RACEHORSE RECORD

JUMPS 2002-2003

Sponsored by:

Editor	Ashley Rumney
Comments by	David Bellingham, Mark Brown, Steffan Edwards
	Walter Glynn, Keith Hewitt, Steve Jones
	Richard Lowther, Ashley Rumney, Ronald Wood
Development	Phillip Lamphee, Dan Di Pol

Published by Raceform Ltd,
Compton, Newbury, Berkshire, RG20 6NL
Tel: 01635 578080
Fax: 01635 578101
Web: www.raceform.co.uk
EMail: rfsubscription@rmgn.co.uk
Printed by William Clowes Ltd, Beccles

ISBN 1-904317-18-9

CONTENTS

Full details of all Raceform services and publications are available from
Raceform, Compton, Newbury, Berkshire RG20 6NL.
Tel: 01635 578080 Fax: 01635 578101.
Web http://www.raceform.co.uk
Email: raceform@raceform.co.uk

Cover Photo: Rhinestone Cowboy (N. Williamson, left),
on his way to beating Thisthatandtother in the
Axminster Kingwell Hurdle at Wincanton.

INTRODUCTION

Raceform's *Racehorse Record* has been designed not only as an historical reference, but also as a guide to the future, with the aim being to provide factual information about individual horses that ran under Jump racing Rules in Britain during the 2002-2003 season, and also to pinpoint conditions that are likely to prove conducive to future success.

For full season's results and ratings, refer to the *Chaseform 2002-2003 Jumps Annual*.

The horses are listed in alphabetical order.

KEY TO HORSE RECORDS

Best Mate (IRE) — Name of horse, plus country of origin suffix in brackets

121   (155h) **178+** — Master Split Second speed rating on left, Raceform rating on right (hurdles ratings in brackets)

8-y-o b g Un Desperado (FR)-Katday (FR) (Miller s Mate)
Miss H C Knight Jim Lewis — Age, colour, sex and pedigree. The sire's name is followed by the dam's name, then the dam's sire's name in brackets

Placings: *11221*/1112/1221-111   (4132) — Trainer's name in bold (plus date of transfer and previous trainer's name if the horse changed stables during the season), followed by the owner's name

2002/03: 20¹GS, 24¹S, 26¹G,

Complete list of the horse's placings, starting with its first recorded race. Bumper outings are in italic, hurdles outings in roman type and chase or hunter chase outings in bold type. A slash '/' or dash '-' indicates a change of season. This is followed in brackets by the Raceform number of the last race in the Form Book in which the horse competed

	Starts	1st	2nd	3rd	Win & Pl
Chases	3	3	0	0	322725
Career Total	16	11	5	0	687354

2002-2003 season's record, broken down into race types followed by career record

178	3/03	Chel	3m2f110yA Ch	GD	£203000
173	12/02	Kemp	3m A Ch	SFT	£87000
175	11/02	Hntg	2m4f110yA Ch	G-S	£32725
176	3/02	Chel	3m2f110yA Ch	GD	£174000
172	11/01	Extr	2m1f110yA HCh	G-F	£21000
167	2/01	Sand	2m4f110yA Ch	HVY	£24000
156	11/00	Chel	2m A Ch	G-S	£15000
151	10/00	Extr	2m1f110yD Ch	GD	£3926
146	4/00	Aint	2m4f A Hdl	GD	£21000
137	12/99	Sand	2m110y D Hdl	G-S	£3680
133	11/99	Chel	2m110y B NHF	GD	£7197
				Total win prize-money £592525	

Career wins, showing (left to right) winning Raceform rating, date of win (month/year), course, distance, race conditions and type, going, win prize money

Going:	Sf: 1-1 GS: 1-1 Gd: 1-1 GF: - Fm: 0-0
Distance:	2m/2m3: 0-0 2m4-2m7: 1-1 **3m+: 2-2**
Track:	LH: 1-1 RH: **2-2** Tight: 0-0 Gall: **2-2**
Aids:	Bl: 0-0 Vi: 0-0 Tstrap: 0-0
Best Rating:	178 3/03 Chel 3m2f110y good Ch

Going record for the season (wins-runs)

Distance record for the season

Track type record for the season

Aids record for the season (blinkers, visor, tongue strap)

Best Raceform rating achieved during the season, followed by the relevant date, course, distance, going and race type

The best staying chaser in the country; has never been out of the first two over hurdles or fences and followed up last season s Cheltenham Gold Cup victory with game success in the King George at Kempton; easy winner of his second Gold Cup in March; has an excellent cruising pace, jumps well, has a fine turn of foot and acts on any ground; effective from 2m 4f to 3m 2f and on any type of track; continues to be the one they all have to beat.

Raceform master comment on selected horses only. (These comments may refer in some instances to races which have already taken place during the 2002-2003 season).

Scale of Weight for Age for Steeple Chases and Hurdle Races
HURDLE RACES

The allowances, assessed in lbs, which three-year-olds and four-year-olds will receive from five-year-olds and upwards

Distance Miles	Age	JAN 1/15	16/31	FEB 1/14	15/29	MAR 1/15	16/31	APR 1/15	16/30	MAY 1/15	16/31	JUNE 1/15	16/30	JULY 1/15	16/31	AUG 1/15	16/31	SEPT 1/15	16/30	OCT 1/15	16/31	NOV 1/15	16/30	DEC 1/15	16/31
2	3	12	11	10	9	8	7	6	5	4	4	3	3	2	2	1	1	-	-	-	-	-	-	-	-
	4	-	-	-	-	-	-	-	-	-	-	-	-	-	-	-	-	-	-	-	-	-	-	-	-
2.5	3	13	12	11	10	9	8	7	6	5	5	4	4	3	3	2	2	1	1	-	-	-	-	-	-
	4	-	-	-	-	-	-	-	-	-	-	-	-	-	-	-	-	-	-	-	-	-	-	-	-
3	3	14	13	12	11	10	10	9	8	7	6	5	5	22	22	21	20	19	18	17	16	15	14	13	-
	4	-	-	-	-	-	-	-	-	-	-	-	-	4	3	3	2	2	1	1	-	-	-	-	-

Scale of Weight for Age for Steeple Chases and Hurdle Races
STEEPLE CHASES

The allowances, assessed in lbs, which four-year-olds and five-year-olds will receive from five-year-olds and upwards

Distance Miles	Age	JAN 1/15	16/31	FEB 1/14	15/29	MAR 1/15	16/31	APR 1/15	16/30	MAY 1/15	16/31	JUNE 1/15	16/30	JULY 1/15	16/31	AUG 1/15	16/31	SEPT 1/15	16/30	OCT 1/15	16/31	NOV 1/15	16/30	DEC 1/15	16/31
2	4	9	8	7	6	5	4	3	3	2	2	1	1	-	-	-	-	-	-	-	-	-	-	-	-
	5	-	-	-	-	-	-	-	-	-	-	-	-	-	-	-	-	-	-	-	-	-	-	-	-
2.5	4	10	9	8	7	6	5	4	4	3	3	2	2	1	1	-	-	-	-	-	-	-	-	-	-
	5	-	-	-	-	-	-	-	-	-	-	-	-	-	-	-	-	-	-	-	-	-	-	-	-
3	4	12	12	11	11	10	10	9	8	7	7	6	5	17	17	16	16	15	15	14	14	13	12	11	10
	5	-	-	-	-	-	-	-	-	-	-	-	-	5	4	4	3	3	2	2	1	1	-	-	-

RACEFORM RATINGS

Raceform Ratings for each horse are listed after the Starting Price and indicate the actual level of performance attained in that race. The figure in the back index represents the BEST public form that Raceform's Handicappers still believe the horse capable of reproducing.

To use the ratings constructively in determining those horses best-in in future events, the following procedures should be followed:

(i) In races where all runners are set to carry the same weight, no calculations are necessary. The horse with the highest rating is best in.

(ii) In races where all runners are set to carry different weights, add one point to the Raceform Rating for every pound less than 12 st to be carried; deduct one point for every pound more than 12 st.

For example,

Horse	Age & Weight	Adjustment from 12st	RR base rating	Adjusted rating
Flagship Uberalles	8-12-00	0	172	172
Edredon Bleu	10-11-12	+2	168	170
Fadalko	9-11-10	+4	168	172
Cenkos	8-11-06	+8	166	174

Therefore Cenkos is top-rated (best-in)

NB No adjustments are made for weight for age in Chaseform ratings. The official weight for age scale is displayed for information purposes while any live weight for age conditions are displayed underneath each individual result.

The following symbols are used in conjunction with the ratings:

++ almost certain to prove better
+ likely to prove better
d disappointing (has run well below best recently)
? form hard to evaluate, may prove unreliable
t tentative rating based on race-time

Weight adjusted ratings for every race are published daily in Raceform Private Handicap, and on our new service, Raceform Private Handicap ONLINE (www.raceform.co.uk). For subscription terms please contact the Subscription Department on (01635) 578080.

REVIEW OF THE SEASON
by David Orton and Richard Lowther

The Open meeting at Cheltenham in November is traditionally the first principal meeting of the National Hunt season. This year, record crowds over the three days saw champion trainer Martin Pipe win the feature Thomas Pink Gold Cup for the third consecutive year. It was the stable s fifth win in the race in last seven runnings. The winner was the nine-year-old Cyfor Malta, who himself was becoming only the fifth horse to win the race twice, under Barry Geraghty at 16/1. Champion jockey Tony McCoy slimmed down to a wafer-thin 10st 1lb so he could ride the favourite, Chicuelo, but the gelding, subject of a massive ante-post gamble and also trained by Pipe, was pulled up after barely jumping a twig.

The final day of the meeting provided some major clues for the season ahead. Rooster Booster, winner of the previous season s County Hurdle at the track, showed he was rapidly improving by romping away with one of the most competitive two-mile handicaps to be contested all season.

Paul Nicholls' Azertyuiop, a five-year-old, advertised his Arkle credentials by beating Golden Alpha in the Grade Two Novice Chase, winning by 16 lengths after a superb leap at the last fence. Last year s Champion bumper runner-up Rhinestone Cowboy, trained by Jonjo O Neill and owned by the Magniers (better known for their exploits in Flat racing), took the Open Bumper in effortless fashion. Ridden on this occasion by the owner s son J. P. Magnier, who was having his first ride in this country and claimed 7lb, 'the Cowboy' looked a very exciting prospect with the Champion Hurdle already mentioned as a likely target.

AMAZING COMEBACK

The defending Stayers Hurdle champion, Baracouda, made an amazing comeback in the Grade Two Ascot Hurdle on November 22nd when notching his tenth straight win. At the start of the race, neither he nor three his rivals had wanted to set the pace, and some 13 seconds elapsed before Tony McCoy, on Mr Cool, stole a lead. It is well known that, while brilliant, Baracouda is also lazy, thus is best coming off a strong pace to keep his interest in a race. All the other jockeys therefore wanted to test the French raider and do this they did, as in Swinley Bottom Mr Cool was at least 35 lengths clear. Indeed even over the last flight the leader was 12 lengths to the good, but Baracouda flew on the run-in to get up by a neck for a remarkable win.

With the abandonment of Ascot s First National Chase the following weekend due to waterlogging, all eyes were on the Peterborough Chase at Huntingdon. Henrietta Knight, who trained Edredon Bleu to a fourth consecutive win in the race the previous year, this time took it with her stable star Best Mate. Making a winning return for his popular owner Jim Lewis, the Gold Cup winner made all under jockey Jim Culloty. He was now to be aimed at the King George at Kempton on Boxing Day.

Away from the racecourse, horse racing was again in the public eye, with the Jockey Club holding hearings into alleged misdemeanours of former riders Dermot Browne and Graham Bradley. Browne, a former champion amateur and later a trainer, who was

already warned off, was banned for another 20 years for admitting during a police inter-view in 2000 to doping 23 horses. Bradley, one of the most colourful and successful jockeys in the sport's history, was warned off for eight years. This came after it was revealed he was guilty of six breaches of the Jockey Club s rules. The ban was one of the longest imposed in over 20 years, and Bradley was also fined £2,500 for offences including bringing racing into disrepute. Best remembered for leading home Michael Dickinson s 'famous five' in the 1983 Cheltenham Gold Cup aboard Bregawn, he also won the 1996 Champion Hurdle on Collier Bay. Since retiring from riding he has set up a bloodstock agency, recruiting horses for jumping from abroad, most notably Seebald, runner-up in the 2002 Arkle at Cheltenham. Despite lodging an immediate appeal which resulted in the ban being reduced to five years, this looked a painful and bitter end to his up and down racing career.

At Newbury in November, the Hennessy meeting provided a feast of top-class jumping. Rhinestone Cowboy made an effortless hurdling debut in the maiden hurdle in the last race of the opening day, jumping accurately and never once coming off the bridle under Norman Williamson. His victory attracted significant Champion Hurdle interest, now that there was no Istabraq to beat.

On the Saturday French raider Jair Du Cochet beat Scots Grey in the Fulke Walwyn Novice Chase, looking potentially top-class in the process. The British press called for his regular rider Jacques Ricou to be replaced by a British jockey, as he would often take a hand off the reins at fences and become unbalanced. Jair Du Cochet's trainer Guillaume Macaire was adamant however that Ricou would continue his association with the novice. The following race on the card, the Grade Two Long Distance Hurdle, was won by 2000 Stayers' Hurdle winner and top-class chaser Bacchanal, who was having only his third start back over hurdles since switching to fences. Nicky Henderson s charge beat Native Emperor by five lengths to increase his options further for the season ahead.

DRAMATIC CONTEST

The Hennessy Cognac Gold Cup produced a dramatic contest. Bottom-weight Be My Royal battled to success over the biggest field for 40 years, beating Gingembre by half a length for Irish trainer Willie Mullins after any number of horses had held a winning chance in the straight. However, he was dismounted after the line by rider David Casey and the next day it emerged that he had sustained a career-ending tendon injury during the race. To add to connections' misery, it later emerged that he was among a host of horses, most of them Irish-trained, who tested positive for morphine, rendering disqualifi-cation virtually inevitable.

Elsewhere that afternoon Intersky Falcon won the Fighting Fifth Hurdle at Newcastle, establishing his Champion Hurdle credentials in the process.

In early December Ireland's favourite hurdler, the evergreen Limestone Lad, took the Grade One Hatton's Grace Hurdle for the third time, looking as good as ever. However, in contrasting style Ned Kelly, a big hope for the Champion Hurdle, dropped away tame-ly to finish a remote third on his reappearance.

The novice hurdling division was starting to look strong and this was emphasised at Sandown when the Jonjo O Neill-trained Coolnagorna beat Thisthatandtother by five lengths in the Grade Two Winter Novices' Hurdle. The last race on the card saw another potential top-notcher in Lord Sam who, after beating the odds-on Inca Trail by three and half lengths, was described by his trainer Victor Dartnall as the best horse he had ever

trained. One of the previous season s better bumper horses, Lord Sam's jumping was messy, yet he powered to victory.

Back in the Emerald Isle, Native Upmanship won his second Grade One John Durkan Memorial Chase, beating Rince Ri in effortless style. The 2001 King George winner First Gold, who was making his comeback after a career-threatening tendon injury, finished back in third.

The following week saw Cheltenham s 40th anniversary two-day pre-Christmas meeting, with the feature race being the Tripleprint Gold Cup worth £100,000. It was won by the Nicky Henderson-trained Fondmort who produced a magnificent jump for Mick Fitzgerald at the last to beat his eight rivals. In the Grade Two Bula Hurdle, Rooster Booster confirmed he was still improving at the age of eight when beating Landing Light by two and a half lengths. The final race went to the progressive staying novice hurdler Iris s Gift, who needed all of champion jockey Tony McCoy s strength in order to beat Ad Hoc in a thrilling finish over three miles.

On the same Saturday, Jonjo O Neill, successful at Cheltenham with Iris s Gift, was making the headlines elsewhere for all the wrong reasons. O Neill was fined for two separate offences over the running and riding of his novice hurdlers Madalyar and Gala Performance at Fakenham and Haydock respectively. The Fakenham incident saw the highest-ever race-day fine imposed by racecourse stewards, as Madalyar's rider was found guilty of 'failure to make sufficient effort to ensure the best possible placing'. O'Neill was fined £3,400; jockey Ron Flavin was suspended for 21 days and the horse was banned from racing for 40 days. Over at Haydock an hour and a half earlier, Gala Performance's connections had been found guilty of schooling the gelding in public. The local stewards handed out a 30-day ban for the horse, and jockey Liam Cooper was suspended for five days.

LIMESTONE ROCKS ON

Mid-December saw Limestone Lad s fourth win of the season and 34th success in total. It was his eighth win at Navan and also equalled the career total of wins recorded by Desert Orchid. Another Bowe family-trained individual also scored at the track as Solerina, a tiny five-year-old mare, completed her hat-trick by readily winning a Grade Three novice hurdle over two and a half miles.

A week later, Baracouda was back at Ascot for his second run of the season and attempting not only to win his 11th successive race, but also his third victory in the Long Walk Hurdle. The race was the mirror image of his previous race, the Ascot Hurdle, as Tony McCoy, on board the highest-rated British staying hurdler Deano s Beeno, poached a massive lead in a small field. Baracouda was again given a mountain to climb, and this time in very testing conditions he failed by a length to peg back the leader. He looked to have had a very hard race, but all credit goes to the victor, who was gaining his first Grade One win.

The Ladbroke Hurdle, worth £100,000, is one of Europe s most valuable handicaps. Formerly run in Ireland at Leopardstown, it moved to Ascot's pre-Christmas meeting in 2001 and was won this season by the novice Chauvinist, trained by Nicky Henderson, who emerged from the fog well clear at the last hurdle and scored by 15 lengths. With stable jockey Mick Fitzgerald unable to do 10st, Norman Williamson rode his third winner of this event and second in succession.

The eagerly-anticipated Pertemps King George VI Chase was next on the agenda at Kempton. The first three home in 2001 re-opposed, and it was the outstanding

Cheltenham Gold Cup winner Best Mate who prevailed, with Tony McCoy aboard as Jim Culloty was suspended. In beating stable companions Marlborough and Bacchanal, with 2001 winner Florida Pearl a well beaten fourth, Best Mate confirmed his position as the best chaser around and McCoy, when asked how good he thought he was, remarked 'I would marry him!'. Earlier McCoy had also reported highly favourably after he had won the opening novice hurdle by 20 lengths on Lord Sam. This was also McCoy's 200th victory of the season.

Intersky Falcon won the Grade One Pertemps Christmas Hurdle in battling style under Charlie Swan. His rider, well qualified in judging Champion Hurdle contenders, suggested the chestnut was ideal for the big race with his front-running tactics. In the Grade One Feltham Novices' Chase, Jair Du Cochet showed his class with a superb round of fencing to beat the ex-French Le Sauvignon. The latter was a high-class hurdler in his native country but tragically, on only his second run for Paul Nicholls, he suffered a heart attack after passing the post and died.

MASSIVE GAMBLE

The Coral Welsh National, over 3m5f at Chepstow, was run in gruelling conditions. It was won by the Jonjo O Neill-trained Mini Sensation, owned by the legendary J. P. McManus. A massive gamble on the day saw him backed from 25/1 in the morning to 8/1 come the off. Mini Sensation thrived on the heavy surface and, under a great ride from Tony Dobbin, beat Chives by seven lengths, looking a genuine contender for the Martell Cognac Grand National at Aintree in April.

Across the Irish Sea at Leopardstown, Beef Or Salmon sprang to prominence in the ante-post market for the Gold Cup with a stylish victory in the Grade One Ericsson Chase over three miles. His trainer Michael Hourigan was in bullish mood afterwards, stating that the novice route would be ignored and that connections of Best Mate should be more worried about his horse than he was of theirs. It certainly seemed that a genuine rival to the reigning champion had emerged. On the same card, Limestone Lad continued his remarkable run with another victory, this time making all in the Grade Two Christmas Hurdle over three miles for his fifth win in a row. News also emerged regarding Ned Kelly, who was to miss the remainder of the season after being found to be lame following his run behind Limestone Lad in the Hatton s Grace Hurdle. Ned Kelly's misfortune left the door open for another of his owners' horses to run in the Champion Hurdle, the novice Rhinestone Cowboy.

The New Year often sees the winter chill kick in and this was again the case, with a total of 12 meetings cancelled between the 6th and 11th of January. With jump racing virtually wiped out All-Weather Flat racing was left to provide the only action.

The first major jump race of 2003, the Victor Chandler Chase at Ascot, was abandoned due to frost, but the following day Leopardstown was able to stage the Pierse Hurdle, a Grade A extended handicap, over two miles and worth 130,000euros. In keeping with the tradition of the race, it had a fiercely competitive field of 28 runners. Home trainer Tony Martin, a master of his trade and in particular at landing a handicap gamble, trained the winner Xenophon. Ridden by Mick Fitzgerald, the gelding was the least experienced in the line-up but that did not stop him recording a smooth two-length win over the British-trained Colourful Life.

The abandonment of the Victor Chandler Chase was Ascot s loss but Kempton s gain, as a replacement event, the Tote Exacta Chase, a Grade Two limited handicap, was run at the Sunbury track's fixture a week later. Young Devereaux, an injury-plagued ten-year-old trained by Paul Nicholls, won the race after a decent battle up the run-in with the Martin Pipe-trained Seebald.

The final race on the card saw Lord Sam gain his third straight win over hurdles, beating a decent field including Ladbroke Hurdle winner Chauvinist and the promising Jonjo O Neill-trained Sh Boom. Jim Culloty, who had won the John Bull Chase aboard Edredon Bleu at Wincanton earlier in the day, flew to Kempton in order to take the ride.

SOLD OUT

On the same day that officials at Cheltenham reported that Gold Cup day at the Festival in March was already sold out, a record 149 entries for the Martell Grand National were announced, 34 of them from Ireland.

The last Saturday in January saw the Pillar Property Chase at Cheltenham and the Great Yorkshire Chase at Doncaster take place. Behrajan, trained by Henry Daly and ridden by Richard Johnson, won a muddling race for the Pillar in good fashion by 14 lengths. The race was marred, however, by the tragic death of Bacchanal, Nicky Henderson s talented charge fallling on the first circuit and breaking a hind leg. Winning rider Richard Johnson completed a double on the card, having earlier won the novices' handicap chase aboard the vastly-improved La Landiere. Trained by Richard Phillips, who was having his best season since leaving Jackdaws Castle in Gloucestershire, the mare won under a welter burden of 11st 12lb to land a fifth win in a row over fences. She was bang on target for either the Cathcart or the SunAlliance Chase at the Festival in March. Not to be outdone, Tony McCoy was also in double form, winning the card's other feature events on Classified in the Grade One Cleeve Hurdle and on course specialist Lady Cricket in the Ladbroke Trophy Chase, both winners being trained by Martin Pipe and owned by David Johnson.

At Doncaster, Pipe was also successful in the Great Yorkshire Chase with Barryscourt Lad, ridden by Rodi Greene, the former point-to-pointer prevailing on the line after a tremendous battle on the run-in with the tough Ryalux. Unfortunately he was dismounted after the line having gone lame, and missed the remainder of the season.

On the Sunday the eagerly anticipated AIG Irish Champion Hurdle saw Limestone Lad, running over an inadequate two-mile trip, lose his first race of the season, going down by a head to the 2002 Supreme Novices' Hurdle winner, Like-A-Butterfly. Trained by Christy Roche and owned by J. P. McManus, the mare was having her first run of the season and knuckled down bravely under Charlie Swan. In the opener on the card, the promising Back In Front, third in the previous season's Champion Bumper at Cheltenham, won the maiden hurdle, while Limestone Lad's stable companion Solerina gave connections some compensation when landing her fifth straight win in the Grade Three Golden Cygnet Novices' Hurdle.

When the Martell Grand National weights were announced, senior National Hunt Handicapper Phil Smith allocated no fewer than 67 horses ten stone or more. The joint top-weights were Irish challenger Florida Pearl and Nicky Henderson s Marlborough, set to shoulder 11st 12lb. It was looking ever more likely that the maximum field of 40 horses would go to post for the four and a half-mile contest. Following the publication of the weights, the bookmakers often report of contenders being backed ante-post, and this

year Irish-trained Monty's Pass and Davids Lad were the subject of strong support. The latter, trained by Tony Martin, had been going well when being brought down with a mile to run the previous season, and Ladbrokes stated they had laid a bet of £25,000 at 20/1 for this year s race.

The richest handicap hurdle in Europe is the Tote Gold Trophy at Newbury, worth a total of £120,000 and usually won by a smart, progressive hurdler. This season 27 runners took part, and Spirit Leader, a seven-year-old mare trained in Ireland by Jessica Harrington, came home ahead of the favourite Non So. An improving sort, Spirit Leader had also won the William Hill Handicap Hurdle at Ascot in December.

Later on the Newbury card, Valley Henry took the Grade Two AON Chase for Paul Nicholls, beating Welsh National runner-up Chives by two and a half lengths. Jumping with more fluency on this better ground, Valley Henry looked a live outsider for the Gold Cup in March.

CHASING SENSATION

Leopardstown's February meeting witnessed Ireland's latest chasing sensation Beef Or Salmon maintain his unbeaten run over fences in the Grade One Hennessy Cognac Gold Cup. Under a cool Timmy Murphy ride, he took it up at the second last fence and went away to beat Colonel Braxton by four lengths. His rise to the top of the chasing ranks was now fully confirmed and Irish punters began dreaming of Gold Cup success come March. Earlier, prolific mare Solerina completed her seven-timer over hurdles with a win in the Grade Two Deloitte And Touche Novices' Hurdle. With her front-running tactics, she looked a mirror image, if on a smaller scale, of stablemate Limestone Lad, and was dubbed Little Limestone by the Irish press. However, she was to be injured after this race, due to a scratch which had been lying dormant since running at Thurles early in the season. That infected her cannon bone on her rear hind leg and she was immediately ruled out for the year ahead.

Jonjo O'Neill was in the headlines again following a hearing at the Jockey Club's headquarters in Portman Square. The Exeter stewards had referred O Neill to the Disciplinary Panel after the running and riding of Top Of The Left in the novice hurdle at their meeting on January 27th. It had been reported that the Jockey Club was seriously considering removing the high-profile trainer's licence, for this third breach of the rules in six weeks, but he was eventually fined £6,000 after it was deemed that the gelding had been schooled in public .

Leading jockey Mick Fitzgerald had the honour of riding the Queen s first winner over jumps in 50 years, when partnering First Love to victory at Folkestone in a novice chase. Trained by Nicky Henderson, the six-year-old son of Bustino had been the last of the Queen Mother's 446 domestic winners. The Queen was to be presented later that month with the Sir Peter O Sullevan Award, in recognition of her outstanding contribution to the sport, an award that in the past was also presented to her mother.

COWBOY SHOOTS TO TOP OF MARKET

With Cheltenham just a month away, further fuel was added to the ante-post fire at Wincanton and at Ascot, where Jonjo O Neill s Keen Leader further cemented his position at the top of the novice chasing tree with an exhibition round of jumping in the Grade Two Amlin Reynoldstown Novices' Chase over three miles. The contest lost much of its appeal however when main rival Jair Du Cochet unseated his unorthodox

rider four out. Nevertheless, both Keen Leader and Jair Du Cochet remained on target for a crack at the Royal & SunAlliance Chase. At Wincanton, Rhinestone Cowboy continued his progression by winning the Grade Two Axminster Kingwell Hurdle, beating fellow novice Thisthatandother by the best part of two lengths with the previous year's Champion Hurdle winner Hors La Loi III back in third. Rhinestone Cowboy was being touted as the natural successor to Istabraq for the Champion Hurdle, yet his trainer Jonjo O Neill refused to reveal his target at the Festival with the novice route still a possible option. Over fences, Azertyuiop made his comeback from a break, scoring in facile manner manner by 25 lengths. He looked very special and was made clear favourite for the Arkle Chase.

The progressive mare La Landiere won the Grade Three Racing Post Chase at Kempton in late February, beating the previous year s winner Gunther McBride by three lengths. Under jockey Warren Marston she secured her sixth consecutive victory since finishing runner-up to Impek on her debut over fences the previous May. She was one of the most improved chasers of the season, and the Cathcart Chase at Cheltenham was now a real target, although connections stated she might be supplemented for the Gold Cup.

Henrietta Knight introduced a promising youngster at Kempton in the shape of Chelsea Bridge, who won the closing bumper on the card. Having his first outing, he came with a storming late run under Jim Culloty to beat Trabolgan by a neck. He looked a bright prospect for novice hurdling in 2003-2004.

At Naas in Ireland Arctic Copper won the Grade Two Newlands Chase over two miles, but it was the performance of Davids Lad, placed last, which caught the eye. The local Stewards determined that the racecourse had been used as a training ground and suspended the horse for 42 days and fined trainer his Tony Martin 1,000euros. The horse was racing over a distance way short of his best and was settled at the back of the field from the off, only to be kept there by pilot Timmy Murphy, who was banned for seven days for insufficient effort. This led to uproar from connections, who desperately tried to find excuses for the run, as the ban meant the horse would be ruled out of the Martell Grand National, for which he had been subject of a major gamble. Appeals were lodged by connections, with the trainer stating that the jockey had been given no specific instructions, and that he should have been more forceful . Eventually, after the owners took the appeal all the way to the High Court, the original verdict was upheld and the lengthy suspension stood.

At the beginning of March Iris s Gift destroyed a select field in the Grade Two Prestige novices' hurdle at Haydock, and confirmed he was bang on target for the Festival. Even more impressive that day was the performance of the Paul Nicholls-trained chaser Shotgun Willy, who took the Red Square Vodka Gold Cup over three and a half miles. Given a never-say-die ride by Ruby Walsh, he was having his first outing for 315 days and became the first horse to win the race under top weight. Shotgun Willy was immediately made favourite for the Grand National in April.

As always, the week before the Cheltenham Festival sees the quality of National Hunt racing dilute, and the public was subjected to some pretty average fare. However, at Sandown on the Saturday before the Festival the Sunderlands Imperial Cup is contested. The sponsors offer a £60,000 bonus if the winning horse can go on to glory in any race at the Festival the following week. This invariably attracts some of the top stables, most notably that of Martin Pipe, who landed the double in 1998 with Blowing Wind. The latter carried the colours of Peter Deal in the County Hurdle. This year he relied on

Korelo, who was backed into favouritism and, after being scrubbed along a mile out, ran on to beat Newhall by six lengths in very testing conditions.

BOOSTER RULES THE ROOST

The Cheltenham Festival, which for many is the most important racing week of the year, continues to grow in stature. With record prize money and all tickets sold out, this was shaping up to be some spectacle.

The feature of day one is the Smurfit Champion Hurdle and, with no Istabraq around, many in the crowd expected the novice Rhinestone Cowboy to emerge as his natural successor. However, it was the vastly-improved grey, Rooster Booster, who won in a style befitting a champion. Trained by Philip Hobbs and ridden by Richard Johnson, the horse confirmed his love affair with the track and powered away to beat Westender by 11 lengths. This was the biggest margin of victory in the race since Istabraq s first win in 1998. Rhinestone Cowboy performed well to finish third, but his jumping was found out in the heat of battle. His stablemate Intersky Falcon was fifth.

The opening Gerrard Wealth Management Supreme Novices' Hurdle was won by the Irish-trained Back In Front who, as favourite, got the punters off to a great start, despite drifting to 3/1. He could be called the winner entering the straight under a typically cool Norman Williamson ride and decimated the field to win by ten lengths.

Next came the Arkle, and another favourite, Azertyuiop, stung the bookmakers having been backed into 5/4. All season Paul Nicholls' five-year-old had remained lightly raced and unbeaten, and he was a most impressive winner. Left in the lead after his stable-mate Le Roi Miguel had fallen at the third fence, he simply had too much speed for his nine rivals and sauntered away to beat Impek by 11 lengths. Jockey Ruby Walsh hailed him as the best two-miler he had ever ridden.

Champion trainer Martin Pipe got off the mark in the fifth race, as Royal Predica took the Fulke Walwyn Kim Muir Challenge Cup Chase for amateur riders. Another wide-margin winner, he beat the well-fancied Ibis Rochelais by ten lengths at 33/1. His jockey Saul McHugh, a 22-year-old Irish amateur, was remarkably gaining his first win under Rules.

FLYER GLIDES IN

Wednesday's feature, the Queen Mother Champion Chase over two miles, was taken in commanding style by the Irish raider Moscow Flyer, winner of the 2002 Arkle Chase. He gave Barry Geraghty his third victory of the meeting, after being left in front at the second last where both Seebald and Latalomne fell. Ironically, Latalomne and rider Vinnie Keane had departed at the same fence when in contention the previous year. Nevertheless Moscow Flyer s performance was a career-best effort and he was a worthy champion.

The opening Royal & SunAlliance Novices' Hurdle looked hot on paper and it lived up to expectations, Irish raider Hardy Eustace, ridden by Kieran Kelly, beating Coolnagorna by two and quarter lengths. In an eventful contest, the runner-up was subsequently disqualified from second spot and placed last, due to his rider Tony Dobbin causing intentional interference to the fourth home Lord Sam at the penultimate flight. The winner was one of many in the line-up that looked grand chasing types.

The Royal & SunAlliance Chase, which usually features the best staying novice chasers around, was won this year by the Philip Hobbs-trained One Knight under Richard

Johnson. The seven-year-old, who made all, survived several mistakes as he beat French challenger Jair Du Cochet, who left it too late, by the best part of two lengths.

The closing contest on day two sees the best of the new talent in the Weatherbys Champion Bumper, a contest that usually throws up numerous clues as to the brightest prospects for the following year. Irish-trained horses had won eight of the previous ten renewals, but this year the first six home were British-trained. Martin Pipe s 2/1 favourite Liberman won all-out from Trabolgan and registered a first victory at the meeting for champion jockey Tony McCoy, who was having a Festival to forget. He had taken three falls and most of his rides had run poorly, so his delight at this win was evident as he punched the air.

ROYAL RETURN

On the Thursday the Queen attended the Festival for the first time in fifty years, and she witnessed Best Mate winning the Tote Gold Cup in fantastic fashion. Rarely in such a high-class event has any horse looked the winner so early on, and not even the departure of second favourite Beef Or Salmon at the third fence could take anything away from the performance of Best Mate, who gave a perfect exhibition of jumping under a confident ride from Jim Culloty and came home ten lengths clear of the runner-up Truckers Tavern. Best Mate became the first horse since L Escargot (1970 and 1971) to win successive Cheltenham Gold Cups and will now try to emulate Arkle by winning three times in as many seasons.

Baracouda successfully defended his Stayers Hurdle crown with a stunning victory over the novice Iris s Gift. The Francois Doumen-trained hurdler was given a tactically superb ride by regular partner Thierry Doumen to win by three-quarters of a length, despite idling when hitting the front before the last. The runner-up confirmed he was a novice of the highest class and looks to have a bright future.

The opener of the last day, the JCB Triumph Hurdle for four-year-olds, is always run at a frantic gallop and it was won this year by Spectroscope, ridden by Barry Geraghty and trained by Jonjo O Neill, who outpointed Well Chief, ridden by Tony McCoy, to win by a head.

The connections of La Landiere opted to run their mare in the Cathcart Chase and the 5/4 favourite did not let them down as she notched her seventh win in a row.

In the 20th and final event of the meeting Barry Geraghty sealed the leading jockey award with victory on Spirit Leader in the Vincent O Brien County Hurdle. The small, but game, mare stormed up the hill to win by a cheeky neck over fellow Irish-trained raider Balapour. This capped a superb week for the Irish and Geraghty in particular.

On the whole the 2003 Cheltenham Festival was the best in recent memory and will take some bettering in the seasons to come. The Festival was, however, a bookmakers' nightmare as ten winning favourites helped punters take millions out of the ring.
Early April sees the start of the north s big National Hunt festival at Aintree. On the Thursday First Gold stormed back to form by taking the Martell Cognac Cup. Winning the race for the second time in three years, the talented French chaser soon bagged the lead and, in first-time blinkers, jumped beautifully to beat Lady Cricket by an easy 14 lengths.

TWO UPMANSHIP

Native Upmanship went one better than at Cheltenham in the Martell Cognac Melling Chase over two and a half miles. At this trip the Irish raider is very hard to beat and he took the race for the second successive season in smooth style under Norman Williamson, with the consistent Seebald comfortably held in second.

Also going one better than at Cheltenham was the Stayers Hurdle runner-up Iris s Gift, who won the Sefton Novices' Hurdle. Setting a relentless gallop, he had his rivals in trouble some way out before making a hash of the final flight, and was ridden out to score by eight lengths from Royal Emperor. This was a season to remember for all concerned with Iris's Gift, whose owner paid just 3,500gns for the grey.

The Friday of the meeting saw leading owner J. P. McManus bag a 1,325/1 treble courtesy of Master Tern, Clan Royal and Patriot Games. The last-named, who won the closing Listed handicap hurdle, was both trained and ridden by Charlie Swan, the legendary Irish jockey best known for his association with three-time Champion Hurdle winner Istabraq, also owned by McManus. This was to be Swan s last winner as a jockey, as he retired from the saddle the following day to concentrate on training.

On Martell Grand National day, the Grade One Martell Cognac Aintree Hurdle went to Irish-trained Sacundai, who inflicted a first defeat of the season on Rooster Booster. Stepping up half a mile in distance, the Champion Hurdle winner was beaten a head, largely due to the fact that his rider Richard Johnson lost his whip when in the lead after the last flight. Take little away, though, from the winner, who looks an improving sort, and whose trainer Edward O Grady stated he would be a Stayers Hurdle candidate next season. He was ridden by Ruby Walsh, who was in outstanding form, winning the first three races on the card.

MASSIVE GAMBLE

The most famous race in the world, the Martell Cognac Grand National, saw a high-class, maximum field of 40 go to post in near perfect conditions. Irish horses had won two of the last four renewals following a long drought, and they added to that this season with Monty s Pass, trained by Jimmy Mangan and ridden by Barry Geraghty. The son of Montelimar gave a foot-perfect exhibition of jumping, beating Supreme Glory by 12 lengths. Monty's Pass was a massive ante-post gamble, netting his owners a reported £1 million. However, there were some other big gambles that stayed in the bookmakers' satchels, much to their relief after the worst Cheltenham Festival in recent memory. The layers' biggest result was the Irish horse Youlneverwalkalone, trained by Christy Roche and owned by J.P. McManus, whose Liverpool-linked name helped fuel a massive gamble down to 8/1. Unfotunately the gelding, who had won the William Hill National Hunt Handicap Chase at Cheltenham, had to be pulled up after fracturing his off-fore cannon bone at an early stage. Favourite Shotgun Willy was also pulled up.

The following Saturday at Ayr the Scottish Grand National was won by the ultra-consistent Ryalux, who beat Martin Pipe s Stormez by a neck in a thrilling finish. Trained by Andy Crook, who has only held a licence for two years, Ryalux has only failed to complete on three of his 28 career starts to date, and has never finished out of the first three when getting round.

Jim Culloty capped a season to remember when winning the Powers Gold Label Irish Grand National aboard the Dessie Hughes-trained Timbera. The race is the richest chase in Ireland and Timbera confirmed his liking for Fairyhouse, as his last four victo-

ries have all been at the course. The 2001 winner Davids Lad, who was now able to race again following his long ban, could only manage fourth on this occasion.

The attheraces Gold Cup brought the curtain down on a spectacular season at Sandown on April 26, Paul Nicholls' Ad Hoc winning the event for the second time in three years. He had been campaigned over hurdles for most of the season, as his trainer did not want to jeopardise his chase mark with the Grand National in mind. However, Ad Hoc unseated his rider at the 19th fence at Aintree, and came here relatively fresh to win his first chase since success in this race in 2001, when it was known as the Whitbread. Always travelling strongly, he stormed up the run-in under Ruby Walsh to beat the luckless Stormez by nine lengths.

The final race of the campaign was won by Skycab, a fitting result as the gelding was the last runner sent out by Josh Gifford, who was retiring after a long career as both jockey and trainer. Gifford, who handed over his Findon yard to his son Nick, will always be associated with 1981 Grand National winner Aldaniti.

Tony McCoy retained his title as Champion Jockey in runaway fashion, riding 257 winners, more than 100 more than nearest rival Richard Johnson, who had suffered a broken leg early in the campaign. In April, Johnson reached the landmark of 1000 career winners in Britain when successful on Quedex at Stratford. Martin Pipe also retained his crown as Champion Trainer, although West Country rival Paul Nicholls put up a good fight to push him close. Marcus Foley was champion conditional.

Another of the select band to have ridden 1000 winners, Adrian Maguire, announced his retirement in October, a serious neck injury incurred the previous March having failed to mend sufficiently. Maguire, one of the best jump jockeys never to have been champion, won the Cheltenham Gold Cup on Cool Ground in 1992. Dean Gallagher, who enjoyed the greatest moment of his career on Hors la Loi III in the 2002 Champion Hurdle, was banned from riding for 18 months in November after testing positive for cocaine. It was his second such offence, and his career in the saddle seemed to be over.

RACEFORM TOP RATED CHASERS

Best Mate (IRE)	188
First Gold (FR)	184
Moscow Flyer (IRE)	184
Edredon Bleu (FR)	182
See More Business (IRE)	181
Tiutchev	180
Behrajan (IRE)	180
Marlborough (IRE)	180
Native Upmanship (IRE)	180
Cyfor Malta (FR)	179
Cenkos (FR)	178
Shotgun Willy (IRE)	178
Hussard Collonges (FR)	178
Bacchanal (IRE)	177
Truckers Tavern (IRE)	177
Kingsmark (IRE)	176
Harbour Pilot (IRE)	176
Valley Henry (IRE)	176
Kadarann (IRE)	176
Azertyuiop (FR)	176
Latalomne (USA)	175
Seebald (GER)	175
Foxchapel King (IRE)	174
Foly Pleasant (FR)	174
Chives (IRE)	174
Lady Cricket (FR)	173
Gingembre (FR)	173
Beef Or Salmon (IRE)	173

RACEFORM TOP RATED HURDLERS

Rooster Booster	178
Baracouda (FR)	176
Limestone Lad (IRE)	174
Deano s Beeno	173
Iris s Gift	173

NB: A ratings revision has reduced the Raceform ratings of all chasers by 10lb as from May 2003.

A Bit Of Fluff

11-y-o b m Green Adventure (USA)-Cantabile (Bustino)
Lady Susan Brooke Lady Susan Brooke

Placings:*000*P/P   (0055)
2002/03: 24^PG,

	Starts	1st	2nd	3rd	Win & Pl
Chases	1	0	0	0	
Career Total	5	0	0	0	

Going: Sf: 0-0 GS: 0-0 Gd: 0-1 GF: - Fm: 0-0
Distance: 2m/2m3: 0-0 2m4-2m7: 0-0 3m+: 0-1
Track: LH: 0-1 RH: 0-0 Tight: 0-1 Gall: 0-0
Aids: Bl: 0-0 Vi: 0-0 Tstrap: 0-0
Best Rating: 78   3/98 Wwck 2m   soft   NHF

A Few Bob Back (IRE)

106   123

7-y-o b g Bob Back (USA)-Kottna (USA) (Lyphard (USA))
D Eddy Brian Chicken

Placings:*0005/5*P41F0012P-1133060   (4553)
2002/03: 22^1S, 20^1S, 21^3GS, 24^3GF, 20^0HY, 24^6S, 22^0G,

	Starts	1st	2nd	3rd	Win & Pl
Hurdles	7	2	0	2	13640
Career Total	21	4	1	2	23329
120	11/02	Ayr	2m4f	C(0-130)HHdl	SFT	£6851
118	11/02	Kels	2m6f110yD(0-125)HHdl	SFT	£4199
108	1/02	Newc	3m	D(0-125)HHdl	SFT	£3542
99	8/01	Slig	2m4f	(0-95)HHdl	SH	£4312
				Total win prize-money £18905		

Going: Sf: 2-4 GS: 0-1 Gd: 0-1 GF: - Fm: 0-1
Distance: 2m/2m3: 0-0 **2m4-2m7: 2-5** 3m+: 0-2
Track: **LH: 2-5** RH: 0-2 **Tight: 1-3** Gall: 0-1
Aids: Bl: 0-0 Vi: 0-0 Tstrap: 0-0
Best Rating: 120 12/02 Muss 3m   gd-fm Hdl

Decent handicap hurdler; acts on a soft surface and stays three miles; has worn cheekpieces and blinkers.

A Piece Of Cake (IRE)

114   147

10-y-o gr g Roselier (FR)-Boreen Bro (Boreen (FR))
Mrs M Reveley Lightbody Celebration Cakes Ltd

Placings:*0*/15F2123131/6F1450-U21U11   (4307)
2002/03: 20^UHY, 20^2S, 20^1HY, 20^UGS, 20^1S, 32^1G,

	Starts	1st	2nd	3rd	Win & Pl
Chases	6	3	1	0	58737
Career Total	23	8	3	2	99213
147	3/03	Kels	4m	C(0-135)HCh	GD	£30856
136	2/03	Ayr	2m4f	B(0-145)HCh	SFT	£13312
136	1/03	Ayr	2m4f	B(0-140)HCh	HVY	£12096
134	2/02	Newc	2m4f	B(0-140)HCh	SFT	£8853
134	4/01	Asct	2m3f110yC(0-130)HCh	SFT	£14040
122	1/01	Newc	2m4f	E Ch	HVY	£3120
110	11/00	Kels	2m6f110yE Ch	SFT	£3315
89	5/00	Weth	2m4f110yD Hdl	G-F	£3432
				Total win prize-money £89026		

Going: Sf: 2-4 GS: 0-1 Gd: 1-1 GF: - Fm: 0-0
Distance: 2m/2m3: 0-0 **2m4-2m7: 2-5** 3m+: 1-1
Track: **LH: 3-6** RH: 0-0 **Tight: 1-1** Gall: 0-0
Aids: Bl: 0-0 Vi: 0-0 Tstrap: 0-0
Best Rating: 147 3/03 Kels 4m   good   Ch

Useful chaser; most of best form over 2m 4f, but managed

---

to win a valuable chase over 4m at Kelso in March 2003; best on soft ground; has tended to make mistakes in the past.

A Right Set Two

99

11-y-o ch g Island Set (USA)-Super Sol (Rolfe (USA))
R M Carson R M Carson

Placings:PF34/12/40/2-PP   (3926)
2002/03: 20^PS, 20^PG,

	Starts	1st	2nd	3rd	Win & Pl
Hurdles	1	0	0	0	0
Chases	1	0	0	0	0
Career Total	11	1	2	1	6296
108	5/99	Hntg	3m	F(0-100)HCh	G-F	£3406
				Total win prize-money £3407		

Going: Sf: 0-1 GS: 0-0 Gd: 0-1 GF: - Fm: 0-0
Distance: 2m/2m3: 0-0 2m4-2m7: 0-0 3m+: 0-0
Track: LH: 0-0 RH: 0-1 Tight: 0-1 Gall: 0-1
Aids: Bl: 0-0 Vi: 0-0 Tstrap: 0-0
Best Rating: 108 5/99 Hntg 3m   gd-fm Ch

A Romp Too Far (IRE)

7-y-o b g Eurobus-Saxa Princess (IRE) (Lancastrian)
K C Bailey Have Fun Racing Partnership

Placings:*0*6-POPP   (4116)
2002/03: 21^PS, 25^PS, 20^PS, 21^PG,

	Starts	1st	2nd	3rd	Win & Pl
Hurdles	4	0	0	0	
Career Total	6	0	0	0	

Going: Sf: 0-3 GS: 0-0 Gd: 0-1 GF: - Fm: 0-0
Distance: 2m/2m3: 0-0 2m4-2m7: 0-3 3m+: 0-1
Track: LH: 0-2 RH: 0-2 Tight: 0-0 Gall: 0-2
Aids: Bl: 0-0 Vi: 0-0 Tstrap: 0-0
Best Rating: 98   10/01 Chel 2m110y   good   NHF

A Thousand Dreams (IRE)

97 (94h)   (70h) 65

13-y-o b g Aristocracy-Ardellis Lady (Pollerton)
L Waring Mrs J Waring

Placings:*0*3446*0/000/0144/0015*P/00P/0006500000065-015PP64P   (1231)
2002/03: 19^0G, 18^1GF, 16^5G, 16^PGF, 16^PGF, 16^6GF, 18^4GF, 16^PFG,

	Starts	1st	2nd	3rd	Win & Pl
Hurdles	2	0	0	0	
Chases	6	3	0	0	2268
Career Total	42	3	0	1	8203
65	6/02	Font	2m2f	G(0-90)HCh	G-F	£2268
95	1/00	Ludl	2m	E Ch	GD	£3209
80	7/98	Wolv	2m	E(0-105)HHdl	G-F	£2144
				Total win prize-money £7622		

Going: Sf: 0-0 GS: 0-0 Gd: 0-3 GF: - Fm: 1-5
Distance: 2m/2m3: 1-7 2m4-2m7: 0-3 3m+: 0-0
Track: LH: 0-6 RH: 0-1 Tight: 1-6 Gall: 0-0
Aids: Bl: 0-0 Vi: 0-0 Tstrap: 0-0
Best Rating: 95   1/00 Ludl 2m   good   Ch

Plating class hurdler who races at around two miles. Has won over fences at two miles. Acts on a sound surface.

A Vendre (FR)

81   65

4-y-o b/br g Kendor (FR)-Waaria (Shareef Dancer (USA))
M C Pipe (C E Brittain 23/9) Eminence Grise Partnership

Placings:4P60   (3445)
2002/03: 17^4GS, 16^PS, 16^6HY, 16^0HY,

	Starts	1st	2nd	3rd	Win & Pl
Hurdles	4	0	0	0	0
Career Total	4	0	0	0	0

Going: Sf: 0-3 GS: 0-1 Gd: 0-0 GF: - Fm: 0-0
Distance: 2m/2m3: 0-4 2m4-2m7: 0-0 3m+: 0-0
Track: LH: 0-3 RH: 0-1 Tight: 0-1 Gall: 0-0
Aids: Bl: 0-0 Vi: 0-0 Tstrap: 0-0
Best Rating: 70   11/02 Tntn 2m1f   gd-sft Hdl

A Verse To Order

12-y-o b g Rymer-Born Bossy (Eborneezer)
Mrs P Ford K R Ford

Placings:*006050*P5/PP-P   (0719)
2002/03: 20^PG,

	Starts	1st	2nd	3rd	Win & Pl
Hurdles	1	0	0	0	
Career Total	11	0	0	0	

Going: Sf: 0-0 GS: 0-0 Gd: 0-1 GF: - Fm: 0-0
Distance: 2m/2m3: 0-0 2m4-2m7: 0-1 3m+: 0-0
Track: LH: 0-0 RH: 0-0 Tight: 0-0 Gall: 0-0
Aids: Bl: 0-0 Vi: 0-0 Tstrap: 0-1
Best Rating: 80   10/97 Tntn 2m1f   gd-fm NHF

A-Time Of Peace (IRE)

10-y-o b m Royal Fountain-Sparkle For Me (Baragoi)
R Lee C R Elliott & R Brereton

Placings:*00*/PPC-P   (0104)
2002/03: 20^PGF,

	Starts	1st	2nd	3rd	Win & Pl
Chases	1	0	0	0	
Career Total	6	0	0	0	

Going: Sf: 0-0 GS: 0-0 Gd: 0-0 GF: - Fm: 0-1
Distance: 2m/2m3: 0-0 2m4-2m7: 0-1 3m+: 0-0
Track: LH: 0-0 RH: 0-1 Tight: 0-1 Gall: 0-0
Aids: Bl: 0-0 Vi: 0-0 Tstrap: 0-0
Best Rating: 82   10/99 Tntn 2m1f   gd-fm NHF

Aavasaksa (FR)

10-y-o b g Dancing Spree (USA)-Afkaza (FR) (Labus (FR))
M F Harris Miss Sam Booker

Placings:F0F/4550P0PP/1145113F324/5R0R/RR   (4345)
2002/03: 16^RS, 16^RGF,

	Starts	1st	2nd	3rd	Win & Pl
Hurdles	2	0	0	0	
Career Total	28	4	1	2	10685
97	9/98	Sedg	2m110y D Ch		G-F	£3510
96	9/98	Font	2m2f110yF Hdl		GD	£2372
100	7/98	Wolv	2m	G Hdl		G-F	£1447

96 7/98 Wolv 2m G Hdl GD £1528
Total win prize-money £8860

Going:	Sf: 0-1	GS: 0-0	Gd: 0-0	GF: -	Fm: 0-1
Distance:	2m/2m3: 0-2	2m4-2m7: 0-0	3m+: 0-0		
Track:	LH: 0-2	RH: 0-0	Tight: 0-0	Gall: 0-0	
Aids:	Bl: 0-0	Vi: 0-0	Tstrap: 0-0		
Best Rating:	104	12/98	NAbb 2m5f110y	soft	Ch

Ababou (FR)

7-y-o ch g Synefos (USA)-Racine Carree (FR) (Dom Racine (FR))
Mrs Lucy Latchford Mrs Lucy Latchford

Placings:00P6/0405046P/6 (4592)
2002/03: 25^{6}G,

	Starts	1st	2nd	3rd	Win & Pl
Chases	1	0	0	0	0
Career Total	13	0	0	0	1008

Going:	Sf: 0-0	GS: 0-0	Gd: 0-1	GF: -	Fm: 0-0
Distance:	2m/2m3: 0-0	2m4-2m7: 0-0	3m+: 0-1		
Track:	LH: 0-1	RH: 0-0	Tight: 0-0	Gall: 0-0	
Aids:	Bl: 0-0	Vi: 0-0	Tstrap: 0-0		
Best Rating:	63	4/03	Hexm 3m1f	good	Ch

Abajany
101   93
9-y-o b g Akarad (FR)-Miss Ivory Coast (USA) (Sir Ivor)
R J Baker M Channon

Placings:P45/260/3/4/03000-060 (0518)
2002/03: 17^{0}GF, 16^{6}G, 17^{0}G,

	Starts	1st	2nd	3rd	Win & Pl
Hurdles	3	0	0	0	0
Career Total	16	0	1	2	3467

Going:	Sf: 0-0	GS: 0-0	Gd: 0-2	GF: -	Fm: 0-1
Distance:	2m/2m3: 0-3	2m4-2m7: 0-0	3m+: 0-0		
Track:	LH: 0-2	RH: 0-1	Tight: 0-1	Gall: 0-0	
Aids:	Bl: 0-0	Vi: 0-0	Tstrap: 0-0		
Best Rating:	106	10/98	Plum 2m1f	good	Hdl

A Flat winner, he has shown bits and pieces of form over timber and looks to need a sound surface.

Abalvino (FR)
111   136
9-y-o ch g Sillery (USA)-Abalvina (FR) (Abdos)
P R Webber I M S Racing & Noel Cronin

Placings:3130/45/F3124321/15132U0-F332210 (4458)
2002/03: 16^{6}FS, 16^{3}S, 16^{8}HY, 16^{2}G, 16^{2}S, 17^{1}S, 16^{0}G,

	Starts	1st	2nd	3rd	Win & Pl
Chases	7	1	2	2	20070
Career Total	28	6	5	7	51533
136 2/03 Newb	2m1f	C(0-135)HCh		SFT	£8190
130 12/01 Strf	2m1f110yD(0-120)HCh			SFT	£8580
130 5/01 Hntg	2m110y	E Ch		GD	£3752
130 4/01 MRas	2m1f110yD Ch			G-S	£4849
117 12/00 Leic	2m	E(0-105)HCh		G-S	£3133
114 1/99 Towc	2m	H NHF		HVY	£1420

Total win prize-money £29924

Going:	Sf: 1-4	GS: 0-1	Gd: 0-2	GF: -	Fm: 0-0
Distance:	2m/2m3: 1-7	2m4-2m7: 0-0	3m+: 0-0		
Track:	LH: 1-6	RH: 0-1	Tight: 0-1	Gall: 1-2	
Aids:	Bl: 0-0	Vi: 0-0	Tstrap: 1-7		

Best Rating: 136 2/03 Newb 2m1f soft Ch
Fair handicap chaser; effective at around two miles and acts on good and soft ground; wears a tongue strap.

Abandon Hope
64f   21f
7-y-o ch m Jupiter Island-Band Of Hope (USA) (Dixieland Band (USA))
W Clay P Riley & N Brown

Placings:0-00 (0560)
2002/03: 16^{8}GS, 17^{0}GF,

	Starts	1st	2nd	3rd	Win & Pl
NH Flat	2	0	0	0	0
Career Total	3	0	0	0	0

Going:	Sf: 0-0	GS: 0-1	Gd: 0-0	GF: -	Fm: 0-1
Distance:	2m/2m3: 0-2	2m4-2m7: 0-0	3m+: 0-0		
Track:	LH: 0-1	RH: 0-1	Tight: 0-1	Gall: 0-0	
Aids:	Bl: 0-0	Vi: 0-0	Tstrap: 0-0		
Best Rating:	21	6/02	Hrfd 2m1f	gd-fm	NHF

Abbey Days (IRE)
93   71
6-y-o ch g Be My Native (USA)-Abbey Emerald (Baptism)
Mrs H Dalton Trevor Hemmings

Placings:40F5 (4635)
2002/03: 16^{4}HY, 16^{0}GS, 19^{6}G, 19^{5}GF,

	Starts	1st	2nd	3rd	Win & Pl
NH Flat	2	0	0	0	0
Hurdles	2	0	0	0	0
Career Total	4	0	0	0	0

Going:	Sf: 0-1	GS: 0-1	Gd: 0-1	GF: -	Fm: 0-1
Distance:	2m/2m3: 0-3	2m4-2m7: 0-1	3m+: 0-0		
Track:	LH: 0-3	RH: 0-1	Tight: 0-1	Gall: 0-1	
Aids:	Bl: 0-0	Vi: 0-0	Tstrap: 0-0		
Best Rating:	77	12/02	Donc 2m110y	gd-sft	NHF

Abbey Lad

13-y-o b g State Diplomacy (USA)-Another Pin (Pinza)
Mrs M Reveley (Ernie Fenwick 29/4) Ernie Fenwick

Placings:2/0-R (0785)
2002/03: 20^{0}G, 26^{8}GF,

	Starts	1st	2nd	3rd	Win & Pl
Chases	2	0	0	0	0
Career Total	3	0	1	0	308

Going:	Sf: 0-0	GS: 0-0	Gd: 0-0	GF: -	Fm: 0-1
Distance:	2m/2m3: 0-0	2m4-2m7: 0-1	3m+: 0-1		
Track:	LH: 0-2	RH: 0-0	Tight: 0-0	Gall: 0-1	
Aids:	Bl: 0-1	Vi: 0-0	Tstrap: 0-0		
Best Rating:	102	3/98	Newc 2m4f	gd-fm	Ch

Abbey's Girl (IRE)

7-y-o b m Elbio-Abbey Trinity (IRE) (Tender King)
K J Burke Kevin M Bourke

Placings:000/00/F (3521)
2002/03: 22^{8}GS,

	Starts	1st	2nd	3rd	Win & Pl
Chases	1	0	0	0	
Career Total	6	0	0	0	

Going:	Sf: 0-0	GS: 0-1	Gd: 0-0	GF: -	Fm: 0-0
Distance:	2m/2m3: 0-0	2m4-2m7: 0-1	3m+: 0-0		
Track:	LH: 0-1	RH: 0-0	Tight: 0-0	Gall: 0-0	
Aids:	Bl: 0-0	Vi: 0-0	Tstrap: 0-0		
Best Rating:	46	4/00	Cork 2m	soft	Hdl

Abbeyknock Boy (IRE)
97(94h)   (75h)80
6-y-o b/br g Alphabatim (USA)-Haha Dash (IRE) (Lord Ha Ha)
M F Harris (Ian Williams 20/12) Pat Owens

Placings:4/04U-0034P00303 (4349)
2002/03: 22^{9}G, 23^{9}GS, 24^{3}G, 22^{4}GF, 24^{8}G, 24^{0}S, 20^{9}GS, 20^{9}GS, 16^{6}G, 24^{3}GF,

	Starts	1st	2nd	3rd	Win & Pl
Hurdles	6	0	0	1	335
Chases	4	0	0	2	1206
Career Total	14	0	0	3	1867

Going:	Sf: 0-1	GS: 0-3	Gd: 0-4	GF: -	Fm: 0-2
Distance:	2m/2m3: 0-1	2m4-2m7: 0-4	3m+: 0-5		
Track:	LH: 0-8	RH: 0-2	Tight: 0-2	Gall: 0-0	
Aids:	Bl: 0-0	Vi: 0-1	Tstrap: 0-0		
Best Rating:	80	3/03	Wwck 3m110y	gd-fm	Ch

Moderate chaser; poor maiden over hurdles; stays three miles; effective at fast ground.

Abbots Court (IRE)
79   63
8-y-o b g Hallowed Turf (USA)-Coronea Sea Queen (IRE) (Bassompierre)
R H Alner H Wellstead

Placings:0/PP-4 (0060)
2002/03: 26^{4}G,

	Starts	1st	2nd	3rd	Win & Pl
Chases	1	0	0	0	260
Career Total	4	0	0	0	260

Going:	Sf: 0-0	GS: 0-0	Gd: 0-1	GF: -	Fm: 0-0
Distance:	2m/2m3: 0-0	2m4-2m7: 0-0	3m+: 0-1		
Track:	LH: 0-0	RH: 0-1	Tight: 0-1	Gall: 0-0	
Aids:	Bl: 0-0	Vi: 0-0	Tstrap: 0-0		
Best Rating:	95	3/01	Hntg 2m110y	soft	NHF

Aberfoyle Park (IRE)
106   117
9-y-o b g Riverhead (USA)-Go For Doe (Whistling Deer)
R H Alner A J Sendell

Placings:34FP (3788)
2002/03: 20^{0}G, 24^{4}G, 21^{8}FGS, 19^{8}G,

	Starts	1st	2nd	3rd	Win & Pl
Chases	4	0	0	1	1145
Career Total	4	0	0	1	1145

Going:	Sf: 0-0	GS: 0-1	Gd: 0-3	GF: -	Fm: 0-1
Distance:	2m/2m3: 0-1	2m4-2m7: 0-2	3m+: 0-1		

Track:	LH: 0-0 RH: 0-4 Tight: 0-0 Gall: 0-0
Aids:	Bl: 0-0 Vi: 0-0 Tstrap: 0-0
Best Rating:	117 11/02 Kemp 3m good Ch

Three-time point winner who was a beaten favourite on his debut under Rules at Kempton in November; has been out of luck since.

Abernant Lady
75   40
6-y-o gr m Absalom-Hosting (Thatching)
A G Newcombe   Derek Walker

Placings:4   (1444)
2002/03: 19⁴F,

	Starts	1st	2nd	3rd	Win & Pl
Hurdles	1	0	0	0	310
Career Total	1	0	0	0	310

Going:	Sf: 0-0 GS: 0-0 Gd: 0-0 GF: - Fm: 0-1
Distance:	2m/2m3: 0-1 2m4-2m7: 0-0 3m+: 0-0
Track:	LH: 0-0 RH: 0-1 Tight: 0-0 Gall: 0-0
Aids:	Bl: 0-0 Vi: 0-0 Tstrap: 0-0
Best Rating:	40 10/02 Extr 2m3f firm Hdl

Aberthatch (FR)
104   102
4-y-o b f Thatching-Academy Angel (FR) (Royal Academy (USA))
M J Ryan   Bernard H Bosomworth

Placings:32   (2233)
2002/03: 16³GS, 16²S,

	Starts	1st	2nd	3rd	Win & Pl
Hurdles	2	0	1	1	2786
Career Total	2	0	1	1	2786

Going:	Sf: 0-1 GS: 0-1 Gd: 0-0 GF: - Fm: 0-0
Distance:	2m/2m3: 0-2 2m4-2m7: 0-0 3m+: 0-0
Track:	LH: 0-0 RH: 0-2 Tight: 0-0 Gall: 0-1
Aids:	Bl: 0-0 Vi: 0-0 Tstrap: 0-0
Best Rating:	98 11/02 Hntg 2m110y gd-sft Hdl

Moderate performer on the Flat, she has shown ability in novice hurdles.

Abinitio Lady (IRE)
98   103
8-y-o br m Be My Native (USA)-Chake-Chake (Goldhill)
Mrs M Reveley   Michael Ahern

Placings:30432/12/32FU-6431   (0581)
2002/03: 16⁶G, 20⁴GS, 16³HY, 16¹G,

	Starts	1st	2nd	3rd	Win & Pl
Hurdles	4	1	0	1	3073
Career Total	15	2	3	4	9659
78	6/02	Hexm	2m110y	E Hdl	GD	£2541
93	7/00	Tipp	2m	NHF	G-F	£3312
			Total win prize-money £5853

Going:	Sf: 0-1 GS: 0-1 Gd: 1-2 GF: - Fm: 0-0
Distance:	2m/2m3: 1-3 2m4-2m7: 0-1 3m+: 0-0
Track:	LH: 1-4 RH: 0-0 Tight: 0-0 Gall: 0-0
Aids:	Bl: 0-0 Vi: 0-0 Tstrap: 0-0
Best Rating:	103 2/02 Hntg 2m110y soft Hdl

Moderate hurdler; fast-ground bumper winner in Ireland; won a weak novices hurdle at Hexham in June 2002; effective at two miles on good ground.

Able Native (IRE)
109(101c)   (95c)111
6-y-o b m Thatching-Native Joy (IRE) (Be My Native (USA))
R C Guest (N B Mason 16/10) N B Mason

Placings:204/0051342122055133-24560616223   (4566)
2002/03: 17²GS, 20⁴G, 16⁵G, 17⁶G, 20⁰G, 20⁶GF, 24¹G, 19⁶G, 16²G, 16²S, 20³GF,

	Starts	1st	2nd	3rd	Win & Pl
Hurdles	7	0	2	1	2885
Chases	4	1	1	0	5669
Career Total	30	4	7	4	24755
95	10/02	Fknm	3m110y	F(0-90)HCh	GD	£4007
113	3/02	Newc	2m4f	E(0-110)HHdl	HVY	£3493
104	1/02	Fknm	2m	E(0-110)HHdl	SFT	£2408
100	10/01	Fknm	2m	F(0-105)HHdl	SFT	£3342
				Total win prize-money £13252

Going:	Sf: 0-1 GS: 0-1 Gd: 1-7 GF: - Fm: 0-2
Distance:	2m/2m3: 0-5 2m4-2m7: 0-5 3m+: 1-1
Track:	LH: 1-8 RH: 0-3 Tight: 1-6 Gall: 0-0
Aids:	Bl: 0-1 Vi: 0-0 Tstrap: 1-7
Best Rating:	113 3/02 Newc 2m4f heavy Hdl

Moderate hurdler; goes well with cut and likes a sharp track; best over two miles, stays two and a half; goes well at Fakenham, where she won over fences in October 2002; acts on ground good and softer.

Ablington Down (IRE)
67   34
8-y-o ch m Camden Town-Quarry Run (Parva Stella)
J W Mullins   Mrs Sally Mullins

Placings:0   (0574)
2002/03: 22⁰G,

	Starts	1st	2nd	3rd	Win & Pl
Hurdles	1	0	0	0	
Career Total	1	0	0	0	

Going:	Sf: 0-0 GS: 0-0 Gd: 0-1 GF: - Fm: 0-0
Distance:	2m/2m3: 0-0 2m4-2m7: 0-1 3m+: 0-0
Track:	LH: 0-1 RH: 0-0 Tight: 0-0 Gall: 0-0
Aids:	Bl: 0-0 Vi: 0-1 Tstrap: 0-0
Best Rating:	34 6/02 NAbb 2m6f good Hdl

Above The Clouds
12-y-o g g Neltino-Goodnight Master (Gay Fandango (USA))
Mrs M Rigg   Mrs M Rigg

Placings:0/P/P/P   (0312)
2002/03: 21⁰PG,

	Starts	1st	2nd	3rd	Win & Pl
Chases	1	0	0	0	
Career Total	4	0	0	0	

Going:	Sf: 0-0 GS: 0-0 Gd: 0-1 GF: - Fm: 0-0
Distance:	2m/2m3: 0-0 2m4-2m7: 0-1 3m+: 0-0
Track:	LH: 0-0 RH: 0-1 Tight: 0-1 Gall: 0-0
Aids:	Bl: 0-0 Vi: 0-0 Tstrap: 0-0
Best Rating:	0 5/02 Folk 2m5f good Ch

Above The Cut (USA)
108   99
11-y-o ch g Topsider (USA)-Placer Queen (Habitat)
C P Morlock   J P M & J W Cook

Placings:25662152/216/64/253606645/22244/0005201421 05-061230363   (4218)
2002/03: 24⁰GF, 19⁶GF, 24¹G, 22²GF, 20³GF, 26⁰GF, 22³GS, 24⁶G, 26³GF,

	Starts	1st	2nd	3rd	Win & Pl
Hurdles	9	1	1	3	4976
Career Total	48	5	11	4	27801
99	7/02	MRas	3m	G(0-95)HHdl	GD	£2289
99	12/01	Tntn	3m110y	D(0-120)HHdl	G-S	£3510
99	10/01	Ludl	3m	F(0-95)HHdl	G-F	£3209
110	5/97	Towc	2m	D(0-120)HHdl	GD	£2840
106	3/97	Ludl	2m	E(0-115)HHdl	G-F	£2584
				Total win prize-money £14433

Going:	Sf: 0-0 GS: 0-1 Gd: 1-2 GF: - Fm: 0-6
Distance:	2m/2m3: 0-1 2m4-2m7: 0-3 3m+: 1-5
Track:	LH: 0-4 RH: 1-5 Tight: 1-5 Gall: 0-1
Aids:	Bl: 0-0 Vi: 0-0 Tstrap: 0-0
Best Rating:	110 5/97 Towc 2m good Hdl

Plating class hurdler; in good form in 2003 registering back-to-back wins at Exeter and Newton Abbot in May and June; fair handicap chaser; does not want the ground too soft; acts on a sound surface; stays 3m 3f.

Absinther
81   66
6-y-o b g Presidium-Heavenly Queen (Scottish Reel)
M R Bosley   Mrs Jean M O Connor

Placings:00   (4117)
2002/03: 16⁶G, 16⁰G,

	Starts	1st	2nd	3rd	Win & Pl
Hurdles	2	0	0	0	
Career Total	2	0	0	0	

Going:	Sf: 0-0 GS: 0-0 Gd: 0-2 GF: - Fm: 0-0
Distance:	2m/2m3: 0-2 2m4-2m7: 0-0 3m+: 0-0
Track:	LH: 0-1 RH: 0-1 Tight: 0-0 Gall: 0-2
Aids:	Bl: 0-0 Vi: 0-0 Tstrap: 0-0
Best Rating:	66 12/02 Newb 2m110y good Hdl

Absolute Majority
89   76
8-y-o ch g Absalom-Shall We Run (Hotfoot)
H S Howe   George Searle

Placings:0/63B/4P   (0925)
2002/03: 17⁴GF, 17⁹GF,

	Starts	1st	2nd	3rd	Win & Pl
Hurdles	2	0	0	0	289
Career Total	6	0	0	1	645

Going:	Sf: 0-0 GS: 0-0 Gd: 0-0 GF: - Fm: 0-2
Distance:	2m/2m3: 0-2 2m4-2m7: 0-0 3m+: 0-0
Track:	LH: 0-2 RH: 0-0 Tight: 0-2 Gall: 0-0
Aids:	Bl: 0-0 Vi: 0-0 Tstrap: 0-1
Best Rating:	87 6/00 NAbb 2m1f gd-fm Hdl

Absolutely Hopeful
89
10-y-o ch g Nearly A Hand-Owena Deep (Deep Run)

C P Morlock Michael Padfield

Placings:304/0/022PP/2FP5556PP/4536410P-FP   (0521)
2002/03: 24FG, 22PG,

	Starts	1st	2nd	3rd	Win & Pl
Hurdles	2	0	0	0	
Career Total	28	1	3	2	6063

89   2/02   Folk   2m6f110y   E(0-110)HHdl
SFT £2555

Total win prize-money £2555

Going:	Sf: 0-0 GS: 0-0 Gd: 0-2 GF: - Fm: 0-0
Distance:	2m/2m3: 0-0 2m4-2m7: 0-1 3m+: 0-1
Track:	LH: 0-2 RH: 0-0 Tight: 0-1 Gall: 0-0
Aids:	Bl: 0-2 Vi: 0-0 Tstrap: 0-2
Best Rating:	89 2/02 Folk 2m6f110y soft Hdl

Abzuson

100

6-y-o b g Abzu-Mellouise (Handsome Sailor)
J R Norton Abzuson Syndicate

Placings:24-16FU2   (3865)
2002/03: 16IG, 16RS, 19FGS, 20UHY, 19QGS,

	Starts	1st	2nd	3rd	Win & Pl
NH Flat	2	1	0	0	1624
Hurdles	3	0	1	0	1144
Career Total	7	1	2	0	3262

102   4/02   Hexm   2m110y   H NHF   GD   £1624
Total win prize-money £1624

Going:	Sf: 0-2 GS: 0-2 Gd: 1-1 GF: - Fm: 0-0
Distance:	2m/2m3: 1-2 2m4-2m7: 0-3 3m+: 0-0
Track:	LH: 1-5 RH: 0-0 Tight: 0-0 Gall: 0-1
Aids:	Bl: 0-0 Vi: 0-0 Tstrap: 0-0
Best Rating:	102 4/02 Hexm 2m110y good NHF

Bumper winner at Hexham, looked a threat when last flight casualty at Newcastle in January; stuck on well when runner-up at Doncaster the following month.

Accademic (IRE)

95   **95**

6-y-o ch g Accordion-Giolla s Bone (Pitpan)
S E H Sherwood Lady Thompson

Placings:05P   (3629)
2002/03: 16QG, 19SGS, 24PS,

	Starts	1st	2nd	3rd	Win & Pl
NH Flat	1	0	0	0	0
Hurdles	2	0	0	0	0
Career Total	3	0	0	0	0

Going:	Sf: 0-1 GS: 0-1 Gd: 0-1 GF: - Fm: 0-0
Distance:	2m/2m3: 0-2 2m4-2m7: 0-0 3m+: 0-1
Track:	LH: 0-0 RH: 0-3 Tight: 0-0 Gall: 0-0
Aids:	Bl: 0-0 Vi: 0-0 Tstrap: 0-0
Best Rating:	95 12/02 Extr 2m3f gd-sft Hdl

Accepting

105   **104**

6-y-o b g Mtoto-D Azy (Persian Bold)
J Mackie Ms Caroline F Breay

Placings:0350   (2494)
2002/03: 22QS, 20QS, 20SS, 19QS,

	Starts	1st	2nd	3rd	Win & Pl
Hurdles	4	0	0	1	506
Career Total	4	0	0	1	506

Moderate hurdler; stayer on the level, and there seems no end to his stamina over jumps; stays three miles-three; acts well on fast ground.

Access Overseas

96   **84d**

6-y-o b m Access Ski-Access Advantage (Infantry)
J D Frost Miss Elaine D Williams

Placings:45/1U4040-3340   (1932)
2002/03: 22QG, 173F, 16QG, 17QGS,

	Starts	1st	2nd	3rd	Win & Pl
Hurdles	4	0	0	2	928
Career Total	12	1	0	2	3203

91   6/01   NAbb   2m1f   G Hdl   GD   £2275
Total win prize-money £2275

Going:	Sf: 0-0 GS: 0-1 Gd: 0-2 GF: - Fm: 0-1
Distance:	2m/2m3: 0-3 2m4-2m7: 0-1 3m+: 0-0
Track:	LH: 0-2 RH: 0-2 Tight: 0-3 Gall: 0-0
Aids:	Bl: 0-0 Vi: 0-0 Tstrap: 0-0
Best Rating:	91 6/01 NAbb 2m1f good Hdl

Plating-class hurdler at around two miles. Acts on good ground.

Accipiter

96f   **102f**

4-y-o b g Polar Falcon (USA)-Accuracy (Gunner B)
G B Balding Miss B Swire

Placings:53   (3789)
2002/03: 16SGS, 17QG,

	Starts	1st	2nd	3rd	Win & Pl
NH Flat	2	0	0	1	293
Career Total	2	0	0	1	293

Going:	Sf: 0-0 GS: 0-1 Gd: 0-1 GF: - Fm: 0-0
Distance:	2m/2m3: 0-2 2m4-2m7: 0-0 3m+: 0-0
Track:	LH: 0-0 RH: 0-2 Tight: 0-0 Gall: 0-0
Aids:	Bl: 0-0 Vi: 0-0 Tstrap: 0-0
Best Rating:	96 2/03 Winc 2m gd-sft NHF

Out of the useful staying mare Accuracy and a half-brother to several decent performers including Brave Tornado; ran a race full of promise on his debut at Wincanton in February and occupied same poistion at Hereford a week later.

Accordion Girl (IRE)

5-y-o b m Accordion-Triple D Or (Golden Love)
J W Mullins Denis J Barry

Placings:3   (4760)
2002/03: 18QGF,

	Starts	1st	2nd	3rd	Win & Pl
NH Flat	1	0	0	1	279
Career Total	1	0	0	1	279

Going:	Sf: 0-0 GS: 0-0 Gd: 0-0 GF: - Fm: 0-1
Distance:	2m/2m3: 0-1 2m4-2m7: 0-0 3m+: 0-0
Track:	LH: 0-1 RH: 0-0 Tight: 0-1 Gall: 0-0
Aids:	Bl: 0-0 Vi: 0-0 Tstrap: 0-0
Best Rating:	78 4/03 Font 2m2f110y gd-fm NHF

Fair debut in a modest bumper at Fontwell in April 2003.

Accystan

86   **77**

8-y-o ch g Efisio-Amia (CAN) (Nijinsky (CAN))
A Crook G Heap

Placings:241204/0/05/000PP-350   (0562)
2002/03: 16QG, 175HY, 19QGF,

	Starts	1st	2nd	3rd	Win & Pl
Hurdles	3	0	0	1	354
Career Total	17	1	2	1	3361

89   11/98   Catt   2m   G Hdl   GD   £1509
Total win prize-money £1509

Going:	Sf: 0-1 GS: 0-0 Gd: 0-1 GF: - Fm: 0-1
Distance:	2m/2m3: 0-2 2m4-2m7: 0-1 3m+: 0-0
Track:	LH: 0-2 RH: 0-1 Tight: 0-2 Gall: 0-0
Aids:	Bl: 0-0 Vi: 0-0 Tstrap: 0-0
Best Rating:	94 2/99 Muss 2m firm Hdl

Acertack (IRE)

89   **65**

6-y-o b g Supreme Leader-Ask The Madam (Strong Gale)
R Rowe Keith Hunter

Placings:000   (3430)
2002/03: 19QGS, 16QG, 18QS,

	Starts	1st	2nd	3rd	Win & Pl
Hurdles	3	0	0	0	
Career Total	3	0	0	0	

Going:	Sf: 0-1 GS: 0-1 Gd: 0-1 GF: - Fm: 0-0
Distance:	2m/2m3: 0-3 2m4-2m7: 0-0 3m+: 0-0
Track:	LH: 0-3 RH: 0-0 Tight: 0-1 Gall: 0-2
Aids:	Bl: 0-0 Vi: 0-0 Tstrap: 0-0
Best Rating:	65 12/02 Newb 2m110y good Hdl

Achilles Wings (USA)

89   **127**

7-y-o b g Irish River (FR)-Shirley Valentine (Shirley Heights)
Miss K M George Exterior Profiles Ltd

Placings:20/43P41U1153-30P   (4475)
2002/03: 16QS, 16QGS, 20PG,

	Starts	1st	2nd	3rd	Win & Pl
Hurdles	3	0	0	1	1243
Career Total	15	3	1	3	16969

127   2/02   Winc   2m   D(0-125)HHdl   SFT   £3514
118   1/02   Winc   2m   D(0-125)HHdl   G-S   £6890
114   11/01   Hrfd   2m3f110yF(0-100)HHdl   GD   £2639
Total win prize-money £13043

Going:	Sf: 0-1 GS: 0-1 Gd: 0-1 GF: - Fm: 0-0
Distance:	2m/2m3: 0-2 2m4-2m7: 0-1 3m+: 0-0
Track:	LH: 0-2 RH: 0-1 Tight: 0-1 Gall: 0-0
Aids:	Bl: 0-0 Vi: 0-0 Tstrap: 0-0
Best Rating:	127 4/02 Chep 2m110y gd-sft Hdl

Decent handicap hurdler; he progressed well in 2001/02, being unfortunate not to complete a four-timer before being outclassed in the Kingwell Hurdle; has found life tough since; suited by two miles on soft ground and a flat, right-handed track.

Ackzo

95   **127**

10-y-o b g Ardross-Trimar Gold (Goldhill)
D McCain Mrs N L Spence

Placings: 3222112/52121P/6P/363PP-4PFP   (3774)
2002/03: 28⁴S, 29³HY, 30⁵G, 25⁵GS,

	Starts	1st	2nd	3rd	Win & Pl
Chases	4	0	0		1048
Career Total	24	4	6	3	79975
139 3/00	Uttx	4m2f		A HCh		GD £43500
120 1/00	Hntg	3m		E Ch		G-S £3562
125 4/99	Carl	2m4f110yE Hdl			GD £2654
125 2/99	Newc	2m4f		E Hdl		G-S £2536

Total win prize-money £52253

Going: Sf: 0-2 GS: 0-1 Gd: 0-1 GF: - Fm: 0-0
Distance: 2m/2m3: 0-0 2m4-2m7: 0-0 3m+: 0-4
Track: LH: 0-4 RH: 0-0 Tight: 0-1 Gall: 0-0
Aids: Bl: 0-4 Vi: 0-0 Tstrap: 0-0
Best Rating: 139 2/02 Newc 4m1f   soft   Ch

Useful staying chaser; at his best on a quick surface; stayed all day; usually wore blinkers. (DEAD)

Acoustic (IRE)
103(79h)   (88h)97
9-y-o br g Orchestra-Rambling Ivy (Mandalus)
O Brennan   Lady Anne Bentinck

Placings: 3/0054-4P446   (4589)
2002/03: 22⁴GS, 25⁵PS, 24⁴G, 23⁴GS, 25⁶G,

	Starts	1st	2nd	3rd	Win & Pl
Chases	5	0	0	0	1112
Career Total	10	0	0	1	1941

Going: Sf: 0-1 GS: 0-2 Gd: 0-2 GF: - Fm: 0-0
Distance: 2m/2m3: 0-0 2m4-2m7: 0-1 3m+: 0-4
Track: LH: 0-3 RH: 0-2 Tight: 0-0 Gall: 0-1
Aids: Bl: 0-0 Vi: 0-0 Tstrap: 0-0
Best Rating: 97 2/03 Leic 2m7f110y gd-sft Ch

A winning point-to-pointer, he has made little impact under Rules so far.

Acquitaine (USA)
68   51
4-y-o f Colonial Affair (USA)-Arctic Eclipse (USA) (Northern Dancer)
A G Newcombe   D Bass

Placings: P0   (1543)
2002/03: 16⁶G, 17⁹F,

	Starts	1st	2nd	3rd	Win & Pl
Hurdles	2	0	0	0	
Career Total	2	0	0	0	

Going: Sf: 0-0 GS: 0-0 Gd: 0-1 GF: - Fm: 0-1
Distance: 2m/2m3: 0-2 2m4-2m7: 0-0 3m+: 0-0
Track: LH: 0-1 RH: 0-0 Tight: 0-2 Gall: 0-0
Aids: Bl: 0-0 Vi: 0-0 Tstrap: 0-0
Best Rating: 51 10/02 Tntn 2m1f   firm   Hdl

Act In Time (IRE)
110(94h)   (95h)113
11-y-o b g Actinium (FR)-Anvil Chorus (Levanter)
T R George   Mrs G C McFerran

Placings: 0P/424/1P2251/515200/4U4415/1P501532-P4   (1801)
2002/03: 24⁵PGS, 26⁴S,

	Starts	1st	2nd	3rd	Win & Pl
Chases	2	0	0	0	388
Career Total	33	6	5	1	52193
118 12/01	Ludl	3m3f110yD(0-120)HCh			GD £7956

---

118 5/01	Sedg	3m4f	D(0-125)HCh	GD	£11163
118 2/01	Fknm	3m110y	F(0-100)HCh	SFT	£4046
121 12/99	Winc	3m1f110yC(0-130)HCh		SFT	£8976
125 4/99	Chel	2m5f	D(0-115)HCh	GD	£5836
106 12/98	Chel	2m5f	E(0-125)HCh	GD	£3452

Total win prize-money £41431

Going: Sf: 0-1 GS: 0-1 Gd: 0-0 GF: - Fm: 0-0
Distance: 2m/2m3: 0-0 2m4-2m7: 0-0 3m+: 0-2
Track: LH: 0-2 RH: 0-0 Tight: 0-2 Gall: 0-0
Aids: Bl: 0-0 Vi: 0-0 Tstrap: 0-0
Best Rating: 125 4/99 Chel 2m5f   good   Ch

Fair chaser; suited by three miles plus and best on good ground; an effective tool around the minor tracks; runner-up in amateur riders' novice hurdle at Exeter April 2003.

Active Account (USA)
74   39
6-y-o b/br g Unaccounted For (USA)-Ameritop (USA) (Topsider (USA))
Mrs H Dalton   Mrs Heather Dalton

Placings: 6P-0   (4117)
2002/03: 16⁶G,

	Starts	1st	2nd	3rd	Win & Pl
Hurdles	1	0	0	0	
Career Total	3	0	0	0	0

Going: Sf: 0-0 GS: 0-0 Gd: 0-1 GF: - Fm: 0-0
Distance: 2m/2m3: 0-1 2m4-2m7: 0-0 3m+: 0-0
Track: LH: 0-0 RH: 0-1 Tight: 0-0 Gall: 0-1
Aids: Bl: 0-0 Vi: 0-0 Tstrap: 0-0
Best Rating: 73 12/01 Muss 2m   good   NHF

Activist
91   100
5-y-o ch g Diesis-Shicklah (USA) (The Minstrel (CAN))
G M Moore   John Robson

Placings: 043326-312   (1498)
2002/03: 20³G, 20¹GF, 20²G,

	Starts	1st	2nd	3rd	Win & Pl
Hurdles	3	1	1		5473
Career Total	9	1	2	3	8822
105 9/02	Prth	2m4f110yD Hdl		G-F	£4290

Total win prize-money £4290

Going: Sf: 0-0 GS: 0-0 Gd: 0-2 GF: - Fm: 1-1
Distance: 2m/2m3: 0-0 2m4-2m7: 1-3 3m+: 0-0
Track: LH: 0-2 RH: 1-1 Tight: 0-0 Gall: 0-0
Aids: Bl: 0-0 Vi: 0-0 Tstrap: 0-0
Best Rating: 106 11/01 Weth 2m   good   Hdl

Winning stayer on the Flat; won at Perth in September 2002; wears cheekpieces; not entirely straightforward.

Ad Hoc (IRE)
115(105h)   (146h)162
9-y-o b g Strong Gale-Knockarctic (Quayside)
P F Nicholls   Sir Robert Ogden

Placings: 3111/FFP521/053B4-51233U1   (4791)
2002/03: 25⁵GS, 24¹HY, 24²G, 24³S, 24³G, 36⁴G, 29¹G,

	Starts	1st	2nd	3rd	Win & Pl
Hurdles	4	1	1		13658
Chases	3	1	0	1	95800
Career Total	22	6	2	4	250361
162 4/03	Sand	3m5f110yA HCh		GD	£87000

---

143 11/02	Asct	3m	D Hdl	HVY	£5109
162 4/01	Sand	3m5f110yA HCh		SFT	£72500
149 4/00	Ayr	3m1f	C HCh	GD	£21970
113 1/00	Ayr	2m5f110yD Ch		SFT	£3945
106 12/99	Leic	2m7f110yE Ch		G-F	£3613

Total win prize-money £194138

Going: Sf: 1-2 GS: 0-1 Gd: 1-4 GF: - Fm: 0-0
Distance: 2m/2m3: 0-0 2m4-2m7: 0-0 3m+: 2-7
Track: LH: 0-5 RH: 2-2 Tight: 0-1 Gall: 0-3
Aids: Bl: 0-0 Vi: 0-0 Tstrap: 0-0
Best Rating: 162 4/03 Sand 3m5f110y good Ch

Smart chaser; full of running when knocked out of the Grand National four out in 2002 and unseated in 2003; confined to hurdles in 2002/3 prior to finishing third in the National Hunt Handicap Chase at Cheltenham; ended season with win in attheraces Gold Cup, a race he won when it was the Whitbread in 2001; stays extended 3m 5f; acts on most types of ground.

Adalie
92(103h)   (91 h)89
9-y-o b m Absalom-Allied Newcastle (Crooner)
P J Hobbs (J Joseph 24/11) Jack Joseph

Placings: 001/0F32-0503213   (4154)
2002/03: 16⁶G, 20⁵G, 16⁶S, 16³HY, 16²GS, 18¹S, 16³G,

	Starts	1st	2nd	3rd	Win & Pl
Hurdles	5	1	0	1	3764
Chases	2	0	1	1	1822
Career Total	14	2	2	3	8750
91 3/03	Font	2m2f110y		F(0-100)HHdl	SFT £3367
105 4/00	NAbb	2m1f	H NHF		HVY £1771

Total win prize-money £5138

Going: Sf: 1-3 GS: 0-1 Gd: 0-3 GF: - Fm: 0-0
Distance: 2m/2m3: 1-6 2m4-2m7: 0-1 3m+: 0-0
Track: LH: 1-6 RH: 0-1 Tight: 1-3 Gall: 0-0
Aids: Bl: 0-0 Vi: 0-0 Tstrap: 0-0
Best Rating: 106 2/00 Kemp 2m   soft   NHF

Bumper winner; moderate hurdler; runner-up on chase debut; acts in soft ground; best at around two and a half miles.

Adalpour (IRE)
97   88+
5-y-o b g Kahyasi-Adalya (IRE) (Darshaan)
Miss J Feilden   Hoofbeats Racing Club

Placings: 02   (2728)
2002/03: 16⁶S, 16²HY,

	Starts	1st	2nd	3rd	Win & Pl
Hurdles	2	0	1	0	674
Career Total	2	0	1	0	674

Going: Sf: 0-2 GS: 0-0 Gd: 0-0 GF: - Fm: 0-0
Distance: 2m/2m3: 0-2 2m4-2m7: 0-0 3m+: 0-0
Track: LH: 0-1 RH: 0-1 Tight: 0-0 Gall: 0-1
Aids: Bl: 0-0 Vi: 0-0 Tstrap: 0-0
Best Rating: 88 12/02 Leic 2m   heavy   Hdl

Adamant Approach (IRE)
(121h)   (152h)150+
9-y-o b g Mandalus-Crash Approach (Crash Course)
W P Mullins   Greenstar Syndicate

Placings: 1/P2422/152413F35-41F1F   (4740a)
2002/03: 16⁴YS, 16¹HY, 16⁶G, 20¹GY, 20⁶G,

	Starts	1st	2nd	3rd	Win & Pl
Chases	5	2	0	0	16341
Career Total	20	5	4	2	99059

129	3/03	Cork	2m4f	Ch	G-Y	£9285
150	12/02	Punc	2m	Ch	HVY	£6773
139	1/02	Leop	2m	(0-140)HHdl	Y-S	£48251
107	10/01	Fair	2m	Hdl	GD	£5564
136	2/00	Leop	2m	NHF	YLD	£4140

Total win prize-money £74016

Going: Sf: 1-1 GS: 0-0 Gd: 0-2 GF: - Fm: 0-0
Distance: 2m/2m3: 1-3 2m4-2m7: 1-2 3m+: 0-0
Track: LH: 0-1 RH: 1-2 Tight: 0-0 Gall: 0-1
Aids: Bl: 0-0 Vi: 0-0 Tstrap: 0-0
Best Rating: 152 3/02 Chel 2m110y gd-sft Hdl

Very promising Irish-trained novice chaser and high-class hurdler; looked likely winner of Supreme Novices Hurdle at Cheltenham Festival in 2002 when falling at last; twice a winner over fences in 2002/2003 and fell in the Arkle in between; stays 2m 4f and suited by cut in the ground; races prominently.

Adamatic (IRE)

12-y-o b g Henbit (USA)-Arpal Magic (Master Owen)
Neil King   Mrs R N Jarvis

Placings: 241323/12213600/3F12U/P202F3/314132110/401 UP66PP/25U40-P   (0209)
2002/03: 16ᴾG,

	Starts	1st	2nd	3rd	Win & Pl
Chases	1	0	0	0	
Career Total	49	9	9	7	46452

125	6/00	Hexm	2m110y	D(0-125)HCh	G-F	£5915
117	10/99	Kels	2m1f	E(0-115)HCh	GD	£3127
109	10/99	Carl	2m	D(0-125)HCh	GD	£4535
107	7/99	Sedg	2m110y	E(0-115)HCh	G-F	£3488
109	6/99	Hexm	2m110y	D(0-125)HCh	SFT	£5572
104	1/98	Muss	2m	E Ch	GD	£2786
102	11/96	Kels	2m2f	D(0-125)HHdl	GD	£2736
75	5/96	Prth	2m110y	D Hdl	FRM	£2905
101	12/95	Muss	2m	H NHF	GD	£1446

Total win prize-money £32512

Going: Sf: 0-0 GS: 0-0 Gd: 0-1 GF: - Fm: 0-0
Distance: 2m/2m3: 0-2 2m4-2m7: 0-0 3m+: 0-0
Track: LH: 0-0 RH: 0-1 Tight: 0-0 Gall: 0-0
Aids: Bl: 0-0 Vi: 0-0 Tstrap: 0-0
Best Rating: 125 6/00 Hexm 2m110y gd-fm Ch

Added Dimension (IRE)
85   **33**
12-y-o b g Top Ville-Lassalia (Sallust)
N A Dunger   N A Dunger

Placings: P/P42636/031112/0/00/303/425014-F00   (4188)
2002/03: 20⁰G, 22⁰S, 28⁰G,

	Starts	1st	2nd	3rd	Win & Pl
Hurdles	3	0	0	0	
Career Total	28	4	3	4	12034

96	12/01	Towc	2m	G(0-95)HHdl	HVY	£1659
111	2/97	Tntn	2m1f	F(0-105)HHdl	GD	£1962
104	2/97	Hrfd	2m1f	F(0-105)HHdl	G-S	£2318
98	1/97	Folk	2m1f110y	F(0-105)HHdl	SFT	£2180

Total win prize-money £8120

Going: Sf: 0-0 GS: 0-0 Gd: 0-2 GF: - Fm: 0-0
Distance: 2m/2m3: 0-0 2m4-2m7: 0-2 3m+: 0-1
Track: LH: 0-1 RH: 0-2 Tight: 0-2 Gall: 0-1
Aids: Bl: 0-0 Vi: 0-0 Tstrap: 0-1
Best Rating: 111 3/97 Hrfd 2m1f good Hdl

Has had a patchy career, with relatively few runs and few wins; has worn a tongue-tie of lat; appears to like Towcester.

Adecco (IRE)
103   **104d**
4-y-o b g Eagle Eyed (USA)-Kharaliya (FR) (Doyoun)
Miss Venetia Williams (C Von Der Recke 24/10) N J Jones

Placings: 16P3   (2768)
2002/03: 16¹F, 16⁶GS, 16ᴾHY, 16³GS,

	Starts	1st	2nd	3rd	Win & Pl
Hurdles	4	1	0	1	4375
Career Total	4	1	0	1	4375

101	10/02	Ludl	2m	E Hdl	FRM	£3523

Total win prize-money £3523

Going: Sf: 0-1 GS: 0-2 Gd: 0-0 GF: - Fm: 1-1
Distance: 2m/2m3: 1-4 2m4-2m7: 0-0 3m+: 0-0
Track: LH: 0-1 RH: 1-3 Tight: 0-1 Gall: 0-0
Aids: Bl: 0-1 Vi: 0-0 Tstrap: 0-0
Best Rating: 101 10/02 Ludl 2m firm Hdl

A winner on the Flat in Germany. Bought by Venetia Williams after making a successful hurdling debut for Christian Von Der Recke at Ludlow October 2002. Found things a lot tougher subsequently.

Adelphi Boy (IRE)
103   **107**
7-y-o ch g Ballad Rock-Toda (Absalom)
M C Chapman   Barry Brown

Placings: 2   (0566)
2002/03: 17²GF,

	Starts	1st	2nd	3rd	Win & Pl
Hurdles	1	0	1	0	772
Career Total	1	0	1	0	772

Going: Sf: 0-0 GS: 0-1 Gd: 0-0 GF: - Fm: 0-0
Distance: 2m/2m3: 0-1 2m4-2m7: 0-0 3m+: 0-0
Track: LH: 0-0 RH: 0-1 Tight: 0-1 Gall: 0-0
Aids: Bl: 0-0 Vi: 0-0 Tstrap: 0-0
Best Rating: 100 6/02 MRas 2m1f110y gd-fm Hdl

Novice hurdler; successful on second start at Perth; acts on fast ground.

Adelphi Theatre (USA)
99   **121**
6-y-o b g Sadler s Wells (USA)-Truly Bound (USA) (In Reality)
R Rowe   The Encore Partnership

Placings: 312100-F600   (4367)
2002/03: 19ᶠGS, 18⁶G, 21⁰G, 20⁰G,

	Starts	1st	2nd	3rd	Win & Pl
Hurdles	4	0	0	0	313
Career Total	10	2	1	1	11796

127	12/01	Font	2m2f110y	C(0-130)HHdl	GD	£6916
128	11/01	Font	2m4f	E Hdl	G-S	£2387

Total win prize-money £9303

Going: Sf: 0-0 GS: 0-1 Gd: 0-3 GF: - Fm: 0-0
Distance: 2m/2m3: 0-2 2m4-2m7: 0-2 3m+: 0-0
Track: LH: 0-2 RH: 0-2 Tight: 0-1 Gall: 0-1
Aids: Bl: 0-0 Vi: 0-0 Tstrap: 0-0
Best Rating: 128 11/01 Font 2m4f gd-sft Hdl

Decent hurdler; winner twice at Fontwell in 2001/02; best suited by two and a half miles and a decent surface.

Adept
89   **58**
4-y-o b f Efisio-Prancing (Prince Sabo)
C W Fairhurst (J Hetherton 20/7) C D Barber-Lomax

Placings: 50   (1304)
2002/03: 16⁵G, 16⁹GF,

	Starts	1st	2nd	3rd	Win & Pl
Hurdles	2	0	0	0	
Career Total	2	0	0	0	

Going: Sf: 0-0 GS: 0-0 Gd: 0-1 GF: - Fm: 0-1
Distance: 2m/2m3: 0-2 2m4-2m7: 0-0 3m+: 0-0
Track: LH: 0-1 RH: 0-1 Tight: 0-0 Gall: 0-0
Aids: Bl: 0-0 Vi: 0-0 Tstrap: 0-0
Best Rating: 58 9/02 Prth 2m110y gd-fm Hdl

Adios Amigo

4-y-o ch g Efisio-Los Alamos (Keen)
A C Whillans (C W Thornton 2/10) E Waugh

Placings: 0   (2247)
2002/03: 16⁰GS,

	Starts	1st	2nd	3rd	Win & Pl
Hurdles	1	0	0	0	
Career Total	1	0	0	0	

Going: Sf: 0-0 GS: 0-1 Gd: 0-0 GF: - Fm: 0-0
Distance: 2m/2m3: 0-1 2m4-2m7: 0-0 3m+: 0-0
Track: LH: 0-1 RH: 0-0 Tight: 0-0 Gall: 0-1
Aids: Bl: 0-0 Vi: 0-0 Tstrap: 0-0
Best Rating: 0 11/02 Newc 2m gd-sft Hdl

Adjawar (IRE)

5-y-o b g Ashkalani (IRE)-Adjriyna (Top Ville)
H Morrison (C A Dwyer 16/5) D J Donner

Placings: P   (2607)
2002/03: 16ᴾS,

	Starts	1st	2nd	3rd	Win & Pl
Hurdles	1	0	0	0	
Career Total	1	0	0	0	

Going: Sf: 0-1 GS: 0-0 Gd: 0-0 GF: - Fm: 0-0
Distance: 2m/2m3: 0-1 2m4-2m7: 0-0 3m+: 0-0
Track: LH: 0-0 RH: 0-1 Tight: 0-0 Gall: 0-0
Aids: Bl: 0-0 Vi: 0-0 Tstrap: 0-0
Best Rating: 2/03 Winc 2m gd-sft Hdl

Adjiram (IRE)
97   **79**
7-y-o b g Be My Guest (USA)-Adjriyna (Top Ville)
D C O Brien   K Marshall

Placings: 2P/0/0406-640   (2058)
2002/03: 20⁶G, 18⁴GF, 16⁰G,

	Starts	1st	2nd	3rd	Win & Pl
Hurdles	3	0	0	0	

Column 1

Career Total	10	0	1	0	744

Going: Sf: 0-0 GS: 0-0 Gd: 0-2 GF: - Fm: 0-1
Distance: 2m/2m3: 0-2 2m4-2m7: 0-1 3m+: 0-0
Track: LH: 0-2 RH: 0-1 Tight: 0-1 Gall: 0-0
Aids: Bl: 0-0 Vi: 0-0 Tstrap: 0-0
Best Rating: 79 6/02 Font 2m2f110y gd-fm Hdl

Admiral Nelson (IRE)

85(78h)   (84h)**60**
8-y-o b/br g Phardante (FR)-Mulberry (IRE) (Denel (FR))
E McNamara Mrs A Long

Placings:605000/2P0P611B000006O   (4201a)
2002/03: 22²G, 20PGF, 20⁰GF, 24FF, 24⁶G, 22¹G, 20¹S, 22BS, 20⁰S, 20⁰S, 20⁰S, 24⁰SH, 22BSH, 24⁰S,

	Starts	1st	2nd	3rd	Win & Pl
Hurdles	11	2	1	0	11564
Chases	4	0	0	0	
Career Total	22	2	1	0	11564
84	11/02 Cork	2m4f	(67-109)HHdl	SFT	£6349
77	10/02 Thur	2m6f	(60-81)HHdl	GD	£4233

Total win prize-money £10583

Going: Sf: 1-7 GS: 0-0 Gd: 1-3 GF: - Fm: 0-3
Distance: 2m/2m3: 0-0 **2m4-2m7: 2-11** 3m+: 0-4
Track: LH: 0-0 RH: **1-5** Tight: 0-1 Gall: 0-0
Aids: Bl: 0-1 Vi: 0-0 Tstrap: 0-0
Best Rating: 90 11/00 Chel 2m110y gd-sft Hdl

Admiral Peary (IRE)

104   **106**
7-y-o b/br g Lord Americo-Arctic Brief (Buckskin (FR))
C R Egerton M Haynes

Placings:33-13PU324611502F   (4759)
2002/03: 16¹GF, 17³GF, 24FGS, 22UGF, 16³G, 17²GF, 16⁴F, 21⁶F, 22¹S, 25¹HY, 19⁵S, 21⁰S, 26²G, 27FGF,

	Starts	1st	2nd	3rd	Win & Pl
NH Flat	2	1	0	1	2476
Hurdles	12	2	2	1	8277
Career Total	16	3	2	4	11230
108	12/02 Plum	3m1f110yE(0-105)HHdl	HVY	£2957
94	11/02 NAbb	2m6f	E(0-100)HHdl	SFT	£2912
86	7/02 Strf	2m110y H NHF	G-F	£2212

Total win prize-money £8082

Going: Sf: 2-4 GS: 0-1 Gd: 0-2 GF: - Fm: 1-7
Distance: 2m/2m3: 1-5 2m4-2m7: 1-5 3m+: 1-4
Track: LH: **1-5** RH: 0-6 **Tight: 1-6** Gall: 0-2
Aids: Bl: 0-0 Vi: 0-0 Tstrap: 0-0
Best Rating: 115 2/02 Font 2m2f110y soft NHF

Modest hurdler; promising efforts in bumpers, but disappointed over hurdles until winning at Newton Abbot in November 2002; followed up in heavy ground at Plumpton in December; effective in soft ground; stays three miles two but effective at shorter.

Admiral Rose

9-y-o b g Handsome Sailor-Rose Ravine (Deep Run)
Mrs Nicholas Jones Mrs Nicholas Jones

Placings:2/1110P/0/UP   (4443)
2002/03: 24UGS, 19PG,

	Starts	1st	2nd	3rd	Win & Pl
Chases	2	0	0	0	

Column 2

Career Total	9	3	1	0	7060
116	11/99 Folk	2m1f110yE Hdl	SFT	£2304
99	11/99 Ludl	2m	E Hdl	GD	£2671
107	5/99 Chep	2m110y H NHF	GD	£1693

Total win prize-money £6668

Going: Sf: 0-0 GS: 0-1 Gd: 0-1 GF: - Fm: 0-0
Distance: 2m/2m3: 0-0 2m4-2m7: 0-1 3m+: 0-1
Track: LH: 0-1 RH: 0-1 Tight: 0-1 Gall: 0-0
Aids: Bl: 0-0 Vi: 0-0 Tstrap: 0-0
Best Rating: 116 11/99 Folk 2m1f110y soft Hdl

Adradee (IRE)

101   **80**
9-y-o b m Ajraas (USA)-Miss Tan A Dee (Tanfirion)
M J Weeden Mrs E A Haycock

Placings:06/00063003<u>2O</u>/261643431116U0/6506036/0604   (4362)
2002/03: 19⁰GS, 17⁶GS, 22⁰S, 19⁴F,

	Starts	1st	2nd	3rd	Win & Pl
Hurdles	4	0	0	0	394
Career Total	37	4	2	5	15041
114	10/99 DRoy	2m	(0-116)HHdl	Y-S	£2464
99	9/99 Clon	2m	(0-102)HHdl	G-F	£2217
95	8/99 Tral	2m	(0-109)HHdl	YLD	£3388
89	6/99 Tral	2m	(0-116)HHdl	GD	£3683

Total win prize-money £11753

Going: Sf: 0-1 GS: 0-2 Gd: 0-0 GF: - Fm: 0-1
Distance: 2m/2m3: 0-1 2m4-2m7: 0-3 3m+: 0-0
Track: LH: 0-0 RH: 0-4 Tight: 0-3 Gall: 0-0
Aids: Bl: 0-0 Vi: 0-0 Tstrap: 0-0
Best Rating: 114 10/99 DRoy 2m yld-sft Hdl

Won four handicap hurdles in Ireland in 1999; disappointing since coming to this country; lightly-raced of late.

Adrians Pride

4-y-o ch f Keen-Pride s Desire (Grey Desire)
N Wilson Mrs Judy Atkinson

Placings:P   (1537)
2002/03: 16PGF,

	Starts	1st	2nd	3rd	Win & Pl
Hurdles	1	0	0	0	
Career Total	1	0	0	0	

Going: Sf: 0-0 GS: 0-0 Gd: 0-0 GF: - Fm: 0-1
Distance: 2m/2m3: 0-1 2m4-2m7: 0-0 3m+: 0-0
Track: LH: 0-1 RH: 0-0 Tight: 0-0 Gall: 0-0
Aids: Bl: 0-0 Vi: 0-0 Tstrap: 0-0
Best Rating: 0 10/02 Weth 2m gd-fm Hdl

Adronikus (IRE)

104   **93**
6-y-o ch g Monsun (GER)-Arionette (Lombard (GER))
D J Wintle Mrs B Grainger

Placings:0P-061130   (4606)
2002/03: 20⁰GF, 16⁸GF, 17¹GF, 16¹G, 16³G, 24⁰G,

	Starts	1st	2nd	3rd	Win & Pl
Hurdles	6	2	0	1	7339
Career Total	8	2	1	0	7339
91	10/02 Fknm	2m	F(0-100)HHdl	GD	£3357
83	7/02 MRas	2m1f110yE(0-105)HHdl	G-F	£3556

Total win prize-money £6913

Going: Sf: 0-0 GS: 0-0 Gd: 1-3 GF: - Fm: 1-3

Column 3

Distance: 2m/2m3: 2-4 2m4-2m7: 0-1 3m+: 0-1
Track: LH: 1-5 RH: 1-1 **Tight: 2-4** Gall: 0-1
Aids: Bl: 2-4 Vi: 0-0 Tstrap: 2-5
Best Rating: 93 10/02 Plum 2m good Hdl

Plating-class hurdler; effective on good or fast ground; best around two miles; winning at Fakenham in October 2002.

Advance East

95   **104**
11-y-o b g Polish Precedent (USA)-Startino (Bustino)
M J M Evans Mrs J Z Munday

Placings:150/23B4U0356/2460133200/23355654123/F/1-P4324   (4023)
2002/03: 20PGS, 19⁴G, 20³S, 16²S, 16⁴S,

	Starts	1st	2nd	3rd	Win & Pl
Chases	5	0	1	1	2618
Career Total	40	4	6	8	25357
93	4/02 Uttx	2m4f	E(0-110)HCh	GD	£3838
90	2/00 Leic	2m	E(0-115)HCh	SFT	£3103
92	2/99 Plum	2m4f	G Hdl	SFT	£2215
112	11/96 Hayd	2m	D Hdl	GD	£3011

Total win prize-money £12168

Going: Sf: 0-3 GS: 0-1 Gd: 0-1 GF: - Fm: 0-0
Distance: 2m/2m3: 0-3 2m4-2m7: 0-2 3m+: 0-0
Track: LH: 0-2 RH: 0-3 Tight: 0-0 Gall: 0-1
Aids: Bl: 0-0 Vi: 0-0 Tstrap: 0-0
Best Rating: 112 11/96 Hayd 2m good Hdl

Fair chaser; suited by soft and good ground and between two/two and a half miles.

Advice Taken (IRE)

6-y-o ch g Rashar (USA)-Cyrenaics (IRE) (Cyrano De Bergerac)
R H Alner (Mrs Pauline Gavin 29/4) P M De Wilde

Placings:36000-PP   (4514)
2002/03: 16⁰HY, 21PG, 22PGF,

	Starts	1st	2nd	3rd	Win & Pl
NH Flat	1	0	0	0	
Hurdles	2	0	0	0	
Career Total	7	0	0	1	452

Going: Sf: 0-1 GS: 0-0 Gd: 0-0 GF: - Fm: 0-1
Distance: 2m/2m3: 0-1 2m4-2m7: 0-2 3m+: 0-0
Track: LH: 0-0 RH: 0-2 Tight: 0-0 Gall: 0-0
Aids: Bl: 0-0 Vi: 0-0 Tstrap: 0-0
Best Rating: 94 10/01 Gway 2m sft-hvy NHF

Advocatus (GER)

91   **73**
5-y-o b g Law Society (USA)-Aguilas (Konigsstuhl (GER))
A G Hobbs Three Counties Racing 2

Placings:54   (4173)
2002/03: 20⁵G, 20⁴S,

	Starts	1st	2nd	3rd	Win & Pl
Hurdles	2	0	0	0	349
Career Total	2	0	0	0	349

Going: Sf: 0-1 GS: 0-0 Gd: 0-1 GF: - Fm: 0-0
Distance: 2m/2m3: 0-0 2m4-2m7: 0-2 3m+: 0-0
Track: LH: 0-1 RH: 0-1 Tight: 0-0 Gall: 0-1
Aids: Bl: 0-0 Vi: 0-0 Tstrap: 0-0
Best Rating: 73 3/03 Hntg 2m4f110y good Hdl

Aegean

114   **112**

9-y-o b g Rock Hopper-Sayulita (Habitat)
Mrs S J Smith Mrs Alicia Skene & W S Skene

Placings:43030/3251112/0332444-P21   (0917)
2002/03: 25^{P}GS, 24^{2}GF, 24^{1}GS,

	Starts	1st	2nd	3rd	Win & Pl
Chases	3	1	1	0	20168
Career Total	22	4	4	5	41777
112	8/02	Prth	3m	C(0-135)HCh	G-S £16968
116	8/00	Worc	2m7f110y		E(0-105)HCh

G-F £3454
| 110 | 7/00 | Worc | 2m7f110y | E Ch | G-F |

£3376
| 96 | 6/00 | Hexm | 3m1f | E(0-105)HCh | G-F £3120 |

Total win prize-money £26920

Going: Sf: 0-0 GS: 1-2 Gd: 0-0 GF: - Fm: 0-1
Distance: 2m/2m3: 0-0 2m4-2m7: 0-0 3m+: 1-3
Track: LH: 0-2 RH: 1-1 Tight: 0-1 Gall: 0-0
Aids: Bl: 0-0 Vi: 0-0 Tstrap: 0-0
Best Rating: 116 10/00 Aint 3m1f good Ch

Modest handicap chaser; effective over three miles; likes a sound surface.

Aegean Pirate (IRE)

76f   **55f**

6-y-o b g Polykratis-Rusheen Na Corra (IRE) (Burslem)
C J Hemsley Keith McKay

Placings:P   (4155)
2002/03: 16^{P}G,

	Starts	1st	2nd	3rd	Win & Pl
NH Flat	1	0	0	0	
Career Total	1	0	0	0	

Going: Sf: 0-0 GS: 0-0 Gd: 0-1 GF: - Fm: 0-0
Distance: 2m/2m3: 0-1 2m4-2m7: 0-0 3m+: 0-0
Track: LH: 0-1 RH: 0-0 Tight: 0-0 Gall: 0-0
Aids: Bl: 0-0 Vi: 0-0 Tstrap: 0-0
Best Rating: 0 3/03 Wwck 2m good NHF

Aelred

109(99h)   (83h)**122**

10-y-o b g Ovac (ITY)-Sponsorship (Sparkler)
R Johnson J L Gledson

Placings:000/556043463642/1212320125/3P23216050-
426323104260   (4751)
2002/03: 18^{4}G, 17^{2}GS, 16^{6}G, 17^{3}S, 16^{2}S, 16^{3}GS, 16^{1}S, 20^{0}G, 17^{5}S, 16^{2}GF, 16^{6}G, 20^{0}G,

	Starts	1st	2nd	3rd	Win & Pl
Hurdles	1	0	0	0	268
Chases	11	1	3	2	12093
Career Total	47	5	10	7	37817
119	12/02	Newc	2m110y	D(0-120)HCh	SFT £5642
116	1/02	Newc	2m110y	E(0-110)HCh	SFT £3370
105	1/01	Newc	2m110y	E(0-110)HCh	SFT £2912
98	5/00	Ctml	2m1f110yF(0-100)HCh	GD	£2990
99	5/00	Kels	2m1f	E Ch	G-S £3445

Total win prize-money £18360

Going: Sf: 1-4 GS: 0-2 Gd: 0-5 GF: - Fm: 0-1
Distance: 2m/2m3: 1-10 2m4-2m7: 0-2 3m+: 0-0
Track: LH: 1-9 RH: 0-3 Tight: 0-5 Gall: 1-2
Aids: Bl: 0-0 Vi: 0-0 Tstrap: 0-3
Best Rating: 120 6/02 Ctml 2m1f110y gd-sft Ch

Fair chaser; best over two miles; suited by cut in the ground; best with forcing tactics; goes well at Newcastle.

Afadan (IRE)

94   **97**

5-y-o br g Royal Academy (USA)-Afasara (IRE) (Shardari)
J R Jenkins St Albans Chasers

Placings:P1PP-0200   (4146)
2002/03: 16^{8}S, 16^{2}GS, 16^{0}GS, 16^{0}G,

	Starts	1st	2nd	3rd	Win & Pl
Hurdles	4	0	1	0	1254
Career Total	8	1	1	0	4780
110	12/01	Sand	2m110y	D Hdl	SFT £3526

Total win prize-money £3526

Going: Sf: 0-1 GS: 0-2 Gd: 0-1 GF: - Fm: 0-0
Distance: 2m/2m3: 0-4 2m4-2m7: 0-0 3m+: 0-0
Track: LH: 0-1 RH: 0-3 Tight: 0-1 Gall: 0-2
Aids: Bl: 0-0 Vi: 0-0 Tstrap: 0-0
Best Rating: 110 11/02 Hntg 2m110y gd-sft Hdl

Moderate hurdler; showed a useful turn of foot to land a novice hurdle at Sandown last season; looked reluctant when runner-up at Huntingdon in November 2002; acts to give underfoot.

Aficionado (IRE)

91   **72**

9-y-o b g Marju (IRE)-Haneena (Habitat)
R Williams R Williams

Placings:3B5560/00060/06064/000/6-6   (0849)
2002/03: 17^{6}GF,

	Starts	1st	2nd	3rd	Win & Pl
Hurdles	1	0	0	0	0
Career Total	21	0	0	1	261

Going: Sf: 0-0 GS: 0-0 Gd: 0-0 GF: - Fm: 0-1
Distance: 2m/2m3: 0-1 2m4-2m7: 0-0 3m+: 0-0
Track: LH: 0-1 RH: 0-0 Tight: 0-1 Gall: 0-0
Aids: Bl: 0-0 Vi: 0-0 Tstrap: 0-0
Best Rating: 73 11/98 Hrfd 2m1f good Hdl

Africa (IRE)

82

6-y-o b m Namaqualand (USA)-Tannerrun (IRE) (Runnett)
A Streeter Malt N Hops

Placings:0/03FF-PP   (0572)
2002/03: 20^{0}G, 16^{P}S,

	Starts	1st	2nd	3rd	Win & Pl
Hurdles	2	0	0	0	
Career Total	7	0	0	1	486

Going: Sf: 0-1 GS: 0-0 Gd: 0-1 GF: - Fm: 0-0
Distance: 2m/2m3: 0-4 2m4-2m7: 0-1 3m+: 0-0
Track: LH: 0-2 RH: 0-2 Tight: 0-0 Gall: 0-0
Aids: Bl: 0-0 Vi: 0-0 Tstrap: 0-0
Best Rating: 82 7/01 Uttx 2m gd-fm Hdl

African Dawn

5-y-o b g Spectrum (IRE)-Lamu Lady (IRE) (Lomond (USA))
P R Webber The Alchemists 2

Placings:P6P   (1891)
2002/03: 17^{P}G, 16^{6}GF, 16^{P}GS,

	Starts	1st	2nd	3rd	Win & Pl
Hurdles	3	0	0	0	196
Career Total	3	0	0	0	196

Going: Sf: 0-0 GS: 0-1 Gd: 0-1 GF: - Fm: 0-1
Distance: 2m/2m3: 0-3 2m4-2m7: 0-0 3m+: 0-0
Track: LH: 0-2 RH: 0-1 Tight: 0-0 Gall: 0-1
Aids: Bl: 0-0 Vi: 0-1 Tstrap: 0-0
Best Rating: 0 11/02 Hntg 2m110y gd-sft Hdl

African Waters (IRE)

98(97h)   (103h)**101+**

6-y-o ch m Be My Native (USA)-Queens Romance (Imperial Fling (USA))
C F Swan Dundrum House Golf Syndicate

Placings:20212403-4241012U054U06   (4203a)
2002/03: 20^{4}SH, 20^{2}G, 20^{4}G, 20^{1}GF, 18^{0}GY, 20^{1}F, 22^{2}GY, 24^{U}SH, 20^{0}HY, 21^{5}G, 20^{4}S, 20^{U}S, 20^{0}HY, 22^{6}S,

	Starts	1st	2nd	3rd	Win & Pl
Hurdles	6	1	1	0	6656
Chases	8	1	1	0	7637
Career Total	22	3	5	1	21709
72	9/02	Clon	2m4f	Ch	FRM £4868
103	7/02	Wxfd	2m4f	Hdl	G-F £3809
93	8/01	Tral	2m	NHF	G-F £3895

Total win prize-money £12573

Going: Sf: 0-5 GS: 0-0 Gd: 0-3 GF: - Fm: 2-2
Distance: 2m/2m3: 0-1 2m4-2m7: 2-12 3m+: 0-1
Track: LH: 0-1 RH: 1-8 Tight: 0-0 Gall: 0-0
Aids: Bl: 0-4 Vi: 0-0 Tstrap: 0-0
Best Rating: 103 7/02 Wxfd 2m4f gd-fm Hdl

Modest Irish chaser; effective at two and a half miles; acts on fast ground.

Afro Man

102   **94**

5-y-o b g Commanche Run-Lady Elle (IRE) (Persian Mews)
C J Mann J E Brown, E Good & R Lucas

Placings:0064   (4212)
2002/03: 18^{0}S, 17^{0}GS, 16^{6}G, 18^{4}G,

	Starts	1st	2nd	3rd	Win & Pl
NH Flat	1	0	0	0	
Hurdles	3	0	0	0	267
Career Total	4	0	0	0	267

Going: Sf: 0-1 GS: 0-1 Gd: 0-2 GF: - Fm: 0-0
Distance: 2m/2m3: 0-4 2m4-2m7: 0-0 3m+: 0-0
Track: LH: 0-2 RH: 0-2 Tight: 0-2 Gall: 0-1
Aids: Bl: 0-0 Vi: 0-0 Tstrap: 0-0
Best Rating: 97 3/03 Font 2m2f110y good Hdl

After Me Boys

114   **124+**

9-y-o b g Arzanni-Realm Wood (Precipice Wood)
Mrs S J Smith Keith Nicholson

Placings:21421/212P-21   (4164)
2002/03: 20^{2}G, 24^{1}GS,

	Starts	1st	2nd	3rd	Win & Pl
Hurdles	2	1	1	0	11641
Career Total	11	4	5	0	25296
124	3/03	Newc	3m	C(0-130)HHdl	G-S £10120
112	8/01	Sthl	2m4f110yE(0-115)HHdl	GF	£2380
110	4/01	MRas	2m3f110yD Hdl	HVY	
£4403109	6/00	Hexm	2mH NHF	G-F £1641	

Total win prize-money £18547

Going: Sf: 0-0 GS: 1-1 Gd: 0-1 GF: - Fm: 0-0

Distance: 2m/2m3: 0-0 2m4-2m7: 0-1 **3m+: 1-1**
Track: **LH: 1-2** RH: 0-0 Tight: 0-0 **Gall: 1-1**
Aids: Bl: 0-0 Vi: 0-0 Tstrap: 0-0
Best Rating: **124** 3/03 Newc 3m   gd-sft Hdl

Fair hurdler; returned after almost a year and a half off after injury when runner-up at Wetherby in February 2003; scored on an easy surface at Newcastle; stays 3m; acts on any ground.

After The Blue (IRE)
87   100
6-y-o b g Last Tycoon-Sudden Interest (FR) (Highest Honor (FR))
C J Mann John & Doreen Tubb

Placings:544442P-F1   (0434)
2002/03: 20^FGF, 20¹GF,

	Starts	1st	2nd	3rd	Win & Pl
Hurdles	2	1	0	0	2499
Career Total	9	1	1	0	3841

100 6/02 Hntg   2m4f110yE Hdl   G-F £2499
                     Total win prize-money £2499

Going: Sf: 0-0 GS: 0-0 Gd: 0-0 GF: - Fm: 1-2
Distance: 2m/2m3: 0-0 **2m4-2m7: 1-2** 3m+: 0-0
Track: LH: 0-0 **RH: 1-2** Tight: 0-0 **Gall: 1-1**
Aids: Bl: 0-0 Vi: 0-0 **Tstrap: 1-2**
Best Rating: **100** 6/02 Hntg 2m4f110y gd-fm Hdl

Modest form in novice hurdles over around two and a half miles.

Afzark
75f   50f
6-y-o b h Afzal-Dark Deb (Black Minstrel)
R H Alner Mrs T M Blair

Placings:00   (3673)
2002/03: 17⁰S, 18⁰GS,

	Starts	1st	2nd	3rd	Win & Pl
NH Flat	2	0	0	0	
Career Total	2	0	0	0	

Going: Sf: 0-1 GS: 0-1 Gd: 0-0 GF: - Fm: 0-0
Distance: 2m/2m3: 0-2 2m4-2m7: 0-0 3m+: 0-0
Track: LH: 0-1 RH: 0-1 Tight: 0-1 Gall: 0-0
Aids: Bl: 0-0 Vi: 0-0 Tstrap: 0-0
Best Rating: **50** 11/02 Hrfd 2m1f   soft NHF

Again An Again (IRE)
(104h)   (93h)**69**
7-y-o b g Montelimar (USA)-Running Board (Deep Run)
S Donohoe Some Day Some Time Syndicate

Placings:0653/0500053F5040-220001103   (1637)
2002/03: 16²GF, 17²YS, 16⁰YS, 20⁰YS, 22⁰G, 17¹G, 16¹F, 16⁰GF, 17³S,

	Starts	1st	2nd	3rd	Win & Pl
NH Flat	1	0	1	0	687
Hurdles	8	2	1	1	9103
Career Total	25	2	2	3	11017

93 9/02 DRoy   2m   (0-116)HHdl FRM £3809
90 9/02 Dpat   2m1f172y (67-102)HHdl GD £3809
                     Total win prize-money £7620

Going: Sf: 0-1 GS: 0-0 Gd: 1-2 GF: - Fm: 1-3
Distance: 2m/2m3: 2-7 2m4-2m7: 0-2 3m+: 0-1
Track: LH: 0-0 RH: 1-3 Tight: 0-0 Gall: 0-0

Aids: Bl: 2-9 Vi: 0-0 Tstrap: 0-0
Best Rating: **108** 4/01 Gowr 2m   yld-sft NHF

Plating-class hurdler; winner twice over hurdles in Ireland in September 2002; handles a bit of cut but looks better suited by faster ground and an easy track.

Agent Provocateur (NZ)
79   66
7-y-o b g Racing Is Fun (USA)-Silver Crest (NZ) (Silver Dream)
S B Clark S B Clark

Placings:3/0F030-   (0006)
2002/03: 20⁰G,

	Starts	1st	2nd	3rd	Win & Pl
Hurdles	1	0	0	0	
Career Total	6	0	2	0	609

Going: Sf: 0-0 GS: 0-0 Gd: 0-1 GF: - Fm: 0-0
Distance: 2m/2m3: 0-0 2m4-2m7: 0-1 3m+: 0-0
Track: LH: 0-1 RH: 0-0 Tight: 0-0 Gall: 0-1
Aids: Bl: 0-0 Vi: 0-0 Tstrap: 0-0
Best Rating: **93** 10/00 Hntg 2m110y gd-fm NHF

Agincourt (IRE)
107(99h)   (79h)**93**
7-y-o b g Alphabatim (USA)-Miss Brantridge (Riboboy (USA))
John R Upson Middleham Park Racing Xxi

Placings:000/065100P-432144   (3993)
2002/03: 21⁴G, 25³HY, 25²S, 24¹S, 24⁴S, 25⁴G,

	Starts	1st	2nd	3rd	Win & Pl
Hurdles	1	0	0	0	0
Chases	5	1	1	1	7587
Career Total	16	2	1	1	10275

91 1/03 Ludl   3m   E(0-105)HCh SFT £4901
79 12/01 Weth   3m1f   F(0-95)HHdl G-S £2688
                     Total win prize-money £7589

Going: Sf: 1-4 GS: 0-0 Gd: 0-2 GF: - Fm: 0-0
Distance: 2m/2m3: 0-0 2m4-2m7: 0-1 **3m+: 1-5**
Track: LH: 0-3 **RH: 1-3** Tight: **1-4** Gall: 0-0
Aids: Bl: 0-0 Vi: 0-0 Tstrap: 0-0
Best Rating: **92** 12/02 MRas 3m1f   soft Ch

Moderate hurdler and chaser; stays three miles; acts on soft ground.

Agitando (IRE)
111   113
7-y-o b g Tenby-Crown Rose (Dara Monarch)
B De Haan The Inspirations Partnership

Placings:511-3030633F   (4734)
2002/03: 16³G, 16⁰S, 16³S, 16⁰G, 16⁶GS, 16³G, 16³G, 16^FGF,

	Starts	1st	2nd	3rd	Win & Pl
Hurdles	8	2	0	4	3452
Career Total	11	2	0	4	9990

122 4/02 MRas 2m1f110yD Hdl   GD £3836
111 4/02 Uttx 2m   E Hdl   GD £2702
                     Total win prize-money £6538

Going: Sf: 0-2 GS: 0-1 Gd: 0-3 GF: - Fm: 0-2
Distance: 2m/2m3: 0-8 2m4-2m7: 0-0 3m+: 0-0
Track: LH: 0-4 RH: 0-4 Tight: 0-2 Gall: 0-1
Aids: Bl: 0-0 Vi: 0-0 Tstrap: 0-0
Best Rating: **122** 12/02 Kemp 2m   soft Hdl

Fair hurdler; best over two miles; acts on soft ground, but much better on a decent surface; has worn cheekpieces.

Ahoopoe
99f   90f
5-y-o ch g Sir Harry Lewis (USA)-Aspark (Sparkler)
Mrs P Robeson Mrs P Robeson

Placings:4   (3930)
2002/03: 16⁴G,

	Starts	1st	2nd	3rd	Win & Pl
NH Flat	1	0	0	0	0
Career Total	1	0	0	0	0

Going: Sf: 0-0 GS: 0-0 Gd: 0-1 GF: - Fm: 0-0
Distance: 2m/2m3: 0-1 2m4-2m7: 0-0 3m+: 0-0
Track: LH: 0-0 RH: 0-1 Tight: 0-0 Gall: 0-1
Aids: Bl: 0-0 Vi: 0-0 Tstrap: 0-0
Best Rating: **90** 3/03 Hntg 2m110y   good NHF

Aifung (IRE)
90   70+
5-y-o ch m Bigstone (IRE)-Palmyra (GER) (Arratos (FR))
R H Buckler Mrs P J Buckler

Placings:2611   (4697)
2002/03: 17²GF, 16⁶G, 16¹GF, 17¹G,

	Starts	1st	2nd	3rd	Win & Pl
NH Flat	4	2	1	0	5226
Career Total	4	2	1	0	5226

100 4/03 NAbb 2m1f   H NHF   GD £2996
90 10/02 Hntg 2m110y   H NHF   G-F £1764
                     Total win prize-money £4760

Going: Sf: 0-0 GS: 0-0 Gd: 1-2 GF: - Fm: 1-2
Distance: **2m/2m3: 2-4** 2m4-2m7: 0-0 3m+: 0-0
Track: LH: 1-2 RH: 1-2 Tight: 1-1 Gall: 1-1
Aids: Bl: 0-0 Vi: 0-0 Tstrap: 0-0
Best Rating: **100** 4/03 NAbb 2m1f   good NHF

Plating-class hurdler; won bumpers at Huntingdon October 2002 and Newton Abbot April 2003; appreciated step up in distance when landing 2m 6f mares only novice hurdle at Newton Abbot in July; stays well; acts on ground good and faster.

Aimees Mark (IRE)
(111h)   (124h)
7-y-o b/br g Jolly Jake (NZ)-Wee Mite (Menelek)
F Flood Raymond McConn

Placings:00004/133F3612-10111400   (4112)
2002/03: 20¹YS, 21⁰GY, 20¹S, 20¹SH, 20¹HY, 20⁴S, 24⁰SH, 21⁰G,

	Starts	1st	2nd	3rd	Win & Pl
Hurdles	8	4	0	0	45078
Career Total	21	6	1	3	59524

123 12/02 Punc 2m4f   HHdl   HVY £9969
121 12/02 Punc 2m4f   (81-123)HHdl SH £11993
109 10/02 Naas 2m4f   HHdl   SFT £13558
102 6/02 Cork 2m4f   (81-123)HHdl Y-S £8972
100 3/02 Fair 2m4f   (67-102)HHdl G-Y £6349
113 10/01 Rosc 2m   NHF   Y-S £3338
                     Total win prize-money £54182

Going: Sf: 2-3 GS: 0-0 Gd: 0-1 GF: - Fm: 0-0
Distance: 2m/2m3: 0-0 **2m4-2m7: 4-7** 3m+: 0-1
Track: LH: 0-2 **RH: 2-3** Tight: 0-0 Gall: 0-1
Aids: Bl: 0-0 Vi: 0-0 Tstrap: 0-0
Best Rating: **125** 3/03 Chel 2m5f   good Hdl

Decent Irish-trained hurdler; suited by two and a half miles and soft ground; has a good strike rate.

Ain Tecbalet (FR)
95   **88**

5-y-o b g Riverquest (FR)-La Chance Au Roy (FR) (Rex Magna (FR))
N J Henderson The French Connection

Placings:40/2224-43130500   (4606)
2002/03: 17⁴G, 19³G, 17¹G, 17³S, 21⁰S, 18⁵HY, 20⁰HY, 24⁰G,

	Starts	1st	2nd	3rd	Win & Pl
Hurdles	5	0	0	0	758
Chases	3	1	0	2	5301
Career Total	14	1	3	2	12960
7/02 Mesl	2m1f110y Ch			GD	£3239
				Total win prize-money £3239	

Going:	Sf: 0-4 GS: 0-0 Gd: 1-4 GF: - Fm: 0-0	
Distance:	2m/2m3: 1-5 2m4-2m7: 0-2 3m+: 0-1	
Track:	LH: 0-3 RH: 0-1 Tight: 0-2 Gall: 0-1	
Aids:	Bl: 0-0 Vi: 0-0 Tstrap: 0-0	
Best Rating:	88 1/03 Font 2m2f110y heavy Hdl	

Ex-French hurdler/chaser; yet to win in this country; may be better suited by decent ground.

Aine Dubh (IRE)
93   **118**

6-y-o b m Bob Back (USA)-Deep Thyne (IRE) (Good Thyne (USA))
Kevin F O Donnell Kevin O Donnell

Placings:4221-30136   (4653a)
2002/03: 16³YS, 16⁰HY, 20¹S, 20³G, 20⁶GF,

	Starts	1st	2nd	3rd	Win & Pl
Hurdles	5	1	0	2	11711
Career Total	9	2	2	2	18421
98 3/03 Tram	2m4f	Hdl		SFT	£5824
99 11/01 Punc	2m	NHF		SFT	£4451
				Total win prize-money £10277	

Going:	Sf: 1-2 GS: 0-0 Gd: 0-1 GF: - Fm: 0-1	
Distance:	2m/2m3: 0-2 2m4-2m7: 1-3 3m+: 0-0	
Track:	LH: 0-1 RH: 0-0 Tight: 0-1 Gall: 0-0	
Aids:	Bl: 0-0 Vi: 0-0 Tstrap: 0-0	
Best Rating:	118 4/03 Aint 2m4f good Hdl	

Irish-trained novice hurdler; easy winner in the mud at Tranmore in March; creditable third in Group Two at Aintree in April 2003.

Air Attache (USA)

8-y-o b g Sky Classic (CAN)-Diplomatic Cover (USA) (Roberto (USA))
K R Pearce (C J Mann 28/7) Keith R Pearce

Placings:1341121/1231   (4678)
2002/03: 16¹GF, 17²G, 21³GF, 19¹GF,

	Starts	1st	2nd	3rd	Win & Pl
Chases	4	2	1	1	6595
Career Total	11	6	2	1	20083
109 4/03 Hrfd	2m3f	H Ch	G-F	£1666	
113 6/02 Hrfd	2m	E Ch	G-F	£3110	
126 8/00 Uttx	2m	D(0-125)HHdl	G-F	£3022	
118 7/00 Worc	2m	D Hdl	G-F	£2899	
112 7/00 NAbb	2m1f	D(0-120)HHdl	G-F	£3018	
104 5/00 MRas	2m1f110yE Hdl		G-F	£2899	
			Total win prize-money £16419		

Going:	Sf: 0-0 GS: 0-0 Gd: 0-1 GF: - Fm: 2-3	
Distance:	2m/2m3: 2-3 2m4-2m7: 0-1 3m+: 0-0	
Track:	LH: 0-2 RH: 2-2 Tight: 0-2 Gall: 0-0	
Aids:	Bl: 0-0 Vi: 0-0 Tstrap: 2-4	
Best Rating:	126 8/00 Uttx 2m gd-fm Hdl	

Useful novice hurdler in 2000; overcame two-year absence to score on chasing debut in June 2002 when trained by Charlie Mann; won hunter chase at Hereford in April 2003 on first run for new yard after long lay-off; effective at up to 2m 4f; suited by fast ground.

Air Control (IRE)
88   **73**

8-y-o b g Executive Perk-Sandy Jayne (IRE) (Royal Fountain)
L Lungo Mrs Barbara Lungo

Placings:4/5/006-0   (3771)
2002/03: 16⁰GS,

	Starts	1st	2nd	3rd	Win & Pl
Hurdles	1	0	0	0	
Career Total	6	0	0	0	0

Going:	Sf: 0-0 GS: 0-1 Gd: 0-0 GF: - Fm: 0-0	
Distance:	2m/2m3: 0-1 2m4-2m7: 0-0 3m+: 0-0	
Track:	LH: 0-1 RH: 0-0 Tight: 0-0 Gall: 0-0	
Aids:	Bl: 0-0 Vi: 0-0 Tstrap: 0-0	
Best Rating:	100 5/00 Uttx 2m good NHF	

Air Of Confusion
95   **93**

5-y-o b g Mr Confusion (IRE)-First Born (Be My Native (USA))
Mrs K Walton Jeff McCarthy

Placings:0   (2117)
2002/03: 17⁰G,

	Starts	1st	2nd	3rd	Win & Pl
NH Flat	1	0	0	0	
Career Total	1	0	0	0	

Going:	Sf: 0-0 GS: 0-0 Gd: 0-1 GF: - Fm: 0-0	
Distance:	2m/2m3: 0-1 2m4-2m7: 0-0 3m+: 0-0	
Track:	LH: 0-0 RH: 0-0 Tight: 0-0 Gall: 0-0	
Aids:	Bl: 0-0 Vi: 0-0 Tstrap: 0-0	
Best Rating:	80 11/02 Aint 2m1f good NHF	

Novice hurdler; strong chasing type; showed promise on hurdles debut; should be suited by a stiffer test of stamina.

Aircon (IRE)
100(70h)   **(44h)89**

8-y-o ch g Moscow Society (USA)-Corrielek (Menelek)
R Dickin G Hutsby

Placings:5/56613/FUF5P300P22-S25PP   (4636)
2002/03: 16⁵G, 19²G, 19⁵S, 28⁰S, 24⁰G,

	Starts	1st	2nd	3rd	Win & Pl
Chases	5	0	1	0	1276
Career Total	22	1	3	2	9952
109 2/01 Wwck	2m4f110y		D Ch	SFT	£5008
			Total win prize-money £5008		

Going:	Sf: 0-2 GS: 0-0 Gd: 0-3 GF: - Fm: 0-0	
Distance:	2m/2m3: 0-3 2m4-2m7: 0-0 3m+: 0-2	
Track:	LH: 0-2 RH: 0-3 Tight: 0-2 Gall: 0-0	
Aids:	Bl: 0-0 Vi: 0-0 Vi: 0-3 Tstrap: 0-0	
Best Rating:	109 5/01 NAbb 3m2f110y gd-fm Ch	

Moderate handicap chaser; does not have the best completion record; stays three miles; regularly visored.

Ajar (IRE)

13-y-o b g Avocat-Door Belle (Fidel)
J W Mullins Col R I Webb-Bowen

Placings:60/32FU/60110215F2/F6103335/0406UO222/U42 111-6LP   (4216)
2002/03: 19⁶G, 24¹-S, 20²G,

	Starts	1st	2nd	3rd	Win & Pl
Chases	3	0	0	0	
Career Total	42	7	7	4	34403
104 3/02 Font	2m4f	H Ch	SFT	£2226	
104 3/02 Sand	2m4f110yH Ch		GD	£3354	
98 2/02 Sand	2m4f110yH Ch		SFT	£2324	
123 12/99 Thur	2m	Hdl	SFT	£6160	
115 3/99 Limk	2m	Ch	SFT	£3989	
116 1/99 Gowr	2m2f	Hdl	SFT	£3437	
112 1/99 Tram	2m	Hdl	SH	£2608	
			Total win prize-money £24102		

Going:	Sf: 0-1 GS: 0-0 Gd: 0-2 GF: - Fm: 0-0	
Distance:	2m/2m3: 0-0 2m4-2m7: 0-2 3m+: 0-1	
Track:	LH: 0-1 RH: 0-1 Tight: 0-1 Gall: 0-0	
Aids:	Bl: 0-0 Vi: 0-1 Tstrap: 0-0	
Best Rating:	132 4/00 Fair 2m soft Hdl	

Fair hunter chaser; ex-Irish; scored twice over two and a half miles at Sandown and once at Fontwell early in 2002; likes the ground good or softer; jumps right-handed.

Akarus (FR)
109   **145**

8-y-o b g Labus (FR)-Meris (FR) (Amarko (FR))
M C Pipe (C Aubert 10/11) A J White

Placings:6040000/030040010F02P0/23320054B655206-00200316P02   (4172)
2002/03: 21⁰VS, 19⁰VS, 21²VS, 22⁰VS, 18⁰VS, 21³VS, 23¹VS, 20⁶HY, 20⁰G, 21⁰GS, 34²S,

	Starts	1st	2nd	3rd	Win & Pl
Hurdles	3	0	0	0	1717
Chases	8	1	2	1	89330
Career Total	47	2	6	4	132305
10/02 Autl	2m7f110y HCh		VS	£48312	
12/00 Pari	2m4f110y Ch		HLD	£4323	
			Total win prize-money £52635		

Going:	Sf: 0-2 GS: 0-1 Gd: 0-1 GF: - Fm: 0-0	
Distance:	2m/2m3: 0-1 2m4-2m7: 0-0 3m+: 1-2	
Track:	LH: 0-5 RH: 0-1 Tight: 0-0 Gall: 0-1	
Aids:	Bl: 0-0 Vi: 0-0 Tstrap: 0-0	
Best Rating:	145 3/03 Uttx 4m2f soft Ch	

Very useful chaser; ran a blinder on only his second start in this country when runner-up in the Midlands National; suited by soft ground.

Akina (NZ)
     81d

12-y-o b g Ivory Hunter (USA)-Wairoa Belle (NZ) (Bold Venture (NZ))
J Neville N Brookes

Placings:1F4F0/F0UP/0FP/FU0F2U2PP-FP   (0123)
2002/03: 20⁶GF, 27⁰GF,

	Starts	1st	2nd	3rd	Win & Pl
Hurdles	2	0	0	0	
Career Total	23	1	2	0	3927
8/98 Awap	1m5f	Hdl	HVY	£2060	
			Total win prize-money £2060		

Going:	Sf: 0-0 GS: 0-0 Gd: 0-1 GF: - Fm: 0-1	
Distance:	2m/2m3: 0-0 2m4-2m7: 0-1 3m+: 0-1	

Track: LH: 0-1 RH: 0-0 Tight: 0-2 Gall: 0-0
Aids: Bl: 0-0 Vi: 0-0 Tstrap: 0-0
Best Rating: 91 3/99 Chep 2m110y   gd-sft   Hdl

Al Mabrook (IRE)
83   88
8-y-o b g Rainbows For Life (CAN)-Sky Lover (Ela-Mana-Mou)
K A Ryan Mrs J Ryan

Placings:2P26332-60P   (3226)
2002/03: 17⁶S, 16⁰G, 21ᴾHY,

	Starts	1st	2nd	3rd	Win & Pl
Hurdles	3	0	0	0	0
Career Total	10	0	3	2	4919

Going: Sf: 0-2 GS: 0-0 Gd: 0-1 GF: - Fm: 0-0
Distance: 2m/2m3: 0-2 2m4-2m7: 0-1 3m+: 0-0
Track: LH: 0-3 RH: 0-0 Tight: 0-0 Gall: 0-0
Aids: Bl: 0-0 Vi: 0-1 Tstrap: 0-0
Best Rating: 88 4/02 Sedg 2m5f110y gd-fm Hdl

Al Skywalker (USA)

10-y-o b g Skywalker (USA)-Bint Alnasr (USA) (Al Nasr (FR))
Jennifer Majette Michael H Watt

Placings:61P/34P11/1P3PP3/32510/1341322-1P1P (2490)
2002/03: 18¹S, 19⁹S, 17¹S, 17⁷G,

	Starts	1st	2nd	3rd	Win & Pl
Hurdles	3	2	0	0	41096
Chases	1	0	0	0	0
Career Total	30	9	3	6	200086
10/02	Fars	2m1f		Hdl	SFT £20548
5/02	Malv	2m2f		Hdl	SFT £20548
11/01	Mntp	2m4f		Hdl	FRM £10000
5/01	Malv	2m2f		Hdl	FRM £20000
3/01	Camd	2m2f		Hdl	FRM £40000
5/99	Malv	2m2f		Hdl	FRM £14457
5/99	Broo	2m2f		Hdl	FRM £3614
4/99	StrH	2m4f		Hdl	FR £7228
11/97	Chto	2m2f		Hdl	GD £2142
				Total win prize-money £138540

Going: Sf: 2-3 GS: 0-0 Gd: 0-1 GF: - Fm: 0-0
Distance: 2m/2m3: 2-4 2m4-2m7: 0-0 3m+: 0-0
Track: LH: 0-1 RH: 0-0 Tight: 0-0 Gall: 0-1
Aids: Bl: 0-0 Vi: 0-0 Tstrap: 0-0
Best Rating: 0 12/02 Chel 2m1f   good   Hdl

Leading US-trained hurdler.

Alagazam
89   67
5-y-o ch g Alhijaz-Maziere (Mazilier (USA))
B I Case Mrs M Howlett

Placings:0-0   (4635)
2002/03: 19⁰GF,

	Starts	1st	2nd	3rd	Win & Pl
Hurdles	1	0	0	0	0
Career Total	2	0	0	0	0

Going: Sf: 0-0 GS: 0-0 Gd: 0-0 GF: - Fm: 0-1
Distance: 2m/2m3: 0-1 2m4-2m7: 0-0 3m+: 0-0
Track: LH: 0-1 RH: 0-0 Tight: 0-0 Gall: 0-0
Aids: Bl: 0-0 Vi: 0-0 Tstrap: 0-0
Best Rating: 44 4/02 Ludl 2m   gd-fm Hdl

Alakdar (CAN)
105(101h)   (77h)98
9-y-o ch g Green Dancer (USA)-Population (General Assembly (USA))
C J Down Ms L Stark

Placings:00/30/0464235/25300/010602F443P-062 (4598)
2002/03: 26⁰S, 24⁶G, 19²GF,

	Starts	1st	2nd	3rd	Win & Pl
Hurdles	3	0	1	0	1104
Career Total	30	1	4	4	9411
88	6/01	NAbb	2m5f110yD	Ch	G-S £4202
			Total win prize-money £4202

Going: Sf: 0-1 GS: 0-0 Gd: 0-1 GF: - Fm: 0-1
Distance: 2m/2m3: 0-1 2m4-2m7: 0-0 3m+: 0-2
Track: LH: 0-0 RH: 0-3 Tight: 0-0 Gall: 0-0
Aids: Bl: 0-0 Vi: 0-0 Tstrap: 0-0
Best Rating: 88 6/01 NAbb 2m5f110y gd-sft   Ch

Moderate chaser; winner on the Flat and over fences; remains a maiden over hurdles; 5lb wrong when wide margin winner of Class F 3m handicap chase at Worcester July 2003; suited by a stamina test.

Alam (USA)
110   114+
4-y-o b g Silver Hawk (USA)-Ghashtah (USA) (Nijinsky (CAN))
P Monteith (E A L Dunlop 3/6) G M Cowan

Placings:2211   (3891)
2002/03: 16²S, 16²GS, 16¹S, 16¹GS,

	Starts	1st	2nd	3rd	Win & Pl
Hurdles	4	2	2	0	9275
Career Total	4	2	2	0	9275
104	3/03	Kels	2m110y	E Hdl	G-S £3627
114	1/03	Ayr	2m	E Hdl	SFT £3510
			Total win prize-money £7137

Going: Sf: 1-2 GS: 1-2 Gd: 0-0 GF: - Fm: 0-0
Distance: 2m/2m3: 2-4 2m4-2m7: 0-0 3m+: 0-0
Track: LH: 2-4 RH: 0-0 Tight: 1-1 Gall: 0-1
Aids: Bl: 0-0 Vi: 0-0 Tstrap: 0-0
Best Rating: 114 1/03 Ayr 2m   soft   Hdl

Excitable type; fair hurdler; runner-up twice before winning decisively at Ayr in January 2003; followed up at Kelso; acts on soft ground.

Albamart Wood
85   80
7-y-o gr g Gran Alba (USA)-Marty s Round (Martinmas)
R J Hodges Lt Col E L Stocker

Placings:F366   (3544)
2002/03: 21ᶠGS, 21³GS, 16⁶S, 19⁶G,

	Starts	1st	2nd	3rd	Win & Pl
Chases	4	0	0	1	1704
Career Total	4	0	0	1	1704

Going: Sf: 0-1 GS: 0-2 Gd: 0-1 GF: - Fm: 0-0
Distance: 2m/2m3: 0-2 2m4-2m7: 0-2 3m+: 0-0
Track: LH: 0-0 RH: 0-4 Tight: 0-1 Gall: 0-0
Aids: Bl: 0-0 Vi: 0-0 Tstrap: 0-2
Best Rating: 80 1/03 Tntn 2m110y soft   Ch

Albamores Madam
101   95
8-y-o gr m Gran Alba (USA)-Lady Gwenmore (Town And Country)

Dr J R J Naylor Howard Smith

Placings:00P32/00435   (4673)
2002/03: 21⁰GS, 22⁰S, 22⁴GF, 25³GF, 26⁵GF,

	Starts	1st	2nd	3rd	Win & Pl
Hurdles	5	0	0	1	415
Career Total	10	0	1	2	1099

Going: Sf: 0-1 GS: 0-1 Gd: 0-0 GF: - Fm: 0-3
Distance: 2m/2m3: 0-0 2m4-2m7: 0-3 3m+: 0-2
Track: LH: 0-0 RH: 0-4 Tight: 0-0 Gall: 0-0
Aids: Bl: 0-0 Vi: 0-0 Tstrap: 0-0
Best Rating: 95 3/03 Plum 3m1f110y gd-fm Hdl

Modest hurdler; acts on a sound surface; stays 3m 1f.

Albermarle (IRE)
92   55
12-y-o ch g Phardante (FR)-Clarahill (Menelek)
M J Gingell Mrs E K Ford

Placings:0/1F31/13450/P2PUF/0/04-PP6   (4683)
2002/03: 21ᴾGS, 20ᴾS, 21⁶GF,

	Starts	1st	2nd	3rd	Win & Pl
Hurdles	1	0	0	0	0
Chases	2	0	0	0	0
Career Total	21	3	1	2	11585
101	5/98	MRas	2m4f	D Ch	G-F £4261
116	4/98	Extr	2m3f110yE Hdl		SFT £2444
109	5/97	Wwck	2m4f110yE Hdl		GD £2761
			Total win prize-money £9466

Going: Sf: 0-1 GS: 0-1 Gd: 0-0 GF: - Fm: 0-1
Distance: 2m/2m3: 0-0 2m4-2m7: 0-3 3m+: 0-1
Track: LH: 0-1 RH: 0-2 Tight: 0-1 Gall: 0-1
Aids: Bl: 0-0 Vi: 0-0 Tstrap: 0-0
Best Rating: 116 4/98 Extr 2m3f110y soft   Hdl

Albert House (IRE)
99f   85f
5-y-o ch g Carroll House-Action Plan (Creative Plan (USA))
R H Alner David O Moon

Placings:00   (4329)
2002/03: 17⁰G, 16⁰G,

	Starts	1st	2nd	3rd	Win & Pl
NH Flat	2	0	0	0	0
Career Total	2	0	0	0	0

Going: Sf: 0-0 GS: 0-0 Gd: 0-2 GF: - Fm: 0-0
Distance: 2m/2m3: 0-2 2m4-2m7: 0-0 3m+: 0-0
Track: LH: 0-1 RH: 0-0 Tight: 0-0 Gall: 0-1
Aids: Bl: 0-0 Vi: 0-0 Tstrap: 0-0
Best Rating: 85 3/03 Newb 2m110y good   NHF

Albert Square (IRE)
93f   85f
6-y-o b g Afflora (IRE)-Place Stephanie (IRE) (Hatim (USA))
R Rowe J C H Berry

Placings:60   (3673)
2002/03: 16⁶GS, 18⁰GS,

	Starts	1st	2nd	3rd	Win & Pl
NH Flat	2	0	0	0	0
Career Total	2	0	0	0	0

Going: Sf: 0-0 GS: 0-2 Gd: 0-0 GF: - Fm: 0-0
Distance: 2m/2m3: 0-2 2m4-2m7: 0-0 3m+: 0-0

Track:	LH: 0-1 RH: 0-1 Tight: 0-1 Gall: 0-0
Aids:	Bl: 0-0 Vi: 0-0 Tstrap: 0-0
Best Rating:	85 1/03 Kemp 2m gd-sft NHF

Albertino Lad

73f   **102f**

6-y-o ch g Mystiko (USA)-Siokra (Kris)
L Lungo R J Gilbert

Placings:5-4   (3775)
2002/03: 16⁴GS,

	Starts	1st	2nd	3rd	Win & Pl
NH Flat	1	0	0	0	0
Career Total	2	0	0	0	0

Going:	Sf: 0-0 GS: 0-1 Gd: 0-0 GF: - Fm: 0-0
Distance:	2m/2m3: 0-1 2m4-2m7: 0-0 3m+: 0-0
Track:	LH: 0-1 RH: 0-0 Tight: 0-0 Gall: 0-0
Aids:	Bl: 0-0 Vi: 0-0 Tstrap: 0-0
Best Rating:	102 2/03 Ayr 2m gd-sft NHF

Albundy (IRE)

98   **86**

4-y-o b g Alzao (USA)-Grove Daffodil (IRE) (Salt Dome (USA))
B Mactaggart (M H Tompkins 30/10) P H Betts (holdings) Ltd

Placings:F640   (4776)
2002/03: 16⁶S, 16⁶GF, 17⁴G, 20⁰G,

	Starts	1st	2nd	3rd	Win & Pl
Hurdles	4	0	0	0	0
Career Total	4	0	0	0	0

Going:	Sf: 0-1 GS: 0-0 Gd: 0-2 GF: - Fm: 0-1
Distance:	2m/2m3: 0-3 2m4-2m7: 0-1 3m+: 0-0
Track:	LH: 0-3 RH: 0-1 Tight: 0-0 Gall: 0-0
Aids:	Bl: 0-0 Vi: 0-0 Tstrap: 0-0
Best Rating:	78 3/03 Weth 2m gd-fm Hdl

Plating-class novice hurdler.

Alcapone (IRE)

114   **(113h)151**

9-y-o b g Roselier (FR)-Ann s Cap (IRE) (Cardinal Flower)
M F Morris Mrs A M Daly

Placings:0F263121436/F55U21F031/34523FPP-031U5PF5624   (4790)
2002/03: 17⁰GY, 20³G, 16¹YS, 20ᵁHY, 20⁵SH, 17ᴾHY, 16ᶠY, 20⁵GY, 25⁶G, 17²GF, 16⁴G,

	Starts	1st	2nd	3rd	Win & Pl
Hurdles	1	0	0	0	0
Chases	10	1	1	1	30562
Career Total	42	5	5	6	91416
152	11/02	Navn	2m		Ch		Y-S	£15950
143	4/01	Fair	2m		Ch		Y-S	£32500
130	12/00	Fair	2m100y		Ch		SFT	£3864
112	2/00	Clon	2m		(0-95)Hdl		SFT	£2760
103	1/00	Tram	2m		Ch		Y-S	£3588

Total win prize-money £58663

Going:	Sf: 0-2 GS: 0-0 Gd: 0-3 GF: - Fm: 0-1
Distance:	2m/2m3: 1-6 2m4-2m7: 0-4 3m+: 0-1
Track:	LH: 1-5 RH: 0-5 Tight: 0-1 Gall: 0-0
Aids:	Bl: 0-0 Vi: 0-0 Tstrap: 0-0
Best Rating:	152 11/02 Navn 2m yld-sft Ch

Very useful Irish chaser; stays three miles but is probably better over slightly shorter trips; suited by cut in the ground.

Alcatras (IRE)

82   **68**

6-y-o b/br g Corrouge (USA)-Kisco (IRE) (Henbit (USA))
B J M Ryall I & Mrs K G Fawcett

Placings:0R0   (3311)
2002/03: 19⁰GS, 16ᴿGS, 19⁰GS,

	Starts	1st	2nd	3rd	Win & Pl
Hurdles	3	0	0	0	
Career Total	3	0	0	0	

Going:	Sf: 0-0 GS: 0-3 Gd: 0-0 GF: - Fm: 0-0
Distance:	2m/2m3: 0-2 2m4-2m7: 0-0 3m+: 0-0
Track:	LH: 0-0 RH: 0-3 Tight: 0-0 Gall: 0-0
Aids:	Bl: 0-0 Vi: 0-0 Tstrap: 0-0
Best Rating:	76 12/02 Extr 2m3f gd-sft Hdl

Alcayde

97   **96**

8-y-o ch g Alhijaz-Lucky Flinders (Free State)
J Akehurst A D Spence

Placings:6/30/5456-2   (1407)
2002/03: 20⁰G,

	Starts	1st	2nd	3rd	Win & Pl
Hurdles	1	0	1	0	896
Career Total	8	0	1	1	1925

Going:	Sf: 0-0 GS: 0-0 Gd: 0-1 GF: - Fm: 0-0
Distance:	2m/2m3: 0-0 2m4-2m7: 0-1 3m+: 0-0
Track:	LH: 0-0 RH: 0-0 Tight: 0-1 Gall: 0-0
Aids:	Bl: 0-0 Vi: 0-0 Tstrap: 0-0
Best Rating:	109 11/00 Asct 2m4f soft Hdl

Moderate maiden hurdler; stays two and a half miles.

Alderbelle

89   **65**

5-y-o b m Alderbrook-Lightning Belle (Belfort (FR))
G M Moore Anmaf Partnership

Placings:66P0   (1371)
2002/03: 17⁶GF, 17⁶G, 22ᴾG, 17⁹GF,

	Starts	1st	2nd	3rd	Win & Pl
NH Flat	1	0	0	0	0
Hurdles	3	0	0	0	0
Career Total	4	0	0	0	0

Going:	Sf: 0-0 GS: 0-0 Gd: 0-2 GF: - Fm: 0-2
Distance:	2m/2m3: 0-3 2m4-2m7: 0-1 3m+: 0-0
Track:	LH: 0-4 RH: 0-0 Tight: 0-4 Gall: 0-0
Aids:	Bl: 0-0 Vi: 0-0 Tstrap: 0-0
Best Rating:	65 8/02 Sedg 2m1f good Hdl

Poor form in bumpers and over hurdles.

Alderfly

77f   **48f**

5-y-o b g Regal Embers (IRE)-Nyika (Town And Country)
J L Spearing Mrs P L Aldersey

Placings:00   (1382)
2002/03: 17⁰G, 17⁰GF,

	Starts	1st	2nd	3rd	Win & Pl
NH Flat	2	0	0	0	0
Career Total	2	0	0	0	0

Going:	Sf: 0-0 GS: 0-0 Gd: 0-1 GF: - Fm: 0-1
Distance:	2m/2m3: 0-2 2m4-2m7: 0-0 3m+: 0-0
Track:	LH: 0-1 RH: 0-1 Tight: 0-1 Gall: 0-0
Aids:	Bl: 0-0 Vi: 0-0 Tstrap: 0-0
Best Rating:	48 10/02 Hrfd 2m1f gd-fm NHF

Alderley Edge

92   **70**

9-y-o gr g Scallywag-Le Madame (Le Bavard (FR))
Keith Thomas Keith Thomas

Placings:3/4FU0004464P   (4710)
2002/03: 24⁴GS, 20ᶠG, 26ᵁGS, 20⁰GF, 22⁰S, 23⁹HY, 24⁴GS, 27⁴S, 24⁶S, 27⁴G, 23ᴾGF,

	Starts	1st	2nd	3rd	Win & Pl
Hurdles	11	0	0	0	312
Career Total	12	0	0	1	550

Going:	Sf: 0-4 GS: 0-3 Gd: 0-2 GF: - Fm: 0-2
Distance:	2m/2m3: 0-0 2m4-2m7: 0-5 3m+: 0-6
Track:	LH: 0-11 RH: 0-0 Tight: 0-4 Gall: 0-1
Aids:	Bl: 0-0 Vi: 0-0 Tstrap: 0-0
Best Rating:	96 5/00 Chep 2m110y firm NHF

Plating-class maiden hurdler.

Aldwych Arrow (IRE)

98   **92**

8-y-o ch g Rainbows For Life (CAN)-Shygate (Shy Groom (USA))
M A Buckley M A Buckley

Placings:0-3126   (1608)
2002/03: 21³G, 17¹GF, 20²GF, 16⁶G,

	Starts	1st	2nd	3rd	Win & Pl
Hurdles	4	1	1	1	4207
Career Total	5	1	1	1	4207
92	10/02	Sedg	2m1f		E Hdl		G-F	£2961

Total win prize-money £2961

Going:	Sf: 0-0 GS: 0-0 Gd: 0-2 GF: - Fm: 1-2
Distance:	2m/2m3: 1-2 2m4-2m7: 0-2 3m+: 0-0
Track:	LH: 1-4 RH: 0-0 Tight: 1-2 Gall: 0-0
Aids:	Bl: 0-0 Vi: 0-0 Tstrap: 0-0
Best Rating:	92 10/02 Hexm 2m4f110y gd-fm Hdl

Moderate hurdler; winner at Sedgefield in October; effective at up to two miles five; may get three miles; acts on a sound surface.

Aleemdar (IRE)

108   **89**

6-y-o b g Doyoun-Aleema (Red God)
Miss K Marks (M J P O Brien 1/8) Nick Shutts

Placings:030500-22110400455   (4704)
2002/03: 16²S, 17²GF, 16¹GY, 17¹G, 16ᴾYS, 16⁴GF, 19⁰S, 17⁰GS, 18⁴G, 17⁹GF, 20⁵G,

	Starts	1st	2nd	3rd	Win & Pl
Hurdles	11	2	2	0	15004
Career Total	17	2	2	1	15484
113	7/02	Klny	2m1f		Hdl		GD	£5503
104	7/02	Naas	2m		Hdl		G-Y	£7196

Total win prize-money £12699

Going:	Sf: 0-2 GS: 0-1 Gd: 1-3 GF: - Fm: 0-3
Distance:	2m/2m3: 2-9 2m4-2m7: 0-2 3m+: 0-0
Track:	LH: 1-5 RH: 0-4 Tight: 0-3 Gall: 0-0
Aids:	Bl: 0-0 Vi: 0-0 Tstrap: 0-0

Best Rating: 113 7/02 Klny 2m1f   good Hdl

Alexander Boyzone (IRE)

9-y-o gr g Mandalus-Fane Bridge (Random Shot)
Miss M E Rowland Paul Mayo

Placings: 30000/3/6-0   (1423)
2002/03: 19⁰GF,

	Starts	1st	2nd	3rd	Win & Pl
Hurdles	1	0	0	0	
Career Total	8	0	0	2	727

Going:	Sf: 0-0 GS: 0-0 Gd: 0-0 GF: - Fm: 0-1
Distance:	2m/2m3: 0-0 2m4-2m7: 0-1 3m+: 0-0
Track:	LH: 0-0 RH: 0-1 Tight: 0-1 Gall: 0-0
Aids:	Bl: 0-0 Vi: 0-0 Tstrap: 0-0
Best Rating: 85	5/00 Punc 2m good NHF

Alexander Park (IRE)

6-y-o b g Yashgan-Lady Laramie (IRE) (Le Bavard (FR))
John R Upson Middleham Park Racing Iv

Placings: P000   (3928)
2002/03: 27⁰S, 20⁰GS, 26⁰G, 26⁰G,

	Starts	1st	2nd	3rd	Win & Pl
Hurdles	4	0	0	0	
Career Total	4	0	0	0	

Going:	Sf: 0-1 GS: 0-1 Gd: 0-2 GF: - Fm: 0-0
Distance:	2m/2m3: 0-0 2m4-2m7: 0-1 3m+: 0-3
Track:	LH: 0-2 RH: 0-2 Tight: 0-2 Gall: 0-1
Aids:	Bl: 0-0 Vi: 0-0 Tstrap: 0-0
Best Rating: 0	3/03 Hntg 3m2f good Hdl

Alf Lauren

100f   **96f**

5-y-o b g Alflora (IRE)-Gokatiego (Huntercombe)
A King Helen Loggin & Richard Preston

Placings: 1   (4322)
2002/03: 17¹G,

	Starts	1st	2nd	3rd	Win & Pl
NH Flat	1	1	0	0	2030
Career Total	1	1	0	0	2030
96 3/03 Bang 2m1f H NHF GD £2030					
Total win prize-money £2030					

Going:	Sf: 0-0 GS: 0-0 Gd: 1-1 GF: - Fm: 0-0
Distance:	2m/2m3: 1-1 2m4-2m7: 0-0 3m+: 0-0
Track:	LH: 1-1 RH: 0-0 Tight: 1-1 Gall: 0-0
Aids:	Bl: 0-0 Vi: 0-0 Tstrap: 0-0
Best Rating: 96	3/03 Bang 2m1f good NHF

Alfa Sunrise

107f   **120f**

6-y-o b g Alflora (IRE)-Gipsy Dawn (Lighter)
R H Buckler Tony Fiorillo

Placings: 5-210   (3782)
2002/03: 16²G, 18¹S, 17⁰GS,

	Starts	1st	2nd	3rd	Win & Pl
NH Flat	3	1	1	0	2796
Career Total	4	1	1	0	2796
120 12/02 Font 2m2f110yH NHF SFT £2226					
Total win prize-money £2226					

Going:	Sf: 1-1 GS: 0-1 Gd: 0-1 GF: - Fm: 0-0
Distance:	2m/2m3: 1-3 2m4-2m7: 0-0 3m+: 0-0
Track:	LH: 1-2 RH: 0-1 Tight: 1-1 Gall: 0-0
Aids:	Bl: 0-0 Vi: 0-0 Tstrap: 0-0
Best Rating: 120	12/02 Font 2m2f110y soft NHF

Fair gelding; stuck on well for second in a Chepstow bumper in October 2002 before bolting up in a similar event at Fontwell; looks a horse with a future.

Alforenka

82f   **88f**

6-y-o ch g Alflora (IRE)-Tochenka (Fine Blue)
H D Daly Anita & Relton Minton

Placings: 06   (3890)
2002/03: 16⁰S, 16⁶G,

	Starts	1st	2nd	3rd	Win & Pl
NH Flat	2	0	0	0	0
Career Total	2	0	0	0	0

Going:	Sf: 0-1 GS: 0-0 Gd: 0-1 GF: - Fm: 0-0
Distance:	2m/2m3: 0-2 2m4-2m7: 0-0 3m+: 0-0
Track:	LH: 0-2 RH: 0-0 Tight: 0-0 Gall: 0-0
Aids:	Bl: 0-0 Vi: 0-0 Tstrap: 0-0
Best Rating: 88	3/03 Hayd 2m good NHF

Alfred The Grey

86(90h)   (85h)**78**

6-y-o gr g Environment Friend-Ranyah (USA) (Our Native (USA))
R Wilman (R Hollinshead 8/6) Saloop

Placings: 60/066P6-001   (0785)
2002/03: 24⁰GF, 24⁰G, 26¹GF,

	Starts	1st	2nd	3rd	Win & Pl
Hurdles	1	0	0	0	
Chases	2	1	0	0	3585
Career Total	10	1	0	0	3585
85 7/02 Sthl 3m2f E Ch G-F £3584					
Total win prize-money £3585					

Going:	Sf: 0-0 GS: 0-0 Gd: 0-1 GF: - Fm: 1-2
Distance:	2m/2m3: 0-0 2m4-2m7: 0-0 3m+: 1-3
Track:	LH: 1-2 RH: 0-1 Tight: 0-0 Gall: 0-0
Aids:	Bl: 0-1 Vi: 0-0 Tstrap: 0-0
Best Rating: 85	7/02 Sthl 3m2f gd-fm Ch

Plating-class chaser; sprang a 33/1 shock when winning a poor three and a quarter mile maiden chase on first outing for new trainer at Southwell July 2002; acts on fast ground.

Alfy Rich

100   **87**

7-y-o b g Alflora (IRE)-Weareagrandmother (Prince Tenderfoot (USA))
P M Rich P M Rich

Placings: 006-P21   (4116)
2002/03: 24²S, 17²S, 21¹G,

	Starts	1st	2nd	3rd	Win & Pl
Hurdles	3	1	1	0	3467
Career Total	6	1	1	0	3467
78 3/03 Hntg 2m5f110yG(0-90)HHdl GD £2555					
Total win prize-money £2555					

Going:	Sf: 0-2 GS: 0-0 Gd: 1-1 GF: - Fm: 0-0
Distance:	2m/2m3: 0-1 2m4-2m7: 1-1 3m+: 0-1
Track:	LH: 0-1 RH: 1-2 Tight: 0-0 Gall: 1-1
Aids:	Bl: 0-0 Vi: 0-0 Tstrap: 0-0
Best Rating: 87	3/03 Extr 2m1f soft Hdl

Plating-class hurdler; improved effort under amateur rider when second at Exeter in March 2003 and followed up with a narrow victory in a Huntingdon seller; effective on good and softer.

Algarve

90   **78**

6-y-o b g Alflora (IRE)-Garvenish (Balinger)
H D Daly Trevor Hemmings

Placings: 600   (4561)
2002/03: 17⁶S, 19⁰S, 20⁰GF,

	Starts	1st	2nd	3rd	Win & Pl
NH Flat	1	0	0	0	0
Hurdles	2	0	0	0	0
Career Total	3	0	0	0	0

Going:	Sf: 0-2 GS: 0-0 Gd: 0-0 GF: - Fm: 0-1
Distance:	2m/2m3: 0-2 2m4-2m7: 0-1 3m+: 0-0
Track:	LH: 0-2 RH: 0-1 Tight: 0-1 Gall: 0-1
Aids:	Bl: 0-0 Vi: 0-0 Tstrap: 0-0
Best Rating: 84	11/02 Hrfd 2m1f soft NHF

Moderate novice hurdler; stays 2m 4f.

Alhaurin

81f   **57f**

4-y-o ch g Classic Cliche (IRE)-Fairey Firefly (Hallgate)
Miss J A Camacho Mrs S Camacho

Placings: 00   (3817)
2002/03: 16⁰GS, 16⁰G,

	Starts	1st	2nd	3rd	Win & Pl
NH Flat	2	0	0	0	
Career Total	2	0	0	0	

Going:	Sf: 0-0 GS: 0-1 Gd: 0-1 GF: - Fm: 0-0
Distance:	2m/2m3: 0-2 2m4-2m7: 0-0 3m+: 0-0
Track:	LH: 0-2 RH: 0-0 Tight: 0-1 Gall: 0-0
Aids:	Bl: 0-0 Vi: 0-0 Tstrap: 0-0
Best Rating: 58	2/03 Weth 2m gd-sft NHF

Alheri

102(99h)   (76h)**70+**

12-y-o gr g Puget (USA)-Miss Haddon (Free Boy)
J A T De Giles J A T De Giles

Placings: 0P6P/3U20/03P-2P03532   (1464)
2002/03: 20²GF, 25⁵G, 21⁰G, 24³GF, 26³GF, 25²F,

	Starts	1st	2nd	3rd	Win & Pl
Hurdles	4	0	1	1	910
Chases	3	0	1	1	1605
Career Total	18	0	3	4	4075

Going:	Sf: 0-0 GS: 0-0 Gd: 0-2 GF: - Fm: 0-5
Distance:	2m/2m3: 0-0 2m4-2m7: 0-3 3m+: 0-4
Track:	LH: 0-4 RH: 0-3 Tight: 0-1 Gall: 0-1
Aids:	Bl: 0-0 Vi: 0-0 Tstrap: 0-0
Best Rating: 76	8/02 Sthl 3m2f gd-fm Hdl

Plating-class hurdler/chaser; stays three miles plus, acts on fast going.

Alice

102   **68**

6-y-o b m Rambo Dancer (CAN)-Cold Line (Exdirectory)
J Hetherton N Hetherton

Placings:*6504*P0P-3   (0878)
2002/03: 21^PGS, 21³G,

	Starts	1st	2nd	3rd	Win & Pl
Hurdles	2	0	0	1	415
Career Total	8	0	0	1	415

Going: Sf: 0-0 GS: 0-1 Gd: 0-1 GF: - Fm: 0-0
Distance: 2m/2m3: 0-0 2m4-2m7: 0-2 3m+: 0-0
Track: LH: 0-1 RH: 0-1 Tight: 0-1 Gall: 0-0
Aids: Bl: 0-0 Vi: 0-0 Tstrap: 0-0
Best Rating: 81   2/02   Fknm   2m   gd-sft   NHF

Moderate form in bumpers so far.

Alice Reigns

98   **75**

6-y-o b m Sir Harry Lewis (USA)-Richards Kate (Fidel)
Mrs A J Perrett S P Tindall

Placings:*1*-4   (1788)
2002/03: 17⁴GS,

	Starts	1st	2nd	3rd	Win & Pl
Hurdles	1	0	0	0	0
Career Total	2	1	0	0	1610
95 1/02 Folk 2m1f110yH NHF			SFT	£1610	
				Total win prize-money £1610	

Going: Sf: 0-0 GS: 0-1 Gd: 0-0 GF: - Fm: 0-0
Distance: 2m/2m3: 0-1 2m4-2m7: 0-0 3m+: 0-0
Track: LH: 0-0 RH: 0-1 Tight: 0-1 Gall: 0-0
Aids: Bl: 0-0 Vi: 0-0 Tstrap: 0-0
Best Rating: 95   1/02   Folk   2m1f110y   soft   NHF

A half-sister to Jane Lechat; bumper winner who became disappointing; won a Folkestone bumper on her debut on soft ground; has the build of a chaser.

Alittlemoreaction

5-y-o b g Alflora (IRE)-Ilderton Road (Noalto)
M J Roberts Mike Roberts

Placings:*000*   (4760)
2002/03: 16⁰G, 17⁰G, 18⁰GF,

	Starts	1st	2nd	3rd	Win & Pl
NH Flat	3	0	0	0	
Career Total	3	0	0	0	

Going: Sf: 0-0 GS: 0-0 Gd: 0-2 GF: - Fm: 0-1
Distance: 2m/2m3: 0-3 2m4-2m7: 0-0 3m+: 0-0
Track: LH: 0-1 RH: 0-2 Tight: 0-2 Gall: 0-1
Aids: Bl: 0-0 Vi: 0-0 Tstrap: 0-0
Best Rating: 0   4/03   Font   2m2f110y   gd-fm   NHF

Alka International

95(105h)   (121h)**116**

11-y-o b g Northern State (USA)-Cachucha (Gay Fandango (USA))
Mrs P Townsley Paul Townsley

Placings:*3240/242P/3212532/262360/11240/0/5246615-5350*   (3670)
2002/03: 17⁵GS, 16³S, 17⁵S, 20⁹GS,

	Starts	1st	2nd	3rd	Win & Pl
Hurdles	1	0	0	0	0

Chases	3	0	0	1	2321
Career Total	38	4	10	5	30981
121	2/02	Plum	2m	D(0-115)HHdl	HVY	£3430
133	12/99	Ling	2m110y	D(0-125)HHdl	SFT	£2851
133	12/99	Font	2m2f110yC(0-130)HHdl	GD	£7002
103	12/97	Hayd	2m	E(0-120)HHdl	SFT	£2221
				Total win prize-money £15506		

Going: Sf: 0-2 GS: 0-2 Gd: 0-0 GF: - Fm: 0-0
Distance: 2m/2m3: 0-3 2m4-2m7: 0-1 3m+: 0-0
Track: LH: 0-1 RH: 0-2 Tight: 0-2 Gall: 0-0
Aids: Bl: 0-2 Vi: 0-0 Tstrap: 0-0
Best Rating: 133   12/99   Kemp   2m   soft   Hdl

Fair, but fragile handicap hurdler; looks best over two miles, but does get further; suited by cut in the ground; often fitted with blinkers.

All Bart Native (IRE)

83   **100**

8-y-o gr g Be My Native (USA)-Bissie s Jayla (Zambrano)
L Wells Mrs Carrie Zetter-Wells

Placings:*4*   (1870)
2002/03: 22⁴GS,

	Starts	1st	2nd	3rd	Win & Pl
Chases	1	0	0	0	313
Career Total	1	0	0	0	313

Going: Sf: 0-0 GS: 0-1 Gd: 0-0 GF: - Fm: 0-0
Distance: 2m/2m3: 0-0 2m4-2m7: 0-1 3m+: 0-0
Track: LH: 0-0 RH: 0-0 Tight: 0-1 Gall: 0-0
Aids: Bl: 0-0 Vi: 0-0 Tstrap: 0-0
Best Rating: 100   11/02   Font   2m6f   gd-sft   Ch

In the frame in staying novice hurdles.

All Bleevable

101   **83**

6-y-o b g Presidium-Eve s Treasure (Bustino)
Mrs S Lamyman Mike & Tony Blee And Roy Allerston

Placings:*6P005/PP20-234*   (4666)
2002/03: 16²G, 16³G, 16⁴G,

	Starts	1st	2nd	3rd	Win & Pl
Hurdles	3	0	1	1	802
Career Total	12	0	2	1	1341

Going: Sf: 0-0 GS: 0-0 Gd: 0-3 GF: - Fm: 0-0
Distance: 2m/2m3: 0-3 2m4-2m7: 0-0 3m+: 0-0
Track: LH: 0-3 RH: 0-0 Tight: 0-3 Gall: 0-0
Aids: Bl: 0-0 Vi: 0-0 Tstrap: 0-0
Best Rating: 80   3/03   Fknm   2m   good   Hdl

Plating-class hurdler; suited by a sharp track and a sound surface.

All Eyez On Me (IRE)

62(86c)   (66c)**52**

6-y-o b g Torus-Ella Rosa (Le Bavard (FR))
Dr P Pritchard A J Whiting

Placings:*000*-FPUUP0P6   (4485)
2002/03: 20^FHY, 23^PS, 20US, 19^UG, 24^PGS, 17⁰G, 21^PGF, 19⁶GF,

	Starts	1st	2nd	3rd	Win & Pl
Hurdles	3	0	0	0	0
Chases	5	0	0	0	0
Career Total	11	0	0	0	0

Going: Sf: 0-3 GS: 0-1 Gd: 0-2 GF: - Fm: 0-2
Distance: 2m/2m3: 0-3 2m4-2m7: 0-3 3m+: 0-2
Track: LH: 0-3 RH: 0-5 Tight: 0-3 Gall: 0-0
Aids: Bl: 0-0 Vi: 0-0 Tstrap: 0-0
Best Rating: 66   1/03   Ludl   2m4f   soft   Ch

All Guns Blazing (IRE)

(104h)   (108h)

7-y-o b g Un Desperado (FR)-Malone Ranger (Noble Philip (USA))
John R Upson The All Guns Blazing Partnership

Placings:*00*P4364-6F   (1796)
2002/03: 20⁶GS, 24^FG,

	Starts	1st	2nd	3rd	Win & Pl
Hurdles	1	0	0	0	0
Chases	1	0	0	0	0
Career Total	9	0	0	1	794

Going: Sf: 0-0 GS: 0-1 Gd: 0-1 GF: - Fm: 0-0
Distance: 2m/2m3: 0-0 2m4-2m7: 0-1 3m+: 0-1
Track: LH: 0-1 RH: 0-1 Tight: 0-1 Gall: 0-0
Aids: Bl: 0-0 Vi: 0-0 Tstrap: 0-0
Best Rating: 101   2/02   Font   2m6f110y   soft   Hdl

In the frame in staying novice hurdles.

All Honey (IRE)

101   **76**

6-y-o ch m Fourstars Allstar (USA)-A Bit Of Honey (The Parson)
Miss K Marks Nick Shutts

Placings:*61*/433540-234540UP0   (4706)
2002/03: 20⁰S, 22³S, 16⁴S, 24⁵S, 20⁴HY, 24⁰S, 20^UG, 25^PS, 20⁰G,

	Starts	1st	2nd	3rd	Win & Pl
Hurdles	7	0	1	1	2320
Chases	2	0	0	0	0
Career Total	17	1	1	3	6999
105	4/01	List	2m	NHF	HVY	£3895
				Total win prize-money £3895		

Going: Sf: 0-7 GS: 0-0 Gd: 0-2 GF: - Fm: 0-0
Distance: 2m/2m3: 0-1 2m4-2m7: 0-5 3m+: 0-3
Track: LH: 0-5 RH: 0-4 Tight: 0-4 Gall: 0-0
Aids: Bl: 0-0 Vi: 0-0 Tstrap: 0-0
Best Rating: 105   4/01   List   2m   heavy   NHF

A bumper winner in Ireland; plating-class hurdler.

All In The Stars (IRE)

87+

5-y-o ch g Fourstars Allstar (USA)-Luton Flyer (Condorcet (FR))
D P Keane Avon Thoroughbreds Ltd

Placings:*0*   (3938)
2002/03: 21⁰GS,

	Starts	1st	2nd	3rd	Win & Pl
Hurdles	1	0	0	0	
Career Total	1	0	0	0	

Going: Sf: 0-0 GS: 0-1 Gd: 0-0 GF: - Fm: 0-0
Distance: 2m/2m3: 0-0 2m4-2m7: 0-1 3m+: 0-0
Track: LH: 0-0 RH: 0-1 Tight: 0-1 Gall: 0-0
Aids: Bl: 0-0 Vi: 0-0 Tstrap: 0-0
Best Rating: 87   3/03   MRas   2m5f110y   gd-sft   Hdl

Point winner in February; third and closing when running out at the last in novices hurdle at Market Rasen two weeks later; stays well.

All Over Now (IRE)
(91h)80

6-y-o b m Broken Hearted-Betty s Girl (Menelek)
Michael Cullen (Miss Venetia Williams 5/7) Frank Clarke

Placings:0R4025 (4178a)
2002/03: 17⁵S, 25⁴S, 16⁴HY, 19⁰S, 20²SH, 20⁵S,

	Starts	1st	2nd	3rd	Win & Pl
NH Flat	3	0	0	0	196
Hurdles	3	0	1	0	1039
Career Total	6	0	1	0	1235

Going: Sf: 0-5 GS: 0-0 Gd: 0-0 GF: - Fm: 0-0
Distance: 2m/2m3: 0-3 2m4-2m7: 0-2 3m+: 0-1
Track: LH: 0-2 RH: 0-0 Tight: 0-2 Gall: 0-0
Aids: Bl: 0-0 Vi: 0-0 Tstrap: 0-0
Best Rating: 91 2/03 Clon 2m4f sft-hvy Hdl

All Points North (IRE)
66 16

4-y-o b g Distinctly North (USA)-Winscarlet North (Garland Knight)
M W Easterby Paul G Jacobs

Placings:0 (0950)
2002/03: 17⁰G,

	Starts	1st	2nd	3rd	Win & Pl
Hurdles	1	0	0	0	
Career Total	1	0	0	0	

Going: Sf: 0-0 GS: 0-0 Gd: 0-1 GF: - Fm: 0-0
Distance: 2m/2m3: 0-1 2m4-2m7: 0-0 3m+: 0-0
Track: LH: 0-1 RH: 0-0 Tight: 0-1 Gall: 0-0
Aids: Bl: 0-0 Vi: 0-0 Tstrap: 0-0
Best Rating: 16 8/02 Sedg 2m1f good Hdl

All Right Clark (IRE)
114 94

10-y-o ch g Tale Quale-Cappahard (Record Run)
N F Glynn N F Glynn

Placings:6F0/063-16014 (1347a)
2002/03: 16¹YS, 17⁶SH, 22⁹GY, 16¹G, 19⁴F,

	Starts	1st	2nd	3rd	Win & Pl
Chases	5	2	0	0	9083
Career Total	11	2	0	1	9647
94 9/02 Uttx 2m	F(0-100)HCh		GD		£3386
72 6/02 Tral 2m	(0-95)HCh		Y-S		£5291
					Total win prize-money £8678

Going: Sf: 0-0 GS: 0-0 Gd: 1-1 GF: - Fm: 0-1
Distance: 2m/2m3: 2-4 2m4-2m7: 0-1 3m+: 0-0
Track: LH: 1-1 RH: 0-1 Tight: 0-0 Gall: 0-0
Aids: Bl: 0-0 Vi: 0-0 Tstrap: 0-0
Best Rating: 94 9/02 Uttx 2m good Ch

Irish chaser, scored over two miles at Uttoxeter in September 2002.

All Sonsilver (FR)
103(86h) (102h)106+

6-y-o b g Son Of Silver-All Licette (FR) (Native Guile (USA))
M Todhunter Sir Robert Ogden

Placings:01-1P2351 (3772)
2002/03: 16¹G, 16⁸G, 20²S, 24³GS, 16⁵G, 21¹GS,

	Starts	1st	2nd	3rd	Win & Pl
Hurdles	1	1	0	0	3360
Chases	5	1	1	1	6692
Career Total	8	3	1	1	13115
106 2/03 Ayr 2m5f110yE(0-105)HCh	G-S				£4114
102 4/02 Hexm 2m110y E(0-110)HHdl	GD				£3360
95 3/02 Kels 2m110y E Hdl	SFT				£3062
					Total win prize-money £10538

Going: Sf: 0-1 GS: 1-2 Gd: 1-3 GF: - Fm: 0-0
Distance: 2m/2m3: 1-3 2m4-2m7: 1-2 3m+: 0-1
Track: LH: 2-6 RH: 0-0 Tight: 0-0 Gall: 0-2
Aids: Bl: 0-0 Vi: 0-0 Tstrap: 0-0
Best Rating: 106 2/03 Ayr 2m5f110y gd-sft Ch

Modest novice chaser; stays two and a half miles; acts with give.

All The Colours (IRE)
(106h) (96h)58

10-y-o br h Classic Secret (USA)-Rainbow Vision (Prince Tenderfoot (USA))
Jonjo O Neill (J E Mulhern 20/7) P Byrne

Placings:213/2246/2/0000-4PF (2080)
2002/03: 22⁴GS, 24²S, 24⁴HY,

	Starts	1st	2nd	3rd	Win & Pl
Chases	3	0	0	0	349
Career Total	15	1	4	1	11098
114 3/97 Leop 2m	NHF		SFT		£3051
					Total win prize-money £3052

Going: Sf: 0-2 GS: 0-1 Gd: 0-0 GF: - Fm: 0-0
Distance: 2m/2m3: 0-0 2m4-2m7: 0-1 3m+: 0-2
Track: LH: 0-1 RH: 0-2 Tight: 0-2 Gall: 0-0
Aids: Bl: 0-0 Vi: 0-0 Tstrap: 0-0
Best Rating: 121 3/97 Chel 2m110y gd-fm NHF

Allanton Brig

7-y-o b g Milieu-Lurdenlaw Rose (New Brig)
R Shiels R Shiels

Placings:0-P (3801)
2002/03: 24²S,

	Starts	1st	2nd	3rd	Win & Pl
Hurdles	1	0	0	0	
Career Total	2	0	0	0	

Going: Sf: 0-1 GS: 0-0 Gd: 0-0 GF: - Fm: 0-0
Distance: 2m/2m3: 0-0 2m4-2m7: 0-0 3m+: 0-1
Track: LH: 0-1 RH: 0-0 Tight: 0-0 Gall: 0-0
Aids: Bl: 0-0 Vi: 0-0 Tstrap: 0-0
Best Rating: 0 2/03 Newc 3m soft Hdl

Alleged Affair (IRE)
88f 89f

6-y-o gr g Safety Catch (USA)-Wren s Princess (Wrens Hill)
O Brennan E G Ashford

Placings:0 (2477)
2002/03: 16⁹GS,

	Starts	1st	2nd	3rd	Win & Pl
NH Flat	1	0	0	0	
Career Total	1	0	0	0	

Going: Sf: 0-0 GS: 0-1 Gd: 0-0 GF: - Fm: 0-0
Distance: 2m/2m3: 0-1 2m4-2m7: 0-0 3m+: 0-0
Track: LH: 0-1 RH: 0-0 Tight: 0-0 Gall: 0-1
Aids: Bl: 0-0 Vi: 0-0 Tstrap: 0-0
Best Rating: 92 12/02 Donc 2m110y gd-sft NHF

Alleged Slave (IRE)
103 110

8-y-o ch g Husyan (USA)-Lek Dawn (Menelek)
A King Mrs Peter Prowting

Placings:2/265 (4173)
2002/03: 24³HY, 24⁶S, 20⁵S,

	Starts	1st	2nd	3rd	Win & Pl
Hurdles	3	0	1	0	790
Career Total	4	0	2	0	1280

Going: Sf: 0-3 GS: 0-0 Gd: 0-0 GF: - Fm: 0-0
Distance: 2m/2m3: 0-0 2m4-2m7: 0-1 3m+: 0-2
Track: LH: 0-2 RH: 0-1 Tight: 0-0 Gall: 0-0
Aids: Bl: 0-0 Vi: 0-0 Tstrap: 0-0
Best Rating: 117 4/00 Hntg 2m110y good NHF

Fair novice hurdler; finished runner-up in a bumper on his debut in April 2000, but was not seen until finishing in the same position in a maiden hurdle at Chepstow in January 2003; well beaten next time; stays three miles and acts on soft ground.

Allegedly Red
95 70

4-y-o ch f Sabrehill (USA)-Tendency (Ballad Rock)
Mrs A Duffield Mrs L J Tounsend

Placings:66F4 (3508)
2002/03: 16⁶G, 16⁹G, 16FHY, 16⁴G,

	Starts	1st	2nd	3rd	Win & Pl
Hurdles	4	0	0	0	0
Career Total	4	0	0	0	0

Going: Sf: 0-1 GS: 0-0 Gd: 0-3 GF: - Fm: 0-0
Distance: 2m/2m3: 0-4 2m4-2m7: 0-0 3m+: 0-0
Track: LH: 0-4 RH: 0-0 Tight: 0-2 Gall: 0-1
Aids: Bl: 0-0 Vi: 0-0 Tstrap: 0-0
Best Rating: 70 11/02 Catt 2m good Hdl

Useless on the level, gave problems before the start on hurdling debut.

Allegiance
72 42

8-y-o b g Rock Hopper-So Precise (FR) (Balidar)
P Wegmann P Wegmann

Placings:P15000532040/004/11626430P/0-0 (4054)
2002/03: 16⁹S,

	Starts	1st	2nd	3rd	Win & Pl
Hurdles	1	0	0	0	
Career Total	26	3	2	2	10600
100 11/00 Wwck 2m	F(0-100)HHdl		HVY		£1940
100 11/00 NAbb 2m1f	F(0-110)HHdl		HVY		£2678
79 9/98 MRas 2m1f110yG Hdl			GD		£1562
					Total win prize-money £6180

Going: Sf: 0-1 GS: 0-0 Gd: 0-0 GF: - Fm: 0-0
Distance: 2m/2m3: 0-1 2m4-2m7: 0-0 3m+: 0-0
Track: LH: 0-1 RH: 0-0 Tight: 0-0 Gall: 0-0
Aids: Bl: 0-0 Vi: 0-0 Tstrap: 0-0
Best Rating: 100 12/00 Chep 2m110y soft Hdl

Aller Moor (IRE)
101   **100**

12-y-o b g Dry Dock-Boggy Peak (Shirley Heights)
C J Gray G Keirle

Placings:060/1122113/5422P/42220P/11P   (4615)
2002/03: 25¹S, 25¹G, 26²G,

	Starts	1st	2nd	3rd	Win & Pl
Chases	3	2	0	0	5075
Career Total	24	6	7	1	36512
100	3/03	Extr	3m1f110yH Ch		GD	5075

100	3/03	Extr	3m1f110yH Ch	GD	
100	3/03	Hrfd	3m1f110yH Ch	SFT	£1526
131	3/98	Winc	3m1f110yD(0-120)HCh	GD	£4384
131	1/98	Winc	3m1f110yC(0-135)HCh	GD	£5225
113	11/97	Winc	3m1f110yE(0-105)HCh	GD	£3550
109	5/97	Strf	3m	H Ch	GD	£2976

Total win prize-money £21210

Going: Sf: 1-1 GS: 0-0 Gd: 1-2 GF: - Fm: 0-0
Distance: 2m/2m3: 0-0 2m4-2m7: 0-0 **3m+: 2-3**
Track: LH: 0-1 **RH: 2-2** Tight: 0-0 Gall: 0-1
Aids: Bl: 0-0 Vi: 0-0 Tstrap: 0-0
Best Rating: **131** 3/98 Winc   3m1f110y good   Ch

Fair handicap chaser at around three miles; returned after an absence of almost two years to win a soft ground hunter chase at Hereford March 2003; followed up on good ground at Exeter next time.

Allez Toujours (IRE)
99   **(58c)**

8-y-o b g Castle Keep-Adapan (Pitpan)
M Sheppard Simon Gegg

Placings:035/5/430PBP3   (4709)
2002/03: 17⁴S, 16³HY, 19⁰S, 19⁸G, 16⁶G, 24³G,

	Starts	1st	2nd	3rd	Win & Pl
Hurdles	4	0	0	2	1178
Chases	3	0	0	0	
Career Total	11	0	0	3	1626

Going: Sf: 0-3 GS: 0-0 Gd: 0-4 GF: - Fm: 0-0
Distance: 2m/2m3: 0-5 2m4-2m7: 0-1 3m+: 0-1
Track: LH: 0-4 RH: 0-3 Tight: 0-1 Gall: 0-0
Aids: Bl: 0-0 Vi: 0-0 Tstrap: 0-0
Best Rating: **104** 12/00 Cork 2m   soft   Hdl

Some ability over hurdles since arriving from Ireland.

Alligator Alley (IRE)

7-y-o ch g Roselier (FR)-Ballyhoura Lady (Green Shoon)
P R Webber Andrew Jenkins

Placings:00P   (3153)
2002/03: 16⁰HY, 19⁰S, 24ᴾHY,

	Starts	1st	2nd	3rd	Win & Pl
NH Flat	2	0	0	0	0
Hurdles	1	0	0	0	
Career Total	3	0	0	0	

Going: Sf: 0-3 GS: 0-0 Gd: 0-0 GF: - Fm: 0-0
Distance: 2m/2m3: 0-2 2m4-2m7: 0-0 3m+: 0-1
Track: LH: 0-3 RH: 0-0 Tight: 0-0 Gall: 0-0
Aids: Bl: 0-0 Vi: 0-1 Tstrap: 0-0
Best Rating: **35** 12/02 Uttx   2m   soft   NHF

Allimac (IRE)
109(102h)   (104h)**123**

6-y-o b g Alphabatim (USA)-Firewood (IRE) (Brush Aside (USA))
Miss H C Knight Mrs T P Radford

Placings:20/2204-1213P1   (4785)
2002/03: 19¹GF, 17²GF, 20¹F, 16³G, 19ᴾG, 20¹G,

	Starts	1st	2nd	3rd	Win & Pl
Chases	6	3	1	1	17062
Career Total	12	3	4	1	19280
105	4/03	MRas	2m4f	D Ch	GD	£5810
123	10/02	Ludl	2m4f	E Ch	FRM	£4108
111	5/02	Hrfd	2m3f	D Ch	G-F	£4875

Total win prize-money £14793

Going: Sf: 0-0 GS: 0-0 Gd: 1-3 GF: - Fm: 2-3
Distance: 2m/2m3: 1-3 **2m4-2m7: 2-3** 3m+: 0-0
Track: LH: 0-1 **RH: 3-5** Tight: 2-3 Gall: 0-0
Aids: Bl: 0-0 Vi: 0-0 Tstrap: 0-0
Best Rating: **123** 11/02 Kemp 2m   good   Ch

Fair novice chaser; won on his chasing debut at Hereford in May 2002; followed up over two and a half miles at Ludlow in October; bled twice before taking a weak event at Market Rasen in April; effective on fast ground.

Allotrope (IRE)

8-y-o b g Nashwan (USA)-Graphite (USA) (Mr Prospector (USA))
Lady Susan Brooke (Mrs M Reveley 6/10) Lady Susan Brooke

Placings:525/3P05430/10-05P   (4565)
2002/03: 24⁰G, 17⁵GS, 24ᴾGF,

	Starts	1st	2nd	3rd	Win & Pl
Hurdles	2	0	0	0	0
Chases	1	0	0	0	0
Career Total	15	1	1	2	4099
86	10/01	Kels	2m6f110yF(0-105)HHdl	GD	£2856

Total win prize-money £2856

Going: Sf: 0-0 GS: 0-1 Gd: 0-1 GF: - Fm: 0-1
Distance: 2m/2m3: 0-1 2m4-2m7: 0-0 3m+: 0-2
Track: LH: 0-1 RH: 0-2 Tight: 0-3 Gall: 0-0
Aids: Bl: 0-2 Vi: 0-0 Tstrap: 0-0
Best Rating: **98** 10/99 Kels 2m6f110y good   Hdl

Allstar Leader (IRE)
97   **83**

6-y-o b g Fourstars Allstar (USA)-Rugged Leader (Supreme Leader)
Seamus O Farrell Seamus O Farrell

Placings:505-0F0000006   (4746a)
2002/03: 16⁰G, 17ᶠY, 16⁰G, 16⁰G, 20⁰YS, 16⁰G, 20⁰SH, 24⁶S, 16⁶G,

	Starts	1st	2nd	3rd	Win & Pl
NH Flat	4	0	0	0	0
Hurdles	5	0	0	0	0
Career Total	12	0	0	0	

Going: Sf: 0-1 GS: 0-0 Gd: 0-5 GF: - Fm: 0-0
Distance: 2m/2m3: 0-6 2m4-2m7: 0-2 3m+: 0-1
Track: LH: 0-1 RH: 0-2 Tight: 0-0 Gall: 0-0
Aids: Bl: 0-0 Vi: 0-0 Tstrap: 0-0
Best Rating: **100** 4/03 Fair   2m   good   NHF

Held in bumpers and maiden hurdle company so far.

Alltime Dancer (IRE)

11-y-o b g Waajib-Dance On Lady (Grundy)
Miss Kate Smyth (Mrs C F Lambert 1/5) Major Charles Lambert

Placings:1213141144/5450003651/6/4540-05   (4031)
2002/03: 33⁰GF, 24⁵S,

	Starts	1st	2nd	3rd	Win & Pl
Chases	2	0	0	0	0
Career Total	27	6	1	2	21185
118	4/97	Plum	2m4f	E(0-115)HHdl	G-F	£2241
114	3/96	Newb	2m110y	D Hdl	G-S	£2941
126	12/95	Sand	2m110y	C Hdl	GD	£3525
126	11/95	Sand	2m110y	C Hdl	G-F	£3355
114	10/95	Extr	2m1f110yE Hdl	GD	£2122
87	7/95	MRas	2m1f110yD Hdl	G-F	£2630

Total win prize-money £16816

Going: Sf: 0-1 GS: 0-0 Gd: 0-0 GF: - Fm: 0-1
Distance: 2m/2m3: 0-0 2m4-2m7: 0-0 3m+: 0-2
Track: LH: 0-1 RH: 0-1 Tight: 0-0 Gall: 0-1
Aids: Bl: 0-0 Vi: 0-0 Tstrap: 0-0
Best Rating: **127** 10/96 Chep 2m110y   good   Hdl

Allude (IRE)
107   **112**

4-y-o b g Darshaan-Ahliyat (USA) (Irish River (FR))
C J Mann (M J Grassick 30/6) Abbott Racing Limited

Placings:36520   (4460)
2002/03: 16³G, 16⁶HY, 17⁵GS, 17²GF, 16⁰G,

	Starts	1st	2nd	3rd	Win & Pl
Hurdles	5	0	1	1	2014
Career Total	5	0	1	1	2014

Going: Sf: 0-1 GS: 0-1 Gd: 0-2 GF: - Fm: 0-1
Distance: 2m/2m3: 0-5 2m4-2m7: 0-0 3m+: 0-0
Track: LH: 0-1 RH: 0-4 Tight: 0-1 Gall: 0-0
Aids: Bl: 0-0 Vi: 0-0 Tstrap: 0-0
Best Rating: **112** 4/03 Aint   2m110y   good   Hdl

Modest hurdler; Flat winner in Ireland; landed novice hurdle at Worcester May 2003; narrow winner of poor event at Cartmel two weeks later; acts on good and good to firm ground.

Almanoso
99   **78**

7-y-o b m Teenoso (USA)-Almanot (Remainder Man)
R Curtis Guildings Racing Club

Placings:6/40550/6230U-P5   (2311)
2002/03: 22ᴾS, 25⁵HY,

	Starts	1st	2nd	3rd	Win & Pl
Hurdles	2	0	0	0	0
Career Total	13	0	1	1	855

Going: Sf: 0-2 GS: 0-0 Gd: 0-0 GF: - Fm: 0-0
Distance: 2m/2m3: 0-0 2m4-2m7: 0-1 3m+: 0-1
Track: LH: 0-1 RH: 0-0 Tight: 0-1 Gall: 0-0
Aids: Bl: 0-0 Vi: 0-0 Tstrap: 0-0
Best Rating: **99** 4/00 Asct   2m110y   soft   NHF

Plating-class staying hurdler, best efforts when ridden from the front.

Almapa

93(105h)   (86h)**85**
11-y-o ch g Absalom-More Fun (Malicious)
R J Baker P Slade

Placings:23341330226333/U4P112334U6/F34213446U4/4
332/343512/4063-0424641462   (1617)
2002/03: 16⁶G, 16⁴G, 17²G, 16⁴GF, 17⁶GF, 16⁴G, 18¹GF, 17⁴F,
19⁶G, 16²F,

	Starts	1st	2nd	3rd	Win & Pl
Hurdles	8	1	1	0	2969
Chases	2	0	1	0	1048
Career Total	60	6	9	16	25275
82	9/02	Font	2m2f110yG(0-95)HHdl	G-F	£2320
96	8/00	NAbb	2m1f	F(0-100)HHdl	GD	£2604
96	10/98	Tntn	2m1f	G(0-90)HHdl	FRM	£1836
94	10/97	Tntn	2m1f	E(0-115)HHdl	FRM	£3737
82	9/97	Strf	2m110y	F Hdl	GD	£1931
81	10/96	Tntn	2m1f	G Hdl	HRD	£2005
				Total win prize-money £14436

Going: Sf: 0-0 GS: 0-0 Gd: 0-4 GF: - Fm: 1-6
Distance: 2m/2m3: 1-10 2m4-2m7: 0-0 3m+: 0-0
Track: LH: 1-7 RH: 0-3 Tight: 1-5 Gall: 0-0
Aids: Bl: 0-1 Vi: 0-0 Tstrap: 0-0
Best Rating: 96 8/00 NAbb 2m1f   good   Hdl

Pays his way in lowly company on fast ground.

Almaravide (GER)

97   **93**
7-y-o ch g Orfano (GER)-Allerleirauh (GER) (Espresso)
M Bradstock P J Constable

Placings:11/44/0   (3288)
2002/03: 17⁹GS,

	Starts	1st	2nd	3rd	Win & Pl
Hurdles	1	0	0	0	
Career Total	5	2	0	0	11145
100	4/00	MRas	2m3f110yD Hdl		SFT	£3253
137	4/00	Chel	2m1f	C Hdl	SFT	£6971
				Total win prize-money £10225

Going: Sf: 0-0 GS: 0-1 Gd: 0-0 GF: - Fm: 0-0
Distance: 2m/2m3: 0-1 2m4-2m7: 0-0 3m+: 0-0
Track: LH: 0-1 RH: 0-0 Tight: 0-0 Gall: 0-1
Aids: Bl: 0-0 Vi: 0-0 Tstrap: 0-0
Best Rating: 137 4/00 Chel 2m1f   soft   Hdl

Fair, lightly-raced hurdler; won his first two races over hurdles in the spring of 2000, but absent for a long time after October of that year; acts on soft ground.

Almashrouk (IRE)

96   **62**
6-y-o ch g Common Grounds-Red Note (Rusticaro (FR))
M E Sowersby (M R Channon 5/7) The Southwold Set

Placings:300050   (4373)
2002/03: 17³GS, 16⁹GS, 16⁶S, 16⁹G, 17⁵G, 17⁹G,

	Starts	1st	2nd	3rd	Win & Pl
Hurdles	6	0	0	1	592
Career Total	6	0	0	1	592

Going: Sf: 0-1 GS: 0-2 Gd: 0-3 GF: - Fm: 0-0
Distance: 2m/2m3: 0-6 2m4-2m7: 0-0 3m+: 0-0
Track: LH: 0-4 RH: 0-2 Tight: 0-4 Gall: 0-1
Aids: Bl: 0-0 Vi: 0-0 Tstrap: 0-0
Best Rating: 62 3/03 MRas 2m1f110y good   Hdl

Plating-class hurdler.

Almazard

74   **41**
6-y-o b g Mazaad-Almanot (Remainder Man)
L Wells Studley Racing Partnership

Placings:000P   (3935)
2002/03: 18⁰S, 16⁰GS, 22²GS, 27⁵S,

	Starts	1st	2nd	3rd	Win & Pl
NH Flat	2	0	0	0	0
Hurdles	2	0	0	0	0
Career Total	4	0	0	0	

Going: Sf: 0-2 GS: 0-2 Gd: 0-0 GF: - Fm: 0-0
Distance: 2m/2m3: 0-2 2m4-2m7: 0-1 3m+: 0-1
Track: LH: 0-2 RH: 0-1 Tight: 0-3 Gall: 0-0
Aids: Bl: 0-2 Vi: 0-0 Tstrap: 0-0
Best Rating: 41 2/03 Font 2m6f110y gd-sft   Hdl

Almire Du Lia (FR)

96   **92**
5-y-o ch g Beyssac (FR)-Lita (FR) (Big John (FR))
Mrs S C Bradburne Hardie, Cochrane, Paterson & Steel

Placings:26512   (4403)
2002/03: 22²S, 22⁶HY, 24⁵S, 20¹GS, 22²GF,

	Starts	1st	2nd	3rd	Win & Pl
Hurdles	5	1	2	0	6644
Career Total	5	1	2	0	6644
92	3/03	Newc	2m4f	E(0-105)HHdl	G-S	£4212
				Total win prize-money £4212

Going: Sf: 0-3 GS: 1-1 Gd: 0-0 GF: - Fm: 0-1
Distance: 2m/2m3: 0-0 2m4-2m7: 1-4 3m+: 0-1
Track: LH: 1-5 RH: 0-0 Tight: 0-0 Gall: 1-1
Aids: Bl: 0-0 Vi: 0-0 Tstrap: 0-0
Best Rating: 92 3/03 Hayd 2m6f   gd-fm   Hdl

Moderate staying novice hurdler; won on handicap debut over two and a half miles; stays further; acts on good to soft or faster; usually wears sheepskin cheekpieces.

Almnadia (IRE)

106   **103**
4-y-o b f Alhaarth (IRE)-Mnaafa (IRE) (Darshaan)
S Gollings (D L Williams 11/9) J Hennessy

Placings:2643126416P035   (4371)
2002/03: 17²GS, 16⁶GF, 17⁴G, 17³GF, 16¹GF, 16²G, 16⁶GS, 16⁴S,
16¹GS, 16⁶S, 16⁵PS, 16³G, 16⁵G,

	Starts	1st	2nd	3rd	Win & Pl
Hurdles	14	2	2	2	17262
Career Total	14	2	2	2	17262
103	12/02	Fknm	2m	E Hdl	G-S	£3465
103	10/02	Chel	2m110y	C Hdl	G-F	£6826
				Total win prize-money £10292

Going: Sf: 0-3 GS: 1-4 Gd: 0-4 GF: - Fm: 1-3
Distance: 2m/2m3: 2-13 2m4-2m7: 0-1 3m+: 0-0
Track: LH: 2-9 RH: 0-5 Tight: 1-5 Gall: 0-0
Aids: Bl: 0-0 Vi: 0-0 Tstrap: 0-0
Best Rating: 103 12/02 Fknm 2m   gd-sft   Hdl

A winner over 12 furlongs on the Flat; sprung a surprise when landing a juvenile hurdle at Cheltenham in October 2002; handles fast ground, not as effective on a soft surface; likes to make the running.

Almontasir (IRE)

35f   **6f**
5-y-o b g Distinctly North (USA)-My Blue (Scenic)

T P McGovern Ahmed Abdel-Khaleq

Placings:PP   (2666)
2002/03: 16⁶G, 18⁸PS,

	Starts	1st	2nd	3rd	Win & Pl
NH Flat	2	0	0	0	
Career Total	2	0	0	0	

Going: Sf: 0-1 GS: 0-0 Gd: 0-0 GF: - Fm: 0-0
Distance: 2m/2m3: 0-2 2m4-2m7: 0-0 3m+: 0-0
Track: LH: 0-2 RH: 0-0 Tight: 0-1 Gall: 0-0
Aids: Bl: 0-0 Vi: 0-0 Tstrap: 0-0
Best Rating: 0 12/02 Font 2m2f110y soft   NHF

Almost Broke

99   **97+**
6-y-o ch g Nearly A Hand-Teletex (Pollerton)
P F Nicholls A G Fear

Placings:2-6F3   (4551)
2002/03: 22⁶GS, 20⁴S, 20³G,

	Starts	1st	2nd	3rd	Win & Pl
Hurdles	3	0	0	1	1178
Career Total	4	0	1	1	1762

Going: Sf: 0-1 GS: 0-1 Gd: 0-1 GF: - Fm: 0-0
Distance: 2m/2m3: 0-0 2m4-2m7: 0-3 3m+: 0-0
Track: LH: 0-3 RH: 0-0 Tight: 0-1 Gall: 0-0
Aids: Bl: 0-0 Vi: 0-0 Tstrap: 0-0
Best Rating: 104 3/02 Ludl 2m   soft   NHF

Just caught on his bumper debut; held over hurdles.

Almost Free

99   **83+**
6-y-o b g Darshaan-Light Fresh Air (USA) (Rahy (USA))
B S Rothwell Ron Macdonald

Placings:P2   (3330)
2002/03: 17⁵PS, 16²G,

	Starts	1st	2nd	3rd	Win & Pl
Hurdles	2	0	1	0	1248
Career Total	2	0	1	0	1248

Going: Sf: 0-1 GS: 0-0 Gd: 0-0 GF: - Fm: 0-0
Distance: 2m/2m3: 0-2 2m4-2m7: 0-0 3m+: 0-0
Track: LH: 0-1 RH: 0-1 Tight: 0-2 Gall: 0-0
Aids: Bl: 0-0 Vi: 0-0 Tstrap: 0-0
Best Rating: 83 1/03 Muss 2m   good   Hdl

Modest novice hurdler, suited by ground good or softer; yet to win over timber.

Almutan Star

8-y-o b m Almutanabbi-Salt Of The Earth (Sterling Bay (SWE))
J Neville A F Syndicate

Placings:P   (0105)
2002/03: 16⁶PGF,

	Starts	1st	2nd	3rd	Win & Pl
Hurdles	1	0	0	0	
Career Total	1	0	0	0	

Going: Sf: 0-0 GS: 0-0 Gd: 0-0 GF: - Fm: 0-1
Distance: 2m/2m3: 0-1 2m4-2m7: 0-0 3m+: 0-0
Track: LH: 0-0 RH: 0-1 Tight: 0-0 Gall: 0-0

Aids: Bl: 0-0 Vi: 0-0 Tstrap: 0-0
Best Rating: 0   5/02 Ludl 2m   gd-fm Hdl

Alpha Blues

105   (115c)**121**

8-y-o ch g Acatenango (GER)-Alpha Belle (GER) (Runnett)
J T R Dreaper Mrs P J Conway

Placings:3264/2211/2-4444003   (4725a)
2002/03: 20⁴HY, 17⁴S, 25⁴S, 20⁴S, 23⁹GS, 16⁹GY, 18³GF,

	Starts	1st	2nd	3rd	Win & Pl
Hurdles	4	0	0	1	1558
Chases	3	0	0	0	1166
Career Total	16	2	4	2	23357
140 4/01	Fair	2m4f	Hdl	SFT	£6677
130 2/01	Fair	2m4f	Hdl	Y-S	£5008
			Total win prize-money £11685		

Going: Sf: 0-4 GS: 0-1 Gd: 0-0 GF: - Fm: 0-1
Distance: 2m/2m3: 0-3 2m4-2m7: 0-2 3m+: 0-1
Track: LH: 0-1 RH: 0-3 Tight: 0-0 Gall: 0-0
Aids: Bl: 0-2 Vi: 0-0 Tstrap: 0-0
Best Rating: 140 5/01 Fair 2m4f   gd-yld Hdl

Useful Irish-trained hurdler/chaser; stays two and a half miles and has been tried at further over fences; suited by soft ground; has worn blinkers.

Alpha Centauri (IRE)

(87h)   (96h)

9-y-o ch g Alphabatim (USA)-Barna Glen (Furry Glen)
Miss Venetia Williams Lady Harris

Placings:0/1P/P5PP   (3110)
2002/03: 21⁵PS, 17⁵GS, 20⁵S, 16⁵S,

	Starts	1st	2nd	3rd	Win & Pl
Hurdles	2	0	0	0	0
Chases	2	0	0	0	0
Career Total	7	1	0	0	3312
104 11/00	Naas	2m	NHF	Y-S	£3312
			Total win prize-money £3312		

Going: Sf: 0-3 GS: 0-1 Gd: 0-0 GF: - Fm: 0-0
Distance: 2m/2m3: 0-2 2m4-2m7: 0-2 3m+: 0-0
Track: LH: 0-2 RH: 0-2 Tight: 0-3 Gall: 0-0
Aids: Bl: 0-0 Vi: 0-0 Tstrap: 0-0
Best Rating: 104 11/00 Naas 2m   yld-sft NHF

Alpha Leather

12-y-o b g Zambrano-Harvey s Choice (Whistlefield)
L P Grassick Postlip Racing

Placings:6400000/B605555/2632P400/306S5064545U0/P6
000-P454   (0883)
2002/03: 24⁵PGF, 21⁴G, 24⁵GF, 24⁴S,

	Starts	1st	2nd	3rd	Win & Pl
Chases	4	0	0	0	691
Career Total	44	0	2	2	3299

Going: Sf: 0-1 GS: 0-0 Gd: 0-1 GF: - Fm: 0-2
Distance: 2m/2m3: 0-0 2m4-2m7: 0-1 3m+: 0-3
Track: LH: 0-3 RH: 0-1 Tight: 0-4 Gall: 0-0
Aids: Bl: 0-0 Vi: 0-0 Tstrap: 0-0
Best Rating: 89 11/95 Uttx 2m   gd-fm NHF

Alpha Noble (GER)

93   **90**

6-y-o b g Lando (GER)-Alpha (GER) (Frontal)
Miss Venetia Williams (P Rau 21/9) Richard Abbott & Mario Stavrou

Placings:4   (2629)
2002/03: 16⁴S,

	Starts	1st	2nd	3rd	Win & Pl
Hurdles	1	0	0	0	0
Career Total	1	0	0	0	0

Going: Sf: 0-1 GS: 0-0 Gd: 0-0 GF: - Fm: 0-0
Distance: 2m/2m3: 0-1 2m4-2m7: 0-0 3m+: 0-0
Track: LH: 0-1 RH: 0-0 Tight: 0-0 Gall: 0-0
Aids: Bl: 0-0 Vi: 0-0 Tstrap: 0-0
Best Rating: 95 12/02 Uttx 2m   soft Hdl

Winner three times on the Flat in Germany; showed some promise though well beaten on debut over hurdles at Uttoxeter in December 2002.

Alpha Romana (IRE)

9-y-o b g Alphabatim (USA)-Stella Romana (Roman Warrior)
Mrs Susan E Busby Mrs Susan E Busby

Placings:06056/0030/P21-1PP0F2   (4487)
2002/03: 16¹GF, 21⁶G, 24⁴S, 16⁶GS, 20⁶GF, 16²GF,

	Starts	1st	2nd	3rd	Win & Pl
Chases	6	1	1	0	4115
Career Total	18	2	2	1	7212
106 5/02	Chel	2m110y	H Ch	G-F	£3675
89 4/02	Fknm	2m5f110yH Ch		GD	£2212
			Total win prize-money £5887		

Going: Sf: 0-1 GS: 0-1 Gd: 0-1 GF: - Fm: 1-3
Distance: 2m/2m3: 1-3 2m4-2m7: 0-2 3m+: 0-1
Track: LH: 1-2 RH: 0-4 Tight: 0-2 Gall: 1-2
Aids: Bl: 0-0 Vi: 0-0 Tstrap: 0-0
Best Rating: 106 5/02 Chel 2m110y gd-fm Ch

Moderate hunter chaser; effective at below three miles; suited by good/fast ground.

Alphabetic

82   **89**

6-y-o ch g Alflora (IRE)-Incamelia (St Columbus)
N J Henderson Mrs D A Henderson

Placings:303   (4444)
2002/03: 17³G, 16⁰S, 16³G,

	Starts	1st	2nd	3rd	Win & Pl
NH Flat	3	0	0	2	633
Career Total	3	0	0	2	633

Going: Sf: 0-1 GS: 0-0 Gd: 0-2 GF: - Fm: 0-0
Distance: 2m/2m3: 0-3 2m4-2m7: 0-0 3m+: 0-0
Track: LH: 0-1 RH: 0-2 Tight: 0-0 Gall: 0-0
Aids: Bl: 0-0 Vi: 0-0 Tstrap: 0-0
Best Rating: 98 4/03 Asct 2m110y good NHF

Fair form in bumpers; shaped as though he needs 3m when third over 2m 4f on hurdling debut at Chepstow May 2003.

Alphamericredonion (IRE)

92   **80+**

7-y-o ch g Naheez (USA)-Radical Sovereign (Radical)

Mrs A Duffield Alphameric Red Onion Ltd

Placings:46606   (2556)
2002/03: 16⁴GF, 16⁶GF, 17⁶G, 16⁰GS, 20⁶GF,

	Starts	1st	2nd	3rd	Win & Pl
NH Flat	4	0	0	0	0
Hurdles	1	0	0	0	0
Career Total	5	0	0	0	0

Going: Sf: 0-0 GS: 0-1 Gd: 0-1 GF: - Fm: 0-3
Distance: 2m/2m3: 0-4 2m4-2m7: 0-1 3m+: 0-0
Track: LH: 0-2 RH: 0-2 Tight: 0-1 Gall: 0-1
Aids: Bl: 0-0 Vi: 0-0 Tstrap: 0-0
Best Rating: 89 11/02 Aint 2m1f   good NHF

Alphasupreme (IRE)

92f   **80f**

6-y-o ch m Alphabatim (USA)-Railway Rabbit (IRE) (Supreme Leader)
Mrs P N Dutfield Simon Dutfield

Placings:45   (1095)
2002/03: 17⁴GF, 17⁵GF,

	Starts	1st	2nd	3rd	Win & Pl
NH Flat	2	0	0	0	0
Career Total	2	0	0	0	0

Going: Sf: 0-0 GS: 0-0 Gd: 0-0 GF: - Fm: 0-2
Distance: 2m/2m3: 0-2 2m4-2m7: 0-0 3m+: 0-0
Track: LH: 0-2 RH: 0-0 Tight: 0-2 Gall: 0-0
Aids: Bl: 0-0 Vi: 0-0 Tstrap: 0-0
Best Rating: 80 7/02 NAbb 2m1f   gd-fm NHF

Alpine Hideaway (IRE)

102   **78**

10-y-o b g Tirol-Arbour (USA) (Graustark)
J S Wainwright Peter Easterby

Placings:534341/1135PP6050/34/0/554000-546   (1705)
2002/03: 17⁵GF, 17⁴G, 17⁶G,

	Starts	1st	2nd	3rd	Win & Pl
Hurdles	3	0	0	0	0
Career Total	28	3	0	4	8832
113 6/98	MRas	2m1f110yE(0-110)HHdl		GD	£2903
112 5/98	Weth	2m	D Hdl	G-F	£2897
102 3/98	Newc	2m	F Hdl	G-F	£1896
			Total win prize-money £7697		

Going: Sf: 0-0 GS: 0-0 Gd: 0-2 GF: - Fm: 0-1
Distance: 2m/2m3: 0-3 2m4-2m7: 0-0 3m+: 0-0
Track: LH: 0-1 RH: 0-2 Tight: 0-3 Gall: 0-0
Aids: Bl: 0-0 Vi: 0-0 Tstrap: 0-0
Best Rating: 113 9/98 Sedg 2m1f   good Hdl

Alpine Message

83f

6-y-o b m Tirol-Jupiter s Message (Jupiter Island)
John Joseph Murphy (S L Keightley 9/5) John Joseph Murphy

Placings:5/600P-0000   (2875a)
2002/03: 16⁶G, 20⁰YS, 16⁶HY, 16⁶HY,

	Starts	1st	2nd	3rd	Win & Pl
NH Flat	2	0	0	0	0
Hurdles	2	0	0	0	0
Career Total	9	0	0	0	0

Going:	Sf: 0-2 GS: 0-0 Gd: 0-1 GF: - Fm: 0-0
Distance:	2m/2m3: 0-3 2m4-2m7: 0-1 3m+: 0-0
Track:	LH: 0-1 RH: 0-0 Tight: 0-1 Gall: 0-0
Aids:	Bl: 0-0 Vi: 0-0 Tstrap: 0-0
Best Rating:	83 11/01 Chel 2m110y good NHF

Alpine Panther (IRE)

10-y-o b g Tirol-Kentucky Wildcat (Be My Guest (USA))
C R Cox C R Cox

Placings:12501/11120F/24F34/PPF50   (4314)
2002/03: 25⁰GF, 22⁰G, 24⁴S, 20⁵GD, 22⁰G,

	Starts	1st	2nd	3rd	Win & Pl
Chases	5	0	0	0	0
Career Total	21	5	3	1	24562
136 12/98 Bang	3m		B(0-140)HHdl	G-S	£6983
130 12/98 Newc	3m		D(0-125)HHdl	SFT	£2773
119 11/98 Plum	2m4f		F Hdl	SFT	£3550
98 4/98 Carl	2m4f110yE Hdl			GD	£2010
111 12/97 Newc	2m		E Hdl	GD	£2274
			Total win prize-money £17590		

Going:	Sf: 0-1 GS: 0-1 Gd: 0-2 GF: - Fm: 0-1
Distance:	2m/2m3: 0-0 2m4-2m7: 0-3 3m+: 0-2
Track:	LH: 0-3 RH: 0-2 Tight: 0-0 Gall: 0-3
Aids:	Bl: 0-1 Vi: 0-0 Tstrap: 0-1
Best Rating:	136 1/99 Chel 2m5f110y gd-sft Hdl

Alpine Prince

77   51

5-y-o b g Rock Hopper-Sweet Lore (Law Society (USA))
R Dickin Mrs M J Field

Placings:00P0   (4486)
2002/03: 14⁰GS, 16⁰S, 19⁰G, 17⁰GF,

	Starts	1st	2nd	3rd	Win & Pl
NH Flat	2	0	0	0	0
Hurdles	2	0	0	0	0
Career Total	4	0	0	0	0

Going:	Sf: 0-1 GS: 0-1 Gd: 0-1 GF: - Fm: 0-1
Distance:	2m/2m3: 0-2 2m4-2m7: 0-1 3m+: 0-0
Track:	LH: 0-1 RH: 0-3 Tight: 0-0 Gall: 0-0
Aids:	Bl: 0-0 Vi: 0-0 Tstrap: 0-0
Best Rating:	52 4/03 Hrfd 2m1f gd-fm Hdl

Alpine Racer (IRE)
81   66

4-y-o b g Lake Coniston (IRE)-Cut No Ice (Great Nephew)
R E Barr Malcolm O Hair

Placings:0040P   (4518)
2002/03: 16⁰S, 16⁰G, 16⁴GS, 19⁰G, 21⁰G,

	Starts	1st	2nd	3rd	Win & Pl
Hurdles	5	0	0	0	294
Career Total	5	0	0	0	294

Going:	Sf: 0-1 GS: 0-1 Gd: 0-3 GF: - Fm: 0-0
Distance:	2m/2m3: 0-4 2m4-2m7: 0-1 3m+: 0-0
Track:	LH: 0-5 RH: 0-0 Tight: 0-4 Gall: 0-1
Aids:	Bl: 0-0 Vi: 0-0 Tstrap: 0-0
Best Rating:	66 12/02 Catt 2m gd-sft Hdl

Poor form in juvenile hurdles.

Alpine Slave

107   112

6-y-o ch g Alflora (IRE)-Celtic Slave (Celtic Cone)
J T Gifford Mrs J T Gifford

Placings:6F13   (4442)
2002/03: 16⁶GS, 21⁴S, 18¹S, 20³G,

	Starts	1st	2nd	3rd	Win & Pl
Hurdles	4	1	0	1	4397
Career Total	4	1	0	1	4397
91 3/03 Font	2m2f110yE Hdl			SFT	£3601
			Total win prize-money £3601		

Going:	Sf: 1-2 GS: 0-1 Gd: 0-1 GF: - Fm: 0-0
Distance:	2m/2m3: 1-2 2m4-2m7: 0-2 3m+: 0-0
Track:	LH: 1-2 RH: 0-2 Tight: 1-2 Gall: 0-0
Aids:	Bl: 0-0 Vi: 0-0 Tstrap: 0-0
Best Rating:	112 4/03 Asct 2m4f good Hdl

Fair hurdler; a winner at Fontwell in 2003; good third in better race next time.

Alqabas (IRE)

91   62

5-y-o b g Nashwan (USA)-Harayir (USA) (Gulch (USA))
M R Hoad Mrs J E Taylor

Placings:UPP5   (4279)
2002/03: 20⁰G, 21⁰HY, 22⁶S, 20⁵GF,

	Starts	1st	2nd	3rd	Win & Pl
Hurdles	4	0	0	0	0
Career Total	4	0	0	0	0

Going:	Sf: 0-2 GS: 0-0 Gd: 0-1 GF: - Fm: 0-1
Distance:	2m/2m3: 0-0 2m4-2m7: 0-4 3m+: 0-0
Track:	LH: 0-2 RH: 0-0 Tight: 0-4 Gall: 0-0
Aids:	Bl: 0-0 Vi: 0-0 Tstrap: 0-0
Best Rating:	62 3/03 Font 2m4f gd-fm Hdl

Alrafid (IRE)

80   74+

4-y-o ch c Halling (USA)-Ginger Tree (USA) (Dayjur (USA))
G L Moore Gillespie Brothers

Placings:6   (3495)
2002/03: 16⁶GS,

	Starts	1st	2nd	3rd	Win & Pl
Hurdles	1	0	0	0	0
Career Total	1	0	0	0	0

Going:	Sf: 0-0 GS: 0-1 Gd: 0-0 GF: - Fm: 0-0
Distance:	2m/2m3: 0-1 2m4-2m7: 0-0 3m+: 0-0
Track:	LH: 0-0 RH: 0-1 Tight: 0-0 Gall: 0-0
Aids:	Bl: 0-0 Vi: 0-0 Tstrap: 0-0
Best Rating:	76 2/03 Kemp 2m gd-sft Hdl

Alscot Foxy Lady (IRE)

82(84h)   (43h)80

6-y-o b m Foxhound (USA)-Arena (Sallust)
R Dickin Warwick Members Two

Placings:0F00-00P   (2731)
2002/03: 16⁰G, 16⁰S, 16⁶HY,

	Starts	1st	2nd	3rd	Win & Pl
Hurdles	3	0	0	0	0
Career Total	7	0	0	0	0

Going:	Sf: 0-2 GS: 0-0 Gd: 0-1 GF: - Fm: 0-0
Distance:	2m/2m3: 0-3 2m4-2m7: 0-0 3m+: 0-0
Track:	LH: 0-1 RH: 0-2 Tight: 0-0 Gall: 0-0
Aids:	Bl: 0-0 Vi: 0-0 Tstrap: 0-0
Best Rating:	47 12/02 Wwck 2m soft Hdl

Plating-class hurdler; not disgraced on chase debut.

Alsina

12-y-o b g Alias Smith (USA)-Tersina (Lighter)
Peter Innes Peter Innes

Placings:P-2PP0   (4506)
2002/03: 25²GS, 25⁰S, 26⁰G, 25⁰G,

	Starts	1st	2nd	3rd	Win & Pl
Chases	4	0	1	0	856
Career Total	5	0	1	0	856

Going:	Sf: 0-1 GS: 0-1 Gd: 0-2 GF: - Fm: 0-0
Distance:	2m/2m3: 0-0 2m4-2m7: 0-0 3m+: 0-4
Track:	LH: 0-3 RH: 0-1 Tight: 0-2 Gall: 0-0
Aids:	Bl: 0-0 Vi: 0-0 Tstrap: 0-0
Best Rating:	89 5/02 Hexm 3m1f gd-sft Ch

Multiple point winner but flopped under Rules on his debut at an advanced age.

Alska (FR)

10-y-o b/br m Leading Counsel (USA)-Kolkwitzia (FR) (The Wonder (FR))
P L Southcombe P L Southcombe

Placings:P00UUP00/332/U05P6P/3U02U-4440   (3592)
2002/03: 21⁴GF, 31⁴G, 24⁴GF, 24⁰S,

	Starts	1st	2nd	3rd	Win & Pl
Chases	4	0	0	0	817
Career Total	26	0	2	3	3346

Going:	Sf: 0-1 GS: 0-0 Gd: 0-1 GF: - Fm: 0-2
Distance:	2m/2m3: 0-0 2m4-2m7: 0-1 3m+: 0-3
Track:	LH: 0-1 RH: 0-3 Tight: 0-0 Gall: 0-0
Aids:	Bl: 0-0 Vi: 0-0 Tstrap: 0-0
Best Rating:	76 5/99 Winc 2m5f firm Ch

Altar Society

30

9-y-o b m Roscoe Blake-Small Money (Altosa Palace)
M J Gingell M J Gingell

Placings:00/540P0P   (0881)
2002/03: 20⁵GS, 20⁴GF, 16⁰S, 25⁴S, 26⁰GF, 22⁴S,

	Starts	1st	2nd	3rd	Win & Pl
Hurdles	6	0	0	0	0
Career Total	8	0	0	0	0

Going:	Sf: 0-3 GS: 0-1 Gd: 0-0 GF: - Fm: 0-2
Distance:	2m/2m3: 0-1 2m4-2m7: 0-3 3m+: 0-2
Track:	LH: 0-5 RH: 0-1 Tight: 0-3 Gall: 0-1
Aids:	Bl: 0-0 Vi: 0-1 Tstrap: 0-0
Best Rating:	45 11/99 Worc 2m gd-sft NHF

Altareek (USA)

93   81

6-y-o b g Alleged (USA)-Black Tulip (FR) (Fabulous Dancer (USA))

J M Jefferson Dean Bostock And Raymond Bostock

Placings:100-3P0 (3830)
2002/03: 19³S, 17⁶S, 16⁹G,

	Starts	1st	2nd	3rd	Win & Pl
Hurdles	3	0	0	1	522
Career Total	6	1	0	1	2265
110 3/02	MRas	2m1f110yH NHF		G-S	£1743
		Total win prize-money £1743

Going: Sf: 0-2 GS: 0-0 Gd: 0-1 GF: - Fm: 0-0
Distance: 2m/2m3: 0-2 2m4-2m7: 0-1 3m+: 0-0
Track: LH: 0-1 RH: 0-2 Tight: 0-2 Gall: 0-0
Aids: Bl: 0-0 Vi: 0-0 Tstrap: 0-0
Best Rating: 110 3/02 MRas 2m1f110y gd-sft NHF

Bumper winner who will need a stamina test over hurdles.

Altay
120   129

6-y-o b g Erin s Isle-Aliuska (IRE) (Fijar Tango (FR))
R A Fahey R M Jeffs & J Potter

Placings:0/1212 (4476)
2002/03: 16¹GF, 19²G, 16¹GF, 16²G,

	Starts	1st	2nd	3rd	Win & Pl
Hurdles	4	2	2	0	20991
Career Total	5	2	2	0	20991
123 3/03	Weth	2m	D(0-125)HHdl	G-F	£6831
109 12/02	Muss	2m	E Hdl	G-F	£4221
		Total win prize-money £11054

Going: Sf: 0-0 GS: 0-0 Gd: 0-2 GF: - Fm: 2-2
Distance: 2m/2m3: 2-4 2m4-2m7: 0-0 3m+: 0-0
Track: LH: 1-3 RH: 1-1 Tight: 1-3 Gall: 0-0
Aids: Bl: 0-0 Vi: 0-0 Tstrap: 0-0
Best Rating: 128 4/03 Aint 2m110y good Hdl

Useful hurdler; better known as a fair middle-distance handicapper on the Flat; has done well in his few outings over hurdles, winning twice and excellent second in valuable handicap at Aintree; suited by two miles and fast ground.

Althrey Ruler (IRE)
108   84

10-y-o b g Phardante (FR)-Keego s Aunt (Tyrant (USA))
F Lloyd (W Clay 3/5) F Lloyd

Placings:0062F/020P1/660/F5P55P440026P-0035P25 (1616)
2002/03: 17⁰G, 16⁰GF, 20³S, 20⁵GF, 24⁶G, 21²F, 24⁵F,

	Starts	1st	2nd	3rd	Win & Pl
Hurdles	7	0	1	1	1779
Career Total	33	1	4	1	7100
97 3/00	Uttx	2m	F(0-100)HHdl	GD	£2789
		Total win prize-money £2790

Going: Sf: 0-1 GS: 0-0 Gd: 0-2 GF: - Fm: 0-4
Distance: 2m/2m3: 0-2 2m4-2m7: 0-3 3m+: 0-2
Track: LH: 0-5 RH: 0-2 Tight: 0-2 Gall: 0-0
Aids: Bl: 0-0 Vi: 0-0 Tstrap: 0-0
Best Rating: 97 3/00 Uttx 2m good Hdl

Plating-class hurdler; acts on good ground; has been tried at up to three miles.

Althrey Torch (IRE)
104   95

11-y-o b g Torus-Keep The Cut (Tarqogan)
W Clay F Lloyd

Placings:6054/2003460/6/P3U260P46-5 (0053)
2002/03: 24⁶G,

	Starts	1st	2nd	3rd	Win & Pl
Hurdles	1	0	0	0	0
Career Total	22	0	2	2	2673

Going: Sf: 0-0 GS: 0-0 Gd: 0-1 GF: - Fm: 0-0
Distance: 2m/2m3: 0-0 2m4-2m7: 0-0 3m+: 0-1
Track: LH: 0-1 RH: 0-0 Tight: 0-1 Gall: 0-0
Aids: Bl: 0-0 Vi: 0-0 Tstrap: 0-0
Best Rating: 95 2/02 Hntg 2m4f110y soft Hdl

Modest hurdler; effective in heavy ground; best formaround two miles.

Altregan Boy (IRE)
103   93

11-y-o b g Lancastrian-Please Oblige (Le Levanstell)
C N Kellett A M Egan

Placings:60000/11B0/F0U020/FP06F/PPP0PP-5UU5134 (2895)
2002/03: 25⁵GS, 25⁵G, 23⁵G, 26⁵G, 28¹S, 25³S, 23⁴S,

	Starts	1st	2nd	3rd	Win & Pl
Chases	7	1	0	1	4981
Career Total	33	3	1	1	13286
93 12/02	MRas	3m4f110yE(0-110)HCh		SFT	£4069
106 5/98	Dund	2m4f153y (0-123)HHdl		G-Y	£5026
104 5/98	Limk	3m	(0-102)HHdl	Y-S	£2382
		Total win prize-money £11478

Going: Sf: 1-3 GS: 0-1 Gd: 0-3 GF: - Fm: 0-0
Distance: 2m/2m3: 0-2 2m4-2m7: 0-1 3m+: 1-6
Track: LH: 0-2 RH: 1-5 Tight: 1-2 Gall: 0-0
Aids: Bl: 0-0 Vi: 0-0 Tstrap: 0-0
Best Rating: 111 4/00 Fair 2m6f yld-sft Hdl

Plating-class chaser; surprise winner from well out of the handicap at Market Rasen in December 2002; acts on soft ground and just stays.

Alvaro (IRE)
104(102c)   (88c)88

6-y-o ch g Priolo (USA)-Gezalle (Shareef Dancer (USA))
D J Wintle (M C Chapman 10/3) Caerphilly Building Supplies Ltd

Placings:60R0/60-03P3313600200003P04 (4673)
2002/03: 16⁹G, 17³GS, 17⁵GF, 16³S, 22³G, 22¹G, 19³GF, 24⁶G, 24⁵G, 24⁶GF, 26²GF, 23⁰G, 23⁹G, 24⁰GS, 16⁰GS, 25³S, 20⁵GS, 24⁰F, 26⁴GF,

	Starts	1st	2nd	3rd	Win & Pl
Hurdles	17	1	1	4	6575
Chases	2	0	0	1	820
Career Total	25	1	1	5	7395
88 8/02	Ctml	2m6f	E Hdl	GD	£3752
		Total win prize-money £3752

Going: Sf: 0-2 GS: 0-4 Gd: 1-7 GF: - Fm: 0-6
Distance: 2m/2m3: 0-5 2m4-2m7: 1-5 3m+: 0-9
Track: LH: 1-12 RH: 0-7 Tight: 1-11 Gall: 0-2
Aids: Bl: 0-0 Vi: 0-0 Tstrap: 0-0
Best Rating: 88 4/03 Hrfd 3m2f gd-fm Hdl

Plating-class hurdler; stays 3m 3f; acts on a sound surface.

Alvino
100   109+

6-y-o b g Alflora (IRE)-Rose Ravine (Deep Run)
Miss H C Knight Martin Broughton

Placings:110-31 (4446)
2002/03: 19³G, 16¹G,

	Starts	1st	2nd	3rd	Win & Pl
Hurdles	2	1	0	1	5467

Career Total	5	3	0	1	17412
109 4/03	Ludl	2m	D Hdl	GD	£4875
130 12/01	Asct	2m110y	B NHF	GD	£10426
114 11/01	Ludl	2m	H NHF	G-F	£1519
		Total win prize-money £16820

Going: Sf: 0-0 GS: 0-0 Gd: 1-2 GF: - Fm: 0-0
Distance: 2m/2m3: 1-1 2m4-2m7: 0-1 3m+: 0-0
Track: LH: 0-0 RH: 1-2 Tight: 0-0 Gall: 0-0
Aids: Bl: 0-0 Vi: 0-0 Tstrap: 0-0
Best Rating: 130 12/01 Asct 2m110y good NHF

Useful bumper performer; suited by ground good or faster; has undergone a wind operation and failed to get home when well beaten third on hurdling bow at Hereford in February; but a much better performance when winning next time at Ludlow.

Always A Gamble
55f

6-y-o br m Lord Americo-Gamblingway (Gambling Debt)
Mrs H Pudd Mrs H Pudd

Placings:0 (0248)
2002/03: 17⁰G,

	Starts	1st	2nd	3rd	Win & Pl
NH Flat	1	0	0	0	
Career Total	1	0	0	0	

Going: Sf: 0-0 GS: 0-0 Gd: 0-1 GF: - Fm: 0-0
Distance: 2m/2m3: 0-1 2m4-2m7: 0-0 3m+: 0-0
Track: LH: 0-0 RH: 0-1 Tight: 0-0 Gall: 0-0
Aids: Bl: 0-0 Vi: 0-0 Tstrap: 0-0
Best Rating: -1 5/02 Extr 2m1f good NHF

Always Rainbows (IRE)
109   127

5-y-o b g Rainbows For Life (CAN)-Maura s Guest (IRE) (Be My Guest (USA))
B S Rothwell (Kevin Prendergast 20/10) J Eddings

Placings:1F1200 (4226)
2002/03: 16¹GS, 16²G, 16¹S, 16²GS, 18⁰GS, 16⁰GF,

	Starts	1st	2nd	3rd	Win & Pl
Hurdles	6	2	1	0	15196
Career Total	6	2	1	0	15196
122 12/02	Weth	2m	D Hdl	SFT	£4615
115 11/02	Weth	2m	D Hdl	G-S	£3981
		Total win prize-money £8596

Going: Sf: 1-1 GS: 1-3 Gd: 0-1 GF: - Fm: 0-1
Distance: 2m/2m3: 2-6 2m4-2m7: 0-0 3m+: 0-0
Track: LH: 2-6 RH: 0-0 Tight: 0-1 Gall: 0-0
Aids: Bl: 0-0 Vi: 1-4 Tstrap: 0-0
Best Rating: 127 2/03 Weth 2m gd-sft Hdl

Useful novice hurdler; suited by 2m and good or soft ground; has worn a visor and blinkers.

Aly Daley (IRE)

15-y-o ch g Roselier (FR)-Roses In June (Timobriol)
D T Greenwood (Mrs Carrie Ford 26/5) Mrs Phyl Robertson

Placings:PP54/33221144/11253524/BFP12/04U5P50/U/U4/0 (0477)
2002/03: 26⁰GS,

	Starts	1st	2nd	3rd	Win & Pl
Chases	1	0	0	0	

Career Total	36	5	5	3	29050		
112 3/98 Newc 3m	D(0-125)HCh	G-F	£3533				
106 11/96 Newc 3m	D(0-125)HCh	G-F	£3501				
109 5/96 Hexm 2m4f110yE(0-100)HCh	SFT	£3343					
107 2/96 Muss 3m	E(0-100)HCh	G-F	£2988				
101 2/96 Sedg 2m5f	E Ch	GD	£3286				

Total win prize-money £16653

Going:	Sf: 0-0 GS: 0-1 Gd: 0-0 GF: - Fm: 0-0
Distance:	2m/2m3: 0-0 2m4-2m7: 0-0 3m+: 0-1
Track:	LH: 0-1 RH: 0-0 Tight: 0-1 Gall: 0-0
Aids:	Bl: 0-0 Vi: 0-0 Tstrap: 0-0
Best Rating:	115 3/98 Newc 3m good Ch

Amacita
101   41

5-y-o b m Shareef Dancer (USA)-Kina (USA) (Bering)
K G Wingrove (J G M O Shea 11/9) M M Foulger

Placings:4P0P0   (4706)
2002/03: 17⁴GF, 17PS, 19⁹G, 26PS, 20⁰G,

	Starts	1st	2nd	3rd	Win & Pl
Hurdles	5	0	0	0	0
Career Total	5	0	0	0	0

Going:	Sf: 0-2 GS: 0-0 Gd: 0-2 GF: - Fm: 0-1
Distance:	2m/2m3: 0-2 2m4-2m7: 0-2 3m+: 0-1
Track:	LH: 0-1 RH: 0-4 Tight: 0-0 Gall: 0-0
Aids:	Bl: 0-0 Vi: 0-0 Tstrap: 0-0
Best Rating:	88 9/02 Hrfd 2m1f gd-fm Hdl

Plating-class hurdler.

Amanda Kasakova
85   51

7-y-o ch m Kasakov-Manna Green (Bustino)
J R Norton Mrs Hazel Tattersall

Placings:0/00   (3911)
2002/03: 19⁰G, 17⁰GS,

	Starts	1st	2nd	3rd	Win & Pl
Hurdles	2	0	0	0	
Career Total	3	0	0	0	

Going:	Sf: 0-0 GS: 0-1 Gd: 0-1 GF: - Fm: 0-0
Distance:	2m/2m3: 0-2 2m4-2m7: 0-0 3m+: 0-0
Track:	LH: 0-1 RH: 0-1 Tight: 0-1 Gall: 0-0
Aids:	Bl: 0-0 Vi: 0-0 Tstrap: 0-0
Best Rating:	74 6/00 Hexm 2m gd-fm NHF

Amandari (FR)
85   70

7-y-o ch g Petit Loup (USA)-Baby Sitting (FR) (Son Of Silver)
Mrs K Walton Mrs K Walton

Placings:P/203PF/066P   (4752)
2002/03: 25⁰G, 20⁶HY, 24⁸S, 24PG,

	Starts	1st	2nd	3rd	Win & Pl
Hurdles	4	0	0	0	0
Career Total	10	0	1	1	1633

Going:	Sf: 0-2 GS: 0-0 Gd: 0-2 GF: - Fm: 0-0
Distance:	2m/2m3: 0-0 2m4-2m7: 0-1 3m+: 0-3
Track:	LH: 0-3 RH: 0-1 Tight: 0-1 Gall: 0-2
Aids:	Bl: 0-0 Vi: 0-0 Tstrap: 0-0
Best Rating:	70 2/03 Newc 3m soft Hdl

Amarettoforanna (IRE)
92   98d

10-y-o b g Satco (FR)-Candy Slam (Candy Cane)
Ferdy Murphy R J V Partnership

Placings:035/32052R0/124/14463500-51P54   (4105)
2002/03: 16⁵S, 21¹GS, 16PS, 19⁵G, 21⁴S,

	Starts	1st	2nd	3rd	Win & Pl
Chases	5	1	0	0	4440
Career Total	26	3	3	3	20366

98 12/02 Fknm 2m5f110yE(0-110)HCh	G-S	£4082	
109 5/01 Ayr 2m	E Ch	G-F	£3471
102 10/00 MRas 2m6f110yE(0-105)HCh	GD	£3900	

Total win prize-money £11453

Going:	Sf: 0-3 GS: 1-1 Gd: 0-1 GF: - Fm: 0-0
Distance:	2m/2m3: 0-3 2m4-2m7: 1-2 3m+: 0-0
Track:	LH: 1-5 RH: 0-0 Tight: 1-3 Gall: 0-1
Aids:	Bl: 0-0 Vi: 0-0 Tstrap: 0-0
Best Rating:	109 5/01 Ayr 2m gd-fm Ch

Moderate front-running chaser; suited by two miles to two miles six, and a sound surface.

Amari (IRE)
75(69h)   (29h)67

8-y-o ch g Grand Plaisir (IRE)-Teazle (Quayside)
A G Hobbs J Parfitt

Placings:5543/P6/5660-00P0   (4221)
2002/03: 16⁰GS, 20⁰G, 26PS, 25⁰GF,

	Starts	1st	2nd	3rd	Win & Pl
Hurdles	3	0	0	0	0
Chases	1	0	0	0	0
Career Total	14	0	0	1	523

Going:	Sf: 0-1 GS: 0-1 Gd: 0-1 GF: - Fm: 0-1
Distance:	2m/2m3: 0-1 2m4-2m7: 0-0 3m+: 0-2
Track:	LH: 0-2 RH: 0-2 Tight: 0-1 Gall: 0-0
Aids:	Bl: 0-0 Vi: 0-0 Tstrap: 0-0
Best Rating:	101 3/00 Uttx 2m4f110y good Hdl

Amarone
94   86

5-y-o b g Young Ern-Tendresse (IRE) (Tender King)
M J Ryan M J R Partnership

Placings:2P100-5P1045   (2320)
2002/03: 16⁵G, 17PG, 16¹GS, 16⁰G, 20⁴GS, 19⁵S,

	Starts	1st	2nd	3rd	Win & Pl
Hurdles	6	1	0	0	2167
Career Total	11	2	1	0	5423

86 10/02 Fknm 2m	G(0-90)HHdl	G-S	£2167
85 2/02 Donc 2m110y G Hdl	SFT	£2404	

Total win prize-money £4572

Going:	Sf: 0-1 GS: 1-2 Gd: 0-3 GF: - Fm: 0-0
Distance:	2m/2m3: 1-4 2m4-2m7: 0-2 3m+: 0-0
Track:	LH: 1-4 RH: 0-2 Tight: 1-5 Gall: 0-0
Aids:	Bl: 0-0 Vi: 1-6 Tstrap: 0-0
Best Rating:	86 10/02 Fknm 2m gd-sft Hdl

Plating-class hurdler, suited by two miles and soft ground.

Amateur Dramatics
50

7-y-o b g Theatrical Charmer-Chaconia Girl (Bay Express)
Mrs P A Tetley Mrs P A Tetley

Placings:0/0P0P4-6   (2415)
2002/03: 18⁶G,

	Starts	1st	2nd	3rd	Win & Pl
Hurdles	1	0	0	0	0
Career Total	7	0	0	0	0

Going:	Sf: 0-0 GS: 0-0 Gd: 0-1 GF: - Fm: 0-0
Distance:	2m/2m3: 0-1 2m4-2m7: 0-0 3m+: 0-0
Track:	LH: 0-1 RH: 0-0 Tight: 0-1 Gall: 0-0
Aids:	Bl: 0-0 Vi: 0-0 Tstrap: 0-0
Best Rating:	50 4/02 Plum 2m5f gd-fm Hdl

Amathus (IRE)
84f   80+f

6-y-o br g New Express-Mistress Sarah (Ashford (USA))
A King The Golden Anorak Partnership

Placings:U3   (1159)
2002/03: 17⁰GF, 17³G,

	Starts	1st	2nd	3rd	Win & Pl
NH Flat	2	0	0	1	312
Career Total	2	0	0	1	312

Going:	Sf: 0-0 GS: 0-0 Gd: 0-1 GF: - Fm: 0-1
Distance:	2m/2m3: 0-2 2m4-2m7: 0-0 3m+: 0-0
Track:	LH: 0-1 RH: 0-1 Tight: 0-2 Gall: 0-0
Aids:	Bl: 0-0 Vi: 0-0 Tstrap: 0-0
Best Rating:	80 9/02 NAbb 2m1f good NHF

Amber Diver (IRE)
(67c)   (21c)49

9-y-o ch g Seclude (USA)-Sugar Beet (Frigid Aire)
J J Lambe Emy Racing Syndicate

Placings:0/0/0P00P0/P03F-P04/0550   (1282a)
2002/03: 24PY, 16⁰GF, 16⁴G, 16⁶S, 20⁵GF, 20⁰F,

	Starts	1st	2nd	3rd	Win & Pl
NH Flat	1	0	0	0	0
Hurdles	2	0	0	0	0
Chases	4	0	0	0	282
Career Total	19	0	0	1	733

Going:	Sf: 0-1 GS: 0-0 Gd: 0-2 GF: - Fm: 0-3
Distance:	2m/2m3: 0-3 2m4-2m7: 0-2 3m+: 0-2
Track:	LH: 0-4 RH: 0-0 Tight: 0-3 Gall: 0-0
Aids:	Bl: 0-6 Vi: 0-0 Tstrap: 0-6
Best Rating:	71 5/99 Navn 2m yld-sft NHF

Amber Go Go
86(86h)   (49 h)46

6-y-o ch m Rudimentary (USA)-Plaything (High Top)
K W Hogg K W Hogg

Placings:0/00PP-0010P4   (4798)
2002/03: 20⁰G, 18⁰G, 17¹GS, 20⁰G, 17PGF, 17⁴GF,

	Starts	1st	2nd	3rd	Win & Pl
Hurdles	6	1	0	0	4173
Career Total	11	1	0	0	4173

71 6/02 Ctml 2m1f110yD Hdl G-S £3913

Total win prize-money £3913

Going:	Sf: 0-0 GS: 1-1 Gd: 0-3 GF: - Fm: 0-2
Distance:	2m/2m3: 1-4 2m4-2m7: 0-2 3m+: 0-0
Track:	LH: 1-5 RH: 0-1 Tight: 1-4 Gall: 0-0
Aids:	Bl: 0-0 Vi: 0-0 Tstrap: 0-0
Best Rating:	71 6/02 Ctml 2m1f110y gd-sft Hdl

Plating-class hurdler; winner on soft ground in June 2002.

Amber Gold

28f

5-y-o b m Tragic Role (USA)-Dark Amber (Formidable (USA))
Mrs S M Johnson Evans, Compton, Matthews & Matthews

Placings:0 (3146)
2002/03: 17⁰S,

	Starts	1st	2nd	3rd	Win & Pl
NH Flat	1	0	0	0	
Career Total	1	0	0	0	

Going:	Sf: 0-1 GS: 0-0 Gd: 0-0 GF: - Fm: 0-0	
Distance:	2m/2m3: 0-1 2m4-2m7: 0-0 3m+: 0-0	
Track:	LH: 0-0 RH: 0-0 Tight: 0-0 Gall: 0-0	
Aids:	Bl: 0-0 Vi: 0-0 Tstrap: 0-0	
Best Rating:	30 1/03 Tntn 2m1f	soft NHF

Amber Lily

85   **58**

11-y-o ch m Librate-Just Bluffing (Green Shoon)
Mrs S M Johnson S J Merrick

Placings:00/0P1P030P000/F263050/P-PPP3F6 (0658)
2002/03: 17⁰GF, 22⁰GS, 19⁹G, 16³S, 16⁷GF, 16⁶GF,

	Starts	1st	2nd	3rd	Win & Pl
Hurdles	6	0	0	1	270
Career Total	27	1	1	3	3259
96	9/99	Hrfd	2m1f		GD £1954

Total win prize-money £1954

Going:	Sf: 0-1 GS: 0-1 Gd: 0-1 GF: - Fm: 0-3
Distance:	2m/2m3: 0-4 2m4-2m7: 0-2 3m+: 0-0
Track:	LH: 0-4 RH: 0-2 Tight: 0-1 Gall: 0-0
Aids:	Bl: 0-2 Vi: 0-0 Tstrap: 0-0
Best Rating:	96 9/99 Hrfd 2m1f good Hdl

Amber Moss

99   **54**

8-y-o ch g Phardante (FR)-Queen s Darling (Le Moss)
Mrs C J Kerr (Mrs S C Bradburne 29/5) Mrs C J Kerr

Placings:0052311/F33U0PF/242P26332P-U646440336 (4773)
2002/03: 25⁴ᵁG, 22⁶GF, 22⁴HY, 21⁶GS, 16⁴GF, 24⁴GS, 24⁰G, 20³S, 20⁶G,

	Starts	1st	2nd	3rd	Win & Pl
Chases	10	0	2	5	2452
Career Total	34	2	5	7	22740
116	4/00	Ayr	2m6f	C HHdl	GD £7488
113	3/00	Uttx	2m4f110yD Hdl		GD £3802

Total win prize-money £11291

Going:	Sf: 0-3 GS: 0-2 Gd: 0-3 GF: - Fm: 0-2
Distance:	2m/2m3: 0-1 2m4-2m7: 0-6 3m+: 0-3
Track:	LH: 0-6 RH: 0-4 Tight: 0-5 Gall: 0-1
Aids:	Bl: 0-0 Vi: 0-0 Tstrap: 0-0
Best Rating:	116 4/00 Ayr 2m6f good Hdl

Amber Prince

69f   **44f**

5-y-o b g Prince Des Coeurs (USA)-Run Amber Run (Run The Gantlet (USA))
P D Evans P D Evans

Placings:0 (4197)
2002/03: 16⁰G,

NH Flat
Career Total

	Starts	1st	2nd	3rd	Win & Pl
NH Flat	1	0	0	0	
Career Total	1	0	0	0	

Going:	Sf: 0-0 GS: 0-0 Gd: 0-1 GF: - Fm: 0-0
Distance:	2m/2m3: 0-1 2m4-2m7: 0-0 3m+: 0-0
Track:	LH: 0-0 RH: 0-1 Tight: 0-0 Gall: 0-0
Aids:	Bl: 0-0 Vi: 0-0 Tstrap: 0-0
Best Rating:	44 3/03 Ludl 2m good NHF

Amberleigh House (IRE)

109(101h)   **(110 h)140**

11-y-o br g Buckskin (FR)-Chancy Gal (Al Sirat (USA))
D McCain Halewood International Ltd

Placings:00/36 f3213144024/2145345B/622F43210/1550P
B/5216501-36324033 (4479)
2002/03: 24³G, 23⁶G, 24³GS, 27²GS, 17⁴GS, 28⁰G, 20³G, 36³G,

	Starts	1st	2nd	3rd	Win & Pl
Hurdles	2	0	0	0	338
Chases	6	0	1	4	85226
Career Total	53	8	8	9	185727
140	4/02	Bang	3m110y	C(0-135)HCh	GD £7572
132	11/01	Aint	3m3f	B HCh	SFT £29000
145	5/00	Punc	2m4f	HCh	GD £11440
143	2/00	Thur	2m4f	Ch	HVY £13000
118	10/98	Gowr	2m1f	Ch	Y-S £2989
129	2/98	Leop	2m	HHdl	Y-S £5956
120	1/98	Navn	2m	Hdl	HVY £2680
111	11/97	Naas	2m	NHF	SH £3051

Total win prize-money £75691

Going:	Sf: 0-0 GS: 0-3 Gd: 0-5 GF: - Fm: 0-0
Distance:	2m/2m3: 0-1 2m4-2m7: 0-1 3m+: 0-6
Track:	LH: 0-7 RH: 0-1 Tight: 0-4 Gall: 0-0
Aids:	Bl: 0-0 Vi: 0-0 Tstrap: 0-0
Best Rating:	145 5/00 Punc 2m4f good Ch

Useful staying handicap chaser; best in decent races receiving weight rather than giving weight away; winner of the Becher Chase in November 2001; finished second in the 2002 Becher Chase and was excellent third in the 2003 Grand National; not very big but jumps well; stays extreme distances.

Ambersong

73   **40**

5-y-o ch g Hernando (FR)-Stygian (USA) (Irish River (FR))
Ian Williams (Mrs N Macauley 16/8) Pursuit Media

Placings:00 (1332)
2002/03: 16⁰G, 16⁰G,

	Starts	1st	2nd	3rd	Win & Pl
Hurdles	2	0	0	0	
Career Total	2	0	0	0	

Going:	Sf: 0-0 GS: 0-0 Gd: 0-2 GF: - Fm: 0-0
Distance:	2m/2m3: 0-2 2m4-2m7: 0-0 3m+: 0-0
Track:	LH: 0-2 RH: 0-0 Tight: 0-1 Gall: 0-0
Aids:	Bl: 0-0 Vi: 0-0 Tstrap: 0-0
Best Rating:	43 9/02 Plum 2m good Hdl

Ambidextrous (IRE)

(102h)   **(80h)**

11-y-o b g Shareef Dancer (USA)-Amber Fizz (USA) (Effervescing (USA))
G J Smith The One Too Many Partnership

Placings:0P66PP/211353/2F0/3F0/60001/45P05P223624/
PP000P3 (1567)
2002/03: 17⁶GF, 20⁶S, 16⁶GF, 20⁰GF, 22⁰GF, 19⁶GF, 22³GS,

	Starts	1st	2nd	3rd	Win & Pl
Hurdles	5	0	0	0	0
Chases	2	0	0	1	698
Career Total	42	3	5	5	13217
100	4/00	Sedg	2m5f110yG(0-100)HHdl	GD	£2054
91	1/97	Hntg	2m110y	E(0-100)HHdl	G-S	£2582
84	12/96	Towc	2m	G(0-95)HHdl	HVY	£2094

Total win prize-money £6732

Going:	Sf: 0-1 GS: 0-1 Gd: 0-0 GF: - Fm: 0-5
Distance:	2m/2m3: 0-3 2m4-2m7: 0-4 3m+: 0-0
Track:	LH: 0-4 RH: 0-3 Tight: 0-4 Gall: 0-0
Aids:	Bl: 0-0 Vi: 0-0 Tstrap: 0-0
Best Rating:	104 5/00 Sedg 2m5f110y gd-fm Hdl

Poor hurdler/chaser.

Ambience

78f   **89f**

6-y-o ch g Wolfhound (USA)-Amber Fizz (USA) (Effervescing (USA))
G A Swinbank Alan Swinbank

Placings:0-50 (4437)
2002/03: 14⁵GF, 16⁹G,

	Starts	1st	2nd	3rd	Win & Pl
NH Flat	2	0	0	0	
Career Total	3	0	0	0	

Going:	Sf: 0-0 GS: 0-0 Gd: 0-1 GF: - Fm: 0-1
Distance:	2m/2m3: 0-2 2m4-2m7: 0-0 3m+: 0-0
Track:	LH: 0-1 RH: 0-0 Tight: 0-0 Gall: 0-0
Aids:	Bl: 0-0 Vi: 0-0 Tstrap: 0-0
Best Rating:	89 3/03 Hrfd 1m6f gd-fm NHF

Ambience Lady

92   **92**

7-y-o b m Batshoof-Upper Caen (High Top)
J W Mullins First Impressions Racing Group 2

Placings:140/4U03P (4626)
2002/03: 18⁴S, 16⁴G, 20⁹G, 19³GF, 17⁶GF,

	Starts	1st	2nd	3rd	Win & Pl
NH Flat	1	0	0	0	0
Hurdles	4	0	0	1	788
Career Total	8	1	0	1	2293
86	1/00	Folk	2m1f110yH NHF		SFT £1505

Total win prize-money £1505

Going:	Sf: 0-1 GS: 0-0 Gd: 0-2 GF: - Fm: 0-2
Distance:	2m/2m3: 0-4 2m4-2m7: 0-1 3m+: 0-0
Track:	LH: 0-2 RH: 0-3 Tight: 0-3 Gall: 0-0
Aids:	Bl: 0-0 Vi: 0-0 Tstrap: 0-0
Best Rating:	92 4/03 Extr 2m3f gd-fm Hdl

Soft ground bumper winner; best effort over hurdles when third in 19 furlong mares only event on firm ground at Exeter April 2003.

Ambleside (IRE)

99   **124d**

12-y-o b g Kambalda-Noellespir (Bargello)
Mrs S D Williams B M Yin

Placings:62140/312403/2U44112/U354122U23/31213125/
34442/0302146-4355P (4624)
2002/03: 26⁴HY, 24³S, 24⁵S, 24⁵S, 26⁶GF,

	Starts	1st	2nd	3rd	Win & Pl
Chases	5	0	0	1	2326
Career Total	53	9	11	9	91520

127	2/02	Sand	3m110y	B(0-140)HCh	SFT	£10695
130	2/00	Chep	3m2f110yC(0-135)HCh		SFT	£6890
131	12/99	Chep	2m3f110yC(0-130)HCh		HVY	£7197
123	12/99	Winc	2m5f	E(0-115)HCh	GD	£3464
125	2/99	Winc	2m5f	D(0-125)HCh	G-S	£7392
115	4/98	Bang	2m1f110yD Ch		SFT	£4221
109	4/98	Tntn	2m110y	D Ch	GD	£3856
119	12/96	Ling	2m110y	C(0-130)HHdl	G-S	£3403
100	2/96	Chep	2m110y	E Hdl	SFT	£2542

Total win prize-money £49664

Going: Sf: 0-4 GS: 0-0 Gd: 0-0 GF: - Fm: 0-1
Distance: 2m/2m3: 0-0 2m4-2m7: 0-0 3m+: 0-5
Track: LH: 0-3 RH: 0-2 Tight: 0-2 Gall: 0-0
Aids: Bl: 0-0 Vi: 0-0 Tstrap: 0-0
Best Rating: 138 4/97 Aint 2m4f good Hdl

Decent chaser; goes well at Chepstow; suited by soft ground and three miles plus.

Ambry
112 **116d**
6-y-o br g Machiavellian (USA)-Alkaffeyeh (IRE) (Sadler s Wells (USA))
G L Moore Raymond Gross, Ms Adrienne Gross

Placings:2124/0230210-116U00 (3751)
2002/03: 18^1GF, 16^1G, 16^6S, 20^4HY, 17^9GS, 21^0G,

	Starts	1st	2nd	3rd	Win & Pl
Hurdles	6	2	0	0	6805
Career Total	17	4	4	1	18685

124	5/02	Towc	2m	D(0-125)HHdl	GD	£3150
124	5/02	Font	2m2f110yD(0-120)HHdl		G-F	£3430
122	3/02	Font	2m2f110yE(0-110)HHdl		SFT	£2646
94	3/01	Plum	2m	E Hdl	HVY	£3304

Total win prize-money £12530

Going: Sf: 0-2 GS: 0-1 Gd: 1-2 GF: - Fm: 1-1
Distance: 2m/2m3: 2-4 2m4-2m7: 0-2 3m+: 0-0
Track: LH: 1-3 RH: 1-2 Tight: 1-2 Gall: 0-2
Aids: Bl: 1-5 Vi: 1-1 Tstrap: 0-0
Best Rating: 124 5/02 Towc 2m good Hdl

Decent handicap hurdler; suited by soft ground; stays to two and a half miles; often blinkered.

Ambushed (IRE)
105 **103**
7-y-o b g Indian Ridge-Surprise Move (IRE) (Simply Great (FR))
P Monteith Allan W Melville

Placings:343/230-F32140 (3156)
2002/03: 16^6G, 16^3GF, 16^1S, 16^4HY, 16^0G,

	Starts	1st	2nd	3rd	Win & Pl
Hurdles	6	1	1	1	11674
Career Total	12	1	2	4	13718

95	11/02	Ayr	2m	D Hdl	SFT	£9200

Total win prize-money £9201

Going: Sf: 1-2 GS: 0-0 Gd: 0-3 GF: - Fm: 0-1
Distance: 2m/2m3: 1-6 2m4-2m7: 0-0 3m+: 0-0
Track: LH: 1-3 RH: 0-3 Tight: 0-2 Gall: 0-0
Aids: Bl: 0-0 Vi: 0-0 Tstrap: 0-0
Best Rating: 103 10/02 Kels 2m110y good Hdl

Moderate hurdler; acts on any ground; winning on soft at Ayr in November 2002.

American President (IRE)
102 **111+**
7-y-o br g Lord Americo-Deceptive Response (Furry Glen)
O Brennan Lady Anne Bentinck

Placings:0050-623 (3265)
2002/03: 16^6G, 16^2S, 19^3GS,

	Starts	1st	2nd	3rd	Win & Pl
Hurdles	3	0	1	1	2322
Career Total	7	0	1	1	2322

Going: Sf: 0-1 GS: 0-1 Gd: 0-1 GF: - Fm: 0-0
Distance: 2m/2m3: 0-2 2m4-2m7: 0-1 3m+: 0-0
Track: LH: 0-3 RH: 0-0 Tight: 0-1 Gall: 0-0
Aids: Bl: 0-0 Vi: 0-0 Tstrap: 0-0
Best Rating: 111 1/03 Donc 2m3f110y gd-sft Hdl

Modest hurdler; lightly-raced; promising efforts around the turn of the year; acts on good ground or softer.

Americanconnection (IRE)
69 **(81c)81**
7-y-o b g Lord Americo-Ballyea Jacki (Straight Lad)
M C Pipe (W P Mullins 21/12) Henderson, George, Pitman

Placings:0/000 (3558)
2002/03: 20^0SH, 20^0S, 20^0HY,

	Starts	1st	2nd	3rd	Win & Pl
Hurdles	2	0	0	0	0
Chases	1	0	0	0	0
Career Total	4	0	0	0	

Going: Sf: 0-2 GS: 0-0 Gd: 0-0 GF: - Fm: 0-0
Distance: 2m/2m3: 0-0 2m4-2m7: 0-3 3m+: 0-0
Track: LH: 0-1 RH: 0-2 Tight: 0-1 Gall: 0-0
Aids: Bl: 0-0 Vi: 0-0 Tstrap: 0-0
Best Rating: 97 4/01 Fair 2m yld-sft NHF

Amica Bella
6-y-o b m Environment Friend-Pontevecchio Bella (Main Reef)
Mrs L C Jewell Helen Clarke And Frank Brawn

Placings:P0-P (3741)
2002/03: 20^0G,

	Starts	1st	2nd	3rd	Win & Pl
Hurdles	1	0	0	0	
Career Total	3	0	0	0	

Going: Sf: 0-0 GS: 0-0 Gd: 0-1 GF: - Fm: 0-0
Distance: 2m/2m3: 0-0 2m4-2m7: 0-1 3m+: 0-0
Track: LH: 0-0 RH: 0-1 Tight: 0-0 Gall: 0-0
Aids: Bl: 0-0 Vi: 0-0 Tstrap: 0-0
Best Rating: 0 2/03 Hntg 2m4f110y good Hdl

Amir Zaman
88 **97+**
5-y-o ch g Salse (USA)-Colorvista (Shirley Heights)
J R Jenkins (J W Payne 9/10) The B C W Partnership

Placings:52 (4001)
2002/03: 16^6G, 16^2S,

	Starts	1st	2nd	3rd	Win & Pl
Hurdles	2	0	1	0	1995
Career Total	2	0	1	0	1995

Going: Sf: 0-1 GS: 0-0 Gd: 0-1 GF: - Fm: 0-0
Distance: 2m/2m3: 0-2 2m4-2m7: 0-0 3m+: 0-0
Track: LH: 0-0 RH: 0-2 Tight: 0-0 Gall: 0-0
Aids: Bl: 0-0 Vi: 0-0 Tstrap: 0-0
Best Rating: 99 3/03 Winc 2m soft Hdl

Fair maiden hurdler; acts on soft ground.

Amitge (FR)
76
9-y-o ch m Vaguely Pleasant (FR)-Ribbon In Her Hair (USA) (Sauce Boat (USA))
Miss Venetia Williams Favourites Racing

Placings:111225P/3536405U/01F1F6/F21111P/4-U (0100)
2002/03: 20^UGF,

	Starts	1st	2nd	3rd	Win & Pl
Chases	1	0	0	0	
Career Total	30	4	3	2	39576

113	12/00	Font	2m2f110yG Hdl		SFT	£2795
110	10/00	Hrfd	2m3f110yG Hdl		GD	£1883
106	8/00	Font	2m2f110yG Hdl		G-F	£2268
105	6/00	Folk	2m1f110yG Hdl		GD	£1554
118	2/00	Wwck	2m4f	D Ch	GD	£4628
112	11/99	Plum	2m4f	E Ch	G-F	£4135
106	10/97	Hrfd	2m1f	E Hdl	G-F	£2220
106	8/97	Worc	2m	E Hdl	GD	£2232
87	8/97	Bang	2m1f	E Hdl	G-F	£2710

Total win prize-money £24426

Going: Sf: 0-0 GS: 0-0 Gd: 0-0 GF: - Fm: 0-1
Distance: 2m/2m3: 0-0 2m4-2m7: 0-1 3m+: 0-0
Track: LH: 0-0 RH: 0-0 Tight: 0-1 Gall: 0-0
Aids: Bl: 0-0 Vi: 0-0 Tstrap: 0-0
Best Rating: 139 2/99 Newb 2m110y good Hdl

Amjad
100 **96d**
6-y-o ch g Cadeaux Genereux-Babita (Habitat)
Miss Kate Milligan Miss Kate Milligan

Placings:F3410-44461660 (3263)
2002/03: 16^4G, 16^4GF, 16^4GS, 19^9GF, 17^1GF, 16^6G, 16^6GS, 16^0GS,

	Starts	1st	2nd	3rd	Win & Pl
Hurdles	8	1	0	0	3408
Career Total	13	2	0	1	6161

92	10/02	Carl	2m1f	E(0-115)HHdl	G-F	£3143
102	12/01	Donc	2m110y	G Hdl	GD	£2331

Total win prize-money £5474

Going: Sf: 0-0 GS: 0-3 Gd: 0-2 GF: - Fm: 1-3
Distance: 2m/2m3: 1-7 2m4-2m7: 0-1 3m+: 0-0
Track: LH: 0-5 RH: 1-3 Tight: 0-2 Gall: 0-2
Aids: Bl: 0-0 Vi: 0-0 Tstrap: 0-0
Best Rating: 102 12/01 Donc 2m110y good Hdl

Moderate hurdler, suited by a sound surface.

Amorello
84f **111+f**
5-y-o b m Be My Native (USA)-Soundsgoodtome (Supreme Leader)
N J Henderson Erik Thorbek

Placings:11 (4611)
2002/03: 17^1S, 17^1G,

	Starts	1st	2nd	3rd	Win & Pl
NH Flat	2	2	0	0	17307
Career Total	2	2	0	0	17307

106	4/03	Chel	2m1f	A NHF	GD £14500
111	1/03	Tntn	2m1f	H NHF	SFT £2807
				Total win prize-money £17307	

Going:	Sf: 1-1 GS: 0-0 Gd: 1-1 GF: - Fm: 0-0
Distance:	2m/2m3: 2-2 2m4-2m7: 0-0 3m+: 0-0
Track:	LH: 1-1 RH: 0-0 Tight: 0-0 Gall: 1-1
Aids:	Bl: 0-0 Vi: 0-0 Tstrap: 0-0
Best Rating:	111 1/03 Tntn 2m1f soft NHF

Won well on her debut in a soft ground Taunton bumper January 2003; confirmed her trainer s opinion that she would be better on a sounder surface when winning Doncaster Bloodstock Sales Mares Only bumper at Cheltenham in April 2003.

Amplifi (IRE)
105   106

6-y-o b g Phardante (FR)-Season s Delight (Idiots Delight)
P J Hobbs   C K Watkins

Placings:20   (3183)
2002/03: 16²S, 16⁰GS,

	Starts	1st	2nd	3rd	Win & Pl
Hurdles	2	0	1	0	1320
Career Total	2	0	1	0	1320

Going:	Sf: 0-1 GS: 0-1 Gd: 0-0 GF: - Fm: 0-0
Distance:	2m/2m3: 0-2 2m4-2m7: 0-0 3m+: 0-0
Track:	LH: 0-1 RH: 0-1 Tight: 0-0 Gall: 0-1
Aids:	Bl: 0-0 Vi: 0-0 Tstrap: 0-0
Best Rating:	106 11/02 Newb 2m110y soft Hdl

Amsara (IRE)
89   53

7-y-o b m Taufan (USA)-Legend Of Spain (USA) (Alleged (USA))
A C Wilson   Cooper Wilson

Placings:0P005F0P0P   (4104)
2002/03: 17⁰GS, 19²G, 17⁰GF, 17⁰G, 17⁵G, 17ᶠGF, 22⁰G, 20⁰HY, 16⁰G, 27ᵖS,

	Starts	1st	2nd	3rd	Win & Pl
Hurdles	10	0	0	0	0
Career Total	10	0	0	0	0

Going:	Sf: 0-2 GS: 0-1 Gd: 0-5 GF: - Fm: 0-2
Distance:	2m/2m3: 0-6 2m4-2m7: 0-3 3m+: 0-1
Track:	LH: 0-9 RH: 0-1 Tight: 0-9 Gall: 0-0
Aids:	Bl: 0-0 Vi: 0-0 Tstrap: 0-0
Best Rating:	72 7/02 Sedg 2m1f gd-fm Hdl

Amusement
87   75d

7-y-o ch g Mystiko (USA)-Jolies Eaux (Shirley Heights)
D G Bridgwater   Daltagh Construction Ltd

Placings:00/200-604P   (4704)
2002/03: 17⁶S, 16⁰GS, 19⁴S, 20ᵖG,

	Starts	1st	2nd	3rd	Win & Pl
Hurdles	4	0	0	0	408
Career Total	9	0	1	0	827

Going:	Sf: 0-2 GS: 0-1 Gd: 0-1 GF: - Fm: 0-0
Distance:	2m/2m3: 0-2 2m4-2m7: 0-2 3m+: 0-0

Track:	LH: 0-2 RH: 0-2 Tight: 0-1 Gall: 0-1
Aids:	Bl: 0-0 Vi: 0-0 Tstrap: 0-0
Best Rating:	89 8/01 Hntg 2m110y gd-fm NHF

Amwell Star (USA)
97   83

5-y-o gr m Silver Buck (USA)-Markham Fair (CAN) (Woodman (USA))
J R Jenkins   Amwell Racing

Placings:F40-3253503F0   (4338)
2002/03: 17³G, 16²G, 16⁵G, 20³HY, 16⁵S, 21⁰GS, 16³GS, 17ᶠG, 20⁰GF,

	Starts	1st	2nd	3rd	Win & Pl
Hurdles	9	0	1	3	2634
Career Total	12	0	1	3	2634

Going:	Sf: 0-2 GS: 0-2 Gd: 0-4 GF: - Fm: 0-1
Distance:	2m/2m3: 0-6 2m4-2m7: 0-3 3m+: 0-0
Track:	LH: 0-4 RH: 0-5 Tight: 0-3 Gall: 0-2
Aids:	Bl: 0-0 Vi: 0-0 Tstrap: 0-0
Best Rating:	87 11/01 Hntg 2m110y good Hdl

Modest hurdler, likely to stay beyond two miles.

Amy's Gift

7-y-o b m Lahib (USA)-Miss Amy Lou (IRE) (Gallic League)
Miss A J Trim   Miss D Miller

Placings:U   (4487)
2002/03: 16ᵁGF,

	Starts	1st	2nd	3rd	Win & Pl
Chases	1	0	0	0	
Career Total	1	0	0	0	

Going:	Sf: 0-0 GS: 0-0 Gd: 0-0 GF: - Fm: 0-0
Distance:	2m/2m3: 0-1 2m4-2m7: 0-0 3m+: 0-0
Track:	LH: 0-0 RH: 0-1 Tight: 0-0 Gall: 0-0
Aids:	Bl: 0-1 Vi: 0-0 Tstrap: 0-0
Best Rating:	0 4/03 Hrfd 2m gd-fm Ch

Anatar (IRE)
111   132

5-y-o b g Caerleon (USA)-Anaza (Darshaan)
M C Pipe   Eminence Grise Partnership

Placings:050-011211001   (4367)
2002/03: 17⁰GF, 17¹G, 16¹G, 16²S, 16¹S, 16¹S, 16⁹G, 21⁰G, 20¹G,

	Starts	1st	2nd	3rd	Win & Pl
Hurdles	9	5	1	0	29135
Career Total	12	5	1	0	29135

132	3/03	Asct	2m4f	C(0-130)HHdl	GD £6971
132	12/02	Uttx	2m	C(0-130)HHdl	SFT £8076
129	12/02	Sand	2m110y	D(0-110)HHdl	SFT £7052
105	10/02	Plum	2m	E(0-100)HHdl	GD £2978
97	9/02	NAbb	2m1f	F(0-100)HHdl	GD £2996
				Total win prize-money £28075	

Going:	Sf: 2-3 GS: 0-0 Gd: 3-5 GF: - Fm: 0-1
Distance:	2m/2m3: 4-7 2m4-2m7: 1-2 3m+: 0-0
Track:	LH: 3-4 RH: 2-5 Tight: 2-2 Gall: 0-1
Aids:	Bl: 0-0 Vi: 0-0 Tstrap: 0-0
Best Rating:	132 3/03 Asct 2m4f good Hdl

Useful hurdler; in good form in 2002/3 but ran as if in the handicapper s grip at Kempton in January; suited by trips of around two miles; suited by ground good or softer.

Anbrooka
88   34

8-y-o ch m Meadowbrook-Angerton Annie (Waterfall)
Mrs H O Graham   R D Graham

Placings:PF665P   (1239)
2002/03: 23ᵖG, 22ᶠGF, 20⁶GS, 20⁶G, 26⁵G, 20ᵖGF,

	Starts	1st	2nd	3rd	Win & Pl
Hurdles	4	0	0	0	0
Chases	2	0	0	0	0
Career Total	6	0	0	0	0

Going:	Sf: 0-0 GS: 0-1 Gd: 0-3 GF: - Fm: 0-2
Distance:	2m/2m3: 0-0 2m4-2m7: 0-4 3m+: 0-2
Track:	LH: 0-3 RH: 0-2 Tight: 0-1 Gall: 0-0
Aids:	Bl: 0-0 Vi: 0-0 Tstrap: 0-0
Best Rating:	42 8/02 Prth 2m4f110y gd-sft Hdl

Andaleer (IRE)
81(97c)   (82c)83

8-y-o b m Phardante (FR)-Dunleer Duchess (Our Mirage)
Mrs H Dalton   M Richards And G Stone

Placings:4/23333-2P   (0654)
2002/03: 20³G, 19²G, 20ᵖGF,

	Starts	1st	2nd	3rd	Win & Pl
Hurdles	2	0	0	1	318
Chases	1	0	1	0	884
Career Total	8	0	2	4	2763

Going:	Sf: 0-0 GS: 0-0 Gd: 0-2 GF: - Fm: 0-1
Distance:	2m/2m3: 0-1 2m4-2m7: 0-2 3m+: 0-0
Track:	LH: 0-2 RH: 0-1 Tight: 0-0 Gall: 0-1
Aids:	Bl: 0-0 Vi: 0-0 Tstrap: 0-0
Best Rating:	93 5/01 Bang 2m1f gd-sft NHF

Plating-class mare; regularly placed over hurdles and on her chasing debut.

Andrew Doble
102   89

4-y-o ch g Sabrehill (USA)-Verchinina (Star Appeal)
Miss Venetia Williams (M A Jarvis 29/5)   Knightsbridge Bc

Placings:600U3130   (3543)
2002/03: 16⁶G, 17⁰G, 16⁰G, 17ᵁS, 16²S, 16¹S, 16³GS, 17⁰G,

	Starts	1st	2nd	3rd	Win & Pl
Hurdles	8	1	0	2	4573
Career Total	8	1	0	2	4573

86	1/03	Fknm	2m	E(0-105)HHdl	SFT £3458
				Total win prize-money £3458	

Going:	Sf: 1-3 GS: 0-1 Gd: 0-4 GF: - Fm: 0-0
Distance:	2m/2m3: 1-8 2m4-2m7: 0-0 3m+: 0-0
Track:	LH: 1-4 RH: 0-4 Tight: 1-2 Gall: 0-0
Aids:	Bl: 0-0 Vi: 0-0 Tstrap: 0-0
Best Rating:	87 1/03 Sthl 2m gd-sft Hdl

Plating-class hurdler; suited by good ground or softer; acts on a sharp track.

Andromache
76   51

4-y-o ch f Hector Protector (USA)-South Sea Bubble (IRE) (Bustino)
G B Balding (L M Cumani 23/11)   J T Brown

Placings:3   (3918)
2002/03: 18³S,

	Starts	1st	2nd	3rd	Win & Pl
Hurdles	1	0	0	1	518
Career Total	1	0	0	1	518

Going: Sf: 0-1 GS: 0-0 Gd: 0-0 GF: - Fm: 0-0
Distance: 2m/2m3: 0-1 2m4-2m7: 0-0 3m+: 0-0
Track: LH: 0-1 RH: 0-0 Tight: 0-1 Gall: 0-0
Aids: Bl: 0-0 Vi: 0-0 Tstrap: 0-0
Best Rating: 45 3/03 Font 2m2f110y soft Hdl

Andromeda (IRE)
85   **64**
4-y-o b f Barathea (IRE)-Royal York (Bustino)
M Todhunter (J Noseda 14/8) Sir Robert Ogden

Placings:0 (1304)
2002/03: 16^0GF,

	Starts	1st	2nd	3rd	Win & Pl
Hurdles	1	0	0	0	
Career Total	1	0	0	0	

Going: Sf: 0-0 GS: 0-0 Gd: 0-0 GF: - Fm: 0-1
Distance: 2m/2m3: 0-1 2m4-2m7: 0-0 3m+: 0-0
Track: LH: 0-0 RH: 0-1 Tight: 0-0 Gall: 0-0
Aids: Bl: 0-0 Vi: 0-0 Tstrap: 0-0
Best Rating: 64 9/02 Prth 2m110y gd-fm Hdl

Andsuephi (IRE)

11-y-o b g Montelimar (USA)-Butler s Daughter (Rhett Butler)
Mrs S A Hodge A H B Hodge

Placings:111140P/13U23/11F40/1P/00P-P (3952)
2002/03: 23^PGS,

	Starts	1st	2nd	3rd	Win & Pl
Chases	1	0	0	0	
Career Total	23	8	1	2	37643
136	5/00 Strf	3m	C(0-135)HCh	G-F	£6337
136	12/99 Leic	2m7f110y	D(0-125)HCh	G-F	£4272
130	11/99 Worc	2m7f110y	C(0-135)HCh	G-S	£5889
131	1/99 Winc	2m5f	D Ch	SFT	£3831
105	12/97 Leic	2m	E Hdl	SFT	£3239
118	10/97 Strf	2m110y	E Hdl	GD	£2670
109	5/97 Winc	2m	H NHF	SFT	£1255
108	5/97 Wwck	2m	H NHF	GD	£1028

Total win prize-money £28525

Going: Sf: 0-0 GS: 0-1 Gd: 0-0 GF: - Fm: 0-0
Distance: 2m/2m3: 0-0 2m4-2m7: 0-0 3m+: 0-1
Track: LH: 0-0 RH: 0-1 Tight: 0-0 Gall: 0-0
Aids: Bl: 0-0 Vi: 0-0 Tstrap: 0-0
Best Rating: 136 5/00 Strf 3m gd-fm Ch

Andy Gin (FR)
89   **104**
4-y-o b g Ski Chief (USA)-Love Love Kate (FR) (Saint Andrews (FR))
P J Hobbs (R Chotard 6/7) Terry Warner

Placings:10 (4130)
2002/03: 17^1GS, 17^0G,

	Starts	1st	2nd	3rd	Win & Pl
Hurdles	2	1	0	0	4784
Career Total	2	1	0	0	4784
104	1/03 Extr	2m1f	D Hdl	G-S	£4784

Total win prize-money £4784

Going: Sf: 0-0 GS: 1-1 Gd: 0-1 GF: - Fm: 0-0
Distance: 2m/2m3: 1-2 2m4-2m7: 0-0 3m+: 0-0
Track: LH: 0-1 RH: 1-1 Tight: 0-0 Gall: 0-1
Aids: Bl: 0-0 Vi: 0-0 Tstrap: 0-0
Best Rating: 104 1/03 Extr 2m1f gd-sft Hdl

Modest juvenile hurdler; winner on debut at Exeter; successful over ten furlongs on Flat in France in 2002: effective on good and soft ground.

Andy's Birthday (IRE)
(74h)   (79h)**103**
12-y-o ch g King Luthier-Clonroche Abendego (Pauper)
Miss S J Wilton John Pointon And Sons

Placings:0P0/1F254P1/P23P6/PP42131-4PP (3500)
2002/03: 24^4S, 26^PHY, 24^PGS,

	Starts	1st	2nd	3rd	Win & Pl
Chases	3	0	0	0	322
Career Total	25	4	3	2	23317
103	3/02 Uttx	2m7f	D(0-115)HCh	HVY	£5068
102	2/02 Kemp	3m	D(0-115)HCh	SFT	£3640
109	4/00 Uttx	3m	D(0-125)HCh	SFT	£4567
107	12/99 Uttx	3m	E(0-105)HCh	SFT	£3288

Total win prize-money £16565

Going: Sf: 0-2 GS: 0-1 Gd: 0-0 GF: - Fm: 0-0
Distance: 2m/2m3: 0-0 2m4-2m7: 0-0 3m+: 0-3
Track: LH: 0-2 RH: 0-1 Tight: 0-1 Gall: 0-0
Aids: Bl: 0-0 Vi: 0-0 Tstrap: 0-1
Best Rating: 109 4/00 Uttx 3m soft Ch

Fair staying chaser when on song. Goes well in soft ground and has benefited from the fitting of a tongue-strap this year.

Angel Delight
105   **97**
7-y-o gr m Seymour Hicks (FR)-Bird s Custard (Birdbrook)
Miss Venetia Williams Croome Cavaliers

Placings:6/560-5510533 (4750)
2002/03: 20^5GF, 21^5S, 21^1GS, 21^0S, 21^5G, 24^3GF, 24^3G,

	Starts	1st	2nd	3rd	Win & Pl
Hurdles	7	1	0	2	9530
Career Total	11	1	0	2	9530
100	2/03 Kemp	2m5f	D(0-115)HHdl	G-S	£6467

Total win prize-money £6467

Going: Sf: 0-2 GS: 1-1 Gd: 0-2 GF: - Fm: 0-2
Distance: 2m/2m3: 0-0 2m4-2m7: 1-5 3m+: 0-2
Track: LH: 0-4 RH: 1-3 Tight: 0-2 Gall: 0-1
Aids: Bl: 0-0 Vi: 0-0 Tstrap: 0-0
Best Rating: 100 2/03 Kemp 2m5f gd-sft Hdl

Modest novice hurdler; stays two miles five; acts on good and yielding ground.

Angel Dust (FR)
(67h)
7-y-o b m Cadoudal (FR)-Silicity (FR) (Son Of Silver)
L J Williams Mrs C M Marles

Placings:0/001R41500/0323PP-PU0 (3854)
2002/03: 19^PGS, 16^UGS, 16^0GS,

	Starts	1st	2nd	3rd	Win & Pl
Chases	3	0	0	0	
Career Total	19	2	1	2	8245
100	12/00 Sthl	2m	E Hdl	SFT	£2331
86	6/00 Prth	2m110y	F(0-100)HHdl	HVY	£3298

Total win prize-money £5630

Going: Sf: 0-0 GS: 0-3 Gd: 0-0 GF: - Fm: 0-0
Distance: 2m/2m3: 0-3 2m4-2m7: 0-0 3m+: 0-0
Track: LH: 0-1 RH: 0-3 Tight: 0-3 Gall: 0-0
Aids: Bl: 0-0 Vi: 0-0 Tstrap: 0-0
Best Rating: 100 12/00 Sthl 2m soft Hdl

Angelena Ballerina
88   **63**
5-y-o b m Roselier (FR)-True Clown (True Song)
N A Twiston-Davies Mr & Mrs Peter Orton

Placings:0F6P (2169)
2002/03: 17^0GS, 20^5S, 17^5G, 21^PGS,

	Starts	1st	2nd	3rd	Win & Pl
NH Flat	1	0	0	0	0
Hurdles	3	0	0	0	0
Career Total	4	0	0	0	0

Going: Sf: 0-1 GS: 0-1 Gd: 0-2 GF: - Fm: 0-0
Distance: 2m/2m3: 0-2 2m4-2m7: 0-2 3m+: 0-0
Track: LH: 0-2 RH: 0-2 Tight: 0-1 Gall: 0-0
Aids: Bl: 0-0 Vi: 0-0 Tstrap: 0-0
Best Rating: 77 5/02 Extr 2m1f good NHF

Angie Gold
84   **53**
6-y-o b m Mesleh-Gold Duchess (Sonnen Gold)
Mrs S J Smith Town Moor Golf Racing Syndicate

Placings:0-00604 (4708)
2002/03: 16^0S, 17^0HY, 16^6GF, 16^0G, 20^4G,

	Starts	1st	2nd	3rd	Win & Pl
NH Flat	3	0	0	0	0
Hurdles	2	0	0	0	0
Career Total	6	0	0	0	0

Going: Sf: 0-2 GS: 0-0 Gd: 0-2 GF: - Fm: 0-1
Distance: 2m/2m3: 0-4 2m4-2m7: 0-1 3m+: 0-0
Track: LH: 0-5 RH: 0-0 Tight: 0-2 Gall: 0-0
Aids: Bl: 0-0 Vi: 0-0 Tstrap: 0-0
Best Rating: 69 3/03 Sthl 2m gd-fm NHF

Maiden hurdler; has not shown much so far.

Angiolini (USA)
88   **85**
6-y-o ch h Woodman (USA)-Danse Royale (IRE) (Caerleon (USA))
N F Glynn N F Glynn

Placings:0/000000-4005 (1352a)
2002/03: 16^5HY, 20^4G, 16^5G, 16^0F, 16^5F,

	Starts	1st	2nd	3rd	Win & Pl
Hurdles	5	0	0	0	0
Career Total	11	0	0	0	0

Going: Sf: 0-1 GS: 0-0 Gd: 0-2 GF: - Fm: 0-2
Distance: 2m/2m3: 0-4 2m4-2m7: 0-1 3m+: 0-0
Track: LH: 0-4 RH: 0-0 Tight: 0-0 Gall: 0-0
Aids: Bl: 0-0 Vi: 0-0 Tstrap: 0-0
Best Rating: 85 5/02 Uttx 2m4f110y good Hdl

Anglanit (CZE)
4-y-o b c Lanitos-Anglointernational (Millfontaine)

M Pitman Ron & Martin Butler

Placings:P   (1756)
2002/03: 16ᴾG,

	Starts	1st	2nd	3rd	Win & Pl
Hurdles	1	0	0	0	
Career Total	1	0	0	0	

Going:	Sf: 0-0 GS: 0-0 Gd: 0-1 GF: - Fm: 0-0
Distance:	2m/2m3: 0-1 2m4-2m7: 0-0 3m+: 0-0
Track:	LH: 0-1 RH: 0-0 Tight: 0-0 Gall: 0-0
Aids:	Bl: 0-0 Vi: 0-0 Tstrap: 0-0
Best Rating:	0 11/02 Wwck 2m good Hdl

Anguilla

97   **75**

8-y-o b g Rudimentary (USA)-More Wise (Ballymore)
P T Dalton Mrs Lucia Farmer

Placings:4/0-0P02   (1236)
2002/03: 16⁰G, 25ᴾG, 20⁰G, 20²G,

	Starts	1st	2nd	3rd	Win & Pl
Hurdles	4	0	1	0	878
Career Total	6	0	1	0	878

Going:	Sf: 0-0 GS: 0-0 Gd: 0-4 GF: - Fm: 0-0
Distance:	2m/2m3: 0-1 2m4-2m7: 0-2 3m+: 0-1
Track:	LH: 0-3 RH: 0-1 Tight: 0-1 Gall: 0-0
Aids:	Bl: 0-0 Vi: 0-0 Tstrap: 0-0
Best Rating:	75 9/02 Worc 2m4f good Hdl

Plating-class hurdler; improved form when narrowly beaten by an odds-on favourite over two and a half miles at Worcester in September 2002; acts on good ground.

Animal Cracker

5-y-o gr m Primo Dominie-Child Star (FR) (Bellypha)
J Balding (R Curtis 12/12) D Marks

Placings:P0   (2452)
2002/03: 17ᴾGS, 17⁰GS,

	Starts	1st	2nd	3rd	Win & Pl
Hurdles	2	0	0	0	
Career Total	2	0	0	0	

Going:	Sf: 0-0 GS: 0-2 Gd: 0-0 GF: - Fm: 0-0
Distance:	2m/2m3: 0-2 2m4-2m7: 0-0 3m+: 0-0
Track:	LH: 0-0 RH: 0-2 Tight: 0-2 Gall: 0-0
Aids:	Bl: 0-0 Vi: 0-0 Tstrap: 0-0
Best Rating:	0 12/02 Tntn 2m1f gd-sft Hdl

Modest sprinter on the level. Pulled up on hurdles debut and tailed off next time out.

Ankles Back (IRE)

                    59

6-y-o b g Seclude (USA)-Pedalo (Legal Tender)
Mrs H Dalton Ray Bailey

Placings:5   (2899)
2002/03: 20⁵S,

	Starts	1st	2nd	3rd	Win & Pl
Chases	1	0	0	0	0
Career Total	1	0	0	0	0

Going:	Sf: 0-1 GS: 0-0 Gd: 0-0 GF: - Fm: 0-0
Distance:	2m/2m3: 0-0 2m4-2m7: 0-1 3m+: 0-0

Track:	LH: 0-0 RH: 0-1 Tight: 0-0 Gall: 0-0
Aids:	Bl: 0-0 Vi: 0-0 Tstrap: 0-0
Best Rating:	64 1/03 Leic 2m4f110y soft Ch

Anna Almost

90   **70**

5-y-o b m Tragic Role (USA)-Princess Hotpot (IRE) (King s Ride)
T Wall D B Roberts

Placings:006-4P3U   (4426)
2002/03: 16⁴GF, 17ᴾS, 17³G, 16ᵁGF,

	Starts	1st	2nd	3rd	Win & Pl
Hurdles	4	0	0	1	374
Career Total	7	0	0	1	374

Going:	Sf: 0-1 GS: 0-0 Gd: 0-1 GF: - Fm: 0-2
Distance:	2m/2m3: 0-4 2m4-2m7: 0-0 3m+: 0-0
Track:	LH: 0-3 RH: 0-1 Tight: 0-3 Gall: 0-0
Aids:	Bl: 0-0 Vi: 0-2 Tstrap: 0-0
Best Rating:	74 4/02 Fknm 2m good NHF

Annadawi

                   78

8-y-o b g Sadler s Wells (USA)-Prayers n Promises (USA) (Foolish Pleasure (USA))
M E Sowersby Paul Clifton

Placings:34/50/00/466-P   (0375)
2002/03: 16ᴾG,

	Starts	1st	2nd	3rd	Win & Pl
Hurdles	1	0	0	0	
Career Total	10	0	0	1	424

Going:	Sf: 0-0 GS: 0-0 Gd: 0-1 GF: - Fm: 0-0
Distance:	2m/2m3: 0-1 2m4-2m7: 0-0 3m+: 0-0
Track:	LH: 0-1 RH: 0-0 Tight: 0-1 Gall: 0-0
Aids:	Bl: 0-0 Vi: 0-0 Tstrap: 0-0
Best Rating:	99 2/99 Thur 2m heavy NHF

Annaghmore Gale (IRE)

9-y-o br g Strong Gale-Kept In The Dark (Kemal (FR))
Miss Sarah George (D T Hughes 29/9) The A J s Partnership

Placings:4/6004O/60F5L6/21C133PSPP-6F232F1P2RU   (4678)
2002/03: 16ᴾY, 24ᶠS, 20²G, 16³GF, 20²GF, 22ᶠGY, 20¹GF, 21ᴾGF, 16²F, 20ᴿGF, 19ᵁGF,

	Starts	1st	2nd	3rd	Win & Pl
Chases	11	1	3	1	12782
Career Total	33	3	4	3	29361
110 8/02	Baln	2m4f	(0-109)HCh	G-F	£7975
112 7/01	Baln	2m1f	Ch	Y-S	£6120
97 5/01	Navn	2m1f	Ch	FRM	£5286
			Total win prize-money £19382		

Going:	Sf: 0-1 GS: 0-0 Gd: 0-1 GF: - Fm: 1-7
Distance:	2m/2m3: 0-2 2m4-2m7: 1-6 3m+: 0-1
Track:	LH: 0-1 RH: 0-6 Tight: 0-1 Gall: 0-0
Aids:	Bl: 0-0 Vi: 0-0 Tstrap: 0-0
Best Rating:	113 8/01 Rosc 2m5f yield Ch

Anne Nutter

4-y-o ch f Kasakov-Bairn Glen (Bairn (USA))
I W McInnes Robert E Cook

Placings:P   (2120)
2002/03: 16ᴾGS,

	Starts	1st	2nd	3rd	Win & Pl
Hurdles	1	0	0	0	
Career Total	1	0	0	0	

Going:	Sf: 0-0 GS: 0-1 Gd: 0-0 GF: - Fm: 0-0
Distance:	2m/2m3: 0-1 2m4-2m7: 0-0 3m+: 0-0
Track:	LH: 0-1 RH: 0-0 Tight: 0-1 Gall: 0-0
Aids:	Bl: 0-0 Vi: 0-0 Tstrap: 0-0
Best Rating:	0 11/02 Fknm 2m gd-sft Hdl

Anne-Lise

78   **81**

5-y-o ch m Inchinor-Red Gloves (Red God)
P D Evans (P M Mooney 6/12) Paul V Jackson

Placings:40   (2629)
2002/03: 16⁴GS, 16⁰S,

	Starts	1st	2nd	3rd	Win & Pl
Hurdles	2	0	0	0	0
Career Total	2	0	0	0	0

Going:	Sf: 0-1 GS: 0-1 Gd: 0-0 GF: - Fm: 0-0
Distance:	2m/2m3: 0-2 2m4-2m7: 0-0 3m+: 0-0
Track:	LH: 0-2 RH: 0-0 Tight: 0-1 Gall: 0-0
Aids:	Bl: 0-0 Vi: 0-0 Tstrap: 0-0
Best Rating:	74 12/02 Sthl 2m gd-sft Hdl

Seven furlong Flat winner in Ireland; looks to struggle to see out two miles over hurdles.

Annie Byers

99   **85**

7-y-o ch m Sula Bula-Tuneful Flutter (Orchestra)
J G Portman M J Vandenberghe

Placings:2004535   (4418)
2002/03: 16²S, 16⁰GS, 21⁰S, 22⁴HY, 19⁵G, 19³G, 22⁵G,

	Starts	1st	2nd	3rd	Win & Pl
NH Flat	2	0	1	0	702
Hurdles	5	0	0	1	1081
Career Total	7	0	1	1	1783

Going:	Sf: 0-3 GS: 0-1 Gd: 0-3 GF: - Fm: 0-0
Distance:	2m/2m3: 0-3 2m4-2m7: 0-4 3m+: 0-0
Track:	LH: 0-2 RH: 0-4 Tight: 0-0 Gall: 0-1
Aids:	Bl: 0-0 Vi: 0-0 Tstrap: 0-0
Best Rating:	101 11/02 Sand 2m110y soft NHF

Showed ability in bumpers but only plating-class form over hurdles.

Annie Fleetwood

93   **87**

5-y-o ch m Anshan-Gold Luck (USA) (Slew O Gold (USA))
C P Morlock J P M & J W Cook

Placings:064   (4514)
2002/03: 16⁰G, 20⁰G, 22⁴GF,

	Starts	1st	2nd	3rd	Win & Pl
NH Flat	1	0	0	0	0
Hurdles	2	0	0	0	0

| Career Total | 3 | 0 | 0 | 0 | 0 |

Going: Sf: 0-0 GS: 0-0 Gd: 0-2 GF: - Fm: 0-1
Distance: 2m/2m3: 0-1 2m4-2m7: 0-2 3m+: 0-0
Track: LH: 0-0 RH: 0-3 Tight: 0-1 Gall: 0-1
Aids: Bl: 0-0 Vi: 0-0 Tstrap: 0-0
Best Rating: 78 4/03 Extr 2m6f110y gd-fm Hdl

Modest form in novice hurdles at up to 2m 6f.

Annie-Jo
82f   **49f**
4-y-o br f Presenting-Lorna s Choice (Oats)
W McKeown Mrs G F White

Placings:000   (4397)
2002/03: 16^0HY, 16^0G, 17^0G,

	Starts	1st	2nd	3rd	Win & Pl
NH Flat	3	0	0	0	
Career Total	3	0	0	0	

Going: Sf: 0-1 GS: 0-0 Gd: 0-2 GF: - Fm: 0-0
Distance: 2m/2m3: 0-3 2m4-2m7: 0-0 3m+: 0-0
Track: LH: 0-2 RH: 0-1 Tight: 0-1 Gall: 0-0
Aids: Bl: 0-0 Vi: 0-0 Tstrap: 0-0
Best Rating: 49 3/03 Carl 2m1f good NHF

Annies Gold (IRE)

7-y-o b m Spanish Place (USA)-Leventos (Le Moss)
Mrs S M Johnson Colin Thomson

Placings:P   (4482)
2002/03: 19^0GF,

	Starts	1st	2nd	3rd	Win & Pl
Hurdles	1	0	0	0	
Career Total	1	0	0	0	

Going: Sf: 0-0 GS: 0-0 Gd: 0-0 GF: - Fm: 0-1
Distance: 2m/2m3: 0-0 2m4-2m7: 0-1 3m+: 0-0
Track: LH: 0-0 RH: 0-1 Tight: 0-0 Gall: 0-0
Aids: Bl: 0-0 Vi: 0-0 Tstrap: 0-0
Best Rating: 0 4/03 Hrfd 2m3f110y gd-fm Hdl

Annodyce
91   **73**
5-y-o b m Faustus (USA)-Coleford (USA) (Secreto (USA))
Miss Z C Davison Auld Firm Partnership

Placings:4-PP5054   (4703)
2002/03: 16^6G, 16^6GS, 16^5HY, 16^0S, 16^4GF, 16^4GF,

	Starts	1st	2nd	3rd	Win & Pl
Hurdles	6	0	0	0	260
Career Total	7	0	0	0	260

Going: Sf: 0-2 GS: 0-1 Gd: 0-1 GF: - Fm: 0-2
Distance: 2m/2m3: 0-6 2m4-2m7: 0-0 3m+: 0-0
Track: LH: 0-5 RH: 0-1 Tight: 0-5 Gall: 0-1
Aids: Bl: 0-0 Vi: 0-0 Tstrap: 0-0
Best Rating: 73 4/03 Plum 2m gd-fm Hdl

Plating-class hurdler; made a promising enough debut at Huntingdon over two miles on good to firm; poor form since.

Anns Girl
99   **87**
10-y-o br m Newski (USA)-Nearly Married (Nearly A Hand)

J C Fox Mrs J A Cleary

Placings:061022413/6563F3P000/2454432111F460/P000-P55000055050   (4256)
2002/03: 16^6GF, 16^5G, 19^5G, 16^6GF, 16^0G, 16^0HY, 16^0S, 22^5GS, 19^5GS, 16^0HY, 17^5S, 17^0G,

	Starts	1st	2nd	3rd	Win & Pl
Hurdles	12	0	0	0	0
Career Total	49	5	4	4	18671
111 10/00 Extr 2m1f D(0-125)HHdl				GD	£3419
105 9/00 Extr 2m1f D(0-120)HHdl				GD	£3159
98 9/00 Worc 2m E(0-115)HHdl				G-F	£2765
104 4/99 NAbb 2m1f E Hdl				GD	£2421
83 6/98 Worc 2m H NHF				GD	£1213
				Total win prize-money	£12979

Going: Sf: 0-4 GS: 0-2 Gd: 0-4 GF: - Fm: 0-2
Distance: 2m/2m3: 0-10 2m4-2m7: 0-2 3m+: 0-0
Track: LH: 0-6 RH: 0-6 Tight: 0-1 Gall: 0-0
Aids: Bl: 0-11 Vi: 0-0 Tstrap: 0-0
Best Rating: 111 11/00 Newb 2m3f soft Hdl

Moderate hurdler; won seller at Worcester May 2003; acts on good ground.

Another Ace (IRE)

6-y-o b g Synefos (USA)-Another Space (Brave Invader (USA))
P D Niven R A Bartlett

Placings:U   (3895)
2002/03: 25^UGS,

	Starts	1st	2nd	3rd	Win & Pl
Chases	1	0	0	0	
Career Total	1	0	0	0	

Going: Sf: 0-0 GS: 0-1 Gd: 0-0 GF: - Fm: 0-0
Distance: 2m/2m3: 0-0 2m4-2m7: 0-0 3m+: 0-1
Track: LH: 0-1 RH: 0-0 Tight: 0-1 Gall: 0-0
Aids: Bl: 0-0 Vi: 0-0 Tstrap: 0-0
Best Rating: 0 3/03 Kels 3m1f gd-sft Ch

Another Arthur

7-y-o ro g Puissance-Traumatic Laura (Pragmatic)
W McKeown Miss Susan J Blain

Placings:54/3/P0   (4433)
2002/03: 18^0S, 16^0G,

	Starts	1st	2nd	3rd	Win & Pl
Hurdles	2	0	0	0	
Career Total	5	0	0	1	349

Going: Sf: 0-1 GS: 0-0 Gd: 0-1 GF: - Fm: 0-0
Distance: 2m/2m3: 0-2 2m4-2m7: 0-0 3m+: 0-0
Track: LH: 0-2 RH: 0-0 Tight: 0-1 Gall: 0-1
Aids: Bl: 0-0 Vi: 0-0 Tstrap: 0-0
Best Rating: 80 5/00 Hexm 2m good Hdl

Another Aspect (IRE)
78   **69**
4-y-o b g Inzar (USA)-The Aspecto Girl (IRE) (Alzao (USA))
J Cullinan Alan Spargo Ltd Toolmakers

Placings:00   (4079)
2002/03: 16^0G, 16^0HY,

	Starts	1st	2nd	3rd	Win & Pl
Hurdles	2	0	0	0	
Career Total	2	0	0	0	

Going: Sf: 0-1 GS: 0-0 Gd: 0-1 GF: - Fm: 0-0
Distance: 2m/2m3: 0-2 2m4-2m7: 0-0 3m+: 0-0
Track: LH: 0-2 RH: 0-0 Tight: 0-1 Gall: 0-1
Aids: Bl: 0-0 Vi: 0-0 Tstrap: 0-0
Best Rating: 72 12/02 Newb 2m110y good Hdl

Another Beeper (IRE)
89   **79**
6-y-o b m Accordion-Raymylettes Niece (IRE) (Dock Leaf)
T G McCourt Martin Leonard O Hanlon

Placings:0-00000P0   (3578)
2002/03: 16^0GF, 16^0S, 18^0YS, 18^0S, 24^0S, 22^PY, 24^0G,

	Starts	1st	2nd	3rd	Win & Pl
NH Flat	1	0	0	0	
Hurdles	6	0	0	0	
Career Total	8	0	0	0	

Going: Sf: 0-3 GS: 0-0 Gd: 0-1 GF: - Fm: 0-1
Distance: 2m/2m3: 0-4 2m4-2m7: 0-1 3m+: 0-2
Track: LH: 0-1 RH: 0-3 Tight: 0-1 Gall: 0-0
Aids: Bl: 0-1 Vi: 0-0 Tstrap: 0-0
Best Rating: 79 11/02 Fair 2m2f soft Hdl

Another Bit
89   **63**
6-y-o ch g Henbit (USA)-Perrinpit Annapolis Vii (Damsire Unregistered)
J C Tuck (Dr P Pritchard 16/1) R Weaver

Placings:U000U4   (4716)
2002/03: 16US, 16^0S, 17^0G, 16^0G, 17^UF, 16^4F,

	Starts	1st	2nd	3rd	Win & Pl
NH Flat	3	0	0	0	
Hurdles	3	0	0	0	
Career Total	6	0	0	0	

Going: Sf: 0-2 GS: 0-0 Gd: 0-2 GF: - Fm: 0-2
Distance: 2m/2m3: 0-6 2m4-2m7: 0-0 3m+: 0-0
Track: LH: 0-1 RH: 0-5 Tight: 0-0 Gall: 0-0
Aids: Bl: 0-0 Vi: 0-0 Tstrap: 0-0
Best Rating: 67 1/03 Ludl 2m soft NHF

Poor form in bumpers and hurdles.

Another Copper
102(82c)   (77c)**90d**
7-y-o ch g Bandmaster (USA)-Letitica (Deep Run)
C J Down (Mrs S D Williams 29/6) Mrs E J Taplin

Placings:301-5FP2F5   (4536)
2002/03: 23^5G, 26^FF, 26^0GF, 24^2S, 26^0GF, 24^5G,

	Starts	1st	2nd	3rd	Win & Pl
Hurdles	3	0	1	0	1325
Chases	3	0	0	0	0
Career Total	9	1	1	1	5315
77 4/02 Extr 2m7f110yE Ch				FRM	£3640
				Total win prize-money	£3640

Going: Sf: 0-1 GS: 0-0 Gd: 0-3 GF: - Fm: 0-2
Distance: 2m/2m3: 0-0 2m4-2m7: 0-0 3m+: 0-6
Track: LH: 0-2 RH: 0-4 Tight: 0-2 Gall: 0-0

Aids: Bl: 0-0 Vi: 0-0 Tstrap: 0-0
Best Rating: 90 3/03 Extr 3m110y soft Hdl

Lightly-raced, he ran well on his hurdling debut at Exeter in October 2001; got off the mark in poor novice chase on his chasing debut at Exeter April 2002; subsequently disappointing over fences; appreciates fast ground.

Another Diamond (IRE)

103   **106+**

5-y-o b m First Trump-Rockin Rosie (Song)
C J Down (L G Cottrell 14/12) G Waterman

Placings:523P1   (4514)
2002/03: 16⁵G, 19²HY, 22³GF, 19PGF, 22¹GF,

	Starts	1st	2nd	3rd	Win & Pl
Hurdles	5	1	1	1	4884
Career Total	5	1	1	1	4884
106 4/03 Extr	2m6f110yF Hdl			G-F	£3052
				Total win prize-money	£3052

Going: Sf: 0-1 GS: 0-0 Gd: 0-1 GF: - Fm: 1-3
Distance: 2m/2m3: 0-1 2m4-2m7: 1-4 3m+: 0-0
Track: LH: 0-0 RH: 1-5 Tight: 0-1 Gall: 0-0
Aids: Bl: 1-1 Vi: 0-0 Tstrap: 0-0
Best Rating: 106 4/03 Extr 2m6f110y gd-fm Hdl

Scored in first-time blinkers in weak extended two and three quarter mile maiden hurdle at Exeter April 2003; seems to act on all types of ground.

Another Dottie (IRE)

10-y-o b g Sharifabad (IRE)-Dottie s Wasp (Tarqogan)
P Butler Mrs E Lucey-Butler

Placings:060F/PP   (2127)
2002/03: 20PG, 21PS,

	Starts	1st	2nd	3rd	Win & Pl
Hurdles	2	0	0	0	
Career Total	6	0	0	0	

Going: Sf: 0-1 GS: 0-0 Gd: 0-1 GF: - Fm: 0-0
Distance: 2m/2m3: 0-0 2m4-2m7: 0-2 3m+: 0-0
Track: LH: 0-1 RH: 0-0 Tight: 0-2 Gall: 0-0
Aids: Bl: 0-0 Vi: 0-0 Tstrap: 0-0
Best Rating: 55 10/99 Thur 2m2f gd-yld NHF

Another Dude (IRE)

102   **115**

6-y-o br g Shardari-Gemma s Fridge (Frigid Aire)
J Howard Johnson Maurice Hutchinson

Placings:0442P-21221P   (4308)
2002/03: 17²G, 16¹G, 19²GS, 16²G, 19¹G, 18PG,

	Starts	1st	2nd	3rd	Win & Pl
Hurdles	6	2	3	0	10626
Career Total	11	2	4	0	11352
109 2/03 Catt	2m3f	E Hdl		GD	£3698
115 11/02 Catt	2m	E(0-100)HHdl		GD	£2908
				Total win prize-money	£6608

Going: Sf: 0-0 GS: 0-1 Gd: 2-5 GF: - Fm: 0-0
Distance: 2m/2m3: 2-6 2m4-2m7: 0-0 3m+: 0-0
Track: LH: 2-5 RH: 0-1 Tight: 2-6 Gall: 0-0
Aids: Bl: 0-0 Vi: 0-0 Tstrap: 0-0
Best Rating: 115 1/03 Muss 2m good Hdl

Novice hurdler; progressive and recorded second success

both at Catterick in February; suited by good ground and will make a chaser in time.

Another Fly

9-y-o b m Buckley-March Fly (Sousa)
A H Mactaggart A H Mactaggart

Placings:0/0-PPF   (1819)
2002/03: 25PGF, 24PS, 25FHY,

	Starts	1st	2nd	3rd	Win & Pl
Hurdles	1	0	0	0	0
Chases	2	0	0	0	0
Career Total	5	0	0	0	

Going: Sf: 0-2 GS: 0-0 Gd: 0-0 GF: - Fm: 0-1
Distance: 2m/2m3: 0-0 2m4-2m7: 0-0 3m+: 0-3
Track: LH: 0-2 RH: 0-1 Tight: 0-1 Gall: 0-0
Aids: Bl: 0-0 Vi: 0-0 Tstrap: 0-0
Best Rating: 39 5/99 Prth 2m110y heavy NHF

Another General (IRE)

107(107h)   (134h)**119+**

8-y-o b g Glacial Storm (USA)-What s In A Name (IRE) (Le Moss)
R T Phillips Paul Duffy, Alan Beard, Brian Beard

Placings:14/1111P-211   (4034)
2002/03: 24²GS, 24¹G, 25¹S,

	Starts	1st	2nd	3rd	Win & Pl
Chases	3	2	1	0	11600
Career Total	10	7	1	0	33430
119 3/03 Ayr	3m1f	D Ch	SFT	£5810	
119 1/03 Donc	3m	E Ch	GD	£4290	
133 3/02 Newb	3m110y	D Hdl	G-S	£4641	
134 2/02 Winc	2m6f	B Hdl	SFT	£9282	
113 1/02 Folk	2m6f110yE Hdl		HVY	£2667	
105 12/01 Leic	2m4f110yD Hdl		HVY	£3588	
116 12/00 Towc	2m	H NHF	HVY	£1652	
			Total win prize-money	£31930	

Going: Sf: 1-1 GS: 0-1 Gd: 1-1 GF: - Fm: 0-0
Distance: 2m/2m3: 0-0 2m4-2m7: 0-0 **3m+: 2-3**
Track: **LH: 2-2** RH: 0-1 Tight: 0-1 **Gall: 1-1**
Aids: Bl: 0-0 Vi: 0-0 Tstrap: 0-0
Best Rating: 134 2/02 Winc 2m6f soft Hdl

Useful novice chaser; also quite decent over hurdles; acts on testing ground but has won on good; stays very well; has the potential to go on to better things.

Another Graduate (IRE)

59f   **45f**

5-y-o ch g Naheez (USA)-Another Daisy (Major Point)
John R Upson The Nap Hand Partnership

Placings:0   (3754)
2002/03: 16⁹G,

	Starts	1st	2nd	3rd	Win & Pl
NH Flat	1	0	0	0	
Career Total	1	0	0	0	

Going: Sf: 0-0 GS: 0-0 Gd: 0-1 GF: - Fm: 0-0
Distance: 2m/2m3: 0-1 2m4-2m7: 0-0 3m+: 0-0
Track: LH: 0-0 RH: 0-1 Tight: 0-0 Gall: 0-0
Aids: Bl: 0-0 Vi: 0-0 Tstrap: 0-0
Best Rating: 45 2/03 Kemp 2m good NHF

Another Helping (FR)

5-y-o gr g Turgeon (USA)-Tabelbala (FR) (Nashamaa)
J R Best Second Helping Associated Group

Placings:0-0P   (4005)
2002/03: 17⁰G, 16PS,

	Starts	1st	2nd	3rd	Win & Pl
NH Flat	2	0	0	0	
Career Total	3	0	0	0	

Going: Sf: 0-1 GS: 0-0 Gd: 0-1 GF: - Fm: 0-0
Distance: 2m/2m3: 0-2 2m4-2m7: 0-0 3m+: 0-0
Track: LH: 0-0 RH: 0-2 Tight: 0-1 Gall: 0-0
Aids: Bl: 0-0 Vi: 0-0 Tstrap: 0-0
Best Rating: 0 3/03 Winc 2m soft NHF

Another Joker

104(107h)   (97h)**102**

8-y-o b g Commanche Run-Just For A Laugh (Idiots Delight)
J L Needham Miss Joanna Needham

Placings:0/20U02-0054   (4195)
2002/03: 16⁰G, 19⁰G, 17⁵G, 16⁴G,

	Starts	1st	2nd	3rd	Win & Pl
Hurdles	3	0	0	0	0
Chases	1	0	0	0	317
Career Total	10	0	2	0	1743

Going: Sf: 0-0 GS: 0-0 Gd: 0-4 GF: - Fm: 0-0
Distance: 2m/2m3: 0-3 2m4-2m7: 0-1 3m+: 0-0
Track: LH: 0-1 RH: 0-3 Tight: 0-1 Gall: 0-0
Aids: Bl: 0-0 Vi: 0-0 Tstrap: 0-0
Best Rating: 102 4/02 Hrfd 2m3f110y good Hdl

Modest novice chaser, acts on fast ground; stays two and a half miles.

Another King

8-y-o ch g Primitive Rising (USA)-Knocksharry (Palm Track)
K W Hogg K W Hogg

Placings:60/6/P0-P   (1071)
2002/03: 22PG,

	Starts	1st	2nd	3rd	Win & Pl
Hurdles	1	0	0	0	0
Career Total	6	0	0	0	0

Going: Sf: 0-0 GS: 0-0 Gd: 0-1 GF: - Fm: 0-0
Distance: 2m/2m3: 0-0 2m4-2m7: 0-1 3m+: 0-0
Track: LH: 0-1 RH: 0-0 Tight: 0-1 Gall: 0-0
Aids: Bl: 0-0 Vi: 0-0 Tstrap: 0-0
Best Rating: 79 10/99 MRas 1m5f110y good NHF

Another Moose (IRE)

102   **114**

8-y-o b g Mister Lord (USA)-Moose (IRE) (Royal Fountain)
Miss E C Lavelle Remenham Racing

Placings:5212/02   (4080)
2002/03: 19⁰GS, 26²S,

	Starts	1st	2nd	3rd	Win & Pl
Chases	2	0	1	0	2054

Career Total	6	1	3	0	6548
130 3/01 Hntg 2m4f110y			E Hdl	SFT	£2327

Total win prize-money £2328

Going: Sf: 0-1 GS: 0-1 Gd: 0-0 GF: - Fm: 0-0
Distance: 2m/2m3: 0-0 2m4-2m7: 0-1 3m+: 0-1
Track: LH: 0-1 RH: 0-1 Tight: 0-1 Gall: 0-0
Aids: Bl: 0-0 Vi: 0-0 Tstrap: 0-0
Best Rating: 130 3/01 Hntg 2m4f110y soft Hdl

Decent novice hurdler early in 2001; has shown ability over fences since returning from a long layoff.

Another Raleagh (IRE)
110(94h)   (123h)**140+**
9-y-o b g Be My Native (USA)-Caffra Mills (Pitpan)
A Ennis A T A Wates

Placings:3/5141/4222-32212   (3498)
2002/03: 16^{3}G, 20^{2}GS, 20^{2}S, 20^{1}G, 20^{2}GS,

	Starts	1st	2nd	3rd	Win & Pl
Chases	5	1	3	1	25641
Career Total	14	3	6	2	38241
136 1/03 Kemp 2m4f110yB(0-140)HCh		GD			£16022
123 4/01 Winc 2m E Hdl		SFT			£3066
109 2/01 Towc 2m E Hdl		HVY			£2506

Total win prize-money £21594

Going: Sf: 0-1 GS: 0-2 Gd: 1-2 GF: - Fm: 0-0
Distance: 2m/2m3: 0-1 **2m4-2m7: 1-4** 3m+: 0-0
Track: LH: 0-1 **RH: 1-4** Tight: 0-0 Gall: 0-1
Aids: Bl: 0-0 Vi: 0-0 Tstrap: 0-0
Best Rating: 140 2/03 Kemp 2m4f110y gd-sft Ch

Useful chaser; ideally suited two and a half miles; ended a frustrating run of placings with a win at Kempton in January 2003; handles both a sound and soft surface; seems best right handed.

Another Sparkle
81f   **72f**
6-y-o gr m Bustino-Sparkling Time (USA) (Olden Times)
Miss Venetia Williams Mrs J K Peutherer

Placings:05   (2450)
2002/03: 16^{0}G, 16^{5}G,

	Starts	1st	2nd	3rd	Win & Pl
NH Flat	2	0	0	0	0
Career Total	2	0	0	0	0

Going: Sf: 0-0 GS: 0-0 Gd: 0-2 GF: - Fm: 0-0
Distance: 2m/2m3: 0-2 2m4-2m7: 0-0 3m+: 0-0
Track: LH: 0-0 RH: 0-2 Tight: 0-0 Gall: 0-0
Aids: Bl: 0-0 Vi: 0-0 Tstrap: 0-0
Best Rating: 72 12/02 Ludl 2m good NHF

Antenne (IRE)
61
6-y-o b m Roakarad-Secrete Envie (USA) (Secreto (USA))
M D Hammond (A Crook 4/5) Hope Springs Eternal

Placings:05056/23453-PP4P   (2180)
2002/03: 24^{P}GS, 22^{P}GS, 20^{4}HY, 20^{P}GS,

	Starts	1st	2nd	3rd	Win & Pl
Hurdles	2	0	0	0	0
Chases	2	0	0	0	271
Career Total	14	0	1	2	4755

Going: Sf: 0-1 GS: 0-3 Gd: 0-0 GF: - Fm: 0-0
Distance: 2m/2m3: 0-0 2m4-2m7: 0-3 3m+: 0-1
Track: LH: 0-3 RH: 0-1 Tight: 0-1 Gall: 0-0
Aids: Bl: 0-1 Vi: 0-1 Tstrap: 0-0
Best Rating: 61 1/02 Sthl 2m gd-sft Hdl

Modest hurdler.

Anthemion (IRE)
90   **62**
6-y-o ch g Night Shift (USA)-New Sensitive (Wattlefield)
Mrs J C McGregor The Coutts McGregor Clan

Placings:0P/FPF-P45P0PP   (4762)
2002/03: 16^{P}GF, 17^{4}GF, 16^{5}S, 16^{P}HY, 16^{0}G, 17^{P}G, 16^{P}G,

	Starts	1st	2nd	3rd	Win & Pl
Hurdles	7	0	0	0	0
Career Total	12	0	0	0	0

Going: Sf: 0-2 GS: 0-0 Gd: 0-3 GF: - Fm: 0-2
Distance: 2m/2m3: 0-7 2m4-2m7: 0-0 3m+: 0-0
Track: LH: 0-3 RH: 0-4 Tight: 0-3 Gall: 0-0
Aids: Bl: 0-0 Vi: 0-0 Tstrap: 0-0
Best Rating: 76 11/02 Ayr 2m soft Hdl

Antonio Mariano (SWE)
91   **113**
12-y-o b g Mango Express-Mango Sampaquita (SWE) (Colombian Friend (USA))
Mrs L C Taylor Mrs Mette Campbell-Andenaes

Placings:1/006/11/1F32F52/3/21-U5   (0558)
2002/03: 16^{U}GS, 19^{G}GF,

	Starts	1st	2nd	3rd	Win & Pl
Chases	2	0	0	0	0
Career Total	18	5	3	2	21931
113 4/02 Font 2m2f D(0-110)HCh		G-F			£3657
108 11/99 Winc 2m D(0-120)HCh		GD			£5095
109 12/97 Folk 2m E(0-100)HCh		GD			£3517
109 11/97 Plum 2m F(0-105)HCh		SFT			£2707
109 4/96 Font 2m2f E Hdl		G-F			£2098

Total win prize-money £17077

Going: Sf: 0-0 GS: 0-1 Gd: 0-0 GF: - Fm: 0-1
Distance: 2m/2m3: 0-2 2m4-2m7: 0-0 3m+: 0-0
Track: LH: 0-1 RH: 0-1 Tight: 0-1 Gall: 0-0
Aids: Bl: 0-0 Vi: 0-0 Tstrap: 0-0
Best Rating: 113 4/02 Font 2m2f gd-fm Ch

Modest handicap chaser; lightly-raced; suited by two miles; stays two miles two; acts on good ground; likes a sharp track.

Antony Ebeneezer
103   **88**
4-y-o ch c Hurricane Sky (AUS)-Captivating (IRE) (Wolfhound (USA))
C R Dore (R C Spicer 27/5) John Purcell

Placings:F50   (1893)
2002/03: 16^{F}GF, 16^{5}G, 16^{9}GS,

	Starts	1st	2nd	3rd	Win & Pl
Hurdles	3	0	0	0	0
Career Total	3	0	0	0	0

Going: Sf: 0-0 GS: 0-0 Gd: 0-1 GF: - Fm: 0-1
Distance: 2m/2m3: 0-3 2m4-2m7: 0-0 3m+: 0-0
Track: LH: 0-2 RH: 0-1 Tight: 0-0 Gall: 0-1
Aids: Bl: 0-0 Vi: 0-0 Tstrap: 0-0
Best Rating: 88 11/02 Wwck 2m good Hdl

Plating-class hurdler; showed significant improvement for being fitted with a tongue tie when readily winning a 2m handicap hurdle at Stratford July 2003; acts on a sound surface; appears to be on the upgrade.

Anxious Moments (IRE)
106   **129**
8-y-o b g Supreme Leader-Ms Brooks (IRE) (Lord Ha Ha)
C F Swan J P McManus

Placings:01/016151-000   (3085a)
2002/03: 16^{0}YS, 16^{0}HY, 16^{0}S,

	Starts	1st	2nd	3rd	Win & Pl
Hurdles	3	0	0	0	0
Career Total	11	4	0	0	64719
129 4/02 Fair 2m HHdl		YLD			£39877
126 12/01 Navn 2m HHdl		YLD			£12580
114 11/01 Cork 2m Hdl		YLD			£6955
112 10/00 Fair 2m NHF		Y-S			£3312

Total win prize-money £62726

Going: Sf: 0-2 GS: 0-0 Gd: 0-0 GF: - Fm: 0-0
Distance: 2m/2m3: 0-3 2m4-2m7: 0-0 3m+: 0-0
Track: LH: 0-1 RH: 0-2 Tight: 0-0 Gall: 0-0
Aids: Bl: 0-0 Vi: 0-0 Tstrap: 0-0
Best Rating: 129 1/03 Leop 2m soft Hdl

Useful hurdler/chaser; good form in 2001/2002; lightly-raced since; suited by soft ground and two miles.

Anzal (IRE)
106   **95+**
5-y-o b g Kahyasi-Anazara (USA) (Trempolino (USA))
D R Gandolfo Peter Melotti & Andy Chalmers

Placings:0-PPPF4016   (4622)
2002/03: 20^{P}GS, 16^{P}GF, 22^{P}G, 17^{F}GS, 20^{4}S, 16^{0}HY, 19^{1}GF, 22^{6}GF,

	Starts	1st	2nd	3rd	Win & Pl
Hurdles	8	1	0	0	3588
Career Total	9	1	0	0	3588
90 4/03 Extr 2m3f F(0-90)HHdl		G-F			£3588

Total win prize-money £3588

Going: Sf: 0-2 GS: 0-2 Gd: 0-1 GF: - Fm: 1-3
Distance: **2m/2m3: 1-4** 2m4-2m7: 0-4 3m+: 0-0
Track: LH: 0-3 **RH: 1-5** Tight: 0-3 Gall: 0-2
Aids: Bl: 0-1 Vi: 0-0 Tstrap: 0-1
Best Rating: 90 4/03 Extr 2m3f gd-fm Hdl

Improving low grade handicap hurdler; benefited from a wind operation with three wins in 2003; a rather in and out performer who apparently needs time between races; suited by a sound surface; effective up to 2m 4f.

Apache Ireland (IRE)
6-y-o b m Mandalus-Brisbee (Prince Bee)
Mrs C J Kerr Mrs C J Kerr

Placings:PP   (4304)
2002/03: 16^{P}G, 22^{P}G,

	Starts	1st	2nd	3rd	Win & Pl
Hurdles	2	0	0	0	
Career Total	2	0	0	0	

Going: Sf: 0-0 GS: 0-0 Gd: 0-2 GF: - Fm: 0-0
Distance: 2m/2m3: 0-1 2m4-2m7: 0-1 3m+: 0-0
Track: LH: 0-2 RH: 0-0 Tight: 0-1 Gall: 0-0
Aids: Bl: 0-0 Vi: 0-0 Tstrap: 0-0
Best Rating: 0   3/03 Kels 2m6f110y good   Hdl

Apadi (USA)
105   97
7-y-o ch g Diesis-Ixtapa (USA) (Chief s Crown (USA))
M C Chapman Barry Brown & Kenny Blanch

Placings:6403/521511620F6000F0-23245U243F36F54255
(4686)
2002/03: 16^2G, 16^3G, 19^2GF, 19^4GF, 17^5GF, 16^UGF, 19^2GS, 21^4GF, 17^3G, 16^FGF, 16^3G, 19^6GF, 16^FG, 16^5GS, 16^4GS, 16^2G, 16^5GF, 17^5GF,

	Starts	1st	2nd	3rd	Win & Pl
Hurdles	18	0	4	3	8858
Career Total	38	3	6	4	19840
102 9/01 Worc	2m	E(0-115)HHdl		G-F	£3083
95 8/01 Ctml	2m1f110y		G(0-90)HHdl	GD	£3657
86 7/01 Sthl	2m	G Hdl		G-F	£1596

Total win prize-money £8338

Going: Sf: 0-0 GS: 0-3 Gd: 0-6 GF: - Fm: 0-9
Distance: 2m/2m3: 0-13 2m4-2m7: 0-5 3m+: 0-0
Track: LH: 0-11 RH: 0-7 Tight: 0-12 Gall: 0-1
Aids: Bl: 0-0 Vi: 0-0 Tstrap: 0-0
Best Rating: 106 10/01 MRas 2m1f110y gd-sft Hdl

Modest and frustrating handicap hurdler; best at two miles on a sound surface; suited by a strong pace but becoming hard to win with.

Aphelion

5-y-o b h Superlative-Starchy Cove (Starch Reduced)
N M Babbage Colin Rashbrook

Placings:P (0613)
2002/03: 16^PGF,

	Starts	1st	2nd	3rd	Win & Pl
Hurdles	1	0	0	0	
Career Total	1	0	0	0	

Going: Sf: 0-0 GS: 0-0 Gd: 0-0 GF: - Fm: 0-1
Distance: 2m/2m3: 0-1 2m4-2m7: 0-0 3m+: 0-0
Track: LH: 0-1 RH: 0-0 Tight: 0-0 Gall: 0-0
Aids: Bl: 0-0 Vi: 0-0 Tstrap: 0-0
Best Rating: 0 6/02 Worc 2m gd-fm Hdl

Apollo Theatre
100f   99f
5-y-o b g Sadler s Wells (USA)-Threatening (Warning)
R Rowe The Encore Partnership II

Placings:533 (4190)
2002/03: 18^5S, 17^3HY, 17^3G,

	Starts	1st	2nd	3rd	Win & Pl
NH Flat	3	0	0	2	579
Career Total	3	0	0	2	579

Going: Sf: 0-2 GS: 0-0 Gd: 0-1 GF: - Fm: 0-0
Distance: 2m/2m3: 0-3 2m4-2m7: 0-0 3m+: 0-0
Track: LH: 0-1 RH: 0-2 Tight: 0-3 Gall: 0-0
Aids: Bl: 0-0 Vi: 0-0 Tstrap: 0-0
Best Rating: 99 3/03 Folk 2m1f110y good NHF

Showed ability in bumpers; acts on soft.

Apple Joe
86(77h)   (41h)90
7-y-o b g Sula Bula-Hazelwain (Hard Fact)
Dr P Pritchard A J Whiting

Placings:FP304-536344 (3552)
2002/03: 23^5G, 24^3GF, 22^6S, 25^3S, 22^4S, 26^4S,

	Starts	1st	2nd	3rd	Win & Pl
Hurdles	1	0	0	0	0
Chases	5	0	0	2	1773
Career Total	11	0	0	3	2513

Going: Sf: 0-4 GS: 0-0 Gd: 0-1 GF: - Fm: 0-1
Distance: 2m/2m3: 0-0 2m4-2m7: 0-2 3m+: 0-4
Track: LH: 0-3 RH: 0-2 Tight: 0-3 Gall: 0-1
Aids: Bl: 0-0 Vi: 0-0 Tstrap: 0-0
Best Rating: 90 12/02 Hrfd 3m1f110y soft Ch

Plating-class performer; yet to win a race; seemingly stays an easy three miles.

Apple John
95(77h)   (26h)97+
14-y-o b g Sula Bula-Hazelwain (Hard Fact)
Dr P Pritchard A J Whiting

Placings:3F/1PUPP/P/050/4P04402142UPU-501P04
(2900)
2002/03: 24^5GF, 23^0G, 251^5S, 26^PHY, 26^0S, 20^4S,

	Starts	1st	2nd	3rd	Win & Pl
Hurdles	1	0	0	0	0
Chases	5	1	0	0	3744
Career Total	30	3	2	1	12553
97 11/02 Hrfd	3m1f110yF(0-90)HCh			SFT	£3474
97 2/02 Font	2m6f	F(0-90)HCh		HVY	£3108
83 3/99 Tntn	3m	H Ch		SFT	£2931

Total win prize-money £9513

Going: Sf: 1-4 GS: 0-0 Gd: 0-1 GF: - Fm: 0-1
Distance: 2m/2m3: 0-0 2m4-2m7: 0-0 **3m+: 1-5**
Track: LH: 0-0 **RH: 1-5** Tight: 0-0 Gall: 0-1
Aids: Bl: 0-0 Vi: 0-0 Tstrap: 0-0
Best Rating: 111 11/96 Kemp 3m gd-sft Ch

A winner over fences, he acts on good and soft ground and is effective at around three miles.

Applemir George
41
8-y-o b g Almushmmir-Lady Sweetapples (Super Song)
Jane Southcombe Mrs J C Duffy

Placings:5/000FP-P (0174)
2002/03: 22^PGF,

	Starts	1st	2nd	3rd	Win & Pl
Hurdles	1	0	0	0	0
Career Total	7	0	0	0	0

Going: Sf: 0-0 GS: 0-0 Gd: 0-0 GF: - Fm: 0-1
Distance: 2m/2m3: 0-0 2m4-2m7: 0-1 3m+: 0-0
Track: LH: 0-0 RH: 0-0 Tight: 0-0 Gall: 0-0
Aids: Bl: 0-0 Vi: 0-1 Tstrap: 0-0
Best Rating: 97 4/01 Tntn 2m1f gd-fm NHF

Applepie Lady (IRE)
99   89
6-y-o b m Lord Americo-Lady Bow (Deep Run)
A J Lidderdale A Franklin

Placings:25-23545 (4511)
2002/03: 17^2G, 16^3G, 21^5GS, 21^4S, 19^5GF,

	Starts	1st	2nd	3rd	Win & Pl
NH Flat	2	0	1	1	758
Hurdles	3	0	0	0	300
Career Total	7	0	2	1	1600

Going: Sf: 0-1 GS: 0-1 Gd: 0-2 GF: - Fm: 0-1
Distance: 2m/2m3: 0-3 2m4-2m7: 0-2 3m+: 0-0
Track: LH: 0-2 RH: 0-3 Tight: 0-1 Gall: 0-0
Aids: Bl: 0-0 Vi: 0-0 Tstrap: 0-0
Best Rating: 96 5/02 Folk 2m1f110y good NHF

Approaching Land (IRE)

8-y-o ch g Dry Dock-Crash Approach (Crash Course)
M W Easterby Major M Watson

Placings:P (0164)
2002/03: 20^PGF,

	Starts	1st	2nd	3rd	Win & Pl
Hurdles	1	0	0	0	
Career Total	1	0	0	0	

Going: Sf: 0-0 GS: 0-0 Gd: 0-0 GF: - Fm: 0-1
Distance: 2m/2m3: 0-0 2m4-2m7: 0-1 3m+: 0-0
Track: LH: 0-1 RH: 0-0 Tight: 0-0 Gall: 0-0
Aids: Bl: 0-0 Vi: 0-0 Tstrap: 0-0
Best Rating: 0 5/02 Weth 2m4f110y gd-fm Hdl

April Ace
74   46
7-y-o ch g First Trump-Champ D Avril (Northfields (USA))
R J Baker Graham Brown

Placings:0-000 (1230)
2002/03: 16^0GF, 16^0S, 16^0G,

	Starts	1st	2nd	3rd	Win & Pl
Hurdles	3	0	0	0	
Career Total	4	0	0	0	

Going: Sf: 0-1 GS: 0-0 Gd: 0-1 GF: - Fm: 0-1
Distance: 2m/2m3: 0-3 2m4-2m7: 0-0 3m+: 0-0
Track: LH: 0-3 RH: 0-0 Tight: 0-2 Gall: 0-0
Aids: Bl: 0-0 Vi: 0-0 Tstrap: 0-0
Best Rating: 48 7/02 Strf 2m110y gd-fm Hdl

April Call

7-y-o b m Gildoran-Cloud Cuckoo (Idiots Delight)
S J Gilmore S J Gilmore

Placings:0/6P-PP (1178)
2002/03: 16^PGF, 16^PGF,

	Starts	1st	2nd	3rd	Win & Pl
Hurdles	2	0	0	0	
Career Total	5	0	0	0	0

Going: Sf: 0-0 GS: 0-0 Gd: 0-0 GF: - Fm: 0-2
Distance: 2m/2m3: 0-2 2m4-2m7: 0-0 3m+: 0-0
Track: LH: 0-2 RH: 0-0 Tight: 0-1 Gall: 0-0
Aids: Bl: 0-0 Vi: 0-0 Tstrap: 0-0
Best Rating: 78 11/01 Tntn 2m1f good NHF

April Louise

98　　　　　　　　　　　65

7-y-o b m Meqdaam (USA)-California Dreamin (Slip Anchor)
T Wall　D Bunn

Placings:0000630/34205051023-4330P　　(4287)
2002/03: 16⁴G, 17³GS, 16³F, 20⁰G, 16⁶GF,

	Starts	1st	2nd	3rd	Win & Pl
Hurdles	5	0	0	2	2502
Career Total	23	1	2	5	15260
109	2/02	Ludl	2m		D(0-115)HHdl SFT £4056

Total win prize-money £4056

Going:	Sf: 0-0 GS: 0-1 Gd: 0-2 GF: - Fm: 0-2
Distance:	2m/2m3: 0-4 2m4-2m7: 0-1 3m+: 0-0
Track:	LH: 0-3 RH: 0-2 Tight: 0-2 Gall: 0-0
Aids:	Bl: 0-0 Vi: 0-0 Tstrap: 0-0
Best Rating:	117 4/02 Aint 2m110y good Hdl

Modest handicapper; acts on soft ground; effective over two miles.

April Spirit

102(94h)　　　　　　(80h)95

8-y-o b m Nomination-Seraphim (FR) (Lashkari)
Mrs S J Smith　Mrs B Ramsden

Placings:06/24533230/03/4051F546-010322035　(2347)
2002/03: 23⁹GF, 23¹G, 23⁹GF, 21³GF, 26²GF, 26²G, 27⁰G, 20³GS, 24⁵GS,

	Starts	1st	2nd	3rd	Win & Pl
Chases	9	1	2	2	7067
Career Total	29	2	4	6	12627
91	7/02	Worc	2m7f110yF(0-100)HCh	GD	£3230
94	8/01	Worc	2m4f110yE(0-105)HCh	G-F	£3484

Total win prize-money £6715

Going:	Sf: 0-0 GS: 0-2 Gd: 1-3 GF: - Fm: 0-4
Distance:	2m/2m3: 0-0 2m4-2m7: 0-2 3m+: 1-7
Track:	LH: 1-9 RH: 0-0 Tight: 0-3 Gall: 0-0
Aids:	Bl: 0-0 Vi: 0-0 Tstrap: 0-0
Best Rating:	95 9/02 Sthl 3m2f good Ch

Moderate staying chaser; stays three miles two; acts on a sound surface.

April Treasure

96　　　　　　　　　(70c)73

8-y-o b m Stani (USA)-Eleri (Rolfe (USA))
Mrs P Ford　W E Donohue

Placings:PP0/P0F25P050P/65005-42P4600P4F　(1454)
2002/03: 16⁴GS, 16²GF, 19⁹S, 16⁴GS, 17⁶GF, 17⁰GF, 16⁹G, 16⁶G, 19⁴GF, 20⁰F,

	Starts	1st	2nd	3rd	Win & Pl
Hurdles	8	0	1	0	1066
Chases	2	0	0	0	0
Career Total	28	0	2	0	1642

Going:	Sf: 0-1 GS: 0-2 Gd: 0-2 GF: - Fm: 0-5
Distance:	2m/2m3: 0-8 2m4-2m7: 0-2 3m+: 0-0
Track:	LH: 0-8 RH: 0-2 Tight: 0-4 Gall: 0-0
Aids:	Bl: 0-0 Vi: 0-0 Tstrap: 0-0
Best Rating:	77 10/00 Strf 2m110y soft Hdl

Plating-class hurdler.

Aqribaa (IRE)

95　　　　　　　　　　68

5-y-o b g Pennekamp (USA)-Karayb (IRE) (Last Tycoon)
A J Lockwood　A J Lockwood

Placings:3P-560　　　　　　　(1527)
2002/03: 17⁵GF, 16⁶GF, 17⁰G,

	Starts	1st	2nd	3rd	Win & Pl
Hurdles	3	0	0	0	0
Career Total	5	0	0	1	486

Going:	Sf: 0-0 GS: 0-0 Gd: 0-1 GF: - Fm: 0-2
Distance:	2m/2m3: 0-3 2m4-2m7: 0-0 3m+: 0-0
Track:	LH: 0-2 RH: 0-1 Tight: 0-2 Gall: 0-0
Aids:	Bl: 0-0 Vi: 0-0 Tstrap: 0-0
Best Rating:	68 9/02 Hexm 2m110y gd-fm Hdl

Aqua Pura (GER)

4-y-o b c Acatenango (GER)-Actraphane (Shareef Dancer (USA))
B J Curley　Mrs B J Curley

Placings:0　　　　　　　　　(2503)
2002/03: 16⁰GS,

	Starts	1st	2nd	3rd	Win & Pl
Hurdles	1	0	0	0	0
Career Total	1	0	0	0	

Going:	Sf: 0-0 GS: 0-1 Gd: 0-0 GF: - Fm: 0-0
Distance:	2m/2m3: 0-1 2m4-2m7: 0-0 3m+: 0-0
Track:	LH: 0-1 RH: 0-0 Tight: 0-1 Gall: 0-0
Aids:	Bl: 0-0 Vi: 0-0 Tstrap: 0-0
Best Rating:	0 12/02 Fknm 2m gd-sft Hdl

Aquarius (IRE)

105　　　　　　　　　　95

5-y-o b g Royal Academy (USA)-Rafha (Kris)
M C Pipe (D Nicholls 3/10)　Done It Again

Placings:12005533　　　　　　(4703)
2002/03: 17¹F, 17²S, 16⁹HY, 24⁰S, 24⁵S, 22⁵F, 17³GF, 16³GF,

	Starts	1st	2nd	3rd	Win & Pl
Hurdles	8	1	1	2	5591
Career Total	8	1	1	2	5591
111	10/02	Tntn	2m1f	E Hdl	FRM £3332

Total win prize-money £3332

Going:	Sf: 0-4 GS: 0-0 Gd: 0-0 GF: - Fm: 1-4
Distance:	2m/2m3: 1-5 2m4-2m7: 0-3 3m+: 0-0
Track:	LH: 0-3 RH: 1-5 Tight: 1-5 Gall: 0-0
Aids:	Bl: 0-0 Vi: 0-1 Tstrap: 0-2
Best Rating:	111 10/02 Tntn 2m1f firm Hdl

Fair hurdler; very useful on the Flat; winner on fast at Taunton in October 2002; suited by fast ground; has failed to stay three miles in soft ground twice; has worn tongue tie and visor; looks to be going the wrong way.

Aquiline

97

5-y-o ch g Sanglamore (USA)-Fantasy Flyer (USA) (Lear Fan (USA))
John A Harris　Risley Hall Partnership

Placings:206-200　　　　　　(3877)
2002/03: 16²GS, 17⁰GS, 19⁰GS,

	Starts	1st	2nd	3rd	Win & Pl
Hurdles	3	0	1	0	884
Career Total	6	0	2	0	2882

Going:	Sf: 0-1 GS: 0-2 Gd: 0-0 GF: - Fm: 0-0
Distance:	2m/2m3: 0-2 2m4-2m7: 0-1 3m+: 0-0

Track:	LH: 0-3 Tight: 0-0 Gall: 0-2
Aids:	Bl: 0-0 Vi: 0-0 Tstrap: 0-0
Best Rating:	100 1/02 Donc 2m110y soft Hdl

Moderate novice hurdler; acts on soft ground.

Ar Muin Na Muice (IRE)

108　　　　　　　　　137+

7-y-o ch m Executive Perk-Raashideah (Dancer s Image (USA))
Jonjo O Neill　Mrs G Smith

Placings:0/111-1F211　　　　　(4326)
2002/03: 20¹S, 24⁵GS, 24²HY, 20¹G, 21¹G,

	Starts	1st	2nd	3rd	Win & Pl
Hurdles	5	3	1	0	40416
Career Total	9	6	1	0	56274
142	3/03	Newb	2m5f	HHdl	GD	£29000
127	2/03	Weth	2m4f110yD Hdl	GD	£5570
104	10/02	Bang	2m4f	D Hdl	SFT	£4264
127	12/01	Leop	2m	NHF	YLD	£6677
118	12/01	Navn	2m	NHF	Y-S	£5564
105	10/01	Gowr	2m	NHF	YLD	£3616

Total win prize-money £54694

Going:	Sf: 1-2 GS: 0-1 Gd: 2-2 GF: - Fm: 0-0
Distance:	2m/2m3: 0-0 2m4-2m7: 3-3 3m+: 0-2
Track:	LH: 3-4 RH: 0-1 Tight: 1-1 Gall: 1-1
Aids:	Bl: 0-0 Vi: 0-0 Tstrap: 0-0
Best Rating:	142 3/03 Newb 2m5f good Hdl

Useful novice hurdler; won the 2003 Mares Final at Newbury; stays three miles; acts in good and heavy ground.

Arabian Goggles

4-y-o ch f Cosmonaut-Jarrettelle (All Systems Go)
H S Howe　Richard Garrard

Placings:4　　　　　　　　　(1366)
2002/03: 17⁴F,

	Starts	1st	2nd	3rd	Win & Pl
Hurdles	1	0	0	0	309
Career Total	1	0	0	0	309

Going:	Sf: 0-0 GS: 0-0 Gd: 0-0 GF: - Fm: 0-1
Distance:	2m/2m3: 0-1 2m4-2m7: 0-0 3m+: 0-0
Track:	LH: 0-0 RH: 0-1 Tight: 0-0 Gall: 0-0
Aids:	Bl: 0-0 Vi: 0-0 Tstrap: 0-0
Best Rating:	0 10/02 Extr 2m1f firm Hdl

Arabian Moon (IRE)

108　　　　　　　　　137

7-y-o ch h Barathea (IRE)-Excellent Alibi (USA) (Exceller (USA))
S Dow　Byerley Bloodstock

Placings:46/111023-110P　　　　(4607)
2002/03: 18¹G, 21¹GF, 21⁰G, 21⁸G,

	Starts	1st	2nd	3rd	Win & Pl
Hurdles	4	2	0	0	15541
Career Total	12	5	1	1	27450
137	10/02	Chel	2m5f	B(0-145)HHdl	G-F	£9323
126	10/02	Font	2m2f110yC(0-130)HHdl	GD	£6217
110	8/01	Uttx	2m4f110yD Hdl	G-F	£3360
110	8/01	Strf	2m6f110yD Hdl	GD	£3523
115	5/01	Fknm	2m7f110yE Hdl	G-F	£2374

Total win prize-money £24798

Going: Sf: 0-0 GS: 0-0 Gd: 1-3 GF: - Fm: 1-1
Distance: 2m/2m3: 1-1 2m4-2m7: 1-3 3m+: 0-0
Track: LH: 2-4 RH: 0-0 Tight: 1-1 Gall: 1-3
Aids: Bl: 0-0 Vi: 0-0 Tstrap: 0-0
Best Rating: 137 10/02 Chel 2m5f   gd-fm Hdl

Useful hurdler; stays three miles, but better over a shorter trip; progressive form in October 2002 with wins at Fontwell and Cheltenham; acts on ground good or faster.

Araf
101   91
4-y-o b g Millkom-Euphyllia (Superpower)
N Wilson (A G Newcombe 7/9) W R S

Placings:0F55   (2610)
2002/03: 16⁹GF, 16ᶠG, 16⁵GS, 16⁵S,

	Starts	1st	2nd	3rd	Win & Pl
Hurdles	4	0	0	0	0
Career Total	4	0	0	0	0

Going: Sf: 0-1 GS: 0-1 Gd: 0-1 GF: - Fm: 0-1
Distance: 2m/2m3: 0-4 2m4-2m7: 0-0 3m+: 0-0
Track: LH: 0-4 RH: 0-0 Tight: 0-1 Gall: 0-1
Aids: Bl: 0-0 Vi: 0-0 Tstrap: 0-0
Best Rating: 85 11/02 Newc 2m   gd-sft Hdl

Selling winner on the Flat; very limited ability over hurdles.

Araglin
81   61
4-y-o b g Sadler s Wells (USA)-River Caro (USA) (Irish River (FR))
Miss S J Wilton John Pointon And Sons

Placings:0F600   (4156)
2002/03: 16⁹G, 17ᶠS, 16⁶S, 19⁹GS, 17⁹G,

	Starts	1st	2nd	3rd	Win & Pl
Hurdles	5	0	0	0	0
Career Total	5	0	0	0	0

Going: Sf: 0-2 GS: 0-1 Gd: 0-2 GF: - Fm: 0-0
Distance: 2m/2m3: 0-4 2m4-2m7: 0-1 3m+: 0-0
Track: LH: 0-3 RH: 0-2 Tight: 0-1 Gall: 0-0
Aids: Bl: 0-3 Vi: 0-0 Tstrap: 0-0
Best Rating: 61 12/02 Wwck 2m   soft Hdl

Araminta

9-y-o ch m Carlingford Castle-Abinovian (Ra Nova)
Mrs L Pomfret Mrs A J Higgins

Placings:000/UB/16634405-0   (4133)
2002/03: 26⁹G,

	Starts	1st	2nd	3rd	Win & Pl
Chases	1	0	0	0	
Career Total	14	1	0	1	3530
87 6/01 Fknm 2m4f	E Hdl			G-F	£2898

Total win prize-money £2898

Going: Sf: 0-0 GS: 0-0 Gd: 0-1 GF: - Fm: 0-0
Distance: 2m/2m3: 0-0 2m4-2m7: 0-0 3m+: 0-0
Track: LH: 0-1 RH: 0-0 Tight: 0-0 Gall: 0-1
Aids: Bl: 0-0 Vi: 0-0 Tstrap: 0-0
Best Rating: 103 3/03 Chel 3m2f1l10y good Ch

Dual point-to-point winner this season; stays three miles; acts on good to soft ground or faster.

Arawak Prince (IRE)
(89c)   (91c)89
7-y-o ch g College Chapel-Alpine Symphony (Northern Dancer)
G Prodromou George Prodromou

Placings:P1045/140P60-124P   (4686)
2002/03: 17¹GF, 16²G, 20⁴GF, 17ᶠGF,

	Starts	1st	2nd	3rd	Win & Pl
Hurdles	2	1	0	0	2223
Chases	2	0	1	0	1548
Career Total	15	3	1	0	8636
89 8/02 Sthl 2m1f	G Hdl			G-F	£2223
106 5/01 Hrfd 2m1f	G(0-95)HHdl			GD	£2100
107 3/00 Plum 2m	E Hdl			GD	£2338

Total win prize-money £6661

Going: Sf: 0-0 GS: 0-0 Gd: 0-1 GF: - Fm: 1-3
Distance: 2m/2m3: 1-3 2m4-2m7: 0-1 3m+: 0-0
Track: LH: 1-2 RH: 0-1 Tight: 0-2 Gall: 0-0
Aids: Bl: 0-0 Vi: 1-4 Tstrap: 0-0
Best Rating: 107 3/00 Plum 2m   good Hdl

Arc En Ciel
74   38
5-y-o b g Rainbow Quest (USA)-Nadia Nerina (CAN) (Northern Dancer)
Mrs L Richards Mrs M J George

Placings:0   (0683)
2002/03: 19⁹GF,

	Starts	1st	2nd	3rd	Win & Pl
Hurdles	1	0	0	0	
Career Total	1	0	0	0	

Going: Sf: 0-0 GS: 0-0 Gd: 0-0 GF: - Fm: 0-1
Distance: 2m/2m3: 0-1 2m4-2m7: 0-0 3m+: 0-0
Track: LH: 0-1 RH: 0-0 Tight: 0-1 Gall: 0-0
Aids: Bl: 0-0 Vi: 0-0 Tstrap: 0-0
Best Rating: 43 7/02 Strf 2m3f   gd-fm Hdl

Arch Stanton (IRE)
95   125
5-y-o b g Lahib (USA)-Sweet Repose (High Top)
W P Mullins John J Brennan

Placings:5322S   (4097)
2002/03: 16⁵S, 16³SH, 16²HY, 16²YS, 16⁵G,

	Starts	1st	2nd	3rd	Win & Pl
Hurdles	5	0	2	1	3993
Career Total	5	0	2	1	3993

Going: Sf: 0-2 GS: 0-0 Gd: 0-1 GF: - Fm: 0-0
Distance: 2m/2m3: 0-5 2m4-2m7: 0-0 3m+: 0-0
Track: LH: 0-4 RH: 0-1 Tight: 0-0 Gall: 0-0
Aids: Bl: 0-0 Vi: 0-0 Tstrap: 0-0
Best Rating: 125 1/03 Leop 2m   yld-sft Hdl

Fair Irish-trained novice hurdler; winner on the Flat; yet to win over timber; suited by 2m and cut in the ground; consistent.

Archbishop
95(73h)   (21h)64
6-y-o ch g Minster Son-Elitist (Keren)
T D Walford G E Dempsey

Placings:0000-520   (1531)

2002/03: 16⁵GF, 22²GF, 21⁹G,

	Starts	1st	2nd	3rd	Win & Pl
Chases	3	0	1	0	1180
Career Total	7	0	1	0	1180

Going: Sf: 0-0 GS: 0-0 Gd: 0-1 GF: - Fm: 0-2
Distance: 2m/2m3: 0-1 2m4-2m7: 0-2 3m+: 0-0
Track: LH: 0-2 RH: 0-1 Tight: 0-2 Gall: 0-0
Aids: Bl: 0-0 Vi: 0-0 Tstrap: 0-0
Best Rating: 67 11/01 Hayd 2m   soft NHF

Very moderate form under all disciplines.

Archer For Four (USA)
84   64
4-y-o b/br g Royal Academy (USA)-Depelchin (USA) (Star De Naskra (USA))
Ferdy Murphy (N Tinkler 29/5) The Aarons Archer Partnership

Placings:000   (2098)
2002/03: 16⁹GF, 16⁵S, 16⁹G,

	Starts	1st	2nd	3rd	Win & Pl
Hurdles	3	0	0	0	
Career Total	3	0	0	0	

Going: Sf: 0-1 GS: 0-1 Gd: 0-1 GF: - Fm: 0-1
Distance: 2m/2m3: 0-3 2m4-2m7: 0-0 3m+: 0-0
Track: LH: 0-3 RH: 0-0 Tight: 0-1 Gall: 0-1
Aids: Bl: 0-1 Vi: 0-0 Tstrap: 0-0
Best Rating: 59 11/02 Newc 2m   soft Hdl

Archie Babe (IRE)
99   107
7-y-o ch g Archway (IRE)-Frensham Manor (Le Johnstan)
J J Quinn Mrs K Mapp

Placings:F44   (3830)
2002/03: 16ᶠGS, 16⁴GS, 16⁴G,

	Starts	1st	2nd	3rd	Win & Pl
Hurdles	3	0	0	0	273
Career Total	3	0	0	0	273

Going: Sf: 0-0 GS: 0-2 Gd: 0-1 GF: - Fm: 0-0
Distance: 2m/2m3: 0-3 2m4-2m7: 0-0 3m+: 0-0
Track: LH: 0-3 RH: 0-0 Tight: 0-0 Gall: 0-1
Aids: Bl: 0-0 Vi: 0-0 Tstrap: 0-0
Best Rating: 107 11/02 Weth 2m   gd-sft Hdl

Modest hurdler; lying second when a faller at the final flight on debut at Wetherby in November; fourth twice since.

Archon (IRE)
87   92
6-y-o ch g Archway (IRE)-Lindas Delight (Batshoof)
Mrs P N Dutfield Simon Dutfield

Placings:20-4   (0735)
2002/03: 17⁴GF,

	Starts	1st	2nd	3rd	Win & Pl
Hurdles	1	0	0	0	289
Career Total	3	0	1	0	941

Going: Sf: 0-0 GS: 0-0 Gd: 0-0 GF: - Fm: 0-1
Distance: 2m/2m3: 0-1 2m4-2m7: 0-0 3m+: 0-0
Track: LH: 0-1 RH: 0-0 Tight: 0-1 Gall: 0-0

Aids: Bl: 0-0 Vi: 0-0 Tstrap: 0-0
Best Rating: 101 6/01 NAbb 2m1f   good   NHF

Arctic Challenge (IRE)

111   131

9-y-o b g Glacial Storm (USA)-Ruckinge Girl (Eborneezer)
K R Burke I & Mrs A Russell

Placings:4/33/3336/2013P01P2-14342P   (4682)
2002/03: 20¹G, 20⁴G, 20³G, 19⁴G, 20²G, 24⁸GF,

	Starts	1st	2nd	3rd	Win & Pl
Chases	6	1	1	1	11213
Career Total	22	3	3	7	25269
126 5/02 Worc 2m4f110yD(0-125)HCh		GD			£4065
111 4/02 Hntg 2m4f110yE Ch		G-F			£3078
129 11/01 Kemp 2m4f110yD Ch		GD			£4936
Total win prize-money £12081					

Going: Sf: 0-0 GS: 0-0 Gd: 1-5 GF: - Fm: 0-1
Distance: 2m/2m3: 0-0 2m4-2m7: 1-5 3m+: 0-1
Track: LH: 1-2 RH: 0-4 Tight: 0-1 Gall: 0-1
Aids: Bl: 0-0 Vi: 0-0 Tstrap: 0-0
Best Rating: 129 2/03 Kemp 2m4f110y good   Ch

Useful handicap chaser; bounced back to form in cheek-pieces when winning 2m 5f handicap at Stratford May 2003; best on ground good or faster; suited by a flat track, has not always been convincing in a tight finish.

Arctic Copper (IRE)
116   147

9-y-o b g Montelimar (USA)-Miss Penguin (General Assembly (USA))
Noel Meade Grand Alliance Racing Club

Placings:02133142/411232122/642F513U45-2225522103   (4654a)
2002/03: 24²G, 16²YS, 24²S, 17⁵HY, 24⁵SH, 20²S, 20²YS, 16¹Y, 20⁶G, 17³GF,

	Starts	1st	2nd	3rd	Win & Pl
Chases	10	1	5	1	58551
Career Total	37	7	12	5	141476
144 2/03 Naas 2m Ch		YLD			£25324
143 1/02 Fair 2m100y Ch		Y-S			£10368
130 2/01 Navn 3m Ch		SFT			£7790
137 10/00 Gowr 2m6f Ch		SFT			£5520
122 5/00 Gowr 2m4f Hdl		Y-S			£3864
109 2/00 Navn 2m2f Hdl		SH			£3588
100 12/99 Navn 2m NHF		HVY			£3080
Total win prize-money £59535					

Going: Sf: 0-3 GS: 0-0 Gd: 0-2 GF: - Fm: 0-1
Distance: 2m/2m3: 1-4 2m4-2m7: 0-3 3m+: 0-3
Track: LH: 1-5 RH: 0-5 Tight: 0-0 Gall: 0-1
Aids: Bl: 0-5 Vi: 0-0 Tstrap: 0-0
Best Rating: 147 4/03 Fair 2m1f   gd-fm   Ch

Useful irish chaser; spent most of the 2000/2001 season being beaten by Sackville in valuable novice chases, but is a useful performer in his own right; some decent efforts since; probably best at distances short of three miles; goes well on easy ground.

Arctic Corner

9-y-o b m Arctic Lord-Chatty Corner (Le Bavard (FR))
N Wilson J McGuinness

Placings:0/PF   (0474)
2002/03: 21PGF, 17FGS,

	Starts	1st	2nd	3rd	Win & Pl
Hurdles	2	0	0	0	
Career Total	3	0	0	0	

Going: Sf: 0-0 GS: 0-1 Gd: 0-0 GF: - Fm: 0-1
Distance: 2m/2m3: 0-1 2m4-2m7: 0-1 3m+: 0-0
Track: LH: 0-2 RH: 0-0 Tight: 0-2 Gall: 0-0
Aids: Bl: 0-0 Vi: 0-0 Tstrap: 0-0
Best Rating: 0 6/02 Ctml 2m1f110y gd-sft Hdl

Arctic Double (IRE)
98   78+

6-y-o b g Insan (USA)-Icy Queen (IRE) (Callernish)
Miss H C Knight T M Curtis

Placings:30-55   (2134)
2002/03: 16⁵G, 21⁵G,

	Starts	1st	2nd	3rd	Win & Pl
Hurdles	2	0	0	0	
Career Total	4	0	0	1	229

Going: Sf: 0-0 GS: 0-0 Gd: 0-2 GF: - Fm: 0-0
Distance: 2m/2m3: 0-1 2m4-2m7: 0-1 3m+: 0-0
Track: LH: 0-0 RH: 0-2 Tight: 0-0 Gall: 0-0
Aids: Bl: 0-0 Vi: 0-0 Tstrap: 0-0
Best Rating: 102 3/02 Sand 2m110y   gd-sft NHF

Arctic Fancy (USA)
108   130

10-y-o ch g Arctic Tern (USA)-Fit And Fancy (USA) (Vaguely Noble)
Miss H C Knight Another Chance Partnership

Placings:21135/12151/63550/4402224-10   (4114)
2002/03: 19¹G, 20⁶G,

	Starts	1st	2nd	3rd	Win & Pl
Chases	2	1	0	0	8301
Career Total	24	6	5	2	44899
130 1/03 Donc 2m3f C(0-130)HCh		GD			£8300
135 4/00 Chep 2m110y E Ch		SFT			£3575
137 1/00 Donc 2m110y D Ch		G-F			£3789
127 11/99 Donc 2m110y E Ch		GD			£2989
125 2/99 Folk 2m1f110yE Hdl		SFT			£2853
119 1/99 Plum 2m1f E Hdl		HVY			£2407
Total win prize-money £23918					

Going: Sf: 0-0 GS: 0-0 Gd: 1-2 GF: - Fm: 0-0
Distance: 2m/2m3: 1-1 2m4-2m7: 0-1 3m+: 0-0
Track: LH: 1-2 RH: 0-0 Tight: 0-0 Gall: 0-0
Aids: Bl: 0-0 Vi: 0-0 Tstrap: 0-0
Best Rating: 139 5/00 Punc 2m   good   Ch

Fair handicap chaser; successful on return in a two and a half mile handicap chase at Doncaster in January; stays three miles; acts on decent and soft ground.

Arctic Gamble
100   102

11-y-o b g Arctic Lord-Honey Gamble (Gambling Debt)
L G Cottrell Miss Sally Lock

Placings:42F-26411   (4717)
2002/03: 23²G, 24⁶GS, 25⁴GS, 24¹F, 25¹F,

	Starts	1st	2nd	3rd	Win & Pl
Chases	5	2	1	0	9813
Career Total	8	2	2	0	11884
102 4/03 Winc 3m1f110yE Ch		FRM			£4137
102 3/03 Tntn 3m F(0-90)HCh		FRM			£3705
Total win prize-money £7842					

Going: Sf: 0-0 GS: 0-2 Gd: 0-1 GF: - Fm: 2-2
Distance: 2m/2m3: 0-0 2m4-2m7: 0-0 3m+: 2-5
Track: LH: 0-0 RH: 2-5 Tight: 1-2 Gall: 0-0
Aids: Bl: 0-0 Vi: 0-0 Tstrap: 0-0
Best Rating: 102 4/03 Winc 3m1f110y firm   Ch

Moderate chaser; broke his duck in modest novices' handicap at Taunton March 2003; followed up next time; stays three miles; appreciates a sound surface.

Arctic Gold (IRE)

(101h)   (96h)54

6-y-o b/br g Arctic Lord-Flashy Gold (Le Bavard (FR))
C F Swan Bhoys Racing Syndicate

Placings:00/424501-P300126   (4583a)
2002/03: 20PG, 17³YS, 17⁰S, 16⁰F, 16¹G, 20²G, 20⁶GF,

	Starts	1st	2nd	3rd	Win & Pl
Hurdles	6	1	1	1	5305
Chases	1	0	0	0	0
Career Total	15	2	2	1	11087
96 10/02 Kels 2m110y D Hdl		GD			£3822
94 4/02 List 2m NHF		G-F			£4233
Total win prize-money £8055					

Going: Sf: 0-1 GS: 0-0 Gd: 1-3 GF: - Fm: 0-2
Distance: 2m/2m3: 1-4 2m4-2m7: 0-3 3m+: 0-0
Track: LH: 1-5 RH: 0-0 Tight: 1-1 Gall: 0-1
Aids: Bl: 0-0 Vi: 0-0 Tstrap: 0-0
Best Rating: 96 10/02 Kels 2m110y   good   Hdl

Irish novice hurdler; suited by two miles and a sound surface; likes to make the running; acts well on a sound surface.

Arctic Grey (IRE)

13-y-o gr g Roselier (FR)-Our Hollow (Wolver Hollow)
Miss A Nolan Mrs P Duncan

Placings:00/000020/F023002/P/P   (0033)
2002/03: 25PGF,

	Starts	1st	2nd	3rd	Win & Pl
Chases	1	0	0	0	
Career Total	17	0	3	1	1755

Going: Sf: 0-0 GS: 0-0 Gd: 0-0 GF: - Fm: 0-1
Distance: 2m/2m3: 0-0 2m4-2m7: 0-0 3m+: 0-1
Track: LH: 0-1 RH: 0-0 Tight: 0-0 Gall: 0-1
Aids: Bl: 0-0 Vi: 0-0 Tstrap: 0-0
Best Rating: 106 1/96 Tram 2m   yield   NHF

Arctic King

10-y-o b g Arctic Lord-Dunsilly Bell (London Bells (CAN))
A M Lloyd A M Lloyd

Placings:06/4636U/02P3F5P/P5P-F   (4026)
2002/03: 25FS,

	Starts	1st	2nd	3rd	Win & Pl
Chases	1	0	0	0	
Career Total	18	0	1	2	2660

Going: Sf: 0-1 GS: 0-0 Gd: 0-0 GF: - Fm: 0-0
Distance: 2m/2m3: 0-0 2m4-2m7: 0-0 3m+: 0-1
Track: LH: 0-0 RH: 0-1 Tight: 0-0 Gall: 0-0
Aids: Bl: 0-0 Vi: 0-0 Tstrap: 0-0
Best Rating: 87 11/00 Hrfd 2m3f   gd-sft   Ch

Arctic Lagoon (IRE)
100   81
4-y-o ch g Bering-Lake Pleasant (IRE) (Elegant Air)
Mrs S C Bradburne (J R Fanshawe 9/6) Strath Pack Partnership

Placings:040P   (4507)
2002/03: 16⁶GS, 16⁴G, 16⁹GF, 16⁶G,

	Starts	1st	2nd	3rd	Win & Pl
Hurdles	4	0	0	0	425
Career Total	4	0	0	0	425

Going: Sf: 0-0 GS: 0-1 Gd: 0-2 GF: - Fm: 0-1
Distance: 2m/2m3: 0-4 2m4-2m7: 0-0 3m+: 0-0
Track: LH: 0-2 RH: 0-2 Tight: 0-3 Gall: 0-0
Aids: Bl: 0-0 Vi: 0-0 Tstrap: 0-1
Best Rating: 81   2/03   Muss   2m   good   Hdl

Plating-class hurdler; still a maiden; appreciated the step up to two and a half miles when second at Perth; suited by a sound surafce.

Arctic Playboy

7-y-o b g Petoski-Arctic Oats (Oats)
G A Swinbank R P Dineen

Placings:0/O3-340   (3987)
2002/03: 16³S, 17⁴GS, 20⁰S,

	Starts	1st	2nd	3rd	Win & Pl
NH Flat	1	0	0	1	286
Hurdles	2	0	0	0	294
Career Total	6	0	0	2	791

Going: Sf: 0-2 GS: 0-1 Gd: 0-0 GF: - Fm: 0-0
Distance: 2m/2m3: 0-2 2m4-2m7: 0-1 3m+: 0-0
Track: LH: 0-2 RH: 0-1 Tight: 0-3 Gall: 0-0
Aids: Bl: 0-0 Vi: 0-0 Tstrap: 0-0
Best Rating: 98   12/02   Newc   2m   soft   NHF

Placed in bumpers but well beaten on debut over hurdles at Bangor in February.

Arctic Sandy (IRE)
105(91h)   (83h)75
13-y-o ch g Sandalay-Reach Here (Hereford)
A Parker Mr & Mrs Raymond Anderson Green

Placings:112/4330/12F1/P6642521/246505460/4P6-4264   (0982)
2002/03: 16⁴G, 20²G, 21⁶GF, 21⁴GF,

	Starts	1st	2nd	3rd	Win & Pl
Chases	4	0	1	0	968
Career Total	35	5	6	2	23206
96 4/00	Kels	2m1f	F(0-110)HCh	SFT	£3945
107 3/98	Newc	2m4f	E Ch	GD	£2814
110 1/98	Muss	2m	D(0-125)HCh	G-S	£3355
116 4/96	Carl	2m1f	H NHF	FRM	£1528
110 10/95	Tipp	2m	NHF	FRM	£3391

Total win prize-money £15035

Going: Sf: 0-0 GS: 0-0 Gd: 0-2 GF: - Fm: 0-2
Distance: 2m/2m3: 0-1 2m4-2m7: 0-3 3m+: 0-0
Track: LH: 0-4 RH: 0-0 Tight: 0-1 Gall: 0-0
Aids: Bl: 0-0 Vi: 0-0 Tstrap: 0-0
Best Rating: 116   4/96   Carl   2m1f   firm   NHF

Arctic Sky (IRE)
108   110+
6-y-o b g Arctic Lord-Lake Garden Park (Comedy Star (USA))
N J Henderson Mrs Christopher Pugh

Placings:0-6122001   (4683)
2002/03: 17⁶G, 17¹GF, 20²GS, 21²S, 21⁹GS, 21⁹G, 21¹¹GF,

	Starts	1st	2nd	3rd	Win & Pl
NH Flat	2	1	0	0	1631
Hurdles	5	1	2	0	5441
Career Total	8	2	2	0	7072
110 4/03	Hntg	2m5f110yE(0-110)HHdl	G-F	£3542
100 6/02	Hrfd	2m1f	N HHF	G-F	£1631

Total win prize-money £5173

Going: Sf: 0-1 GS: 0-2 Gd: 0-2 GF: - Fm: 2-2
Distance: 2m/2m3: 1-2 2m4-2m7: 1-5 3m+: 0-0
Track: LH: 0-1 RH: 2-5 Tight: 0-1 Gall: 1-1
Aids: Bl: 0-0 Vi: 0-0 Tstrap: 0-0
Best Rating: 110   4/03   Hntg   2m5f110y   gd-fm   Hdl

Bumper winner at Hereford in June 2002; improved effort to make all in 2m 6f handicap hurdle on fast ground at Huntingdon in April; will make a chaser in time.

Arctic Spirit
102(94h)   (65h)103
8-y-o b g Arctic Lord-Dickies Girl (Saxon Farm)
R Dickin The Lordy Racing Partnership

Placings:0P005/60246532/0001U1F561-2P031636 (4398)
2002/03: 19²GF, 20^PGF, 16⁶G, 16³GS, 16¹GS, 16⁶S, 18³GF, 16⁶GF,

	Starts	1st	2nd	3rd	Win & Pl
Chases	8	1	1	2	6039
Career Total	31	4	3	3	18021
103 10/03	Sthl	2m	F(0-105)HCh	G-S	£3374
103 4/02	Towc	2m110y	E(0-105)HCh	GD	£4202
96 12/01	Leic	2m	E(0-105)HCh	G-F	£3146
82 11/01	Wwck	2m110y	F(0-100)HCh	GD	£2562

Total win prize-money £13284

Going: Sf: 0-1 GS: 1-2 Gd: 0-1 GF: - Fm: 0-4
Distance: 2m/2m3: 1-7 2m4-2m7: 0-1 3m+: 0-0
Track: LH: 1-4 RH: 0-3 Tight: 1-4 Gall: 0-1
Aids: Bl: 0-0 Vi: 0-0 Tstrap: 0-0
Best Rating: 103   1/03   Sthl   2m   gd-sft   Ch

Modest handicap chaser; best at around two miles; likes to dominate.

Arctic Splash
98   71
8-y-o ch m St Ninian-Arctic Oats (Oats)
G A Swinbank R P Dineen

Placings:2343454/5/0P0402-6   (0615)
2002/03: 16²G, 20⁶GF,

	Starts	1st	2nd	3rd	Win & Pl
Hurdles	2	0	1	0	514
Career Total	15	0	2	2	1320

Going: Sf: 0-0 GS: 0-0 Gd: 0-1 GF: - Fm: 0-1
Distance: 2m/2m3: 0-1 2m4-2m7: 0-1 3m+: 0-0
Track: LH: 0-2 RH: 0-0 Tight: 0-0 Gall: 0-1
Aids: Bl: 0-0 Vi: 0-0 Tstrap: 0-0
Best Rating: 90   11/99   Hexm   2m   good   NHF

Arctic Star

8-y-o b g Polar Falcon (USA)-Three Stars (Star Appeal)
V Thompson V Thompson

Placings:0F/00205640/P   (0083)
2002/03: 25^PGS,

	Starts	1st	2nd	3rd	Win & Pl
Chases	1	0	0	0	
Career Total	11	0	1	0	748

Going: Sf: 0-0 GS: 0-1 Gd: 0-0 GF: - Fm: 0-0
Distance: 2m/2m3: 0-0 2m4-2m7: 0-0 3m+: 0-1
Track: LH: 0-0 RH: 0-0 Tight: 0-0 Gall: 0-0
Aids: Bl: 0-0 Vi: 0-0 Tstrap: 0-0
Best Rating: 74   12/99   Muss   2m   gd-sft   Hdl

Arctic Times (IRE)

7-y-o ch g Montelimar (USA)-Miss Penguin (General Assembly (USA))
Eugene M O Sullivan Trevor Hemmings

Placings:40/0F40-212   (4480)
2002/03: 24²SH, 24¹Y, 25²G,

	Starts	1st	2nd	3rd	Win & Pl
Chases	3	1	2	0	9684
Career Total	9	1	2	0	9684
100 3/03	Limk	3m	Ch	YLD	£5152

Total win prize-money £5153

Going: Sf: 0-0 GS: 0-0 Gd: 0-1 GF: - Fm: 0-0
Distance: 2m/2m3: 0-0 2m4-2m7: 0-0 3m+: 1-3
Track: LH: 0-1 RH: 1-2 Tight: 0-1 Gall: 0-0
Aids: Bl: 0-0 Vi: 0-0 Tstrap: 0-0
Best Rating: 103   4/03   Aint   3m1f   good   Ch

Point winner in Ireland; has shown fair form in hunter chases; runner-up to a smart-type at Aintree in April 2003.

Arctictaldi (IRE)
87(93h)   (88h)100
13-y-o br g Cataldi-Arctic Sue (Arctic Slave)
M J M Evans M J M Evans

Placings:00/P40/F/6P5U3/2F15322214412/2312234PPP3-0504   (2896)
2002/03: 17⁰GS, 16⁵G, 17⁰G, 16⁴S,

	Starts	1st	2nd	3rd	Win & Pl
Hurdles	1	0	0	0	0
Chases	3	0	0	0	258
Career Total	39	4	8	5	25107
106 8/01	Ctml	2m1f110yD(0-120)HCh	GD	£5292
100 3/01	Muss	2m1f110yF(0-105)HCh	HVY	£3360
104 12/00	Sedg	2m110y F(0-105)HCh	SFT	£3591
105 10/00	Sthl	2m	F(0-100)HCh	G-S	£2164

Total win prize-money £14408

Going: Sf: 0-1 GS: 0-1 Gd: 0-2 GF: - Fm: 0-0
Distance: 2m/2m3: 0-4 2m4-2m7: 0-0 3m+: 0-0
Track: LH: 0-2 RH: 0-2 Tight: 0-1 Gall: 0-0
Aids: Bl: 0-0 Vi: 0-0 Tstrap: 0-0
Best Rating: 106   11/01   Sedg   2m110y   soft   Ch

Moderate chaser; consistent; goes well on a sharp track; prone to jumping errors.

Ard Na Carrig (IRE)

10-y-o ch g Mister Lord (USA)-Coxtown Lass (IRE) (Selko)
M Sheppard Simon Gegg

Placings:0/0/P/4/PP-3   (1454)
2002/03: 20³F,

	Starts	1st	2nd	3rd	Win & Pl
Chases	1	0	0	1	672
Career Total	7	0	0	1	957

Going: Sf: 0-0 GS: 0-0 Gd: 0-0 GF: - Fm: 0-1
Distance: 2m/2m3: 0-0 2m4-2m7: 0-1 3m+: 0-0
Track: LH: 0-0 RH: 0-1 Tight: 0-1 Gall: 0-0
Aids: Bl: 0-0 Vi: 0-0 Tstrap: 0-0
Best Rating: 2   12/98 Wxfd 2m   sft-hvy Ch

Ardan Glas (IRE)
71f   116f
6-y-o ch g Safety Catch (USA)-Jude s Hollow (IRE) (Hollow Hand)
P M J Doyle   J Gleeson

Placings:3/5-50   (1995)
2002/03: 16⁵G, 16⁰GS,

	Starts	1st	2nd	3rd	Win & Pl
NH Flat	2	0	0	0	
Career Total	4	0	0	1	423

Going: Sf: 0-0 GS: 0-1 Gd: 0-1 GF: - Fm: 0-0
Distance: 2m/2m3: 0-2 2m4-2m7: 0-0 3m+: 0-0
Track: LH: 0-1 RH: 0-0 Tight: 0-0 Gall: 0-0
Aids: Bl: 0-0 Vi: 0-0 Tstrap: 0-0
Best Rating: 116   4/01 Cork 2m   yld-sft NHF

Has run well in bumpers in Ireland, but still a maiden.

Ardashir (FR)
70   57
4-y-o b g Simon Du Desert (FR)-Antea (FR) (Esprit Du Nord (USA))
N A Twiston-Davies (Robert Collet 24/6) Miss Caroline Wilson

Placings:0P   (4084)
2002/03: 16⁰G, 16ᴾGS,

	Starts	1st	2nd	3rd	Win & Pl
Hurdles	2	0	0	0	
Career Total	2	0	0	0	

Going: Sf: 0-0 GS: 0-1 Gd: 0-1 GF: - Fm: 0-0
Distance: 2m/2m3: 0-2 2m4-2m7: 0-0 3m+: 0-0
Track: LH: 0-2 RH: 0-0 Tight: 0-1 Gall: 0-1
Aids: Bl: 0-0 Vi: 0-0 Tstrap: 0-0
Best Rating: 55   12/02 Newb 2m110y   good Hdl

Middle-distance winner on the Flat in France; well beaten on hurdling debut in this country.

Ardbei (IRE)
14-y-o ch g Le Bavard (FR)-Blackrath Girl (Bargello)
G W Thomas   G W Thomas

Placings:04   (0218)
2002/03: 25⁰GF, 25⁴G,

	Starts	1st	2nd	3rd	Win & Pl
Chases	2	0	0	0	0
Career Total	2	0	0	0	0

Going: Sf: 0-0 GS: 0-0 Gd: 0-1 GF: - Fm: 0-0
Distance: 2m/2m3: 0-0 2m4-2m7: 0-0 3m+: 0-2

Track: LH: 0-1 RH: 0-1 Tight: 0-0 Gall: 0-1
Aids: Bl: 0-0 Vi: 0-0 Tstrap: 0-0
Best Rating: 0   5/02 Hrfd 3m1f110y good   Ch

Arden Hills (IRE)
104   85
9-y-o b g Supreme Leader-Pisa (IRE) (Carlingford Castle)
J D Frost   Christine And Aubrey Loze

Placings:RBP-0R614   (4692)
2002/03: 21⁰S, 20ᴾS, 19⁰GS, 16¹HY, 22⁴G,

	Starts	1st	2nd	3rd	Win & Pl
Hurdles	4	1	0	0	2729
Chases	1	0	0	0	
Career Total	8	1	0	0	2729

85   2/03   Chep   2m110y   G(0-90)HHdl   HVY   £2450
Total win prize-money £2450

Going: Sf: 1-3 GS: 0-1 Gd: 0-1 GF: - Fm: 0-0
Distance: 2m/2m3: 1-2 2m4-2m7: 0-3 3m+: 0-0
Track: LH: 1-3 RH: 0-1 Tight: 0-2 Gall: 0-0
Aids: Bl: 0-0 Vi: 0-0 Tstrap: 0-0
Best Rating: 85   2/03   Chep   2m110y   heavy   Hdl

Plating-class hurdler; failed to complete on each of his four starts over fences; won a selling hurdle at Chepstow in February 2003; suited by soft ground; seems to handle a faster surface but probably needs further than 2m on it.

Ardent Scout
109   145
11-y-o b g Ardross-Vidette (Billion (USA))
Mrs S J Smith   Mrs Alicia Skene & W S Skene

Placings:53F013104B/1U31P32PP/32134/123PP/3403P50 -1332120   (3886)
2002/03: 24¹G, 25³G, 32³GF, 22²S, 27¹GS, 28²HY, 28⁴G,

	Starts	1st	2nd	3rd	Win & Pl
Chases	7	2	2	2	75291
Career Total	43	8	5	11	127996

145	11/02	Aint	3m3f	B HCh	G-S	£37700
115	5/02	Uttx	3m	B HCh	GD	£11485
129	11/00	Ayr	3m1f	C(0-135)HCh	G-S	£6942
114	11/99	Bang	3m110y	C(0-130)HCh	HVY	£6087
133	12/98	Weth	3m1f	D Ch	SFT	£3756
115	11/98	Carl	2m4f110yD Ch		SFT	£3501
114	12/97	Weth	2m4f110yD(0-110)HHdl		SFT	£3304
96	11/97	Carl	2m4f110yE Hdl		GD	£2500

Total win prize-money £75277

Going: Sf: 0-2 GS: 1-1 Gd: 1-3 GF: - Fm: 0-1
Distance: 2m/2m3: 0-0 2m4-2m7: 0-0 3m+: 2-6
Track: LH: 2-6 RH: 0-0 Tight: 1-2 Gall: 0-0
Aids: Bl: 0-0 Vi: 0-0 Tstrap: 0-0
Best Rating: 145   11/02 Aint   3m3f   gd-sft Ch

Useful staying handicap chaser; sound jumper; goes well in testing conditions; won the Becher Chase at Aintree in November 2002.

Ardfinnan (IRE)
(90c)   (101c)97
10-y-o b g Torus-O Tuk Deep (Deep Run)
Ian Williams   Willsford Racing Incorporated

Placings:220/52U41/235032/632F/3P0P00-3   (0198)
2002/03: 21³F,

	Starts	1st	2nd	3rd	Win & Pl
Hurdles	1	0	0	1	374
Career Total	25	1	6	5	11982

111   4/99   Hntg   2m5f110yE Hdl   G-F   £2962
Total win prize-money £2962

Track: LH: 0-1 RH: 0-1 Tight: 0-0 Gall: 0-1
Aids: Bl: 0-0 Vi: 0-0 Tstrap: 0-0
Best Rating: 117   11/99 Wwck 2m   good   Ch

Moderate hurdler/chaser; stays two miles five; acts on fast ground.

Ardmayle (IRE)
9-y-o b g Be My Native (USA)-Serena Bay (Furry Glen)
Mrs Richard Arthur   Mrs Richard Arthur

Placings:PP-4   (4107)
2002/03: 27⁴S,

	Starts	1st	2nd	3rd	Win & Pl
Chases	1	0	0	0	0
Career Total	3	0	0	0	0

Going: Sf: 0-1 GS: 0-0 Gd: 0-0 GF: - Fm: 0-0
Distance: 2m/2m3: 0-0 2m4-2m7: 0-0 3m+: 0-1
Track: LH: 0-1 RH: 0-0 Tight: 0-1 Gall: 0-0
Aids: Bl: 0-0 Vi: 0-0 Tstrap: 0-0
Best Rating: 72   3/03 Sedg 3m3f   soft   Ch

Ardour Glowing
9-y-o b m Ardross-Albaciyna (Hotfoot)
D A Rees   D Rees

Placings:2126/21111/FP   (2104)
2002/03: 24ᶠGS, 26ᴾGS,

	Starts	1st	2nd	3rd	Win & Pl
Hurdles	2	0	0		
Career Total	11	5	3	0	13918

110	7/00	NAbb	3m3f	E Hdl	G-F	£2873
129	7/00	Worc	3m	E Hdl	GD	£2352
107	6/00	NAbb	2m6f	D Hdl	G-F	£2856
116	6/00	Uttx	3m110y	E Hdl	G-F	£2474
100	2/00	Font	2m2f110yH NHF		G-S	£1578

Total win prize-money £12135

Going: Sf: 0-0 GS: 0-2 Gd: 0-0 GF: - Fm: 0-0
Distance: 2m/2m3: 0-0 2m4-2m7: 0-0 3m+: 0-2
Track: LH: 0-1 RH: 0-1 Tight: 0-1 Gall: 0-1
Aids: Bl: 0-0 Vi: 0-0 Tstrap: 0-0
Best Rating: 129   7/00 Worc 3m   good   Hdl

Ardwelshin (FR)
34
5-y-o b g Ajdayt (USA)-Reem Dubai (IRE) (Nashwan (USA))
B G Powell (Kevin Prendergast 9/9) Nil Desperandum

Placings:0P   (4328)
2002/03: 16⁰G, 16ᴾG,

	Starts	1st	2nd	3rd	Win & Pl
Hurdles	2	0	0	0	
Career Total	2	0	0	0	

Going: Sf: 0-0 GS: 0-0 Gd: 0-2 GF: - Fm: 0-0
Distance: 2m/2m3: 0-2 2m4-2m7: 0-0 3m+: 0-0
Track: LH: 0-2 RH: 0-0 Tight: 0-0 Gall: 0-2
Aids: Bl: 0-0 Vi: 0-0 Tstrap: 0-0
Best Rating: 0   3/03 Newb 2m110y   good Hdl

Argeegee

5-y-o b g Terimon-Lunar Missile (Cruise Missile)
S Gollings R G Gibney

Placings:500   (3938)
2002/03: 16⁵GF, 17⁰G, 21⁰GS,

	Starts	1st	2nd	3rd	Win & Pl
NH Flat	2	0	0	0	0
Hurdles	1	0	0	0	0
Career Total	3	0	0	0	0

Going: Sf: 0-0 GS: 0-1 Gd: 0-1 GF: - Fm: 0-1
Distance: 2m/2m3: 0-2 2m4-2m7: 0-1 3m+: 0-0
Track: LH: 0-0 RH: 0-3 Tight: 0-2 Gall: 0-1
Aids: Bl: 0-0 Vi: 0-0 Tstrap: 0-0
Best Rating: 88   10/02   Hntg   2m110y   gd-fm   NHF

Argento
104   117
6-y-o b g Weldnaas (USA)-Four M S (Majestic Maharaj)
G M Moore J B Wallwin

Placings:654-32311222662   (4591)
2002/03: 16³G, 16²G, 17³G, 16¹GF, 17¹G, 17²G, 16²G, 16²S, 16⁶GS, 19⁶GS, 16²G,

	Starts	1st	2nd	3rd	Win & Pl
Hurdles	11	2	5	2	13598
Career Total	14	2	5	2	13598
108	10/02	Sedg	2m1f	E Hdl	GD	£3307
97	10/02	Hexm	2m110y	E Hdl	G-F	£2877

Total win prize-money £6185

Going: Sf: 0-1 GS: 0-2 Gd: 1-7 GF: - Fm: 1-1
Distance: 2m/2m3: 2-10 2m4-2m7: 0-1 3m+: 0-0
Track: LH: 2-11 RH: 0-0 Tight: 1-4 Gall: 0-0
Aids: Bl: 0-0 Vi: 0-0 Tstrap: 0-0
Best Rating: 117   4/03   Hexm   2m110y   good   Hdl

Fair hurdler; best over trips of around two miles; handles cut in the ground, but best on good or faster; goes well on undulating tracks.

Argy Bargy (IRE)
67f   31f
6-y-o b g Lord Americo-Bargy Fancy (Crash Course)
J Wade John Wade

Placings:0   (1533)
2002/03: 17⁰G,

	Starts	1st	2nd	3rd	Win & Pl
NH Flat	1	0	0	0	
Career Total	1	0	0	0	

Going: Sf: 0-0 GS: 0-0 Gd: 0-1 GF: - Fm: 0-0
Distance: 2m/2m3: 0-1 2m4-2m7: 0-0 3m+: 0-0
Track: LH: 0-1 RH: 0-0 Tight: 0-1 Gall: 0-0
Aids: Bl: 0-0 Vi: 0-0 Tstrap: 0-0
Best Rating: 34   10/02   Sedg   2m1f   good   NHF

Arijaz
53f   93f
6-y-o b g Teenoso (USA)-Zajira (IRE) (Ela-Mana-Mou)
P R Webber Zajira Racing

Placings:6-4   (4431)
2002/03: 18⁴GF,

	Starts	1st	2nd	3rd	Win & Pl
NH Flat	1	0	0	0	274

Career Total   2   0   0   0   274

Going: Sf: 0-0 GS: 0-0 Gd: 0-0 GF: - Fm: 0-1
Distance: 2m/2m3: 0-1 2m4-2m7: 0-0 3m+: 0-0
Track: LH: 0-1 RH: 0-0 Tight: 0-0 Gall: 0-0
Aids: Bl: 0-0 Vi: 0-0 Tstrap: 0-0
Best Rating: 93   3/03   Plum   2m2f   gd-fm   NHF

Arizona (IRE)
94   76
5-y-o b g Sadler s Wells (USA)-Marie De Beaujeu (FR) (Kenmare (FR))
B S Rothwell F S W Partnership

Placings:0   (3965)
2002/03: 16⁰S,

	Starts	1st	2nd	3rd	Win & Pl
Hurdles	1	0	0	0	
Career Total	1	0	0	0	

Going: Sf: 0-1 GS: 0-0 Gd: 0-0 GF: - Fm: 0-0
Distance: 2m/2m3: 0-1 2m4-2m7: 0-0 3m+: 0-0
Track: LH: 0-1 RH: 0-0 Tight: 0-1 Gall: 0-0
Aids: Bl: 0-0 Vi: 0-0 Tstrap: 0-0
Best Rating: 76   3/03   Catt   2m   soft   Hdl

Well beaten on hurdling debut.

Arjaypear (IRE)
90   71
4-y-o b g Petardia-Lila Pedigo (IRE) (Classic Secret (USA))
John R Upson T R Pearson

Placings:P50   (1004)
2002/03: 17⁰GS, 16⁵GS, 17⁰GF,

	Starts	1st	2nd	3rd	Win & Pl
Hurdles	3	0	0	0	0
Career Total	3	0	0	0	0

Going: Sf: 0-0 GS: 0-2 Gd: 0-0 GF: - Fm: 0-1
Distance: 2m/2m3: 0-3 2m4-2m7: 0-0 3m+: 0-0
Track: LH: 0-2 RH: 0-1 Tight: 0-3 Gall: 0-0
Aids: Bl: 0-2 Vi: 0-0 Tstrap: 0-0
Best Rating: 53   8/02   Bang   2m1f   gd-fm   Hdl

Showed improved form when staying on 50/1 second in modest 2m novice hurdle at Worcester July 2003; may appreciated a longer trip.

Arlequin De Sou (FR)
109(88h)   (89h)131
9-y-o b g Sir Brink (FR)-Colombine (USA) (Empery (USA))
P J Hobbs Mrs Karola Vann

Placings:1141356/2112P5/1321433F/002-1F206   (4603)
2002/03: 22¹G, 21²G, 21²HY, 21⁹GS, 26⁶G,

	Starts	1st	2nd	3rd	Win & Pl
Chases	5	1	1	0	9771
Career Total	29	8	5	4	63043
131	10/02	Hayd	2m4f	D(0-125)HCh	GD	£5206
137	12/00	Chel	2m5f	E(0-125)HCh	SFT	£7247
121	11/00	Winc	2m6f	E(0-115)HHdl	G-S	£4426
116	2/00	Font	2m6f110yD(0-125)HHdl		G-S	£5499
105	2/00	Chep	2m4f	D(0-125)HHdl	SFT	£3087
	12/98	Autl	2m1f110y	Ch	HVY	£6566
	11/98	Engh	2m2f	Ch	VS	£6566
	10/98	Autl	2m4f110y	Ch	HLD	£6566

Total win prize-money £45167

Argeegee
Career Total   2   0   0   0   274

Going: Sf: 0-0 GS: 0-0 Gd: 0-0 GF: - Fm: 0-1
Distance: 2m/2m3: 0-1 2m4-2m7: 0-0 3m+: 0-0
Track: LH: 0-1 RH: 0-0 Tight: 0-0 Gall: 0-0
Aids: Bl: 0-0 Vi: 0-0 Tstrap: 0-0
Best Rating: 93   3/03   Plum   2m2f   gd-fm   NHF

Going: Sf: 0-1 GS: 0-1 Gd: 1-3 GF: - Fm: 0-0
Distance: 2m/2m3: 0-0 2m4-2m7: 1-4 3m+: 0-1
Track: LH: 1-5 RH: 0-0 Tight: 0-0 Gall: 0-4
Aids: Bl: 1-5 Vi: 0-0 Tstrap: 0-0
Best Rating: 137   12/00   Chel   2m5f   soft   Ch

Useful chaser; best when bullying the opposition from the front; caught up the hill at Cheltenham on New Year s Day 2003; wears blinkers; suited by trips of around two and a half miles on easy and good ground.

Arm And A Leg (IRE)
100   88
8-y-o ch g Petardia-Ikala (Lashkari)
Mrs D A Hamer (H L Davies 10/5) H L Davies

Placings:50F/P0F1340   (1597)
2002/03: 16ᴾGF, 16⁰GF, 20ᶠG, 16¹GS, 17³GF, 16⁴GF, 19⁶G,

	Starts	1st	2nd	3rd	Win & Pl
Hurdles	6	1	0	1	2885
Chases	1	0	0	0	
Career Total	10	1	0	1	2885
88	8/02	Worc	2m	G(0-90)HHdl	G-S	£1986

Total win prize-money £1987

Going: Sf: 0-0 GS: 1-1 Gd: 0-2 GF: - Fm: 0-4
Distance: 2m/2m3: 1-6 2m4-2m7: 0-1 3m+: 0-0
Track: LH: 1-6 RH: 0-1 Tight: 0-1 Gall: 0-1
Aids: Bl: 0-0 Vi: 0-0 Tstrap: 0-0
Best Rating: 88   10/02   Chep   2m110y   gd-fm   Hdl

Plating-class hurdler; best around two miles; acts on most ground.

Armada's Secret (IRE)
97f   91f
5-y-o b g Un Desperado (FR)-Brigette s Secret (Good Thyne (USA))
K C Bailey Mrs N L Spence

Placings:5P   (4122)
2002/03: 16⁵S, 16ᴾG,

	Starts	1st	2nd	3rd	Win & Pl
NH Flat	2	0	0	0	0
Career Total	2	0	0	0	0

Going: Sf: 0-1 GS: 0-0 Gd: 0-1 GF: - Fm: 0-0
Distance: 2m/2m3: 0-2 2m4-2m7: 0-0 3m+: 0-0
Track: LH: 0-0 RH: 0-2 Tight: 0-0 Gall: 0-1
Aids: Bl: 0-0 Vi: 0-0 Tstrap: 0-0
Best Rating: 91   1/03   Ludl   2m   soft   NHF

A half-brother to two and a half mile hunter chase winner Secret Streams.

Armageddon
                             84
6-y-o b g Deploy-Arusha (IRE) (Dance Of Life (USA))
O Sherwood Raymond Tooth

Placings:12/P6-50P   (4194)
2002/03: 19⁵GS, 24⁰GS, 21ᴾG,

	Starts	1st	2nd	3rd	Win & Pl
Hurdles	3	0	0	0	0
Career Total	7	1	1	0	4004
108	1/01	Chep	2m110y	H NHF	G-S	£1484

Total win prize-money £1484

Going: Sf: 0-0 GS: 0-2 Gd: 0-1 GF: - Fm: 0-0
Distance: 2m/2m3: 0-0 2m4-2m7: 0-2 3m+: 0-1
Track: LH: 0-1 RH: 0-2 Tight: 0-0 Gall: 0-0
Aids: Bl: 0-0 Vi: 0-0 Tstrap: 0-0
Best Rating: 110 2/01 Newb 2m110y soft NHF

A useful bumper winner early in 2001, was pulled up on his hurdling debut after a year s absence. Has won on good to soft ground.

Armaguedon (FR)
109f **127f**
5-y-o b g Garde Royale-Miss Dundee (FR) (Esprit Du Nord (USA))
L Lungo Ashleybank Investments Limited

Placings:3-1130 (4481)
2002/03: 14^{1}GS, 14^{1}GS, 16^{3}HY, 17^{0}G,

	Starts	1st	2nd	3rd	Win & Pl	
NH Flat	4	2	0	1	7104	
Career Total	5	2	0	2	7582	
127	12/02 Ayr	1m6f	H NHF		G-S	£2618
125	11/02 Newc	1m6f	H NHF		G-S	£2646
					Total win prize-money	£5264

Going: Sf: 0-1 GS: 2-2 Gd: 0-1 GF: - Fm: 0-0
Distance: 2m/2m3: 0-2 2m4-2m7: 0-0 3m+: 0-0
Track: LH: 2-3 RH: 0-0 Tight: 0-0 Gall: 0-0
Aids: Bl: 0-0 Vi: 0-0 Tstrap: 0-0
Best Rating: 127 12/02 Ayr 1m6f gd-sft NHF

Useful bumper performer; won two 14f bumpers in the north; pulled too hard in heavy ground in a Chepstow Grade Two.

Armaturk (FR)
103(123h) (151h)**151**
6-y-o ch g Baby Turk-Armalita (FR) (Goodland (FR))
P F Nicholls B C Marshall

Placings:332111/3121131-342100 (4647a)
2002/03: 17^{3}G, 16^{4}G, 16^{2}HY, 21^{1}GS, 20^{0}G, 21^{0}G,

	Starts	1st	2nd	3rd	Win & Pl	
Chases	6	1	1	1	26594	
Career Total	19	8	3	5	142883	
144	2/03 Winc	2m5f	B Ch		G-S	£11979
151	4/02 Aint	2m	A Ch		GD	£46500
142	2/02 Wwck	2m110y	A Ch		SFT	£18000
139	12/01 Newb	2m2f110yD Ch			GD	£5905
151	10/01 Kemp	2m	B Hdl		G-S	£6890
130	4/01 Kemp	2m	D Hdl		GD	£3939
128	4/01 Plum	2m	E Hdl		HVY	£2513
	1/01 Pau	2m110y	Hdl		SFT	£6305
					Total win prize-money	£102032

Going: Sf: 0-1 GS: 1-1 Gd: 0-4 GF: - Fm: 0-0
Distance: 2m/2m3: 0-3 2m4-2m7: 1-3 3m+: 0-0
Track: LH: 0-3 RH: 1-2 Tight: 0-0 Gall: 0-2
Aids: Bl: 0-0 Vi: 0-0 Tstrap: 0-0
Best Rating: 151 12/02 Weth 2m heavy Ch

Smart chaser; French import; high-class novice in 2001/02, finishing third in the Arkle before beating Seebald at Aintree; finished runner-up in a valuable prize at Wetherby on Boxing Day 2002 before winning at Wincanton; effective at two miles but stays two miles five and versatile regarding ground; likes to front run.

Arms Acrossthesea
92 **86**
4-y-o b g Namaqualand (USA)-Zolica (Beveled (USA))
F P Murtagh J Clayton

Placings:F54P45 (2304)

2002/03: 16^{6}G, 16^{5}GF, 16^{4}F, 16^{6}G, 16^{4}G, 16^{5}GS,

	Starts	1st	2nd	3rd	Win & Pl
Hurdles	6	0	0	0	271
Career Total	6	0	0	0	271

Going: Sf: 0-0 GS: 0-1 Gd: 0-3 GF: - Fm: 0-2
Distance: 2m/2m3: 0-6 2m4-2m7: 0-0 3m+: 0-0
Track: LH: 0-5 RH: 0-1 Tight: 0-3 Gall: 0-0
Aids: Bl: 0-0 Vi: 0-0 Tstrap: 0-0
Best Rating: 86 11/02 Catt 2m good Hdl

Yet to prove he stays two miles over hurdles.

Aroseforclare
87 **31**
7-y-o b m Royal Vulcan-Lovelyroseofclare (Torus)
Miss K M George Kevin David Kerslake

Placings:06/000-0PU (4798)
2002/03: 21^{0}S, 20^{9}S, 17^{U}GF,

	Starts	1st	2nd	3rd	Win & Pl
Hurdles	3	0	0	0	
Career Total	8	0	0	0	0

Going: Sf: 0-2 GS: 0-0 Gd: 0-0 GF: - Fm: 0-1
Distance: 2m/2m3: 0-1 2m4-2m7: 0-2 3m+: 0-0
Track: LH: 0-1 RH: 0-1 Tight: 0-2 Gall: 0-0
Aids: Bl: 0-0 Vi: 0-0 Tstrap: 0-0
Best Rating: 62 5/01 Extr 2m1f firm NHF

Poor hurdler; shown little so far.

Arribilo (GER)
107 (90c)**91**
9-y-o b g Top Ville-Arborea (GER) (Priamos (GER))
B P J Baugh (P R Johnson 9/6) I J Hooper

Placings:0/P62P045-265PF031 (4679)
2002/03: 16^{2}GF, 16^{6}GS, 16^{5}HY, 16^{4}S, 16^{6}G, 16^{0}S, 17^{3}GF, 16^{1}GF,

	Starts	1st	2nd	3rd	Win & Pl	
Hurdles	7	1	1	1	3876	
Chases	1	0	0	0	0	
Career Total	16	1	2	1	4557	
91	4/03 Hntg	2m110y G(0-90)HHdl		G-F	£2413	
				Total win prize-money	£2414	

Going: Sf: 0-3 GS: 0-1 Gd: 0-1 GF: - Fm: 1-3
Distance: 2m/2m3: 1-8 2m4-2m7: 0-0 3m+: 0-0
Track: LH: 0-3 RH: 1-5 Tight: 0-2 Gall: 1-1
Aids: Bl: 0-2 Vi: 0-0 Tstrap: 0-0
Best Rating: 91 4/03 Hntg 2m110y gd-fm Hdl

Modest form over hurdles, including claimers; took a selling handicap hurdle on fast ground at Huntingdon in April; best over two miles.

Arrows Gold
88 **78**
5-y-o b g Sure Blade (USA)-Gamefull Gold (Mummy s Game)
D M Grissell Mrs Caroline Martin

Placings:0F60 (4186)
2002/03: 17^{0}HY, 17^{6}HY, 20^{6}S, 17^{0}G,

	Starts	1st	2nd	3rd	Win & Pl
Hurdles	4	0	0	0	0
Career Total	4	0	0	0	0

Going: Sf: 0-3 GS: 0-0 Gd: 0-1 GF: - Fm: 0-0
Distance: 2m/2m3: 0-3 2m4-2m7: 0-1 3m+: 0-0

Track: LH: 0-0 RH: 0-3 Tight: 0-4 Gall: 0-0
Aids: Bl: 0-0 Vi: 0-0 Tstrap: 0-0
Best Rating: 78 12/02 Folk 2m1f110y heavy Hdl

Art Expert (FR)
92
5-y-o b g Pursuit Of Love-Celtic Wing (Midyan (USA))
Mrs N Macauley Classic Glass & Dishwashing Systems Ltd

Placings:P0 (4337)
2002/03: 17^{5}GF, 16^{0}GF,

	Starts	1st	2nd	3rd	Win & Pl
Hurdles	2	0	0	0	
Career Total	2	0	0	0	

Going: Sf: 0-0 GS: 0-0 Gd: 0-0 GF: - Fm: 0-2
Distance: 2m/2m3: 0-2 2m4-2m7: 0-0 3m+: 0-0
Track: LH: 0-1 RH: 0-1 Tight: 0-0 Gall: 0-1
Aids: Bl: 0-0 Vi: 0-0 Tstrap: 0-0
Best Rating: 73 3/03 Hntg 2m110y gd-fm Hdl

Art Nouveau
78f **53f**
5-y-o b m Cyrano De Bergerac-Norska (Northfields (USA))
J A Moore Mrs J M Moore

Placings:0-0 (0409)
2002/03: 17^{0}GF,

	Starts	1st	2nd	3rd	Win & Pl
NH Flat	1	0	0	0	
Career Total	2	0	0	0	

Going: Sf: 0-0 GS: 0-0 Gd: 0-0 GF: - Fm: 0-1
Distance: 2m/2m3: 0-1 2m4-2m7: 0-0 3m+: 0-0
Track: LH: 0-0 RH: 0-1 Tight: 0-1 Gall: 0-0
Aids: Bl: 0-0 Vi: 0-0 Tstrap: 0-0
Best Rating: 52 6/02 MRas 2m1f110y gd-fm NHF

Artemesia
103(101h) (101h)**101+**
8-y-o b m Teenoso (USA)-Annicombe Run (Deep Run)
Ferdy Murphy Beautifully Bred Partnership

Placings:3/024/03U6R4-2120001 (4668)
2002/03: 20^{2}G, 23^{1}GS, 24^{2}G, 22^{0}G, 21^{0}G, 19^{0}S, 20^{1}G,

	Starts	1st	2nd	3rd	Win & Pl	
Hurdles	7	2	2	0	7602	
Career Total	17	2	3	2	8891	
91	4/03 Fknm	2m4f	E(0-105)HHdl		GD	£3423
91	5/02 Fknm	2m7f110yE(0-100)HHdl			G-S	£2996
					Total win prize-money	£6419

Going: Sf: 0-1 GS: 1-1 Gd: 1-5 GF: - Fm: 0-0
Distance: 2m/2m3: 0-0 2m4-2m7: 1-5 3m+: 1-2
Track: LH: 2-7 RH: 0-0 Tight: 2-4 Gall: 0-1
Aids: Bl: 0-0 Vi: 0-0 Tstrap: 0-0
Best Rating: 102 1/01 Fknm 2m soft NHF

Plating-class handicap hurdler; good second on her first try over fences at Hexham in June; stays three miles and acts on a good or slightly softer surface; goes well at Fakenham; game.

Artemise (FR)
69 **82**
5-y-o b m Cyborg (FR)-Articule (FR) (Art Francais (USA))

A King Mrs Anthony West

Placings:00P2P (4626)
2002/03: 16⁰HY, 16⁶GS, 17⁶S, 16²GF, 17⁶GF,

	Starts	1st	2nd	3rd	Win & Pl
NH Flat	2	0	0	0	0
Hurdles	3	0	1	0	863
Career Total	5	0	1	0	863

Going: Sf: 0-2 GS: 0-1 Gd: 0-0 GF: - Fm: 0-2
Distance: 2m/2m3: 0-5 2m4-2m7: 0-0 3m+: 0-0
Track: LH: 0-4 RH: 0-1 Tight: 0-2 Gall: 0-1
Aids: Bl: 0-0 Vi: 0-0 Tstrap: 0-0
Best Rating: 82 3/03 Wwck 2m gd-fm Hdl

Modest novice hurdler.

Arthur Porter

10-y-o ch g Crawter-Chetsford Water (Sir Lark)
P R Hedger Ms L Angell

Placings:6P-P (0274)
2002/03: 17⁶S,

	Starts	1st	2nd	3rd	Win & Pl
Chases	1	0	0	0	
Career Total	3	0	0	0	0

Going: Sf: 0-1 GS: 0-0 Gd: 0-0 GF: - Fm: 0-0
Distance: 2m/2m3: 0-1 2m4-2m7: 0-0 3m+: 0-0
Track: LH: 0-1 RH: 0-0 Tight: 0-1 Gall: 0-0
Aids: Bl: 0-0 Vi: 0-0 Tstrap: 0-0
Best Rating: 0 5/02 Bang 2m1f110y soft Ch

Arthurs Kingdom (IRE)
99   79

7-y-o b g Roi Danzig (USA)-Merrie Moment (IRE) (Taufan (USA))
Miss Kate Milligan Dr Roy Palmer

Placings:603450/05325105P-P2053310 (4267)
2002/03: 24⁶G, 27²G, 22⁶G, 24⁵GF, 27³G, 27³S, 27¹S, 24⁶GF,

	Starts	1st	2nd	3rd	Win & Pl
Hurdles	8	1	1	2	3913
Career Total	23	2	2	4	8037
79 3/03 Sedg 3m3f110yG(0-90)HHdl				SFT	£2443
79 8/01 Ctml 2m6f yG(0-90)HHdl				G-S	£2772
				Total win prize-money	£5215

Going: Sf: 1-2 GS: 0-0 Gd: 0-4 GF: - Fm: 0-2
Distance: 2m/2m3: 0-0 2m4-2m7: 0-1 3m+: 1-7
Track: LH: 1-7 RH: 0-1 Tight: 1-7 Gall: 0-0
Aids: Bl: 0-0 Vi: 0-0 Tstrap: 0-0
Best Rating: 90 9/00 Sedg 2m1f soft Hdl

Plating-class staying hurdler, stays marathon trips; seems to handle any ground; has worn cheekpieces.

Aruba Dam (IRE)
77f   51f

5-y-o br m Be My Native (USA)-Arumah (Arapaho)
P F Nicholls Mrs Kathy Stuart

Placings:0 (4005)
2002/03: 16⁰S,

	Starts	1st	2nd	3rd	Win & Pl
NH Flat	1	0	0	0	
Career Total	1	0	0	0	

Going: Sf: 0-1 GS: 0-0 Gd: 0-0 GF: - Fm: 0-0
Distance: 2m/2m3: 0-1 2m4-2m7: 0-0 3m+: 0-0
Track: LH: 0-0 RH: 0-1 Tight: 0-2 Gall: 0-0
Aids: Bl: 0-0 Vi: 0-0 Tstrap: 0-0
Best Rating: 51 3/03 Winc 2m soft NHF

Arvi's Way
95f

6-y-o b g Alflora (IRE)-Gentle Madam (Camden Town)
Mrs S J Smith Mrs Alicia Skene & W S Skene

Placings:6-0 (2117)
2002/03: 17⁰G,

	Starts	1st	2nd	3rd	Win & Pl
NH Flat	1	0	0	0	
Career Total	2	0	0	0	

Going: Sf: 0-0 GS: 0-0 Gd: 0-1 GF: - Fm: 0-0
Distance: 2m/2m3: 0-1 2m4-2m7: 0-0 3m+: 0-0
Track: LH: 0-0 RH: 0-0 Tight: 0-0 Gall: 0-0
Aids: Bl: 0-0 Vi: 0-0 Tstrap: 0-0
Best Rating: 95 4/02 Carl 2m1f good NHF

Asador (FR)
104   141

7-y-o ch g Kadounor (FR)-Apos (FR) (Baillamont (USA))
P F Nicholls Darren C Mercer

Placings:1110/1F1P-1FF0 (3518)
2002/03: 19¹HY, 19⁶HY, 16⁶HY, 20⁴GS,

	Starts	1st	2nd	3rd	Win & Pl
Hurdles	1	0	0	0	0
Chases	3	1	0	0	7345
Career Total	12	6	0	0	39006
137 11/02 Chep 2m3f110yC(0-130)HCh				HVY	£7345
130 2/02 Plum 2m1f E Ch				HVY	£3360
130 12/01 NAbb 2m110y D Ch				HVY	£3740
2/00 Ange 2m1f110y Hdl				VS	£10567
1/00 Pau 2m2f Hdl				VS	£7535
12/99 Pau 2m110y Hdl				HVY	£6459
				Total win prize-money	£39006

Going: Sf: 1-3 GS: 0-1 Gd: 0-0 GF: - Fm: 0-0
Distance: 2m/2m3: 0-1 2m4-2m7: 1-3 3m+: 0-0
Track: LH: 1-4 RH: 0-0 Tight: 0-0 Gall: 0-0
Aids: Bl: 0-0 Vi: 0-0 Tstrap: 0-0
Best Rating: 141 1/03 Chep 2m110y heavy Ch

Very useful chaser/hurdler; effective at two to two and a half miles; suited by a left-handed track; well suited by soft ground; not a good jumper of fences.

Asas
95   (99h)85

9-y-o b g Nashwan (USA)-Oumaldaaya (USA) (Nureyev (USA))
D G McArdle Topline Syndicate

Placings:000/00010110300/564401204000/01PU046P-50 (1291a)
2002/03: 21⁵G, 16⁰F,

	Starts	1st	2nd	3rd	Win & Pl
Hurdles	1	0	0	0	
Chases	0	0	0	0	
Career Total	36	5	1	1	18982
84 5/01 Dund 2m1f (0-102)HCh				FRM	£5842
100 7/00 Dund 2m4f153y (0-109)HHdl				FRM	£3036
88 9/99 Dund 2m135y (0-95)HHdl				FRM	£2217
99 8/99 Dund 2m135y (0-95)HHdl				FRM	£3696
82 7/99 Dund 2m135y (0-95)HHdl				G-F	£2209
				Total win prize-money	£17003

Going: Sf: 0-0 GS: 0-0 Gd: 0-1 GF: - Fm: 0-1
Distance: 2m/2m3: 0-1 2m4-2m7: 0-1 3m+: 0-0
Track: LH: 0-2 RH: 0-0 Tight: 0-1 Gall: 0-0
Aids: Bl: 0-1 Vi: 0-1 Tstrap: 0-0
Best Rating: 105 7/00 Dund 2m4f153y gd-fm Hdl

Ascot Touch (IRE)

7-y-o b/br g Architect (USA)-Ascot Touchseal (NZ) (Mayo Mellay (NZ))
J A Moore J A Moore

Placings:0/050605 (4797)
2002/03: 17⁰G, 27⁵S, 26⁰G, 24⁶GF, 25⁰G, 27⁵GF,

	Starts	1st	2nd	3rd	Win & Pl
NH Flat	1	0	0	0	
Hurdles	2	0	0	0	
Chases	3	0	0	0	
Career Total	7	0	0	0	

Going: Sf: 0-1 GS: 0-0 Gd: 0-3 GF: - Fm: 0-2
Distance: 2m/2m3: 0-1 2m4-2m7: 0-0 3m+: 0-5
Track: LH: 0-3 RH: 0-2 Tight: 0-2 Gall: 0-1
Aids: Bl: 0-0 Vi: 0-1 Tstrap: 0-0
Best Rating: 87 1/01 Ayr 2m gd-sft NHF

Ash Branch (IRE)
101   81

9-y-o ch g Shardari-Etnas Princess (The Parson)
Sir John Barlow Bt Sir John & Lady Barlow

Placings:0/500P-1 (1010)
2002/03: 20¹GF,

	Starts	1st	2nd	3rd	Win & Pl
Hurdles	1	1	0	0	3052
Career Total	6	1	0	0	3052
81 8/02 Bang 2m4f E Hdl				G-F	£3052
				Total win prize-money	£3052

Going: Sf: 0-0 GS: 0-0 Gd: 0-0 GF: - Fm: 1-1
Distance: 2m/2m3: 0-0 2m4-2m7: 1-1 3m+: 0-0
Track: LH: 1-1 RH: 0-0 Tight: 1-1 Gall: 0-0
Aids: Bl: 0-0 Vi: 0-0 Tstrap: 0-0
Best Rating: 81 8/02 Bang 2m4f gd-fm Hdl

Poor hurdler.

Ashbury Star (NZ)
104(101h)   (105h)70

8-y-o ch g Sumayr-Piaf s Star (NZ) (Famous Star)
Mrs N Smith Tony Hayward

Placings:P1/3040234202-205P44 (4756)
2002/03: 18²GF, 17⁰GS, 17⁵S, 16⁷S, 17⁴HY, 18⁴GF,

	Starts	1st	2nd	3rd	Win & Pl
Chases	6	0	1	0	1520
Career Total	18	1	5	2	9047
103 4/01 Plum 2m E Hdl				HVY	£2723
				Total win prize-money	£2723

Going: Sf: 0-3 GS: 0-1 Gd: 0-0 GF: - Fm: 0-2
Distance: 2m/2m3: 0-6 2m4-2m7: 0-0 3m+: 0-0
Track: LH: 0-3 RH: 0-1 Tight: 0-6 Gall: 0-0
Aids: Bl: 0-0 Vi: 0-0 Tstrap: 0-0
Best Rating: 105 6/01 NAbb 2m1f good Hdl

Modest hurdler, has done enough over fences to suggest

that he can add to his tally; acts in soft ground. Suited by two miles.

Ashfield Jake (IRE)

(62h)
11-y-o br g Jolly Jake (NZ)-Ashfield Rose (Mon Capitaine)
S T Lewis Simon T Lewis

Placings:0U00P-PP (0740)
2002/03: 20PS, 25PG,

	Starts	1st	2nd	3rd	Win & Pl
Hurdles	2	0	0	0	
Career Total	7	0	0	0	

Going: Sf: 0-1 GS: 0-0 Gd: 0-1 GF: - Fm: 0-0
Distance: 2m/2m3: 0-0 2m4-2m7: 0-1 3m+: 0-1
Track: LH: 0-2 RH: 0-0 Tight: 0-2 Gall: 0-0
Aids: Bl: 0-0 Vi: 0-0 Tstrap: 0-0
Best Rating: 37 5/01 Hntg 2m4f110y good Hdl

Ashgan (IRE)

106(107h) (120h)110+
10-y-o br g Yashgan-Nicky s Dilemma (Kambalda)
Mrs H Dalton A J & Mrs L Brazier

Placings:2FP215P/4P5P115/P113/41-1P1224500 (2327)
2002/03: 20¹GF, 24PGF, 20¹GF, 21²G, 20PGF, 21⁴G, 23⁵G, 24⁰G, 16⁰GS,

	Starts	1st	2nd	3rd	Win & Pl
Hurdles	2	1	0	0	3582
Chases	7	1	2	0	8006
Career Total	29	8	4	1	31749
114 7/02 Worc	2m4f	D(0-115)HHdl	G-F	£3581	
110 6/02 Worc	2m4f110yD(0-120)HCh	G-F	£4114		
108 5/01 Hntg	2m4f110yE Ch	G-F	£3262		
118 8/00 Bang	2m4f110yD(0-100)HCh	GD	£4251		
123 7/00 Sedg	2m5f110yD(0-125)HHdl	G-F	£3139		
114 3/00 Folk	2m6f110yF(0-110)HHdl	GD	£2416		
118 2/00 MRas	2m5f110yF(0-110)HHdl	G-S	£1921		
98 3/99 Hntg	2m5f110yE Hdl	G-S	£2740		
Total win prize-money £25428					

Going: Sf: 0-0 GS: 0-1 Gd: 0-4 GF: - Fm: 2-4
Distance: 2m/2m3: 0-1 **2m4-2m7: 2-5** 3m+: 0-3
Track: **LH: 2-7** RH: 0-2 Tight: 0-4 Gall: 0-0
Aids: Bl: 0-0 Vi: 0-1 Tstrap: 0-0
Best Rating: 123 7/00 Sedg 2m5f110y gd-fm Hdl

Modest handicap hurdler/chaser; best at distances short of three miles; acts on fast ground but was successful on good to soft in his younger days.

Ashgar (USA)

100(103c) (98c)107
7-y-o ch g Bien Bien (USA)-Ardisia (USA) (Affirmed (USA))
M D Hammond (P J Hobbs 31/8) Jay Dee Bloodstock Limited

Placings:2/1124023-314F2P2261P5P (4767)
2002/03: 23³G, 26¹G, 32⁴GF, 26FGF, 26²GF, 22PGF, 21²GF, 20²GF, 20⁶GS, 23¹HY, 24PS, 20PG,

	Starts	1st	2nd	3rd	Win & Pl
Hurdles	5	1	0	0	2216
Chases	8	3	1	3	10604
Career Total	21	4	6	2	22883
107 11/02 Weth	2m7f	G Hdl	HVY	£2215	
93 5/02 Uttx	3m2f	E Ch	GD	£3391	
109 11/01 Ludl	2m5f	E Hdl	G-F	£2803	
109 11/01 Ludl	2m5f	E Hdl	G-F	£2712	
Total win prize-money £11125					

Going: Sf: 1-2 GS: 0-1 Gd: 1-4 GF: - Fm: 0-6
Distance: 2m/2m3: 0-0 2m4-2m7: 1-7 3m+: 1-6
Track: LH: 2-6 RH: 0-6 Tight: 0-3 Gall: 0-0
Aids: **Bl: 2-11** Vi: 0-0 Tstrap: 0-0
Best Rating: 122 4/02 Chel 3m gd-fm Hdl

Modest hurdler; has not looked a natural over fences; quirky sort; needs a lot of driving; best on fast ground; has won at up to three and a quarter miles.

Ashley Brook (IRE)

108f 112f
5-y-o ch g Magical Wonder (USA)-Seamill (IRE) (Lafontaine (USA))
K Bishop Mrs E K Ellis

Placings:23410 (4481)
2002/03: 17²G, 14³GS, 13⁴S, 16¹S, 17⁰G,

	Starts	1st	2nd	3rd	Win & Pl
NH Flat	5	1	1	1	1043
Career Total	5	1	1	1	1043
112 01/03 Ludl	2mNHF		S	£803	
Total win prize-money £803					

Going: Sf: 1-2 GS: 0-1 Gd: 0-2 GF: - Fm: 0-0
Distance: **2m/2m3: 1-3** 2m4-2m7: 0-0 3m+: 0-0
Track: LH: 0-2 **RH: 1-2** Tight: 0-1 Gall: 0-0
Aids: Bl: 0-0 Vi: 0-0 Tstrap: 0-0
Best Rating: 112 1/03 Ludl 2m soft NHF

Modest performer; gained due reward for some consistent efforts when dead-heating in Ludlow bumper January 2003; acts on easy ground.

Ashley Muck

104(95h) (126h)122
10-y-o b g Gunner B-Miss Muck (Balinger)
M C Pipe Matt Archer & Miss Jean Broadhurst

Placings:U5/32F12/3/50P13/21111123-F443 (4388)
2002/03: 20FGS, 20⁴HY, 20⁴GS, 23³F,

	Starts	1st	2nd	3rd	Win & Pl
Chases	4	0	0	1	2343
Career Total	25	7	4	5	45381
136 9/01 Uttx	2m5f	D(0-125)HCh	GD	£4920	
136 8/01 Uttx	2m5f	C(0-135)HCh	G-F	£5872	
136 8/01 NAbb	2m5f110yD Ch	GD	£3721		
131 7/01 NAbb	2m5f110yE Ch	G-F	£3376		
112 6/01 NAbb	2m5f110yD Ch	G-F	£3840		
123 3/01 Strf	2m110y D(0-125)HHdl	SFT	£7436		
126 11/98 Extr	2m1f	E Hdl	SFT	£2805	
Total win prize-money £31973					

Going: Sf: 0-1 GS: 0-2 Gd: 0-0 GF: - Fm: 0-1
Distance: 2m/2m3: 0-2 2m4-2m7: 0-3 3m+: 0-1
Track: LH: 0-2 RH: 0-2 Tight: 0-1 Gall: 0-1
Aids: Bl: 0-0 Vi: 0-0 Tstrap: 0-0
Best Rating: 136 9/01 Uttx 2m5f good Ch

Fair handicap chaser; has plenty of ability, but has temperament problems and sometimes loses ground at the start; acts on fast ground; suited by trips of around two and a half miles.

Ashleybank House (IRE)

74 91
6-y-o b g Lord Americo-Deep Perk (IRE) (Deep Run)
L Lungo Ashleybank Investments Limited

Placings:045 (4225)
2002/03: 16⁰GS, 16⁴HY, 20⁵GF,

	Starts	1st	2nd	3rd	Win & Pl
NH Flat	2	0	0	0	
Hurdles	1	0	0	0	
Career Total	3	0	0	0	

Going: Sf: 0-1 GS: 0-1 Gd: 0-0 GF: - Fm: 0-1
Distance: 2m/2m3: 0-2 2m4-2m7: 0-1 3m+: 0-0
Track: LH: 0-3 RH: 0-0 Tight: 0-0 Gall: 0-0
Aids: Bl: 0-0 Vi: 0-0 Tstrap: 0-0
Best Rating: 103 1/03 Newc 2m heavy NHF

Plating-class performer; big, chasing-type; showed some ability in bumpers and ran with credit on hurdling bow at Wetherby in March; acts on soft ground; will be suited by a stiff test of stamina.

Ashman (IRE)

92(92c) (84+c)73
10-y-o b g Ashmolean (USA)-Rhein Maiden (Rheingold)
R N Bevis The Wirral Optimists

Placings:5/0F01216/04/F0PP-P635F0P (1563)
2002/03: 17PS, 16SGF, 16³S, 16SGF, 17FG, 16SF, 17PG,

	Starts	1st	2nd	3rd	Win & Pl
Hurdles	5	0	0	1	723
Chases	2	0	0	0	0
Career Total	21	2	1	1	8084
123 3/00 Bang	2m1f	E Hdl	GD	£3038	
113 2/00 Hrfd	2m1f	F(0-100)HHdl	GD	£2884	
Total win prize-money £5922					

Going: Sf: 0-2 GS: 0-0 Gd: 0-2 GF: - Fm: 0-3
Distance: 2m/2m3: 0-7 2m4-2m7: 0-0 3m+: 0-0
Track: LH: 0-4 RH: 0-3 Tight: 0-3 Gall: 0-1
Aids: Bl: 0-0 Vi: 0-0 Tstrap: 0-6
Best Rating: 123 3/00 Bang 2m1f good Hdl

Plating-class performer; former successful pointer; a keen sort; top of the ground performer; successful twice at two miles one; prone to the odd mistake.

Ashnaya (FR)

100 98+
5-y-o b m Ashkalani (IRE)-Upend (Main Reef)
W Storey B P Bradshaw

Placings:06-5F21PP0 (2141)
2002/03: 16SG, 16FGS, 17²G, 17¹G, 20PS, 21PS, 16PGS,

	Starts	1st	2nd	3rd	Win & Pl
Hurdles	7	1	1	0	4562
Career Total	9	1	1	0	4562
91 8/02 Ctml	2m1f110yE(0-100)HHdl	GD	£3738		
Total win prize-money £3738					

Going: Sf: 0-2 GS: 0-2 Gd: 1-3 GF: - Fm: 0-0
Distance: **2m/2m3: 1-5** 2m4-2m7: 0-2 3m+: 0-0
Track: **LH: 1-5** RH: 0-2 Tight: 1-3 Gall: 0-1
Aids: Bl: 0-2 Vi: 0-0 Tstrap: 0-0
Best Rating: 91 8/02 Ctml 2m1f110y good Hdl

Plating-class hurdler; stays two and a half miles; acts on most types of ground.

Ashton Vale

101 98
4-y-o ch g Ashkalani (IRE)-My Valentina (Royal Academy (USA))
P F Nicholls (R Hannon 14/8) The Hill Top Partnership

Placings:1231533 (4793)
2002/03: 17¹G, 17²G, 16³GF, 16¹F, 16⁵F, 16³F, 17³GF,

	Starts	1st	2nd	3rd	Win & Pl
Hurdles	7	2	1	3	9121
Career Total	7	2	1	3	9121
97 10/02 Winc 2m	E Hdl			FRM	£3108
100 9/02 NAbb 2m1f	E Hdl			GD	£3136

Total win prize-money £6245

Going: Sf: 0-0 GS: 0-0 Gd: 1-2 GF: - Fm: 1-5
Distance: 2m2m3: 2-7 2m4-2m7: 0-0 3m+: 0-0
Track: LH: 1-4 RH: 1-3 Tight: 1-3 Gall: 0-0
Aids: Bl: 0-0 Vi: 0-0 Tstrap: 1-5
Best Rating: 101 10/02 Chep 2m110y gd-fm Hdl

Modest juvenile hurdler; made a winning debut over hurdles at Newton Abbot in August 2002 and won a non-event at Wincanton in October; best on a sound surface; usually wears a tongue tie.

Ashtoreth (IRE)
99   70
4-y-o ch f Ashkalani (IRE)-Sally Chase (Sallust)
D McCain (G A Butler 4/7) D McCain

Placings:3P02PP5   (4675)
2002/03: 17^3G, 17^PGF, 17^0G, 16^2S, 16^PS, 17^PS, 17^5GF,

	Starts	1st	2nd	3rd	Win & Pl
Hurdles	7	0	1	1	1260
Career Total	7	0	1	1	1260

Going: Sf: 0-3 GS: 0-0 Gd: 0-2 GF: - Fm: 0-2
Distance: 2m2m3: 0-7 2m4-2m7: 0-0 3m+: 0-0
Track: LH: 0-4 RH: 0-3 Tight: 0-4 Gall: 0-0
Aids: Bl: 0-0 Vi: 0-0 Tstrap: 0-0
Best Rating: 69 9/02 Bang 2m1f good Hdl

Plating-class maiden hurdler.

Ashwell Boy (IRE)

12-y-o b g Strong Gale-Billys Pet (Le Moss)
B R Summers (M C Pipe 17/5) A B S Racing

Placings:125/0F1052F/14PF261/P11F334223/11142313/5 22F2/F00/23125-PP   (4390)
2002/03: 16^PG, 19^PF,

	Starts	1st	2nd	3rd	Win & Pl
Chases	2	0	0	0	
Career Total	50	11	11	6	109902
133 10/01 Kemp 2m	B(0-140)HCh			G-S	£8957
138 3/99 Newb 2m4f	C(0-135)HCh			SFT	£7035
131 10/98 Chep 2m3f110y	C(0-130)HCh			GD	£5085
142 5/98 Strf 2m5f110y	D Ch			GD	£3730
114 5/98 Strf 2m5f110y	D Ch			FRM	£4068
131 10/97 NAbb 2m110y	E Ch			G-F	£2859
131 9/97 Strf 2m4f	D Ch			GD	£3890
127 4/97 Chep 2m	B HHdl			G-F	£4674
125 5/96 Winc 2m	E Hdl			FRM	£2442
127 1/96 Asct 2m110y	D Hdl			SFT	£3988
102 3/95 Newb 2m110y	H NHF			GD	£2248

Total win prize-money £48981

Going: Sf: 0-0 GS: 0-0 Gd: 0-1 GF: - Fm: 0-1
Distance: 2m2m3: 0-1 2m4-2m7: 0-1 3m+: 0-0
Track: LH: 0-1 RH: 0-0 Tight: 0-1 Gall: 0-0
Aids: Bl: 0-0 Vi: 0-1 Tstrap: 0-0
Best Rating: 142 5/98 Strf 2m5f110y good Ch

Formerly useful chaser; not easy to train or a straightforward ride; suited by fast ground; has been fitted with a visor of late.

Asian Persuasion (IRE)
90   44
4-y-o gr g Danehill Dancer (IRE)-Kaitlin (IRE) (Salmon Leap (USA))
B A Pearce (E L James 17/10) Fred Camis

Placings:30254P00   (4143)
2002/03: 16^3GF, 17^0G, 16^2F, 17^5F, 16^4S, 16^PGS, 17^0GS, 16^0G,

	Starts	1st	2nd	3rd	Win & Pl
Hurdles	8	0	1	1	1932
Career Total	8	0	1	1	1932

Going: Sf: 0-1 GS: 0-2 Gd: 0-2 GF: - Fm: 0-3
Distance: 2m2m3: 0-8 2m4-2m7: 0-0 3m+: 0-0
Track: LH: 0-3 RH: 0-5 Tight: 0-4 Gall: 0-0
Aids: Bl: 0-0 Vi: 0-0 Tstrap: 0-0
Best Rating: 70 10/02 Tntn 2m1f firm Hdl

Plating-class hurdler; acts on fast ground.

Ask For Luck (IRE)
83   86
6-y-o b g Camden Town-French Thistle (Kemal (FR))
J G Portman Anthony Boswood

Placings:00B3   (3901)
2002/03: 16^0S, 20^0HY, 16^BG, 24^3S,

	Starts	1st	2nd	3rd	Win & Pl
NH Flat	1	0	0	0	0
Hurdles	3	0	0	1	811
Career Total	4	0	0	1	811

Going: Sf: 0-3 GS: 0-0 Gd: 0-1 GF: - Fm: 0-0
Distance: 2m2m3: 0-2 2m4-2m7: 0-1 3m+: 0-1
Track: LH: 0-4 RH: 0-0 Tight: 0-0 Gall: 0-2
Aids: Bl: 0-0 Vi: 0-0 Tstrap: 0-0
Best Rating: 94 12/02 Wwck 2m soft NHF

Modest novice hurdler; stays three miles.

Ask Henry (IRE)
104   130
7-y-o b/br g Jolly Jake (NZ)-Pineway Vii (Damsire Unregistered)
P F Nicholls Mrs Marianne G Barber

Placings:22120P   (4613)
2002/03: 22^2GS, 21^2GS, 26^1HY, 24^2G, 32^0G, 25^PG,

	Starts	1st	2nd	3rd	Win & Pl
Chases	6	1	3	0	10072
Career Total	6	1	3	0	10072
123 1/03 Chep 3m2f110y	E Ch			HVY	£4173

Total win prize-money £4173

Going: Sf: 1-1 GS: 0-2 Gd: 0-3 GF: - Fm: 0-0
Distance: 2m2m3: 0-0 2m4-2m7: 0-0 3m+: 1-4
Track: LH: 1-5 RH: 0-1 Tight: 0-0 Gall: 0-4
Aids: Bl: 0-0 Vi: 0-0 Tstrap: 0-0
Best Rating: 130 2/03 Newb 3m good Ch

Very useful novice chaser; half-brother to Valley Henry; stays 3m 2f; acts on testing ground.

Ask Mary

6-y-o b m Endoli (USA)-Gold Nite (Nesselrode (USA))
O O Neill Ivor Potter

Placings:0040   (4733)
2002/03: 16^0S, 16^0G, 16^4GF, 16^0GF,

	Starts	1st	2nd	3rd	Win & Pl
NH Flat	3	0	0	0	0
Hurdles	1	0	0	0	0
Career Total	4	0	0	0	0

Going: Sf: 0-1 GS: 0-0 Gd: 0-0 GF: - Fm: 0-2
Distance: 2m2m3: 0-4 2m4-2m7: 0-0 3m+: 0-0
Track: LH: 0-1 RH: 0-3 Tight: 0-0 Gall: 0-0
Aids: Bl: 0-0 Vi: 0-0 Tstrap: 0-0
Best Rating: 65 3/03 Ludl 2m gd-fm NHF

Ask Me What (IRE)
97   98
6-y-o b m Shernazar-Laffan s Bridge (IRE) (Mandalus)
Miss Venetia Williams The Turf Club

Placings:4-143120   (4326)
2002/03: 17^1HY, 17^4S, 20^3HY, 17^1S, 21^2S, 21^0G,

	Starts	1st	2nd	3rd	Win & Pl
NH Flat	2	1	0	0	1918
Hurdles	4	1	1	1	5044
Career Total	7	2	1	1	7647
98 3/03 Bang 2m1f	E Hdl			SFT	£3432
102 12/02 Folk 2m1f110y	H NHF			HVY	£1918

Total win prize-money £5350

Going: Sf: 2-5 GS: 0-0 Gd: 0-1 GF: - Fm: 0-0
Distance: 2m2m3: 2-3 2m4-2m7: 0-3 3m+: 0-1
Track: LH: 1-4 RH: 1-1 Tight: 2-3 Gall: 0-1
Aids: Bl: 0-0 Vi: 0-0 Tstrap: 0-0
Best Rating: 102 1/03 Tntn 2m1f soft NHF

Fair novice hurdler; comfortable winner at Bangor in March 2003; effective at two miles but stays further; acts on soft ground.

Ask The Natives (IRE)
99   (124h)131+
9-y-o br g Be My Native (USA)-Ask The Lady (Over The River (FR))
P F Nicholls Paul K Barber

Placings:21/11/FF4B3/P5-1325   (3283)
2002/03: 22^1GS, 20^3GS, 24^2S, 21^5GS,

	Starts	1st	2nd	3rd	Win & Pl
Chases	4	1	1	1	17672
Career Total	15	4	2	2	33517
118 11/02 Font 2m6f	E Ch			G-S	£4062
126 12/99 Chel 2m1f	C Hdl			GD	£5459
126 11/99 Extr 2m3f	D Hdl			G-S	£3522
109 3/99 Winc 2m	H NHF			GD	£1682

Total win prize-money £14727

Going: Sf: 0-1 GS: 1-3 Gd: 0-0 GF: - Fm: 0-0
Distance: 2m2m3: 0-0 2m4-2m7: 1-3 3m+: 0-1
Track: LH: 0-2 RH: 0-1 Tight: 1-1 Gall: 0-2
Aids: Bl: 0-0 Vi: 0-0 Tstrap: 0-0
Best Rating: 131 12/02 Kemp 3m soft Ch

Useful novice chaser; made an unfortunate start to his chasing career, taking two heavy falls in November 2000; third in a valuable handicap hurdle at Aintree in April 2001, but off the track after October that year; scored on his reappearance over a year later over two miles six on good to soft ground; fair efforts since; stays three miles; acts on good to soft ground.

Asking

97   88

11-y-o b g Skyliner-Ma Famille (Welsh Saint)
M Bradstock Miss J C Blackwell

Placings:34613/02/520/5P/243F0/3240/20164-0024200
(4004)
2002/03: 20⁰G, 17⁰GS, 22²GS, 19⁴S, 24²S, 22⁰HY, 22⁰S,

	Starts	1st	2nd	3rd	Win & Pl
Hurdles	7	0	2	0	1212
Career Total	33	2	7	4	11575
95 12/01 MRas	2m3f110yG(0-95)HHdl		SFT		£1575
90 11/95 MRas	2m1f110yD Hdl		G-F		£3134
		Total win prize-money £4709			

Going: Sf: 0-4 GS: 0-2 Gd: 0-1 GF: - Fm: 0-0
Distance: 2m/2m3: 0-1 2m4-2m7: 0-5 3m+: 0-1
Track: LH: 0-2 RH: 0-5 Tight: 0-6 Gall: 0-0
Aids: Bl: 0-0 Vi: 0-2 Tstrap: 0-0
Best Rating: 95 12/01 MRas 2m3f110y soft Hdl

Plating-class hurdler; stays three miles; handles any ground but best on soft; sometimes wears a visor.

Asparagus (IRE)

109(114h)   (115h)127

9-y-o b g Roselier (FR)-Arctic Bead (IRE) (Le Moss)
M Sheppard Simon Gegg

Placings:23FF/F1434211-232331
(4175)
2002/03: 16²S, 17³GS, 16²HY, 19³S, 17³S, 21¹S,

	Starts	1st	2nd	3rd	Win & Pl
Chases	6	1	2	3	17512
Career Total	18	4	4	5	31937
127 3/03 Uttx	2m5f	C(0-135)HCh		SFT	£9399
115 3/02 Uttx	2m	F(0-100)HCh		HVY	£3445
110 3/02 Chep	2m110y	F(0-95)HCh		SFT	£2989
115 11/01 Uttx	2m	E Hdl		HVY	£2730
		Total win prize-money £18563			

Going: Sf: 1-5 GS: 0-1 Gd: 0-0 GF: - Fm: 0-0
Distance: 2m/2m3: 0-5 2m4-2m7: 1-1 3m+: 0-0
Track: LH: 1-5 RH: 0-1 Tight: 0-1 Gall: 0-2
Aids: Bl: 0-0 Vi: 0-0 Tstrap: 1-6
Best Rating: 127 3/03 Uttx 2m5f soft Ch

Useful chaser; loves the mud; usually wears a tongue tie; effective at up to two miles five.

Assured Movements (USA)

107   84

7-y-o b g Northern Flagship (USA)-Love At Dawn (USA) (Grey Dawn Ii)
Mrs D A Hamer Twelly Davies

Placings:623F02/4035/0312-4
(0246)
2002/03: 16²GS, 22⁴G,

	Starts	1st	2nd	3rd	Win & Pl
Hurdles	2	0	1	0	735
Career Total	15	1	3	3	6677
91 4/02 Chep	2m110y E Hdl		G-F		£2856
		Total win prize-money £2856			

Going: Sf: 0-0 GS: 0-1 Gd: 0-1 GF: - Fm: 0-0
Distance: 2m/2m3: 0-1 2m4-2m7: 0-1 3m+: 0-0
Track: LH: 0-0 RH: 0-2 Tight: 0-0 Gall: 0-0
Aids: Bl: 0-0 Vi: 0-0 Tstrap: 0-2
Best Rating: 95 5/02 Extr 2m6f110y good Hdl

Modest hurdler; suited by two miles; acts on fast and soft ground.

Assured Physique

86   74

6-y-o b g Salse (USA)-Metaphysique (FR) (Law Society (USA))
R J Baker Graham Brown

Placings:0045-65006
(4597)
2002/03: 16⁶GF, 17⁵S, 20⁰GF, 16⁰GF, 17⁶GF,

	Starts	1st	2nd	3rd	Win & Pl
Hurdles	5	0	0	0	0
Career Total	9	0	0	0	0

Going: Sf: 0-1 GS: 0-0 Gd: 0-0 GF: - Fm: 0-4
Distance: 2m/2m3: 0-4 2m4-2m7: 0-1 3m+: 0-0
Track: LH: 0-2 RH: 0-3 Tight: 0-1 Gall: 0-0
Aids: Bl: 0-4 Vi: 0-0 Tstrap: 0-0
Best Rating: 81 4/02 Extr 2m1f firm Hdl

Modest performer on Flat and over hurdles.

Asta La Vista (GER)

88   89+

5-y-o b h Nebos (GER)-Aminata (GER) (Local Suitor (USA))
C Von Der Recke H Bartelt & W Molitor

Placings:5
(3101)
2002/03: 16⁵S,

	Starts	1st	2nd	3rd	Win & Pl
Hurdles	1	0	0	0	0
Career Total	1	0	0	0	0

Going: Sf: 0-1 GS: 0-0 Gd: 0-0 GF: - Fm: 0-0
Distance: 2m/2m3: 0-1 2m4-2m7: 0-0 3m+: 0-0
Track: LH: 0-1 RH: 0-0 Tight: 0-1 Gall: 0-0
Aids: Bl: 0-0 Vi: 0-0 Tstrap: 0-0
Best Rating: 89 1/03 Plum 2m soft Hdl

Astafort (FR)

100   82

4-y-o ch g Kendor (FR)-Tres Chic (USA) (Northern Fashion (USA))
A C Whillans Mrs Murray Scott

Placings:043025U
(4033)
2002/03: 16⁰G, 16⁴S, 16³S, 16⁶S, 20²HY, 17⁵GS, 16⁰S,

	Starts	1st	2nd	3rd	Win & Pl
Hurdles	7	0	1	1	1440
Career Total	7	0	1	1	1440

Going: Sf: 0-5 GS: 0-1 Gd: 0-1 GF: - Fm: 0-0
Distance: 2m/2m3: 0-6 2m4-2m7: 0-1 3m+: 0-0
Track: LH: 0-6 RH: 0-1 Tight: 0-0 Gall: 0-0
Aids: Bl: 0-0 Vi: 0-0 Tstrap: 0-0
Best Rating: 86 1/03 Ayr 2m soft Hdl

Plating-class; fair efforts over hurdles in ordinary company, looking likely to appreciate a longer trip; effective at two miles though; acts on good ground.

Aston Mara

102   103

6-y-o b g Bering-Coigach (Niniski (USA))
M A Buckley Mrs D J Buckley

Placings:42003/0144230624-504036
(2180)
2002/03: 20⁵GS, 20⁰G, 20⁴GF, 24⁰GF, 23³HY, 20⁶GS,

	Starts	1st	2nd	3rd	Win & Pl
Hurdles	6	0	0	1	633

Career Total	21	1	3	3	7583
101 6/01 Prth	2m4f110y		E Hdl		FRM
£2961					
		Total win prize-money £2961			

Going: Sf: 0-1 GS: 0-2 Gd: 0-1 GF: - Fm: 0-2
Distance: 2m/2m3: 0-0 2m4-2m7: 0-5 3m+: 0-1
Track: LH: 0-4 RH: 0-2 Tight: 0-2 Gall: 0-1
Aids: Bl: 0-0 Vi: 0-0 Tstrap: 0-0
Best Rating: 101 9/01 MRas 2m3f110y soft Hdl

Moderate hurdler; best at around two and a half miles, but stays three; suited by fast ground.

Astormydayiscoming

104   81

5-y-o b g Alhaatmi-Valentine Song (Pas De Seul)
W M Brisbourne Out Of The Frying Pan Partnership

Placings:2442
(1926)
2002/03: 16²GF, 20⁴GS, 22⁴G, 16²GS,

	Starts	1st	2nd	3rd	Win & Pl
Hurdles	4	0	2	0	1613
Career Total	4	0	2	0	1613

Going: Sf: 0-0 GS: 0-2 Gd: 0-1 GF: - Fm: 0-1
Distance: 2m/2m3: 0-2 2m4-2m7: 0-2 3m+: 0-0
Track: LH: 0-3 RH: 0-1 Tight: 0-2 Gall: 0-0
Aids: Bl: 0-0 Vi: 0-0 Tstrap: 0-0
Best Rating: 87 11/02 Ludl 2m gd-sft Hdl

Plating-class hurdler; best at two miles; acts on fast and easy ground; has worncheekpieces.

Astral Prince

(93h)   (62h)58+

5-y-o ch g Efisio-Val D Erica (Ashmore (FR))
A Crook D E Reeves & P W Colley

Placings:006-0460
(1563)
2002/03: 16⁰G, 17⁴G, 17⁶G, 17⁰G,

	Starts	1st	2nd	3rd	Win & Pl
Hurdles	4	0	0	0	0
Career Total	7	0	0	0	0

Going: Sf: 0-0 GS: 0-0 Gd: 0-4 GF: - Fm: 0-0
Distance: 2m/2m3: 0-4 2m4-2m7: 0-0 3m+: 0-0
Track: LH: 0-3 RH: 0-1 Tight: 0-2 Gall: 0-0
Aids: Bl: 0-0 Vi: 0-0 Tstrap: 0-1
Best Rating: 71 4/02 Sedg 2m1f gd-fm Hdl

Astro Lines (IRE)

99(96h)   (63+h)96

9-y-o ch g Classic Secret (USA)-Fado s Delight (Orchestra)
Ferdy Murphy K Lee and I Davies

Placings:F134431/33/14F/46P505-34
(0740)
2002/03: 22³GF, 25⁴G,

	Starts	1st	2nd	3rd	Win & Pl
Hurdles	1	0	0	0	0
Chases	1	0	0	1	543
Career Total	20	3	0	5	11842
95 11/00 Newc	2m4f	E Ch		SFT	£3279
121 3/98 Kels	2m2f	E Hdl		GD	£2318
106 9/97 Fair	2m	Hdl		G-Y	£3051
		Total win prize-money £8650			

Going: Sf: 0-0 GS: 0-0 Gd: 0-1 GF: - Fm: 0-1
Distance: 2m/2m3: 0-0 2m4-2m7: 0-1 3m+: 0-1
Track: LH: 0-1 RH: 0-1 Tight: 0-2 Gall: 0-0

Aids: Bl: 0-0 Vi: 0-0 Tstrap: 0-0
Best Rating: 122 4/99 Kels 2m110y gd-fm Hdl

Modest chaser/hurdler; suited by cut in the ground.

At The Double
46   **76**
7-y-o b g Sure Blade (USA)-Moheli (Ardross)
P Winkworth Adrian Lindsay Smith, Bob Keen

Placings:0/40065-6   **(1747)**
2002/03: 21⁶S,

	Starts	1st	2nd	3rd	Win & Pl
Hurdles	1	0	0	0	0
Career Total	7	0	0	0	0

Going: Sf: 0-1 GS: 0-0 Gd: 0-0 GF: - Fm: 0-0
Distance: 2m/2m3: 0-0 2m4-2m7: 0-1 3m+: 0-0
Track: LH: 0-1 RH: 0-0 Tight: 0-1 Gall: 0-0
Aids: Bl: 0-0 Vi: 0-1 Tstrap: 0-0
Best Rating: 76 4/02 Towc 3m good Hdl

Atalanta Surprise (IRE)
98   **79**
6-y-o ch g Phardante (FR)-Curragh Breeze (Furry Glen)
R H Buckler Martyn Forrester

Placings:003640PP   **(4310)**
2002/03: 18⁰GF, 16⁶S, 18³HY, 18⁶HY, 21⁴S, 20⁰HY, 26⁰S, 24⁰G,

	Starts	1st	2nd	3rd	Win & Pl
NH Flat	3	0	0	1	339
Hurdles	5	0	0	0	369
Career Total	8	0	0	1	708

Going: Sf: 0-6 GS: 0-0 Gd: 0-1 GF: - Fm: 0-1
Distance: 2m/2m3: 0-4 2m4-2m7: 0-2 3m+: 0-2
Track: LH: 0-5 RH: 0-3 Tight: 0-4 Gall: 0-1
Aids: Bl: 0-0 Vi: 0-0 Tstrap: 0-0
Best Rating: 85 12/02 Plum 2m2f heavy NHF

Atalya
100(95h)   (102h)**85**
6-y-o ch g Afzal-Sandy Looks (Music Boy)
S T Lewis (S E H Sherwood 7/2) W E Catstrey

Placings:0024313/23P-40P33   **(4485)**
2002/03: 16⁴S, 17⁰S, 17⁶S, 16³GF, 19³GF,

	Starts	1st	2nd	3rd	Win & Pl
Hurdles	2	0	0	0	0
Chases	3	0	0	2	1477
Career Total	15	1	2	5	7072
88 1/01 Winc 2m		F Hdl		SFT	£2513

Total win prize-money £2513

Going: Sf: 0-3 GS: 0-0 Gd: 0-0 GF: - Fm: 0-2
Distance: 2m/2m3: 0-5 2m4-2m7: 0-0 3m+: 0-0
Track: LH: 0-2 RH: 0-0 Tight: 0-2 Gall: 0-0
Aids: Bl: 0-0 Vi: 0-0 Tstrap: 0-0
Best Rating: 102 5/01 Hntg 2m110y gd-fm Hdl

Plating-class hurdler/chaser; suited by soft ground; handles fast; has been inclined to be let down by his jumping over fences.

Atavistic (IRE)
105   **136**
11-y-o b g Architect (USA)-Saceili (Saher)

P J Hobbs Mrs Jill Emery, Mr A Staple, Mr E Morris

Placings:*0210*/3P13F/12111P/1PF1/35B12PP/22223P0-16P **(3142)**
2002/03: 28¹GS, 29⁶S, 27⁰PS,

	Starts	1st	2nd	3rd	Win & Pl
Chases	3	1	0	0	5729
Career Total	36	10	7	4	71718
134 10/02 Strf	3m4f	D(0-125)HCh	G-S	£5330
136 1/01 Tntn	3m3f	C(0-130)HCh	SFT	£7150
139 1/00 Tntn	3m3f	C(0-130)HCh	G-S	£6955
125 11/99 NAbb	3m2f110yD(0-120)HCh	SFT	£3838
126 2/99 Tntn	3m	D Ch	G-S	£4572
127 2/99 NAbb	3m2f110yE Ch	HVY	£2892
110 1/99 Kemp	3m110y D(0-120)HHdl	SFT	£5503
106 10/98 Font	2m6f110y(0-115)HHdl	GD	£2302
97 1/97 Tntn	2m3f110yE Hdl	GD	£1945
111 3/96 Ayr	2m	H NHF	GD	£1250

Total win prize-money £41739

Going: Sf: 0-2 GS: 1-1 Gd: 0-0 GF: - Fm: 0-0
Distance: 2m/2m3: 0-0 2m4-2m7: 0-0 3m+: 1-3
Track: LH: 1-2 RH: 0-1 Tight: 1-3 Gall: 0-0
Aids: Bl: 0-0 Vi: 0-0 Tstrap: 0-0
Best Rating: 139 1/00 Tntn 3m3f gd-sft Ch

Useful chaser; successful seasonal debut when winning handicap at Stratford October 2002; goes well on sharp tracks, but can make mistakes; goes well fresh, stays three and a half miles plus; acts on soft ground; considered best when conceding weight to inferior rivals.

Athenian Law
104   **105+**
6-y-o br g Darshaan-Titania s Way (Fairy King (USA))
P J Hobbs Richard Green (fine Paintings)

Placings:*11*-3   **(4754)**
2002/03: 16³G,

	Starts	1st	2nd	3rd	Win & Pl
Hurdles	1	0	0	1	1093
Career Total	3	2	0	1	5685
95 11/01 MRas	2m1f110yE Hdl	G-S	£2996
99 10/01 Hrfd	2m1f	H NHF	GD	£1596

Total win prize-money £4592

Going: Sf: 0-0 GS: 0-0 Gd: 0-1 GF: - Fm: 0-0
Distance: 2m/2m3: 0-1 2m4-2m7: 0-0 3m+: 0-0
Track: LH: 0-0 RH: 0-1 Tight: 0-0 Gall: 0-0
Aids: Bl: 0-0 Vi: 0-0 Tstrap: 0-0
Best Rating: 101 4/03 Prth 2m110y good Hdl

Modest hurdler; made winning debut in Hereford bumper October 2001; odds-on when making successful transition to hurdles in weak event at Market Rasen the following month; not seen until third in Perth handicap April 2003; pulled up after losing action at Newton Abbot in May; bounced back when narrowly beaten at Worcester in July; effective at 2m; acts on a sound surface.

Athirty (IRE)
74f   **66f**
6-y-o ch g Denel (FR)-Terrific Temp (Kemal (FR))
C Tizzard Mrs P Tizzard

Placings:*0*-0   **(1855)**
2002/03: 16⁶G,

	Starts	1st	2nd	3rd	Win & Pl
NH Flat	1	0	0	0	
Career Total	2	0	0	0	

Going: Sf: 0-0 GS: 0-0 Gd: 0-1 GF: - Fm: 0-0
Distance: 2m/2m3: 0-1 2m4-2m7: 0-0 3m+: 0-0

Track: LH: 0-0 RH: 0-1 Tight: 0-0 Gall: 0-0
Aids: Bl: 0-0 Vi: 0-0 Tstrap: 0-0
Best Rating: 66 3/02 Winc 2m soft NHF

Athleague Guest (IRE)
101(109h)   (107h)**70**
10-y-o b g Be My Guest (USA)-Santella Bell (Ballad Rock)
A Sadik A Sadik

Placings:4/3162P/060/16FP6332-P03P4F55 **(4271)**
2002/03: 24⁶GS, 20⁰G, 20⁰S, 25⁰G, 19⁴GS, 20⁰GS, 24⁰GS,

	Starts	1st	2nd	3rd	Win & Pl
Chases	8	0	0	1	692
Career Total	25	2	2	4	13999
98 10/01 Uttx	2m4f110yC(0-130)HHdl	G-S	£6500
107 2/98 Naas	2m	Hdl	SFT	£2680

Total win prize-money £9180

Going: Sf: 0-1 GS: 0-4 Gd: 0-3 GF: - Fm: 0-0
Distance: 2m/2m3: 0-0 2m4-2m7: 0-5 3m+: 0-3
Track: LH: 0-7 RH: 0-1 Tight: 0-2 Gall: 0-1
Aids: Bl: 0-1 Vi: 0-0 Tstrap: 0-0
Best Rating: 113 2/98 Naas 2m4f yield Hdl

Plating-class chaser; suited by cut in the ground; stays two and a half miles.

Athnowen (IRE)
111   **95**
11-y-o b g Lord Americo-Lady Bluebird (Arapaho)
J R Payne R J Payne

Placings:PF6510U2344/05365FU/P0P1-2F6322R2 **(4694)**
2002/03: 19⁰G, 25⁰G, 24⁶S, 20⁰S, 16⁰G, 16²S, 19⁰G, 21²G,

	Starts	1st	2nd	3rd	Win & Pl
Chases	8	0	4	1	5523
Career Total	30	2	5	3	14009
84 3/02 NAbb	2m5f110yG(0-95)HCh	GD	£2282
95 1/00 Hrfd	2m	E(0-105)HCh	G-S	£3103

Total win prize-money £5386

Going: Sf: 0-3 GS: 0-0 Gd: 0-5 GF: - Fm: 0-0
Distance: 2m/2m3: 0-2 2m4-2m7: 0-4 3m+: 0-2
Track: LH: 0-2 RH: 0-6 Tight: 0-2 Gall: 0-0
Aids: Bl: 0-0 Vi: 0-0 Tstrap: 0-0
Best Rating: 101 3/00 Tntn 2m3f good Ch

Plating-class chaser; stays two miles six, effective at shorter; acts on most types of ground.

Atlantic Crossing (IRE)
109   **113+**
6-y-o b g Roselier (FR)-Ocean Mist (IRE) (Crash Course)
P Beaumont N W A Bannister

Placings:000-U110   **(3265)**
2002/03: 20⁰S, 20¹HY, 20¹G, 19⁰GS,

	Starts	1st	2nd	3rd	Win & Pl
Hurdles	4	2	0	0	7631
Career Total	7	2	0	0	7631
112 12/02 Hayd	2m4f	D Hdl	GD	£4056
113 11/02 Carl	2m4f	E Hdl	HVY	£3575

Total win prize-money £7631

Going: Sf: 1-2 GS: 0-1 Gd: 1-1 GF: - Fm: 0-0
Distance: 2m/2m3: 0-0 2m4-2m7: 2-4 3m+: 0-0
Track: LH: 1-3 RH: 1-1 Tight: 0-0 Gall: 0-0
Aids: Bl: 0-0 Vi: 0-0 Tstrap: 0-0
Best Rating: 113 11/02 Carl 2m4f heavy Hdl

Modest hurdler; showed his first real sign of form when making all to win a novice hurdle at Carlisle in November 2002; followed up in game fashion over Haydock s brush hurdles; stays two and a half miles; looks to have a future.

Atlantic Drift (IRE)
67

9-y-o b g Commanche Run-Cantafleur (Cantab)
J A Moore J A Moore

Placings:53/6430/U060R0-0   (0186)
2002/03: 24⁰G,

	Starts	1st	2nd	3rd	Win & Pl
Hurdles	1	0	0	0	
Career Total	13	0	0	2	822

Going:	Sf: 0-0 GS: 0-0 Gd: 0-1 GF: - Fm: 0-0
Distance:	2m/2m3: 0-0 2m4-2m7: 0-0 3m+: 0-1
Track:	LH: 0-1 RH: 0-0 Tight: 0-0 Gall: 0-0
Aids:	Bl: 0-0 Vi: 0-0 Tstrap: 0-0
Best Rating:	100 11/99 Chep 2m110y gd-sft NHF

Atlantic Hawk
100f   88f

5-y-o b g Daar Alzamaan (IRE)-Pyewacket (Belfort (FR))
Ferdy Murphy R Sunter

Placings:045   (4560)
2002/03: 16⁰HY, 16⁴GF, 16⁵GD,

	Starts	1st	2nd	3rd	Win & Pl
NH Flat	3	0	0	0	0
Career Total	3	0	0	0	0

Going:	Sf: 0-1 GS: 0-0 Gd: 0-1 GF: - Fm: 0-1
Distance:	2m/2m3: 0-3 2m4-2m7: 0-0 3m+: 0-0
Track:	LH: 0-3 RH: 0-0 Tight: 0-0 Gall: 0-0
Aids:	Bl: 0-0 Vi: 0-0 Tstrap: 0-0
Best Rating:	88 4/03 Ayr 2m good NHF

Bumper performer; has shown promise in three starts; will have to learn to settle better.

Atlantic Lady (GER)
92   89

5-y-o br m Dashing Blade-Atlantic City (GER) (Medicus (GER))
Mrs N S Sharpe (C Von Der Recke 21/12) J Pritchard

Placings:3F2F6P0   (4626)
2002/03: 17³S, 16⁵G, 16²S, 20⁵S, 16⁶S, 19⁵S, 17⁰GF,

	Starts	1st	2nd	3rd	Win & Pl
Hurdles	7	0	1	1	1350
Career Total	7	0	1	1	1350

Going:	Sf: 0-5 GS: 0-0 Gd: 0-1 GF: - Fm: 0-1
Distance:	2m/2m3: 0-5 2m4-2m7: 0-2 3m+: 0-0
Track:	LH: 0-2 RH: 0-1 Tight: 0-1 Gall: 0-0
Aids:	Bl: 0-0 Vi: 0-0 Tstrap: 0-0
Best Rating:	89 12/02 Uttx 2m soft Hdl

Plating-class hurdler; best on soft.

Atlantic Power
101(88h)   (37h)79

10-y-o gr g Golden Lahab (USA)-She Say She Will (Roselier (FR))

W Storey Thistle And Rose Racing

Placings:0300655/531352/210/0PF0-P2P663PP   (3353)
2002/03: 24ᴾGS, 20²GS, 21ᴾG, 21⁶G, 25⁶HY, 24³GS, 25ᴾS, 24ᴾHY,

	Starts	1st	2nd	3rd	Win & Pl
Hurdles	2	0	0	0	0
Chases	6	0	1	1	2972
Career Total	28	2	3	4	10707
101 6/00 Prth	3m110y	F(0-110)HHdl		HVY	£2691
95 2/00 Ayr	2m4f	F(0-95)HHdl		HVY	£2730
			Total win prize-money £5421

Going:	Sf: 0-3 GS: 0-3 Gd: 0-2 GF: - Fm: 0-0
Distance:	2m/2m3: 0-0 2m4-2m7: 0-3 3m+: 0-5
Track:	LH: 0-6 RH: 0-2 Tight: 0-3 Gall: 0-2
Aids:	Bl: 0-0 Vi: 0-0 Tstrap: 0-0
Best Rating:	101 6/00 Prth 3m110y heavy Hdl

Plating-class maiden chaser; stays well.

Atlantic Prince (IRE)
73   55

7-y-o b g Fairy King (USA)-Idle Chat (USA) (Assert)
Mrs K M Lamb Mrs K M Lamb

Placings:00/P0/06006P00U-0   (0373)
2002/03: 18⁰G,

	Starts	1st	2nd	3rd	Win & Pl
Hurdles	1	0	0	0	
Career Total	14	0	0	0	0

Going:	Sf: 0-0 GS: 0-0 Gd: 0-1 GF: - Fm: 0-0
Distance:	2m/2m3: 0-1 2m4-2m7: 0-0 3m+: 0-0
Track:	LH: 0-1 RH: 0-0 Tight: 0-1 Gall: 0-0
Aids:	Bl: 0-0 Vi: 0-0 Tstrap: 0-0
Best Rating:	55 9/01 Sedg 2m1f gd-fm Hdl

Atlantic Rhapsody (FR)
(108h)   (132h)66

6-y-o b g Machiavellian (USA)-First Waltz (FR) (Green Dancer (USA))
T M Walsh Atlantic Racing Ltd

Placings:311663-50054   (4741a)
2002/03: 18⁵S, 16⁰HY, 16⁹G, 16⁵HY, 16⁴G,

	Starts	1st	2nd	3rd	Win & Pl
Hurdles	5	0	0	0	438
Career Total	11	2	0	2	20200
123 1/02 Naas	2m	Hdl		SH	£7975
106 1/02 Punc	2m	Hdl		Y-S	£5503
			Total win prize-money £13478

Going:	Sf: 0-3 GS: 0-0 Gd: 0-2 GF: - Fm: 0-0
Distance:	2m/2m3: 0-5 2m4-2m7: 0-0 3m+: 0-0
Track:	LH: 0-3 RH: 0-2 Tight: 0-0 Gall: 0-1
Aids:	Bl: 0-0 Vi: 0-0 Tstrap: 0-0
Best Rating:	132 4/02 Fair 2m yield Hdl

Useful hurdler; effective over two miles; he acts on a soft surface.

Atlanticus (IRE)
97(93h)   (102h)84

7-y-o b g King s Lake (USA)-Amazonia (GER) (Alpenkonig (GER))
C Grant (B J Curley 9/10) Paul & Anne Sellars

Placings:06004350-14   (3163)
2002/03: 20¹G, 19⁴G,

	Starts	1st	2nd	3rd	Win & Pl
Hurdles	1	1	0	0	2216
Chases	1	0	0	0	527
Career Total	10	1	0	1	3831
84 10/02 Fknm	2m4f	G Hdl		GD	£2215
			Total win prize-money £2216

Going:	Sf: 0-0 GS: 0-0 Gd: 1-2 GF: - Fm: 0-0
Distance:	2m/2m3: 0-1 2m4-2m7: 1-1 3m+: 0-0
Track:	LH: 1-2 RH: 0-0 Tight: 1-2 Gall: 0-0
Aids:	Bl: 0-0 Vi: 0-0 Tstrap: 0-0
Best Rating:	102 12/01 Leop 2m yield Hdl

Plating-class hurdler; had spells in Germany and Ireland before winning a selling hurdle at Fakenham in October on his first start for Barney Curley; changed stables and little impact on chasing bow.

Atlastaboy (IRE)
103   108

7-y-o b g Phardante (FR)-Corcaigh (Town And Country)
T R George Timothy N Chick

Placings:33561   (3744)
2002/03: 16³S, 20³S, 22⁵HY, 24⁶S, 26¹G,

	Starts	1st	2nd	3rd	Win & Pl
NH Flat	1	0	0	1	351
Hurdles	4	1	0	1	5581
Career Total	5	1	0	2	5932
108 2/03 Hntg	3m2f	D(0-115)HHdl		GD	£4979
			Total win prize-money £4979

Going:	Sf: 0-4 GS: 0-0 Gd: 1-1 GF: - Fm: 0-0
Distance:	2m/2m3: 0-1 2m4-2m7: 0-2 3m+: 1-2
Track:	LH: 0-1 RH: 1-4 Tight: 0-2 Gall: 1-1
Aids:	Bl: 0-0 Vi: 0-0 Tstrap: 0-0
Best Rating:	108 2/03 Hntg 3m2f good Hdl

Modest hurdler; goes well on good ground; stays very well.

Atomic Breeze (IRE)
105   78

9-y-o b/br g Strong Gale-Atomic Lady (Over The River (FR))
D M Forster D M Forster

Placings:0P/0P/0P3P-F45PP423P51   (4662)
2002/03: 24ᴾG, 20ᶠGF, 22⁴G, 16⁵GF, 20ᴾGS, 26ᴾGF, 27⁴G, 28²GF, 27³G, 20⁵GF, 26¹GF,

	Starts	1st	2nd	3rd	Win & Pl
Chases	12	1	1	1	8253
Career Total	19	1	1	2	8851
78 4/03 Carl	3m2f	F(0-95)HCh		G-F	£5954
			Total win prize-money £5954

Going:	Sf: 0-0 GS: 0-1 Gd: 0-5 GF: - Fm: 1-6
Distance:	2m/2m3: 0-1 2m4-2m7: 0-4 3m+: 1-7
Track:	LH: 0-8 RH: 1-4 Tight: 0-5 Gall: 0-1
Aids:	Bl: 0-0 Vi: 0-0 Tstrap: 0-0
Best Rating:	88 4/02 Sedg 2m5f gd-fm Ch

Plating-class staying chaser, ran quite well in the autumn of 2002; got off the mark at Carlisle in April 2003; stays three miles-three; acts on a sound surface.

Attack
86   88+

7-y-o gr g Sabrehill (USA)-Butsova (Formidable (USA))
Mrs A L M King (Mrs John Harrington 16/11) Aiden Murphy

Placings:0010   (1967)

2002/03: 16⁰GF, 16⁰GY, 16¹GF, 16⁰GS,

	Starts	1st	2nd	3rd	Win & Pl
NH Flat	1	0	0	0	0
Hurdles	3	1	0	0	6350
Career Total	4	1	0	0	6350
88	10/02 Limk	2m	Hdl	G-F	£6349

Total win prize-money £6350

Going:	Sf: 0-0 GS: 0-1 Gd: 0-0 GF: - Fm: 1-2
Distance:	2m/2m3: 1-4 2m4-2m7: 0-0 3m+: 0-0
Track:	LH: 0-1 RH: 0-0 Tight: 0-0 Gall: 0-0
Aids:	Bl: 0-0 Vi: 0-0 Tstrap: 1-3
Best Rating:	88 10/02 Limk 2m gd-fm Hdl

Plating-class ex-Irish novice hurdler; made all at Limerick in October 2002; has been running on the All-Weather over here.

Atticus Finch (IRE)
98(93h)   (91h)**88**

6-y-o b g Witness Box (USA)-Dramatic Loop (IRE) (Balinger)
Mrs M Stirk Mrs M Stirk

Placings:3544P31UF   (4783)
2002/03: 20³GF, 16⁵G, 20⁴S, 16⁴G, 25⁵G, 20³S, 16¹GF, 17⁰G, 17⁵G,

	Starts	1st	2nd	3rd	Win & Pl
Hurdles	3	0	0	0	295
Chases	6	1	0	2	5934
Career Total	9	1	0	2	6229
88	3/03 Weth	2m	E(0-105)HCh	G-F	£4017

Total win prize-money £4017

Going:	Sf: 0-2 GS: 0-0 Gd: 0-5 GF: - Fm: 1-2
Distance:	2m/2m3: 1-5 2m4-2m7: 0-3 3m+: 0-1
Track:	LH: 1-7 RH: 0-2 Tight: 0-5 Gall: 0-0
Aids:	Bl: 0-0 Vi: 0-0 Tstrap: 0-0
Best Rating:	91 10/02 Hayd 2m good Hdl

Moderate chaser; winning pointer; back over two miles when winning at Wetherby in March; stays two and a half miles; keen sort; chancy jumper; took an intermediate hurdle over mini-fences at Southwell in May.

Atum Re (IRE)
98(107h)   (117+h)**110**

6-y-o br g Be My Native (USA)-Collopy s Cross (Pragmatic)
P R Webber Paul Green

Placings:10-P165   (4412)
2002/03: 16ᴾS, 16¹GS, 18⁶GS, 17⁵G,

	Starts	1st	2nd	3rd	Win & Pl
Hurdles	4	1	0	0	6138
Career Total	6	2	0	0	7741
117	2/03 Winc	2m	D Hdl	G-S	£5687
108	12/01 Ludl	2m	H NHF	GD	£1603

Total win prize-money £7291

Going:	Sf: 0-1 GS: 1-2 Gd: 0-1 GF: - Fm: 0-0
Distance:	2m/2m3: 1-4 2m4-2m7: 0-0 3m+: 0-0
Track:	LH: 0-1 RH: 1-3 Tight: 0-2 Gall: 0-0
Aids:	Bl: 0-0 Vi: 0-0 Tstrap: 0-0
Best Rating:	117 2/03 Winc 2m gd-sft Hdl

Fair novice hurdler; best over two miles; acts on good and good to soft ground.

Auburn Spirit
109   (69h)**91**

8-y-o ch g Teamster-Spirit Of Youth (Kind Of Hush)
M D I Usher (G Brown 18/12) G A Summers

Placings:04/5000/514306/6031463-FP2621   (4702)
2002/03: 24ᶠGS, 26ᴾS, 26²S, 26⁶GS, 24⁴HY, 26¹GF,

	Starts	1st	2nd	3rd	Win & Pl
Chases	6	1	2	0	5276
Career Total	25	3	2	3	12407
91	4/03 Plum	3m2f	F(0-90)HCh	G-F	£3360
91	2/02 Hrfd	2m3f	E(0-105)HCh	HVY	£3237
68	11/00 Winc	2m6f	F(0-100)HHdl	SFT	£2639

Total win prize-money £9236

Going:	Sf: 0-3 GS: 0-2 Gd: 0-0 GF: - Fm: 1-1
Distance:	2m/2m3: 0-0 2m4-2m7: 0-0 3m+: 1-6
Track:	LH: 1-3 RH: 0-2 Tight: 1-5 Gall: 0-0
Aids:	Bl: 0-0 Vi: 0-0 Tstrap: 0-0
Best Rating:	91 4/03 Plum 3m2f gd-fm Ch

Moderate chaser; stays three and a quarter miles; acts on most ground.

Auchonvillers
77   **68+**

6-y-o b g Deploy-Forbearance (Bairn (USA))
Mrs H Dalton (B A McMahon 1/5) Major W R Paton-Smith And Partners

Placings:45   (1236)
2002/03: 16⁴GF, 20⁵G,

	Starts	1st	2nd	3rd	Win & Pl
Hurdles	2	0	0	0	277
Career Total	2	0	0	0	277

Going:	Sf: 0-0 GS: 0-0 Gd: 0-1 GF: - Fm: 0-1
Distance:	2m/2m3: 0-1 2m4-2m7: 0-1 3m+: 0-0
Track:	LH: 0-2 RH: 0-0 Tight: 0-0 Gall: 0-0
Aids:	Bl: 0-0 Vi: 0-0 Tstrap: 0-0
Best Rating:	68 7/02 Worc 2m gd-fm Hdl

Audacter (IRE)
111   **125**

10-y-o b g Strong Gale-Sue s A Lady (Le Moss)
L Wells Mrs Carrie Zetter-Wells

Placings:20/430/1223/1543/321-31126PF   (2552)
2002/03: 25³GS, 22¹GF, 22¹G, 24²GF, 24⁶GS, 20⁶GS, 21ᶠS,

	Starts	1st	2nd	3rd	Win & Pl
Chases	7	2	1	1	16310
Career Total	23	5	5	5	54304
125	10/02 Font	2m6f	D(0-120)HCh	GD	£4842
117	8/02 Font	2m6f	E(0-110)HCh	G-F	£4114
110	10/01 Extr	2m7f110yD Ch		G-S	£4192
150	5/00 Hayd	2m7f110yB Hdl		GD	£7085
117	1/00 Kemp	2m5f	C(0-130)HHdl	GD	£7052

Total win prize-money £27289

Going:	Sf: 0-1 GS: 0-3 Gd: 1-1 GF: - Fm: 1-2
Distance:	2m/2m3: 0-0 2m4-2m7: 2-4 3m+: 0-3
Track:	LH: 0-1 RH: 0-4 Tight: 2-4 Gall: 0-1
Aids:	Bl: 0-0 Vi: 0-0 Tstrap: 0-0
Best Rating:	150 5/00 Hayd 2m7f110y good Hdl

Useful chaser; one-time very useful staying hurdler; relatively lightly raced over fences; has improvement in him; effective on fast ground; stays three miles.

Audiostreetdotcom
110   **98**

6-y-o ch g Risk Me (FR)-Ballagarrow Girl (North Stoke)
G B Balding Audiostreetdotcom Partnership

Placings:426/0U34236441-4603015306326   (4563)
2002/03: 20⁴G, 22⁶S, 21⁰G, 22³G, 20⁵S, 19¹HY, 21⁵S, 21³HY,

20⁰HY, 21⁶HY, 22³S, 21²S, 24⁶GF,

	Starts	1st	2nd	3rd	Win & Pl
Hurdles	13	1	1	3	6691
Career Total	26	2	3	5	13572
98	12/02 Newb	2m3f	E(0-110)HHdl	HVY	£3150
98	3/02 NAbb	2m6f	E(0-105)HHdl	GD	£3136

Total win prize-money £6286

Going:	Sf: 1-9 GS: 0-0 Gd: 0-3 GF: - Fm: 0-1
Distance:	2m/2m3: 1-1 2m4-2m7: 0-11 3m+: 0-1
Track:	LH: 1-13 RH: 0-0 Tight: 0-7 Gall: 1-2
Aids:	Bl: 0-0 Vi: 0-0 Tstrap: 0-0
Best Rating:	105 1/01 Wwck 2m soft Hdl

Moderate hurdler; has ability but also a few quirks; suited by soft ground; stays two miles-six; wears sheepskin cheek-pieces.

Auditty (IRE)
100   **108**

10-y-o b g Montelimar (USA)-Tax Code (Workboy)
W Jenks (A L T Moore 11/10) Michael Stoddart

Placings:060/0605F/F410150/P1521565/2310121U0P-24334504   (4398)
2002/03: 16²G, 20⁴GF, 16³G, 17³GF, 16⁴S, 20⁵GS, 20⁰S, 16⁴GF,

	Starts	1st	2nd	3rd	Win & Pl
Chases	8	0	1	2	5202
Career Total	41	7	4	3	46946
121	9/01 List	2m	(0-130)HCh	G-F	£7790
121	8/01 Tram	2m	(0-109)HCh	GD	£7233
108	6/01 Tram	2m	(0-123)HCh	FRM	£6399
109	8/00 Tram	2m4f	(0-109)HCh	G-F	£5520
85	6/00 Dund	2m1f	(0-102)HCh	G-Y	£4140
92	10/99 Navn	2m1f	(0-102)HCh	GD	£3388
82	9/99 Dund	2m3f	(0-102)HCh	FRM	£2464

Total win prize-money £36935

Going:	Sf: 0-2 GS: 0-1 Gd: 0-2 GF: - Fm: 0-3
Distance:	2m/2m3: 0-5 2m4-2m7: 0-3 3m+: 0-0
Track:	LH: 0-1 RH: 0-2 Tight: 0-1 Gall: 0-0
Aids:	Bl: 0-0 Vi: 0-0 Tstrap: 0-0
Best Rating:	121 7/02 Tipp 2m4f gd-fm Ch

Moderate former Irish chaser; loves fast ground; effective at up to two and a half miles.

Augathella
82f   **73f**

6-y-o b g Out Of Hand-Choral Work (Song)
W S Kittow Mrs S Kittow

Placings:40   (1606)
2002/03: 17⁴G, 16⁰G,

	Starts	1st	2nd	3rd	Win & Pl
NH Flat	2	0	0	0	0
Career Total	2	0	0	0	0

Going:	Sf: 0-0 GS: 0-0 Gd: 0-2 GF: - Fm: 0-0
Distance:	2m/2m3: 0-2 2m4-2m7: 0-0 3m+: 0-0
Track:	LH: 0-2 RH: 0-0 Tight: 0-1 Gall: 0-0
Aids:	Bl: 0-0 Vi: 0-0 Tstrap: 0-0
Best Rating:	73 9/02 NAbb 2m1f good NHF

Augustus Macrae
86f   **81f**

6-y-o b g Theatrical Charmer-More Wise (Ballymore)
Mrs L Richards Jonathan Knight

Placings:0   (0149)
2002/03: 16⁰GF,

	Starts	1st	2nd	3rd	Win & Pl
NH Flat	1	0	0	0	
Career Total	1	0	0	0	

Going: Sf: 0-0 GS: 0-0 Gd: 0-0 GF: - Fm: 0-1
Distance: 2m/2m3: 0-1 2m4-2m7: 0-0 3m+: 0-0
Track: LH: 0-1 RH: 0-0 Tight: 0-0 Gall: 0-0
Aids: Bl: 0-0 Vi: 0-0 Tstrap: 0-0
Best Rating: 81 5/02 Chep 2m110y gd-fm NHF

Auk

95   64

8-y-o ch g Absalom-Lady Stock (Crofter (USA))
Mrs P Robeson Mrs P Robeson

Placings: 0P/0P0613F0-6054P40   (4116)
2002/03: 16⁶HY, 17⁰S, 16⁵S, 17⁴GS, 16⁶HY, 16⁴GS, 21⁰G,

	Starts	1st	2nd	3rd	Win & Pl
Hurdles	7	0	0	0	0
Career Total	17	1	0	1	2365

72 1/02 Leic 2m   G(0-90)HHdl   SFT £1939
Total win prize-money £1939

Going: Sf: 0-4 GS: 0-2 Gd: 0-1 GF: - Fm: 0-0
Distance: 2m/2m3: 0-6 2m4-2m7: 0-1 3m+: 0-0
Track: LH: 0-3 RH: 0-4 Tight: 0-1 Gall: 0-1
Aids: Bl: 0-0 Vi: 0-0 Tstrap: 0-0
Best Rating: 72 1/02 Towc 2m   heavy Hdl

Plating-class hurdler; free-running; handles testing ground; effective over two miles.

Auld Nick (IRE)

85f   85f

5-y-o b g Old Vic-Grey Tor (Ahonoora)
M C Pipe Sean Lucey

Placings: 0   (2378)
2002/03: 16⁰S,

	Starts	1st	2nd	3rd	Win & Pl
NH Flat	1	0	0	0	
Career Total	1	0	0	0	

Going: Sf: 0-1 GS: 0-0 Gd: 0-0 GF: - Fm: 0-0
Distance: 2m/2m3: 0-1 2m4-2m7: 0-0 3m+: 0-0
Track: LH: 0-1 RH: 0-0 Tight: 0-0 Gall: 0-0
Aids: Bl: 0-0 Vi: 0-0 Tstrap: 0-0
Best Rating: 85 12/02 Wwck 2m   soft NHF

Auld Thynes Sake (IRE)

98f   102f

6-y-o b g Good Thyne (USA)-La Fairy (IRE) (Lafontaine (USA))
Mrs Merrita Jones Speed 2911 Ltd

Placings: 430   (4329)
2002/03: 17⁴G, 16³G, 16⁰G,

	Starts	1st	2nd	3rd	Win & Pl
NH Flat	3	0	0	1	635
Career Total	3	0	0	1	635

Going: Sf: 0-0 GS: 0-0 Gd: 0-3 GF: - Fm: 0-0
Distance: 2m/2m3: 0-3 2m4-2m7: 0-0 3m+: 0-0
Track: LH: 0-2 RH: 0-1 Tight: 0-0 Gall: 0-1
Aids: Bl: 0-0 Vi: 0-0 Tstrap: 0-0
Best Rating: 102 10/02 Chel 2m110y good NHF

Promising efforts in bumpers.

Aunt Elsie (IRE)

93   84

6-y-o b m Norwich-Shayista (Tap On Wood)
E Sheehy (V Bowens 17/8) A P Brady

Placings: 0/00021-33P5P   (2265)
2002/03: 18³GF, 16⁵S, 16PYS, 16⁶GF, 16PHY,

	Starts	1st	2nd	3rd	Win & Pl
Hurdles	5	0	0	2	945
Career Total	11	1	1	2	5328

97 3/02 Tram 2m   NHF   SH £3598
Total win prize-money £3598

Going: Sf: 0-2 GS: 0-0 Gd: 0-0 GF: - Fm: 0-2
Distance: 2m/2m3: 0-5 2m4-2m7: 0-0 3m+: 0-0
Track: LH: 0-1 RH: 0-2 Tight: 0-1 Gall: 0-0
Aids: Bl: 0-0 Vi: 0-0 Tstrap: 0-1
Best Rating: 97 3/02 Tram 2m   sft-hvy NHF

Aunt Hilda

96   73

4-y-o b f Distant Relative-Aloha Jane (USA) (Hawaii)
M F Harris (J L Dunlop 3/8) Mrs Susan Keable

Placings: 503330PP   (3236)
2002/03: 17⁵G, 17⁰GF, 17³GF, 17³F, 16³GS, 16⁹GS, 17PS, 16PS,

	Starts	1st	2nd	3rd	Win & Pl
Hurdles	8	0	0	3	1319
Career Total	8	0	0	3	1319

Going: Sf: 0-2 GS: 0-2 Gd: 0-1 GF: - Fm: 0-3
Distance: 2m/2m3: 0-8 2m4-2m7: 0-0 3m+: 0-0
Track: LH: 0-2 RH: 0-6 Tight: 0-5 Gall: 0-1
Aids: Bl: 0-5 Vi: 0-1 Tstrap: 0-0
Best Rating: 80 11/02 Hntg 2m110y gd-sft Hdl

Plating-class hurdler; placed in low-grade juvenile hurdles and beaten in sellers.

Auntie Bob

57f

5-y-o b m Overbury (IRE)-Kadari (Commanche Run)
W Clay G A Greaves

Placings: 5-00   (0560)
2002/03: 16⁰G, 17⁰GF,

	Starts	1st	2nd	3rd	Win & Pl
NH Flat	2	0	0	0	
Career Total	3	0	0	0	0

Going: Sf: 0-0 GS: 0-0 Gd: 0-1 GF: - Fm: 0-1
Distance: 2m/2m3: 0-2 2m4-2m7: 0-0 3m+: 0-0
Track: LH: 0-1 RH: 0-1 Tight: 0-0 Gall: 0-0
Aids: Bl: 0-0 Vi: 0-0 Tstrap: 0-0
Best Rating:

Aussi Don (IRE)

7-y-o ch g Accordion-Maryland Flagship (Persian Bold)
P F Nicholls (V Bowens 10/9) A P Brady

Placings: 00/0B   (3141)
2002/03: 16⁰HY, 17⁸S,

	Starts	1st	2nd	3rd	Win & Pl
NH Flat	1	0	0	0	0

Hurdles	1	0	0	0	0
Career Total	4	0	0	0	

Going: Sf: 0-2 GS: 0-0 Gd: 0-0 GF: - Fm: 0-0
Distance: 2m/2m3: 0-2 2m4-2m7: 0-0 3m+: 0-0
Track: LH: 0-0 RH: 0-1 Tight: 0-1 Gall: 0-0
Aids: Bl: 0-0 Vi: 0-0 Tstrap: 0-0
Best Rating: 84 3/00 Bang 2m1f   good NHF

Autcaesar Autnihil (IRE)

93(82h)   (82h)70

8-y-o b g Supreme Leader-Monagey (Pimpernel s Tune)
A G Juckes (Noel T Chance 22/5) Whistlejacket Partnership

Placings: 000-6P4F   (4321)
2002/03: 23⁶G, 24PS, 23⁴S, 24FG,

	Starts	1st	2nd	3rd	Win & Pl
Chases	4	0	0	0	323
Career Total	7	0	0	0	323

Going: Sf: 0-2 GS: 0-0 Gd: 0-2 GF: - Fm: 0-0
Distance: 2m/2m3: 0-0 2m4-2m7: 0-0 3m+: 0-4
Track: LH: 0-2 RH: 0-2 Tight: 0-2 Gall: 0-0
Aids: Bl: 0-0 Vi: 0-0 Tstrap: 0-0
Best Rating: 82 3/02 Newb 2m5f   soft Hdl

Autumn Fantasy (USA)

96   85

4-y-o b c Lear Fan (USA)-Autumn Glory (USA) (Graustark)
B Ellison (J H M Gosden 1/10) Ashley Carr

Placings: 6003   (4406)
2002/03: 16⁶GS, 16⁰GS, 16⁹G, 20³G,

	Starts	1st	2nd	3rd	Win & Pl
Hurdles	4	0	0	1	542
Career Total	4	0	0	1	542

Going: Sf: 0-0 GS: 0-2 Gd: 0-2 GF: - Fm: 0-0
Distance: 2m/2m3: 0-3 2m4-2m7: 0-1 3m+: 0-0
Track: LH: 0-4 RH: 0-0 Tight: 0-0 Gall: 0-0
Aids: Bl: 0-0 Vi: 0-0 Tstrap: 0-0
Best Rating: 86 1/03 Donc 2m110y gd-sft Hdl

Moderate novice hurdler; stays two and a half miles; effective on good ground.

Autumn Rain (USA)

99   97+

6-y-o br g Dynaformer (USA)-Edda (USA) (Ogygian (USA))
D L Williams (N A Callaghan 4/7) Ridgeway Farm Racing

Placings: P063   (2636)
2002/03: 22PGS, 16⁰GS, 21⁶S, 25³S,

	Starts	1st	2nd	3rd	Win & Pl
Hurdles	4	0	0	1	456
Career Total	4	0	0	1	456

Going: Sf: 0-2 GS: 0-2 Gd: 0-0 GF: - Fm: 0-0
Distance: 2m/2m3: 0-1 2m4-2m7: 0-2 3m+: 0-1
Track: LH: 0-3 RH: 0-1 Tight: 0-1 Gall: 0-1
Aids: Bl: 0-0 Vi: 0-0 Tstrap: 0-0
Best Rating: 97 12/02 Wwck 3m1f   soft Hdl

Moderate hurdler; fair handicapper on the Flat; has shown ability over hurdles.

Autumn Stroll (IRE)
96f   102+f
5-y-o ch g Toulon-Bermuda Castle (Carlingford Castle)
C F Swan   Sean Harrington

Placings:*010*   (3160)
2002/03: 16⁰GS, 16¹GF, 16⁰G,

	Starts	1st	2nd	3rd	Win & Pl
NH Flat	3	1	0	0	2968
Career Total	3	1	0	0	2968
102	12/02 Muss	2m		H NHF	G-F £2968

Total win prize-money £2968

Going:	Sf: 0-0 GS: 0-1 Gd: 0-1 GF: - Fm: 1-1
Distance:	2m/2m3: 1-3 2m4-2m7: 0-0 3m+: 0-0
Track:	LH: 0-1 RH: 1-2 Tight: 1-2 Gall: 0-0
Aids:	Bl: 0-0 Vi: 0-0 Tstrap: 0-0
Best Rating:	102 12/02 Muss 2m gd-fm NHF

Moderate bumper performer; got off the mark on his second start in a Musselburgh bumper in December; disappointing on a return there the following month; acts on fast ground.

Avadi (IRE)
85f   72f
5-y-o b g Un Desperado (FR)-Flamewood (Touching Wood (USA))
Mrs H Dalton   Mrs Julie Martin

Placings:*0*   (4628)
2002/03: 17⁰GF,

	Starts	1st	2nd	3rd	Win & Pl
NH Flat	1	0	0	0	
Career Total	1	0	0	0	

Going:	Sf: 0-0 GS: 0-0 Gd: 0-0 GF: - Fm: 0-1
Distance:	2m/2m3: 0-1 2m4-2m7: 0-0 3m+: 0-0
Track:	LH: 0-1 RH: 0-0 Tight: 0-1 Gall: 0-0
Aids:	Bl: 0-0 Vi: 0-0 Tstrap: 0-0
Best Rating:	72 4/03 NAbb 2m1f gd-fm NHF

Avalanche (FR)
112(101h)   (102h)133
6-y-o gr g Highest Honor (FR)-Fairy Gold (Golden Fleece (USA))
J R Best   The Downhill Partnership

Placings:200/U3P-1F120U4   (4792)
2002/03: 20¹S, 21ᶠGS, 20¹GS, 20²G, 22⁰HY, 20ᵁG, 20⁴G,

	Starts	1st	2nd	3rd	Win & Pl
Hurdles	1	0	0	0	
Chases	6	2	1	0	20924
Career Total	13	2	1	0	23600
124	2/03 Kemp	2m4f110yC(0-135)HCh	G-S	£9657
111	1/03 Leic	2m4f110yE Ch	SFT	£4927

Total win prize-money £14584

Going:	Sf: 1-2 GS: 1-2 Gd: 0-3 GF: - Fm: 0-0
Distance:	2m/2m3: 0-0 2m4-2m7: 2-7 3m+: 0-0
Track:	LH: 0-1 RH: 2-6 Tight: 0-1 Gall: 0-0
Aids:	Bl: 0-0 Vi: 0-0 Tstrap: 0-0
Best Rating:	133 2/03 Kemp 2m4f110y good Ch

Fair hurdler/chaser; made a good start over fences at Leicester in January 2003 and won a good handicap at Kempton next time of what looked a lenient mark; stays two and a half miles, acts on soft ground; appears best going right-handed.

Avalon Buck (IRE)
106   102
10-y-o b g Buckskin (FR)-Lilly s Way (Golden Love)
Miss Venetia Williams   Miss Suzannah Cotterill

Placings:1/2211134/1PP-F0   (4029)
2002/03: 25ᶠG, 24⁰S,

	Starts	1st	2nd	3rd	Win & Pl
Chases	2	0	0	0	
Career Total	13	5	2	1	16299
123	12/01 Sthl	3m110y E Ch	SFT	£3475
116	2/01 Uttx	2m4f110yD Hdl	SFT	£3475
111	1/01 Chep	2m4f	E Hdl	G-S £2439
124	1/01 Extr	2m4f	E Hdl	HVY £2136
110	12/99 Wwck	2m	H NHF	SFT £1912

Total win prize-money £13440

Going:	Sf: 0-1 GS: 0-0 Gd: 0-1 GF: - Fm: 0-0
Distance:	2m/2m3: 0-0 2m4-2m7: 0-0 3m+: 0-2
Track:	LH: 0-1 RH: 0-2 Tight: 0-1 Gall: 0-0
Aids:	Bl: 0-0 Vi: 0-0 Tstrap: 0-0
Best Rating:	124 1/01 Extr 2m1f heavy Hdl

Moderate performer; a winner of a bumper and three hurdles, he made an impressive start to his chasing career when winning easily at Southwell but subsequently; stays three miles plus; suited by soft ground.

Avanti Express (IRE)
101   125+
13-y-o b g Supreme Leader-Muckride Lady (Deep Run)
Miss E C Lavelle   Mrs Sarah Stevens

Placings:2/2210/2421311/1/2243250/6/36-11P   (2240)
2002/03: 17¹G, 17¹GS, 17ᴾGS,

	Starts	1st	2nd	3rd	Win & Pl
Chases	3	2	0	0	12149
Career Total	26	7	8	3	44147
125	10/02 Strf	2m1f110yD(0-125)HCh	G-S	£6753
114	10/02 Strf	2m1f110yD(0-120)HCh	GD	£5395
125	4/99 MRas	2m1f110yD(0-120)HCh	GD	£3925
112	4/98 Worc	2m	E Ch	G-S	£3206
129	4/98 MRas	2m1f110yD Ch	SFT	£4027
126	3/98 Tntn	2m3f	D Ch	G-S	£4369
113	2/97 Hrfd	2m1f	E Hdl	SFT	£2347

Total win prize-money £30024

Going:	Sf: 0-0 GS: 1-2 Gd: 1-1 GF: - Fm: 0-0
Distance:	2m/2m3: 2-3 2m4-2m7: 0-0 3m+: 0-0
Track:	LH: 2-3 RH: 0-0 Tight: 2-2 Gall: 0-1
Aids:	Bl: 0-0 Vi: 0-0 Tstrap: 0-0
Best Rating:	132 5/99 Aint 2m gd-sft Ch

Useful handicap chaser; off the track for 22 months until reappearing at Sandown in March 2002; bounced back to form with two victories over the extended two miles at Stratford in October; effective at between two and three miles; acts on good and soft ground.

Avebury
97(105h)   (98h)90
7-y-o b g Fairy King (USA)-Circle Of Chalk (FR) (Kris)
G M Moore   The Tupgill Partnership

Placings:20/33110   (1087)
2002/03: 16³G, 16³GS, 17¹GF, 17¹G, 16⁰GF,

	Starts	1st	2nd	3rd	Win & Pl
Hurdles	5	2	0	2	6769
Career Total	7	2	1	2	7213
98	8/02 Sedg	2m1f	E Hdl	GD	£2905
95	7/02 Sedg	2m1f	E Hdl	G-F	£2954

Total win prize-money £5859

Going:	Sf: 0-0 GS: 0-1 Gd: 1-2 GF: - Fm: 1-2
Distance:	2m/2m3: 2-5 2m4-2m7: 0-0 3m+: 0-0
Track:	LH: 2-3 RH: 0-2 Tight: 2-3 Gall: 0-1
Aids:	Bl: 0-0 Vi: 0-0 Tstrap: 2-2
Best Rating:	105 12/00 Muss 2m good NHF

Plating-class hurdler; lightly-raced; scored back to back wins at Sedgefield in the summer of 2002; suited by trips around two miles.

Avec Plaisir (IRE)

8-y-o ch g Grand Plaisir (IRE)-Ballinellard Lady (Fine Blade (USA))
T R George   Mrs Christine Davies

Placings:0/52/PPP   (2845)
2002/03: 22ᴾGS, 24ᴾGS, 25ᴾS,

	Starts	1st	2nd	3rd	Win & Pl
Chases	3	0	0	0	
Career Total	6	0	1	0	1072

Going:	Sf: 0-1 GS: 0-2 Gd: 0-0 GF: - Fm: 0-0
Distance:	2m/2m3: 0-0 2m4-2m7: 0-1 3m+: 0-2
Track:	LH: 0-2 RH: 0-1 Tight: 0-0 Gall: 0-3
Aids:	Bl: 0-0 Vi: 0-0 Tstrap: 0-0
Best Rating:	110 1/01 Donc 3m110y good Hdl

Avitta (IRE)
108   97
4-y-o b f Pennekamp (USA)-Alinova (USA) (Alleged (USA))
Miss Venetia Williams (H-A Pantall 14/6) P A Deal

Placings:12   (3554)
2002/03: 16¹S, 16²HY,

	Starts	1st	2nd	3rd	Win & Pl
Hurdles	2	1	1	0	5969
Career Total	2	1	1	0	5969
102	1/03 Fknm	2m	D Hdl	SFT	£4881

Total win prize-money £4882

Going:	Sf: 1-2 GS: 0-0 Gd: 0-0 GF: - Fm: 0-0
Distance:	2m/2m3: 1-2 2m4-2m7: 0-0 3m+: 0-0
Track:	LH: 1-2 RH: 0-0 Tight: 1-2 Gall: 0-0
Aids:	Bl: 0-0 Vi: 0-0 Tstrap: 0-0
Best Rating:	102 1/03 Fknm 2m soft Hdl

Fair novice hurdler; acts on soft ground; effective over two miles.

Awesome Wells (IRE)
96   82+
9-y-o b g Sadler s Wells (USA)-Shadywood (Habitat)
D J Wintle   M Tuerks

Placings:P/P-044P1   (4054)
2002/03: 19⁰GF, 17⁴S, 20⁴GS, 17ᴾGS, 16¹S,

	Starts	1st	2nd	3rd	Win & Pl
Hurdles	5	1	0	0	3212
Career Total	7	1	0	0	3212
82	3/03 Wwck	2m	F(0-100)HHdl	SFT	£2838

Total win prize-money £2839

Going:	Sf: 1-2 GS: 0-2 Gd: 0-0 GF: - Fm: 0-1
Distance:	2m/2m3: 1-3 2m4-2m7: 0-2 3m+: 0-0
Track:	LH: 1-3 RH: 0-2 Tight: 0-2 Gall: 0-0
Aids:	Bl: 0-0 Vi: 0-0 Tstrap: 1-3

Best Rating: 82 3/03 Wwck 2m   soft   Hdl

Plating-class hurdler; limited ability over hurdles; suited by cut in the ground

Ay Carumba

6-y-o b g Seymour Hicks (FR)-Aldington Peach (Creetown)
J F Panvert J F Panvert

Placings:*U000*   (4122)
2002/03: 16^U_G, 18^0HY, 16^0HY, 16^0_G,

	Starts	1st	2nd	3rd	Win & Pl
NH Flat	4	0	0	0	
Career Total	4	0	0	0	

Going: Sf: 0-2 GS: 0-0 Gd: 0-2 GF: - Fm: 0-0
Distance: 2m/2m3: 0-4 2m4-2m7: 0-0 3m+: 0-0
Track: LH: 0-2 RH: 0-2 Tight: 0-1 Gall: 0-1
Aids: Bl: 0-0 Vi: 0-0 Tstrap: 0-0
Best Rating: 0 3/03 Hntg 2m110y   good   NHF

Aye Surely (IRE)
84(106h)   (98h)98
9-y-o b g Legal Circles (USA)-Uno Navarro (Raga Navarro (ITY))
Mrs A M Thorpe (Michael Hourigan 16/3) Don Jones

Placings:12506/034/0U0F40P-01F0BFF405442   (4623)
2002/03: 16^0GY, 20^1S, 22^FY, 22^0HY, 19^BF, 17^FS, 21^FS, 20^4HY, 16^0S, 16^5SH, 17^4S, 20^4G, 27^2GF,

	Starts	1st	2nd	3rd	Win & Pl
Hurdles	3	0	1	0	1210
Chases	10	1	0	0	8722
Career Total	28	2	2	1	14384
110 7/02 Limk	2m4f		(0-109)HCh	SFT	£7619
93 6/99 Slig	2m		Hdl	HVY	£2209
					Total win prize-money £9830

Going: Sf: 1-6 GS: 0-0 Gd: 0-1 GF: - Fm: 0-2
Distance: 2m/2m3: 0-6 **2m4-2m7: 1-6** 3m+: 0-1
Track: LH: 0-1 RH: 1-7 Tight: 0-2 Gall: 0-0
Aids: Bl: 1-10 Vi: 0-0 Tstrap: 0-0
Best Rating: 110 7/02 Limk 2m4f   soft   Ch

Modest ex-Irish hurdler; showed little on British debut, but better effort when chasing home fair sort next time in a Newton Abbot claimer; usually wore blinkers in Ireland but left off so far by current connections.

Azertyuiop (FR)
115(113h)   (162h)166+
6-y-o b g Baby Turk-Temara (FR) (Rex Magna (FR))
P F Nicholls J Hales

Placings:112/1545-1111   (4098)
2002/03: 17^1GS, 16^1GS, 16^1GS, 16^1G,

	Starts	1st	2nd	3rd	Win & Pl
Chases	4	4	0	0	115736
Career Total	11	7	1	0	193360
166 3/03 Chel	2m	A Ch		GD	£81200
159 2/03 Winc	2m	C Ch		G-S	£8946
160 11/02 Chel	2m	A Ch		G-S	£17400
125 10/02 MRas	2m1f110yC Ch			G-S	£8190
162 11/01 Winc	2m	A HHdl		GD	£15000
155 2/01 Winc	2m	A Hdl		GD	£21000
10/00 Autl	1m7f	Hdl		VS	£13449
					Total win prize-money £165185

Going: Sf: 0-0 GS: 3-3 Gd: 1-1 GF: - Fm: 0-0
Distance: 2m/2m3: 4-4 2m4-2m7: 0-0 3m+: 0-0

Track: LH: 2-2 RH: 2-2 Tight: 1-1 Gall: 2-2
Aids: Bl: 0-0 Vi: 0-0 Tstrap: 0-0
Best Rating: 166 3/03 Chel 2m   good   Ch

Top-class novice chaser; formerly high-class hurdler; wide-margin winner of all four outings over fences including Arkle Challenge Trophy at Cheltenham by 11l from Impek; suited by 2m; acts on good and soft ground; jumps well; races keenly; a Queen Mother Chase prospect.

Aztec Rule (IRE)
                                                    87
10-y-o b g Strong Gale-Monksville (Monksfield)
R Curtis Eddie Gloyne

Placings:503P/022/F5-P   (0969)
2002/03: 22^PGS,

	Starts	1st	2nd	3rd	Win & Pl
Hurdles	1	0	0	0	
Career Total	10	0	2	1	1932

Going: Sf: 0-0 GS: 0-1 Gd: 0-0 GF: - Fm: 0-0
Distance: 2m/2m3: 0-0 2m4-2m7: 0-1 3m+: 0-0
Track: LH: 0-1 RH: 0-0 Tight: 0-1 Gall: 0-0
Aids: Bl: 0-0 Vi: 0-0 Tstrap: 0-0
Best Rating: 94 12/99 Donc 2m4f   gd-fm   Hdl

B B Boy
82   84
7-y-o br g Arctic Lord-Belle Muguet (Bargello)
K C Bailey T Benfield And Mr W Brown

Placings:00-PF44   (4341)
2002/03: 25^PG, 16^FG, 20^4G, 20^4GF,

	Starts	1st	2nd	3rd	Win & Pl
Chases	4	0	0	0	577
Career Total	6	0	0	0	577

Going: Sf: 0-0 GS: 0-0 Gd: 0-3 GF: - Fm: 0-1
Distance: 2m/2m3: 0-1 2m4-2m7: 0-2 3m+: 0-1
Track: LH: 0-1 RH: 0-3 Tight: 0-0 Gall: 0-3
Aids: Bl: 0-0 Vi: 0-0 Tstrap: 0-0
Best Rating: 88 3/03 Hntg 2m4f110y good   Ch

B So Bold

9-y-o b g Never So Bold-Gunner Girl (Gunner B)
J Neville Ian Muir

Placings:0/5P   (0053)
2002/03: 24^PG,

	Starts	1st	2nd	3rd	Win & Pl
Hurdles	1	0	0	0	
Career Total	3	0	0	0	0

Going: Sf: 0-0 GS: 0-0 Gd: 0-1 GF: - Fm: 0-0
Distance: 2m/2m3: 0-0 2m4-2m7: 0-0 3m+: 0-1
Track: LH: 0-1 RH: 0-0 Tight: 0-1 Gall: 0-0
Aids: Bl: 0-0 Vi: 0-0 Tstrap: 0-0
Best Rating: 78 11/99 Ludl 2m   good   NHF

Baba Au Rhum (IRE)
(99h)   (100h)130
11-y-o ch g Baba Karam-Spring About (Hard Fought)
Ian Williams The Duck Racing Partnership

Placings:P6/124/P411/133/41334-05   (0787)
2002/03: 17^0GF, 17^5GF,

	Starts	1st	2nd	3rd	Win & Pl
Hurdles	2	0	0	0	0
Career Total	19	5	1	4	24728
120 7/01 Sthl	2m	F(0-105)HCh		G-F	£4134
120 10/00 MRas	2m1f110yD(0-120)HHdl			GD	£7020
111 3/99 Ludl	2m	E(0-115)HHdl		GD	£2866
105 10/98 Ludl	2m	E Hdl		G-F	£2402
110 9/97 Worc	2m	D Ch		GD	£3728
					Total win prize-money £20151

Going: Sf: 0-0 GS: 0-0 Gd: 0-0 GF: - Fm: 0-2
Distance: 2m/2m3: 0-2 2m4-2m7: 0-0 3m+: 0-0
Track: LH: 0-1 RH: 0-1 Tight: 0-1 Gall: 0-0
Aids: Bl: 0-0 Vi: 0-0 Tstrap: 0-0
Best Rating: 122 9/01 Strf 2m1f110y gd-fm Ch

Useful handicapper on the Flat; lightly raced; best at around two miles; acts on a sound surface.

Babarullah
61f   23f
5-y-o ch g Lucky Wednesday-Hantergantic (Van Der Linden (FR))
B R Foster Michael Brownrigg

Placings:0   (4542)
2002/03: 16^0G,

	Starts	1st	2nd	3rd	Win & Pl
NH Flat	1	0	0	0	
Career Total	1	0	0	0	

Going: Sf: 0-0 GS: 0-0 Gd: 0-0 GF: - Fm: 0-0
Distance: 2m/2m3: 0-1 2m4-2m7: 0-0 3m+: 0-0
Track: LH: 0-0 RH: 0-1 Tight: 0-0 Gall: 0-0
Aids: Bl: 0-0 Vi: 0-0 Tstrap: 0-0
Best Rating: 23 4/03 Ludl 2m   good   NHF

Baby Gee
105   92
9-y-o ch m King Among Kings-Market Blues (Porto Bello)
D W Whillans Chas N Whillans

Placings:004/011123-412   (3868)
2002/03: 16^4HY, 17^1HY, 16^2GS,

	Starts	1st	2nd	3rd	Win & Pl
Hurdles	3	1	1	0	9311
Career Total	12	4	2	1	18036
91 2/03 Sedg	2m1f	E(0-110)HHdl		HVY	£4745
81 2/02 Muss	2m	E(0-105)HHdl		G-S	£2996
80 1/02 Newc	2m	E(0-100)HHdl		SFT	£2534
73 1/02 Catt	2m	G(0-90)HHdl		G-S	£1764
					Total win prize-money £12039

Going: Sf: 1-2 GS: 0-1 Gd: 0-0 GF: - Fm: 0-0
Distance: **2m/2m3: 1-3** 2m4-2m7: 0-0 3m+: 0-0
Track: **LH: 1-3** RH: 0-0 Tight: 1-1 Gall: 0-1
Aids: Bl: 0-0 Vi: 0-0 Tstrap: 0-0
Best Rating: 92 2/03 Donc 2m110y   gd-sft Hdl

Plating-class hurdler; stays two miles four; seems to go on any ground.

Baby John (IRE)
(100h)   (98h)63
10-y-o ch g Celio Rufo-Kings Princess (King s Ride)
Mrs Sarah Horner-Harker Mrs Sarah Horner-Harker

Placings:0/33PF/324513/34350-5FP   (1708)

2002/03: 20⁵G, 25ᶠG, 27ᴾG,

	Starts	1st	2nd	3rd	Win & Pl
Chases	3	0	0	0	0
Career Total	19	1	1	6	8782
109 11/00 Tntn	2m3f	D(0-105)HCh		GD	£4793

Total win prize-money £4794

Going: Sf: 0-0 GS: 0-0 Gd: 0-3 GF: - Fm: 0-0
Distance: 2m/2m3: 0-2 2m4-2m7: 0-1 3m+: 0-2
Track: LH: 0-3 RH: 0-0 Tight: 0-2 Gall: 0-0
Aids: Bl: 0-0 Vi: 0-0 Tstrap: 0-0
Best Rating: 109 11/00 Tntn 2m3f   gd-sft Ch

Bacardi Boy (IRE)
102(109h)   (112h)100
7-y-o b g Lord Americo-Little Welly (Little Buskins)
T R George Allan Stennett & Terry Warner

Placings: 13332-130   (4171)
2002/03: 24¹HY, 24³GS, 22⁰S,

	Starts	1st	2nd	3rd	Win & Pl
Hurdles	3	1	0	1	3457
Career Total	8	2	1	4	10367
112 1/03 Chep	3m	F Hdl		HVY	£2772
118 11/01 Carl	2m1f	H NHF		SFT	£1610

Total win prize-money £4382

Going: Sf: 1-2 GS: 0-1 Gd: 0-0 GF: - Fm: 0-0
Distance: 2m/2m3: 0-0 2m4-2m7: 0-1 3m+: 1-2
Track: LH: 1-2 RH: 0-1 Tight: 0-1 Gall: 0-0
Aids: Bl: 0-0 Vi: 0-0 Tstrap: 0-0
Best Rating: 126 12/01 Chep 2m110y gd-sft NHF

Useful novice hurdler; bumper winner; just denied when third on chasing bow at Uttoxeter in May; has disappointed since; stays three miles plus; best on soft ground.

Baccarat (IRE)
100   95
9-y-o b g Bob Back (USA)-Sarahlee (Sayyaf)
T J Fitzgerald (J G Fitzgerald 8/2) J S Murdoch

Placings: 1230/4/F33/3-PP3P   (4773)
2002/03: 16ᴾG, 23³G, 20³GF, 20⁰G,

	Starts	1st	2nd	3rd	Win & Pl
Chases	4	0	0	1	627
Career Total	13	1	1	5	4926
115 12/98 Donc	2m110y	H NHF		GD	£1413

Total win prize-money £1413

Going: Sf: 0-0 GS: 0-0 Gd: 0-3 GF: - Fm: 0-1
Distance: 2m/2m3: 0-1 2m4-2m7: 0-2 3m+: 0-1
Track: LH: 0-2 RH: 0-1 Tight: 0-1 Gall: 0-0
Aids: Bl: 0-0 Vi: 0-0 Tstrap: 0-1
Best Rating: 123 3/99 Chel 2m110y gd-sft NHF

Modest chaser; lightly raced; looked a promising novice chaser at one stage but pulled up on first two outings this time; ran a lot better when modest third at Wetherby in March 2003.

Bacchanal (IRE)
118(114h)   (161+h)170
9-y-o ch g Bob Back (USA)-Justitia (Dunbeath (USA))
N J Henderson Lady Lloyd Webber

Placings: 2115/121/4111F0/1310-13F   (3285)
2002/03: 24¹S, 24³S, 25ᶠGS,

	Starts	1st	2nd	3rd	Win & Pl
Hurdles	1	1	0	0	17400
Chases	2	0	0	1	16500
Career Total	20	10	2	2	262798

---

160 11/02 Newb	3m110y	A Hdl		SFT	£17400
168 2/02 Newb	3m	A Ch		SFT	£34800
162 12/01 Sand	3m110y	B Ch		G-S	£10816
162 2/01 Asct	3m110y	A Ch		SFT	£22925
162 12/00 Kemp	3m	A Ch		G-S	£26200
155 11/00 Newb	2m4f	C Ch		G-S	£7772
168 3/00 Chel	3m	A Hdl		G-F	£66700
163 11/99 Newb	2m110y	A(0-145)Hdl		G-S	£13090
159 3/99 Chep	2m110y	B Hdl		SFT	£13550
134 2/99 Sand	3m110y	D Hdl		G-S	£3009

Total win prize-money £216262

Going: Sf: 1-2 GS: 0-1 Gd: 0-0 GF: - Fm: 0-0
Distance: 2m/2m3: 0-0 2m4-2m7: 0-0 3m+: 1-3
Track: LH: 1-2 RH: 0-1 Tight: 0-0 Gall: 1-2
Aids: Bl: 0-1 Vi: 0-0 Tstrap: 0-0
Best Rating: 168 2/02 Newb 3m   soft Ch

Top-class chaser/hurdler; decisive winner of the 2000 Stayers Hurdle at Cheltenham; subsequently mixed hurdling and chasing and showed top-class form under both codes; landed the 2000 Grade One Feltham Novices Chase at Kempton and the 2002 Aon Chase at Newbury; made a winning return over hurdles at Newbury in November 2002 before finishing third in the King George; sadly destroyed after a fall at Cheltenham in January 2003. (DEAD)

Bachelors Pad
100   80d
9-y-o b g Pursuit Of Love-Note Book (Mummy s Pet)
Miss S J Wilton John Pointon And Sons

Placings: 05/00155361030-026040   (4711)
2002/03: 21⁰G, 16²S, 17⁶GS, 16⁰G, 17⁴G, 16⁰GF,

	Starts	1st	2nd	3rd	Win & Pl
Hurdles	6	0	1	0	560
Career Total	19	2	1	2	5089
86 12/01 Strf	2m110y	G(0-95)HHdl		SFT	£2002
86 10/01 Fknm	2m	G(0-90)HHdl		SFT	£1862

Total win prize-money £3865

Going: Sf: 0-1 GS: 0-1 Gd: 0-3 GF: - Fm: 0-1
Distance: 2m/2m3: 0-5 2m4-2m7: 0-1 3m+: 0-0
Track: LH: 0-5 RH: 0-1 Tight: 0-4 Gall: 0-0
Aids: Bl: 0-0 Vi: 0-0 Tstrap: 0-0
Best Rating: 86 12/01 Strf 2m110y soft Hdl

Moderate hurdler, he acts on soft ground and is effective over two miles.

Bachiana (FR)
87
6-y-o ch m Exit To Nowhere (USA)-Etoile D Ocean (USA) (Northern Dancer)
M C Pipe Ray Ransom

Placings: P/0450P-P3   (0895)
2002/03: 16ᴾGF, 24³S,

	Starts	1st	2nd	3rd	Win & Pl
Hurdles	2	0	0	1	344
Career Total	8	0	0	1	344

Going: Sf: 0-1 GS: 0-0 Gd: 0-0 GF: - Fm: 0-1
Distance: 2m/2m3: 0-1 2m4-2m7: 0-0 3m+: 0-1
Track: LH: 0-2 RH: 0-0 Tight: 0-1 Gall: 0-0
Aids: Bl: 0-0 Vi: 0-0 Tstrap: 0-1
Best Rating: 87 12/01 NAbb 2m1f   heavy NHF

Back In Front (IRE)
115   158+
6-y-o br g Bob Back (USA)-Storm Front (IRE) (Strong Gale)
E J O Grady D Cox

Placings: 1130-2111   (4097)
2002/03: 16²SH, 16¹YS, 20¹S, 16¹G,

	Starts	1st	2nd	3rd	Win & Pl
Hurdles	4	3	1	0	81393
Career Total	8	5	1	1	97552
158 3/03 Chel	2m110y	A Hdl		GD	£58000
149 2/03 Limk	2m4f	Hdl		SFT	£7616
130 1/03 Leop	2m	Hdl		Y-S	£7616
131 11/01 Chel	2m110y	A NHF		GD	£8814
111 7/01 Naas	2m	NHF		GD	£3895

Total win prize-money £85943

Going: Sf: 1-1 GS: 0-0 Gd: 1-1 GF: - Fm: 0-0
Distance: 2m/2m3: 2-3 2m4-2m7: 1-1 3m+: 0-0
Track: LH: 2-2 RH: 1-2 Tight: 0-0 Gall: 0-0
Aids: Bl: 0-0 Vi: 0-0 Tstrap: 0-0
Best Rating: 158 3/03 Chel 2m110y good Hdl

Smart Irish-trained novice hurdler; easy winner of the Supreme Novices at 2003 Cheltenham Festival; bumper winner; suited to 2m and ground good or softer.

Back To Ben Alder (IRE)
105f   118f
6-y-o b/br g Bob Back (USA)-Winter Fox (Martinmas)
N J Henderson Mrs Christopher Hanbury

Placings: 10   (4115)
2002/03: 16¹GS, 16⁰G,

	Starts	1st	2nd	3rd	Win & Pl
NH Flat	2	1	0	0	2394
Career Total	2	1	0	0	2394
118 1/03 Kemp	2m	H NHF		G-S	£2394

Total win prize-money £2394

Going: Sf: 0-0 GS: 1-1 Gd: 0-1 GF: - Fm: 0-0
Distance: 2m/2m3: 1-2 2m4-2m7: 0-0 3m+: 0-0
Track: LH: 0-1 RH: 1-1 Tight: 0-0 Gall: 0-0
Aids: Bl: 0-0 Vi: 0-0 Tstrap: 0-0
Best Rating: 118 1/03 Kemp 2m   gd-sft NHF

Fair bumper performer; easy winner on his debut; well beaten in the Cheltenham bumper; handles easy ground.

Backbeat (IRE)
101   111
6-y-o ch g Bob Back (USA)-Pinata (Deep Run)
D R C Elsworth W V & Mrs E S Robins

Placings: 240-41P   (4442)
2002/03: 16⁴GS, 19¹S, 20ᴾG,

	Starts	1st	2nd	3rd	Win & Pl
Hurdles	3	1	0	0	5985
Career Total	6	1	1	0	5985
111 2/03 Newb	2m3f	D Hdl		SFT	£5583

Total win prize-money £5584

Going: Sf: 1-1 GS: 0-1 Gd: 0-1 GF: - Fm: 0-0
Distance: 2m/2m3: 1-2 2m4-2m7: 0-1 3m+: 0-0
Track: LH: 1-1 RH: 0-2 Tight: 0-0 Gall: 1-1
Aids: Bl: 0-0 Vi: 0-0 Tstrap: 0-0
Best Rating: 121 12/01 Asct 2m110y good NHF

Fair hurdler; a change of tactics to front running resulted in him hacking up in a moderate novice event at Newbury in February; beaten next time; effective on good/soft ground.

Backcraft (IRE)
105   113+
5-y-o b g Bob Back (USA)-Bawnanell (Viking (USA))

L Lungo M Magowan

Placings:313-14P6P0P   (4509)
2002/03: 16¹GF, 19⁴GF, 16ᴾS, 16⁶HY, 22ᴾGS, 18⁰G, 22ᴾG,

	Starts	1st	2nd	3rd	Win & Pl
Hurdles	7	1	0	0	3872
Career Total	10	2	0	2	8245
120 5/02	Weth 2m		D(0-115)HHdl	G-F	£3447
102 3/02	Kels 2m2f		E Hdl	HVY	£2786
			Total win prize-money		£6234

Going: Sf: 0-2 GS: 0-1 Gd: 0-2 GF: - Fm: 1-2
Distance: 2m/2m3: 1-4 2m4-2m7: 0-3 3m+: 0-0
Track: LH: 1-6 RH: 0-1 Tight: 0-5 Gall: 0-0
Aids: Bl: 0-0 Vi: 0-0 Tstrap: 0-0
Best Rating: 120 5/02   Weth 2m   gd-fm   Hdl

Modest hurdler; stays two and a half miles; seems to go on any ground.

Backed To Exact (IRE)

9-y-o b g War Hero-Panning (Pitpan)
J R Cornwall M Thornton

Placings:3P   (0434)
2002/03: 20³GS, 20ᴾGF,

	Starts	1st	2nd	3rd	Win & Pl
Hurdles	2	0	0	1	427
Career Total	2	0	0	1	427

Going: Sf: 0-0 GS: 0-1 Gd: 0-0 GF: - Fm: 0-1
Distance: 2m/2m3: 0-0 2m4-2m7: 0-2 3m+: 0-0
Track: LH: 0-1 RH: 0-1 Tight: 0-1 Gall: 0-1
Aids: Bl: 0-0 Vi: 0-0 Tstrap: 0-0
Best Rating: 0   6/02   Hntg   2m4f110y   gd-fm   Hdl

Backscratcher
97   73

9-y-o b g Backchat (USA)-Tiernee Quintana (Artaius (USA))
John R Upson The Fourways Partnership

Placings:000/0406003   (4786)
2002/03: 16⁹G, 16⁴GS, 17⁰S, 20⁶S, 21⁹G, 20⁰GF, 22³G,

	Starts	1st	2nd	3rd	Win & Pl
Hurdles	7	0	0	1	449
Career Total	10	0	0	1	449

Going: Sf: 0-2 GS: 0-1 Gd: 0-3 GF: - Fm: 0-1
Distance: 2m/2m3: 0-3 2m4-2m7: 0-4 3m+: 0-0
Track: LH: 0-2 RH: 0-3 Tight: 0-4 Gall: 0-1
Aids: Bl: 0-1 Vi: 0-0 Tstrap: 0-0
Best Rating: 75   4/03   MRas   2m6f   good   Hdl

Backsheesh (IRE)

8-y-o b g Bob Back (USA)-Kottna (USA) (Lyphard (USA))
G Tuer G Tuer

Placings:00/0406 14/062406/0341-P   (4133)
2002/03: 26ᴾG,

	Starts	1st	2nd	3rd	Win & Pl
Chases	1	0	0	0	
Career Total	19	2	1	1	6510
106 3/02	MRas 3m1f		H Ch	G-S	£1528
99 4/00	DRoy 2m		NHF	G-F	£2760
			Total win prize-money		£4288

Going: Sf: 0-0 GS: 0-0 Gd: 0-1 GF: - Fm: 0-0
Distance: 2m/2m3: 0-0 2m4-2m7: 0-0 3m+: 0-1
Track: LH: 0-1 RH: 0-0 Tight: 0-0 Gall: 0-1
Aids: Bl: 0-0 Vi: 0-0 Tstrap: 0-1
Best Rating: 106 3/02   MRas 3m1f   gd-sft   Ch

Backview
104   94

11-y-o ch g Backchat (USA)-Book Review (Balidar)
I A Wood (M Salaman 23/1) Miss Amanda Jones

Placings:0/56/14/0/0/000/031643P0-32P   (3557)
2002/03: 24³S, 21²HY, 22ᴾHY,

	Starts	1st	2nd	3rd	Win & Pl
Hurdles	3	0	1	1	1102
Career Total	21	2	1	3	5032
94 1/02	Sedg	2m5f110yG(0-90)HHdl	HVY	£1701
91 4/98	Hrfd	2m1f G Hdl	SFT	£1698
			Total win prize-money		£3399

Going: Sf: 0-3 GS: 0-0 Gd: 0-0 GF: - Fm: 0-0
Distance: 2m/2m3: 0-0 2m4-2m7: 0-2 3m+: 0-1
Track: LH: 0-1 RH: 0-2 Tight: 0-2 Gall: 0-0
Aids: Bl: 0-0 Vi: 0-0 Tstrap: 0-3
Best Rating: 94   1/03   Wwck   2m5f   heavy   Hdl

Selling hurdler; ran out a ready winner at Sedgefield in January 2002; stays three miles; acts on heavy ground.

Baclama (FR)
105(101c)   (113c)107

7-y-o b m Siam (USA)-Santa Ana Wind (USA) (Empery (USA))
M C Pipe Glenmore Investments Ltd

Placings:50121206/PP0P/21003512014PF34-045063   (1285)
2002/03: 16⁹GF, 20⁴G, 16⁵S, 16⁰GS, 17⁶GF, 18³GF,

	Starts	1st	2nd	3rd	Win & Pl
Hurdles	6	0	0	1	1146
Career Total	33	5	4	3	34502
103 11/01	Font	2m2f F(0-110)HCh	G-S	£3290
93 8/01	Font	2m2f110yG Hdl	G-F	£2341
89 5/01	Hrfd	2m3f110yG Hdl	GD	£2380
11/99	Autl	2m2f Hdl	HLD	£6997
10/99	Autl	2m2f Hdl	HVY	£6997
			Total win prize-money		£22006

Going: Sf: 0-1 GS: 0-1 Gd: 0-1 GF: - Fm: 0-3
Distance: 2m/2m3: 0-5 2m4-2m7: 0-1 3m+: 0-0
Track: LH: 0-6 RH: 0-0 Tight: 0-2 Gall: 0-0
Aids: Bl: 0-0 Vi: 0-2 Tstrap: 0-0
Best Rating: 107 5/01   Tntn   2m3f110y   firm   Hdl

Modest hurdler/chaser; stays two miles three furlongs; acts on most types of ground.

Badda Bing (IRE)
68   72

6-y-o b g Marju (IRE)-Entracte (Henbit (USA))
Miss G Lee Aidan J Ryan

Placings:0/006F-00P   (2914a)
2002/03: 16⁹GS, 16⁹HY, 16ᴾHY,

	Starts	1st	2nd	3rd	Win & Pl
Hurdles	3	0	0	0	
Career Total	8	0	0	0	

Going: Sf: 0-2 GS: 0-1 Gd: 0-0 GF: - Fm: 0-0
Distance: 2m/2m3: 0-3 2m4-2m7: 0-0 3m+: 0-0
Track: LH: 0-1 RH: 0-0 Tight: 0-0 Gall: 0-0

Going: Sf: 0-0 GS: 0-0 Gd: 0-1 GF: - Fm: 0-0
Distance: 2m/2m3: 0-0 2m4-2m7: 0-0 3m+: 0-1
Track: LH: 0-1 RH: 0-0 Tight: 0-0 Gall: 0-1
Aids: Bl: 0-0 Vi: 0-0 Tstrap: 0-1
Best Rating: 106 3/02   MRas 3m1f   gd-sft   Ch

Baden Vugie (IRE)
84(90h)   (47h)48

6-y-o bl g Hamas (IRE)-Bag Lady (Be My Guest (USA))
S T Lewis (H D Daly 3/1) Simon T Lewis

Placings:00/000-0045   (4349)
2002/03: 16⁰G, 20⁰GS, 20⁴S, 24⁵GF,

	Starts	1st	2nd	3rd	Win & Pl
Chases	4	0	0	0	374
Career Total	9	0	0	0	374

Going: Sf: 0-1 GS: 0-1 Gd: 0-1 GF: - Fm: 0-1
Distance: 2m/2m3: 0-1 2m4-2m7: 0-2 3m+: 0-1
Track: LH: 0-2 RH: 0-2 Tight: 0-2 Gall: 0-0
Aids: Bl: 0-0 Vi: 0-0 Tstrap: 0-0
Best Rating: 58   2/01   Wwck   2m   soft   NHF

Badger Beer

11-y-o b g Town And Country-Panda Pops (Cornuto)
J W Dufosee Mrs R H Woodhouse

Placings:4/43P/20P/014P0B4-3P   (0316)
2002/03: 21³GF, 21ᴾG,

	Starts	1st	2nd	3rd	Win & Pl
Chases	2	0	0	1	1046
Career Total	16	1	1	2	4065
95 5/01	Winc 2m5f		H Ch	G-F	£2222
			Total win prize-money		£2223

Going: Sf: 0-0 GS: 0-0 Gd: 0-1 GF: - Fm: 0-1
Distance: 2m/2m3: 0-0 2m4-2m7: 0-0 3m+: 0-0
Track: LH: 0-0 RH: 0-2 Tight: 0-1 Gall: 0-0
Aids: Bl: 0-0 Vi: 0-0 Tstrap: 0-2
Best Rating: 98   4/02   Extr   2m7f110y   firm   Ch

Hunter chaser; likes fast ground; stays well.

Badgers Glory
75   62

7-y-o gr/ro g Neltino-Shedid (St Columbus)
G P Enright Frederick Gray

Placings:00PP4P-4P   (0785)
2002/03: 26ᴾG, 20⁴GF, 26ᴾGF,

	Starts	1st	2nd	3rd	Win & Pl
Chases	3	0	0	0	217
Career Total	8	0	0	0	480

Going: Sf: 0-0 GS: 0-0 Gd: 0-1 GF: - Fm: 0-2
Distance: 2m/2m3: 0-0 2m4-2m7: 0-1 3m+: 0-2
Track: LH: 0-2 RH: 0-2 Tight: 0-2 Gall: 0-0
Aids: Bl: 0-2 Vi: 0-0 Tstrap: 0-0
Best Rating: 71   5/01   Folk   2m1f110y   gd-sft   NHF

Badworth Gale (IRE)
95   61

9-y-o br g Strong Gale-Badsworth Madam (Over The River (FR))
K C Bailey Dennis Yardy

Placings:P64/0P   (0982)

2002/03: 22QGF, 21PGF,

	Starts	1st	2nd	3rd	Win & Pl
Chases	2	0	0	0	
Career Total	5	0	0	0	269

Going: Sf: 0-0 GS: 0-0 Gd: 0-0 GF: - Fm: 0-2
Distance: 2m/2m3: 0-0 2m4-2m7: 0-2 3m+: 0-0
Track: LH: 0-1 RH: 0-1 Tight: 0-1 Gall: 0-0
Aids: Bl: 0-0 Vi: 0-0 Tstrap: 0-0
Best Rating: 61 6/02 MRas 2m6f110y gd-fm Ch

Bahamian Heir (IRE)
74   49
4-y-o b c Lake Coniston (IRE)-Bally Souza (IRE) (Alzao (USA))
N Wilson (D Nicholls 9/1) Mrs N C Wilson

Placings:00 (4156)
2002/03: 16QGS, 17QG,

	Starts	1st	2nd	3rd	Win & Pl
Hurdles	2	0	0	0	
Career Total	2	0	0	0	

Going: Sf: 0-0 GS: 0-1 Gd: 0-1 GF: - Fm: 0-0
Distance: 2m/2m3: 0-2 2m4-2m7: 0-0 3m+: 0-0
Track: LH: 0-1 RH: 0-1 Tight: 0-1 Gall: 0-1
Aids: Bl: 0-0 Vi: 0-0 Tstrap: 0-0
Best Rating: 50 1/03 Donc 2m110y gd-sft Hdl

Bahamian Sun
4-y-o b g Bahamian Bounty-Dear Person (Rainbow Quest (USA))
F Jordan F K Jennings

Placings:6 (2207)
2002/03: 17⁶S,

	Starts	1st	2nd	3rd	Win & Pl
Hurdles	1	0	0	0	0
Career Total	1	0	0	0	0

Going: Sf: 0-1 GS: 0-0 Gd: 0-0 GF: - Fm: 0-0
Distance: 2m/2m3: 0-1 2m4-2m7: 0-0 3m+: 0-0
Track: LH: 0-1 RH: 0-0 Tight: 0-1 Gall: 0-0
Aids: Bl: 0-0 Vi: 0-0 Tstrap: 0-0
Best Rating: 0 11/02 Bang 2m1f soft Hdl

Baie D'Along (FR)
4-y-o b f Tel Quel (FR)-County Kerry (FR) (Comrade In Arms)
N J Hawke Mrs D R Whigham

Placings:5 (4697)
2002/03: 17⁵G,

	Starts	1st	2nd	3rd	Win & Pl
NH Flat	1	0	0	0	0
Career Total	1	0	0	0	0

Going: Sf: 0-0 GS: 0-0 Gd: 0-1 GF: - Fm: 0-0
Distance: 2m/2m3: 0-1 2m4-2m7: 0-0 3m+: 0-0
Track: LH: 0-1 RH: 0-0 Tight: 0-1 Gall: 0-0
Aids: Bl: 0-0 Vi: 0-0 Tstrap: 0-0
Best Rating: 0 4/03 NAbb 2m1f good NHF

Bailey's Bro (IRE)
6-y-o br g Castle Keep-Boreen Bro (Boreen (FR))
M Bradstock The Frankly Intolerable

Placings:0P (3928)
2002/03: 16⁰HY, 26PG,

	Starts	1st	2nd	3rd	Win & Pl
NH Flat	1	0	0	0	0
Hurdles	1	0	0	0	0
Career Total	2	0	0	0	

Going: Sf: 0-1 GS: 0-0 Gd: 0-1 GF: - Fm: 0-0
Distance: 2m/2m3: 0-1 2m4-2m7: 0-0 3m+: 0-1
Track: LH: 0-1 RH: 0-1 Tight: 0-0 Gall: 0-2
Aids: Bl: 0-0 Vi: 0-0 Tstrap: 0-0
Best Rating: 64 12/02 Newb 2m110y heavy NHF

Bailey's Of Cashel (IRE)
8-y-o ch g Husyan (USA)-Ballyharron (Deep Run)
L Wells David Cox & P B Davis Insurance Services

Placings:00/P (0909)
2002/03: 24PGS,

	Starts	1st	2nd	3rd	Win & Pl
Hurdles	1	0	0	0	
Career Total	3	0	0	0	

Going: Sf: 0-0 GS: 0-1 Gd: 0-0 GF: - Fm: 0-0
Distance: 2m/2m3: 0-0 2m4-2m7: 0-0 3m+: 0-0
Track: LH: 0-0 RH: 0-1 Tight: 0-1 Gall: 0-0
Aids: Bl: 0-0 Vi: 0-0 Tstrap: 0-0
Best Rating: 97 5/00 Punc 2m good NHF

Baileys Prize (USA)
99   95
6-y-o ch g Mister Baileys-Mar Mar (USA) (Forever Casting (USA))
C J Gray A C Heal

Placings:6434020 (3427)
2002/03: 17⁶G, 17⁴S, 17³GS, 19⁴GS, 19⁰S, 19²GS, 18⁰S,

	Starts	1st	2nd	3rd	Win & Pl
Hurdles	7	0	1	1	1753
Career Total	7	0	1	1	1753

Going: Sf: 0-3 GS: 0-3 Gd: 0-1 GF: - Fm: 0-0
Distance: 2m/2m3: 0-6 2m4-2m7: 0-1 3m+: 0-0
Track: LH: 0-2 RH: 0-5 Tight: 0-4 Gall: 0-0
Aids: Bl: 0-0 Vi: 0-0 Tstrap: 0-0
Best Rating: 95 1/03 Extr 2m3f gd-sft Hdl

Bairon (FR)
95   108+
5-y-o b g Subotica (FR)-Advantage (FR) (Antheus (USA))
P F Nicholls Derek Millard

Placings:11 (0735)
2002/03: 17¹G, 17¹GF,

	Starts	1st	2nd	3rd	Win & Pl
Hurdles	2	2	0	0	6741
Career Total	2	2	0	0	6741

108 7/02 NAbb 2m1f D Hdl G-F £3752
113 6/02 NAbb 2m1f E Hdl GD £2989
Total win prize-money £6741

Going: Sf: 0-0 GS: 0-0 Gd: 1-1 GF: - Fm: 1-1
Distance: 2m/2m3: 2-2 2m4-2m7: 0-0 3m+: 0-0
Track: LH: 2-2 RH: 0-0 Tight: 2-2 Gall: 0-0
Aids: Bl: 0-0 Vi: 0-0 Tstrap: 0-0
Best Rating: 113 6/02 NAbb 2m1f good Hdl

Modest hurdler; twice a winner over a mile and a half in the French Provinces; successful on his first two starts over hurdles at Newton Abbot in the summer of 2002; acts on a sound surface.

Bak On Board
7-y-o b g Sula Bula-Kirstins Pride (Silly Prices)
Mrs S Gardner D V Gardner

Placings:000/05P35-P (0246)
2002/03: 22PG,

	Starts	1st	2nd	3rd	Win & Pl
Hurdles	1	0	0	0	
Career Total	9	0	0	1	400

Going: Sf: 0-0 GS: 0-0 Gd: 0-1 GF: - Fm: 0-0
Distance: 2m/2m3: 0-0 2m4-2m7: 0-1 3m+: 0-0
Track: LH: 0-0 RH: 0-1 Tight: 0-0 Gall: 0-0
Aids: Bl: 0-0 Vi: 0-0 Tstrap: 0-0
Best Rating: 74 1/01 Kemp 2m soft NHF

Bak To Bill
(116h)   (122 h)84+
8-y-o b g Nicholas Bill-Kirstins Pride (Silly Prices)
Mrs S Gardner D V Gardner

Placings:4/63ROP2PP/2062P3065425412-2321234 (4400)
2002/03: 22²S, 22³HY, 22²S, 20¹HY, 21²G, 22³S, 22⁴GF,

	Starts	1st	2nd	3rd	Win & Pl
Hurdles	7	1	3	2	18155
Career Total	31	2	8	4	26276

115 1/03 Leic 2m4f110yD(0-120)HHdl HVY £6909
105 3/02 Winc 2m6f F(0-100)HHdl GD £3402
Total win prize-money £10312

Going: Sf: 1-5 GS: 0-0 Gd: 0-1 GF: - Fm: 0-1
Distance: 2m/2m3: 0-0 2m4-2m7: 1-7 3m+: 0-0
Track: LH: 0-4 RH: 1-3 Tight: 0-2 Gall: 0-0
Aids: Bl: 0-0 Vi: 0-0 Tstrap: 0-0
Best Rating: 122 3/03 Uttx 2m6f110y soft Hdl

Fair, progressive handicap hurdler; acts on good and heavy ground; effective at two miles four to two miles six; goes well for his lady rider.

Bakiri (IRE)
99   82+
5-y-o b g Doyoun-Bakiya (USA) (Trempolino (USA))
R T Phillips Mrs Claire Smith

Placings:000 (3091)
2002/03: 16⁰GS, 16⁰S, 19⁰GS,

	Starts	1st	2nd	3rd	Win & Pl
Hurdles	3	0	0	0	
Career Total	3	0	0	0	

Going: Sf: 0-1 GS: 0-2 Gd: 0-0 GF: - Fm: 0-0
Distance: 2m/2m3: 0-2 2m4-2m7: 0-1 3m+: 0-0
Track: LH: 0-3 RH: 0-0 Tight: 0-0 Gall: 0-1
Aids: Bl: 0-0 Vi: 0-0 Tstrap: 0-0

Best Rating: 67 1/03 Donc 2m3f110y gd-sft Hdl

Bal De Nuit (FR)
107   **119**

4-y-o gr g Balleroy (USA)-Eoline (FR) (In Fijar (USA))
P F Nicholls (J Bertran De Balanda 6/11) Mrs Monica Hackett

Placings:F0321F1 (4605)
2002/03: 15FS, 15DVS, 173HO, 172HY, 161G, 16FGS, 171G,

	Starts	1st	2nd	3rd	Win & Pl
Hurdles	4	2	0	0	14999
Chases	3	0	1	1	11767
Career Total	7	2	1	1	26766
119 4/03	Chel	2m1f	B Hdl	GD	£9744
119 1/03	Kemp	2m	D Hdl	GD	£5255

Total win prize-money £14999

Going: Sf: 0-2 GS: 0-1 Gd: 2-2 GF: - Fm: 0-0
Distance: 2m/2m3: 2-5 2m4-2m7: 0-0 3m+: 0-0
Track: LH: 1-1 RH: 1-2 Tight: 0-0 Gall: 1-1
Aids: Bl: 0-0 Vi: 0-0 Tstrap: 0-0
Best Rating: 119 4/03 Chel 2m1f good Hdl

Fair novice hurdler; placed over fences in France; won juvenile hurdle at Kempton on British debut, but fell next time; back off the mark next time at Cheltenham in April; effective over two miles on good ground; acts in soft.

Balakar (IRE)
109   **96**

7-y-o b g Doyoun-Balaniya (USA) (Diesis)
M F Harris D M Robb

Placings:0/05043/P30101 (4631)
2002/03: 16PS, 163GS, 21DS, 161GF, 19DGF, 161GF,

	Starts	1st	2nd	3rd	Win & Pl
Hurdles	6	2	0	2	8218
Career Total	12	2	0	2	8798
96 4/03	Plum	2m	F(0-90)Hdl	G-F	£2618
92 3/03	Wwck	2m	D(0-120)HHdl	G-F	£4823

Total win prize-money £7441

Going: Sf: 0-2 GS: 0-1 Gd: 0-0 GF: - Fm: 2-3
Distance: 2m/2m3: 2-5 2m4-2m7: 0-1 3m+: 0-0
Track: LH: 2-5 RH: 0-1 Tight: 1-2 Gall: 0-0
Aids: Bl: 0-0 Vi: 0-0 Tstrap: 1-1
Best Rating: 103 10/00 Punc 2m gd-yld Hdl

Moderate hurdler; effective in soft and fast ground ; suited by trips of around two miles.

Balanak (USA)
96

12-y-o b g Shahrastani (USA)-Banque Privee (USA) (Private Account (USA))
D R Gandolfo M A Dore

Placings:11104/400000/351F/5354404/042214203/34/0612
262/22455P-03 (0492)
2002/03: 22DGS, 203HY,

	Starts	1st	2nd	3rd	Win & Pl
Hurdles	2	0	0	1	526
Career Total	48	6	8	5	36849
96 12/00	Folk	2m6f110yF(0-105)HHdl	HVY	£1890
111 8/98	Ctml	2m6f	D(0-120)HHdl	G-S	£2878
124 11/96	Wwck	2m3f	D(0-145)HHdl	GD	£5052
131 2/95	Kemp	2m	A Hdl	HVY	£8438
129 1/95	Wind	2m	D Hdl	SFT	£3113
110 1/95	Towc	2m	E Hdl	HVY	£2267

Total win prize-money £23640

Going: Sf: 0-1 GS: 0-1 Gd: 0-0 GF: - Fm: 0-0
Distance: 2m/2m3: 0-0 2m4-2m7: 0-2 3m+: 0-0
Track: LH: 0-2 RH: 0-1 Tight: 0-1 Gall: 0-0
Aids: Bl: 0-0 Vi: 0-0 Tstrap: 0-0
Best Rating: 131 2/95 Kemp 2m heavy Hdl

Balapour (IRE)
119   **137**

5-y-o b g Kahyasi-Balaniya (USA) (Diesis)
Patrick O Brady Miss Rita Shah

Placings:51031000423-0U534BF20F (4742a)
2002/03: 16DYS, 20UYS, 20SSH, 20SYS, 164HY, 16BS, 20FHY,
172G, 20RG, 16FG,

	Starts	1st	2nd	3rd	Win & Pl
Hurdles	10	0	1	1	16785
Career Total	21	2	2	3	53527
119 12/01	Fair	2m	Hdl	YLD	£13104
111 9/01	Fair	2m	Hdl	FRM	£5564

Total win prize-money £18670

Going: Sf: 0-3 GS: 0-0 Gd: 0-3 GF: - Fm: 0-0
Distance: 2m/2m3: 0-5 2m4-2m7: 0-5 3m+: 0-0
Track: LH: 0-6 RH: 0-4 Tight: 0-1 Gall: 0-1
Aids: Bl: 0-0 Vi: 0-0 Tstrap: 0-9
Best Rating: 137 3/03 Chel 2m1f good Hdl

Fairly useful Irish-trained hurdler; stayed on into creditable fourth in 2002 Triumph Hurdle, and showed his liking for the track when returning to finish runner-up in the County Hurdle in 2003; does not have a great winning record but does not get his conditions very often; best form over 2m; seems best on a sound surface and in a strongly-run race.

Bali Breeze (IRE)
70   **38**

4-y-o gr f Common Grounds-Bahia Laura (FR) (Bellypha)
T G McCourt (Kevin Prendergast 31/10) Fergal Gaughran

Placings:UP0 (3579)
2002/03: 16UHY, 16PS, 16DG,

	Starts	1st	2nd	3rd	Win & Pl
Hurdles	3	0	0	0	
Career Total	3	0	0	0	

Going: Sf: 0-2 GS: 0-0 Gd: 0-1 GF: - Fm: 0-0
Distance: 2m/2m3: 0-3 2m4-2m7: 0-0 3m+: 0-0
Track: LH: 0-2 RH: 0-1 Tight: 0-1 Gall: 0-0
Aids: Bl: 0-0 Vi: 0-0 Tstrap: 0-0
Best Rating: 38 2/03 Muss 2m good Hdl

Bali Strong (IRE)
102   **101**

9-y-o b g Strong Gale-Greavesfind (The Parson)
Ferdy Murphy Geoff Hubbard Racing

Placings:243662U1/32110646/6/024-4625 (1478)
2002/03: 24RG, 27BGF, 212GF, 26SGF,

	Starts	1st	2nd	3rd	Win & Pl
Hurdles	4	0	1	0	939
Career Total	24	3	5	2	14800
114 11/99	Kemp	3m110y	D(0-120)HHdl	GD	£3485
111 10/99	Plum	3m1f110yD(0-125)HHdl	G-F	£3187
108 4/99	Hntg	2m5f110yE(0-115)HHdl	GD	£2722

Total win prize-money £9396

Going: Sf: 0-0 GS: 0-0 Gd: 0-1 GF: - Fm: 0-3
Distance: 2m/2m3: 0-0 2m4-2m7: 0-1 3m+: 0-3
Track: LH: 0-2 RH: 0-2 Tight: 0-0 Gall: 0-2
Aids: Bl: 0-0 Vi: 0-0 Tstrap: 0-4

Best Rating: 114 11/99 Kemp 3m110y good Hdl

Moderate hurdler; stays three miles one; best on a sound surface.

Balinahinch Castle (IRE)
108   **120**

6-y-o b g Good Thyne (USA)-Emerald Flair (Flair Path)
Mrs L B Normile (Jonjo O Neill 4/11) K J Fehilly

Placings:11P5 (4764)
2002/03: 221G, 251G, 24PG, 24SG,

	Starts	1st	2nd	3rd	Win & Pl
Hurdles	4	2	0	0	7535
Career Total	4	2	0	0	7535
120 11/02	Wwck	3m1f	D Hdl	GD	£3835
120 10/02	Extr	2m6f110yE Hdl	GD	£3377

Total win prize-money £7213

Going: Sf: 0-0 GS: 0-0 Gd: 2-4 GF: - Fm: 0-0
Distance: 2m/2m3: 0-0 2m4-2m7: 1-1 3m+: 1-3
Track: LH: 1-2 RH: 1-2 Tight: 0-1 Gall: 0-0
Aids: Bl: 0-0 Vi: 0-0 Tstrap: 0-0
Best Rating: 120 11/02 Wwck 3m1f good Hdl

Fair hurdler; ex-Irish pointer, stayed on well to win a novice hurdle at Exeter on his British debut and put up another staying performance to win at Warwick; stays beyond three miles and is a chaser in the making; clearly prefers good ground.

Balisteros (FR)
99(103c)   (104c)**63**

14-y-o b g Bad Conduct (USA)-Oldburry (FR) (Fin Bon)
Mrs B K Thomson Mrs B K Thomson

Placings:00/005FU50/2/35/112/124F4P/2353-3 (4520)
2002/03: 273G,

	Starts	1st	2nd	3rd	Win & Pl
Chases	1	0	0	1	217
Career Total	26	3	4	4	14683
117 5/00	Uttx	3m2f	H Ch	G-F	£3393
103 3/00	Kels	3m1f	H Ch	G-S	£1960
105 2/00	Sedg	2m5f	H Ch	G-S	£1582

Total win prize-money £6936

Going: Sf: 0-0 GS: 0-0 Gd: 0-1 GF: - Fm: 0-0
Distance: 2m/2m3: 0-0 2m4-2m7: 0-0 3m+: 0-1
Track: LH: 0-1 RH: 0-0 Tight: 0-1 Gall: 0-0
Aids: Bl: 0-0 Vi: 0-0 Tstrap: 0-0
Best Rating: 118 6/00 Strf 3m4f good Ch

Fair pointer/hunter chaser; prolific points winner in his prime, but in the veteran stage now; showed he is still capable of winning when landing fast-run 3m ladies event at Stratford May 2003; can make mistakes; stays well; seems to go on any ground.

Balkirk
97   **89d**

6-y-o ch g Selkirk (USA)-Balenare (Pharly (FR))
G L Moore The Friday Night Racing Club

Placings:006-443PP (3550)
2002/03: 164G, 164G, 163S, 16PS, 16PHY,

	Starts	1st	2nd	3rd	Win & Pl
Hurdles	5	0	0	1	1763
Career Total	8	0	0	1	1763

Going: Sf: 0-3 GS: 0-0 Gd: 0-2 GF: - Fm: 0-0

Distance: 2m/2m3: 0-5 2m4-2m7: 0-0 3m+: 0-0
Track: LH: 0-1 RH: 0-4 Tight: 0-1 Gall: 0-0
Aids: BI: 0-0 Vi: 0-0 Tstrap: 0-0
Best Rating: 89   12/02   Sand   2m110y   soft   Hdl

Ball Games
91   **79**
5-y-o b g Mind Games-Deb s Ball (Glenstal (USA))
D Moffatt   Cartmel Bloodstock

Placings:00-553   (1076)
2002/03: 16⁵GF, 17⁵HY, 17³G,

	Starts	1st	2nd	3rd	Win & Pl
Hurdles	3	0	0	1	560
Career Total	5	0	0	1	560

Going: Sf: 0-1 GS: 0-0 Gd: 0-1 GF: - Fm: 0-1
Distance: 2m/2m3: 0-3 2m4-2m7: 0-0 3m+: 0-0
Track: LH: 0-3 RH: 0-0 Tight: 0-2 Gall: 0-0
Aids: BI: 0-0 Vi: 0-1 Tstrap: 0-0
Best Rating: 84   8/02   Ctml   2m1f110y   good   Hdl

Modest novice hurdler.

Ball O Malt (IRE)
(105h)   **(109h)85**
7-y-o b g Star Quest-Vera Dodd (IRE) (Riot Helmet)
Ronald O Leary   Declan J Kinahan

Placings:0421054   (4068a)
2002/03: 20⁰F, 18⁴YS, 20²S, 17¹GS, 20⁰HY, 18⁵YS, 24⁴HY,

	Starts	1st	2nd	3rd	Win & Pl
NH Flat	5	1	1	0	3535
Hurdles	2	0	0	0	286
Career Total	7	1	1	0	3821
115 12/02 Bang	2m1f		H NHF	G-S	£1940

Total win prize-money £1940

Going: Sf: 0-3 GS: 1-1 Gd: 0-0 GF: - Fm: 0-1
Distance: **2m/2m3: 1-3** 2m4-2m7: 0-3 3m+: 0-1
Track: LH: **1-2** RH: 0-0 Tight: **1-1** Gall: 0-0
Aids: BI: 0-0 Vi: 0-0 Tstrap: 0-0
Best Rating: 115   12/02   Bang   2m1f   gd-sft   NHF

Plating-class performer; runner-up in a bumper at Galway before winning a similar event very easily at Bangor in December 2002; held over hurdles so far.

Balla D'Aire (IRE)
       57
8-y-o b/br g Balla Cove-Silius (Junius (USA))
K F Clutterbuck   K F Clutterbuck

Placings:324/P0044/00545P/5-P   (0699)
2002/03: 17ᴾGF,

	Starts	1st	2nd	3rd	Win & Pl
Chases	1	0	0	0	
Career Total	16	0	1	1	1385

Going: Sf: 0-0 GS: 0-0 Gd: 0-0 GF: - Fm: 0-1
Distance: 2m/2m3: 0-1 2m4-2m7: 0-0 3m+: 0-0
Track: LH: 0-0 RH: 0-1 Tight: 0-1 Gall: 0-0
Aids: BI: 0-0 Vi: 0-0 Tstrap: 0-0
Best Rating: 91   2/99   Plum   2m1f   gd-sft   Hdl

Ballad Minstrel (IRE)
85   **49**
11-y-o gr g Ballad Rock-Sashi Woo (Rusticaro (FR))

T J Fitzgerald (J G Fitzgerald 26/2) Mrs C C Longstaff

Placings:14/20/301B4/22122213/30F0/P0014/0   (3833)
2002/03: 20⁰G,

	Starts	1st	2nd	3rd	Win & Pl
Chases	1	0	0	0	
Career Total	27	5	6	3	30080
122	2/01	Weth	2m	E(0-115)HCh	SFT	£3484
126	3/99	Bang	2m4f110yC(0-130)HCh	SFT	£5680
124	12/98	Catt	2m	E Ch	GD	£3148
107	2/98	Newc	2m	E Hdl	GD	£2442
110	2/96	Hayd	2m	H NHF	HVY	£1745

Total win prize-money £16501

Going: Sf: 0-0 GS: 0-0 Gd: 0-1 GF: - Fm: 0-0
Distance: 2m/2m3: 0-0 2m4-2m7: 0-1 3m+: 0-0
Track: LH: 0-1 RH: 0-0 Tight: 0-1 Gall: 0-0
Aids: BI: 0-0 Vi: 0-0 Tstrap: 0-0
Best Rating: 126   3/99   Bang   2m4f110y   soft   Ch

Balladeer (IRE)
101   **108**
5-y-o b g King s Theatre (IRE)-Carousel Music (On Your Mark)
Miss H C Knight (J W Hills 19/10) Scott Hardy Partnership

Placings:F3226   (4473)
2002/03: 17ᶠGS, 16³S, 21²GS, 19²GS, 24⁶G,

	Starts	1st	2nd	3rd	Win & Pl
Hurdles	5	0	2	1	5545
Career Total	5	0	2	1	5545

Going: Sf: 0-1 GS: 0-3 Gd: 0-1 GF: - Fm: 0-0
Distance: 2m/2m3: 0-2 2m4-2m7: 0-2 3m+: 0-0
Track: LH: 0-2 RH: 0-3 Tight: 0-2 Gall: 0-1
Aids: BI: 0-0 Vi: 0-0 Tstrap: 0-0
Best Rating: 108   3/03   Donc   2m3f110y   gd-sft   Hdl

Fair handicapper on the Flat; has shown promise over hurdles; suited by two and a half miles; acts on any ground.

Ballard Connection
4-y-o ch f Danzig Connection (USA)-Ballard Lady (IRE) (Ballad Rock)
J S Wainwright   J S Wainwright

Placings:PP   (3912)
2002/03: 16ᴾS, 17ᴾGS,

	Starts	1st	2nd	3rd	Win & Pl
Hurdles	2	0	0	0	
Career Total	2	0	0	0	

Going: Sf: 0-1 GS: 0-1 Gd: 0-0 GF: - Fm: 0-0
Distance: 2m/2m3: 0-2 2m4-2m7: 0-0 3m+: 0-0
Track: LH: 0-1 RH: 0-1 Tight: 0-1 Gall: 0-0
Aids: BI: 0-0 Vi: 0-0 Tstrap: 0-0
Best Rating: 0   3/03   Carl   2m1f   gd-sft   Hdl

Ballards Boy (FR)
70   **60**
4-y-o b g Sleeping Car (FR)-Anita (FR) (Olmeto)
N J Pomfret   Mrs Liz Deacon

Placings:0   (4269)
2002/03: 16⁰GF,

	Starts	1st	2nd	3rd	Win & Pl
NH Flat	1	0	0	0	
Career Total	1	0	0	0	

Going: Sf: 0-0 GS: 0-0 Gd: 0-0 GF: - Fm: 0-1
Distance: 2m/2m3: 0-0 2m4-2m7: 0-0 3m+: 0-0
Track: LH: 0-1 RH: 0-0 Tight: 0-1 Gall: 0-0
Aids: BI: 0-0 Vi: 0-0 Tstrap: 0-0
Best Rating: 56   3/03   Sthl   2m   gd-fm   NHF

Ballet Red
       57
6-y-o b m Sea Raven (IRE)-Cailin Rua (IRE) (Montelimar (USA))
R D Wylie   Dennis Patrick Flynn

Placings:000/024-P   (0263)
2002/03: 16⁶G,

	Starts	1st	2nd	3rd	Win & Pl
Hurdles	1	0	0	0	
Career Total	7	0	1	0	1147

Going: Sf: 0-0 GS: 0-0 Gd: 0-1 GF: - Fm: 0-0
Distance: 2m/2m3: 0-0 2m4-2m7: 0-0 3m+: 0-0
Track: LH: 0-1 RH: 0-0 Tight: 0-1 Gall: 0-0
Aids: BI: 0-0 Vi: 0-0 Tstrap: 0-0
Best Rating: 57   9/01   Sedg   2m5f110y   good   Hdl

Ballina
11-y-o b g Ayyabaan-Nicolene (Nice Music)
J G M O Shea   S Gallagher

Placings:60/0666/U45/P   (0817)
2002/03: 20ᴾGF,

	Starts	1st	2nd	3rd	Win & Pl
Hurdles	1	0	0	0	
Career Total	10	0	0	0	278

Going: Sf: 0-0 GS: 0-0 Gd: 0-0 GF: - Fm: 0-1
Distance: 2m/2m3: 0-0 2m4-2m7: 0-1 3m+: 0-0
Track: LH: 0-1 RH: 0-0 Tight: 0-0 Gall: 0-0
Aids: BI: 0-0 Vi: 0-0 Tstrap: 0-0
Best Rating: 80   5/97   Chep   2m110y   gd-sft   NHF

Ballincara (IRE)
10-y-o b g Broadsword (USA)-Four Sport (Swing Easy (USA))
Miss L Blackford (E J O Grady 28/7) R C Skinner

Placings:PP/0/300PRP-15004P   (4390)
2002/03: 20¹YS, 18⁵S, 20⁴G, 17³G, 20⁴GF, 19ᴾF,

	Starts	1st	2nd	3rd	Win & Pl
Chases	6	1	0	0	6209
Career Total	15	1	0	1	6914
80 5/02 Clon	2m4f		C(0-109)HCh	Y-S	£5926

Total win prize-money £5926

Going: Sf: 0-1 GS: 0-0 Gd: 0-0 GF: - Fm: 0-2
Distance: 2m/2m3: 0-2 **2m4-2m7: 1-4** 3m+: 0-0
Track: LH: 0-0 **RH: 1-4** Tight: 0-0 Gall: 0-0
Aids: BI: 0-0 Vi: 0-0 Tstrap: 0-0
Best Rating: 97   11/01   Naas   2m   yield   Ch

Ballinclay King (IRE)
118   **145**
9-y-o b g Asir-Clonroche Artic (Pauper)

Ferdy Murphy I Guise, B Leatherday & N L Spence

Placings:*14*/115102/**1314214**/04PP-P3314P   (4479)
2002/03: 20PS, 253S, 253G, 211HY, 214GS, 36PG,

	Starts	1st	2nd	3rd	Win & Pl
Hurdles	1	0	0	0	0
Chases	5	1	0	2	31493
Career Total	25	8	2	3	109085
145	1/03	Chel	2m5f	B HCh	HVY £23200
152	4/01	Aint	2m	A Ch	HVY £46500
144	12/00	Ayr	2m	D Ch	SFT £3705
145	10/00	Weth	2m	E Ch	G-S £3206
131	2/00	Ayr	2m4f	E Hdl	HVY £2747
116	12/99	Hayd	2m	D Hdl	HVY £3322
122	11/99	Ayr	2m	E Hdl	GD £2670
130	4/99	Ayr	2m	H NHF	SFT £3548
				Total win prize-money £88900	

Going:	Sf: 1-3 GS: 0-1 Gd: 0-2 GF: - Fm: 0-0
Distance:	2m/2m3: 0-0 2m4-2m7: 1-3 3m+: 0-3
Track:	LH: 1-6 RH: 0-0 Tight: 0-1 Gall: 1-3
Aids:	Bl: 0-0 Vi: 0-0 Tstrap: 0-0
Best Rating:	152 4/01 Aint 2m heavy Ch

Very useful chaser; lost his way at the start of 2002, but was back to his very best a year later; suited by soft ground; best at two and a half miles.

Ballinure Boy (IRE)

10-y-o b g Meneval (USA)-Sweet Cahore (General Ironside)
Mrs S J Hickman   Mrs N E Turtle

Placings:1   (0315)
2002/03: 211G,

	Starts	1st	2nd	3rd	Win & Pl
Chases	1	1	0	0	1430
Career Total	1	1	0	0	1430
90	5/02	Folk	2m5f	H Ch	GD £1430
			Total win prize-money £1430		

Going:	Sf: 0-0 GS: 0-0 Gd: 1-1 GF: - Fm: 0-0
Distance:	2m/2m3: 0-0 2m4-2m7: 1-1 3m+: 0-0
Track:	LH: 0-0 RH: 1-1 Tight: 1-1 Gall: 0-0
Aids:	Bl: 0-0 Vi: 0-0 Tstrap: 0-0
Best Rating:	90 5/02 Folk 2m5f good Ch

Comfortable winner of a maiden hunter chase at Folkestone in May 2002.

Bally Lira
107   121

11-y-o b m Lir-Ballyorney Girl (New Member)
S C Burrough (P R Rodford 23/1) Victor Thorne

Placings:*633045521*/24P36541U33/6343P242/322635101/65U0356-505135   (4151)
2002/03: 265HY, 320GS, 265S, 261HY, 303S, 295G,

	Starts	1st	2nd	3rd	Win & Pl
Chases	6	1	0	1	10367
Career Total	50	5	6	11	43056
121	2/03	Chep	3m21110yC(0-135)HCh	HVY £8303
109	4/01	Extr	3m11f110yE(0-115)HCh	SFT £4355
115	3/01	Wwck	3m2f	F(0-100)HCh	HVY £2786
97	3/99	Chep	3m	D Ch	HVY £3870
89	3/98	Extr	2m7f	D(0-125)HHdl	G-S £3353
			Total win prize-money £22668		

Going:	Sf: 1-4 GS: 0-1 Gd: 0-1 GF: - Fm: 0-0
Distance:	2m/2m3: 0-0 2m4-2m7: 0-0 3m+: 1-6
Track:	LH: 1-4 RH: 0-2 Tight: 0-1 Gall: 0-0
Aids:	Bl: 0-0 Vi: 0-0 Tstrap: 0-0
Best Rating:	121 2/03 Chep 3m2f110y heavy Ch

Fair chaser; stays forever, but is painfully slow and would ideally like five miles in treacle; she managed a couple of wins early in 2001 when she was able to take advantage of the leaders falling in a heap; won easily when leading all the way at Chepstow in February 2003, causing a shock under a fine ride from 13lb out of the handicap.

Bally's Bak
72   25

5-y-o ch m Bob Back (USA)-Whatagale (Strong Gale)
Mrs S J Smith   Formulated Polymer Products Ltd

Placings:03500   (4661)
2002/03: 160GS, 163HY, 165G, 169GF, 170GF,

	Starts	1st	2nd	3rd	Win & Pl
NH Flat	4	0	0	1	271
Hurdles	1	0	0	0	0
Career Total	5	0	0	1	271

Going:	Sf: 0-1 GS: 0-1 Gd: 0-1 GF: - Fm: 0-2
Distance:	2m/2m3: 0-5 2m4-2m7: 0-0 3m+: 0-0
Track:	LH: 0-4 RH: 0-1 Tight: 0-1 Gall: 0-0
Aids:	Bl: 0-0 Vi: 0-0 Tstrap: 0-0
Best Rating:	80 1/03 Newc 2m heavy NHF

Plating-class mare; well beaten third in a bumper at Newcastle in January and on hurdling debut.

Ballybay Demense (IRE)
98   91+

7-y-o b/br g Bob Back (USA)-Coach Road (Brave Invader (USA))
L A Dace   New World Racing

Placings:UU53   (3746)
2002/03: 26US, 24UGS, 21US, 243G,

	Starts	1st	2nd	3rd	Win & Pl
Chases	4	0	0	1	496
Career Total	4	0	0	1	496

Going:	Sf: 0-2 GS: 0-1 Gd: 0-1 GF: - Fm: 0-0
Distance:	2m/2m3: 0-0 2m4-2m7: 0-1 3m+: 0-3
Track:	LH: 0-1 RH: 0-3 Tight: 0-2 Gall: 0-1
Aids:	Bl: 0-0 Vi: 0-0 Tstrap: 0-0
Best Rating:	91 2/03 Hntg 3m good Ch

Plating-class, lightly-raced chaser; has only completed twice, but has shown promise.

Ballybough Rasher (IRE)
109(101h)   (108h)126

8-y-o b g Broken Hearted-Chat Her Up (Proverb)
J Howard Johnson   Comtake-Welding Engineering Specialists

Placings:0001/1F121PP-3U1UP4P   (4469)
2002/03: 203GF, 22US, 201G, 26UGS, 24PG, 324G, 25PG,

	Starts	1st	2nd	3rd	Win & Pl
Chases	7	1	0	1	11550
Career Total	18	5	1	1	30580
135	11/02	Aint	2m4f	D(0-125)HCh	GD £7215
130	1/02	Donc	3m	D Ch	GD £4273
122	10/01	Aint	3m1f	C Ch	GD £7252
108	5/01	Hexm	3m	F(0-100)HHdl	G-F £2231
100	2/01	Catt	3m1f110yF(0-100)HHdl	SFT £2002
			Total win prize-money £22975		

Going:	Sf: 0-1 GS: 0-1 Gd: 1-4 GF: - Fm: 0-1

Distance:	2m/2m3: 0-0 2m4-2m7: 1-3 3m+: 0-4
Track:	LH: 1-7 RH: 0-0 Tight: 1-4 Gall: 0-2
Aids:	Bl: 0-0 Vi: 0-0 Tstrap: 0-0
Best Rating:	135 11/02 Aint 2m4f good Ch

Useful chaser; effective from two and a half to three miles; acts on any ground; does tend to make mistakes and not altogether consistent.

Ballybrophy (IRE)
113   119+

8-y-o gr g Roselier (FR)-Bavardmore (Le Bavard (FR))
S E H Sherwood   Keith Berry

Placings:P10/211   (4057)
2002/03: 262GS, 241GS, 291GS,

	Starts	1st	2nd	3rd	Win & Pl
Chases	3	2	1	0	13519
Career Total	6	3	1	0	16154
119	3/03	Wwck	3m5f	D(0-125)HCh	G-S £6886
115	2/03	Asct	3m110y	E(0-110)HCh	G-S £5616
103	12/00	Hntg	3m2f	H Ch	HVY £2634
			Total win prize-money £15138		

Going:	Sf: 0-1 GS: 2-2 Gd: 0-0 GF: - Fm: 0-0
Distance:	2m/2m3: 0-0 2m4-2m7: 0-0 3m+: 2-3
Track:	LH: 1-2 RH: 1-1 Tight: 0-0 Gall: 0-0
Aids:	Bl: 0-0 Vi: 0-0 Tstrap: 0-0
Best Rating:	119 3/03 Wwck 3m5f gd-sft Ch

Fair chaser; impressed with his sound jumping when winning a three mile handicap chase at Ascot in February 2003; went on to complete hat-trick, and is progressive; stays 3m 5f; suited by soft ground.

Ballycassidy (IRE)
117(109h)   (131dh)143+

7-y-o br g Insan (USA)-Bitofabreeze (IRE) (Callernish)
A King   G C Mordaunt,C G Clarke,Hon D Whitfeld

Placings:2233/111F2310-2220   (4609)
2002/03: 202GS, 242G, 242GS, 240G,

	Starts	1st	2nd	3rd	Win & Pl
Hurdles	1	0	0	0	0
Chases	3	0	3	0	4394
Career Total	16	4	6	3	33983
131	1/02	Hntg	3m2f	A Hdl	G-S £12127
129	6/01	Strf	3m3f	D(0-125)HHdl	G-F £3666
122	5/01	Strf	2m6f110yD Hdl	GD £3900
108	5/01	Hrld	3m2f	E Hdl	GD £2800
			Total win prize-money £22494		

Going:	Sf: 0-0 GS: 0-2 Gd: 0-2 GF: - Fm: 0-0
Distance:	2m/2m3: 0-0 2m4-2m7: 0-1 3m+: 0-3
Track:	LH: 0-2 RH: 0-2 Tight: 0-2 Gall: 0-2
Aids:	Bl: 0-1 Vi: 0-0 Tstrap: 0-0
Best Rating:	131 1/02 Hntg 3m2f gd-sft Hdl

Very useful hurdler/useful chaser; formerly with Alan King; off the mark on debut for new yard in novice chase June 2003; followed up at Stratford before landing valuable Market Rasen handicap; effective at 2m4f and 3m; acts on most types of ground; has worn blinkers.

Ballydavid (IRE)
98   65

11-y-o b g Lord Americo-Arctic Bavard (Le Bavard (FR))
G B Balding   Mrs Alurie O Sullivan

Placings:300/405PP/5-4   (4706)
2002/03: 204G,

	Starts	1st	2nd	3rd	Win & Pl
Hurdles	1	0	0	0	0

Career Total   10   0   0   1   350

Going: Sf: 0-0 GS: 0-0 Gd: 0-1 GF: - Fm: 0-0
Distance: 2m/2m3: 0-0 2m4-2m7: 0-1 3m+: 0-0
Track: LH: 0-1 RH: 0-0 Tight: 0-0 Gall: 0-0
Aids: Bl: 0-0 Vi: 0-0 Tstrap: 0-0
Best Rating: 88   2/98   Sedg   2m5f110y   good   Hdl

Plating-class-hurdler at around two and a half miles.

Ballygarvan (IRE)

(79h)   (93h) 132
8-y-o br g King Luthier-Lackengarra Wood (Prince Regent (FR))
T R George   Jobs Racing

Placings:550520/242/31-F   (1852)
2002/03: 25^{F}G,

	Starts	1st	2nd	3rd	Win & Pl
Chases	1	0	0	0	
Career Total	12	1	3	1	5095
132 10/01 Weth 3m1f	F Ch			GD	£2288
				Total win prize-money	£2288

Going: Sf: 0-0 GS: 0-0 Gd: 0-1 GF: - Fm: 0-0
Distance: 2m/2m3: 0-0 2m4-2m7: 0-0 3m+: 0-1
Track: LH: 0-0 RH: 0-1 Tight: 0-0 Gall: 0-0
Aids: Bl: 0-0 Vi: 0-0 Tstrap: 0-0
Best Rating: 132 10/01 Weth 3m1f   good   Ch

Useful chaser; ex-Irish; placed over hurdles before winning on his chase debut at Wetherby in October 2001; missed the rest of the season; suffered a fatal fall on his first start for Tom George at Wincanton in November 2002. (DEAD)

Ballygobackwards (IRE)

84   75
11-y-o b g Lord Americo-Bargy Fancy (Crash Course)
C T Pogson   C T Pogson

Placings:34432043/PU3P4PP40/PP0P0P20-6F   (0185)
2002/03: 16^{R}G, 16^{F}G,

	Starts	1st	2nd	3rd	Win & Pl
Hurdles	2	0	0	0	0
Career Total	27	0	2	4	4989

Going: Sf: 0-0 GS: 0-0 Gd: 0-2 GF: - Fm: 0-0
Distance: 2m/2m3: 0-0 2m4-2m7: 0-0 3m+: 0-0
Track: LH: 0-2 RH: 0-0 Tight: 0-1 Gall: 0-0
Aids: Bl: 0-0 Vi: 0-0 Tstrap: 0-0
Best Rating: 88 1/00 Sthl 2m   gd-sft   Ch

Plating-class hurdler/chaser; still a maiden; suited by fast ground.

Ballyharry (IRE)

13-y-o b g Phardante (FR)-Oakville Lady (Menelek)
P Grindey   Peter Grindey

Placings:5P2603/PP3/FP/P-P   (1819)
2002/03: 25^{P}HY,

	Starts	1st	2nd	3rd	Win & Pl
Chases	1	0	0	0	
Career Total	13	0	1	2	1243

Going: Sf: 0-1 GS: 0-0 Gd: 0-0 GF: - Fm: 0-0
Distance: 2m/2m3: 0-0 2m4-2m7: 0-0 3m+: 0-1

Track: LH: 0-1 RH: 0-0 Tight: 0-0 Gall: 0-0
Aids: Bl: 0-0 Vi: 0-0 Tstrap: 0-0
Best Rating: 80   1/98   Ling   2m7f   gd-sft   Hdl

Ballykettrail (IRE)
106   120
7-y-o b h Catrail (USA)-Ballykett Lady (USA) (Sir Ivor)
Jonjo O Neill (C Roche 9/2) J P McManus

Placings:33/11124-350006002   (4639)
2002/03: 16°YS, 20^{S}G, 16°S, 16°S, 16°S, 16°YS, 16°HY, 16°S, 16^{2}GF,

	Starts	1st	2nd	3rd	Win & Pl
Hurdles	9	0	1	1	2201
Career Total	16	3	2	3	20603
119 8/01 Baln	2m4f	Hdl		GD	£4451
112 7/01 Klny	2m1f	NHF		GD	£4451
115 6/01 Naas	2m	NHF		G-Y	£3895
			Total win prize-money		£12799

Going: Sf: 0-5 GS: 0-0 Gd: 0-1 GF: - Fm: 0-1
Distance: 2m/2m3: 0-8 2m4-2m7: 0-1 3m+: 0-0
Track: LH: 0-4 RH: 0-3 Tight: 0-1 Gall: 0-0
Aids: Bl: 0-0 Vi: 0-0 Tstrap: 0-4
Best Rating: 127 12/01 Leop 2m   yield   Hdl

Won two bumpers and a two and a half mile maiden hurdle in Ireland in 2001; promising first run for Jonjo O Neill when second to Ragdale Hall at Stratford April 2003; unsuited by soft ground; seems sure to win races for his new stable.

Ballykissann
99   62
8-y-o ch g Ballacashtal (CAN)-Mybella Ann (Anfield)
J C Tuck   Paul De Weck

Placings:P02P0P/604640P/0/00000300-4PP550P (2061)
2002/03: 16^{R}GF, 22^{P}GF, 22^{P}G, 16^{S}F, 19^{S}F, 19°GF, 17^{P}S,

	Starts	1st	2nd	3rd	Win & Pl
Hurdles	7	0	0	0	0
Career Total	29	0	1	1	675

Going: Sf: 0-1 GS: 0-0 Gd: 0-1 GF: - Fm: 0-5
Distance: 2m/2m3: 0-3 2m4-2m7: 0-4 3m+: 0-0
Track: LH: 0-2 RH: 0-5 Tight: 0-4 Gall: 0-1
Aids: Bl: 0-0 Vi: 0-0 Tstrap: 0-0
Best Rating: 75   11/98   Tntn   2m1f   good   Hdl

Ballyknock Rose (IRE)

8-y-o ch m Cardinal Flower-Annamkerrig (Stetchworth (USA))
L P Grassick (T R George 23/2) Nettleton Harts

Placings:PPP   (4708)
2002/03: 16^{P}HY, 19^{P}G, 20^{P}G,

	Starts	1st	2nd	3rd	Win & Pl
Hurdles	2	0	0	0	0
Chases	1	0	0	0	0
Career Total	3	0	0	0	

Going: Sf: 0-1 GS: 0-0 Gd: 0-2 GF: - Fm: 0-0
Distance: 2m/2m3: 0-1 2m4-2m7: 0-2 3m+: 0-0
Track: LH: 0-2 RH: 0-1 Tight: 0-0 Gall: 0-0
Aids: Bl: 0-0 Vi: 0-0 Tstrap: 0-0
Best Rating: 0   4/03   Uttx   2m4f110y   good   Hdl

Ballyknokan Lad (IRE)

98   73
9-y-o ch g Yashgan-Peace River (IRE) (Over The River (FR))
Denis P Murphy   Murphy s Syndicate

Placings:00P02-053   (0922)
2002/03: 22°YS, 17^{S}SH, 26^{3}GF,

	Starts	1st	2nd	3rd	Win & Pl
Chases	3	0	0	1	419
Career Total	8	0	1	1	1646

Going: Sf: 0-0 GS: 0-0 Gd: 0-0 GF: - Fm: 0-1
Distance: 2m/2m3: 0-1 2m4-2m7: 0-1 3m+: 0-1
Track: LH: 0-1 RH: 0-0 Tight: 0-1 Gall: 0-0
Aids: Bl: 0-0 Vi: 0-0 Tstrap: 0-3
Best Rating: 73   8/02   NAbb   3m2f110y   gd-fm   Ch

Modest Irish chaser; third at Newton Abbot in the summer of 2002.

Ballylesson (IRE)
101   85
8-y-o b g Erdelistan (FR)-Three Dieu (Three Dons)
S H Shirley-Beavan   Mrs S H Shirley-Beavan

Placings:30SFP   (3505)
2002/03: 18^{S}G, 20°GF, 21^{S}GF, 24^{F}G, 20^{P}HY,

	Starts	1st	2nd	3rd	Win & Pl
Hurdles	4	0	0	1	536
Chases	1	0	0	0	0
Career Total	5	0	0	1	536

Going: Sf: 0-1 GS: 0-0 Gd: 0-2 GF: - Fm: 0-2
Distance: 2m/2m3: 0-1 2m4-2m7: 0-3 3m+: 0-1
Track: LH: 0-4 RH: 0-1 Tight: 0-3 Gall: 0-0
Aids: Bl: 0-0 Vi: 0-0 Tstrap: 0-0
Best Rating: 85   5/02   Kels   2m2f   good   Hdl

Ballyline (IRE)
103   92
12-y-o b g Electric-Miss Dikler (Tepukei)
B G Powell   The 49 Partnership

Placings:F20122F23PP24/F1234612B/F321025P330/P062
P0/35245-5P   (0389)
2002/03: 24^{S}G, 25^{P}GS,

	Starts	1st	2nd	3rd	Win & Pl
Chases	2	0	0	0	0
Career Total	46	4	11	6	49146
120 10/98 Worc	2m7f110yC(0-135)HCh		GD	£4796
117 3/98 Uttx	2m5f	C(0-135)HCh	GD	£7132
111 11/97 Kels	2m6f110yC(0-135)HCh		GD	£5158
90 10/96 Weth	2m	D(0-105)HCh	GD	£3561
		Total win prize-money		£20648

Going: Sf: 0-0 GS: 0-1 Gd: 0-1 GF: - Fm: 0-0
Distance: 2m/2m3: 0-0 2m4-2m7: 0-0 3m+: 0-2
Track: LH: 0-2 RH: 0-0 Tight: 0-1 Gall: 0-0
Aids: Bl: 0-0 Vi: 0-0 Tstrap: 0-0
Best Rating: 123 4/98 Aint 2m6f   soft   Ch

Plating-class, front-running chaser; having his first run for a year and a half when third at Wetherby in November 2001; has run fairly well since, but has not won since October 1998; best on good ground; stays three miles.

Ballylusky (IRE)

114   (101c)**124**

6-y-o b g Lord Americo-Blackbushe Place (IRE) (Buckskin (FR))
Jonjo O Neill (David Wachman 18/5) Black Sheep Racing

Placings:5/001232**F3UF**62-523112340   (4102)
2002/03: 24⁵Y, 22²YS, 20³G, 20¹GS, 21¹GS, 20²G, 21³S, 22⁴HY, 25⁰G,

	Starts	1st	2nd	3rd	Win & Pl
Hurdles	8	2	1	2	29006
Chases	1	0	1	0	933
Career Total	**22**	**3**	**5**	**4**	**41180**
124 11/02 MRas	2m5f110yB HHdl			G-S	£10075
120 11/02 Weth	2m4f110yC(0-130)HHdl			G-S	£7046
100 9/01 List	2m	Hdl		G-F	£5842
			Total win prize-money £22964		

Going:	Sf: 0-2 GS: 2-2 Gd: 0-3 GF: - Fm: 0-0
Distance:	2m/2m3: 0-0 **2m4-2m7: 2-7** 3m+: 0-0
Track:	LH: 1-5 RH: 1-2 **Tight: 1-2** Gall: 0-2
Aids:	Bl: 0-0 Vi: 0-0 Tstrap: 0-0
Best Rating:	**124** 2/03 Sand 2m6f heavy Hdl

Ex-Irish; decent hurdler/moderate chaser; stays two and a half miles; appreciates being ridden aggresively; acts on any ground; tough.

Ballymore Rover (IRE)

(83h)   (59h)

9-y-o b g Euphemism-Tots Paradise (Roi Guillaume (FR))
Mrs A C Tate Richard Tate

Placings:45606/0U0-50PP   (0610)
2002/03: 22⁵G, 24⁰G, 24²G, 23⁰GF,

	Starts	1st	2nd	3rd	Win & Pl
Hurdles	3	0	0	0	0
Chases	1	0	0	0	0
Career Total	**12**	**0**	**0**	**0**	**0**

Going:	Sf: 0-0 GS: 0-0 Gd: 0-3 GF: - Fm: 0-1
Distance:	2m/2m3: 0-0 2m4-2m7: 0-1 3m+: 0-3
Track:	LH: 0-3 RH: 0-1 Tight: 0-1 Gall: 0-0
Aids:	Bl: 0-0 Vi: 0-0 Tstrap: 0-0
Best Rating:	**97** 5/00 Worc 2m good NHF

Ballynattin Blue (IRE)

104   **116**

10-y-o ch g Good Thyne (USA)-Ballynattin Moss (Le Moss)
J N R Billinge Sceptre House Golf Society

Placings:505410/410P4/14P6-360   (2563)
2002/03: 24³S, 22⁶S, 24⁰GS,

	Starts	1st	2nd	3rd	Win & Pl
Hurdles	3	0	0	1	728
Career Total	**18**	**3**	**1**	**1**	**15802**
116 10/01 Aint	3m110y C(0-135)HHdl		GD	£6870
111 1/01 Ayr	3m110y F(0-100)HHdl		SFT	£3094
102 3/00 Kels	2m6f110yE Hdl		G-S	£2044
		Total win prize-money £12009		

Going:	Sf: 0-2 GS: 0-1 Gd: 0-0 GF: - Fm: 0-0
Distance:	2m/2m3: 0-0 2m4-2m7: 0-1 3m+: 0-2
Track:	LH: 0-3 RH: 0-0 Tight: 0-1 Gall: 0-0
Aids:	Bl: 0-0 Vi: 0-0 Tstrap: 0-0
Best Rating:	**116** 10/01 Aint 3m110y good Hdl

He stays three miles over hurdles and acts on good and soft

---

ground. Suited by racing prominently and a left-handed galloping track.

Ballyrobert (IRE)

94(95h)   (89 h)**80**

6-y-o b/br g Bob s Return (IRE)-Line Abreast (High Line)
N A Gaselee The Saxon Partnership

Placings:40460   (4056)
2002/03: 21⁴S, 16⁰S, 16⁴S, 20⁶GS, 20⁰GS,

	Starts	1st	2nd	3rd	Win & Pl
Hurdles	2	0	0	0	347
Chases	3	0	0	0	367
Career Total	**5**	**0**	**0**	**0**	**714**

Going:	Sf: 0-3 GS: 0-2 Gd: 0-0 GF: - Fm: 0-0
Distance:	2m/2m3: 0-2 2m4-2m7: 0-3 3m+: 0-0
Track:	LH: 0-2 RH: 0-3 Tight: 0-0 Gall: 0-1
Aids:	Bl: 0-0 Vi: 0-0 Tstrap: 0-0
Best Rating:	**89** 11/02 Kemp 2m5f soft Hdl

Ballysicyos (FR)

105   (130c)**133**

8-y-o b g Nikos-Bally Duke (FR) (Iron Duke (FR))
M C Pipe Mrs P A Deal

Placings:FFF304152/240/11**F0U6**/1P665163-03006 (4609)
2002/03: 24⁰G, 24³S, 25⁰G, 24⁰G, 24⁶G,

	Starts	1st	2nd	3rd	Win & Pl
Hurdles	5	0	0	1	1542
Career Total	**31**	**5**	**2**	**3**	**39399**
142 2/02 Wwck	3m1f	D(0-125)HHdl	SFT	£5200
120 5/01 Extr	3m1f110yE(0-115)HCh	FRM	£4680
126 11/00 Plum	2m4f	D Ch	SFT	£3948
142 10/00 Strf	2m3f	C(0-135)HHdl	SFT	£5118
114 2/99 Ludl	2m	E Hdl	GD	£2038
		Total win prize-money £20986		

Going:	Sf: 0-1 GS: 0-0 Gd: 0-4 GF: - Fm: 0-0
Distance:	2m/2m3: 0-0 2m4-2m7: 0-0 3m+: 0-5
Track:	LH: 0-4 RH: 0-1 Tight: 0-1 Gall: 0-3
Aids:	Bl: 0-0 Vi: 0-0 Tstrap: 0-0
Best Rating:	**142** 2/02 Wwck 3m1f soft Hdl

Useful staying hurdler; winner at Warwick in February 2002; has been tried over fences with limited success; stays three miles plus and has won on fast ground and soft; has worn blinkers.

Ballystone (IRE)

111(102h)   (112 h)**126**

10-y-o ch g Roselier (FR)-Gusserane Princess (Paddy s Stream)
L Lungo Andrew W B Duncan & S E Constable

Placings:266**F2**/1121P/2U10-P2U21U12   (4619)
2002/03: 25⁶GS, 24²S, 31⁰GS, 22²HY, 24¹GF, 24⁰S, 24¹S, 24²GF,

	Starts	1st	2nd	3rd	Win & Pl
Hurdles	3	1	2	0	5562
Chases	5	1	1	0	10979
Career Total	**22**	**6**	**7**	**0**	**38997**
112 3/03 Carl	3m110y E Hdl		SFT	£3542
123 12/02 Muss	3m	D(0-120)HCh	G-F	£6678
126 12/01 Catt	3m1f110yD(0-120)HCh	GD	£4982
122 2/01 Carl	3m2f	D(0-125)HCh	SFT	£4270
122 11/00 Newc	3m	D Ch	SFT	£4580
117 11/00 Carl	2m5f110yD(0-110)HCh	SFT	£3861
		Total win prize-money £27915		

Going:	Sf: 1-3 GS: 0-3 Gd: 0-0 GF: - Fm: 1-2

Distance:	2m/2m3: 0-0 2m4-2m7: 0-1 **3m+: 2-7**
Track:	LH: 0-3 **RH: 2-5 Tight: 1-4** Gall: 0-0
Aids:	Bl: 0-0 Vi: 0-1 Tstrap: 0-0
Best Rating:	**126** 4/03 Carl 3m gd-fm Ch

Decent staying chaser/hurdler; tends to make the odd mistake over fences and was put back over hurdles in the autumn of 2002 before scoring over three miles over fences at Musselburgh; reverted to hurdles to win at Carlisle; stays three and a quarter miles; has won on soft ground and good to firm.

Ballyvaddy (IRE)

110(107h)   (115+h)**92**

7-y-o gr g Roselier (FR)-Bodalmore Kit (Bargello)
G B Balding Lady G Wates

Placings:0/4UP312-120431   (4540)
2002/03: 21¹G, 25²HY, 21⁰GS, 22⁴S, 20³G, 21¹G,

	Starts	1st	2nd	3rd	Win & Pl
Hurdles	6	2	1	1	13581
Career Total	**13**	**3**	**2**	**2**	**20409**
115 4/03 Ludl	2m5f	D(0-120)HHdl	GD	£5499
101 10/02 Kemp	2m5f	D(0-125)HHdl	GD	£5073
96 4/02 Winc	2m6f	E(0-105)HHdl	GD	£3458
		Total win prize-money £14030		

Going:	Sf: 0-2 GS: 0-1 Gd: 2-3 GF: - Fm: 0-0
Distance:	2m/2m3: 0-0 **2m4-2m7: 2-5** 3m+: 0-1
Track:	LH: 0-1 **RH: 2-5** Tight: 0-0 Gall: 0-1
Aids:	Bl: 0-0 **Vi: 1-2** Tstrap: 0-0
Best Rating:	**115** 4/03 Ludl 2m5f good Hdl

Moderate hurdler/chaser; lightly-raced; scored at Kempton on his return in October; well backed when winning 21 furlong handicap at Ludlow April 2003; consistent; stays two miles-six, acts on good ground, has worn a visor and sheepskin cheekpieces.

Ballywalter (IRE)

99   **81**

7-y-o ch g Commanche Run-Call Me Honey (Le Bavard (FR))
N A Gaselee (I R Ferguson 18/5) N A Gaselee

Placings:F 55055   (4428)
2002/03: 22⁼GF, 17⁵YS, 21⁵S, 21⁰S, 21⁵S, 25⁵GF,

	Starts	1st	2nd	3rd	Win & Pl
NH Flat	1	0	0	0	0
Hurdles	5	0	0	0	0
Career Total	**6**	**0**	**0**	**0**	**0**

Going:	Sf: 0-3 GS: 0-0 Gd: 0-0 GF: - Fm: 0-2
Distance:	2m/2m3: 0-1 2m4-2m7: 0-4 3m+: 0-1
Track:	LH: 0-3 RH: 0-0 Tight: 0-1 Gall: 0-1
Aids:	Bl: 0-0 Vi: 0-0 Tstrap: 0-0
Best Rating:	**81** 3/03 Plum 3m1f110y gd-fm Hdl

Balnagreine (IRE)

108   **94**

10-y-o b g Strong Gale-Regent Miss (Prince Regent (FR))
J Mackie Peter McMahon

Placings:0460/00000/50F000/32U-2P0   (0565)
2002/03: 24²G, 24³GF, 22⁰GF,

	Starts	1st	2nd	3rd	Win & Pl
Chases	3	0	1	0	1144
Career Total	**21**	**0**	**2**	**1**	**2474**

Going:	Sf: 0-0 GS: 0-1 Gd: 0-1 GF: - Fm: 0-1

Distance: 2m/2m3: 0-0 2m4-2m7: 0-1 3m+: 0-2
Track: LH: 0-2 RH: 0-1 Tight: 0-3 Gall: 0-0
Aids: Bl: 0-0 Vi: 0-0 Tstrap: 0-0
Best Rating: 94 5/02 Sthl 3m110y good Ch

Moderate ex-Irish chaser; stays three miles; suited by fast ground.

Baloo

105   110+

7-y-o b g Morpeth-Moorland Nell (Neltino)
J D Frost Cloud Nine-Premier Cru

Placings:3540550/3364104-1340   (2177)
2002/03: 27¹GF, 24³G, 22⁴S, 24⁰HY,

	Starts	1st	2nd	3rd	Win & Pl
Hurdles	4	1	0	1	4039
Career Total	18	2	0	4	7657

102 7/02 NAbb 3m3f E(0-105)HHdl G-F £2933
87 11/01 Extr 2m6f110y E(0-105)HHdl
G-F £2520

Total win prize-money £5453

Going: Sf: 0-2 GS: 0-0 Gd: 0-1 GF: - Fm: 1-1
Distance: 2m/2m3: 0-0 2m4-2m7: 0-1 3m+: 1-3
Track: LH: 1-4 RH: 0-0 Tight: 1-2 Gall: 0-0
Aids: Bl: 0-0 Vi: 0-0 Tstrap: 0-0
Best Rating: 102 7/02 NAbb 3m3f gd-fm Hdl

Modest hurdler; stays 3m 3f; likes top of the ground.

Balsox

7-y-o b g Alzao (USA)-Bobbysoxer (Valiyar)
B G Powell Nil Desperandum

Placings:20/40/P-PP   (0324)
2002/03: 16ᴾGS, 19ᴾG, 20ᴾG,

	Starts	1st	2nd	3rd	Win & Pl
Hurdles	2	0	0	0	
Chases	1	0	0	0	
Career Total	7	0	1	0	650

Going: Sf: 0-0 GS: 0-1 Gd: 0-2 GF: - Fm: 0-0
Distance: 2m/2m3: 0-2 2m4-2m7: 0-1 3m+: 0-0
Track: LH: 0-1 RH: 0-2 Tight: 0-0 Gall: 0-0
Aids: Bl: 0-1 Vi: 0-0 Tstrap: 0-0
Best Rating: 87 11/00 Chel 2m110y gd-sft Hdl

Baltic Magic (IRE)

79   102

9-y-o b g Yashgan-Woolly (Giolla Mear)
J L Spearing The Square Milers

Placings:5P0P431PF/02P134P-0   (0216)
2002/03: 19⁰G,

	Starts	1st	2nd	3rd	Win & Pl
Hurdles	1	0	0	0	
Career Total	17	2	1	2	12284

93 1/02 Hrfd 2m3f110yE Hdl SFT £2849
107 1/01 Tram 2m4f Ch SH £6677

Total win prize-money £9526

Going: Sf: 0-0 GS: 0-0 Gd: 0-1 GF: - Fm: 0-0
Distance: 2m/2m3: 0-0 2m4-2m7: 0-1 3m+: 0-0
Track: LH: 0-0 RH: 0-1 Tight: 0-0 Gall: 0-0
Aids: Bl: 0-1 Vi: 0-0 Tstrap: 0-0
Best Rating: 109 1/01 Thur 3m heavy Ch

Baluchi Way

81f   61f

7-y-o b m Nomadic Way (USA)-Kakapo (Oats)
P Beaumont P Jackson

Placings:0⁰0   (0409)
2002/03: 17⁰S, 17⁰GF,

	Starts	1st	2nd	3rd	Win & Pl
NH Flat	2	0	0	0	
Career Total	2	0	0	0	

Going: Sf: 0-1 GS: 0-0 Gd: 0-0 GF: - Fm: 0-1
Distance: 2m/2m3: 0-2 2m4-2m7: 0-0 3m+: 0-0
Track: LH: 0-1 RH: 0-1 Tight: 0-2 Gall: 0-0
Aids: Bl: 0-0 Vi: 0-0 Tstrap: 0-0
Best Rating: 61 6/02 MRas 2m1f110y gd-fm NHF

Banjo Hill

112(104h)   (100h)116+

9-y-o b g Arctic Lord-Just Hannah (Macmillion)
Miss E C Lavelle (C Weedon 12/12) John B Hobbs

Placings:454000016/12200/1/P-2353325511   (4614)
2002/03: 18²GF, 20³GF, 18⁵G, 22³GF, 22³G, 20²GS, 20⁵GS, 20⁵G, 20¹GF, 21¹G,

	Starts	1st	2nd	3rd	Win & Pl
Hurdles	5	0	1	3	2204
Chases	5	2	1	0	18880
Career Total	26	5	4	3	31550

115 4/03 Chel 2m5f D(0-115)HCh GD £13050
115 3/03 Hntg 2m4f110yF(0-95)HCh G-F £3601
105 5/00 Extr 2m6f D(0-120)HHdl FRM £3692
99 9/99 Font 2m6f110yE(0-115)HHdl GD £2267
89 4/99 Winc 2m6f F(0-105)HHdl GD £2570

Total win prize-money £25181

Going: Sf: 0-0 GS: 0-2 Gd: 1-4 GF: - Fm: 1-4
Distance: 2m/2m3: 0-2 2m4-2m7: 2-8 3m+: 0-0
Track: LH: 1-8 RH: 1-2 Tight: 0-0 Gall: 2-3
Aids: Bl: 0-0 Vi: 0-0 Tstrap: 0-0
Best Rating: 115 4/03 Chel 2m5f good Ch

Moderate hurdler/chaser; won novices handicap chase in March 2003 on first run for Emma Lavelle; overcame a 14lb rise in the weights when following up at Cheltenham next time and completed the hat-trick at Exeter; stays nearly three miles; effective at 2m4f; acts on a sound surface.

Banjo Island (IRE)

5-y-o br m Warcraft (USA)-Mandalaw (IRE) (Mandalus)
G L Moore John B Hobbs

Placings:050   (2662)
2002/03: 16⁰G, 17⁵HY, 18⁰S,

	Starts	1st	2nd	3rd	Win & Pl
NH Flat	2	0	0	0	0
Hurdles	1	0	0	0	0
Career Total	3	0	0	0	0

Going: Sf: 0-2 GS: 0-0 Gd: 0-1 GF: - Fm: 0-0
Distance: 2m/2m3: 0-2 2m4-2m7: 0-0 3m+: 0-0
Track: LH: 0-1 RH: 0-2 Tight: 0-2 Gall: 0-0
Aids: Bl: 0-0 Vi: 0-0 Tstrap: 0-0
Best Rating: 80 11/02 Winc 2m good NHF

Bank On Lady

70f   38f

5-y-o ch m Dromod Hill-Sail On Lady (New Member)
R J Smith J De Lisle Wells

Placings:000   (4542)
2002/03: 16⁰S, 16⁰GF, 16⁰G,

	Starts	1st	2nd	3rd	Win & Pl
NH Flat	3	0	0	0	
Career Total	3	0	0	0	

Going: Sf: 0-1 GS: 0-0 Gd: 0-1 GF: - Fm: 0-1
Distance: 2m/2m3: 0-3 2m4-2m7: 0-0 3m+: 0-0
Track: LH: 0-1 RH: 0-2 Tight: 0-0 Gall: 0-0
Aids: Bl: 0-0 Vi: 0-0 Tstrap: 0-0
Best Rating: 38 3/03 Wwck 2m soft NHF

Bankersdraft

93   62

8-y-o ch g Mazaad-Overdraft (Bustino)
R C Guest N B Mason

Placings:0PP6/PP0-6F3   (4341)
2002/03: 16⁶S, 24⁶G, 20³GF,

	Starts	1st	2nd	3rd	Win & Pl
Chases	3	0	0	1	554
Career Total	10	0	0	1	554

Going: Sf: 0-1 GS: 0-0 Gd: 0-1 GF: - Fm: 0-1
Distance: 2m/2m3: 0-1 2m4-2m7: 0-1 3m+: 0-1
Track: LH: 0-1 RH: 0-2 Tight: 0-1 Gall: 0-2
Aids: Bl: 0-0 Vi: 0-0 Tstrap: 0-0
Best Rating: 62 3/03 Hntg 2m4f110y gd-fm Ch

Plating-class novice chaser.

Banner Gale (IRE)

(85h)   (42h)

14-y-o b g Strong Gale-Tipperary Special (Wrekin Rambler)
Dr P Pritchard Mrs T Pritchard

Placings:53/5150520/3405P3/22201/0P360540/4610U3/0/F4P55P   (4348)
2002/03: 20⁰GS, 21⁴HY, 21ᴾGS, 24⁵HY, 25⁵GS, 20ᴾGF,

	Starts	1st	2nd	3rd	Win & Pl
Hurdles	1	0	0	0	
Chases	5	0	0	5	1960
Career Total	41	3	4	5	16377

106 9/99 NAbb 3m2f110yD(0-120)HCh G-F £4123
105 10/94 Tipp 2m NHF SFT £3261

Total win prize-money £7386

Going: Sf: 0-2 GS: 0-3 Gd: 0-0 GF: - Fm: 0-1
Distance: 2m/2m3: 0-0 2m4-2m7: 0-4 3m+: 0-2
Track: LH: 0-5 RH: 0-1 Tight: 0-0 Gall: 0-3
Aids: Bl: 0-0 Vi: 0-0 Tstrap: 0-0
Best Rating: 120 12/96 Leop 3m yield Ch

Moderate chaser; scored on fast ground over the extended three and a quarter miles at Newton Abbot in September 1999; lightly-raced and held since; acts on a sound surface.

Banneret (USA)

10-y-o b g Imperial Falcon (CAN)-Dashing Partner (Formidable (USA))
F L Matthews (T Wall 6/5) F L Matthews

Placings:334/0/FRF-06R   (4390)

2002/03: 21FGS, 20QG, 16RGF, 19RF,

	Starts	1st	2nd	3rd	Win & Pl
Hurdles	3	0	0	0	0
Chases	1	0	0	0	0
Career Total	10	0	0	2	450

Going: Sf: 0-0 GS: 0-1 Gd: 0-1 GF: - Fm: 0-2
Distance: 2m/2m3: 0-0 2m4-2m7: 0-3 3m+: 0-0
Track: LH: 0-1 RH: 0-3 Tight: 0-1 Gall: 0-0
Aids: Bl: 0-1 Vi: 0-0 Tstrap: 0-0
Best Rating: 83 1/00 Ludl 2m gd-sft Hdl

Bansha House

11-y-o ch g Ardross-Proverbial Rose (Proverb)
Mrs Caroline Chadney Mrs D Brown

Placings:03/PB/31/PP (4451)
2002/03: 25PS, 24PG,

	Starts	1st	2nd	3rd	Win & Pl
Chases	2	0	0	0	0
Career Total	8	1	0	2	3479

105 5/00 Hntg 2m4f110yE Hdl G-S £2777
Total win prize-money £2778

Going: Sf: 0-1 GS: 0-0 Gd: 0-1 GF: - Fm: 0-0
Distance: 2m/2m3: 0-0 2m4-2m7: 0-0 3m+: 0-2
Track: LH: 0-0 RH: 0-2 Tight: 0-1 Gall: 0-0
Aids: Bl: 0-0 Vi: 0-0 Tstrap: 0-0
Best Rating: 105 5/00 Hntg 2m4f110y gd-sft Hdl

Barabaschi
82 45
7-y-o b g Elmaamul (USA)-Hills Presidium (Presidium)
R N Bevis (D Nicholls 6/8) Peter J Doyle

Placings:0 (1575)
2002/03: 16QG,

	Starts	1st	2nd	3rd	Win & Pl
Hurdles	1	0	0	0	0
Career Total	1	0	0	0	0

Going: Sf: 0-0 GS: 0-0 Gd: 0-1 GF: - Fm: 0-0
Distance: 2m/2m3: 0-1 2m4-2m7: 0-0 3m+: 0-0
Track: LH: 0-1 RH: 0-0 Tight: 0-1 Gall: 0-0
Aids: Bl: 0-0 Vi: 0-0 Tstrap: 0-0
Best Rating: 51 10/02 Strf 2m110y good Hdl

Baracouda (FR)
126 176+
8-y-o b g Alesso (USA)-Peche Aubar (FR) (Zino)
F Doumen J P McManus

Placings:52/112211111/1111-121 (4131)
2002/03: 201HY, 252S, 241G,

	Starts	1st	2nd	3rd	Win & Pl
Hurdles	3	2	1	0	117060
Career Total	18	13	4	0	512588

176 3/03 Chel 3m A Hdl GD £85260
158 11/02 Asct 2m4f A Hdl HVY £18600
171 3/02 Chel 3m A Hdl GD £72500
156 2/02 Kemp 3m110y A Hdl G-S £15000
176 12/01 Asct 3m1f110yA Hdl GD £33000
171 11/01 Asct 2m4f A Hdl GD £15600
155 4/01 Sand 3m A Hdl G-S £37700
     3/01 Autl 2m3f110y Hdl HVY £31038
161 2/01 Font 2m4f B Hdl G-S £14365
175 12/00 Asct 3m1f110yA Hdl HVY £33000
11/00 Autl 2m4f110y Hdl HVY £48031
7/00 Autl 2m2f Hdl HLD £14409
5/00 Autl 2m3f110y HHdl VS £25937
Total win prize-money £444440

Going: Sf: 1-2 GS: 0-0 Gd: 1-1 GF: - Fm: 0-0
Distance: 2m/2m3: 0-0 2m4-2m7: 1-1 3m+: 1-2
Track: LH: 1-1 RH: 1-2 Tight: 0-0 Gall: 1-1
Aids: Bl: 0-0 Vi: 0-0 Tstrap: 0-0
Best Rating: 176 3/03 Chel 3m good Hdl

The Champion staying hurdler; he won ten consecutive races over hurdles including two Long Walk Hurdles at Ascot and the 2002 Stayers Hurdle at the Festival; given a lot to do at Ascot in his first two starts of the 2002/03 season, just getting up to win the first, but being beaten by Deano s Beeno on his attempt to win a third Long Walk; bounced back to win Stayers again at Cheltenham; acts on any ground; not a straightforward ride.

Baran Itsu
80 39
9-y-o br g Itsu (USA)-Adelbaran (FR) (No Pass No Sale)
B J Llewellyn F H Williams

Placings:0/00PP/6F5P (0981)
2002/03: 21RG, 16FGF, 245S, 17PGF,

	Starts	1st	2nd	3rd	Win & Pl
Chases	4	0	0	0	0
Career Total	9	0	0	0	0

Going: Sf: 0-1 GS: 0-0 Gd: 0-1 GF: - Fm: 0-2
Distance: 2m/2m3: 0-2 2m4-2m7: 0-1 3m+: 0-1
Track: LH: 0-4 RH: 0-0 Tight: 0-2 Gall: 0-0
Aids: Bl: 0-0 Vi: 0-0 Tstrap: 0-0
Best Rating: 41 7/02 Strf 2m5f110y good Ch

Baranndee (IRE)
72(102h) (86h)81
8-y-o b m Jurado (USA)-Last Princess (Le Prince)
A J Martin William Flood

Placings:000/0-12000606 (3534a)
2002/03: 221GF, 242GG, 179S, 180S, 209S, 204S, 206S,

	Starts	1st	2nd	3rd	Win & Pl
Hurdles	2	1	1	0	4648
Chases	6	0	0	0	0
Career Total	12	1	1	0	4648

84 5/02 DRoy 2m6f Hdl G-F £3809
Total win prize-money £3810

Going: Sf: 0-6 GS: 0-1 Gd: 0-0 GF: - Fm: 1-1
Distance: 2m/2m3: 0-3 2m4-2m7: 1-3 3m+: 0-2
Track: LH: 0-0 RH: 0-2 Tight: 0-0 Gall: 0-0
Aids: Bl: 0-0 Vi: 0-0 Tstrap: 0-0
Best Rating: 88 6/02 Prth 3m110y gd-sft Hdl

Barbizon (NZ)
97(95h) (87h)96
9-y-o b g Oregon (USA)-Fleece Tum (NZ) (Umteen (NZ))
B De Haan Plough Racing

Placings:0660/3F01/1PF/60P-1 (2133)
2002/03: 201G,

	Starts	1st	2nd	3rd	Win & Pl
Chases	1	1	0	0	4173
Career Total	15	3	0	1	9170

96 11/02 Ludl 2m4f E(0-105)HCh GD £4173
96 5/00 Ludl 2m5f E(0-105)HHdl GD £2600
96 4/00 Towc 2m5f F Hdl GD £1909
Total win prize-money £8683

Going: Sf: 0-0 GS: 0-0 Gd: 1-1 GF: - Fm: 0-0
Distance: 2m/2m3: 0-0 2m4-2m7: 1-1 3m+: 0-0
Track: LH: 0-0 RH: 1-1 Tight: 1-1 Gall: 0-0
Aids: Bl: 0-0 Vi: 0-0 Tstrap: 1-1
Best Rating: 96 11/02 Ludl 2m4f good Ch

Moderate chaser/hurdler; returning from a long lay-off to win a novices handicap chase in November 2002; effective at two and a half miles; acts on a sound surface.

Barbury Hill (IRE)
91 74
7-y-o b g Rashar (USA)-Supreme Rehearsal (IRE) (Supreme Leader)
A King Mrs A Shutes,Mrs L Field & J E Brown

Placings:656-060 (4482)
2002/03: 19QGS, 16RGF, 19QGF,

	Starts	1st	2nd	3rd	Win & Pl
Hurdles	3	0	0	0	0
Career Total	6	0	0	0	0

Going: Sf: 0-0 GS: 0-1 Gd: 0-0 GF: - Fm: 0-2
Distance: 2m/2m3: 0-1 2m4-2m7: 0-2 3m+: 0-0
Track: LH: 0-1 RH: 0-2 Tight: 0-0 Gall: 0-0
Aids: Bl: 0-0 Vi: 0-0 Tstrap: 0-0
Best Rating: 87 11/01 NAbb 2m1f good NHF

Barcelona
109 116
6-y-o b g Barathea (IRE)-Pipitina (Bustino)
G L Moore RFG Investments Ltd

Placings:1406541-52464030 (4441)
2002/03: 225GF, 212G, 164S, 206GS, 214S, 219G, 203G, 209G,

	Starts	1st	2nd	3rd	Win & Pl
Hurdles	8	0	1	1	3736
Career Total	15	2	1	1	23978

110 4/02 Asct 2m4f B Hdl G-F £17400
115 10/01 Font 2m2f110yE Hdl G-S £2460
Total win prize-money £19861

Going: Sf: 0-2 GS: 0-1 Gd: 0-4 GF: - Fm: 0-1
Distance: 2m/2m3: 0-1 2m4-2m7: 0-7 3m+: 0-0
Track: LH: 0-2 RH: 0-6 Tight: 0-2 Gall: 0-0
Aids: Bl: 0-3 Vi: 0-0 Tstrap: 0-0
Best Rating: 116 11/02 Sand 2m110y soft Hdl

Fair hurdler; fair stayer on the level; stays two and a half miles; does not want the ground too soft.

Barcham Again (IRE)
107 97
6-y-o b g Aristocracy-Dante s Thatch (IRE) (Phardante (FR))
K C Bailey D Allen

Placings:02P (3672)
2002/03: 16QG, 212G, 22PGS,

	Starts	1st	2nd	3rd	Win & Pl
NH Flat	1	0	0	0	0
Hurdles	2	0	1	0	1096
Career Total	3	0	1	0	1096

Going: Sf: 0-0 GS: 0-1 Gd: 0-2 GF: - Fm: 0-0
Distance: 2m/2m3: 0-1 2m4-2m7: 0-2 3m+: 0-0
Track: LH: 0-1 RH: 0-2 Tight: 0-1 Gall: 0-0

Aids: Bl: 0-0 Vi: 0-0 Tstrap: 0-0
Best Rating: 97 11/02 Ludl 2m5f good Hdl

Moderate hurdler; stayed on into second on his hurdles debut.

Bard Of Drumcoo (IRE)

8-y-o ch g Orange Reef-Sporting Houdini (Monseigneur (USA))
M A Kemp Mr & Mrs J R M Ridge

Placings:0P6-F6 (4671)
2002/03: 21^{F}G, 24^{6}G,

	Starts	1st	2nd	3rd	Win & Pl
Chases	2	0	0	0	0
Career Total	5	0	0	0	

Going: Sf: 0-0 GS: 0-0 Gd: 0-2 GF: - Fm: 0-0
Distance: 2m/2m3: 0-0 2m4-2m7: 0-1 3m+: 0-1
Track: LH: 0-2 RH: 0-0 Tight: 0-2 Gall: 0-0
Aids: Bl: 0-0 Vi: 0-0 Tstrap: 0-0
Best Rating: 69 4/03 Fknm 3m110y good Ch

Barden Lady
64

6-y-o b m Presidium-Pugilistic (Hard Fought)
H D Daly D G Blagden

Placings:P05P-P (0447)
2002/03: 21^{P}GS, 19^{P}G,

	Starts	1st	2nd	3rd	Win & Pl
Hurdles	2	0	0	0	
Career Total	5	0	0	0	0

Going: Sf: 0-0 GS: 0-1 Gd: 0-1 GF: - Fm: 0-0
Distance: 2m/2m3: 0-0 2m4-2m7: 0-2 3m+: 0-0
Track: LH: 0-0 RH: 0-2 Tight: 0-0 Gall: 0-0
Aids: Bl: 0-0 Vi: 0-0 Tstrap: 0-0
Best Rating: 64 4/02 Hrfd 2m1f gd-fm Hdl

Bardon Boy

9-y-o ch g Rakaposhi King-Paper Dice (Le Dauphin)
Mrs Monica Tory Mrs Monica Tory & Norman Tory

Placings:U03P0/45FF54/P (0218)
2002/03: 25^{P}G,

	Starts	1st	2nd	3rd	Win & Pl
Chases	1	0	0	0	
Career Total	12	0	0	1	662

Going: Sf: 0-0 GS: 0-0 Gd: 0-1 GF: - Fm: 0-0
Distance: 2m/2m3: 0-0 2m4-2m7: 0-0 3m+: 0-1
Track: LH: 0-0 RH: 0-1 Tight: 0-0 Gall: 0-0
Aids: Bl: 0-0 Vi: 0-0 Tstrap: 0-0
Best Rating: 79 7/00 Sthl 3m110y gd-fm Ch

Bareme (FR)
112 122+

4-y-o b g Homme De Loi (IRE)-Roxa (FR) (Kenmare (FR))
N J Henderson Raymond Tooth

Placings:61 (3494)

2002/03: 16^{6}G, 16^{1}GS,

	Starts	1st	2nd	3rd	Win & Pl
Hurdles	2	1	0	0	5028
Career Total	2	1	0	0	5028
122 2/03 Kemp 2m		D Hdl		G-S	£5027

Total win prize-money £5028

Going: Sf: 0-0 GS: 1-1 Gd: 0-1 GF: - Fm: 0-0
Distance: 2m/2m3: 1-2 2m4-2m7: 0-0 3m+: 0-0
Track: LH: 0-0 RH: 1-2 Tight: 0-0 Gall: 0-0
Aids: Bl: 0-0 Vi: 0-0 Tstrap: 0-0
Best Rating: 122 2/03 Kemp 2m gd-sft Hdl

Useful juvenile hurdler; pulled too hard on debut; successful at Kempton on second run; acts in yielding ground.

Barito (GER)
105(101h) (126h)126

6-y-o b g Winged Love (IRE)-Blumme (CHI) (Jadar (CHI))
C Von Der Recke (F Doumen 21/7) Gestut Karlshof

Placings:31121301560-4216 (4085)
2002/03: 18^{4}S, 17^{2}S, 20^{1}S, 20^{6}GS,

	Starts	1st	2nd	3rd	Win & Pl
Hurdles	1	0	0	0	1340
Chases	3	1	1	0	9388
Career Total	15	5	2	2	34968
126 1/03 Plum 2m4f		D Ch		SFT	£8260
126 12/01 Kemp 2m		B Hdl		GD	£7085
9/01 Maia 2m110y		Hdl		GD	£6212
7/01 Aabe 2m1f		HHdl		SFT	£1607
7/01 Aabe 2m1f		Hdl		SFT	£1607

Total win prize-money £24771

Going: Sf: 1-3 GS: 0-1 Gd: 0-0 GF: - Fm: 0-0
Distance: 2m/2m3: 0-2 2m4-2m7: 1-2 3m+: 0-0
Track: LH: 1-3 RH: 0-1 Tight: 1-3 Gall: 0-0
Aids: Bl: 0-0 Vi: 0-0 Tstrap: 0-0
Best Rating: 126 1/03 Plum 2m4f soft Ch

Decent novice chaser; acts on soft ground; stays two miles four.

Barkingatthemoon
89

9-y-o b g Seymour Hicks (FR)-China s Way (USA) (Native Uproar (USA))
J Mackie Fools Who Dream

Placings:4/050044/22/3-P (3367)
2002/03: 20^{P}GS,

	Starts	1st	2nd	3rd	Win & Pl
Hurdles	1	0	0	0	
Career Total	11	0	2	1	1719

Going: Sf: 0-0 GS: 0-1 Gd: 0-0 GF: - Fm: 0-0
Distance: 2m/2m3: 0-0 2m4-2m7: 0-1 3m+: 0-0
Track: LH: 0-1 RH: 0-0 Tight: 0-1 Gall: 0-0
Aids: Bl: 0-0 Vi: 0-0 Tstrap: 0-0
Best Rating: 101 12/98 Donc 2m110y good NHF

Barley Meadow (IRE)
92(78c) (51c)70

11-y-o ch g Phardante (FR)-Foredefine (Bonne Noel)
R Ford The Haydock Club

Placings:650000/000UP002065/30U35002141612433/452
51464/4325562P6005/1530220P0P60-3U030 (0562)
2002/03: 20^{3}G, 16^{U}GF, 21^{6}G, 16^{3}GS, 19^{0}GF,

	Starts	1st	2nd	3rd	Win & Pl
Hurdles	4	0	0	1	372
Chases	1	0	0	1	716
Career Total	71	5	8	8	17801
79 7/01 MRas 2m5f110yG(0-90)HHdl				G-S	£1624
98 7/99 Worc 2m		G Hdl		G-F	£1730
92 11/98 Ludl 2m		G(0-95)HHdl		GD	£1660
91 10/98 Hexm 2m		G Hdl		GD	£2158
82 9/98 Worc 2m		G(0-90)HHdl		G-F	£2460

Total win prize-money £9632

Going: Sf: 0-0 GS: 0-1 Gd: 0-2 GF: - Fm: 0-2
Distance: 2m/2m3: 0-2 2m4-2m7: 0-3 3m+: 0-0
Track: LH: 0-1 RH: 0-4 Tight: 0-2 Gall: 0-1
Aids: Bl: 0-1 Vi: 0-3 Tstrap: 0-5
Best Rating: 98 7/99 Worc 2m gd-fm Hdl

Plating-class hurdler; stays two miles five; likes decent ground; wears a visor and sometimes tongue-tied.

Barn Dancer (IRE)

8-y-o b m Cataldi-Dancing Gale (Strong Gale)
G P Kelly G P Kelly

Placings:00P0/F-PP (1705)
2002/03: 16^{P}GS, 17^{P}G,

	Starts	1st	2nd	3rd	Win & Pl
Hurdles	2	0	0	0	
Career Total	7	0	0	0	

Going: Sf: 0-0 GS: 0-1 Gd: 0-1 GF: - Fm: 0-0
Distance: 2m/2m3: 0-0 2m4-2m7: 0-0 3m+: 0-0
Track: LH: 0-2 RH: 0-0 Tight: 0-2 Gall: 0-0
Aids: Bl: 0-0 Vi: 0-0 Tstrap: 0-0
Best Rating: 59 7/00 Rosc 2m gd-fm NHF

Barnards Green (IRE)
80 79

5-y-o ch g Florida Son-Pearly Castle (IRE) (Carlingford Castle)
R H Alner T H Chadney

Placings:0 (3754)
2002/03: 16^{6}G,

	Starts	1st	2nd	3rd	Win & Pl
NH Flat	1	0	0	0	
Career Total	1	0	0	0	

Going: Sf: 0-0 GS: 0-0 Gd: 0-1 GF: - Fm: 0-0
Distance: 2m/2m3: 0-1 2m4-2m7: 0-0 3m+: 0-0
Track: LH: 0-0 RH: 0-1 Tight: 0-0 Gall: 0-0
Aids: Bl: 0-0 Vi: 0-0 Tstrap: 0-0
Best Rating: 79 2/03 Kemp 2m good NHF

Barnburgh Boy
95 (117h)124

9-y-o ch g Shalford (IRE)-Tuxford Hideaway (Cawston s Clown)
Miss Venetia Williams Mrs H Spencer

Placings:513P4222/422111212/205/2134216/360F-PF03104 (1007)
2002/03: 20^{P}S, 17^{F}GF, 20^{U}GF, 17^{3}GF, 17^{1}S, 18^{0}VS, 20^{4}GF,

	Starts	1st	2nd	3rd	Win & Pl
Hurdles	2	0	0	1	826
Chases	5	1	0	0	5662

Career Total	38	8	10	4	51899
119 7/02	MRas	2m1f110yD(0-115)HCh		SFT	£5132
124 2/01	Hntg	2m110y D(0-120)HCh		G-S	£4231
116 11/00	MRas	2m1f110yD(0-120)HCh		G-S	£5379
119 3/99	Newc	2m110y E Ch		SFT	£3420
107 2/99	Catt	2m D Ch		GD	£4302
112 2/99	Muss	2m E Ch		GD	£2788
104 1/99	Catt	2m D Ch		SFT	£3684
100 12/97	Weth	2m D Hdl		SFT	£3127
		Total win prize-money £32065			

Going: Sf: 1-2 GS: 0-0 Gd: 0-0 GF: - Fm: 0-4
Distance: 2m/2m3: 1-4 2m4-2m7: 0-3 3m+: 0-0
Track: LH: 0-5 RH: 1-2 Tight: 1-4 Gall: 0-0
Aids: Bl: 0-0 Vi: 0-0 Tstrap: 0-0
Best Rating: 128 2/99 Newc 2m110y gd-sft Ch

Fair chaser; finished alone at Market Rasen in July 2002; stays and extended two miles one; acts on good/good to soft ground.

Barneysian

(89h) (74h)
7-y-o b g Petoski-Rosemoss (Le Moss)
R Dickin Mrs Margaret James

Placings:*0/05-000* (3882)
2002/03: 21⁰GS, 17⁰GS, 16⁰GS,

	Starts	1st	2nd	3rd	Win & Pl
Hurdles	3	0	0	0	
Career Total	6	0	0	0	0

Going: Sf: 0-0 GS: 0-3 Gd: 0-0 GF: - Fm: 0-0
Distance: 2m/2m3: 0-2 2m4-2m7: 0-1 3m+: 0-0
Track: LH: 0-2 RH: 0-1 Tight: 0-1 Gall: 0-1
Aids: Bl: 0-0 Vi: 0-0 Tstrap: 0-0
Best Rating: 74 2/02 MRas 2m3f110y gd-sft Hdl

Baron Allfours

95 74

11-y-o gr g Baron Blakeney-Georgian Quickstep (Dubassoff (USA))
Miss Z C Davison The Secret Circle

Placings:*0/0P/2U25F3PP/PPPPPP34454P2F-P* (4702)
2002/03: 26⁰GF,

	Starts	1st	2nd	3rd	Win & Pl
Chases	1	0	0	0	
Career Total	26	0	3	2	4412

Going: Sf: 0-0 GS: 0-0 Gd: 0-0 GF: - Fm: 0-1
Distance: 2m/2m3: 0-2 2m4-2m7: 0-0 3m+: 0-1
Track: LH: 0-1 RH: 0-0 Tight: 0-1 Gall: 0-0
Aids: Bl: 0-0 Vi: 0-0 Tstrap: 0-0
Best Rating: 86 7/00 MRas 2m6f110y good Ch

Modest maiden chaser, stays three miles plus.

Baron Crocodile

83 67

5-y-o b g Puissance-Glow Again (The Brianstan)
M Todhunter (Mrs E Slack 1/8) A Slack

Placings:*0P* (0875)
2002/03: 17⁰GF, 17ᴾG,

	Starts	1st	2nd	3rd	Win & Pl
Hurdles	2	0	0	0	
Career Total	2	0	0	0	0

Going: Sf: 0-0 GS: 0-0 Gd: 0-1 GF: - Fm: 0-1
Distance: 2m/2m3: 0-2 2m4-2m7: 0-0 3m+: 0-0
Track: LH: 0-2 RH: 0-0 Tight: 0-2 Gall: 0-0
Aids: Bl: 0-0 Vi: 0-0 Tstrap: 0-2
Best Rating: 69 7/02 Sedg 2m1f gd-fm Hdl

Baron Monty (IRE)

97f 117f

5-y-o b g Supreme Leader-Lady Shoco (Montekin)
C Grant Trevor Hemmings

Placings:*51120* (4481)
2002/03: 16⁵S, 16¹HY, 16¹HY, 17²S, 17⁰G,

	Starts	1st	2nd	3rd	Win & Pl
NH Flat	5	2	1	0	4360
Career Total	5	2	1	0	4360
117 2/03 Ayr	2m	H NHF		HVY	£1897
108 1/03 Ayr	2m	H NHF		HVY	£1911
		Total win prize-money £3808			

Going: Sf: 2-4 GS: 0-0 Gd: 0-1 GF: - Fm: 0-0
Distance: 2m/2m3: 2-5 2m4-2m7: 0-0 3m+: 0-0
Track: LH: 2-3 RH: 0-0 Tight: 0-0 Gall: 0-0
Aids: Bl: 0-0 Vi: 0-0 Tstrap: 0-0
Best Rating: 117 3/03 Carl 2m1f soft NHF

Fair bumper performer; half-brother to Tonoco; improved from his debut to win twice on testing ground at Ayr early in 2003.

Baron Windrush

61f

5-y-o b g Alderbrook-Dame Scarlet (Blakeney)
N A Twiston-Davies The Double Octagon Partnership

Placings:*0* (2172)
2002/03: 14⁰GS,

	Starts	1st	2nd	3rd	Win & Pl
NH Flat	1	0	0	0	
Career Total	1	0	0	0	

Going: Sf: 0-0 GS: 0-1 Gd: 0-0 GF: - Fm: 0-0
Distance: 2m/2m3: 0-0 2m4-2m7: 0-0 3m+: 0-0
Track: LH: 0-1 RH: 0-0 Tight: 0-0 Gall: 0-0
Aids: Bl: 0-0 Vi: 0-0 Tstrap: 0-0
Best Rating: 62 11/02 Wwck 1m6f gd-sft NHF

Barontina

7-y-o br m Baron Blakeney-Berina (Goldhills Pride)
H H G Owen H H G Owen

Placings:*P* (0823)
2002/03: 16ᴾGF,

	Starts	1st	2nd	3rd	Win & Pl
NH Flat	1	0	0	0	
Career Total	1	0	0	0	

Going: Sf: 0-0 GS: 0-0 Gd: 0-0 GF: - Fm: 0-1
Distance: 2m/2m3: 0-1 2m4-2m7: 0-0 3m+: 0-0
Track: LH: 0-1 RH: 0-0 Tight: 0-0 Gall: 0-0
Aids: Bl: 0-0 Vi: 0-0 Tstrap: 0-0
Best Rating: 0 7/02 Worc 2m gd-fm NHF

Barracat (IRE)

94f 110+f

6-y-o b g Good Thyne (USA)-Helens Fashion (IRE) (Over The River (FR))

B W Hills D C G Gyle-Thompson

Placings:*1* (0219)
2002/03: 17¹G,

	Starts	1st	2nd	3rd	Win & Pl
NH Flat	1	1	0	0	1803
Career Total	1	1	0	0	1803
110 5/02 Hrfd	2m1f	H NHF		GD	£1802
		Total win prize-money £1803			

Going: Sf: 0-0 GS: 0-0 Gd: 1-1 GF: - Fm: 0-0
Distance: 2m/2m3: 1-1 2m4-2m7: 0-0 3m+: 0-0
Track: LH: 0-0 RH: 1-1 Tight: 0-0 Gall: 0-0
Aids: Bl: 0-0 Vi: 0-0 Tstrap: 0-0
Best Rating: 110 5/02 Hrfd 2m1f good NHF

Modest bumper performer; showed turn of foot to win bumper in May 2002; absent since.

Barrelbio (IRE)

104(94c) (99c)118

8-y-o b g Elbio-Esther (Persian Bold)
F P Murtagh Mrs M E James

Placings:*30P/6442040/222111551004/421333U61134220P P5-606P* (1307)
2002/03: 22ᴿGS, 20⁰GF, 21⁶G, 24ᴾGF,

	Starts	1st	2nd	3rd	Win & Pl
Hurdles	4	0	0	0	0
Career Total	44	7	7	5	37532
123 10/01 Sedg	2m5f110yD(0-125)HHdl		GD	£3171
115 9/01 Sedg	2m5f110yD(0-120)HHdl		GD	£3337
115 6/01 Prth	2m4f110yD(0-125)HHdl		G-F	£3406
116 12/00 Weth	2m D(0-135)HHdl		SFT	£4940
117 7/00 Worc	2m4f E Hdl		G-F	£2387
106 7/00 Wolv	2m E Hdl		G-S	£2298
100 6/00 Prth	2m4f110yD Hdl		GD	£3435
		Total win prize-money £22976			

Going: Sf: 0-0 GS: 0-1 Gd: 0-1 GF: - Fm: 0-2
Distance: 2m/2m3: 0-0 2m4-2m7: 0-3 3m+: 0-1
Track: LH: 0-2 RH: 0-2 Tight: 0-2 Gall: 0-0
Aids: Bl: 0-0 Vi: 0-0 Tstrap: 0-0
Best Rating: 123 11/01 MRas 2m5f110y gd-sft Hdl

Fair hurdler; suited by decent ground and hold-up tactics; has shown consistent form in modest handicap hurdles; acts on most types of ground; most effective over trips of around two and a half miles.

Barren Lands

103(114h) (120h)121

8-y-o b g Green Desert (USA)-Current Raiser (Filiberto (USA))
K Bishop Mrs E K Ellis

Placings:*62314102/031P106/2004342F22-15615* (2486)
2002/03: 16¹G, 17⁵G, 21⁶GF, 19¹S, 16⁵G,

	Starts	1st	2nd	3rd	Win & Pl
Hurdles	1	1	0	0	6148
Chases	4	1	0	0	7366
Career Total	30	6	6	3	37724
121 11/02 Hrfd	2m3f	D(0-115)HCh	SFT	£6773
121 5/02 Aint	2m110y	B(0-145)HHdl	GD	£6148
116 1/01 Tntn	2m1f	D(0-120)HHdl	SFT	£3575
116 10/00 Winc	2m	D(0-110)HHdl	G-S	£3250
104 1/00 Tntn	2m1f	D(0-120)HHdl	G-S	£3526
109 12/99 Winc	2m	F(0-100)HHdl	SFT	£2402
		Total win prize-money £25674			

Going: Sf: 1-1 GS: 0-0 Gd: 1-3 GF: - Fm: 0-1
Distance: 2m/2m3: 2-4 2m4-2m7: 0-1 3m+: 0-0
Track: LH: 1-4 RH: 1-1 Tight: 1-3 Gall: 0-0
Aids: Bl: 0-0 Vi: 0-0 Tstrap: 0-0

Best Rating: 121 11/02 Hrfd 2m3f   soft   Ch

Fair hurdler; best on a right-handed track; suited by two miles with give in the ground; landed a Hereford handicap in November 2002.

Barresbo

104   122

9-y-o b g Barrys Gamble-Bo Babbity (Strong Gale)
A C Whillans E Waugh

Placings:0/2023044/1/22302142-12   **(3518)**
2002/03: 22¹GS, 20²GS,

	Starts	1st	2nd	3rd	Win & Pl
Hurdles	2	1	1	0	5578
Career Total	19	3	7	2	19464
111 5/02	Kels	2m6f110yD(0-125)HHdl	G-S	£3458
115 2/02	Ayr	2m4f	F(0-95)HHdl	HVY	£3150
104 4/01	Prth	2m110y	G Hdl	HVY	£3614

Total win prize-money £10222

Going: Sf: 0-0 GS: 1-2 Gd: 0-0 GF: - Fm: 0-0
Distance: 2m/2m3: 0-0 **2m4-2m7: 1-2** 3m+: 0-0
Track: **LH: 1-2** RH: 0-0 **Tight: 1-1** Gall: 0-0
Aids: Bl: 0-0 Vi: 0-0 Tstrap: 0-0
Best Rating: 122 2/03 Hayd 2m4f   gd-sft   Hdl

Fair hurdler; likes to race prominently; effective at up to three miles; likes soft ground but handles faster.

Barrosa

83   58+

4-y-o b f Sabrehill (USA)-Shehana (USA) (The Minstrel (CAN))
Miss K M George A B Parr

Placings:6   **(1004)**
2002/03: 17⁶GF,

	Starts	1st	2nd	3rd	Win & Pl
Hurdles	1	0	0	0	0
Career Total	1	0	0	0	0

Going: Sf: 0-0 GS: 0-0 Gd: 0-0 GF: - Fm: 0-1
Distance: 2m/2m3: 0-1 2m4-2m7: 0-0 3m+: 0-0
Track: LH: 0-1 RH: 0-0 Tight: 0-1 Gall: 0-0
Aids: Bl: 0-0 Vi: 0-0 Tstrap: 0-0
Best Rating: 58 8/02 Bang 2m1f   gd-fm   Hdl

Barrow (SWI)

99   97

6-y-o br g Caerleon (USA)-Bestow (Shirley Heights)
Ferdy Murphy Janet And Myrtle

Placings:4324/2-01   **(4681)**
2002/03: 16⁰GF, 21¹GF,

	Starts	1st	2nd	3rd	Win & Pl
Hurdles	2	1	0	0	3626
Career Total	7	1	2	1	7124
97 4/03	Hntg	2m5f110yE Hdl	G-F	£3626

Total win prize-money £3626

Going: Sf: 0-0 GS: 0-0 Gd: 0-0 GF: - Fm: 1-2
Distance: 2m/2m3: 0-1 **2m4-2m7: 1-1** 3m+: 0-0
Track: LH: 0-0 RH: 1-2 Tight: 0-0 Gall: 1-2
Aids: Bl: 0-0 Vi: 0-0 Tstrap: 0-0
Best Rating: 113 5/01 Ayr 2m6f   gd-fm   Hdl

Modest novice hurdler; finally broke his duck in poor company on fast ground at Huntingdon in April; suited by two mile six and will stay well.

Barrow Drive

120(101h)   (140h)145

7-y-o b g Gunner B-Fille De Soleil (Sunyboy)
Anthony Mullins (C Byrnes 30/7) Mrs B Lenihan

Placings:3111166-F2111112213   **(4110)**
2002/03: 21⁵S, 17²SH, 20¹YS, 22¹Y, 17¹S, 20¹G, 20¹S, 20²SH, 20²S, 21¹YS, 24³G,

	Starts	1st	2nd	3rd	Win & Pl
Chases	11	6	3	1	131188
Career Total	18	10	3	2	163710
145 2/03	Leop	2m5f	Ch	Y-S	£44318
139 11/02	Punc	2m4f	Ch	SFT	£15398
137 10/02	Gowr	2m4f	Ch	GD	£15950
109 9/02	Gway	2m1f	Ch	SFT	£7975
120 7/02	Gway	2m6f	Ch	YLD	£10368
104 7/02	Kbgn	2m4f	Ch	Y-S	£6561
140 12/01	Cork	3m	Hdl	Y-S	£15725
125 11/01	Cork	2m	Hdl	Y-S	£6677
120 9/01	Gway	2m5f	NHF	GD	£5842
114 8/01	Kbgn	2m3f	NHF	GD	£3895

Total win prize-money £132713

Going: Sf: 2-4 GS: 0-0 Gd: 1-2 GF: - Fm: 0-0
Distance: 2m/2m3: 1-2 **2m4-2m7: 5-8** 3m+: 0-1
Track: LH: 1-2 **RH: 4-6** Tight: 0-0 Gall: 0-1
Aids: Bl: 0-0 Vi: 0-0 **Tstrap: 6-8**
Best Rating: 145 3/03 Chel 3m110y   good   Ch

Useful, progressive Irish -trained novice chaser; has a good strike rate; won Grade One P. J. Moriarty Chase at Leopardstown; effective at up to 2m 6f; acts on soft ground; wears a tongue tie.

Barryscourt Lad (IRE)

112   129+

9-y-o b g Glacial Storm (USA)-Clonana (Le Bavard (FR))
M C Pipe (D Pipe 1/5) Roseberry Racing

Placings:2252-2F1   **(3292)**
2002/03: 33²GF, 25⁵S, 24¹G,

	Starts	1st	2nd	3rd	Win & Pl
Chases	3	1	1	0	34291
Career Total	7	1	4	0	39713
131 1/03	Donc	3m	A(0-145)HCh	GF	£32567

Total win prize-money £32567

Going: Sf: 0-1 GS: 0-0 Gd: 1-1 GF: - Fm: 0-1
Distance: 2m/2m3: 0-0 2m4-2m7: 0-0 **3m+: 1-3**
Track: **LH: 1-3** RH: 0-0 Tight: 0-0 **Gall: 1-3**
Aids: Bl: 0-0 Vi: 0-0 Tstrap: 0-0
Best Rating: 131 1/03 Donc 3m   good   Ch

Useful chaser; promising hunter chaser in 2002; unlucky when falling at the last in a novice handicap at Cheltenham in December; rallied bravely to take the Great Yorkshire Chase at Doncaster the following month; finished very sore and is likely to be on the sidelines for quite a while.

Barton

104   (170h)140

10-y-o ch g Port Etienne (FR)-Peanuts (FR) (Mistigri)
T D Easterby Sir Stanley Clarke

Placings:O2/1111111/12514/2111101-0366   **(4457)**
2002/03: 24⁰GS, 20³GS, 21⁶G, 25⁶G,

	Starts	1st	2nd	3rd	Win & Pl
Chases	4	0	0	1	5524
Career Total	25	14	3	1	291881
160 4/02	Aint	3m1f	A Ch	GD	£46500
139 1/02	Newc	2m4f	A Ch	SFT	£14875
139 12/01	Weth	2m	C Ch	G-S	£6376
147 12/01	Newc	3m	C Ch	G-S	£6711
129 11/01	Newc	2m4f	E Ch	GD	£3110
170 4/01	Aint	2m4f	A Hdl	HVY	£71400
163 11/00	Newc	2m	A Hdl	SFT	£22200
163 4/99	Aint	2m4f	A Hdl	GD	£17850
160 3/99	Chel	2m5f	A Hdl	G-S	£45960
158 1/99	Donc	2m4f	A Hdl	GD	£10087
149 12/98	Sand	2m6f	A Hdl	GD	£9689
148 11/98	Uttx	2m4f110yA Hdl	GD	£9419
119 10/98	Weth	2m7f	C Hdl	SFT	£4185
113 10/98	Weth	2m4f110yD Hdl	GD	£3037

Total win prize-money £271404

Going: Sf: 0-0 GS: 0-2 Gd: 0-2 GF: - Fm: 0-0
Distance: 2m/2m3: 0-0 2m4-2m7: 0-2 3m+: 0-2
Track: LH: 0-4 RH: 0-0 Tight: 0-1 Gall: 0-1
Aids: Bl: 0-0 Vi: 0-0 Tstrap: 0-0
Best Rating: 170 4/01 Aint 2m4f   heavy   Hdl

Formerly top-class hurdler/very useful novice chaser; won the Royal and SunAlliance Hurdle at the Cheltenham Festival in 2001 and the Grade Two Mildmay Novices Chase at Aintree in April 2002; not at his best in 2002/2003, although showed signs of a return to form at Cheltenham; acts on good and soft ground; stays three miles.

Barton Bandit

97   (78h)90

7-y-o ch g Sula Bula-Yamrah (Milford)
D McCain D McCain

Placings:4/0P4PF4-522PP4P   **(1097)**
2002/03: 16⁶G, 20²G, 20⁴GF, 16⁶GF, 20⁴S, 26⁶GF,

	Starts	1st	2nd	3rd	Win & Pl
Chases	7	0	2	0	2293
Career Total	14	0	2	0	2900

Going: Sf: 0-1 GS: 0-0 Gd: 0-2 GF: - Fm: 0-4
Distance: 2m/2m3: 0-2 2m4-2m7: 0-0 3m+: 0-1
Track: LH: 0-6 RH: 0-1 Tight: 0-5 Gall: 0-0
Aids: Bl: 0-0 Vi: 0-0 Tstrap: 0-7
Best Rating: 90 5/02 Aint 2m4f   good   Ch

Moderate novice chaser; rather clumsy jumper.

Barton Baron (IRE)

89f   72f

5-y-o b g Phardante (FR)-Boolavogue (IRE) (Torus)
D P Keane Sir Stanley Clarke

Placings:00   **(4444)**
2002/03: 16⁰GS, 16⁸G,

	Starts	1st	2nd	3rd	Win & Pl
NH Flat	2	0	0	0	
Career Total	2	0	0	0	

Going: Sf: 0-0 GS: 0-1 Gd: 0-1 GF: - Fm: 0-0
Distance: 2m/2m3: 0-2 2m4-2m7: 0-0 3m+: 0-0
Track: LH: 0-0 RH: 0-2 Tight: 0-0 Gall: 0-0
Aids: Bl: 0-0 Vi: 0-0 Tstrap: 0-0
Best Rating: 71 1/03 Kemp 2m   gd-sft   NHF

Barton Bog (IRE)

(96h)   (89h)86

9-y-o gr g Roselier (FR)-Al s Niece (Al Sirat (USA))
J R Cornwall J R Cornwall

Placings:630232/23523P0-5   **(1759)**
2002/03: 26⁶G,

	Starts	1st	2nd	3rd	Win & Pl
Chases	1	0	0	0	0
Career Total	14	0	4	4	5398

Going: Sf: 0-0 GS: 0-0 Gd: 0-1 GF: - Fm: 0-0
Distance: 2m/2m3: 0-0 2m4-2m7: 0-0 3m+: 0-1
Track: LH: 0-1 RH: 0-0 Tight: 0-0 Gall: 0-0
Aids: Bl: 0-0 Vi: 0-0 Tstrap: 0-0
Best Rating: 89 4/01 Prth 3m110y heavy Hdl

Plating-class chaser; winning point-to-pointer; needs staying distances over fences; suited by soft ground; acts on a sound surface as well; stays three miles.

Barton Dante
105   111
6-y-o b m Phardante (FR)-Cindie Girl (Orchestra)
M W Easterby Sir Stanley Clarke

Placings:22/2f31210-3U   (4367)
2002/03: 16³GF, 20⁴G,

	Starts	1st	2nd	3rd	Win & Pl
Hurdles	2	0	0	1	1051
Career Total	11	3	4	2	10172

107	1/02	Sedg	2m5f110yE Hdl		HVY	£2450
105	11/01	Catt	2m3f	F Hdl	G-F	£1907
97	10/01	Bang	2m1f	H NHF	GD	£1767

Total win prize-money £6126

Going: Sf: 0-0 GS: 0-0 Gd: 0-1 GF: - Fm: 0-1
Distance: 2m/2m3: 0-1 2m4-2m7: 0-1 3m+: 0-0
Track: LH: 0-1 RH: 0-1 Tight: 0-0 Gall: 0-0
Aids: Bl: 0-0 Vi: 0-0 Tstrap: 0-0
Best Rating: 111 3/03 Weth 2m gd-fm Hdl

Modest hurdler; stays two and a half miles; acts on any ground.

Barton Dream (IRE)
97   76?
7-y-o b g Le Bavard (FR)-Tax Dream (IRE) (Electric)
John Allen Nic Allen

Placings:0000-6FP5F   (0727)
2002/03: 22⁵GF, 22²GF, 24⁴G, 19⁵GF, 22²GF,

	Starts	1st	2nd	3rd	Win & Pl
Hurdles	5	0	0	0	0
Career Total	9	0	0	0	0

Going: Sf: 0-0 GS: 0-0 Gd: 0-1 GF: - Fm: 0-4
Distance: 2m/2m3: 0-1 2m4-2m7: 0-3 3m+: 0-1
Track: LH: 0-5 RH: 0-0 Tight: 0-4 Gall: 0-0
Aids: Bl: 0-0 Vi: 0-0 Tstrap: 0-0
Best Rating: 72 6/02 Strf 2m6f110y gd-fm Hdl

Barton Gate
5-y-o b g Rock Hopper-Ruth s River (Young Man (FR))
M W Easterby Sir Stanley Clarke

Placings:5036   (4355)
2002/03: 17⁵GF, 16⁶GS, 17³HY, 20⁶GF,

	Starts	1st	2nd	3rd	Win & Pl
NH Flat	3	0	0	1	288
Hurdles	1	0	0	0	0
Career Total	4	0	0	1	288

Going: Sf: 0-1 GS: 0-1 Gd: 0-0 GF: - Fm: 0-2
Distance: 2m/2m3: 0-3 2m4-2m7: 0-1 3m+: 0-0
Track: LH: 0-2 RH: 0-2 Tight: 0-1 Gall: 0-1
Aids: Bl: 0-1 Vi: 0-0 Tstrap: 0-0
Best Rating: 85 2/03 Sedg 2m1f heavy NHF

Best effort in bumpers so far was when third at Sedgefield in February; acts well on soft; has worn a visor.

Barton Hill
91   106
6-y-o b g Nicholas Bill-Home From The Hill (IRE) (Jareer (USA))
T D Easterby Sir Stanley Clarke

Placings:5P04   (4176)
2002/03: 17⁵G, 20PGS, 19⁰G, 16⁴S,

	Starts	1st	2nd	3rd	Win & Pl
NH Flat	1	0	0	0	0
Hurdles	3	0	0	0	395
Career Total	4	0	0	0	395

Going: Sf: 0-1 GS: 0-1 Gd: 0-2 GF: - Fm: 0-0
Distance: 2m/2m3: 0-3 2m4-2m7: 0-1 3m+: 0-0
Track: LH: 0-4 RH: 0-0 Tight: 0-2 Gall: 0-1
Aids: Bl: 0-0 Vi: 0-0 Tstrap: 0-0
Best Rating: 106 3/03 Uttx 2m soft Hdl

Barton Nic
111(97c)   (64c)100
10-y-o b g Nicholas Bill-Dutch Majesty (Horning)
D P Keane Conkwell Grange Stud Ltd

Placings:4625/0/0P/2F-51315   (3824)
2002/03: 20⁵S, 24¹S, 24³HY, 16¹HY, 26⁵GS,

	Starts	1st	2nd	3rd	Win & Pl
Hurdles	4	2	0	1	5607
Chases	1	0	0	0	0
Career Total	14	2	2	1	6357

100	2/03	Plum	2m	F(0-90)HHdl	HVY	£2576
84	12/02	Uttx	3m110y	F(0-100)HHdl	SFT	£2653

Total win prize-money £5229

Going: Sf: 2-4 GS: 0-1 Gd: 0-0 GF: - Fm: 0-0
Distance: 2m/2m3: 1-1 2m4-2m7: 0-1 3m+: 1-3
Track: LH: 2-5 RH: 0-0 Tight: 1-1 Gall: 0-1
Aids: Bl: 1-2 Vi: 0-0 Tstrap: 0-0
Best Rating: 102 2/99 Sedg 2m1f good NHF

Moderate hurdler; has won over two and three miles; goes well on a soft surface; often fitted with either sheepskin cheekpieces or blinkers.

Barton Saint (NZ)
92(94h)   (65h)85
8-y-o ch g St Hilarion (USA)-Aquatramp (NZ) (Pevero)
P R Rodford Les Trott

Placings:P00/0-053P242PP   (1785)
2002/03: 21⁰GF, 25⁵G, 21³GF, 21PGF, 21²G, 19⁴GF, 26²G, 25PG, 25PGF,

	Starts	1st	2nd	3rd	Win & Pl
Hurdles	1	0	0	0	0
Chases	8	0	2	1	3216
Career Total	13	0	2	1	3216

Going: Sf: 0-0 GS: 0-0 Gd: 0-4 GF: - Fm: 0-5
Distance: 2m/2m3: 0-0 2m4-2m7: 0-5 3m+: 0-4
Track: LH: 0-7 RH: 0-2 Tight: 0-5 Gall: 0-0
Aids: Bl: 0-0 Vi: 0-0 Tstrap: 0-1
Best Rating: 85 10/02 Sthl 3m2f good Ch

Plating-class chaser; winning pointer; has made the frame under Rules but looks painfully slow; best over trips short of three miles.

Basford Boy
86   72+
4-y-o b g Tragic Role (USA)-Legatee (Risk Me (FR))
A Streeter Boler Stanley Racing

Placings:2   (1323)
2002/03: 17²GF,

	Starts	1st	2nd	3rd	Win & Pl
Hurdles	1	0	1	0	584
Career Total	1	0	1	0	584

Going: Sf: 0-0 GS: 0-0 Gd: 0-0 GF: - Fm: 0-1
Distance: 2m/2m3: 0-1 2m4-2m7: 0-0 3m+: 0-0
Track: LH: 0-0 RH: 0-0 Tight: 0-1 Gall: 0-0
Aids: Bl: 0-0 Vi: 0-0 Tstrap: 0-0
Best Rating: 72 9/02 MRas 2m1f110y gd-fm Hdl

Basil
101(59h)   (7h)86
10-y-o br g Lighter-Thrupence (Royal Highway)
R H Buckler Mrs C J Dunn

Placings:PU00/RU3P5-0531F   (4253)
2002/03: 26⁰G, 22⁵G, 22³HY, 26¹S, 23FG,

	Starts	1st	2nd	3rd	Win & Pl
Hurdles	1	0	0	0	0
Chases	4	1	0	1	4033
Career Total	14	1	0	2	4680

86	1/03	Wwck	3m2f	F(0-95)HCh	SFT	£3556

Total win prize-money £3556

Going: Sf: 1-2 GS: 0-0 Gd: 0-3 GF: - Fm: 0-0
Distance: 2m/2m3: 0-0 2m4-2m7: 0-2 3m+: 1-3
Track: LH: 1-1 RH: 0-2 Tight: 0-2 Gall: 0-1
Aids: Bl: 1-2 Vi: 0-0 Tstrap: 0-0
Best Rating: 86 1/03 Wwck 3m2f soft Ch

Modest handicap chaser; ended long losing run when successful at Warwick in January 2003; acts in testing conditions; stays three and a quarter miles.

Bassano (USA)
92   83
9-y-o b g Alwasmi (USA)-Marittima (USA) (L Emigrant (USA))
S C Burrough (P R Rodford 16/1) Mrs Christine Priest

Placings:5644/40/63322P5/6304   (4095)
2002/03: 24⁶G, 26³HY, 19⁰G, 24⁴HY,

	Starts	1st	2nd	3rd	Win & Pl
Chases	4	0	0	1	568
Career Total	17	0	2	3	3541

Going: Sf: 0-3 GS: 0-0 Gd: 0-1 GF: - Fm: 0-0
Distance: 2m/2m3: 0-1 2m4-2m7: 0-0 3m+: 0-3
Track: LH: 0-2 RH: 0-2 Tight: 0-3 Gall: 0-0
Aids: Bl: 0-0 Vi: 0-0 Tstrap: 0-0
Best Rating: 107 1/01 Font 2m6f110y soft Hdl

Bassenhally
95   103
13-y-o ch g Celtic Cone-Milly Kelly (Murrayfield)
Mrs P Sly Thorney Racing Club

Placings:00/4F2263/10UP306/F11441U/612/11PP6P/P/12
P-43 (2237)
2002/03: 24⁴GS, 23³G,

	Starts	1st	2nd	3rd	Win & Pl
Chases	2	0	0	1	923
Career Total	37	8	4	3	38832
103	10/01	Fknm	3m110y	F(0-110)HCh	SFT	£4760
120	12/99	Fknm	3m110y	D(0-120)HCh	GD	£4905
120	10/99	Fknm	3m110y	F(0-110)HCh	GD	£4606
117	10/98	Fknm	3m110y	E(0-110)HCh	GD	£4597
108	3/98	Fknm	2m5f110yD(0-120)HCh	GD	£4265
108	12/97	MRas	3m1f	E(0-105)HCh	HVY	£3434
110	11/97	MRas	3m1f	E(0-105)HCh	GD	£3678
87	11/96	Uttx	2m	E(0-100)HHdl	GD	£2347

Total win prize-money £32598

Going:	Sf: 0-0 GS: 0-1 Gd: 0-1 GF: - Fm: 0-0
Distance:	2m/2m3: 0-0 2m4-2m7: 0-0 3m+: 0-2
Track:	LH: 0-1 RH: 0-1 Tight: 0-1 Gall: 0-0
Aids:	Bl: 0-0 Vi: 0-0 Tstrap: 0-0
Best Rating:	122 11/98 Hntg 3m gd-sft Ch

Moderate veteran handicap chaser; goes well at Fakenham; seems to run his best races when fresh; handles good ground or softer; often front runs.

Bathsheba

4-y-o b f Overbury (IRE)-Winnow (Oats)
J Gallagher Miss Marie Steele

Placings:0 (3556)
2002/03: 18⁰HY,

	Starts	1st	2nd	3rd	Win & Pl
NH Flat	1	0	0	0	
Career Total	1	0	0	0	

Going:	Sf: 0-1 GS: 0-0 Gd: 0-0 GF: - Fm: 0-0
Distance:	2m/2m3: 0-0 2m4-2m7: 0-0 3m+: 0-0
Track:	LH: 0-1 RH: 0-0 Tight: 0-0 Gall: 0-0
Aids:	Bl: 0-0 Vi: 0-0 Tstrap: 0-0
Best Rating:	0 2/03 Plum 2m2f heavy NHF

Bathwick Annie
108 97

7-y-o ch m Sula Bula-Lily Mab (FR) (Prince Mab (FR))
D P Keane W Clifford

Placings:24035 (4004)
2002/03: 20²S, 20⁴S, 20⁰HY, 21³S, 22⁵S,

	Starts	1st	2nd	3rd	Win & Pl
Hurdles	5	0	1	1	1656
Career Total	5	0	1	1	1656

Going:	Sf: 0-5 GS: 0-0 Gd: 0-0 GF: - Fm: 0-0
Distance:	2m/2m3: 0-0 2m4-2m7: 0-5 3m+: 0-0
Track:	LH: 0-3 RH: 0-2 Tight: 0-2 Gall: 0-0
Aids:	Bl: 0-0 Vi: 0-0 Tstrap: 0-0
Best Rating:	97 12/02 Chep 2m4f soft Hdl

Moderate hurdler; former maiden pointer; looked an unlucky loser when narrowly beaten on hurdling debut over two and a half miles at Chepstow; has failed to progress.

Batman Senora (FR)
112(103h) (109h)

7-y-o b g Chamberlin (FR)-Cartza (FR) (Carmarthen (FR))
Ian Williams (P Rago 24/11) G Polinski

Placings:0004655423F145/0514025650000/004600043341
465431-430320401 (4561)
2002/03: 22⁴VS, 29³VS, 22⁰VS, 20³VS, 19²VS, 22⁰VS, 27⁴HY,
20⁰HY, 20¹GF,

	Starts	1st	2nd	3rd	Win & Pl
Hurdles	4	1	1	1	12457
Chases	5	0	0	1	61196
Career Total	54	5	3	6	228676
109	4/03	Bang	2m4f	E Hdl	G-F	£3721
	4/02	Autl	2m7f110y	Ch	VS	£14723
	12/01	Cagn	2m3f	Ch	GD	£7786
	6/00	Autl	2m1f110y	HCh	VS	£19212
	3/00	Autl	2m1f110y	Ch	VS	£11527

Total win prize-money £56970

Going:	Sf: 0-2 GS: 0-0 Gd: 0-0 GF: - Fm: 1-1
Distance:	2m/2m3: 0-0 2m4-2m7: 1-7 3m+: 0-2
Track:	LH: 1-9 RH: 0-0 Tight: 1-1 Gall: 0-0
Aids:	Bl: 1-7 Vi: 0-0 Tstrap: 0-0
Best Rating:	119 11/02 Autl 2m4f110y heavy Hdl

Ex-French chaser; stays at least three miles; acts on heavy ground; often blinkered; ran well in top French races in the spring.

Batoutoftheblue

10-y-o br g Batshoof-Action Belle (Auction Ring (USA))
G A Swinbank Mrs I Gibson

Placings:333220/2B3/1-P (1384)
2002/03: 16⁵GF,

	Starts	1st	2nd	3rd	Win & Pl
Hurdles	1	0	0	0	0
Career Total	11	1	3	4	7265
120	5/01	Ayr	2m6f	E Hdl	G-F	£2968

Total win prize-money £2968

Going:	Sf: 0-0 GS: 0-0 Gd: 0-0 GF: - Fm: 0-1
Distance:	2m/2m3: 0-1 2m4-2m7: 0-0 3m+: 0-0
Track:	LH: 0-1 RH: 0-0 Tight: 0-0 Gall: 0-0
Aids:	Bl: 0-0 Vi: 0-0 Tstrap: 0-0
Best Rating:	120 5/01 Ayr 2m6f gd-fm Hdl

Batswing
107(110h) (130dh)134

8-y-o b g Batshoof-Magic Milly (Simply Great (FR))
B Ellison Ashley Carr

Placings:13/4/21B3/300112041-6PO405 (4458)
2002/03: 16⁸GS, 20⁰GS, 16⁰S, 16⁴G, 16⁵G,

	Starts	1st	2nd	3rd	Win & Pl
Hurdles	1	0	0	0	0
Chases	5	0	0	0	3256
Career Total	22	5	2	3	44228
134	4/02	Punc	2m	(0-127)HCh	G-Y	£9969
114	1/02	Muss	2m	E Ch	SFT	£3107
107	1/02	Muss	2m	D Ch	GD	£4192
122	2/01	Donc	2m110y	C(0-130)HHdl	GD	£5534
113	3/99	Trntn	2m3f110yE Hdl	SFT	£2452

Total win prize-money £25257

Going:	Sf: 0-1 GS: 0-2 Gd: 0-3 GF: - Fm: 0-0
Distance:	2m/2m3: 0-5 2m4-2m7: 0-1 3m+: 0-0
Track:	LH: 0-4 RH: 0-2 Tight: 0-2 Gall: 0-2
Aids:	Bl: 0-0 Vi: 0-0 Tstrap: 0-0
Best Rating:	134 4/02 Punc 2m gd-yld Ch

Decent chaser; acts well with cut in the ground; two miles is his trip; has worn blinkers and cheekpieces.

Batten Down (IRE)
95 74

5-y-o b g Glacial Storm (USA)-Dikler Gale (IRE) (Strong Gale)
Jonjo O Neill J P McManus

Placings:000 (4191)
2002/03: 16⁰GS, 25⁰G, 16⁰G,

	Starts	1st	2nd	3rd	Win & Pl
NH Flat	1	0	0	0	0
Hurdles	2	0	0	0	0
Career Total	3	0	0	0	

Going:	Sf: 0-0 GS: 0-1 Gd: 0-2 GF: - Fm: 0-0
Distance:	2m/2m3: 0-2 2m4-2m7: 0-0 3m+: 0-1
Track:	LH: 0-2 RH: 0-1 Tight: 0-1 Gall: 0-1
Aids:	Bl: 0-0 Vi: 0-0 Tstrap: 0-0
Best Rating:	86 12/02 Donc 2m110y gd-sft NHF

Irish point winner but has shown little here so far.

Battle Line
91 80

4-y-o b g Brief Truce (USA)-Forest Heights (Slip Anchor)
E McNamara Aidan J Ryan

Placings:00B00 (3605a)
2002/03: 16⁰HY, 16⁰GS, 16⁸HY, 16⁰S, 16⁰SH,

	Starts	1st	2nd	3rd	Win & Pl
Hurdles	5	0	0	0	
Career Total	5	0	0	0	

Going:	Sf: 0-3 GS: 0-1 Gd: 0-0 GF: - Fm: 0-0
Distance:	2m/2m3: 0-5 2m4-2m7: 0-0 3m+: 0-0
Track:	LH: 0-1 RH: 0-2 Tight: 0-0 Gall: 0-0
Aids:	Bl: 0-0 Vi: 0-0 Tstrap: 0-0
Best Rating:	80 2/03 Punc 2m soft Hdl

Battle Warning
114 119

8-y-o b g Warning-Royal Ballet (IRE) (Sadler s Wells (USA))
P Bowen P Bowen

Placings:2P1224P (4606)
2002/03: 19²G, 24⁸G, 19¹GS, 20³HY, 22²GS, 21⁴G, 24⁰G,

	Starts	1st	2nd	3rd	Win & Pl
Hurdles	7	1	3	0	18433
Career Total	7	1	3	0	18433
119	1/03	Donc	2m3f110yE Hdl	G-S	£3532

Total win prize-money £3533

Going:	Sf: 0-1 GS: 1-2 Gd: 0-4 GF: - Fm: 0-0
Distance:	2m/2m3: 0-0 2m4-2m7: 1-5 3m+: 0-2
Track:	LH: 1-4 RH: 0-3 Tight: 0-0 Gall: 0-2
Aids:	Bl: 0-1 Vi: 0-0 Tstrap: 0-0
Best Rating:	119 2/03 Winc 2m6f gd-sft Hdl

Fair staying novice hurdler; winning stayer on the Flat; scored narrowly over hurdles at Doncaster in January 2003; stays 2m 6f; handles cut in the ground; won in first time blinkers latest.

Bay Island (IRE)
104 105

7-y-o b/br g Treasure Hunter-Wild Deer (Royal Buck)
Mrs H Dalton B Perkins

Placings:PP5-11132P (4271)
2002/03: 24¹S, 26¹G, 23¹GF, 24³GS, 25²G, 24⁸G,

	Starts	1st	2nd	3rd	Win & Pl
Chases	6	3	1	1	13679
Career Total	9	3	1	1	13679

105 11/02 Leic 2m7f110y E(0-105)HCh G-F £4065
102 11/02 Wwck 3m2f E(0-105)HCh GD £3558
98 10/02 Bang 3m110y E(0-105)HCh SFT £4186
Total win prize-money £11811

Going: Sf: 1-1 GS: 0-1 Gd: 1-3 GF: - Fm: 1-1
Distance: 2m/2m3: 0-0 2m4-2m7: 0-0 3m+: 3-6
Track: LH: 2-3 RH: 1-3 Tight: 1-1 Gall: 0-1
Aids: Bl: 0-0 Vi: 0-0 Tstrap: 3-5
Best Rating: 105 12/02 Hntg 3m gd-sft Ch

Modest chaser; Irish point winner, had achieved little over fences until winning a poor race at Bangor in October and went on to complete a hat-trick; excellent second at Hereford in February after a break; stays well and suited by forcing tactics.

Bay Legend (IRE)

5-y-o b g Toulon-Kabarda (Relkino)
M Pitman Simpsonair Worldwide Distribution Ltd

Placings:0 (0063)
2002/03: 17⁰G,

	Starts	1st	2nd	3rd	Win & Pl
NH Flat	1	0	0	0	
Career Total	1	0	0	0	

Going: Sf: 0-0 GS: 0-0 Gd: 0-1 GF: - Fm: 0-0
Distance: 2m/2m3: 0-1 2m4-2m7: 0-0 3m+: 0-0
Track: LH: 0-0 RH: 0-1 Tight: 0-1 Gall: 0-0
Aids: Bl: 0-0 Vi: 0-0 Tstrap: 0-0
Best Rating:

Bay Magic (IRE)
101(96c) (106c)82
10-y-o b g Ela-Mana-Mou-Come In (Be My Guest (USA))
Miss Lucinda V Russell (J Howard Johnson 8/11) A R Trotter

Placings:61/4502245000/32/2P4344/2545-31F5424625 (4753)
2002/03: 20³S, 20¹HY, 22FHY, 21⁵GS, 21⁴S, 24²HY, 24⁴S, 20⁶GS, 25²S, 24⁵G,

	Starts	1st	2nd	3rd	Win & Pl
Hurdles	4	0	1	1	2233
Chases	6	1	1	0	5994
Career Total	34	2	7	3	18080

106 11/02 Hexm 2m4f110yE(0-105)HCh HVY £3523
112 9/97 List 2m NHF SFT £3730
Total win prize-money £7253

Going: Sf: 1-7 GS: 0-2 Gd: 0-1 GF: - Fm: 0-0
Distance: 2m/2m3: 0-0 2m4-2m7: 1-6 3m+: 0-4
Track: LH: 1-7 RH: 0-3 Tight: 0-1 Gall: 0-0
Aids: Bl: 0-0 Vi: 0-0 Tstrap: 0-0
Best Rating: 112 5/98 Leop 2m gd-fm NHF

Mainly consistent, he proved he goes on heavy ground, but the fact that he has yet to win in 19 outings over hurdles is a bit of a concern.

Bay Of Dreams
90 75
4-y-o ch g Salse (USA)-Cantico (Green Dancer (USA))
R M Stronge (I A Balding 13/5) Mrs C C Regalado-Gonzalez

Placings:46000 (4186)
2002/03: 16⁴S, 17⁶GS, 16⁰GS, 17⁰G, 17⁰G,

	Starts	1st	2nd	3rd	Win & Pl
Hurdles	5	0	0	0	0
Career Total	5	0	0	0	0

Going: Sf: 0-1 GS: 0-2 Gd: 0-2 GF: - Fm: 0-0
Distance: 2m/2m3: 0-5 2m4-2m7: 0-0 3m+: 0-0
Track: LH: 0-2 RH: 0-3 Tight: 0-1 Gall: 0-0
Aids: Bl: 0-0 Vi: 0-0 Tstrap: 0-0
Best Rating: 75 1/03 Extr 2m1f gd-sft Hdl

Bay Of Plenty
93 79
9-y-o b m Teenoso (USA)-Bara Peg (Random Shot)
P J Hobbs J M Davidson

Placings:00/S00330/6F (0447)
2002/03: 16⁶GF, 19FG,

	Starts	1st	2nd	3rd	Win & Pl
Hurdles	2	0	0	0	0
Career Total	10	0	0	2	1292

Going: Sf: 0-0 GS: 0-0 Gd: 0-1 GF: - Fm: 0-1
Distance: 2m/2m3: 0-1 2m4-2m7: 0-0 3m+: 0-0
Track: LH: 0-1 RH: 0-1 Tight: 0-0 Gall: 0-0
Aids: Bl: 0-0 Vi: 0-0 Tstrap: 0-0
Best Rating: 87 11/00 Tntn 2m3f110y gd-sft Hdl

Bdellium
97f 83f
5-y-o b m Royal Vulcan-Kelly s Logic (Netherkelly)
B I Case Neil Hutley

Placings:00 (4162)
2002/03: 16⁶G, 17⁰G,

	Starts	1st	2nd	3rd	Win & Pl
NH Flat	2	0	0	0	
Career Total	2	0	0	0	

Going: Sf: 0-0 GS: 0-0 Gd: 0-2 GF: - Fm: 0-0
Distance: 2m/2m3: 0-2 2m4-2m7: 0-0 3m+: 0-0
Track: LH: 0-0 RH: 0-2 Tight: 0-1 Gall: 0-1
Aids: Bl: 0-0 Vi: 0-0 Tstrap: 0-0
Best Rating: 83 3/03 MRas 2m1f110y good NHF

Be A Better Boy

7-y-o b g Primitive Rising (USA)-Carat Stick (Gold Rod)
J B Walton Messrs F T Walton

Placings:P (0481)
2002/03: 24PGS,

	Starts	1st	2nd	3rd	Win & Pl
Hurdles	1	0	0	0	
Career Total	1	0	0	0	

Going: Sf: 0-0 GS: 0-1 Gd: 0-0 GF: - Fm: 0-0
Distance: 2m/2m3: 0-0 2m4-2m7: 0-0 3m+: 0-0
Track: LH: 0-0 RH: 0-1 Tight: 0-0 Gall: 0-0
Aids: Bl: 0-0 Vi: 0-0 Tstrap: 0-0
Best Rating:

Be Fair
104 110+
5-y-o br g Blushing Flame (USA)-Tokyo (Mtoto)
D E Cantillon Mrs Edward Cantillon

Placings:1-11402 (4481)
2002/03: 17¹G, 16¹G, 16⁴G, 16⁶G, 17²G,

	Starts	1st	2nd	3rd	Win & Pl
NH Flat	5	2	1	0	11774
Career Total	6	3	1	0	13566

117 9/02 Worc 2m H NHF GD £1990
117 9/02 NAbb 2m1f H NHF GD £2184
104 4/02 Hntg 2m110y H NHF G-F £1792
Total win prize-money £5966

Going: Sf: 0-0 GS: 0-0 Gd: 2-5 GF: - Fm: 0-0
Distance: 2m/2m3: 2-5 2m4-2m7: 0-0 3m+: 0-0
Track: LH: 2-4 RH: 0-0 Tight: 1-1 Gall: 0-1
Aids: Bl: 0-0 Vi: 0-0 Tstrap: 0-0
Best Rating: 128 4/03 Aint 2m1f good NHF

Modest novice hurdler; won his first three bumpers and finished well clear of the others when runner-up in Grade Two bumper at Aintree; successful on hurdles bow and won just as easy next time; pacey sort and should make a very useful novice hurdler.

Be My Adelina (IRE)
95f 105+f
5-y-o b m Be My Native (USA)-Adelinas Leader (IRE) (Supreme Leader)
P F Nicholls Jeffrey Hordle

Placings:3 (4600)
2002/03: 17³GF,

	Starts	1st	2nd	3rd	Win & Pl
NH Flat	1	0	0	1	432
Career Total	1	0	0	1	432

Going: Sf: 0-0 GS: 0-0 Gd: 0-0 GF: - Fm: 0-1
Distance: 2m/2m3: 0-1 2m4-2m7: 0-0 3m+: 0-0
Track: LH: 0-0 RH: 0-1 Tight: 0-0 Gall: 0-0
Aids: Bl: 0-0 Vi: 0-0 Tstrap: 0-0
Best Rating: 90 4/03 Extr 2m1f gd-fm NHF

Modest bumper performer; just tapped for speed in slowly-run bumper at Exeter on her debut; won at Bangor next time.

Be My Destiny (IRE)
107 115
6-y-o b g Be My Native (USA)-Miss Cali (Young Man (FR))
M Pitman Mrs Elizabeth Pearce

Placings:206-02125 (4048)
2002/03: 16⁶G, 17²HY, 17¹HY, 17²HY, 20⁵HY,

	Starts	1st	2nd	3rd	Win & Pl
Hurdles	5	1	2	0	6737
Career Total	8	1	3	0	7185

115 1/03 Folk 2m1f110y E Hdl HVY £3577
Total win prize-money £3577

Going: Sf: 1-4 GS: 0-0 Gd: 0-1 GF: - Fm: 0-0
Distance: 2m/2m3: 1-4 2m4-2m7: 0-1 3m+: 0-0
Track: LH: 0-0 RH: 1-5 Tight: 1-3 Gall: 0-0
Aids: Bl: 0-0 Vi: 0-0 Tstrap: 0-0
Best Rating: 115 2/03 Folk 2m1f110y heavy Hdl

Fair novice hurdler; effective on testing ground at around two miles; keen sort; a chaser in the making.

Be My Dream (IRE)

8-y-o b g Be My Native (USA)-Dream Toi (Carlburg)
R J Webb (Jonjo O Neill 26/8) C W Booth

Placings:06/31132-2122254   (4059)
2002/03: 23²G, 24¹HY, 24²S, 26²G, 25²G, 27⁵G, 26⁴GS,

	Starts	1st	2nd	3rd	Win & Pl
Chases	7	1	4	0	8881
Career Total	14	3	5	2	19001
117 6/02 Uttx	3m		D Ch	HVY	£4147
111 10/01 Weth	3m1f		F(0-90)HHdl	GD	£2492
111 10/01 MRas	3m		F(0-100)HHdl	G-S	£2712

Total win prize-money £9352

Going:	Sf: 1-2 GS: 0-1 Gd: 0-4 GF: - Fm: 0-0
Distance:	2m/2m3: 0-0 2m4-2m7: 0-0 3m+: 1-7
Track:	LH: 1-4 RH: 0-2 Tight: 0-3 Gall: 0-0
Aids:	Bl: 0-0 Vi: 0-0 Tstrap: 0-0
Best Rating:	117 8/02 Bang 3m110y soft Ch

Modest hunter chaser; stays well; acts on good ground.

Be My Friend (IRE)
111   111+

7-y-o b g Be My Native (USA)-Miss Lamb (Relkino)
Mrs H Dalton J Hales

Placings:351   (4316)
2002/03: 17³GS, 19⁵GS, 17¹G,

	Starts	1st	2nd	3rd	Win & Pl
Hurdles	3	1	0	1	4504
Career Total	3	1	0	1	4504
115 3/03 Bang 2m1f		E Hdl		GD	£3916

Total win prize-money £3916

Going:	Sf: 0-0 GS: 0-2 Gd: 1-1 GF: - Fm: 0-0
Distance:	2m/2m3: 1-2 2m4-2m7: 0-1 3m+: 0-0
Track:	LH: 1-3 RH: 0-0 Tight: 1-2 Gall: 0-0
Aids:	Bl: 0-0 Vi: 0-0 Tstrap: 0-0
Best Rating:	115 3/03 Bang 2m1f good Hdl

Fair hurdler; scored on third attempt at Bangor in march 2003; has only raced on good or softer.

Be My Manager (IRE)
108   127

8-y-o b g Be My Native (USA)-Fahy Quay (Quayside)
Miss H C Knight The Earl Cadogan

Placings:2143/11/P4F-5303000   (4472)
2002/03: 21⁵G, 24³G, 25⁰G, 21³HY, 21⁰GS, 24⁰G, 21⁰G,

	Starts	1st	2nd	3rd	Win & Pl
Chases	7	0	2	3	3977
Career Total	16	3	1	3	29716
146 1/01 Chel	2m5f		C HCh	SFT	£11212
120 10/00 Tntn	2m3f		D Ch	GD	£5642
117 1/00 Leic	2m4f110yD Hdl			SFT	£3705

Total win prize-money £20560

Going:	Sf: 0-1 GS: 0-1 Gd: 0-5 GF: - Fm: 0-0
Distance:	2m/2m3: 0-0 2m4-2m7: 0-4 3m+: 0-3
Track:	LH: 0-7 RH: 0-0 Tight: 0-2 Gall: 0-5
Aids:	Bl: 0-0 Vi: 0-0 Tstrap: 0-0
Best Rating:	146 1/01 Chel 2m5f soft Ch

Decent chaser; rather disappointing in 2002/3; acts on good ground; stays three miles.

Be My Royal (IRE)
105   (148h)151

9-y-o b g Be My Native (USA)-Royal Rehearsal (Pamroy)
W P Mullins Mrs V O Leary

Placings:1/3/11102/FFU3UPUF-13111   (2243)
2002/03: 16¹S, 21³S, 20¹YS, 28¹S, 26¹GS,

	Starts	1st	2nd	3rd	Win & Pl
Chases	5	4	0	1	94925
Career Total	20	8	1	3	132812
151 11/02 Newb	3m2f110yA HCh			G-S	£60900
135 11/02 Cork	3m4f		(0-140)HCh	SFT	£19938
124 10/02 Thur	2m4f		Ch	Y-S	£7975
110 5/02 Wxfd	2m		Ch	SFT	£4868
153 12/00 Thur	3m		Hdl	SFT	£7800
133 11/00 Cork	3m		Hdl	SFT	£4692
130 10/00 Wxfd	3m		Hdl	HVY	£4416
111 4/99 Fair	2m		NHF	YLD	£6138

Total win prize-money £116728

Going:	Sf: 2-3 GS: 1-1 Gd: 0-0 GF: - Fm: 0-0
Distance:	2m/2m3: 1-1 2m4-2m7: 1-2 3m+: 2-2
Track:	LH: 1-1 RH: 1 Tight: 0-0 Gall: 1-1
Aids:	Bl: 0-0 Vi: 0-0 Tstrap: 0-0
Best Rating:	153 12/00 Thur 3m soft Hdl

Smart staying chaser; former decent novice hurdler; winning the Cork National and scoring a memorable win in the Hennessy, in which he suffered career-ending tendon injury; reportedly failed a drugs test post race; stayed well; acted on a soft surface.

Be Upstanding
103(104h)   (106h)111

8-y-o ch g Hubbly Bubbly (USA)-Two Travellers (Deep Run)
Ferdy Murphy M Holmes

Placings:UF/01345-6331021S   (4775)
2002/03: 16⁶G, 17³S, 21³S, 21¹S, 21⁰GS, 24²G, 24¹G, 24⁵G,

	Starts	1st	2nd	3rd	Win & Pl
Hurdles	1	0	0	0	
Chases	7	2	1	2	11639
Career Total	15	3	1	3	15429
120 4/03 Uttx	3m		E(0-110)HCh	GD	£4416
111 1/03 Fknm	2m5f110yE(0-100)HCh			SFT	£3806
86 2/02 Fknm	2m4f		D Hdl	G-S	£3343

Total win prize-money £11566

Going:	Sf: 1-3 GS: 0-1 Gd: 1-4 GF: - Fm: 0-0
Distance:	2m/2m3: 0-2 2m4-2m7: 1-3 3m+: 1-3
Track:	LH: 2-6 RH: 0-2 Tight: 1-3 Gall: 0-0
Aids:	Bl: 0-0 Vi: 0-0 Tstrap: 0-0
Best Rating:	120 4/03 Uttx 3m good Ch

Modest novice chaser; stays 3m; acts on soft ground; on the upgrade.

Beacon Hill Lass

5-y-o b m Reprimand-Wild Moon (USA) (Arctic Tern (USA))
R Ford D C Fillingham

Placings:PPU   (0892)
2002/03: 16ᴾGF, 21ᴾGF, 17ᵁS,

	Starts	1st	2nd	3rd	Win & Pl
Hurdles	3	0	0	0	
Career Total	3	0	0	0	

Going:	Sf: 0-1 GS: 0-0 Gd: 0-0 GF: - Fm: 0-2
Distance:	2m/2m3: 0-2 2m4-2m7: 0-1 3m+: 0-0
Track:	LH: 0-3 RH: 0-0 Tight: 0-3 Gall: 0-0
Aids:	Bl: 0-0 Vi: 0-0 Tstrap: 0-0

Best Rating: 0   8/02   Bang 2m1f   soft   Hdl

Beacon Vale (IRE)

7-y-o ch g Forest Wind (USA)-Pam Story (Sallust)
G Barnett W G Galley

Placings:P   (1488)
2002/03: 20ᴾGS,

	Starts	1st	2nd	3rd	Win & Pl
Hurdles	1	0	0	0	
Career Total	1	0	0	0	

Going:	Sf: 0-0 GS: 0-1 Gd: 0-0 GF: - Fm: 0-0
Distance:	2m/2m3: 0-0 2m4-2m7: 0-1 3m+: 0-0
Track:	LH: 0-1 RH: 0-0 Tight: 0-1 Gall: 0-0
Aids:	Bl: 0-0 Vi: 0-0 Tstrap: 0-0
Best Rating:	0 10/02 Bang 2m4f gd-sft Hdl

Beamish (IRE)

9-y-o ch g Caesar Imperator (FR)-Super Slaney (Brave Invader (USA))
P C Ritchens P Ritchens

Placings:3404/PP-PU   (3313)
2002/03: 19ᴾS, 23ᵁPS,

	Starts	1st	2nd	3rd	Win & Pl
Chases	2	0	0	0	
Career Total	8	0	0	1	575

Going:	Sf: 0-1 GS: 0-1 Gd: 0-0 GF: - Fm: 0-0
Distance:	2m/2m3: 0-1 2m4-2m7: 0-0 3m+: 0-1
Track:	LH: 0-0 RH: 0-2 Tight: 0-1 Gall: 0-0
Aids:	Bl: 0-0 Vi: 0-0 Tstrap: 0-0
Best Rating:	108 7/00 Worc 2m good NHF

Beanboy

5-y-o ch g Clantime-Lady Blues Singer (Chief Singer)
Mrs S Lamyman P Lamyman

Placings:PP   (1625)
2002/03: 17ᴾGF, 20ᴾGS,

	Starts	1st	2nd	3rd	Win & Pl
Hurdles	2	0	0	0	
Career Total	2	0	0	0	

Going:	Sf: 0-0 GS: 0-1 Gd: 0-0 GF: - Fm: 0-1
Distance:	2m/2m3: 0-0 2m4-2m7: 0-1 3m+: 0-0
Track:	LH: 0-1 RH: 0-1 Tight: 0-2 Gall: 0-0
Aids:	Bl: 0-0 Vi: 0-0 Tstrap: 0-0
Best Rating:	0 10/02 Fknm 2m4f gd-sft Hdl

Bear On Board (IRE)
108   118

8-y-o b g Black Monday-Under The River (Over The River (FR))
A King J E Brown

Placings:122/P3312   (4174)
2002/03: 24ᴾHY, 25³S, 23⁰S, 24¹S, 26²S,

	Starts	1st	2nd	3rd	Win & Pl
Chases	5	1	1	2	13089

Career Total	8	2	3	2	18442
114 3/03 Bang 3m110y D(0-120)HCh				SFT	£5838
115 11/00 Uttx 2m6f110yE Hdl				HVY	£2485

Total win prize-money £8323

Going: Sf: 1-5 GS: 0-0 Gd: 0-0 GF: - Fm: 0-0
Distance: 2m/2m3: 0-0 2m4-2m7: 0-0 3m+: 1-5
Track: LH: 1-3 RH: 0-0 Tight: 1-3 Gall: 0-0
Aids: Bl: 0-0 Vi: 0-0 Tstrap: 0-0
Best Rating: 124 2/01 Asct 3m   heavy Hdl

Fair chaser; formerly useful novice hurdler but suffered an injury; pulled up on his chasing debut in November 2002; progressed to win at Bangor in March 2003; stays three miles; effective in soft ground.

Beasley
92   74
4-y-o b g First Trump-Le Shuttle (Presidium)
M Pitman Shared Options

Placings:F43004   (2610)
2002/03: 16FGS, 18⁴G, 16³F, 16⁹G, 18⁹G, 16⁴S,

	Starts	1st	2nd	3rd	Win & Pl
Hurdles	6	0	0	1	444
Career Total	6	0	0	1	444

Going: Sf: 0-1 GS: 0-1 Gd: 0-3 GF: - Fm: 0-1
Distance: 2m/2m3: 0-6 2m4-2m7: 0-0 3m+: 0-0
Track: LH: 0-3 RH: 0-1 Tight: 0-4 Gall: 0-0
Aids: Bl: 0-0 Vi: 0-1 Tstrap: 0-0
Best Rating: 71 12/02 Uttx 2m   soft Hdl

Poor selling hurdler.

Beat The Heat (IRE)
103   110+
5-y-o b g Salse (USA)-Summer Trysting (USA) (Alleged (USA))
Jedd O Keeffe John Haythorne & June Wheelhouse

Placings:3235   (3164)
2002/03: 16³GS, 17²S, 16³GF, 16⁵G,

	Starts	1st	2nd	3rd	Win & Pl
Hurdles	4	0	1	2	3025
Career Total	4	0	1	2	3025

Going: Sf: 0-1 GS: 0-1 Gd: 0-1 GF: - Fm: 0-0
Distance: 2m/2m3: 0-4 2m4-2m7: 0-0 3m+: 0-0
Track: LH: 0-3 RH: 0-1 Tight: 0-3 Gall: 0-0
Aids: Bl: 0-1 Vi: 0-0 Tstrap: 0-0
Best Rating: 112 1/03 Catt 2m   good Hdl

Modest hurdler; Flat winner, has shown a fair level of ability over hurdles but well beaten on handicap bow.

Beat The Retreat
88(95h)   (90h)91
8-y-o b g Terimon-Carpet Slippers (Daring March)
A King Mrs Peter Mason

Placings:43/33-3PP3P02   (4680)
2002/03: 22³G, 20PGS, 16PGS, 17³GS, 16PGF, 17⁹GF, 20²GF,

	Starts	1st	2nd	3rd	Win & Pl
Hurdles	6	0	0	2	1149
Chases	1	0	1	0	1188
Career Total	11	0	1	5	3938

Going: Sf: 0-0 GS: 0-3 Gd: 0-1 GF: - Fm: 0-3
Distance: 2m/2m3: 0-4 2m4-2m7: 0-3 3m+: 0-0

Track: LH: 0-3 RH: 0-4 Tight: 0-0 Gall: 0-1
Aids: Bl: 0-0 Vi: 0-0 Tstrap: 0-0
Best Rating: 107 1/02 Hntg 2m110y gd-sft Hdl

Modest maiden hurdler; runner-up on debut over fences at Huntingdon in April; effective at up to two miles six; acts on good and soft ground.

Beat The Ring (IRE)
91   92+
5-y-o br g Tagula (IRE)-Pursue (Auction Ring (USA))
C A Dwyer Mrs K W Sneath

Placings:644-3   (0170)
2002/03: 16³G,

	Starts	1st	2nd	3rd	Win & Pl
Hurdles	1	0	0	1	349
Career Total	4	0	0	1	349

Going: Sf: 0-0 GS: 0-0 Gd: 0-1 GF: - Fm: 0-0
Distance: 2m/2m3: 0-1 2m4-2m7: 0-0 3m+: 0-0
Track: LH: 0-1 RH: 0-0 Tight: 0-1 Gall: 0-0
Aids: Bl: 0-0 Vi: 0-0 Tstrap: 0-0
Best Rating: 93 5/02 Sthl 2m   good Hdl

Moderate hurdler; may struggle to stay two miles over hurdles; could do better in novice handicaps.

Beau Brun (FR)
7-y-o b/br g Cadoudal (FR)-Atakaia (FR) (Ataxerxes (GER))
Graeme Roe Roe Racing Ltd

Placings:P53/P-PP   (1244)
2002/03: 22PGS, 24PG,

	Starts	1st	2nd	3rd	Win & Pl
Hurdles	2	0	0	0	
Career Total	6	0	0	1	675

Going: Sf: 0-0 GS: 0-0 Gd: 0-1 GF: - Fm: 0-0
Distance: 2m/2m3: 0-0 2m4-2m7: 0-1 3m+: 0-1
Track: LH: 0-2 RH: 0-0 Tight: 0-1 Gall: 0-0
Aids: Bl: 0-0 Vi: 0-0 Tstrap: 0-0
Best Rating: 55 11/99 2m110y   good Hdl

Beau Castle (IRE)
11-y-o b g Castle Keep-Temba (Beau Chapeau)
Mrs K Lawther S M Atkins

Placings:6/4PP416/00/U4PP   (4314)
2002/03: 20UGF, 214G, 16PGS, 22PG,

	Starts	1st	2nd	3rd	Win & Pl
Chases	4	0	0	0	0
Career Total	13	1	0	0	2390
88 8/99 Font 2m6f110y				F(0-100)HHdl	
G-F £2390					

Total win prize-money £2390

Going: Sf: 0-0 GS: 0-1 Gd: 0-2 GF: - Fm: 0-1
Distance: 2m/2m3: 0-1 2m4-2m7: 0-0 3m+: 0-0
Track: LH: 0-1 RH: 0-3 Tight: 0-1 Gall: 0-2
Aids: Bl: 0-0 Vi: 0-0 Tstrap: 0-0
Best Rating: 89 6/98 Worc 2m   gd-fm NHF

Beau Jake (IRE)
96(93h)   (79h)99
8-y-o b g Jolly Jake (NZ)-Cool Mary (Beau Charmeur (FR))

N M Babbage John Cantrill

Placings:44003000-55F63   (4447)
2002/03: 16⁵S, 24⁵S, 26FS, 26⁶GF, 24³G,

	Starts	1st	2nd	3rd	Win & Pl
Hurdles	1	0	0	0	0
Chases	4	0	0	1	900
Career Total	13	0	0	2	1301

Going: Sf: 0-3 GS: 0-0 Gd: 0-1 GF: - Fm: 0-1
Distance: 2m/2m3: 0-1 2m4-2m7: 0-0 3m+: 0-4
Track: LH: 0-0 RH: 0-4 Tight: 0-4 Gall: 0-0
Aids: Bl: 0-0 Vi: 0-0 Tstrap: 0-0
Best Rating: 104 5/01 Hntg 2m110y gd-fm NHF

Beau Roberto
87   94
9-y-o b g Robellino (USA)-Night Jar (Night Shift (USA))
J S Goldie J W Armstrong

Placings:54/25   (1959)
2002/03: 22²GF, 20⁵S,

	Starts	1st	2nd	3rd	Win & Pl
Hurdles	2	0	1	0	1060
Career Total	4	0	1	0	1060

Going: Sf: 0-1 GS: 0-0 Gd: 0-0 GF: - Fm: 0-1
Distance: 2m/2m3: 0-0 2m4-2m7: 0-2 3m+: 0-0
Track: LH: 0-2 RH: 0-0 Tight: 0-1 Gall: 0-0
Aids: Bl: 0-0 Vi: 0-0 Tstrap: 0-0
Best Rating: 105 11/99 Ayr 2m   good Hdl

Moderate novice hurdler; returned from a long break to make the frame at Kelso in October 2002; likely to prove best around two and a half miles.

Beau Torero (FR)
92(93h)   (83dh)82
5-y-o gr g True Brave (USA)-Brave Lola (FR) (Dom Pasquini (FR))
Mrs L C Taylor Miss M Talbot

Placings:3000005   (4523)
2002/03: 16³GF, 12⁰G, 16⁹GS, 16⁰GS, 20PHY, 16⁹G, 16⁵G,

	Starts	1st	2nd	3rd	Win & Pl
NH Flat	2	0	0	1	252
Hurdles	4	0	0	0	
Chases	1	0	0	0	0
Career Total	7	0	0	1	252

Going: Sf: 0-1 GS: 0-2 Gd: 0-3 GF: - Fm: 0-1
Distance: 2m/2m3: 0-5 2m4-2m7: 0-1 3m+: 0-0
Track: LH: 0-3 RH: 0-4 Tight: 0-0 Gall: 0-2
Aids: Bl: 0-0 Vi: 0-0 Tstrap: 0-0
Best Rating: 93 10/02 Hntg 2m110y gd-fm NHF

Plating-class novice chaser/hurdler; did not jump well on his chase debut.

Beau Tudor (IRE)
9-y-o b g Aragon-Sunley Silks (Formidable (USA))
Miss L C Siddall Miss L C Siddall

Placings:P   (3965)
2002/03: 16PS,

	Starts	1st	2nd	3rd	Win & Pl
Hurdles	1	0	0	0	
Career Total	1	0	0	0	

Beauchamp Oracle
79f   64f

6-y-o gr g Mystiko (USA)-Beauchamp Cactus (Niniski (USA))
A J Chamberlain   A J Chamberlain

Placings:0   (1696)
2002/03: 16⁰G,

	Starts	1st	2nd	3rd	Win & Pl
NH Flat	1	0	0	0	
Career Total	1	0	0	0	

Going: Sf: 0-0 GS: 0-0 Gd: 0-1 GF: - Fm: 0-0
Distance: 2m/2m3: 0-1 2m4-2m7: 0-0 3m+: 0-0
Track: LH: 0-1 RH: 0-0 Tight: 0-0 Gall: 0-0
Aids: Bl: 0-0 Vi: 0-0 Tstrap: 0-0
Best Rating: 64   10/02 Chel   2m110y   good   NHF

Beaufort Zero
97   80

9-y-o br g Strong Gale-Miss Roulette (Mummy s Game)
C P Morlock   Sir Peter Miller

Placings:60/5/P/5P   (4709)
2002/03: 25⁵G, 24⁸G,

	Starts	1st	2nd	3rd	Win & Pl
Hurdles	2	0	0	0	0
Career Total	6	0	0	0	0

Going: Sf: 0-0 GS: 0-0 Gd: 0-2 GF: - Fm: 0-0
Distance: 2m/2m3: 0-0 2m4-2m7: 0-0 3m+: 0-2
Track: LH: 0-2 RH: 0-0 Tight: 0-0 Gall: 0-0
Aids: Bl: 0-0 Vi: 0-0 Tstrap: 0-0
Best Rating: 99   1/99   Donc   2m110y   good   NHF

Beauly (IRE)
101   72

8-y-o b g Beau Sher-Woodland Theory (Sheer Grit)
J G M O Shea   K A Wells

Placings:00013   (4598)
2002/03: 20⁵S, 20⁹S, 20⁹HY, 17¹F, 19³GF,

	Starts	1st	2nd	3rd	Win & Pl
Hurdles	5	1	0	1	4566
Career Total	5	1	0	1	4566
72 3/03 Extr 2m1f E(0-100)HHdl FRM £4013					
Total win prize-money £4014					

Going: Sf: 0-3 GS: 0-0 Gd: 0-0 GF: - Fm: 1-2
Distance: 2m/2m3: 1-2 2m4-2m7: 0-3 3m+: 0-0
Track: LH: 0-3 RH: 1-2 Tight: 0-0 Gall: 0-0
Aids: Bl: 0-0 Vi: 0-0 Tstrap: 0-0
Best Rating: 72   4/03   Extr   2m3f   gd-fm   Hdl

Plating-class hurdler; marked improvement when 50/1 winner of 17 furlong novices' handicap on firm ground at Exeter March 2003; acts on fast ground; should be suited by a return to a longer trip.

Beausejour (USA)
102   87+

5-y-o ch m Diesis-Libeccio (NZ) (Danzatore (CAN))
B G Powell   Miss K Mundy

Placings:F500   (4371)
2002/03: 16⁸GS, 20⁵S, 16⁰S, 16⁹G,

	Starts	1st	2nd	3rd	Win & Pl
Hurdles	4	0	0	0	0

Going: Sf: 0-1 GS: 0-0 Gd: 0-0 GF: - Fm: 0-0
Distance: 2m/2m3: 0-1 2m4-2m7: 0-0 3m+: 0-0
Track: LH: 0-1 RH: 0-0 Tight: 0-1 Gall: 0-0
Aids: Bl: 0-0 Vi: 0-0 Tstrap: 0-0
Best Rating: 0   3/03   Catt   2m   soft   Hdl

Beauanarrow (IRE)
(77h)   (80h)**95**

8-y-o b g Beau Sher-Ardnasagh Rose (Crash Course)
N M Babbage   John Cantrill

Placings:21/31642-F   (0073)
2002/03: 19⁶GF,

	Starts	1st	2nd	3rd	Win & Pl
Chases	1	0	0	0	
Career Total	8	2	2	1	5844
104 12/01 Ludl 2m H NHF GD £1981					
102 4/01 MRas 2m1f110yH NHF HVY £1764					
Total win prize-money £3745					

Going: Sf: 0-0 GS: 0-0 Gd: 0-0 GF: - Fm: 0-1
Distance: 2m/2m3: 0-1 2m4-2m7: 0-0 3m+: 0-0
Track: LH: 0-0 RH: 0-1 Tight: 0-0 Gall: 0-0
Aids: Bl: 0-0 Vi: 0-0 Tstrap: 0-0
Best Rating: 107   11/01   Ludl   2m   gd-fm   NHF

Moderate hurdler; previously fair bumper performer; effective at around two miles, he acts on good and heavy ground.

Beauchamp Magic
88   57

8-y-o b g Northern Park (USA)-Beauchamp Buzz (High Top)
K R Burke (M D I Usher 11/11)   Regency Red Partnership

Placings:0P/0/600   (4104)
2002/03: 16⁶GF, 19⁰GS, 27⁰S,

	Starts	1st	2nd	3rd	Win & Pl
Hurdles	3	0	0	0	0
Career Total	6	0	0	0	0

Going: Sf: 0-1 GS: 0-1 Gd: 0-0 GF: - Fm: 0-1
Distance: 2m/2m3: 0-1 2m4-2m7: 0-1 3m+: 0-1
Track: LH: 0-2 RH: 0-1 Tight: 0-2 Gall: 0-0
Aids: Bl: 0-0 Vi: 0-0 Tstrap: 0-0
Best Rating: 75   10/00   Font   2m4f   good   Hdl

Beauchamp Nyx
70   19

7-y-o b m Northern Park (USA)-Beauchamp Image (Midyan (USA))
P A Pritchard   P A Pritchard

Placings:30   (1826)
2002/03: 24³GF, 22⁰S,

	Starts	1st	2nd	3rd	Win & Pl
Hurdles	2	0	0	1	638
Career Total	2	0	0	1	638

Going: Sf: 0-1 GS: 0-0 Gd: 0-0 GF: - Fm: 0-1
Distance: 2m/2m3: 0-2 2m4-2m7: 0-1 3m+: 0-1
Track: LH: 0-1 RH: 0-1 Tight: 0-1 Gall: 0-0
Aids: Bl: 0-0 Vi: 0-0 Tstrap: 0-0
Best Rating: 31   11/02   Uttx   2m6f110y   soft   Hdl

Tailed off on her hurdling debut.

Career Total   4   0   0   0   0

Going: Sf: 0-2 GS: 0-1 Gd: 0-1 GF: - Fm: 0-0
Distance: 2m/2m3: 0-3 2m4-2m7: 0-1 3m+: 0-0
Track: LH: 0-1 RH: 0-2 Tight: 0-2 Gall: 0-0
Aids: Bl: 0-0 Vi: 0-0 Tstrap: 0-0
Best Rating: 64   3/03   Winc   2m   soft   Hdl

GPlating-class hurdler; got off the mark in 2m novices' claiming hurdle at Worcester June 2003; acts on fast ground; best at 2m; inclined to run too freely.

Beaver Lodge (IRE)
100(105h)   (120 h)109

6-y-o gr g Grand Lodge (USA)-Thistlewood (Kalamoun)
C J Mann   Granville J Harper

Placings:0234/445011-61400   (4367)
2002/03: 21⁸GS, 19¹GS, 22⁴GS, 20⁹G, 20⁰G,

	Starts	1st	2nd	3rd	Win & Pl
Hurdles	5	1	0	0	6856
Career Total	15	3	1	1	16485
119 12/02 MRas 2m3f110yD(0-125)HHdl G-S £5037					
113 4/02 Bang 2m4f E Hdl GD £3962					
112 4/02 MRas 2m3f110yD(0-120)HHdl G-F £3500					
Total win prize-money £12500					

Going: Sf: 0-0 GS: 1-3 Gd: 0-2 GF: - Fm: 0-0
Distance: 2m/2m3: 0-0 **2m4-2m7: 1-5** 3m+: 0-0
Track: LH: 0-2 **RH: 1-3** Tight: **1-1** Gall: 0-1
Aids: Bl: 0-0 Vi: 0-0 Tstrap: 0-0
Best Rating: 120   3/03   Asct   2m4f   good   Hdl

Fair, ex-Irish handicap hurdler; did well in this country in 2002, improving gradually and winning three times; just held on chasing debut at Market Rasen in July 2003; eventually well beaten by Stromness over 3m next time; suited by trips of around 2m 4f; goes on any ground.

Beckdale
94   66

7-y-o b g Perpendicular-Knocksharry (Palm Track)
Andrew Turnell   Dr John Hollowood

Placings:3224000/FP6P10-P365P   (3226)
2002/03: 16⁸GF, 16³HY, 17⁶S, 17⁵GS, 21⁵HY,

	Starts	1st	2nd	3rd	Win & Pl
Hurdles	5	0	0	1	316
Career Total	18	1	2	2	4298
89 3/02 Sedg 2m1f E(0-105)HHdl SFT £2541					
Total win prize-money £2541					

Going: Sf: 0-3 GS: 0-1 Gd: 0-0 GF: - Fm: 0-1
Distance: 2m/2m3: 0-4 2m4-2m7: 0-1 3m+: 0-0
Track: LH: 0-4 RH: 0-1 Tight: 0-3 Gall: 0-0
Aids: Bl: 0-0 Vi: 0-0 Tstrap: 0-0
Best Rating: 110   12/00   Donc   2m110y   heavy   NHF

Plating-class hurdler; took advantage of a lenient mark to take a two mile novices handicap at Sedgefield in March but out of form since.

Beckley (IRE)
96   100

7-y-o b g Phardante (FR)-Baybush (Boreen (FR))
C Grant   J Henderson (co Durham)

Placings:2306-4F1   (4776)
2002/03: 16⁴GS, 20⁴HY, 20¹G,

	Starts	1st	2nd	3rd	Win & Pl
Hurdles	3	1	0	0	5941
Career Total	7	1	1	1	6617

| 100 | 4/03 | Prth | 2m4f110yD(0-110)HHdl | GD | £5941 |

Total win prize-money £5941

Going: Sf: 0-1 GS: 0-1 Gd: 1-1 GF: - Fm: 0-0
Distance: 2m/2m3: 0-1 2m4-2m7: 1-2 3m+: 0-0
Track: LH: 0-2 RH: 1-1 Tight: 0-1 Gall: 0-1
Aids: Bl: 0-0 Vi: 0-0 Tstrap: 0-0
Best Rating: 100 4/03 Prth 2m4f110y good Hdl

Moderate hurdler; half-brother to Sparky Gayle; showed ability in bumpers; got off the mark over hurdles at Perth in April 2003; stays two and ahalf miles; suited by a sound surface.

Beckon
97   77+
7-y-o ch m Beveled (USA)-Carolynchristensen (Sweet Revenge)
R Wilman (B R Johnson 7/10) Mrs Joanna Hughes

Placings:3   (1428)
2002/03: 16³GF,

	Starts	1st	2nd	3rd	Win & Pl
Hurdles	1	0	0	1	418
Career Total	1	0	0	1	418

Going: Sf: 0-0 GS: 0-0 Gd: 0-0 GF: - Fm: 0-1
Distance: 2m/2m3: 0-1 2m4-2m7: 0-0 3m+: 0-0
Track: LH: 0-1 RH: 0-0 Tight: 0-1 Gall: 0-0
Aids: Bl: 0-0 Vi: 0-0 Tstrap: 0-0
Best Rating: 77 10/02 Plum 2m gd-fm Hdl

Plating-class performer, showed ability on hurdling debut.

Bed Bug (FR)
98   99+
5-y-o b g Double Bed (FR)-Cotation (FR) (Recitation (USA))
N J Henderson The Barrow Boys Iv

Placings:045031   (4669)
2002/03: 16⁹G, 16⁴GS, 19²S, 19⁰S, 16³GF, 16¹G,

	Starts	1st	2nd	3rd	Win & Pl
NH Flat	2	0	0	0	
Hurdles	4	1	0	1	6015
Career Total	6	1	0	1	6015

100 4/03 Fknm 2m D(0-110)HHdl GD £5445
Total win prize-money £5446

Going: Sf: 0-2 GS: 0-1 Gd: 1-2 GF: - Fm: 0-1
Distance: 2m/2m3: 0-4 2m4-2m7: 0-1 3m+: 0-0
Track: LH: 1-3 RH: 0-3 Tight: 1-2 Gall: 0-3
Aids: Bl: 0-0 Vi: 0-0 Tstrap: 0-0
Best Rating: 100 4/03 Fknm 2m good Hdl

Moderate novice hurdler; effective at two miles on a sound surface; seemed not to stay when tried over 2m 3f.

Bede (IRE)
89(98h)   (92h)77
7-y-o b g Spanish Place (USA)-Midnight Oil (Menelek)
P J Hobbs M G St Quinton

Placings:6650-0   (0039)
2002/03: 19⁰G,

	Starts	1st	2nd	3rd	Win & Pl
Chases	1	0	0	0	
Career Total	5	0	0	0	

Going: Sf: 0-0 GS: 0-0 Gd: 0-1 GF: - Fm: 0-0
Distance: 2m/2m3: 0-2 2m4-2m7: 0-1 3m+: 0-0
Track: LH: 0-0 RH: 0-1 Tight: 0-0 Gall: 0-0
Aids: Bl: 0-0 Vi: 0-0 Tstrap: 0-0
Best Rating: 95 5/01 Extr 2m1f good NHF

Bedford Leader
68   32
5-y-o b m Bedford (USA)-Neladar (Ardar)
A P Jones B W Bedford

Placings:00   (3556)
2002/03: 16⁹HY, 18⁰HY,

	Starts	1st	2nd	3rd	Win & Pl
NH Flat	2	0	0	0	
Career Total	2	0	0	0	

Going: Sf: 0-2 GS: 0-0 Gd: 0-0 GF: - Fm: 0-0
Distance: 2m/2m3: 0-2 2m4-2m7: 0-0 3m+: 0-0
Track: LH: 0-2 RH: 0-0 Tight: 0-0 Gall: 0-1
Aids: Bl: 0-0 Vi: 0-0 Tstrap: 0-0
Best Rating: 31 2/03 Plum 2m2f heavy NHF

Bee An Bee (IRE)
105   115
6-y-o b g Phardante (FR)-Portia s Delight (IRE) (The Parson)
P Winkworth Stan Moore

Placings:2200-6421024F   (4442)
2002/03: 20⁶G, 22⁴GS, 16²S, 17¹GS, 17⁹GS, 20²HY, 21⁴S, 20⁷G,

	Starts	1st	2nd	3rd	Win & Pl
Hurdles	8	1	2	0	6967
Career Total	12	1	4	0	7907

106 12/02 Extr 2m1f E(0-100)HHdl G-S £3486
Total win prize-money £3486

Going: Sf: 0-3 GS: 1-3 Gd: 0-2 GF: - Fm: 0-0
Distance: 2m/2m3: 1-3 2m4-2m7: 0-5 3m+: 0-0
Track: LH: 0-4 RH: 1-4 Tight: 0-3 Gall: 0-0
Aids: Bl: 0-0 Vi: 0-2 Tstrap: 0-0
Best Rating: 115 2/03 Plum 2m5f soft Hdl

Modest handicapper; bred to make a chaser but has run well over timber; suited by two to two and a half miles; acts well on soft ground.

Beechbrook Gale (IRE)
60   83
7-y-o b g Toulon-Swan Upping (Lord Gayle (USA))
John R Upson Jim Bath & Martin Tucker

Placings:5FP3-F6   (2331)
2002/03: 25²G, 21⁶GS,

	Starts	1st	2nd	3rd	Win & Pl
Chases	2	0	0	0	
Career Total	6	0	0	1	943

Going: Sf: 0-0 GS: 0-1 Gd: 0-1 GF: - Fm: 0-0
Distance: 2m/2m3: 0-0 2m4-2m7: 0-1 3m+: 0-0
Track: LH: 0-0 RH: 0-2 Tight: 0-1 Gall: 0-0
Aids: Bl: 0-0 Vi: 0-0 Tstrap: 0-0
Best Rating: 83 3/02 Towc 2m110y gd-sft Ch

Beeches Girl
97   82
8-y-o b m Lord Americo-Phyll-Tarquin (Tarqogan)
R Dickin E R C Beech & B Wilkinson

Placings:060P/50PF65-P445P3334   (4320)
2002/03: 19⁶G, 22⁴GF, 17⁴G, 20⁵HY, 21⁶G, 16³HY, 16³HY, 16³S, 17⁴G,

	Starts	1st	2nd	3rd	Win & Pl
Hurdles	8	0	0	3	1764
Chases	1	0	0	0	0
Career Total	19	0	0	3	1764

Going: Sf: 0-4 GS: 0-0 Gd: 0-4 GF: - Fm: 0-1
Distance: 2m/2m3: 0-6 2m4-2m7: 0-3 3m+: 0-0
Track: LH: 0-3 RH: 0-6 Tight: 0-2 Gall: 0-0
Aids: Bl: 0-1 Vi: 0-0 Tstrap: 0-0
Best Rating: 82 12/02 Leic 2m heavy Hdl

Moderate hurdler.

Beechwood
96f   107f
5-y-o b g Fraam-Standard Rose (Ile De Bourbon (USA))
Miss H C Knight Peter Taplin

Placings:4434   (4197)
2002/03: 16⁴G, 16⁴GS, 16³GS, 16⁴G,

	Starts	1st	2nd	3rd	Win & Pl
NH Flat	4	0	0	1	353
Career Total	4	0	0	1	353

Going: Sf: 0-0 GS: 0-2 Gd: 0-2 GF: - Fm: 0-0
Distance: 2m/2m3: 0-4 2m4-2m7: 0-0 3m+: 0-0
Track: LH: 0-1 RH: 0-3 Tight: 0-0 Gall: 0-1
Aids: Bl: 0-0 Vi: 0-0 Tstrap: 0-0
Best Rating: 107 2/03 Winc 2m gd-sft NHF

Has shown ability on all starts in bumpers.

Beedulup
103(90c)   (30c)80
8-y-o br g Perpendicular-Biloela (Nicholas Bill)
P Wegmann (J A Moore 24/10) P Wegmann

Placings:040/P/5P06122254   (4704)
2002/03: 21⁵GS, 16⁸GS, 21⁰S, 21⁶G, 22¹G, 22²GF, 20²GF, 21²G, 21⁵F, 20⁴G,

	Starts	1st	2nd	3rd	Win & Pl
Hurdles	8	1	3	0	5348
Chases	2	0	0	0	0
Career Total	14	1	3	0	5348

69 8/02 Ctml 2m6f G(0-90)HHdl GD £2772
Total win prize-money £2772

Going: Sf: 0-1 GS: 0-1 Gd: 1-4 GF: - Fm: 0-4
Distance: 2m/2m3: 0-1 2m4-2m7: 1-9 3m+: 0-0
Track: LH: 1-7 RH: 0-3 Tight: 1-7 Gall: 0-0
Aids: Bl: 0-0 Vi: 0-0 Tstrap: 0-0
Best Rating: 98 1/00 Newc 2m soft NHF

Beef Or Salmon (IRE)
115(94h)   (118h)163+
7-y-o ch g Cajetano (USA)-Farinella (IRE) (Salmon Leap (USA))
Michael Hourigan B J Craig

Placings:312²F11050-1111F   (4132)
2002/03: 20¹HY, 16¹S, 24¹HY, 24¹YS, 26²G,

	Starts	1st	2nd	3rd	Win & Pl
Chases	5	4	0	0	165297
Career Total	14	7	1	1	187104

163 2/03 Leop 3m Ch Y-S £67597
163 12/02 Leop 3m Ch HVY £59815
146 12/02 Cork 2m Ch SFT £15950
152 11/02 Clon 2m4f Ch HVY £21932
118 1/02 Gowr 2m2f Hdl HVY £7975
120 1/02 Cork 2m NHF SFT £4868
123 11/01 Clon 2m NHF SFT £4173
Total win prize-money £182313

Going: Sf: 3-3 GS: 0-0 Gd: 0-0 GF: - Fm: 0-0
Distance: 2m/2m3: 1-1 2m4-2m7: 1-1 **3m+: 2-3**
Track: **LH: 2-3** RH: 1-1 Tight: 0-0 Gall: 0-1
Aids: Bl: 0-0 Vi: 0-0 Tstrap: 0-0
Best Rating: 163 2/03 Leop 3m yld-sft Ch

High-class Irish-trained chaser; has progressed quickly in his first season over fences in 2002/03 to become the rising star of Irish chasing; won his first four chases, culminating in the Ericsson Chase and Hennessy Gold Cup at Leopardstown; well fancied for Cheltenham Gold Cup, but fell at the second; stays 3m, effective at shorter, goes well in soft and heavy ground; usually held up and has a turn of foot; still progressing, held in the highest regard by connections and could be anything.

Beefy
75f
7-y-o ch g Shining Jewel-Cherry Sip (Nearly A Hand)
J R Best F J Mills

Placings:50 (0724)
2002/03: 16^{5}G, 16^{9}G,

	Starts	1st	2nd	3rd	Win & Pl
NH Flat	2	0	0	0	0
Career Total	2	0	0	0	0

Going: Sf: 0-0 GS: 0-0 Gd: 0-1 GF: - Fm: 0-1
Distance: 2m/2m3: 0-2 2m4-2m7: 0-0 3m+: 0-0
Track: LH: 0-1 RH: 0-0 Tight: 0-0 Gall: 0-0
Aids: Bl: 0-0 Vi: 0-0 Tstrap: 0-0
Best Rating: 75 7/02 Strf 2m110y gd-fm NHF

Beefy Nova
108 84
11-y-o ch g Ra Nova-Cherry Sip (Nearly A Hand)
G H Yardley Philip Jones

Placings:3322032/50642P/UU4415150/2FP2/3604405 (4738)
2002/03: 20^{3}S, 20^{6}S, 20^{0}S, 20^{4}G, 24^{4}G, 24^{0}G, 24^{5}GF,

	Starts	1st	2nd	3rd	Win & Pl
Chases	7	0	0	1	654
Career Total	33	2	6	4	18471
117 2/00 Ludl	2m4f	D(0-125)HCh	G-F		£4095
114 12/99 Hrfd	2m3f	D(0-110)HCh	HVY		£4344

Total win prize-money £8440

Going: Sf: 0-3 GS: 0-0 Gd: 0-3 GF: - Fm: 0-1
Distance: 2m/2m3: 0-0 2m4-2m7: 0-4 3m+: 0-3
Track: LH: 0-3 RH: 0-4 Tight: 0-2 Gall: 0-2
Aids: Bl: 0-0 Vi: 0-0 Tstrap: 0-0
Best Rating: 120 11/00 Aint 2m4f gd-sft Ch

Plating-class chaser; stays two and a half miles; acts on both extremes of going.

Beethoven (IRE)
104 121
7-y-o b/br g Yashgan-Adare Princess (Paico)
Noel T Chance T Collins

Placings:12/31P-5 (2362)
2002/03: 20^{6}S,

	Starts	1st	2nd	3rd	Win & Pl
Hurdles	1	0	0	0	658
Career Total	6	2	1	1	14536
119 12/01 Asct	2m4f	B Hdl	GD		£10348
126 2/01 Asct	2m110y	H NHF	HVY		£2485

Total win prize-money £12833

Going: Sf: 0-1 GS: 0-0 Gd: 0-0 GF: - Fm: 0-0
Distance: 2m/2m3: 0-0 2m4-2m7: 0-1 3m+: 0-0
Track: LH: 0-1 RH: 0-0 Tight: 0-0 Gall: 0-0
Aids: Bl: 0-0 Vi: 0-0 Tstrap: 0-0
Best Rating: 126 3/01 Sand 2m110y heavy NHF

Fair hurdler; useful bumper performer who won well at Ascot on his hurdling debut in December 2001; has had his problems and been lightly raced since; acts on good ground or easier.

Before The Mast (IRE)
105f 117f
6-y-o br g Broken Hearted-Kings Reserve (King s Ride)
Noel T Chance A D Weller

Placings:2-3 (1606)
2002/03: 16^{3}G,

	Starts	1st	2nd	3rd	Win & Pl
NH Flat	1	0	0	1	285
Career Total	2	0	1	1	935

Going: Sf: 0-0 GS: 0-0 Gd: 0-1 GF: - Fm: 0-0
Distance: 2m/2m3: 0-1 2m4-2m7: 0-0 3m+: 0-0
Track: LH: 0-1 RH: 0-0 Tight: 0-0 Gall: 0-0
Aids: Bl: 0-0 Vi: 0-0 Tstrap: 0-0
Best Rating: 117 2/02 Sand 2m110y soft NHF

Promising efforts in bumpers.

Begsy's Bullet
98(103h) (85+h)85d
8-y-o b m Primitive Rising (USA)-Seeker s Sister (Ashmore (FR))
D McCain Mrs D McCain

Placings:020251/0F1502 (4105)
2002/03: 16^{6}S, 20^{5}S, 21^{1}HY, 17^{5}HY, 20^{0}S, 21^{2}S,

	Starts	1st	2nd	3rd	Win & Pl
Hurdles	3	1	0	0	3465
Chases	3	0	1	0	1433
Career Total	12	2	3	0	11044
85 1/03 Sedg	2m5f110yE Hdl	HVY			£3465
81 2/01 Sedg	2m5f	D Ch	SFT		£4740

Total win prize-money £8205

Going: Sf: 1-6 GS: 0-0 Gd: 0-0 GF: - Fm: 0-0
Distance: 2m/2m3: 0-2 2m4-2m7: 1-4 3m+: 0-0
Track: **LH: 1-6** RH: 0-0 **Tight: 1-4** Gall: 0-1
Aids: Bl: 0-0 Vi: 0-0 Tstrap: 0-0
Best Rating: 85 1/03 Sedg 2m5f110y heavy Hdl

Moderate hurdler/chaser; landed a modest mares only novices hurdle at Sedgefield in January; acts on soft ground.

Behari (IRE)
83 60
9-y-o b g Kahyasi-Berhala (IRE) (Doyoun)
F M Barton F M Barton

Placings:000/04222F550/33F423345/000P005-0P4UP0406P (1244)
2002/03: 20^{0}G, 19^{0}G, 23^{4}G, 21^{U}GS, 23^{0}GF, 20^{0}G, 21^{4}GF, 20^{0}G, 20^{6}GF, 24^{0}PG,

	Starts	1st	2nd	3rd	Win & Pl
Hurdles	6	0	0	0	0
Chases	4	0	0	0	239
Career Total	38	0	4	4	4801

Going: Sf: 0-0 GS: 0-1 Gd: 0-6 GF: - Fm: 0-3
Distance: 2m/2m3: 0-1 2m4-2m7: 0-7 3m+: 0-2
Track: LH: 0-9 RH: 0-1 Tight: 0-3 Gall: 0-0
Aids: Bl: 0-0 Vi: 0-0 Tstrap: 0-5
Best Rating: 88 8/00 Bang 2m4f good Hdl

Behavingbadly (IRE)
107(106h) (125h)125
8-y-o b g Lord Americo-Audrey s Turn (Strong Gale)
A Parker R A Bartlett

Placings:521122-03F43210 (4307)
2002/03: 20^{0}S, 25^{3}S, 24^{4}GS, 20^{4}S, 25^{3}HY, 25^{2}GS, 25^{1}S, 32^{0}G,

	Starts	1st	2nd	3rd	Win & Pl
Chases	8	1	1	2	10255
Career Total	14	3	4	2	20685
125 3/03 Ayr	3m1f	D(0-125)HCh	SFT		£6531
112 1/02 Catt	3m1f110yE Hdl		G-S		£2807
95 12/01 Hexm	3m	E Hdl	SFT		£2439

Total win prize-money £11778

Going: Sf: 1-5 GS: 0-2 Gd: 0-1 GF: - Fm: 0-0
Distance: 2m/2m3: 0-0 2m4-2m7: 0-2 3m+: 1-6
Track: LH: 1-7 RH: 0-1 Tight: 0-2 Gall: 0-2
Aids: Bl: 0-0 Vi: 0-0 Tstrap: 0-0
Best Rating: 125 3/03 Ayr 3m1f soft Ch

Useful ex-Irish chaser/ hurdler; gets three miles; suited by soft ground.

Behrajan (IRE)
121(105h) (152h)170
8-y-o b g Arazi (USA)-Behera (Mill Reef (USA))
H D Daly The Behrajan Partnership

Placings:11215/52113/112213/33212P-61150 (4479)
2002/03: 24^{6}S, 24^{1}S, 25^{1}GS, 26^{5}G, 36^{0}G,

	Starts	1st	2nd	3rd	Win & Pl
Chases	5	2	0	0	89350
Career Total	27	11	6	4	250774
170 1/03 Chel	3m1f110yA Ch		G-S		£49600
166 12/02 Asct	3m110y A HCh		SFT		£31000
168 12/01 Weth	3m1f	A HCh	G-S		£19053
144 3/01 Hntg	3m	E Ch	SFT		£3562
122 11/00 Extr	2m7f110yD Ch		G-S		£5330
140 10/00 Weth	3m1f	D Ch	G-S		£4186
164 1/00 Hayd	2m7f110yA Hdl		SFT		£15000
167 12/99 Chel	3m	B Hdl	SFT		£8286
138 2/99 Wwck	2m4f110yB Hdl		G-S		£7385
138 1/99 Sand	2m110y A Hdl		SFT		£15699
125 12/98 Wwck	2m	E Hdl	G-S		£2792

Total win prize-money £161896

Going: Sf: 1-2 GS: 1-1 Gd: 0-2 GF: - Fm: 0-0
Distance: 2m/2m3: 0-0 2m4-2m7: 0-0 3m+: 2-5
Track: LH: 1-4 RH: 1-1 Tight: 0-1 Gall: 1-2
Aids: Bl: 0-0 Vi: 0-0 Tstrap: 0-0
Best Rating: 170 1/03 Chel 3m1f110y gd-sft Ch

Top-class chaser; runner-up in the Hennessys at both Newbury and Leopardstown in 2001/2; disappointed in the 2002 Gold Cup; won a valuable Ascot handicap in December before producing best ever performance when

making all to beat Foly Pleasant in the Pillar at Cheltenham; stayed on into fifth in Cheltenham Gold Cup; suited by 3m plus and easy ground; an out and out galloper; does not find a great deal when in front.

Behzad (IRE)

104   **83**

4-y-o b g Kahyasi-Behriya (IRE) (Kenmare (FR))
D McCain Daren Brown

Placings:*30*   (4481)
2002/03: 17³G, 17⁰G,

	Starts	1st	2nd	3rd	Win & Pl
NH Flat	2	0	0	1	290
Career Total	2	0	0	1	290

Going: Sf: 0-0 GS: 0-0 Gd: 0-2 GF: - Fm: 0-0
Distance: 2m/2m3: 0-2 2m4-2m7: 0-0 3m+: 0-0
Track: LH: 0-1 RH: 0-0 Tight: 0-1 Gall: 0-0
Aids: Bl: 0-0 Vi: 0-0 Tstrap: 0-0
Best Rating: 87 3/03 Bang 2m1f   good NHF

Showed a little ability in bumpers; well beaten on hurdling debut.

Bekstar

102   **101d**

8-y-o br m Nicholas Bill-Murex (Royalty)
J C Tuck J C Tuck

Placings:*400/0064/0031F46-41255000*   (4566)
2002/03: 22⁴GF, 22¹G, 22²G, 17⁵G, 20⁵GS, 24⁰G, 19⁰F, 20⁰GF,

	Starts	1st	2nd	3rd	Win & Pl
Hurdles	8	1	1	0	3585
Career Total	22	2	1	1	5953
100	6/02	NAbb	2m6f	E(0-105)HHdl	GD	£2639
91	10/01	Extr	2m3f	G(0-95)HHdl	G-F	£1792

Total win prize-money £4431

Going: Sf: 0-0 GS: 0-1 Gd: 1-4 GF: - Fm: 0-3
Distance: 2m/2m3: 0-1 **2m4-2m7: 1-6** 3m+: 0-1
Track: LH: 1-4 RH: 0-4 Tight: 1-5 Gall: 0-0
Aids: Bl: 0-0 Vi: 0-0 Tstrap: 0-0
Best Rating: 101 6/02 NAbb 2m6f   good Hdl

Moderate hurdler; stays two miles six, acts on fast ground.

Belarus (IRE)

11-y-o b g Waajib-Kavali (Blakeney)
Mrs T White Mrs Susan Ashburner

Placings:*50P0U0/6P/2/R*   (4255)
2002/03: 25⁰G,

	Starts	1st	2nd	3rd	Win & Pl
Chases	1	0	0	0	
Career Total	10	0	1	0	474

Going: Sf: 0-0 GS: 0-0 Gd: 0-1 GF: - Fm: 0-0
Distance: 2m/2m3: 0-0 2m4-2m7: 0-0 3m+: 0-1
Track: LH: 0-0 RH: 0-1 Tight: 0-0 Gall: 0-0
Aids: Bl: 0-0 Vi: 0-0 Tstrap: 0-0
Best Rating: 89 5/00 Hrfd 3m1f110y gd-sft Ch

Belisario (IRE)

108   **120**

9-y-o b/br g Distinctly North (USA)-Bold Kate (Bold Lad (IRE))

M W Easterby Paul G Jacobs

Placings:*413/562/1F/3131-30*   (4165)
2002/03: 20³G, 24⁰GS,

	Starts	1st	2nd	3rd	Win & Pl
Chases	2	0	0	1	866
Career Total	14	4	1	4	13469
115	3/02	Donc	3m	E Ch		SFT	£3302
119	1/02	Weth	2m7f110yE Ch		G-S	£3363
112	10/00	Weth	2m7f	F(0-100)HHdl	G-S	£1970
106	3/98	MRas	1m5f110yH NHF		G-S	£1287

Total win prize-money £9924

Going: Sf: 0-0 GS: 0-1 Gd: 0-1 GF: - Fm: 0-0
Distance: 2m/2m3: 0-0 2m4-2m7: 0-1 3m+: 0-1
Track: LH: 0-2 RH: 0-0 Tight: 0-0 Gall: 0-1
Aids: Bl: 0-0 Vi: 0-0 Tstrap: 0-0
Best Rating: 123 2/02 Hayd 2m6f   heavy Ch

Fair novice chaser; has taken well to fences but does not stand much racing; acts on good to soft; stays 3m.

Belitlir

(49h)   (37h)**70**

11-y-o b m Lir-Kimberley Ann (St Columbus)
Miss S Young B R J Young

Placings:*0/00/P5542-0454*   (0869)
2002/03: 22⁰G, 21⁴GS, 26⁵G, 21⁴GF,

	Starts	1st	2nd	3rd	Win & Pl
Hurdles	1	0	0	0	0
Chases	3	0	0	0	681
Career Total	12	0	1	0	2288

Going: Sf: 0-0 GS: 0-1 Gd: 0-2 GF: - Fm: 0-1
Distance: 2m/2m3: 0-0 2m4-2m7: 0-3 3m+: 0-1
Track: LH: 0-3 RH: 0-1 Tight: 0-3 Gall: 0-0
Aids: Bl: 0-0 Vi: 0-0 Tstrap: 0-0
Best Rating: 70 2/02 Tntn 3m   soft Ch

Bell Lane Lad (IRE)

101   **86+**

6-y-o b g Wakashan-Busti Lass (IRE) (Bustineto)
A King (J R Jenkins 17/12) Jack McGrath

Placings:*0-000P1*   (4566)
2002/03: 16⁰GS, 22⁰GS, 20⁵S, 22ᴾHY, 20¹GF,

	Starts	1st	2nd	3rd	Win & Pl
NH Flat	1	0	0	0	
Hurdles	4	1	0	0	5519
Career Total	6	1	0	0	5519
86	4/03	Bang	2m4f	F(0-100)HHdl	G-F	£5518

Total win prize-money £5519

Going: Sf: 0-2 GS: 0-2 Gd: 0-0 GF: - Fm: 1-1
Distance: 2m/2m3: 0-1 **2m4-2m7: 1-4** 3m+: 0-0
Track: LH: 1-3 RH: 0-2 Tight: 1-4 Gall: 0-0
Aids: Bl: 0-0 Vi: 0-0 Tstrap: 0-0
Best Rating: 86 4/03 Bang 2m4f   gd-fm Hdl

Bell Tex (IRE)

95   **63**

11-y-o br g Orchestra-Lyngard (Balliol)
J C Fox Shirley M & Peter G Palmer

Placings:*P/P040/2-0*   (4598)
2002/03: 19⁰GF,

	Starts	1st	2nd	3rd	Win & Pl
Hurdles	1	0	0	0	
Career Total	7	0	1	0	582

Going: Sf: 0-0 GS: 0-0 Gd: 0-0 GF: - Fm: 0-1
Distance: 2m/2m3: 0-1 2m4-2m7: 0-0 3m+: 0-0
Track: LH: 0-0 RH: 0-1 Tight: 0-0 Gall: 0-0
Aids: Bl: 0-0 Vi: 0-0 Tstrap: 0-0
Best Rating: 85 5/01 Folk 2m4f110y gd-fm Hdl

Bell Tor (IRE)

92   **85**

6-y-o b m King s Ride-Shannon Juliette (Julio Mariner)
D R Gandolfo Starlight Racing

Placings:*6-PP26*   (4315)
2002/03: 20⁵S, 20ᴾGS, 20²S, 19⁶G,

	Starts	1st	2nd	3rd	Win & Pl
Hurdles	4	0	1	0	1042
Career Total	5	0	1	0	1042

Going: Sf: 0-0 GS: 0-1 Gd: 0-1 GF: - Fm: 0-0
Distance: 2m/2m3: 0-1 2m4-2m7: 0-3 3m+: 0-0
Track: LH: 0-2 RH: 0-1 Tight: 0-1 Gall: 0-2
Aids: Bl: 0-0 Vi: 0-0 Tstrap: 0-0
Best Rating: 88 6/01 Worc 2m   good NHF

Moderate novice hurdler; hung left and just beaten at Fontwell in February 2003; stays two and a half miles.

Bella Brio (IRE)

81f   **55f**

5-y-o b m Shernazar-Spin A Coin (Torus)
G A Harker Geoff Bonson and Ian Townsend

Placings:*050*   (4437)
2002/03: 17⁰GF, 17⁵GF, 16⁰G,

	Starts	1st	2nd	3rd	Win & Pl
NH Flat	3	0	0	0	0
Career Total	3	0	0	0	0

Going: Sf: 0-0 GS: 0-0 Gd: 0-1 GF: - Fm: 0-2
Distance: 2m/2m3: 0-3 2m4-2m7: 0-0 3m+: 0-0
Track: LH: 0-2 RH: 0-1 Tight: 0-2 Gall: 0-0
Aids: Bl: 0-0 Vi: 0-0 Tstrap: 0-0
Best Rating: 55 7/02 Sedg 2m1f   gd-fm NHF

Bella Mary

87(94h)   **72**

8-y-o b m Derrylin-Pro-Token (Proverb)
C T Pogson C T Pogson

Placings:*0P0/4P320P0P*   (4798)
2002/03: 19⁴GF, 20ᴾS, 16²S, 16²GS, 16⁰HY, 16ᴾG, 21⁰S, 17ᴾGF,

	Starts	1st	2nd	3rd	Win & Pl
Hurdles	8	0	1	1	1765
Career Total	11	0	1	1	1765

Going: Sf: 0-4 GS: 0-1 Gd: 0-1 GF: - Fm: 0-2
Distance: 2m/2m3: 0-5 2m4-2m7: 0-3 3m+: 0-0
Track: LH: 0-7 RH: 0-1 Tight: 0-6 Gall: 0-0
Aids: Bl: 0-0 Vi: 0-0 Tstrap: 0-0
Best Rating: 82 12/02 Stfnl 2m   gd-sft Hdl

Placed in novices hurdles but is only very moderate.

Bella's Princess

9-y-o b/br m Broadsword (USA)-Kathy Cook (Glenstal (USA))

R J Smith R Smith

Placings:60/6P6 (1244)
2002/03: 20^6G, 20^7GF, 24^6G,

	Starts	1st	2nd	3rd	Win & Pl
Hurdles	3	0	0	0	0
Career Total	5	0	0	0	0

Going: Sf: 0-0 GS: 0-0 Gd: 0-2 GF: - Fm: 0-1
Distance: 2m/2m3: 0-0 2m4-2m7: 0-2 3m+: 0-1
Track: LH: 0-3 RH: 0-0 Tight: 0-0 Gall: 0-0
Aids: Bl: 0-0 Vi: 0-0 Tstrap: 0-0
Best Rating: 78 12/98 Hrfd 2m1f good NHF

Bellacaccia (IRE)
98   90+
7-y-o ch m Beau Sher-Game Gambler (IRE) (Long Pond)
C W Thornton D B Dennison

Placings:4/324-64BF03 (4434)
2002/03: 21^6G, 16^4G, 20^8S, 20^5S, 20^9GS, 20^3G,

	Starts	1st	2nd	3rd	Win & Pl
Hurdles	6	0	0	1	655
Career Total	10	0	1	2	1393

Going: Sf: 0-2 GS: 0-1 Gd: 0-3 GF: - Fm: 0-0
Distance: 2m/2m3: 0-1 2m4-2m7: 0-5 3m+: 0-0
Track: LH: 0-6 RH: 0-0 Tight: 0-2 Gall: 0-1
Aids: Bl: 0-0 Vi: 0-0 Tstrap: 0-0
Best Rating: 99 10/01 Carl 2m1f gd-sft NHF

Fair hurdler; stays three miles; has won on fast ground; probably better with cut.

Belle D'Anjou (FR)
102   100
6-y-o b m Saint Cyrien (FR)-Epsibelle (IRE) (Darshaan)
P J Hobbs (M C Pipe 4/5) Network Training

Placings:4/211111530/1101B3-0P60 (4136)
2002/03: 16^0G, 16^2GF, 17^8G, 17^9G,

	Starts	1st	2nd	3rd	Win & Pl
Hurdles	3	0	0	0	0
Chases	1	0	0	0	0
Career Total	20	8	1	2	48116
131	12/01	Newb	2m110y	B Hdl	G-S £7250
135	11/01	Tntn	2m3f110yD(0-120)HHdl		G-S £3633
120	10/01	Chep	2m3f	HHdl	GD £9834
109	9/00	Plum	2m	C Hdl	GD £4845
112	9/00	Strf	2m110y	E Hdl	GD £2795
109	8/00	NAbb	2m1f	E Hdl	G-F £2506
104	8/00	Bang	2m1f	E Hdl	GD £2886
	6/00	Autl	1m7f	Hdl	VS £6244

Total win prize-money £39995

Going: Sf: 0-0 GS: 0-0 Gd: 0-3 GF: - Fm: 0-1
Distance: 2m/2m3: 0-4 2m4-2m7: 0-0 3m+: 0-0
Track: LH: 0-4 RH: 0-0 Tight: 0-2 Gall: 0-1
Aids: Bl: 0-0 Vi: 0-0 Tstrap: 0-0
Best Rating: 135 11/01 Tntn 2m3f110y gd-sft Hdl

Moderate hurdler; ex-French; stays two miles three, but effective at shorter; acts well on good and good to soft ground.

Belle D'Orsini (FR)
41
8-y-o ch m Le Nain Jaune (FR)-Ma Belle (FR) (Lightning (FR))
Jonjo O Neill V N Stroud

Placings:3F/41P30F/22311/0-F (1572)
2002/03: 19^6G,

	Starts	1st	2nd	3rd	Win & Pl
Hurdles	1	0	0	0	
Career Total	15	3	2	3	13755
132	1/01	Donc	2m4f	C(0-135)HHdl	GD £5430
120	1/01	Donc	2m4f	E(0-115)HHdl	GD £2733
109	5/99	Ctml	2m1f110y	G Hdl	G-F £2556

Total win prize-money £10721

Going: Sf: 0-0 GS: 0-0 Gd: 0-1 GF: - Fm: 0-0
Distance: 2m/2m3: 0-1 2m4-2m7: 0-0 3m+: 0-0
Track: LH: 0-1 RH: 0-0 Tight: 0-1 Gall: 0-0
Aids: Bl: 0-0 Vi: 0-0 Tstrap: 0-0
Best Rating: 132 1/01 Donc 2m4f good Hdl

Fatally injured at Stratford in October 2002. (DEAD)

Belle Derriere

8-y-o b m Kylian (USA)-Metannee (The Brianstan)
J A Danahar J A Danahar

Placings:2141/60PP-B (4089)
2002/03: 24^8GS,

	Starts	1st	2nd	3rd	Win & Pl
Chases	1	0	0	0	
Career Total	9	2	1	0	5794
121	12/99	Leic	2m	E Hdl	GD £3340
100	10/99	Ludl	2m	H NHF	G-F £1721

Total win prize-money £5061

Going: Sf: 0-0 GS: 0-1 Gd: 0-0 GF: - Fm: 0-0
Distance: 2m/2m3: 0-0 2m4-2m7: 0-0 3m+: 0-1
Track: LH: 0-1 RH: 0-0 Tight: 0-1 Gall: 0-0
Aids: Bl: 0-0 Vi: 0-0 Tstrap: 0-0
Best Rating: 121 12/99 Leic 2m good Hdl

Bellefleur
89   76+
6-y-o b m Alflora (IRE)-Isabeau (Law Society (USA))
J M Jefferson Pryke Hygiene Group,J Wilkinson,B Wade

Placings:055-045P3 (3996)
2002/03: 20^0HY, 20^4GS, 16^5G, 25^5G, 20^3G,

	Starts	1st	2nd	3rd	Win & Pl
Hurdles	5	0	0	1	822
Career Total	8	0	0	1	822

Going: Sf: 0-1 GS: 0-1 Gd: 0-3 GF: - Fm: 0-0
Distance: 2m/2m3: 0-1 2m4-2m7: 0-3 3m+: 0-1
Track: LH: 0-5 RH: 0-0 Tight: 0-2 Gall: 0-1
Aids: Bl: 0-0 Vi: 0-0 Tstrap: 0-0
Best Rating: 81 2/02 Donc 2m110y soft NHF

Plating-class hurdler; has shown only moderate form; suited by cut in the ground.

Bellino Empresario (IRE)
88   67
5-y-o b g Robellino (USA)-The Last Empress (IRE) (Last Tycoon)
B Llewellyn (I A Wood 28/8) Mrs M Llewellyn

Placings:P (4641)
2002/03: 19^0GF,

	Starts	1st	2nd	3rd	Win & Pl
Hurdles	1	0	0	0	
Career Total	1	0	0	0	

Going: Sf: 0-0 GS: 0-0 Gd: 0-0 GF: - Fm: 0-1
Distance: 2m/2m3: 0-1 2m4-2m7: 0-0 3m+: 0-0
Track: LH: 0-1 RH: 0-0 Tight: 0-1 Gall: 0-0
Aids: Bl: 0-0 Vi: 0-0 Tstrap: 0-0
Best Rating: 0 4/03 Strf 2m3f gd-fm Hdl

Selling hurdler; keen sort and not getting home at present.

Bellino Spirit (IRE)
96(95h)   (74h)86
7-y-o b m Robellino (USA)-Working Model (Ile De Bourbon (USA))
M Todhunter Tim Kilroe

Placings:00/F4P3-02051P (4105)
2002/03: 20^0S, 20^2GS, 20^9GS, 25^5S, 21^1HY, 21^8S,

	Starts	1st	2nd	3rd	Win & Pl
Hurdles	3	0	1	0	834
Chases	3	1	0	0	5558
Career Total	12	1	1	1	6772
86	2/03	Sedg	2m5f	D Ch	HVY £5557

Total win prize-money £5558

Going: Sf: 1-4 GS: 0-2 Gd: 0-0 GF: - Fm: 0-0
Distance: 2m/2m3: 0-0 2m4-2m7: 1-5 3m+: 0-1
Track: LH: 1-6 RH: 0-0 Tight: 1-2 Gall: 0-1
Aids: Bl: 0-0 Vi: 0-0 Tstrap: 0-0
Best Rating: 86 2/03 Sedg 2m5f heavy Ch

Moderate novice hurdler/chaser; won a weak chase at Sedgefield in February; acts on soft and heavy ground; stays over two and a half miles.

Bellmanear
85f   63f
5-y-o b m Alflora (IRE)-Mirthful (Will Somers)
M F Harris Let s Live Racing

Placings:00 (4542)
2002/03: 16^0GF, 16^0G,

	Starts	1st	2nd	3rd	Win & Pl
NH Flat	2	0	0	0	
Career Total	2	0	0	0	

Going: Sf: 0-0 GS: 0-0 Gd: 0-1 GF: - Fm: 0-1
Distance: 2m/2m3: 0-2 2m4-2m7: 0-0 3m+: 0-0
Track: LH: 0-0 RH: 0-2 Tight: 0-0 Gall: 0-1
Aids: Bl: 0-0 Vi: 0-0 Tstrap: 0-0
Best Rating: 63 3/03 Hntg 2m110y gd-fm NHF

Belloc
75
8-y-o gr g Arzanni-Princess Story (Prince De Galles)
Mrs D Haine Mrs Solna Thomson Jones

Placings:0/2200P/4P-P (2104)
2002/03: 26^8GS,

	Starts	1st	2nd	3rd	Win & Pl
Hurdles	1	0	0	0	
Career Total	9	0	2	0	868

Going: Sf: 0-0 GS: 0-1 Gd: 0-0 GF: - Fm: 0-0
Distance: 2m/2m3: 0-0 2m4-2m7: 0-0 3m+: 0-1
Track: LH: 0-0 RH: 0-1 Tight: 0-0 Gall: 0-1
Aids: Bl: 0-0 Vi: 0-0 Tstrap: 0-0
Best Rating: 95 11/00 Wwck 2m heavy NHF

Belski

105
100

10-y-o br g Arctic Lord-Bellekino (Relkino)
C Tizzard (Mrs Laura J Young 22/5) The Butterwick Syndicate

Placings:2P222   (1038)
2002/03: 25²G, 26⁶G, 21²GF, 16²GF, 20²GF,

	Starts	1st	2nd	3rd	Win & Pl
Chases	5	0	4	0	4638
Career Total	5	0	4	0	4638

Going: Sf: 0-0 GS: 0-0 Gd: 0-2 GF: - Fm: 0-3
Distance: 2m/2m3: 0-1 2m4-2m7: 0-2 3m+: 0-2
Track: LH: 0-3 RH: 0-1 Tight: 0-3 Gall: 0-0
Aids: Bl: 0-0 Vi: 0-0 Tstrap: 0-0
Best Rating: 100 8/02 Font 2m4f   gd-fm Ch

Moderate chaser; winning pointer; runner-up in novice chases in the summer of 2002; stays three miles.

Belvento (IRE)

101
94+

11-y-o b g Strong Gale-Salufair (Salluceva)
J T Gifford (N J Gifford 22/5) Mrs Jean Plackett

Placings:00/5050/PF4/P/1P2P4   (4632)
2002/03: 26¹G, 20⁶S, 20²G, 24⁶G, 26⁴GF,

	Starts	1st	2nd	3rd	Win & Pl
Chases	5	1	1	0	2204
Career Total	15	1	1	0	2417
101 5/02	Folk	3m2f	H Ch	GD	£1436

Total win prize-money £1437

Going: Sf: 0-1 GS: 0-0 Gd: 1-3 GF: - Fm: 0-1
Distance: 2m/2m3: 0-2 2m4-2m7: 0-0 3m+: 1-3
Track: LH: 0-2 RH: 1-2 Tight: 1-3 Gall: 0-0
Aids: Bl: 0-0 Vi: 0-0 Tstrap: 0-0
Best Rating: 101 5/02 Folk 3m2f   good Ch

Modest chaser; prolific winner between the flags; stays three miles two; suited by a sound surface.

Belvoir (IRE)

8-y-o b g Husyan (USA)-Coumeenoole Lady (The Parson)
Miss Lucinda V Russell Peter J S Russell

Placings:0   (1958)
2002/03: 16⁰S,

	Starts	1st	2nd	3rd	Win & Pl
Hurdles	1	0	0	0	
Career Total	1	0	0	0	

Going: Sf: 0-1 GS: 0-0 Gd: 0-0 GF: - Fm: 0-0
Distance: 2m/2m3: 0-1 2m4-2m7: 0-0 3m+: 0-0
Track: LH: 0-1 RH: 0-0 Tight: 0-0 Gall: 0-0
Aids: Bl: 0-0 Vi: 0-0 Tstrap: 0-0
Best Rating: 0 11/02 Ayr 2m   soft Hdl

Ben Ewar

104
121

9-y-o b g Old Vic-Sunset Reef (Mill Reef (USA))
K O Cunningham-Brown A J Richards

Placings:16501/035-4P5P0423   (4780)
2002/03: 16⁴G, 20⁶S, 21⁵S, 16⁶G, 20⁰HY, 20⁴G, 16²G, 16³GF,

	Starts	1st	2nd	3rd	Win & Pl
Hurdles	8	0	1	1	9572

Career Total   16   2   1   2   44896
4/01 Engh 2m1f110y Hdl   HVY £19399
128 12/00 Asct 2m110y A Hdl   HVY £9600
Total win prize-money £28999

Going: Sf: 0-3 GS: 0-0 Gd: 0-4 GF: - Fm: 0-1
Distance: 2m/2m3: 0-4 2m4-2m7: 0-4 3m+: 0-0
Track: LH: 0-3 RH: 0-5 Tight: 0-0 Gall: 0-0
Aids: Bl: 0-0 Vi: 0-0 Tstrap: 0-1
Best Rating: 139 3/02 Chel 2m1f   good Hdl

Fair hurdler; ex-French; formerly high-class performer on the Flat and over hurdles; stays two and a half miles and handles most types of ground; not the most trustworthy and is one to steer clear of; handles most ground.

Ben More

88
70

5-y-o b g Seymour Hicks (FR)-Stac-Pollaidh (Tina s Pet)
J S King Miss S Douglas-Pennant

Placings:35042   (4757)
2002/03: 16³GF, 17⁵G, 19⁰S, 19⁴F, 22²GF,

	Starts	1st	2nd	3rd	Win & Pl
NH Flat	2	0	0	1	269
Hurdles	3	0	1	0	1406
Career Total	5	0	1	1	1675

Going: Sf: 0-1 GS: 0-0 Gd: 0-1 GF: - Fm: 0-3
Distance: 2m/2m3: 0-3 2m4-2m7: 0-2 3m+: 0-0
Track: LH: 0-2 RH: 0-3 Tight: 0-2 Gall: 0-0
Aids: Bl: 0-0 Vi: 0-0 Tstrap: 0-0
Best Rating: 90 12/02 Hrfd 2m1f   good NHF

Plating-class novice hurdler; stays two miles-six; best on a sound surface.

Benbecula (IRE)

109
116+

6-y-o b g Glacial Storm (USA)-Lough View (Radical)
P R Webber J Dougall

Placings:20-53223   (4048)
2002/03: 16⁵S, 16³HY, 19²GS, 21²S, 20³HY,

	Starts	1st	2nd	3rd	Win & Pl
Hurdles	5	0	2	2	10086
Career Total	7	0	3	2	10851

Going: Sf: 0-4 GS: 0-1 Gd: 0-0 GF: - Fm: 0-0
Distance: 2m/2m3: 0-2 2m4-2m7: 0-3 3m+: 0-0
Track: LH: 0-4 RH: 0-1 Tight: 0-1 Gall: 0-2
Aids: Bl: 0-0 Vi: 0-1 Tstrap: 0-0
Best Rating: 116 3/03 Sand 2m4f110y heavy Hdl

Fair hurdler; placed in bumpers and novices hurdles; stays two miles five; potential chaser.

Benbow

95
80

6-y-o ch g Gunner B-Juno Away (Strong Gale)
F Jordan D Pugh

Placings:0534   (4536)
2002/03: 16⁰G, 26⁵GF, 24³GF, 24⁴G,

	Starts	1st	2nd	3rd	Win & Pl
NH Flat	1	0	0	0	0
Hurdles	3	0	0	1	918
Career Total	4	0	0	1	918

Going: Sf: 0-0 GS: 0-0 Gd: 0-2 GF: - Fm: 0-2

Distance: 2m/2m3: 0-1 2m4-2m7: 0-0 3m+: 0-3
Track: LH: 0-1 RH: 0-3 Tight: 0-1 Gall: 0-0
Aids: Bl: 0-0 Vi: 0-0 Tstrap: 0-0
Best Rating: 80 4/03 Ludl 3m   good Hdl

Benbradagh (IRE)

9-y-o b g Mister Lord (USA)-Meenia (Black Minstrel)
B W Duke Cotswold Coppington Connection

Placings:P/35P/PP00-P   (0505)
2002/03: 24⁰G,

	Starts	1st	2nd	3rd	Win & Pl
Hurdles	1	0	0	0	
Career Total	9	0	0	1	366

Going: Sf: 0-0 GS: 0-0 Gd: 0-1 GF: - Fm: 0-0
Distance: 2m/2m3: 0-0 2m4-2m7: 0-0 3m+: 0-1
Track: LH: 0-1 RH: 0-0 Tight: 0-0 Gall: 0-0
Aids: Bl: 0-0 Vi: 0-0 Tstrap: 0-0
Best Rating: 95 12/00 MRas 2m3f110y gd-sft Hdl

Benbyas

114
140

6-y-o b g Rambo Dancer (CAN)-Light The Way (Nicholas Bill)
D Carroll (J L Eyre 6/5) C H Stephenson & Partners

Placings:223/21113340-4013250   (4112)
2002/03: 16⁴GS, 16⁰S, 16¹S, 16³HY, 17²GS, 16⁵G, 21⁰G,

	Starts	1st	2nd	3rd	Win & Pl
Hurdles	7	1	1	1	29623
Career Total	18	4	4	4	76763
140 12/02	Donc	2m110y	B(0-140)HHdl	SFT	£8151
133 12/01	Chel	2m1f	C(0-135)HHdl	GD	£17875
113 11/01	Weth	2m	D Hdl	GD	£3948
117 11/01	Weth	2m	C Hdl	GD	£5635

Total win prize-money £35610

Going: Sf: 1-3 GS: 0-2 Gd: 0-2 GF: - Fm: 0-0
Distance: 2m/2m3: 1-6 2m4-2m7: 0-1 3m+: 0-0
Track: LH: 1-6 RH: 0-1 Tight: 0-0 Gall: 1-5
Aids: Bl: 0-0 Vi: 0-0 Tstrap: 0-0
Best Rating: 140 2/03 Newb 2m110y   good Hdl

Very useful front-running hurdler; won two novice events at Wetherby in 2001 before taking a handicap hurdle at Cheltenham in battling fashion; consistent efforts since and returned to winning form at Doncaster in December. 2002. A brave sort who has twice run well in the Tote Gold Trophy; suited by the minimum trip and good ground.

Benefit

94(102c)
(86c)87

9-y-o b g Primitive Rising (USA)-Sobriquet (Roan Rocket)
Miss L C Siddall Mrs D Ibbotson

Placings:34/213040206/13534P5-P043P2F100   (4786)
2002/03: 25⁰GS, 24⁰G, 23⁴G, 20³GS, 24⁴S, 21²S, 24⁴G, 22¹G, 22⁰G, 22⁰G,

	Starts	1st	2nd	3rd	Win & Pl
Hurdles	4	1	0	0	4797
Chases	6	0	1	1	2226
Career Total	28	3	3	5	16386
87 3/03	MRas	2m6f	D(0-115)HHdl	GD	£4797
89 5/01	Wwck	2m5f	F(0-90)HHdl	GD	£2597
103 6/00	Uttx	2m4f110yD Hdl		GD	£2947

Total win prize-money £10342

Going: Sf: 0-2 GS: 0-2 Gd: 1-6 GF: - Fm: 0-0

Distance: 2m/2m3: 0-0 **2m4-2m7: 1-5** 3m+: 0-5
Track: LH: 0-6 RH: 0-1 Tight: 0-3 Gall: 0-0
Aids: Bl: 0-0 Vi: 0-0 Tstrap: 0-0
Best Rating: 103 6/00 Uttx 2m4f110y good Hdl

Plating-class hurdler/chaser; tends to run in snatches; his narrow victory at Market Rasen in March ending a long losing sequence; stays two miles six; best on good ground.

Bengal Boy

100(100h)   (86h)85

7-y-o b g Gildoran-Bengal Lady (Celtic Cone)
P Beaumont Brandsby Racing

Placings:0004P/PP46P2U5315-03U246645664   (4794)
2002/03: 16⁰GS, 16³GF, 17ᵁGS, 17²G, 20⁴GS, 17⁶S, 16⁶HY, 16⁴G, 16⁵G, 19⁶S, 16⁶G, 21⁴GF,

	Starts	1st	2nd	3rd	Win & Pl
Hurdles	9	0	1	1	1906
Chases	3	0	0	0	338
Career Total	28	1	2	2	8537
97	3/02	Bang	2m1f110y		D Ch SFT
£4340					

Total win prize-money £4340

Going: Sf: 0-3 GS: 0-3 Gd: 0-4 GF: - Fm: 0-2
Distance: 2m/2m3: 0-10 2m4-2m7: 0-2 3m+: 0-0
Track: LH: 0-9 RH: 0-3 Tight: 0-6 Gall: 0-1
Aids: Bl: 0-0 Vi: 0-0 Tstrap: 0-0
Best Rating: 98 6/02 Ctml 2m1f110y good Hdl

Moderate hurdler/chaser; prone to jumping errors and made mistakes before winning a terrible Bangor novice chase by a wide margin in March 2002; handles soft and fast ground and should stay two and a half miles.

Benick (IRE)

10-y-o b g Yashgan-Sounds Symphonic (Orchestra)
N A Twiston-Davies M P Wareing & D J Owen

Placings:PF/0F112P53P/0P05-PP   (1850)
2002/03: 24ᴾS, 25ᴾG,

	Starts	1st	2nd	3rd	Win & Pl
Chases	2	0	0	0	
Career Total	17	2	1	1	5701
107	11/00	Sedg	3m3f110yE Hdl		SFT £2348
107	11/00	Chep	3m	F Hdl	SFT £1883

Total win prize-money £4232

Going: Sf: 0-1 GS: 0-0 Gd: 0-1 GF: - Fm: 0-0
Distance: 2m/2m3: 0-0 2m4-2m7: 0-0 3m+: 0-2
Track: LH: 0-1 RH: 0-1 Tight: 0-1 Gall: 0-0
Aids: Bl: 0-1 Vi: 0-0 Tstrap: 0-0
Best Rating: 107 11/00 Plum 3m1f110y heavy Hdl

Benjamin (IRE)

83   63

5-y-o b g Night Shift (USA)-Best Academy (USA) (Roberto (USA))
Jane Southcombe (P Mitchell 5/7) Ray Bown

Placings:00PP0   (4270)
2002/03: 17⁰F, 16⁰G, 17ᴾS, 17ᴾS, 16⁰G,

	Starts	1st	2nd	3rd	Win & Pl
Hurdles	5	0	0	0	
Career Total	5	0	0	0	

Going: Sf: 0-2 GS: 0-0 Gd: 0-2 GF: - Fm: 0-1
Distance: 2m/2m3: 0-5 2m4-2m7: 0-0 3m+: 0-0
Track: LH: 0-3 RH: 0-2 Tight: 0-3 Gall: 0-0

Aids: Bl: 0-0 Vi: 0-0 Tstrap: 0-2
Best Rating: 63 3/03 Chep 2m110y good Hdl

Bennie's Pride (IRE)

107(94h)   (107h)120d

7-y-o b g Welsh Term-Mugs Away (Mugatpura)
E J O Grady T B Conroy

Placings:042024300-102310035214400F   (4064a)
2002/03: 16¹SH, 17⁰S, 16²YS, 20³GY, 20¹GF, 21⁰GY, 22⁰G, 22³G, 24⁵S, 24²F, 20¹YS, 20⁴GS, 24⁴HY, 24⁰S, 18⁰S, 24⁴HY,

	Starts	1st	2nd	3rd	Win & Pl
NH Flat	2	1	0	0	3387
Hurdles	7	1	1	2	6577
Chases	7	1	1	0	11788
Career Total	25	3	4	3	24504
120	11/02	Clon	2m4f	Ch	Y-S £6349
105	7/02	Baln	2m4f	Hdl	G-F £4021
95	5/02	Clon	2m	NHF	SH £3386

Total win prize-money £13758

Going: Sf: 0-6 GS: 0-1 Gd: 0-2 GF: - Fm: 1-2
Distance: 2m/2m3: 0-2 **2m4-2m7: 2-7** 3m+: 0-5
Track: LH: 0-4 **RH: 1-3** Tight: 0-0 Gall: 0-1
Aids: Bl: 0-0 Vi: 0-0 Tstrap: 0-0
Best Rating: 120 11/02 Clon 2m4f yld-sft Ch

Benny The Vice (USA)

89   68

4-y-o ch g Benny The Dip (USA)-Vice On Ice (USA) (Vice Regent (CAN))
Mrs A Duffield E Grayson

Placings:00   (2098)
2002/03: 16⁰S, 16⁰G,

	Starts	1st	2nd	3rd	Win & Pl
Hurdles	2	0	0	0	
Career Total	2	0	0	0	

Going: Sf: 0-1 GS: 0-0 Gd: 0-1 GF: - Fm: 0-0
Distance: 2m/2m3: 0-2 2m4-2m7: 0-0 3m+: 0-0
Track: LH: 0-2 RH: 0-0 Tight: 0-1 Gall: 0-0
Aids: Bl: 0-1 Vi: 0-0 Tstrap: 0-0
Best Rating: 68 11/02 Ayr 2m soft Hdl

Benrajah (IRE)

110   100

6-y-o b g Lord Americo-Andy s Fancy (IRE) (Andretti)
H D Daly The Behrajan Partnership

Placings:2-335013   (4673)
2002/03: 20³G, 20³S, 20⁵S, 21⁰S, 25¹GF, 26³GF,

	Starts	1st	2nd	3rd	Win & Pl
Hurdles	6	1	0	3	5315
Career Total	7	1	1	3	5801
100	3/03	Wwck	3m1f	E Hdl	G-F £3571

Total win prize-money £3572

Going: Sf: 0-3 GS: 0-0 Gd: 0-1 GF: - Fm: 1-2
Distance: 2m/2m3: 0-0 2m4-2m7: 0-4 **3m+: 1-2**
Track: **LH: 1-3** RH: 0-3 Tight: 0-0 Gall: 0-1
Aids: Bl: 0-0 Vi: 0-0 Tstrap: 0-0
Best Rating: 108 10/02 Chep 2m4f good Hdl

Modest novice hurdler; acts on fast ground; stays three miles.

Bens Big

7-y-o br g Vouchsafe-Strathdearn (Saritamer (USA))
Mrs S J Smith Mrs Enid Brindle

Placings:PP   (1897)
2002/03: 20ᴾS, 21ᴾS,

	Starts	1st	2nd	3rd	Win & Pl
Chases	2	0	0	0	
Career Total	2	0	0	0	

Going: Sf: 0-2 GS: 0-0 Gd: 0-0 GF: - Fm: 0-0
Distance: 2m/2m3: 0-2 2m4-2m7: 0-2 3m+: 0-0
Track: LH: 0-1 RH: 0-1 Tight: 0-1 Gall: 0-0
Aids: Bl: 0-0 Vi: 0-0 Tstrap: 0-2
Best Rating: 0 11/02 Sedg 2m5f soft Ch

Benson (IRE)

109(75h)   (82h)105

8-y-o b/br g Hawkstone (IRE)-Erin St Helen (IRE) (Seclude (USA))
H D Daly Alpha Gold Partnership

Placings:4P5/6-1530F1P   (4614)
2002/03: 19¹G, 20⁵S, 20³GS, 20⁰GS, 20⁶G, 20¹GF, 21⁰G,

	Starts	1st	2nd	3rd	Win & Pl
Chases	7	2	0	1	10990
Career Total	11	2	0	1	10990
105	3/03	Wwck	2m4f110yD(0-120)HCh		G-F 5754
112	10/02	Hrfd	2m3f	E(0-105)HCh	GD £4160

Total win prize-money £9914

Going: Sf: 0-1 GS: 0-2 Gd: 1-3 GF: - Fm: 1-1
Distance: 2m/2m3: 1-1 2m4-2m7: 1-6 3m+: 0-0
Track: LH: 1-3 RH: 1-4 Tight: 0-2 Gall: 0-1
Aids: Bl: 0-0 Vi: 0-0 Tstrap: 0-0
Best Rating: 112 10/02 Hrfd 2m3f good Ch

Modest chaser; effective at two and a half miles; acts on good and fast ground; jumping has room for improvement.

Bentyheath Lane

104   73

6-y-o b g Puissance-Eye Sight (Roscoe Blake)
M Mullineaux The Hon Mrs S Pakenham

Placings:500P-P32200   (1380)
2002/03: 16ᴾGS, 16³GF, 17²GF, 16²GF, 20⁰G, 17⁰GF,

	Starts	1st	2nd	3rd	Win & Pl
Hurdles	6	0	2	1	2680
Career Total	10	0	2	1	2680

Going: Sf: 0-1 GS: 0-1 Gd: 0-1 GF: - Fm: 0-4
Distance: 2m/2m3: 0-5 2m4-2m7: 0-1 3m+: 0-0
Track: LH: 0-5 RH: 0-1 Tight: 0-3 Gall: 0-0
Aids: Bl: 0-0 Vi: 0-0 Tstrap: 0-0
Best Rating: 73 8/02 Uttx 2m gd-fm Hdl

Poor novice hurdler.

Benvolio

91(80h)   (69h)55

6-y-o br g Cidrax (FR)-Miss Capulet (Commanche Run)
C N Kellett 7 A.D. Racing

Placings:0P000000/00000PP-0R3P5P4P5PP4   (4264)
2002/03: 19⁰G, 23⁰G, 21³GS, 23⁰G, 21⁵GF, 24ᴾS, 20⁴S, 20ᴾS, 24⁵S, 25ᴾG, 23ᴾGS, 20⁴GF,

	Starts	1st	2nd	3rd	Win & Pl
Chases	12	0	0	1	1283

Career Total 27 0 0 1 1283

Going:	Sf: 0-4 GS: 0-2 Gd: 0-4 GF: - Fm: 0-2
Distance:	2m/2m3: 0-1 2m4-2m7: 0-6 3m+: 0-5
Track:	LH: 0-7 RH: 0-5 Tight: 0-2 Gall: 0-0
Aids:	Bl: 0-0 Vi: 0-0 Tstrap: 0-0
Best Rating:	69 5/01 Hrfd 2m3f110y good Hdl

Berewolf (IRE)

(91h)   (93h)**54**
9-y-o b g Commanche Run-Iron Star (General Ironside)
J T Gifford The Arkle Bar Partnership

Placings:5/4/06000B0F-0   (0102)
2002/03: 22⁰GF,

	Starts	1st	2nd	3rd	Win & Pl
Hurdles	1	0	0	0	
Career Total	11	0	0	0	218

Going:	Sf: 0-0 GS: 0-0 Gd: 0-0 GF: - Fm: 0-1
Distance:	2m/2m3: 0-0 2m4-2m7: 0-1 3m+: 0-0
Track:	LH: 0-1 RH: 0-0 Tight: 0-1 Gall: 0-0
Aids:	Bl: 0-1 Vi: 0-0 Tstrap: 0-0
Best Rating:	102 3/99 Asct 2m110y gd-fm NHF

Bergamo

103   92
7-y-o b g Robellino (USA)-Pretty Thing (Star Appeal)
B Ellison Rasen Goes Racing

Placings:0324P/21423124-526054   (4795)
2002/03: 21⁵G, 16²GF, 16⁶G, 21⁰G, 20⁵G, 21⁴GF,

	Starts	1st	2nd	3rd	Win & Pl
Hurdles	6	0	1	0	2321
Career Total	19	2	5	2	16664
109	3/02	Fknm	2m	D(0-120)HHdl	GD	£5408
103	12/01	Muss	2m4f	E Hdl	GD	£3052

Total win prize-money £8460

Going:	Sf: 0-0 GS: 0-0 Gd: 0-4 GF: - Fm: 0-2
Distance:	2m/2m3: 0-2 2m4-2m7: 0-4 3m+: 0-0
Track:	LH: 0-5 RH: 0-1 Tight: 0-3 Gall: 0-0
Aids:	Bl: 0-5 Vi: 0-0 Tstrap: 0-0
Best Rating:	109 9/02 Prth 2m110y gd-fm Hdl

Plating-class hurdler; fair performer at his best; suited by a sound surface and a sharp track; goes well at Musselburgh; wears blinkers or cheekpieces; usually held up.

Bering Gifts (IRE)

8-y-o b g Bering-Bobbysoxer (Valiyar)
Mrs T J Hill (C J Mann 11/10) Alan Hill

Placings:6/3601F0/10512140-0414034235   (4667)
2002/03: 18⁰GF, 17⁴GF, 16¹GF, 16⁴GF, 16⁰G, 16³GF, 16⁴GF, 21²G, 19³F, 21⁵G,

	Starts	1st	2nd	3rd	Win & Pl
Hurdles	7	1	0	1	5124
Chases	3	0	1	1	1210
Career Total	25	5	2	3	17923
118	6/02	Strf	2m110y	D(0-120)HHdl	G-F	£3562
118	8/01	Hntg	2m110y	F(0-110)HHdl	G-F	£1946
107	7/01	NAbb	2m1f	D(0-120)HHdl	G-F	£3114
113	5/01	Hntg	2m110y	E Hdl	G-F	£3136
100	8/00	Worc	2m	F Hdl	G-F	£1897

Total win prize-money £13655

Going: Sf: 0-0 GS: 0-0 Gd: 0-3 GF: - Fm: 1-7

Distance:	2m/2m3: 1-7 2m4-2m7: 0-3 3m+: 0-0
Track:	LH: 1-6 RH: 0-4 Tight: 1-5 Gall: 0-2
Aids:	Bl: 0-0 Vi: 0-0 Tstrap: 0-0
Best Rating:	118 7/02 Strf 2m110y gd-fm Hdl

Formerly fair handicap hurdler for Charlie Mann; likes fast ground; needs to be produced late; placed in hunter chases at Fakenham and Exeter March 2000; likely to prove best at distances around two and a half miles.

Berkeley Frontier (IRE)

(81c)   (73c)**99**
10-y-o ch g Imperial Frontier (USA)-Harristown Rose (Miami Springs)
N A Twiston-Davies Mrs C Twiston-Davies

Placings:200/6PF135/U252461/05U53/06PP0201-PP   (3744)
2002/03: 24ᴾGS, 26ᴾG,

	Starts	1st	2nd	3rd	Win & Pl
Hurdles	2	0	0	0	
Career Total	31	3	4	2	12900
99	4/02	Towc	3m	E(0-105)HHdl	GD	£2681
110	3/00	Winc	2m	D(0-125)HHdl	G-S	£2977
94	3/99	Towc	2m	E(0-105)HHdl	GD	£2617

Total win prize-money £8276

Going:	Sf: 0-0 GS: 0-1 Gd: 0-1 GF: - Fm: 0-0
Distance:	2m/2m3: 0-2 2m4-2m7: 0-0 3m+: 0-2
Track:	LH: 0-1 RH: 0-1 Tight: 0-1 Gall: 0-1
Aids:	Bl: 0-0 Vi: 0-0 Tstrap: 0-0
Best Rating:	118 5/00 Towc 2m gd-fm Hdl

Moderate handicap hurdler; acts on good and good to soft ground; effective between two and three miles; goes well at Towcester.

Berkeley Hall

104   85
6-y-o b m Saddlers Hall (IRE)-Serious Affair (Valiyar)
R Lee (B Palling 20/9) Richard Edwards

Placings:60   (4733)
2002/03: 16⁶G, 16⁰GF,

	Starts	1st	2nd	3rd	Win & Pl
Hurdles	2	0	0	0	0
Career Total	2	0	0	0	0

Going:	Sf: 0-0 GS: 0-0 Gd: 0-1 GF: - Fm: 0-1
Distance:	2m/2m3: 0-2 2m4-2m7: 0-0 3m+: 0-0
Track:	LH: 0-1 RH: 0-1 Tight: 0-0 Gall: 0-0
Aids:	Bl: 0-0 Vi: 0-0 Tstrap: 0-0
Best Rating:	75 3/03 Ludl 2m good Hdl

Plating-class hurdler; runner-up in 2m mares-only novices' seller at Stratford May 2003.

Berlin Blue

106(92h)   132
10-y-o b g Belmez (USA)-Blue Brocade (Reform)
R M Stronge Peter J Douglas Engineering

Placings:444F0/52116/642322/4111/54-03PF   (4557)
2002/03: 21⁰S, 24³G, 25ᴾG, 33ᶠG,

	Starts	1st	2nd	3rd	Win & Pl
Hurdles	1	0	0	0	0
Chases	3	0	0	1	3065
Career Total	26	5	4	2	50609
129	7/00	Uttx	4m110y	B(0-140)HCh	G-F	£26000
115	6/00	Uttx	3m	D Ch	G-F	£3718

110	5/00	Uttx	3m2f	E Ch	G-F	£3159
119	3/99	Newb	3m110y	D Hdl	G-F	£2997
113	2/99	Hntg	2m4f110yE(0-105)HHdl	G-S	£2808

Total win prize-money £38683

Going:	Sf: 0-1 GS: 0-0 Gd: 0-3 GF: - Fm: 0-0
Distance:	2m/2m3: 0-0 2m4-2m7: 0-1 3m+: 0-3
Track:	LH: 0-4 RH: 0-0 Tight: 0-1 Gall: 0-2
Aids:	Bl: 0-0 Vi: 0-0 Tstrap: 0-0
Best Rating:	129 7/00 Uttx 4m110y gd-fm Ch

Fair hurdler/decent chaser; scored a hat-trick over fences at Uttoxeter in the summer of 2000; lightly raced since; stays four miles; best on good ground or faster; sound jumper.

Bermuda Bay (IRE)

57f   24f
6-y-o b m Be My Native (USA)-Von Carty (IRE) (Supreme Leader)
N J Henderson Brian & Gwen Griffiths

Placings:0   (0907)
2002/03: 16⁰G,

	Starts	1st	2nd	3rd	Win & Pl
NH Flat	1	0	0	0	
Career Total	1	0	0	0	

Going:	Sf: 0-0 GS: 0-0 Gd: 0-1 GF: - Fm: 0-0
Distance:	2m/2m3: 0-1 2m4-2m7: 0-0 3m+: 0-0
Track:	LH: 0-1 RH: 0-0 Tight: 0-0 Gall: 0-0
Aids:	Bl: 0-0 Vi: 0-0 Tstrap: 0-0
Best Rating:	24 8/02 Worc 2m good NHF

Bermuda Blue

101   87+
7-y-o gr g Arzanni-Calora (USA) (Private Account (USA))
M C Pipe D A Johnson

Placings:3   (0488)
2002/03: 24³HY,

	Starts	1st	2nd	3rd	Win & Pl
Hurdles	1	0	0	1	367
Career Total	1	0	0	1	367

Going:	Sf: 0-1 GS: 0-0 Gd: 0-0 GF: - Fm: 0-0
Distance:	2m/2m3: 0-0 2m4-2m7: 0-0 3m+: 0-1
Track:	LH: 0-1 RH: 0-0 Tight: 0-0 Gall: 0-0
Aids:	Bl: 0-0 Vi: 0-0 Tstrap: 0-0
Best Rating:	87 6/02 Uttx 3m110y heavy Hdl

Bernardon (GER)

110   131
7-y-o b g Suave Dancer (USA)-Bejaria (GER) (Konigstuhl (GER))
M C Pipe The Macca & Growler Partnership

Placings:1F0-124000P0   (4049)
2002/03: 16¹S, 17²GF, 17⁴G, 16⁰HY, 16⁹G, 16⁰G, 16ᴾS, 16⁰HY,

	Starts	1st	2nd	3rd	Win & Pl
Hurdles	8	1	1	0	16222
Career Total	11	2	1	0	20037
136	6/02	Worc	2m	B(0-140)HHdl	SFT	£13897
111	2/02	Tntn	2m1f	D Hdl	SFT	£3815

Total win prize-money £17712

Going:	Sf: 1-4 GS: 0-0 Gd: 0-3 GF: - Fm: 0-1
Distance:	2m/2m3: 1-8 2m4-2m7: 0-0 3m+: 0-0
Track:	LH: 1-5 RH: 0-3 Tight: 0-1 Gall: 0-2
Aids:	Bl: 0-0 Vi: 0-0 Tstrap: 0-0

Best Rating: 136 8/02 Sthl 2m1f gd-fm Hdl

Useful ex-German hurdler; acts best on soft ground; effective at around two miles; has worn a visor.

Berrington (NZ)

6-y-o b g Fort Prospect (USA)-Calamity (NZ) (Bally Royal)
B P J Baugh M W & A N Harris

Placings:00-P (1400)
2002/03: 16PGF,

	Starts	1st	2nd	3rd	Win & Pl
Hurdles	1	0	0	0	
Career Total	3	0	0	0	

Going: Sf: 0-0 GS: 0-0 Gd: 0-0 GF: - Fm: 0-1
Distance: 2m/2m3: 0-1 2m4-2m7: 0-0 3m+: 0-0
Track: LH: 0-0 RH: 0-0 Tight: 0-0 Gall: 0-0
Aids: Bl: 0-0 Vi: 0-0 Tstrap: 0-0
Best Rating: 50 12/01 Ludl 2m good NHF

Beseiged (USA)
105 114+

6-y-o ch g Cadeaux Genereux-Munnaya (USA) (Nijinsky (CAN))
R A Fahey Mike Caulfield

Placings:525-111 (4688)
2002/03: 161GF, 161GS, 191GF,

	Starts	1st	2nd	3rd	Win & Pl
NH Flat	1	1	0	0	2345
Hurdles	2	2	0	0	8218
Career Total	6	3	1	0	11029
114	4/03	MRas	2m3f110yD Hdl		G-F	£5320
102	6/02	Prth	2m110y E Hdl		G-S	£2898
98	5/02	Prth	2m110y H NHF		G-F	£2345

Total win prize-money £10563

Going: Sf: 0-0 GS: 1-1 Gd: 0-0 GF: - Fm: 2-2
Distance: 2m/2m3: 2-2 2m4-2m7: 1-1 3m+: 0-0
Track: LH: 0-0 RH: 3-3 Tight: 1-1 Gall: 0-0
Aids: Bl: 0-0 Vi: 0-0 Tstrap: 0-0
Best Rating: 114 4/03 MRas 2m3f110y gd-fm Hdl

Modest novice hurdler; fair form in bumpers, winning at Perth in May 2002; off the mark over hurdles at the same course the following month and returned from nearly a year off to win at Market Rasen; suited by a sound surface.

Beside Himself (IRE)

10-y-o b g Brush Aside (USA)-Lady Torsil (Torus)
N M Lampard Miss Z L Urquhart

Placings:0U/P (3955)
2002/03: 20PGS,

	Starts	1st	2nd	3rd	Win & Pl
Chases	1	0	0	0	
Career Total	3	0	0	0	

Going: Sf: 0-0 GS: 0-1 Gd: 0-0 GF: - Fm: 0-0
Distance: 2m/2m3: 0-0 2m4-2m7: 0-1 3m+: 0-0
Track: LH: 0-0 RH: 0-1 Tight: 0-1 Gall: 0-0
Aids: Bl: 0-0 Vi: 0-0 Tstrap: 0-0
Best Rating: 0 3/03 Leic 2m4f110y gd-sft Ch

Beso Mi Rapido
67f 30f

5-y-o b m Alderbrook-Love You Madly (IRE) (Bob Back (USA))
M C Pipe Mrs Alison C Farrant

Placings:00 (4005)
2002/03: 17PGS, 16PS,

	Starts	1st	2nd	3rd	Win & Pl
NH Flat	2	0	0	0	
Career Total	2	0	0	0	

Going: Sf: 0-1 GS: 0-1 Gd: 0-0 GF: - Fm: 0-0
Distance: 2m/2m3: 0-2 2m4-2m7: 0-0 3m+: 0-0
Track: LH: 0-0 RH: 0-2 Tight: 0-0 Gall: 0-0
Aids: Bl: 0-0 Vi: 0-0 Tstrap: 0-0
Best Rating: 30 3/03 Winc 2m soft NHF

Bessie Bunter
95 63

7-y-o b m Rakaposhi King-Black H Penny (Town And Country)
J A B Old Bessie Bunter Partnership

Placings:500-55006 (4091)
2002/03: 19SGS, 16PS, 16PHY, 24PS, 19PHY,

	Starts	1st	2nd	3rd	Win & Pl
Hurdles	5	0	0	0	0
Career Total	8	0	0	0	

Going: Sf: 0-4 GS: 0-1 Gd: 0-0 GF: - Fm: 0-0
Distance: 2m/2m3: 0-2 2m4-2m7: 0-2 3m+: 0-1
Track: LH: 0-2 RH: 0-3 Tight: 0-3 Gall: 0-0
Aids: Bl: 0-0 Vi: 0-0 Tstrap: 0-0
Best Rating: 82 12/02 Chep 2m110y soft Hdl

Best Available (IRE)
104(105h) (102h)95

8-y-o b g Accordion-Grangeshoon (Green Shoon)
P J Hobbs Aiden Murphy

Placings:30/P3150-2FP (0391)
2002/03: 19QGF, 23FG, 21PG,

	Starts	1st	2nd	3rd	Win & Pl
Chases	3	0	1	0	1500
Career Total	10	1	1	2	7085
102	2/02	Tntn	2m3f110yD Hdl		SFT	£4556

Total win prize-money £4557

Going: Sf: 0-0 GS: 0-0 Gd: 0-2 GF: - Fm: 0-1
Distance: 2m/2m3: 0-1 2m4-2m7: 0-0 3m+: 0-1
Track: LH: 0-1 RH: 0-1 Tight: 0-1 Gall: 0-0
Aids: Bl: 0-0 Vi: 0-0 Tstrap: 0-0
Best Rating: 102 5/02 Hrfd 2m3f gd-fm Ch

Moderate hurdler/chaser; got off the mark at Taunton in February 2002; runner-up on his chasing debut; stays two and a half miles; suited by soft ground; not entirely straightforward.

Best Mate (IRE)
121 (155h)178+

8-y-o b g Un Desperado (FR)-Katday (FR) (Miller s Mate)
Miss H C Knight Jim Lewis

Placings:/1221/1112/1221-111 (4132)
2002/03: 201GS, 241S, 261G,

	Starts	1st	2nd	3rd	Win & Pl
Chases	3	3	0	0	322725

Career Total		16	11	5	0	687354
178	3/03	Chel	3m2f110yA Ch		GD	£203000
173	12/02	Kemp	3m A Ch		SFT	£87000
175	11/02	Hntg	2m4f110yA Ch		G-S	£32725
176	3/02	Chel	3m2f110yA Ch		GD	£174000
172	11/01	Extr	2m1f110yA HCh		G-F	£21000
167	2/01	Sand	2m4f110yA Ch		HVY	£24000
156	11/00	Chel	2m A Ch		G-S	£15000
151	10/00	Extr	2m1f110yD Ch		GD	£3926
146	4/00	Aint	2m4f A Hdl		GD	£21000
137	12/99	Sand	2m110y D Hdl		G-S	£3680
133	11/99	Chel	2m110y B NHF		GD	£7197

Total win prize-money £592529

Going: Sf: 1-1 GS: 1-1 Gd: 1-1 GF: - Fm: 0-0
Distance: 2m/2m3: 0-0 2m4-2m7: 1-1 3m+: 2-2
Track: LH: 1-1 RH: 2-2 Tight: 0-0 Gall: 2-2
Aids: Bl: 0-0 Vi: 0-0 Tstrap: 0-0
Best Rating: 178 3/03 Chel 3m2f110y good Ch

The best staying chaser in the country; has never been out of the first two over hurdles or fences and followed up last season s Cheltenham Gold Cup victory with game success in the King George at Kempton; easy winner of his second Gold Cup in March; has an excellent cruising pace, jumps well, has a fine turn of foot and acts on any ground; effective from 2m 4f to 3m 2f and on any type of track; continues to be the one they all have to beat.

Best Wait (IRE)
107(97c) (86c)115

6-y-o b m Insan (USA)-Greek Melody (IRE) (Trojan Fort)
P F Nicholls (T Hogan 11/10) J M Ryan

Placings:61241530305F0-614263 (4549)
2002/03: 17SG, 161GY, 164S, 162GF, 166G, 163G,

	Starts	1st	2nd	3rd	Win & Pl
Hurdles	6	1	1	1	10140
Career Total	19	3	2	3	30583
108	9/02	Rosc	2m	(74-116)HHdl	G-Y	£4239
105	10/01	Limk	2m	Hdl	YLD	£8387
101	7/01	Cork	2m	NHF	FRM	£5564

Total win prize-money £18191

Going: Sf: 0-1 GS: 0-0 Gd: 0-3 GF: - Fm: 0-1
Distance: 2m/2m3: 1-6 2m4-2m7: 0-0 3m+: 0-0
Track: LH: 0-2 RH: 0-3 Tight: 0-0 Gall: 0-0
Aids: Bl: 0-0 Vi: 0-0 Tstrap: 1-6
Best Rating: 125 12/01 Fair 2m yield Hdl

Fair hurdler; ex-Irish; effective at two miles and seems to handle any ground; wears a tongue tie.

Besuto (IRE)

6-y-o br g Fourstars Allstar (USA)-Mabbots Own (Royal Trip)
A King Mrs M C Sweeney

Placings:456 (2609)
2002/03: 174GS, 205S, 206S,

	Starts	1st	2nd	3rd	Win & Pl
NH Flat	1	0	0	0	0
Hurdles	2	0	0	0	0
Career Total	3	0	0	0	

Going: Sf: 0-2 GS: 0-1 Gd: 0-0 GF: - Fm: 0-0
Distance: 2m/2m3: 0-1 2m4-2m7: 0-2 3m+: 0-0
Track: LH: 0-1 RH: 0-1 Tight: 0-0 Gall: 0-0
Aids: Bl: 0-0 Vi: 0-0 Tstrap: 0-0
Best Rating: 89 11/02 Tntn 2m1f gd-sft NHF

Betabatim (IRE)

(100h)   (94h)**94**

8-y-o b g Alphabatim (USA)-Lucy Platter (FR) (Record Token)
J E Brockbank J E Brockbank

Placings:*5*/P/P0FP54-155**UP**   (3892)
2002/03: 16[1]GS, 16[5]GF, 18[5]G, 17[U]S, 17[P]GS,

	Starts	1st	2nd	3rd	Win & Pl
Hurdles	3	1	0	0	2940
Chases	2	0	0	0	0
Career Total	13	1	0	0	2940
94 5/02	Kels	2m110y E Hdl		G-S	£2940

Total win prize-money £2940

Going:	Sf: 0-1 GS: 1-2 Gd: 0-1 GF: - Fm: 0-1
Distance:	2m/2m3: 1-5 2m4-2m7: 0-0 3m+: 0-0
Track:	LH: 1-4 RH: 0-0 Tight: 1-4 Gall: 0-0
Aids:	Bl: 0-0 Vi: 0-0 Tstrap: 0-0
Best Rating:	95 4/00 Carl 2m1f gd-sft NHF

Moderate hurdler; best at around two miles; suited by cut in the ground.

Better Days (IRE)

(105h)   (122h)

7-y-o b g Supreme Leader-Kilkilrun (Deep Run)
N J Henderson Trevor Hemmings

Placings:*2*/160-P   (2628)
2002/03: 21[P]S,

	Starts	1st	2nd	3rd	Win & Pl
Chases	1	0	0	0	
Career Total	5	1	1	0	5157
115 11/01	Aint	2m110y D Hdl		G-S	£4212

Total win prize-money £4212

Going:	Sf: 0-1 GS: 0-0 Gd: 0-0 GF: - Fm: 0-0
Distance:	2m/2m3: 0-0 2m4-2m7: 0-1 3m+: 0-0
Track:	LH: 0-1 RH: 0-0 Tight: 0-0 Gall: 0-0
Aids:	Bl: 0-0 Vi: 0-0 Tstrap: 0-0
Best Rating:	115 11/01 Aint 2m110y gd-sft Hdl

Better Moment (IRE)

106   (92+c)**97+**

6-y-o b g Turtle Island (IRE)-Snoozeandyoulose (IRE) (Scenic)
M C Pipe M C Pipe

Placings:0105434/3U2-2441615364   (2941)
2002/03: 20[2]G, 16[4]G, 17[4]S, 16[1]GF, 20[5]GF, 17[1]GF, 17[5]GF, 17[3]F, 19[6]GF, 16[4]S,

	Starts	1st	2nd	3rd	Win & Pl
Hurdles	9	2	1	1	6078
Chases	1	0	0	0	0
Career Total	20	3	2	3	9167
96 7/02	NAbb	2m1f	F(0-90)Hdl	G-F	£2653
96 6/02	Worc	2m	G Hdl		G-F	£2054
86 1/01	Catt	2m	G Hdl		G-S	£1596

Total win prize-money £6304

Going:	Sf: 0-2 GS: 0-0 Gd: 0-2 GF: - Fm: 2-6
Distance:	2m/2m3: 2-7 2m4-2m7: 0-3 3m+: 0-0
Track:	LH: 2-6 RH: 0-4 Tight: 1-4 Gall: 0-0
Aids:	Bl: 0-0 Vi: 2-10 Tstrap: 0-0
Best Rating:	97 10/02 Extr 2m1f firm Hdl

Selling hurdler; best at around 2m; acts on fast ground but has scored on good to soft.

Better Thyne (IRE)

108   (121c)**108**

7-y-o ch g Good Thyne (USA)-Cailin Cainnteach (Le Bavard (FR))
V R A Dartnall R F Woodward

Placings:P3310-1UF6P   (3778)
2002/03: 24[1]GS, 26[U]HY, 23[F]GS, 24[6]G, 24[P]GS,

	Starts	1st	2nd	3rd	Win & Pl
Hurdles	3	1	0	0	4443
Chases	2	0	0	0	0
Career Total	10	2	0	2	7367
108 12/02	Tntn	3m110y D(0-120)HHdl	G-S	£4277
102 1/02	Uttx	3m110y F Hdl		HVY	£1974

Total win prize-money £6251

Going:	Sf: 0-1 GS: 1-3 Gd: 0-1 GF: - Fm: 0-0
Distance:	2m/2m3: 0-0 2m4-2m7: 0-0 3m+: 1-5
Track:	LH: 0-2 RH: 1-3 Tight: 1-1 Gall: 0-1
Aids:	Bl: 0-0 Vi: 0-0 Tstrap: 0-0
Best Rating:	121 1/03 Extr 2m7f110y gd-sft Ch

Modest hurdler; casualty on his first two starts over fences; does not do anything quickly but stays particularly well; loves the mud.

Bewleys Hotels (IRE)

94(101h)   (97h)**95**

7-y-o ch g Muharib (USA)-Alchymya (Cosmo)
Mrs M Reveley Bewley s Hotels, Glasgow (bsh Ltd)

Placings:3-324   (2102)
2002/03: 16[3]G, 16[2]G, 16[4]G,

	Starts	1st	2nd	3rd	Win & Pl
Hurdles	2	0	1	1	1956
Chases	1	0	0	0	369
Career Total	4	0	1	2	2584

Going:	Sf: 0-0 GS: 0-0 Gd: 0-3 GF: - Fm: 0-0
Distance:	2m/2m3: 0-3 2m4-2m7: 0-0 3m+: 0-0
Track:	LH: 0-3 RH: 0-0 Tight: 0-0 Gall: 0-0
Aids:	Bl: 0-0 Vi: 0-0 Tstrap: 0-0
Best Rating:	97 11/02 Hayd 2m good Hdl

Moderate hurdler/chaser; lightly raced; showed ability when fourth on chasing debut at Catterick in November; can do better over further.

Beyond Borders (USA)

99   96

5-y-o b/br g Pleasant Colony (USA)-Welcome Proposal (Be My Guest (USA))
S Gollings (D K Weld 26/9) Quickfall Racing

Placings:236-0032064626   (4345)
2002/03: 17[3]G, 18[2]GY, 16[3]S, 16[2]F, 16[9]GS, 16[6]GS, 20[4]HY, 16[5]GS, 16[2]GS, 16[6]GS,

	Starts	1st	2nd	3rd	Win & Pl
Hurdles	10	0	2	1	3179
Career Total	13	0	3	2	4829

Going:	Sf: 0-2 GS: 0-4 Gd: 0-1 GF: - Fm: 0-2
Distance:	2m/2m3: 0-9 2m4-2m7: 0-1 3m+: 0-0
Track:	LH: 0-7 RH: 0-1 Tight: 0-1 Gall: 0-2
Aids:	Bl: 0-8 Vi: 0-0 Tstrap: 0-0
Best Rating:	113 2/03 Naas 2m heavy Hdl

Modest hurdler; ex-Irish; effective at two miles.

Beyond Control (IRE)

105(103c)   (109c)**126**

8-y-o b g Supreme Leader-Bucktina (Buckskin (FR))
C Tizzard (P F Nicholls 14/1) Anthony Knott

Placings:F31P-PU1101P   (4439)
2002/03: 26[P]S, 23[U]GS, 22[1]HY, 24[1]GS, 23[9]GS, 22[1]HY, 24[P]G,

	Starts	1st	2nd	3rd	Win & Pl
Hurdles	5	3	0	0	16858
Chases	2	0	0	0	0
Career Total	11	4	0	1	20555
126 3/03	Sand	2m6f	D(0-120)HHdl	HVY	£9419
126 1/03	Kemp	3m110y	D(0-120)HHdl	G-S	£5073
112 1/03	Folk	2m6f110yG Hdl		HVY	£2366
112 2/02	Tntn	3m110y E Hdl		SFT	£3087

Total win prize-money £19945

Going:	Sf: 2-3 GS: 1-3 Gd: 0-1 GF: - Fm: 0-0
Distance:	2m/2m3: 0-0 2m4-2m7: 2-2 3m+: 1-5
Track:	LH: 0-2 RH: 3-5 Tight: 1-2 Gall: 0-0
Aids:	Bl: 0-0 Vi: 0-0 Tstrap: 0-0
Best Rating:	126 3/03 Sand 2m6f heavy Hdl

Useful staying hurdler/ modest chaser; not always the most fluent jumper of fences; has been a revelation since going back hurdling winning three of last five starts; stays three miles plus; well suited by soft ground.

Beyond The Pale (IRE)

105   115+

5-y-o gr g Be My Native (USA)-Cyrano Imperial (IRE) (Cyrano De Bergerac)
Noel T Chance A D Weller

Placings:40-151   (2770)
2002/03: 17[1]G, 16[5]GS, 16[1]HY,

	Starts	1st	2nd	3rd	Win & Pl
NH Flat	2	1	0	0	2437
Hurdles	1	1	0	0	4368
Career Total	5	2	0	0	6805
115 12/02	Newb	2m110y	D Hdl	HVY	£4368
110 10/02	Sedg	2m1f	H NHF	GD	£1981

Total win prize-money £6349

Going:	Sf: 1-1 GS: 0-1 Gd: 1-1 GF: - Fm: 0-0
Distance:	2m/2m3: 2-3 2m4-2m7: 0-0 3m+: 0-0
Track:	LH: 2-3 RH: 0-0 Tight: 1-1 Gall: 1-1
Aids:	Bl: 0-0 Vi: 0-0 Tstrap: 0-0
Best Rating:	115 12/02 Newb 2m110y heavy Hdl

Useful novice hurdler; bumper winner; suited by 2m and ground good or softer.

Bezwell Blue

78f   36f

4-y-o ch f Bluebird (USA)-Willisa (Polar Falcon (USA))
Mrs J C McGregor Corsby Racing

Placings:0   (3583)
2002/03: 16[6]G,

	Starts	1st	2nd	3rd	Win & Pl
NH Flat	1	0	0	0	
Career Total	1	0	0	0	

Going:	Sf: 0-0 GS: 0-0 Gd: 0-1 GF: - Fm: 0-0
Distance:	2m/2m3: 0-1 2m4-2m7: 0-0 3m+: 0-0
Track:	LH: 0-0 RH: 0-1 Tight: 0-1 Gall: 0-0
Aids:	Bl: 0-0 Vi: 0-0 Tstrap: 0-0
Best Rating:	36 2/03 Muss 2m good NHF

Bhutan (IRE)
103   114
8-y-o b g Polish Patriot (USA)-Bustinetta (Bustino)
G L Moore (D J Wintle 10/12) Nigel Shields

Placings:3P624/21113/1000/4141556-51235   (4294)
2002/03: 18⁵GS, 16¹S, 18²G, 16³GS, 16⁵GF,

	Starts	1st	2nd	3rd	Win & Pl
Hurdles	5	1	1	1	4215
Career Total	26	7	3	3	30399
107 11/02 Chep	2m110y G Hdl			SFT	£2282
130 11/01 Font	2m2f110yF Hdl			G-S	£2352
129 10/01 Plum	2m F Hdl			SFT	£2310
130 10/00 Kels	2m110y D(0-120)HHdl			GD	£7117
127 12/99 Weth	2m C(0-135)HHdl			G-S	£4760
116 11/99 Newc	2m E(0-115)HHdl			G-S	£2232
87 6/99 MRas	2m1f110yE Hdl			GD	£2652

Total win prize-money £23707

Going:	Sf: 1-1 GS: 0-2 Gd: 0-1 GF: - Fm: 0-1
Distance:	2m/2m3: 1-5 2m4-2m7: 0-0 3m+: 0-0
Track:	LH: 1-4 RH: 0-1 Tight: 0-3 Gall: 0-0
Aids:	Bl: 0-0 Vi: 0-0 Tstrap: 0-0
Best Rating:	130 11/01 Font 2m2f110y gd-sft Hdl

Fair hurdler; acts on fast and soft ground; stays two and a half miles; prolific winner on the All-Weather; not the most trustworthy of individuals.

Bicycle Thief (IRE)
106(103h)   (116h)123
10-y-o ch g Archway (IRE)-Push Bike (Ballad Rock)
Miss Venetia Williams B Moore & E C Stephens

Placings:52/13110/0014/0046-F32231   (4321)
2002/03: 17ᶠS, 21³S, 21²GS, 20²GS, 19³S, 24¹G,

	Starts	1st	2nd	3rd	Win & Pl
Chases	6	1	2	2	11006
Career Total	21	5	3	3	36630
110 3/03 Bang	3m110y D Ch			GD	£5950
138 3/01 Ling	2m3f110yB(0-140)HHdl			HVY	£14040
127 1/00 Kemp	2m5f D Hdl			GD	£3835
125 12/99 Hrfd	2m3f110yE Hdl			HVY	£2850
129 12/99 Hrfd	2m3f110yE Hdl			GD	£2682

Total win prize-money £29357

Going:	Sf: 0-3 GS: 0-2 Gd: 1-1 GF: - Fm: 0-0
Distance:	2m/2m3: 0-1 2m4-2m7: 0-4 3m+: 1-1
Track:	LH: 1-3 RH: 0-2 Tight: 1-3 Gall: 0-0
Aids:	Bl: 0-0 Vi: 0-0 Tstrap: 0-0
Best Rating:	138 3/01 Ling 2m3f110y heavy Hdl

Fair handicap hurdler; fair novice chaser, but not a natural over fences; suited by trips of around two and a half miles; acts in soft ground; inconsistent.

Bid For Fame (USA)
105   99
6-y-o b/br g Quest For Fame-Shroud (USA) (Vaguely Noble)
N J Henderson (T G Mills 20/9) Elite Racing Club

Placings:43   (4311)
2002/03: 21⁴G, 21³G,

	Starts	1st	2nd	3rd	Win & Pl
Hurdles	2	0	0	1	1567
Career Total	2	0	0	1	1567

Going:	Sf: 0-0 GS: 0-0 Gd: 0-2 GF: - Fm: 0-0
Distance:	2m/2m3: 0-0 2m4-2m7: 0-2 3m+: 0-0
Track:	LH: 0-1 RH: 0-1 Tight: 0-0 Gall: 0-1
Aids:	Bl: 0-0 Vi: 0-0 Tstrap: 0-0
Best Rating:	99 3/03 Newb 2m5f good Hdl

Fair novice hurdler; has run well over 2m 5f, but may be better over shorter; handles fast ground.

Bid Me Welcome
81
7-y-o b g Alzao (USA)-Blushing Barada (USA) (Blushing Groom (FR))
Miss D A McHale (Mrs J R Ramsden 26/8) Andrew Sim

Placings:2   (1100)
2002/03: 17²GF,

	Starts	1st	2nd	3rd	Win & Pl
Hurdles	1	0	1	0	635
Career Total	1	0	1	0	635

Going:	Sf: 0-0 GS: 0-0 Gd: 0-0 GF: - Fm: 0-1
Distance:	2m/2m3: 0-1 2m4-2m7: 0-0 3m+: 0-0
Track:	LH: 0-1 RH: 0-0 Tight: 0-0 Gall: 0-0
Aids:	Bl: 0-0 Vi: 0-0 Tstrap: 0-0
Best Rating:	81 8/02 Sthl 2m1f gd-fm Hdl

Moderate Flat stayer, runner-up in seller on hurdling debut; acts on fast ground.

Big Joe Dakara
81   53
8-y-o b g Akarad (FR)-Ruling Honor (USA) (Hero s Honor (USA))
J Mackie Scattered Friends Partnership

Placings:00/PP45   (0817)
2002/03: 20ᴾGS, 24ᴾHY, 20⁴GS, 20⁵GF,

	Starts	1st	2nd	3rd	Win & Pl
Hurdles	4	0	0	0	0
Career Total	6	0	0	0	0

Going:	Sf: 0-1 GS: 0-2 Gd: 0-0 GF: - Fm: 0-1
Distance:	2m/2m3: 0-0 2m4-2m7: 0-3 3m+: 0-1
Track:	LH: 0-4 RH: 0-0 Tight: 0-0 Gall: 0-0
Aids:	Bl: 0-0 Vi: 0-0 Tstrap: 0-0
Best Rating:	60 1/01 Catt 2m gd-sft NHF

Big Max
106(104h)   (113h)100
8-y-o b g Rakaposhi King-Edwina s Dawn (Space King)
Miss K M George Exterior Profiles Ltd

Placings:0P414/1231/364P013-2P4U53P   (3625)
2002/03: 20²GS, 21ᴾG, 20⁴G, 24ᵁG, 24⁵GS, 24³S, 24ᴾGS,

	Starts	1st	2nd	3rd	Win & Pl
Hurdles	1	0	0	0	0
Chases	6	1	1	2	2348
Career Total	23	4	2	4	19708
100 3/02 MRas	2m5f110yD(0-120)HHdl			G-S	£4069
113 4/01 Muss	3m			F(0-100)HHdl	G-F £3251
104 10/00 MRas	3m			F(0-100)HHdl	GD £2646
85 1/00 Muss	2m4f			F(0-100)HHdl	GD £3493

Total win prize-money £13461

Going:	Sf: 0-1 GS: 0-3 Gd: 0-3 GF: - Fm: 0-0
Distance:	2m/2m3: 0-0 2m4-2m7: 0-3 3m+: 0-4
Track:	LH: 0-4 RH: 0-7 Tight: 0-6 Gall: 0-0
Aids:	Bl: 0-0 Vi: 0-0 Tstrap: 0-0
Best Rating:	113 4/01 Muss 3m gd-fm Hdl

Moderate chaser/modest hurdler; free-runner; stays three miles; seems to appreciate a sharp right-handed track and good or fast ground.

Big Quick (IRE)
102   101
8-y-o ch g Glacial Storm (USA)-Furryvale (Furry Glen)
L Wells R A Gadd

Placings:32-22002314   (4759)
2002/03: 20²GF, 20²GS, 22²G, 20⁰S, 22²GS, 21³GF, 24¹GF, 27⁴GF,

	Starts	1st	2nd	3rd	Win & Pl
Hurdles	8	1	3	1	8765
Career Total	10	1	4	2	9718
101 4/03 Extr	3m110y E(0-110)HHdl			G-F	£4810

Total win-money £4810

Going:	Sf: 0-1 GS: 0-2 Gd: 0-1 GF: - Fm: 1-4
Distance:	2m/2m3: 0-0 2m4-2m7: 0-6 3m+: 1-2
Track:	LH: 0-4 RH: 1-2 Tight: 0-6 Gall: 0-1
Aids:	Bl: 0-0 Vi: 0-0 Tstrap: 0-0
Best Rating:	102 5/01 NAbb 2m1f gd-fm NHF

Moderate hurdler; despite his saddle having slipped badly lost his maiden tag over hurdles in 3m fast ground handicap at Exeter April 2003.

Big Star (IRE)
79f   59f
6-y-o ro g Fourstars Allstar (USA)-Dame Blakeney (IRE) (Blakeney)
J S Haldane Gordon E Davidson

Placings:0'00   (4039)
2002/03: 16⁰HY, 16⁰S,

	Starts	1st	2nd	3rd	Win & Pl
NH Flat	2	0	0	0	
Career Total	3	0	0	0	

Going:	Sf: 0-2 GS: 0-0 Gd: 0-0 GF: - Fm: 0-0
Distance:	2m/2m3: 0-2 2m4-2m7: 0-0 3m+: 0-0
Track:	LH: 0-2 RH: 0-0 Tight: 0-0 Gall: 0-0
Aids:	Bl: 0-0 Vi: 0-0 Tstrap: 0-0
Best Rating:	66 4/01 Muss 2m1f gd-fm NHF

Big Wheel
98(92c)   (89+c)103
8-y-o ch g Mujtahid (USA)-Numuthej (USA) (Nureyev (USA))
N G Richards Jim Ennis

Placings:45/1041113/F001P3P/F512   (4795)
2002/03: 16ᶠS, 16⁵S, 17¹G, 21²GF,

	Starts	1st	2nd	3rd	Win & Pl
Hurdles	2	1	0	0	4126
Chases	2	0	0	0	
Career Total	20	6	1	2	16227
97 3/03 Sedg	2m1f			G(0-90)HHdl	GD £2408
105 1/01 Tntn	2m3f110yF(0-105)HHdl			SFT	£2604
103 3/00 Ludl	2m			F Hdl	GD £2730
109 3/00 Hrfd	2m1f			G Hdl	GD £2128
100 1/00 Winc	2m			F Hdl	G-S £1939
102 11/99 Ludl	2m			G Hdl	GD £1968

Total win prize-money £13777

Going:	Sf: 0-2 GS: 0-0 Gd: 1-1 GF: - Fm: 0-1
Distance:	2m/2m3: 1-3 2m4-2m7: 0-1 3m+: 0-0
Track:	LH: 1-3 RH: 0-1 Tight: 1-2 Gall: 0-0
Aids:	Bl: 0-0 Vi: 0-0 Tstrap: 0-0
Best Rating:	109 3/00 Hrfd 2m1f good Hdl

Selling-class hurdler; multiple winner at that level; effective on a sound surface or softer; stays two miles-three but outstayed when tried over an extended two miles-five; well suited by a sharp track.

Bignoyse (IRE)

10-y-o b g Little Bighorn-Black River Lady (River Beauty)
C R Wilson Bill Martin

Placings:P/PPP-P6P   (0331)
2002/03: 24PGS, 20PGF, 20PG,

	Starts	1st	2nd	3rd	Win & Pl
Hurdles	3	0	0	0	0
Career Total	7	0	0	0	0

Going: Sf: 0-0 GS: 0-1 Gd: 0-1 GF: - Fm: 0-1
Distance: 2m/2m3: 0-0 2m4-2m7: 0-2 3m+: 0-1
Track: LH: 0-3 RH: 0-0 Tight: 0-0 Gall: 0-0
Aids: Bl: 0-2 Vi: 0-1 Tstrap: 0-0
Best Rating: 0   5/02 Weth 2m4f110y good Hdl

Bigwig (IRE)
104   81
10-y-o ch g Thatching-Sabaah (USA) (Nureyev (USA))
G L Moore Mrs Elizabeth Kiernan

Placings:6504/405P0034/511562026/62O250411/06F3301
2/044060116-005300004   (4629)
2002/03: 21SG, 19OGF, 16OS, 22SHY, 19SHY, 21OS, 21OHY, 21OG,
21OGF, 214GF,

	Starts	1st	2nd	3rd	Win & Pl
Hurdles	10	0	0	1	450
Career Total	56	7	5	4	23368
99	4/02	Plum	2m5f	E(0-105)HHdl	G-F	£2975
95	3/02	Plum	2m5f	F(0-90)Hdl	G-S	£1928
104	4/01	Plum	2m5f	F(0-105)HHdl	HVY	£2901
110	4/00	Plum	2m5f	F(0-105)HHdl	G-S	£2800
110	4/00	Plum	2m5f	F Hdl	G-S	£2758
97	8/98	Worc	2m2f	E(0-115)HHdl	GD	£2442
78	5/98	Hntg	2m110y	G(0-95)HHdl	G-F	£1716
				Total win prize-money £17523

Going: Sf: 0-5 GS: 0-0 Gd: 0-2 GF: - Fm: 0-3
Distance: 2m/2m3: 0-3 2m4-2m7: 0-7 3m+: 0-0
Track: LH: 0-8 RH: 0-2 Tight: 0-8 Gall: 0-2
Aids: Bl: 0-10 Vi: 0-0 Tstrap: 0-0
Best Rating: 110 4/00 Plum 2m5f   gd-sft Hdl

Plating-class hurdler; fair sort at best, but on the decline now; course specialist a Plumpton; suited by testing ground, but acts on faster; usually wears blinkers; best in the spring.

Bill Owen
91   85
7-y-o ch g Nicholas Bill-Pollys Owen (Master Owen)
D P Keane Roger/Mary Barton & Wadswickcountrystore

Placings:P54   (4569)
2002/03: 21PGS, 19SG, 244G,

	Starts	1st	2nd	3rd	Win & Pl
Chases	3	0	0	0	435
Career Total	3	0	0	0	435

Going: Sf: 0-0 GS: 0-1 Gd: 0-2 GF: - Fm: 0-0
Distance: 2m/2m3: 0-0 2m4-2m7: 0-2 3m+: 0-1
Track: LH: 0-1 RH: 0-2 Tight: 0-1 Gall: 0-0
Aids: Bl: 0-0 Vi: 0-0 Tstrap: 0-0
Best Rating: 85 3/03 Asct 2m3f110y good Ch

Bill's Echo
82f   77f
4-y-o br g Double Eclipse (IRE)-Bit On Edge (Henbit (USA))

P Monteith Burns Partnership

Placings:5504   (4039)
2002/03: 14SGS, 16SHY, 16OGS, 16⁴S,

	Starts	1st	2nd	3rd	Win & Pl
NH Flat	4	0	0	0	0
Career Total	4	0	0	0	0

Going: Sf: 0-2 GS: 0-2 Gd: 0-0 GF: - Fm: 0-0
Distance: 2m/2m3: 0-3 2m4-2m7: 0-0 3m+: 0-0
Track: LH: 0-4 RH: 0-0 Tight: 0-0 Gall: 0-0
Aids: Bl: 0-0 Vi: 0-0 Tstrap: 0-0
Best Rating: 77 3/03 Ayr 2m soft NHF

Billesley Belle

6-y-o ch m Sula Bula-Tara Vii (Damsire Unregistered)
A J Wilson H Fentum

Placings:00   (4350)
2002/03: 17OS, 16OGF,

	Starts	1st	2nd	3rd	Win & Pl
NH Flat	2	0	0	0	0
Career Total	2	0	0	0	0

Going: Sf: 0-1 GS: 0-0 Gd: 0-0 GF: - Fm: 0-1
Distance: 2m/2m3: 0-2 2m4-2m7: 0-0 3m+: 0-0
Track: LH: 0-1 RH: 0-1 Tight: 0-0 Gall: 0-0
Aids: Bl: 0-0 Vi: 0-0 Tstrap: 0-0
Best Rating: 0 3/03 Wwck 2m gd-fm NHF

Billie John (IRE)
107(106h)   (103+h)115+
8-y-o ch g Boyne Valley-Lovestream (Sandy Creek)
Mrs K Walton Mrs Patricia M Wilson

Placings:0/60620-14241   (1229)
2002/03: 16¹G, 20⁴GF, 19²GF, 17⁴G, 17¹G,

	Starts	1st	2nd	3rd	Win & Pl
Hurdles	5	2	1	0	7642
Career Total	11	2	2	0	8502
103	9/02	Bang	2m1f	D Hdl	GD	£3818
96	5/02	Hexm	2m110y	E Hdl	GD	£2548
				Total win prize-money £6367

Going: Sf: 0-0 GS: 0-0 Gd: 2-3 GF: - Fm: 0-2
Distance: 2m/2m3: 2-3 2m4-2m7: 0-2 3m+: 0-0
Track: LH: 2-4 RH: 0-1 Tight: 1-3 Gall: 0-0
Aids: Bl: 0-0 Vi: 0-0 Tstrap: 0-0
Best Rating: 103 9/02 Bang 2m1f good Hdl

Modest chaser; acts on fast ground; best at around two miles.

Billy Ballbreaker (IRE)
90   70
7-y-o br g Good Thyne (USA)-Droichead Dhamhile (IRE) (The Parson)
P F Nicholls A G Fear

Placings:50-6   (4251)
2002/03: 17⁶G,

	Starts	1st	2nd	3rd	Win & Pl
Hurdles	1	0	0	0	0
Career Total	3	0	0	0	0

Billy Nomaite
107   119+
9-y-o ch g Komaite (USA)-Lucky Monashka (Lucky Wednesday)
Mrs S J Smith R Preston

Placings:66020U4600P/2211351/162/63F-2F1U   (0796)
2002/03: 20²S, 20⁶G, 201GF, 20UGS,

	Starts	1st	2nd	3rd	Win & Pl
Chases	4	1	1	0	12580
Career Total	28	5	5	2	30561
119	6/02	MRas	2m4f	C(0-135)HCh	G-F	£10349
113	10/00	Kels	2m1f	E Ch	SFT	£3510
113	12/99	Uttx	2m	C(0-130)HHdl	SFT	£5135
110	9/99	Worc	2m	E(0-115)HHdl	G-F	£2250
100	8/99	Strf	2m110y	F(0-105)HHdl	GD	£1976
				Total win prize-money £23223

Going: Sf: 0-1 GS: 0-1 Gd: 0-1 GF: - Fm: 1-1
Distance: 2m/2m3: 0-0 2m4-2m7: 1-4 3m+: 0-0
Track: LH: 0-2 RH: 1-2 Tight: 1-3 Gall: 0-0
Aids: Bl: 0-0 Vi: 0-0 Tstrap: 0-0
Best Rating: 119 6/02 MRas 2m4f gd-fm Ch

Fair chaser; keen sort; has been successful over hurdles and fences; acts on most types of ground; stays two and a half miles.

Bin It (IRE)
101   119
7-y-o b m Supreme Leader-Castle Stream (Paddy s Stream)
C J Mann John Seth-Smith

Placings:3235/F2121220-25   (2043)
2002/03: 24²S, 22⁵HY,

	Starts	1st	2nd	3rd	Win & Pl
Hurdles	2	0	1	0	1668
Career Total	14	2	6	2	16577
119	1/02	Hrfd	2m3f110yE(0-110)HHdl	SFT	£3475
108	11/01	Towc	2m5f	D Hdl	SFT	£3913
				Total win prize-money £7389

Going: Sf: 0-2 GS: 0-0 Gd: 0-0 GF: - Fm: 0-0
Distance: 2m/2m3: 0-0 2m4-2m7: 0-1 3m+: 0-1
Track: LH: 0-2 RH: 0-0 Tight: 0-1 Gall: 0-0
Aids: Bl: 0-0 Vi: 0-0 Tstrap: 0-0
Best Rating: 119 11/02 Uttx 3m110y soft Hdl

Fair hurdler; has proven admirably consistent over hurdles, showing progressive form in the process; stays three miles; likes soft ground.

Bindaree (IRE)
115(91h)   (112+h)139
9-y-o ch g Roselier (FR)-Flowing Tide (Main Reef)
N A Twiston-Davies H R Mould

Placings:31111240/1213U124U/0533601-0FU2406 (4479)
2002/03: 25OGS, 27⁵FGS, 26UGS, 26²S, 24⁴GS, 28OG, 36⁶G,

	Starts	1st	2nd	3rd	Win & Pl
Hurdles	1	0	0	0	0
Chases	6	0	0	1	20800
Career Total	31	8	4	4	419316
148	4/02	Aint	4m4f	A HCh	GD	£290000

144	1/01	Asct	3m110y	B Ch	G-S	£8807
133	11/00	Chep	2m3f110yA	Ch	SFT	£18000
136	9/00	Prth	2m4f110yD	Ch	HVY	£4771
153	12/99	Chel	2m5f110yA	Hdl	SFT	£16375
153	12/99	Chel	3m	A Hdl	G-S	£9525
141	11/99	Chep	3m	B Hdl	SFT	£7132
135	10/99	Carl	3m110y	E Hdl	GD	£2346

Total win prize-money £356958

Going:	Sf: 0-1 GS: 0-4 Gd: 0-2 GF: - Fm: 0-0
Distance:	2m/2m3: 0-0 2m4-2m7: 0-0 3m+: 0-7
Track:	LH: 0-7 RH: 0-0 Tight: 0-2 Gall: 0-1
Aids:	Bl: 0-0 Vi: 0-0 Tstrap: 0-0
Best Rating:	153 12/99 Chel 2m5f110y soft Hdl

Very useful chaser; winner of the Grand National in 2002, emphasising that he jumps well and stays forever; suited by going left-handed; effective on good and soft ground; largely out of form this time but ran much better when managing sixth in this year s Grand National after two bad mistakes.

Bindy Bondy
81 52

6-y-o b m Beveled (USA)-Rockmount Rose (Proverb)
J R Best Mrs V Palmer

Placings:000P (4426)
2002/03: 17^0HY, 16^0GS, 16^0GF,

	Starts	1st	2nd	3rd	Win & Pl
NH Flat	3	0	0	0	0
Hurdles	1	0	0	0	0
Career Total	4	0	0	0	

Going:	Sf: 0-1 GS: 0-1 Gd: 0-1 GF: - Fm: 0-1
Distance:	2m/2m3: 0-4 2m4-2m7: 0-0 3m+: 0-0
Track:	LH: 0-1 RH: 0-3 Tight: 0-2 Gall: 0-0
Aids:	Bl: 0-0 Vi: 0-0 Tstrap: 0-0
Best Rating:	82 2/03 Ludl 2m good NHF

Binny Bay
101(99h) (85 h)90

7-y-o b m Karinga Bay-Binny Grove (Sunyboy)
D McCain D McCain

Placings:000030034612-15623443 (4562)
2002/03: 20^1S, 26^5HY, 21^6S, 16^2S, 16^3S, 16^4HY, 20^4GF, 17^3GF,

	Starts	1st	2nd	3rd	Win & Pl
Hurdles	3	1	0	0	3724
Chases	5	0	1	2	2846
Career Total	20	2	2	4	10040

90	5/02	Bang	2m4f	D(0-110)HHdl	SFT £3724
85	4/02	Uttx	2m	G Hdl	G-F £1946

Total win prize-money £5670

Going:	Sf: 1-6 GS: 0-0 Gd: 0-0 GF: - Fm: 0-2
Distance:	2m/2m3: 0-4 2m4-2m7: 1-3 3m+: 0-1
Track:	LH: 1-8 RH: 0-0 Tight: 1-7 Gall: 0-0
Aids:	Bl: 0-0 Vi: 0-0 Tstrap: 1-8
Best Rating:	90 4/03 Bang 2m1f110y gd-fm Ch

Plating-class chaser/hurdler; got up in final stride to land two-mile seller at Uttoxeter in April 2002; appeared to settle better with the aid of a tongue-tie and a new bit; added to that in better company at Bangor the next month; stays two and a half miles; acts on soft ground; well beaten over fences so far.

Bint St James
84 58+

8-y-o b m Shareef Dancer (USA)-St James s Antigua (IRE) (Law Society (USA))

W Clay Mrs Janet Dutton

Placings:550/P4U3F0P01P/402FPP0-005 (2202)
2002/03: 20^0Q, 23^0HY, 16^2S,

	Starts	1st	2nd	3rd	Win & Pl
Hurdles	3	0	0	0	0
Career Total	23	1	1	1	2443

85 11/99 MRas 2m3f110yG(0-90)HHdl G-S £1490
Total win prize-money £1490

Going:	Sf: 0-2 GS: 0-0 Gd: 0-1 GF: - Fm: 0-0
Distance:	2m/2m3: 0-1 2m4-2m7: 0-2 3m+: 0-0
Track:	LH: 0-3 RH: 0-0 Tight: 0-1 Gall: 0-0
Aids:	Bl: 0-0 Vi: 0-0 Tstrap: 0-0
Best Rating:	85 11/99 MRas 2m3f110y gd-sft Hdl

Birchall Belle (IRE)
79f 60f

5-y-o b m Presenting-Queenford Belle (Celtic Cone)
Mrs H Dalton Mrs Claire Massey

Placings:0 (3747)
2002/03: 16^0G,

	Starts	1st	2nd	3rd	Win & Pl
NH Flat	1	0	0	0	0
Career Total	1	0	0	0	

Going:	Sf: 0-0 GS: 0-0 Gd: 0-1 GF: - Fm: 0-0
Distance:	2m/2m3: 0-1 2m4-2m7: 0-0 3m+: 0-0
Track:	LH: 0-0 RH: 0-1 Tight: 0-0 Gall: 0-1
Aids:	Bl: 0-0 Vi: 0-0 Tstrap: 0-0
Best Rating:	60 2/03 Hntg 2m110y good NHF

Bird King

6-y-o b g Rakaposhi King-Miss Wrensborough (Buckskin (FR))
D R Gandolfo Starlight Racing

Placings:0-UP (1748)
2002/03: 21^UG, 21^PS,

	Starts	1st	2nd	3rd	Win & Pl
Hurdles	2	0	0	0	
Career Total	3	0	0	0	

Going:	Sf: 0-1 GS: 0-0 Gd: 0-1 GF: - Fm: 0-0
Distance:	2m/2m3: 0-0 2m4-2m7: 0-2 3m+: 0-0
Track:	LH: 0-2 RH: 0-0 Tight: 0-2 Gall: 0-0
Aids:	Bl: 0-0 Vi: 0-0 Tstrap: 0-0
Best Rating:	0 11/02 Plum 2m5f soft Hdl

Birotex Boy (IRE)
88 89d

10-y-o b g Meneval (USA)-Ballymorris Belle (Laurence O)
M W Easterby Birotex

Placings:00063/2/50/0P2P/R5333P-0P4 (2068)
2002/03: 16^6S, 16^6S, 17^4GS,

	Starts	1st	2nd	3rd	Win & Pl
Chases	3	0	0	0	369
Career Total	21	0	2	4	3541

Going:	Sf: 0-2 GS: 0-1 Gd: 0-0 GF: - Fm: 0-0
Distance:	2m/2m3: 0-3 2m4-2m7: 0-0 3m+: 0-0
Track:	LH: 0-1 RH: 0-0 Tight: 0-2 Gall: 0-0
Aids:	Bl: 0-1 Vi: 0-0 Tstrap: 0-0
Best Rating:	94 5/98 Hexm 2m good Hdl

Plating-class maiden over hurdles and fences; acts on good and soft ground.

Birth Of The Blues
79 40

7-y-o ch g Efisio-Great Steps (Vaigly Great)
A Charlton Miss Juliet E Reed

Placings:P000/0 (1285)
2002/03: 18^0GF,

	Starts	1st	2nd	3rd	Win & Pl
Hurdles	1	0	0	0	
Career Total	5	0	0	0	

Going:	Sf: 0-0 GS: 0-0 Gd: 0-0 GF: - Fm: 0-1
Distance:	2m/2m3: 0-1 2m4-2m7: 0-0 3m+: 0-0
Track:	LH: 0-1 RH: 0-0 Tight: 0-1 Gall: 0-0
Aids:	Bl: 0-0 Vi: 0-0 Tstrap: 0-0
Best Rating:	57 12/00 Fknm 2m gd-sft Hdl

Bishlir
58f

5-y-o gr g Lir-Rose Park Dancer Vii (Damsire Unregistered)
Miss K M George Miss S J Gillbard

Placings:0 (3673)
2002/03: 18^0GS,

	Starts	1st	2nd	3rd	Win & Pl
NH Flat	1	0	0	0	
Career Total	1	0	0	0	

Going:	Sf: 0-0 GS: 0-1 Gd: 0-0 GF: - Fm: 0-0
Distance:	2m/2m3: 0-1 2m4-2m7: 0-0 3m+: 0-0
Track:	LH: 0-1 RH: 0-0 Tight: 0-1 Gall: 0-0
Aids:	Bl: 0-0 Vi: 0-0 Tstrap: 0-0
Best Rating:	0 2/03 Font 2m2f110y gd-sft NHF

Bishop's Blade
75 60

6-y-o b g Sure Blade (USA)-Myrtilla (Beldale Flutter (USA))
M Hill Edward Retter

Placings:0 (3311)
2002/03: 19^0GS,

	Starts	1st	2nd	3rd	Win & Pl
Hurdles	1	0	0	0	
Career Total	1	0	0	0	

Going:	Sf: 0-0 GS: 0-1 Gd: 0-0 GF: - Fm: 0-0
Distance:	2m/2m3: 0-1 2m4-2m7: 0-0 3m+: 0-0
Track:	LH: 0-0 RH: 0-1 Tight: 0-0 Gall: 0-0
Aids:	Bl: 0-1 Vi: 0-0 Tstrap: 0-0
Best Rating:	60 1/03 Extr 2m3f gd-sft Hdl

Bishop's Bridge (IRE)
91f 78f

5-y-o b g Norwich-River Swell (IRE) (Over The River (FR))
C P Morlock S Kimber

Placings:0 (3322)
2002/03: 16^0GS,

	Starts	1st	2nd	3rd	Win & Pl
NH Flat	1	0	0	0	
Career Total	1	0	0	0	

Bit O Magic (IRE)
110   107

11-y-o ch g Henbit (USA)-Arpal Magic (Master Owen)
Ferdy Murphy Geoff Adam

Placings:1/20/4F15344/650/31/**U2P41-323030F122F**
(4751)
2002/03: 17³GS, 17²G, 16³G, 16⁰G, 19³G, 19⁰S, 20ᶠG, 20¹G, 17²S, 17²G, 20ᶠG,

	Starts	1st	2nd	3rd	Win & Pl
Chases	11	1	3	3	12160
Career Total	31	5	5	5	25298
107 1/03 Muss	2m4f		E(0-110)HCh	GD	£5343
101 4/02 Hntg	2m110y	D(0-115)HCh	G-F	£4059
101 10/00 Kels	2m2f	F(0-110)HHdl	SFT	£1879
88 12/98 Muss	2m4f	E Hdl	GD	£2262
99 5/96 Prth	2m110y	H NHF	FRM	£1966
			Total win prize-money £15510		

Going: Sf: 0-2 GS: 0-1 Gd: 1-8 GF: - Fm: 0-0
Distance: 2m/2m3: 0-8 **2m4-2m7: 1-3** 3m+: 0-0
Track: LH: 0-4 **RH: 1-7 Tight: 1-6** Gall: 0-0
Aids: Bl: 0-2 Vi: 0-0 Tstrap: 0-0
Best Rating: 107 4/03 Kels 2m1f good Ch

Modest handicap chaser; winner at Musselburgh in January; stays two miles four; seems to act on most ground; has worn blinkers.

Bit O' Gold
52   1

5-y-o b g Henbit (USA)-Run Of Gold (Deep Run)
Mrs K B Mactaggart (Denys Smith 25/7) Mrs J Roncoroni

Placings:0000
(4665)
2002/03: 16⁰G, 16⁰GF, 17⁰GF, 17⁰GF,

	Starts	1st	2nd	3rd	Win & Pl
NH Flat	4	0	0	0	
Career Total	4	0	0	0	

Going: Sf: 0-0 GS: 0-0 Gd: 0-1 GF: - Fm: 0-3
Distance: 2m/2m3: 0-4 2m4-2m7: 0-0 3m+: 0-0
Track: LH: 0-2 RH: 0-1 Tight: 0-1 Gall: 0-0
Aids: Bl: 0-0 Vi: 0-0 Tstrap: 0-0
Best Rating: 55 6/02 Hexm 2m110y good NHF

Bit O'Speed (IRE)

12-y-o b g Henbit (USA)-Speedy Debbie (Pollerton)
Mrs S Richardson James Richardson

Placings:0/00/143331/525545PP/42/13
(4640)
2002/03: 24¹G, 21³G,

	Starts	1st	2nd	3rd	Win & Pl
Chases	2	1	0	1	3434
Career Total	24	3	2	4	10839
106 4/03 Strf	3m	H Ch	GD	£2898
108 9/97 Gway	2m1f	Ch	Y-S	£3391
90 5/97 Dpat	2m1f172y Hdl		GD	£1695
			Total win prize-money £7985		

Going: Sf: 0-0 GS: 0-0 Gd: 1-2 GF: - Fm: 0-0
Distance: 2m/2m3: 0-0 2m4-2m7: 0-1 **3m+: 1-1**
Track: **LH: 1-2** RH: 0-0 **Tight: 1-2** Gall: 0-0
Aids: Bl: 0-0 Vi: 0-0 Tstrap: 0-0
Best Rating: 115 5/98 Wxfd 2m4f good Ch

Hunter chaser; winning hurdler and chaser in his native Ireland; made all to land a Stratford hunter chase in April 2003; found 2m 5f inadequate when third at the same venue a week later; suited by a sound surface and three miles.

Bit Of A Gem

7-y-o b m Henbit (USA)-Krystle Saint (St Columbus)
K A Morgan D J Wheatley

Placings:000P
(4715)
2002/03: 16⁸G, 16⁹G, 20⁸GF, 20ᶠGF,

	Starts	1st	2nd	3rd	Win & Pl
NH Flat	2	0	0	0	0
Hurdles	2	0	0	0	0
Career Total	4	0	0	0	0

Going: Sf: 0-0 GS: 0-0 Gd: 0-2 GF: - Fm: 0-2
Distance: 2m/2m3: 0-2 2m4-2m7: 0-2 3m+: 0-0
Track: LH: 0-3 RH: 0-1 Tight: 0-0 Gall: 0-0
Aids: Bl: 0-0 Vi: 0-0 Tstrap: 0-0
Best Rating: 68 7/02 Worc 2m good NHF

Bit Of A Snob
(59h)   (19h)98

12-y-o b g St Columbus-Classey (Dubassoff (USA))
J S King Miss S Douglas-Pennant

Placings:PP02043/1P1313P/P01-PPP0
(0658)
2002/03: 19ᴾG, 16ᴾGS, 16ᴾGF, 16⁹GF,

	Starts	1st	2nd	3rd	Win & Pl
Hurdles	1	0	0	0	0
Chases	3	0	0	0	0
Career Total	21	4	1	3	14662
98 8/01 Hntg	2m110y	F(0-100)HCh	G-F	£2660
104 8/00 NAbb	2m110y	F(0-110)HCh	GD	£4065
98 6/00 Hrfd	2m	E Ch	G-F	£3110
100 5/00 Winc	2m	E Hdl	FRM	£2751
			Total win prize-money £12587		

Going: Sf: 0-0 GS: 0-1 Gd: 0-1 GF: - Fm: 0-2
Distance: 2m/2m3: 0-3 2m4-2m7: 0-1 3m+: 0-0
Track: LH: 0-2 RH: 0-2 Tight: 0-1 Gall: 0-1
Aids: Bl: 0-2 Vi: 0-0 Tstrap: 0-0
Best Rating: 104 8/00 NAbb 2m110y good Ch

Bit Of Minster
(96h)   (60h)92

7-y-o b g Minster Son-Bit On Edge (Henbit (USA))
P Monteith Burns Partnership

Placings:0P/0043442-P
(0182)
2002/03: 25ᴾG,

	Starts	1st	2nd	3rd	Win & Pl
Chases	1	0	0	0	0
Career Total	10	0	1	1	2048

Going: Sf: 0-0 GS: 0-0 Gd: 0-1 GF: - Fm: 0-0
Distance: 2m/2m3: 0-0 2m4-2m7: 0-0 3m+: 0-1
Track: LH: 0-1 RH: 0-0 Tight: 0-0 Gall: 0-0
Aids: Bl: 0-0 Vi: 0-0 Tstrap: 0-0
Best Rating: 92 4/02 Hexm 3m1f good Ch

Modest hurdler, yet to prove he truly gets three miles.

Bitofamixup (IRE)

12-y-o br g Strong Gale-Geeaway (Gala Performance (USA))
M J Roberts Mike Roberts

Placings:011/12122/164U/P2PP/63P3-06UU
(4459)
2002/03: 24⁶GS, 24⁶GF, 25ᵁG, 21ᵁG,

Going: Sf: 0-0 GS: 0-1 Gd: 0-0 GF: - Fm: 0-0
Distance: 2m/2m3: 0-1 2m4-2m7: 0-0 3m+: 0-0
Track: LH: 0-0 RH: 0-1 Tight: 0-0 Gall: 0-0
Aids: Bl: 0-0 Vi: 0-0 Tstrap: 0-0
Best Rating: 78 1/03 Kemp 2m   gd-sft NHF

Bishopstone Belle

6-y-o b m Formidable (USA)-Relatively Easy (Relkino)
J A Moore J A Moore

Placings:P/PP-P
(1165)
2002/03: 21ᴾG,

	Starts	1st	2nd	3rd	Win & Pl
Hurdles	1	0	0	0	
Career Total	4	0	0	0	

Going: Sf: 0-0 GS: 0-0 Gd: 0-1 GF: - Fm: 0-0
Distance: 2m/2m3: 0-0 2m4-2m7: 0-0 3m+: 0-0
Track: LH: 0-1 RH: 0-0 Tight: 0-1 Gall: 0-0
Aids: Bl: 0-0 Vi: 0-0 Tstrap: 0-0
Best Rating: 0 9/02 Sedg 2m5f110y good Hdl

Bison King (IRE)
99f   100f

6-y-o b g King s Ride-Valantonia (IRE) (Over The River (FR))
C R Egerton Mrs Evelyn Hankinson

Placings:20
(2477)
2002/03: 16²G, 16⁰GS,

	Starts	1st	2nd	3rd	Win & Pl
NH Flat	2	0	1	0	714
Career Total	2	0	1	0	714

Going: Sf: 0-0 GS: 0-1 Gd: 0-1 GF: - Fm: 0-0
Distance: 2m/2m3: 0-2 2m4-2m7: 0-0 3m+: 0-0
Track: LH: 0-1 RH: 0-1 Tight: 0-0 Gall: 0-1
Aids: Bl: 0-0 Vi: 0-0 Tstrap: 0-0
Best Rating: 100 11/02 Ludl 2m   good NHF

Scopey sort, runner-up in a bumper on his debut.

Bisquet-De-Bouche
101   72

9-y-o ch m Most Welcome-Larive (Blakeney)
A W Carroll Martin Brook

Placings:0/0202B12P/63641/35-05P5P
(3992)
2002/03: 20⁶G, 24⁵G, 21ᴾS, 20⁶GS, 25ᴾG,

	Starts	1st	2nd	3rd	Win & Pl
Hurdles	4	0	0	0	0
Chases	1	0	0	0	0
Career Total	21	2	3	2	9190
97 4/01 Winc	2m6f	F(0-105)HHdl	SFT	£3724
87 2/00 Catt	3m1f110yF(0-100)HHdl	GD	£2012
			Total win prize-money £5737		

Going: Sf: 0-1 GS: 0-1 Gd: 0-3 GF: - Fm: 0-0
Distance: 2m/2m3: 0-0 2m4-2m7: 0-3 3m+: 0-2
Track: LH: 0-4 RH: 0-1 Tight: 0-2 Gall: 0-0
Aids: Bl: 0-0 Vi: 0-0 Tstrap: 0-0
Best Rating: 97 4/01 Winc 2m6f   soft Hdl

Plating-class hurdler; possibly a shade unlucky when close third despite finishing lame in 2m 6f selling handicap Newton Abbot May 2003; never a factor when tried over fences; best on a sound surface; stays three miles.

	Starts	1st	2nd	3rd	Win & Pl
Chases	4	0	0	0	0
Career Total	**24**	**5**	**4**	**2**	**34611**

140	5/98	Worc	2m7f110yE Ch		GD	£3566
131	2/98	Font	3m2f110yD Ch		GD	£3975
126	5/97	Bang	3m110y	H Ch	GD	£1548
137	4/97	Aint	3m1f	B Ch	GD	£7107
108	2/97	Hntg	3m	H Ch	G-S	£1262

Total win prize-money £17459

Going: Sf: 0-0 GS: 0-1 Gd: 0-2 GF: - Fm: 0-1
Distance: 2m/2m3: 0-0 2m4-2m7: 0-1 3m+: 0-3
Track: LH: 0-4 RH: 0-0 Tight: 0-4 Gall: 0-0
Aids: Bl: 0-1 Vi: 0-0 Tstrap: 0-2
Best Rating: **146** 4/98 Ayr 3m1f good Ch

Formerly smart hunter chaser; seems to have benefitted from having his tongue tied again and won hunter chase at Folkestone May 2003; showed he is still a force to be reckoned with when springing 25/1 surprise in Horse and Hound Cup at Stratford next time.

Bitter Sweet

106 **104**

7-y-o gr m Deploy-Julia Flyte (Drone (USA))
J L Spearing Masonaires

Placings:000/132403-2224135 **(4571)**
2002/03: 16^{2}GF, 16^{2}G, 17^{2}GF, 17^{4}GS, 16^{1}G, 16^{3}GS, 16^{5}GF,

	Starts	1st	2nd	3rd	Win & Pl
Hurdles	7	1	3	1	9266
Career Total	**16**	**2**	**4**	**3**	**14070**

103	11/02	Wwck	2m	D(0-125)HHdl	GD	£3770
83	9/01	Worc	2m	E Hdl	G-F	£2443

Total win prize-money £6213

Going: Sf: 0-0 GS: 0-2 Gd: 1-2 GF: - Fm: 0-3
Distance: **2m/2m3: 1-7** 2m4-2m7: 0-0 3m+: 0-0
Track: **LH: 1-4** RH: 0-3 Tight: 0-3 Gall: 0-2
Aids: Bl: 0-0 Vi: 0-0 Tstrap: 0-0
Best Rating: **104** 11/02 Hntg 2m110y gd-sft Hdl

Moderate handicap hurdler; running well in the autumn of 2002 and gained a deserved victory at Warwick in November; suited by good or faster ground; likes to be produced late.

Bivacastle

7-y-o ch m Carlingford Castle-Bivadell (Bivouac)
B N Pollock Stuart A Blyth

Placings:P **(4708)**
2002/03: 20^{P}G,

	Starts	1st	2nd	3rd	Win & Pl
Hurdles	1	0	0	0	
Career Total	**1**	**0**	**0**	**0**	

Going: Sf: 0-0 GS: 0-0 Gd: 0-1 GF: - Fm: 0-0
Distance: 2m/2m3: 0-0 2m4-2m7: 0-1 3m+: 0-0
Track: LH: 0-1 RH: 0-0 Tight: 0-0 Gall: 0-0
Aids: Bl: 0-0 Vi: 0-0 Tstrap: 0-0
Best Rating: **0** 4/03 Uttx 2m4f110y good Hdl

Black Beatle

8-y-o b g Roscoe Blake-Rose Albertine (Record Token)
S H Shirley-Beavan J E M Vestey

Placings:P **(1562)**
2002/03: 22^{P}G,

	Starts	1st	2nd	3rd	Win & Pl
Hurdles	1	0	0	0	
Career Total	**1**	**0**	**0**	**0**	

Going: Sf: 0-0 GS: 0-0 Gd: 0-1 GF: - Fm: 0-0
Distance: 2m/2m3: 0-0 2m4-2m7: 0-1 3m+: 0-0
Track: LH: 0-1 RH: 0-0 Tight: 0-1 Gall: 0-0
Aids: Bl: 0-0 Vi: 0-0 Tstrap: 0-0
Best Rating: **0** 10/02 Kels 2m6f110y good Hdl

Black Bullet (NZ)

107 **118**

10-y-o br g Silver Pistol (AUS)-Monte D Oro (NZ) (Cache Of Gold (USA))
Mrs J Candlish (A Streeter 6/6) Martin Jump

Placings:0/034162/3F2113/2U02/PP-323511P551 **(4023)**
2002/03: 16^{3}GS, 16^{2}G, 16^{3}HY, 19^{5}G, 16^{1}S, 16^{1}G, 16^{P}S, 16^{5}S, 16^{5}G, 16^{1}S,

	Starts	1st	2nd	3rd	Win & Pl
Chases	10	3	1	2	19103
Career Total	**29**	**6**	**5**	**5**	**38244**

118	3/03	Hrfd	2m	E(0-110)HCh	SFT	£4104
112	12/02	Hayd	2m	D(0-125)HCh	GD	£6825
106	11/02	Newc	2m110y	D(0-115)HCh	SFT	£4693
106	2/00	Leic	2m	E Ch	SFT	£4750
109	2/00	Newc	2m110y	E Ch	SFT	£2983
102	12/98	MRas	2m1f110yD Hdl		SFT	£3029

Total win prize-money £26386

Going: Sf: 2-5 GS: 0-1 Gd: 1-4 GF: - Fm: 0-0
Distance: **2m/2m3: 3-10** 2m4-2m7: 0-0 3m+: 0-0
Track: **LH: 2-4** RH: 1-6 Tight: 0-0 **Gall: 1-2**
Aids: Bl: 0-0 Vi: 0-0 Tstrap: 0-0
Best Rating: **118** 3/03 Hrfd 2m soft Ch

Fair two-mile handicap chaser; goes well in the mud; likes to make the running.

Black Dante (IRE)

(129h)

9-y-o b g Phardante (FR)-Orchardstown (Pollerton)
P J Hobbs Peter Luff

Placings:2512/PR **(3318)**
2002/03: 26^{P}GS, 24^{R}GS,

	Starts	1st	2nd	3rd	Win & Pl
Chases	2	0	0	0	
Career Total	**6**	**1**	**2**	**0**	**6805**

108	1/01	Hayd	2m6f	D Hdl	SFT	£3542

Total win prize-money £3542

Going: Sf: 0-0 GS: 0-2 Gd: 0-0 GF: - Fm: 0-0
Distance: 2m/2m3: 0-0 2m4-2m7: 0-0 3m+: 0-2
Track: LH: 0-1 RH: 0-1 Tight: 0-0 Gall: 0-0
Aids: Bl: 0-0 Vi: 0-0 Tstrap: 0-0
Best Rating: **129** 4/01 Asct 3m heavy Hdl

Black Frost (IRE)

105 **115**

7-y-o ch g Glacial Storm (USA)-Black Tulip (Pals Passage)
Mrs S J Smith Trevor Hemmings

Placings:23/50-351P1 **(4659)**
2002/03: 20^{3}GS, 16^{5}G, 20^{1}GS, 20^{P}GS, 20^{1}GF,

	Starts	1st	2nd	3rd	Win & Pl
Hurdles	5	2	0	1	9231
Career Total	**9**	**2**	**1**	**2**	**9961**

99	4/03	Carl	2m4f	E Hdl	G-F	£3500
115	1/03	Hayd	2m4f	D Hdl	G-S	£5083

Total win prize-money £8583

Going: Sf: 0-0 GS: 1-3 Gd: 0-1 GF: - Fm: 1-1
Distance: 2m/2m3: 0-1 **2m4-2m7: 2-4** 3m+: 0-0
Track: LH: 1-4 RH: 1-1 Tight: 0-2 Gall: 0-0
Aids: Bl: 0-0 Vi: 0-0 Tstrap: 0-0
Best Rating: **115** 1/03 Hayd 2m4f gd-sft Hdl

Modest novice hurdler; stays two and a half miles; handles any ground; looks a real stayer.

Black Kite (IRE)

4-y-o br g Desert King (IRE)-Snoozeandyoulose (IRE) (Scenic)
H J Manners H J Manners

Placings:0P **(3805)**
2002/03: 16^{0}G, 21^{P}S,

	Starts	1st	2nd	3rd	Win & Pl
NH Flat	1	0	0	0	0
Hurdles	1	0	0	0	0
Career Total	**2**	**0**	**0**	**0**	

Going: Sf: 0-1 GS: 0-0 Gd: 0-1 GF: - Fm: 0-0
Distance: 2m/2m3: 0-1 2m4-2m7: 0-1 3m+: 0-0
Track: LH: 0-2 RH: 0-0 Tight: 0-1 Gall: 0-1
Aids: Bl: 0-0 Vi: 0-0 Tstrap: 0-0
Best Rating: **36** 2/03 Newb 2m110y good NHF

Black Rainbow (IRE)

93 **66**

5-y-o br m Definite Article-Inonder (Belfort (FR))
T J Etherington (A Dickman 18/5) S Calladene

Placings:43-03000 **(4337)**
2002/03: 16^{0}G, 17^{3}S, 19^{0}GS, 16^{0}HY, 16^{0}GF,

	Starts	1st	2nd	3rd	Win & Pl
NH Flat	2	0	0	1	253
Hurdles	3	0	0	0	0
Career Total	**7**	**0**	**0**	**2**	**491**

Going: Sf: 0-2 GS: 0-1 Gd: 0-1 GF: - Fm: 0-1
Distance: 2m/2m3: 0-5 2m4-2m7: 0-0 3m+: 0-0
Track: LH: 0-4 RH: 0-1 Tight: 0-2 Gall: 0-2
Aids: Bl: 0-0 Vi: 0-0 Tstrap: 0-0
Best Rating: **88** 5/02 Bang 2m1f soft NHF

Has looked devoid of pace in mares only bumpers.

Black Secret

76

10-y-o br m Gildoran-Polypodium (Politico (USA))
R J Baker T Hubbard

Placings:1/2/P0/50-3 **(0719)**
2002/03: 20^{3}G,

	Starts	1st	2nd	3rd	Win & Pl
Hurdles	1	0	0	1	406
Career Total	**7**	**1**	**1**	**1**	**2071**

104	3/98	Folk	2m1f110yH NHF	GD	£1308

Total win prize-money £1308

Going: Sf: 0-0 GS: 0-0 Gd: 0-1 GF: - Fm: 0-0
Distance: 2m/2m3: 0-0 2m4-2m7: 0-1 3m+: 0-0
Track: LH: 0-1 RH: 0-0 Tight: 0-0 Gall: 0-0
Aids: Bl: 0-0 Vi: 0-0 Tstrap: 0-0
Best Rating: **104** 11/98 Extr 2m1f soft NHF

Black Stripe Lady
83f   85f
5-y-o b m Karinga Bay-Garvenish (Balinger)
M Todhunter Black Stripe Racing

Placings:44   (4594)
2002/03: 16⁴G, 16⁴G,

	Starts	1st	2nd	3rd	Win & Pl
NH Flat	2	0	0	0	0
Career Total	2	0	0	0	0

Going: Sf: 0-0 GS: 0-0 Gd: 0-2 GF: - Fm: 0-0
Distance: 2m/2m3: 0-2 2m4-2m7: 0-0 3m+: 0-0
Track: LH: 0-2 RH: 0-0 Tight: 0-0 Gall: 0-0
Aids: Bl: 0-0 Vi: 0-0 Tstrap: 0-0
Best Rating: 85 3/03 Hayd 2m   good NHF

Blackberry Way

9-y-o ch m Almoojid-Prickly Path (Royal Match)
Ms Louise Cullen Chris And Stella Watson

Placings:P/5-13435   (4541)
2002/03: 20¹GF, 25³GS, 24⁴GS, 22³G, 24⁵G,

	Starts	1st	2nd	3rd	Win & Pl
Chases	5	1	0	2	1852
Career Total	7	1	0	2	1852
78 5/02 Hntg 2m4f110yH Ch		G-F		£1352	
			Total win prize-money £1352		

Going: Sf: 0-0 GS: 0-2 Gd: 0-2 GF: - Fm: 1-1
Distance: 2m/2m3: 0-0 2m4-2m7: 1-2 3m+: 0-3
Track: LH: 0-1 RH: 1-4 Tight: 0-2 Gall: 1-2
Aids: Bl: 0-0 Vi: 0-0 Tstrap: 0-0
Best Rating: 91 3/03 Newb 2m6f110y good Ch

Lightly-raced ex-pointer; appreciates fast ground; won over two and a half miles at Huntingdon in May 2002.

Blackchurch Mist (IRE)
106   113
6-y-o b m Erin s Isle-Diandra (Shardari)
B W Duke Brendan W Duke Racing

Placings:0-30332P11P5   (4610)
2002/03: 18⁰G, 16³GF, 16⁶G, 16³F, 20³G, 22²G, 21PGS, 22¹GS, 20¹G, 20PGF, 21⁵G,

	Starts	1st	2nd	3rd	Win & Pl
NH Flat	4	0	0	2	592
Hurdles	7	2	1	1	9341
Career Total	11	2	1	3	9932
99 3/03 Folk 2m4f110yE Hdl		GD		£3542	
98 12/02 Winc 2m6f E(0-100)HHdl		G-S	£3388		
			Total win prize-money £6931		

Going: Sf: 0-0 GS: 1-2 Gd: 1-6 GF: - Fm: 0-3
Distance: 2m/2m3: 0-4 2m4-2m7: 2-7 3m+: 0-0
Track: LH: 0-5 RH: 2-6 Tight: 1-2 Gall: 0-3
Aids: Bl: 0-0 Vi: 0-0 Tstrap: 2-7
Best Rating: 104 4/03 Chel 2m5f110y good Hdl

Moderate hurdler; stays two and three quarter miles over hurdles; usually raced prominently; suffers from breathing trouble; is usually tongue tied.

Blackcountry Lad

8-y-o b g Henbit (USA)-Cupids Bower (Owen Dudley)
A P James T N Siviter

Placings:O00/PP   (2565)
2002/03: 19PG, 17PGS,

	Starts	1st	2nd	3rd	Win & Pl
Hurdles	2	0	0	0	
Career Total	5	0	0	0	

Going: Sf: 0-0 GS: 0-1 Gd: 0-1 GF: - Fm: 0-0
Distance: 2m/2m3: 0-1 2m4-2m7: 0-1 3m+: 0-0
Track: LH: 0-1 RH: 0-1 Tight: 0-1 Gall: 0-0
Aids: Bl: 0-0 Vi: 0-0 Tstrap: 0-0
Best Rating: 17 12/00 Hrfd 2m1f   heavy NHF

Blackjack Lir

9-y-o b g Lir-Miss Black Glama (Derrylin)
P R Rodford P R Rodford

Placings:0-P   (0345)
2002/03: 22PGS,

	Starts	1st	2nd	3rd	Win & Pl
Hurdles	1	0	0	0	
Career Total	2	0	0	0	

Going: Sf: 0-0 GS: 0-1 Gd: 0-0 GF: - Fm: 0-0
Distance: 2m/2m3: 0-0 2m4-2m7: 0-1 3m+: 0-0
Track: LH: 0-1 RH: 0-0 Tight: 0-1 Gall: 0-0
Aids: Bl: 0-0 Vi: 0-0 Tstrap: 0-0
Best Rating:

Blackout (IRE)
99   70
8-y-o b g Black Monday-Fine Bess (Fine Blade (USA))
J Barclay Jim Barclay

Placings:6/0605PP/45435   (4038)
2002/03: 21⁴S, 21⁵GS, 24⁵S, 20³HY, 16⁵S,

	Starts	1st	2nd	3rd	Win & Pl
Chases	5	0	0	1	2177
Career Total	12	0	0	1	2177

Going: Sf: 0-4 GS: 0-1 Gd: 0-0 GF: - Fm: 0-0
Distance: 2m/2m3: 0-1 2m4-2m7: 0-3 3m+: 0-1
Track: LH: 0-5 RH: 0-0 Tight: 0-0 Gall: 0-0
Aids: Bl: 0-0 Vi: 0-0 Tstrap: 0-0
Best Rating: 83 1/01 Ayr 3m110y gd-sft Hdl

Modest hurdler/novice chaser; yet to win a race of any sort.

Blakeney Coast (IRE)
101(89h)   (75+h)91+
6-y-o b g Satco (FR)-Up to More Trix (IRE) (Torus)
Mrs M Reveley Cristiana s Crew

Placings:660-056PP32   (4588)
2002/03: 20⁰S, 20⁵GS, 16⁶G, 16PG, 21PGS, 16³GF, 20²G,

	Starts	1st	2nd	3rd	Win & Pl
Hurdles	2	0	0	0	0
Chases	5	0	1	1	1605
Career Total	10	0	1	1	1605

Going: Sf: 0-1 GS: 0-2 Gd: 0-3 GF: - Fm: 0-1
Distance: 2m/2m3: 0-3 2m4-2m7: 0-4 3m+: 0-0
Track: LH: 0-7 RH: 0-0 Tight: 0-1 Gall: 0-3
Aids: Bl: 0-0 Vi: 0-0 Tstrap: 0-0
Best Rating: 91 12/01 Hntg 2m110y gd-sft NHF

Plating-class hurdler; off the mark over fences in a one-sided match at Wetherby in May; acts on firm ground; jumps soundly.

Blakeney Hill

8-y-o ch m Baron Blakeney-Hillgate Lady (Rustingo)
Mrs N S Sharpe Miss M J Ward

Placings:00P-P   (0072)
2002/03: 26PGF,

	Starts	1st	2nd	3rd	Win & Pl
Hurdles	1	0	0	0	
Career Total	4	0	0	0	

Going: Sf: 0-0 GS: 0-0 Gd: 0-0 GF: - Fm: 0-1
Distance: 2m/2m3: 0-0 2m4-2m7: 0-0 3m+: 0-1
Track: LH: 0-0 RH: 0-1 Tight: 0-0 Gall: 0-0
Aids: Bl: 0-0 Vi: 0-0 Tstrap: 0-0
Best Rating: 17 12/01 Hrfd 2m1f   soft NHF

Blakey (IRE)

7-y-o b g Maledetto (IRE)-Villars (Home Guard (USA))
Mrs N S Sharpe M D Jones

Placings:P/PP   (0614)
2002/03: 20PGF, 20PGF,

	Starts	1st	2nd	3rd	Win & Pl
Hurdles	2	0	0	0	
Career Total	3	0	0	0	

Going: Sf: 0-0 GS: 0-0 Gd: 0-0 GF: - Fm: 0-2
Distance: 2m/2m3: 0-0 2m4-2m7: 0-2 3m+: 0-0
Track: LH: 0-2 RH: 0-0 Tight: 0-0 Gall: 0-0
Aids: Bl: 0-0 Vi: 0-0 Tstrap: 0-1
Best Rating: 0 6/02 Worc 2m4f   gd-fm Hdl

Blank Cheque

13-y-o b g Idiots Delight-Quickapenny (Espresso)
J J Coates J J Coates

Placings:503P/3/3/4/0-5   (0210)
2002/03: 25⁵S,

	Starts	1st	2nd	3rd	Win & Pl
Chases	1	0	0	0	0
Career Total	9	0	0	3	1131

Going: Sf: 0-1 GS: 0-0 Gd: 0-0 GF: - Fm: 0-0
Distance: 2m/2m3: 0-0 2m4-2m7: 0-0 3m+: 0-1
Track: LH: 0-0 RH: 0-1 Tight: 0-0 Gall: 0-0
Aids: Bl: 0-0 Vi: 0-0 Tstrap: 0-0
Best Rating: 104 4/98 Chel 3m1f110y good Ch

Blasket Sound (IRE)
100   100
11-y-o b g Lancastrian-June s Friend (Laurence O)
D J Wintle R H L Barnes

Placings:541235331/464UP64320145FU/45PU3F1143/264
221P0/20P0P216-00253   (4083)
2002/03: 27⁰GF, 26⁰GS, 22²HY, 22⁵HY, 25³HY,

	Starts	1st	2nd	3rd	Win & Pl
Hurdles	5	0	1	1	1049

Career Total	55	7	8	7	32472
100 2/02 Hntg 3m2f E(0-110)HHdl SFT					£2576
113 3/01 Hntg 3m2f F(0-110)HHdl SFT					£2051
105 3/00 Towc 3m1f D(0-120)HCh SFT					£3848
100 3/00 Chep 3m2f110yE(0-115)HCh HVY					£2879
104 1/99 Naas 3m (0-116)HCh HVY					£3989
101 4/98 Clon 3m Ch HVY					£1935
104 11/97 Limk 2m4f Hdl HVY					£2712
				Total win prize-money	£19994

Going: Sf: 0-3 GS: 0-1 Gd: 0-0 GF: - Fm: 0-1
Distance: 2m/2m3: 0-0 2m4-2m7: 0-2 3m+: 0-3
Track: LH: 0-1 RH: 0-3 Tight: 0-3 Gall: 0-1
Aids: Bl: 0-0 Vi: 0-0 Tstrap: 0-0
Best Rating: 113 3/01 Hntg 3m2f soft Hdl

Modest staying hurdler; acts on an easy surface; best around 3m 2f.

Blayney Dancer 32

6-y-o b g Contract Law (USA)-Lady Poly (Dunbeath (USA))
Jonjo O Neill Mrs M Liston

Placings:2015/0-0 (0625)
2002/03: 17⁰GF,

	Starts	1st	2nd	3rd	Win & Pl
Hurdles	1	0	0	0	
Career Total	6	1	1	0	4273
96 10/00 Kemp 2m D Hdl G-S					£3412
				Total win prize-money	£3413

Going: Sf: 0-0 GS: 0-0 Gd: 0-0 GF: - Fm: 0-1
Distance: 2m/2m3: 0-1 2m4-2m7: 0-0 3m+: 0-0
Track: LH: 0-0 RH: 0-1 Tight: 0-1 Gall: 0-0
Aids: Bl: 0-0 Vi: 0-0 Tstrap: 0-0
Best Rating: 96 10/00 Kemp 2m gd-sft Hdl

Blazing Batman 93(105h) (74h)97

10-y-o ch g Shaab-Cottage Blaze (Sunyboy)
Dr P Pritchard Jumping Jokers

Placings:50/42/F/FP04/PU415P41542PP0-444632360 (4623)
2002/03: 20⁴GS, 23⁴S, 17⁴G, 24⁶G, 17³S, 25²G, 24³GS, 26⁶GF, 27⁶GF,

	Starts	1st	2nd	3rd	Win & Pl
Hurdles	7	0	1	2	2280
Chases	2	0	0	0	848
Career Total	32	2	3	2	15322
93 11/01 Fknm 3m5f110yF(0-100)HCh SFT					£4123
93 7/01 Sthl 3m110y E Ch G-F					£3406
				Total win prize-money	£7530

Going: Sf: 0-2 GS: 0-2 Gd: 0-3 GF: - Fm: 0-2
Distance: 2m/2m3: 0-2 2m4-2m7: 0-1 3m+: 0-6
Track: LH: 0-6 RH: 0-3 Tight: 0-3 Gall: 0-1
Aids: Bl: 0-0 Vi: 0-0 Tstrap: 0-0
Best Rating: 101 1/01 Weth 2m4f110y heavy Ch

Plating-class staying chaser/ hurdler.

Blazing Court (IRE) 63f 22f

6-y-o ch g Roselier (FR)-The Blazing Star (Proverb)
D J Wintle Court Roof Tiling Ltd

Placings:0 (3322)
2002/03: 16⁹GS,

	Starts	1st	2nd	3rd	Win & Pl
NH Flat	1	0	0	0	
Career Total	1	0	0	0	

Going: Sf: 0-0 GS: 0-1 Gd: 0-0 GF: - Fm: 0-0
Distance: 2m/2m3: 0-1 2m4-2m7: 0-0 3m+: 0-0
Track: LH: 0-0 RH: 0-1 Tight: 0-0 Gall: 0-0
Aids: Bl: 0-0 Vi: 0-0 Tstrap: 0-0
Best Rating: 22 1/03 Kemp 2m gd-sft NHF

Blazing Miracle

11-y-o b m Shaab-Cottage Blaze (Sunyboy)
G Chambers Mrs C L Heard

Placings:U50P6/440520F5/03/0/1 (0371)
2002/03: 26¹S,

	Starts	1st	2nd	3rd	Win & Pl
Chases	1	1	0	0	3335
Career Total	17	1	1	1	5115
85 5/02 NAbb 3m2f110yH Ch SFT					£3334
				Total win prize-money	£3335

Going: Sf: 1-1 GS: 0-0 Gd: 0-0 GF: - Fm: 0-0
Distance: 2m/2m3: 0-0 2m4-2m7: 0-0 3m+: 1-1
Track: LH: 1-1 RH: 0-0 Tight: 1-1 Gall: 0-0
Aids: Bl: 0-0 Vi: 0-0 Tstrap: 0-0
Best Rating: 85 5/02 NAbb 3m2f110y soft Ch

Moderate hunter chaser; stayed on well from what appeared to be a hopeless position when winning three and a quarter mile hunter chase at Newton Abbot May 2002; acts on soft ground.

Blazing Saddles (IRE) 76 58

4-y-o b g Sadler s Wells (USA)-Dalawara (IRE) (Top Ville)
P R Hedger (I A Balding 21/10) Mrs Gina Webster

Placings:002 (4698)
2002/03: 18⁰G, 17⁰G, 16²GF,

	Starts	1st	2nd	3rd	Win & Pl
Hurdles	3	0	1	0	1075
Career Total	3	0	1	0	1075

Going: Sf: 0-0 GS: 0-0 Gd: 0-2 GF: - Fm: 0-1
Distance: 2m/2m3: 0-3 2m4-2m7: 0-0 3m+: 0-0
Track: LH: 0-2 RH: 0-1 Tight: 0-3 Gall: 0-0
Aids: Bl: 0-0 Vi: 0-0 Tstrap: 0-0
Best Rating: 58 4/03 Plum 2m gd-fm Hdl

Poor hurdler; yet to show any worthwhile form; has worn cheekpieces.

Bless Yourself (IRE) 73 56

7-y-o b g Shardari-Wee Madge (Apollo Eight)
D McCain John Singleton

Placings:0-06P (3493)
2002/03: 16⁰GS, 20⁶HY, 17⁵GS,

	Starts	1st	2nd	3rd	Win & Pl
Hurdles	3	0	0	0	
Career Total	4	0	0	0	

Going: Sf: 0-1 GS: 0-2 Gd: 0-0 GF: - Fm: 0-0
Distance: 2m/2m3: 0-2 2m4-2m7: 0-1 3m+: 0-0
Track: LH: 0-2 RH: 0-1 Tight: 0-1 Gall: 0-0
Aids: Bl: 0-0 Vi: 0-0 Tstrap: 0-0
Best Rating: 56 11/02 Ludl 2m gd-sft Hdl

Bleu Superbe (FR) 110 144

8-y-o b g Epervier Bleu-Brett s Dream (FR) (Pharly (FR))
Miss Venetia Williams P A Deal, A Hirschfeld & J Tyndall

Placings:111113/F603P122/5PPP13P/F3P-11PP11PPP (4458)
2002/03: 16¹G, 16¹G, 20⁰GS, 20⁰G, 17¹GS, 16¹G, 16⁰HY, 16⁰G, 16⁰G,

	Starts	1st	2nd	3rd	Win & Pl
Chases	9	4	0	0	33929
Career Total	33	11	2	4	142113
144 1/03 Donc 2m110y B(0-150)HCh GD					£13585
142 11/02 Newb 2m1f C(0-135)HCh G-S					£9326
144 5/02 Towc 2m110y C(0-135)HCh GD					£5850
131 5/02 Aint 2m D(0-125)HCh GD					£5167
140 3/01 Hayd 2m D(0-120)HCh HVY					£7117
1/00 Cagn 2m7f Ch SFT					£21133
3/99 Pau 2m2f110y Ch VS					£7535
1/99 Pau 2m2f Hdl VS					£15070
1/99 Pau 2m2f Hdl HVY					£7535
12/98 Bord 2m2f Hdl VS					£5051
11/98 Bord 2m2f Hdl VS					£3030
				Total win prize-money	£100401

Going: Sf: 0-1 GS: 1-2 Gd: 3-6 GF: - Fm: 0-0
Distance: 2m/2m3: 4-7 2m4-2m7: 0-2 3m+: 0-0
Track: LH: 3-5 RH: 1-4 Tight: 1-3 Gall: 2-3
Aids: Bl: 0-0 Vi: 0-0 Tstrap: 0-0
Best Rating: 144 1/03 Donc 2m110y good Ch

Very useful handicap chaser; has a habit of either winning or pulling up; has won on decent and soft ground; best at two miles.

Blood Sub (IRE) 103 111+

6-y-o b g Roselier (FR)-Clearwater Glen (Furry Glen)
Jonjo O Neill J P McManus

Placings:251 (4173)
2002/03: 17²S, 22⁵GS, 20¹S,

	Starts	1st	2nd	3rd	Win & Pl
NH Flat	1	0	1	0	554
Hurdles	2	1	0	0	4537
Career Total	3	1	1	0	5091
111 3/03 Uttx 2m4f110yE Hdl SFT					£4537
				Total win prize-money	£4537

Going: Sf: 1-2 GS: 0-1 Gd: 0-0 GF: - Fm: 0-0
Distance: 2m/2m3: 0-1 2m4-2m7: 1-2 3m+: 0-0
Track: LH: 1-1 RH: 0-2 Tight: 0-1 Gall: 0-0
Aids: Bl: 0-0 Vi: 0-0 Tstrap: 0-0
Best Rating: 111 3/03 Uttx 2m4f110y soft Hdl

Modest hurdler; runner-up in a Folkestone bumper on his debut; got off the mark on second attempt over hurdles; stays two and a half miles; acts on soft ground.

Blooming Amazing 77 59

9-y-o b g Mazilier (USA)-Cornflower Blue (Tymavos)
D Burchell Three Acres Racing

Placings:0/000 (0658)
2002/03: 17⁰G, 16⁰GF, 20⁰GF,

	Starts	1st	2nd	3rd	Win & Pl
Hurdles	3	0	0	0	
Career Total	4	0	0	0	

Going:	Sf: 0-0 GS: 0-0 Gd: 0-1 GF: - Fm: 0-2
Distance:	2m/2m3: 0-3 2m4-2m7: 0-0 3m+: 0-0
Track:	LH: 0-3 RH: 0-0 Tight: 0-1 Gall: 0-0
Aids:	Bl: 0-0 Vi: 0-0 Tstrap: 0-0
Best Rating:	**61** 10/99 MRas 2m1f110y good Hdl

Blossom Whispers
92   80

6-y-o b m Ezzoud (IRE)-Springs Welcome (Blakeney)
Mrs M Reveley (C A Cyzer 6/8) The Chest Pains Syndicate

Placings:053006F   (4710)
2002/03: 19⁰GS, 16⁵HY, 17⁹HY, 21⁰GS, 20⁰S, 27⁶S, 23ᶠGF,

	Starts	1st	2nd	3rd	Win & Pl
Hurdles	7	0	0	1	697
Career Total	7	0	0	1	697

Going:	Sf: 0-4 GS: 0-2 Gd: 0-0 GF: - Fm: 0-1
Distance:	2m/2m3: 0-2 2m4-2m7: 0-4 3m+: 0-1
Track:	LH: 0-5 RH: 0-2 Tight: 0-3 Gall: 0-2
Aids:	Bl: 0-0 Vi: 0-0 Tstrap: 0-0
Best Rating:	**80** 4/03 Weth 2m7f gd-fm Hdl

Plating-class hurdler; looked sure to be involved in the finish before falling two out in a seller at Wetherby in April 2003; suited by a test of stamina.

Blow Wind Blow (IRE)
95   (61c)82

9-y-o b/br g Strong Gale-Phargara (IRE) (Phardante (FR))
Jonjo O Neill J P McManus

Placings:000 f34/01/3413F0F/00-000   (3778)
2002/03: 25⁰HY, 20⁰HY, 24⁰GS,

	Starts	1st	2nd	3rd	Win & Pl
Hurdles	3	0	0	0	
Career Total	20	3	0	3	31302
104 9/00	Gway 3m			(0-123)HHdl	YLD £4140
90 8/99	Gway 2m2f			(67-102)HHdl	G-F £17343
92 9/98	List 2m			NHF	G-Y £3885
				Total win prize-money £25370	

Going:	Sf: 0-2 GS: 0-1 Gd: 0-0 GF: - Fm: 0-0
Distance:	2m/2m3: 0-0 2m4-2m7: 0-1 3m+: 0-2
Track:	LH: 0-1 RH: 0-2 Tight: 0-0 Gall: 0-0
Aids:	Bl: 0-0 Vi: 0-0 Tstrap: 0-0
Best Rating:	**118** 11/00 Chel 2m5f gd-sft Hdl

Blowing Away (IRE)
83(96h)   (56h)64

9-y-o b/br m Last Tycoon-Taken By Force (Persian Bold)
Julian Poulton (J E Long 30/5) Mrs Elizabeth Reed

Placings:301/6365F-664300   (4157)
2002/03: 16⁶G, 17⁶GF, 18⁴GF, 24³F, 20⁰G, 17⁰G,

	Starts	1st	2nd	3rd	Win & Pl
Hurdles	5	0	0	1	489
Chases	1	0	0	0	
Career Total	14	1	0	3	2945
71 3/98	Uttx 2m			G Hdl	GD £1595
				Total win prize-money £1595	

Going:	Sf: 0-0 GS: 0-0 Gd: 0-3 GF: - Fm: 0-3
Distance:	2m/2m3: 0-4 2m4-2m7: 0-1 3m+: 0-1
Track:	LH: 0-2 RH: 0-4 Tight: 0-3 Gall: 0-2
Aids:	Bl: 0-0 Vi: 0-0 Tstrap: 0-1
Best Rating:	**80** 2/98 Catt 2m good Hdl

Selling class over hurdles and on the Flat. Tried at up to three miles.

Blowing Kisses

4-y-o b f Missed Flight-Blowing Bubbles (Native Admiral (USA))
M Mullineaux Mrs A Meller

Placings:0   (2574)
2002/03: 12⁰G,

	Starts	1st	2nd	3rd	Win & Pl
NH Flat	1	0	0	0	
Career Total	1	0	0	0	

Going:	Sf: 0-0 GS: 0-0 Gd: 0-0 GF: - Fm: 0-0
Distance:	2m/2m3: 0-0 2m4-2m7: 0-0 3m+: 0-0
Track:	LH: 0-0 RH: 0-0 Tight: 0-0 Gall: 0-0
Aids:	Bl: 0-0 Vi: 0-0 Tstrap: 0-0
Best Rating:	**0** 12/02 Newb 1m4f110y good NHF

Blowing Rock (IRE)
100   126d

11-y-o b g Strong Gale-Poor Elsie (Crash Course)
Miss H C Knight Mrs Peter Andrews

Placings:562/P21404/S1F0423/2U24212/1U340/2122501-
644P   (2077)
2002/03: 23⁶G, 21⁴GF, 26⁴G, 25ᴾGS,

	Starts	1st	2nd	3rd	Win & Pl
Chases	4	0	0	0	1146
Career Total	39	6	10	2	41252
126 4/02	Hntg 3m			D(0-120)HCh	G-F £3952
121 5/01	Hrfd			3m1f110yE(0-115)HCh	GD £4338
106 5/00	MRas 3m1f			E(0-115)HCh	G-F £4290
102 11/99	Leic			2m7f110yE(0-115)HCh	G-F £3525
102 5/98	Towc 2m6f			E(0-100)HCh	G-F £3315
104 10/97	Chel			2m110y D Hdl	G-F £2918
				Total win prize-money £22340	

Going:	Sf: 0-0 GS: 0-1 Gd: 0-2 GF: - Fm: 0-1
Distance:	2m/2m3: 0-0 2m4-2m7: 0-1 3m+: 0-3
Track:	LH: 0-2 RH: 0-2 Tight: 0-1 Gall: 0-0
Aids:	Bl: 0-0 Vi: 0-0 Tstrap: 0-0
Best Rating:	**126** 4/02 Hntg 3m gd-fm Ch

Useful handicap chaser; spring and autumn horse; inclined to run in snatches; best in small fields and needs a decent surface; usually kept to right-handed tracks; stays three miles.

Blowing Wind (FR)
106   147d

10-y-o b/br g Fabulous Dancer (USA)-Bassita (Bustino)
M C Pipe P A Deal

Placings:02403111/4F2B0/4112106/303113/P513-36000
                                                      (4479)
2002/03: 27³GS, 21⁶HY, 21⁰GS, 20⁰G, 36⁶G,

	Starts	1st	2nd	3rd	Win & Pl
Chases	5	0	0	1	7750
Career Total	35	9	3	6	286039
147 3/02	Chel			2m4f110yA HCh	G-S £45500
134 2/01	Sand 2m			B HCh	HVY £10071
147 1/01	Donc			2m3f110yC(0-130)HCh	GD £6545
140 2/00	Asct			2m3f110yB Ch	G-S £10114
138 1/00	Leic 2m			E Ch	GD £3315
118 12/99	Ludl 2m			E Ch	G-S £3048
155 4/98	Ayr 2m			A HHdl	GD £15669
156 3/98	Chel 2m1f			A HHdl	GD £26974
147 3/98	Sand			2m110y B(0-150)HHdl	SFT £21495

Total win prize-money £142735

Going:	Sf: 0-1 GS: 0-2 Gd: 0-2 GF: - Fm: 0-0
Distance:	2m/2m3: 0-0 2m4-2m7: 0-3 3m+: 0-2
Track:	LH: 0-5 RH: 0-0 Tight: 0-2 Gall: 0-3
Aids:	Bl: 0-0 Vi: 0-0 Tstrap: 0-0
Best Rating:	**158** 2/99 Hayd 2m soft Hdl

Very useful chaser; third in the 2001 Grand National, he was below his best in 2002 until running out a surprise winner of the Mildmay of Flete at the Festival; seemed not to fully see out the trip when a remote third in the 2002 Grand National; below his best so far this term though again completed the course in the Grand National; acts on good, soft and heavy ground.

Blue Americo (IRE)
99f   85f

5-y-o b g Lord Americo-Princess Menelek (Menelek)
P F Nicholls Mrs Angela Tincknell

Placings:0   (4329)
2002/03: 16⁰G,

	Starts	1st	2nd	3rd	Win & Pl
NH Flat	1	0	0	0	
Career Total	1	0	0	0	

Going:	Sf: 0-0 GS: 0-0 Gd: 0-0 GF: - Fm: 0-0
Distance:	2m/2m3: 0-1 2m4-2m7: 0-0 3m+: 0-0
Track:	LH: 0-1 RH: 0-0 Tight: 0-0 Gall: 0-1
Aids:	Bl: 0-0 Vi: 0-0 Tstrap: 0-0
Best Rating:	**85** 3/03 Newb 2m110y good NHF

Blue Canyon (IRE)
94f   90f

5-y-o b g Phardante (FR)-Miss Gosling (Prince Bee)
B De Haan Willsford Racing Incorporated

Placings:00   (4155)
2002/03: 16⁰S, 16⁰G,

	Starts	1st	2nd	3rd	Win & Pl
NH Flat	2	0	0	0	
Career Total	2	0	0	0	

Going:	Sf: 0-1 GS: 0-0 Gd: 0-0 GF: - Fm: 0-0
Distance:	2m/2m3: 0-2 2m4-2m7: 0-0 3m+: 0-0
Track:	LH: 0-2 RH: 0-0 Tight: 0-0 Gall: 0-1
Aids:	Bl: 0-0 Vi: 0-0 Tstrap: 0-0
Best Rating:	**90** 3/03 Wwck 2m good NHF

Blue Derby (IRE)
85   69

5-y-o b g Supreme Leader-Minigirls Niece (IRE) (Strong Gale)
P J Hobbs Mrs Angela Tincknell

Placings:01   (4364)
2002/03: 16⁰S, 17¹F,

	Starts	1st	2nd	3rd	Win & Pl
NH Flat	2	1	0	0	1869
Career Total	2	1	0	0	1869
84 3/03	Tntn 2m1f			H NHF	FRM £1869
				Total win prize-money £1869	

Going:	Sf: 0-1 GS: 0-0 Gd: 0-0 GF: - Fm: 1-1
Distance:	2m/2m3: 1-2 2m4-2m7: 0-0 3m+: 0-0
Track:	LH: 0-1 RH: 0-0 Tight: 0-0 Gall: 0-0
Aids:	Bl: 0-0 Vi: 0-0 Tstrap: 0-0
Best Rating:	**84** 3/03 Tntn 2m1f firm NHF

Plating-class performer; closely related to smart hurdler Minorettes Girl who is the dam of Shotgun Willy; made all in firm ground bumper at Taunton March 2003; disappointing on hurdling debut the following month.

Blue Endeavour (IRE)

94f   92f

5-y-o b g Endeavour (USA)-Jingle Bells (FR) (In The Mood (FR))
P F Nicholls Mrs Angela Tincknell

Placings:4   (4628)
2002/03: 17⁴GF,

	Starts	1st	2nd	3rd	Win & Pl
NH Flat	1	0	0	0	0
Career Total	1	0	0	0	0

Going: Sf: 0-0 GS: 0-0 Gd: 0-0 GF: - Fm: 0-1
Distance: 2m/2m3: 0-1 2m4-2m7: 0-0 3m+: 0-0
Track: LH: 0-1 RH: 0-0 Tight: 0-1 Gall: 0-0
Aids: Bl: 0-0 Vi: 0-0 Tstrap: 0-0
Best Rating: 92 4/03 NAbb 2m1f   gd-fm NHF

From good jumping family; tapped for speed when fourth in first two bumpers; likely to need further over obstacles.

Blue Irish (IRE)

(105h)   (95h)95

12-y-o gr g Roselier (FR)-Grannie No (Brave Invader (USA))
Ferdy Murphy Miss J V Morgan

Placings:2066353/141/41/4FPP3UP/U/F-4260262 (4104)
2002/03: 25⁴GF, 27²G, 24⁶GS, 27⁰S, 27²HY, 24⁶HY, 27²S,

	Starts	1st	2nd	3rd	Win & Pl
Hurdles	6	0	3	0	2496
Chases	1	0	0	0	418
Career Total	28	3	4	3	22816
120	11/98	Carl	3m2f	C(0-130)HCh	HVY £4856
125	2/98	Naas	3m	Ch	Y-S £5956
118	11/97	Navn	2m4f	Ch	HVY £4069

Total win prize-money £14882

Going: Sf: 0-4 GS: 0-1 Gd: 0-1 GF: - Fm: 0-1
Distance: 2m/2m3: 0-0 2m4-2m7: 0-0 3m+: 0-7
Track: LH: 0-7 RH: 0-0 Tight: 0-6 Gall: 0-1
Aids: Bl: 0-0 Vi: 0-0 Tstrap: 0-0
Best Rating: 128 11/99 DRoy 3m1f   soft Ch

Moderate hurdler; one-time useful chaser in Ireland; runner-up in old boys chase at Cartmel in May; stays well; goes best at Sedgefield.

Blue Jar

66   36

5-y-o b g Royal Abjar (USA)-Artist s Glory (Rarity)
M Mullineaux T Clarke

Placings:00-PBPP   (4316)
2002/03: 20⁸S, 16⁸G, 16⁸S, 17⁸G,

	Starts	1st	2nd	3rd	Win & Pl
Hurdles	4	0	0	0	0
Career Total	6	0	0	0	0

Going: Sf: 0-2 GS: 0-0 Gd: 0-2 GF: - Fm: 0-0
Distance: 2m/2m3: 0-3 2m4-2m7: 0-1 3m+: 0-0
Track: LH: 0-3 RH: 0-1 Tight: 0-2 Gall: 0-1
Aids: Bl: 0-0 Vi: 0-0 Tstrap: 0-0
Best Rating: 65 3/02 Hntg 2m110y   gd-fm NHF

Blue Leader (IRE)

76   49

4-y-o b c Cadeaux Genereux-Blue Duster (USA) (Danzig (USA))
G Brown (E A L Dunlop 22/10) Mrs Amanda Killick

Placings:000P   (4391)
2002/03: 16⁰HY, 16⁰S, 16⁰GS, 17ᴾF,

	Starts	1st	2nd	3rd	Win & Pl
Hurdles	4	0	0	0	0
Career Total	4	0	0	0	0

Going: Sf: 0-2 GS: 0-1 Gd: 0-0 GF: - Fm: 0-1
Distance: 2m/2m3: 0-4 2m4-2m7: 0-0 3m+: 0-0
Track: LH: 0-2 RH: 0-2 Tight: 0-1 Gall: 0-1
Aids: Bl: 0-0 Vi: 0-0 Tstrap: 0-0
Best Rating: 49 2/03 Sand 2m110y   heavy Hdl

Blue Legend (IRE)

76   28

6-y-o b m Blues Traveller (IRE)-Swoon Along (Dunphy)
B Mactaggart John Mc C Hodge

Placings:PF0   (1562)
2002/03: 16ᴾGF, 16ᶠG, 22⁰G,

	Starts	1st	2nd	3rd	Win & Pl
Hurdles	3	0	0	0	0
Career Total	3	0	0	0	0

Going: Sf: 0-0 GS: 0-0 Gd: 0-2 GF: - Fm: 0-1
Distance: 2m/2m3: 0-2 2m4-2m7: 0-1 3m+: 0-0
Track: LH: 0-2 RH: 0-1 Tight: 0-1 Gall: 0-0
Aids: Bl: 0-0 Vi: 0-0 Tstrap: 0-3
Best Rating: 19 10/02 Kels 2m6f110y   good Hdl

Blue Lizard (IRE)

87   53

6-y-o b g Roselier (FR)-Rathsallagh Tartan (Strong Gale)
Ferdy Murphy A Bloom

Placings:40   (3801)
2002/03: 23⁴GS, 24⁰S,

	Starts	1st	2nd	3rd	Win & Pl
Hurdles	2	0	0	0	306
Career Total	2	0	0	0	306

Going: Sf: 0-1 GS: 0-1 Gd: 0-0 GF: - Fm: 0-0
Distance: 2m/2m3: 0-0 2m4-2m7: 0-1 3m+: 0-1
Track: LH: 0-2 RH: 0-0 Tight: 0-0 Gall: 0-1
Aids: Bl: 0-0 Vi: 0-0 Tstrap: 0-0
Best Rating: 53 12/02 Weth 2m7f   gd-sft Hdl

Blue Momma (IRE)

86   70

4-y-o b f Petardia-Heads We Called (IRE) (Bluebird (USA))
M C Pipe (P R Webber 13/5) J D Travellers

Placings:P200   (4693)
2002/03: 16ᴾHY, 17²S, 19⁰HY, 17⁰G,

	Starts	1st	2nd	3rd	Win & Pl
Hurdles	4	0	1	0	718
Career Total	4	0	1	0	718

Going: Sf: 0-3 GS: 0-0 Gd: 0-1 GF: - Fm: 0-0
Distance: 2m/2m3: 0-3 2m4-2m7: 0-1 3m+: 0-0

Blue Morning

73f   61f

5-y-o b m Balnibarbi-Bad Start (USA) (Bold Bidder)
Mrs J C McGregor Mrs Daphne Pease

Placings:00   (4397)
2002/03: 16⁰HY, 17⁰G,

	Starts	1st	2nd	3rd	Win & Pl
NH Flat	2	0	0	0	0
Career Total	2	0	0	0	0

Going: Sf: 0-1 GS: 0-0 Gd: 0-1 GF: - Fm: 0-0
Distance: 2m/2m3: 0-2 2m4-2m7: 0-0 3m+: 0-0
Track: LH: 0-1 RH: 0-1 Tight: 0-0 Gall: 0-0
Aids: Bl: 0-0 Vi: 0-0 Tstrap: 0-0
Best Rating: 61 2/03 Ayr 2m   heavy NHF

Blue Native

88f   72f

6-y-o br m Be My Native (USA)-Supreme Wings (IRE) (Supreme Leader)
R J Hodges Mrs Angela Tincknell

Placings:0   (4155)
2002/03: 16⁰G,

	Starts	1st	2nd	3rd	Win & Pl
NH Flat	1	0	0	0	0
Career Total	1	0	0	0	0

Going: Sf: 0-0 GS: 0-0 Gd: 0-1 GF: - Fm: 0-0
Distance: 2m/2m3: 0-2 2m4-2m7: 0-0 3m+: 0-0
Track: LH: 0-1 RH: 0-0 Tight: 0-0 Gall: 0-0
Aids: Bl: 0-0 Vi: 0-0 Tstrap: 0-0
Best Rating: 72 3/03 Wwck 2m   good NHF

Blue Planet (IRE)

95   96

5-y-o b g Bluebird (USA)-Millie Musique (Miller s Mate)
P G Murphy Miss J Collison

Placings:30-442   (3923)
2002/03: 21⁴G, 20⁴GS, 20²S,

	Starts	1st	2nd	3rd	Win & Pl
Hurdles	3	0	1	0	770
Career Total	5	0	1	1	1313

Going: Sf: 0-1 GS: 0-1 Gd: 0-1 GF: - Fm: 0-0
Distance: 2m/2m3: 0-0 2m4-2m7: 0-3 3m+: 0-0
Track: LH: 0-1 RH: 0-0 Tight: 0-3 Gall: 0-0
Aids: Bl: 0-0 Vi: 0-0 Tstrap: 0-0
Best Rating: 96 3/03 Font 2m4f   soft Hdl

Blue Ride (IRE)

111   126+

6-y-o b m King s Ride-Charmere s Beauty (IRE) (Phardante (FR))
P F Nicholls Mrs Angela Tincknell

Placings: 1-21131 (4610)
2002/03: 19^2GS, 16^1GS, 22^1GS, 21^3G, 21^1G,

	Starts	1st	2nd	3rd	Win & Pl
Hurdles	5	3	1	1	31999
Career Total	6	4	1	1	34222

130	4/03	Chel	2m5f110yA	HHdl	GD	£16240
121	2/03	Winc	2m6f	D Hdl	G-S	£5369
98	12/02	Winc	2m	E Hdl	G-S	£3010
96	4/02	Ludl	2m	H NHF	G-F	£2222

Total win prize-money £26842

Going: Sf: 0-0 GS: 2-3 Gd: 1-2 GF: - Fm: 0-0
Distance: 2m/2m3: 1-1 2m4-2m7: 2-4 3m+: 0-0
Track: LH: 1-2 RH: 2-3 Tight: 0-1 Gall: 1-2
Aids: Bl: 0-0 Vi: 0-0 Tstrap: 0-0
Best Rating: 130 4/03 Chel 2m5f110y good Hdl

Useful novice hurdler; winner twice at Wincanton; landed Listed mares only handicap at Cheltenham April 2003; stays two miles six; acts on fast and yielding ground; set to go chasing next season.

Blue Shannon (IRE)
79f — 92f
5-y-o b m Be My Native (USA)-Shannon Foam (Le Bavard (FR))
P F Nicholls   Mrs Angela Tincknell

Placings: 204 (4697)
2002/03: 16^2GF, 17^0G, 17^4G,

	Starts	1st	2nd	3rd	Win & Pl
NH Flat	3	0	1	0	734
Career Total	3	0	1	0	734

Going: Sf: 0-0 GS: 0-0 Gd: 0-2 GF: - Fm: 0-0
Distance: 2m/2m3: 0-3 2m4-2m7: 0-0 3m+: 0-0
Track: LH: 0-2 RH: 0-1 Tight: 0-1 Gall: 0-1
Aids: Bl: 0-0 Vi: 0-0 Tstrap: 0-0
Best Rating: 92 3/03 Ludl 2m gd-fm NHF

Blue Streak (IRE)
103 — 100
6-y-o ch g Bluebird (USA)-Fleet Amour (USA) (Afleet (CAN))
G L Moore (K Bell 19/8) D R Hunnisett

Placings: 4162160 (3937)
2002/03: 16^4G, 16^1GF, 16^6G, 16^2S, 16^1S, 16^4HY, 18^0S,

	Starts	1st	2nd	3rd	Win & Pl
Hurdles	7	2	1	0	6868
Career Total	7	2	1	0	6868

| 100 | 11/02 | Plum | 2m | E(0-110)HHdl | SFT | £3094 |
| 100 | 10/02 | Plum | 2m | F Hdl | G-F | £2926 |

Total win prize-money £6020

Going: Sf: 1-4 GS: 0-0 Gd: 0-2 GF: - Fm: 1-1
Distance: 2m/2m3: 2-7 2m4-2m7: 0-0 3m+: 0-0
Track: LH: 2-7 RH: 0-0 Tight: 2-7 Gall: 0-0
Aids: Bl: 0-0 Vi: 0-0 Tstrap: 0-0
Best Rating: 100 11/02 Plum 2m soft Hdl

Claiming-class hurdler, suited by two miles and fast ground.

Blue Style (IRE)
91 — 70
7-y-o ch g Bluebird (USA)-Style For Life (IRE) (Law Society (USA))
P Burgoyne   M Mason

Placings: 0200 (1932)
2002/03: 19^0S, 18^2GF, 16^0G, 17^0GS,

	Starts	1st	2nd	3rd	Win & Pl
Hurdles	4	0	1	0	660
Career Total	4	0	1	0	660

Going: Sf: 0-1 GS: 0-1 Gd: 0-1 GF: - Fm: 0-1
Distance: 2m/2m3: 0-4 2m4-2m7: 0-0 3m+: 0-1
Track: LH: 0-3 RH: 0-1 Tight: 0-4 Gall: 0-0
Aids: Bl: 0-1 Vi: 0-0 Tstrap: 0-0
Best Rating: 70 8/02 Font 2m2f110y gd-fm Hdl

Bluebell Hill
6-y-o b m Puget (USA)-Fooling With Fire (Idiots Delight)
Mrs L Williamson   Miss Judy Eaton

Placings: 60P0 (4320)
2002/03: 17^6HY, 17^0HY, 19^PGF, 17^0G,

	Starts	1st	2nd	3rd	Win & Pl
NH Flat	2	0	0	0	0
Hurdles	2	0	0	0	0
Career Total	4	0	0	0	0

Going: Sf: 0-2 GS: 0-0 Gd: 0-1 GF: - Fm: 0-0
Distance: 2m/2m3: 0-3 2m4-2m7: 0-1 3m+: 0-0
Track: LH: 0-3 RH: 0-1 Tight: 0-3 Gall: 0-0
Aids: Bl: 0-0 Vi: 0-0 Tstrap: 0-0
Best Rating: 73 1/03 Sedg 2m1f heavy NHF

Bluebell Wedding
8-y-o b m Henbit (USA)-Ina s Farewell (Random Shot)
J Barclay   John Dudgeon

Placings: 0/P (0616)
2002/03: 20^PGF,

	Starts	1st	2nd	3rd	Win & Pl
Hurdles	1	0	0	0	
Career Total	2	0	0	0	

Going: Sf: 0-0 GS: 0-0 Gd: 0-0 GF: - Fm: 0-1
Distance: 2m/2m3: 0-0 2m4-2m7: 0-1 3m+: 0-0
Track: LH: 0-1 RH: 0-0 Tight: 0-0 Gall: 0-0
Aids: Bl: 0-0 Vi: 0-0 Tstrap: 0-0
Best Rating: 0 6/02 Hexm 2m4f110y gd-fm Hdl

Blues Of The Night
7-y-o gr m Petong-Candane (Danehill (USA))
R Johnson   Robert Johnson

Placings: P0/0P (1735)
2002/03: 16^0G, 16^PS,

	Starts	1st	2nd	3rd	Win & Pl
Hurdles	2	0	0	0	
Career Total	4	0	0	0	

Going: Sf: 0-1 GS: 0-0 Gd: 0-1 GF: - Fm: 0-0
Distance: 2m/2m3: 0-0 2m4-2m7: 0-3 3m+: 0-0
Track: LH: 0-2 RH: 0-0 Tight: 0-0 Gall: 0-0
Aids: Bl: 0-0 Vi: 0-0 Tstrap: 0-0
Best Rating: 18 11/99 Newc 2m good Hdl

Blues Story (FR)
92 — 92
5-y-o b g Pistolet Bleu (IRE)-Herbe Sucree (FR) (Tiffauges)
P R Webber   D Heath

Placings: 00-44 (4051)
2002/03: 18^4HY, 16^4HY,

	Starts	1st	2nd	3rd	Win & Pl
NH Flat	1	0	0	0	278
Hurdles	1	0	0	0	378
Career Total	4	0	0	0	655

Going: Sf: 0-2 GS: 0-0 Gd: 0-0 GF: - Fm: 0-0
Distance: 2m/2m3: 0-2 2m4-2m7: 0-0 3m+: 0-0
Track: LH: 0-1 RH: 0-1 Tight: 0-0 Gall: 0-0
Aids: Bl: 0-0 Vi: 0-0 Tstrap: 0-0
Best Rating: 76 2/03 Plum 2m2f heavy NHF

Well beaten in bumpers and over hurdles; has shown some ability.

Blueshaan (IRE)
97(107h) — (85h)75
10-y-o b g Darshaan-Pale Blue (Kris)
Mrs A M Thorpe (Dr P Pritchard 4/5) Mrs A M Thorpe

Placings: 03/1U2P35/P6P/PP00006-1360 (1378)
2002/03: 17^1GF, 16^3GF, 19^6GF, 19^0GS,

	Starts	1st	2nd	3rd	Win & Pl
Hurdles	1	1	0	0	2450
Chases	3	0	0	1	420
Career Total	22	2	1	3	7204

| 85 | 5/02 | Hrfd | 2m1f | G(0-95)HHdl | G-F | £2450 |
| 120 | 10/98 | Chep | 2m4f110yE Hdl | | G-S | £1982 |

Total win prize-money £4432

Going: Sf: 0-0 GS: 0-0 Gd: 0-0 GF: - Fm: 1-4
Distance: 2m/2m3: 1-4 2m4-2m7: 0-0 3m+: 0-0
Track: LH: 0-0 RH: 1-4 Tight: 0-0 Gall: 0-1
Aids: Bl: 0-0 Vi: 0-0 Tstrap: 0-0
Best Rating: 120 10/98 Chep 2m4f110y gd-sft Hdl

Plating-class chaser/hurdler; has dropped steadily in the weights and landed a weak selling hurdle in May 2002; stays two miles four; handles fast and easy ground

Blunham Hill (IRE)
100 — 101
5-y-o ch g Over The River (FR)-Bronach (Beau Charmeur (FR))
John R Upson   Ian N Mallett

Placings: 53P5 (3852)
2002/03: 20^5S, 20^3G, 20^PGS, 24^5GS,

	Starts	1st	2nd	3rd	Win & Pl
Hurdles	4	0	0	1	624
Career Total	4	0	0	1	624

Going: Sf: 0-1 GS: 0-2 Gd: 0-1 GF: - Fm: 0-0
Distance: 2m/2m3: 0-0 2m4-2m7: 0-3 3m+: 0-1
Track: LH: 0-3 RH: 0-1 Tight: 0-1 Gall: 0-0
Aids: Bl: 0-0 Vi: 0-0 Tstrap: 0-0
Best Rating: 101 12/02 Hayd 2m4f good Hdl

Moderate hurdler; showed a fair bit of promise over Haydock s brush hurdles in late 2002; effective over two and a half miles.

Blushing Spur

5-y-o b g Flying Spur (AUS)-Bogus John (CAN) (Blushing John (USA))
A Charlton (D Shaw 17/2) Allan Darke

Placings:UP　　　　　　　　　　　　　　(2629)
2002/03: 16^UG, 16^PS,

	Starts	1st	2nd	3rd	Win & Pl
Hurdles	2	0	0	0	
Career Total	2	0	0	0	

Going: Sf: 0-1 GS: 0-0 Gd: 0-1 GF: - Fm: 0-0
Distance: 2m/2m3: 0-2 2m4-2m7: 0-0 3m+: 0-0
Track: LH: 0-2 RH: 0-0 Tight: 0-0 Gall: 0-1
Aids: Bl: 0-0 Vi: 0-1 Tstrap: 0-0
Best Rating: 0　12/02　Uttx　2m　　　soft　　Hdl

Blyth Brook

11-y-o b g Meadowbrook-The Bean-Goose (King Sitric)
W T Reed (Miss S E Forster 21/6) Mrs S A Sutton

Placings:000/25P2/65-03P　　　　　　(4480)
2002/03: 20⁰GF, 24³G, 25^PG,

	Starts	1st	2nd	3rd	Win & Pl
Chases	3	0	0	1	409
Career Total	12	0	2	1	2243

Going: Sf: 0-0 GS: 0-0 Gd: 0-2 GF: - Fm: 0-1
Distance: 2m/2m3: 0-0 2m4-2m7: 0-1 3m+: 0-2
Track: LH: 0-2 RH: 0-1 Tight: 0-2 Gall: 0-0
Aids: Bl: 0-0 Vi: 0-0 Tstrap: 0-0
Best Rating: 105　4/01　Ayr　3m3f110y good　　Ch

Fair hunter chaser; effective from two and a half miles upwards and suited by fast ground; can be headstrong.

Blythe Lady
92　　　　　　　　　　　　　　　　　　87

9-y-o b m Warrshan (USA)-Aldwick Colonnade (Kind Of Hush)
T Wall John Reynolds & Derek Dean

Placings:264302P/P302/3F43400FP/223000-
40P35P5P0PP　　　　　　　　　　　　(4704)
2002/03: 16⁴S, 16⁹GF, 20^PG, 16³GF, 20⁵F, 24^PS, 16⁵HY, 20^PGS, 16⁰S, 16^PS, 20^PG.

	Starts	1st	2nd	3rd	Win & Pl
Hurdles	7	0	0	1	500
Chases	4	0	0	0	0
Career Total	37	0	5	6	6180

Going: Sf: 0-5 GS: 0-1 Gd: 0-2 GF: - Fm: 0-3
Distance: 2m/2m3: 0-6 2m4-2m7: 0-4 3m+: 0-1
Track: LH: 0-8 RH: 0-3 Tight: 0-3 Gall: 0-0
Aids: Bl: 0-4 Vi: 0-0 Tstrap: 0-0
Best Rating: 93　3/00　Uttx　2m4f110y good　Hdl

Bneya (FR)

6-y-o b m Hero's Honor (USA)-Khariyada (FR) (Akarad (FR))
Mrs M Reveley David J Jackson

Placings:3F20/0224-P　　　　　　　　(2382)
2002/03: 23^PGS,

	Starts	1st	2nd	3rd	Win & Pl
Hurdles	1	0	0	0	
Career Total	9	0	3	1	30652

Going: Sf: 0-0 GS: 0-1 Gd: 0-0 GF: - Fm: 0-0
Distance: 2m/2m3: 0-2 2m4-2m7: 0-1 3m+: 0-0
Track: LH: 0-1 RH: 0-0 Tight: 0-0 Gall: 0-0
Aids: Bl: 0-0 Vi: 0-1 Tstrap: 0-0
Best Rating: 0　12/02　Weth　2m7f　　gd-sft　Hdl

Bo Dancer (IRE)
103　　　　　　　　　　　　　　　　　94

9-y-o ch g Magical Wonder (USA)-Pitty Pal (USA) (Caracolero (USA))
Mrs E Slack A Slack

Placings:00/10/211/060/064-2211334334　(1418)
2002/03: 20⁴G, 24²G, 27²G, 17¹G, 16¹GF, 21³GF, 27³G, 17⁴G, 20³GF, 24³GF, 22⁴GF,

	Starts	1st	2nd	3rd	Win & Pl
Hurdles	11	2	2	4	11529
Career Total	23	5	3	4	19061
94	6/02	Hexm	2m110y	D(0-115)HHdl	G-F	£3346
93	6/02	Ctml	2m1f110yD(0-120)HHdl	GD	£3458
101	12/99	Catt	2m3f	F(0-110)HHdl	G-F	£1924
97	11/99	Carl	2m4f110yF(0-105)HHdl	G-S	£2430
83	11/98	Hexm	2m4f110yE	Hdl	HVY	£2553
				Total win prize-money £13711		

Going: Sf: 0-0 GS: 0-0 Gd: 1-6 GF: - Fm: 1-5
Distance: 2m/2m3: 2-3 2m4-2m7: 0-4 3m+: 0-4
Track: LH: 2-10 RH: 0-1 Tight: 1-6 Gall: 0-1
Aids: Bl: 0-0 Vi: 0-0 Tstrap: 0-0
Best Rating: 101　12/99　Catt　2m3f　　gd-fm　Hdl

Moderate hurdler; consistent; stays two and a half miles; acts on any ground; needs to come late with one sharp run.

Bo Squidley

6-y-o b m Karinga Bay-Martins Lottee (Martinmas)
Mrs S Gardner Ms Kay Julian

Placings:U/R　　　　　　　　　　　　(0629)
2002/03: 16US, 22^RGF,

	Starts	1st	2nd	3rd	Win & Pl
NH Flat	1	0	0	0	0
Hurdles	1	0	0	0	0
Career Total	2	0	0	0	

Going: Sf: 0-1 GS: 0-0 Gd: 0-0 GF: - Fm: 0-1
Distance: 2m/2m3: 0-1 2m4-2m7: 0-1 3m+: 0-0
Track: LH: 0-2 RH: 0-0 Tight: 0-1 Gall: 0-0
Aids: Bl: 0-0 Vi: 0-0 Tstrap: 0-0
Best Rating: 0　6/02　NAbb　2m6f　　gd-fm　Hdl

Board Walk (IRE)
99　　　　　　　　　　　　　　　　102

8-y-o b g Commanche Run-Swift Tide (Hard Boy)
Mrs M Reveley Mrs M Hoey

Placings:0P0/P3F1U-32　　　　　　　(2001)
2002/03: 22³G, 22²S,

	Starts	1st	2nd	3rd	Win & Pl
Chases	2	0	1	1	1913
Career Total	10	1	1	2	5831
102	1/02	Newc	3m	F(0-100)HCh	SFT	£3496
				Total win prize-money £3497		

Going: Sf: 0-1 GS: 0-0 Gd: 0-1 GF: - Fm: 0-0
Distance: 2m/2m3: 0-0 2m4-2m7: 0-2 3m+: 0-0
Track: LH: 0-2 RH: 0-0 Tight: 0-0 Gall: 0-0
Aids: Bl: 0-0 Vi: 0-0 Tstrap: 0-0
Best Rating: 102　11/02　Hayd　2m6f　　soft　　Ch

Moderate chaser; enormous, lightly-raced gelding; suited by a test of stamina; handles soft ground.

Boardroom Dancer (IRE)

6-y-o b g Executive Perk-Dancing Course (IRE) (Crash Course)
D J Caro D J Caro

Placings:466　　　　　　　　　　　　(4527)
2002/03: 18⁴S, 16⁶S, 20⁶G,

	Starts	1st	2nd	3rd	Win & Pl
NH Flat	2	0	0	0	0
Hurdles	1	0	0	0	0
Career Total	3	0	0	0	0

Going: Sf: 0-2 GS: 0-0 Gd: 0-1 GF: - Fm: 0-0
Distance: 2m/2m3: 0-2 2m4-2m7: 0-1 3m+: 0-0
Track: LH: 0-2 RH: 0-1 Tight: 0-1 Gall: 0-0
Aids: Bl: 0-0 Vi: 0-0 Tstrap: 0-0
Best Rating: 74　12/02　Font　2m2f110y soft　NHF

Boardwalk Knight (IRE)
98?

6-y-o b g Shardari-Takhiyra (Vayrann)
M Todhunter (D T Hughes 7/10) Abbadis Racing Club

Placings:002F-0100P　　　　　　　　(2103)
2002/03: 16⁹GY, 16¹GY, 16⁹Y, 16⁶G, 16^PG,

	Starts	1st	2nd	3rd	Win & Pl
Hurdles	5	1	0	0	3810
Career Total	9	1	1	0	5100
92	8/02	Wxfd	2m	Hdl	G-Y	£3809
				Total win prize-money £3810		

Going: Sf: 0-0 GS: 0-0 Gd: 0-2 GF: - Fm: 0-0
Distance: 2m/2m3: 1-5 2m4-2m7: 0-0 3m+: 0-0
Track: LH: 0-1 RH: 0-0 Tight: 0-1 Gall: 0-0
Aids: Bl: 0-0 Vi: 0-0 Tstrap: 0-0
Best Rating: 98　10/02　Rosc　2m　　good　Hdl

Moderate hurdler; ex-Irish; acts on easy ground.

Boater
98　　　　　　　　　　　　　　　　76

9-y-o b g Batshoof-Velvet Beret (IRE) (Dominion)
R J Baker Christine And Aubrey Loze

Placings:23/42P61/02211402/3F5/032252426-16F4 (4625)
2002/03: 17¹GS, 16⁶S, 22^FGF, 17⁴GF,

	Starts	1st	2nd	3rd	Win & Pl
Hurdles	4	1	0	0	2940
Career Total	31	4	9	3	22865
111	5/02	NAbb	2m1f	E(0-105)HHdl	G-S	£2562
118	8/99	NAbb	2m1f	C(0-130)HHdl	GD	£4662
112	7/99	NAbb	2m1f	F(0-100)HHdl	G-F	£2640
99	4/99	Tntn	2m1f	F(0-100)HHdl	G-S	£1966
				Total win prize-money £11830		

Going: Sf: 0-1 GS: 1-1 Gd: 0-0 GF: - Fm: 0-2
Distance: 2m/2m3: 1-3 2m4-2m7: 0-1 3m+: 0-0
Track: LH: 1-4 RH: 0-0 Tight: 1-3 Gall: 0-0

Aids: **Bl:** 1-4 **Vi:** 0-0 **Tstrap:** 0-0
Best Rating: 122 7/00   NAbb 2m1f   gd-fm   Hdl

Fair handicap hurdler; suited by fast ground but acts on easier; returned after a five month absence to narrowly win a Class E handicap at Newton Abbot May 2002; lightly raced since; usually wears blinkers.

Bob Ar Aghaidh (IRE)

103   111

7-y-o b g Bob Back (USA)-Shuil Ar Aghaidh (The Parson)
A J Lidderdale George Ward

Placings:260-5232   (3153)
2002/03: 22⁵S, 20²S, 22³HY, 24²HY,

	Starts	1st	2nd	3rd	Win & Pl
Hurdles	4	0	2	1	2419
Career Total	7	0	3	1	3112

Going: Sf: 0-4 GS: 0-0 Gd: 0-0 GF: - Fm: 0-0
Distance: 2m/2m3: 0-0 2m4-2m7: 0-3 3m+: 0-0
Track: LH: 0-3 RH: 0-1 Tight: 0-1 Gall: 0-0
Aids: Bl: 0-0 Vi: 0-0 Tstrap: 0-0
Best Rating: 111 1/03   Chep 3m   heavy   Hdl

Modest hurdler; out of the 1993 Stayers Hurdle winner; has shown ability in bumpers and over hurdles.

Bob Le Gaoth (IRE)

83

7-y-o br g Bob Back (USA)-Shuil Le Gaoth (IRE) (Strong Gale)
A J Lidderdale Bonusprint

Placings:31/U-F   (1748)
2002/03: 21ᶠS,

	Starts	1st	2nd	3rd	Win & Pl
Hurdles	1	0	0	0	
Career Total	4	1	0	1	2830
110 4/01	NAbb 2m1f	H NHF		SFT	£2450
				Total win prize-money £2450

Going: Sf: 0-1 GS: 0-0 Gd: 0-0 GF: - Fm: 0-0
Distance: 2m/2m3: 0-0 2m4-2m7: 0-1 3m+: 0-0
Track: LH: 0-1 RH: 0-0 Tight: 0-1 Gall: 0-0
Aids: Bl: 0-0 Vi: 0-0 Tstrap: 0-0
Best Rating: 110 4/01   NAbb 2m1f   soft   NHF

Bob The Piler

99   95

7-y-o b g Jendali (USA)-Laxay (Laxton)
N G Richards Taranto De Pol

Placings:415/4   (2191)
2002/03: 17⁴HY,

	Starts	1st	2nd	3rd	Win & Pl
Hurdles	1	0	0	0	0
Career Total	4	1	0	0	1589
108 2/01	Sedg 2m1f	H NHF		SFT	£1589
				Total win prize-money £1589

Going: Sf: 0-1 GS: 0-0 Gd: 0-0 GF: - Fm: 0-0
Distance: 2m/2m3: 0-1 2m4-2m7: 0-0 3m+: 0-0
Track: LH: 0-0 RH: 0-1 Tight: 0-0 Gall: 0-0
Aids: Bl: 0-0 Vi: 0-0 Tstrap: 0-0
Best Rating: 109 4/01   Aint 2m1f   heavy   NHF

Bob's Buster

93(105c)   (92c)61

7-y-o b g Bob s Return (IRE)-Saltina (Bustino)
R Johnson Mrs Geraldine Jones

Placings:FP0/02053444/252F4331-3045   (2102)
2002/03: 16³G, 16⁶G, 16⁴HY, 16⁵G,

	Starts	1st	2nd	3rd	Win & Pl
Hurdles	3	0	0	1	480
Chases	1	0	0	0	0
Career Total	23	1	3	4	9204
90 4/02	Hexm 2m110y	E(0-110)HHdl		GD	£3052
				Total win prize-money £3052

Going: Sf: 0-1 GS: 0-0 Gd: 0-3 GF: - Fm: 0-0
Distance: 2m/2m3: 0-4 2m4-2m7: 0-0 3m+: 0-0
Track: LH: 0-4 RH: 0-0 Tight: 0-2 Gall: 0-0
Aids: Bl: 0-0 Vi: 0-0 Tstrap: 0-0
Best Rating: 92 11/02   Catt 2m   good   Ch

Plating-class chaser; has shown ability in ordinary company in hurdles and novice chases; acts on a sound surface.

Bob's Gone (IRE)

105   105

5-y-o ch g Eurobus-Bob s Girl (IRE) (Bob Back (USA))
R J Smith (Miss F M Crowley 26/7) R Smith

Placings:F35241P-U044   (4683)
2002/03: 20ᵁG, 22⁰G, 24⁴GF, 21⁴GF,

	Starts	1st	2nd	3rd	Win & Pl
Hurdles	4	0	0	0	442
Career Total	11	1	1	0	9079
105 12/01	Limk 2m	Hdl		SFT	£6120
				Total win prize-money £6121

Going: Sf: 0-0 GS: 0-0 Gd: 0-2 GF: - Fm: 0-0
Distance: 2m/2m3: 0-0 2m4-2m7: 0-3 3m+: 0-1
Track: LH: 0-0 RH: 0-1 Tight: 0-0 Gall: 0-1
Aids: Bl: 0-0 Vi: 0-0 Tstrap: 0-0
Best Rating: 105 12/01   Limk 2m   soft   Hdl

Moderate hurdler; won over two miles on the Flat in Ireland; lightly-raced since landing two mile Limerick maiden hurdle December 2001; landed gamble when making most in 2m 6f Stratford handicap July 2003; stays well; likes cut in the ground.

Bobalong (IRE)

81f   85f

6-y-o b g Bob s Return (IRE)-Northern Wind (Northfields (USA))
C P Morlock Pell-Mell Partners

Placings:0   (3782)
2002/03: 17⁰GS,

	Starts	1st	2nd	3rd	Win & Pl
NH Flat	1	0	0	0	
Career Total	1	0	0	0	

Going: Sf: 0-0 GS: 0-1 Gd: 0-0 GF: - Fm: 0-0
Distance: 2m/2m3: 0-1 2m4-2m7: 0-0 3m+: 0-0
Track: LH: 0-0 RH: 0-1 Tight: 0-0 Gall: 0-0
Aids: Bl: 0-0 Vi: 0-0 Tstrap: 0-0
Best Rating: 85 2/03   Extr 2m1f   gd-sft   NHF

Bobanvi

102   68

5-y-o b m Timeless Times (USA)-Bobanlyn (IRE) (Dance Of Life (USA))

J S Wainwright S Pedersen

Placings:0002044P-P2500063   (4710)
2002/03: 20ᴾGS, 16²G, 16⁵HY, 16⁵GS, 16⁹G, 17⁹G, 16⁶G, 23⁹GF,

	Starts	1st	2nd	3rd	Win & Pl
Hurdles	8	0	1	1	1211
Career Total	16	0	2	1	1877

Going: Sf: 0-1 GS: 0-2 Gd: 0-4 GF: - Fm: 0-1
Distance: 2m/2m3: 0-6 2m4-2m7: 0-2 3m+: 0-0
Track: LH: 0-6 RH: 0-2 Tight: 0-3 Gall: 0-3
Aids: Bl: 0-0 Vi: 0-0 Tstrap: 0-0
Best Rating: 73 11/01   Weth 2m   good   Hdl

Moderate hurdler; yet to win a race; often wears cheekpieces.

Bobaway (IRE)

6-y-o br g Bob Back (USA)-Baybush (Boreen (FR))
A J Lidderdale Tripleprint

Placings:0-0P   (2945)
2002/03: 17⁰GS, 21ᴾS,

	Starts	1st	2nd	3rd	Win & Pl
NH Flat	1	0	0	0	0
Hurdles	1	0	0	0	0
Career Total	3	0	0	0	

Going: Sf: 0-1 GS: 0-1 Gd: 0-0 GF: - Fm: 0-0
Distance: 2m/2m3: 0-1 2m4-2m7: 0-1 3m+: 0-0
Track: LH: 0-1 RH: 0-1 Tight: 0-1 Gall: 0-0
Aids: Bl: 0-0 Vi: 0-0 Tstrap: 0-0
Best Rating: 74 3/02   Newb 2m110y   gd-sft   NHF

Bobayaro (IRE)

103(105h)   (108h)132+

7-y-o b g Bob Back (USA)-Instanter (Morston (FR))
N G Richards It s A Bargain Syndicate

Placings:2/6413321-232F421   (4753)
2002/03: 20²G, 20³GS, 24²GS, 24⁴G, 25⁴GS, 25²G, 24¹G,

	Starts	1st	2nd	3rd	Win & Pl
Hurdles	1	0	1	0	1104
Chases	6	1	2	1	13662
Career Total	15	3	5	3	25932
97 4/03	Prth	3m	C Ch	GD	£9065
108 4/02	Prth	2m4f110yD Hdl		GD	£3718
99 9/01	Gway	2m	NHF	G-F	£5008
				Total win prize-money £17791

Going: Sf: 0-0 GS: 0-3 Gd: 1-4 GF: - Fm: 0-0
Distance: 2m/2m3: 0-0 2m4-2m7: 0-0 **3m+:** 1-5
Track: LH: 0-4 **RH:** 1-3 Tight: 0-4 Gall: 0-1
Aids: Bl: 0-0 Vi: 0-0 Tstrap: 0-0
Best Rating: 116 12/02   Muss 3m   gd-sft   Ch

Fair chaser; successful over hurdles; rattled up a hat-trick between April and June 2003; stays 3 miles; best on decent ground.

Bobbi Rose Red

102   76

6-y-o ch m Bob Back (USA)-Lady Rosanna (Kind Of Hush)
P T Dalton Mrs Julie Martin

Placings:536-05F4   (4153)
2002/03: 16⁶GS, 16⁹GS, 19⁵G, 24ᶠGS, 25⁴G,

	Starts	1st	2nd	3rd	Win & Pl
NH Flat	2	0	0	0	0

| Hurdles | 3 | 0 | 0 | 0 | 0 |
| Career Total | 7 | 0 | 0 | 1 | 223 |

Going: Sf: 0-0 GS: 0-3 Gd: 0-2 GF: - Fm: 0-0
Distance: 2m/2m3: 0-2 2m4-2m7: 0-1 3m+: 0-2
Track: LH: 0-3 RH: 0-2 Tight: 0-0 Gall: 0-0
Aids: Bl: 0-0 Vi: 0-0 Tstrap: 0-0
Best Rating: 83　3/02　Towc　2m　　soft　NHF

Plating-class novice hurdler; stays three miles.

Bobbie James (IRE)

7-y-o ch g Roselier (FR)-Brown Forest (Brave Invader (USA))
J Mackie Mrs D E H Turner

Placings:00　　　　　　　　　　　　　　　　　(1811)
2002/03: 16⁰G, 16⁰G,

	Starts	1st	2nd	3rd	Win & Pl
NH Flat	2	0	0	0	
Career Total	2	0	0	0	

Going: Sf: 0-0 GS: 0-0 Gd: 0-2 GF: - Fm: 0-0
Distance: 2m/2m3: 0-2 2m4-2m7: 0-0 3m+: 0-0
Track: LH: 0-2 RH: 0-0 Tight: 0-0 Gall: 0-0
Aids: Bl: 0-0 Vi: 0-0 Tstrap: 0-0
Best Rating: 59　10/02　Chel　2m110y　good　NHF

Bobby Blakeney
86　　　　　　45

8-y-o gr g Baron Blakeney-Coming Out (Fair Season)
Miss L V Davis Miss Louise Davis

Placings:P　　　　　　　　　　　　　　　　(4527)
2002/03: 20ᶠG,

	Starts	1st	2nd	3rd	Win & Pl
Hurdles	1	0	0	0	
Career Total	1	0	0	0	

Going: Sf: 0-0 GS: 0-0 Gd: 0-1 GF: - Fm: 0-0
Distance: 2m/2m3: 0-0 2m4-2m7: 0-1 3m+: 0-0
Track: LH: 0-1 RH: 0-0 Tight: 0-0 Gall: 0-0
Aids: Bl: 0-0 Vi: 0-0 Tstrap: 0-0
Best Rating: 0　4/03　Uttx　2m4f110y　good　Hdl

Bobby Grant
116　　　　　153

12-y-o ch g Gunner B-Goldaw (Gala Performance (USA))
P Beaumont John J Thompson

Placings:3⁄1115/2/2F2310/121124/251/6-3240　(3886)
2002/03: 24³S, 24²G, 28⁴HY, 28⁶G,

	Starts	1st	2nd	3rd	Win & Pl
Chases	4	0	1	1	20750
Career Total	26	8	7	3	132102

163	12/00	Hayd	3m	A Ch		HVY	£25200
153	1/00	Hayd	3m	B(0-140)HCh		SFT	£8827
160	12/99	Hayd	3m	A Ch		HVY	£25000
137	11/99	Newc	3m	D(0-125)HCh		GD	£3810
142	1/99	Newc	2m4f	A Ch		SFT	£12834
112	2/97	Newc	2m4f	E Hdl		GD	£2473
101	1/97	Weth	2m4f110yE Hdl			GD	£2587
100	12/96	Hexm	2m	H NHF		G-S	£1406
					Total win prize-money £82139		

Going: Sf: 0-2 GS: 0-0 Gd: 0-2 GF: - Fm: 0-0
Distance: 2m/2m3: 0-0 2m4-2m7: 0-0 3m+: 0-4

Track: LH: 0-4 RH: 0-0 Tight: 0-0 Gall: 0-0
Aids: Bl: 0-4 Vi: 0-0 Tstrap: 0-0
Best Rating: 163　12/00　Hayd　3m　　heavy　Ch

Smart staying chaser; lightly raced these days; stays beyond three miles; effective in soft ground; goes well at Haydock.

Bobosh
108　　　　　103

7-y-o b g Devil s Jump-Jane Craig (Rapid Pass)
R Dickin Haydn Gott

Placings:00/0⁄0250255234040210-504440　(1943)
2002/03: 16⁰GS, 21⁵GF, 19⁰GF, 26⁴GF, 18⁴GF, 16⁴G, 21⁰G,

	Starts	1st	2nd	3rd	Win & Pl
Hurdles	7	0	0	0	943
Career Total	25	1	4	1	11971

| 102 | 4/02 | Ludl | 2m5f | D(0-120)HHdl | G-F | £4336 |
| | | | | Total win prize-money £4337 | | |

Going: Sf: 0-0 GS: 0-1 Gd: 0-2 GF: - Fm: 0-4
Distance: 2m/2m3: 0-4 2m4-2m7: 0-2 3m+: 0-1
Track: LH: 0-4 RH: 0-3 Tight: 0-2 Gall: 0-1
Aids: Bl: 0-0 Vi: 0-0 Tstrap: 0-0
Best Rating: 102　4/02　Ludl　2m5f　　gd-fm　Hdl

Moderate hurdler; stays two miles five; seems to act on any surface; lacks a change of gear.

Bobsbest (IRE)
108(83c)　　　(59c)84

7-y-o b g Lashkari-Bobs (Warpath)
R Dickin R A Jefferies

Placings:0400/06634040-5200P0F1P2　(4786)
2002/03: 17⁵GF, 20²G, 16⁰GS, 19⁰S, 26⁸S, 19⁰G, 16ᶠG, 22¹G, 22ᵖGF, 22²G,

	Starts	1st	2nd	3rd	Win & Pl
Hurdles	8	1	2	0	4895
Chases	2	1	2	1	
Career Total	22	1	2	1	5525

| 75 | 3/03 | MRas | 2m6f | F(0-95)HHdl | GD | £3241 |
| | | | | Total win prize-money £3241 | | |

Going: Sf: 0-2 GS: 0-1 Gd: 1-5 GF: - Fm: 0-2
Distance: 2m/2m3: 0-5 2m4-2m7: 1-4 3m+: 0-1
Track: LH: 0-4 RH: 0-4 Tight: 0-1 Gall: 0-0
Aids: Bl: 0-0 Vi: 0-0 Tstrap: 0-0
Best Rating: 88　10/00　Chel　2m110y　good　NHF

Plating-class hurdler/chaser; stays well and suited by decent ground; has worn visor.

Bodfari Creek
104　　　　　98

6-y-o ch g In The Wings-Cormorant Creek (Gorytus (USA))
P R Webber Bodfari Stud Ltd

Placings:1-2F　　　　　　　　　　　　(1085)
2002/03: 17²S, 16ᶠGF,

	Starts	1st	2nd	3rd	Win & Pl
Hurdles	2	0	1	0	1308
Career Total	3	1	1	0	3240

| 98 | 3/02 | Hayd | 2m | H NHF | GD | £1932 |
| | | | | Total win prize-money £1932 | | |

Going: Sf: 0-1 GS: 0-0 Gd: 0-0 GF: - Fm: 0-1
Distance: 2m/2m3: 0-2 2m4-2m7: 0-0 3m+: 0-0
Track: LH: 0-1 RH: 0-1 Tight: 0-1 Gall: 0-0
Aids: Bl: 0-0 Vi: 0-0 Tstrap: 0-0
Best Rating: 98　8/02　Bang　2m1f　　soft　Hdl

Moderate hurdler; successful on debut in Haydock bumper March 2002; failed to achieve much with back-to-back wins at Worcester over 3m in the summer of 2003; stays 3m; acts on fast ground; consistent.

Bodfari Rose
102　　　　　92

4-y-o ch f Indian Ridge-Royale Rose (FR) (Bering)
A Bailey (W J Haggas 2/7) Mrs J Bailey

Placings:332P　　　　　　　　　　　(4033)
2002/03: 17³S, 16³HY, 17²GS, 16⁶PS,

	Starts	1st	2nd	3rd	Win & Pl
Hurdles	4	0	1	2	1952
Career Total	4	0	1	2	1952

Going: Sf: 0-3 GS: 0-1 Gd: 0-0 GF: - Fm: 0-0
Distance: 2m/2m3: 0-4 2m4-2m7: 0-0 3m+: 0-0
Track: LH: 0-2 RH: 0-2 Tight: 0-1 Gall: 0-0
Aids: Bl: 0-1 Vi: 0-0 Tstrap: 0-0
Best Rating: 89　3/03　Carl　2m1f　　gd-sft　Hdl

Moderate maiden hurdler; regularly in the frame without getting her head in front.

Bodfari Signet
112　　　　　102

7-y-o ch g King s Signet (USA)-Darakah (Doulab (USA))
Mrs S C Bradburne Strath Pack Partnership

Placings:4130P/00F316/4F541422246-212455065233
　　　　　　　　　　　　　　　　　　(4767)
2002/03: 20²GS, 20¹GF, 16²GS, 24⁴GF, 16⁵G, 20⁵GS, 16⁹G, 22⁶GS, 20⁵GF, 20²G, 20³GF, 20³G,

	Starts	1st	2nd	3rd	Win & Pl
Hurdles	12	1	3	2	10835
Career Total	34	4	6	4	26116

104	5/02	Prth	2m4f110yE(0-110)HHdl	G-F	£4182
103	12/01	Muss	2m1f	G(0-95)HHdl	G-F	£2341
92	4/01	Muss	2m1f	F(0-100)HHdl	G-F	£3230
91	9/99	Strf	2m110y	E Hdl	G-F	£3096
				Total win prize-money £12853		

Going: Sf: 0-0 GS: 0-4 Gd: 0-4 GF: - Fm: 1-4
Distance: 2m/2m3: 0-3 2m4-2m7: 1-8 3m+: 0-1
Track: LH: 0-4 RH: 1-8 Tight: 0-4 Gall: 0-0
Aids: Bl: 0-0 Vi: 0-0 Tstrap: 0-0
Best Rating: 109　3/02　Kels　2m110y　soft　Hdl

Fair hurdler; bets at two and a half miles, acts on any ground, likes Musselburgh.

Boheidel (GER)
68　　　　　51+

5-y-o b h Dashing Blade-Birthday Party (FR) (Windwurf (GER))
M C Pipe (H Hesse 27/8) Peter Braun

Placings:0　　　　　　　　　　　　　(1603)
2002/03: 16⁰G,

	Starts	1st	2nd	3rd	Win & Pl
Hurdles	1	0	0	0	
Career Total	1	0	0	0	

Going: Sf: 0-0 GS: 0-0 Gd: 0-1 GF: - Fm: 0-0
Distance: 2m/2m3: 0-1 2m4-2m7: 0-0 3m+: 0-0
Track: LH: 0-1 RH: 0-0 Tight: 0-0 Gall: 0-0
Aids: Bl: 0-0 Vi: 0-0 Tstrap: 0-0
Best Rating: 40　10/02　Chep　2m110y　good　Hdl

Bohill Lad (IRE)

104(105c)   (120c)**117**
9-y-o b g Contract Law (USA)-La Sass (Sassafras (FR))
J D Frost Mrs J McCormack

Placings:000/44400000/U343P3015/1534422UP/12122631
2-513PP60501   (4596)
2002/03: 16⁶GS, 16¹GF, 17³G, 16⁶GS, 19⁶GS, 16⁶GS, 16⁰GS,
16⁵GS, 17⁰G, 19¹GF,

	Starts	1st	2nd	3rd	Win & Pl
Hurdles	7	1	0	1	5840
Chases	3	1	0	0	4531
Career Total	48	7	6	6	37486
117 4/03	Extr	2m3f	D(0-125)HHdl	G-F	£4810
120 7/02	NAbb	2m110y	D(0-125)HCh	G-F	£4530
118 3/02	Extr	2m3f	D(0-115)HHdl	GD	£3542
120 7/01	NAbb	2m110y	D Ch	GD	£4057
105 6/01	NAbb	2m1f	F(0-105)HHdl	G-F	£3073
103 5/00	Extr	2m1f	E(0-115)HHdl	G-F	£3201
97 3/00	Tntn	2m1f	G Hdl	GD	£1526
			Total win prize-money £24740		

Going: Sf: 0-0 GS: 0-6 Gd: 0-2 GF: - Fm: 2-2
Distance: 2m/2m3: 2-9 2m4-2m7: 0-1 3m+: 0-0
Track: LH: 1-4 RH: 1-6 Tight: 1-5 Gall: 0-1
Aids: Bl: 0-0 Vi: 0-0 Tstrap: 0-0
Best Rating: 120 7/02 NAbb 2m110y   gd-fm   Ch

Fair hurdler/chaser; mixes hurdling and chasing these days and is a fair tool under both codes around the minor tracks; suited by two to two and a half miles and though he has run well on soft ground, is better on faster; benefitted from a change of tactics when making all in 2m 3f handicap hurdle at Exeter April 2003; ran much better than finishing position suggests next time.

Bold Bishop (IRE)

122f   **140f**
6-y-o b g Religiously (USA)-Ladybojangles (IRE) (Buckskin (FR))
Jonjo O Neill (J I A Charlton 17/11) Mrs G Smith

Placings:1-404   (4115)
2002/03: 16⁴GS, 16⁰G, 16⁴G,

	Starts	1st	2nd	3rd	Win & Pl
NH Flat	3	0	0	0	2911
Career Total	4	1	0	0	4850
111 4/02	Weth	2m	H NHF	G-F	£1939
			Total win prize-money £1939		

Going: Sf: 0-0 GS: 0-1 Gd: 0-2 GF: - Fm: 0-0
Distance: 2m/2m3: 0-3 2m4-2m7: 0-0 3m+: 0-0
Track: LH: 0-3 RH: 0-0 Tight: 0-0 Gall: 0-1
Aids: Bl: 0-1 Vi: 0-0 Tstrap: 0-0
Best Rating: 140 3/03 Chel 2m110y   good   NHF

Useful bumper horse; fourth in Champion Bumper at Cheltenham.

Bold Cardowan (IRE)

108   **86**
7-y-o b g Persian Bold-Moving Trend (IRE) (Be My Guest (USA))
John Berry J McCarthy

Placings:340/036201-13P00305   (4217)
2002/03: 20¹G, 24¹GS, 20³G, 20⁰GS, 20⁰G, 25⁰G, 19³S, 21⁰HY,
22⁶G,

	Starts	1st	2nd	3rd	Win & Pl
Hurdles	8	2	0	2	5722
Chases	1	0	0	0	0

Career Total   17   2   1   4   7110
93 5/02 Hexm 3m   E Hdl   G-S   £2702
91 4/02 Newc 2m4f   F(0-90)Hdl   GD   £2226
                    Total win prize-money £4928

Going: Sf: 0-2 GS: 1-2 Gd: 1-5 GF: - Fm: 0-0
Distance: 2m/2m3: 0-1 2m4-2m7: 1-6 3m+: 1-2
Track: LH: 2-8 RH: 0-1 Tight: 0-2 Gall: 1-1
Aids: Bl: 0-0 Vi: 0-0 Tstrap: 0-0
Best Rating: 93 6/02 Hexm 2m4f110y good   Hdl

Fair hurdler at his best, stays three miles and effective on good ground; finds nothing off the bridle and needs plenty of kidding.

Bold Decision

75f   **54f**
5-y-o ch g Bold Arrangement-Cap That (Derek H)
J R Turner Yarm Racing Partnership

Placings:00   (3412)
2002/03: 16⁰G, 16⁰GS,

	Starts	1st	2nd	3rd	Win & Pl
NH Flat	2	0	0	0	
Career Total	2	0	0	0	

Going: Sf: 0-0 GS: 0-1 Gd: 0-1 GF: - Fm: 0-0
Distance: 2m/2m3: 0-2 2m4-2m7: 0-0 3m+: 0-0
Track: LH: 0-2 RH: 0-0 Tight: 0-1 Gall: 0-0
Aids: Bl: 0-0 Vi: 0-0 Tstrap: 0-0
Best Rating: 55 2/03 Weth 2m   gd-sft   NHF

Bold Doll (IRE)

81   **61**
4-y-o b/br f Dolphin Street (FR)-Bold Miss (Bold Lad (IRE))
Mrs P N Dutfield Simon Dutfield

Placings:U03   (1366)
2002/03: 17⁰GF, 16⁰G, 17³F,

	Starts	1st	2nd	3rd	Win & Pl
Hurdles	3	0	0	1	618
Career Total	3	0	0	1	618

Going: Sf: 0-0 GS: 0-0 Gd: 0-1 GF: - Fm: 0-2
Distance: 2m/2m3: 0-3 2m4-2m7: 0-0 3m+: 0-0
Track: LH: 0-2 RH: 0-1 Tight: 0-1 Gall: 0-0
Aids: Bl: 0-0 Vi: 0-0 Tstrap: 0-0
Best Rating: 61 10/02 Extr 2m1f   firm   Hdl

Bold Hunter

100(94h)   (58h)**86**
9-y-o b g Polish Precedent (USA)-Pumpona (USA) (Sharpen Up)
M J M Evans M J M Evans

Placings:0U/2126453/06404P53/00P035-1353F5P5 (4223)
2002/03: 17¹G, 17⁰GF, 19⁴G, 16³S, 17⁴HY, 16⁴GS, 17⁴S, 16⁵GF,

	Starts	1st	2nd	3rd	Win & Pl
Chases	8	1	0	2	5629
Career Total	31	2	2	5	10939
84 5/02	Bang	2m1f110yE(0-100)HCh	GD	£4329
96 8/99	Strf	2m110y E Hdl	GD	£2537
		Total win prize-money £6867		

Going: Sf: 0-3 GS: 0-1 Gd: 1-2 GF: - Fm: 0-0
Distance: 2m/2m3: 1-8 2m4-2m7: 0-0 3m+: 0-0
Track: LH: 1-4 RH: 0-4 Tight: 1-4 Gall: 0-0
Aids: Bl: 0-0 Vi: 0-0 Tstrap: 0-0
Best Rating: 97 8/99 NAbb 2m1f   good   Hdl

Modest winning chaser. Got off the mark at Bangor in May 2002.

Bold Investor

114(107h)   (129h)**144+**
6-y-o b g Anshan-Shirlstar Investor (Some Hand)
Jonjo O Neill Mrs A R Thompson

Placings:F412306/31416-113P02   (4461)
2002/03: 20¹S, 24¹G, 24³S, 24²G, 24⁰G, 20²G,

	Starts	1st	2nd	3rd	Win & Pl
Chases	6	2	1	1	24093
Career Total	18	5	2	3	40432
140 11/02	Kemp	3m	D Ch	GD	£5005
125 10/02	Carl	2m4f	D Ch	SFT	£5928
129 3/02	Sand	2m6f	D(0-120)HHdl	G-S	£7280
120 1/02	Donc	2m4f	E(0-110)HHdl	GD	£3104
105 11/00	Newc	2m	E Hdl	SFT	£2415
		Total win prize-money £23733		

Going: Sf: 1-2 GS: 0-0 Gd: 1-4 GF: - Fm: 0-0
Distance: 2m/2m3: 0-0 2m4-2m7: 1-2 3m+: 1-4
Track: LH: 0-2 RH: 2-4 Tight: 0-1 Gall: 0-1
Aids: Bl: 0-0 Vi: 0-0 Tstrap: 0-0
Best Rating: 144 4/03 Aint 2m4f   good   Ch

Very useful novice chaser; winner over fences at Carlisle and Kempton; runner-up in valuable novices handicap at Aintree in April; effective over three miles; acts in good and soft ground.

Bold Jogger (IRE)

85   **75d**
6-y-o b g Persian Bold-Mouette (FR) (Fabulous Dancer (USA))
N A Graham J P Kok

Placings:000   (3864)
2002/03: 16⁰G, 16⁰S, 19⁰GS,

	Starts	1st	2nd	3rd	Win & Pl
Hurdles	3	0	0	0	
Career Total	3	0	0	0	

Going: Sf: 0-1 GS: 0-1 Gd: 0-1 GF: - Fm: 0-0
Distance: 2m/2m3: 0-2 2m4-2m7: 0-1 3m+: 0-0
Track: LH: 0-2 RH: 0-1 Tight: 0-0 Gall: 0-2
Aids: Bl: 0-0 Vi: 0-0 Tstrap: 0-0
Best Rating: 75 12/02 Newb 2m110y   good   Hdl

Bold King (FR)

103(104h)   (100h)**111**
8-y-o gr g Turgeon (USA)-Vanila Fudge (USA) (Bold Bidder)
Ian Williams Favourites Racing

Placings:1050000/46112/11235/5413212035-
3P230001341   (4707)
2002/03: 25³GS, 24²GF, 24²G, 28³S, 27⁰G, 24⁰G, 26⁰G, 21¹G,
24³F, 26⁴GF, 26¹G,

	Starts	1st	2nd	3rd	Win & Pl
Hurdles	4	1	1	0	4342
Chases	7	1	0	3	9170
Career Total	38	9	5	6	54234
111 4/03	Uttx	3m2f	E(0-110)HCh	GD	£5381
92 3/03	Wwck	2m5f	F Hdl	GD	£2702
114 1/02	Ludl	3m	D(0-115)HHdl	GD	£3415
109 11/01	Extr	2m3f	D(0-125)HHdl	G-F	£3510
127 11/00	Leic	2m	E Ch	G-S	£3022
107 10/00	Towc	2m110y	D Ch	GD	£3835
101 3/00	Ludl	2m	F(0-105)HHdl	GD	£4111
101 3/00	Hntg	2m110y	F(0-110)HHdl	G-F	£1806
6/98	Autl	1m7f	Hdl	VS	£10101
		Total win prize-money £37885		

Going: Sf: 0-1 GS: 0-1 Gd: 2-6 GF: - Fm: 0-3
Distance: 2m/2m3: 0-0 2m4-2m7: 1-1 3m+: 1-10
Track: LH: 2-4 RH: 0-7 Tight: 0-5 Gall: 0-2
Aids: Bl: 0-0 Vi: 0-3 Tstrap: 0-0
Best Rating: 127 11/00 Newb 2m1f   heavy Ch

Moderate hurdler/chaser; stays three miles plus and appreciates decent ground.

Bold McLaughlan

5-y-o b g Mind Games-Stoneydale (Tickled Pink)
Miss M Bragg W H Whitley

Placings:PP-P   (1376)
2002/03: 19PGF,

	Starts	1st	2nd	3rd	Win & Pl
Hurdles	1	0	0	0	
Career Total	3	0	0	0	

Going: Sf: 0-0 GS: 0-0 Gd: 0-0 GF: - Fm: 0-1
Distance: 2m/2m3: 0-0 2m4-2m7: 0-0 3m+: 0-0
Track: LH: 0-0 RH: 0-1 Tight: 0-0 Gall: 0-0
Aids: Bl: 0-0 Vi: 0-0 Tstrap: 0-0
Best Rating: 0 10/02 Hrfd 2m3f110y gd-fm Hdl

Bold Momento
95f   69f
4-y-o b g Never So Bold-Native Of Huppel (IRE) (Be My Native (USA))
B De Haan William A Tyrer

Placings:0   (4329)
2002/03: 16QG,

	Starts	1st	2nd	3rd	Win & Pl
NH Flat	1	0	0	0	
Career Total	1	0	0	0	

Going: Sf: 0-0 GS: 0-0 Gd: 0-1 GF: - Fm: 0-0
Distance: 2m/2m3: 0-1 2m4-2m7: 0-0 3m+: 0-0
Track: LH: 0-1 RH: 0-0 Tight: 0-0 Gall: 0-1
Aids: Bl: 0-0 Vi: 0-0 Tstrap: 0-0
Best Rating: 69 3/03 Newb 2m110y good NHF

Bold Navigator
103   99
13-y-o b g Lighter-Drummond Lass (Peacock (FR))
A M Crow A M Crow

Placings:P/0/5-P141U   (4589)
2002/03: 20PG, 251G, 244S, 241S, 25UG,

	Starts	1st	2nd	3rd	Win & Pl
Chases	5	2	0	0	7561
Career Total	8	2	0	0	7561
99	3/03	Carl	3m	F(0-95)HCh	SFT	£3513
85	10/02	Hexm	3m1f	E Ch	GD	£3780
				Total win prize-money £7293		

Going: Sf: 1-2 GS: 0-0 Gd: 1-3 GF: - Fm: 0-0
Distance: 2m/2m3: 0-0 2m4-2m7: 0-1 3m+: 2-4
Track: LH: 1-4 RH: 1-1 Tight: 0-0 Gall: 0-0
Aids: Bl: 0-0 Vi: 0-0 Tstrap: 0-0
Best Rating: 99 3/03 Carl 3m   soft Ch

Ex-eventer and point-to-pointer, successful in a very weak novice chase at Hexham in October and took a weak handicap chase at Carlisle in March; stays three miles; acts on good/good to soft ground.

Bold Precedent

6-y-o b g Polish Precedent (USA)-Shining Water (USA) (Riverman (USA))
J R Best (R J White 8/8) D S Nevison

Placings:P   (1447)
2002/03: 20PG,

	Starts	1st	2nd	3rd	Win & Pl
Hurdles	1	0	0	0	
Career Total	1	0	0	0	

Going: Sf: 0-0 GS: 0-0 Gd: 0-1 GF: - Fm: 0-0
Distance: 2m/2m3: 0-0 2m4-2m7: 0-1 3m+: 0-0
Track: LH: 0-1 RH: 0-0 Tight: 0-1 Gall: 0-0
Aids: Bl: 0-0 Vi: 0-0 Tstrap: 0-0
Best Rating: 0 10/02 Fknm 2m4f   good Hdl

Bold Raider

6-y-o b g Rudimentary (USA)-Spanish Heart (King Of Spain)
I A Balding The Farleigh Court Racing Partnership

Placings:P   (2365)
2002/03: 16PS,

	Starts	1st	2nd	3rd	Win & Pl
Hurdles	1	0	0	0	
Career Total	1	0	0	0	

Going: Sf: 0-1 GS: 0-0 Gd: 0-0 GF: - Fm: 0-0
Distance: 2m/2m3: 0-1 2m4-2m7: 0-0 3m+: 0-0
Track: LH: 0-1 RH: 0-0 Tight: 0-0 Gall: 0-0
Aids: Bl: 0-0 Vi: 0-0 Tstrap: 0-0
Best Rating: 0 12/02 Chep 2m110y soft Hdl

Bold Statement

11-y-o ch g Kris-Bold Fantasy (Bold Lad (IRE))
S Flook S Flook

Placings:52/01U4512/11253U31/23145UF/U0   (4451)
2002/03: 25UG, 24QG,

	Starts	1st	2nd	3rd	Win & Pl
Chases	2	0	0	0	
Career Total	26	6	4	3	23538
110	12/98	Tntn	3m	E(0-110)HCh	GD	£3317
109	4/98	Prth	3m	D(0-110)HCh	HVY	£5196
115	5/97	Ctml	2m1f110yE Hdl		GD	£3072
119	5/97	Hexm	2m	E Hdl	G-F	£2607
105	3/97	Hexm	2m	E Hdl	SFT	£2917
104	11/96	Hexm	2m	H NHF	GD	£1343
				Total win prize-money £18454		

Going: Sf: 0-0 GS: 0-0 Gd: 0-2 GF: - Fm: 0-0
Distance: 2m/2m3: 0-0 2m4-2m7: 0-0 3m+: 0-2
Track: LH: 0-0 RH: 0-2 Tight: 0-1 Gall: 0-0
Aids: Bl: 0-0 Vi: 0-0 Tstrap: 0-2
Best Rating: 119 5/97 Hexm 2m   gd-fm Hdl

Winner of a couple of weak points in the spring of 2003.

Bold Tactics (IRE)

7-y-o br g Jurado (USA)-Bold Lyndsey (Be My Native (USA))
F A Hutsby K Hutsby

Placings:235   (4255)

2002/03: 252S, 233GS, 255G,

	Starts	1st	2nd	3rd	Win & Pl
Chases	3	0	1	1	777
Career Total	3	0	1	1	777

Going: Sf: 0-1 GS: 0-1 Gd: 0-1 GF: - Fm: 0-0
Distance: 2m/2m3: 0-0 2m4-2m7: 0-0 3m+: 0-3
Track: LH: 0-0 RH: 0-3 Tight: 0-1 Gall: 0-0
Aids: Bl: 0-0 Vi: 0-0 Tstrap: 0-0
Best Rating: 86 2/03 Folk 3m1f   soft Ch

Promising pointer/hunter chaser.

Bolder Alexander (IRE)
96   63
6-y-o b g Persian Bold-Be Yourself (USA) (Noalcoholic (FR))
F Jordan M W Doyle

Placings:600000-P0   (0770)
2002/03: 22PGF, 20QF,

	Starts	1st	2nd	3rd	Win & Pl
Hurdles	2	0	0	0	
Career Total	8	0	0	0	0

Going: Sf: 0-0 GS: 0-0 Gd: 0-0 GF: - Fm: 0-2
Distance: 2m/2m3: 0-0 2m4-2m7: 0-2 3m+: 0-0
Track: LH: 0-2 RH: 0-0 Tight: 0-1 Gall: 0-0
Aids: Bl: 0-0 Vi: 0-0 Tstrap: 0-0
Best Rating: 63 11/01 Strf 2m110y soft Hdl

Bolshie Baron
85   67
14-y-o b g Baron Blakeney-Contrary Lady (Conwyn)
M F Harris E O Steward

Placings:6620422/P0P50P/4/P2PP/43P3-B6P   (0189)
2002/03: 33BGF, 25BGF, 30PGF,

	Starts	1st	2nd	3rd	Win & Pl
Chases	3	0	0	0	0
Career Total	25	0	4	2	5405

Going: Sf: 0-0 GS: 0-0 Gd: 0-0 GF: - Fm: 0-3
Distance: 2m/2m3: 0-0 2m4-2m7: 0-0 3m+: 0-3
Track: LH: 0-1 RH: 0-2 Tight: 0-0 Gall: 0-2
Aids: Bl: 0-0 Vi: 0-0 Tstrap: 0-3
Best Rating: 82 5/00 Folk 3m7f   good Ch

A modest pointer and poor hunter.

Bolshoi Ballet
106   99
5-y-o b g Dancing Spree (USA)-Broom Isle (Damister (USA))
J Mackie The M A S Partnership

Placings:050P1   (3902)
2002/03: 16QHY, 16PS, 16QGS, 20PGS, 161S,

	Starts	1st	2nd	3rd	Win & Pl
Hurdles	5	1	0	0	5272
Career Total	5	1	0	0	5272
99	3/03	Newb	2m110y	D(0-110)HHdl	SFT	£5271
				Total win prize-money £5272		

Going: Sf: 1-3 GS: 0-2 Gd: 0-0 GF: - Fm: 0-0
Distance: 2m/2m3: 1-4 2m4-2m7: 0-1 3m+: 0-0
Track: LH: 1-4 RH: 0-1 Tight: 0-1 Gall: 1-2
Aids: Bl: 0-0 Vi: 0-0 Tstrap: 0-0

Best Rating: 99 3/03 Newb 2m110y soft Hdl

Moderate hurdler; won weak race at Newbury March 2003; acts on soft ground.

Bolt Action (IRE)
100 ... 128

7-y-o br g Phardante (FR)-Ebony Jane (Roselier (FR))
P F Nicholls C G Roach

Placings:1P (3189)
2002/03: 20¹HY, 22ᴾGS,

	Starts	1st	2nd	3rd	Win & Pl
Hurdles	2	1	0	0	4043
Career Total	2	1	0	0	4043

128 12/02 Chep 2m4f D Hdl HVY £4043
Total win prize-money £4043

Going: Sf: 1-1 GS: 0-1 Gd: 0-0 GF: - Fm: 0-0
Distance: 2m/2m3: 0-0 **2m4-2m7: 1-2** 3m+: 0-0
Track: LH: 1-1 RH: 0-1 Tight: 0-0 Gall: 0-0
Aids: Bl: 0-0 Vi: 0-0 Tstrap: 0-0
Best Rating: 128 12/02 Chep 2m4f heavy Hdl

Useful hurdler; winning pointer; made an impressive debut over hurdles at Chepstow in December 2002; fatally injured at Wincanton the following month. (DEAD)

Bolton Barrie (IRE)
92 ... 82

5-y-o b g Broken Hearted-Ballyduggan Queen (IRE) (King Luthier)
R C Guest (N B Mason 12/11) Glenn Roberts

Placings:0630 (4778)
2002/03: 16⁹GS, 16⁶G, 16³G, 16⁰G,

	Starts	1st	2nd	3rd	Win & Pl
NH Flat	4	0	0	1	272
Career Total	4	0	0	1	272

Going: Sf: 0-0 GS: 0-1 Gd: 0-3 GF: - Fm: 0-0
Distance: 2m/2m3: 0-4 2m4-2m7: 0-0 3m+: 0-0
Track: LH: 0-3 RH: 0-1 Tight: 0-2 Gall: 0-0
Aids: Bl: 0-0 Vi: 0-0 Tstrap: 0-0
Best Rating: 96 4/03 Hexm 2m110y good NHF

Bolton Forest (IRE)

10-y-o b g Be My Native (USA)-Tickenor Wood (Le Bavard (FR))
C Storey Mrs C Strang Steel

Placings:0/12200/04413055P/51/16204/6-50 (0377)
2002/03: 25⁵G, 25⁰GF,

	Starts	1st	2nd	3rd	Win & Pl
Chases	2	0	0	0	0
Career Total	25	4	3	1	17093

115 5/00 MRas 2m6f110y E Ch G-F £3526
107 4/00 Font 2m4f F(0-100)HHdl GD £2744
93 7/98 Limk 2m2f Hdl YLD £2989
100 9/97 List 2m NHF G-Y £4069
Total win prize-money £13328

Going: Sf: 0-0 GS: 0-0 Gd: 0-1 GF: - Fm: 0-1
Distance: 2m/2m3: 0-0 2m4-2m7: 0-0 3m+: 0-2
Track: LH: 0-2 RH: 0-0 Tight: 0-2 Gall: 0-0
Aids: Bl: 0-0 Vi: 0-0 Tstrap: 0-0
Best Rating: 115 5/00 MRas 2m6f110y gd-fm Ch

Boltoutoftheblue
71 ... 65

4-y-o ch g Bluegrass Prince (IRE)-Forget To Remindme (Forzando)
J S Moore W J S Ratcliffe

Placings:56 (1153)
2002/03: 18⁵G, 17⁶G,

	Starts	1st	2nd	3rd	Win & Pl
Hurdles	2	0	0	0	0
Career Total	2	0	0	0	0

Going: Sf: 0-0 GS: 0-1 Gd: 0-2 GF: - Fm: 0-0
Distance: 2m/2m3: 0-2 2m4-2m7: 0-0 3m+: 0-0
Track: LH: 0-2 RH: 0-0 Tight: 0-2 Gall: 0-0
Aids: Bl: 0-0 Vi: 0-2 Tstrap: 0-0
Best Rating: 65 8/02 Font 2m2f110y good Hdl

Bomb Alaska
57

8-y-o br g Polar Falcon (USA)-So True (So Blessed)
G B Balding Miss B Swire

Placings:60-P (2239)
2002/03: 16²S,

	Starts	1st	2nd	3rd	Win & Pl
Hurdles	1	0	0	0	
Career Total	3	0	0	0	188

Going: Sf: 0-1 GS: 0-0 Gd: 0-0 GF: - Fm: 0-0
Distance: 2m/2m3: 0-1 2m4-2m7: 0-0 3m+: 0-0
Track: LH: 0-1 RH: 0-0 Tight: 0-0 Gall: 0-1
Aids: Bl: 0-0 Vi: 0-0 Tstrap: 0-0
Best Rating: 57 12/01 Newb 2m110y good Hdl

Bomba Charger

11-y-o b g Prince Of Peace-Lady Guinevere (Tormento)
Mrs R Welch Mrs R Welch

Placings:06/P03PF6/4/0/24 (3950)
2002/03: 26²S, 23⁴GS,

	Starts	1st	2nd	3rd	Win & Pl
Chases	2	0	1	0	1193
Career Total	12	0	1	1	1447

Going: Sf: 0-1 GS: 0-1 Gd: 0-0 GF: - Fm: 0-0
Distance: 2m/2m3: 0-0 2m4-2m7: 0-0 3m+: 0-2
Track: LH: 0-1 RH: 0-1 Tight: 0-1 Gall: 0-0
Aids: Bl: 0-0 Vi: 0-0 Tstrap: 0-0
Best Rating: 89 5/00 Chep 3m firm Ch

Bonfire Night (IRE)
81 ... 61

7-y-o b m Air Display (USA)-Smokey Path (IRE) (Scallywag)
D J Wintle Lavender Hill Stud L L C

Placings:0 (0328)
2002/03: 16⁰G,

	Starts	1st	2nd	3rd	Win & Pl
NH Flat	1	0	0	0	
Career Total	1	0	0	0	

Going: Sf: 0-0 GS: 0-0 Gd: 0-1 GF: - Fm: 0-0
Distance: 2m/2m3: 0-1 2m4-2m7: 0-0 3m+: 0-0

Track: LH: 0-1 RH: 0-0 Tight: 0-0 Gall: 0-0
Aids: Bl: 0-0 Vi: 0-0 Tstrap: 0-0
Best Rating: 39 5/02 Worc 2m good NHF

Bongo Fury (FR)
108 ... 112

4-y-o b f Sillery (USA)-Nativelee (FR) (Giboulee (CAN))
M C Pipe (J E Pease 25/5) Lord Donoughmore & Countess Donoughmore

Placings:221121210 (3999)
2002/03: 16²G, 17²F, 16¹F, 16¹G, 16²GS, 16¹S, 16²HY, 16¹HY, 16⁶S,

	Starts	1st	2nd	3rd	Win & Pl
Hurdles	9	4	4	0	26490
Career Total	9	4	4	0	26490

112 2/03 Sand 2m110y D Hdl HVY £5209
112 12/02 Sand 2m110y D Hdl SFT £5375
102 10/02 Strf 2m110y E(0-100)HHdl GD £3523
89 10/02 Ludl 2m E Hdl FRM £3464
Total win prize-money £17574

Going: Sf: 2-4 GS: 0-1 Gd: 1-2 GF: - Fm: 1-2
Distance: **2m/2m3: 4-9** 2m4-2m7: 0-0 3m+: 0-0
Track: LH: 1-3 **RH: 3-6** Tight: 1-1 Gall: 0-0
Aids: Bl: 0-0 Vi: 4-8 Tstrap: 0-0
Best Rating: 112 2/03 Sand 2m110y heavy Hdl

Fair novice hurdler; acts on both fast and testing ground; best at around two miles; usually visored.

Bonny Boy (IRE)
75

8-y-o b g Bustino-Dingle Bay (Petingo)
D A Rees D Rees

Placings:2/03P (4113)
2002/03: 24⁰HY, 26³S, 32ᴾG,

	Starts	1st	2nd	3rd	Win & Pl
Hurdles	1	0	0	0	0
Chases	2	0	0	1	726
Career Total	4	0	1	1	1430

Going: Sf: 0-2 GS: 0-0 Gd: 0-1 GF: - Fm: 0-0
Distance: 2m/2m3: 0-0 2m4-2m7: 0-0 3m+: 0-3
Track: LH: 0-2 RH: 0-0 Tight: 0-1 Gall: 0-1
Aids: Bl: 0-0 Vi: 0-3 Tstrap: 0-0
Best Rating: 75 3/03 Font 3m2f110y soft Ch

Bonnybridge (IRE)
(17h)75

6-y-o ch m Zaffaran (USA)-Oralee (Prominer)
Liam Lennon Liam Lennon

Placings:0040055 (4454a)
2002/03: 16⁶G, 16⁶F, 17⁴GF, 16⁴G, 17⁰S, 20⁵G, 20⁵G,

	Starts	1st	2nd	3rd	Win & Pl
NH Flat	4	0	0	0	196
Hurdles	1	0	0	0	0
Chases	2	0	0	0	0
Career Total	7	0	0	0	196

Going: Sf: 0-1 GS: 0-0 Gd: 0-4 GF: - Fm: 0-2
Distance: 2m/2m3: 0-5 2m4-2m7: 0-2 3m+: 0-0
Track: LH: 0-0 RH: 0-4 Tight: 0-1 Gall: 0-0
Aids: Bl: 0-0 Vi: 0-0 Tstrap: 0-0
Best Rating: 77 2/03 Muss 2m good NHF

Bonus Bridge (IRE)
111(100h)   (108h)115
8-y-o b g Executive Perk-Corivia (Over The River (FR))
H D Daly   Lady Knutsford

Placings:34/123P4-25222   (4438)
2002/03: 16²G, 16⁵G, 19²GS, 19²S, 24²G,

	Starts	1st	2nd	3rd	Win & Pl
Chases	5	0	4	0	7610
Career Total	12	1	5	2	12784
103	10/01 Hrfd	2m1f	E Hdl		SFT £3328

Total win prize-money £3329

Going:	Sf: 0-1 GS: 0-1 Gd: 0-3 GF: - Fm: 0-0
Distance:	2m/2m3: 0-2 2m4-2m7: 0-2 3m+: 0-1
Track:	LH: 0-1 RH: 0-4 Tight: 0-0 Gall: 0-0
Aids:	Bl: 0-0 Vi: 0-0 Tstrap: 0-0
Best Rating:	123 1/03 Extr 2m3f110y gd-sft Ch

Fair hurdler/decent novice chaser; acts on soft ground, but handles a sounder surface; stays two miles three.

Bonus Trix (IRE)
87   93
7-y-o b g Executive Perk-Black Trix (Peacock (FR))
A J Lidderdale   Team George I

Placings:P/10-06P   (3173)
2002/03: 16⁵GS, 17⁶GS, 20⁸GS,

	Starts	1st	2nd	3rd	Win & Pl
Hurdles	3	0	0	0	
Career Total	6	1	0	0	1666
95	5/01 Bang	2m1f	H NHF	GD £1666	

Total win prize-money £1666

Going:	Sf: 0-0 GS: 0-3 Gd: 0-0 GF: - Fm: 0-0
Distance:	2m/2m3: 0-2 2m4-2m7: 0-1 3m+: 0-0
Track:	LH: 0-3 RH: 0-0 Tight: 0-1 Gall: 0-0
Aids:	Bl: 0-0 Vi: 0-0 Tstrap: 0-0
Best Rating:	95 3/02 Newb 2m110y gd-sft NHF

Boogy Woogy

7-y-o ch g Rock Hopper-Primulette (Mummy s Pet)
Robert Bowling (T D Easterby 16/10) A Bowling

Placings:312/13P00643/450-33243   (4089)
2002/03: 21³GF, 21³GF, 23²GF, 25⁴GS, 24³GS,

	Starts	1st	2nd	3rd	Win & Pl
Chases	5	0	1	3	3299
Career Total	19	2	2	6	16490
125	10/00 Weth	2m	D(0-125)HHdl	G-S £2957	
90	11/99 MRas	2m1f110yD Hdl		G-S £3504	

Total win prize-money £6462

Going:	Sf: 0-0 GS: 0-2 Gd: 0-0 GF: - Fm: 0-3
Distance:	2m/2m3: 0-0 2m4-2m7: 0-2 3m+: 0-3
Track:	LH: 0-4 RH: 0-0 Tight: 0-4 Gall: 0-0
Aids:	Bl: 0-5 Vi: 0-0 Tstrap: 0-0
Best Rating:	125 10/00 Weth 2m gd-sft Hdl

Hunter chaser; winning hurdler at around two miles; effective on any ground; often looks out of love with the game.

Book's Way
81   52
7-y-o br g Afzal-In A Whirl (USA) (Island Whirl (USA))
Paul Hamer (Mrs D A Hamer 28/6) Gwynne Phillips

Placings:006/PP   (4736)
2002/03: 22⁸GF, 24⁸GF,

	Starts	1st	2nd	3rd	Win & Pl
Hurdles	1	0	0	0	0
Chases	1	0	0	0	0
Career Total	5	0	0	0	0

Going:	Sf: 0-0 GS: 0-0 Gd: 0-0 GF: - Fm: 0-2
Distance:	2m/2m3: 0-0 2m4-2m7: 0-1 3m+: 0-1
Track:	LH: 0-2 RH: 0-0 Tight: 0-1 Gall: 0-0
Aids:	Bl: 0-0 Vi: 0-0 Tstrap: 0-0
Best Rating:	38 11/99 Hrfd 2m1f good Hdl

Books Law

5-y-o b g Contract Law (USA)-In A Whirl (USA) (Island Whirl (USA))
Mrs D A Hamer   Power Units (1953) Ltd

Placings:PP   (1575)
2002/03: 17⁸GF, 16⁸G,

	Starts	1st	2nd	3rd	Win & Pl
Hurdles	2	0	0	0	
Career Total	2	0	0	0	

Going:	Sf: 0-0 GS: 0-0 Gd: 0-1 GF: - Fm: 0-1
Distance:	2m/2m3: 0-2 2m4-2m7: 0-0 3m+: 0-0
Track:	LH: 0-2 RH: 0-0 Tight: 0-2 Gall: 0-0
Aids:	Bl: 0-0 Vi: 0-0 Tstrap: 0-0
Best Rating:	0 10/02 Strf 2m110y good Hdl

Boom Or Bust (IRE)
79   88
4-y-o ch g Entrepreneur-Classic Affair (USA) (Trempolino (USA))
Miss K M George (A Berry 21/9) The Westwoods

Placings:5P3FP   (4637)
2002/03: 16⁵GF, 17³PS, 17³F, 16⁶G, 16⁸GF,

	Starts	1st	2nd	3rd	Win & Pl
Hurdles	5	0	0	1	930
Career Total	5	0	0	1	930

Going:	Sf: 0-1 GS: 0-0 Gd: 0-1 GF: - Fm: 0-3
Distance:	2m/2m3: 0-5 2m4-2m7: 0-0 3m+: 0-0
Track:	LH: 0-2 RH: 0-3 Tight: 0-2 Gall: 0-0
Aids:	Bl: 0-0 Vi: 0-0 Tstrap: 0-0
Best Rating:	88 4/03 Ludl 2m good Hdl

Improved effort despite being flattered by his proximity to the first two on firm ground third start.

Borani
96   118
8-y-o b g Shirley Heights-Ower (IRE) (Lomond (USA))
S Gollings   Mrs E Houlton

Placings:0/00/B1F361-0   (0795)
2002/03: 17⁰GS,

	Starts	1st	2nd	3rd	Win & Pl
Hurdles	1	0	0	0	
Career Total	10	2	0	1	8265
118	4/02 Strf	2m110y	D(0-110)HHdl	GD £3783	
105	2/02 Sand	2m110y	D(0-115)HHdl	SFT £3672	

Total win prize-money £7456

Going:	Sf: 0-0 GS: 0-1 Gd: 0-0 GF: - Fm: 0-0
Distance:	2m/2m3: 0-1 2m4-2m7: 0-0 3m+: 0-0
Track:	LH: 0-0 RH: 0-1 Tight: 0-1 Gall: 0-0
Aids:	Bl: 0-0 Vi: 0-0 Tstrap: 0-0

	Starts	1st	2nd	3rd	Win & Pl
Hurdles	1	0	0	0	0
Chases	1	0	0	0	0
Career Total	5	0	0	0	0

Best Rating: 118 4/02 Strf 2m110y good Hdl
Fair hurdler; twice a winner over hurdles early in 2002; a very difficult ride who needs to be produced right on the line; best a two miles; acts on any ground.

Border Burn
90   65
9-y-o ch g Safawan-Burning Ryme (Rymer)
N M L Ewart   N M L Ewart

Placings:6P/450-40   (0182)
2002/03: 25⁴GS, 25⁰G,

	Starts	1st	2nd	3rd	Win & Pl
Chases	2	0	0	0	214
Career Total	7	0	0	0	214

Going:	Sf: 0-0 GS: 0-1 Gd: 0-1 GF: - Fm: 0-0
Distance:	2m/2m3: 0-0 2m4-2m7: 0-0 3m+: 0-2
Track:	LH: 0-2 RH: 0-0 Tight: 0-0 Gall: 0-0
Aids:	Bl: 0-1 Vi: 0-0 Tstrap: 0-0
Best Rating:	81 5/02 Hexm 3m1f gd-sft Ch

Border Farmer (IRE)
81   35
10-y-o b g Riverhead (USA)-Double Figures (FR) (Double Form)
James Richardson   James Richardson

Placings:006/04P/06/U26-U   (4541)
2002/03: 24ᵁG,

	Starts	1st	2nd	3rd	Win & Pl
Chases	1	0	0	0	
Career Total	12	0	1	0	530

Going:	Sf: 0-0 GS: 0-0 Gd: 0-1 GF: - Fm: 0-0
Distance:	2m/2m3: 0-0 2m4-2m7: 0-0 3m+: 0-1
Track:	LH: 0-0 RH: 0-1 Tight: 0-1 Gall: 0-0
Aids:	Bl: 0-0 Vi: 0-0 Tstrap: 0-0
Best Rating:	79 5/01 Strf 3m gd-fm Ch

Border Glen
72   41
7-y-o b g Selkirk (USA)-Sulitelma (USA) (The Minstrel (CAN))
P Wegmann (J J Bridger 30/6) P Wegmann

Placings:PP060   (4641)
2002/03: 17⁸GS, 17⁸S, 17⁰G, 16⁶G, 19⁰GF,

	Starts	1st	2nd	3rd	Win & Pl
Hurdles	5	0	0	0	0
Career Total	5	0	0	0	0

Going:	Sf: 0-1 GS: 0-1 Gd: 0-2 GF: - Fm: 0-1
Distance:	2m/2m3: 0-5 2m4-2m7: 0-0 3m+: 0-0
Track:	LH: 0-2 RH: 0-3 Tight: 0-2 Gall: 0-0
Aids:	Bl: 0-2 Vi: 0-2 Tstrap: 0-0
Best Rating:	41 4/03 Ludl 2m good Hdl

Border Light

10-y-o ch g Lighter-Border Cherry (Deep Run)
H J Manners   H J Manners

Placings:0/0/45P/03PP-3P   (4480)

2002/03: 26⁹S, 25ᴾG,

	Starts	1st	2nd	3rd	Win & Pl
Chases	2	0	0	1	260
Career Total	11	0	0	2	1069

Going: Sf: 0-1 GS: 0-0 Gd: 0-1 GF: - Fm: 0-0
Distance: 2m/2m3: 0-0 2m4-2m7: 0-0 3m+: 0-2
Track: LH: 0-2 RH: 0-0 Tight: 0-2 Gall: 0-0
Aids: Bl: 0-0 Vi: 0-0 Tstrap: 0-0
Best Rating: 83   3/03   Plum   3m2f   soft   Ch

Winning pointer; yet to win under Rules; stays three miles; acts well on both good and soft ground.

Border Native

7-y-o ch g Distinct Native-Sanjo (Kafu)
A Parker The Border Natives

Placings:PP   (4435)
2002/03: 24ᴾHY, 20ᴾG,

	Starts	1st	2nd	3rd	Win & Pl
Hurdles	2	0	0	0	
Career Total	2	0	0	0	

Going: Sf: 0-1 GS: 0-0 Gd: 0-1 GF: - Fm: 0-0
Distance: 2m/2m3: 0-0 2m4-2m7: 0-0 3m+: 0-1
Track: LH: 0-2 RH: 0-0 Tight: 0-0 Gall: 0-1
Aids: Bl: 0-0 Vi: 0-0 Tstrap: 0-0
Best Rating: 0   4/03   Newc   2m4f   good   Hdl

Border Nomad

70   40

9-y-o b m Nomadic Way (USA)-Ascot Lass (Touching Wood (USA))
M A Barnes P T H Osborne

Placings:5050   (1731)
2002/03: 17⁵G, 17⁰G, 20⁵GF, 22⁰S,

	Starts	1st	2nd	3rd	Win & Pl
Hurdles	4	0	0	0	0
Career Total	4	0	0	0	0

Going: Sf: 0-1 GS: 0-0 Gd: 0-2 GF: - Fm: 0-1
Distance: 2m/2m3: 0-2 2m4-2m7: 0-2 3m+: 0-0
Track: LH: 0-4 RH: 0-0 Tight: 0-3 Gall: 0-0
Aids: Bl: 0-0 Vi: 0-0 Tstrap: 0-0
Best Rating: 40   10/02   Hexm   2m4f110y   gd-fm   Hdl

Border Run

80(81c)   (41c)57

6-y-o b g Missed Flight-Edraianthus (Windjammer (USA))
M Mullineaux P T Hollins

Placings:0031300/PPPF5P-P00P000   (4116)
2002/03: 17ᴾG, 16⁰G, 16⁰S, 17ᴾHY, 16⁰S, 21⁰G,

	Starts	1st	2nd	3rd	Win & Pl
Hurdles	3	0	0	0	0
Chases	4	0	0	0	0
Career Total	**20**	**1**	**0**	**2**	**3574**
78	12/00 Ludl	2m		G Hdl	SFT £2853
			Total win prize-money £2854		

Going: Sf: 0-3 GS: 0-0 Gd: 0-4 GF: - Fm: 0-0
Distance: 2m/2m3: 0-5 2m4-2m7: 0-2 3m+: 0-0
Track: LH: 0-3 RH: 0-0 Tight: 0-2 Gall: 0-2
Aids: Bl: 0-2 Vi: 0-0 Tstrap: 0-0
Best Rating: 84   1/01   Tntn   2m1f   heavy   Hdl

Border Star (IRE)

103   94+

6-y-o b g Parthian Springs-Tengello (Bargello)
J M Jefferson Mrs Kathleen Campey

Placings:O655005-461436   (2379)
2002/03: 16⁴GF, 18⁶G, 16¹GS, 16⁴G, 16⁹GS, 20⁶GS,

	Starts	1st	2nd	3rd	Win & Pl
Hurdles	6	1	0	1	4067
Career Total	**13**	**1**	**0**	**1**	**4067**
87	8/02 Strf	2m110y	E(0-105)HHdl	G-S	£3601
			Total win prize-money £3601		

Going: Sf: 0-0 GS: 1-3 Gd: 0-2 GF: - Fm: 0-1
Distance: 2m/2m3: 1-5 2m4-2m7: 0-1 3m+: 0-0
Track: LH: 1-6 RH: 0-0 Tight: 1-2 Gall: 0-1
Aids: Bl: 0-0 Vi: 0-0 Tstrap: 0-0
Best Rating: 94   11/02   Newc   2m   gd-sft   Hdl

Moderate hurdler; limited ability in novice hurdles around two miles before winning at Stratford in August 2002; handles soft ground.

Borehill Joker

(108h)   (86 h)97

7-y-o ch g Pure Melody (USA)-Queen Matilda (Castle Keep)
E Haddock Miss H M Newell

Placings:3/0021P3062115/4154524522366-140P030
                                             (4119)
2002/03: 16⁶GS, 16¹S, 16⁴G, 17⁰GS, 17ᴾGS, 16⁰HY, 16⁹G,

	Starts	1st	2nd	3rd	Win & Pl
Hurdles	8	1	0	1	4469
Career Total	**33**	**5**	**5**	**4**	**17677**
104	5/02	Towc	2m	D(0-120)HHdl	SFT £3740
104	10/01	Sthl	2m	F(0-105)HHdl	GD £2240
102	1/01	Leic	2m	F Hdl	HVY £2646
101	1/01	Leic	2m	G(0-90)HHdl	HVY £1967
89	10/00	Towc	2m	G Hdl	G-S £1575
			Total win prize-money £12169		

Going: Sf: 1-3 GS: 0-3 Gd: 0-2 GF: - Fm: 0-0
Distance: 2m/2m3: 1-8 2m4-2m7: 0-0 3m+: 0-0
Track: LH: 0-2 RH: 1-6 Tight: 0-1 Gall: 0-2
Aids: Bl: 0-0 Vi: 0-0 Tstrap: 1-8
Best Rating: 104   5/02   Towc   2m   good   Hdl

Plating-class hurdler, suited by a right-handed track and soft ground.

Boring Goring (IRE)

104(107h)   (90h)90

9-y-o b g Aristocracy-Coolrusk (IRE) (Millfontaine)
Miss A M Newton-Smith The Goring Hotel and S Gordon-Watson

Placings:40/0P2P54/44FF/PUF2161-0B4320   (4429)
2002/03: 24⁰GF, 20⁸G, 20⁴G, 20³GF, 25²GF, 21⁰GF,

	Starts	1st	2nd	3rd	Win & Pl
Hurdles	3	0	0	0	459
Chases	3	0	1	1	1874
Career Total	**25**	**2**	**3**	**1**	**9850**
90	3/02 Plum	2m5f	E Hdl	GD	£2719
90	11/01 Extr	2m6f110yF(0-100)HHdl	G-F	£2727
		Total win prize-money £5447		

Going: Sf: 0-0 GS: 0-0 Gd: 0-2 GF: - Fm: 0-4
Distance: 2m/2m3: 0-0 2m4-2m7: 0-4 3m+: 0-2
Track: LH: 0-4 RH: 0-1 Tight: 0-3 Gall: 0-0
Aids: Bl: 0-0 Vi: 0-0 Tstrap: 0-6
Best Rating: 95   2/99   Folk   2m1f110y   soft   NHF

Moderate hurdler; controversial winner at Exeter in

November 2001; scored on his own merits at Plumpton over Easter; has shown ability over fences; stays two miles five furlongs; likes good/fast ground.

Born Of Fubar

88

9-y-o gr g North Col-Scallykath (Scallywag)
B J M Ryall B J M Ryall

Placings:06/3F/5000F-P   (0609)
2002/03: 16ᴾGF,

	Starts	1st	2nd	3rd	Win & Pl
Hurdles	1	0	0	0	
Career Total	10	0	0	1	391

Going: Sf: 0-0 GS: 0-0 Gd: 0-0 GF: - Fm: 0-1
Distance: 2m/2m3: 0-1 2m4-2m7: 0-0 3m+: 0-0
Track: LH: 0-1 RH: 0-0 Tight: 0-0 Gall: 0-0
Aids: Bl: 0-0 Vi: 0-0 Tstrap: 0-0
Best Rating: 93   11/99   Tntn   2m1f   good   Hdl

Borora

70   54

4-y-o gr g Shareef Dancer (USA)-Bustling Nelly (Bustino)
D E Cantillon (I A Balding 3/10) Mrs E M Clarke

Placings:0   (2182)
2002/03: 16⁰GS,

	Starts	1st	2nd	3rd	Win & Pl
Hurdles	1	0	0	0	
Career Total	1	0	0	0	

Going: Sf: 0-0 GS: 0-1 Gd: 0-0 GF: - Fm: 0-0
Distance: 2m/2m3: 0-1 2m4-2m7: 0-0 3m+: 0-0
Track: LH: 0-1 RH: 0-0 Tight: 0-0 Gall: 0-0
Aids: Bl: 0-0 Vi: 0-0 Tstrap: 0-0
Best Rating: 57   11/02   Weth   2m   gd-sft   Hdl

Borrisheen Bay

83

8-y-o b g Arctic Lord-Soraway (Choral Society)
Mrs Richard Arthur Mrs Richard Arthur

Placings:FF6P6F20P6-P   (0066)
2002/03: 21ᴾGF,

	Starts	1st	2nd	3rd	Win & Pl
Hurdles	1	0	0	0	
Career Total	11	0	1	0	780

Going: Sf: 0-0 GS: 0-0 Gd: 0-0 GF: - Fm: 0-1
Distance: 2m/2m3: 0-0 2m4-2m7: 0-1 3m+: 0-0
Track: LH: 0-1 RH: 0-0 Tight: 0-1 Gall: 0-0
Aids: Bl: 0-0 Vi: 0-0 Tstrap: 0-1
Best Rating: 83   11/01   Catt   3m1f110y   gd-fm   Hdl

Maiden hurdler.

Bosphorus

58f

4-y-o b g Polish Precedent (USA)-Ancara (Dancing Brave (USA))
D G Bridgwater Led Astray Again Partnership

Placings:0   (2574)
2002/03: 12⁰G,

	Starts	1st	2nd	3rd	Win & Pl
NH Flat	1	0	0	0	

Career Total   1   0   0   0

Going:	Sf: 0-0 GS: 0-0 Gd: 0-1 GF: - Fm: 0-0
Distance:	2m/2m3: 0-0 2m4-2m7: 0-0 3m+: 0-0
Track:	LH: 0-1 RH: 0-0 Tight: 0-0 Gall: 0-0
Aids:	Bl: 0-0 Vi: 0-0 Tstrap: 0-0
Best Rating:	58 12/02 Newb 1m4f110y good NHF

Boss Doyle (IRE)
110   157

11-y-o b g Lapierre-Prolific Scot (Northern Guest (USA))
M F Morris Mrs A M Daly

Placings:4221201/**1111211F**/242P0/14215/P153225/1320-242   **(2812a)**
2002/03: 25²GS, 24⁴S, 24²HY,

	Starts	1st	2nd	3rd	Win & Pl
Hurdles	3	0	2	0	13928
Career Total	39	12	12	2	169691
158 11/01	Weth	3m1f	A Hdl	GD	£13200
153 10/00	Weth	3m1f	A Hdl	SFT	£13200
140 1/00	Leop	2m6f	(0-140)HHdl	YLD	£4692
152 11/99	Navn	3m	HHdl	Y-S	£7392
166 4/98	Aint	3m1f	A Ch	SFT	£26344
144 3/98	Fair	3m1f	HCh	YLD	£8739
156 12/97	Leop	3m	Ch	HVY	£6782
130 10/97	Gowr	2m2f	Ch	G-F	£3051
112 10/97	Thur	2m6f	Ch	YLD	£2543
110 9/97	List	2m6f	Ch	G-Y	£4069
116 3/97	Thur	3m	Hdl	GD	£2712
118 1/97	Thur	2m	Hdl	GD	£2204
			Total win prize-money £94931		

Going:	Sf: 0-2 GS: 0-1 Gd: 0-0 GF: - Fm: 0-0
Distance:	2m/2m3: 0-0 2m4-2m7: 0-0 3m+: 0-3
Track:	LH: 0-3 RH: 0-0 Tight: 0-0 Gall: 0-1
Aids:	Bl: 0-3 Vi: 0-0 Tstrap: 0-0
Best Rating:	166 4/98 Aint 3m1f soft Ch

High-class hurdler; proved a revelation when switched to fences, scoring six of his first seven outings; his lack of size and scope made life tougher at the top level and he reverted successfully to hurdles in the 1999/2000 season; won the West Yorkshire Hurdle at Wetherby in 2000 & 2001; best when fresh; liked cut in the ground; stayed three miles one; has been retired.

Boss Morton (IRE)
101   70

12-y-o b g Tremblant-Sandy Kelly (Ovac (ITY))
S G Chadwick S Chadwick

Placings:0051F000/4/U0U0P/FU0P2316F33402P/6UU/003F/00600P-3022   **(4710)**
2002/03: 17³HY, 19⁴GF, 20²GF, 23²GF,

	Starts	1st	2nd	3rd	Win & Pl
Hurdles	4	0	2	1	1728
Career Total	46	2	4	5	11872
89 7/98	Klny	2m1f	(0-102)HCh	G-F	£3288
107 9/95	Gway	2m	Hdl	G-F	£3391
			Total win prize-money £6679		

Going:	Sf: 0-1 GS: 0-0 Gd: 0-0 GF: - Fm: 0-3
Distance:	2m/2m3: 0-1 2m4-2m7: 0-3 3m+: 0-0
Track:	LH: 0-3 RH: 0-1 Tight: 0-2 Gall: 0-0
Aids:	Bl: 0-0 Vi: 0-0 Tstrap: 0-4
Best Rating:	107 9/95 Gway 2m gd-fm Hdl

Boss Royal

(103h)   (90h)**77**

6-y-o ch g Afzal-Born Bossy (Eborneezer)

S T Lewis (S E H Sherwood 10/2) W E Catstrey

Placings:P/0003P341-**PFU**   **(4346)**
2002/03: 22PGF, 19FG, 16UGF,

	Starts	1st	2nd	3rd	Win & Pl
Hurdles	1	0	0	0	0
Chases	2	0	0	0	0
Career Total	12	1	0	2	6022
90 4/02	Bang	2m4f	F(0-100)HHdl	GD	£5245
			Total win prize-money £5246		

Going:	Sf: 0-0 GS: 0-0 Gd: 0-1 GF: - Fm: 0-2
Distance:	2m/2m3: 0-2 2m4-2m7: 0-1 3m+: 0-0
Track:	LH: 0-1 RH: 0-2 Tight: 0-0 Gall: 0-0
Aids:	Bl: 0-0 Vi: 0-0 Tstrap: 0-3
Best Rating:	90 4/02 Bang 2m4f good Hdl

Very modest hurdler, likes to front run. Appreciated the step up to two and a half miles when getting off the mark in a handicap at Bangor in April and will make a chaser in time.

Boss Tweed (IRE)
95   91

6-y-o b g Persian Bold-Betty Kenwood (Dominion)
B Mactaggart Graeme Renton

Placings:02-46   **(4762)**
2002/03: 16⁴G, 16⁶G,

	Starts	1st	2nd	3rd	Win & Pl
Hurdles	2	0	0	0	640
Career Total	4	0	1	0	1832

Going:	Sf: 0-0 GS: 0-0 Gd: 0-2 GF: - Fm: 0-0
Distance:	2m/2m3: 0-2 2m4-2m7: 0-0 3m+: 0-0
Track:	LH: 0-1 RH: 0-1 Tight: 0-1 Gall: 0-0
Aids:	Bl: 0-0 Vi: 0-0 Tstrap: 0-2
Best Rating:	104 5/02 Kels 2m110y good Hdl

Plating-class hurdler; suited by good ground; only raced at two miles; usually wears tongue tie.

Boston Lass
107(99h)   (72h)**85**

6-y-o br m Terimon-Larksmore (Royal Fountain)
R D E Woodhouse M K Oldham

Placings:4004P063-0452302**P**   **(4170)**
2002/03: 24⁰GF, 25⁴GF, 24⁵S, 21²S, 20⁰GS, 21²HY, 21PS,

	Starts	1st	2nd	3rd	Win & Pl
Hurdles	6	0	1	1	1425
Chases	2	0	1	0	1710
Career Total	16	0	2	2	3484

Going:	Sf: 0-5 GS: 0-1 Gd: 0-0 GF: - Fm: 0-0
Distance:	2m/2m3: 0-0 2m4-2m7: 0-4 3m+: 0-4
Track:	LH: 0-6 RH: 0-2 Tight: 0-4 Gall: 0-0
Aids:	Bl: 0-0 Vi: 0-0 Tstrap: 0-0
Best Rating:	85 2/03 Sedg 2m5f heavy Ch

Moderate hurdler/chaser; stays three miles, but may prefer shorter; suited by soft.

Bosuns Mate

10-y-o ch g Yachtsman (USA)-Langton Lass (Nearly A Hand)
M Keighley M Keighley

Placings:41/1211200/0U361231/FPPF032/P1656-123   **(4059)**
2002/03: 20¹S, 23²GS, 26³GS,

	Starts	1st	2nd	3rd	Win & Pl
Chases	3	1	1	1	4271
Career Total	32	8	5	4	72304
90 2/03	Sand	2m4f110yH Ch		SFT	£2373
126 10/01	Extr	3m1f110yD(0-120)HCh		G-F	£5440
145 4/00	Sand	3m110y B Ch		SFT	£16883
145 3/00	Bang	3m110y D Ch		GD	£4719
137 1/99	Newb	3m110y C Hdl		HVY	£4781
137 12/98	Chel	3m A Hdl		GD	£9375
113 5/98	Worc	2m H NHF		G-F	£1560
101 3/98	Ludl	2m H NHF		GD	£1203
			Total win prize-money £46336		

Going:	Sf: 1-1 GS: 0-2 Gd: 0-0 GF: - Fm: 0-0
Distance:	2m/2m3: 0-0 2m4-2m7: 1-1 3m+: 0-2
Track:	LH: 0-1 RH: 1-2 Tight: 0-0 Gall: 0-0
Aids:	Bl: 0-0 Vi: 0-0 Tstrap: 0-0
Best Rating:	145 4/00 Sand 3m110y soft Ch

Smart novice chaser in 1999-2000; now a useful hunter chaser; possibly best in the spring; stays well and won a fair hunter chase at Sandown in February 2003; acts on any ground.

Bosworth Boy

5-y-o b g Deploy-Krill (Kris)
Ian Williams John L Marriott

Placings:630-0   **(2322)**
2002/03: 17⁰S,

	Starts	1st	2nd	3rd	Win & Pl
Hurdles	1	0	0	0	
Career Total	4	0	0	1	387

Going:	Sf: 0-1 GS: 0-0 Gd: 0-0 GF: - Fm: 0-0
Distance:	2m/2m3: 0-1 2m4-2m7: 0-0 3m+: 0-0
Track:	LH: 0-0 RH: 0-1 Tight: 0-1 Gall: 0-0
Aids:	Bl: 0-0 Vi: 0-0 Tstrap: 0-0
Best Rating:	87 4/02 Asct 2m110y gd-fm NHF

Bouchasson (FR)
113   129

10-y-o b g Big John (FR)-Kizil Ayak (FR) (Stratege (USA))
P J Hobbs Allan Stennett

Placings:051P/0311/42234U4/5P03/00312000-2U266   **(1548)**
2002/03: 24²GF, 26UG, 24²GS, 23RG, 24⁶F,

	Starts	1st	2nd	3rd	Win & Pl
Chases	5	0	2	0	8335
Career Total	32	4	5	4	83024
129 11/01	Kemp	2m4f110yB(0-140)HCh	GD	£8999
144 4/99	Punc	2m4f HCh	YLD	£12718
144 4/99	Ayr	2m4f A Ch	SFT	£15840
1/98	Cagn	2m110y HHdl	GD	£6566
		Total win prize-money £44124		

Going:	Sf: 0-0 GS: 0-1 Gd: 0-2 GF: - Fm: 0-2
Distance:	2m/2m3: 0-0 2m4-2m7: 0-0 3m+: 0-5
Track:	LH: 0-3 RH: 0-2 Tight: 0-1 Gall: 0-0
Aids:	Bl: 0-3 Vi: 0-2 Tstrap: 0-0
Best Rating:	144 4/99 Punc 2m4f yield Ch

Useful chaser; benefited from a drop in the handicap when winning at Kempton in November 2001; rising back up the weights again seems to have found him out; effective at up to three miles; suited by right-handed tracks..

Boulevard Bay (IRE)
96   84

12-y-o b g Royal Fountain-Cairita (Pitcairn)

Mrs P Robeson Mrs P Robeson

Placings:0/F0FP3P1316/41/3623/55500613-2   (0110)
2002/03: 16²GS,

	Starts	1st	2nd	3rd	Win & Pl
Chases	1	0	1	0	1060
Career Total	26	4	2	5	18536
80	2/02	Leic	2m	F(0-90)HCh	SFT	£3010
106	11/99	Towc	2m110y	D(0-120)HCh	GD	£3722
107	3/99	Ling	2m	F(0-110)HCh	G-S	£3501
107	2/99	Leic	2m1f	E Ch	G-S	£3080

Total win prize-money £13313

Going: Sf: 0-0 GS: 0-1 Gd: 0-0 GF: - Fm: 0-0
Distance: 2m/2m3: 0-1 2m4-2m7: 0-0 3m+: 0-0
Track: LH: 0-0 RH: 0-0 Tight: 0-0 Gall: 0-0
Aids: Bl: 0-1 Vi: 0-0 Tstrap: 0-0
Best Rating: 110 1/99 Leic   2m4f110y   gd-sft   Ch

Fair chaser, he acts on ground with some ease, but cannot cope with very soft ground and is most effective over two miles.

Boulta (IRE)

9-y-o ch g Commanche Run-Boulta View (Beau Chapeau)
Mrs Clare Moore (J S Haldane 7/7) Mrs Clare Moore

Placings:0-250P02   (4506)
2002/03: 20²GF, 25⁵GF, 26⁹GS, 20⁰G, 25⁰S, 25²G,

	Starts	1st	2nd	3rd	Win & Pl
Chases	6	0	2	0	1720
Career Total	7	0	2	0	1720

Going: Sf: 0-1 GS: 0-1 Gd: 0-2 GF: - Fm: 0-2
Distance: 2m/2m3: 0-0 2m4-2m7: 0-2 3m+: 0-4
Track: LH: 0-4 RH: 0-2 Tight: 0-5 Gall: 0-0
Aids: Bl: 0-0 Vi: 0-0 Tstrap: 0-0
Best Rating: 91 5/02 Prth   2m4f110y   gd-fm   Ch

Modest hunter chaser; handles any ground; has worn a tongue tie and cheekpieces.

Bounce Back (USA)

108(115h)   (153h)146

7-y-o ch g Trempolino (USA)-Lattaquie (FR) (Fast Topaze (USA))
M C Pipe Mrs Belinda Harvey

Placings:21F/1332224/2321433561-0P6   (4791)
2002/03: 26⁹GS, 29²HY, 29⁶G,

	Starts	1st	2nd	3rd	Win & Pl
Chases	3	0	0	0	2250
Career Total	23	4	6	5	257757
156	4/02	Sand	3m5f110yA HCh	GD	£72500
139	12/01	Chep	2m3f110yD Ch	SFT	£4124
	5/00	Autl	2m3f110y Hdl	VS	£28818
	3/00	Engh	2m2f	Hdl	HLD	£11527

Total win prize-money £116969

Going: Sf: 0-1 GS: 0-1 Gd: 0-1 GF: - Fm: 0-0
Distance: 2m/2m3: 0-0 2m4-2m7: 0-0 3m+: 0-3
Track: LH: 0-2 RH: 0-1 Tight: 0-0 Gall: 0-1
Aids: Bl: 0-0 Vi: 0-0 Tstrap: 0-0
Best Rating: 156 4/02 Sand   3m5f110y   good   Ch

Smart chaser; formerly a high-class hurdler in France; won a novice chase at Chepstow in December 2001; did not look a natural over fences; after a couple of runs over hurdles, he proved a revelation when stepped up to three miles five in the Attheraces Gold Cup at Sandown in April 2002; well held in light campaign in 2002/3; ideally suited by at least three miles; acts on good and soft ground.

Bound

116   124

5-y-o b g Kris-Tender Moment (IRE) (Caerleon (USA))
Mrs L Wadham Dingley Dell Racing Ltd

Placings:3P203112-3023000   (4323)
2002/03: 16³GF, 16⁰GF, 16²G, 17³G, 16⁹HY, 16⁰G,

	Starts	1st	2nd	3rd	Win & Pl
Hurdles	7	0	1	2	5896
Career Total	15	2	3	4	15252
110	4/02	Plum	2m	E Hdl	G-F	£2698
106	3/02	MRas	2m1f110yD Hdl	G-S	£3672

Total win prize-money £6372

Going: Sf: 0-1 GS: 0-0 Gd: 0-4 GF: - Fm: 0-2
Distance: 2m/2m3: 0-7 2m4-2m7: 0-0 3m+: 0-0
Track: LH: 0-5 RH: 0-2 Tight: 0-0 Gall: 0-2
Aids: Bl: 0-0 Vi: 0-0 Tstrap: 0-7
Best Rating: 124 12/02 Chel   2m1f   good   Hdl

Fair handicap hurdler; suited by forcing tactics; effective over two miles; acts on fast and easy ground; wears a tongue tie.

Boundtohonour (IRE)

79(90h)   (35h)46

11-y-o b g Rashar (USA)-Densidal (Tanfirion)
Ian Williams Newhaven Racing Club

Placings:3006/40P/F5P0P/F2166154/33PP51P450/6PP-000P   (4409)
2002/03: 27⁰G, 26⁹GS, 20⁰G, 25⁰G,

	Starts	1st	2nd	3rd	Win & Pl
Hurdles	2	0	0	0	0
Chases	2	0	0	0	0
Career Total	37	3	1	3	11180
94	12/00	Hntg	3m	F(0-110)HCh	HVY	£2925
90	3/00	Sedg	2m5f	F(0-110)HCh	G-F	£3500
94	12/99	Folk	2m6f110yF(0-105)HHdl	SFT	£1960

Total win prize-money £8385

Going: Sf: 0-0 GS: 0-1 Gd: 0-3 GF: - Fm: 0-0
Distance: 2m/2m3: 0-0 2m4-2m7: 0-1 3m+: 0-3
Track: LH: 0-2 RH: 0-2 Tight: 0-1 Gall: 0-2
Aids: Bl: 0-0 Vi: 0-2 Tstrap: 0-0
Best Rating: 94 12/00 Hntg   3m   heavy   Ch

Bourbon Manhattan

119f   136f

5-y-o b g Alflora (IRE)-Vanina Ii (FR) (Italic (FR))
A King Susan And Vanessa Clinton

Placings:116   (4115)
2002/03: 17¹GS, 16¹S, 16⁶G,

	Starts	1st	2nd	3rd	Win & Pl
NH Flat	3	2	0	0	6284
Career Total	3	2	0	0	6284
129	3/03	Newb	2m110y	H NHF	SFT	£3248
110	11/02	Tntn	2m1f	H NHF	G-S	£2436

Total win prize-money £5684

Going: Sf: 1-1 GS: 1-1 Gd: 0-1 GF: - Fm: 0-0
Distance: 2m/2m3: 2-3 2m4-2m7: 0-0 3m+: 0-0
Track: LH: 1-2 RH: 0-0 Tight: 0-0 Gall: 1-1
Aids: Bl: 0-0 Vi: 0-0 Tstrap: 0-0
Best Rating: 134 3/03 Chel   2m110y   good   NHF

Very useful bumper horse, winner of first two starts and sixth at Cheltenham.

Bow Rocky

10-y-o b g Failiq (FR)-Just Maunby (Derek H)
Mrs J A Saunders Roy Hartop

Placings:4   (1755)
2002/03: 16⁴G,

	Starts	1st	2nd	3rd	Win & Pl
Chases	1	0	0	0	361
Career Total	1	0	0	0	361

Going: Sf: 0-0 GS: 0-0 Gd: 0-1 GF: - Fm: 0-0
Distance: 2m/2m3: 0-1 2m4-2m7: 0-0 3m+: 0-0
Track: LH: 0-1 RH: 0-0 Tight: 0-0 Gall: 0-0
Aids: Bl: 0-0 Vi: 0-0 Tstrap: 0-0
Best Rating: 0   11/02 Wwck   2m110y   good   Ch

Bow Strada

112(114h)   (135h)136

6-y-o ch g Rainbow Quest (USA)-La Strada (Niniski (USA))
P J Hobbs M J Tuckey

Placings:23/11F01-2231014   (4554)
2002/03: 20²GF, 17²G, 19³G, 16¹GF, 21⁰G, 19¹G, 20⁴G,

	Starts	1st	2nd	3rd	Win & Pl
Hurdles	2	0	1	0	2200
Chases	5	2	1	1	13598
Career Total	14	5	3	2	31351
136	3/03	Asct	2m3f110yD Ch	GD	£5356
130	11/02	Leic	2m	E Ch	G-F	£4046
135	4/02	Extr	2m3f	D(0-125)HHdl	FRM	£3575
121	12/01	Tntn	2m1f	D Hdl	G-S	£5528
123	12/01	Donc	2m110y	E Hdl	GD	£3290

Total win prize-money £21795

Going: Sf: 0-0 GS: 0-0 Gd: 1-5 GF: - Fm: 1-2
Distance: 2m/2m3: 1-2 2m4-2m7: 1-5 3m+: 0-0
Track: LH: 0-3 RH: 2-4 Tight: 0-0 Gall: 0-1
Aids: Bl: 0-0 Vi: 0-0 Tstrap: 0-0
Best Rating: 136 3/03 Asct   2m3f110y   good   Ch

Useful handicap hurdler/novice chaser; stays two and a half miles; suited by a sound surface.

Bowcliffe Court (IRE)

98   64

11-y-o b g Slip Anchor-Res Nova (USA) (Blushing Groom (FR))
G H Jones John Priday Construction Ltd

Placings:P130/6443/511/P600-0   (0074)
2002/03: 17⁰GF,

	Starts	1st	2nd	3rd	Win & Pl
Hurdles	1	0	0	0	
Career Total	16	3	0	2	10295
113	12/98	Leic	2m	E(0-110)HHdl	SFT	£3028
104	12/98	Leic	2m	E(0-110)HHdl	G-S	£2206
98	12/96	Chep	2m110y	D Hdl	SFT	£2693

Total win prize-money £7928

Going: Sf: 0-0 GS: 0-0 Gd: 0-0 GF: - Fm: 0-1
Distance: 2m/2m3: 0-1 2m4-2m7: 0-0 3m+: 0-0
Track: LH: 0-0 RH: 0-1 Tight: 0-0 Gall: 0-0
Aids: Bl: 0-0 Vi: 0-0 Tstrap: 0-1
Best Rating: 113 12/98 Leic   2m   soft   Hdl

Bowden Vulcan

80f   54f

5-y-o b g Royal Vulcan-No Grandad (Strong Gale)

B N Pollock C M Wilson

Placings:0   (4322)
2002/03: 17⁰G,

	Starts	1st	2nd	3rd	Win & Pl
NH Flat	1	0	0	0	
Career Total	1	0	0	0	

Going:	Sf: 0-0 GS: 0-0 Gd: 0-1 GF: - Fm: 0-0
Distance:	2m/2m3: 0-1 2m4-2m7: 0-0 3m+: 0-0
Track:	LH: 0-1 RH: 0-0 Tight: 0-1 Gall: 0-0
Aids:	Bl: 0-0 Vi: 0-0 Tstrap: 0-0
Best Rating:	54 3/03 Bang 2m1f good NHF

Bowleaze (IRE)
98f   94+f
4-y-o br g Right Win (IRE)-Mrs Cullen (Over The River (FR))
R H Alner Martin Short

Placings:1   (4601)
2002/03: 17¹GF,

	Starts	1st	2nd	3rd	Win & Pl
NH Flat	1	1	0	0	3262
Career Total	1	1	0	0	3262
91	4/03 Extr	2m1f	H NHF		G-F £3262
			Total win prize-money £3262

Going:	Sf: 0-0 GS: 0-0 Gd: 0-0 GF: - Fm: 1-1
Distance:	2m/2m3: 1-1 2m4-2m7: 0-0 3m+: 0-0
Track:	LH: 0-0 RH: 1-1 Tight: 0-0 Gall: 0-0
Aids:	Bl: 0-0 Vi: 0-0 Tstrap: 0-0
Best Rating:	91 4/03 Extr 2m1f gd-fm NHF

Easy winner of six-runner fast ground bumper on his debut at Exeter April 2003.

Bowles Patrol (IRE)
100(91h)   (75h)95
11-y-o gr g Roselier (FR)-Another Dud (Le Bavard (FR))
John R Upson Bill Ellis

Placings:00F3/00022/3/UP12134414/12235FP31/1U36523
5/0P61103-545F   (4259)
2002/03: 24⁵GS, 27⁴GS, 25⁵G, 27⁷FG,

	Starts	1st	2nd	3rd	Win & Pl
Chases	4	0	0	0	530
Career Total	48	8	6	8	38159
103	12/01 Tntn	3m	F(0-105)HCh	G-S	£3802
98	11/01 Sedg	3m3f	F(0-105)HCh	SFT	£2863
111	5/00 Hntg	2m5f110yF(0-110)HHdl		SFT	£2710
112	4/00 MRas	2m5f110yF(0-100)HHdl		SFT	£1542
101	11/99 NAbb	2m5f110yF(0-100)HCh		SFT	£3120
107	3/99 Newb	2m5f	E(0-115)HNHF		SFT	£3057
91	12/98 Plum	3m110y	(0-105)HHdl	G-S	£2775
86	11/98 Carl	2m4f110yE(0-100)HHdl		SFT	£2402
			Total win prize-money £22274

Going:	Sf: 0-0 GS: 0-2 Gd: 0-2 GF: - Fm: 0-0
Distance:	2m/2m3: 0-0 2m4-2m7: 0-0 3m+: 0-4
Track:	LH: 0-2 RH: 0-2 Tight: 0-3 Gall: 0-1
Aids:	Bl: 0-0 Vi: 0-0 Tstrap: 0-0
Best Rating:	112 1/01 Leic 2m4f110y heavy Hdl

Staying chaser, genuine if a little one-paced.

Bowling Beauty
77   36
5-y-o br m Alderbrook-Bowling Fort (Bowling Pin)
Miss S E Forster A G & Mrs E J Bell

Placings:6   (4411)

2002/03: 16⁶G,

	Starts	1st	2nd	3rd	Win & Pl
NH Flat	1	0	0	0	0
Career Total	1	0	0	0	0

Going:	Sf: 0-0 GS: 0-0 Gd: 0-1 GF: - Fm: 0-0
Distance:	2m/2m3: 0-1 2m4-2m7: 0-0 3m+: 0-0
Track:	LH: 0-1 RH: 0-0 Tight: 0-0 Gall: 0-0
Aids:	Bl: 0-0 Vi: 0-0 Tstrap: 0-0
Best Rating:	76 3/03 Hexm 2m110y good NHF

Box Builder
(104h)   (110h)72
6-y-o ch g Fraam-Ena Olley (Le Moss)
B G Powell M Hutchinson

Placings:4025-122410P   (2373)
2002/03: 20¹G, 20²GS, 24²GF, 23⁴G, 22¹GF, 21⁰GS, 26⁵GS,

	Starts	1st	2nd	3rd	Win & Pl
Hurdles	5	2	2	0	8198
Chases	2	0	0	0	311
Career Total	11	2	3	0	9284
102	8/02 NAbb	2m6f	E Hdl	G-F	£2898
110	5/02 Aint	2m4f	D Hdl	GD	£3588
			Total win prize-money £6486

Going:	Sf: 0-0 GS: 0-3 Gd: 1-2 GF: - Fm: 1-2
Distance:	2m/2m3: 0-0 2m4-2m7: 2-4 3m+: 0-3
Track:	LH: 2-7 RH: 0-0 Tight: 2-2 Gall: 0-1
Aids:	Bl: 0-0 Vi: 0-0 Tstrap: 2-7
Best Rating:	110 6/02 Worc 3m gd-fm Hdl

Plating-class hurdler; effective at around two miles six furlongs; acts on a sound surface; did not take to chasing when tried in August 2002; regularly tongue tied.

Boxer's Double
83(87c)   (49c)56
6-y-o ch g Petoski-Grayrose Double (Celtic Cone)
G A Ham K C White

Placings:6000PP-P05340060R   (4627)
2002/03: 20⁰GF, 20⁰G, 19⁵F, 19³F, 19⁴G, 16⁹GS, 16⁰HY, 19⁶GS, 24⁰F, 21⁶GF,

	Starts	1st	2nd	3rd	Win & Pl
Hurdles	8	0	0	1	278
Chases	2	0	0	0	0
Career Total	16	0	0	1	278

Going:	Sf: 0-1 GS: 0-2 Gd: 0-2 GF: - Fm: 0-5
Distance:	2m/2m3: 0-3 2m4-2m7: 0-6 3m+: 0-1
Track:	LH: 0-4 RH: 0-6 Tight: 0-5 Gall: 0-0
Aids:	Bl: 0-1 Vi: 0-2 Tstrap: 0-0
Best Rating:	76 10/01 Hrfd 2m1f good NHF

Boyne Banks (IRE)
89   92d
8-y-o ch g Boyne Valley-Pallatess (Pall Mall)
N A Twiston-Davies James Cheetham

Placings:P-640P   (3824)
2002/03: 24⁶GS, 16⁴GS, 20⁰S, 26⁸GS,

	Starts	1st	2nd	3rd	Win & Pl
Chases	4	0	0	0	392
Career Total	5	0	0	0	392

Going:	Sf: 0-1 GS: 0-3 Gd: 0-0 GF: - Fm: 0-0
Distance:	2m/2m3: 0-1 2m4-2m7: 0-1 3m+: 0-2

Track:	LH: 0-3 RH: 0-1 Tight: 0-1 Gall: 0-0
Aids:	Bl: 0-0 Vi: 0-0 Tstrap: 0-0
Best Rating:	92 12/02 Wwck 3m110y gd-sft Ch

Boyzontoowa (IRE)
113
11-y-o b g Beau Sher-Lindabell (Over The River (FR))
W Storey John J Maguire

Placings:06000/12332P4/6F160012/PF01232/4133UP/4P2
-P   (2139)
2002/03: 20⁰GS,

	Starts	1st	2nd	3rd	Win & Pl
Hurdles	1	0	0	0	
Career Total	37	6	5	5	26802
110	6/00 Prth	3m	E(0-115)HCh	HVY	£4810
110	1/00 Catt	3m1f110yF(0-105)HCh	GD	£2730
99	4/99 Hexm	2m4f110yF(0-105)HCh	GD	£3160
88	12/98 Catt	2m3f	(0-120)HCh	GD	£3571
84	11/97 Hexm	2m4f110yG(0-90)HHdl	G-F	£1725
			Total win prize-money £15996

Going:	Sf: 0-0 GS: 0-1 Gd: 0-0 GF: - Fm: 0-0
Distance:	2m/2m3: 0-0 2m4-2m7: 0-1 3m+: 0-0
Track:	LH: 0-1 RH: 0-0 Tight: 0-0 Gall: 0-1
Aids:	Bl: 0-0 Vi: 0-0 Tstrap: 0-0
Best Rating:	110 11/00 Newc 2m4f soft Ch

Modest staying chaser; wins in his turn; best with some cut in the ground; consistent.

Bozo (IRE)
12-y-o b g Kefaah (USA)-Hossvend (Malinowski (USA))
N Parker (B J M Ryall 1/5) Mrs R E Parker

Placings:30/30022F20P/33PP30/321U415/02P3P0/24PP3
3P06-0P6   (4572)
2002/03: 19⁹G, 19³PF, 24⁶G,

	Starts	1st	2nd	3rd	Win & Pl
Chases	3	0	0	0	0
Career Total	42	2	6	9	21868
104	4/00 Ludl	2m4f	D(0-120)HCh	GD	£5476
108	11/99 Tntn	2m3f	C Ch	GD	£6045
			Total win prize-money £11522

Going:	Sf: 0-0 GS: 0-0 Gd: 0-2 GF: - Fm: 0-1
Distance:	2m/2m3: 0-0 2m4-2m7: 0-2 3m+: 0-1
Track:	LH: 0-1 RH: 0-2 Tight: 0-1 Gall: 0-0
Aids:	Bl: 0-0 Vi: 0-0 Tstrap: 0-0
Best Rating:	121 3/97 Chel 2m110y gd-fm NHF

Bracey Run (IRE)
103   106
13-y-o b g The Parson-Outdoor Ivy (Deep Run)
A J Lidderdale Bonusprint

Placings:2/31334P/FF/33203/311U/40004-41426   (1871)
2002/03: 17⁴S, 20¹GS, 20⁴S, 20²GS, 22⁶GS,

	Starts	1st	2nd	3rd	Win & Pl
Hurdles	5	1	1	0	3916
Career Total	28	4	3	7	24775
112	5/02 Sthl	2m4f110yE(0-105)HHdl	G-S	£2639
126	5/00 Uttx	2m4f110yB(0-140)HHdl	G-F	£6227
119	5/00 Hrfd	2m3f110yD(0-120)HHdl	GD	£3269
110	12/97 Towc	2m	E Hdl	SFT	£2705
			Total win prize-money £14842

Going:	Sf: 0-2 GS: 1-3 Gd: 0-0 GF: - Fm: 0-0
Distance:	2m/2m3: 0-1 2m4-2m7: 1-4 3m+: 0-0
Track:	LH: 1-5 RH: 0-0 Tight: 1-4 Gall: 0-0

Aids: BI: 0-0 Vi: 0-0 Tstrap: 0-0
Best Rating: 130 2/98 Chep 2m4f110y gd-sft Hdl

Modest veteran hurdler; on the downgrade; had slipped to a useful mark when winning moderate handicap at Southwell in May 2002; third in same race this time; acts on all types of ground.

Braceys Girl (IRE)
89   71
6-y-o b/br m Be My Native (USA)-Minigirls Niece (IRE) (Strong Gale)
D Brace David Brace

Placings:*360053-P0*   (1006)
2002/03: 20PS, 20QGF,

	Starts	1st	2nd	3rd	Win & Pl
Hurdles	2	0	0	0	
Career Total	8	0	0	2	810

Going: Sf: 0-1 GS: 0-0 Gd: 0-0 GF: - Fm: 0-1
Distance: 2m/2m3: 0-0 2m4-2m7: 0-2 3m+: 0-0
Track: LH: 0-2 RH: 0-0 Tight: 0-1 Gall: 0-0
Aids: BI: 0-0 Vi: 0-0 Tstrap: 0-1
Best Rating: 77 10/01 Chep 2m110y soft NHF

Bracken Fire

9-y-o b m Jupiter Island-Dragon Fire (Dragonara Palace (USA))
G F H Charles-Jones R A Hughes

Placings:*F6P0P*   (3777)
2002/03: 19FGS, 16RGS, 19PGS, 17QS, 17PGS,

	Starts	1st	2nd	3rd	Win & Pl
Hurdles	5	0	0	0	0
Career Total	5	0	0	0	0

Going: Sf: 0-1 GS: 0-4 Gd: 0-0 GF: - Fm: 0-0
Distance: 2m/2m3: 0-4 2m4-2m7: 0-1 3m+: 0-0
Track: LH: 0-0 RH: 0-5 Tight: 0-2 Gall: 0-0
Aids: BI: 0-0 Vi: 0-0 Tstrap: 0-0
Best Rating: 0 2/03 Extr 2m1f gd-sft Hdl

Brackenheath (IRE)

12-y-o b g Le Moss-Stable Lass (Golden Love)
Mrs D M Grissell John Grist

Placings:*0220/F142120/P022F240/3F5/PP/1R-3P* (3562)
2002/03: 21³G, 25PS,

	Starts	1st	2nd	3rd	Win & Pl
Chases	2	0	0	1	282
Career Total	28	3	7	2	24850
100 5/01 Folk	3m2f	H Ch		GD	£1462
118 2/98 Folk	2m6f110yE Hdl		G-F	£2731
109 11/97 Asct	3m	C Hdl		SFT	£3582
			Total win prize-money £7778		

Going: Sf: 0-1 GS: 0-0 Gd: 0-1 GF: - Fm: 0-0
Distance: 2m/2m3: 0-0 2m4-2m7: 0-1 3m+: 0-1
Track: LH: 0-0 RH: 0-2 Tight: 0-2 Gall: 0-0
Aids: BI: 0-2 Vi: 0-0 Tstrap: 0-0
Best Rating: 139 4/98 Aint 3m110y soft Hdl

Formerly useful hurdler.chaser, now hunter chasing. Best on a sound surface although handles softer, likes Folkestone.

Brackney Boy (IRE)
103   (92c)89
9-y-o b g Zaffaran (USA)-Donard Lily (Master Buck)
I A Duncan Dr Stephen Sinclair

Placings:*5220/001246-F60F30*   (4333a)
2002/03: 16FG, 20RS, 25DYS, 18FHY, 25³S, 24QGY,

	Starts	1st	2nd	3rd	Win & Pl
Hurdles	1	0	0	0	0
Chases	5	0	0	1	830
Career Total	16	1	3	1	13823
102 11/01 DRoy	2m6f	Hdl		YLD	£6677
			Total win prize-money £6677		

Going: Sf: 0-3 GS: 0-0 Gd: 0-1 GF: - Fm: 0-0
Distance: 2m/2m3: 0-2 2m4-2m7: 0-1 3m+: 0-3
Track: LH: 0-2 RH: 0-2 Tight: 0-1 Gall: 0-0
Aids: BI: 0-0 Vi: 0-0 Tstrap: 0-0
Best Rating: 112 11/01 Navn 3m yld-sft Hdl

Brad
94f   97f
5-y-o b g Deploy-Celia Brady (Last Tycoon)
P R Webber Mrs David Blackburn

Placings:*20-5*   (2178)
2002/03: 16⁵HY,

	Starts	1st	2nd	3rd	Win & Pl
NH Flat	1	0	0	0	0
Career Total	3	0	1	0	662

Going: Sf: 0-1 GS: 0-0 Gd: 0-0 GF: - Fm: 0-0
Distance: 2m/2m3: 0-1 2m4-2m7: 0-0 3m+: 0-0
Track: LH: 0-1 RH: 0-0 Tight: 0-0 Gall: 0-0
Aids: BI: 0-0 Vi: 0-0 Tstrap: 0-0
Best Rating: 97 11/02 Chep 2m110y heavy NHF

Showed promise in bumper on heavy ground.

Bradley My Boy (IRE)
93   81
7-y-o ch g Treasure Hunter-Clonaslee Baby (Konigssee)
Mrs A M Naughton (V Bowens 13/9) W M Wanless

Placings:*45/10050-000FP5*   (4616)
2002/03: 16DYS, 16QS, 16QGF, 18FG, 20PG, 175GF,

	Starts	1st	2nd	3rd	Win & Pl
Hurdles	5	0	0	0	0
Chases	1	0	0	0	0
Career Total	13	1	0	0	1886
103 5/01 NAbb	2m1f	H NHF		G-F	£1694
			Total win prize-money £1694		

Going: Sf: 0-1 GS: 0-0 Gd: 0-0 GF: 0-2 GF: - Fm: 0-0
Distance: 2m/2m3: 0-5 2m4-2m7: 0-1 3m+: 0-0
Track: LH: 0-2 RH: 0-1 Tight: 0-0 Gall: 0-0
Aids: BI: 0-0 Vi: 0-0 Tstrap: 0-3
Best Rating: 103 5/01 NAbb 2m1f gd-fm NHF

Moderate ex-Irish hurdler; poor form since arriving in Britain.

Bradley Wood
76   41
8-y-o b g Primitive Rising (USA)-Synonymous (New Member)
Mrs Jane Galpin H T Pelham

Placings:*0PUP*   (1798)

2002/03: 18QGF, 18PG, 17UF, 17PS,

	Starts	1st	2nd	3rd	Win & Pl
Hurdles	4	0	0	0	
Career Total	4	0	0	0	

Going: Sf: 0-1 GS: 0-0 Gd: 0-1 GF: - Fm: 0-2
Distance: 2m/2m3: 0-4 2m4-2m7: 0-0 3m+: 0-0
Track: LH: 0-3 RH: 0-1 Tight: 0-4 Gall: 0-0
Aids: BI: 0-2 Vi: 0-0 Tstrap: 0-0
Best Rating: 41 9/02 Font 2m2f110y gd-fm Hdl

Bradogue (IRE)

6-y-o b g Nucleon (USA)-Waweewawoo (IRE) (Rusticaro (FR))
F Lloyd F Lloyd

Placings:*P*   (2565)
2002/03: 17PGS,

	Starts	1st	2nd	3rd	Win & Pl
Hurdles	1	0	0	0	
Career Total	1	0	0	0	

Going: Sf: 0-0 GS: 0-1 Gd: 0-0 GF: - Fm: 0-0
Distance: 2m/2m3: 0-1 2m4-2m7: 0-0 3m+: 0-0
Track: LH: 0-1 RH: 0-0 Tight: 0-1 Gall: 0-0
Aids: BI: 0-0 Vi: 0-0 Tstrap: 0-1
Best Rating: 0 12/02 Bang 2m1f gd-sft Hdl

Brady Boys (USA)
98   87
6-y-o b g Cozzene (USA)-Elvia (USA) (Roberto (USA))
J G M O Shea D Cound and R Davies

Placings:*5P-4042010*   (4450)
2002/03: 17⁴G, 17QS, 16⁴S, 16²S, 16QS, 17¹HY, 21QG,

	Starts	1st	2nd	3rd	Win & Pl
Hurdles	7	1	1	0	3260
Career Total	9	1	1	0	3260
87 3/03 Tntn	2m1f	G Hdl		HVY	£2373
			Total win prize-money £2373		

Going: Sf: 1-5 GS: 0-0 Gd: 0-2 GF: - Fm: 0-0
Distance: 2m/2m3: 1-6 2m4-2m7: 0-1 3m+: 0-0
Track: LH: 0-2 RH: 1-5 Tight: 1-2 Gall: 0-0
Aids: BI: 0-0 Vi: 0-0 Tstrap: 0-0
Best Rating: 87 3/03 Tntn 2m1f heavy Hdl

Plating-class hurdler; inconsistent and runs best when fresh; acts on soft ground.

Braeburn
95
8-y-o b g Petoski-Great Granny Smith (Fine Blue)
R T Phillips Mrs T Stopford-Sackville

Placings:*2P-FP*   (4327)
2002/03: 16FS, 18PG,

	Starts	1st	2nd	3rd	Win & Pl
Chases	2	0	0	0	
Career Total	4	0	1	0	1242

Going: Sf: 0-1 GS: 0-0 Gd: 0-0 GF: - Fm: 0-0
Distance: 2m/2m3: 0-2 2m4-2m7: 0-0 3m+: 0-0
Track: LH: 0-1 RH: 0-1 Tight: 0-0 Gall: 0-1
Aids: BI: 0-0 Vi: 0-0 Tstrap: 0-0
Best Rating: 95 3/02 Ludl 3m gd-sft Ch

Bramblehill Duke (IRE)

113   **140**

11-y-o b g Kambalda-Scat-Cat (Furry Glen)
Miss Venetia Williams South Wales Shower Supplies T/a Faucets

Placings: *143P/11331/F2R21/5P1165/03P20-312000F*
                                              (4479)
2002/03: 24³GF, 24¹HY, 25²G, 26⁶S, 24⁰HY, 24⁰G, 36⁶G,

	Starts	1st	2nd	3rd	Win & Pl
Chases	7	1	1	1	18641
Career Total	32	8	4	5	64145

135	11/02	Bang	3m110y	C(0-130)HCh	HVY	£7377
135	1/01	Wwck	2m4f110yC(0-135)HCh	SFT	£8424
140	1/01	Uttx	2m4f	B(0-140)HCh	HVY	£10426
125	2/00	Hayd	2m6f	C Ch	HVY	£7315
119	11/98	Newb	2m5f	E(0-110)HHdl	GD	£3566
109	5/98	Towc	2m	E Hdl	G-F	£2460
109	5/98	Chep	2m110y	E(0-100)HHdl	GD	£2416
107	11/97	Hayd	2m	H NHF	GD	£1278
				Total win prize-money £43263		

Going: Sf: 1-3 GS: 0-0 Gd: 0-3 GF: - Fm: 0-1
Distance: 2m/2m3: 0-0 2m4-2m7: 0-0 3m+: 1-7
Track: LH: 1-6 RH: 0-1 Tight: 1-2 Gall: 0-3
Aids: Bl: 0-0 Vi: 0-0 Tstrap: 0-0
Best Rating: 140 12/02 Chel 3m1f110y good Ch

Useful handicap chaser; stays three miles, although effective at shorter; acts on most types of ground.

Bramlynn Brook (FR)

102f   **100f**

5-y-o ch g Apple Tree (FR)-Sainte Lys (FR) (Don Roberto (USA))
Miss Venetia Williams Christopher Drury

Placings: *522*   (3556)
2002/03: 12⁵GS, 17²GS, 18²HY,

	Starts	1st	2nd	3rd	Win & Pl
NH Flat	3	0	2	0	1665
Career Total	3	0	2	0	1665

Going: Sf: 0-1 GS: 0-2 Gd: 0-0 GF: - Fm: 0-0
Distance: 2m/2m3: 0-0 2m4-2m7: 0-0 3m+: 0-0
Track: LH: 0-3 RH: 0-0 Tight: 0-1 Gall: 0-0
Aids: Bl: 0-0 Vi: 0-0 Tstrap: 0-0
Best Rating: 100 2/03 Plum 2m2f heavy NHF

Moderate bumper performer; runner-up behind a useful sort in a bumper at Bangor in December on only second start-again filled that position at Plumpton in February.; looks essentially a stayer; acts well on soft ground; should improve on what he has done so far.

Brand New Dance

9-y-o b g Gildoran-Starawak (Star Appeal)
D J Wintle J P Dickinson

Placings: *23/P-P*   (0217)
2002/03: 17⁰G,

	Starts	1st	2nd	3rd	Win & Pl
Hurdles	1	0	0	0	
Career Total	4	0	1	1	976

Going: Sf: 0-0 GS: 0-0 Gd: 0-1 GF: - Fm: 0-0

Distance: 2m/2m3: 0-1 2m4-2m7: 0-0 3m+: 0-0
Track: LH: 0-0 RH: 0-1 Tight: 0-0 Gall: 0-0
Aids: Bl: 0-0 Vi: 0-0 Tstrap: 0-1
Best Rating: 115 9/00 Rosc 2m good Hdl

Brandsby Stripe

100(94h)   (72h)**69**

8-y-o ch g Nomadic Way (USA)-I m Fine (Fitzwilliam (USA))
P Beaumont Brandsby Racing 2

Placings: *0/60P4*   (4108)
2002/03: 17⁶HY, 19⁰GS, 20⁴HY, 17⁴S,

	Starts	1st	2nd	3rd	Win & Pl
Hurdles	4	0	0	0	0
Career Total	5	0	0	0	0

Going: Sf: 0-3 GS: 0-1 Gd: 0-0 GF: - Fm: 0-0
Distance: 2m/2m3: 0-2 2m4-2m7: 0-2 3m+: 0-0
Track: LH: 0-2 RH: 0-2 Tight: 0-2 Gall: 0-0
Aids: Bl: 0-0 Vi: 0-0 Tstrap: 0-0
Best Rating: 74 3/03 Sedg 2m1f soft Hdl

Plating-class maiden hurdler.

Brankley Boy

87f   **108f**

5-y-o ch g Afzal-Needwood Fortune (Tycoon Ii)
N J Henderson Gary Stewart

Placings: *1*   (3644)
2002/03: 16¹GS,

	Starts	1st	2nd	3rd	Win & Pl
NH Flat	1	1	0	0	2468
Career Total	1	1	0	0	2468
108	2/03	Winc	2m	H NHF	G-S	£2467
				Total win prize-money £2468		

Going: Sf: 0-0 GS: 1-1 Gd: 0-0 GF: - Fm: 0-0
Distance: 2m/2m3: 1-1 2m4-2m7: 0-0 3m+: 0-0
Track: LH: 0-0 RH: 1-1 Tight: 0-0 Gall: 0-0
Aids: Bl: 0-0 Vi: 0-0 Tstrap: 0-0
Best Rating: 108 2/03 Winc 2m gd-sft NHF

A half-brother to Lady Rebecca, put up a resolute performance to win a bumper on his debut.

Brassis Hill (IRE)

12-y-o b g Marktingo-Mystery Woman (Tula Rocket)
Miss A M Newton-Smith The Sleeping Partnership

Placings: *0/40400/1655/6020P/2/3234/5300P3-6* (0058)
2002/03: 16⁶G,

	Starts	1st	2nd	3rd	Win & Pl
Chases	1	0	0	0	
Career Total	27	1	3	4	6868
95	5/97	Clon	2m	NHF	GD	£2204
				Total win prize-money £2204		

Going: Sf: 0-0 GS: 0-0 Gd: 0-1 GF: - Fm: 0-0
Distance: 2m/2m3: 0-1 2m4-2m7: 0-0 3m+: 0-0
Track: LH: 0-0 RH: 0-0 Tight: 0-0 Gall: 0-0
Aids: Bl: 0-0 Vi: 0-0 Tstrap: 0-1
Best Rating: 95 5/97 Clon 2m good NHF

Brave Caradoc (IRE)

80f   **79f**

5-y-o b g Un Desperado (FR)-Drivers Bureau (Proverb)

G L Moore M K George

Placings: *3*   (4053)
2002/03: 16³HY,

	Starts	1st	2nd	3rd	Win & Pl
NH Flat	1	0	0	1	341
Career Total	1	0	0	1	341

Brave Effect (IRE)

95   **102**

7-y-o br g Bravefoot-Crupney Lass (Ardoon)
M Todhunter P E Sowerby, K A Sowerby, R E Bell

Placings: *2-0P4401*   (4621)
2002/03: 16⁶G, 20⁶HY, 19⁴GS, 16⁴S, 16⁶G, 20¹GF,

	Starts	1st	2nd	3rd	Win & Pl
Hurdles	6	1	1	0	4206
Career Total	7	1	1	0	5056
102	4/03	Carl	2m4f	E(0-105)HHdl	G-F	£3934
				Total win prize-money £3934		

Going: Sf: 0-2 GS: 0-1 Gd: 0-2 GF: - Fm: 1-1
Distance: 2m/2m3: 0-3 2m4-2m7: 1-3 3m+: 0-0
Track: LH: 0-5 RH: 1-1 Tight: 0-2 Gall: 0-0
Aids: Bl: 0-0 Vi: 0-0 Tstrap: 0-1
Best Rating: 102 4/03 Carl 2m4f gd-fm Hdl

Moderate hurdler; promising debut in a novices hurdle at Carlisle in April 2002; failed to build on that until winning a weak novices handicap at Carlisle in April 2003; stays two and a half miles; suited by a sound surface; has worn a tongue strap.

Brave King (IRE)

98   **74**

10-y-o b g King s Ride-Arumah (Arapaho)
Ronald Thompson B Bruce

Placings: *1/6P5/5-0*   (2471)
2002/03: 16⁰G,

	Starts	1st	2nd	3rd	Win & Pl
Hurdles	1	0	0	0	
Career Total	6	1	0	0	1371
107	4/98	Towc	2m	H NHF	SFT	£1371
				Total win prize-money £1371		

Going: Sf: 0-0 GS: 0-0 Gd: 0-1 GF: - Fm: 0-0
Distance: 2m/2m3: 0-1 2m4-2m7: 0-0 3m+: 0-0
Track: LH: 0-1 RH: 0-0 Tight: 0-0 Gall: 0-1
Aids: Bl: 0-0 Vi: 0-0 Tstrap: 0-0
Best Rating: 107 4/98 Towc 2m soft NHF

Brave Knight

75

6-y-o b g Presidium-Agnes Jane (Sweet Monday)
N Bycroft Piers Casimir-Mrowczynski

Placings: *5-2PP*   (2896)
2002/03: 17²GS, 16⁶G, 16⁶S,

	Starts	1st	2nd	3rd	Win & Pl
Chases	3	0	1	0	2520
Career Total	4	0	1	0	2520

Going:	Sf: 0-1 GS: 0-1 Gd: 0-1 GF: - Fm: 0-0
Distance:	2m/2m3: 0-3 2m4-2m7: 0-0 3m+: 0-0
Track:	LH: 0-1 RH: 0-2 Tight: 0-2 Gall: 0-0
Aids:	Bl: 0-0 Vi: 0-0 Tstrap: 0-0
Best Rating:	75 10/02 MRas 2m1f110y gd-sft Ch

Poor maiden on the Flat; has been beaten over hurdles, over fences and in a point-to-point.

Brave Lord (IRE)

84   94+

6-y-o ch g Mister Lord (USA)-Artic Squaw (IRE) (Buckskin (FR))
L Lungo Solway Stayers

Placings:6   (3991)
2002/03: 17⁶S,

	Starts	1st	2nd	3rd	Win & Pl
NH Flat	1	0	0	0	0
Career Total	1	0	0	0	0

Going:	Sf: 0-1 GS: 0-0 Gd: 0-0 GF: - Fm: 0-0
Distance:	2m/2m3: 0-1 2m4-2m7: 0-0 3m+: 0-0
Track:	LH: 0-0 RH: 0-1 Tight: 0-0 Gall: 0-0
Aids:	Bl: 0-0 Vi: 0-0 Tstrap: 0-0
Best Rating:	93 3/03 Carl 2m1f soft NHF

Brave Spirit (FR)

5-y-o b g Legend Of France (USA)-Guerre Ou Paix (FR) (Comrade In Arms)
Ian Williams Sir Robert Ogden

Placings:00   (4442)
2002/03: 16⁹S, 20⁹G,

	Starts	1st	2nd	3rd	Win & Pl
NH Flat	1	0	0	0	0
Hurdles	1	0	0	0	0
Career Total	2	0	0		0

Going:	Sf: 0-1 GS: 0-0 Gd: 0-1 GF: - Fm: 0-0
Distance:	2m/2m3: 0-1 2m4-2m7: 0-0 3m+: 0-0
Track:	LH: 0-1 RH: 0-0 Tight: 0-0 Gall: 0-1
Aids:	Bl: 0-0 Vi: 0-0 Tstrap: 0-0
Best Rating:	68 3/03 Newb 2m110y soft NHF

Brave Vision

104   87

7-y-o b g Clantime-Kinlet Vision (IRE) (Vision (USA))
A C Whillans Mrs S Harrow

Placings:F/534622/54U556221-163055   (3896)
2002/03: 16¹G, 16⁶GF, 20³GS, 16⁹HY, 17⁵HY, 22⁵GS,

	Starts	1st	2nd	3rd	Win & Pl
Hurdles	6	1	0	4	3316
Career Total	22	2	4	2	10965
100	5/02	Kels	2m110y E(0-120)HHdl	GD	£2793
93	3/02	Kels	2m110y E(0-110)HHdl	SFT	£3435
				Total win prize-money £6228	

Going:	Sf: 0-2 GS: 0-2 Gd: 1-1 GF: - Fm: 0-1
Distance:	2m/2m3: 1-4 2m4-2m7: 0-2 3m+: 0-0
Track:	LH: 1-4 RH: 0-0 Tight: 1-3 Gall: 0-1
Aids:	Bl: 0-0 Vi: 0-0 Tstrap: 0-0
Best Rating:	100 5/02 Kels 2m110y good Hdl

Plating-class hurdler, consistent, if somewhat fustrating; appears best at the minimum trip; effective on most ground but best with some cut.

Bravo

103   92+

5-y-o b/br g Efisio-Apache Squaw (Be My Guest (USA))
J Mackie Paul D Leech

Placings:4-04001   (4338)
2002/03: 16⁵S, 19⁴GS, 17⁰GS, 20⁰GS, 20¹GF,

	Starts	1st	2nd	3rd	Win & Pl
Hurdles	5	1	0	0	3708
Career Total	6	1	0	0	4208
93	3/03	Hntg	2m4f110yE(0-100)HHdl	G-F	£3708
				Total win prize-money £3708	

Going:	Sf: 0-1 GS: 0-3 Gd: 0-0 GF: - Fm: 1-1
Distance:	2m/2m3: 0-2 2m4-2m7: 1-3 3m+: 0-0
Track:	LH: 0-3 RH: 1-2 Tight: 0-2 Gall: 1-3
Aids:	Bl: 0-0 Vi: 1-2 Tstrap: 0-0
Best Rating:	93 3/03 Hntg 2m4f110y gd-fm Hdl

Moderate novice hurdler; stays 2m 4f; acts on fast ground; successful in a visor.

Brazil (IRE)

60   86

5-y-o b g Germany (USA)-Alberta Rose (IRE) (Phardante (FR))
T R George Mrs Sharon C Nelson

Placings:000   (4772)
2002/03: 12⁰G, 16⁹G, 16⁰G,

	Starts	1st	2nd	3rd	Win & Pl
NH Flat	2	0	0	0	0
Hurdles	1	0	0	0	0
Career Total	3	0	0		0

Going:	Sf: 0-0 GS: 0-0 Gd: 0-3 GF: - Fm: 0-0
Distance:	2m/2m3: 0-2 2m4-2m7: 0-0 3m+: 0-0
Track:	LH: 0-1 RH: 0-2 Tight: 0-1 Gall: 0-0
Aids:	Bl: 0-0 Vi: 0-0 Tstrap: 0-0
Best Rating:	78 12/02 Newb 1m4f110y good NHF

Brea Hill

78

10-y-o b g Brotherly (USA)-Top Feather (High Top)
Ferdy Murphy A W K Merriam

Placings:650/635F3UP/P/P42U6F26-P   (0025)
2002/03: 25⁵G,

	Starts	1st	2nd	3rd	Win & Pl
Chases	1	0	0	0	
Career Total	20	0	2	2	2826

Going:	Sf: 0-0 GS: 0-0 Gd: 0 GF: - Fm: 0-0
Distance:	2m/2m3: 0-0 2m4-2m7: 0-0 3m+: 0-1
Track:	LH: 0-1 RH: 0-0 Tight: 0-0 Gall: 0-0
Aids:	Bl: 0-0 Vi: 0-0 Tstrap: 0-1
Best Rating:	99 12/98 Newc 2m soft NHF

Break Dancer (IRE)

4-y-o b g Danehill Dancer (IRE)-Peep Of Day (USA) (Lypheor)
M J Roberts Mike Roberts

Placings:PPP   (4184)
2002/03: 18⁵G, 17⁵HY, 17⁵G,

	Starts	1st	2nd	3rd	Win & Pl
Hurdles	3	0	0	0	

| Career Total | 3 | 0 | 0 |

Going:	Sf: 0-1 GS: 0-0 Gd: 0-2 GF: - Fm: 0-0
Distance:	2m/2m3: 0-3 2m4-2m7: 0-0 3m+: 0-0
Track:	LH: 0-1 RH: 0-2 Tight: 0-3 Gall: 0-0
Aids:	Bl: 0-1 Vi: 0-0 Tstrap: 0-0
Best Rating:	0 3/03 Folk 2m1f110y good Hdl

Breaking Breeze (IRE)

109(105h)   (105h)114+

8-y-o b g Mandalus-Knockacool Breeze (Buckskin (FR))
J S King H Porter, N Rich, V Askew

Placings:1040/321400-014311   (1199)
2002/03: 19⁰G, 20¹GF, 21⁴GF, 21³GF, 20¹GF, 19¹GF,

	Starts	1st	2nd	3rd	Win & Pl
Hurdles	1	0	0	0	
Chases	5	3	0	1	12061
Career Total	16	5	1	2	21161
114	9/02	Hrfd	2m3f	E(0-110)HCh	G-F	£4338
105	8/02	Hntg	2m4f110y E Ch	G-F	£3487
105	6/02	Hntg	2m4f110y E Ch	G-F	£2977
103	12/01	Ludl	2m	E(0-115)HHdl	GD	£4046
111	8/00	Cork	2m	NHF	Y-S	£3588
				Total win prize-money £18437	

Going:	Sf: 0-0 GS: 0-0 Gd: 0-1 GF: - Fm: 3-5
Distance:	2m/2m3: 1-1 2m4-2m7: 2-5 3m+: 0-0
Track:	LH: 0-2 RH: 3-4 Tight: 0-1 Gall: 2-2
Aids:	Bl: 0-0 Vi: 0-0 Tstrap: 0-0
Best Rating:	114 9/02 Hrfd 2m3f gd-fm Ch

Modest chaser; improved over hurdles to win a two-mile handicap in December 2001; acts on good ground; winning novice chaser in the summer of 2002.

Breathtaking View (USA)

107   89

7-y-o b g Country Pine (USA)-Lituya Bay (USA) (Empery (USA))
G Prodromou Mrs B Macalister

Placings:5003   (4669)
2002/03: 17⁵HY, 19⁰G, 20⁴G, 16³G,

	Starts	1st	2nd	3rd	Win & Pl
Hurdles	4	0	0	1	838
Career Total	4	0	0	1	838

Going:	Sf: 0-1 GS: 0-0 Gd: 0-3 GF: - Fm: 0-0
Distance:	2m/2m3: 0-3 2m4-2m7: 0-1 3m+: 0-0
Track:	LH: 0-2 RH: 0-0 Tight: 0-3 Gall: 0-1
Aids:	Bl: 0-0 Vi: 0-0 Tstrap: 0-0
Best Rating:	75 4/03 Fknm 2m good Hdl

Plating-class; took a selling hurdle at Market Rasen in June; just held on in a better race there three weeks later; stays two and a half miles; acts on a sound surface.

Brenda's Delight (IRE)

87   31

5-y-o b m Blues Traveller (IRE)-Tara s Delight (Dunbeath (USA))
P Butler E H Whatmough

Placings:P5-U0P   (1788)

Career Total   3   0   0   0

2002/03: 16⁵G, 18ᵁG, 16⁰G, 17ᴾGS,

	Starts	1st	2nd	3rd	Win & Pl
Hurdles	4	0	0	0	0
Career Total	5	0	0	0	0

Going:	Sf: 0-0 GS: 0-1 Gd: 0-3 GF: - Fm: 0-0
Distance:	2m/2m3: 0-4 2m4-2m7: 0-0 3m+: 0-0
Track:	LH: 0-3 RH: 0-1 Tight: 0-4 Gall: 0-0
Aids:	Bl: 0-0 Vi: 0-0 Tstrap: 0-0
Best Rating:	46 4/02 Plum 2m good Hdl

Brereton (IRE)

102(97h)   (83h)106

7-y-o b g Be My Native (USA)-Society News (Law Society (USA))
N J Henderson Pump & Plant Services Ltd

Placings:205-400   (4606)
2002/03: 20⁴S, 21⁰S, 24⁰G,

	Starts	1st	2nd	3rd	Win & Pl
Hurdles	3	0	0	0	0
Career Total	6	0	1	0	488

Going:	Sf: 0-2 GS: 0-0 Gd: 0-1 GF: - Fm: 0-0
Distance:	2m/2m3: 0-0 2m4-2m7: 0-2 3m+: 0-1
Track:	LH: 0-2 RH: 0-1 Tight: 0-0 Gall: 0-1
Aids:	Bl: 0-0 Vi: 0-0 Tstrap: 0-0
Best Rating:	120 12/01 Wwck 2m soft NHF

Moderate hurdler; encouraging debut in a Warwick bumper; looked to need further when fifth on his hurdles bow over two miles five; acts on soft ground; has suffered from breathing problems.

Breteche (FR)

8-y-o b m Fijar Tango (FR)-Foinery (Reference Point)
Miss C Newman C G Newman

Placings:2F064120452/30130/061P6PP346U636/004-P
                                               (0245)
2002/03: 25ᴾG,

	Starts	1st	2nd	3rd	Win & Pl
Chases	1	0	0	0	
Career Total	36	3	3	4	11528
86	5/00	NAbb	2m110y	D Ch	G-F	£3750
86	5/99	Ctml	2m1f110yG(0-100)HHdl	GD	£3503
74	1/99	Folk	2m1f110y	G Hdl	HVY	£1618

Total win prize-money £8873

Going:	Sf: 0-0 GS: 0-0 Gd: 0-1 GF: - Fm: 0-0
Distance:	2m/2m3: 0-0 2m4-2m7: 0-0 3m+: 0-1
Track:	LH: 0-0 RH: 0-1 Tight: 0-0 Gall: 0-0
Aids:	Bl: 0-0 Vi: 0-0 Tstrap: 0-0
Best Rating:	86 5/00 NAbb 2m110y gd-fm Ch

Breuddwyd Lyn

64

5-y-o br g Awesome-Royal Resort (King Of Spain)
D Burchell Lyn Phillips

Placings:0PF   (4191)
2002/03: 16⁰G, 16ᴾS, 16ᶠG,

	Starts	1st	2nd	3rd	Win & Pl
NH Flat	1	0	0	0	
Hurdles	2	0	0	0	
Career Total	3	0	0	0	

Going:	Sf: 0-0 GS: 0-0 Gd: 0-0 GF: 0-1 Fm: 0-0
Distance:	2m/2m3: 0-3 2m4-2m7: 0-0 3m+: 0-0
Track:	LH: 0-1 RH: 0-2 Tight: 0-1 Gall: 0-0
Aids:	Bl: 0-0 Vi: 0-0 Tstrap: 0-0
Best Rating:	64 3/03 Ludl 2m good Hdl

Brewster (IRE)

98   113

6-y-o b g Roselier (FR)-Aelia Paetina (Buckskin (FR))
Ian Williams (I Buchanan 29/4) Mr & Mrs John Poynton

Placings:1-322   (2713)
2002/03: 16¹HY, 20³S, 20²S, 20⁰HY,

	Starts	1st	2nd	3rd	Win & Pl
NH Flat	1	1	0	0	3387
Hurdles	3	0	2	1	3145
Career Total	4	1	2	1	6532
117	4/02	Slig	2m		NHF	HVY	£3386

Total win prize-money £3387

Going:	Sf: 1-4 GS: 0-0 Gd: 0-0 GF: - Fm: 0-0
Distance:	2m/2m3: 1-1 2m4-2m7: 0-3 3m+: 0-0
Track:	LH: 0-2 RH: 0-1 Tight: 0-0 Gall: 0-0
Aids:	Bl: 0-0 Vi: 0-0 Tstrap: 0-0
Best Rating:	117 4/02 Slig 2m heavy NHF

Modest hurdler; Irish bumper winne; has run well in novice hurdles in this country; effective in testing ground.

Brian James

98(77c)   (24c)86

9-y-o ch g River God (USA)-Rose Orchard (Rouser)
F P Murtagh Brian Callaghan

Placings:04PPP/45216FP3/23332-040PP3P   (4374)
2002/03: 21⁰G, 27⁴S, 27⁰S, 24ᴾHY, 27ᴾHY, 27³S, 27ᴾG,

	Starts	1st	2nd	3rd	Win & Pl
Hurdles	6	0	0	1	741
Chases	1	0	0	0	0
Career Total	25	1	3	5	7226
102	12/00	Sedg	3m3f110yE Hdl		SFT	£2380

Total win prize-money £2380

Going:	Sf: 0-5 GS: 0-0 Gd: 0-2 GF: - Fm: 0-0
Distance:	2m/2m3: 0-0 2m4-2m7: 0-1 3m+: 0-6
Track:	LH: 0-7 RH: 0-0 Tight: 0-6 Gall: 0-0
Aids:	Bl: 0-0 Vi: 0-0 Tstrap: 0-0
Best Rating:	102 11/01 Sedg 3m3f110y good Hdl

Moderate staying hurdler; stays extreme distances; has worn cheekpieces.

Briar (CZE)

103   94

4-y-o b c House Rules (USA)-Bright Angel (ATA) (Antuco (GER))
M Pitman C B Hoffman

Placings:04143420   (4325)
2002/03: 16⁰GF, 16⁴GS, 17¹S, 16⁴HY, 17³HY, 21⁴S, 20²HY, 19⁰G,

	Starts	1st	2nd	3rd	Win & Pl
Hurdles	8	1	1	1	6264
Career Total	8	1	1	1	6264
94	11/02	Folk	2m1f110yE Hdl		SFT	£3094

Total win prize-money £3094

Going:	Sf: 1-5 GS: 0-1 Gd: 0-1 GF: - Fm: 0-1
Distance:	2m/2m3: 1-6 2m4-2m7: 0-0 3m+: 0-0
Track:	LH: 0-2 RH: 1-6 Tight: 1-2 Gall: 0-2
Aids:	Bl: 0-0 Vi: 0-0 Tstrap: 0-0
Best Rating:	94 3/03 Sand 2m4f110y heavy Hdl

Moderate hurdler; got off the mark at Folkestone in November 2002; has been unable to follow up since.; should be suited by further in time.

Briar Rose (IRE)

98   72

8-y-o gr m Roselier (FR)-Born Lucky (Deep Run)
N M L Ewart N M L Ewart

Placings:PP00/P6P023   (4409)
2002/03: 21ᴾS, 25⁶S, 21ᴾHY, 24⁰S, 32²S, 25³G,

	Starts	1st	2nd	3rd	Win & Pl
Chases	6	0	1	1	1554
Career Total	10	0	1	1	1554

Going:	Sf: 0-5 GS: 0-0 Gd: 0-1 GF: - Fm: 0-0
Distance:	2m/2m3: 0-0 2m4-2m7: 0-2 3m+: 0-4
Track:	LH: 0-5 RH: 0-1 Tight: 0-2 Gall: 0-0
Aids:	Bl: 0-0 Vi: 0-0 Tstrap: 0-0
Best Rating:	59 2/01 Sedg 2m5f110y soft Hdl

Briar's Mist (IRE)

103(90h)   (103h)103

6-y-o gr g Roselier (FR)-Claycastle (IRE) (Carlingford Castle)
Miss H C Knight Trevor Hemmings

Placings:0035-4FP3   (4321)
2002/03: 21⁴HY, 26⁶GS, 19ᴾHY, 24³G,

	Starts	1st	2nd	3rd	Win & Pl
Chases	4	0	0	1	1432
Career Total	8	0	0	2	2015

Going:	Sf: 0-2 GS: 0-1 Gd: 0-1 GF: - Fm: 0-0
Distance:	2m/2m3: 0-0 2m4-2m7: 0-2 3m+: 0-2
Track:	LH: 0-4 RH: 0-0 Tight: 0-2 Gall: 0-0
Aids:	Bl: 0-0 Vi: 0-0 Tstrap: 0-0
Best Rating:	103 3/03 Bang 3m110y good Ch

Moderate hurdler/chaser; has shown ability over hurdles and fences at up to three miles.

Bric A Brac

74   30

6-y-o ch m Minster Son-Greenhill s Girl (Radetzky)
W G Young W G Young

Placings:000-0   (4772)
2002/03: 16⁰G,

	Starts	1st	2nd	3rd	Win & Pl
Hurdles	1	0	0	0	
Career Total	4	0	0	0	

Going:	Sf: 0-0 GS: 0-0 Gd: 0-0 GF: 0-1 Fm: 0-0
Distance:	2m/2m3: 0-1 2m4-2m7: 0-0 3m+: 0-0
Track:	LH: 0-0 RH: 0-1 Tight: 0-0 Gall: 0-0
Aids:	Bl: 0-0 Vi: 0-0 Tstrap: 0-0
Best Rating:	0 4/03 Prth 2m110y good Hdl

Bridal White

(51c)   (61c)

7-y-o b m Robellino (USA)-Alwatar (USA) (Caerleon (USA))
M Wigham Charles Alan McKechnie

Placings:60/5P-P   (2301)
2002/03: 16ᴾGS,

	Starts	1st	2nd	3rd	Win & Pl
Hurdles	1	0	0	0	
Career Total	5	0	0	0	0

Going: Sf: 0-0 GS: 0-1 Gd: 0-0 GF: - Fm: 0-0
Distance: 2m/2m3: 0-1 2m4-2m7: 0-0 3m+: 0-0
Track: LH: 0-1 RH: 0-0 Tight: 0-1 Gall: 0-0
Aids: Bl: 0-0 Vi: 0-0 Tstrap: 0-0
Best Rating: 65   11/99   Hntg   2m110y   gd-fm   Hdl

Bridgend Blue (IRE)
96   66

7-y-o b g Up And At Em-Sperrin Mist (Camden Town)
J S Hubbuck   J S Hubbuck

Placings:53P/P60P00P06P050-0505   (1528)
2002/03: 16⁰G, 17⁹GF, 16⁵GF, 22⁹GF, 21⁵G,

	Starts	1st	2nd	3rd	Win & Pl
Hurdles	5	0	0	0	
Career Total	20	0	0	1	341

Going: Sf: 0-0 GS: 0-0 Gd: 0-2 GF: - Fm: 0-3
Distance: 2m/2m3: 0-3 2m4-2m7: 0-2 3m+: 0-0
Track: LH: 0-5 RH: 0-0 Tight: 0-3 Gall: 0-1
Aids: Bl: 0-0 Vi: 0-0 Tstrap: 0-0
Best Rating: 71   9/99   Hntg   2m110y   good   Hdl

Modest hurdler.

Brief Dance (IRE)
108   116

6-y-o b g Brief Truce (USA)-Serenad Dancer (FR) (Antheus (USA))
P J Hobbs (P Hughes 17/8)   N Elliott

Placings:5BF4BF4346-1FF1203   (2327)
2002/03: 16¹GY, 17⁵YS, 16⁵SH, 16¹G, 16²F, 16⁹GF, 16³GS,

	Starts	1st	2nd	3rd	Win & Pl
Hurdles	7	2	1	1	9953
Career Total	17	2	1	2	11542
108 6/02	Tram	2m	Hdl	GD	£3809
86 5/02	Baln	2m	Hdl	G-Y	£4233
			Total win prize-money £8043		

Going: Sf: 0-0 GS: 0-1 Gd: 1-1 GF: - Fm: 0-2
Distance: 2m/2m3: 2-7 2m4-2m7: 0-0 3m+: 0-0
Track: LH: 0-1 RH: 0-1 Tight: 0-0 Gall: 0-0
Aids: Bl: 0-0 Vi: 0-0 Tstrap: 0-0
Best Rating: 116   12/02   Winc   2m   gd-sft   Hdl

Fair hurdler; formerly trained in Ireland; has been successful twice in novice company over two miles; handles good and soft ground.

Brigade Charge (USA)
114   125

8-y-o b h Affirmed (USA)-Fairy Footsteps (Mill Reef (USA))
C Roche   J P McManus

Placings:40/30022132/4/2B11-63   (3305a)
2002/03: 20⁶GS, 19³S,

	Starts	1st	2nd	3rd	Win & Pl
Chases	2	0	0	1	2278
Career Total	17	3	4	3	43119
125 3/02	Navn	2m1f	Ch	SH	£6773
115 2/02	Fair	2m2f	Ch	SFT	£7831
115 12/99	Leop	2m	Hdl	SH	£4620
			Total win prize-money £19225		

Going: Sf: 0-1 GS: 0-1 Gd: 0-0 GF: - Fm: 0-0
Distance: 2m/2m3: 0-1 2m4-2m7: 0-1 3m+: 0-0
Track: LH: 0-2 RH: 0-0 Tight: 0-0 Gall: 0-1
Aids: Bl: 0-0 Vi: 0-0 Tstrap: 0-0
Best Rating: 129   5/00   Hayd   2m   good   Hdl

Useful hurdler/chaser in Ireland; stays two miles two; acts in soft ground.

Brigadier Du Bois (FR)

4-y-o gr g Apeldoorn (FR)-Artic Night (FR) (Kaldoun (FR))
Mrs L Wadham   Hebomapa

Placings:2030   (4460)
2002/03: 16²S, 16⁰HY, 17³HY, 16⁰G,

	Starts	1st	2nd	3rd	Win & Pl
Hurdles	4	0	1	1	8079
Career Total	4	0	1	1	8079

Going: Sf: 0-3 GS: 0-0 Gd: 0-1 GF: - Fm: 0-0
Distance: 2m/2m3: 0-4 2m4-2m7: 0-0 3m+: 0-0
Track: LH: 0-1 RH: 0-0 Tight: 0-1 Gall: 0-0
Aids: Bl: 0-0 Vi: 0-0 Tstrap: 0-0
Best Rating: 0   4/03   Aint   2m110y   good   Hdl

Has been placed on the Flat and over hurdles in France; acts on soft ground.

Brigante Girl (IRE)
105f   105+f

5-y-o b m Old Vic-Strong Winds (IRE) (Strong Gale)
N G Richards   Kevin Johnston

Placings:23   (2391)
2002/03: 17²GS, 14³GS,

	Starts	1st	2nd	3rd	Win & Pl
NH Flat	2	0	1	1	909
Career Total	2	0	1	1	909

Going: Sf: 0-0 GS: 0-2 Gd: 0-0 GF: - Fm: 0-0
Distance: 2m/2m3: 0-1 2m4-2m7: 0-0 3m+: 0-0
Track: LH: 0-2 RH: 0-0 Tight: 0-1 Gall: 0-0
Aids: Bl: 0-0 Vi: 0-0 Tstrap: 0-0
Best Rating: 100   10/02   Bang   2m1f   gd-sft   NHF

Modest mare; beat the others out of sight when well beaten by the promising Priests Bridge in a Bangor bumper October 2002; fair run next time; has only raced on easy ground.

Briggs Turn
83   68

9-y-o b g Rudimentary (USA)-Turnabout (Tyrnavos)
Mrs Merrita Jones   Nick Kearns

Placings:P/562221220/300/031-0   (4088)
2002/03: 16⁰GS,

	Starts	1st	2nd	3rd	Win & Pl
Hurdles	1	0	0	0	
Career Total	17	2	5	2	9054
107 1/02	Ludl	2m	G(0-95)HHdl	GD	£2107
96 12/98	Ludl	2m	E(0-110)HHdl	G-S	£2722
			Total win prize-money £4830		

Going: Sf: 0-0 GS: 0-1 Gd: 0-0 GF: - Fm: 0-0
Distance: 2m/2m3: 0-1 2m4-2m7: 0-0 3m+: 0-0
Track: LH: 0-1 RH: 0-0 Tight: 0-0 Gall: 0-0
Aids: Bl: 0-0 Vi: 0-0 Tstrap: 0-0

Best Rating: 107   1/02   Ludl   2m   good   Hdl

Plating-class hurdler; better horse on good ground; best at two miles.

Bright Approach (IRE)

10-y-o gr g Roselier (FR)-Dysart Lady (King s Ride)
Mrs O Bush   J H Burbidge

Placings:5/141P66-12122   (4451)
2002/03: 33¹GF, 31²G, 27¹G, 26²G, 24²G,

	Starts	1st	2nd	3rd	Win & Pl
Chases	5	2	3	0	19485
Career Total	12	4	3	0	26999
112 2/03	Ludl	3m3f110yH Ch		GD	£3010
121 5/02	Chel	4m1f	H Ch	G-F	£5603
103 5/01	Chel	4m1f	H Ch	GD	£5528
98 5/01	Extr	2m7f110yH Ch		GD	£1715
			Total win prize-money £15856		

Going: Sf: 0-0 GS: 0-0 Gd: 1-4 GF: - Fm: 1-1
Distance: 2m/2m3: 0-0 2m4-2m7: 0-0 3m+: 2-5
Track: LH: 1-4 RH: 1-3 Tight: 1-3 Gall: 1-2
Aids: Bl: 0-0 Vi: 0-0 Tstrap: 0-0
Best Rating: 133   3/03   Chel   3m2f110y   good   Ch

Useful hunter chaser, in good form in 2003 when runner-up in the Cheltenham Foxhunters and Horse and Hound Cup ; stays 4m; needs a test of stamina; likes fast ground.

Bright Beacon

9-y-o br g Lighter-Pennulli (Sir Nulli)
Evan Williams   Mrs P Tollit

Placings:P/4   (4089)
2002/03: 24⁴GS,

	Starts	1st	2nd	3rd	Win & Pl
Chases	1	0	0	0	273
Career Total	2	0	0	0	273

Going: Sf: 0-0 GS: 0-1 Gd: 0-0 GF: - Fm: 0-0
Distance: 2m/2m3: 0-0 2m4-2m7: 0-0 3m+: 0-1
Track: LH: 0-1 RH: 0-0 Tight: 0-1 Gall: 0-0
Aids: Bl: 0-0 Vi: 0-0 Tstrap: 0-0
Best Rating: 60   3/03   Strf   3m   gd-sft   Ch

Bright Destiny
95   57

12-y-o br g Destroyer-Bright Suggestion (Magnate)
J S Goldie   Mrs C Brown

Placings:000P/0446P05P031F6/646/352251321340/36P1P
246/3PPP4P04P04/46515346P-04P5PP   (3774)
2002/03: 25⁰GS, 25⁴S, 20⁵S, 24⁵HY, 25⁵HY, 25⁵GS,

	Starts	1st	2nd	3rd	Win & Pl
Chases	6	0	0	0	277
Career Total	66	5	4	7	45991
94 2/02	Ayr	3m1f	D(0-120)HCh	HVY	£7560
103 2/00	Ayr	3m1f	D(0-120)HCh	HVY	£10980
107 3/99	Ayr	3m1f	D(0-125)HCh	SFT	£6020
105 2/99	Ayr	3m1f	E(0-115)HCh	SFT	£3548
88 3/97	Hexm	3m1f	G(0-90)HCh	SFT	£2357
			Total win prize-money £30465		

Going: Sf: 0-4 GS: 0-2 Gd: 0-0 GF: - Fm: 0-0
Distance: 2m/2m3: 0-0 2m4-2m7: 0-1 3m+: 0-5
Track: LH: 0-6 RH: 0-0 Tight: 0-0 Gall: 0-1

Aids: BI: 0-0 Vi: 0-1 Tstrap: 0-0
Best Rating: 107 3/99 Kels 4m   good   Ch

Bright November

12-y-o b g Niniski (USA)-Brigata (Brigadier Gerard)
D R Gandolfo Mrs C Skipworth

Placings:05522216/110/3F/2P/11115/24P-F   (0338)
2002/03: 16^{F}G,

	Starts	1st	2nd	3rd	Win & PI
Chases	1	0	0	0	
Career Total	24	7	5	1	41539
134	2/01	Asct	2m3f110yB Ch		SFT £10166
130	11/00	Kemp	2m	D Ch	SFT £4251
134	11/00	Kemp	2m4f110yD Ch		SFT £5096
124	10/00	Hrfd	2m	F(0-110)HCh	GD £3711
118	4/98	Uttx	2m	B(0-140)HHdl	G-S £5003
107	4/98	Hrfd	2m1f	F(0-105)HHdl	SFT £3048
91	4/96	Hrfd	2m3f110yF(0-95)HHdl		G-F £2906

Total win prize-money £34183

Going: Sf: 0-0 GS: 0-0 Gd: 0-1 GF: - Fm: 0-0
Distance: 2m/2m3: 0-1 2m4-2m7: 0-0 3m+: 0-0
Track: LH: 0-0 RH: 0-1 Tight: 0-0 Gall: 0-0
Aids: BI: 0-0 Vi: 0-0 Tstrap: 0-0
Best Rating: 134 2/01 Asct 2m3f110y soft Ch

Formerly useful chaser; now hunter chasing and pointing; smart front runner; best going right-handed and races enthusiastically; acts on an easy surface.

Bright Question
64

6-y-o ch g Nashwan (USA)-Ozone Friendly (USA) (Green Forest (USA))
Mrs Merrita Jones Speed 2911 Ltd

Placings:00P0-P   (0417)
2002/03: 16^{P}GF,

	Starts	1st	2nd	3rd	Win & PI
Hurdles	1	0	0	0	
Career Total	5	0	0	0	

Going: Sf: 0-0 GS: 0-0 Gd: 0-0 GF: - Fm: 0-0
Distance: 2m/2m3: 0-1 2m4-2m7: 0-0 3m+: 0-0
Track: LH: 0-1 RH: 0-0 Tight: 0-1 Gall: 0-0
Aids: BI: 0-0 Vi: 0-0 Tstrap: 0-0
Best Rating: 64 4/02 Wwck 2m   gd-fm   Hdl

Bright Steel (IRE)
78   52

6-y-o gr g Roselier (FR)-Ikeathy (Be Friendly)
A Parker Mr & Mrs Raymond Anderson Green

Placings:0-00   (4014)
2002/03: 16^{0}HY, 16^{0}S,

	Starts	1st	2nd	3rd	Win & PI
Hurdles	2	0	0	0	
Career Total	3	0	0	0	

Going: Sf: 0-2 GS: 0-0 Gd: 0-0 GF: - Fm: 0-0
Distance: 2m/2m3: 0-2 2m4-2m7: 0-0 3m+: 0-0
Track: LH: 0-2 RH: 0-0 Tight: 0-1 Gall: 0-0
Aids: BI: 0-0 Vi: 0-0 Tstrap: 0-0
Best Rating: 58 12/01 Muss 2m   good   NHF

Brighter Shade (IRE)
108

13-y-o b g Sheer Grit-Shady Doorknocker (Mon Capitaine)
Mrs Sarah L Dent The Blue Bell Partnership

Placings:16121/32F52241/U425UP6/513220/3   (0166)
2002/03: 25^{3}GF,

	Starts	1st	2nd	3rd	Win & PI
Chases	1	0	0	1	221
Career Total	27	5	7	3	27934
114	6/99	Prth	3m	D(0-125)HCh	SFT £4201
122	4/98	Uttx	2m4f	C(0-135)HCh	G-S £4810
119	3/97	Weth	2m4f110yD Ch		GD £3652
117	2/97	Newc	2m4f	E Ch	GD £2862
102	10/96	Sedg	2m1f	H NHF	G-F £1070

Total win prize-money £16598

Going: Sf: 1-2 GS: 0-0 Gd: 0-0 GF: - Fm: 0-1
Distance: 2m/2m3: 0-0 2m4-2m7: 0-0 3m+: 0-1
Track: LH: 0-1 RH: 0-0 Tight: 0-0 Gall: 0-0
Aids: BI: 0-0 Vi: 0-0 Tstrap: 0-0
Best Rating: 124 2/98 Newc 2m4f   good   Ch

Prolific point winner.

Britannia Mills

12-y-o gr m Nordico (USA)-May Fox (Healaugh Fox)
D Burchell Don Gould

Placings:F2/01633023P03060P0/P56/23/1F6160000PF2/0
012S6000/20065300/000000-PP05   (1412)
2002/03: 22^{P}G, 17^{P}G, 21^{0}G, 22^{5}G,

	Starts	1st	2nd	3rd	Win & PI
Hurdles	4	0	0	0	0
Career Total	62	4	6	6	15532
78	8/99	Ctml	2m6f	G(0-90)HHdl	GD £2864
80	8/98	Ctml	2m6f	G(0-90)HHdl	GD £2262
86	6/98	Uttx	2m4f110yG(0-90)HHdl		GD £1752
84	8/95	Ctml	2m1f110yG(0-90)HHdl		FRM £2324

Total win prize-money £9203

Going: Sf: 0-0 GS: 0-0 Gd: 0-4 GF: - Fm: 0-0
Distance: 2m/2m3: 0-1 2m4-2m7: 0-3 3m+: 0-0
Track: LH: 0-4 RH: 0-0 Tight: 0-4 Gall: 0-0
Aids: BI: 0-2 Vi: 0-0 Tstrap: 0-0
Best Rating: 89 1/96 MRas 3m   gd-fm   Hdl

British Volunteer (IRE)
107   96

7-y-o br g Executive Perk-Dante Light (IRE) (Phardante (FR))
C J Mann Roy Wright And The Volunteers

Placings:0/33P-3   (2134)
2002/03: 21^{3}G,

	Starts	1st	2nd	3rd	Win & PI
Hurdles	1	0	0	1	548
Career Total	5	0	0	3	1295

Going: Sf: 0-0 GS: 0-0 Gd: 0-1 GF: - Fm: 0-0
Distance: 2m/2m3: 0-0 2m4-2m7: 0-1 3m+: 0-0
Track: LH: 0-0 RH: 0-1 Tight: 0-0 Gall: 0-0
Aids: BI: 0-0 Vi: 0-0 Tstrap: 0-0
Best Rating: 96 11/02 Ludl 2m5f   good   Hdl

Moderate hurdler; s promise on hurdling debut and again in November 2002 after 11 months off.

Broadbrook Lass
108   111+

9-y-o ch m Broadsword (USA)-Netherbrook Lass (Netherkelly)
Mrs H Dalton Michael H Ings

Placings:21F1P   (4483)
2002/03: 24^{2}HY, 21^{1}GS, 24^{F}G, 20^{1}S, 25^{P}GF,

	Starts	1st	2nd	3rd	Win & PI
Chases	5	2	1	0	10243
Career Total	5	2	1	0	10243
105	8/02	Bang	2m4f110yD Ch		SFT £4845
111	6/02	Uttx	2m5f	D Ch	G-S £4121

Total win prize-money £8967

Going: Sf: 1-2 GS: 1-1 Gd: 0-1 GF: - Fm: 0-1
Distance: 2m/2m3: 0-0 2m4-2m7: 2-2 3m+: 0-3
Track: LH: 2-4 RH: 0-1 Tight: 1-2 Gall: 0-0
Aids: BI: 0-0 Vi: 0-0 Tstrap: 0-0
Best Rating: 111 6/02 Uttx 2m5f   gd-sft   Ch

Dual winning pointer; won a couple of novice chases on soft ground at around two and a half miles in the summer of 2002; acts on any ground; a bit of a tail swisher; possibly unsuited to right-handed courses.

Broadgate Flyer (IRE)
110(98h)   (84h)101

9-y-o b g Silver Kite (USA)-Fabulous Pet (Somethingfabulous (USA))
Miss Lucinda V Russell (D A Lamb 28/1) D G Pryde

Placings:343165/R05P00UF/4005P450616/P6026/P54620
0P-5330U441   (4620)
2002/03: 17^{5}GF, 16^{3}GF, 16^{3}G, 16^{0}GS, 16^{U}GF, 20^{4}G, 20^{4}G, 20^{1}GF,

	Starts	1st	2nd	3rd	Win & PI
Hurdles	1	0	0	0	
Chases	7	1	0	2	6326
Career Total	46	3	2	4	15691
84	4/03	Carl	2m4f	E(0-110)HCh	G-F £4348
80	3/00	Sedg	2m110y D Ch		G-F £4119
72	10/97	Kels	2m110y	E Hdl	FRM £2192

Total win prize-money £10661

Going: Sf: 0-0 GS: 0-1 Gd: 0-3 GF: - Fm: 1-4
Distance: 2m/2m3: 0-5 2m4-2m7: 1-3 3m+: 0-0
Track: LH: 0-4 RH: 1-4 Tight: 0-6 Gall: 0-0
Aids: BI: 0-0 Vi: 0-0 Tstrap: 1-8
Best Rating: 84 4/03 Carl 2m4f   gd-fm   Ch

Plating-class chaser; stays three miles; very much suited by fast ground; usually tongue tied.

Broadnard
104   98

9-y-o b g Ardross-Broadhurst (Workboy)
Mrs P Sly Malt Partnership

Placings:200/2104P/43   (2238)
2002/03: 20^{4}S, 24^{3}S,

	Starts	1st	2nd	3rd	Win & PI
Hurdles	2	0	0	1	889
Career Total	10	1	2	1	13472
103	12/99	Chel	2m1f	D(0-120)HHdl	SFT £10552

Total win prize-money £10553

Going: Sf: 0-2 GS: 0-0 Gd: 0-0 GF: - Fm: 0-0
Distance: 2m/2m3: 0-0 2m4-2m7: 0-1 3m+: 0-1
Track: LH: 0-1 RH: 0-1 Tight: 0-0 Gall: 0-0
Aids: BI: 0-0 Vi: 0-0 Tstrap: 0-0
Best Rating: 106 1/99 Donc 2m110y   gd-sft   Hdl

Won an ordinary novice handicap at Cheltenham on the last day of the 20th century, but has had problems and been lightly raced since.

Brockton Mist (IRE)
104(105h)   (114 h)**123d**
8-y-o ch g Mister Lord (USA)-Glens Princess (Prince Hansel)
P J Hobbs Mrs D A La Trobe

Placings:2/050-21122F3U3   (4599)
2002/03: 20²G, 23¹G, 24¹GF, 24²G, 24²G, 26²FG, 25³S, 24⁴UG, 24³GF,

	Starts	1st	2nd	3rd	Win & Pl
Hurdles	4	2	1	1	9171
Chases	5	0	2	1	3787
Career Total	13	2	4	2	13458
100	9/02	Prth	3m110y	E Hdl	G-F £4134
114	5/02	Weth	2m7f	D Hdl	GD £3535
				Total win prize-money £7669

Going:	Sf: 0-1 GS: 0-0 Gd: 1-6 GF: - Fm: 1-2
Distance:	2m/2m3: 0-0 2m4-2m7: 1-2 3m+: 1-7
Track:	LH: 1-4 RH: 1-4 Tight: 0-3 Gall: 0-0
Aids:	Bl: 0-0 Vi: 0-0 Tstrap: 0-0
Best Rating:	123 11/02 Hayd 3m good Ch

Fair chaser; half-brother to Grand National winner Papillon; won 3m novice hurdles at Wetherby and Perth 2002; subsequently become disappointing over fences; acts on ground good and faster.

Broctune Line
44
9-y-o ch g Safawan-Ra Ra (Lord Gayle (USA))
Mrs P Ford M Sweeney

Placings:2006/P/04000P3/0/00P-P   (0111)
2002/03: 16⁶GS,

	Starts	1st	2nd	3rd	Win & Pl
Hurdles	1	0	0	0	
Career Total	17	0	1	1	1177

Going:	Sf: 0-0 GS: 0-1 Gd: 0-0 GF: - Fm: 0-0
Distance:	2m/2m3: 0-1 2m4-2m7: 0-0 3m+: 0-0
Track:	LH: 0-1 RH: 0-1 Tight: 0-0 Gall: 0-0
Aids:	Bl: 0-0 Vi: 0-0 Tstrap: 0-0
Best Rating:	87 11/97 Weth 2m gd-sft Hdl

Broguestown Breeze (IRE)
104(90h)   (92h)**100**
10-y-o b g Montelimar (USA)-Spin A Coin (Torus)
L A Dace Danny O Sullivan

Placings:0321/P00P25/34PP/3-2   (1583)
2002/03: 26²G,

	Starts	1st	2nd	3rd	Win & Pl
Chases	1	0	1	0	1700
Career Total	16	1	3	3	8099
105	1/99	DRoy	2m4f	Ch	HVY £3376
				Total win prize-money £3376

Going:	Sf: 0-0 GS: 0-0 Gd: 0-1 GF: - Fm: 0-2
Distance:	2m/2m3: 0-0 2m4-2m7: 0-0 3m+: 0-1
Track:	LH: 0-1 RH: 0-0 Tight: 0-1 Gall: 0-0
Aids:	Bl: 0-0 Vi: 0-0 Tstrap: 0-0
Best Rating:	105 1/99 DRoy 2m4f heavy Ch

Moderate chaser/hurdler; ran a blinder at Plumpton after a a long break when going down by a short head in a handicap chasestays two miles four; acts on testing ground.

Broke Road (IRE)
105(109c)   (107+c)**110**
7-y-o b g Deploy-Shamaka (Kris)
Mrs H Dalton Stephen Appelbee

Placings:44315/06403P1/0522P6110-1261244   (1218)
2002/03: 16¹GS, 16²S, 16⁶GS, 16¹G, 16²GF, 17⁴GF, 17⁴G,

	Starts	1st	2nd	Win & Pl
Hurdles	3	0	1	2013
Chases	4	2	1	7524
Career Total	28	6	4	28421
107	7/02	Worc	2m	E Ch	GD £3497
91	5/02	Fknm	2m110y	E Ch	G-S £2967
110	2/02	Fknm	2m	D(0-115)HHdl	G-S £3334
105	1/02	Catt	2m	E(0-110)HHdl	G-S £7280
97	2/01	Fknm	2m	E(0-115)HHdl	SFT £3292
98	3/00	Fknm	2m	E Hdl	GD £2320
				Total win prize-money £22693

Going:	Sf: 0-1 GS: 1-2 Gd: 1-2 GF: - Fm: 0-2
Distance:	2m/2m3: 2-7 2m4-2m7: 0-0 3m+: 0-0
Track:	LH: 2-7 RH: 0-0 Tight: 1-3 Gall: 0-0
Aids:	Bl: 0-0 Vi: 0-0 Tstrap: 0-0
Best Rating:	110 7/02 Strf 2m110y gd-fm Hdl

Modest chaser/hurdler; winner twice over hurdles at the start of 2002; made a successful debut over fences at Fakenham in May and won again over fences at Worcester in July; suited by a sharp left-handed track; handles fast ground but suited by good ground or softer.

Broken Arrow (IRE)
95   **99**
6-y-o b g Sri Pekan (USA)-Domniga (IRE) (Be My Guest (USA))
A J Lidderdale Bernard Gover Bloodstock Trading Ltd

Placings:1/004-06   (0407)
2002/03: 17⁵S, 17⁶GF,

	Starts	1st	2nd	3rd	Win & Pl
Hurdles	2	0	0	0	
Career Total	6	1	0	0	1568
105	4/01	Tntn	2m1f	H NHF	G-F £1568
				Total win prize-money £1568

Going:	Sf: 0-1 GS: 0-0 Gd: 0-0 GF: - Fm: 0-1
Distance:	2m/2m3: 0-2 2m4-2m7: 0-0 3m+: 0-0
Track:	LH: 0-1 RH: 0-1 Tight: 0-2 Gall: 0-0
Aids:	Bl: 0-0 Vi: 0-0 Tstrap: 0-2
Best Rating:	105 4/01 Tntn 2m1f gd-fm NHF

Fast-ground bumper winner, given too much to do on his hurdling debut. Wears a tongue tie.

Broken Dream (IRE)
96(104h)   (97h)**112**
6-y-o b g Broken Hearted-A Little Further (Mandalus)
Miss H C Knight Ms Linda Agran

Placings:204-23UP   (4569)
2002/03: 20²HY, 20³S, 19⁴UG, 24²FG,

	Starts	1st	2nd	3rd	Win & Pl
Chases	4	0	1	1	2054
Career Total	7	0	2	1	2985

Going:	Sf: 0-2 GS: 0-0 Gd: 0-2 GF: - Fm: 0-0
Distance:	2m/2m3: 0-1 2m4-2m7: 0-2 3m+: 0-1
Track:	LH: 0-2 RH: 0-2 Tight: 0-3 Gall: 0-0

Aids: Bl: 0-0 Vi: 0-0 Tstrap: 0-0
Best Rating: 112 12/02 Plum 2m4f heavy Ch

Fair novice hurdler/chaser; suited by decent ground and around two miles four over hurdles and fences.

Broken Knights (IRE)
87   **116+**
6-y-o ch g Broken Hearted-Knight s Row (Le Bavard (FR))
N G Richards The Broken Knights

Placings:1211   (4590)
2002/03: 16¹S, 16²GS, 20¹HY, 20¹G,

	Starts	1st	2nd	3rd	Win & Pl
NH Flat	2	1	1	0	2784
Hurdles	2	2	0	0	7475
Career Total	4	3	1	0	10258
109	4/03	Hexm	2m4f110yE Hdl	GD £3678
116	1/03	Ayr	2m4f	E Hdl	HVY £3796
112	11/02	Ayr	2m	H NHF	SFT £2012
				Total win prize-money £9488

Going:	Sf: 2-2 GS: 0-1 Gd: 1-1 GF: - Fm: 0-0
Distance:	2m/2m3: 1-2 2m4-2m7: 2-2 3m+: 0-0
Track:	LH: 3-4 RH: 0-0 Tight: 0-0 Gall: 0-1
Aids:	Bl: 0-0 Vi: 0-0 Tstrap: 0-0
Best Rating:	116 1/03 Ayr 2m4f heavy Hdl

Useful novice hurdler; bumper winner; stays two and a half miles and is best with cut in the ground; likely to go on to better things.

Bromley's Daughter
84   **51**
7-y-o b m Minster Son-Bromley Rose (Rubor)
R Ford A Eubank

Placings:00000   (4621)
2002/03: 16⁰GF, 16⁰G, 17⁰GS, 20⁰G, 20⁰GF,

	Starts	1st	2nd	3rd	Win & Pl
NH Flat	1	0	0	0	0
Hurdles	4	0	0	0	0
Career Total	5	0	0	0	

Going:	Sf: 0-0 GS: 0-1 Gd: 0-2 GF: - Fm: 0-2
Distance:	2m/2m3: 0-3 2m4-2m7: 0-2 3m+: 0-0
Track:	LH: 0-2 RH: 0-3 Tight: 0-2 Gall: 0-0
Aids:	Bl: 0-0 Vi: 0-0 Tstrap: 0-0
Best Rating:	77 12/02 Muss 2m gd-fm NHF

Bronhallow
108(97h)   (60h)**88**
10-y-o b g Belmez (USA)-Grey Twig (Godswalk (USA))
Mrs Barbara Waring R Parker,E Davies,L Nicholls,Mrs R Field

Placings:50P0025P/023P43355P4125/4356556/46433/00P 000634   (4483)
2002/03: 24⁰S, 24⁰GS, 20⁰PS, 23⁰S, 21⁰HY, 22⁰HY, 20⁰GS, 24³GF, 25⁴GF,

	Starts	1st	2nd	3rd	Win & Pl
Hurdles	6	0	0	0	0
Chases	3	0	0	1	1110
Career Total	43	1	3	7	8434
101	4/99	Uttx	3m110y	F(0-100)HHdl	G-S £3061
				Total win prize-money £3061

Going:	Sf: 0-5 GS: 0-2 Gd: 0-0 GF: - Fm: 0-2
Distance:	2m/2m3: 0-0 2m4-2m7: 0-4 3m+: 0-5

Track: LH: 0-4 RH: 0-5 Tight: 0-2 Gall: 0-1
Aids: Bl: 0-4 Vi: 0-2 Tstrap: 0-9
Best Rating: 102 11/99 Uttx 3m110y soft Hdl

Plating-class hurdler/novice chaser; acts on most ground; has worn blinkers; stays 3m.

Bronze Light

78   44

5-y-o ch m Moscow Society (USA)-Barton Bay (IRE) (Kambalda)
M J Roberts Mike Roberts

Placings:00P0   (4187)
2002/03: 12⁰GS, 16⁰GS, 20⁰G, 20⁰G,

	Starts	1st	2nd	3rd	Win & Pl
NH Flat	2	0	0	0	0
Hurdles	2	0	0	0	0
Career Total	4	0	0		0

Going: Sf: 0-0 GS: 0-2 Gd: 0-2 GF: - Fm: 0-0
Distance: 2m/2m3: 0-1 2m4-2m7: 0-2 3m+: 0-0
Track: LH: 0-1 RH: 0-3 Tight: 0-1 Gall: 0-2
Aids: Bl: 0-0 Vi: 0-0 Tstrap: 0-0
Best Rating: 83 11/02 Newb 1m4f110y gd-sft NHF

Bronzesmith

105(99h)   110

7-y-o b g Greensmith-Bronze Age (Celtic Cone)
B J M Ryall Mrs M E Ash

Placings:062/13-3F24   (4368)
2002/03: 16³G, 19⁴GS, 16²S, 19⁴G,

	Starts	1st	2nd	3rd	Win & Pl
Chases	4	0	1	1	3133
Career Total	9	1	2	2	7225
89	10/01 Extr	2m1f	E Hdl	G-F	£2765
				Total win prize-money	£2765

Going: Sf: 0-0 GS: 0-1 Gd: 0-2 GF: - Fm: 0-0
Distance: 2m/2m3: 0-3 2m4-2m7: 0-1 3m+: 0-0
Track: LH: 0-0 RH: 0-4 Tight: 0-1 Gall: 0-1
Aids: Bl: 0-0 Vi: 0-0 Tstrap: 0-0
Best Rating: 110 1/03 Hntg 2m110y soft Ch

Modest chaser; won 2m 1f novice hurdle on fast ground at Exeter October 2001; disappointing over fences but is not badly handicapped now on some of his form; best at up to 2m 4f.

Brook Bee

87   72

11-y-o br g Meadowbrook-Brown Bee Iii (Marcus Superbus)
T H Caldwell (M J Caldwell 18/5) M J Caldwell

Placings:63/5POF3231/331P5/01P16FRP/U/6P   (0401)
2002/03: 24⁶S, 25⁰GF,

	Starts	1st	2nd	3rd	Win & Pl
Chases	2	0	0	0	0
Career Total	26	4	1	5	14633
105	12/99 Plum	3m2f	F(0-100)Ch	GD	£2900
102	10/99 Towc	3m1f	F(0-110)HCh	GD	£2869
94	10/98 Towc	3m1f	D(0-110)HCh	GD	£2747
96	4/98 Plum	3m1f110yE Ch		G-S	£3040
				Total win prize-money	£11556

Going: Sf: 0-1 GS: 0-0 Gd: 0-0 GF: - Fm: 0-1
Distance: 2m/2m3: 0-0 2m4-2m7: 0-0 3m+: 0-2
Track: LH: 0-2 RH: 0-0 Tight: 0-1 Gall: 0-0
Aids: Bl: 0-0 Vi: 0-0 Tstrap: 0-0
Best Rating: 109 5/98 Towc 3m1f gd-fm Ch

Brook Street

91   65

6-y-o b g Cruise Missile-Sweet Spice (Native Bazaar)
C Tizzard The Butterwick Syndicate

Placings:45-06   (2127)
2002/03: 18⁵G, 16⁹GF, 21⁶S,

	Starts	1st	2nd	3rd	Win & Pl
NH Flat	2	0	0	0	0
Hurdles	1	0	0	0	0
Career Total	4	0	0		0

Going: Sf: 0-1 GS: 0-0 Gd: 0-1 GF: - Fm: 0-1
Distance: 2m/2m3: 0-2 2m4-2m7: 0-1 3m+: 0-0
Track: LH: 0-3 RH: 0-0 Tight: 0-1 Gall: 0-0
Aids: Bl: 0-0 Vi: 0-0 Tstrap: 0-0
Best Rating: 89 3/02 Winc 2m soft NHF

Brook Tean

84   65

9-y-o b m River God (USA)-Saucy Eater (Saucy Kit)
W M Brisbourne R W Adams

Placings:2F05/5P   (4527)
2002/03: 17⁵G, 20⁰G,

	Starts	1st	2nd	3rd	Win & Pl
Hurdles	2	0	0	0	0
Career Total	6	0	1		487

Going: Sf: 0-0 GS: 0-0 Gd: 0-2 GF: - Fm: 0-0
Distance: 2m/2m3: 0-1 2m4-2m7: 0-1 3m+: 0-0
Track: LH: 0-2 RH: 0-0 Tight: 0-1 Gall: 0-0
Aids: Bl: 0-0 Vi: 0-0 Tstrap: 0-0
Best Rating: 100 10/00 Bang 2m1f soft NHF

Brooklands Lad

103   96

6-y-o b g North Col-Sancal (Whistlefield)
J W Mullins B R Edgeley

Placings:4002   (4635)
2002/03: 16⁴GF, 17⁰G, 19⁰S, 19²GF,

	Starts	1st	2nd	3rd	Win & Pl
NH Flat	2	0	0	0	0
Hurdles	2	0	1	0	860
Career Total	4	0	1	0	860

Going: Sf: 0-1 GS: 0-0 Gd: 0-1 GF: - Fm: 0-2
Distance: 2m/2m3: 0-4 2m4-2m7: 0-0 3m+: 0-0
Track: LH: 0-3 RH: 0-1 Tight: 0-1 Gall: 0-1
Aids: Bl: 0-0 Vi: 0-0 Tstrap: 0-0
Best Rating: 96 4/03 Strf 2m3f gd-fm Hdl

Moderate novice hurdler; looked set to score when run out of it by Quedex in 2m 3f maiden hurdle at Stratford April 2003; can go one better in similar company; unsuited by soft ground.

Brooklyn Boy

79f   52f

6-y-o ch h Meadowbrook-Blue Ivory Vii (Damsire Unregistered)
J C Tuck The Japica Partnership

Placings:600   (2064)
2002/03: 17⁶G, 17⁰GF, 17⁰S,

	Starts	1st	2nd	3rd	Win & Pl
NH Flat	3	0	0	0	0

Career Total 3 0 0 0 0

Going: Sf: 0-1 GS: 0-0 Gd: 0-1 GF: - Fm: 0-1
Distance: 2m/2m3: 0-3 2m4-2m7: 0-0 3m+: 0-0
Track: LH: 0-1 RH: 0-2 Tight: 0-1 Gall: 0-0
Aids: Bl: 0-0 Vi: 0-0 Tstrap: 0-0
Best Rating: 52 10/02 Hrld 2m1f gd-fm NHF

Brooklyn Breeze (IRE)

108   133+

6-y-o b/br g Be My Native (USA)-Moss Gale (Strong Gale)
L Lungo Ashleybank Investments Limited

Placings:4-1111   (4764)
2002/03: 17¹G, 16¹G, 20¹G, 24¹G,

	Starts	1st	2nd	3rd	Win & Pl
NH Flat	1	1	0	0	3357
Hurdles	3	3	0	0	19196
Career Total	5	4	0	0	22552
133	4/03 Prth	3m110y C Hdl	GD		£7482
124	4/03 Ayr	2m4f	C Hdl	GD	£7657
95	1/03 Muss	2m	E Hdl	GD	£4056
107	11/02 Aint	2m1f	H NHF	GD	£3356
				Total win prize-money	£22553

Going: Sf: 0-0 GS: 0-0 Gd: 4-4 GF: - Fm: 0-0
Distance: 2m/2m3: 2-2 2m4-2m7: 1-1 3m+: 1-1
Track: LH: 1-1 RH: 2-2 Tight: 1-1 Gall: 0-0
Aids: Bl: 0-0 Vi: 0-0 Tstrap: 0-0
Best Rating: 133 4/03 Prth 3m110y good Hdl

Useful novice hurdler; bumper winner; stays three miles; suited by good ground; likes to be held up; progressive.

Brooklyn's Gold (USA)

118   130

8-y-o b g Seeking The Gold (USA)-Brooklyn s Dance (FR) (Shirley Heights)
Ian Williams Terry Warner

Placings:0/60F1254222-12144133   (4476)
2002/03: 17¹G, 16²GS, 16¹GS, 16⁴GS, 16¹G, 16³G, 16³G,

	Starts	1st	2nd	3rd	Win & Pl
Hurdles	8	3	1	2	34000
Career Total	19	4	5	2	44771
126	2/03 Kemp	2m	C(0-135)HHdl	GD	£10092
118	11/02 Hntg	2m110y	D(0-120)HHdl	G-S	£8326
117	10/02 Hrfd	2m1f	D(0-120)HHdl	GD	£3955
107	1/02 Wwck	2m	D(0-110)HHdl	SFT	£5174
				Total win prize-money	£27548

Going: Sf: 0-1 GS: 1-3 Gd: 2-4 GF: - Fm: 0-0
Distance: 2m/2m3: 3-8 2m4-2m7: 0-0 3m+: 0-0
Track: LH: 0-3 RH: 3-5 Tight: 0-1 Gall: 1-3
Aids: Bl: 0-0 Vi: 0-0 Tstrap: 0-0
Best Rating: 130 4/03 Aint 2m110y good Hdl

Decent handicap hurdler; very consistent in 2002/3; suited by two miles and good ground.

Brooksby Whorlton (IRE)

103   95d

9-y-o b g Commanche Run-Superlee (IRE) (Le Moss)
G A Harker M F Spence

Placings:4/11/0PP00/P3PP0F-01PP6   (4518)

2002/03: 20⁰S, 21¹S, 21ᴾS, 20ᴾG, 21⁶G,

	Starts	1st	2nd	3rd	Win & Pl
Hurdles	5	1	0	0	2646
Career Total	19	3	0	1	7235
95	12/02 Sedg	2m5f110yF(0-90)Hdl		SFT	£2646
107	12/99 Sedg	2m5f110yE Hdl		SFT	£1940
95	11/99 Kels	2m2f	E Hdl	GD	£2416

Total win prize-money £7002

Going: Sf: 1-3 GS: 0-0 Gd: 0-2 GF: - Fm: 0-0
Distance: 2m/2m3: 0-0 **2m4-2m7: 1-5** 3m+: 0-0
Track: LH: **1-5** RH: 0-0 Tight: **1-3** Gall: 0-2
Aids: Bl: 0-1 Vi: 0-0 Tstrap: 0-0
Best Rating: 107 12/99 Sedg 2m5f110y soft Hdl

Selling-class hurdler; won at Sedgefield in December 2002, but is not the most reliable; stays two miles five; acts on soft ground, usually wears blinkers or cheekpieces.

Brooksie

104   **102**

8-y-o b g Efisio-Elkie Brooks (Relkino)
Miss K M George Exterior Profiles Ltd

Placings:00030330/64366P0/313663262/00023463P31-2511   (0733)
2002/03: 17²G, 17⁵GF, 16¹G, 17¹GF,

	Starts	1st	2nd	3rd	Win & Pl
Hurdles	4	2	1	0	8470
Career Total	39	4	4	10	20453
102	7/02 NAbb	2m1f	D(0-120)HHdl	G-F	£3546
102	7/02 Worc	2m	D(0-115)HHdl	GD	£3591
102	4/02 Tntn	2m1f	E(0-110)HHdl	GD	£2674
91	1/01 Tntn	2m3f110yG Hdl		HVY	£1596

Total win prize-money £11407

Going: Sf: 0-0 GS: 0-0 Gd: 1-2 GF: - Fm: 1-2
Distance: **2m/2m3: 2-4** 2m4-2m7: 0-0 3m+: 0-0
Track: LH: **2-4** RH: 0-0 Tight: 1-3 Gall: 0-0
Aids: Bl: 0-0 **Vi: 2-4** Tstrap: 0-0
Best Rating: 102 7/02 NAbb 2m1f gd-fm Hdl

Moderate hurdler; effective between two and a half miles; appears to like Taunton; had a modest strike-rate until landing consecutive handicaps at Worcester and Newton Abbot in July 2002; seems to handle most types of ground.

Broom Close (IRE)

94(104h)   (89 h)**90**

9-y-o b g Yashgan-Pick Nine (Tumble Wind (USA))
R Johnson Jack Thornton

Placings:4P/0-1265414   (4141)
2002/03: 20¹S, 20²GS, 20⁶S, 16⁵HY, 16⁴HY, 20¹S, 24⁴S,

	Starts	1st	2nd	3rd	Win & Pl
Hurdles	4	2	1	0	6799
Chases	3	0	0	0	305
Career Total	10	2	1	0	7104
89	2/03 Newc	2m4f	F(0-90)HHdl	SFT	£2765
82	10/02 Carl	2m4f	E(0-105)HHdl	SFT	£3206

Total win prize-money £5971

Going: Sf: 2-6 GS: 0-1 Gd: 0-0 GF: - Fm: 0-0
Distance: 2m/2m3: 0-0 **2m4-2m7: 2-4** 3m+: 0-1
Track: LH: **1-5** RH: 1-2 Tight: 0-0 **Gall: 1-4**
Aids: Bl: 0-0 Vi: 0-0 Tstrap: 0-0
Best Rating: 90 1/03 Newc 2m110y heavy Ch

Moderate handicap hurdler; winner at Carlisle and Newcastle this time; best at up to two and a half miles.

Brother Ernest

73

8-y-o b/br g Phardante (FR)-Minerstown (IRE) (Miners Lamp)
Ferdy Murphy Exors Of The Late G A Hubbard

Placings:0000/PUP/506-P   (0379)
2002/03: 21ᴾG,

	Starts	1st	2nd	3rd	Win & Pl
Hurdles	1	0	0	0	
Career Total	11	0	0	0	0

Going: Sf: 0-0 GS: 0-0 Gd: 0-1 GF: - Fm: 0-0
Distance: 2m/2m3: 0-0 2m4-2m7: 0-1 3m+: 0-0
Track: LH: 0-0 RH: 0-1 Tight: 0-0 Gall: 0-1
Aids: Bl: 0-0 Vi: 0-0 Tstrap: 0-1
Best Rating: 84 1/00 Hntg 2m110y good NHF

Brother Joe (NZ)

100(118h)   (144 h)**128+**

9-y-o ch g Hula Town (NZ)-Olivia Rose (NZ) (Travolta (FR))
P J Hobbs Sir Robert Ogden

Placings:2111/F55F1/123U023-16P05P   (4607)
2002/03: 25¹GS, 24⁵S, 25ᴾS, 24⁰G, 24⁵G, 21ᴾG,

	Starts	1st	2nd	3rd	Win & Pl
Hurdles	6	1	0	0	18850
Career Total	22	6	3	2	75978
160	11/02 Weth	3m1f	A Hdl	G-S	£17400
155	10/01 Chel	2m5f	B(0-145)HHdl	GD	£9282
142	4/01 Ayr	2m6f	B(0-150)HHdl	GD	£7124
140	4/00 Ayr	2m6f	B HHdl	GD	£6988
140	3/00 Chep	2m4f	B(0-140)HHdl	G-S	£6825
110	11/99 Twth	2m4f110yF Hdl		G-S	£1499

Total win prize-money £49119

Going: Sf: 0-2 GS: 1-1 Gd: 0-3 GF: - Fm: 0-0
Distance: 2m/2m3: 0-0 2m4-2m7: 0-1 **3m+: 1-5**
Track: LH: **1-4** RH: 0-2 Tight: 0-0 Gall: 0-3
Aids: Bl: 0-1 Vi: 0-0 Tstrap: 0-0
Best Rating: 160 11/02 Weth 3m1f gd-sft Hdl

Useful chaser/smart hurdler when in the mood; best effort a 15l defeat of Boss Doyle in Grade Two staying hurdle at Wetherby in November 2002; disappointing since and clearly quirky; eventually well beaten runner-up on chasing debut at Worcester May 2003 after jumping right-handed when getting tired; successful when dropped back to 2m at the same course next time, and followed up over 2m 5f at Uttoxeter; gets 3m on a sound surface but does not want it too soft; goes well fresh; none to trust.

Brother Ted

69   **49**

6-y-o b g Henbit (USA)-Will Be Wanton (Palm Track)
J K Cresswell J K S Cresswell

Placings:0500   (3998)
2002/03: 17⁰GF, 16⁵GF, 17⁰G, 16⁶G,

	Starts	1st	2nd	3rd	Win & Pl
NH Flat	4	0	0	0	0
Career Total	4	0	0	0	0

Going: Sf: 0-0 GS: 0-0 Gd: 0-2 GF: - Fm: 0-2
Distance: 2m/2m3: 0-4 2m4-2m7: 0-0 3m+: 0-0
Track: LH: 0-1 RH: 0-2 Tight: 0-2 Gall: 0-0
Aids: Bl: 0-0 Vi: 0-0 Tstrap: 0-1
Best Rating: 86 7/02 Strf 2m110y gd-fm NHF

Browjoshy (IRE)

(105h)   (112h)**106**

10-y-o b g Zaffaran (USA)-Keeping Company (Kings Company)
K C Bailey (M Pitman 17/5) B D L Racing

Placings:5/3F00/410353/321135P/3P1P0/60P653-0F5P   (2467)
2002/03: 27⁰GF, 27ᶠGS, 28⁵S, 31ᴾGS,

	Starts	1st	2nd	3rd	Win & Pl
Hurdles	1	0	0	0	0
Chases	3	0	0	0	524
Career Total	33	4	1	7	64413
144	1/01 Wwck	3m2f	B(0-150)HCh	SFT	£27391
130	2/00 Uttx	3m2f	C HCh	SFT	£15570
132	1/01 Folk	2m5f	D(0-110)HCh	G-S	£3993
107	11/98 Twtc	2m5f	F HHdl	SFT	£2092

Total win prize-money £49048

Going: Sf: 0-1 GS: 0-2 Gd: 0-0 GF: - Fm: 0-1
Distance: 2m/2m3: 0-0 2m4-2m7: 0-0 3m+: 0-4
Track: LH: 0-4 RH: 0-0 Tight: 0-2 Gall: 0-0
Aids: Bl: 0-3 Vi: 0-0 Tstrap: 0-0
Best Rating: 144 1/01 Wwck 3m2f soft Ch

Modest handicap chaser; useful a couple of seasons ago; has rather lost his way; stays well; best on soft ground.

Brown Chieftain (IRE)

10-y-o b g Meneval (USA)-Brown Trout (IRE) (Beau Charmeur (FR))
A W G Geering A W G Geering

Placings:00000/P   (0371)
2002/03: 26ᴾS,

	Starts	1st	2nd	3rd	Win & Pl
Chases	1	0	0	0	
Career Total	6	0	0	0	

Going: Sf: 0-1 GS: 0-0 Gd: 0-0 GF: - Fm: 0-0
Distance: 2m/2m3: 0-0 2m4-2m7: 0-0 3m+: 0-1
Track: LH: 0-1 RH: 0-0 Tight: 0-1 Gall: 0-0
Aids: Bl: 0-0 Vi: 0-0 Tstrap: 0-0
Best Rating: 56 8/00 Kbgn 2m4f gd-fm Ch

Brown Esquire

12-y-o b g Broadleaf-Ana Brown (Souvran)
Miss G Dewhurst Miss G Dewhurst

Placings:0PP/PP/2-6P   (3548)
2002/03: 24⁶G, 25ᴾG,

	Starts	1st	2nd	3rd	Win & Pl
Chases	2	0	0	0	0
Career Total	8	0	1	0	751

Going: Sf: 0-0 GS: 0-0 Gd: 0-2 GF: - Fm: 0-0
Distance: 2m/2m3: 0-0 2m4-2m7: 0-0 3m+: 0-1
Track: LH: 0-1 RH: 0-0 Tight: 0-1 Gall: 0-0
Aids: Bl: 0-0 Vi: 0-0 Tstrap: 0-0
Best Rating: 89 4/02 Ludl 3m gd-fm Ch

Brown Owl

9-y-o b m Petoski-Laura Grey (Cantab)

W G M Turner Mrs H Fullerton

Placings:PP/P (0732)
2002/03: 21^{P}GF,

	Starts	1st	2nd	3rd	Win & Pl
Chases	1	0	0	0	
Career Total	3	0	0	0	

Going: Sf: 0-0 GS: 0-0 Gd: 0-0 GF: - Fm: 0-1
Distance: 2m/2m3: 0-0 2m4-2m7: 0-0 3m+: 0-0
Track: LH: 0-1 RH: 0-0 Tight: 0-1 Gall: 0-0
Aids: Bl: 0-0 Vi: 0-0 Tstrap: 0-0
Best Rating: 0   7/02   NAbb   2m5f110y   gd-fm   Ch

Brown Teddy

102 **102+**
6-y-o b g Afzal-Quadrapol (Pollerton)
R Ford G B Barlow

Placings:4-044115 (4435)
2002/03: 17^{0}G, 17^{4}GS, 16^{4}GF, 16^{1}G, 16^{1}G, 20^{5}G,

	Starts	1st	2nd	3rd	Win & Pl
NH Flat	1	0	0	0	
Hurdles	5	2	0	0	7062
Career Total	7	2	0	0	7062
102 3/03	Hntg	2m110y	F(0-100)HHdl		GD £2681
97 1/03	Muss	2m	E Hdl		GD £4056

Total win prize-money £6737

Going: Sf: 0-0 GS: 0-1 Gd: 2-4 GF: - Fm: 0-1
Distance: 2m/2m3: 2-5 2m4-2m7: 0-1 3m+: 0-0
Track: LH: 0-1 RH: 2-5 Tight: 1-4 Gall: 1-2
Aids: Bl: 0-0 Vi: 0-0 Tstrap: 0-0
Best Rating: 102 3/03   Hntg   2m110y   good   Hdl

Modest hurdler; chasing bred; won novice hurdles in early 2003 over two miles; acts on good ground; likes a sharp, right-handed track; promises to stay further.

Brownie Returns (IRE)

104 (78h)**102**
10-y-o b g Dry Dock-What A Brownie (Strong Gale)
M F Morris Mrs A M Daly

Placings:00/30033U0UU0/00P1S03P/PP4/F00PF126054-00410641P012 (4657a)
2002/03: 25^{9}G, 22^{0}GY, 25^{4}YS, 25^{1}GF, 24^{0}G, 28^{6}S, 24^{4}S, 25^{1}S, 24^{5}S, 24^{0}S, 24^{1}Y, 25^{2}GF,

	Starts	1st	2nd	3rd	Win & Pl
Hurdles	1	0	0	0	0
Chases	11	3	1	0	26594
Career Total	46	5	2	4	40174
102 3/03	Limk	3m	(0-135)HCh	YLD £13717
102 12/02	Folk	3m1f	E(0-110)HCh	SFT £4007
91 8/02	Kbgn	3m1f	(0-95)HCh	G-F £5714
94 11/01	Thur	2m6f	(0-109)HCh	Y-S £5564
100 11/99	Clon	2m4f	(0-109)HCh	Y-S £3542

Total win prize-money £32547

Going: Sf: 1-5 GS: 0-0 Gd: 0-2 GF: - Fm: 1-2
Distance: 2m/2m3: 0-0 2m4-2m7: 0-1 3m+: 3-11
Track: LH: 0-2 RH: 2-4 Tight: 1-1 Gall: 0-0
Aids: Bl: 3-10 Vi: 0-0 Tstrap: 0-0
Best Rating: 106 5/98   Clon   2m4f   good   Hdl

Moderate handicap chaser; stays three miles; acts well with cut in the ground; wears blinkers.

Browns Delight

65 **32**
6-y-o b m Runnett-Fearless Princess (Tyrnavos)

Mrs A C Tate B Staight

Placings:PPP0P00-0 (0040)
2002/03: 17^{0}G,

	Starts	1st	2nd	3rd	Win & Pl
Hurdles	1	0	0	0	
Career Total	8	0	0	0	

Going: Sf: 0-0 GS: 0-0 Gd: 0-1 GF: - Fm: 0-0
Distance: 2m/2m3: 0-1 2m4-2m7: 0-0 3m+: 0-0
Track: LH: 0-0 RH: 0-1 Tight: 0-0 Gall: 0-0
Aids: Bl: 0-0 Vi: 0-0 Tstrap: 0-0
Best Rating: 33   4/02   Uttx   2m   gd-fm   Hdl

Bruern (IRE)

79f **59f**
6-y-o b g Aahsaylad-Bob s Girl (IRE) (Bob Back (USA))
Mrs Mary Hambro Richard Hambro

Placings:0 (3528)
2002/03: 16^{0}G,

	Starts	1st	2nd	3rd	Win & Pl
NH Flat	1	0	0	0	
Career Total	1	0	0	0	

Going: Sf: 0-0 GS: 0-0 Gd: 0 GF: - Fm: 0-0
Distance: 2m/2m3: 0-1 2m4-2m7: 0-0 3m+: 0-0
Track: LH: 0-1 RH: 0-0 Tight: 0-0 Gall: 0-1
Aids: Bl: 0-0 Vi: 0-0 Tstrap: 0-0
Best Rating: 59   2/03   Newb   2m110y   good   NHF

Brumalis (NZ)

11-y-o b g High Ice (USA)-Kerry Sue (NZ) (Knighthood (NZ))
Miss Laura Cottam K J Condliffe

Placings:4503P6/6PP6FP53P602/UF3PP/00-U (0317)
2002/03: 34^{U}G,

	Starts	1st	2nd	3rd	Win & Pl
Chases	1	0	0	0	
Career Total	26	0	1	3	3031

Going: Sf: 0-0 GS: 0-0 Gd: 0-0 GF: 0-1 Fm: - 0-0
Distance: 2m/2m3: 0-0 2m4-2m7: 0-0 3m+: 0-1
Track: LH: 0-1 RH: 0-1 Tight: 0-0 Gall: 0-0
Aids: Bl: 0-1 Vi: 0-0 Tstrap: 0-0
Best Rating: 87   4/99   Bang   3m   gd-sft   Hdl

Bruno Paillard

78f **57f**
6-y-o ch g Minster Son-Chasers Bar (Oats)
J R Turner J E Swiers

Placings:0 (0627)
2002/03: 17^{0}GF,

	Starts	1st	2nd	3rd	Win & Pl
NH Flat	1	0	0	0	
Career Total	1	0	0	0	

Going: Sf: 0-0 GS: 0-0 Gd: 0-0 GF: - Fm: 0-1
Distance: 2m/2m3: 0-1 2m4-2m7: 0-0 3m+: 0-0
Track: LH: 0-0 RH: 0-0 Tight: 0-1 Gall: 0-0
Aids: Bl: 0-0 Vi: 0-0 Tstrap: 0-0
Best Rating: 57   6/02   MRas   2m1f110y   gd-fm   NHF

Brush A King

103 **93**
8-y-o b g Derrylin-Colonial Princess (Roscoe Blake)
C T Pogson C T Pogson

Placings:560^{1}03/0PP-3PP046151 (4795)
2002/03: 20^{3}GF, 21^{P}GF, 20^{P}GF, 19^{0}S, 24^{4}S, 24^{6}HY, 19^{1}G, 21^{5}G, 21^{1}GF,

	Starts	1st	2nd	3rd	Win & Pl
Hurdles	9	2	0	1	8550
Career Total	17	2	0	2	8817
89 4/03	Sedg	2m5f110yG(0-100)HHdl	G-F £5584
78 2/03	Catt	2m3f	G(0-90)HHdl	GD £2450

Total win prize-money £8035

Going: Sf: 0-3 GS: 0-0 Gd: 1-2 GF: - Fm: 1-4
Distance: 2m/2m3: 1-1 2m4-2m7: 1-6 3m+: 0-2
Track: LH: 2-7 RH: 0-2 Tight: 2-2 Gall: 0-2
Aids: Bl: 0-0 Vi: 0-0 Tstrap: 0-0
Best Rating: 96   11/00   Weth   2m   heavy   NHF

Plating-class hurdler; stays two miles-five; suited by a sound surface; scored at Catterick in February 2003, and took a valuable seller at Sedgefield in April.

Brush The Ark

92 **97+**
9-y-o b m Brush Aside (USA)-Expensive Lark (Sir Lark)
J S Smith Donald Smith

Placings:125/362PP04-3222 (1849)
2002/03: 26^{3}GF, 23^{3}GS, 26^{2}GF, 22^{2}G,

	Starts	1st	2nd	3rd	Win & Pl
Hurdles	4	0	3	1	3480
Career Total	14	1	5	2	7226
100 10/00	Bang	2m1f	H NHF	SFT £1704

Total win prize-money £1705

Going: Sf: 0-0 GS: 0-1 Gd: 0-1 GF: - Fm: 0-2
Distance: 2m/2m3: 0-0 2m4-2m7: 0-1 3m+: 0-3
Track: LH: 0-1 RH: 0-3 Tight: 0-1 Gall: 0-0
Aids: Bl: 0-0 Vi: 0-0 Tstrap: 0-0
Best Rating: 100   10/00   Bang   2m1f   soft   NHF

Moderate hurdler; bumper winner; acts on soft ground; stays well.

Brush With Fame (IRE)

88(91c) (64c)**23**
11-y-o b g Brush Aside (USA)-Cheeney s Gift (Quayside)
G J Smith Mrs Michelle Adamson

Placings:3/0U0536/111F2P6/151361P/52235/0P-0P (0986)
2002/03: 24^{0}G, 26^{P}GF,

	Starts	1st	2nd	3rd	Win & Pl
Hurdles	2	0	0	0	
Career Total	30	6	3	4	21212
85 11/99	Wwck	3m1f110yE(0-115)HCh	GD £3080
97 9/99	NAbb	3m2f110yE Ch	G-F £3036
95 7/99	Worc	3m	D(0-125)HHdl	G-F £2968
97 9/98	Worc	3m	E(0-100)HHdl	G-F £2460
97 8/98	Worc	3m	F(0-95)HHdl	G-F £1954
94 7/98	NAbb	2m6f	E(0-100)HHdl	G-F £2670

Total win prize-money £16169

Going: Sf: 0-0 GS: 0-0 Gd: 0-1 GF: - Fm: 0-1
Distance: 2m/2m3: 0-0 2m4-2m7: 0-0 3m+: 0-2
Track: LH: 0-1 RH: 0-1 Tight: 0-1 Gall: 0-0
Aids: Bl: 0-0 Vi: 0-0 Tstrap: 0-0
Best Rating: 102   4/97   Worc   2m   gd-fm   NHF

Bruthuinne (IRE)
105   111d
8-y-o ch g Vaquillo (USA)-Portane Miss (Salluceva)
B G Powell Martin Broughton

Placings:63/34/4PU3223P-114F   (2258)
2002/03: 25¹GF, 26¹G, 26⁴GS, 25⁶S,

	Starts	1st	2nd	3rd	Win & Pl
Chases	4	2	0	0	10243
Career Total	16	2	2	4	16162
111 10/02 Plum	3m2f	D(0-120)HCh		GD	£5950
95 10/02 Hrfd	3m1f110yE Ch			G-F	£3874

Total win prize-money £9825

Going:	Sf: 0-1 GS: 0-1 Gd: 1-1 GF: - Fm: 1-1
Distance:	2m/2m3: 0-0 2m4-2m7: 0-0 **3m+: 2-4**
Track:	LH: 1-2 RH: 1-2 **Tight: 1-3** Gall: 0-0
Aids:	Bl: 0-0 Vi: 0-0 Tstrap: 0-0
Best Rating:	**111** 10/02 Plum 3m2f good Ch

Modest chaser; half-brother to Aghawadda Gold; broke his duck in three-runner 25 furlong novice chase at Hereford October 2002; followed up with a game performance when winning at Plumpton; seems to act on most types of ground; better on a decent surface.

Bryants Rooney

7-y-o ch g Prince Rooney (IRE)-Forever Blushing (Blushing Scribe (USA))
Miss M P Bryant Miss M Bryant

Placings:0   (0436)
2002/03: 16⁶GF,

	Starts	1st	2nd	3rd	Win & Pl
NH Flat	1	0	0	0	
Career Total	1	0	0	0	

Going:	Sf: 0-0 GS: 0-0 Gd: 0-0 GF: - Fm: 0-1
Distance:	2m/2m3: 0-1 2m4-2m7: 0-0 3m+: 0-0
Track:	LH: 0-0 RH: 0-0 Tight: 0-0 Gall: 0-0
Aids:	Bl: 0-0 Vi: 0-0 Tstrap: 0-0
Best Rating:	**0** 6/02 Hntg 2m110y gd-fm NHF

Buadhach (IRE)

7-y-o b g Petoski-Viking Rocket (Viking (USA))
M A Hill M A Hill

Placings:P20/0P0210P0-0   (4678)
2002/03: 19⁰GF,

	Starts	1st	2nd	3rd	Win & Pl
Chases	1	0	0	0	
Career Total	12	1	2	0	4643
84 11/01 Ayr	2m4f	D(0-110)HHdl	G-S	£3402

Total win prize-money £3402

Going:	Sf: 0-0 GS: 0-0 Gd: 0-0 GF: - Fm: 0-1
Distance:	2m/2m3: 0-1 2m4-2m7: 0-0 3m+: 0-0
Track:	LH: 0-0 RH: 0-1 Tight: 0-0 Gall: 0-0
Aids:	Bl: 0-0 Vi: 0-0 Tstrap: 0-0
Best Rating:	**103** 6/00 Hexm 2m4f gd-fm NHF

Bualadhbos (IRE)
67   54
4-y-o b g Royal Applause-Goodnight Girl (IRE) (Alzao (USA))
F Jordan F K Jennings

Placings:6   (1893)
2002/03: 16⁶GS,

	Starts	1st	2nd	3rd	Win & Pl
Hurdles	1	0	0	0	0
Career Total	1	0	0	0	0

Going:	Sf: 0-0 GS: 0-1 Gd: 0-0 GF: - Fm: 0-0
Distance:	2m/2m3: 0-1 2m4-2m7: 0-0 3m+: 0-0
Track:	LH: 0-0 RH: 0-1 Tight: 0-0 Gall: 0-1
Aids:	Bl: 0-0 Vi: 0-0 Tstrap: 0-0
Best Rating:	**48** 11/02 Hntg 2m110y gd-sft Hdl

Buccaneer Boy (IRE)
85   95
10-y-o b g Buckskin (FR)-Shady Miss (Mandamus)
Ian Williams Mrs Rosemary Paterson

Placings:F22/21143/35   (3489)
2002/03: 30⁹GS, 30⁵S,

	Starts	1st	2nd	3rd	Win & Pl
Chases	2	0	0	1	1233
Career Total	10	2	3	2	14330
120 1/01 Extr	2m7f110yE Ch		HVY	£3815
109 12/00 Extr	2m7f110yE(0-105)HCh	HVY	£3854

Total win prize-money £7671

Going:	Sf: 0-1 GS: 0-1 Gd: 0-0 GF: - Fm: 0-0
Distance:	2m/2m3: 0-0 2m4-2m7: 0-0 3m+: 0-2
Track:	LH: 0-1 RH: 0-1 Tight: 0-1 Gall: 0-0
Aids:	Bl: 0-1 Vi: 0-1 Tstrap: 0-0
Best Rating:	**120** 1/01 Extr 2m7f110y heavy Ch

Moderate chaser; successful pointer; won two novice events at Exeter; on testing ground; rested after injuring himself at Sandown in February 2001; has struggled since his return.

Buck's Palace

10-y-o ch g Buckley-Lady Geneva (Royalty)
B Mactaggart The Potassium Partnership

Placings:f216144/223P3/1312/33-PP   (4353)
2002/03: 20⁵S, 23⁷GF,

	Starts	1st	2nd	3rd	Win & Pl
Chases	2	0	0	0	
Career Total	20	5	4	5	31403
126 10/00 Ludl	3m	E Ch		G-F	£3328
105 5/00 Ludl	2m4f	D Ch		GD	£4257
116 2/99 Uttx	3m110y	C Hdl		HVY	£5295
121 11/98 Winc	2m6f	C Hdl		GD	£4279
109 5/98 Hrfd	2m1f	H NHF		GD	£1229

Total win prize-money £18390

Going:	Sf: 0-1 GS: 0-0 Gd: 0-0 GF: - Fm: 0-1
Distance:	2m/2m3: 0-0 2m4-2m7: 0-1 3m+: 0-1
Track:	LH: 0-1 RH: 0-0 Tight: 0-0 Gall: 0-1
Aids:	Bl: 0-0 Vi: 0-0 Tstrap: 0-0
Best Rating:	**126** 11/00 Ludl 3m good Ch

Fair handicap chaser; something of a quirky character; won twice on good ground at Ludlow in 2000; has left Paul Nicholls and is not one to trust.

Buckby Lane
106   120+
7-y-o b g Nomadic Way (USA)-Buckby Folly (Netherkelly)
P R Webber Mrs P Starkey

Placings:4P-2U311   (4602)

2002/03: 21²S, 21ᵁHY, 21³S, 21¹HY, 21¹G,

	Starts	1st	2nd	3rd	Win & Pl
Hurdles	5	2	1	1	23079
Career Total	5	2	1	1	23079
126 4/03 Chel	2m5f110yB Hdl		GD	£17400
120 3/03 Plum	2m5f	E Hdl		HVY	£3474

Total win prize-money £20874

Going:	Sf: 1-4 GS: 0-0 Gd: 1-1 GF: - Fm: 0-0
Distance:	2m/2m3: 0-0 **2m4-2m7: 2-5** 3m+: 0-0
Track:	**LH: 2-4** RH: 0-1 Tight: 1-3 Gall: 1-1
Aids:	Bl: 0-0 Vi: 0-0 Tstrap: 0-0
Best Rating:	**126** 4/03 Chel 2m5f110y good Hdl

Decent hurdler; still progressing; stays 2m 5f and acts on good and soft ground; suited by forcing tactics; looks sure to make a nice chaser.

Buckland Boy

6-y-o b g Rakaposhi King-Lichen Moss (Le Moss)
P Haskins N B Jones

Placings:P   (4736)
2002/03: 24⁰PGF,

	Starts	1st	2nd	3rd	Win & Pl
Chases	1	0	0	0	
Career Total	1	0	0	0	

Going:	Sf: 0-0 GS: 0-0 Gd: 0-0 GF: - Fm: 0-1
Distance:	2m/2m3: 0-0 2m4-2m7: 0-0 3m+: 0-1
Track:	LH: 0-1 RH: 0-0 Tight: 0-0 Gall: 0-0
Aids:	Bl: 0-0 Vi: 0-0 Tstrap: 0-0
Best Rating:	**0** 4/03 Chep 3m gd-fm Ch

Buckland Knight (IRE)
86   101
7-y-o b/br g Commanche Run-Myra Gaye (Buckskin (FR))
D M Grissell Mrs R M Hepburn

Placings:400/U1P-0PU5P   (2982)
2002/03: 17⁰G, 21ᴾG, 22ᵁHY, 19⁵HY, 20ᴾHY,

	Starts	1st	2nd	3rd	Win & Pl
Hurdles	5	0	0	0	
Career Total	11	1	0	0	2744
115 1/02 Folk	2m1f110yE Hdl		HVY	£2744

Total win prize-money £2744

Going:	Sf: 0-3 GS: 0-0 Gd: 0-2 GF: - Fm: 0-0
Distance:	2m/2m3: 0-2 2m4-2m7: 0-3 3m+: 0-0
Track:	LH: 0-1 RH: 0-3 Tight: 0-3 Gall: 0-1
Aids:	Bl: 0-3 Vi: 0-0 Tstrap: 0-0
Best Rating:	**115** 1/02 Folk 2m1f110y heavy Hdl

Moderate hurdler; caused a 100/1 surprise when winning at Folkestone in January 2002; very much suited by heavy ground.

Bucks View (IRE)

13-y-o b g Buckskin (FR)-Our View (Our Mirage)
G D Hanmer H R Hocknell

Placings:4-FU   (0395)
2002/03: 24⁴S, 28ᵁG,

	Starts	1st	2nd	3rd	Win & Pl
Chases	2	0	0	0	
Career Total	3	0	0	0	0

Going: Sf: 0-1 GS: 0-0 Gd: 0-1 GF: - Fm: 0-0
Distance: 2m/2m3: 0-0 2m4-2m7: 0-0 3m+: 0-2
Track: LH: 0-0 RH: 0-0 Tight: 0-2 Gall: 0-0
Aids: Bl: 0-0 Vi: 0-0 Tstrap: 0-0
Best Rating: 99 5/02 Strf   3m4f   good   Ch

Buckskin Lad (IRE)
106   87
8-y-o b/br g Buckskin (FR)-Loverush (Golden Love)
C Roberts (J Neville 7/3) A J Harkins

Placings:2/6PP126   (4428)
2002/03: 24⁶G, 22⁷GS, 20ᴾHY, 25¹G, 26²S, 25⁶GF,

	Starts	1st	2nd	3rd	Win & Pl
Hurdles	6	1	1	0	4432
Career Total	7	1	2	0	4866

87 2/03 Catt   3m1f110yE(0-100)HHdl   GD £3562
                                Total win prize-money £3562

Going: Sf: 0-2 GS: 0-1 Gd: 1-2 GF: - Fm: 0-1
Distance: 2m/2m3: 0-0 2m4-2m7: 0-2 3m+: 1-4
Track: LH: 1-4 RH: 0-1 Tight: 1-3 Gall: 0-0
Aids: Bl: 0-0 Vi: 0-0 Tstrap: 0-0
Best Rating: 97 5/00 Worc   2m   gd-fm NHF

Plating-class hurdler; shock winner at Catterick in February 2003 appreciating the better ground; good effort when second under a penalty on softer ground at Hereford next time; stays three miles plus.

Buddhi (IRE)

5-y-o b g Be My Native (USA)-Paean Express (IRE) (Paean)
M Pitman Mrs T Brown

Placings:P   (2117)
2002/03: 17ᴾG,

	Starts	1st	2nd	3rd	Win & Pl
NH Flat	1	0	0	0	
Career Total	1	0	0	0	

Going: Sf: 0-0 GS: 0-0 Gd: 0-1 GF: - Fm: 0-0
Distance: 2m/2m3: 0-1 2m4-2m7: 0-0 3m+: 0-0
Track: LH: 0-0 RH: 0-0 Tight: 0-0 Gall: 0-0
Aids: Bl: 0-0 Vi: 0-0 Tstrap: 0-0
Best Rating: 0 11/02 Aint   2m1f   good   NHF

Buddy Diver
59   52
10-y-o br g Revlow-Rely-On-Pearl (Deep Diver)
C J Gray Tony Hutchings

Placings:0PP/6-0   (3825)
2002/03: 16⁰GS,

	Starts	1st	2nd	3rd	Win & Pl
Hurdles	1	0	0	0	
Career Total	5	0	0	0	0

Going: Sf: 0-0 GS: 0-1 Gd: 0-0 GF: - Fm: 0-0
Distance: 2m/2m3: 0-1 2m4-2m7: 0-0 3m+: 0-0
Track: LH: 0-1 RH: 0-0 Tight: 0-0 Gall: 0-0
Aids: Bl: 0-0 Vi: 0-0 Tstrap: 0-0
Best Rating: 52 4/02 Hrfd   2m1f   gd-fm Hdl

Buddy Girie

10-y-o b g Lord Bud-Hatsu-Girie (Ascertain (USA))

P Cornforth J Cornforth

Placings:F/4   (4261)
2002/03: 27⁴G,

	Starts	1st	2nd	3rd	Win & Pl
Chases	1	0	0	0	0
Career Total	2	0	0	0	0

Going: Sf: 0-0 GS: 0-0 Gd: 0-1 GF: - Fm: 0-0
Distance: 2m/2m3: 0-0 2m4-2m7: 0-0 3m+: 0-0
Track: LH: 0-1 RH: 0-0 Tight: 0-1 Gall: 0-0
Aids: Bl: 0-0 Vi: 0-0 Tstrap: 0-0
Best Rating: 87 3/03 Sedg   3m3f   good   Ch

Multiple point winner but one paced under Rules.

Bude
103   94
4-y-o gr g Environment Friend-Gay Da Cheen (IRE) (Tenby)
S A Brookshaw L Briggs

Placings:52466001P23   (4616)
2002/03: 17⁵G, 16²F, 17⁴G, 16⁸G, 20⁶G, 16⁰G, 16⁰HY, 16¹G, 19ᴾG, 16²G, 17³GF,

	Starts	1st	2nd	3rd	Win & Pl
Hurdles	11	1	2	1	6913
Career Total	11	1	2	1	6913

85 3/03 Ludl 2m   E(0-105)HHdl GD £4017
                                Total win prize-money £4017

Going: Sf: 0-1 GS: 0-0 Gd: 1-8 GF: - Fm: 0-2
Distance: 2m/2m3: 1-10 2m4-2m7: 0-1 3m+: 0-0
Track: LH: 0-5 RH: 1-6 Tight: 0-2 Gall: 0-2
Aids: Bl: 1-6 Vi: 0-0 Tstrap: 0-0
Best Rating: 94 4/03 Carl   2m1f   gd-fm Hdl

Moderate hurdler; won weak four-year-old handicap over two miles at Ludlow March 2003; acts on ground good and faster; usually wears blinkers.

Bugsy Malone
77f   58f
5-y-o b g Sir Harry Lewis (USA)-Aisholt (Avocat)
M R Bosley John E McClenaghan

Placings:000   (2574)
2002/03: 16⁰GF, 16⁰GS, 12⁰G,

	Starts	1st	2nd	3rd	Win & Pl
NH Flat	3	0	0	0	
Career Total	3	0	0	0	

Going: Sf: 0-0 GS: 0-1 Gd: 0-1 GF: - Fm: 0-1
Distance: 2m/2m3: 0-2 2m4-2m7: 0-0 3m+: 0-0
Track: LH: 0-2 RH: 0-1 Tight: 0-0 Gall: 0-1
Aids: Bl: 0-0 Vi: 0-1 Tstrap: 0-0
Best Rating: 58 12/02 Hntg   2m110y   gd-sft NHF

Builders Mate

9-y-o b g Cruise Missile-Crossing Star Vii (Damsire Unregistered)
S J Marshall S J Marshall

Placings:PP   (3225)
2002/03: 27ᴾS, 27ᴾHY,

	Starts	1st	2nd	3rd	Win & Pl
Chases	2	0	0	0	
Career Total	2	0	0	0	

Going: Sf: 0-2 GS: 0-0 Gd: 0-0 GF: - Fm: 0-0
Distance: 2m/2m3: 0-0 2m4-2m7: 0-0 3m+: 0-2
Track: LH: 0-2 RH: 0-0 Tight: 0-2 Gall: 0-0
Aids: Bl: 0-0 Vi: 0-0 Tstrap: 0-0
Best Rating: 0   1/03   Sedg   3m3f   heavy Ch

Bullet

8-y-o b g Alhijaz-Beacon (High Top)
Mrs H Dalton Mrs Rita Butler & Mrs Gabrielle McNeela

Placings:0   (1568)
2002/03: 19⁰G,

	Starts	1st	2nd	3rd	Win & Pl
Hurdles	1	0	0	0	
Career Total	1	0	0	0	

Going: Sf: 0-0 GS: 0-0 Gd: 0-1 GF: - Fm: 0-0
Distance: 2m/2m3: 0-0 2m4-2m7: 0-1 3m+: 0-0
Track: LH: 0-0 RH: 0-1 Tight: 0-0 Gall: 0-0
Aids: Bl: 0-0 Vi: 0-0 Tstrap: 0-0
Best Rating: 0 10/02 MRas 2m3f110y good   Hdl

Bullfinch
100   122
10-y-o ch g Anshan-Lambay (Lorenzaccio)
R T Phillips Paul Duffy, Alan Beard, Brian Beard

Placings:5526/1316/**UP03P**014/1120P0/64144P005-45436
                                                 (1088)
2002/03: 27⁴GF, 22⁵G, 27⁴GF, 27³GF, 26⁶GF,

	Starts	1st	2nd	3rd	Win & Pl
Hurdles	5	0	0	1	806
Career Total	36	6	2	3	21836

122	6/01	NAbb	2m6f	D(0-120)HHdl	G-S	£3368
118	8/00	Uttx	3m110y	D(0-120)HHdl	G-F	£3059
112	5/00	Chep	3m	E(0-115)HHdl	FRM	£2726
112	4/00	Tntn	3m110y	G(0-95)HHdl	G-S	£1722
100	7/98	Worc	2m	E Hdl	G-F	£2512
104	5/98	MRas	2m1f110yE Hdl		G-F	£2862
				Total win prize-money £16252

Going: Sf: 0-0 GS: 0-0 Gd: 0-1 GF: - Fm: 0-4
Distance: 2m/2m3: 0-0 2m4-2m7: 0-1 3m+: 0-4
Track: LH: 0-4 RH: 0-1 Tight: 0-4 Gall: 0-1
Aids: Bl: 0-0 Vi: 0-0 Tstrap: 0-0
Best Rating: 122 6/01 NAbb 3m3f   gd-fm Hdl

Fair staying hurdler; stays three miles; has won on fast ground and good to soft.

Bunbury
90(94c)   (91c)76
10-y-o ch g Gildoran-Metaxa (Khalkis)
E L James E James

Placings:546/06U/2P5   (3825)
2002/03: 17²HY, 20ᴾS, 16⁵GS,

	Starts	1st	2nd	3rd	Win & Pl
Hurdles	1	0	0	0	
Chases	2	0	1	0	1302
Career Total	9	0	1	0	1302

Going: Sf: 0-2 GS: 0-1 Gd: 0-0 GF: - Fm: 0-0
Distance: 2m/2m3: 0-2 2m4-2m7: 0-1 3m+: 0-0
Track: LH: 0-3 RH: 0-0 Tight: 0-1 Gall: 0-0
Aids: Bl: 0-0 Vi: 0-0 Tstrap: 0-0
Best Rating: 98 12/00 Extr   2m6f110y heavy Hdl

Plating-class chaser; runner-up in a novice chase in November 2002 having been off the track for nearly two years; suited by testing ground.

Bungee Jumper
111   104+
13-y-o b g Idiots Delight-Catherine Bridge (Pitpan)
P L Clinton Trevor Farrow

Placings:20/002/2113/00/P40/42P26P0/2F431/3/P-P
(4706)
2002/03: 20PG,

	Starts	1st	2nd	3rd	Win & Pl
Hurdles	1	0	0	0	
Career Total	29	3	6	3	14991
105 7/99 Strf	2m1f110yD Ch			GD	£4318
104 10/95 Ludl	2m	E Hdl		FRM	£2332
97 9/95 Hntg	2m110y E Hdl			G-F	£2442
			Total win prize-money £9094		

Going:	Sf: 0-0 GS: 0-0 Gd: 0-1 GF: - Fm: 0-0
Distance:	2m/2m3: 0-0 2m4-2m7: 0-1 3m+: 0-0
Track:	LH: 0-1 RH: 0-0 Tight: 0-0 Gall: 0-0
Aids:	Bl: 0-0 Vi: 0-0 Tstrap: 0-0
Best Rating:	109 5/00 Worc 2m gd-fm Ch

Moderate chaser; one-time fairly useful novice for Tim Forster; back to form after a long spell in the doldrums when winning modest handicap chase at Uttoxeter in June; best at two miles; likes fast ground.

Bunkum
105   125
5-y-o b g Robellino (USA)-Spinning Mouse (Bustino)
R Lee John Jackson And Maggie Pope

Placings:441-1
(3447)
2002/03: 201HY,

	Starts	1st	2nd	3rd	Win & Pl
Hurdles	1	1	0	0	5025
Career Total	4	2	0	0	7692
122 2/03 Chep	2m4f	D(0-125)HHdl	HVY	£5024
118 3/02 Chep	2m110y E Hdl		SFT	£2667
			Total win prize-money £7692	

Going:	Sf: 1-1 GS: 0-0 Gd: 0-0 GF: - Fm: 0-0
Distance:	2m/2m3: 0-0 2m4-2m7: 1-1 3m+: 0-0
Track:	LH: 1-1 RH: 0-0 Tight: 0-0 Gall: 0-0
Aids:	Bl: 0-0 Vi: 0-0 Tstrap: 0-0
Best Rating:	122 2/03 Chep 2m4f heavy Hdl

Fair hurdler; effective at two and a half miles; acts on soft/heavy ground.

Bunratty Castle (IRE)
111   (114h)130+
8-y-o b g Supreme Leader-Shannon Foam (Le Bavard (FR))
P F Nicholls T J Hawkins, D J Nichols, A J White

Placings:212/4P42323-1U1
(2330)
2002/03: 201GS, 21UG, 251GS,

	Starts	1st	2nd	3rd	Win & Pl
Chases	3	2	0	0	12565
Career Total	13	3	4	2	26287
130 12/02 Winc	3m1f110yD(0-120)HCh	G-S	£7052
105 10/02 Strf	2m4f D Ch	G-S	£5512
115 1/01 Cork	2m Hdl	SFT	£4729
		Total win prize-money £17295	

Going:	Sf: 0-0 GS: 2-2 Gd: 0-1 GF: - Fm: 0-0
Distance:	2m/2m3: 0-0 2m4-2m7: 1-2 3m+: 1-1

Track: LH: 1-1 RH: 1-2 **Tight: 1-2** Gall: 0-0
Aids: Bl: 0-0 Vi: 0-0 Tstrap: 0-0
Best Rating: 130 12/02 Winc   3m1f110y   gd-sft   Ch

Useful chaser; useful novice hurdler when with Tony Mullins in Ireland; bought for 27,000gns and now with Paul Nicholls; inclined to make the odd jumping error; left clear at the second last to win a two and a half mile novice chase at Stratford in October 2002; ridden to get the trip when successful over three miles one at Wincanton in December; acts on soft ground.

Burcot Girl (IRE)
68   21
6-y-o b m Petardia-Phoenix Forli (USA) (Forli (ARG))
Mrs A C Tate M Tate

Placings:P0-0PP0
(2288)
2002/03: 16PG, 16PG, 16PG, 17PG,

	Starts	1st	2nd	3rd	Win & Pl
Hurdles	4	0	0	0	
Career Total	6	0	0	0	

Going:	Sf: 0-0 GS: 0-0 Gd: 0-3 GF: - Fm: 0-1
Distance:	2m/2m3: 0-4 2m4-2m7: 0-0 3m+: 0-0
Track:	LH: 0-1 RH: 0-3 Tight: 0-1 Gall: 0-0
Aids:	Bl: 0-0 Vi: 0-0 Tstrap: 0-0
Best Rating:	25 12/02 Hrfd 2m1f good Hdl

Burdens Girl
53
6-y-o ch m Alflora (IRE)-Dalbeattie (Phardante (FR))
H D Daly Furrows Ltd

Placings:44-00
(3865)
2002/03: 164GS, 210S, 19OGS,

	Starts	1st	2nd	3rd	Win & Pl
NH Flat	1	0	0	0	0
Hurdles	2	0	0	0	0
Career Total	4	0	0	0	0

Going:	Sf: 0-1 GS: 0-2 Gd: 0-0 GF: - Fm: 0-0
Distance:	2m/2m3: 0-2 2m4-2m7: 0-2 3m+: 0-0
Track:	LH: 0-1 RH: 0-2 Tight: 0-0 Gall: 0-0
Aids:	Bl: 0-0 Vi: 0-0 Tstrap: 0-0
Best Rating:	89 2/02 Ludl 2m good NHF

Burgundy Lace (USA)
99   89
4-y-o b f Lord Avie (USA)-Oro Bianco (USA) (Lyphard s Wish (FR))
Mrs L Wadham (J E Pease 9/11) The Salmon Racing Partnership

Placings:46P
(3554)
2002/03: 164GS, 165S, 16PHY,

	Starts	1st	2nd	3rd	Win & Pl
Hurdles	3	0	0	0	570
Career Total	3	0	0	0	570

Going:	Sf: 0-3 GS: 0-0 Gd: 0-0 GF: - Fm: 0-0
Distance:	2m/2m3: 0-3 2m4-2m7: 0-0 3m+: 0-0
Track:	LH: 0-2 RH: 0-1 Tight: 0-2 Gall: 0-0
Aids:	Bl: 0-0 Vi: 0-0 Tstrap: 0-0
Best Rating:	87 12/02 Kemp 2m soft Hdl

Burlu (FR)
9-y-o ch g Garde Royale-Acquevillaise (FR) (Un Prince (FR))
M C Pipe Fabien Ouaki

Placings:05524/200F2P/05635432000446/6113F20/61112 210-PFP
(4791)
2002/03: 24PG, 36FG, 29PG,

	Starts	1st	2nd	3rd	Win & Pl
Chases	3	0	0	0	
Career Total	43	6	7	3	59825
3/02 Autl	2m2f110y Ch	HVY	£6184
1/02 Pau	2m2f110y Ch	VS	£4382
1/02 Pau	2m2f110y Ch	GD	£6816
1/02 Pau	2m2f110y Ch	VS	£6817
1/01 Pau	2m7f Ch	HVY	£3880
1/01 Pau	2m2f110y Ch	HLD	£3880
		Total win prize-money £31960	

Going:	Sf: 0-0 GS: 0-0 Gd: 0-3 GF: - Fm: 0-0
Distance:	2m/2m3: 0-0 2m4-2m7: 0-0 3m+: 0-0
Track:	LH: 0-2 RH: 0-0 Tight: 0-1 Gall: 0-1
Aids:	Bl: 0-3 Vi: 0-0 Tstrap: 0-0
Best Rating:	0 4/03 Sand 3m5f110y good Ch

Ex-French chaser; stays two miles seven but most effective at two and a quarter; acts on testing ground; often wears blinkers; stiff tasks in 2002/3, and fell at Becher s second time around in the National.

Burning Truth (USA)
99(105h)   (115h)113
9-y-o ch g Known Fact (USA)-Galega (Sure Blade (USA))
M Sheppard (Mrs A Duffield 22/6) G Jones

Placings:0/0/4512114
(4639)
2002/03: 164G, 165G, 171GF, 162F, 161F, 161GF, 164GF,

	Starts	1st	2nd	3rd	Win & Pl
Hurdles	7	3	1	0	16756
Career Total	9	3	1	0	16756
115 4/03 Strf	2m110y D(0-120)HHdl	G-F	£5512
104 10/02 Ludl	2m D(0-120)HHdl	FRM	£6776
99 10/02 Hrfd	2m1f E(0-100)HHdl	G-F	£3034
		Total win prize-money £15323	

Going:	Sf: 0-0 GS: 0-0 Gd: 0-2 GF: - Fm: 3-5
Distance:	2m/2m3: 3-7 2m4-2m7: 0-0 3m+: 0-0
Track:	LH: 1-4 RH: 2-3 Tight: 1-3 Gall: 0-0
Aids:	Bl: 0-0 Vi: 0-0 Tstrap: 0-0
Best Rating:	115 4/03 Strf 2m110y gd-fm Hdl

Fair front-running hurdler; won at Ludlow and Hereford in October 2002 and returned from a break to win at Stratford in April 2003; runner-up on first three starts over fences and deserves to go one better; suited by fast ground which helps him stay 2m.

Burra Sahib
(74h)   (50h)
7-y-o b g First Trump-Old Flower (Persian Bold)
P C Ritchens Fraser Miller Racing

Placings:P0-034P
(0993)
2002/03: 22OG, 213GS, 264G, 26PGF,

	Starts	1st	2nd	3rd	Win & Pl
Hurdles	1	0	0	0	0
Chases	3	0	0	1	950
Career Total	6	0	0	1	950

Going:	Sf: 0-0 GS: 0-1 Gd: 0-2 GF: - Fm: 0-1
Distance:	2m/2m3: 0-0 2m4-2m7: 0-2 3m+: 0-2

Track: LH: 0-3 RH: 0-1 Tight: 0-3 Gall: 0-0
Aids: Bl: 0-0 Vi: 0-0 Tstrap: 0-1
Best Rating: 50 4/02 Strf 2m6f110y good Hdl

Burry Brave

4-y-o b g Presidium-Keep Mum (Mummy s Pet)
J S Goldie Patrick H Marron

Placings:P   (2768)
2002/03: 16PGS,

	Starts	1st	2nd	3rd	Win & Pl
Hurdles	1	0	0	0	
Career Total	1	0	0	0	

Going: Sf: 0-0 GS: 0-1 Gd: 0-0 GF: - Fm: 0-0
Distance: 2m/2m3: 0-1 2m4-2m7: 0-0 3m+: 0-0
Track: LH: 0-0 RH: 0-1 Tight: 0-1 Gall: 0-0
Aids: Bl: 0-0 Vi: 0-0 Tstrap: 0-0
Best Rating: 0   12/02 Muss 2m   gd-sft Hdl

Burundi (IRE)

102(111h)   (120 h)108
9-y-o b g Danehill (USA)-Sofala (Home Guard (USA))
A W Carroll K Marshall, M Lennon

Placings:1162/P40/223P436-1305F01205   (4607)
2002/03: 17¹G, 19³GS, 16⁵S, 16⁵G, 19⁹F G, 16⁰S, 20¹G, 20²G, 20⁹G, 21⁵G,

	Starts	1st	2nd	3rd	Win & Pl
Hurdles	7	2	1	1	10981
Chases	3	0	0	0	396
Career Total	24	4	4	3	24374
120 2/03	Weth	2m4f110yD(0-125)HHdl		GD	£4940
120 5/02	Folk	2m1f110yE(0-110)HHdl		GD	£2968
120 12/98	Leic	2m	E Hdl	G-S	£2882
109 11/98	Leic	2m	E Hdl	SFT	£2903

Total win prize-money £13693

Going: Sf: 0-2 GS: 0-1 Gd: 2-7 GF: - Fm: 0-0
Distance: 2m/2m3: 1-6 2m4-2m7: 1-4 3m+: 0-0
Track: LH: 1-7 RH: 1-3 Tight: 1-2 Gall: 0-2
Aids: Bl: 0-1 Vi: 0-0 Tstrap: 0-0
Best Rating: 120 3/03 Chep 2m4f   good   Hdl

Modest hurdler; stays two and a half miles and suited by good ground; best when held up; has been let down by his jumping over fences and has twice been reported to have suffered from breathing problems; got his act together when pipping odds on Tamango in extended 2m 1f novices chase at Stratford July 2003; acts on ground good and softer.

Burwood Breeze (IRE)

104(98h)   (100h)110
7-y-o b g Fresh Breeze (USA)-Shuil Le Cheile (Quayside)
T R George David & Lesley Byrne

Placings:544420-F552   (4078)
2002/03: 20FS, 25⁵S, 20⁵GS, 20²S,

	Starts	1st	2nd	3rd	Win & Pl
Chases	4	0	1	0	1723
Career Total	10	0	2	0	3125

Going: Sf: 0-3 GS: 0-1 Gd: 0-0 GF: - Fm: 0-0
Distance: 2m/2m3: 0-0 2m4-2m7: 0-3 3m+: 0-1
Track: LH: 0-3 RH: 0-1 Tight: 0-1 Gall: 0-1
Aids: Bl: 0-0 Vi: 0-1 Tstrap: 0-0

Best Rating: 103 3/03 Plum 2m4f   soft   Ch

Fair novice chaser; suited by two and a half miles and acts on soft ground.

Bus

90(69h)   (54h)96
8-y-o ch g Weld-Roaring Breeze (Roaring Riva)
Mrs L Williamson M Williamson

Placings:000P0/106F040/34F2   (0739)
2002/03: 17³GF, 16⁴S, 17F G, 16²G,

	Starts	1st	2nd	3rd	Win & Pl
Hurdles	1	0	0	1	317
Chases	3	0	1	0	1340
Career Total	16	1	1	1	3577
70 5/00	Hexm	2m	F(0-95)HHdl	GD	£1919

Total win prize-money £1919

Going: Sf: 0-1 GS: 0-0 Gd: 0-2 GF: - Fm: 0-1
Distance: 2m/2m3: 0-4 2m4-2m7: 0-0 3m+: 0-1
Track: LH: 0-4 RH: 0-0 Tight: 0-4 Gall: 0-0
Aids: Bl: 0-0 Vi: 0-0 Tstrap: 0-0
Best Rating: 96 7/02 Strf 2m1f110y good   Ch

Moderate hurdler, suited by fast ground.

Bush Hill Bandit (IRE)

8-y-o b/br g Executive Perk-Baby Isle (Menelek)
Mrs Anne-Marie Hays C J Hays

Placings:06/006/P-1   (4671)
2002/03: 24¹G,

	Starts	1st	2nd	3rd	Win & Pl
Chases	1	1	0	0	2878
Career Total	7	1	0	0	2878
94 4/03	Fknm	3m110y	H Ch	GD	£2878

Total win prize-money £2878

Going: Sf: 0-0 GS: 0-0 Gd: 1-1 GF: - Fm: 0-0
Distance: 2m/2m3: 0-0 2m4-2m7: 0-0 3m+: 1-1
Track: LH: 1-1 RH: 0-0 Tight: 1-1 Gall: 0-0
Aids: Bl: 0-0 Vi: 0-0 Tstrap: 0-0
Best Rating: 94 4/03 Fknm 3m110y   good   Ch

Modest pointer/hunter chaser; completed a hat-trick on hunter-chase debut at Fakenham in April 2003; stays three miles; best on a sound surface.

Bush Park (IRE)

106(104h)   (102h)115
8-y-o b g Be My Native (USA)-By All Means (Pitpan)
R H Alner H Wellstead

Placings:325/3503/0012312310-014B310F   (4694)
2002/03: 24⁰GF, 21¹GF, 19⁴G, 20RGS, 20³G, 20¹HY, 20⁹G, 21F G,

	Starts	1st	2nd	3rd	Win & Pl
Hurdles	1	0	0	0	0
Chases	7	2	0	1	14789
Career Total	25	5	3	6	31684
123 12/02	Plum	2m4f	D(0-125)HCh	HVY	£5362
117 10/02	Uttx	2m5f	D(0-125)HCh	G-F	£7800
102 3/02	Winc	2m	E(0-105)HHdl	SFT	£2730
112 11/01	Hrld	2m3f	E(0-115)HCh	GD	£3435
101 10/01	Sthl	2m	F(0-100)HCh	GD	£2756

Total win prize-money £22084

Going: Sf: 1-1 GS: 0-1 Gd: 0-4 GF: - Fm: 1-2
Distance: 2m/2m3: 0-0 2m4-2m7: 2-7 3m+: 0-1
Track: LH: 2-7 RH: 0-1 Tight: 1-3 Gall: 0-1

Aids: Bl: 0-0 Vi: 0-0 Tstrap: 0-0
Best Rating: 123 12/02 Plum 2m4f   heavy   Ch

Fair chaser; winner over both hurdles and fences; stays two and a half miles; a sound jumper who handles good ground or softer; tried in a visor after falling at Newton Abbot April 2003.

Bushehr (IRE)

100(96c)   (80c)90
11-y-o b g Persian Bold-Shejrah (USA) (Northjet)
Mrs A M Thorpe Mrs A M Thorpe

Placings:30500245/4/40-U3U223   (1083)
2002/03: 16UGF, 16³GF, 16UGF, 22²GS, 22⁰GF, 20³GF,

	Starts	1st	2nd	3rd	Win & Pl
Hurdles	3	0	2	1	1990
Chases	3	0	0	1	492
Career Total	17	0	3	3	3896

Going: Sf: 0-0 GS: 0-1 Gd: 0-0 GF: - Fm: 0-5
Distance: 2m/2m3: 0-3 2m4-2m7: 0-3 3m+: 0-0
Track: LH: 0-4 RH: 0-2 Tight: 0-2 Gall: 0-2
Aids: Bl: 0-0 Vi: 0-0 Tstrap: 0-0
Best Rating: 93 10/95 Carl 2m1f   gd-fm   Hdl

Moderate chaser/hurdler; handles fast ground; suited by soft.

Bushido (IRE)

104   104
4-y-o br g Brief Truce (USA)-Pheopotstown (Henbit (USA))
Mrs S J Smith (D K Weld 18/8) Mrs B Ramsden

Placings:0221213   (4637)
2002/03: 16⁰GF, 16²G, 16²GS, 17¹GS, 17²G, 16¹G, 16³GF,

	Starts	1st	2nd	3rd	Win & Pl
Hurdles	7	2	3	1	11585
Career Total	7	2	3	1	11585
104 3/03	Hexm	2m110y	E Hdl	GD	£3887
95 3/03	Carl	2m1f	F Hdl	G-S	£2660

Total win prize-money £6547

Going: Sf: 0-0 GS: 1-2 Gd: 1-3 GF: - Fm: 0-2
Distance: 2m/2m3: 2-7 2m4-2m7: 0-0 3m+: 0-0
Track: LH: 1-5 RH: 1-1 Tight: 0-4 Gall: 0-0
Aids: Bl: 0-0 Vi: 0-0 Tstrap: 0-0
Best Rating: 104 4/03 Strf 2m110y   gd-fm   Hdl

Fair novice hurdler; off the mark in a tight finish at Carlisle in March and creditable effort next time before notching second win at Hexham the same month; acts on good and good to soft; should stay further than two miles.

Business

4-y-o br c Bluegrass Prince (IRE)-Dancing Doll (USA) (Buckfinder (USA))
G A Ham (I A Wood 5/5) All For One

Placings:PPR   (3252)
2002/03: 18²GF, 16PGS, 16RHY,

	Starts	1st	2nd	3rd	Win & Pl
Hurdles	3	0	0	0	
Career Total	3	0	0	0	

Going: Sf: 0-1 GS: 0-1 Gd: 0-0 GF: - Fm: 0-1
Distance: 2m/2m3: 0-2 2m4-2m7: 0-0 3m+: 0-0
Track: LH: 0-2 RH: 0-1 Tight: 0-1 Gall: 0-0
Aids: Bl: 0-0 Vi: 0-1 Tstrap: 0-0
Best Rating: 0   1/03 Wwck 2m   heavy   Hdl

Business Class (NZ)
103(90h)   (76h)**107**

11-y-o b g Accountant (NZ)-Fury s Princess (NZ) (Our Kungfu (NZ))
Mrs M Reveley Ernie Fenwick

Placings:5531104-212F063P3   (4787)
2002/03: 20²GS, 22¹GF, 22²G, 24⁴GS, 16⁶GS, 19⁶G, 20³GS, 21¹PG, 20³G,

	Starts	1st	2nd	3rd	Win & Pl
Hurdles	2	0	0	0	0
Chases	7	1	2	2	7506
Career Total	16	3	2	3	16535
106	6/02	MRas	2m6f110yF(0-100)HCh	G-F	£3526
105	4/02	Sedg	2m5f	D Ch	G-F	£3883
94	3/02	Catt	2m	D Ch	G-S	£4192

Total win prize-money £11603

Going:	Sf: 0-0 GS: 0-4 Gd: 0-4 GF: - Fm: 0-0
Distance:	2m2/m3: 0-2 **2m4-2m7: 1-6** 3m+: 0-1
Track:	LH: 0-4 RH: **1-5** Tight: **1-7** Gall: 0-0
Aids:	Bl: 0-0 Vi: 0-0 Tstrap: 0-0
Best Rating:	**109** 7/02 MRas 2m6f110y good Ch

Modest chaser; former three-day eventer; jumps soundly and took two modest novice chases in the spring of 2002; stays two miles six; unraced on ground softer than good to soft.

Busky Gorse
59

7-y-o gr m Scallywag-Miss Anax (Anax)
P Beaumont Josttigo Racing

Placings:0/R0-0P   (0566)
2002/03: 17⁰G, 17PGF,

	Starts	1st	2nd	3rd	Win & Pl
Hurdles	2	0	0	0	
Career Total	5	0	0	0	

Going:	Sf: 0-0 GS: 0-0 Gd: 0-1 GF: - Fm: 0-1
Distance:	2m2/m3: 0-2 2m4-2m7: 0-0 3m+: 0-0
Track:	LH: 0-1 RH: 0-1 Tight: 0-2 Gall: 0-0
Aids:	Bl: 0-0 Vi: 0-0 Tstrap: 0-0
Best Rating:	**32** 1/01 Catt 2m gd-sft NHF

Bustamante

7-y-o ch g Sir Harry Lewis (USA)-Carribean Sound (Good Times (ITY))
P Monteith Hamilton House Limited

Placings:0-U   (1984)
2002/03: 16US,

	Starts	1st	2nd	3rd	Win & Pl
Chases	1	0	0	0	
Career Total	2	0	0	0	

Going:	Sf: 0-1 GS: 0-0 Gd: 0-0 GF: - Fm: 0-0
Distance:	2m2/m3: 0-1 2m4-2m7: 0-0 3m+: 0-0
Track:	LH: 0-1 RH: 0-0 Tight: 0-1 Gall: 0-0
Aids:	Bl: 0-0 Vi: 0-0 Tstrap: 0-0
Best Rating:	**0** 11/02 Ayr 2m soft Ch

Busted Flat (IRE)
109   **90**

10-y-o br g Bustino-Trailing Rose (Undulate (USA))
Mrs M Reveley R Burridge

Placings:000V/4131F/50/6-0P016   (3744)
2002/03: 20⁰GS, 20PGS, 19⁹S, 23¹GS, 26⁶G,

	Starts	1st	2nd	3rd	Win & Pl
Hurdles	5	1	0	0	5005
Career Total	17	3	0	1	10150
90	2/03	Weth	2m7f	D(0-115)HHdl	G-S	£5005
106	1/00	Weth	2m4f110yF(0-105)HHdl	SFT	£2170
85	11/99	Weth	2m4f110yF(0-110)HHdl	GD	£2304

Total win prize-money £9479

Going:	Sf: 0-1 GS: 1-3 Gd: 0-1 GF: - Fm: 0-0
Distance:	2m2/m3: 0-0 **2m4-2m7: 1-4** 3m+: 0-1
Track:	**LH: 1-4** RH: 0-1 Tight: 0-0 Gall: 0-1
Aids:	Bl: 0-0 Vi: 0-0 Tstrap: 0-0
Best Rating:	**106** 2/00 Weth 2m7f soft Hdl

Plating-class hurdler; emerged from the wilderness to pull off a shock win in a handicap hurdle run in testing conditions at Wetherby in February; stays nearly three miles.

Buster Clyde (IRE)
73f   **56f**

6-y-o b g Bustomi-The Red Mare (Sagaro)
J R Bewley R Bewley

Placings:0   (2518)
2002/03: 16⁰S,

	Starts	1st	2nd	3rd	Win & Pl
NH Flat	1	0	0	0	
Career Total	1	0	0	0	

Going:	Sf: 0-1 GS: 0-0 Gd: 0-0 GF: - Fm: 0-0
Distance:	2m2/m3: 0-1 2m4-2m7: 0-0 3m+: 0-0
Track:	LH: 0-1 RH: 0-0 Tight: 0-0 Gall: 0-0
Aids:	Bl: 0-0 Vi: 0-0 Tstrap: 0-0
Best Rating:	**56** 12/02 Newc 2m soft NHF

Bustisu
89f   **82f**

6-y-o b m Rakaposhi King-Tasmin Gayle (IRE) (Strong Gale)
D J Wintle John W Egan

Placings:63   (2259)
2002/03: 16⁶G, 17³HY,

	Starts	1st	2nd	3rd	Win & Pl
NH Flat	2	0	0	1	274
Career Total	2	0	0	1	274

Going:	Sf: 0-1 GS: 0-0 Gd: 0-0 GF: - Fm: 0-0
Distance:	2m2/m3: 0-2 2m4-2m7: 0-0 3m+: 0-0
Track:	LH: 0-1 RH: 0-1 Tight: 0-1 Gall: 0-0
Aids:	Bl: 0-0 Vi: 0-0 Tstrap: 0-0
Best Rating:	**82** 12/02 Folk 2m1f110y heavy NHF

Bustling Rio (IRE)
85(96c)   (109c)**123**

7-y-o b g Up And At Em-Une Venitienne (FR) (Green Dancer (USA))
P C Haslam Rio Stainless Engineering Limited

Placings:111/14120-0   (1741)
2002/03: 20⁰GS,

	Starts	1st	2nd	3rd	Win & Pl
Hurdles	1	0	0	0	
Career Total	9	5	1	0	17751
99	3/02	Hntg	2m4f110yE Ch	G-F	£3035
99	11/01	Newc	2m4f	E Ch	G-S	£3168

124	1/01	Weth	2m7f	E Hdl	HVY	£2660
120	10/00	Aint	2m4f	E Hdl	GD	£3120
113	10/00	MRas	2m3f110yE Hdl	GD	£2912

Total win prize-money £14897

Going:	Sf: 0-0 GS: 1-0 Gd: 0-0 GF: - Fm: 0-0
Distance:	2m2/m3: 0-0 2m4-2m7: 0-1 3m+: 0-0
Track:	LH: 0-1 RH: 0-0 Tight: 0-0 Gall: 0-0
Aids:	Bl: 0-0 Vi: 0-0 Tstrap: 0-0
Best Rating:	**124** 1/01 Weth 2m7f heavy Hdl

Useful chaser; modest hurdler; winner on the Flat on both turf and sand; very versatile; probably best over trips of around two and a half miles though he does stay further; acts on any ground.

Butterwick Chief
99   **68**

6-y-o b g Be My Chief (USA)-Swift Return (Double Form)
R A Fahey P S Cresswell

Placings:000-P3   (2688)
2002/03: 18PHY, 17³GS,

	Starts	1st	2nd	3rd	Win & Pl
Hurdles	2	0	0	1	347
Career Total	5	0	0	1	347

Going:	Sf: 0-1 GS: 0-1 Gd: 0-0 GF: - Fm: 0-0
Distance:	2m2/m3: 0-2 2m4-2m7: 0-0 3m+: 0-0
Track:	LH: 0-1 RH: 0-1 Tight: 0-2 Gall: 0-0
Aids:	Bl: 0-0 Vi: 0-1 Tstrap: 0-0
Best Rating:	**68** 12/02 MRas 2m1f110y gd-sft Hdl

Plating-class hurdler, seems to appreciate soft ground.

Buz Kiri (USA)
88   **79**

5-y-o b g Gulch (USA)-Whitecorners (USA) (Caro)
A W Carroll Serafino Agodino

Placings:0   (3847)
2002/03: 16⁰G,

	Starts	1st	2nd	3rd	Win & Pl
Hurdles	1	0	0	0	
Career Total	1	0	0	0	

Going:	Sf: 0-0 GS: 0-0 Gd: 0-1 GF: - Fm: 0-0
Distance:	2m2/m3: 0-1 2m4-2m7: 0-0 3m+: 0-0
Track:	LH: 0-0 RH: 0-1 Tight: 0-0 Gall: 0-0
Aids:	Bl: 0-0 Vi: 0-0 Tstrap: 0-1
Best Rating:	**75** 2/03 Ludl 2m good Hdl

Buzybakson (IRE)
97   **102+**

6-y-o b/br g Bob Back (USA)-Middle Verde (USA) (Sham (USA))
A M Hales Andrew L Cohen

Placings:06F13   (2985)
2002/03: 16⁰G, 16⁶GF, 20⁶HY, 19¹GS, 22³HY,

	Starts	1st	2nd	3rd	Win & Pl
NH Flat	2	0	0	0	0
Hurdles	3	1	0	1	3478
Career Total	5	1	0	1	3478
102	12/02	MRas	2m3f110yF Hdl	G-S	£2964

Total win prize-money £2965

Going:	Sf: 0-2 GS: 1-1 Gd: 0-1 GF: - Fm: 0-1
Distance:	2m2/m3: 0-2 **2m4-2m7: 1-3** 3m+: 0-1
Track:	LH: 0-2 RH: **1-2** Tight: **1-3** Gall: 0-0

Aids: Bl: 0-0 Vi: 0-0 Tstrap: 0-0
Best Rating: 102 12/02 MRas 2m3f110y gd-sft Hdl

Moderate hurdler; lightly raced; won an ordinary event on testing ground at Market Rasen in December 2002.

By Definition (IRE)
73   35
5-y-o gr m Definite Article-Miss Goodbody (Castle Keep)
J M Bradley Paul De Weck

Placings: P0P   (2671)
2002/03: 16⁶G, 16⁶G, 17⁵S,

	Starts	1st	2nd	3rd	Win & Pl
Hurdles	3	0	0	0	
Career Total	3	0	0	0	

Going: Sf: 0-1 GS: 0-0 Gd: 0-2 GF: - Fm: 0-0
Distance: 2m/2m3: 0-3 2m4-2m7: 0-0 3m+: 0-0
Track: LH: 0-0 RH: 0-3 Tight: 0-0 Gall: 0-0
Aids: Bl: 0-0 Vi: 0-0 Tstrap: 0-0
Best Rating: 35 12/02 Ludl 2m   good   Hdl

By Degree (IRE)
107   125
7-y-o gr g Roselier (FR)-Decent Enough (Decent Fellow)
R J Hodges Fieldspring Racing

Placings: 00-5F221   (3948)
2002/03: 16⁵G, 22⁶GS, 22²GS, 24²S, 24¹S,

	Starts	1st	2nd	3rd	Win & Pl
NH Flat	1	0	0	0	
Hurdles	4	1	2	0	9413
Career Total	7	1	2	0	9413
94	3/03	Extr	3m110y	E Hdl	SFT £4306
				Total win prize-money £4306

Going: Sf: 1-2 GS: 0-2 Gd: 0-1 GF: - Fm: 0-0
Distance: 2m/2m3: 0-1 2m4-2m7: 0-2 3m+: 1-2
Track: LH: 0-0 RH: 1-5 Tight: 0-0 Gall: 0-0
Aids: Bl: 0-0 Vi: 0-0 Tstrap: 0-0
Best Rating: 123 2/03 Asct 3m   soft   Hdl

Useful hurdler; Irish pointing winner; finished second to a couple of leading staying novice hurdlers before winning a slowly-run minor event on soft ground at Exeter.

By N By (IRE)
93f
7-y-o b g Un Desperado (FR)-Andonova (Prince Tenderfoot (USA))
Miss Venetia Williams The Down South Syndicate

Placings: 00-   (0013)
2002/03: 18⁰G,

	Starts	1st	2nd	3rd	Win & Pl
NH Flat	1	0	0	0	
Career Total	2	0	0	0	

Going: Sf: 0-0 GS: 0-0 Gd: 0-1 GF: - Fm: 0-0
Distance: 2m/2m3: 0-1 2m4-2m7: 0-0 3m+: 0-0
Track: LH: 0-1 RH: 0-0 Tight: 0-0 Gall: 0-0
Aids: Bl: 0-0 Vi: 0-0 Tstrap: 0-0
Best Rating: 93 1/02 Kemp 2m   soft   NHF

Bygone
94f   89f
5-y-o b g Past Glories-Meltonby (Sayf El Arab (USA))

J Hetherton N Hetherton

Placings: 2   (0834)
2002/03: 17²GF,

	Starts	1st	2nd	3rd	Win & Pl
NH Flat	1	0	1	0	526
Career Total	1	0	1	0	526

Going: Sf: 0-0 GS: 0-0 Gd: 0-0 GF: - Fm: 0-1
Distance: 2m/2m3: 0-1 2m4-2m7: 0-0 3m+: 0-0
Track: LH: 0-1 RH: 0-0 Tight: 0-1 Gall: 0-0
Aids: Bl: 0-0 Vi: 0-0 Tstrap: 0-0
Best Rating: 89 7/02 Sedg 2m1f   gd-fm   NHF

Encouraging debut in a Sedgefield bumper.

Byron Lamb
106(108h)   (122h)135+
6-y-o b g Rambo Dancer (CAN)-Caroline Lamb (Hotfoot)
N G Richards Edward Melville

Placings: 73111-12121   (4407)
2002/03: 16¹GS, 21²GS, 16¹HY, 17²GS, 16¹G,

	Starts	1st	2nd	3rd	Win & Pl
Chases	5	3	2	0	17868
Career Total	10	7	2	1	29164
127	3/03	Hexm	2m110y	E Ch	GD £3880
119	1/03	Ayr	2m	D Ch	HVY £5453
122	12/02	Ayr	2m	D Ch	G-S £4914
113	3/02	Carl	2m1f	E Hdl	G-S £3094
122	3/02	Ayr	2m	D Hdl	SFT £3465
112	3/02	Ayr	2m	F Hdl	HVY £2478
112	11/01	Ayr	2m	H NHF	G-S £1788
				Total win prize-money £25075

Going: Sf: 1-1 GS: 1-3 Gd: 1-1 GF: - Fm: 0-0
Distance: 2m/2m3: 3-4 2m4-2m7: 0-1 3m+: 0-0
Track: LH: 3-5 RH: 0-0 Tight: 0-1 Gall: 0-0
Aids: Bl: 0-0 Vi: 0-0 Tstrap: 0-0
Best Rating: 135 3/03 Kels 2m1f   gd-sft   Ch

Very useful novice chaser; formerly decent hurdler; good record at Ayr; adequate rather than good jumper; best over 2m and did not seem to stay when tried over farther; suited by cut in the ground.

C'Est Deja Vu (IRE)
91   83
7-y-o b g Phardante (FR)-Quayside Romance (Quayside)
P F Nicholls C R Barnett

Placings: 05F660-4   (0123)
2002/03: 27⁴GF,

	Starts	1st	2nd	3rd	Win & Pl
Hurdles	1	0	0	0	0
Career Total	7	0	0	0	0

Going: Sf: 0-0 GS: 0-0 Gd: 0-0 GF: - Fm: 0-1
Distance: 2m/2m3: 0-0 2m4-2m7: 0-0 3m+: 0-1
Track: LH: 0-0 RH: 0-0 Tight: 0-1 Gall: 0-0
Aids: Bl: 0-0 Vi: 0-0 Tstrap: 0-0
Best Rating: 93 11/01 Plum 2m2f   gd-sft   NHF

Ca Ne Fait Rien (IRE)
80f   85f
7-y-o gr g Denel (FR)-Fairytale-Ending (Sweet Story)
N M Babbage Ford Associated Racing Team Ii

Placings: 04-4   (0205)

2002/03: 16⁴GF,

	Starts	1st	2nd	3rd	Win & Pl
NH Flat	1	0	0	0	0
Career Total	3	0	0	0	0

Going: Sf: 0-0 GS: 0-0 Gd: 0-0 GF: - Fm: 0-1
Distance: 2m/2m3: 0-1 2m4-2m7: 0-0 3m+: 0-0
Track: LH: 0-1 RH: 0-0 Tight: 0-0 Gall: 0-0
Aids: Bl: 0-0 Vi: 0-0 Tstrap: 0-0
Best Rating: 85 5/02 Worc 2m   gd-fm   NHF

Caballe (USA)
103   71
6-y-o ch m Opening Verse (USA)-Attirance (FR) (Crowned Prince (USA))
Dr P Pritchard (N J Henderson 28/2) B S Hicks

Placings: 133350-14050005   (4625)
2002/03: 16¹GS, 16⁴S, 16⁹GS, 21⁵S, 17⁰G, 19⁰GS, 17⁰G, 17⁵GF,

	Starts	1st	2nd	3rd	Win & Pl
Hurdles	8	1	0	0	4076
Career Total	14	2	0	3	7781
106	11/02	Hntg	2m110y	D(0-115)HHdl	G-S £4075
114	12/01	Plum	2m	E Hdl	SFT £2492
				Total win prize-money £6568

Going: Sf: 0-2 GS: 1-3 Gd: 0-2 GF: - Fm: 0-1
Distance: 2m/2m3: 1-6 2m4-2m7: 0-2 3m+: 0-0
Track: LH: 0-4 RH: 1-4 Tight: 0-3 Gall: 1-2
Aids: Bl: 0-2 Vi: 0-0 Tstrap: 0-0
Best Rating: 114 12/01 Bang 2m1f   gd-sft   Hdl

Modest handicap hurdler at her best;. effective over two miles and acts on a soft surface.

Cabaret Quest
(96h)   (62h)
7-y-o ch g Pursuit Of Love-Cabaret Artiste (Shareef Dancer (USA))
J M Bradley Miss S Howell

Placings: 0P40F-0FP   (0659)
2002/03: 16⁰G, 16⁶GF, 16⁰GF,

	Starts	1st	2nd	3rd	Win & Pl
Hurdles	1	0	0	0	0
Chases	2	0	0	0	0
Career Total	8	0	0	0	0

Going: Sf: 0-0 GS: 0-0 Gd: 0-1 GF: - Fm: 0-2
Distance: 2m/2m3: 0-3 2m4-2m7: 0-0 3m+: 0-0
Track: LH: 0-3 RH: 0-0 Tight: 0-1 Gall: 0-0
Aids: Bl: 0-0 Vi: 0-0 Tstrap: 0-1
Best Rating: 68 9/01 Worc 2m   gd-fm   Hdl

Cabille (FR)
11-y-o ch g Lesotho (USA)-Ironique (FR) (Riverman (USA))
H H G Owen H H G Owen

Placings: 023P/0P40/PU   (3821)
2002/03: 20⁰S, 23⁰GS,

	Starts	1st	2nd	3rd	Win & Pl
Chases	2	0	0	0	0
Career Total	10	0	1	1	1788

Going: Sf: 0-1 GS: 0-1 Gd: 0-0 GF: - Fm: 0-0
Distance: 2m/2m3: 0-0 2m4-2m7: 0-1 3m+: 0-0
Track: LH: 0-1 RH: 0-1 Tight: 0-0 Gall: 0-0
Aids: Bl: 0-0 Vi: 0-0 Tstrap: 0-0
Best Rating: 94 3/98 Donc 2m110y   soft   Ch

Cades Bay

12-y-o b g Unfuwain (USA)-Antilla (Averof)
Miss L Gardner D V Gardner

Placings:0/00F3/5P/0F/P0U55500-0   (0029)
2002/03: 21⁰GF,

	Starts	1st	2nd	3rd	Win & Pl
Chases	1	0	0	0	
Career Total	19	0	0	2	695

Going: Sf: 0-0 GS: 0-0 Gd: 0-0 GF: - Fm: 0-1
Distance: 2m/2m3: 0-0 2m4-2m7: 0-1 3m+: 0-0
Track: LH: 0-1 RH: 0-0 Tight: 0-0 Gall: 0-1
Aids: Bl: 0-1 Vi: 0-0 Tstrap: 0-0
Best Rating: 92   10/95 Extr 2m1f110y good Hdl

Cadougold (FR)

102(84h)   (59h)134
12-y-o b g Cadoudal (FR)-Fontaine Aux Faons (FR) (Nadjar (FR))
Miss K Marks (M C Pipe 23/8) Nick Shutts

Placings:F316511/00253/34141/22022/2/1P1F13/1434P34
2-455F   (1208)
2002/03: 23⁴G, 22⁵GF, 18⁵GF, 21⁶G,

	Starts	1st	2nd	3rd	Win & Pl
Hurdles	1	0	0	0	0
Chases	3	0	0	0	532
Career Total	41	9	7	6	133455
137 5/01	NAbb	2m5f110yE Ch		G-F	£3614
114 4/01	Hayd	2m	C Ch	SFT	£6776
124 3/01	Wwck	2m4f110yE Ch		HVY	£3133
130 11/00	Tntn	2m3f	C Ch	G-S	£6080
148 4/97	Aint	2m4f	B HHdl	GD	£12653
139 12/96	Chep	2m4f110yB(0-140)HHdl		SFT	£4935
99 4/95	Chep	2m110y	E Hdl	GD	£2500
112 4/95	Chep	2m110y	E Hdl	FRM	£2794
124 3/95	Wind	2m4f	E Hdl	HVY	£2267

Total win prize-money £44755

Going: Sf: 0-0 GS: 0-0 Gd: 0-2 GF: - Fm: 0-2
Distance: 2m/2m3: 0-1 2m4-2m7: 0-2 3m+: 0-1
Track: LH: 0-2 RH: 0-1 Tight: 0-2 Gall: 0-0
Aids: Bl: 0-0 Vi: 0-1 Tstrap: 0-0
Best Rating: 153   4/98 Chep 2m110y heavy Hdl

Useful hurdler/ chaser; effective on a variety of ground; has a high cruising speed; effective at around two and a half miles but has shown he stays three; claimed out of Martin Pipe s yard in August 2002.

Cadrillon (FR)

13-y-o br g Le Pontet (FR)-Jenvraie (FR) (Night And Day)
Miss J E Foster Yorkshire Point-to-Point Club

Placings:4000F4/0/13P45326P0/54P4545443P/6464P2550
P0P/PP-52P   (4261)
2002/03: 25⁵GF, 26²GS, 27⁵G,

	Starts	1st	2nd	3rd	Win & Pl
Chases	3	0	1	0	780
Career Total	45	1	3	3	9145
93 5/98	Hexm	3m1f	H Ch	G-S	£2583

Total win prize-money £2583

Going: Sf: 0-0 GS: 0-1 Gd: 0-1 GF: - Fm: 0-1
Distance: 2m/2m3: 0-0 2m4-2m7: 0-0 3m+: 0-3
Track: LH: 0-3 RH: 0-0 Tight: 0-2 Gall: 0-0
Aids: Bl: 0-2 Vi: 0-0 Tstrap: 0-0
Best Rating: 93   5/98 Hexm 3m1f   gd-sft Ch

Plating-class chaser but better pointer; stays really well.

Cadw (IRE)

89(71h)   (47h)42
8-y-o b g Cadeaux Genereux-Night Jar (Night Shift (USA))
R Dickin Harborne House Racing

Placings:0/0-606   (4223)
2002/03: 16⁵HY, 16⁹GS, 16⁶GF,

	Starts	1st	2nd	3rd	Win & Pl
Hurdles	2	0	0	0	0
Chases	1	0	0	0	0
Career Total	5	0	0	0	0

Going: Sf: 0-1 GS: 0-1 Gd: 0-0 GF: - Fm: 0-1
Distance: 2m/2m3: 0-3 2m4-2m7: 0-0 3m+: 0-0
Track: LH: 0-1 RH: 0-2 Tight: 0-0 Gall: 0-1
Aids: Bl: 0-0 Vi: 0-0 Tstrap: 0-0
Best Rating: 47   3/01 MRas 2m1f110y gd-sft Hdl

Caernomore

5-y-o b g Caerleon (USA)-Nuryana (Nureyev (USA))
W G M Turner (P C Haslam 15/2) Michael Kelly

Placings:P   (4675)
2002/03: 17⁵GF,

	Starts	1st	2nd	3rd	Win & Pl
Hurdles	1	0	0	0	
Career Total	1	0	0	0	

Going: Sf: 0-0 GS: 0-0 Gd: 0-0 GF: - Fm: 0-0
Distance: 2m/2m3: 0-1 2m4-2m7: 0-0 3m+: 0-0
Track: LH: 0-0 RH: 0-1 Tight: 0-0 Gall: 0-0
Aids: Bl: 0-0 Vi: 0-0 Tstrap: 0-0
Best Rating: 0   4/03 Hrfd 2m1f   gd-fm Hdl

Caesar's Palace (GER)

107   106
6-y-o ch g Lomitas-Caraveine (FR) (Nikos)
Miss Lucinda V Russell (M C Pipe 10/8) Brahms & Liszt

Placings:111156/25000P4410-1231626024   (4618)
2002/03: 24¹GF, 24²GS, 24³G, 22¹GS, 24⁶GF, 24²S, 22⁶HY, 23⁹S, 22²S, 20⁴GF,

	Starts	1st	2nd	3rd	Win & Pl
Hurdles	10	2	3	1	10829
Career Total	26	7	4	1	33358
96 8/02	Strf	2m6f110yF Hdl		G-S	£3073
127 5/02	Chep	3m	E(0-115)HHdl	G-F	£2681
125 4/02	Extr	3m110y	D(0-120)HHdl	FRM	£5401
124 12/00	Chel	2m1f	B Hdl	SFT	£7150
119 11/00	Newb	2m110y	D Hdl	SFT	£3887
119 9/00	Plum	2m	E Hdl	G-F	£2352
105 8/00	Font	2m2f110yE Hdl		G-F	£2254

Total win prize-money £26799

Going: Sf: 0-4 GS: 1-2 Gd: 0-1 GF: - Fm: 1-3
Distance: 2m/2m3: 0-0 2m4-2m7: 1-4 3m+: 1-6
Track: LH: 2-8 RH: 0-2 Tight: 1-4 Gall: 0-0
Aids: Bl: 0-0 Vi: 2-4 Tstrap: 0-0
Best Rating: 127   5/02 Chep 3m   gd-fm Hdl

Modest hurdler; prolific novice hurdle winner for Martin Pipe in 2000; won at Exeter and Chepstow when stepped up to three miles in the spring of 2002 amd won a Stratford claimer in August, held since for a new stable; at his best

---

when making the running; usually wears visor, blinkers or cheekpieces.

Cage Aux Folles (IRE)

91   73
8-y-o b g Kenmare (FR)-Ivory Thread (USA) (Sir Ivor)
R Lee The Cage Aux Folles Partnership

Placings:403/P3032534451/4511P31443021/0P-0005   (4283)
2002/03: 17⁰HY, 19⁰G, 16⁹GS, 16⁵GF,

	Starts	1st	2nd	3rd	Win & Pl
Hurdles	4	0	0	0	0
Career Total	33	5	2	6	22402
120 4/01	NAbb	2m1f	E(0-115)HHdl	SFT	£5590
117 10/00	Bang	2m1f	F(0-110)HHdl	SFT	£4309
107 7/00	Worc	2m	E(0-115)HHdl	G-F	£3464
108 6/00	NAbb	2m1f	F(0-105)HHdl	G-F	£2597
96 4/00	Winc	2m	F(0-110)HHdl	G-S	£2247

Total win prize-money £18209

Going: Sf: 0-1 GS: 0-1 Gd: 0-1 GF: - Fm: 0-1
Distance: 2m/2m3: 0-3 2m4-2m7: 0-1 3m+: 0-0
Track: LH: 0-2 RH: 0-2 Tight: 0-2 Gall: 0-0
Aids: Bl: 0-0 Vi: 0-2 Tstrap: 0-1
Best Rating: 120   4/01 NAbb 2m1f   soft Hdl

Caher Society (IRE)

11-y-o ch g Moscow Society (USA)-Dame s Delight (Ballymoss)
Paul Morris R D J Swinburne

Placings:0/05/P33P0P/35F/261P-40   (0395)
2002/03: 16⁴G, 28⁹G,

	Starts	1st	2nd	3rd	Win & Pl
Chases	2	0	0	0	
Career Total	18	1	1	3	5322
106 3/02	Ludl	2m4f	H Ch	SFT	£2786

Total win prize-money £2786

Going: Sf: 0-0 GS: 0-0 Gd: 0-2 GF: - Fm: 0-0
Distance: 2m/2m3: 0-1 2m4-2m7: 0-0 3m+: 0-1
Track: LH: 0-1 RH: 0-1 Tight: 0-1 Gall: 0-0
Aids: Bl: 0-0 Vi: 0-0 Tstrap: 0-0
Best Rating: 106   3/02 Ludl 2m4f   soft Ch

Modest pointer/hunter chaser.

Cahors (IRE)

10-y-o b g Mandalus-Croom River (IRE) (Over The River (FR))
J J Boulter J J Boulter

Placings:1/F42/6   (4314)
2002/03: 22⁶G,

	Starts	1st	2nd	3rd	Win & Pl
Chases	1	0	0	0	0
Career Total	5	1	1	0	3042
114 3/00	Tntn	3m	H Ch	GD	£1964

Total win prize-money £1964

Going: Sf: 0-0 GS: 0-0 Gd: 0-0 GF: - Fm: 0-0
Distance: 2m/2m3: 0-0 2m4-2m7: 0-0 3m+: 0-1
Track: LH: 0-1 RH: 0-0 Tight: 0-0 Gall: 0-1
Aids: Bl: 0-1 Vi: 0-0 Tstrap: 0-0
Best Rating: 114   3/00 Tntn 3m   good Ch

Caitriona's Choice (IRE)
107   **119**

12-y-o b g Carmelite House (USA)-Muligatawny (Malacate (USA))
P Monteith (Michael Cunningham 25/1) The Dregs Of Humanity

Placings:165322/0223162316/06/0604022/512/B0/6453B6
04-16062P0   (4763)
2002/03: 17¹SH, 16⁶HY, 17⁰SH, 20⁶S, 16²HY, 16ᴾHY, 16⁶G,

	Starts	1st	2nd	3rd	Win & Pl
Chases	7	1	1		8439
Career Total	45	5	9	4	34911
109	6/02	Navn	2m1f	(0-116)HCh	SH	£6773
96	7/99	Gway	2m1f	Ch	G-F	£4910
123	1/97	Punc	2m	(0-116)HHdl	YLD	£3051
110	10/96	Rosc	2m	Hdl	YLD	£4237
116	5/95	Baln	2m	NHF	GD	£2204

Total win prize-money £21177

Going: Sf: 0-4 GS: 0-0 Gd: 0-1 GF: - Fm: 0-0
Distance: 2m/2m3: 1-6 2m4-2m7: 0-1 3m+: 0-0
Track: LH: 1-4 RH: 0-2 Tight: 0-1 Gall: 0-0
Aids: Bl: 0-0 Vi: 0-0 Tstrap: 1-7
Best Rating: 123 1/97 Punc 2m   yield   Hdl

Modest chaser, formerly trained in Ireland; won on fast ground and with cut; suited by two miles.

Calamint
57   **19**

4-y-o gr g Kaldoun (FR)-Coigach (Niniski (USA))
K C Bailey (J R Fanshawe 14/8) Sootys Racing Club

Placings:00P   (3571)
2002/03: 16⁶S, 17⁰HY, 16ᴾHY,

	Starts	1st	2nd	3rd	Win & Pl
Hurdles	3	0	0	0	
Career Total	3	0	0	0	

Going: Sf: 0-3 GS: 0-0 Gd: 0-0 GF: - Fm: 0-0
Distance: 2m/2m3: 0-3 2m4-2m7: 0-0 3m+: 0-0
Track: LH: 0-1 RH: 0-2 Tight: 0-1 Gall: 0-0
Aids: Bl: 0-0 Vi: 0-0 Tstrap: 0-0
Best Rating: 19 12/02 Wwck 2m   soft   Hdl

Calatagan (IRE)
96   **111+**

4-y-o ch g Danzig Connection (USA)-Calachuchi (Martinmas)
J M Jefferson (Miss J A Camacho 26/8) Mr & Mrs J M Davenport

Placings:1F   (2768)
2002/03: 16¹GS, 16ᶠGS,

	Starts	1st	2nd	3rd	Win & Pl
Hurdles	2	1	0	0	3835
Career Total	2	1	0	0	3835
111	12/02	Catt	2m	D Hdl	G-S	£3835

Total win prize-money £3835

Going: Sf: 0-0 GS: 1-2 Gd: 0-0 GF: - Fm: 0-0
Distance: 2m/2m3: 1-2 2m4-2m7: 0-0 3m+: 0-0
Track: LH: 1-1 RH: 0-1 Tight: 1-2 Gall: 0-0
Aids: Bl: 0-0 Vi: 0-0 Tstrap: 0-0
Best Rating: 111 12/02 Catt 2m   gd-sft   Hdl

Modest hurdler, keen sort, runaway winner on hurdling debut at Catterick in December; acts on good to soft.

Calcot Flyer
102   **89**

5-y-o br g Anshan-Lady Catcher (Free Boy)
A King Miss J M Bodycote

Placings:00   (4090)
2002/03: 16⁹GS, 16⁹GS,

	Starts	1st	2nd	3rd	Win & Pl
NH Flat	2	0	0	0	
Career Total	2	0	0	0	

Going: Sf: 0-0 GS: 0-2 Gd: 0-0 GF: - Fm: 0-0
Distance: 2m/2m3: 0-2 2m4-2m7: 0-0 3m+: 0-0
Track: LH: 0-1 RH: 0-0 Tight: 0-1 Gall: 0-0
Aids: Bl: 0-0 Vi: 0-0 Tstrap: 0-0
Best Rating: 92 1/03 Hayd 2m   gd-sft   NHF

Showed little in bumpers but shaped better on hurdling bow.

Caldamus

11-y-o gr g Scallywag-Portodamus (Porto Bello)
Miss S Waugh Miss R D Elliott

Placings:465/3514/B46/P2-1   (4003)
2002/03: 25¹S,

	Starts	1st	2nd	3rd	Win & Pl
Chases	1	1	0	0	1456
Career Total	13	2	1	1	5609
99	3/03	Winc	3m1f110yH Ch	SFT	£1456
110	2/99	Sedg	2m5f110yE Hdl	GD	£2582

Total win prize-money £4039

Going: Sf: 1-1 GS: 0-0 Gd: 0-0 GF: - Fm: 0-0
Distance: 2m/2m3: 0-0 2m4-2m7: 0-0 3m+: 1-1
Track: LH: 0-0 RH: 1-1 Tight: 0-0 Gall: 0-0
Aids: Bl: 0-0 Vi: 0-0 Tstrap: 0-0
Best Rating: 110 2/99 Sedg 2m5f110y good Hdl

Fair form in point-to-points and hunter chases; effective from 2m 4f to 3m; handles soft ground, but best on good.

Calfstown Lord
77

11-y-o b g Arctic Lord-Calfstown Maid (Master Buck)
C J Gray P Popham, F D Popham, T Bartlett

Placings:005/02220P/P/04FU604023-U0   (0243)
2002/03: 22ᵁGS, 23⁹G,

	Starts	1st	2nd	3rd	Win & Pl
Chases	2	0	0	0	
Career Total	22	0	4	1	5889

Going: Sf: 0-0 GS: 0-1 Gd: 0-1 GF: - Fm: 0-0
Distance: 2m/2m3: 0-0 2m4-2m7: 0-1 3m+: 0-1
Track: LH: 0-0 RH: 0-2 Tight: 0-0 Gall: 0-0
Aids: Bl: 0-2 Vi: 0-0 Tstrap: 0-0
Best Rating: 99 2/00 Tntn 3m   soft   Ch

Moderate chaser; stays three miles; handles any ground; has worn headgear.

Caliban (IRE)
105   **113**

5-y-o ch g Rainbows For Life (CAN)-Amour Toujours (IRE) (Law Society (USA))
Ian Williams Jim Edmunds

Placings:522224323445-612   (4703)
2002/03: 20⁶G, 16¹G, 16²GF,

	Starts	1st	2nd	3rd	Win & Pl
Hurdles	3	1	1	0	4091
Career Total	15	1	6	2	9261
113	11/02 Hayd	2m	E(0-105)HHdl	GD	£3052

Total win prize-money £3052

Going: Sf: 0-0 GS: 0-0 Gd: 1-2 GF: - Fm: 0-1
Distance: 2m/2m3: 1-2 2m4-2m7: 0-1 3m+: 0-0
Track: LH: 1-3 RH: 0-0 Tight: 0-1 Gall: 0-0
Aids: Bl: 0-0 Vi: 0-0 Tstrap: 0-0
Best Rating: 113 11/02 Hayd 2m   good   Hdl

Fair hurdler; regularly in the frame in juvenile hurdles in 2001/2; off the mark at Haydock in November 2002; looks best suited by good ground or softer; suited by trips of around two miles.

Calinash (IRE)
79   **83**

9-y-o b g Insan (USA)-Hi Cal (Callernish)
Mrs L Williamson John Riley

Placings:P54P30   (2942)
2002/03: 20ᴾGS, 16⁵G, 17⁴S, 21ᴾS, 17⁹HY, 20⁰GS,

	Starts	1st	2nd	3rd	Win & Pl
Hurdles	1	0	0	0	0
Chases	5	0	0	1	1067
Career Total	6	0	0	1	1067

Going: Sf: 0-3 GS: 0-2 Gd: 0-1 GF: - Fm: 0-0
Distance: 2m/2m3: 0-3 2m4-2m7: 0-3 3m+: 0-0
Track: LH: 0-5 RH: 0-1 Tight: 0-5 Gall: 0-0
Aids: Bl: 0-0 Vi: 0-0 Tstrap: 0-0
Best Rating: 83 10/02 Bang 2m1f110y soft   Ch

Very moderate novice chaser.

Calitas (FR)

4-y-o b g Solido (FR)-Callistine (FR) (Arctic Tern (USA))
G A Harker G R Orchard

Placings:314P   (3579)
2002/03: 15³F, 16¹G, 17⁴HY, 16ᴾG,

	Starts	1st	2nd	3rd	Win & Pl
Hurdles	3	1	0	1	5705
Chases	1	0	0	0	2448
Career Total	4	1	0	1	8153
	10/02 Fntb	2m	Hdl	GD	£4417

Total win prize-money £4417

Going: Sf: 0-1 GS: 0-0 Gd: 1-2 GF: - Fm: 0-1
Distance: 2m/2m3: 1-3 2m4-2m7: 0-0 3m+: 0-0
Track: LH: 0-0 RH: 0-1 Tight: 0-1 Gall: 0-0
Aids: Bl: 0-0 Vi: 0-0 Tstrap: 0-0
Best Rating: 0 2/03 Muss 2m   good   Hdl

Ex-French hurdler/chaser; broke a leg on his British debut at Musselburgh in February 2003. (DEAD)

Caliwag (IRE)
86(85h)   (74h)**98**

7-y-o b g Lahib (USA)-Mitsubishi Style (Try My Best (USA))
Jamie Poulton Lottie Collins Partnership

Placings:006-3   (4047)
2002/03: 16⁵S,

	Starts	1st	2nd	3rd	Win & Pl
Chases	1	0	0	1	1023
Career Total	4	0	0	1	1023

Going: Sf: 0-1 GS: 0-0 Gd: 0-0 GF: - Fm: 0-0
Distance: 2m/2m3: 0-0 2m4-2m7: 0-0 3m+: 0-0
Track: LH: 0-0 RH: 0-1 Tight: 0-0 Gall: 0-0
Aids: Bl: 0-0 Vi: 0-0 Tstrap: 0-0
Best Rating: 98 3/03 Sand 2m   soft   Ch

Plating-class performer on the Flat; showed little in novice hurdles in 2000/1; well beaten on chasing debut.

Calko

85   55

6-y-o ch g Timeless Times (USA)-Jeethgaya (USA) (Critique (USA))
R Wilman R Wilman

Placings:65   (1100)
2002/03: 16^{R}S, 17^{S}GF,

	Starts	1st	2nd	3rd	Win & Pl
Hurdles	2	0	0	0	0
Career Total	2	0	0	0	0

Going: Sf: 0-1 GS: 0-0 Gd: 0-0 GF: - Fm: 0-1
Distance: 2m/2m3: 0-2 2m4-2m7: 0-0 3m+: 0-0
Track: LH: 0-2 RH: 0-0 Tight: 0-1 Gall: 0-0
Aids: Bl: 0-0 Vi: 0-0 Tstrap: 0-0
Best Rating: 55 8/02 Sthl 2m1f   gd-fm   Hdl

Call Me Jack (IRE)

97(93c)   (97c)94

7-y-o b g Lord Americo-Tawney Rose (Tarqogan)
J Hetherton R G Fell

Placings:6/026521/431F-P3F2   (4257)
2002/03: 16^{P}G, 17^{H}Y, 20^{F}G, 16^{2}G,

	Starts	1st	2nd	3rd	Win & Pl
Hurdles	3	0	0	1	730
Chases	1	0	1	0	1245
Career Total	15	2	3	2	10110
102	11/01	Sedg	2m1f	E(0-115)HHdl	SFT	£2338
97	4/01	Prth	2m110y D Hdl	HVY	£3332
				Total win prize-money £5670		

Going: Sf: 0-1 GS: 0-0 Gd: 0-3 GF: - Fm: 0-0
Distance: 2m/2m3: 0-3 2m4-2m7: 0-1 3m+: 0-0
Track: LH: 0-4 RH: 0-0 Tight: 0-3 Gall: 0-0
Aids: Bl: 0-0 Vi: 0-0 Tstrap: 0-2
Best Rating: 108 3/01 MRas 2m1f110y gd-sft Hdl

Modest hurdler/novice chaser; suited by two miles over hurdles in soft ground.

Call Me Sonic

86(88h)   (92h)74

7-y-o b g Henbit (USA)-Call-Me-Dinky (Mart Lane)
R H Alner (C A Fuller 4/3) C A Fuller

Placings:0P45-3P5   (4695)
2002/03: 22^{3}GF, 20^{P}GS, 16^{5}G,

	Starts	1st	2nd	3rd	Win & Pl
Hurdles	1	0	0	1	0
Chases	2	0	0	0	0
Career Total	7	0	0	1	0

Going: Sf: 0-0 GS: 0-1 Gd: 0-1 GF: - Fm: 0-1
Distance: 2m/2m3: 0-1 2m4-2m7: 0-2 3m+: 0-0
Track: LH: 0-1 RH: 0-2 Tight: 0-1 Gall: 0-0
Aids: Bl: 0-0 Vi: 0-0 Tstrap: 0-0
Best Rating: 92 4/02 Winc 2m   good   Hdl

Has shown only moderate form over hurdles at fences.

Call My Guest (IRE)

102

13-y-o b g Be My Guest (USA)-Overcall (Bustino)
R E Peacock Derek and Jean Clee

Placings:2232322P/2211310212/54F0/5220005F4/23/U41
P13F053/66U046231/34F404/5503-P   (1640)
2002/03: 21^{P}G,

	Starts	1st	2nd	3rd	Win & Pl
Hurdles	1	0	0	0	
Career Total	63	7	13	9	55283
110	4/00	Ludl	2m5f	D(0-120)HHdl	G-S	£4160
121	7/98	MRas	2m1f110yC(0-135)HHdl	G-F	£10317
121	6/98	Worc	2m4f	D(0-120)HHdl	GD	£2979
134	4/95	Weth	2m4f110yC(0-135)HHdl	GD	£4207
132	3/95	Weth	2m4f110yD(0-125)HHdl	SFT	£2924
125	11/94	Weth	2m4f110y HHdl	G-S	£2807
113	11/94	Carl	2m4f110y Hdl	GD	£2233
				Total win prize-money £29631		

Going: Sf: 0-0 GS: 0-0 Gd: 0-1 GF: - Fm: 0-0
Distance: 2m/2m3: 0-2 2m4-2m7: 0-1 3m+: 0-0
Track: LH: 0-0 RH: 0-1 Tight: 0-1 Gall: 0-0
Aids: Bl: 0-0 Vi: 0-0 Tstrap: 0-0
Best Rating: 134 5/95 Asct 2m4f   gd-fm   Hdl

Moderate handicap hurdler in his younger days; retains ability; effective at two and a half miles; does not want the ground too soft.

Call The Shots (IRE)

97

14-y-o br g Callermish-Golden Strings (Perspex)
J Wade John Wade

Placings:0U0000/0033/412U/421/P/PPPPP/6531/61-P   (0695)
2002/03: 22^{P}G,

	Starts	1st	2nd	3rd	Win & Pl
Chases	1	0	0	0	
Career Total	30	4	2	3	21011
97	9/01	Sedg	3m3f	E(0-115)HCh	G-F	£3542
91	10/99	Sedg	3m3f	F(0-130)HCh	G-F	£3022
110	3/97	Kels	3m4f	C(0-130)HCh	GD	£6775
106	1/96	Sedg	3m3f	E Ch	G-F	£3647
				Total win prize-money £16987		

Going: Sf: 0-0 GS: 0-0 Gd: 0-0 GF: - Fm: 0-0
Distance: 2m/2m3: 0-0 2m4-2m7: 0-0 3m+: 0-1
Track: LH: 0-0 RH: 0-0 Tight: 0-1 Gall: 0-0
Aids: Bl: 0-0 Vi: 0-0 Tstrap: 0-0
Best Rating: 110 3/97 Kels 3m4f   good   Ch

Calladine (IRE)

142

7-y-o b g Erin s Isle-Motus (Anfield)
C Roche S J Murphy

Placings:1F6000/031613/50-4U3   (3647a)
2002/03: 24^{4}YS, 16^{U}G, 16^{3}Y,

	Starts	1st	2nd	3rd	Win & Pl
Hurdles	3	0	0	1	3766
Career Total	17	3	0	3	37751
145	12/00	Leop	3m	HHdl	SH	£7176
131	11/00	Naas	2m4f	HHdl	Y-S	£10400
127	12/99	Leop	2m	Hdl	SH	£14508
				Total win prize-money £32085		

Going: Sf: 0-0 GS: 0-0 Gd: 0-0 GF: 0-1 Fm: 0-0
Distance: 2m/2m3: 0-2 2m4-2m7: 0-0 3m+: 0-1
Track: LH: 0-2 RH: 0-0 Tight: 0-0 Gall: 0-1
Aids: Bl: 0-0 Vi: 0-0 Tstrap: 0-0

Best Rating: 145 12/00 Leop 3m   sft-hvy Hdl

Useful Irish-trained hurdler; stays three miles but effective at two; acts on both fast and soft ground; has a decent turn of foot and is often held up.

Called To The Bar

90   87

10-y-o b g Legal Bwana-Miss Gaylord (Cavo Doro)
P M Rich B Meadmore

Placings:0UP/P011/P2   (4004)
2002/03: 24^{P}GS, 22^{2}S,

	Starts	1st	2nd	3rd	Win & Pl
Hurdles	2	0	1	0	956
Career Total	9	2	1	0	5221
94	3/00	Folk	3m4f	F(0-100)HHdl	G-F	£1881
76	3/00	Hrfd	3m2f	F(0-95)HHdl	GD	£2383
				Total win prize-money £4266		

Going: Sf: 0-1 GS: 0-1 Gd: 0-0 GF: - Fm: 0-0
Distance: 2m/2m3: 0-0 2m4-2m7: 0-1 3m+: 0-1
Track: LH: 0-0 RH: 0-2 Tight: 0-0 Gall: 0-0
Aids: Bl: 0-0 Vi: 0-0 Tstrap: 0-0
Best Rating: 94 3/00 Folk 3m4f   gd-fm   Hdl

Formerly a modest staying handicap hurdler; lightly raced since 2000.

Calleva Star (IRE)

12-y-o b g Over The River (FR)-Ask The Madam (Strong Gale)
Mrs F E Needham Michael D Abrahams

Placings:6P/442342/332413/P3F431FP/4U3/PB0U02-6P
                                               (0189)
2002/03: 25^{6}GS, 30^{P}GF,

	Starts	1st	2nd	3rd	Win & Pl
Chases	2	0	0	0	0
Career Total	33	2	4	7	16140
102	3/99	Plum	3m1f110yE(0-125)HCh	HVY	£3420
102	3/98	Plum	3m1f110yE Ch	GD	£3130
				Total win prize-money £6550		

Going: Sf: 0-0 GS: 0-1 Gd: 0-0 GF: - Fm: 0-1
Distance: 2m/2m3: 0-0 2m4-2m7: 0-0 3m+: 0-2
Track: LH: 0-1 RH: 0-1 Tight: 0-1 Gall: 0-1
Aids: Bl: 0-0 Vi: 0-0 Tstrap: 0-0
Best Rating: 106 12/97 Uttx 3m   soft   Ch

Fair pointer who generally struggles in hunter chases.

Callfourseasons (IRE)

11-y-o b g Euphemism-Home And Dry (Crash Course)
M Mullineaux R Williamson

Placings:66/56041160/14P16/51PPP/P-PUPP   (0731)
2002/03: 20^{P}GS, 24^{U}S, 20^{P}GF, 22^{P}GF,

	Starts	1st	2nd	3rd	Win & Pl
Hurdles	1	0	0	0	0
Chases	3	0	0	0	0
Career Total	25	5	0	0	16185
125	12/00	Sthl	3m110y E(0-115)HCh	SFT	£2798
125	3/00	Bang	3m110y D(0-125)HCh	SFT	£4777
111	11/99	Hayd	2m6f	E(0-115)HCh	GD	£3922
110	11/98	Kels	2m6f110yE(0-100)HHdl	SFT	£2290
97	10/98	Weth	3m1f	F(0-105)HHdl	GD	£1917
				Total win prize-money £15706		

Going:	Sf: 0-1 GS: 0-2 Gd: 0-0 GF: - Fm: 0-1
Distance:	2m/2m3: 0-0 2m4-2m7: 0-3 3m+: 0-1
Track:	LH: 0-4 RH: 0-0 Tight: 0-3 Gall: 0-0
Aids:	Bl: 0-0 Vi: 0-0 Tstrap: 0-0
Best Rating:	125 12/00 Sthl 3m110y soft Ch

Calling Brave (IRE)
111   132
7-y-o ch g Bob Back (USA)-Queenie Kelly (The Parson)
N J Henderson   Sir Robert Ogden

Placings: 1420-1U12200   (4456)
2002/03: 16¹G, 20ᵁS, 19¹G, 21²HY, 21²G, 21⁰G, 24⁰G,

	Starts	1st	2nd	3rd	Win & Pl
Hurdles	7	2	2		19474
Career Total	11	3	3	0	23148
124	12/02	Newb	2m3f		D Hdl	GD	£4927
114	11/02	Kemp	2m		D Hdl	GD	£4251
132	11/01	Aint	2m1f		H NHF	G-S	£2149

Total win prize-money £11327

Going:	Sf: 0-2 GS: 0-0 Gd: 2-5 GF: - Fm: 0-0
Distance:	2m/2m3: 2-2 2m4-2m7: 0-4 3m+: 0-1
Track:	LH: 1-4 RH: 1-3 Tight: 0-1 Gall: 1-3
Aids:	Bl: 0-0 Vi: 0-0 Tstrap: 0-0
Best Rating:	132 2/03 Kemp 2m5f good Hdl

Very useful novice hurdler; half-brother to Queens Harbour and Ottowa; formerly a fair performer in bumpers; needs good ground; stays well.

Calon Lan (IRE)
103   92
12-y-o b g Bustineto-Cherish (Bargello)
R Williams   R Williams

Placings: 3/F/4P13/233P12/41545/1/0P004P-PP24 (0997)
2002/03: 17²GF, 20⁰GF, 21²GF, 21⁴GF,

	Starts	1st	2nd	3rd	Win & Pl
Hurdles	1	0	0	0	0
Chases	3	0	1	0	1750
Career Total	28	4	3	4	29380
105	3/01	Hntg	2m110y	D(0-125)HCh	SFT	£4108
116	10/99	Strf	2m1f110yD(0-120)HCh	G-F	£3821
109	4/99	Ayr	2m	C Ch	HVY	£5865
112	3/98	Newb	2m110y	C Hdl	SFT	£4237

Total win prize-money £18031

Going:	Sf: 0-0 GS: 0-0 Gd: 0-0 GF: - Fm: 0-4
Distance:	2m/2m3: 0-1 2m4-2m7: 0-3 3m+: 0-0
Track:	LH: 0-3 RH: 0-1 Tight: 0-3 Gall: 0-0
Aids:	Bl: 0-1 Vi: 0-0 Tstrap: 0-0
Best Rating:	125 11/98 Chep 2m3f110y gd-sft Ch

Plating-class chaser; stays two miles five; best on a sound surface; has worn blinkers.

Camaderry (IRE)
85   85+
5-y-o ch g Dr Devious (IRE)-Rathvindon (Realm)
Noel T Chance   Mrs M C Sweeney

Placings: 63   (0384)
2002/03: 18⁶GF, 16³G,

	Starts	1st	2nd	3rd	Win & Pl
Hurdles	2	0	0	1	354
Career Total	2	0	0	1	354

Going:	Sf: 0-0 GS: 0-0 Gd: 0-1 GF: - Fm: 0-1
Distance:	2m/2m3: 0-2 2m4-2m7: 0-0 3m+: 0-0
Track:	LH: 0-1 RH: 0-1 Tight: 0-1 Gall: 0-1

Aids:	Bl: 0-0 Vi: 0-0 Tstrap: 0-0
Best Rating:	85 5/02 Font 2m2f110y gd-fm Hdl

Camair Commander (IRE)
89   61
5-y-o b g Beau Sher-Miss Josephine (IRE) (Kemal (FR))
W McKeown   Colin W German

Placings: 0-000P60   (4258)
2002/03: 16⁶GS, 20⁰HY, 24⁰S, 20⁰S, 17⁶S, 17⁰G,

	Starts	1st	2nd	3rd	Win & Pl
Hurdles	6	0	0	0	0
Career Total	7	0	0	0	0

Going:	Sf: 0-4 GS: 0-1 Gd: 0-1 GF: - Fm: 0-0
Distance:	2m/2m3: 0-3 2m4-2m7: 0-2 3m+: 0-1
Track:	LH: 0-5 RH: 0-1 Tight: 0-2 Gall: 0-3
Aids:	Bl: 0-1 Vi: 0-0 Tstrap: 0-0
Best Rating:	63 3/03 Sedg 2m1f good Hdl

Camair Crusader (IRE)
100(72c)   (82c)82
9-y-o br g Jolly Jake (NZ)-Sigrid s Dream (USA) (Triple Bend (USA))
F P Murtagh   Colin W German

Placings: 00/00P6F0245/33232S414/P6FF0441-00030 (3799)
2002/03: 16¹G, 16⁰GS, 19⁰GF, 21⁰G, 21³G, 16⁰S,

	Starts	1st	2nd	3rd	Win & Pl
Hurdles	6	1	0	1	2109
Career Total	33	2	3	4	6855
86	4/02	Newc	2m	G(0-95)HHdl	GD	£1799
91	4/01	MRas	2m1f110yG Hdl	G-S	£1890

Total win prize-money £3689

Going:	Sf: 0-1 GS: 0-1 Gd: 1-3 GF: - Fm: 0-1
Distance:	2m/2m3: 1-3 2m4-2m7: 0-3 3m+: 0-0
Track:	LH: 1-5 RH: 0-1 Tight: 0-3 Gall: 1-2
Aids:	Bl: 0-0 Vi: 0-0 Tstrap: 0-0
Best Rating:	93 9/00 Sedg 2m1f soft Hdl

Camaraderie
100   92
7-y-o b g Most Welcome-Secret Valentine (Wollow)
A G Juckes (Mrs M Reveley 4/10)   Mrs K C Price

Placings: 010/6-2214   (4445)
2002/03: 16²G, 16²GF, 16¹G, 16⁴G,

	Starts	1st	2nd	3rd	Win & Pl
Hurdles	4	1	2	0	3772
Career Total	8	2	2	0	6145
92	3/03	Chep	2m110y	G Hdl	GD	£2366
104	10/00	Kels	2m110y	G Hdl	SFT	£2373

Total win prize-money £4739

Going:	Sf: 0-0 GS: 0-0 Gd: 1-3 GF: - Fm: 0-1
Distance:	2m/2m3: 1-4 2m4-2m7: 0-0 3m+: 0-0
Track:	LH: 1-3 RH: 0-1 Tight: 0-0 Gall: 0-0
Aids:	Bl: 0-1 Vi: 0-0 Tstrap: 0-0
Best Rating:	104 10/00 Kels 2m110y soft Hdl

Moderate hurdler; in fairly good form during 2003.

Cambio (IRE)
103   91+
5-y-o b g Turtle Island (IRE)-Motley (Rainbow Quest (USA))
B R Johnson   Mrs Beryl Williams

Placings: 64-610   (1967)
2002/03: 17⁶G, 20¹S, 16⁰GS,

	Starts	1st	2nd	3rd	Win & Pl
Hurdles	3	1	0	0	2513
Career Total	5	1	0	0	2513
91	6/02	Worc	2m4f	F(0-100)HHdl	SFT	£2513

Total win prize-money £2513

Going:	Sf: 1-1 GS: 0-1 Gd: 0-1 GF: - Fm: 0-0
Distance:	2m/2m3: 0-2 2m4-2m7: 1-1 3m+: 0-0
Track:	LH: 1-2 RH: 0-1 Tight: 0-1 Gall: 0-0
Aids:	Bl: 0-0 Vi: 0-0 Tstrap: 0-0
Best Rating:	91 6/02 Worc 2m4f soft Hdl

Plating-class hurdler; did not jump fluently on first two hurdles starts but off the mark at Worcester in June 2002.

Cambrian Dawn
(113h)   (122h)122+
9-y-o b g Danehill (USA)-Welsh Daylight (Welsh Pageant)
Jonjo O Neill   Out The Box Racing

Placings: 41/41123/1-0FU   (3318)
2002/03: 20⁰GS, 25⁶G, 24ᵁGS,

	Starts	1st	2nd	3rd	Win & Pl
Hurdles	1	0	0	0	0
Chases	2	0	0	0	0
Career Total	14	4	1	1	13462
122	4/02	Prth	2m4f110yC(0-130)HHdl	GD	£5931
108	1/00	Catt	3m1f110yE Hdl	GD	£2817
113	11/99	Hexm	2m	H NHF	GD	£1595
113	4/99	Hexm	2m	H NHF	GD	£1640

Total win prize-money £11985

Going:	Sf: 0-0 GS: 0-1 Gd: 0-2 GF: - Fm: 0-0
Distance:	2m/2m3: 0-0 2m4-2m7: 0-1 3m+: 0-2
Track:	LH: 0-1 RH: 0-2 Tight: 0-1 Gall: 0-0
Aids:	Bl: 0-0 Vi: 0-0 Tstrap: 0-0
Best Rating:	122 12/02 Hrfd 3m1f110y good Ch

Decent handicap hurdler, off the track more than two years until winning at Perth in April 2002. Effective at two and a half miles.

Camden Dolphin (IRE)
6-y-o gr m Camden Town-Ackle Backle (Furry Glen)
B A Pearce   Mark Hoaren

Placings: 0-0P   (4212)
2002/03: 16⁰G, 18⁷G,

	Starts	1st	2nd	3rd	Win & Pl
NH Flat	1	0	0	0	0
Hurdles	1	0	0	0	0
Career Total	3	0	0	0	0

Going:	Sf: 0-0 GS: 0-0 Gd: 0-2 GF: - Fm: 0-0
Distance:	2m/2m3: 0-2 2m4-2m7: 0-0 3m+: 0-0
Track:	LH: 0-2 RH: 0-0 Tight: 0-1 Gall: 0-1
Aids:	Bl: 0-0 Vi: 0-0 Tstrap: 0-0
Best Rating:	39 3/02 Wwck 2m gd-sft NHF

Camden King (IRE)

(99h)   (61h)
8-y-o b/br g Camden Town-Valerie Owens (IRE)
(Lancastrian)
T P McGovern Wellpool Ltd And Mark Holman

Placings:00/3455/604-P   (0175)
2002/03: 16⁴GS, 21⁹GF,

	Starts	1st	2nd	3rd	Win & Pl
Hurdles	1	0	0	0	0
Chases	1	0	0	0	0
Career Total	10	0	0	1	250

Going: Sf: 0-0 GS: 0-1 Gd: 0-0 GF: - Fm: 0-1
Distance: 2m/2m3: 0-1 2m4-2m7: 0-1 3m+: 0-0
Track: LH: 0-0 RH: 0-2 Tight: 0-0 Gall: 0-0
Aids: Bl: 0-0 Vi: 0-0 Tstrap: 0-0
Best Rating: 94 5/00 Folk 2m1f110y good NHF

Camden Tanner (IRE)

(113h)   (134h)**127+**
7-y-o b g Camden Town-Poor Elsie (Crash Course)
Robert Tyner Famous Lads Syndicate

Placings:50611/112255-2320   (4112)
2002/03: 24²HY, 16³S, 22²HY, 21⁹G,

	Starts	1st	2nd	3rd	Win & Pl
Hurdles	4	0	2	1	22594
Career Total	15	4	4	1	50046
109 11/01 Cork 2m		(0-116)HHdl		YLD	£6955
104 10/01 Tipp 2m		(0-109)HHdl		HVY	£4729
113 1/01 Cork 2m		NHF		SFT	£4451
113 12/00 Cork 2m		NHF		SFT	£3588
				Total win prize-money £19726	

Going: Sf: 0-3 GS: 0-0 Gd: 0-1 GF: - Fm: 0-0
Distance: 2m/2m3: 0-1 2m4-2m7: 0-2 3m+: 0-1
Track: LH: 0-2 RH: 0-1 Tight: 0-0 Gall: 0-1
Aids: Bl: 0-0 Vi: 0-0 Tstrap: 0-0
Best Rating: 134 2/03 Sand 2m6f heavy Hdl

Decent Irish hurdler; has only ever won over two miles; suited by soft ground.

Camdenation (IRE)

104   94
7-y-o b g Camden Town-Out The Nav (IRE) (Over The River
(FR))
J T Gifford Unstable Companions

Placings:50-012350   (3668)
2002/03: 16⁹G, 22¹GS, 22⁹HY, 20⁴S, 20⁵S, 22⁰GS,

	Starts	1st	2nd	3rd	Win & Pl
Hurdles	6	1	1	1	4797
Career Total	8	1	1	1	4797
102 11/02 Folk	2m6f110yE Hdl			G-S	£2989
				Total win prize-money £2989	

Going: Sf: 0-3 GS: 1-2 Gd: 0-1 GF: - Fm: 0-0
Distance: 2m/2m3: 0-1 2m4-2m7: 1-5 3m+: 0-0
Track: LH: 0-2 RH: 1-3 Tight: 1-5 Gall: 0-1
Aids: Bl: 0-0 Vi: 0-0 Tstrap: 0-0
Best Rating: 102 11/02 Folk 2m6f110y gd-sft Hdl

Cameron Bridge (IRE)

105(109h)   (108h)**124**
7-y-o b g Camden Town-Arctic Raheen (Over The River
(FR))
P J Hobbs The Country Side

Placings:F5/55532112-F363541414   (4779)
2002/03: 17⁵G, 16³G, 20⁶G, 19³GS, 16⁵G, 16⁴GS, 19¹S, 16⁴G,
19¹GF, 20⁴GF,

	Starts	1st	2nd	3rd	Win & Pl
Hurdles	2	0	0	1	545
Chases	8	2	0	1	13727
Career Total	20	4	2	3	22470
107 4/03 Hrfd	2m3f	E Ch		G-F	£5187
115 3/03 Extr	2m3f110yE Ch			SFT	£4901
101 1/02 Winc	2m	E Hdl		G-S	£3136
105 1/02 Winc	2m	E(0-110)HHdl		GD	£2989
				Total win prize-money £16213	

Going: Sf: 1-1 GS: 0-2 Gd: 0-5 GF: - Fm: 1-2
Distance: 2m/2m3: 1-7 2m4-2m7: 1-3 3m+: 0-0
Track: LH: 0-0 RH: 2-10 Tight: 0-3 Gall: 0-0
Aids: Bl: 0-0 Vi: 0-0 Tstrap: 0-0
Best Rating: 124 3/03 Asct 2m good Ch

Fair novice chaser; suited by trips of around two and a half miles and acts on any ground.

Cameron Jack

100(101c)   (64c)**96+**
8-y-o b g Elmaamul (USA)-Ile De Reine (Ile De Bourbon
(USA))
Miss Kate Milligan The Aunts

Placings:2/0/0/5U36P2   (4378)
2002/03: 17⁵G, 22⁴G, 16³HY, 24⁶G, 20⁸S, 21²G,

	Starts	1st	2nd	3rd	Win & Pl
Hurdles	2	0	0	0	0
Chases	4	0	1	1	1469
Career Total	8	0	2	1	2181

Going: Sf: 0-2 GS: 0-0 Gd: 0-4 GF: - Fm: 0-0
Distance: 2m/2m3: 0-2 2m4-2m7: 0-3 3m+: 0-1
Track: LH: 0-5 RH: 0-1 Tight: 0-4 Gall: 0-0
Aids: Bl: 0-0 Vi: 0-0 Tstrap: 0-0
Best Rating: 85 4/00 Sedg 2m1f good Hdl

Plating-class chaser; low grade hurdler; poor jumper; rejuvenated since switching back to hurdles with back-to-back wins over 3m2f at Southwell July 2003; acts on good ground; stays well.

Camerosa

7-y-o b g Risk Me (FR)-High Heather (Shirley Heights)
A D Smith Duckhaven Stud

Placings:0P   (2778)
2002/03: 16⁰S, 17⁷S,

	Starts	1st	2nd	3rd	Win & Pl
Hurdles	2	0	0	0	
Career Total	2	0	0	0	

Going: Sf: 0-2 GS: 0-0 Gd: 0-0 GF: - Fm: 0-0
Distance: 2m/2m3: 0-2 2m4-2m7: 0-0 3m+: 0-0
Track: LH: 0-1 RH: 0-1 Tight: 0-1 Gall: 0-0
Aids: Bl: 0-0 Vi: 0-0 Tstrap: 0-0
Best Rating: 0 2/03 Hrfd 3m2f good Hdl

Camitrov (FR)

13-y-o b g Sharken (FR)-Emitrovna (FR) (Buisson D Or)
G R Kerr G R Kerr

Placings:11341/42/55/3/243F/1/2UP-6   (0190)
2002/03: 24⁶GF,

	Starts	1st	2nd	3rd	Win & Pl
Chases	1	0	0	0	0
Career Total	19	4	3	3	48501
118 3/00 Sand	3m110y E Ch			GD	£6380
125 4/95 Punc	2m4f	Ch		YLD	£12871
97 12/94 MRas	2m1f110y	Ch		SFT	£4056
112 11/94 Wwck	2m	Ch		G-S	£3600
				Total win prize-money £26908	

Going: Sf: 0-0 GS: 0-0 Gd: 0-0 GF: - Fm: 0-0
Distance: 2m/2m3: 0-0 2m4-2m7: 0-0 3m+: 0-1
Track: LH: 0-0 RH: 0-1 Tight: 0-0 Gall: 0-1
Aids: Bl: 0-0 Vi: 0-0 Tstrap: 0-0
Best Rating: 144 3/95 Chel 2m soft Ch

Formerly a useful chaser, but is now just an ordinary pointer/hunter.

Camp Hill

100(93h)   (94h)**94d**
9-y-o gr g Ra Nova-Baytino (Neltino)
J S Haldane Mrs Hugh Fraser

Placings:00/6P00/P5542/50436U42F-P60412U23   (3772)
2002/03: 25⁵GS, 18⁶S, 20⁹S, 21⁴GS, 20¹S, 25²S, 24⁰HY, 20²HY,
21³GS,

	Starts	1st	2nd	3rd	Win & Pl
Hurdles	2	0	0	0	0
Chases	7	1	2	1	8199
Career Total	29	1	4	2	11511
94 12/02 Ayr	2m4f	F(0-90)Ch		SFT	£3038
				Total win prize-money £3038	

Going: Sf: 1-6 GS: 0-3 Gd: 0-0 GF: - Fm: 0-0
Distance: 2m/2m3: 0-1 **2m4-2m7:** 1-5 3m+: 0-3
Track: **LH:** 1-9 RH: 0-0 Tight: 0-1 Gall: 0-2
Aids: Bl: 0-0 Vi: 0-0 Tstrap: 0-0
Best Rating: 94 12/02 Ayr 2m4f soft Ch

Moderate chaser, surprise winner of a poor chase at Ayr in late 2002. Stays two and a half miles plus; suited by soft ground.

Camp Nou (IRE)

105   115
6-y-o b g Sadler s Wells (USA)-Campestral (USA) (Alleged
(USA))
Jonjo O Neill M Tabor

Placings:3/0405-F1103   (3915)
2002/03: 20⁵S, 24¹GS, 22¹HY, 24⁰G, 24³GS,

	Starts	1st	2nd	3rd	Win & Pl
Hurdles	5	2	0	1	10156
Career Total	10	2	0	2	10785
115 11/02 NAbb	2m6f	D(0-125)HHdl		HVY	£3693
115 11/02 Sthl	3m110y	D(0-115)HHdl		G-S	£5622
				Total win prize-money £9316	

Going: Sf: 1-2 GS: 1-2 Gd: 0-1 GF: - Fm: 0-0
Distance: 2m/2m3: 0-0 2m4-2m7: 1-2 3m+: 1-3
Track: **LH:** 2-3 RH: 0-2 **Tight:** 2-2 Gall: 0-1
Aids: Bl: 0-0 Vi: 0-0 Tstrap: 0-1
Best Rating: 115 11/02 NAbb 2m6f heavy Hdl

Fair staying hurdler, he has benefited from being given a stamina test and got off the mark over hurdles over three

miles at Southwell in November; defied a penalty in heavy ground over slightly shorter at Newton Abbot next time.

Campaign Trail (IRE)

103   **125+**

5-y-o b g Sadler s Wells (USA)-Campestral (USA) (Alleged (USA))

Jonjo O Neill M Tabor

Placings:5660-11   (3367)
2002/03: 17¹S, 20¹GS,

	Starts	1st	2nd	3rd	Win & Pl
Hurdles	2	2	0	0	8970
Career Total	6	2	0	0	8970
117 1/03 Sthl	2m4f110yD Hdl			G-S	£5070
125 10/02 Carl	2m1f	D(0-115)HHdl		SFT	£3900
		Total win prize-money £8970

Going:	Sf: 1-1 GS: 1-1 Gd: 0-0 GF: - Fm: 0-0
Distance:	2m/2m3: 1-1 2m4-2m7: 1-1 3m+: 0-0
Track:	LH: 1-1 RH: 1-1 Tight: 1-1 Gall: 0-0
Aids:	Bl: 0-0 Vi: 0-0 Tstrap: 0-0
Best Rating:	125 10/02 Carl 2m1f soft Hdl

Decent, progressive hurdler; made a successful debut in handicap company at Carlisle in October 2002 and followed up very easily in novice company at Southwell; suited by soft ground and stays 2m 4f.

Camus Des Mottes (FR)

56

7-y-o b g Africanus (FR)-Camille Des Mottes (FR) (Abdonski (FR))

Dr P Pritchard The Retreat Racing Club

Placings:46/056PF6/PP-P6P   (0412)
2002/03: 22⁶G, 16⁶F, 19⁹GF,

	Starts	1st	2nd	Win & Pl
Hurdles	2	0	0	0
Chases	1	0	0	0
Career Total	13	0	0	753

Going:	Sf: 0-0 GS: 0-0 Gd: 0-1 GF: - Fm: 0-2
Distance:	2m/2m3: 0-2 2m4-2m7: 0-1 3m+: 0-0
Track:	LH: 0-3 RH: 0-0 Tight: 0-1 Gall: 0-0
Aids:	Bl: 0-1 Vi: 0-0 Tstrap: 0-0
Best Rating:	90 2/01 Ludl 2m4f good Ch

Can Cortana (IRE)

76   **83**

7-y-o b g Supreme Leader-Glen Boosh (Furry Glen)

T D Easterby David & Steven Dudley

Placings:0430-P5   (1542)
2002/03: 20⁷GF, 25⁵GF,

	Starts	1st	2nd	3rd	Win & Pl
Hurdles	2	0	0	0	0
Career Total	6	0	0	1	492

Going:	Sf: 0-0 GS: 0-0 Gd: 0-0 GF: - Fm: 0-2
Distance:	2m/2m3: 0-0 2m4-2m7: 0-1 3m+: 0-1
Track:	LH: 0-2 RH: 0-0 Tight: 0-0 Gall: 0-0
Aids:	Bl: 0-0 Vi: 0-0 Tstrap: 0-0
Best Rating:	83 11/01 MRas 2m1f110y gd-sft Hdl

Can't Be Scrabble

93   **89+**

10-y-o b g Gargoor-Scribble Along (Supergrey)

R J Down J Selby

Placings:F   (4487)
2002/03: 16⁶GF,

	Starts	1st	2nd	3rd	Win & Pl
Chases	1	0	0	0	
Career Total	1	0	0	0	

Going:	Sf: 0-0 GS: 0-0 Gd: 0-0 GF: - Fm: 0-1
Distance:	2m/2m3: 0-1 2m4-2m7: 0-0 3m+: 0-0
Track:	LH: 0-0 RH: 0-1 Tight: 0-0 Gall: 0-0
Aids:	Bl: 0-0 Vi: 0-0 Tstrap: 0-0
Best Rating:	0 4/03 Hrfd 2m gd-fm Ch

Canada

109   **140+**

5-y-o b g Ezzoud (IRE)-Chancel (USA) (Al Nasr (FR))

M C Pipe W J Gredley

Placings:1P-243   (4475)
2002/03: 16²GS, 16⁴HY, 20³G,

	Starts	1st	2nd	3rd	Win & Pl
Hurdles	3	0	1	1	8454
Career Total	5	1	1	1	12357
109 2/02 Hayd	2m		D Hdl	HVY	£3902
		Total win prize-money £3903

Going:	Sf: 0-1 GS: 0-1 Gd: 0-1 GF: - Fm: 0-0
Distance:	2m/2m3: 0-2 2m4-2m7: 0-1 3m+: 0-0
Track:	LH: 0-2 RH: 0-1 Tight: 0-1 Gall: 0-0
Aids:	Bl: 0-0 Vi: 0-0 Tstrap: 0-0
Best Rating:	126 4/03 Aint 2m4f good Hdl

Useful hurdler; has run with credit in the face of some very stiff tasks; easy winner at Market Rasen in July; stays 2m 6f; seems to handle any ground.

Canada Road (IRE)

75f   **87f**

5-y-o b g Great Marquess-New Technique (FR) (Formidable (USA))

R J Smith Oliver Ryan, Kieran Ryan, Janet Baker

Placings:5   (4685)
2002/03: 16⁵GF,

	Starts	1st	2nd	3rd	Win & Pl
NH Flat	1	0	0	0	0
Career Total	1	0	0	0	0

Going:	Sf: 0-0 GS: 0-0 Gd: 0-0 GF: - Fm: 0-1
Distance:	2m/2m3: 0-1 2m4-2m7: 0-0 3m+: 0-0
Track:	LH: 0-0 RH: 0-1 Tight: 0-0 Gall: 0-1
Aids:	Bl: 0-0 Vi: 0-0 Tstrap: 0-0
Best Rating:	87 4/03 Hntg 2m110y gd-fm NHF

Well beaten in a bumper.

Canadiane (FR)

112(102h)   (123h)**120**

8-y-o ch m Nikos-Carmonera (FR) (Carmont (FR))

M C Pipe D A Johnson

Placings:664F/454562125/06503242P4-312121323133244121U5 (4596)
2002/03: 17³G, 20¹GF, 20²GS, 19¹G, 17²GF, 17¹G, 21³GF, 16²GF, 17³S, 20¹GF, 23³G, 19³GF, 21²G, 20⁴G, 16⁴GS, 17¹S, 18²S, 16¹GF,

Canal End (IRE)

100   **90**

6-y-o b g Montelimar (USA)-Miss Cripps (IRE) (Lafontaine (USA))

Jonjo O Neill (C Roche 21/12) Mrs Jonjo O Neill

Placings:000026   (4566)
2002/03: 18⁰S, 18⁵S, 18⁰S, 20⁰S, 25²G, 20⁶GF,

	Starts	1st	2nd	3rd	Win & Pl
Hurdles	6	0	1	0	1068
Career Total	6	0	1	0	1068

Going:	Sf: 0-4 GS: 0-0 Gd: 0-1 GF: - Fm: 0-1
Distance:	2m/2m3: 0-2 2m4-2m7: 0-2 3m+: 0-1
Track:	LH: 0-3 RH: 0-2 Tight: 0-2 Gall: 0-0
Aids:	Bl: 0-0 Vi: 0-0 Tstrap: 0-0
Best Rating:	90 4/03 Bang 2m4f gd-fm Hdl

Cancun Caribe (IRE)

96   **97+**

6-y-o ch g Port Lucaya-Miss Tuko (Good Times (ITY))

J D Frost (K McAuliffe 5/5) Dapper Racing Syndicate

Placings:001   (4220)
2002/03: 17⁰S, 19⁰GS, 19¹GF,

	Starts	1st	2nd	3rd	Win & Pl
Hurdles	3	1	0	0	2359
Career Total	3	1	0	0	2359
97 3/03 Hrfd	2m3f110yG Hdl			G-F	£2359
		Total win prize-money £2359

Going:	Sf: 0-1 GS: 0-1 Gd: 0-0 GF: - Fm: 1-1
Distance:	2m/2m3: 0-2 2m4-2m7: 1-1 3m+: 0-0
Track:	LH: 0-0 RH: 1-3 Tight: 0-1 Gall: 0-0
Aids:	Bl: 0-0 Vi: 0-0 Tstrap: 0-0
Best Rating:	97 3/03 Hrfd 2m3f110y gd-fm Hdl

Candarli (IRE)

105   **114**

7-y-o ch g Polish Precedent (USA)-Calounia (IRE) (Pharly (FRI))

D R Gandolfo A E Frost

Placings:5/301-302P   (4449)
2002/03: 16³GS, 16⁵S, 17²G, 16⁵G,

21⁰G, 19⁵GF,

	Starts	1st	2nd	3rd	Win & Pl
Hurdles	2	1	0	0	5168
Chases	18	5	5	5	37779
Career Total	43	7	9	6	69494
120 3/03 Hayd	2m	D(0-120)HCh	G-F	£8368
123 1/03 Tntn	2m1f	D(0-120)HHdl	SFT	£5167
120 8/02 Font	2m4f	E Ch	G-F	£4431
118 7/02 Strf	2m1f110yE Ch		GD	£3640
112 6/02 Hrfd	2m3f	E Ch	GD	£3045
102 5/02 Ludl	2m4f	D Ch	G-F	£4026
120 12/99 Chep	2m110y	D Hdl	G-S	£3347
		Total win prize-money £32027

Going:	Sf: 1-3 GS: 0-2 Gd: 2-7 GF: - Fm: 3-8
Distance:	2m/2m3: 4-11 2m4-2m7: 2-8 3m+: 0-1
Track:	LH: 2-11 RH: 3-8 Tight: 4-11 Gall: 0-0
Aids:	Bl: 0-0 Vi: 0-0 Tstrap: 0-0
Best Rating:	123 1/03 Tntn 2m1f soft Hdl

Fair chaser/hurdler; did well in ordinary company over fences in the summer and autumn of 2002; won back over hurdles early in 2003; stays two and a half miles; acts on most ground; jumps well; tough and consistent.

Column 1

	Starts	1st	2nd	3rd	Win & Pl
Hurdles	4	0	1	1	2759
Career Total	8	1	1	2	9151

106 3/02 Winc 2m   D(0-125)HHdl   GD   £5261
Total win prize-money £5262

Going:	Sf: 0-1 GS: 0-1 Gd: 0-2 GF: - Fm: 0-0
Distance:	2m/2m3: 0-4 2m4-2m7: 0-0 3m+: 0-0
Track:	LH: 0-0 RH: 0-4 Tight: 0-0 Gall: 0-1
Aids:	Bl: 0-0 Vi: 0-0 Tstrap: 0-0
Best Rating:	114 3/03 Extr 2m1f good Hdl

Fair hurdler; acts on good ground; effective over two miles.

Candour

76   32

4-y-o b f So Factual (USA)-Outward s Gal (Ashmore (FR))
Mrs D Haine G Haine

Placings:00   (2503)
2002/03: 16⁰GS, 16⁰GS,

	Starts	1st	2nd	3rd	Win & Pl
Hurdles	2	0	0	0	
Career Total	2	0	0	0	

Going:	Sf: 0-0 GS: 0-2 Gd: 0-0 GF: - Fm: 0-0
Distance:	2m/2m3: 0-2 2m4-2m7: 0-0 3m+: 0-0
Track:	LH: 0-2 RH: 0-0 Tight: 0-2 Gall: 0-0
Aids:	Bl: 0-0 Vi: 0-0 Tstrap: 0-0
Best Rating:	38 11/02 Fknm 2m gd-sft Hdl

Candy Anchor (FR)

87   71

4-y-o b f Slip Anchor-Kandavu (Safawan)
Andrew Reid (J G Given 17/9) A S Reid

Placings:5PP   (2610)
2002/03: 17¹S, 18PG, 16PS,

	Starts	1st	2nd	3rd	Win & Pl
Hurdles	3	0	0	0	0
Career Total	3	0	0	0	0

Going:	Sf: 0-2 GS: 0-0 Gd: 0-1 GF: - Fm: 0-0
Distance:	2m/2m3: 0-3 2m4-2m7: 0-0 3m+: 0-0
Track:	LH: 0-2 RH: 0-1 Tight: 0-2 Gall: 0-0
Aids:	Bl: 0-0 Vi: 0-0 Tstrap: 0-0
Best Rating:	71 11/02 Folk 2m1f110y soft Hdl

Cannon Bridge (IRE)

94   70

5-y-o ch g Definite Article-Hit For Six (Tap On Wood)
D Shaw J C Fretwell

Placings:6-2   (0567)
2002/03: 16²GS,

	Starts	1st	2nd	3rd	Win & Pl
Hurdles	1	0	1	0	762
Career Total	2	0	1	0	762

Going:	Sf: 0-0 GS: 0-1 Gd: 0-0 GF: - Fm: 0-0
Distance:	2m/2m3: 0-1 2m4-2m7: 0-0 3m+: 0-0
Track:	LH: 0-1 RH: 0-0 Tight: 0-0 Gall: 0-0
Aids:	Bl: 0-0 Vi: 0-0 Tstrap: 0-0
Best Rating:	70 6/02 Uttx 2m gd-sft Hdl

Canny Chiftane

79   30

7-y-o b g Be My Chief (USA)-Prudence (Grundy)

Column 2

Miss C J E Caroe Miss C J E Caroe

Placings:04461/30PP5/0P0PP16400P-P   (0088)
2002/03: 20PG,

	Starts	1st	2nd	3rd	Win & Pl
Hurdles	1	0	0	0	
Career Total	22	2	0	1	4135

86 11/01 Fknm 2m4f   G(0-95)HHdl   SFT £1867
77 4/00 Newc 2m   F Hdl   G-S £1897
Total win prize-money £3765

Going:	Sf: 0-0 GS: 0-0 Gd: 0-1 GF: - Fm: 0-0
Distance:	2m/2m3: 0-0 2m4-2m7: 0-1 3m+: 0-0
Track:	LH: 0-1 RH: 0-0 Tight: 0-0 Gall: 0-0
Aids:	Bl: 0-1 Vi: 0-0 Tstrap: 0-0
Best Rating:	86 11/01 Fknm 2m4f soft Hdl

Plating-class hurdler; suited by cut in the ground. Stays two and a half miles, often wears a visor.

Canon Barney (IRE)

107   (111h) 118+

8-y-o b/br g Salluceva-Debbie s Candy (Candy Cane)
Jonjo O Neill J P McManus

Placings:3F/64153F41-3U41   (4174)
2002/03: 17³S, 20ᵁS, 17⁴S, 26¹S,

	Starts	1st	2nd	3rd	Win & Pl
Chases	4	1	0	1	13542
Career Total	14	3	0	3	26687

118 3/03 Uttx 3m2f   B HCh   SFT £12342
111 2/02 Navn 2m   Hdl   SFT £5503
102 11/01 Navn 2m   NHF   YLD £5008
Total win prize-money £22853

Going:	Sf: 1-4 GS: 0-0 Gd: 0-0 GF: - Fm: 0-0
Distance:	2m/2m3: 0-2 2m4-2m7: 0-1 3m+: 1-1
Track:	LH: 1-3 RH: 0-1 Tight: 0-2 Gall: 0-0
Aids:	Bl: 0-0 Vi: 0-0 Tstrap: 0-0
Best Rating:	118 3/03 Uttx 3m2f soft Ch

Modest chaser; stays three miles two; acts on soft ground; suited by forcing tactics.

Canon McCarthy (IRE)

96   89

7-y-o ch g Be My Native (USA)-Archetype (Over The River (FR))
A W Carroll Gary J Roberts

Placings:34563/0332-246   (3264)
2002/03: 25²G, 20⁴GS, 24⁶G,

	Starts	1st	2nd	3rd	Win & Pl
Chases	3	0	1	0	1830
Career Total	12	0	2	4	5515

Going:	Sf: 0-0 GS: 0-1 Gd: 0-2 GF: - Fm: 0-0
Distance:	2m/2m3: 0-0 2m4-2m7: 0-1 3m+: 0-2
Track:	LH: 0-1 RH: 0-2 Tight: 0-1 Gall: 0-1
Aids:	Bl: 0-0 Vi: 0-0 Tstrap: 0-0
Best Rating:	96 10/00 Font 2m4f good Hdl

Moderate form in novice and handicaps chases. Stays three miles.

Canovas Kingdom

5-y-o ch g Aragon-Joan s Venture (Beldale Flutter (USA))
Bob Jones Bob Jones

Column 3

Placings:P   (1890)
2002/03: 16PGS,

	Starts	1st	2nd	3rd	Win & Pl
Hurdles	1	0	0	0	
Career Total	1	0	0	0	

Going:	Sf: 0-0 GS: 0-1 Gd: 0-0 GF: - Fm: 0-0
Distance:	2m/2m3: 0-1 2m4-2m7: 0-0 3m+: 0-0
Track:	LH: 0-0 RH: 0-1 Tight: 0-0 Gall: 0-1
Aids:	Bl: 0-0 Vi: 0-0 Tstrap: 0-0
Best Rating:	0 11/02 Hntg 2m110y gd-sft Hdl

Cantarinho

5-y-o b g Alderbrook-Hot Hostess (Silly Season)
M A Kemp M A Kemp

Placings:2   (4667)
2002/03: 21²G,

	Starts	1st	2nd	3rd	Win & Pl
Chases	1	0	1	0	630
Career Total	1	0	1	0	630

Going:	Sf: 0-0 GS: 0-0 Gd: 0-1 GF: - Fm: 0-0
Distance:	2m/2m3: 0-0 2m4-2m7: 0-1 3m+: 0-0
Track:	LH: 0-1 RH: 0-0 Tight: 0-1 Gall: 0-0
Aids:	Bl: 0-0 Vi: 0-0 Tstrap: 0-0
Best Rating:	72 4/03 Fknm 2m5f110y good Ch

Moderate pointer/hunter; stays three miles; suited by a sound surface.

Cantenac Brown (IRE)

8-y-o ch g Ikdam-Mossbrook (Le Moss)
J J Boulter J J Boulter

Placings:6   (4552)
2002/03: 27⁶G,

	Starts	1st	2nd	3rd	Win & Pl
Chases	1	0	0	0	0
Career Total	1	0	0	0	0

Going:	Sf: 0-0 GS: 0-0 Gd: 0-0 GF: - Fm: 0-0
Distance:	2m/2m3: 0-0 2m4-2m7: 0-0 3m+: 0-1
Track:	LH: 0-0 RH: 0-0 Tight: 0-0 Gall: 0-1
Aids:	Bl: 0-0 Vi: 0-0 Tstrap: 0-0
Best Rating:	45 4/03 Ayr 3m3f110y good Ch

Canterbury (IRE)

85   75

10-y-o b g King s Ride-Private Dancer (Deep Run)
R J Baker Churchgoers Anonymous

Placings:0P/02/6-4P   (0923)
2002/03: 20⁴GF, 22PGF,

	Starts	1st	2nd	3rd	Win & Pl
Hurdles	2	0	0	0	0
Career Total	7	0	1	0	552

Going:	Sf: 0-0 GS: 0-0 Gd: 0-0 GF: - Fm: 0-2
Distance:	2m/2m3: 0-0 2m4-2m7: 0-2 3m+: 0-0
Track:	LH: 0-2 RH: 0-0 Tight: 0-1 Gall: 0-0
Aids:	Bl: 0-0 Vi: 0-0 Tstrap: 0-0
Best Rating:	75 4/01 Extr 2m1f gd-sft Hdl

Canterbury Jack (IRE)

103   **103**

6-y-o b g Supreme Leader-Crest Of The Hill (Prince Regent (FR))
M C Pipe   P J Finn

Placings: 0/223   (1460)
2002/03: 24²G, 22²F, 22³F,

	Starts	1st	2nd	3rd	Win & Pl
Hurdles	3	0	2	1	2024
Career Total	4	0	2	1	2024

Going: Sf: 0-0 GS: 0-0 Gd: 0-1 GF: - Fm: 0-2
Distance: 2m/2m3: 0-0 2m4-2m7: 0-2 3m+: 0-1
Track: LH: 0-1 RH: 0-2 Tight: 0-0 Gall: 0-0
Aids: Bl: 0-0 Vi: 0-0 Tstrap: 0-0
Best Rating: 103   9/02   Worc   3m   good   Hdl

The winner of four points in Ireland in 2002 was bought for 15,000gns. Decent efforts in staying novice hurdles before looking reluctant in a first-time visor at Wincanton in October 2002. Handles fast ground.

Cantys Brig (IRE)

85   **49**

6-y-o gr g Roselier (FR)-Call Catherine (IRE) (Strong Gale)
Miss L C Siddall   Mrs D Ibbotson

Placings: 060030   (4435)
2002/03: 16⁵G, 16⁶GS, 16⁹GS, 16⁰HY, 25³S, 20⁰G,

	Starts	1st	2nd	3rd	Win & Pl
NH Flat	4	0	0	0	0
Hurdles	2	0	0	1	514
Career Total	6	0	0	1	514

Going: Sf: 0-2 GS: 0-2 Gd: 0-2 GF: - Fm: 0-0
Distance: 2m/2m3: 0-4 2m4-2m7: 0-1 3m+: 0-1
Track: LH: 0-6 RH: 0-0 Tight: 0-1 Gall: 0-1
Aids: Bl: 0-0 Vi: 0-0 Tstrap: 0-0
Best Rating: 59   1/03   Newc   2m   heavy   NHF

Canyoubatim (IRE)

97   **73**

9-y-o b g Alphabatim (USA)-Boat Whistle (Amoristic (USA))
Dr P Pritchard   Docs R Us

Placings: 6/F04P-5P23446654P   (3922)
2002/03: 21⁵GF, 24⁰F, 26²GF, 26³GF, 24⁴GF, 24⁴G, 20⁶GS, 16⁶S, 21⁵G, 19⁴S, 22⁵S,

	Starts	1st	2nd	3rd	Win & Pl
Hurdles	1	0	0	0	0
Chases	10	0	1	1	3924
Career Total	16	0	1	1	3924

Going: Sf: 0-3 GS: 0-1 Gd: 0-2 GF: - Fm: 0-5
Distance: 2m/2m3: 0-2 2m4-2m7: 0-4 3m+: 0-5
Track: LH: 0-9 RH: 0-2 Tight: 0-4 Gall: 0-4
Aids: Bl: 0-0 Vi: 0-0 Tstrap: 0-0
Best Rating: 107   10/00   Chel   3m1f110y   good   Hdl

Very moderate chaser, best efforts on fast ground.

Cap In Hand

85   **55**

11-y-o ch g Nearly A Hand-Beringa Bee (Sunley Builds)
Mrs S J Smith   A P Russell

Placings: 00/F0/50/153/400   (4706)
2002/03: 20⁴GF, 20⁰G, 20⁰G,

	Starts	1st	2nd	3rd	Win & Pl
Hurdles	3	0	0	0	0
Career Total	12	1	0	1	2046
82	9/00	Sedg	2m5f110y		G(0-95)HHdl
GD	£1673				

Total win prize-money £1673

Going: Sf: 0-0 GS: 0-0 Gd: 0-2 GF: - Fm: 0-1
Distance: 2m/2m3: 0-0 2m4-2m7: 0-3 3m+: 0-0
Track: LH: 0-3 RH: 0-0 Tight: 0-0 Gall: 0-1
Aids: Bl: 0-0 Vi: 0-0 Tstrap: 0-0
Best Rating: 82   9/00   Sedg   2m5f110y   good   Hdl

Cap It If You Can (IRE)

95   **86**

10-y-o b m Capitano-Lady Of Tara (Deep Run)
T H Caldwell   Mrs C J Cadwaladr

Placings: 00502001210/62U3364/03PP3621P25/P5042P/0 1306PU643053540-22P0PP   (4566)
2002/03: 21²GF, 24²S, 22⁵GF, 19⁰G, 20⁰G, 20⁰GF,

	Starts	1st	2nd	3rd	Win & Pl
Hurdles	6	0	2	0	1450
Career Total	57	4	8	7	21327
96	5/01	Hntg	2m5f110yF(0-110)HHdl	G-F	£2018
100	2/00	Carl	2m1f	D(0-120)HHdl	HVY	£3074
109	3/98	Wxfd	2m4f	(0-116)HHdl	SH	£2382
99	2/98	Gowr	2m	Hdl	YLD	£2680

Total win prize-money £10157

Going: Sf: 0-1 GS: 0-0 Gd: 0-2 GF: - Fm: 0-3
Distance: 2m/2m3: 0-0 2m4-2m7: 0-5 3m+: 0-3
Track: LH: 0-3 RH: 0-3 Tight: 0-2 Gall: 0-1
Aids: Bl: 0-0 Vi: 0-0 Tstrap: 0-0
Best Rating: 109   3/98   Wxfd   2m4f   sft-hvy   Hdl

Plating-class handicap hurdler, suited by around two and a half miles.

Capacoostic

81   **51**

6-y-o ch m Savahra Sound-Cocked Hat Girl (Ballacashtal (CAN))
A G Juckes (S R Bowring 11/7)   C A Cavanagh

Placings: 00   (4320)
2002/03: 16⁰G, 17⁰G,

	Starts	1st	2nd	3rd	Win & Pl
Hurdles	2	0	0	0	
Career Total	2	0	0	0	

Going: Sf: 0-0 GS: 0-0 Gd: 0-2 GF: - Fm: 0-0
Distance: 2m/2m3: 0-2 2m4-2m7: 0-0 3m+: 0-0
Track: LH: 0-1 RH: 0-1 Tight: 0-1 Gall: 0-0
Aids: Bl: 0-0 Vi: 0-0 Tstrap: 0-0
Best Rating: 51   12/02   Ludl   2m   good   Hdl

Cape Canaveral (IRE)

99   **114d**

4-y-o b g Sadler s Wells (USA)-Emmaline (USA) (Affirmed (USA))
G L Moore (A P O Brien 5/6)   Gillespie Brothers

Placings: 20555   (4325)
2002/03: 18²G, 16⁰G, 16⁵HY, 16⁵S, 19⁵G,

	Starts	1st	2nd	3rd	Win & Pl
Hurdles	5	0	1	0	1123
Career Total	5	0	1	0	1123

Going: Sf: 0-2 GS: 0-0 Gd: 0-3 GF: - Fm: 0-0
Distance: 2m/2m3: 0-5 2m4-2m7: 0-0 3m+: 0-0
Track: LH: 0-3 RH: 0-2 Tight: 0-1 Gall: 0-2
Aids: Bl: 0-0 Vi: 0-0 Tstrap: 0-0
Best Rating: 114   12/02   Font   2m2f110y   good   Hdl

Fair hurdler; is becoming disappointing.

Cape Coral

80f   **53f**

6-y-o ch m Henbit (USA)-Celtic Deep (Celtic Cone)
A Parker   S R Galloway

Placings: 0   (1477)
2002/03: 17⁰GF,

	Starts	1st	2nd	3rd	Win & Pl
NH Flat	1	0	0	0	
Career Total	1	0	0	0	

Going: Sf: 0-0 GS: 0-0 Gd: 0-0 GF: - Fm: 0-1
Distance: 2m/2m3: 0-1 2m4-2m7: 0-0 3m+: 0-0
Track: LH: 0-0 RH: 0-1 Tight: 0-0 Gall: 0-0
Aids: Bl: 0-0 Vi: 0-0 Tstrap: 0-0
Best Rating: 53   10/02   Carl   2m1f   gd-fm   NHF

Cape Stormer (IRE)

109(105h)   (109+h)**124**

8-y-o b g Be My Native (USA)-My Sunny South (Strong Gale)
P F Nicholls (Miss H C Knight 7/5)   Mrs Toni S Tipper

Placings: 0P225-121316102   (4720)
2002/03: 20¹GF, 19²GF, 20¹G, 25³G, 20¹G, 24⁶G, 22¹G, 20⁰G, 22²F,

	Starts	1st	2nd	3rd	Win & Pl
Hurdles	2	1	1	0	3606
Chases	7	3	1	1	28160
Career Total	14	4	4	1	33332
124	3/03	Newb	2m6f110yD(0-120)HCh	GD	£7085
121	12/02	Ludl	2m4f	D(0-120)HCh	GD	£6695
121	10/02	Chel	2m4f110yD(0-110)HCh	GD	£9700
109	5/02	Font	2m4f	E Hdl	GF	£2593

Total win prize-money £26074

Going: Sf: 0-0 GS: 0-0 Gd: 3-6 GF: - Fm: 1-3
Distance: 2m/2m3: 0-0 2m4-2m7: 4-7 3m+: 0-2
Track: LH: 2-4 RH: 1-4 Tight: 2-4 Gall: 2-2
Aids: Bl: 0-0 Vi: 0-0 Tstrap: 0-0
Best Rating: 124   3/03   Newb   2m6f110y   good   Ch

Decent novice chaser; effective from 2m 4f to 2m 6f and well suited by a sound surface; consistent.

Capital Lad (IRE)

64   **33**

5-y-o br g Charnwood Forest (IRE)-Casla (Lomond (USA))
G Brown   Capital Accomodation Ltd

Placings: F0   (0647)
2002/03: 16²GF, 16⁰GF,

	Starts	1st	2nd	3rd	Win & Pl
Hurdles	2	0	0	0	
Career Total	2	0	0	0	

Going: Sf: 0-0 GS: 0-0 Gd: 0-0 GF: - Fm: 0-2

Distance: 2m/2m3: 0-2 2m4-2m7: 0-0 3m+: 0-0
Track: LH: 0-2 RH: 0-0 Tight: 0-1 Gall: 0-0
Aids: Bl: 0-0 Vi: 0-0 Tstrap: 0-0
Best Rating: 38 6/02 Strf 2m110y gd-fm Hdl

Cappa Hill (IRE)

7-y-o ch g Dromod Hill-Swatter (IRE) (Over The River (FR))
Mrs A M Thorpe Just Maybe Club

Placings:PPP   (4347)
2002/03: 24PGS, 24PG, 25PGF,

	Starts	1st	2nd	3rd	Win & Pl
Hurdles	3	0	0	0	
Career Total	3	0	0	0	

Going: Sf: 0-0 GS: 0-1 Gd: 0-1 GF: - Fm: 0-1
Distance: 2m/2m3: 0-0 2m4-2m7: 0-0 3m+: 0-3
Track: LH: 0-2 RH: 0-1 Tight: 0-0 Gall: 0-0
Aids: Bl: 0-0 Vi: 0-0 Tstrap: 0-0
Best Rating: 0 3/03 Wwck 3m1f gd-fm Hdl

Cappadrummin (IRE)
95   110

6-y-o ch g Bob Back (USA)-Out And About (Orchestra)
N J Henderson Lady Lloyd Webber

Placings:1-5F   (3871)
2002/03: 16⁵S, 19FS,

	Starts	1st	2nd	3rd	Win & Pl
Hurdles	2	0	0	0	294
Career Total	3	1	0	0	2856
112 2/02 Kemp 2m		H NHF		GD	£2562

Total win prize-money £2562

Going: Sf: 0-2 GS: 0-0 Gd: 0-0 GF: - Fm: 0-0
Distance: 2m/2m3: 0-2 2m4-2m7: 0-0 3m+: 0-0
Track: LH: 0-2 RH: 0-0 Tight: 0-0 Gall: 0-2
Aids: Bl: 0-0 Vi: 0-0 Tstrap: 0-0
Best Rating: 112 2/02 Kemp 2m good NHF

A brother to the smart chaser Whattabob, he is a good-ground bumper winner and ran a promising race on his hurdling debut.

Capricorn
95   101

5-y-o b g Minster Son-Loch Scavaig (IRE) (The Parson)
W McKeown Ian Ives

Placings:40-5232   (4228)
2002/03: 20⁵HY, 24²S, 24³S, 25²GF,

	Starts	1st	2nd	3rd	Win & Pl
Hurdles	4	0	2	1	2620
Career Total	6	0	2	1	2620

Going: Sf: 0-3 GS: 0-0 Gd: 0-0 GF: - Fm: 0-1
Distance: 2m/2m3: 0-0 2m4-2m7: 0-1 3m+: 0-3
Track: LH: 0-3 RH: 0-1 Tight: 0-0 Gall: 0-1
Aids: Bl: 0-1 Vi: 0-0 Tstrap: 0-0
Best Rating: 101 1/03 Ayr 2m4f heavy Hdl

Fair maiden hurdler, best effort when runner-up to an easy winner at Wetherby in March when blinkered; stays three miles.

Capricorn Princess
85(113h)   (124h)87+

9-y-o b m Nicholas Bill-Yamrah (Milford)
B D Leavy Capricorn Hospitality

Placings:00P635/424112/0230P5-1   (4524)
2002/03: 16¹G,

	Starts	1st	2nd	3rd	Win & Pl
Hurdles	1	1	0	0	5879
Career Total	19	3	3	2	18242
124 4/03 Uttx 2m		D(0-125)HHdl	GD	£5878
95 8/00 Bang 2m1f		D Hdl	GD	£3477
93 7/00 Uttx 2m		E(0-105)HHdl	G-F	£3552

Total win prize-money £12909

Going: Sf: 0-0 GS: 0-0 Gd: 1-1 GF: - Fm: 0-0
Distance: 2m/2m3: 1-1 2m4-2m7: 0-0 3m+: 0-0
Track: LH: 1-1 RH: 0-0 Tight: 0-0 Gall: 0-0
Aids: Bl: 0-0 Vi: 0-0 Tstrap: 1-1
Best Rating: 124 4/03 Uttx 2m good Hdl

Fair hurdler; landed a touch on return from injury at Uttoxeter in April 2003; finished lame when well-beaten second on chase debut; suited by a sound surface; best at around two miles.

Capriolo (IRE)
105   102

7-y-o ch g Priolo (USA)-Carroll s Canyon (IRE) (Hatim (USA))
P G Murphy (J C Fox 18/7) S J Kingshott

Placings:040P-4213235050   (4429)
2002/03: 17⁴GS, 16²G, 16¹S, 18³GS, 21²HY, 20³HY, 18⁵S, 21⁰HY, 21⁵S, 21⁰GF,

	Starts	1st	2nd	3rd	Win & Pl
Hurdles	10	1	2	2	6247
Career Total	14	1	2	2	6872
104 11/02 Plum 2m		F Hdl	SFT	£2968

Total win prize-money £2968

Going: Sf: 1-6 GS: 0-2 Gd: 0-1 GF: - Fm: 0-1
Distance: 2m/2m3: 1-5 2m4-2m7: 0-5 3m+: 0-0
Track: LH: 1-9 RH: 0-0 Tight: 0-0 Gall: 0-0
Aids: Bl: 0-1 Vi: 0-0 Tstrap: 0-0
Best Rating: 105 11/02 Font 2m2f110y gd-sft Hdl

Moderate hurdler; middle-distance performer on the Flat; won 2m Plumpton claimer November 2002; returned to form with a couple of good seconds at Fontwell May 2003; acts on any ground.

Captain Bravado (IRE)
78   53

9-y-o b g Torus-Miss Bavard (Le Bavard (FR))
D J Caro J A S Hardcastle

Placings:P-0   (0089)
2002/03: 22⁰G,

	Starts	1st	2nd	3rd	Win & Pl
Hurdles	1	0	0	0	
Career Total	2	0	0	0	

Going: Sf: 0-0 GS: 0-0 Gd: 0-1 GF: - Fm: 0-0
Distance: 2m/2m3: 0-0 2m4-2m7: 0-1 3m+: 0-0
Track: LH: 0-1 RH: 0-0 Tight: 0-0 Gall: 0-0
Aids: Bl: 0-0 Vi: 0-0 Tstrap: 0-0
Best Rating: 53 5/02 Uttx 2m6f110y good Hdl

Captain Clooney (IRE)
100   94

10-y-o b g Supreme Leader-Capincur Lady (Over The River (FR))
N R Mitchell Michael Green

Placings:4251000/40/5P/0PU-1FP   (3552)
2002/03: 26¹HY, 25²S, 26²PS,

	Starts	1st	2nd	3rd	Win & Pl
Chases	3	1	0	0	4069
Career Total	18	2	1	0	9276
94 12/02 Plum 3m2f		F(0-100)HCh	HVY	£4069
116 1/99 Punc 3m		Hdl	HVY	£3989

Total win prize-money £8059

Going: Sf: 1-3 GS: 0-0 Gd: 0-0 GF: - Fm: 0-0
Distance: 2m/2m3: 0-0 2m4-2m7: 0-0 3m+: 1-3
Track: LH: 1-2 RH: 0-1 Tight: 1-3 Gall: 0-0
Aids: Bl: 0-0 Vi: 0-0 Tstrap: 0-0
Best Rating: 116 1/99 Punc 3m heavy Hdl

Moderate chaser; improved form to win at Plumpton in December 2002; acts in heavy ground; stays three and a quarter miles.

Captain Flinders (IRE)
96f   106f

6-y-o b g Satco (FR)-Auburn Queen (Kinglet)
C J Mann P M Warren

Placings:02   (2444)
2002/03: 16⁰GS, 16²GS,

	Starts	1st	2nd	3rd	Win & Pl
NH Flat	2	0	1	0	566
Career Total	2	0	1	0	566

Going: Sf: 0-0 GS: 0-2 Gd: 0-0 GF: - Fm: 0-0
Distance: 2m/2m3: 0-2 2m4-2m7: 0-0 3m+: 0-0
Track: LH: 0-1 RH: 0-1 Tight: 0-0 Gall: 0-1
Aids: Bl: 0-0 Vi: 0-0 Tstrap: 0-0
Best Rating: 106 11/02 Chel 2m110y gd-sft NHF

Has shown good form in bumpers.

Captain Jake

8-y-o b g Phardante (FR)-Cherry Crest (Pollerton)
H D Daly Mrs Jane Lane

Placings:66/PP   (3826)
2002/03: 22PGS, 24PGS,

	Starts	1st	2nd	3rd	Win & Pl
Chases	2	0	0	0	
Career Total	4	0	0	0	0

Going: Sf: 0-0 GS: 0-2 Gd: 0-0 GF: - Fm: 0-0
Distance: 2m/2m3: 0-0 2m4-2m7: 0-0 3m+: 0-1
Track: LH: 0-2 RH: 0-0 Tight: 0-0 Gall: 0-0
Aids: Bl: 0-0 Vi: 0-0 Tstrap: 0-0
Best Rating: 86 1/01 Hayd 2m6f soft Hdl

Captain O'Neill
101(99c)   (91c)90

9-y-o b g Welsh Captain-The Last Tune (Gunner B)
J G M O Shea Gary Roberts

Placings:600P303P/36/001PPOP-51034F323P0F002
(3445)
2002/03: 17⁵GF, 20¹GF, 24⁹G, 20³G, 16⁴GF, 21ᶠGF, 23³GF, 24²S, 20³G, 23ᴾG, 24⁰HY, 17ᶠGS, 19⁰S, 16⁰S, 16²HY,

	Starts	1st	2nd	3rd	Win & Pl
Hurdles	8	1	1	0	2779
Chases	7	0	1	3	3260
Career Total	32	2	2	6	8963
87	5/02 Chep	2m4f	G(0-90)HHdl	G-F	£2079
90	12/01 Chep	2m4f	G Hdl	SFT	£1946

Total win prize-money £4025

Going: Sf: 0-5 GS: 0-1 Gd: 0-4 GF: - Fm: 1-5
Distance: 2m/2m3: 0-5 2m4-2m7: 1-5 3m+: 0-5
Track: LH: 1-12 RH: 0-3 Tight: 0-3 Gall: 0-0
Aids: Bl: 0-0 Vi: 0-1 Tstrap: 0-0
Best Rating: 91 8/02 Worc 2m4f110y good Ch

Plating-class hurdler; won twice over 2m 4f at Chepstow; struggles to stay 3m over fences.

Captain Robin (IRE)
95   88
9-y-o b g Supreme Leader-Gentle Madam (Camden Town)
N A Twiston-Davies H R Mould

Placings:102/04P (3629)
2002/03: 20⁰S, 24⁴HY, 24ᴾS,

	Starts	1st	2nd	3rd	Win & Pl
Hurdles	3	0	0	0	0
Career Total	6	1	1	0	2653
106	11/99 NAbb	2m1f	H NHF	G-S	£1945

Total win prize-money £1945

Going: Sf: 0-3 GS: 0-0 Gd: 0-0 GF: - Fm: 0-0
Distance: 2m/2m3: 0-0 2m4-2m7: 0-1 3m+: 0-2
Track: LH: 0-2 RH: 0-1 Tight: 0-0 Gall: 0-0
Aids: Bl: 0-0 Vi: 0-0 Tstrap: 0-0
Best Rating: 106 3/00 Newb 2m110y soft NHF

Fair bumper performer but has struggled over hurdles; effective at around two miles; acts well with cut in the ground.

Captain Ron (IRE)

7-y-o b g Marju (IRE)-Callas Star (Chief Singer)
S Lloyd N E Powell

Placings:0-0 (4678)
2002/03: 19⁰GF,

	Starts	1st	2nd	3rd	Win & Pl
Chases	1	0	0	0	
Career Total	2	0	0	0	

Going: Sf: 0-0 GS: 0-0 Gd: 0-0 GF: - Fm: 0-1
Distance: 2m/2m3: 0-0 2m4-2m7: 0-0 3m+: 0-0
Track: LH: 0-0 RH: 0-1 Tight: 0-0 Gall: 0-0
Aids: Bl: 0-0 Vi: 0-0 Tstrap: 0-0
Best Rating: 47 7/01 Strf 2m6f110y gd-fm Hdl

Captain Scotland
74   32
4-y-o b g Beveled (USA)-Little Egret (Carwhite)
D J S Ffrench Davis Norcosse Partnership

Placings:0 (1844)
2002/03: 16⁰S,

	Starts	1st	2nd	3rd	Win & Pl
Hurdles	1	0	0	0	
Career Total	1	0	0	0	

Going: Sf: 0-1 GS: 0-0 Gd: 0-0 GF: - Fm: 0-0
Distance: 2m/2m3: 0-1 2m4-2m7: 0-0 3m+: 0-0
Track: LH: 0-0 RH: 0-1 Tight: 0-0 Gall: 0-0
Aids: Bl: 0-0 Vi: 0-0 Tstrap: 0-0
Best Rating: 48 11/02 Sand 2m10y soft Hdl

Captain Valiant (IRE)
99f   99f
5-y-o b g Supreme Leader-Anna Valley (Gleason (USA))
G B Balding Miss B Swire

Placings:032 (4542)
2002/03: 13⁰S, 16³G, 16²G,

	Starts	1st	2nd	3rd	Win & Pl
NH Flat	3	0	1	1	1115
Career Total	3	0	1	1	1115

Going: Sf: 0-1 GS: 0-0 Gd: 0-2 GF: - Fm: 0-0
Distance: 2m/2m3: 0-2 2m4-2m7: 0-0 3m+: 0-0
Track: LH: 0-0 RH: 0-3 Tight: 0-0 Gall: 0-0
Aids: Bl: 0-0 Vi: 0-0 Tstrap: 0-0
Best Rating: 99 4/03 Ludl 2m good NHF

Good jumping pedigree; twice placed in modest bumpers at Ludlow spring 2003.

Captain Zinzan (NZ)
113(99c)   (101c)128+
8-y-o b g Zabeel (NZ)-Lady Springfield (NZ) (Sharivari (USA))
L A Dace (Mrs A J Perrett 22/3) The Tuesday Syndicate

Placings:44/121/2-33F543 (4639)
2002/03: 16³GF, 20³GS, 20ᶠGS, 18⁵G, 16⁴G, 16³GF,

	Starts	1st	2nd	3rd	Win & Pl
Hurdles	2	0	0	1	1198
Chases	4	0	0	2	1442
Career Total	12	2	2	3	9451
119	1/01 Donc	2m110y	E Hdl	GD	£3080
108	8/00 Hntg	2m110y	H NHF	G-F	£1477

Total win prize-money £4557

Going: Sf: 0-0 GS: 0-2 Gd: 0-2 GF: - Fm: 0-2
Distance: 2m/2m3: 0-4 2m4-2m7: 0-2 3m+: 0-0
Track: LH: 0-3 RH: 0-3 Tight: 0-0 Gall: 0-2
Aids: Bl: 0-0 Vi: 0-0 Tstrap: 0-0
Best Rating: 119 1/01 Donc 2m110y good Hdl

Fair hurdler; remarkable improvement over hurdles in June 2003 and hacked up when completing a hat-trick; has managed to keep ahead of the Handicapper despite having gone up over a stone; seems sure to be in for another hefty rise in the ratings; best on a sound surface; stays 2m 4f.

Captain's Leap (IRE)
93   90
7-y-o ch g Grand Plaisir (IRE)-Ballingowan Star (Le Moss)
L Lungo J Regan

Placings:216-5 (2140)
2002/03: 16⁵GS,

	Starts	1st	2nd	3rd	Win & Pl
Hurdles	1	0	0	0	
Career Total	4	1	1	0	2002
99	12/01 Muss	2m	H NHF	GD	£1554

Total win prize-money £1554

Going: Sf: 0-0 GS: 0-1 Gd: 0-0 GF: - Fm: 0-0
Distance: 2m/2m3: 0-1 2m4-2m7: 0-0 3m+: 0-0
Track: LH: 0-1 RH: 0-0 Tight: 0-0 Gall: 0-1
Aids: Bl: 0-0 Vi: 0-0 Tstrap: 0-0
Best Rating: 102 3/02 Ayr 2m soft NHF

A well regarded individual. He was runner-up on his bumper debut at Sedgefield in November 2001 on good ground, and got off the mark at Musselburgh the following month.

Captain's Walk
56   32
7-y-o b g Seymour Hicks (FR)-Mayina (Idiots Delight)
P Bowen John O Sullivan

Placings:60/40P-P6 (4077)
2002/03: 24ᴾGS, 21⁶HY,

	Starts	1st	2nd	3rd	Win & Pl
Hurdles	2	0	0	0	0
Career Total	7	0	0	0	0

Going: Sf: 0-1 GS: 0-1 Gd: 0-0 GF: - Fm: 0-0
Distance: 2m/2m3: 0-0 2m4-2m7: 0-1 3m+: 0-1
Track: LH: 0-1 RH: 0-0 Tight: 0-2 Gall: 0-0
Aids: Bl: 0-0 Vi: 0-0 Tstrap: 0-0
Best Rating: 95 5/01 Hntg 2m110y gd-fm NHF

Captains Table
109   118
10-y-o b g Welsh Captain-Wensum Girl (Ballymoss)
R Dickin Les Pike

Placings:6-21P223F (4638)
2002/03: 16²GF, 16¹G, 20ᴾS, 16²G, 16²GS, 20³GF, 17ᶠG,

	Starts	1st	2nd	3rd	Win & Pl
Chases	7	1	3	1	9551
Career Total	7	1	3	1	9551
111	12/02 Donc	2m110y	D Ch	GD	£4741

Total win prize-money £4741

Going: Sf: 0-1 GS: 0-1 Gd: 1-3 GF: - Fm: 0-2
Distance: 2m/2m3: 1-5 2m4-2m7: 0-2 3m+: 0-0
Track: LH: 1-4 RH: 0-3 Tight: 0-1 Gall: 1-2
Aids: Bl: 0-0 Vi: 0-0 Tstrap: 0-0
Best Rating: 118 2/03 Leic 2m gd-sft Ch

Fair chaser; ex-eventer; jumped soundly when making all in novices chase at Doncaster in December 2002; acts on a sound surface; likes to make the running; effective at two miles.

Captaintwothousand
100(107h)   (92h)98
8-y-o b g Milieu-Royal Scarlet (Royal Fountain)
C W Fairhurst Mrs A M Leggett

Placings:0/2P6U50/0P22123-52566 (3165)
2002/03: 20⁵GS, 17²S, 17⁵S, 16⁶HY, 16⁶G,

	Starts	1st	2nd	3rd	Win & Pl
Chases	5	0	1	0	1472
Career Total	19	1	5	1	7364
92	3/02 Catt	2m3f	F(0-100)HHdl	G-S	£2096

Total win prize-money £2097

Moderate chaser, ran much better race over fences on second start when runner-up at Market Rasen in December.

Caracciola (GER)
107   120
6-y-o b g Lando (GER)-Capitolina (FR) (Empery (USA))
N J Henderson P J D Pottinger

Placings:21313P   (4470)
2002/03: 16²S, 16¹G, 16⁹S, 16¹G, 16³G, 16⁶G,

	Starts	1st	2nd	3rd	Win & Pl
Hurdles	6	2	1	2	17712
Career Total	6	2	1	2	17712
120	2/03	Newb	2m110y	C Hdl	GD £7384
113	12/02	Newb	2m110y	D Hdl	GD £4738

Total win prize-money £12123

Going: Sf: 0-2 GS: 0-0 Gd: 2-4 GF: - Fm: 0-0
Distance: 2m/2m3: 2-6 2m4-2m7: 0-0 3m+: 0-0
Track: LH: 2-4 RH: 0-2 Tight: 0-1 Gall: 2-2
Aids: Bl: 0-0 Vi: 0-0 Tstrap: 0-0
Best Rating: 120 2/03 Newb 2m110y good Hdl

Decent novice hurdler; ex-German; both wins so far at
Newbury; best over two miles; acts on good or soft ground;
suited by waiting tactics.

Caracciola (NZ)
92   75
7-y-o ch g Fiesta Star (AUS)-Striking Princess (NZ) (Straight
Strike (USA))
J L Spearing J Westwood

Placings:0PP-P20P0   (4465)
2002/03: 16⁵GF, 16²HY, 17⁰G, 26⁶S, 24⁰F,

	Starts	1st	2nd	3rd	Win & Pl
Hurdles	5	0	1	0	1075
Career Total	8	0	1	0	1075

Going: Sf: 0-2 GS: 0-0 Gd: 0-1 GF: - Fm: 0-2
Distance: 2m/2m3: 0-3 2m4-2m7: 0-0 3m+: 0-2
Track: LH: 0-1 RH: 0-4 Tight: 0-1 Gall: 0-0
Aids: Bl: 0-0 Vi: 0-0 Tstrap: 0-0
Best Rating: 75 1/03 Leic 2m heavy Hdl

Very moderate hurdler.

Caramelle (IRE)
7-y-o ch m Be My Guest (USA)-Lobbino (Bustino)
J D Czerpak Stampede Racing

Placings:04P/PP   (0393)
2002/03: 17⁵S, 16⁶GF,

	Starts	1st	2nd	3rd	Win & Pl
Hurdles	2	0	0	0	
Career Total	5	0	0	0	220

Going: Sf: 0-1 GS: 0-0 Gd: 0-0 GF: - Fm: 0-1
Distance: 2m/2m3: 0-2 2m4-2m7: 0-0 3m+: 0-0
Track: LH: 0-2 RH: 0-0 Tight: 0-2 Gall: 0-0
Aids: Bl: 0-0 Vi: 0-0 Tstrap: 0-0
Best Rating: 77 12/00 Leic 2m heavy Hdl

Carandrew (FR)
78   89
10-y-o b g Saint Andrews (FR)-Cara Maria (FR) (Cadoudal
(FR))
D M Lloyd D M Lloyd

Placings:0/0166541/00F4121FU2/2354050P/11114500051
1-03F   (3245)
2002/03: 16⁰G, 22³HY, 21⁵HY,

	Starts	1st	2nd	3rd	Win & Pl
Hurdles	3	0	0	1	338
Career Total	41	10	3	2	55000
136	4/02	Chep	2m110y	C(0-130)HHdl	G-F £5509
127	4/02	Chep	2m110y	F Hdl	G-S £1897
136	5/01	Folk	2m1f110yF(0-110)HHdl	G-F £2982
110	5/01	Extr	2m1f	E(0-115)HHdl	FRM £3108
120	5/01	Sthl	2m1f	F(0-105)HHdl	G-F £2086
106	5/01	Tntn	2m1f	F(0-100)HHdl	FRM £2107
136	2/00	Plum	2m1f	E Ch	HVY £3585
120	1/00	Extr	2m7f110yD Ch	HVY £5040
5/99	Autl	2m1f110y HHdl		VS £10764
9/98	Nior	2m3f	Hdl	SFT £3030

Total win prize-money £40108

Going: Sf: 0-2 GS: 0-0 Gd: 0-1 GF: - Fm: 0-0
Distance: 2m/2m3: 0-1 2m4-2m7: 0-2 3m+: 0-0
Track: LH: 0-1 RH: 0-2 Tight: 0-2 Gall: 0-0
Aids: Bl: 0-0 Vi: 0-0 Tstrap: 0-0
Best Rating: 136 4/02 Chep 2m110y gd-fm Hdl

Plating-class hurdler; winner over hurdles in France and
England, he has also won over fences. He completed a four-
timer over hurdles in the spring of 2001, but shot up the
handicap as a result and his two victories at Chepstow in
April 2002 were in weak events. Suited by two miles and
fast ground.

Carapuce (FR)
84   87
4-y-o ch g Bigstone (IRE)-Treasure City (FR) (Moulin)
L Lungo (H-A Pantall 16/6) Mr & Mrs Raymond Anderson
Green

Placings:50B0   (4590)
2002/03: 16⁵G, 16⁸GS, 20⁰G,

	Starts	1st	2nd	3rd	Win & Pl
Hurdles	4	0	0	0	0
Career Total	4	0	0	0	0

Going: Sf: 0-0 GS: 0-2 Gd: 0-2 GF: - Fm: 0-0
Distance: 2m/2m3: 0-3 2m4-2m7: 0-1 3m+: 0-0
Track: LH: 0-2 RH: 0-2 Tight: 0-3 Gall: 0-0
Aids: Bl: 0-0 Vi: 0-0 Tstrap: 0-0
Best Rating: 87 12/02 Muss 2m gd-sft Hdl

Carbonado
9-y-o b g Anshan-Virevoite (Shareef Dancer (USA))
H R Tuck Mrs M J Tuck

Placings:546F0/42-42PP5   (4451)
2002/03: 21⁴GF, 24²GF, 25⁵G, 25⁹G, 24⁵G,

	Starts	1st	2nd	3rd	Win & Pl
Chases	5	0	1	0	962
Career Total	12	0	2	0	1762

Going: Sf: 0-0 GS: 0-0 Gd: 0-3 GF: - Fm: 0-2
Distance: 2m/2m3: 0-0 2m4-2m7: 0-1 3m+: 0-4
Track: LH: 0-1 RH: 0-4 Tight: 0-2 Gall: 0-1
Aids: Bl: 0-0 Vi: 0-0 Tstrap: 0-1
Best Rating: 95 5/02 Ludl 3m gd-fm Ch

Hunter chaser, effective over three miles on a sound surface.

Carbury Cross (IRE)
103(87h)   (105h)120
9-y-o b g Mandalus-Brickey Gazette (Fine Blade (USA))
Jonjo O Neill Anne Duchess Of Westminster

Placings:41306/211/111/62021U6-P6P00P0   (4479)
2002/03: 25⁹G, 26⁶GS, 24⁴S, 24⁰G, 28⁹G, 24⁴G, 36⁴G,

	Starts	1st	2nd	3rd	Win & Pl
Chases	7	0	0	0	1575
Career Total	25	7	3	1	89358
153	4/02	Aint	3m1f	B HCh	GD £26000
134	4/01	Ayr	3m1f	B HCh	G-F £21385
130	2/01	Donc	3m	E Ch	GD £3225
124	1/01	Muss	3m	E Ch	G-S £3575
122	11/99	Hayd	2m7f110yD(0-120)HHdl	GD £3078
126	10/99	Carl	3m110y	E(0-115)HHdl	GD £2402
108	1/99	Weth	2m4f110yD Hdl	SFT £3116

Total win prize-money £62782

Going: Sf: 0-1 GS: 0-1 Gd: 0-5 GF: - Fm: 0-0
Distance: 2m/2m3: 0-0 2m4-2m7: 0-0 3m+: 0-7
Track: LH: 0-4 RH: 0-3 Tight: 0-1 Gall: 0-2
Aids: Bl: 0-4 Vi: 0-0 Tstrap: 0-0
Best Rating: 153 11/02 Newb 3m2f110y gd-sft. Ch

Very useful handicap chaser; winner of a valuable event at
Aintree in April 2002; well below par in 2002/3 but creditable
seventh in the Grand National; normally a sound jumper;
stays at least three and a half miles; acts on fast and soft
ground; often blinkered.

Cardinal Error
68f   29f
5-y-o ch g Pure Melody (USA)-Shy Marianet (IRE) (Shy
Groom (USA))
John A Harris Mrs P C Bowles

Placings:00   (4269)
2002/03: 16⁹G, 16⁸GF,

	Starts	1st	2nd	3rd	Win & Pl
NH Flat	2	0	0	0	
Career Total	2	0	0	0	

Going: Sf: 0-0 GS: 0-0 Gd: 0-1 GF: - Fm: 0-1
Distance: 2m/2m3: 0-2 2m4-2m7: 0-0 3m+: 0-0
Track: LH: 0-1 RH: 0-1 Tight: 0-1 Gall: 0-1
Aids: Bl: 0-0 Vi: 0-0 Tstrap: 0-0
Best Rating: 29 3/03 Sthl 2m gd-fm NHF

Cardinal Mark (IRE)
106(106h)   (103h)87
9-y-o b g Ardross-Sister Of Gold (The Parson)
Mrs S J Smith G T Pierse

Placings:1P013/60/41300635FF002P-46430   (3802)
2002/03: 26⁴HY, 27⁶S, 25⁴GS, 24³HY, 20⁰S,

	Starts	1st	2nd	3rd	Win & Pl
Chases	5	0	0	1	1400
Career Total	26	3	1	4	18930
114	5/01	Baln	2m4f	Ch	G-Y £5286
89	3/00	Clon	2m	Hdl	G-Y £2980
101	10/99	Cork	2m1f	NHF	Y-S £3388

Total win prize-money £11655

Going: Sf: 0-4 GS: 0-0 Gd: 0-0 GF: - Fm: 0-0
Distance: 2m/2m3: 0-0 2m4-2m7: 0-1 3m+: 0-4
Track: LH: 0-4 RH: 0-1 Tight: 0-2 Gall: 0-2
Aids: Bl: 0-0 Vi: 0-0 Tstrap: 0-0
Best Rating: 114 5/01 Baln 2m4f gd-yld Ch

Moderate ex-Irish chaser, suited by three miles plus and cut
in the ground.

Cardinal Way (IRE)
10-y-o b/br g Cardinal Flower-Loving Way (Golden Love)

Mrs Julie Read A F J J Moss

Placings:66/4/P-P   (0187)
2002/03: 20PGF,

	Starts	1st	2nd	3rd	Win & Pl
Chases	1	0	0	0	
Career Total	5	0	0	0	0

Going:	Sf: 0-0 GS: 0-0 Gd: 0-0 GF: - Fm: 0-1
Distance:	2m/2m3: 0-0 2m4-2m7: 0-1 3m+: 0-0
Track:	LH: 0-0 RH: 0-1 Tight: 0-0 Gall: 0-1
Aids:	Bl: 0-0 Vi: 0-0 Tstrap: 0-0
Best Rating:	89 3/98 Font 2m2f110y gd-fm Hdl

Carew

96(87h)   (59h)70+
7-y-o b g Minster Son-The White Lion (Flying Tyke)
C Grant   D Vic Roper

Placings:52B/40-004   (1370)
2002/03: 17OG, 17PGF, 214GF,

	Starts	1st	2nd	3rd	Win & Pl
Hurdles	3	0	0	0	
Career Total	8	0	1	0	450

Going:	Sf: 0-0 GS: 0-0 Gd: 0-1 GF: - Fm: 0-2
Distance:	2m/2m3: 0-2 2m4-2m7: 0-1 3m+: 0-0
Track:	LH: 0-3 RH: 0-0 Tight: 0-3 Gall: 0-0
Aids:	Bl: 0-0 Vi: 0-0 Tstrap: 0-0
Best Rating:	102 12/00 Muss 2m good NHF

Plating-class novice hurdler; remote second behind very easy winner on his chasing bow at Cartmel in July.

Carew Lad

83   60+
7-y-o b g Arzanni-Miss Skindles (Taufan (USA))
Mrs D A Hamer   Mrs Mandy Hinchliffe

Placings:6   (0724)
2002/03: 16RG,

	Starts	1st	2nd	3rd	Win & Pl
NH Flat	1	0	0	0	0
Career Total	1	0	0	0	0

Going:	Sf: 0-0 GS: 0-0 Gd: 0-1 GF: - Fm: 0-0
Distance:	2m/2m3: 0-1 2m4-2m7: 0-0 3m+: 0-0
Track:	LH: 0-1 RH: 0-0 Tight: 0-0 Gall: 0-0
Aids:	Bl: 0-0 Vi: 0-0 Tstrap: 0-0
Best Rating:	81 7/02 Worc 2m good NHF

Careysville (IRE)

101   112
12-y-o b g Carmelite House (USA)-Kavali (Blakeney)
Miss Venetia Williams   Miss V M Williams

Placings:6500P/06/5F11PF5/2101/F424/3/02-52P   (4765)
2002/03: 245S, 242S, 31PG,

	Starts	1st	2nd	3rd	Win & Pl
Chases	3	0	1	0	2508
Career Total	28	4	4	1	30113
129	3/99	Newb	3m	C(0-135)HCh	SFT	£5524
129	1/99	Folk	3m2f	D(0-125)HCh	SFT	£7335
118	1/98	Ludl	3m	E(0-115)HCh	SFT	£3048
122	12/97	Font	3m2f110yE(0-100)HCh	SFT	£3603

Total win prize-money £19511

Going:	Sf: 0-2 GS: 0-0 Gd: 0-1 GF: - Fm: 0-0

Distance:	2m/2m3: 0-0 2m4-2m7: 0-0 3m+: 0-3
Track:	LH: 0-0 RH: 0-2 Tight: 0-0 Gall: 0-0
Aids:	Bl: 0-0 Vi: 0-0 Tstrap: 0-0
Best Rating:	129 3/99 Newb 3m soft Ch

Moderate chaser; runner-up in the Grand Military Gold Cup in both 2002 and 2003; stays 3m 4f and is effective on soft ground.

Cariad Preseli (IRE)

81   51
8-y-o b m Jurado (USA)-Big Sally (Salluceva)
S G Griffiths   S G Griffiths

Placings:0/650   (4320)
2002/03: 19RGF, 19SG, 17OG,

	Starts	1st	2nd	3rd	Win & Pl
Hurdles	3	0	0	0	0
Career Total	4	0	0	0	0

Going:	Sf: 0-0 GS: 0-0 Gd: 0-2 GF: - Fm: 0-1
Distance:	2m/2m3: 0-1 2m4-2m7: 0-2 3m+: 0-0
Track:	LH: 0-1 RH: 0-0 Tight: 0-1 Gall: 0-0
Aids:	Bl: 0-0 Vi: 0-0 Tstrap: 0-2
Best Rating:	86 4/01 Tntn 2m1f gd-fm NHF

Caribbean Cove (IRE)

100   109+
5-y-o gr g Norwich-Peaceful Rose (Roselier (FR))
Miss H C Knight   Trevor Hemmings

Placings:00031   (4567)
2002/03: 16OGS, 16OGS, 19OGS, 193S, 201GF,

	Starts	1st	2nd	3rd	Win & Pl
NH Flat	2	0	0	0	0
Hurdles	3	1	0	1	4580
Career Total	5	1	0	1	4580
109	4/03	Bang	2m4f		E Hdl	G-F	£3721

Total win prize-money £3721

Going:	Sf: 0-2 GS: 0-2 Gd: 0-0 GF: - Fm: 1-1
Distance:	2m/2m3: 0-4 2m4-2m7: 1-1 3m+: 0-0
Track:	LH: 1-3 RH: 0-2 Tight: 1-1 Gall: 0-1
Aids:	Bl: 0-0 Vi: 0-0 Tstrap: 0-0
Best Rating:	109 4/03 Bang 2m4f gd-fm Hdl

Modest form to date, although did appear suited by the step up to two miles three at Newbury in February.

Caribbean Summer

71   30
6-y-o b g Bold Arrangement-Poppadom (Rapid River)
J R Turner   Mrs Sylvia Blakeley

Placings:6P   (1633)
2002/03: 17OGF, 24PS,

	Starts	1st	2nd	3rd	Win & Pl
Hurdles	2	0	0	0	0
Career Total	2	0	0	0	0

Going:	Sf: 0-1 GS: 0-0 Gd: 0-0 GF: - Fm: 0-1
Distance:	2m/2m3: 0-1 2m4-2m7: 0-0 3m+: 0-1
Track:	LH: 0-0 RH: 0-2 Tight: 0-0 Gall: 0-0
Aids:	Bl: 0-0 Vi: 0-0 Tstrap: 0-0
Best Rating:	36 10/02 Carl 2m1f gd-fm Hdl

Caribbean Dream

8-y-o ch m Afzal-Lovelek (Golden Love)
G E Jones   G Elwyn Jones

Placings:P   (4022)
2002/03: 19PS,

	Starts	1st	2nd	3rd	Win & Pl
Hurdles	1	0	0	0	
Career Total	1	0	0	0	

Going:	Sf: 0-1 GS: 0-0 Gd: 0-0 GF: - Fm: 0-0
Distance:	2m/2m3: 0-0 2m4-2m7: 0-1 3m+: 0-0
Track:	LH: 0-0 RH: 0-1 Tight: 0-0 Gall: 0-0
Aids:	Bl: 0-0 Vi: 0-0 Tstrap: 0-0
Best Rating:	0 3/03 Hrfd 2m3f110y soft Hdl

Carl's Boy

7-y-o ch g Itsu (USA)-Adelbaran (FR) (No Pass No Sale)
F H Williams (B J Llewellyn 18/7) F H Williams

Placings:F353/55002/3P25   (4487)
2002/03: 203G, 16PGF, 162GF, 165GF,

	Starts	1st	2nd	3rd	Win & Pl
Hurdles	1	0	1	0	1160
Chases	3	0	0	1	487
Career Total	13	0	2	3	2883

Going:	Sf: 0-0 GS: 0-0 Gd: 0-1 GF: - Fm: 0-3
Distance:	2m/2m3: 0-3 2m4-2m7: 0-1 3m+: 0-0
Track:	LH: 0-2 RH: 0-2 Tight: 0-0 Gall: 0-1
Aids:	Bl: 0-0 Vi: 0-0 Tstrap: 0-0
Best Rating:	87 1/01 Ludl 2m soft Hdl

Carling Elect

7-y-o ch m Carlingford Castle-Electress (Baron Blakeney)
R H P Williams   J S Payne

Placings:00054P-U   (4736)
2002/03: 24UGF,

	Starts	1st	2nd	3rd	Win & Pl
Chases	1	0	0	0	
Career Total	7	0	0	0	0

Going:	Sf: 0-0 GS: 0-0 Gd: 0-0 GF: - Fm: 0-1
Distance:	2m/2m3: 0-0 2m4-2m7: 0-0 3m+: 0-1
Track:	LH: 0-1 RH: 0-0 Tight: 0-0 Gall: 0-0
Aids:	Bl: 0-0 Vi: 0-0 Tstrap: 0-1
Best Rating:	67 1/02 Ludl 2m5f good Hdl

Carlingbrook

69
9-y-o ch g Carlingford Castle-Siliferous (Sandy Creek)
T R George   Mrs Sharon C Nelson

Placings:54/P4-P   (2200)
2002/03: 16PS,

	Starts	1st	2nd	3rd	Win & Pl
Hurdles	1	0	0	0	
Career Total	5	0	0	0	491

Going:	Sf: 0-1 GS: 0-0 Gd: 0-0 GF: - Fm: 0-0
Distance:	2m/2m3: 0-1 2m4-2m7: 0-0 3m+: 0-0

Track: LH: 0-1 RH: 0-0 Tight: 0-0 Gall: 0-0
Aids: Bl: 0-0 Vi: 0-0 Tstrap: 0-0
Best Rating: 100 2/00 Asct 2m110y soft NHF

Carlovent (FR)
113   142
8-y-o b g Cadoudal (FR)-Carlaya (FR) (Carmarthen (FR))
M C Pipe C M, B J & R F Batterham

Placings:11F113/1111FF11160/514PU612/543535034-5034P50133   (4789)
2002/03: 24⁵S, 25⁹GS, 20³HY, 22⁴GS, 22³HY, 20⁵S, 25⁹G, 24¹G, 24³G, 24³GF,

	Starts	1st	2nd	3rd	Win & Pl
Hurdles	10	1	0	3	36366
Career Total	44	14	1	7	179311

142	4/03	Aint	3m110y A HHdl	GD	£23200
149	4/01	Aint	3m110y B HHdl	SFT	£26000
144	11/00	Asct	2m B HCh	G-S	£13312
136	11/99	Chep	2m110y B Hdl	G-S	£6710
147	11/99	Chep	2m4f B HHdl	SFT	£22073
142	10/99	Chep	2m110y B HHdl	SFT	£6710
134	7/99	Wolv	2m4f110yC(0-130)HHdl	G-F	£6563
	6/99	Autl	2m110y Ch	SFT	£6997
	6/99	Toul	2m110y Hdl	GD	£3767
	5/99	Dax	2m3f Ch	SFT	£3767
	10/98	Mesl	2m110y Ch	HVY	£3535
	9/98	Jarn	2m Hdl	GD	£1515
	7/98	Pomp	1m5f110y Hdl	GD	£2828
	6/98	Pomp	1m5f110y Hdl	GD	£2525

Total win prize-money £129503

Going: Sf: 0-4 GS: 0-2 Gd: 1-3 GF: - Fm: 0-1
Distance: 2m/2m3: 0-0 2m4-2m7: 0-4 3m+: 1-6
Track: LH: 1-5 RH: 0-4 Tight: 1-1 Gall: 0-3
Aids: Bl: 0-0 Vi: 1-4 Tstrap: 0-0
Best Rating: 150 2/02 Sand 2m6f soft Hdl

Very useful hurdler/chaser; he is a multiple winner in both France and here; took a three-mile handicap hurdle at Aintree for the second time in three years in April 2003; acts on any ground; best at around three miles; reportedly blind in one eye; has been let down by his hurdling.

Carlton Climber
97f   116f
5-y-o b g Carlton (GER)-High Climber (Mandrake Major)
Mrs S J Smith Mrs S Smith

Placings:1   (3357)
2002/03: 16¹HY,

	Starts	1st	2nd	3rd	Win & Pl
NH Flat	1	1	0	0	1869
Career Total	1	1	0	0	1869

116	1/03	Newc	2m	H NHF	HVY	£1869

Total win prize-money £1869

Going: Sf: 1-1 GS: 0-0 Gd: 0-0 GF: - Fm: 0-0
Distance: 2m/2m3: 1-1 2m4-2m7: 0-0 3m+: 0-0
Track: LH: 1-1 RH: 0-0 Tight: 0-0 Gall: 0-0
Aids: Bl: 0-0 Vi: 0-0 Tstrap: 0-0
Best Rating: 116 1/03 Newc 2m heavy NHF

Won on his racecourse debut in a bumper at Newcastle in January 2003 but collapsed and died in the unsaddling enclosure. (DEAD)

Carly Bay
99   86
5-y-o b m Carlton (GER)-Polly Minor (Sunley Builds)
G P Enright A O Ashford

Placings:0-44415   (3934)
2002/03: 18⁹G, 17⁴GS, 17⁴HY, 18⁴S, 16¹HY, 20⁵S,

	Starts	1st	2nd	3rd	Win & Pl
NH Flat	2	0	0	0	0
Hurdles	4	1	0	0	3801
Career Total	6	1	0	0	3801

91	2/03	Plum	2m	E Hdl	HVY	£3532

Total win prize-money £3533

Going: Sf: 1-4 GS: 0-1 Gd: 0-1 GF: - Fm: 0-0
Distance: 2m/2m3: 1-5 2m4-2m7: 0-1 3m+: 0-0
Track: LH: 1-3 RH: 0-2 Tight: 1-5 Gall: 0-0
Aids: Bl: 0-0 Vi: 0-0 Tstrap: 0-0
Best Rating: 91 2/03 Plum 2m heavy Hdl

Modest novice hurdler; got off the mark in an ordinary novice hurdle at Plumpton; acts on heavy ground; effective over two miles.

Carlyta
107   74
7-y-o ch m Carlingford Castle-Baryta (Nishapour (FR))
J T Gifford Lime Street Racing Syndicate

Placings:0P4PP-53   (2075)
2002/03: 17⁵GS, 16⁹GS,

	Starts	1st	2nd	3rd	Win & Pl
Hurdles	2	0	0	1	538
Career Total	7	0	0	1	538

Going: Sf: 0-0 GS: 0-2 Gd: 0-0 GF: - Fm: 0-0
Distance: 2m/2m3: 0-2 2m4-2m7: 0-0 3m+: 0-0
Track: LH: 0-0 RH: 0-2 Tight: 0-1 Gall: 0-0
Aids: Bl: 0-0 Vi: 0-0 Tstrap: 0-0
Best Rating: 80 11/02 Winc 2m gd-sft Hdl

Carna Too
72   60
6-y-o br m Afzal-H And K Punter (Mandalus)
C J Drewe Rw2

Placings:00-00P0   (4290)
2002/03: 16⁹GS, 18⁶S, 19⁶S, 22⁹GF,

	Starts	1st	2nd	3rd	Win & Pl
Hurdles	4	0	0	0	
Career Total	6	0	0	0	

Going: Sf: 0-2 GS: 0-1 Gd: 0-0 GF: - Fm: 0-0
Distance: 2m/2m3: 0-2 2m4-2m7: 0-1 3m+: 0-0
Track: LH: 0-1 RH: 0-3 Tight: 0-1 Gall: 0-0
Aids: Bl: 0-0 Vi: 0-0 Tstrap: 0-0
Best Rating: 60 2/03 Font 2m2f110y soft Hdl

Carnacrack
108   93+
9-y-o b g Le Coq D Or-Carney (New Brig)
Miss S E Forster Joe Storey

Placings:21021F4033   (4503)
2002/03: 22²GF, 26¹G, 27⁰G, 28²S, 25¹HY, 30⁶GS, 24⁴S, 26⁶S, 25³G, 25³G,

	Starts	1st	2nd	3rd	Win & Pl
Chases	10	2	2	2	11920
Career Total	10	2	2	2	11920

95	11/02	Kels	3m1f	F(0-100)Hch	HVY	£4026
86	6/02	Ctml	3m2f	E Ch	GD	£3146

Total win prize-money £7173

Going: Sf: 1-4 GS: 0-1 Gd: 1-4 GF: - Fm: 0-1

Distance: 2m/2m3: 0-0 2m4-2m7: 0-1 3m+: 2-9
Track: LH: 2-9 RH: 0-1 Tight: 2-7 Gall: 0-2
Aids: Bl: 0-0 Vi: 0-0 Tstrap: 0-0
Best Rating: 95 11/02 Kels 3m1f heavy Ch

Moderate chaser; stays three miles plus; suited by some cut; returned to form when successfull at Cartmel in July.

Carnage (IRE)
94   87+
6-y-o b g Catrail (USA)-Caranina (USA) (Caro)
P Bowen (C Drew 16/1) The Galloping Punters

Placings:54   (4733)
2002/03: 20⁵GF, 16⁴GF,

	Starts	1st	2nd	3rd	Win & Pl
Hurdles	2	0	0	0	273
Career Total	2	0	0	0	273

Going: Sf: 0-0 GS: 0-0 Gd: 0-0 GF: - Fm: 0-2
Distance: 2m/2m3: 0-1 2m4-2m7: 0-1 3m+: 0-0
Track: LH: 0-2 RH: 0-0 Tight: 0-1 Gall: 0-0
Aids: Bl: 0-0 Vi: 0-0 Tstrap: 0-0
Best Rating: 87 4/03 Chep 2m110y gd-fm Hdl

Modest hurdler; paid the penalty for forcing a strong pace when well-backed on second start in Chepstow maiden April 2003.

Carnoustie (USA)
100   92
5-y-o gr m Ezzoud (IRE)-Sarba (USA) (Persepolis (FR))
R T Phillips Dozen Dreamers Partnership

Placings:3-3412403521   (4086)
2002/03: 17³GS, 16⁴HY, 17¹GF, 19²GF, 22⁴GF, 17⁰G, 17³GS, 16⁵GS, 19²GS, 19¹GS,

	Starts	1st	2nd	3rd	Win & Pl
Hurdles	10	2	2	2	8886
Career Total	11	2	2	2	9322

89	3/03	Strf	2m3f	G Hdl	G-S	£2947
98	6/02	NAbb	2m1f	D Hdl	G-F	£3419

Total win prize-money £6366

Going: Sf: 0-1 GS: 1-4 Gd: 0-2 GF: - Fm: 1-3
Distance: 2m/2m3: 2-8 2m4-2m7: 0-2 3m+: 0-0
Track: LH: 2-6 RH: 0-4 Tight: 2-6 Gall: 0-0
Aids: Bl: 0-0 Vi: 0-0 Tstrap: 0-0
Best Rating: 98 6/02 NAbb 2m1f gd-fm Hdl

Moderate novice hurdler; stays two and a half miles; has worn cheekpieces..

Carole's Dove
92   68
7-y-o b m Manhal-Nimble Dove (Starch Reduced)
C J Price Ryan Price

Placings:605P365-00   (2779)
2002/03: 17⁰S, 24⁰S,

	Starts	1st	2nd	3rd	Win & Pl
Hurdles	2	0	0	0	
Career Total	9	0	0	1	497

Going: Sf: 0-2 GS: 0-0 Gd: 0-0 GF: - Fm: 0-0
Distance: 2m/2m3: 0-1 2m4-2m7: 0-0 3m+: 0-1
Track: LH: 0-0 RH: 0-2 Tight: 0-1 Gall: 0-0
Aids: Bl: 0-0 Vi: 0-0 Tstrap: 0-0
Best Rating: 71 12/01 Chep 2m110y soft Hdl

Caroline's Rose
69   26
5-y-o br m Fraam-Just Rosie (Sula Bula)
A P Jones The Lambourn Racing Club

Placings:0   (1250)
2002/03: 16⁰G,

	Starts	1st	2nd	3rd	Win & Pl
NH Flat	1	0	0	0	
Career Total	1	0	0	0	

Going: Sf: 0-0 GS: 0-0 Gd: 0-1 GF: - Fm: 0-0
Distance: 2m/2m3: 0-1 2m4-2m7: 0-0 3m+: 0-0
Track: LH: 0-1 RH: 0-0 Tight: 0-0 Gall: 0-0
Aids: Bl: 0-0 Vi: 0-0 Tstrap: 0-0
Best Rating: 15   9/02   Worc   2m   good   NHF

Carousing
93   106
6-y-o b g Selkirk (USA)-Moon Carnival (Be My Guest (USA))
Mrs J C McGregor (Mrs D Thomson 23/5) Carousing Partners

Placings:54522/440-640   (2556)
2002/03: 20⁶S, 16⁴HY, 20⁰GF,

	Starts	1st	2nd	3rd	Win & Pl
Hurdles	3	0	0	0	281
Career Total	11	0	2	0	1475

Going: Sf: 0-2 GS: 0-0 Gd: 0-0 GF: - Fm: 0-1
Distance: 2m/2m3: 0-1 2m4-2m7: 0-2 3m+: 0-0
Track: LH: 0-2 RH: 0-1 Tight: 0-2 Gall: 0-0
Aids: Bl: 0-0 Vi: 0-0 Tstrap: 0-0
Best Rating: 106   10/01   Aint   2m4f   good   Hdl

Modest hurdler; winning stayer on the Flat, he has shown ability over hurdles; likes good ground.

Carpet Princess (IRE)
105   91
5-y-o gr/ro m Prince Of Birds (USA)-Krayyalei (IRE) (Krayyan)
Mrs P N Dutfield Axminster Carpets Ltd

Placings:132640   (2781)
2002/03: 20¹GF, 24³GF, 17²F, 20⁶GS, 16⁴GS, 19⁰S,

	Starts	1st	2nd	3rd	Win & Pl
Hurdles	6	1	1	1	4790
Career Total	6	1	1	1	4790

79   8/02   Bang   2m4f   E Hdl   G-F   £3066
Total win prize-money £3066

Going: Sf: 0-1 GS: 0-2 Gd: 0-0 GF: - Fm: 1-3
Distance: 2m/2m3: 0-2 2m4-2m7: 1-3 3m+: 0-1
Track: LH: 1-2 RH: 0-4 Tight: 1-2 Gall: 0-0
Aids: Bl: 0-0 Vi: 0-0 Tstrap: 0-0
Best Rating: 91   11/02   Winc   2m   gd-sft   Hdl

Moderate hurdler; probably did not achieve much when making a successful debut in a two and a half mile maiden hurdle at Bangor August 2002, and ran better in defeat subsequently; handles fast and easy ground.

Carraca (IRE)
88   65
5-y-o b g Alzao (USA)-Honey Bun (Unfuwain (USA))
Mrs A M Thorpe S A Douch

Placings:6RP   (0649)
2002/03: 19⁶GF, 16ᴿGF, 17ᴾGF,

	Starts	1st	2nd	3rd	Win & Pl
Hurdles	3	0	0	0	0
Career Total	3	0	0	0	0

Going: Sf: 0-0 GS: 0-0 Gd: 0-0 GF: - Fm: 0-3
Distance: 2m/2m3: 0-2 2m4-2m7: 0-1 3m+: 0-0
Track: LH: 0-2 RH: 0-1 Tight: 0-1 Gall: 0-0
Aids: Bl: 0-0 Vi: 0-0 Tstrap: 0-0
Best Rating: 65   5/02   Hrfd   2m3f110y   gd-fm   Hdl

Carradium
(98h)   (77h)
7-y-o b g Presidium-Carrapateira (Gunner B)
R Shiels R Shiels

Placings:0/P000044-4000P   (1897)
2002/03: 20⁴G, 16⁴G, 16⁹GF, 16⁰G, 16⁰S, 21ᴾS,

	Starts	1st	2nd	3rd	Win & Pl
Hurdles	5	0	0	0	0
Chases	1	0	0	0	0
Career Total	13	0	0	0	0

Going: Sf: 0-2 GS: 0-0 Gd: 0-3 GF: - Fm: 0-1
Distance: 2m/2m3: 0-4 2m4-2m7: 0-2 3m+: 0-0
Track: LH: 0-5 RH: 0-1 Tight: 0-4 Gall: 0-1
Aids: Bl: 0-0 Vi: 0-0 Tstrap: 0-6
Best Rating: 77   5/02   Kels   2m110y   good   Hdl

Carriage Ride (IRE)
67   16
5-y-o b g Tidaro (USA)-Casakurali (Gleason (USA))
N G Richards James Callow & David Wesley Yates

Placings:0   (4749)
2002/03: 20⁰G,

	Starts	1st	2nd	3rd	Win & Pl
Hurdles	1	0	0	0	0
Career Total	1	0	0	0	0

Going: Sf: 0-0 GS: 0-0 Gd: 0-1 GF: - Fm: 0-0
Distance: 2m/2m3: 0-0 2m4-2m7: 0-1 3m+: 0-0
Track: LH: 0-0 RH: 0-1 Tight: 0-0 Gall: 0-0
Aids: Bl: 0-0 Vi: 0-0 Tstrap: 0-0
Best Rating: 16   4/03   Prth   2m4f110y   good   Hdl

Carrick Troop (IRE)
110   126d
10-y-o gr g Roselier (FR)-Over The Pond (IRE) (Over The River (FR))
Mrs M Reveley Major J C K Young

Placings:P4/6B112/322PPU3P/P13B114-1430504 (3872)
2002/03: 16¹G, 16⁴GS, 16³G, 20⁰G, 16⁵G, 16⁰S, 17⁴S,

	Starts	1st	2nd	3rd	Win & Pl
Chases	7	1	0	1	10720
Career Total	29	6	3	4	51534

125   11/02   Weth   2m   C(0-135)HCh   GD   £8200
126   3/02   Newb   2m2f110yD(0-125)HCh   G-S   £7182
118   3/02   Newb   2m1f   C(0-135)HCh   SFT   £8268
114   12/01   Hayd   2m   D(0-125)HCh   SFT   £9051
116   1/00   Sedg   3m3f   F(0-105)HCh   SFT   £2873
110   12/99   MRas   3m1f   E(0-105)HCh   G-S   £3481
Total win prize-money £39057

Going: Sf: 0-2 GS: 0-1 Gd: 1-4 GF: - Fm: 0-0
Distance: 2m/2m3: 1-6 2m4-2m7: 0-1 3m+: 0-0
Track: LH: 1-5 RH: 0-2 Tight: 0-0 Gall: 0-2
Aids: Bl: 0-0 Vi: 0-0 Tstrap: 0-0
Best Rating: 126   12/02   Hayd   2m   good   Ch

Decent handicap chaser who used to race over three miles plus but now seems perfectly capable at trips around two miles; suited by soft ground; needs a strong pace in order to show his best.

Carried Interest (IRE)
108
9-y-o br g Celio Rufo-Laurie Belle (Boreen (FR))
D J Caro Mrs J D Kington

Placings:33/5333/106462/24P344-P   (1622)
2002/03: 24ᴾGS,

	Starts	1st	2nd	3rd	Win & Pl
Chases	1	0	0	0	
Career Total	19	1	2	6	10508

117   12/00   Hntg   3m   E(0-105)HCh   SFT   £3289
Total win prize-money £3290

Going: Sf: 0-0 GS: 0-1 Gd: 0-0 GF: - Fm: 0-0
Distance: 2m/2m3: 0-0 2m4-2m7: 0-0 3m+: 0-1
Track: LH: 0-1 RH: 0-0 Tight: 0-1 Gall: 0-0
Aids: Bl: 0-0 Vi: 0-0 Tstrap: 0-0
Best Rating: 117   4/01   Font   2m6f   good   Ch

Fair chaser who stays well and is versatile with regard to ground conditions. Has lost his way somewhat this year.

Carrigafoyle
101   80
8-y-o b g Young Senor (USA)-Miss Skindles (Taufan (USA))
O Brennan O Brennan

Placings:40/06-02050PP   (4666)
2002/03: 17⁰S, 16²S, 19⁰GS, 16⁵GS, 19⁰GS, 17ᴾG, 16ᴾG,

	Starts	1st	2nd	3rd	Win & Pl
Hurdles	7	0	1	0	886
Career Total	11	0	1	0	886

Going: Sf: 0-2 GS: 0-3 Gd: 0-2 GF: - Fm: 0-0
Distance: 2m/2m3: 0-5 2m4-2m7: 0-2 3m+: 0-0
Track: LH: 0-5 RH: 0-2 Tight: 0-4 Gall: 0-2
Aids: Bl: 0-0 Vi: 0-0 Tstrap: 0-0
Best Rating: 93   1/03   Donc   2m110y   gd-sft   Hdl

Moderate hurdler; acts on a soft surface; has never raced beyond two miles three; still a maiden.

Carroll's Dove
5-y-o ch m Carroll House-Dancing Dove (IRE) (Denel (FR))
M C Pipe Paul Murphy

Placings:30P   (3111)
2002/03: 16³G, 17⁰S, 22ᴾHY,

	Starts	1st	2nd	3rd	Win & Pl
NH Flat	2	0	0	1	433
Hurdles	1	0	0	0	0
Career Total	3	0	0	1	433

Going: Sf: 0-2 GS: 0-0 Gd: 0-1 GF: - Fm: 0-0
Distance: 2m/2m3: 0-2 2m4-2m7: 0-1 3m+: 0-0
Track: LH: 0-0 RH: 0-3 Tight: 0-1 Gall: 0-0
Aids: Bl: 0-0 Vi: 0-0 Tstrap: 0-0

Best Rating: **86** 12/02 Ludl 2m   good NHF

Third in a bumper on her debut; held subsequently.

Carroll's Gold (IRE)
94   **74**
5-y-o br g Carroll House-Missfethard-On-Sea (Deep Run)
E L James Mrs M M Stobart

Placings:*500*   (2574)
2002/03: 17⁵G, 16⁰G, 12⁰G,

	Starts	1st	2nd	3rd	Win & Pl
NH Flat	3	0	0	0	0
Career Total	3	0	0	0	0

Going: Sf: 0-0 GS: 0-0 Gd: 0-3 GF: - Fm: 0-0
Distance: 2m2m3: 0-2 2m4-2m7: 0-0 3m+: 0-0
Track: LH: 0-1 RH: 0-1 Tight: 0-0 Gall: 0-0
Aids: Bl: 0-0 Vi: 0-0 Tstrap: 0-0
Best Rating: **93** 5/02 Extr 2m1f   good NHF

Poor form in bumpers; well beaten runner-up on hurdling debut at Uttoxeter in July.

Carryonharry (IRE)
108   (132h)**133**
9-y-o gr g Roselier (FR)-Bluebell Avenue (Boreen Beag)
M C Pipe Drs D Silk J Castro M Gillard P Walker

Placings:*663113/1133/1110F-P10P46P*   (4557)
2002/03: 25⁵GS, 24¹S, 24⁰G, 24⁴S, 24⁴G, 24⁶G, 33⁵PG,

	Starts	1st	2nd	3rd	Win & Pl
Chases	7	1	0	4	34750
Career Total	22	8	0	4	70469

133	12/02	Kemp	3m	C(0-135)HChl	SFT	£29000
124	12/01	Extr	2m7f110yD Ch		GD	£5538
122	11/01	Extr	2m7f110yD Ch		G-F	£5681
133	11/01	Font	2m6f	E Ch	G-S	£3185
133	11/00	Chep	3m	C(0-130)HHdl	HVY	£5057
130	11/00	Newb	3m110y	D(0-120)HHdl	SFT	£4212
114	2/00	Wwck	2m4f110yD Hdl		GD	£3685
106	1/00	Plum	2m5f	E Hdl	SFT	£2415
				Total win prize-money £58774		

Going: Sf: 1-2 GS: 0-1 Gd: 0-4 GF: - Fm: 0-0
Distance: 2m2m3: 0-0 2m4-2m7: 0-0 **3m+: 1-7**
Track: LH: 0-3 **RH: 1-4** Tight: 0-0 Gall: 0-2
Aids: Bl: 0-0 Vi: 0-3 Tstrap: 0-0
Best Rating: **133** 3/03 Chel 3m110y   good Ch

Fair chaser; effective at three miles; has won on good and soft ground; has worn a visor.

Case Of Poteen (IRE)
103   **90**
7-y-o b/br m Witness Box (USA)-On The Hooch (Over The River (FR))
Mrs S C Bradburne Mrs P Grant

Placings:*60/3232503/043246-FC4230*   (4304)
2002/03: 20⁶G, 24⁶GF, 24⁴HY, 20²GS, 22³S, 22⁰G,

	Starts	1st	2nd	3rd	Win & Pl
Hurdles	6	0	1	1	2008
Career Total	21	0	4	5	6269

Going: Sf: 0-2 GS: 0-1 Gd: 0-2 GF: - Fm: 0-1
Distance: 2m2m3: 0-0 2m4-2m7: 0-4 3m+: 0-2
Track: LH: 0-5 RH: 0-1 Tight: 0-1 Gall: 0-0
Aids: Bl: 0-0 Vi: 0-0 Tstrap: 0-0

Best Rating: **103** 1/01 Newc 2m4f   heavy Hdl

Moderate staying hurdler who continues to fall short; fully exposed.

Cash 'n Carrots
62   **21**
4-y-o b g Missed Flight-Rhiannon (Welsh Pageant)
R C Harper R C Harper

Placings:*0000*   (4272)
2002/03: 13⁰S, 16⁰S, 16⁰GS, 16⁰G,

	Starts	1st	2nd	3rd	Win & Pl
NH Flat	3	0	0	0	0
Hurdles	1	0	0	0	0
Career Total	4	0	0	0	0

Going: Sf: 0-2 GS: 0-1 Gd: 0-1 GF: - Fm: 0-0
Distance: 2m2m3: 0-3 2m4-2m7: 0-0 3m+: 0-0
Track: LH: 0-1 RH: 0-3 Tight: 0-0 Gall: 0-0
Aids: Bl: 0-0 Vi: 0-0 Tstrap: 0-0
Best Rating: **40** 12/02 Extr 1m5f   soft NHF

Cash 'N' Credit
96(100h)   (70h)**78**
5-y-o b m Homo Sapien-Not Enough (Balinger)
R Dickin Mrs J M Mann

Placings:*00-534*   (4641)
2002/03: 16⁵GS, 16³GF, 19⁴GF,

	Starts	1st	2nd	3rd	Win & Pl
Hurdles	3	0	0	1	498
Career Total	5	0	0	1	498

Going: Sf: 0-0 GS: 0-1 Gd: 0-0 GF: - Fm: 0-2
Distance: 2m2m3: 0-3 2m4-2m7: 0-0 3m+: 0-0
Track: LH: 0-3 RH: 0-0 Tight: 0-3 Gall: 0-0
Aids: Bl: 0-0 Vi: 0-0 Tstrap: 0-0
Best Rating: **70** 3/03 Sthl 2m   gd-fm Hdl

Plating-class hurdler; stepped up on previous efforts when making winning debut over fences off low weight in 2m novices handicap at Worcester June 2003; disappointing off an 8lb higher mark over the same course and distance next time; acts on a sound surface.

Cash For Questions (IRE)
99   **92**
11-y-o b g Supreme Leader-Deep Dollar (Deep Run)
R A Fahey P S Cresswell

Placings:*03/41/5016/U0/P-0531P04*   (4710)
2002/03: 16⁰G, 20⁵GF, 20⁰GS, 19¹GS, 20²G, 20⁰G, 23⁴GF,

	Starts	1st	2nd	3rd	Win & Pl
Hurdles	7	1	0	1	4720
Career Total	18	3	0	2	10742

89	1/03	Donc	2m3f110yE(0-110)HHdl	G-S	£4303
110	1/00	Donc	2m4f	E(0-115)HHdl	GD	£2951
91	12/98	Catt	2m3f	E Hdl	GD	£2584
				Total win prize-money £9838		

Going: Sf: 0-0 GS: 1-2 Gd: 0-3 GF: - Fm: 0-2
Distance: 2m2m3: 0-1 **2m4-2m7: 1-6** 3m+: 0-0
Track: **LH: 1-6** RH: 0-1 Tight: 0-0 Gall: 0-0
Aids: Bl: 0-0 Vi: 0-0 Tstrap: 0-0
Best Rating: **110** 1/00 Donc 2m4f   good Hdl

Veteran hurdler; game winner at Doncaster in January.

Cash Return
84   **43**
4-y-o b f Bob s Return (IRE)-We Re In The Money (Billion (USA))
B G Powell Berkeley Square Racing

Placings:*00000*   (3672)
2002/03: 14⁰GS, 12⁰G, 19⁰S, 22⁰GS, 22⁰GS,

	Starts	1st	2nd	3rd	Win & Pl
NH Flat	2	0	0	0	0
Hurdles	3	0	0	0	0
Career Total	5	0	0	0	0

Going: Sf: 0-1 GS: 0-3 Gd: 0-1 GF: - Fm: 0-0
Distance: 2m2m3: 0-2 2m4-2m7: 0-3 3m+: 0-0
Track: LH: 0-3 RH: 0-2 Tight: 0-2 Gall: 0-0
Aids: Bl: 0-1 Vi: 0-0 Tstrap: 0-0
Best Rating: **57** 12/02 Newb 1m4f110y   good NHF

Cashaban
81   **70**
10-y-o ch g Ballacashtal (CAN)-Portway Anna (Hot Brandy)
J S Smith Michael J Smith

Placings:*00UPP3/PP/24/F0P-00*   (0419)
2002/03: 16⁰G, 17⁰HY,

	Starts	1st	2nd	3rd	Win & Pl
Hurdles	2	0	0		
Career Total	15	0	1	1	1210

Going: Sf: 0-1 GS: 0-0 Gd: 0-1 GF: - Fm: 0-0
Distance: 2m2m3: 0-2 2m4-2m7: 0-0 3m+: 0-0
Track: LH: 0-2 RH: 0-0 Tight: 0-2 Gall: 0-0
Aids: Bl: 0-1 Vi: 0-0 Tstrap: 0-0
Best Rating: **82** 5/00 Strf 2m110y   good Hdl

Cashaplenty
79   **56**
10-y-o ch g Ballacashtal (CAN)-Storm Of Plenty (Billion (USA))
J W Unett J R Salter

Placings:*P0/0/0P4141146/4F500/0*   (0349)
2002/03: 16⁰G,

	Starts	1st	2nd	3rd	Win & Pl
Hurdles	1	0	0	0	
Career Total	18	3	0	0	6881

105	12/98	Donc	2m110y	F(0-100)HHdl	GD	£2232
101	11/98	Wwck	2m	F(0-100)HHdl	SFT	£2227
87	11/98	Uttx	2m	E(0-100)HHdl	SFT	£2421
				Total win prize-money £6881		

Going: Sf: 0-0 GS: 0-0 Gd: 0-0 GF: - Fm: 0-0
Distance: 2m2m3: 0-0 2m4-2m7: 0-0 3m+: 0-0
Track: LH: 0-1 RH: 0-0 Tight: 0-1 Gall: 0-0
Aids: Bl: 0-0 Vi: 0-0 Tstrap: 0-0
Best Rating: **105** 12/98 Donc 2m110y   good Hdl

Cashel Dancer
100   **82**
4-y-o b f Bishop Of Cashel-Dancing Debut (Polar Falcon (USA))
S A Brookshaw Ken Edwards

Placings:*440*   (1806)
2002/03: 16⁴G, 16⁴F, 16⁰G,

	Starts	1st	2nd	3rd	Win & Pl
Hurdles	3	0	0	0	584

Career Total	3	0	0	0	584

Going: Sf: 0-0 GS: 0-0 Gd: 0-2 GF: - Fm: 0-1
Distance: 2m/2m3: 0-3 2m4-2m7: 0-0 3m+: 0-0
Track: LH: 0-2 RH: 0-1 Tight: 0-0 Gall: 0-0
Aids: Bl: 0-0 Vi: 0-0 Tstrap: 0-0
Best Rating: 77   10/02   Ludl   2m   firm   Hdl

In the frame in weak novice hurdles before accounting for a depleted field at Uttoxeter in June 2003; stays two and a half miles.

Cashew Kid (IRE)

6-y-o b g Persian Mews-No Honey (Dual)
S E H Sherwood (Miss K Marks 19/6) D Lodder

Placings:60-0PP   (4285)
2002/03: 17⁰G, 20ᴾGF, 21ᴾGF,

	Starts	1st	2nd	3rd	Win & Pl
NH Flat	1	0	0	0	0
Hurdles	2	0	0	0	0
Career Total	5	0	0	0	0

Going: Sf: 0-0 GS: 0-0 Gd: 0-1 GF: - Fm: 0-2
Distance: 2m/2m3: 0-1 2m4-2m7: 0-2 3m+: 0-0
Track: LH: 0-1 RH: 0-2 Tight: 0-0 Gall: 0-0
Aids: Bl: 0-0 Vi: 0-0 Tstrap: 0-0
Best Rating: 70   5/02   Extr   2m1f   good   NHF

Casing (IRE)

5-y-o gr m Case Law-Singhana (IRE) (Mouktar)
F Jordan The Fab Five

Placings:P   (2166)
2002/03: 16ᴾGS,

	Starts	1st	2nd	3rd	Win & Pl
Hurdles	1	0	0	0	0
Career Total	1	0	0	0	0

Going: Sf: 0-0 GS: 0-1 Gd: 0-0 GF: 0-0 Fm: 0-0
Distance: 2m/2m3: 0-1 2m4-2m7: 0-0 3m+: 0-0
Track: LH: 0-1 RH: 0-0 Tight: 0-0 Gall: 0-0
Aids: Bl: 0-0 Vi: 0-0 Tstrap: 0-0
Best Rating: 0   11/02   Wwck   2m   gd-sft   Hdl

Caspar's Date
90f   82f

6-y-o ch g Afzal-Rabdanna (Rabdan)
J Gallagher Smith Wadley Homes Ltd

Placings:0-60   (1382)
2002/03: 16⁶G, 17⁰GF,

	Starts	1st	2nd	3rd	Win & Pl
NH Flat	2	0	0	0	0
Career Total	3	0	0	0	0

Going: Sf: 0-0 GS: 0-0 Gd: 0-1 GF: - Fm: 0-1
Distance: 2m/2m3: 0-2 2m4-2m7: 0-0 3m+: 0-0
Track: LH: 0-1 RH: 0-1 Tight: 0-0 Gall: 0-0
Aids: Bl: 0-0 Vi: 0-0 Tstrap: 0-0
Best Rating: 82   10/02   Hrfd   2m1f   gd-fm   NHF

Is out of a half-sister to Floyd. Staying on well and would have finished third had he not broken down in the closing stages on bumper debut at Hereford October 2002.

Cassia Green
98   98+

9-y-o gr g Scallywag-Casa s Star (Top Star)
Mrs H Dalton (R N Bevis 3/6) Mrs J Greenway

Placings:P6-6F31   (4154)
2002/03: 19⁶G, 21ᶠS, 20³GS, 16¹G,

	Starts	1st	2nd	3rd	Win & Pl
Chases	4	1	0	1	4176
Career Total	6	1	0	1	4176
98	3/03	Wwck	2m110y F(0-95)HCh	GD	£3514
			Total win prize-money		£3514

Going: Sf: 0-1 GS: 0-1 Gd: 1-2 GF: - Fm: 0-0
Distance: 2m/2m3: 1-2 2m4-2m7: 0-2 3m+: 0-0
Track: LH: 1-2 RH: 0-2 Tight: 0-0 Gall: 0-0
Aids: Bl: 0-0 Vi: 0-0 Tstrap: 0-0
Best Rating: 98   3/03   Wwck   2m110y   good   Ch

Winning pointer; likes to force the pace; held a winning lead when crashing out two out in a modest handicap chase at Uttoxeter in June 2002; badly hampered when close third at Leicester in February 2003; won two mile handicap at Warwick in fast time on good ground in March; likely to prove best at distances up to two and a half miles.

Cassia Heights
112(88h)   (79h)114

8-y-o b g Montelimar (USA)-Cloncoose (IRE) (Remainder Man)
S A Brookshaw B Ridge & D Hewitt

Placings:000/0200P/0542U4P311331-22422426304 (4619)
2002/03: 24²GS, 22²G, 24⁴G, 24²S, 27²G, 24⁴S, 24²G, 24⁶G, 24³GF, 21⁰G, 24⁴GF,

	Starts	1st	2nd	3rd	Win & Pl
Chases	11	0	5	1	17409
Career Total	32	3	7	4	36931
111	3/02	Hayd	3m	D(0-125)HCh	GD	£7085
91	1/02	Donc	3m	D(0-115)HCh	SFT	£4290
92	1/02	Ludl	3m	E(0-105)HCh	GD	£3581
				Total win prize-money		£14957

Going: Sf: 0-2 GS: 0-1 Gd: 0-6 GF: - Fm: 0-2
Distance: 2m/2m3: 0-0 2m4-2m7: 0-2 3m+: 0-9
Track: LH: 0-7 RH: 0-4 Tight: 0-5 Gall: 0-1
Aids: Bl: 0-0 Vi: 0-0 Tstrap: 0-11
Best Rating: 114   2/03   Ludl   3m   good   Ch

Fair handicap chaser; consistent form in 2002/3; acts on good and soft ground; stays three miles plus; seems suited by a flat track; regularly tongue tied.

Castanet
93   82

4-y-o b f Pennekamp (USA)-Addaya (IRE) (Persian Bold)
A E Price (W J Haggas 4/12) Mrs Carol Davis

Placings:246   (4605)
2002/03: 17²S, 16⁴GF, 17⁶G,

	Starts	1st	2nd	3rd	Win & Pl
Hurdles	3	0	1	0	1706
Career Total	3	0	1	0	1706

Going: Sf: 0-1 GS: 0-0 Gd: 0-1 GF: - Fm: 0-1
Distance: 2m/2m3: 0-3 2m4-2m7: 0-0 3m+: 0-0
Track: LH: 0-3 RH: 0-0 Tight: 0-0 Gall: 0-1
Aids: Bl: 0-0 Vi: 0-0 Tstrap: 0-0
Best Rating: 82   3/03   Hayd   2m   gd-fm   Hdl

Plating-class maiden on the Flat; respectable effort on hurdles debut, but too keen on fast ground next time.

Castle Clear (IRE)
110(100c)   (73c)82

10-y-o b g Castle Keep-Rose Of Allendale (Green Shoon)
Mrs S C Bradburne R Hilley

Placings:1/0320/F523/UU12P343U014/U560/0663313313-32000F020   (3154)
2002/03: 20³GF, 20²GS, 22⁰GF, 22⁰G, 22⁰S, 20ᶠS, 20⁰GS, 20²S, 20⁰G,

	Starts	1st	2nd	3rd	Win & Pl
Hurdles	7	0	1	1	1480
Chases	2	0	1	0	2085
Career Total	44	5	5	10	26263
89	4/02	Kels	2m6f110yD(0-120)HHdl	G-F	£3465
89	12/01	Ayr	2m4f	F(0-105)HHdl	SFT	£3052
92	1/00	Sthl	2m4f110yE(0-115)HCh	G-S	£3313
97	6/99	Perth	2m	E Ch	SFT	£3452
112	3/97	Ayr	2m	H NHF	SFT	£1035
				Total win prize-money		£14319

Going: Sf: 0-3 GS: 0-2 Gd: 0-2 GF: - Fm: 0-2
Distance: 2m/2m3: 0-0 2m4-2m7: 0-9 3m+: 0-0
Track: LH: 0-6 RH: 0-3 Tight: 0-4 Gall: 0-1
Aids: Bl: 0-0 Vi: 0-0 Tstrap: 0-0
Best Rating: 112   3/97   Ayr   2m   soft   NHF

Plating-class hurdler; winning chaser, he has looked happier back over hurdles of late. Stays two miles-six, acts on any ground.

Castle Folly (IRE)
97   91+

11-y-o b g Carlingford Castle-Air Plane (Arratos (FR))
J White Nick Quesnel

Placings:P/0P4-F3211   (1411)
2002/03: 21ᶠHY, 21³G, 26²GF, 21¹G, 22¹G,

	Starts	1st	2nd	3rd	Win & Pl
Chases	5	2	1	1	8789
Career Total	9	2	1	1	9008
91	10/02	Font	2m6f	F(0-95)HCh	GD	£3745
88	9/02	Sthl	2m5f110yE Ch	GD	£3506
				Total win prize-money		£7252

Going: Sf: 0-1 GS: 0-0 Gd: 2-3 GF: - Fm: 0-1
Distance: 2m/2m3: 0-0 2m4-2m7: 2-4 3m+: 0-1
Track: LH: 1-4 RH: 0-0 Tight: 1-3 Gall: 0-0
Aids: Bl: 2-4 Vi: 0-0 Tstrap: 0-0
Best Rating: 91   10/02   Font   2m6f   good   Ch

Multiple winning pointer who likes to force the pace and stays three and a quarter miles. Off the mark under rules in weak contest at Southwell and followed up at Fontwell in October.

Castle Friend
95   78+

8-y-o b g Durgam (USA)-Furry Friend (USA) (Bold Bidder)
F S Storey F S Storey

Placings:240/04-P554   (0876)
2002/03: 16ᴾG, 16⁵GF, 17⁵GF, 17⁴G,

	Starts	1st	2nd	3rd	Win & Pl
Hurdles	4	0	0	0	748
Career Total	9	0	1	0	748

Going: Sf: 0-0 GS: 0-0 Gd: 0-2 GF: - Fm: 0-2
Distance: 2m/2m3: 0-4 2m4-2m7: 0-0 3m+: 0-0
Track: LH: 0-4 RH: 0-0 Tight: 0-2 Gall: 0-0
Aids: Bl: 0-0 Vi: 0-0 Tstrap: 0-0
Best Rating: 90   9/98   Sedg   2m1f   gd-fm   Hdl

Castle Owen (IRE)

100(88h)   (81h)**105**

11-y-o b g Castle Keep-Lady Owenette (IRE) (Salluceva)
Mrs A C Hamilton Mr & Mrs Gavin Hamilton

Placings:*11343/5111402/F135/020U4*   (1388)
2002/03: 16⁶G, 16²GS, 16⁹G, 16⁰GF, 16⁴GF,

	Starts	1st	2nd	3rd	Win & Pl
Hurdles	2	0	0	0	0
Chases	3	0	1	0	1656
Career Total	**21**	**6**	**2**	**3**	**21485**
111 11/99 Hrfd	3m1f110yD Ch		GD		£3525
126 1/99 Hntg	2m5f110yD(0-120)HHdl		SFT		£3247
126 12/98 Hntg	2m5f110yF(0-100)HHdl		SFT		£2472
115 12/98 Ludl	2m5f110yE(0-105)HHdl		G-S		£2444
128 11/97 Winc	2m	H NHF		GD	£1201
114 5/97 Hrfd	2m1f	H NHF		GD	£1030
		Total win prize-money £13920			

Going:	Sf: 0-0 GS: 0-1 Gd: 0-2 GF: - Fm: 0-2
Distance:	2m/2m3: 0-0 2m4-2m7: 0-0 3m+: 0-0
Track:	LH: 0-3 RH: 0-2 Tight: 0-1 Gall: 0-0
Aids:	Bl: 0-0 Vi: 0-0 Tstrap: 0-0
Best Rating:	128 4/99 Chel 3m good Hdl

Modest chaser/hurdler; has run in points; best at around two miles; handles good ground or softer.

Castle Prince (IRE)

102   **114**

9-y-o b g Homo Sapien-Lisaleen Lady (Miners Lamp)
R J Hodges Miss R Dobson

Placings:*66000/2432F2/33144515-23455U34002*   (4719)
2002/03: 16²F, 16³GF, 17⁴G, 16⁵GS, 20⁵GS, 16⁰GS, 21³GS, 17⁴G, 16⁰S, 16⁰G, 16²F,

	Starts	1st	2nd	3rd	Win & Pl
Chases	11	0	2	2	15507
Career Total	**30**	**2**	**5**	**5**	**30598**
115 4/02 Winc	2m	D(0-115)HCh	GD	£4368
102 1/02 Folk	2m	E(0-105)HCh	SFT	£3367
		Total win prize-money £7735			

Going:	Sf: 0-1 GS: 0-4 Gd: 0-3 GF: - Fm: 0-3
Distance:	2m/2m3: 0-9 2m4-2m7: 0-2 3m+: 0-0
Track:	LH: 0-3 RH: 0-8 Tight: 0-0 Gall: 0-3
Aids:	Bl: 0-0 Vi: 0-0 Tstrap: 0-0
Best Rating:	140 4/02 Sand 2m good Ch

Fair handicap chaser; usually out of his depth in small-field conditions events; suited by two to two and a half miles; acts on any ground.

Castle Richard (IRE)

103   **112**

6-y-o gr g Sexton Blake-Miss McCormick (IRE) (Roselier (FR))
G M Moore Mrs Mary And Miss Susan Hatfield

Placings:*6512P*   (3989)
2002/03: 17⁶G, 20⁵S, 21¹S, 20²HY, 24⁵S,

	Starts	1st	2nd	3rd	Win & Pl
NH Flat	1	0	0	0	
Hurdles	4	1	1	0	4508
Career Total	**5**	**1**	**1**	**0**	**4508**
112 12/02 Sedg	2m5f110yE Hdl		SFT		£3388
		Total win prize-money £3388			

Going:	Sf: 1-4 GS: 0-0 Gd: 0-1 GF: - Fm: 0-0
Distance:	2m/2m3: 0-1 2m4-2m7: 1-3 3m+: 0-1
Track:	LH: 1-4 RH: 0-1 Tight: 1-2 Gall: 0-1

Aids: Bl: 0-0 Vi: 0-0 Tstrap: 0-0
Best Rating: 112 2/03 Ayr 2m4f heavy Hdl

Fair novice hurdler, stays two miles five, acts on a soft surface.

Castle River (USA)

67   **51**

4-y-o b g Irish River (FR)-Castellina (USA) (Danzig Connection (USA))
B G Powell (B W Hills 24/10) Mrs Rachel A Powell

Placings:*0*   (2568)
2002/03: 16⁰G,

	Starts	1st	2nd	3rd	Win & Pl
Hurdles	1	0	0	0	
Career Total	**1**	**0**	**0**	**0**	

Going:	Sf: 0-0 GS: 0-0 Gd: 0-1 GF: - Fm: 0-0
Distance:	2m/2m3: 0-0 2m4-2m7: 0-0 3m+: 0-0
Track:	LH: 0-1 RH: 0-0 Tight: 0-0 Gall: 0-1
Aids:	Bl: 0-0 Vi: 0-0 Tstrap: 0-0
Best Rating:	49 12/02 Newb 2m110y good Hdl

Castlebridge

91   **54**

6-y-o b g Batshoof-Super Sisters (AUS) (Call Report (USA))
K R Burke (M D I Usher 24/10) P Sweeting

Placings:*3/0-0300*   (3825)
2002/03: 16⁰G, 20³HY, 21⁰HY, 16⁰GS,

	Starts	1st	2nd	3rd	Win & Pl
Hurdles	4	0	0	1	330
Career Total	**6**	**0**	**0**	**2**	**650**

Going:	Sf: 0-2 GS: 0-1 Gd: 0-1 GF: - Fm: 0-0
Distance:	2m/2m3: 0-2 2m4-2m7: 0-2 3m+: 0-0
Track:	LH: 0-4 RH: 0-1 Tight: 0-1 Gall: 0-2
Aids:	Bl: 0-0 Vi: 0-3 Tstrap: 0-0
Best Rating:	68 8/00 Bang 2m1f good Hdl

Bad selling hurdler.

Castleford (IRE)

96f   **101f**

5-y-o b g Be My Native (USA)-Commanche Bay (IRE) (Commanche Run)
P J Hobbs Mrs D Whateley, Mrs L Field & D Green

Placings:*05*   (4275)
2002/03: 16⁰G, 16⁵G,

	Starts	1st	2nd	3rd	Win & Pl
NH Flat	2	0	0	0	0
Career Total	**2**	**0**	**0**	**0**	**0**

Going:	Sf: 0-0 GS: 0-0 Gd: 0-2 GF: - Fm: 0-0
Distance:	2m/2m3: 0-2 2m4-2m7: 0-0 3m+: 0-0
Track:	LH: 0-1 RH: 0-1 Tight: 0-0 Gall: 0-0
Aids:	Bl: 0-0 Vi: 0-0 Tstrap: 0-0
Best Rating:	101 3/03 Chep 2m110y good NHF

Out of an unraced half-sister to Topsham Bay, showed ability on his bumper debut.

Castlehale (IRE)

10-y-o ch g Over The River (FR)-Ann s Fancy (River Knight (FR))

A W Congdon D T Hooper

Placings:060/50F/P/2P   (0395)
2002/03: 19²G, 28⁰PG,

	Starts	1st	2nd	3rd	Win & Pl
Chases	2	0	1	0	488
Career Total	**9**	**0**	**1**	**0**	**488**

Going:	Sf: 0-0 GS: 0-0 Gd: 0-2 GF: - Fm: 0-0
Distance:	2m/2m3: 0-0 2m4-2m7: 0-1 3m+: 0-1
Track:	LH: 0-1 RH: 0-1 Tight: 0-1 Gall: 0-1
Aids:	Bl: 0-2 Vi: 0-0 Tstrap: 0-0
Best Rating:	74 5/02 Extr 2m3f110y good Ch

Modest pointer/hunter chaser, suited by a sound surface. Usually wears blinkers.

Castlemore (IRE)

100f   **102f**

5-y-o b g Be My Native (USA)-Parsonetta (The Parson)
P J Hobbs Castlemore Securities Limited

Placings:*44*   (4005)
2002/03: 16⁴G, 16⁴S,

	Starts	1st	2nd	3rd	Win & Pl
NH Flat	2	0	0	0	0
Career Total	**2**	**0**	**0**	**0**	**0**

Going:	Sf: 0-1 GS: 0-0 Gd: 0-1 GF: - Fm: 0-0
Distance:	2m/2m3: 0-2 2m4-2m7: 0-0 3m+: 0-0
Track:	LH: 0-0 RH: 0-2 Tight: 0-0 Gall: 0-0
Aids:	Bl: 0-0 Vi: 0-0 Tstrap: 0-0
Best Rating:	102 3/03 Winc 2m soft NHF

Ability in bumpers.

Castleshane (IRE)

113   **134**

6-y-o b g Kris-Ahbab (IRE) (Ajdal (USA))
S Gollings W Hobson,J King,G King,P Winfrow

Placings:2340P/F51242053-2501   (4734)
2002/03: 16²G, 16⁵GS, 17⁰G, 16¹GF,

	Starts	1st	2nd	3rd	Win & Pl
Hurdles	4	1	1	0	16181
Career Total	**18**	**2**	**4**	**4**	**35443**
134 4/03 Chep	2m110y C(0-135)HHdl	G-F	£7231
106 10/01 Chel	2m110y D Hdl	GD	£7345
	Total win prize-money £14576		

Going:	Sf: 0-0 GS: 0-1 Gd: 0-2 GF: - Fm: 1-1
Distance:	2m/2m3: 1-4 2m4-2m7: 0-0 3m+: 0-0
Track:	LH: 1-3 RH: 0-1 Tight: 0-0 Gall: 0-2
Aids:	Bl: 0-0 Vi: 0-0 Tstrap: 0-0
Best Rating:	134 4/03 Chep 2m110y gd-fm Hdl

Useful hurdler; not too bad on the Flat either; likes his own way out in front, otherwise he can tend to sulk; suited by two miles and a sound surface.

Catch Ball

99   **136**

7-y-o ch m Prince Sabo-Canoodle (Warpath)
W P Mullins Mrs P M Byrne

Placings:4326/433111145F2/P0240-60555   (3257a)
2002/03: 20⁶YS, 24⁰S, 24⁵YS, 24⁵HY, 24⁵SH,

	Starts	1st	2nd	3rd	Win & Pl
Hurdles	5	0	0	0	
Career Total	**25**	**4**	**3**	**3**	**34158**
124 12/00 Navn	3m	HHdl	HVY	£7176

126	11/00	Clon	2m4f	(0-109)HHdl	HVY	£3312
106	10/00	Fair	2m4f	(0-116)HHdl	Y-S	£3312
100	10/00	Fair	2m4f	(0-95)HHdl	G-Y	£3588
				Total win prize-money £17388		

Going:	Sf: 0-2 GS: 0-0 Gd: 0-0 GF: - Fm: 0-0
Distance:	2m/2m3: 0-0 2m4-2m7: 0-1 3m+: 0-4
Track:	LH: 0-4 RH: 0-0 Tight: 0-0 Gall: 0-1
Aids:	Bl: 0-0 Vi: 0-0 Tstrap: 0-0
Best Rating:	136 12/02 Navn 3m yld-sft Hdl

Once very useful hurdler; progressed through 2000/01 season culminating in 3 1/2l defeat by Limestone Lad (giving 20lb) at Navan; haslost her way since; stays 3m and is effective with cut in the ground.

Catch The Perk (IRE)

90   **74**

6-y-o b g Executive Perk-Kilbally Quilty (IRE) (Montelimar (USA))
Miss Lucinda V Russell A A Bissett

Placings:6425046   (4661)
2002/03: 16⁶G, 16⁴GF, 16²GF, 16⁵G, 16⁰G, 20⁴G, 17⁶GF,

	Starts	1st	2nd	3rd	Win & Pl
NH Flat	4	0	1	0	848
Hurdles	3	0	0	0	589
Career Total	7	0	1	0	1437

Going:	Sf: 0-0 GS: 0-0 Gd: 0-4 GF: - Fm: 0-3
Distance:	2m/2m3: 0-6 2m4-2m7: 0-1 3m+: 0-0
Track:	LH: 0-4 RH: 0-3 Tight: 0-2 Gall: 0-0
Aids:	Bl: 0-0 Vi: 0-0 Tstrap: 0-0
Best Rating:	98 12/02 Muss 2m gd-fm NHF

Exposed in bumpers.

Catch Them All (IRE)

54   **65**

6-y-o br g Mandalus-Only Flower (Warpath)
J Howard Johnson (C F Swan 5/8) P Reilly

Placings:0-00005PP   (3811)
2002/03: 16⁰YS, 19⁰YS, 16⁰S, 24⁰G, 17⁵S, 20⁵S, 25⁵G,

	Starts	1st	2nd	3rd	Win & Pl
NH Flat	2	0	0	0	0
Hurdles	5	0	0	0	0
Career Total	8	0	0	0	0

Going:	Sf: 0-3 GS: 0-0 Gd: 0-2 GF: - Fm: 0-0
Distance:	2m/2m3: 0-4 2m4-2m7: 0-1 3m+: 0-2
Track:	LH: 0-3 RH: 0-1 Tight: 0-2 Gall: 0-1
Aids:	Bl: 0-2 Vi: 0-0 Tstrap: 0-0
Best Rating:	84 7/02 Kbgn 2m3f yld-sft NHF

Catchatan (IRE)

112   **98**

8-y-o b g Cataldi-Snowtan (IRE) (Tanfirion)
P R Webber Dennis Yardy

Placings:P4/P21045   (4121)
2002/03: 20⁴GS, 23²G, 16¹GS, 20⁵GS, 16⁴GS, 20⁵G,

	Starts	1st	2nd	3rd	Win & Pl
Chases	6	1	1	0	6438
Career Total	8	1	1	0	6438
98	12/02	Leic	2m	D(0-110)HCh	G-S	£4849
				Total win prize-money £4849		

Going:	Sf: 0-0 GS: 1-4 Gd: 0-2 GF: - Fm: 0-0
Distance:	2m/2m3: 1-2 2m4-2m7: 0-3 3m+: 0-1
Track:	LH: 0-0 RH: 1-6 Tight: 0-0 Gall: 0-2
Aids:	Bl: 0-0 Vi: 0-0 Tstrap: 1-5
Best Rating:	99 12/02 Leic 2m7f110y good Ch

Ran well at a big price when runner-up in a novice chase at Leicester and got his head in front when dropped back to two miles in December; disappointing since.

Cateel Bay

91   **61**

5-y-o ch m Most Welcome-Calachuchi (Martinmas)
H Alexander Mrs C D Bruce

Placings:06U06P00   (4143)
2002/03: 17⁰GS, 16⁶G, 16⁰GF, 17⁰GS, 16⁶G, 16⁶G, 16⁰S, 16⁰G,

	Starts	1st	2nd	3rd	Win & Pl
Hurdles	8	0	0	0	0
Career Total	8	0	0	0	0

Going:	Sf: 0-1 GS: 0-2 Gd: 0-4 GF: - Fm: 0-1
Distance:	2m/2m3: 0-8 2m4-2m7: 0-0 3m+: 0-0
Track:	LH: 0-7 RH: 0-1 Tight: 0-7 Gall: 0-0
Aids:	Bl: 0-0 Vi: 0-0 Tstrap: 0-0
Best Rating:	62 1/03 Catt 2m good Hdl

Catherine's Way (IRE)

11-y-o b g Mandalus-Sharp Approach (Crash Course)
Neil King Mrs P K J Brightwell

Placings:0/405F/42141/1P/U4/2P5-PP   (0368)
2002/03: 16⁶G, 21⁸S,

	Starts	1st	2nd	3rd	Win & Pl
Chases	2	0	0	0	
Career Total	19	3	2	0	12875
120	2/00	MRas	2m6f110yD(0-125)HCh	G-S	£4536
115	3/99	Leic	2m4f110yE(0-105)HCh	SFT	£3496
111	12/98	Hntg	2m110y E(0-105)HCh	SFT	£2901
				Total win prize-money £10934		

Going:	Sf: 0-1 GS: 0-0 Gd: 0-1 GF: - Fm: 0-0
Distance:	2m/2m3: 0-1 2m4-2m7: 0-1 3m+: 0-0
Track:	LH: 0-1 RH: 0-1 Tight: 0-1 Gall: 0-0
Aids:	Bl: 0-0 Vi: 0-0 Tstrap: 0-0
Best Rating:	120 2/00 MRas 2m6f110y gd-sft Ch

Front-running hunter chaser, suited by cut and goes well fresh.

Caucasian (IRE)

90f   **72f**

5-y-o gr g Leading Counsel (USA)-Kemal s Princess (Kemal (FR))
Ian Williams Ian Williams

Placings:0   (3930)
2002/03: 16⁰G,

	Starts	1st	2nd	3rd	Win & Pl
NH Flat	1	0	0	0	
Career Total	1	0	0	0	

Going:	Sf: 0-0 GS: 0-0 Gd: 0-1 GF: - Fm: 0-0
Distance:	2m/2m3: 0-1 2m4-2m7: 0-0 3m+: 0-0
Track:	LH: 0-0 RH: 0-1 Tight: 0-1 Gall: 0-1
Aids:	Bl: 0-0 Vi: 0-0 Tstrap: 0-0

Best Rating:	72 3/03 Hntg 2m110y good NHF

Caught'n The Slips (IRE)

69f

7-y-o br m Roselier (FR)-Bold Glen (Bold Owl)
D J Caro The Yes - No - Wait Sorries

Placings:0   (0686)
2002/03: 16⁰GF,

	Starts	1st	2nd	3rd	Win & Pl
NH Flat	1	0	0	0	
Career Total	1	0	0	0	

Going:	Sf: 0-0 GS: 0-0 Gd: 0-0 GF: - Fm: 0-1
Distance:	2m/2m3: 0-1 2m4-2m7: 0-0 3m+: 0-0
Track:	LH: 0-0 RH: 0-1 Tight: 0-0 Gall: 0-0
Aids:	Bl: 0-0 Vi: 0-0 Tstrap: 0-0
Best Rating:	69 7/02 Strf 2m110y gd-fm NHF

Caversfield

52

8-y-o ch g Tina s Pet-Canoodle (Warpath)
J M Bradley S E Hall

Placings:00004/0   (3825)
2002/03: 16⁰GS,

	Starts	1st	2nd	3rd	Win & Pl
Hurdles	1	0	0	0	
Career Total	6	0	0	0	0

Going:	Sf: 0-0 GS: 0-1 Gd: 0-0 GF: - Fm: 0-0
Distance:	2m/2m3: 0-1 2m4-2m7: 0-0 3m+: 0-0
Track:	LH: 0-1 RH: 0-0 Tight: 0-0 Gall: 0-0
Aids:	Bl: 0-0 Vi: 0-0 Tstrap: 0-0
Best Rating:	70 11/99 Wwck 2m good Hdl

Cavvies Niece

5-y-o b m Ballet Royal (USA)-Cavisoir (Afzal)
H J Manners H J Manners

Placings:0P   (1036)
2002/03: 16⁰G, 18⁸PGF,

	Starts	1st	2nd	3rd	Win & Pl
NH Flat	1	0	0	0	0
Hurdles	1	0	0	0	0
Career Total	2	0	0	0	

Going:	Sf: 0-0 GS: 0-0 Gd: 0-1 GF: - Fm: 0-1
Distance:	2m/2m3: 0-2 2m4-2m7: 0-0 3m+: 0-0
Track:	LH: 0-2 RH: 0-0 Tight: 0-1 Gall: 0-0
Aids:	Bl: 0-0 Vi: 0-0 Tstrap: 0-1
Best Rating:	0 8/02 Font 2m2f110y gd-fm Hdl

Cayman Went

87f   **95f**

4-y-o b g Bering-Bonne Ile (Ile De Bourbon (USA))
C C Bealby Irvin S Naylor

Placings:350   (4444)
2002/03: 12³G, 16⁵G, 16⁰G,

	Starts	1st	2nd	3rd	Win & Pl
NH Flat	3	0	0	1	401

| Career Total | 3 | 0 | 0 | 1 | 401 |

Going: Sf: 0-0 GS: 0-0 Gd: 0-3 GF: - Fm: 0-0
Distance: 2m/2m3: 0-2 2m4-2m7: 0-0 3m+: 0-0
Track: LH: 0-2 RH: 0-1 Tight: 0-1 Gall: 0-0
Aids: Bl: 0-2 Vi: 0-0 Tstrap: 0-0
Best Rating: 95 12/02 Newb 1m4f110y good NHF

Showed a fair level of ability when third on debut in bumper at Newbury in December but hung badly and most disappointing next time.

Cead Mile Failte
65   69
8-y-o ch g Most Welcome-Avionne (Derrylin)
B J Llewellyn B W Parren

Placings:P0400U0-0   (1441)
2002/03: 19⁰F,

	Starts	1st	2nd	3rd	Win & PI
Hurdles	1	0	0	0	
Career Total	8	0	0	0	

Going: Sf: 0-0 GS: 0-0 Gd: 0-0 GF: - Fm: 0-1
Distance: 2m/2m3: 0-2 2m4-2m7: 0-0 3m+: 0-0
Track: LH: 0-0 RH: 0-1 Tight: 0-1 Gall: 0-0
Aids: Bl: 0-0 Vi: 0-0 Tstrap: 0-0
Best Rating: 69 10/01 Strf 2m110y gd-sft Hdl

Ceanannas Mor (IRE)
108   113
9-y-o b g Strong Gale-Game Sunset (Menelek)
N J Henderson Major Christopher Hanbury

Placings:033/14FF/164032-54PP   (4472)
2002/03: 31⁵GS, 24⁴GS, 24⁵FG, 21⁵FG,

	Starts	1st	2nd	3rd	Win & PI
Chases	4	0	0	3	1669
Career Total	17	2	1	3	33604
132 10/01 Kemp 3m	B(0-145)HCh			G-S	£17400
120 11/00 Leic 2m7f110yE Ch				G-S	£3302
				Total win prize-money	£20702

Going: Sf: 0-0 GS: 0-2 Gd: 0-2 GF: - Fm: 0-0
Distance: 2m/2m3: 0-4 2m4-2m7: 0-1 3m+: 0-3
Track: LH: 0-2 RH: 0-2 Tight: 0-1 Gall: 0-0
Aids: Bl: 0-0 Vi: 0-0 Tstrap: 0-0
Best Rating: 132 3/02 Chel 3m110y gd-sft Ch

Modest handicap chaser; best at around three miles; acts on good/good to soft ground; not at his best in 2002/3.

Cearnach
87   55
5-y-o b g Night Shift (USA)-High Matinee (Shirley Heights)
J M Bradley Leeway Group Limited

Placings:PP55P000   (4220)
2002/03: 16⁶G, 16⁶G, 17⁵S, 21⁵HY, 16⁶HY, 17⁰S, 16⁰GS, 19⁰GF,

	Starts	1st	2nd	3rd	Win & PI
Hurdles	8	0	0	0	0
Career Total	8	0	0	0	0

Going: Sf: 0-4 GS: 0-1 Gd: 0-2 GF: - Fm: 0-1
Distance: 2m/2m3: 0-4 2m4-2m7: 0-2 3m+: 0-0
Track: LH: 0-3 RH: 0-5 Tight: 0-5 Gall: 0-0
Aids: Bl: 0-1 Vi: 0-0 Tstrap: 0-0

Cedar
81   80
6-y-o gr g Absalom-Setai s Palace (Royal Palace)
R Dickin D J Jackson

Placings:F4   (4574)
2002/03: 20⁶GF, 22⁴GF,

	Starts	1st	2nd	3rd	Win & PI
Hurdles	2	0	0	0	328
Career Total	2	0	0	0	328

Going: Sf: 0-0 GS: 0-0 Gd: 0-0 GF: - Fm: 0-2
Distance: 2m/2m3: 0-0 2m4-2m7: 0-2 3m+: 0-0
Track: LH: 0-2 RH: 0-0 Tight: 0-2 Gall: 0-0
Aids: Bl: 0-0 Vi: 0-0 Tstrap: 0-0
Best Rating: 80 4/03 Strf 2m6f110y gd-fm Hdl

Cedar Broom (IRE)
101   72
10-y-o b g Brush Aside (USA)-Flash N Run (Record Run)
E R Clough E R Clough

Placings:6/2234F30/20165/P6F4P3P   (1199)
2002/03: 20⁵PS, 16⁶GF, 21⁵GF, 20⁴G, 20⁵GS, 20³G, 19⁵GF,

	Starts	1st	2nd	3rd	Win & PI
Hurdles	1	0	0	0	0
Chases	6	0	0	1	790
Career Total	20	1	3	3	6107
87 6/00 Uttx 2m	E Hdl			G-F	£2621
				Total win prize-money	£2622

Going: Sf: 0-1 GS: 0-1 Gd: 0-2 GF: - Fm: 0-3
Distance: 2m/2m3: 0-2 2m4-2m7: 0-5 3m+: 0-0
Track: LH: 0-6 RH: 0-1 Tight: 0-1 Gall: 0-0
Aids: Bl: 0-0 Vi: 0-0 Tstrap: 0-0
Best Rating: 104 10/99 Tntn 2m1f gd-fm NHF

Cedar Chief
6-y-o b g Saddlers Hall (IRE)-Dame Ashfield (Grundy)
R J O Sullivan R O S Racing

Placings:243044/F45410PF026-6U0   (0665)
2002/03: 26⁶G, 23⁰G, 22⁰GF,

	Starts	1st	2nd	3rd	Win & PI
Hurdles	1	0	0	0	0
Chases	2	0	1	2	3099
Career Total	20	1	2	2	3099
85 10/01 Folk 2m6f110yG(0-95)HHdl				HVY	£1561
				Total win prize-money	£1561

Going: Sf: 0-0 GS: 0-0 Gd: 0-2 GF: - Fm: 0-1
Distance: 2m/2m3: 0-0 2m4-2m7: 0-1 3m+: 0-2
Track: LH: 0-2 RH: 0-1 Tight: 0-1 Gall: 0-0
Aids: Bl: 0-2 Vi: 0-0 Tstrap: 0-0
Best Rating: 85 10/01 Folk 2m6f110y heavy Hdl

Cedar Flag (IRE)
75   68
9-y-o br g Jareer (USA)-Sasha Lea (Cawston s Clown)
L A Dace Luke Dace

Placings:0/0/306-P0   (0429)
2002/03: 20⁰GF, 18⁰GF,

Hurdles	2	0	0	0	
Career Total	7	0	0	1	389

Going: Sf: 0-0 GS: 0-0 Gd: 0-0 GF: - Fm: 0-2
Distance: 2m/2m3: 0-1 2m4-2m7: 0-1 3m+: 0-0
Track: LH: 0-1 RH: 0-0 Tight: 0-2 Gall: 0-0
Aids: Bl: 0-0 Vi: 0-0 Tstrap: 0-0
Best Rating: 74 10/99 Hntg 2m110y gd-fm NHF

Cedar Green
108   125
9-y-o br g Bustino-Explosiva (USA) (Explodent (USA))
K C Bailey J Perriss

Placings:0/P41R23PP/F12126-3512   (3946)
2002/03: 25⁵HY, 29⁵GS, 26¹GS, 30²S,

	Starts	1st	2nd	3rd	Win & PI
Chases	4	1	1	1	10837
Career Total	19	4	4	2	31813
125 2/03 Font 3m2f110yD(0-125)HCh				G-S	£5668
119 1/02 Carl 3m4f	C(0-130)Ch			SFT	£7020
109 12/01 Wwck 3m2f	D(0-120)HCh			SFT	£3932
113 12/00 Towc 2m6f	D Ch			HVY	£4130
				Total win prize-money	£20751

Going: Sf: 0-2 GS: 1-2 Gd: 0-0 GF: - Fm: 0-0
Distance: 2m/2m3: 0-0 2m4-2m7: 0-0 3m+: 1-4
Track: LH: 0-2 RH: 0-0 Tight: 1-1 Gall: 0-0
Aids: Bl: 1-4 Vi: 0-0 Tstrap: 0-0
Best Rating: 125 3/03 Extr 3m6f110y soft Ch

Decent chaser; has scored several times in the mud, but does not always look the most reliable ride; stays extreme distances; scored at Fontwell in February 2003; good second off 7lb higher mark in Devon National at Exeter next time; wears blinkers.

Cedar Grove
88   70
6-y-o b g Shirley Heights-Trojan Desert (Troy)
John A Harris Paddy Barrett

Placings:00   (2728)
2002/03: 16⁰S, 16⁰HY,

	Starts	1st	2nd	3rd	Win & PI
Hurdles	2	0	0	0	
Career Total	2	0	0	0	

Going: Sf: 0-2 GS: 0-0 Gd: 0-0 GF: - Fm: 0-0
Distance: 2m/2m3: 0-2 2m4-2m7: 0-0 3m+: 0-0
Track: LH: 0-1 RH: 0-1 Tight: 0-0 Gall: 0-1
Aids: Bl: 0-0 Vi: 0-0 Tstrap: 0-1
Best Rating: 66 12/02 Donc 2m110y soft Hdl

Cedar Master (IRE)
101   96
6-y-o b g Soviet Lad (USA)-Samriah (IRE) (Wassl)
R J O Sullivan Robert Allen

Placings:03246   (0886)
2002/03: 17⁰G, 16³G, 20²GF, 16⁴GF, 19⁶S,

	Starts	1st	2nd	3rd	Win & PI
Hurdles	5	0	1	1	1498
Career Total	5	0	1	1	1498

Going: Sf: 0-1 GS: 0-0 Gd: 0-2 GF: - Fm: 0-2
Distance: 2m/2m3: 0-4 2m4-2m7: 0-0 3m+: 0-0

Track: LH: 0-4 RH: 0-1 Tight: 0-2 Gall: 0-0
Aids: Bl: 0-1 Vi: 0-0 Tstrap: 0-0
Best Rating: 102 5/02   Worc   2m   good   Hdl

Moderate novice hurdler; regularly placed, but yet to win; suited by a sound surface.

Cedar Square (IRE)
105   110

12-y-o b g Dancing Dissident (USA)-Friendly Ann (Artaius (USA))
V R A Dartnall Nick Viney

Placings:0/F/1/1U0P5112/32641/P/P2UP4-2233   (1039)
2002/03: 25²G, 21²GS, 24³S, 22³GF,

	Starts	1st	2nd	3rd	Win & Pl
Chases	4	0	2	2	4371
Career Total	26	5	5	3	33177
128 2/00	Kemp	3m	D(0-125)HCh	GD	£7150
124 4/99	Bang	3m110y	D(0-125)HCh	G-S	£7782
124 4/99	Hntg	3m	D(0-120)HCh	G-F	£4287
118 5/98	Aint	3m1f	H Ch	G-F	£1781
110 4/98	Chel	2m5f	H Ch	GD	£1961

Total win prize-money £22963

Going: Sf: 0-1 GS: 0-1 Gd: 0-1 GF: - Fm: 0-1
Distance: 2m/2m3: 0-0 2m4-2m7: 0-2 3m+: 0-2
Track: LH: 0-3 RH: 0-0 Tight: 0-4 Gall: 0-0
Aids: Bl: 0-2 Vi: 0-0 Tstrap: 0-0
Best Rating: 129 11/98   Newb   2m4f   soft   Ch

He is an effective handicap chaser at a modest level. Suited by trips just short of three miles but does stay that trip on an easy track. Acts on good/good to soft ground.

Celebration Town (IRE)
98   88+

6-y-o b/br g Case Law-Battle Queen (Kind Of Hush)
N G Richards (D Morris 9/8) Greystoke Stables Ltd

Placings:00   (4762)
2002/03: 16⁰GS, 16⁰G,

	Starts	1st	2nd	3rd	Win & Pl
Hurdles	2	0	0	0	
Career Total	2	0	0	0	

Going: Sf: 0-0 GS: 0-1 Gd: 0-1 GF: - Fm: 0-0
Distance: 2m/2m3: 0-2 2m4-2m7: 0-0 3m+: 0-0
Track: LH: 0-1 RH: 0-1 Tight: 0-0 Gall: 0-1
Aids: Bl: 0-0 Vi: 0-0 Tstrap: 0-0
Best Rating: 87 3/03   Newc   2m   gd-sft   Hdl

Moderate novice hurdler; formerly useful on the Flat; narrow winner of a slowly-run handicap at Hexham in June 2003; has limited stamina.

Celibate (IRE)
118   137

12-y-o ch g Shy Groom (USA)-Dance Alone (USA) (Monteverdi)
C J Mann Stamford Bridge Partnership

Placings:25213664/0521210446F0/2111123F2/1545124/02
31531/33433226B/03P1355265/10403236P-34   (2056)
2002/03: 21³G, 20⁴G,

	Starts	1st	2nd	3rd	Win & Pl
Chases	2	0	0	1	5256
Career Total	73	13	13	13	269696
143 10/01	Winc	2m5f	A HCh	GD	£21000
147 12/00	Asct	2m	B HCh	SFT	£9339

---

157 4/99	Punc	2m	Ch	YLD	£32098
157 2/99	Newb	2m1f	A Ch	G-S	£18503
160 12/97	Asct	2m	B HCh	G-S	£9403
153 10/97	Kemp	2m	B(0-150)HCh	GD	£4429
134 11/96	Chel	2m	A Ch	GD	£11780
120 10/96	Chel	2m	D Ch	FRM	£3701
134 10/96	Kemp	2m	D Ch	GD	£3436
110 9/96	Worc	2m	D Ch	G-F	£3562
122 12/95	Hayd	2m	C(0-135)HHdl	GD	£3728
117 11/95	Towc	2m	D(0-120)HHdl	G-F	£2756
108 11/94	Clon	2m	Hdl	SFT	£2120

Total win prize-money £125857

Going: Sf: 0-0 GS: 0-0 Gd: 0-2 GF: - Fm: 0-0
Distance: 2m/2m3: 0-0 2m4-2m7: 0-2 3m+: 0-0
Track: LH: 0-0 RH: 0-2 Tight: 0-0 Gall: 0-0
Aids: Bl: 0-0 Vi: 0-0 Tstrap: 0-0
Best Rating: 161 1/98   Asct   2m   soft   Ch

Useful chaser; admirably consistent, although not as good as he once was; has struggled against the very best two-milers in the last couple of seasons; stepped up to around two and a half miles for the first half of 2001 and made a winning reappearance over two miles five at Wincanton in October of that year, the furthest he has won over; has won on soft and good ground and likes to front-run.

Celioso (IRE)
85(103h)   (84 h)92+

6-y-o b g Celio Rufo-Bettons Rose (Roselier (FR))
Mrs S J Smith (A Crook 3/5) Leigh Musketeer Racing Club

Placings:00P-P4414   (4709)
2002/03: 21⁵GF, 17⁴S, 25⁴G, 24¹G, 24⁴G,

	Starts	1st	2nd	3rd	Win & Pl
Hurdles	5	1	0	0	3968
Career Total	8	1	0	0	3968
84 3/03	Carl	3m110y	E(0-105)HHdl	GD	£3668

Total win prize-money £3668

Going: Sf: 0-1 GS: 0-0 Gd: 1-3 GF: - Fm: 0-1
Distance: 2m/2m3: 0-1 2m4-2m7: 0-1 3m+: 1-3
Track: LH: 0-3 RH: 1-2 Tight: 0-3 Gall: 0-0
Aids: Bl: 0-0 Vi: 0-0 Tstrap: 0-0
Best Rating: 84 3/03   Carl   3m110y   good   Hdl

Modest novice hurdler; in better form of late and took a stayers handicap at Carlisle in March; suited by decent ground.

Celony
97   70

6-y-o b m Primitive Rising (USA)-Lapopie (Deep Run)
C P Morlock Dwight Makins

Placings:00P-4   (0143)
2002/03: 20⁴GF,

	Starts	1st	2nd	3rd	Win & Pl
Hurdles	1	0	0	0	282
Career Total	4	0	0	0	282

Going: Sf: 0-0 GS: 0-0 Gd: 0-0 GF: - Fm: 0-1
Distance: 2m/2m3: 0-0 2m4-2m7: 0-1 3m+: 0-0
Track: LH: 0-1 RH: 0-0 Tight: 0-0 Gall: 0-0
Aids: Bl: 0-0 Vi: 0-0 Tstrap: 0-0
Best Rating: 75 11/01   Wwck   2m   good   NHF

Celtic Blaze (IRE)
87   85

4-y-o b f Charente River (IRE)-Firdaunt (Tanfirion)
B S Rothwell (Seamus Fahey 7/10) Cleaning And Paper Disposables Ltd

---

Placings:22   (2768)
2002/03: 16²GS, 16²GS,

	Starts	1st	2nd	3rd	Win & Pl
Hurdles	2	0	2	0	2884
Career Total	2	0	2	0	2884

Going: Sf: 0-0 GS: 0-2 Gd: 0-0 GF: - Fm: 0-0
Distance: 2m/2m3: 0-2 2m4-2m7: 0-0 3m+: 0-0
Track: LH: 0-1 RH: 0-1 Tight: 0-1 Gall: 0-0
Aids: Bl: 0-0 Vi: 0-0 Tstrap: 0-0
Best Rating: 85 12/02   Muss   2m   gd-sft   Hdl

Plating-class hurdler; placed in juvenile hurdles in the autumn of 2002 on easy ground before returning to the Flat.

Celtic Bounty (IRE)
(64h)   (37h)

7-y-o b g Treasure Hunter-Welsh Glen (Furry Glen)
R J Hodges Roger Raison

Placings:0/00-PP   (3315)
2002/03: 16⁰S, 19⁰GS,

	Starts	1st	2nd	3rd	Win & Pl
Hurdles	1	0	0	0	0
Chases	1	0	0	0	0
Career Total	5	0	0	0	

Going: Sf: 0-1 GS: 0-0 Gd: 0-0 GF: - Fm: 0-0
Distance: 2m/2m3: 0-0 2m4-2m7: 0-1 3m+: 0-0
Track: LH: 0-1 RH: 0-1 Tight: 0-0 Gall: 0-0
Aids: Bl: 0-0 Vi: 0-0 Tstrap: 0-0
Best Rating: 75 12/00   Hntg   2m110y   heavy   NHF

Celtic Dancer (IRE)
94   79

4-y-o b g Sadler s Wells (USA)-Noora Abu (Ahonoora)
Jonjo O Neill (J S Bolger 25/5) Rojari Syndicate

Placings:5000P   (3875)
2002/03: 16⁵S, 16⁰G, 16⁰GS, 17⁰G, 21⁰S,

	Starts	1st	2nd	3rd	Win & Pl
Hurdles	5	0	0	0	0
Career Total	5	0	0	0	0

Going: Sf: 0-2 GS: 0-1 Gd: 0-2 GF: - Fm: 0-0
Distance: 2m/2m3: 0-4 2m4-2m7: 0-1 3m+: 0-0
Track: LH: 0-3 RH: 0-2 Tight: 0-0 Gall: 0-2
Aids: Bl: 0-1 Vi: 0-0 Tstrap: 0-1
Best Rating: 77 12/02   Newb   2m110y   good   Hdl

Celtic Duke

11-y-o b g Strong Gale-Celtic Cygnet (Celtic Cone)
J M Turner J M Turner

Placings:030/2363/13521/212/2PP/2   (4671)
2002/03: 24²G,

	Starts	1st	2nd	3rd	Win & Pl
Chases	1	0	1	0	
Career Total	19	3	6	4	22835
114 11/99	Kels	3m4f	D(0-120)HCh	GD	£3779
105 4/99	Kels	3m1f	D(0-120)HCh	G-F	£4071
90 6/98	Prth	3m	D Ch	G-F	£3501

Total win prize-money £11352

Going: Sf: 0-0 GS: 0-0 Gd: 0-1 GF: - Fm: 0-0
Distance: 2m/2m3: 0-0 2m4-2m7: 0-0 3m+: 0-1

Track: LH: 0-1 RH: 0-0 Tight: 0-1 Gall: 0-0
Aids: Bl: 0-0 Vi: 0-0 Tstrap: 0-0
Best Rating: 114 5/00 Sedg 3m4f   gd-fm Ch

Moderate hunter chaser/point-to-pointer; former staying handicapper; stays three miles; goes well on top of the ground.

Celtic Flow

81   58

5-y-o b m Primitive Rising (USA)-Celtic Lane (Welsh Captain)
C R Wilson W R Wilson

Placings:5006   (4103)
2002/03: 17⁵HY, 16⁸G, 24⁰S, 21⁶S,

	Starts	1st	2nd	3rd	Win & Pl
NH Flat	1	0	0	0	0
Hurdles	3	0	0	0	0
Career Total	4	0	0	0	0

Going: Sf: 0-3 GS: 0-0 Gd: 0-1 GF: - Fm: 0-0
Distance: 2m/2m3: 0-2 2m4-2m7: 0-1 3m+: 0-1
Track: LH: 0-4 RH: 0-0 Tight: 0-3 Gall: 0-1
Aids: Bl: 0-0 Vi: 0-0 Tstrap: 0-0
Best Rating: 75 1/03 Sedg 2m1f   heavy NHF

Celtic Justice (IRE)

99   113

8-y-o br g Mister Lord (USA)-Just Ginger (The Parson)
R J Hodges Fieldspring Racing

Placings:5/04016055-510   (0439)
2002/03: 19⁶G, 17¹S, 20⁴G,

	Starts	1st	2nd	3rd	Win & Pl
Hurdles	3	1	0	0	2296
Career Total	12	2	0	0	5698
112 5/02 NAbb	2m1f		G Hdl		SFT £2296
113 12/01 Chep	2m110y		B Hdl		SFT £3402
				Total win prize-money £5698

Going: Sf: 1-1 GS: 0-0 Gd: 0-2 GF: - Fm: 0-0
Distance: 2m/2m3: 1-1 2m4-2m7: 0-2 3m+: 0-0
Track: LH: 1-2 RH: 0-1 Tight: 1-1 Gall: 0-0
Aids: Bl: 0-0 Vi: 0-0 Tstrap: 0-0
Best Rating: 113 12/01 Chep 2m110y   soft Hdl

Modest hurdler; winning Irish pointer; winner of a small race at Chepstow and a seller at Newton Abbot on soft ground.

Celtic Legend (FR)

90   82

4-y-o br g Celtic Swing-Another Legend (USA) (Lyphard s Wish (FR))
Mrs M Reveley (Mme C Head-Maarek 6/5) P D Savill

Placings:064   (4306)
2002/03: 16⁰GS, 17⁶GS, 18⁴G,

	Starts	1st	2nd	3rd	Win & Pl
Hurdles	3	0	0	0	322
Career Total	3	0	0	0	322

Going: Sf: 0-0 GS: 0-2 Gd: 0-1 GF: - Fm: 0-0
Distance: 2m/2m3: 0-3 2m4-2m7: 0-0 3m+: 0-0
Track: LH: 0-2 RH: 0-1 Tight: 0-1 Gall: 0-1
Aids: Bl: 0-0 Vi: 0-0 Tstrap: 0-1
Best Rating: 82 3/03 Kels 2m2f   good Hdl

Plating-class juvenile hurdler; well beaten so far; might do better in handicap company in due course.

Celtic Pride (IRE)

102(99h)   (137h)117

8-y-o gr g Roselier (FR)-Grannie No (Brave Invader (USA))
Jonjo O Neill Walters Plant Hire Ltd

Placings:0110/P10-3   (1807)
2002/03: 24³G,

	Starts	1st	2nd	3rd	Win & Pl
Chases	1	0	0	1	780
Career Total	8	3	0	1	21248
137 2/02 Hayd	2m7f110yB HHdl			HVY £8782
125 1/01 Navn	2m6f		Hdl		SFT £6677
110 1/01 Fair	2m6f		Hdl		HVY £5008
				Total win prize-money £20468

Going: Sf: 0-0 GS: 0-0 Gd: 0-1 GF: - Fm: 0-0
Distance: 2m/2m3: 0-2 2m4-2m7: 0-0 3m+: 0-1
Track: LH: 0-1 RH: 0-0 Tight: 0-0 Gall: 0-0
Aids: Bl: 0-0 Vi: 0-0 Tstrap: 0-0
Best Rating: 137 2/02 Hayd 2m7f110y   heavy Hdl

Fair hurdler/chaser; decent Irish novice hurdler in 2000/2001; won 3m handicap hurdle at Haydock Febaruary 2002; lightly-raced since; modest form in 3m novice chases.

Celtic Rover

5-y-o b g Celtic Swing-Lady Sabo (Prince Sabo)
C R Dore (C A Dwyer 7/9) John Purcell

Placings:PP-P   (1890)
2002/03: 16⁶GS,

	Starts	1st	2nd	3rd	Win & Pl
Hurdles	1	0	0	0	
Career Total	3	0	0	0	

Going: Sf: 0-0 GS: 0-1 Gd: 0-0 GF: - Fm: 0-0
Distance: 2m/2m3: 0-1 2m4-2m7: 0-0 3m+: 0-0
Track: LH: 0-0 RH: 0-1 Tight: 0-0 Gall: 0-1
Aids: Bl: 0-0 Vi: 0-0 Tstrap: 0-0
Best Rating: 0 11/02 Hntg 2m110y   gd-sft Hdl

Celtic Season

11-y-o b g Vital Season-Welsh Flower (Welsh Saint)
C W Loggin Richard West

Placings:6/505/2F1P04/12U14P3/F3PF52P12/P042-5P0
                                                       (0416)
2002/03: 21⁵GF, 25⁵PS, 24⁹GF,

	Starts	1st	2nd	3rd	Win & Pl
Chases	3	0	0	0	0
Career Total	33	4	5	2	22764
116 3/01 Hntg	3m		F(0-110)HCh		SFT £2625
116 12/99 Ling	2m4f110yC(0-130)HCh			SFT £5766
116 9/99 Hntg	2m4f110yD(0-125)HCh			GF £4055
120 1/99 Leic	2m4f110yF(0-100)HCh			SFT £2427
				Total win prize-money £14873

Going: Sf: 0-1 GS: 0-0 Gd: 0-0 GF: - Fm: 0-2
Distance: 2m/2m3: 0-0 2m4-2m7: 0-1 3m+: 0-2
Track: LH: 0-2 RH: 0-1 Tight: 0-1 Gall: 0-1
Aids: Bl: 0-0 Vi: 0-0 Tstrap: 0-3
Best Rating: 120 1/99 Leic 2m4f110y   soft Ch

Celtic Song (IRE)

74   92

7-y-o b g Cataldi-Iron Mariner (IRE) (Mandalus)
P F Nicholls Formpave Ltd

Placings:306F/10   (4391)
2002/03: 22¹F, 17⁰F,

	Starts	1st	2nd	3rd	Win & Pl
Hurdles	2	1	0	0	2982
Career Total	6	1	0	1	3271
92 10/02 Winc	2m6f		E Hdl		FRM £2982
				Total win prize-money £2982

Going: Sf: 0-0 GS: 0-0 Gd: 0-0 GF: - Fm: 1-2
Distance: 2m/2m3: 0-1 2m4-2m7: 1-1 3m+: 0-0
Track: LH: 0-0 RH: 1-2 Tight: 0-0 Gall: 0-0
Aids: Bl: 0-0 Vi: 0-0 Tstrap: 0-0
Best Rating: 99 4/01 Winc 2m   soft Hdl

Lightly-raced novice hurdler. Stays two miles and six and acts on fast ground.

Celtic Star (IRE)

105   106

5-y-o b g Celtic Swing-Recherchee (Rainbow Quest (USA))
Nick Williams Mrs Jane Kelly

Placings:3243226-0313P66   (1931)
2002/03: 16⁰GS, 17³GF, 18¹GF, 18³G, 19⁰G, 16⁶G, 24⁶GS,

	Starts	1st	2nd	3rd	Win & Pl
Hurdles	7	1	0	2	5910
Career Total	14	1	3	4	10259
100 9/02 Font	2m2f110yE Hdl			G-F £3136
				Total win prize-money £3136

Going: Sf: 0-0 GS: 0-2 Gd: 0-3 GF: - Fm: 1-2
Distance: 2m/2m3: 1-6 2m4-2m7: 0-3 3m+: 0-1
Track: LH: 1-5 RH: 0-2 Tight: 1-5 Gall: 0-0
Aids: Bl: 0-0 Vi: 1-4 Tstrap: 0-0
Best Rating: 106 10/02 Font 2m2f110y   good Hdl

Moderate hurdler, got off the mark at Fontwell in September 2002 on fast ground over two miles two.

Celtic Tanner (IRE)

78f   74f

4-y-o b g Royal Abjar (USA)-Mills Pride (IRE) (Posen (USA))
D J Wintle D J Wintle

Placings:0   (3754)
2002/03: 16⁰G,

	Starts	1st	2nd	3rd	Win & Pl
NH Flat	1	0	0	0	
Career Total	1	0	0	0	

Going: Sf: 0-0 GS: 0-0 Gd: 0-1 GF: - Fm: 0-0
Distance: 2m/2m3: 0-1 2m4-2m7: 0-0 3m+: 0-0
Track: LH: 0-0 RH: 0-1 Tight: 0-0 Gall: 0-0
Aids: Bl: 0-0 Vi: 0-0 Tstrap: 0-0
Best Rating: 74 2/03 Kemp 2m   good NHF

Celtic Vision (IRE)

107   120+

7-y-o b g Be My Native (USA)-Dream Run (Deep Run)
Jonjo O Neill Mrs J Doyle & Mrs P Shanahan

Placings:3/1020-212P1   (4308)
2002/03: 17²GS, 20¹GS, 20²S, 20⁰HY, 18¹G,

	Starts	1st	2nd	3rd	Win & Pl
Hurdles	5	2	2	0	16541
Career Total	10	3	3	1	19612
120 3/03 Kels	2m2f		C(0-135)HHdl		GD £10257
117 11/02 Sthl	2m4f110yD Hdl			G-S £4212
112 12/01 NAbb	2m1f		H NHF		HVY £2317
				Total win prize-money £16786

Going: Sf: 0-2 GS: 1-2 Gd: 1-1 GF: - Fm: 0-0
Distance: 2m/2m3: 1-2 2m4-2m7: 1-3 3m+: 0-0
Track: LH: 2-4 RH: 0-1 Tight: 2-3 Gall: 0-0
Aids: Bl: 0-0 Vi: 0-0 Tstrap: 1-4
Best Rating: 120 3/03 Kels 2m2f good Hdl

Bumper winner; decent novice hurdler; stays two and a half miles and suited by cut in the ground; has worn a tongue tie.

Cenkos (FR)

117(99h)   (129h)168

9-y-o ch g Nikos-Vincenza (Grundy)
P F Nicholls Mrs J Stewart

Placings:111/4/PF1F121121/244423P/14444351-12342
       (4790)
2002/03: 16¹S, 17²G, 16³G, 20⁴G, 16²G,

	Starts	1st	2nd	3rd	Win & Pl
Chases	5	1	2	1	127500
Career Total	34	11	6	3	419389
168	12/02	Sand	2m	A Ch	SFT	£59500
166	4/02	Sand	2m	B Ch	GD	£44625
154	5/01	Wwck	2m110y	B Ch	G-F	£10952
155	4/00	Aint	2m	A Ch	GD	£36000
158	2/00	Wwck	2m	A Ch	SFT	£14410
152	1/00	Kemp	2m	D Ch	GF	£5908
140	12/99	Sthl	2m	B(0-140)HCh	SFT	£8651
123	12/99	Plum	2m1f	E Ch	GD	£2900
	4/98	Engh	2m1f	Hdl	HVY	£15152
	3/98	Engh	2m2f	Hdl	VS	£10101
	3/98	Engh	2m110y	Hdl	HLD	£10101

Total win prize-money £218302

Going: Sf: 1-1 GS: 0-0 Gd: 0-4 GF: - Fm: 0-0
Distance: 2m/2m3: 1-4 2m4-2m7: 0-1 3m+: 0-0
Track: LH: 0-3 RH: 1-2 Tight: 0-1 Gall: 0-2
Aids: Bl: 0-0 Vi: 0-0 Tstrap: 0-0
Best Rating: 168 4/03 Sand 2m good Ch

Top-class chaser; third in the last two runnings of the Queen Mother Champion Chase; best at two miles; acts on any ground; goes well at Sandown; needs the sun on his back.

Centaur Express

81(90h)   (89h)52

11-y-o b g Siberian Express (USA)-Gay Twenties (Lord Gayle (USA))
Mrs J Candlish (A Streeter 3/5) Centaur Racing Ltd

Placings:34321F112/11030/526012U3/514311/3U533/05-P5
       (2068)
2002/03: 20PG, 17SGS,

	Starts	1st	2nd	3rd	Win & Pl
Chases	2	0	0	0	0
Career Total	37	9	4	8	35068
122	3/99	Leic	2m1f	E(0-115)HCh	HVY	£3548
122	1/99	Leic	2m1f	E(0-115)HCh	SFT	£2768
110	11/98	MRas	2m1f110yD(0-120)HCh	HVY	£3675
126	3/98	Bang	2m1f110yD Ch	G-S	£3436
123	12/96	MRas	2m1f110yD(0-120)HHdl	GD	£2945
122	11/96	Bang	2m1f	D(0-110)HHdl	G-S	£3176
118	3/96	Newb	2m110y	C(0-135)HHdl	HVY	£3395
100	3/96	Catt	2m	E Hdl	GD	£2374
87	1/96	Catt	2m	G(0-90)HHdl	GD	£2392

Total win prize-money £27711

Going: Sf: 0-0 GS: 0-1 Gd: 0-1 GF: - Fm: 0-0
Distance: 2m/2m3: 0-1 2m4-2m7: 0-1 3m+: 0-0
Track: LH: 0-1 RH: 0-1 Tight: 0-2 Gall: 0-0
Aids: Bl: 0-0 Vi: 0-0 Tstrap: 0-0
Best Rating: 126 4/98 MRas 2m1f110y soft Ch

Centaur Spirit

83

6-y-o b g Distant Relative-Winnie Reckless (Local Suitor (USA))
A Streeter Centaur Racing Ltd

Placings:4/54-P   (1563)
2002/03: 17PG,

	Starts	1st	2nd	3rd	Win & Pl
Hurdles	1	0	0	0	
Career Total	4	0	0	0	220

Going: Sf: 0-0 GS: 0-0 Gd: 0-1 GF: - Fm: 0-0
Distance: 2m/2m3: 0-0 2m4-2m7: 0-0 3m+: 0-0
Track: LH: 0-0 RH: 0-1 Tight: 0-0 Gall: 0-0
Aids: Bl: 0-0 Vi: 0-0 Tstrap: 0-0
Best Rating: 90 11/00 Leic 2m heavy Hdl

Centax (CZE)

9-y-o ch g Lincoln (CZE)-Centaurea (CZE) (Chiavari)
Z Semenka Inpost Uherske Hradiste

Placings:06014/P/132-10240   (1940)
2002/03: 22¹G, 29⁴G, 25²S, 34⁴HY, 31⁰GS,

	Starts	1st	2nd	3rd	Win & Pl
Chases	5	1	1	0	6821
Career Total	14	3	2	1	9942
5/02	Pard	2m6f110y Ch	GD	£966
9/01	Pard	2m7f	Ch	GD	£722
9/99	Pard	2m1f110y Ch	GD	£350

Total win prize-money £2038

Going: Sf: 0-2 GS: 0-1 Gd: 1-2 GF: - Fm: 0-0
Distance: 2m/2m3: 0-0 2m4-2m7: 1-1 3m+: 0-4
Track: LH: 0-3 RH: 0-0 Tight: 0-0 Gall: 0-0
Aids: Bl: 0-0 Vi: 0-0 Tstrap: 0-0
Best Rating: 0 11/02 Chel 3m7f gd-sft Ch

Czech-trained gelding. He finished fourth in the cross-country Velka Pardubicka of 2002.

Central Committee (IRE)

105   111

8-y-o ch g Royal Academy (USA)-Idle Chat (USA) (Assert)
R T Phillips The Escape Committee

Placings:464B5P/21/56113314   (3943)
2002/03: 22⁵GF, 20⁶GF, 20¹G, 21¹G, 19³GS, 22¹GS, 24⁴GS,

	Starts	1st	2nd	3rd	Win & Pl
Hurdles	8	3	0	2	14473
Career Total	16	4	1	2	17577
111	2/03	Font	2m6f110yE(0-110)HHdl	G-S	£4173
98	10/02	Sedg	2m5f110yE(0-105)HHdl	GD	£3391
98	9/02	Bang	2m4f	E(0-110)HHdl	GD	£5187
103	6/00	Worc	2m4f	E Hdl	GF	£2506

Total win prize-money £15258

Going: Sf: 0-0 GS: 1-3 Gd: 2-3 GF: - Fm: 0-2
Distance: 2m/2m3: 0-0 2m4-2m7: 3-6 3m+: 0-2
Track: LH: 3-6 RH: 0-0 Tight: 3-5 Gall: 0-0
Aids: Bl: 0-0 Vi: 0-0 Tstrap: 0-0
Best Rating: 111 3/03 MRas 3m gd-sft Hdl

Modest hurdler; has had injury and wind problems; suited by two and a half miles and fast ground; game sort.

Ceresfield (NZ)

104(102h)   (99h)110

7-y-o br m Westminster (NZ)-Audrey Rose (NZ) (Blue Razor (USA))
R C Guest (N B Mason 4/12) Keith Middleton

Placings:63341-245052   (4711)
2002/03: 14²F, 13⁴HY, 20⁵F, 16⁰HY, 16⁵GS, 16²GF,

	Starts	1st	2nd	3rd	Win & Pl
Hurdles	5	0	2	0	1482
Chases	1	0	0	0	71
Career Total	11	1	2	2	3357
4/02	Araw	1m6f	Hdl	FRM	£1250

Total win prize-money £1250

Going: Sf: 0-2 GS: 0-1 Gd: 0-0 GF: - Fm: 0-3
Distance: 2m/2m3: 0-3 2m4-2m7: 0-1 3m+: 0-0
Track: LH: 0-3 RH: 0-0 Tight: 0-1 Gall: 0-0
Aids: Bl: 0-0 Vi: 0-0 Tstrap: 0-0
Best Rating: 99 4/03 Weth 2m gd-fm Hdl

Moderate hurdler; winner on the Flat and over fences in New Zeland; winner on an impressive chasing bow at Hexham in April, jumping well and winning easily; could not defy 12lb ride in the weights next time; simple task at Cartmel in July; best at around two miles.

Cereus (USA)

4-y-o ch g Gilded Time (USA)-Dayflower (USA) (Majestic Light (USA))
Miss J S Davis (Ian Williams 14/12) Miss J Davis

Placings:PP   (3870)
2002/03: 16PGS, 16PS,

	Starts	1st	2nd	3rd	Win & Pl
Hurdles	2	0	0	0	
Career Total	2	0	0	0	

Going: Sf: 0-1 GS: 0-1 Gd: 0-0 GF: - Fm: 0-0
Distance: 2m/2m3: 0-2 2m4-2m7: 0-0 3m+: 0-0
Track: LH: 0-1 RH: 0-1 Tight: 0-0 Gall: 0-2
Aids: Bl: 0-0 Vi: 0-0 Tstrap: 0-0
Best Rating: 0 2/03 Newb 2m110y soft Hdl

Cerulean

31f

5-y-o ch g Polar Falcon (USA)-Billie Blue (Ballad Rock)
Dr J D Scargill R A Dalton

Placings:0-   (0013)
2002/03: 18⁰G,

	Starts	1st	2nd	3rd	Win & Pl
NH Flat	1	0	0	0	
Career Total	1	0	0	0	

Going: Sf: 0-0 GS: 0-0 Gd: 0-1 GF: - Fm: 0-0
Distance: 2m/2m3: 0-2 2m4-2m7: 0-0 3m+: 0-0
Track: LH: 0-1 RH: 0-0 Tight: 0-0 Gall: 0-0
Aids: Bl: 0-0 Vi: 0-0 Tstrap: 0-0
Best Rating: 31 4/02 Plum 2m2f good NHF

Cerulean Rose

4-y-o ch f Bluegrass Prince (IRE)-Elegant Rose (Noalto)
A W Carroll Rob Willis

Placings:0   (1918)

2002/03: 16⁰GS,

	Starts	1st	2nd	3rd	Win & Pl
Hurdles	1	0	0	0	
Career Total	1	0	0	0	

Going:	Sf: 0-0 GS: 0-1 Gd: 0-0 GF: - Fm: 0-0
Distance:	2m/2m3: 0-1 2m4-2m7: 0-0 3m+: 0-0
Track:	LH: 0-1 RH: 0-0 Tight: 0-0 Gall: 0-1
Aids:	Bl: 0-0 Vi: 0-0 Tstrap: 0-1
Best Rating:	0 11/02 Newb 2m110y gd-sft Hdl

Cesaria (FR)
107(100c)   (89+c)123
6-y-o b m Highest Honor (FR)-Cat Storm (CAN) (Storm Cat (USA))
M C Pipe Joe Moran

Placings:2310211500-245P   (3249)
2002/03: 16²GS, 18⁴G, 19⁵GS, 25⁵HY,

	Starts	1st	2nd	3rd	Win & Pl
Hurdles	3	0	1	0	3604
Chases	1	0	0	0	0
Career Total	14	3	3	1	27522
126 2/02 Plum	2m		E Hdl	HVY	£2583
133 12/01 Leic	2m		E Hdl	G-S	£3167
9/01 Autl	2m2f		Hdl	VS	£10669
			Total win prize-money £16420		

Going:	Sf: 0-1 GS: 0-2 Gd: 0-1 GF: - Fm: 0-0
Distance:	2m/2m3: 0-2 2m4-2m7: 0-1 3m+: 0-1
Track:	LH: 0-2 RH: 0-2 Tight: 0-1 Gall: 0-1
Aids:	Bl: 0-0 Vi: 0-1 Tstrap: 0-0
Best Rating:	133 12/01 Leic 2m gd-sft Hdl

Fair hurdler; French import, she just lost out at Plumpton on her British debut before winning easily at Leicester in December 2001; fortunate winner at Plumpton next time, she may not want the ground too testing; decent reappearance when runner-up in a fair handicap hurdle at Huntingdon in November; suited by two miles; has won on soft ground and good.

Cetti's Warbler
84f   78f
5-y-o gr m Sir Harry Lewis (USA)-Sedge Warbler (Scallywag)
Mrs P Robeson Mrs P Robeson

Placings:0   (2378)
2002/03: 16⁶S,

	Starts	1st	2nd	3rd	Win & Pl
NH Flat	1	0	0	0	
Career Total	1	0	0	0	

Going:	Sf: 0-1 GS: 0-0 Gd: 0-0 GF: - Fm: 0-0
Distance:	2m/2m3: 0-1 2m4-2m7: 0-0 3m+: 0-0
Track:	LH: 0-1 RH: 0-0 Tight: 0-0 Gall: 0-0
Aids:	Bl: 0-0 Vi: 0-0 Tstrap: 0-0
Best Rating:	78 12/02 Wwck 2m soft NHF

Chabibi
4-y-o br f Mark Of Esteem (IRE)-Nunsharpa (Sharpo)
T H Caldwell R S G Jones

Placings:P   (3368)
2002/03: 16⁰GS,

	Starts	1st	2nd	3rd	Win & Pl
Hurdles	1	0	0	0	

Career Total   1   0   0   0

Going:	Sf: 0-0 GS: 0-1 Gd: 0-0 GF: - Fm: 0-0
Distance:	2m/2m3: 0-1 2m4-2m7: 0-0 3m+: 0-0
Track:	LH: 0-1 RH: 0-0 Tight: 0-1 Gall: 0-0
Aids:	Bl: 0-0 Vi: 0-0 Tstrap: 0-0
Best Rating:	0 1/03 Sthl 2m gd-sft Hdl

Chabrimal Minster
101   99
6-y-o b g Minster Son-Bromley Rose (Rubor)
R Ford B Mills, C Roberts, M & M Burrows

Placings:2   (3987)
2002/03: 20²S,

	Starts	1st	2nd	3rd	Win & Pl
Hurdles	1	0	1	0	1028
Career Total	1	0	1	0	1028

Going:	Sf: 0-1 GS: 0-0 Gd: 0-0 GF: - Fm: 0-0
Distance:	2m/2m3: 0-0 2m4-2m7: 0-1 3m+: 0-0
Track:	LH: 0-0 RH: 0-1 Tight: 0-0 Gall: 0-0
Aids:	Bl: 0-0 Vi: 0-0 Tstrap: 0-0
Best Rating:	99 3/03 Carl 2m4f soft Hdl

Exceeded stable expectations when running well at 50-1 on his racecourse debut.

Chadswell (IRE)
104(104c)   (108c)108
10-y-o b g Lord Americo-Marita Ann (Crozier)
R Ford Mike Proudfoot Partnership

Placings:543461/10P/24F531142-1P2P03   (3986)
2002/03: 26¹HY, 28⁸S, 27²S, 26⁶HY, 24⁶S, 26⁵S,

	Starts	1st	2nd	3rd	Win & Pl
Hurdles	2	1	0	0	4745
Chases	4	0	1	1	1935
Career Total	24	5	3	3	23719
108 6/02 Ctml	3m2f	D(0-125)HHdl	HVY	£4745
108 3/02 Sedg	3m4f	D(0-115)HCh	SFT	£4007
101 2/02 Sedg	3m3f	E(0-110)HCh	SFT	£3297
102 5/00 Ctml	2m6f	F(0-95)HHdl	G-S	£3068
99 4/00 Carl	2m4f110yE Hdl		G-S	£2562
		Total win prize-money £17679		

Going:	Sf: 1-6 GS: 0-0 Gd: 0-0 GF: - Fm: 0-0
Distance:	2m/2m3: 0-0 2m4-2m7: 0-0 3m+: 1-6
Track:	LH: 1-4 RH: 0-2 Tight: 1-4 Gall: 0-1
Aids:	Bl: 0-0 Vi: 0-0 Tstrap: 0-0
Best Rating:	108 11/02 Sedg 3m3f soft Ch

Modest chaser/hurdler. Needs three miles plus and soft ground. Likes a sharp track.

Chain Line
13-y-o br g Relkino-Housemistress (New Member)
J W F Aynsley J W F Aynsley

Placings:0/060/0P0/PP5/400P000/1FP0PFP/00P5P/F5PP-0FPPPP   (3967)
2002/03: 16⁰G, 16⁶GF, 16⁶G, 16⁶GS, 19⁶G, 19⁶S,

	Starts	1st	2nd	3rd	Win & Pl
Hurdles	6	0	0	0	
Career Total	39	1	0	0	2668
88 6/99 Hexm	2m	E Hdl	G-F	£2668
		Total win prize-money £2668		

Going:	Sf: 0-1 GS: 0-1 Gd: 0-3 GF: - Fm: 0-1

Distance:	2m/2m3: 0-6 2m4-2m7: 0-0 3m+: 0-0
Track:	LH: 0-5 RH: 0-1 Tight: 0-3 Gall: 0-0
Aids:	Bl: 0-0 Vi: 0-0 Tstrap: 0-0
Best Rating:	88 6/99 Hexm 2m gd-fm Hdl

Chalcedony
106(84h)   (100h)107
7-y-o ch g Highest Honor (FR)-Sweet Holland (USA) (Alydar (USA))
R Rowe Brian Thrift

Placings:603136/3F0PP4-132311   (1678)
2002/03: 20¹GF, 20³GF, 20²GF, 20³G, 20¹GF, 16¹GF,

	Starts	1st	2nd	3rd	Win & Pl
Chases	6	3	1	2	19595
Career Total	18	4	1	5	24427
112 10/02 Chel	2m	C Ch	G-F	£9718
103 10/02 Plum	2m4f	E Ch	G-F	£4298
102 6/02 Font	2m4f	E Ch	G-F	£2821
102 2/01 Plum	2m	E(0-115)HHdl	SFT	£3526
		Total win prize-money £20364		

Going:	Sf: 0-0 GS: 0-0 Gd: 0-1 GF: - Fm: 3-5
Distance:	2m/2m3: 1-1 2m4-2m7: 2-5 3m+: 0-0
Track:	LH: 2-3 RH: 0-0 Tight: 2-5 Gall: 1-1
Aids:	Bl: 0-0 Vi: 0-0 Tstrap: 0-0
Best Rating:	112 10/02 Chel 2m gd-fm Ch

Fair novice chaser; effective from two to two and a half miles; suited by fast ground; likes to race prominently.

Chalford Oaks
6-y-o ch g High Adventure-Soulieana (Manado)
T R Greathead Mrs S Greathead

Placings:P/PO   (3349)
2002/03: 19⁵S, 16⁵HY,

	Starts	1st	2nd	3rd	Win & Pl
Hurdles	2	0	0	0	
Career Total	3	0	0	0	

Going:	Sf: 0-2 GS: 0-0 Gd: 0-0 GF: - Fm: 0-0
Distance:	2m/2m3: 0-1 2m4-2m7: 0-0 3m+: 0-0
Track:	LH: 0-0 RH: 0-2 Tight: 0-0 Gall: 0-0
Aids:	Bl: 0-0 Vi: 0-0 Tstrap: 0-0
Best Rating:	0 1/03 Leic 2m heavy Hdl

Challenor
70   54
5-y-o ch g Casteddu-Expletive (Shiny Tenth)
Ian Williams Pump & Plant Services Ltd

Placings:00P   (3926)
2002/03: 16⁰GS, 16⁰S, 20⁰G,

	Starts	1st	2nd	3rd	Win & Pl
Hurdles	3	0	0	0	
Career Total	3	0	0	0	

Going:	Sf: 0-1 GS: 0-1 Gd: 0-1 GF: - Fm: 0-0
Distance:	2m/2m3: 0-2 2m4-2m7: 0-1 3m+: 0-0
Track:	LH: 0-1 RH: 0-2 Tight: 0-0 Gall: 0-2
Aids:	Bl: 0-0 Vi: 0-0 Tstrap: 0-0
Best Rating:	54 12/02 Wwck 2m soft Hdl

Champagne Harry
106   114
5-y-o b g Sir Harry Lewis (USA)-Sparkling Cinders (Netherkelly)

N A Twiston-Davies H R Mould

Placings:*30U*   **(4635)**
2002/03: 17³S, 16⁰GS, 19ᵁGF,

	Starts	1st	2nd	3rd	Win & Pl
NH Flat	2	0	0	1	269
Hurdles	1	0	0	0	0
Career Total	3	0	0	1	269

Going:	Sf: 0-1 GS: 0-1 Gd: 0-0 GF: - Fm: 0-1
Distance:	2m/2m3: 0-3 2m4-2m7: 0-0 3m+: 0-0
Track:	LH: 0-3 RH: 0-0 Tight: 0-2 Gall: 0-0
Aids:	Bl: 0-0 Vi: 0-0 Tstrap: 0-0
Best Rating:	94 11/02 Chel 2m110y gd-sft NHF

Modest hurdler; novice hurdle winner at Hereford in May 2003; improved on that effort when runner-up under a penalty in bad ground at Uttoxeter a week later; easy winner of weak event at Worcester in June; narrowly beaten under triple penalty when stepped up to 3m at the same course next time.

Champagne Lil
112   107
6-y-o gr m Terimon-Sparkling Cinders (Netherkelly)
N A Twiston-Davies Mrs E M Bathurst

Placings:*4fU53-6042P3*   **(4752)**
2002/03: 17⁶G, 20⁰GS, 22⁴GS, 21²PS, 24³G,

	Starts	1st	2nd	3rd	Win & Pl
Hurdles	6	0	1	1	3777
Career Total	11	1	1	2	5981
96	10/01	Chep	2m110y H NHF		GD £1617

Total win prize-money £1617

Going:	Sf: 0-1 GS: 0-3 Gd: 0-2 GF: - Fm: 0-0
Distance:	2m/2m3: 0-1 2m4-2m7: 0-4 3m+: 0-1
Track:	LH: 0-1 RH: 0-5 Tight: 0-0 Gall: 0-1
Aids:	Bl: 0-0 Vi: 0-0 Tstrap: 0-0
Best Rating:	96 10/01 Chep 2m110y good NHF

Moderate hurdler; stays three miles; acts on a sound surface, but is effective with cut in the ground.

Chan Move
101   73
11-y-o b g Move Off-Kanisa (Chantro)
W J Smith W J Smith

Placings:*000/0P000F0PP0/PP/P025520/P00/00R-5* **(2514)**
2002/03: 20⁵S,

	Starts	1st	2nd	3rd	Win & Pl
Hurdles	1	0	0	0	0
Career Total	29	0	2	0	986

Going:	Sf: 0-1 GS: 0-0 Gd: 0-0 GF: - Fm: 0-0
Distance:	2m/2m3: 0-0 2m4-2m7: 0-1 3m+: 0-0
Track:	LH: 0-1 RH: 0-0 Tight: 0-0 Gall: 0-1
Aids:	Bl: 0-0 Vi: 0-0 Tstrap: 0-0
Best Rating:	84 4/00 Newc 2m gd-sft Hdl

Chance Investment
86   70
6-y-o b m Homo Sapien-Edithmead (IRE) (Shardari)
R Ford Richard Ford

Placings:*004P2P-30*   **(1072)**
2002/03: 16³GF, 17⁰G,

	Starts	1st	2nd	3rd	Win & Pl
Hurdles	2	0	0	1	294

Career Total	8	0	1	1	1066

Going:	Sf: 0-0 GS: 0-0 Gd: 0-1 GF: - Fm: 0-1
Distance:	2m/2m3: 0-2 2m4-2m7: 0-0 3m+: 0-0
Track:	LH: 0-2 RH: 0-0 Tight: 0-1 Gall: 0-0
Aids:	Bl: 0-0 Vi: 0-0 Tstrap: 0-0
Best Rating:	70 4/02 Sedg 2m1f gd-fm Hdl

Plating-class, lightly-raced hurdler; seems suited by a sound surface.

Chancers Dante (IRE)
108   92+
7-y-o b g Phardante (FR)-Own Acre (Linacre)
Ferdy Murphy Mrs P B Symes

Placings:*f0003-06P0*   **(4168)**
2002/03: 23⁰G, 26⁶GS, 25ᴾHY, 20⁰GS,

	Starts	1st	2nd	3rd	Win & Pl
Hurdles	4	0	0	0	0
Career Total	9	1	0	1	5080
101	6/01	Cork	2m4f	NHF	GD £4729

Total win prize-money £4730

Going:	Sf: 0-1 GS: 0-2 Gd: 0-1 GF: - Fm: 0-0
Distance:	2m/2m3: 0-0 2m4-2m7: 0-2 3m+: 0-2
Track:	LH: 0-2 RH: 0-1 Tight: 0-0 Gall: 0-2
Aids:	Bl: 0-0 Vi: 0-0 Tstrap: 0-0
Best Rating:	101 6/01 Cork 2m4f good NHF

Plating-class hurdler; stays three miles; effective on ground from good to heavy.

Chancit
72   33
4-y-o b f Piccolo-Polly Worth (Wolver Hollow)
M E Sowersby (Andrew Reid 12/7) A Milner

Placings:*0P*   **(2300)**
2002/03: 17⁰GF, 16ᴾGS,

	Starts	1st	2nd	3rd	Win & Pl
Hurdles	2	0	0	0	
Career Total	2	0	0	0	

Going:	Sf: 0-0 GS: 0-1 Gd: 0-0 GF: - Fm: 0-1
Distance:	2m/2m3: 0-2 2m4-2m7: 0-0 3m+: 0-0
Track:	LH: 0-1 RH: 0-1 Tight: 0-2 Gall: 0-0
Aids:	Bl: 0-0 Vi: 0-0 Tstrap: 0-0
Best Rating:	33 9/02 MRas 2m1f110y gd-fm Hdl

Chancy Charly (IRE)
10-y-o b g King s Ride-Lady Siobhan (Laurence O)
S Gollings Mrs E Houlton

Placings:*31C2/PPP*   **(0570)**
2002/03: 22ᴾG, 24ᴾGS, 24ᴾS,

	Starts	1st	2nd	3rd	Win & Pl
Hurdles	2	0	0	0	0
Chases	1	0	0	0	0
Career Total	7	1	1	1	4705
96	2/00	Newc	3m	E Ch	SFT £2970

Total win prize-money £2971

Going:	Sf: 0-1 GS: 0-1 Gd: 0-1 GF: - Fm: 0-0
Distance:	2m/2m3: 0-0 2m4-2m7: 0-1 3m+: 0-2
Track:	LH: 0-3 RH: 0-0 Tight: 0-1 Gall: 0-0
Aids:	Bl: 0-0 Vi: 0-0 Tstrap: 0-0

Best Rating: 108 2/00 Donc 3m   good   Ch

Change Of Image
69   20
5-y-o b m Spectrum (IRE)-Reveuse Du Soir (Vision (USA))
J R Weymes (H R A Cecil 12/6) Jeff Isteed

Placings:*0*   **(2099)**
2002/03: 19⁰G,

	Starts	1st	2nd	3rd	Win & Pl
Hurdles	1	0	0	0	
Career Total	1	0	0	0	

Going:	Sf: 0-0 GS: 0-0 Gd: 0-1 GF: - Fm: 0-0
Distance:	2m/2m3: 0-1 2m4-2m7: 0-0 3m+: 0-0
Track:	LH: 0-1 RH: 0-0 Tight: 0-1 Gall: 0-0
Aids:	Bl: 0-0 Vi: 0-0 Tstrap: 0-0
Best Rating:	20 11/02 Catt 2m3f good Hdl

Channahrlie (IRE)
112(107h)   (93h)96
9-y-o gr g Celio Rufo-Derravarragh Lady (IRE) (Radical)
R Dickin J C Clemmow

Placings:*034/20610/551224PF16-02222221PP*   **(4765)**
2002/03: 25³GF, 24²GF, 24²F, 26²G, 23²GF, 23²G, 24²GS, 24¹GF, 24ᴾGF, 31ᴾG,

	Starts	1st	2nd	3rd	Win & Pl
Hurdles	1	0	1	0	988
Chases	9	1	5	0	10541
Career Total	28	4	9	1	27466
91	3/03	Sthl	3m110y	E(0-110)HCh	G-F £4347
93	4/02	Hrfd	3m2f	E(0-105)HHdl	G-F £2912
90	8/01	Bang	3m110y	D(0-125)HCh	GD £5382
90	12/00	Leic	2m	D(0-110)HCh	G-S £4241

Total win prize-money £16882

Going:	Sf: 0-0 GS: 0-1 Gd: 0-3 GF: - Fm: 1-6
Distance:	2m/2m3: 0-0 2m4-2m7: 0-0 3m+: 1-10
Track:	LH: 1-3 RH: 0-6 Tight: 1-3 Gall: 0-0
Aids:	Bl: 0-0 Vi: 0-0 Tstrap: 0-0
Best Rating:	96 2/03 Asct 3m110y gd-sft Ch

Modest hurdler/chaser; had made a habit of finishing runner-up before winning a handicap chase at Southwell in March 2003; effective at around three miles; acts on good and fast ground.

Chantessa Sioux
5-y-o b m Paley Prince (USA)-Legendary Lady (Reprimand)
W G M Turner I E Chant

Placings:*P*   **(0269)**
2002/03: 16ᴾGF,

	Starts	1st	2nd	3rd	Win & Pl
Hurdles	1	0	0	0	
Career Total	1	0	0	0	

Going:	Sf: 0-0 GS: 0-0 Gd: 0-0 GF: - Fm: 0-1
Distance:	2m/2m3: 0-1 2m4-2m7: 0-0 3m+: 0-0
Track:	LH: 0-1 RH: 0-0 Tight: 0-1 Gall: 0-0
Aids:	Bl: 0-0 Vi: 0-0 Tstrap: 0-0
Best Rating:	0 5/02 Strf 2m110y gd-fm Hdl

Chanticlier
95   113+
6-y-o b g Roselier (FR)-Cherry Crest (Pollerton)

K C Bailey Mrs Jane Lane

Placings:2-65 (2491)
2002/03: 21⁶GS, 24⁵G,

	Starts	1st	2nd	3rd	Win & Pl
Hurdles	2	0	0	0	877
Career Total	3	0	1	0	1606

Going: Sf: 0-0 GS: 0-1 Gd: 0-1 GF: - Fm: 0-0
Distance: 2m/2m3: 0-0 2m4-2m7: 0-1 3m+: 0-1
Track: LH: 0-2 RH: 0-0 Tight: 0-0 Gall: 0-2
Aids: Bl: 0-0 Vi: 0-0 Tstrap: 0-0
Best Rating: 116 3/02 Sand 2m110y gd-sft NHF

Modest hurdler; gave a hotpot a real fright on his debut in a Sandown bumper and was not disgraced on his hurdling debut; highly tried first two starts over hurdles; third when dropped in class over 3m 2f at Hereford May 2003.

Chantilly Lady
77   43
10-y-o ch m Rising-Ladiz (Persian Bold)
M J Weeden Just Racing

Placings:0/5P/52/P0 (2332)
2002/03: 16⁷GS, 22⁵GS,

	Starts	1st	2nd	3rd	Win & Pl
Hurdles	2	0	0	0	
Career Total	7	0	1	0	716

Going: Sf: 0-0 GS: 0-2 Gd: 0-0 GF: - Fm: 0-0
Distance: 2m/2m3: 0-1 2m4-2m7: 0-1 3m+: 0-0
Track: LH: 0-0 RH: 0-2 Tight: 0-0 Gall: 0-0
Aids: Bl: 0-0 Vi: 0-0 Tstrap: 0-0
Best Rating: 90 3/01 Extr 2m1f heavy Hdl

Chaos Theory
100(105c)   (127c)111
8-y-o b g Jupiter Island-Indian Orchid (Warpath)
Mrs M Reveley R Burridge

Placings:U/40F113/63600/0FP1FP4F-6600 (4354)
2002/03: 16⁶GS, 16⁶GS, 16⁶G, 20⁹GF,

	Starts	1st	2nd	3rd	Win & Pl
Hurdles	4	0	0	0	
Career Total	24	3	0	2	11842
117 12/01 Muss 2m4f D Ch				G-F	£4270
122 1/00 Hntg 2m110y D Hdl				GD	£3346
104 1/00 Muss 2m E Hdl				SFT	£2772
			Total win prize-money £10389		

Going: Sf: 0-0 GS: 0-2 Gd: 0-0 GF: - Fm: 0-1
Distance: 2m/2m3: 0-3 2m4-2m7: 0-1 3m+: 0-0
Track: LH: 0-1 RH: 0-3 Tight: 0-1 Gall: 0-2
Aids: Bl: 0-3 Vi: 0-0 Tstrap: 0-0
Best Rating: 126 12/00 Hntg 2m110y soft Hdl

Notched up his only two successes in his three-year career in chasing company in January 2000, on right-handed tracks. Seems to have struggled with a stiff mark since. Took a crashing fall at Kempton in October 2001, then won on his chasing debut but has gone the wrong way since. Races mainly between two and two and a half miles.

Chaparro Amargoso (IRE)
112(104h)   (86h)110
10-y-o b g Ela-Mana-Mou-Champanera (Top Ville)
B Ellison E J Berry

Placings:1/3/3P6/12F43446052-12334 (0951)
2002/03: 16¹GF, 16²G, 16³G, 16³GS, 21⁴G,

	Starts	1st	2nd	3rd	Win & Pl
Chases	5	1	1	2	7911
Career Total	21	3	3	5	16667
104 5/02 Weth 2m D(0-115)HCh				G-F	£4069
108 7/01 Sedg 2m110y E Ch				G-F	£3152
110 10/97 Hexm 2m H NHF				G-F	£1187
			Total win prize-money £8409		

Going: Sf: 0-0 GS: 0-1 Gd: 0-3 GF: - Fm: 1-1
Distance: 2m/2m3: 1-4 2m4-2m7: 0-1 3m+: 0-0
Track: LH: 1-5 RH: 0-0 Tight: 0-3 Gall: 0-0
Aids: Bl: 0-0 Vi: 0-0 Tstrap: 0-0
Best Rating: 110 7/02 Wolv 2m gd-sft Ch

A consistent performer in modest handicap chases, he is best suited by two miles and fast ground.

Chapel Royale (IRE)
95   88
6-y-o gr g College Chapel-Merci Royale (Fairy King (USA))
Jedd O Keeffe (D Nicholls 29/9) J Potts

Placings:000 (3965)
2002/03: 16⁹GS, 16⁹G, 16⁹S,

	Starts	1st	2nd	3rd	Win & Pl
Hurdles	3	0	0	0	
Career Total	3	0	0	0	

Going: Sf: 0-1 GS: 0-1 Gd: 0-1 GF: - Fm: 0-0
Distance: 2m/2m3: 0-3 2m4-2m7: 0-0 3m+: 0-0
Track: LH: 0-3 RH: 0-0 Tight: 0-1 Gall: 0-0
Aids: Bl: 0-0 Vi: 0-0 Tstrap: 0-0
Best Rating: 88 2/03 Weth 2m good Hdl

Modest handicapper on the Flat; no worthwhile form over hurdles.

Chapeltown (IRE)
11-y-o b g Denel (FR)-Lady Dunsford (Torus)
N J Henderson Newbury Racehorse Owners Group Ii

Placings:066630/213/1513/41-U (4323)
2002/03: 16ᵁG,

	Starts	1st	2nd	3rd	Win & Pl
Hurdles	1	0	0	0	
Career Total	16	4	1	3	24006
135 11/01 Newb 2m3f C(0-135)HHdl				GD	£7150
130 3/01 Newb 2m110y D Hdl				HVY	£4738
135 11/00 Newb 2m110y C Hdl				HVY	£5720
99 5/98 DRoy 2m NHF				GD	£1489
			Total win prize-money £19098		

Going: Sf: 0-0 GS: 0-0 Gd: 0-1 GF: - Fm: 0-0
Distance: 2m/2m3: 0-1 2m4-2m7: 0-0 3m+: 0-0
Track: LH: 0-1 RH: 0-0 Tight: 0-0 Gall: 0-1
Aids: Bl: 0-0 Vi: 0-0 Tstrap: 0-0
Best Rating: 135 11/01 Newb 2m3f good Hdl

Useful hurdler; very lightly raced in recent years; goes well at Newbury; effective on good and heavy ground; stays two miles three furlongs.

Charalambous (USA)
87   92+
6-y-o b g Hermitage (USA)-Hula Lei (USA) (State Dinner (USA))

C L Popham Mrs A E Baker

Placings:020/46 (1230)
2002/03: 16⁴S, 16⁸G,

	Starts	1st	2nd	3rd	Win & Pl
Hurdles	2	0	0	0	0
Career Total	5	0	1	0	718

Going: Sf: 0-1 GS: 0-0 Gd: 0-1 GF: - Fm: 0-0
Distance: 2m/2m3: 0-2 2m4-2m7: 0-0 3m+: 0-0
Track: LH: 0-2 RH: 0-0 Tight: 0-0 Gall: 0-0
Aids: Bl: 0-0 Vi: 0-0 Tstrap: 0-0
Best Rating: 90 8/02 Worc 2m soft Hdl

Lightly-raced, has shown modest ability over hurdles.

Charge Card
68f   33f
5-y-o b h Zafonic (USA)-Prophecy (IRE) (Warning)
Miss M E Rowland Miss M E Rowland

Placings:0 (0409)
2002/03: 17⁰GF,

	Starts	1st	2nd	3rd	Win & Pl
NH Flat	1	0	0	0	
Career Total	1	0	0	0	

Going: Sf: 0-0 GS: 0-0 Gd: 0-0 GF: - Fm: 0-0
Distance: 2m/2m3: 0-1 2m4-2m7: 0-0 3m+: 0-0
Track: LH: 0-0 RH: 0-1 Tight: 0-1 Gall: 0-0
Aids: Bl: 0-0 Vi: 0-0 Tstrap: 0-0
Best Rating: 33 6/02 MRas 2m1f110y gd-fm NHF

Charlatan (IRE)
84   77
5-y-o b g Charnwood Forest (IRE)-Taajreh (IRE) (Mtoto)
M J Gingell (Mrs C A Dunnett 29/11) Andy Middleton

Placings:000 (3741)
2002/03: 16⁹S, 16⁹HY, 20⁹G,

	Starts	1st	2nd	3rd	Win & Pl
Hurdles	3	0	0	0	
Career Total	3	0	0	0	

Going: Sf: 0-2 GS: 0-0 Gd: 0-1 GF: - Fm: 0-0
Distance: 2m/2m3: 0-2 2m4-2m7: 0-1 3m+: 0-0
Track: LH: 0-0 RH: 0-3 Tight: 0-0 Gall: 0-2
Aids: Bl: 0-0 Vi: 0-0 Tstrap: 0-0
Best Rating: 77 1/03 Hntg 2m110y soft Hdl

Charles Spencelayh (IRE)
78   70
7-y-o b g Tenby-Legit (IRE) (Runnett)
J G M O Shea (M C Pipe 8/5) Mick Fletcher

Placings:5P600-P5 (2175)
2002/03: 20⁰GF, 16⁶S,

	Starts	1st	2nd	3rd	Win & Pl
Hurdles	2	0	0	0	0
Career Total	7	0	0	0	0

Going: Sf: 0-1 GS: 0-0 Gd: 0-0 GF: - Fm: 0-1
Distance: 2m/2m3: 0-1 2m4-2m7: 0-1 3m+: 0-0
Track: LH: 0-2 RH: 0-0 Tight: 0-0 Gall: 0-0
Aids: Bl: 0-0 Vi: 0-1 Tstrap: 0-0

Best Rating: 91   1/02   Tntn   2m1f   soft   Hdl

Charlie Bubbles (IRE)

68f   **49f**

6-y-o b g Un Desperado (FR)-Bounty (IRE) (Cataldi)
B De Haan   Flora Charlie Limited

Placings:0   (0523)
2002/03: 17^0G,

	Starts	1st	2nd	3rd	Win & Pl
NH Flat	1	0	0	0	
Career Total	1	0	0	0	

Going: Sf: 0-0 GS: 0-0 Gd: 0-1 GF: - Fm: 0-0
Distance: 2m/2m3: 0-1 2m4-2m7: 0-0 3m+: 0-0
Track: LH: 0-1 RH: 0-0 Tight: 0-1 Gall: 0-0
Aids: Bl: 0-0 Vi: 0-0 Tstrap: 0-0
Best Rating: 49 6/02 NAbb 2m1f good NHF

Charlie Chang (IRE)

(82h)   (38h)**90**

10-y-o b g Don t Forget Me-East River (FR) (Arctic Tern (USA))
A G Juckes   David Workman

Placings:6002/3P001160/0P/004**P14-F**   (0114)
2002/03: 25^FGS,

	Starts	1st	2nd	3rd	Win & Pl
Chases	1	0	0	0	
Career Total	21	3	1	1	10788
90	3/02 Bang	3m110y	D Ch	SFT	£4410
90	3/99 Wwck	2m	F(0-100)HHdl	SFT	£2110
86	2/99 Folk	2m1f110y0(0-90)HHdl		G-S	£1660
			Total win prize-money		£8180

Going: Sf: 0-0 GS: 0-1 Gd: 0-0 GF: - Fm: 0-0
Distance: 2m/2m3: 0-0 2m4-2m7: 0-0 3m+: 0-1
Track: LH: 0-0 RH: 0-1 Tight: 0-0 Gall: 0-0
Aids: Bl: 0-0 Vi: 0-0 Tstrap: 0-0
Best Rating: 90 3/02 Bang 3m110y soft Ch

Modest novice chaser who won a farcical event at Bangor in 2002 over an extended three miles. Goes well in soft ground.

Charlie Hawes (IRE)

14-y-o b g Euphemism-Eyecap (King s Ride)
Miss Gillian A Russell   Miss Gillian A Russell

Placings:0006FP/505P40/000040/PU   (4314)
2002/03: 24^PS, 22^UG,

	Starts	1st	2nd	3rd	Win & Pl
Chases	2	0	0	0	
Career Total	20	0	0	0	0

Going: Sf: 0-1 GS: 0-0 Gd: 0-1 GF: - Fm: 0-0
Distance: 2m/2m3: 0-2 2m4-2m7: 0-1 3m+: 0-1
Track: LH: 0-2 RH: 0-0 Tight: 0-0 Gall: 0-2
Aids: Bl: 0-0 Vi: 0-0 Tstrap: 0-0
Best Rating: 79 12/97 Folk 2m6f110y good Hdl

Charlie Kennet

91   **88**

5-y-o b g Pyramus (USA)-Evaporate (Insan (USA))

D G Bridgwater   The Rule Racing Syndicate

Placings:224400   (2499)
2002/03: 16^2GF, 17^2GF, 16^4F, 16^4G, 16^6GS, 20^9GS,

	Starts	1st	2nd	3rd	Win & Pl
NH Flat	4	0	2	0	1054
Hurdles	2	0	0	0	0
Career Total	6	0	2	0	1054

Going: Sf: 0-0 GS: 0-2 Gd: 0-1 GF: - Fm: 0-3
Distance: 2m/2m3: 0-5 2m4-2m7: 0-1 3m+: 0-0
Track: LH: 0-4 RH: 0-2 Tight: 0-1 Gall: 0-0
Aids: Bl: 0-0 Vi: 0-0 Tstrap: 0-0
Best Rating: 100 10/02 Chep 2m110y good NHF

Has shown decent form in finishing runner-up in two decent bumpers. Disappointing at Ludlow third start.

Charlie Pickle (USA)

100

5-y-o b g Ghazi (USA)-Dancing Vaguely (USA) (Vaguely Noble)
C C Bealby   Foreneish Racing

Placings:2244   (3089)
2002/03: 16^2GF, 16^2GS, 16^4GS, 19^4GS,

	Starts	1st	2nd	3rd	Win & Pl
NH Flat	3	0	2	0	1012
Hurdles	1	0	0	0	272
Career Total	4	0	2	0	1283

Going: Sf: 0-0 GS: 0-3 Gd: 0-0 GF: - Fm: 0-1
Distance: 2m/2m3: 0-3 2m4-2m7: 0-1 3m+: 0-0
Track: LH: 0-3 RH: 0-1 Tight: 0-2 Gall: 0-1
Aids: Bl: 0-0 Vi: 0-0 Tstrap: 0-0
Best Rating: 101 1/03 Donc 2m3f110y gd-sft Hdl

Ha shown some ability in bumpers and made a pleasing debut over hurdles at Doncaster in January.

Charlie Siddle

85(96h)   (67h)**80**

9-y-o b g Thowra (FR)-Figrant (USA) (L Emigrant (USA))
Miss K M George   A B Parr

Placings:54P/F5/4546044P-0P   (0175)
2002/03: 17^0G, 21^PGF,

	Starts	1st	2nd	3rd	Win & Pl
Chases	2	0	0	0	
Career Total	15	0	0	0	837

Going: Sf: 0-0 GS: 0-0 Gd: 0-1 GF: - Fm: 0-1
Distance: 2m/2m3: 0-1 2m4-2m7: 0-1 3m+: 0-0
Track: LH: 0-1 RH: 0-1 Tight: 0-1 Gall: 0-0
Aids: Bl: 0-0 Vi: 0-1 Tstrap: 0-0
Best Rating: 80 4/01 Extr 2m3f110y soft Ch

Charlie Strong (IRE)

10-y-o b g Strong Gale-The Village Vixen (Buckskin (FR))
R Kelvin-Hughes   R Kelvin-Hughes

Placings:6/1/63-1P   (0414)
2002/03: 21^{11}G, 28^2GF,

	Starts	1st	2nd	3rd	Win & Pl
Chases	2	1	0	0	6796
Career Total	6	2	0	1	8908
108	5/02 Winc	2m5f	H Ch	G-F	£6795

109	4/01 Extr	2m7f110yH Ch		G-S	£1790
		Total win prize-money			£8587

Going: Sf: 0-0 GS: 0-0 Gd: 0-0 GF: - Fm: 1-2
Distance: 2m/2m3: 0-0 2m4-2m7: 1-1 3m+: 0-1
Track: LH: 0-1 RH: 1-1 Tight: 0-1 Gall: 0-0
Aids: Bl: 0-0 Vi: 0-0 Tstrap: 0-0
Best Rating: 109 4/01 Extr 2m7f110y gd-sft Ch

Fair winning pointer/hunter. Easy winner of 21 furlong of a weakly contested event at Wincanton May 2002. Best on goodish ground.

Charlie Taylor (IRE)

70   **57**

7-y-o ch g Insan (USA)-Gusserane Lark (Napoleon Bonaparte)
C N Kellett   Sean A Taylor

Placings:0/0-00   (2200)
2002/03: 16^5S, 16^0S,

	Starts	1st	2nd	3rd	Win & Pl
Hurdles	2	0	0	0	
Career Total	4	0	0	0	

Going: Sf: 0-2 GS: 0-0 Gd: 0-0 GF: - Fm: 0-0
Distance: 2m/2m3: 0-2 2m4-2m7: 0-0 3m+: 0-0
Track: LH: 0-2 RH: 0-0 Tight: 0-0 Gall: 0-0
Aids: Bl: 0-0 Vi: 0-0 Tstrap: 0-0
Best Rating: 57 11/02 Uttx 2m soft Hdl

Charlieadams (IRE)

13-y-o b g Carlingford Castle-Lucy Platter (FR) (Record Token)
J F W Muir (L Lungo 19/10)   J F W Muir

Placings:0/000P0/2/4U3/50F3/O116UUP-2FU1112226   (4261)
2002/03: 21^2GF, 16^6G, 20^UGF, 21^{11}GF, 21^1G, 20^1G, 24^2GF, 25^2G, 21^2S, 27^6G,

	Starts	1st	2nd	3rd	Win & Pl
Chases	10	3	4	0	21256
Career Total	31	5	5	2	26011
110	8/02 Prth	2m4f110yD(0-115)HCh	GD	£6760
114	8/02 Sedg	2m5f D(0-120)HCh	GD	£4784
101	7/02 Sedg	2m5f E(0-110)HCh	G-F	£4124
88	5/01 Hexm	2m4f110yH Ch	G-F	£1337
88	5/01 Prth	2m4f110yH Ch	SFT	£2317
		Total win prize-money		£19322

Going: Sf: 0-1 GS: 0-0 Gd: 2-5 GF: - Fm: 1-4
Distance: 2m/2m3: 0-2 2m4-2m7: 3-6 3m+: 0-3
Track: LH: 2-7 RH: 1-3 Tight: 2-5 Gall: 0-0
Aids: Bl: 0-0 Vi: 0-0 Tstrap: 0-0
Best Rating: 114 10/02 Kels 3m1f good Ch

Modest chaser who has improved since being trained professionally, winning three times in the summer of 2002. Suited by two and a half miles. Goes on most ground but best form has been on a sound surface.

Charliemoore

99   **90**

7-y-o ch g Karinga Bay-Your Care (FR) (Caerwent)
G L Moore   Bryan Pennick

Placings:010-000   (3753)
2002/03: 18^0G, 16^0S, 19^0G, 21^0G,

	Starts	1st	2nd	3rd	Win & Pl
NH Flat	1	0	0	0	0

Hurdles	3	0	0	0	0
Career Total	6	1	0	0	1712

90 4/02 Plum 2m2f   H NHF   G-F   £1711

Total win prize-money £1712

Going:	Sf: 0-1 GS: 0-0 Gd: 0-3 GF: - Fm: 0-0
Distance:	2m/2m3: 0-3 2m4-2m7: 0-1 3m+: 0-0
Track:	LH: 0-3 RH: 0-1 Tight: 0-0 Gall: 0-2
Aids:	Bl: 0-0 Vi: 0-0 Tstrap: 0-0
Best Rating:	90 12/02 Newb 2m3f good Hdl

Charlies Future

108   107

5-y-o b g Democratic (USA)-Fausterelie (Faustus (USA))
S C Burrough (P R Rodford 6/1) M L Lewis-Jones

Placings:55003-0640215   (4441)
2002/03: 24⁰S, 22⁶S, 19⁴GS, 22⁰HY, 19²S, 19¹HY, 20⁵G,

	Starts	1st	2nd	3rd	Win & Pl
Hurdles	7	1	1	0	5132
Career Total	12	1	1	1	5580

107 3/03 Tntn   2m3f110y   E(0-105)HHdl
HVY £3887

Total win prize-money £3887

Going:	Sf: 1-5 GS: 0-1 Gd: 0-1 GF: - Fm: 0-0
Distance:	2m/2m3: 0-1 2m4-2m7: 1-5 3m+: 0-1
Track:	LH: 0-2 RH: 1-5 Tight: 1-3 Gall: 0-0
Aids:	Bl: 0-0 Vi: 0-0 Tstrap: 0-0
Best Rating:	108 4/03 Asct 2m4f good Hdl

Modest hurdler; easy winner of ordinary handicap at Taunton March 2003; acts on soft ground; stays two miles six.

Charliesmedarlin

103   90+

12-y-o b g Macmillion-Top Cover (High Top)
Mrs Barbara Waring E S Chivers

Placings:00/P/4UPL06P3P/30/11/U   (4636)
2002/03: 24⁰G,

	Starts	1st	2nd	3rd	Win & Pl
Chases	1	0	0	0	
Career Total	17	2	0	2	8895

104 7/00 Strf   2m5f110yE(0-105)HCh   G-F £3428
91   7/00 Worc   2m7f110yF(0-110)HCh   GD   £4306

Total win prize-money £7735

Going:	Sf: 0-0 GS: 0-0 Gd: 0-1 GF: - Fm: 0-0
Distance:	2m/2m3: 0-0 2m4-2m7: 0-0 3m+: 0-1
Track:	LH: 0-1 RH: 0-0 Tight: 0-1 Gall: 0-0
Aids:	Bl: 0-0 Vi: 0-0 Tstrap: 0-0
Best Rating:	104 7/00 Strf 2m5f110y gd-fm Ch

Moderate handicap chaser; off course for nearly three years after winning back-to-back handicaps July 2000; failed to complete first three starts after comeback; much better effort having been dropped 15lb when third at Newton Abbot June 2003; scored from 6lb out of the handicap at Uttoxeter next time; stays 3m; acts on a sound surface.

Charm Offensive

85   74

5-y-o b m Zieten (USA)-Shoag (USA) (Affirmed (USA))
C J Gray (S R Bowring 12/7) What Racing

Placings:500   (3779)
2002/03: 17⁵S, 17⁰S, 19⁹GS,

	Starts	1st	2nd	3rd	Win & Pl
Hurdles	3	0	0	0	0
Career Total	3	0	0	0	0

Going:	Sf: 0-2 GS: 0-1 Gd: 0-0 GF: - Fm: 0-0
Distance:	2m/2m3: 0-3 2m4-2m7: 0-0 3m+: 0-0
Track:	LH: 0-3 RH: 0-3 Tight: 0-2 Gall: 0-0
Aids:	Bl: 0-0 Vi: 0-0 Tstrap: 0-0
Best Rating:	74 12/02 Tntn 2m1f soft Hdl

Charming Admiral (IRE)

99(86h)   (86h)99

10-y-o b g Shareef Dancer (USA)-Lilac Charm (Bustino)
Mrs A Duffield The Old Spice Girls

Placings:4312013/3014F2/116P/50-51P61   (4142)
2002/03: 17⁵S, 25¹GS, 27⁸S, 26⁶S, 20¹S,

	Starts	1st	2nd	3rd	Win & Pl
Hurdles	1	0	0	0	0
Chases	4	2	0	0	7469
Career Total	24	7	2	3	27484

99   3/03 Hexm   2m4f110yF(0-100)HCh   SFT £3276
92   12/02 Catt 3m1f110yE(0-110)HCh   G-S £4192
109 9/00 Sedg   2m5f   E(0-115)HCh   SFT £4153
109 8/00 Ctml   2m5f110yF(0-110)HCh   G-S £3461
100 2/99 Carl   2m4f110yD Ch   HVY £3964
126 4/98 Kels   2m110y D(0-125)HHdl   HVY £2762
124 1/98 Catt   2m3f   E Hdl   G-S £2092

Total win prize-money £23903

Going:	Sf: 1-4 GS: 1-1 Gd: 0-0 GF: - Fm: 0-0
Distance:	2m/2m3: 0-1 2m4-2m7: 1-1 3m+: 1-3
Track:	LH: 2-5 RH: 0-0 Tight: 1-3 Gall: 0-0
Aids:	Bl: 2-5 Vi: 0-0 Tstrap: 0-0
Best Rating:	126 4/98 Kels 2m110y heavy Hdl

Versatile-type, moderate chaser; emerged from the wilderness, making the most of a good opportunity when successful at Catterick in December; came from an impossible position when adding to his record at Hexham in March; stays really well but is unreliable.

Charming Jack

6-y-o b g Charmer-No Fizz (Broadsword (USA))
D M Grissell The Hon Mrs C Cameron

Placings:0FP   (3805)
2002/03: 17⁰GS, 16⁶GS, 21⁸S,

	Starts	1st	2nd	3rd	Win & Pl
NH Flat	1	0	0	0	0
Hurdles	2	0	0	0	0
Career Total	3	0	0	0	

Going:	Sf: 0-1 GS: 0-2 Gd: 0-0 GF: - Fm: 0-0
Distance:	2m/2m3: 0-2 2m4-2m7: 0-1 3m+: 0-0
Track:	LH: 0-2 RH: 0-1 Tight: 0-2 Gall: 0-1
Aids:	Bl: 0-0 Vi: 0-0 Tstrap: 0-1
Best Rating:	0 2/03 Plum 2m5f soft Hdl

Charmouth Forest

100   79

7-y-o ch g Lir-Crimson Lady (Crimson Beau)
C J Gray D J Staddon

Placings:00/650-55564   (4622)
2002/03: 19⁵GS, 19²S, 17⁵GS, 22⁶S, 22⁴GF,

	Starts	1st	2nd	3rd	Win & Pl
Hurdles	5	0	0	0	456
Career Total	10	0	0	0	456

Going:	Sf: 0-1 GS: 0-2 Gd: 0-1 GF: - Fm: 0-1
Distance:	2m/2m3: 0-2 2m4-2m7: 0-3 3m+: 0-0
Track:	LH: 0-2 RH: 0-3 Tight: 0-3 Gall: 0-0
Aids:	Bl: 0-0 Vi: 0-0 Tstrap: 0-0
Best Rating:	82 1/03 Extr 2m3f gd-sft Hdl

Moderate hurdler; yet to make the frame.

Charnwood Street (IRE)

95   73

4-y-o b g Charnwood Forest (IRE)-La Vigie (King Of Clubs)
D Shaw Swann Racing Ltd

Placings:005   (4156)
2002/03: 16⁰GS, 16⁰GS, 17⁵G,

	Starts	1st	2nd	3rd	Win & Pl
Hurdles	3	0	0	0	0
Career Total	3	0	0	0	0

Going:	Sf: 0-0 GS: 0-2 Gd: 0-1 GF: - Fm: 0-0
Distance:	2m/2m3: 0-3 2m4-2m7: 0-0 3m+: 0-0
Track:	LH: 0-2 RH: 0-1 Tight: 0-2 Gall: 0-1
Aids:	Bl: 0-0 Vi: 0-0 Tstrap: 0-0
Best Rating:	74 1/03 Donc 2m110y gd-sft Hdl

Charter Ridge (IRE)

10-y-o b g Glacial Storm (USA)-Pure Spec (Fine Blade (USA))
Jonjo O Neill Anne Duchess Of Westminster

Placings:103611/5BF4/11P312442/PP-P   (1725)
2002/03: 24⁴GS,

	Starts	1st	2nd	3rd	Win & Pl
Chases	1	0	0	0	
Career Total	22	6	2	2	34611

133 10/00 Aint 3m1f   C Ch   GD   £6870
118 5/00 Aint   3m1f   D(0-120)HCh   G-F £4228
123 5/00 Weth   3m1f   D(0-110)HCh   G-F £5265
109 4/99 Bang   3m   E Hdl   G-S £2990
102 4/99 Bang   2m4f   E Hdl   GD   £2486
102 6/98 Clon   2m4f   NHF   GD   £2382

Total win prize-money £24223

Going:	Sf: 0-0 GS: 0-1 Gd: 0-0 GF: - Fm: 0-0
Distance:	2m/2m3: 0-0 2m4-2m7: 0-0 3m+: 0-1
Track:	LH: 0-0 RH: 0-0 Tight: 0-0 Gall: 0-0
Aids:	Bl: 0-0 Vi: 0-0 Tstrap: 0-0
Best Rating:	135 11/00 Newb 3m gd-sft Ch

Charter Royal (FR)

91(102c)   (71dc)59

8-y-o b g Royal Charter (FR)-Tadjmine (FR) (Tadj (FR))
A R Dicken Ron Affleck

Placings:650/050300/2241F0F/60145053400U-P63P00P
                                          (3803)
2002/03: 20⁰G, 20⁶S, 16⁸S, 21⁸S, 20⁰G, 24⁰G, 20⁸S,

	Starts	1st	2nd	3rd	Win & Pl
Hurdles	3	0	0	0	0
Chases	4	0	0	1	521
Career Total	35	2	2	3	8105

80   11/01 Sedg   2m110y F(0-100)HCh   SFT £2520
80   1/01 Catt   2m   F(0-100)HCh   G-S £2401

Total win prize-money £4922

Going:	Sf: 0-4 GS: 0-0 Gd: 0-3 GF: - Fm: 0-1
Distance:	2m/2m3: 0-1 2m4-2m7: 0-5 3m+: 0-1

Track: LH: 0-5 RH: 0-2 Tight: 0-4 Gall: 0-2
Aids: Bl: 0-0 Vi: 0-0 Tstrap: 0-0
Best Rating: 84 10/00 Carl 2m   gd-sft Ch

Chase The Sunset (IRE)
87   78

5-y-o ch g Un Desperado (FR)-Cherry Chase (IRE) (Red Sunset)
Miss H C Knight Jim Lewis

Placings:04   (2194)
2002/03: 17[0]GS, 17[4]GS,

	Starts	1st	2nd	3rd	Win & Pl
NH Flat	1	0	0	0	0
Hurdles	1	0	0	0	332
Career Total	2	0	0	0	332

Going: Sf: 0-0 GS: 0-1 Gd: 0-1 GF: - Fm: 0-0
Distance: 2m/2m3: 0-2 2m4-2m7: 0-0 3m+: 0-0
Track: LH: 0-1 RH: 0-0 Tight: 0-0 Gall: 0-0
Aids: Bl: 0-0 Vi: 0-0 Tstrap: 0-0
Best Rating: 78 11/02 Tntn 2m1f   gd-sft Hdl

Chasing The Wind
11

8-y-o b m Henbit (USA)-Deep In The Arctic (Deep Run)
Mrs L Wadham Mrs C M Cooke

Placings:P-0   (1220)
2002/03: 16[0]GS, 21[0]G,

	Starts	1st	2nd	3rd	Win & Pl
Hurdles	2	0	0	0	
Career Total	2	0	0	0	

Going: Sf: 0-0 GS: 0-1 Gd: 0-1 GF: - Fm: 0-0
Distance: 2m/2m3: 0-1 2m4-2m7: 0-1 3m+: 0-0
Track: LH: 0-1 RH: 0-0 Tight: 0-0 Gall: 0-0
Aids: Bl: 0-0 Vi: 0-0 Tstrap: 0-0
Best Rating: 11 9/02 Sthl 2m5f110y good Hdl

Chateau Burf
69f   52f

7-y-o ch g Cruise Missile-Headstrong Miss (Le Bavard (FR))
D G Bridgwater H Burford

Placings:00   (0560)
2002/03: 17[0]G, 17[0]GF,

	Starts	1st	2nd	3rd	Win & Pl
NH Flat	2	0	0	0	
Career Total	2	0	0	0	

Going: Sf: 0-0 GS: 0-0 Gd: 0-1 GF: - Fm: 0-1
Distance: 2m/2m3: 0-2 2m4-2m7: 0-0 3m+: 0-0
Track: LH: 0-0 RH: 0-2 Tight: 0-0 Gall: 0-0
Aids: Bl: 0-0 Vi: 0-0 Tstrap: 0-0
Best Rating: 52 5/02 Hrfd 2m1f   good NHF

Chateau Rose (IRE)
105(109h)   (107h)116

7-y-o b g Roselier (FR)-Claycastle (IRE) (Carlingford Castle)
N A Gaselee The Southern Set

Placings:30/32220-43133U   (4312)
2002/03: 22[4]GS, 26[9]HY, 23[1]S, 26[3]S, 24[3]S, 22[0]G,

	Starts	1st	2nd	3rd	Win & Pl
Hurdles	1	0	0	0	0
Chases	5	1	0	3	6937
Career Total	13	1	3	5	10393

116 1/03 Leic 2m7f110yE Ch   SFT £4192
Total win prize-money £4193

Going: Sf: 1-4 GS: 0-1 Gd: 0-1 GF: - Fm: 0-0
Distance: 2m/2m3: 0-2 2m4-2m7: 0-2 3m+: 1-4
Track: LH: 0-4 RH: 1-2 Tight: 0-2 Gall: 0-1
Aids: Bl: 0-0 Vi: 0-0 Tstrap: 0-0
Best Rating: 116 3/03 Sand 3m110y soft Ch

Modest hurdler/chaser; got off the mark when winning at Leicester in January 2003; needs soft ground; stays well.

Chater Flair
97   102

6-y-o b g Efisio-Native Flair (Be My Native (USA))
D Burchell (C J Mann 1/6) Arran Hughes

Placings:2-U20   (2499)
2002/03: 24[U]GF, 22[2]GF, 20[0]GS,

	Starts	1st	2nd	3rd	Win & Pl
Hurdles	3	0	1	0	1345
Career Total	4	0	2	0	2590

Going: Sf: 0-0 GS: 0-1 Gd: 0-0 GF: - Fm: 0-2
Distance: 2m/2m3: 0-2 2m4-2m7: 0-2 3m+: 0-1
Track: LH: 0-2 RH: 0-1 Tight: 0-2 Gall: 0-0
Aids: Bl: 0-0 Vi: 0-0 Tstrap: 0-0
Best Rating: 102 6/02 Strf 2m6f110y gd-fm Hdl

Runner-up in both completed starts over hurdles. Stays well and acts on fast ground.

Chatergold (IRE)
97(110c)   (95c)75

11-y-o b g Posen (USA)-Fiodoir (Weavers Hall)
P Wegmann P Wegmann

Placings:00P/P5P4P53/320UU26/013041U2244155/20S15 P425O6PP4-0P3044   (1058)
2002/03: 22[0]G, 20[2]GS, 20[3]G, 20[0]G, 22[4]GS, 24[4]GF,

	Starts	1st	2nd	3rd	Win & Pl
Hurdles	5	0	0	1	277
Chases	1	0	0	0	
Career Total	51	4	6	4	20629

95 7/01 Wolv 3m1f E(0-115)HCh G-F £4065
95 12/00 Folk 2m F(0-95)HCh SFT £3042
90 9/00 Font 3m2f110yE(0-105)HCh G-S £3055
79 5/00 Extr 2m3f H Ch G-F £1485
Total win prize-money £11648

Going: Sf: 0-0 GS: 0-2 Gd: 0-3 GF: - Fm: 0-1
Distance: 2m/2m3: 0-0 2m4-2m7: 0-5 3m+: 0-1
Track: LH: 0-6 RH: 0-0 Tight: 0-3 Gall: 0-0
Aids: Bl: 0-0 Vi: 0-0 Tstrap: 0-0
Best Rating: 99 4/99 Strf 3m   gd-sft Ch

A modest hurdler/chaser suited by three miles and fast ground, although handles softer.

Chauvinist (IRE)
111   145

8-y-o b g Roselier (FR)-Sacajawea (Tanfirion)
N J Henderson Mrs E Roberts & Nick Roberts

Placings:1/224-11303   (4097)
2002/03: 16[1]S, 16[1]HY, 21[3]S, 16[0]G, 16[3]G,

	Starts	1st	2nd	3rd	Win & Pl
Hurdles	5	2	0	2	75653
Career Total	9	3	2	2	83724

145 12/02 Asct 2m110y A(0-150)HHdl HVY £58000
121 11/02 Newb 2m110y D Hdl SFT £4290
118 2/01 Kemp 2m H NHF G-S £2541
Total win prize-money £64831

Going: Sf: 2-2 GS: 0-0 Gd: 0-3 GF: - Fm: 0-0
Distance: 2m/2m3: 2-4 2m4-2m7: 0-1 3m+: 0-0
Track: LH: 1-3 RH: 1-2 Tight: 0-0 Gall: 1-2
Aids: Bl: 0-0 Vi: 0-0 Tstrap: 0-0
Best Rating: 145 12/02 Asct 2m110y heavy Hdl

Very useful novice hurdler; winner of the 2002 Ladbroke Hurdle at Ascot and third in the Supreme Novices at Cheltenham; stays 2m 4f although probably best over shorter; suited by soft ground.

Chelsea Bridge (IRE)
91f   107+f

5-y-o b g Over The River (FR)-Anguillita (IRE) (King Of Clubs)
Miss H C Knight The Earl Cadogan

Placings:1   (3754)
2002/03: 16[1]G,

	Starts	1st	2nd	3rd	Win & Pl
NH Flat	1	1	0	0	3916
Career Total	1	1	0	0	3916

107 2/03 Kemp 2m H NHF GD £3916
Total win prize-money £3916

Going: Sf: 0-0 GS: 0-0 Gd: 1-1 GF: - Fm: 0-0
Distance: 2m/2m3: 1-1 2m4-2m7: 0-0 3m+: 0-0
Track: LH: 0-0 RH: 1-1 Tight: 0-0 Gall: 0-0
Aids: Bl: 0-0 Vi: 0-0 Tstrap: 0-0
Best Rating: 107 2/03 Kemp 2m   good NHF

Jumping-bred bumper performer; made a winning debut in a decent Kempton bumper in February 2003.

Chem's Truce (IRE)
103   113

6-y-o b g Brief Truce (USA)-In The Rigging (USA) (Topsider (USA))
Miss Venetia Williams O P Dakin

Placings:P60-1226   (1967)
2002/03: 16[1]G, 17[2]S, 16[2]G, 16[6]GS,

	Starts	1st	2nd	3rd	Win & Pl
Hurdles	4	1	2	0	5286
Career Total	7	1	2	0	5286

107 10/02 Hayd 2m E(0-105)HHdl   £3080
Total win prize-money £3080

Going: Sf: 0-1 GS: 0-1 Gd: 1-2 GF: - Fm: 0-0
Distance: 2m/2m3: 1-4 2m4-2m7: 0-0 3m+: 0-0
Track: LH: 1-4 RH: 0-0 Tight: 0-1 Gall: 0-0
Aids: Bl: 0-0 Vi: 0-0 Tstrap: 0-0
Best Rating: 113 11/02 Chel 2m110y gd-sft Hdl

A decent middle-distance handicapper on the Flat for William Muir, he travelled well before being pulled up on his hurdling debut when he was reported to have lost his action, but ran better next time. Winner on his return this season, he should have won next time. Possibly at his best on fast ground.

Chequered Flag
(109h)100   (101h)100

8-y-o ch m Deploy-Monza (Hotfoot)

P R Webber   Mrs D Barnett

Placings:4/46/0125420-F   (0624)
2002/03: 17FGF,

	Starts	1st	2nd	3rd	Win & Pl
Chases	1	0	0	0	
Career Total	11	1	2	0	5637
95 7/01 Wolv 2m			E Hdl		G-S £2374

Total win prize-money £2374

Going: Sf: 0-0 GS: 0-0 Gd: 0-0 GF: - Fm: 0-1
Distance: 2m/2m3: 0-1 2m4-2m7: 0-0 3m+: 0-0
Track: LH: 0-0 RH: 0-1 Tight: 0-1 Gall: 0-0
Aids: Bl: 0-0 Vi: 0-0 Tstrap: 0-0
Best Rating: 101 9/01 Bang 2m4f good Hdl

Chercher L'Amour (FR)

95   76

4-y-o b f Charnwood Forest (IRE)-Recherchee (Rainbow Quest (USA))
Mrs M Reveley (Mme C Head-Maarek 13/8) A Frame

Placings:5000   (4262)
2002/03: 16SG, 16GS, 16GS, 17GG,

	Starts	1st	2nd	3rd	Win & Pl
Hurdles	4	0	0	0	
Career Total	4	0	0	0	0

Going: Sf: 0-0 GS: 0-2 Gd: 0-2 GF: - Fm: 0-0
Distance: 2m/2m3: 0-4 2m4-2m7: 0-0 3m+: 0-0
Track: LH: 0-4 RH: 0-0 Tight: 0-1 Gall: 0-1
Aids: Bl: 0-0 Vi: 0-0 Tstrap: 0-0
Best Rating: 76 11/02 Newc 2m gd-sft Hdl

Chergan (IRE)

110   122

10-y-o b g Yashgan-Cherry Bright (IRE) (Miners Lamp)
Mrs S C Bradburne Copland, Hardie And Steel

Placings:PF3/P35042U222/23P42114P/32P62222214-51152360202   (4763)
2002/03: 16SG, 161GF, 201GF, 16GS, 242GF, 243GS, 206G, 200G, 162GF, 210G, 162G,

	Starts	1st	2nd	3rd	Win & Pl
Chases	11	2	3	1	28523
Career Total	44	5	15	5	64623
122 10/02 Weth 2m4f110yB(0-145)HCh				G-F	£10888
114 9/02 Prth 2m D(0-115)HCh				G-F	£8151
116 3/02 Hayd 2m D(0-120)HCh				GD	£7052
116 1/01 Muss 2m4f F(0-110)HCh				G-S	£4858
106 1/01 Muss 2m4f F(0-110)HCh				GD	£3601

Total win prize-money £34553

Going: Sf: 0-0 GS: 0-2 Gd: 0-5 GF: - Fm: 2-4
Distance: 2m/2m3: 1-5 2m4-2m7: 1-4 3m+: 0-2
Track: LH: 1-6 RH: 1-5 Tight: 0-4 Gall: 0-1
Aids: Bl: 0-0 Vi: 0-0 Tstrap: 0-0
Best Rating: 122 4/03 Prth 2m good Ch

Fair handicap chaser; effective at two to three miles, but is possibly best over two and a half; acts on any ground but best on a sound surface; in good form in the autumn of 2002.

Cherokee Boy

124

11-y-o gr g Mirror Boy-Cherry Side (General Ironside)
B J M Ryall Hunt & Co (bournemouth) Ltd

Placings:2433P121/62111R0/05P/11220626-PP   (0662)
2002/03: 25PGF, 32PGF,

	Starts	1st	2nd	3rd	Win & Pl
Chases	2	0	0	0	
Career Total	28	7	6	2	38233
123 5/01 Winc 3m1f110yD(0-120)HCh				G-F	£4699
117 5/01 Hrfd 3m1f110yF(0-105)HCh				GD	£3900
117 2/00 Wwck 3m5f F(0-110)HCh				GD	£3048
101 11/99 Tntn 3m3f D(0-125)HCh				GD	£6937
98 10/99 Winc 3m1f110yF(0-110)HCh				G-F	£4260
97 4/99 Font 3m2f110yE Ch				GD	£2867
87 3/99 Font 3m2f110yE Ch				G-F	£2985

Total win prize-money £28700

Going: Sf: 0-0 GS: 0-0 Gd: 0-0 GF: - Fm: 0-2
Distance: 2m/2m3: 0-0 2m4-2m7: 0-0 3m+: 0-2
Track: LH: 0-0 RH: 0-1 Tight: 0-0 Gall: 0-0
Aids: Bl: 0-0 Vi: 0-0 Tstrap: 0-0
Best Rating: 124 12/01 Extr 4m gd-sft Ch

A decent staying handicap chaser at the minor tracks. Ideally served by fast ground and a right-handed course.

Cherry Brandy

85   86

7-y-o ch g Elmaamul (USA)-Brand (Shareef Dancer (USA))
Miss H C Knight The Copper Horse Syndicate

Placings:43/1/P6   (3182)
2002/03: 19PG, 21PG,

	Starts	1st	2nd	3rd	Win & Pl
Hurdles	2	0	0	0	322
Career Total	5	1	0	1	2060
100 5/00 Worc 2m			H NHF		G-F £1519

Total win prize-money £1519

Going: Sf: 0-0 GS: 0-0 Gd: 0-2 GF: - Fm: 0-0
Distance: 2m/2m3: 0-2 2m4-2m7: 0-1 3m+: 0-0
Track: LH: 0-1 RH: 0-1 Tight: 0-0 Gall: 0-1
Aids: Bl: 0-0 Vi: 0-0 Tstrap: 0-0
Best Rating: 110 4/00 Asct 2m110y soft NHF

Cherry Gold

9-y-o b g Rakaposhi King-Merry Cherry (Deep Run)
Evan Williams R Mason

Placings:1   (4736)
2002/03: 241GF,

	Starts	1st	2nd	3rd	Win & Pl
Chases	1	1	0	0	3406
Career Total	1	1	0	0	3406
105 4/03 Chep 3m			H Ch		G-F £3406

Total win prize-money £3406

Going: Sf: 0-0 GS: 0-0 Gd: 0-0 GF: - Fm: 1-1
Distance: 2m/2m3: 0-0 2m4-2m7: 0-0 3m+: 1-1
Track: LH: 1-1 RH: 0-0 Tight: 0-0 Gall: 0-0
Aids: Bl: 0-0 Vi: 0-0 Tstrap: 0-0
Best Rating: 105 4/03 Chep 3m gd-fm Ch

Prolific winner between the flags; made a successful debut under Rules when winning the final of a point-to-point series at Chepstow April 2003; had less to do when following up at the same course next time; acts on a sound surface.

Cherry Tart (IRE)

104(104c)   (105c)100

9-y-o b m Persian Mews-Cherry Avenue (King s Ride)
R Ford A Eyres D F Price A Woods

Placings:6P3503P205/U4U1023/3112213-2613   (1530)
2002/03: 16²G, 20⁶GF, 20¹GS, 21³G,

	Starts	1st	2nd	3rd	Win & Pl
Hurdles	3	0	1	1	1580
Chases	1	1	0	0	6776
Career Total	28	5	5	6	29476
105 6/02 Prth 2m4f110yE(0-110)HCh				G-S	£6776
98 3/02 Hexm 2m110y E(0-110)HHdl				HVY	£2425
105 6/01 Prth 2m4f110yF(0-110)HCh				G-F	£5434
97 5/01 Prth 2m4f110yF(0-90)HHdl				G-F	£3262
91 1/01 Newc 2m110y E(0-105)HCh				HVY	£3061

Total win prize-money £20960

Going: Sf: 0-0 GS: 1-1 Gd: 0-2 GF: - Fm: 0-1
Distance: 2m/2m3: 0-1 2m4-2m7: 1-3 3m+: 0-0
Track: LH: 0-2 RH: 1-2 Tight: 0-1 Gall: 0-0
Aids: Bl: 0-0 Vi: 0-0 Tstrap: 0-0
Best Rating: 105 6/02 Prth 2m4f110y gd-sft Ch

Modest handicap chaser/hurdler. Effective on good/heavy. Stays 2m4f well and likes to front run.

Chesnut Wood

9-y-o ch g Tigerwood-Sally Haven (Haven)
Miss Beth Roberts Miss Beth Roberts

Placings:F   (4736)
2002/03: 24FGF,

	Starts	1st	2nd	3rd	Win & Pl
Chases	1	0	0	0	
Career Total	1	0	0	0	

Going: Sf: 0-0 GS: 0-0 Gd: 0-0 GF: - Fm: 0-1
Distance: 2m/2m3: 0-0 2m4-2m7: 0-0 3m+: 0-1
Track: LH: 0-1 RH: 0-0 Tight: 0-0 Gall: 0-0
Aids: Bl: 0-0 Vi: 0-0 Tstrap: 0-0
Best Rating: 0 4/03 Chep 3m gd-fm Ch

Chester Park

80f   53f

5-y-o ch g King s Signet (USA)-Good Skills (Bustino)
K Bishop K Bishop

Placings:0   (4628)
2002/03: 17OGF,

	Starts	1st	2nd	3rd	Win & Pl
NH Flat	1	0	0	0	
Career Total	1	0	0	0	

Going: Sf: 0-0 GS: 0-0 Gd: 0-0 GF: - Fm: 0-1
Distance: 2m/2m3: 0-1 2m4-2m7: 0-0 3m+: 0-0
Track: LH: 0-1 RH: 0-0 Tight: 0-1 Gall: 0-0
Aids: Bl: 0-0 Vi: 0-0 Tstrap: 0-0
Best Rating: 53 4/03 NAbb 2m1f gd-fm NHF

Chevalier Bayard (IRE)

105   91

10-y-o br g Strong Gale-Flying Pegus (Beau Chapeau)
J R Adam James R Adam

Placings:06P/0433F/32/260/36U-2412031346   (4393)
2002/03: 22²GF, 24⁴GF, 21¹G, 20²GF, 20⁰G, 20³S, 20¹G, 20³G, 19⁴G, 20⁶G,

	Starts	1st	2nd	3rd	Win & Pl
Chases	10	2	2	2	11952
Career Total	26	2	4	6	16520

91   1/03   Muss   2m4f   E(0-110)HCh   GD   £4686
89   9/02   Sthl   2m5f110y   F(0-95)HCh
GD   £3459

Total win prize-money £8146

Going:	Sf: 0-1 GS: 0-0 Gd: 2-6 GF: - Fm: 0-3
Distance:	2m/2m3: 0-1 **2m4-2m7: 2-8** 3m+: 0-1
Track:	LH: 1-5 RH: 1-5 **Tight: 1-3** Gall: 0-2
Aids:	Bl: 1-2 Vi: 1-6 Tstrap: 0-0
Best Rating:	96 12/00 Donc 2m110y heavy Ch

Modest handicap chaser; has been lightly raced over the last couple of seasons, but managed to make all to win a terrible race at Southwell in September and won again at Musselburgh in January; best trip seems to be around two and a half miles and suited by a sound surface.

Chevalier Errant (IRE)

109   119

10-y-o b g Strong Gale-Luminous Run (Deep Run)
J R Adam   James R Adam

Placings:0531/235**3**335**32**/24114326/11B-1U05F605

(3846)
2002/03: 21¹¹GF, 20¹¹UGd, 24⁰F, 24⁵GF, 20⁵GS, 20⁶GS, 24⁰G, 24⁵G,

	Starts	1st	2nd	3rd	Win & Pl
Chases	8	1	0		10859
Career Total	32	6	4	7	54962
128	6/02	Strf		2m5f110yB(0-140)HCh	G-F	£10108
128	6/01	MRas		2m4f	C(0-135)HCh	G-F	£10476
128	6/01	Strf		2m1f110yC(0-135)HCh	G-F	£6864
120	12/00	Donc		2m110y	C(0-130)HCh	HVY	£6022
119	11/00	Ayr		2m	C(0-130)HCh	SFT	£6118
102	4/99	Kels		2m110y	E Hdl	G-S	£3025

Total win prize-money £42615

Going:	Sf: 0-0 GS: 0-2 Gd: 0-2 GF: - Fm: 1-4
Distance:	2m/2m3: 0-0 **2m4-2m7: 1-4** 3m+: 0-4
Track:	**LH: 1-4** RH: 0-4 Tight: 1-3 Gall: 0-2
Aids:	Bl: 0-0 Vi: 0-0 Tstrap: 0-0
Best Rating:	128 6/02 Strf 2m5f110y gd-fm Ch

Useful handicap chaser at his best; stays two and three quarter miles; acts on good/good to firm ground.

Chevet Boy (IRE)

5-y-o b g Welsh Term-Sizzle (High Line)
J Howard Johnson   D M Gibbons

Placings:F

(4225)
2002/03: 20⁰GF,

	Starts	1st	2nd	3rd	Win & Pl
Hurdles	1	0	0	0	
Career Total	1	0	0	0	

Going:	Sf: 0-0 GS: 0-0 Gd: 0-0 GF: - Fm: 0-1
Distance:	2m/2m3: 0-0 2m4-2m7: 0-1 3m+: 0-0
Track:	LH: 0-1 RH: 0-0 Tight: 0-0 Gall: 0-0
Aids:	Bl: 0-0 Vi: 0-0 Tstrap: 0-0
Best Rating:	0 3/03 Weth 2m4f110y gd-fm Hdl

Chevet Girl (IRE)

106   (102c)116

8-y-o ch m Roselier (FR)-Vulcash (IRE) (Callernish)
J Howard Johnson   D M Gibbons

Placings:0663/5115510-1PF003

(4663)
2002/03: 16¹G, 16PGS, 16²G, 16⁰GF, 16⁰G, 17³GF,

	Starts	1st	2nd	3rd	Win & Pl
Hurdles	5	1	0	1	3774
Chases	1	0	0	0	0
Career Total	17	4	0	2	13153
116	11/02	Weth	2m	E(0-110)HHdl	GD	£3066
99	4/02	Kels	2m110y	D(0-125)HHdl	G-F	£3591
103	11/01	Weth	2m	E(0-105)HHdl	GD	£3052
85	10/01	Carl	2m1f	E(0-115)HHdl	G-S	£2441

Total win prize-money £12151

Going:	Sf: 0-0 GS: 0-1 Gd: 1-3 GF: - Fm: 0-2
Distance:	**2m/2m3: 1-6** 2m4-2m7: 0-0 3m+: 0-0
Track:	**LH: 1-3** RH: 0-3 Tight: 0-2 Gall: 0-1
Aids:	Bl: 0-0 Vi: 0-0 Tstrap: 0-0
Best Rating:	116 11/02 Weth 2m good Hdl

Modest handicap hurdler; best over two miles on a sound surface; fell on her chasing debut; goes well fresh.

Cheyenne Chief

102   95d

4-y-o b c Be My Chief (USA)-Cartuccia (IRE) (Doyoun)
G M Moore   John Lishman

Placings:524F1440P

(4228)
2002/03: 17⁵G, 17²GF, 17⁴G, 20²GF, 16¹S, 16⁴GS, 16⁴HY, 24⁰G, 25PGF,

	Starts	1st	2nd	3rd	Win & Pl
Hurdles	9	1	1	0	4874
Career Total	9	1	1	0	4874
96	11/02	Newc	2m	E Hdl	SFT	£3423

Total win prize-money £3423

Going:	Sf: 1-2 GS: 0-1 Gd: 0-3 GF: - Fm: 0-3
Distance:	**2m/2m3: 1-6** 2m4-2m7: 0-1 3m+: 0-2
Track:	**LH: 1-7** RH: 0-2 Tight: 0-0 Gall: 1-2
Aids:	Bl: 0-1 Vi: 0-0 Tstrap: 0-0
Best Rating:	96 11/02 Newc 2m soft Hdl

Slow maiden on the Flat and took a modest juvenile hurdle at Newcastle in November.

Chicago Bulls (IRE)

106   126

5-y-o b g Darshaan-Celestial Melody (USA) (The Minstrel (CAN))
A King   Mrs Mark Powell

Placings:54455110-232400

(4112)
2002/03: 20²S, 22³S, 20²S, 20⁴GS, 22⁰HY, 21⁰G,

	Starts	1st	2nd	3rd	Win & Pl
Hurdles	6	0	2	1	15272
Career Total	14	2	2	1	22193
120	3/02	Ludl	2m5f	E Hdl	SFT	£3125
113	2/02	Donc	2m4f	E Hdl	SFT	£3164

Total win prize-money £6290

Going:	Sf: 0-4 GS: 0-1 Gd: 0-1 GF: - Fm: 0-0
Distance:	2m/2m3: 0-0 2m4-2m7: 0-6 3m+: 0-0
Track:	LH: 0-5 RH: 0-1 Tight: 0-0 Gall: 0-1
Aids:	Bl: 0-0 Vi: 0-0 Tstrap: 0-0
Best Rating:	126 1/03 Hayd 2m4f gd-sft Hdl

Fair hurdler, twice successful in staying juvenile hurdles in the spring of 2002; promising reappearance when second on handicap debut in Tote Silver Trophy at Chepstow in November and has continued to run well since; stays two miles six; acts on soft ground.

Chicuelo (FR)

111(97h)   (96h)146

7-y-o b g Mansonnien (FR)-Dovapas (FR) (Paseo (FR))
M C Pipe   Mrs Belinda Harvey

Placings:03/512F023/222433210/225025-1P11P01 (4389)
2002/03: 20¹GS, 20PGS, 19¹GS, 24¹S, 24PG, 21⁰G, 25¹F,

	Starts	1st	2nd	3rd	Win & Pl
Hurdles	1	0	0	0	
Chases	6	4	0	0	63448
Career Total	31	6	9	4	207700
146	3/03	Extr		3m1f110yD Ch	FRM	£7046
143	1/03	Hntg	3m	E Ch	SFT	£5208
141	12/02	Asct		2m3f110yB(0-140)HCh	G-S	£13494
146	7/02	MRas	2m4f	B(0-140)HCh	G-S	£37700
	4/01	Autl	2m2f	Hdl	HVY	£14549
	7/99	Autl	1m1f110y	Hdl	HLD	£10764

Total win prize-money £88761

Going:	Sf: 1-1 GS: 2-3 Gd: 0-2 GF: - Fm: 1-1
Distance:	2m/2m3: 0-0 2m4-2m7: 2-4 3m+: 2-3
Track:	LH: 0-2 **RH: 4-5** Tight: 1-1 Gall: 1-3
Aids:	Bl: 0-0 Vi: 0-0 **Tstrap: 4-7**
Best Rating:	146 3/03 Extr 3m1f110y firm Ch

Very useful chaser; ex-French; effective from two and a half to three miles; appears to handle all types of going; suited by flat tracks; sometimes makes mistakes and has disappointed in both the Thomas Pink and Racing Post Trophy last season; won four runner extended three mile novices chase at Exeter March 2003; suited by small fields and going right-handed; usually wears a visor.

Chief Cashier

112   126

8-y-o b g Persian Bold-Kentfield (Busted)
G B Balding   The Tachyarrhythmias

Placings:404/45/32641105014

(4608)
2002/03: 16³GS, 16²GS, 16⁶S, 16⁴S, 16¹S, 16¹GS, 17⁰GS, 16⁵G, 16⁰S, 16¹G, 17⁴G,

	Starts	1st	2nd	3rd	Win & Pl
Hurdles	11	3	1	1	21137
Career Total	16	3	1	1	23489
126	4/03	Ludl		D(0-125)HHdl	GD	£5850
119	1/03	Winc	2m	D(0-125)HHdl	G-S	£6496
110	1/03	Ludl	2m	E(0-105)HHdl	SFT	£3896

Total win prize-money £16243

Going:	Sf: 1-4 GS: 1-4 Gd: 1-3 GF: - Fm: 0-0
Distance:	**2m/2m3: 3-11** 2m4-2m7: 0-0 3m+: 0-0
Track:	LH: 0-4 **RH: 3-7** Tight: 0-0 Gall: 0-3
Aids:	Bl: 0-0 Vi: 0-0 Tstrap: 0-0
Best Rating:	126 4/03 Ludl 2m good Hdl

Decent hurdler; acts with give in the ground and on a sound surface; looks best over two miles on a sharp track.

Chief Chippie

81(105h)   (78h)63

10-y-o b g Mandalus-Little Katrina (Little Buskins)
P Needham   P Needham

Placings:00P0/P03PP00/**P53P0U5PP**/453P5304P/00/P461
PP56-5P6

(0619)
2002/03: 23⁶G, 25PGF, 25⁵GF,

	Starts	1st	2nd	3rd	Win & Pl
Chases	3	0	0	0	
Career Total	42	1	0	4	4072
78	12/01	Catt	2m3f	F(0-100)HHdl	GD	£2023

Total win prize-money £2023

Going:	Sf: 0-0 GS: 0-0 Gd: 0-1 GF: - Fm: 0-2
Distance:	2m/2m3: 0-0 2m4-2m7: 0-0 3m+: 0-3
Track:	LH: 0-2 RH: 0-0 Tight: 0-0 Gall: 0-0
Aids:	Bl: 0-0 Vi: 0-0 Tstrap: 0-0
Best Rating:	90 2/00 Carl 2m4f110y heavy Hdl

Chief Monte (IRE)
90(76h)   (67h)60+
8-y-o b g Montelimar (USA)-Giollaretta (Giolla Mear)
Mrs S J Smith J Henderson (co Durham)

Placings:00/P0-465P   (2102)
2002/03: 19⁴GF, 25⁵GF, 16⁵S, 16⁶G,

	Starts	1st	2nd	3rd	Win & Pl
Hurdles	2	0	0	0	0
Chases	2	0	0	0	
Career Total	8	0	0	0	

Going:	Sf: 0-1 GS: 0-0 Gd: 0-1 GF: - Fm: 0-2
Distance:	2m/2m3: 0-2 2m4-2m7: 0-1 3m+: 0-1
Track:	LH: 0-2 RH: 0-2 Tight: 0-2 Gall: 0-0
Aids:	Bl: 0-0 Vi: 0-0 Tstrap: 0-0
Best Rating:	68 10/02 Carl 2m soft Ch

Chief Mouse
99   (63h)70
10-y-o b g Be My Chief (USA)-Top Mouse (High Top)
B D Leavy J A Provan

Placings:12106P111/5634030/P05424310000/PU155/3313
21/P-035063   (1217)
2002/03: 20⁰GS, 20³GF, 24⁵GF, 24⁹GF, 21⁶GF, 26³G,

	Starts	1st	2nd	3rd	Win & Pl
Hurdles	1	0	0	0	0
Chases	5	0	0	2	1251
Career Total	46	9	3	8	42465
104	7/00	Strf	3m	D(0-120)HCh	G-F	£4810
101	6/00	Uttx	2m	D(0-120)HCh	G-F	£3692
89	10/99	Ludl	2m4f	D(0-110)HCh	G-F	£4162
90	9/98	Bang	2m4f	E(0-110)HHdl	GD	£3631
108	4/97	Asct	2m110y	D(0-110)HHdl	G-F	£3420
108	4/97	Chel	2m4f110yC HHdl		G-F	£4788
90	3/97	Ludl	2m	F Hdl	G-F	£2094
106	11/96	MRas	2m1f110yD Hdl		GD	£3148
88	8/96	Hrfd	2m1f	E Hdl	G-F	£2444
				Total win prize-money £32190

Going:	Sf: 0-0 GS: 0-0 Gd: 0-1 GF: - Fm: 0-4
Distance:	2m/2m3: 0-0 2m4-2m7: 0-3 3m+: 0-3
Track:	LH: 0-6 RH: 0-0 Tight: 0-2 Gall: 0-0
Aids:	Bl: 0-0 Vi: 0-0 Tstrap: 0-1
Best Rating:	109 1/97 Tntn 2m1f good Hdl

Regressive handicap chaser. Acts on good and good to firm ground, he is effective from two miles to three miles.

Chief Witness (IRE)
102   121+
7-y-o b g Witness Box (USA)-Rosies Sister (IRE) (Deep Run)
Noel T Chance Michael French

Placings:111   (4153)
2002/03: 23¹S, 22¹GS, 25¹G,

	Starts	1st	2nd	3rd	Win & Pl
Hurdles	3	3	0	0	10536
Career Total	3	3	0	0	10536
114	3/03	Wwck	3m1f	E Hdl	GD	£3738
118	2/03	Font	2m6f110yE Hdl		G-S	£4173
124	1/03	Fknm	2m7f110yF Hdl		SFT	£2625
				Total win prize-money £10536

Going:	Sf: 1-1 GS: 1-1 Gd: 1-1 GF: - Fm: 0-0
Distance:	2m/2m3: 0-0 2m4-2m7: 1-1 3m+: 2-2
Track:	LH: 3-3 RH: 0-0 Tight: 2-2 Gall: 0-0
Aids:	Bl: 0-0 Vi: 0-0 Tstrap: 0-0
Best Rating:	124 1/03 Fknm 2m7f110y soft Hdl

Fair novice hurdler, winning all three of his starts; stays three miles; best on soft ground; looks a useful novice chaser in the making.

Chieftain's Crown (USA)
83   64
12-y-o ch g Chief s Crown (USA)-Simple Taste (USA) (Sharpen Up)
Mrs H M Bridges Mrs H M Bridges

Placings:5P2111/6564/1244/P-50   (0192)
2002/03: 20⁵GF, 21⁰GF,

	Starts	1st	2nd	3rd	Win & Pl
Hurdles	2	0	0	0	0
Career Total	17	4	2	0	10986
94	5/97	Font	2m2f110yE(0-110)HHdl	G-F	£2241
95	5/96	Plum	2m4f	E(0-115)HHdl	FRM	£2259
95	4/96	Plum	2m4f	E(0-110)HHdl	FRM	£2574
95	4/96	Plum	2m4f	E Hdl	G-F	£2490
				Total win prize-money £9565

Going:	Sf: 0-0 GS: 0-0 Gd: 0-0 GF: - Fm: 0-2
Distance:	2m/2m3: 0-0 2m4-2m7: 0-2 3m+: 0-0
Track:	LH: 0-0 RH: 0-1 Tight: 0-1 Gall: 0-1
Aids:	Bl: 0-0 Vi: 0-0 Tstrap: 0-0
Best Rating:	95 5/96 Plum 2m4f firm Hdl

Chili Pepper
62   24
6-y-o gr m Chilibang-Game Germaine (Mummy s Game)
P R Wood Mrs R Auchterlounie

Placings:P0PP   (3814)
2002/03: 16⁵S, 17⁰HY, 16⁶G, 16⁶G,

	Starts	1st	2nd	3rd	Win & Pl
Hurdles	4	0	0	0	0
Career Total	4	0	0	0	0

Going:	Sf: 0-2 GS: 0-0 Gd: 0-2 GF: - Fm: 0-0
Distance:	2m/2m3: 0-0 2m4-2m7: 0-0 3m+: 0-0
Track:	LH: 0-4 RH: 0-0 Tight: 0-3 Gall: 0-0
Aids:	Bl: 0-0 Vi: 0-0 Tstrap: 0-0
Best Rating:	24 1/03 Sedg 2m1f heavy Hdl

Chilli Jo
83   60
11-y-o b g Latest Model-Arctic Caper (Pardigras)
D D Scott Mrs M Fooks

Placings:PP/P-PP60R   (0850)
2002/03: 23⁵G, 16⁵S, 16⁶GF, 21⁰GF, 16⁶GF,

	Starts	1st	2nd	3rd	Win & Pl
Chases	5	0	0	0	0
Career Total	8	0	0	0	0

Going:	Sf: 0-1 GS: 0-0 Gd: 0-1 GF: - Fm: 0-3
Distance:	2m/2m3: 0-3 2m4-2m7: 0-1 3m+: 0-1
Track:	LH: 0-4 RH: 0-1 Tight: 0-4 Gall: 0-0
Aids:	Bl: 0-0 Vi: 0-0 Tstrap: 0-0
Best Rating:	60 6/02 NAbb 2m110y gd-fm Ch

Chinese Cracker
5-y-o b g King s Signet (USA)-Heart Broken (Bustino)
J R Norton Michael Ng

Placings:P   (2517)
2002/03: 16²PS,

	Starts	1st	2nd	3rd	Win & Pl
Hurdles	1	0	0	0	
Career Total	1	0	0	0	

Going:	Sf: 0-1 GS: 0-0 Gd: 0-0 GF: - Fm: 0-0
Distance:	2m/2m3: 0-1 2m4-2m7: 0-0 3m+: 0-0
Track:	LH: 0-1 RH: 0-0 Tight: 0-0 Gall: 0-1
Aids:	Bl: 0-0 Vi: 0-0 Tstrap: 0-0
Best Rating:	0 12/02 Newc 2m soft Hdl

Chives (IRE)
123   164
8-y-o b g Good Thyne (USA)-Chatty Actress (Le Bavard (FR))
Miss H C Knight Trevor Hemmings

Placings:15/11/31F133-2220P   (4479)
2002/03: 24²S, 29²HY, 24²G, 26³G, 36P G,

	Starts	1st	2nd	3rd	Win & Pl
Chases	5	0	3	0	43400
Career Total	15	5	3	3	76565
133	2/02	Winc	3m1f110yD Ch		SFT	£4368
126	12/01	Strf	3m	D Ch	SFT	£5154
130	11/00	Kemp	2m5f	D Hdl	SFT	£3753
105	10/00	Hrfd	2m1f	E Hdl	GD	£2684
116	2/00	Sand	2m110y	H NHF	SFT	£1746
				Total win prize-money £17709

Going:	Sf: 0-2 GS: 0-0 Gd: 0-3 GF: - Fm: 0-0
Distance:	2m/2m3: 0-0 2m4-2m7: 0-0 3m+: 0-5
Track:	LH: 0-5 RH: 0-0 Tight: 0-1 Gall: 0-2
Aids:	Bl: 0-0 Vi: 0-0 Tstrap: 0-0
Best Rating:	164 12/02 Chep 3m5f110y heavy Ch

High-class staying chaser; scored twice over fences in the 2001/2002 in season and ran a blinder to finish third in the Royal & SunAlliance Chase at the Festival; runner-up in his first two starts of this term, including under a big weight in the Welsh National; faded into seventh in the Cheltenham Gold Cup; blundered badly early on and broke a blood vessel when soon pulled up in the Grand National; suited by soft and heavy ground; stays at least 3m 5f; honest and genuine.

Chivite (IRE)
104   111+
4-y-o b g Alhaarth (IRE)-Laura Margaret (Persian Bold)
K R Burke (Mrs A J Perrett 4/10) I Russell

Placings:023   (4148)
2002/03: 16⁰G, 16²GS, 16³G,

	Starts	1st	2nd	3rd	Win & Pl
Hurdles	3	0	1	1	1620
Career Total	3	0	1	1	1620

Going:	Sf: 0-0 GS: 0-1 Gd: 0-2 GF: - Fm: 0-0
Distance:	2m/2m3: 0-3 2m4-2m7: 0-0 3m+: 0-0
Track:	LH: 0-2 RH: 0-1 Tight: 0-2 Gall: 0-0
Aids:	Bl: 0-0 Vi: 0-0 Tstrap: 0-0
Best Rating:	97 3/03 Kels 2m110y gd-sft Hdl

Appreciated longer trip and showed improved form when winning 2m 5f novice hurdle at Huntingdon May 2003; easy task when wide margin winner of a poor event at Uttoxeter in July; acts on fast ground.

Chivvy Charver (IRE)

69 76

6-y-o ch g Commanche Run-Claddagh Pride (Bargello)
G A Swinbank Ward And Gartzen

Placings:*46-*00P (0418)
2002/03: 16^{0}G, 20^{0}G, 22^{P}HY,

	Starts	1st	2nd	3rd	Win & Pl
Hurdles	3	0	0	0	
Career Total	**5**	**0**	**0**	**0**	**0**

Going: Sf: 0-1 GS: 0-0 Gd: 0-2 GF: - Fm: 0-0
Distance: 2m/2m3: 0-1 2m4-2m7: 0-2 3m+: 0-0
Track: LH: 0-3 RH: 0-0 Tight: 0-1 Gall: 0-0
Aids: Bl: 0-0 Vi: 0-0 Tstrap: 0-0
Best Rating: **89** 4/02 Carl 2m1f good NHF

Cho Polu (IRE)

99 106

6-y-o ch g Un Desperado (FR)-Rainbow Alliance (IRE) (Golden Love)
P J Hobbs M J Tuckey

Placings:*0-*25220 (3282)
2002/03: 17^{2}G, 21^{5}GS, 16^{2}S, 17^{2}S, 17^{0}GS,

	Starts	1st	2nd	3rd	Win & Pl
Hurdles	5	0	3	0	6119
Career Total	**6**	**0**	**3**	**0**	**6119**

Going: Sf: 0-2 GS: 0-2 Gd: 0-1 GF: - Fm: 0-0
Distance: 2m/2m3: 0-4 2m4-2m7: 0-1 3m+: 0-0
Track: LH: 0-3 RH: 0-2 Tight: 0-0 Gall: 0-2
Aids: Bl: 0-2 Vi: 0-0 Tstrap: 0-0
Best Rating: **106** 12/02 Chel 2m1f soft Hdl

Fair novice hurdle, but not an easy ride.

Chocolate Soldier (IRE)

106f 91f

5-y-o ch g Mister Lord (USA)-Traditional Lady (Carlingford Castle)
T P Tate T P Tate

Placings:*05* (4594)
2002/03: 16^{0}G, 16^{5}G,

	Starts	1st	2nd	3rd	Win & Pl
NH Flat	2	0	0	0	0
Career Total	**2**	**0**	**0**	**0**	**0**

Going: Sf: 0-0 GS: 0-0 Gd: 0-2 GF: - Fm: 0-0
Distance: 2m/2m3: 0-2 2m4-2m7: 0-0 3m+: 0-0
Track: LH: 0-2 RH: 0-0 Tight: 0-0 Gall: 0-0
Aids: Bl: 0-0 Vi: 0-0 Tstrap: 0-0
Best Rating: **72** 4/03 Hexm 2m110y good NHF

Moderate performer; showed signs of temperament in point-to-points; made all in a poor bumper at Sedgefield in July; handles fast ground.

Choice Cut (IRE)

10-y-o b g Tirol-Lancette (Double Jump)
T H Caldwell T H Caldwell

Placings:*305/335426/21U0/5/P* (3952)
2002/03: 23^{P}GS,

	Starts	1st	2nd	3rd	Win & Pl
Chases	1	0	0	0	
Career Total	**15**	**1**	**2**	**3**	**5127**

95	6/99	Uttx	3m110y	E Hdl	GD	£2389

Total win prize-money £2390

Going: Sf: 0-0 GS: 0-1 Gd: 0-0 GF: - Fm: 0-0
Distance: 2m/2m3: 0-0 2m4-2m7: 0-0 3m+: 0-1
Track: LH: 0-0 RH: 0-1 Tight: 0-0 Gall: 0-0
Aids: Bl: 0-0 Vi: 0-0 Tstrap: 0-0
Best Rating: **106** 4/99 Carl 2m4f110y good Hdl

Choisty (IRE)

99 91

13-y-o ch g Callernish-Rosemount Rose (Ashmore (FR))
H E Haynes H Edward Haynes

Placings:5C32/2UF11U/F1FP/4PR041U1/22142F/0/PPP21 P3-P4 (4057)
2002/03: 24^{P}GS, 29^{4}GS,

	Starts	1st	2nd	3rd	Win & Pl
Hurdles	1	0	0	0	0
Chases	1	0	0	0	530
Career Total	**38**	**7**	**6**	**2**	**59366**

120	3/02	Wwck	3m5f	C(0-135)HCh	GD	£6857
135	1/00	Wwck	3m5f	B(0-145)HCh	SFT	£14014
126	5/99	Hrfd	3m1f110y	E(0-115)HCh	GD	£3525
131	3/99	Chep	3m	D(0-120)HCh	G-S	£7002
123	3/98	Wwck	3m5f	C(0-135)HCh	SFT	£8550
117	1/97	Weth	3m1f	E Ch	GD	£3077
108	1/97	Carl	3m	D Ch	GD	£3842

Total win prize-money £46871

Going: Sf: 0-0 GS: 0-2 Gd: 0-0 GF: - Fm: 0-0
Distance: 2m/2m3: 0-0 2m4-2m7: 0-0 3m+: 0-2
Track: LH: 0-2 RH: 0-0 Tight: 0-0 Gall: 0-0
Aids: Bl: 0-0 Vi: 0-0 Tstrap: 0-0
Best Rating: **135** 3/00 Wwck 3m5f soft Ch

He has enjoyed a fair amount of success in staying handicap chases over the years, but did not take to Aintree when tried in three consecutive Grand Nationals, falling twice and unseating once. Showed his first form for nearly two years when second at Warwick in February 2002 and took the Warwick National for the second time in five years.

Chop-Chop (IRE)

88 84

9-y-o b/br g Be My Native (USA)-Arctic Bavard (Le Bavard (FR))
D C Turner Mrs M E Turner

Placings:*0/P/0PPU4650/030400P3-3PF6* (1545)
2002/03: 17^{3}GF, 17^{P}G, 17^{F}F, 17^{6}F,

	Starts	1st	2nd	3rd	Win & Pl
Hurdles	4	0	0	1	315
Career Total	**22**	**0**	**0**	**3**	**1624**

Going: Sf: 0-0 GS: 0-0 Gd: 0-1 GF: - Fm: 0-3
Distance: 2m/2m3: 0-4 2m4-2m7: 0-0 3m+: 0-0
Track: LH: 0-2 RH: 0-2 Tight: 0-3 Gall: 0-0
Aids: Bl: 0-0 Vi: 0-0 Tstrap: 0-4
Best Rating: **90** 10/00 Extr 2m1f good Hdl

Chopneyev (FR)

114 145

5-y-o b g Goldneyev (USA)-Pierre De Soleil (FR) (Jefferson (ZIM))
R T Phillips Mrs Claire Smith

Placings:20-211120 (4102)
2002/03: 20^{2}HY, 20^{1}S, 24^{1}HY, 22^{1}HY, 20^{2}S, 25^{0}G,

	Starts	1st	2nd	3rd	Win & Pl
Hurdles	6	3	2	0	58183
Career Total	**8**	**3**	**3**	**0**	**59283**

131	2/03	Sand	2m6f	A HHdl	HVY	£34800
126	1/03	Ayr	3m110y	D Hdl	HVY	£4764
124	12/02	Uttx	2m4f110y	D(0-120)HHdl	SFT	£6760

Total win prize-money £46325

Going: Sf: 3-5 GS: 0-0 Gd: 0-1 GF: - Fm: 0-0
Distance: 2m/2m3: 0-0 **2m4-2m7: 2-4** 3m+: 1-2
Track: **LH: 2-4** RH: 1-2 Tight: 0-0 Gall: 0-1
Aids: Bl: 0-0 Vi: 0-0 Tstrap: 0-0
Best Rating: **145** 2/03 Asct 2m4f soft Hdl

Useful, progressive staying novice hurdler; good second in competitive handicap at Ascot in February a fair representation of his ability; stays 3m; prefers testing conditions.

Chopwell Fabrics (IRE)

66 36

5-y-o b g Thatching-Maridana (USA) (Nijinsky (CAN))
J Howard Johnson Durham Drapes Ltd

Placings:PP-50P0 (2301)
2002/03: 16^{5}GF, 17^{0}G, 27^{P}S, 16^{0}GS,

	Starts	1st	2nd	3rd	Win & Pl
Hurdles	4	0	0	0	0
Career Total	**6**	**0**	**0**	**0**	**0**

Going: Sf: 0-1 GS: 0-1 Gd: 0-1 GF: - Fm: 0-1
Distance: 2m/2m3: 0-3 2m4-2m7: 0-0 3m+: 0-1
Track: LH: 0-4 RH: 0-0 Tight: 0-3 Gall: 0-0
Aids: Bl: 0-0 Vi: 0-0 Tstrap: 0-0
Best Rating: **38** 10/02 Sedg 2m1f good Hdl

Chotapeg

6-y-o b g Sulaafah (USA)-Totally Tiddly (French Vine)
P Wegmann (J A Moore 31/10) P Wegmann

Placings:*0*PP0 (4086)
2002/03: 17^{0}G, 17^{P}G, 16^{P}G, 19^{0}GS,

	Starts	1st	2nd	3rd	Win & Pl
NH Flat	2	0	0	0	0
Hurdles	2	0	0	0	0
Career Total	**4**	**0**	**0**	**0**	

Going: Sf: 0-0 GS: 0-1 Gd: 0-3 GF: - Fm: 0-0
Distance: 2m/2m3: 0-4 2m4-2m7: 0-0 3m+: 0-0
Track: LH: 0-3 RH: 0-1 Tight: 0-3 Gall: 0-1
Aids: Bl: 0-0 Vi: 0-0 Tstrap: 0-0
Best Rating: **0** 3/03 Strf 2m3f gd-sft Hdl

Chris And Ryan (IRE)

70f 46f

5-y-o b g Goldmark (USA)-Beautyofthepeace (IRE) (Exactly Sharp (USA))
R Allan Ian R Flannigan

Placings:*0* (1309)
2002/03: 16^{0}GF,

	Starts	1st	2nd	3rd	Win & Pl
NH Flat	1	0	0	0	

Career Total   1   0   0   0

Going:	Sf: 0-0 GS: 0-0 Gd: 0-0 GF: - Fm: 0-1
Distance:	2m/2m3: 0-1 2m4-2m7: 0-0 3m+: 0-0
Track:	LH: 0-0 RH: 0-1 Tight: 0-0 Gall: 0-0
Aids:	Bl: 0-0 Vi: 0-0 Tstrap: 0-0
Best Rating:	49 9/02 Prth 2m110y gd-fm NHF

Christmas Truce (IRE)
94   85

4-y-o b g Brief Truce (USA)-Superflash (Superlative)
M H Tompkins Raceworld

Placings: 4   (4156)
2002/03: 17⁴G,

	Starts	1st	2nd	3rd	Win & Pl
Hurdles	1	0	0	0	372
Career Total	1	0	0	0	372

Going:	Sf: 0-0 GS: 0-0 Gd: 0-1 GF: - Fm: 0-0
Distance:	2m/2m3: 0-1 2m4-2m7: 0-0 3m+: 0-0
Track:	LH: 0-0 RH: 0-1 Tight: 0-1 Gall: 0-0
Aids:	Bl: 0-0 Vi: 0-0 Tstrap: 0-0
Best Rating:	85 3/03 MRas 2m1f110y good Hdl

Fair middle-distance handicapper on the Flat; laboured fourth in ordinary juvenile hurdle at Market Rasen in March.

Christopher
105   116

6-y-o gr g Arzanni-Forest Nymph (NZ) (Oak Ridge (FR))
P J Hobbs Allan Stennett

Placings: 10263-114F0   (2199)
2002/03: 17¹G, 20¹G, 20⁴G, 21ᶠG, 19⁰GS,

	Starts	1st	2nd	3rd	Win & Pl
Hurdles	5	2	0	0	5916
Career Total	10	3	1	1	9256
116 5/02 Uttx	2m4f110y			E Hdl	GD £2667
112 5/02 Extr	2m1f			E Hdl	GD £2856
101 5/01 Hrfd	2m1f			H NHF	GD £1956

Total win prize-money £7480

Bumper winner, appreciated a sound surface when winning a novices hurdle at Exeter May 2002. Followed up at Uttoxeter, acts on good ground, stays two and a half miles. Should progress to better things.

Christy Jnr (IRE)
88(90h)   (67h)52

9-y-o b g Andretti-Rare Currency (Rarity)
C J Teague Mrs J H Burn

Placings: 0/00/0045   (4710)
2002/03: 17⁰G, 20⁰S, 24⁴GF, 23⁵GF,

	Starts	1st	2nd	3rd	Win & Pl
Hurdles	4	0	0	0	0
Career Total	7	0	0	0	0

Going:	Sf: 0-1 GS: 0-0 Gd: 0-1 GF: - Fm: 0-2
Distance:	2m/2m3: 0-1 2m4-2m7: 0-2 3m+: 0-1
Track:	LH: 0-4 RH: 0-0 Tight: 0-2 Gall: 0-1

Aids: Bl: 0-0 Vi: 0-0 Tstrap: 0-0
Best Rating: 79   4/99   Clon   2m4f   heavy   Hdl

Christy's Pride (IRE)
83(97h)   (109h)101

11-y-o ch m Kambalda-Caddy Shack (Precipice Wood)
C Weedon Bill Hinge

Placings: 05/512321/P4-40   (4113)
2002/03: 20⁴GS, 32⁰G,

	Starts	1st	2nd	3rd	Win & Pl
Chases	2	0	0	0	438
Career Total	12	2	2	1	12896
109 4/01 Asct	3m		C(0-135)HHdl	HVY	£6288
104 1/01 Font	2m6f110yF(0-90)HHdl			SFT	£2562

Total win prize-money £8851

Going:	Sf: 0-0 GS: 0-1 Gd: 0-1 GF: - Fm: 0-0
Distance:	2m/2m3: 0-0 2m4-2m7: 0-1 3m+: 0-1
Track:	LH: 0-1 RH: 0-1 Tight: 0-1 Gall: 0-1
Aids:	Bl: 0-0 Vi: 0-0 Tstrap: 0-0
Best Rating:	109 4/01 Asct 3m heavy Hdl

Chunito
93   49

8-y-o b g Beveled (USA)-Wasimah (Caerleon (USA))
D M Lloyd D M Lloyd

Placings: 240000/6/4454/P-00P   (4706)
2002/03: 16⁰GS, 24⁰F, 20ᵖG,

	Starts	1st	2nd	3rd	Win & Pl
Hurdles	3	0	0	0	
Career Total	15	0	1	0	598

Going:	Sf: 0-0 GS: 0-1 Gd: 0-1 GF: - Fm: 0-1
Distance:	2m/2m3: 0-1 2m4-2m7: 0-1 3m+: 0-1
Track:	LH: 0-2 RH: 0-1 Tight: 0-1 Gall: 0-0
Aids:	Bl: 0-0 Vi: 0-0 Tstrap: 0-0
Best Rating:	90 9/98 NAbb 2m1f gd-fm Hdl

Churchtown Glen (IRE)
100(89h)   (78h)88

10-y-o b/br g Be My Native (USA)-Hill Side Glen (Goldhill)
Ian Williams C J Tipton

Placings: 0163533/130115002/533133334P/P233F050P/31 PP26-54654   (4349)
2002/03: 25⁵GF, 25⁴S, 23⁶G, 24⁵G, 24⁴GF,

	Starts	1st	2nd	3rd	Win & Pl
Chases	5	0	0	0	547
Career Total	46	6	3	13	40864
101 11/01 Uttx	3m2f	F(0-95)HCh		SFT	£3031
98 11/99 Newb	2m4f	D Ch		G-F	£5336
117 12/98 Hayd	2m4f	B HHdl		SFT	£6827
117 11/98 Hayd	2m6f	B HHdl		HVY	£5022
118 10/98 Strf	2m3f	C(0-135)HHdl		GD	£3743
97 11/97 Ludl	2m5f110yE Hdl			GD	£2346

Total win prize-money £26305

Going:	Sf: 0-1 GS: 0-0 Gd: 0-2 GF: - Fm: 0-2
Distance:	2m/2m3: 0-0 2m4-2m7: 0-0 3m+: 0-5
Track:	LH: 0-1 RH: 0-4 Tight: 0-0 Gall: 0-1
Aids:	Bl: 0-0 Vi: 0-0 Tstrap: 0-0
Best Rating:	119 5/99 Uttx 3m110y good Hdl

Modest chaser; stays three miles plus; has had breathing problems; acts on soft/heavy ground; has won on faster.

Churlish Lad (IRE)
94f

6-y-o b g Commanche Run-Pennyala (Skyliner)
M Bradstock The Frankly Intolerable

Placings: 1-U   (0219)
2002/03: 18¹G, 17ᵁG,

	Starts	1st	2nd	3rd	Win & Pl
NH Flat	2	1	0	0	1708
Career Total	2	1	0	0	1708
94 4/02 Plum	2m2f	H NHF		GD	£1708

Total win prize-money £1708

Going:	Sf: 0-0 GS: 0-0 Gd: 1-2 GF: - Fm: 0-0
Distance:	2m/2m3: 1-2 2m4-2m7: 0-0 3m+: 0-0
Track:	LH: 1-1 RH: 0-1 Tight: 0-0 Gall: 0-0
Aids:	Bl: 0-0 Vi: 0-0 Tstrap: 0-0
Best Rating:	94 4/02 Plum 2m2f good NHF

Winner of a Plumpton bumper on his debut; whipped round at the start next time; acts on good ground.

Cill Churnain (IRE)
96(113h)   (127 h)120+

10-y-o b/br g Arctic Cider (USA)-The Dozer (IRE) (Bulldozer)
Mrs S J Smith Keith Middleton

Placings: PO/PUR2U3U2O24531-421131124   (1991)
2002/03: 24⁴GS, 26²GS, 24¹GF, 21¹GF, 21³G, 21¹G, 20²GS, 214⁰G,

	Starts	1st	2nd	3rd	Win & Pl
Hurdles	9	4	2	1	22896
Career Total	25	5	5	3	29823
109 9/02 Worc	2m4f	C(0-135)HHdl		GD	£5968
118 9/02 Sthl	2m5f110yD(0-125)HHdl			GD	£5109
108 7/02 Sedg	2m5f110yD(0-125)HHdl			G-F	£3672
110 6/02 Worc	3m	E Hdl		G-F	£2632
108 3/02 Sedg	2m5f	E Ch		SFT	£3051

Total win prize-money £20434

Going:	Sf: 0-0 GS: 0-4 Gd: 2-3 GF: - Fm: 2-2
Distance:	2m/2m3: 0-0 2m4-2m7: 3-5 3m+: 1-3
Track:	LH: 4-9 RH: 0-0 Tight: 1-4 Gall: 0-1
Aids:	Bl: 0-0 Vi: 0-0 Tstrap: 0-0
Best Rating:	127 11/02 Weth 2m4f110y gd-sft Hdl

Useful handicap hurdler / chaser; back over fences after a successfull spell over hurdles when easy winner at Uttoxeter in July; stays 3m but effective over shorter; handles the soft but is considered best on a sounder surface.

Cillamon
91f   85f

6-y-o b m Terimon-Dubacilla (Dubasoff (USA))
L G Cottrell Henry T Cole

Placings: 6   (0149)
2002/03: 16⁶GF,

	Starts	1st	2nd	3rd	Win & Pl
NH Flat	1	0	0	0	0
Career Total	1	0	0	0	0

Going:	Sf: 0-0 GS: 0-0 Gd: 0-0 GF: - Fm: 0-1
Distance:	2m/2m3: 0-1 2m4-2m7: 0-0 3m+: 0-0
Track:	LH: 0-1 RH: 0-0 Tight: 0-0 Gall: 0-0
Aids:	Bl: 0-0 Vi: 0-0 Tstrap: 0-0
Best Rating:	85 5/02 Chep 2m110y gd-fm NHF

Daughter of high-class chaser Dubacilla; won 2m 4f point February 2003.

Cimarrone Cove (IRE)

111   **127**

8-y-o b g Roselier (FR)-Sugarstown (Sassafras (FR))
N J Henderson (M Pitman 17/5) Philip Matton

Placings:2/4124/P4611F3/3606P-532FP   (3444)
2002/03: 25⁵G, 24³HY, 24²GS, 27⁶S, 26⁶HY,

	Starts	1st	2nd	3rd	Win & Pl
Chases	5	0	1	1	3010
Career Total	22	3	3	3	19958
130	12/00	Newb	3m	D Ch		SFT	£4348
119	12/00	Donc	3m	D Ch		HVY	£5118
114	12/99	Hntg	3m2f	E Hdl		G-S	£2757
				Total win prize-money £12226			

Going: Sf: 0-3 GS: 0-1 Gd: 0-1 GF: - Fm: 0-0
Distance: 2m/2m3: 0-0 2m4-2m7: 0-0 3m+: 0-5
Track: LH: 0-2 RH: 0-3 Tight: 0-2 Gall: 0-0
Aids: Bl: 0-1 Vi: 0-0 Tstrap: 0-0
Best Rating: 130 2/01 Newb 3m   soft   Ch

Fair staying handicap chaser, suited by soft ground. has worn headgear. Now with Nicky Henderson and is back to near best.

Cindesti (IRE)

(69h)   (44h)**92**

7-y-o b g Barathea (IRE)-Niamh Cinn Oir (IRE) (King Of Clubs)
C N Kellett   J E Titley

Placings:614/50/4U66-P   (2067)
2002/03: 21⁵GS,

	Starts	1st	2nd	3rd	Win & Pl
Hurdles	1	0	0	0	
Career Total	10	1	0	0	2801
115	2/00	Donc	2m4f	E Hdl		GD	£2380
				Total win prize-money £2380			

Going: Sf: 0-0 GS: 0-1 Gd: 0-0 GF: - Fm: 0-0
Distance: 2m/2m3: 0-0 2m4-2m7: 0-1 3m+: 0-0
Track: LH: 0-0 RH: 0-1 Tight: 0-0 Gall: 0-0
Aids: Bl: 0-0 Vi: 0-0 Tstrap: 0-0
Best Rating: 115 2/00 Donc 2m4f   good   Hdl

Cinnamon Club

11-y-o b m Derrylin-Cinnamon Run (Deep Run)
Mrs Ruth Hayter   Mrs A Villar

Placings:05/25533/5001U/P   (4147)
2002/03: 21⁵G,

	Starts	1st	2nd	3rd	Win & Pl
Chases	1	0	0	0	
Career Total	13	1	1	2	3170
87	6/98	Worc	2m	F Hdl		GD	£2136
				Total win prize-money £2136			

Going: Sf: 0-0 GS: 0-0 Gd: 0-0 GF: - Fm: 0-0
Distance: 2m/2m3: 0-0 2m4-2m7: 0-1 3m+: 0-0
Track: LH: 0-1 RH: 0-0 Tight: 0-1 Gall: 0-0
Aids: Bl: 0-0 Vi: 0-0 Tstrap: 0-1
Best Rating: 94 5/97 Hrfd 2m1f   good   NHF

Cinnamon Line

102   **99**

7-y-o ch g Derrylin-Cinnamon Run (Deep Run)
R H Alner   Club Ten

Placings:24/3350-6F35   (4252)
2002/03: 22⁶GS, 24⁴HY, 24³S, 22⁵G,

	Starts	1st	2nd	3rd	Win & Pl
Hurdles	4	0	0	1	580
Career Total	10	0	1	3	2264

Going: Sf: 0-2 GS: 0-1 Gd: 0-1 GF: - Fm: 0-0
Distance: 2m/2m3: 0-0 2m4-2m7: 0-2 3m+: 0-2
Track: LH: 0-1 RH: 0-3 Tight: 0-1 Gall: 0-0
Aids: Bl: 0-0 Vi: 0-0 Tstrap: 0-0
Best Rating: 110 3/01   Newb   2m110y   heavy   NHF

Moderate hurdler; chaser in the making; has not translated his bumper form to hurdles; better effort when third in a three mile handicap at Taunton January 2003; acts on soft/heavy ground.

Cionn Mhalanna (IRE)

63f   **91f**

5-y-o b g Corrouge (USA)-Pennyland (Le Bavard (FR))
P Beaumont   D R Brown & Miss E E Toland

Placings:05   (4593)
2002/03: 17⁰GS, 16⁵G,

	Starts	1st	2nd	3rd	Win & Pl
NH Flat	2	0	0	0	
Career Total	2	0	0	0	0

Going: Sf: 0-0 GS: 0-1 Gd: 0-1 GF: - Fm: 0-0
Distance: 2m/2m3: 0-2 2m4-2m7: 0-0 3m+: 0-0
Track: LH: 0-1 RH: 0-1 Tight: 0-0 Gall: 0-0
Aids: Bl: 0-0 Vi: 0-0 Tstrap: 0-0
Best Rating: 97 3/03 Carl 2m1f   gd-sft   NHF

Circle Of Wolves

96   **91**

5-y-o ch g Wolfhound (USA)-Misty Halo (High Top)
M J Gingell (Bob Jones 14/3) Mrs J M Penney

Placings:5543-545205003   (4574)
2002/03: 19⁵G, 22⁴S, 16⁵GS, 16²S, 16⁹GS, 20⁵S, 16⁹G, 20⁰GF, 22³GF,

	Starts	1st	2nd	3rd	Win & Pl
Hurdles	9	0	1	1	1802
Career Total	13	0	1	2	4196

Going: Sf: 0-3 GS: 0-2 Gd: 0-2 GF: - Fm: 0-2
Distance: 2m/2m3: 0-4 2m4-2m7: 0-5 3m+: 0-0
Track: LH: 0-5 RH: 0-3 Tight: 0-5 Gall: 0-2
Aids: Bl: 0-0 Vi: 0-0 Tstrap: 0-0
Best Rating: 91 1/03 Donc 2m110y   gd-sft   Hdl

Moderate hurdler; suited by cut in the ground.

Circumstance

5-y-o ch m Beveled (USA)-Instant Pleasure (Baim (USA))
N A Graham   Rush Green Partnership

Placings:UP   (0352)
2002/03: 17⁰G, 20⁰GS,

	Starts	1st	2nd	3rd	Win & Pl
Hurdles	2	0	0	0	
Career Total	2	0	0	0	

Going: Sf: 0-0 GS: 0-1 Gd: 0-1 GF: - Fm: 0-0
Distance: 2m/2m3: 0-1 2m4-2m7: 0-1 3m+: 0-0
Track: LH: 0-1 RH: 0-1 Tight: 0-2 Gall: 0-0
Aids: Bl: 0-0 Vi: 0-0 Tstrap: 0-0
Best Rating:

Cisco

90   **52**

5-y-o b g Shambo-School Run (Deep Run)
Andrew Turnell   Dr John Hollowood

Placings:050-66U50   (4168)
2002/03: 16⁶GS, 20⁶GS, 20⁰GS, 17⁵S, 20⁰GS,

	Starts	1st	2nd	3rd	Win & Pl
Hurdles	5	0	0	0	0
Career Total	8	0	0	0	0

Going: Sf: 0-1 GS: 0-4 Gd: 0-0 GF: - Fm: 0-0
Distance: 2m/2m3: 0-2 2m4-2m7: 0-3 3m+: 0-0
Track: LH: 0-4 RH: 0-1 Tight: 0-1 Gall: 0-3
Aids: Bl: 0-2 Vi: 0-0 Tstrap: 0-0
Best Rating: 68   11/02 Hntg   2m110y   gd-sft   Hdl

Cita Verda (FR)

115   **125**

5-y-o b m Take Risks (FR)-Mossita (FR) (Tip Moss (FR))
P Monteith   Mr & Mrs Raymond Anderson Green

Placings:1102-3155411   (4549)
2002/03: 16³G, 16¹GF, 20⁵G, 17⁵G, 20⁴GS, 16¹HY, 16¹G,

	Starts	1st	2nd	3rd	Win & Pl
Hurdles	7	3	0	1	28987
Career Total	11	5	1	1	36265
122	4/03	Ayr	2m	B HHdl		GD	£17664
119	1/03	Ayr	2m	D(0-120)HHdl	HVY	£5278
119	5/02	Prth	2m110y	E Hdl		G-F	£2978
115	3/02	Ayr	2m	E Hdl		HVY	£3024
85	2/02	Muss	2m	E Hdl		SFT	£2660
				Total win prize-money £31605			

Going: Sf: 1-1 GS: 0-1 Gd: 1-4 GF: - Fm: 1-1
Distance: 2m/2m3: 3-5 2m4-2m7: 0-2 3m+: 0-0
Track: LH: 2-5 RH: 1-2 Tight: 0-3 Gall: 0-1
Aids: Bl: 0-0 Vi: 0-0 Tstrap: 0-0
Best Rating: 122 4/03 Ayr   2m   good   Hdl

Useful handicap hurdler; completed a hat trick at the start of 2003; stays two miles and acts on any ground.

Citius (IRE)

(92h)   (89h)**111**

7-y-o b g Supreme Leader-Fancy Me Not (IRE) (Bulldozer)
R Rowe   Tom Perkins

Placings:213/00613-P   (2573)
2002/03: 22⁰G,

	Starts	1st	2nd	3rd	Win & Pl
Chases	1	0	0	0	
Career Total	9	2	1	2	9244
111	1/02	Winc	2m5f	D Ch		G-S	£4387
115	1/01	Folk	2m1f110y	E Hdl		HVY	£2541
				Total win prize-money £6929			

Going: Sf: 0-0 GS: 0-0 Gd: 0-1 GF: - Fm: 0-0
Distance: 2m/2m3: 0-0 2m4-2m7: 0-1 3m+: 0-0
Track: LH: 0-1 RH: 0-0 Tight: 0-0 Gall: 0-1
Aids: Bl: 0-0 Vi: 0-0 Tstrap: 0-0
Best Rating: 115 1/01 Folk   2m1f110y   heavy   Hdl

Successful over hurdles in January 2001, he has also been

successful over fences. Effective from two to two miles five, he acts on a soft surface.

City Gent

104(93h)   87

9-y-o b g Primitive Rising (USA)-Classy Lassy (Class Distinction)
N Wilson J McGuinness

Placings:050SF/PUF535/2364P211/665PP400-5534U42
(4787)
2002/03: 16⁵G, 20⁵GS, 16³S, 17⁴G, 20∪G, 17⁴G, 20²G,

	Starts	1st	2nd	3rd	Win & Pl
Hurdles	1	0	0	0	0
Chases	6	0	1	1	2753
Career Total	34	2	3	3	14959
98	4/01	MRas	2m1f110yE(0-105)HCh	HVY	£3932
98	2/01	Muss	2m	D(0-110)HCh	GD	£4823

Total win prize-money £8756

Going:	Sf: 0-1 GS: 0-1 Gd: 0-5 GF: - Fm: 0-0
Distance:	2m/2m3: 0-4 2m4-2m7: 0-3 3m+: 0-0
Track:	LH: 0-2 RH: 0-5 Tight: 0-3 Gall: 0-0
Aids:	Bl: 0-0 Vi: 0-0 Tstrap: 0-0
Best Rating:	98 4/01 MRas 2m1f110y heavy Ch

Plating-class chaser; best at two miles but stays further.

City Kid (DEN)

11-y-o ch g Village Star (FR)-Irish Lute (Luthier)
Rune Haugen Ms Liv Saether Myskja

Placings:115/12/14/2/4435   (2467)
2002/03: 21⁴S, 22⁴G, 21³HY, 31⁵GS,

	Starts	1st	2nd	3rd	Win & Pl
Chases	4	0	0	1	3182
Career Total	12	4	2	1	23343
8/99	Ovrl	2m5f	Ch	GD	£3155
6/98	Stro	2m5f	Ch	GD	£8416
8/97	Ovrl	2m	Hdl	GD	£1837
7/97	Ovrl	2m	Hdl	GD	£1837

Total win prize-money £15245

Going:	Sf: 0-2 GS: 0-1 Gd: 0-1 GF: - Fm: 0-0
Distance:	2m/2m3: 0-0 2m4-2m7: 0-3 3m+: 0-1
Track:	LH: 0-1 RH: 0-0 Tight: 0-0 Gall: 0-0
Aids:	Bl: 0-0 Vi: 0-0 Tstrap: 0-0
Best Rating:	0 12/02 Chel 3m7f gd-sft Ch

Norwegian-trained chaser. Best over two and a half miles.

City Poser (IRE)

95(103h)   (116h)108+

8-y-o b g Posen (USA)-Citissima (Simbir)
Simon Earle The Plum Merchants

Placings:0002/41440/50641-2F42   (1570)
2002/03: 24²GF, 27⁵GF, 24⁴YS, 24²G,

	Starts	1st	2nd	3rd	Win & Pl
Hurdles	3	0	1	0	2098
Chases	1	0	1	0	1726
Career Total	18	2	3	0	13751
116	4/02	Wwck	3m1f	D(0-115)HHdl	G-F	£4309
96	9/00	Baln	2m	(0-102)HHdl	SFT	£3588

Total win prize-money £7898

Going:	Sf: 0-0 GS: 0-0 Gd: 0-1 GF: - Fm: 0-2
Distance:	2m/2m3: 0-0 2m4-2m7: 0-0 3m+: 0-4
Track:	LH: 0-3 RH: 0-1 Tight: 0-2 Gall: 0-0
Aids:	Bl: 0-0 Vi: 0-0 Tstrap: 0-0
Best Rating:	116 5/02 Strf 3m3f gd-fm Hdl

Modest handicap hurdler; handles soft ground but is suited by faster; stays three miles; promising chase debut in October 2002.

City Reach

81   66

7-y-o b g Petong-Azola (IRE) (Alzao (USA))
Miss M Bragg (P J Makin 18/11) W H Whitley

Placings:PP   (3141)
2002/03: 17⁵S, 17⁶S,

	Starts	1st	2nd	3rd	Win & Pl
Hurdles	2	0	0	0	
Career Total	2	0	0	0	

Going:	Sf: 0-2 GS: 0-0 Gd: 0-0 GF: - Fm: 0-0
Distance:	2m/2m3: 0-2 2m4-2m7: 0-0 3m+: 0-0
Track:	LH: 0-0 RH: 0-0 Tight: 0-2 Gall: 0-0
Aids:	Bl: 0-0 Vi: 0-0 Tstrap: 0-2
Best Rating:	0 1/03 Tntn 2m1f soft Hdl

City Standard (IRE)

7-y-o b g Rainbow Quest (USA)-City Fortress (Troy)
M F Harris M Harris

Placings:546P-PP   (3811)
2002/03: 19⁶G, 25⁶G,

	Starts	1st	2nd	3rd	Win & Pl
Hurdles	2	0	0	0	
Career Total	6	0	0	0	0

Going:	Sf: 0-0 GS: 0-0 Gd: 0-2 GF: - Fm: 0-0
Distance:	2m/2m3: 0-0 2m4-2m7: 0-1 3m+: 0-1
Track:	LH: 0-1 RH: 0-1 Tight: 0-1 Gall: 0-0
Aids:	Bl: 0-0 Vi: 0-0 Tstrap: 0-0
Best Rating:	98 6/01 Strf 2m110y gd-fm Hdl

Civil Gent (IRE)

64   31

4-y-o ch g Flying Spur (AUS)-Calamity Kate (IRE) (Fairy King (USA))
M E Sowersby J Payne

Placings:0FP0   (3864)
2002/03: 16⁶G, 16⁵GS, 17⁵S, 19⁰GS,

	Starts	1st	2nd	3rd	Win & Pl
Hurdles	4	0	0	0	
Career Total	4	0	0	0	

Going:	Sf: 0-1 GS: 0-2 Gd: 0-1 GF: - Fm: 0-0
Distance:	2m/2m3: 0-3 2m4-2m7: 0-1 3m+: 0-0
Track:	LH: 0-3 RH: 0-1 Tight: 0-1 Gall: 0-0
Aids:	Bl: 0-0 Vi: 0-0 Tstrap: 0-0
Best Rating:	25 2/03 Donc 2m3f110y gd-sft Hdl

Clair Valley

99   90

9-y-o b m Ardross-Annicombe Run (Deep Run)
Ferdy Murphy Miss J V Morgan

Placings:3045/65P/0326-15   (0764)
2002/03: 25¹S, 27⁵GF,

	Starts	1st	2nd	3rd	Win & Pl
Hurdles	2	1	0	0	2891

Career Total	13	1	1	2	4317
90	7/02	Wolv	3m1f	E Hdl	SFT	£2891

Total win prize-money £2891

Going:	Sf: 1-1 GS: 0-0 Gd: 0-0 GF: - Fm: 0-1
Distance:	2m/2m3: 0-0 2m4-2m7: 0-0 3m+: 1-2
Track:	LH: 1-2 RH: 0-0 Tight: 1-2 Gall: 0-0
Aids:	Bl: 0-0 Vi: 0-0 Tstrap: 0-0
Best Rating:	90 7/02 Sedg 3m3f110y gd-fm Hdl

Some ability in novice hurdles until winning at Wolverhampton in July 2002. Stays three miles and goes on any ground.

Claire's Nomad

7-y-o b g Nomadic Way (USA)-Clairet (Sagaro)
J S Wainwright Philip E Clark

Placings:6   (0510)
2002/03: 20⁶G,

	Starts	1st	2nd	3rd	Win & Pl
Hurdles	1	0	0	0	0
Career Total	1	0	0	0	0

Going:	Sf: 0-0 GS: 0-0 Gd: 0-1 GF: - Fm: 0-0
Distance:	2m/2m3: 0-0 2m4-2m7: 0-1 3m+: 0-0
Track:	LH: 0-1 RH: 0-0 Tight: 0-0 Gall: 0-0
Aids:	Bl: 0-0 Vi: 0-0 Tstrap: 0-0
Best Rating:	0 6/02 Worc 2m4f good Hdl

Clan Royal (FR)

105   (104h)133+

8-y-o b g Chef De Clan Ii (FR)-Allee Du Roy (FR) (Rex Magna (FR))
Jonjo O Neill J P McManus

Placings:00/311332/1343-351411   (4472)
2002/03: 19³G, 16⁵G, 18¹S, 16⁴S, 20¹S, 21¹G,

	Starts	1st	2nd	3rd	Win & Pl
Chases	6	3	0	1	56511
Career Total	18	6	1	6	74480
133	4/03	Aint	2m5f110y	B(0-150)HCh	GD	£40600
123	3/03	Newb	2m4f	D(0-125)HCh	SFT	£10037
117	2/03	Font	2m2f	E(0-105)HCh	SFT	£4046
112	6/01	Navn	2m1f	(0-116)HCh	FRM	£6955
101	7/00	Baln	2m1f	Ch	G-F	£3588
103	7/00	Bell	2m1f	Hdl	G-F	£3174

Total win prize-money £68402

Going:	Sf: 2-3 GS: 0-0 Gd: 1-3 GF: - Fm: 0-0
Distance:	2m/2m3: 1-4 2m4-2m7: 2-2 3m+: 0-0
Track:	LH: 2-3 RH: 0-2 Tight: 2-2 Gall: 1-1
Aids:	Bl: 0-0 Vi: 0-0 Tstrap: 0-0
Best Rating:	133 4/03 Aint 2m5f110y good Ch

Decent ex-Irish chaser; took the Topham Chase at Aintree in April; stays two miles five but effective at shorter; acts on any ground, but better on soft.

Claras Pride (IRE)

87   69

11-y-o b g Be My Native (USA)-Our Hollow (Wolver Hollow)
M S Wilesmith M S Wilesmith

Placings:00655/0/F-5   (0508)
2002/03: 23⁵G,

	Starts	1st	2nd	3rd	Win & Pl
Chases	1	0	0	0	0
Career Total	8	0	0	0	0

Going:	Sf: 0-0 GS: 0-0 Gd: 0-1 GF: - Fm: 0-0
Distance:	2m/2m3: 0-0 2m4-2m7: 0-0 3m+: 0-1
Track:	LH: 0-1 RH: 0-0 Tight: 0-0 Gall: 0-0
Aids:	Bl: 0-0 Vi: 0-0 Tstrap: 0-0
Best Rating:	88 7/98 Wxfd 2m good NHF

Clarendon (IRE)

(107h)   (112 h)**95+**

7-y-o ch g Forest Wind (USA)-Sparkish (IRE) (Persian Bold)
P J Hobbs The Plus Fours

Placings:43/11-1000   (3727)
2002/03: 16¹GF, 16⁰G, 16⁰GS, 16⁰G,

	Starts	1st	2nd	3rd	Win & Pl
Hurdles	4	1	0	0	6832
Career Total	8	3	0	1	13662
125 7/02 Strf	2m110y	D(0-125)HHdl		G-F	£6831
108 6/01 NAbb	2m1f	D Hdl		G-F	£3554
106 6/01 Worc	2m	E Hdl		G-F	£2562

Total win prize-money £12948

Going:	Sf: 0-0 GS: 0-1 Gd: 0-2 GF: - Fm: 1-1
Distance:	2m/2m3: 1-4 2m4-2m7: 0-0 3m+: 0-0
Track:	LH: 1-1 RH: 0-3 Tight: 1-1 Gall: 0-0
Aids:	Bl: 0-0 Vi: 0-0 Tstrap: 0-0
Best Rating:	125 7/02 Strf 2m110y gd-fm Hdl

Fair hurdler; runner-up in claimer at Newton Abbot June 2003; well-backed when falling at the last with a length lead on chasing debut at the same course next time; appreciates fast ground; effective at around 2m.

Clashbridane (IRE)

11-y-o b g Lancastrian-Castleview Rose (Master Buck)
Mrs G B Walford Mrs G B Walford

Placings:P/P2043P-5   (0503)
2002/03: 26⁵G,

	Starts	1st	2nd	3rd	Win & Pl
Chases	1	0	0	0	0
Career Total	8	0	1	1	993

Going:	Sf: 0-0 GS: 0-0 Gd: 0-1 GF: - Fm: 0-0
Distance:	2m/2m3: 0-0 2m4-2m7: 0-0 3m+: 0-1
Track:	LH: 0-1 RH: 0-0 Tight: 0-1 Gall: 0-0
Aids:	Bl: 0-0 Vi: 0-0 Tstrap: 0-0
Best Rating:	83 4/02 Carl 3m2f gd-sft Ch

Class Of Ninetytwo (IRE)

14-y-o b g Lancastrian-Lothian Lassie (Precipice Wood)
S Wynne J E Stockton

Placings:050/65000/P11113/212/PF5P/P/P21-23P (3962)
2002/03: 34²G, 26³GS, 24⁴S,

	Starts	1st	2nd	3rd	Win & Pl
Chases	3	0	1	1	1277
Career Total	28	6	4	2	30781
92 3/02 Bang	3m110y	H Ch		SFT	£1498
127 11/96 Wwck	3m2f	B(0-145)HCh		GD	£6736
124 2/96 Chep	3m2f110yD(0-125)HCh			SFT	£4099
119 1/96 Leic	3m	F(0-105)HCh		GD	£3236
110 12/95 Ludl	3m	F(0-100)HCh		G-F	£2775
113 11/95 Wwck	3m2f	D Ch		GD	£3756

Total win prize-money £22100

Going:	Sf: 0-1 GS: 0-1 Gd: 0-1 GF: - Fm: 0-0
Distance:	2m/2m3: 0-0 2m4-2m7: 0-0 3m+: 0-3
Track:	LH: 0-3 RH: 0-0 Tight: 0-2 Gall: 0-0
Aids:	Bl: 0-0 Vi: 0-0 Tstrap: 0-0
Best Rating:	127 11/96 Wwck 3m2f good Ch

One-time fair staying handicapper; modest hunter chaser these days; likes to dominate; stays very well.

Classic China

96f   100f

6-y-o ch m Karinga Bay-Chanelle (The Parson)
J W Mullins Amesbury China

Placings:22   (3113)
2002/03: 18²S, 17²HY,

	Starts	1st	2nd	3rd	Win & Pl
NH Flat	2	0	2	0	1174
Career Total	2	0	2	0	1174

Going:	Sf: 0-2 GS: 0-0 Gd: 0-0 GF: - Fm: 0-0
Distance:	2m/2m3: 0-0 2m4-2m7: 0-0 3m+: 0-0
Track:	LH: 0-1 RH: 0-1 Tight: 0-2 Gall: 0-0
Aids:	Bl: 0-0 Vi: 0-0 Tstrap: 0-0
Best Rating:	100 1/03 Folk 2m1f110y heavy NHF

Classic Conkers (IRE)

99   92

9-y-o b g Conquering Hero (USA)-Erck (Sun Prince)
Miss J Feilden Steven Rees

Placings:0/234   (2499)
2002/03: 20²GS, 20³HY, 20⁴GS,

	Starts	1st	2nd	3rd	Win & Pl
Hurdles	3	0	1	1	1599
Career Total	4	0	1	1	1599

Going:	Sf: 0-1 GS: 0-2 Gd: 0-0 GF: - Fm: 0-0
Distance:	2m/2m3: 0-0 2m4-2m7: 0-3 3m+: 0-0
Track:	LH: 0-3 RH: 0-0 Tight: 0-2 Gall: 0-0
Aids:	Bl: 0-0 Vi: 0-0 Tstrap: 0-0
Best Rating:	92 11/02 Weth 2m4f110y heavy Hdl

Modest on the Flat, he has shown some ability in his few attempts over hurdles. Needs at least two and a half miles.

Classic Eagle

63

10-y-o b g Unfuwain (USA)-La Lutine (My Swallow)
Miss J Feilden (N A Graham 3/5) Steve Rees Racing
Classic Eagle

Placings:013102P/42316245/F0/4/00-4   (0492)
2002/03: 20⁴HY,

	Starts	1st	2nd	3rd	Win & Pl
Hurdles	1	0	0	0	263
Career Total	21	3	3	2	13265
123 11/98 Hntg	2m110y	E(0-115)HHdl		G-S	£2600
115 2/98 Fknm	2m	E(0-115)HHdl		G-F	£2985
120 12/97 Catt	2m	E Hdl		G-S	£2038

Total win prize-money £7623

Going:	Sf: 0-1 GS: 0-0 Gd: 0-0 GF: - Fm: 0-0
Distance:	2m/2m3: 0-0 2m4-2m7: 0-1 3m+: 0-0
Track:	LH: 0-1 RH: 0-0 Tight: 0-0 Gall: 0-0
Aids:	Bl: 0-0 Vi: 0-0 Tstrap: 0-0
Best Rating:	125 3/99 Asct 2m110y gd-fm Hdl

Classic Example

4-y-o ch c Mark Of Esteem (IRE)-Classic Form (IRE) (Alzao (USA))
Miss S J Wilton (E A L Dunlop 7/10) John Pointon And Sons

Placings:PF   (4316)
2002/03: 16⁰GS, 17⁰G,

	Starts	1st	2nd	3rd	Win & Pl
Hurdles	2	0	0	0	
Career Total	2	0	0	0	

Going:	Sf: 0-0 GS: 0-1 Gd: 0-1 GF: - Fm: 0-0
Distance:	2m/2m3: 0-2 2m4-2m7: 0-0 3m+: 0-0
Track:	LH: 0-1 RH: 0-1 Tight: 0-1 Gall: 0-0
Aids:	Bl: 0-0 Vi: 0-0 Tstrap: 0-0
Best Rating:	0 3/03 Bang 2m1f good Hdl

Classic Fable (IRE)

60

11-y-o b m Lafontaine (USA)-Rathmill Syke (True Song)
J L Needham J L Needham

Placings:0/P/P00646PUF4-P   (0123)
2002/03: 27⁶GF,

	Starts	1st	2nd	3rd	Win & Pl
Hurdles	1	0	0	0	
Career Total	13	0	0	0	

Going:	Sf: 0-0 GS: 0-0 Gd: 0-0 GF: - Fm: 0-1
Distance:	2m/2m3: 0-0 2m4-2m7: 0-0 3m+: 0-1
Track:	LH: 0-0 RH: 0-0 Tight: 0-1 Gall: 0-0
Aids:	Bl: 0-0 Vi: 0-0 Tstrap: 0-1
Best Rating:	60 3/02 Bang 2m1f soft Hdl

Classic Jazz (NZ)

104

8-y-o br g Paris Opera (AUS)-Johnny Loves Jazz (NZ) (Virginia Privateer (USA))
N J Henderson Michael Buckley

Placings:1-P   (3288)
2002/03: 17⁵GS,

	Starts	1st	2nd	3rd	Win & Pl
Hurdles	1	0	0	0	
Career Total	2	1	0	0	2562
104 6/01 Worc	2m	E Hdl		G-F	£2562

Total win prize-money £2562

Going:	Sf: 0-0 GS: 0-1 Gd: 0-0 GF: - Fm: 0-0
Distance:	2m/2m3: 0-1 2m4-2m7: 0-0 3m+: 0-0
Track:	LH: 0-1 RH: 0-0 Tight: 0-0 Gall: 0-1
Aids:	Bl: 0-0 Vi: 0-0 Tstrap: 0-0
Best Rating:	104 6/01 Worc 2m gd-fm Hdl

Moderate hurdler; Flat winner in New Zealand; won novice hurdle on British debut in the summer of 2001; off the track a long time afterwards; effective at two miles; acts on fast ground.

Classic Lash (IRE)

110(100h)   (92h)**103+**

7-y-o b g Classic Cheer (IRE)-Khaiylasha (IRE) (Kahyasi)
P Needham (P J Rothwell 26/10) P Needham

Placings:000030216F0300-P05502114P35312 (4660)
2002/03: 20⁰HY, 24⁰YS, 20⁵GF, 20⁵G, 22⁹GF, 24²G, 22¹GF, 24¹G,

20⁴YS, 27ᴾS, 21³S, 16⁵G, 21³G, 21¹G, 20²GF,

	Starts	1st	2nd	3rd	Win & Pl
Hurdles	10	2	1	0	11475
Chases	5	1	1	2	6555
Career Total	**29**	**4**	**3**	**4**	**24490**
102 4/03 Sedg 2m5f	E Ch			GD	£4056
92 10/02 Limk 3m	(60-95)HHdl			GD	£6561
85 10/02 Dpat 2m6f	(60-95)HHdl			G-F	£3809
93 9/01 DRoy 3m	(0-102)HHdl			FRM	£3895

Total win prize-money £18322

Going:	Sf: 0-3 GS: 0-0 Gd: 2-6 GF: - Fm: 1-4
Distance:	2m/2m3: 0-2 2m4-2m7: 2-10 3m+: 1-4
Track:	LH: 1-6 RH: 0-1 Tight: 1-5 Gall: 0-0
Aids:	Bl: 0-0 Vi: 0-0 Tstrap: 0-0
Best Rating:	102 4/03 Sedg 2m5f good Ch

Moderate chaser; winning hurdler in his native Ireland; off the mark over fences when successful at Sedgefield in April; stays three miles, best on a sound surface.

Classic Native (IRE)
115f   131f
5-y-o b g Be My Native (USA)-Thats Irish (Furry Glen)
Jonjo O Neill   Ray & Sue Dodd Partnership

Placings:101   (4481)
2002/03: 16¹S, 16⁹G, 17¹G,

	Starts	1st	2nd	3rd	Win & Pl
NH Flat	3	2	0	0	19402
Career Total	**3**	**2**	**0**	**0**	**19402**
131 4/03 Aint 2m1f	A NHF			GD	£17400
113 12/02 Wwck 2m	H NHF			SFT	£2002

Total win prize-money £19402

Going:	Sf: 1-1 GS: 0-0 Gd: 1-2 GF: - Fm: 0-0
Distance:	2m/2m3: 2-3 2m4-2m7: 0-0 3m+: 0-0
Track:	LH: 1-2 RH: 0-0 Tight: 0-0 Gall: 0-0
Aids:	Bl: 0-0 Vi: 0-0 Tstrap: 0-0
Best Rating:	131 4/03 Aint 2m1f good NHF

Very useful bumper horse; followed up a Warwick first time out success with victory in Grade 2 bumper at Aintree; should stay well.

Classic Note (IRE)
111   104
8-y-o b m Classic Secret (USA)-Fovea (IRE) (Sarab)
A J Martin   Old Century Syndicate

Placings:000/U/2 1-1005   (4742a)
2002/03: 16¹GS, 19⁰S, 16⁹S, 16⁵G,

	Starts	1st	2nd	3rd	Win & Pl
Hurdles	4	1	0	0	10440
Career Total	**11**	**2**	**1**	**0**	**14329**
110 11/02 Chel 2m110y	D(0-110)HHdl			G-S	£10440
100 10/01 Dpat 2m1f172y				NHF	G-Y £2921

Total win prize-money £13361

Going:	Sf: 0-2 GS: 1-1 Gd: 0-1 GF: - Fm: 0-0
Distance:	2m/2m3: 1-4 2m4-2m7: 0-0 3m+: 0-0
Track:	LH: 1-3 RH: 0-1 Tight: 0-0 Gall: 0-0
Aids:	Bl: 0-0 Vi: 0-0 Tstrap: 0-0
Best Rating:	110 11/02 Chel 2m110y gd-sft Hdl

Winner of a Downpatrick bumper in October 2001, he got off the mark over hurdles in a novice handicap at Cheltenham in November 2002. Effective with cut in the ground over two miles.

Classic Rock
80f   71f
4-y-o b g Classic Cliche (IRE)-Ruby Vision (IRE) (Vision (USA))
J W Unett   G J G Roberts

Placings:00   (3174)
2002/03: 12⁰GS, 16⁹GS,

	Starts	1st	2nd	3rd	Win & Pl
NH Flat	2	0	0	0	
Career Total	**2**	**0**	**0**	**0**	

Going:	Sf: 0-0 GS: 0-2 Gd: 0-0 GF: - Fm: 0-0
Distance:	2m/2m3: 0-1 2m4-2m7: 0-0 3m+: 0-0
Track:	LH: 0-2 RH: 0-0 Tight: 0-0 Gall: 0-0
Aids:	Bl: 0-0 Vi: 0-0 Tstrap: 0-0
Best Rating:	78 11/02 Newb 1m4f110y gd-sft NHF

Classical Ben
102f   103f
5-y-o ch g Most Welcome-Stoproveritate (Scorpio (FR))
R A Fahey   J D Clark And Partners

Placings:31   (4594)
2002/03: 16³G, 16¹G,

	Starts	1st	2nd	3rd	Win & Pl
NH Flat	2	1	0	1	2198
Career Total	**2**	**1**	**0**	**1**	**2198**
97 4/03 Hexm 2m110y	H NHF			GD	£1904

Total win prize-money £1904

Going:	Sf: 0-0 GS: 0-0 Gd: 1-2 GF: - Fm: 0-0
Distance:	2m/2m3: 1-2 2m4-2m7: 0-0 3m+: 0-0
Track:	LH: 1-2 RH: 0-0 Tight: 0-1 Gall: 0-0
Aids:	Bl: 0-0 Vi: 0-0 Tstrap: 0-0
Best Rating:	97 4/03 Hexm 2m110y good NHF

Moderate bumper winner; acts on good ground.

Classified (IRE)
113   155
7-y-o b g Roselier (FR)-Treidlia (Mandalus)
M C Pipe   D A Johnson

Placings:0/11111141-2114   (4131)
2002/03: 21²G, 21¹GS, 20¹GS, 24⁴G,

	Starts	1st	2nd	3rd	Win & Pl
Hurdles	4	2	1	0	79773
Career Total	**13**	**9**	**1**	**0**	**159518**
147 2/03 Font 2m4f	A Hdl			G-S	£23200
152 1/03 Chel 2m5f110yA Hdl				G-S	£44625
155 4/02 Aint 2m4f	A Hdl			GD	£29000
141 2/02 Sand 2m6f	B Hdl			SFT	£7215
145 1/02 Wwck 2m5f	A Hdl			SFT	£12000
144 12/01 Newb 2m5f	A Hdl			GD	£16660
121 12/01 Plum 2m5f	E Hdl			GD	£2544
124 12/01 Towc 2m	H NHF			HVY	£2261
108 10/01 Gowr 2m4f	NHF			GD	£5564

Total win prize-money £143071

Going:	Sf: 0-0 GS: 2-2 Gd: 0-2 GF: - Fm: 0-0
Distance:	2m/2m3: 0-0 2m4-2m7: 2-3 3m+: 0-1
Track:	LH: 1-3 RH: 0-0 Tight: 1-1 Gall: 1-3
Aids:	Bl: 0-0 Vi: 0-0 Tstrap: 0-0
Best Rating:	155 3/03 Chel 3m good Hdl

Smart staying hurdler; winner of the Cleeve Hurdle at Cheltenham in January and the falsely-run National Spirit Hurdle at Fontwell in February; stays 2m 5f; held over 3m 1f when fourth in the Stayers Hurdle; acts on good and heavy; suited by coming from off a fast pace; genuine.

Classify
95f   86f
4-y-o b g Classic Cliche (IRE)-Slmaat (Sharpo)
P F Nicholls   C R Barnett

Placings:32   (4601)
2002/03: 16³GF, 17²GF,

	Starts	1st	2nd	3rd	Win & Pl
NH Flat	2	0	1	1	1265
Career Total	**2**	**0**	**1**	**1**	**1265**

Going:	Sf: 0-0 GS: 0-0 Gd: 0-0 GF: - Fm: 0-2
Distance:	2m/2m3: 0-2 2m4-2m7: 0-0 3m+: 0-0
Track:	LH: 0-0 RH: 0-2 Tight: 0-0 Gall: 0-0
Aids:	Bl: 0-0 Vi: 0-0 Tstrap: 0-0
Best Rating:	86 4/03 Extr 2m1f gd-fm NHF

Placed in two fast ground bumpers.

Classy Clare
5-y-o b m Nicholas Bill-Clare s Choice (Pragmatic)
J M Bradley   John Brookman

Placings:PP   (4626)
2002/03: 17⁵S, 17⁰GF,

	Starts	1st	2nd	3rd	Win & Pl
Hurdles	2	0	0	0	
Career Total	**2**	**0**	**0**	**0**	

Going:	Sf: 0-1 GS: 0-0 Gd: 0-0 GF: - Fm: 0-1
Distance:	2m/2m3: 0-2 2m4-2m7: 0-0 3m+: 0-0
Track:	LH: 0-1 RH: 0-1 Tight: 0-1 Gall: 0-0
Aids:	Bl: 0-0 Vi: 0-0 Tstrap: 0-0
Best Rating:	0 4/03 NAbb 2m1f gd-fm Hdl

Classy Clarence (IRE)
87f   76f
6-y-o ch g Un Desperado (FR)-Winscarlet North (Garland Knight)
A J Lidderdale   J Fishpool

Placings:0   (4155)
2002/03: 16⁹G,

	Starts	1st	2nd	3rd	Win & Pl
NH Flat	1	0	0	0	
Career Total	**1**	**0**	**0**	**0**	

Going:	Sf: 0-0 GS: 0-0 Gd: 0-1 GF: - Fm: 0-0
Distance:	2m/2m3: 0-1 2m4-2m7: 0-0 3m+: 0-0
Track:	LH: 0-1 RH: 0-0 Tight: 0-0 Gall: 0-0
Aids:	Bl: 0-0 Vi: 0-0 Tstrap: 0-0
Best Rating:	76 3/03 Wwck 2m good NHF

Claude (IRE)
54f
5-y-o g Hamas (IRE)-Tigora (Ahonoora)
B Palling (Mrs A J Bowlby 8/8)   Mrs R M Williams

Placings:0   (0560)
2002/03: 17⁰GF,

	Starts	1st	2nd	3rd	Win & Pl
NH Flat	1	0	0	0	
Career Total	**1**	**0**	**0**	**0**	

Going:	Sf: 0-0 GS: 0-0 Gd: 0-0 GF: - Fm: 0-1
Distance:	2m/2m3: 0-1 2m4-2m7: 0-0 3m+: 0-0
Track:	LH: 0-0 RH: 0-1 Tight: 0-0 Gall: 0-0
Aids:	Bl: 0-0 Vi: 0-0 Tstrap: 0-0
Best Rating:	

Claude Greengrass

107   **105+**

7-y-o ch g Shalford (IRE)-Rainbow Brite (BEL) (Captain s Treasure)
Jonjo O Neill (Francis Berry 1/11) J P McManus

Placings:0000000-0215F2   (4027)
2002/03: 16⁹HY, 16⁶YS, 16²G, 16¹GS, 20⁵GS, 16⁶G, 16²HY,

	Starts	1st	2nd	3rd	Win & Pl
Hurdles	7	1	2	0	7266
Career Total	13	1	2	0	7266
97	1/03	Donc	2m110y F(0-100)HHdl		G-S	£3630

Total win prize-money £3630

Going:	Sf: 0-2 GS: 1-2 Gd: 0-2 GF: - Fm: 0-0
Distance:	2m/2m3: 1-6 2m4-2m7: 0-1 3m+: 0-0
Track:	LH: 1-4 RH: 0-1 Tight: 0-2 Gall: 1-1
Aids:	Bl: 0-2 Vi: 0-0 Tstrap: 0-0
Best Rating:	105 2/03 Weth 2m good Hdl

Moderate hurdler; narrowly failed to land a gamble at Catterick prior to winning at Doncaster a week later; blinkered for the first time, clear when falling at the last at Wetherby in February; best over two miles; suited by cut in the ground.

Claudias Rainbow

6-y-o br m Alflora (IRE)-By The Lake (Tyrant (USA))
R C Guest (N B Mason 8/2) N B Mason

Placings:0P0P   (3834)
2002/03: 16⁰GS, 19⁰GS, 16⁰G, 20⁰G,

	Starts	1st	2nd	3rd	Win & Pl
NH Flat	1	0	0	0	
Hurdles	3	0	0	0	
Career Total	4	0	0	0	

Going:	Sf: 0-0 GS: 0-2 Gd: 0-2 GF: - Fm: 0-0
Distance:	2m/2m3: 0-2 2m4-2m7: 0-2 3m+: 0-0
Track:	LH: 0-4 RH: 0-0 Tight: 0-1 Gall: 0-1
Aids:	Bl: 0-0 Vi: 0-0 Tstrap: 0-0
Best Rating:	64 12/02 Donc 2m110y gd-sft NHF

Claudius Tertius

98   **75+**

6-y-o b g Rudimentary (USA)-Sanctuary Cove (Habitat)
N B Mason N B Mason

Placings:050000/0P1P00P-P6130   (1052)
2002/03: 16⁵GS, 17⁵GS, 17¹G, 21³G, 22⁰G,

	Starts	1st	2nd	3rd	Win & Pl
Hurdles	5	1	0	1	2233
Career Total	18	2	0	1	4449
75	8/02	Sedg	2m1f	G(0-90)HHdl	GD	£1953
67	8/01	Sedg	2m5f110yF(0-100)HHdl		G-F	£2215

Total win prize-money £4169

Going:	Sf: 0-0 GS: 0-1 Gd: 1-3 GF: - Fm: 0-1
Distance:	2m/2m3: 1-3 2m4-2m7: 0-2 3m+: 0-0
Track:	LH: 1-4 RH: 0-1 Tight: 1-4 Gall: 0-0
Aids:	Bl: 1-3 Vi: 0-0 Tstrap: 1-3
Best Rating:	75 8/02 Sedg 2m5f110y good Hdl

Plating-class handicap hurdler. Goes well round Sedgefield. Stays two miles five. Acts on a sound surface.

Claymore (IRE)

108(106h)   (128h)**140**

7-y-o b g Broadsword (USA)-Mazza (Mazilier (USA))

O Sherwood B T Stewart-Brown

Placings:010F12P3-314131UP   (4175)
2002/03: 20³GS, 16¹HY, 16⁴G, 19¹HY, 22³GS, 12¹GS, 18¹S, 21³S,

	Starts	1st	2nd	3rd	Win & Pl
Chases	8	3	0	2	24867
Career Total	16	5	1	3	33808
140	2/03	Hayd	2m6f	D Ch	G-S	£5551
140	12/02	Chep	2m3f110yC(0-135)HCh	HVY	£9984
140	11/02	Uttx	2m	D Ch	HVY	£5252
115	1/02	Font	2m2f110yE Hdl	GD	£2730
111	11/01	Plum	2m2f	H NHF	G-S	£1652

Total win prize-money £25169

Going:	Sf: 2-4 GS: 1-3 Gd: 0-1 GF: - Fm: 0-0
Distance:	2m/2m3: 1-3 2m4-2m7: 2-5 3m+: 0-0
Track:	LH: 3-7 RH: 0-1 Tight: 0-0 Gall: 0-2
Aids:	Bl: 0-0 Vi: 0-0 Tstrap: 0-0
Best Rating:	140 2/03 Hayd 2m6f gd-sft Ch

Very useful novice chaser; effective at two to miles six; acts on good ground and softer; tends to make mistakes.

Clear Away (IRE)

87   **64**

6-y-o b g Clearly Bust-Twinkle Bright (USA) (Star De Naskra (USA))
P G Murphy A Lowrie & Mrs J Lowrie

Placings:4   (1246)
2002/03: 24⁴G,

	Starts	1st	2nd	3rd	Win & Pl
Hurdles	1	0	0	0	0
Career Total	1	0	0	0	0

Going:	Sf: 0-0 GS: 0-0 Gd: 0-1 GF: - Fm: 0-0
Distance:	2m/2m3: 0-0 2m4-2m7: 0-1 3m+: 0-0
Track:	LH: 0-1 RH: 0-0 Tight: 0-0 Gall: 0-0
Aids:	Bl: 0-0 Vi: 0-0 Tstrap: 0-0
Best Rating:	64 9/02 Worc 3m good Hdl

Clear Dawn (IRE)

108   (95h)**111**

8-y-o b g Clearly Bust-Cobra Queen (Dawn Review)
J M Jefferson Mr & Mrs J M Davenport

Placings:P66/530331035/331-62300   (4528)
2002/03: 24⁶GF, 24²GS, 20³G, 24⁰S, 24⁰G,

	Starts	1st	2nd	3rd	Win & Pl
Chases	5	0	1	3	3809
Career Total	20	2	1	7	13878
100	10/01	Weth	2m7f110yE(0-105)HCh	GD	£3542
100	1/01	Muss	3m	F(0-105)HHdl	GD	£3721

Total win prize-money £7264

Going:	Sf: 0-1 GS: 0-1 Gd: 0-2 GF: - Fm: 0-1
Distance:	2m/2m3: 0-2 2m4-2m7: 0-1 3m+: 0-4
Track:	LH: 0-2 RH: 0-3 Tight: 0-3 Gall: 0-1
Aids:	Bl: 0-0 Vi: 0-0 Tstrap: 0-0
Best Rating:	111 1/03 Muss 2m4f good Ch

Modest chaser; stays three miles; best on good ground

Clear Skies (IRE)

88   **121**

10-y-o b g Phardante (FR)-Fighting Doleila (Humdoleila)
N A Gaselee Mrs R W S Baker

Placings:0/343/2535/52/132-B0   (2105)
2002/03: 20⁶GS, 20⁰GS,

	Starts	1st	2nd	3rd	Win & Pl
Chases	2	0	0	0	

	Career Total	15	1	3	4	12165
110	2/02	Leic	2m	E Ch	SFT	£3419

Total win prize-money £3419

Going:	Sf: 0-0 GS: 0-2 Gd: 0-0 GF: - Fm: 0-0
Distance:	2m/2m3: 0-0 2m4-2m7: 0-2 3m+: 0-0
Track:	LH: 0-1 RH: 0-1 Tight: 0-0 Gall: 0-2
Aids:	Bl: 0-0 Vi: 0-0 Tstrap: 0-0
Best Rating:	121 3/02 Sand 2m good Ch

Fair chaser; made a winning reappearance in February 2002; acts on soft ground and is effective at two miles.

Cleopatras Therapy (IRE)

99f   **91f**

6-y-o b g Gone Fishin-Nec Precario (Krayyan)
Ian Williams C M Kinane

Placings:152   (4122)
2002/03: 16¹S, 16⁵GS, 16²G,

	Starts	1st	2nd	3rd	Win & Pl
NH Flat	3	1	1	0	3402
Career Total	3	1	1	0	3402
90	1/03	Ludl	2m	H NHF	SFT	£2828

Total win prize-money £2828

Going:	Sf: 1-1 GS: 0-1 Gd: 0-1 GF: - Fm: 0-0
Distance:	2m/2m3: 1-3 2m4-2m7: 0-0 3m+: 0-0
Track:	LH: 0-1 RH: 1-2 Tight: 0-0 Gall: 0-1
Aids:	Bl: 0-0 Vi: 0-0 Tstrap: 0-0
Best Rating:	91 3/03 Hntg 2m110y good NHF

Made a winning debut in a Ludlow bumper in January but too keen and well beaten under a penalty.

Clever Fella

94f   **71f**

4-y-o ch g Elmaamul (USA)-Festival Of Magic (USA) (Clever Trick (USA))
M Dods M J K Dods

Placings:0   (3160)
2002/03: 16⁰G,

	Starts	1st	2nd	3rd	Win & Pl
NH Flat	1	0	0	0	
Career Total	1	0	0	0	

Going:	Sf: 0-0 GS: 0-0 Gd: 0-1 GF: - Fm: 0-0
Distance:	2m/2m3: 0-0 2m4-2m7: 0-0 3m+: 0-0
Track:	LH: 0-0 RH: 0-1 Tight: 0-1 Gall: 0-0
Aids:	Bl: 0-0 Vi: 0-0 Tstrap: 0-0
Best Rating:	71 1/03 Muss 2m good NHF

Clever Thyne (IRE)

102   **105**

6-y-o b g Good Thyne (USA)-Clever Milly (Precipice Wood)
H D Daly Mrs Geoffrey Churton

Placings:4555-2F23F4   (4318)
2002/03: 22²GS, 24⁴FG, 21²GS, 21³G, 21⁴FG, 24⁴G,

	Starts	1st	2nd	3rd	Win & Pl
Hurdles	5	0	2	1	2964
Chases	1	0	0	0	0
Career Total	10	0	2	1	2964

Going:	Sf: 0-0 GS: 0-1 Gd: 0-5 GF: - Fm: 0-0
Distance:	2m/2m3: 0-0 2m4-2m7: 0-4 3m+: 0-2
Track:	LH: 0-3 RH: 0-3 Tight: 0-2 Gall: 0-0

Aids: Bl: 0-0 Vi: 0-0 Tstrap: 0-2
Best Rating: 105 11/02 Ludl 2m5f   gd-sft Hdl

Moderate hurdler; appreciated a longer trip when winning 3m 2f maiden hurdle at Hereford May 2003; has been let down by his hurdling in the past and fell in his only novice chase to date.

Cleymor House (IRE)

87   **54**

5-y-o ch g Duky-Deise Lady (Le Bavard (FR))
John R Upson Ian N Mallett

Placings:000   (3850)
2002/03: 21⁰S, 16⁰HY, 19⁰GS,

	Starts	1st	2nd	3rd	Win & Pl
Hurdles	3	0	0	0	
Career Total	3	0	0	0	

Going: Sf: 0-2 GS: 0-1 Gd: 0-0 GF: - Fm: 0-0
Distance: 2m/2m3: 0-1 2m4-2m7: 0-2 3m+: 0-0
Track: LH: 0-1 RH: 0-2 Tight: 0-1 Gall: 0-0
Aids: Bl: 0-0 Vi: 0-0 Tstrap: 0-0
Best Rating: 58 2/03 Sand 2m110y   heavy Hdl

Clifton Fox

104   **122+**

11-y-o b g Deploy-Loveskate (USA) (Overskate (CAN))
Jonjo O Neill J P McManus

Placings:12/02   (3447)
2002/03: 16⁰G, 20²HY,

	Starts	1st	2nd	3rd	Win & Pl
Hurdles	2	0	1	0	1546
Career Total	4	1	2	0	7401
129 12/99 Newc	2m	D Hdl		SFT	£3745
			Total win prize-money £3745		

Going: Sf: 0-1 GS: 0-0 Gd: 0-1 GF: - Fm: 0-0
Distance: 2m/2m3: 0-1 2m4-2m7: 0-1 3m+: 0-0
Track: LH: 0-1 RH: 0-1 Tight: 0-0 Gall: 0-0
Aids: Bl: 0-0 Vi: 0-0 Tstrap: 0-0
Best Rating: 129 12/99 Newc 2m   soft Hdl

A Cambridgeshire and November Handicap winner on the Flat, he won a novice hurdle very impressively at Newcastle on his jumping debut in December 1999 after a three-year absence during which he had been fired, but only ran once more in January 2000 and was absent again for around three years until coming back in 2003, where he finished runner-up on second run.

Clifton Mist

104   **91**

7-y-o gr m Lyphento (USA)-Brave Maiden (Three Legs)
H S Howe Richard Garrard

Placings:U5P5/R44/600445600-1P100   (4602)
2002/03: 19¹F, 19⁵GS, 19¹S, 21⁰GS, 21⁰G,

	Starts	1st	2nd	3rd	Win & Pl
Hurdles	5	2	0	0	5703
Career Total	21	2	0	0	6657
91 12/02 Tntn	2m3f110yF(0-95)HHdl			SFT	£3757
85 10/02 Tntn	2m3f110yG(0-90)HHdl			FRM	£1946
		Total win prize-money £5703			

Going: Sf: 1-1 GS: 0-2 Gd: 0-1 GF: - Fm: 1-1
Distance: 2m/2m3: 0-0 2m4-2m7: 2-5 3m+: 0-0
Track: LH: 0-1 RH: 2-4 Tight: 2-3 Gall: 0-1

Aids: Bl: 0-0 Vi: 0-0 Tstrap: 0-0
Best Rating: 91 12/02 Tntn 2m3f110y soft Hdl

Plating-class hurdler, stays two and a half miles, acts on fast ground.

Clingstone

97   **98d**

7-y-o b m Henbit (USA)-Linen Leaf (Bold Owl)
T R George Timothy N Chick

Placings:06-25P   (3958)
2002/03: 16²GS, 20⁵G, 17⁵S,

	Starts	1st	2nd	3rd	Win & Pl
Hurdles	3	0	1	0	860
Career Total	5	0	1	0	860

Going: Sf: 0-1 GS: 0-1 Gd: 0-1 GF: - Fm: 0-0
Distance: 2m/2m3: 0-2 2m4-2m7: 0-1 3m+: 0-0
Track: LH: 0-1 RH: 0-2 Tight: 0-2 Gall: 0-0
Aids: Bl: 0-0 Vi: 0-0 Tstrap: 0-0
Best Rating: 98 12/02 Winc 2m   gd-sft Hdl

She looked to need a greater test of stamina after her two bumpers when touched off at Wincanton in December but disappointing next time.

Clod Hopper (IRE)

13-y-o gr g Roselier (FR)-Clodagh Lady (Boreen (FR))
Ian Williams M Murphy

Placings:00P/0P32/10312/61F4P36/15/1U440/P   (0684)
2002/03: 24⁰G,

	Starts	1st	2nd	3rd	Win & Pl
Chases	1	0	0	0	
Career Total	27	5	2	3	22316
97 5/00 Towc	3m1f	E(0-115)HCh		G-F	£3276
97 3/00 Ludl	3m	E(0-115)HCh		GD	£6201
100 12/98 Ludl	2m4f	D(0-115)HCh		G-S	£3696
88 1/97 Winc	2m6f	F(0-105)HHdl		G-F	£2372
80 11/96 Asct	2m4f	D(0-105)HHdl		G-F	£3591
		Total win prize-money £19137			

Going: Sf: 0-0 GS: 0-0 Gd: 0-1 GF: - Fm: 0-0
Distance: 2m/2m3: 0-0 2m4-2m7: 0-0 3m+: 0-1
Track: LH: 0-1 RH: 0-0 Tight: 0-0 Gall: 0-0
Aids: Bl: 0-0 Vi: 0-0 Tstrap: 0-0
Best Rating: 100 12/98 Ludl 2m4f   gd-sft Ch

Clodagh Valley (IRE)

8-y-o b g Doubletour (USA)-Raise A Princess (USA) (Raise A Native)
R J Bevis Carden Arms Racing Club

Placings:0344/000000/P-P0   (0208)
2002/03: 24⁴G, 22⁰G,

	Starts	1st	2nd	3rd	Win & Pl
Chases	2	0	0	0	
Career Total	13	0	0	1	680

Going: Sf: 0-0 GS: 0-0 Gd: 0-2 GF: - Fm: 0-0
Distance: 2m/2m3: 0-0 2m4-2m7: 0-1 3m+: 0-1
Track: LH: 0-1 RH: 0-1 Tight: 0-1 Gall: 0-0
Aids: Bl: 0-0 Vi: 0-0 Tstrap: 0-0
Best Rating: 89 3/00 Thur 2m   soft NHF

Clodoald (FR)

86(109h)   (110+h)**65**

6-y-o b g Beaudelaire (USA)-Mint Stick (FR) (Tropular)
M C Pipe Stef Stefanou

Placings:6/02F032255640132000/302300000P44-
2P41113B   (1943)
2002/03: 16²GF, 20⁵S, 22⁴GF, 16¹GF, 20¹GF, 20¹GF, 21⁸G,

	Starts	1st	2nd	3rd	Win & Pl
Hurdles	8	3	1	0	10519
Career Total	39	4	6	5	38900
110 9/02 Hntg	2m4f110yD(0-120)HHdl		G-F	£4114
106 8/02 Worc	2m4f	G Hdl		GD	£2934
109 7/02 Uttx	2m	G(0-95)HHdl		G-F	£2086
12/00 Engh	2m1f			Ch	HVY	£6244
		Total win prize-money £15379			

Going: Sf: 0-1 GS: 0-0 Gd: 1-2 GF: - Fm: 2-5
Distance: 2m/2m3: 1-3 **2m4-2m7: 2-6** 3m+: 0-0
Track: LH: **2-7** RH: 1-1 Tight: 0-2 **Gall: 1-2**
Aids: Bl: 0-0 Vi: 0-0 Tstrap: 0-0
Best Rating: 110 10/02 Chep 2m4f   gd-fm Hdl

Fair form in selling and handicap hurdles, acts on a sound surface and stays two miles five furlongs.

Clonmel's Minella (IRE)

115   **121**

12-y-o b g Strong Gale-Martones Chance (Golden Love)
Michael Hourigan John J Nallen

Placings:1/130/U40F/211F320U   (1035a)
2002/03: 21²GF, 19¹F, 22¹G, 18⁵S, 24³HY, 19²S, 32⁰G, 20⁰GF,

	Starts	1st	2nd	3rd	Win & Pl
Chases	8	2	1	1	29520
Career Total	16	4	2	2	38643
99 10/02 Cork	2m6f	(0-116)HCh		GD	£7975
91 9/02 List	2m3f	(0-95)HCh		FRM	£6984
126 1/00 Naas	2m	Hdl		SH	£4416
116 4/98 List	2m4f	NHF		Y-S	£2978
		Total win prize-money £22354			

Going: Sf: 0-3 GS: 0-0 Gd: 1-2 GF: - Fm: 1-3
Distance: 2m/2m3: 1-3 2m4-2m7: 1-3 3m+: 0-2
Track: LH: 0-4 RH: 0-1 Tight: 0-0 Gall: 0-1
Aids: Bl: 0-0 Vi: 0-0 Tstrap: 0-0
Best Rating: 126 1/00 Naas 2m   sft-hvy Hdl

Fair Irish chaser at up to two and three-quarter miles; effective on most ground.

Clonroche Vinyls (IRE)

101   **89**

8-y-o ch m Rashar (USA)-Clonroche Beggar (Pauper)
Ferdy Murphy Nicholas Butterly

Placings:f3024-630605   (4752)
2002/03: 24⁶S, 16³HY, 20⁰GS, 22⁶G, 22⁰G, 24⁵G,

	Starts	1st	2nd	3rd	Win & Pl
Hurdles	6	0	0	1	529
Career Total	11	1	1	2	3364
100 12/01 Folk	2m1f110yH NHF			HVY	£1589
		Total win prize-money £1589			

Going: Sf: 0-2 GS: 0-1 Gd: 0-3 GF: - Fm: 0-0
Distance: 2m/2m3: 0-1 2m4-2m7: 0-3 3m+: 0-2
Track: LH: 0-4 RH: 0-2 Tight: 0-2 Gall: 0-1
Aids: Bl: 0-0 Vi: 0-0 Tstrap: 0-0
Best Rating: 101 3/02 Towc 2m5f   soft Hdl

Plating-class hurdler; heavy ground bumper winner, best effort over hurdles when third at Newcastle in January.

Clonshire Paddy (IRE)

103(93h)   (82h)98

7-y-o gr g Roselier (FR)-Gusserane Princess (Paddy s Stream)

C Grant   Lord Daresbury & J E Greenall

Placings:64/62503/F-032U5F00   (4141)
2002/03: 23⁰G, 25³HY, 22³HY, 27⁰US, 25⁵S, 25⁶GS, 22⁰GS, 24⁰S,

	Starts	1st	2nd	3rd	Win & Pl
Hurdles	3	0	0	0	0
Chases	5	0	1	1	1699
Career Total	16	0	2	2	3033

Going:	Sf: 0-5 GS: 0-2 Gd: 0-1 GF: - Fm: 0-0
Distance:	2m/2m3: 0-0 2m4-2m7: 0-3 3m+: 0-5
Track:	LH: 0-8 RH: 0-0 Tight: 0-3 Gall: 0-0
Aids:	Bl: 0-0 Vi: 0-0 Tstrap: 0-0
Best Rating:	108 12/02 Kels 2m6f110y heavy R

Moderate staying novice chaser; stays three miles plus; appreciates testing ground.

Cloth Of Gold

101   122

6-y-o b g Barathea (IRE)-Bustinetta (Bustino)

Lady Herries   Mrs H A Cameron-Rose

Placings:461-1   (0578)
2002/03: 22¹G,

	Starts	1st	2nd	3rd	Win & Pl
Hurdles	1	1	0	0	3310
Career Total	4	2	0	0	6145
122	6/02	NAbb	2m6f	D(0-120)HHdl	GD	£3309
96	4/02	Hntg	2m5f110yE Hdl	G-F	£2835
			Total win prize-money £6145		

Going:	Sf: 0-0 GS: 0-0 Gd: 1-1 GF: - Fm: 0-0
Distance:	2m/2m3: 0-0 2m4-2m7: 1-1 3m+: 0-0
Track:	LH: 1-1 RH: 0-0 Tight: 1-1 Gall: 0-0
Aids:	Bl: 0-0 Vi: 0-0 Tstrap: 0-0
Best Rating:	122 6/02 NAbb 2m6f good Hdl

Cloudkicker (IRE)

(92h)   (50h)83

10-y-o b g Dry Dock-Last Sprite (Tug Of War)

Miss Venetia Williams   A J Roberts

Placings:346P/52F-FU0P   (2781)
2002/03: 26⁶HY, 21ᵁGS, 22⁰GS, 19⁰S,

	Starts	1st	2nd	3rd	Win & Pl
Hurdles	2	0	0	0	0
Chases	2	0	0	0	0
Career Total	11	0	1	1	1198

Going:	Sf: 0-2 GS: 0-2 Gd: 0-0 GF: - Fm: 0-0
Distance:	2m/2m3: 0-0 2m4-2m7: 0-3 3m+: 0-1
Track:	LH: 0-1 RH: 0-3 Tight: 0-2 Gall: 0-0
Aids:	Bl: 0-0 Vi: 0-0 Tstrap: 0-0
Best Rating:	100 12/99 Uttx 2m soft NHF

Cloudy Creek (IRE)

99(102h)   (99h)107

9-y-o gr g Roselier (FR)-Jacob s Creek (IRE) (Buckskin (FR))

Miss H C Knight   Chamberlain Addiscott Silk Partnership

Placings:10-4F6P   (3851)
2002/03: 24⁴GS, 24⁴S, 20⁶GS, 24⁰GS,

	Starts	1st	2nd	3rd	Win & Pl
Chases	4	0	0	0	375
Career Total	6	1	0	0	2864
99	3/02	Plum	2m5f	E Hdl		G-S	£2488
			Total win prize-money £2489			

Going:	Sf: 0-1 GS: 0-3 Gd: 0-0 GF: - Fm: 0-0
Distance:	2m/2m3: 0-0 2m4-2m7: 0-1 3m+: 0-3
Track:	LH: 0-0 RH: 0-4 Tight: 0-2 Gall: 0-1
Aids:	Bl: 0-0 Vi: 0-0 Tstrap: 0-0
Best Rating:	107 12/02 Tntn 3m gd-sft Ch

Former point winner, won his hurdle debut over two miles five on easy ground. Has shown ability over fences. Likes to race prominently.

Cloudy Grey (IRE)

109f   131f

6-y-o gr g Roselier (FR)-Dear Limousin (Pollerton)

Miss E C Lavelle   Mrs J R Lavelle & Mrs A Hepworth

Placings:4112   (3528)
2002/03: 16⁴S, 17¹G, 16¹GS, 16²G,

	Starts	1st	2nd	3rd	Win & Pl
NH Flat	4	2	1	0	8481
Career Total	4	2	1	0	8481
128	1/03	Hayd	2m	H NHF	G-S	£2121
109	12/02	Hrfd	2m1f	H NHF	GD	£1960
			Total win prize-money £4081		

Going:	Sf: 0-1 GS: 1-1 Gd: 1-2 GF: - Fm: 0-0
Distance:	2m/2m3: 2-4 2m4-2m7: 0-0 3m+: 0-0
Track:	LH: 1-2 RH: 1-2 Tight: 0-0 Gall: 0-1
Aids:	Bl: 0-0 Vi: 0-0 Tstrap: 0-0
Best Rating:	131 2/03 Newb 2m110y good NHF

Showed promise but ran very green on his debut in a Sandown bumper; easy winner next time. Won well under a penalty at Haydock next time. His trainer was later reported as saying that he is potentially the best horse she has ever trained.

Club Royal

100(96h)   (80 h)80+

6-y-o b g Alflora (IRE)-Miss Club Royal (Avocat)

D McCain   Halewood International Ltd

Placings:P6402   (4661)
2002/03: 17⁷G, 16⁶GS, 17⁴GS, 17⁰G, 17²GF,

	Starts	1st	2nd	3rd	Win & Pl
Hurdles	5	0	1	0	1282
Career Total	5	0	1	0	1282

Going:	Sf: 0-1 GS: 0-2 Gd: 0-1 GF: - Fm: 0-0
Distance:	2m/2m3: 0-5 2m4-2m7: 0-0 3m+: 0-0
Track:	LH: 0-3 RH: 0-2 Tight: 0-3 Gall: 0-0
Aids:	Bl: 0-0 Vi: 0-0 Tstrap: 0-0
Best Rating:	80 4/03 Carl 2m1f gd-fm Hdl

Plating-class novice hurdler; won a weak novices hurdle at Sedgefield in May; third on debut over fences at Market Rasen the following month; stays two and a half miles.

Co Optimist

99   98+

6-y-o b g Homo Sapien-Tapua Taranata (IRE) (Mandalus)

N A Twiston-Davies   The Co-Optimistic Partnership

Placings:15064-5325   (3523)
2002/03: 17⁵G, 22³GS, 26²S, 24⁵G,

	Starts	1st	2nd	3rd	Win & Pl
Hurdles	4	0	1	1	1704
Career Total	9	1	1	1	3244
103	10/01	MRas	2m1f110yH NHF	GD	£1540
			Total win prize-money £1540		

Going:	Sf: 0-1 GS: 0-1 Gd: 0-2 GF: - Fm: 0-0
Distance:	2m/2m3: 0-1 2m4-2m7: 0-1 3m+: 0-2
Track:	LH: 0-1 RH: 0-3 Tight: 0-0 Gall: 0-1
Aids:	Bl: 0-0 Vi: 0-0 Tstrap: 0-0
Best Rating:	103 10/01 MRas 2m1f110y good NHF

Disappointing after winning a bumper at Market Rasen on his debut, but running quite well over hurdles late in 2002. Stays three miles.

Coachman (IRE)

68f   29f

5-y-o b g King s Ride-Royal Shares (IRE) (Royal Fountain)

J Howard Johnson   J Howard Johnson

Placings:0   (4665)
2002/03: 17⁰GF,

	Starts	1st	2nd	3rd	Win & Pl
NH Flat	1	0	0	0	
Career Total	1	0	0	0	

Going:	Sf: 0-0 GS: 0-0 Gd: 0-0 GF: - Fm: 0-1
Distance:	2m/2m3: 0-1 2m4-2m7: 0-0 3m+: 0-0
Track:	LH: 0-0 RH: 0-1 Tight: 0-0 Gall: 0-0
Aids:	Bl: 0-0 Vi: 0-0 Tstrap: 0-0
Best Rating:	29 4/03 Carl 2m1f gd-fm NHF

Coastguard (IRE)

92(95h)   (90h)89

9-y-o b g Satco (FR)-Godlike (Godswalk (USA))

C J Mann   The Coastlyne Partnership

Placings:526311P/53UP214651-3U3003P   (4765)
2002/03: 24³S, 22ᵁS, 21³S, 22⁰GS, 24⁰GS, 22³S, 31⁰G,

	Starts	1st	2nd	3rd	Win & Pl
Hurdles	1	0	0	0	0
Chases	6	0	0	3	2053
Career Total	24	4	2	5	21020
105	3/02	Newb	2m6f110yD(0-120)HCh	G-S	£7247
101	12/01	Strf	2m5f110yF(0-110)HCh	SFT	£3549
97	3/01	Plum	2m5f	F(0-90)Hdl	HVY	£2320
96	2/01	Folk	2m6f110yF(0-110)HHdl	HVY	£1985
			Total win prize-money £15103		

Going:	Sf: 0-4 GS: 0-2 Gd: 0-1 GF: - Fm: 0-0
Distance:	2m/2m3: 0-0 2m4-2m7: 0-4 3m+: 0-3
Track:	LH: 0-2 RH: 0-4 Tight: 0-2 Gall: 0-1
Aids:	Bl: 0-7 Vi: 0-0 Tstrap: 0-0
Best Rating:	105 3/02 Newb 2m6f110y gd-sft Ch

Modest handicap chaser; suited by two and half to three miles and soft ground.

Coastward (IRE)

7-y-o b g Scenic-Sarakarta (USA) (Trempolino (USA))

P R Hedger   Chris Silverthorne

Placings:46/P   (0057)
2002/03: 17⁰G,

	Starts	1st	2nd	3rd	Win & Pl
Hurdles	1	0	0	0	
Career Total	3	0	0	0	192

Going:	Sf: 0-0 GS: 0-0 Gd: 0-1 GF: - Fm: 0-0			
Distance:	2m/2m3: 0-1 2m4-2m7: 0-0 3m+: 0-0			
Track:	LH: 0-0 RH: 0-1 Tight: 0-1 Gall: 0-0			
Aids:	Bl: 0-0 Vi: 0-0 Tstrap: 0-0			
Best Rating:	**96** 1/00 Leop 2m		yield	NHF

Cobbet (CZE)

112(110h)   (127h)**126**

7-y-o b g Favoured Nations (IRE)-Creace (CZE) (Sirano (CZE))

T R George Timothy N Chick

Placings:101122344-62331   (4612)

2002/03: 17⁶GF, 16²GF, 16³GF, 16³GS, 16¹G,

	Starts	1st	2nd	3rd	Win & Pl
Hurdles	1	0	0	0	0
Chases	4	1	1	2	17598
Career Total	14	4	3	3	31112
126	4/03 Chel 2m110y C(0-135)HCh	£12760			
115	10/01 Winc 2m F(0-110)HHdl	GD £3250			
104	10/01 Winc 2m F(0-100)HHdl	G-F £2485			
100	5/01 Fknm 2m G Hdl	G-F £1596			
	Total win prize-money £20091				

Going:	Sf: 0-0 GS: 0-1 Gd: 1-1 GF: - Fm: 0-3			
Distance:	2m/2m3: 1-5 2m4-2m7: 0-0 3m+: 0-3			
Track:	LH: 1-2 RH: 0-3 Tight: 0-1 Gall: 1-2			
Aids:	Bl: 0-0 Vi: 0-0 Tstrap: 0-0			
Best Rating:	**126** 4/03 Chel 2m110y good Ch			

Fair novice chaser; ex-Polish-trained; landed a hat-trick of chases between April and June 2003; two miles is his trip; best on decent ground; goes well fresh.

Cobreces

101   **123+**

5-y-o b g Environment Friend-Oleada (IRE) (Tirol)

P F Nicholls (M Rolland 1/12) Gerry Mizel & Terry Warner

Placings:1143-13005211   (4281)

2002/03: 18¹VS, 17³VS, 20⁰VS, 20⁰VS, 18⁵HY, 16²S, 20¹G, 20¹GF,

	Starts	1st	2nd	3rd	Win & Pl
Hurdles	1	0	0	0	1380
Chases	7	3	1	1	27788
Career Total	12	5	1	2	66209
118	3/03 Font D Ch	G-F £6104			
123	3/03 Wwck 2m4f110yE Ch	GD £4252			
	5/02 Autl 2m2f Ch	VS £12368			
	11/01 Autl 1m7f Hdl	VS £12124			
	10/01 Autl 1m7f Hdl	VS £14549			
	Total win prize-money £49398				

Going:	Sf: 0-2 GS: 0-0 Gd: 1-1 GF: - Fm: 1-1			
Distance:	2m/2m3: 1-4 2m4-2m7: 2-4 3m+: 0-0			
Track:	LH: 1-1 RH: 0-1 Tight: 1-2 Gall: 0-0			
Aids:	Bl: 0-0 Vi: 0-0 Tstrap: 0-0			
Best Rating:	**123** 3/03 Wwck 2m4f110y good Ch			

Decent novice chaser; acts on both fast and soft ground; effective at around two and a half miles.

Cock A Hoop

101   **91**

9-y-o b g Roscoe Blake-Rose Delight (Idiots Delight)

C J Mann Mrs Nicholas Jones

Placings:PP/1/P-22P4   (1200)

2002/03: 24²GF, 22²GF, 27⁰GF, 26⁴GF,

	Starts	1st	2nd	3rd	Win & Pl
Hurdles	4	0	2	0	1783
Career Total	8	1	2	0	4608

92	6/00 Hrfd 3m2f E Hdl	G-F £2824		
	Total win prize-money £2824			

Going:	Sf: 0-0 GS: 0-0 Gd: 0-0 GF: - Fm: 0-4			
Distance:	2m/2m3: 0-0 2m4-2m7: 0-1 3m+: 0-3			
Track:	LH: 0-3 RH: 0-1 Tight: 0-2 Gall: 0-0			
Aids:	Bl: 0-0 Vi: 0-0 Tstrap: 0-0			
Best Rating:	**92** 6/02 NAbb 2m6f gd-fm Hdl			

Lightly raced hurdler; stays three miles and acts on fast ground.

Cock Of The North (IRE)

100   **102**

6-y-o b g Supreme Leader-Our Quest (Private Walk)

C R Egerton Charles Egerton

Placings:2   (2669)

2002/03: 19²S,

	Starts	1st	2nd	3rd	Win & Pl
Hurdles	1	0	1	0	1030
Career Total	1	0	1	0	1030

Going:	Sf: 0-1 GS: 0-0 Gd: 0-0 GF: - Fm: 0-0			
Distance:	2m/2m3: 0-0 2m4-2m7: 0-1 3m+: 0-0			
Track:	LH: 0-0 RH: 0-1 Tight: 0-0 Gall: 0-0			
Aids:	Bl: 0-0 Vi: 0-0 Tstrap: 0-0			
Best Rating:	**102** 12/02 Hrfd 2m3f110y soft Hdl			

A half-brother to Rough Quest, he shaped with promise on his debut.

Cock Of The Roost (IRE)

82   **58**

6-y-o b g Executive Perk-Sly Maid (Rapid River)

S T Lewis Simon T Lewis

Placings:00050P0P6   (3350)

2002/03: 16⁹G, 16⁰GF, 16⁹G, 17⁵GF, 17⁰G, 20⁰GS, 16⁰S, 20⁰HY, 20⁶HY,

	Starts	1st	2nd	3rd	Win & Pl
NH Flat	4	0	0	0	0
Hurdles	5	0	0	0	0
Career Total	9	0	0	0	0

Going:	Sf: 0-3 GS: 0-1 Gd: 0-3 GF: - Fm: 0-2			
Distance:	2m/2m3: 0-6 2m4-2m7: 0-3 3m+: 0-0			
Track:	LH: 0-5 RH: 0-4 Tight: 0-1 Gall: 0-0			
Aids:	Bl: 0-0 Vi: 0-0 Tstrap: 0-4			
Best Rating:	**76** 10/02 Hrfd 2m1f gd-fm NHF			

Cockatoo Ridge

106f   **91f**

6-y-o ch g Riverwise (USA)-Came Cottage (Nearly A Hand)

N R Mitchell Mrs E Mitchell

Placings:051   (4760)

2002/03: 16⁹GS, 16⁵S, 18¹GF,

	Starts	1st	2nd	3rd	Win & Pl
NH Flat	3	1	0	0	1953
Career Total	3	1	0	0	1953
91	4/03 Font 2m2f110yH NHF	G-F £1953			
	Total win prize-money £1953				

Going:	Sf: 0-1 GS: 0-1 Gd: 0-0 GF: - Fm: 1-1			
Distance:	2m/2m3: 1-3 2m4-2m7: 0-0 3m+: 0-0			
Track:	LH: 1-1 RH: 0-2 Tight: 1-1 Gall: 0-0			

Aids:	Bl: 0-0 Vi: 0-0 Tstrap: 0-0			
Best Rating:	**91** 4/03 Font 2m2f110y gd-fm NHF			

Moderate bumper performer; scored at Fontwell in April 2003; acts on fast ground.

Cockney Rainbow (IRE)

94   **77+**

6-y-o b m Rainbows For Life (CAN)-Cockney Ground (IRE) (Common Grounds)

R H Alner P M De Wilde

Placings:4P44   (2706)

2002/03: 20⁴S, 22⁰G, 20⁴S, 16⁴GS,

	Starts	1st	2nd	3rd	Win & Pl
Hurdles	4	0	0	0	656
Career Total	4	0	0	0	656

Going:	Sf: 0-2 GS: 0-1 Gd: 0-1 GF: - Fm: 0-0			
Distance:	2m/2m3: 0-1 2m4-2m7: 0-3 3m+: 0-0			
Track:	LH: 0-1 RH: 0-3 Tight: 0-1 Gall: 0-0			
Aids:	Bl: 0-0 Vi: 0-0 Tstrap: 0-0			
Best Rating:	**77** 12/02 Winc 2m gd-sft Hdl			

Very good rules debut when promising fourth to a really good mare. Will stay further and looks useful.

Cocksure (IRE)

8-y-o b g Nomination-Hens Grove (Alias Smith (USA))

B J Llewellyn Miss Emily Jane Jones

Placings:U62000/0034000/50P0/P   (0957)

2002/03: 16⁰GS,

	Starts	1st	2nd	3rd	Win & Pl
Hurdles	1	0	0	0	0
Career Total	18	0	1	1	979

Going:	Sf: 0-0 GS: 0-1 Gd: 0-0 GF: - Fm: 0-0			
Distance:	2m/2m3: 0-1 2m4-2m7: 0-0 3m+: 0-0			
Track:	LH: 0-1 RH: 0-0 Tight: 0-0 Gall: 0-0			
Aids:	Bl: 0-0 Vi: 0-0 Tstrap: 0-0			
Best Rating:	**97** 11/98 Fair 2m yld-sft Hdl			

Code Sign (USA)

102   **96+**

4-y-o b g Gulch (USA)-Karasavina (IRE) (Sadler s Wells (USA))

P J Hobbs (J H M Gosden 5/10) Denise Winton and Elizabeth Hodgson

Placings:600   (3776)

2002/03: 17⁶S, 17⁰S, 17⁰GS,

	Starts	1st	2nd	3rd	Win & Pl
Hurdles	3	0	0	0	0
Career Total	3	0	0	0	0

Going:	Sf: 0-2 GS: 0-1 Gd: 0-0 GF: - Fm: 0-0			
Distance:	2m/2m3: 0-3 2m4-2m7: 0-0 3m+: 0-0			
Track:	LH: 0-0 RH: 0-3 Tight: 0-2 Gall: 0-0			
Aids:	Bl: 0-0 Vi: 0-0 Tstrap: 0-0			
Best Rating:	**66** 2/03 Extr 2m1f gd-sft Hdl			

Moderate hurdler; frustrating maiden on the Flat; took advantage of being handicapped on unsuitably soft ground when winning over two miles at Worcester May 2003; beaten off an 11lb higher mark next time.

Cody

85   **64**

4-y-o ch c Zilzal (USA)-Ibtihaj (USA) (Raja Baba (USA))
G A Ham   P A Dales

Placings:000000   (4622)
2002/03: 16⁰GS, 17⁰GS, 17⁰GS, 16⁰G, 19⁰G, 22⁰GF,

	Starts	1st	2nd	3rd	Win & Pl
Hurdles	6	0	0	0	
Career Total	6	0	0	0	

Going:	Sf: 0-1 GS: 0-2 Gd: 0-2 GF: - Fm: 0-1
Distance:	2m/2m3: 0-5 2m4-2m7: 0-1 3m+: 0-0
Track:	LH: 0-3 RH: 0-3 Tight: 0-1 Gall: 0-1
Aids:	Bl: 0-0 Vi: 0-0 Tstrap: 0-0
Best Rating:	64 2/03 Extr 2m1f gd-sft Hdl

Moderate hurdler; limited promise so far.

Cold Comfort

74

11-y-o b g Arctic Lord-Main Brand (Main Reef)
I R Brown   I R Brown

Placings:U6-F   (0554)
2002/03: 19FGF,

	Starts	1st	2nd	3rd	Win & Pl
Hurdles	1	0	0	0	
Career Total	3	0	0	0	0

Going:	Sf: 0-0 GS: 0-0 Gd: 0-0 GF: 0-1 Fm: 0-1
Distance:	2m/2m3: 0-0 2m4-2m7: 0-1 3m+: 0-0
Track:	LH: 0-0 RH: 0-1 Tight: 0-0 Gall: 0-0
Aids:	Bl: 0-0 Vi: 0-0 Tstrap: 0-0
Best Rating:	74 4/02 Chep 2m110y gd-fm Hdl

Coleham

83f   **60f**

5-y-o b m Saddlers Hall (IRE)-Katie Scarlett (Lochnager)
W M Brisbourne   John Pugh

Placings:14-2   (0436)
2002/03: 16²GF,

	Starts	1st	2nd	3rd	Win & Pl
NH Flat	1	0	1	0	445
Career Total	3	1	1	0	2478
94	2/02	Ludl	2m	H NHF	GD £2033
				Total win prize-money £2034	

Going:	Sf: 0-0 GS: 0-0 Gd: 0-0 GF: 0-1 Fm: 0-1
Distance:	2m/2m3: 0-1 2m4-2m7: 0-0 3m+: 0-0
Track:	LH: 0-0 RH: 0-1 Tight: 0-0 Gall: 0-1
Aids:	Bl: 0-0 Vi: 0-0 Tstrap: 0-0
Best Rating:	94 3/02 Ludl 2m soft NHF

Ready winner on her bumper debut.

Colette (IRE)

101

6-y-o b m Nicolotte-Ascensiontide (Ela-Mana-Mou)
S T Lewis   Simon T Lewis

Placings:23/4065F023000412-P   (0051)
2002/03: 20PG,

	Starts	1st	2nd	3rd	Win & Pl
Hurdles	1	0	0	0	
Career Total	17	1	3	2	4845
82	3/02	Plum	2m5f	G(0-90)HHdl	GD £2107
				Total win prize-money £2107	

Going:	Sf: 0-0 GS: 0-0 Gd: 0-1 GF: - Fm: 0-0
Distance:	2m/2m3: 0-0 2m4-2m7: 0-1 3m+: 0-0
Track:	LH: 0-3 RH: 0-3 Tight: 0-1 Gall: 0-1
Aids:	Bl: 0-0 Vi: 0-0 Tstrap: 0-0
Best Rating:	101 4/01 Plum 2m heavy Hdl

Modest hurdler, stays two miles five furlongs.

Colin's Hope

5-y-o b g Then Again-Bahawir Pour (USA) (Green Dancer (USA))
M J Gingell (M W Easterby 31/10)   Axe And Compass

Placings:6-006P0   (3742)
2002/03: 17⁰G, 17⁰G, 18⁶HY, 22PHY, 16⁰G,

	Starts	1st	2nd	3rd	Win & Pl
NH Flat	3	0	0	0	0
Hurdles	2	0	0	0	0
Career Total	6	0	0	0	0

Going:	Sf: 0-2 GS: 0-0 Gd: 0-3 GF: - Fm: 0-0
Distance:	2m/2m3: 0-4 2m4-2m7: 0-1 3m+: 0-0
Track:	LH: 0-3 RH: 0-2 Tight: 0-4 Gall: 0-1
Aids:	Bl: 0-0 Vi: 0-0 Tstrap: 0-0
Best Rating:	72 10/02 Sedg 2m1f good NHF

Collective Dream

8-y-o b g North Col-Tournanova (High Line)
R Curtis   Collective Dreamers

Placings:P   (3901)
2002/03: 24PS,

	Starts	1st	2nd	3rd	Win & Pl
Hurdles	1	0	0	0	
Career Total	1	0	0	0	

Going:	Sf: 0-1 GS: 0-0 Gd: 0-0 GF: - Fm: 0-0
Distance:	2m/2m3: 0-0 2m4-2m7: 0-0 3m+: 0-1
Track:	LH: 0-1 RH: 0-0 Tight: 0-0 Gall: 0-1
Aids:	Bl: 0-0 Vi: 0-0 Tstrap: 0-0
Best Rating:	0 3/03 Newb 3m110y soft Hdl

College City (IRE)

103   **88**

4-y-o b g College Chapel-Polish Crack (IRE) (Polish Patriot (USA))
R C Guest (N B Mason 17/1)   Mrs Anna Kenny

Placings:00012   (3967)
2002/03: 16⁰GS, 16⁰G, 16⁰G, 16¹S, 19²S,

	Starts	1st	2nd	3rd	Win & Pl
Hurdles	5	1	1	0	3153
Career Total	5	1	1	0	3153
88	2/03	Newc	2m	G(0-95)HHdl	SFT £2387
				Total win prize-money £2387	

Going:	Sf: 1-2 GS: 0-1 Gd: 0-2 GF: - Fm: 0-0
Distance:	2m/2m3: 1-5 2m4-2m7: 0-0 3m+: 0-0
Track:	LH: 1-4 RH: 0-1 Tight: 0-3 Gall: 1-2
Aids:	Bl: 0-0 Vi: 0-0 Tstrap: 0-0
Best Rating:	88 2/03 Newc 2m soft Hdl

Plating-class; runaway winner of a selling hurdle at Newcastle in February and runner-up in better event at Catterick a week later.

Colliers Court

85f   **86f**

6-y-o b g Puget (USA)-Rag Time Belle (Raga Navarro (ITY))
Mrs L Williamson   The Castle Bend Syndicate

Placings:600   (3570)
2002/03: 16⁶S, 16⁰GS, 17⁰HY,

	Starts	1st	2nd	3rd	Win & Pl
NH Flat	3	0	0	0	0
Career Total	3	0	0	0	0

Going:	Sf: 0-2 GS: 0-1 Gd: 0-0 GF: - Fm: 0-0
Distance:	2m/2m3: 0-3 2m4-2m7: 0-0 3m+: 0-0
Track:	LH: 0-3 RH: 0-0 Tight: 0-1 Gall: 0-0
Aids:	Bl: 0-0 Vi: 0-0 Tstrap: 0-0
Best Rating:	86 12/02 Uttx 2m soft NHF

Colliers Quay (IRE)

107   **113**

7-y-o b g Warcraft (USA)-Francois s Crumpet (IRE) (Strong Gale)
Miss Venetia Williams (M J P O Brien 1/8)   The Quay Quintet

Placings:60-001412050   (3133)
2002/03: 18⁰S, 16⁰S, 24¹GF, 20⁴YS, 26¹G, 21²G, 21⁰G, 24⁵GS, 24⁸S,

	Starts	1st	2nd	3rd	Win & Pl
NH Flat	1	0	0	0	0
Hurdles	8	2	1	0	11885
Career Total	11	2	1	0	11885
110	9/02	Sthl	3m2f	E Hdl	GD £2891
106	7/02	Cork	3m	Hdl	G-F £7619
				Total win prize-money £10511	

Going:	Sf: 0-3 GS: 0-1 Gd: 1-3 GF: - Fm: 1-1
Distance:	2m/2m3: 0-2 2m4-2m7: 0-3 3m+: 2-4
Track:	LH: 1-2 RH: 0-4 Tight: 0-2 Gall: 0-0
Aids:	Bl: 0-0 Vi: 0-0 **Tstrap: 1-2**
Best Rating:	113 10/02 Plum 2m5f good Hdl

Had won a couple of novice hurdles prior to finding his penalty too much at Plumpton when running into a decent rival.

Colline De Feu

103   **99**

6-y-o b m Sabrehill (USA)-Band Of Fire (USA) (Chief s Crown (USA))
Mrs P Sly   David L Bayliss

Placings:061064-24533   (3117)
2002/03: 16²HY, 19⁴GS, 16⁵HY, 16³HY, 21³S,

	Starts	1st	2nd	3rd	Win & Pl
Hurdles	5	0	1	2	2075
Career Total	11	1	1	2	5466
95	1/02	Fknm	2m4f	D Hdl	SFT £3391
				Total win prize-money £3392	

Going:	Sf: 0-4 GS: 0-1 Gd: 0-0 GF: - Fm: 0-0
Distance:	2m/2m3: 0-4 2m4-2m7: 0-1 3m+: 0-0
Track:	LH: 0-2 RH: 0-3 Tight: 0-0 Gall: 0-1
Aids:	Bl: 0-0 Vi: 0-0 Tstrap: 0-0
Best Rating:	99 12/02 Leic 2m heavy Hdl

Moderate hurdler; won a weak Fakenham novices hurdle in January 2002 on testing ground.

Colnside Bonnie

98   **93**

5-y-o ch m Afzal-Armagnac Messenger (Pony Express)
B G Powell (H E Haynes 1/6) A Cutler

Placings:*2-540*FP2512F   (4511)
2002/03: 16²GS, 16⁵GF, 174ᶠGF, 17⁰HY, 19ᶠGS, 22ᴾGS, 17²S,
19⁵HY, 16¹GF, 17²F, 19ᶠGF,

	Starts	1st	2nd	3rd	Win & Pl
NH Flat	4	0	1	0	496
Hurdles	7	1	2	0	5781
Career Total	**11**	**1**	**3**	**0**	**6277**
89 3/03 Winc 2m		E(0-105)HHdl		G-F	£3489

Total win prize-money £3490

Going:	Sf: 0-3 GS: 0-3 Gd: 0-0 GF: - Fm: 1-5
Distance:	2m/2m3: 1-9 2m4-2m7: 0-2 3m+: 0-0
Track:	LH: 0-2 RH: 1-9 Tight: 0-4 Gall: 0-0
Aids:	Bl: 0-0 Vi: 0-0 Tstrap: 0-0
Best Rating:	93 3/03 Extr 2m1f firm Hdl

Front-runner; appreciated faster ground when winning two
mile novice handicap hurdle at Wincanton March 2003; possibly unlucky not to follow up under a penalty in a similar
event at Exeter the following week.

Colombe D'Or

104   **73+**

6-y-o gr g Petong-Deep Divide (Nashwan (USA))
M C Chapman Rasen Goes Racing

Placings:*04/*3063050-00056   (0908)
2002/03: 16⁰G, 17⁰GF, 17⁰GF, 16⁵GF, 17⁵GS,

	Starts	1st	2nd	3rd	Win & Pl
Hurdles	5	0	0	0	0
Career Total	**14**	**0**	**0**	**2**	**847**

Going:	Sf: 0-0 GS: 0-1 Gd: 0-1 GF: - Fm: 0-3
Distance:	2m/2m3: 0-5 2m4-2m7: 0-0 3m+: 0-3
Track:	LH: 0-2 RH: 0-3 Tight: 0-4 Gall: 0-0
Aids:	Bl: 0-1 Vi: 0-0 Tstrap: 0-0
Best Rating:	79 11/01 Hntg 2m110y good Hdl

Colombian Green (IRE)

103(113h)   (123h)**113**

9-y-o b g Sadler s Wells (USA)-Sharaya (USA) (Youth
(USA))
D R Gandolfo Starlight Racing

Placings:*0/2*F242/1346-3634P4   (4052)
2002/03: 16³GS, 16⁶HY, 17³GS, 20⁴S, 20ᴾS, 16⁴S,

	Starts	1st	2nd	3rd	Win & Pl
Hurdles	2	0	0	1	1038
Chases	4	0	1	3	3199
Career Total	**16**	**1**	**3**	**3**	**12418**
123 10/01 Hrfd 2m1f		D(0-120)HHdl		SFT	£3311

Total win prize-money £3311

Going:	Sf: 0-4 GS: 0-2 Gd: 0-0 GF: - Fm: 0-0
Distance:	2m/2m3: 0-4 2m4-2m7: 0-2 3m+: 0-0
Track:	LH: 0-4 RH: 0-6 Tight: 0-1 Gall: 0-0
Aids:	Bl: 0-0 Vi: 0-0 Tstrap: 0-0
Best Rating:	123 11/01 Asct 2m110y good Hdl

Fair novice chaser/decent winning hurdler; acts on soft
ground and is suited by around two miles; regularly held up;
fell on his chasing debut; better effort on his next try over
fences two years later, but well beaten in two starts since.

Colonel Braxton (IRE)

113   (151h)**158**

8-y-o b g Buckskin (FR)-Light The Lamp (Miners Lamp)
D T Hughes Mrs John Magnier

Placings:*162/*6111/B215-42120   (4132)
2002/03: 20⁴SH, 24²HY, 17¹S, 24²YS, 26⁹G,

	Starts	1st	2nd	3rd	Win & Pl
Hurdles	1	0	0	0	1380
Chases	4	1	2	0	47842
Career Total	**16**	**6**	**4**	**0**	**141703**
150 1/03 Fair	2m1f	Ch		SFT	£10551
143 2/02 Naas	2m4f	Ch		HVY	£15153
151 4/01 Fair	2m4f	Hdl		SFT	£35000
151 2/01 Leop	2m2f	Hdl		HVY	£23588
139 1/01 Naas	2m3f	Hdl		SFT	£5564
125 12/99 Leop	2m	NHF		SH	£4620

Total win prize-money £94480

Going:	Sf: 1-2 GS: 0-0 Gd: 0-1 GF: - Fm: 0-0
Distance:	2m/2m3: 1-1 2m4-2m7: 0-1 3m+: 0-3
Track:	LH: 0-3 RH: 1-2 Tight: 0-0 Gall: 0-1
Aids:	Bl: 0-0 Vi: 0-0 Tstrap: 0-0
Best Rating:	160 12/02 Leop 3m heavy Ch

High-class chaser; best form this term in comprehensive
defeats by Beef Or Salmon in the Ericsson and Hennessy
Cognac Gold Cups; effective at between 2m and 3m; acts on
a sound surface but handles soft/heavy ground.

Colonel Brown (IRE)

77   **19**

7-y-o b g Scenic-Musical Smoke (IRE) (Orchestra)
O O Neill R S And R J Lanchbury

Placings:*0/*0006000/5201P4-P6P   (0884)
2002/03: 17ᴾGF, 16⁶G, 17ᴾS,

	Starts	1st	2nd	3rd	Win & Pl
Hurdles	2	0	0	0	0
Chases	1	0	0	0	0
Career Total	**17**	**1**	**1**	**0**	**6170**
99 7/01 Dund	2m1f	Ch		FRM	£5008

Total win prize-money £5008

Going:	Sf: 0-1 GS: 0-0 Gd: 0-1 GF: - Fm: 0-1
Distance:	2m/2m3: 0-3 2m4-2m7: 0-0 3m+: 0-0
Track:	LH: 0-2 RH: 0-1 Tight: 0-3 Gall: 0-0
Aids:	Bl: 0-0 Vi: 0-0 Tstrap: 0-0
Best Rating:	99 7/01 Dund 2m1f firm Ch

Colonel Custer

8-y-o ch g Komaite (USA)-Mohican (Great Nephew)
R Brotherton Binding Matters Ltd

Placings:P-0   (0143)
2002/03: 20⁰GF,

	Starts	1st	2nd	3rd	Win & Pl
Hurdles	1	0	0	0	
Career Total	**2**	**0**	**0**	**0**	

Going:	Sf: 0-0 GS: 0-0 Gd: 0-0 GF: - Fm: 0-1
Distance:	2m/2m3: 0-0 2m4-2m7: 0-1 3m+: 0-0
Track:	LH: 0-1 RH: 0-0 Tight: 0-0 Gall: 0-0
Aids:	Bl: 0-0 Vi: 0-0 Tstrap: 0-0
Best Rating:	0 5/02 Chep 2m4f gd-fm Hdl

Colonel Frank

103   **113**

6-y-o b g Toulon-Fit For Firing (FR) (In Fijar (USA))
B G Powell The Hambledon Hunters

Placings:*0-*34612   (4527)
2002/03: 17³GS, 16⁴S, 19⁶G, 18¹G, 20²G,

	Starts	1st	2nd	3rd	Win & Pl
NH Flat	1	0	0	0	263
Hurdles	4	1	1	0	4899
Career Total	**6**	**1**	**1**	**1**	**5162**
111 3/03 Font	2m2f110yE Hdl		GD	£3464	

Total win prize-money £3465

Going:	Sf: 0-1 GS: 0-1 Gd: 1-3 GF: - Fm: 0-0
Distance:	2m/2m3: 1-4 2m4-2m7: 0-1 3m+: 0-0
Track:	LH: 1-4 RH: 0-1 Tight: 1-2 Gall: 0-2
Aids:	Bl: 0-0 Vi: 0-0 Tstrap: 0-0
Best Rating:	113 4/03 Uttx 2m4f110y good Hdl

Fair novice hurdler; front runner; stays 2m 4f; suited by a
sound surface.

Colonel Kurtz (USA)

5-y-o b g Slip Anchor-Rustaka (USA) (Riverman (USA))
John Berry The 1997 Partnership

Placings:P   (0765)
2002/03: 21ᴾGF,

	Starts	1st	2nd	3rd	Win & Pl
Hurdles	1	0	0	0	
Career Total	**1**	**0**	**0**	**0**	

Going:	Sf: 0-0 GS: 0-0 Gd: 0-0 GF: - Fm: 0-1
Distance:	2m/2m3: 0-0 2m4-2m7: 0-1 3m+: 0-0
Track:	LH: 0-1 RH: 0-0 Tight: 0-1 Gall: 0-0
Aids:	Bl: 0-0 Vi: 0-0 Tstrap: 0-0
Best Rating:	0 7/02 Sedg 2m5f110y gd-fm Hdl

Colonel Mustard

78   **33**

7-y-o ch g Keen-Juliet Bravo (Glow (USA))
Mrs H E Rees (P G Murphy 29/7) Mrs H E Rees

Placings:P/0000   (4217)
2002/03: 16⁰GF, 16⁹G, 17⁰S, 22⁰G,

	Starts	1st	2nd	3rd	Win & Pl
Hurdles	4	0	0	0	
Career Total	**5**	**0**	**0**	**0**	

Going:	Sf: 0-1 GS: 0-0 Gd: 0-2 GF: - Fm: 0-1
Distance:	2m/2m3: 0-3 2m4-2m7: 0-1 3m+: 0-0
Track:	LH: 0-3 RH: 0-1 Tight: 0-2 Gall: 0-1
Aids:	Bl: 0-0 Vi: 0-0 Tstrap: 0-0
Best Rating:	61 6/02 Worc 2m gd-fm Hdl

Colonel North (IRE)

(79h)   (55h)

7-y-o b g Distinctly North (USA)-Tricky (Song)
David Pearson David Pearson

Placings:4/00006   (3266)
2002/03: 20⁰GS, 16⁹G, 20⁰G, 17⁰S, 16⁶G,

	Starts	1st	2nd	3rd	Win & Pl
Hurdles	4	0	0	0	0
Chases	1	0	0	0	0
Career Total	**6**	**0**	**0**	**0**	**212**

Going:	Sf: 0-1 GS: 0-1 Gd: 0-3 GF: - Fm: 0-0
Distance:	2m/2m3: 0-3 2m4-2m7: 0-2 3m+: 0-0
Track:	LH: 0-5 RH: 0-0 Tight: 0-3 Gall: 0-1
Aids:	Bl: 0-0 Vi: 0-0 Tstrap: 0-0
Best Rating:	87 8/00 Worc 2m gd-fm Hdl

Colonial Rule (USA)
102   94

6-y-o b g Pleasant Colony (USA)-Musicale (USA) (The Minstrel (CAN))
Mrs L B Normile (Jonjo O Neill 12/3) A K Collins

Placings:022F1P/P-02P433P2P0   **(4795)**
2002/03: 20⁰G, 22²GF, 21²GS, 21⁴HY, 22³HY, 26³G, 22²S, 21²G, 24¹⁰G, 21⁰GF,

	Starts	1st	2nd	3rd	Win & Pl
Hurdles	10	0	2	2	2605
Career Total	17	1	4	2	5329
93 2/01 Catt 2m3f G(0-90)HHdl SFT £1708					
				Total win prize-money £1708	

Going:	Sf: 0-3 GS: 0-1 Gd: 0-4 GF: - Fm: 0-0
Distance:	2m/2m3: 0-0 2m4-2m7: 0-8 3m+: 0-2
Track:	LH: 0-4 RH: 0-6 Tight: 0-4 Gall: 0-2
Aids:	Bl: 0-3 Vi: 0-1 Tstrap: 0-3
Best Rating:	94 3/03 Hntg 2m5f110y good Hdl

Moderate hurdler; has been tried in blinkers and a visor; looks best at around two miles six, but stays further; acts on testing ground.

Colonial Sunrise (USA)
88   91

6-y-o b g Pleasant Colony (USA)-Dancing Reef (USA) (Danzig (USA))
T D Easterby Elite Racing Club

Placings:342/434-302   **(1980)**
2002/03: 16³GS, 16⁰G, 16²HY,

	Starts	1st	2nd	3rd	Win & Pl
Hurdles	3	0	1	1	1304
Career Total	9	0	2	3	2628

Going:	Sf: 0-1 GS: 0-1 Gd: 0-1 GF: - Fm: 0-0
Distance:	2m/2m3: 0-3 2m4-2m7: 0-0 3m+: 0-0
Track:	LH: 0-3 RH: 0-0 Tight: 0-1 Gall: 0-0
Aids:	Bl: 0-0 Vi: 0-0 Tstrap: 0-0
Best Rating:	95 4/01 MRas 1m5f110y gd-sft NHF

Colonial Sunset (IRE)
103₍₉₉ₕ₎   ₍₉₃ₕ₎105

9-y-o b g Lancastrian-Thai Nang (Tap On Wood)
Dr P Pritchard A J Whiting

Placings:200/0212P60/000/000/2-P500552320236   **(4430)**
2002/03: 21²G, 24²GF, 20⁶G, 20⁰GS, 24⁴G, 18⁵GF, 17⁵F, 16²G, 16⁵GF, 17²S, 20⁶G, 18²S, 16³HY, 20⁶GF,

	Starts	1st	2nd	3rd	Win & Pl
Hurdles	6	0	1	0	714
Chases	8	0	3	2	7224
Career Total	29	1	7	2	14750
106 12/98 Leop 2m Hdl SFT £4184					
				Total win prize-money £4185	

| Going: | Sf: 0-3 GS: 0-1 Gd: 0-5 GF: - Fm: 0-5 |
| Distance: | 2m/2m3: 0-7 2m4-2m7: 0-5 3m+: 0-2 |

Track:	LH: 0-9 RH: 0-4 Tight: 0-8 Gall: 0-1
Aids:	Bl: 0-3 Vi: 0-0 Tstrap: 0-0
Best Rating:	118 1/99 Leop 2m heavy Hdl

Plating-class hurdler; fair chaser; acts on soft ground; stays two and a half miles.

Colorado Falls (IRE)
106   103+

5-y-o b g Nashwan (USA)-Ballet Shoes (IRE) (Ela-Mana-Mou)
P Monteith J W D Campbell

Placings:1   **(0423)**
2002/03: 17¹HY,

	Starts	1st	2nd	3rd	Win & Pl
Hurdles	1	1	0	0	3458
Career Total	1	1	0	0	3458
103 6/02 Ctml 2m1f110yD Hdl HVY £3458					
				Total win prize-money £3458	

Going:	Sf: 1-1 GS: 0-0 Gd: 0-0 GF: - Fm: 0-0
Distance:	2m/2m3: 1-1 2m4-2m7: 0-0 3m+: 0-0
Track:	LH: 1-1 RH: 0-0 Tight: 1-1 Gall: 0-0
Aids:	Bl: 0-0 Vi: 0-0 Tstrap: 0-0
Best Rating:	103 6/02 Ctml 2m1f110y heavy Hdl

Won on his hurdling debut on heavy ground in June 2002; absent subsequently.

Colourful Life (IRE)
111₍₁₀₆c₎   ₍₁₃₂c₎125

7-y-o ch g Rainbows For Life (CAN)-Rasmara (Kalaglow)
Mrs M Reveley Andy Peake & David Jackson

Placings:4225/1U1F14F114-5022606   **(4475)**
2002/03: 16⁵HY, 21⁰GS, 16²GS, 16²S, 20⁶S, 16⁰G, 20⁶G,

	Starts	1st	2nd	3rd	Win & Pl
Hurdles	7	0	2	0	19739
Career Total	21	5	4	0	56793
116 2/02 Kemp 2m C(0-135)HHdl G-S £10920					
111 2/02 Newc 2m B HHdl SFT £8489					
120 11/01 Uttx 2m D Ch HVY £4944					
122 11/01 Weth 2m4f110yD(0-115)HCh GD £5372					
96 5/01 Weth 2m4f110yD Hdl GD £4011					
				Total win prize-money £33736	

Going:	Sf: 0-3 GS: 0-2 Gd: 0-2 GF: - Fm: 0-0
Distance:	2m/2m3: 0-4 2m4-2m7: 0-3 3m+: 0-0
Track:	LH: 0-5 RH: 0-1 Tight: 0-1 Gall: 0-2
Aids:	Bl: 0-0 Vi: 0-0 Tstrap: 0-0
Best Rating:	125 1/03 Leop 2m soft Hdl

Fair hurdler/chaser; runner-up in 2003 Pierce Hurdle; effective at up to two and a half miles; acts on most types of ground.

Colquhoun
105   110

9-y-o b g Rakaposhi King-Red Rambler (Rymer)
T R George B A Kilpatrick

Placings:2P5P1P/P2/F2U   **(4313)**
2002/03: 19²FG, 20²GS, 18⁰UG,

	Starts	1st	2nd	3rd	Win & Pl
Chases	3	0	1	0	1295
Career Total	11	1	3	0	6244
117 3/00 Chep 2m4f D Hdl G-S £3191					
				Total win prize-money £3192	

Going:	Sf: 0-0 GS: 0-1 Gd: 0-2 GF: - Fm: 0-0
Distance:	2m/2m3: 0-2 2m4-2m7: 0-1 3m+: 0-0
Track:	LH: 0-2 RH: 0-1 Tight: 0-0 Gall: 0-1

| Aids: | Bl: 0-0 Vi: 0-0 Tstrap: 0-0 |
| Best Rating: | 117 3/00 Chep 2m4f   gd-sft Hdl |

Modest novice chaser; regularly placed without winning; chancey jumper; stays 2m 6f

Columbus (IRE)
117   113

6-y-o b g Sadler s Wells (USA)-Northern Script (USA) (Arts And Letters (USA))
Mrs J Candlish (C Grant 11/10) Racing For You Limited

Placings:32126P/4262222   **(4563)**
2002/03: 17⁴GF, 19²S, 20⁶HY, 19²G, 19²S, 22²GF, 24²GF,

	Starts	1st	2nd	3rd	Win & Pl
Hurdles	7	0	5	0	9344
Career Total	13	1	7	1	14635
93 1/01 Ayr 2m E Hdl SFT £2814					
				Total win prize-money £2814	

Going:	Sf: 0-3 GS: 0-0 Gd: 0-1 GF: - Fm: 0-3
Distance:	2m/2m3: 0-1 2m4-2m7: 0-5 3m+: 0-1
Track:	LH: 0-2 RH: 0-5 Tight: 0-1 Gall: 0-0
Aids:	Bl: 0-1 Vi: 0-6 Tstrap: 0-0
Best Rating:	112 4/03 Bang 3m gd-fm Hdl

Modest hurdler at around two and a half miles; has frequently changed stables; suited by cut in the ground, but also handles a sound surface; by no means reliable; usually wears a visor.

Colvada

7-y-o b m North Col-Prevada (Soldier Rose)
P G Murphy (A King 23/11) The Virtual Partnership

Placings:FPP-PP   **(3429)**
2002/03: 20⁰GS, 22⁵S,

	Starts	1st	2nd	3rd	Win & Pl
Hurdles	1	0	0	0	0
Chases	1	0	0	0	0
Career Total	5	0	0	0	

Going:	Sf: 0-1 GS: 0-1 Gd: 0-0 GF: - Fm: 0-0
Distance:	2m/2m3: 0-0 2m4-2m7: 0-2 3m+: 0-0
Track:	LH: 0-1 RH: 0-1 Tight: 0-1 Gall: 0-1
Aids:	Bl: 0-0 Vi: 0-0 Tstrap: 0-0
Best Rating:	88 1/02 Hrfd 2m3f110y soft Hdl

Comanche War Paint (IRE)
103₍₈₈h₎   ₍94 h₎106

6-y-o b g Commanche Run-Galeshula (Strong Gale)
P F Nicholls Tony Fear & Tim Hawkins

Placings:62F   **(3599)**
2002/03: 22⁶HY, 23²S, 24⁵S,

	Starts	1st	2nd	3rd	Win & Pl
Hurdles	2	0	1	0	750
Chases	1	0	0	0	0
Career Total	3	0	1	0	750

Going:	Sf: 0-3 GS: 0-0 Gd: 0-0 GF: - Fm: 0-0
Distance:	2m/2m3: 0-0 2m4-2m7: 0-1 3m+: 0-2
Track:	LH: 0-1 RH: 0-2 Tight: 0-3 Gall: 0-0
Aids:	Bl: 0-0 Vi: 0-0 Tstrap: 0-0
Best Rating:	94 1/03 Fknm 2m7f110y soft Hdl

Modest hurdler/chaser; acts on decent ground; stays three miles one.

Combe Castle

99   **49**

8-y-o gr g Carlingford Castle-Silver Cirrus (General Ironside)
K C Bailey The Norfolk Neighbours

Placings:/0OUPP-U0R6P   (3108)
2002/03: 23^UG, 24^OGS, 24^RS, 23⁶S, 21^PS,

	Starts	1st	2nd	3rd	Win & Pl
Chases	5	0	0	0	0
Career Total	10	0	0	0	0

Going:	Sf: 0-3 GS: 0-1 Gd: 0-1 GF: - Fm: 0-0
Distance:	2m/2m3: 0-0 2m4-2m7: 0-0 3m+: 0-4
Track:	LH: 0-1 RH: 0-4 Tight: 0-1 Gall: 0-1
Aids:	Bl: 0-0 Vi: 0-0 Tstrap: 0-0
Best Rating:	49 1/03 Leic 2m7f110y soft Ch

Combined Venture (IRE)

96(93h)   (65h)**81**

7-y-o b h Dolphin Street (FR)-Centinela (Caerleon (USA))
G J Smith Mrs Joanne Woods

Placings:F002U/P-PP05PP0   (2688)
2002/03: 16^PS, 17^PGF, 17⁰G, 17⁵GS, 17^PGS, 20^PGS, 17⁰GS,

	Starts	1st	2nd	3rd	Win & Pl
Hurdles	7	0	0	0	0
Career Total	13	0	1	0	446

Going:	Sf: 0-0 GS: 0-3 Gd: 0-3 GF: - Fm: 0-1
Distance:	2m/2m3: 0-6 2m4-2m7: 0-1 3m+: 0-0
Track:	LH: 0-3 RH: 0-4 Tight: 0-4 Gall: 0-0
Aids:	Bl: 0-0 Vi: 0-0 Tstrap: 0-1
Best Rating:	70 3/01 MRas 2m1f110y good Hdl

Come In Moscow (IRE)

103   (84h)**99**

7-y-o ch m Over The River (FR)-Kiria Mou (USA) (To-Agori-Mou)
John Joseph Murphy John Joseph Murphy

Placings:506/000104/00543PU3-2P6P31RF4   (4649a)
2002/03: 20²S, 20^PSH, 20⁶SH, 24^PHY, 17³S, 20¹S, 24^PHY, 21^FG, 24⁴GF,

	Starts	1st	2nd	3rd	Win & Pl
Chases	9	1	1	1	27098
Career Total	26	1	2	3	34507
118	1/03	Thur	2m4f		Ch	SFT	£21103
96	12/00	Cork	2m		Hdl	SFT	£3864

Total win prize-money £24968

Going:	Sf: 1-5 GS: 0-0 Gd: 0-1 GF: - Fm: 0-1
Distance:	2m/2m3: 0-1 2m4-2m7: 1-5 3m+: 0-3
Track:	LH: 0-3 RH: 1-5 Tight: 0-1 Gall: 0-0
Aids:	Bl: 0-0 Vi: 0-0 Tstrap: 0-0
Best Rating:	118 1/03 Thur 2m4f soft Ch

Fair Irish chaser; best at two and a half miles; likes soft ground.

Come On Boy

9-y-o ch g Henbit (USA)-Miss Rewarde (Andy Rew)
Mark Doyle Mrs Pat Mullen

Placings:P   (4026)
2002/03: 25^PS,

	Starts	1st	2nd	3rd	Win & Pl
Chases	1	0	0	0	
Career Total	1	0	0	0	

Going:	Sf: 0-1 GS: 0-0 Gd: 0-0 GF: - Fm: 0-0
Distance:	2m/2m3: 0-0 2m4-2m7: 0-0 3m+: 0-1
Track:	LH: 0-0 RH: 0-1 Tight: 0-0 Gall: 0-0
Aids:	Bl: 0-0 Vi: 0-0 Tstrap: 0-0
Best Rating:	0 3/03 Hrfd 2m1f110y soft Ch

Come On George (IRE)

7-y-o b g Barathea (IRE)-Lacovia (USA) (Majestic Light (USA))
Mark Doyle Ms S A Gray

Placings:00P/0/P   (0383)
2002/03: 24^PG,

	Starts	1st	2nd	3rd	Win & Pl
Chases	1	0	0	0	
Career Total	5	0	0	0	

Going:	Sf: 0-0 GS: 0-0 Gd: 0-0 GF: - Fm: 0-0
Distance:	2m/2m3: 0-0 2m4-2m7: 0-0 3m+: 0-1
Track:	LH: 0-0 RH: 0-1 Tight: 0-0 Gall: 0-1
Aids:	Bl: 0-0 Vi: 0-0 Tstrap: 0-0
Best Rating:	57 2/00 Wwck 2m good Hdl

Comedy Gayle

16-y-o b g Lir-Follifoot s Folly (Comedy Star (USA))
Ms Sue Willcock Ms Sue Willcock

Placings:600/P13/3U2P/21PP/P15P012-P   (0032)
2002/03: 21^PGF,

	Starts	1st	2nd	3rd	Win & Pl
Chases	1	0	0	0	
Career Total	22	4	3	2	14620
105	8/01	NAbb	2m5f110y	F(0-90)Ch	GD	£2926
105	5/01	Font	2m6f	E(0-115)HCh	G-F	£3500
109	5/99	Strf	3m	H Ch	GD	£3668
113	3/98	NAbb	2m5f110y	H Ch	SFT	£1004

Total win prize-money £11099

Going:	Sf: 0-0 GS: 0-0 Gd: 0-0 GF: - Fm: 0-1
Distance:	2m/2m3: 0-0 2m4-2m7: 0-1 3m+: 0-0
Track:	LH: 0-1 RH: 0-0 Tight: 0-0 Gall: 0-1
Aids:	Bl: 0-0 Vi: 0-0 Tstrap: 0-0
Best Rating:	113 3/98 NAbb 2m5f110y soft Ch

Comeoutofthefog (IRE)

8-y-o b g Mujadil (USA)-Local Belle (Ballymore)
Mrs P Ford Chris Nenadich

Placings:P   (0692)
2002/03: 16^PS,

	Starts	1st	2nd	3rd	Win & Pl
Hurdles	1	0	0	0	
Career Total	1	0	0	0	

| Going: | Sf: 0-1 GS: 0-0 Gd: 0-0 GF: - Fm: 0-0 |

Distance:	2m/2m3: 0-1 2m4-2m7: 0-0 3m+: 0-0
Track:	LH: 0-1 RH: 0-0 Tight: 0-1 Gall: 0-0
Aids:	Bl: 0-0 Vi: 0-0 Tstrap: 0-0
Best Rating:	0 7/02 Wolv 2m soft Hdl

Comeragh Gale (IRE)

93   **100**

10-y-o br g Strong Gale-Comeragh Princess (Le Moss)
V R A Dartnall Nick Viney

Placings:020/40P6-1UP4   (0653)
2002/03: 22¹G, 22^UG, 22^PG, 22⁴GF,

	Starts	1st	2nd	3rd	Win & Pl
Hurdles	4	1	0	0	2450
Career Total	11	1	1	0	3162
100	5/02	Extr	2m6f110yF	Hdl	GD	£2450

Total win prize-money £2450

Going:	Sf: 0-0 GS: 0-0 Gd: 1-3 GF: - Fm: 0-1
Distance:	2m/2m3: 0-0 **2m4-2m7:** 1-4 3m+: 0-0
Track:	LH: 0-2 RH: **1-2** Tight: 0-2 Gall: 0-0
Aids:	**Bl:** 1-4 Vi: 0-0 Tstrap: 0-0
Best Rating:	100 5/02 Extr 2m6f110y good Hdl

Moderate hurdler; point-to-point winner; wore blinkers when winning 22 furlong amateur riders novices hurdle at Exeter on good ground May 2002.

Comete Du Lac (FR)

88   **82**

6-y-o b m Comte Du Bourg (FR)-Line Du Nord (FR) (Esprit Du Nord (USA))
M D Hammond (J Ortet 18/9) Andy Peake & David Jackson

Placings:FF/P46234FF4F/2112121P-313F24R0   (2766)
2002/03: 17³, 18¹VS, 21³VS, 21^FVS, 17²S, 16⁴S, 16^PGS, 20^RGS,

	Starts	1st	2nd	3rd	Win & Pl
Hurdles	1	0	0	0	
Chases	7	1	1	2	24576
Career Total	28	5	5	3	52423
6/02	Autl	2m2f110y	Ch		VS	£12368
12/01	Cagn	2m2f	Hdl		SFT	£6719
10/01	Toul	2m2f	Ch		GD	£4850
8/01	Auri	2m1f110y	Ch		GD	£1649
7/01	Auri	2m1f110y	Ch		GD	£1649

Total win prize-money £27235

Going:	Sf: 0-2 GS: 0-2 Gd: 0-0 GF: - Fm: 0-0
Distance:	**2m/2m3:** 1-5 2m4-2m7: 0-3 3m+: 0-0
Track:	LH: 0-2 RH: 0-1 Tight: 0-1 Gall: 0-0
Aids:	**Bl:** 1-3 Vi: 0-1 Tstrap: 0-0
Best Rating:	87 11/02 Ayr 2m soft Ch

Formerly trained in France where he was successful over hurdles and four times over fences, mostly around two miles two. Refused to race on British debut. Acts on good and soft ground.

Comex Flyer (IRE)

111(107c)   (110+c)**143**

6-y-o ch g Prince Of Birds (USA)-Smashing Pet (Mummy s Pet)
P F Nicholls Neil Smith

Placings:F/1243111120-31143132532F   (4136)
2002/03: 16³GF, 16¹G, 16¹GF, 19⁴GF, 20³S, 21¹S, 22³GS, 20²GS, 21⁵GS, 20³GS, 20²G, 17^FG,

	Starts	1st	2nd	3rd	Win & Pl
Hurdles	8	1	2	3	29028
Chases	4	2	0	1	14493

Career Total	23	8	4	5	71039	
145 12/02 Wwck	2m5f	B(0-150)HHdl	SFT	£8625		
0 10/02 Kemp	2m	D Ch	G-F	£7280		
107 10/02 Fknm	2m110y	D Ch	GD	£6045		
135 10/01 Font	2m2f110yB HHdl		SFT	£12342		
115 9/01 Font	2m2f110yE Hdl		G-F	£3150		
120 8/01 Font	2m2f110yE(0-115)HHdl		G-F	£2397		
120 8/01 Worc	2m	E Hdl	G-F	£2954		
112 5/01 Sthl	2m	E Hdl	G-F	£2527		
				Total win prize-money £45322		

Going: Sf: 1-2 GS: 0-4 Gd: 1-3 GF: - Fm: 1-3
Distance: 2m/2m3: 2-5 2m4-2m7: 1-7 3m+: 0-0
Track: LH: 2-8 RH: 1-3 Tight: 1-3 Gall: 0-2
Aids: Bl: 0-0 Vi: 0-0 Tstrap: 1-8
Best Rating: 145 1/03 Hayd 2m4f   gd-sft   Hdl

Very useful hurdler/fair chaser; won five times over hurdles in 2001 and then won twice over fences in the autumn of 2002, though one was a walkover; slipped and lost confidence when well beaten at odds-on next time; switched back successfully to hurdles in December 2002, and had continued to perform consistently in 2003; useful company; acts on any ground; wears a tongue tie.

Comfortable Call
105   77
5-y-o ch g Nashwan (USA)-High Standard (Kris)
H Alexander   Paul J Dixon

Placings:6P00431   (4782)
2002/03: 26⁶GS, 17ᴾGF, 19⁰G, 16⁰G, 16⁴S, 17³G, 17¹G,

	Starts	1st	2nd	3rd	Win & Pl
Hurdles	7	1	0	1	2752
Career Total	7	1	0	1	2752
74 4/03 MRas	2m1f110yG(0-95)HHdl		GD	2399	
				Total win prize-money £2400	

Going: Sf: 0-1 GS: 0-1 Gd: 1-4 GF: - Fm: 0-1
Distance: 2m/2m3: 1-5 2m4-2m7: 0-1 3m+: 0-1
Track: LH: 0-3 RH: 1-4 Tight: 1-6 Gall: 0-1
Aids: Bl: 0-0 Vi: 0-0 Tstrap: 1-3
Best Rating: 77 3/03 MRas 2m1f110y   good   Hdl

Plating-class hurdler; handed a seller when clear leader fell at the last at Market Rasen in April; has run well since; stays two and a half miles.

Coming Through (IRE)
92   68
11-y-o ch g Le Bavard (FR)-Gay Countess (Master Buck)
T Wall   D Pugh

Placings:PPPP-4PPPP35   (1005)
2002/03: 17⁴G, 21ᴾS, 16ᴾGF, 21ᴾGF, 23ᴾGF, 20³S, 20⁵GF,

	Starts	1st	2nd	3rd	Win & Pl
Chases	7	0	0	1	1079
Career Total	11	0	0	1	1079

Going: Sf: 0-2 GS: 0-0 Gd: 0-1 GF: - Fm: 0-4
Distance: 2m/2m3: 0-2 2m4-2m7: 0-4 3m+: 0-1
Track: LH: 0-7 RH: 0-0 Tight: 0-4 Gall: 0-0
Aids: Bl: 0-0 Vi: 0-0 Tstrap: 0-0
Best Rating: 68 8/02 Bang 2m4f110y   soft   Ch

Commanche Court (IRE)
116(116h)   (135h)162
10-y-o ch h Commanche Run-Sorceress (FR) (Fabulous Dancer (USA))

T M Walsh   D F Desmond

Placings:111/21064/121134/332B1/1342P/5530242P-3163   (4457)
2002/03: 16³SH, 20¹YS, 26⁶G, 25³G,

	Starts	1st	2nd	3rd	Win & Pl
Chases	4	1	0	2	36750
Career Total	36	10	6	7	376363
157 2/03 Navn	2m4f	HCh	Y-S	12662	
152 5/00 Punc	3m1f	Ch	GD	£59520	
164 4/00 Fair	3m5f	HCh	G-Y	£62680	
147 12/98 Leop	3m	Hdl	SH	£8445	
156 12/98 Navn	2m4f	Hdl	HVY	£14076	
153 10/98 Navn	2m4f	Hdl	HVY	£9853	
150 12/97 Leop	2m	HHdl	HVY	£6782	
135 3/97 Chel	2m1f	A Hdl	GD	£44289	
130 2/97 Punc	2m	Hdl	SFT	£6782	
130 2/97 Leop	2m	Hdl	G-Y	£6782	
				Total win prize-money £231873	

Going: Sf: 0-0 GS: 0-0 Gd: 0-2 GF: - Fm: 0-0
Distance: 2m/2m3: 0-0 2m4-2m7: 1-1 3m+: 0-2
Track: LH: 1-3 RH: 0-1 Tight: 0-1 Gall: 0-1
Aids: Bl: 0-0 Vi: 0-0 Tstrap: 0-0
Best Rating: 174 3/02 Chel 3m2f110y   good   Ch

High-class chaser; runner-up to Best Mate in 2002 Cheltenham Gold Cup, sixth in the 2003 Gold Cup; stays 3m 5f; acts on most types of ground, reportedly suited by fast ground; probably as good as ever given the right conditions.

Commanche Drums (IRE)
99   88
9-y-o b g Commanche Run-Mabbots Own (Royal Trip)
O Brennan   O Brennan

Placings:50/340P-5634   (4418)
2002/03: 19⁵GS, 17⁶G, 20³GF, 22⁴G,

	Starts	1st	2nd	3rd	Win & Pl
Hurdles	4	0	0	1	571
Career Total	10	0	0	2	979

Going: Sf: 0-0 GS: 0-1 Gd: 0-2 GF: - Fm: 0-1
Distance: 2m/2m3: 0-1 2m4-2m7: 0-3 3m+: 0-0
Track: LH: 0-1 RH: 0-2 Tight: 0-1 Gall: 0-1
Aids: Bl: 0-0 Vi: 0-0 Tstrap: 0-0
Best Rating: 89 3/03 Hntg 2m4f110y   gd-fm   Hdl

Moderate novice hurdler.

Commanche General (IRE)
103   97
6-y-o b g Commanche Run-Shannon Amber (IRE) (Phardante (FR))
J F Panvert   J F Panvert

Placings:00-443P0614   (4450)
2002/03: 17⁴G, 16⁴GS, 22³GS, 20ᴾHY, 19⁰GS, 24⁶GS, 21¹GS, 21⁴G,

	Starts	1st	2nd	3rd	Win & Pl
NH Flat	2	0	0	0	0
Hurdles	6	1	0	1	4182
Career Total	10	1	0	1	4182
97 3/03 MRas	2m5f110yE Hdl		G-S	3380	
				Total win prize-money £3380	

Going: Sf: 0-1 GS: 1-5 Gd: 0-2 GF: - Fm: 0-0
Distance: 2m/2m3: 0-2 2m4-2m7: 1-5 3m+: 0-1
Track: LH: 0-3 RH: 1-5 Tight: 1-4 Gall: 0-0
Aids: Bl: 0-0 Vi: 0-0 Tstrap: 0-0

Best Rating: 97 3/03 MRas 2m5f110y gd-sft Hdl

Moderate novice hurdler; all the way winner at Market Rasen in March 2003; suited by cut; stays two miles five.

Commanche Hero (IRE)
110(105h)   (89 h)96
10-y-o ch g Cardinal Flower-Fair Bavard (Le Bavard (FR))
R J Price   Pete Holder

Placings:104/64F0043/00/00F3F46334-3P050123   (4636)
2002/03: 22³GF, 22ᴾG, 24⁰G, 17⁵S, 20⁰GS, 24¹G, 24²G, 24³G,

	Starts	1st	2nd	3rd	Win & Pl
Hurdles	3	0	0	1	366
Chases	5	1	1	1	5339
Career Total	30	2	1	6	9181
85 3/03 Hntg	3m	F(0-95)HCh	GD	£3477	
103 1/98 Font	2m2f	H NHF	SFT	£1434	
				Total win prize-money £4912	

Going: Sf: 0-1 GS: 0-1 Gd: 1-5 GF: - Fm: 0-1
Distance: 2m/2m3: 0-2 2m4-2m7: 0-3 3m+: 1-4
Track: LH: 0-4 RH: 1-4 Tight: 0-3 Gall: 1-1
Aids: Bl: 0-0 Vi: 0-0 Tstrap: 0-0
Best Rating: 103 1/98 Font 2m2f   soft   NHF

He made a successful debut in a bumper in January 1998, but it took until March 2003 for him to win another race; stays three miles over fences; acts on good ground and softer.

Commanche Jim (IRE)
109(101h)   (103h)120+
7-y-o b g Commanche Run-On A Dream (Balinger)
R H Alner   David O Moon

Placings:5/0/04344145P0-4F215116   (4174)
2002/03: 24⁴F, 21ᴾS, 26²HY, 21¹S, 26⁵S, 24¹S, 26¹S, 26⁶S,

	Starts	1st	2nd	3rd	Win & Pl
Hurdles	2	0	0	0	385
Chases	6	3	1	0	15096
Career Total	19	4	1	0	18626
120 3/03 Font	3m2f110yE(0-110)HCh		SFT	£4381	
107 2/03 Tntn	3m	D(0-115)HCh	SFT	£5765	
103 12/02 Folk	2m5f	F(0-95)HCh	SFT	£3493	
101 12/01 Plum	3m1f110yE(0-105)HHdl		SFT	£2418	
				Total win prize-money £16060	

Going: Sf: 3-7 GS: 0-0 Gd: 0-0 GF: - Fm: 0-1
Distance: 2m/2m3: 0-0 2m4-2m7: 1-2 3m+: 2-6
Track: LH: 0-3 RH: 2-4 Tight: 3-5 Gall: 0-0
Aids: Bl: 0-0 Vi: 0-0 Tstrap: 0-0
Best Rating: 120 3/03 Font 3m2f110y   soft   Ch

Fair novice chaser; progressive; stays an extended 3m 2f; acts in the mud.

Commanche Pride (IRE)
97(83h)   (92h)82
9-y-o b g Commanche Run-Galla s Pride (Quayside)
E McNamara   Sean Curran

Placings:0060/0005445P/F02036U303500/022053PU352 23-0036   (1122a)
2002/03: 22⁰G, 20⁰YS, 20³GF, 16⁶G,

	Starts	1st	2nd	3rd	Win & Pl
Hurdles	2	0	0	0	0
Chases	2	0	0	1	663

Career Total   43   0   5   7   10034

Going:	Sf: 0-0 GS: 0-0 Gd: 0-2 GF: - Fm: 0-1
Distance:	2m/2m3: 0-1 2m4-2m7: 0-3 3m+: 0-0
Track:	LH: 0-1 RH: 0-1 Tight: 0-0 Gall: 0-0
Aids:	Bl: 0-0 Vi: 0-0 Tstrap: 0-0
Best Rating:	96 8/00 Tral 2m yld-sft Ch

Commanche Quest (IRE)

107(102h)   (104h)111

7-y-o b g Commanche Run-Conna Dodger (IRE) (Kemal (FR))
Mrs M Reveley The Eleven O Clock Club

Placings:642534-35F6P34   (3913)
2002/03: 20³S, 20⁵S, 25⁵S, 20⁶GS, 20⁰GS, 25³GS, 20⁴S,

	Starts	1st	2nd	3rd	Win & Pl
Hurdles	4	0	0	1	590
Chases	3	0	1	1	945
Career Total	**13**	**0**	**1**	**3**	**4963**

Going:	Sf: 0-4 GS: 0-3 Gd: 0-0 GF: - Fm: 0-0
Distance:	2m/2m3: 0-0 2m4-2m7: 0-5 3m+: 0-2
Track:	LH: 0-6 RH: 0-1 Tight: 0-0 Gall: 0-0
Aids:	Bl: 0-1 Vi: 0-0 Tstrap: 0-0
Best Rating:	111 2/03 Ayr 3m1f gd-sft Ch

Modest form over hurdles; has shown some ability over fences. Stays three miles; acts with give.

Commanche Summer

100(104c)   (76c)83

9-y-o b m Commanche Run-Royal Typhoon (Royal Fountain)
J D Frost E M Treneer

Placings:0U23/6/460P4/40P40436-046330   (4627)
2002/03: 22⁰GS, 22⁴GS, 24⁶S, 17³S, 25³S, 21⁹GF,

	Starts	1st	2nd	3rd	Win & Pl
Hurdles	4	0	0	1	456
Chases	2	0	0	1	618
Career Total	**24**	**0**	**1**	**4**	**4123**

Going:	Sf: 0-3 GS: 0-2 Gd: 0-0 GF: - Fm: 0-1
Distance:	2m/2m3: 0-1 2m4-2m7: 0-3 3m+: 0-2
Track:	LH: 0-1 RH: 0-5 Tight: 0-2 Gall: 0-0
Aids:	Bl: 0-0 Vi: 0-0 Tstrap: 0-0
Best Rating:	83 10/01 Bang 2m4f110y good Ch

Maiden selling hurdler/chaser; paid the penalty in the ratings for a good effort from a stone out of the handicap in 3m amateur riders hurdle at Chepstow May 2003; seems to handle all types of ground.

Commanche Wind (IRE)

105   94

8-y-o b g Commanche Run-Delko (Decent Fellow)
E W Tuer E Tuer

Placings:0/0060300/5F-101324P   (4776)
2002/03: 21¹GF, 24⁹G, 20¹GS, 19³GF, 21²GF, 21⁴G, 20⁹G,

	Starts	1st	2nd	3rd	Win & Pl
Hurdles	7	2	1	1	8002
Career Total	**17**	**2**	**1**	**2**	**8338**

---

107   5/02   Weth   2m4f110yD(0-120)HHdl   G-S   £3360
96   5/02   Sedg   2m5f110yE Hdl   G-F   £2569
                Total win prize-money £5929

Going:	Sf: 0-0 GS: 1-1 Gd: 0-3 GF: - Fm: 1-3
Distance:	2m/2m3: 0-0 **2m4-2m7: 2-6** 3m+: 0-1
Track:	**LH: 2-5** RH: 0-2 **Tight: 1-4** Gall: 0-0
Aids:	Bl: 0-0 Vi: 0-0 Tstrap: 0-0
Best Rating:	107 7/02 Sedg 2m5f110y gd-fm Hdl

Modest hurdler, stays two and a half miles.

Commandant (IRE)

10-y-o b g Good Thyne (USA)-Slave Run (Deep Run)
C C Bealby Mrs J Knight

Placings:0/430P/UP   (1531)
2002/03: 21ᵁG, 21ᴾG,

	Starts	1st	2nd	3rd	Win & Pl
Chases	2	0	0	0	
Career Total	**7**	**0**	**0**	**1**	**260**

Going:	Sf: 0-0 GS: 0-0 Gd: 0-2 GF: - Fm: 0-0
Distance:	2m/2m3: 0-0 2m4-2m7: 0-2 3m+: 0-0
Track:	LH: 0-2 RH: 0-0 Tight: 0-1 Gall: 0-0
Aids:	Bl: 0-1 Vi: 0-0 Tstrap: 0-0
Best Rating:	103 11/99 Weth 2m good NHF

Commander Glen (IRE)

11-y-o b g Glenstal (USA)-Une Parisienne (FR) (Bolkonski)
J W Hughes J W Hughes

Placings:251351/5546366/51406/P101455/22/P4-U (4552)
2002/03: 27ᵁG,

	Starts	1st	2nd	3rd	Win & Pl
Chases	1	0	0	0	
Career Total	**30**	**5**	**3**	**2**	**23992**

101   8/99   Prth   3m   E(0-115)HCh   G-F   £4182
101   6/99   Sthl   3m110y   F(0-105)HCh   G-F   £3074
105   9/98   Prth   2m4f110yD Ch   GD   £4182
101   12/96   Muss   2m4f   E(0-100)HHdl   G-F   £2542
86   10/96   Kels   2m2f   E Hdl   FRM   £1884
            Total win prize-money £15864

Going:	Sf: 0-0 GS: 0-0 Gd: 0-1 GF: - Fm: 0-0
Distance:	2m/2m3: 0-0 2m4-2m7: 0-0 3m+: 0-1
Track:	LH: 0-1 RH: 0-0 Tight: 0-0 Gall: 0-0
Aids:	Bl: 0-0 Vi: 0-0 Tstrap: 0-0
Best Rating:	105 9/98 Prth 2m4f110y good Ch

Commasarris

11-y-o gr g Joli Wasfi (USA)-Lucy Aura (Free State)
Mrs S Wall Mrs S Wall

Placings:6/P/P2   (0315)
2002/03: 22ᴾG, 21²G,

	Starts	1st	2nd	3rd	Win & Pl
Chases	2	0	1	0	440
Career Total	**4**	**0**	**1**	**0**	**440**

Going:	Sf: 0-0 GS: 0-0 Gd: 0-2 GF: - Fm: 0-0
Distance:	2m/2m3: 0-0 2m4-2m7: 0-2 3m+: 0-0
Track:	LH: 0-0 RH: 0-0 Tight: 0-1 Gall: 0-0
Aids:	Bl: 0-0 Vi: 0-0 Tstrap: 0-1

Best Rating: 85   5/02   Folk   2m5f   good   Ch

Commissar (IRE)

4-y-o b g Common Grounds-Trescalini (IRE) (Sadler s Wells (USA))
J J Bridger (R Charlton 23/10) Mrs Julie l Lankshear

Placings:F   (3494)
2002/03: 16ᶠGS,

	Starts	1st	2nd	3rd	Win & Pl
Hurdles	1	0	0	0	
Career Total	**1**	**0**	**0**	**0**	

Going:	Sf: 0-0 GS: 0-1 Gd: 0-0 GF: - Fm: 0-0
Distance:	2m/2m3: 0-1 2m4-2m7: 0-0 3m+: 0-0
Track:	LH: 0-0 RH: 0-0 Tight: 0-0 Gall: 0-0
Aids:	Bl: 0-0 Vi: 0-0 Tstrap: 0-0
Best Rating:	0 2/03 Kemp 2m gd-sft Hdl

Common Girl (IRE)

102f   87f

5-y-o gr m Roselier (FR)-Rumups Debut (IRE) (Good Thyne (USA))
O Brennan J W Hardy

Placings:53   (4672)
2002/03: 16⁵GF, 16³G,

	Starts	1st	2nd	3rd	Win & Pl
NH Flat	2	0	0	1	272
Career Total	**2**	**0**	**0**	**1**	**272**

Going:	Sf: 0-0 GS: 0-0 Gd: 0-1 GF: - Fm: 0-1
Distance:	2m/2m3: 0-2 2m4-2m7: 0-0 3m+: 0-0
Track:	LH: 0-1 RH: 0-1 Tight: 0-1 Gall: 0-1
Aids:	Bl: 0-0 Vi: 0-0 Tstrap: 0-0
Best Rating:	87 4/03 Fknm 2m good NHF

Moderate bumper performer; has shown some ability on a sound surface.

Compadre

92   84

5-y-o gr g Environment Friend-Cardinal Press (Sharrood (USA))
P Beaumont J Stephenson

Placings:P   (4590)
2002/03: 20ᴾG,

	Starts	1st	2nd	3rd	Win & Pl
Hurdles	1	0	0	0	
Career Total	**1**	**0**	**0**	**0**	

Going:	Sf: 0-0 GS: 0-0 Gd: 0-1 GF: - Fm: 0-0
Distance:	2m/2m3: 0-0 2m4-2m7: 0-1 3m+: 0-0
Track:	LH: 0-1 RH: 0-0 Tight: 0-0 Gall: 0-0
Aids:	Bl: 0-0 Vi: 0-0 Tstrap: 0-0
Best Rating:	0 4/03 Hexm 2m4f110y good Hdl

Novice hurdler; effective at two miles; acts on good and good to firm; should do better in handicaps.

Compton Amica (IRE)

104   96d

7-y-o gr m High Estate-Nephrite (Godswalk (USA))
K Bishop Mrs E K Ellis

Placings:0061P2P/0P20-45533002   (4096)
2002/03: 24⁴GS, 16⁵G, 19⁵GS, 16³S, 17³GS, 19⁰GS, 17⁰G, 19²HY,

	Starts	1st	2nd	3rd	Win & Pl
Hurdles	8	0	1	2	1903
Career Total	19	1	3	2	5816

86 12/00 Winc 2m F(0-95)HHdl G-S £2625
Total win prize-money £2625

Going:	Sf: 0-2 GS: 0-4 Gd: 0-2 GF: - Fm: 0-0
Distance:	2m/2m3: 0-6 2m4-2m7: 0-1 3m+: 0-1
Track:	LH: 0-3 RH: 0-5 Tight: 0-2 Gall: 0-0
Aids:	Bl: 0-0 Vi: 0-0 Tstrap: 0-0
Best Rating:	96 12/02 Bang 2m1f gd-sft Hdl

Moderate handicap hurdler at around two miles on soft ground; goes well at Wincanton.

Compton Chick (IRE)

98(99h)   (96dh)92

5-y-o b m Dolphin Street (FR)-Cecina (Welsh Saint)
J W Mullins New Forest Racing Partnership

Placings:355-42542044   (4755)
2002/03: 18⁴GF, 18²GF, 16⁵G, 22⁴GS, 20²HY, 22⁰GS, 20⁴HY, 18⁴GF,

	Starts	1st	2nd	3rd	Win & Pl
Hurdles	8	0	2	0	2226
Career Total	11	0	2	1	2524

Going:	Sf: 0-2 GS: 0-2 Gd: 0-1 GF: - Fm: 0-3
Distance:	2m/2m3: 0-4 2m4-2m7: 0-4 3m+: 0-0
Track:	LH: 0-4 RH: 0-4 Tight: 0-4 Gall: 0-0
Aids:	Bl: 0-0 Vi: 0-0 Tstrap: 0-2
Best Rating:	96 11/02 Leic 2m4f110y heavy Hdl

Plating-class hurdler; won weak novice event on chase debut; good effort on return to hurdles after unseating over fences; acts on fast ground; stays 2m 4f.

Comte De Chambord

28

7-y-o gr g Baron Blakeney-Show Rose (Coliseum)
Mark Campion A M Campion

Placings:305   (0834)
2002/03: 16³S, 16⁰G, 17⁵GF,

	Starts	1st	2nd	3rd	Win & Pl
NH Flat	3	0	0	1	218
Career Total	3	0	0	1	218

Going:	Sf: 0-1 GS: 0-0 Gd: 0-1 GF: - Fm: 0-0
Distance:	2m/2m3: 0-3 2m4-2m7: 0-0 3m+: 0-0
Track:	LH: 0-3 RH: 0-0 Tight: 0-0 Gall: 0-0
Aids:	Bl: 0-0 Vi: 0-0 Tstrap: 0-0
Best Rating:	92 6/02 Worc 2m soft NHF

Showed little in bumpers; tailed off on hurdling debut at Wetherby in May.

Concerto Collonges (FR)

13-y-o br g El Badr-Mariane Collonge (FR) (Cap Martin (FR))
Miss A Armitage O R M Hartley

Placings:1/052/0-6   (0166)

2002/03: 25⁶GF,

	Starts	1st	2nd	3rd	Win & Pl
Chases	1	0	0	0	0
Career Total	6	1	1	0	2308

89 4/00 Carl 3m2f H Ch G-S £1363
Total win prize-money £1364

Going:	Sf: 0-0 GS: 0-0 Gd: 0-0 GF: - Fm: 0-1
Distance:	2m/2m3: 0-0 2m4-2m7: 0-0 3m+: 0-1
Track:	LH: 0-1 RH: 0-1 Tight: 0-0 Gall: 0-0
Aids:	Bl: 0-0 Vi: 0-0 Tstrap: 0-0
Best Rating:	89 4/01 Prth 3m7f heavy Ch

Consistent pointer who pays his way. Needs soft ground.

Conchita

90f   107+f

6-y-o b m St Ninian-Carnetto (Le Coq D Or)
G A Harker Mrs G E Brewis

Placings:331   (4411)
2002/03: 16³HY, 17³GS, 16¹G,

	Starts	1st	2nd	3rd	Win & Pl
NH Flat	3	1	0	2	2591
Career Total	3	1	0	2	2591

102 3/03 Hexm 2m110y H NHF GD £2037
Total win prize-money £2037

Going:	Sf: 0-1 GS: 0-1 Gd: 1-1 GF: - Fm: 0-0
Distance:	2m/2m3: 1-3 2m4-2m7: 0-0 3m+: 0-0
Track:	LH: 1-2 RH: 0-1 Tight: 0-0 Gall: 0-0
Aids:	Bl: 0-0 Vi: 0-0 Tstrap: 0-0
Best Rating:	102 3/03 Hexm 2m110y good NHF

Modest performer; third first time in a bumper at Newcastle in January and occupied same position at Carlisle two months later; has since won twice at Hexham; should make her mark over hurdles in time.

Condoyle (IRE)

89(98h)   (86h)64+

10-y-o b g Rare One-Worthy Gale (Strong Gale)
R J Baker Percy Buckingham

Placings:F5B4335056-64P2   (1602)
2002/03: 20⁶G, 25⁴GF, 25⁶G, 19²G,

	Starts	1st	2nd	3rd	Win & Pl
Chases	4	0	1	0	1048
Career Total	14	0	1	2	2132

Going:	Sf: 0-0 GS: 0-0 Gd: 0-3 GF: - Fm: 0-1
Distance:	2m/2m3: 0-0 2m4-2m7: 0-2 3m+: 0-2
Track:	LH: 0-2 RH: 0-2 Tight: 0-0 Gall: 0-0
Aids:	Bl: 0-0 Vi: 0-0 Tstrap: 0-0
Best Rating:	86 7/01 Worc 2m4f good Hdl

Plating-class chaser, wears headgear.

Conquer (IRE)

105

8-y-o b g Phardante (FR)-Tullow Performance (Gala Performance (USA))
H D Daly M Ward-Thomas

Placings:334/3-UP   (3137)
2002/03: 24ᵁG, 24²S,

	Starts	1st	2nd	3rd	Win & Pl
Chases	2	0	0	0	0
Career Total	6	0	0	3	1429

Going:	Sf: 0-1 GS: 0-0 Gd: 0-1 GF: - Fm: 0-0

Distance:	2m/2m3: 0-0 2m4-2m7: 0-0 3m+: 0-2
Track:	LH: 0-1 RH: 0-1 Tight: 0-1 Gall: 0-1
Aids:	Bl: 0-0 Vi: 0-0 Tstrap: 0-0
Best Rating:	105 9/01 Hrfd 3m1f110y gd-fm Ch

Moderate chaser; point-to-point winner; has shown a tendency to jump left-handed; stays three miles plus.

Conroy

102   93+

4-y-o b g Greensmith-Highland Spirit (Scottish Reel)
F Jordan D Ancil

Placings:453   (4542)
2002/03: 12⁴GS, 14⁵GS, 16³G,

	Starts	1st	2nd	3rd	Win & Pl
NH Flat	3	0	0	1	418
Career Total	3	0	0	1	418

Going:	Sf: 0-0 GS: 0-2 Gd: 0-1 GF: - Fm: 0-0
Distance:	2m/2m3: 0-1 2m4-2m7: 0-0 3m+: 0-0
Track:	LH: 0-2 RH: 0-1 Tight: 0-0 Gall: 0-0
Aids:	Bl: 0-0 Vi: 0-0 Tstrap: 0-0
Best Rating:	87 4/03 Ludl 2m good NHF

Fair jumping pedigree; has not performed at all badly in bumper and hurdle races.

Contact (IRE)

78   88

6-y-o br g Grand Lodge (USA)-Pink Cashmere (IRE) (Polar Falcon (USA))
M Wigham D Hassan

Placings:5   (2682)
2002/03: 16⁵S,

	Starts	1st	2nd	3rd	Win & Pl
Hurdles	1	0	0	0	284
Career Total	1	0	0	0	284

Going:	Sf: 0-1 GS: 0-0 Gd: 0-0 GF: - Fm: 0-0
Distance:	2m/2m3: 0-1 2m4-2m7: 0-0 3m+: 0-0
Track:	LH: 0-0 RH: 0-1 Tight: 0-0 Gall: 0-0
Aids:	Bl: 0-0 Vi: 0-0 Tstrap: 0-0
Best Rating:	88 12/02 Kemp 2m soft Hdl

Modest performer on the Flat at around a mile.

Contes (IRE)

106(81h)   (98h)112

11-y-o b g Lafontaine (USA)-Dara s Diocese (Bishop Of Orange)
P R Hedger P R Hedger

Placings:353P1P51/0F/2000-3F14P   (0632)
2002/03: 20³GF, 20⁵S, 22¹GF, 20⁴G, 21⁹GF,

	Starts	1st	2nd	3rd	Win & Pl
Chases	5	1	0	1	8050
Career Total	19	3	1	3	18689

93 6/02 Font 2m6f D(0-125)HCh G-F £6922
114 4/00 Font 2m6f C Ch GD £7052
117 2/00 Folk 2m5f F(0-90)HCh G-S £2452
Total win prize-money £16429

Going:	Sf: 0-1 GS: 0-0 Gd: 0-1 GF: - Fm: 1-3
Distance:	2m/2m3: 0-0 2m4-2m7: 1-5 3m+: 0-0
Track:	LH: 0-3 RH: 0-0 Tight: 1-4 Gall: 0-0
Aids:	Bl: 1-5 Vi: 0-0 Tstrap: 0-0
Best Rating:	117 2/00 Folk 2m5f gd-sft Ch

Modest chaser at up to three miles, lightly raced in recent

years. Improved form since wearing blinkers and was clear when falling at the last over two and a half miles at Bangor May 2002.

Conti D'Estruval (FR)

13-y-o b g Synefos (USA)-Barbara Conti (ITY) (Teodoro Trivulzio)
Mrs P Smith Terry E G Smith

Placings:003UP03/230316F51111/523UP53435/PP23/12/P R/PP   (0209)
2002/03: 21PGF, 16PG,

		Starts	1st	2nd	3rd	Win & Pl
Chases		2	0	0		0
Career Total		39	6	4	8	33801
95	5/99 Ludl	2m4f	H Ch		G-F	£1339
126	4/96 Strf	2m4f	C(0-135)HCh		G-F	£4861
116	4/96 Extr	2m4f	2m3f110yC(0-130)HCh	G-F	£4828
111	4/96 Ludl	2m4f	D(0-125)HCh		G-F	£4104
112	3/96 Hntg	2m4f110yD(0-125)HCh	GD		£3598
105	11/95 Winc	2m5f	D(0-125)HCh		G-F	£5253
		Total win prize-money £23985				

Going: Sf: 0-0 GS: 0-0 Gd: 0-1 GF: - Fm: 0-1
Distance: 2m/2m3: 0-1 2m4-2m7: 0-1 3m+: 0-0
Track: LH: 0-1 RH: 0-1 Tight: 0-0 Gall: 0-1
Aids: Bl: 0-0 Vi: 0-0 Tstrap: 0-0
Best Rating: 126 8/96 Uttx   2m4f   gd-fm   Ch

Contract Scotland (IRE)

102(103h)   (100h)98
8-y-o br g Religiously (USA)-Stroked Again (On Your Mark)
L Lungo Contract Scotland Limited

Placings:000/5204211-1562   (4356)
2002/03: 201G, 271G, 225S, 226S, 202GF,

		Starts	1st	2nd	3rd	Win & Pl
Hurdles		4	2	0		6183
Chases		1	0	1	0	1254
Career Total		14	3	3	0	12413
100	5/02 Kels	3m3f	E(0-100)HHdl	GD	£3523
94	4/02 Newc	2m4f	E(0-100)HHdl	GD	£2660
92	4/02 Hexm	2m4f110yE(0-105)HHdl	G-F	£2919
		Total win prize-money £9102				

Going: Sf: 0-2 GS: 0-0 Gd: 2-2 GF: - Fm: 0-1
Distance: 2m/2m3: 0-0 2m4-2m7: 1-4 3m+: 1-1
Track: LH: 2-5 RH: 0-0 Tight: 1-2 Gall: 1-1
Aids: Bl: 0-0 Vi: 0-0 Tstrap: 0-0
Best Rating: 100 5/02 Kels   3m3f   good   Hdl

Fair handicap hurdler; runner-up on chasing bow at Wetherby in March; prefers a fast surface.

Control Man (IRE)

115f   133+f
5-y-o ch g Glacial Storm (USA)-Got To Fly (IRE) (Kemal (FR))
M C Pipe D A Johnson

Placings:115   (3528)
2002/03: 181HY, 161HY, 165G,

		Starts	1st	2nd	3rd	Win & Pl
NH Flat		3	2	0	0	12473
Career Total		3	2	0	0	12473
131	12/02 Chep	2m110y	A NHF		HVY	£9600
116	12/02 Plum	2m2f	N NHF		HVY	£2373
		Total win prize-money £11973				

Cook O'Hawick (IRE)

94   82
6-y-o b g King s Ride-Miner s Yank (Miners Lamp)
L Lungo Ashleybank Investments Limited

Placings:050   (4504)
2002/03: 16QG, 165S, 16QG,

		Starts	1st	2nd	3rd	Win & Pl
NH Flat		1	0	0	0	0
Hurdles		2	0	0	0	0
Career Total		3	0	0	0	0

Going: Sf: 0-1 GS: 0-0 Gd: 0-2 GF: - Fm: 0-0
Distance: 2m/2m3: 0-3 2m4-2m7: 0-0 3m+: 0-0
Track: LH: 0-2 RH: 0-1 Tight: 0-2 Gall: 0-0
Aids: Bl: 0-0 Vi: 0-0 Tstrap: 0-0
Best Rating: 82 1/03 Muss   2m   good   NHF

Cookies Bank

64f
5-y-o b g Broadsword (USA)-Kitty Come Home (Monsanto (FR))
Mrs S D Williams Berry Racing

Placings:5   (4364)
2002/03: 175F,

		Starts	1st	2nd	3rd	Win & Pl
NH Flat		1	0	0	0	0
Career Total		1	0	0	0	0

Going: Sf: 0-0 GS: 0-0 Gd: 0-0 GF: - Fm: 0-1
Distance: 2m/2m3: 0-1 2m4-2m7: 0-0 3m+: 0-0
Track: LH: 0-0 RH: 0-0 Tight: 0-0 Gall: 0-0
Aids: Bl: 0-0 Vi: 0-0 Tstrap: 0-0
Best Rating: 64 3/03 Tntn   2m1f   firm   NHF

Cool Archie

10-y-o b g Roscoe Blake-Echo Lake (Tycoon Ii)
M Mullineaux Michael Mullineaux

Placings:P-6   (1615)
2002/03: 206F,

		Starts	1st	2nd	3rd	Win & Pl
Chases		1	0	0	0	0
Career Total		2	0	0	0	0

Going: Sf: 0-0 GS: 0-0 Gd: 0-0 GF: - Fm: 0-1
Distance: 2m/2m3: 0-0 2m4-2m7: 0-1 3m+: 0-0
Track: LH: 0-0 RH: 0-1 Tight: 0-1 Gall: 0-0
Aids: Bl: 0-0 Vi: 0-0 Tstrap: 0-0
Best Rating: 0 10/02 Ludl   2m4f   firm   Ch

Cool Border

(98h)   (85dh)
8-y-o gr m Grey Desire-Irish Orchid (Free State)
M Bradstock J G St P Burridge

Placings:65/026P-060R   (3746)
2002/03: 20QGS, 226HY, 20QS, 24RG,

		Starts	1st	2nd	3rd	Win & Pl
Hurdles		3	0	0	0	0
Chases		1	0	0	0	0
Career Total		10	0	1	0	1108

Going: Sf: 0-2 GS: 0-1 Gd: 0-1 GF: - Fm: 0-0
Distance: 2m/2m3: 0-0 2m4-2m7: 0-3 3m+: 0-1
Track: LH: 0-0 RH: 0-4 Tight: 0-1 Gall: 0-2
Aids: Bl: 0-1 Vi: 0-0 Tstrap: 0-0
Best Rating: 98 5/00 Bang   2m1f   good   NHF

Cool Chilli

86   49
5-y-o gr g Gran Alba (USA)-Miss Flossa (FR) (Big John (FR))
N J Pomfret R P Brett

Placings:500-UP0060   (4679)
2002/03: 16UGS, 19PS, 16QGS, 17QGS, 16QG, 16QGF,

		Starts	1st	2nd	3rd	Win & Pl
Hurdles		6	0	0	0	0
Career Total		9	0	0	0	0

Going: Sf: 0-1 GS: 0-3 Gd: 0-1 GF: - Fm: 0-0
Distance: 2m/2m3: 0-5 2m4-2m7: 0-1 3m+: 0-0
Track: LH: 0-2 RH: 0-4 Tight: 0-2 Gall: 0-3
Aids: Bl: 0-0 Vi: 0-0 Tstrap: 0-3
Best Rating: 81 3/02 Hntg   2m110y   gd-fm   NHF

Plating-class hurdler; showed some promise in bumpers in 2002; poor form since.

Cool Cossack (IRE)

101f   98f
6-y-o ch g Moscow Society (USA)-Knockacool Breeze (Buckskin (FR))
Mrs S J Smith Trevor Hemmings

Placings:2   (4665)
2002/03: 172GF,

		Starts	1st	2nd	3rd	Win & Pl
NH Flat		1	0	1	0	606
Career Total		1	0	1	0	606

Going: Sf: 0-0 GS: 0-0 Gd: 0-0 GF: - Fm: 0-1
Distance: 2m/2m3: 0-1 2m4-2m7: 0-0 3m+: 0-0
Track: LH: 0-0 RH: 0-1 Tight: 0-0 Gall: 0-0
Aids: Bl: 0-0 Vi: 0-0 Tstrap: 0-0
Best Rating: 98 4/03 Carl   2m1f   gd-fm   NHF

Half-brother to winning hurdler/chaser Breaking Breeze; showed plenty of promise on bumper debut in April 2003.

Cool Degree (IRE)

53f   94f
5-y-o br g Arctic Lord-Ballyfin Maid (IRE) (Boreen (FR))
Ferdy Murphy Trevor Hemmings

Placings:44   (4685)
2002/03: 174S, 164GF,

		Starts	1st	2nd	3rd	Win & Pl
NH Flat		2	0	0	0	0

Career Total   2   0   0   0   0

Going: Sf: 0-1 GS: 0-0 Gd: 0-0 GF: - Fm: 0-1
Distance: 2m/2m3: 0-2 2m4-2m7: 0-0 3m+: 0-0
Track: LH: 0-0 RH: 0-2 Tight: 0-0 Gall: 0-1
Aids: Bl: 0-0 Vi: 0-0 Tstrap: 0-0
Best Rating: 94 3/03 Carl 2m1f   soft   NHF

Well beaten fourth in weak bumper on debut.

Cool Frolic (IRE)

9-y-o br g Strong Gale-Delia Murphy (Golden Love)
O Brennan   Mrs Pat Brennan

Placings:0/P   (0330)
2002/03: 23PG,

	Starts	1st	2nd	3rd	Win & Pl
Chases	1	0	0	0	
Career Total	2	0	0	0	

Going: Sf: 0-0 GS: 0-0 Gd: 0-1 GF: - Fm: 0-0
Distance: 2m/2m3: 0-0 2m4-2m7: 0-0 3m+: 0-1
Track: LH: 0-0 RH: 0-0 Tight: 0-0 Gall: 0-0
Aids: Bl: 0-0 Vi: 0-0 Tstrap: 0-0
Best Rating: 0 5/02 Weth 2m7f110y good   Ch

Cool Investment (IRE)

104(108h)   (109 h)125+
6-y-o b g Prince Of Birds (USA)-Superb Investment (IRE) (Hatim (USA))
R M Stronge   A P Holland

Placings:4003333-40211   (2774)
2002/03: 20⁴GS, 21⁰G, 20³HY, 24¹GS, 22¹S,

	Starts	1st	2nd	3rd	Win & Pl
Hurdles	2	0	0	0	330
Chases	3	2	1	0	14806
Career Total	12	2	1	4	17619

125 12/02 Newb 2m6f110yD(0-110)HCh SFT £5421
119 12/02 Wwck 3m110y C Ch   G-S £7735
Total win prize-money £13156

Going: Sf: 1-2 GS: 1-2 Gd: 0-1 GF: - Fm: 0-0
Distance: 2m/2m3: 0-0 2m4-2m7: 1-4 3m+: 1-1
Track: LH: 2-4 RH: 0-1 Tight: 0-1 **Gall: 1-2**
Aids: Bl: 0-0 Vi: 0-0 Tstrap: 0-0
Best Rating: 125 12/02 Newb 2m6f110y soft   Ch

Fair novice chaser; winning at Warwick and Newbury in December 2002; stays two miles six; acts on most types of ground but suited by soft.

Cool Million

74   75
10-y-o ch g Derrylin-Goldaw (Gala Performance (USA))
Mrs H M Bridges   Mrs H M Bridges

Placings:U-5PP   (2585)
2002/03: 22⁵GS, 25PG, 23PS,

	Starts	1st	2nd	3rd	Win & Pl
Chases	3	0	0	0	0
Career Total	4	0	0	0	0

Going: Sf: 0-0 GS: 0-2 Gd: 0-1 GF: - Fm: 0-0
Distance: 2m/2m3: 0-0 2m4-2m7: 0-1 3m+: 0-2
Track: LH: 0-0 RH: 0-2 Tight: 0-1 Gall: 0-0

Cool Miner (IRE)

89   69
11-y-o b g Miners Lamp-Coolafinka (IRE) (Strong Statement (USA))
J Wade   John Wade

Placings:065P/40P4/21020/0P0P-00   (0694)
2002/03: 20⁰G, 24⁰G,

	Starts	1st	2nd	3rd	Win & Pl
Hurdles	2	0	0	0	
Career Total	19	1	2	0	4273

89 5/00 Hexm 2m4f110yE(0-105)HHdl GD £2347
Total win prize-money £2347

Going: Sf: 0-0 GS: 0-0 Gd: 0-2 GF: - Fm: 0-0
Distance: 2m/2m3: 0-0 2m4-2m7: 0-1 3m+: 0-1
Track: LH: 0-1 RH: 0-1 Tight: 0-1 Gall: 0-0
Aids: Bl: 0-0 Vi: 0-0 Tstrap: 0-0
Best Rating: 89 5/00 Hexm 2m4f110y good   Hdl

Cool Monty (IRE)

103(101h)   (122h)103
9-y-o ch g Montelimar (USA)-Rose Ground (Over The River (FR))
I A Balding   Guy Luck

Placings:0/44/202-P1P   (2724)
2002/03: 16PHY, 17¹S, 20PS,

	Starts	1st	2nd	3rd	Win & Pl
Hurdles	1	0	0	0	0
Chases	2	1	0	0	4784
Career Total	9	1	2	0	8209

103 12/02 MRas 2m1f110yD Ch   SFT £4784
Total win prize-money £4784

Going: Sf: 1-3 GS: 0-0 Gd: 0-0 GF: - Fm: 0-0
Distance: 2m/2m3: 1-2 2m4-2m7: 0-1 3m+: 0-0
Track: LH: 0-0 RH: 1-3 Tight: 1-1 Gall: 0-0
Aids: Bl: 0-0 Vi: 0-0 Tstrap: 0-0
Best Rating: 122 12/01 Sand 2m110y soft   Hdl

Moderate chaser; Irish point winner, all-the-way winner of a novices chase at Market Rasen in December 2002. Suited by soft ground.

Cool Roxy

106   105
6-y-o b g Environment Friend-Roxy River (Ardross)
A G Blackmore   A G Blackmore

Placings:00F-P444412216   (4602)
2002/03: 16PGF, 16⁴GF, 16⁴GF, 16⁴G, 16⁴G, 16¹GS, 20⁶GS, 21²S, 16¹G, 21⁶G,

	Starts	1st	2nd	3rd	Win & Pl
Hurdles	10	2	2	0	12915
Career Total	13	2	2	0	12915

105 3/03 Fknm 2m D(0-120)HHdl GD £6207
95 11/02 Fknm 2m E(0-105)HHdl G-S £3415
Total win prize-money £9624

Going: Sf: 0-1 GS: 1-2 Gd: 1-4 GF: - Fm: 0-3
Distance: 2m/2m3: 2-7 2m4-2m7: 0-3 3m+: 0-0
Track: LH: 2-8 RH: 0-2 Tight: 2-6 Gall: 0-4
Aids: Bl: 0-0 Vi: 0-0 Tstrap: 0-0
Best Rating: 105 3/03 Fknm 2m   good   Hdl

Modest novice hurdler; stays two miles five; acts on most ground; likes to race prominently.

Cool Song

88   80
7-y-o ch g Michelozzo (USA)-Vi s Delight (New Member)
D J Caro   M J Weaver

Placings:5-55   (2004)
2002/03: 17⁵G, 17⁵S,

	Starts	1st	2nd	3rd	Win & Pl
NH Flat	1	0	0	0	0
Hurdles	1	0	0	0	0
Career Total	3	0	0	0	0

Going: Sf: 0-1 GS: 0-0 Gd: 0-1 GF: - Fm: 0-0
Distance: 2m/2m3: 0-2 2m4-2m7: 0-0 3m+: 0-0
Track: LH: 0-0 RH: 0-2 Tight: 0-2 Gall: 0-0
Aids: Bl: 0-0 Vi: 0-0 Tstrap: 0-0
Best Rating: 91 10/02 MRas 2m1f110y good   NHF

Cool Spot (IRE)

(78h)   (37h)
15-y-o ch g Boyne Valley-Beagle Bay (Deep Run)
J R Best   Dave Howe

Placings:F2/P/54232141/F12123F/32P143/42322456U/0   (0698)
2002/03: 17⁰GF,

	Starts	1st	2nd	3rd	Win & Pl
Hurdles	1	0	0	0	
Career Total	34	5	9	5	45133

109 2/00 Sand 2m4f110y   C(0-130)HCh
G-S £7052
104 2/99 Hrfd 2m F(0-100)HCh GD £7327
101 12/98 Folk 2m F(0-100)HCh G-S £2929
92 4/98 MRas 2m1f110yD(0-120)HCh SFT £4151
89 3/98 MRas 2m1f110yE(0-110)HCh G-S £3094
Total win prize-money £24558

Going: Sf: 0-0 GS: 0-0 Gd: 0-0 GF: - Fm: 0-1
Distance: 2m/2m3: 0-1 2m4-2m7: 0-0 3m+: 0-0
Track: LH: 0-0 RH: 0-1 Tight: 0-1 Gall: 0-0
Aids: Bl: 0-0 Vi: 0-0 Tstrap: 0-0
Best Rating: 118 2/01 Sand 2m   heavy   Ch

He is difficult to win with (finds little off the bridle) but races consistently and pays his way in place money. Effective up to two and a half miles, he has reached the veteran stage and could struggle next term.

Coole Abbey (IRE)

11-y-o b g Viteric (FR)-Eleanors Joy (Sheer Grit)
Mrs Clare Moore   Mrs Clare Moore

Placings:F12/1622/112/2/2200-32211   (4169)
2002/03: 25³GS, 25²G, 22²GF, 24¹G, 24¹GS,

	Starts	1st	2nd	3rd	Win & Pl
Chases	5	2	2	1	5712
Career Total	20	6	9	1	18371

110 3/03 Newc 3m H Ch   G-S £1519
110 2/03 Muss 3m H Ch   GD £2863
115 3/00 MRas 3m1f H Ch   G-F £1610
116 2/00 Muss 3m H Ch   G-S £2310
120 2/99 Muss 3m H Ch   G-F £1940
120 3/98 Newc 2m4f H Ch   G-F £1023
Total win prize-money £11266

Going: Sf: 0-0 GS: 1-2 Gd: 1-2 GF: - Fm: 0-1
Distance: 2m/2m3: 0-2 2m4-2m7: 0-1 3m+: 2-4
Track: LH: 1-3 RH: 1-2 Tight: 1-4 Gall: 1-1
Aids: Bl: 0-0 Vi: 0-0 Tstrap: 0-0
Best Rating: 120 2/99 Muss 3m   gd-fm   Ch

Fair hunter chaser; stays three miles; has won on a soft surface, but has a better record on decent ground; goes well fresh.

Coole Spirit (IRE)
102   134+

10-y-o b g All Haste (USA)-Chocolatebiscuit (Biskrah)
Miss E C Lavelle Coole And The Gang

Placings:2105/4323F/11-1P   (4172)
2002/03: 24¹GS, 34^PS,

		Starts	1st	2nd	3rd	Win & Pl
Chases		2	1	0	0	10871
Career Total		13	4	2	2	26110
134	1/03 Kemp 3m	D(0-125)HCh	G-S	£10871
123	11/01 Uttx	E Ch	SFT	£3523
112	11/01 Font	3m2f110yE Ch	G-S	£3120
108	12/99 Leic	2m4f110yD Hdl	GD	£3665
		Total win prize-money £21179

Going: Sf: 0-1 GS: 1-1 Gd: 0-0 GF: - Fm: 0-0
Distance: 2m/2m3: 0-0 2m4-2m7: 0-0 3m+: 1-2
Track: LH: 0-1 RH: 1-1 Tight: 0-0 Gall: 0-0
Aids: Bl: 0-0 Vi: 0-0 Tstrap: 0-0
Best Rating: 134 1/03 Kemp 3m   gd-sft   Ch

Very useful handicap chaser; returned from a lengthy absence to win at Kempton in January 2003; stays beyond three miles; effective on soft ground.

Cooling Off (IRE)
100   91

6-y-o b m Brief Truce (USA)-Lovers Parlour (Beldale Flutter (USA))
J R Jenkins American Horse Racing Club Ltd

Placings:214405P-6PP1550   (4214)
2002/03: 16^PGS, 20^PG, 16^PS, 20^PGS, 18¹G, 16⁵GS, 16⁵GS, 18⁰G,

		Starts	1st	2nd	3rd	Win & Pl
Hurdles		8	1	0	0	2219
Career Total		14	2	1	0	6248
95	12/02 Font	2m2f110yG Hdl	GD	£2219
102	10/01 Fknm	2m4f	D Hdl	SFT	£3326
		Total win prize-money £5545

Going: Sf: 0-1 GS: 0-4 Gd: 1-3 GF: - Fm: 0-0
Distance: 2m/2m3: 1-6 2m4-2m7: 0-2 3m+: 0-0
Track: LH: 1-6 RH: 0-2 Tight: 1-5 Gall: 0-1
Aids: Bl: 0-0 Vi: 1-6 Tstrap: 0-0
Best Rating: 102 10/01 Fknm 2m4f   soft   Hdl

Won a two and a half mile soft ground novices hurdle at Fakenham in October 2001, but lost her form subsequently; won a weak selling hurdle from the front at Fontwell in December 2002.

Coolnagorna (IRE)
120   160

6-y-o b/br g Warcraft (USA)-Mandalaw (IRE) (Mandalus)
Jonjo O Neill Mrs G Smith

Placings:P51¹6-21110F   (4462)
2002/03: 22²S, 20¹S, 20¹S, 21¹HY, 21⁰G, 20^FG,

		Starts	1st	2nd	3rd	Win & Pl
Hurdles		6	3	1	0	40109
Career Total		11	5	1	0	49290
160	12/02 Newb	2m5f	A Hdl	HVY	£20300
160	12/02 Sand	2m4f110yA Hdl	SFT	£14500
142	11/02 Chep	2m4f	D Hdl	SFT	£4231
110	11/01 Cork	2m	NHF	Y-S	£5008
101	11/01 Cork	2m	NHF	YLD	£4173
		Total win prize-money £48213

Going: Sf: 3-4 GS: 0-0 Gd: 0-2 GF: - Fm: 0-0
Distance: 2m/2m3: 0-0 2m4-2m7: 3-6 3m+: 0-0
Track: LH: 2-5 RH: 1-1 Tight: 0-1 Gall: 1-2
Aids: Bl: 0-0 Vi: 0-0 Tstrap: 0-0
Best Rating: 160 12/02 Newb 2m5f   heavy   Hdl

Smart novice hurdler; suited by testing ground; stayed 2m 6f; impressive winner of decent novice hurdles before fine effort to finish second in the the Royal & SunAlliance Novices Hurdle at the 2003 Festival; infront when falling fatally at Aintree. (DEAD)

Coolsan (IRE)
104   115

8-y-o b g Insan (USA)-Coolreagh Princess (Raise You Ten)
R H Alner H V Perry

Placings:1/0P3-211PP   (3523)
2002/03: 22²G, 21¹S, 25¹S, 24^PGS, 24^PG,

		Starts	1st	2nd	3rd	Win & Pl
Hurdles		5	2	1	0	7304
Career Total		9	3	1	0	12302
115	12/02 Wwck	3m1f	E Hdl	SFT	£3192
103	11/02 Plum	2m5f	E Hdl	SFT	£3146
114	4/01 Cork	2m4f	NHF	SFT	£4451
		Total win prize-money £10791

Going: Sf: 2-2 GS: 0-1 Gd: 0-2 GF: - Fm: 0-0
Distance: 2m/2m3: 0-0 2m4-2m7: 1-2 3m+: 1-3
Track: LH: 2-4 RH: 0-1 Tight: 1-1 Gall: 0-2
Aids: Bl: 0-0 Vi: 0-0 Tstrap: 0-0
Best Rating: 115 12/02 Wwck 3m1f   soft   Hdl

Fair hurdler; won a Cork bumper for Donal Hassett on his debut in April 2001; third in a maiden hurdle in March 2002, his first form in Britain; winner at Plumpton and Warwick before Christmas; stays three miles; acts on soft ground.

Coolteen Hero (IRE)
101   84

13-y-o b g King Luthier-Running Stream (Paddy s Stream)
R H Alner J Browne,Mrs C Robertson,Mrs E Woodhouse

Placings:612U5U12212/F11222F3233/315B534FP/F52120
3235/431432253/05425113063-00F32431FF   (2667)
2002/03: 19⁰G, 25⁰G, 24^FGF, 25³F, 24²GF, 25⁴GF, 23³GF, 23¹G,
22^RG, 26^PS,

		Starts	1st	2nd	3rd	Win & Pl
Chases		10	1	1	2	6344
Career Total		71	11	15	14	61690
84	11/02 Leic	2m7f110yF(0-100)HCh	GD	£3425
91	11/01 Leic	2m7f110yF(0-105)HCh	G-F	£3020
92	11/01 Chep	3m	F(0-110)HCh	G-S	£2555
106	11/00 Leic	2m4f110yF(0-100)HCh	G-S	£2889
110	11/99 Hrfd	2m3f	F(0-110)HCh	GD	£3525
113	11/98 Plum	2m	E(0-115)HCh	SFT	£3452
116	10/97 Bang	3m1f110yE(0-115)HCh	GD	£4135
112	9/97 Extr	2m1f110yE(0-115)HCh	G-F	£3436
106	4/97 Extr	2m3f110yD(0-125)HCh	FRM	£3629
100	2/97 Plum	2m	E Ch	G-S	£3183
80	10/96 Tntn	2m110y E Ch	G-F	£2828
		Total win prize-money £36082

Going: Sf: 0-1 GS: 0-0 Gd: 1-4 GF: - Fm: 0-5
Distance: 2m/2m3: 0-0 2m4-2m7: 0-2 3m+: 1-8
Track: LH: 0-0 RH: 1-8 Tight: 0-4 Gall: 0-1
Aids: Bl: 0-0 Vi: 0-0 Tstrap: 0-1
Best Rating: 119 3/98 Folk 2m   good   Ch

Plating-class chaser; veteran front-running handicapper; stays three miles; acts on a sound surface, but handles soft.

Coombs Spinney

6-y-o b g Homo Sapien-Woodram Delight (Idiots Delight)
Mrs P Sly R M Micklethwait

Placings:00-0   (2218)
2002/03: 16⁰S,

		Starts	1st	2nd	3rd	Win & Pl
Hurdles		1	0	0	0	
Career Total		3	0	0	0	

Going: Sf: 0-1 GS: 0-0 Gd: 0-0 GF: - Fm: 0-0
Distance: 2m/2m3: 0-1 2m4-2m7: 0-0 3m+: 0-0
Track: LH: 0-1 RH: 0-0 Tight: 0-0 Gall: 0-1
Aids: Bl: 0-0 Vi: 0-0 Tstrap: 0-0
Best Rating: 53 3/02 MRas 2m1f110y gd-sft NHF

Cootehill Boy (IRE)
(98h)   (87h)

9-y-o br g Strong Gale-Orospring (Tesoro Mio)
W Storey John J Maguire

Placings:0/0500/011133/6642-PUF   (0583)
2002/03: 20²G, 24^PG, 22^UGF, 20^FG,

		Starts	1st	2nd	3rd	Win & Pl
Hurdles		2	0	1	0	636
Chases		2	0	0	0	0
Career Total		17	2	1	2	6461
90	8/00 Prth	3m110y F(0-100)HHdl	GD	£2990
93	8/00 Sedg	2m5f110yF(0-100)HHdl	GD	£2226
		Total win prize-money £5216

Going: Sf: 0-0 GS: 0-0 Gd: 0-3 GF: - Fm: 0-1
Distance: 2m/2m3: 0-0 2m4-2m7: 0-3 3m+: 0-1
Track: LH: 0-4 RH: 0-0 Tight: 0-2 Gall: 0-0
Aids: Bl: 0-0 Vi: 0-4 Tstrap: 0-0
Best Rating: 95 10/00 Weth 2m7f   gd-sft   Hdl

Copeland
105   160

8-y-o b g Generous (IRE)-Whitehaven (Top Ville)
M C Pipe Professor D B A Silk & Mrs Heather Silk

Placings:211202/3635053/211202U1-0F62   (4780)
2002/03: 16⁰G, 16^FG, 20⁶G, 16²GF,

		Starts	1st	2nd	3rd	Win & Pl
Hurdles		4	0	1	0	15450
Career Total		25	5	7	3	227150
163	4/02 Sand	2m110y B Hdl	GD	£35700
163	2/02 Newb	2m110y A HHdl	SFT	£63800
163	1/02 Chel	2m1f	B(0-145)HHdl	HVY	£10257
143	12/99 Sand	2m110y B HHdl	G-S	£34900
128	11/99 Wwck	2m2f110y	D Hdl	£19950
£4146					
		Total win prize-money £148803

Going: Sf: 0-0 GS: 0-0 Gd: 0-3 GF: - Fm: 0-1
Distance: 2m/2m3: 0-3 2m4-2m7: 0-1 3m+: 0-0
Track: LH: 0-3 RH: 0-1 Tight: 0-1 Gall: 0-0
Aids: Bl: 0-0 Vi: 0-4 Tstrap: 0-0
Best Rating: 163 4/02 Sand 2m110y   good   Hdl

High-class hurdler; winner of the 2002 Tote Gold Trophy and short-head second to Intersky Falcon in Masai Hurdle at Sandown in April 2002; off the track for 10 months subsequently and not in the same form since returning; best over 2m; suited by the ground good or softer; usually wears a visor.

Coppeen Sam (IRE)

86(87h)   (68h)**84+**

8-y-o b g Samhoi (USA)-Castleview Rose (Master Buck)
Miss Jacqueline S Doyle The 1st Flemington Partnership

Placings:3430/000-5   (2774)
2002/03: 22⁵S,

	Starts	1st	2nd	3rd	Win & Pl
Chases	1	0	0	0	0
Career Total	8	0	0	2	582

Going:	Sf: 0-1 GS: 0-0 Gd: 0-0 GF: - Fm: 0-0
Distance:	2m/2m3: 0-0 2m4-2m7: 0-1 3m+: 0-0
Track:	LH: 0-1 RH: 0-0 Tight: 0-0 Gall: 0-1
Aids:	Bl: 0-0 Vi: 0-0 Tstrap: 0-0
Best Rating:	100 12/00 Hntg 2m110y heavy NHF

Moderate novice hurdler, stays two miles seven-plus, suited by soft ground, has worn blinkers.

Copper Moss

104   **93**

5-y-o ch g Le Moss-Shiona Anne (Royal Fountain)
N W Alexander Nicholas Alexander

Placings:0-00P425   (4551)
2002/03: 14⁰GS, 16⁰HY, 20ᴾHY, 20⁴GS, 16²S, 20⁵G,

	Starts	1st	2nd	3rd	Win & Pl
NH Flat	2	0	0	0	0
Hurdles	4	0	1	0	1039
Career Total	7	0	1	0	1039

Going:	Sf: 0-3 GS: 0-2 Gd: 0-1 GF: - Fm: 0-0
Distance:	2m/2m3: 0-2 2m4-2m7: 0-3 3m+: 0-0
Track:	LH: 0-6 RH: 0-0 Tight: 0-0 Gall: 0-0
Aids:	Bl: 0-0 Vi: 0-0 Tstrap: 0-0
Best Rating:	93 3/03 Ayr 2m soft Hdl

Copper Shell

103(67h)   (46h)**93**

9-y-o ch g Beveled (USA)-Luly My Love (Hello Gorgeous (USA))
Miss A M Newton-Smith (G L Moore 22/5) Brighton Racing Club

Placings:5P230/400604/504/51210P/553P26-340320   (3929)
2002/03: 16³G, 16⁴G, 16⁰S, 21³S, 16²HY, 20⁰G,

	Starts	1st	2nd	3rd	Win & Pl
Hurdles	1	0	0	0	0
Chases	5	0	1	2	2033
Career Total	32	2	4	4	12807
107	4/01 Plum	2m1f		E Ch	SFT £3883
100	1/01 Folk	2m		E(0-105)HCh	HVY £2912
					Total win prize-money £6796

Going:	Sf: 0-3 GS: 0-0 Gd: 0-3 GF: - Fm: 0-0
Distance:	2m/2m3: 0-4 2m4-2m7: 0-2 3m+: 0-0
Track:	LH: 0-2 RH: 0-4 Tight: 0-4 Gall: 0-1
Aids:	Bl: 0-0 Vi: 0-0 Tstrap: 0-5
Best Rating:	107 4/01 Plum 2m1f soft Ch

Mderate chaser; winner on the Flat and over fences; wears a tongue strap; acts on a soft surface; is effective at around two miles.

Copperbeech (IRE)

9-y-o ch m Common Grounds-Caimanite (Tap On Wood)

H H G Owen J P Owen

Placings:5/P   (0613)
2002/03: 16ᴾGF,

	Starts	1st	2nd	3rd	Win & Pl
Hurdles	1	0	0		
Career Total	2	0	0	0	0

Going:	Sf: 0-0 GS: 0-0 Gd: 0-0 GF: - Fm: 0-1
Distance:	2m/2m3: 0-1 2m4-2m7: 0-0 3m+: 0-0
Track:	LH: 0-1 RH: 0-0 Tight: 0-0 Gall: 0-0
Aids:	Bl: 0-0 Vi: 0-0 Tstrap: 0-0
Best Rating:	0 6/02 Worc 2m gd-fm Hdl

Coppermalt (USA)

83   **76+**

5-y-o b g Affirmed (USA)-Poppy Carew (IRE) (Danehill (USA))
P J Hobbs (P W Harris 14/8) Mrs A M Palmer

Placings:3   (0818)
2002/03: 16³GF,

	Starts	1st	2nd	3rd	Win & Pl
Hurdles	1	0	0	1	554
Career Total	1	0	0	1	554

Going:	Sf: 0-0 GS: 0-0 Gd: 0-0 GF: - Fm: 0-1
Distance:	2m/2m3: 0-1 2m4-2m7: 0-0 3m+: 0-0
Track:	LH: 0-1 RH: 0-0 Tight: 0-0 Gall: 0-0
Aids:	Bl: 0-0 Vi: 0-0 Tstrap: 0-0
Best Rating:	76 7/02 Worc 2m gd-fm Hdl

Copperpot (IRE)

76   **78**

6-y-o ch g Treasure Hunter-Merillion (Touch Paper)
N G Richards Trevor Hemmings

Placings:0555-   (0001)
2002/03: 20⁵G,

	Starts	1st	2nd	3rd	Win & Pl
Hurdles	1	0	0	0	0
Career Total	4	0	0	0	0

Going:	Sf: 0-0 GS: 0-0 Gd: 0-0 GF: - Fm: 0-0
Distance:	2m/2m3: 0-0 2m4-2m7: 0-1 3m+: 0-0
Track:	LH: 0-1 RH: 0-0 Tight: 0-0 Gall: 0-1
Aids:	Bl: 0-0 Vi: 0-0 Tstrap: 0-0
Best Rating:	78 4/02 Carl 2m4f good Hdl

Copplestone (IRE)

102   **103**

7-y-o b g Second Set (IRE)-Queen Of The Brush (Averof)
W Storey B P Bradshaw

Placings:44-4612U54P   (4258)
2002/03: 16⁴S, 17⁶S, 16¹GS, 16²S, 21ᵁS, 19⁵G, 19⁴S, 17ᴾG,

	Starts	1st	2nd	3rd	Win & Pl
Hurdles	8	1	1	0	4533
Career Total	10	1	1	0	4533
87	12/02 Catt	2m		G(0-95)HHdl	G-S £3623
					Total win prize-money £3624

Going:	Sf: 0-5 GS: 1-1 Gd: 0-2 GF: - Fm: 0-0
Distance:	2m/2m3: 1-7 2m4-2m7: 0-1 3m+: 0-0
Track:	LH: 1-8 RH: 0-0 Tight: 1-7 Gall: 0-1
Aids:	Bl: 0-0 Vi: 0-0 Tstrap: 0-0
Best Rating:	90 12/02 Newc 2m soft Hdl

Moderate hurdler, likes a left-handed track and goes well at Catterick; suited by two miles; acts on any ground; wears cheekpieces.

Copsale Lad

103   **105+**

6-y-o ch g Karinga Bay-Squeaky Cottage (True Song)
Miss H C Knight Swallow Partnership

Placings:5P   (2602)
2002/03: 16⁵S, 20ᴾS,

	Starts	1st	2nd	3rd	Win & Pl
Hurdles	2	0	0	0	0
Career Total	2	0	0	0	0

Going:	Sf: 0-2 GS: 0-0 Gd: 0-0 GF: - Fm: 0-0
Distance:	2m/2m3: 0-1 2m4-2m7: 0-1 3m+: 0-0
Track:	LH: 0-1 RH: 0-1 Tight: 0-0 Gall: 0-1
Aids:	Bl: 0-0 Vi: 0-0 Tstrap: 0-0
Best Rating:	105 11/02 Newb 2m110y soft Hdl

Coquelles (FR)

92(110h)   (97h)**95**

7-y-o b m In The Wings-La Toja (FR) (Gift Card (FR))
R M Stronge A P Holland

Placings:6/P5/0521-54F14P   (4170)
2002/03: 24⁵GS, 20⁴GS, 19⁵S, 19¹G, 20⁴G, 21ᴾS,

	Starts	1st	2nd	3rd	Win & Pl
Hurdles	3	1	0	0	5083
Chases	3	0	0	0	762
Career Total	13	2	1	0	10033
97	2/03 Hrfd	2m3f110yD(0-115)HHdl		GD	£5083
87	3/02 Tntn	2m3f110yE(0-105)HHdl		SFT	£3486
					Total win prize-money £8569

Going:	Sf: 0-2 GS: 0-2 Gd: 1-2 GF: - Fm: 0-0
Distance:	2m/2m3: 0-0 2m4-2m7: 1-5 3m+: 0-1
Track:	LH: 0-2 RH: 1-4 Tight: 0-3 Gall: 0-0
Aids:	Bl: 0-0 Vi: 0-0 Tstrap: 0-0
Best Rating:	97 2/03 Hrfd 2m3f110y good Hdl

Modest hurdler, stays two and a half miles; acts on good and soft ground; has shown a little ability over fences.

Coral Island

106(93h)   (93h)**113+**

9-y-o b g Charmer-Misowni (Niniski (USA))
R M Stronge Mrs Bernice Stronge

Placings:1130/00600/F016100/001412164P-5U663P1   (4313)
2002/03: 20⁵GS, 31ᵁGS, 16⁶GS, 24ᴿGS, 20³S, 24ᴾGS, 18¹G,

	Starts	1st	2nd	3rd	Win & Pl
Chases	7	1	0	1	8866
Career Total	33	8	1	2	35779
113	3/03 Newb	2m3f110yD(0-125)HCh		GD	£7085
128	1/02 Donc	2m3f110yD Ch		SFT	£4431
117	12/01 Plum	2m1f		D Ch	GD	£4030
114	12/01 Wwck	2m110y		D Ch	SFT	£4004
117	12/99 Font	2m6f110yC(0-130)HHdl		G-S	£4742
106	10/99 Font	2m6f110yE(0-115)HHdl		GF	£2285
103	9/97 Sedg	2m1f		E Hdl	G-F	£2320
103	8/97 Prth	2m110y		E Hdl	GD	£2276
					Total win prize-money £31174

Going:	Sf: 0-1 GS: 0-5 Gd: 1-1 GF: - Fm: 0-0
Distance:	2m/2m3: 1-2 2m4-2m7: 0-2 3m+: 0-3
Track:	LH: 1-7 RH: 0-0 Tight: 0-3 Gall: 1-2
Aids:	Bl: 0-0 Vi: 0-0 Tstrap: 0-0
Best Rating:	128 1/02 Donc 2m3f110y soft Ch

Fair chaser; effective at up to two miles six; acts on any ground.

Coralinga

80   **45**

6-y-o b m Terimon-Kintra (Sunyboy)
Miss E C Lavelle Mrs Julien Turner

Placings:2-P0P   (4595)
2002/03: 19PS, 26OG, 22PGF,

	Starts	1st	2nd	3rd	Win & Pl
Hurdles	3	0	0	0	
Career Total	4	0	1	0	489

Going:	Sf: 0-1 GS: 0-0 Gd: 0-1 GF: - Fm: 0-1
Distance:	2m/2m3: 0-0 2m4-2m7: 0-2 3m+: 0-1
Track:	LH: 0-0 RH: 0-3 Tight: 0-0 Gall: 0-1
Aids:	BI: 0-0 Vi: 0-0 Tstrap: 0-0
Best Rating:	71 4/02 Plum 2m2f gd-fm NHF

Showed promise on bumper debut.

Corbie Abbey (IRE)

(99h)   (97h)**85**

8-y-o b g Glacial Storm (USA)-Dromoland Lady (Pollerton)
P Beaumont J Stephenson

Placings:600/0P6P0/300F4-P   (1568)
2002/03: 19PG,

	Starts	1st	2nd	3rd	Win & Pl
Hurdles	1	0	0	0	
Career Total	14	0	0	1	429

Going:	Sf: 0-0 GS: 0-0 Gd: 0-1 GF: - Fm: 0-0
Distance:	2m/2m3: 0-0 2m4-2m7: 0-1 3m+: 0-0
Track:	LH: 0-0 RH: 0-1 Tight: 0-0 Gall: 0-0
Aids:	BI: 0-0 Vi: 0-0 Tstrap: 0-0
Best Rating:	97 4/01 Ayr 2m good Hdl

Corbie's Glen

101(90h)   (77h)**80**

9-y-o b m Broadsword (USA)-Celestial Bride (Godswalk (USA))
B Mactaggart Mrs M Marshall

Placings:00065/404-2   (1414)
2002/03: 25PGF,

	Starts	1st	2nd	3rd	Win & Pl
Chases	1	0	1	0	1248
Career Total	9	0	1	0	1806

Going:	Sf: 0-0 GS: 0-0 Gd: 0-0 GF: - Fm: 0-1
Distance:	2m/2m3: 0-0 2m4-2m7: 0-0 3m+: 0-1
Track:	LH: 0-1 RH: 0-0 Tight: 0-1 Gall: 0-0
Aids:	BI: 0-0 Vi: 0-0 Tstrap: 0-0
Best Rating:	80 10/02 Kels 3m1f gd-fm Ch

Cordilla (IRE)

89f   **96f**

5-y-o b g Accordion-Tumble Heather (Tumble Wind (USA))
N G Richards Trevor Hemmings

Placings:2   (4039)
2002/03: 16PS,

	Starts	1st	2nd	3rd	Win & Pl
NH Flat	1	0	1	0	633

Career Total   1   0   1   0   633

Going:	Sf: 0-1 GS: 0-0 Gd: 0-0 GF: - Fm: 0-0
Distance:	2m/2m3: 0-1 2m4-2m7: 0-0 3m+: 0-0
Track:	LH: 0-1 RH: 0-0 Tight: 0-0 Gall: 0-0
Aids:	BI: 0-0 Vi: 0-0 Tstrap: 0-0
Best Rating:	96 3/03 Ayr 2m soft NHF

Core Of Silver (IRE)

87f   **60f**

4-y-o b g Nucleon (USA)-My Silversmith (IRE) (Cyrano De Bergerac)
P Monteith Mrs G Smyth

Placings:0   (4778)
2002/03: 16OG,

	Starts	1st	2nd	3rd	Win & Pl
NH Flat	1	0	0	0	
Career Total	1	0	0	0	

Going:	Sf: 0-0 GS: 0-0 Gd: 0-1 GF: - Fm: 0-0
Distance:	2m/2m3: 0-1 2m4-2m7: 0-0 3m+: 0-0
Track:	LH: 0-0 RH: 0-1 Tight: 0-0 Gall: 0-0
Aids:	BI: 0-0 Vi: 0-0 Tstrap: 0-0
Best Rating:	60 4/03 Prth 2m110y good NHF

Cork Harbour (FR)

70   **31**

7-y-o ch g Grand Lodge (USA)-Irish Sea (Irish River (FR))
P Bowen (Mrs N Smith 17/10) Marshall James

Placings:6/00   (3597)
2002/03: 17OS, 17OS,

	Starts	1st	2nd	3rd	Win & Pl
Hurdles	2	0	0	0	
Career Total	3	0	0	0	0

Going:	Sf: 0-2 GS: 0-0 Gd: 0-0 GF: - Fm: 0-0
Distance:	2m/2m3: 0-2 2m4-2m7: 0-0 3m+: 0-0
Track:	LH: 0-0 RH: 0-2 Tight: 0-2 Gall: 0-0
Aids:	BI: 0-0 Vi: 0-0 Tstrap: 0-0
Best Rating:	75 1/01 Tntn 2m1f soft Hdl

Selling-class hurdler; jinked and gave his rider no chance when sent off favourite at Sedgefield in July.

Corkan (IRE)

111   **71**

9-y-o b g Torus-Broad Tab (Cantab)
J Cullinan Mrs E Reid

Placings:066P/533P4/2P441-125P   (1164)
2002/03: 26IGF, 24PGF, 24SG, 27PG,

	Starts	1st	2nd	3rd	Win & Pl
Chases	4	1	1	0	4457
Career Total	18	2	2	2	9891
91 5/02 Font 3m2f110y					E(0-105)HCh
G-F £3514					
83 3/02 Plum 3m2f					F(0-95)HCh GD £2509

Total win prize-money £6023

Going:	Sf: 0-0 GS: 0-0 Gd: 0-2 GF: - Fm: 1-2
Distance:	2m/2m3: 0-0 2m4-2m7: 0-0 3m+: 1-4
Track:	LH: 0-2 RH: 0-1 Tight: 1-3 Gall: 0-1
Aids:	BI: 0-0 Vi: 0-0 Tstrap: 0-0
Best Rating:	91 6/02 Hntg 3m gd-fm Ch

Plating-class chaser; ex-Irish gelding; stays around three and a quarter miles; acts on good ground.

Corletto (POL)

103(109h)   (91h)**99**

6-y-o b g Professional (IRE)-Cortesia (POL) (Who Knows)
T R George B A Kilpatrick

Placings:P65115-3203P   (4154)
2002/03: 17OG, 16PG, 17OGS, 16SGS, 16PG,

	Starts	1st	2nd	3rd	Win & Pl
Chases	5	0	1	2	2738
Career Total	11	2	1	2	9568
91 4/02 Hrfd 2m1f					D(0-115)HHdl G-F £3896
85 3/02 Tntn 2m1f					F(0-95)HHdl SFT £2933

Total win prize-money £6830

Going:	Sf: 0-0 GS: 0-2 Gd: 0-3 GF: - Fm: 0-0
Distance:	2m/2m3: 0-5 2m4-2m7: 0-0 3m+: 0-0
Track:	LH: 0-3 RH: 0-2 Tight: 0-2 Gall: 0-0
Aids:	BI: 0-0 Vi: 0-0 Tstrap: 0-0
Best Rating:	95 11/02 MRas 2m1f110y gd-sft Ch

Moderate chaser; best at around two miles.

Cornish Gale (IRE)

92(103c)   (133c)**110+**

9-y-o br g Strong Gale-Seanaphobal Lady (Kambalda)
P F Nicholls C G Roach

Placings:0/22P/53111-PF0   (4612)
2002/03: 20PG, 18FG, 16OG,

	Starts	1st	2nd	3rd	Win & Pl
Chases	3	0	0	0	
Career Total	12	3	2	1	29958
126 12/01 Asct 2m					C(0-125)HCh GD £10166
139 11/01 Chel 2m4f110yB Ch					GD £12754
123 11/01 Extr 2m3f110yD Ch					G-F £5395

Total win prize-money £28315

Going:	Sf: 0-0 GS: 0-0 Gd: 0-3 GF: - Fm: 0-0
Distance:	2m/2m3: 0-2 2m4-2m7: 0-1 3m+: 0-0
Track:	LH: 0-2 RH: 0-1 Tight: 0-0 Gall: 0-2
Aids:	BI: 0-0 Vi: 0-0 Tstrap: 0-0
Best Rating:	139 11/01 Chel 2m4f110y good Ch

Useful chaser, reverted to hurdles winning twice in novice company at Wincanton in May; long odds-on when turned over at Wetherby later the same mont; stays two miles six but effective at shorter; needs decent ground.

Cornish Rebel (IRE)

115f   **138f**

6-y-o br g Un Desperado (FR)-Katday (FR) (Miller s Mate)
P F Nicholls C G Roach

Placings:10   (4115)
2002/03: 16IG, 16OG,

	Starts	1st	2nd	3rd	Win & Pl
NH Flat	2	1	0	0	11600
Career Total	2	1	0	0	11600
138 2/03 Newb 2m110y A NHF					GD £11600

Total win prize-money £11600

Going:	Sf: 0-0 GS: 0-0 Gd: 1-2 GF: - Fm: 0-0
Distance:	2m/2m3: 1-2 2m4-2m7: 0-0 3m+: 0-0
Track:	LH: 1-2 RH: 0-0 Tight: 0-0 Gall: 1-1
Aids:	BI: 0-0 Vi: 0-0 Tstrap: 0-0
Best Rating:	138 2/03 Newb 2m110y good NHF

Very useful bumper performer; full-brother to Best Mate and Inca Trail who cost Ir£110,000, he was a very impressive winner of a Grade Two Newbury bumper on his debut, despite hanging; well beaten in Champion Bumper at Cheltenham.

Corporate Player (IRE)

92f   **84f**

5-y-o b g Zaffaran (USA)-Khazna (Stanford)
Noel T Chance   A D Weller

Placings:6   (4190)
2002/03: 17⁶G,

	Starts	1st	2nd	3rd	Win & Pl
NH Flat	1	0	0	0	0
Career Total	1	0	0	0	0

Going:	Sf: 0-0 GS: 0-0 Gd: 0-1 GF: - Fm: 0-0
Distance:	2m/2m3: 0-1 2m4-2m7: 0-0 3m+: 0-0
Track:	LH: 0-0 RH: 0-1 Tight: 0-1 Gall: 0-0
Aids:	Bl: 0-0 Vi: 0-0 Tstrap: 0-1
Best Rating:	84 3/03 Folk 2m1f110y good NHF

Corrare (IRE)

95   **68**

6-y-o b m Corrouge (USA)-Granig Rarity (Rarity)
J R Boyle   John Hopkins (t/a South Hatch Racing)

Placings:0P03   (4629)
2002/03: 16⁰S, 20⁰S, 20⁰G, 21³GF,

	Starts	1st	2nd	3rd	Win & Pl
Hurdles	4	0	0	1	350
Career Total	4	0	0	1	350

Going:	Sf: 0-2 GS: 0-0 Gd: 0-1 GF: - Fm: 0-1
Distance:	2m/2m3: 0-1 2m4-2m7: 0-3 3m+: 0-0
Track:	LH: 0-2 RH: 0-1 Tight: 0-4 Gall: 0-0
Aids:	Bl: 0-0 Vi: 0-0 Tstrap: 0-0
Best Rating:	68 4/03 Plum 2m5f gd-fm Hdl

Poor hurdler; first sign of ability when third in a moderate Plumpton seller in first-time blinkers in April 2003.

Correct And Right (IRE)

101   **94**

4-y-o b f Great Commotion (USA)-Miss Hawkins (Modern Dancer)
J W Mullins   Seamus Mullins

Placings:30205014   (4515)
2002/03: 16³G, 16⁰G, 17²S, 17⁰GS, 22⁵GS, 19⁰HY, 16¹GF, 17⁴GF,

	Starts	1st	2nd	3rd	Win & Pl
Hurdles	8	1	1	1	4685
Career Total	8	1	1	1	4685
85 3/03 Wwck 2m		F Hdl		G-F	£3020

Total win prize-money £3021

Going:	Sf: 0-2 GS: 0-2 Gd: 0-2 GF: - Fm: 1-2
Distance:	2m/2m3: 1-6 2m4-2m7: 0-2 3m+: 0-0
Track:	LH: 1-3 RH: 0-5 Tight: 0-3 Gall: 0-1
Aids:	Bl: 0-0 Vi: 0-0 Tstrap: 0-0
Best Rating:	94 1/03 Chel 2m1f gd-sft Hdl

Moderate hurdler; failed to achieve much when winning two mile maiden hurdle at Warwick March 2003; acts on good to firm.

Corrib Lad (IRE)

102f   **106f**

5-y-o b/br g Supreme Leader-Nun So Game (The Parson)
P J Hobbs   Ms C Hehir

Placings:03   (4155)
2002/03: 16⁰HY, 16³G,

	Starts	1st	2nd	3rd	Win & Pl
NH Flat	2	0	0	1	303
Career Total	2	0	0	1	303

Going:	Sf: 0-1 GS: 0-0 Gd: 0-1 GF: - Fm: 0-0
Distance:	2m/2m3: 0-2 2m4-2m7: 0-0 3m+: 0-0
Track:	LH: 0-1 RH: 0-1 Tight: 0-0 Gall: 0-0
Aids:	Bl: 0-0 Vi: 0-0 Tstrap: 0-0
Best Rating:	106 3/03 Wwck 2m good NHF

Modest bumper performer; virtually ran off the course on his bumper debut at Sandown February 2003; close third despite jinking at the wing of the final flight in a competitive bumper at Warwick next time; apparently not straight forward; he clearly possesses ability.

Corrib Supreme (IRE)

102   **90**

8-y-o b g Supreme Leader-Black Pit (Black Minstrel)
A J Martin   Southsea Syndicate

Placings:0/3500005-050   (4772)
2002/03: 16⁰YS, 16⁵HY, 16⁰G,

	Starts	1st	2nd	3rd	Win & Pl
Hurdles	3	0	0	0	
Career Total	11	0	0	1	367

Going:	Sf: 0-1 GS: 0-0 Gd: 0-1 GF: - Fm: 0-0
Distance:	2m/2m3: 0-3 2m4-2m7: 0-0 3m+: 0-0
Track:	LH: 0-2 RH: 0-1 Tight: 0-0 Gall: 0-0
Aids:	Bl: 0-0 Vi: 0-0 Tstrap: 0-0
Best Rating:	107 5/01 Gowr 2m yield NHF

Moderate Irish-trained maiden hurdler.

Corroboree (IRE)

103   **97**

6-y-o b g Corrouge (USA)-Laura s Toi (Quayside)
N A Twiston-Davies   The Corroborators

Placings:32000-10   (1943)
2002/03: 16¹S, 21⁰G,

	Starts	1st	2nd	3rd	Win & Pl
Hurdles	2	1	0	0	3445
Career Total	7	1	1	1	4369
99 11/02 Kemp 2m		E(0-110)	HHdl	SFT	£3445

Total win prize-money £3445

Going:	Sf: 1-1 GS: 0-0 Gd: 0-1 GF: - Fm: 0-0
Distance:	2m/2m3: 1-1 2m4-2m7: 0-1 3m+: 0-0
Track:	LH: 0-0 RH: 1-1 Tight: 0-0 Gall: 0-1
Aids:	Bl: 0-0 Vi: 0-0 Tstrap: 0-0
Best Rating:	107 11/01 Aint 2m1f gd-sft NHF

Moderate hurdler; has shown promise in bumpers; disappointed over hurdles early in 2002 when the stable was out of form; got off the mark in a small Kempton handicap on testing ground; effective at two miles; may get further.

Corston Joker

13-y-o b g Idiots Delight-Corston Lass (Menelek)
J M Turner   J M Turner

Placings:0P6PU/F00313P/111121/R1R2/R02R/P5/1R
                         (0314)

2002/03: 24¹G, 31ᴿG,

	Starts	1st	2nd	3rd	Win & Pl
Chases	2	1	0	0	1501
Career Total	30	8	3	2	36306
98 5/02 Fknm	3m110y H Ch			GD	£1500
131 5/98 Bang	2m4f110yD(0-120)HCh			GD	£4260
138 4/98 Prth	2m4f110yD(0-125)HCh			GD	£5865
131 3/98 Newc	2m4f D(0-125)HCh			G-F	£3468
117 12/97 Newc	2m4f C(0-130)HCh			GD	£4674
117 11/97 Catt	2m3f E(0-115)HCh			GD	£3148
114 11/97 Carl	2m4f110yC(0-135)HCh			FRM	£4682
107 3/97 Newc	2m4f E Ch			GD	£2849

Total win prize-money £30451

Going:	Sf: 0-0 GS: 0-0 Gd: 1-2 GF: - Fm: 0-0
Distance:	2m/2m3: 0-0 2m4-2m7: 0-0 3m+: 1-2
Track:	LH: 1-1 RH: 0-1 Tight: 1-2 Gall: 0-0
Aids:	Bl: 0-0 Vi: 0-0 Tstrap: 0-0
Best Rating:	138 4/98 Prth 2m4f110y good Ch

Corundum (USA)

4-y-o b g Benny The Dip (USA)-Santi Sana (Formidable (USA))
D E Cantillon   Mrs Julie Mitchell

Placings:P   (1641)
2002/03: 16ᴾG,

	Starts	1st	2nd	3rd	Win & Pl
Hurdles	1	0	0	0	
Career Total	1	0	0	0	

Going:	Sf: 0-0 GS: 0-0 Gd: 0-1 GF: - Fm: 0-0
Distance:	2m/2m3: 0-1 2m4-2m7: 0-0 3m+: 0-0
Track:	LH: 0-0 RH: 0-1 Tight: 0-0 Gall: 0-0
Aids:	Bl: 0-0 Vi: 0-0 Tstrap: 0-1
Best Rating:	0 10/02 Kemp 2m good Hdl

Corunna

6-y-o b g Puissance-Kind Of Shy (Kind Of Hush)
R Johnson (A Berry 18/11)   Foster Watson

Placings:PP   (4433)
2002/03: 17ᴾGS, 16ᴾG,

	Starts	1st	2nd	3rd	Win & Pl
Hurdles	2	0	0	0	
Career Total	2	0	0	0	

Going:	Sf: 0-0 GS: 0-1 Gd: 0-1 GF: - Fm: 0-0
Distance:	2m/2m3: 0-2 2m4-2m7: 0-0 3m+: 0-0
Track:	LH: 0-1 RH: 0-1 Tight: 0-1 Gall: 0-1
Aids:	Bl: 0-0 Vi: 0-0 Tstrap: 0-0
Best Rating:	0 4/03 Newc 2m good Hdl

Cosi Fan Tutte

94   **93+**

5-y-o b g Inchinor-Bumpkin (Free State)
M C Pipe (B Hanbury 8/9)   Stuart M Mercer

Placings:5   (2193)
2002/03: 17⁵GS,

	Starts	1st	2nd	3rd	Win & Pl
Hurdles	1	0	0	0	0
Career Total	1	0	0	0	0

Going:	Sf: 0-0 GS: 0-1 Gd: 0-0 GF: - Fm: 0-0

Distance:	2m/2m3: 0-1 2m4-2m7: 0-0 3m+: 0-0
Track:	LH: 0-0 RH: 0-1 Tight: 0-1 Gall: 0-0
Aids:	Bl: 0-0 Vi: 0-1 Tstrap: 0-0
Best Rating:	93 11/02 Tntn 2m1f gd-sft Hdl

Cosmic Case

112   **109**

8-y-o b m Casteddu-La Fontainova (IRE) (Lafontaine (USA))
J S Goldie The Cosmic Cases

Placings:4000560416/53225101P/12B110665   **(4754)**
2002/03: 16¹GS, 20²G, 20⁸G, 16¹GF, 16¹GF, 20⁰G, 19⁶S, 20⁶GS, 16⁵G,

	Starts	1st	2nd	3rd	Win & Pl
Hurdles	9	3	1	0	21021
Career Total	28	6	3	1	34093

105	10/02	Kels	2m110y	D(0-120)HHdl	G-F	£8053
103	9/02	Prth	2m110y	D(0-115)HHdl	G-F	£5564
94	8/02	Prth	2m110y	D(0-115)HHdl	G-S	£5434
94	2/01	Kels	2m2f	E(0-115)HHdl	SFT	£6500
94	12/00	Muss	2m	G(0-95)HHdl	GD	£2331
92	2/00	Catt	2m	F(0-95)Hdl	GD	£1928

Total win prize-money £29812

Going:	Sf: 0-1 GS: 1-2 Gd: 0-4 GF: - Fm: 2-2
Distance:	2m/2m3: 3-4 2m4-2m7: 0-5 3m+: 0-0
Track:	LH: 1-4 RH: 2-5 Tight: 1-4 Gall: 0-0
Aids:	Bl: 0-0 Vi: 0-0 Tstrap: 0-0
Best Rating:	105 10/02 Kels 2m110y gd-fm Hdl

Modest hurdler; tends to mix hurdling with Flat; stays two and a half miles, handles most ground; best going right-handed.

Cosmic Flight (IRE)

81   **41**

7-y-o b g Torus-Palatine Lady (Pauper)
Noel T Chance Top Flight Racing

Placings:0/50-30P   **(1178)**
2002/03: 16³GF, 20⁰GF, 16⁰GF,

	Starts	1st	2nd	3rd	Win & Pl
NH Flat	1	0	0	1	260
Hurdles	2	0	0	0	0
Career Total	6	0	0	1	260

Going:	Sf: 0-0 GS: 0-0 Gd: 0-0 GF: - Fm: 0-3
Distance:	2m/2m3: 0-2 2m4-2m7: 0-1 3m+: 0-0
Track:	LH: 0-3 RH: 0-0 Tight: 0-1 Gall: 0-0
Aids:	Bl: 0-0 Vi: 0-0 Tstrap: 0-0
Best Rating:	84 7/02 Worc 2m gd-fm NHF

Cosmic Ranger

100   **64**

5-y-o b g Magic Ring (IRE)-Lismore (Relkino)
H Alexander Mrs Sheila Macleod

Placings:6P0400   **(4258)**
2002/03: 19⁶GF, 16⁶S, 16⁰G, 17⁴HY, 16⁰S, 17⁰G,

	Starts	1st	2nd	3rd	Win & Pl
Hurdles	6	0	0	0	0
Career Total	6	0	0	0	0

Going:	Sf: 0-3 GS: 0-0 Gd: 0-0 GF: - Fm: 0-1
Distance:	2m/2m3: 0-5 2m4-2m7: 0-1 3m+: 0-0
Track:	LH: 0-4 RH: 0-2 Tight: 0-5 Gall: 0-0
Aids:	Bl: 0-0 Vi: 0-0 Tstrap: 0-0
Best Rating:	64 3/03 Sedg 2m1f good Hdl

First worthwhile form when runner-up in selling handicap hurdle at Cartmel in May.

Cosmic Song

99   **80**

6-y-o b m Cosmonaut-Hotaria (Sizzling Melody)
R M Whitaker Country Lane Partnership

Placings:P4   **(3368)**
2002/03: 16ᴾGS, 16⁴GS,

	Starts	1st	2nd	3rd	Win & Pl
Hurdles	2	0	0	0	0
Career Total	2	0	0	0	0

Going:	Sf: 0-0 GS: 0-2 Gd: 0-0 GF: - Fm: 0-0
Distance:	2m/2m3: 0-2 2m4-2m7: 0-0 3m+: 0-0
Track:	LH: 0-2 RH: 0-0 Tight: 0-2 Gall: 0-0
Aids:	Bl: 0-0 Vi: 0-0 Tstrap: 0-0
Best Rating:	66 1/03 Sthl 2m gd-sft Hdl

Winner of three selling races on the Flat; best race over hurdles on third start when well beaten fourth at Wetherby in May.

Cosmo Jack (IRE)

7-y-o b g Balla Cove-Foolish Law (IRE) (Law Society (USA))
S Flook S Flook

Placings:5101110/0PPP0/3PP-F   **(0108)**
2002/03: 24ᶠGF,

	Starts	1st	2nd	3rd	Win & Pl
Chases	1	0	0	0	
Career Total	16	4	0	1	9191

96	1/00	Tntn	2m1f	E(0-105)HHdl	SFT	£2601
104	1/00	Leic	2m	G Hdl	SFT	£1904
86	12/99	Ludl	2m	F Hdl	G-S	£2766
85	11/99	Catt	2m	G Hdl	G-F	£1605

Total win prize-money £8877

Going:	Sf: 0-0 GS: 0-0 Gd: 0-0 GF: - Fm: 0-1
Distance:	2m/2m3: 0-0 2m4-2m7: 0-0 3m+: - 0-1
Track:	LH: 0-0 RH: 0-0 Tight: 0-1 Gall: 0-0
Aids:	Bl: 0-0 Vi: 0-0 Tstrap: 0-0
Best Rating:	104 1/00 Leic 2m soft Hdl

Cosmocrat

103   **99**

5-y-o b g Cosmonaut-Bella Coola (Northern State (USA))
C G Cox S Barrow,G O Toole,G Whyte & Friends

Placings:6F-200F   **(3902)**
2002/03: 16²HY, 16⁰S, 17⁰GS, 16ᶠS,

	Starts	1st	2nd	3rd	Win & Pl
Hurdles	4	0	1	0	1093
Career Total	6	0	1	0	1093

Going:	Sf: 0-3 GS: 0-1 Gd: 0-0 GF: - Fm: 0-0
Distance:	2m/2m3: 0-4 2m4-2m7: 0-0 3m+: 0-0
Track:	LH: 0-3 RH: 0-1 Tight: 0-0 Gall: 0-2
Aids:	Bl: 0-0 Vi: 0-0 Tstrap: 0-0
Best Rating:	99 1/03 Chel 2m1f gd-sft Hdl

Moderate hurdler; fair miler on the Flat; acts in soft ground.

Cosmosonic

4-y-o ch f Cosmonaut-Double Birthday (Cavo Doro)
W Storey M D Townson

Placings:PP	**(4517)**
2002/03: 16ᴾG, 17ᴾG,	

	Starts	1st	2nd	3rd	Win & Pl
Hurdles	2	0	0	0	
Career Total	2	0	0	0	

Going:	Sf: 0-0 GS: 0-0 Gd: 0-2 GF: - Fm: 0-0
Distance:	2m/2m3: 0-2 2m4-2m7: 0-0 3m+: 0-0
Track:	LH: 0-2 RH: 0-0 Tight: 0-1 Gall: 0-0
Aids:	Bl: 0-0 Vi: 0-0 Tstrap: 0-0
Best Rating:	0 4/03 Sedg 2m1f good Hdl

Cotebrook

4-y-o ch g First Trump-Chantelys (Ballacashtal (CAN))
J M Jefferson Yorkshire Racing Club Owners Group

Placings:P   **(1806)**
2002/03: 16ᴾG,

	Starts	1st	2nd	3rd	Win & Pl
Hurdles	1	0	0	0	
Career Total	1	0	0	0	

Going:	Sf: 0-0 GS: 0-0 Gd: 0-1 GF: - Fm: 0-0
Distance:	2m/2m3: 0-1 2m4-2m7: 0-0 3m+: 0-0
Track:	LH: 0-1 RH: 0-0 Tight: 0-0 Gall: 0-0
Aids:	Bl: 0-0 Vi: 0-0 Tstrap: 0-0
Best Rating:	0 11/02 Hayd 2m good Hdl

Cotopaxi (IRE)

104   **133**

7-y-o b g Turtle Island (IRE)-Ullapool (Dominion)
Miss Venetia Williams (Michael Cunningham 19/5) Mrs Kathy Stuart

Placings:061440/4015500/004400-0513114   **(1838)**
2002/03: 16⁰S, 16⁵S, 20¹G, 17³GS, 19¹GS, 17¹GF, 20⁴S,

	Starts	1st	2nd	3rd	Win & Pl
Hurdles	7	3	0	1	22210
Career Total	26	5	0	1	33305

130	8/02	Sthl	2m	C(0-130)HHdl	G-F	£5882
129	8/02	MRas	2m3f	110yC(0-130)HHdl	G-S	£6130
116	7/02	Wolv	2m4f	110yD(0-125)HHdl	GD	£4046
121	8/00	Gway	2m	Hdl	G-Y	£4692
103	11/99	Navn	2m	Hdl	Y-S	£4004

Total win prize-money £24756

Going:	Sf: 0-3 GS: 1-2 Gd: 1-1 GF: - Fm: 1-1
Distance:	2m/2m3: 1-4 2m4-2m7: 2-3 3m+: 0-0
Track:	LH: 2-5 RH: 1-2 Tight: 2-3 Gall: 0-0
Aids:	Bl: 0-0 Vi: 0-0 Tstrap: 0-0
Best Rating:	130 11/02 Chep 2m4f soft Hdl

Ex-Irish, he is an effective sort in modest handicap hurdles. Suited by good or softer ground and two and a half miles.

Cottstown Boy (IRE)

102(100c)   (102c)**109**

12-y-o ch g King Luthier-Ballyanihan (Le Moss)
Mrs S C Bradburne The Hon Thomas Cochrane

Placings:003045/3FUF62U32U23111/304146102255/51FP 0613653/P40363033/532113253PP60-3   **(0253)**
2002/03: 24³GF,

	Starts	1st	2nd	3rd	Win & Pl
Hurdles	1	0	0	1	635

Career Total		67	9	7	15	53691
89	10/01 Sthl	3m110y	F(0-110)HCh		GD	£2562
92	9/01 Prth	3m	F(0-100)HCh		GD	£5655
118	12/99 Ayr	2m4f	D(0-125)HHdl		HVY	£2986
95	8/99 Prth	3m	D Ch		G-F	£4401
117	12/98 Ayr	2m4f	D(0-125)HHdl		HVY	£2901
115	11/98 Ayr	2m4f	C(0-135)HHdl		G-S	£4825
108	4/98 Prth	2m4f110y	D(0-110)HHdl		HVY	£4744
107	4/98 Prth	3m110y	E(0-110)HHdl		GD	£3902
101	3/98 Kels	2m6f110y	E Hdl		GD	£2010

Total win prize-money £33988

Going: Sf: 0-0 GS: 0-0 Gd: 0-0 GF: - Fm: 0-1
Distance: 2m/2m3: 0-0 2m4-2m7: 0-0 3m+: 0-1
Track: LH: 0-0 RH: 0-1 Tight: 0-0 Gall: 0-0
Aids: Bl: 0-0 Vi: 0-0 Tstrap: 0-0
Best Rating: 118 11/00 Ayr 2m4f soft Hdl

Modest hurdler/chaser, made a winning return to fences in September 2001 over three miles and followed up the following month at Southwell. Suited by three miles and good ground.

Could Be Anything

6-y-o b m Homo Sapien-Our Chrisy (Carlburg)
R T Phillips Horwath Franchising Ltd

Placings:0U (3138)
2002/03: 16⁰G, 21ᵁS,

	Starts	1st	2nd	3rd	Win & Pl
NH Flat	1	0	0	0	0
Hurdles	1	0	0	0	
Career Total	2	0	0	0	

Going: Sf: 0-1 GS: 0-0 Gd: 0-0 GF: - Fm: 0-0
Distance: 2m/2m3: 0-1 2m4-2m7: 0-0 3m+: 0-0
Track: LH: 0-0 RH: 0-2 Tight: 0-0 Gall: 0-0
Aids: Bl: 0-0 Vi: 0-0 Tstrap: 0-0
Best Rating: 65 11/02 Ludl 2m good NHF

Could It Be Legal
80f   76f
6-y-o b g Roviris-Miss Gaylord (Cavo Doro)
P M Rich B Meadmore

Placings:0 (2378)
2002/03: 16⁰S,

	Starts	1st	2nd	3rd	Win & Pl
NH Flat	1	0	0	0	
Career Total	1	0	0	0	

Going: Sf: 0-1 GS: 0-0 Gd: 0-0 GF: - Fm: 0-0
Distance: 2m/2m3: 0-1 2m4-2m7: 0-0 3m+: 0-0
Track: LH: 0-1 RH: 0-0 Tight: 0-0 Gall: 0-0
Aids: Bl: 0-0 Vi: 0-0 Tstrap: 0-0
Best Rating: 76 12/02 Wwck 2m soft NHF

Couldn't Be Phar (IRE)
74f   33f
6-y-o ch g Phardante (FR)-Queenford Belle (Celtic Cone)
D R Gandolfo Starlight Racing

Placings:00 (3673)
2002/03: 18⁰S, 18⁰GS,

	Starts	1st	2nd	3rd	Win & Pl
NH Flat	2	0	0	0	

Career Total		2	0	0	0	

Going: Sf: 0-1 GS: 0-1 Gd: 0-0 GF: - Fm: 0-0
Distance: 2m/2m3: 0-2 2m4-2m7: 0-0 3m+: 0-0
Track: LH: 0-2 RH: 0-0 Tight: 0-1 Gall: 0-0
Aids: Bl: 0-0 Vi: 0-0 Tstrap: 0-0
Best Rating: 33 11/02 Plum 2m2f soft NHF

Couloir
99(94c)   (104c)96
7-y-o gr m Gran Alba (USA)-Hollow Creek (Tarqogan)
H Morrison The Most Welcome Partnership

Placings:6/46002166-5PP54B (4786)
2002/03: 16⁵G, 20²⁰GS, 20²G, 16⁵G, 174GF, 22⁸G,

	Starts	1st	2nd	3rd	Win & Pl
Hurdles	3	0	0	0	573
Chases	3	0	0	0	0
Career Total	15	1	0	0	3873
85	4/02 Winc 2m	E(0-110)HHdl	GD	£2520	

Total win prize-money £2520

Going: Sf: 0-0 GS: 0-1 Gd: 0-4 GF: - Fm: 0-1
Distance: 2m/2m3: 0-3 2m4-2m7: 0-3 3m+: 0-0
Track: LH: 0-0 RH: 0-5 Tight: 0-1 Gall: 0-1
Aids: Bl: 0-0 Vi: 0-0 Tstrap: 0-0
Best Rating: 104 11/02 Kemp 2m good Ch

Broke her duck at the seventh attempt over hurdles when dropped back to the minimum trip; effective on good and slightly softer.

Coulters Candy
92   92
5-y-o ch g Clantime-Heldigvis (Hot Grove)
A C Whillans 7 Up Partnership

Placings:200506 (4772)
2002/03: 16²G, 17⁰HY, 16⁹GS, 16⁵GF, 16⁰G, 16⁶G,

	Starts	1st	2nd	3rd	Win & Pl
NH Flat	4	0	1	0	515
Hurdles	2	0	0	0	0
Career Total	6	0	1	0	515

Going: Sf: 0-1 GS: 0-1 Gd: 0-3 GF: - Fm: 0-1
Distance: 2m/2m3: 0-6 2m4-2m7: 0-0 3m+: 0-0
Track: LH: 0-5 RH: 0-1 Tight: 0-2 Gall: 0-0
Aids: Bl: 0-0 Vi: 0-0 Tstrap: 0-0
Best Rating: 93 7/02 Worc 2m good NHF

Modest form in bumpers, suited by fast ground.

Coulthard (IRE)
85(109h)   (112h)89
10-y-o ch g Glenstal (USA)-Royal Aunt (Martinmas)
Mrs P Sly R Brazier

Placings:033/52332FF4151/612162/0320/000F/234353F0-330423 (3745)
2002/03: 16²GS, 16³HY, 17⁰G, 16⁴S, 16²S, 16⁹G,

	Starts	1st	2nd	3rd	Win & Pl
Hurdles	4	0	1	2	3717
Chases	2	0	0	1	1400
Career Total	42	4	3	11	37643
130	1/99 Wwck 2m	D(0-125)HHdl	SFT	£2838	
121	11/98 Towc 2m	D(0-125)HHdl	SFT	£2745	
112	4/98 Asct 2m110y	D(0-110)HHdl	SFT	£3647	
109	3/98 Limk 2m	(0-123)HHdl	SFT	£3573	

Total win prize-money £12806

Going: Sf: 0-4 GS: 0-0 Gd: 0-2 GF: - Fm: 0-0
Distance: 2m/2m3: 0-6 2m4-2m7: 0-0 3m+: 0-0
Track: LH: 0-2 RH: 0-4 Tight: 0-1 Gall: 0-2
Aids: Bl: 0-0 Vi: 0-0 Tstrap: 0-0
Best Rating: 130 1/00 Chel 2m1f gd-sft Hdl

Fair hurdler, modest chaser; acts well with cut in the ground and is best over two miles.

Count Can Do (IRE)
92   110
4-y-o br c Doyoun-Countess Candy (Great Nephew)
F Doumen Comtesse C A Armand

Placings:153F (2568)
2002/03: 16¹HY, 17⁵HY, 16³G, 19⁵VS,

	Starts	1st	2nd	3rd	Win & Pl
Hurdles	4	1	0	1	12335
Career Total	4	1	0	1	12335
	11/02 Engh 2m110y	Hdl	HVY	£10601	

Total win prize-money £10601

Going: Sf: 1-2 GS: 0-0 Gd: 0-1 GF: - Fm: 0-0
Distance: 2m/2m3: 1-3 2m4-2m7: 0-1 3m+: 0-0
Track: LH: 1-3 RH: 0-0 Tight: 0-0 Gall: 0-1
Aids: Bl: 1-4 Vi: 0-0 Tstrap: 0-0
Best Rating: 108 12/02 Newb 2m110y good Hdl

Winner on the Flat and over hurdles in France; third in a good race on British debut, usually blinkered.

Count Keni
81   57
8-y-o ch g Formidable (USA)-Flying Amy (Norwich (USA))
Mrs K B Mactaggart Mrs J Roncoroni

Placings:0P/000/00/65-0366 (4660)
2002/03: 22⁰GF, 25³G, 25⁶GS, 20⁶GF,

	Starts	1st	2nd	3rd	Win & Pl
Chases	4	0	0	1	540
Career Total	13	0	0	1	540

Going: Sf: 0-0 GS: 0-1 Gd: 0-1 GF: - Fm: 0-2
Distance: 2m/2m3: 0-0 2m4-2m7: 0-2 3m+: 0-2
Track: LH: 0-3 RH: 0-1 Tight: 0-2 Gall: 0-0
Aids: Bl: 0-0 Vi: 0-0 Tstrap: 0-0
Best Rating: 57 3/03 Kels 3m1f gd-sft Ch

Modest pointer, has looked one paced under Rules.

Count Oski
108(97h)   (92h)100
7-y-o b g Petoski-Sea Countess (Ercolano (USA))
M J Ryan The Laodiceans

Placings:0/05500-0FF541P (4614)
2002/03: 19⁰G, 21⁵FS, 17⁵S, 25⁵G, 24⁴G, 24¹G, 21⁵G,

	Starts	1st	2nd	3rd	Win & Pl
Hurdles	1	0	0	0	0
Chases	6	1	0	1	5884
Career Total	13	1	0	0	5884
100	3/03 Asct 3m110y	D(0-110)HCh	GD	£5460	

Total win prize-money £5460

Going: Sf: 0-1 GS: 0-1 Gd: 1-5 GF: - Fm: 0-0
Distance: 2m/2m3: 0-1 2m4-2m7: 0-3 3m+: 1-3
Track: LH: 0-2 RH: 1-5 Tight: 0-3 Gall: 0-2
Aids: Bl: 0-0 Vi: 0-0 Tstrap: 0-0
Best Rating: 100 3/03 Asct 3m110y good Ch

Count Tallahassee

74   **49+**

6-y-o ch g Dervish-Give Me An Answer (True Song)
J Parkes Mrs I M Moore

Placings:00/0P-0   (0157)
2002/03: 17⁰G,

	Starts	1st	2nd	3rd	Win & Pl
Chases	1	0	0	0	
Career Total	5	0	0	0	

Going: Sf: 0-0 GS: 0-0 Gd: 0-1 GF: - Fm: 0-0
Distance: 2m/2m3: 0-1 2m4-2m7: 0-0 3m+: 0-0
Track: LH: 0-1 RH: 0-0 Tight: 0-1 Gall: 0-0
Aids: Bl: 0-0 Vi: 0-0 Tstrap: 0-0
Best Rating: 54 2/01 Weth 2m   soft NHF

Count Tony

90   **111**

9-y-o ch g Keen-Turtle Dove (Gyr (USA))
P Bowen Brian Collett

Placings:412165/1200/02210P/2P0/5F0F30-P   (0216)
2002/03: 19ᴾG,

	Starts	1st	2nd	3rd	Win & Pl
Hurdles	1	0	0	0	
Career Total	26	4	5	1	22013
117 6/99	Worc	2m4f	C(0-135)HHdl	G-F	£4705
112 5/98	Prth	2m110y	E Hdl	G-F	£2598
110 2/98	Catt	2m	E Hdl	GD	£2332
108 11/97	Ayr	2m	E Hdl	G-S	£2262

Total win prize-money £11897

Going: Sf: 0-0 GS: 0-0 Gd: 0-1 GF: - Fm: 0-0
Distance: 2m/2m3: 0-0 2m4-2m7: 0-1 3m+: 0-0
Track: LH: 0-0 RH: 0-1 Tight: 0-0 Gall: 0-0
Aids: Bl: 0-0 Vi: 0-0 Tstrap: 0-0
Best Rating: 117 6/99 Worc 2m4f   gd-fm Hdl

Moderate handicap hurdler; best on fast ground at around two and a half miles; lightly-raced of late and has obviously been difficult to train.

Countback (FR)

82f   **78f**

4-y-o b g Anabaa (USA)-Count Me Out (FR) (Kaldoun (FR))
C C Bealby Blake Kennedy Partnership

Placings:6   (4788)
2002/03: 17⁶G,

	Starts	1st	2nd	3rd	Win & Pl
NH Flat	1	0	0	0	0
Career Total	1	0	0	0	0

Going: Sf: 0-0 GS: 0-0 Gd: 0-1 GF: - Fm: 0-0
Distance: 2m/2m3: 0-1 2m4-2m7: 0-0 3m+: 0-0
Track: LH: 0-0 RH: 0-1 Tight: 0-1 Gall: 0-0
Aids: Bl: 0-0 Vi: 0-0 Tstrap: 0-0
Best Rating: 78 4/03 MRas 2m1f110y good NHF

Raced keenly when well beaten on debut in modest bumper at Market Rasen in April.

Countess Camilla

105f   **110+f**

6-y-o br m Bob s Return (IRE)-Forest Pride (IRE) (Be My Native (USA))
K C Bailey The Fingers Crossed partnership

Placings:411   (3747)
2002/03: 16⁴GS, 17¹HY, 16¹G,

	Starts	1st	2nd	3rd	Win & Pl
NH Flat	3	2	0	0	3871
Career Total	3	2	0	0	3871
110 2/03	Hntg	2m110y	H NHF	GD	£1988
110 1/03	Folk	2m1f110yH NHF		HVY	£1883

Total win prize-money £3871

Going: Sf: 1-1 GS: 0-1 Gd: 1-1 GF: - Fm: 0-0
Distance: 2m/2m3: 2-3 2m4-2m7: 0-0 3m+: 0-0
Track: LH: 0-1 RH: 2-2 Tight: 1-1 Gall: 1-1
Aids: Bl: 0-0 Vi: 0-0 Tstrap: 0-0
Best Rating: 110 2/03 Hntg 2m110y   good NHF

Decent bumper performer; chasing type; acts on both good and heavy ground.

Country Boy

12-y-o b g Town And Country-Hollomoore (Moorestyle)
Steve Cheatle Tarragon Racing li

Placings:0000/36003/46F624243P/60030/54PP-P02 (0383)
2002/03: 21ᴾGF, 26⁰G, 24²G,

	Starts	1st	2nd	3rd	Win & Pl
Chases	3	0	1	0	342
Career Total	31	0	3	4	3668

Going: Sf: 0-0 GS: 0-0 Gd: 0-2 GF: - Fm: 0-1
Distance: 2m/2m3: 0-0 2m4-2m7: 0-1 3m+: 0-2
Track: LH: 0-1 RH: 0-2 Tight: 0-1 Gall: 0-2
Aids: Bl: 0-0 Vi: 0-0 Tstrap: 0-0
Best Rating: 90 4/00 Hrld 2m1f   good Hdl

Country Chef

13

7-y-o b g Henbit (USA)-Witney Girl (Le Bavard (FR))
John Allen Dingley Dell Racing Ltd

Placings:560-PPP   (2447)
2002/03: 16ᴾGS, 21ᴾGS, 21ᴾG,

	Starts	1st	2nd	3rd	Win & Pl
Hurdles	3	0	0	0	
Career Total	6	0	0	0	0

Going: Sf: 0-0 GS: 0-2 Gd: 0-1 GF: - Fm: 0-0
Distance: 2m/2m3: 0-1 2m4-2m7: 0-2 3m+: 0-0
Track: LH: 0-0 RH: 0-3 Tight: 0-0 Gall: 0-0
Aids: Bl: 0-0 Vi: 0-0 Tstrap: 0-0
Best Rating: 83 11/01 Sedg 2m1f   good NHF

Country Kris

94   **77**

11-y-o b g Town And Country-Mariban (Mummy s Pet)
B J M Ryall B J M Ryall

Placings:042/4240/3622/0202PP66/560/0201000-00 (3944)
2002/03: 21⁰G, 19⁰GS, 17⁰S,

	Starts	1st	2nd	3rd	Win & Pl
Hurdles	3	0	0	0	
Career Total	31	1	7	1	7484
104 10/01	Strf	2m110y	F(0-100)HHdl	G-S	£2303

Total win prize-money £2303

Going: Sf: 0-1 GS: 0-1 Gd: 0-1 GF: - Fm: 0-0
Distance: 2m/2m3: 0-1 2m4-2m7: 0-2 3m+: 0-0
Track: LH: 0-1 RH: 0-2 Tight: 0-2 Gall: 0-0
Aids: Bl: 0-0 Vi: 0-0 Tstrap: 0-0

Best Rating: 106 11/99 Extr 2m6f   gd-sft Hdl

Country Rose

(68h)   (19h)

7-y-o ch m Carlingford Castle-Clover Song (True Song)
Mrs P Townsley The Village Idiot Partnership

Placings:U00-06   (2128)
2002/03: 17⁰G, 17⁶S,

	Starts	1st	2nd	3rd	Win & Pl
Hurdles	1	0	0	0	0
Chases	1	0	0	0	0
Career Total	5	0	0	0	0

Going: Sf: 0-1 GS: 0-0 Gd: 0-1 GF: - Fm: 0-0
Distance: 2m/2m3: 0-2 2m4-2m7: 0-0 3m+: 0-0
Track: LH: 0-1 RH: 0-1 Tight: 0-2 Gall: 0-0
Aids: Bl: 0-0 Vi: 0-0 Tstrap: 0-0
Best Rating: 42 4/02 Chel 2m1f   good NHF

Countrywide Star (IRE)

91   **68**

5-y-o ch g Common Grounds-Silver Slipper (Indian Ridge)
C N Kellett J E Titley

Placings:0P-030P   (2731)
2002/03: 18⁰GF, 16³G, 16⁹HY, 16ᴾHY,

	Starts	1st	2nd	3rd	Win & Pl
Hurdles	4	0	0	1	430
Career Total	6	0	0	1	430

Going: Sf: 0-2 GS: 0-0 Gd: 0-1 GF: - Fm: 0-1
Distance: 2m/2m3: 0-4 2m4-2m7: 0-0 3m+: 0-0
Track: LH: 0-3 RH: 0-1 Tight: 0-2 Gall: 0-0
Aids: Bl: 0-0 Vi: 0-0 Tstrap: 0-0
Best Rating: 68 10/02 Strf 2m110y   good Hdl

Lightly raced hurdler, third in a ladies race in October 2002.

County Classic

80f

4-y-o b f Noble Patriarch-Cumbrian Rhapsody (Sharrood (USA))
T D Easterby M H Easterby

Placings:2   (2142)
2002/03: 14²GS,

	Starts	1st	2nd	3rd	Win & Pl
NH Flat	1	0	1	0	756
Career Total	1	0	1	0	756

Going: Sf: 0-0 GS: 0-1 Gd: 0-0 GF: - Fm: 0-0
Distance: 2m/2m3: 0-0 2m4-2m7: 0-0 3m+: 0-0
Track: LH: 0-1 RH: 0-0 Tight: 0-0 Gall: 0-0
Aids: Bl: 0-0 Vi: 0-0 Tstrap: 0-0
Best Rating: 80 11/02 Newc 1m6f   gd-sft NHF

Finished runner-up to a good sort on debut.

County Derry

10-y-o b g Derrylin-Colonial Princess (Roscoe Blake)
J Scott G T Lever

Placings:PP/14523-1425   (4133)

2002/03: 25¹S, 28⁴GF, 26²HY, 26⁵G,

	Starts	1st	2nd	3rd	Win & Pl
Chases	4	1	1	0	9664
Career Total	11	2	2	1	14189

132	5/02	Towc	3m1f	H Ch	SFT £6857
100	5/01	Strf	3m4f	H Ch	G-F £2614

Total win prize-money £9473

Going: Sf: 1-2 GS: 0-0 Gd: 0-1 GF: - Fm: 0-1
Distance: 2m/2m3: 0-0 2m4-2m7: 0-0 3m+: 1-4
Track: LH: 0-3 RH: 1-1 Tight: 0-1 Gall: 0-1
Aids: Bl: 0-0 Vi: 0-0 Tstrap: 0-0
Best Rating: 132 2/03 Chep 3m2f110y heavy Ch

Useful pointer/ hunter chaser; fifth in 2003 Cheltenham Foxhunters ; acts on any ground; has been let down on occasions by his jumping.

County Flyer

106(95h)   (77+h)**95**

10-y-o b g Cruise Missile-Random Select (Random Shot)
J S Smith R J Heathman (county Contractors) Ltd

Placings:00/P0/43003/44461-P56   (4528)
2002/03: 24²G, 19⁵G, 24⁶G,

	Starts	1st	2nd	3rd	Win & Pl
Chases	3	0	0	0	0
Career Total	17	1	0	2	5453

91	12/01	Extr	2m7f110yE(0-105)HCh	G-S	£3796

Total win prize-money £3796

Going: Sf: 0-0 GS: 0-0 Gd: 0-3 GF: - Fm: 0-0
Distance: 2m/2m3: 0-0 2m4-2m7: 0-1 3m+: 0-2
Track: LH: 0-1 RH: 0-2 Tight: 0-0 Gall: 0-1
Aids: Bl: 0-0 Vi: 0-0 Tstrap: 0-1
Best Rating: 99 3/99 Asct 2m110y gd-fm NHF

Moderate chaser; given a year off after finishing lame when landing a weak novices chase at Exeter in December 2001; won competitive Class E 3m 1f handicap at Hereford May 2003; runner up over hurdles at Cartmel later the same month; suited by soft ground; stays well.

Courage Under Fire

112(91h)   (90h)**124**

8-y-o b g Risk Me (FR)-Dreamtime Quest (Blakeney)
C C Bealby T P Radford

Placings:0/65P05/01/53P3336122P-1213P   (2691)
2002/03: 25¹GS, 24²GS, 26¹GS, 25³GS, 33⁶PS,

	Starts	1st	2nd	3rd	Win & Pl
Chases	5	2	1	1	18795
Career Total	24	4	3	5	29279

124	11/02	Font	3m2f110yD(0-125)HCh	G-S	£5726
121	10/02	MRas	3m1f	C(0-130)HCh	G-S £10335
118	2/02	MRas	2m6f110yE(0-105)HCh	SFT	£3444
102	4/01	Fknm	3m110y	H Ch	G-S	£2200

Total win prize-money £21706

Going: Sf: 0-1 GS: 2-4 Gd: 0-0 GF: - Fm: 0-0
Distance: 2m/2m3: 0-0 2m4-2m7: 0-0 3m+: 2-5
Track: LH: 0-2 RH: 1-2 Tight: 2-4 Gall: 0-0
Aids: Bl: 2-5 Vi: 0-0 Tstrap: 0-0
Best Rating: 124 11/02 Font 3m2f110y gd-sft Ch

Handicap chaser, stays well and best with cut in the ground. Goes well at Market Rasen.

Courser's Cove

85

6-y-o b g Sir Harry Lewis (USA)-Pearl Cove (Town And Country)
Mrs P Robeson Mrs P Robeson

Placings:020-4P   (4285)
2002/03: 16⁴GS, 21³GF,

	Starts	1st	2nd	3rd	Win & Pl
NH Flat	1	0	0	0	0
Hurdles	1	0	0	0	0
Career Total	5	0	1	0	458

Going: Sf: 0-0 GS: 0-1 Gd: 0-0 GF: - Fm: 0-1
Distance: 2m/2m3: 0-1 2m4-2m7: 0-1 3m+: 0-0
Track: LH: 0-0 RH: 0-2 Tight: 0-0 Gall: 0-0
Aids: Bl: 0-0 Vi: 0-0 Tstrap: 0-0
Best Rating: 98 1/02 Hntg 2m110y gd-sft NHF

Has shown promise in bumpers. Acts on good to soft ground.

Coursing Run (IRE)

103(100h)   (117h)**112+**

7-y-o ch g Glacial Storm (USA)-Let The Hare Run (IRE) (Tale Quale)
H D Daly The Hon Mrs A E Heber-Percy

Placings:21P5-1   (1905)
2002/03: 24¹GS,

	Starts	1st	2nd	3rd	Win & Pl
Chases	1	1	0	0	4424
Career Total	5	2	1	0	9038

112	11/02	Sthl	3m110y	E Ch	G-S	£4424
117	11/01	Chep	2m4f	D Hdl	SFT	£3493

Total win prize-money £7918

Going: Sf: 0-0 GS: 1-1 Gd: 0-0 GF: - Fm: 0-0
Distance: 2m/2m3: 0-0 2m4-2m7: 0-0 3m+: 1-1
Track: LH: 1-1 RH: 0-0 Tight: 1-1 Gall: 0-0
Aids: Bl: 0-0 Vi: 0-0 Tstrap: 0-0
Best Rating: 117 11/01 Chep 2m4f soft Hdl

Fair novice hurdler, he made a winning debut over fences in a non-event at Southwell in November 2002. Stays well.

Court Champagne

105   **98**

7-y-o b m Batshoof-Fairfield s Breeze (Buckskin (FR))
R J Price Derek & Cheryl Holder

Placings:611P6/0143-B60F2   (4704)
2002/03: 16⁸GS, 19⁵S, 17⁰G, 20⁵GF, 20²G,

	Starts	1st	2nd	3rd	Win & Pl
Hurdles	5	0	1	0	962
Career Total	14	3	1	1	11377

91	5/01	Wwck	2m	E(0-115)HHdl	G-F	£2625
96	2/01	Ludl	2m	E(0-115)HHdl	G-S	£4124
76	6/00	Strf	2m110y	D Hdl	GD	£3250

Total win prize-money £9999

Going: Sf: 0-1 GS: 0-1 Gd: 0-2 GF: - Fm: 0-0
Distance: 2m/2m3: 0-2 2m4-2m7: 0-3 3m+: 0-0
Track: LH: 0-3 RH: 0-2 Tight: 0-2 Gall: 0-1
Aids: Bl: 0-0 Vi: 0-0 Tstrap: 0-0
Best Rating: 96 2/01 Ludl 2m gd-sft Hdl

Moderate hurdler; won in the mud in game style at Uttoxeter in May; equally effective on fast ground; effective over two miles but stays further.

Court Dreaming

6-y-o b m Alflora (IRE)-Court Town (Camden Town)
D R Gandolfo P G Kennedy

Placings:0-P   (3113)

2002/03: 16⁰GS, 17⁸HY,

	Starts	1st	2nd	3rd	Win & Pl
NH Flat	2	0	0	0	
Career Total	2	0	0	0	

Going: Sf: 0-1 GS: 0-1 Gd: 0-0 GF: - Fm: 0-0
Distance: 2m/2m3: 0-2 2m4-2m7: 0-0 3m+: 0-0
Track: LH: 0-0 RH: 0-2 Tight: 0-1 Gall: 0-0
Aids: Bl: 0-0 Vi: 0-0 Tstrap: 0-0
Best Rating: 0 1/03 Folk 2m1f110y heavy NHF

Court Empress

76f   **49f**

6-y-o ch m Emperor Fountain-Tudor Sunset (Sunyboy)
P D Purdy P D Purdy

Placings:0   (4155)
2002/03: 16⁰G,

	Starts	1st	2nd	3rd	Win & Pl
NH Flat	1	0	0	0	
Career Total	1	0	0	0	

Going: Sf: 0-0 GS: 0-0 Gd: 0-1 GF: - Fm: 0-0
Distance: 2m/2m3: 0-1 2m4-2m7: 0-0 3m+: 0-0
Track: LH: 0-1 RH: 0-0 Tight: 0-0 Gall: 0-0
Aids: Bl: 0-0 Vi: 0-0 Tstrap: 0-0
Best Rating: 49 3/03 Wwck 2m good NHF

Court In The Act (IRE)

89   **80**

7-y-o b m Commanche Run-Princess Andromeda (Corvaro (USA))
J W Mullins Ian F Sandell

Placings:40060/6420-66431   (0788)
2002/03: 17⁸G, 26⁵G, 22⁴G, 22³GF, 21¹GF,

	Starts	1st	2nd	3rd	Win & Pl
Hurdles	5	1	0	1	2391
Career Total	14	1	1	1	3263

80	7/02	Sthl	2m5f110yG Hdl	G-F	£1922

Total win prize-money £1923

Going: Sf: 0-0 GS: 0-0 Gd: 0-3 GF: - Fm: 1-2
Distance: 2m/2m3: 0-1 2m4-2m7: 1-3 3m+: 0-1
Track: LH: 1-3 RH: 0-2 Tight: 0-2 Gall: 0-1
Aids: Bl: 0-0 Vi: 0-0 Tstrap: 0-0
Best Rating: 80 7/02 Sthl 2m5f110y gd-fm Hdl

Plating-class hurdler; won poor novices seller over just short of two and three quarter miles at Southwell July 2002.

Court Nanny

9-y-o ch m Nicholas Bill-Tudor Sunset (Sunyboy)
P D Purdy P D Purdy

Placings:0/0/FP-P   (3334)
2002/03: 24⁵PS,

	Starts	1st	2nd	3rd	Win & Pl
Hurdles	1	0	0	0	
Career Total	5	0	0	0	

Going: Sf: 0-1 GS: 0-0 Gd: 0-0 GF: - Fm: 0-0
Distance: 2m/2m3: 0-0 2m4-2m7: 0-0 3m+: 0-1
Track: LH: 0-0 RH: 0-1 Tight: 0-1 Gall: 0-0
Aids: Bl: 0-0 Vi: 0-0 Tstrap: 0-0

Best Rating: **76** 4/00 Font 2m2f110y good NHF

Court Of Appeal
86   **102**

6-y-o ch g Bering-Hiawatha s Song (USA) (Chief s Crown (USA))
B Ellison Spring Cottage Syndicate No 2

Placings:105-0   (0795)
2002/03: 17⁰GS,

	Starts	1st	2nd	3rd	Win & Pl
Hurdles	1	0	0	0	
Career Total	4	1	0	0	2744
108 1/02 Muss 2m			E Hdl		GD £2744

Total win prize-money £2744

Going:	Sf: 0-0 GS: 0-1 Gd: 0-0 GF: - Fm: 0-0
Distance:	2m/2m3: 0-1 2m4-2m7: 0-0 3m+: 0-0
Track:	LH: 0-1 RH: 0-1 Tight: 0-1 Gall: 0-0
Aids:	Bl: 0-0 Vi: 0-0 Tstrap: 0-0
Best Rating:	**108** 1/02 Muss 2m good Hdl

A fair Flat handicapper, made a winning hurdles debut at Musselburgh in January 2002 but held since. Suited by good ground and two miles, but may not want it much faster.

Court Of Justice (USA)
110   **105**

7-y-o b g Alleged (USA)-Captive Island (Northfields (USA))
K A Morgan Mrs P A L Butler

Placings:142/246-143   (3994)
2002/03: 16¹HY, 20⁴HY, 16²G,

	Starts	1st	2nd	3rd	Win & Pl
Hurdles	3	1	0	1	3674
Career Total	9	2	2	1	10037
103 12/02 Leic 2m			G Hdl		HVY £2359
113 11/00 Weth 2m			D Hdl		SFT £3308

Total win prize-money £5668

Going:	Sf: 1-2 GS: 0-0 Gd: 0-1 GF: - Fm: 0-0
Distance:	2m/2m3: 1-2 2m4-2m7: 0-1 3m+: 0-0
Track:	LH: 0-2 RH: 1-1 Tight: 1-0 Gall: 0-0
Aids:	Bl: 0-0 Vi: 0-0 Tstrap: 0-0
Best Rating:	**117** 12/01 Sthl 2m4f110y soft Hdl

Fair hurdler; stays two to two and a half miles; suited by soft ground.

Courtcard

4-y-o b f Persian Bold-Hafhafah (Shirley Heights)
Mrs Lucinda Featherstone Heart Of England Racing

Placings:P   (0971)
2002/03: 16⁰GS,

	Starts	1st	2nd	3rd	Win & Pl
Hurdles	1	0	0	0	
Career Total	1	0	0	0	

Going:	Sf: 0-0 GS: 0-1 Gd: 0-0 GF: 0-0
Distance:	2m/2m3: 0-1 2m4-2m7: 0-0 3m+: 0-0
Track:	LH: 0-1 RH: 0-0 Tight: 0-1 Gall: 0-0
Aids:	Bl: 0-0 Vi: 0-0 Tstrap: 0-0
Best Rating:	**0** 8/02 Strf 2m110y gd-sft Hdl

Courtledge
100(97h)   (78h)**102**

8-y-o b g Unfuwain (USA)-Tremellick (Mummy s Pet)
M J Gingell Going Grey Partnership

Placings:P605040601163-314PPPP   (2121)
2002/03: 20³G, 21³G, 20¹GS, 21⁴GF, 24⁶G, 22⁶G, 24⁶GS, 24⁶GS,

	Starts	1st	2nd	3rd	Win & Pl
Chases	8	1	0	2	4624
Career Total	20	3	0	2	12904
102 7/02 Wolv 2m4f110yE(0-105)HCh				G-S	£3604
102 4/02 Fknm 2m5f110yE(0-110)HCh				GD	£4114
91 3/02 Fknm 3m110y D Ch				GD	£4165

Total win prize-money £11884

Going:	Sf: 0-0 GS: 1-3 Gd: 0-4 GF: - Fm: 0-1
Distance:	2m/2m3: 0-0 2m4-2m7: 1-5 3m+: 0-3
Track:	LH: 1-7 RH: 0-0 Tight: 1-7 Gall: 0-0
Aids:	Bl: 0-0 Vi: 0-0 Tstrap: 0-0
Best Rating:	**102** 7/02 Wolv 2m4f110y gd-sft Ch

A fair handicap chaser. Effective from two and a half to three miles and the ground good or softer.

Covent Garden
118   **132+**

5-y-o b g Sadler s Wells (USA)-Temple Row (Ardross)
J Howard Johnson Ada Partnership

Placings:U60-11111   (3894)
2002/03: 16¹GF, 20¹GF, 20¹G, 24¹GF, 18¹GS,

	Starts	1st	2nd	3rd	Win & Pl
Hurdles	5	5	0	0	44367
Career Total	5	5	0	0	44367
132 3/03 Kels 2m2f			A Hdl	G-S	£17400
129 12/02 Muss 3m			D(0-125)HHdl	G-F	£6760
121 11/02 Aint 2m4f			C(0-130)HHdl	GD	£14300
104 10/02 Carl 2m4f			E(0-100)HHdl	G-F	£2931
78 10/02 Hexm 2m110y			E(0-100)HHdl	G-F	£2975

Total win prize-money £44367

Going:	Sf: 0-0 GS: 1-1 Gd: 1-1 GF: - Fm: 3-3
Distance:	2m/2m3: 2-2 2m4-2m7: 2-2 3m+: 1-1
Track:	LH: 3-3 RH: 2-2 Tight: 3-3 Gall: 0-0
Aids:	Bl: 0-0 Vi: 0-0 Tstrap: 0-0
Best Rating:	**132** 3/03 Kels 2m2f gd-sft Hdl

Useful hurdler; winner on the Flat; completed a fine five-timer in 2002/3 despite a huge rise in the handicap, won a Grade 2 event on last occasion; effective at between two and three miles; especially effective on fast ground.

Cowboyboots (IRE)
102   **115**

5-y-o b g Lord Americo-Little Welly (Little Buskins)
L Wells Hills, Smith And Wearne

Placings:523-3213P   (3629)
2002/03: 21³G, 21²S, 22¹HY, 24³GS, 24⁶S,

	Starts	1st	2nd	3rd	Win & Pl
Hurdles	5	1	1	2	8250
Career Total	8	1	2	3	9027
115 1/03 Font 2m6f110yE Hdl				HVY	£3591

Total win prize-money £3591

Going:	Sf: 1-3 GS: 0-1 Gd: 0-1 GF: - Fm: 0-0
Distance:	2m/2m3: 0-0 2m4-2m7: 1-3 3m+: 0-2
Track:	LH: 1-4 RH: 0-1 Tight: 1-3 Gall: 0-1
Aids:	Bl: 0-0 Vi: 0-0 Tstrap: 0-0
Best Rating:	**115** 1/03 Font 2m6f110y heavy Hdl

Useful hurdler; won a novice event at Fontwell in January 2003; stays three miles; acts in testing ground.

Coxwell Footman
(79h)   (42h)

7-y-o b g Infantry-Coxwell Quick Step (Balinger)
Mrs L C Taylor Mrs P A Allsopp

Placings:0F0P-0P   (3788)
2002/03: 17⁰S, 19⁰G,

	Starts	1st	2nd	3rd	Win & Pl
Hurdles	1	0	0	0	0
Chases	1	0	0	0	0
Career Total	6	0	0	0	

Going:	Sf: 0-1 GS: 0-0 Gd: 0-1 GF: - Fm: 0-0
Distance:	2m/2m3: 0-2 2m4-2m7: 0-0 3m+: 0-0
Track:	LH: 0-0 RH: 0-2 Tight: 0-0 Gall: 0-0
Aids:	Bl: 0-0 Vi: 0-1 Tstrap: 0-0
Best Rating:	**83** 1/02 Ludl 2m good NHF

Coy Lad (IRE)
                                                          65

6-y-o ch g Be My Native (USA)-Don t Tutch Me (The Parson)
J G Fitzgerald Mr & Mrs Raymond Anderson Green

Placings:44-64   (2769)
2002/03: 16⁶S, 16⁴GS,

	Starts	1st	2nd	3rd	Win & Pl
NH Flat	2	0	0	0	318
Career Total	4	0	0	0	1143

Going:	Sf: 0-1 GS: 0-1 Gd: 0-0 GF: - Fm: 0-0
Distance:	2m/2m3: 0-2 2m4-2m7: 0-0 3m+: 0-0
Track:	LH: 0-1 RH: 0-1 Tight: 0-1 Gall: 0-0
Aids:	Bl: 0-0 Vi: 0-0 Tstrap: 0-0
Best Rating:	**106** 2/02 Newb 2m10y soft NHF

Crack Regiment (IRE)
101   **92**

11-y-o b g Lafontaine (USA)-Princess Crack (IRE) (Buckskin (FR))
R H Buckler Twentyman

Placings:P4/3F2/022F/5P00-4224263505   (4020)
2002/03: 26⁴GF, 24²G, 24²HY, 20⁴S, 24²GF, 26⁶GF, 24³GS, 24⁵G, 22⁵S, 26⁵S,

	Starts	1st	2nd	3rd	Win & Pl
Hurdles	8	0	3	0	2492
Chases	2	0	0	1	632
Career Total	23	0	6	2	7638

Going:	Sf: 0-4 GS: 0-1 Gd: 0-2 GF: - Fm: 0-3
Distance:	2m/2m3: 0-0 2m4-2m7: 0-1 3m+: 0-8
Track:	LH: 0-5 RH: 0-5 Tight: 0-3 Gall: 0-1
Aids:	Bl: 0-0 Vi: 0-0 Tstrap: 0-0
Best Rating:	**112** 11/00 Newb 2m5f soft Hdl

A former winning point-to-pointer. Moderate maiden over hurdles and fences.

Cracking Dawn (IRE)
107(111h)   (132h)**135+**

8-y-o b g Be My Native (USA)-Rare Coin (Kemal (FR))
R H Alner Peter Bonner

Placings:0/012-1　　　　　　　　(1807)
2002/03: 24¹G,

	Starts	1st	2nd	3rd	Win & Pl
Chases	1	1	0	0	5460
Career Total	5	2	1	0	10118
135 11/02 Hayd	3m		D Ch		GD £5460
125 2/02 Font	2m6f110y			E Hdl	SFT £3332

Total win prize-money £8792

Going: Sf: 0-0 GS: 0-0 Gd: 1-1 GF: - Fm: 0-0
Distance: 2m/2m3: 0-0 2m4-2m7: 0-0 3m+: 1-1
Track: LH: 1-1 RH: 0-0 Tight: 0-0 Gall: 0-0
Aids: Bl: 0-0 Vi: 0-0 Tstrap: 0-0
Best Rating: 135 11/02 Hayd 3m　good　Ch

Useful chaser; winner of Irish point-to-points; won a Fontwell novice hurdle on his British debut; jumped well to win at Haydock on his chasing debut; stays well.

Crackrattle (IRE)

9-y-o ch g Montelimar (USA)-Gaye Le Moss (Le Moss)
B N Pollock Mrs P Polito, L Stilwell, S P Russel

Placings:6/P-60　　　　　　　　(4516)
2002/03: 17⁶G, 21⁰G,

	Starts	1st	2nd	3rd	Win & Pl
Chases	2	0	0	0	0
Career Total	4	0	0	0	0

Going: Sf: 0-0 GS: 0-0 Gd: 0-2 GF: - Fm: 0-0
Distance: 2m/2m3: 0-1 2m4-2m7: 0-1 3m+: 0-0
Track: LH: 0-2 RH: 0-0 Tight: 0-2 Gall: 0-0
Aids: Bl: 0-0 Vi: 0-0 Tstrap: 0-2
Best Rating: 66 4/99 Towc 2m　good NHF

Cracow (IRE)

88(91c)　　　　　　　　(83c)80

6-y-o b g Polish Precedent (USA)-Height Of Secrecy (Shirley Heights)
N J Hawke The Cornish Crac Partnership

Placings:00P004-0205　　　　　　(0872)
2002/03: 16⁶GF, 16²G, 16⁹GF, 17⁵GF,

	Starts	1st	2nd	3rd	Win & Pl
Hurdles	2	0	0	0	0
Chases	2	0	1	0	974
Career Total	10	0	1	0	974

Going: Sf: 0-0 GS: 0-0 Gd: 0-1 GF: - Fm: 0-3
Distance: 2m/2m3: 0-4 2m4-2m7: 0-0 3m+: 0-0
Track: LH: 0-3 RH: 0-1 Tight: 0-2 Gall: 0-0
Aids: Bl: 0-2 Vi: 0-0 Tstrap: 0-0
Best Rating: 83 6/02 Hrfd 2m　good Ch

Modest form over hurdles at two miles to two miles-five on good ground. Runner-up on his chase debut.

Crafty Monkey (IRE)

89f　　　　　　　　87+f

6-y-o b g Warcraft (USA)-Mikey s Monkey (Monksfield)
M Pitman G Pascoe & S Brewer

Placings:6　　　　　　　　(1627)
2002/03: 16⁶GS,

	Starts	1st	2nd	3rd	Win & Pl
NH Flat	1	0	0	0	0
Career Total	1	0	0	0	0

Craigary

79(95c)　　　　　　　　(74c)71

12-y-o b g Dunbeath (USA)-Velvet Pearl (Record Token)
D A Nolan James A Cringan

Placings:00/000064/060/3211406/00F03/6033256/03P440
650/64530300P000-P0　　　　　　(0251)
2002/03: 21⁰GF, 16⁹GF,

	Starts	1st	2nd	3rd	Win & Pl
Hurdles	1	0	0	0	0
Chases	1	0	0	0	0
Career Total	53	2	2	7	8999
92 12/97 Catt	2m3f		E(0-110)HHdl		GD £2220
92 11/97 Sedg	2m1f		G(0-95)HHdl		GD £1842

Total win prize-money £4062

Going: Sf: 0-0 GS: 0-0 Gd: 0-0 GF: - Fm: 0-2
Distance: 2m/2m3: 0-1 2m4-2m7: 0-1 3m+: 0-0
Track: LH: 0-1 RH: 0-1 Tight: 0-1 Gall: 0-0
Aids: Bl: 0-0 Vi: 0-0 Tstrap: 0-0
Best Rating: 92 12/97 Catt 2m3f　good Hdl

Mixes chasing hurdling and Flat racing, but has not won over jumps since 1997.

Cramond (IRE)

91f　　　　　　　　87f

5-y-o br g Lord Americo-Rullahola (Blue Rullah)
A Parker R A Bartlett

Placings:6　　　　　　　　(4560)
2002/03: 16⁶G,

	Starts	1st	2nd	3rd	Win & Pl
NH Flat	1	0	0	0	0
Career Total	1	0	0	0	0

Going: Sf: 0-0 GS: 0-0 Gd: 0-1 GF: - Fm: 0-0
Distance: 2m/2m3: 0-1 2m4-2m7: 0-0 3m+: 0-0
Track: LH: 0-1 RH: 0-0 Tight: 0-0 Gall: 0-0
Aids: Bl: 0-0 Vi: 0-0 Tstrap: 0-0
Best Rating: 87 4/03 Ayr 2m　good NHF

Cranborne (IRE)

29f

6-y-o b m King s Ride-Random Wind (Random Shot)
B G Powell D & J Newell

Placings:00　　　　　　　　(3146)
2002/03: 18⁰HY, 17⁰S,

	Starts	1st	2nd	3rd	Win & Pl
NH Flat	2	0	0	0	0
Career Total	2	0	0	0	0

Going: Sf: 0-2 GS: 0-0 Gd: 0-0 GF: - Fm: 0-0
Distance: 2m/2m3: 0-2 2m4-2m7: 0-0 3m+: 0-0
Track: LH: 0-1 RH: 0-0 Tight: 0-1 Gall: 0-0
Aids: Bl: 0-0 Vi: 0-0 Tstrap: 0-0
Best Rating: 31 1/03 Tntn 2m1f　soft NHF

Crane Beach

81f　　　　　　　　53f

5-y-o b m Afzal-Indian Cruise (Cruise Missile)

B W Duke Susan Livesey, Ian Griffiths

Placings:00　　　　　　　　(4343)
2002/03: 16⁹S, 16⁰GF,

	Starts	1st	2nd	3rd	Win & Pl
NH Flat	2	0	0	0	
Career Total	2	0	0	0	

Going: Sf: 0-1 GS: 0-0 Gd: 0-0 GF: - Fm: 0-1
Distance: 2m/2m3: 0-2 2m4-2m7: 0-0 3m+: 0-0
Track: LH: 0-1 RH: 0-1 Tight: 0-0 Gall: 0-1
Aids: Bl: 0-0 Vi: 0-0 Tstrap: 0-0
Best Rating: 53 3/03 Hntg 2m110y　gd-fm NHF

Crarae Jack

89f　　　　　　　　83f

5-y-o gr g Gran Alba (USA)-Double Dose (Al Sirat (USA))
H P Hogarth Hogarth Racing

Placings:0　　　　　　　　(4560)
2002/03: 16⁰G,

	Starts	1st	2nd	3rd	Win & Pl
NH Flat	1	0	0	0	0
Career Total	1	0	0	0	0

Going: Sf: 0-0 GS: 0-0 Gd: 0-1 GF: - Fm: 0-0
Distance: 2m/2m3: 0-1 2m4-2m7: 0-0 3m+: 0-0
Track: LH: 0-1 RH: 0-0 Tight: 0-0 Gall: 0-0
Aids: Bl: 0-0 Vi: 0-0 Tstrap: 0-1
Best Rating: 83 4/03 Ayr 2m　good NHF

Crazy Horse (IRE)

107　　　　　　　　140

10-y-o b g Little Bighorn-Our Dorcet (Condorcet (FR))
L Lungo Ashleybank Investments Limited

Placings:P101/2211213/5U2220/3U31/1-P6P　　(4131)
2002/03: 20⁰GS, 20⁶G, 24⁹G,

	Starts	1st	2nd	3rd	Win & Pl
Hurdles	3	0	0	0	390
Career Total	25	7	6	3	76596
152 5/01 Hayd	2m7f110y	B Hdl		GD	£10237
159 4/01 Aint	2m4f	B HHdl		SFT	£26000
150 3/99 Kels	2m2f	B Hdl		SFT	£13680
125 1/99 Kels	2m110y	D Hdl		HVY	£2932
133 12/98 Ayr	2m	E Hdl		HVY	£2682
120 4/98 Ayr	2m	H NHF		GD	£3598
128 2/98 Weth	2m	H NHF		GD	£1434

Total win prize-money £60566

Going: Sf: 0-0 GS: 0-1 Gd: 0-2 GF: - Fm: 0-0
Distance: 2m/2m3: 0-0 2m4-2m7: 0-2 3m+: 0-1
Track: LH: 0-3 RH: 0-0 Tight: 0-0 Gall: 0-1
Aids: Bl: 0-0 Vi: 0-0 Tstrap: 0-0
Best Rating: 159 4/01 Aint 2m4f　soft Hdl

Smart hurdler who has been lightly raced over the years; won valuable handicap at Aintree and decent hurdle at Haydock in 2001; off the track for nearly two years prior to return in January 2003; stays three miles; acts on good and soft ground; has to be produced late; one to watch until showing signs of retaining ability.

Crazy Like A Fool (IRE)

4-y-o b g Charnwood Forest (IRE)-Shanghai Girl (Distant Relative)

B Mactaggart Miss Charlotte Mooney

Placings:*P*   (4411)
2002/03: 16PG,

	Starts	1st	2nd	3rd	Win & Pl
NH Flat	1	0	0	0	
Career Total	1	0	0	0	

Going:	Sf: 0-0 GS: 0-0 Gd: 0-1 GF: - Fm: 0-0
Distance:	2m/2m3: 0-1 2m4-2m7: 0-0 3m+: 0-0
Track:	LH: 0-1 RH: 0-0 Tight: 0-0 Gall: 0-0
Aids:	Bl: 0-0 Vi: 0-0 Tstrap: 0-0
Best Rating:	0 3/03 Hexm 2m110y good NHF

Crazy Mazie

84   69

6-y-o b m Risk Me (FR)-Post Impressionist (IRE) (Ahonoora)
K A Morgan K A Morgan

Placings:*6663-004F*   (4786)
2002/03: 16DG, 21DGS, 204G, 22FG,

	Starts	1st	2nd	3rd	Win & Pl
Hurdles	4	0	0	0	273
Career Total	8	0	0	1	530

Going:	Sf: 0-0 GS: 0-1 Gd: 0-3 GF: - Fm: 0-0
Distance:	2m/2m3: 0-1 2m4-2m7: 0-3 3m+: 0-0
Track:	LH: 0-1 RH: 0-2 Tight: 0-3 Gall: 0-0
Aids:	Bl: 0-0 Vi: 0-0 Tstrap: 0-0
Best Rating:	83 4/02 MRas 2m1f110y good NHF

Cream Gorse

(97h)   (85h) 100d

7-y-o ch m Alflora (IRE)-Celtic Slave (Celtic Cone)
H D Daly B G Hellyer

Placings:*5/55440-FF6P*   (3785)
2002/03: 25FG, 24FG, 25RG, 25PG,

	Starts	1st	2nd	3rd	Win & Pl
Chases	4	0	0	0	
Career Total	10	0	0	0	571

Going:	Sf: 0-0 GS: 0-0 Gd: 0-4 GF: - Fm: 0-0
Distance:	2m/2m3: 0-0 2m4-2m7: 0-0 3m+: 0-4
Track:	LH: 0-1 RH: 0-2 Tight: 0-1 Gall: 0-0
Aids:	Bl: 0-0 Vi: 0-0 Tstrap: 0-0
Best Rating:	100 10/02 Hrfd 3m1f110y good Ch

Chasing type who has shown some ability in novice hurdles. Just about to lose second place when falling at the penultimate fence on chasing debut over an extended three miles at Hereford October 2002.

Creative Time (IRE)

103(78h)   (66h)115

7-y-o b g Houmayoun (FR)-Creative Princess (IRE) (Creative Plan (USA))
Miss H C Knight Mrs G M Sturges & H Stephen Smith

Placings:*3334-20P*   (3846)
2002/03: 242GS, 24DG, 24PG,

	Starts	1st	2nd	3rd	Win & Pl
Chases	3	0	1	0	2096
Career Total	7	0	1	3	4213

Going:	Sf: 0-0 GS: 0-1 Gd: 0-2 GF: - Fm: 0-0
Distance:	2m/2m3: 0-0 2m4-2m7: 0-0 3m+: 0-3

Track:	LH: 0-1 RH: 0-2 Tight: 0-2 Gall: 0-1
Aids:	Bl: 0-0 Vi: 0-0 Tstrap: 0-0
Best Rating:	115 1/03 Ludl 3m gd-sft Ch

Fair novice chaser; has shown form over at up to three miles on both fast and soft ground.

Credenza Moment

64

5-y-o b g Pyramus (USA)-Mystoski (Petoski)
M Madgwick W V Roker

Placings:*P50000-0PP*   (4094)
2002/03: 16DS, 24PS, 17PHY,

	Starts	1st	2nd	3rd	Win & Pl
Hurdles	3	0	0	0	0
Career Total	9	0	0	0	0

Going:	Sf: 0-3 GS: 0-0 Gd: 0-0 GF: - Fm: 0-0
Distance:	2m/2m3: 0-2 2m4-2m7: 0-0 3m+: 0-1
Track:	LH: 0-1 RH: 0-2 Tight: 0-2 Gall: 0-0
Aids:	Bl: 0-0 Vi: 0-0 Tstrap: 0-0
Best Rating:	78 11/01 Sand 2m110y gd-sft Hdl

Creek Tower

74f

6-y-o b g Rainbow Quest (USA)-Pass The Peace (Alzao (USA))
C J Price Glyn Byard

Placings:*00-P*   (1250)
2002/03: 16PG,

	Starts	1st	2nd	3rd	Win & Pl
NH Flat	1	0	0	0	
Career Total	3	0	0	0	

Going:	Sf: 0-0 GS: 0-0 Gd: 0-1 GF: - Fm: 0-0
Distance:	2m/2m3: 0-1 2m4-2m7: 0-0 3m+: 0-0
Track:	LH: 0-1 RH: 0-0 Tight: 0-0 Gall: 0-0
Aids:	Bl: 0-0 Vi: 0-0 Tstrap: 0-0
Best Rating:	74 3/02 Strf 2m110y gd-sft NHF

Cregg House (IRE)

107(101h)   (115 h)137

8-y-o ch g King Persian-Loyal River (Over The River (FR))
P Mullins Mrs Kathleen Kennedy

Placings:*0223446/3F421136/PP4024222R-310324532P0604R5*   (4725a)
2002/03: 16DY, 16IS, 16DG, 20DF, 20DG, 16DVS, 24DS, 20DHY, 16DY, 24PHY, 24DSH, 22DSH, 20DHY, 20DG, 36RG, 18DGF,

	Starts	1st	2nd	3rd	Win & Pl
Hurdles	7	1	1	1	8267
Chases	9	2	2	4	14854
Career Total	41	3	9	6	75680
113	6/02	Navn	2m		Hdl	SFT	£5714
116	2/01	Fair	3m1f		HCh	YLD	£10483
104	1/01	Fair	2m5f120y Ch			HVY	£5564
					Total win prize-money £21764		

Going:	Sf: 1-5 GS: 0-0 Gd: 0-4 GF: - Fm: 0-2
Distance:	2m/2m3: 1-6 2m4-2m7: 0-6 3m+: 0-4
Track:	LH: 1-5 RH: 0-6 Tight: 0-1 Gall: 0-1
Aids:	Bl: 0-1 Vi: 0-0 Tstrap: 0-0
Best Rating:	156 3/02 Chel 2m5f good Ch

Useful Irish chaser; runner-up in the Cathcart in 2002, and ran well at the Festival in 2003 when fourth in the Mildmay Of Flete; travels well but tends to find little off the bridle; suited by cut in the ground; best at two to two and a half miles.

Creon

109(102c)   (119c)130

8-y-o b g Saddlers Hall (IRE)-Creake (Derring Do)
Jonjo O Neill J P McManus

Placings:*004/04P120/0003F05001164/3002430061-016*   (4102)
2002/03: 24DS, 241HY, 25RG,

	Starts	1st	2nd	3rd	Win & Pl
Hurdles	3	1	0	0	7059
Career Total	35	5	3	2	30536
130	11/02	Chep	3m	C(0-130)HHdl	HVY	£6158
109	4/02	Prth	3m2f110yF(0-90)HCh	GD	£5330
134	1/01	Kemp	3m110y	D(0-120)HHdl	SFT	£5187
134	12/00	Weth	2m7f	C(0-130)HHdl	SFT	£4992
90	9/99	Baln	2m	Hdl	G-F	£2957
					Total win prize-money £24625	

Going:	Sf: 1-2 GS: 0-0 Gd: 0-1 GF: - Fm: 0-0
Distance:	2m/2m3: 0-0 2m4-2m7: 0-0 3m+: 1-3
Track:	LH: 1-3 RH: 0-0 Tight: 0-0 Gall: 0-1
Aids:	Bl: 0-0 Vi: 0-0 Tstrap: 0-0
Best Rating:	134 1/01 Kemp 3m110y soft Hdl

Decent hurdler/moderate chaser who looks very good on his day but cannot always reproduce it; bolted up over hurdles in November 2002; acts on soft ground but handles faster; stays three miles two.

Cresswell Cherry (IRE)

102   104

8-y-o b m Camden Town-Cherry Country (Town And Country)
N A Twiston-Davies James Cheetham

Placings:*34P/2021636-224P0*   (3843)
2002/03: 212G, 242GS, 204S, 24PGS, 24DG,

	Starts	1st	2nd	3rd	Win & Pl
Hurdles	4	0	2	0	3324
Chases	1	0	0	0	0
Career Total	15	1	4	2	8883
93	1/02	Towc	2m	E(0-110)HHdl	HVY	£2978
				Total win prize-money £2979		

Going:	Sf: 0-1 GS: 0-2 Gd: 0-2 GF: - Fm: 0-0
Distance:	2m/2m3: 0-0 2m4-2m7: 0-2 3m+: 0-3
Track:	LH: 0-0 RH: 0-5 Tight: 0-3 Gall: 0-0
Aids:	Bl: 0-0 Vi: 0-0 Tstrap: 0-0
Best Rating:	104 11/02 Extr 3m110y gd-sft Hdl

An ex-pointer, moderate handicap hurdler, she acts on heavy ground and is effective over two miles, but stays further.

Cresswell Gold

100   77

6-y-o b m Homo Sapien-Running For Gold (Rymer)
D A Rees D A Rees & P Harris

Placings:*0-05P6PPP*   (3923)
2002/03: 16DG, 16RG, 20PGS, 20RS, 22PGS, 20PHY, 20PS,

	Starts	1st	2nd	3rd	Win & Pl
NH Flat	1	0	0	0	0
Hurdles	6	0	0	0	0
Career Total	8	0	0	0	0

Going:	Sf: 0-3 GS: 0-2 Gd: 0-2 GF: - Fm: 0-0
Distance:	2m/2m3: 0-2 2m4-2m7: 0-5 3m+: 0-0
Track:	LH: 0-5 RH: 0-1 Tight: 0-2 Gall: 0-0
Aids:	Bl: 0-0 Vi: 0-0 Tstrap: 0-0

Best Rating: 84 12/02 Chep 2m4f   soft   Hdl

Beat sole surviving rival in maiden point June 2002; plating-class hurdler.

Cresswell Quay
109   108+
10-y-o g Bold Fox-Karatina (FR) (Dilettante Ii)
P Bowen Bruce McKay

Placings:60/50650/5/4313/F46P-11121   (3112)
2002/03: 26¹HY, 26¹G, 22¹G, 24²S, 25¹S,

	Starts	1st	2nd	3rd	Win & Pl
Chases	5	4	1	0	20696
Career Total	21	5	1	2	25041

111	1/03	Folk	3m1f	E(0-110)HCh SFT	£8173
102	12/02	Font	2m6f	F(0-90)HCh GD	£4104
84	11/02	Wwck	3m2f	F(0-95)HCh GD	£3083
105	11/02	NAbb	3m2f110y	(0-105)HCh HVY	£4261
94	7/00	Wolv	3m1f	E Hdl G-S	£2293

Total win prize-money £21918

Going: Sf: 2-3 GS: 0-0 Gd: 2-2 GF: - Fm: 0-0
Distance: 2m/2m3: 0-0 2m4-2m7: 1-1 3m+: 3-4
Track: LH: 2-3 RH: 1-1 Tight: 3-3 Gall: 0-0
Aids: Bl: 0-0 Vi: 0-0 Tstrap: 0-0
Best Rating: 111 1/03 Folk 3m1f   soft   Ch

Modest staying chaser; he has formed a formidable partnership with Timmy Murphy who is unbeaten in four starts on him in 2002/2003; needs to be produced with precise timing; suited by three miles and soft ground.

Crewski
8-y-o br g Newski (USA)-Darlin Again (Jolly Me)
H J Manners H J Manners

Placings:P   (0029)
2002/03: 21PGF,

	Starts	1st	2nd	3rd	Win & Pl
Chases	1	0	0	0	
Career Total	1	0	0	0	

Going: Sf: 0-0 GS: 0-0 Gd: 0-0 GF: - Fm: 0-1
Distance: 2m/2m3: 0-0 2m4-2m7: 0-1 3m+: 0-0
Track: LH: 0-1 RH: 0-0 Tight: 0-0 Gall: 0-0
Aids: Bl: 0-0 Vi: 0-0 Tstrap: 0-0
Best Rating:

Criminal Silk
88   69
8-y-o b m Tragic Role (USA)-See You In Court (London Gazette)
S J Gilmore L G Kimber

Placings:060/006-0P   (0340)
2002/03: 16⁰GF, 24PG,

	Starts	1st	2nd	3rd	Win & Pl
Hurdles	2	0	0	0	
Career Total	8	0	0	0	0

Going: Sf: 0-0 GS: 0-0 Gd: 0-1 GF: - Fm: 0-1
Distance: 2m/2m3: 0-1 2m4-2m7: 0-0 3m+: 0-1
Track: LH: 0-0 RH: 0-2 Tight: 0-0 Gall: 0-1
Aids: Bl: 0-0 Vi: 0-0 Tstrap: 0-0
Best Rating: 91 12/00 Donc 2m110y   heavy   NHF

Crimson Brocade
85   81
12-y-o b m Daring March-Stellaris (Star Appeal)
Mrs K J Tutty N D Tutty

Placings:50/4P/55PP-0   (0163)
2002/03: 20⁰GF,

	Starts	1st	2nd	3rd	Win & Pl
Chases	1	0	0	0	
Career Total	9	0	0	0	248

Going: Sf: 0-0 GS: 0-0 Gd: 0-0 GF: - Fm: 0-1
Distance: 2m/2m3: 0-0 2m4-2m7: 0-1 3m+: 0-0
Track: LH: 0-1 RH: 0-0 Tight: 0-0 Gall: 0-0
Aids: Bl: 0-0 Vi: 0-0 Tstrap: 0-0
Best Rating: 81 11/01 Weth 3m1f   good   Ch

Crimson Pirate (IRE)
107   104+
6-y-o b g Phardante (FR)-Stroked Again (On Your Mark)
B De Haan Flora Charlie Limited

Placings:0-21   (4117)
2002/03: 16²G, 16¹G,

	Starts	1st	2nd	3rd	Win & Pl
Hurdles	2	1	1	0	5052
Career Total	3	1	1	0	5052

111	3/03	Hntg	2m110y	E Hdl GD	£3743

Total win prize-money £3744

Going: Sf: 0-0 GS: 0-0 Gd: 1-2 GF: - Fm: 0-0
Distance: 2m/2m3: 1-2 2m4-2m7: 0-0 3m+: 0-0
Track: LH: 0-0 RH: 1-2 Tight: 0-0 Gall: 1-1
Aids: Bl: 0-0 Vi: 0-0 Tstrap: 0-0
Best Rating: 111 3/03 Hntg 2m110y   good   Hdl

Lightly-raced novice hurdler; made all to win over an extended two miles at Huntingdon in March; stays two miles; acts on good ground reportedly unsuited by heavy.

Crinan (IRE)
87f   59f
5-y-o ch g Carroll House-Esther (Persian Bold)
Mrs P Sly Mrs V M Edmonson

Placings:00   (4788)
2002/03: 16⁰G, 17⁰G,

	Starts	1st	2nd	3rd	Win & Pl
NH Flat	2	0	0	0	
Career Total	2	0	0	0	

Going: Sf: 0-0 GS: 0-0 Gd: 0-2 GF: - Fm: 0-0
Distance: 2m/2m3: 0-2 2m4-2m7: 0-0 3m+: 0-0
Track: LH: 0-1 RH: 0-1 Tight: 0-0 Gall: 0-1
Aids: Bl: 0-0 Vi: 0-0 Tstrap: 0-0
Best Rating: 59 3/03 Newb 2m110y   good   NHF

Cristal Lady
5-y-o b m Broadsword (USA)-Lots Of Luck (Neltino)
R Wilman J T Billson

Placings:0   (4343)
2002/03: 16⁰GF,

	Starts	1st	2nd	3rd	Win & Pl
NH Flat	1	0	0	0	
Career Total	1	0	0	0	

Going: Sf: 0-0 GS: 0-0 Gd: 0-0 GF: - Fm: 0-1
Distance: 2m/2m3: 0-1 2m4-2m7: 0-0 3m+: 0-0
Track: LH: 0-1 RH: 0-1 Tight: 0-0 Gall: 0-1
Aids: Bl: 0-0 Vi: 0-0 Tstrap: 0-0
Best Rating: 0 3/03 Hntg 2m110y   gd-fm   NHF

Cristoforo (IRE)
100   71+
6-y-o b g Perugino (USA)-Red Barons Lady (IRE) (Electric)
B J Curley P Byrne

Placings:000-0   (1716)
2002/03: 16⁰G,

	Starts	1st	2nd	3rd	Win & Pl
Hurdles	1	0	0	0	
Career Total	4	0	0	0	

Going: Sf: 0-0 GS: 0-0 Gd: 0-1 GF: - Fm: 0-0
Distance: 2m/2m3: 0-1 2m4-2m7: 0-0 3m+: 0-0
Track: LH: 0-1 RH: 0-0 Tight: 0-0 Gall: 0-0
Aids: Bl: 0-0 Vi: 0-0 Tstrap: 0-0
Best Rating: 40 10/02 Strf 2m110y   good   Hdl

Cristophe
95   72
5-y-o b g Kris-Our Shirley (Shirley Heights)
Mrs B K Thomson (A Crook 3/5) Mrs B K Thomson

Placings:000P0-360224   (4518)
2002/03: 21³HY, 20⁶S, 19⁰S, 17²G, 17²G, 21⁴G,

	Starts	1st	2nd	3rd	Win & Pl
Hurdles	6	0	2	1	1723
Career Total	11	0	2	1	1723

Going: Sf: 0-3 GS: 0-0 Gd: 0-3 GF: - Fm: 0-0
Distance: 2m/2m3: 0-3 2m4-2m7: 0-3 3m+: 0-0
Track: LH: 0-6 RH: 0-0 Tight: 0-5 Gall: 0-1
Aids: Bl: 0-0 Vi: 0-0 Tstrap: 0-0
Best Rating: 72 4/03 Sedg 2m5f110y   good   Hdl

Plating-class hurdler; runner-up in two selling races at Sedgefield this spring; stays two miles five; suited by a sound surface; has worn blinkers and a visor.

Cristys Picnic (IRE)
13-y-o b g Tremblant-My Maizey (Buckskin (FR))
G M Spencer G F Smith

Placings:06/43060/000P412/30P113P/02330400/35P6P66
5RU/06P/P-P4   (0108)
2002/03: 21PGF, 24⁴GF,

	Starts	1st	2nd	3rd	Win & Pl
Chases	2	0	0	0	
Career Total	45	3	2	6	24034

116	7/97	Tipp	2m4f	HCh GD	£6782
107	7/97	Kbgn	2m7f	HCh GD	£8762
88	4/97	Navn	2m4f	Ch FRM	£3051

Total win prize-money £18596

Going: Sf: 0-0 GS: 0-0 Gd: 0-0 GF: - Fm: 0-2
Distance: 2m/2m3: 0-0 2m4-2m7: 0-1 3m+: 0-1
Track: LH: 0-1 RH: 0-1 Tight: 0-1 Gall: 0-1
Aids: Bl: 0-1 Vi: 0-0 Tstrap: 0-0
Best Rating: 116 7/97 Tipp 2m4f   good   Ch

Career Total   1   0   0   0

Croaghnacree (IRE)

6-y-o b m Mister Lord (USA)-Castle Flame (IRE)
(Carlingford Castle)
S J Marshall S J Marshall

Placings:*00P*   (3911)
2002/03: 16OS, 16^OHY, 17^PGS.

	Starts	1st	2nd	3rd	Win & Pl
NH Flat	2	0	0	0	0
Hurdles	1	0	0	0	0
Career Total	3	0	0	0	

Going: Sf: 0-2 GS: 0-1 Gd: 0-0 GF: - Fm: 0-0
Distance: 2m/2m3: 0-3 2m4-2m7: 0-0 3m+: 0-0
Track: LH: 0-2 RH: 0-1 Tight: 0-0 Gall: 0-0
Aids: Bl: 0-0 Vi: 0-0 Tstrap: 0-0
Best Rating: 51 1/03 Newc 2m   heavy NHF

Croc An Oir (IRE)
72(84c)   (58c)**69**
6-y-o ch g Treasure Hunter-Cool Mary (Beau Charmeur
(FR))
Miss Venetia Williams (Cathal McCarthy 17/11) Mrs E
Murdoch Freud & Sir Clement Freud

Placings:*03*   (3932)
2002/03: 16^OHY, 20³S,

	Starts	1st	2nd	3rd	Win & Pl
NH Flat	1	0	0	0	0
Chases	1	0	0	1	623
Career Total	2	0	0	1	623

Going: Sf: 0-2 GS: 0-0 Gd: 0-0 GF: - Fm: 0-0
Distance: 2m/2m3: 0-1 2m4-2m7: 0-1 3m+: 0-0
Track: LH: 0-1 RH: 0-0 Tight: 0-1 Gall: 0-1
Aids: Bl: 0-0 Vi: 0-0 Tstrap: 0-0
Best Rating: 73 12/02 Newb 2m110y heavy NHF

Poor novice hurdler; stays really well.

Croc En Bouche (USA)
89f   **81f**
4-y-o b g Broad Brush (USA)-Supercook (USA) (Best Turn
(USA))
Mrs H Dalton G A Roberts

Placings:*00*   (4542)
2002/03: 16^OGF, 16^OG,

	Starts	1st	2nd	3rd	Win & Pl
NH Flat	2	0	0	0	0
Career Total	2	0	0	0	

Going: Sf: 0-0 GS: 0-0 Gd: 0-1 GF: - Fm: 0-0
Distance: 2m/2m3: 0-2 2m4-2m7: 0-0 3m+: 0-0
Track: LH: 0-1 RH: 0-1 Tight: 0-1 Gall: 0-0
Aids: Bl: 0-0 Vi: 0-0 Tstrap: 0-0
Best Rating: 73 4/03 Ludl 2m   good NHF

Crocadee
                                                  144
10-y-o b g Rakaposhi King-Raise The Dawn (Rymer)
Miss Venetia Williams Favourites Racing

Placings:*20/12/*1121016/**311FU**212/F   (2243)

2002/03: 26^FGS,

	Starts	1st	2nd	3rd	Win & Pl
Chases	1	0	0	0	
Career Total	20	8	5	1	79611
150 2/01 Kemp	2m4f110yA Ch			GD	£13200
140 12/00 Hayd	2m	A Ch		HVY	£12000
145 11/00 Hayd	2m4f	B Ch		HVY	£11180
143 2/00 Hntg	2m4f110yB Hdl		SFT	£6968
142 2/00 Leic	2m4f110yD Hdl		G-S	£4446
152 11/99 Hayd	2m4f	C Hdl		G-S	£5472
113 11/99 Hayd	2m4f	D Hdl		GD	£3095
129 3/99 Bang	2m1f	H NHF		G-S	£1630
			Total win prize-money £57991

Going: Sf: 0-0 GS: 0-1 Gd: 0-0 GF: - Fm: 0-0
Distance: 2m/2m3: 0-0 2m4-2m7: 0-0 3m+: 0-1
Track: LH: 0-1 RH: 0-1 Tight: 0-0 Gall: 0-1
Aids: Bl: 0-0 Vi: 0-0 Tstrap: 0-0
Best Rating: 152 2/01 Sand 2m4f110y heavy Ch

He was a useful novice chaser, winning three times in his first camapign over the larger obstacles, but his jumping let him down more than once and he fell on his only attempt at three miles. He unfortunately missed the next season after picking up a tendon injury. Fell in the Hennessy on his return.

Crocodiles Den (IRE)

7-y-o b g Alphabatim (USA)-Misty Gold (Arizona Duke)
R Wilman Richard R H Whiting

Placings:*00-*3UP   (3231)
2002/03: 20³F, 24^UGS, 23^PS,

	Starts	1st	2nd	3rd	Win & Pl
Hurdles	1	0	0	0	0
Chases	2	0	0	1	632
Career Total	5	0	0	1	632

Going: Sf: 0-1 GS: 0-1 Gd: 0-0 GF: - Fm: 0-1
Distance: 2m/2m3: 0-0 2m4-2m7: 0-1 3m+: 0-2
Track: LH: 0-2 RH: 0-1 Tight: 0-3 Gall: 0-0
Aids: Bl: 0-0 Vi: 0-0 Tstrap: 0-0
Best Rating: 71 5/01 Klny 2m1f   good NHF

Croker (IRE)
105   **100**
8-y-o ch g Rainbows For Life (CAN)-Almagest (Dike (USA))
S T Lewis Simon T Lewis

Placings:4313/3344/P66033P/0001400-311200   (3576)
2002/03: 17³GF, 16¹HY, 17¹GS, 16²HY, 19⁰GS, 16⁰HY,

	Starts	1st	2nd	3rd	Win & Pl
Hurdles	6	2	1		6925
Career Total	28	4	1	7	14446
100 12/02 Bang	2m1f	F(0-100)HHdl		G-S	£2404
89 12/02 Leic	2m	F(0-105)HHdl		HVY	£3031
81 8/01 Bang	2m1f	G(0-95)HHdl		GD	£2383
110 11/98 Uttx	2m	E Hdl		SFT	£2295
			Total win prize-money £10115

Going: Sf: 1-3 GS: 1-2 Gd: 0-0 GF: - Fm: 0-1
Distance: **2m/2m3: 2-6** 2m4-2m7: 0-0 3m+: 0-0
Track: LH: 1-1 RH: 1-5 **Tight: 1-2** Gall: 0-0
Aids: Bl: 0-0 Vi: 0-0 Tstrap: 0-0
Best Rating: 113 12/98 Wwck 2m   gd-sft Hdl

A fair sort in modest handicap hurdles, he managed to win one at Leicester in December and followed up with an all-the-way success at Bangor two weeks later. Suited by two miles.

Cromarty Rules
85   **55**
6-y-o b g Anshan-Cromarty (Shareef Dancer (USA))
N B Mason N B Mason

Placings:00P   (1183)
2002/03: 16⁰G, 16⁰G, 21^PG,

	Starts	1st	2nd	3rd	Win & Pl
Hurdles	3	0	0	0	
Career Total	3	0	0	0	

Going: Sf: 0-0 GS: 0-0 Gd: 0-3 GF: - Fm: 0-0
Distance: 2m/2m3: 0-2 2m4-2m7: 0-1 3m+: 0-0
Track: LH: 0-3 RH: 0-0 Tight: 0-2 Gall: 0-0
Aids: Bl: 0-0 Vi: 0-0 Tstrap: 0-2
Best Rating: 59 5/02 Sthl 2m   good Hdl

Cromer Pier
100   **83**
8-y-o b g Reprimand-Fleur Du Val (Valiyar)
G Fierro G Fierro

Placings:605001/PP0P1002P00/0-00   (2202)
2002/03: 17⁰G, 16⁰S,

	Starts	1st	2nd	3rd	Win & Pl
Hurdles	2	0	0	0	
Career Total	20	2	1	0	3544
83 10/00 MRas	2m1f110yG(0-95)HHdl		GD	£1456
93 4/00 MRas	2m1f110yG Hdl		SFT	£1519
			Total win prize-money £2975

Going: Sf: 0-1 GS: 0-0 Gd: 0-1 GF: - Fm: 0-0
Distance: 2m/2m3: 0-2 2m4-2m7: 0-0 3m+: 0-0
Track: LH: 0-1 RH: 0-1 Tight: 0-0 Gall: 0-0
Aids: Bl: 0-0 Vi: 0-0 Tstrap: 0-0
Best Rating: 93 4/00 MRas 2m1f110y soft Hdl

Plating-class hurdler; stays 2m 4f.

Cromwell (IRE)
88   (69h)**79**
8-y-o b g Last Tycoon-Catherine Parr (USA) (Riverman
(USA))
M C Chapman Sir Stanley Clarke

Placings:*06054/*344111453640644551/*323**612441P61410/
0236P-UPP   (4414)
2002/03: 24US, 33^PS, 22^PG,

	Starts	1st	2nd	3rd	Win & Pl
Chases	3	0	0	0	
Career Total	46	8	3	5	38931
113 3/01 MRas	3m1f	D Ch		HVY	£5303
107 2/01 Catt	3m1f110yE Ch		SFT	£3745
107 11/00 MRas	3m1f	E(0-115)HCh		G-S	£4329
102 10/00 MRas	3m1f	D Ch		GD	£5096
107 4/00 MRas	3m3f110yD Hdl		SFT	£3000
103 8/99 MRas	3m	D Hdl		G-F	£3109
103 7/99 MRas	2m1f110yD Hdl		G-F	£3070
106 7/99 MRas	2m5f110yE Hdl		G-F	£2316
			Total win prize-money £29970

Going: Sf: 0-2 GS: 0-0 Gd: 0-1 GF: - Fm: 0-0
Distance: 2m/2m3: 0-0 2m4-2m7: 0-1 3m+: 0-2
Track: LH: 0-1 RH: 0-2 Tight: 0-2 Gall: 0-0
Aids: Bl: 0-2 Vi: 0-0 Tstrap: 0-0
Best Rating: 113 5/01 Weth 3m1f   firm Ch

Plating-class chaser; multiple course winner at Market Rasen; seems able to cope with most surfaces; stays well.

Crosby Don

98(81h)   (33h)**75**

8-y-o b g Alhijaz-Evening Star (Red Sunset)
J R Weymes Don Raper

Placings:6034P0/06FF6/434/5B0002   (4785)
2002/03: 16⁵HY, 20⁸GS, 20⁶S, 19⁰S, 16⁹G, 20²G,

	Starts	1st	2nd	3rd	Win & Pl
Hurdles	4	0	0	0	0
Chases	2	0	1	0	1660
Career Total	20	0	1	2	2692

Going:	Sf: 0-3 GS: 0-1 Gd: 0-2 GF: - Fm: 0-0
Distance:	2m/2m3: 0-3 2m4-2m7: 0-3 3m+: 0-0
Track:	LH: 0-5 RH: 0-1 Tight: 0-2 Gall: 0-1
Aids:	Bl: 0-0 Vi: 0-0 Tstrap: 0-0
Best Rating:	92 11/98 Newc 2m good Hdl

Poor novice hurdler, novice chaser.

Crosby Donjohn

91   **67**

6-y-o ch g Magic Ring (IRE)-Ovideo (Domynsky)
J R Weymes Don Raper

Placings:0PP   (3965)
2002/03: 16⁰G, 19⁸G, 16⁸S,

	Starts	1st	2nd	3rd	Win & Pl
Hurdles	3	0	0	0	
Career Total	3	0	0	0	

Going:	Sf: 0-1 GS: 0-0 Gd: 0-2 GF: - Fm: 0-0
Distance:	2m/2m3: 0-3 2m4-2m7: 0-0 3m+: 0-0
Track:	LH: 0-2 RH: 0-1 Tight: 0-3 Gall: 0-0
Aids:	Bl: 0-0 Vi: 0-0 Tstrap: 0-0
Best Rating:	67 1/03 Muss 2m good Hdl

Cross The Rubicon (IRE)

                                75

12-y-o ch g Over The River (FR)-One Way Only (Le Bavard (FR))
G A Harker P I Harker

Placings:0/P334P/P32P/5P3/P/U03P35-PP (0182)
2002/03: 25ᴾG, 25ᴾG,

	Starts	1st	2nd	3rd	Win & Pl
Chases	2	0	0	0	
Career Total	22	0	1	6	4410

Going:	Sf: 0-0 GS: 0-0 Gd: 0-2 GF: - Fm: 0-0
Distance:	2m/2m3: 0-0 2m4-2m7: 0-0 3m+: 0-2
Track:	LH: 0-2 RH: 0-0 Tight: 0-0 Gall: 0-0
Aids:	Bl: 0-2 Vi: 0-0 Tstrap: 0-0
Best Rating:	97 3/98 NAbb 3m2f110y soft Ch

Crossbow Creek

110f   **116f**

5-y-o b g Lugana Beach-Roxy River (Ardross)
M G Rimell Mrs M R T Rimell

Placings:10   (4115)
2002/03: 16¹GS, 16⁰G,

	Starts	1st	2nd	3rd	Win & Pl
NH Flat	2	1	0	0	2436
Career Total	2	1	0	0	2436

---

111 2/03 Weth 2m   H NHF   G-S £2436
                     Total win prize-money £2436

Going:	Sf: 0-0 GS: 1-1 Gd: 0-1 GF: - Fm: 0-0
Distance:	2m/2m3: 1-2 2m4-2m7: 0-0 3m+: 0-0
Track:	LH: 1-2 RH: 0-0 Tight: 0-0 Gall: 0-0
Aids:	Bl: 0-0 Vi: 0-0 Tstrap: 0-0
Best Rating:	116 3/03 Chel 2m110y good NHF

Fair bumper horse; big sort, scored in decisive fashion on racecourse debut in a bumper at Wetherby in February.

Crow Creek (IRE)

93f   **85f**

5-y-o br g Presenting-Rossacrowe Gale (IRE) (Strong Gale)
B N Doran Mrs Shirley Clifford-Thorp

Placings:3   (4737)
2002/03: 16³GF,

	Starts	1st	2nd	3rd	Win & Pl
NH Flat	1	0	0	1	288
Career Total	1	0	0	1	288

Going:	Sf: 0-0 GS: 0-0 Gd: 0-0 GF: - Fm: 0-1
Distance:	2m/2m3: 0-1 2m4-2m7: 0-0 3m+: 0-0
Track:	LH: 0-1 RH: 0-0 Tight: 0-0 Gall: 0-0
Aids:	Bl: 0-0 Vi: 0-0 Tstrap: 0-0
Best Rating:	85 4/03 Chep 2m110y gd-fm NHF

Crownfield

104   **99**

4-y-o b g Blushing Flame (USA)-Chief Island (Be My Chief (USA))
Mrs M Reveley Bill Brown

Placings:04P02   (4637)
2002/03: 16⁰S, 16⁴GS, 20ᴾGS, 16⁰GF, 16²GF,

	Starts	1st	2nd	3rd	Win & Pl
Hurdles	5	0	1	0	5154
Career Total	5	0	1	0	5154

Going:	Sf: 0-1 GS: 0-2 Gd: 0-0 GF: - Fm: 0-2
Distance:	2m/2m3: 0-4 2m4-2m7: 0-1 3m+: 0-0
Track:	LH: 0-5 RH: 0-0 Tight: 0-1 Gall: 0-1
Aids:	Bl: 0-0 Vi: 0-0 Tstrap: 0-0
Best Rating:	99 4/03 Strf 2m110y gd-fm Hdl

Moderate hurdler; improving and opened account over hurdles on firm ground at Wetherby in May 2003.

Crowning Glory

84   **30**

9-y-o b m Rakaposhi King-Miss Lizzie (Push On)
Mrs D A Hamer The Tally Ho Partnership

Placings:50/P0-P6   (0447)
2002/03: 17ᴾG, 19⁶G,

	Starts	1st	2nd	3rd	Win & Pl
Hurdles	2	0	0	0	
Career Total	6	0	0	0	

Going:	Sf: 0-0 GS: 0-0 Gd: 0-0 GF: - Fm: 0-0
Distance:	2m/2m3: 0-1 2m4-2m7: 0-1 3m+: 0-0
Track:	LH: 0-0 RH: 0-2 Tight: 0-0 Gall: 0-0
Aids:	Bl: 0-0 Vi: 0-0 Tstrap: 0-0
Best Rating:	78 12/99 Hrfd 2m1f good NHF

Cruagh Express (IRE)

105   **88**

7-y-o b g Unblest-Cry In The Dark (Godswalk (USA))
G L Moore E Farncombe

Placings:13P-2   (1571)
2002/03: 16²G,

	Starts	1st	2nd	3rd	Win & Pl
Hurdles	1	0	1	0	658
Career Total	4	1	1	1	3443
88 11/01 Plum 2m	F Hdl			G-S	£2331

                     Total win prize-money £2331

Going:	Sf: 0-0 GS: 0-0 Gd: 0-1 GF: - Fm: 0-0
Distance:	2m/2m3: 0-1 2m4-2m7: 0-0 3m+: 0-0
Track:	LH: 0-1 RH: 0-0 Tight: 0-1 Gall: 0-0
Aids:	Bl: 0-0 Vi: 0-0 Tstrap: 0-1
Best Rating:	92 10/02 Strf 2m110y good Hdl

A fair handicapper at around a mile on the Flat. Had no problem with stamina when he won on his hurdles debut at Plumpton in November 2001. Reported to have made a noise though. Runner-up in a seller on his return to hurdles in October 2002.

Cruise Around

11-y-o b g Cruise Missile-New Cherry (New Brig)
A R Dicken Stephen Ramsay

Placings:6   (1240)
2002/03: 20⁶GF,

	Starts	1st	2nd	3rd	Win & Pl
Hurdles	1	0	0	0	0
Career Total	1	0	0	0	0

Going:	Sf: 0-0 GS: 0-0 Gd: 0-0 GF: - Fm: 0-1
Distance:	2m/2m3: 0-0 2m4-2m7: 0-1 3m+: 0-0
Track:	LH: 0-1 RH: 0-0 Tight: 0-0 Gall: 0-0
Aids:	Bl: 0-0 Vi: 0-0 Tstrap: 0-0
Best Rating:	0 9/02 Hexm 2m4f110y gd-fm Hdl

Crunchy (IRE)

106   **100**

5-y-o ch g Common Grounds-Credit Crunch (IRE) (Caerleon (USA))
B Ellison (J A R Toller 24/10) The Half Moon Club

Placings:024   (4316)
2002/03: 16⁰S, 16²S, 17⁴G,

	Starts	1st	2nd	3rd	Win & Pl
Hurdles	3	0	1	0	1418
Career Total	3	0	1	0	1418

Going:	Sf: 0-2 GS: 0-0 Gd: 0-1 GF: - Fm: 0-0
Distance:	2m/2m3: 0-3 2m4-2m7: 0-0 3m+: 0-0
Track:	LH: 0-3 RH: 0-0 Tight: 0-2 Gall: 0-1
Aids:	Bl: 0-0 Vi: 0-0 Tstrap: 0-3
Best Rating:	100 3/03 Catt 2m soft Hdl

Moderate hurdler; appreciated the better ground and just held at bay in novices hurdle at Catterick in March; had been in good form on the All-Weather previously; best at around two miles; acts on fast ground.

Crusoe (IRE)

87   **45**

6-y-o b g Turtle Island (IRE)-Self Reliance (Never So Bold)

A Sadik A Sadik

Placings:P0004P-0   (2061)
2002/03: 17⁰S,

	Starts	1st	2nd	3rd	Win & Pl
Hurdles	1	0	0	0	
Career Total	7	0	0	0	0

Going:	Sf: 0-1 GS: 0-0 Gd: 0-0 GF: - Fm: 0-0
Distance:	2m/2m3: 0-1 2m4-2m7: 0-0 3m+: 0-0
Track:	LH: 0-0 RH: 0-1 Tight: 0-0 Gall: 0-0
Aids:	Bl: 0-0 Vi: 0-0 Tstrap: 0-0
Best Rating:	49 11/02 Hrfd 2m1f soft Hdl

Cruz Santa
108   60
10-y-o b m Lord Bud-Linpac Mapleleaf (Dominion)
Mrs M Reveley The Mary Reveley Racing Club

Placings:R/230233453500/23U/10222332/121434-312F50
      (3864)
2002/03: 22³GS, 22¹GF, 24²G, 20²S, 22⁵S, 19⁰GS,

	Starts	1st	2nd	3rd	Win & Pl
Hurdles	6	1	1	1	4061
Career Total	36	4	9	9	23130
111	7/02	Strf	2m6f110yG Hdl		G-F	£2275
103	11/01	Weth	2m7f	G Hdl	GD	£2338
102	10/01	Carl	2m1f	E(0-115)HHdl	SFT	£2968
85	5/00	Ctml	2m1f110yG Hdl		G-F	£2436

Total win prize-money £10017

Going:	Sf: 0-2 GS: 0-2 Gd: 0-1 GF: - Fm: 1-1
Distance:	2m/2m3: 0-0 **2m4-2m7: 1-5** 3m+: 0-1
Track:	**LH: 1-6** RH: 0-0 **Tight: 1-3** Gall: 0-0
Aids:	Bl: 0-0 Vi: 0-0 Tstrap: 0-0
Best Rating:	111 9/02 Uttx 3m110y good Hdl

She has had such a frustrating career with a plethora of
major placings, but very few actual wins. Best held up, she
is suited by a good pace and her easy wins in sellers indicate she is slightly better than that grade. Stays two miles
seven an acts on any ground.

Crystal D'Ainay (FR)
101   125+
4-y-o b g Saint Preuil (FR)-Guendale (FR) (Cadoudal (FR))
A King (G Macaire 22/12) Mrs Jeni Fisher

Placings:4112212   (4462)
2002/03: 16⁴S, 18¹HO, 18¹HO, 17²S, 16²G, 16¹S, 20²G,

	Starts	1st	2nd	3rd	Win & Pl
Hurdles	5	2	2	0	23674
Chases	2	1	1	0	8540
Career Total	7	3	3	0	32214
125	3/03	Uttx	2m	D Hdl	SFT	£5128
	12/02	Ange	2m2f110y	Ch	HLD	£4712
	11/02	Bord	2m2f	Hdl	HLD	£4417

Total win prize-money £14258

Going:	Sf: 1-3 GS: 0-0 Gd: 0-2 GF: - Fm: 0-0
Distance:	**2m/2m3: 3-6** 2m4-2m7: 0-1 3m+: 0-0
Track:	**LH: 1-3** RH: 0-0 Tight: 0-1 Gall: 0-0
Aids:	Bl: 0-0 Vi: 0-0 Tstrap: 0-0
Best Rating:	125 3/03 Uttx 2m soft Hdl

Fair hurdler; winning hurdler in France; won easily at
Uttoxeter on second British run; runner-up in Grade 2 event
at Aintree; stays two mile four; effective in soft ground.

Crystal Vein

5-y-o gr g Miners Lamp-Crystal Comet (Cosmo)

B G Powell Victor G Palmer

Placings:0U0-PPP   (3183)
2002/03: 19⁰G, 19⁰S, 16²GS,

	Starts	1st	2nd	3rd	Win & Pl
Hurdles	3	0	0	0	
Career Total	6	0	0	0	

Going:	Sf: 0-1 GS: 0-1 Gd: 0-1 GF: - Fm: 0-0
Distance:	2m/2m3: 0-2 2m4-2m7: 0-1 3m+: 0-0
Track:	LH: 0-1 RH: 0-0 Tight: 0-1 Gall: 0-1
Aids:	Bl: 0-0 Vi: 0-0 Tstrap: 0-0
Best Rating:	60 3/02 Strf 2m110y gd-sft NHF

Cudlic Candyfloss
(88h)   (68h)75
10-y-o b m Abutammam-Cudlic Cream (No Evil)
P Bowen Mrs L J Williams

Placings:066P60P/P3/60504P0-F   (0092)
2002/03: 20⁰F,

	Starts	1st	2nd	3rd	Win & Pl
Chases	1	0	0	0	
Career Total	17	0	0	1	235

Going:	Sf: 0-0 GS: 0-0 Gd: 0-1 GF: - Fm: 0-0
Distance:	2m/2m3: 0-0 2m4-2m7: 0-0 3m+: 0-0
Track:	LH: 0-1 RH: 0-0 Tight: 0-0 Gall: 0-0
Aids:	Bl: 0-0 Vi: 0-0 Tstrap: 0-0
Best Rating:	81 11/99 Extr 2m1f gd-sft NHF

Cullen Road (IRE)
93   76
5-y-o b g Wakashan-My Wings (Erin s Hope)
J R Jenkins Jack McGrath

Placings:6005F5   (4186)
2002/03: 16⁶GF, 16⁰GS, 16⁰S, 20⁵GS, 16⁰G, 17⁵G,

	Starts	1st	2nd	3rd	Win & Pl
NH Flat	2	0	0	0	0
Hurdles	4	0	0	0	0
Career Total	6	0	0	0	0

Going:	Sf: 0-1 GS: 0-2 Gd: 0-2 GF: - Fm: 0-0
Distance:	2m/2m3: 0-5 2m4-2m7: 0-1 3m+: 0-0
Track:	LH: 0-3 RH: 0-3 Tight: 0-3 Gall: 0-2
Aids:	Bl: 0-0 Vi: 0-0 Tstrap: 0-0
Best Rating:	86 10/02 Hntg 2m110y gd-fm NHF

Modest form in bumpers and novice hurdles; best on a
sound surface.

Cullian
107   95
6-y-o b m Missed Flight-Diamond Gig (Pitskelly)
Mrs N Smith The Cullian Partnership

Placings:0504-1P01   (3807)
2002/03: 17¹GS, 18⁵S, 19⁰GS, 21¹S,

	Starts	1st	2nd	3rd	Win & Pl
Hurdles	4	2	0	0	6565
Career Total	8	2	0	0	6565
94	2/03	Plum	2m5f	E(0-105)HHdl	SFT	£3523
95	11/02	Folk	2m1f110yE Hdl		G-S	£3041

Total win prize-money £6565

Going:	Sf: 1-2 GS: 1-2 Gd: 0-0 GF: - Fm: 0-0
Distance:	2m/2m3: 1-3 2m4-2m7: 1-1 3m+: 0-0

Track:	LH: 1-2 RH: 1-2 **Tight: 2-3** Gall: 0-0
Aids:	Bl: 0-0 Vi: 0-0 Tstrap: 0-0
Best Rating:	95 11/02 Folk 2m1f110y gd-sft Hdl

Modest novice hurdler; stays two miles five; effective in soft
ground; has worn cheekpieces.

Culminate
81   66
6-y-o ch g Afzal-Straw Blade (Final Straw)
J E Long J King

Placings:00   (2548)
2002/03: 17⁹GS, 17⁰HY,

	Starts	1st	2nd	3rd	Win & Pl
Hurdles	2	0	0	0	
Career Total	2	0	0	0	

Going:	Sf: 0-1 GS: 0-1 Gd: 0-0 GF: - Fm: 0-0
Distance:	2m/2m3: 0-2 2m4-2m7: 0-0 3m+: 0-0
Track:	LH: 0-0 RH: 0-2 Tight: 0-2 Gall: 0-0
Aids:	Bl: 0-0 Vi: 0-0 Tstrap: 0-0
Best Rating:	66 11/02 Tntn 2m1f gd-sft Hdl

Cumbrian Knight (IRE)
97   106
5-y-o b g Presenting-Crashrun (Crash Course)
J M Jefferson Cumbrian Industrials Ltd

Placings:4231440   (3816)
2002/03: 16⁴GF, 16²GF, 17³G, 16¹G, 16⁴GS, 16⁴GS, 19⁰G,

	Starts	1st	2nd	3rd	Win & Pl
NH Flat	4	1	1	1	3280
Hurdles	3	0	0	0	401
Career Total	7	1	1	1	3681
97	11/02	Hayd	2m	H NHF	GD	£2138

Total win prize-money £2139

Going:	Sf: 0-0 GS: 0-0 Gd: 0-2 GF: - Fm: 0-2
Distance:	2m/2m3: 1-7 2m4-2m7: 0-0 3m+: 0-0
Track:	LH: 1-5 RH: 0-2 Tight: 0-2 Gall: 0-0
Aids:	Bl: 0-0 Vi: 0-0 Tstrap: 0-0
Best Rating:	106 2/03 Hayd 2m gd-sft Hdl

Promise in bumpers on fast ground, before getting off the
mark at Haydock in November 2002.

Cupboard Lover
113   131
7-y-o ch g Risk Me (FR)-Galejade (Sharrood (USA))
N J Henderson Mrs Lesley Lockwood and Mrs Judy
Mihalop

Placings:2150/042201004-33   (3727)
2002/03: 16⁵S, 16⁴G,

	Starts	1st	2nd	3rd	Win & Pl
Hurdles	2	0	0	2	4052
Career Total	15	2	3	2	20198
126	12/01	Kemp	2m5f	C(0-135)HHdl	GD	£7410
120	1/01	Tntn	2m1f	E Hdl	SFT	£2680

Total win prize-money £10090

Going:	Sf: 0-1 GS: 0-0 Gd: 0-1 GF: - Fm: 0-0
Distance:	2m/2m3: 0-2 2m4-2m7: 0-0 3m+: 0-0
Track:	LH: 0-1 RH: 0-1 Tight: 0-0 Gall: 0-0
Aids:	Bl: 0-0 Vi: 0-0 Tstrap: 0-0
Best Rating:	131 2/03 Kemp 2m good Hdl

A useful handicapper on the Flat, he mixes hurdling with

racing on the level these days;acts on most types of ground, but probably at his best with cut; stays two miles five furlongs; suited by a sharp, right-handed track.

Curly Spencer (IRE)
110(100h)　　　　　　　　　　　(116 h)121

9-y-o br g Yashgan-Tim s Brief (Avocat)
A Parker　Mr & Mrs Raymond Anderson Green

Placings:00/543051100/1U/PF2422-51114　　(3893)
2002/03: 24⁵GF, 20¹GS, 20¹GS, 20¹S, 22⁴GS,

	Starts	1st	2nd	3rd	Win & Pl
Hurdles	1	1	0	0	2898
Chases	4	2	0	0	19499
Career Total	24	6	3	1	37336
121	1/03	Ayr	2m4f	C(0-130)HCh	SFT	£8034
113	11/02	Newc	2m4f	D(0-125)HCh	G-S	£10582
116	11/02	Carl	2m4f	E(0-100)HHdl	G-S	£2898
116	2/01	Carl	2m4f110yF(0-100)HCh	HVY	£3721
109	3/00	Hexm	2m4f110yF(0-100)HCh	SFT	£3107
103	3/00	Carl	2m	E(0-115)HCh	HVY	£3380

Total win prize-money £31722

Going:	Sf: 1-1 GS: 2-3 Gd: 0-0 GF: - Fm: 0-1
Distance:	2m/2m3: 0-0 2m4-2m7: 3-4 3m+: 0-1
Track:	LH: 2-3 RH: 1-2 Tight: 0-1 Gall: 1-1
Aids:	Bl: 0-0 Vi: 0-0 Tstrap: 0-0
Best Rating:	121　1/03　Ayr　2m4f　soft　Ch

Decent chaser; best over two and a half miles; suited by cut in the ground; suited by forcing tactics; still improving.

Curtins Hill (IRE)
109(103h)　　　　　　　　　　　(107 h)107

9-y-o b g Roi Guillaume (FR)-Kinallen Lady (IRE) (Abednego)
T R George　Mrs Henry Pitman

Placings:0050-611402　　　　　　　(4692)
2002/03: 16⁵S, 21¹G, 17¹S, 24⁴G, 18⁶S, 22²G,

	Starts	1st	2nd	3rd	Win & Pl
Hurdles	6	2	1	0	14187
Career Total	10	2	1	0	14187
107	12/02	Chel	2m1f	D(0-100)HHdl	SFT	£9265
98	12/02	Ludl	2m5f	E(0-105)HHdl	GD	£3484

Total win prize-money £12749

Going:	Sf: 1-3 GS: 0-0 Gd: 1-3 GF: - Fm: 0-0
Distance:	2m/2m3: 1-3 2m4-2m7: 1-2 3m+: 0-1
Track:	LH: 1-4 RH: 1-2 Tight: 0-3 Gall: 1-1
Aids:	Bl: 0-0 Vi: 0-0 Tstrap: 0-0
Best Rating:	107　4/03　NAbb　2m6f　good　Hdl

Modest ex-Irish hurdler; winner of a weak event at Ludlow in December 2002; followed up at Cheltenham on New Year's Eve; effective at two miles to two miles five; acts on good and soft ground.

Cuthill Hope (IRE)
113　　　　　　　　　　　　　119+

12-y-o gr g Peacock (FR)-Sicilian Princess (Sicilian Prince)
A C Whillans & Stephen Gilchrist

Placings:441/331F6F1/143O/12U/50P1P5-531　(1732)
2002/03: 25⁵GS, 25³GF, 22¹S,

	Starts	1st	2nd	3rd	Win & Pl
Chases	3	1	0	1	7465
Career Total	36	7	1	4	36080
119	11/02	Kels	2m6f110yD(0-120)HCh	SFT	£6773
119	3/02	Kels	3m1f	D(0-120)HCh	SFT	£5427
118	11/00	Ayr	2m4f	D(0-120)HCh	G-S	£3750
114	5/98	Aint	2m	D(0-125)HCh	G-F	£4622
126	4/98	Kels	2m1f	D-Ch	SFT	£3403

| 126 | 1/98 | Donc | 2m3f110yD Ch | GD | £4237 |
| 105 | 3/97 | Plum | 2m1f | E Hdl | G-S | £2553 |

Total win prize-money £30768

Going:	Sf: 1-1 GS: 2-3 Gd: 0-0 GF: - Fm: 0-1
Distance:	2m/2m3: 0-0 2m4-2m7: 1-1 3m+: 0-2
Track:	LH: 1-3 RH: 0-0 Tight: 1-3 Gall: 0-0
Aids:	Bl: 0-0 Vi: 0-0 Tstrap: 0-0
Best Rating:	126　4/98　Kels　2m1f　soft　Ch

Useful handicap chaser. Stays three miles plus. Acts on a sound surface and with cut. Missed all of 1999 and most of 2000 due to injury. Won at Kelso in March 2002. Likes to make the running.

Cyanara
101(103h)　　　　　　　　　　　(61h)92

7-y-o b m Jupiter Island-Shamana (Broadsword) (USA)
Dr P Pritchard　Mrs Grace-Ann Hanney

Placings:0/P/P061P00P0-00O0　　　　(4692)
2002/03: 16⁵S, 16⁰HY, 17⁰S, 22⁰G,

	Starts	1st	2nd	3rd	Win & Pl
Hurdles	4	0	0	0	
Career Total	15	1	0	0	3234
76	11/01	Fknm	2m	E(0-105)HHdl	SFT	£3234

Total win prize-money £3234

Going:	Sf: 0-3 GS: 0-0 Gd: 0-1 GF: - Fm: 0-0
Distance:	2m/2m3: 0-3 2m4-2m7: 0-1 3m+: 0-0
Track:	LH: 0-3 RH: 0-1 Tight: 0-1 Gall: 0-0
Aids:	Bl: 0-0 Vi: 0-0 Tstrap: 0-0
Best Rating:	76　11/01　Fknm　2m　soft　Hdl

Cybele Eria (FR)
100(113h)　　　　　　　　　　　(117h)105

6-y-o b m Johann Quatz (FR)-Money Can t Buy (Thatching)
N J Henderson　The Studwell Partnership

Placings:23/2241-F25003212　　　　(4689)
2002/03: 17⁵S, 17²G, 16⁵G, 16⁰GS, 17⁰S, 17³S, 16²G, 16¹GF, 17²G,

	Starts	1st	2nd	3rd	Win & Pl
Hurdles	5	0	1	0	1217
Chases	4	1	2	1	8023
Career Total	15	2	6	2	15810
89	3/03	Wwck	2m110y E Ch	G-F	£4036
117	3/02	Hrfd	2m1f	E Hdl	SFT	£2849

Total win prize-money £6886

Going:	Sf: 0-3 GS: 0-0 Gd: 0-4 GF: - Fm: 1-1
Distance:	2m/2m3: 1-9 2m4-2m7: 0-0 3m+: 0-0
Track:	LH: 1-4 RH: 0-5 Tight: 0-5 Gall: 0-1
Aids:	Bl: 0-0 Vi: 0-0 Tstrap: 0-0
Best Rating:	117　11/02　Hayd　2m　good　Hdl

Modest hurdler/novice chaser; acts on soft ground; does not find much off the bridle.

Cyfor Malta (FR)
111　　　　　　　　　　　　　169

10-y-o b g Cyborg (FR)-Force Nine (FR) (Luthier)
M C Pipe　D A Johnson

Placings:32111211/11/3/1402P-14U　　(3285)
2002/03: 20¹GS, 21⁴G, 25⁵UG,

	Starts	1st	2nd	3rd	Win & Pl
Chases	3	1	0	0	63000
Career Total	19	9	3	2	305361
169	11/02	Chel	2m4f110yA HCh	G-S	£58000
162	12/01	Newb	2m4f	B(0-145)HCh	SFT	£20300
169	1/99	Chel	3m1f110y	A Ch	SFT	

£18390
163	11/98	Chel	2m4f110yA HCh	GD	£47260
158	4/98	Aint	2m6f	B(0-145)HCh	SFT	£25072
147	3/98	Chel	2m5f	B Ch	GD	£33500
146	1/98	Sand	2m4f110yD Ch	G-S	£4485
	11/97	Autl	2m4f110y Ch	HLD	£22447
	10/97	Autl	2m1f110y Ch	VS	£13468

Total win prize-money £242923

Going:	Sf: 0-0 GS: 1-2 Gd: 0-1 GF: - Fm: 0-0
Distance:	2m/2m3: 0-0 2m4-2m7: 1-2 3m+: 0-1
Track:	LH: 1-3 RH: 0-0 Tight: 0-0 Gall: 1-3
Aids:	Bl: 0-0 Vi: 0-0 Tstrap: 0-0
Best Rating:	169　11/02　Chel　2m4f110y　gd-sft　Ch

Top-class chaser; landed the Murphy s Gold Cup and the Pillar Chase in 1998/9; a leg injury then kept him off the track for two years; back to his best on his seasonal debut in November 2002 when landing the Thomas Pink, four years on from his first success in the same race; held in the Tripleprint off a 10lb higher mark; acts on an easy surface; stays 3m 1f, although he is effective at shorter; has worn a visor.

Cyfrinach Lyn
84f　　　　　　　　　　　　　68f

5-y-o b m Awesome-Blue Corn (Henbit (USA))
D Burchell　Lyn Phillips

Placings:0　　　　　　　　　　(4197)
2002/03: 16⁰G,

	Starts	1st	2nd	3rd	Win & Pl
NH Flat	1	0	0	0	
Career Total	1	0	0	0	

Going:	Sf: 0-0 GS: 0-0 Gd: 0-1 GF: - Fm: 0-0
Distance:	2m/2m3: 0-1 2m4-2m7: 0-0 3m+: 0-0
Track:	LH: 0-0 RH: 0-1 Tight: 0-0 Gall: 0-0
Aids:	Bl: 0-0 Vi: 0-0 Tstrap: 0-0
Best Rating:	68　3/03　Ludl　2m　good　NHF

Cyindien (FR)
103　　　　　　　　　　　　　107

6-y-o b/br g Cyborg (FR)-Indiana Rose (FR) (Cadoudal (FR))
Miss Venetia Williams　Sir Robert Ogden

Placings:5-222　　　　　　　　(2636)
2002/03: 22⁵GS, 17²S, 25²S,

	Starts	1st	2nd	3rd	Win & Pl
Hurdles	3	0	3	0	2674
Career Total	4	0	3	0	2674

Going:	Sf: 0-2 GS: 0-1 Gd: 0-0 GF: - Fm: 0-0
Distance:	2m/2m3: 0-1 2m4-2m7: 0-1 3m+: 0-0
Track:	LH: 0-2 RH: 0-1 Tight: 0-2 Gall: 0-0
Aids:	Bl: 0-0 Vi: 0-0 Tstrap: 0-0
Best Rating:	107　12/02　Wwck　3m1f　soft　Hdl

Runner-up on his first three starts over hurdles. Stays three miles, acts with cut in the ground.

Cynara
90

5-y-o b m Imp Society (USA)-Reina (Homeboy)
G M Moore　A J Racehorses

Placings:01003-U　　　　　　　(1704)
2002/03: 27⁰UG,

	Starts	1st	2nd	3rd	Win & Pl
Hurdles	1	0	0	0	

Career Total	6	1	0	1	3027
90 12/01 MRas 2m1f110y				E Hdl	SFT
£2653					
				Total win prize-money £2653

Going:	Sf: 0-0 GS: 0-0 Gd: 0-1 GF: - Fm: 0-0
Distance:	2m/2m3: 0-0 2m4-2m7: 0-0 3m+: 0-1
Track:	LH: 0-1 RH: 0-0 Tight: 0-1 Gall: 0-0
Aids:	Bl: 0-0 Vi: 0-0 Tstrap: 0-0
Best Rating:	90 3/02 Sedg 2m5f110y soft Hdl

Cynosure

6-y-o b g Runnett-Polly Two (Reesh)
J R Weymes B B Pratt

Placings:5P   (0618)
2002/03: 16⁵G, 16ᴾGF,

	Starts	1st	2nd	3rd	Win & Pl
Hurdles	2	0	0	0	0
Career Total	2	0	0	0	0

Going:	Sf: 0-0 GS: 0-0 Gd: 0-0 GF: 0-1 Fm: 0-1
Distance:	2m/2m3: 0-2 2m4-2m7: 0-0 3m+: 0-0
Track:	LH: 0-2 RH: 0-0 Tight: 0-0 Gall: 0-0
Aids:	Bl: 0-0 Vi: 0-0 Tstrap: 0-0
Best Rating:	0 6/02 Hexm 2m110y gd-fm Hdl

Cyrium (IRE)
91f   80f

4-y-o b g Woodborough (USA)-Jarmar Moon (Unfuwain (USA))
R F Fisher Great Head House Estates Limited

Placings:0   (4788)
2002/03: 17⁰G,

	Starts	1st	2nd	3rd	Win & Pl
NH Flat	1	0	0	0	
Career Total	1	0	0	0	

Going:	Sf: 0-0 GS: 0-0 Gd: 0-1 GF: - Fm: 0-0
Distance:	2m/2m3: 0-1 2m4-2m7: 0-0 3m+: 0-0
Track:	LH: 0-0 RH: 0-1 Tight: 0-0 Gall: 0-0
Aids:	Bl: 0-0 Vi: 0-0 Tstrap: 0-0
Best Rating:	56 4/03 MRas 2m1f110y good NHF

Czar Of Peace (IRE)
109   119

5-y-o ch h Brief Truce (USA)-Metroella (IRE) (Entitled)
W P Mullins M J Hanrahan

Placings:314052-02454P0   (3078a)
2002/03: 16⁰YS, 16²G, 16⁴F, 16⁵G, 16⁴HY, 16ᴾHY, 20⁰S,

	Starts	1st	2nd	3rd	Win & Pl
Hurdles	7	0	1	0	5706
Career Total	13	1	2	1	15444
119 10/01 Gway 2m			Hdl	SH	£6399
			Total win prize-money £6399

Going:	Sf: 0-3 GS: 0-0 Gd: 0-2 GF: - Fm: 0-1
Distance:	2m/2m3: 0-6 2m4-2m7: 0-1 3m+: 0-0
Track:	LH: 0-2 RH: 0-2 Tight: 0-0 Gall: 0-0
Aids:	Bl: 0-0 Vi: 0-0 Tstrap: 0-0
Best Rating:	119 4/02 Punc 2m gd-yld Hdl

Winning Irish hurdler. Effective at around two miles. Goes well with cut in the ground.

D J Flippance (IRE)
108(104h)   (94h)117

8-y-o b g Orchestra-Jane Bond (Good Bond)
A Parker Mr & Mrs Raymond Anderson Green

Placings:006/503/25312PP-311   (2250)
2002/03: 24³S, 28¹S, 30¹QS,

	Starts	1st	2nd	3rd	Win & Pl
Hurdles	1	0	0	1	466
Chases	2	2	0	0	10449
Career Total	16	3	2	3	17340
117 11/02 Newc 3m6f	E(0-110)HCh	G-S	£5703
105 11/02 Kels 3m4f	E(0-110)HCh	SFT	£4745
98 2/02 Muss 3m	E Ch	SFT	£3388
		Total win prize-money £13837

Going:	Sf: 1-2 GS: 1-1 Gd: 0-0 GF: - Fm: 0-0
Distance:	2m/2m3: 0-0 2m4-2m7: 0-0 3m+: 2-3
Track:	LH: 2-2 RH: 0-1 Tight: 1-1 Gall: 1-1
Aids:	Bl: 0-0 Vi: 0-0 Tstrap: 0-0
Best Rating:	117 11/02 Newc 3m6f gd-sft Ch

Fair form over fences at the start of 2002 before losing his way. Had a pipe-opener over hurdles in October and then reverted with success to the larger obstacles at Kelso in November and folowed up at Newcastle two weeks later.. Suited by soft ground and stays well.

D'Argent (IRE)
96   119

6-y-o gr g Roselier (FR)-Money Galore (IRE) (Monksfield)
A King Nigel Bunter

Placings:0211-00   (4441)
2002/03: 20⁶GS, 20⁹G,

	Starts	1st	2nd	3rd	Win & Pl
Hurdles	2	0	0	0	
Career Total	6	2	1	0	6711
119 3/02 Extr 2m3f	E Hdl	GD	£2842
119 3/02 Donc 2m4f	E Hdl	SFT	£3122
		Total win prize-money £5964

Going:	Sf: 0-0 GS: 0-0 Gd: 0-1 GF: - Fm: 0-0
Distance:	2m/2m3: 0-0 2m4-2m7: 0-2 3m+: 0-0
Track:	LH: 0-1 RH: 0-1 Tight: 0-0 Gall: 0-0
Aids:	Bl: 0-0 Vi: 0-0 Tstrap: 0-0
Best Rating:	119 3/02 Extr 2m3f good Hdl

Improving with every outing and won twice in March 2002. Stays two and a half miles, handles good ground or softer. Will make a nice chaser in time.

D-Day-Smoke

9-y-o ch g Cigar-Little Pockthorpe (Morston (FR))
A Streeter Norman Wolstencroft

Placings:P   (1207)
2002/03: 16ᴾG,

	Starts	1st	2nd	3rd	Win & Pl
Hurdles	1	0	0	0	
Career Total	1	0	0	0	

Going:	Sf: 0-0 GS: 0-0 Gd: 0-1 GF: - Fm: 0-0
Distance:	2m/2m3: 0-1 2m4-2m7: 0-0 3m+: 0-0
Track:	LH: 0-1 RH: 0-0 Tight: 0-0 Gall: 0-0
Aids:	Bl: 0-0 Vi: 0-0 Tstrap: 0-0
Best Rating:	0 9/02 Uttx 2m good Hdl

Da Buick (IRE)

5-y-o b g Turtle Island (IRE)-Kindness Itself (IRE) (Ahonoora)
S J Magnier Fergus Jones

Placings:P   (1900)
2002/03: 17ᴾS,

	Starts	1st	2nd	3rd	Win & Pl
Hurdles	1	0	0	0	
Career Total	1	0	0	0	

Going:	Sf: 0-1 GS: 0-0 Gd: 0-0 GF: - Fm: 0-0
Distance:	2m/2m3: 0-1 2m4-2m7: 0-0 3m+: 0-0
Track:	LH: 0-1 RH: 0-0 Tight: 0-1 Gall: 0-0
Aids:	Bl: 0-0 Vi: 0-0 Tstrap: 0-0
Best Rating:	0 11/02 Sedg 2m1f soft Hdl

Dabarpour (IRE)
104(84c)   (69c)96

7-y-o b/br g Alzao (USA)-Dabara (IRE) (Shardari)
Ian Williams Terry Warner

Placings:4050/32500/120003124-14624   (1618)
2002/03: 16¹F, 16⁴GF, 16⁶GF, 16²GF, 16⁴F,

	Starts	1st	2nd	3rd	Win & Pl
Hurdles	5	1	1	0	5201
Career Total	23	3	4	2	14503
112 5/02 Wwck 2m	D(0-115)HHdl	FRM	£3349
103 11/01 Hntg 2m110y	E(0-115)HHdl	GD	£2429
100 6/01 Strf 2m110y	E(0-105)HHdl	G-F	£3209
		Total win prize-money £8989

Going:	Sf: 0-0 GS: 0-0 Gd: 0-0 GF: - Fm: 1-5
Distance:	2m/2m3: 1-5 2m4-2m7: 0-0 3m+: 0-0
Track:	LH: 1-4 RH: 0-1 Tight: 0-2 Gall: 0-0
Aids:	Bl: 0-0 Vi: 0-0 Tstrap: 1-3
Best Rating:	112 5/02 Wwck 2m firm Hdl

Modest handicap hurdler; disappointing in only start over fences; acts on fast ground; seems best at around 2m.

Dabus
100   98

8-y-o b g Kris-Licorne (Sadler s Wells (USA))
M C Chapman Alan Mann

Placings:PP03606/125211425/3202303F   (2689)
2002/03: 17³GS, 17²GF, 17⁰G, 19²GF, 17³GF, 16⁰G, 16³G, 17ᶠS,

	Starts	1st	2nd	3rd	Win & Pl
Hurdles	7	0	2	3	3193
Chases	1	0	0	0	0
Career Total	24	3	5	4	17726
111 7/00 Sthl 2m	D(0-120)HHdl	G-F	£5499
111 7/00 MRas 2m1f110y	E(0-105)HHdl	GD	£2886
91 5/00 Strf 2m110y	F(0-100)HHdl	GD	£2982
		Total win prize-money £11367

Going:	Sf: 0-1 GS: 0-1 Gd: 0-3 GF: - Fm: 0-3
Distance:	2m/2m3: 0-7 2m4-2m7: 0-1 3m+: 0-0
Track:	LH: 0-3 RH: 0-5 Tight: 0-5 Gall: 0-0
Aids:	Bl: 0-0 Vi: 0-0 Tstrap: 0-0
Best Rating:	111 7/00 Strf 2m3f gd-fm Hdl

Plating-class, tempermanetal hurdler; has been known to refuse to race.

Daddy Dancer (FR)

12-y-o b g Italic (FR)-Tresse D Or (FR) (Northern Treat (USA))

Martin Jones R F Jones

Placings:4/60F362/3F33P3P/643P/6/F-PP   (0317)
2002/03: 33PGF, 34PG,

	Starts	1st	2nd	3rd	Win & Pl
Chases	2	0	0	0	
Career Total	22	0	1	6	5729

Going: Sf: 0-0 GS: 0-0 Gd: 0-1 GF: - Fm: 0-1
Distance: 2m/2m3: 0-0 2m4-2m7: 0-0 3m+: 0-2
Track: LH: 0-2 RH: 0-0 Tight: 0-0 Gall: 0-1
Aids: Bl: 0-0 Vi: 0-0 Tstrap: 0-0
Best Rating: 103 2/99 Leic 2m4f110y gd-sft Ch

Dads Lad (IRE)
103   **82**
9-y-o b g Supreme Leader-Furryvale (Furry Glen)
Miss Suzy Smith (H D Daly 24/5) Miss Suzy Smith

Placings:4334/304514-03F4B3   (4095)
2002/03: 25DG, 24³GS, 24FGS, 254S, 25BS, 24³HY,

	Starts	1st	2nd	3rd	Win & Pl
Chases	6	0	0	2	1891
Career Total	16	1	0	5	9297

100 3/02 Bang 3m110y D(0-110)HCh SFT £4231
Total win prize-money £4232

Going: Sf: 0-3 GS: 0-2 Gd: 0-1 GF: - Fm: 0-0
Distance: 2m/2m3: 0-0 2m4-2m7: 0-0 3m+: 0-6
Track: LH: 0-2 RH: 0-4 Tight: 0-5 Gall: 0-0
Aids: Bl: 0-4 Vi: 0-0 Tstrap: 0-0
Best Rating: 103 2/01 Tntn 3m heavy Ch

Modest handicap chaser, suited by soft ground, stays 3m; wears blinkers.

Daffanarc
25f   **65f**
5-y-o b m Weld-Flower Of Tintern (Free State)
P F Nicholls Win-A-Lot Syndicate

Placings:0   (4600)
2002/03: 17DGF,

	Starts	1st	2nd	3rd	Win & Pl
NH Flat	1	0	0	0	
Career Total	1	0	0	0	

Going: Sf: 0-0 GS: 0-0 Gd: 0-0 GF: - Fm: 0-1
Distance: 2m/2m3: 0-1 2m4-2m7: 0-0 3m+: 0-0
Track: LH: 0-0 RH: 0-1 Tight: 0-0 Gall: 0-0
Aids: Bl: 0-0 Vi: 0-0 Tstrap: 0-0
Best Rating: 65 4/03 Extr 2m1f gd-fm NHF

Daimajin (IRE)
84   **57**
4-y-o b g Dr Devious (IRE)-Arrow Field (USA) (Sunshine Forever (USA))
R H Alner (B G Powell 4/1) John Baker

Placings:00   (4270)
2002/03: 16PS, 16DG,

	Starts	1st	2nd	3rd	Win & Pl
Hurdles	2	0	0	0	
Career Total	2	0	0	0	

Going: Sf: 0-1 GS: 0-0 Gd: 0-1 GF: - Fm: 0-0
Distance: 2m/2m3: 0-2 2m4-2m7: 0-0 3m+: 0-0
Track: LH: 0-1 RH: 0-1 Tight: 0-0 Gall: 0-0
Aids: Bl: 0-0 Vi: 0-0 Tstrap: 0-0
Best Rating: 57 3/03 Chep 2m110y good Hdl

Dainty Man (IRE)
11-y-o b/br g Cardinal Flower-Web Of Gold (Bustineto)
Mrs A R Hewitt Miss M A De Quincey

Placings:P5/6P/06   (4541)
2002/03: 20DGS, 24⁶G,

	Starts	1st	2nd	3rd	Win & Pl
Chases	2	0	0	0	0
Career Total	6	0	0	0	0

Going: Sf: 0-0 GS: 0-1 Gd: 0-1 GF: - Fm: 0-0
Distance: 2m/2m3: 0-0 2m4-2m7: 0-1 3m+: 0-1
Track: LH: 0-0 RH: 0-2 Tight: 0-1 Gall: 0-0
Aids: Bl: 0-0 Vi: 0-0 Tstrap: 0-0
Best Rating: 85 5/00 Chel 2m5f good Ch

Daisy Leigh
83   **52**
9-y-o b m Crested Lark-Mrs Pepperpot (Kinglet)
G B Balding A K Leigh

Placings:0PP   (3475)
2002/03: 24DGS, 23PGS, 25PGS,

	Starts	1st	2nd	3rd	Win & Pl
Chases	3	0	0	0	
Career Total	3	0	0	0	

Going: Sf: 0-0 GS: 0-3 Gd: 0-0 GF: - Fm: 0-0
Distance: 2m/2m3: 0-0 2m4-2m7: 0-0 3m+: 0-3
Track: LH: 0-0 RH: 0-3 Tight: 0-1 Gall: 0-0
Aids: Bl: 0-0 Vi: 0-0 Tstrap: 0-0
Best Rating: 52 12/02 Tntn 3m gd-sft Ch

Dajazar (IRE)
74   (95dc)**32**
7-y-o b g Seattle Dancer (USA)-Dajarra (IRE) (Blushing Groom (FR))
Miss V Scott (A Scott 7/4) Mr & Mrs Aynsley & M Abercrombie

Placings:0530P/2310023-030412P00   (4774)
2002/03: 16DGF, 19³YS, 16⁶Gd, 16⁴GF, 22¹G, 20²GF, 24PGF, 22⁰G, 27⁰G,

	Starts	1st	2nd	3rd	Win & Pl
Hurdles	8	1	0	1	8138
Chases	1	0	1	0	1227
Career Total	21	2	3	4	16409

106 8/02 Tral 2m6f (81-123)HHdl GD £7407
107 7/01 Dund 2m135y Hdl FRM £3895
Total win prize-money £11303

Going: Sf: 0-0 GS: 0-0 Gd: 1-3 GF: - Fm: 0-5
Distance: 2m/2m3: 0-4 2m4-2m7: 1-3 3m+: 0-2
Track: LH: 0-1 RH: 0-0 Tight: 0-1 Gall: 0-0
Aids: Bl: 1-5 Vi: 0-0 Tstrap: 1-3
Best Rating: 116 2/01 Naas 2m sft-hvy Hdl

Dalby Of York
88   **56**
7-y-o ch g Polar Falcon (USA)-Miller s Creek (USA) (Star De Naskra (USA))

M E Sowersby M E Sowersby

Placings:P-5P   (2160)
2002/03: 23⁵HY, 27PS,

	Starts	1st	2nd	3rd	Win & Pl
Hurdles	2	0	0	0	0
Career Total	3	0	0	0	0

Going: Sf: 0-2 GS: 0-0 Gd: 0-0 GF: - Fm: 0-0
Distance: 2m/2m3: 0-0 2m4-2m7: 0-1 3m+: 0-1
Track: LH: 0-2 RH: 0-0 Tight: 0-1 Gall: 0-0
Aids: Bl: 0-0 Vi: 0-0 Tstrap: 0-0
Best Rating: 56 11/02 Weth 2m7f heavy Hdl

Dalcassian Buck (IRE)
100(99h)   (93 h)**86**
9-y-o ch g Buckskin (FR)-Menebeans (IRE) (Duky)
C L Popham (K C Bailey 24/5) The Four Bucks

Placings:F4P6P1-446PP4F   (3475)
2002/03: 16¹GS, 21⁴GF, 24⁴G, 22⁶GS, 27PS, 22PGS, 19⁴S, 25FGS,

	Starts	1st	2nd	3rd	Win & Pl
Hurdles	6	1	0	0	3397
Chases	2	0	0	0	439
Career Total	13	1	0	0	4070

93 4/02 Towc 2m E Hdl G-S £3146
Total win prize-money £3147

Going: Sf: 0-2 GS: 1-4 Gd: 0-1 GF: - Fm: 0-1
Distance: 2m/2m3: 1-2 2m4-2m7: 0-3 3m+: 0-3
Track: LH: 0-1 RH: 1-7 Tight: 0-2 Gall: 0-1
Aids: Bl: 0-0 Vi: 0-0 Tstrap: 0-0
Best Rating: 93 5/02 Towc 3m good Hdl

Modest hurdler/chaser, won a weak novices hurdle at Towcester in April 2002. Effective at a stiff two miles.

Dale Creek (IRE)
97   **95**
8-y-o b g Mandalus-Typhoon Signal (Aristocracy)
R H Alner (Henry De Bromhead 13/9) David O Moon

Placings:0/0PF0/0U60/54256415-FPPU042   (3314)
2002/03: 24FGF, 25PYS, 22PGF, 25¼GF, 24⁰G, 24⁴S, 25²GS,

	Starts	1st	2nd	3rd	Win & Pl
Chases	7	0	1	0	2174
Career Total	24	1	2	0	10174

95 8/01 Kbgn 3m1f Ch GD £6677
Total win prize-money £6677

Going: Sf: 0-1 GS: 0-1 Gd: 0-1 GF: - Fm: 0-3
Distance: 2m/2m3: 0-0 2m4-2m7: 0-1 3m+: 0-6
Track: LH: 0-0 RH: 0-4 Tight: 0-1 Gall: 0-0
Aids: Bl: 0-0 Vi: 0-0 Tstrap: 0-0
Best Rating: 99 6/01 Kbgn 3m3f good NHF

Ex-Irish staying chaser, possibly best in good ground.

Dalligan (IRE)
108   **99+**
9-y-o b g Executive Perk-Comeragh Queen (The Parson)
D E Cantillon (N J Pewter 11/5) N J Pewter

Placings:6U-413   (0491)
2002/03: 20⁴GF, 24¹GS, 24³HY,

	Starts	1st	2nd	3rd	Win & Pl
Chases	3	1	0	1	6176
Career Total	5	1	0	1	6176

99 5/02 Fknm 3m110y D(0-115)HCh G-S £5434

Total win prize-money £5434

Going:	Sf: 0-1 GS: 1-1 Gd: 0-0 GF: - Fm: 0-1
Distance:	2m/2m3: 0-0 2m4-2m7: 0-1 3m+: 1-2
Track:	LH: 1-2 RH: 0-1 Tight: 1-1 Gall: 0-1
Aids:	Bl: 0-0 Vi: 0-0 Tstrap: 0-0
Best Rating:	99 5/02 Fknm 3m110y gd-sft Ch

Modest pointer/hunter chaser, is best with cut in the ground.

Dalus Park (IRE)

8-y-o b g Mandalus-Pollerton Park (Pollerton)
Mrs Antonia Bealby   Exors Of The Late R E N Gardiner

Placings:2-20   (0395)
2002/03: 22²G, 28⁰G,

	Starts	1st	2nd	3rd	Win & Pl
Chases	2	0	1	0	876
Career Total	3	0	2	0	1534

Going:	Sf: 0-0 GS: 0-0 Gd: 0-2 GF: - Fm: 0-0
Distance:	2m/2m3: 0-0 2m4-2m7: 0-1 3m+: 0-1
Track:	LH: 0-1 RH: 0-1 Tight: 0-1 Gall: 0-0
Aids:	Bl: 0-0 Vi: 0-0 Tstrap: 0-0
Best Rating:	103 5/02 Towc 2m6f good Ch

Winning pointer, he shaped with promise on his debut over regulation fences. Acts with cut.

Dam The Breeze
109(111c)   (117c)111
10-y-o b g Ikdam-Cool Breeze (Windjammer (USA))
Evan Williams   Kevin Glastonbury

Placings:FPP/45F21601/112-0F   (4459)
2002/03: 24⁰GS, 21²FG,

	Starts	1st	2nd	3rd	Win & Pl
Chases	2	0	0	0	
Career Total	16	4	2	0	17018
111	5/01	Hntg	3m2f	F(0-95)HHdl	G-F	£2520
111	5/01	Hntg	3m	E(0-115)HCh	GD	£4329
105	4/01	MRas	3m1f	F(0-95)Ch	G-S	£3906
113	8/00	Worc	2m7f110yE Ch			£3347

Total win prize-money £14103

Going:	Sf: 0-0 GS: 0-1 Gd: 0-1 GF: - Fm: 0-0
Distance:	2m/2m3: 0-0 2m4-2m7: 0-1 3m+: 0-1
Track:	LH: 0-1 RH: 0-1 Tight: 0-2 Gall: 0-0
Aids:	Bl: 0-0 Vi: 0-0 Tstrap: 0-0
Best Rating:	113 1/02 Winc 3m1f110y good Ch

Modest staying hurdler/chaser; stays 3m 2f; appreciates a decent surface; front runner.

Dame Fonteyn
100   96
6-y-o b m Suave Dancer (USA)-Her Honour (Teenoso (USA))
C Tizzard   Mrs Sarah Tizzard

Placings:300/30F245243-0442605   (4290)
2002/03: 22⁰GF, 19⁴S, 16⁴S, 16²HY, 21⁶GS, 17⁰GS, 22⁵GF,

	Starts	1st	2nd	3rd	Win & Pl
Hurdles	7	0	1	0	1391
Career Total	19	0	3	3	3971

Going:	Sf: 0-3 GS: 0-2 Gd: 0-0 GF: - Fm: 0-0
Distance:	2m/2m3: 0-4 2m4-2m7: 0-3 3m+: 0-0
Track:	LH: 0-2 RH: 0-5 Tight: 0-1 Gall: 0-0
Aids:	Bl: 0-0 Vi: 0-0 Tstrap: 0-0

Best Rating: 96 1/03 Chep 2m110y heavy Hdl

Stays two miles six furlongs. Best on easy ground although has yet to lose her maiden tag over hurdles.

Damien's Choice (IRE)
111(102h)   (108h)113
11-y-o b g Erin s Hope-Reenoga (Tug Of War)
G A Swinbank (Ferdy Murphy 30/4)   M Sawers

Placings:264/43/525P0P240/04126/40650/21P11226-652UF55211   (4763)
2002/03: 16⁶G, 17⁵GF, 17²GS, 16⁴G, 20⁴GS, 16⁵GS, 17⁵S, 16²GF, 17¹G, 16¹G,

	Starts	1st	2nd	3rd	Win & Pl
Hurdles	1	0	0	0	0
Chases	9	2	2	0	18364
Career Total	44	6	9	2	37770
113	4/03	Prth	2m	D(0-125)HCh	GD	£8255
108	4/03	Kels	2m1f	E(0-110)HCh	GD	£6948
102	12/01	Catt	2m	F(0-100)HCh	SFT	£3965
94	11/01	Sedg	2m110y	F(0-100)HCh	SFT	£2884
108	6/01	Hexm	2m	E(0-115)HHdl	GD	£2366
81	11/99	Kels	2m110y	F(0-95)HHdl	GD	£3039

Total win prize-money £27458

Going:	Sf: 0-1 GS: 0-3 Gd: 2-4 GF: - Fm: 0-2
Distance:	2m/2m3: 2-9 2m4-2m7: 0-1 3m+: 0-0
Track:	LH: 1-6 RH: 1-4 Tight: 1-6 Gall: 0-2
Aids:	Bl: 0-0 Vi: 0-0 Tstrap: 0-0
Best Rating:	113 4/03 Prth 2m good Ch

Modest chaser, best over two miles; acts on any ground; had his usual cheekpieces left off when winning at Kelso in April 2003, but followed up at Perth with them re-applied.

Damiens Pride (IRE)

13-y-o b g Bulldozer-Riopoless (Royal And Regal (USA))
Mrs S J Batchelor   Mrs S J Batchelor

Placings:302P-213F   (4390)
2002/03: 21²GF, 19¹G, 21³S, 19⁵F,

	Starts	1st	2nd	3rd	Win & Pl
Chases	4	1	1	1	4003
Career Total	8	1	2	2	4880
92	5/02	Extr	2m3f110yH Ch		GD	£1586

Total win prize-money £1586

Going:	Sf: 0-1 GS: 0-0 Gd: 1-1 GF: - Fm: 0-2
Distance:	2m/2m3: 0-0 2m4-2m7: 1-4 3m+: 0-0
Track:	LH: 0-2 RH: 1-2 Tight: 0-1 Gall: 0-1
Aids:	Bl: 0-0 Vi: 0-0 Tstrap: 0-0
Best Rating:	100 5/02 Chel 2m5f gd-fm Ch

Damus (GER)
105(98h)   (118h)122
9-y-o br g Surumu (GER)-Dawn Side (CAN) (Bold Forbes (USA))
Ian Williams   Favourites Racing

Placings:203/1322U/1311300/1221P5-F624443   (4570)
2002/03: 17⁵GF, 16⁵GF, 16²GF, 16⁴G, 19⁴G, 18⁴G, 20³G,

	Starts	1st	2nd	3rd	Win & Pl
Hurdles	1	0	0	0	0
Chases	6	0	1	1	5945
Career Total	28	6	6	5	51955
130	12/01	Sthl	2m	B(0-140)HCh	GD	£13848
118	10/01	MRas	2m1f110yD(0-120)HHdl		G-S	£5551
130	12/00	Plum	2m110y	E Ch		G-S	£3003

128	7/00	Wolv	2m	C(0-135)HCh	G-S	£7928
115	5/00	Hrfd	2m	E Ch		G-S	£3051
123	10/99	Plum	2m	E(0-105)HHdl	G-F	£3176

Total win prize-money £36559

Going:	Sf: 0-0 GS: 0-0 Gd: 0-4 GF: - Fm: 0-3
Distance:	2m/2m3: 0-6 2m4-2m7: 0-1 3m+: 0-0
Track:	LH: 0-6 RH: 0-1 Tight: 0-2 Gall: 0-1
Aids:	Bl: 0-0 Vi: 0-0 Tstrap: 0-0
Best Rating:	130 6/02 Strf 2m1f110y gd-fm Ch

Fair handicap chaser, jumps well; effective over hurdles too; unlikely to stay much beyond two miles; acts on good to soft ground.

Dan De Lion

4-y-o b c Danzig Connection (USA)-Fiorini (Formidable (USA))
Jedd O Keeffe   Wetherby Racing Bureau 49

Placings:P   (1304)
2002/03: 16⁹GF,

	Starts	1st	2nd	3rd	Win & Pl
Hurdles	1	0	0	0	
Career Total	1	0	0	0	

Going:	Sf: 0-0 GS: 0-0 Gd: 0-0 GF: - Fm: 0-1
Distance:	2m/2m3: 0-1 2m4-2m7: 0-0 3m+: 0-0
Track:	LH: 0-0 RH: 0-1 Tight: 0-0 Gall: 0-0
Aids:	Bl: 0-0 Vi: 0-0 Tstrap: 0-0
Best Rating:	0 9/02 Prth 2m110y gd-fm Hdl

Dan De Man (IRE)
101(107h)   (71 h)71
12-y-o b g Phardante (FR)-Slave De (Arctic Slave)
Miss L C Siddall   Miss L C Siddall

Placings:05/060F5/3P0151225/41123360/4560404P51/040P400/3P100024000-P0P065P2   (4163)
2002/03: 16²GF, 16⁰G, 20⁵GS, 20⁰G, 22⁶S, 20⁰S, 20²FS, 16²GS,

	Starts	1st	2nd	3rd	Win & Pl
Hurdles	3	0	0	0	
Chases	5	0	0	0	1333
Career Total	61	6	5	4	23273
92	11/01	Hayd	2m4f	F(0-110)HHdl	SFT	£2758
97	4/00	Newc	2m110y	E Ch		G-S	£3458
115	12/98	Newc	2m	E(0-110)HHdl	SFT	£2211
112	11/98	Weth	2m4f110yE(0-110)HHdl		GD	£2407
97	1/98	Donc	2m110y	F(0-110)HHdl	GD	£2356
84	12/97	Newc	2m	F(0-110)HHdl	GD	£1934

Total win prize-money £15127

Going:	Sf: 0-3 GS: 0-2 Gd: 0-2 GF: - Fm: 0-1
Distance:	2m/2m3: 0-3 2m4-2m7: 0-5 3m+: 0-0
Track:	LH: 0-8 RH: 0-0 Tight: 0-0 Gall: 0-2
Aids:	Bl: 0-0 Vi: 0-0 Tstrap: 0-0
Best Rating:	117 1/00 Weth 2m soft Hdl

Moderate hurdler/chaser; generally inconsistent; effective on a soft surface; stays 2m 4f.

Dance Free (USA)
52   74
5-y-o b g Fly So Free (USA)-Dances With Music (USA) (Sovereign Dancer (USA))
I R Brown (M J Grassick 6/9)   I R Brown

Placings:0-500   (4358)
2002/03: 16⁵S, 16⁰GF, 19⁰F,

	Starts	1st	2nd	3rd	Win & Pl
Hurdles	3	0	0	0	

Career Total   4   0   0   0

Going: Sf: 0-1 GS: 0-0 Gd: 0-0 GF: - Fm: 0-2
Distance: 2m/2m3: 0-2 2m4-2m7: 0-1 3m+: 0-0
Track: LH: 0-0 RH: 0-1 Tight: 0-1 Gall: 0-0
Aids: Bl: 0-0 Vi: 0-0 Tstrap: 0-0
Best Rating: 74 3/02 Leop 2m   heavy Hdl

Dance In Tune

87(107h)   (105 h)**99**
6-y-o ch g Mujtahid (USA)-Dancing Prize (IRE) (Sadler s Wells (USA))
P J Hobbs Major And Mrs P I C Payne

Placings:11643   (4625)
2002/03: 17¹GF, 16¹GF, 16⁶GF, 174F, 173GF,

	Starts	1st	2nd	3rd	Win & Pl
Hurdles	5	2	0	1	7679
Career Total	5	2	0	1	7679
111 8/02 Worc 2m		E Hdl		G-F	£3157
102 8/02 NAbb 2m1f		D Hdl		G-F	£3766

Total win prize-money £6923

Going: Sf: 0-0 GS: 0-0 Gd: 0-0 GF: - Fm: 2-5
Distance: 2m/2m3: 2-5 2m4-2m7: 0-0 3m+: 0-0
Track: LH: 2-3 RH: 0-2 Tight: 1-3 Gall: 0-0
Aids: Bl: 0-0 Vi: 0-0 Tstrap: 0-0
Best Rating: 111 8/02 Worc 2m   gd-fm Hdl

Fair hurdler; off the track for two years before making a winning hurdles debut at Newton Abbot in August 2002; followed up with an easy win at Worcester later that month; disappointing since; promising debut over fences when third in 2m handicap chase at Newton Abbot May 2003; seems sure to improve; suited by fast ground; may require a stiffer 2m now.

Dance Of Life

96   **78**
4-y-o b f Shareef Dancer (USA)-Regan (USA) (Lear Fan (USA))
S Gollings Christopher Shirley Brasher

Placings:P600F   (4782)
2002/03: 17PS, 16⁶GS, 16⁰HY, 16⁰G, 17FG,

	Starts	1st	2nd	3rd	Win & Pl
Hurdles	5	0	0	0	0
Career Total	5	0	0	0	0

Going: Sf: 0-2 GS: 0-1 Gd: 0-2 GF: - Fm: 0-0
Distance: 2m/2m3: 0-5 2m4-2m7: 0-0 3m+: 0-0
Track: LH: 0-2 RH: 0-3 Tight: 0-4 Gall: 0-0
Aids: Bl: 0-3 Vi: 0-0 Tstrap: 0-0
Best Rating: 78 4/03 MRas 2m1f110y good Hdl

Plating-class hurdler; in a seller for the first time was clear when falling at the last at Market Rasen in April.

Dancer Polish (POL)

102   **100**
5-y-o b g Professional (IRE)-Doloreska (POL) (Who Knows)
A Sadik A Sadik

Placings:4213P5   (2107)
2002/03: 16⁴GF, 16²G, 16¹GF, 20³GS, 16PHY, 16⁵GS,

	Starts	1st	2nd	3rd	Win & Pl
Hurdles	6	1	1	1	4546
Career Total	6	1	1	1	4546
100 10/02 Uttx 2m		E Hdl		G-F	£3250

Total win prize-money £3250

Going: Sf: 0-1 GS: 0-2 Gd: 0-1 GF: - Fm: 1-2
Distance: 2m/2m3: 1-5 2m4-2m7: 0-1 3m+: 0-0
Track: LH: 1-5 RH: 0-1 Tight: 0-1 Gall: 0-1
Aids: Bl: 0-0 Vi: 0-0 Tstrap: 0-0
Best Rating: 100 10/02 Uttx 2m   gd-fm Hdl

A dual winner on the Flat in Poland. Finished a moderate fourth on his hurdling debut at Uttoxeter August 2002. Off the mark in modest company on a return visit there in October over two miles on good ground.

Dances With Rivers

87f   **54f**
4-y-o b f River Falls-Make Merry (IRE) (Dunbeath (USA))
Mrs M Reveley Falcon Assets

Placings:0   (3583)
2002/03: 16⁰G,

	Starts	1st	2nd	3rd	Win & Pl
NH Flat	1	0	0	0	
Career Total	1	0	0	0	

Going: Sf: 0-0 GS: 0-0 Gd: 0-1 GF: - Fm: 0-0
Distance: 2m/2m3: 0-1 2m4-2m7: 0-0 3m+: 0-0
Track: LH: 0-0 RH: 0-1 Tight: 0-1 Gall: 0-0
Aids: Bl: 0-0 Vi: 0-0 Tstrap: 0-0
Best Rating: 54 2/03 Muss 2m   good NHF

Dancetillyoudrop (IRE)

12-y-o b g Clearly Bust-Keep Dancing (Lord Gayle (USA))
P F Nicholls Derek Millard

Placings:12522/3F1342FP2/FF2P110446/F24313/P313201532/5P122-11U3PP   (3848)
2002/03: 31¹G, 26¹G, 32UGF, 26³GF, 25PS, 27PG,

	Starts	1st	2nd	3rd	Win & Pl
Chases	6	2	0	1	8881
Career Total	51	10	11	8	54816
114 6/02 NAbb 3m2f110yD(0-120)HCh			GD	£4305
111 5/02 Folk 3m7f		H Ch			£3484
112 2/02 Plum 3m2f		H Ch		HVY	£1148
112 11/00 Font 3m2f110yD(0-125)HCh			HVY	£3955
114 5/00 Font 3m2f110yF(0-105)HCh			GD	£2990
114 11/99 Winc 3m1f110yD(0-125)HCh			GD	£7035
107 1/99 Winc 3m1f110yE(0-115)HCh			SFT	£3454
116 1/99 Font 3m1f110yE(0-125)HCh			SFT	£4352
105 11/97 Worc 2m4f110yE(0-105)HCh			SFT	£3125
106 6/96 Naas 2m		NHF		YLD	£2824

Total win prize-money £36675

Going: Sf: 0-1 GS: 0-0 Gd: 2-3 GF: - Fm: 0-2
Distance: 2m/2m3: 0-0 2m4-2m7: 0-0 3m+: 2-6
Track: LH: 1-2 RH: 1-3 Tight: 2-5 Gall: 0-0
Aids: Bl: 0-0 Vi: 0-0 Tstrap: 0-1
Best Rating: 120 4/98 Font 3m2f110y soft Ch

Fair hunter chaser nowadays; stays well; effective in most types of ground.

Dancing Bay

105   **127**
6-y-o b g Suave Dancer (USA)-Kabayil (Dancing Brave (USA))
N J Henderson Elite Racing Club

Placings:2F-1410   (4049)
2002/03: 16¹S, 16⁴GS, 21¹S, 16⁰HY,

	Starts	1st	2nd	3rd	Win & Pl
Hurdles	4	2	0	0	13948

Career Total 6 2 1 0 15043
122 2/03 Plum 2m5f C Hdl SFT £6857
127 1/03 Plum 2m D Hdl SFT £5590
Total win prize-money £12448

Going: Sf: 2-3 GS: 0-1 Gd: 0-0 GF: - Fm: 0-0
Distance: 2m/2m3: 1-3 2m4-2m7: 1-1 3m+: 0-0
Track: LH: 2-3 RH: 0-1 Tight: 2-2 Gall: 0-0
Aids: Bl: 0-0 Vi: 0-0 Tstrap: 0-0
Best Rating: 127 1/03 Plum 2m   soft Hdl

Decent staying handicapper on the level; decent handicap hurdler; effective at up to two miles five; acts on soft ground.

Dancing Dolphin (IRE)

93   **66**
4-y-o b f Dolphin Street (FR)-Dance Model (Unfuwain (USA))
Julian Poulton Meddler Racing

Placings:300   (1641)
2002/03: 16³G, 16⁶G, 16⁰G,

	Starts	1st	2nd	3rd	Win & Pl
Hurdles	3	0	0	1	634
Career Total	3	0	0	1	634

Going: Sf: 0-0 GS: 0-0 Gd: 0-2 GF: - Fm: 0-1
Distance: 2m/2m3: 0-3 2m4-2m7: 0-0 3m+: 0-0
Track: LH: 0-2 RH: 0-1 Tight: 0-0 Gall: 0-0
Aids: Bl: 0-0 Vi: 0-0 Tstrap: 0-0
Best Rating: 66 9/02 Uttx 2m   good Hdl

Dancing Fosenby

7-y-o b g Terimon-Wave Dancer (Dance In Time (CAN))
D McCain D McCain

Placings:4PP0043-604   (0739)
2002/03: 20⁶G, 17⁰HY, 16⁴G,

	Starts	1st	2nd	3rd	Win & Pl
Hurdles	2	0	0	0	0
Chases	1	0	0	0	269
Career Total	10	0	0	1	769

Going: Sf: 0-1 GS: 0-0 Gd: 0-2 GF: - Fm: 0-0
Distance: 2m/2m3: 0-2 2m4-2m7: 0-1 3m+: 0-0
Track: LH: 0-3 RH: 0-0 Tight: 0-3 Gall: 0-0
Aids: Bl: 0-0 Vi: 0-0 Tstrap: 0-0
Best Rating: 66 4/02 Ludl 2m   good Hdl

Dancing Pearl

108   **97**
5-y-o ch m Dancing Spree (USA)-Elegant Rose (Noalto)
C J Price J E Heymans

Placings:344-44116   (4549)
2002/03: 16⁴HY, 174GS, 16¹GS, 16¹GF, 16⁶G,

	Starts	1st	2nd	3rd	Win & Pl
Hurdles	5	2	0	0	7758
Career Total	8	2	0	1	9442
92 3/03 Sthl 2m		E Hdl		G-F	£3486
97 1/03 Sthl 2m		E Hdl		G-S	£3542

Total win prize-money £7028

Going: Sf: 0-1 GS: 1-2 Gd: 0-1 GF: - Fm: 1-1
Distance: 2m/2m3: 2-5 2m4-2m7: 0-0 3m+: 0-0
Track: LH: 2-4 RH: 0-1 Tight: 2-3 Gall: 0-0

Aids: Bl: 0-0 Vi: 0-0 Tstrap: 0-0
Best Rating: 106 4/02 Chel 2m1f   good NHF

Half-sister to useful sprinter Bowden Rose, she has shown some ability in bumpers but achieved little over hurdles so far, although she did win a weak mares only event at Southwell in January.

Dancing Shirley

87   60

5-y-o b m Dancing Spree (USA)-High Heather (Shirley Heights)
T P McGovern T P McGovern

Placings: 40-0   (1582)
2002/03: 21⁰G,

	Starts	1st	2nd	3rd	Win & Pl
Hurdles	1	0	0	0	
Career Total	3	0	0	0	0

Going: Sf: 0-0 GS: 0-0 Gd: 0-1 GF: - Fm: 0-0
Distance: 2m/2m3: 0-0 2m4-2m7: 0-0 3m+: 0-0
Track: LH: 0-1 RH: 0-0 Tight: 0-1 Gall: 0-0
Aids: Bl: 0-0 Vi: 0-0 Tstrap: 0-0
Best Rating: 80 3/02 Hntg 2m110y   gd-fm NHF

Bred for speed rather than stamina. Showed ability on debut.

Dancing Water

102   111

4-y-o gr g Halling (USA)-Gleaming Water (Kalaglow)
Patrick O Brady (R F Johnson Houghton 16/10) Miss Rita Shah

Placings: 003   (4084)
2002/03: 16⁰S, 16⁰YS, 16³GS,

	Starts	1st	2nd	3rd	Win & Pl
Hurdles	3	0	0	1	858
Career Total	3	0	0	1	858

Going: Sf: 0-1 GS: 0-1 Gd: 0-0 GF: - Fm: 0-0
Distance: 2m/2m3: 0-3 2m4-2m7: 0-0 3m+: 0-0
Track: LH: 0-2 RH: 0-1 Tight: 0-0 Gall: 0-0
Aids: Bl: 0-0 Vi: 0-0 Tstrap: 0-0
Best Rating: 111 2/03 Fair 2m   yld-sft Hdl

Modest novice hurdler; maiden on the Flat; placed on third start over hurdles at Stratford.

Dande's Rambo

(80h)   (100h)

6-y-o gr g Rambo Dancer (CAN)-Kajetana (FR) (Caro)
P R Hedger Noel Cronin

Placings: 5-F   (3496)
2002/03: 20ᶠGS,

	Starts	1st	2nd	3rd	Win & Pl
Chases	1	0	0	0	
Career Total	2	0	0	0	0

Going: Sf: 0-0 GS: 0-1 Gd: 0-0 GF: - Fm: 0-0
Distance: 2m/2m3: 0-0 2m4-2m7: 0-1 3m+: 0-0
Track: LH: 0-0 RH: 0-1 Tight: 0-0 Gall: 0-0
Aids: Bl: 0-0 Vi: 0-0 Tstrap: 0-0
Best Rating: 100 5/01 Font 2m2f110y gd-fm Hdl

Dandonell (IRE)

(102h)   (94h)

9-y-o b g Ajraas (USA)-Courtown Bay (Don)
J C Tuck Mrs Erica Griffiths

Placings: 0254/02P662/6/5115P01P3-4F   (0244)
2002/03: 22⁴G, 25ᶠG,

	Starts	1st	2nd	3rd	Win & Pl
Hurdles	1	0	0	0	0
Chases	1	0	0	0	0
Career Total	22	3	3	1	11277
94	12/01 Extr	2m6f110yE(0-115)HHdl	G-S	£3206
94	5/01 Font	2m6f110yE(0-115)HHdl	G-F	£2534
82	5/01 Extr	2m6f110yF(0-100)HHdl	FRM	£2716
		Total win prize-money £8456		

Going: Sf: 0-0 GS: 0-0 Gd: 0-2 GF: - Fm: 0-0
Distance: 2m/2m3: 0-0 2m4-2m7: 0-1 3m+: 0-1
Track: LH: 0-0 RH: 0-2 Tight: 0-0 Gall: 0-0
Aids: Bl: 0-0 Vi: 0-0 Tstrap: 0-0
Best Rating: 94 12/01 Extr 2m6f110y gd-sft Hdl

Three times successful at around two and three-quarter miles over hurdles including two wins at Exeter. Seems to act on anything but extremes of going.

Dandy Lad (IRE)

97f   96f

6-y-o b g Zaffaran (USA)-Gerdando Lady (IRE) (Exhibitioner)
O Sherwood O M C Sherwood

Placings: 65   (4431)
2002/03: 16⁶G, 18⁵GF,

	Starts	1st	2nd	3rd	Win & Pl
NH Flat	2	0	0	0	0
Career Total	2	0	0	0	0

Going: Sf: 0-0 GS: 0-0 Gd: 0-1 GF: - Fm: 0-1
Distance: 2m/2m3: 0-2 2m4-2m7: 0-0 3m+: 0-0
Track: LH: 0-2 RH: 0-0 Tight: 0-0 Gall: 0-0
Aids: Bl: 0-0 Vi: 0-0 Tstrap: 0-0
Best Rating: 96 3/03 Wwck 2m   good NHF

Dandy Regent

9-y-o b g Green Desert (USA)-Tahilla (Moorestyle)
C J Price (John A Harris 26/8) Glyn Byard

Placings: P   (2671)
2002/03: 17ᴾS,

	Starts	1st	2nd	3rd	Win & Pl
Hurdles	1	0	0	0	0
Career Total	1	0	0	0	0

Going: Sf: 0-1 GS: 0-0 Gd: 0-0 GF: - Fm: 0-0
Distance: 2m/2m3: 0-1 2m4-2m7: 0-0 3m+: 0-0
Track: LH: 0-0 RH: 0-1 Tight: 0-0 Gall: 0-0
Aids: Bl: 0-0 Vi: 0-0 Tstrap: 0-0
Best Rating: 0 12/02 Hrfd 2m1f   soft Hdl

Daneswood

92   69

4-y-o b g Be My Chief (USA)-Floria Tosca (Petong)
K F Clutterbuck (P W D Arcy 3/10) K F Clutterbuck

Placings: 4   (1336)
2002/03: 16⁴GF,

	Starts	1st	2nd	3rd	Win & Pl
Hurdles	1	0	0	0	0
Career Total	1	0	0	0	0

Going: Sf: 0-0 GS: 0-0 Gd: 0-0 GF: - Fm: 0-1
Distance: 2m/2m3: 0-1 2m4-2m7: 0-0 3m+: 0-0
Track: LH: 0-0 RH: 0-0 Tight: 0-0 Gall: 0-1
Aids: Bl: 0-0 Vi: 0-0 Tstrap: 0-0
Best Rating: 70 9/02 Hntg 2m110y   gd-fm Hdl

Dangerous Deploy

(100h)   (75h)

6-y-o b g Deploy-Emily-Mou (IRE) (Cadeaux Genereux)
Miss K M George A M Wellstead

Placings: 40554/P4-00F   (3932)
2002/03: 19⁰S, 16⁰HY, 20ᶠS,

	Starts	1st	2nd	3rd	Win & Pl
Hurdles	2	0	0	0	0
Chases	1	0	0	0	0
Career Total	10	0	0	0	235

Going: Sf: 0-3 GS: 0-0 Gd: 0-0 GF: - Fm: 0-0
Distance: 2m/2m3: 0-1 2m4-2m7: 0-2 3m+: 0-0
Track: LH: 0-1 RH: 0-1 Tight: 0-2 Gall: 0-0
Aids: Bl: 0-0 Vi: 0-2 Tstrap: 0-0
Best Rating: 75 11/01 Strf 2m6f110y soft Hdl

Very moderate form at up to three miles over hurdles.

Dangerousdanmagru (IRE)

101   105

7-y-o b g Forest Wind (USA)-Blue Bell Girl (Blakeney)
N F Glynn N F Glynn

Placings: 210/405412-1054064   (2630)
2002/03: 20¹S, 20⁰YS, 17⁵G, 20⁴S, 16⁰S, 20⁶S, 20⁴S,

	Starts	1st	2nd	3rd	Win & Pl
Hurdles	7	1	0	0	6814
Career Total	16	3	2	0	22703
110	5/02 Cork	2m4f	(0-109)HHdl	SFT	£5926
104	3/02 Cork	2m	(0-109)HHdl	G-Y	£6349
113	11/99 DRoy	2m	Hdl	SFT	£6160
		Total win prize-money £18437		

Going: Sf: 1-5 GS: 0-0 Gd: 0-1 GF: - Fm: 0-0
Distance: 2m/2m3: 0-2 2m4-2m7: 1-5 3m+: 0-0
Track: LH: 0-2 RH: 0-0 Tight: 0-0 Gall: 0-0
Aids: Bl: 0-0 Vi: 0-0 Tstrap: 0-0
Best Rating: 113 11/99 DRoy 2m   soft Hdl

Showed good form in Irish Juvenile hurdles in 99 but was then absent for a long time. Has won a few times since being back in handicap hurdles over two and a half miles on soft ground.

Dangerously Good

97   121

5-y-o b g Shareef Dancer (USA)-Ecologically Kind (Alleged (USA))
R C Guest (D Morris 8/12) N J Jones

Placings: 50   (4097)
2002/03: 19⁵G, 16⁰G,

	Starts	1st	2nd	3rd	Win & Pl
Hurdles	2	0	0	0	0
Career Total	2	0	0	0	0

Going: Sf: 0-0 GS: 0-0 Gd: 0-2 GF: - Fm: 0-0
Distance: 2m/2m3: 0-2 2m4-2m7: 0-0 3m+: 0-0
Track: LH: 0-2 RH: 0-0 Tight: 0-1 Gall: 0-0
Aids: Bl: 0-0 Vi: 0-1 Tstrap: 0-0
Best Rating: 121 3/03 Chel 2m110y good Hdl

Lightly-raced performer on the Flat; has won on sand in Spain; showed ability on hurdling debut at Catterick in February and can do better; has worn cheekpieces.

Daniels Hymn

(112h) (115h)105
8-y-o b g Prince Daniel (USA)-French Spirit (FR) (Esprit Du Nord (USA))
Miss F M Crowley Top Marques Syndicate

Placings:2/212-344P21 (4650a)
2002/03: 18^{3}YS, 22^{4}S, 21^{4}GS, 24^{4}PYS, 16^{2}G, 20^{1}F,

	Starts	1st	2nd	3rd	Win & Pl
Hurdles	6	1	1	1	8566
Career Total	10	2	4	1	16074

106 4/03 Cork 2m4f Hdl FRM £5824
106 6/01 Navn 2m NHF G-F £3895
Total win prize-money £9720

Going: Sf: 0-1 GS: 0-1 Gd: 0-1 GF: - Fm: 1-1
Distance: 2m/2m3: 0-2 2m4-2m7: 1-3 3m+: 0-1
Track: LH: 0-1 RH: 0-1 Tight: 0-0 Gall: 0-1
Aids: Bl: 0-0 Vi: 0-0 Tstrap: 0-0
Best Rating: 127 7/01 Tipp 2m4f gd-fm NHF

Danimas (IRE)

102 (74c)100
6-y-o b g Foxhound (USA)-Cerosia (Pitskelly)
B G Powell (C F Swan 10/3) Seamus Mannion

Placings:00/0-40163F (4315)
2002/03: 18^{4}S, 16^{0}S, 16^{1}G, 18^{6}HY, 17^{3}HY, 19^{6}G,

	Starts	1st	2nd	3rd	Win & Pl
Hurdles	5	1	0	1	7372
Chases	1	0	0	0	
Career Total	9	1	0	1	7372

100 2/03 Muss 2m D(0-120)HHdl GD £6708
Total win prize-money £6708

Going: Sf: 0-4 GS: 0-0 Gd: 1-2 GF: - Fm: 0-0
Distance: 2m/2m3: 1-6 2m4-2m7: 0-0 3m+: 0-0
Track: LH: 0-1 RH: 1-4 Tight: 1-2 Gall: 0-1
Aids: Bl: 0-0 Vi: 0-0 Tstrap: 0-0
Best Rating: 100 2/03 Muss 2m good Hdl

Moderate Irish-trained hurdler; effective over two miles; acts well on good ground.

Danny's Chapel (IRE)

4-y-o b g College Chapel-Blue Sioux (Indian Ridge)
J Neville Robert Bernard

Placings:0 (3930)
2002/03: 16^{0}G,

	Starts	1st	2nd	3rd	Win & Pl
NH Flat	1	0	0	0	
Career Total	1	0	0	0	

Going: Sf: 0-0 GS: 0-0 Gd: 0-1 GF: - Fm: 0-0
Distance: 2m/2m3: 0-1 2m4-2m7: 0-0 3m+: 0-0
Track: LH: 0-0 RH: 0-0 Tight: 0-0 Gall: 0-1
Aids: Bl: 0-0 Vi: 0-0

Danse Slave (FR)

100 90
4-y-o b f Broadway Flyer (USA)-Snow Girl (FR) (River Mist (USA))
R H Alner S W D Partnership

Placings:024021 (4511)
2002/03: 12^{4}GS, 16^{2}S, 17^{4}GS, 17^{0}GS, 17^{2}GF, 19^{1}GF,

	Starts	1st	2nd	3rd	Win & Pl
NH Flat	1	0	0	0	0
Hurdles	5	1	2	0	7472
Career Total	6	1	2	0	7472

86 4/03 Extr 2m3f D Hdl G-F £5122
Total win prize-money £5122

Going: Sf: 0-1 GS: 0-3 Gd: 0-0 GF: - Fm: 1-2
Distance: 2m/2m3: 1-5 2m4-2m7: 0-0 3m+: 0-0
Track: LH: 0-2 RH: 1-4 Tight: 0-0 Gall: 0-0
Aids: Bl: 0-0 Vi: 0-0 Tstrap: 0-0
Best Rating: 90 12/02 Wwck 2m soft Hdl

Built on some fair performances when winning 19 furlong mares only novices hurdle at Exeter on fast ground April 2003.

Dante's Battle (IRE)

93(108c) 78
11-y-o b/br g Phardante (FR)-No Battle (Khalkis)
Miss K Marks (Noel Meade 2/8) Nick Shutts

Placings:060/20220/011403200/11244/110/02F32F-455P (1112)
2002/03: 16^{4}GF, 17^{5}Y, 17^{5}GF, 21^{2}GF,

	Starts	1st	2nd	3rd	Win & Pl
Hurdles	2	0	0	0	920
Chases	2	0	0	0	
Career Total	35	6	7	2	38929

133 5/00 Rosc 2m5f Ch FRM £5536
117 5/00 Tipp 2m4f Ch FRM £4140
131 6/99 Gowr 2m (0-140)HHdl GD £6138
110 5/99 Baln 2m1f Ch GD £3683
121 7/98 Naas 2m (0-123)HHdl GD £2989
108 6/98 Thur 2m Hdl GD £1935
Total win prize-money £24422

Going: Sf: 0-0 GS: 0-0 Gd: 0-0 GF: - Fm: 0-3
Distance: 2m/2m3: 0-3 2m4-2m7: 0-1 3m+: 0-0
Track: LH: 0-2 RH: 0-1 Tight: 0-0 Gall: 0-0
Aids: Bl: 0-0 Vi: 0-0 Tstrap: 0-0
Best Rating: 133 8/01 Gway 2m1f gd-yld Ch

Dante's Brook (IRE)

93 82
9-y-o ch g Phardante (FR)-Arborfield Brook (Over The River (FR))
B Mactaggart Jim Jeffrey

Placings:0/5600/343P0/334P (1721)
2002/03: 16^{3}GF, 16^{3}G, 17^{4}G, 25^{3}PG,

	Starts	1st	2nd	3rd	Win & Pl
Chases	4	0	0	2	1804
Career Total	14	0	0	4	2879

Going: Sf: 0-0 GS: 0-0 Gd: 0-0 GF: - Fm: 0-1
Distance: 2m/2m3: 0-3 2m4-2m7: 0-0 3m+: 0-1
Track: LH: 0-3 RH: 0-1 Tight: 0-1 Gall: 0-0
Aids: Bl: 0-0 Vi: 0-0 Tstrap: 0-4
Best Rating: 86 5/00 Kels 2m110y gd-fm Hdl

Danteco

106(104h) (95h)100
8-y-o gr g Phardante (FR)-Up Cooke (Deep Run)
Miss Kate Milligan Mrs J M L Milligan

Placings:3/6056/P00O-1FF14212P4 (4620)
2002/03: 16^{0}G, 20^{1}GF, 20^{6}GF, 21^{F}GF, 21^{1}G, 22^{4}G, 21^{2}G, 20^{1}GF, 21^{2}GF, 21^{P}G, 20^{4}GF,

	Starts	1st	2nd	3rd	Win & Pl
Hurdles	3	1	1	0	3731
Chases	8	2	1	0	7458
Career Total	19	3	2	1	11412

94 9/02 Hexm 2m4f110yE(0-110)HCh G-F £3503
95 8/02 Sedg 2m5f110yE(0-100)HHdl GD £2905
94 6/02 Hexm 2m4f110yF Ch G-F £2184
Total win prize-money £8593

Going: Sf: 0-0 GS: 0-0 Gd: 1-5 GF: - Fm: 2-6
Distance: 2m/2m3: 0-1 2m4-2m7: 3-10 3m+: 0-0
Track: LH: 3-10 RH: 0-1 Tight: 1-6 Gall: 0-1
Aids: Bl: 0-0 Vi: 0-0 Tstrap: 0-0
Best Rating: 100 10/02 Sedg 2m5f gd-fm Ch

Modest chaser/hurdler; headstrong type; equally effective over hurdles and fences; stays two miles five furlongs; acts on a sound surface.

Dantes Venture (IRE)

102 99
6-y-o b g Phardante (FR)-Fast Adventure (Deep Run)
D J Caro Mrs J F Billington

Placings:005-223020 (4563)
2002/03: 17^{2}G, 21^{2}S, 20^{3}S, 21^{0}G, 24^{2}G, 24^{0}GF,

	Starts	1st	2nd	3rd	Win & Pl
Hurdles	6	0	3	1	4120
Career Total	9	0	3	1	4120

Going: Sf: 0-2 GS: 0-0 Gd: 0-3 GF: - Fm: 0-1
Distance: 2m/2m3: 0-1 2m4-2m7: 0-3 3m+: 0-0
Track: LH: 0-2 RH: 0-4 Tight: 0-1 Gall: 0-0
Aids: Bl: 0-0 Vi: 0-0 Tstrap: 0-0
Best Rating: 106 11/02 Kemp 2m5f soft Hdl

Continues to knock on the door in long distance novice hurdles and was second for the fourth time at Hereford May 2003.

Dantes Wager (IRE)

94 87
7-y-o b g Phardante (FR)-Gales Wager (Strong Gale)
Miss G Browne Miss S Pilkington

Placings:55P (4310)
2002/03: 16^{5}HY, 22^{5}GS, 24^{P}G,

	Starts	1st	2nd	3rd	Win & Pl
NH Flat	1	0	0	0	0
Hurdles	2	0	0	0	399
Career Total	3	0	0	0	399

Going: Sf: 0-1 GS: 0-1 Gd: 0-1 GF: - Fm: 0-0
Distance: 2m/2m3: 0-1 2m4-2m7: 0-1 3m+: 0-0
Track: LH: 0-2 RH: 0-1 Tight: 0-0 Gall: 0-2
Aids: Bl: 0-0 Vi: 0-0 Tstrap: 0-0
Best Rating: 82 2/03 Winc 2m6f gd-sft Hdl

Dantie Boy (IRE)

105(109h)   (116h)122

7-y-o br g Phardante (FR)-Ballybride Gale (IRE) (Strong Gale)
P J Hobbs Mrs Anona Taylor

Placings:521-51213266   (4614)
2002/03: 22⁵G, 20¹G, 19²F, 19¹GF, 21³G, 19²F, 21⁶GF, 21⁶G,

	Starts	1st	2nd	3rd	Win & Pl
Hurdles	4	1	1	0	4648
Chases	4	1	1	1	8162
Career Total	11	3	3	1	16694
122	10/02	Tntn	2m3f	D Ch	G-F £5427
86	9/02	Worc	2m4f	E Hdl	GD £3073
109	4/02	Extr	2m6f110yE Hdl	FRM £3071

Total win prize-money £11573

Going:	Sf: 0-0 GS: 0-0 Gd: 1-4 GF: - Fm: 1-4
Distance:	2m/2m3: 1-2 2m4-2m7: 1-6 3m+: 0-0
Track:	LH: 1-4 RH: 1-4 **Tight: 1-5** Gall: 0-1
Aids:	Bl: 0-0 Vi: 0-0 Tstrap: 0-0
Best Rating:	122 11/02 Folk 2m5f good Ch

A fair sort over hurdles; won on second start over the larger obstacles at Taunton in October 2002; let down by his jumping next time; suited by two and a half miles; acts on fast ground.

Danton (IRE)

102   96

5-y-o ch g Cadeaux Genereux-Royal Circle (Sadler s Wells (USA))
Miss S J Wilton (M Johnston 20/5) John Pointon And Sons

Placings:64F   (3262)
2002/03: 16⁶G, 16⁴S, 16ᶠGS,

	Starts	1st	2nd	3rd	Win & Pl
Hurdles	3	0	0	0	0
Career Total	3	0	0	0	0

Going:	Sf: 0-1 GS: 0-1 Gd: 0-1 GF: - Fm: 0-0
Distance:	2m/2m3: 0-3 2m4-2m7: 0-0 3m+: 0-0
Track:	LH: 0-3 RH: 0-0 Tight: 0-0 Gall: 0-1
Aids:	Bl: 0-0 Vi: 0-0 Tstrap: 0-0
Best Rating:	96 11/02 Uttx 2m soft Hdl

Danzig Flyer (IRE)

90   43

8-y-o b g Roi Danzig (USA)-Fenland Express (IRE) (Reasonable (FR))
M Mullineaux Mrs Renee Farrington-Kirkham

Placings:000/6P0/600-0F   (0799)
2002/03: 16⁰GF, 21ᶠS,

	Starts	1st	2nd	3rd	Win & Pl
Hurdles	2	0	0	0	
Career Total	11	0	0	0	0

Going:	Sf: 0-1 GS: 0-0 Gd: 0-0 GF: - Fm: 0-1
Distance:	2m/2m3: 0-1 2m4-2m7: 0-0 3m+: 0-0
Track:	LH: 0-1 RH: 0-0 Tight: 0-1 Gall: 0-0
Aids:	Bl: 0-0 Vi: 0-0 Tstrap: 0-0
Best Rating:	65 11/01 Strf 2m110y soft Hdl

Danzig Island (IRE)

98(83h)   (101h)101

12-y-o b g Roi Danzig (USA)-Island Morn (USA) (Our Native (USA))

Mrs H Dalton Mrs S Barber And A B Wood

Placings:443/15013/0F/2P0P/213/P1/2010125-0   (0351)
2002/03: 24⁰GS,

	Starts	1st	2nd	3rd	Win & Pl
Chases	1	0	0	0	
Career Total	27	6	4	3	23388
101	3/02	Leic	2m4f110yE(0-110)HCh	SFT £3318
94	6/01	Worc	2m4f110yD(0-110)HCh	GD £4290
101	4/01	Weth	2m7f	G(0-90)HHdl	G-S £2744
101	3/00	Plum	3m1f110yF(0-100)HHdl	GD £2268
107	2/96	Ludl	2m5f110yE Hdl	GD £2542
100	11/95	Nott	2m5f110yE Hdl	G-F £2461

Total win prize-money £17623

Going:	Sf: 0-0 GS: 0-1 Gd: 0-0 GF: - Fm: 0-0
Distance:	2m/2m3: 0-0 2m4-2m7: 0-0 3m+: 0-1
Track:	LH: 0-1 RH: 0-0 Tight: 0-0 Gall: 0-0
Aids:	Bl: 0-0 Vi: 0-0 Tstrap: 0-0
Best Rating:	107 2/96 Ludl 2m5f110y good Hdl

Winning handicapper over fences on good to soft ground. Has won over three miles, but looks best suited to two and a half of late, particularly when given an uncontested lead. Has had a patchy career due to a series of different injuries, and connections believe he is a horse for a summer campaign.

Daprika (FR)

100   106

5-y-o b m Epervier Bleu-Kaprika (FR) (Cadoudal (FR))
N J Henderson (J Bertran De Balanda 16/9) Thurloe Thoroughbreds V

Placings:454636-154   (3114)
2002/03: 17¹VS, 16⁵S, 16⁴S,

	Starts	1st	2nd	3rd	Win & Pl
Hurdles	2	0	0	0	
Chases	1	1	0	0	14724
Career Total	9	1	0	0	23927
	9/02	Engh	2m1f	Ch	VS £14724

Total win prize-money £14724

Going:	Sf: 0-2 GS: 0-0 Gd: 0-0 GF: - Fm: 0-0
Distance:	2m/2m3: 1-3 2m4-2m7: 0-0 3m+: 0-0
Track:	LH: 0-1 RH: 0-1 Tight: 0-1 Gall: 0-1
Aids:	Bl: 0-0 Vi: 0-0 Tstrap: 0-0
Best Rating:	106 1/03 Hntg 2m110y soft Hdl

Ex-French hurdler/chaser; scored at Enghien in September 2002; modest efforts over hurdles in this country to date.

Darak (IRE)

83   62

7-y-o b g Doyoun-Dararita (IRE) (Halo (USA))
Mrs K J Tutty (Ferdy Murphy 11/5) N D Tutty

Placings:0000150F/40000-B00F4   (1528)
2002/03: 17⁸GF, 16⁸G, 27⁰GF, 21ᶠG, 21⁴G,

	Starts	1st	2nd	3rd	Win & Pl
Hurdles	5	0	0	0	
Career Total	18	1	0	0	3299
92	8/00	Ctml	2m1f110yG(0-90)HHdl	G-S £3298

Total win prize-money £3299

Going:	Sf: 0-0 GS: 0-0 Gd: 0-3 GF: - Fm: 0-2
Distance:	2m/2m3: 0-2 2m4-2m7: 0-2 3m+: 0-1
Track:	LH: 0-5 RH: 0-0 Tight: 0-4 Gall: 0-0
Aids:	Bl: 0-0 Vi: 0-0 Tstrap: 0-0
Best Rating:	92 8/00 Ctml 2m1f110y gd-sft Hdl

Darapour (IRE)

109   139

9-y-o b g Fairy King (USA)-Dawala (IRE) (Lashkari)
Jonjo O Neill J P McManus

Placings:21034/64420/5404/202F/2311546P-P1B   (2466)
2002/03: 20ᴾS, 201GS, 24ᴮG,

	Starts	1st	2nd	3rd	Win & Pl
Hurdles	3	1	0	0	5265
Career Total	29	4	5	2	43056
139	12/02	Sthl	2m4f110yD(0-125)HHdl	G-S £5265
118	8/01	Gway	2m	Hdl	G-Y £6955
135	5/01	Clon	2m4f	Hdl	G-F £4173
132	1/98	Leop	2m	Hdl	Y-S £3573

Total win prize-money £19968

Going:	Sf: 0-1 GS: 1-1 Gd: 0-1 GF: - Fm: 0-0
Distance:	2m/2m3: 0-0 **2m4-2m7: 1-2** 3m+: 0-1
Track:	**LH: 1-3** RH: 0-0 Tight: 1-1 Gall: 0-1
Aids:	Bl: 0-0 Vi: 0-0 Tstrap: 0-0
Best Rating:	139 12/02 Sthl 2m4f110y gd-sft Hdl

A smart hurdler at his very best, he stays well but does not find much off the bridle. Best with ease in the ground, he has won at up to two and a half miles and bounced back to score in facile fashion over that trip at Southwell in December. Fatally injured at Cheltenham. (DEAD)

Daraydan (IRE)

11-y-o b g Kahyasi-Delsy (FR) (Abdos)
D Pipe M C Pipe

Placings:16130321/111400/**11P**506002/021153003/621/0-U   (0317)
2002/03: 34ᵁG,

	Starts	1st	2nd	3rd	Win & Pl
Chases	1	0	0	0	
Career Total	37	11	4	4	73348
115	4/01	NAbb	3m3f	F Hdl	SFT £2331
144	10/99	Chel	3m3f	B(0-145)HHdl	GD £6911
140	6/99	Uttx	2m6f110yB(0-140)HHdl	G-F £5771
104	7/98	Wolv	2m4f110yE Ch	G-F £2959
96	7/98	Worc	2m	E Ch	GD £3345
151	12/97	Chel	2m4f110yB Hdl	G-F £10260
125	11/97	Newb	2m5f	B Hdl	GD £5344
151	10/97	Chel	2m5f	B(0-145)HHdl	G-F £4751
137	4/97	Asct	2m4f	C Hdl	G-F £3728
125	12/96	Chel	2m1f	C Hdl	G-F £3810
121	11/96	Leic	2m	E Hdl	G-S £2924

Total win prize-money £52138

Going:	Sf: 0-0 GS: 0-0 Gd: 0-1 GF: - Fm: 0-0
Distance:	2m/2m3: 0-0 2m4-2m7: 0-0 3m+: 0-1
Track:	LH: 0-1 RH: 0-0 Tight: 0-0 Gall: 0-0
Aids:	Bl: 0-0 Vi: 0-0 Tstrap: 0-0
Best Rating:	151 12/97 Chel 2m4f110y good Hdl

Dardanus

(100h)   (103+h)100+

5-y-o ch g Komaite (USA)-Dance On A Cloud (USA) (Capote (USA))
C J Mann (R J White 7/7) M J & C G Cruddace

Placings:14220   (1692)
2002/03: 18¹GF, 19⁴GF, 18²GF, 18²G, 16⁰G,

	Starts	1st	2nd	3rd	Win & Pl
Hurdles	5	1	2	0	4752
Career Total	5	1	2	0	4752
100	8/02	Font	2m2f110yE Hdl	G-F £2968

Total win prize-money £2968

Going: Sf: 0-0 GS: 0-0 Gd: 0-2 GF: - Fm: 1-3
Distance: 2m/2m3: 1-4 2m4-2m7: 0-1 3m+: 0-0
Track: LH: 1-4 RH: 0-1 Tight: 1-3 Gall: 0-0
Aids: Bl: 0-1 Vi: 0-0 Tstrap: 0-0
Best Rating: 103 10/02 Font 2m2f110y good Hdl

Fair middle-distance handicapper on the Flat; made a winning debut over hurdles in August 2002; slightly disappointing when only fourth next time, but has since bounced back to form at Fontwell; in third place when falling at the last on chasing debut in 2m 4f handicap at Worcester May 2003.

Dare

96   (94c)92

8-y-o b g Beveled (USA)-Run Amber Run (Run The Gantlet (USA))
R Lee J E Potter

Placings:0P/014/2222266/0F211024-04365000   (4058)
2002/03: 17⁰GS, 16⁴S, 20³S, 16⁶S, 15⁵GS, 16⁹HY, 19⁹G, 21⁰S,

	Starts	1st	2nd	3rd	Win & Pl
Hurdles	5	0	0	0	0
Chases	3	0	1		1199
Career Total	28	3	7	1	15528
107 11/01 NAbb	2m1f	F(0-110)HHdl		GD	£2569
112 11/01 Uttx	2m	F(0-110)HHdl		SFT	£2611
79 1/00 Wwck	2m	E(0-105)HHdl		SFT	£2870

Total win prize-money £8050

Going: Sf: 0-5 GS: 0-1 Gd: 0-2 GF: - Fm: 0-0
Distance: 2m/2m3: 0-5 2m4-2m7: 0-3 3m+: 0-0
Track: LH: 0-5 RH: 0-3 Tight: 0-3 Gall: 0-1
Aids: Bl: 0-0 Vi: 0-0 Tstrap: 0-7
Best Rating: 112 4/02 Uttx 2m good Hdl

A fair handicap hurdler at up to two and a half miles. Has won on good but prefers soft ground. Needs a strong pace. Has shown next to nothing so far over fences.

Daretobedifferent (IRE)

84   63

5-y-o ch g Aristocracy-Telmary (Guillaume Tell (USA))
Miss H C Knight Willsford Racing Incorporated

Placings:00FP   (4310)
2002/03: 21⁰GS, 21⁰GS, 22⁶GS, 24⁰G,

	Starts	1st	2nd	3rd	Win & Pl
Hurdles	4	0	0	0	
Career Total	4	0	0	0	

Going: Sf: 0-0 GS: 0-3 Gd: 0-1 GF: - Fm: 0-0
Distance: 2m/2m3: 0-0 2m4-2m7: 0-0 3m+: 0-1
Track: LH: 0-1 RH: 0-3 Tight: 0-0 Gall: 0-1
Aids: Bl: 0-0 Vi: 0-0 Tstrap: 0-0
Best Rating: 94 2/03 Extr 2m6f110y gd-sft Hdl

Darialann (IRE)

(112h)   (129h)114?

8-y-o b g Kahyasi-Delsy (FR) (Abdos)
O Brennan (A L T Moore 2/11) John Sheridan

Placings:6142/4200/5120006-U1F35PP   (4524)
2002/03: 17⁰US, 16¹YS, 17⁵FY, 17³GF, 16⁵YS, 18⁵S, 16⁹HY,

	Starts	1st	2nd	3rd	Win & Pl
Hurdles	2	1	0	0	6985
Chases	5	0	0	1	601
Career Total	22	3	3	1	34278
129 7/02 Gway	2m	Hdl		Y-S	£6984
116 9/01 DRoy	2m	Hdl		FRM	£4173

---

117 1/00 Punc 2m Hdl SFT £3312

Total win prize-money £14470

Going: Sf: 0-2 GS: 0-0 Gd: 0-1 GF: - Fm: 0-1
Distance: 2m/2m3: 1-7 2m4-2m7: 0-0 3m+: 0-0
Track: LH: 0-1 RH: 1-3 Tight: 0-0 Gall: 0-0
Aids: Bl: 1-5 Vi: 0-0 Tstrap: 0-0
Best Rating: 132 8/01 Gway 2m gd-yld Hdl

Darien

92   73

9-y-o b g Sadler s Wells (USA)-Aryenne (FR) (Green Dancer (USA))
R J Price Price Is Right Partnership

Placings:232P03/40   (3263)
2002/03: 19⁴HY, 16⁹GS,

	Starts	1st	2nd	3rd	Win & Pl
Hurdles	2	0	0	0	0
Career Total	8	0	2	2	2650

Going: Sf: 0-1 GS: 0-1 Gd: 0-0 GF: - Fm: 0-0
Distance: 2m/2m3: 0-2 2m4-2m7: 0-0 3m+: 0-0
Track: LH: 0-2 RH: 0-0 Tight: 0-0 Gall: 0-2
Aids: Bl: 0-0 Vi: 0-0 Tstrap: 0-0
Best Rating: 103 12/98 Chep 2m110y good Hdl

Darina's Boy

105   113

7-y-o b g Sula Bula-Glebelands Girl (Burslem)
L Wells L Wells

Placings:3121206   (4789)
2002/03: 18³S, 21¹S, 24²GS, 24¹S, 27²GF, 24⁰G, 24⁶GF,

	Starts	1st	2nd	3rd	Win & Pl
NH Flat	1	0	0	1	318
Hurdles	6	2	2	0	13566
Career Total	7	2	2	1	13884
113 3/03 Bang	3m	D(0-125)HHdl		SFT	£4745
92 1/03 Plum	2m5f	D Hdl		SFT	£4797

Total win prize-money £9542

Going: Sf: 2-3 GS: 0-1 Gd: 0-1 GF: - Fm: 0-2
Distance: 2m/2m3: 0-1 2m4-2m7: 1-1 3m+: 1-5
Track: LH: 2-4 RH: 0-1 Tight: 2-4 Gall: 0-1
Aids: Bl: 0-0 Vi: 0-0 Tstrap: 0-0
Best Rating: 113 3/03 Font 3m3f gd-fm Hdl

Fair hurdler; stays three miles three; acts on decent and soft ground; progressive.

Daring Native (IRE)

10-y-o b/br g Be My Native (USA)-Scarlet Tina (Dusky Boy)
J M Ratcliffe (P J Millington 26/5) J M Ratcliffe

Placings:000PP4/033/P-0   (0503)
2002/03: 26⁰G,

	Starts	1st	2nd	3rd	Win & Pl
Chases	1	0	0	0	
Career Total	11	0	0	2	1113

Going: Sf: 0-0 GS: 0-0 Gd: 0-1 GF: - Fm: 0-0
Distance: 2m/2m3: 0-0 2m4-2m7: 0-0 3m+: 0-1
Track: LH: 0-1 RH: 0-0 Tight: 0-0 Gall: 0-0
Aids: Bl: 0-0 Vi: 0-0 Tstrap: 0-0
Best Rating: 82 2/01 Weth 3m1f soft Ch

Daring News

97   70

8-y-o b g Risk Me (FR)-Hot Sunday Sport (Star Appeal)
O O Neill Michael J Brown

Placings:01U5/52/0P/6-006P   (4571)
2002/03: 19⁹GS, 19⁹GS, 16⁶GF, 16⁶GF,

	Starts	1st	2nd	3rd	Win & Pl
Hurdles	4	0	0	0	
Career Total	13	1	1	0	2612
83 3/99 Towc	2m	G Hdl		GD	£1674

Total win prize-money £1674

Going: Sf: 0-0 GS: 0-2 Gd: 0-0 GF: - Fm: 0-2
Distance: 2m/2m3: 0-3 2m4-2m7: 0-1 3m+: 0-0
Track: LH: 0-2 RH: 0-1 Tight: 0-2 Gall: 0-0
Aids: Bl: 0-0 Vi: 0-0 Tstrap: 0-0
Best Rating: 89 6/99 Worc 2m4f gd-fm Hdl

Daring Thomas

96

8-y-o b g Derrylin-Dawn Encounter (Rymer)
D M Grissell Barry & Baroness Noakes

Placings:0455443/5-P   (1727)
2002/03: 20⁰GS,

	Starts	1st	2nd	3rd	Win & Pl
Hurdles	1	0	0	0	
Career Total	9	0	0	1	377

Going: Sf: 0-0 GS: 0-1 Gd: 0-0 GF: - Fm: 0-0
Distance: 2m/2m3: 0-0 2m4-2m7: 0-1 3m+: 0-0
Track: LH: 0-0 RH: 0-1 Tight: 0-0 Gall: 0-0
Aids: Bl: 0-0 Vi: 0-0 Tstrap: 0-0
Best Rating: 96 4/01 Font 2m6f110y good Hdl

Daringly

85   85

14-y-o b g Daring March-Leylandia (Wolver Hollow)
G F Bridgwater (Michael Appleby 4/5) Michael Appleby

Placings:0001503P0P404/UPF24/P0000P/612P/4P/5P/PP
P004P6/P5605350/522340P05203P5P0-P54P00P (1041)
2002/03: 25⁶GF, 21⁵G, 22⁴GF, 24⁶GF, 21⁰GF, 26⁹GF, 26⁶GF,

	Starts	1st	2nd	3rd	Win & Pl
Chases	7	0	0	0	533
Career Total	71	2	5	4	14493
88 6/96 MRas	2m6f110yD(0-105)HCh		G-F	£4107
80 11/93 Uttx	2m	Hdl		GD	£1864

Total win prize-money £5972

Going: Sf: 0-0 GS: 0-0 Gd: 0-1 GF: - Fm: 0-6
Distance: 2m/2m3: 0-0 2m4-2m7: 0-3 3m+: 0-4
Track: LH: 0-4 RH: 0-1 Tight: 0-5 Gall: 0-0
Aids: Bl: 0-0 Vi: 0-0 Tstrap: 0-0
Best Rating: 93 11/93 Newb 2m5f good Hdl

Moderate, veteran chaser with a poor strike rate. Best on fast ground.

Dark Buccaneer

30f

5-y-o b g Sovereign Water (FR)-Some Cherry (Some Hand)
J Wade John Wade

Placings:0   (1982)
2002/03: 16⁹HY,

	Starts	1st	2nd	3rd	Win & Pl
NH Flat	1	0	0	0	

Career Total	1	0	0	0

Going: Sf: 0-1 GS: 0-0 Gd: 0-0 GF: - Fm: 0-0
Distance: 2m/2m3: 0-1 2m4-2m7: 0-0 3m+: 0-0
Track: LH: 0-1 RH: 0-0 Tight: 0-0 Gall: 0-0
Aids: Bl: 0-0 Vi: 0-0 Tstrap: 0-0
Best Rating: 30 11/02 Weth 2m   heavy NHF

Dark Character
107f   99f

4-y-o b g Reprimand-Poyle Jezebelle (Sharpo)
G A Swinbank Leading Star Racing Group

Placings:216   (4481)
2002/03: 16²GS, 16¹GF, 17⁶G,

	Starts	1st	2nd	3rd	Win & Pl
NH Flat	3	1	1	0	2993
Career Total	3	1	1	0	2993
99	3/03	Sthl	2m	H NHF	G-F	£1967

Total win prize-money £1967

Going: Sf: 0-0 GS: 0-1 Gd: 0-1 GF: - Fm: 1-1
Distance: 2m/2m3: 1-3 2m4-2m7: 0-0 3m+: 0-0
Track: LH: 1-2 RH: 0-0 Tight: 1-1 Gall: 0-0
Aids: Bl: 0-0 Vi: 0-0 Tstrap: 0-0
Best Rating: 99 4/03 Aint 2m1f   good NHF

Made up for an unlucky defeat on debut when clear-cut winner of a bumper at Southwell in March.

Dark Crusader (IRE)
95

8-y-o br g Cajetano (USA)-Glissade (Furry Glen)
Miss Lucinda V Russell Brahms & Liszt

Placings:42204P/4311PP/44PPP-P   (1111)
2002/03: 24⁰GF,

	Starts	1st	2nd	3rd	Win & Pl
Hurdles	1	0	0	0	
Career Total	18	2	2	1	7782
118	12/00	Folk	2m4f110yE Hdl	HVY	£2621
118	11/00	Towc	2m5f	E Hdl	£2275

Total win prize-money £4897

Going: Sf: 0-0 GS: 0-0 Gd: 0-0 GF: - Fm: 0-0
Distance: 2m/2m3: 0-0 2m4-2m7: 0-0 3m+: 0-1
Track: LH: 0-1 RH: 0-0 Tight: 0-0 Gall: 0-0
Aids: Bl: 0-1 Vi: 0-0 Tstrap: 0-0
Best Rating: 118 12/00 Folk 2m4f110y heavy Hdl

Dark Fairy
98   118+

5-y-o br m Tragic Role (USA)-Sharp Fairy (Sharpo)
M C Pipe D A Johnson

Placings:12403-33314   (1404)
2002/03: 16³S, 16²GF, 20³G, 22¹GF, 20⁴GF,

	Starts	1st	2nd	3rd	Win & Pl
Hurdles	5	1	0	3	8514
Career Total	10	2	1	4	13708
118	7/02	NAbb	2m6f	C(0-130)HHdl	G-F	£6325
111	10/01	Hrfd	2m1f	E Hdl	G-S	£2593

Total win prize-money £8919

Going: Sf: 0-1 GS: 0-0 Gd: 0-1 GF: - Fm: 1-3
Distance: 2m/2m3: 0-2 2m4-2m7: 1-3 3m+: 0-0
Track: LH: 1-5 RH: 0-0 Tight: 1-3 Gall: 0-0
Aids: Bl: 0-0 Vi: 0-0 Tstrap: 0-0
Best Rating: 118 7/02 NAbb 2m6f   gd-fm Hdl

Bought for 21,000gns after winning a ten-furlong seller at Leicester in September 2001, she won on her hurdling debut at Hereford, but her limitations have been exposed subsequently. Landed an uncompetitive event when stepped up to 22 furlongs at Newton Abbot July 2002. Seems to handle most types of ground.

Dark Island

8-y-o b g Silver Season-Isle Maree (Star Appeal)
Mary Meek Mrs Mary Meek

Placings:P   (3901)
2002/03: 24ᴾS,

	Starts	1st	2nd	3rd	Win & Pl
Hurdles	1	0	0	0	
Career Total	1	0	0	0	

Going: Sf: 0-1 GS: 0-0 Gd: 0-0 GF: - Fm: 0-0
Distance: 2m/2m3: 0-0 2m4-2m7: 0-0 3m+: 0-0
Track: LH: 0-1 RH: 0-0 Tight: 0-0 Gall: 0-1
Aids: Bl: 0-0 Vi: 0-0 Tstrap: 0-0
Best Rating: 0 4/03 Extr 2m6f110y gd-fm Hdl

Dark Mandate (IRE)

5-y-o b/br m Mandalus-Ceoltoir Dubh (Black Minstrel)
J S Haldane Mrs Hugh Fraser

Placings:P   (4504)
2002/03: 16ᴾG,

	Starts	1st	2nd	3rd	Win & Pl
Hurdles	1	0	0	0	
Career Total	1	0	0	0	

Going: Sf: 0-0 GS: 0-0 Gd: 0-1 GF: - Fm: 0-0
Distance: 2m/2m3: 0-0 2m4-2m7: 0-0 3m+: 0-0
Track: LH: 0-1 RH: 0-0 Tight: 0-0 Gall: 0-0
Aids: Bl: 0-0 Vi: 0-0 Tstrap: 0-0
Best Rating: 0 4/03 Kels 2m110y good Hdl

Dark Room (IRE)
106   116

6-y-o b g Toulon-Maudlin Bridge (IRE) (Strong Gale)
Jonjo O Neill J P McManus

Placings:U-6U51223P0   (4307)
2002/03: 20⁶S, 22ᵁGS, 21⁵HY, 25¹S, 24²S, 24²GS, 22³S, 32ᴾG, 32⁰G,

	Starts	1st	2nd	3rd	Win & Pl
Chases	9	1	2	1	8396
Career Total	10	1	2	1	8396
112	12/02	MRas	3m1f	E(0-105)HCh	SFT	£4212

Total win prize-money £4212

Going: Sf: 1-5 GS: 0-2 Gd: 0-2 GF: - Fm: 0-0
Distance: 2m/2m3: 0-0 2m4-2m7: 0-0 3m+: 1-5
Track: LH: 0-4 RH: 1-4 Tight: 1-5 Gall: 0-2
Aids: Bl: 0-0 Vi: 0-0 Tstrap: 0-0
Best Rating: 116 2/03 Newb 2m6f110y soft Ch

Fair novice chaser; stays well; acts on soft ground.

Dark Shadows
101   101

8-y-o b g Machiavellian (USA)-Instant Desire (USA) (Northern Dancer)

W Storey D O Cremin

Placings:4020/066-2PP2   (4225)
2002/03: 16²GS, 16ᴾGS, 16ᴾS, 20²GF,

	Starts	1st	2nd	3rd	Win & Pl
Hurdles	4	0	2	0	1733
Career Total	11	0	3	0	2229

Going: Sf: 0-1 GS: 0-2 Gd: 0-0 GF: - Fm: 0-1
Distance: 2m/2m3: 0-3 2m4-2m7: 0-1 3m+: 0-0
Track: LH: 0-3 RH: 0-1 Tight: 0-1 Gall: 0-1
Aids: Bl: 0-0 Vi: 0-0 Tstrap: 0-0
Best Rating: 106 3/00 MRas 1m5f110y gd-fm NHF

Returned to form when runner-up in a modest novices hurdle run on fast ground at Wetherby in March.

Dark Society
87

5-y-o b g Imp Society (USA)-No Candles Tonight (Star Appeal)
A W Carroll Group 1 Racing (1994) Ltd

Placings:26523023-4P   (3598)
2002/03: 16⁴HY, 17ᴾS,

	Starts	1st	2nd	3rd	Win & Pl
Hurdles	2	0	0	0	269
Career Total	10	0	3	2	2461

Going: Sf: 0-2 GS: 0-0 Gd: 0-0 GF: - Fm: 0-0
Distance: 2m/2m3: 0-2 2m4-2m7: 0-0 3m+: 0-0
Track: LH: 0-0 RH: 0-2 Tight: 0-1 Gall: 0-0
Aids: Bl: 0-0 Vi: 0-0 Tstrap: 0-0
Best Rating: 87 4/02 Sedg 2m1f   gd-fm Hdl

Moderate two-mile hurdler. Can travel well in his races but tends to find little under pressure. Suited by soft ground.

Dark Victor (IRE)
92   84

7-y-o b g Cadeaux Genereux-Dimmer (Kalaglow)
D Shaw The Higham Partnership

Placings:30/05050   (3508)
2002/03: 16³S, 16⁵S, 16⁹S, 16²G, 16⁰G,

	Starts	1st	2nd	3rd	Win & Pl
Hurdles	5	0	0	0	0
Career Total	7	0	0	1	247

Going: Sf: 0-3 GS: 0-0 Gd: 0-2 GF: - Fm: 0-0
Distance: 2m/2m3: 0-5 2m4-2m7: 0-0 3m+: 0-0
Track: LH: 0-5 RH: 0-0 Tight: 0-0 Gall: 0-1
Aids: Bl: 0-0 Vi: 0-0 Tstrap: 0-0
Best Rating: 91 1/00 Catt 2m   good NHF

Moderate handicapper on the Flat, well beaten on all starts over hurdles.

Dark'n Sharp (GER)
109(116h)   (134h)155

8-y-o b g Sharpo-Daytona Beach (GER) (Konigsstuhl (GER))
R T Phillips Ascot Five Plus One

Placings:11316/F2311-3F332U   (4604)
2002/03: 16³GS, 16ᶠS, 16³G, 16³G, 16²G, 21ᵁG,

	Starts	1st	2nd	3rd	Win & Pl
Hurdles	1	0	0	1	5500
Chases	5	0	1	2	32450
Career Total	16	5	2	5	101854

117	4/02	Ayr	2m	C Ch	GD	£6191
151	4/02	Aint	2m	A HCh	GD	£34800
129	2/01	Newc	2m	B HHdl	HVY	£8329
125	12/00	Donc	2m110y	E Hdl	G-S	£2978
109	11/00	Newc	2m	D Hdl	G-S	£3016

Total win prize-money £55316

Going:	Sf: 0-1 GS: 0-1 Gd: 0-4 GF: - Fm: 0-0
Distance:	2m/2m3: 0-5 2m4-2m7: 0-1 3m+: 0-0
Track:	LH: 0-4 RH: 0-2 Tight: 0-1 Gall: 0-2
Aids:	Bl: 0-0 Vi: 0-0 Tstrap: 0-0
Best Rating:	155 4/03 Aint 2m good Ch

Smart chaser; won over fences at Aintree and Ayr in 2002 and third in the Grand Annual at the Cheltenham Festival; creditable third to Young Devereaux in Grade Two chase at Kempton this season before repeating his third place at the Festival; yet to prove he stays further than two miles; best on good ground, although does handle soft.

Darmil (IRE)

110

10-y-o br g Welsh Term-Ballinkillen (Levmoss)
I A Duncan M J Millar

Placings:050510/F0F51002/F320PP/1-P   (3324)
2002/03: 20PG,

	Starts	1st	2nd	3rd	Win & Pl
Chases	1	0	0	0	
Career Total	22	3	2	1	16283
110	10/01	Dpat	3m	(0-102)HCh	G-Y	£4173
104	1/00	Fair	2m5f110y	Ch	SFT	£3864
101	4/99	DRoy	3m	Hdl	YLD	£3069

Total win prize-money £11106

Going:	Sf: 0-0 GS: 0-0 Gd: 0-1 GF: - Fm: 0-0
Distance:	2m/2m3: 0-0 2m4-2m7: 0-1 3m+: 0-0
Track:	LH: 0-0 RH: 0-1 Tight: 0-0 Gall: 0-0
Aids:	Bl: 0-0 Vi: 0-0 Tstrap: 0-0
Best Rating:	110 10/01 Dpat 3m gd-yld Ch

Darnley

103   104

6-y-o b/br g Henbit (USA)-Reeling (Relkino)
J N R Billinge Sceptre House Golf Society

Placings:0-0PF34   (4772)
2002/03: 16QG, 17PS, 16FS, 16QG, 16QG,

	Starts	1st	2nd	3rd	Win & Pl
NH Flat	1	0	0	0	
Hurdles	4	0	0	1	1571
Career Total	6	0	0	1	1571

Going:	Sf: 0-2 GS: 0-0 Gd: 0-3 GF: - Fm: 0-0
Distance:	2m/2m3: 0-5 2m4-2m7: 0-0 3m+: 0-0
Track:	LH: 0-3 RH: 0-2 Tight: 0-1 Gall: 0-0
Aids:	Bl: 0-0 Vi: 0-0 Tstrap: 0-0
Best Rating:	104 4/03 Ayr 2m good Hdl

Moderate novice hurdler; best efforts on good ground.

Darrell Boy (IRE)

80   74

8-y-o b g Commanche Run-Free For Ever (Little Buskins)
J R Norton L & R Racing

Placings:00/04P50P33P1-65   (3124)
2002/03: 20⁶HY, 20⁵HY,

	Starts	1st	2nd	3rd	Win & Pl
Hurdles	2	0	0	0	0
Career Total	14	1	0	2	2360

74	3/02	Sedg	3m3f110yG(0-90)HHdl	SFT	£1841

Total win prize-money £1841

Going:	Sf: 0-2 GS: 0-0 Gd: 0-0 GF: - Fm: 0-0
Distance:	2m/2m3: 0-0 2m4-2m7: 0-2 3m+: 0-0
Track:	LH: 0-1 RH: 0-1 Tight: 0-0 Gall: 0-1
Aids:	Bl: 0-0 Vi: 0-2 Tstrap: 0-0
Best Rating:	91 5/01 Newc 2m gd-fm NHF

Plating-class hurdler, often wears blinkers or visor. Successful over a marathon trip at Sedgefield in March 2002.

Dash For Gold

95   65

4-y-o gr f Highest Honor (FR)-Dashing Water (Dashing Blade)
J Hetherton R G Fell

Placings:0P4044000   (4262)
2002/03: 16QGF, 16PGS, 16⁴S, 16QG, 17⁴S, 21⁴HY, 20⁰S, 17QGS, 17QG,

	Starts	1st	2nd	3rd	Win & Pl
Hurdles	9	0	0	0	0
Career Total	9	0	0	0	0

Going:	Sf: 0-4 GS: 0-2 Gd: 0-2 GF: - Fm: 0-1
Distance:	2m/2m3: 0-7 2m4-2m7: 0-2 3m+: 0-0
Track:	LH: 0-7 RH: 0-2 Tight: 0-5 Gall: 0-2
Aids:	Bl: 0-2 Vi: 0-0 Tstrap: 0-0
Best Rating:	77 11/02 Newc 2m soft Hdl

Dash Of Magic

68   32

5-y-o b m Magic Ring (IRE)-Praglia (IRE) (Darshaan)
J Hetherton 21st Century Racing

Placings:0   (3830)
2002/03: 16QG,

	Starts	1st	2nd	3rd	Win & Pl
Hurdles	1	0	0	0	0
Career Total	1	0	0	0	0

Going:	Sf: 0-0 GS: 0-0 Gd: 0-1 GF: - Fm: 0-0
Distance:	2m/2m3: 0-1 2m4-2m7: 0-0 3m+: 0-0
Track:	LH: 0-1 RH: 0-0 Tight: 0-0 Gall: 0-0
Aids:	Bl: 0-0 Vi: 0-0 Tstrap: 0-0
Best Rating:	32 2/03 Weth 2m good Hdl

Plating-class handicapper on the Flat; no wrothwhile form over hurdles.

Dashing Dollar (IRE)

85   52

12-y-o b g Lord Americo-Cora Swan (Tarqogan)
J R Payne R J Payne

Placings:0/06 f120/440/1/F00113/0U0065/10P405020-5PF0P5   (4692)
2002/03: 22⁵G, 27PS, 22FG, 19⁰GS, 24PGS, 22⁵G,

	Starts	1st	2nd	3rd	Win & Pl
Hurdles	6	0	0	0	0
Career Total	38	6	2	1	23712
119	5/01	Extr	2m6f110yE(0-115)HHdl	G-S	£3346
121	4/00	Extr	3m3f110yD(0-125)HHdl	HVY	£3753
114	3/00	Extr	2m7f	E(0-115)HHdl	G-S	£3315
116	11/98	Wind	2m6f110yD(0-125)HHdl	GD	£5303
114	11/96	Clon	2m	Hdl	Y-S	£2295
118	11/96	Clon	2m	NHF	YLD	£2648

Total win prize-money £20661

Going:	Sf: 0-1 GS: 0-2 Gd: 0-3 GF: - Fm: 0-0
Distance:	2m/2m3: 0-1 2m4-2m7: 0-3 3m+: 0-2
Track:	LH: 0-3 RH: 0-3 Tight: 0-3 Gall: 0-0
Aids:	Bl: 0-0 Vi: 0-0 Tstrap: 0-0
Best Rating:	121 4/00 Extr 2m3f110y heavy Hdl

Fairly useful handicap hurdler who is versatile as regards ground and stays two miles-six. Goes particularly well at Exeter.

Dashing Home (IRE)

113   127

4-y-o b g Lahib (USA)-Dashing Rose (Mashhor Dancer (USA))
Noel Meade Mrs P Towey

Placings:213301   (4724a)
2002/03: 16²G, 16¹HY, 16²S, 16³HY, 17QG, 16¹GF,

	Starts	1st	2nd	3rd	Win & Pl
Hurdles	6	2	1	2	20292
Career Total	6	2	1	2	20292
122	4/03	Fair	2m	Hdl	G-F	£9496
110	11/02	DRoy	2m	Hdl	HVY	£6349

Total win prize-money £15847

Going:	Sf: 1-3 GS: 0-1 Gd: 0-0 GF: - Fm: 1-1
Distance:	2m/2m3: 2-6 2m4-2m7: 0-0 3m+: 0-0
Track:	LH: 0-2 RH: 1-2 Tight: 0-0 Gall: 0-1
Aids:	Bl: 0-0 Vi: 0-0 Tstrap: 0-0
Best Rating:	124 3/03 Chel 2m1f good Hdl

Useful juvenile hurdler; acts in heavy ground; effective over two miles.

Dashing Steve

75   45

4-y-o b g Danzig Connection (USA)-Blazing Sunset (Blazing Saddles (AUS))
Mrs A M Thorpe (M D Hammond 28/1) D A Jones

Placings:00P   (4733)
2002/03: 16QG, 16QGS, 16PGF,

	Starts	1st	2nd	3rd	Win & Pl
Hurdles	3	0	0	0	
Career Total	3	0	0	0	

Going:	Sf: 0-0 GS: 0-1 Gd: 0-1 GF: - Fm: 0-1
Distance:	2m/2m3: 0-3 2m4-2m7: 0-0 3m+: 0-0
Track:	LH: 0-3 RH: 0-0 Tight: 0-2 Gall: 0-0
Aids:	Bl: 0-0 Vi: 0-0 Tstrap: 0-0
Best Rating:	45 11/02 Catt 2m good Hdl

Dat My Horse (IRE)

101(105h)   (122h)99

9-y-o b g All Haste (USA)-Toposki (FR) (Top Ville)
P G Murphy A Lowrie & Mrs J Lowrie

Placings:F5/P/FF-111023034P   (3846)
2002/03: 26¹GF, 24¹G, 24¹GF, 24⁸GF, 25²GF, 19³G, 22⁰HY, 23³GS, 20⁴S, 24P,

	Starts	1st	2nd	3rd	Win & Pl
Hurdles	7	3	1	1	12739
Chases	3	0	0	1	1230
Career Total	15	3	1	2	13969
122	6/02	MRas	3m	E Hdl	G-F	£2565
113	5/02	Towc	3m	D Hdl	GD	£3250
116	5/02	Hrld	3m2f	D Hdl	G-F	£3150

Total win prize-money £8966

Going:	Sf: 0-2 GS: 0-1 Gd: 1-3 GF: - Fm: 2-4

Distance: 2m/2m3: 0-0 2m4-2m7: 0-3 3m+: 3-7
Track: LH: 0-2 RH: 3-8 Tight: 1-5 Gall: 0-1
Aids: Bl: 0-0 Vi: 0-0 Tstrap: 0-0
Best Rating: 122 11/02 Hrfd 2m3f110y good Hdl

Winning pointer; modest hurdler; stays 3m 2f; acts on fast ground, handles softer.

Daughter In Law (IRE)

95   66

10-y-o b m Law Society (USA)-Colonial Line (USA) (Plenty Old (USA))
Miss C J E Caroe Miss C J E Caroe

Placings:P0040P3/0035P000/33205500/0400600/P2P-604P   (0770)
2002/03: 21PGS, 21⁶G, 19⁰GF, 24⁴G, 20PGF,

	Starts	1st	2nd	3rd	Win & Pl
Hurdles	5	0	0	0	0
Career Total	37	0	2	4	2223

Going: Sf: 0-0 GS: 0-1 Gd: 0-2 GF: - Fm: 0-2
Distance: 2m/2m3: 0-0 2m4-2m7: 0-4 3m+: 0-1
Track: LH: 0-2 RH: 0-3 Tight: 0-1 Gall: 0-1
Aids: Bl: 0-0 Vi: 0-0 Tstrap: 0-5
Best Rating: 81 5/99 Towc 2m soft Hdl

Plating-class hurdler. Best at around two and a half miles, likes fast ground, usually tongue tied.

Dave The Bank

8-y-o ch g Desert Dirham (USA)-L Ancressaan (Dalsaan)
T H Caldwell R Cabrera-Vargas

Placings:P/P   (3367)
2002/03: 20PGS,

	Starts	1st	2nd	3rd	Win & Pl
Hurdles	1	0	0	0	
Career Total	2	0	0	0	

Going: Sf: 0-0 GS: 0-1 Gd: 0-0 GF: - Fm: 0-0
Distance: 2m/2m3: 0-0 2m4-2m7: 0-0 3m+: 0-0
Track: LH: 0-1 RH: 0-0 Tight: 0-1 Gall: 0-0
Aids: Bl: 0-0 Vi: 0-0 Tstrap: 0-0
Best Rating: 0 1/03 Sthl 2m4f110y gd-sft Hdl

Davenport Democrat (IRE)

97f   111+f

5-y-o ch h Fourstars Allstar (USA)-Storm Court (IRE) (Glacial Storm (USA))
W P Mullins Mrs N O Callaghan

Placings:010   (4115)
2002/03: 16⁶S, 16¹YS, 16⁶G,

	Starts	1st	2nd	3rd	Win & Pl
NH Flat	3	1	0	0	4481
Career Total	3	1	0	0	4481
111 2/03 Fair 2m			NHF	Y-S	£4480

Total win prize-money £4481

Going: Sf: 0-1 GS: 0-0 Gd: 0-0 GF: 0-1 Fm: 0-0
Distance: 2m/2m3: 1-3 2m4-2m7: 0-0 3m+: 0-0
Track: LH: 0-1 RH: 1-1 Tight: 0-0 Gall: 0-0
Aids: Bl: 0-0 Vi: 0-0 Tstrap: 0-0
Best Rating: 111 2/03 Fair 2m yld-sft NHF

Davenport Milenium (IRE)

123   158

7-y-o b g Insan (USA)-Society Belle (Callernish)
W P Mullins Mrs N O Callaghan

Placings:12/1F5111-3   (2684)
2002/03: 16³S,

	Starts	1st	2nd	3rd	Win & Pl
Hurdles	1	0	0	1	8250
Career Total	9	5	1	1	116991
158 4/02 Punc 2m		Hdl		G-Y	£49693
154 4/02 Punc 2m4f		Hdl		GD	£34233
140 3/02 Fair 2m2f		Hdl		G-Y	£7975
120 12/01 Fair 2m2f		Hdl		YLD	£6677
132 2/01 Leop 2m		NHF		HVY	£5564

Total win prize-money £104143

Going: Sf: 0-1 GS: 0-0 Gd: 0-0 GF: - Fm: 0-0
Distance: 2m/2m3: 0-2 2m4-2m7: 0-0 3m+: 0-0
Track: LH: 0-0 RH: 0-1 Tight: 0-0 Gall: 0-0
Aids: Bl: 0-0 Vi: 0-0 Tstrap: 0-0
Best Rating: 158 4/02 Punc 2m gd-yld Hdl

High-class Irish hurdler; scored three times in the spring of 2002 including two Grade Ones within the space of three days at the Punchestown Festival; finished 9l 3rd to Intersky Falcon in Christmas Hurdle at Kempton on his return; reportedly does not want the ground too soft; effective from 2m to 2m 4f; met a setback early in 2003.

Davoski

105(101h)   (122h)155

9-y-o b g Niniski (USA)-Pamela Peach (Habitat)
Miss Venetia Williams Sir Robert Ogden

Placings:113132142210/1/16120/34-13430   (3525)
2002/03: 16¹GS, 16³G, 16⁴S, 16³HY, 16⁹G,

	Starts	1st	2nd	3rd	Win & Pl
Hurdles	1	0	0	0	0
Chases	4	1	0	2	27363
Career Total	25	9	4	5	100044
155 11/02 Asct 2m		A(0-150)HCh		G-S	£17835
152 12/00 Chel 2m110y		B HCh		SFT	£13663
140 10/00 Strf 2m5f110yC(0-135)HCh				SFT	£6890
134 10/99 Fknm 2m5f110yC Ch				GD	£8135
136 4/99 Uttx 2m		C(0-135)HHdl		G-S	£5083
134 1/99 Kemp 2m		D Hdl		SFT	£2944
121 11/98 NAbb 2m1f		E(0-110)HHdl		SFT	£2684
114 10/98 Uttx 2m		E Hdl		GD	£2431
98 9/98 Hrfd 2m1f		E Hdl		G-F	£2430

Total win prize-money £62097

Going: Sf: 0-2 GS: 1-1 Gd: 0-2 GF: - Fm: 0-0
Distance: 2m/2m3: 1-5 2m4-2m7: 0-3 3m+: 0-0
Track: LH: 0-3 RH: 1-2 Tight: 0-0 Gall: 0-2
Aids: Bl: 0-0 Vi: 0-0 Tstrap: 0-0
Best Rating: 155 11/02 Asct 2m gd-sft Ch

Very useful chaser; developed into a real good handicapper in 2000/2001 before being sidelined for a year with leg trouble; returned with a good third in the Victor Chandler in January 2002; won on his reappearance at Ascot this season; stays two miles five, but seems most effective at the minimum trip; effective on all grounds; best when fresh.

Davy's Image

9-y-o ch g Milieu-Reigate Head (Timber King)
B Bousfield Mrs D A Bousfield

Placings:0P/PP-P   (2103)

Dawn Court

74   40

6-y-o b m Rakaposhi King-Herald The Dawn (Dubassoff (USA))
R H Alner Mrs U Wainwright

Placings:0-P00   (4290)
2002/03: 19PGS, 19⁰S, 22⁰GF,

	Starts	1st	2nd	3rd	Win & Pl
Hurdles	3	0	0	0	
Career Total	4	0	0	0	

Going: Sf: 0-1 GS: 0-1 Gd: 0-0 GF: - Fm: 0-1
Distance: 2m/2m3: 0-0 2m4-2m7: 0-3 3m+: 0-0
Track: LH: 0-0 RH: 0-3 Tight: 0-2 Gall: 0-0
Aids: Bl: 0-0 Vi: 0-0 Tstrap: 0-0
Best Rating: 52 4/02 Font 2m2f110y gd-fm NHF

Dawn Fox (IRE)

72   54

7-y-o ch m Phardante (FR)-Golden Vixen (Goldhill)
N G Ayliffe D T Hooper

Placings:06-P60P   (1812)
2002/03: 17PS, 19⁶GF, 17⁰GF, 17PG,

	Starts	1st	2nd	3rd	Win & Pl
Hurdles	4	0	0	0	0
Career Total	6	0	0	0	0

Going: Sf: 0-1 GS: 0-0 Gd: 0-1 GF: - Fm: 0-2
Distance: 2m/2m3: 0-3 2m4-2m7: 0-1 3m+: 0-0
Track: LH: 0-2 RH: 0-2 Tight: 0-2 Gall: 0-0
Aids: Bl: 0-0 Vi: 0-0 Tstrap: 0-0
Best Rating: 54 7/02 NAbb 2m1f gd-fm Hdl

Dawn's Cognac (IRE)

10-y-o b g Glacial Storm (USA)-Misty Venture (Foggy Bell)
D Brace David Brace

Placings:U/PP   (3674)
2002/03: 24PG, 26PGS,

	Starts	1st	2nd	3rd	Win & Pl
Chases	2	0	0	0	
Career Total	3	0	0	0	

Going: Sf: 0-0 GS: 0-1 Gd: 0-1 GF: 0-0 Fm: 0-0
Distance: 2m/2m3: 0-0 2m4-2m7: 0-0 3m+: 0-2
Track: LH: 0-1 RH: 0-1 Tight: 0-1 Gall: 0-0
Aids: Bl: 0-0 Vi: 0-0 Tstrap: 0-0
Best Rating: 0 2/03 Font 3m2f110y gd-sft Ch

Day Du Roy (FR)

5-y-o b g Ajdayt (USA)-Rose Pomme (FR) (Rose Laurel)
Jonjo O Neill (F Danloux 23/11) Mrs Mo Done

Placings:001PP (3442)
2002/03: 18^{0}VS, 17^{0}VS, 19^{1}HO, 19^{P}G, 16^{P}HY,

	Starts	1st	2nd	3rd	Win & Pl
Hurdles	1	0	0	0	
Chases	4	1	0	0	4712
Career Total	**5**	**1**	**0**	**0**	**4712**
11/02 Fntb	2m3f	Ch		HLD	£4712
				Total win prize-money	£4712

Going: Sf: 0-1 GS: 0-0 Gd: 0-1 GF: - Fm: 0-0
Distance: 2m/2m3: 1-5 2m4-2m7: 0-0 3m+: 0-0
Track: LH: 0-2 RH: 0-0 Tight: 0-0 Gall: 0-0
Aids: Bl: 0-0 Vi: 0-0 Tstrap: 0-0
Best Rating: 0 3/03 Bang 3m110y good Ch

Winner of a four-year-olds chase in France in November. Started favourite at Doncaster in January but pulled too hard then blundered and was pulled up.

Day Lewis

7-y-o b g Golden Heights-Darling Dianne (IRE) (Burslem)
Jonjo O Neill Day Lewis Group

Placings:0P (1601)
2002/03: 17^{0}G, 20^{P}G,

	Starts	1st	2nd	3rd	Win & Pl
NH Flat	1	0	0	0	0
Hurdles	1	0	0	0	
Career Total	**2**	**0**	**0**	**0**	

Going: Sf: 0-0 GS: 0-0 Gd: 0-2 GF: - Fm: 0-0
Distance: 2m/2m3: 0-1 2m4-2m7: 0-1 3m+: 0-0
Track: LH: 0-1 RH: 0-1 Tight: 0-0 Gall: 0-0
Aids: Bl: 0-0 Vi: 0-0 Tstrap: 0-0
Best Rating: 77 5/02 Extr 2m1f good NHF

Daytime Dawn (IRE)

12-y-o b g Rashar (USA)-Ard Clos (Ardoon)
R N C Wale (Mrs P Robeson 19/7) R N C Wale

Placings:F0/564/00/U1/1/0/4-PP (4288)
2002/03: 17^{P}GF, 20^{P}GF,

	Starts	1st	2nd	3rd	Win & Pl
Chases	2	0	0	0	
Career Total	**14**	**2**	**0**	**0**	**4455**
108 4/00 Hrfd	2m	H Ch		GD	£2012
88 4/99 Hrfd	2m3f	H Ch		G-F	£2442
				Total win prize-money	£4455

Going: Sf: 0-0 GS: 0-0 Gd: 0-0 GF: - Fm: 0-2
Distance: 2m/2m3: 0-1 2m4-2m7: 0-0 3m+: 0-0
Track: LH: 0-1 RH: 0-1 Tight: 0-1 Gall: 0-0
Aids: Bl: 0-0 Vi: 0-0 Tstrap: 0-0
Best Rating: 108 4/00 Hrfd 2m good Ch

Dazzling Rio (IRE)

99   94
4-y-o b g Ashkalani (IRE)-Dazzling Fire (IRE) (Bluebird (USA))
P C Haslam Rio Stainless Engineering Limited

Placings:P2634 (2473)
2002/03: 16^{P}GF, 16^{2}GF, 16^{8}GF, 16^{3}G, 16^{4}G,

	Starts	1st	2nd	3rd	Win & Pl
Hurdles	5	0	1	1	1575
Career Total	**5**	**0**	**1**	**1**	**1575**

Going: Sf: 0-0 GS: 0-0 Gd: 0-2 GF: - Fm: 0-3
Distance: 2m/2m3: 0-5 2m4-2m7: 0-0 3m+: 0-0
Track: LH: 0-4 RH: 0-1 Tight: 0-3 Gall: 0-1
Aids: Bl: 0-0 Vi: 0-0 Tstrap: 0-0
Best Rating: 94 11/02 Catt 2m good Hdl

Returned after a barren spell when narrowly denied in novices hurdle at Cartmel in July.

Db My Son

99   (70h) 110+
7-y-o b g Gildoran-Rolling Dice (Balinger)
P F Nicholls (V Bowens 28/9) A P Brady

Placings:000P-F02146F10 (3136)
2002/03: 24^{F}S, 16^{3}GF, 16^{2}GF, 20^{1}G, 17^{4}S, 24^{6}G, 19^{F}F, 19^{1}S, 20^{P}S,

	Starts	1st	2nd	3rd	Win & Pl
Chases	9	2	1	0	11356
Career Total	**13**	**2**	**1**	**0**	**11356**
110 12/02 Tntn	2m3f	F(0-95)HCh		SFT	£4420
103 8/02 Tral	2m4f	Ch		GD	£5291
				Total win prize-money	£9711

Going: Sf: 1-4 GS: 0-0 Gd: 1-2 GF: - Fm: 0-3
Distance: 2m/2m3: 1-5 2m4-2m7: 1-2 3m+: 0-2
Track: LH: 0-0 RH: 1-3 Tight: 1-2 Gall: 0-0
Aids: Bl: 0-0 Vi: 0-0 Tstrap: 0-0
Best Rating: 110 12/02 Tntn 2m3f soft Ch

Ex-Irish, he won a novice chase at Taunton on his British debut. Acts on good and soft ground.

Dd's Glenalla (IRE)

102f   90f
6-y-o b m Be My Native (USA)-Willowho Pride (Arapaho)
N A Twiston-Davies (I R Ferguson 21/6) Mrs Caroline Beresford-Wylie

Placings:0620P (4611)
2002/03: 16^{6}S, 17^{P}HY, 18^{2}S, 16^{9}S, 17^{P}G,

	Starts	1st	2nd	3rd	Win & Pl
NH Flat	5	0	1	0	552
Career Total	**5**	**0**	**1**	**0**	**552**

Going: Sf: 0-4 GS: 0-0 Gd: 0-1 GF: - Fm: 0-0
Distance: 2m/2m3: 0-5 2m4-2m7: 0-0 3m+: 0-0
Track: LH: 0-3 RH: 0-1 Tight: 0-2 Gall: 0-1
Aids: Bl: 0-0 Vi: 0-0 Tstrap: 0-0
Best Rating: 90 2/03 Font 2m2f110y soft NHF

Modest bumper form.

De Oralie (IRE)

100   72
10-y-o ch g Tremblant-Tsing Tao (He Loves Me)
A J Lockwood A J Lockwood

Placings:0000/360350/00PF65/U0/PP-003 (0625)
2002/03: 17^{0}GF, 17^{0}GF, 17^{3}GF,

	Starts	1st	2nd	3rd	Win & Pl
Hurdles	3	0	0	1	250
Career Total	**23**	**0**	**0**	**3**	**848**

Going: Sf: 0-0 GS: 0-0 Gd: 0-0 GF: - Fm: 0-3
Distance: 2m/2m3: 0-3 2m4-2m7: 0-0 3m+: 0-0
Track: LH: 0-0 RH: 0-3 Tight: 0-3 Gall: 0-0
Aids: Bl: 0-0 Vi: 0-0 Tstrap: 0-0
Best Rating: 92 5/98 Klny 2m1f yld-sft NHF

Headstrong plater.

Dead Aim (IRE)

(87h)   (63h)
9-y-o b g Sadler s Wells (USA)-Dead Certain (Absalom)
N Wilson Mrs Karan Ridley

Placings:53/44/2P/P60F (4589)
2002/03: 17^{P}HY, 17^{6}GS, 20^{9}G, 25^{F}G,

	Starts	1st	2nd	3rd	Win & Pl
Hurdles	3	0	0	0	0
Chases	1	0	0	0	
Career Total	**10**	**0**	**1**	**1**	**1223**

Going: Sf: 0-1 GS: 0-1 Gd: 0-2 GF: - Fm: 0-0
Distance: 2m/2m3: 0-2 2m4-2m7: 0-1 3m+: 0-1
Track: LH: 0-3 RH: 0-1 Tight: 0-2 Gall: 0-1
Aids: Bl: 0-0 Vi: 0-0 Tstrap: 0-0
Best Rating: 90 9/00 Sedg 2m1f good Hdl

Dead-Eyed Dick (IRE)

102(82h)   (76h) 109d
7-y-o b g Un Desperado (FR)-Glendale Charmer (Down The Hatch)
Nick Williams Mrs Jane Williams

Placings:00/05P-01FP6P (4095)
2002/03: 24^{9}G, 23^{1}GS, 21^{F}G, 22^{P}S, 24^{6}S, 24^{P}HY,

	Starts	1st	2nd	3rd	Win & Pl
Hurdles	1	0	0	0	0
Chases	5	1	0	0	4466
Career Total	**11**	**1**	**0**	**0**	**4466**
102 12/02 Extr	2m7f110yD(0-105)HCh			G-S	£4465
				Total win prize-money	£4466

Going: Sf: 0-3 GS: 1-1 Gd: 0-2 GF: - Fm: 0-0
Distance: 2m/2m3: 0-0 2m4-2m7: 0-0 3m+: 1-4
Track: LH: 0-2 RH: 1-3 Tight: 0-3 Gall: 0-1
Aids: Bl: 0-0 Vi: 0-0 Tstrap: 0-0
Best Rating: 109 12/02 Chel 2m5f good Ch

Got off the mark on his chasing debut in a small novice handicap at Exeter December 2002. Still going well when falling three out in Class B novice event at Cheltenham next time.

Deadly Doris

86   63
9-y-o b m Ron s Victory (USA)-Camp Chair (Ela-Mana-Mou)
N A Smith Stan Hey And Partners

Placings:540/55600/5042U25355/15655-40P (4566)
2002/03: 16^{4}GS, 16^{P}HY, 20^{P}GF,

	Starts	1st	2nd	3rd	Win & Pl
Hurdles	3	0	0	0	0
Career Total	**26**	**1**	**2**	**1**	**4195**
92 11/01 Towc	2m	E Hdl		SFT	£2618
				Total win prize-money	£2618

Going: Sf: 0-1 GS: 0-1 Gd: 0-0 GF: - Fm: 0-1
Distance: 2m/2m3: 0-2 2m4-2m7: 0-1 3m+: 0-0
Track: LH: 0-1 RH: 0-2 Tight: 0-1 Gall: 0-0
Aids: Bl: 0-0 Vi: 0-0 Tstrap: 0-0
Best Rating: 94 1/99 Hntg 2m110y soft NHF

Modest hurdler, suited by two miles and soft ground; has worn blinkers.

Dealer Del
111   103+
9-y-o b g Deltic (USA)-No Deal (Sharp Deal)
C J Down Mrs Hazel Leeves

Placings:053-51P2UP   (4483)
2002/03: 21⁵GF, 22¹G, 28PG, 24²GS, 32UG, 25PGF,

	Starts	1st	2nd	3rd	Win & Pl
Chases	6	1	1	0	4202
Career Total	9	1	1	1	4693
103 5/02 Towc 2m6f	H Ch			GD	£2847

Total win prize-money £2847

Going:	Sf: 0-0 GS: 0-1 Gd: 1-3 GF: - Fm: 0-2
Distance:	2m/2m3: 0-0 2m4-2m7: 1-2 3m+: 0-4
Track:	LH: 0-4 RH: 1-3 Tight: 0-2 Gall: 0-2
Aids:	Bl: 0-0 Vi: 0-0 Tstrap: 0-0
Best Rating:	103 2/03 Tntn 3m gd-sft Ch

Moderate hunter/handicap chaser; pulled up between winning at Hereford and Newton Abbot in May/June 2003; stays 3m 2f; acts on any ground; inconsistent and suffers from back problems.

Dealer's Choice (IRE)
105(103h)   (109+h)121
9-y-o gr g Roselier (FR)-Cam Flower Vii (Damsire Unregistered)
M Pitman P Duffy, G King, D Roberts, B Savage

Placings:1/2F65F5/U/261P1P-21PFU   (4570)
2002/03: 22²GS, 21¹S, 24PS, 20FGS, 20UG,

	Starts	1st	2nd	3rd	Win & Pl
Hurdles	1	0	1	0	968
Chases	4	1	0	0	5200
Career Total	19	4	3	0	18738
121 12/02 Folk 2m5f	D(0-120)HCh	SFT		£5200
121 3/02 Ludl 2m4f	D(0-115)HCh	SFT		£5148
108 12/01 Ludl 2m4f	F(0-95)HCh		GD	£3887
97 4/99 Font 2m2f110yH	NHF		GD	£1567

Total win prize-money £15802

Going:	Sf: 1-2 GS: 0-2 Gd: 0-1 GF: - Fm: 0-0
Distance:	2m/2m3: 0-0 2m4-2m7: 1-4 3m+: 0-1
Track:	LH: 0-2 RH: 1-3 Tight: 1-2 Gall: 0-1
Aids:	Bl: 0-0 Vi: 0-0 Tstrap: 0-0
Best Rating:	121 12/02 Folk 2m5f soft Ch

Decent chaser, but just modest hurdler; stays two miles five furlongs; suited by an easy surface and a sharp track.

Deano's Beeno
127   160
11-y-o b g Far North (CAN)-Sans Dot (Busted)
M C Pipe Axom

Placings:105/111/2105/12215/1210/00-23121612   (4789)
2002/03: 23²G, 24³S, 25¹S, 23²GS, 24¹G, 24⁴G, 24²GI,

	Starts	1st	2nd	3rd	Win & Pl
Hurdles	8	3	3	1	117151
Career Total	29	12	7	1	232841
160 4/03 Asct	3m	A Hdl	GD	£23200
160 2/03 Kemp	3m110y	A Hdl	GD	£23800
173 12/02 Asct	3m1f110yA Hdl	SFT	£40200
176 11/01 Donc	3m110y	A Hdl	GD	£15780
176 11/00 Newb	3m110y	A Hdl	SFT	£13800
153 2/00 Newb	3m	C Ch	G-S	£6474

---

176 11/99 Newb	3m110y	A Hdl	G-S	£13100
174 1/99 Hayd	2m7f110yA Hdl	SFT	£12440
153 12/97 Bang	3m	B(0-140)HHdl	GD	£4783
154 11/97 Hayd	2m6f	B HHdl	SFT	£4883
148 11/97 NAbb	2m6f	D(0-125)HHdl	SFT	£2762
134 12/96 NAbb	2m1f	D Hdl	SFT	£2911

Total win prize-money £164135

Going:	Sf: 1-2 GS: 0-1 Gd: 2-4 GF: - Fm: 0-1
Distance:	2m/2m3: 0-0 2m4-2m7: 0-0 3m+: 3-8
Track:	LH: 0-4 RH: 3-3 Tight: 0-0 Gall: 0-2
Aids:	Bl: 0-0 Vi: 0-0 Tstrap: 0-0
Best Rating:	176 1/01 Donc 3m110y good Hdl

High-class staying hurdler; took the scalp of Baracouda in the Long Walk Hurdle at Ascot in December 2002 under an inspired McCoy ride and landed Grade 2 Rendlesham Hurdle at Kempton in February; returned to Ascot to land the Long Distance Hurdle in April; often shows signs of temperament; best on a flat, left-handed track; goes well fresh; needs to dominate.

Dear Deal
108   123
10-y-o b g Sharp Deal-The Deer Hound (Cash And Carry)
C Tizzard J A G Meaden

Placings:665/2443/11/32P4-2220S22P   (2585)
2002/03: 26²GF, 23²G, 26²G, 32UGF, 26⁵GF, 26²S, 25²GS, 23PGS,

	Starts	1st	2nd	3rd	Win & Pl
Chases	8	0	5	0	7192
Career Total	21	2	7	2	17811
121 10/00 Winc	2m6f	E Hdl	G-S	£2506
118 9/00 Extr	2m6f110yE Hdl	GD	£2632

Total win prize-money £5138

Going:	Sf: 0-1 GS: 0-2 Gd: 0-2 GF: - Fm: 0-3
Distance:	2m/2m3: 0-0 2m4-2m7: 0-0 3m+: 0-3
Track:	LH: 0-3 RH: 0-3 Tight: 0-4 Gall: 0-0
Aids:	Bl: 0-2 Vi: 0-0 Tstrap: 0-0
Best Rating:	123 12/02 Winc 3m1f110y gd-sft Ch

Formerly a useful hurdler, he missed the whole of 2001, but has shown ability over fences since returning in January 2002. Stays three miles plus, is suited by soft ground, but has won no faster.

Dear Lord (IRE)
82   61
6-y-o ch g Mister Lord (USA)-Carange (Known Fact (USA))
Mrs A M Thorpe Mrs Sarajane Holden

Placings:0P0P   (3933)
2002/03: 25⁰S, 19PGS, 20⁰G, 22PS,

	Starts	1st	2nd	3rd	Win & Pl
Hurdles	3	0	0	0	0
Chases	1	0	0	0	0
Career Total	4	0	0	0	0

Going:	Sf: 0-2 GS: 0-0 Gd: 0-1 GF: - Fm: 0-0
Distance:	2m/2m3: 0-0 2m4-2m7: 0-3 3m+: 0-1
Track:	LH: 0-2 RH: 0-2 Tight: 0-1 Gall: 0-1
Aids:	Bl: 0-0 Vi: 0-0 Tstrap: 0-0
Best Rating:	61 2/03 Hntg 2m4f110y good Hdl

Deb's Son
96   86
6-y-o b g Minster Son-Deb s Ball (Glenstal (USA))
James Moffatt (D Moffatt 16/12) Mr & Mrs A G Milligan

Placings:32403/613040-6P01   (4518)

2002/03: 17⁶GS, 22PHY, 21⁰G, 21¹G,

	Starts	1st	2nd	3rd	Win & Pl
Hurdles	4	1	0	0	2352
Career Total	15	2	1	3	7568
86 4/03 Sedg	2m5f110yG(0-100)HHdl	GD	£2352
100 8/01 Ctml	2m6f	E Hdl	G-S	£3115

Total win prize-money £5467

Going:	Sf: 0-1 GS: 0-1 Gd: 1-2 GF: - Fm: 0-0
Distance:	2m/2m3: 0-1 2m4-2m7: 1-3 3m+: 0-0
Track:	LH: 1-3 RH: 0-1 Tight: 1-3 Gall: 0-0
Aids:	Bl: 0-0 Vi: 1-1 Tstrap: 0-0
Best Rating:	100 8/01 Ctml 2m6f gd-sft Hdl

Modest hurdler, won a seller in first-time visor at Sedgefield in April 2003; stays two miles-six plus, suited by cut in the ground; has worn cheekpieces.

Decisive
69   67
4-y-o b g Alhaarth (IRE)-Alys (Blakeney)
P R Webber (W J Haggas 2/10) Peter S Jensen

Placings:0   (3392)
2002/03: 16⁰HY,

	Starts	1st	2nd	3rd	Win & Pl
Hurdles	1	0	0	0	
Career Total	1	0	0	0	

Going:	Sf: 0-1 GS: 0-0 Gd: 0-0 GF: - Fm: 0-0
Distance:	2m/2m3: 0-0 2m4-2m7: 0-0 3m+: 0-0
Track:	LH: 0-0 RH: 0-1 Tight: 0-0 Gall: 0-0
Aids:	Bl: 0-0 Vi: 0-0 Tstrap: 0-0
Best Rating:	67 2/03 Sand 2m110y heavy Hdl

Moderate middle-distance maiden on the Flat.

Deckie (IRE)
108(102h)   (110h)111
8-y-o b g Be My Native (USA)-Shannon Spray (Le Bavard (FR))
C Roche J P McManus

Placings:0006003/11F0-063310353   (2407a)
2002/03: 24⁰S, 22⁶G, 22³GY, 23³F, 20¹GF, 16⁸G, 16³S, 25⁵G, 16³SH,

	Starts	1st	2nd	3rd	Win & Pl
Hurdles	2	0	0	0	
Chases	7	1	0	4	9110
Career Total	20	3	0	5	20804
106 9/02 Kbgn	2m4f	Ch	G-F	£5291
110 8/01 Gway	2m2f	(0-116)HHdl	G-Y	£6677
129 7/01 Tipp	2m4f	NHF	G-F	£4451

Total win prize-money £16420

Going:	Sf: 0-2 GS: 0-0 Gd: 0-3 GF: - Fm: 1-2
Distance:	2m/2m3: 0-3 2m4-2m7: 1-4 3m+: 0-0
Track:	LH: 0-2 RH: 0-1 Tight: 0-1 Gall: 0-0
Aids:	Bl: 0-0 Vi: 0-0 Tstrap: 1-1
Best Rating:	129 7/01 Tipp 2m4f gd-fm NHF

Modest Irish handicapper, stays two and a half miles, acts on any ground.

Decoded
102   85
7-y-o ch g Deploy-Golden Panda (Music Boy)
C Grant Mrs H E Aitkin

Placings:431260/56/663F65-14P   (3162)
2002/03: 25¹GF, 27⁴S, 25PG,

	Starts	1st	2nd	3rd	Win & Pl
Chases	3	1	0	0	4317

Career Total	17	2	1	2	9221
85	10/02 Kels	3m1f	E Ch	G-F	£4056
94	1/00 Ayr	2m4f	E Hdl	SFT	£2723
			Total win prize-money £6779		

Going: Sf: 0-1 GS: 0-0 Gd: 0-1 GF: - Fm: 1-1
Distance: 2m/2m3: 0-0 2m4-2m7: 0-0 3m+: 1-3
Track: LH: 1-3 RH: 0-0 Tight: 1-3 Gall: 0-0
Aids: Bl: 0-0 Vi: 0-0 Tstrap: 0-0
Best Rating: 94 1/00 Ayr 2m4f soft Hdl

Plating-class chaser; stays three miles one furlong; acts on any ground; has worn cheekpieces.

Deep King (IRE)

8-y-o b/br g King s Ride-Splendid Run (Deep Run)
J W Mullins (Martin M Treacy 10/9) Miss Dinah Wilkins

Placings:143OUP3 (4630)
2002/03: 20¹GF, 23⁴F, 17³S, 20⁰S, 20⁰S, 25ᵖG, 17³GF,

	Starts	1st	2nd	3rd	Win & Pl
Chases	7	1	0	2	7394
Career Total	7	1	0	2	7394
80	7/02 Wxfd 2m4f	Ch		G-F	£5291
		Total win prize-money £5291			

Going: Sf: 0-3 GS: 0-0 Gd: 0-1 GF: - Fm: 1-3
Distance: 2m/2m3: 0-2 2m4-2m7: 1-4 3m+: 0-1
Track: LH: 0-2 RH: 1-4 Tight: 0-2 Gall: 0-0
Aids: Bl: 0-0 Vi: 0-0 Tstrap: 1-2
Best Rating: 100 8/02 Tipp 2m7f firm Ch

Modest chaser; winner over fences in Ireland; no promise in this country; stays two and a half miles.

Deep Sigh

6-y-o b g Weld-At Long Last (John French)
D R Gandolfo Mrs John Lee

Placings:50P (3784)
2002/03: 17⁵HY, 18⁰HY, 19ᵖG,

	Starts	1st	2nd	3rd	Win & Pl
NH Flat	2	0	0	0	0
Hurdles	1	0	0	0	0
Career Total	3	0	0	0	0

Going: Sf: 0-2 GS: 0-0 Gd: 0-1 GF: - Fm: 0-0
Distance: 2m/2m3: 0-2 2m4-2m7: 0-1 3m+: 0-0
Track: LH: 0-2 RH: 0-1 Tight: 0-1 Gall: 0-0
Aids: Bl: 0-0 Vi: 0-0 Tstrap: 0-0
Best Rating: 84 11/02 NAbb 2m1f heavy NHF

Deep Sunset (IRE)
110(100c)   (117+c)128
7-y-o b m Supreme Leader-Twinkle Sunset (Deep Run)
N J Henderson R A Ballin

Placings:132/2144-4451F22 (4610)
2002/03: 16⁴HY, 16⁴S, 16⁵G, 20¹G, 21ᶠS, 16²G, 21²G,

	Starts	1st	2nd	3rd	Win & Pl
Hurdles	5	0	2	0	18155
Chases	2	1	0	0	6760
Career Total	14	3	4	1	39336
117	2/03 Ludl	2m4f	D Ch	GD	£6760
106	12/01 Hntg	2m4f110yD Hdl		G-S	£3601
103	12/00 Ludl	2m	H NHF	SFT	£1708
			Total win prize-money £12069		

Going: Sf: 0-3 GS: 0-0 Gd: 1-4 GF: - Fm: 0-0

Distance: 2m/2m3: 0-4 2m4-2m7: 1-3 3m+: 0-0
Track: LH: 0-3 RH: 1-4 Tight: 1-1 Gall: 0-1
Aids: Bl: 0-0 Vi: 0-0 Tstrap: 0-0
Best Rating: 128 1/03 Kemp 2m good Hdl

Fair handicap hurdler; made a winning chase debut in February 2003; fell next time so returned to hurdles to finish runner-up at Ayr and Cheltenham in April; suited by two and a half miles; acts on good and soft ground.

Deep Water (USA)
109(110h)   (122h)128
9-y-o b g Diesis-Water Course (USA) (Irish River (FR))
M D Hammond The County Set

Placings:1121/5/410/0211F0P/03336-4032411 (4229)
2002/03: 20⁴GS, 20⁰G, 16³GS, 16²GS, 20⁴GS, 17¹S, 16¹GF,

	Starts	1st	2nd	3rd	Win & Pl
Hurdles	5	0	1	1	4556
Chases	2	2	0	0	10722
Career Total	27	8	3	4	86050
128	3/03 Weth	2m	D(0-120)HCh	G-F	£5378
126	3/03 MRas	2m1f110yD(0-120)HCh	SFT	£5343
123	12/00 MRas	2m1f110yD Ch	SFT	£5421
115	11/00 Catt	2m	D Ch	GD	£4173
140	2/00 Hayd	2m	B Hdl	SFT	£14490
146	4/98 Aint	2m110y A Hdl	GD	£28334
126	2/98 Kels	2m110y C Hdl	G-S	£4065
100	1/98 Kels	2m110y D Hdl	HVY	£3025
			Total win prize-money £70230		

Going: Sf: 1-1 GS: 0-4 Gd: 0-1 GF: - Fm: 1-1
Distance: 2m/2m3: 2-4 2m4-2m7: 0-3 3m+: 0-0
Track: LH: 0-1 RH: 1-1 Tight: 1-2 Gall: 0-0
Aids: Bl: 0-0 Vi: 0-0 Tstrap: 0-0
Best Rating: 146 4/98 Aint 2m110y good Hdl

Fair hurdler/chaser nowadays; back over fences when successful at Market Rasen in March and followed up in game fashion at Wetherby two weeks later; stays two and a half miles plus; acts on good and soft ground.

Deepritive

6-y-o b m Primitive Rising (USA)-Last Of The Deep (IRE) (Deep Run)
R Hollinshead M A Connors

Placings:000-P (4641)
2002/03: 19ᵖGF,

	Starts	1st	2nd	3rd	Win & Pl
Hurdles	1	0	0	0	
Career Total	4	0	0	0	

Going: Sf: 0-0 GS: 0-0 Gd: 0-0 GF: 0-0 Fm: 0-1
Distance: 2m/2m3: 0-1 2m4-2m7: 0-0 3m+: 0-0
Track: LH: 0-1 RH: 0-0 Tight: 0-1 Gall: 0-0
Aids: Bl: 0-0 Vi: 0-0 Tstrap: 0-0
Best Rating: 77 3/02 MRas 2m1f110y gd-sft NHF

Chasing-bred who has shown some ability in bumpers.

Deer Dolly (IRE)

6-y-o b m Welsh Term-Wild Deer (Royal Buck)
P Butler Mrs E Lucey-Butler

Placings:P (4277)
2002/03: 20ᵖGF,

	Starts	1st	2nd	3rd	Win & Pl
Hurdles	1	0	0	0	
Career Total	1	0	0	0	

Going: Sf: 0-0 GS: 0-0 Gd: 0-0 GF: - Fm: 0-1
Distance: 2m/2m3: 0-0 2m4-2m7: 0-1 3m+: 0-0
Track: LH: 0-0 RH: 0-0 Tight: 0-1 Gall: 0-0
Aids: Bl: 0-0 Vi: 0-0 Tstrap: 0-0
Best Rating: 0 3/03 Font 2m4f gd-fm Hdl

Deer Park Lass (IRE)
91(95h)   (72h)82
11-y-o ch m Mister Lord (USA)-Adare Flore (IRE) (Fairbairn)
R Johnson Mrs C Lawson-Croome

Placings:5B/P/0RP06R025244-P00 (2305)
2002/03: 16⁴G, 21ᵖS, 19⁰G, 16⁰GS,

	Starts	1st	2nd	3rd	Win & Pl
Hurdles	2	0	0	0	0
Chases	2	0	0	0	228
Career Total	18	0	2	0	2999

Going: Sf: 0-1 GS: 0-1 Gd: 0-2 GF: - Fm: 0-0
Distance: 2m/2m3: 0-3 2m4-2m7: 0-1 3m+: 0-0
Track: LH: 0-4 RH: 0-0 Tight: 0-3 Gall: 0-1
Aids: Bl: 0-0 Vi: 0-0 Tstrap: 0-0
Best Rating: 82 3/02 Sedg 2m110y soft Ch

Still a maiden over hurdles and fences, but acts on soft ground and is effective over two miles.

Deferlant (FR)
106(108c)   (116c)108
6-y-o ch g Bering-Sail Storm (USA) (Topsider (USA))
Mrs H Dalton Mrs G McNeela

Placings:123120/622224300-342111F40040F (4712)
2002/03: 17³GF, 17⁴G, 21²GF, 17¹G, 16¹GS, 20¹GS, 16ᶠG, 16⁴GS, 17⁰GS, 19⁰G, 16⁴GF, 16⁰GF, 16ᶠGF,

	Starts	1st	2nd	3rd	Win & Pl
Hurdles	4	0	0	0	763
Chases	9	3	1	1	17405
Career Total	28	5	7	3	34945
125	8/02 Worc	2m4f110yE Ch	G-S	£3575
101	8/02 Prth	2m	D Ch	G-S	£6695
114	7/02 Strf	2m1f110yD Ch	GD	£4728
115	12/00 Newb	2m110y D Hdl	SFT	£3786
110	7/00 MRas	2m1f110yD Hdl	G-F	£3477
			Total win prize-money £22263		

Going: Sf: 0-0 GS: 2-4 Gd: 1-4 GF: - Fm: 0-5
Distance: 2m/2m3: 2-10 2m4-2m7: 1-3 3m+: 0-0
Track: LH: 2-9 RH: 1-4 Tight: 1-5 Gall: 0-1
Aids: Bl: 0-0 Vi: 3-13 Tstrap: 0-0
Best Rating: 130 8/01 Strf 2m110y gd-fm Hdl

Fair hurdler, decent chaser; often finishes weakly over fences; stays in excess of two and a half miles; usually visored, generally jumps well.

Definite Flash (IRE)
69   44
5-y-o b m Definite Article-Superflash (Superlative)
M Wellings The 1471 Racing Partnership

Placings:0P (3864)
2002/03: 16⁶GS, 19ᵖGS,

	Starts	1st	2nd	3rd	Win & Pl
Hurdles	2	0	0	0	
Career Total	2	0	0	0	

Going: Sf: 0-0 GS: 0-2 Gd: 0-0 GF: - Fm: 0-0
Distance: 2m/2m3: 0-1 2m4-2m7: 0-1 3m+: 0-0
Track: LH: 0-2 RH: 0-0 Tight: 0-0 Gall: 0-0
Aids: Bl: 0-0 Vi: 0-0 Tstrap: 0-0
Best Rating: 44 2/03 Hayd 2m   gd-sft Hdl

Definite Return (IRE)

5-y-o ch m Definite Article-Keen Note (Sharpo)
D J Wintle D J Wintle

Placings:P   (4021)
2002/03: 17PS,

	Starts	1st	2nd	3rd	Win & Pl
Hurdles	1	0	0	0	
Career Total	1	0	0	0	

Going: Sf: 0-1 GS: 0-0 Gd: 0-0 GF: - Fm: 0-0
Distance: 2m/2m3: 0-1 2m4-2m7: 0-0 3m+: 0-0
Track: LH: 0-0 RH: 0-0 Tight: 0-0 Gall: 0-0
Aids: Bl: 0-0 Vi: 0-0 Tstrap: 0-0
Best Rating: 0 3/03 Hrfd 2m1f   soft Hdl

Del Trotter (IRE)

103(98c)   (113c)99
8-y-o b g King Luthier-Arctic Alice (Brave Invader (USA))
J Howard Johnson Group Captain J A Prideaux

Placings:006140/50000S01-F163435   (4795)
2002/03: 17FS, 16¹S, 17RS, 17³S, 16⁴G, 16³G, 21SGF,

	Starts	1st	2nd	3rd	Win & Pl
Hurdles	5	0	0	2	897
Chases	2	1	0	0	4056
Career Total	21	3	0	2	15945
113	11/02	Sedg	2m110y	E(0-110)HCh	SFT	£4056
113	3/02	Wxfd	2m	Ch	SFT	£7407
108	12/00	Clon	2m	NHF	SH	£3312

Total win prize-money £14776

Going: Sf: 1-4 GS: 0-0 Gd: 0-2 GF: - Fm: 0-1
Distance: 2m/2m3: 1-6 2m4-2m7: 0-1 3m+: 0-0
Track: LH: 1-7 RH: 0-0 Tight: 1-5 Gall: 0-1
Aids: Bl: 0-0 Vi: 0-0 Tstrap: 0-0
Best Rating: 113 11/02 Sedg 2m110y   soft Ch

Modest ex-Irish hurdler/chaser; scored on his second start over fences in this country at Sedgefield in November 2002; subsequently reverted to hurdles; seemingly better on a soft surface.

Delaware (FR)

108(99c)   (144c)112d
7-y-o ch g Garde Royale-L Indienne (FR) (Le Nain Jaune (FR))
M C Pipe Sandicroft Stud II

Placings:2/4/005U1B21F/62F-0322112304   (2307)
2002/03: 17⁰G, 20³G, 17²S, 17²G, 22¹GF, 22¹S, 24²GF, 21³G, 18⁰GS, 21⁴HY,

	Starts	1st	2nd	3rd	Win & Pl
Hurdles	10	2	3	2	10498
Career Total	24	4	6	2	33126
97	8/02	Strf	2m6f110yD	Hdl	SFT	£4043
112	6/02	NAbb	2m6f	E(0-105)HHdl	G-F	£2618
113	2/01	Ludl	2m4f	E Ch	GD	£3484
	7/00	Autl	2m1f110y	Ch	HVY	£6244

Total win prize-money £16389

Going: Sf: 1-3 GS: 0-1 Gd: 0-4 GF: - Fm: 1-2
Distance: 2m/2m3: 0-4 2m4-2m7: 2-5 3m+: 0-1
Track: LH: 2-9 RH: 0-1 Tight: 2-7 Gall: 0-0
Aids: Bl: 0-0 Vi: 2-10 Tstrap: 0-0
Best Rating: 134 2/02 Winc 2m5f   gd-sft Ch

Modest hurdler/chaser; French import; effective over fences and hurdles, stays two and three-quarter miles; has won on all types of ground; usually visored.

Delaware Bay

99   87
4-y-o ch g Karinga Bay-Galacia (IRE) (Gallic League)
R H Alner A P Hedditch

Placings:0545   (2781)
2002/03: 17⁰G, 16⁵GS, 16⁴GS, 19⁵S,

	Starts	1st	2nd	3rd	Win & Pl
Hurdles	4	0	0	0	0
Career Total	4	0	0	0	0

Going: Sf: 0-1 GS: 0-2 Gd: 0-1 GF: - Fm: 0-0
Distance: 2m/2m3: 0-3 2m4-2m7: 0-1 3m+: 0-0
Track: LH: 0-0 RH: 0-4 Tight: 0-0 Gall: 0-0
Aids: Bl: 0-0 Vi: 0-0 Tstrap: 0-0
Best Rating: 87 12/02 Winc 2m   gd-sft Hdl

Delgany Royal (IRE)

112(108h)   (117h)123
11-y-o b g Denel (FR)-Glen Of Erin (Furry Glen)
D T Hughes Glen Devlin

Placings:00P1PP0/440F06/P23U11212350P/6310P04-64364U45600   (4499a)
2002/03: 16⁸YS, 24⁴S, 22³S, 24⁶HY, 24⁴S, 24⁰G, 28⁴SH, 28⁵S, 20⁶Y, 24⁰GY, 24⁰GY,

	Starts	1st	2nd	3rd	Win & Pl
Hurdles	3	0	0	1	515
Chases	8	0	0	0	5056
Career Total	44	5	3	4	54256
131	12/01	Fair	3m1f	HCh	YLD	£15725
118	12/00	Leop	2m5f	(0-116)HCh	SH	£6072
114	11/00	Punc	2m2f	(0-116)HCh	HVY	£4968
109	10/00	Fair	2m4f	(0-109)HCh	GD	£3312
99	2/99	Gowr	2m2f	Ch	SH	£5217

Total win prize-money £35296

Going: Sf: 0-5 GS: 0-0 Gd: 0-1 GF: - Fm: 0-0
Distance: 2m/2m3: 0-2 2m4-2m7: 0-2 3m+: 0-8
Track: LH: 0-6 RH: 0-1 Tight: 0-0 Gall: 0-1
Aids: Bl: 0-0 Vi: 0-0 Tstrap: 0-0
Best Rating: 131 12/01 Fair 3m1f   yield Ch

Best at around three miles, he has a good weight-carrying record and is suited by testing conditions. Jumps soundly.

Deliceo (IRE)

97   89
10-y-o br g Roselier (FR)-Grey s Delight (Decent Fellow)
M Sheppard The Blues Partnership

Placings:1/0035204/36332412P4P/21462443FP-U14010   (4192)
2002/03: 25PGS, 24US, 19¹G, 20⁴GF, 19⁰S, 20¹GS, 20⁰G,

	Starts	1st	2nd	3rd	Win & Pl
Hurdles	1	0	0	0	0
Chases	6	2	0	0	9367
Career Total	35	5	5	5	27294
89	2/03	Leic	2m4f110yE(0-105)HCh	G-S	£4953
82	11/02	Hrfd	2m3f	E(0-105)HCh	GD	£4147
84	11/01	Towc	2m6f	F(0-105)HCh	SFT	£3753

| 89 | 12/00 | Ludl | 2m4f | D(0-115)HCh | SFT | £5012 |
| 92 | 10/98 | Carl | 2m1f | H NHF | GD | £1255 |

Total win prize-money £19122

Going: Sf: 0-2 GS: 1-2 Gd: 1-2 GF: - Fm: 0-1
Distance: 2m/2m3: 1-1 2m4-2m7: 1-4 3m+: 0-2
Track: LH: 0-1 RH: 2-6 Tight: 0-2 Gall: 0-0
Aids: Bl: 0-0 Vi: 0-0 Tstrap: 0-0
Best Rating: 92 10/98 Carl 2m1f   good NHF

Moderate chaser; stays three miles; suited by soft ground.

Delilah Blue (NZ)

106   108
10-y-o b m High Ice (USA)-Calamity (NZ) (Bally Royal)
S A Brookshaw Brian Davies

Placings:50/004/120P31U0/01FP33-2   (0092)
2002/03: 20²G,

	Starts	1st	2nd	3rd	Win & Pl
Chases	1	0	1	0	951
Career Total	20	3	2	3	14055
108	6/01	Hrfd	2m3f	F(0-110)HCh	FRM	£3552
108	11/00	Ludl	2m	E(0-105)HCh	GD	£3406
95	5/00	Chep	2m110y	E(0-105)HHdl	FRM	£2516

Total win prize-money £9475

Going: Sf: 0-0 GS: 0-0 Gd: 0-1 GF: - Fm: 0-0
Distance: 2m/2m3: 0-0 2m4-2m7: 0-1 3m+: 0-0
Track: LH: 0-1 RH: 0-0 Tight: 0-0 Gall: 0-0
Aids: Bl: 0-0 Vi: 0-0 Tstrap: 0-0
Best Rating: 108 6/01 Hrfd 2m3f   firm Ch

Moderate chaser, stays two and a half miles and acts on a sound surface.

Dellone

93(90c)   (62c)65
11-y-o b g Gunner B-Coire Vannich (Celtic Cone)
T R George M C Houghton

Placings:R/F4/62U32P32P/6441041F6-00U44U   (4119)
2002/03: 17⁰HY, 16⁰HY, 16¹US, 19⁴S, 16⁴HY, 16⁰UG,

	Starts	1st	2nd	3rd	Win & Pl
Hurdles	5	0	0	0	310
Chases	0	0	0	0	0
Career Total	27	3	2	2	9352
92	2/02	Hrfd	2m1f	E(0-100)HHdl	HVY	£2702
88	12/01	Hrfd	2m1f	E(0-105)HHdl	SFT	£2418

Total win prize-money £5121

Going: Sf: 0-5 GS: 0-0 Gd: 0-1 GF: - Fm: 0-0
Distance: 2m/2m3: 0-5 2m4-2m7: 0-1 3m+: 0-0
Track: LH: 0-2 RH: 0-4 Tight: 0-3 Gall: 0-1
Aids: Bl: 0-0 Vi: 0-0 Tstrap: 0-0
Best Rating: 92 2/02 Folk 2m1f110y   soft Hdl

Plating-class hurdler and a moderate maiden over fences; effective at around two miles one; acts well on a soft surface; likes to make the running.

Delmonte (IRE)

(97h)   (62h)
7-y-o b g Montekin-Delway (Fidel)
J J Lambe (H Smyth 26/8) Leslie Lowry

Placings:00/0000/P-0000P   (1860a)
2002/03: 20⁴G, 24⁰YS, 22⁰F, 20⁰GF, 20⁰HY,

	Starts	1st	2nd	3rd	Win & Pl
Hurdles	4	0	0	0	0
Chases	1	0	0	0	0
Career Total	12	0	0	0	0

Going: Sf: 0-1 GS: 0-0 Gd: 0-1 GF: - Fm: 0-2
Distance: 2m/2m3: 0-0 2m4-2m7: 0-4 3m+: 0-1
Track: LH: 0-1 RH: 0-0 Tight: 0-0 Gall: 0-0
Aids: Bl: 0-1 Vi: 0-0 Tstrap: 0-0
Best Rating: 86   11/00   DRoy   2m   yld-sft   Hdl

Delphi

97   90

7-y-o ch g Grand Lodge (USA)-Euridice (IRE) (Woodman (USA))
B G Powell (C Collins 7/10) Philip Banfield

Placings:2/F60/34500-450000003   (4681)
2002/03: 16⁴G, 20⁵G, 20⁹GY, 16⁹F, 20⁹G, 19⁹S, 22⁹GS, 21⁹S, 21³GF,

	Starts	1st	2nd	3rd	Win & Pl
Hurdles	9	0	0	1	739
Career Total	18	0	1	2	2333

Going: Sf: 0-2 GS: 0-1 Gd: 0-3 GF: - Fm: 0-2
Distance: 2m/2m3: 0-2 2m4-2m7: 0-7 3m+: 0-0
Track: LH: 0-2 RH: 0-2 Tight: 0-2 Gall: 0-2
Aids: Bl: 0-2 Vi: 0-2 Tstrap: 0-2
Best Rating: 106   9/01   List   2m   gd-fm   Hdl

Moderate novice hurdler; lacks scope.

Deltas First

(84h)   (72h)
7-y-o b g Nile Delta (IRE)-Shalabia (Fast Topaze (USA))
D C Turner (R D E Woodhouse 7/11) Mrs M E Turner

Placings:0/P6-3PPP   (3947)
2002/03: 22³GF, 21⁹G, 16⁹G, 19⁹S,

	Starts	1st	2nd	3rd	Win & Pl
Hurdles	1	0	0	0	0
Chases	3	0	0	1	590
Career Total	7	0	0	1	590

Going: Sf: 0-1 GS: 0-0 Gd: 0-2 GF: - Fm: 0-1
Distance: 2m/2m3: 0-1 2m4-2m7: 0-3 3m+: 0-0
Track: LH: 0-2 RH: 0-2 Tight: 0-2 Gall: 0-0
Aids: Bl: 0-0 Vi: 0-0 Tstrap: 0-0
Best Rating: 72   8/01   Sedg   2m1f   gd-fm   Hdl

Very moderate form so far.

Demasta (NZ)

98   131

12-y-o ch g Northerly Native (USA)-Hit It Gold (AUS) (Hit It Benny (AUS))
N J Henderson Michael Buckley

Placings:1113/1/114/11611-1PP445   (4612)
2002/03: 16¹F, 20²⁰GS, 16²G, 16⁴G, 16⁴G,

	Starts	1st	2nd	3rd	Win & Pl
Chases	6	1	0	0	17411
Career Total	19	11	0	1	84986

140	5/02	Wwck	2m110y	B Ch		FRM	£11816
140	4/02	Sand	2m	B(0-145)HCh		GD	£17400
132	4/02	Chel	2m110y	C(0-135)HCh		GD	£12662
123	7/01	MRas	2m4f	D Ch		GD	£5466
114	6/01	NAbb	2m110y	D Ch		G-F	£3876
	8/99	Maia	2m1f110y	Hdl		GD	£8201
	8/99	Maia	2m1f110y	Hdl		GD	£7290
	5/99	Elle	1m6f175y	Hdl		SFT	£2381
	9/97	Awap	1m5f	Hdl		SFT	£2048
	9/97	Araw	1m6f	Hdl		SFT	£1775
	8/97	Hast	1m4f110y	Hdl		G-S	£2101

Total win prize-money £75018

Going: Sf: 0-0 GS: 0-1 Gd: 0-4 GF: - Fm: 1-1
Distance: 2m/2m3: 1-5 2m4-2m7: 0-1 3m+: 0-0
Track: LH: 1-3 RH: 0-3 Tight: 0-1 Gall: 0-2
Aids: Bl: 0-0 Vi: 0-0 Tstrap: 0-0
Best Rating: 140   5/02   Wwck   2m110y   firm   Ch

Very useful handicap chaser; likes to force the pace; can go well fresh; effective at up to two and a half miles on ground good or faster.

Demi Beau

114   126

5-y-o b g Dr Devious (IRE)-Charming Life (NZ) (Sir Tristram)
C J Mann (W Jarvis 26/10) Hugh Villiers

Placings:144   (4547)
2002/03: 16¹GS, 16⁴G, 16⁴G,

	Starts	1st	2nd	3rd	Win & Pl
Hurdles	3	1	0	0	5632
Career Total	3	1	0	0	5632
126	1/03	Donc	2m110y	E Hdl		G-S	£3562

Total win prize-money £3562

Going: Sf: 0-0 GS: 1-1 Gd: 0-2 GF: - Fm: 0-0
Distance: 2m/2m3: 1-3 2m4-2m7: 0-0 3m+: 0-0
Track: LH: 1-2 RH: 0-1 Tight: 0-0 Gall: 1-1
Aids: Bl: 0-0 Vi: 0-0 Tstrap: 0-0
Best Rating: 126   1/03   Donc   2m110y   gd-sft   Hdl

Decent, lightly-raced hurdler; winning handicapper on the Flat; suited by 2m and acts on any ground; likes to race prominently.

Dempsey (IRE)

89f   105f

5-y-o b g Lord Americo-Kyle Cailin (Over The River (FR))
M Pitman Mrs T Brown

Placings:3P0   (4481)
2002/03: 16²G, 16⁹G, 17⁹G,

	Starts	1st	2nd	3rd	Win & Pl
NH Flat	3	0	0	1	603
Career Total	3	0	0	1	603

Going: Sf: 0-0 GS: 0-0 Gd: 0-3 GF: - Fm: 0-0
Distance: 2m/2m3: 0-3 2m4-2m7: 0-0 3m+: 0-0
Track: LH: 0-1 RH: 0-1 Tight: 0-0 Gall: 0-0
Aids: Bl: 0-0 Vi: 0-0 Tstrap: 0-0
Best Rating: 105   2/03   Kemp   2m   good   NHF

Full-brother to former useful Irish-trained chaser Puget Blue; made an encouraging debut in a bumper at Kempton in February 2003.

Denada

104   117

7-y-o ch g Bob Back (USA)-Alavie (FR) (Quart De Vin (FR))
Mrs Susan Nock Gerard Nock

Placings:2F3P   (3831)
2002/03: 26²GS, 24²F, 24³G, 25⁹G,

	Starts	1st	2nd	3rd	Win & Pl
Chases	4	0	1	1	2765
Career Total	4	0	1	1	2765

Going: Sf: 0-0 GS: 0-1 Gd: 0-3 GF: - Fm: 0-0
Distance: 2m/2m3: 0-0 2m4-2m7: 0-0 3m+: 0-4
Track: LH: 0-4 RH: 0-0 Tight: 0-0 Gall: 0-2
Aids: Bl: 0-0 Vi: 0-0 Tstrap: 0-0
Best Rating: 117   2/03   Newb   3m   good   Ch

Point-to-point winner in Ireland; placed in novice chases; stays three miles.

Denarius (USA)

96   110

8-y-o b g Silver Hawk (USA)-Ambrosine (USA) (Mr Prospector (USA))
G A Swinbank S V Rutter

Placings:11/0/13PP3/23525P-0040531   (2699)
2002/03: 17⁰S, 16⁹G, 16⁴HY, 25⁹G, 17⁵HY, 16³HY, 21¹S,

	Starts	1st	2nd	3rd	Win & Pl
Hurdles	7	1	0	1	4035
Career Total	21	4	2	4	12447
110	12/02	Sedg	2m5f110yE(0-110)HHdl		SFT	£3300
103	11/00	Catt	2m3f	E Hdl		G-S	£1858
111	4/99	Carl	2m1f	H NHF		GD	£1682
96	3/99	Carl	2m1f	H NHF		SFT	£1430

Total win prize-money £8274

Going: Sf: 1-5 GS: 0-0 Gd: 0-2 GF: - Fm: 0-0
Distance: 2m/2m3: 0-5 2m4-2m7: 1-1 3m+: 0-1
Track: LH: 1-4 RH: 0-3 Tight: 1-2 Gall: 0-0
Aids: Bl: 0-0 Vi: 0-0 Tstrap: 0-0
Best Rating: 114   5/01   Hexm   2m4f110y   soft   Hdl

Modest hurdler/chaser, stays two and a half miles, often wears a tongue tie.

Dene View (IRE)

98(105h)   (98h)98

8-y-o br g Good Thyne (USA)-The Furnituremaker (Mandalus)
R A Fahey C H Stevens

Placings:00/00/4433305P-1312P3   (4715)
2002/03: 19¹GS, 21³S, 16¹G, 19²G, 18⁵G, 20³GF,

	Starts	1st	2nd	3rd	Win & Pl
Hurdles	3	1	0	2	3840
Chases	3	1	1	0	5299
Career Total	18	2	1	4	10272
95	1/03	Donc	2m110y	E(0-105)HCh		GD	£4110
98	12/02	Catt	2m3f	E(0-110)HHdl		G-S	£2929

Total win prize-money £7041

Going: Sf: 0-1 GS: 1-1 Gd: 1-3 GF: - Fm: 0-1
Distance: 2m/2m3: 2-4 2m4-2m7: 0-2 3m+: 0-0
Track: LH: 2-6 RH: 0-0 Tight: 1-2 Gall: 1-2
Aids: Bl: 0-0 Vi: 0-0 Tstrap: 0-0
Best Rating: 98   2/03   Donc   2m3f   good   Ch

Modest hurdler/chaser, shock winner back over hurdles at Catterick in December; opened his account over fences with a narrow success at Doncaster the following month.

Deneises Blossom (IRE)

97(102h)   (71h)75

10-y-o b m Beau Sher-Lindabell (Over The River (FR))
W Storey John J Maguire

Placings:45B/P/6024003503-0623463204B0   (4588)
2002/03: 20³G, 24⁰G, 16⁶G, 17²HY, 22³G, 20⁴G, 16⁶G, 17³G, 27²G, 24⁰G, 27⁴S, 27⁶G, 20⁹G,

	Starts	1st	2nd	3rd	Win & Pl
Hurdles	7	0	1	2	1774
Chases	6	0	1	1	1617
Career Total	26	0	3	4	4721

Going: Sf: 0-2 GS: 0-0 Gd: 0-11 GF: - Fm: 0-0
Distance: 2m/2m3: 0-4 2m4-2m7: 0-4 3m+: 0-5

Track: LH: 0-12 RH: 0-1 Tight: 0-9 Gall: 0-1
Aids: Bl: 0-0 Vi: 0-0 Tstrap: 0-0
Best Rating: 81 1/02 Newc 2m   soft   Hdl

Moderate maiden hurdler/chaser, stays two miles-six, appreciates cut in the ground.

Denel Lady (IRE)

9-y-o ch m Denel (FR)-Lough Hill Lady (Cantab)
R Dickin J Hanna & R A Hancocks

Placings:00PP64P/0F/4P   (0269)
2002/03: 20⁴GF, 16⁰GF,

	Starts	1st	2nd	3rd	Win & Pl
Hurdles	1	0	0	0	0
Chases	1	0	0	0	310
Career Total	11	0	0	0	310

Going: Sf: 0-0 GS: 0-0 Gd: 0-0 GF: - Fm: 0-2
Distance: 2m/2m3: 0-1 2m4-2m7: 0-1 3m+: 0-0
Track: LH: 0-1 RH: 0-1 Tight: 0-2 Gall: 0-0
Aids: Bl: 0-0 Vi: 0-0 Tstrap: 0-0
Best Rating: 68 5/99 Bang 2m1f   good   NHF

Denise Best (IRE)
100   72

5-y-o ch m Goldmark (USA)-Titchwell Lass (Lead On Time (USA))
Miss K M George Exterior Profiles Ltd

Placings:26   (4793)
2002/03: 20²GF, 17⁶GF,

	Starts	1st	2nd	3rd	Win & Pl
Hurdles	2	0	1	0	872
Career Total	2	0	1	0	872

Going: Sf: 0-0 GS: 0-0 Gd: 0-0 GF: - Fm: 0-2
Distance: 2m/2m3: 0-1 2m4-2m7: 0-1 3m+: 0-0
Track: LH: 0-2 RH: 0-0 Tight: 0-2 Gall: 0-0
Aids: Bl: 0-0 Vi: 0-0 Tstrap: 0-0
Best Rating: 72 8/02 Bang 2m4f   gd-fm   Hdl

Dennett Lough (IRE)

12-y-o b g Torus-Monica s Pet (Sovereign Gleam)
C Storey Mrs A D Wauchope

Placings:FB/26F/53/52250-F   (0085)
2002/03: 25⁵GS,

	Starts	1st	2nd	3rd	Win & Pl
Chases	1	0	0	0	
Career Total	13	0	3	1	2187

Going: Sf: 0-0 GS: 0-1 Gd: 0-0 GF: - Fm: 0-0
Distance: 2m/2m3: 0-0 2m4-2m7: 0-0 3m+: 0-1
Track: LH: 0-1 RH: 0-0 Tight: 0-0 Gall: 0-0
Aids: Bl: 0-0 Vi: 0-0 Tstrap: 0-0
Best Rating: 95 5/99 Kels 3m1f   gd-fm   Ch

Modest staying pointer/hunter chaser, suited by fast ground although handles softer.

Denney's Well (IRE)
93   69+

8-y-o ch g Good Thyne (USA)-Julias Well (Golden Love)

H D Daly (G D Hanmer 8/6) Patrick Burling Developments Ltd

Placings:35   (2208)
2002/03: 26³G, 24⁵HY,

	Starts	1st	2nd	3rd	Win & Pl
Chases	2	0	0	1	354
Career Total	2	0	0	1	354

Going: Sf: 0-1 GS: 0-0 Gd: 0-1 GF: - Fm: 0-0
Distance: 2m/2m3: 0-1 2m4-2m7: 0-0 3m+: 0-0
Track: LH: 0-2 RH: 0-0 Tight: 0-2 Gall: 0-0
Aids: Bl: 0-0 Vi: 0-0 Tstrap: 0-0
Best Rating: 69 6/02 Ctml 3m2f   good   Ch

Deoch An Dorais (IRE)
106(96h)   (115h)111

8-y-o b g Supreme Leader-General Rain (General Ironside)
N J Henderson Park Lane Racing AG Switzerland

Placings:6/0053122/33/3F00-2U22UP   (4438)
2002/03: 16²G, 20⁰S, 23⁶S, 16²G, 22⁰G, 24⁶G,

	Starts	1st	2nd	3rd	Win & Pl
Chases	6	0	3	0	4249
Career Total	20	1	5	4	13300
101 1/00 Naas 2m		NHF		SFT	£3312
			Total win prize-money		£3312

Going: Sf: 0-3 GS: 0-0 Gd: 0-3 GF: - Fm: 0-0
Distance: 2m/2m3: 0-2 2m4-2m7: 0-2 3m+: 0-2
Track: LH: 0-2 RH: 0-4 Tight: 0-0 Gall: 0-2
Aids: Bl: 0-0 Vi: 0-0 Tstrap: 0-0
Best Rating: 115 12/01 Newb 2m110y   soft   Hdl

Fair hurdler/chaser; strong sort; has suffered from back problems; best at around two miles on an easy surface.

Deputy Leader (IRE)

11-y-o b g Florida Son-Larne (Giolla Mear)
Keith Thomas (K Hunter 1/6) Keith Thomas

Placings:5365/F/4U660F   (1074)
2002/03: 20⁴GF, 20⁰GF, 16⁶GF, 21⁵G, 16⁰G, 21⁵FG,

	Starts	1st	2nd	3rd	Win & Pl
Hurdles	1	0	0	0	0
Chases	5	0	0	0	0
Career Total	11	0	0	1	182

Going: Sf: 0-0 GS: 0-0 Gd: 0-3 GF: - Fm: 0-3
Distance: 2m/2m3: 0-2 2m4-2m7: 0-3 3m+: 0-0
Track: LH: 0-6 RH: 0-0 Tight: 0-4 Gall: 0-0
Aids: Bl: 0-0 Vi: 0-0 Tstrap: 0-0
Best Rating: 107 12/97 Towc 2m   soft   NHF

Derby Heights

10-y-o br g Golden Heights-Elvonera (Elvis)
R J Smith Mrs V J Emms

Placings:0P   (2445)
2002/03: 16⁰GS, 16⁰PG,

	Starts	1st	2nd	3rd	Win & Pl
Hurdles	2	0	0	0	
Career Total	2	0	0	0	

Going: Sf: 0-0 GS: 0-1 Gd: 0-1 GF: - Fm: 0-0
Distance: 2m/2m3: 0-2 2m4-2m7: 0-0 3m+: 0-0
Track: LH: 0-1 RH: 0-1 Tight: 0-0 Gall: 0-0
Aids: Bl: 0-0 Vi: 0-0 Tstrap: 0-0
Best Rating: 0 12/02 Ludl 2m   good   Hdl

Dere Lyn
98   78

5-y-o b g Awesome-Our Resolution (Caerleon (USA))
D Burchell Lyn Phillips

Placings:000-016   (0500)
2002/03: 16⁶GF, 22¹GS, 22⁶G,

	Starts	1st	2nd	3rd	Win & Pl
Hurdles	3	1	0	0	2408
Career Total	6	1	0	0	2408
81 5/02 NAbb 2m6f		G(0-95)HHdl		G-S	£2408
			Total win prize-money		£2408

Going: Sf: 0-0 GS: 1-1 Gd: 0-1 GF: - Fm: 0-1
Distance: 2m/2m3: 0-0 1 **2m4-2m7:** 1-2 3m+: 0-0
Track: LH: 1-3 RH: 0-0 Tight: 1-2 Gall: 0-0
Aids: Bl: 0-1 Vi: 0-0 Tstrap: 0-0
Best Rating: 81 5/02 NAbb 2m6f   gd-sft   Hdl

Moderate form in novice hurdles.

Derek Trotter

4-y-o b g Cosmonaut-Cinderella Derek (Hittite Glory)
A D Smith Miss Kerensa Pluess

Placings:0   (4760)
2002/03: 18⁰GF,

	Starts	1st	2nd	3rd	Win & Pl
NH Flat	1	0	0	0	
Career Total	1	0	0	0	

Going: Sf: 0-0 GS: 0-0 Gd: 0-0 GF: - Fm: 0-1
Distance: 2m/2m3: 0-0 2m4-2m7: 0-0 3m+: 0-0
Track: LH: 0-1 RH: 0-0 Tight: 0-1 Gall: 0-0
Aids: Bl: 0-0 Vi: 0-0 Tstrap: 0-0
Best Rating: 0 4/03 Font 2m2f110y   gd-fm   NHF

Derivative (IRE)
107   112

5-y-o b/br g Erin s Isle-Our Hope (Dancing Brave (USA))
Miss Venetia Williams P Ryan

Placings:20-32615   (4032)
2002/03: 16³S, 16²HY, 17⁶GS, 20¹HY, 20⁵HY,

	Starts	1st	2nd	3rd	Win & Pl
Hurdles	5	1	1	1	5844
Career Total	7	1	2	1	7236
106 2/03 Ayr 2m4f E Hdl				HVY	£3640
			Total win prize-money		£3640

Going: Sf: 1-4 GS: 0-1 Gd: 0-0 GF: - Fm: 0-0
Distance: 2m/2m3: 0-3 **2m4-2m7:** 1-2 3m+: 0-0
Track: LH: 1-4 RH: 0-1 Tight: 0-0 Gall: 0-2
Aids: Bl: 0-0 Vi: 0-0 Tstrap: 0-0
Best Rating: 112 12/02 Newb 2m110y   heavy   Hdl

Modest hurdler; stays two and a half miles; handles good but appreciates much softer ground.

Derring Bridge
104(99c)   (107c)103

13-y-o b g Derring Rose-Bridge Ash (Normandy)

Mrs S M Johnson I K Johnson   Total win prize-money £14714

Placings:0P51U0F/040055P4/031U654300642/223111321
1436/4222221143/4002113342120F/1244435F/63514R0-
31RP   **(1200)**
2002/03: 24³GS, 24¹G, 24ᴿGF, 26ᴾGF,

	Starts	1st	2nd	3rd	Win & Pl
Hurdles	4	1	0	1	6464
Career Total	84	15	13	11	86272
103 8/02	Worc	3m	C(0-135)HHdl	GD	£5921
102 7/01	Worc	3m	D(0-125)HHdl	GD	£4017
116 6/00	Worc	2m7f110yC(0-135)HCh	G-F	£7046
114 4/99	Hntg	3m	E(0-115)HCh	GD	£3601
106 7/99	NAbb	3m2f110yD(0-125)HCh	G-F	£3543
116 7/99	NAbb	2m7f110yF(0-110)HCh	G-F	£2497
109 9/98	NAbb	3m2f110yD(0-110)HCh	G-F	£3355
98 4/98	Worc	2m7f110yE Ch	G-F	£2951
107 9/97	MRas	3m	C(0-130)HHdl	GD	£3717
111 9/97	NAbb	3m3f	D(0-120)HHdl	GD	£2655
104 7/97	Worc	3m	D(0-120)HHdl	G-F	£2756
107 6/97	Uttx	3m110y	D(0-125)HHdl	GD	£3436
111 6/97	Sthl	3m110y	E(0-110)HHdl	G-S	£2390
91 6/96	Sthl	3m110y	E(0-110)HHdl	GD	£2624
87 3/95	Ludl	2m5f110yE Hdl	G-S	£2626

Total win prize-money £53569

Going: Sf: 0-0 GS: 0-1 Gd: 1-1 GF: - Fm: 0-2
Distance: 2m/2m3: 0-0 2m4-2m7: 0-0 3m+: 1-4
Track: LH: 1-3 RH: 0-1 Tight: 0-1 Gall: 0-0
Aids: Bl: 0-0 Vi: 0-0 Tstrap: 0-0
Best Rating: 116 6/00 Worc 2m7f110y gd-fm Ch

Moderate hurdler now in the veteran stage; out and out stayer; goes well on fast ground; good record at Worcester and nearly landed the same event for the third time in six years when narrowly beaten at his favourite course July 2003.

Derring Dove

11-y-o b g Derring Rose-Shadey Dove (Deadly Nightshade)
H W Lavis H W Lavis

Placings:0/P05/P/4432P/400-P233   **(4541)**
2002/03: 26ᴾHY, 25²S, 24³G, 24³G,

	Starts	1st	2nd	3rd	Win & Pl
Chases	4	0	1	2	1372
Career Total	17	0	2	3	2680

Going: Sf: 0-2 GS: 0-0 Gd: 0-2 GF: - Fm: 0-0
Distance: 2m/2m3: 0-0 2m4-2m7: 0-0 3m+: 0-4
Track: LH: 0-2 RH: 0-2 Tight: 0-1 Gall: 0-0
Aids: Bl: 0-0 Vi: 0-0 Tstrap: 0-0
Best Rating: 99 2/01 Ludl 3m gd-sft Ch

Maiden hunter chaser; completed a hat-trick in point-to-points in 1999; improved effort when runner-up in soft ground at Hereford March 2003; stays three miles.

Derrintogher Yank (IRE)

111   **123+**

9-y-o b g Lord Americo-Glenmalur (Black Minstrel)
S E H Sherwood Con O Connor

Placings:23/411221/05/P1   **(2135)**
2002/03: 21ᴾG, 24¹G,

	Starts	1st	2nd	3rd	Win & Pl
Chases	2	1	0	0	5473
Career Total	12	4	3	1	18116
123 11/02	Ludl	3m	D Ch	GD	£5473
126 3/00	Strf	2m6f110yD Hdl	GD	£3971
127 11/99	Kemp	2m5f	D Hdl	GD	£3217
112 10/99	Chep	2m4f	E Hdl	GD	£2052

Going: Sf: 0-0 GS: 0-0 Gd: 1-2 GF: - Fm: 0-0
Distance: 2m/2m3: 0-0 2m4-2m7: 0-1 3m+: 1-1
Track: LH: 0-1 RH: 1-1 Tight: 1-2 Gall: 0-0
Aids: Bl: 0-0 Vi: 0-0 Tstrap: 0-0
Best Rating: 133 11/99 Winc 2m6f good Hdl

Did well in novice hurdles in 1999/2000, but was injured early the following season. Made all in a novice chase in November 2002. Effective at three miles.

Derry Ann

74   **78**

7-y-o b m Derrylin-Ancat Girl (Politico (USA))
G P Kelly Mrs H Ratcliffe

Placings:040-330   **(2099)**
2002/03: 16³GF, 16³GS, 19⁰G,

	Starts	1st	2nd	3rd	Win & Pl
NH Flat	1	0	0	1	281
Hurdles	2	0	0	1	618
Career Total	6	0	0	2	899

Going: Sf: 0-0 GS: 0-1 Gd: 0-1 GF: - Fm: 0-1
Distance: 2m/2m3: 0-3 2m4-2m7: 0-0 3m+: 0-0
Track: LH: 0-3 RH: 0-0 Tight: 0-2 Gall: 0-0
Aids: Bl: 0-0 Vi: 0-0 Tstrap: 0-0
Best Rating: 91 5/02 Chep 2m110y gd-fm NHF

Glimmer of ability in bumpers.

Derry Dice

68   **74**

7-y-o b g Derrylin-Paper Dice (Le Dauphin)
C T Pogson C T Pogson

Placings:00460U   **(4681)**
2002/03: 16⁰HY, 16⁰GS, 16⁴G, 16⁶G, 20⁰GF, 21ᵁGF,

	Starts	1st	2nd	3rd	Win & Pl
NH Flat	4	0	0	0	0
Hurdles	2	0	0	0	0
Career Total	6	0	0	0	0

Going: Sf: 0-1 GS: 0-1 Gd: 0-2 GF: - Fm: 0-2
Distance: 2m/2m3: 0-4 2m4-2m7: 0-2 3m+: 0-0
Track: LH: 0-4 RH: 0-2 Tight: 0-2 Gall: 0-2
Aids: Bl: 0-5 Vi: 0-0 Tstrap: 0-0
Best Rating: 85 1/03 Sthl 2m good NHF

Derryquin

96   **99+**

8-y-o b g Lion Cavern (USA)-Top Berry (High Top)
P L Gilligan Lady Bland

Placings:142   **(1219)**
2002/03: 17ᵀGF, 17⁴G, 17²G,

	Starts	1st	2nd	3rd	Win & Pl
Hurdles	3	1	1	0	4603
Career Total	3	1	1	0	4603
99 7/02	NAbb	2m1f	D Hdl	G-F	£3757

Total win prize-money £3757

Going: Sf: 0-0 GS: 0-0 Gd: 0-2 GF: - Fm: 1-1
Distance: 2m/2m3: 1-3 2m4-2m7: 0-0 3m+: 0-0
Track: LH: 1-3 RH: 0-0 Tight: 1-2 Gall: 0-0
Aids: Bl: 0-1 Vi: 0-0 Tstrap: 0-0
Best Rating: 99 9/02 Sthl 2m1f good Hdl

A fair mile handicapper on the Flat. Overcame some novicey jumping early on to make quite an impressive winning debut

over hurdles at Newton Abbot July 2002 but well beaten next time under a penalty.

Derryrose

10-y-o br g Derrylin-Levantine Rose (Levanter)
R J Kyle R J Kyle

Placings:6P526P30U/5P430P0/3-51   **(0161)**
2002/03: 25⁵GS, 25¹G,

	Starts	1st	2nd	3rd	Win & Pl
Chases	2	1	0	0	1960
Career Total	19	1	1	3	3697
100 5/02	Kels	3m1f	H Ch	GD	£1960

Total win prize-money £1960

Going: Sf: 0-0 GS: 0-1 Gd: 1-1 GF: - Fm: 0-0
Distance: 2m/2m3: 0-0 2m4-2m7: 0-0 3m+: 1-2
Track: LH: 1-2 RH: 0-0 Tight: 1-1 Gall: 0-0
Aids: Bl: 0-0 Vi: 0-0 Tstrap: 0-0
Best Rating: 100 5/02 Kels 3m1f good Ch

Moderate hunter chaser; stays three miles one; acts on a sound surface.

Dervalloc (IRE)

6-y-o b g Zaffaran (USA)-Keeping Company (Kings Company)
P Winkworth P Winkworth

Placings:04   **(3948)**
2002/03: 16⁰HY, 24⁴S,

	Starts	1st	2nd	3rd	Win & Pl
NH Flat	1	0	0	0	0
Hurdles	1	0	0	0	331
Career Total	2	0	0	0	331

Going: Sf: 0-2 GS: 0-0 Gd: 0-0 GF: - Fm: 0-0
Distance: 2m/2m3: 0-1 2m4-2m7: 0-0 3m+: 0-1
Track: LH: 0-0 RH: 0-2 Tight: 0-0 Gall: 0-0
Aids: Bl: 0-0 Vi: 0-0 Tstrap: 0-0
Best Rating: 86 2/03 Sand 2m110y heavy NHF

Desailly

104   **127**

9-y-o ch g Teamster-G W Superstar (Rymer)
G B Balding The Team

Placings:452/3U3U1-22564   **(4002)**
2002/03: 22²S, 25²GS, 24⁵S, 23⁶S, 21⁴S,

	Starts	1st	2nd	3rd	Win & Pl
Chases	5	0	2	0	6449
Career Total	13	1	3	2	14928
122 3/02	Extr	2m7f110yD(0-125)HCh	GD	£4914

Total win prize-money £4914

Going: Sf: 0-4 GS: 0-1 Gd: 0-0 GF: - Fm: 0-0
Distance: 2m/2m3: 0-0 2m4-2m7: 0-2 3m+: 0-3
Track: LH: 0-1 RH: 0-4 Tight: 0-0 Gall: 0-1
Aids: Bl: 0-0 Vi: 0-0 Tstrap: 0-0
Best Rating: 124 12/02 Extr 3m1f110y gd-sft Ch

Fair chaser; lightly raced; stays three miles; acts well on good ground.

Desert Air (JPN)

109   **121**

4-y-o ch g Desert King (IRE)-Greek Air (IRE) (Ela-Mana-Mou)

M C Pipe (P F I Cole 23/9) Mrs Belinda Harvey

Placings:213   (3494)
2002/03: 16²S, 17¹S, 16³GS,

	Starts	1st	2nd	3rd	Win & Pl
Hurdles	3	1	1	1	6352
Career Total	3	1	1	1	6352
115 1/03 Tntn	2m1f		E Hdl	SFT	£4530

Total win prize-money £4531

Going:	Sf: 1-2 GS: 0-1 Gd: 0-0 GF: - Fm: 0-0
Distance:	2m/2m3: 1-3 2m4-2m7: 0-0 3m+: 0-0
Track:	LH: 0-0 RH: 1-3 Tight: 1-1 Gall: 0-1
Aids:	Bl: 0-0 Vi: 1-2 Tstrap: 0-0
Best Rating:	121 2/03 Kemp 2m gd-sft Hdl

Useful juvenile hurdler; effective in soft ground; tends to jump to the right.

Desert Arc (IRE)
98f   101f

5-y-o b g Spectrum (IRE)-Bint Albadou (IRE) (Green Desert (USA))
A M Balding (Jonjo O Neill 2/3) D J Deer

Placings:40   (3917)
2002/03: 16⁴G, 17⁰GS,

	Starts	1st	2nd	3rd	Win & Pl
NH Flat	2	0	0	0	318
Career Total	2	0	0	0	318

Going:	Sf: 0-0 GS: 0-1 Gd: 0-1 GF: - Fm: 0-0
Distance:	2m/2m3: 0-2 2m4-2m7: 0-0 3m+: 0-0
Track:	LH: 0-1 RH: 0-1 Tight: 0-1 Gall: 0-0
Aids:	Bl: 0-0 Vi: 0-0 Tstrap: 0-0
Best Rating:	101 10/02 Chel 2m110y good NHF

Good fourth in warm bumper at Cheltenham in October but bitter disapointment when next seen out at Carlisle in March (odds-on).

Desert Boot
76   83

8-y-o gr g High Kicker (USA)-Desert Mist (Sharrood (USA))
T H Caldwell T H Caldwell

Placings:60/0/U/P0PP-4PP   (0986)
2002/03: 23⁴GF, 24⁶GF, 26⁶GF,

	Starts	1st	2nd	3rd	Win & Pl
Hurdles	1	0	0	0	0
Chases	2	0	0	0	413
Career Total	11	0	0	0	413

Going:	Sf: 0-0 GS: 0-0 Gd: 0-0 GF: - Fm: 0-3
Distance:	2m/2m3: 0-0 2m4-2m7: 0-0 3m+: 0-3
Track:	LH: 0-3 RH: 0-0 Tight: 0-1 Gall: 0-0
Aids:	Bl: 0-0 Vi: 0-0 Tstrap: 0-0
Best Rating:	83 5/02 Worc 2m7f110y gd-fm Ch

Desert City
76   74

4-y-o b g Darnay-Oasis (Valiyar)
P R Webber (R Hannon 16/10) The Huntingdon Hopefuls

Placings:003   (4539)
2002/03: 16⁰GS, 16⁰GS, 16³G,

	Starts	1st	2nd	3rd	Win & Pl
Hurdles	3	0	0	1	644
Career Total	3	0	0	1	644

Going:	Sf: 0-0 GS: 0-2 Gd: 0-1 GF: - Fm: 0-0
Distance:	2m/2m3: 0-3 2m4-2m7: 0-0 3m+: 0-0
Track:	LH: 0-1 RH: 0-2 Tight: 0-0 Gall: 0-1
Aids:	Bl: 0-0 Vi: 0-0 Tstrap: 0-0
Best Rating:	74 1/03 Donc 2m110y gd-sft Hdl

Well held over hurdles so far.

Desert Moss

6-y-o b g Le Moss-Super Gambler (Lighter)
N B Mason N B Mason

Placings:0   (0267)
2002/03: 20⁰G,

	Starts	1st	2nd	3rd	Win & Pl
Hurdles	1	0	0	0	
Career Total	1	0	0	0	

Going:	Sf: 0-0 GS: 0-0 Gd: 0-0 GF: - Fm: 0-0
Distance:	2m/2m3: 0-0 2m4-2m7: 0-0 3m+: 0-0
Track:	LH: 0-1 RH: 0-0 Tight: 0-0 Gall: 0-0
Aids:	Bl: 0-0 Vi: 0-0 Tstrap: 0-0
Best Rating:	0 5/02 Aint 2m4f good Hdl

Desert Traveller (IRE)
92   62

5-y-o b g Desert Style (IRE)-Cellatica (USA) (Sir Ivor)
R J Baker R J Baker

Placings:00P000-04   (1365)
2002/03: 22⁰GF, 22⁴F,

	Starts	1st	2nd	3rd	Win & Pl
Hurdles	2	0	0	0	0
Career Total	8	0	0	0	0

Going:	Sf: 0-0 GS: 0-0 Gd: 0-0 GF: - Fm: 0-2
Distance:	2m/2m3: 0-0 2m4-2m7: 0-2 3m+: 0-0
Track:	LH: 0-1 RH: 0-1 Tight: 0-0 Gall: 0-0
Aids:	Bl: 0-0 Vi: 0-0 Tstrap: 0-0
Best Rating:	62 10/02 Extr 2m6f110y firm Hdl

Desire Me
72   35

5-y-o b m Silca Blanka (IRE)-Dazzle Me (Kalaglow)
A D Smith Duckhaven Stud

Placings:0   (0040)
2002/03: 17⁰G,

	Starts	1st	2nd	3rd	Win & Pl
Hurdles	1	0	0	0	
Career Total	1	0	0	0	

Going:	Sf: 0-0 GS: 0-0 Gd: 0-0 GF: - Fm: 0-0
Distance:	2m/2m3: 0-1 2m4-2m7: 0-0 3m+: 0-0
Track:	LH: 0-0 RH: 0-1 Tight: 0-0 Gall: 0-0
Aids:	Bl: 0-0 Vi: 0-0 Tstrap: 0-0
Best Rating:	35 5/02 Extr 2m1f good Hdl

Desmond Tutu (IRE)
109   110

6-y-o b g Be My Native (USA)-Amy Fairy (The Parson)
P F Nicholls D J Nichols

Placings:1-12232121   (4718)
2002/03: 16¹G, 17²S, 16²GS, 19³GS, 18²G, 19¹F, 22²GF, 22¹F,

	Starts	1st	2nd	3rd	Win & Pl
NH Flat	1	1	0	0	1995
Hurdles	7	2	4	1	13896
Career Total	9	4	4	1	17956
110 4/03 Winc	2m6f	E Hdl		FRM	£3647
84 3/03 Extr	2m3f	E Hdl		FRM	£5011
119 10/02 Chep	2m110y	H NHF		GD	£1995
113 4/02 Font	2m2f110yH NHF			G-F	£2065

Total win prize-money £12719

Going:	Sf: 0-1 GS: 0-2 Gd: 1-2 GF: - Fm: 2-3
Distance:	2m/2m3: 2-5 2m4-2m7: 1-3 3m+: 0-0
Track:	LH: 1-2 RH: 2-6 Tight: 0-3 Gall: 0-0
Aids:	Bl: 0-0 Vi: 0-0 Tstrap: 0-0
Best Rating:	119 10/02 Chep 2m110y good NHF

Fair novice hurdler; stays 2m 6f; best on ground good or faster; set to go novice chasing shortly.

Desperate Measures
89(104h)   (73h)53

7-y-o ch m Kasakov-Precious Ballerina (Ballacashtal (CAN))
Miss Lucinda V Russell A D Stewart

Placings:04050-U363P   (1056)
2002/03: 16⁰GF, 20³GS, 17⁶GF, 16³GS, 17⁰G,

	Starts	1st	2nd	3rd	Win & Pl
Hurdles	5	0	0	2	1164
Career Total	10	0	0	2	1164

Going:	Sf: 0-0 GS: 0-2 Gd: 0-1 GF: - Fm: 0-2
Distance:	2m/2m3: 0-0 2m4-2m7: 0-1 3m+: 0-0
Track:	LH: 0-2 RH: 0-3 Tight: 0-2 Gall: 0-0
Aids:	Bl: 0-0 Vi: 0-0 Tstrap: 0-0
Best Rating:	92 12/01 Muss 2m1f gd-fm NHF

Has shown limited ability in bumpers and hurdles. Seems suited by fast ground.

Destin D'Estruval (FR)

12-y-o b g Port Etienne (FR)-Vocation (FR) (Toujours Pret (USA))
A W Congdon C J Britton

Placings:22254/234351/2114F0320FP4/512041/24FP6/P/0   (4390)

2002/03: 19⁰F,

	Starts	1st	2nd	3rd	Win & Pl
Chases	1	0	0	0	
Career Total	36	5	8	3	35178
101 4/99 Strf	2m5f110yH Ch			G-S	£2250
114 2/99 Bang	2m4f110yH Ch			G-S	£1544
146 10/97 Worc	2m4f110yC(0-135)HCh			SFT	£4605
142 5/97 Worc	2m4f110yD(0-125)HCh			SFT	£3614
139 4/97 Ayr	2m4f	B HCh		GD	£7390

Total win prize-money £19404

Going:	Sf: 0-0 GS: 0-0 Gd: 0-0 GF: - Fm: 0-1
Distance:	2m/2m3: 0-0 2m4-2m7: 0-1 3m+: 0-0
Track:	LH: 0-0 RH: 0-1 Tight: 0-0 Gall: 0-0
Aids:	Bl: 0-0 Vi: 0-0 Tstrap: 0-0
Best Rating:	146 10/97 Worc 2m4f110y soft Ch

Destiny Calls

95   **95**

13-y-o ch g Lord Avie (USA)-Miss Renege (USA) (Riva Ridge (USA))
N A Gaselee   Simon Harrap

Placings:2211/2220U/1131321/252/44444/51/31L401R1R/60241/04456-4P   (0774)
2002/03: 20⁶G, 21⁴GF, 23ᴾGF,

	Starts	1st	2nd	3rd	Win & Pl
Chases	3	0	0	0	266
Career Total	47	11	9	3	82024

133	8/00	Uttx	2m5f	C(0-135)HCh	G-F	£6114
138	11/99	Newb	2m4f	D(0-125)HCh	G-F	£6254
138	8/99	Uttx	2m5f	C(0-135)HCh	G-F	£5772
134	5/99	Strf	2m5f110yC(0-135)HCh		GD	£5998
125	3/99	Newb	2m4f	C(0-135)HCh	G-F	£7699
129	4/96	Sand	2m4f110yC HCh		G-F	£13851
114	11/95	Wwck	2m	D Ch		GD	£3802
118	10/95	Bang	2m1f110yD Ch		GD	£3631
111	5/95	Wwck	2m	C(0-130)HHdl		G-F	£3525
94	4/94	Uttx	2m	Hdl		GD	£1987
89	3/94	Newb	2m110y	Hdl		GD	£2840

Total win prize-money £61477

Going:	Sf: 0-0 GS: 0-0 Gd: 0-0 GF: - Fm: 0-2
Distance:	2m/2m3: 0-0 2m4-2m7: 0-2 3m+: 0-1
Track:	LH: 0-3 RH: 0-0 Tight: 0-2 Gall: 0-0
Aids:	Bl: 0-0 Vi: 0-0 Tstrap: 0-0
Best Rating:	138 11/99 Newb 2m4f gd-fm Ch

Formerly fair chaser, best at two and ahalf miles on fast ground, he has refused to race in his time and is far from straightforward, but did nothing wrong when winning gamely at Uttoxeter in August 2000. Not seen out again for 14 months, he struggled in handicaps since but has taken a big drop in the ratings as a result.

Destructive (USA)

75   **44**

5-y-o b/br g Dehere (USA)-Respectability (USA) (His Majesty (USA))
J Mackie   Trying To Buy Fun Partnership

Placings:P0FP   (4116)
2002/03: 19ᴾG, 20⁰G, 19ᶠGS, 21ᴾG,

	Starts	1st	2nd	3rd	Win & Pl
Hurdles	4	0	0	0	
Career Total	4	0	0	0	

Going:	Sf: 0-0 GS: 0-1 Gd: 0-3 GF: - Fm: 0-0
Distance:	2m/2m3: 0-0 2m4-2m7: 0-4 3m+: 0-0
Track:	LH: 0-1 RH: 0-3 Tight: 0-1 Gall: 0-2
Aids:	Bl: 0-3 Vi: 0-0 Tstrap: 0-0
Best Rating:	44 2/03 Hntg 2m4f110y good Hdl

Detonateur (FR)

109   **106d**

5-y-o b g Pistolet Bleu (IRE)-Soviet Princess (IRE) (Soviet Lad (USA))
Ian Williams   Mr & Mrs John Poynton

Placings:020-054302   (4784)
2002/03: 16⁰GS, 16⁵G, 16⁴S, 16³S, 16⁰G, 19²G,

	Starts	1st	2nd	3rd	Win & Pl
Hurdles	6	0	1	1	4946
Career Total	9	0	2	1	6061

Going:	Sf: 0-2 GS: 0-1 Gd: 0-3 GF: - Fm: 0-0
Distance:	2m/2m3: 0-5 2m4-2m7: 0-1 3m+: 0-0

Track:	LH: 0-4 RH: 0-2 Tight: 0-1 Gall: 0-1
Aids:	Bl: 0-0 Vi: 0-0 Tstrap: 0-0
Best Rating:	116 3/02 Chel 2m110y gd-sft Hdl

Fair hurdler at his best; French import; suited by soft ground; yet to win a race, but has faced some stiff tasks; tends to race freely and looked most reluctant at Southwell in May (long odds-on but well beaten sixth).

Detroit Davy (IRE)

12-y-o b g Detroit Sam (FR)-Pretty Damsel (Prince Hansel)
D W Oakes   N G Anderson

Placings:440/U/2P/6U3/P   (0029)
2002/03: 21ᴾGF,

	Starts	1st	2nd	3rd	Win & Pl
Chases	1	0	0	0	
Career Total	10	0	1	1	1361

Going:	Sf: 0-0 GS: 0-0 Gd: 0-0 GF: - Fm: 0-1
Distance:	2m/2m3: 0-0 2m4-2m7: 0-1 3m+: 0-0
Track:	LH: 0-1 RH: 0-0 Tight: 0-0 Gall: 0-1
Aids:	Bl: 0-0 Vi: 0-0 Tstrap: 0-0
Best Rating:	106 2/96 Asct 2m110y soft NHF

Devil's Run (IRE)

105(106h)   (112h)**114**

7-y-o b g Commanche Run-She Devil (Le Moss)
J Wade   John Wade

Placings:004/0331134-6F423212   (4395)
2002/03: 21⁶G, 20ᶠGS, 21⁴GS, 20⁴HY, 27³HY, 20²S, 21¹S, 20²G,

	Starts	1st	2nd	3rd	Win & Pl
Hurdles	1	0	0	0	
Chases	7	3	1	1	10285
Career Total	18	3	3	4	22711

112	3/03	Sedg	2m5f	E(0-110)HCh	SFT	£4657
112	2/02	Newc	2m4f	B(0-140)HHdl	SFT	£6753
108	1/02	Weth	2m4f110yD(0-115)HHdl		G-S	£3500

Total win prize-money £14911

Going:	Sf: 1-4 GS: 0-2 Gd: 0-2 GF: - Fm: 0-0
Distance:	2m/2m3: 0-0 2m4-2m7: 1-7 3m+: 0-1
Track:	LH: 1-5 RH: 0-0 Tight: 1-3 Gall: 0-1
Aids:	Bl: 0-0 Vi: 0-0 Tstrap: 0-0
Best Rating:	114 3/03 Carl 2m4f soft Ch

Novice chaser; winner twice over hurdles; broke his duck over fences when successful at Sedgefield in March; acts on soft and looked unsuited by fast when disapointing runner-up at Carlisle two weeks later; stays 2m 5f.

Devon Abbot

5-y-o br g Bishop Of Cashel-Final Attraction (Jalmood (USA))
R J Hodges   The Black Diamonds

Placings:00   (2339)
2002/03: 17⁰GS, 13⁰S,

	Starts	1st	2nd	3rd	Win & Pl
NH Flat	2	0	0	0	
Career Total	2	0	0	0	

Going:	Sf: 0-1 GS: 0-1 Gd: 0-0 GF: - Fm: 0-0
Distance:	2m/2m3: 0-2 2m4-2m7: 0-0 3m+: 0-0
Track:	LH: 0-0 RH: 0-1 Tight: 0-0 Gall: 0-0
Aids:	Bl: 0-0 Vi: 0-0 Tstrap: 0-0
Best Rating:	0 12/02 Extr 1m5f soft NHF

Devon Dream (IRE)

79   **46**

7-y-o b g Paris House-Share The Vision (Vision (USA))
R J Baker (J M Bradley 26/8)   Mrs Maureen Shenkin

Placings:0P   (1800)
2002/03: 20⁰G, 17ᴾS,

	Starts	1st	2nd	3rd	Win & Pl
Hurdles	2	0	0	0	
Career Total	2	0	0	0	

Going:	Sf: 0-1 GS: 0-0 Gd: 0-1 GF: - Fm: 0-0
Distance:	2m/2m3: 0-1 2m4-2m7: 0-1 3m+: 0-0
Track:	LH: 0-1 RH: 0-0 Tight: 0-2 Gall: 0-0
Aids:	Bl: 0-1 Vi: 0-0 Tstrap: 0-0
Best Rating:	46 10/02 Font 2m4f good Hdl

Devon View (IRE)

109   **139**

9-y-o b g Jolly Jake (NZ)-Skipaside (Quayside)
P F Nicholls   Derek Millard

Placings:P/212122-3113U32   (4792)
2002/03: 19³G, 16¹S, 16¹GS, 16³HY, 16ᵁS, 19³G, 20²G,

	Starts	1st	2nd	3rd	Win & Pl
Chases	7	2	1	3	23597
Career Total	14	4	5	3	36247

137	12/02	Wwck	2m110y	C(0-130)HCh	G-S	£7345
136	11/02	Chep	2m110y	D(0-120)HCh	SFT	£4758
113	3/02	Chep	2m3f110yE Ch		SFT	£3081
129	2/02	Leic	2m	E Ch		SFT	£3406

Total win prize-money £18590

Going:	Sf: 1-3 GS: 1-1 Gd: 0-3 GF: - Fm: 0-0
Distance:	2m/2m3: 2-5 2m4-2m7: 0-2 3m+: 0-0
Track:	LH: 2-4 RH: 0-3 Tight: 0-0 Gall: 0-0
Aids:	Bl: 0-0 Vi: 0-0 Tstrap: 0-0
Best Rating:	139 4/03 Sand 2m4f110y good Ch

Very useful handicap chaser; stays two and a half miles; effective at shorter; acts on soft ground; likes to race prominently.

Devonshire (IRE)

10-y-o b/br g King s Ride-Lispatrick Lass (Kambalda)
D Lowe   D Lowe

Placings:3/23312/2/P/24   (4026)
2002/03: 27²GS, 25⁴S,

	Starts	1st	2nd	3rd	Win & Pl
Chases	2	0	1	0	860
Career Total	9	1	4	2	7083

104	1/99	MRas	2m3f110yE Hdl		SFT	£3134

Total win prize-money £3134

Going:	Sf: 0-1 GS: 0-0 Gd: 0-1 GF: - Fm: 0-0
Distance:	2m/2m3: 0-0 2m4-2m7: 0-0 3m+: 0-2
Track:	LH: 0-0 RH: 0-2 Tight: 0-1 Gall: 0-0
Aids:	Bl: 0-0 Vi: 0-0 Tstrap: 0-0
Best Rating:	104 1/99 MRas 2m3f110y soft Hdl

Modest hunter chaser; prone to jumping errors.

Devote

94   **95**

5-y-o b g Pennekamp (USA)-Radiant Bride (USA) (Blushing Groom (FR))
B J Llewellyn   The Welsh Valleys Syndicate

Placings:35420213-003422   (4272)
2002/03: 19⁹GS, 22⁰HY, 17³GS, 19⁴GS, 17²HY, 16²G,

	Starts	1st	2nd	3rd	Win & Pl
Hurdles	6	0	2	1	1713
Career Total	14	1	4	3	7785
95 2/02 Tntn	2m3f110yE(0-110)HHdl	SFT			£3388

Total win prize-money £3388

Going: Sf: 0-3 GS: 0-2 Gd: 0-1 GF: - Fm: 0-0
Distance: 2m/2m3: 0-3 2m4-2m7: 0-3 3m+: 0-0
Track: LH: 0-1 RH: 0-5 Tight: 0-5 Gall: 0-0
Aids: Bl: 0-6 Vi: 0-0 Tstrap: 0-0
Best Rating: 95 3/03 Chep 2m110y good Hdl

Selling handicap hurdler; not the most fluent jumper, he has a mischievous streak in him but stays all day and won his debut in handicap company; likes to dominate.

Di's Dilemma

100f   92f

5-y-o b m Teenoso (USA)-Reve En Rose (Revlow)
C C Bealby   T W R Bayley

Placings:30   (4672)
2002/03: 17³G, 16⁹G,

	Starts	1st	2nd	3rd	Win & Pl
NH Flat	2	0	0	1	263
Career Total	2	0	0	1	263

Going: Sf: 0-0 GS: 0-0 Gd: 0-2 GF: - Fm: 0-0
Distance: 2m/2m3: 0-2 2m4-2m7: 0-0 3m+: 0-0
Track: LH: 0-1 RH: 0-1 Tight: 0-2 Gall: 0-0
Aids: Bl: 0-0 Vi: 0-0 Tstrap: 0-0
Best Rating: 92 3/03 MRas 2m1f110y good NHF

Stoutly-bred, close third in ordinary mares only bumper on debut at Market Rasen in March; well beaten on a sound surface subsequently.

Diamant Noir

102f   103f

5-y-o b m Sir Harry Lewis (USA)-Free Travel (Royalty)
Jonjo O Neill   D J Burke

Placings:211   (4404)
2002/03: 16²G, 16¹S, 16¹GF,

	Starts	1st	2nd	3rd	Win & Pl
NH Flat	3	2	1	0	5440
Career Total	3	2	1	0	5440
103 3/03 Hayd	2m	H NHF		G-F	£2870
108 3/03 Wwck	2m	H NHF		SFT	£2002

Total win prize-money £4872

Going: Sf: 1-1 GS: 0-0 Gd: 0-1 GF: - Fm: 1-1
Distance: 2m/2m3: 2-3 2m4-2m7: 0-0 3m+: 0-0
Track: LH: 2-2 RH: 0-1 Tight: 0-0 Gall: 0-1
Aids: Bl: 0-0 Vi: 0-0 Tstrap: 0-0
Best Rating: 108 3/03 Wwck 2m soft NHF

Fair bumper performer; runner-up on her debut in a bumper on good ground before winning on soft and fast; has a fair turn of foot.

Diamond Cottage (IRE)

107   86

8-y-o b g Peacock (FR)-Sea Bright (IRE) (King s Ride)
R Johnson   J L Gledson

Placings:0/00P2-254   (1863)
2002/03: 24²GS, 25⁵GS, 24⁴GS,

	Starts	1st	2nd	3rd	Win & Pl
Hurdles	3	0	1	0	1048
Career Total	8	0	2	0	1905

Going: Sf: 0-0 GS: 0-3 Gd: 0-0 GF: - Fm: 0-0
Distance: 2m/2m3: 0-0 2m4-2m7: 0-3 3m+: - 0-3
Track: LH: 0-2 RH: 0-1 Tight: 0-0 Gall: 0-0
Aids: Bl: 0-0 Vi: 0-0 Tstrap: 0-1
Best Rating: 86 5/02 Hexm 3m gd-sft Hdl

Moderate hurdler.

Diamond Darren (IRE)

100   88

4-y-o ch g Dolphin Street (FR)-Deerussa (IRE) (Jareer (USA))
R D E Woodhouse (John Berry 23/11)   M A Sawyer

Placings:434230   (2098)
2002/03: 17⁴GS, 17³G, 17⁴G, 16²GF, 16³F, 16⁰G,

	Starts	1st	2nd	3rd	Win & Pl
Hurdles	6	0	1	2	2149
Career Total	6	0	1	2	2149

Going: Sf: 0-0 GS: 0-1 Gd: 0-3 GF: - Fm: 0-2
Distance: 2m/2m3: 0-6 2m4-2m7: 0-0 3m+: 0-0
Track: LH: 0-3 RH: 0-3 Tight: 0-4 Gall: 0-1
Aids: Bl: 0-0 Vi: 0-0 Tstrap: 0-0
Best Rating: 88 10/02 Ludl 2m firm Hdl

Poor maiden on the Flat but already a better hurdler.

Diamond Dazzler

69f   70f

5-y-o br g Sula Bula-Dancing Diamond (IRE) (Alzao (USA))
D P Keane   Conkwell Grange Stud Ltd

Placings:00   (3563)
2002/03: 16⁰GS, 17⁰HY,

	Starts	1st	2nd	3rd	Win & Pl
NH Flat	2	0	0	0	
Career Total	2	0	0	0	

Going: Sf: 0-1 GS: 0-1 Gd: 0-0 GF: - Fm: 0-0
Distance: 2m/2m3: 0-2 2m4-2m7: 0-0 3m+: 0-0
Track: LH: 0-0 RH: 0-2 Tight: 0-1 Gall: 0-1
Aids: Bl: 0-0 Vi: 0-0 Tstrap: 0-1
Best Rating: 70 2/03 Folk 2m1f110y heavy NHF

Diamond Dynasty

81   62

6-y-o b g Son Pardo-Reperage (USA) (Key To Content (USA))
J N R Billinge   Fife Foxhounds Racing

Placings:000PP-P000   (4772)
2002/03: 16⁵S, 16⁰G, 16⁹G, 16⁰G,

	Starts	1st	2nd	3rd	Win & Pl
Hurdles	4	0	0	0	
Career Total	9	0	0	0	

Going: Sf: 0-1 GS: 0-0 Gd: 0-3 GF: - Fm: 0-0
Distance: 2m/2m3: 0-4 2m4-2m7: 0-0 3m+: 0-0
Track: LH: 0-2 RH: 0-2 Tight: 0-1 Gall: 0-0
Aids: Bl: 0-0 Vi: 0-0 Tstrap: 0-0
Best Rating: 62 4/03 Prth 2m110y good Hdl

Diamond Hall

106(100h)   (102h)86

10-y-o b g Lapierre-Willitwin (Majestic Maharaj)
R D Tudor (N A Twiston-Davies 5/7)   R D Tudor

Placings:51/1200/3/1/40P633F-UP5235050303   (4614)
2002/03: 17⁴G, 16⁸GF, 24⁵G, 19²G, 19³GF, 20⁵GS, 16⁰G, 16⁵S, 20⁰S, 17³S, 20⁰GS, 21³G,

	Starts	1st	2nd	3rd	Win & Pl
Hurdles	1	0	0	0	0
Chases	11	0	1	3	5259
Career Total	27	3	2	6	12929
102 5/99 Strf	2m110y F(0-100)HHdl	G-S			£2682
91 10/97 Ludl	2m	H NHF		G-F	£1213
86 4/97 Chep	2m110y H NHF	FRM			£1686

Total win prize-money £5582

Going: Sf: 0-3 GS: 0-2 Gd: 0-5 GF: - Fm: 0-2
Distance: 2m/2m3: 0-7 2m4-2m7: 0-4 3m+: 0-1
Track: LH: 0-8 RH: 0-4 Tight: 0-4 Gall: 0-2
Aids: Bl: 0-0 Vi: 0-0 Tstrap: 0-0
Best Rating: 102 5/01 Sedg 2m1f good Hdl

Fair hurdler; best effort over fences when third in 2m 5f novices handicap at Cheltenham in April when 8lb wrong .

Diamond Jobe (IRE)

86   74

4-y-o ch g College Chapel-Dazzling Maid (IRE) (Tate Gallery (USA))
J Hetherton   Diamond Racing Ltd

Placings:6   (3579)
2002/03: 16⁶G,

	Starts	1st	2nd	3rd	Win & Pl
Hurdles	1	0	0	0	0
Career Total	1	0	0	0	0

Going: Sf: 0-0 GS: 0-0 Gd: 0-1 GF: - Fm: 0-0
Distance: 2m/2m3: 0-1 2m4-2m7: 0-0 3m+: 0-0
Track: LH: 0-0 RH: 0-1 Tight: 0-1 Gall: 0-0
Aids: Bl: 0-0 Vi: 0-0 Tstrap: 0-0
Best Rating: 75 2/03 Muss 2m good Hdl

Diamond Joshua (IRE)

105

5-y-o b g Mujadil (USA)-Elminya (IRE) (Sure Blade (USA))
M E Sowersby (John Berry 6/7)   The Prize Guys Partnership

Placings:1333P-6040P3   (4354)
2002/03: 21⁶S, 17⁰HY, 16⁴GS, 16⁰GS, 20⁶G, 20³GF,

	Starts	1st	2nd	3rd	Win & Pl
Hurdles	6	0	0	1	1395
Career Total	11	1	0	4	17301
101 10/01 Weth	2m	D Hdl		GD	£3843

Total win prize-money £3843

Going: Sf: 0-2 GS: 0-2 Gd: 0-1 GF: - Fm: 0-1
Distance: 2m/2m3: 0-3 2m4-2m7: 0-3 3m+: 0-0
Track: LH: 0-6 RH: 0-0 Tight: 0-0 Gall: 0-2
Aids: Bl: 0-0 Vi: 0-0 Tstrap: 0-4
Best Rating: 131 3/02 Chel 2m1f good Hdl

Fair hurdler at his best; staying-on third in the Triumph Hurdle in 2002; has changed stables and found things tough since; best avoided; stays 2m 4f.

Diamond Max (IRE)

97 99

5-y-o b g Nicolotte-Kawther (Tap On Wood)
P D Evans Diamond Racing Ltd

Placings:4 **(2507)**
2002/03: 16^{4}G,

	Starts	1st	2nd	3rd	Win & Pl
Hurdles	1	0	0	0	313
Career Total	1	0	0	0	313

Going: Sf: 0-0 GS: 0-0 Gd: 0-1 GF: - Fm: 0-0
Distance: 2m/2m3: 0-1 2m4-2m7: 0-0 3m+: 0-0
Track: LH: 0-1 RH: 0-0 Tight: 0-0 Gall: 0-0
Aids: Bl: 0-0 Vi: 0-0 Tstrap: 0-0
Best Rating: **99** 12/02 Hayd 2m good Hdl

Diamond Monroe (IRE)

98 86

7-y-o ch g Treasure Hunter-Star Of Monroe (Derring Rose)
N J Henderson Newbury Racehorse Owners Group

Placings:50552 **(4709)**
2002/03: 21^{5}S, 21^{0}GS, 24^{5}S, 19^{5}G, 24^{2}G,

	Starts	1st	2nd	3rd	Win & Pl
Hurdles	5	0	1	0	1054
Career Total	5	0	1	0	1054

Going: Sf: 0-2 GS: 0-1 Gd: 0-2 GF: - Fm: 0-0
Distance: 2m/2m3: 0-1 2m4-2m7: 0-2 3m+: 0-2
Track: LH: 0-4 RH: 0-1 Tight: 0-0 Gall: 0-3
Aids: Bl: 0-0 Vi: 0-0 Tstrap: 0-0
Best Rating: **86** 4/03 Uttx 3m110y good Hdl

Moderate hurdler; limited promise so far; stays three miles; acts on good ground.

Diamond Sal

101f 101+f

5-y-o b m Bob Back (USA)-Fortune s Girl (Ardross)
Mrs M Reveley R Haggas

Placings:2 **(3412)**
2002/03: 16^{2}GS,

	Starts	1st	2nd	3rd	Win & Pl
NH Flat	1	0	1	0	696
Career Total	1	0	1	0	696

Going: Sf: 0-0 GS: 0-1 Gd: 0-0 GF: - Fm: 0-0
Distance: 2m/2m3: 0-1 2m4-2m7: 0-0 3m+: 0-0
Track: LH: 0-1 RH: 0-0 Tight: 0-0 Gall: 0-0
Aids: Bl: 0-0 Vi: 0-0 Tstrap: 0-0
Best Rating: **102** 2/03 Weth 2m gd-sft NHF

Finished clear second best on racecourse debut in a bumper at Wetherby in February.

Diamond Tipped

5-y-o ch m Sure Blade (USA)-Locket (Precocious)
M R Bosley Jeff Plumb

Placings:00 **(0737)**
2002/03: 17^{0}S, 17^{0}GF,

	Starts	1st	2nd	3rd	Win & Pl
NH Flat	2	0	0	0	
Career Total	2	0	0	0	

Going: Sf: 0-1 GS: 0-0 Gd: 0-0 GF: - Fm: 0-1
Distance: 2m/2m3: 0-2 2m4-2m7: 0-0 3m+: 0-0
Track: LH: 0-2 RH: 0-0 Tight: 0-2 Gall: 0-0
Aids: Bl: 0-0 Vi: 0-0 Tstrap: 0-0
Best Rating: **0** 7/02 NAbb 2m1f gd-fm NHF

Diamond Vein

87f 86f

4-y-o b c Green Dancer (USA)-Blushing Sunrise (USA) (Cox s Ridge (USA))
P A Blockley (R Wilman 11/2) J Lavelle

Placings:0010 **(4275)**
2002/03: 14^{0}GS, 16^{0}G, 17^{1}HY, 16^{0}G,

	Starts	1st	2nd	3rd	Win & Pl
NH Flat	4	1	0	0	2016
Career Total	4	1	0	0	2016

86 2/03 Sedg 2m1f H NHF HVY £2016
Total win prize-money £2016

Going: Sf: 1-1 GS: 0-1 Gd: 0-2 GF: - Fm: 0-0
Distance: **2m/2m3: 1-3** 2m4-2m7: 0-0 3m+: 0-0
Track: **LH: 1-4** RH: 0-0 **Tight: 1-2** Gall: 0-0
Aids: Bl: 0-0 Vi: 0-0 Tstrap: 0-0
Best Rating: **86** 2/03 Sedg 2m1f heavy NHF

Winner of a modest bumper; acts on soft ground.

Diamonds Will Do (IRE)

108 108

6-y-o b m Bigstone (IRE)-Clear Ability (IRE) (Be My Guest (USA))
Miss Venetia Williams (M J P O Brien 24/7) Geraldine Mapp & Lawrence Degville

Placings:65510-05423300 **(4159)**
2002/03: 19^{0}GF, 19^{5}GF, 21^{4}G, 17^{2}S, 16^{3}GS, 21^{3}S, 21^{0}HY, 22^{0}G,

	Starts	1st	2nd	3rd	Win & Pl
Hurdles	8	0	1	2	3170
Career Total	13	1	1	2	6980

104 3/02 DRoy 2m Hdl G-Y £3809
Total win prize-money £3810

Going: Sf: 0-3 GS: 0-1 Gd: 0-2 GF: - Fm: 0-2
Distance: 2m/2m3: 0-3 2m4-2m7: 0-5 3m+: 0-0
Track: LH: 0-5 RH: 0-2 Tight: 0-5 Gall: 0-0
Aids: Bl: 0-0 Vi: 0-0 Tstrap: 0-0
Best Rating: **108** 12/02 Fknm 2m gd-sft Hdl

Staying hurdler who does not possess much in the way of acceleration and is best forcing the pace.

Diceman (IRE)

105(80h) (109h)115

8-y-o b g Supreme Leader-Henry s Gamble (IRE) (Carlingford Castle)
Mrs S J Smith John Veitch,Graham Allen,Patrick Veitch

Placings:332/3/0-12311 **(4166)**
2002/03: 19^{1}GS, 19^{2}G, 22^{3}GS, 20^{1}S, 20^{1}GS,

	Starts	1st	2nd	3rd	Win & Pl
Hurdles	1	1	0	0	3178
Chases	4	2	1	1	11233
Career Total	10	3	2	4	16088

115 3/03 Newc 2m4f E Ch G-S £4017
115 3/03 Carl 2m4f E Ch SFT £4212
109 12/02 Donc 2m3f110yE Hdl G-S £3178
Total win prize-money £11407

Going: Sf: 1-1 GS: 2-3 Gd: 0-1 GF: - Fm: 0-0
Distance: 2m/2m3: 0-1 **2m4-2m7: 3-4** 3m+: 0-0
Track: **LH: 2-4** RH: 1-1 Tight: 0-0 **Gall: 1-1**
Aids: Bl: 0-0 Vi: 0-0 Tstrap: 0-0
Best Rating: **115** 3/03 Newc 2m4f gd-sft Ch

Fair chaser; winning hurdler; twice a winner in March 2003; stays two and a half miles; acts on soft ground.

Dick McCarthy (IRE)

106 95

11-y-o b g Lancastrian-Waltzing Shoon (Green Shoon)
R Rowe Anthony D Kerman

Placings:50050/0222/003/132162310/2360/424226322-335P522 **(4761)**
2002/03: 26^{3}G, 24^{3}GS, 24^{5}S, 26^{P}GS, 26^{5}S, 21^{2}GF, 26^{2}GF,

	Starts	1st	2nd	3rd	Win & Pl
Chases	7	0	2	2	3569
Career Total	41	3	13	7	35013

115 3/00 Newb 2m6f110yD(0-120)HCh G-F £7247
115 12/99 Plum 2m1f E Ch SFT £3895
106 10/99 Plum 2m4f D(0-115)HCh G-F £5365
Total win prize-money £16509

Going: Sf: 0-2 GS: 0-2 Gd: 0-1 GF: - Fm: 0-2
Distance: 2m/2m3: 0-0 2m4-2m7: 0-1 3m+: 0-6
Track: LH: 0-1 RH: 0-3 Tight: 0-5 Gall: 0-1
Aids: Bl: 0-1 Vi: 0-0 Tstrap: 0-0
Best Rating: **118** 1/00 Plum 2m4f soft Ch

Fair chaser; stays three miles plus; acts on any ground; consistently placed but difficult to win with.

Dick The Taxi

102(93h) (130h)87+

9-y-o b g Karlinsky (USA)-Another Galaxy (IRE) (Anita s Prince)
R J Smith Dicks Backers

Placings:101/0321P1/0P6-61P **(0514)**
2002/03: 16^{6}G, 16^{1}GF, 16^{P}S,

	Starts	1st	2nd	3rd	Win & Pl
Hurdles	3	1	0	0	6997
Career Total	15	5	1	1	17339

120 6/02 Strf 2m110y C(0-135)HHdl G-F £6838
130 4/01 Fknm 2m D(0-110)HHdl G-S £3291
117 2/01 Tntn 2m1f E Hdl HVY £2702
122 4/00 MRas 1m5f110yH NHF SFT £1533
119 5/99 Worc 2m H NHF G-S £1735
Total win prize-money £16099

Going: Sf: 0-1 GS: 0-0 Gd: 0-1 GF: - Fm: 1-1
Distance: **2m/2m3: 1-3** 2m4-2m7: 0-0 3m+: 0-0
Track: **LH: 1-3** RH: 0-0 **Tight: 1-2** Gall: 0-0
Aids: Bl: 0-0 Vi: 0-0 Tstrap: 0-0
Best Rating: **130** 4/01 Fknm 2m gd-sft Hdl

Fair hurdler; winner on the Flat; too keen and let down by jumping on chasing bow; best over 2m; acts on any ground.

Dick Turpin (USA)

109 109

9-y-o br g Red Ransom (USA)-Turn To Money (USA) (Turn To Mars (USA))
Mrs L Wadham The Dyball Partnership

Placings:P/31602412 **(4669)**
2002/03: 20^{3}GS, 20^{1}GS, 16^{6}GS, 19^{0}GS, 16^{2}S, 16^{4}G, 17^{1}G, 16^{2}G,

	Starts	1st	2nd	3rd	Win & Pl
Hurdles	8	2	2	1	16120

Career Total	9	2	2	1	16120
100 3/03 MRas 2m1f110yD(0-120)HHdl				GD	£8437
96 12/02 Fknm 2m4f E Hdl				G-S	£3475
				Total win prize-money	£11913

Going: Sf: 0-1 GS: 1-4 Gd: 1-3 GF: - Fm: 0-0
Distance: 2m/2m3: 1-5 2m4-2m7: 1-3 3m+: 0-0
Track: LH: 1-6 RH: 1-2 **Tight: 2-6** Gall: 0-0
Aids: Bl: 0-0 Vi: 0-0 Tstrap: 0-0
Best Rating: 103 4/03 Fknm 2m   good   Hdl

Moderate hurdler; stays two and a half miles; acts on good and good to soft ground.

Did'ntsleepawink (IRE)

(93h)   (80h)
7-y-o b g Dromod Hill-Kamalee (Kambalda)
Jonjo O Neill J P McManus

Placings:00056 2-5050   (2471)
2002/03: 17⁵G, 16⁰G, 16⁵G, 16⁹G,

	Starts	1st	2nd	3rd	Win & Pl
Hurdles	4	0	0	0	0
Career Total	10	0	1	0	1472

Going: Sf: 0-0 GS: 0-0 Gd: 0-4 GF: - Fm: 0-0
Distance: 2m/2m3: 0-4 2m4-2m7: 0-0 3m+: 0-0
Track: LH: 0-3 RH: 0-1 Tight: 0-0 Gall: 0-1
Aids: Bl: 0-0 Vi: 0-0 Tstrap: 0-0
Best Rating: 105 4/02 Fair 2m   yield   NHF

Ex-Irish hurdler, showed in bumpers he has an engine but yet to show much over timber.

Didifon

104(107h)   (116h)110
8-y-o b g Zafonic (USA)-Didicoy (USA) (Danzig (USA))
N P McCormack (Noel Meade 9/5) Mrs D McCormack

Placings:0/61506/360000-603312   (4432)
2002/03: 16⁶GS, 16⁰GS, 16³G, 16³S, 16¹G, 16²G,

	Starts	1st	2nd	3rd	Win & Pl
Hurdles	2	0	0	0	750
Chases	4	1	1	2	7356
Career Total	18	2	1	3	16166
110 3/03 Sedg 2m110y E Ch				GD	£4665
119 11/00 DRoy 2m				Y-S	£5520
				Total win prize-money	£10186

Going: Sf: 0-1 GS: 0-2 Gd: 1-3 GF: - Fm: 0-0
Distance: 2m/2m3: 1-6 2m4-2m7: 0-0 3m+: 0-0
Track: LH: 1-6 RH: 0-0 **Tight: 1-2** Gall: 0-3
Aids: Bl: 0-0 Vi: 0-0 Tstrap: 0-0
Best Rating: 122 10/01 Gway 2m   sft-hvy   Hdl

Moderate chaser; best at around two miles; likes fast ground; usually wears cheekpieces.

Die Fledermaus (IRE)

105(85h)   85+
9-y-o b g Batshoof-Top Mouse (High Top)
D J Wintle L & P Partnership

Placings:60F0/23440/3113124/141231200/363024105-214P04P   (2632)
2002/03: 20²GF, 25¹G, 24⁴G, 20⁵G, 20⁹GS, 25⁴S, 20⁵S,

	Starts	1st	2nd	3rd	Win & Pl
Hurdles	1	0	0	0	456
Chases	6	1	1	0	6502

Career Total	41	8	6	6	42347
110 7/02 Wolv 3m1f D(0-115)HCh				GD	£4928
109 11/01 Tntn 3m F(0-105)HCh				GD	£3080
108 8/00 Sthl 3m110y E(0-115)HCh				GD	£4357
115 7/00 Wolv 2m4f110yD(0-125)HHdl				GD	£6711
105 6/00 NAbb 2m5f110yD Ch				G-F	£3760
111 10/99 Chep 2m4f D(0-125)HHdl				SFT	£3062
106 8/99 Ctml 2m6f E Hdl				GD	£2915
104 8/99 Bang 2m4f E Hdl				GD	£1882
				Total win prize-money	£30697

Going: Sf: 0-2 GS: 0-1 Gd: 1-3 GF: - Fm: 0-1
Distance: 2m/2m3: 0-3 2m4-2m7: 0-4 **3m+: 1-3**
Track: **LH: 1-5** RH: 0-2 **Tight: 1-2** Gall: 0-1
Aids: Bl: 0-2 Vi: 0-0 Tstrap: 0-0
Best Rating: 115 7/00 Wolv 2m4f110y   good   Hdl

Useful hurdler, equally effective over fences. Suited by two and a half over hurdles and three miles over fences. Acts on most surfaces.

Digdaga (USA)

4-y-o b/br f Machiavellian (USA)-Baaderah (IRE) (Cadeaux Genereux)
Mrs S Lamyman Nigel And Sarah Underwood

Placings:P   (3236)
2002/03: 16⁰S,

	Starts	1st	2nd	3rd	Win & Pl
Hurdles	1	0	0	0	
Career Total	1	0	0	0	

Going: Sf: 0-1 GS: 0-0 Gd: 0-0 GF: - Fm: 0-0
Distance: 2m/2m3: 0-1 2m4-2m7: 0-0 3m+: 0-0
Track: LH: 0-1 RH: 0-0 Tight: 0-1 Gall: 0-0
Aids: Bl: 0-0 Vi: 0-0 Tstrap: 0-0
Best Rating: 0   1/03 Fknm 2m   soft   Hdl

Dihatjum

102   108
6-y-o b g Mujtahid (USA)-Rosie Potts (Shareef Dancer (USA))
R M Flower M Lickert

Placings:21P001-53355   (1481)
2002/03: 17⁵G, 18³GF, 16³GF, 18⁵G, 16⁵GF,

	Starts	1st	2nd	3rd	Win & Pl
Hurdles	5	0	0	2	1677
Career Total	11	2	1	2	8313
104 4/02 Plum 2m E(0-110)HHdl				G-F	£3374
104 9/01 Plum 2m E Hdl				G-S	£2506
				Total win prize-money	£5880

Going: Sf: 0-0 GS: 0-0 Gd: 0-2 GF: - Fm: 0-3
Distance: 2m/2m3: 0-5 2m4-2m7: 0-0 3m+: 0-0
Track: LH: 0-3 RH: 0-2 Tight: 0-4 Gall: 0-1
Aids: Bl: 0-0 Vi: 0-0 Tstrap: 0-0
Best Rating: 108 7/02 Strf 2m110y   gd-fm   Hdl

A moderate handicapper on the Flat, ran really well on his hurdling debut at Plumpton in September and got off the mark at the same track two weeks later. Also won his first race of 2002 there.

Diletia

101   102
6-y-o b m Dilum (USA)-Miss Laetitia (IRE) (Entitled)
R H Alner T H Chadney

Placings:25246/656262F-32113B50122   (4599)

2002/03: 24³G, 20²GF, 22¹F, 19¹F, 25³G, 22⁸GS, 22⁵GS, 24⁰S, 22¹G, 24²GF, 24²GF,

	Starts	1st	2nd	3rd	Win & Pl
Hurdles	11	3	3	2	17098
Career Total	23	7	7	2	20958
102 3/03 Extr 2m6f110yE(0-105)HHdl				GD	£4273
88 10/02 Extr 2m3f D Hdl				FRM	£4030
102 10/02 Extr 2m6f110yE Hdl				FRM	£3360
				Total win prize-money	£11664

Going: Sf: 0-1 GS: 0-2 Gd: 1-3 GF: - Fm: 2-5
Distance: 2m/2m3: 1-1 **2m4-2m7: 2-5** 3m+: 0-5
Track: LH: 0-0 **RH: 3-10** Tight: 0-1 Gall: 0-1
Aids: Bl: 0-0 Vi: 0-0 Tstrap: 0-0
Best Rating: 104 11/00 Hrfd 2m1f   gd-sft   Hdl

Modest handicap hurdler; acts on ground good or faster; stays at least two and three quarter miles; all three of her wins have come at Exeter.

Dilly

86   83
5-y-o br m Dilum (USA)-Princess Rosananti (IRE) (Shareef Dancer (USA))
P R Chamings Mrs J E L Wright

Placings:4P5P   (1231)
2002/03: 18⁴GF, 16⁶GF, 18⁵GF, 16⁸G,

	Starts	1st	2nd	3rd	Win & Pl
Hurdles	4	0	0	0	0
Career Total	4	0	0	0	0

Going: Sf: 0-0 GS: 0-0 Gd: 0-1 GF: - Fm: 0-3
Distance: 2m/2m3: 0-4 2m4-2m7: 0-0 3m+: 0-0
Track: LH: 0-4 RH: 0-0 Tight: 0-3 Gall: 0-0
Aids: Bl: 0-0 Vi: 0-0 Tstrap: 0-0
Best Rating: 83   6/02 Font 2m2f110y   gd-fm   Hdl

Dim Byd

4-y-o ch g So Factual (USA)-Time Clash (Timeless Times (USA))
P D Williams Mrs D J Hughes

Placings:P   (1393)
2002/03: 16⁰GF,

	Starts	1st	2nd	3rd	Win & Pl
Hurdles	1	0	0	0	
Career Total	1	0	0	0	

Going: Sf: 0-0 GS: 0-0 Gd: 0-0 GF: - Fm: 0-1
Distance: 2m/2m3: 0-1 2m4-2m7: 0-0 3m+: 0-0
Track: LH: 0-1 RH: 0-0 Tight: 0-0 Gall: 0-0
Aids: Bl: 0-0 Vi: 0-0 Tstrap: 0-0
Best Rating: 0   10/02 Chep 2m110y   gd-fm   Hdl

Dingo Dancer

109   103+
10-y-o b g Dancing High-Some Shiela (Remainder Man)
J P Dodds J R Jeffreys

Placings:4000054/11P00/PP12-15P3513   (2305)
2002/03: 17¹G, 22⁵GS, 16⁶G, 17³GF, 21⁵GF, 19¹G, 16³GS,

	Starts	1st	2nd	3rd	Win & Pl
Chases	7	2	0	2	10180
Career Total	23	5	1	2	21797
103 11/02 Catt 2m3f D(0-115)HCh				GD	£4868
103 5/02 Kels 2m1f D Ch				GD	£4069
94 4/02 Kels 2m1f E(0-110)HCh				G-F	£4407

86	5/00	Prth	2m110y	E(0-105)HHdl	G-S	£3454
78	5/00	Newc	2m4f	E(0-105)HHdl	G-F	£2590
				Total win prize-money		£19390

Going:	Sf: 0-0 Gd: 2-3 GF: 0-3
Distance:	2m/2m3: 2-5 2m4-2m7: 0-2 3m+: 0-0
Track:	LH: 2-6 RH: 0-1 Tight: 2-6 Gall: 0-0
Aids:	Bl: 0-0 Vi: 0-0 Tstrap: 0-0
Best Rating:	103 12/02 Catt 2m gd-sft Ch

Modest handicap chaser successful on his return after a break at Catterick in November 2002. Best over two and a half miles.

Dinky Dora
96 **82**

10-y-o ch m Gunner B-Will Be Wanton (Palm Track)
J K Cresswell J K S Cresswell

Placings:020/4000/61555PP326/5065/05455/136-5P00 (2067)
2002/03: 22⁵GF, 22ᴾGF, 20⁰G, 21⁹GS,

	Starts	1st	2nd	3rd	Win & Pl
Hurdles	4	0	0	0	0
Career Total	33	2	2	2	6577
87 6/01 MRas 2m3f110yG(0-90)HHdl				G-F	£1736
93 5/98 Worc 2m4f E(0-100)HHdl				G-F	£2862
				Total win prize-money	£4599

Going:	Sf: 0-0 GS: 0-2 Gd: 0-1 GF: - Fm: 0-1
Distance:	2m/2m3: 0-0 2m4-2m7: 0-4 3m+: 0-0
Track:	LH: 0-3 RH: 0-1 Tight: 0-3 Gall: 0-0
Aids:	Bl: 0-0 Vi: 0-0 Tstrap: 0-0
Best Rating:	99 12/97 Uttx 2m gd-sft NHF

Dinofelis
105 **81**

5-y-o b g Rainbow Quest (USA)-Revonda (IRE) (Sadler s Wells (USA))
W M Brisbourne Mark Brisbourne

Placings:6PPP02 (4666)
2002/03: 16⁶F, 16ᴾG, 16ᴾGS, 16ᴾG, 16⁰G, 16²G,

	Starts	1st	2nd	3rd	Win & Pl
Hurdles	6	0	1	0	676
Career Total	6	0	1	0	676

Going:	Sf: 0-0 GS: 0-1 Gd: 0-4 GF: - Fm: 0-1
Distance:	2m/2m3: 0-6 2m4-2m7: 0-0 3m+: 0-0
Track:	LH: 0-3 RH: 0-3 Tight: 0-2 Gall: 0-0
Aids:	Bl: 0-0 Vi: 0-0 Tstrap: 0-1
Best Rating:	72 4/03 Fknm 2m good Hdl

Poor plater; best efforts on fast ground and sharp tracks.

Dinsey Finnegan (IRE)

8-y-o b g Fresh Breeze (USA)-Rose Of Solway (Derring Rose)
Simon Bloss (N W Padfield 22/5) J G Phillips

Placings:00/P4 (3954)
2002/03: 21ᴾG, 20⁴GS,

	Starts	1st	2nd	3rd	Win & Pl
Chases	2	0	0	0	167
Career Total	4	0	0	0	167

Going:	Sf: 0-0 GS: 0-1 Gd: 0-1 GF: - Fm: 0-0

Dionn Righ (IRE)
103 **111**

8-y-o b g Asir-Happy Eliza (Laurence O)
J Howard Johnson Gordon Brown/bert Watson

Placings:4U-P11P2 (4797)
2002/03: 25⁵G, 27¹HY, 27¹HY, 32²G, 27²GF,

	Starts	1st	2nd	3rd	Win & Pl
Chases	5	2	1	0	9734
Career Total	7	2	1	0	9894
111 2/03 Sedg 3m3f E Ch				HVY	£4046
105 12/02 Sedg 3m3f E Ch				SFT	£4351
				Total win prize-money	£8398

Going:	Sf: 2-2 GS: 0-0 Gd: 0-2 GF: - Fm: 0-1
Distance:	2m/2m3: 0-0 2m4-2m7: 0-0 3m+: 2-5
Track:	LH: 2-5 RH: 0-0 Tight: 2-3 Gall: 0-1
Aids:	Bl: 0-0 Vi: 0-0 Tstrap: 0-0
Best Rating:	111 2/03 Sedg 3m3f heavy Ch

Modest novice chaser; outslogged rivals when winning at Sedgefield in February; stays three miles-three; acts on soft ground but handles faster.

Diorama (GER)
89 **81**

8-y-o b m Bakharoff (USA)-Dosha (FR) (Sharpman)
L A Dace Mrs K Tobin And Miss R Kennedy

Placings:0/000605/0000-160P04F (4428)
2002/03: 21¹S, 22⁶G, 24⁰S, 22ᴾHY, 21⁰S, 21⁴G, 25ᶠGF,

	Starts	1st	2nd	3rd	Win & Pl
Hurdles	7	1	0	0	3066
Career Total	18	1	0	0	3066
86 11/02 Plum 2m5f F(0-90)HHdl				SFT	£3066
				Total win prize-money	£3066

Going:	Sf: 1-4 GS: 0-0 Gd: 0-2 GF: - Fm: 0-1
Distance:	2m/2m3: 0-0 2m4-2m7: 1-5 3m+: 0-2
Track:	LH: 1-4 RH: 0-0 Tight: 1-3 Gall: 0-2
Aids:	Bl: 0-1 Vi: 0-0 Tstrap: 0-2
Best Rating:	86 11/02 Plum 2m5f soft Hdl

Plating-class hurdler; landed a gamble in ordinary handicap hurdle at Plumpton in November.

Direct Access (IRE)
107 **147+**

8-y-o ch g Roselier (FR)-Spanish Flame (IRE) (Spanish Place (USA))
L Lungo Ashleybank Investments Limited

Placings:1111/11F24-1P (2243)
2002/03: 25¹S, 26ᴾGS,

	Starts	1st	2nd	3rd	Win & Pl
Chases	2	1	0	0	8015
Career Total	11	7	1	0	49678
147 11/02 Kels 3m1f C(0-130)HCh				SFT	£8014
136 11/01 Carl 2m4f D Ch				HVY	£5187
113 11/01 Carl 2m D Ch				SFT	£4823
143 3/01 Sand 2m4f110yA HHdl				HVY	£18560
143 2/01 Kels 2m6f110yE Hdl				SFT	£2730
142 1/01 Ayr 2m4f				G-S	£3423
122 12/00 Ayr 2m4f E Hdl				SFT	£2380
				Total win prize-money	£45118

Going:	Sf: 1-1 GS: 0-1 Gd: 0-0 GF: - Fm: 0-0
Distance:	2m/2m3: 0-0 2m4-2m7: 0-2 3m+: 0-0
Track:	LH: 0-0 RH: 0-2 Tight: 0-1 Gall: 0-0
Aids:	Bl: 0-0 Vi: 0-1 Tstrap: 0-0
Best Rating:	82 3/03 Leic 2m4f110y gd-sft Ch

Very useful novice chaser in 2001/2; made a winning return at Kelso but pulled up in the Hennessy; stays three miles plus, acts on soft ground.

Direct Bearing (IRE)
117 **131**

6-y-o b g Polish Precedent (USA)-Uncertain Affair (IRE) (Darshaan)
D K Weld Dr Michael Smurfit

Placings:1/1024-2006 (4136)
2002/03: 16²YS, 16⁰S, 20ᴾYS, 17⁶G,

	Starts	1st	2nd	3rd	Win & Pl
Hurdles	4	0	1	0	2595
Career Total	9	2	2	0	18181
117 1/02 Leop 2m Hdl				HVY	£7619
113 1/01 Fair 2m NHF				SFT	£4451
				Total win prize-money	£12072

Going:	Sf: 0-1 GS: 0-0 Gd: 0-1 GF: - Fm: 0-0
Distance:	2m/2m3: 0-3 2m4-2m7: 0-1 3m+: 0-0
Track:	LH: 0-2 RH: 0-2 Tight: 0-0 Gall: 0-1
Aids:	Bl: 0-1 Vi: 0-0 Tstrap: 0-0
Best Rating:	131 3/03 Chel 2m1f good Hdl

Useful hurdler; effective over two miles, but likely to get further in time; acts on ground ranging from good to heavy.

Direct Descendant (IRE)
90 **89**

4-y-o ch g Be My Guest (USA)-Prague Spring (Salse (USA))
J J Quinn Dwayne Woods

Placings:1003 (2473)
2002/03: 17¹GF, 16⁰GF, 16⁰G, 16³G,

	Starts	1st	2nd	3rd	Win & Pl
Hurdles	4	1	0	1	2476
Career Total	4	1	0	1	2476
74 9/02 MRas 2m1f110yG Hdl				G-F	£2044
				Total win prize-money	£2044

Going:	Sf: 0-0 GS: 0-0 Gd: 0-2 GF: - Fm: 1-2
Distance:	2m/2m3: 1-4 2m4-2m7: 0-0 3m+: 0-0
Track:	LH: 0-3 RH: 1-1 Tight: 1-2 Gall: 0-1
Aids:	Bl: 0-0 Vi: 0-0 Tstrap: 0-0
Best Rating:	89 11/02 Catt 2m good Hdl

Winning selling hurdler.

Direct Route (IRE)
154

12-y-o b g Executive Perk-Mursuma (Rarity)
J Howard Johnson Chris Heron

Placings:111211232/411513P2/121UF11/2124313/22421/5 43/P (2498)
2002/03: 16ᴾS,

	Starts	1st	2nd	3rd	Win & Pl
Hurdles	1	0	0	0	
Career Total	40	15	10	5	384687
166 4/00 Aint 2m4f A Ch				GD	£60000
159 4/99 Aint 2m4f A Ch				GD	£50575
161 12/98 Sand 2m A Ch				GD	£35727
146 4/98 Punc 2m Ch				HVY	£18869
153 4/98 Aint 2m A Ch				GD	£33254
145 12/97 Sand 2m A Ch				GD	£12560

103	10/97	Weth	2m	D Ch	G-F	£3712
139	1/97	Kels	2m110y	B HHdl	GD	£4769
129	11/96	Newc	2m	B(0-145)HHdl	GD	£4824
130	11/96	Weth	2m	C(0-135)HHdl	GD	£3710
116	2/96	Kels	2m2f	D(0-110)HHdl	SFT	£2913
112	1/96	Muss	2m	F Hdl	GD	£2263
109	11/95	Catt	2m	H NHF	G-F	£1150
109	10/95	Carl	2m1f	H NHF	G-F	£1150
105	5/95	MRas	1m5f110yH NHF		G-F	£1350
					Total win prize-money £235833	

Going: Sf: 0-1 GS: 0-0 Gd: 0-0 GF: - Fm: 0-0
Distance: 2m/2m3: 0-1 2m4-2m7: 0-0 3m+: 0-0
Track: LH: 0-1 RH: 0-0 Tight: 0-0 Gall: 0-1
Aids: Bl: 0-0 Vi: 0-0 Tstrap: 0-0
Best Rating: 168 12/98 Weth 2m   soft   Ch

A top notch chaser at up to two and a half miles, he won the Mumm Melling Chase at Aintree in both 1999 and 2000. He needs decent groun. Retired.

Direction
100f   97f

5-y-o b m Lahib (USA)-Theme (IRE) (Sadler s Wells (USA))
K A Morgan J Sheridan,G S Alcock,Miss S M Cosgrove

Placings:1-0240   (4611)
2002/03: 17⁰S, 16²G, 17⁴G, 17⁰G,

	Starts	1st	2nd	3rd	Win & Pl
NH Flat	4	0	1	0	866
Career Total	5	1	1	0	2483
93	3/02	MRas	2m1f110yH NHF		G-S	£1617
				Total win prize-money £1617		

Going: Sf: 0-1 GS: 0-0 Gd: 0-3 GF: - Fm: 0-0
Distance: 2m/2m3: 0-4 2m4-2m7: 0-0 3m+: 0-0
Track: LH: 0-2 RH: 0-0 Tight: 0-2 Gall: 0-1
Aids: Bl: 0-0 Vi: 0-0 Tstrap: 0-0
Best Rating: 97 3/03 MRas 2m1f110y good NHF

Took a mares bumper by a decisive margin on her debut at Market Rasen in March 2002 and close fourth under her penalty in same event this time round.

Dirk Cove (IRE)
106(90h)   (89h)108

9-y-o ch g Montelimar (USA)-Another Miller (Gala Performance (USA))
R Rowe Dr B Alexander

Placings:543/11205/36-334P405341   (4758)
2002/03: 24³G, 26⁹GS, 26⁴S, 24⁰G, 24⁴GS, 21⁰HY, 24⁵G, 25³G, 24⁴G, 22¹GF,

	Starts	1st	2nd	3rd	Win & Pl
Hurdles	2	0	0	0	390
Chases	8	1	0	3	7526
Career Total	20	3	1	5	16655
108	4/03	Font	2m6f	E Ch	G-F	£4371
107	12/00	Nttn	3m110y	D(0-120)HHdl	SFT	£3575
104	11/00	Towc	2m5f	E(0-115)HHdl	SFT	£2240
				Total win prize-money £10186		

Going: Sf: 0-2 GS: 0-2 Gd: 0-5 GF: - Fm: 1-1
Distance: 2m/2m3: 0-0 2m4-2m7: 1-2 3m+: 0-8
Track: LH: 0-4 RH: 0-4 Tight: 1-6 Gall: 0-2
Aids: Bl: 1-6 Vi: 0-0 Tstrap: 0-0
Best Rating: 113 1/01 Kemp 3m110y soft Hdl

Modest staying hurdler/chaser, suited by soft ground, but acts on a sound surface; stays three miles.

Dirty Sanchez

5-y-o b g Manhal-Lady Poly (Dunbeath (USA))
Jamie Poulton Robert Townsend

Placings:00   (0725)
2002/03: 18⁰GF, 16⁰GF,

	Starts	1st	2nd	3rd	Win & Pl
NH Flat	1	0	0	0	0
Hurdles	1	0	0	0	0
Career Total	2	0	0	0	

Going: Sf: 0-0 GS: 0-0 Gd: 0-0 GF: - Fm: 0-2
Distance: 2m/2m3: 0-2 2m4-2m7: 0-0 3m+: 0-0
Track: LH: 0-2 RH: 0-0 Tight: 0-2 Gall: 0-0
Aids: Bl: 0-0 Vi: 0-0 Tstrap: 0-0
Best Rating: 0 7/02 Strf 2m110y gd-fm Hdl

Discreet Girl

4-y-o b f Mistertopogigo (IRE)-Pillow Talk (IRE) (Taufan (USA))
Mrs S Lamyman P Lamyman

Placings:00P   (4672)
2002/03: 14⁰GS, 17⁰G, 16²G,

	Starts	1st	2nd	3rd	Win & Pl
NH Flat	3	0	0	0	
Career Total	3	0	0	0	

Going: Sf: 0-0 GS: 0-1 Gd: 0-2 GF: - Fm: 0-0
Distance: 2m/2m3: 0-2 2m4-2m7: 0-0 3m+: 0-0
Track: LH: 0-2 RH: 0-1 Tight: 0-2 Gall: 0-0
Aids: Bl: 0-0 Vi: 0-0 Tstrap: 0-0
Best Rating: 0 4/03 Fknm 2m   good   NHF

Dispol Foxtrot
79   40

5-y-o ch m Alhijaz-Foxtrot Pie (Shernazar)
A Scott (T D Barron 20/9) Miss Victoria Scott Jnr

Placings:P0   (3816)
2002/03: 16³PHY, 19⁰G,

	Starts	1st	2nd	3rd	Win & Pl
Hurdles	2	0	0	0	
Career Total	2	0	0	0	

Going: Sf: 0-1 GS: 0-0 Gd: 0-1 GF: - Fm: 0-0
Distance: 2m/2m3: 0-2 2m4-2m7: 0-0 3m+: 0-0
Track: LH: 0-2 RH: 0-0 Tight: 0-1 Gall: 0-1
Aids: Bl: 0-0 Vi: 0-0 Tstrap: 0-0
Best Rating: 45 2/03 Catt 2m3f   good   Hdl

Dispol Rock (IRE)
105   97

7-y-o b g Ballad Rock-Havana Moon (Ela-Mana-Mou)
Dr P Pritchard (T D Barron 15/5) Dr P Pritchard

Placings:5U00F543310   (4484)
2002/03: 21⁵G, 18⁰G, 16⁰G, 16⁰G, 16⁴S, 16⁵S, 16⁴GS, 16³HY, 16³GS, 17¹HY, 17⁰GF,

	Starts	1st	2nd	3rd	Win & Pl
Hurdles	11	1	0	2	7076
Career Total	11	1	0	2	7076
97	3/03	Tntn	2m1f	F(0-95)HHdl	HVY	£4371
				Total win prize-money £4371		

Going: Sf: 1-4 GS: 0-2 Gd: 0-4 GF: - Fm: 0-1
Distance: 2m/2m3: 1-10 2m4-2m7: 0-1 3m+: 0-0
Track: LH: 0-7 RH: 1-4 Tight: 1-3 Gall: 0-0
Aids: Bl: 0-0 Vi: 0-0 Tstrap: 0-0
Best Rating: 97 3/03 Tntn 2m1f   heavy   Hdl

Plating-class hurdler; easy winner of weak extended two mile handicap at Taunton March 2003; acts on soft ground.

Distant Romance

6-y-o br m Phardante (FR)-Rhine Aria (Workboy)
Miss Z C Davison The Merry Monks

Placings:0P   (2233)
2002/03: 16⁰S, 16⁶S,

	Starts	1st	2nd	3rd	Win & Pl
NH Flat	1	0	0	0	0
Hurdles	1	0	0	0	0
Career Total	2	0	0	0	

Going: Sf: 0-2 GS: 0-0 Gd: 0-0 GF: - Fm: 0-0
Distance: 2m/2m3: 0-2 2m4-2m7: 0-0 3m+: 0-0
Track: LH: 0-0 RH: 0-2 Tight: 0-0 Gall: 0-0
Aids: Bl: 0-0 Vi: 0-0 Tstrap: 0-0
Best Rating: 20 11/02 Sand 2m110y soft NHF

Distant Sky (USA)
76   80

6-y-o ch g Distant View (USA)-Nijinsky Star (USA) (Nijinsky (CAN))
P Mitchell Richard J Cohen

Placings:B00   (3182)
2002/03: 17⁸GS, 16⁰S, 21⁰G,

	Starts	1st	2nd	3rd	Win & Pl
Hurdles	3	0	0	0	
Career Total	3	0	0	0	

Going: Sf: 0-1 GS: 0-1 Gd: 0-1 GF: - Fm: 0-0
Distance: 2m/2m3: 0-2 2m4-2m7: 0-1 3m+: 0-0
Track: LH: 0-0 RH: 0-3 Tight: 0-1 Gall: 0-0
Aids: Bl: 0-0 Vi: 0-0 Tstrap: 0-0
Best Rating: 80 12/02 Kemp 2m   soft   Hdl

Still a maiden on the Flat. Brought down at the first on his hurdles bow.

Distant Storm
100   95

10-y-o ch g Pharly (FR)-Candle In The Wind (Thatching)
B J Llewellyn Miss Emily Jane Jones

Placings:23/5435PP111222313/5233423P233502/3324021232165333/336546056/31P3232P3-4563104652035 (4668)
2002/03: 19⁴G, 19⁵GF, 22⁶GF, 22⁴GF, 18¹GF, 19⁰GF, 16⁴GF, 19⁶G, 22⁵GS, 20²GS, 16⁰GS, 21³G, 20⁵G,

	Starts	1st	2nd	3rd	Win & Pl
Hurdles	13	1	1	2	3981
Career Total	78	8	15	23	51235
71	8/02	Font	2m2f110yG Hdl		G-F	£2310
106	6/01	MRas	2m3f110yD(0-120)HHdl		G-F	£3598
117	12/99	Chep	2m110y	C(0-135)HHdl	HVY	£8247
102	10/99	Winc	2m6f	F(0-105)HHdl	GD	£2892
102	3/98	Hntg	2m110y	E(0-110)HHdl	GD	£2250
90	11/97	Winc	2m	E(0-100)HHdl	GD	£2248
93	11/97	Uttx	2m	E(0-100)HHdl	GD	£2449
78	10/97	Extr	2m1f110yG(0-95)HHdl		GD	£1812
				Total win prize-money £25806		

Going: Sf: 0-0 GS: 0-3 Gd: 0-4 GF: - Fm: 1-6
Distance: 2m/2m3: 1-4 2m4-2m7: 0-9 3m+: 0-0
Track: LH: 1-8 RH: 0-5 Tight: 1-8 Gall: 0-1
Aids: Bl: 1-13 Vi: 0-0 Tstrap: 1-13
Best Rating: 117 6/00　Strf　2m110y　good　Hdl

Selling-class hurdler; effective at various trips and handles most surfaces; usually wears blinkers and a tongue tie; goes well for Emily Jones.

Distant Thunder (IRE)

104f　　　　　　　　　　　101f

5-y-o b g Phardante (FR)-Park Breeze (IRE) (Strong Gale)
R H Alner　Old Moss Farm

Placings:24　　　　　　　　　　(3754)
2002/03: 16²GS, 16⁴G,

	Starts	1st	2nd	3rd	Win & Pl
NH Flat	2	0	1	0	982
Career Total	2	0	1	0	982

Going: Sf: 0-0 GS: 0-1 Gd: 0-1 GF: - Fm: 0-0
Distance: 2m/2m3: 0-2 2m4-2m7: 0-0 3m+: 0-0
Track: LH: 0-0 RH: 0-2 Tight: 0-0 Gall: 0-0
Aids: Bl: 0-0 Vi: 0-0 Tstrap: 0-0
Best Rating: 101 2/03　Kemp 2m　good　NHF

Half-brother to Moving Earth and hurdles winner Fork Lightning; fair form in two Kempton bumpers early in 2003.

Distillery (USA)

72　　　　　　　　　　　54

5-y-o ch g Mister Baileys-Respectable (USA) (Northrop (USA))
J G M O Shea　Gary Roberts

Placings:6P　　　　　　　　　　(0882)
2002/03: 16⁶GF, 16⁰S,

	Starts	1st	2nd	3rd	Win & Pl
Hurdles	2	0	0	0	0
Career Total	2	0	0	0	0

Going: Sf: 0-1 GS: 0-0 Gd: 0-0 GF: - Fm: 0-1
Distance: 2m/2m3: 0-2 2m4-2m7: 0-0 3m+: 0-0
Track: LH: 0-2 RH: 0-0 Tight: 0-2 Gall: 0-0
Aids: Bl: 0-0 Vi: 0-1 Tstrap: 0-0
Best Rating: 56 7/02　Strf　2m110y　gd-fm　Hdl

Distinctive (IRE)

14-y-o ch g Orchestra-Zimuletta (Distinctly (USA))
Mrs Caroline Chadney　Mrs D J Jackson

Placings:54/F0300/06F315/1P62135/31U11P4/5P4/6FPP/4
0/23/11-P　　　　　　　　　　(0032)
2002/03: 21ᴾGF,

	Starts	1st	2nd	3rd	Win & Pl
Chases	1	0	0	0	
Career Total	41	8	2	5	29577
101	4/02	Bang	3m110y	H Ch	GD	£1883
108	5/01	Wwck	2m4f110y	H Ch	G-F	£1281
	2/97	Hntg	2m4f110yD(0-120)HCh	GD	£3582
	2/97	Strf	2m5f110yD(0-125)HCh	GD	£3582
	12/96	Bang	2m4f110yD(0-120)HCh	GD	£4065
	2/96	Leic	3m	E(0-110)HCh	G-S	£3479
	12/95	Bang	2m4f110yD(0-120)HCh	G-S	£3793
	3/95	Nott	2m5f110yE Ch	G-S	£2846

Total win prize-money £24514

Going: Sf: 0-0 GS: 0-0 Gd: 0-0 GF: - Fm: 0-1
Distance: 2m/2m3: 0-0 2m4-2m7: 0-1 3m+: 0-0
Track: LH: 0-1 RH: 0-0 Tight: 0-0 Gall: 0-1
Aids: Bl: 0-0 Vi: 0-0 Tstrap: 0-0
Best Rating: 108 5/01　Wwck　2m4f110y　gd-fm　Ch

Sprightly veteran hunter chaser, very tough and needs fast ground.

Distinctly Well (IRE)

69　　　　　　　　　　　50

6-y-o b g Distinctly North (USA)-Brandywell (Skyliner)
B A McMahon　The Bears Syndicate

Placings:000　　　　　　　　　　(3262)
2002/03: 16⁰GS, 16⁰S, 16⁰GS,

	Starts	1st	2nd	3rd	Win & Pl
Hurdles	3	0	0	0	
Career Total	3	0	0	0	

Going: Sf: 0-1 GS: 0-2 Gd: 0-0 GF: - Fm: 0-0
Distance: 2m/2m3: 0-3 2m4-2m7: 0-0 3m+: 0-0
Track: LH: 0-3 RH: 0-0 Tight: 0-0 Gall: 0-1
Aids: Bl: 0-0 Vi: 0-0 Tstrap: 0-0
Best Rating: 50 12/02　Wwck　2m　soft　Hdl

Distingo (FR)

107　　　　　　　　　　　111

6-y-o b/br g Courtroom (FR)-Quinte Au Roi (FR) (Prince Regent (FR))
Mrs L Wadham (J F Bernard 29/6)　R B Holt

Placings:23P　　　　　　　　　　(3810)
2002/03: 16²GS, 17³S, 16ᴾS,

	Starts	1st	2nd	3rd	Win & Pl
Hurdles	3	0	1	1	1663
Career Total	3	0	1	1	1663

Going: Sf: 0-2 GS: 0-1 Gd: 0-0 GF: - Fm: 0-0
Distance: 2m/2m3: 0-3 2m4-2m7: 0-0 3m+: 0-0
Track: LH: 0-1 RH: 0-2 Tight: 0-2 Gall: 0-1
Aids: Bl: 0-0 Vi: 0-0 Tstrap: 0-0
Best Rating: 111 2/03　Tntn　2m1f　soft　Hdl

Successful on the Flat in France; showed a fair level of ability over hurdles, but pulled up after suffering an injury at Plumpton in February 2003. (DEAD)

Diva

113　　　　　　　　　　　114+

6-y-o b m Exit To Nowhere (USA)-Opera Lover (IRE) (Sadler s Wells (USA))
A King　Mrs Joy Fenton And Partners

Placings:1324/40-P41　　　　　　　　　　(1481)
2002/03: 17ᴾGF, 16⁴GF, 16¹GF,

	Starts	1st	2nd	3rd	Win & Pl
Hurdles	3	1	0	0	8404
Career Total	9	2	1	1	12752
114	10/02	Hntg	2m110y	C(0-130)HHdl	G-F	£8034
119	10/00	Hrfd	2m1f	E Hdl	GD	£2583

Total win prize-money £10617

Going: Sf: 0-0 GS: 0-0 Gd: 0-0 GF: - Fm: 1-3
Distance: 2m/2m3: 1-3 2m4-2m7: 0-0 3m+: 0-0
Track: LH: 0-2 RH: 1-1 Tight: 0-1 Gall: 1-1
Aids: Bl: 0-0 Vi: 0-0 Tstrap: 0-0
Best Rating: 119 10/00　Hrfd　2m1f　good　Hdl

Fairly useful hurdler on her day, but has stamina limitations and needs a sharp track and good ground or faster to shine. Given a fine tactical ride when winning at Huntingdon in October 2002.

Divet Hill

9-y-o b g Milieu-Bargello s Lady (Bargello)
Mrs A Hamilton　Ian Hamilton

Placings:5P/4O12221133-1122311141514　　　(4640)
2002/03: 25¹GS, 20¹GF, 25²GF, 16²G, 20³GF, 21¹GF, 21¹GF,
20¹G, 21⁴GS, 25¹GF, 22⁵GS, 21¹G, 21⁴G,

	Starts	1st	2nd	3rd	Win & Pl
Hurdles	4	3	0		9923
Chases	9	4	2	1	41477
Career Total	25	10	5	3	66786
120	4/03	Aint	2m5f110yB Ch	GD	£24375
126	10/02	Kels	3m1f	D(0-125)HCh	G-F	£5434
104	8/02	Prth	2m4f110yD Hdl	GD	£4043
104	7/02	Sedg	2m5f110yE Hdl	G-F	£2940
92	7/02	Sedg	2m5f110yE Hdl	G-F	£2940
124	5/02	Prth	2m4f110yD(0-115)HCh	G-F	£5512
104	5/02	Hexm	3m1f	H Ch	G-S	£2310
121	9/01	Sedg	2m5f	E Ch	G-F	£3282
98	8/01	Prth	2m	D Ch	GD	£4056
115	5/01	Newc	3m	E Ch	G-F	£3668

Total win prize-money £58561

Going: Sf: 0-0 GS: 1-2 Gd: 2-5 GF: - Fm: 4-6
Distance: 2m/2m3: 0-1 2m4-2m7: 5-9 3m+: 2-3
Track: LH: 5-11 RH: 2-2 Tight: 4-8 Gall: 0-0
Aids: Bl: 0-0 Vi: 0-0 Tstrap: 0-0
Best Rating: 126 10/02　Kels　3m1f　gd-fm　Ch

Useful front-running hurdler/hunter chaser, effective at two and a half to three miles plus; good jumper and excelled himself when taking the Foxhunters at Aintree; may have found the race coming too soon when disappointing at Stratford next time; suited by fast ground; genuine sort.

Divine Mist (IRE)

94+

6-y-o br g Roselier (FR)-Tate Divinity (IRE) (Tate Gallery (USA))
Jonjo O Neill　Trevor Hemmings

Placings:00-20F　　　　　　　　　　(3780)
2002/03: 16²GS, 19⁰GS, 22ᶠGS,

	Starts	1st	2nd	3rd	Win & Pl
NH Flat	1	0	1	0	574
Hurdles	2	0	0	0	0
Career Total	5	0	1	0	574

Going: Sf: 0-0 GS: 0-3 Gd: 0-0 GF: - Fm: 0-0
Distance: 2m/2m3: 0-1 2m4-2m7: 0-2 3m+: 0-0
Track: LH: 0-2 RH: 0-1 Tight: 0-1 Gall: 0-0
Aids: Bl: 0-0 Vi: 0-0 Tstrap: 0-0
Best Rating: 94 2/03　Extr　2m6f110y　gd-sft　Hdl

Divorce Action (IRE)

96(77c)　　　　　(75c)117

7-y-o b g Common Grounds-Overdue Reaction (Be My Guest (USA))
R M Stronge　Kevin Elliott

Placings:26510/406/413456-53304　　　(0787)
2002/03: 16⁵F, 20³GS, 19³GF, 20⁰S, 17⁴GF,

	Starts	1st	2nd	3rd	Win & Pl
Hurdles	5	0	0	2	1638

Career Total	19	2	1	3	14204
117 7/01 Sthl	2m	D(0-120)HHdl	G-F	£5395	
99 3/00 Newb	2m110y	D(0-120)HHdl	G-F	£5362	

Total win prize-money £10758

Going: Sf: 0-1 GS: 0-1 Gd: 0-0 GF: - Fm: 0-3
Distance: 2m/2m3: 0-2 2m4-2m7: 0-3 3m+: 0-0
Track: LH: 0-4 RH: 0-1 Tight: 0-2 Gall: 0-0
Aids: Bl: 0-0 Vi: 0-0 Tstrap: 0-0
Best Rating: 117 7/01 Sthl 2m gd-fm Hdl

Fair handicap hurdler at the minimum trip on fast ground.

Divulge (USA)
104(81c)   (74c)88
6-y-o b g Diesis-Avira (Dancing Brave (USA))
A Crook (M D Hammond 30/6) Jay Dee Bloodstock Limited

Placings:000/03F6-FU425530   (1325)
2002/03: 16FS, 16UGF, 164GF, 172G, 165GS, 175G, 173G, 170GF,

	Starts	1st	2nd	3rd	Win & Pl
Hurdles	6	0	1	0	1120
Chases	2	0	0	1	469
Career Total	15	0	1	2	1984

Going: Sf: 0-1 GS: 0-1 Gd: 0-3 GF: - Fm: 0-3
Distance: 2m/2m3: 0-8 2m4-2m7: 0-3 3m+: 0-0
Track: LH: 0-6 RH: 0-2 Tight: 0-3 Gall: 0-0
Aids: Bl: 0-0 Vi: 0-0 Tstrap: 0-0
Best Rating: 91 11/01 Strf 2m110y soft Hdl

Frustrating plating-class hurdler/chaser who has let been down his jumping on early chasing starts.

Dix Bay
81(104h)   (111h)75+
8-y-o b g Teenoso (USA)-Cooks Lawn (The Parson)
M W Easterby Mrs E J Wright & Mr & Mrs A D Bairstow

Placings:042/1213/2061-U5P   (3798)
2002/03: 19UG, 16SG, 20PS,

	Starts	1st	2nd	3rd	Win & Pl
Chases	3	0	0	0	
Career Total	14	3	3	1	12649
112 4/02 Weth	2m4f110y			D(0-115)HHdl G-F £4277	
106 1/01 Weth	2m4f110y			D Hdl G-S £3759	
108 10/00 MRas	2m1f110y			H NHF GD £1554	

Total win prize-money £9590

Going: Sf: 0-1 GS: 0-0 Gd: 0-2 GF: - Fm: 0-0
Distance: 2m/2m3: 0-2 2m4-2m7: 0-1 3m+: 0-0
Track: LH: 0-3 RH: 0-0 Tight: 0-2 Gall: 0-1
Aids: Bl: 0-0 Vi: 0-0 Tstrap: 0-0
Best Rating: 112 4/02 Weth 2m4f110y gd-fm Hdl

Modest hurdler, he is effective at up to two and a half miles and acts on most going. Can go well fresh and was reappearing after a break when successful at Wetherby in April 2002. Early casualty on chasing bow.

Dixcart Valley
94(101h)   (75h)65
7-y-o b g Carlingford Castle-Renshaw Wood (Ascertain (USA))
P Beaumont The Foulrice Twenty

Placings:PP5500P   (4589)
2002/03: 19PGS, 27PS, 255G, 255G, 250G, 200GS, 25PG,

	Starts	1st	2nd	3rd	Win & Pl
Hurdles	6	0	0	0	0
Chases	1	0	0	0	0
Career Total	7	0	0	0	0

Going: Sf: 0-1 GS: 0-2 Gd: 0-4 GF: - Fm: 0-0
Distance: 2m/2m3: 0-1 2m4-2m7: 0-0 3m+: 0-5
Track: LH: 0-7 RH: 0-0 Tight: 0-5 Gall: 0-1
Aids: Bl: 0-0 Vi: 0-0 Tstrap: 0-0
Best Rating: 75 2/03 Catt 3m1f110y good Hdl

Poor novice hurdler/chaser.

Dixon Varner (IRE)
13-y-o b g Sheer Grit-Raise The Bells (Belfalas)
Mrs D M Grissell F Marshall

Placings:F/F1F1/1/P13/2   (0062)
2002/03: 262G,

	Starts	1st	2nd	3rd	Win & Pl
Chases	1	0	1	0	331
Career Total	10	4	1	1	22321
128 2/99 Thur	3m			HVY	£3222
114 5/97 Kbgn	3m1f	Ch		GD	£2204
127 4/97 Punc	3m1f	Ch		GD	£12871
110 2/97 Thur	3m	Ch		SFT	£3391

Total win prize-money £21689

Going: Sf: 0-0 GS: 0-0 Gd: 0-1 GF: - Fm: 0-0
Distance: 2m/2m3: 0-0 2m4-2m7: 0-0 3m+: 0-1
Track: LH: 0-0 RH: 0-1 Tight: 0-1 Gall: 0-0
Aids: Bl: 0-0 Vi: 0-0 Tstrap: 0-0
Best Rating: 128 2/99 Thur 3m heavy Ch

Former Irish hunter chaser. Fair form in points, best on good ground or softer.

Dizzy Lad (IRE)
91   81
7-y-o b g Alphabatim (USA)-Court Session (Seymour Hicks (FR))
J S King Terry Bailey

Placings:06/4   (4634)
2002/03: 214GF,

	Starts	1st	2nd	3rd	Win & Pl
Hurdles	1	0	0	0	268
Career Total	3	0	0	0	268

Going: Sf: 0-0 GS: 0-0 Gd: 0-0 GF: - Fm: 0-1
Distance: 2m/2m3: 0-0 2m4-2m7: 0-1 3m+: 0-0
Track: LH: 0-1 RH: 0-0 Tight: 0-1 Gall: 0-0
Aids: Bl: 0-0 Vi: 0-0 Tstrap: 0-0
Best Rating: 92 4/01 Font 2m2f110y good Hdl

Poor form in novice hurdles at up to 2m 5f.

Dizzy Tart (IRE)
104   95
4-y-o b f Definite Article-Tizzy (Formidable (USA))
Mrs P N Dutfield Darren C Mercer

Placings:23102035   (4573)
2002/03: 172G, 163G, 161GF, 169G, 162GS, 160GS, 173G, 165GF,

	Starts	1st	2nd	3rd	Win & Pl
Hurdles	8	1	2	2	6203
Career Total	8	1	2	2	6203
85 9/02 Hntg	2m110y E Hdl			G-F	£3031

Total win prize-money £3031

Going: Sf: 0-0 GS: 0-2 Gd: 0-4 GF: - Fm: 1-2
Distance: 2m/2m3: 1-8 2m4-2m7: 0-0 3m+: 0-0
Track: LH: 0-3 RH: 1-5 Tight: 0-2 Gall: 1-1
Aids: Bl: 0-0 Vi: 0-0 Tstrap: 0-0
Best Rating: 92 2/03 Hrfd 2m1f good Hdl

Plating-class hurdler, acts on a sound surface; effective at around two miles; usually held up.

Dizzy's Dream (IRE)
110f   121f
5-y-o b g Shernazar-Balingale (Balinger)
Noel Meade Kevin C O Sullivan

Placings:10
2002/03: 161S, 160G,   (4115)

	Starts	1st	2nd	3rd	Win & Pl
NH Flat	2	1	0	0	5825
Career Total	2	1	0	0	5825
121 2/03 Leop	2m	NHF		SFT	£5824

Total win prize-money £5825

Going: Sf: 1-1 GS: 0-0 Gd: 0-1 GF: - Fm: 0-0
Distance: 2m/2m3: 1-2 2m4-2m7: 0-0 3m+: 0-0
Track: LH: 0-1 RH: 0-0 Tight: 0-0 Gall: 0-0
Aids: Bl: 0-0 Vi: 0-0 Tstrap: 0-0
Best Rating: 121 2/03 Leop 2m soft NHF

Djc The Blue (IRE)
10-y-o gr g Young Man (FR)-Polocracy (IRE) (Aristocracy)
J Hetherton R G Fell

Placings:0/00P/00-PP   (0385)
2002/03: 24PGS, 25PGS,

	Starts	1st	2nd	3rd	Win & Pl
Hurdles	2	0	0	0	
Career Total	8	0	0	0	

Going: Sf: 0-0 GS: 0-2 Gd: 0-0 GF: - Fm: 0-0
Distance: 2m/2m3: 0-0 2m4-2m7: 0-0 3m+: 0-2
Track: LH: 0-2 RH: 0-0 Tight: 0-0 Gall: 0-0
Aids: Bl: 0-0 Vi: 0-0 Tstrap: 0-0
Best Rating: 63 5/99 Naas 2m gd-fm NHF

Djeddah (FR)
114   132
12-y-o b g Shafoun (FR)-Union Jack Iii (FR) (Mister Jack (FR))
F Doumen Haras D Ecouves

Placings:3244/11130P1132/53405PR2P6/453P14/F113050 /6P0440UP/03R0106U-P34205050   (4479)
2002/03: 29PVS, 223VS, 224VS, 202GS, 22PVS, 255G, 250G, 245G, 36PG,

	Starts	1st	2nd	3rd	Win & Pl
Hurdles	1	0	1	0	2061
Chases	8	0	0	1	23327
Career Total	62	9	4	8	391825
136 11/01 Asct	3m110y B(0-150)HCh			GD	£10198
9/99 Autl	2m5f110y Ch			SFT	£26911
7/99 Autl	2m6f	Ch		SFT	£32293

4/99	Nanc	2m5f	Ch	SFT	£10764
2/97	Asct	3m110y	A Ch	G-F	£15875
12/96	Kemp	3m	Ch	G-F	£23100
9/96	Autl	2m2f	HHdl	VS	£31620
6/96	Autl	2m5f110y	Ch		£19762

Total win prize-money £183699

Going: Sf: 0-0 GS: 0-1 Gd: 0-4 GF: - Fm: 0-0
Distance: 2m/2m3: 0-0 2m4-2m7: 0-4 3m+: 0-5
Track: LH: 0-7 RH: 0-1 Tight: 0-1 Gall: 0-2
Aids: Bl: 0-9 Vi: 0-0 Tstrap: 0-0
Best Rating: 150 2/98 Sand 3m110y gd-fm Ch

Decent French-trained chaser; won at Ascot in November 2001; held here and in France since; needs a sound surface to produce his best; stays three miles; normally runs in blinkers.

Do It On Dani
107   **125**

8-y-o br m Weld-Dark City (Sweet Monday)
Mrs A M Thorpe   Mrs A M Thorpe

Placings:34050/6042342-2312214110P64   (4609)
2002/03: 26²GF, 26³G, 27¹GF, 27²GF, 22²GS, 24¹GF, 224³G,
24¹GF, 25¹G, 25⁰GS, 24²HY, 24⁶G, 24⁴G,

		Starts	1st	2nd	3rd	Win & Pl
Hurdles		13	4	3	1	25976
Career Total		25	4	5	3	27874
120	10/02	Plum	3m1f110yD(0-120)HHdl	GD	£4108
112	4/02	MRas	3m	C(0-135)HHdl	G-F	£8235
104	8/02	Uttx	3m110y E Hdl	G-F	£3328
95	6/02	NAbb	3m3f	C(0-130)HHdl	G-F	£5044

Total win prize-money £20717

Going: Sf: 0-1 GS: 0-2 Gd: 1-5 GF: - Fm: 3-5
Distance: 2m/2m3: 0-0 2m4-2m7: 0-2 3m+: 4-11
Track: LH: 2-9 RH: 1-3 Tight: 2-6 Gall: 0-3
Aids: Bl: 0-0 Vi: 0-0 Tstrap: 0-0
Best Rating: 120 10/02 Plum 3m1f110y good Hdl

Fair hurdler; in good form in 2002 and shot up the ratings after four victories; stays beyond 3m; acts on fast ground; consistent; does not look a natural chaser.

Do Keep Up
99   **78**

6-y-o g Missed Flight-Aimee Jane (USA) (Our Native (USA))
N P Littmoden   W R Hornby

Placings:00-P000   (4292)
2002/03: 20⁰HY, 20⁰GS, 16⁸G, 16⁸GF,

		Starts	1st	2nd	3rd	Win & Pl
Hurdles		4	0	0	0	
Career Total		6	0	0	0	

Going: Sf: 0-1 GS: 0-1 Gd: 0-1 GF: - Fm: 0-1
Distance: 2m/2m3: 0-2 2m4-2m7: 0-2 3m+: 0-0
Track: LH: 0-1 RH: 0-3 Tight: 0-1 Gall: 0-1
Aids: Bl: 0-0 Vi: 0-0 Tstrap: 0-0
Best Rating: 78 2/03 Hntg 2m110y good Hdl

Do L'Enfant D'Eau (FR)
114   **134**

4-y-o ch g Minds Music (USA)-L Eau Sauvage (Saumarez)
P J Hobbs (J-P Totain 14/5)   Terry Warner

Placings:3-3131431110   (4460)

2002/03: 17³VS, 17¹S, 16³S, 17¹HY, 19⁴S, 20³GS, 17¹G, 16¹S,
16¹G, 16⁹G,

		Starts	1st	2nd	3rd	Win & Pl
Hurdles		10	5	0	3	47128
Career Total		11	5	0	4	51079
134	3/03	Wwck	2m	B HHdl	GD	£17991
127	3/03	Newb	2m110y	C(0-130)HHdl	SFT	£12272
119	2/03	Hrfd	2m1f	D(0-110)HHdl	GD	£4745
100	12/02	Folk	2m1f110yE Hdl	HVY	£3643
96	11/02	Hrfd	2m1f	E Hdl	SFT	£3475

Total win prize-money £42130

Going: Sf: 3-5 GS: 0-1 Gd: 2-3 GF: - Fm: 0-0
Distance: 2m/2m3: 5-8 2m4-2m7: 0-2 3m+: 0-0
Track: LH: 2-4 RH: 3-5 Tight: 1-4 Gall: 1-1
Aids: Bl: 0-0 Vi: 0-0 Tstrap: 0-0
Best Rating: 134 3/03 Wwck 2m good Hdl

French import; progressive juvenile hurdler; completed a hat-trick in four-year-old handicaps in the spring of 2003; effective in soft ground but handles good; genuine sort.

Do Ye Know Wha (IRE)
99   **122**

11-y-o b g Ajraas (USA)-Norton Princess (Wolver Hollow)
R Curtis   Eddie Gloyne

Placings:21230/0/1124/1442PP4/313/P4340-50P   (0837)
2002/03: 20⁵G, 22⁰G, 22²GF,

		Starts	1st	2nd	3rd	Win & Pl
Hurdles		3	0	0	0	
Career Total		28	5	4	4	33245
125	10/00	Ludl	3m	E(0-115)HHdl	G-F	£4485
107	9/99	Hntg	3m	E Ch	GD	£2968
118	10/98	Chep	2m4f110yE Hdl	G-S	£1996
115	10/98	Bang	2m4f	E Hdl	GD	£2358
119	10/96	Naas	2m	NHF	GD	£3530

Total win prize-money £15338

Going: Sf: 0-0 GS: 0-0 Gd: 0-2 GF: - Fm: 0-1
Distance: 2m/2m3: 0-0 2m4-2m7: 0-3 3m+: 0-0
Track: LH: 0-3 RH: 0-0 Tight: 0-2 Gall: 0-0
Aids: Bl: 0-2 Vi: 0-0 Tstrap: 0-0
Best Rating: 132 12/98 Sand 2m6f good Hdl

Fair hurdler, stays three miles and acts on a sound surface.

Dobbiesgardenworld (IRE)
97f   **110f**

6-y-o b g Great Marquess-Rosy Posy (IRE) (Roselier (FR))
L Lungo   Ashleybank Investments Limited

Placings:133   (3991)
2002/03: 16¹S, 16³HY, 17³S,

		Starts	1st	2nd	3rd	Win & Pl
NH Flat		3	1	0	2	2548
Career Total		3	1	0	2	2548
104	12/02	Newc	2m	H NHF	SFT	£2002

Total win prize-money £2002

Going: Sf: 1-3 GS: 0-0 Gd: 0-0 GF: - Fm: 0-0
Distance: 2m/2m3: 1-3 2m4-2m7: 0-0 3m+: 0-0
Track: LH: 1-2 RH: 0-1 Tight: 0-0 Gall: 0-0
Aids: Bl: 0-0 Vi: 0-0 Tstrap: 0-0
Best Rating: 110 3/03 Carl 2m1f soft NHF

Fair Irish bumper winner; successful on debut at Newcastle; acts on soft ground.

Doberman (IRE)
103   **83**

8-y-o br g Dilum (USA)-Switch Blade (IRE) (Robellino (USA))
W M Brisbourne   Mrs I M Folkes

Placings:520/43   (3135)
2002/03: 16⁴S, 16³S,

		Starts	1st	2nd	3rd	Win & Pl
Hurdles		2	0	0	1	749
Career Total		5	0	1	1	1441

Going: Sf: 0-2 GS: 0-0 Gd: 0-0 GF: - Fm: 0-0
Distance: 2m/2m3: 0-2 2m4-2m7: 0-0 3m+: 0-0
Track: LH: 0-0 RH: 0-2 Tight: 0-0 Gall: 0-0
Aids: Bl: 0-2 Vi: 0-0 Tstrap: 0-0
Best Rating: 84 12/99 Ludl 2m good Hdl

Plating-class hurdler, not one to trust.

Doc Ryan's
99   **87**

9-y-o b g Damister (USA)-Jolimo (Fortissimo)
B J Llewellyn   William Vaughan

Placings:2PP/212440/6   (0902)
2002/03: 20⁶G,

		Starts	1st	2nd	3rd	Win & Pl
Hurdles		1	0	0	0	0
Career Total		10	1	3	0	6874
117	10/99	Fknm	2m	D Hdl	GD	£3007

Total win prize-money £3008

Going: Sf: 0-0 GS: 0-0 Gd: 0-1 GF: - Fm: 0-0
Distance: 2m/2m3: 0-0 2m4-2m7: 0-1 3m+: 0-0
Track: LH: 0-1 RH: 0-0 Tight: 0-0 Gall: 0-0
Aids: Bl: 0-1 Vi: 0-0 Tstrap: 0-0
Best Rating: 117 10/99 Fknm 2m good Hdl

Docklands Limo
99   **104**

10-y-o b h Most Welcome-Bugle Sound (Bustino)
G F Bridgwater   John Marks

Placings:2102/4365501/2-00P   (3405)
2002/03: 16⁸GS, 17⁰G, 22²HY,

		Starts	1st	2nd	3rd	Win & Pl
Hurdles		3	0	0	0	
Career Total		15	2	3	1	46365
143	4/01	Aint	2m110y	B HHdl	HVY	£26000
124	3/00	Newb	2m110y	D Hdl	G-F	£3867

Total win prize-money £29868

Going: Sf: 0-1 GS: 0-1 Gd: 0-1 GF: - Fm: 0-0
Distance: 2m/2m3: 0-2 2m4-2m7: 0-1 3m+: 0-0
Track: LH: 0-3 RH: 0-0 Tight: 0-0 Gall: 0-1
Aids: Bl: 0-0 Vi: 0-0 Tstrap: 0-0
Best Rating: 143 5/01 Hayd 2m good Hdl

A useful handicap hurdler who gained his biggest victory at Aintree on Grand National day 2001 when winning a valuable handicap hurdle over two miles in desperate conditions, and ran a very good race at Haydock after that when second. Lightly raced since.

Doctor Bravious (IRE)

10-y-o b g Priolo (USA)-Sharp Slipper (Sharpo)
Jamie Poulton   Chris Steward & Christina Taylor

Placings:033P0/0402440115342/P1253/0P/P5P-   (0011)
2002/03: 21^PG,

	Starts	1st	2nd	3rd	Win & Pl
Hurdles	1	0	0	0	
Career Total	28	3	3	4	13168

98	12/99	Plum	2m5f	E(0-115)HHdl	GD	£2320
97	2/99	Plum	2m1f	E(0-115)HHdl	SFT	£5199
86	1/99	Tntn	2m1f	G Hdl	SFT	£1509

Total win prize-money £9028

Going:	Sf: 0-0 GS: 0-0 Gd: 0-1 GF: - Fm: 0-0
Distance:	2m/2m3: 0-0 2m4-2m7: 0-1 3m+: 0-0
Track:	LH: 0-1 RH: 0-0 Tight: 0-1 Gall: 0-0
Aids:	Bl: 0-0 Vi: 0-0 Tstrap: 0-0
Best Rating:	100 4/99 Plum 2m4f good Hdl

Doctor Dove
44
9-y-o ch g St Enodoc-Saucy Dove (Saucy Kit)
C J Price   J P Price

Placings:33/5/0-P   (0742)
2002/03: 20^PG,

	Starts	1st	2nd	3rd	Win & Pl
Hurdles	1	0	0	0	
Career Total	5	0	0	2	471

Going:	Sf: 0-0 GS: 0-0 Gd: 0-1 GF: - Fm: 0-0
Distance:	2m/2m3: 0-0 2m4-2m7: 0-1 3m+: 0-0
Track:	LH: 0-1 RH: 0-0 Tight: 0-0 Gall: 0-0
Aids:	Bl: 0-0 Vi: 0-0 Tstrap: 0-0
Best Rating:	90 4/00 NAbb 2m1f heavy NHF

Doctor Green (FR)
46   99
10-y-o b g Green Desert (USA)-Highbrow (Shirley Heights)
M C Pipe   M C Pipe

Placings:1114354P/561406154021/2542/3634320F5530-
0P   (0994)
2002/03: 16^OGS, 22^PGF,

	Starts	1st	2nd	3rd	Win & Pl
Hurdles	2	0	0		
Career Total	38	6	4	5	19663

113	4/00	Extr	2m1f110yG(0-95)HHdl	HVY	£2044
98	12/99	Tntn	2m3f110yG Hdl	G-S	£1523
106	10/99	Strf	2m110y G Hdl	G-S	£1744
111	10/96	Chel	2m110y C Hdl	G-F	£3468
109	10/96	Wwck	2m	D Hdl	FRM	£3109
103	10/96	Extr	2m1f110yE Hdl	GD	£1969

Total win prize-money £13858

Going:	Sf: 0-0 GS: 0-1 Gd: 0-0 GF: - Fm: 0-1
Distance:	2m/2m3: 0-1 2m4-2m7: 0-0 3m+: 0-0
Track:	LH: 0-2 RH: 0-0 Tight: 0-1 Gall: 0-0
Aids:	Bl: 0-0 Vi: 0-2 Tstrap: 0-0
Best Rating:	119 5/00 Uttx 2m4f110y good Hdl

Fair plater, likes to front-run, suited by cut in the ground.
Has won from two miles to two miles three furlongs.

Doctor John
103   96
6-y-o ch g Handsome Sailor-Bollin Sophie (Efisio)
Andrew Turnell   Dr John Hollowood

Placings:6-050   (4252)
2002/03: 16^OGS, 19^SGS, 22^OG,

	Starts	1st	2nd	3rd	Win & Pl
Hurdles	3	0	0	0	0

Career Total   4   0   0   0   0

Going:	Sf: 0-0 GS: 0-2 Gd: 0-1 GF: - Fm: 0-0
Distance:	2m/2m3: 0-1 2m4-2m7: 0-2 3m+: 0-0
Track:	LH: 0-2 RH: 0-1 Tight: 0-0 Gall: 0-1
Aids:	Bl: 0-0 Vi: 0-0 Tstrap: 0-0
Best Rating:	96 1/03 Donc 2m110y gd-sft Hdl

Plater on the Flat; no real promise over hurdles.

Doctor Wood
100   78
8-y-o b g Joligeneration-Ladywood (Doctor Wall)
Miss V A Stephens   D G Stephens

Placings:10P-50032   (3549)
2002/03: 17^SG, 17^OGF, 22^OGS, 19^SS, 17^OG,

	Starts	1st	2nd	3rd	Win & Pl
Hurdles	5	0	1	1	1420
Career Total	8	1	1	1	3804

92	11/01	Tntn	2m1f	H NHF	GD	£2383

Total win prize-money £2384

Going:	Sf: 0-1 GS: 0-1 Gd: 0-2 GF: - Fm: 0-1
Distance:	2m/2m3: 0-3 2m4-2m7: 0-2 3m+: 0-0
Track:	LH: 0-2 RH: 0-3 Tight: 0-3 Gall: 0-0
Aids:	Bl: 0-0 Vi: 0-0 Tstrap: 0-0
Best Rating:	92 11/01 Tntn 2m1f good NHF

Plating-class hurdler; stays two and a half miles.

Doe Nal Rua (IRE)
85   89
6-y-o b g Mister Lord (USA)-Phardante Girl (IRE)
(Phardante (FR))
T D Easterby   The G-Guck Group

Placings:30003   (3566)
2002/03: 16^OHY, 16OS, 16^OGS, 19^OGS, 21^OHY,

	Starts	1st	2nd	3rd	Win & Pl
NH Flat	2	0	0	1	354
Hurdles	3	0	0	1	517
Career Total	5	0	0	2	871

Going:	Sf: 0-3 GS: 0-2 Gd: 0-0 GF: - Fm: 0-0
Distance:	2m/2m3: 0-3 2m4-2m7: 0-2 3m+: 0-0
Track:	LH: 0-5 RH: 0-0 Tight: 0-1 Gall: 0-1
Aids:	Bl: 0-0 Vi: 0-0 Tstrap: 0-0
Best Rating:	89 2/03 Sedg 2m5f110y heavy Hdl

Fair form in bumpers/hurdlers; acts on soft ground.

Does It Matter
(59h)   (24h)
6-y-o b g Carlingford Castle-Flopsy Mopsy (Full Of Hope)
P C Ritchens   John Pearl

Placings:000P   (3871)
2002/03: 17^OG, 17^OGF, 16^OGF, 19OS,

	Starts	1st	2nd	3rd	Win & Pl
NH Flat	3	0	0	0	0
Hurdles	1	0	0	0	0
Career Total	4	0	0	0	

Going:	Sf: 0-1 GS: 0-0 Gd: 0-1 GF: - Fm: 0-2
Distance:	2m/2m3: 0-4 2m4-2m7: 0-0 3m+: 0-0
Track:	LH: 0-1 RH: 0-2 Tight: 0-1 Gall: 0-1
Aids:	Bl: 0-0 Vi: 0-0 Tstrap: 0-0
Best Rating:	62 7/02 Strf 2m110y gd-fm NHF

Career Total   4   0   0   0   0

Going:	Sf: 0-0 GS: 0-2 Gd: 0-1 GF: - Fm: 0-0
Distance:	2m/2m3: 0-1 2m4-2m7: 0-2 3m+: 0-0
Track:	LH: 0-2 RH: 0-1 Tight: 0-0 Gall: 0-1
Aids:	Bl: 0-0 Vi: 0-0 Tstrap: 0-0
Best Rating:	96 1/03 Donc 2m110y gd-sft Hdl

Doigts D'Or (FR)
98   90+
8-y-o b g Sanglamore (USA)-Doigts De Fee (USA)
(L Emigrant (USA))
P R Webber   Mrs Fiona Gregory

Placings:502/15040/5/44   (2942)
2002/03: 16⁴HY, 20⁴GS,

	Starts	1st	2nd	3rd	Win & Pl
Chases	2	0	0		811
Career Total	11	1	1	0	4415

110	11/99	Hntg	2m110y E Hdl	GD	£2635

Total win prize-money £2635

Going:	Sf: 0-1 GS: 0-1 Gd: 0-0 GF: - Fm: 0-0
Distance:	2m/2m3: 0-1 2m4-2m7: 0-1 3m+: 0-0
Track:	LH: 0-1 RH: 0-1 Tight: 0-1 Gall: 0-0
Aids:	Bl: 0-0 Vi: 0-0 Tstrap: 0-0
Best Rating:	110 1/00 Kemp 2m good Hdl

Winning novice hurdler but poor novice chaser; best over
two miles; acts on fast ground.

Doire-Chrinn (IRE)
101   96
7-y-o b/br m Unblest-Princess Monarch (IRE) (Fairy King
(USA))
D P Kelly   Emmet Quinn

Placings:4330-40646   (3973a)
2002/03: 16⁴YS, 16^OGS, 16⁸S, 16⁸HY,

	Starts	1st	2nd	3rd	Win & Pl
Hurdles	5	0	0	0	781
Career Total	9	0	0	2	2193

Going:	Sf: 0-3 GS: 0-1 Gd: 0-0 GF: - Fm: 0-0
Distance:	2m/2m3: 0-5 2m4-2m7: 0-0 3m+: 0-0
Track:	LH: 0-4 RH: 0-0 Tight: 0-0 Gall: 0-0
Aids:	Bl: 0-0 Vi: 0-0 Tstrap: 0-0
Best Rating:	114 11/01 Punc 2m soft Hdl

Winner on the Flat, but is a maiden over hurdles.

Doli Cygnus
103f   95f
5-y-o gr m Bedford (USA)-Damsong (Petong)
E L James   Mrs D Hardy

Placings:53   (2064)
2002/03: 16⁵G, 17³S,

	Starts	1st	2nd	3rd	Win & Pl
NH Flat	2	0	0	1	268
Career Total	2	0	0	1	268

Going:	Sf: 0-1 GS: 0-0 Gd: 0-0 GF: - Fm: 0-0
Distance:	2m/2m3: 0-2 2m4-2m7: 0-0 3m+: 0-0
Track:	LH: 0-1 RH: 0-1 Tight: 0-0 Gall: 0-0
Aids:	Bl: 0-0 Vi: 0-0 Tstrap: 0-0
Best Rating:	95 11/02 Hrfd 2m1f soft NHF

Staying on well in bumpers on her first two runs.

Dollar Law
107   112
7-y-o ch g Selkirk (USA)-Western Heights (Shirley Heights)
R J Price   The Cleobury Partnership

Placings:433323441U   (4316)
2002/03: 16⁴GS, 16⁸S, 16³S, 17³GS, 17²GS, 16³S, 16⁴GS, 16⁴GS,
16¹G, 17^UG,

Career Total   4   0   0   0   0

	Starts	1st	2nd	3rd	Win & Pl
Hurdles	10	1	1	4	11605
Career Total	10	1	1	4	11605
104 3/03	Chep	2m110y	D Hdl	GD	£5053

Total win prize-money £5054

Going:	Sf: 0-3 GS: 0-5 Gd: 1-2 GF: - Fm: 0-0
Distance:	2m/2m3: 1-10 2m4-2m7: 0-0 3m+: 0-0
Track:	LH: 1-9 RH: 0-1 Tight: 0-3 Gall: 0-1
Aids:	Bl: 0-0 Vi: 0-0 Tstrap: 0-3
Best Rating:	112 3/03 Strf 2m110y gd-sft Hdl

Modest maiden hurdler; ran well in handicaps early in 2003; suited by soft ground and trips around two miles; wears a tongue tie; has worn sheepskin cheekpieces.

Dolly Mop
81   56
7-y-o b m Nearly A Hand-Roving Seal (Privy Seal)
B J M Ryall D R Bell

Placings:0-560   (4366)
2002/03: 17⁵GS, 20⁶S, 20⁹G,

	Starts	1st	2nd	3rd	Win & Pl
Hurdles	3	0	0	0	0
Career Total	4	0	0	0	0

Going:	Sf: 0-1 GS: 0-1 Gd: 0-1 GF: - Fm: 0-0
Distance:	2m/2m3: 0-1 2m4-2m7: 0-2 3m+: 0-0
Track:	LH: 0-1 RH: 0-2 Tight: 0-1 Gall: 0-0
Aids:	Bl: 0-0 Vi: 0-0 Tstrap: 0-0
Best Rating:	69 10/01 Extr 2m1f gd-sft NHF

Dolphinelle (IRE)
83   65
7-y-o b g Dolphin Street (FR)-Mamie s Joy (Prince Tenderfoot (USA))
Jamie Poulton Chris Steward

Placings:050/34P0003-00006   (3804)
2002/03: 16⁹GF, 16⁶GF, 16⁹S, 16⁰S, 16⁶S,

	Starts	1st	2nd	3rd	Win & Pl
Hurdles	5	0	0	0	0
Career Total	15	0	0	2	668

Going:	Sf: 0-3 GS: 0-0 Gd: 0-0 GF: - Fm: 0-2
Distance:	2m/2m3: 0-5 2m4-2m7: 0-0 3m+: 0-0
Track:	LH: 0-5 RH: 0-0 Tight: 0-4 Gall: 0-0
Aids:	Bl: 0-1 Vi: 0-0 Tstrap: 0-0
Best Rating:	93 12/00 Kemp 2m gd-sft Hdl

Dom Shadeed
71   57
8-y-o b g Shadeed (USA)-Fair Dominion (Dominion)
R J Baker Graham Brown

Placings:60/0R   (4256)
2002/03: 16⁹S, 17⁸G,

	Starts	1st	2nd	3rd	Win & Pl
Hurdles	2	0	0	0	0
Career Total	4	0	0	0	0

Going:	Sf: 0-1 GS: 0-0 Gd: 0-1 GF: - Fm: 0-0
Distance:	2m/2m3: 0-2 2m4-2m7: 0-0 3m+: 0-0
Track:	LH: 0-1 RH: 0-1 Tight: 0-0 Gall: 0-0
Aids:	Bl: 0-0 Vi: 0-0 Tstrap: 0-0
Best Rating:	61 9/99 Tntn 2m3f110y gd-fm Hdl

Domappel
104
11-y-o b g Domynsky-Appelania (Star Appeal)
M C Banks M C Banks

Placings:5106/153213/004/633230/243/42-PF   (0336)
2002/03: 20⁸GF, 20⁶G,

	Starts	1st	2nd	3rd	Win & Pl
Chases	2	0	0	0	
Career Total	26	3	4	6	27639
119 3/97	Uttx	2m4f110yB HHdl	GD	£10065
118 11/96	Wwck	2m3f D(0-125)HHdl	GD	£2908
116 12/95	Hayd	2m D Hdl	GD	£2957

Total win prize-money £15931

Going:	Sf: 0-0 GS: 0-0 Gd: 0-1 GF: - Fm: 0-1
Distance:	2m/2m3: 0-0 2m4-2m7: 0-2 3m+: 0-0
Track:	LH: 0-1 RH: 0-0 Tight: 0-0 Gall: 0-0
Aids:	Bl: 0-0 Vi: 0-0 Tstrap: 0-0
Best Rating:	122 12/98 Donc 2m4f good Hdl

Modest hurdler/chaser, on a long losing run and lightly-raced of late. Suited by a sound surface.

Dome
92   89
5-y-o b/br g Be My Chief (USA)-Round Tower (High Top)
S Dow Troubleshooters

Placings:4P6-306   (0642)
2002/03: 18³GF, 20⁶GF, 22⁶GF,

	Starts	1st	2nd	3rd	Win & Pl
Hurdles	3	0	0	1	348
Career Total	6	0	0	1	619

Going:	Sf: 0-0 GS: 0-0 Gd: 0-0 GF: - Fm: 0-3
Distance:	2m/2m3: 0-1 2m4-2m7: 0-2 3m+: 0-0
Track:	LH: 0-3 RH: 0-0 Tight: 0-2 Gall: 0-0
Aids:	Bl: 0-0 Vi: 0-0 Tstrap: 0-2
Best Rating:	89 6/02 Font 2m2f110y gd-fm Hdl

Domenico (IRE)
109   110
5-y-o b g Sadler s Wells (USA)-Russian Ballet (USA) (Nijinsky (CAN))
J R Jenkins (P R Webber 19/10) American Horse Racing Club Ltd

Placings:02-1535   (4081)
2002/03: 16¹S, 20⁵S, 16³GS, 16⁵HY,

	Starts	1st	2nd	3rd	Win & Pl
Hurdles	4	1	0	1	4815
Career Total	6	1	1	1	5577
110 11/02	Uttx	2m	E Hdl	SFT	£3643

Total win prize-money £3644

Going:	Sf: 1-3 GS: 0-1 Gd: 0-0 GF: - Fm: 0-0
Distance:	2m/2m3: 1-3 2m4-2m7: 0-1 3m+: 0-0
Track:	LH: 1-3 RH: 0-1 Tight: 0-1 Gall: 0-1
Aids:	Bl: 0-0 Vi: 0-0 Tstrap: 0-0
Best Rating:	110 11/02 Uttx 2m soft Hdl

Irish maiden winner on the Flat. Highly tried on his hurdles debut on his debut in this country. Won an ordinary novice at Utttoxeter on his reappearance in November 2002. Acts on good ground and soft.

Dominikus
109(105h)   (105h)125+
6-y-o b g Second Set (IRE)-Dolce Vita (GER) (Windwurf (GER))

Ferdy Murphy The Aarons Archer Partnership

Placings:405/116066420-5212   (0891)
2002/03: 16⁵GF, 20²GF, 20¹G, 20²S,

	Starts	1st	2nd	3rd	Win & Pl
Chases	4	1	2	0	6485
Career Total	16	3	3	0	13271
106 7/02	MRas	2m4f	E Ch	GD	£3997
89 6/01	Hexm	2m	D Hdl	GD	£3353
89 5/01	Hexm	2m	F(0-95)HHdl	FRM	£2017

Total win prize-money £9368

Going:	Sf: 0-1 GS: 0-0 Gd: 1-1 GF: - Fm: 0-2
Distance:	2m/2m3: 0-1 2m4-2m7: 1-3 3m+: 0-0
Track:	LH: 0-2 RH: 1-2 Tight: 1-2 Gall: 0-0
Aids:	Bl: 0-0 Vi: 0-0 Tstrap: 0-0
Best Rating:	115 6/02 Hexm 2m4f110y gd-fm Ch

Fair chaser; stays three miles; acts on fast ground.

Dominion Prince
5-y-o b g First Trump-Lammastide (Martinmas)
D Mullarkey D J Dugdale

Placings:0   (4337)
2002/03: 16⁰GF,

	Starts	1st	2nd	3rd	Win & Pl
Hurdles	1	0	0	0	
Career Total	1	0	0	0	

Going:	Sf: 0-0 GS: 0-0 Gd: 0-0 GF: - Fm: 0-1
Distance:	2m/2m3: 0-1 2m4-2m7: 0-0 3m+: 0-0
Track:	LH: 0-0 RH: 0-1 Tight: 0-0 Gall: 0-1
Aids:	Bl: 0-0 Vi: 0-0 Tstrap: 0-1
Best Rating:	0 3/03 Hntg 2m110y gd-fm Hdl

Domquista D'Or
106   66
6-y-o b g Superpower-Gild The Lily (Ile De Bourbon (USA))
G A Ham Colin B Taylor

Placings:P0653035-P032PP50   (4450)
2002/03: 20⁰G, 17⁰GS, 16³GF, 16²S, 17⁰G, 19⁰GF, 19⁵GF, 21⁰G,

	Starts	1st	2nd	3rd	Win & Pl
Hurdles	8	0	1	1	942
Career Total	16	0	1	3	1788

Going:	Sf: 0-1 GS: 0-1 Gd: 0-3 GF: - Fm: 0-3
Distance:	2m/2m3: 0-4 2m4-2m7: 0-4 3m+: 0-0
Track:	LH: 0-5 RH: 0-3 Tight: 0-3 Gall: 0-0
Aids:	Bl: 0-2 Vi: 0-0 Tstrap: 0-0
Best Rating:	82 7/02 Uttx 2m gd-fm Hdl

Still a maiden over jumps. Best efforts have come at around two miles on soft ground.

Don Fernando
103   133
4-y-o b c Zilzal (USA)-Teulada (USA) (Riverman (USA))
M C Pipe (E A L Dunlop 14/9) Lucayan Stud

Placings:112B0   (4470)
2002/03: 16¹GS, 17¹G, 17²GS, 17⁸G, 16⁸G,

	Starts	1st	2nd	3rd	Win & Pl
Hurdles	5	2	1	0	27726
Career Total	5	2	1	0	27726
133 12/02	Chel	2m1f	A Hdl	GD	£11600
127 11/02	Chel	2m110y	B Hdl	G-S	£9526

Total win prize-money £21126

Going: Sf: 0-0 GS: 1-2 Gd: 1-3 GF: - Fm: 0-0
Distance: 2m/2m3: 2-5 2m4-2m7: 0-0 3m+: 0-0
Track: LH: 2-5 RH: 0-0 Tight: 0-1 **Gall:** 1-3
Aids: Bl: 0-0 Vi: 0-0 Tstrap: 0-0
Best Rating: 133 12/02 Chel 2m1f   good   Hdl

One of the leading juvenile hurdlers; suited by two miles; acts well with cut in the ground; has worn a visor, but very game; goes well at Cheltenham, although brought down there in the Triumph Hurdle.

Don Ido (ARG)
100   89
7-y-o b g Lazy Boy (ARG)-She s Goy You (ARG) (Indalecio (ARG))
J A B Old W E Sturt

Placings:U-435   (1682)
2002/03: 17⁴F, 16³G, 16⁵GF,

	Starts	1st	2nd	3rd	Win & Pl
Hurdles	3	0	0	1	1009
Career Total	4	0	0	1	1009

Going: Sf: 0-0 GS: 0-0 Gd: 0-1 GF: - Fm: 0-2
Distance: 2m/2m3: 0-3 2m4-2m7: 0-0 3m+: 0-0
Track: LH: 0-2 RH: 0-1 Tight: 0-1 Gall: 0-0
Aids: Bl: 0-0 Vi: 0-0 Tstrap: 0-0
Best Rating: 89 10/02 Chel 2m110y   gd-fm   Hdl

A winner on the Flat in Argentina. Let down by jumping on hurdling debut at Taunton April 2002 but ran a promising race at Stratford in October.

Don Royal

9-y-o b g Rakaposhi King-Donna Farina (Little Buskins)
J Scott G T Lever

Placings:3PP   (4480)
2002/03: 25³S, 20⁴S, 25⁵G,

	Starts	1st	2nd	3rd	Win & Pl
Chases	3	0	0	1	428
Career Total	3	0	0	1	428

Going: Sf: 0-2 GS: 0-0 Gd: 0-1 GF: - Fm: 0-0
Distance: 2m/2m3: 0-0 2m4-2m7: 0-1 3m+: 0-2
Track: LH: 0-1 RH: 0-2 Tight: 0-1 Gall: 0-0
Aids: Bl: 0-0 Vi: 0-0 Tstrap: 0-0
Best Rating: 82 5/02 Towc 3m1f   soft   Ch

Don Valentino (POL)
71   36
4-y-o ch g Duke Valentino-Dona (POL) (Dakota)
T R George Sir Stanley Clarke

Placings:0   (3776)
2002/03: 17⁰GS,

	Starts	1st	2nd	3rd	Win & Pl
Hurdles	1	0	0	0	
Career Total	1	0	0	0	

Going: Sf: 0-0 GS: 0-1 Gd: 0-0 GF: - Fm: 0-0
Distance: 2m/2m3: 0-1 2m4-2m7: 0-0 3m+: 0-0
Track: LH: 0-0 RH: 0-1 Tight: 0-0 Gall: 0-0
Aids: Bl: 0-0 Vi: 0-0 Tstrap: 0-0
Best Rating: 39 2/03 Extr 2m1f   gd-sft   Hdl

Don't Sioux Me (IRE)
111   109
5-y-o b g Sadler s Wells (USA)-Commanche Belle (Shirley Heights)
C R Dore (H R A Cecil 26/10) L Cohen

Placings:623   (4522)
2002/03: 16⁶G, 16²GF, 16³G,

	Starts	1st	2nd	3rd	Win & Pl
Hurdles	3	0	1	1	1663
Career Total	3	0	1	1	1663

Going: Sf: 0-0 GS: 0-0 Gd: 0-2 GF: - Fm: 0-1
Distance: 2m/2m3: 0-3 2m4-2m7: 0-0 3m+: 0-0
Track: LH: 0-1 RH: 0-2 Tight: 0-0 Gall: 0-2
Aids: Bl: 0-0 Vi: 0-0 Tstrap: 0-0
Best Rating: 95 4/03 Uttx 2m   good   Hdl

Modest hurdler, effective over two miles and handles most types of ground; sometimes tongue tied; consistent.

Don't Tell Jr (IRE)
100   102
9-y-o b g Mister Lord (USA)-Middle Third (Miners Lamp)
Ferdy Murphy Geoff Hubbard Racing

Placings:0PP6/65/321-32   (2119)
2002/03: 24³GS, 29²GS,

	Starts	1st	2nd	3rd	Win & Pl
Chases	2	0	1	1	2240
Career Total	11	1	2	2	6759
102 2/02 Plum 3m2f		E Ch		HVY	£3055
		Total win prize-money £3055			

Going: Sf: 0-0 GS: 0-2 Gd: 0-0 GF: - Fm: 0-0
Distance: 2m/2m3: 0-0 2m4-2m7: 0-0 3m+: 0-2
Track: LH: 0-1 RH: 0-1 Tight: 0-1 Gall: 0-0
Aids: Bl: 0-0 Vi: 0-0 Tstrap: 0-0
Best Rating: 102 11/02 Fknm 3m5f110y gd-sft   Ch

Came into his own when tried over fences and got off the mark at Plumpton in February 2002. Stays beyond three miles and goes very well with plenty of cut.

Dona Ferentis (IRE)

8-y-o b m Homo Sapien-Greek Tan (Pitpan)
S Flook D F Quinlan

Placings:PP/40FP-P   (3951)
2002/03: 16²GS,

	Starts	1st	2nd	3rd	Win & Pl
Chases	1	0	0	0	
Career Total	7	0	0	0	0

Going: Sf: 0-0 GS: 0-1 Gd: 0-0 GF: - Fm: 0-0
Distance: 2m/2m3: 0-1 2m4-2m7: 0-0 3m+: 0-0
Track: LH: 0-0 RH: 0-1 Tight: 0-0 Gall: 0-0
Aids: Bl: 0-1 Vi: 0-0 Tstrap: 0-1
Best Rating: 88 5/01 Hntg 2m110y gd-fm   Hdl

Donadino (IRE)
111(97h)   (98h)122
10-y-o br g Be My Native (USA)-Atteses (Smooth Stepper)
Jonjo O Neill (C F Swan 29/8) J P McManus

Placings:25/20F14/31313/B143/1FU06B-3P103   (1335)
2002/03: 20³S, 20³GS, 17¹Y, 16⁶F, 20³GF,

	Starts	1st	2nd	3rd	Win & Pl
Hurdles	1	0	0	1	687
Chases	4	1	0	1	15586
Career Total	27	6	2	6	49595
122 8/02	Gway 2m1f	HCh		YLD	£14355
120 5/01	Rosc 2m5f	Ch		G-F	£7862
110 6/00	Rosc 2m	Hdl		GD	£3864
97 3/00	Naas 2m	Ch		Y-S	£4736
123 9/99	Baln 2m1f	Ch		G-F	£6160
117 3/99	Leop 2m	Hdl		YLD	£3069
		Total win prize-money £40049			

Going: Sf: 0-1 GS: 0-1 Gd: 0-0 GF: - Fm: 0-2
Distance: 2m/2m3: 1-2 2m4-2m7: 0-3 3m+: 0-0
Track: LH: 0-2 RH: 1-3 Tight: 0-1 Gall: 0-1
Aids: Bl: 0-0 Vi: 0-0 Tstrap: 0-0
Best Rating: 130 5/00 Punc 2m   gd-fm   Ch

Fair chaser at around two and a half miles, suited by fast ground but acts on softer.

Donallach Mor (IRE)

11-y-o b g Phardante (FR)-Panalee (Pitpan)
Mrs S H Shirley-Beavan (S H Shirley-Beavan 19/10) Mrs Charles Sample

Placings:1/11P0/2/2P-P4P   (4508)
2002/03: 25⁵PG, 24⁴S, 27⁵PG,

	Starts	1st	2nd	3rd	Win & Pl
Chases	3	0	0	0	314
Career Total	11	3	2	0	13355
111 10/99	Towc 2m6f	E Ch		GD	£2739
126 5/99	Strf 3m4f	H Ch		GD	£6414
104 4/99	Hntg 3m	H Ch		GD	£1475
		Total win prize-money £10628			

Going: Sf: 0-1 GS: 0-0 Gd: 0-2 GF: - Fm: 0-3
Distance: 2m/2m3: 0-0 2m4-2m7: 0-0 3m+: 0-3
Track: LH: 0-2 RH: 0-1 Tight: 0-2 Gall: 0-0
Aids: Bl: 0-0 Vi: 0-0 Tstrap: 0-0
Best Rating: 126 5/99 Strf 3m4f   good   Ch

A former hunter chaser, he acts on good ground and goes well over two miles and six furlongs plus. Lightly raced in recent seasons.

Donatus (IRE)
97   103
7-y-o b g Royal Academy (USA)-La Dame Du Lac (USA) (Round Table)
Miss K M George (S Dow 29/4) Exterior Profiles Ltd

Placings:22240/41P/0SPP3F-2463P   (0773)
2002/03: 16⁶G, 16²GF, 17⁴G, 20⁶GF, 16³G, 20⁰GF,

	Starts	1st	2nd	3rd	Win & Pl
Hurdles	6	0	1	1	2657
Career Total	19	1	4	2	10377
111 10/00	Fknm 2m4f	D Hdl		GD	£2990
		Total win prize-money £2990			

Going: Sf: 0-0 GS: 0-0 Gd: 0-3 GF: - Fm: 0-3
Distance: 2m/2m3: 0-4 2m4-2m7: 0-2 3m+: 0-0
Track: LH: 0-6 RH: 0-0 Tight: 0-3 Gall: 0-0
Aids: Bl: 0-0 Vi: 0-0 Tstrap: 0-0
Best Rating: 130 3/00 Chel 2m1f   gd-fm   Hdl

Frustrating sort over hurdles, often there or thereabouts but on a long losing run. Still better than he was on the Flat.

Donegal Shore (IRE)
84   73
4-y-o b c Mujadil (USA)-Distant Shore (IRE) (Jareer (USA))

Mrs J Candlish (B W Hills 17/8) Racing For You Limited

Placings:000P   (4525)
2002/03: 16⁵S, 19⁰G, 17⁰GS, 16ᴾG,

	Starts	1st	2nd	3rd	Win & Pl
Hurdles	4	0	0	0	
Career Total	4	0	0	0	

Going:	Sf: 0-1 GS: 0-1 Gd: 0-2 GF: - Fm: 0-0
Distance:	2m2m3: 0-3 2m4-2m7: 0-1 3m+: 0-0
Track:	LH: 0-2 RH: 0-2 Tight: 0-0 Gall: 0-0
Aids:	Bl: 0-0 Vi: 0-0 Tstrap: 0-2
Best Rating:	70 3/03 Carl 2m1f gd-sft Hdl

A winner over five furlongs on the Flat, he has yet to prove he stays further than six. Hampered early on and never got into the race on his hurdling debut at Warwick.

Donie Dooley (IRE)
95   91+
5-y-o ch g Be My Native (USA)-Bridgeofallen (IRE) (Torus)
P T Dalton Mrs Julie Martin

Placings:43-0   (3890)
2002/03: 16⁰G,

	Starts	1st	2nd	3rd	Win & Pl
NH Flat	1	0	0	0	
Career Total	3	0	0	1	1853

Going:	Sf: 0-0 GS: 0-0 Gd: 0-1 GF: - Fm: 0-0
Distance:	2m/2m3: 0-1 2m4-2m7: 0-0 3m+: 0-0
Track:	LH: 0-1 RH: 0-0 Tight: 0-0 Gall: 0-0
Aids:	Bl: 0-0 Vi: 0-0 Tstrap: 0-0
Best Rating:	93 3/02 Limk 2m soft NHF

Novice hurdler; ex-Irish ; won at Uttoxeter in June; stays 2m 4f; acts on fast ground.

Donnabella
76   38
6-y-o b m Bustino-Howanever (Buckskin (FR))
John R Upson (R J Hodges 22/10) Mrs R E Tate

Placings:00   (4187)
2002/03: 17⁰G, 20⁰G,

	Starts	1st	2nd	3rd	Win & Pl
NH Flat	1	0	0	0	0
Hurdles	1	0	0	0	0
Career Total	2	0	0	0	

Going:	Sf: 0-0 GS: 0-0 Gd: 0-2 GF: - Fm: 0-0
Distance:	2m/2m3: 0-1 2m4-2m7: 0-1 3m+: 0-0
Track:	LH: 0-0 RH: 0-0 Tight: 0-1 Gall: 0-0
Aids:	Bl: 0-0 Vi: 0-0 Tstrap: 0-0
Best Rating:	48 10/02 Extr 2m1f good NHF

Donnini (IRE)
100   57
6-y-o ch g Kris-La Luna (USA) (Lyphard (USA))
B D Leavy (Miss K Marks 14/9) Alexander Gould

Placings:23F65P00P   (4525)
2002/03: 17²G, 17³GF, 16⁵S, 18⁶GF, 16⁵G, 16ᴾG, 16⁹GS, 17⁰G, 16ᴾG,

	Starts	1st	2nd	3rd	Win & Pl
Hurdles	9	0	1	1	1488
Career Total	9	0	1	1	1488

Going:	Sf: 0-1 GS: 0-1 Gd: 0-5 GF: - Fm: 0-2
Distance:	2m/2m3: 0-9 2m4-2m7: 0-0 3m+: 0-0
Track:	LH: 0-7 RH: 0-2 Tight: 0-2 Gall: 0-1
Aids:	Bl: 0-0 Vi: 0-0 Tstrap: 0-1
Best Rating:	98 7/02 NAbb 2m1f gd-fm Hdl

Modest novice hurdler, has promise on all starts over timber.

Donnybrook (IRE)
107   116
10-y-o ch g Riot Helmet-Evening Bun (Baragoi)
R D E Woodhouse R Smith,D Hall,D Thompson,Mrs C Clarke

Placings:00/433P042/151144300/3221315/P40240/503403
410-04514404   (4175)
2002/03: 16⁰GF, 25⁴G, 20⁵S, 20¹G, 20⁴GS, 24⁴G, 20⁰G, 21⁴S,

	Starts	1st	2nd	3rd	Win & Pl
Chases	8	1	0	0	9556
Career Total	48	7	4	7	56314

116	11/02	Hayd	D(0-125)HCh		GD	£4803
116	3/02	Newc	2m110y	D(0-125)HCh	HVY	£4728
121	1/00	Newc	2m4f	A Ch	SFT	£19500
115	12/99	Uttx	2m	D Ch	SFT	£4182
102	10/98	Weth	2m	E(0-105)HHdl	SFT	£3174
93	10/98	MRas	2m3f110yE Hdl		SFT	£2845
95	5/98	Hexm	2m	E Hdl	GD	£2033
				Total win prize-money £41269		

Going:	Sf: 0-2 GS: 0-1 Gd: 1-4 GF: - Fm: 0-1
Distance:	2m/2m3: 0-1 2m4-2m7: 1-5 3m+: 0-2
Track:	LH: 1-8 RH: 0-0 Tight: 0-2 Gall: 0-2
Aids:	Bl: 0-0 Vi: 0-0 Tstrap: 0-0
Best Rating:	121 1/00 Newc 2m4f soft Ch

Fair handicap chaser; jumps well; best on soft ground; stays three miles; by no means consistent.

Dooley Gate
74f   58f
6-y-o b g Petoski-High B (Gunner B)
F P Murtagh F P Murtagh

Placings:0   (2518)
2002/03: 16⁶S,

	Starts	1st	2nd	3rd	Win & Pl
NH Flat	1	0	0	0	
Career Total	1	0	0	0	

Going:	Sf: 0-1 GS: 0-0 Gd: 0-0 GF: - Fm: 0-0
Distance:	2m/2m3: 0-1 2m4-2m7: 0-0 3m+: 0-0
Track:	LH: 0-1 RH: 0-0 Tight: 0-0 Gall: 0-0
Aids:	Bl: 0-0 Vi: 0-0 Tstrap: 0-0
Best Rating:	58 12/02 Newc 2m soft NHF

Doon Run (IRE)
(111h)   (100h)**106**
9-y-o ch g Commanche Run-Paupers Spring (Pauper)
B G Powell (Michael Hourigan 4/5) The L L C J Partnership

Placings:4⁄24400/40612312205P/30/0304F0002-03P   (2217)
2002/03: 24⁰Y, 25³HY, 22⁵S,

	Starts	1st	2nd	3rd	Win & Pl
Hurdles	2	0	0	1	663
Chases	1	0	0	0	0
Career Total	32	2	5	4	16460
110	12/99 Thur	2m	Hdl		SFT	£3696
106	10/99 Cork	2m	NHF		Y-S	£3234
				Total win prize-money £6930		

Going:	Sf: 0-2 GS: 0-0 Gd: 0-0 GF: - Fm: 0-0
Distance:	2m/2m3: 0-0 2m4-2m7: 0-1 3m+: 0-2
Track:	LH: 0-1 RH: 0-1 Tight: 0-0 Gall: 0-1
Aids:	Bl: 0-0 Vi: 0-0 Tstrap: 0-0
Best Rating:	115 1/00 Navn 2m2f soft Hdl

Moderate hurdler/chaser. Has not won since 1999. Acts on soft ground.

Doran's Day (IRE)
96   90
6-y-o b g Gildoran-Inverdonan (Our Mirage)
Mrs H Dalton Trevor Hemmings

Placings:005-3P   (1786)
2002/03: 19³GF, 22ᴾGS,

	Starts	1st	2nd	3rd	Win & Pl
Hurdles	2	0	0	1	450
Career Total	5	0	0	1	450

Going:	Sf: 0-0 GS: 0-1 Gd: 0-0 GF: - Fm: 0-1
Distance:	2m/2m3: 0-2 2m4-2m7: 0-2 3m+: 0-0
Track:	LH: 0-0 RH: 0-2 Tight: 0-1 Gall: 0-0
Aids:	Bl: 0-0 Vi: 0-0 Tstrap: 0-0
Best Rating:	90 5/02 Hrfd 2m3f110y gd-fm Hdl

Dorans Gold
108(94h)   (81h)131d
9-y-o b g Gildoran-Cindie Girl (Orchestra)
P F Nicholls Mel Fordham S Fisher M Harper H Johnson

Placings:2/1P50/11F2F42/12P-1P120   (4101)
2002/03: 20¹S, 20ᴾG, 20¹GS, 20²GS, 24⁰G,

	Starts	1st	2nd	3rd	Win & Pl
Chases	5	2	1	0	22111
Career Total	20	6	5	0	81796
133	12/02	Wwck	2m4f110yC(0-130)HCh		G-S	£11235
130	10/02	Bang	2m4f110yD(0-125)HCh		SFT	£6727
124	7/01	MRas	2m4f	B(0-140)HCh	G-S	£37297
118	10/00	Hntg	2m4f110yE Ch		G-F	£2951
103	5/00	Extr	2m3f	E(0-105)HCh	GD	£3136
112	11/99	Aint	2m110y	D Hdl	GD	£3993
				Total win prize-money £65341		

Going:	Sf: 1-1 GS: 1-2 Gd: 0-2 GF: - Fm: 0-0
Distance:	2m/2m3: 0-0 2m4-2m7: 2-4 3m+: 0-1
Track:	LH: 2-4 RH: 0-1 Tight: 1-1 Gall: 0-1
Aids:	Bl: 0-0 Vi: 0-0 Tstrap: 0-0
Best Rating:	133 12/02 Wwck 2m4f110y gd-sft Ch

Decent chaser; best over two and a half miles; suited by soft ground.

Dorans Pride (IRE)
14-y-o ch g Orchestra-Marians Pride (Pry)
Michael Hourigan T J Doran

Placings:1/1222111F/12211142/11/11111F31/1115134/112
103/421P12236/B21323333/40-2F   (4133)
2002/03: 24²YS, 26ᶠG,

	Starts	1st	2nd	3rd	Win & Pl
Chases	2	0	1	0	1766
Career Total	62	27	13	9	632538
147	11/00	Clon	2m4f	Ch		SFT	£15600
150	1/00	Navn	2m4f	HHdl		SFT	£5520
147	11/99	Clon	2m4f	Ch		Y-S	£17410
171	12/98	Leop	3m	Ch		SH	£45217
171	11/98	Clon	2m4f	Ch		SFT	£11956
162	10/98	Gowr	2m4f	Ch		SFT	£16891

168	2/98	Leop	3m	Ch	Y-S	£50434
168	12/97	Fair	2m4f	Ch	GD	£23564
175	11/97	Clon	2m4f	Ch	SFT	£13564
175	9/97	List	3m	HCh	YLD	£30693
153	4/97	Leop	2m4f	Ch	G-F	£22871
164	2/97	Leop	2m5f	Ch	G-Y	£9653
142	12/96	Leop	3m	Ch	G-Y	£7061
159	12/96	Fair	2m4f	Ch	YLD	£23453
138	11/96	Punc	2m4f	Ch	YLD	£7123
148	12/95	Fair	2m4f	Hdl	YLD	£27722
147	11/95	Navn	2m4f	Hdl	GD	£6782
167	3/95	Chel	3m	A Hdl	SFT	£47422
157	2/95	Punc	3m	Hdl	HVY	£9579
158	12/94	Leop	2m6f	Hdl	HVY	£6523
148	11/94	Navn	2m4f	Hdl	G-Y	£6523
139	2/94	Punc	2m2f110y	Hdl	SFT	£6571
142	2/94	Fair	2m2f	Hdl	HVY	£3942
131	1/94	Naas	2m3f	HHdl	HVY	£6571
110	9/93	List	2m	Hdl	SFT	£4134
	4/93	Baln	2m	NHF	SFT	£2411
				Total win prize-money £429202		

Going: Sf: 0-0 GS: 0-0 Gd: 0-1 GF: - Fm: 0-0
Distance: 2m2m3: 0-0 2m4-2m7: 0-0 3m+: 0-2
Track: LH: 0-2 RH: 0-0 Tight: 0-0 Gall: 0-1
Aids: Bl: 0-0 Vi: 0-0 Tstrap: 0-0
Best Rating: 175 3/98 Chel 3m2f110y good Ch

A marvellous veteran, he was top class over both hurdles and fences in his prime; a three-time point-to-point winner in Ireland in 2003, he tragically broke a leg in a fall in the Cheltenham Foxhunters . (DEAD)

Doreen's Dream (IRE)

5-y-o ch m Moscow Society (USA)-Sister Gabrielle (IRE) (Buckskin (FR))
G B Balding G E Heard

Placings:0P   (3554)
2002/03: 16⁰HY, 16ᴾHY,

	Starts	1st	2nd	3rd	Win & Pl
NH Flat	1	0	0	0	0
Hurdles	1	0	0	0	0
Career Total	2	0	0	0	0

Going: Sf: 0-2 GS: 0-0 Gd: 0-0 GF: - Fm: 0-0
Distance: 2m2m3: 0-2 2m4-2m7: 0-0 3m+: 0-0
Track: LH: 0-2 RH: 0-0 Tight: 0-1 Gall: 0-1
Aids: Bl: 0-0 Vi: 0-0 Tstrap: 0-0
Best Rating: 0 2/03 Plum 2m heavy Hdl

Dorset Fern (IRE)

92(96h)   (76h)47
7-y-o b m Tirol-La Duse (Junius (USA))
G B Balding Miss M Lane

Placings:060/00/00000003UP0-P203004   (4223)
2002/03: 17ᴾGF, 17²GS, 19⁵S, 19³GS, 16⁹HY, 19⁹GS, 16⁴GF,

	Starts	1st	2nd	3rd	Win & Pl
Hurdles	6	0	1	1	861
Chases	1	0	0	0	339
Career Total	23	0	1	2	1428

Going: Sf: 0-2 GS: 0-3 Gd: 0-0 GF: - Fm: 0-2
Distance: 2m2m3: 0-5 2m4-2m7: 0-2 3m+: 0-0
Track: LH: 0-1 RH: 0-6 Tight: 0-3 Gall: 0-0
Aids: Bl: 0-0 Vi: 0-0 Tstrap: 0-0
Best Rating: 76 12/02 Tntn 2m3f110y gd-sft Hdl

Plating-class maiden. Looks slow.

Dottie Digger (IRE)

74   57
4-y-o b f Catrail (USA)-Hint-Of-Romance (IRE) (Treasure Kay)
Miss Lucinda V Russell (I Semple 2/11) Dig In Racing

Placings:00B6P   (4762)
2002/03: 16⁹GS, 16⁹G, 16ᴮGS, 18⁶G, 16ᴾG,

	Starts	1st	2nd	3rd	Win & Pl
Hurdles	5	0	0	0	0
Career Total	5	0	0	0	0

Going: Sf: 0-0 GS: 0-2 Gd: 0-3 GF: - Fm: 0-0
Distance: 2m2m3: 0-5 2m4-2m7: 0-0 3m+: 0-0
Track: LH: 0-2 RH: 0-3 Tight: 0-4 Gall: 0-0
Aids: Bl: 0-0 Vi: 0-0 Tstrap: 0-0
Best Rating: 53 3/03 Kels 2m2f good Hdl

Double Account (FR)

118(105c)   (112c)122
8-y-o b g Sillery (USA)-Fabulous Account (USA) (Private Account (USA))
C J Mann M J & C G Cruddace

Placings:3/120500165/3024040/103321-105   (4553)
2002/03: 21¹G, 22⁰HY, 22⁵G,

	Starts	1st	2nd	3rd	Win & Pl
Hurdles	3	1	0	0	13340
Career Total	26	5	3	4	40178
122	2/03	Kemp	2m5f	C(0-130)HHdl	GD £13340
96	5/01	Clon	2m2f	Ch	GD £5286
108	1/00	Punc	2m	(0-137)HHdl	Y-S £4968
104	5/99	Navn	2m	Hdl	GD £5524
				Total win prize-money £29119	

Going: Sf: 0-1 GS: 0-0 Gd: 1-2 GF: - Fm: 0-0
Distance: 2m2m3: 0-0 2m4-2m7: 1-3 3m+: 0-0
Track: LH: 0-1 RH: 1-2 Tight: 0-0 Gall: 0-0
Aids: Bl: 0-0 Vi: 0-0 Tstrap: 0-0
Best Rating: 122 2/03 Kemp 2m5f good Hdl

Ex-Irish hurdler/chaser; dead-heated at Plumpton in September 2001; returned from 17 months off to win a Kempton handicap hurdle; effective over two and a half miles and on good or easy ground.

Double Agent

100
10-y-o ch g Niniski (USA)-Rexana (Relko)
Miss A M Newton-Smith E J Farrant

Placings:611F03/50315360/3002562/3/0P5013-P   (0123)
2002/03: 27³GF,

	Starts	1st	2nd	3rd	Win & Pl
Hurdles	1	0	0	0	0
Career Total	29	4	2	6	14670
100	1/02	Folk	2m6f110yG Hdl		SFT £2275
103	12/97	Newc	2m4f	C(0-135)HHdl	GD £3273
105	2/97	Muss	2m	E(0-105)HHdl	GD £2560
103	2/97	Muss	2m	E Hdl	G-F £2399
				Total win prize-money £10508	

Going: Sf: 0-0 GS: 0-0 Gd: 0-0 GF: - Fm: 0-1
Distance: 2m2m3: 0-0 2m4-2m7: 0-0 3m+: 0-1
Track: LH: 0-0 RH: 0-0 Tight: 0-1 Gall: 0-0
Aids: Bl: 0-0 Vi: 0-0 Tstrap: 0-0
Best Rating: 105 4/97 Prth 2m110y good Hdl

A fair hurdler on good ground a few years ago, he has suf-

fered with injury and had little racing recently. Made most to win at Folkestone in January 2002. Acts on a sound surface but has won in heavy ground.

Double Bid

81   39
6-y-o b g Rudimentary (USA)-Bidweaya (USA) (Lear Fan (USA))
Mrs N S Sharpe K Morgan

Placings:3F01P0/6P000U-PPP50   (2130)
2002/03: 17ᴾGF, 16ᴾGF, 17ᴾG, 17⁵G, 24⁰G,

	Starts	1st	2nd	3rd	Win & Pl
Hurdles	5	0	0	0	0
Career Total	17	1	0	1	2461
92	2/01	Donc	2m110y G Hdl		GD £1985
				Total win prize-money £1985	

Going: Sf: 0-0 GS: 0-0 Gd: 0-3 GF: - Fm: 0-2
Distance: 2m2m3: 0-0 2m4-2m7: 0-0 3m+: 0-1
Track: LH: 0-1 RH: 0-4 Tight: 0-0 Gall: 0-1
Aids: Bl: 0-1 Vi: 0-0 Tstrap: 0-4
Best Rating: 92 2/01 Donc 2m110y good Hdl

Double Blade

106   121
8-y-o b g Kris-Sesame (Derrylin)
Mrs M Reveley The Mary Reveley Racing Club

Placings:11110/4300/313-5113   (1539)
2002/03: 16⁵G, 16¹GF, 17¹GF, 16³GF,

	Starts	1st	2nd	3rd	Win & Pl
Hurdles	4	2	0	1	8343
Career Total	16	7	0	4	31993
121	10/02	Sedg	2m1f	F Hdl	G-F £2646
114	9/02	Prth	2m110y	F Hdl	G-F £4199
123	11/01	Weth	2m	C(0-135)HHdl	GD £5395
130	11/99	Sedg	2m1f	C Hdl	GD £4696
130	10/99	Weth	2m	C Hdl	GD £4955
119	10/99	Sedg	2m1f	E Hdl	G-F £2635
106	9/99	Sedg	2m1f	E Hdl	G-F £2407
				Total win prize-money £26935	

Going: Sf: 0-0 GS: 0-0 Gd: 0-0 GF: - Fm: 2-3
Distance: 2m2m3: 2-4 2m4-2m7: 0-0 3m+: 0-0
Track: LH: 1-3 RH: 0-1 Tight: 1-2 Gall: 0-0
Aids: Bl: 0-0 Vi: 0-0 Tstrap: 0-0
Best Rating: 130 10/00 Weth 2m gd-sft Hdl

A useful novice hurdler back in 1999, not as good these days but has a fair amount of ability and is a force in claiming company; suited by a sound surface; usually held up and doesn t always find as much as expected off the bridle.

Double Bogey Blues (IRE)

101   (108²h)108
7-y-o b g Celio Rufo-Belmount Star (IRE) (Good Thyne (USA))
M Mullineaux (M F Morris 17/5) The Hon Mrs S Pakenham

Placings:05/41F6054P03-565121P   (4401)
2002/03: 24⁵S, 26⁶GS, 24⁵S, 25¹G, 25⁵S, 24¹GF, 24ᴾGF,

	Starts	1st	2nd	3rd	Win & Pl
Chases	7	2	1	0	11818
Career Total	19	3	1	1	18954
108	3/03	Ludl	3m	D Ch	G-F £5740
108	2/03	Hrfd	3m1f110yE(0-105)HCh	GD £4212
105	11/01	Thur	2m6f	Hdl	Y-S £5564
				Total win prize-money £15517	

Going: Sf: 0-3 GS: 0-1 Gd: 1-1 GF: - Fm: 1-2
Distance: 2m/2m3: 0-0 2m4-2m7: 0-0 **3m+: 2-7**
Track: LH: 0-4 **RH: 2-2 Tight: 1-1** Gall: 0-0
Aids: Bl: 0-0 Vi: 0-0 Tstrap: 0-0
Best Rating: **108** 3/03 Ludl 3m   gd-fm Ch

Modest ex-Irish chaser; broke his duck here in a novices handicap chase at Hereford in February and added to that at Ludlow; stays well and acts on most types of ground.

Double Bubble (IRE)

5-y-o b/br g Mandalus-Double Talk (Dublin Taxi)
C N Kellett Rob Woodward

Placings:0   (2292)
2002/03: 17⁰G,

	Starts	1st	2nd	3rd	Win & Pl
NH Flat	1	0	0	0	
Career Total	1	0	0	0	

Going: Sf: 0-0 GS: 0-0 Gd: 0-1 GF: - Fm: 0-0
Distance: 2m/2m3: 0-1 2m4-2m7: 0-0 3m+: 0-0
Track: LH: 0-1 RH: 0-1 Tight: 0-0 Gall: 0-0
Aids: Bl: 0-0 Vi: 0-0 Tstrap: 0-0
Best Rating: **0** 12/02 Hrfd 2m1f   good NHF

Double Destiny
96   94

7-y-o b g Anshan-Double Gift (Cragador)
Miss E C Lavelle (D K Ivory 29/7) Mrs P Scott-Dunn

Placings:025   (4733)
2002/03: 16⁰GF, 17²GF, 16⁵GF,

	Starts	1st	2nd	3rd	Win & Pl
Hurdles	3	0	1	0	1255
Career Total	3	0	1	0	1255

Going: Sf: 0-0 GS: 0-0 Gd: 0-0 GF: - Fm: 0-3
Distance: 2m/2m3: 0-3 2m4-2m7: 0-0 3m+: 0-0
Track: LH: 0-1 RH: 0-2 Tight: 0-0 Gall: 0-1
Aids: Bl: 0-0 Vi: 0-0 Tstrap: 0-0
Best Rating: **88** 4/03 Extr 2m1f   gd-fm Hdl

Stepped up on hurdling debut when second to easy winner Double Honour at Exeter; adopted front-running tactics in first-time cheekpieces when stepped up to 2m 3f at Exeter May 2003.

Double Diplomacy

7-y-o b g State Diplomacy (USA)-Malmo (Free State)
P Beaumont Mrs E Dixon

Placings:PPP   (3154)
2002/03: 21⁸S, 19⁸GS, 20⁸G,

	Starts	1st	2nd	3rd	Win & Pl
Hurdles	3	0	0	0	
Career Total	3	0	0	0	

Going: Sf: 0-1 GS: 0-1 Gd: 0-1 GF: - Fm: 0-0
Distance: 2m/2m3: 0-0 2m4-2m7: 0-0 3m+: 0-0
Track: LH: 0-1 RH: 0-2 Tight: 0-3 Gall: 0-0
Aids: Bl: 0-1 Vi: 0-0 Tstrap: 0-0
Best Rating: **0** 1/03 Muss 2m4f   good Hdl

Double Em
86   58

4-y-o b g Balnibarbi-Something Speedy (IRE) (Sayf El Arab (USA))
C W Fairhurst David Bartlett

Placings:P00   (1323)
2002/03: 17⁸GS, 17⁰G, 17⁰GF,

	Starts	1st	2nd	3rd	Win & Pl
Hurdles	3	0	0	0	
Career Total	3	0	0	0	

Going: Sf: 0-0 GS: 0-1 Gd: 0-1 GF: - Fm: 0-1
Distance: 2m/2m3: 0-3 2m4-2m7: 0-0 3m+: 0-0
Track: LH: 0-1 RH: 0-2 Tight: 0-3 Gall: 0-0
Aids: Bl: 0-0 Vi: 0-0 Tstrap: 0-0
Best Rating: **58** 8/02 Sedg 2m1f   good Hdl

Double Emblem (IRE)
74f   52f

6-y-o ch m Weld-Sultry (Sula Bula)
W M Brisbourne Michael Brownrigg

Placings:0   (1063)
2002/03: 16⁰GF,

	Starts	1st	2nd	3rd	Win & Pl
NH Flat	1	0	0	0	
Career Total	1	0	0	0	

Going: Sf: 0-0 GS: 0-0 Gd: 0-0 GF: - Fm: 0-1
Distance: 2m/2m3: 0-1 2m4-2m7: 0-0 3m+: 0-0
Track: LH: 0-1 RH: 0-0 Tight: 0-0 Gall: 0-0
Aids: Bl: 0-0 Vi: 0-0 Tstrap: 0-0
Best Rating: **61** 8/02 Worc 2m   gd-fm NHF

Double Fun (HOL)
97   102

4-y-o b c Bretigny (FR)-Rising Stream (Pharly (FR))
C Von Der Recke Biesdeel Stud

Placings:206   (4084)
2002/03: 16²GS, 16⁰S, 16⁰GS,

	Starts	1st	2nd	3rd	Win & Pl
Hurdles	3	0	1	0	1364
Career Total	3	0	1	0	1364

Going: Sf: 0-1 GS: 0-2 Gd: 0-0 GF: - Fm: 0-0
Distance: 2m/2m3: 0-3 2m4-2m7: 0-0 3m+: 0-0
Track: LH: 0-2 RH: 0-1 Tight: 0-1 Gall: 0-1
Aids: Bl: 0-0 Vi: 0-0 Tstrap: 0-0
Best Rating: **102** 11/02 Asct 2m110y   gd-sft Hdl

Modest juvenile hurdler; winner on the Flat in Holland.

Double Honour (FR)
108   122

5-y-o gr g Highest Honor (FR)-Silver Cobra (USA) (Silver Hawk (USA))
P J Hobbs (M Johnston 19/10) The 4th Middleham Partnership

Placings:11301   (4510)
2002/03: 16¹S, 19¹GS, 21³G, 21⁰G, 17¹GF,

	Starts	1st	2nd	3rd	Win & Pl
Hurdles	5	3	0	1	12853

Career Total	5	3	0	1	12853
118	4/03	Extr	2m1f	E Hdl	G-F £4078
140	1/03	Extr	2m3f	E Hdl	G-S £3808
132	1/03	Hntg	2m110y	E Hdl	SFT £3668

Total win prize-money £11555

Going: Sf: 1-1 GS: 1-1 Gd: 0-2 GF: - Fm: 1-1
Distance: **2m/2m3: 3-3** 2m4-2m7: 0-2 3m+: 0-0
Track: LH: 0-1 **RH: 3-4** Tight: 0-0 Gall: 1-2
Aids: Bl: 0-0 Vi: 0-0 Tstrap: 0-0
Best Rating: **140** 1/03 Extr 2m3f   gd-sft Hdl

Smart stayer on the Flat; winner of his first two starts over hurdles but beaten in a better race next time; easy task when winning at Exeter; stays 2m 3f and acts on any ground, but probably at his best on a soft surface; suited by forcing tactics.

Double Rich

10-y-o ch g Rich Charlie-Spartona (Cisto (FR))
David M Easterby Lord Daresbury

Placings:UP   (4261)
2002/03: 25⁰GS, 27⁰G,

	Starts	1st	2nd	3rd	Win & Pl
Chases	2	0	0	0	
Career Total	2	0	0	0	

Going: Sf: 0-0 GS: 0-1 Gd: 0-1 GF: - Fm: 0-0
Distance: 2m/2m3: 0-0 2m4-2m7: 0-0 3m+: 0-2
Track: LH: 0-1 RH: 0-1 Tight: 0-2 Gall: 0-0
Aids: Bl: 0-0 Vi: 0-0 Tstrap: 0-0
Best Rating: **0** 3/03 Sedg 3m3f   good Ch

Double Spey
95   95

4-y-o b g Atraf-Yankee Special (Bold Lad (IRE))
P C Haslam Mrs B M Hawkins & A Dixon

Placings:40   (3891)
2002/03: 16⁴GF, 16⁰GS,

	Starts	1st	2nd	3rd	Win & Pl
Hurdles	2	0	0	0	303
Career Total	2	0	0	0	303

Going: Sf: 0-0 GS: 0-1 Gd: 0-0 GF: - Fm: 0-1
Distance: 2m/2m3: 0-2 2m4-2m7: 0-0 3m+: 0-0
Track: LH: 0-2 RH: 0-0 Tight: 0-1 Gall: 0-0
Aids: Bl: 0-0 Vi: 0-0 Tstrap: 0-0
Best Rating: **95** 10/02 Weth 2m   gd-fm Hdl

Double Tee (IRE)
(92c)   (35c)77

7-y-o br g Jurado (USA)-Monkeylane (Monksfield)
N J Hawke Mrs June Dodd

Placings:60/000660UP-0P   (0246)
2002/03: 24⁰GF, 22⁰G,

	Starts	1st	2nd	3rd	Win & Pl
Hurdles	1	0	0	0	0
Chases	1	0	0	0	0
Career Total	12	0	0	0	0

Going: Sf: 0-0 GS: 0-0 Gd: 0-1 GF: - Fm: 0-1
Distance: 2m/2m3: 0-0 2m4-2m7: 0-1 3m+: 0-1
Track: LH: 0-0 RH: 0-2 Tight: 0-1 Gall: 0-0
Aids: Bl: 0-0 Vi: 0-1 Tstrap: 0-0

Best Rating: **77**   12/01   Winc   2m6f   good   Hdl

Double Wish (IRE)
79   **61**

5-y-o b h Barathea (IRE)-Love Bateta (IRE) (Caerleon (USA))
Miss M E Rowland   Miss M E Rowland

Placings:P0   (4486)
2002/03: 21PHY, 17OGF,

	Starts	1st	2nd	3rd	Win & Pl
Hurdles	2	0	0	0	
Career Total	2	0	0	0	

Going:	Sf: 0-1 GS: 0-0 Gd: 0-0 GF: - Fm: 0-1
Distance:	2m2m3: 0-2 2m4-2m7: 0-1 3m+: 0-0
Track:	LH: 0-1 RH: 0-1 Tight: 0-1 Gall: 0-0
Aids:	Bl: 0-0 Vi: 0-1 Tstrap: 0-0
Best Rating:	29 4/03 Hrfd 2m1f gd-fm Hdl

Double You Cubed
97   **59**

9-y-o b g Destroyer-Bright Suggestion (Magnate)
J S Goldie   Mrs D I Goldie

Placings:P5PP-5U   (4592)
2002/03: 25SG, 25UG,

	Starts	1st	2nd	3rd	Win & Pl
Chases	2	0	0	0	0
Career Total	6	0	0	0	0

Going:	Sf: 0-0 GS: 0-0 Gd: 0-2 GF: - Fm: 0-0
Distance:	2m2m3: 0-0 2m4-2m7: 0-0 3m+: 0-2
Track:	LH: 0-2 RH: 0-0 Tight: 0-0 Gall: 0-0
Aids:	Bl: 0-0 Vi: 0-0 Tstrap: 0-0
Best Rating:	48 3/03 Hexm 3m1f good Ch

Plating-class chaser; poor form to date.

Douceur Des Songes (FR)
102   (69c)**87**

6-y-o b m Art Francais (USA)-Ma Poetesse (FR) (Sorrento (FR))
M C Pipe   Yvonne & The Toy Boys

Placings:4004/P002331-123245P23P06   (4700)
2002/03: 161HY, 16²G, 173GF, 19²GF, 174G, 245GF, 21PS, 16²S, 183G, 24PS, 21OS, 216GF,

	Starts	1st	2nd	3rd	Win & Pl
Hurdles	10	1	3	2	7169
Chases	2	0	0	0	0
Career Total	23	2	4	4	18934
105	6/02	Uttx	2m	D Hdl	HVY £3454
105	4/02	Font	2m2f110y		E Hdl G-F £2709

Total win prize-money £6164

Going:	Sf: 1-5 GS: 0-0 Gd: 0-3 GF: - Fm: 0-4
Distance:	2m2m3: 1-6 2m4-2m7: 0-4 3m+: 0-2
Track:	LH: 1-8 RH: 0-4 Tight: 0-7 Gall: 0-0
Aids:	Bl: 0-0 Vi: 0-0 Tstrap: 0-0
Best Rating:	112 7/02 Worc 2m good Hdl

Fair form in France over hurdles and fences, she won a maiden hurdle at Fontwell in April 2002 and followed up at Uttoxeter, but has been a bit disappointing since. Acts on any ground.

Douze Douze (FR)
111   **159**

7-y-o ch g Saint Cyrien (FR)-Kitkelly (FR) (Tamelo (FR))
G Macaire   F Videaud

Placings:131/1121/12PU1   (3628)
2002/03: 181HO, 20²GS, 24PS, 19UGS, 181VS,

	Starts	1st	2nd	3rd	Win & Pl
Hurdles	2	2	0	0	15049
Chases	3	0	1	0	12100
Career Total	12	7	2	1	149259
	3/03	Autl	2m2f	Hdl	VS £11221
	11/02	Chol	2m2f110y	Hdl	HLD £3828
165	11/00	Autl	2m6f	Ch	HVY £57637
	9/00	Bord	2m2f	Ch	FRM £3362
	9/00	Autl	2m4f110y	Ch	VS £14409
	10/99	Autl	2m1f110y	Ch	VS £12917
	5/99	Autl	2m1f110y	Hdl	VS £12917

Total win prize-money £116291

Going:	Sf: 0-1 GS: 0-2 Gd: 0-0 GF: - Fm: 0-0
Distance:	2m2m3: 2-2 2m4-2m7: 0-2 3m+: 0-1
Track:	LH: 0-0 RH: 0-3 Tight: 0-0 Gall: 0-1
Aids:	Bl: 0-0 Vi: 0-0 Tstrap: 0-1
Best Rating:	165 11/00 Autl 2m6f heavy Ch

Winning hurdler/chaser in France in the mud, never finishing out of the first three in all his starts over there. Finished runner-up to Best Mate on his British debut in the Peterborough Chase at Huntingdon, but jumped clumsily. Pulled up in the King George. Stays two miles six over fences.

Dove From Above
98(95c)   (67c)**65**

10-y-o b g Henbit (USA)-Sally s Dove (Celtic Cone)
R J Price   Mrs Chris Davies

Placings:0400/0P06/40200416F/P/F06F-040P   (1789)
2002/03: 26OGF, 22⁴GF, 26OGF, 22PGS,

	Starts	1st	2nd	3rd	Win & Pl
Hurdles	4	0	0	0	0
Career Total	26	1	1	0	3828
79	10/99	Ludl	2m5f	E(0-105)HHdl	G-F £2766

Total win prize-money £2766

Going:	Sf: 0-0 GS: 0-1 Gd: 0-0 GF: - Fm: 0-3
Distance:	2m2m3: 0-0 2m4-2m7: 0-2 3m+: 0-2
Track:	LH: 0-1 RH: 0-3 Tight: 0-2 Gall: 0-2
Aids:	Bl: 0-1 Vi: 0-0 Tstrap: 0-0
Best Rating:	90 9/97 Hntg 2m110y gd-fm NHF

Dovetto

14-y-o ch g Riberetto-Shadey Dove (Deadly Nightshade)
C J Price   Mrs M Price

Placings:0/555/0/0/30/0464102422/3544442312/06353P12 55/50200031/3420P36P5-P   (0114)
2002/03: 25PGS,

	Starts	1st	2nd	3rd	Win & Pl
Chases	1	0	0	0	
Career Total	56	4	8	8	26088
87	4/01	Plum	2m4f	F(0-100)HCh	SFT £3542
85	3/00	Hrfd	2m	E(0-115)HCh	GD £4381
86	3/99	Chep	2m3f110yD(0-110)HCh	G-S	£3772
86	1/98	Extr	2m2f	E(0-100)HHdl	HVY £2565

Total win prize-money £14261

Going:	Sf: 0-0 GS: 0-1 Gd: 0-0 GF: - Fm: 0-0
Distance:	2m2m3: 0-0 2m4-2m7: 0-0 3m+: 0-1
Track:	LH: 0-0 RH: 0-1 Tight: 0-0 Gall: 0-0
Aids:	Bl: 0-0 Vi: 0-0 Tstrap: 0-0

Best Rating: **91**   2/99   Carl   2m   heavy   Ch

A half-brother to Flakey Dove, he is an ordinary handicap chaser at around two and a half miles, effective in soft ground.

Down (FR)

12-y-o b g Le Nain Jaune (FR)-Izoba (FR) (Bamako Iii)
R Waley-Cohen   Robert Waley-Cohen

Placings:0P0   (4459)
2002/03: 33OGF, 26PHY, 21OG,

	Starts	1st	2nd	3rd	Win & Pl
Chases	3	0	0	0	
Career Total	3	0	0	0	

Going:	Sf: 0-1 GS: 0-0 Gd: 0-1 GF: - Fm: 0-1
Distance:	2m2m3: 0-0 2m4-2m7: 0-1 3m+: 0-2
Track:	LH: 0-3 RH: 0-0 Tight: 0-1 Gall: 0-1
Aids:	Bl: 0-0 Vi: 0-0 Tstrap: 0-0
Best Rating:	78 4/03 Aint 2m5f110y good Ch

Decent point-to-pointer; lightly raced under Rules.

Downpour (USA)
101   **114**

5-y-o b g Torrential (USA)-Juliac (USA) (Accipiter (USA))
Ian Williams   Favourites Racing

Placings:0-103   (3877)
2002/03: 191GF, 16OG, 19³GS,

	Starts	1st	2nd	3rd	Win & Pl
Hurdles	3	1	0	1	4189
Career Total	4	1	0	1	4189
100	5/02	Hrfd	2m3f110yD Hdl	G-F	£3150

Total win prize-money £3150

Going:	Sf: 0-0 GS: 0-1 Gd: 0-1 GF: - Fm: 1-1
Distance:	2m2m3: 0-1 2m4-2m7: 1-2 3m+: 0-0
Track:	LH: 0-2 RH: 1-1 Tight: 0-0 Gall: 0-1
Aids:	Bl: 0-0 Vi: 0-0 Tstrap: 0-0
Best Rating:	114 3/03 Donc 2m3f110y gd-sft Hdl

Fair novice hurdler; successfull at Hereford in May; stays 2m 4f and suited by fast ground.

Doyenne
93   **74**

9-y-o gr m Mystiko (USA)-No Chili (Glint Of Gold)
J Neville   J Milton

Placings:015/03P0U/P/20   (1172)
2002/03: 22²GF, 22OGF,

	Starts	1st	2nd	3rd	Win & Pl
Hurdles	2	0	1	0	636
Career Total	11	1	1	1	3761
99	2/98	Donc	2m4f	E Hdl	G-F £2343

Total win prize-money £2343

Going:	Sf: 0-0 GS: 0-0 Gd: 0-0 GF: - Fm: 0-2
Distance:	2m2m3: 0-0 2m4-2m7: 0-2 3m+: 0-0
Track:	LH: 0-2 RH: 0-0 Tight: 0-2 Gall: 0-0
Aids:	Bl: 0-0 Vi: 0-0 Tstrap: 0-2
Best Rating:	110 11/98 Wind 2m6f110y good Hdl

Very moderate hurdler/ point-to-pointer nowadays.

Dr Billy (IRE)

9-y-o b g Dry Dock-Carrigconeen (Beau Charmeur (FR))

A Kirtley A Kirtley

Placings:00000/BP/6   (4506)
2002/03: 25⁶G,

	Starts	1st	2nd	3rd	Win & Pl
Chases	1	0	0	0	0
Career Total	8	0	0	0	0

Going:	Sf: 0-0 GS: 0-0 Gd: 0-1 GF: - Fm: 0-0
Distance:	2m/2m3: 0-0 2m4-2m7: 0-0 3m+: 0-1
Track:	LH: 0-1 RH: 0-0 Tight: 0-1 Gall: 0-0
Aids:	Bl: 0-0 Vi: 0-0 Tstrap: 0-0
Best Rating:	73 4/03 Kels 3m1f good Ch

Dr Charlie

101   107

5-y-o ch g Dr Devious (IRE)-Miss Toot (Ardross)
C J Mann Martin Myers

Placings:61-55404   (4159)
2002/03: 19⁵GS, 22²S, 20⁴HY, 19⁰G, 22⁴G,

	Starts	1st	2nd	3rd	Win & Pl
Hurdles	5	0	0	0	756
Career Total	7	1	0	0	3678
101 4/02 Wwck 2m3f		E Hdl		G-F	£2922

Total win prize-money £2923

Going:	Sf: 0-2 GS: 0-1 Gd: 0-2 GF: - Fm: 0-0
Distance:	2m/2m3: 0-0 2m4-2m7: 0-0 3m+: 0-0
Track:	LH: 0-3 RH: 0-1 Tight: 0-0 Gall: 0-1
Aids:	Bl: 0-0 Vi: 0-0 Tstrap: 0-0
Best Rating:	104 3/03 MRas 2m6f good Hdl

Fair hurdler, stays two and a half miles; effective on most types of ground.

Dr Deductible

11-y-o b g Derrylin-Tantrum (Leading Man)
J E Brockbank Mrs J E Brockbank

Placings:PP3UFP5/5   (0402)
2002/03: 20⁵GF,

	Starts	1st	2nd	3rd	Win & Pl
Chases	1	0	0	0	0
Career Total	8	0	0	1	412

Going:	Sf: 0-0 GS: 0-0 Gd: 0-0 GF: - Fm: 0-1
Distance:	2m/2m3: 0-0 2m4-2m7: 0-0 3m+: 0-0
Track:	LH: 0-1 RH: 0-0 Tight: 0-0 Gall: 0-0
Aids:	Bl: 0-0 Vi: 0-0 Tstrap: 0-0
Best Rating:	74 4/00 Carl 2m4f110y gd-sft Ch

Modest hunter chaser; stays three miles; acts well on fast ground.

Dr Jazz (NZ)

89   113d

11-y-o ch g First Norman (USA)-Almacenista (NZ) (Nuage D Or (USA))
M C Pipe P A Deal

Placings:21F1236/424221/56300/0PP65P-0   (0573)
2002/03: 17⁰G,

	Starts	1st	2nd	3rd	Win & Pl
Hurdles	1	0	0	0	
Career Total	25	3	5	2	20683
135 4/00 Uttx 2m		C(0-135)HHdl		HVY	£5245
123 1/99 Folk 2m1f110yE Hdl				HVY	£2488
7/98 Puke 1m5f110y Hdl				HVY	£1144

A Kirtley   Total win prize-money £8878

Going:	Sf: 0-0 GS: 0-0 Gd: 0-1 GF: - Fm: 0-0
Distance:	2m/2m3: 0-1 2m4-2m7: 0-0 3m+: 0-0
Track:	LH: 0-1 RH: 0-0 Tight: 0-1 Gall: 0-0
Aids:	Bl: 0-0 Vi: 0-1 Tstrap: 0-0
Best Rating:	135 4/00 Uttx 2m heavy Hdl

Dr Raj

64f

4-y-o ch g In The Wings-Tawaaded (IRE) (Nashwan (USA))
B A McMahon C G Conway

Placings:0   (3883)
2002/03: 16⁰GS,

	Starts	1st	2nd	3rd	Win & Pl
NH Flat	1	0	0	0	
Career Total	1	0	0	0	

Going:	Sf: 0-0 GS: 0-1 Gd: 0-0 GF: - Fm: 0-0
Distance:	2m/2m3: 0-1 2m4-2m7: 0-0 3m+: 0-0
Track:	LH: 0-1 RH: 0-0 Tight: 0-0 Gall: 0-1
Aids:	Bl: 0-0 Vi: 0-0 Tstrap: 0-0
Best Rating:	0 3/03 Donc 2m110y gd-sft NHF

Unraced on the Flat.

Dr Strangelove (IRE)

5-y-o ch g Dr Devious (IRE)-Renzola (Dragonara Palace (USA))
P R Johnson (M D Hammond 24/9) Mrs L V Durnall

Placings:PP-P0   (2941)
2002/03: 17²G, 16⁰S,

	Starts	1st	2nd	3rd	Win & Pl
Hurdles	2	0	0	0	
Career Total	4	0	0	0	

Going:	Sf: 0-1 GS: 0-0 Gd: 0-1 GF: - Fm: 0-0
Distance:	2m/2m3: 0-2 2m4-2m7: 0-0 3m+: 0-0
Track:	LH: 0-0 RH: 0-2 Tight: 0-0 Gall: 0-0
Aids:	Bl: 0-1 Vi: 0-0 Tstrap: 0-0
Best Rating:	0 1/03 Ludl 2m soft Hdl

Dragon Hunter (IRE)

(103h)   (110h)

8-y-o b g Welsh Term-Sahob (Roselier (FR))
C R Egerton J Douglas & T Davis

Placings:421P-F   (2373)
2002/03: 26⁶GS,

	Starts	1st	2nd	3rd	Win & Pl
Chases	1	0	0	0	
Career Total	5	1	1	0	3783
110 3/02 Font 3m3f		E Hdl		SFT	£2509

Total win prize-money £2510

Going:	Sf: 0-0 GS: 0-1 Gd: 0-0 GF: - Fm: 0-0
Distance:	2m/2m3: 0-0 2m4-2m7: 0-0 3m+: 0-1
Track:	LH: 0-1 RH: 0-0 Tight: 0-0 Gall: 0-0
Aids:	Bl: 0-0 Vi: 0-0 Tstrap: 0-0
Best Rating:	110 3/02 Font 3m3f soft Hdl

Novice hurdler, stays extreme distances.

Dragon King

111   100

11-y-o b g Rakaposhi King-Dunsilly Bell (London Bells (CAN))
P Bowen R Greenway

Placings:2/050046110/032031353302/5P33231311303304
53U440220/22253250400/04131103-4042142414F1 (4761)
2002/03: 20⁴G, 22⁰GF, 26⁴GF, 21²GF, 21¹GF, 26⁴HY, 22²HY, 20⁴S, 22¹S, 20⁴GS, 21²G, 26¹GF,

	Starts	1st	2nd	3rd	Win & Pl
Chases	12	3	2	0	12184
Career Total	78	12	12	16	58257
100 4/03 Font 3m2f110yF(0-100)HCh				G-F	£3374
99 2/03 Font 2m6f F(0-90)HCh				SFT	£3381
80 7/02 NAbb 2m5f110yF(0-90)Ch				G-F	£2947
92 9/01 MRas 3m1f F(0-110)HCh				G-F	£4114
92 8/01 NAbb 3m2f110yF(0-100)HCh				G-F	£2947
86 7/01 Worc 4m110yF(0-100)HCh				SFT	£2975
111 9/99 Sedg 2m5f D(0-120)HCh				G-F	£3699
111 9/99 NAbb 2m5f110yD(0-125)HCh				G-F	£3765
90 8/99 NAbb 2m110y D Ch				GD	£3838
98 11/98 Wind 2m E(0-110)HHdl				G-S	£2880
94 3/98 Tntn 2m1f F(0-95)HHdl				G-S	£2050
84 3/98 Tntn 2m1f F(0-105)HHdl				G-S	£1903

Total win prize-money £37874

Going:	Sf: 1-4 GS: 0-1 Gd: 0-2 GF: - Fm: 2-5
Distance:	2m/2m3: 0-0 2m4-2m7: 2-9 3m+: 1-3
Track:	LH: 1-6 RH: 0-2 Tight: 3-7 Gall: 0-0
Aids:	Bl: 2-4 Vi: 0-0 Tstrap: 0-0
Best Rating:	111 9/99 Sedg 2m5f gd-fm Ch

Modest chaser; very sound jumper; stays three miles-two; acts on fast ground and with give.

Dragon Lord

9-y-o b g Warning-Cockatoo Island (High Top)
Mrs Alison Hickman Mrs Alison Hickman

Placings:1/220236/6/4F/F   (0315)
2002/03: 21⁶FG,

	Starts	1st	2nd	3rd	Win & Pl
Chases	1	0	0	0	
Career Total	11	1	3	1	3468
104 2/98 Ling 2m110y H NHF				GD	£1339

Total win prize-money £1340

Going:	Sf: 0-0 GS: 0-0 Gd: 0-1 GF: - Fm: 0-0
Distance:	2m/2m3: 0-0 2m4-2m7: 0-1 3m+: 0-0
Track:	LH: 0-0 RH: 0-1 Tight: 0-1 Gall: 0-0
Aids:	Bl: 0-0 Vi: 0-0 Tstrap: 0-0
Best Rating:	106 11/98 Chel 2m110y gd-sft NHF

Dragut Torghoud (IRE)

98   89

7-y-o b g Persian Mews-Artist s Jewel (Le Moss)
N M Babbage Ford Associated Racing Team li

Placings:4P462   (4450)
2002/03: 16⁴G, 22²G, 20⁴S, 20⁶GS, 21²G,

	Starts	1st	2nd	3rd	Win & Pl
NH Flat	1	0	0	0	0
Hurdles	4	0	1	0	2049
Career Total	5	0	1	0	2049

Going:	Sf: 0-1 GS: 0-1 Gd: 0-3 GF: - Fm: 0-0
Distance:	2m/2m3: 0-1 2m4-2m7: 0-4 3m+: 0-0

Track: LH: 0-3 RH: 0-2 Tight: 0-2 Gall: 0-0
Aids: Bl: 0-0 Vi: 0-0 Tstrap: 0-0
Best Rating: 89 4/03 Ludl 2m5f good Hdl

Moderate novice hurdler; first form when chasing home fair sort at Ludlow in April 2003; stays two miles five.

Drakestone

108   98

12-y-o b g Motivate-Lyricist (Averof)
R L Brown R L Brown

Placings:06034/030033/52/306/F3U54P0113/2/4013440P2
-0   (3543)
2002/03: 17⁰G,

	Starts	1st	2nd	3rd	Win & Pl
Hurdles	1	0	0		
Career Total	37	3	3	8	13895
103 8/01 Worc 2m4f	F Hdl			G-F	£1897
97 2/00 Bang 2m1f	F(0-110)HHdl			G-S	£3623
75 1/00 Hrfd 2m1f	F Hdl			G-S	£2324
			Total win prize-money £7845		

Going: Sf: 0-0 GS: 0-0 Gd: 0-1 GF: - Fm: 0-0
Distance: 2m/2m3: 0-1 2m4-2m7: 0-0 3m+: 0-0
Track: LH: 0-0 RH: 0-1 Tight: 0-0 Gall: 0-0
Aids: Bl: 0-0 Vi: 0-0 Tstrap: 0-0
Best Rating: 105 10/01 Chep 2m4f good Hdl

Moderate handicap hurdler; returned as good as ever after a year off with leg trouble with wins at Hereford in May and June 2003; stays 2m 4f, suited by a sound surface although has won with cut in the ground.

Drama King

98   86

11-y-o b g Tragic Role (USA)-Consistent Queen (Queens Hussar)
B J Llewellyn Alan J Williams

Placings:F5142/0612/501/00P/36416500P-05P15040
                                                      (3825)
2002/03: 20⁰G, 20⁵GF, 22ᴾGS, 16¹S, 17⁵GS, 21⁰HY, 16⁴HY,
16⁰GS,

	Starts	1st	2nd	3rd	Win & Pl
Hurdles	8	1	0	0	1960
Career Total	32	5	2	1	12902
86 11/02 Uttx 2m	G(-90)HHdl		SFT	£1960	
96 12/01 Folk 2m4f110yF(0-100)HHdl		SFT	£1820		
96 1/00 Uttx 2m4f110yG(0-95)HHdl		SFT	£2191		
100 7/98 Worc 2m4f	E(0-115)HHdl		G-F	£2337	
95 3/98 Strf 2m3f	G Hdl		GD	£2901	
			Total win prize-money £11211		

Going: Sf: 1-3 GS: 0-3 Gd: 0-1 GF: - Fm: 0-1
Distance: 2m/2m3: 1-4 2m4-2m7: 0-4 3m+: 0-0
Track: LH: 1-8 RH: 0-0 Tight: 0-4 Gall: 0-0
Aids: Bl: 1-6 Vi: 0-0 Tstrap: 0-0
Best Rating: 100 7/98 Strf 2m6f110y gd-fm Hdl

A plating-class hurdler, winner at Uttoxeter in November. Acts on any ground and stays two and a half miles. Has a tendency to find little off the bridle.

Dramatic Miss

8-y-o b m Deploy-Stos (IRE) (Bluebird (USA))
R J Price Stephen J Fletcher

Placings:00-0P   (1232)
2002/03: 16⁰S, 16ᴾG,

	Starts	1st	2nd	3rd	Win & Pl
Hurdles	2	0	0	0	

Career Total   4   0   0   0

Going: Sf: 0-1 GS: 0-0 Gd: 0-1 GF: - Fm: 0-0
Distance: 2m/2m3: 0-2 2m4-2m7: 0-0 3m+: 0-0
Track: LH: 0-2 RH: 0-0 Tight: 0-0 Gall: 0-0
Aids: Bl: 0-0 Vi: 0-0 Tstrap: 0-0
Best Rating: 54 6/01 MRas 2m1f110y gd-fm NHF

Dramatic Quest

95   106

6-y-o b g Zafonic (USA)-Ultra Finesse (USA) (Rahy (USA))
Ian Williams M Murphy

Placings:4106-5P20   (4752)
2002/03: 19⁵S, 20ᴾS, 20²G, 24⁰G,

	Starts	1st	2nd	3rd	Win & Pl
Hurdles	4	0	1	0	728
Career Total	8	1	1	0	4200
113 1/02 Donc 2m110y	D Hdl		SFT	£3472	
			Total win prize-money £3472		

Going: Sf: 0-2 GS: 0-0 Gd: 0-2 GF: - Fm: 0-0
Distance: 2m/2m3: 0-0 2m4-2m7: 0-3 3m+: 0-1
Track: LH: 0-1 RH: 0-3 Tight: 0-0 Gall: 0-1
Aids: Bl: 0-1 Vi: 0-0 Tstrap: 0-0
Best Rating: 113 1/02 Donc 2m110y soft Hdl

Fair hurdler; effective over two miles, but stays further, goes well on soft ground, but effective on decent ground.

Dream A Dream

4-y-o b f Emperor Jones (USA)-Thornbury (IRE) (Tender King)
G C H Chung (Mrs D Haine 29/9) Mrs Susan Mountain

Placings:0   (1336)
2002/03: 16⁰GF,

	Starts	1st	2nd	3rd	Win & Pl
Hurdles	1	0	0	0	
Career Total	1	0	0	0	

Going: Sf: 0-0 GS: 0-0 Gd: 0-0 GF: - Fm: 0-1
Distance: 2m/2m3: 0-1 2m4-2m7: 0-0 3m+: 0-0
Track: LH: 0-0 RH: 0-1 Tight: 0-0 Gall: 0-1
Aids: Bl: 0-0 Vi: 0-0 Tstrap: 0-0
Best Rating: 0 9/02 Hntg 2m110y gd-fm Hdl

Dream Of Nurmi

(108h)   (121h)132

9-y-o ch g Pursuit Of Love-Finlandaise (FR) (Arctic Tern (USA))
Mrs S J Smith Mrs Jacqueline Conroy

Placings:11/R21R05/0600/51115U44P31-3P   (0271)
2002/03: 20⁰G, 24ᴾGF,

	Starts	1st	2nd	3rd	Win & Pl
Hurdles	1	0	0	1	1612
Chases	1	0	0	0	0
Career Total	25	7	1	2	34554
132 4/02 Prth 2m4f110yD(0-125)HCh		GD	£8684		
115 7/01 Strf 2m5f110yD Ch		G-F	£4147		
115 6/01 Hexm 2m4f110yE Ch		GD	£3243		
113 5/01 Weth 2m4f110yD Ch		FRM	£4368		
132 12/99 Wwck 2m D(0-125)HHdl		SFT	£3899		
112 4/99 Hntg 2m110y E Hdl		GD	£2757		
112 4/99 Ludl 2m E Hdl		GD	£2640		
			Total win prize-money £29740		

Going: Sf: 0-0 GS: 0-0 Gd: 0-1 GF: - Fm: 0-1
Distance: 2m/2m3: 0-0 2m4-2m7: 0-1 3m+: 0-1
Track: LH: 0-2 RH: 0-0 Tight: 0-1 Gall: 0-0
Aids: Bl: 0-0 Vi: 0-0 Tstrap: 0-0
Best Rating: 132 4/02 Prth 2m4f110y good Ch

A capable hurdler on his day, he refused to jump off on several occasions in the past, but his new yard seem to have sweetened him up. Took well to fences during the summer of 2001, completing a hat-trick, although he was well held until winning at Perth in April. Best on a sound surface.

Dream On Then

7-y-o ch m Royal Vulcan-Dreamside (Quayside)
John R Upson Sidney J Smith

Placings:0   (0269)
2002/03: 16⁰GF,

	Starts	1st	2nd	3rd	Win & Pl
Hurdles	1	0	0	0	
Career Total	1	0	0	0	

Going: Sf: 0-0 GS: 0-0 Gd: 0-0 GF: - Fm: 0-1
Distance: 2m/2m3: 0-1 2m4-2m7: 0-0 3m+: 0-0
Track: LH: 0-1 RH: 0-0 Tight: 0-1 Gall: 0-0
Aids: Bl: 0-0 Vi: 0-0 Tstrap: 0-0
Best Rating: 0 5/02 Strf 2m110y gd-fm Hdl

Dream On Willie (IRE)

98(104h)   (83dh)84

6-y-o b g Synefos (USA)-Mrs Mahon s Toy (IRE) (Roselier (FR))
E A Elliott Eric A Elliott

Placings:62035   (4159)
2002/03: 22⁶S, 20ᴾHY, 20⁰GS, 20³GS, 22⁵G,

	Starts	1st	2nd	3rd	Win & Pl
Hurdles	5	0	1	1	1854
Career Total	5	0	1	1	1854

Going: Sf: 0-2 GS: 0-2 Gd: 0-1 GF: - Fm: 0-0
Distance: 2m/2m3: 0-0 2m4-2m7: 0-5 3m+: 0-0
Track: LH: 0-1 RH: 0-3 Tight: 0-2 Gall: 0-0
Aids: Bl: 0-0 Vi: 0-0 Tstrap: 0-0
Best Rating: 101 11/02 Carl 2m4f heavy Hdl

Modest novice hurdler/chaser; appreciates a test of stamina.

Dream With Me (FR)

101(112h)   (124 h)130+

6-y-o b g Johann Quatz (FR)-Midnight Ride (FR) (Fast Topaze (USA))
M C Pipe Dr G Madan Mohan

Placings:256-111116P0   (4476)
2002/03: 16¹GF, 16¹GF, 19¹GF, 17¹GS, 16¹GS, 16⁶GS, 21ᴾG,
16⁰G,

	Starts	1st	2nd	3rd	Win & Pl
Hurdles	8	5	0	0	24899
Career Total	11	5	1	0	25679
138 11/02 Asct 2m110y C(0-135)HHdl		G-S	£6743		
129 10/02 Bang 2m1f D(0-115)HHdl		G-S	£7312		
115 10/02 Hrfd 2m3f110yE Hdl		G-F	£3024		
105 8/02 Uttx 2m E Hdl		G-F	£3454		
121 6/02 Strf 2m110y E(0-105)HHdl		G-F	£3614		
			Total win prize-money £24150		

Going: Sf: 0-0 GS: 2-3 Gd: 0-2 GF: - Fm: 3-3
Distance: 2m/2m3: 4-6 2m4-2m7: 1-2 3m+: 0-0
Track: LH: 3-6 RH: 2-2 Tight: 2-3 Gall: 0-1
Aids: Bl: 0-0 Vi: 0-0 Tstrap: 4-7
Best Rating: 138 11/02 Asct 2m110y gd-sft Hdl

Useful ex-French novice hurdler; won his first five starts of the 2002/2003 season; won three-runner novice chase at Market Rasen May 2003; seemed to find 21 furlongs too far next time; effective on fast and yielding ground; stays 2m 4f; wears a tongue tie.

Dreamie Battle
96   66

5-y-o br m Makbul-Highland Rossie (Pablond)
R Hollinshead Tim Leadbeater

Placings:00-53455U0   (4486)
2002/03: 16⁵GF, 16³GS, 16⁴S, 16⁵GF, 16⁵S, 16ᵁG, 17⁰GF,

	Starts	1st	2nd	3rd	Win & Pl
Hurdles	7	0	0	1	415
Career Total	9	0	0	1	415

Going: Sf: 0-2 GS: 0-1 Gd: 0-1 GF: - Fm: 0-3
Distance: 2m/2m3: 0-7 2m4-2m7: 0-0 3m+: 0-0
Track: LH: 0-5 RH: 0-2 Tight: 0-4 Gall: 0-0
Aids: Bl: 0-0 Vi: 0-0 Tstrap: 0-0
Best Rating: 83 2/02 Ludl 2m good Hdl

Little form to get excited about over hurdles so far and seems to struggle to last out two miles.

Drom Wood (IRE)
101(99h)   84

7-y-o ch g Be My Native (USA)-Try Your Case (Proverb)
T R George Mrs M Devine

Placings:0104-0F   (4622)
2002/03: 16⁸S, 22ᶠGF,

	Starts	1st	2nd	3rd	Win & Pl
Hurdles	1	0	0	0	0
Chases	1	0	0	0	0
Career Total	6	1	0	0	4113
100 7/01 Bell 2m1f	NHF			G-F	£3756

Total win prize-money £3756

Going: Sf: 0-1 GS: 0-0 Gd: 0-0 GF: - Fm: 0-1
Distance: 2m/2m3: 0-1 2m4-2m7: 0-0 3m+: 0-0
Track: LH: 0-2 RH: 0-0 Tight: 0-1 Gall: 0-0
Aids: Bl: 0-0 Vi: 0-0 Tstrap: 0-0
Best Rating: 100 7/01 Bell 2m1f gd-fm NHF

Moderate hurdler and chaser; won a bumper in his native Ireland; showed little in two starts over hurdles; well beaten on chase debut in November 2002, but improved in next chase where the ground was much better; stays two and a half miles, should get further; acts well and seems best served by fast ground.

Drombeag (IRE)
92f   108f

5-y-o b g Presenting-Bula Beag (IRE) (Brush Aside) (USA)
Jonjo O Neill J P McManus

Placings:31   (3991)
2002/03: 17³GS, 17¹S,

	Starts	1st	2nd	3rd	Win & Pl
NH Flat	2	1	0	1	2226
Career Total	2	1	0	1	2226
108 3/03 Carl 2m1f	H NHF			SFT	£1932

Total win prize-money £1932

Going: Sf: 1-1 GS: 0-1 Gd: 0-0 GF: - Fm: 0-0
Distance: 2m/2m3: 1-2 2m4-2m7: 0-0 3m+: 0-0
Track: LH: 0-0 RH: 1-2 Tight: 0-0 Gall: 0-0
Aids: Bl: 0-0 Vi: 0-0 Tstrap: 0-0
Best Rating: 108 3/03 Carl 2m1f soft NHF

Third on his debut in a bumper; should make a hurdler.

Dromod Point (IRE)
14-y-o ch g Dromod Hill-Bright Point (Shackleton)
Mrs N K Case Mrs N K Case

Placings:43/5030/0060/555P/U6/3F4/P   (0179)
2002/03: 21ᴾGF,

	Starts	1st	2nd	3rd	Win & Pl
Chases	1	0	0	0	
Career Total	20	0	0	3	1486

Going: Sf: 0-0 GS: 0-0 Gd: 0-0 GF: - Fm: 0-1
Distance: 2m/2m3: 0-0 2m4-2m7: 0-1 3m+: 0-0
Track: LH: 0-0 RH: 0-1 Tight: 0-0 Gall: 0-0
Aids: Bl: 0-1 Vi: 0-0 Tstrap: 0-0
Best Rating: 76 4/96 Tipp 2m gd-yld Hdl

Druid's Glen (IRE)
110(102h)   (114h)135

7-y-o ch g Un Desperado (FR)-Fais Vite (USA) (Sharpen Up)
Jonjo O Neill J P McManus

Placings:253411-11P202   (4416)
2002/03: 25¹S, 24¹GS, 20ᴾS, 20²G, 32⁰G, 25²G,

	Starts	1st	2nd	3rd	Win & Pl
Chases	6	2	2	0	18963
Career Total	12	4	3	1	29162
135 12/02 Sthl 3m110y	E Ch			G-S	£4389
121 11/02 MRas 3m1f	D Ch			SFT	£4793
114 4/02 Strf 2m6f110y	E Hdl			GD	£3220
113 3/02 Strf 2m6f110y	D Hdl			G-S	£4173

Total win prize-money £16576

Going: Sf: 1-2 GS: 1-1 Gd: 0-3 GF: - Fm: 0-0
Distance: 2m/2m3: 0-0 2m4-2m7: 0-2 3m+: 2-4
Track: LH: 1-2 RH: 1-4 Tight: 2-3 Gall: 0-1
Aids: Bl: 0-0 Vi: 0-0 Tstrap: 0-0
Best Rating: 135 2/03 Kemp 2m4f110y good Ch

Useful novice chaser; looks best over three miles but effective at shorter; suited by a sharp track; acts on good and soft ground.

Drum Battle
96   102

11-y-o ch g Bold Arrangement-Cannon Boy (USA) (Canonero (USA))
P F Nicholls (W G M Turner 7/5) David Chown

Placings:4233/P61422/52P300351/65211/PPU3004P/U4F2 3F21PP-356   (4624)
2002/03: 26⁵GS, 28⁵G, 26⁶GF,

	Starts	1st	2nd	3rd	Win & Pl
Chases	3	0	0	1	828
Career Total	45	5	7	7	25549
105 2/02 Wwck 3m5f	E(0-110)HCh			HVY	£4506
119 1/99 Font 3m2f110y	E Ch			SFT	£2802
114 12/98 Hrfd 3m1f110y	D Ch			SFT	£3728
101 4/98 Plum 2m4f	E(0-115)HHdl			G-S	£2490
92 2/97 Ludl 2m5f110y	E Hdl			G-S	£2444

Total win prize-money £15972

Going: Sf: 0-0 GS: 0-1 Gd: 0-1 GF: - Fm: 0-1
Distance: 2m/2m3: 0-0 2m4-2m7: 0-0 3m+: 0-3
Track: LH: 0-2 RH: 0-0 Tight: 0-2 Gall: 0-0
Aids: Bl: 0-0 Vi: 0-0 Tstrap: 0-2
Best Rating: 119 1/99 Font 3m2f110y soft Ch

Modest chaser; won a point-to-point in January 2003; stays well and handles heavy ground, but not the best of jumpers; usually wears tongue tie.

Drum Majorette
98   95+

8-y-o ch m Infantry-Smart Chick (True Song)
B G Powell C A Cavanagh

Placings:44-551   (3429)
2002/03: 22⁵G, 22⁵HY, 22¹S,

	Starts	1st	2nd	3rd	Win & Pl
Hurdles	3	1	0	0	2471
Career Total	5	1	0	0	2471
102 2/03 Font 2m6f110y	G Hdl			SFT	£2471

Total win prize-money £2471

Going: Sf: 1-2 GS: 0-0 Gd: 0-1 GF: - Fm: 0-0
Distance: 2m/2m3: 0-0 2m4-2m7: 1-3 3m+: 0-0
Track: LH: 1-1 RH: 0-2 Tight: 1-2 Gall: 0-0
Aids: Bl: 0-0 Vi: 0-0 Tstrap: 0-0
Best Rating: 102 2/03 Font 2m6f110y soft Hdl

Fair plater over hurdles, acts in soft ground and stays two and three-quarter miles.

Drumdoney (IRE)
97   89

8-y-o br g Dromod Hill-Stradbally Bay (Shackleton)
R H Alner J P M & J W Cook

Placings:6F-3P   (2057)
2002/03: 25³G, 24ᶠPG,

	Starts	1st	2nd	3rd	Win & Pl
Chases	2	0	0	1	739
Career Total	4	0	0	1	739

Going: Sf: 0-0 GS: 0-0 Gd: 0-2 GF: - Fm: 0-0
Distance: 2m/2m3: 0-0 2m4-2m7: 0-0 3m+: 0-2
Track: LH: 0-0 RH: 0-2 Tight: 0-0 Gall: 0-0
Aids: Bl: 0-0 Vi: 0-0 Tstrap: 0-0
Best Rating: 93 10/02 Winc 3m1f110y good Ch

Drumlin (IRE)
8-y-o b g Glacial Storm (USA)-Shannon Lough (IRE) (Deep Run)
J M Turner J M Turner

Placings:54O21/525P/6-6   (4667)
2002/03: 21⁶G,

	Starts	1st	2nd	3rd	Win & Pl
Chases	1	0	0	0	0
Career Total	11	1	2	0	4330
114 1/00 Plum 2m	E Hdl			SFT	£2747

Total win prize-money £2748

Going: Sf: 0-0 GS: 0-0 Gd: 0-1 GF: - Fm: 0-0
Distance: 2m/2m3: 0-0 2m4-2m7: 0-1 3m+: 0-0
Track: LH: 0-1 RH: 0-0 Tight: 0-1 Gall: 0-0
Aids: Bl: 0-0 Vi: 0-0 Tstrap: 0-0
Best Rating: 124 12/99 Uttx 2m soft Hdl

Dry Highline (IRE)

11-y-o b g Dry Dock-Fandango Girl (Last Fandango)
Mrs Ruth Hayter Mrs A Villar

Placings:*0/05*P*44*/PF-F   (0191)
2002/03: 24FGF,

	Starts	1st	2nd	3rd	Win & Pl
Chases	1	0	0	0	
Career Total	9	0	0	0	268

Going:	Sf: 0-0 GS: 0-0 Gd: 0-0 GF: - Fm: 0-1
Distance:	2m/2m3: 0-0 2m4-2m7: 0-0 3m+: 0-1
Track:	LH: 0-0 RH: 0-1 Tight: 0-0 Gall: 0-1
Aids:	Bl: 0-0 Vi: 0-0 Tstrap: 0-0
Best Rating:	95 4/99 Clon 2m4f heavy Hdl

Front-running pointer/hunter chaser who has won on good and heavy ground. Not a totally reliable jumper but has a good record when completing.

Dual Star (IRE)
103(84h)   (99h)99
8-y-o b g Warning-Sizes Vary (Be My Guest (USA))
P J Hobbs (S Donohoe 7/5) Mrs S L Hobbs

Placings:0040/410P/040266051500/0306006200F46F-011P53046   (2065)
2002/03: 20PGY, 161GF, 161GF, 16PGF, 165G, 163G, 190GF, 194GS, 256S,

	Starts	1st	2nd	3rd	Win & Pl
Hurdles	1	0	0	0	0
Chases	8	2	0	1	7998
Career Total	43	4	2	2	15967
94 8/02 NAbb 2m110y E(0-110)HCh			G-F	£3675	
89 7/02 NAbb 2m110y F(0-100)HCh			G-F	£3283	
105 10/00 Dpat 2m1f172y (0-102)HHdl			YLD	£2345	
86 8/99 Dpat 2m1f87y Hdl			G-F	£2002	
			Total win prize-money £11306		

Going:	Sf: 0-1 GS: 0-1 Gd: 0-2 GF: - Fm: 2-4
Distance:	**2m/2m3:** 2-6 2m4-2m7: 0-2 3m+: 0-1
Track:	**LH:** 2-4 RH: 0-4 Tight: 2-5 Gall: 0-0
Aids:	Bl: 0-0 Vi: 0-0 **Tstrap:** 2-9
Best Rating:	105 10/00 Dpat 2m1f172y yield Hdl

Moderate chaser; effective at two miles; acts on fast ground.

Dubai Seven Stars
120   121
5-y-o ch m Suave Dancer (USA)-Her Honour (Teenoso (USA))
M C Pipe Mrs Alison C Farrant

Placings:1P10-2400   (4475)
2002/03: 242S, 214S, 250G, 200G,

	Starts	1st	2nd	3rd	Win & Pl
Hurdles	4	0	1	0	3785
Career Total	8	2	1	0	8856
103 1/02 Tntn 2m1f E Hdl			SFT	£2631	
115 12/01 Plum 2m E Hdl			GD	£2439	
			Total win prize-money £5071		

Going:	Sf: 0-2 GS: 0-0 Gd: 0-2 GF: - Fm: 0-0
Distance:	2m/2m3: 0-0 2m4-2m7: 0-2 3m+: 0-0
Track:	LH: 0-4 RH: 0-0 Tight: 0-1 Gall: 0-1
Aids:	Bl: 0-0 Vi: 0-0 Tstrap: 0-0
Best Rating:	130 11/02 Chep 3m soft Hdl

Decent hurdler; effective over two but stays three miles; third in the 2002 Cesarewitch on the Flat; has won on good ground and heavy.

Dublin Lights (IRE)
(72c)   (54c)
8-y-o b/br g Electric-Whosview (Fine Blade (USA))
J I A Charlton J I A Charlton

Placings:0/P00-P   (0084)
2002/03: 24PGS,

	Starts	1st	2nd	3rd	Win & Pl
Hurdles	1	0	0	0	
Career Total	5	0	0	0	

Going:	Sf: 0-0 GS: 0-1 Gd: 0-0 GF: - Fm: 0-0
Distance:	2m/2m3: 0-0 2m4-2m7: 0-0 3m+: 0-1
Track:	LH: 0-1 RH: 0-0 Tight: 0-0 Gall: 0-0
Aids:	Bl: 0-0 Vi: 0-0 Tstrap: 0-0
Best Rating:	70 5/00 Dpat 2m1f172y gd-fm NHF

Lightly-raced and well held in a bumper and chases.

Duc De Coigny

8-y-o b g Damister (USA)-Shercol (Monseigneur (USA))
M Mullineaux Michael Mullineaux

Placings:0-PPPU   (3966)
2002/03: 20PHY, 16PS, 19PG, 16US,

	Starts	1st	2nd	3rd	Win & Pl
Hurdles	1	0	0	0	0
Chases	3	0	0	0	
Career Total	5	0	0	0	

Going:	Sf: 0-3 GS: 0-0 Gd: 0-1 GF: - Fm: 0-0
Distance:	2m/2m3: 0-3 2m4-2m7: 0-1 3m+: 0-0
Track:	LH: 0-1 RH: 0-3 Tight: 0-1 Gall: 0-0
Aids:	Bl: 0-0 Vi: 0-0 Tstrap: 0-0
Best Rating:	0 3/03 Catt 2m soft Ch

Duchamp (USA)
108(104h)   (110h)119
6-y-o b g Pine Bluff (USA)-Higher Learning (USA) (Fappiano (USA))
A M Balding (I A Balding 7/12) R & E H Investments Ltd

Placings:35/21213132F-5425U04F2   (4313)
2002/03: 215G, 204GS, 202G, 165GS, 21UHY, 190G, 204G, 19FG, 182G,

	Starts	1st	2nd	3rd	Win & Pl
Hurdles	1	0	0	0	0
Chases	8	3	2	0	7565
Career Total	20	3	5	3	24004
131 12/01 Donc 2m3f110yD Ch			GD	£4407	
110 11/01 Towc 2m110y E Ch			SFT	£3822	
110 5/01 Font 2m2f110yE Hdl			G-F	£2418	
			Total win prize-money £10648		

Going:	Sf: 0-1 GS: 0-2 Gd: 0-6 GF: - Fm: 0-0
Distance:	2m/2m3: 0-4 2m4-2m7: 0-5 3m+: 0-0
Track:	LH: 0-7 RH: 0-2 Tight: 0-0 Gall: 0-2
Aids:	Bl: 0-0 Vi: 0-6 Tstrap: 0-0
Best Rating:	131 11/02 Kemp 2m4f110y good Ch

Decent chaser; winner on the Flat, over hurdles and fences; stays 3m 3f; has worn a visor.

Dudleys Delight

4-y-o b f Makbul-Steadfast Elite (IRE) (Glenstal (USA))
M C Pipe (R Guest 23/9) Eminence Grise Partnership

Placings:P   (2059)
2002/03: 17PS,

	Starts	1st	2nd	3rd	Win & Pl
Hurdles	1	0	0	0	
Career Total	1	0	0	0	

Going:	Sf: 0-1 GS: 0-0 Gd: 0-0 GF: - Fm: 0-0
Distance:	2m/2m3: 0-1 2m4-2m7: 0-0 3m+: 0-0
Track:	LH: 0-0 RH: 0-1 Tight: 0-0 Gall: 0-0
Aids:	Bl: 0-0 Vi: 0-0 Tstrap: 0-0
Best Rating:	0 11/02 Hrfd 2m1f soft Hdl

Duds (IRE)

4-y-o ch g Definite Article-Domino s Nurse (Dom Racine (FR))
F P Murtagh Play Fair Partnership

Placings:P   (1224)
2002/03: 17PG,

	Starts	1st	2nd	3rd	Win & Pl
Hurdles	1	0	0	0	
Career Total	1	0	0	0	

Going:	Sf: 0-0 GS: 0-0 Gd: 0-1 GF: - Fm: 0-0
Distance:	2m/2m3: 0-1 2m4-2m7: 0-0 3m+: 0-0
Track:	LH: 0-1 RH: 0-0 Tight: 0-1 Gall: 0-0
Aids:	Bl: 0-0 Vi: 0-0 Tstrap: 0-0
Best Rating:	0 9/02 Bang 2m1f good Hdl

Duke Of Buckingham (IRE)
108   117
7-y-o b g Phardante (FR)-Deselby s Choice (Crash Course)
P R Webber C W Booth

Placings:3/3-2344   (2849)
2002/03: 19PGF, 203G, 214G, 164S,

	Starts	1st	2nd	3rd	Win & Pl
Chases	4	0	1	1	5908
Career Total	6	0	1	3	6413

Going:	Sf: 0-1 GS: 0-0 Gd: 0-2 GF: - Fm: 0-1
Distance:	2m/2m3: 0-2 2m4-2m7: 0-2 3m+: 0-0
Track:	LH: 0-2 RH: 0-2 Tight: 0-2 Gall: 0-2
Aids:	Bl: 0-0 Vi: 0-0 Tstrap: 0-0
Best Rating:	117 12/02 Chel 2m110y soft Ch

Useful chaser; modest form in bumpers before winning a point in the spring of 2002; seemingly improved over fences of late, taking notable scalp of Santenay before bolting up next time; disappointed in hot handicap; best at around two miles; acts on a sound surface.

Duke Of Earl (IRE)
100   121
4-y-o ch g Ali-Royal (IRE)-Faye (Monsanto (FR))
S Kirk Speedith Group

Placings:15330   (4130)
2002/03: 161GS, 175G, 16PHY, 163G, 170G,

	Starts	1st	2nd	3rd	Win & Pl
Hurdles	5	1	0	2	14997
Career Total	5	1	0	2	14997
115 11/02 Hntg 2m110y B Hdl			G-S	£10374	
			Total win prize-money £10374		

Going: Sf: 0-1 GS: 1-1 Gd: 0-3 GF: - Fm: 0-0
Distance: 2m/2m3: 1-5 2m4-2m7: 0-0 3m+: 0-0
Track: LH: 0-2 RH: 1-3 Tight: 0-0 Gall: 1-3
Aids: Bl: 0-0 Vi: 0-0 Tstrap: 0-0
Best Rating: 121 12/02 Chel 2m1f   good   Hdl

Fair juvenile hurdler; seems best suited by decent ground, although has run well on heavy.

Dulas Bay
126

9-y-o b g Selkirk (USA)-Ivory Gull (USA) (Storm Bird (CAN))
M Pitman   C B Hoffman

Placings:23313/P36P0/6/1F1F30/61314400-4   (1847)
2002/03: 20⁴GS,

	Starts	1st	2nd	3rd	Win & Pl
Chases	1	0	0	0	651
Career Total	26	5	1	6	40798

126 1/02 Wwck 2m4f110yC(0-135)HCh SFT £7312
120 11/01 Sand 2m4f110yC(0-135)HCh G-S £8190
120 1/01 Kemp 2m4f110yD(0-115)HCh SFT £5164
112 1/01 Ludl 2m4f E(0-105)HCh SFT £3464
108 4/98 Weth 2m D Hdl G-S £3125
Total win prize-money £27257

Going: Sf: 0-0 GS: 0-1 Gd: 0-0 GF: - Fm: 0-0
Distance: 2m/2m3: 0-0 2m4-2m7: 0-1 3m+: 0-0
Track: LH: 0-0 RH: 0-1 Tight: 0-0 Gall: 0-0
Aids: Bl: 0-0 Vi: 0-0 Tstrap: 0-0
Best Rating: 126 1/02 Wwck 2m4f110y soft Ch

A useful handicap chaser, he goes well fresh and stays two and a half miles plus. Usually held up. At his best on soft ground.

Duma Tau (IRE)
72   36

7-y-o gr g Executive Perk-Di s Wag (Scallywag)
J T Gifford Mrs S N J Embiricos

Placings:P-00   (3871)
2002/03: 21⁹GS, 19⁰S,

	Starts	1st	2nd	3rd	Win & Pl
Hurdles	2	0	0	0	
Career Total	3	0	0	0	

Going: Sf: 0-1 GS: 0-1 Gd: 0-0 GF: - Fm: 0-0
Distance: 2m/2m3: 0-1 2m4-2m7: 0-1 3m+: 0-0
Track: LH: 0-1 RH: 0-1 Tight: 0-0 Gall: 0-1
Aids: Bl: 0-0 Vi: 0-0 Tstrap: 0-0
Best Rating: 36 2/03 Newb 2m3f soft Hdl

Dumadic
85   56

6-y-o b g Nomadic Way (USA)-Duright (Dubassoff (USA))
T D Walford Peter Sawney

Placings:0/30P-0   (0171)
2002/03: 16⁹G,

	Starts	1st	2nd	3rd	Win & Pl
Hurdles	1	0	0	0	
Career Total	5	0	0	1	253

Going: Sf: 0-0 GS: 0-0 Gd: 0-1 GF: - Fm: 0-0
Distance: 2m/2m3: 0-1 2m4-2m7: 0-0 3m+: 0-0
Track: LH: 0-1 RH: 0-0 Tight: 0-0 Gall: 0-0
Aids: Bl: 0-0 Vi: 0-0 Tstrap: 0-0
Best Rating: 88 3/02 Sthl 2m heavy NHF

Dumaran (IRE)
99   119+

5-y-o b g Be My Chief (USA)-Pine Needle (Kris)
A M Balding (I A Balding 20/12) R & E H Investments Ltd

Placings:015P   (3282)
2002/03: 16⁰S, 16¹S, 16⁵S, 17ᴾGS,

	Starts	1st	2nd	3rd	Win & Pl
Hurdles	4	1	0	0	4759
Career Total	4	1	0	0	4759

119 12/02 Wwck 2m   D Hdl   SFT   £4134
Total win prize-money £4134

Going: Sf: 1-3 GS: 0-1 Gd: 0-0 GF: - Fm: 0-0
Distance: 2m/2m3: 1-4 2m4-2m7: 0-0 3m+: 0-0
Track: LH: 1-3 RH: 0-1 Tight: 0-0 Gall: 0-2
Aids: Bl: 0-0 Vi: 0-0 Tstrap: 0-0
Best Rating: 119 12/02 Wwck 2m soft Hdl

Fair novice hurdler; effective over two miles and acts on soft ground; likes to race prominently.

Dun An Doras (IRE)
105   101

7-y-o br g Glacial Storm (USA)-Doorslammer (Avocat)
J D Frost Cloud Nine-Premier Cru

Placings:0/0-502354   (4252)
2002/03: 17⁵G, 20⁰S, 17²GS, 19³GS, 20⁵HY, 22⁴G,

	Starts	1st	2nd	3rd	Win & Pl
Hurdles	6	0	1	1	1889
Career Total	8	0	1	1	1889

Going: Sf: 0-3 GS: 0-1 Gd: 0-2 GF: - Fm: 0-0
Distance: 2m/2m3: 0-3 2m4-2m7: 0-3 3m+: 0-0
Track: LH: 0-3 RH: 0-3 Tight: 0-1 Gall: 0-0
Aids: Bl: 0-0 Vi: 0-0 Tstrap: 0-0
Best Rating: 98 3/03 Extr 2m6f110y good Hdl

Modest hurdler; won maiden point in Ireland; won weakly contested 2m 6f novice hurdle at Newton Abbot June 2003; effective with cut in the ground but did win on good to firm.

Dun Distinctly (IRE)
83(83h)   (66h)71

6-y-o b g Distinctly North (USA)-Dunbally (Dunphy)
P C Haslam Lady Kitson

Placings:310P/5000-60   (0420)
2002/03: 16⁶G, 17⁰HY,

	Starts	1st	2nd	3rd	Win & Pl
Chases	2	0	0	0	
Career Total	10	1	0	1	1899

95 11/00 Catt 2m   G Hdl   GD   £1554
Total win prize-money £1554

Going: Sf: 0-1 GS: 0-0 Gd: 0-1 GF: - Fm: 0-0
Distance: 2m/2m3: 0-2 2m4-2m7: 0-0 3m+: 0-0
Track: LH: 0-2 RH: 0-0 Tight: 0-0 Gall: 0-0
Aids: Bl: 0-0 Vi: 0-0 Tstrap: 0-0
Best Rating: 95 11/00 Catt 2m good Hdl

Duncrievie Gale

6-y-o gr g Gildoran-The Whirlie Weevil (Scallywag)
Mrs L B Normile Robertson McCallum

Placings:0-P   (1633)
2002/03: 24ᴾS,

	Starts	1st	2nd	3rd	Win & Pl
Hurdles	1	0	0	0	
Career Total	2	0	0	0	

Going: Sf: 0-1 GS: 0-0 Gd: 0-0 GF: - Fm: 0-0
Distance: 2m/2m3: 0-0 2m4-2m7: 0-0 3m+: 0-1
Track: LH: 0-0 RH: 0-1 Tight: 0-0 Gall: 0-0
Aids: Bl: 0-0 Vi: 0-0 Tstrap: 0-0
Best Rating: 80 4/02 Ayr 2m good NHF

Dundonald
79   50

4-y-o ch g Magic Ring (IRE)-Cal Norma s Lady (IRE) (Lyphard s Special (USA))
P D Niven (I Semple 11/3) Laumar Racing

Placings:00   (4517)
2002/03: 16⁰GF, 17⁰G,

	Starts	1st	2nd	3rd	Win & Pl
Hurdles	2	0	0	0	
Career Total	2	0	0	0	

Going: Sf: 0-0 GS: 0-0 Gd: 0-1 GF: - Fm: 0-1
Distance: 2m/2m3: 0-2 2m4-2m7: 0-0 3m+: 0-0
Track: LH: 0-2 RH: 0-0 Tight: 0-1 Gall: 0-0
Aids: Bl: 0-0 Vi: 0-0 Tstrap: 0-0
Best Rating: 50 4/03 Sedg 2m1f good Hdl

Dungarvans Choice (IRE)
111(101c)   (126c)139

8-y-o ch g Orchestra-Marys Gift (Monksfield)
N J Henderson Elite Racing Club

Placings:2O14/2110-2P12   (4171)
2002/03: 19²S, 19ᴾHY, 21¹S, 22²S,

	Starts	1st	2nd	3rd	Win & Pl
Hurdles	2	1	1	0	9381
Chases	2	0	1	0	1472
Career Total	12	4	4	0	21759

132 2/03 Newb 2m5f D(0-125)HHdl SFT £5882
124 2/02 Sand 2m110y D Hdl HVY £4660
126 1/02 Hntg 2m110y E Hdl G-S £2569
109 1/01 Chep 2m110y H NHF G-S £1491
Total win prize-money £14604

Going: Sf: 1-4 GS: 0-0 Gd: 0-0 GF: - Fm: 0-0
Distance: 2m/2m3: 0-0 2m4-2m7: 1-4 3m+: 0-0
Track: LH: 1-4 RH: 0-0 Tight: 0-0 Gall: 1-1
Aids: Bl: 0-0 Vi: 0-0 Tstrap: 0-0
Best Rating: 139 3/03 Uttx 2m6f110y soft Hdl

Decent form in bumpers and over hurdles; did not take to jumping fences; effective at up to two and a half miles; appreciates cut in the ground.

Dunkerron
99   80

6-y-o b g Pursuit Of Love-Top Berry (High Top)
J Joseph Jack Joseph

Placings:3P053-5002530P   (1716)
2002/03: 16⁵GF, 16⁰G, 20⁵S, 16²G, 16⁵GF, 20³GF, 17⁰GF, 16ᴾG,

	Starts	1st	2nd	3rd	Win & Pl
Hurdles	8	0	1	1	1284
Career Total	13	0	1	3	2198

Going: Sf: 0-1 GS: 0-0 Gd: 0-3 GF: - Fm: 0-4
Distance: 2m/2m3: 0-6 2m4-2m7: 0-2 3m+: 0-0

Track: LH: 0-6 RH: 0-1 Tight: 0-3 Gall: 0-0
Aids: Bl: 0-1 Vi: 0-0 Tstrap: 0-0
Best Rating: 88 12/01 Chep 2m110y   soft   Hdl

Modest hurdler; took advantage of a lenient mark when beating a large field in 2m Huntingdon conditional seller May 2003; suited by a sound surface and a positive ride.

Dunlea (IRE)
109   97
7-y-o b h Common Grounds-No Distractions (Tap On Wood)
John G Carr A-One Syndicate

Placings:0053310/00003/0000-6400   (3129a)
2002/03: 16⁶GF, 21⁴G, 22⁰S, 18⁰S,

	Starts	1st	2nd	3rd	Win & Pl
Hurdles	4	0	0	0	949
Career Total	20	1	0	3	6569
87	3/00 Navn 2m		Hdl	YLD	£4416

Total win prize-money £4416

Going: Sf: 0-2 GS: 0-0 Gd: 0-1 GF: - Fm: 0-1
Distance: 2m/2m3: 0-2 2m4-2m7: 0-2 3m+: 0-0
Track: LH: 0-2 RH: 0-2 Tight: 0-0 Gall: 0-1
Aids: Bl: 0-0 Vi: 0-0 Tstrap: 0-0
Best Rating: 108 10/00 Cork 2m1f   soft   Hdl

Dunmanus Bay (IRE)
105(104h)   (86h)96
6-y-o gr g Mandalus-Baby Fane (IRE) (Buckskin (FR))
R H Alner (B G Powell 25/11) John Baker

Placings:0330F6   (4370)
2002/03: 22⁰G, 22³GF, 22³GS, 23⁰G, 24⁰G, 24⁰G,

	Starts	1st	2nd	3rd	Win & Pl
Hurdles	3	0	0	2	1077
Chases	3	0	0	0	
Career Total	6	0	0	2	1077

Going: Sf: 0-0 GS: 0-1 Gd: 0-4 GF: - Fm: 0-1
Distance: 2m/2m3: 0-0 2m4-2m7: 0-3 3m+: 0-3
Track: LH: 0-3 RH: 0-3 Tight: 0-3 Gall: 0-0
Aids: Bl: 0-0 Vi: 0-0 Tstrap: 0-0
Best Rating: 86 5/02 Strf   2m6f110y   gd-fm   Hdl

Modest placed form over hurdles; let down by his jumping over fences until transformed by a visor when winning Class F 2m 3f handicap at Exeter April 2003; acts on good ground.

Dunnicks Chance
84   71
8-y-o b m Greensmith-Field Chance (Whistlefield)
F G Tucker F G Tucker

Placings:0F50/60-P3P6002   (4626)
2002/03: 19⁰GS, 16³GS, 16⁵HY, 22⁶GS, 19⁰G, 22⁰GF, 17²GF,

	Starts	1st	2nd	3rd	Win & Pl
Hurdles	7	0	1	1	1537
Career Total	13	0	1	1	1537

Going: Sf: 0-1 GS: 0-3 Gd: 0-1 GF: - Fm: 0-2
Distance: 2m/2m3: 0-3 2m4-2m7: 0-4 3m+: 0-0
Track: LH: 0-2 RH: 0-5 Tight: 0-2 Gall: 0-0
Aids: Bl: 0-0 Vi: 0-0 Tstrap: 0-0
Best Rating: 71 4/03 NAbb 2m1f   gd-fm   Hdl

Poor hurdler; handed second place in a maiden hurdle at Newton Abbot in April 2003.

Dunnicks Field
82   55
7-y-o b g Greensmith-Field Chance (Whistlefield)
F G Tucker F G Tucker

Placings:000-6P   (3310)
2002/03: 17⁶S, 19⁰GS,

	Starts	1st	2nd	3rd	Win & Pl
Hurdles	2	0	0	0	0
Career Total	5	0	0	0	

Going: Sf: 0-1 GS: 0-1 Gd: 0-0 GF: - Fm: 0-0
Distance: 2m/2m3: 0-2 2m4-2m7: 0-0 3m+: 0-0
Track: LH: 0-0 RH: 0-2 Tight: 0-0 Gall: 0-0
Aids: Bl: 0-0 Vi: 0-0 Tstrap: 0-0
Best Rating: 90 2/02 Asct 2m110y   soft   NHF

Dunnicks Trust
61f   54f
5-y-o b g Greensmith-Country Magic (National Trust)
F G Tucker F G Tucker

Placings:00   (4005)
2002/03: 16⁰GS, 16⁵S,

	Starts	1st	2nd	3rd	Win & Pl
NH Flat	2	0	0	0	
Career Total	2	0	0	0	

Going: Sf: 0-1 GS: 0-1 Gd: 0-0 GF: - Fm: 0-0
Distance: 2m/2m3: 0-2 2m4-2m7: 0-0 3m+: 0-0
Track: LH: 0-0 RH: 0-2 Tight: 0-0 Gall: 0-0
Aids: Bl: 0-0 Vi: 0-0 Tstrap: 0-0
Best Rating: 54 2/03 Winc 2m   gd-sft NHF

Dunnicks View
98   80
14-y-o b g Sula Bula-Country Magic (National Trust)
F G Tucker F G Tucker

Placings:55/6050/P0P02/P43/3U3403P/F4F34622435/456
2165P33/6521026/000222536-6355   (4624)
2002/03: 26⁶G, 19³GS, 25⁵GF, 26⁵GF,

	Starts	1st	2nd	3rd	Win & Pl
Chases	4	0	0	1	548
Career Total	62	2	9	10	23622
87	12/00 Tntn	3m	F(0-105)HCh	SFT	£3461
91	1/00 Tntn	3m	F(0-95)HCh	SFT	£3077

Total win prize-money £6539

Going: Sf: 0-0 GS: 0-1 Gd: 0-1 GF: - Fm: 0-2
Distance: 2m/2m3: 0-1 2m4-2m7: 0-0 3m+: 0-3
Track: LH: 0-2 RH: 0-2 Tight: 0-2 Gall: 0-0
Aids: Bl: 0-0 Vi: 0-0 Tstrap: 0-0
Best Rating: 100 1/94 Chel 2m1f   soft   Hdl

Modest staying chaser, tends to reserve his best for Taunton; stays three and a quarter miles; acts on soft ground.

Dunowen (IRE)
(103h)   (83h)99
8-y-o b g Be My Native (USA)-Lulu Buck (Buckskin (FR))
T E Hyde Mrs T E Hyde

Placings:0U4/00040463-3221F   (4113)
2002/03: 20³HY, 20²S, 20⁴S, 20¹S, 32⁶G,

	Starts	1st	2nd	3rd	Win & Pl
Hurdles	2	0	1	1	2143

Chases   3   1   1   0   8279
Career Total 16   1   2   2   11930
| 99 | 2/03 Limk | 2m4f | (0-109)HCh | SFT | £6720 |

Total win prize-money £6721

Going: Sf: 1-4 GS: 0-0 Gd: 0-1 GF: - Fm: 0-0
Distance: 2m/2m3: 0-0 2m4-2m7: 1-4 3m+: 0-1
Track: LH: 0-1 RH: 1-3 Tight: 0-0 Gall: 0-1
Aids: Bl: 1-3 Vi: 0-0 Tstrap: 0-0
Best Rating: 99 2/03 Limk 2m4f   soft   Ch

Dunraven
108(94c)   (82c)85
8-y-o b g Perpendicular-Politique (Politico (USA))
M J Gingell Fare Dealing Partnership

Placings:6F6/0503P500-401104033U3   (4684)
2002/03: 25⁰G, 16⁴G, 16⁰G, 17¹G, 16¹GS, 20⁰GS, 16⁴GS, 16⁰G,
16²S, 16³S, 16⁰G, 16³GF,

	Starts	1st	2nd	3rd	Win & Pl
Hurdles	9	2	0	1	6815
Chases	3	0	0	2	1570
Career Total	22	2	0	4	8739
85	10/02 Fknm	2m	E(0-105)HHdl	G-S	£3740
85	10/02 Sthl	2m1f	G(0-95)HHdl	GD	£2317

Total win prize-money £6058

Going: Sf: 0-2 GS: 1-3 Gd: 1-6 GF: - Fm: 0-1
Distance: 2m/2m3: 2-10 2m4-2m7: 0-1 3m+: 0-1
Track: LH: 2-8 RH: 0-3 Tight: 1-4 Gall: 0-2
Aids: Bl: 0-0 Vi: 0-0 Tstrap: 0-0
Best Rating: 85 11/02 Fknm 2m   gd-sft Hdl

Modest handicap hurdler; little impact so far over fences; best at 2m; suited by give underfoot.

Dunrig (IRE)
8-y-o b g King s Ride-Belon Brig (New Brig)
L Lungo (John Paul Berry 3/5) David Coltman

Placings:P221   (4506)
2002/03: 24⁰S, 25²GS, 25²G, 25¹G,

	Starts	1st	2nd	3rd	Win & Pl
Chases	4	1	2	0	4494
Career Total	4	1	2	0	4494
85	4/03 Kels	3m1f	H Ch	GD	£2847

Total win prize-money £2847

Going: Sf: 0-1 GS: 0-1 Gd: 1-2 GF: - Fm: 0-0
Distance: 2m/2m3: 0-0 2m4-2m7: 0-0 3m+: 1-4
Track: LH: 1-3 RH: 0-1 Tight: 1-3 Gall: 0-0
Aids: Bl: 0-0 Vi: 0-0 Tstrap: 0-0
Best Rating: 101 3/03 Kels 3m1f   good   Ch

Winning pointer; runner-up in two hunter chases before getting off the mark at Kelso; stays three miles one well; acts with cut in the ground.

Dunsfold Dazzler
11-y-o b m Phardante (FR)-Rositary (FR) (Trenel)
Mrs Mair Hughes B R Hughes

Placings:P   (0031)
2002/03: 33⁰GF,

	Starts	1st	2nd	3rd	Win & Pl
Chases	1	0	0	0	
Career Total	1	0	0	0	

Going: Sf: 0-0 GS: 0-0 Gd: 0-0 GF: - Fm: 0-1

Distance: 2m/2m3: 0-0 2m4-2m7: 0-0 3m+: 0-1
Track: LH: 0-1 RH: 0-0 Tight: 0-0 Gall: 0-1
Aids: Bl: 0-0 Vi: 0-0 Tstrap: 0-0
Best Rating:

Dunsford Hall (IRE)

9-y-o gr g Top Of The World-Dark Fluff (Mandalus)
R N Bevis   R N Bevis

Placings:PP   (1246)
2002/03: 26PG, 24PG,

	Starts	1st	2nd	3rd	Win & Pl
Hurdles	2	0	0	0	
Career Total	2	0	0	0	

Going: Sf: 0-0 GS: 0-0 Gd: 0-2 GF: - Fm: 0-0
Distance: 2m/2m3: 0-0 2m4-2m7: 0-0 3m+: 0-2
Track: LH: 0-2 RH: 0-0 Tight: 0-0
Aids: Bl: 0-0 Vi: 0-0 Tstrap: 0-0
Best Rating: 0   9/02 Worc 3m   good   Hdl

Dunster Castle

110(99h)   (106h)**119**
8-y-o ch g Carlingford Castle-Gay Edition (New Member)
P J Hobbs   Mrs D L Whateley

Placings: 1/25F/32631-3P21   (4447)
2002/03: 24³G, 24PG, 21²S, 24¹G,

	Starts	1st	2nd	3rd	Win & Pl
Chases	4	1	1	1	8878
Career Total	13	3	3	3	16242
118	4/03	Ludl	3m	D Ch	GD	£6300
105	4/02	Winc	2m6f	E Hdl	GD	£3052
105	3/00	Chep	2m110y	H NHF	GD	£1757

Total win prize-money £11109

Going: Sf: 0-1 GS: 0-0 Gd: 1-3 GF: - Fm: 0-0
Distance: 2m/2m3: 0-0 2m4-2m7: 0-0 3m+: 1-3
Track: LH: 0-1 RH: 1-3 Tight: 1-2 Gall: 0-1
Aids: Bl: 0-0 Vi: 0-0 Tstrap: 0-0
Best Rating: 118 4/03 Ludl 3m   good   Ch

Fair hurdler/chaser; acts on good ground; stays three miles.

Dunston Ace

9-y-o b g Sizzling Melody-Miss Vaigly Blue (Vaigly Great)
B D Leavy   Paul Hollinshead

Placings:0PPP-P   (0685)
2002/03: 21PG,

	Starts	1st	2nd	3rd	Win & Pl
Chases	1	0	0	0	
Career Total	5	0	0	0	

Going: Sf: 0-0 GS: 0-0 Gd: 0-1 GF: - Fm: 0-0
Distance: 2m/2m3: 0-0 2m4-2m7: 0-1 3m+: 0-0
Track: LH: 0-1 RH: 0-0 Tight: 0-1 Gall: 0-0
Aids: Bl: 0-0 Vi: 0-0 Tstrap: 0-0
Best Rating: 0   7/02 Strf 2m5f110y   good   Ch

Dunston Bill

105(81h)   (73h)**122**
9-y-o b g Sizzling Melody-Fardella (ITY) (Molvedo)
C J Mann   All For One And One For All Partnership

Placings:624/20P31/325P041/642144124F-21U23P (4175)
2002/03: 20²GS, 22¹S, 20US, 20²GS, 20³HY, 21PS,

	Starts	1st	2nd	3rd	Win & Pl
Chases	6	1	2	1	12156
Career Total	31	5	7	3	35134
122	11/02	MRas	2m6f110yD(0-120)HCh	SFT	£5512
119	1/02	Kemp	2m4f110yD(0-115)HCh	SFT	£5096
112	12/01	NAbb	2m5f110yE(0-105)HCh	HVY	£3427
106	4/00	Hrfd	2m1f	E(0-115)HHdl	GD	£4082
98	4/99	Towc	2m	F(0-105)HHdl	SFT	£1933

Total win prize-money £20050

Going: Sf: 1-4 GS: 0-2 Gd: 0-0 GF: - Fm: 0-0
Distance: 2m/2m3: 0-0 2m4-2m7: 1-6 3m+: 0-0
Track: LH: 0-3 RH: 1-4 Tight: 1-2 Gall: 0-0
Aids: Bl: 1-6 Vi: 0-0 Tstrap: 0-0
Best Rating: 122 11/02 MRas 2m6f110y soft   Ch

Fair chaser; best over trips around two and a half miles or a bit further; suited by cut in the ground; suited by sharp tracks; best going right-handed; usually wears blinkers.

Dunston Durgam (IRE)

88   **59**
9-y-o b g Durgam (USA)-Blazing Sunset (Blazing Saddles (AUS))
R Hollinshead   Mrs H J Bannister

Placings:P000/U4F/FP00   (1207)
2002/03: 22FGF, 22PGS, 16⁰GF, 16⁰G,

	Starts	1st	2nd	3rd	Win & Pl
Hurdles	4	0	0	0	
Career Total	11	0	0	0	0

Going: Sf: 0-0 GS: 0-1 Gd: 0-1 GF: - Fm: 0-2
Distance: 2m/2m3: 0-0 2m4-2m7: 0-2 3m+: 0-0
Track: LH: 0-4 RH: 0-0 Tight: 0-2 Gall: 0-0
Aids: Bl: 0-0 Vi: 0-0 Tstrap: 0-0
Best Rating: 58   9/02 Uttx 2m   good   Hdl

Dunston Gold

80(94c)   (64+c)**59**
9-y-o ch g Risk Me (FR)-Maria Whittaker (Cure The Blues (USA))
G Barnett   J C Bradbury

Placings:50-02FP   (0986)
2002/03: 22⁰G, 21²S, 25FGF, 26PGF,

	Starts	1st	2nd	3rd	Win & Pl
Hurdles	2	0	0	0	
Chases	2	0	1	0	764
Career Total	6	0	1	0	764

Going: Sf: 0-1 GS: 0-0 Gd: 0-1 GF: - Fm: 0-2
Distance: 2m/2m3: 0-0 2m4-2m7: 0-2 3m+: 0-2
Track: LH: 0-3 RH: 0-1 Tight: 0-0 Gall: 0-0
Aids: Bl: 0-0 Vi: 0-0 Tstrap: 0-0
Best Rating: 64   6/02 Uttx 2m5f   soft   Ch

Modest pointer, has shown little under Rules.

Dunston Heath (IRE)

93   **71**
10-y-o b g Durgam (USA)-Yola (IRE) (Last Tycoon)
B D Leavy   Barry Leavy

Placings:0P40000/500163/60020241P/4004P-4P0 (4116)
2002/03: 22⁴GS, 24PGS, 21⁰G,

	Starts	1st	2nd	3rd	Win & Pl
Hurdles	2	0	0	0	0
Chases	1	0	0	0	0
Career Total	30	2	1	1	10092
87	4/00	Bang	2m4f	F(0-100)HHdl	G-S	£5167
84	3/99	Hntg	2m5f110yG(0-90)HHdl	G-S	£2458

Total win prize-money £7626

Going: Sf: 0-0 GS: 0-2 Gd: 0-1 GF: - Fm: 0-0
Distance: 2m/2m3: 0-0 2m4-2m7: 0-2 3m+: 0-1
Track: LH: 0-2 RH: 0-1 Tight: 0-2 Gall: 0-1
Aids: Bl: 0-0 Vi: 0-0 Tstrap: 0-2
Best Rating: 87   4/00 Bang 2m4f   gd-sft   Hdl

Dunston Slick

63(91c)   (93c)**64**
10-y-o ch g Weld-Havrin Princess (Scallywag)
W Clay   M Braycotton

Placings:0P/005000U60000-0   (0658)
2002/03: 16⁰GF,

	Starts	1st	2nd	3rd	Win & Pl
Hurdles	1	0	0	1	
Career Total	15	0	0	0	

Going: Sf: 0-0 GS: 0-0 Gd: 0-0 GF: - Fm: 0-1
Distance: 2m/2m3: 0-1 2m4-2m7: 0-0 3m+: 0-0
Track: LH: 0-1 RH: 0-0 Tight: 0-0 Gall: 0-0
Aids: Bl: 0-0 Vi: 0-0 Tstrap: 0-0
Best Rating: 83 12/01 Ludl 2m   good   Ch

Durham Glint

12-y-o b g Glint Of Gold-Jem Jen (Great Nephew)
Mrs J E Speight   Eddy Luke

Placings:0000/F/P   (0503)
2002/03: 26PG,

	Starts	1st	2nd	3rd	Win & Pl
Chases	1	0	0	0	
Career Total	6	0	0	0	

Going: Sf: 0-0 GS: 0-0 Gd: 0-0 GF: - Fm: 0-0
Distance: 2m/2m3: 0-0 2m4-2m7: 0-0 3m+: 0-1
Track: LH: 0-1 RH: 0-0 Tight: 0-1 Gall: 0-0
Aids: Bl: 0-0 Vi: 0-0 Tstrap: 0-0
Best Rating: 76   5/95 MRas 1m5f110y gd-fm   NHF

Duringthenight (IRE)

104f   **96f**
4-y-o b g Namaqualand (USA)-Legend Of Spain (USA) (Alleged (USA))
G A Swinbank   Miss Sally R Haynes

Placings:6222   (4778)
2002/03: 17⁶G, 16²G, 16²G, 16²G,

	Starts	1st	2nd	3rd	Win & Pl
NH Flat	4	0	3	0	2138
Career Total	4	0	3	0	2138

Going: Sf: 0-0 GS: 0-1 Gd: 0-3 GF: - Fm: 0-0
Distance: 2m/2m3: 0-4 2m4-2m7: 0-0 3m+: 0-0
Track: LH: 0-2 RH: 0-2 Tight: 0-0 Gall: 0-0

Aids: Bl: 0-0 Vi: 0-0 Tstrap: 0-0
Best Rating: 96 4/03 Prth 2m110y good NHF

Modest bumper performer; runner-up three times in spring of 2003; acts on good ground.

Durlston Bay
103   104
6-y-o b g Welsh Captain-Nelliellamay (Super Splash (USA))
S Dow Sandbaggers Club

Placings:4P5P6-321   (0410)
2002/03: 17³G, 17²G, 22¹GF,

	Starts	1st	2nd	3rd	Win & Pl
Hurdles	3	1	1	1	5597
Career Total	8	1	1	1	5597
104 6/02 Strf 2m6f110yD Hdl				G-F	£4371
				Total win prize-money	£4371

Going: Sf: 0-0 GS: 0-0 Gd: 0-2 GF: - Fm: 1-1
Distance: 2m/2m3: 0-2 2m4-2m7: 1-1 3m+: 0-0
Track: LH: 1-1 RH: 0-1 Tight: 1-2 Gall: 0-0
Aids: Bl: 0-0 Vi: 0-0 Tstrap: 0-0
Best Rating: 104 6/02 Strf 2m6f110y gd-fm Hdl

Modest hurdler, stays well and acts on fast ground.

Dushaan
76   23
8-y-o ch g Anshan-Soon To Be (Hot Spark)
Mrs L B Normile Out The Box Racing

Placings:5/3400405P1/10P-0   (2165)
2002/03: 17⁰S,

	Starts	1st	2nd	3rd	Win & Pl
Hurdles	1	0	0	0	
Career Total	14	2	1		6333
96 5/01 Prth 2m110y	HHdl			SFT	£3445
96 4/01 Weth 2m	F(0-100)HHdl			G-S	£2614
				Total win prize-money	£6060

Going: Sf: 0-1 GS: 0-0 Gd: 0-0 GF: - Fm: 0-0
Distance: 2m/2m3: 0-1 2m4-2m7: 0-0 3m+: 0-0
Track: LH: 0-1 RH: 0-0 Tight: 0-1 Gall: 0-0
Aids: Bl: 0-0 Vi: 0-0 Tstrap: 0-0
Best Rating: 101 5/00 Prth 2m110y gd-sft NHF

Moderate hurdler, showed progressive form in the spring of 2001, winning at Wetherby and Perth. Suited by soft ground.

Dusk Duel (USA)
(86h)   (108h)159
8-y-o b g Kris-Night Secret (Nijinsky (CAN))
N J Henderson Anthony Speelman

Placings:10/2110/3112/30-0   (4323)
2002/03: 16⁶G,

	Starts	1st	2nd	3rd	Win & Pl
Hurdles	1	0	0	0	
Career Total	13	5	2	2	53891
139 12/00 Kemp 2m	B Ch			G-S	£8437
148 12/00 Chel 2m5f	B Ch			SFT	£11340
141 2/00 Weth 2m	A Hdl			SFT	£9600
149 1/00 Asct 2m110y	C Hdl			SFT	£4914
107 3/99 Sand 2m110y	H NHF			SFT	£1619
				Total win prize-money	£35911

Going: Sf: 0-0 GS: 0-0 Gd: 0 GF: - Fm: 0-0
Distance: 2m/2m3: 0-0 2m4-2m7: 0-0 3m+: 0-0
Track: LH: 0-1 RH: 0-0 Tight: 0-0 Gall: 0-1
Aids: Bl: 0-0 Vi: 0-0 Tstrap: 0-0
Best Rating: 149 11/01 Asct 2m3f110y good Ch

Smart chaser/very useful hurdler, he won novice chases at Cheltenham and Kempton in the winter of 2000; good return at Ascot in November 2001, but beaten over three miles next time and missed the rest of the season; well beaten when returned to hurdles for reappearance in March 2003; acts on soft ground; has worn visor.

Dusky Blue (IRE)
89   75+
4-y-o b g Bluebird (USA)-Massada (Most Welcome)
Jonjo O Neill Mrs G Smith

Placings:P3   (0890)
2002/03: 17⁶GS, 17³S,

	Starts	1st	2nd	3rd	Win & Pl
Hurdles	2	0	0	1	450
Career Total	2	0	0	1	450

Going: Sf: 0-1 GS: 0-1 Gd: 0-0 GF: - Fm: 0-0
Distance: 2m/2m3: 0-2 2m4-2m7: 0-0 3m+: 0-0
Track: LH: 0-1 RH: 0-1 Tight: 0-2 Gall: 0-0
Aids: Bl: 0-1 Vi: 0-0 Tstrap: 0-1
Best Rating: 75 8/02 Bang 2m1f soft Hdl

Dusky Light
93   83
5-y-o b m Gildoran-Starawak (Star Appeal)
P F Nicholls Richard Barber

Placings:34   (2197)
2002/03: 17³GS, 19⁴GS,

	Starts	1st	2nd	3rd	Win & Pl
NH Flat	1	0	0	0	348
Hurdles	1	0	0	0	470
Career Total	2	0	0	1	818

Going: Sf: 0-0 GS: 0-2 Gd: 0-0 GF: - Fm: 0-0
Distance: 2m/2m3: 0-2 2m4-2m7: 0-0 3m+: 0-0
Track: LH: 0-0 RH: 0-1 Tight: 0-1 Gall: 0-0
Aids: Bl: 0-0 Vi: 0-0 Tstrap: 0-0
Best Rating: 90 11/02 Tntn 2m1f gd-sft NHF

Dusty Democrat
97   74+
5-y-o b g Democratic (USA)-Two Shots (Dom Racine (FR))
W G M Turner T.O.C.S. Ltd

Placings:0005656P-46024   (1546)
2002/03: 17⁴GF, 17⁶GF, 16⁰G, 16²F, 19⁴F,

	Starts	1st	2nd	3rd	Win & Pl
Hurdles	5	0	1	0	875
Career Total	13	0	1	0	875

Going: Sf: 0-0 GS: 0-0 Gd: 0-0 GF: - Fm: 0-4
Distance: 2m/2m3: 0-4 2m4-2m7: 0-1 3m+: 0-0
Track: LH: 0-2 RH: 0-3 Tight: 0-1 Gall: 0-0
Aids: Bl: 0-0 Vi: 0-1 Tstrap: 0-0
Best Rating: 74 10/02 Ludl 2m firm Hdl

Selling hurdler. Proved no match for the useful Iorana when runner-up at Ludlow October 2002.

Dusty Star
4-y-o b f Danzig Connection (USA)-Sindos (Busted)
W G M Turner T.O.C.S. Ltd

Placings:U0   (1614)
2002/03: 17⁰F, 16⁰F,

	Starts	1st	2nd	3rd	Win & Pl
Hurdles	2	0	0	0	
Career Total	2	0	0	0	

Dusty Too
82   43
5-y-o gr m Terimon-Princess Florine (USA) (Our Native (USA))
Mrs A J Perrett S P Tindall

Placings:1140   (2572)
2002/03: 16¹G, 16¹GF, 16⁴G, 19⁰G,

	Starts	1st	2nd	3rd	Win & Pl
NH Flat	3	2		0	4154
Hurdles	1	0		0	0
Career Total	4	2		0	4154
97 8/02 Worc 2m	H NHF			G-F	£1887
101 8/02 Worc 2m	H NHF			GD	£2266
				Total win prize-money	£4154

Going: Sf: 0-0 GS: 0-0 Gd: 1-3 GF: - Fm: 1-1
Distance: 2m/2m3: 2-4 2m4-2m7: 0-0 3m+: 0-0
Track: LH: 2-4 RH: 0-0 Tight: 0-0 Gall: 0-1
Aids: Bl: 0-0 Vi: 0-0 Tstrap: 0-0
Best Rating: 101 8/02 Worc 2m good NHF

A half-sister to a couple of bumper winners in Ireland one of which went on to score twice over hurdles. Narrow winner of a Worcester bumper on her debut when she defeated a rival with some good form to his name. Followed up in easier race at same course next time. Held subsequently.

Dutch Dyane
98   85
10-y-o b m Midyan (USA)-Double Dutch (Nicholas Bill)
G P Enright L Fuller, Miss P Ross, Neil Kenworthy

Placings:0024/4331/1531F2/34040P/3P0-00P1P (2053)
2002/03: 22⁶GF, 20⁰S, 21⁰GF, 22¹S, 24⁰G,

	Starts	1st	2nd	3rd	Win & Pl
Hurdles	5	1	0	0	3705
Career Total	30	4	3	5	20175
80 11/02 Sand 2m6f	E(0-105)HHdl			SFT	£3705
108 1/00 Leic 2m6f	E(0-115)HHdl			SFT	£5492
96 11/99 Font 2m6f110y	F(0-110)HHdl			SFT	£2320
94 11/98 Leic 2m4f110y	E(0-100)HHdl			SFT	£2882
				Total win prize-money	£14400

Going: Sf: 1-2 GS: 0-0 Gd: 0-1 GF: - Fm: 0-2
Distance: 2m/2m3: 0-0 2m4-2m7: 1-4 3m+: 0-1
Track: LH: 0-3 RH: 1-2 Tight: 0-2 Gall: 0-0
Aids: Bl: 0-0 Vi: 0-0 Tstrap: 0-0
Best Rating: 112 11/00 Newb 2m3f soft Hdl

Very moderate hurdler, she was winning her first race in almost three years at Sandown in November 2002. Stays two miles-six and appreciates soft ground.

Dynamic Lifter (IRE)
104   95
5-y-o ch g Be My Native (USA)-Best Trump (Le Bavard (FR))

Jonjo O Neill J P McManus

Placings:006032   (4267)
2002/03: 16⁹GS, 21⁰S, 21⁶S, 20⁹HY, 25³G, 24²GF,

	Starts	1st	2nd	3rd	Win & Pl
NH Flat	1	0	0	0	0
Hurdles	5	0	1	1	1459
Career Total	6	0	1	1	1459

Going: Sf: 0-3 GS: 0-1 Gd: 0-1 GF: - Fm: 0-1
Distance: 2m/2m3: 0-1 2m4-2m7: 0-3 3m+: 0-2
Track: LH: 0-4 RH: 0-2 Tight: 0-3 Gall: 0-0
Aids: Bl: 0-1 Vi: 0-0 Tstrap: 0-0
Best Rating: 95   3/03   Weth   3m1f   good   Hdl

Moderate hurdler; stays 3m 3f; acts on fast ground; running well in the summer of 2003.

Earl Sigurd (IRE)
109   106
5-y-o ch g High Kicker (USA)-My Kind (Mon Tresor)
L Lungo Queens House

Placings:3131-00P   (4591)
2002/03: 16⁹GS, 20⁹G, 16⁶G,

	Starts	1st	2nd	3rd	Win & Pl
Hurdles	3	0	0	0	
Career Total	7	2	0	2	7409
103	12/01	Catt	2m	D Hdl	SFT £3997
88	10/01	Kels	2m110y	E Hdl	GD £2618
			Total win prize-money £6616		

Going: Sf: 0-0 GS: 0-1 Gd: 0-2 GF: - Fm: 0-0
Distance: 2m/2m3: 0-2 2m4-2m7: 0-1 3m+: 0-0
Track: LH: 0-2 RH: 0-1 Tight: 0-0 Gall: 0-0
Aids: Bl: 0-1 Vi: 0-0 Tstrap: 0-0
Best Rating: 103 12/01 Catt 2m   soft   Hdl

Moderate hurdler; best at two miles; has won on a sound surface and soft ground.

Earl Token

7-y-o b g Primitive Rising (USA)-Lady Token (Roscoe Blake)
R J Armson R J Armson

Placings:PP   (0387)
2002/03: 26²G, 20⁰GS,

	Starts	1st	2nd	3rd	Win & Pl
Chases	2	0	0	0	
Career Total	2	0	0	0	

Going: Sf: 0-0 GS: 0-1 Gd: 0-1 GF: - Fm: 0-0
Distance: 2m/2m3: 0-0 2m4-2m7: 0-1 3m+: 0-1
Track: LH: 0-2 RH: 0-0 Tight: 0-0 Gall: 0-0
Aids: Bl: 0-0 Vi: 0-0 Tstrap: 0-0
Best Rating: 0   5/02   Weth   2m4f110y   gd-sft   Ch

Earl's Kitchen
100f   115f
6-y-o ch g Karinga Bay-Rempstone (Coronash)
C Tizzard Mrs J E Purdie

Placings:2100   (3673)
2002/03: 16²HY, 18¹HY, 16⁰G, 18⁰GS,

	Starts	1st	2nd	3rd	Win & Pl
NH Flat	4	1	1	0	2632
Career Total	4	1	1	0	2632
115	1/03	Font	2m2f110yH NHF	HVY £1946	
			Total win prize-money £1946		

Going: Sf: 1-2 GS: 0-1 Gd: 0-1 GF: - Fm: 0-0
Distance: 2m/2m3: 1-4 2m4-2m7: 0-0 3m+: 0-0
Track: LH: 1-4 RH: 0-0 Tight: 1-2 Gall: 0-1
Aids: Bl: 0-0 Vi: 0-0 Tstrap: 0-0
Best Rating: 115 1/03 Font 2m2f110y heavy NHF

Ex-pointer; winner of a heavy-ground bumper in January 2003

Early Dawn

9-y-o ch m Rakaposhi King-Early Run (Deep Run)
Miss T McCurrich (C Grant 1/8) Mrs S Cartridge

Placings:PP-140PP0   (4390)
2002/03: 21¹GF, 20⁴G, 17⁰HY, 20⁰GS, 20⁰GF, 19⁰F,

	Starts	1st	2nd	3rd	Win & Pl
Chases	6	1	0	0	3325
Career Total	8	1	0	0	3325
75	5/02	Sedg	2m5f	E Ch	G-F £3022
			Total win prize-money £3023		

Going: Sf: 0-1 GS: 0-1 Gd: 0-1 GF: - Fm: 1-3
Distance: 2m/2m3: 0-0 1 2m4-2m7: 1-5 3m+: 0-0
Track: LH: 1-3 RH: 0-3 Tight: 1-3 Gall: 0-0
Aids: Bl: 0-0 Vi: 0-0 Tstrap: 0-0
Best Rating: 75   5/02   Sedg   2m5f   gd-fm   Ch

Early Edition
96   89
7-y-o b g Primitive Rising (USA)-Ottery News (Pony Express)
O J Carter O J Carter

Placings:PF   (4554)
2002/03: 22²PG, 20²FG,

	Starts	1st	2nd	3rd	Win & Pl
Chases	2	0	0	0	
Career Total	2	0	0	0	

Going: Sf: 0-0 GS: 0-0 Gd: 0-2 GF: - Fm: 0-0
Distance: 2m/2m3: 0-0 2m4-2m7: 0-2 3m+: 0-0
Track: LH: 0-2 RH: 0-0 Tight: 0-0 Gall: 0-1
Aids: Bl: 0-0 Vi: 0-0 Tstrap: 0-0
Best Rating: 0   4/03   Ayr   2m4f   good   Ch

Early Morning Call (IRE)

11-y-o ch g Henbit (USA)-Golonig (Goldhill)
D P Keane (Paul Keane 1/5) The It s My Job Partnership

Placings:3/232/2P-PP   (4761)
2002/03: 33⁰GF, 26²FG,

	Starts	1st	2nd	3rd	Win & Pl
Chases	2	0	0	0	
Career Total	8	0	3	2	3283

Going: Sf: 0-0 GS: 0-0 Gd: 0-0 GF: - Fm: 0-2
Distance: 2m/2m3: 0-0 2m4-2m7: 0-0 3m+: 0-2
Track: LH: 0-1 RH: 0-0 Tight: 0-1 Gall: 0-1
Aids: Bl: 0-0 Vi: 0-0 Tstrap: 0-0
Best Rating: 82   8/98   Hntg   2m4f110y   gd-fm   Ch

Early Riser

5-y-o b m Primitive Rising (USA)-Coneygree (Northern State (USA))

C C Bealby P M Bradley

Placings:00-P   (0407)
2002/03: 17⁶GF,

	Starts	1st	2nd	3rd	Win & Pl
Hurdles	1	0	0	0	
Career Total	3	0	0	0	

Going: Sf: 0-0 GS: 0-0 Gd: 0-0 GF: - Fm: 0-1
Distance: 2m/2m3: 0-1 2m4-2m7: 0-0 3m+: 0-0
Track: LH: 0-0 RH: 0-1 Tight: 0-1 Gall: 0-0
Aids: Bl: 0-0 Vi: 0-0 Tstrap: 0-0
Best Rating: 50   3/02   MRas   2m1f110y   gd-sft   NHF

Early Start
105f   102+f
5-y-o ch m Husyan (USA)-Gipsy Dawn (Lighter)
J W Mullins Adam Day

Placings:13   (4611)
2002/03: 18¹S, 17³G,

	Starts	1st	2nd	3rd	Win & Pl
NH Flat	2	1	0	1	4682
Career Total	2	1	0	1	4682
102	2/03	Font	2m2f110yH NHF	SFT £1932	
			Total win prize-money £1932		

Going: Sf: 1-1 GS: 0-0 Gd: 0-1 GF: - Fm: 0-0
Distance: 2m/2m3: 1-2 2m4-2m7: 0-0 3m+: 0-0
Track: LH: 1-2 RH: 0-0 Tight: 1-1 Gall: 0-1
Aids: Bl: 0-0 Vi: 0-0 Tstrap: 0-0
Best Rating: 102 2/03 Font 2m2f110y soft NHF

Won a soft ground Fontwell bumper on her debut in February 2003; creditable third in mares only Listed event at Cheltenham in April on a sounder surface.

Earthmover (IRE)

12-y-o ch g Mister Lord (USA)-Clare s Crystal (Tekoah)
P F Nicholls R M Penny

Placings:11111/FU0P/511536F/112233U0/1342P3-P11411
                                                   (4615)
2002/03: 24²G, 25¹GS, 26¹HY, 26⁴G, 27¹G, 26¹G,

	Starts	1st	2nd	3rd	Win & Pl
Chases	6	4	0	0	15360
Career Total	36	14	3	5	141570
139	4/03	Chel	3m2f110yH Ch	GD	£6698
140	4/03	Ayr	3m3f110yH Ch	GD	£3575
134	2/03	Chep	3m2f110yH Ch	HVY	£1561
140	2/03	Weth	3m1f	H Ch	G-S	£1526
150	10/01	Chep	3m	B(0-145)HCh	GD	£9937
152	5/00	Weth	3m1f	B(0-145)HCh	G-S	£9486
148	5/00	Chep	3m	B(0-145)HCh	FRM	£8703
151	11/99	Chep	3m	B(0-150)HHdl	SFT	£6824
141	10/99	Chel	3m1f110yD Hdl	GD	£4531
159	3/98	Chel	3m2f110yB Ch	GD	£18957
133	3/98	Newb	3m	H Ch	SFT	£1576
127	2/98	Wwck	3m2f	H Ch	GD	£1086
119	5/97	Strf	3m4f	H Ch	GD	£4272
112	5/97	Chep	3m	H Ch	G-S	£3434
			Total win prize-money £82171		

Going: Sf: 1-1 GS: 1-1 Gd: 2-4 GF: - Fm: 0-0
Distance: 2m/2m3: 0-0 2m4-2m7: 0-0 3m+: 4-6
Track: LH: 4-6 RH: 0-0 Tight: 0-0 Gall: 1-2
Aids: Bl: 0-0 Vi: 0-0 Tstrap: 0-0
Best Rating: 159 3/98 Chel 3m2f110y good Ch

Smart staying chaser; winner of the 1998 Foxhunters at Cheltenham; back in hunter chase company in 2003, suc-

cessful at Wetherby, Chepstow, Ayr and Cheltenham; twice a winner early in the new campaign; needs a left-handed track; stays well.

Easibrook Jane
100   81

5-y-o b m Alderbrook-Relatively Easy (Relkino)
C Tizzard R G Tizzard

Placings:05320   (4187)
2002/03: 13⁰S, 17⁵S, 16³HY, 19²S, 20⁰G,

	Starts	1st	2nd	3rd	Win & Pl
NH Flat	2	0	0	0	0
Hurdles	3	0	1	1	2158
Career Total	5	0	1	1	2158

Going: Sf: 0-4 GS: 0-0 Gd: 0-1 GF: - Fm: 0-0
Distance: 2m/2m3: 0-3 2m4-2m7: 0-1 3m+: 0-0
Track: LH: 0-1 RH: 0-3 Tight: 0-2 Gall: 0-0
Aids: Bl: 0-0 Vi: 0-0 Tstrap: 0-0
Best Rating: 81 3/03 Extr 2m3f   soft   Hdl

Moderate novice hurdler; stays 19 furlongs; has shown form on a soft surface.

East Hill (IRE)
102   103

7-y-o b g Satco (FR)-Sharmalyne (FR) (Melyno)
G B Balding Mr & Mrs Tony Geake

Placings:341/2240-40452   (4315)
2002/03: 16⁴G, 22⁰S, 21⁴S, 21⁵G, 19²G,

	Starts	1st	2nd	3rd	Win & Pl
Hurdles	5	0	1	0	1683
Career Total	12	1	3	1	6237
106 4/01 Font 2m2f110yH NHF				GD	£1914

Total win prize-money £1915

Going: Sf: 0-2 GS: 0-0 Gd: 0-3 GF: - Fm: 0-0
Distance: 2m/2m3: 0-2 2m4-2m7: 0-3 3m+: 0-0
Track: LH: 0-2 RH: 0-3 Tight: 0-0 Gall: 0-2
Aids: Bl: 0-0 Vi: 0-0 Tstrap: 0-0
Best Rating: 107 11/01 Kemp 2m5f   good   Hdl

Fair novice hurdler; bumper winner; stays 2m 3f and best on good ground.

East Tycoon (IRE)
105   122+

4-y-o ch g Bigstone (IRE)-Princesse Sharpo (USA) (Trempolino (USA))
Jonjo O Neill (M J Grassick 10/11) Mrs G Smith

Placings:141   (4084)
2002/03: 16¹GS, 16⁴G, 16¹GS,

	Starts	1st	2nd	3rd	Win & Pl
Hurdles	3	2	0	0	14299
Career Total	3	2	0	0	14299
122 3/03 Strf	2m110y D Hdl			G-S	£5577
120 1/03 Donc	2m110y C Hdl			G-S	£7221

Total win prize-money £12799

Going: Sf: 0-0 GS: 2-2 Gd: 0-1 GF: - Fm: 0-0
Distance: 2m/2m3: 2-3 2m4-2m7: 0-0 3m+: 0-0
Track: LH: 2-2 RH: 0-1 Tight: 1-1 Gall: 1-1
Aids: Bl: 1-1 Vi: 0-0 Tstrap: 0-0
Best Rating: 122 3/03 Strf 2m110y   gd-sft   Hdl

Decent ex-Irish hurdler; acts on a sound surface; effective at two miles; has worn blinkers.

Easter Present (IRE)
102f   98f

4-y-o br g Presenting-Spring Fiddler (IRE) (Fidel)
Miss H C Knight Mrs R A Humphries

Placings:3   (4005)
2002/03: 16³S,

	Starts	1st	2nd	3rd	Win & Pl
NH Flat	1	0	0	1	285
Career Total	1	0	0	1	285

Going: Sf: 0-1 GS: 0-0 Gd: 0-0 GF: - Fm: 0-0
Distance: 2m/2m3: 0-1 2m4-2m7: 0-0 3m+: 0-0
Track: LH: 0-0 RH: 0-0 Tight: 0-0 Gall: 0-0
Aids: Bl: 0-0 Vi: 0-0 Tstrap: 0-0
Best Rating: 98 3/03 Winc 2m   soft   NHF

Placed in a bumper.

Eastern Prophets
75   55+

10-y-o b g Emarati (USA)-Four Love (Pas De Seul)
Jedd O Keeffe Wetherby Racing Bureau 54

Placings:0   (0658)
2002/03: 16⁰GF,

	Starts	1st	2nd	3rd	Win & Pl
Hurdles	1	0	0	0	0
Career Total	1	0	0	0	0

Going: Sf: 0-0 GS: 0-0 Gd: 0-0 GF: - Fm: 0-1
Distance: 2m/2m3: 0-1 2m4-2m7: 0-0 3m+: 0-0
Track: LH: 0-1 RH: 0-0 Tight: 0-0 Gall: 0-0
Aids: Bl: 0-0 Vi: 0-0 Tstrap: 0-0
Best Rating: 55 6/02 Worc 2m   gd-fm Hdl

Eastern Red
61   27

5-y-o b m Contract Law (USA)-Gagajulu (Al Hareb (USA))
Miss M Bragg Friends Of Rock Park

Placings:PF-0   (3598)
2002/03: 17⁰S,

	Starts	1st	2nd	3rd	Win & Pl
Hurdles	1	0	0	0	0
Career Total	3	0	0	0	0

Going: Sf: 0-1 GS: 0-0 Gd: 0-0 GF: - Fm: 0-0
Distance: 2m/2m3: 0-1 2m4-2m7: 0-0 3m+: 0-0
Track: LH: 0-0 RH: 0-1 Tight: 0-1 Gall: 0-0
Aids: Bl: 0-0 Vi: 0-0 Tstrap: 0-0
Best Rating: 27 2/03 Tntn 2m1f   soft   Hdl

Eastern Tribute (USA)
114   125

7-y-o b g Affirmed (USA)-Mia Duchessa (USA) (Nijinsky (CAN))
A C Whillans John J Elliot

Placings:33F44/51410202/033225P42-1U42601FP (4037)
2002/03: 18¹GS, 16⁰UGS, 22⁴S, 16²S, 20⁶G, 16⁰S, 20¹HY, 20⁷GS, 20⁷PS,

	Starts	1st	2nd	3rd	Win & Pl
Hurdles	9	2	1	0	17928

Career Total
	31	4	6	4	35424
122 1/03 Ayr	2m4f	B(0-150)HHdl		HVY	£10159
113 5/02 Kels	2m2f	D(0-125)HHdl		G-S	£6201
110 1/01 Ayr	2m	D(0-125)HHdl		SFT	£3388
98 11/00 Ayr	2m	E Hdl		SFT	£1974

Total win prize-money £21723

Going: Sf: 1-5 GS: 1-3 Gd: 0-1 GF: - Fm: 0-0
Distance: 2m/2m3: 1-4 2m4-2m7: 1-5 3m+: 0-0
Track: LH: 2-8 RH: 0-1 Tight: 1-4 Gall: 0-0
Aids: Bl: 0-0 Vi: 0-0 Tstrap: 0-0
Best Rating: 122 1/03 Ayr 2m4f   heavy   Hdl

Fair handicap hurdler, he is suited by a soft surface and is effective at up to two and a half miles.

Easternking
94   71+

4-y-o ch f Sabrehill (USA)-Kshessinskaya (Hadeer)
J S Wainwright Peter Easterby

Placings:0056520   (4418)
2002/03: 16⁰S, 16⁰GS, 17⁵S, 16⁶HY, 16⁵S, 19²G, 22⁰G,

	Starts	1st	2nd	3rd	Win & Pl
Hurdles	7	0	1	0	700
Career Total	7	0	1	0	700

Going: Sf: 0-4 GS: 0-1 Gd: 0-2 GF: - Fm: 0-0
Distance: 2m/2m3: 0-6 2m4-2m7: 0-1 3m+: 0-0
Track: LH: 0-5 RH: 0-1 Tight: 0-3 Gall: 0-2
Aids: Bl: 0-0 Vi: 0-4 Tstrap: 0-0
Best Rating: 71 2/03 Catt 2m3f   good   Hdl

Poor form in juvenile hurdles; runner-up in a seller at Catterick in February.

Easton Gale
104   132

9-y-o b g Strong Gale-Laurello (Bargello)
Ferdy Murphy Geoff Hubbard Racing

Placings:05252/1PPP/1113F/16-P13   (2500)
2002/03: 24⁵GF, 24¹GS, 24³GS,

	Starts	1st	2nd	3rd	Win & Pl
Chases	3	1	0	1	6038
Career Total	19	6	2	2	33860
125 11/02 Fknm	3m110y	D(0-120)HCh		G-S	£5018
123 11/01 Fknm	3m110y	D(0-120)HCh		SFT	£4669
123 10/00 Fknm	2m5f110yC Ch			GD	£6548
118 6/00 Fknm	3m110y	E(0-115)HCh		GD	£5271
104 5/00 Towc	2m6f	C Ch		GF	£2983
120 10/99 Uttx	2m6f110yC Hdl			G-S	£5204

Total win prize-money £29696

Going: Sf: 0-0 GS: 1-2 Gd: 0-0 GF: - Fm: 0-1
Distance: 2m/2m3: 0-0 2m4-2m7: 0-0 3m+: 1-3
Track: LH: 1-2 RH: 0-1 Tight: 1-2 Gall: 0-0
Aids: Bl: 0-0 Vi: 0-0 Tstrap: 0-0
Best Rating: 125 12/02 Fknm 3m110y   gd-sft   Ch

Fair chaser, lightly-raced of late. Goes well at Fakenham, acts on most ground. Stays three miles.

Eastwell Manor
97   72

5-y-o b g Dancing Spree (USA)-Kinchenjunga (Darshaan)
Miss M Bragg Friends Of Rock Park

Placings:PP-3F   (1060)
2002/03: 17³GF, 16⁶GF,

	Starts	1st	2nd	3rd	Win & Pl
Hurdles	2	0	0	1	579

Career Total	4	0	0	1	579

Going: Sf: 0-0 GS: 0-0 Gd: 0-0 GF: - Fm: 0-2
Distance: 2m/2m3: 0-2 2m4-2m7: 0-0 3m+: 0-0
Track: LH: 0-2 RH: 0-0 Tight: 0-1 Gall: 0-0
Aids: Bl: 0-0 Vi: 0-0 Tstrap: 0-0
Best Rating: 72 8/02 NAbb 2m1f   gd-fm   Hdl

Eastwood Drifter (USA)

(104h)   (78h)
6-y-o ch g Woodman (USA)-Mandarina (USA) (El Gran Senor (USA))
B G Powell The Late Carmine Giannini And Son

Placings:0P5/05-632P6   (1247)
2002/03: 16⁶G, 16³GS, 22²GF, 22ᴾGF, 23⁸G,

	Starts	1st	2nd	3rd	Win & Pl
Hurdles	4	0	1	1	1168
Chases	1	0	0	0	0
Career Total	10	0	1	1	1168

Going: Sf: 0-0 GS: 0-1 Gd: 0-1 GF: - Fm: 0-3
Distance: 2m/2m3: 0-2 2m4-2m7: 0-2 3m+: 0-1
Track: LH: 0-5 RH: 0-0 Tight: 0-2 Gall: 0-0
Aids: Bl: 0-0 Vi: 0-0 Tstrap: 0-0
Best Rating: 78 8/02 Font 2m6f110y gd-fm   Hdl

Lightly-raced selling hurdler, suited by fast ground. Stays well.

Easy Company (IRE)
92   64

7-y-o ch g Commanche Run-Thistle Chat (Le Bavard (FR))
H E Haynes N D Edden

Placings:03P   (0683)
2002/03: 16⁶GF, 20³GS, 19ᴾGF,

	Starts	1st	2nd	3rd	Win & Pl
NH Flat	1	0	0	0	0
Hurdles	2	0	0	1	471
Career Total	3	0	0	1	471

Going: Sf: 0-0 GS: 0-1 Gd: 0-0 GF: - Fm: 0-2
Distance: 2m/2m3: 0-2 2m4-2m7: 0-1 3m+: 0-0
Track: LH: 0-3 RH: 0-0 Tight: 0-1 Gall: 0-0
Aids: Bl: 0-0 Vi: 0-0 Tstrap: 0-0
Best Rating: 67 5/02 Worc 2m   gd-fm NHF

Easy Squeezy

(92h)   (72h)
6-y-o b g Alflora (IRE)-Easy Horse (FR) (Carmarthen (FR))
N A Twiston-Davies The Yes - No - Wait Sorries

Placings:500   (4749)
2002/03: 16⁵G, 22ᵁGS, 20ᵁG,

	Starts	1st	2nd	3rd	Win & Pl
NH Flat	1	0	0	0	0
Hurdles	2	0	0	0	0
Career Total	3	0	0	0	0

Going: Sf: 0-0 GS: 0-1 Gd: 0-0 GF: - Fm: 0-0
Distance: 2m/2m3: 0-1 2m4-2m7: 0-2 3m+: 0-0
Track: LH: 0-2 RH: 0-1 Tight: 0-2 Gall: 0-0
Aids: Bl: 0-0 Vi: 0-0 Tstrap: 0-0
Best Rating: 87 1/03 Sthl 2m   good NHF

Plating-class hurdler; benefited from waiting tactics when a strong finishing third in 2m 6f novice hurdle at Stratford May 2003; tried to run out next time; should stay 3m; acts on fast ground.

Easy Tiger (FR)
91f   76f

5-y-o ch g Sillery (USA)-Extreme Dream (FR) (Zino)
N J Henderson Team Tiger

Placings:0-5   (0063)
2002/03: 17⁵G,

	Starts	1st	2nd	3rd	Win & Pl
NH Flat	1	0	0	0	0
Career Total	2	0	0	0	0

Going: Sf: 0-0 GS: 0-0 Gd: 0-1 GF: - Fm: 0-0
Distance: 2m/2m3: 0-1 2m4-2m7: 0-0 3m+: 0-0
Track: LH: 0-0 RH: 0-1 Tight: 0-1 Gall: 0-0
Aids: Bl: 0-0 Vi: 0-0 Tstrap: 0-0
Best Rating: 76 5/02 Folk 2m1f110y good NHF

Eau De Cologne
114   139

11-y-o b g Persian Bold-No More Rosies (Warpath)
B G Powell Dr M Evans

Placings:3212/1F2342611/42/2116/42113/20P32UP-66340502112   (4714)
2002/03: 24⁵GF, 25⁶G, 25³GS, 25⁴GS, 24⁰S, 25⁵GS, 24⁰G, 21²S, 24¹G, 24¹GF, 25²GF,

	Starts	1st	2nd	3rd	Win & Pl
Chases	11	2	2	1	33958
Career Total	42	10	11	5	141111
139 3/03	Hayd	3m	D(0-125)HCh	G-F	£8628
126 3/03	Newb	3m	C(0-135)HCh	GD	£16158
149 3/01	Asct	2m3f110yB HCh		SFT	£10088
143 12/00	Kemp	3m	C(0-130)HCh	G-S	£11310
144 3/00	Newb	3m	C(0-140)HCh	GF	£10520
137 3/00	Winc	2m5f	D Ch	G-S	£4387
138 4/98	Asct	3m	B HHdl	SFT	£5193
141 2/98	Newb	3m110y	C(0-130)HHdl	GD	£4130
115 5/97	Hrfd	2m3f110yE Hdl		GD	£2070
109 3/97	Plum	2m4f	E Hdl	G-F	£2826

Total win prize-money £75314

Going: Sf: 0-2 GS: 0-3 Gd: 1-3 GF: - Fm: 1-3
Distance: 2m/2m3: 0-0 2m4-2m7: 0-1 3m+: 2-10
Track: LH: 2-3 RH: 0-8 Tight: 0-1 Gall: 1-1
Aids: Bl: 0-3 Vi: 2-3 Tstrap: 0-0
Best Rating: 149 2/02 Kemp 3m   good   Ch

Useful handicap chaser; stays three miles one; acts on good and soft ground; goes well in a visor; established a good partnership with young James Davies in early 2003.

Eau So Sloe

12-y-o b g Baron Blakeney-Final Attraction (Jalmood (USA))
F L Matthews Mrs L Danton

Placings:5/0PF4F4P/2/PP0P/PPPP/PPPUP-0PP00 (4678)
2002/03: 16⁰GF, 34ᴾG, 27ᴾG, 16⁶GF, 19⁰GF,

	Starts	1st	2nd	3rd	Win & Pl
Chases	5	0	0	0	0
Career Total	27	0	1	0	1075

Going: Sf: 0-0 GS: 0-0 Gd: 0-2 GF: - Fm: 0-3
Distance: 2m/2m3: 0-3 2m4-2m7: 0-0 3m+: 0-2
Track: LH: 0-2 RH: 0-3 Tight: 0-1 Gall: 0-1

Aids: Bl: 0-4 Vi: 0-0 Tstrap: 0-0
Best Rating: 90 12/95 Folk 2m1f110y good NHF

Ebinzayd (IRE)
111   123

7-y-o b g Tenby-Sharakawa (IRE) (Darshaan)
L Lungo Miss S Blumberg

Placings:0/12113/2U0-20500   (3832)
2002/03: 18²GS, 16⁰G, 20⁵GS, 20⁹HY, 20⁰G,

	Starts	1st	2nd	3rd	Win & Pl
Hurdles	5	0	1	0	1908
Career Total	14	3	3	1	13834
119 4/01	Muss	2m1f	D Hdl	G-F	£3822
109 1/01	Muss	2m	E Hdl	G-S	£2254
116 11/00	Kels	2m110y E Hdl		SFT	£2964

Total win prize-money £9040

Going: Sf: 0-1 GS: 0-2 Gd: 0-2 GF: - Fm: 0-0
Distance: 2m/2m3: 0-2 2m4-2m7: 0-3 3m+: 0-0
Track: LH: 0-5 RH: 0-0 Tight: 0-0 Gall: 0-1
Aids: Bl: 0-0 Vi: 0-0 Tstrap: 0-0
Best Rating: 126 6/01 Prth 2m4f110y gd-fm Hdl

Fair hurdler; stays two and a half miles; acts on any ground; jumped badly when tried over fences.

Ebony Light (IRE)
107(102h)   (101h) 130

7-y-o br g Buckskin (FR)-Amelioras Daughter (General Ironside)
D McCain Roger Bellamy

Placings:40213-3334F1F114   (4174)
2002/03: 20³GS, 25³GS, 20³S, 20⁴S, 20⁵S, 20¹HY, 25⁵HY, 20¹S, 20¹S, 26⁴S,

	Starts	1st	2nd	3rd	Win & Pl
Hurdles	3	0	0	3	1597
Chases	7	3	0	0	18636
Career Total	15	4	1	4	24131
130 3/03	Carl	2m4f	C Ch	SFT	£9065
125 2/03	Newc	2m4f	C Ch	SFT	£4134
110 1/03	Newc	2m4f	E Ch	HVY	£4026
100 3/02	Uttx	3m110y E Hdl		HVY	£2702

Total win prize-money £19928

Going: Sf: 3-8 GS: 0-2 Gd: 0-0 GF: - Fm: 0-0
Distance: 2m/2m3: 0-0 2m4-2m7: 3-7 3m+: 0-3
Track: LH: 2-9 RH: 1-1 Tight: 0-2 Gall: 2-2
Aids: Bl: 0-0 Vi: 0-0 Tstrap: 0-0
Best Rating: 130 3/03 Carl 2m4f   soft   Ch

Fair, front-running chaser; stays three miles plus; handles testing conditions.

Echo Du Lac (FR)
108(113h)   (113h) 116

7-y-o b g Matahawk-Love Dream (FR) (Platonic Love)
A King Jerry Wright

Placings:46/3P10/P3-F1P234   (4312)
2002/03: 20ᴾGS, 24¹GS, 25ᴾS, 24²S, 24³GS, 22⁴G,

	Starts	1st	2nd	3rd	Win & Pl
Chases	6	1	1	1	8239
Career Total	14	2	1	3	8081
116 12/02	Sthl	3m110y	D(0-115)HCh	G-S	£5148
110 3/01	Ling	2m110y	E(0-105)HHdl	HVY	£2933

Total win prize-money £8081

Going: Sf: 0-2 GS: 1-3 Gd: 0-1 GF: - Fm: 0-0
Distance: 2m/2m3: 0-0 2m4-2m7: 0-0 3m+: 1-4
Track: LH: 1-3 RH: 0-3 Tight: 1-2 Gall: 0-3

Aids: Bl: 0-0 Vi: 0-0 Tstrap: 0-3
Best Rating: 116 1/03 Hntg 3m   soft   Ch

He cannot have the ground too soft and relished the bottomless ground when winning over hurdles at Lingfield in March 2001. Gave a polished performance when opening his account over fences at Southwell in December 2002.

Echo's Of Dawn (IRE)
88   123

11-y-o ch g Duky-Nicenames (IRE) (Decent Fellow)
John R Upson Middleham Park Racing Xvii

Placings:UP532/4112U153/1626P-31P0P   (4175)
2002/03: 24³HY, 24¹S, 28³HY, 24⁰S, 21PS,

	Starts	1st	2nd	3rd	Win & Pl
Chases	5	1	0	1	6868
Career Total	23	5	3	3	39723
123	12/02	Uttx	3m	D(0-125)HCh	SFT	£5733
124	11/01	Bang	3m110y	C(0-130)HCh	SFT	£6955
124	1/00	Ludl	3m	E(0-105)HCh	GD	£3818
117	11/99	Uttx	2m5f	E(0-115)HCh	G-S	£4182
109	11/99	Uttx	2m4f	E(0-105)HCh	SFT	£2957
				Total win prize-money £23646		

Going: Sf: 1-5 GS: 0-0 Gd: 0-0 GF: - Fm: 0-0
Distance: 2m/2m3: 0-0 2m4-2m7: 0-1 3m+: 1-4
Track: LH: 1-4 RH: 0-1 Tight: 0-1 Gall: 0-0
Aids: Bl: 0-0 Vi: 0-0 Tstrap: 0-0
Best Rating: 124 2/02 Sand 3m110y gd-sft Ch

Fair three-mile chaser. Goes on good ground or softer. Returned from a long absence with a win at Bangor in November 2001. Turned in a game effort from the front when winning again at Uttoxeter in December 2002.

Eckleys Pride
84   42

6-y-o b g Michelozzo (USA)-Marnie s Girl (Crooner)
C W Thornton W E Robson

Placings:545   (1423)
2002/03: 17⁵GF, 17⁴GF, 19⁵GF,

	Starts	1st	2nd	3rd	Win & Pl
NH Flat	2	0	0	0	0
Hurdles	1	0	0	0	0
Career Total	3	0	0	0	0

Going: Sf: 0-0 GS: 0-0 Gd: 0-0 GF: - Fm: 0-3
Distance: 2m/2m3: 0-2 2m4-2m7: 0-1 3m+: 0-0
Track: LH: 0-1 RH: 0-2 Tight: 0-3 Gall: 0-0
Aids: Bl: 0-0 Vi: 0-0 Tstrap: 0-0
Best Rating: 89 6/02 MRas 2m1f110y gd-fm NHF

Ecuyer Du Roi (FR)
113

7-y-o b g Roi De Rome (USA)-Mill s Cambric (FR) (Iron Duke (FR))
M C Pipe R Stanley

Placings:1522F6P/2P121-P   (0244)
2002/03: 25PG,

	Starts	1st	2nd	3rd	Win & Pl
Chases	1	0	0	0	
Career Total	13	3	4	0	26245
113	4/02	Plum	3m5f	D(0-115)HCh	G-F	£4875
107	6/01	NAbb	3m2f110yF(0-110)HCh	G-F	£3010
	5/99	Engh	1m7f	Hdl	VS	£6997
				Total win prize-money £14882		

Going: Sf: 0-0 GS: 0-0 Gd: 0-1 GF: - Fm: 0-0
Distance: 2m/2m3: 0-0 2m4-2m7: 0-0 3m+: 0-1
Track: LH: 0-0 RH: 0-1 Tight: 0-0 Gall: 0-0
Best Rating: 113 4/02 Plum 3m5f   gd-fm   Ch

Lightly raced staying chaser up to three miles five. Likes a sound surface.

Ede'lff
104   96

6-y-o b m Tragic Role (USA)-Flying Amy (Norwick (USA))
W G M Turner Hawks And Doves Racing Syndicate

Placings:P400/5-656U2141130   (4287)
2002/03: 16⁶G, 16⁵G, 16⁶S, 17⁰UGS, 17²G, 16¹G, 17⁴S, 16¹S, 16¹HY, 16³G, 16⁹GF,

	Starts	1st	2nd	3rd	Win & Pl
Hurdles	11	3	1	1	10657
Career Total	16	3	1	1	10657
95	2/03	Leic	2m	F Hdl	HVY	£3503
85	1/03	Ludl	2m	G(75-95)Hdl	SFT	£3104
83	12/02	Ludl	2m	F Hdl	GD	£3115
				Total win prize-money £9724		

Going: Sf: 2-4 GS: 0-1 Gd: 1-5 GF: - Fm: 0-1
Distance: 2m/2m3: 3-11 2m4-2m7: 0-0 3m+: 0-0
Track: LH: 0-3 RH: 3-8 Tight: 0-4 Gall: 0-0
Aids: Bl: 0-0 Vi: 0-0 Tstrap: 3-6
Best Rating: 96 2/03 Catt 2m   good   Hdl

Moderate hurdler; successful three times in selling and plating company; effective at two miles; acts on good and soft ground.

Eden Dancer
(96h)   (80h)

11-y-o b g Shareef Dancer (USA)-Dash (Connaught)
B Ellison (M C Pipe 9/8) Geoffrey Hamilton

Placings:32241/1333003/21124FF506/64P0/1011412/3101 1234/01156PP-P3PP5400U   (2323)
2002/03: 20PGF, 16³G, 21PGF, 20PS, 21⁵G, 16⁴GF, 17⁹GF, 16⁹GS, 22US,

	Starts	1st	2nd	3rd	Win & Pl
Hurdles	5	0	0	0	323
Chases	4	0	0	1	900
Career Total	57	13	6	8	66291
127	8/01	Bang	2m4f110yD(0-125)HCh	GD	£7020
123	6/01	Worc	2m4f110yC(0-130)HCh	GD	£6873
123	9/00	Plum	2m1f	E Ch	GD	£3780
115	9/00	Sedg	2m110y	E Ch	GD	£3607
127	6/00	MRas	2m1f110yD Ch	G-F	£5992
127	10/99	Ludl	2m	D(0-120)HHdl	G-F	£3680
125	7/99	MRas	2m1f110yB(0-140)HHdl	G-F	£10220
121	7/99	MRas	2m1f110yF(0-105)HHdl	G-F	£1928
114	5/99	Extr	2m1f	G(0-95)HHdl	G-F	£1968
105	9/97	Prth	2m110y	F Hdl	G-F	£2283
104	8/97	Sedg	2m1f	F Hdl	G-F	£2020
104	5/96	Prth	2m110y	D Hdl	G-F	£2736
110	2/96	Muss	2m	E Hdl	G-F	£2630
				Total win prize-money £54741		

Going: Sf: 0-2 GS: 0-1 Gd: 0-2 GF: - Fm: 0-4
Distance: 2m/2m3: 0-4 2m4-2m7: 0-5 3m+: 0-0
Track: LH: 0-4 RH: 0-4 Tight: 0-4 Gall: 0-0
Aids: Bl: 0-0 Vi: 0-0 Tstrap: 0-0
Best Rating: 127 8/01 Bang 2m4f110y good   Ch

A tough front runner, he is suited by fast ground and had a successful time summer jumping in 2001, but has lost his way since. Best around at two and a half miles, he is useful when allowed to bully inferior opposition.

Edgar Gink (IRE)

9-y-o ch g Step Together (USA)-Turbo Run (Deep Run)
L Corcoran The A T P Racing Partnership

Placings:5P/4P53-23   (4480)
2002/03: 24²F, 25³G,

	Starts	1st	2nd	3rd	Win & Pl
Chases	2	0	1	1	2734
Career Total	8	0	1	2	3357

Going: Sf: 0-0 GS: 0-0 Gd: 0-1 GF: - Fm: 0-1
Distance: 2m/2m3: 0-0 2m4-2m7: 0-0 3m+: 0-2
Track: LH: 0-1 RH: 0-1 Tight: 0-2 Gall: 0-0
Aids: Bl: 0-0 Vi: 0-0 Tstrap: 0-0
Best Rating: 100 4/03 Aint 3m1f   good   Ch

Won weak point March 2003; unlucky not to win Taunton hunter chase eight days later when over confidently ridden; acts on ground good and faster.

Edgatorius (IRE)

7-y-o b g Phardante (FR)-Silent Shot (Random Shot)
B Smart Mrs Julie Martin

Placings:0-P   (3265)
2002/03: 19PGS,

	Starts	1st	2nd	3rd	Win & Pl
Hurdles	1	0	0	0	
Career Total	2	0	0	0	

Going: Sf: 0-0 GS: 0-1 Gd: 0-0 GF: - Fm: 0-0
Distance: 2m/2m3: 0-0 2m4-2m7: 0-1 3m+: 0-0
Track: LH: 0-1 RH: 0-0 Tight: 0-0 Gall: 0-0
Aids: Bl: 0-0 Vi: 0-0 Tstrap: 0-0
Best Rating: 91 3/02 Hayd 2m   good   NHF

Edgely (IRE)

8-y-o b g Warcraft (USA)-Clodagh s Treasure (Tarqogan)
K G Wingrove L T Woodhouse

Placings:0-PPP   (4709)
2002/03: 21PG, 17PGF, 24PG,

	Starts	1st	2nd	3rd	Win & Pl
Hurdles	3	0	0	0	
Career Total	4	0	0	0	

Going: Sf: 0-0 GS: 0-0 Gd: 0-2 GF: - Fm: 0-1
Distance: 2m/2m3: 0-2 2m4-2m7: 0-1 3m+: 0-1
Track: LH: 0-2 RH: 0-1 Tight: 0-0 Gall: 0-0
Aids: Bl: 0-2 Vi: 0-0 Tstrap: 0-0
Best Rating: 0 4/03 Uttx 3m110y good   Hdl

Edginswell Lass
51f   76f

5-y-o b m Morpeth-Oribi Gorge (IRE) (Heraldiste (USA))
J D Frost Terry Sanders

Placings:00   (1598)
2002/03: 16⁹GF, 17⁹G,

	Starts	1st	2nd	3rd	Win & Pl
NH Flat	2	0	0	0	
Career Total	2	0	0	0	

Going: Sf: 0-0 GS: 0-0 Gd: 0-1 GF: - Fm: 0-1
Distance: 2m/2m3: 0-2 2m4-2m7: 0-0 3m+: 0-0
Track: LH: 0-0 RH: 0-2 Tight: 0-0 Gall: 0-1
Aids: Bl: 0-0 Vi: 0-0 Tstrap: 0-0
Best Rating: 76   10/02   Hntg   2m110y   gd-fm   NHF

Edmo Heights

118   **124**

7-y-o ch g Keen-Bodham (Bustino)
T D Easterby   Edmolift Uk Ltd

Placings:13/4P2111154O   (4754)
2002/03: 16⁴G, 16⁶PGS, 19²GS, 16¹G, 16¹G, 16¹G, 16⁵GF, 16⁴G, 16⁰G,

	Starts	1st	2nd	3rd	Win & Pl
Hurdles	9	3	1	0	20544
Career Total	11	4	1	1	23428

120	2/03	Catt	2m	C(0-130)HHdl	GD	£6948
111	1/03	Catt	2m	E(0-110)HHdl	GD	£7085
103	12/02	Hayd	2m	E(0-110)HHdl	GD	£3192
98	8/00	Sedg	2m1f	E Hdl	GD	£2338

Total win prize-money £19564

Going: Sf: 0-0 GS: 0-2 Gd: 3-6 GF: - Fm: 0-1
Distance: 2m/2m3: 3-9 2m4-2m7: 0-0 3m+: 0-0
Track: LH: 3-7 RH: 0-2 Tight: 2-4 Gall: 0-1
Aids: Bl: 0-0 Vi: 0-0 Tstrap: 0-0
Best Rating: 122   4/03   Aint   2m110y   good   Hdl

Fair hurdler; completed a hat trick in modest company in the middle of the 2002/2003 season; made all at Aintree in May; effective at around two miles; acts on good ground.

Edredon Bleu (FR)

117   **168**

11-y-o b g Grand Tresor (FR)-Nuit Bleue Iii (FR) (Le Pontet (FR))
Miss H C Knight   Jim Lewis

Placings:1520P/41111F/41212/51331/3161/1243-121166   (4471)
2002/03: 17¹G, 16²S, 21¹GS, 21¹GS, 16⁶G, 20⁶G,

	Starts	1st	2nd	3rd	Win & Pl
Chases	6	3	1	0	80331
Career Total	35	15	5	4	503619

165	1/03	Winc	2m5f	B Ch	G-S	£16042
168	12/02	Winc	2m5f	B Ch	G-S	£11928
172	11/02	Extr	2m4f110yA H Ch		GD	£24360
168	11/01	Hntg	2m4f110yA Ch		G-S	£30000
164	4/01	Sand	2m	A Ch		G-S	£49300
168	11/00	Hntg	2m4f110yA Ch		G-S	£27000
166	3/00	Chel	2m	A Ch		GD	£107300
163	11/99	Hntg	2m4f110yA Ch		G-F	£23750
167	2/99	Sand	2m	B HCh		GD	£8036
164	11/98	Hntg	2m4f110yA Ch		GD	£18211
154	3/98	Chel	2m110y B HCh		GD	£29611
152	2/98	Sand	2m	B(0-145)HCh		G-F	£7578
142	12/97	Kemp	2m4f110yB HCh		SFT	£12741
138	12/97	Leic	2m4f110yC(0-130)HCh		GD	£4945

Total win prize-money £370805

Going: Sf: 0-1 GS: 2-2 Gd: 1-3 GF: - Fm: 0-0
Distance: 2m/2m3: 1-3 2m4-2m7: 2-3 3m+: 0-0
Track: LH: 0-2 RH: 3-4 Tight: 0-1 Gall: 0-1
Aids: Bl: 0-0 Vi: 0-0 Tstrap: 3-6
Best Rating: 172   11/02   Extr   2m1f110y   good   Ch

Top-class chaser, winner of the Queen Mother Champion Chase in 2000; not helped by the softish ground when fourth in the 2002 running; winner three times in 2003/3, below form on soft ground behind Cenkos at Sandown; stays two and a half miles (won four successive runnings of the Peterborough Chase at Huntingdon); good jumper; his

---

attacking style of racing is best suited to fast conditions; wears a tongue tie.

Effectual

103(103h)   (134h)**115+**

10-y-o b g Efisio-Moharabuiee (Pas De Seul)
Miss Venetia Williams   B C Dice

Placings:311211145/3311564/201255343/20/6600-35501   (3921)
2002/03: 23³G, 25⁵G, 21⁵G, 23⁹GS, 26¹S,

	Starts	1st	2nd	3rd	Win & Pl
Hurdles	3	0	0	1	2605
Chases	2	1	0	0	5082
Career Total	36	9	4	6	93648

115	3/03	Font	3m2f110yE Ch		SFT	£5082
156	12/99	Chep	3m	B HHdl	GD	£6911
140	1/99	Font	2m2f110yC(0-130)HHdl	SFT	£4735
138	12/98	Donc	2m110y B HHdl	GD	£5020
136	3/98	Chep	2m110y B Hdl	SFT	£13745
132	3/98	Donc	2m110y C(0-135)Hdl	SFT	£4090
130	2/98	Weth	2m	B(0-145)HHdl	GD	£5455
127	12/97	Tntn	2m1f	D Hdl	GD	£3018
125	12/97	NAbb	2m1f	E Hdl	HVY	£2148

Total win prize-money £50207

Going: Sf: 1-1 GS: 0-1 Gd: 0-3 GF: - Fm: 0-0
Distance: 2m/2m3: 0-2 2m4-2m7: 0-1 3m+: 1-4
Track: LH: 0-2 RH: 0-2 Tight: 1-1 Gall: 0-0
Aids: Bl: 0-0 Vi: 0-0 Tstrap: 0-0
Best Rating: 159   5/00   Punc   3m   good   Hdl

Decent hurdler; has not always looked a straightforward ride; fourth to Bacchanal in the 2000 Stayers Hurdle at the Cheltenham Festival, but has not looked the same horse since returning from a year off with a tendon injury; stays three miles; has won on good and soft ground.

Effie Gray

90   **56**

4-y-o b f Sri Pekan (USA)-Rose Bouquet (General Assembly (USA))
P Monteith (P W Harris 11/7)   Mrs Maud Monteith

Placings:0046   (2300)
2002/03: 16⁰GF, 16⁰GF, 16⁴S, 16⁶GS,

	Starts	1st	2nd	3rd	Win & Pl
Hurdles	4	0	0	0	0
Career Total	4	0	0	0	0

Going: Sf: 0-1 GS: 0-1 Gd: 0-0 GF: - Fm: 0-2
Distance: 2m/2m3: 0-4 2m4-2m7: 0-0 3m+: 0-0
Track: LH: 0-3 RH: 0-1 Tight: 0-3 Gall: 0-0
Aids: Bl: 0-0 Vi: 0-0 Tstrap: 0-0
Best Rating: 51   10/02   Kels   2m110y   gd-fm   Hdl

Very moderate novice hurdler; easily best effort when close third at Sedgefield in July.

Effrontery (IRE)

10-y-o ch g Lanfranco-Arctic Raheen (Over The River (FR))
A J Chamberlain   A J Chamberlain

Placings:00/4/0/P   (0512)
2002/03: 16⁵S,

	Starts	1st	2nd	3rd	Win & Pl
Hurdles	1	0	0	0	0
Career Total	5	0	0	0	220

Going: Sf: 0-1 GS: 0-0 Gd: 0-0 GF: - Fm: 0-0

Distance: 2m/2m3: 0-1 2m4-2m7: 0-0 3m+: 0-0
Track: LH: 0-1 RH: 0-0 Tight: 0-0 Gall: 0-0
Aids: Bl: 0-0 Vi: 0-0 Tstrap: 0-0
Best Rating: 79   9/98   MRas   1m5f110y   good   NHF

Effusive

90(94h)   (126dh)**94**

10-y-o b g Phardante (FR)-Bubbling (Tremblant)
Jonjo O Neill   J P McManus

Placings:24/15/5561213/BF6020-6P   (2327)
2002/03: 16⁶S, 16⁸PGS,

	Starts	1st	2nd	3rd	Win & Pl
Hurdles	2	0	0	0	0
Career Total	19	3	3	1	13365

126	8/00	Rosc	2m	(0-116)HHdl	FRM	£4140
121	7/00	Klny	2m1f	(0-102)HHdl	GD	£3312
92	8/99	Wxfd	2m	Hdl	GD	£2679

Total win prize-money £10132

Going: Sf: 0-1 GS: 0-1 Gd: 0-0 GF: - Fm: 0-0
Distance: 2m/2m3: 0-2 2m4-2m7: 0-0 3m+: 0-0
Track: LH: 0-0 RH: 0-2 Tight: 0-0 Gall: 0-0
Aids: Bl: 0-0 Vi: 0-0 Tstrap: 0-0
Best Rating: 126   8/01   Naas   2m   gd-yld   Hdl

Ex-Irish handicap hurdler, effective at around two miles on good ground or faster. Now with Jonjo O Neill.

Egypt

104   **88**

5-y-o b g Green Desert (USA)-Just You Wait (Nonoalco (USA))
Miss K Marks   Nick Shutts

Placings:P66554-0515P343412F   (1381)
2002/03: 17⁰GF, 16⁵GF, 16¹HY, 16⁵GF, 16⁸PG, 16⁴GF, 16³GF, 16⁴GS, 20¹GF, 19²GF, 19²GF,

	Starts	1st	2nd	3rd	Win & Pl
Hurdles	12	2	1	2	10389
Career Total	18	2	1	2	10389

86	8/02	Font	2m4f	F(0-90)HHdl	G-F	£3094
87	6/02	Uttx	2m	E(0-110)HHdl	HVY	£5083

Total win prize-money £8177

Going: Sf: 1-1 GS: 0-1 Gd: 0-2 GF: - Fm: 1-8
Distance: 2m/2m3: 1-9 2m4-2m7: 1-3 3m+: 0-0
Track: LH: 1-8 RH: 0-3 Tight: 1-5 Gall: 0-0
Aids: Bl: 0-0 Vi: 1-3 Tstrap: 0-0
Best Rating: 91   9/02   Hrfd   2m3f110y   gd-fm   Hdl

Has shown only moderate form over hurdles, winning twice in the summer of 2002.

Egypt Point (IRE)

84   **61**

6-y-o b g Jurado (USA)-Cherry Jubilee (Le Bavard (FR))
D G Bridgwater   Long Hill Partnership

Placings:0-6   (2205)
2002/03: 20⁶S,

	Starts	1st	2nd	3rd	Win & Pl
Hurdles	1	0	0	0	0
Career Total	2	0	0	0	0

Going: Sf: 0-1 GS: 0-0 Gd: 0-0 GF: - Fm: 0-0
Distance: 2m/2m3: 0-0 2m4-2m7: 0-1 3m+: 0-0
Track: LH: 0-1 RH: 0-0 Tight: 0-0 Gall: 0-0
Aids: Bl: 0-0 Vi: 0-0 Tstrap: 0-0
Best Rating: 72   4/02   MRas   2m1f110y   good   NHF

Ei Ei

114(107h)   (121 h)**148+**
8-y-o b g North Briton-Branitska (Mummy s Pet)
M C Chapman Mrs S M Richards

Placings:0641121111540246032-3512463514215113061
(4781)
2002/03: 20³GF, 20⁵G, 17¹GS, 20²GF, 16⁴GS, 20⁶GS, 17³G, 17⁵GF, 16¹G, 17⁴GF, 17²GS, 16¹GS, 16⁵HY, 16¹GS, 16¹GS, 16³S, 16⁰GS, 16⁶G, 16¹GF,

	Starts	1st	2nd	3rd	Win & Pl
Hurdles	4	2	0	0	11893
Chases	15	4	2	3	52198
Career Total	38	12	5	4	90591
135	4/03	Sand	2m	B(0-145)HCh	G-F	£18600
121	1/03	Sthl	2m	E(0-110)HHdl	G-S	£3605
103	12/02	Hntg	2m110y	D(0-125)HHdl	G-S	£8287
140	11/02	Sthl	2m	C(0-130)HCh	G-S	£10010
129	9/02	Worc	2m	C(0-135)HCh	GD	£7174
130	6/02	Ctml	2m1f110yD(0-125)HCh	G-S	£4355
128	10/01	Sthl	2m	E(0-115)HCh	GD	£3386
112	10/01	Sedg	2m110y	G(0-115)HCh	GD	£3265
127	9/01	MRas	2m4f	F(0-110)HCh	SFT	£3916
129	9/01	Strf	2m1f110yD(0-115)HCh	G-F	£4127
92	8/01	Sthl	2m	F(0-100)HCh	G-F	£2775
91	7/01	Strf	2m110y	G Hdl	G-F	£1967

Total win prize-money £71473

Going: Sf: 0-2 GS: 4-8 Gd: 1-4 GF: - Fm: 1-5
Distance: 2m/2m3: 6-15 2m4-2m7: 0-4 3m+: 0-0
Track: LH: 4-12 RH: 2-7 Tight: 3-11 Gall: 1-1
Aids: Bl: 0-0 Vi: 0-0 Tstrap: 0-0
Best Rating: 140 11/02 Sthl 2m gd-sft Ch

Modest performer over hurdles; useful over fences; tough and consistent front runner; best at around two miles, but stays two and a half; does not want the ground too soft.

Eibh'n Abbie

74   **40**
4-y-o b g Forzando-Brookhead Lady (Petong)
P D Evans P D Evans

Placings:6   (0890)
2002/03: 17⁶S,

	Starts	1st	2nd	3rd	Win & Pl
Hurdles	1	0	0	0	0
Career Total	1	0	0	0	0

Going: Sf: 0-1 GS: 0-0 Gd: 0-0 GF: - Fm: 0-0
Distance: 2m/2m3: 0-1 2m4-2m7: 0-0 3m+: 0-0
Track: LH: 0-1 RH: 0-0 Tight: 0-0 Gall: 0-0
Aids: Bl: 0-0 Vi: 0-0 Tstrap: 0-0
Best Rating: 40 8/02 Bang 2m1f soft Hdl

Eight (IRE)

90   **65**
7-y-o ch g Thatching-Up To You (Sallust)
C G Cox Charles Curtis

Placings:P-00   (4191)
2002/03: 16⁶GS, 16⁰G,

	Starts	1st	2nd	3rd	Win & Pl
Hurdles	2	0	0	0	0
Career Total	3	0	0	0	0

Going: Sf: 0-0 GS: 0-1 Gd: 0-1 GF: - Fm: 0-0
Distance: 2m/2m3: 0-2 2m4-2m7: 0-0 3m+: 0-0
Track: LH: 0-0 RH: 0-2 Tight: 0-0 Gall: 0-1
Aids: Bl: 0-0 Vi: 0-0 Tstrap: 0-0

Best Rating: 65 3/03 Ludl 2m   good Hdl

Eilean

81f   **76f**
5-y-o b m Jurado (USA)-Upper Mount Street (IRE) (Strong Gale)
C P Morlock Mrs Hugh Maitland-Jones

Placings:000   (0660)
2002/03: 16⁰G, 17⁹G, 16⁹GF,

	Starts	1st	2nd	3rd	Win & Pl
NH Flat	3	0	0	0	
Career Total	3	0	0	0	

Going: Sf: 0-0 GS: 0-0 Gd: 0-2 GF: - Fm: 0-1
Distance: 2m/2m3: 0-3 2m4-2m7: 0-0 3m+: 0-0
Track: LH: 0-3 RH: 0-0 Tight: 0-1 Gall: 0-0
Aids: Bl: 0-1 Vi: 0-0 Tstrap: 0-0
Best Rating: 76 5/02 Worc 2m   good NHF

Eileen Alanna (IRE)

101   **75**
11-y-o b m Rashar (USA)-Kilcotty Wonder (Peacock (FR))
G F Edwards G F Edwards

Placings:02244244FP0P/4621660P/00124-62P04006
(4623)
2002/03: 27⁶G, 27²S, 26⁶GS, 22⁰GS, 24⁴S, 22⁰S, 24⁰F, 27⁶GF,

	Starts	1st	2nd	3rd	Win & Pl
Hurdles	8	0	1	0	540
Career Total	33	2	6	0	8605
78	11/01	Sedg	3m3f110yF(0-100)HHdl	GD	£2198
98	11/00	MRas	2m5f110yF Hdl	G-S	£1951

Total win prize-money £4150

Going: Sf: 0-3 GS: 0-2 Gd: 0-1 GF: - Fm: 0-2
Distance: 2m/2m3: 0-0 2m4-2m7: 0-2 3m+: 0-6
Track: LH: 0-4 RH: 0-4 Tight: 0-6 Gall: 0-1
Aids: Bl: 0-0 Vi: 0-0 Tstrap: 0-0
Best Rating: 98 11/00 MRas 2m5f110y gd-sft Hdl

A frustrating sort, she has been placed numerous times and, bar two modest hurdle wins, has proved short of toe at the business end. She prefers to be held up, stays three miles three furlongs and is suited by cut in the ground.

El Bandito (IRE)

111(97h)   (87h)**100**
9-y-o ch g Un Desperado (FR)-Red Marble (Le Bavard (FR))
R Lee (J Howard Johnson 3/5) The Another Comedy Partnership

Placings:52/1330/4P55F00-PP11   (4273)
2002/03: 21⁸GF, 20⁶G, 20¹GS, 19¹G,

	Starts	1st	2nd	3rd	Win & Pl
Chases	4	2	0	0	9922
Career Total	17	3	1	2	12886
100	3/03	Chep	2m3f110yD(0-110)HCh	GD	£5622
88	2/03	Leic	2m4f110yF(0-95)HCh	G-S	£4299
105	5/00	Extr	2m1f H NHF	G-F	£1767

Total win prize-money £11691

Going: Sf: 0-0 GS: 1-1 Gd: 1-2 GF: - Fm: 0-1
Distance: 2m/2m3: 0-0 2m4-2m7: 2-4 3m+: 0-0
Track: LH: 1-2 RH: 1-2 Tight: 0-2 Gall: 0-0
Aids: Bl: 0-0 Vi: 0-0 Tstrap: 0-0
Best Rating: 111 5/00 Worc 2m   good NHF

Modest chaser who caused a shock when winning a moderate contest at Leicester in February 2003 and followed up at Chepstow. Needs decent ground.

El Cordobes (IRE)

106   **98**
12-y-o b g Torus-Queens Tricks (Le Bavard (FR))
Mrs J R Buckley Mrs J R Buckley

Placings:3/005000/0/2P55445/13154213/32010/6654P400-14P421F3433
(4670)
2002/03: 21¹G, 19⁴GF, 21⁸G, 21⁴GS, 20²GS, 22¹S, 16⁵S, 17³S, 20⁴GS, 22³G, 21³G,

	Starts	1st	2nd	3rd	Win & Pl
Chases	11	2	1	3	15146
Career Total	47	6	4	7	36046
98	12/02	MRas	2m6f110yD(0-120)HCh	SFT	£5894
90	5/02	Fknm	2m5f110yF(0-100)HCh	GD	£3444
98	10/00	Fknm	2m5f110yF(0-100)HCh	GD	£3563
94	3/00	Donc	2m110y D(0-110)HCh	G-S	£4134
92	9/99	Hntg	2m110y E(0-115)HCh	G-F	£3109
94	5/99	Hntg	2m4f110yF(0-100)HCh	G-F	£3406

Total win prize-money £23552

Going: Sf: 1-3 GS: 0-3 Gd: 1-4 GF: - Fm: 0-1
Distance: 2m/2m3: 0-3 2m4-2m7: 2-8 3m+: 0-0
Track: LH: 1-5 RH: 1-6 Tight: 2-8 Gall: 0-1
Aids: Bl: 0-0 Vi: 0-0 Tstrap: 0-0
Best Rating: 98 4/03 Fknm 2m5f110y good Ch

Moderate handicap chaser; headstrong front-runner; effective from two miles to two miles six furlongs; acts on a sound surface, but also effective with cut in the ground.

El Divino (GER)

59   **93**
8-y-o b g Platini (GER)-Eivissa (GER) (Frontal)
Ian Williams Favourites Racing

Placings:F55-0   (0567)
2002/03: 16⁰GS,

	Starts	1st	2nd	3rd	Win & Pl
Hurdles	1	0	0	0	
Career Total	4	0	0	0	0

Going: Sf: 0-0 GS: 0-1 Gd: 0-0 GF: - Fm: 0-0
Distance: 2m/2m3: 0-1 2m4-2m7: 0-0 3m+: 0-0
Track: LH: 0-1 RH: 0-0 Tight: 0-0 Gall: 0-0
Aids: Bl: 0-0 Vi: 0-0 Tstrap: 0-0
Best Rating: 93 3/02 Winc 2m   good Hdl

Group winner on the Flat in Germany but has yet to show anything like that level of ability over hurdles. Capable of better and will be interesting when qualified for handicaps. Goes well in soft ground.

El Don

91(84h)   (62h)**61**
11-y-o b g High Kicker (USA)-Madam Gerard (Brigadier Gerard)
B Scriven B Scriven

Placings:0/12214P13/55142/P0F/FP600/F5F0/00-P0P
(4693)
2002/03: 17⁸G, 17⁰G, 17⁸G,

	Starts	1st	2nd	3rd	Win & Pl
Hurdles	3	0	0	0	
Career Total	31	4	3	1	18037
111	10/97	Font	2m2f110yD(0-125)HHdl	GD	£3416
113	4/97	Chep	2m4f110yC(0-135)HHdl	FRM	£3533
104	11/96	Weth	2m	B(0-145)HHdl	GD	£4825
104	5/96	Font	2m2f	E Hdl	G-F	£2427

Total win prize-money £14202

Going: Sf: 0-0 GS: 0-0 Gd: 0-3 GF: - Fm: 0-0
Distance: 2m/2m3: 0-3 2m4-2m7: 0-0 3m+: 0-0

Track: LH: 0-3 RH: 0-0 Tight: 0-3 Gall: 0-0
Aids: Bl: 0-0 Vi: 0-0 Tstrap: 0-0
Best Rating: 114 4/99 Fknm 2m4f   good   Hdl

El Hamra (IRE)

5-y-o gr g Royal Abjar (USA)-Cherlinoa (FR) (Crystal Palace (FR))
M J Haynes (B A McMahon 8/10) Porthilly Partners

Placings:0   (3560)
2002/03: 17⁰HY,

	Starts	1st	2nd	3rd	Win & Pl
Hurdles	1	0	0	0	
Career Total	1	0	0	0	

Going: Sf: 0-1 GS: 0-0 Gd: 0-0 GF: - Fm: 0-0
Distance: 2m/2m3: 0-1 2m4-2m7: 0-0 3m+: 0-0
Track: LH: 0-0 RH: 0-1 Tight: 0-1 Gall: 0-0
Aids: Bl: 0-0 Vi: 0-0 Tstrap: 0-0
Best Rating: 0 2/03 Folk 2m1f110y heavy Hdl

El Hombre

85f   89f

5-y-o b g Afzal-Dunsilly Bell (London Bells (CAN))
C C Bealby Michael Hill

Placings:03   (2505)
2002/03: 14⁰GS, 16³GS,

	Starts	1st	2nd	3rd	Win & Pl
NH Flat	2	0	0	1	287
Career Total	2	0	0	1	287

Going: Sf: 0-0 GS: 0-2 Gd: 0-0 GF: - Fm: 0-0
Distance: 2m/2m3: 0-1 2m4-2m7: 0-0 3m+: 0-0
Track: LH: 0-2 RH: 0-0 Tight: 0-1 Gall: 0-0
Aids: Bl: 0-0 Vi: 0-0 Tstrap: 0-0
Best Rating: 89 12/02 Fknm 2m   gd-sft NHF

El Hombre Del Rio (IRE)

107   100

6-y-o ch g Over The River (FR)-Hug In A Fog (IRE) (Strong Gale)
R H Alner Perpetual Pub s Lazy Punters Black Book

Placings:0P-242232   (4310)
2002/03: 17³HY, 24⁴GS, 24²S, 24²GS, 26³G, 24²G,

	Starts	1st	2nd	3rd	Win & Pl
Hurdles	6	0	4	1	6358
Career Total	8	0	4	1	6358

Going: Sf: 0-2 GS: 0-2 Gd: 0-2 GF: - Fm: 0-0
Distance: 2m/2m3: 0-1 2m4-2m7: 0-0 3m+: 0-5
Track: LH: 0-3 RH: 0-3 Tight: 0-3 Gall: 0-1
Aids: Bl: 0-0 Vi: 0-0 Tstrap: 0-0
Best Rating: 104 3/02 Newb 2m110y gd-sft NHF

Fair staying novice hurdler; stays 3m plus; handles good ground, but better with some cut; lacks pace and should have a future over fences when faced with a severe test of stamina.

El Monty (IRE)

                                   126

8-y-o b g Montelimar (USA)-Tax Code (Workboy)

R H Alner The Collars And Cuffs Partnership

Placings:25/46/12-P   (2371)
2002/03: 22³S,

	Starts	1st	2nd	3rd	Win & Pl
Hurdles	1	0	0	0	
Career Total	7	1	2	0	4539
111 12/01 Folk	2m1f110y			E Hdl	SFT
£2555					

Total win prize-money £2555

Going: Sf: 0-1 GS: 0-0 Gd: 0-0 GF: - Fm: 0-0
Distance: 2m/2m3: 0-0 2m4-2m7: 0-1 3m+: 0-0
Track: LH: 0-0 RH: 0-1 Tight: 0-0 Gall: 0-0
Aids: Bl: 0-0 Vi: 0-0 Tstrap: 0-0
Best Rating: 126 3/02 Chep 2m4f   gd-sft Hdl

Fair hurdler, the booking of McCoy was noteworthy when he beat a long odds-on favourite after a two-year break in December 2001. Good run next time. Acts on soft ground.

El Pedro

90   87

4-y-o b g Piccolo-Standard Rose (Ile De Bourbon (USA))
M R Channon Peter Taplin

Placings:000   (3109)
2002/03: 16⁰S, 16⁰G, 17⁰HY,

	Starts	1st	2nd	3rd	Win & Pl
Hurdles	3	0	0	0	
Career Total	3	0	0	0	

Going: Sf: 0-2 GS: 0-0 Gd: 0-1 GF: - Fm: 0-0
Distance: 2m/2m3: 0-3 2m4-2m7: 0-0 3m+: 0-0
Track: LH: 0-2 RH: 0-1 Tight: 0-1 Gall: 0-2
Aids: Bl: 0-0 Vi: 0-0 Tstrap: 0-0
Best Rating: 79 12/02 Newb 2m110y good Hdl

El Penyon

6-y-o b g Rock Hopper-Capel Lass (The Brianstan)
J W Mullins Patrick Everard

Placings:000   (4444)
2002/03: 16⁰G, 17⁰S, 16⁰G,

	Starts	1st	2nd	3rd	Win & Pl
NH Flat	3	0	0	0	
Career Total	3	0	0	0	

Going: Sf: 0-1 GS: 0-0 Gd: 0-2 GF: - Fm: 0-0
Distance: 2m/2m3: 0-3 2m4-2m7: 0-0 3m+: 0-0
Track: LH: 0-0 RH: 0-3 Tight: 0-0 Gall: 0-0
Aids: Bl: 0-0 Vi: 0-0 Tstrap: 0-0
Best Rating: 55 11/02 Winc 2m   good NHF

El Vaquero (IRE)

98f   102f

5-y-o ch g Un Desperado (FR)-Marble Fontaine (Lafontaine (USA))
Miss H C Knight T M Curtis

Placings:10   (4481)
2002/03: 16¹GS, 17⁰G,

	Starts	1st	2nd	3rd	Win & Pl
NH Flat	2	1	0	0	1981
Career Total	2	1	0	0	1981
102 12/02 Hntg	2m110y H NHF			G-S	£1981

Total win prize-money £1981

Going: Sf: 1-1 GS: 1-1 Gd: 0-1 GF: - Fm: 0-0
Distance: 2m/2m3: 1-2 2m4-2m7: 0-0 3m+: 0-0
Track: LH: 0-0 RH: 1-1 Tight: 0-0 Gall: 1-1
Aids: Bl: 0-0 Vi: 0-0 Tstrap: 0-0
Best Rating: 102 12/02 Hntg 2m110y   gd-sft NHF

Got off the mark at the first attempt in a decent bumper over two miles. Acts on good to soft ground.

El Viejo (IRE)

                                   120

6-y-o b g Norwich-Shuil Na Gale (Strong Gale)
L Wells Mrs Carrie Zetter-Wells

Placings:33/311P2P-3P   (1321)
2002/03: 21³G, 24PGF,

	Starts	1st	2nd	3rd	Win & Pl
Hurdles	2	0	0	1	786
Career Total	10	2	1	4	13505
120 11/01 Asct	2m4f			C Hdl	GD £4966
110 11/01 Sand	2m110y			H NHF	G-S £2425

Total win prize-money £7392

Going: Sf: 0-0 GS: 0-0 Gd: 0-1 GF: - Fm: 0-1
Distance: 2m/2m3: 0-0 2m4-2m7: 0-1 3m+: 0-1
Track: LH: 0-1 RH: 0-1 Tight: 0-1 Gall: 0-1
Aids: Bl: 0-0 Vi: 0-0 Tstrap: 0-0
Best Rating: 120 9/02 Sthl 2m5f110y good Hdl

Fair hurdler; bred to stay; placed in some decent bumpers before winning one in good style at Sandown in November 2001. Followed up with hurdles debut win in decent company, but pulled up after being struck into at Market Rasen. Suited by at least two and a half miles over hurdles.

El Zito (IRE)

76   69

6-y-o b g Mukaddamah (USA)-Samite (FR) (Tennyson (FR))
R Brotherton Roy Brotherton

Placings:16245/1-P0   (2639)
2002/03: 19PGS, 16⁰S,

	Starts	1st	2nd	3rd	Win & Pl
Hurdles	2	0	0	0	
Career Total	8	2	1	0	7713
122 5/01 Folk	2m1f110yF(0-110)HHdl			G-S	£3620
107 12/00 Folk	2m1f110yE Hdl			HVY	£2730

Total win prize-money £6351

Going: Sf: 0-1 GS: 0-1 Gd: 0-0 GF: - Fm: 0-0
Distance: 2m/2m3: 0-1 2m4-2m7: 0-1 3m+: 0-0
Track: LH: 0-1 RH: 0-1 Tight: 0-1 Gall: 0-0
Aids: Bl: 0-0 Vi: 0-0 Tstrap: 0-1
Best Rating: 122 5/01 Folk 2m1f110y gd-sft Hdl

Plating-class hurdler, suited by soft ground, usually wears a tongue tie.

Ela Agapi Mou (USA)

(96h)   (92h)

10-y-o b g Storm Bird (CAN)-Vaguar (USA) (Vaguely Noble)
R S Brookhouse R S Brookhouse

Placings:2511/1031001003/1310P330/U4000P3/33055420 P2334/2606-06P   (0508)
2002/03: 20⁰GF, 24⁶G, 23PG,

	Starts	1st	2nd	3rd	Win & Pl
Hurdles	2	0	0	0	0
Chases	1	0	0	0	0
Career Total	49	7	4	10	35112
134 11/98 Newb	2m5f			C(0-135)HHdl	G-S £4958

130	10/98	Plum	2m4f	E(0-115)HHdl	G-F	£2802
125	2/98	Kemp	2m5f	D(0-125)HHdl	GD	£3420
129	11/97	Asct	2m110y	B(0-145)HHdl	SFT	£6664
101	5/97	Font	2m2f110yE Hdl		G-F	£2302
128	3/97	Ling	2m3f110yD Hdl		G-S	£3400
115	3/97	Font	2m2f110yD Hdl		GD	£2906

Total win prize-money £26456

Going: Sf: 0-0 GS: 0-0 Gd: 0-2 GF: - Fm: 0-1
Distance: 2m/2m3: 0-0 2m4-2m7: 0-1 3m+: 0-2
Track: LH: 0-3 RH: 0-0 Tight: 0-0 Gall: 0-0
Aids: Bl: 0-0 Vi: 0-0 Tstrap: 0-0
Best Rating: 134 11/98 Newb 2m5f gd-sft Hdl

Modest hurdler, not as good as he was. Seems to handle any ground and stays three miles.

Ela D'Argent (IRE)
106   102
4-y-o b f Ela-Mana-Mou-Petite-D-Argent (Noalto)
M C Pipe (P Monteith 18/7) E Nisbet

Placings:U11051   (4425)
2002/03: 17^{U}G, 16^{1}GF, 16^{1}GF, 16^{9}G, 16^{5}S, 16^{1}GF,

	Starts	1st	2nd	3rd	Win & Pl
Hurdles	6	3	0	0	11027
Career Total	6	3	0	0	11027

102	3/03	Plum	2m	F Hdl	G-F	£2765
102	10/02	Chep	2m110y	D Hdl	G-F	£4075
101	9/02	Prth	2m110y	D Hdl	G-F	£4186

Total win prize-money £11027

Going: Sf: 0-1 GS: 0-0 Gd: 0-2 GF: - Fm: 3-3
Distance: 2m/2m3: 3-6 2m4-2m7: 0-0 3m+: 0-0
Track: LH: 2-5 RH: 1-1 Tight: 1-3 Gall: 0-0
Aids: Bl: 0-0 Vi: 0-0 Tstrap: 0-0
Best Rating: 102 3/03 Plum 2m gd-fm Hdl

Moderate hurdler; front-runner; did not achieve much when winning Plumpton claimer March 2003; acts on fast ground; effective at two miles.

Ela Jay
4-y-o b f Double Eclipse (IRE)-Papirusa (IRE) (Pennine Walk)
H Morrison (G A Butler 21/10) J & L Wetherald - M & M Glover

Placings:U   (2637)
2002/03: 16^{U}S,

	Starts	1st	2nd	3rd	Win & Pl
Hurdles	1	0	0	0	
Career Total	1	0	0	0	

Going: Sf: 0-1 GS: 0-0 Gd: 0-0 GF: - Fm: 0-0
Distance: 2m/2m3: 0-1 2m4-2m7: 0-0 3m+: 0-0
Track: LH: 0-1 RH: 0-0 Tight: 0-0 Gall: 0-0
Aids: Bl: 0-0 Vi: 0-0 Tstrap: 0-0
Best Rating:

Ela La Senza (IRE)
112   91+
6-y-o br g Lord Americo-Diamond Glow (Kalaglow)
N A Twiston-Davies Xunely Limited

Placings:45560U   (3595)
2002/03: 17^{4}GS, 16^{5}GS, 17^{5}S, 17^{9}GS, 20^{U}HY,

	Starts	1st	2nd	3rd	Win & Pl
Hurdles	6	0	0	0	240
Career Total	6	0	0	0	240

Going: Sf: 0-3 GS: 0-3 Gd: 0-0 GF: - Fm: 0-0
Distance: 2m/2m3: 0-5 2m4-2m7: 0-1 3m+: 0-0
Track: LH: 0-3 RH: 0-3 Tight: 0-1 Gall: 0-2
Aids: Bl: 0-0 Vi: 0-0 Tstrap: 0-0
Best Rating: 82 12/02 Chel 2m1f soft Hdl

Plating-class hurdler; off the mark at Worcester June 2003; stays 2m 4f; acts on soft and fast ground.

Ela Re
111   107+
4-y-o ch g Sabrehill (USA)-Lucia Tarditi (FR) (Crystal Glitters (USA))
C R Dore (G Prodromou 14/12) L Cohen

Placings:02O30   (4637)
2002/03: 16^{9}GS, 17^{2}G, 16°GF, 17^{3}G, 16°GF,

	Starts	1st	2nd	3rd	Win & Pl
Hurdles	5	0	1	1	2571
Career Total	5	0	1	1	2571

Going: Sf: 0-0 GS: 0-1 Gd: 0-2 GF: - Fm: 0-2
Distance: 2m/2m3: 0-5 2m4-2m7: 0-0 3m+: 0-0
Track: LH: 0-3 RH: 0-2 Tight: 0-4 Gall: 0-0
Aids: Bl: 0-0 Vi: 0-0 Tstrap: 0-0
Best Rating: 105 3/03 MRas 2m1f110y good Hdl

Modest hurdler; in good form in the spring of 2003; goes well at Market Rasen; suited by trips of around two miles and effective on good ground.

Elaando
95(97c)   (89+c)105
8-y-o b g Darshaan-Evocatrice (Persepolis (FR))
Mrs Merrita Jones Nick Kearns

Placings:561/1314504351/0/2-PP33P   (1640)
2002/03: 16^{P}S, 20^{P}G, 22^{3}GF, 19^{3}F, 21^{P}G,

	Starts	1st	2nd	3rd	Win & Pl
Hurdles	3	0	0	1	658
Chases	2	0	0	1	633
Career Total	20	4	1	4	14030

115	4/00	Towc	2m	D(0-125)HHdl	GD	£3133
112	6/99	MRas	2m3f110yF(0-105)HHdl		G-F	£2442
110	5/99	Extr	2m1f	F(0-100)HHdl	FRM	£2810
94	4/99	Folk	2m1f110yE Hdl		G-F	£2264

Total win prize-money £10651

Going: Sf: 0-1 GS: 0-0 Gd: 0-2 GF: - Fm: 0-2
Distance: 2m/2m3: 0-2 2m4-2m7: 0-3 3m+: 0-0
Track: LH: 0-0 RH: 0-5 Tight: 0-2 Gall: 0-0
Aids: Bl: 0-0 Vi: 0-0 Tstrap: 0-0
Best Rating: 115 4/00 Towc 2m good Hdl

Fair hurdler, best on a sound surface. He has had injury problems, but is particularly effective in the summer and is suited by two miles plus.

Electric Nellie
87f   85f
6-y-o gr m Neltino-Alternation (FR) (Electric)
S Gollings Mrs Lin Hesketh

Placings:U5030   (4611)
2002/03: 17^{U}GS, 16^{5}G, 16^{9}GS, 16^{3}G, 17°GS,

	Starts	1st	2nd	3rd	Win & Pl
NH Flat	5	0	0	1	447
Career Total	5	0	0	1	447

Going: Sf: 0-0 GS: 0-2 Gd: 0-3 GF: - Fm: 0-0
Distance: 2m/2m3: 0-5 2m4-2m7: 0-0 3m+: 0-0
Track: LH: 0-4 RH: 0-1 Tight: 0-1 Gall: 0-1
Aids: Bl: 0-0 Vi: 0-0 Tstrap: 0-0
Best Rating: 85 2/03 Ludl 2m good NHF

Modest form in bumpers.

Elegant Clutter (IRE)
79   64
5-y-o b g Petorius-Mountain Hop (IRE) (Tirol)
R N Bevis Kelvin Briggs

Placings:0655-0P   (4525)
2002/03: 16^{5}S, 16^{P}G,

	Starts	1st	2nd	3rd	Win & Pl
Hurdles	2	0	0	0	
Career Total	6	0	0	0	

Going: Sf: 0-1 GS: 0-0 Gd: 0-1 GF: - Fm: 0-0
Distance: 2m/2m3: 0-2 2m4-2m7: 0-0 3m+: 0-0
Track: LH: 0-2 RH: 0-0 Tight: 0-0 Gall: 0-0
Aids: Bl: 0-0 Vi: 0-0 Tstrap: 0-0
Best Rating: 96 11/01 Thur 2m yld-sft Hdl

Elegant Fan (USA)
29
8-y-o b/br g Lear Fan (USA)-Elegance (USA) (Providential)
Mrs K M Lamb Mrs K M Lamb

Placings:000/00P00/P44640000P/P6PPP0P-00   (0579)
2002/03: 20^{P}G, 16^{9}G, 20^{9}G,

	Starts	1st	2nd	3rd	Win & Pl
Hurdles	3	0	0	0	
Career Total	27	0	0	0	212

Going: Sf: 0-0 GS: 0-0 Gd: 0-3 GF: - Fm: 0-0
Distance: 2m/2m3: 0-1 2m4-2m7: 0-2 3m+: 0-0
Track: LH: 0-3 RH: 0-0 Tight: 0-0 Gall: 0-1
Aids: Bl: 0-0 Vi: 0-0 Tstrap: 0-0
Best Rating: 70 4/99 Sedg 2m1f firm Hdl

Elegant Knight
60   14
6-y-o ch g Elegant Monarch-Night Bloomer (USA) (Told (USA))
R H Alner (Mrs S Gardner 9/11) Dartmoor Pixies Racing Club

Placings:000   (4270)
2002/03: 16^{9}G, 17°G, 16^{9}G,

	Starts	1st	2nd	3rd	Win & Pl
NH Flat	2	0	0	0	
Hurdles	1	0	0	0	
Career Total	3	0	0	0	

Going: Sf: 0-0 GS: 0-1 Gd: 0-2 GF: - Fm: 0-0
Distance: 2m/2m3: 0-3 2m4-2m7: 0-0 3m+: 0-0
Track: LH: 0-1 RH: 0-2 Tight: 0-0 Gall: 0-0
Aids: Bl: 0-0 Vi: 0-0 Tstrap: 0-0
Best Rating: 75 11/02 Winc 2m good NHF

Elenas River (IRE)
109(108h)   (112h)112
7-y-o br g Over The River (FR)-Elena s Beauty (Tarqogan)

Miss H C Knight Ian David Limited

Placings:556/02213-FU4023   **(4512)**
2002/03: 24FG, 20US, 24⁴G, 23⁹S, 22²G, 24³GF,

	Starts	1st	2nd	3rd	Win & Pl
Hurdles	1	0	0	1	1054
Chases	5	0	1	0	2822
Career Total	**14**	**1**	**3**	**2**	**15004**
99	2/02	Ludl	2m5f	D(0-120)HHdl	GD	£5187

Total win prize-money £5187

Going:	Sf: 0-2 GS: 0-0 Gd: 0-3 GF: - Fm: 0-1
Distance:	2m/2m3: 0-0 2m4-2m7: 0-2 3m+: 0-4
Track:	LH: 0-2 RH: 0-4 Tight: 0-1 Gall: 0-1
Aids:	Bl: 0-0 Vi: 0-0 Tstrap: 0-0
Best Rating:	117 11/01 NAbb 2m5f110y good Ch

Fair over hurdles, but taking time to adapt to fences; stays 2m 5f and suited by good ground.

Elfeet Bay (IRE)
98(92h)   (71h)83
8-y-o b g Yashgan-Marjoram (Warpath)
Mrs L Williamson Mrs J E Webster

Placings:0000⁶/00/60   **(4567)**
2002/03: 17⁶G, 20⁰GF,

	Starts	1st	2nd	3rd	Win & Pl
Hurdles	2	0	0	0	0
Career Total	**9**	**0**	**0**	**0**	**0**

Going:	Sf: 0-0 GS: 0-0 Gd: 0-1 GF: - Fm: 0-1
Distance:	2m/2m3: 0-1 2m4-2m7: 0-1 3m+: 0-0
Track:	LH: 0-2 RH: 0-0 Tight: 0-2 Gall: 0-0
Aids:	Bl: 0-0 Vi: 0-0 Tstrap: 0-0
Best Rating:	86 3/00 Thur 2m good NHF

Poor hurdler; runner-up in modest chase at Cartmel in May.

Elgar
103   94
6-y-o ch g Alflora (IRE)-School Run (Deep Run)
G H Yardley Mrs S Tainton

Placings:02-0   **(3926)**
2002/03: 20⁰G,

	Starts	1st	2nd	3rd	Win & Pl
Hurdles	1	0	0	0	0
Career Total	**3**	**0**	**1**	**0**	**1568**

Going:	Sf: 0-0 GS: 0-0 Gd: 0-1 GF: - Fm: 0-0
Distance:	2m/2m3: 0-0 2m4-2m7: 0-1 3m+: 0-0
Track:	LH: 0-0 RH: 0-1 Tight: 0-0 Gall: 0-1
Aids:	Bl: 0-0 Vi: 0-0 Tstrap: 0-0
Best Rating:	109 3/02 Hayd 2m6f good Hdl

Chasing-type, runner up on his first outing over hurdles but lightly-raced since.

Eljay's Boy
97f   97f
5-y-o b g Sir Harry Lewis (USA)-Woodland Flower (Furry Glen)
P F Nicholls Stephen Purdew and Des Nichols

Placings:02   **(4628)**
2002/03: 16⁵GS, 17²GF,

	Starts	1st	2nd	3rd	Win & Pl
NH Flat	2	0	1	0	916
Career Total	**2**	**0**	**1**	**0**	**916**

Going:	Sf: 0-0 GS: 0-1 Gd: 0-0 GF: - Fm: 0-1
Distance:	2m/2m3: 0-2 2m4-2m7: 0-0 3m+: 0-0
Track:	LH: 0-1 RH: 0-1 Tight: 0-1 Gall: 0-0
Aids:	Bl: 0-0 Vi: 0-0 Tstrap: 0-0
Best Rating:	97 4/03 NAbb 2m1f gd-fm NHF

Half-brother to Stamparland Hill; well backed when beaten in a bumper on his debut; benefitted from the experience when second at Newton Abbot after.

Eljutan (IRE)
82   102
5-y-o b g Namaqualand (USA)-Camarat (Ahonoora)
J Joseph Jack Joseph

Placings:134-0   **(3427)**
2002/03: 18⁰S,

	Starts	1st	2nd	3rd	Win & Pl
Hurdles	1	0	0	0	
Career Total	**4**	**1**	**0**	**1**	**4163**
102	9/01	Plum	2m	E Hdl	G-F	£2478

Total win prize-money £2478

Going:	Sf: 0-1 GS: 0-0 Gd: 0-0 GF: - Fm: 0-0
Distance:	2m/2m3: 0-1 2m4-2m7: 0-0 3m+: 0-0
Track:	LH: 0-1 RH: 0-0 Tight: 0-1 Gall: 0-0
Aids:	Bl: 0-0 Vi: 0-0 Tstrap: 0-0
Best Rating:	102 10/01 Chel 2m110y good Hdl

Comfortable winner on his hurdles debut at Plumpton, was found out in better class and may need further.

Ell-Emm-Ess

8-y-o b m Golden Heights-Four M S (Majestic Maharaj)
Mrs N S Sharpe M D Jones

Placings:0/P-PFP   **(1057)**
2002/03: 24⁰GF, 20⁰G, 20⁰PGF,

	Starts	1st	2nd	3rd	Win & Pl
Hurdles	3	0	0	0	
Career Total	**5**	**0**	**0**	**0**	

Going:	Sf: 0-0 GS: 0-0 Gd: 0-1 GF: - Fm: 0-2
Distance:	2m/2m3: 0-0 2m4-2m7: 0-2 3m+: 0-1
Track:	LH: 0-3 RH: 0-0 Tight: 0-0 Gall: 0-0
Aids:	Bl: 0-0 Vi: 0-0 Tstrap: 0-0
Best Rating:	20 2/00 Wwck 2m good NHF

Ella Carisa
68   34
4-y-o b f Elmaamul (USA)-Salty Girl (IRE) (Scenic)
A Charlton Lenan Pipco Limited

Placings:60   **(2417)**
2002/03: 16⁶GS, 18⁰G,

	Starts	1st	2nd	3rd	Win & Pl
Hurdles	2	0	0	0	0
Career Total	**2**	**0**	**0**	**0**	**0**

Going:	Sf: 0-0 GS: 0-1 Gd: 0-1 GF: - Fm: 0-0
Distance:	2m/2m3: 0-2 2m4-2m7: 0-0 3m+: 0-0
Track:	LH: 0-2 RH: 0-0 Tight: 0-1 Gall: 0-1
Aids:	Bl: 0-0 Vi: 0-0 Tstrap: 0-0
Best Rating:	34 11/02 Newb 2m110y gd-sft Hdl

Ellamine
108(90c)   (98c)85
9-y-o b m Warrshan (USA)-Anhaar (Ela-Mana-Mou)

M C Pipe Orchard Partnership

Placings:621322/3/0400440122143F00-130222P05 **(4513)**
2002/03: 22¹GF, 16³GF, 20⁰G, 17²F, 17²F, 17²GF, 19⁵S, 17⁰GS, 19⁵GF,

	Starts	1st	2nd	3rd	Win & Pl
Hurdles	9	1	3	1	6256
Career Total	**32**	**4**	**8**	**4**	**17971**
105	6/02	NAbb	2m6f	G(0-95)HHdl	G-F	£2317
98	10/01	Strf	2m110y	G Hdl	G-S	£2023
99	9/01	Font	2m2f110yG(0-95)HHdl	G-F	£2436
94	7/98	Wolv	2m	E Hdl	GD	£2207

Total win prize-money £8983

Going:	Sf: 0-1 GS: 0-1 Gd: 0-1 GF: - Fm: 1-6
Distance:	2m/2m3: 0-6 2m4-2m7: 1-3 3m+: 0-0
Track:	LH: 1-3 RH: 0-6 Tight: 1-5 Gall: 0-0
Aids:	Bl: 0-0 Vi: 0-2 Tstrap: 1-5
Best Rating:	105 6/02 NAbb 2m6f gd-fm Hdl

Selling-class hurdler, stays two miles six; acts on most surfaces, often tongue tied; did not take to fences when tried in December 2001.

Elle Roseador
105f   80f
4-y-o b f El Conquistador-The Hon Rose (Baron Blakeney)
M Madgwick Mrs Monica Yates

Placings:42   **(4760)**
2002/03: 16⁴GF, 18²GF,

	Starts	1st	2nd	3rd	Win & Pl
NH Flat	2	0	1	0	558
Career Total	**2**	**0**	**1**	**0**	**558**

Going:	Sf: 0-0 GS: 0-0 Gd: 0-0 GF: - Fm: 0-2
Distance:	2m/2m3: 0-2 2m4-2m7: 0-0 3m+: 0-0
Track:	LH: 0-1 RH: 0-1 Tight: 0-1 Gall: 0-0
Aids:	Bl: 0-0 Vi: 0-0 Tstrap: 0-0
Best Rating:	80 4/03 Font 2m2f110y gd-fm NHF

Modest bumper performer; acts on fast ground.

Elle Royal (IRE)
92   69
4-y-o br f Ali-Royal (IRE)-Silvretta (IRE) (Tirol)
T P McGovern The Green And Gold Partnership

Placings:05U0   **(4186)**
2002/03: 17⁰HY, 16⁵HY, 18US, 17⁰G,

	Starts	1st	2nd	3rd	Win & Pl
Hurdles	4	0	0	0	0
Career Total	**4**	**0**	**0**	**0**	**0**

Going:	Sf: 0-3 GS: 0-0 Gd: 0-1 GF: - Fm: 0-0
Distance:	2m/2m3: 0-2 2m4-2m7: 0-0 3m+: 0-0
Track:	LH: 0-2 RH: 0-2 Tight: 0-4 Gall: 0-0
Aids:	Bl: 0-0 Vi: 0-0 Tstrap: 0-0
Best Rating:	63 3/03 Folk 2m1f110y good Hdl

Ellen's Rock
7f
5-y-o b m Rock Hopper-Hellene (Dominion)
Paul Johnson P and Mrs D M Johnson

Placings:0   **(2142)**
2002/03: 14⁰GS,

	Starts	1st	2nd	3rd	Win & Pl
NH Flat	1	0	0	0	
Career Total	**1**	**0**	**0**	**0**	

Going: Sf: 0-0 GS: 0-1 Gd: 0-0 GF: - Fm: 0-0
Distance: 2m/2m3: 0-0 2m4-2m7: 0-0 3m+: 0-0
Track: LH: 0-1 RH: 0-0 Tight: 0-0 Gall: 0-0
Aids: Bl: 0-0 Vi: 0-0 Tstrap: 0-0
Best Rating: 7 11/02 Newc 1m6f gd-sft NHF

Ellie Moss
86f   71f
5-y-o b m Le Moss-Kayella (Fine Blade (USA))
R Dickin Mrs J Cumiskey

Placings:0   (4060)
2002/03: 16⁰S,

	Starts	1st	2nd	3rd	Win & Pl
NH Flat	1	0	0	0	
Career Total	1	0	0	0	

Going: Sf: 0-1 GS: 0-0 Gd: 0-0 GF: - Fm: 0-0
Distance: 2m/2m3: 0-1 2m4-2m7: 0-0 3m+: 0-0
Track: LH: 0-1 RH: 0-0 Tight: 0-0 Gall: 0-0
Aids: Bl: 0-0 Vi: 0-0 Tstrap: 0-0
Best Rating: 79 3/03 Wwck 2m soft NHF

Ello Ollie (IRE)
101(105c)   (101c)94
8-y-o b g Roselier (FR)-Kayanna (Torenaga)
Andrew Turnell Dr John Hollowood

Placings:3022U50/06P1F222-5   (0186)
2002/03: 20²G, 24⁵G,

	Starts	1st	2nd	3rd	Win & Pl
Hurdles	2	0	1	0	760
Career Total	16	1	5	1	8441
91 1/02 Leic	2m7f110yF(0-95)HCh		GD	£3913	

Total win prize-money £3913

Going: Sf: 0-0 GS: 0-0 Gd: 0-2 GF: - Fm: 0-0
Distance: 2m/2m3: 0-0 2m4-2m7: 0-1 3m+: 0-1
Track: LH: 0-2 RH: 0-0 Tight: 0-0 Gall: 0-1
Aids: Bl: 0-2 Vi: 0-0 Tstrap: 0-0
Best Rating: 99 2/00 Newc 2m4f soft Hdl

Moderate handicap hurdler/chaser, effective over three miles and acts on good ground. Has won in blinkers.

Elsaroni
96(98h)   (92h)65
9-y-o ch g Primitive Rising (USA)-Malmo (Free State)
P Beaumont Mrs E Dixon

Placings:0/00P/56454P-6   (0163)
2002/03: 20⁶GF,

	Starts	1st	2nd	3rd	Win & Pl
Chases	1	0	0	0	0
Career Total	11	0	0	0	0

Going: Sf: 0-0 GS: 0-0 Gd: 0-0 GF: - Fm: 0-1
Distance: 2m/2m3: 0-0 2m4-2m7: 0-1 3m+: 0-0
Track: LH: 0-1 RH: 0-0 Tight: 0-0 Gall: 0-0
Aids: Bl: 0-0 Vi: 0-0 Tstrap: 0-0
Best Rating: 92 4/02 Weth 2m4f110y good Hdl

Showed little over hurdles but looks more of a chaser.

Eltigri (FR)
105   121
11-y-o b g Mistigri-Obepine Ii (FR) (Quart De Vin (FR))

A Ennis A T A Wates

Placings:231/4/031/1P1P/10/51   (2775)
2002/03: 24⁵GS, 24¹S,

	Starts	1st	2nd	3rd	Win & Pl
Chases	2	1	0	0	10725
Career Total	15	6	1	2	45966
121 12/02 Newb 3m	D(0-125)HCh	SFT	£10725		
121 2/01 Hayd 3m	B(0-140)HCh	HVY	£9700		
117 2/00 Sand 3m110y	B(0-145)HCh	G-S	£10517		
119 1/00 Folk 3m2f	E(0-115)HCh	G-S	£7085		
124 3/99 Leic	2m7f110yE(0-115)HCh	HVY	£3860		
11/96 Nant	2m2f110y Ch	HVY	£3535		

Total win prize-money £45424

Going: Sf: 1-1 GS: 0-1 Gd: 0-0 GF: - Fm: 0-0
Distance: 2m/2m3: 0-0 2m4-2m7: 0-0 3m+: 1-2
Track: LH: 1-1 RH: 0-1 Tight: 0-0 Gall: 1-1
Aids: Bl: 0-0 Vi: 0-0 Tstrap: 0-0
Best Rating: 124 3/99 Leic 2m7f110y heavy Ch

Lightly raced, he is useful but inconsistent. Returned from a long absence at Sandown in December 2002. Suited by soft ground, he jumps soundly and goes very well fresh.

Eluna
105(103c)   (94+c)112
5-y-o ch m Unfuwain (USA)-Elisha (GER) (Konigsstuhl (GER))
Ian Williams Mr & Mrs John Poynton

Placings:21100-45P6   (4610)
2002/03: 16⁴G, 19⁵GS, 20⁴S, 21⁶G,

	Starts	1st	2nd	3rd	Win & Pl
Hurdles	2	0	0	0	420
Chases	2	0	0	0	551
Career Total	9	2	1	0	6666
124 2/02 Wwck 2m	E Hdl	HVY	£2954		
124 1/02 Wwck 2m	E Hdl	HVY	£2740		

Total win prize-money £5695

Going: Sf: 0-1 GS: 0-1 Gd: 0-2 GF: - Fm: 0-0
Distance: 2m/2m3: 0-1 2m4-2m7: 0-3 3m+: 0-0
Track: LH: 0-2 RH: 0-2 Tight: 0-0 Gall: 0-1
Aids: Bl: 0-0 Vi: 0-0 Tstrap: 0-1
Best Rating: 124 2/02 Wwck 2m heavy Hdl

Ex-German-trained filly; won twice at Warwick at the start of 2002; joined Ian Williams and has struggled both over hurdles and fences; acts on heavy ground.

Elvera
94f   87f
5-y-o b m Elmaamul (USA)-Bewitch (Idiots Delight)
J M Bradley Miss Derien Edwards

Placings:00   (4600)
2002/03: 16⁰G, 17⁰GF,

	Starts	1st	2nd	3rd	Win & Pl
NH Flat	2	0	0	0	
Career Total	2	0	0	0	

Going: Sf: 0-0 GS: 0-0 Gd: 0-1 GF: - Fm: 0-1
Distance: 2m/2m3: 0-2 2m4-2m7: 0-0 3m+: 0-0
Track: LH: 0-0 RH: 0-2 Tight: 0-0 Gall: 0-0
Aids: Bl: 0-0 Vi: 0-0 Tstrap: 0-0
Best Rating: 87 3/03 Ludl 2m good NHF

Elvis
100(102c)   (97c)95
10-y-o b g Southern Music-Tyqueen (Tycoon Ii)

L Wells The Chap Quartet

Placings:60/P0P/660511/003/233F-F406B02   (4631)
2002/03: 20⁶FGS, 21¹⁴HY, 18⁰S, 18⁶S, 18⁶GF, 16²GF,

	Starts	1st	2nd	3rd	Win & Pl
Hurdles	6	0	1	0	748
Chases	1	0	0	0	0
Career Total	25	2	2	3	9277
98 12/99 Font	2m2f110yD(0-120)HHdl	G-S	£3070		
101 12/99 Font	2m2f110yG Hdl	GD	£2867		

Total win prize-money £5939

Going: Sf: 0-3 GS: 0-1 Gd: 0-1 GF: - Fm: 0-2
Distance: 2m/2m3: 0-5 2m4-2m7: 0-2 3m+: 0-0
Track: LH: 0-5 RH: 0-2 Tight: 0-6 Gall: 0-0
Aids: Bl: 0-0 Vi: 0-0 Tstrap: 0-0
Best Rating: 101 5/01 NAbb 2m1f gd-fm Hdl

Moderate hurdler; stays two miles-two; suited by good or slightly softer; has been tried unsuccessfully over fences; does not find much for pressure.

Elvis (FR)
97   106
7-y-o ch g Red Paradise-Safari Liz (USA) (Hawaii)
R Waley-Cohen Robert Waley-Cohen

Placings:504404/22   (0646)
2002/03: 21²GS, 24²GF,

	Starts	1st	2nd	3rd	Win & Pl
Chases	2	0	2	0	2368
Career Total	8	0	2	0	8181

Going: Sf: 0-0 GS: 0-1 Gd: 0-0 GF: - Fm: 0-1
Distance: 2m/2m3: 0-0 2m4-2m7: 0-1 3m+: 0-1
Track: LH: 0-2 RH: 0-0 Tight: 0-1 Gall: 0-0
Aids: Bl: 0-0 Vi: 0-0 Tstrap: 0-0
Best Rating: 106 6/02 Strf 3m gd-fm Ch

Winning pointer who has shown promise in novice chases.

Elvis Reigns
105(85h)   (92h)99
7-y-o b g Rock City-Free Rein (Sagaro)
M D Hammond (Ferdy Murphy 15/1) A G Chappell

Placings:231UPP00/P/004-0135624403533   (4712)
2002/03: 16⁶GF, 17¹HY, 20³S, 20⁵HY, 16⁶GS, 16²S, 16⁴G, 16⁴HY, 16⁴G, 16³G, 16⁵S, 16³GF, 16³GF,

	Starts	1st	2nd	3rd	Win & Pl
Hurdles	1	0	0	0	0
Chases	12	1	1	4	8795
Career Total	25	2	2	5	30646
106 6/02 Ctml	2m1f110yE(0-100)HCh	HVY	£3419		
7/99 Autl	2m1f110y Hdl	SFT	£11840		

Total win prize-money £15259

Going: Sf: 1-6 GS: 0-1 Gd: 0-3 GF: - Fm: 0-3
Distance: 2m/2m3: 1-11 2m4-2m7: 0-2 3m+: 0-0
Track: LH: 1-8 RH: 0-5 Tight: 1-5 Gall: 0-2
Aids: Bl: 0-1 Vi: 0-0 Tstrap: 0-0
Best Rating: 106 7/02 Limk 2m4f soft Ch

Moderate chaser; effective at 2m to 2m 4f; has worn blinkers and cheekpieces.

Em's Royalty
99   101
6-y-o b g Royal Fountain-Gaelic Empress (Regular Guy)
A Parker J John Paterson

Placings:3   (3504)

2002/03: 20³HY,

	Starts	1st	2nd	3rd	Win & Pl
Hurdles	1	0	0	1	560
Career Total	1	0	0	1	560

Going:	Sf: 0-1 GS: 0-0 Gd: 0-0 GF: - Fm: 0-0
Distance:	2m/2m3: 0-0 2m4-2m7: 0-1 3m+: 0-0
Track:	LH: 0-1 RH: 0-0 Tight: 0-0 Gall: 0-0
Aids:	Bl: 0-0 Vi: 0-0 Tstrap: 0-0
Best Rating:	101 2/03 Ayr 2m4f heavy Hdl

Showed ability when third in a heavy ground novice hurdle on debut.

Emali

84   **31**

6-y-o b g Emarati (USA)-Princess Poquito (Hard Fought)
Mrs H E Rees   Mrs H E Rees

Placings:PP/PP4   (4464)
2002/03: 17ᴾF, 16ᴾS, 19⁴F,

	Starts	1st	2nd	3rd	Win & Pl
Hurdles	1	0	0	0	0
Chases	2	0	0	0	428
Career Total	5	0	0	0	428

Going:	Sf: 0-1 GS: 0-0 Gd: 0-0 GF: - Fm: 0-2
Distance:	2m/2m3: 0-3 2m4-2m7: 0-0 3m+: 0-0
Track:	LH: 0-0 RH: 0-3 Tight: 0-2 Gall: 0-0
Aids:	Bl: 0-0 Vi: 0-0 Tstrap: 0-3
Best Rating:	42 4/03 Tntn 2m3f firm Ch

Emerald Mist (IRE)

92   **68**

4-y-o b f Sacrament-Jade s Gem (Sulaafah (USA))
G B Balding   Baldings (training) Ltd

Placings:5066O   (4629)
2002/03: 17⁵GS, 19⁹G, 18⁶S, 19⁶GF, 21⁰GF,

	Starts	1st	2nd	3rd	Win & Pl
Hurdles	5	0	0	0	0
Career Total	5	0	0	0	0

Going:	Sf: 0-1 GS: 0-1 Gd: 0-1 GF: - Fm: 0-2
Distance:	2m/2m3: 0-2 2m4-2m7: 0-3 3m+: 0-0
Track:	LH: 0-2 RH: 0-3 Tight: 0-3 Gall: 0-0
Aids:	Bl: 0-0 Vi: 0-0 Tstrap: 0-0
Best Rating:	68 4/03 Plum 2m5f gd-fm Hdl

Emley

50

7-y-o b m Safawan-Bit Of A State (Free State)
N Wilson   J Wilkins

Placings:0   (0768)
2002/03: 17⁰GF,

	Starts	1st	2nd	3rd	Win & Pl
Hurdles	1	0	0	0	0
Career Total	1	0	0	0	0

Going:	Sf: 0-0 GS: 0-0 Gd: 0-0 GF: - Fm: 0-1
Distance:	2m/2m3: 0-1 2m4-2m7: 0-0 3m+: 0-0
Track:	LH: 0-1 RH: 0-0 Tight: 0-1 Gall: 0-0
Aids:	Bl: 0-0 Vi: 0-0 Tstrap: 0-0
Best Rating:	0 7/02 Sedg 2m1f gd-fm Hdl

Emma Hamilton

6-y-o b m Karinga Bay-Tharita (Thatch (USA))
C J Gray   A C Heal

Placings:600P   (4386)
2002/03: 16⁶GF, 17⁰GF, 16⁰S, 19ᴾF,

	Starts	1st	2nd	3rd	Win & Pl
NH Flat	3	0	0	0	0
Hurdles	1	0	0	0	0
Career Total	4	0	0	0	0

Going:	Sf: 0-1 GS: 0-0 Gd: 0-0 GF: - Fm: 0-3
Distance:	2m/2m3: 0-4 2m4-2m7: 0-0 3m+: 0-0
Track:	LH: 0-2 RH: 0-2 Tight: 0-1 Gall: 0-0
Aids:	Bl: 0-0 Vi: 0-0 Tstrap: 0-0
Best Rating:	71 6/02 Worc 2m gd-fm NHF

Emotional Moment (IRE)

114   **143**

6-y-o b g Religiously (USA)-Rosceen Bui (IRE) (Phardante (FR))
T J Taaffe   Watercork Syndicate

Placings:0606611136-1114144   (4475)
2002/03: 16¹YS, 16¹HY, 16¹YS, 16⁴S, 24¹YS, 21⁴G, 20⁴G,

	Starts	1st	2nd	3rd	Win & Pl
Hurdles	7	4	0	0	72983
Career Total	17	7	0	1	91264
143	2/03	Navn	3m		Hdl	Y-S	£21103
126	12/02	Navn	2m		HHdl	Y-S	£11963
117	11/02	DRoy	2m	(0-135)HHdl	HVY	£25920
110	10/02	Wxfd	2m	(74-102)HHdl	Y-S	£5291
98	1/02	Gowr	2m1f	(0-116)HHdl	HVY	£7619
100	1/02	DRoy	2m	(60-88)HHdl	SFT	£3809
82	12/01	Limk	2m	(0-102)HHdl	SFT	£6120

Total win prize-money £81829

Going:	Sf: 1-2 GS: 0-0 Gd: 0-2 GF: - Fm: 0-0
Distance:	2m/2m3: 3-4 2m4-2m7: 0-2 3m+: 1-1
Track:	LH: 2-5 RH: 0-0 Tight: 0-1 Gall: 0-1
Aids:	Bl: 0-0 Vi: 0-0 Tstrap: 0-0
Best Rating:	143 2/03 Navn 3m yld-sft Hdl

Very useful hurdler; acts well on a soft surface; goes well over two miles but landed a Grade Three at Navan when stepped up to three miles; seemed to handle faster conditions in the 2003 Coral Cup; progressive.

Empereur River (FR)

11-y-o b g Riverquest (FR)-Nuit Des Fanges (FR) (Trac)
J Ortet   P Matran

Placings:3P5/1304551363P/U353643123/224/11211/F3F2 23312331/42F1F3212-F4251543P   (4479)
2002/03: 26ᶠG, 29⁴G, 25²G, 30⁵S, 25¹S, 28⁵HY, 31⁴VS, 23³S, 36ᴾG,

	Starts	1st	2nd	3rd	Win & Pl
Chases	9	1	1	2	25139
Career Total	62	12	11	15	207155
	12/02	Pau	3m1f	Ch		SFT	£7480
	2/02	Mont	2m7f	Ch		VS	£7596
	12/01	Pau	3m1f	Ch		SFT	£7012
	4/01	Pau	3m1f	Ch		G-S	£6790
	1/01	Pau	3m5f	Ch			£7759
	4/00	Pau	3m1f	Ch			£6724
	2/00	Pau	2m7f	Ch			£4322

Total win prize-money £72024

Going:	Sf: 1-4 GS: 0-0 Gd: 0-4 GF: - Fm: 0-0
Distance:	2m/2m3: 0-0 2m4-2m7: 0-1 3m+: 1-8
Track:	LH: 0-1 RH: 0-0 Tight: 0-1 Gall: 0-0
Aids:	Bl: 0-0 Vi: 0-0 Tstrap: 0-0
Best Rating:	0 4/03 Aint 4m4f good Ch

Decent chaser in France; acts well on soft; stays three miles plus.

Emperor Ross (IRE)

112(101h)   (111h)**132**

8-y-o b/br g Roselier (FR)-Gilded Empress (Menelek)
N G Richards   James Callow & David Wesley Yates

Placings:30/33-111F1P2   (4751)
2002/03: 25¹GS, 24¹GS, 20¹GF, 32ᶠGF, 27¹GF, 24ᴾGS, 20⁴G,

	Starts	1st	2nd	3rd	Win & Pl
Chases	7	4	1	0	22569
Career Total	11	4	1	3	24147
129	7/02	Sedg	3m3f	D Ch		G-F	£4693
132	6/02	Hexm	2m4f110y E Ch		G-F	£3237
127	6/02	Prth	3m	D(0-115)HCh	G-S	£6711
112	5/02	Hexm	3m1f	E Ch		G-S	£3185

Total win prize-money £17826

Going:	Sf: 0-0 GS: 2-3 Gd: 0-1 GF: - Fm: 2-3
Distance:	2m/2m3: 0-0 2m4-2m7: 1-2 3m+: 3-5
Track:	LH: 3-3 RH: 1-3 Tight: 1-1 Gall: 0-0
Aids:	Bl: 0-0 Vi: 0-0 Tstrap: 4-7
Best Rating:	132 4/03 Prth 2m4f110y good Ch

Placed in points, hurdles and chases, he has reportedly had breathing problems. Improved form over fences in 2002. Stays three and a half miles, acts on any ground.

Emperor's Magic (IRE)

105   **123**

12-y-o ch g Over The River (FR)-Sengirrefcha (Reformed Character)
R C Guest (N B Mason 4/12)   N B Mason

Placings:63/2/33523/512404/1U13421F3-F61431235   (4775)
2002/03: 24ᶠGS, 22⁶S, 24¹S, 19⁴G, 25³GS, 20¹GS, 22²G, 24³GF, 24⁵G,

	Starts	1st	2nd	3rd	Win & Pl
Chases	9	2	1	2	16752
Career Total	32	6	5	8	46100
112	3/03	MRas	2m4f	E(0-110)HCh	G-S	£4371
115	11/02	Newc	3m	D(0-125)HCh	SFT	£5720
111	3/02	MRas	2m6f110yD(0-120)HCh	SFT	£4771
110	12/01	Catt	3m1f110yF(0-110)HCh	SFT	£4290
98	11/01	Carl	2m4f	E(0-115)HCh	SFT	£6955
97	2/01	Carl	2m4f110yF(0-105)HCh	SFT	£3575

Total win prize-money £29682

Going:	Sf: 1-2 GS: 1-3 Gd: 0-3 GF: - Fm: 0-1
Distance:	2m/2m3: 0-1 2m4-2m7: 1-3 3m+: 1-5
Track:	LH: 1-6 RH: 1-3 Tight: 1-7 Gall: 1-1
Aids:	Bl: 0-0 Vi: 0-0 Tstrap: 1-2
Best Rating:	123 3/03 MRas 2m6f110y good Ch

Fair chaser; stays three miles one furlong but effective over shorter; acts on soft ground; has worn a tongue tie.

Emphatic (IRE)

105   **107**

8-y-o ch g Ela-Mana-Mou-Sally Rose (Sallust)
J G Portman   Hockham Racing

Placings: 00352/1401000/02015/234125   (4759)
2002/03: 22²GS, 22³S, 22⁴GS, 26¹G, 26²GF, 27⁵GF,

	Starts	1st	2nd	3rd	Win & Pl
Hurdles	6	1	2	1	6365
Career Total	23	4	4	2	19751
107	3/03	Hntg	3m2f	E(0-110)HHdl	GD	£3458
113	3/01	Font	2m6f110yF(0-100)HHdl	HVY	£2457
113	1/00	Sand	2m6f	D(0-110)HHdl	SFT	£5278
109	11/99	Newb	3m110y	D(0-110)HHdl	G-F	£3496

Total win prize-money £14689

Going: Sf: 0-1 GS: 0-2 Gd: 1-1 GF: - Fm: 0-2
Distance: 2m/2m3: 0-0 2m4-2m7: 0-3 3m+: 1-3
Track: LH: 0-2 RH: 1-3 Tight: 0-3 Gall: 1-2
Aids: Bl: 1-6 Vi: 0-0 Tstrap: 0-0
Best Rating: 113 3/01 Font 2m6f110y heavy Hdl

Modest staying handicap hurdler, well suited by testing ground; usually wears blinkers or a visor.

Empire Park

109   (101c)120

8-y-o b g Tragic Role (USA)-Millaine (Formidable (USA))
C R Egerton Elite Racing Club

Placings: 12/F512311214P3520-3111601P005   (3943)
2002/03: 21³GF, 20¹S, 26¹GF, 22¹S, 22⁶S, 24⁰G, 21¹S, 22ᴾHY, 24⁰G, 24⁰GS, 24⁵GS,

	Starts	1st	2nd	3rd	Win & Pl
Hurdles	11	4	0	1	16301
Career Total	28	9	4	3	32750
120	1/03	Hntg	2m5f110yD(0-110)HHdl	SFT	£4953
120	11/02	NAbb	2m6f	C(0-130)HHdl	SFT	£5973
102	8/02	Sthl	3m2f	F Hdl	G-F	£2541
112	8/02	Worc	2m4f	F Hdl	SFT	£2268
120	12/01	Newb	2m3f	F(0-110)HHdl	GD	£3276
120	11/01	Towc	2m	G Hdl	SFT	£1946
100	10/01	Hrfd	2m3f110y	G Hdl	G-S	£1949
114	9/01	Prth	2m110y	F Hdl	GD	£2975
93	7/99	MRas	2m1f110yF Hdl	G-F	£1452

Total win prize-money £27335

Going: Sf: 3-5 GS: 0-2 Gd: 0-2 GF: - Fm: 1-2
Distance: 2m/2m3: 0-0 2m4-2m7: 3-6 3m+: 1-5
Track: LH: 3-8 RH: 1-3 Tight: 1-3 Gall: 1-3
Aids: Bl: 4-11 Vi: 0-0 Tstrap: 0-0
Best Rating: 120 1/03 Hntg 2m5f110y soft Hdl

Fair staying hurdler and a consistent sort in modest handicaps; effective at up to three miles two furlongs; acts on most types of ground; usually wears blinkers; has run poorly of late.

Empress Alice

6-y-o b m Petoski-Blue Empress (Blue Cashmere)
Dr P Pritchard (R E Peacock 24/7) Four For Fun

Placings: 0-RPP   (1843)
2002/03: 16ᴿGF, 16ᴾGF, 16ᴾGS,

	Starts	1st	2nd	3rd	Win & Pl
Hurdles	2	0	0	0	0
Chases	1	0	0	0	0
Career Total	4	0	0	0	

Going: Sf: 0-0 GS: 0-1 Gd: 0-0 GF: - Fm: 0-2
Distance: 2m/2m3: 0-3 2m4-2m7: 0-0 3m+: 0-0
Track: LH: 0-2 RH: 0-1 Tight: 0-0 Gall: 0-0
Aids: Bl: 0-0 Vi: 0-0 Tstrap: 0-0
Best Rating: 0 11/02 Sand 2m gd-sft Ch

Empress Streamline

7-y-o b m Emperor Fountain-Judys Line (Capricorn Line)
R H Alner Miss S Waterman

Placings: 0/UPP   (3474)
2002/03: 17ᵁGS, 16ᴾGS, 22ᴾGS,

	Starts	1st	2nd	3rd	Win & Pl
Hurdles	3	0	0	0	
Career Total	4	0	0	0	

Going: Sf: 0-0 GS: 0-3 Gd: 0-0 GF: - Fm: 0-0
Distance: 2m/2m3: 0-2 2m4-2m7: 0-1 3m+: 0-0
Track: LH: 0-0 RH: 0-3 Tight: 0-1 Gall: 0-0
Aids: Bl: 0-0 Vi: 0-0 Tstrap: 0-0
Best Rating: 0 2/03 Winc 2m6f gd-sft Hdl

En El Em Flyer

102   70

8-y-o b g Seymour Hicks (FR)-Sound N Rhythm (Tudor Rhythm)
R Curtis Keith J Bradley/gordon Houldsworth

Placings: 60000P-023   (2613)
2002/03: 22⁵S, 25²ᴾHY, 24³S,

	Starts	1st	2nd	3rd	Win & Pl
Hurdles	3	0	1	1	1224
Career Total	9	0	1	1	1224

Going: Sf: 0-3 GS: 0-0 Gd: 0-0 GF: - Fm: 0-0
Distance: 2m/2m3: 0-0 2m4-2m7: 0-1 3m+: 0-2
Track: LH: 0-1 RH: 0-1 Tight: 0-0 Gall: 0-0
Aids: Bl: 0-0 Vi: 0-0 Tstrap: 0-0
Best Rating: 81 6/01 Worc 2m gd-fm NHF

Poor handicap hurdler, suited by three miles.

Enchanted Cottage

97

11-y-o b g Governor General-Mitsubishi Colour (Cut Above)
D M Grissell Pleisure Ltd

Placings: 00P535/12216/F30/0P6364P55/60/62410P3-5P00R   (4629)
2002/03: 21⁵GF, 20ᴾHY, 22⁰HY, 21⁰GD, 21ᴿGF,

	Starts	1st	2nd	3rd	Win & Pl
Hurdles	5	0	0	0	0
Career Total	37	3	3	4	10776
80	10/01	Font	2m4f	G(0-95)HHdl	G-S	£2299
97	3/97	Hexm	2m4f110yE(0-100)HHdl	SFT	£2794
81	2/97	Catt	2m3f	E(0-105)HHdl	GD	£2211

Total win prize-money £7306

Going: Sf: 0-2 GS: 0-0 Gd: 0-0 GF: - Fm: 0-3
Distance: 2m/2m3: 0-0 2m4-2m7: 0-5 3m+: 0-0
Track: LH: 0-3 RH: 0-2 Tight: 0-4 Gall: 0-0
Aids: Bl: 0-0 Vi: 0-0 Tstrap: 0-0
Best Rating: 97 3/97 Hexm 2m4f110y soft Hdl

Plating-class hurdler, stays two and a half miles plus. Suited by fast ground but handles some cut.

Enchanted Flight

72   39

7-y-o b m Access Travel-Fair Enchantress (Enchantment)
C N Kellett Peter J Hammersley

Placings: 0P5P   (0727)
2002/03: 16⁴G, 20ᴾGS, 19⁵GF, 22ᴾGF,

	Starts	1st	2nd	3rd	Win & Pl
Hurdles	4	0	0	0	0
Career Total	4	0	0	0	0

Encore Cadoudal (FR)

101   104

5-y-o b g Cadoudal (FR)-Maousse (FR) (Labus (FR))
M C Pipe D A Johnson

Placings: 20-6305   (4292)
2002/03: 20⁶GS, 16³G, 19⁰GS, 16⁵GF,

	Starts	1st	2nd	3rd	Win & Pl
Hurdles	4	0	0	1	769
Career Total	6	0	1	1	1437

Going: Sf: 0-0 GS: 0-2 Gd: 0-1 GF: - Fm: 0-1
Distance: 2m/2m3: 0-3 2m4-2m7: 0-1 3m+: 0-0
Track: LH: 0-1 RH: 0-2 Tight: 0-2 Gall: 0-0
Aids: Bl: 0-0 Vi: 0-0 Tstrap: 0-0
Best Rating: 107 3/03 Winc 2m gd-fm Hdl

A half-brother to dual winning hurdler Maousse Honor. Made an encouraging bumper debut at Haydock in January 2002 and third over hurdles in November. Keen sort.

End Of An Error

106   79

4-y-o b f Charmer-Needwood Poppy (Rolfe (USA))
M C Chapman G McCowan

Placings: 004   (4686)
2002/03: 16ᴿHY, 16⁰G, 17ᴿGF,

	Starts	1st	2nd	3rd	Win & Pl
Hurdles	3	0	0	0	0
Career Total	3	0	0	0	0

Going: Sf: 0-1 GS: 0-0 Gd: 0-1 GF: - Fm: 0-1
Distance: 2m/2m3: 0-3 2m4-2m7: 0-0 3m+: 0-0
Track: LH: 0-1 RH: 0-2 Tight: 0-1 Gall: 0-0
Aids: Bl: 0-0 Vi: 0-0 Tstrap: 0-0
Best Rating: 72 4/03 MRas 2m1f110y gd-fm Hdl

Plater; changed hands after a wide margin success at Market Rasen in July; easy winner for new connections in non-seller at Sedgefield in July; suited by three miles.

Engaged

8-y-o b g St Ninian-Betrothed (Aglojo)
T D Walford John A Cooper

Placings: P/F-UF   (4166)
2002/03: 20ᵁS, 20ᶠGS,

	Starts	1st	2nd	3rd	Win & Pl
Chases	2	0	0	0	
Career Total	4	0	0	0	

Going: Sf: 0-1 GS: 0-1 Gd: 0-0 GF: - Fm: 0-0
Distance: 2m/2m3: 0-0 2m4-2m7: 0-2 3m+: 0-0
Track: LH: 0-1 RH: 0-0 Tight: 0-0 Gall: 0-1

Aids: Bl: 0-0 Vi: 0-0 Tstrap: 0-0
Best Rating: 0   3/03   Newc 2m4f   gd-sft   Ch

Enhancer
105f   111+f
5-y-o b g Zafonic (USA)-Ypha (USA) (Lyphard (USA))
G A Swinbank Mrs H Whitaker

Placings: 1-11   (4230)
2002/03: 16¹GF, 16¹GF,

	Starts	1st	2nd	3rd	Win & Pl
NH Flat	2	2	0	0	3766
Career Total	3	3	0	0	5632
111	3/03	Weth 2m	H NHF	G-F	£1932
103	9/02	Hexm 2m110y	H NHF	G-F	£1834
99	2/02	Muss 2m	H NHF	SFT	£1865

Total win prize-money £5632

Going: Sf: 0-0 GS: 0-0 Gd: 0-0 GF: - Fm: 2-2
Distance: 2m/2m3: 2-2 2m4-2m7: 0-0 3m+: 0-0
Track: LH: 2-2 RH: 0-0 Tight: 0-0 Gall: 0-0
Aids: Bl: 0-0 Vi: 0-0 Tstrap: 0-0
Best Rating: 111   3/03   Weth 2m   gd-fm   NHF

A half-brother to useful jumper Redemption, he won a weak bumper on his debut at Musselburgh and followed up at Hexham last year; back in action after a six month break when a wide margin winner at Wetherby in March; clearly at least useful.

Enitsag (FR)
102   104
4-y-o ch g Pistolet Bleu (IRE)-Rosala (FR) (Lashkari)
M C Pipe D A Johnson

Placings: 111601   (4625)
2002/03: 12¹GS, 13¹S, 17¹GS, 17⁶GS, 16⁰G, 17¹GF,

	Starts	1st	2nd	3rd	Win & Pl
NH Flat	2	2	0	0	5758
Hurdles	4	2	0	0	8735
Career Total	6	4	0	0	14492
102	4/03	NAbb 2m1f	D(0-115)HHdl	G-F	£4912
97	2/03	Bang 2m1f	E Hdl	S-F	£3822
100	12/02	Extr 1m5f	H NHF	SFT	£2733
100	11/02	Newb 1m4f110yH NHF		G-S	£3024

Total win prize-money £14493

Going: Sf: 1-1 GS: 2-3 Gd: 0-1 GF: - Fm: 1-1
Distance: 2m/2m3: 2-4 2m4-2m7: 0-0 3m+: 0-0
Track: LH: 3-3 RH: 1-3 Tight: 2-2 Gall: 0-0
Aids: Bl: 0-0 Vi: 0-0 Tstrap: 0-0
Best Rating: 102   4/03   NAbb 2m1f   gd-fm   Hdl

Modest hurdler; dual bumper winner at less than two miles; scrambled home when winning at Bangor on hurdles debut; showed signs of temperament when beaten in handicaps after; given a change of tactics to make all at Newton Abbot in April 2003; acts on soft and fast ground.

Ennel Boy (IRE)
109(103h)   (113h)116
10-y-o ch g Torus-Golden Symphony (Le Moss)
N M Babbage Provex Products Ltd

Placings: 0/0/PP04/312-23P5   (4789)
2002/03: 24²G, 27³GF, 24⁶G, 24⁵GF,

	Starts	1st	2nd	3rd	Win & Pl
Hurdles	4	0	1	1	5591
Career Total	13	1	2	2	9586
100	5/01	Hntg	3m2f	E(0-105)HHdl	G-F	£2565

Total win prize-money £2566

Going: Sf: 0-0 GS: 0-0 Gd: 0-2 GF: - Fm: 0-2
Distance: 2m/2m3: 0-0 2m4-2m7: 0-0 3m+: 0-4
Track: LH: 0-2 RH: 0-0 Tight: 0-1 Gall: 0-2
Aids: Bl: 0-0 Vi: 0-0 Tstrap: 0-0
Best Rating: 113   4/03   Sand   3m   gd-fm   Hdl

Fair hurdler; won 21 furlong novices handicap chase at Stratford May 2003; seemed to find the same trip on the short side at Newton Abbot next time; stays 3m plus; acts on fast ground; lightly raced in recent seasons.

Enrique (GER)
141
8-y-o ch g Niniski (USA)-Eicidora (GER) (Surumu (GER))
P J Hobbs Sir Robert Ogden

Placings: 1220113/5211F/4P125-P   (4557)
2002/03: 33⁵G,

	Starts	1st	2nd	3rd	Win & Pl
Chases	1	0	0	0	
Career Total	18	6	4	1	52144
139	12/01	Winc	3m1f110yD(0-125)HCh	GD	£9148
141	11/00	Ludl	3m	D Ch	GD	£4446
128	11/00	Ludl	2m4f	E Ch	GD	£3552
137	3/00	Ling	2m3f110yC(0-135)HHdl	GD	£14885
133	3/00	Sand	2m110y E(0-115)HHdl	GD	£4212
113	11/99	NAbb	2m1f	E Hdl	SFT	£2422

Total win prize-money £38667

Going: Sf: 0-0 GS: 0-0 Gd: 0-1 GF: - Fm: 0-0
Distance: 2m/2m3: 0-0 2m4-2m7: 0-0 3m+: 0-1
Track: LH: 0-1 RH: 0-0 Tight: 0-0 Gall: 0-0
Aids: Bl: 0-0 Vi: 0-0 Tstrap: 0-0
Best Rating: 141   4/02   Aint   3m1f   good   Ch

Very useful handicap chaser; stays 3m 1f; effective on fast ground; acts on soft.

Entertainer (IRE)
110(86c)   (75c)103
7-y-o b g Be My Guest (USA)-Green Wings (General Assembly (USA))
A R Dicken (P F Nicholls 23/1) Ron Affleck

Placings: 22/1F2401/001-0052646   (4754)
2002/03: 24⁰S, 20⁰S, 20⁵S, 21²HY, 20⁶S, 18⁴G, 16⁶G,

	Starts	1st	2nd	3rd	Win & Pl
Hurdles	6	0	1	0	1552
Chases	1	0	0	0	0
Career Total	18	3	4	0	16587
135	11/00	Worc	2m4f	C(0-135)HHdl	GD	£5519
126	4/01	Winc	2m	E Hdl	SFT	£3493
126	5/00	Font	2m2f110yE Hdl	GD	£2450

Total win prize-money £11463

Going: Sf: 0-5 GS: 0-0 Gd: 0-2 GF: - Fm: 0-0
Distance: 2m/2m3: 0-2 2m4-2m7: 0-4 3m+: 0-1
Track: LH: 0-4 RH: 0-2 Tight: 0-3 Gall: 0-0
Aids: Bl: 0-1 Vi: 0-0 Tstrap: 0-0
Best Rating: 135   6/01   Worc   2m4f   good   Hdl

Formerly fair hurdler, now on the downgrade; best at around two and a half miles; acts on good but has won on softer.

Entree (FR)
95f   85f
4-y-o b f Ela-Mana-Mou-Easter Baby (Derrylin)
P D Cundell Mrs Sara Wickins

Placings: 62   (4060)
2002/03: 12⁶GS, 16²S,

	Starts	1st	2nd	3rd	Win & Pl
NH Flat	2	0	1	0	572

Career Total 2   0   1   0   572

Going: Sf: 0-1 GS: 0-1 Gd: 0-0 GF: - Fm: 0-0
Distance: 2m/2m3: 0-1 2m4-2m7: 0-0 3m+: 0-0
Track: LH: 0-2 RH: 0-0 Tight: 0-0 Gall: 0-0
Aids: Bl: 0-0 Vi: 0-0 Tstrap: 0-0
Best Rating: 90   3/03   Wwck 2m   soft   NHF

Twice placed in bumpers; wore blinkers third start.

Envious
109   73
4-y-o ch g Hernando (FR)-Prima Verde (Leading Counsel (USA))
R Allan Mrs Rita Cioffi

Placings: 600   (1944)
2002/03: 16⁶GF, 16⁰GF, 16⁰S,

	Starts	1st	2nd	3rd	Win & Pl
Hurdles	3	0	0	0	0
Career Total	3	0	0	0	0

Going: Sf: 0-1 GS: 0-0 Gd: 0-0 GF: - Fm: 0-2
Distance: 2m/2m3: 0-3 2m4-2m7: 0-0 3m+: 0-0
Track: LH: 0-2 RH: 0-1 Tight: 0-0 Gall: 0-0
Aids: Bl: 0-0 Vi: 0-0 Tstrap: 0-0
Best Rating: 73   9/02   Prth   2m110y   gd-fm   Hdl

Moderate novice; best efforts when runner-up at Cartmel in July and Sedgefield a week later.

Environment Audit
102   93
4-y-o ch g Kris-Bold And Beautiful (Bold Lad (IRE))
J R Jenkins (B W Hills 8/7) American Horse Racing Club Ltd

Placings: 0442064   (3924)
2002/03: 16⁰G, 16⁴S, 16²S, 17⁹HY, 16⁶HY, 16⁴G,

	Starts	1st	2nd	3rd	Win & Pl
Hurdles	7	0	1	0	2591
Career Total	7	0	1	0	2591

Going: Sf: 0-4 GS: 0-1 Gd: 0-2 GF: - Fm: 0-0
Distance: 2m/2m3: 0-7 2m4-2m7: 0-0 3m+: 0-0
Track: LH: 0-1 RH: 0-6 Tight: 0-0 Gall: 0-1
Aids: Bl: 0-0 Vi: 0-0 Tstrap: 0-0
Best Rating: 95   12/02   Sand   2m110y   soft   Hdl

A winner on the level at ten furlongs. Showed ability when fourth on second out over hurdles in November and then when second at Sandown in December.

Enzo De Baune (FR)
110   101
6-y-o b g En Calcat (FR)-Pure Moon (FR) (Pure Flight (USA))
G A Harker Lord Bolton

Placings: 5403F-06P4444U21   (4660)
2002/03: 17⁰G, 18⁶HY, 21³HY, 24⁴VS, 20⁴S, 16⁴S, 16⁰UG, 21²G, 20¹GF,

	Starts	1st	2nd	3rd	Win & Pl
Chases	10	1	1	0	7346
Career Total	15	1	1	1	8975
101	4/03	Carl	2m4f	E(0-100)HCh	G-F	£4485

Total win prize-money £4485

Going: Sf: 0-5 GS: 0-0 Gd: 0-3 GF: - Fm: 1-1
Distance: 2m/2m3: 0-5 2m4-2m7: 1-4 3m+: 0-1

Track: LH: 0-5 **RH: 1-1** Tight: 0-2 Gall: 0-2
Aids: Bl: 0-1 Vi: 0-0 Tstrap: 0-0
Best Rating: 101 4/03 Carl 2m4f   gd-fm   Ch

Moderate novice chaser; jumped right when runner-up at Sedgefield in April, but won well at Carlisle; stays two miles five; acts on a sound surface; has worn blinkers; best going right-handed and making the running.

Eoins Pride (IRE)

108   (64h) 116

8-y-o b g Houmayoun (FR)-Cheeky Chic (Laurence O)
E Bolger Patrick Kearns

Placings:3/011-6406042F0P   (4204a)
2002/03: 24⁶S, 20⁴VS, 16⁹G, 21⁶GF, 24⁰F, 31⁴GS, 31²GS, 18⁶SH, 24⁰S, 20⁶S,

	Starts	1st	2nd	3rd	Win & Pl
Hurdles	1	0	0	0	0
Chases	9	0	1	0	7163
Career Total	**14**	**2**	**1**	**1**	**16952**
100 4/02 Fair	2m4f	Ch	YLD	£4656
100 1/02 Thur	3m	Ch	HVY	£4656

Total win prize-money £9312

Going: Sf: 0-3 GS: 0-2 Gd: 0-1 GF: - Fm: 0-2
Distance: 2m/2m3: 0-2 2m4-2m7: 0-3 3m+: 0-5
Track: LH: 0-3 RH: 0-5 Tight: 0-0 Gall: 0-0
Aids: Bl: 0-0 Vi: 0-0 Tstrap: 0-2
Best Rating: 116 12/02 Chel 3m7f   gd-sft   Ch

Fair Irish chaser; stays four miles; suited by soft ground.

Epervier D'Or (FR)

109   142

5-y-o b g Epervier Bleu-Magdor (FR) (Magwal (FR))
P F Nicholls D J & F A Jackson

Placings:12-11125   (3748)
2002/03: 16¹G, 17¹GS, 16¹S, 16²G, 20⁵G,

	Starts	1st	2nd	3rd	Win & Pl
Chases	5	3	1	0	34213
Career Total	**7**	**4**	**2**	**0**	**49247**
136 12/02 Kemp	2m	B Ch	SFT	£13082
130 12/02 Extr	2m1f110y	C Ch	G-S	£10432
120 11/02 Weth	2m	E Ch	GD	£4112
11/01 Engh	2m1f110y		Hdl	HVY	£9699

Total win prize-money £37327

Going: Sf: 1-1 GS: 1-1 Gd: 1-3 GF: - Fm: 0-0
Distance: 2m/2m3: 3-4 2m4-2m7: 0-1 3m+: 0-0
Track: LH: 1-1 RH: 2-4 Tight: 0-0 Gall: 0-0
Aids: Bl: 0-0 Vi: 0-0 **Tstrap: 2-4**
Best Rating: 136 1/03 Kemp 2m   good   Ch

Useful ex-French novice chaser; won his first three starts over fences before going down to Farmer Jack (giving 8lb) at Kempton in January; all form around 2m; effective on good and soft ground; usually wears a tongue-tie; likes to race prominently; has broken blood-vessels.

Epicure (FR)

106   92

6-y-o b/br g Northern Crystal-L Epicurienne (FR) (Rex Magna (FR))
M C Pipe Mrs Belinda Harvey

Placings:0000-1112P500PP   (3856)
2002/03: 17¹S, 17¹GF, 20¹S, 17²GF, 20⁰GF, 16⁵S, 17⁰S, 17⁰S, 19⁵S, 17⁵GS,

	Starts	1st	2nd	3rd	Win & Pl
Hurdles	10	3	1	0	12477
Career Total	**14**	**3**	**1**	**0**	**12477**
117 8/02 Bang	2m4f	D(0-115)HHdl	SFT	£4868

---

117 6/02 NAbb	2m1f	E(0-105)HHdl	G-F	£3031
112 5/02 NAbb	2m1f	D Hdl	SFT	£3419

Total win prize-money £11319

Going: Sf: 2-6 GS: 0-1 Gd: 0-0 GF: - Fm: 1-3
Distance: 2m/2m3: 2-7 2m4-2m7: 1-3 3m+: 0-0
Track: LH: 3-6 RH: 0-4 **Tight: 3-7** Gall: 0-1
Aids: Bl: 0-0 Vi: 0-0 Tstrap: 0-0
Best Rating: 117 8/02 NAbb 2m1f   gd-fm   Hdl

Showed marked improvement since joining Martin Pipe and completed a hat-trick during the summer of 2002; handles most types of ground; pulled up as if something was amiss at Worcester in August and did not run that well at Sandown next time; beaten favourite in valuable Uttoxeter seller May 2003.

Epitre (FR)

90   110

6-y-o b g Common Grounds-Epistolienne (Law Society (USA))
M F Harris (A Fabre 31/10) Let s Live Racing

Placings:60P   (3629)
2002/03: 16⁶GS, 16⁰GS, 24⁰S,

	Starts	1st	2nd	3rd	Win & Pl
Hurdles	3	0	0	0	600
Career Total	**3**	**0**	**0**	**0**	**600**

Going: Sf: 0-1 GS: 0-2 Gd: 0-0 GF: - Fm: 0-0
Distance: 2m/2m3: 0-2 2m4-2m7: 0-0 3m+: 0-1
Track: LH: 0-2 RH: 0-1 Tight: 0-0 Gall: 0-0
Aids: Bl: 0-0 Vi: 0-0 Tstrap: 0-0
Best Rating: 107 1/03 Hayd 2m   gd-sft   Hdl

Listed class stayer on the Flat in France; 46l 6th of 7 to Flame Creek in Grade Two Hurdle at Haydock pick of poor form over hurdles in this country.

Epop (IRE)

83   51

6-y-o b g Religiously (USA)-General Rain (General Ironside)
J Howard Johnson Dick Thackeray

Placings:000PP   (3811)
2002/03: 22⁰S, 20⁰S, 16⁰G, 24⁰HY, 25⁰G,

	Starts	1st	2nd	3rd	Win & Pl
Hurdles	5	0	0	0	
Career Total	**5**	**0**	**0**	**0**	

Going: Sf: 0-4 GS: 0-0 Gd: 0-1 GF: - Fm: 0-0
Distance: 2m/2m3: 0-2 2m4-2m7: 0-2 3m+: 0-2
Track: LH: 0-5 RH: 0-0 Tight: 0-2 Gall: 0-3
Aids: Bl: 0-0 Vi: 0-0 Tstrap: 0-0
Best Rating: 51 12/02 Newc 2m   soft   Hdl

Epsilo De La Ronce (FR)

11-y-o b/br g Le Riverain (FR)-India Rosa (FR) (Carnaval)
S Flook S Flook

Placings:61440PF250/4/56210/215F2P40P-11262154
                                            (4678)
2002/03: 21¹GF, 20¹F, 21²S, 22⁶GS, 20²GS, 20¹GF, 21⁵G, 19⁴GF,

	Starts	1st	2nd	3rd	Win & Pl
Chases	8	3	2	0	12188
Career Total	**33**	**6**	**6**	**0**	**24493**
107 3/03 Ludl	2m4f	H Ch	G-F	£3167

---

103 5/02 Wwck	2m4f110yH Ch		FRM	£1260
109 5/02 Chel	2m5f	H Ch	G-F	£3902
109 5/01 Strf	3m	H Ch	G-S	£3523
109 4/01 Asct	2m3f110yH Ch		SFT	£3227
9/98 Pmnl	2m2f110y Ch		GD	£2727

Total win prize-money £17808

Going: Sf: 0-1 GS: 0-2 Gd: 0-1 GF: - Fm: 3-4
Distance: 2m/2m3: 0-1 **2m4-2m7: 3-7** 3m+: 0-0
Track: LH: 2-5 RH: 1-3 Tight: 1-3 Gall: 1-1
Aids: Bl: 0-0 Vi: 0-0 Tstrap: 0-0
Best Rating: 109 5/02 Chel 2m5f   gd-fm   Ch

Fair hunter chaser; acts on fast and yielding ground; stays 3m, but more effective over shorter.

Equal Balance

64   35

5-y-o ch g Pivotal-Thatcher s Era (IRE) (Never So Bold)
C J Hemsley Mrs M L Sell

Placings:F00   (1603)
2002/03: 19⁶GF, 16⁰G, 16⁰G,

	Starts	1st	2nd	3rd	Win & Pl
Hurdles	3	0	0	0	
Career Total	**3**	**0**	**0**	**0**	

Going: Sf: 0-0 GS: 0-0 Gd: 0-2 GF: - Fm: 0-1
Distance: 2m/2m3: 0-2 2m4-2m7: 0-1 3m+: 0-0
Track: LH: 0-2 RH: 0-1 Tight: 0-1 Gall: 0-0
Aids: Bl: 0-0 Vi: 0-0 Tstrap: 0-0
Best Rating: 27 9/02 Plum 2m   good   Hdl

Equiname

89   74

6-y-o b g Rock Hopper-Bayrouge (IRE) (Gorytus (USA))
J G M O Shea Mrs Ruth Nelmes, C L Dubois & N Nelmes

Placings:0200-00P06   (4116)
2002/03: 20⁰S, 17⁰GS, 24⁴HY, 16⁰GS, 21⁶G,

	Starts	1st	2nd	3rd	Win & Pl
Hurdles	5	0	0	0	
Career Total	**9**	**0**	**1**	**0**	**568**

Going: Sf: 0-2 GS: 0-2 Gd: 0-1 GF: - Fm: 0-0
Distance: 2m/2m3: 0-2 2m4-2m7: 0-2 3m+: 0-1
Track: LH: 0-4 RH: 0-1 Tight: 0-1 Gall: 0-1
Aids: Bl: 0-0 Vi: 0-0 Tstrap: 0-0
Best Rating: 99 1/02 Hayd 2m   soft   NHF

Improved on debut effort to finish second in a bumper at Newcastle. Acts on soft ground and is effective at two miles.

Equivocal (IRE)

106   102

7-y-o ch g Roselier (FR)-Coral Cluster (Jasmine Star)
M F Morris Sir Anthony O Reilly

Placings:05-54U0323004   (4300a)
2002/03: 20⁵G, 16⁴S, 19⁴S, 16⁹S, 17³HY, 22²S, 24³YS, 24⁰S, 18⁰S, 24⁴Y,

	Starts	1st	2nd	3rd	Win & Pl
Hurdles	10	0	1	2	2945
Career Total	**12**	**0**	**1**	**2**	**2945**

Going: Sf: 0-7 GS: 0-0 Gd: 0-0 GF: - Fm: 0-0
Distance: 2m/2m3: 0-5 2m4-2m7: 0-2 3m+: 0-3
Track: LH: 0-3 RH: 0-3 Tight: 0-1 Gall: 0-0
Aids: Bl: 0-0 Vi: 0-0 Tstrap: 0-0

Column 1

Best Rating: 104 1/03 Navn 2m6f   soft   Hdl

Irish-trained maiden hurdler.

Ercon (IRE)

5-y-o ch g Thatching-Certain Impression (USA) (Forli (ARG))
R Hollinshead C Forster

Placings: 06PP   (3515)
2002/03: 17⁰GF, 17⁶GF, 19⁰GS, 16⁰GS,

	Starts	1st	2nd	3rd	Win & Pl
NH Flat	2	0	0	0	0
Hurdles	2	0	0	0	0
Career Total	4	0	0	0	0

Going: Sf: 0-0 GS: 0-2 Gd: 0-0 GF: - Fm: 0-2
Distance: 2m/2m3: 0-3 2m4-2m7: 0-1 3m+: 0-0
Track: LH: 0-2 RH: 0-2 Tight: 0-1 Gall: 0-0
Aids: Bl: 0-0 Vi: 0-0 Tstrap: 0-0
Best Rating: 72 6/02 Hrfd 2m1f   gd-fm NHF

Eric's Charm (FR)
109f   113f

5-y-o b g Nikos-Ladoun (FR) (Kaldoun (FR))
O Sherwood M St Quinton & P Deal

Placings: 115   (4481)
2002/03: 18¹G, 16¹G, 17⁵G,

	Starts	1st	2nd	3rd	Win & Pl
NH Flat	3	2	0	0	4698
Career Total	3	2	0	0	4698
113 3/03 Hntg 2m110y H NHF				GD	£2009
110 2/03 Font 2m2f110yH NHF				G-S	£1939
			Total win prize-money £3948		

Going: Sf: 0-0 GS: 1-1 Gd: 1-2 GF: - Fm: 0-0
Distance: 2m/2m3: 2-3 2m4-2m7: 0-0 3m+: 0-0
Track: LH: 1-1 RH: 1-1 Tight: 1-1 Gall: 1-1
Aids: Bl: 0-0 Vi: 0-0 Tstrap: 0-0
Best Rating: 113 3/03 Hntg 2m110y   good NHF

Half-brother to Monkerhostin; won bumpers on early in 2003 before being beaten at Aintree; acts on good and good to soft ground.

Erics Way
82   52

6-y-o b g Man Among Men (IRE)-Gypsy Crystal (USA) (Flying Saucer)
P R Rodford E T Wey

Placings: 000-P55   (1154)
2002/03: 22ᴾG, 20⁵S, 22⁵G,

	Starts	1st	2nd	3rd	Win & Pl
Hurdles	3	0	0	0	0
Career Total	6	0	0	0	0

Going: Sf: 0-1 GS: 0-0 Gd: 0-1 GF: - Fm: 0-1
Distance: 2m/2m3: 0-0 2m4-2m7: 0-3 3m+: 0-0
Track: LH: 0-3 RH: 0-0 Tight: 0-2 Gall: 0-0
Aids: Bl: 0-0 Vi: 0-0 Tstrap: 0-0
Best Rating: 73 10/01 Chel 2m110y   good NHF

Erin Alley (IRE)
94   81

10-y-o ch g Be My Native (USA)-Cousin Flo (True Song)

Column 2

D J Wintle L & P Partnership

Placings: 55005/P3P/P/022F1P-553   (4078)
2002/03: 19⁵G, 21⁵S, 20³S,

	Starts	1st	2nd	3rd	Win & Pl
Chases	3	0	0	1	626
Career Total	18	1	2	2	5477
85 1/02 Plum 2m4f F(0-90)HCh				HVY	£2847
			Total win prize-money £2847		

Going: Sf: 0-2 GS: 0-0 Gd: 0-1 GF: - Fm: 0-0
Distance: 2m/2m3: 0-1 2m4-2m7: 0-2 3m+: 0-0
Track: LH: 0-1 RH: 0-0 Tight: 0-2 Gall: 0-0
Aids: Bl: 0-0 Vi: 0-0 Tstrap: 0-0
Best Rating: 104 12/97 Towc 2m   soft   NHF

Modest chaser, stays two and a half miles and acts in the mud.

Erins Lass (IRE)
106   91

6-y-o b m Erin s Isle-Amative (Beau Charmeur (FR))
R Dickin Stratford Members Club

Placings: 00P6-02206   (2168)
2002/03: 19⁰GF, 17²GF, 19²GF, 23⁹G, 19⁶GS,

	Starts	1st	2nd	3rd	Win & Pl
Hurdles	5	0	2	0	2128
Career Total	9	0	2	0	2128

Going: Sf: 0-0 GS: 0-1 Gd: 0-1 GF: - Fm: 0-3
Distance: 2m/2m3: 0-4 2m4-2m7: 0-1 3m+: 0-0
Track: LH: 0-4 RH: 0-1 Tight: 0-3 Gall: 0-0
Aids: Bl: 0-0 Vi: 0-0 Tstrap: 0-0
Best Rating: 79 7/02 Strf 2m3f   gd-fm Hdl

Moderate hurdler; successful at Market Rasen in June; finished fast and just failed to follow up there two weeks later.

Erne Lady (IRE)

6-y-o b m Mandalus-Clonalig Lady (Deep Run)
Mrs L C Taylor Mrs David Plunkett

Placings: P   (3499)
2002/03: 24ᴾGS,

	Starts	1st	2nd	3rd	Win & Pl
Hurdles	1	0	0	0	0
Career Total	1	0	0	0	0

Going: Sf: 0-0 GS: 0-1 Gd: 0-0 GF: - Fm: 0-0
Distance: 2m/2m3: 0-0 2m4-2m7: 0-0 3m+: 0-1
Track: LH: 0-0 RH: 0-1 Tight: 0-0 Gall: 0-0
Aids: Bl: 0-0 Vi: 0-0 Tstrap: 0-0
Best Rating: 0 2/03 Kemp 3m110y   gd-sft Hdl

Ernest Llewellyn

6-y-o b g Afzal-Little Gift (Broadsword (USA))
O O Neill P J R Gardner

Placings: 0   (4542)
2002/03: 16⁰G,

	Starts	1st	2nd	3rd	Win & Pl
NH Flat	1	0	0	0	0
Career Total	1	0	0	0	0

Going: Sf: 0-0 GS: 0-0 Gd: 0-0 GF: - Fm: 0-0
Distance: 2m/2m3: 0-1 2m4-2m7: 0-0 3m+: 0-0

Column 3

Track: LH: 0-0 RH: 0-1 Tight: 0-0 Gall: 0-0
Aids: Bl: 0-0 Vi: 0-0 Tstrap: 0-0
Best Rating: 0   4/03 Ludl 2m   good NHF

Ernest William (IRE)
96(95h)   (108h)102

11-y-o b/br g Phardante (FR)-Minerstown (IRE) (Miners Lamp)
J A Supple (Ferdy Murphy 12/12) Geoff Hubbard Racing

Placings: 0/0F450/11F141/1/52311U-P3PP4462   (4670)
2002/03: 16ᴾG, 21³G, 21ᴾG, 20ᴾGS, 20⁴GS, 21⁴GS, 21²G,

	Starts	1st	2nd	3rd	Win & Pl
Hurdles	3	0	0	1	1060
Chases	5	0	1	0	2023
Career Total	27	7	2	2	34734
117 4/02 MRas 2m6f110yD(0-120)HCh				GD	£6890
95 4/02 MRas 2m1f110yD Ch				GD	£4088
115 4/01 Prth 2m4f110yC(0-130)HHdl				HVY	£5882
117 3/98 Ling 2m3f110yC(0-135)HHdl				GD	£4889
115 2/98 Hntg 2m5f110yC(0-110)HHdl				GD	£2652
100 12/97 Hntg 2m5f110yF(0-100)HHdl				G-S	£2244
93 12/97 Wwck 2m3f C(0-100)HHdl				GD	£2640
			Total win prize-money £29290		

Going: Sf: 0-0 GS: 0-3 Gd: 0-5 GF: - Fm: 0-0
Distance: 2m/2m3: 0-1 2m4-2m7: 0-7 3m+: 0-0
Track: LH: 0-4 RH: 0-4 Tight: 0-3 Gall: 0-2
Aids: Bl: 0-1 Vi: 0-0 Tstrap: 0-0
Best Rating: 117 4/02 MRas 2m6f110y good   Ch

Moderate chaser; comfortable winner of a novices chase and a handicap at Market Rasen in April 2002; stays two and three-quarter miles; acts on a sound surface but handles heavy.

Errand Boy
                 124

9-y-o b g Ardross-Love Match (USA) (Affiliate (USA))
Mrs S J Smith Trevor Hemmings

Placings: 12/161F115/F422U0/2U4222344-F   (0090)
2002/03: 26ᶠG,

	Starts	1st	2nd	3rd	Win & Pl
Chases	1	0	0	0	
Career Total	25	5	7	1	53045
132 3/00 Sand 2m4f110yA HHdl				GD	£16800
132 2/00 Newc 2m C HHdl				HVY	£7085
103 12/99 Catt 2m3f E Hdl				G-F	£1940
105 10/99 Sthl 2m E Hdl				G-S	£2192
119 3/99 Catt 2m H NHF				SFT	£1525
			Total win prize-money £29542		

Going: Sf: 0-0 GS: 0-0 Gd: 0-1 GF: - Fm: 0-0
Distance: 2m/2m3: 0-0 2m4-2m7: 0-0 3m+: 0-1
Track: LH: 0-1 RH: 0-0 Tight: 0-0 Gall: 0-0
Aids: Bl: 0-0 Vi: 0-0 Tstrap: 0-0
Best Rating: 148 4/00 Aint 3m110y good Hdl

A winner of a bumper and four novice hurdles including the 2000 EBF Final, he has some fair form over fences, but keeps on finding one or two too good. Acts on most types of ground and is effective at up to two miles four furlongs. Not the best of jumpers and likes to dominate.

Errigal (FR)
96   62

8-y-o ch g Murmure (FR)-Miss Big John (FR) (Big John (FR))
K C Bailey The Wild Rover Racing Partnership

Placings: 4245104/34P4PF45/00-000P   (3744)

2002/03: 16⁰HY, 22⁰S, 24⁰S, 26ᴾG,

	Starts	1st	2nd	3rd	Win & Pl
Hurdles	4	0	0	0	
Career Total	21	1	1	1	5232
91	1/99	Fknm	2m4f		D Hdl	G-S	£2692

Total win prize-money £2693

Going: Sf: 0-3 GS: 0-0 Gd: 0-1 GF: - Fm: 0-0
Distance: 2m/2m3: 0-1 2m4-2m7: 0-1 3m+: 0-2
Track: LH: 0-0 RH: 0-4 Tight: 0-0 Gall: 0-1
Aids: Bl: 0-0 Vi: 0-0 Tstrap: 0-0
Best Rating: 96 11/00 Wwck 3m110y   heavy   Ch

Erris Express (IRE)
100   91
5-y-o ch h Definite Article-Postie (Sharpo)
J J Quinn Erris Boys

Placings:000   (3830)
2002/03: 16⁰S, 16⁰GS, 16⁰G,

	Starts	1st	2nd	3rd	Win & Pl
NH Flat	1	0	0	0	0
Hurdles	2	0	0	0	
Career Total	3	0	0	0	

Going: Sf: 0-1 GS: 0-1 Gd: 0-1 GF: - Fm: 0-0
Distance: 2m/2m3: 0-3 2m4-2m7: 0-0 3m+: 0-0
Track: LH: 0-3 RH: 0-0 Tight: 0-0 Gall: 0-1
Aids: Bl: 0-0 Vi: 0-0 Tstrap: 0-0
Best Rating: 91 1/03 Donc 2m110y   gd-sft   Hdl

Erro Codigo
95   56
8-y-o b g Formidable (USA)-Home Wrecker (DEN)
(Affiliation Order (USA))
F P Murtagh Mrs Anna Kenny

Placings:0500660/26-0550F04P0   (2301)
2002/03: 17⁰HY, 17⁵G, 16⁵GF, 17⁰G, 17⁷G, 16⁰GF, 16⁴GF, 17ᴾG, 16⁰GS,

	Starts	1st	2nd	3rd	Win & Pl
Hurdles	9	0	0	0	0
Career Total	18	0	1	0	576

Going: Sf: 0-1 GS: 0-1 Gd: 0-4 GF: - Fm: 0-3
Distance: 2m/2m3: 0-9 2m4-2m7: 0-0 3m+: 0-0
Track: LH: 0-9 RH: 0-0 Tight: 0-6 Gall: 0-0
Aids: Bl: 0-0 Vi: 0-0 Tstrap: 0-0
Best Rating: 76 6/02 Hexm 2m110y   gd-fm   Hdl

Escort
103   100
7-y-o b g Most Welcome-Benazir (High Top)
W Clay The Escort Partnership

Placings:2P4/06512533/303P-004464   (0902)
2002/03: 24⁰G, 20⁰G, 22⁴GF, 24⁴G, 16⁸GF, 20⁴G,

	Starts	1st	2nd	3rd	Win & Pl
Hurdles	6	0	0	0	0
Career Total	21	1	2	4	6541
94	12/00	Weth	2m4f110yD(0-110)HHdl	SFT	£3250

Total win prize-money £3250

Going: Sf: 0-0 GS: 0-0 Gd: 0-4 GF: - Fm: 0-2
Distance: 2m/2m3: 0-1 2m4-2m7: 0-3 3m+: 0-2
Track: LH: 0-5 RH: 0-1 Tight: 0-1 Gall: 0-0
Aids: Bl: 0-0 Vi: 0-5 Tstrap: 0-0
Best Rating: 100 5/01 Sthl 3m110y   firm   Hdl

A winner on the Flat, he has been successful over hurdles on soft ground and is effective over two miles four.

Esendi
74   98
8-y-o b g Buckley-Cagaleena (Cagirama)
Miss Venetia Williams T England

Placings:0/P445-U0   (4004)
2002/03: 22⁰HY, 22⁰S,

	Starts	1st	2nd	3rd	Win & Pl
Hurdles	1	0	0	0	
Chases	1	0	0	0	
Career Total	7	0	0	0	375

Going: Sf: 0-2 GS: 0-0 Gd: 0-0 GF: - Fm: 0-0
Distance: 2m/2m3: 0-0 2m4-2m7: 0-2 3m+: 0-0
Track: LH: 0-0 RH: 0-1 Tight: 0-1 Gall: 0-0
Aids: Bl: 0-0 Vi: 0-0 Tstrap: 0-0
Best Rating: 98 10/01 Hrfd 2m1f   soft   Hdl

Moderate form in bumpers and novice hurdles.

Eshbran Lad
100f   88f
6-y-o b g Golden Lahab (USA)-Lansdowne Lady (Orange Bay)
R C Guest P J Harle

Placings:50   (4788)
2002/03: 16⁵GF, 17⁰G,

	Starts	1st	2nd	3rd	Win & Pl
NH Flat	2	0	0	0	0
Career Total	2	0	0	0	0

Going: Sf: 0-0 GS: 0-0 Gd: 0-1 GF: - Fm: 0-1
Distance: 2m/2m3: 0-2 2m4-2m7: 0-0 3m+: 0-0
Track: LH: 0-1 RH: 0-1 Tight: 0-1 Gall: 0-0
Aids: Bl: 0-0 Vi: 0-0 Tstrap: 0-0
Best Rating: 88 3/03 Weth 2m   gd-fm   NHF

Made a pleasing debut when staying on fifth in bumper at Wetherby in March; capable of better in time.

Esher Common (IRE)
92   84
5-y-o b g Common Grounds-Alsahah (IRE) (Unfuwain (USA))
C J Price (D E Cantillon 11/7) Leahall Lodge Racing 1

Placings:00   (3115)
2002/03: 16⁰HY, 16⁰S,

	Starts	1st	2nd	3rd	Win & Pl
Hurdles	2	0	0	0	0
Career Total	2	0	0	0	0

Going: Sf: 0-2 GS: 0-0 Gd: 0-0 GF: - Fm: 0-0
Distance: 2m/2m3: 0-2 2m4-2m7: 0-0 3m+: 0-0
Track: LH: 0-1 RH: 0-1 Tight: 0-0 Gall: 0-2
Aids: Bl: 0-0 Vi: 0-0 Tstrap: 0-2
Best Rating: 84 12/02 Newb 2m110y   heavy   Hdl

Eskleybrook
114(101h)   (88h)153
10-y-o b g Arzanni-Crystal Run Vii (Damsire Unregistered)
V Y Gethin V Y Gethin

Placings:00/P54PP111/1132/11F/4F30U6-11P   (4134)
2002/03: 16¹HY, 16¹G, 16ᴾG,

	Starts	1st	2nd	3rd	Win & Pl
Chases	3	2	0	0	24919
Career Total	26	9	1	2	67543
153	2/03	Kemp	2m	B Ch		GD	£12435
153	2/03	Sand	2m	B HCh		HVY	£12483
149	2/01	Sand	2m	C(0-135)HCh		SFT	£8580
139	1/01	Kemp	2m	D(0-120)HCh		SFT	£5668
123	10/99	Extr	2m1f	E(0-115)HCh		GD	£4143
119	5/99	Strf	2m1f110yC(0-130)HCh			GD	£5725
111	4/99	Bang	2m1f110yF(0-100)HCh			G-S	£4260
134	4/99	Wwck	2m	E(0-115)HCh		SFT	£3028
99	4/99	Hrfd	2m	F(0-110)HCh		G-F	£3550

Total win prize-money £59873

Going: Sf: 1-1 GS: 0-0 Gd: 1-2 GF: - Fm: 0-0
Distance: 2m/2m3: 2-3 2m4-2m7: 0-0 3m+: 0-0
Track: LH: 0-1 RH: 2-2 Tight: 0-0 Gall: 0-1
Aids: Bl: 0-0 Vi: 0-0 Tstrap: 0-0
Best Rating: 153 2/03 Kemp 2m   good   Ch

Smart front-running handicap chaser; caused a surprise when winning a good race at 50/1 at Sandown in February; followed up in conditions event at Kempton; suited by two miles; looks especially suited by soft conditions but acts on good ground too.

Esp Hill
39f   72f
5-y-o ch m Moscow Society (USA)-Heatheridge (IRE) (Carlingford Castle)
L Lungo The Timbertops

Placings:56   (4594)
2002/03: 17⁵G, 16⁶G,

	Starts	1st	2nd	3rd	Win & Pl
NH Flat	2	0	0	0	0
Career Total	2	0	0	0	0

Going: Sf: 0-0 GS: 0-0 Gd: 0-2 GF: - Fm: 0-0
Distance: 2m/2m3: 0-2 2m4-2m7: 0-0 3m+: 0-0
Track: LH: 0-1 RH: 0-1 Tight: 0-0 Gall: 0-0
Aids: Bl: 0-0 Vi: 0-0 Tstrap: 0-0
Best Rating: 72 3/03 Carl 2m1f   good   NHF

Backward-type; beaten a fair way when third in bumper at Hexham in April on third start.

Esperanza Iv (FR)
107   99
11-y-o b m Quart De Vin (FR)-Relizane Iii (FR) (Diaghilev)
M J Roberts Mike Roberts

Placings:6501P3133P/3/2U221434/51243/P26-P233   (0570)
2002/03: 24ᴾGS, 24²GS, 28³G, 24³S,

	Starts	1st	2nd	3rd	Win & Pl
Hurdles	1	0	0	0	0
Chases	3	0	1	2	3040
Career Total	31	4	6	8	28550
105	11/00	Leic	2m7f110yF(0-110)HCh	G-S	£2687
90	2/00	Fknm	3m110y	F(0-100)HCh	GD	£4270
99	2/98	Plum	3m1f110yE Ch		GD	£3263
87	11/97	Towc	3m	D HHdl	GD	£2714

Total win prize-money £12936

Going: Sf: 0-1 GS: 0-2 Gd: 0-1 GF: - Fm: 0-0
Distance: 2m/2m3: 0-0 2m4-2m7: 0-0 3m+: 0-4
Track: LH: 0-3 RH: 0-1 Tight: 0-2 Gall: 0-0
Aids: Bl: 0-0 Vi: 0-0 Tstrap: 0-0
Best Rating: 105 12/00 Leic 2m7f110y   gd-sft   Ch

Consistent if modest handicap chaser. Stays three miles and acts on good to soft ground.

Esprit De Cotte (FR)

11-y-o b g Lute Antique (FR)-Rafale De Cotte (FR) (Italic (FR))
R Gurney (R Parker 26/5) Mrs J M Newsome & Mrs A A Gurney

Placings:1/123/1/3321/2FPP40FP/P06U/450   (4459)
2002/03: 26⁴G, 245F, 21⁰G,

		Starts	1st	2nd	3rd	Win & Pl
Chases		3	0	0	0	0
Career Total		24	4	3	3	62757
113	4/99	Strf	2m6f110yE	Hdl	G-S	£2178
	2/98	Autl	2m6f	Ch	VS	£10101
	5/96	Autl	2m1f110y	Ch	VS	£15810
	1/96	Pau	2m1f	Ch	HVY	£6588
			Total win prize-money £34677

Going:	Sf: 0-0 GS: 0-0 Gd: 0-2 GF: - Fm: 0-1	
Distance:	2m/2m3: 0-0 2m4-2m7: 0-1 3m+: 0-2	
Track:	LH: 0-1 RH: 0-2 Tight: 0-3 Gall: 0-0	
Aids:	Bl: 0-0 Vi: 0-0 Tstrap: 0-0	
Best Rating:	145 11/99 Worc 2m7f110y gd-sft Ch	

Former ex-French chaser, now pointing and hunter/chasing; seems best on easy ground; sometimes wears blinkers.

Ess Of Norway (FR)
96   88

4-y-o gr g Linamix (FR)-Tres De Cem (NOR) (Rainbow Quest (USA))
J C Tuck J C Tuck

Placings:60   (4191)
2002/03: 16⁶S, 16⁰G,

	Starts	1st	2nd	3rd	Win & Pl
Hurdles	2	0	0	0	0
Career Total	2	0	0	0	0

Going:	Sf: 0-1 GS: 0-0 Gd: 0-0 GF: - Fm: 0-0
Distance:	2m/2m3: 0-2 2m4-2m7: 0-0 3m+: 0-0
Track:	LH: 0-1 RH: 0-1 Tight: 0-0 Gall: 0-1
Aids:	Bl: 0-0 Vi: 0-0 Tstrap: 0-0
Best Rating:	88 2/03 Newb 2m110y soft Hdl

Essie
84   48

6-y-o b m Ezzoud (IRE)-Safari Park (Absalom)
Miss M E Rowland Ms D A Stevens

Placings:0   (0407)
2002/03: 17⁰GF,

	Starts	1st	2nd	3rd	Win & Pl
Hurdles	1	0	0	0	0
Career Total	1	0	0	0	0

Going:	Sf: 0-0 GS: 0-0 Gd: 0-0 GF: - Fm: 0-1
Distance:	2m/2m3: 0-1 2m4-2m7: 0-0 3m+: 0-0
Track:	LH: 0-0 RH: 0-1 Tight: 0-1 Gall: 0-0
Aids:	Bl: 0-0 Vi: 0-0 Tstrap: 0-0
Best Rating:	44 6/02 MRas 2m1f110y gd-fm Hdl

Estabella (IRE)
    64

6-y-o ch m Mujtahid (USA)-Lady In Green (Shareef Dancer (USA))

M Wellings J R Sutcliffe

Placings:P0/P0   (2471)
2002/03: 22PG, 16⁰G,

	Starts	1st	2nd	3rd	Win & Pl
Hurdles	2	0	0	0	0
Career Total	4	0	0	0	0

Going:	Sf: 0-0 GS: 0-0 Gd: 0-2 GF: - Fm: 0-0
Distance:	2m/2m3: 0-1 2m4-2m7: 0-1 3m+: 0-0
Track:	LH: 0-1 RH: 0-1 Tight: 0-0 Gall: 0-1
Aids:	Bl: 0-0 Vi: 0-0 Tstrap: 0-0
Best Rating:	64 4/01 Kemp 2m good Hdl

Esters Boy
83   74

5-y-o b g Sure Blade (USA)-Moheli (Ardross)
P G Murphy J Cooper

Placings:000   (4446)
2002/03: 16⁰G, 17⁰G, 16⁰G,

	Starts	1st	2nd	3rd	Win & Pl
NH Flat	2	0	0	0	0
Hurdles	1	0	0	0	0
Career Total	3	0	0	0	0

Going:	Sf: 0-0 GS: 0-0 Gd: 0-3 GF: - Fm: 0-0
Distance:	2m/2m3: 0-3 2m4-2m7: 0-0 3m+: 0-0
Track:	LH: 0-1 RH: 0-2 Tight: 0-0 Gall: 0-0
Aids:	Bl: 0-0 Vi: 0-0 Tstrap: 0-0
Best Rating:	76 9/02 Worc 2m good NHF

Estuary (USA)
101   91

8-y-o ch g Riverman (USA)-Ocean Ballad (Grundy)
Ms A E Embiricos D W Haggie

Placings:6/300-6323   (1218)
2002/03: 16⁶GF, 16³GF, 16²GF, 17³G,

	Starts	1st	2nd	3rd	Win & Pl
Hurdles	4	0	1	2	1679
Career Total	8	0	1	3	2026

Going:	Sf: 0-0 GS: 0-0 Gd: 0-1 GF: - Fm: 0-3
Distance:	2m/2m3: 0-4 2m4-2m7: 0-0 3m+: 0-0
Track:	LH: 0-3 RH: 0-0 Tight: 0-1 Gall: 0-1
Aids:	Bl: 0-0 Vi: 0-0 Tstrap: 0-0
Best Rating:	91 8/02 Hntg 2m110y gd-fm Hdl

He has shown some ability in a bumper and over hurdles, and should be able to make his mark when the ground is fast.

Estupendo (IRE)
102   91

6-y-o b g Tidaro (USA)-Spendapromise (Goldhill)
L Wells David Cox

Placings:00-04PU   (3827)
2002/03: 20⁰GS, 224HY, 21PHY, 24UGS,

	Starts	1st	2nd	3rd	Win & Pl
Hurdles	4	0	0	0	0
Career Total	6	0	0	0	0

Going:	Sf: 0-2 GS: 0-2 Gd: 0-0 GF: - Fm: 0-0
Distance:	2m/2m3: 0-0 2m4-2m7: 0-3 3m+: 0-1
Track:	LH: 0-2 RH: 0-1 Tight: 0-2 Gall: 0-0
Aids:	Bl: 0-1 Vi: 0-0 Tstrap: 0-0

Best Rating: 91 12/02 Folk 2m6f110y heavy Hdl

Eternal Spring (IRE)
97   149

6-y-o b g Persian Bold-Emerald Waters (King s Lake (USA))
J R Fanshawe Paul Green

Placings:043/2142-F14FF   (3640)
2002/03: 16FGS, 21¹G, 24⁴S, 21FGS, 16FGS,

		Starts	1st	2nd	3rd	Win & Pl
Hurdles		5	1	0	0	14003
Career Total		12	2	2	1	39729
149	12/02	Chel	2m5f110yB Hdl	GD	£12958
137	2/02	Newb	2m110y C Hdl	SFT	£6344
		Total win prize-money £19302

Going:	Sf: 0-1 GS: 0-3 Gd: 1-1 GF: - Fm: 0-0
Distance:	2m/2m3: 0-2 2m4-2m7: 1-2 3m+: 0-1
Track:	LH: 1-4 RH: 0-1 Tight: 0-0 Gall: 1-3
Aids:	Bl: 0-0 Vi: 0-0 Tstrap: 0-1
Best Rating:	149 12/02 Chel 2m5f110y good Hdl

Smart hurdler; acts on ground ranging from good to heavy; stays two miles five, but effective over shorter; has worn a tongue tie.

Ettrick (NZ)
108   94

8-y-o b g Hereward The Wake (USA)-Kardinia (NZ) (Creag-An-Sgor)
Mrs Barbara Waring Nicholson McCormack Shapter Frost

Placings:3P5/445PP6P0-1420   (0623)
2002/03: 17¹GF, 16⁴G, 17²G, 17⁰GF,

		Starts	1st	2nd	3rd	Win & Pl
Hurdles		4	1	1	1	3940
Career Total		15	1	1	1	4916
94	5/02	Hrfd	2m1f	E(0-105)HHdl	G-F	£3150
			Total win prize-money £3150

Going:	Sf: 0-0 GS: 0-0 Gd: 0-2 GF: - Fm: 1-2
Distance:	2m/2m3: 1-4 2m4-2m7: 0-0 3m+: 0-0
Track:	LH: 0-1 RH: 1-3 Tight: 0-1 Gall: 0-0
Aids:	Bl: 0-0 Vi: 0-0 Tstrap: 0-0
Best Rating:	94 6/02 Hrfd 2m1f good Hdl

Modest hurdler, suited by two miles and fast ground. Not the most consistent.

Euro Bleu (FR)
105   112

5-y-o b g Franc Bleu Argent (USA)-Princess Card (FR) (Gift Card (FR))
Mrs L Wadham (E Lemartinel 25/1) Hebomapa

Placings:0510   (4462)
2002/03: 18⁰VS, 16⁵HY, 17¹VS, 20⁰G,

		Starts	1st	2nd	3rd	Win & Pl
Hurdles		4	1	0	0	7841
Career Total		4	1	0	0	7841
	1/03	Pau	2m1f110y Hdl	VS	£7169
			Total win prize-money £7169

Going:	Sf: 0-1 GS: 0-0 Gd: 0-1 GF: - Fm: 0-0
Distance:	2m/2m3: 1-3 2m4-2m7: 0-0 3m+: 0-0
Track:	LH: 0-1 RH: 0-0 Tight: 0-1 Gall: 0-0
Aids:	Bl: 0-0 Vi: 0-0 Tstrap: 0-0
Best Rating:	67 4/03 Aint 2m4f good Hdl

Winning hurdler in France; runner-up on second outing here at Uttoxeter in April; suited by soft ground and will stay three miles.

Europa

106   **150**

7-y-o b g Jupiter Island-Dublin Ferry (Celtic Cone)
T P Tate B T Stewart-Brown

Placings: *15/1112/1312FP2-1131F*   (4114)
2002/03: 16¹GF, 19¹GS, 16³G, 19¹G, 20°FG,

	Starts	1st	2nd	3rd	Win & Pl
Chases	5	3	0	1	25617
Career Total	18	9	3	2	50250
150	3/03	Donc	2m3f	C(0-135)HCh	GD £10101
142	12/02	Donc	2m3f	C(0-135)HCh	G-S £8096
119	5/02	Prth	2m	D Ch	G-F £5330
137	1/02	Catt	2m3f	D Ch	G-S £6279
120	12/01	Hexm	2m110y	E Ch	SFT £3003
131	2/01	Bang	2m1f	E Hdl	HVY £2744
143	1/01	Donc	2m4f	D Hdl	GD £4007
112	11/00	Wwck	2m	N Hdl	HVY £1575
119	3/00	Donc	2m110y	H NHF	GD £1631

Total win prize-money £42767

Going: Sf: 0-0 GS: 1-1 Gd: 1-3 GF: - Fm: 1-1
Distance: 2m/2m3: 3-4 2m4-2m7: 0-1 3m+: 0-0
Track: LH: 2-4 RH: 1-1 Tight: 0-0 Gall: 0-2
Aids: Bl: 0-0 Vi: 0-0 Tstrap: 0-0
Best Rating: 150 3/03 Donc 2m3f   good   Ch

Very useful chaser; has a fine wins-to-runs ratio over hurdles and fences; stays two and half miles; handles any going but prefers decent ground.

Eveies Boy (IRE)

8-y-o b g Shardari-Bloomfield (IRE) (Alzao (USA))
Richard Mathias J F Apperley

Placings: 00/040S/FP-3   (4487)
2002/03: 16³GF,

	Starts	1st	2nd	3rd	Win & Pl
Chases	1	0	0	1	220
Career Total	9	0	0	1	387

Going: Sf: 0-0 GS: 0-0 Gd: 0-0 GF: - Fm: 0-1
Distance: 2m/2m3: 0-1 2m4-2m7: 0-0 3m+: 0-0
Track: LH: 0-0 RH: 0-1 Tight: 0-0 Gall: 0-0
Aids: Bl: 0-0 Vi: 0-0 Tstrap: 0-0
Best Rating: 72 4/03 Hrfd 2m   gd-fm   Ch

Even More (IRE)

104   **101**

8-y-o b g Husyan (USA)-Milan Moss (Le Moss)
R H Alner G Keirle

Placings: 02P33   (4438)
2002/03: 23°GS, 25²GS, 32°G, 25³F, 24³G,

	Starts	1st	2nd	3rd	Win & Pl
Chases	5	0	1	2	4383
Career Total	5	0	1	2	4383

Going: Sf: 0-0 GS: 0-2 Gd: 0-2 GF: - Fm: 0-1
Distance: 2m/2m3: 0-0 2m4-2m7: 0-0 3m+: 0-5
Track: LH: 0-1 RH: 0-4 Tight: 0-0 Gall: 0-1
Aids: Bl: 0-0 Vi: 0-0 Tstrap: 0-0
Best Rating: 113 2/03 Winc 3m1f110y gd-sft Ch

Decent chaser; stays well; acts on good ground; has shown promise over fences.

Evening Out

Placings: 0   (0623)
2002/03: 16°GF,

	Starts	1st	2nd	3rd	Win & Pl
NH Flat	1	0	0	0	
Career Total	1	0	0	0	

6-y-o b g Charmer-Princess Dancer (Alzao (USA))
P D Williams Mrs Denise Williams

Going: Sf: 0-0 GS: 0-0 Gd: 0-0 GF: - Fm: 0-1
Distance: 2m/2m3: 0-1 2m4-2m7: 0-0 3m+: 0-0
Track: LH: 0-1 RH: 0-0 Tight: 0-0 Gall: 0-0
Aids: Bl: 0-0 Vi: 0-0 Tstrap: 0-0
Best Rating: 0 7/02 Worc 2m   gd-fm NHF

Evening Splash (IRE)

86   **54**

7-y-o b m Royal Fountain-Red Dusk (Deep Run)
Mrs J K M Oliver The Bank Partnership

Placings: 5-000P   (2923)
2002/03: 17°S, 22°S, 17°HY, 22°HY,

	Starts	1st	2nd	3rd	Win & Pl
NH Flat	1	0	0	0	0
Hurdles	3	0	0	0	0
Career Total	5	0	0	0	0

Going: Sf: 0-4 GS: 0-0 Gd: 0-0 GF: - Fm: 0-0
Distance: 2m/2m3: 0-2 2m4-2m7: 0-2 3m+: 0-0
Track: LH: 0-2 RH: 0-2 Tight: 0-1 Gall: 0-0
Aids: Bl: 0-0 Vi: 0-0 Tstrap: 0-0
Best Rating: 89 3/02 Ayr 2m   heavy NHF

Ever Blessed (IRE)

93   **111**

11-y-o b g Lafontaine (USA)-Sanctify (Joshua)
P J Hobbs Stewart Andrew

Placings: 12/3/232/2111F/11P/P-U0   (2243)
2002/03: 24°S, 26³GS,

	Starts	1st	2nd	3rd	Win & Pl
Chases	2	0	0	0	
Career Total	17	6	4	2	77457
155	11/99	Newb	3m2f110yA HCh		G-S £48880
137	10/99	Chep	3m	B(0-145)HCh	SFT £8533
134	3/99	Bang	3m110y	D Ch	SFT £4548
110	3/99	Towc	2m6f	E Ch	SFT £3028
132	1/99	Leic	2m7f110yF Ch		SFT £2212
117	2/96	Asct	2m110y	H NHF	SFT £2851

Total win prize-money £70054

Going: Sf: 0-1 GS: 0-1 Gd: 0-0 GF: - Fm: 0-0
Distance: 2m/2m3: 0-0 2m4-2m7: 0-0 3m+: 0-2
Track: LH: 0-2 RH: 0-0 Tight: 0-0 Gall: 0-1
Aids: Bl: 0-0 Vi: 0-0 Tstrap: 0-0
Best Rating: 155 11/99 Newb 3m2f110y gd-sft Ch

A smart handicapper, he won the 1999 Hennessy for Mark Pitman. Never easy to train, he was deliberately sent to the 2000 Gold Cup without a prep race, but found conditions too fast and was pulled up, reportedly injuring his off-fore knee. Pulled up on his return after nearly two years off, and unseated on his first run of 2002/2003. Acts on soft ground and stays three and a quarter miles.

Ever Present (IRE)

107   **122**

5-y-o ch g Presenting-My Grand Rose (IRE) (Executive Perk)
A King Ramsay Donald Brown

Placings: 51245   (3850)
2002/03: 18°S, 17¹S, 17²GS, 17⁴GS, 19⁵GS,

	Starts	1st	2nd	3rd	Win & Pl
NH Flat	1	0	0	0	
Hurdles	4	1	1	0	5046
Career Total	5	1	1	0	5046
109	11/02	Bang	2m1f	E Hdl	SFT £3178

Total win prize-money £3178

Going: Sf: 1-2 GS: 0-3 Gd: 0-0 GF: - Fm: 0-0
Distance: 2m/2m3: 1-4 2m4-2m7: 0-1 3m+: 0-0
Track: LH: 1-4 RH: 0-1 Tight: 1-3 Gall: 0-1
Aids: Bl: 0-0 Vi: 0-0 Tstrap: 0-0
Best Rating: 122 1/03 Chel 2m1f   gd-sft Hdl

Fair novice hurdler; suited by trips of around two miles; best on soft ground.

Everready

103f   **97f**

5-y-o b g Afzal-Sister Shot (Celtic Cone)
P J Hobbs Ms C Hehir

Placings: 0-43   (4090)
2002/03: 18⁴GS, 16³GS,

	Starts	1st	2nd	3rd	Win & Pl
NH Flat	2	0	0	1	542
Career Total	3	0	0	1	542

Going: Sf: 0-0 GS: 0-2 Gd: 0-0 GF: - Fm: 0-0
Distance: 2m/2m3: 0-2 2m4-2m7: 0-0 3m+: 0-0
Track: LH: 0-1 RH: 0-0 Tight: 0-1 Gall: 0-0
Aids: Bl: 0-0 Vi: 0-0 Tstrap: 0-0
Best Rating: 99 3/03 Strf 2m110y gd-sft NHF

Out of a full-sister to Champion Hurdle winner Celtic Shot; has shown ability in bumers on easy ground.

Eviyrn (IRE)

82   **66**

7-y-o b g In The Wings-Evrana (USA) (Nureyev (USA))
J R Jenkins S C Finance Limited

Placings: 65056/0143500P/32FP-00P   (4217)
2002/03: 16°HY, 22°S, 22°G,

	Starts	1st	2nd	3rd	Win & Pl
Hurdles	3	0	0	0	
Career Total	20	1	1	2	4497
86	10/00	Plum	2m	E(0-105)HHdl	SFT £2576

Total win prize-money £2576

Going: Sf: 0-2 GS: 0-0 Gd: 0-1 GF: - Fm: 0-0
Distance: 2m/2m3: 0-1 2m4-2m7: 0-2 3m+: 0-0
Track: LH: 0-1 RH: 0-2 Tight: 0-1 Gall: 0-0
Aids: Bl: 0-0 Vi: 0-0 Tstrap: 0-0
Best Rating: 90 12/00 Donc 2m110y heavy Hdl

Evolution (IRE)

98   **54**

6-y-o b m Phardante (FR)-Cape Breeze (IRE) (Strong Gale)
M J Gingell (G H Yardley 12/12) The Equus Club

Placings: 56/40034-6066050   (4428)
2002/03: 20°S, 21°GS, 19°GS, 23°S, 22°HY, 20°GF, 25°GF,

	Starts	1st	2nd	3rd	Win & Pl
Hurdles	7	0	0	0	0
Career Total	14	0	0	1	636

Going: Sf: 0-3 GS: 0-2 Gd: 0-0 GF: - Fm: 0-2
Distance: 2m/2m3: 0-0 2m4-2m7: 0-5 3m+: 0-2
Track: LH: 0-2 RH: 0-4 Tight: 0-4 Gall: 0-1
Aids: Bl: 0-1 Vi: 0-0 Tstrap: 0-0
Best Rating: 79 2/01 Wwck 2m soft NHF

Evolution Lad (IRE)
90   59
7-y-o b g Sharp Charter-Neatly Does It (IRE) (Camden Town)
D J Caro Evolution Films Limited

Placings:1300P-P06 (1932)
2002/03: 19⁹GF, 21⁰F, 17⁶GS,

	Starts	1st	2nd	3rd	Win & Pl
Hurdles	3	0	0	0	0
Career Total	8	1	0	1	1995
91 10/01 Ludl 2m H NHF				G-F	£1750

Total win prize-money £1750

Going: Sf: 0-0 GS: 0-1 Gd: 0-0 GF: - Fm: 0-2
Distance: 2m/2m3: 0-1 2m4-2m7: 0-2 3m+: 0-0
Track: LH: 0-0 RH: 0-3 Tight: 0-1 Gall: 0-0
Aids: Bl: 0-0 Vi: 0-0 Tstrap: 0-0
Best Rating: 91 10/01 Ludl 2m gd-fm NHF

Ewar Bold
102   90
10-y-o b g Bold Arrangement-Monaneigue Lady (Julio Mariner)
K G Wingrove L T Woodhouse

Placings:U06655P43/0/P/F/03F01-2646P (4347)
2002/03: 21¹GS, 16²GS, 24⁸G, 19⁴G, 25⁶G, 25⁵GF,

	Starts	1st	2nd	3rd	Win & Pl
Hurdles	6	1	1	0	2557
Career Total	22	1	1	2	3091
90 4/02 Towc 2m5f G Hdl				G-S	£1981

Total win prize-money £1981

Going: Sf: 0-0 GS: 1-2 Gd: 0-3 GF: - Fm: 0-1
Distance: 2m/2m3: 0-1 2m4-2m7: 1-2 3m+: 0-3
Track: LH: 0-2 RH: 1-4 Tight: 0-0 Gall: 0-0
Aids: Bl: 0-0 Vi: 0-0 Tstrap: 1-6
Best Rating: 90 6/02 Hrfd 2m3f110y good Hdl

Selling-class hurdler, suited by cut in the ground.

Exact (FR)
11-y-o ch g Beyssac (FR)-Valse De Sienne (FR) (Petit Montmorency (USA))
Mrs R L Elliot (N P Williams 1/5) Miss V A Russell

Placings:PPP4/U655034/1/P35-5 (4508)
2002/03: 25⁵G,

	Starts	1st	2nd	3rd	Win & Pl
Chases	1	0	0	0	0
Career Total	16	1	0	2	3971
103 5/99 Chep 3m E(0-115)HHdl				GD	£2542

Total win prize-money £2542

Going: Sf: 0-0 GS: 0-0 Gd: 0-1 GF: - Fm: 0-0
Distance: 2m/2m3: 0-0 2m4-2m7: 0-0 3m+: 0-1
Track: LH: 0-1 RH: 0-0 Tight: 0-1 Gall: 0-0
Aids: Bl: 0-0 Vi: 0-0 Tstrap: 0-0

Best Rating: 106 4/99 Uttx 2m4f gd-sft Ch

Modest pointer/hunter chaser. Suited by good ground or faster and front-running tactics. Wears blinkers and has worn a tongue tie.

Exalted (IRE)
95   80
10-y-o b g High Estate-Heavenward (USA) (Conquistador Cielo (USA))
T A K Cuthbert Mrs Elva Maxwell & Roy Thorburn

Placings:240/12046R30/56506423235126/03202104/4025 6/45035F-600 (4475)
2002/03: 24⁸GS, 20⁹G, 20⁰G,

	Starts	1st	2nd	3rd	Win & Pl
Hurdles	3	0	0	0	0
Career Total	47	3	8	5	24116
118 1/00 Ayr 2m4f B(0-145)HHdl				SFT	£6899
106 2/99 Ayr 2m4f F(0-95)HHdl				SFT	£2878
109 10/97 Hrfd 2m1f E Hdl				G-F	£2290

Total win prize-money £12068

Going: Sf: 0-0 GS: 0-1 Gd: 0-2 GF: - Fm: 0-0
Distance: 2m/2m3: 0-0 2m4-2m7: 0-2 3m+: 0-1
Track: LH: 0-1 RH: 0-2 Tight: 0-1 Gall: 0-0
Aids: Bl: 0-0 Vi: 0-0 Tstrap: 0-0
Best Rating: 119 1/01 Ayr 2m4f gd-sft Hdl

He is a bit of a character and not the most reliable of sorts. Stays well and acts in soft ground. Mixes turf Flat racing with hurdling. Suited by a strong pace.

Excellent Vibes (IRE)
97   75
5-y-o b g Doyoun-Hawait Al Barr (Green Desert (USA))
J L Spearing Thomas D Goodman

Placings:060 (4536)
2002/03: 16⁰S, 19⁶F, 24⁰G,

	Starts	1st	2nd	3rd	Win & Pl
NH Flat	1	0	0	0	0
Hurdles	2	0	0	0	0
Career Total	3	0	0	0	0

Going: Sf: 0-1 GS: 0-0 Gd: 0-1 GF: - Fm: 0-1
Distance: 2m/2m3: 0-1 2m4-2m7: 0-1 3m+: 0-1
Track: LH: 0-0 RH: 0-3 Tight: 0-1 Gall: 0-0
Aids: Bl: 0-0 Vi: 0-1 Tstrap: 0-0
Best Rating: 43 4/03 Ludl 3m good Hdl

Executive Choice (IRE)
97   58
9-y-o b g Don t Forget Me-Shadia (USA) (Naskra (USA))
B Ellison (Miss V Haigh 29/4) Sporting Occasions Racing No 3

Placings:26/12142400/3061U12405/05405UPP0B6-0P04P (1705)
2002/03: 16⁶G, 19⁰GF, 21⁸PG, 22⁰G, 17⁴GF, 17⁰PG,

	Starts	1st	2nd	3rd	Win & Pl
Career Total	36	4	4	1	11666
109 12/00 Fknm 2m G(0-95)HHdl				G-S	£1802
102 11/00 Sedg 2m1f G(0-95)HHdl				SFT	£1631
105 8/99 Ctml 2m1f110yE(0-105)HHdl				GD	£2302
100 7/99 Sedg 2m1f E Hdl				G-F	£2512

Total win prize-money £8250

Executive Decision (IRE)
107(109h)   (121h)123
9-y-o ch g Classic Music (USA)-Bengala (FR) (Hard To Beat)
Mrs L Wadham Ms K J Austin

Placings:116/2055150/14/F/6U26-PP263133 (4612)
2002/03: 20⁰PG, 16⁶PS, 16²GS, 16⁶S, 17³HY, 16¹G, 16³S, 16³G,

	Starts	1st	2nd	3rd	Win & Pl
Hurdles	5	0	1	1	2463
Chases	3	1	0	2	10078
Career Total	25	5	3	3	32740
127 2/03 Hntg 2m110y D(0-120)HCh				GD	£6630
129 11/99 NAbb 2m110y E Ch				SFT	£3156
133 3/99 Chep 2m110y C(0-130)HHdl				HVY	£4417
117 2/98 Navn 2m Hdl				SFT	£5956
119 12/97 Leop 2m Hdl				HVY	£4069

Total win prize-money £24230

Going: Sf: 0-4 GS: 0-1 Gd: 1-3 GF: - Fm: 0-0
Distance: 2m/2m3: 1-7 2m4-2m7: 0-1 3m+: 0-0
Track: LH: 0-3 RH: 1-5 Tight: 0-2 Gall: 1-2
Aids: Bl: 0-0 Vi: 1-7 Tstrap: 0-0
Best Rating: 133 3/99 Chel 2m1f gd-sft Hdl

Fair hurdler, decent chaser; best over two miles; acts on ground ranging from good to heavy; has worn blinkers and a visor.

Executive Flyer (IRE)
91   (16h)70+
12-y-o ch g Executive Perk-Luton Flyer (Condorcet (FR))
Mrs A M Thorpe Mrs A M Thorpe

Placings:100P/PU0001/40/0203U6/0-0665 (1059)
2002/03: 17⁰GG, 16⁶GF, 17⁶GF, 20⁵G,

	Starts	1st	2nd	3rd	Win & Pl
Hurdles	1	0	0	0	0
Chases	3	0	0	0	0
Career Total	23	2	1	1	7362
87 4/99 Wxfd 2m (0-102)HHdl				Y-S	£2455
108 9/95 List 2m NHF				GD	£3730

Total win prize-money £6185

Going: Sf: 0-0 GS: 0-0 Gd: 0-1 GF: - Fm: 0-3
Distance: 2m/2m3: 0-3 2m4-2m7: 0-1 3m+: 0-0
Track: LH: 0-3 RH: 0-1 Tight: 0-2 Gall: 0-0
Aids: Bl: 0-0 Vi: 0-0 Tstrap: 0-0
Best Rating: 108 9/95 List 2m good NHF

Executive Mistress (IRE)
52f   42f
6-y-o ch m Executive Perk-Buckland Filleigh (IRE) (Buckskin (FR))
P R Rodford M Lewis-Jones, J Beer, Mrs J Dacey

Placings:0 (0328)
2002/03: 16⁰G,

	Starts	1st	2nd	3rd	Win & Pl
NH Flat	1	0	0	0	

Career Total	1	0	0	0

Going: Sf: 0-0 GS: 0-0 Gd: 0-1 GF: - Fm: 0-0
Distance: 2m/2m3: 0-1 2m4-2m7: 0-0 3m+: 0-0
Track: LH: 0-1 RH: 0-0 Tight: 0-0 Gall: 0-0
Aids: Bl: 0-0 Vi: 0-0 Tstrap: 0-0
Best Rating: 42 5/02 Worc 2m   good NHF

Executive Network

5-y-o b g Silca Blanka (IRE)-Scene Stealer (Scenic)
A D Smith Duckhaven Stud

Placings:P   (4251)
2002/03: 17PG,

	Starts	1st	2nd	3rd	Win & Pl
Hurdles	1	0	0	0	
Career Total	1	0	0	0	

Going: Sf: 0-0 GS: 0-0 Gd: 0-1 GF: - Fm: 0-0
Distance: 2m/2m3: 0-1 2m4-2m7: 0-0 3m+: 0-0
Track: LH: 0-0 RH: 0-1 Tight: 0-0 Gall: 0-0
Aids: Bl: 0-0 Vi: 0-0 Tstrap: 0-0
Best Rating: 0 3/03 Extr 2m1f   good Hdl

Executive Office (IRE)
97   91

10-y-o bl g Executive Perk-Lilly s Pride (IRE) (Long Pond)
S T Lewis Simon T Lewis

Placings:0000/6/5230435/PPF-P114P   (3959)
2002/03: 25PHY, 20¹S, 20¹S, 20⁴GS, 24PS,

	Starts	1st	2nd	3rd	Win & Pl
Hurdles	1	0	0	0	0
Chases	4	2	0	0	8800
Career Total	20	2	1	2	10872
91	2/03	Leic	2m4f110yE(0-105)HCh	SFT	£4927
81	1/03	Wwck	2m4f110yF(0-90)HCh	SFT	£3542

Total win prize-money £8469

Going: Sf: 2-4 GS: 0-1 Gd: 0-0 GF: - Fm: 0-0
Distance: 2m/2m3: 0-0 **2m4-2m7:** 2-3 3m+: 0-2
Track: LH: 1-2 RH: 1-2 Tight: 0-0 Gall: 0-0
Aids: Bl: 0-0 Vi: 0-0 Tstrap: 0-0
Best Rating: 93 10/00 Extr 2m7f110y good Ch

Moderate hurdler/chaser; seemingly best on soft ground; two and a half miles seems his ideal trip.

Executive Question (IRE)
65f   18f

5-y-o ch g Executive Perk-Fair Survival (IRE) (Le Moss)
A Robson A Robson

Placings:0   (4778)
2002/03: 16⁰G,

	Starts	1st	2nd	3rd	Win & Pl
NH Flat	1	0	0	0	
Career Total	1	0	0	0	

Going: Sf: 0-0 GS: 0-0 Gd: 0-1 GF: - Fm: 0-0
Distance: 2m/2m3: 0-1 2m4-2m7: 0-0 3m+: 0-0
Track: LH: 0-0 RH: 0-1 Tight: 0-0 Gall: 0-0
Aids: Bl: 0-0 Vi: 0-0 Tstrap: 0-0
Best Rating: 18 4/03 Prth 2m110y good NHF

Exhibit (IRE)
79   53

5-y-o b g Royal Academy (USA)-Juno Madonna (IRE) (Sadler s Wells (USA))
N J Hawke (R Hannon 14/10) Truscotts (Barnstaple) Ltd - Peugeot

Placings:P   (4001)
2002/03: 16PS,

	Starts	1st	2nd	3rd	Win & Pl
Hurdles	1	0	0	0	
Career Total	1	0	0	0	

Going: Sf: 0-1 GS: 0-0 Gd: 0-0 GF: - Fm: 0-0
Distance: 2m/2m3: 0-1 2m4-2m7: 0-0 3m+: 0-0
Track: LH: 0-0 RH: 0-1 Tight: 0-0 Gall: 0-0
Aids: Bl: 0-0 Vi: 0-0 Tstrap: 0-0
Best Rating: 0 3/03 Winc 2m   soft Hdl

Existential (FR)
103   120

8-y-o b g Exit To Nowhere (USA)-Lyceana (USA) (Super Concorde (USA))
P F Nicholls H B Geddes

Placings:5/32P3P/2/4-135215   (3889)
2002/03: 21¹GS, 20³GS, 225S, 24²S, 24¹GS, 225S,

	Starts	1st	2nd	3rd	Win & Pl
Chases	6	2	1	1	10534
Career Total	14	2	3	3	13083
120	2/03	Kemp	3m	E(0-115)HCh	G-S	£4329
120	10/02	Fknm	2m5f110y		F(0-100)HCh	

G-S £3779

Total win prize-money £8109

Going: Sf: 0-2 GS: 2-3 Gd: 0-1 GF: - Fm: 0-0
Distance: 2m/2m3: 0-0 2m4-2m7: 1-4 3m+: 1-2
Track: LH: 1-4 RH: 0-2 Tight: **1-3** Gall: 0-1
Aids: Bl: 0-0 Vi: 0-0 Tstrap: 0-0
Best Rating: 120 2/03 Kemp 3m   gd-sft Ch

Fair handicap chaser. Suited by trips of around two and a half miles to three miles. Acts on a soft surface.

Exit Swinger (FR)
115(99h)   (139h)150

8-y-o b g Exit To Nowhere (USA)-Morganella (FR) (D Arras (FR))
M C Pipe Sandicroft Stud I

Placings:26/5F306431221051/263F/316420-U0403 (4472)
2002/03: 20UGS, 21³G, 21⁴HY, 16⁶G, 21³G,

	Starts	1st	2nd	3rd	Win & Pl
Chases	5	0	0	1	9700
Career Total	31	4	5	5	114449
155	12/01	Newb	2m1f	C(0-135)HCh	SFT	£9510
136	4/00	Sand	2m110yC HCh		SFT	£17517
136	2/00	Chep	2m4f	D Hdl	SFT	£3334
	12/99	Autl	2m1f110y Ch		HLD	£6997

Total win prize-money £37360

Going: Sf: 0-1 GS: 0-1 Gd: 0-3 GF: - Fm: 0-0
Distance: 2m/2m3: 0-1 2m4-2m7: 0-4 3m+: 0-0
Track: LH: 0-5 RH: 0-0 Tight: 0-0 Gall: 0-4
Aids: Bl: 0-0 Vi: 0-0 Tstrap: 0-0
Best Rating: 155 3/02 Chel 2m110y good Ch

Useful hurdler/smart chaser; a winner over fences in France, he has won two chases in this country, but best runs have included two placings in the Thomas Pink Gold Cup and a third in the Topham at Aintree in April; looks handicapped to the hilt; unproven beyond two and a half miles; likes to get his toe in.

Exit To Wave (FR)
120   146d

7-y-o ch g Exit To Nowhere (USA)-Hereke (Blakeney)
P F Nicholls Malcolm Pearce & Gerry Mizel Ii

Placings:11111P344/P1F1P142U/440-4320PUP   (4557)
2002/03: 24⁴S, 20³GS, 24²S, 24⁰G, 34PS, 21UG, 33PG,

	Starts	1st	2nd	3rd	Win & Pl
Chases	7	0	1	1	17600
Career Total	28	8	2	2	88268
148	3/01	Wwck	2m110y	B HCh	HVY	£10717
136	1/01	Asct	2m	A Ch	G-S	£15000
125	11/00	Wwck	2m110y	D Ch	HVY	£4039
	12/99	Cagn	2m2f	Hdl	SFT	£7685
	12/99	Bord	2m2f	Hdl	GD	£3842
	11/99	Bord	2m2f	Hdl	VS	£3445
	10/99	Bord	2m110y	Hdl	HVY	£3767
	10/99	Mtbn	2m1f110y	Hdl	SFT	£2368

Total win prize-money £50863

Going: Sf: 0-3 GS: 0-1 Gd: 0-3 GF: - Fm: 0-0
Distance: 2m/2m3: 0-0 2m4-2m7: 0-2 3m+: 0-5
Track: LH: 0-5 RH: 0-2 Tight: 0-1 Gall: 0-1
Aids: Bl: 0-0 Vi: 0-0 Tstrap: 0-7
Best Rating: 150 11/01 Weth 2m4f110y good Ch

Useful handicap chaser; just failed at Ascot in December 2002; best on a soft surface; stays three miles; wears a tongue tie.

Exodous (ARG)
102   97

7-y-o ch g Equalize (USA)-Empire Glory (ARG) (Good Manners (USA))
J A B Old W E Sturt

Placings:65-303   (4371)
2002/03: 16³GS, 16⁰GF, 16³G,

	Starts	1st	2nd	3rd	Win & Pl
Hurdles	3	0	0	2	1243
Career Total	5	0	0	2	1243

Going: Sf: 0-0 GS: 0-1 Gd: 0-1 GF: - Fm: 0-1
Distance: 2m/2m3: 0-3 2m4-2m7: 0-0 3m+: 0-0
Track: LH: 0-2 RH: 0-1 Tight: 0-0 Gall: 0-0
Aids: Bl: 0-0 Vi: 0-0 Tstrap: 0-0
Best Rating: 97 3/03 Asct 2m110y good Hdl

Won six times on the Flat in Argentina at up to a mile and a half. Now with Jim Old, has only shown moderate form over hurdles.

Exotic Profiles

9-y-o ch m Minster Son-Ragroyal (Royal Palace)
Miss K M George R E Baskerville

Placings:00/060516/PR   (0180)
2002/03: 17PG, 22RGF,

	Starts	1st	2nd	3rd	Win & Pl
Hurdles	1	0	0	0	0
Chases	1	0	0	0	0
Career Total	10	1	0	0	1837
77	11/99	NAbb	2m1f	G Hdl	SFT	£1837

Total win prize-money £1837

Going: Sf: 0-0 GS: 0-0 Gd: 0-1 GF: - Fm: 0-1
Distance: 2m/2m3: 0-1 2m4-2m7: 0-1 3m+: 0-0
Track: LH: 0-2 RH: 0-2 Tight: 0-0 Gall: 0-0

Aids: Bl: 0-0 Vi: 0-0 Tstrap: 0-0
Best Rating: 77   11/99   NAbb   2m1f   soft   Hdl

Expense Account (IRE)

(96h)   (67h)
9-y-o b m Executive Perk-Cranagh Lady (Le Bavard (FR))
Mrs H Dalton   Paul O Connell & Aidan Walls

Placings: 00/50PB-UP   (0215)
2002/03: 20ᵁGF, 25ᴾG,

	Starts	1st	2nd	3rd	Win & Pl
Chases	2	0	0	0	
Career Total	8	0	0	0	0

Going: Sf: 0-0 GS: 0-0 Gd: 0-1 GF: - Fm: 0-1
Distance: 2m/2m3: 0-0 2m4-2m7: 0-1 3m+: 0-1
Track: LH: 0-0 RH: 0-2 Tight: 0-1 Gall: 0-0
Aids: Bl: 0-1 Vi: 0-0 Tstrap: 0-0
Best Rating: 67   11/01   Towc   2m5f   soft   Hdl

Exstoto

106   114
6-y-o b g Mtoto-Stoproveritate (Scorpio (FR))
R A Fahey   J D Clark And Partners

Placings: 4/101313F241-523P263   (4713)
2002/03: 20⁵GS, 21²GS, 19³GS, 20ᴾS, 20²GF, 22⁶GF, 20³GF,

	Starts	1st	2nd	3rd	Win & Pl
Hurdles	7	0	2	2	7359
Career Total	18	4	3	4	22687
108	4/02	Weth	2m4f110yB(0-145)HHdl	GD	£5109
113	10/01	MRas	2m3f110yD Hdl	G-S	£3430
97	7/01	Sedg	2m1f	H NHF	£1536
97	5/01	Sthl	2m	H NHF	£1564

Total win prize-money £11641

Going: Sf: 0-1 GS: 0-3 Gd: 0-0 GF: - Fm: 0-3
Distance: 2m/2m3: 0-0 2m4-2m7: 0-7 3m+: 0-0
Track: LH: 0-5 RH: 0-2 Tight: 0-1 Gall: 0-0
Aids: Bl: 0-0 Vi: 0-0 Tstrap: 0-0
Best Rating: 114   3/03   Weth   2m4f110y   gd-fm   Hdl

Fair hurdler; dual bumper winner on fast ground; stays two and three quarter miles; effective on good or softer ground.

Exterior Profiles (IRE)

99
13-y-o b g Good Thyne (USA)-Best Of Kin (Pry)
Miss K M George   Miss K George

Placings: 1/121550F3/1F4U3F/F/P150552U43263604234-5P005F   (3933)
2002/03: 19⁶GS, 19ᴾS, 16⁶S, 19⁰GS, 22⁵GS, 22ᶠS,

	Starts	1st	2nd	3rd	Win & Pl
Hurdles	6	0	0	0	
Career Total	41	5	4	5	16069
100	5/01	Hexm	2m4f110yE(0-115)HHdl	G-F	£1949
114	5/96	Uttx	2m4f110yD Hdl	G-F	£2871
115	11/95	Kemp	2m	D Hdl	GD	£2780
111	5/95	Wwck	2m	H NHF	G-F	£1602
111	4/95	Ayr	2m	H NHF	G-F	£1329

Total win prize-money £10532

Going: Sf: 0-3 GS: 0-3 Gd: 0-0 GF: - Fm: 0-0
Distance: 2m/2m3: 0-2 2m4-2m7: 0-4 3m+: 0-0
Track: LH: 0-2 RH: 0-4 Tight: 0-3 Gall: 0-0
Aids: Bl: 0-0 Vi: 0-0 Tstrap: 0-0

Best Rating: 127   3/97   Wwck   2m4f110y   good   Ch

Plating-class hurdler, suited by two and a half miles and stays three. Likes to make the running.

Extra Cache (NZ)

98(109h)   (121h)117
10-y-o br g Cache Of Gold (USA)-Gizmo (NZ) (Jubilee Wine (USA))
O Brennan   Lady Anne Bentinck

Placings: 3/1432/114643-42U14211   (4680)
2002/03: 16⁴F, 21²S, 21ᵁS, 19¹GS, 19⁴G, 23²G, 20¹G, 20¹GF,

	Starts	1st	2nd	3rd	Win & Pl
Chases	8	3	2	0	16660
Career Total	19	6	3	3	27232
110	4/03	Hntg	2m4f110yE Ch	G-F	£4158
114	3/03	Hntg	2m4f110yE Ch	GD	£3900
117	12/02	Donc	2m3f	D Ch	G-S	£4918
121	5/01	Weth	2m	E(0-115)HHdl	FRM	£2562
114	5/01	Weth	2m	E(0-115)HHdl	GD	£2632
108	5/00	Towc	2m	E Hdl	G-F	£2534

Total win prize-money £20705

Going: Sf: 0-2 GS: 1-1 Gd: 1-3 GF: - Fm: 1-2
Distance: 2m/2m3: 1-3 2m4-2m7: 2-4 3m+: 0-1
Track: LH: 1-5 RH: 2-2 Tight: 0-2 Gall: 2-2
Aids: Bl: 0-0 Vi: 0-0 Tstrap: 0-0
Best Rating: 121   5/01   Weth   2m   firm   Hdl

Winner three times over hurdles and opened his account over fences at Doncaster in December 2002; has since scored twice at Huntingdon; stays two and a half miles; acts on most types of ground.

Extra Jack (FR)

109(79h)   (89h)139
11-y-o b g Neustrien (FR)-Union Jack Iii (FR) (Mister Jack (FR))
P F Nicholls   Sir Robert Ogden

Placings: 511/P/0450/12061011031231/0PF1/511420-5425550   (4472)
2002/03: 20⁵S, 20⁴GS, 20²HY, 20⁵G, 16⁵HY, 17⁵S, 21⁰G,

	Starts	1st	2nd	3rd	Win & Pl
Hurdles	1	0	0	0	0
Chases	6	0	1	0	7281
Career Total	39	11	4	2	135825
151	12/01	Chep	2m3f110yC(0-135)HCh	G-S	£10270
147	11/01	Chep	2m3f110yC(0-130)HCh	SFT	£7322
144	4/01	Prth	2m	B(0-150)HCh	HVY	£9818
123	4/00	Strf	2m6f110yE Hdl	GD	£2646
	12/99	Cagn	2m5f110y Hdl	GD	£6459
	11/99	Autl	2m3f	Ch	HLD	£6997
	10/99	Autl	2m3f	Ch	HVY	£6997
	9/99	Autl	2m2f110y	Ch	VS	£6997
	6/99	Autl	2m2f110y	Ch	VS	£6997
	4/97	Autl	2m5f110y	HCh	VS	£22447
	3/97	Autl	2m6f	Ch	VS	£11223

Total win prize-money £98175

Going: Sf: 0-4 GS: 0-1 Gd: 0-2 GF: - Fm: 0-0
Distance: 2m/2m3: 0-2 2m4-2m7: 0-5 3m+: 0-0
Track: LH: 0-5 RH: 0-2 Tight: 0-1 Gall: 0-2
Aids: Bl: 0-7 Vi: 0-0 Tstrap: 0-0
Best Rating: 151   3/02   Donc   2m3f110y   gd-sft   Ch

Very useful handicap chaser; probably best at around two and a half miles these days; goes well in testing conditions and usually wears blinkers.

Extra Proud

105(104h)   (95h)108
9-y-o ch g Dancing High-Spring Onion (King Sitric)
W Amos   W Amos

Placings: 6F62/60/2PF102-U1U14322   (4620)
2002/03: 24ᵁGF, 22¹GF, 21ᵁGF, 21¹GF, 20⁴G, 24³GF, 20²G, 20²GF,

	Starts	1st	2nd	3rd	Win & Pl
Chases	8	2	2	1	13012
Career Total	20	3	5	1	18365
108	7/02	Strf	2m5f110yE(0-105)HCh	G-F	£4290
95	5/02	Kels	2m6f110yD Ch	G-F	£4176
95	12/01	Muss	2m4f	E Hdl	GD	£3052

Total win prize-money £11518

Going: Sf: 0-0 GS: 0-0 Gd: 0-2 GF: - Fm: 2-6
Distance: 2m/2m3: 0-0 2m4-2m7: 2-6 3m+: 0-2
Track: LH: 2-3 RH: 0-5 Tight: 2-2 Gall: 0-0
Aids: Bl: 0-0 Vi: 0-0 Tstrap: 2-8
Best Rating: 108   4/03   Carl   2m4f   gd-fm   Ch

Fair chaser; suited by around two and a half miles; acts on a sound surface; not the most fluent of jumpers; wears tongue tie.

Extra Stout (IRE)

11-y-o ch g Buckskin (FR)-Bold Strike (FR) (Bold Lad (USA))
Miss J M Furness   J C Clark

Placings: 0/060P/F/114/4PP/P/05B0-0   (4508)
2002/03: 25⁰G,

	Starts	1st	2nd	3rd	Win & Pl
Chases	1	0	0	0	
Career Total	18	2	0	0	11337
101	4/99	Aint	3m1f	B Ch	GD	£8537
97	3/99	Sand	3m110y	H Ch	GD	£2042

Total win prize-money £10580

Going: Sf: 0-0 GS: 0-0 Gd: 0-1 GF: - Fm: 0-0
Distance: 2m/2m3: 0-0 2m4-2m7: 0-0 3m+: 0-1
Track: LH: 0-1 RH: 0-0 Tight: 0-1 Gall: 0-0
Aids: Bl: 0-0 Vi: 0-0 Tstrap: 0-0
Best Rating: 101   4/99   Aint   3m1f   good   Ch

Eye Of The Tiger (IRE)

106   101
7-y-o ch g Regular Guy-Banner Lady (Milan)
S A Kirk   K J Martin

Placings: 51-0403000   (4553)
2002/03: 16⁰HY, 17⁴YS, 20⁶S, 20³S, 24⁰SH, 24⁰GY, 22⁰G,

	Starts	1st	2nd	3rd	Win & Pl
Hurdles	7	0	0	1	1974
Career Total	9	1	0	1	5784
105	3/02	DRoy	2m	Hdl	SFT	£3809

Total win prize-money £3810

Going: Sf: 0-3 GS: 0-0 Gd: 0-1 GF: - Fm: 0-0
Distance: 2m/2m3: 0-2 2m4-2m7: 0-0 3m+: 0-0
Track: LH: 0-3 RH: 0-2 Tight: 0-0 Gall: 0-0
Aids: Bl: 0-0 Vi: 0-0 Tstrap: 0-0
Best Rating: 105   3/02   DRoy   2m   soft   Hdl

Eyes Dont Lie (IRE)

93   78
5-y-o b g Namaqualand (USA)-Avidal Park (Horage)

D A Nolan Mrs J McFadyen-Murray

Placings:54034P-65400   (2556)
2002/03: 17⁶HY, 20⁵GS, 22⁴GF, 22⁰G, 20⁰GF,

	Starts	1st	2nd	3rd	Win & Pl
Hurdles	5	0	0	0	265
Career Total	11	0	0	1	721

Going: Sf: 0-1 GS: 0-1 Gd: 0-1 GF: - Fm: 0-2
Distance: 2m/2m3: 0-1 2m4-2m7: 0-0 3m+: 0-0
Track: LH: 0-3 RH: 0-2 Tight: 0-4 Gall: 0-0
Aids: Bl: 0-0 Vi: 0-1 Tstrap: 0-1
Best Rating: 78 10/02 Kels 2m6f110y gd-fm Hdl

Modest hurdler, usually wears a tongue tie, has worn blinkers.

Eyes To The Right (IRE)

101   73d

4-y-o ch g Eagle Eyed (USA)-Capable Kate (IRE) (Alzao (USA))
A J Chamberlain (P S McEntee 2/4) Lord Goldicote

Placings:6P0645U   (4698)
2002/03: 16⁶GS, 16⁶S, 16⁰S, 16⁶G, 16⁴G, 16⁵G, 16⁰GF,

	Starts	1st	2nd	3rd	Win & Pl
Hurdles	7	0	0	0	0
Career Total	7	0	0	0	0

Going: Sf: 0-2 GS: 0-1 Gd: 0-3 GF: - Fm: 0-1
Distance: 2m/2m3: 0-7 2m4-2m7: 0-0 3m+: 0-0
Track: LH: 0-3 RH: 0-4 Tight: 0-3 Gall: 0-1
Aids: Bl: 0-0 Vi: 0-0 Tstrap: 0-0
Best Rating: 73 3/03 Hntg 2m110y good Hdl

Plating-class gelding; best at around two miles; acts on good ground.

Eyze (IRE)

95   82

7-y-o b g Lord Americo-Another Raheen (IRE) (Sandalay)
B Mactaggart (E J O Grady 28/7) Stoneage Paving

Placings:0-U6P6FP0   (3896)
2002/03: 17⁰S, 16⁶YS, 20⁰GF, 16⁶G, 20⁶GF, 24⁴PHY, 22⁰GS,

	Starts	1st	2nd	3rd	Win & Pl
Hurdles	4	0	0	0	0
Chases	3	0	0	0	0
Career Total	8	0	0	0	0

Going: Sf: 0-2 GS: 0-1 Gd: 0-1 GF: - Fm: 0-2
Distance: 2m/2m3: 0-3 2m4-2m7: 0-3 3m+: 0-1
Track: LH: 0-3 RH: 0-2 Tight: 0-1 Gall: 0-0
Aids: Bl: 0-0 Vi: 0-0 Tstrap: 0-0
Best Rating: 90 7/02 Limk 2m yld-sft Hdl

Ex Irish; moderate form so far in Britain; connections yet to establish a suitable trip for him; acts on soft ground.

Fabrezan (FR)

101   89

4-y-o b g Nikos-Fabulous Secret (FR) (Fabulous Dancer (USA))
Nick Williams Mrs Jane Kelly

Placings:P3633P   (2781)
2002/03: 17⁰GF, 17³G, 16⁶G, 16³G, 19³S, 19⁶S,

	Starts	1st	2nd	3rd	Win & Pl
Hurdles	6	0	0	3	1394

	Career Total	6	0	0	3	1394

Going: Sf: 0-2 GS: 0-0 Gd: 0-3 GF: - Fm: 0-1
Distance: 2m/2m3: 0-5 2m4-2m7: 0-1 3m+: 0-0
Track: LH: 0-2 RH: 0-4 Tight: 0-3 Gall: 0-0
Aids: Bl: 0-0 Vi: 0-0 Tstrap: 0-0
Best Rating: 89 10/02 Kemp 2m good Hdl

Won modest 2m 4f novice hurdle at Worcester July 2003; considered best with some cut in the ground.

Facts Not Fiction (IRE)

99   119

9-y-o b/br g Phardante (FR)-Facts n Fancies (Furry Glen)
F Doumen Peter Hans Vogt

Placings:44/35453F52/0200010F6/2010U31050/0423F366 14-1P0000   (3621)
2002/03: 20¹G, 21⁸PG, 20⁸VH, 24⁰G, 20⁸VH, 19⁰VS,

	Starts	1st	2nd	3rd	Win & Pl
Hurdles	5	1	0	0	8589
Chases	1	0	0	0	0
Career Total	45	5	4	5	106368

	5/02	Badn	2m4f165y Hdl		GD	£8589
	3/02	Autl	2m3f110y HHdl		HVY	£10012
138	12/00	Kemp	2m5f	C(0-135)HHdl	VS	£7670
	10/00	Autl	2m3f110y HHdl		VS	£8646
117	2/00	Newb	3m110y D Hdl		G-S	£4680

Total win prize-money £39597

Going: Sf: 0-2 GS: 0-0 Gd: 1-3 GF: - Fm: 0-0
Distance: 2m/2m3: 0-0 2m4-2m7: 1-5 3m+: 0-0
Track: LH: 0-3 RH: 0-1 Tight: 0-0 Gall: 0-1
Aids: Bl: 1-4 Vi: 0-0 Tstrap: 0-0
Best Rating: 138 12/00 Kemp 2m5f gd-sft Hdl

French-trained hurdler, winner twice in this country in 2000 and on heavy ground at Auteuil in March 2002. He stays three miles and loves the mud.

Fadalko (FR)

109   142

10-y-o b g Cadoudal (FR)-Kalliste (FR) (Calicot (FR))
P F Nicholls Sir Robert Ogden

Placings:2111/25P6210/11512U2F/122112/33620314-5250U6   (4604)
2002/03: 21⁵G, 21²GS, 19⁵GS, 20⁰G, 36⁰U, 21⁵G,

	Starts	1st	2nd	3rd	Win & Pl
Chases	6	0	1	0	9158
Career Total	39	11	10	3	350416

163	4/02	Chel	2m5f	A Ch	G-F	£24562
168	4/01	Aint	2m4f	A Ch	SFT	£74400
161	12/00	Winc	2m5f	B Ch	G-S	£9642
157	10/00	Winc	2m5f	A HCh	G-S	£21000
162	2/00	Uttx	2m	C HCh	SFT	£7020
145	11/99	Chel	2m	A Ch	GD	£13100
140	10/99	Bang	2m1f110yD Ch		SFT	£4130
145	4/99	Ayr	2m	A HHdl	SFT	£15385
	3/98	Autl	2m2f	Hdl	VS	£30303
	12/97	Autl	2m1f110y Hdl		HLD	£16835
	11/97	Autl	2m1f110y Hdl		VS	£11223

Total win prize-money £227602

Going: Sf: 0-0 GS: 0-2 Gd: 0-4 GF: - Fm: 0-0
Distance: 2m/2m3: 0-0 2m4-2m7: 0-5 3m+: 0-1
Track: LH: 0-4 RH: 0-2 Tight: 0-0 Gall: 0-3
Aids: Bl: 0-1 Vi: 0-0 Tstrap: 0-0
Best Rating: 168 4/01 Aint 2m4f soft Ch

Smart chaser; best at two to two and a half miles; a genuine sort, handles all grounds; has shown his best form in the spring.

Faddad (USA)

95   85

7-y-o b g Irish River (FR)-Miss Mistletoes (IRE) (The Minstrel (CAN))
D C O Brien J S Court

Placings:0/0-50P   (4186)
2002/03: 17⁵G, 16⁰G, 17⁵G,

	Starts	1st	2nd	3rd	Win & Pl
Hurdles	3	0	0	0	0
Career Total	5	0	0	0	0

Going: Sf: 0-0 GS: 0-0 Gd: 0-3 GF: - Fm: 0-0
Distance: 2m/2m3: 0-3 2m4-2m7: 0-0 3m+: 0-0
Track: LH: 0-0 RH: 0-3 Tight: 0-2 Gall: 0-0
Aids: Bl: 0-0 Vi: 0-0 Tstrap: 0-0
Best Rating: 85 5/02 Folk 2m1f110y good Hdl

Fadoudal Du Cochet (FR)

112   (140h)149

10-y-o b g Cadoudal (FR)-Eau De Vie (FR) (Dhaudevi (FR))
A L T Moore Sir Anthony O Reilly

Placings:0023/2131134/14312/0115/321133-3302P (4134)
2002/03: 16⁸YS, 16³S, 16⁰G, 16²Y, 16⁸PG,

	Starts	1st	2nd	3rd	Win & Pl
Chases	5	0	1	2	11820
Career Total	31	9	5	9	135463

143	3/02	Chel	2m	110y A HCh	GD	£39000
140	2/02	Gowr	2m	Hdl	SFT	£23926
143	1/01	Navn	2m1f	(0-123)HCh	SFT	£6677
128	12/00	Punc	2m	(0-123)HCh	SH	£6072
125	2/00	Punc	2m	Ch	SFT	£10440
111	10/99	Navn	2m1f	Ch	Y-S	£4312
134	1/99	Naas	2m	Hdl	HVY	£6138
134	1/99	Thur	2m	Hdl	HVY	£4296
106	11/98	Cork	2m	Hdl	SFT	£2391

Total win prize-money £103214

Going: Sf: 0-1 GS: 0-0 Gd: 0-2 GF: - Fm: 0-0
Distance: 2m/2m3: 0-5 2m4-2m7: 0-0 3m+: 0-0
Track: LH: 0-3 RH: 0-1 Tight: 0-0 Gall: 0-1
Aids: Bl: 0-0 Vi: 0-0 Tstrap: 0-0
Best Rating: 149 2/03 Naas 2m yield Ch

Fair hurdler/useful chaser in Ireland; acts well on a soft surface; best at two miles; game winner of the Grand Annual Chase at the 2002 Cheltenham Festival on good ground.

Fair Enough (IRE)

(99h)   (83h)

8-y-o b m Phardante (FR)-Woodford Princess (Menelek)
R Rowe Mr & Mrs Robin Lamb

Placings:4400600-6003   (4759)
2002/03: 17⁶GS, 16⁰GS, 21⁰GS, 27³GF,

	Starts	1st	2nd	3rd	Win & Pl
Hurdles	4	0	0	1	1056
Career Total	11	0	0	1	1604

Going: Sf: 0-0 GS: 0-3 Gd: 0-0 GF: - Fm: 0-1
Distance: 2m/2m3: 0-2 2m4-2m7: 0-1 3m+: 0-1
Track: LH: 0-0 RH: 0-3 Tight: 0-2 Gall: 0-0
Aids: Bl: 0-0 Vi: 0-0 Tstrap: 0-0
Best Rating: 89 5/01 Tipp 2m2f heavy NHF

Plating-class hurdler; stays three miles-three; best on a sound surface.

Fair Exchange

10-y-o b g Bustino-Sharp Vixen (Laurence O)
Mrs M G Sheppard M G Sheppard

Placings:1   (4417)
2002/03: 25¹G,

	Starts	1st	2nd	3rd	Win & Pl
Chases	1	1	0	0	1242
Career Total	1	1	0	0	1242
92 3/03 MRas 3m1f		H Ch		GD	£1241

Total win prize-money £1242

Going:	Sf: 0-0 GS: 0-0 Gd: 1-1 GF: - Fm: 0-0
Distance:	2m/2m3: 0-0 2m4-2m7: 0-0 **3m+: 1-1**
Track:	LH: 0-0 **RH: 1-1** Tight: **1-1** Gall: 0-0
Aids:	Bl: 0-0 Vi: 0-0 Tstrap: 0-0
Best Rating:	92 3/03 MRas 3m1f good Ch

Prolific point winner; fortuitous winner of a hunter chase at Market Rasen in March on first try under Rules.

Fair Prospect
102   106

7-y-o b g Sir Harry Lewis (USA)-Fair Sara (Mcindoe)
P F Nicholls (J A Glover 24/11) Fourstar Partners

Placings:15-F41   (4527)
2002/03: 16²GS, 16⁴G, 20¹G,

	Starts	1st	2nd	3rd	Win & Pl
Hurdles	3	1	0	0	4249
Career Total	5	2	0	0	5859
106 4/03 Uttx	2m4f110yE Hdl		GD	£3864
102 6/01 Hexm	2m	H NHF	G-S	£1610

Total win prize-money £5474

Going:	Sf: 0-0 GS: 0-1 Gd: 1-2 GF: - Fm: 0-0
Distance:	2m/2m3: 0-2 **2m4-2m7: 1-1** 3m+: 0-0
Track:	**LH: 1-3** RH: 0-0 Tight: 0-1 Gall: 0-0
Aids:	Bl: 0-0 Vi: 0-0 Tstrap: 0-0
Best Rating:	106 4/03 Uttx 2m4f110y good Hdl

Fair novice hurdler; winner at Uttoxeter in April 2003; followed up easily against weak opposition at Wetherby the following month; flopped there a week later; stays well; suited by decent ground.

Fair Question (IRE)
106   104

5-y-o b g Rainbow Quest (USA)-Fair Of The Furze (Ela-Mana-Mou)
Miss Venetia Williams (J L Dunlop 25/5) The MerseyClyde Partnership

Placings:P642   (4316)
2002/03: 16⁶GS, 16⁶GS, 17⁴GS, 17²G,

	Starts	1st	2nd	3rd	Win & Pl
Hurdles	4	0	1	0	1205
Career Total	4	0	1	0	1205

Going:	Sf: 0-0 GS: 0-3 Gd: 0-1 GF: - Fm: 0-0
Distance:	2m/2m3: 0-4 2m4-2m7: 0-0 3m+: 0-0
Track:	LH: 0-2 RH: 0-2 Tight: 0-2 Gall: 0-1
Aids:	Bl: 0-0 Vi: 0-0 Tstrap: 0-0
Best Rating:	104 3/03 Bang 2m1f good Hdl

Listed-class stayer on the Flat; has shown ability over hurdles; tends to race a bit freely; has shown form on most types of ground.

Fair Sprite (IRE)
97   82

6-y-o ch g Over The River (FR)-Saucy Sprite (Balliol)
R H Alner Lady Talbot Of Malahide

Placings:5P   (3151)
2002/03: 23⁵GS, 26ᴾHY,

	Starts	1st	2nd	3rd	Win & Pl
Chases	2	0	0	0	0
Career Total	2	0	0	0	0

Going:	Sf: 0-1 GS: 0-1 Gd: 0-0 GF: - Fm: 0-0
Distance:	2m/2m3: 0-0 2m4-2m7: 0-0 3m+: 0-2
Track:	LH: 0-1 RH: 0-1 Tight: 0-0 Gall: 0-0
Aids:	Bl: 0-0 Vi: 0-0 Tstrap: 0-0
Best Rating:	82 12/02 Extr 2m7f110y gd-sft Ch

Fair Wind (IRE)

11-y-o b g Strong Gale-Corcomroe (Busted)
Mrs H Bartlett Mrs H Bartlett

Placings:31/P164-2PRP   (4133)
2002/03: 26²GF, 26ᴾHY, 24⁴RS, 26ᴾG,

	Starts	1st	2nd	3rd	Win & Pl
Chases	4	0	1	0	1660
Career Total	10	2	1	1	6173
115 2/02 Wwck	3m2f	H Ch	HVY	£1330
115 4/01 Extr	2m7f110yH Ch		SFT	£2271

Total win prize-money £3602

Going:	Sf: 0-2 GS: 0-0 Gd: 0-1 GF: - Fm: 0-1
Distance:	2m/2m3: 0-0 2m4-2m7: 0-0 3m+: 0-4
Track:	LH: 0-4 RH: 0-0 Tight: 0-0 Gall: 0-3
Aids:	Bl: 0-1 Vi: 0-0 Tstrap: 0-0
Best Rating:	117 3/02 Chel 3m2f110y good Ch

Fairmead Princess

5-y-o b m Rudimentary (USA)-Lessons Lass (IRE) (Doyoun)
M J Gingell C N & Mrs A V Roberts

Placings:00P-   (0008)
2002/03: 16ᴾG,

	Starts	1st	2nd	3rd	Win & Pl
Hurdles	1	0	0	0	
Career Total	3	0	0	0	

Going:	Sf: 0-0 GS: 0-0 Gd: 0-1 GF: - Fm: 0-0
Distance:	2m/2m3: 0-1 2m4-2m7: 0-0 3m+: 0-0
Track:	LH: 0-1 RH: 0-0 Tight: 0-1 Gall: 0-0
Aids:	Bl: 0-0 Vi: 0-0 Tstrap: 0-0
Best Rating:	

Fairtoto
94   94d

7-y-o b g Mtoto-Fairy Feet (Sadler s Wells (USA))
D J Wintle Mrs Joan L Egan

Placings:650/51222/22203-060   (3843)
2002/03: 21¹G, 20⁶HY, 24⁰G,

	Starts	1st	2nd	3rd	Win & Pl
Hurdles	3	0	0	0	
Career Total	16	1	6	1	9039
106 7/00 Strf	2m6f110yD Hdl		G-F	£3266

Total win prize-money £3266

Fairwood Heart (IRE)

(108h)   (126h)**87**

6-y-o b/b g Broken Hearted-Bowery Lass (IRE) (Abednego)
P J Rothwell Tom Stronge

Placings:14-1233301524   (4456)
2002/03: 16¹SH, 16²S, 17³G, 16³F, 20³HY, 16⁶S, 22¹YS, 24⁵SH, 23²GS, 24⁴G,

	Starts	1st	2nd	3rd	Win & Pl
Hurdles	10	2	2	3	21374
Career Total	12	3	2	3	25983
115 1/03 Leop	2m	(74-116)HHdl	Y-S	£8441
108 6/02 Baln	2m	Hdl	SH	£4021
105 5/01 Klny	2m1f	NHF	G-F	£4173

Total win prize-money £16636

Going:	Sf: 0-3 GS: 0-1 Gd: 0-2 GF: - Fm: 0-1
Distance:	2m/2m3: 1-5 2m4-2m7: 1-2 3m+: 0-3
Track:	**LH: 1-4** RH: 0-2 Tight: 0-1 Gall: 0-0
Aids:	Bl: 0-0 Vi: 0-0 Tstrap: 0-0
Best Rating:	126 4/03 Aint 3m110y good Hdl

Fair Irish-trained hurdler; stays three miles; acts on soft ground.

Fait Le Jojo (FR)
110(111h)   (148h)**133**

6-y-o b g Pistolet Bleu (IRE)-Pretty Davis (USA) (Trempolino (USA))
P J Hobbs Jay Dee Bloodstock Limited

Placings:12F26/0322501-01U411FF   (4548)
2002/03: 16⁰G, 16¹GF, 17ᵁGS, 16⁴GS, 16¹GS, 16¹G, 20ᶠG, 16ᶠG,

	Starts	1st	2nd	3rd	Win & Pl
Hurdles	1	0	0	0	0
Chases	7	3	0	0	15592
Career Total	20	5	4	1	65356
133 3/03 Ludl	2m	E Ch	GD	£4121
130 1/03 Ludl	2m	E Ch	G-S	£5096
121 10/02 Uttx	2m	B Ch	G-F	£4875
145 4/02 Asct	2m110y	B(0-140)HHdl	G-F	£7156
135 11/00 Asct	2m110y	B Hdl	SFT	£8073

Total win prize-money £29322

Going:	Sf: 0-0 GS: 1-3 Gd: 1-4 GF: - Fm: 1-1
Distance:	**2m/2m3: 3-7** 2m4-2m7: 0-1 3m+: 0-0
Track:	LH: 1-5 **RH: 2-3** Tight: **2-4** Gall: 0-1
Aids:	Bl: 0-0 Vi: 0-0 Tstrap: 0-0
Best Rating:	145 4/02 Asct 2m110y gd-fm Hdl

Useful handicap hurdler/novice chaser; has taken fairly well to chasing in 2002/03, winning three times; suited by two miles and is best suited by decent ground; likes to force the pace.

Falchion
101(105h)   (110h)**110**

8-y-o b g Broadsword (USA)-Fastlass (Celtic Cone)
J R Bewley R Bewley

Placings:6/56025/1352-3233F2U   (4305)
2002/03: 20³GS, 21²S, 16³HY, 20³HY, 20ᶠHY, 20²S, 25ᵁG,

	Starts	1st	2nd	3rd	Win & Pl
Hurdles	1	0	0	1	438
Chases	6	0	2	2	4125
Career Total	17	1	4	4	11769

106 11/01 Ayr 2m6f   E Hdl   G-S £2597
Total win prize-money £2597

Going: Sf: 0-5 GS: 0-1 Gd: 0-1 GF: - Fm: 0-0
Distance: 2m/2m3: 0-1 2m4-2m7: 0-5 3m+: 0-1
Track: LH: 0-7 RH: 0-0 Tight: 0-1 Gall: 0-2
Aids: Bl: 0-0 Vi: 0-0 Tstrap: 0-7
Best Rating: 110 3/03 Ayr 2m4f soft Ch

Winning hurdler; good efforts over fences, but keeps finding one too good; stays 3m 1f.

Falcon Du Coteau (FR)
95(88h)   (67h)119
10-y-o b g Apeldoorn (FR)-Ifrika (FR) (Bamako Iii)
A J Martin Lyreen Syndicate

Placings:000460/102/60/03131213F-0000050   (4727a)
2002/03: 16GS, 20GS, 19GS, 18GSH, 17GGY, 21SG, 29GG,

	Starts	1st	2nd	3rd	Win & Pl
Hurdles	2	0	0	0	0
Chases	5	0	0	0	1750
Career Total	27	4	2	3	37584

115 1/02 Leop 2m3f (0-130)HCh HVY £13957
110 12/01 Punc 2m   (0-116)HCh SFT £7862
101 11/01 Clon 2m1f (0-102)HCh YLD £5008
87 5/99 Gowr 2m   (0-102)HHdl GD   £3069
Total win prize-money £29897

Going: Sf: 0-3 GS: 0-0 Gd: 0-2 GF: - Fm: 0-0
Distance: 2m/2m3: 0-4 2m4-2m7: 0-2 3m+: 0-1
Track: LH: 0-3 RH: 0-3 Tight: 0-1 Gall: 0-0
Aids: Bl: 0-4 Vi: 0-0 Tstrap: 0-0
Best Rating: 119 4/03 Aint 2m5f110y good Ch

Fair handicap chaser, he is effective at around two miles and stays further; acts well with cut in the ground; likes to make the running; wears blinkers.

Falcon Georgie
86   44
4-y-o b f Sri Pekan (USA)-Georgia Stephens (USA) (The Minstrel (CAN))
Miss B Sanders J M Quinn

Placings:4P5   (4755)
2002/03: 18GS, 17GG, 18GGF,

	Starts	1st	2nd	3rd	Win & Pl
Hurdles	3	0	0	0	259
Career Total	3	0	0	0	259

Going: Sf: 0-1 GS: 0-0 Gd: 0-1 GF: - Fm: 0-1
Distance: 2m/2m3: 0-3 2m4-2m7: 0-0 3m+: 0-0
Track: LH: 0-2 RH: 0-1 Tight: 0-3 Gall: 0-0
Aids: Bl: 0-0 Vi: 0-0 Tstrap: 0-0
Best Rating: 44 4/03 Font 2m2f110y gd-fm Hdl

Falcon Ridge
98   87
9-y-o ch g Seven Hearts-Glen Kella Manx (Tickled Pink)
Miss E C Lavelle J R Lavelle

Placings:6454133/244/P/P42-3P   (0736)
2002/03: 16GS, 16GGF,

	Starts	1st	2nd	3rd	Win & Pl
Chases	2	0	0	1	480
Career Total	16	1	2	3	5405

102 3/99 Tntn 2m1f   F(0-105)HHdl SFT £1962
Total win prize-money £1963

Going: Sf: 0-0 GS: 0-0 Gd: 0-0 GF: - Fm: 0-2
Distance: 2m/2m3: 0-2 2m4-2m7: 0-0 3m+: 0-0
Track: LH: 0-2 RH: 0-0 Tight: 0-2 Gall: 0-0
Aids: Bl: 0-0 Vi: 0-0 Tstrap: 0-0
Best Rating: 102 5/99 Worc 2m4f gd-fm Hdl

Modest chaser, stays two miles-five and acts on a sound surface.

Falmer For All (IRE)
98f   84f
5-y-o b g Warcraft (USA)-Sunset Walk (Le Bavard (FR))
T P McGovern T C Gilligan

Placings:55   (4350)
2002/03: 18GS, 16GGF,

	Starts	1st	2nd	3rd	Win & Pl
NH Flat	2	0	0	0	0
Career Total	2	0	0	0	0

Going: Sf: 0-0 GS: 0-0 Gd: 0-0 GF: - Fm: 0-1
Distance: 2m/2m3: 0-2 2m4-2m7: 0-0 3m+: 0-0
Track: LH: 0-2 RH: 0-0 Tight: 0-1 Gall: 0-0
Aids: Bl: 0-0 Vi: 0-0 Tstrap: 0-0
Best Rating: 84 2/03 Font 2m2f110y gd-sft NHF

False Tail (IRE)
                                  88
11-y-o b g Roselier (FR)-Its Good Ere (Import)
J J Lambe (Gerard Cully 2/11) M Futter

Placings:1P/4P/PFU   (4531a)
2002/03: 25PYS, 26FG, 24UGF,

	Starts	1st	2nd	3rd	Win & Pl
Chases	3	0	0	0	
Career Total	7	1	0	0	1606

110 5/98 Chep 3m   H Ch   GD £1203
Total win prize-money £1204

Going: Sf: 0-0 GS: 0-0 Gd: 0-1 GF: - Fm: 0-1
Distance: 2m/2m3: 0-0 2m4-2m7: 0-0 3m+: 0-3
Track: LH: 0-1 RH: 0-2 Tight: 0-0 Gall: 0-1
Aids: Bl: 0-0 Vi: 0-0 Tstrap: 0-0
Best Rating: 110 5/98 Chep 3m good Ch

Fair Irish point-to-pointer; not so effective in hunter chases; stays three miles; acts on an easy surface.

Famfoni (FR)
109(98h)   (96h)116
10-y-o ch g Pamponi (FR)-India Rosa (FR) (Carnaval)
K C Bailey The Propelers Partnership

Placings:322/424/43452/2/15-341   (1940)
2002/03: 27GF, 28G, 31GS,

	Starts	1st	2nd	3rd	Win & Pl
Hurdles	1	0	0	1	498
Chases	2	1	0	0	19683
Career Total	17	2	5	3	39519

119 11/02 Chel 3m7f   B Ch   G-S £19314
110 3/02 Ludl 3m   D Ch   G-S £4036
Total win prize-money £23351

Going: Sf: 0-0 GS: 1-1 Gd: 0-1 GF: - Fm: 0-0
Distance: 2m/2m3: 0-0 2m4-2m7: 0-0 3m+: 1-3
Track: LH: 1-3 RH: 0-0 Tight: 0-2 Gall: 0-0
Aids: Bl: 0-0 Vi: 0-0 Tstrap: 0-0
Best Rating: 119 11/02 Chel 3m7f gd-sft Ch

Useful staying chaser. Has worn blinkers and visor but won without them in spring of 2002. A bit of a monkey at home by all accounts, he is difficult to train, but he did win a cross country chase at Cheltenham in November. Acts on soft/heavy ground.

Fami (FR)
                                  104
10-y-o ch g Le Nain Jaune (FR)-Quimie Ii (FR) (Barbotan (FR))
Miss Venetia Williams Len Jakeman

Placings:U310/024UUU13F/1F5/035U-P (0268)
2002/03: 27PGF,

	Starts	1st	2nd	3rd	Win & Pl
Hurdles	1	0	0	0	
Career Total	21	3	1	3	12088

107 11/00 Hrfd 2m3f   E(0-115)HCh SFT £3731
100 1/00 Font 3m2f110yF(0-100)HCh GD £2843
99 4/99 Bang   2m4f   E Hdl   GD   £2486
Total win prize-money £9061

Going: Sf: 0-0 GS: 0-0 Gd: 0-0 GF: - Fm: 0-1
Distance: 2m/2m3: 0-2 2m4-2m7: 0-0 3m+: 0-1
Track: LH: 0-1 RH: 0-0 Tight: 0-0 Gall: 0-0
Aids: Bl: 0-0 Vi: 0-0 Tstrap: 0-0
Best Rating: 107 11/00 Hrfd 2m3f soft Ch

Modest staying chaser, suited by soft ground.

Familie Footsteps
(104h)   (106h)
9-y-o b g Primitive Rising (USA)-Ramilie (Rambah)
G A Swinbank Miss A H Sykes

Placings:0/4/3500/311F2-5   (0167)
2002/03: 16GF,

	Starts	1st	2nd	3rd	Win & Pl
Hurdles	1	0	0	0	0
Career Total	12	2	1	2	7444

102 8/01 Sedg 2m1f   D Hdl   G-F £3265
94 7/01 Sedg   2m1f   E Hdl   G-F £2523
Total win prize-money £5790

Going: Sf: 0-0 GS: 0-0 Gd: 0-0 GF: - Fm: 0-0
Distance: 2m/2m3: 0-1 2m4-2m7: 0-0 3m+: 0-0
Track: LH: 0-1 RH: 0-0 Tight: 0-0 Gall: 0-0
Aids: Bl: 0-0 Vi: 0-0 Tstrap: 0-0
Best Rating: 106 9/01 Sedg 2m1f good Hdl

Successful in two hurdle races on fast ground.

Family Business (IRE)
7-y-o ch g Over The River (FR)-Morego (Way Up North)
D Pipe (M C Pipe 9/5) Mrs Caroline Donnan & P J Finn

Placings:20/4121203-423FBFF   (4615)
2002/03: 24G, 25GS, 24S, 24FS, 26G, 21FG, 26FG,

	Starts	1st	2nd	3rd	Win & Pl
Chases	7	0	1	1	1786
Career Total	16	2	4	2	15490

1/02 Sthl 3m110y E Ch   G-S £4824
132 12/01 Leic 2m7f110yE Ch GD £3146
Total win prize-money £7970

Going: Sf: 0-2 GS: 0-1 Gd: 0-4 GF: - Fm: 0-0
Distance: 2m/2m3: 0-0 2m4-2m7: 0-1 3m+: 0-6
Track: LH: 0-4 RH: 0-3 Tight: 0-2 Gall: 0-2
Aids: Bl: 0-2 Vi: 0-1 Tstrap: 0-0
Best Rating: 132 12/01 Leic 2m7f110y good Ch

Fair chaser; acts on good or easy ground and is effective at around three miles; winning pointer in 2003.

Family Venture (IRE)

110   **107**

6-y-o br g Montelimar (USA)-Well Honey (Al Sirat (USA))
Ferdy Murphy The Family Venture Partnership

Placings:036132   (3578)
2002/03: 16⁰G, 24³GS, 19⁶GS, 24¹G, 24³G, 24²G,

	Starts	1st	2nd	3rd	Win & Pl
Hurdles	6	1	1	2	6794
Career Total	6	1	1	2	6794
101 1/03 Muss 3m E(0-105)HHdl GD £4163					

Total win prize-money £4163

Going: Sf: 0-0 GS: 0-2 Gd: 1-4 GF: - Fm: 0-0
Distance: 2m/2m3: 0-2 2m4-2m7: 0-0 3m+: 1-4
Track: LH: 0-2 RH: 1-4 Tight: 1-4 Gall: 0-0
Aids: Bl: 0-0 Vi: 0-0 Tstrap: 0-1
Best Rating: 107 2/03 Muss 3m   good Hdl

Modest hurdler; Irish point winner, stays three miles and best on good ground; sometimes wears a tongue-tie.

Fandango De Chassy (FR)

103(110c)   (107c)**106**

10-y-o b g Brezzo (FR)-Laita De Mercurey (FR) (Dom Luc (FR))
Mrs L Wadham C J Hays

Placings:0000/35FU052/211122211P6/PPP/3451110321-P2520P34P   (4563)
2002/03: 25ᴾGS, 26²S, 26⁵HY, 30²GS, 24⁰G, 33⁵PS, 25³HY, 26⁴G, 24⁵GF,

	Starts	1st	2nd	3rd	Win & Pl
Hurdles	4	0	0	1	795
Chases	5	0	2	0	6656
Career Total	44	9	8	4	55196
107 3/02 Towc 3m1f F(0-100)HCh G-S £3559					
113 12/01 Towc 3m E(0-115)HHdl HVY £5248					
110 11/01 Towc 3m D(0-120)HHdl SFT £5362					
108 11/01 Towc 3m F(0-90)Hdl SFT £2362					
100 1/00 Naas 3m (0-116)HCh SH £6072					
95 1/00 Fair 3m1f (0-123)HCh SFT £8320					
103 6/99 Prth 3m110y F(0-110)HHdl SFT £2879					
91 6/99 Prth 2m4f110yF(0-95)HCh G-S £3582					
109 5/99 DRoy 3m Hdl SFT £3069					

Total win prize-money £40458

Going: Sf: 0-4 GS: 0-2 Gd: 0-2 GF: - Fm: 0-1
Distance: 2m/2m3: 0-0 2m4-2m7: 0-0 3m+: 0-9
Track: LH: 0-3 RH: 0-6 Tight: 0-3 Gall: 0-3
Aids: Bl: 0-0 Vi: 0-1 Tstrap: 0-0
Best Rating: 116 1/02 Wwck 3m1f   heavy Hdl

Modest handicap chaser, a real stayer; suited by soft ground and a stiff track.

Fanfaron (FR)

10-y-o b g Sarpedon (FR)-Ocana Iv (FR) (Monsieur X)
Paul Phillips Miss Sally Bond

Placings:3/21/123R22/25251/2366R4/1B5-260F   (4255)
2002/03: 25²GF, 25⁶S, 24⁰GS, 25⁵G,

	Starts	1st	2nd	3rd	Win & Pl
Chases	4	0	1	0	700
Career Total	27	4	8	3	27239
113 2/02 Tntn 3m H Ch SFT £3094					
136 4/00 Plum 2m4f F(0-110)HCh SFT £3250					
140 11/98 MRas 2m4f E Ch HVY £3093					
9/97 Bord 2m2f Hdl SFT £3367					

Total win prize-money £12804

Going: Sf: 0-1 GS: 0-1 Gd: 0-1 GF: - Fm: 0-1
Distance: 2m/2m3: 0-0 2m4-2m7: 0-0 3m+: 0-4
Track: LH: 0-0 RH: 0-4 Tight: 0-1 Gall: 0-0
Aids: Bl: 0-0 Vi: 0-0 Tstrap: 0-0
Best Rating: 140 4/99 Sand 2m4f110y   good Ch

Modest hunter chaser/pointer; stays three miles; acts on good ground but best on soft; inclined to jump right-handed.

Fanion De Nourry (FR)

10-y-o ch g Bad Conduct (USA)-Ottomane (FR) (Quart De Vin (FR))
E Haddock Miss H M Newell

Placings:4FF/OP040O/0P5/12P0/00P-F6P   (0317)
2002/03: 33ᶠGF, 25⁶S, 34ᴾG,

	Starts	1st	2nd	3rd	Win & Pl
Chases	3	0	0	0	
Career Total	22	1	1	0	2464
101 5/00 Towc 3m1f H Ch G-F £1568					

Total win prize-money £1568

Going: Sf: 0-1 GS: 0-0 Gd: 0-1 GF: - Fm: 0-0
Distance: 2m/2m3: 0-0 2m4-2m7: 0-0 3m+: 0-3
Track: LH: 0-2 RH: 0-1 Tight: 0-0 Gall: 0-1
Aids: Bl: 0-0 Vi: 0-0 Tstrap: 0-0
Best Rating: 108 5/00 Uttx 4m2f   gd-fm Ch

Fantasmic

104   **103**

7-y-o ch g Broadsword (USA)-Squeaky Cottage (True Song)
A M Hales Andrew L Cohen

Placings:40-P3012   (4602)
2002/03: 19⁵GS, 16³S, 16⁰S, 16¹G, 21²G,

	Starts	1st	2nd	3rd	Win & Pl
Hurdles	5	1	1	1	10929
Career Total	7	1	1	1	10929
102 4/03 Uttx 2m E Hdl GD £3675					

Total win prize-money £3675

Going: Sf: 0-2 GS: 0-1 Gd: 1-2 GF: - Fm: 0-0
Distance: 2m/2m3: 1-4 2m4-2m7: 0-1 3m+: 0-0
Track: LH: 1-5 RH: 0-1 Tight: 0-0 Gall: 0-2
Aids: Bl: 0-0 Vi: 0-0 Tstrap: 0-0
Best Rating: 104 4/03 Chel 2m5f110y   good Hdl

Modest hurdler; got off the mark on good ground at Uttoxeter in April 2003; effective from two miles to two miles five; looks a chaser in the making.

Fantastic Champion (IRE)

110   **118**

4-y-o b g Entrepreneur-Reine Mathilde (USA) (Vaguely Noble)
Mrs L Wadham (P W D Arcy 8/7) Champion And The Fantastics

Placings:022   (3494)
2002/03: 16⁶G, 16²G, 16²GS,

	Starts	1st	2nd	3rd	Win & Pl
Hurdles	3	0	2	0	3164
Career Total	3	0	2	0	3164

Going: Sf: 0-0 GS: 0-1 Gd: 0-2 GF: - Fm: 0-0
Distance: 2m/2m3: 0-3 2m4-2m7: 0-0 3m+: 0-0
Track: LH: 0-1 RH: 0-2 Tight: 0-0 Gall: 0-1
Aids: Bl: 0-0 Vi: 0-0 Tstrap: 0-0
Best Rating: 118 2/03 Kemp 2m   gd-sft Hdl

Decent juvenile hurdler; goes well on good and good to soft ground; effective over two miles.

Far Ahead

75   **49**

11-y-o b g Soviet Star (USA)-Cut Ahead (Kalaglow)
D Carroll Sunpak Potatoes

Placings:41146/P00   (3567)
2002/03: 16⁶PGS, 16⁰GS, 17⁰HY,

	Starts	1st	2nd	3rd	Win & Pl
Hurdles	3	0	0	0	
Career Total	8	2	0	0	5418
122 3/97 Newc 2m E Hdl GD £2452					
103 2/97 Muss 2m E Hdl GD £1720					

Total win prize-money £4173

Going: Sf: 0-1 GS: 0-2 Gd: 0-0 GF: - Fm: 0-0
Distance: 2m/2m3: 0-3 2m4-2m7: 0-0 3m+: 0-0
Track: LH: 0-3 RH: 0-0 Tight: 0-2 Gall: 0-1
Aids: Bl: 0-0 Vi: 0-0 Tstrap: 0-0
Best Rating: 127 4/97 Aint 2m4f   good Hdl

Far Bridge (IRE)

(76h)   (57h)

8-y-o ch g Phardante (FR)-Droichidin (Good Thyne (USA))
P Wegmann P Wegmann

Placings:6/00P-6P   (4705)
2002/03: 17⁶GF, 21⁵PG,

	Starts	1st	2nd	3rd	Win & Pl
Chases	2	0	0	0	0
Career Total	6	0	0	0	0

Going: Sf: 0-0 GS: 0-0 Gd: 0-1 GF: - Fm: 0-0
Distance: 2m/2m3: 0-1 2m4-2m7: 0-0 3m+: 0-0
Track: LH: 0-2 RH: 0-0 Tight: 0-1 Gall: 0-0
Aids: Bl: 0-0 Vi: 0-0 Tstrap: 0-0
Best Rating: 59 3/01 Extr 2m3f   heavy Hdl

Far Dawn (USA)

102   **109**

10-y-o b g Sunshine Forever (USA)-Dawn s Reality (USA) (In Reality)
J Gallagher John L Marriott

Placings:11422/230002P/34061/5/32/61P2   (4732)
2002/03: 23⁶GS, 24¹GF, 25⁶G, 24⁵GF,

	Starts	1st	2nd	3rd	Win & Pl
Chases	4	1	1	0	5099
Career Total	24	4	6	3	40478
85 3/03 Sthl 3m110y E Ch G-F £3841					
123 4/99 Chel 3m B(0-140)HHdl GD £10845					
118 12/96 Sand 2m110y D Hdl GD £2905					
87 11/96 Wind 2m E Hdl GD £2687					

Total win prize-money £20280

Going: Sf: 0-0 GS: 0-1 Gd: 0-1 GF: - Fm: 1-2
Distance: 2m/2m3: 0-0 2m4-2m7: 0-0 3m+: 1-4
Track: LH: 1-3 RH: 0-1 Tight: 1-2 Gall: 0-0
Aids: Bl: 0-0 Vi: 0-0 Tstrap: 0-0

Best Rating: 132 10/97 Chep 2m110y   gd-fm   Hdl

Useful fast-ground hurdler for Amanda Perrett; made promising chase debut for Ian Williams debut after an absence of nearly two years; way below form on first run for John Gallagher after similar absence; won four-runner extended 3m novice chase at Southwell March 2003; acts on ground good and faster.

Far Glen (IRE)

8-y-o b g Phardante (FR)-Asigh Glen (Furry Glen)
R D E Woodhouse   R D E Woodhouse

Placings:FPP/553P50063-2F2   (4552)
2002/03: 21²GF, 25⁵G, 27²G,

	Starts	1st	2nd	3rd	Win & Pl
Hurdles	1	0	1	0	752
Chases	2	0	1	0	1100
Career Total	15	0	2	2	2678

Going: Sf: 0-0 GS: 0-0 Gd: 0-2 GF: - Fm: 0-1
Distance: 2m/2m3: 0-0 2m4-2m7: 0-1 3m+: 0-2
Track: LH: 0-3 RH: 0-0 Tight: 0-1 Gall: 0-0
Aids: Bl: 0-0 Vi: 0-0 Tstrap: 0-0
Best Rating: 97 4/03 Ayr   3m3f110y good   Ch

Moderate form over hurdles to date; chancy jumper and has yet to complete over fences; stays two and a half miles plus, acts on fast ground.

Far Horizon (IRE)
109   130
9-y-o b g Phardante (FR)-Polly Puttens (Pollerton)
N J Henderson   Lady Tennant

Placings:12/222/213P   (4442)
2002/03: 16²S, 20¹S, 21³G, 20³G,

	Starts	1st	2nd	3rd	Win & Pl
Hurdles	4	1	1	1	9693
Career Total	9	2	5	1	18698
128 12/02 Asct	2m4f	C Hdl		SFT	£7133
122 5/99 Hrfd	2m1f	H NHF		G-S	£1651

Total win prize-money £8785

Going: Sf: 1-2 GS: 0-0 Gd: 0-2 GF: - Fm: 0-0
Distance: 2m/2m3: 0-1 2m4-2m7: 1-3 3m+: 0-0
Track: LH: 0-1 RH: 1-3 Tight: 0-0 Gall: 0-1
Aids: Bl: 0-0 Vi: 0-0 Tstrap: 0-0
Best Rating: 130 1/03 Kemp 2m5f   good   Hdl

Decent novice hurdler; suited by two and a half miles and soft ground.

Far Pavilions
107   131
4-y-o b g Halling (USA)-Flambera (FR) (Akarad (FR))
G A Swinbank (Mrs J R Ramsden 27/9)   J David Abell

Placings:1111P   (4460)
2002/03: 16¹GS, 16¹GS, 16¹G, 16¹G, 16⁶G,

	Starts	1st	2nd	3rd	Win & Pl
Hurdles	5	4	0	0	25048
Career Total	5	4	0	0	25048
131 3/03 Hayd	2m	B Hdl		GD	£10166
119 2/03 Muss	2m	D Hdl		GD	£5525
121 12/02 Muss	2m	D Hdl		G-S	£5538
107 12/02 Catt	2m	D Hdl		G-S	£3818

Total win prize-money £25048

Going: Sf: 0-0 GS: 2-2 Gd: 2-3 GF: - Fm: 0-0
Distance: 2m/2m3: 4-5 2m4-2m7: 0-0 3m+: 0-0

Track: LH: 2-3 RH: 2-2 Tight: 3-4 Gall: 0-0
Aids: Bl: 0-0 Vi: 0-0 Tstrap: 0-0
Best Rating: 131 3/03 Hayd 2m   good   Hdl

Useful juvenile hurdler; best over two miles and acts on any ground; unbeaten over hurdles so far and looks progressive but ran badly and was pulled up at Aintree.

Faraway John (IRE)

5-y-o b g Farhaan-Indiana Dancer (Hallgate)
G P Enright   Neil Kenworthy

Placings:P   (2310)
2002/03: 16⁵HY,

	Starts	1st	2nd	3rd	Win & Pl
Hurdles	1	0	0	0	
Career Total	1	0	0	0	

Going: Sf: 0-1 GS: 0-0 Gd: 0-0 GF: - Fm: 0-0
Distance: 2m/2m3: 0-1 2m4-2m7: 0-0 3m+: 0-0
Track: LH: 0-1 RH: 0-0 Tight: 0-1 Gall: 0-0
Aids: Bl: 0-0 Vi: 0-0 Tstrap: 0-0
Best Rating: 0   12/02 Plum 2m   heavy   Hdl

Fard Du Moulin Mas (FR)
95(81h)   (92h)108
10-y-o b/br g Morespeed-Soiree D Ex (FR) (Kashtan (FR))
M E D Francis   Mrs Merrick Francis Iii

Placings:13/1P3P/0054PP6/6325116F/0PP/4P50-F5P
                                           (2573)
2002/03: 21⁶G, 20⁵GS, 22²G,

	Starts	1st	2nd	3rd	Win & Pl
Chases	3	0	0	0	
Career Total	31	4	1	3	71065
136 11/99 Sand	2m4f110yC(0-130)HCh		GD	£7002
137 10/99 Worc	2m4f	C(0-135)HHdl	G-F	£5084
9/97 Autl	2m2f	Ch		SFT	£13468
3/97 Autl	2m1f110y Hdl			Y-S	£11223

Total win prize-money £36778

Going: Sf: 0-0 GS: 0-1 Gd: 0-2 GF: - Fm: 0-0
Distance: 2m/2m3: 0-0 2m4-2m7: 0-3 3m+: 0-0
Track: LH: 0-1 RH: 0-2 Tight: 0-0 Gall: 0-2
Aids: Bl: 0-0 Vi: 0-0 Tstrap: 0-0
Best Rating: 137 10/99 Worc 2m4f   gd-fm   Hdl

Ex-French, he was going like a winner when falling in the valuable Tote Silver Cup at Ascot in December 1999, suffering a career-threatening injury. has struggled for form since. Best trip around two and a half miles. Has done most of his winning on good to soft.

Fare Dealing (IRE)
100(106h)   (97h)95
10-y-o b g Tremblant-Charming Whisper (Deep Run)
M J Gingell   Fare Dealing Partnership

Placings:34B450/FF/4312P0321-05622003   (2350)
2002/03: 21¹G, 18⁰GF, 22⁵GF, 16⁶G, 17²G, 16²G, 20⁰G, 20⁰G, 20³GS,

	Starts	1st	2nd	3rd	Win & Pl
Hurdles	6	1	0	1	3309
Chases	3	0	2	0	3120
Career Total	25	2	4	4	11819
102 4/02 Plum	2m5f	E(0-110)HHdl	GD	£2499
97 12/01 Sthl	2m4f110yE(0-105)HHdl	GD	£2478

Total win prize-money £4977

Track: LH: 2-3 RH: 2-2 Tight: 3-4 Gall: 0-0
Aids: Bl: 0-0 Vi: 0-0 Tstrap: 0-0
Best Rating: 131 3/03 Hayd 2m   good   Hdl
Distance: 2m2m3: 0-4 2m4-2m7: 1-5 3m+: 0-0
Track: LH: 1-9 RH: 0-0 Tight: 1-7 Gall: 0-1
Aids: Bl: 0-0 Vi: 0-0 Tstrap: 0-0
Best Rating: 102 4/02 Plum 2m5f   good   Hdl

Modest hurdler, stays two and three-quarter miles. Made a promising return to fences over an insufficient trip in September. Suited by good ground. Front runner.

Farfields Prince
89(102c)   (117c)73
11-y-o b g Weldnaas (USA)-Coca (Levmoss)
K G Wingrove   K O Warner

Placings:2115230/05U4/F1422255/P16F-0000   (0658)
2002/03: 16⁹GF, 19⁹G, 20⁵S, 16⁹GF,

	Starts	1st	2nd	3rd	Win & Pl
Hurdles	4	0	0	0	
Career Total	27	4	5	1	17750
107 9/01 Plum	2m1f	F(0-110)HCh	G-F	£3307
96 5/00 Hexm	2m110y	E Ch	GD	£2204
117 10/98 Weth	2m	C Hdl	GD	£4081
112 10/98 Hexm	2m	E Hdl	GD	£2490

Total win prize-money £12084

Going: Sf: 0-1 GS: 0-0 Gd: 0-1 GF: - Fm: 0-2
Distance: 2m/2m3: 0-2 2m4-2m7: 0-2 3m+: 0-0
Track: LH: 0-3 RH: 0-1 Tight: 0-0 Gall: 0-0
Aids: Bl: 0-2 Vi: 0-0 Tstrap: 0-0
Best Rating: 117 4/99 Weth 2m   gd-fm   Hdl

Farinel
(118h)   (131h)110
7-y-o b g In The Wings-Dame De L Oise (USA) (Riverman (USA))
A L T Moore   J P McManus

Placings:0/3004/4512212P-360000   (4475)
2002/03: 24³S, 20⁶YS, 20⁵S, 16⁰YS, 25⁰G, 20⁰G,

	Starts	1st	2nd	3rd	Win & Pl
Hurdles	4	0	0	1	1561
Chases	2	0	0	0	
Career Total	19	2	3	2	42195
123 1/02 Leop	3m	HHdl	Y-S	£15950
106 8/01 Kbgn	2m3f	(0-116)HHdl	GD	£7233

Total win prize-money £23185

Going: Sf: 0-2 GS: 0-0 Gd: 0-2 GF: - Fm: 0-0
Distance: 2m/2m3: 0-0 2m4-2m7: 0-3 3m+: 0-0
Track: LH: 0-5 RH: 0-0 Tight: 0-1 Gall: 0-1
Aids: Bl: 0-1 Vi: 0-0 Tstrap: 0-0
Best Rating: 131 11/02 Chep 3m   soft   Hdl

Useful Irish handicap hurdler; stays three miles; acts on good and yielding ground.

Farington Lodge (IRE)
80f
5-y-o b g Simply Great (FR)-Lodge Party (IRE) (Strong Gale)
Jonjo O Neill   Trevor Hemmings

Placings:0   (2574)
2002/03: 12⁰G,

	Starts	1st	2nd	3rd	Win & Pl
NH Flat	1	0	0	0	
Career Total	1	0	0	0	

Going: Sf: 0-0 GS: 0-0 Gd: 0-1 GF: - Fm: 0-0
Distance: 2m/2m3: 0-0 2m4-2m7: 0-0 3m+: 0-0
Track: LH: 0-1 RH: 0-0 Tight: 0-0 Gall: 0-0
Aids: Bl: 0-0 Vi: 0-0 Tstrap: 0-0
Best Rating: 80 12/02 Newb 1m4f110y good NHF

Farmer Jack

109(115h)   (135h)**154**
7-y-o b g Afflora (IRE)-Cheryls Pet (IRE) (General Ironside)
J W Mullins Peter Partridge

Placings:/4511420-4111243   (4554)
2002/03: 19⁴G, 19¹GS, 16¹G, 16¹G, 20²HY, 16⁴G, 20³G,

	Starts	1st	2nd	3rd	Win & Pl
Chases	7	3	1	1	54410
Career Total	15	6	2	1	73565
154	1/03	Kemp	2m	B Ch	GD £15446
145	12/02	Hayd	2m	C Ch	GD £9187
130	11/02	Tntn	2m3f	D Ch	G-S £6352
135	1/02	Asct	2m4f	C Hdl	G-S £5304
110	12/01	Extr	2m3f	E Hdl	GD £2922
105	4/01	Tntn	2m1f	H NHF	G-F £1568

Total win prize-money £40781

Going: Sf: 0-1 GS: 1-1 Gd: 2-5 GF: - Fm: 0-0
Distance: 2m/2m3: 3-4 2m4-2m7: 0-3 3m+: 0-0
Track: LH: 1-3 RH: 2-4 Tight: 1-1 Gall: 0-1
Aids: Bl: 0-0 Vi: 0-0 Tstrap: 0-0
Best Rating: 154 1/03 Kemp 2m good Ch

High-class novice chaser; formerly very useful hurdler; impressive winner of novice events at Taunton, Haydock and Kempton (beat Epervier D Or 6l conceding 8lb) before going down by 3l to Tarxien in Scilly Isles Novice Chase at Sandown (not quite stay 2m 4f in heavy ground); fourth in Arkle at Cheltenham; suited by 2m and gets 2m 4f on decent ground; acts on good and soft ground; has a good cruising speed and generally jumps well.

Farmer Josh

(91h)   (47h)
9-y-o b g Dancing High-Millie Duffer (Furry Glen)
Miss L V Davis (A Streeter 12/5) Miss Louise Davis

Placings:000P/50405PP/P/00   (4706)
2002/03: 16⁰G, 20⁰G,

	Starts	1st	2nd	3rd	Win & Pl
Hurdles	2	0	0	0	0
Career Total	14	0	0	0	0

Going: Sf: 0-0 GS: 0-0 Gd: 0-2 GF: - Fm: 0-0
Distance: 2m/2m3: 0-1 2m4-2m7: 0-1 3m+: 0-0
Track: LH: 0-2 RH: 0-0 Tight: 0-1 Gall: 0-0
Aids: Bl: 0-0 Vi: 0-0 Tstrap: 0-0
Best Rating: 73 4/99 MRas 2m3f110y good Hdl

Farne Isle

99f   98f
4-y-o ch f Midnight Legend-Biloela (Nicholas Bill)
G A Harker M F Spence

Placings:1650   (4611)
2002/03: 17¹HY, 16⁶G, 17⁵G, 17⁰G,

	Starts	1st	2nd	3rd	Win & Pl
NH Flat	4	1	0	0	1855
Career Total	4	1	0	0	1855
98	1/03	Sedg	2m1f	H NHF	HVY £1855

Total win prize-money £1855

Going: Sf: 1-1 GS: 0-0 Gd: 0-3 GF: - Fm: 0-0

Distance: 2m/2m3: 1-4 2m4-2m7: 0-0 3m+: 0-0
Track: LH: 1-2 RH: 0-2 Tight: 1-3 Gall: 0-1
Aids: Bl: 0-0 Vi: 0-0 Tstrap: 0-0
Best Rating: 98 1/03 Sedg 2m1f heavy NHF

Bumper winner on her debut at Sedgefield in January.

Farrago

36f
5-y-o b m Bold Arrangement-Farah (Lead On Time (USA))
J R Turner J R Turner

Placings:66   (1824)
2002/03: 17⁶GS, 16⁶HY,

	Starts	1st	2nd	3rd	Win & Pl
NH Flat	2	0	0	0	0
Career Total	2	0	0	0	0

Going: Sf: 0-1 GS: 0-1 Gd: 0-0 GF: - Fm: 0-0
Distance: 2m/2m3: 0-2 2m4-2m7: 0-0 3m+: 0-0
Track: LH: 0-2 RH: 0-0 Tight: 0-1 Gall: 0-0
Aids: Bl: 0-0 Vi: 0-0 Tstrap: 0-0
Best Rating: 36 11/02 Hexm 2m110y heavy NHF

Fas

64
7-y-o ch g Weldnaas (USA)-Polly s Teahouse (Shack (USA))
Mrs K Walton (C W Fairhurst 30/4) F & T Walton

Placings:4-0P   (3325)
2002/03: 16⁰G, 16⁶G,

	Starts	1st	2nd	3rd	Win & Pl
Hurdles	2	0	0	0	0
Career Total	3	0	0	0	0

Going: Sf: 0-0 GS: 0-0 Gd: 0-2 GF: - Fm: 0-0
Distance: 2m/2m3: 0-2 2m4-2m7: 0-0 3m+: 0-0
Track: LH: 0-1 RH: 0-1 Tight: 0-1 Gall: 0-0
Aids: Bl: 0-0 Vi: 0-0 Tstrap: 0-0
Best Rating: 64 4/02 Sedg 2m1f gd-fm Hdl

Fasgo (IRE)

106(84h)   (110h)**126**
8-y-o b g Montelimar (USA)-Action Plan (Creative Plan (USA))
P F Nicholls F A Smith

Placings:1P31P0-2F235   (3444)
2002/03: 25²GS, 30⁶GS, 29²GS, 26³S, 26⁵HY,

	Starts	1st	2nd	3rd	Win & Pl
Chases	5	0	2	1	7631
Career Total	11	2	2	2	15609
118	2/02	Sand	3m110y	D(0-115)HCh	SFT £5005
110	11/01	Chep	3m	F Hdl	G-S £1918

Total win prize-money £6923

Going: Sf: 0-2 GS: 0-3 Gd: 0-0 GF: - Fm: 0-0
Distance: 2m/2m3: 0-0 2m4-2m7: 0-0 3m+: 0-5
Track: LH: 0-3 RH: 0-2 Tight: 0-1 Gall: 0-2
Aids: Bl: 0-1 Vi: 0-0 Tstrap: 0-0
Best Rating: 126 12/02 Wwck 3m5f gd-sft Ch

Fair handicap chaser, he acts on good and soft ground. Stays well.

Fashion House

7-y-o b m Homo Sapien-High Heels (IRE) (Supreme Leader)
S Pike Stewart Pike

Placings:50-0552   (4541)
2002/03: 17⁰G, 22⁵GF, 22⁵G, 24²G,

	Starts	1st	2nd	3rd	Win & Pl
Hurdles	3	0	0	0	0
Chases	1	0	1	0	848
Career Total	6	0	1	0	848

Going: Sf: 0-0 GS: 0-0 Gd: 0-3 GF: - Fm: 0-1
Distance: 2m/2m3: 0-1 2m4-2m7: 0-2 3m+: 0-1
Track: LH: 0-1 RH: 0-3 Tight: 0-2 Gall: 0-0
Aids: Bl: 0-0 Vi: 0-0 Tstrap: 0-0
Best Rating: 92 4/03 Ludl 3m good Ch

Won two points in March 2003; a shade unlucky not to complete a hat-trick in modest hunter chase at Ludlow next month.

Fashion Victim

105   **84**
8-y-o b g High Estate-Kirkby Belle (Bay Express)
Mrs A C Tate J A Simpson

Placings:00/464F550/400150-000P0146L   (1896)
2002/03: 16⁸GF, 16⁰G, 17⁰GF, 17⁶GF, 16⁹G, 19¹GF, 21⁴F, 17⁵GF, 16³GS,

	Starts	1st	2nd	3rd	Win & Pl
Hurdles	9	1	0	0	5102
Career Total	24	2	0	0	7601
91	10/02	Hrfd	2m3f110yE(0-110)HHdl	G-F £4844
91	10/01	Hrfd	2m1f	F(0-100)HHdl	GD £2499

Total win prize-money £7343

Going: Sf: 0-0 GS: 0-1 Gd: 0-2 GF: - Fm: 1-6
Distance: 2m/2m3: 0-7 2m4-2m7: 1-2 3m+: 0-0
Track: LH: 0-4 RH: 1-5 Tight: 0-2 Gall: 0-1
Aids: Bl: 0-0 Vi: 0-0 Tstrap: 0-1
Best Rating: 91 10/02 Hrfd 2m3f110y gd-fm Hdl

Modest handicap hurdler. Bounced back to form after a wind operation when registering his second course victory in a four-runner race at Hereford October 2002. Can be tricky at the start.

Fassan (IRE)

11-y-o br g Contract Law (USA)-Persian Susan (USA) (Herbager)
Mrs K J Tutty (A Crook 3/6) N D Tutty

Placings:F232/523024/03222166/34224/12321P/54663664 3/P5424P-P6   (3513)
2002/03: 21⁸PS, 28⁶G,

	Starts	1st	2nd	3rd	Win & Pl
Chases	2	0	0	0	0
Career Total	47	3	12	7	36782
104	2/00	Hayd	2m	C HCh	SFT £6041
104	11/99	Aint	2m	D(0-115)HCh	GD £9187
110	3/98	Catt	2m	E Hdl	SFT £2598

Total win prize-money £17828

Going: Sf: 0-1 GS: 0-0 Gd: 0-1 GF: - Fm: 0-0
Distance: 2m/2m3: 0-0 2m4-2m7: 0-1 3m+: 0-1
Track: LH: 0-2 RH: 0-0 Tight: 0-1 Gall: 0-0
Aids: Bl: 0-1 Vi: 0-0 Tstrap: 0-0
Best Rating: 112 2/97 Weth 2m soft Hdl

Fast Flowing

5-y-o b m Sovereign Water (FR)-Spartona (Cisto (FR))
J Wade John Wade

Placings:0P   (1820)
2002/03: 17⁰GF, 20ᴾHY,

	Starts	1st	2nd	3rd	Win & Pl
NH Flat	1	0	0	0	0
Hurdles	1	0	0	0	0
Career Total	2	0	0		0

Going: Sf: 0-1 GS: 0-0 Gd: 0-0 GF: - Fm: 0-1
Distance: 2m/2m3: 0-1 2m4-2m7: 0-0 3m+: 0-0
Track: LH: 0-1 RH: 0-1 Tight: 0-0 Gall: 0-0
Aids: Bl: 0-0 Vi: 0-0 Tstrap: 0-0
Best Rating: 52 10/02 Carl 2m1f   gd-fm NHF

Fast King (FR)
94   101

5-y-o b g Housamix (FR)-Fast Girl (FR) (Gay Minstrel (FR))
P J Hobbs The Kingpins

Placings:3105-05100F   (4695)
2002/03: 20⁰G, 17⁵HY, 19¹GS, 19⁰S, 17⁰GS, 16ᶠG,

	Starts	1st	2nd	3rd	Win & Pl
Hurdles	5	1	0	0	4342
Chases	1	0	0	0	0
Career Total	10	2	0	1	7784
96	12/02 Tntn	2m3f110yD(0-120)HHdl		G-S	£4342
90	11/01 Bang	2m1f	E Hdl	G-S	£2691
			Total win prize-money £7034		

Going: Sf: 0-2 GS: 1-2 Gd: 0-2 GF: - Fm: 0-0
Distance: 2m/2m3: 0-3 2m4-2m7: 1-3 3m+: 0-0
Track: LH: 0-3 RH: 1-3 Tight: 1-5 Gall: 0-0
Aids: Bl: 1-6 Vi: 0-0 Tstrap: 0-0
Best Rating: 101 11/01 Asct 2m1y good Hdl

Modest ex-French hurdler, suited by soft ground.

Fast Mix (FR)
102   103

4-y-o gr g Linamix (FR)-Fascinating Hill (FR) (Danehill (USA))
M C Pipe (A Fabre 27/5) Jim Weeden

Placings:1P2F2   (4363)
2002/03: 16¹GS, 16ᴾHY, 16²HY, 20ᴾHY, 17²F,

	Starts	1st	2nd	3rd	Win & Pl
Hurdles	5	1	2	0	6443
Career Total	5	1	2	0	6443
103	11/02 Newb	2m110y	D Hdl	G-S	£4101
			Total win prize-money £4102		

Going: Sf: 0-3 GS: 1-1 Gd: 0-0 GF: - Fm: 0-1
Distance: 2m/2m3: 1-4 2m4-2m7: 0-1 3m+: 0-0
Track: LH: 1-4 RH: 0-1 Tight: 0-2 Gall: 1-1
Aids: Bl: 0-0 Vi: 0-0 Tstrap: 0-0
Best Rating: 103 1/03 Plum 2m   heavy Hdl

Hacked up on debut when winning a poor juvenile hurdle at Newbury in November 2002, but failed to handle heavy ground next time, although ran better on it on his handicap debut subsequently; possibly unlucky when second on fast ground in juvenile event at Taunton March 2003.

Fatal Flaw (USA)
87   95

6-y-o b g Hansel (USA)-Fateful (USA) (Topsider (USA))

A Ennis (D Shaw 1/3) Equine America (UK) Ltd

Placings:5150-P564   (4282)
2002/03: 16ᴾGS, 16⁵GF, 16⁶G, 18⁴GF,

	Starts	1st	2nd	3rd	Win & Pl
Hurdles	1	0	0	0	0
Chases	3	0	0	0	435
Career Total	8	1	0	0	8966
1/02 Pau	2m3f	Hdl		VS	£7012
			Total win prize-money £7012		

Going: Sf: 0-0 GS: 0-1 Gd: 0-1 GF: - Fm: 0-2
Distance: 2m/2m3: 0-4 2m4-2m7: 0-1 3m+: 0-0
Track: LH: 0-0 RH: 0-3 Tight: 0-1 Gall: 0-0
Aids: Bl: 0-0 Vi: 0-0 Tstrap: 0-2
Best Rating: 99 11/02 Leic 2m   good Ch

A winner on the Flat in France, but down the field on his hurdles debut and novice chases.

Fate A Compli (IRE)

8-y-o ch g Over The River (FR)-Oh Clare (Laurence O)
R H Alner T J Summerfield

Placings:0P/P-   (0009)
2002/03: 26ᴾG,

	Starts	1st	2nd	3rd	Win & Pl
Chases	1	0	0	0	
Career Total	3	0	0	0	

Going: Sf: 0-0 GS: 0-0 Gd: 0-1 GF: - Fm: 0-0
Distance: 2m/2m3: 0-0 2m4-2m7: 0-0 3m+: 0-0
Track: LH: 0-1 RH: 0-0 Tight: 0-1 Gall: 0-0
Aids: Bl: 0-0 Vi: 0-0 Tstrap: 0-0
Best Rating: 72 9/00 Chep 2m110y good NHF

Fatehalkhair (IRE)
113(109h)   (125h)128

11-y-o ch g Kris-Midway Lady (USA) (Alleged (USA))
B Ellison R Wagner

Placings:3232/11021134F1F/163301P0/04/011F521464/01
0P5421-1304P5   (4796)
2002/03: 21¹GF, 24³G, 24⁰G, 25⁴G, 33ᴾG, 28⁵GF,

	Starts	1st	2nd	3rd	Win & Pl
Hurdles	1	1	0	0	3741
Chases	5	0	0	1	6022
Career Total	49	13	5	6	84179
123	7/02	Sedg	2m5f110yD(0-120)HHdl	G-F	£3740
135	4/02	Sedg	3m4f	D(0-125)HCh	G-F	£14105
125	11/01	Sedg	2m5f110yB HHdl	SFT	£8438
125	12/00	Sedg	2m5f	E Ch	SFT	£3168
125	8/00	Sedg	2m110y	E Ch	GD	£3042
106	7/00	Sedg	2m110y	E Ch	FRM	£3168
131	2/99	Sedg	2m1f	D(0-125)HHdl	GD	£5836
120	7/98	Sedg	2m5f110yD(0-120)HHdl	G-F	£2843
117	2/98	Sedg	2m1f	D(0-125)HHdl	GD	£2952
105	10/97	Sedg	2m5f110yD(0-125)HHdl	G-F	£3685
106	9/97	Sedg	2m1f	E Hdl	G-F	£2320
101	5/97	Sedg	2m1f	F(0-100)HHdl	G-F	£2248
96	5/97	Sedg	2m1f	E Hdl	G-F	£2320
			Total win prize-money £57870			

Going: Sf: 0-0 GS: 0-0 Gd: 0-4 GF: - Fm: 1-2
Distance: 2m/2m3: 0-0 2m4-2m7: 1-1 3m+: 0-5
Track: LH: 1-6 RH: 0-0 Tight: 1-3 Gall: 0-2
Aids: Bl: 0-0 Vi: 0-0 Tstrap: 0-0
Best Rating: 135 4/02 Sedg 3m4f   gd-fm Ch

Useful chaser/fair hurdler; versatile performer; difficult to beat at Sedgefield where he has gained all of his jumps

---

wins; stays three and a half miles; suited by a sound surface; Flat winner in 2002.

Father D (IRE)
101   97d

8-y-o b g Mister Lord (USA)-Abrahams Cross (IRE) (Bustomi)
R H Buckler C T & A Samways

Placings:03P2401-F00014   (4631)
2002/03: 17ᶠG, 16⁰G, 17⁰GS, 17⁹G, 19¹GF, 16⁴GF,

	Starts	1st	2nd	3rd	Win & Pl
Hurdles	6	1	0	0	3835
Career Total	13	2	1	1	7657
97	4/03	Extr	2m3f	F(0-90)HHdl	G-F	£3835
100	4/02	Uttx	2m	E Hdl	GD	£2702
			Total win prize-money £6537		

Going: Sf: 0-0 GS: 0-1 Gd: 0-3 GF: - Fm: 1-2
Distance: 2m/2m3: 1-6 2m4-2m7: 0-0 3m+: 0-0
Track: LH: 0-2 RH: 1-4 Tight: 0-2 Gall: 0-0
Aids: Bl: 0-0 Vi: 0-0 Tstrap: 0-0
Best Rating: 105 12/01 NAbb 2m1f   heavy NHF

Moderate novice hurdler; keen front-running sort; won over two miles at Uttoxeter in April 2002; returned to form when winning at Exeter April 2003; acts on ground good and faster.

Father Mulcahy
76(102h)   66

7-y-o b g Safawan-Constant Delight (Never So Bold)
D McCain Mrs I P Gregson

Placings:43/3020-PP34P   (3487)
2002/03: 20ᴾG, 17ᴾHY, 16²S, 16⁴HY, 17ᴾS,

	Starts	1st	2nd	3rd	Win & Pl
Hurdles	1	0	0	0	0
Chases	4	0	0	1	1252
Career Total	11	0	1	3	3589

Going: Sf: 0-4 GS: 0-0 Gd: 0-1 GF: - Fm: 0-0
Distance: 2m/2m3: 0-4 2m4-2m7: 0-1 3m+: 0-0
Track: LH: 0-5 RH: 0-0 Tight: 0-3 Gall: 0-0
Aids: Bl: 0-2 Vi: 0-0 Tstrap: 0-0
Best Rating: 100 3/02 Uttx 2m4f110y heavy Hdl

Novice hurdler, returned from 684 days off to run a creditable third at Towcester in January 2002; suited by heavy ground; no impact over fences so far.

Father Paddy
102(98c)   (90+c)104

8-y-o ch g Minster Son-Sister Claire (Quayside)
T J Fitzgerald (J G Fitzgerald 18/1) P McMahon

Placings:321/6/5063-32   (4260)
2002/03: 19³G, 21²G,

	Starts	1st	2nd	3rd	Win & Pl
Hurdles	1	0	1	0	1002
Chases	1	0	0	1	1054
Career Total	10	1	2	3	7670
107	3/00	Carl	2m1f	H NHF	G-S	£4446
			Total win prize-money £4446		

Going: Sf: 0-0 GS: 0-0 Gd: 0-2 GF: - Fm: 0-0
Distance: 2m/2m3: 0-1 2m4-2m7: 0-1 3m+: 0-0
Track: LH: 0-2 RH: 0-0 Tight: 0-2 Gall: 0-0
Aids: Bl: 0-0 Vi: 0-0 Tstrap: 0-0
Best Rating: 107 3/00 Carl 2m1f   gd-sft NHF

Lightly-raced bumper winner who has shown only moderate form over hurdles and fences.

Father Rector (IRE)

14-y-o b g The Parson-Mwanamio (Sole Mio (USA))
R Tate (Mrs F E Needham 1/6) William Lamarque

Placings:05/5056f12U350/504303P/64263211461016/13F/
111P/240141550/5/41043-116F   (0684)
2002/03: 25¹GF, 22¹GF, 20⁶GF, 24⁶G,

	Starts	1st	2nd	3rd	Win & Pl
Chases	4	2	0	0	3304
Career Total	60	15	4	6	62032
104 6/02	MRas	2m6f110yH Ch		G-F	£1757
105 5/02	Weth	3m1f	H Ch	G-F	£1547
113 5/01	MRas	2m6f110yH Ch		GD	£2460
126 10/99	Strf	2m5f110yC(0-135)HCh	G-F	£8008
125 6/99	Worc	2m4f110yD(0-120)HCh	G-F	£3923
129 10/98	Winc	2m5f	E(0-115)HCh	G-F	£4580
124 5/98	MRas	2m6f110yH Ch		G-F	£2052
117 5/98	Hrfd	2m3f	H Ch	GD	£1830
122 2/98	Hrdg	3m	H Ch	GD	£1213
104 3/97	Thur	2m6f	Ch	GD	£2712
117 9/96	List	3m	HHdl	G-F	£7371
117 8/96	Tram	2m4f	(0-109)HHdl	GD	£2824
110 8/96	Gway	2m5f190y HHdl	G-F	£9974
114 11/94	Clon	3m	Hdl	HVY	£2120
11/94	Clon	2m	NHF	Y-S	£2446

Total win prize-money £54822

Going: Sf: 0-0 GS: 0-0 Gd: 0-1 GF: - Fm: 2-3
Distance: 2m/2m3: 0-0 2m4-2m7: 1-2 3m+: 1-2
Track: LH: 1-3 RH: 1-1 Tight: 1-2 Gall: 0-0
Aids: Bl: 0-0 Vi: 0-0 Tstrap: 0-0
Best Rating: 129 5/99 Uttx 2m4f   gd-fm Ch

Veteran pointer/hunter chaser, suited by fast ground; stays three miles plus, but looks better at shorter.

Fatherly Chat (IRE)

7-y-o b g Supreme Leader-Frozen Ground (Arctic Slave)
R T Phillips Ascot Five Plus One

Placings:0P   (3153)
2002/03: 16⁰GS, 24ᴾHY,

	Starts	1st	2nd	3rd	Win & Pl
NH Flat	1	0	0	0	0
Hurdles	1	0	0	0	0
Career Total	2	0	0		

Going: Sf: 0-1 GS: 0-1 Gd: 0-0 GF: - Fm: 0-0
Distance: 2m/2m3: 0-1 2m4-2m7: 0-0 3m+: 0-1
Track: LH: 0-2 RH: 0-0 Tight: 0-1 Gall: 0-0
Aids: Bl: 0-0 Vi: 0-0 Tstrap: 0-0
Best Rating: 67 11/02 Sthl 2m   gd-sft NHF

Fathom

5-y-o ch g Zafonic (USA)-River Lullaby (USA) (Riverman (USA))
Mrs L B Normile K J Fehilly

Placings:00   (4778)
2002/03: 17⁰G, 16⁰G,

	Starts	1st	2nd	3rd	Win & Pl
NH Flat	2	0	0	0	
Career Total	2	0	0		

Going: Sf: 0-0 GS: 0-0 Gd: 0-2 GF: - Fm: 0-0
Distance: 2m/2m3: 0-2 2m4-2m7: 0-0 3m+: 0-0
Track: LH: 0-0 RH: 0-1 Tight: 0-0 Gall: 0-0

Aids: Bl: 0-0 Vi: 0-0 Tstrap: 0-0
Best Rating: 70 4/03 Prth 2m110y   good NHF

Faugere

79   108
7-y-o ch g Jupiter Island-Pinch (Ardross)
P F Nicholls J J Boulter

Placings:26   (4310)
2002/03: 20²HY, 24⁶G,

	Starts	1st	2nd	3rd	Win & Pl
Hurdles	2	0	1	0	1054
Career Total	2	0	1	0	1054

Going: Sf: 0-1 GS: 0-0 Gd: 0-1 GF: - Fm: 0-0
Distance: 2m/2m3: 0-0 2m4-2m7: 0-1 3m+: 0-1
Track: LH: 0-1 RH: 0-1 Tight: 0-1 Gall: 0-1
Aids: Bl: 0-0 Vi: 0-0 Tstrap: 0-0
Best Rating: 108 2/03 Folk 2m4f110y heavy Hdl

Ex-pointer; showed promise in a maiden hurdle on testing ground; stays two and a half miles.

Faustino

99   89
11-y-o br g Faustus (USA)-Hot Case (Upper Case (USA))
D M Grissell The Rooster Club

Placings:501631/142010022/43F12323/4B5/U35332F/51P
PP/236-3   (0127)
2002/03: 26³GF,

	Starts	1st	2nd	3rd	Win & Pl
Chases	1	0	0	1	502
Career Total	42	6	7	9	30390
85 6/00	Prth	2m4f110yF(0-110)HCh	SFT	£4771
79 9/97	Extr	2m3f	D Ch	G-F	£3501
113 8/96	Hrfd	2m3f110yD(0-125)HHdl	G-F	£2864
108 5/96	Ludl	2m	E Hdl	G-F	£2285
117 4/96	Asct	2m110y D(0-110)HHdl	G-F	£3517
105 3/96	Winc	2m	E Hdl	G-F	£2232

Total win prize-money £19172

Going: Sf: 0-0 GS: 0-0 Gd: 0-0 GF: - Fm: 0-1
Distance: 2m/2m3: 0-0 2m4-2m7: 0-0 3m+: 0-1
Track: LH: 0-0 RH: 0-0 Tight: 0-1 Gall: 0-0
Aids: Bl: 0-0 Vi: 0-0 Tstrap: 0-0
Best Rating: 117 4/96 Asct 2m110y gd-fm Hdl

Formerly a useful chaser on firm ground, he has since proved himself on easy going and is versatile as regards trip. He is reported to have had breathing problems.

Favoured Option (IRE)

113(72h)   (20h)122
8-y-o ch g Glacial Storm (USA)-Hot House Flower (Derring Rose)
Ian Williams K A Cosby

Placings:006/P20351/0F634321P-U52222211   (4619)
2002/03: 25ᴾGS, 23⁴U, 25⁵GF, 24²GS, 25²S, 25²GS, 23²GS, 29²G,
25¹GF, 24¹GF,

	Starts	1st	2nd	3rd	Win & Pl
Chases	10	2	5	0	28197
Career Total	27	4	7	3	41167
122 4/03	Carl	3m	D(0-125)HCh	G-F	£13975
122 4/03	Hrfd	3m1f110yE(0-110)HCh	G-F	£6097
106 4/02	Carl	3m2f	D(0-115)HCh	G-F	£7003
97 2/01	Folk	2m6f110yE Hdl	HVY	£2544

Total win prize-money £29621

Going: Sf: 0-1 GS: 0-4 Gd: 0-2 GF: - Fm: 2-3
Distance: 2m/2m3: 0-0 2m4-2m7: 0-0 3m+: 2-10
Track: LH: 0-3 RH: 2-7 Tight: 0-2 Gall: 0-1
Aids: Bl: 0-0 Vi: 0-0 Tstrap: 0-0
Best Rating: 122 4/03 Carl 3m   gd-fm Ch

Fair chaser; ended a frustrating run of seconds when winning a weakly contested extended three mile handicap at Hereford April 2003 and followed up at Carlisle two weeks later, seems weighted up to the hilt now; stays three and a half miles; suited by fast ground, but effective with cut.

Fawn Prince (IRE)

(85c)   (83c)
10-y-o b g Electric-Regent Star (Prince Regent (FR))
S G Chadwick S Chadwick

Placings:10/6000/10/530/02630P66-P   (3963)
2002/03: 16ᴾS,

	Starts	1st	2nd	3rd	Win & Pl
Hurdles	1	0	0	0	
Career Total	20	2	1	2	6544
103 7/98	Bell	2m1f	Hdl	G-F	£2391
106 1/97	Leop	2m	NHF	G-Y	£3051

Total win prize-money £5443

Going: Sf: 0-1 GS: 0-0 Gd: 0-0 GF: - Fm: 0-0
Distance: 2m/2m3: 0-1 2m4-2m7: 0-0 3m+: 0-0
Track: LH: 0-1 RH: 0-0 Tight: 0-1 Gall: 0-0
Aids: Bl: 0-0 Vi: 0-0 Tstrap: 0-0
Best Rating: 106 1/97 Leop 2m   gd-yld NHF

Fayalie (IRE)

8-y-o b m Classic Memory-Much Obliged (Crash Course)
Miss V J Parvin J H Hewitt

Placings:0/000/P   (4261)
2002/03: 27ᴾG,

	Starts	1st	2nd	3rd	Win & Pl
Chases	1	0	0	0	
Career Total	5	0	0		

Going: Sf: 0-0 GS: 0-0 Gd: 0-1 GF: - Fm: 0-0
Distance: 2m/2m3: 0-0 2m4-2m7: 0-0 3m+: 0-1
Track: LH: 0-1 RH: 0-0 Tight: 0-1 Gall: 0-0
Aids: Bl: 0-0 Vi: 0-0 Tstrap: 0-0
Best Rating: 64 11/00 DRoy 2m   yld-sft NHF

Fayrway Rhythm (IRE)

79   36
6-y-o b g Fayruz-The Way She Moves (North Stoke)
Ian Emmerson Ms Josie Swinburn

Placings:06/3446031230-06   (4663)
2002/03: 22⁰G, 17⁶GF,

	Starts	1st	2nd	3rd	Win & Pl
Hurdles	2	0	0	0	
Career Total	14	1	1	3	4555
103 11/01	Tntn	2m1f	G(0-90)HHdl	GD	£1732

Total win prize-money £1733

Going: Sf: 0-0 GS: 0-2 Gd: 0-1 GF: - Fm: 0-1
Distance: 2m/2m3: 0-1 2m4-2m7: 0-1 3m+: 0-0
Track: LH: 0-1 RH: 0-1 Tight: 0-0 Gall: 0-0
Aids: Bl: 0-0 Vi: 0-2 Tstrap: 0-0
Best Rating: 103 11/01 Carl 2m1f   heavy Hdl

Placed form over hurdles. Has become disappointing and dropped to claiming company to get off the mark at the ninth attempt at Taunton in November. Good effort for new yard next time. Runs in blinkers or a visor.

Feanor

105   **95+**

5-y-o b m Presidium-Nouvelle Cuisine (Yawa)
Mrs S A Watt Major E J Watt

Placings:5F653P133-UPPP0   (4711)
2002/03: 16^U^G, 16^P^G, 16^P^S, 16^P^G, 16^0^GF,

	Starts	1st	2nd	3rd	Win & Pl
Hurdles	5	0	0	0	
Career Total	14	1	0	3	4372

95 1/02 Catt 2m   E Hdl   SFT £2723
Total win prize-money £2723

Going: Sf: 0-1 GS: 0-0 Gd: 0-3 GF: - Fm: 0-1
Distance: 2m/2m3: 0-5 2m4-2m7: 0-0 3m+: 0-1
Track: LH: 0-5 RH: 0-1 Tight: 0-1 Gall: 0-0
Aids: Bl: 0-0 Vi: 0-0 Tstrap: 0-0
Best Rating: 95 1/02 Catt 2m   soft Hdl

Moderate form shown over hurdles before getting off the mark at Catterick in January 2002; in good form in the summer of 2003 with a win in weak event at Southwell with a good third in better company at Worcester; scored again back at Southwell next time; effective at 2m; seems to handle all types of ground.

Fear Siuil (IRE)

111   **115**

10-y-o b g Strong Gale-Astral River (Over The River (FR))
Nick Williams (D M Forster 8/5) Mrs Jane Kelly

Placings:0P0/54P/P/P1FPP3-4212P34   (1644)
2002/03: 16^4^GF, 16^2^GF, 20^1^GF, 17^4^S, 21^P^GF, 17^3^G, 16^4^GF,

	Starts	1st	2nd	3rd	Win & Pl
Chases	7	1	2	1	13234
Career Total	20	2	2	2	19154

110 7/02 Strf 2m4f D(0-125)HCh G-F £8190
110 11/01 Catt 2m3f E(0-115)HCh G-F £5027
Total win prize-money £13218

Going: Sf: 0-1 GS: 0-0 Gd: 0-1 GF: - Fm: 1-5
Distance: 2m/2m3: 0-5 2m4-2m7: 1-2 3m+: 0-0
Track: LH: 1-6 RH: 0-1 Tight: 1-4 Gall: 0-0
Aids: Bl: 0-0 Vi: 0-0 Tstrap: 1-7
Best Rating: 116 8/02 Strf 2m1f110y soft Ch

Moderate handicap chaser, stays two and a half miles and is suited by a sharp track; best on a sound surface; has worn a tongue tie.

Fearless Mel (IRE)

105   **107**

9-y-o b g Mandalus-Milan Pride (Northern Guest) (USA))
Mrs H Dalton Mrs W D Leppington

Placings:0/32   (4321)
2002/03: 20^9^GS, 24^2^G,

	Starts	1st	2nd	3rd	Win & Pl
Chases	2	0	1	1	2034
Career Total	3	0	1	1	2034

Going: Sf: 0-0 GS: 0-1 Gd: 0-1 GF: - Fm: 0-0
Distance: 2m/2m3: 0-0 2m4-2m7: 0-1 3m+: 0-1
Track: LH: 0-1 RH: 0-1 Tight: 0-1 Gall: 0-0
Aids: Bl: 0-0 Vi: 0-0 Tstrap: 0-0
Best Rating: 107 3/03 Bang 3m110y good Ch

Feel The Pride (IRE)

103   **112+**

5-y-o b m Persian Bold-Nordic Pride (Horage)
Jonjo O Neill (J S Bolger 23/6) Mrs M Liston

Placings:3   (1779)
2002/03: 19^3^GS,

	Starts	1st	2nd	3rd	Win & Pl
Hurdles	1	0	0	1	840
Career Total	1	0	0	1	840

Going: Sf: 0-0 GS: 0-0 Gd: 0-0 GF: - Fm: 0-0
Distance: 2m/2m3: 0-1 2m4-2m7: 0-0 3m+: 0-0
Track: LH: 0-0 RH: 0-0 Tight: 0-0 Gall: 0-0
Aids: Bl: 0-0 Vi: 0-0 Tstrap: 0-0
Best Rating: 103 11/02 Extr   2m3f   gd-sft Hdl

Fair Flat form in Ireland; completed a hat-trick in novice hurdles in the summer of 2003; acts on fast ground.

Feeling Fizzical

5-y-o b g Feelings (FR)-Stepdaughter (Relkino)
Mrs J C McGregor Mrs Dorothy Thomson

Placings:PP   (4376)
2002/03: 24^P^S, 27^P^G,

	Starts	1st	2nd	3rd	Win & Pl
Hurdles	2	0	0	0	
Career Total	2	0	0	0	

Going: Sf: 0-1 GS: 0-0 Gd: 0-1 GF: - Fm: 0-0
Distance: 2m/2m3: 0-0 2m4-2m7: 0-0 3m+: 0-0
Track: LH: 0-2 RH: 0-0 Tight: 0-1 Gall: 0-0
Aids: Bl: 0-0 Vi: 0-0 Tstrap: 0-0
Best Rating: 0   3/03 Sedg 3m3f110y good Hdl

Felix Darby (IRE)

109(94h)   (73 h)**85**

8-y-o b g Buckskin (FR)-Cool Anne (Orchardist)
Miss G Browne Ms Pat Treacy

Placings:44542   (4738)
2002/03: 21^4^S, 20^4^S, 24^5^GS, 29^4^G, 24^2^GF,

	Starts	1st	2nd	3rd	Win & Pl
Hurdles	3	0	0	0	320
Chases	2	0	1	0	1609
Career Total	5	0	1	0	1929

Going: Sf: 0-2 GS: 0-1 Gd: 0-1 GF: - Fm: 0-1
Distance: 2m/2m3: 0-0 2m4-2m7: 0-2 3m+: 0-3
Track: LH: 0-4 RH: 0-1 Tight: 0-1 Gall: 0-0
Aids: Bl: 0-0 Vi: 0-0 Tstrap: 0-0
Best Rating: 85 4/03 Chep 3m   gd-fm Ch

Placed in Irish points but very modest form over hurdles; not disgraced in 21 furlong handicap chase on fencing debut at Warwick March 2003; stays well; acts on fast ground; seems sure to win in the novice ranks.

Felix Randal (IRE)

93(103h)   (98h)**92+**

7-y-o ch g Be My Native (USA)-Odd Sox (FR) (Main Reef)
Jonjo O Neill Anne Duchess Of Westminster

Placings:06P0P12-30P2   (4221)
2002/03: 23^3^G, 24^0^GS, 22^P^GS, 25^2^GF,

	Starts	1st	2nd	3rd	Win & Pl
Hurdles	3	0	1	0	655

Chases (Feel The Pride continued)

Chases	1	0	1	0	1060
Career Total	11	1	2	1	7229

98 4/02 Ludl 2m5f   E(0-105)HHdl GD £3900
Total win prize-money £3900

Going: Sf: 0-0 GS: 0-2 Gd: 0-1 GF: - Fm: 0-1
Distance: 2m/2m3: 0-0 2m4-2m7: 0-1 3m+: 0-3
Track: LH: 0-2 RH: 0-2 Tight: 0-1 Gall: 0-0
Aids: Bl: 0-1 Vi: 0-0 Tstrap: 0-1
Best Rating: 98 10/02 Hayd 2m7f110y good Hdl

Had shown modest form in first five starts until taking advantage of move into handicap company with comfortable success at Ludlow in April 2002. Decent reappearance when third in a handicap at Haydock. Decent ground seems to suit and two mile four plus.

Felloo (IRE)

14-y-o br g Decent Fellow-Cuckaloo (Master Buck)
Mrs R E Walker (J Taylor 12/5) John Eaton

Placings:440/45PP/6425/5/2P/P   (0319)
2002/03: 26^P^G,

	Starts	1st	2nd	3rd	Win & Pl
Chases	1	0	0	0	
Career Total	15	0	2	0	2509

Going: Sf: 0-0 GS: 0-0 Gd: 0-1 GF: - Fm: 0-0
Distance: 2m/2m3: 0-0 2m4-2m7: 0-0 3m+: 0-0
Track: LH: 0-1 RH: 0-0 Tight: 0-0 Gall: 0-0
Aids: Bl: 0-0 Vi: 0-0 Tstrap: 0-0
Best Rating: 100 3/96 Sand 2m110y soft Hdl

Felony (IRE)

89   **62**

8-y-o ch g Pharly (FR)-Scales Of Justice (Final Straw)
L P Grassick Baskerville Racing Club

Placings:P0063/1/P-00PP45   (4149)
2002/03: 20^0^G, 17^0^G, 17^0^G, 26^P^S, 16^4^S, 21^5^G,

	Starts	1st	2nd	3rd	Win & Pl
Hurdles	6	0	0	0	0
Career Total	13	1	0	1	1865

82 5/99 Hrfd 2m3f110yG Hdl   G-S £1658
Total win prize-money £1658

Going: Sf: 0-2 GS: 0-0 Gd: 0-4 GF: - Fm: 0-0
Distance: 2m/2m3: 0-3 2m4-2m7: 0-2 3m+: 0-1
Track: LH: 0-3 RH: 0-3 Tight: 0-0 Gall: 0-0
Aids: Bl: 0-0 Vi: 0-0 Tstrap: 0-2
Best Rating: 82 5/99 Hrfd   2m3f110y gd-sft Hdl

Fen Gypsy

74   **60**

5-y-o b g Nashwan (USA)-Didicoy (USA) (Danzig (USA))
P D Evans Thats Racing Partnership

Placings:00   (2570)
2002/03: 16^0^G, 16^0^G,

	Starts	1st	2nd	3rd	Win & Pl
Hurdles	2	0	0	0	
Career Total	2	0	0	0	

Going: Sf: 0-0 GS: 0-0 Gd: 0-2 GF: - Fm: 0-0
Distance: 2m/2m3: 0-2 2m4-2m7: 0-0 3m+: 0-0
Track: LH: 0-1 RH: 0-1 Tight: 0-0 Gall: 0-1
Aids: Bl: 0-0 Vi: 0-0 Tstrap: 0-2
Best Rating: 60 12/02 Ludl 2m   good Hdl

Fern Lord (IRE)

96   **114+**

6-y-o ch h Mister Lord (USA)-Deep Fern (Deep Run)
Jonjo O Neill Mrs L Busteed

Placings:051   (3901)
2002/03: 24⁰GS, 21⁵G, 24¹S,

	Starts	1st	2nd	3rd	Win & Pl
Hurdles	3	1	0	0	5567
Career Total	3	1	0	0	5567
114 3/03 Newb 3m110y D Hdl			SFT		£5271

Total win prize-money £5272

Going: Sf: 1-1 GS: 0-1 Gd: 0-1 GF: - Fm: 0-0
Distance: 2m/2m3: 0-0 2m4-2m7: 0-1 3m+: 1-2
Track: LH: 1-1 RH: 0-2 Tight: 0-0 Gall: 1-1
Aids: Bl: 0-0 Vi: 0-0 Tstrap: 0-0
Best Rating: 114 3/03 Newb 3m110y soft Hdl

Novice hurdler; easy winner at Newbury in March 2003; stays three miles plus; effective in soft ground.

Fernleigh

6-y-o b g Another Sam-Price Of Sentiment (IRE) (Trojan Fen)
M J Gingell Basil White

Placings:0P   (0700)
2002/03: 16⁰S, 19ᴾGF,

	Starts	1st	2nd	3rd	Win & Pl
NH Flat	1	0	0	0	
Hurdles	1	0	0	0	0
Career Total	2	0	0	0	

Going: Sf: 0-1 GS: 0-0 Gd: 0-0 GF: - Fm: 0-1
Distance: 2m/2m3: 0-1 2m4-2m7: 0-1 3m+: 0-0
Track: LH: 0-1 RH: 0-1 Tight: 0-0 Gall: 0-0
Aids: Bl: 0-0 Vi: 0-0 Tstrap: 0-0
Best Rating: 0 7/02 MRas 2m3f110y gd-fm Hdl

Ferrets Hill (IRE)

92(92h)   (84 h)**76**

7-y-o br g Good Thyne (USA)-Doolin Lake (IRE) (Salluceva)
Ferdy Murphy Mrs T H Barclay/Mrs F D McInnes Skinner

Placings:20-4P34P45   (4166)
2002/03: 20⁴GF, 20ᴾGS, 20³GS, 23⁴S, 25ᴾG, 25⁴S, 20⁵GS,

	Starts	1st	2nd	3rd	Win & Pl
Hurdles	5	0	0	1	798
Chases	2	0	0	0	410
Career Total	9	0	1	1	1623

Going: Sf: 0-2 GS: 0-3 Gd: 0-1 GF: - Fm: 0-1
Distance: 2m/2m3: 0-0 2m4-2m7: 0-4 3m+: 0-3
Track: LH: 0-6 RH: 0-1 Tight: 0-5 Gall: 0-1
Aids: Bl: 0-0 Vi: 0-0 Tstrap: 0-0
Best Rating: 96 10/01 Fknm 2m soft NHF

Ferzao (IRE)

97   **107+**

6-y-o b g Alzao (USA)-Fer De Lance (IRE) (Diesis)
C J Mann Derek Crowson

Placings:522   (0647)
2002/03: 17⁵GF, 17²GF, 16²GF,

	Starts	1st	2nd	3rd	Win & Pl
Hurdles	3	0	2	0	2200

Career Total   3   0   2   0   2200

Going: Sf: 0-0 GS: 0-0 Gd: 0-0 GF: - Fm: 0-3
Distance: 2m/2m3: 0-3 2m4-2m7: 0-0 3m+: 0-0
Track: LH: 0-2 RH: 0-1 Tight: 0-3 Gall: 0-0
Aids: Bl: 0-0 Vi: 0-0 Tstrap: 0-3
Best Rating: 112 6/02 Strf 2m110y gd-fm Hdl

Stepped up on hurdling debut when second to the useful Tactful Remark at Newton Abbot June 2002. Too much to do next time, but is capable of going one better.

Festival Flyer

96   **98**

8-y-o b g Alhijaz-Odilese (Mummy s Pet)
Miss M Bragg W H Whitley

Placings:P/4541/P34-01   (4512)
2002/03: 22⁰GF, 24¹GF,

	Starts	1st	2nd	3rd	Win & Pl
Hurdles	2	1	0	0	6851
Career Total	10	2	0	1	10329
98 4/03 Extr 3m110y D(0-120)HHdl	G-F				£6851
98 8/00 NAbb 2m6f D Hdl	G-F				£2910

Total win prize-money £9762

Going: Sf: 0-0 GS: 0-0 Gd: 0-0 GF: - Fm: 1-2
Distance: 2m/2m3: 0-0 2m4-2m7: 0-1 3m+: 1-1
Track: LH: 0-1 RH: 1-1 Tight: 0-1 Gall: 0-0
Aids: Bl: 0-0 Vi: 0-0 Tstrap: 0-0
Best Rating: 98 4/03 Extr 3m110y gd-fm Hdl

Staying hurdler, returned after nine month absence to win slowly run three mile hurdle at Exeter April 2003; acts well on good or faster ground.

Fey Macha (IRE)

88   **114**

8-y-o b m Phardante (FR)-West Lodge (Deep Run)
Paul A Roche Gerard Halley

Placings:014043-0612120   (1990)
2002/03: 22⁰G, 20⁶GF, 24¹G, 20²G, 19¹GF, 20²F, 21⁰GS,

	Starts	1st	2nd	3rd	Win & Pl
Hurdles	7	2	2	0	13969
Career Total	13	3	2	1	20594
102 8/02 Kbgn 2m3f Hdl	G-F				£5079
96 8/02 Cork 3m Hdl	GD				£5503
99 8/01 Gway 2m2f NHF	G-Y				£5564

Total win prize-money £16148

Going: Sf: 0-0 GS: 0-1 Gd: 1-3 GF: - Fm: 1-3
Distance: 2m/2m3: 1-1 2m4-2m7: 0-5 3m+: 1-1
Track: LH: 0-1 RH: 0-0 Tight: 0-0 Gall: 0-1
Aids: Bl: 0-0 Vi: 0-0 Tstrap: 0-0
Best Rating: 114 9/02 Tipp 2m4f firm Hdl

Twice a winner over hurdles, he stays well, having won over three miles, and acts on a sound surface.

Fiche And Chips

76   **57**

4-y-o b c Distant Relative-Moorefield Girl (IRE) (Gorytus (USA))
A Dickman G N Gregoriou

Placings:00   (1537)
2002/03: 16⁰GF, 16⁰GF,

	Starts	1st	2nd	3rd	Win & Pl
Hurdles	2	0	0	0	
Career Total	2	0	0	0	

Going: Sf: 0-0 GS: 0-0 Gd: 0-0 GF: - Fm: 0-2
Distance: 2m/2m3: 0-2 2m4-2m7: 0-0 3m+: 0-0
Track: LH: 0-2 RH: 0-0 Tight: 0-1 Gall: 0-0
Aids: Bl: 0-0 Vi: 0-1 Tstrap: 0-0
Best Rating: 57 10/02 Weth 2m gd-fm Hdl

Fiddlers Elbow

7-y-o ch g Jester-Swallow This (Town Crier)
J R Jenkins P T Griffith

Placings:O0F   (2016)
2002/03: 16⁰GF, 17⁰GS, 16ᶠHY,

	Starts	1st	2nd	3rd	Win & Pl
NH Flat	2	0	0	0	0
Hurdles	1	0	0	0	0
Career Total	3	0	0	0	

Going: Sf: 0-1 GS: 0-1 Gd: 0-0 GF: - Fm: 0-1
Distance: 2m/2m3: 0-3 2m4-2m7: 0-0 3m+: 0-0
Track: LH: 0-0 RH: 0-3 Tight: 0-1 Gall: 0-1
Aids: Bl: 0-0 Vi: 0-0 Tstrap: 0-0
Best Rating: 0 11/02 Leic 2m heavy Hdl

Field Master (IRE)

108   **100**

6-y-o ch g Foxhound (USA)-Bold Avril (IRE) (Persian Bold)
C J Gray Ken Mantyk

Placings:425/5O0U4656216040-53112P4   (4387)
2002/03: 16⁵G, 16³F, 19¹GF, 19¹GS, 19²GS, 20⁵S, 22⁴F,

	Starts	1st	2nd	3rd	Win & Pl
Hurdles	7	2	1	1	7963
Career Total	24	3	3	1	12012
100 11/02 Tntn 2m3f110yE(0-110)HHdl	G-S				£3276
90 10/02 Tntn 2m3f110yF(0-100)HHdl	G-F				£2341
90 12/01 Extr 2m3f F(0-95)HHdl	G-S				£2464

Total win prize-money £8082

Going: Sf: 0-1 GS: 1-2 Gd: 0-1 GF: - Fm: 1-3
Distance: 2m/2m3: 0-2 2m4-2m7: 2-5 3m+: 0-0
Track: LH: 0-1 RH: 2-6 Tight: 2-3 Gall: 0-0
Aids: Bl: 0-0 Vi: 0-1 Tstrap: 0-0
Best Rating: 100 11/02 Tntn 2m3f110y gd-sft Hdl

Fair form in modest handicap hurdles in the south west. Suited by trips of around two and a half miles.

Fielding's Hay (IRE)

104(102h)   (85h)**93**

7-y-o b m Supreme Leader-Kates Fling (USA) (Quiet Fling (USA))
Mrs J Candlish (A Streeter 22/5) Greencard Golfers

Placings:0/134U55-0P0642   (4707)
2002/03: 20⁰G, 22ᴾGS, 20⁵S, 25⁶S, 24⁴G, 26²G,

	Starts	1st	2nd	3rd	Win & Pl
Hurdles	1	0	0	0	
Chases	5	0	1	0	1906
Career Total	13	1	1	1	3793
108 5/01 Sthl 2m H NHF	G-F				£1561

Total win prize-money £1561

Going: Sf: 0-2 GS: 0-1 Gd: 0-3 GF: - Fm: 0-0
Distance: 2m/2m3: 0-0 2m4-2m7: 0-3 3m+: 0-3
Track: LH: 0-4 RH: 0-2 Tight: 0-0 Gall: 0-0
Aids: Bl: 0-0 Vi: 0-1 Tstrap: 0-0
Best Rating: 108 5/01 Sthl 2m gd-fm NHF

Fair form in bumpers, not as good over hurdles or fences; stays beyond three miles.

Fier Goumier (FR)
106   **112**
8-y-o b g Chef De Clan Ii (FR)-Azilal (FR) (Rex Magna (FR))
Jonjo O Neill (A L T Moore 29/8) J P McManus

Placings:6S2/61405/211P34-000   (3752)
2002/03: 22⁰Y, 20⁰GF, 20⁰G,

	Starts	1st	2nd	3rd	Win & Pl
Chases	3	0	0	0	
Career Total	17	3	2	1	28795
114 7/01 Tipp	2m4f		HCh	GD	£13104
105 6/01 Kbgn	2m4f	(0-116)HCh		GD	£7862
73 6/00 Kbgn	2m4f		Ch		G-F	£3450
			Total win prize-money £24418		

Going:	Sf: 0-0 GS: 0-0 Gd: 0-1 GF: - Fm: 0-1
Distance:	2m/2m3: 0-0 2m4-2m7: 0-3 3m+: 0-0
Track:	LH: 0-0 RH: 0-2 Tight: 0-0 Gall: 0-0
Aids:	Bl: 0-0 Vi: 0-0 Tstrap: 0-0
Best Rating:	114 7/01 Tipp 2m4f good Ch

Fair ex-Irish chaser; won three times over 2m 4f over fences on good ground; now with Jonjo O Neill.

Fierce Money

7-y-o b g Nicholas Bill-Nut Tree (King Of Spain)
R T Phillips Richard Phillips

Placings:4-0P   (4595)
2002/03: 16⁰GF, 22⁰GF,

	Starts	1st	2nd	3rd	Win & Pl
NH Flat	1	0	0	0	0
Hurdles	1	0	0	0	0
Career Total	3	0	0	0	0

Going:	Sf: 0-0 GS: 0-0 Gd: 0-0 GF: - Fm: 0-2
Distance:	2m/2m3: 0-1 2m4-2m7: 0-1 3m+: 0-0
Track:	LH: 0-1 RH: 0-1 Tight: 0-0 Gall: 0-0
Aids:	Bl: 0-0 Vi: 0-0 Tstrap: 0-0
Best Rating:	93 4/02 Ludl 2m gd-fm NHF

Fiery Creek
84   **57**
6-y-o ch m Moscow Society (USA)-Deep Creek (Deep Run)
D J Wintle John W Egan

Placings:30-000   (3441)
2002/03: 16⁰GS, 17⁰G, 20⁰HY,

	Starts	1st	2nd	3rd	Win & Pl
NH Flat	2	0	0	0	0
Hurdles	1	0	0	0	0
Career Total	5	0	0	1	271

Going:	Sf: 0-1 GS: 0-1 Gd: 0-1 GF: - Fm: 0-0
Distance:	2m/2m3: 0-2 2m4-2m7: 0-1 3m+: 0-0
Track:	LH: 0-2 RH: 0-1 Tight: 0-0 Gall: 0-0
Aids:	Bl: 0-0 Vi: 0-0 Tstrap: 0-0
Best Rating:	89 2/02 Wwck 2m heavy NHF

Fiery Peace
101   **97**
6-y-o ch g Tina s Pet-Burning Mirage (Pamroy)
H D Daly R M Kirkland

Placings:5P0-65F0   (2943)
2002/03: 17⁰G, 16⁵G, 16⁶G, 16⁰S,

	Starts	1st	2nd	3rd	Win & Pl
Hurdles	4	0	0	0	0

Career Total   7   0   0   0   0

Returned after six-month absence to finish good second to Jollyolly in 2m 3f Class E novices hurdle at Hereford June 2003; disappointing when finding nothing off the bridle next time.

Fife And Drum (USA)
42
6-y-o b/br g Rahy (USA)-Fife (IRE) (Lomond (USA))
J Akehurst Last Order s Partnership

Placings:000-P   (0417)
2002/03: 16⁶GF,

	Starts	1st	2nd	3rd	Win & Pl
Hurdles	1	0	0	0	
Career Total	4	0	0	0	

Going:	Sf: 0-0 GS: 0-0 Gd: 0-0 GF: - Fm: 0-1
Distance:	2m/2m3: 0-1 2m4-2m7: 0-0 3m+: 0-0
Track:	LH: 0-1 RH: 0-0 Tight: 0-1 Gall: 0-0
Aids:	Bl: 0-0 Vi: 0-0 Tstrap: 0-0
Best Rating:	42 12/01 Extr 2m3f good Hdl

Fifteen Reds
71(103h)   (84 h)**51**
8-y-o b g Jumbo Hirt (USA)-Dominance (Dominion)
F S Storey F S Storey

Placings:20/56/460/60635-255301550   (4590)
2002/03: 21²GF, 17⁵GF, 20⁵GF, 21³GF, 24⁰GF, 24¹G, 20⁵S, 27⁵S, 20⁰G,

	Starts	1st	2nd	3rd	Win & Pl
Hurdles	9	1	1	1	3422
Career Total	21	1	2	2	4184
87 10/02 Hexm 3m		F(0-100)HHdl	GD	£2170	
		Total win prize-money £2170			

Going:	Sf: 0-2 GS: 0-0 Gd: 1-2 GF: - Fm: 0-5
Distance:	2m/2m3: 0-1 2m4-2m7: 0-5 3m+: 1-3
Track:	LH: 1-8 RH: 0-1 Tight: 0-4 Gall: 0-0
Aids:	Bl: 0-0 Vi: 0-0 Tstrap: 0-0
Best Rating:	90 1/99 MRas 1m5f110y soft NHF

Modest, staying novice hurdler, had plenty of chances before winning a three-horse affair at Hexham.

Fifth Generation (IRE)
111(105c)   (95c)**94**
13-y-o b g Bulldozer-Fragrant s Last (Little Buskins)
Dr P Pritchard The B A R Partnership (purton)

Placings:40/2/4U4/6335F/01111/30F/6U00026F00/P544254
010/05P524P0U2131O443035-3602103040020   (4693)
2002/03: 16⁵GS, 16³F, 17⁶GS, 17⁰GF, 22²GF, 16¹GF, 17⁰G, 19³S, 16⁸GS, 16⁴GS, 16⁰GS, 17⁰G, 16²GF, 17⁰G,

	Starts	1st	2nd	3rd	Win & Pl
Hurdles	14	1	2	2	10056
Career Total	72	8	7	8	37603
94 7/02 Strf	2m110y	F(0-110)HHdl	G-F	£4056	
96 1/02 Uttx	2m	F(0-90)Hdl	HVY	£1946	

---

90 12/01 Leic	2m4f110yG(0-90)HHdl	HVY	£1988
96 4/01 NAbb	2m6f	E(0-105)HHdl	SFT	£3136
114 12/97 Limk	2m4f	(0-123)HCh	HVY	£3391
107 12/97 Clon	2m4f	(0-102)HCh	HVY	£3899
95 12/97 Thur	2m2f	(0-109)HCh	SFT	£2204
93 11/97 Clon	2m4f	(0-109)HCh	HVY	£3391
		Total win prize-money £24012		

Going:	Sf: 0-1 GS: 0-5 Gd: 0-3 GF: - Fm: 1-5
Distance:	2m/2m3: 1-12 2m4-2m7: 0-2 3m+: 0-0
Track:	LH: 1-10 RH: 0-4 Tight: 1-6 Gall: 0-1
Aids:	Bl: 0-0 Vi: 0-0 Tstrap: 0-0
Best Rating:	114 12/97 Limk 2m4f heavy Ch

Veteran front-running hurdler/chaser, acts on any ground; appears to be most effective at two miles to two miles four furlongs in moderate company.

Fiftysevenchannels (IRE)

14-y-o b g Bustineto-Allitess (Mugatpura)
Miss A Armitage John A Cooper

Placings:1224/2111P2444/510301P/2521533/0521/3/P0-
FP   (0477)
2002/03: 25⁰GS, 26⁰GS,

	Starts	1st	2nd	3rd	Win & Pl
Chases	2	0	0	0	
Career Total	36	8	7	4	62981
127 11/98 Fair	2m	HCh	Y-S	£5978
110 11/97 Chel	3m7f	B Ch	G-F	£17668
131 2/97 Fair	2m	HCh	G-Y	£6782
130 11/96 Leop	2m1f	HCh	YLD	£4546
125 1/96 Fair	2m	(0-120)HCh	Y-S	£3177
130 1/96 Tram	2m6f	Ch	YLD	£3712
105 5/95 Weth	2m4f110yH Ch		GD	£2010
107 2/95 Hrfd	3m1f110yH Ch		HVY	£1968
		Total win prize-money £45844		

Going:	Sf: 0-0 GS: 0-1 Gd: 0-0 GF: - Fm: 0-1
Distance:	2m/2m3: 0-0 2m4-2m7: 0-0 3m+: 0-2
Track:	LH: 0-2 RH: 0-0 Tight: 0-2 Gall: 0-0
Aids:	Bl: 0-2 Vi: 0-0 Tstrap: 0-0
Best Rating:	133 5/97 Strf 2m1f110y good Ch

Once smart hunter but is now a veteran. Acts on any ground.

Figawin
93
8-y-o b g Rudimentary (USA)-Dear Person (Rainbow Quest (USA))
R Wilman Mr C A Walton

Placings:5540066/625F3453/230U060363F1/52-50 (1899)
2002/03: 22⁵S, 27⁰S,

	Starts	1st	2nd	3rd	Win & Pl
Chases	2	0	0	0	
Career Total	31	1	3	5	9095
90 4/01 Fknm	2m5f110yF(0-110)HCh	G-S	£4231	
		Total win prize-money £4232		

Going:	Sf: 0-2 GS: 0-0 Gd: 0-0 GF: - Fm: 0-0
Distance:	2m/2m3: 0-0 2m4-2m7: 0-1 3m+: 0-0
Track:	LH: 0-2 RH: 0-0 Tight: 0-2 Gall: 0-0
Aids:	Bl: 0-0 Vi: 0-0 Tstrap: 0-0
Best Rating:	93 10/01 Fknm 3m110y soft Ch

Moderate chaser, suited to soft ground. Goes well at Fakenham.

Fille D'Argent (IRE)

4-y-o gr f Desert Style (IRE)-Talina (General Assembly (USA))
Mrs P N Dutfield Chris Scott

Placings:0   (1004)
2002/03: 17⁰GF,

	Starts	1st	2nd	3rd	Win & Pl
Hurdles	1	0	0	0	
Career Total	1	0	0	0	

Going:	Sf: 0-0 GS: 0-0 Gd: 0-0 GF: - Fm: 0-1		
Distance:	2m/2m3: 0-1 2m4-2m7: 0-0 3m+: 0-0		
Track:	LH: 0-1 RH: 0-0 Tight: 0-0 Gall: 0-0		
Aids:	Bl: 0-0 Vi: 0-0 Tstrap: 0-0		
Best Rating:	0 8/02 Bang 2m1f gd-fm Hdl		

Filou Du Bois (FR)

10-y-o b g Shafoun (FR)-Jamaica (FR) (Tryptic)
Ms A E Embiricos Ms A E Embiricos

Placings:05020/P26400/P   (0321)
2002/03: 26⁰G,

	Starts	1st	2nd	3rd	Win & Pl
Chases	1	0	0	0	
Career Total	12	0	2	0	2128

Going:	Sf: 0-0 GS: 0-0 Gd: 0-1 GF: - Fm: 0-0
Distance:	2m/2m3: 0-0 2m4-2m7: 0-0 3m+: 0-1
Track:	LH: 0-1 RH: 0-0 Tight: 0-0 Gall: 0-0
Aids:	Bl: 0-1 Vi: 0-0 Tstrap: 0-0
Best Rating:	93 2/99 Leic 2m1f gd-sft Ch

Fils De Cresson (IRE)

90   98

13-y-o b g Torus-Hellfire Hostess (Lucifer (USA))
J R Adam James R Adam

Placings:63/F54P34/F/P33124136/5P3344/05/5221-4P
    (1490)
2002/03: 16⁴GS, 17⁵GS,

	Starts	1st	2nd	3rd	Win & Pl
Chases	2	0	0	0	265
Career Total	32	3	3	7	20808
98 4/02	Weth	2m	F(0-100)HCh	G-F	£3486
119 3/99	Ayr	2m	D(0-125)HCh	SFT	£4337
107 12/98	Catt	2m	E Ch	GD	£2753

Total win prize-money £10578

Going:	Sf: 0-0 GS: 0-2 Gd: 0-0 GF: - Fm: 0-0
Distance:	2m/2m3: 0-2 2m4-2m7: 0-0 3m+: 0-0
Track:	LH: 0-1 RH: 0-1 Tight: 0-1 Gall: 0-0
Aids:	Bl: 0-0 Vi: 0-0 Tstrap: 0-2
Best Rating:	119 3/99 Ayr 2m soft Ch

Moderate two-mile chaser, acts on any ground.

Filscot

11-y-o b g Scottish Reel-Filliode (Mossberry)
Mrs S S Harbour (C P Morlock 10/8) P J Morgan

Placings:261/F443/31400124/25422224023/5F21244303P/5
030P34-12436144P2   (4640)

Fin Bec (FR)

106   105

10-y-o b g Tip Moss (FR)-Tourbrune (FR) (Pamponi (FR))
A P Jones P Newell

Placings:30/235332/3411PU/35125621UP/35P24046-
3UPPP1541   (4690)
2002/03: 23³G, 20ᵁGS, 22ᴾS, 21ᴾS, 24ᴾS, 20¹S, 23⁵S, 22⁴G,
25¹G,

	Starts	1st	2nd	3rd	Win & Pl
Chases	9	2	0	1	11101
Career Total	41	6	5	8	37362
108 4/03	MRas	3m1f	F(0-95)Ch	GD	£3720
104 1/03	Leic	2m4f110yE(0-105)HCh	SFT	£5512
106 1/01	Folk	3m2f	F(0-100)HCh	HVY	£2520
111 10/00	Sthl	3m110y	E Hdl	HVY	£2710
106 3/00	Sand	3m110y	D(0-115)HCh	GD	£5027
106 2/00	Leic	2m4f110yF(0-95)HCh	SFT	£3526

Total win prize-money £23018

Going:	Sf: 1-5 GS: 0-1 Gd: 1-3 GF: - Fm: 0-0
Distance:	2m/2m3: 0-0 2m4-2m7: 1-5 3m+: 1-4
Track:	LH: 0-3 RH: 2-6 Tight: 1-3 Gall: 0-3
Aids:	Bl: 2-8 Vi: 0-0 Tstrap: 0-0
Best Rating:	111 10/00 Sthl 3m110y heavy Hdl

Fair chaser; stays three miles but effective over shorter; suited by soft ground; has worn blinkers and sheepskin cheekpieces.

Final Chance

84(84h)   (70h)70

9-y-o ch m Nader-Milly s Chance (Mljet)
C Tizzard L G Tizzard

Placings:000/6/60-064U   (1698)
2002/03: 19⁰F, 19⁶F, 19⁴F, 19ᵁGF,

	Starts	1st	2nd	3rd	Win & Pl
Hurdles	2	0	0	0	
Chases	2	0	0	0	419
Career Total	10	0	0	0	419

Going:	Sf: 0-0 GS: 0-0 Gd: 0-0 GF: - Fm: 0-4
Distance:	2m/2m3: 0-4 2m4-2m7: 0-0 3m+: 0-0
Track:	LH: 0-0 RH: 0-4 Tight: 0-2 Gall: 0-0
Aids:	Bl: 0-0 Vi: 0-0 Tstrap: 0-0
Best Rating:	74 1/99 Font 2m2f110y soft NHF

2002/03: 25⁴GS, 25¹G, 20²G, 25⁴G, 20³GF, 23⁶GF, 24¹G, 24⁴S,
23⁴GS, 22ᴾG, 21²G,

	Starts	1st	2nd	3rd	Win & Pl
Chases	11	2	2	1	14777
Career Total	53	6	11	8	39374
100 7/02	Strf	3m	D(0-115)HCh	GD	£6942
100 5/02	Hrfd	3m1f110yF(0-95)HCh	GD	£3926
113 10/00	Ludl	2m4f	E Ch	G-F	£3081
105 2/99	Kemp	2m5f	D(0-120)HHdl	GD	£3680
108 5/98	Hntg	2m4f110yE Hdl	G-F	£2530
103 4/97	NAbb	2m1f	H NHF	FRM	£1278

Total win prize-money £21437

Going:	Sf: 0-1 GS: 0-2 Gd: 2-6 GF: - Fm: 0-2
Distance:	2m/2m3: 0-0 2m4-2m7: 0-4 **3m+: 2-7**
Track:	LH: 1-6 RH: 1-4 **Tight: 1-4** Gall: 0-1
Aids:	Bl: 0-3 Vi: 0-1 Tstrap: 0-0
Best Rating:	116 11/99 Leic 2m7f110y gd-fm Ch

Modest chaser; caught last strides after a mistake two out in 2m 5f hunter chase at Stratford April 2003; best on a sound surface; stays three miles.

Final Escapade

10-y-o ch g St Columbus-Country Princess (Country Retreat)
C Wadland Mrs E M Wharton

Placings:P-0   (3954)
2002/03: 20⁰GS,

	Starts	1st	2nd	3rd	Win & Pl
Chases	1	0	0	0	
Career Total	2	0	0	0	

Going:	Sf: 0-0 GS: 0-1 Gd: 0-0 GF: - Fm: 0-0
Distance:	2m/2m3: 0-0 2m4-2m7: 0-1 3m+: 0-0
Track:	LH: 0-0 RH: 0-1 Tight: 0-0 Gall: 0-0
Aids:	Bl: 0-0 Vi: 0-0 Tstrap: 0-0
Best Rating:	0 3/03 Leic 2m4f110y gd-sft Ch

Final Lap

98   51

7-y-o b g Batshoof-Lap Of Honour (Final Straw)
S T Lewis Simon T Lewis

Placings:0PP/6U000P040-600P15P023335000   (4486)
2002/03: 17⁶S, 19⁹G, 16⁹GF, 20⁶G, 16¹S, 16⁵GS, 16⁶G, 17⁹F,
19²F, 16³G, 16³G, 17³G, 17⁵GS, 17⁰G, 16⁹GS, 17⁰GF,

	Starts	1st	2nd	3rd	Win & Pl
Hurdles	16	1	1	3	3802
Career Total	28	1	1	3	3802
72 8/02	Strf	2m110y	G Hdl	SFT	£2254

Total win prize-money £2254

Going:	Sf: 1-2 GS: 0-3 Gd: 0-7 GF: - Fm: 0-4
Distance:	**2m/2m3: 1-13** 2m4-2m7: 0-3 3m+: 0-0
Track:	**LH: 1-9** RH: 0-7 **Tight: 1-7** Gall: 0-0
Aids:	Bl: 0-3 Vi: 0-1 Tstrap: 0-0
Best Rating:	78 11/02 Hrfd 2m1f good Hdl

Has had extensive treatment for back problems and sprang a surprise when 25/1 winner of Stratford seller in August 2002. Acts on soft ground.

Final Match

5-y-o b m Derrylin-Furstin (Furry Glen)
T Wall D Pugh

Placings:00   (0660)
2002/03: 16⁹S, 16⁰GF,

	Starts	1st	2nd	3rd	Win & Pl
NH Flat	2	0	0	0	
Career Total	2	0	0	0	

Going:	Sf: 0-1 GS: 0-0 Gd: 0-0 GF: - Fm: 0-1
Distance:	2m/2m3: 0-2 2m4-2m7: 0-0 3m+: 0-0
Track:	LH: 0-2 RH: 0-0 Tight: 0-0 Gall: 0-0
Aids:	Bl: 0-0 Vi: 0-0 Tstrap: 0-0
Best Rating:	0 6/02 Worc 2m gd-fm NHF

Final View (FR)

4-y-o b g Distant View (USA)-Unafurtivalagrima (USA) (Quest For Fame)
T Wall (M Zilber 24/6) V and J Properties

Placings:0   (2059)
2002/03: 17⁰S,

	Starts	1st	2nd	3rd	Win & Pl
Hurdles	1	0	0	0	

Career Total   1   0   0   0

Going: Sf: 0-1 GS: 0-0 Gd: 0-0 GF: - Fm: 0-0
Distance: 2m2m3: 0-1 2m4-2m7: 0-0 3m+: 0-0
Track: LH: 0-0 RH: 0-1 Tight: 0-0 Gall: 0-0
Aids: Bl: 0-0 Vi: 0-0 Tstrap: 0-0
Best Rating: 0   11/02 Hrfd 2m1f   soft   Hdl

Finbar's Law
98   93
6-y-o b g Contract Law (USA)-De Valera (Faustus (USA))
R Johnson   Mrs June Quinn

Placings:P/O6-P04P01   (4408)
2002/03: 16PG, 16OG, 214GS, 24PS, 22OG, 161G,

	Starts	1st	2nd	3rd	Win & Pl
Hurdles	6	1	0	0	3918
Career Total	9	1	0	0	3918
89 3/03 Hexm 2m110y E Hdl				GD	£3658

Total win prize-money £3658

Going: Sf: 0-1 GS: 0-1 Gd: 1-4 GF: - Fm: 0-0
Distance: 2m/2m3: 1-3 2m4-2m7: 0-2 3m+: 0-1
Track: LH: 1-4 RH: 0-2 Tight: 0-4 Gall: 0-0
Aids: Bl: 0-0 Vi: 0-0 Tstrap: 1-6
Best Rating: 89 3/03 Hexm 2m110y   good   Hdl

Find The Lady (IRE)

9-y-o b m Montelimar (USA)-Run Lizzy Run (IRE)
(Dunbeath (USA))
Stephen McCormick   Stephen McCormick

Placings:000P/PP   (0392)
2002/03: 21PG, 24PG,

	Starts	1st	2nd	3rd	Win & Pl
Chases	2	0	0	0	
Career Total	6	0	0	0	

Going: Sf: 0-0 GS: 0-0 Gd: 0-2 GF: - Fm: 0-0
Distance: 2m/2m3: 0-0 2m4-2m7: 0-1 3m+: 0-1
Track: LH: 0-1 RH: 0-1 Tight: 0-2 Gall: 0-0
Aids: Bl: 0-0 Vi: 0-0 Tstrap: 0-0
Best Rating: 41 3/99 Tram 2m4f   yld-sft   Hdl

Fine Times

9-y-o b g Timeless Times (USA)-Marfen (Lochnager)
Milson Robinson   Milson Robinson

Placings:0P/0P/1-5   (0068)
2002/03: 21SGF,

	Starts	1st	2nd	3rd	Win & Pl
Chases	1	0	0	0	
Career Total	6	1	0	0	1091
87 4/02 MRas 3m1f H Ch				GD	£1090

Total win prize-money £1091

Going: Sf: 0-0 GS: 0-0 Gd: 0-0 GF: - Fm: 0-1
Distance: 2m/2m3: 0-0 2m4-2m7: 0-1 3m+: 0-0
Track: LH: 0-1 RH: 0-0 Tight: 0-0 Gall: 0-0
Aids: Bl: 0-0 Vi: 0-0 Tstrap: 0-1
Best Rating: 87 4/02 MRas 3m1f   good   Ch

Modest pointer, won a hunter chase at Market Rasen in
April 2002. Acts on a sound surface.

Finest Of Men

7-y-o b g Tina's Pet-Merry Missus (Bargello)
J B Walton   Messrs F T Walton

Placings:0/305-0   (0083)
2002/03: 25OGS,

	Starts	1st	2nd	3rd	Win & Pl
Chases	1	0	0	0	
Career Total	5	0	0	1	267

Going: Sf: 0-0 GS: 0-1 Gd: 0-0 GF: - Fm: 0-0
Distance: 2m/2m3: 0-0 2m4-2m7: 0-0 3m+: 0-1
Track: LH: 0-1 RH: 0-0 Tight: 0-0 Gall: 0-0
Aids: Bl: 0-0 Vi: 0-0 Tstrap: 0-0
Best Rating: 80 2/02 Muss 2m   soft   NHF

A half-brother to the useful staying chaser Merry Master. He
will not come into his own until he tackles fences.

Finnigan's Lot (IRE)

9-y-o b g Lancastrian-Light Bidder (Auction Ring (USA))
E L James   E James

Placings:00/PP   (0311)
2002/03: 21PGF, 26PG,

	Starts	1st	2nd	3rd	Win & Pl
Chases	2	0	0	0	
Career Total	4	0	0	0	

Going: Sf: 0-0 GS: 0-0 Gd: 0-1 GF: - Fm: 0-1
Distance: 2m/2m3: 0-0 2m4-2m7: 0-1 3m+: 0-1
Track: LH: 0-1 RH: 0-1 Tight: 0-1 Gall: 0-1
Aids: Bl: 0-2 Vi: 0-0 Tstrap: 0-1
Best Rating: 83 11/98 Wwck 2m   soft   NHF

Finzi (IRE)
79f   44f
5-y-o b g Zaffaran (USA)-Sporting Talent (IRE) (Seymour
Hicks (FR))
D J Caro   The Meld Partnership

Placings:00   (4444)
2002/03: 16OS, 16OG,

	Starts	1st	2nd	3rd	Win & Pl
NH Flat	2	0	0	0	
Career Total	2	0	0	0	

Going: Sf: 0-1 GS: 0-0 Gd: 0-1 GF: - Fm: 0-0
Distance: 2m/2m3: 0-2 2m4-2m7: 0-0 3m+: 0-0
Track: LH: 0-0 RH: 0-2 Tight: 0-0 Gall: 0-0
Aids: Bl: 0-0 Vi: 0-0 Tstrap: 0-0
Best Rating: 44 4/03 Asct 2m110y   good   NHF

Fiolino (FR)
(102h)   (74h)
10-y-o b g Bayolidaan (FR)-Vellea (FR) (Cap Martin (FR))
M W Easterby   Mrs M E Curtis

Placings:0440/04062/P61P55323-PFP0   (3510)
2002/03: 20PGS, 24FS, 25PG, 25OG,

	Starts	1st	2nd	3rd	Win & Pl
Hurdles	2	0	0	0	0
Chases	2	0	0	0	0
Career Total	22	1	2	2	5781
95 12/01 Uttx 3m E(0-105)HCh				SFT	£3159

Total win prize-money £3159

Going: Sf: 0-1 GS: 0-1 Gd: 0-2 GF: - Fm: 0-0
Distance: 2m/2m3: 0-0 2m4-2m7: 0-1 3m+: 0-3
Track: LH: 0-4 RH: 0-0 Tight: 0-2 Gall: 0-1
Aids: Bl: 0-0 Vi: 0-0 Tstrap: 0-0
Best Rating: 99 3/02 Hexm 4m   heavy   Ch

Fionnula's Rainbow (IRE)
99(110c)   (68c)81
8-y-o ch m Rainbows For Life (CAN)-Bon Retour (Sallust)
S T Lewis   Simon T Lewis

Placings:052526631/2202/14435/2141140P3P4-
6P643006205   (3600)
2002/03: 20⁶S, 24²GS, 20⁶GF, 16⁴G, 19³GF, 19⁰GS, 19⁰GS,
22⁶GS, 20²HY, 21⁰HY, 24⁵S,

	Starts	1st	2nd	3rd	Win & Pl
Hurdles	10	0	1	1	1404
Chases	1	0	0	0	0
Career Total	40	5	7	4	27636
125 12/01 Hntg 2m4f110yD Ch				G-S	£3987
125 11/01 Fknm 2m5f110yD Ch				SFT	£3767
113 9/01 Hntg 2m4f110yD(0-120)HHdl				GD	£4134
113 11/00 Winc 2m E(0-115)HHdl				SFT	£3698
92 4/99 Wxfd 2m Hdl				Y-S	£2455

Total win prize-money £18043

Going: Sf: 0-4 GS: 0-4 Gd: 0-1 GF: - Fm: 0-2
Distance: 2m/2m3: 0-2 2m4-2m7: 0-7 3m+: 0-2
Track: LH: 0-5 RH: 0-6 Tight: 0-6 Gall: 0-1
Aids: Bl: 0-1 Vi: 0-0 Tstrap: 0-0
Best Rating: 125 12/01 Hntg 2m4f110y gd-sft Ch

Consistent ex-Irish hurdler, she took well to fences in
2001/2002. Best with cut in the ground. Stays two miles five.

Fiori
113(109h)   (134h)125
7-y-o b g Anshan-Fen Princess (IRE) (Trojan Fen)
P C Haslam   Wilson Imports I

Placings:2/13211/40061610-10023F   (4773)
2002/03: 17¹G, 17⁰S, 16⁰G, 16²G, 17³S, 20⁶G,

	Starts	1st	2nd	3rd	Win & Pl
Chases	6	1	1	1	6767
Career Total	20	6	3	2	23729
102 10/02 Kels 2m1f D Ch				GD	£4680
130 11/01 Carl 2m1f D(0-120)HHdl				HVY	£3311
130 3/01 MRas 2m1f110yD Hdl				G-S	£3822
122 2/01 Uttx 2m D Hdl				SFT	£2859
134 12/00 Hayd 2m D Hdl				HVY	£3250

Total win prize-money £17923

Going: Sf: 0-2 GS: 0-0 Gd: 1-4 GF: - Fm: 0-0
Distance: 2m/2m3: 1-5 2m4-2m7: 0-1 3m+: 0-0
Track: LH: 1-4 RH: 0-2 Tight: 1-3 Gall: 0-0
Aids: Bl: 0-0 Vi: 0-0 Tstrap: 0-0
Best Rating: 134 2/02 Wwck 2m   soft   Hdl

Fair hurdler/chaser; goes well in testing ground but acts on
faster; best at around two miles although stays two and a
half.

Fire Angel

6-y-o ch m Henbit (USA)-Stane Street (IRE) (Gorytus
(USA))
R T Phillips   Ford Associated Racing Team III

Placings:0P   (3138)

2002/03: 16⁰GS, 21ᴾS,

	Starts	1st	2nd	3rd	Win & Pl
NH Flat	1	0	0	0	0
Hurdles	1	0	0	0	0
Career Total	2	0	0	0	

Going:	Sf: 0-1 GS: 0-1 Gd: 0-0 GF: - Fm: 0-0
Distance:	2m/2m3: 0-1 2m4-2m7: 0-1 3m+: 0-0
Track:	LH: 0-1 RH: 0-1 Tight: 0-0 Gall: 0-0
Aids:	Bl: 0-0 Vi: 0-0 Tstrap: 0-0
Best Rating:	55 11/02 Weth 2m gd-sft NHF

Fire In Ice

4-y-o f Missed Flight-Boulabas (IRE) (Nashamaa)
B P J Baugh   C Harrison

Placings: PFUUU   (4539)
2002/03: 17³S, 17ᶠGF, 17ᵁF, 16ᵁGF, 16ᵁG,

	Starts	1st	2nd	3rd	Win & Pl
Hurdles	5	0	0	0	
Career Total	5	0	0	0	

Going:	Sf: 0-1 GS: 0-0 Gd: 0-1 GF: - Fm: 0-3
Distance:	2m/2m3: 0-5 2m4-2m7: 0-0 3m+: 0-0
Track:	LH: 0-2 RH: 0-3 Tight: 0-2 Gall: 0-0
Aids:	Bl: 0-0 Vi: 0-0 Tstrap: 0-0
Best Rating:	0 4/03 Ludl 2m good Hdl

Fire Ranger
86   **67**

7-y-o ch m Presidium-Regal Flame (Royalty)
J D Frost   P A Tylor

Placings: 52445   (4222)
2002/03: 17⁵G, 17²GF, 16⁴GF, 19⁴S, 17⁵GF,

	Starts	1st	2nd	3rd	Win & Pl
NH Flat	3	0	1	0	642
Hurdles	2	0	0	0	404
Career Total	5	0	1	0	1046

Going:	Sf: 0-1 GS: 0-0 Gd: 0-1 GF: - Fm: 0-3
Distance:	2m/2m3: 0-5 2m4-2m7: 0-0 3m+: 0-0
Track:	LH: 0-2 RH: 0-3 Tight: 0-2 Gall: 0-1
Aids:	Bl: 0-0 Vi: 0-0 Tstrap: 0-0
Best Rating:	88 7/02 NAbb 2m1f gd-fm NHF

Improved on debut when runner-up in Newton Abbot bumper July 2002; subsequently disappointing over hurdles.

Fireaway
(106h)   (117h)**104+**

9-y-o b g Infantry-Handymouse (Nearly A Hand)
O Brennan   Mrs Pat Brennan

Placings: 1132/12362-4   (2496)
2002/03: 19⁴GS,

	Starts	1st	2nd	3rd	Win & Pl
Chases	1	0	0	0	378
Career Total	10	3	3	2	12746
104	12/01	Donc	2m110y	E Hdl	GD	£3276
126	12/00	Donc	2m110y	H NHF	HVY	£1736
114	5/00	Chep	2m110y	H NHF	FRM	£1662

Total win prize-money £6675

Going:	Sf: 0-0 GS: 0-1 Gd: 0-0 GF: - Fm: 0-0
Distance:	2m/2m3: 0-1 2m4-2m7: 0-0 3m+: 0-0
Track:	LH: 0-1 RH: 0-0 Tight: 0-0 Gall: 0-0

Aids:	Bl: 0-0 Vi: 0-0 Tstrap: 0-0
Best Rating:	126 12/00 Chep 2m110y soft NHF

A decent bumper horse turned novice hurdler, but has not built on his victory at Doncaster in 2001. Possibly found two and a half miles beyond him when well beaten on chasing debut at Doncaster in December.

Fireball Macnamara (IRE)
103(106h)   (113h)**124**

7-y-o b g Lord Americo-Glint Of Baron (Glint Of Gold)
M Pitman   J C Hitchins

Placings: 56/4/01421024100-22212PP   (4461)
2002/03: 16²G, 21²GS, 19²GS, 19¹G, 19²GS, 20ᴾGS, 20ᴾG,

	Starts	1st	2nd	3rd	Win & Pl
Chases	7	1	4	0	12376
Career Total	21	4	6	0	34181
124	1/03	Donc	2m3f	D Ch	GD	£6987
113	11/01	Chel	2m110y	A Hdl	GD	£15000
112	8/01	Sthl	2m	E Hdl	G-F	£2450
103	5/01	Hntg	2m110y	E Hdl	G-F	£2429

Total win prize-money £26867

Going:	Sf: 0-0 GS: 0-3 Gd: 1-4 GF: - Fm: 0-0
Distance:	2m/2m3: 1-4 2m4-2m7: 0-3 3m+: 0-0
Track:	LH: 1-7 RH: 0-0 Tight: 0-3 Gall: 0-0
Aids:	Bl: 0-0 Vi: 0-0 Tstrap: 0-0
Best Rating:	124 1/03 Donc 2m3f good Ch

Fair hurdler; yet to be out of the two in five starts over fences, getting off the mark at Doncaster in January; seemingly better on a sound surface but does act well enough on soft; stays two miles three.

Fireside Legend (IRE)
92   **62**

4-y-o b g College Chapel-Miss Sandman (Manacle)
Miss M P Bryant (W G M Turner 13/2)   Miss M Bryant

Placings: 005O44650B   (4698)
2002/03: 16⁹G, 16⁹GS, 16⁵G, 16⁰S, 16⁴HY, 16⁴HY, 17⁶S, 16⁵HY, 22⁰G, 16⁸GF,

	Starts	1st	2nd	3rd	Win & Pl
Hurdles	10	0	0	0	0
Career Total	10	0	0	0	0

Going:	Sf: 0-5 GS: 0-1 Gd: 0-3 GF: - Fm: 0-1
Distance:	2m/2m3: 0-9 2m4-2m7: 0-1 3m+: 0-0
Track:	LH: 0-7 RH: 0-3 Tight: 0-5 Gall: 0-1
Aids:	Bl: 0-7 Vi: 0-0 Tstrap: 0-1
Best Rating:	72 12/02 Winc 2m gd-sft Hdl

Selling hurdler, only poor form so far.

Firestone (GER)
110   **101**

6-y-o b g Dictator s Song (USA)-Fatinizza (IRE) (Niniski (USA))
A W Carroll   K Marshall

Placings: 50P24131-50036242   (4625)
2002/03: 16⁵S, 16⁰G, 16⁰S, 16³G, 16⁶GS, 16²G, 16⁴GF, 17²GF,

	Starts	1st	2nd	3rd	Win & Pl
Hurdles	8	0	2	1	4416
Career Total	16	2	3	1	14664
103	3/02	Chep	2m110y	C(0-130)HHdl	G-S	£6825
88	2/02	Plum	2m	F(0-90)HHdl	HVY	£1949

Total win prize-money £8775

Going:	Sf: 0-2 GS: 0-1 Gd: 0-3 GF: - Fm: 0-2
Distance:	2m/2m3: 0-8 2m4-2m7: 0-0 3m+: 0-0
Track:	LH: 0-5 RH: 0-3 Tight: 0-2 Gall: 0-1
Aids:	Bl: 0-0 Vi: 0-0 Tstrap: 0-5
Best Rating:	103 3/02 Chep 2m110y gd-sft Hdl

Moderate hurdler; suited by soft ground; likes to be held up; best at two miles; has had bleeding and breathing problems; has worn a tongue tie.

Firey Senorita (IRE)
77   **72**

6-y-o b m Great Commotion (USA)-Spanish Rose (Belmez (USA))
L A Dace   R P Behan

Placings: 000/0050-P0   (0429)
2002/03: 23ᴾGS, 18⁰GF,

	Starts	1st	2nd	3rd	Win & Pl
Hurdles	2	0	0	0	
Career Total	9	0	0	0	

Going:	Sf: 0-0 GS: 0-1 Gd: 0-0 GF: - Fm: 0-1
Distance:	2m/2m3: 0-1 2m4-2m7: 0-0 3m+: 0-1
Track:	LH: 0-2 RH: 0-0 Tight: 0-2 Gall: 0-0
Aids:	Bl: 0-0 Vi: 0-0 Tstrap: 0-0
Best Rating:	72 11/01 Naas 2m yld-sft Hdl

Firey Steel (IRE)
105   **100**

6-y-o gr g Roselier (FR)-Charming Mo (IRE) (Callernish)
A J Martin   K C Syndicate

Placings: 0-50546   (3520)
2002/03: 20⁵SH, 16⁰S, 22⁵S, 24⁴YS, 20⁶GS,

	Starts	1st	2nd	3rd	Win & Pl
Hurdles	5	0	0	0	698
Career Total	6	0	0	0	698

Going:	Sf: 0-2 GS: 0-1 Gd: 0-0 GF: - Fm: 0-0
Distance:	2m/2m3: 0-1 2m4-2m7: 0-3 3m+: 0-1
Track:	LH: 0-2 RH: 0-3 Tight: 0-2 Gall: 0-0
Aids:	Bl: 0-0 Vi: 0-0 Tstrap: 0-0
Best Rating:	100 1/03 Punc 3m yld-sft Hdl

Firinn
                 61

8-y-o b g Phardante (FR)-Viking Rocket (Viking (USA))
A M Crow   Mrs P C Stirling

Placings: 50/2P   (3166)
2002/03: 24²GS, 25ᴾG,

	Starts	1st	2nd	3rd	Win & Pl
Hurdles	2	0	1	0	1105
Career Total	4	0	1	0	1105

Going:	Sf: 0-0 GS: 0-1 Gd: 0-1 GF: - Fm: 0-0
Distance:	2m/2m3: 0-0 2m4-2m7: 0-0 3m+: 0-2
Track:	LH: 0-1 RH: 0-1 Tight: 0-1 Gall: 0-0
Aids:	Bl: 0-0 Vi: 0-0 Tstrap: 0-0
Best Rating:	88 10/00 Carl 2m1f gd-sft NHF

Well beaten second on hurdling debut at Carlisle in November 2002.

First Alliance (IRE)
76   **67**

6-y-o b g Caerleon (USA)-Lady Liberty (NZ) (Noble Bijou (USA))

E W Tuer (K A Morgen 22/5) E Tuer

Placings:55/050050-P0   (0615)
2002/03: 20^P G, 20^Q GF,

	Starts	1st	2nd	3rd	Win & Pl
Hurdles	2	0	0	0	
Career Total	10	0	0	0	0

Going:	Sf: 0-0 GS: 0-0 Gd: 0-1 GF: - Fm: 0-1
Distance:	2m/2m3: 0-0 2m4-2m7: 0-2 3m+: 0-0
Track:	LH: 0-2 RH: 0-0 Tight: 0-0 Gall: 0-0
Aids:	Bl: 0-0 Vi: 0-0 Tstrap: 0-0
Best Rating:	81 3/01 MRas 2m1f110y good NHF

First Base
92   77

4-y-o ch g First Trump-Rose Music (Luthier)
R E Barr Malcolm O Hair

Placings:0P3   (4517)
2002/03: 16^D GS, 16^P GF, 17^3 G,

	Starts	1st	2nd	3rd	Win & Pl
Hurdles	3	0	0	1	506
Career Total	3	0	0	1	506

Going:	Sf: 0-0 GS: 0-1 Gd: 0-1 GF: - Fm: 0-1
Distance:	2m/2m3: 0-3 2m4-2m7: 0-0 3m+: 0-0
Track:	LH: 0-3 RH: 0-0 Tight: 0-2 Gall: 0-0
Aids:	Bl: 0-0 Vi: 0-0 Tstrap: 0-0
Best Rating:	77 4/03 Sedg 2m1f good Hdl

Plating-class novice hurdler; best effort when third in a poor contest at Sedgefield in April 2003; may do better when stepped up in trip; has worn cheekpieces.

First Day Cover (IRE)
89   89

7-y-o b g Toulon-Bilberry (Nicholas Bill)
Noel T Chance A D Weller

Placings:51-4604   (4217)
2002/03: 17^4 HY, 20^6 HY, 21^0 G, 22^4 G,

	Starts	1st	2nd	3rd	Win & Pl
Hurdles	4	0	0	0	0
Career Total	6	1	0	0	1558
97 12/01 Plum 2m2f			H NHF	SFT	£1557
				Total win prize-money £1558

Going:	Sf: 0-2 GS: 0-0 Gd: 0-2 GF: - Fm: 0-0
Distance:	2m/2m3: 0-1 2m4-2m7: 0-3 3m+: 0-0
Track:	LH: 0-1 RH: 0-3 Tight: 0-3 Gall: 0-0
Aids:	Bl: 0-0 Vi: 0-0 Tstrap: 0-0
Best Rating:	97 12/01 Plum 2m2f soft NHF

Benefited from his debut to land a Plumpton bumper. Looks a staying type.

First Embrace
102   91

7-y-o b g Faustus (USA)-Legal Embrace (CAN) (Legal Bid (USA))
K Bell North Farm Stud

Placings:2226/24U5055-05   (1547)
2002/03: 24^0 G, 24^5 F,

	Starts	1st	2nd	3rd	Win & Pl
Hurdles	2	0	0	0	0
Career Total	13	0	4	0	2052

Going: Sf: 0-0 GS: 0-0 Gd: 0-1 GF: - Fm: 0-1
Distance: 2m/2m3: 0-0 2m4-2m7: 0-0 3m+: 0-2
Track: LH: 0-1 RH: 0-1 Tight: 0-1 Gall: 0-0
Aids: Bl: 0-0 Vi: 0-0 Tstrap: 0-0
Best Rating: 108 5/00 Hntg 2m110y gd-sft NHF

Moderate form in bumpers and hurdles at around two miles.

First Flight
(109c)114

7-y-o br g Neltino-The Beginning (Goldhill)
K C Bailey Major Basil Heaton

Placings:3/4220-FP   (4153)
2002/03: 19^F GS, 25^P G,

	Starts	1st	2nd	3rd	Win & Pl
Hurdles	1	0	0	0	0
Chases	1	0	0	0	0
Career Total	7	0	2	1	3083

Going:	Sf: 0-0 GS: 0-0 Gd: 0-1 GF: - Fm: 0-0
Distance:	2m/2m3: 0-0 2m4-2m7: 0-1 3m+: 0-1
Track:	LH: 0-1 RH: 0-1 Tight: 0-0 Gall: 0-0
Aids:	Bl: 0-0 Vi: 0-0 Tstrap: 0-0
Best Rating:	114 2/02 Kemp 3m110y soft Hdl

Has shown plenty of promise in a handful of novice hurdles without winning; acts with cut and stays three miles.

First Gold (FR)
120(121h)   (151h)174

10-y-o b g Shafoun (FR)-Nuit D Or Ii (FR) (Pot D Or (FR))
F Doumen J P McManus

Placings:6242111F/1/F2/32111121U/534-303P1   (4457)
2002/03: 20^3 SH, 24^0 HY, 25^3 GS, 26^P G, 25^1 G,

	Starts	1st	2nd	3rd	Win & Pl
Chases	5	1	0	2	96369
Career Total	28	10	5	4	693261
174 4/03 Aint 3m1f	A Ch			GD	£87000
178 4/01 Aint 3m1f	A Ch			SFT	£71400
178 12/00 Kemp 3m	A Ch			G-S	£87000
180 11/00 Autl 3m3f110y	Ch			HVY	£84534
10/00 Autl 2m6f	Ch			VS	£38425
9/00 Autl 2m4f110y	Hdl			VS	£10567
5/98 Autl 3m5f	Ch			SFT	£121212
3/98 Autl 2m5f110y	HCh			VS	£35353
2/98 Autl 2m2f110y	Ch			VS	£10101
1/98 Pau 2m4f110y	Ch			SFT	£5051
				Total win prize-money £550643

Going:	Sf: 0-1 GS: 0-1 Gd: 1-2 GF: - Fm: 0-0
Distance:	2m/2m3: 0-0 2m4-2m7: 0-0 3m+: 1-4
Track:	LH: 1-3 RH: 0-2 Tight: 1-1 Gall: 0-1
Aids:	Bl: 1-1 Vi: 0-0 Tstrap: 0-0
Best Rating:	180 11/00 Autl 3m3f110y heavy Ch

Smart French chaser; won the King George VI Chase and the Martell Cup in 2000/01; ran away with the same Aintree race this time when blinkered for the first time; suited by a sharp three miles; best form with cut in the ground.

First Grey
86f   81f

4-y-o gr f Environment Friend-Myrtilla (Beldale Flutter (USA))
E W Tuer E Tuer

Placings:0420   (3917)
2002/03: 14^0 GS, 16^4 HY, 17^2 HY, 17^0 GS,

	Starts	1st	2nd	3rd	Win & Pl
NH Flat	4	0	1	0	576

Career Total   4   0   1   0   576

Going:	Sf: 0-2 GS: 0-2 Gd: 0-0 GF: - Fm: 0-0
Distance:	2m/2m3: 0-3 2m4-2m7: 0-0 3m+: 0-0
Track:	LH: 0-3 RH: 0-1 Tight: 0-1 Gall: 0-0
Aids:	Bl: 0-0 Vi: 0-0 Tstrap: 0-0
Best Rating:	87 3/03 Carl 2m1f gd-sft NHF

Runner-up at Sedgefield in February.

First Judgement (IRE)
93   72

7-y-o b g Leading Counsel (USA)-Star Gold (Bonne Noel)
J W Mullins Adam Day

Placings:00-5   (1592)
2002/03: 22^5 G,

	Starts	1st	2nd	3rd	Win & Pl
Hurdles	1	0	0	0	0
Career Total	3	0	0	0	0

Going:	Sf: 0-0 GS: 0-0 Gd: 0-1 GF: - Fm: 0-0
Distance:	2m/2m3: 0-0 2m4-2m7: 0-1 3m+: 0-0
Track:	LH: 0-0 RH: 0-1 Tight: 0-0 Gall: 0-0
Aids:	Bl: 0-0 Vi: 0-0 Tstrap: 0-0
Best Rating:	87 10/02 Extr 2m6f110y good Hdl

First Love
119(109h)   (138h)138+

7-y-o br g Bustino-First Romance (Royalty)
N J Henderson The Queen

Placings:2121/1221-2212   (4047)
2002/03: 16^2 HY, 18^2 S, 21^1 S, 16^2 S,

	Starts	1st	2nd	3rd	Win & Pl
Chases	4	1	3	0	9681
Career Total	12	5	7	0	29019
138 2/03 Folk 2m5f	E Ch			SFT	£4046
116 3/02 Sand 2m110y	D Hdl			G-S	£4524
138 12/01 Sand 2m110y	D Hdl			SFT	£4524
128 4/01 Asct 2m110y	H NHF			HVY	£2583
123 2/01 Towc 2m	H NHF			HVY	£1575
				Total win prize-money £17252

Going:	Sf: 1-4 GS: 0-0 Gd: 0-0 GF: - Fm: 0-0
Distance:	2m/2m3: 0-3 **2m4-2m7:** 1-1 3m+: 0-0
Track:	LH: 0-2 **RH: 1-2** Tight: 1-1 Gall: 0-1
Aids:	Bl: 0-0 Vi: 0-0 Tstrap: 0-0
Best Rating:	138 2/03 Folk 2m5f soft Ch

A big, strong gelding, useful novice chaser/hurdler; showed plenty of ability to win two bumpers and two hurdle races at around two miles; beaten on first two runs over fences despite jumping well; got off the mark at Folkestone in February 2003; stays at least two and a half miles and appears to appreciate cut in the ground; all his wins have been on right-handed tracks.

First Officer (USA)
104(94h)   (93h)93

6-y-o b g Lear Fan (USA)-Trampoli (USA) (Trempolino (USA))
C C Bealby K McGeorge & T Radford

Placings:0/6505P32   (4632)
2002/03: 16^6 GS, 20^5 GS, 20^0 GS, 19^5 GS, 20^P GS, 25^3 G, 26^2 GF,

	Starts	1st	2nd	3rd	Win & Pl
Hurdles	4	0	0	0	0

Chases	3	0	1	1	2012
Career Total	8	0	1	1	2012

Going: Sf: 0-0 GS: 0-5 Gd: 0-1 GF: - Fm: 0-1
Distance: 2m/2m3: 0-1 2m4-2m7: 0-4 3m+: 0-2
Track: LH: 0-3 RH: 0-3 Tight: 0-4 Gall: 0-0
Aids: Bl: 0-2 Vi: 0-0 Tstrap: 0-0
Best Rating: 93   11/02   Weth   2m   gd-sft   Hdl

Plating-class chaser; fair stayer on the Flat, limited ability over hurdles; off the mark over fences at Southwell in May; stays well; acts on good to soft and good to firm; has worn blinkers.

First Touch (IRE)

9-y-o br g Montelimar (USA)-Jennycomequick (Furry Glen)
M R Bosley First Touch

Placings:0/PP   (2570)
2002/03: 21PS, 16PG,

	Starts	1st	2nd	3rd	Win & Pl
Hurdles	2	0	0	0	
Career Total	3	0	0	0	

Going: Sf: 0-1 GS: 0-0 Gd: 0-1 GF: - Fm: 0-0
Distance: 2m/2m3: 0-1 2m4-2m7: 0-1 3m+: 0-0
Track: LH: 0-2 RH: 0-0 Tight: 0-0 Gall: 0-1
Aids: Bl: 0-0 Vi: 0-0 Tstrap: 0-1
Best Rating: 114   11/00   Chel   2m110y   gd-sft   NHF

First Truth

110   **93**

6-y-o b g Rudimentary (USA)-Pursuit Of Truth (USA) (Irish River (FR))
Mrs H Dalton   Ray Bailey

Placings:20063-31   (0277)
2002/03: 17³G, 17¹S,

	Starts	1st	2nd	3rd	Win & Pl
Hurdles	2	1	0	1	5073
Career Total	7	1	1	2	6337
111	5/02	Bang	2m1f		D(0-120)HHdl	SFT £4407

Total win prize-money £4407

Going: Sf: 1-1 GS: 0-0 Gd: 0-1 GF: - Fm: 0-0
Distance: 2m/2m3: 1-2 2m4-2m7: 0-0 3m+: 0-0
Track: LH: 1-2 RH: 0-0 Tight: 1-2 Gall: 0-0
Aids: Bl: 0-0 Vi: 0-0 Tstrap: 0-0
Best Rating: 111   5/02   Bang   2m1f   soft   Hdl

Fair efforts over hurdles to date at around two miles, including winning at Bangor. Gives the impression a stiffer test would suit. Acts on soft ground.

Fisher Street

100(89h)   (59h)**97+**

8-y-o gr g Tigani-Pricket Walk (Amboise)
Mrs S C Bradburne   Mrs C J Kerr

Placings:00/025044013031PP-41   (0376)
2002/03: 20⁴GF, 25¹GF,

	Starts	1st	2nd	3rd	Win & Pl
Chases	2	1	0	0	4922
Career Total	18	3	1	2	14389
97	5/02	Kels	3m1f	D(0-115)HCh	G-F	£4498
97	3/02	Newc	2m4f	E Ch	HVY	£3415
92	12/01	Muss	2m	F(0-95)HCh	G-F	£3052

Total win prize-money £10966

Fishki's Lad

103   **105**

8-y-o b g Casteddu-Fishki (Niniski (USA))
E W Tuer (M D Hammond 15/7)   Shore Property

Placings:3310/2061512/04432/00P0P-213024   (4509)
2002/03: 20²G, 24¹G, 25³G, 19⁴GS, 24²S, 24²G,

	Starts	1st	2nd	3rd	Win & Pl
Hurdles	6	1	2	1	4295
Career Total	27	4	5	4	15946
102	6/02	Hexm	3m	F(0-100)HHdl	GD	£2320
103	4/00	Hexm	2m4f110yD(0-125)HHdl	GD	£3172
102	2/00	Muss	3m	E Hdl	GD	£2450
97	3/99	Hexm	2m	H NHF	G-S	£1556

Total win prize-money £9500

Going: Sf: 0-1 GS: 0-1 Gd: 1-4 GF: - Fm: 0-0
Distance: 2m/2m3: 0-0 2m4-2m7: 0-0 3m+: 1-3
Track: LH: 1-6 RH: 0-0 Tight: 0-2 Gall: 0-0
Aids: Bl: 1-3 Vi: 0-0 Tstrap: 0-0
Best Rating: 107   1/01   Muss   3m   gd-sft   Hdl

Modest handicap hurdler; acts on good ground and stays three miles.

Five Pence

72   **36**

7-y-o b g Henbit (USA)-Le Saule D Or (Sonnen Gold)
P Winkworth   Bill Naylor

Placings:00   (2588)
2002/03: 16⁰S, 19⁰GS,

	Starts	1st	2nd	3rd	Win & Pl
Hurdles	2	0	0	0	
Career Total	2	0	0	0	

Going: Sf: 0-1 GS: 0-1 Gd: 0-0 GF: - Fm: 0-0
Distance: 2m/2m3: 0-2 2m4-2m7: 0-0 3m+: 0-0
Track: LH: 0-1 RH: 0-1 Tight: 0-0 Gall: 0-1
Aids: Bl: 0-0 Vi: 0-0 Tstrap: 0-0
Best Rating: 36   11/02   Newb   2m110y   soft   Hdl

Flag Fen (USA)

105   **86**

12-y-o b/br g Riverman (USA)-Damascus Flag (USA) (Damascus (USA))
H J Collingridge   H J Collingridge

Placings:310/4F602-4565   (4666)
2002/03: 16⁴GS, 16⁵GS, 16⁶G, 16⁵G,

	Starts	1st	2nd	3rd	Win & Pl
Hurdles	4	0	0	0	288
Career Total	12	1	1	0	3579
110	12/00	Fknm	2m	E Hdl	G-S	£1764

Total win prize-money £1764

Going: Sf: 0-0 GS: 0-2 Gd: 0-2 GF: - Fm: 0-0
Distance: 2m/2m3: 0-4 2m4-2m7: 0-0 3m+: 0-0
Track: LH: 0-4 RH: 0-0 Tight: 0-4 Gall: 0-0
Aids: Bl: 0-0 Vi: 0-0 Tstrap: 0-0
Best Rating: 110   12/00   Fknm   2m   gd-sft   Hdl

Going: Sf: 0-0 GS: 0-0 Gd: 0-0 GF: - Fm: 1-2
Distance: 2m/2m3: 0-0 2m4-2m7: 0-1 3m+: 1-1
Track: LH: 1-1 RH: 0-1 Tight: 1-1 Gall: 0-0
Aids: Bl: 0-0 Vi: 1-1 Tstrap: 0-0
Best Rating: 97   5/02   Kels   3m1f   gd-fm   Ch

A fair novice hurdler in 2001/2. Switched his attentions to fencing; stays three miles one; acts on soft ground; jumps soundly.

Plating-class hurdler; at the veteran stage; suited by a sharp track and cut in the ground; goes well at Fakenham.

Flagship Uberalles (IRE)

114   **156**

9-y-o br g Accordion-Fourth Degree (Oats)
P J Hobbs   J P McManus

Placings:113/22121111/11213PP/1244/112-4P5   (4111)
2002/03: 16⁴S, 24PS, 16⁵G,

	Starts	1st	2nd	3rd	Win & Pl
Chases	3	0	0	0	11250
Career Total	28	13	6	2	497626
170	3/02	Chel	2m	A Ch	G-S	£127600
170	12/01	Sand	2m	A Ch	G-S	£46400
173	12/00	Chel	2m110y	A Ch	SFT	£31900
167	2/00	Newb	2m1f	A Ch	G-S	£25350
166	12/99	Sand	2m	A Ch	GD	£38700
158	11/99	Extr	2m1f	A HCh	G-S	£19050
151	4/99	Aint	2m	A Ch	G-S	£32725
157	3/99	Chel	2m	A Ch	G-S	£57300
144	2/99	Wwck	2m	A Ch	G-S	£16224
131	1/99	Kemp	2m	D Ch	SFT	£4810
131	12/98	Extr	2m1f110yC Ch	G-S	£5114
99	3/98	Limk	2m	Hdl	YLD	£3573
113	3/98	Navn	2m	Hdl	Y-S	£2680

Total win prize-money £411428

Going: Sf: 0-2 GS: 0-0 Gd: 0-1 GF: - Fm: 0-0
Distance: 2m/2m3: 0-2 2m4-2m7: 0-0 3m+: 0-1
Track: LH: 0-1 RH: 0-2 Tight: 0-0 Gall: 0-1
Aids: Bl: 0-1 Vi: 0-0 Tstrap: 0-0
Best Rating: 173   12/00   Chel   2m110y   soft   Ch

Top-class two-mile chaser; winner of the 2002 Champion Chase at the Cheltenham Festival; has failed to reproduce his best this term, jumping sketchily and finishing a well beaten 4th to Cenkos in the Tingle Creek at Sandown and running poorly in the King George at Kempton (beaten before the trip became an issue); suited by some cut in the ground and all best form around 2m; not the greatest jumper among the top 2m chasers and has a history of back problems; goes well fresh.

Flahive's First

112(108h)   (65 h)**106**

9-y-o ch g Interrex (CAN)-Striking Image (IRE) (Flash Of Steel)
D Burchell   Don Gould

Placings:F043206/0000203314100403 36F44U0255/34130 P/P502P/PF0420-2223525311404UP0366464   (4676)
2002/03: 17²G, 17²S, 17⁹HY, 16³S, 16⁵G, 16²GF, 20⁵G, 20³GS, 17¹G, 17¹G, 16⁴GS, 16⁹S, 19⁴S, 21⁰GS, 19⁵S, 17⁰S, 16³GS, 18⁶S, 19⁶HY, 20⁴G, 17⁶GF, 19⁴GF,

	Starts	1st	2nd	3rd	Win & Pl
Hurdles	2	0	0	0	0
Chases	20	2	4	3	16490
Career Total	72	5	9	10	29753
95	8/02	Ctml	2m1f110yD(0-115)HCh	GD	£5590
92	8/02	Ctml	2m1f110yF(0-95)HCh	GD	£3484
87	6/99	Worc	2m	F(0-105)HHdl	G-S	£1957
84	8/98	Ctml	2m1f110yG(0-90)HHdl	G-F	£2432
80	8/98	Worc	2m	G Hdl	GD	£1520

Total win prize-money £14984

Going: Sf: 0-9 GS: 0-4 Gd: 2-6 GF: - Fm: 0-3
Distance: 2m/2m3: 2-16 2m4-2m7: 0-6 3m+: 0-0
Track: LH: 2-13 RH: 0-8 Tight: 2-11 Gall: 0-0
Aids: Bl: 0-0 Vi: 0-0 Tstrap: 0-0
Best Rating: 95   8/02   Ctml   2m1f110y   good   Ch

Moderate chaser; has scored four times over the extended

two miles at Cartmel; stays two miles four; best on good or faster ground.

Flame Creek (IRE)
105(124h)   (158 h)**125+**
7-y-o b g Shardari-Sheila s Pet (IRE) (Welsh Term)
Noel T Chance Martin Wesson Partners

Placings: 1/21-1110P   (4555)
2002/03: 16¹G, 17¹HY, 16¹GS, 16⁰G, 16ᴾG,

	Starts	1st	2nd	3rd	Win & Pl
Hurdles	5	3	0	0	46820
Career Total	8	5	1	0	58286
158	1/03	Hayd	2m	A Hdl	G-S £23200
147	1/03	Chel	2m11f	B(0-150)HHdl	HVY £15300
136	5/02	Kels	2m110y	B Hdl	GD £8320
138	4/02	Chel	2m11f	B Hdl	GD £9009
119	4/01	Winc	2m	H NHF	SFT £1673

Total win prize-money £57502

Going:	Sf: 1-1 GS: 1-1 Gd: 1-3 GF: - Fm: 0-0
Distance:	2m/2m3: 3-5 2m4-2m7: 0-0 3m+: 0-0
Track:	LH: 3-5 RH: 0-0 Tight: 1-1 Gall: 1-1
Aids:	Bl: 0-0 Vi: 0-0 Tstrap: 0-0
Best Rating:	158 1/03 Hayd 2m gd-sft Hdl

High-class hurdler; impressive in a decent handicap at Cheltenham at the start of 2003 and again won well in muddling Grade Two Champion Hurdle Trial at Haydock; well beaten in Champion Hurdle; did not jump well in the Scottish Champion Hurdle on ground he is reported to prefer; made a winning chase debut at Bangor in May but did not jump that well; again did not impress with his fencing when following up in facile fashion at Wetherby a week later; suited by 2m; effective on heavy ground but ideally suited by a sound surface.

Flame Of Zara
101f   **95f**
4-y-o ch f Blushing Flame (USA)-Sierra Madrona (USA) (Woodman (USA))
Mrs M Reveley R Meredith

Placings: 4222   (4611)
2002/03: 12⁴G, 16²G, 16²GF, 17²G,

	Starts	1st	2nd	3rd	Win & Pl
NH Flat	4	0	3	0	6898
Career Total	4	0	3	0	6898

Going:	Sf: 0-0 GS: 0-0 Gd: 0-3 GF: - Fm: 0-1
Distance:	2m/2m3: 0-3 2m4-2m7: 0-0 3m+: 0-0
Track:	LH: 0-4 RH: 0-0 Tight: 0-1 Gall: 0-1
Aids:	Bl: 0-0 Vi: 0-0 Tstrap: 0-0
Best Rating:	95 4/03 Chel 2m1f good NHF

Progressive form in bumpers; best effort when runner-up in Listed mares only event at Cheltenham April 2003; acts on ground good and faster.

Flamebird (IRE)
97   **92**
6-y-o b m Mukaddamah (USA)-Flamenco (USA) (Dance Spell (USA))
Jonjo O Neill Mrs L R Lovell

Placings: F3   (0177)
2002/03: 17ᶠG, 16³GF,

	Starts	1st	2nd	3rd	Win & Pl
Hurdles	2	0	0	1	384
Career Total	2	0	0	1	384

Going:	Sf: 0-0 GS: 0-0 Gd: 0-1 GF: - Fm: 0-1
Distance:	2m/2m3: 0-2 2m4-2m7: 0-0 3m+: 0-0
Track:	LH: 0-0 RH: 0-2 Tight: 0-0 Gall: 0-0
Aids:	Bl: 0-0 Vi: 0-0 Tstrap: 0-0
Best Rating:	92 5/02 Winc 2m gd-fm Hdl

Has shown ability in modest hurdling company.

Flamenca (USA)
99   **61**
4-y-o b f Diesis-Highland Ceilidh (IRE) (Scottish Reel)
R Allan Allan A Grant

Placings: 0326P06543   (4798)
2002/03: 17⁰G, 17³G, 16²GF, 16⁶S, 16ᴾGS, 16⁰GS, 16⁰GS, 18⁶G, 16⁴G, 17³GF,

	Starts	1st	2nd	3rd	Win & Pl
Hurdles	10	0	1	2	2506
Career Total	10	0	1	2	2506

Going:	Sf: 0-1 GS: 0-3 Gd: 0-4 GF: - Fm: 0-2
Distance:	2m/2m3: 0-10 2m4-2m7: 0-0 3m+: 0-0
Track:	LH: 0-1 RH: 0-0 Tight: 0-6 Gall: 0-1
Aids:	Bl: 0-0 Vi: 0-3 Tstrap: 0-0
Best Rating:	81 3/03 Hexm 2m110y good Hdl

Plating-class hurdler; moody sort; poor form when placed in juvenile hurdles in 2002/03; acts on a sound surface.

Flaming Cheek
95   **83+**
5-y-o b g Blushing Flame (USA)-Rueful Lady (Streetfighter)
A G Blackmore A G Blackmore

Placings: 40456   (4148)
2002/03: 17⁴S, 16⁰GS, 16⁴S, 16⁵G, 16⁶G,

	Starts	1st	2nd	3rd	Win & Pl
NH Flat	4	0	0	0	0
Hurdles	1	0	0	0	0
Career Total	5	0	0	0	0

Going:	Sf: 0-2 GS: 0-1 Gd: 0-2 GF: - Fm: 0-0
Distance:	2m/2m3: 0-5 2m4-2m7: 0-0 3m+: 0-0
Track:	LH: 0-1 RH: 0-4 Tight: 0-2 Gall: 0-2
Aids:	Bl: 0-0 Vi: 0-0 Tstrap: 0-0
Best Rating:	87 3/03 Hntg 2m110y good NHF

Very modest form in bumpers and over hurdles.

Flaming Heck
                                    84f
6-y-o b g Dancing High-Heckley Spark (Electric)
Mrs L B Normile D A Whitaker

Placings: 3   (0026)
2002/03: 16³G,

	Starts	1st	2nd	3rd	Win & Pl
NH Flat	1	0	0	1	232
Career Total	1	0	0	1	232

Going:	Sf: 0-0 GS: 0-0 Gd: 0-1 GF: - Fm: 0-0
Distance:	2m/2m3: 0-1 2m4-2m7: 0-0 3m+: 0-0
Track:	LH: 0-1 RH: 0-0 Tight: 0-0 Gall: 0-0
Aids:	Bl: 0-0 Vi: 0-0 Tstrap: 0-0
Best Rating:	84 4/02 Hexm 2m110y good NHF

Flaming Spirt
4-y-o b f Blushing Flame (USA)-Fair Test (Fair Season)
J S Moore W J Wyatt

Placings: UP   (2715)
2002/03: 16ᵁG, 16ᴾHY,

	Starts	1st	2nd	3rd	Win & Pl
Hurdles	2	0	0	0	
Career Total	2	0	0	0	

Going:	Sf: 0-1 GS: 0-0 Gd: 0-1 GF: - Fm: 0-0
Distance:	2m/2m3: 0-2 2m4-2m7: 0-0 3m+: 0-0
Track:	LH: 0-2 RH: 0-0 Tight: 0-0 Gall: 0-1
Aids:	Bl: 0-0 Vi: 0-0 Tstrap: 0-0
Best Rating:	0 12/02 Chep 2m110y heavy Hdl

Flash Gordon
111   **109**
9-y-o ch g Gildoran-Florence May (Grange Melody)
Mrs S Richardson R G Fairbarns

Placings: 0/1/51-FPU   (4636)
2002/03: 20ᶠS, 21ᴾGS, 24ᵁG,

	Starts	1st	2nd	3rd	Win & Pl
Chases	3	0	0	0	
Career Total	7	2	0	0	7670
109	3/02	Hrfd	2m	D(0-115)HCh	GD £4524
99	4/01	Tntn	2m3f	E Ch	G-F £3146

Total win prize-money £7670

Going:	Sf: 0-1 GS: 0-1 Gd: 0-1 GF: - Fm: 0-0
Distance:	2m/2m3: 0-0 2m4-2m7: 0-2 3m+: 0-1
Track:	LH: 0-1 RH: 0-2 Tight: 0-1 Gall: 0-0
Aids:	Bl: 0-0 Vi: 0-0 Tstrap: 0-0
Best Rating:	109 3/02 Hrfd 2m good Ch

Modest chaser; likes to front run; effective at up to 2m 4f; sometimes gives problems at the start; lightly raced.

Flash Of Memory
86   **83**
6-y-o b m Rock Hopper-Mystic Memory (Ela-Mana-Mou)
P D Niven (R A Fahey 7/7) Carnoustie Racing Club Ltd

Placings: 5212-30   (1743)
2002/03: 20³GF, 16⁰GS,

	Starts	1st	2nd	3rd	Win & Pl
Hurdles	2	0	0	1	603
Career Total	6	1	2	1	3314
99	12/01	Muss	2m1f	H NHF	G-F £1582

Total win prize-money £1582

Going:	Sf: 0-0 GS: 0-1 Gd: 0-0 GF: - Fm: 0-1
Distance:	2m/2m3: 0-1 2m4-2m7: 0-1 3m+: 0-0
Track:	LH: 0-2 RH: 0-0 Tight: 0-0 Gall: 0-0
Aids:	Bl: 0-0 Vi: 0-0 Tstrap: 0-0
Best Rating:	99 2/02 Muss 2m soft NHF

Second in a bumper on her second start, she got off the mark in a similar race at Musselburgh. Runner-up there under her penalty. Fair run on her hurdling debut in October 2002.

Flashant
87   **48**
8-y-o ch g Henbit (USA)-La Furze (Winden)
A W Carroll A Bayman

Placings: 000/4001/P0/00-P54   (0908)

2002/03: 16⁰GS, 24ᴾG, 20⁵GF, 17⁴GS,

	Starts	1st	2nd	3rd	Win & Pl
Hurdles	4	0	0	0	0
Career Total	14	1	0	0	2562
84	3/00	Sedg	2m1f	E(0-105)HHdl	G-F £2282

Total win prize-money £2282

Going: Sf: 0-0 GS: 0-2 Gd: 0-1 GF: - Fm: 0-1
Distance: 2m2m3: 0-2 2m4-2m7: 0-1 3m+: 0-1
Track: LH: 0-2 RH: 0-2 Tight: 0-1 Gall: 0-0
Aids: Bl: 0-1 Vi: 0-0 Tstrap: 0-0
Best Rating: 84 3/00 Sedg 2m1f gd-fm Hdl

Flat Mate (IRE)

(50h)

6-y-o br g Supreme Leader-Lady Nethertown (Windjammer (USA))
Mrs S J Smith Trevor Hemmings

Placings:0P0F (3913)
2002/03: 16⁰G, 20ᴾHY, 19⁰GS, 20ᶠS,

	Starts	1st	2nd	3rd	Win & Pl
NH Flat	1	0	0	0	
Hurdles	2	0	0	0	
Chases	1	0	0	0	
Career Total	4	0	0		

Going: Sf: 0-2 GS: 0-1 Gd: 0-1 GF: - Fm: 0-0
Distance: 2m2m3: 0-1 2m4-2m7: 0-3 3m+: 0-0
Track: LH: 0-2 RH: 0-2 Tight: 0-0 Gall: 0-0
Aids: Bl: 0-0 Vi: 0-0 Tstrap: 0-0
Best Rating: 50 1/03 Donc 2m3f110y gd-sft Hdl

Flat Stanley

72   27

4-y-o b g Celtic Swing-Cool Grey (Absalom)
R Bastiman John Endersby

Placings:P (3089)
2002/03: 19ᴾGS,

	Starts	1st	2nd	3rd	Win & Pl
Hurdles	1	0	0	0	
Career Total	1	0	0	0	

Going: Sf: 0-0 GS: 0-1 Gd: 0-0 GF: - Fm: 0-0
Distance: 2m2m3: 0-0 2m4-2m7: 0-1 3m+: 0-0
Track: LH: 0-1 RH: 0-0 Tight: 0-0 Gall: 0-0
Aids: Bl: 0-0 Vi: 0-0 Tstrap: 0-0
Best Rating: 0 1/03 Donc 2m3f110y gd-sft Hdl

Flat Top

96   117

12-y-o b g Blakeney-New Edition (Great Nephew)
M W Easterby Major M Watson

Placings:21F4/P6200P/F4P042P4/2P5F2P1113/U2134431
12/P353/12253302FP/522P0313-5UU0 (3351)
2002/03: 20⁵G, 25ᵁGS, 25ᵁGS, 24⁰GF,

	Starts	1st	2nd	3rd	Win & Pl
Chases	4	0	0	0	
Career Total	66	9	12	9	71462
117	3/02	Newb	3m	C(0-135)HCh	G-S £15636
113	10/00	Hexm	2m4f110yE(0-115)HCh		HVY £2847
121	3/99	Newc	3m	E(0-115)HCh	GD £2788
121	3/99	Newc	3m	D(0-125)HCh	SFT £8609
110	12/98	Catt	3m1f110yE(0-115)HHdl		GD £2486
125	4/98	Hexm	3m1f	E Ch	HVY £3154
125	4/98	Chel	2m5f	D(0-115)HCh	HVY £5402

| 113 | 4/98 | Weth | 2m4f110yD Ch | G-S | £3684 |
| 3/95 | Hexm | 3m | E Hdl | HVY | £2304 |

Total win prize-money £46912

Going: Sf: 0-1 GS: 0-2 Gd: 0-1 GF: - Fm: 0-0
Distance: 2m2m3: 0-0 2m4-2m7: 0-1 3m+: 0-3
Track: LH: 0-4 RH: 0-0 Tight: 0-1 Gall: 0-1
Aids: Bl: 0-0 Vi: 0-0 Tstrap: 0-0
Best Rating: 125 4/98 Sand 2m4f110y gd-sft Ch

Fair chaser, stays three miles and suited by soft ground.

Flaviatore

94   85

5-y-o b h Deploy-Trundley Wood (Wassl)
Mario Hofer Stall Lucky Owner

Placings:0P (4117)
2002/03: 16⁰GS, 16ᴾG,

	Starts	1st	2nd	3rd	Win & Pl
Hurdles	2	0	0	0	
Career Total	2	0	0	0	

Going: Sf: 0-0 GS: 0-1 Gd: 0-1 GF: - Fm: 0-0
Distance: 2m2m3: 0-2 2m4-2m7: 0-0 3m+: 0-0
Track: LH: 0-0 RH: 0-2 Tight: 0-0 Gall: 0-1
Aids: Bl: 0-0 Vi: 0-0 Tstrap: 0-0
Best Rating: 85 2/03 Winc 2m gd-sft Hdl

Flaxley Abbey

85   65

6-y-o gr m Arzanni-Dunbrody Abbey (Proverb)
J D Frost David G Jones

Placings:0-00P50 (4595)
2002/03: 17⁰G, 17⁰GF, 19⁰S, 17⁵GF, 22⁰GF,

	Starts	1st	2nd	3rd	Win & Pl
NH Flat	2	0	0	0	0
Hurdles	3	0	0	0	0
Career Total	6	0	0	0	0

Going: Sf: 0-1 GS: 0-0 Gd: 0-1 GF: - Fm: 0-3
Distance: 2m2m3: 0-4 2m4-2m7: 0-1 3m+: 0-0
Track: LH: 0-2 RH: 0-3 Tight: 0-2 Gall: 0-0
Aids: Bl: 0-0 Vi: 0-0 Tstrap: 0-0
Best Rating: 78 7/02 NAbb 2m1f gd-fm NHF

Flaxley Wood

105   129

12-y-o b/br g Kambalda-Coolbawn Run (Deep Run)
R H Buckler Mrs D A La Trobe

Placings:50/6541P/134132126/1112P4/112F4P/504-210 (1396)
2002/03: 22⁰GF, 21¹GF, 24⁰GF,

	Starts	1st	2nd	3rd	Win & Pl
Chases	3	1	1	0	10199
Career Total	34	10	5	2	64443
121	8/02	Uttx	2m5f	C(0-135)HCh	G-F £8069
128	10/00	Chel	2m4f110yC(0-135)HCh		GD £10676
125	10/00	Sthl	2m4f110yC(0-130)HHdl		HVY £6873
130	1/99	Chel	2m5f	C HCh	SFT £7360
103	8/98	Worc	2m7f110yD Ch		GD £3767
103	7/98	Worc	2m7f110yE Ch		G-F £3257
108	2/98	Font	2m6f110yD(0-120)HHdl		GD £3080
	12/97	Font	2m6f110yD(0-120)HHdl		SFT £3021
	10/97	Strf	2m6f110yD(0-125)HHdl		GD £2784
	1/97	Plum	2m4f	E(0-110)HHdl	GD £2490

Total win prize-money £51381

Flecthefawna (IRE)

91   82

7-y-o b h Glacial Storm (USA)-Lady Sperrin (Abednego)
L A Dace Churchfields Partnership

Placings:004 (3319)
2002/03: 17⁰S, 18⁰HY, 21⁴GS,

	Starts	1st	2nd	3rd	Win & Pl
NH Flat	2	0	0	0	0
Hurdles	1	0	0	0	436
Career Total	3	0	0	0	436

Going: Sf: 0-2 GS: 0-1 Gd: 0-0 GF: - Fm: 0-0
Distance: 2m2m3: 0-2 2m4-2m7: 0-1 3m+: 0-0
Track: LH: 0-1 RH: 0-2 Tight: 0-1 Gall: 0-0
Aids: Bl: 0-0 Vi: 0-0 Tstrap: 0-0
Best Rating: 82 1/03 Kemp 2m5f gd-sft Hdl

Fleet Lad (USA)

67

8-y-o b g Afleet (CAN)-Temperence Cordial (USA) (Temperence Hill (USA))
J D Frost J E Blake

Placings:31PP/500-P (0633)
2002/03: 17ᴾGF,

	Starts	1st	2nd	3rd	Win & Pl
Hurdles	1	0	0		
Career Total	8	1	0	1	3377
80	8/99	Tral	2m1f	NHF	YLD £3080

Total win prize-money £3080

Going: Sf: 0-0 GS: 0-0 Gd: 0-0 GF: - Fm: 0-1
Distance: 2m2m3: 0-1 2m4-2m7: 0-0 3m+: 0-0
Track: LH: 0-1 RH: 0-0 Tight: 0-1 Gall: 0-0
Aids: Bl: 0-0 Vi: 0-0 Tstrap: 0-0
Best Rating: 80 8/99 Tral 2m1f yield NHF

Going: Sf: 0-0 GS: 0-0 Gd: 0-0 GF: - Fm: 1-3
Distance: 2m2m3: 0-0 2m4-2m7: 1-2 3m+: 0-1
Track: LH: 1-2 RH: 0-0 Tight: 0-1 Gall: 0-0
Aids: Bl: 0-0 Vi: 0-0 Tstrap: 0-0
Best Rating: 135 1/01 Chel 2m5f soft Ch

He is a useful chaser and effective from two and a half to three miles on any ground. Best when ridden aggressively, he goes well when fresh and has recorded four of his successes after a break of 120 days or longer.

Flemming (USA)

88   60

6-y-o ch g Green Dancer (USA)-La Groupie (FR) (Groom Dancer (USA))
A G Juckes Ten Out Of Ten Racing Partnership

Placings:P66 (1195)
2002/03: 17ᴾG, 20ᴿGF, 19ᴿGF,

	Starts	1st	2nd	3rd	Win & Pl
Hurdles	3	0	0	0	0
Career Total	3	0	0	0	0

Going: Sf: 0-0 GS: 0-0 Gd: 0-1 GF: - Fm: 0-2
Distance: 2m2m3: 0-1 2m4-2m7: 0-2 3m+: 0-0
Track: LH: 0-1 RH: 0-2 Tight: 0-0 Gall: 0-0
Aids: Bl: 0-2 Vi: 0-0 Tstrap: 0-0
Best Rating: 60 8/02 Worc 2m4f gd-fm Hdl

Fleur

65   **39**

7-y-o b m Petoski-Mizzie Lizzie (Netherkelly)
J Gallagher M K Florey

Placings:*50*-0PP   (2169)
2002/03: 16³GS, 16⁰G, 16ᴾGS, 21ᴾGS,

	Starts	1st	2nd	3rd	Win & Pl
NH Flat	1	0	0	0	0
Hurdles	3	0	0	0	0
Career Total	5	0	0	0	0

Going: Sf: 0-0 GS: 0-3 Gd: 0-1 GF: - Fm: 0-0
Distance: 2m/2m3: 0-3 2m4-2m7: 0-1 3m+: 0-0
Track: LH: 0-2 RH: 0-2 Tight: 0-0 Gall: 0-1
Aids: Bl: 0-0 Vi: 0-0 Tstrap: 0-0
Best Rating: 79 4/02 Wwck 2m   gd-fm NHF

Fleur De Marechal

78(97h)   (74h)**77**

8-y-o br m Greensmith-Welsh Flower (Welsh Saint)
J W Mullins Patrick Everard

Placings:*05300*/34404P/553**U3-3F2PF3P**   (1196)
2002/03: 20³G, 21ᶠG, 25²GF, 23ᴾG, 21ᶠGF, 22³G, 25ᴾGF,

	Starts	1st	2nd	3rd	Win & Pl
Chases	7	0	1	2	1979
Career Total	23	0	1	6	3723

Going: Sf: 0-0 GS: 0-0 Gd: 0-4 GF: - Fm: 0-3
Distance: 2m/2m3: 0-0 2m4-2m7: 0-1 3m+: 0-0
Track: LH: 0-4 RH: 0-2 Tight: 0-2 Gall: 0-0
Aids: Bl: 0-0 Vi: 0-4 Tstrap: 0-0
Best Rating: 93 11/99 Hrfd 2m1f   good NHF

Modest novice chaser. May be best at trips short of three
miles.

Flexible Concience (IRE)

86   **93**

8-y-o br g Glacial Storm (USA)-Philly Athletic (Sit In The
Corner (USA))
J A B Old Willie Robertson/nigel Dempster

Placings:*004*-6   (2214)
2002/03: 21⁶S,

	Starts	1st	2nd	3rd	Win & Pl
Hurdles	1	0	0	0	0
Career Total	4	0	0	0	0

Going: Sf: 0-1 GS: 0-0 Gd: 0-0 GF: - Fm: 0-0
Distance: 2m/2m3: 0-0 2m4-2m7: 0-1 3m+: 0-0
Track: LH: 0-1 RH: 0-0 Tight: 0-0 Gall: 0-1
Aids: Bl: 0-0 Vi: 0-0 Tstrap: 0-0
Best Rating: 93 3/02 Towc 2m5f   gd-sft Hdl

Lightly-raced individual at up to two miles five. Modest form
to date.

Flight Command

105f   **102f**

5-y-o ch g Gunner B-Wing On (Quayside)
P Beaumont N W A Bannister

Placings:*1*   (4778)
2002/03: 16¹G,

	Starts	1st	2nd	3rd	Win & Pl
NH Flat	1	1	0	0	3542
Career Total	1	1	0	0	3542
102 4/03 Prth 2m110y H NHF				GD	£3542
Total win prize-money £3542					

Going: Sf: 0-0 GS: 0-0 Gd: 1-1 GF: - Fm: 0-0
Distance: **2m/2m3: 1-1** 2m4-2m7: 0-0 3m+: 0-0
Track: LH: 0-0 **RH: 1-1** Tight: 0-0 Gall: 0-0
Aids: Bl: 0-0 Vi: 0-0 Tstrap: 0-0
Best Rating: 102 4/03 Prth 2m110y   good NHF

Bred to be a chaser; made successful debut in a Perth
bumper in April 2003; acts on good ground.

Flight To Tuscany

81   **60**

5-y-o b m Bonny Scot (IRE)-Tuscan Butterfly (Beldale
Flutter (USA))
J M Bradley J M Bradley

Placings:0   (1230)
2002/03: 16⁰G,

	Starts	1st	2nd	3rd	Win & Pl
Hurdles	1	0	0	0	
Career Total	1	0	0	0	

Going: Sf: 0-0 GS: 0-0 Gd: 0-0 GF: - Fm: 0-0
Distance: 2m/2m3: 0-1 2m4-2m7: 0-0 3m+: 0-0
Track: LH: 0-1 RH: 0-0 Tight: 0-0 Gall: 0-0
Aids: Bl: 0-0 Vi: 0-0 Tstrap: 0-0
Best Rating: 60 9/02 Worc 2m   good   Hdl

Flighty Leader (IRE)

99   **66**

11-y-o b g Supreme Leader-Flighty Ann (The Parson)
P Spottiswood P Spottiswood

Placings:033044/140533/46423F5/30600-040   (0615)
2002/03: 27⁰G, 24⁴GS, 20⁰GF,

	Starts	1st	2nd	3rd	Win & Pl
Hurdles	3	0	0	0	0
Career Total	27	1	1	6	5789
101 10/99 Kels 2m6f110yG Hdl				GD	£1954
Total win prize-money £1954					

Going: Sf: 0-0 GS: 0-1 Gd: 0-1 GF: - Fm: 0-0
Distance: 2m/2m3: 0-0 2m4-2m7: 0-1 3m+: 0-2
Track: LH: 0-2 RH: 0-1 Tight: 0-1 Gall: 0-0
Aids: Bl: 0-0 Vi: 0-0 Tstrap: 0-0
Best Rating: 101 10/99 Kels 2m6f110y good   Hdl

Poor selling hurdler; stays two mile six.

Flinders

95(96h)   (81h)**85**

8-y-o b m Henbit (USA)-Stupid Cupid (Idiots Delight)
R Rowe Leith Hill Chasers

Placings:*363*/4300/3054550-5102P   (4702)
2002/03: 17⁵G, 25¹G, 22⁰G, 24²F, 26ᴾGF,

	Starts	1st	2nd	3rd	Win & Pl
Chases	5	1	1	0	5339
Career Total	19	1	1	4	6399
80 11/02 Folk 3m1f F(0-95)HCh				GD	£4199
Total win prize-money £4199					

Going: Sf: 0-0 GS: 0-0 Gd: 1-3 GF: - Fm: 0-2
Distance: 2m/2m3: 0-1 2m4-2m7: 0-1 **3m+: 1-3**
Track: LH: 0-0 **RH: 1-2** Tight: 1-5 Gall: 0-0
Aids: Bl: 0-0 Vi: 0-0 Tstrap: 0-0

Best Rating: 97 1/00 Folk 2m1f110y soft   NHF

A maiden over hurdles, she got off the mark over fences on
her first attempt beyond three miles in a modest novices
handicap at Folkestone in November 2002; acts on ground
good or faster.

Flinders Chase

107   **107**

8-y-o gr g Terimon-Proverbial Rose (Proverb)
C J Mann P M Warren

Placings:*41*/3U-3333223U   (4002)
2002/03: 17³GS, 16³G, 20³HY, 18³G, 16²S, 20²GS, 24³S, 21ᵁS,

	Starts	1st	2nd	3rd	Win & Pl
Chases	8	0	2	5	7157
Career Total	12	1	2	6	11557
113 11/00 MRas 2m1f110yD Hdl				SFT	£3225
Total win prize-money £3225					

Going: Sf: 0-4 GS: 0-2 Gd: 0-2 GF: - Fm: 0-0
Distance: 2m/2m3: 0-4 2m4-2m7: 0-3 3m+: 0-1
Track: LH: 0-3 RH: 0-5 Tight: 0-4 Gall: 0-1
Aids: Bl: 0-0 Vi: 0-0 Tstrap: 0-0
Best Rating: 123 11/00 Chel 2m110y   gd-sft NHF

Modest chaser; frustrating type; suited by soft ground; stays
two and a half miles.

Flinski (IRE)

93   **81**

8-y-o b g Warcraft (USA)-Rose Almond (Stanford)
J P Broderick J P Broderick

Placings:*0*/406334P6/23600-00500250   (4585a)
2002/03: 16⁰S, 18⁰YS, 16⁵S, 16⁰S, 16⁰HY, 20²Y, 20⁵F, 20⁰GF,

	Starts	1st	2nd	3rd	Win & Pl
Hurdles	8	0	1	0	935
Career Total	22	0	2	3	3099

Going: Sf: 0-4 GS: 0-0 Gd: 0-0 GF: - Fm: 0-2
Distance: 2m/2m3: 0-5 2m4-2m7: 0-3 3m+: 0-0
Track: LH: 0-2 RH: 0-4 Tight: 0-0 Gall: 0-0
Aids: Bl: 0-0 Vi: 0-0 Tstrap: 0-3
Best Rating: 96 9/01 List 2m   gd-fm NHF

Flite Of Araby

6-y-o b g Green Desert (USA)-Allegedly Blue (USA)
(Alleged (USA))
N J Hawke N J McMullan

Placings:P0   (3332)
2002/03: 17ᴾGS, 17⁰S,

	Starts	1st	2nd	3rd	Win & Pl
Hurdles	2	0	0	0	
Career Total	2	0	0	0	

Going: Sf: 0-1 GS: 0-1 Gd: 0-0 GF: - Fm: 0-0
Distance: 2m/2m3: 0-2 2m4-2m7: 0-0 3m+: 0-0
Track: LH: 0-0 RH: 0-2 Tight: 0-2 Gall: 0-0
Aids: Bl: 0-0 Vi: 0-0 Tstrap: 0-0
Best Rating: 0 1/03 Tntn 2m1f   soft   Hdl

Flood's Fancy

10-y-o gr m Then Again-Port Na Blath (On Your Mark)

B R Foster Michael Brownrigg

Placings:025/0/30P/P065F/P   (4446)
2002/03: 16PG,

	Starts	1st	2nd	3rd	Win & Pl
Hurdles	1	0	0	0	
Career Total	13	0	1	1	1016

Going: Sf: 0-0 GS: 0-0 Gd: 0-1 GF: - Fm: 0-0
Distance: 2m/2m3: 0-1 2m4-2m7: 0-0 3m+: 0-0
Track: LH: 0-0 RH: 0-1 Tight: 0-0 Gall: 0-0
Aids: Bl: 0-0 Vi: 0-0 Tstrap: 0-1
Best Rating: 80   10/96 Worc 2m   gd-fm   Hdl

Flora Muck

91(96h)   (82h)**64**
7-y-o b m Alflora (IRE)-Muckertoo (Sagaro)
N A Twiston-Davies The Yes - No - Wait Sorries

Placings:46060-123FU5   (4024)
2002/03: 241GS, 222S, 253S, 19FG, 26UGS, 255S,

	Starts	1st	2nd	3rd	Win & Pl
Hurdles	2	1	1	0	3111
Chases	4	0	0	1	617
Career Total	11	1	1	1	3727
82 5/02 Towc 3m		F(0-100)HHdl		G-S	£2278

Total win prize-money £2279

Going: Sf: 0-3 GS: 1-2 Gd: 0-1 GF: - Fm: 0-0
Distance: 2m/2m3: 0-1 2m4-2m7: 0-1 3m+: 1-4
Track: LH: 0-2 RH: 1-4 Tight: 0-2 Gall: 0-0
Aids: Bl: 0-0 Vi: 0-0 Tstrap: 0-0
Best Rating: 88   10/01 Bang 2m1f   good   NHF

Modest hurdler, stays well.

Flora Poste

77   **30**
7-y-o ch m Alflora (IRE)-Preachers Popsy (The Parson)
J C Tuck Piers F Dibben

Placings:6/40-050   (4252)
2002/03: 17PS, 16SGS, 22PG,

	Starts	1st	2nd	3rd	Win & Pl
Hurdles	3	0	0	0	0
Career Total	6	0	0	0	0

Going: Sf: 0-0 GS: 0-1 Gd: 0-1 GF: - Fm: 0-0
Distance: 2m/2m3: 0-2 2m4-2m7: 0-1 3m+: 0-0
Track: LH: 0-0 RH: 0-3 Tight: 0-0 Gall: 0-0
Aids: Bl: 0-0 Vi: 0-0 Tstrap: 0-0
Best Rating: 77   3/01 Newb 2m1y10y   heavy   NHF

Flora Princess

71(98h)   (94h)**53**
6-y-o b m Alflora (IRE)-Rakaposhi Queen (Rakaposhi King)
A King Mrs D J Hues

Placings:0/550333-030   (2414)
2002/03: 222G, 213GS, 20PG,

	Starts	1st	2nd	3rd	Win & Pl
Hurdles	1	0	0	0	0
Chases	2	0	0	1	746
Career Total	10	0	0	4	2448

Going: Sf: 0-0 GS: 0-1 Gd: 0-2 GF: - Fm: 0-0
Distance: 2m/2m3: 0-0 2m4-2m7: 0-3 3m+: 0-0
Track: LH: 0-0 RH: 0-2 Tight: 0-1 Gall: 0-0

Aids: Bl: 0-0 Vi: 0-0 Tstrap: 0-0
Best Rating: 94   3/02 Hrfd 2m3f110y soft   Hdl

Modest form over hurdles, stays two and a half miles.

Floral Leader

7-y-o b m Alflora (IRE)-Inch Ahead (IRE) (Over The River (FR))
C N Kellett Mrs Helen Herrick

Placings:000P-U   (0053)
2002/03: 24UG,

	Starts	1st	2nd	3rd	Win & Pl
Hurdles	1	0	0	0	
Career Total	5	0	0	0	

Going: Sf: 0-0 GS: 0-0 Gd: 0-1 GF: - Fm: 0-0
Distance: 2m/2m3: 0-0 2m4-2m7: 0-0 3m+: 0-1
Track: LH: 0-1 RH: 0-0 Tight: 0-1 Gall: 0-0
Aids: Bl: 0-0 Vi: 0-0 Tstrap: 0-0
Best Rating: 49   1/02 Towc 2m   heavy   NHF

Florenzar (IRE)

77   **62**
5-y-o b m Inzar (USA)-Nurse Tyra (USA) (Dr Blum (USA))
Miss Sheena West Miss Elaine Parry

Placings:6   (0425)
2002/03: 186GF,

	Starts	1st	2nd	3rd	Win & Pl
Hurdles	1	0	0	0	0
Career Total	1	0	0	0	0

Going: Sf: 0-0 GS: 0-0 Gd: 0-0 GF: - Fm: 0-1
Distance: 2m/2m3: 0-1 2m4-2m7: 0-0 3m+: 0-0
Track: LH: 0-1 RH: 0-0 Tight: 0-1 Gall: 0-0
Aids: Bl: 0-0 Vi: 0-0 Tstrap: 0-0
Best Rating: 62   6/02 Font 2m2f110y gd-fm   Hdl

Florida (IRE)

5-y-o b m Sri Pekan (USA)-Florinda (CAN) (Vice Regent (CAN))
I A Wood Neardown Stables

Placings:P5-P   (2671)
2002/03: 17PS,

	Starts	1st	2nd	3rd	Win & Pl
Hurdles	1	0	0	0	
Career Total	3	0	0	0	0

Going: Sf: 0-1 GS: 0-0 Gd: 0-0 GF: - Fm: 0-0
Distance: 2m/2m3: 0-1 2m4-2m7: 0-0 3m+: 0-0
Track: LH: 0-0 RH: 0-1 Tight: 0-0 Gall: 0-0
Aids: Bl: 0-0 Vi: 0-0 Tstrap: 0-0
Best Rating: 0   12/02 Hrfd 2m1f   soft   Hdl

Moderate maiden over hurdles.

Florida Pearl (IRE)

114   **153**
11-y-o b g Florida Son-Ice Pearl (Flatbush)
W P Mullins Mrs V O Leary

Placings:11/111/F132/12112/42212/3114011-44P0 (4111)

2002/03: 244S, 244S, 24PYS, 16PG,

	Starts	1st	2nd	3rd	Win & Pl
Chases	4	0	0	0	10077
Career Total	30	14	6	2	797252
170 4/02 Punc 3m1f		Ch		GD	£60858
174 4/02 Aint 3m1f		A Ch		GD	£69600
172 12/01 Kemp 3m		A Ch		GD	£87000
166 12/01 Punc 2m4f		Ch		SFT	£36693
163 2/01 Leop 3m		Ch		HVY	£55443
164 2/00 Leop 3m		Ch		YLD	£53680
161 1/00 Leop 2m3f		HCh		YLD	£7800
160 11/99 DRoy 3m1f		Ch		SFT	£55803
168 2/99 Leop 3m		Ch		SFT	£54464
171 3/98 Chel 3m110y		A Ch		GD	£54817
150 2/98 Leop 2m5f		Ch		Y-S	£28260
155 12/97 Leop 2m3f		Ch		HVY	£4069
136 3/97 Chel 2m110y		A NHF		G-F	£18760
134 12/96 Leop 2m		NHF		YLD	£4237

Total win prize-money £591489

Going: Sf: 0-2 GS: 0-0 Gd: 0-1 GF: - Fm: 0-0
Distance: 2m/2m3: 0-1 2m4-2m7: 0-0 3m+: 0-3
Track: LH: 0-2 RH: 0-1 Tight: 0-0 Gall: 0-1
Aids: Bl: 0-0 Vi: 0-0 Tstrap: 0-0
Best Rating: 174   4/02 Aint 3m1f   good   Ch

Top-class chaser; won the King George at Kempton, the Martell Cup at Aintree and the Punchestown Heineken Gold Cup in 2001/2; well below form this term and found to be suffering from a respiratory problem after being pulled up at Leopardstown; effective from 2m 4f to 3m, may not stay farther; acts on any ground but best efforts on a good or good to soft; seems to do well when racing prominently.

Florida Rain (IRE)

103   **93**
7-y-o b g Florida Son-Ameretto (Stetchworth (USA))
Mrs M Reveley Andy Peake & David Jackson

Placings:00/34-01   (2302)
2002/03: 16PGS, 191GS,

	Starts	1st	2nd	3rd	Win & Pl
Hurdles	2	1	0	0	3024
Career Total	6	1	0	1	3271
101 12/02 Catt 2m3f		E Hdl		G-S	£3024

Total win prize-money £3024

Going: Sf: 0-0 GS: 1-2 Gd: 0-0 GF: - Fm: 0-0
Distance: 2m/2m3: 1-2 2m4-2m7: 0-0 3m+: 0-0
Track: LH: 1-2 RH: 0-0 Tight: 1-1 Gall: 0-0
Aids: Bl: 0-0 Vi: 0-0 Tstrap: 0-0
Best Rating: 101   12/02 Catt 2m3f   gd-sft   Hdl

A chaser in the making. Best effort when third in a bumper on good to soft on his third start. Narrow winner at Catterick in December, should improve again.

Florries Son

105(108h)   (121 h)**125**
8-y-o b g Minster Son-Florrie Palmer (Deadly Nightshade)
M Todhunter Mrs F M Gray

Placings:2111312   (4553)
2002/03: 202G, 241GF, 221G, 231G, 203S, 251GF, 222G,

	Starts	1st	2nd	3rd	Win & Pl
Hurdles	7	4	2	1	18405
Career Total	7	4	2	1	18405
120 3/03 Weth 3m1f		E Hdl		G-F	£3425
119 11/02 Weth 2m7f		F(0-100)HHdl		GD	£2362
90 10/02 Kels 2m6f110yE Hdl				GD	£3809
85 10/02 Hexm 3m		E Hdl		G-F	£2835

Total win prize-money £12433

Going: Sf: 0-1 GS: 0-0 Gd: 2-4 GF: - Fm: 2-2

Distance: 2m/2m3: 0-0 2m4-2m7: 2-5 3m+: 2-2
Track: LH: 4-7 RH: 0-0 **Tight: 1-1** Gall: 0-0
Aids: Bl: 0-0 Vi: 0-0 Tstrap: 0-0
Best Rating: 121 4/03 Ayr 2m6f   good   Hdl

Fair novice chaser; progressive novice hurdler winning four times in 2002/2003; successful on chasing debut and should prove useful in that sphere; stays three miles; acts on a sound surface.

Flossy Tops
101   93
5-y-o b m Gildoran-Right You Be (Sunyboy)
R D E Woodhouse David Scott

Placings:20-50105   (3996)
2002/03: 17⁵GS, 17⁰S, 20¹HY, 20⁰G, 20⁵G,

	Starts	1st	2nd	3rd	Win & Pl
NH Flat	2	0	0	0	0
Hurdles	3	1	0	0	3206
Career Total	7	1	1	0	3758
93 11/02 Weth	2m4f110yE Hdl		HVY	£3206	
Total win prize-money £3206					

Going: Sf: 1-2 GS: 0-1 Gd: 0-2 GF: - Fm: 0-0
Distance: 2m/2m3: 0-2 **2m4-2m7: 1-3** 3m+: 0-0
Track: **LH: 1-4** RH: 0-0 Tight: 0-0 Gall: 0-0
Aids: Bl: 0-0 Vi: 0-0 Tstrap: 0-0
Best Rating: 93 11/02 Weth 2m4f110y heavy Hdl

Switch to hurdling proved a successful one and she shaped as though she will stay further than two and a half miles when successful at Wetherby in November.

Flower Of Pitcur
102f   96f
6-y-o b g Allflora (IRE)-Coire Vannich (Celtic Cone)
T R George Mrs Strachan,L-Palmer,Parkinson,J Morris

Placings:1P0   (4778)
2002/03: 16¹G, 17ᴾG, 16⁰G,

	Starts	1st	2nd	3rd	Win & Pl
NH Flat	3	1	0	0	2079
Career Total	3	1	0	0	2079
96 3/03 Hntg	2m110y H NHF		GD	£2079	
Total win prize-money £2079					

Going: Sf: 0-0 GS: 0-0 Gd: 1-3 GF: - Fm: 0-0
Distance: **2m/2m3: 1-3** 2m4-2m7: 0-0 3m+: 0-0
Track: LH: 0-0 **RH: 1-2** Tight: 0-0 **Gall: 1-1**
Aids: Bl: 0-0 Vi: 0-0 Tstrap: 0-0
Best Rating: 96 3/03 Hntg 2m110y good NHF

Moderate bumper winner; acts on good ground.

Fluff 'N' Puff
103(84h)   (66h)103
9-y-o ch g Nicholas Bill-Puff Puff (All Systems Go)
J S King Dajam Ltd

Placings:003/062/0PF32F53-3124P2235   (4614)
2002/03: 21³G, 24¹G, 24²GS, 25⁴S, 25ᴾGS, 21²GS, 24²G, 21³GF, 21⁵G,

	Starts	1st	2nd	3rd	Win & Pl
Chases	9	1	3	2	14915
Career Total	23	1	5	5	17939
97 11/02 Ludl	3m	E(0-110)HCh	GD	£5473	
Total win prize-money £5473					

Going: Sf: 0-1 GS: 0-3 Gd: 1-4 GF: - Fm: 0-1
Distance: 2m/2m3: 0-0 2m4-2m7: 0-4 3m+: 1-5
Track: LH: 0-2 **RH: 1-7 Tight: 1-1** Gall: 0-4
Aids: Bl: 0-0 Vi: 0-0 Tstrap: 0-0

Best Rating: 103 3/03 Winc 2m5f   gd-fm   Ch

Modest handicap chaser; has placed form over hurdles and fences and was a lucky winner of a handicap chase in November 2002; has run well since though; best on a decent surface; stays three miles but possibly best suited to shorter.

Flush (FR)
97(92h)   (88+h)89
8-y-o b/br m Warning-Garden Pink (FR) (Bellypha)
Miss S J Wilton John Pointon And Sons

Placings:154543/35112324/4/014534   (4523)
2002/03: 16⁰GS, 17¹G, 16⁴G, 20⁵GS, 17³GS, 16⁴G,

	Starts	1st	2nd	3rd	Win & Pl
Hurdles	3	1	0	0	2258
Chases	3	0	0	1	1192
Career Total	21	4	2	4	14057
81 12/02 Hrfd	2m1f	G Hdl		GD	£1946
109 2/00 Donc	2m110y	G Hdl		GD	£1540
109 2/00 Ludl	2m	G Hdl		G-F	£2282
107 1/99 Wwck	2m	E Hdl		SFT	£2617
Total win prize-money £8386					

Going: Sf: 0-0 GS: 0-3 Gd: 1-3 GF: - Fm: 0-0
Distance: **2m/2m3: 1-5** 2m4-2m7: 0-1 3m+: 0-0
Track: LH: 0-0 **RH: 1-5** Tight: 0-2 Gall: 0-0
Aids: Bl: 0-0 Vi: 0-0 Tstrap: 0-0
Best Rating: 113 5/00 Uttx 2m   good   Hdl

Moderate chaser; acts on good and good to soft; yet to prove she stays two miles four.

Fly Buy Dubai
63   42
4-y-o b g Salse (USA)-Her Honour (Teenoso (USA))
M C Pipe (M L W Bell 13/6) Mrs Alison C Farrant

Placings:56   (4463)
2002/03: 19⁵F, 17⁶F,

	Starts	1st	2nd	3rd	Win & Pl
Hurdles	2	0	0	0	0
Career Total	2	0	0	0	0

Going: Sf: 0-0 GS: 0-0 Gd: 0-0 GF: - Fm: 0-2
Distance: 2m/2m3: 0-1 2m4-2m7: 0-1 3m+: 0-0
Track: LH: 0-0 RH: 0-2 Tight: 0-2 Gall: 0-0
Aids: Bl: 0-0 Vi: 0-2 Tstrap: 0-0
Best Rating: 51 4/03 Tntn 2m1f   firm   Hdl

Failed to see out two and a half miles when visored for his hurdling debut.

Fly For Paddy
89f   78f
5-y-o b g Michelozzo (USA)-Tirley Pop Eye (Cruise Missile)
Mrs H Dalton B Perkins

Placings:30-40   (2292)
2002/03: 17⁴S, 17⁰G,

	Starts	1st	2nd	3rd	Win & Pl
NH Flat	2	0	0	0	0
Career Total	4	0	0	1	316

Going: Sf: 0-1 GS: 0-0 Gd: 0-1 GF: - Fm: 0-0
Distance: 2m/2m3: 0-2 2m4-2m7: 0-0 3m+: 0-0
Track: LH: 0-1 RH: 0-1 Tight: 0-1 Gall: 0-0
Aids: Bl: 0-0 Vi: 0-0 Tstrap: 0-0
Best Rating: 78 12/02 Hrfd 2m1f   good   NHF

Third in bumper on racecourse debut.

Fly Kicker
94   78
6-y-o ch g High Kicker (USA)-Double Birthday (Cavo Doro)
W Storey (E J Alston 16/8) M D Townson

Placings:300P30   (4434)
2002/03: 17³G, 17⁰S, 16⁶GS, 25ᴾG, 17³G, 20⁰G,

	Starts	1st	2nd	3rd	Win & Pl
Hurdles	6	0	0	2	817
Career Total	6	0	0	2	817

Going: Sf: 0-1 GS: 0-1 Gd: 0-4 GF: - Fm: 0-0
Distance: 2m/2m3: 0-4 2m4-2m7: 0-1 3m+: 0-1
Track: LH: 0-6 RH: 0-0 Tight: 0-4 Gall: 0-2
Aids: Bl: 0-0 Vi: 0-0 Tstrap: 0-0
Best Rating: 71 3/03 Sedg 2m1f   good   Hdl

Plating-class hurdler; yet to prove he stays further than two miles one; acts on good ground.

Flying Bold (IRE)
102   90
8-y-o ch g Persian Bold-Princess Reema (USA) (Affirmed (USA))
N G Ayliffe Mrs M A Barrett

Placings:0/33103120/0530/304000-640150   (2453)
2002/03: 20⁶GS, 17⁴G, 17⁰GF, 22¹GF, 26⁵G, 19⁰GS,

	Starts	1st	2nd	3rd	Win & Pl
Hurdles	6	1	0	0	2198
Career Total	25	3	1	5	8134
90 8/02 NAbb	2m6f	G(0-95)HHdl	G-F	£2198	
89 1/00 Catt	2m3f	G(0-90)HHdl	GD	£1620	
86 10/99 Kels	2m110y	G Hdl	GD	£2010	
Total win prize-money £5829					

Going: Sf: 0-0 GS: 0-1 Gd: 0-2 GF: - Fm: 1-3
Distance: 2m/2m3: 0-2 **2m4-2m7: 1-3** 3m+: 0-1
Track: **LH: 1-4** RH: 0-2 **Tight: 1-4** Gall: 0-0
Aids: Bl: 0-3 Vi: 0-0 Tstrap: 0-0
Best Rating: 94 2/00 Catt 2m3f   good   Hdl

Selling hurdler, stays two miles six furlongs on a sound surface.

Flying First (IRE)
87   51
8-y-o b g Executive Perk-Rule The Waves (Deep Run)
T D McCarthy A D Spence

Placings:020/PP   (3920)
2002/03: 20ᴾGS, 18ᴾS,

	Starts	1st	2nd	3rd	Win & Pl
Hurdles	2	0	0	0	
Career Total	5	0	1	0	490

Going: Sf: 0-1 GS: 0-1 Gd: 0-0 GF: - Fm: 0-0
Distance: 2m/2m3: 0-1 2m4-2m7: 0-1 3m+: 0-0
Track: LH: 0-1 RH: 0-0 Tight: 0-2 Gall: 0-0
Aids: Bl: 0-0 Vi: 0-0 Tstrap: 0-0
Best Rating: 100 3/00 Folk 2m1f110y gd-fm NHF

Flying Fortress
97(98h)   (85 h)88
6-y-o b g Petoski-Misty Fort (Menelek)
H D Daly J B Sumner

Placings:06-30003P   (4273)
2002/03: 16³G, 21⁰G, 17⁰GS, 17⁰G, 16³G, 19ᴾG,

	Starts	1st	2nd	3rd	Win & Pl
Hurdles	4	0	0	1	674
Chases	2	0	0	1	624
Career Total	8	0	0	2	1298

Going:	Sf: 0-0 GS: 0-1 Gd: 0-5 GF: - Fm: 0-0
Distance:	2m/2m3: 0-4 2m4-2m7: 0-2 3m+: 0-0
Track:	LH: 0-3 RH: 0-3 Tight: 0-0 Gall: 0-2
Aids:	Bl: 0-0 Vi: 0-0 Tstrap: 0-0
Best Rating:	88 3/03 Hntg 2m110y good Ch

Shaped well in a novice hurdle at Haydock in November 2002. has shown ability over fences.

Flying Fortune (IRE)
101   108
7-y-o b g Jolly Jake (NZ)-Dynamite Flyer (USA) (Explodent (USA))
N M Babbage Provex Products Ltd

Placings:*00354-1432*   (4606)
2002/03: 22^{1}G, 24^{4}GS, 24^{3}G, 24^{2}G,

	Starts	1st	2nd	3rd	Win & Pl
Hurdles	4	1	1	1	8606
Career Total	9	1	1	2	9435
102 10/02	Winc	2m6f		E Hdl	GD £3374
			Total win prize-money £3374		

Going:	Sf: 0-0 GS: 0-1 Gd: 1-3 GF: - Fm: 0-0
Distance:	2m/2m3: 0-0 2m4-2m7: 1-0 3m+: 0-3
Track:	LH: 0-2 RH: 1-2 Tight: 0-1 Gall: 0-2
Aids:	Bl: 0-0 Vi: 0-0 Tstrap: 0-0
Best Rating:	108 4/03 Chel 3m good Hdl

Fair staying hurdler; stays three miles and handles cut in the ground, but looks better on a sounder surface.

Flying Gunner
112   111
12-y-o ch g Gunner B-Dans Le Vent (Pollerton)
A King R Maryan Green

Placings:*632F3/2212215/5P4B34*035/1121100/64041P4/3 205/00-0450   (3523)
2002/03: 24^{0}G, 24^{4}GS, 25^{5}HY, 24^{0}G,

	Starts	1st	2nd	3rd	Win & Pl
Hurdles	4	0	0	0	579
Career Total	45	7	7	5	54408
140 2/00	Newb	3m110y	C(0-130)HHdl	G-S	£5947
135 2/99	Newb	3m110y	C(0-130)HHdl	G-S	£4731
132 1/99	Uttx	3m110y	C(0-135)HHdl	SFT	£7545
128 11/98	Chep	3m	C(0-130)HHdl	G-S	£5199
122 11/98	Newb	3m110y	C(0-135)HHdl	G-S	£5021
111 2/97	Hntg	3m2f	E Hdl	G-S	£2600
114 11/96	Chep	3m	D Hdl	G-S	£2823
			Total win prize-money £33868		

Going:	Sf: 0-2 GS: 0-1 Gd: 0-1 GF: - Fm: 0-0
Distance:	2m/2m3: 0-0 2m4-2m7: 0-0 3m+: 0-4
Track:	LH: 0-4 RH: 0-0 Tight: 0-1 Gall: 0-1
Aids:	Bl: 0-0 Vi: 0-0 Tstrap: 0-0
Best Rating:	140 11/00 Chel 3m1f110y gd-sft Hdl

Particularly lazy, he needs plenty of driving. Once a decent staying handicap hurdler, he has been lightly raced of late. Best over three miles with cut in the ground and has a good record at Newbury.

Flying High (IRE)
100(98h)   (87h)90
8-y-o b g Fayruz-Shayista (Tap On Wood)
M Todhunter B Batey

Placings:00/0P/054246*201362-335500*   (1237)
2002/03: 20^{3}G, 16^{3}GF, 21^{5}G, 21^{5}GF, 17^{0}GF, 16^{9}GF,

	Starts	1st	2nd	3rd	Win & Pl
Hurdles	2	0	0	0	0
Chases	4	0	0	2	1212
Career Total	22	1	0	2	6629
84 8/01	Sedg	2m110y	E Ch	G-F	£2912
			Total win prize-money £2912		

Going:	Sf: 0-0 GS: 0-0 Gd: 0-2 GF: - Fm: 0-4
Distance:	2m/2m3: 0-3 2m4-2m7: 0-3 3m+: 0-0
Track:	LH: 0-6 RH: 0-0 Tight: 0-3 Gall: 0-0
Aids:	Bl: 0-0 Vi: 0-1 Tstrap: 0-0
Best Rating:	90 10/01 Sedg 2m110y good Ch

Flying Maria

12-y-o gr m Neltino-Flying Mistress (Lear Jet)
J S Papworth J S Papworth

Placings:*2F5242P/113/*UP/P-P   (0176)
2002/03: 21^{P}GF,

	Starts	1st	2nd	3rd	Win & Pl
Chases	1	0	0	0	
Career Total	14	2	3	1	5865
100 3/00	NAbb	2m5f110y	H Ch	GD	£1482
113 3/00	Ludl	2m4f	H Ch	SFT	£2436
			Total win prize-money £3918		

Going:	Sf: 0-0 GS: 0-0 Gd: 0-0 GF: - Fm: 0-1
Distance:	2m/2m3: 0-0 2m4-2m7: 0-1 3m+: 0-0
Track:	LH: 0-0 RH: 0-1 Tight: 0-0 Gall: 0-0
Aids:	Bl: 0-0 Vi: 0-0 Tstrap: 0-0
Best Rating:	113 3/00 Ludl 2m4f soft Ch

Flying Spirit (IRE)
96   74
4-y-o b g Flying Spur (AUS)-All Laughter (Vision (USA))
M H Tompkins Mrs Nicola Guest

Placings:*56*   (4686)
2002/03: 16^{5}G, 17^{6}GF,

	Starts	1st	2nd	3rd	Win & Pl
Hurdles	2	0	0	0	0
Career Total	2	0	0	0	0

Going:	Sf: 0-0 GS: 0-0 Gd: 0-1 GF: - Fm: 0-1
Distance:	2m/2m3: 0-2 2m4-2m7: 0-0 3m+: 0-0
Track:	LH: 0-1 RH: 0-1 Tight: 0-2 Gall: 0-0
Aids:	Bl: 0-0 Vi: 0-0 Tstrap: 0-0
Best Rating:	74 3/03 Fknm 2m good Hdl

Flying Veil

9-y-o gr g Neltino-Take The Veil (Monksfield)
Mrs D M Grissell Chartwell Racing

Placings:*60/*P/0-F   (0311)
2002/03: 26^{F}G,

	Starts	1st	2nd	3rd	Win & Pl
Chases	1	0	0	0	
Career Total	5	0	0	0	0

Going:	Sf: 0-0 GS: 0-0 Gd: 0-1 GF: - Fm: 0-0
Distance:	2m/2m3: 0-0 2m4-2m7: 0-0 3m+: 0-1
Track:	LH: 0-0 RH: 0-1 Tight: 0-1 Gall: 0-0
Aids:	Bl: 0-0 Vi: 0-0 Tstrap: 0-0

Best Rating: 69 5/01 Folk 2m1f110y gd-sft Hdl

Flyoff (IRE)
69
6-y-o b g Mtoto-Flyleaf (FR) (Persian Bold)
K A Morgan Harmer Personal Care Ltd

Placings:*6-60*   (1230)
2002/03: 16^{6}GF, 16^{9}G,

	Starts	1st	2nd	3rd	Win & Pl
Hurdles	2	0	0	0	0
Career Total	3	0	0	0	0

Going:	Sf: 0-0 GS: 0-0 Gd: 0-1 GF: - Fm: 0-1
Distance:	2m/2m3: 0-2 2m4-2m7: 0-0 3m+: 0-0
Track:	LH: 0-2 RH: 0-0 Tight: 0-0 Gall: 0-0
Aids:	Bl: 0-0 Vi: 0-0 Tstrap: 0-0
Best Rating:	69 3/02 Carl 2m1f gd-sft Hdl

Flyover
99   73
6-y-o b m Presidium-Flash-By (Ilium)
J C Fox Miss Sarah-Jane Durman

Placings:*00056*   (4693)
2002/03: 16^{0}G, 16^{0}S, 20^{0}G, 16^{5}G, 17^{6}G,

	Starts	1st	2nd	3rd	Win & Pl
Hurdles	5	0	0	0	0
Career Total	5	0	0	0	0

Going:	Sf: 0-1 GS: 0-0 Gd: 0-4 GF: - Fm: 0-0
Distance:	2m/2m3: 0-4 2m4-2m7: 0-1 3m+: 0-0
Track:	LH: 0-3 RH: 0-2 Tight: 0-0 Gall: 0-1
Aids:	Bl: 0-0 Vi: 0-0 Tstrap: 0-0
Best Rating:	73 4/03 NAbb 2m1f good Hdl

Fnan
(116h)   (138h)132
7-y-o b g Generous (IRE)-Rafha (Kris)
Noel Meade D P Sharkey

Placings:21112P/F/4*2000153-0*P1100   (4475)
2002/03: 23^{D}YS, 22^{P}GY, 22^{1}GF, 20^{1}GF, 24^{0}F, 20^{0}G,

	Starts	1st	2nd	3rd	Win & Pl
Hurdles	1	0	0	0	0
Chases	5	2	0	0	25920
Career Total	20	6	3	1	55616
114 8/02	Tral	2m4f	HCh	G-F	£17944
103 8/02	Tram	2m6f	HCh	G-Y	£7975
138 3/02	Fair	2m2f	Hdl	G-Y	£7975
125 6/00	Wxfd	2m4f	Hdl	G-Y	£3588
114 5/00	Fair	2m	Hdl	G-Y	£3864
114 5/00	Navn	2m2f	Hdl	G-Y	£3588
			Total win prize-money £44935		

Going:	Sf: 0-0 GS: 0-0 Gd: 0-1 GF: - Fm: 2-3
Distance:	2m/2m3: 0-0 2m4-2m7: 2-5 3m+: 0-1
Track:	LH: 0-2 RH: 1-2 Tight: 0-1 Gall: 0-0
Aids:	Bl: 0-0 Vi: 0-0 Tstrap: 0-0
Best Rating:	138 4/02 Punc 3m good Hdl

Fair Irish-trained chaser; effective at two and a half miles; acts on good and fast ground.

Foggy (IRE)
85   (80c)60
10-y-o gr g Merrymount-Rosy Waters (Roselier (FR))

J R Norton Miss A J Hurst

Placings:0000061/2451/040/UPP060-65P   (3803)
2002/03: 23⁶HY, 21⁵S, 20⁸S,

	Starts	1st	2nd	3rd	Win & Pl
Hurdles	3	0	0	0	
Career Total	23	2	1	0	6006
101	3/00	Hexm 3m		F(0-100)HHdl	SFT	£2159
89	4/99	Towc 2m5f		E(0-105)HHdl	SFT	£2862

Total win prize-money £5023

Going: Sf: 0-3 GS: 0-0 Gd: 0-0 GF: - Fm: 0-0
Distance: 2m/2m3: 0-0 2m4-2m7: 0-3 3m+: 0-0
Track: LH: 0-3 RH: 0-0 Tight: 0-1 Gall: 0-1
Aids: Bl: 0-0 Vi: 0-0 Tstrap: 0-0
Best Rating: 101 3/00 Hexm 3m   soft   Hdl

Follow De Call

13-y-o b g Callernish-Designer (Celtic Cone)
Michael Blake Michael Blake

Placings:00/003F00003/54202325110632/5535433244F14/
40646000/60P/P03-0   (0193)
2002/03: 20⁰F,

	Starts	1st	2nd	3rd	Win & Pl
Chases	1	0	0	0	
Career Total	53	3	5	8	16557
85	1/99	Uttx	2m	F(0-110)HCh	SFT	£2710
91	10/97	Bang	2m1f		GD	£2274
89	9/97	Bang	2m1f	D Hdl	GD	£2788

Total win prize-money £7772

Going: Sf: 0-0 GS: 0-0 Gd: 0-0 GF: - Fm: 0-1
Distance: 2m/2m3: 0-0 2m4-2m7: 0-1 3m+: 0-0
Track: LH: 0-1 RH: 0-0 Tight: 0-0 Gall: 0-0
Aids: Bl: 0-0 Vi: 0-0 Tstrap: 0-0
Best Rating: 92 5/98 Bang 2m1f110y gd-sft Ch

Follow Jean

7-y-o b m Perpendicular-Ask Jean (Ascertain (USA))
M E Sowersby M E Sowersby

Placings:00-P   (0021)
2002/03: 20⁰G,

	Starts	1st	2nd	3rd	Win & Pl
Hurdles	1	0	0	0	
Career Total	3	0	0	0	

Going: Sf: 0-0 GS: 0-0 Gd: 0-1 GF: - Fm: 0-0
Distance: 2m/2m3: 0-0 2m4-2m7: 0-1 3m+: 0-0
Track: LH: 0-1 RH: 0-0 Tight: 0-0 Gall: 0-0
Aids: Bl: 0-0 Vi: 0-0 Tstrap: 0-0
Best Rating: 68 2/02 Muss 2m   soft   NHF

Follow Me
101   93

7-y-o ch g Keen-Fairlead (Slip Anchor)
F P Murtagh (Jonjo O Neill 15/11) D O Connor

Placings:4034/2211P6/1002230-5000   (4260)
2002/03: 25⁵HY, 21⁰G, 24⁵G, 21⁰G,

	Starts	1st	2nd	3rd	Win & Pl
Hurdles	4	0	0	0	
Career Total	21	3	4	2	14780
104	10/01	Sthl	3m110y	D(0-120)HHdl	GD	£3474
110	11/00	Hayd	2m4f	F(0-110)HHdl	HVY	£2590
100	10/00	Carl	2m1f	E(0-115)HHdl	G-S	£2664

Total win prize-money £8728

Going: Sf: 0-1 GS: 0-1 Gd: 0-2 GF: - Fm: 0-0
Distance: 2m/2m3: 0-0 2m4-2m7: 0-3 3m+: 0-2
Track: LH: 0-2 RH: 0-2 Tight: 0-1 Gall: 0-1
Aids: Bl: 0-0 Vi: 0-0 Tstrap: 0-0
Best Rating: 110 3/02 Bang 3m   soft   Hdl

Fairly useful handicap hurdler who does not do anything
quickly, stays three miles, acts on most types of ground.

Follow The Flow (IRE)
102   84

7-y-o ch g Over The River (FR)-October Lady (Lucifer
(USA))
P A Pritchard Woodland Generators

Placings:4P3P004   (4140)
2002/03: 24⁴HY, 24⁸GF, 25⁵S, 27⁷G, 26⁰S, 26⁰GS, 32⁴S,

	Starts	1st	2nd	3rd	Win & Pl
Chases	7	0	0	1	1349
Career Total	7	0	0	1	1349

Going: Sf: 0-4 GS: 0-1 Gd: 0-1 GF: - Fm: 0-1
Distance: 2m/2m3: 0-0 2m4-2m7: 0-0 3m+: 0-7
Track: LH: 0-5 RH: 0-2 Tight: 0-3 Gall: 0-0
Aids: Bl: 0-0 Vi: 0-0 Tstrap: 0-0
Best Rating: 56 1/03 Wwck 3m2f   soft   Ch

Plating-class chaser; stays three miles plus; effective on
good ground.

Follow The Trend (IRE)
98(88h)   (67h)103

9-y-o br g Beau Sher-Newgate Princess (Prince Regent
(FR))
Miss A M Newton-Smith Brighton Racing Club

Placings:503405/63D1U1UF/P5544112P-641044   (4633)
2002/03: 21⁶G, 21⁴S, 20¹S, 24⁹GS, 20⁴GS, 20⁴GF,

	Starts	1st	2nd	3rd	Win & Pl
Hurdles	2	0	0	0	
Chases	4	1	0	0	3817
Career Total	29	5	1	2	16800
103	1/03	Leic	2m4f110y	F(0-95)HCh	SFT	£3503
98	2/02	Hntg	2m4f110y	F(0-95)HCh	SFT	£2688
89	1/02	Folk	2m5f	F(0-95)HCh	SFT	£3376
89	2/01	Folk	2m5f	F(0-90)HCh	SFT	£2520
88	1/01	Folk	2m5f	E(0-90)HCh	SFT	£1929

Total win prize-money £14018

Going: Sf: 1-2 GS: 0-2 Gd: 0-1 GF: - Fm: 0-1
Distance: 2m/2m3: 0-0 2m4-2m7: 1-5 3m+: 0-1
Track: LH: 0-3 RH: 1-3 Tight: 0-3 Gall: 0-0
Aids: Bl: 0-0 Vi: 0-0 Tstrap: 0-0
Best Rating: 103 1/03 Leic 2m4f110y soft   Ch

Modest handicap chaser; goes well right-handed; suited by
two miles five; best on soft ground; wears sheepskin side-
burns due to lack of concentration, according to his trainer;
usually hits form at the beginning of the year.

Follow Up
77f   108f

5-y-o b g Phardante (FR)-Dashing March (Daring March)
N J Henderson B T Stewart-Brown

Placings:42   (1923)
2002/03: 16⁴G, 12²GS,

	Starts	1st	2nd	3rd	Win & Pl
NH Flat	2	0	1	0	864
Career Total	2	0	1	0	864

Going: Sf: 0-0 GS: 0-1 Gd: 0-1 GF: - Fm: 0-0
Distance: 2m/2m3: 0-1 2m4-2m7: 0-0 3m+: 0-0
Track: LH: 0-2 RH: 0-0 Tight: 0-0 Gall: 0-0
Aids: Bl: 0-0 Vi: 0-0 Tstrap: 0-0
Best Rating: 113 11/02 Newb 1m4f110y gd-sft NHF

Fourth on debut but finished a good runner-up next time.

Follow Your Star

5-y-o ch g Pursuit Of Love-Possessive Artiste (Shareef
Dancer (USA))
P W Harris (P J Hobbs 28/7) Mrs P W Harris

Placings:P   (0780)
2002/03: 16⁰GF,

	Starts	1st	2nd	3rd	Win & Pl
Hurdles	1	0	0	0	
Career Total	1	0	0	0	

Going: Sf: 0-0 GS: 0-0 Gd: 0-0 GF: - Fm: 0-1
Distance: 2m/2m3: 0-1 2m4-2m7: 0-0 3m+: 0-0
Track: LH: 0-1 RH: 0-0 Tight: 0-0 Gall: 0-0
Aids: Bl: 0-0 Vi: 0-0 Tstrap: 0-0
Best Rating: 0 7/02 NAbb 2m1f   gd-fm   Hdl

Maiden on the Flat, he lost his action and had to be pulled
up on his hurdling bow.

Folly Road (IRE)

13-y-o b g Mister Lord (USA)-Lady Can (Cantab)
D L Williams Miss L Horner

Placings:541015FF/0/23115/P353U13412/404PPP202P0/0
S4240P4U513-44620   (4459)
2002/03: 25⁴GS, 24⁴S, 24⁶S, 22²G, 21⁰G,

	Starts	1st	2nd	3rd	Win & Pl
Chases	5	0	1	0	1101
Career Total	52	7	6	5	71313
114	3/02	Sand	3m110y	E Ch	GD	£7182
118	4/00	Chep	3m	E(0-115)HCh	SFT	£3324
118	2/00	MRas	3m4f110y	D(0-120)HCh	G-S	£4192
122	12/98	Folk	3m2f	D(0-125)HCh	G-S	£7580
118	11/98	Wwck	3m2f	C(0-130)HCh	SFT	£4926
118	1/97	Folk	3m	Ch	YLD	£3051
99	11/96	Naas	3m4f	Hdl	YLD	£3177

Total win prize-money £33437

Going: Sf: 0-2 GS: 0-1 Gd: 0-2 GF: - Fm: 0-0
Distance: 2m/2m3: 0-0 2m4-2m7: 0-2 3m+: 0-3
Track: LH: 0-2 RH: 0-3 Tight: 0-1 Gall: 0-1
Aids: Bl: 0-0 Vi: 0-0 Tstrap: 0-0
Best Rating: 122 12/98 Folk 3m2f   gd-sft   Ch

Formerly a useful staying chaser, but now a modest performer in hunter chases; lacks pace and requires extreme
distances.

Foly Pleasant (FR)
115   164

9-y-o ch g Vaguely Pleasant (FR)-Jeffologie (FR) (Jefferson
(ZIM))
Miss H C Knight Jim Lewis & Friends

Placings:1/111P1/122/22/1210P-4220   (4100)
2002/03: 20⁴GS, 21²G, 25²GS, 24⁰G,

Column 1

	Starts	1st	2nd	3rd	Win & Pl
Chases	4	0	2		44600
Career Total	20	8	7	0	151960

164	1/02	Chel	2m5f	A HCh	HVY £32500
145	10/01	Strf	2m5f110yC(0-135)HCh	G-S	£6838
	5/99	Dax	2m1f110y Hdl	SFT	£4306
	4/99	Pau	2m4f110y Hdl	VS	£4306
	1/99	Pau	2m2f Hdl	VS	£15070
	1/99	Pau	2m2f Hdl	HVY	£7535
	12/98	Pau	2m2f110y Ch	SFT	£5382
	4/98	Pau	2m2f110y Ch	SFT	£4

Total win prize-money £75941

Going: Sf: 0-0 GS: 0-2 Gd: 0-2 GF: - Fm: 0-0
Distance: 2m/2m3: 0-0 2m4-2m7: 0-2 3m+: 0-2
Track: LH: 0-4 RH: 0-0 Tight: 0-0 Gall: 0-4
Aids: Bl: 0-0 Vi: 0-0 Tstrap: 0-4
Best Rating: 164 12/02 Chel 2m5f   good   Ch

Very useful handicap chaser; good efforts at Cheltenham in 2002/3, in the frame in the Thomas Pink, the Tripleprint and the Pillar Chase; effective between 2m 4f and 3m 1f; acts on a sound surface, reportedly prefers an easy one; wears a tongue tie.

Fond Farewell (IRE)
94(96h)   (92h)82
8-y-o b m Phardante (FR)-Doorslammer (Avocat)
K C Bailey Mrs J Way

Placings:00/6/6343640-4   (1850)
2002/03: 254G,

	Starts	1st	2nd	3rd	Win & Pl
Chases	1	0	0	0	784
Career Total	11	0	0	2	1571

Going: Sf: 0-0 GS: 0-0 Gd: 0-1 GF: - Fm: 0-0
Distance: 2m/2m3: 0-0 2m4-2m7: 0-0 3m+: 0-1
Track: LH: 0-0 RH: 0-1 Tight: 0-0 Gall: 0-0
Aids: Bl: 0-0 Vi: 0-0 Tstrap: 0-0
Best Rating: 92 3/02 Wwck 3m1f   gd-sft   Hdl

Lightly-raced, yet to get off the mark. Stays three miles plus.

Fondmort (FR)
118   158
7-y-o b g Cyborg (FR)-Hansie (FR) (Sukawa (FR))
N J Henderson W J Brown

Placings:30/214132P/1P1153-31F022   (4604)
2002/03: 213GS, 211G, 16FG, 24PG, 20PG, 212G,

	Starts	1st	2nd	3rd	Win & Pl
Chases	6	1	2	1	88899
Career Total	21	6	4	4	173912

158	12/02	Chel	2m5f	A HCh	GD £58000
146	12/01	Kemp	2m	B Ch	GD £11287
150	12/01	Sand	2m	A Ch	G-S £18000
140	10/01	Kemp	2m	D Ch	G-S £4914
130	12/00	Kemp	2m	B Hdl	G-S £7215
	9/00	Autl	2m2f	Hdl	VS £14409

Total win prize-money £113826

Going: Sf: 0-0 GS: 0-1 Gd: 1-5 GF: - Fm: 0-0
Distance: 2m/2m3: 0-1 2m4-2m7: 1-4 3m+: 0-1
Track: LH: 1-3 RH: 0-3 Tight: 0-0 Gall: 1-3
Aids: Bl: 0-0 Vi: 0-0 Tstrap: 0-0
Best Rating: 158 3/03 Chel 2m4f110y good   Ch

Smart chaser; did well over fences in his novice season with three wins, but finished lame in the 2002 Arkle; returned to form to win the Tripleprint Gold Cup at Cheltenham in December, but took a heavy fall at Kempton and appeared not to stay 3m at same track in February; runner-up in

Column 2

Mildmay of Flete at Cheltenham; acts on good ground or slightly softer; stays around 2m 4f.

Football Crazy (IRE)
86   61+
4-y-o b g Mujadil (USA)-Schonbein (IRE) (Persian Heights)
N A Callaghan John Livock

Placings:5   (2120)
2002/03: 165GS,

	Starts	1st	2nd	3rd	Win & Pl
Hurdles	1	0	0	0	0
Career Total	1	0	0	0	0

Going: Sf: 0-0 GS: 0-1 Gd: 0-0 GF: - Fm: 0-0
Distance: 2m/2m3: 0-1 2m4-2m7: 0-0 3m+: 0-0
Track: LH: 0-1 RH: 0-0 Tight: 0-0 Gall: 0-0
Aids: Bl: 0-0 Vi: 0-0 Tstrap: 0-0
Best Rating: 67 11/02 Fknm 2m   gd-sft   Hdl

Did not appear to stay on jumps debut.

For Cathal (IRE)

12-y-o b g Legal Circles (USA)-Noble For Stamps (Deep Run)
Mrs Sarah L Dent John Mackley

Placings:231/1211/44F2326/P/622P24-44   (0166)
2002/03: 254G, 254GF,

	Starts	1st	2nd	3rd	Win & Pl
Chases	2	0	0	0	0
Career Total	23	4	7	2	25745

118	4/98	Newc	3m	E Hdl	SFT £2274
117	3/98	Sedg	3m4f	C(0-130)HCh	G-S £10601
104	11/97	Newc	3m	E Hdl	GD £2253
100	2/97	Newc	3m	E Ch	GD £2901

Total win prize-money £18030

Going: Sf: 0-0 GS: 0-1 Gd: 0-0 GF: - Fm: 0-1
Distance: 2m/2m3: 0-0 2m4-2m7: 0-0 3m+: 0-2
Track: LH: 0-2 RH: 0-0 Tight: 0-1 Gall: 0-0
Aids: Bl: 0-0 Vi: 0-0 Tstrap: 0-0
Best Rating: 118 2/99 Weth 2m7f   good   Hdl

One-time useful chaser but in his dotage is a slow hunter chaser.

For William

17-y-o b g Whistling Deer-Pampered Sue (Pampered King)
Mrs M Rigg Mrs M Rigg

Placings:0/321421042143353230/01F66012P442402U36/P12U44F3412155/0424F/P030/U/P   (0313)
2002/03: 25PG,

	Starts	1st	2nd	3rd	Win & Pl
Chases	1	0	0	0	
Career Total	62	8	10	8	56672

129	3/93	Leop	3m	HCh	YLD £4451
127	2/93	Punc	3m2f110y	HCh	SFT £7419
120	8/92	Tral	2m4f	HCh	SFT £7738
	8/91	Tral	2m4f	Ch	G-F £2875
	6/91	Tral	2m6f	HHdl	GD £1916
	11/90	Naas	2m	Hdl	SFT £2679
	8/90	Tral	2m1f	NHF	GD £2924
	5/90	Naas	2m	NHF	G-F £1341

Total win prize-money £31347

Going: Sf: 0-0 GS: 0-0 Gd: 0-1 GF: - Fm: 0-0
Distance: 2m/2m3: 0-0 2m4-2m7: 0-0 3m+: 0-1
Track: LH: 0-0 RH: 0-0 Tight: 0-1 Gall: 0-0

Column 3

Aids: Bl: 0-0 Vi: 0-0 Tstrap: 0-0
Best Rating: 130 9/93 List 3m   soft   Ch

For Your Ears Only (IRE)
85   62
7-y-o b g Be My Native (USA)-Sister Ida (Bustino)
A Parker Mr & Mrs Raymond Anderson Green

Placings:3/00-30   (2556)
2002/03: 163GF, 200GF,

	Starts	1st	2nd	3rd	Win & Pl
NH Flat	1	0	0	1	261
Hurdles	1	0	0	0	0
Career Total	5	0	0	2	734

Going: Sf: 0-0 GS: 0-0 Gd: 0-0 GF: - Fm: 0-2
Distance: 2m/2m3: 0-1 2m4-2m7: 0-1 3m+: 0-0
Track: LH: 0-1 RH: 0-0 Tight: 0-1 Gall: 0-0
Aids: Bl: 0-0 Vi: 0-0 Tstrap: 0-0
Best Rating: 96 10/02 Hexm 2m110y   gd-fm   NHF

Forbes Park
89
8-y-o b g Alzao (USA)-Rose Alto (Adonijah)
M J Coombe J Coombe

Placings:0-P3   (0613)
2002/03: 23PG, 163GF,

	Starts	1st	2nd	3rd	Win & Pl
Hurdles	2	0	0	1	335
Career Total	3	0	0	1	335

Going: Sf: 0-0 GS: 0-0 Gd: 0-1 GF: - Fm: 0-1
Distance: 2m/2m3: 0-1 2m4-2m7: 0-0 3m+: 0-1
Track: LH: 0-2 RH: 0-0 Tight: 0-1 Gall: 0-0
Aids: Bl: 0-0 Vi: 0-0 Tstrap: 0-0
Best Rating: 76 6/02 Worc 2m   gd-fm   Hdl

Foreman (GER)
112   147
5-y-o ch h Monsun (GER)-Fleurie (GER) (Dashing Blade)
T Doumen (F Doumen 10/11) Ecurie Passing

Placings:113232314   (4109)
2002/03: 171G, 161G, 193VS, 182VS, 193VS, 202HY, 163S, 211G, 214G,

	Starts	1st	2nd	3rd	Win & Pl
Hurdles	9	3	2	3	75451
Career Total	9	3	2	3	75451

141	2/03	Kemp	2m5f	C Hdl	GD £6844
	5/02	Badn	2m110y Hdl	GD	£6748
98	5/02	Folk	2m1f110yE Hdl	GD	£2870

Total win prize-money £16462

Going: Sf: 0-2 GS: 0-0 Gd: 3-4 GF: - Fm: 0-0
Distance: 2m/2m3: 2-4 2m4-2m7: 1-5 3m+: 0-0
Track: LH: 0-4 RH: 2-3 Tight: 1-1 Gall: 0-1
Aids: Bl: 0-0 Vi: 0-0 Tstrap: 0-0
Best Rating: 143 3/03 Chel 2m5f   good   Hdl

Useful French-trained novice hurdler; effective at around 2m, but stays 2m 5f; handles soft ground, but best on good; likes to be held up.

Foreshore Man
88 (34h)**85**
12-y-o b g Derrylin-Royal Birthday (St Paddy)
B S Rothwell J Eddings

Placings:60/420**B3U**/332**U4**/0541314440/0366P526-6
(2162)
2002/03: 16⁶S,

	Starts	1st	2nd	3rd	Win & Pl
Chases	1	0	0	0	0
Career Total	32	2	3	5	18729
93 12/00 Hayd	2m6f		D(0-115)HCh	HVY	£6058
85 11/00 Weth	2m4f110y	D(0-110)HCh	HVY	£5291
			Total win prize-money £11349		

Going:	Sf: 0-1 GS: 0-0 Gd: 0-0 GF: - Fm: 0-0
Distance:	2m/2m3: 0-1 2m4-2m7: 0-0 3m+: 0-0
Track:	LH: 0-1 RH: 0-0 Tight: 0-1 Gall: 0-0
Aids:	Bl: 0-0 Vi: 0-1 Tstrap: 0-0
Best Rating:	98 1/00 Weth 2m4f110y soft Ch

Fair handicap chaser, effective at up to two miles-six. Suited by plenty of cut.

Forest Dante (IRE)
97 **81**
10-y-o ch g Phardante (FR)-Mossy Mistress (IRE) (Le Moss)
F Kirby Fred Kirby

Placings:6000F/602F1043/S1131PF/435231FP2-
U630P5U4 (4796)
2002/03: 22**U**G, 19⁶G, 22³S, 19⁰G, 21²G, 20⁵G, 20**U**G, 28⁴GF,

	Starts	1st	2nd	3rd	Win & Pl
Hurdles	1	0	0	0	0
Chases	7	0	0	1	1886
Career Total	37	3	3	5	36324
112 1/02 Catt	2m3f	D(0-120)HCh	SFT	£4062
109 11/00 Catt	2m3f	E(0-115)HCh	GD	£5005
112 10/00 Sthl	2m4f110y	D(0-120)HCh	HVY	£6808
105 9/00 MRas	2m4f	F(0-110)HCh	G-F	£4251
87 1/00 Catt	2m	E(0-105)HCh	GD	£4264
		Total win prize-money £24392		

Going:	Sf: 0-1 GS: 0-0 Gd: 0-6 GF: - Fm: 0-1
Distance:	2m/2m3: 0-2 2m4-2m7: 0-5 3m+: 0-1
Track:	LH: 0-6 RH: 0-2 Tight: 0-5 Gall: 0-0
Aids:	Bl: 0-0 Vi: 0-0 Tstrap: 0-0
Best Rating:	112 3/02 MRas 2m6f110y soft Ch

Moderate chaser; a big, able jumper at his best; best at around two and a half miles; acts on any ground; goes well at Catterick.

Forest Flora
93(86h) (47h)**77**
9-y-o b m King s Ride-Celtic Flora (Celtic Cone)
J W Mullins New Forest Racing Partnership

Placings:00**U**460/B2312P34442362/030P/60**F**0-05440566
(1331)
2002/03: 21⁰GF, 20⁵G, 23⁴G, 21⁴GF, 23⁹GF, 21⁵GF, 25⁶GF, 21⁶G,

	Starts	1st	2nd	3rd	Win & Pl
Hurdles	1	0	0	0	0
Chases	7	0	0	4	639
Career Total	36	1	4	4	7636
86 9/99 Worc	3m	E(0-105)HHdl	G-F	£2425
		Total win prize-money £2425		

Going:	Sf: 0-0 GS: 0-0 Gd: 0-3 GF: - Fm: 0-5
Distance:	2m/2m3: 0-0 2m4-2m7: 0-5 3m+: 0-3
Track:	LH: 0-5 RH: 0-2 Tight: 0-3 Gall: 0-0
Aids:	Bl: 0-0 Vi: 0-1 Tstrap: 0-0
Best Rating:	88 4/00 NAbb 2m6f heavy Hdl

Forest Fountain (IRE)
12-y-o b/br g Royal Fountain-Forest Gale (Strong Gale)
Mrs H L Needham J D Callow

Placings:P/P/35B/31/4330P510-545 (0317)
2002/03: 33⁵GF, 30⁴GF, 34⁵G,

	Starts	1st	2nd	3rd	Win & Pl
Chases	3	0	0	0	0
Career Total	18	2	0	4	8843
90 4/02 Ludl	3m	H Ch	G-F	£2628
107 5/00 Strf	3m	H Ch	G-F	£2951
		Total win prize-money £5580		

Going:	Sf: 0-0 GS: 0-0 Gd: 0-1 GF: - Fm: 0-2
Distance:	2m/2m3: 0-0 2m4-2m7: 0-0 3m+: 0-3
Track:	LH: 0-2 RH: 0-1 Tight: 0-0 Gall: 0-2
Aids:	Bl: 0-0 Vi: 0-0 Tstrap: 0-0
Best Rating:	111 5/99 Strf 3m4f good Ch

A winner of point-to-points and over fences, he acts on most types of ground and is effective at around three miles.

Forest Green Flyer
101 **73d**
7-y-o b m Syrtos-Bolton Flyer (Aragon)
O O Neill T Horsley

Placings:60000/046/406255P0P-05100025P (3944)
2002/03: 21⁵GS, 19⁰G, 16⁵G, 17¹GS, 16⁹S, 24⁰S, 16⁹S, 16²HY,
16⁵HY, 17⁸S,

	Starts	1st	2nd	3rd	Win & Pl
Hurdles	10	1	1	0	2786
Career Total	26	1	2	0	3375
73 11/02 Tntn	2m1f	G(0-90)HHdl	G-S	£2019
		Total win prize-money £2020		

Going:	Sf: 0-6 GS: 1-2 Gd: 0-2 GF: - Fm: 0-0
Distance:	2m/2m3: 1-7 2m4-2m7: 0-2 3m+: 0-1
Track:	LH: 0-3 RH: 1-7 Tight: 1-3 Gall: 0-0
Aids:	Bl: 0-0 Vi: 0-0 Tstrap: 0-0
Best Rating:	80 2/02 Ludl 2m soft Hdl

Selling-class hurdler.

Forest Gunner
106(107h) (123h)**125**
9-y-o ch g Gunner B-Gouly Duff (Party Mink)
R Ford John Gilsenan

Placings:40/36/1213125-112 (2502)
2002/03: 21¹G, 21¹GS, 24²GS,

	Starts	1st	2nd	3rd	Win & Pl
Chases	3	2	1	0	10507
Career Total	14	5	3	2	22412
125 11/02 Fknm	2m5f110y		D Ch	G-S	£5096
112 10/02 Sedg	2m5f	E Ch	GD	£4147
123 1/02 Weth	2m7f	E Hdl	G-S	£2681
123 11/01 MRas	2m5f110y	F Hdl	G-S	£2254
120 5/01 Aint	2m4f	D Hdl	GD	£3584
		Total win prize-money £17762		

Going:	Sf: 0-0 GS: 1-2 Gd: 1-1 GF: - Fm: 0-0
Distance:	2m/2m3: 0-0 2m4-2m7: 2-2 3m+: 0-1
Track:	LH: 2-3 RH: 0-0 Tight: 2-3 Gall: 0-0
Aids:	Bl: 0-0 Vi: 0-0 Tstrap: 0-0
Best Rating:	125 12/02 Fknm 3m110y gd-sft Ch

A fair hurdler who has had his problems with injury, he has shown what he is capable of in 2001. Well suited by sharp tracks, and appreciates good ground or slightly softer. Likes to front run and stays two miles seven. He has impressed over fences with a handful of wins, jumping well and galloping on strongly.

Forest Heath (IRE)
103 **82**
6-y-o gr g Common Grounds-Caroline Lady (JPN) (Caro)
H J Collingridge Bockmer Partnership

Placings:5-056 (4573)
2002/03: 16⁹G, 16⁵GF, 16⁶GF,

	Starts	1st	2nd	3rd	Win & Pl
Hurdles	3	0	0	0	0
Career Total	4	0	0	0	0

Going:	Sf: 0-0 GS: 0-0 Gd: 0-1 GF: - Fm: 0-2
Distance:	2m/2m3: 0-3 2m4-2m7: 0-0 3m+: 0-0
Track:	LH: 0-2 RH: 0-1 Tight: 0-1 Gall: 0-1
Aids:	Bl: 0-0 Vi: 0-0 Tstrap: 0-0
Best Rating:	82 4/03 Strf 2m110y gd-fm Hdl

Forest Ivory (NZ)
105 **91**
12-y-o ch g Ivory Hunter (USA)-Fair And Square (NZ) (Crown Lease)
Dr P Pritchard (R D Wylie 13/3) Lady Maria Coventry

Placings:1220/11241/F112/4333460/53235/30/00P3600-
002450056 (4607)
2002/03: 24⁰S, 25⁰G, 27²S, 23⁴HY, 27⁵HY, 26⁰G, 24⁰S, 24⁵GF,
21⁶G,

	Starts	1st	2nd	3rd	Win & Pl
Hurdles	9	0	1	0	2186
Career Total	43	6	6	7	96255
141 11/97 Bang	3m110y	D Ch	SFT	£3842
115 11/97 Weth	3m1f	D Ch	G-S	£3600
144 4/97 Aint	3m110y	A Hdl	GD	£21532
122 12/96 Worc	2m4f	E Hdl	G-S	£2915
119 11/96 Towc	2m5f	F Hdl	GD	£1849
121 11/95 Worc	2m	H NHF	SFT	£1455
		Total win prize-money £35194		

Going:	Sf: 0-5 GS: 0-0 Gd: 0-3 GF: - Fm: 0-1
Distance:	2m/2m3: 0-0 2m4-2m7: 0-2 3m+: 0-7
Track:	LH: 0-7 RH: 0-2 Tight: 0-3 Gall: 0-2
Aids:	Bl: 0-3 Vi: 0-0 Tstrap: 0-0
Best Rating:	145 12/97 Kemp 3m soft Ch

Smart in his peak but only selling class now; stays really well; suited by testing conditions.

Forest Thyne (IRE)
(92h) (68h)**78**
9-y-o ch g Good Thyne (USA)-Tullow Performance (Gala Performance (USA))
J R Jenkins Jack McGrath

Placings:320/023450/5/PPFP0P4-4 (0152)
2002/03: 23⁴G,

	Starts	1st	2nd	3rd	Win & Pl
Hurdles	1	0	0	0	0
Career Total	18	0	2	2	2352

Going:	Sf: 0-0 GS: 0-0 Gd: 0-1 GF: - Fm: 0-0
Distance:	2m/2m3: 0-0 2m4-2m7: 0-0 3m+: 0-1
Track:	LH: 0-1 RH: 0-0 Tight: 0-1 Gall: 0-0
Aids:	Bl: 0-0 Vi: 0-1 Tstrap: 0-0

Best Rating: 101 11/98 Worc 2m   heavy NHF

Forest Tune (IRE)
106   **114**

5-y-o b g Charnwood Forest (IRE)-Swift Chorus (Music Boy)
B Hanbury The Acorn Partnership

Placings:20212   (4446)
2002/03: 16²GS, 16⁰G, 16²S, 16¹GF, 16²G,

	Starts	1st	2nd	3rd	Win & Pl
Hurdles	5	1	3	0	8180
Career Total	5	1	3	0	8180

114 3/03 Ludl 2m   E(0-105)HHdl G-F £4940
Total win prize-money £4940

Going:	Sf: 0-1 GS: 0-1 Gd: 0-2 GF: - Fm: 1-1
Distance:	2m/2m3: 1-5 2m4-2m7: 0-0 3m+: 0-0
Track:	LH: 0-2 RH: 1-3 Tight: 0-1 Gall: 0-2
Aids:	Bl: 0-0 Vi: 0-0 Tstrap: 0-0
Best Rating:	114 3/03 Ludl 2m gd-fm Hdl

Modest mile handicapper on the flat, runner-up at Huntingdon in November, winner next time before finding a useful horse too good the time after.

Forestry
(98h)   (65h)**48**

9-y-o b g Highest Honor (FR)-Arboretum (IRE) (Green Desert (USA))
J G M O Shea N M Lowe

Placings:0/P05303/6PPP3   (0739)
2002/03: 17⁹GF, 22⁸GS, 19⁹G, 21⁸G, 16³G,

	Starts	1st	2nd	3rd	Win & Pl
Hurdles	3	0	0	0	
Chases	2	0	0	1	538
Career Total	12	0	0	3	1144

Going:	Sf: 0-0 GS: 0-1 Gd: 0-3 GF: - Fm: 0-1
Distance:	2m/2m3: 0-2 2m4-2m7: 0-3 3m+: 0-0
Track:	LH: 0-3 RH: 0-2 Tight: 0-3 Gall: 0-0
Aids:	Bl: 0-0 Vi: 0-0 Tstrap: 0-0
Best Rating:	87 2/99 Hrfd 2m1f good Hdl

Forever Dream
98f   **98+f**

5-y-o b g Afzal-Quadrapol (Pollerton)
P J Hobbs A Stevens & W Mckibbin

Placings:6251   (4296)
2002/03: 17⁶GS, 16²GS, 16⁵GS, 16¹GF,

	Starts	1st	2nd	3rd	Win & Pl
NH Flat	4	1	1	0	3015
Career Total	4	1	1	0	3015

98 3/03 Winc 2m   H NHF G-F £2331
Total win prize-money £2331

Going:	Sf: 0-0 GS: 0-3 Gd: 0-0 GF: - Fm: 1-1
Distance:	2m/2m3: 1-4 2m4-2m7: 0-0 3m+: 0-0
Track:	LH: 0-0 RH: 1-2 Tight: 0-0 Gall: 0-0
Aids:	Bl: 0-0 Vi: 0-0 Tstrap: 0-0
Best Rating:	98 3/03 Winc 2m gd-fm NHF

Bumper winner; seems to act on fast and easy ground.

Forever Noble (IRE)
99   **82**

10-y-o b g Forzando-Pagan Queen (Vaguely Noble)

R Allan Mrs Florence C Ratter

Placings:32/620/1P222241/F352U3/1/6505-0   (4505)
2002/03: 17⁰G,

	Starts	1st	2nd	3rd	Win & Pl
Chases	1	0	0	0	
Career Total	25	3	7	3	19116

125 10/00 Fknm 3m110y F(0-110)HCh GD £4602
116 4/99 Weth 2m4f110yD Hdl G-F £3436
103 11/98 Hntg 2m110y E Hdl G-S £2110
Total win prize-money £10148

Going:	Sf: 0-0 GS: 0-0 Gd: 0-1 GF: - Fm: 0-0
Distance:	2m/2m3: 0-2 2m4-2m7: 0-0 3m+: 0-0
Track:	LH: 0-1 RH: 0-0 Tight: 0-1 Gall: 0-0
Aids:	Bl: 0-0 Vi: 0-0 Tstrap: 0-0
Best Rating:	125 10/00 Fknm 3m110y good Ch

Plating-class hurdler/chaser; stays three miles; acts on good/good to soft ground.

Forever Posh
67f   **49f**

6-y-o b m Rakaposhi King-B Final (Gunner B)
Mrs S M Johnson P J Allen

Placings:0   (3849)
2002/03: 16⁹G,

	Starts	1st	2nd	3rd	Win & Pl
NH Flat	1	0	0	0	
Career Total	1	0	0	0	

Going:	Sf: 0-0 GS: 0-0 Gd: 0-1 GF: - Fm: 0-0
Distance:	2m/2m3: 0-1 2m4-2m7: 0-0 3m+: 0-0
Track:	LH: 0-0 RH: 0-1 Tight: 0-0 Gall: 0-0
Aids:	Bl: 0-0 Vi: 0-0 Tstrap: 0-0
Best Rating:	49 2/03 Ludl 2m good NHF

Fork Lightning (IRE)
107   **120**

7-y-o gr g Roselier (FR)-Park Breeze (IRE) (Strong Gale)
A King Mr & Mrs F C Welch

Placings:441321   (4606)
2002/03: 20⁴HY, 19⁴G, 21¹GS, 22³GS, 20²G, 24¹G,

	Starts	1st	2nd	3rd	Win & Pl
Hurdles	6	2	1	1	19049
Career Total	6	2	1	1	19049

120 4/03 Chel 3m D(0-120)HHdl GD £10483
110 1/03 Kemp 2m5f D Hdl G-S £5664
Total win prize-money £16148

Going:	Sf: 0-1 GS: 1-2 Gd: 1-3 GF: - Fm: 0-0
Distance:	2m/2m3: 0-0 2m4-2m7: 1-5 3m+: 1-1
Track:	LH: 1-2 RH: 1-4 Tight: 0-1 Gall: 1-1
Aids:	Bl: 0-0 Vi: 0-0 Tstrap: 0-0
Best Rating:	120 4/03 Chel 3m good Hdl

Fair hurdler; stays two miles five; acts on good and yielding ground.

Forlorn Hope

6-y-o b g Tragic Role (USA)-Rum N Raisin (Rakaposhi King)
B D Leavy A J McMullan

Placings:P0   (4522)
2002/03: 16⁵S, 16⁰G,

	Starts	1st	2nd	3rd	Win & Pl
Hurdles	2	0	0	0	
Career Total	2	0	0	0	

Going:	Sf: 0-1 GS: 0-0 Gd: 0-1 GF: - Fm: 0-0
Distance:	2m/2m3: 0-2 2m4-2m7: 0-0 3m+: 0-0
Track:	LH: 0-1 RH: 0-1 Tight: 0-0 Gall: 0-1
Aids:	Bl: 0-0 Vi: 0-0 Tstrap: 0-0
Best Rating:	0 4/03 Uttx 2m good Hdl

Formal Bid (USA)
110   **123**

6-y-o b g Dynaformer (USA)-Fantastic Bid (USA) (Auction Ring (USA))
C C Bealby Michael Hill

Placings:2522P3-31301223   (3627)
2002/03: 16³GS, 16²S, 19¹G, 20³GS, 16⁹GS, 20¹HY, 19²GS, 20²HY, 20³S,

	Starts	1st	2nd	3rd	Win & Pl
Hurdles	9	2	2	4	19853
Career Total	14	2	5	4	22528

110 12/02 Leic 2m4f110yD Hdl HVY £4940
118 10/02 MRas 2m3f110yE Hdl GD £3710
Total win prize-money £8650

Going:	Sf: 1-4 GS: 0-4 Gd: 1-1 GF: - Fm: 0-0
Distance:	2m/2m3: 0-3 2m4-2m7: 2-6 3m+: 0-0
Track:	LH: 0-1 RH: 2-8 Tight: 1-2 Gall: 0-1
Aids:	Bl: 0-0 Vi: 0-0 Tstrap: 0-0
Best Rating:	121 2/03 Asct 2m4f soft Hdl

Decent hurdler; acts on good ground or softer; effective at around two and a half miles.

Formal Invitation (IRE)

14-y-o ch g Be My Guest (USA)-Clarista (USA) (Riva Ridge (USA))
David Maybury David Maybury

Placings:322114/211/112/2PP/P4/0-0F   (0416)
2002/03: 21⁰GF, 24⁵GF,

	Starts	1st	2nd	3rd	Win & Pl
Chases	2	0	0	0	
Career Total	20	6	5	1	21737

133 5/97 Strf 2m5f110yD Ch GD £3548
126 5/97 Uttx 2m4f D(0-125)HCh G-S £3517
127 4/97 Chel 2m5f D Ch G-F £3397
125 3/97 MRas 2m4f D Ch G-F £3773
93 3/93 Wolv 2m110y Hdl G-F £1484
87 3/93 Ludl 2m Hdl G-F £1475
Total win prize-money £17196

Going:	Sf: 0-0 GS: 0-0 Gd: 0-0 GF: - Fm: 0-2
Distance:	2m/2m3: 0-0 2m4-2m7: 0-1 3m+: 0-1
Track:	LH: 0-2 RH: 0-0 Tight: 0-1 Gall: 0-1
Aids:	Bl: 0-0 Vi: 0-0 Tstrap: 0-0
Best Rating:	133 5/97 Strf 2m5f110y good Ch

Formidable Flame
90   **60**

10-y-o ch g Formidable (USA)-Madiyla (Darshaan)
C Tizzard G B J Humphries

Placings:P0/50P6/00064/2P65P00/04P   (0994)
2002/03: 17⁰GF, 22⁴GF, 22⁶GF,

	Starts	1st	2nd	3rd	Win & Pl
Hurdles	3	0	0	0	0
Career Total	20	0	1	0	524

Going: Sf: 0-0 GS: 0-0 Gd: 0-0 GF: - Fm: 0-3
Distance: 2m/2m3: 0-1 2m4-2m7: 0-2 3m+: 0-0
Track: LH: 0-3 RH: 0-0 Tight: 0-3 Gall: 0-0
Aids: Bl: 0-1 Vi: 0-0 Tstrap: 0-0
Best Rating: 75   5/00   Extr   2m1f   firm   Hdl

Formidable Stella
68f   24f
7-y-o b m Formidable (USA)-Stellajoe (Le Dauphin)
Miss Z C Davison Rags to Riches

Placings:000   (0436)
2002/03: 17⁰G, 17⁰G, 16⁰GF,

	Starts	1st	2nd	3rd	Win & Pl
NH Flat	3	0	0	0	
Career Total	3	0	0	0	

Going: Sf: 0-0 GS: 0-0 Gd: 0-2 GF: - Fm: 0-1
Distance: 2m/2m3: 0-3 2m4-2m7: 0-0 3m+: 0-0
Track: LH: 0-0 RH: 0-3 Tight: 0-1 Gall: 0-1
Aids: Bl: 0-0 Vi: 0-0 Tstrap: 0-0
Best Rating: 39   5/02   Extr   2m1f   good   NHF

Fornaught Alliance (IRE)

10-y-o br g Zaffaran (USA)-Carrick Shannon (Green Shoon)
G Tuer Yarm Skip Alliance

Placings:533/5050356/52223522B23005/2142253/006R611
45-320   (4508)
2002/03: 21³S, 27²G, 25⁰G,

	Starts	1st	2nd	3rd	Win & Pl
Chases	3	0	1	1	708
Career Total	43	3	10	7	33681
97	3/02	Sedg	2m5f	D(0-120)HCh	SFT	£3987
97	2/02	Sedg	3m3f110yE(0-110)HHdl	SFT	£5488
114	11/00	Hayd	2m6f	D(0-120)HCh	SFT	£8060

Total win prize-money £17536

Going: Sf: 0-1 GS: 0-0 Gd: 0-2 GF: - Fm: 0-0
Distance: 2m/2m3: 0-0 2m4-2m7: 0-1 3m+: 0-2
Track: LH: 0-3 RH: 0-0 Tight: 0-2 Gall: 0-0
Aids: Bl: 0-3 Vi: 0-0 Tstrap: 0-0
Best Rating: 114   1/01   Fknm   3m110y   soft   Ch

Versatile, if quirky, sort who is suited by three miles.

Forrest Tribe (IRE)
102   98
10-y-o b/br g Be My Native (USA)-Island Bridge (Mandalus)
W Jenks Mrs Douglas Graham

Placings:0644/140/234143P4/55020PF/500636232-3
(0075)
2002/03: 25³GF,

	Starts	1st	2nd	3rd	Win & Pl
Chases	1	0	0	1	600
Career Total	32	2	4	5	19325
112	2/00	Kels	2m6f110yC(0-130)HCh	G-S	£7621
115	3/99	Ayr	2m4f	E Ch	SFT	£2898

Total win prize-money £10519

Going: Sf: 0-0 GS: 0-0 Gd: 0-0 GF: - Fm: 0-0
Distance: 2m/2m3: 0-0 2m4-2m7: 0-0 3m+: 0-1
Track: LH: 0-0 RH: 0-1 Tight: 0-0 Gall: 0-0
Aids: Bl: 0-0 Vi: 0-0 Tstrap: 0-0
Best Rating: 115   3/99   Ayr   2m4f   soft   Ch

Ex-Irish chaser, effective over three miles and best with a bit of cut.

Forthechop
90   59
6-y-o b g Minshaanshu Amad (USA)-Cousin Jenny (Midyan (USA))
R C Harper R C Harper

Placings:4P000-4P65   (3550)
2002/03: 17⁴GS, 16⁵HY, 16⁵HY,

	Starts	1st	2nd	3rd	Win & Pl
Hurdles	4	0	0	0	0
Career Total	9	0	0	0	274

Going: Sf: 0-3 GS: 0-1 Gd: 0-0 GF: - Fm: 0-0
Distance: 2m/2m3: 0-4 2m4-2m7: 0-0 3m+: 0-0
Track: LH: 0-2 RH: 0-2 Tight: 0-2 Gall: 0-0
Aids: Bl: 0-0 Vi: 0-0 Tstrap: 0-0
Best Rating: 59   11/02   Tntn   2m1f   gd-sft   Hdl

Fortunate Dave (USA)
105   107
4-y-o b g Lear Fan (USA)-Lady Ameriflora (USA) (Lord Avie (USA))
Ian Williams M N Dennis

Placings:10232420   (4776)
2002/03: 16¹G, 16⁸GS, 17²S, 18³G, 16²G, 16⁴G, 17²G, 20⁶G,

	Starts	1st	2nd	3rd	Win & Pl
Hurdles	8	1	3	1	8943
Career Total	8	1	3	1	8943
102	11/02	Wwck	2m	D Hdl	GD	£4013

Total win prize-money £4014

Going: Sf: 0-1 GS: 0-1 Gd: 1-6 GF: - Fm: 0-0
Distance: 2m/2m3: 1-7 2m4-2m7: 0-1 3m+: 0-0
Track: LH: 1-6 RH: 0-2 Tight: 0-3 Gall: 0-1
Aids: Bl: 0-0 Vi: 0-0 Tstrap: 0-0
Best Rating: 107   3/03   Hntg   2m110y   good   Hdl

Modest hurdler; made a winning debut over hurdles in November 2002 and struggled under a penalty since; handles good ground or softer.

Fortune Island (IRE)
106   116+
4-y-o b g Turtle Island (IRE)-Blue Kestrel (IRE) (Bluebird (USA))
M C Pipe (C F Wall 26/8) J M Brown & M J Blackburn

Placings:P10   (4130)
2002/03: 16⁵GS, 17¹GS, 17⁰G,

	Starts	1st	2nd	3rd	Win & Pl
Hurdles	3	1	0	0	3523
Career Total	3	1	0	0	3523
112	2/03	Extr	2m1f	E Hdl	G-S	£3523

Total win prize-money £3523

Going: Sf: 0-0 GS: 1-2 Gd: 0 GF: - Fm: 0-0
Distance: 2m/2m3: 1-3 2m4-2m7: 0-0 3m+: 0-0
Track: LH: 0-1 RH: 1-2 Tight: 0-0 Gall: 0-1
Aids: Bl: 0-0 Vi: 0-0 Tstrap: 0-0
Best Rating: 116   3/03   Chel   2m1f   good   Hdl

Fair hurdler; effective over two miles; acts on good to soft ground.

Fortune's Fool
101   66
4-y-o b g Zilzal (USA)-Peryllys (Warning)
I A Brown I A Brown

Placings:P604   (4782)
2002/03: 16⁵GS, 17⁶G, 17⁰G, 17⁴G,

	Starts	1st	2nd	3rd	Win & Pl
Hurdles	4	0	0	0	0
Career Total	4	0	0	0	0

Going: Sf: 0-0 GS: 0-1 Gd: 0-3 GF: - Fm: 0-0
Distance: 2m/2m3: 0-4 2m4-2m7: 0-0 3m+: 0-0
Track: LH: 0-2 RH: 0-2 Tight: 0-4 Gall: 0-0
Aids: Bl: 0-0 Vi: 0-0 Tstrap: 0-0
Best Rating: 66   4/03   MRas   2m1f110y   good   Hdl

Plating-class novice hurdler.

Forty Love (IRE)
8-y-o b g Second Set (IRE)-Pharjoy (FR) (Pharly (FR))
Miss J Fisher Miss J Fisher

Placings:42511/F   (0260)
2002/03: 20⁵GF,

	Starts	1st	2nd	3rd	Win & Pl
Chases	1	0	0	0	
Career Total	6	2	1	0	8863
98	2/99	Muss	2m4f	E(0-100)HHdl	GD	£5537
93	1/99	Muss	2m	G(0-95)HHdl	G-S	£2490

Total win prize-money £8027

Going: Sf: 0-0 GS: 0-0 Gd: 0-0 GF: - Fm: 0-1
Distance: 2m/2m3: 0-0 2m4-2m7: 0-1 3m+: 0-0
Track: LH: 0-0 RH: 0-1 Tight: 0-0 Gall: 0-0
Aids: Bl: 0-0 Vi: 0-0 Tstrap: 0-0
Best Rating: 98   2/99   Muss   2m4f   good   Hdl

Forum Chris (IRE)
101   119+
6-y-o ch g Trempolino (USA)-Memory Green (USA) (Green Forest (USA))
Mrs S J Smith Mrs Jacqueline Conroy

Placings:111   (0817)
2002/03: 22¹HY, 20¹GF, 20¹GF,

	Starts	1st	2nd	3rd	Win & Pl
Hurdles	3	3	0	0	8970
Career Total	3	3	0	0	8970
115	7/02	Worc	2m4f	E Hdl	G-F	£2877
119	6/02	Hexm	2m4f110yE Hdl	G-F	£2583
97	6/02	Ctml	2m6f	D Hdl	HVY	£3510

Total win prize-money £8970

Going: Sf: 1-1 GS: 0-0 Gd: 0-0 GF: - Fm: 2-2
Distance: 2m/2m3: 0-0 2m4-2m7: 3-3 3m+: 0-0
Track: LH: 3-3 RH: 0-0 Tight: 1-1 Gall: 0-0
Aids: Bl: 0-0 Vi: 0-0 Tstrap: 0-0
Best Rating: 119   6/02   Hexm   2m4f110y   gd-fm   Hdl

Dual winner on the Flat at three, has won all three starts in novice hurdles and looks a fair prospect.

Forza Glory
95   81+
4-y-o ch f Forzando-Glory Isle (Hittite Glory)
Miss B Sanders Mrs J Laycock & A C Verdie

Placings:3054   (3248)

2002/03: 17³S, 16⁰S, 16⁵S, 16⁴HY,

	Starts	1st	2nd	3rd	Win & Pl
Hurdles	4	0	0	1	709
Career Total	4	0	0	1	709

Going: Sf: 0-4 GS: 0-0 Gd: 0-0 GF: - Fm: 0-0
Distance: 2m/2m3: 0-4 2m4-2m7: 0-0 3m+: 0-0
Track: LH: 0-3 RH: 0-1 Tight: 0-2 Gall: 0-1
Aids: Bl: 0-0 Vi: 0-0 Tstrap: 0-0
Best Rating: 75   11/02 Folk   2m1f110y   soft   Hdl

Modest novice hurdler on soft ground.

Forzacurity

95   82

4-y-o ch g Forzando-Nice Lady (Connaught)
J L Spearing The Square Milers

Placings:65   (2207)
2002/03: 17⁶S, 17⁵S,

	Starts	1st	2nd	3rd	Win & Pl
Hurdles	2	0	0	0	0
Career Total	2	0	0	0	0

Going: Sf: 0-1 GS: 0-0 Gd: 0-1 GF: - Fm: 0-0
Distance: 2m/2m3: 0-2 2m4-2m7: 0-0 3m+: 0-0
Track: LH: 0-1 RH: 0-1 Tight: 0-1 Gall: 0-0
Aids: Bl: 0-0 Vi: 0-0 Tstrap: 0-0
Best Rating: 82   11/02 Bang   2m1f   soft   Hdl

Three times a winner at between seven furlongs and a mile.
Failed to prove he gets the trip on hurdling debut at Hereford
October 2002.

Fosse Hill

95   93

6-y-o b g Bustino-Amber s Image (Billion (USA))
Miss H C Knight Lord Vestey

Placings:10-6   (0177)
2002/03: 16⁶GF,

	Starts	1st	2nd	3rd	Win & Pl
Hurdles	1	0	0	0	0
Career Total	3	1	0	0	1712
106 11/01 Ludl 2m H NHF G-F £1711					
Total win prize-money £1712					

Going: Sf: 0-0 GS: 0-0 Gd: 0-0 GF: - Fm: 0-1
Distance: 2m/2m3: 0-1 2m4-2m7: 0-0 3m+: 0-0
Track: LH: 0-0 RH: 0-1 Tight: 0-0 Gall: 0-0
Aids: Bl: 0-0 Vi: 0-0 Tstrap: 0-0
Best Rating: 106   11/01 Ludl   2m   gd-fm NHF

Made a winning bumper debut at Ludlow, but well beaten on
hurdling debut.

Fossy Bear

11-y-o br m Lir-Full Spirit (Bay Spirit)
Miss S Young B R J Young

Placings:F/P/4   (4255)
2002/03: 25⁴G,

	Starts	1st	2nd	3rd	Win & Pl
Chases	1	0	0	0	273
Career Total	3	0	0	0	273

Going: Sf: 0-0 GS: 0-0 Gd: 0-1 GF: - Fm: 0-0
Distance: 2m/2m3: 0-0 2m4-2m7: 0-0 3m+: 0-1
Track: LH: 0-0 RH: 0-1 Tight: 0-0 Gall: 0-0

Aids: Bl: 0-0 Vi: 0-0 Tstrap: 0-0
Best Rating: 80   3/03   Extr   3m1f110y   good   Ch

Unlucky only to have won four of her last five points; highly
tried in hunter chase at Exeter March 2003.

Foster

88f   69f

4-y-o b g Teenoso (USA)-Glorious Jane (Hittite Glory)
M F Harris The Golden Anorak Partnership

Placings:0P   (4737)
2002/03: 16⁶G, 16⁶GF,

	Starts	1st	2nd	3rd	Win & Pl
NH Flat	2	0	0	0	
Career Total	2	0	0	0	

Going: Sf: 0-0 GS: 0-0 Gd: 0-1 GF: - Fm: 0-1
Distance: 2m/2m3: 0-2 2m4-2m7: 0-0 3m+: 0-0
Track: LH: 0-2 RH: 0-0 Tight: 0-0 Gall: 0-0
Aids: Bl: 0-0 Vi: 0-0 Tstrap: 0-0
Best Rating: 69   3/03   Wwck   2m   good   NHF

Foston Second (IRE)

77   68

6-y-o ch m Lycius (USA)-Gentle Guest (IRE) (Be My Guest (USA))
C Weedon Atlantic Foods Ltd

Placings:360-   (0008)
2002/03: 16⁰G,

	Starts	1st	2nd	3rd	Win & Pl
Hurdles	1	0	0	0	
Career Total	3	0	0	1	283

Going: Sf: 0-0 GS: 0-0 Gd: 0-1 GF: - Fm: 0-0
Distance: 2m/2m3: 0-1 2m4-2m7: 0-0 3m+: 0-0
Track: LH: 0-1 RH: 0-0 Tight: 0-1 Gall: 0-0
Aids: Bl: 0-0 Vi: 0-0 Tstrap: 0-0
Best Rating: 68   12/01 Leic   2m   good   Hdl

Fou Doux (FR)

(88h)   (70h)

7-y-o b g Le Grillon Ii (FR)-Folie Douce (FR) (Fast (FR))
P W Hiatt (D G Bridgwater 24/5) Paul Porter

Placings:4221/2/PP-3PU0P0   (3741)
2002/03: 16⁹G, 20⁰G, 16¹⁵S, 25⁹S, 20⁹G,

	Starts	1st	2nd	3rd	Win & Pl
Hurdles	3	0	0	1	266
Chases	3	0	0	0	
Career Total	13	3	1	3	12890
12/99 Pau 2m110y Hdl VS £5920					
Total win prize-money £5920					

Going: Sf: 0-3 GS: 0-0 Gd: 0-3 GF: - Fm: 0-0
Distance: 2m/2m3: 0-3 2m4-2m7: 0-2 3m+: 0-1
Track: LH: 0-0 RH: 0-5 Tight: 0-1 Gall: 0-0
Aids: Bl: 0-1 Vi: 0-0 Tstrap: 0-1
Best Rating: 70   5/02   Towc   2m   good   Hdl

Fouette

59

5-y-o b m Saddlers Hall (IRE)-Tight Spin (High Top)
J Howard Johnson J Howard Johnson

Placings:004F-P   (0080)
2002/03: 16⁶GS,

	Starts	1st	2nd	3rd	Win & Pl
Hurdles	1	0	0	0	
Career Total	5	0	0	0	0

Going: Sf: 0-0 GS: 0-1 Gd: 0-0 GF: - Fm: 0-0
Distance: 2m/2m3: 0-1 2m4-2m7: 0-0 3m+: 0-0
Track: LH: 0-1 RH: 0-0 Tight: 0-0 Gall: 0-0
Aids: Bl: 0-0 Vi: 0-0 Tstrap: 0-0
Best Rating: 59   3/02   Kels   2m2f   heavy   Hdl

Fountain Bank (IRE)

100(106c)   (80c)102+

10-y-o b g Lafontaine (USA)-Clogrecon Lass (Raise You Ten)
M J Gingell T Alexander And G S Plastow

Placings:30/4046/P3F/21112441P4660-U561340PPP3   (4706)
2002/03: 24⁴G, 24⁵GS, 20⁶GF, 23¹G, 26³GF, 23⁴G, 22⁰GF, 23⁸GF, 21⁸GS, 21⁸GF, 20³G,

	Starts	1st	2nd	3rd	Win & Pl
Hurdles	4	0	0	1	359
Chases	7	1	0	1	5033
Career Total	33	5	2	4	19200
104 8/02 Worc 2m7f110yE Ch GD £4036					
109 9/01 Font 2m6f110yF(0-110)HHdl G-F £2688					
108 6/01 Strf 2m6f110yF(0-95)HHdl G-F £2443					
101 6/01 Worc 2m4f F(0-110)HHdl G-F £2562					
95 6/01 Fknm 2m7f110yF(0-100)HHdl G-F £3003					
Total win prize-money £14733					

Going: Sf: 0-0 GS: 0-2 Gd: 1-4 GF: - Fm: 0-5
Distance: 2m/2m3: 0-0 2m4-2m7: 0-0 **3m+:** 1-6
Track: **LH:** 1-10 RH: 0-0 Tight: 0-5 Gall: 0-0
Aids: Bl: 0-0 **Vi:** 1-9 Tstrap: 0-0
Best Rating: 109   9/01   Font   2m6f110y   gd-fm   Hdl

Plating-class hurdler/chaser; acts on decent ground; stays
three miles.

Fountain Bid (IRE)

11-y-o b g Royal Fountain-Lilford Castle (Carlingford Castle)
R Dean Richard Dean

Placings:02123/0340424244500/P444U4F06205P44/3P03 5345PP4446PR/P   (0311)
2002/03: 26⁰G,

	Starts	1st	2nd	3rd	Win & Pl
Chases	1	0	0	0	
Career Total	50	1	5	5	9390
94 4/98 Font 2m2f110yF Hdl G-S £2072					
Total win prize-money £2072					

Going: Sf: 0-0 GS: 0-0 Gd: 0-1 GF: - Fm: 0-0
Distance: 2m/2m3: 0-0 2m4-2m7: 0-0 3m+: 0-1
Track: LH: 0-0 RH: 0-1 Tight: 0-1 Gall: 0-0
Aids: Bl: 0-1 Vi: 0-0 Tstrap: 0-0
Best Rating: 97   4/98   Plum   2m4f   gd-sft   Hdl

Fountain Brig

99(98h)   (70h)79

7-y-o b/br g Royal Fountain-Lillie s Brig (New Brig)
N W Alexander (N Alexander 26/12) Alexander Family

Placings:06053-0P336   (3772)
2002/03: 20⁰GS, 24⁶HY, 24³HY, 20³HY, 21⁶GS,

	Starts	1st	2nd	3rd	Win & Pl
Hurdles	4	0	0	2	1201
Chases	1	0	0	0	0
Career Total	10	0	0	3	1697

Going: Sf: 0-3 GS: 0-2 Gd: 0-0 GF: - Fm: 0-0
Distance: 2m/2m3: 0-0 2m4-2m7: 0-3 3m+: 0-2
Track: LH: 0-5 RH: 0-0 Tight: 0-0 Gall: 0-0
Aids: Bl: 0-0 Vi: 0-0 Tstrap: 0-0
Best Rating: 79 2/03 Ayr 2m5f110y gd-sft Ch

Little sign of ability so far.

Four Men (IRE)

6-y-o b g Nicolotte-Sound Pet (Runnett)
Miss K M George Stableline

Placings:P-P (1091)
2002/03: 17PGF,

	Starts	1st	2nd	3rd	Win & Pl
Hurdles	1	0	0	0	
Career Total	2	0	0	0	

Going: Sf: 0-0 GS: 0-0 Gd: 0-0 GF: - Fm: 0-1
Distance: 2m/2m3: 0-1 2m4-2m7: 0-0 3m+: 0-0
Track: LH: 0-1 RH: 0-0 Tight: 0-1 Gall: 0-0
Aids: Bl: 0-0 Vi: 0-0 Tstrap: 0-0
Best Rating: 0 8/02 NAbb 2m1f gd-fm Hdl

Four Mile Clump
96(91h)   (96h)87

9-y-o b g Petoski-Rare Luck (Rare One)
P J Jones P J Jones

Placings:0P0R3/PP/23P11-43PP00 (4759)
2002/03: 254GS, 263HY, 25PS, 24FGS, 25QGF, 27QGF,

	Starts	1st	2nd	3rd	Win & Pl
Hurdles	1	0	0	0	0
Chases	5	0	0	1	1115
Career Total	18	2	1	3	12532
107 12/01 Hrfd	3m1f110yF(0-100)HCh			GD	£7068
95 11/01 Hrfd	3m1f110yF(0-90)HCh			GD	£2796
				Total win prize-money	£9866

Going: Sf: 0-2 GS: 0-2 Gd: 0-0 GF: - Fm: 0-2
Distance: 2m/2m3: 0-0 2m4-2m7: 0-0 3m+: 0-6
Track: LH: 0-0 RH: 0-5 Tight: 0-3 Gall: 0-0
Aids: Bl: 0-0 Vi: 0-1 Tstrap: 0-0
Best Rating: 107 12/01 Hrfd 3m1f110y good Ch

Showed improved form to win twice at Hereford late in 2001. Well held on return after a year off. Suited by forcing tactics.

Four Of A Kind
71f

5-y-o b g Most Welcome-Pegs (Mandrake Major)
C W Thornton Guy Reed

Placings:00-0 (0026)
2002/03: 16QG,

	Starts	1st	2nd	3rd	Win & Pl
NH Flat	1	0	0	0	
Career Total	3	0	0	0	

Going: Sf: 0-0 GS: 0-0 Gd: 0-1 GF: - Fm: 0-0
Distance: 2m/2m3: 0-1 2m4-2m7: 0-0 3m+: 0-0
Track: LH: 0-1 RH: 0-0 Tight: 0-0 Gall: 0-0
Aids: Bl: 0-0 Vi: 0-0 Tstrap: 0-0

Best Rating: 71 4/02 Ayr 2m good NHF

Four To Win (IRE)
91(94h)   (88h)95

7-y-o b g Tremblant-Ballybeg Rose (IRE) (Roselier (FR))
Miss Jacqueline S Doyle Cover Point Racing

Placings:0460P-FPF (4695)
2002/03: 20FGS, 21PS, 16FG,

	Starts	1st	2nd	3rd	Win & Pl
Chases	3	0	0	0	
Career Total	8	0	0	0	0

Going: Sf: 0-1 GS: 0-1 Gd: 0-1 GF: - Fm: 0-0
Distance: 2m/2m3: 0-2 2m4-2m7: 0-0 3m+: 0-0
Track: LH: 0-1 RH: 0-2 Tight: 0-2 Gall: 0-1
Aids: Bl: 0-2 Vi: 0-0 Tstrap: 0-0
Best Rating: 88 1/02 Hntg 2m110y gd-sft Hdl

Fourloch (IRE)
66

5-y-o b m Fourstars Allstar (USA)-Loch Wee (IRE) (Colmore Row)
N G Richards Mrs Linda Bott

Placings:0 (0474)
2002/03: 17QGS,

	Starts	1st	2nd	3rd	Win & Pl
Hurdles	1	0	0	0	
Career Total	1	0	0	0	

Going: Sf: 0-0 GS: 0-1 Gd: 0-0 GF: - Fm: 0-0
Distance: 2m/2m3: 0-1 2m4-2m7: 0-0 3m+: 0-0
Track: LH: 0-1 RH: 0-0 Tight: 0-1 Gall: 0-0
Aids: Bl: 0-0 Vi: 0-0 Tstrap: 0-0
Best Rating: 0 6/02 Ctml 2m1f110y gd-sft Hdl

Fours Are Wild (IRE)
71   65

10-y-o ch g Montelimar (USA)-Lousion (Lucifer (USA))
K C Bailey Mrs Amelia Dalton

Placings:0/0011P2/P/P0PU4-0 (0555)
2002/03: 25QGF,

	Starts	1st	2nd	3rd	Win & Pl
Chases	1	0	0	0	
Career Total	14	2	1	0	10122
123 11/99 Weth	2m4f110yD(0-110)HCh			GD	£3899
110 11/99 Kemp	2m4f110yD Ch			GD	£4611
				Total win prize-money	£8510

Going: Sf: 0-0 GS: 0-0 Gd: 0-0 GF: - Fm: 0-1
Distance: 2m/2m3: 0-0 2m4-2m7: 0-0 3m+: 0-3
Track: LH: 0-0 RH: 0-1 Tight: 0-0 Gall: 0-0
Aids: Bl: 0-1 Vi: 0-0 Tstrap: 0-0
Best Rating: 123 11/99 Weth 2m4f110y good Ch

Fourspice Allspice (IRE)
74   67

5-y-o b m Fourstars Allstar (USA)-A Dhahirah (Beldale Flutter (USA))
B R Millman (J W Mullins 9/11) Terry Cooper

Placings:5546PU0 (3598)
2002/03: 18GGF, 175GF, 164GF, 16RG, 22PG, 19UGS, 17QS,

	Starts	1st	2nd	3rd	Win & Pl
NH Flat	3	0	0	0	
Hurdles	4	0	0	0	
Career Total	7	0	0	0	0

Going: Sf: 0-1 GS: 0-1 Gd: 0-2 GF: - Fm: 0-3
Distance: 2m/2m3: 0-6 2m4-2m7: 0-1 3m+: 0-0
Track: LH: 0-1 RH: 0-5 Tight: 0-2 Gall: 0-0
Aids: Bl: 0-0 Vi: 0-0 Tstrap: 0-0
Best Rating: 84 5/02 Font 2m2f110y gd-fm NHF

Fox In The Box
104   106

6-y-o gr g Supreme Leader-Charlotte Gray (Rolfe (USA))
R H Alner Peter Bonner

Placings:046-41P5 (4442)
2002/03: 224GS, 201S, 20PHY, 20GG,

	Starts	1st	2nd	3rd	Win & Pl
Hurdles	4	1	0	0	3428
Career Total	7	1	0	0	3428
102 12/02 Chep	2m4f E Hdl			SFT	£2919
				Total win prize-money	£2919

Going: Sf: 1-2 GS: 0-1 Gd: 0-1 GF: - Fm: 0-0
Distance: 2m/2m3: 0-0 2m4-2m7: 1-4 3m+: 0-0
Track: LH: 1-1 RH: 0-3 Tight: 0-0 Gall: 0-0
Aids: Bl: 0-0 Vi: 0-0 Tstrap: 0-0
Best Rating: 106 11/02 Winc 2m6f gd-sft Hdl

Fair bumper/hurdler; would have been closer but for a blunder two out when fourth over 22 furlongs on hurdling debut at Wincanton November 2002; narrow winner after some novicey jumping over two and a half miles in the Chepstow mud; considered a three mile chaser in the making.

Foxchapel King (IRE)
113   128

10-y-o b g Jolly Jake (NZ)-Monatrim (Le Moss)
M F Morris Sir Anthony O Reilly

Placings:11166P/122FF114/0314322/2610P2/61110U-P1424U00 (4791)
2002/03: 24PS, 251S, 244HY, 242S, 244SH, 24UG, 24QGY, 29QG,

	Starts	1st	2nd	3rd	Win & Pl
Chases	8	1	1	0	31713
Career Total	41	12	7	2	307938
151 11/02 Fair	3m1f HCh			SFT	£15153
160 12/01 Leop	3m Ch			YLD	£60282
151 11/01 DRoy	3m Ch			Y-S	£53225
151 10/01 Limk	3m HCh			YLD	£26209
151 11/00 Chel	3m3f110yB HCh			G-S	£32500
143 11/99 Navn	3m HCh			YLD	£29017
133 4/99 Cork	3m Ch			SFT	£11562
117 2/99 Clon	2m4f Ch			SFT	£4296
107 10/98 Thur	2m6f Ch			GD	£3138
137 12/97 Leop	2m4f Hdl			HVY	£4069
121 11/97 Naas	2m Hdl			SH	£3051
98 11/97 Clon	2m Hdl			G-Y	£2543
				Total win prize-money	£245052

Going: Sf: 1-4 GS: 0-0 Gd: 0-2 GF: - Fm: 0-0
Distance: 2m/2m3: 0-0 2m4-2m7: 0-0 3m+: 1-8
Track: LH: 0-3 RH: 1-3 Tight: 0-0 Gall: 0-1
Aids: Bl: 0-0 Vi: 0-0 Tstrap: 0-0
Best Rating: 164 1/03 Leop 3m soft Ch

High-class Irish chaser; stays three and a half miles; likes to get his toe in but has never won on heavy ground over fences.

Foxchapel Queen (IRE)

101f   **105f**

5-y-o b/br m Over The River (FR)-Glencairn Lass (Buckskin (FR))
N J Henderson Paul Green

Placings:2-235   (4611)
2002/03: 18²HY, 16³GF, 17⁵G,

	Starts	1st	2nd	3rd	Win & Pl
NH Flat	3	0	1	1	1591
Career Total	4	0	2	1	2818

Going: Sf: 0-1 GS: 0-0 Gd: 0-1 GF: - Fm: 0-1
Distance: 2m/2m3: 0-3 2m4-2m7: 0-0 3m+: 0-0
Track: LH: 0-3 RH: 0-0 Tight: 0-1 Gall: 0-1
Aids: Bl: Rtchns Vi: 0-0 Tstrap: 0-0
Best Rating: 105 1/03 Font 2m2f110y heavy NHF

Modest bumper performer; placed in all three starts on varying ground; lacks a turn of foot.

Foxes Fandango

83   **51**

6-y-o br g Munjarid-The Pride Of Pokey (Uncle Pokey)
N A Gaselee Dean Woodley

Placings:00   (4117)
2002/03: 16⁰GS, 16⁰G,

	Starts	1st	2nd	3rd	Win & Pl
NH Flat	1	0	0	0	0
Hurdles	1	0	0	0	0
Career Total	2	0	0	0	0

Going: Sf: 0-0 GS: 0-1 Gd: 0-1 GF: - Fm: 0-0
Distance: 2m/2m3: 0-2 2m4-2m7: 0-0 3m+: 0-0
Track: LH: 0-0 RH: 0-2 Tight: 0-0 Gall: 0-1
Aids: Bl: 0-0 Vi: 0-0 Tstrap: 0-0
Best Rating: 93 2/03 Winc 2m gd-sft NHF

Foxhall Lady

75   **37**

6-y-o gr m Lyphento (USA)-Carmel (Malaspina)
J C Tuck Robert House

Placings:000   (4222)
2002/03: 17⁰G, 19⁰GS, 17⁰GF,

	Starts	1st	2nd	3rd	Win & Pl
NH Flat	1	0	0	0	0
Hurdles	2	0	0	0	0
Career Total	3	0	0	0	0

Going: Sf: 0-0 GS: 0-1 Gd: 0-1 GF: - Fm: 0-1
Distance: 2m/2m3: 0-3 2m4-2m7: 0-0 3m+: 0-0
Track: LH: 0-0 RH: 0-3 Tight: 0-0 Gall: 0-0
Aids: Bl: 0-0 Vi: 0-0 Tstrap: 0-0
Best Rating: 37 2/03 Extr 2m3f gd-sft Hdl

Foxies Lad

101(78h)   **71**

12-y-o b g Then Again-Arctic Sands (Riboboy (USA))
C J Gray P Popham, F D Popham, T Bartlett

Placings:4/34002323/4P/22230/3510P6/05U06U   (4735)
2002/03: 19⁰S, 20⁵S, 22ᵁS, 24⁰S, 21⁶GF, 19ᵁGF,

	Starts	1st	2nd	3rd	Win & Pl
Hurdles	1	0	0	0	0

Chases	5	0	0	0	0
Career Total	28	1	5	5	13369
100 2/01 Winc 2m	C Ch		GD £6077		

Total win prize-money £6078

Going: Sf: 0-4 GS: 0-0 Gd: 0-0 GF: - Fm: 0-2
Distance: 2m/2m3: 0-0 2m4-2m7: 0-5 3m+: 0-1
Track: LH: 0-3 RH: 0-2 Tight: 0-4 Gall: 0-0
Aids: Bl: 0-1 Vi: 0-0 Tstrap: 0-0
Best Rating: 110 3/97 Newb 2m5f good Hdl

Won Class C 2m novice chase at Wincanton February 2001; has often been let down by his jumping since.

Foxmeade Dancer

69   **45**

5-y-o b g Lyphento (USA)-Georgian Quickstep (Dubassoff (USA))
P C Ritchens Mrs A E Morton

Placings:0PP6F   (2061)
2002/03: 16⁰GF, 19⁰S, 16⁶GF, 19⁶G, 17⁶S,

	Starts	1st	2nd	3rd	Win & Pl
NH Flat	1	0	0	0	0
Hurdles	4	0	0	0	0
Career Total	5	0	0	0	0

Going: Sf: 0-2 GS: 0-0 Gd: 0-1 GF: - Fm: 0-2
Distance: 2m/2m3: 0-3 2m4-2m7: 0-1 3m+: 0-0
Track: LH: 0-3 RH: 0-2 Tight: 0-2 Gall: 0-0
Aids: Bl: 0-0 Vi: 0-0 Tstrap: 0-0
Best Rating: 71 5/02 Chep 2m110y gd-fm NHF

Foxs Shadow

8-y-o gr m Neltino-Change Of Fortune (Broadsword (USA))
John A Harris R H Fox

Placings:PP0   (3095)
2002/03: 16⁶S, 20ᴾHY, 16⁰GS,

	Starts	1st	2nd	3rd	Win & Pl
Hurdles	3	0	0	0	0
Career Total	3	0	0	0	0

Going: Sf: 0-2 GS: 0-1 Gd: 0-0 GF: - Fm: 0-0
Distance: 2m/2m3: 0-2 2m4-2m7: 0-1 3m+: 0-0
Track: LH: 0-1 RH: 0-2 Tight: 0-0 Gall: 0-1
Aids: Bl: 0-0 Vi: 0-0 Tstrap: 0-0
Best Rating: 0 1/03 Donc 2m110y gd-sft Hdl

Foxy Lad

78   **45**

7-y-o ch g Bob s Return (IRE)-Shy Hiker (Netherkelly)
Graeme Roe M J Lilley

Placings:0/500-PP00   (2438)
2002/03: 16⁶G, 22ᴾGS, 20⁰G, 21⁰GS,

	Starts	1st	2nd	3rd	Win & Pl
Hurdles	4	0	0	0	
Career Total	8	0	0	0	0

Going: Sf: 0-0 GS: 0-2 Gd: 0-2 GF: - Fm: 0-0
Distance: 2m/2m3: 0-1 2m4-2m7: 0-3 3m+: 0-0
Track: LH: 0-1 RH: 0-2 Tight: 0-2 Gall: 0-1
Aids: Bl: 0-0 Vi: 0-0 Tstrap: 0-0
Best Rating: 67 8/01 Worc 2m gd-fm NHF

Fraamtastic

90   **56**

6-y-o b m Fraam-Fading (Pharly (FR))
B A Pearce Richard J Gray

Placings:RPPP/506   (3554)
2002/03: 17⁵HY, 16⁶HY, 16⁶HY,

	Starts	1st	2nd	3rd	Win & Pl
Hurdles	3	0	0	0	0
Career Total	7	0	0	0	0

Going: Sf: 0-3 GS: 0-0 Gd: 0-0 GF: - Fm: 0-0
Distance: 2m/2m3: 0-3 2m4-2m7: 0-0 3m+: 0-0
Track: LH: 0-1 RH: 0-2 Tight: 0-2 Gall: 0-0
Aids: Bl: 0-0 Vi: 0-0 Tstrap: 0-0
Best Rating: 56 12/02 Folk 2m1f110y heavy Hdl

Fragrant Rose

103   **110**

7-y-o b m Alflora (IRE)-Levantine Rose (Levanter)
Miss H C Knight David Jenks

Placings:1316-113621   (4708)
2002/03: 17¹G, 19¹GS, 19³S, 21⁶G, 19²GF, 20¹G,

	Starts	1st	2nd	3rd	Win & Pl
Hurdles	6	3	1	1	15931
Career Total	10	5	1	2	20059
108 4/03 Uttx	2m4f110yE Hdl		GD £3535		
109 11/02 Tntn	2m3f110yC Hdl		G-S £6110		
97 11/02 Hrfd	2m1f E Hdl		GD £3445		
116 1/02 Tntn	2m1f H NHF		SFT £2114		
110 11/01 Hrfd	2m1f H NHF		GD £1631		

Total win prize-money £16835

Going: Sf: 0-1 GS: 1-1 Gd: 2-3 GF: - Fm: 0-1
Distance: 2m/2m3: 1-2 **2m4-2m7: 2-4** 3m+: 0-0
Track: LH: 1-2 **RH: 2-4** Tight: 1-1 Gall: 0-1
Aids: Bl: 0-0 Vi: 0-0 Tstrap: 0-0
Best Rating: 116 1/02 Tntn 2m1f soft NHF

Fair novice hurdler; stays two miles three; acts on good and soft ground.

Frances Bertha

72f   **49f**

6-y-o ch m Dervish-Glenside Charley (Chas Sawyer)
Mrs H Dalton Lowcross Racing Club

Placings:00   (1250)
2002/03: 16⁶GF, 16⁰G,

	Starts	1st	2nd	3rd	Win & Pl
NH Flat	2	0	0	0	0
Career Total	2	0	0	0	

Going: Sf: 0-0 GS: 0-0 Gd: 0-0 GF: - Fm: 0-1
Distance: 2m/2m3: 0-2 2m4-2m7: 0-0 3m+: 0-0
Track: LH: 0-2 RH: 0-0 Tight: 0-0 Gall: 0-0
Aids: Bl: 0-0 Vi: 0-0 Tstrap: 0-0
Best Rating: 58 8/02 Worc 2m gd-fm NHF

Francines-Boy (IRE)

101   **111**

7-y-o b g Namaqualand (USA)-Nancy Drew (Sexton Blake)
C Roche Miss K McGann

Placings:121321/41630/324-420   (3724a)
2002/03: 20⁴G, 21²HY, 18⁶S,

	Starts	1st	2nd	3rd	Win & Pl
Chases	3	0	1	0	2886

Career Total	17	4	4	3		29542
102	1/01	Tram	2m4f	Ch	HVY	£5564
120	2/00	Navn	2m	Hdl	SH	£4416
117	11/99	Punc	2m	Hdl	YLD	£3388
95	8/99	Tram	2m	Hdl	G-F	£3080
				Total win prize-money £16449		

Going: Sf: 0-2 GS: 0-0 Gd: 0-1 GF: - Fm: 0-0
Distance: 2m/2m3: 0-1 2m4-2m7: 0-2 3m+: 0-0
Track: LH: 0-2 RH: 0-0 Tight: 0-1 Gall: 0-0
Aids: Bl: 0-0 Vi: 0-0 Tstrap: 0-0
Best Rating: 125 12/99 Leop 2m   sft-hvy Hdl

Switched to fences at an early stage, he strung together some respectable efforts and should develop into a fair staying handicapper this term.

Francolino (FR)
89(94h)   (10h)70
10-y-o b g Useful (FR)-Quintefeuille Ii (FR) (Kashtan (FR))
N A Gaselee Barry Marsden

Placings:4321350/45314/2P442/2541512/41PP04P/P040-0P53   (4633)
2002/03: 22³GS, 22⁸S, 20⁵GF, 20³GF,

	Starts	1st	2nd	3rd	Win & Pl
Hurdles	2	0	0	0	0
Chases	2	0	0	1	480
Career Total	39	5	5	4	60311
130	10/00	Plum	2m4f	D(0-125)HCh	SFT	£4480
	4/00	Pmnl	2m3f	Ch	SFT	£2882
	2/00	Pau	2m3f	Ch	SFT	£3842
	11/97	Ange	2m5f	Ch	VS	£9540
	1/97	Pau	2m2f110y	Ch	VS	£5612
				Total win prize-money £26356		

Going: Sf: 0-1 GS: 0-1 Gd: 0-0 GF: - Fm: 0-2
Distance: 2m/2m3: 0-0 2m4-2m7: 0-4 3m+: 0-0
Track: LH: 0-3 RH: 0-1 Tight: 0-3 Gall: 0-0
Aids: Bl: 0-0 Vi: 0-0 Tstrap: 0-0
Best Rating: 130 10/00 Plum 2m4f   soft Ch

Moderate hurdler/chaser; poor form since returning to the course after more than a year off; has worn cheekpieces and blinkers; does not appear to stay 3m.

Francoskid (IRE)
108   102
11-y-o ch g Kambalda-Serocco Wind (Roi Guillaume (FR))
Liam Lennon (T J Kidd 6/7) Liam Lennon

Placings:O144/00/63355230342025321/145/005B/5000-3015166   (4383a)
2002/03: 20³G, 20⁰S, 20¹S, 24⁵S, 24¹G, 28⁶S, 24⁶G,

	Starts	1st	2nd	3rd	Win & Pl
Chases	7	2	0	1	9718
Career Total	41	5	4	6	24186
102	2/03	Muss	3m	F(0-95)HCh	GD	£4163
94	12/02	DRoy	2m4f	(0-95)HCh	SFT	£4868
103	5/99	Gowr	2m4f	(0-102)HCh	GD	£3069
100	4/99	Gowr	2m6f	(0-102)HCh	SFT	£3683
96	7/96	Naas	2m	NHF	GD	£2824
				Total win prize-money £18608		

Going: Sf: 1-4 GS: 0-0 Gd: 1-3 GF: - Fm: 0-0
Distance: 2m/2m3: 0-2 2m4-2m7: 1-3 3m+: 1-4
Track: LH: 0-0 RH: 1-3 Tight: 1-1 Gall: 0-0
Aids: Bl: 0-0 Vi: 0-0 Tstrap: 0-0
Best Rating: 103 5/99 Gowr 2m4f   good Ch

Moderate chaser; trained in Northern Ireland; stays three miles and best on good ground; not very big and possibly not up to carrying very big weights.

Frankie Anson
89(103h)   (90h)56
6-y-o b g Anshan-Smilingatstrangers (Macmillion)
M D Hammond (M W Easterby 18/1) Frank Hanson

Placings:50-41040041   (4710)
2002/03: 16⁴GF, 17¹GF, 16⁶GS, 19⁴S, 16⁵S, 16⁰G, 16⁴G, 23¹GF,

	Starts	1st	2nd	3rd	Win & Pl
NH Flat	2	1	0	0	2030
Hurdles	6	1	0	0	2689
Career Total	10	2	0	0	4719
90	4/03	Weth	2m7f	G(0-90)HHdl	G-F	£2422
102	10/02	MRas	2m1f110y		H NHF	G-F	£2030
				Total win prize-money £4452		

Going: Sf: 0-2 GS: 0-1 Gd: 0-2 GF: - Fm: 2-3
Distance: 2m/2m3: 1-6 2m4-2m7: 1-2 3m+: 0-0
Track: LH: 1-6 RH: 1-2 Tight: 1-3 Gall: 0-1
Aids: Bl: 0-0 Vi: 0-0 Tstrap: 0-0
Best Rating: 102 10/02 MRas 2m1f110y gd-fm NHF

Moderate hurdler; made all to win a modest bumper at Market Rasen in October 2002; broke the course record when stepped up in trip to win over two miles seven at Wetherby in April 2003; suited by a sound surface; fatally injured on chase debut in July. (DEAD)

Frankie's River
101   92
6-y-o b g Over The River (FR)-Up The Junction (IRE) (Treasure Kay)
R H Alner Paul Murphy & Frank Watson

Placings:462-24   (0488)
2002/03: 20²GF, 24⁴HY,

	Starts	1st	2nd	3rd	Win & Pl
Hurdles	2	0	1	0	1126
Career Total	5	0	2	0	2269

Going: Sf: 0-1 GS: 0-0 Gd: 0-0 GF: - Fm: 0-1
Distance: 2m/2m3: 0-0 2m4-2m7: 0-1 3m+: 0-1
Track: LH: 0-2 RH: 0-0 Tight: 0-0 Gall: 0-0
Aids: Bl: 0-0 Vi: 0-0 Tstrap: 0-0
Best Rating: 107 12/01 Wwck 2m   soft NHF

Appeared on the upgrade when well beaten second to odds-on favourite under tender handling at Uttoxeter in April. Fair effort next time, stays two and a half miles.

Frankincense (IRE)
103   92
7-y-o gr g Paris House-Mistral Wood (USA) (Far North (CAN))
A J Lockwood Chester Bosomworth

Placings:6230-05616PP   (4795)
2002/03: 16⁰GS, 17⁵GS, 21⁵S, 21¹HY, 25⁶G, 21⁶P, 21⁶GF,

	Starts	1st	2nd	3rd	Win & Pl
Hurdles	7	1	0	0	2373
Career Total	11	1	1	1	3670
92	1/03	Sedg	2m5f110yG(0-90)HHdl		HVY	£2373
				Total win prize-money £2373		

Going: Sf: 1-2 GS: 0-2 Gd: 0-2 GF: - Fm: 0-1
Distance: 2m/2m3: 0-2 2m4-2m7: 1-4 3m+: 0-1
Track: LH: 1-6 RH: 0-1 Tight: 1-6 Gall: 0-0
Aids: Bl: 0-0 Vi: 0-0 Tstrap: 0-0
Best Rating: 92 1/03 Sedg 2m5f110y heavy Hdl

Plating-class hurdler; winner on the Flat in Germany, he showed improved form to take a bad ground selling hurdle at Sedgefield in January 2003.

Franklin-D
7-y-o ch g Democratic (USA)-English Mint (Jalmood (USA))
J R Jenkins Mrs Stella Peirce

Placings:P   (0690)
2002/03: 16⁸PGS,

	Starts	1st	2nd	3rd	Win & Pl
Hurdles	1	0	0	0	
Career Total	1	0	0	0	

Going: Sf: 0-0 GS: 0-1 Gd: 0-0 GF: - Fm: 0-0
Distance: 2m/2m3: 0-1 2m4-2m7: 0-0 3m+: 0-0
Track: LH: 0-1 RH: 0-0 Tight: 0-0 Gall: 0-0
Aids: Bl: 0-0 Vi: 0-0 Tstrap: 0-0
Best Rating: 0   7/02 Wolv 2m   gd-sft Hdl

Frantic Tan (IRE)
114
11-y-o ch g Zaffaran (USA)-Brownskin (Buckskin (FR))
D J Caro The Bunkers Hill Mob

Placings:613/4/012/U211U6/6PUUP-46PPF   (4087)
2002/03: 24⁴G, 29⁶HY, 26⁶HY, 30⁶G, 24⁴GS,

	Starts	1st	2nd	3rd	Win & Pl
Chases	5	0	0	0	1973
Career Total	23	4	2	1	89636
157	2/01	Hayd	3m4f110yA HCh		SFT	£58000
147	2/00	Newb	3m	C Ch	SFT	£6972
116	2/00	Hayd	2m6f	D Hdl	SFT	£3412
131	2/98	Newb	2m110y	H NHF	GD	£6937
				Total win prize-money £75323		

Going: Sf: 0-2 GS: 0-1 Gd: 0-2 GF: - Fm: 0-0
Distance: 2m/2m3: 0-0 2m4-2m7: 0-0 3m+: 0-5
Track: LH: 0-5 RH: 0-0 Tight: 0-2 Gall: 0-1
Aids: Bl: 0-1 Vi: 0-0 Tstrap: 0-0
Best Rating: 157 2/01 Hayd 3m4f110y soft Ch

One-time very useful staying chaser but is now looking a light of former days.

Fraternize
94   80d
5-y-o ch g Spectrum (IRE)-Proud Titania (IRE) (Fairy King (USA))
M C Pipe (S Dow 23/8) A J Lomas

Placings:40545RRP   (4094)
2002/03: 16⁴GS, 17⁹G, 19⁵GS, 16⁴HY, 16⁵S, 16⁶HY, 17⁷RGS, 17⁶HY,

	Starts	1st	2nd	3rd	Win & Pl
Hurdles	8	0	0	0	0
Career Total	8	0	0	0	0

Going: Sf: 0-4 GS: 0-3 Gd: 0-1 GF: - Fm: 0-0
Distance: 2m/2m3: 0-7 2m4-2m7: 0-1 3m+: 0-0
Track: LH: 0-1 RH: 0-7 Tight: 0-2 Gall: 0-0
Aids: Bl: 0-0 Vi: 0-7 Tstrap: 0-0
Best Rating: 80 1/03 Ludl 2m   soft Hdl

Frazer Island (IRE)
102
14-y-o br g Phardante (FR)-Avransha (Random Shot)
M A Allen Mr & Mrs Sherwood

Placings:50⁵F0/22122U1/1U4F0344/P4420BF/2253/4-PP   (2312)

2002/03: 24PGS, 26PHY,

	Starts	1st	2nd	3rd	Win & Pl
Chases	2	0	0	0	
Career Total	34	3	7	2	31975
131 10/97 Chep	2m3f110yC(0-130)HCh			GD	£4393
132 4/97 Plum	3m1f110yE Ch			G-F	£3176
132 2/97 Hntg	2m4f110yE Ch			G-S	£3023
			Total win prize-money		£10593

Going: Sf: 0-1 GS: 0-1 Gd: 0-0 GF: - Fm: 0-0
Distance: 2m/2m3: 0-0 2m4-2m7: 0-0 3m+: 0-2
Track: LH: 0-1 RH: 0-1 Tight: 0-1 Gall: 0-1
Aids: Bl: 0-0 Vi: 0-0 Tstrap: 0-0
Best Rating: 135 3/97 Asct 2m3f110y good Ch

Frazer's Lad
102   84
6-y-o b g Whittingham (IRE)-Loch Tain (Lochnager)
M E Sowersby A Milner

Placings:P000P-P2151643   (4782)
2002/03: 21PGF, 16²G, 16¹G, 16⁵G, 17⁹GF, 17⁶GF, 16⁴GF, 17³G,

	Starts	1st	2nd	3rd	Win & Pl
Hurdles	8	2	1	1	4771
Career Total	13	2	1	1	4771
84 6/02 MRas	2m1f110yG(0-90)HHdl			G-F	£1750
82 6/02 Hexm	2m110y F(0-95)HHdl			GD	£1970
			Total win prize-money		£3721

Going: Sf: 0-0 GS: 0-0 Gd: 1-4 GF: - Fm: 1-4
Distance: 2m/2m3: 2-7 2m4-2m7: 0-1 3m+: 0-0
Track: LH: 1-6 RH: 1-2 Tight: 1-4 Gall: 0-0
Aids: Bl: 2-4 Vi: 0-4 Tstrap: 0-0
Best Rating: 84 6/02 MRas 2m1f110y gd-fm Hdl

Plating-class hurdler, in good heart in the summer of 2002; usually wears blinkers or a visor.

Fred's In The Know
106(105h)   114+
8-y-o ch g Interrex (CAN)-Lady Vynz (Whitstead)
N Waggott N Waggott

Placings:52/23212300/54222P-2421U1   (4138)
2002/03: 20²S, 20⁴G, 16²G, 16¹G, 20⁴S, 16¹S,

	Starts	1st	2nd	3rd	Win & Pl
Hurdles	2	0	1	0	3208
Chases	4	2	1	0	9657
Career Total	22	3	9	2	25431
114 3/03 Hexm	2m110y E Ch			SFT	£3861
110 2/03 Weth	2m E Ch			GD	£4111
131 12/00 Leic	2m4f110yD Hdl			HVY	£3848
			Total win prize-money		£11820

Going: Sf: 1-3 GS: 0-0 Gd: 1-3 GF: - Fm: 0-0
Distance: 2m/2m3: 2-3 2m4-2m7: 0-3 3m+: 0-0
Track: LH: 2-5 RH: 0-1 Tight: 0-2 Gall: 0-0
Aids: Bl: 0-0 Vi: 0-0 Tstrap: 0-0
Best Rating: 131 1/01 Newc 2m4f soft Hdl

Fair handicap hurdler; excellent second on debut over fences at Catterick in February and off the mark at Wetherby two weeks later; simple task when following up at Hexham in March; better suited by two and a half miles.

Freddie Taylor
42
6-y-o b g Sula Bula-Clowater Lady (IRE) (Orchestra)
J C McConnochie J C McConnochie

Placings:40F0/0P-PP   (0510)
2002/03: 17PG, 20PG,

	Starts	1st	2nd	3rd	Win & Pl
Hurdles	2	0	0	0	
Career Total	8	0	0	0	0

Going: Sf: 0-0 GS: 0-0 Gd: 0-2 GF: - Fm: 0-0
Distance: 2m/2m3: 0-1 2m4-2m7: 0-1 3m+: 0-0
Track: LH: 0-1 RH: 0-1 Tight: 0-1 Gall: 0-0
Aids: Bl: 0-0 Vi: 0-0 Tstrap: 0-0
Best Rating: 84 2/01 Winc 2m good NHF

Freddie's Comet (IRE)
100   92
7-y-o b g Freddie s Star-Baltimore Bay (Bishop Of Orange)
John R Upson Middleham Park Racing Vii

Placings:U0/PP433-160P   (1197)
2002/03: 16³GS, 17¹GF, 17⁶GF, 17⁹GF, 19PGF,

	Starts	1st	2nd	3rd	Win & Pl
Hurdles	5	1	0	1	2479
Career Total	11	1	0	2	3101
88 6/02 MRas	2m1f110y F(0-100)HHdl			G-F	£2029
			Total win prize-money		£2029

Going: Sf: 0-0 GS: 0-1 Gd: 0-0 GF: - Fm: 1-4
Distance: 2m/2m3: 1-4 2m4-2m7: 0-1 3m+: 0-0
Track: LH: 0-0 RH: 1-5 Tight: 1-3 Gall: 0-0
Aids: Bl: 0-0 Vi: 0-0 Tstrap: 0-0
Best Rating: 97 11/00 Ludl 2m good NHF

Modest hurdler, stays two and a half miles, not an easy ride.

Freddy Flintstone
96(95h)   (85h)90
6-y-o b g Bigstone (IRE)-Daring Ditty (Daring March)
D W P Arbuthnot Lady Whent

Placings:62-0   (2446)
2002/03: 16⁹G,

	Starts	1st	2nd	3rd	Win & Pl
Chases	1	0	0	0	
Career Total	3	0	1	0	790

Going: Sf: 0-0 GS: 0-0 Gd: 0-1 GF: - Fm: 0-0
Distance: 2m/2m3: 0-0 2m4-2m7: 0-0 3m+: 0-0
Track: LH: 0-0 RH: 0-1 Tight: 0-1 Gall: 0-0
Aids: Bl: 0-0 Vi: 0-0 Tstrap: 0-0
Best Rating: 90 12/02 Ludl 2m good Ch

Fair effort on second appearance over hurdles at Exeter in October. Handles fast ground.

Frederic Forever (IRE)
104   119
5-y-o b g Exit To Nowhere (USA)-Sarooh s Love (USA) (Nureyev (USA))
P J Hobbs Mrs D A Winton

Placings:11215225-22   (1395)
2002/03: 16²GF, 16²GF,

	Starts	1st	2nd	3rd	Win & Pl
Hurdles	2	0	2	0	4544
Career Total	13	3	5	0	17773
107 10/01 Chep	2m110y D Hdl			GD	£3464
108 9/01 NAbb	2m1f E Hdl			G-F	£2863
96 8/01 Font	2m2f110yE Hdl			G-F	£2324
			Total win prize-money		£8652

Going: Sf: 0-0 GS: 0-0 Gd: 0-0 GF: - Fm: 0-2
Distance: 2m/2m3: 0-2 2m4-2m7: 0-0 3m+: 0-0
Track: LH: 0-2 RH: 0-0 Tight: 0-1 Gall: 0-0
Aids: Bl: 0-0 Vi: 0-0 Tstrap: 0-0
Best Rating: 119 10/02 Chep 2m110y gd-fm Hdl

Useful juvenile hurdler in the autumn of 2001, he made a decent return to action in September 2002. Suited by good ground or faster.

Free Gift
71f   45f
5-y-o b g Presenting-Gladtogetit (Green Shoon)
R H Alner T Chadney, D Guyer, V Howard, P Tozer

Placings:00   (4329)
2002/03: 16⁹S, 16⁹G,

	Starts	1st	2nd	3rd	Win & Pl
NH Flat	2	0	0	0	
Career Total	2	0	0	0	

Going: Sf: 0-1 GS: 0-0 Gd: 0-1 GF: - Fm: 0-0
Distance: 2m/2m3: 0-2 2m4-2m7: 0-0 3m+: 0-0
Track: LH: 0-2 RH: 0-0 Tight: 0-0 Gall: 0-2
Aids: Bl: 0-0 Vi: 0-0 Tstrap: 0-0
Best Rating: 38 3/03 Newb 2m110y soft NHF

Free Return (IRE)
95(103h)   (111 h)102
8-y-o ch g Magical Wonder (USA)-Free Reserve (USA) (Tom Rolfe)
Noel T Chance Mrs Jill Cox

Placings:2133/050-331515335   (4295)
2002/03: 19³GS, 20³GF, 22¹G, 25⁵G, 17¹G, 16⁵S, 19³G, 20³GS, 21⁵GF,

	Starts	1st	2nd	3rd	Win & Pl
Hurdles	5	2	0	2	8328
Chases	4	0	0	2	1492
Career Total	16	3	1	6	12367
111 12/02 Hrfd	2m1f E(0-105)HHdl			GD	£2940
105 10/02 Font	2m6f110yD(0-120)HHdl			GD	£4309
95 8/00 NAbb	2m1f H NHF			GD	£1491
			Total win prize-money		£8741

Going: Sf: 0-1 GS: 0-1 Gd: 2-4 GF: - Fm: 0-3
Distance: 2m/2m3: 1-3 2m4-2m7: 1-5 3m+: 0-1
Track: LH: 1-2 RH: 1-6 Tight: 1-2 Gall: 0-1
Aids: Bl: 0-0 Vi: 0-0 Tstrap: 0-0
Best Rating: 111 12/02 Hrfd 2m1f good Hdl

Modest novice chaser; successful at trips between two miles one and two miles six over hurdles; best effort over fences when third at Hereford in February but disappointing since.

Free To Run (IRE)
107   (43h)106
9-y-o b g Satco (FR)-Lady Oats (Oats)
Mrs S J Smith Mrs S Smith

Placings:00040/100/40030044F/0045344-4121323134123   (2762)
2002/03: 25⁴G, 21¹HY, 20²G, 25¹GF, 22³G, 27²GF, 21³G, 26¹G, 24³GS, 24⁴GF, 22¹S, 24²S, 24³S,

	Starts	1st	2nd	3rd	Win & Pl
Chases	13	4	3	4	22977
Career Total	37	5	3	6	27523
106 11/02 Hayd	2m6f E(0-105)HCh			SFT	£3614
107 8/02 Ctml	3m2f E Ch			GD	£4192
103 6/02 Hexm	3m1f E(0-105)HCh			G-F	£3133

107 6/02 Ctml 2m5f110yE Ch HVY £3374
80 5/99 Dpat 2m1f172y NHF GD £1994
Total win prize-money £16309

Going: Sf: 2-4 GS: 0-1 Gd: 1-5 GF: - Fm: 1-3
Distance: 2m/2m3: 0-0 2m4-2m7: 2-5 3m+: 2-8
Track: LH: 4-12 RH: 0-1 Tight: 2-6 Gall: 0-2
Aids: Bl: 0-0 Vi: 0-0 Tstrap: 0-0
Best Rating: 107 12/02 Newc 3m soft Ch

Modest ex-Irish chaser; best at around 3m; jumps well and has won three times for amateur Sam Beddoes.

Free Will

(92h) (92h)
6-y-o ch g Indian Ridge-Free Guest (Be My Guest (USA))
A Scott A & J Scott Ltd

Placings:20P-5P (0952)
2002/03: 16^5G, 16^6PG,

	Starts	1st	2nd	3rd	Win & Pl
Hurdles	1	0	0	0	0
Chases	1	0	0	0	0
Career Total	5	0	1	0	697

Going: Sf: 0-0 GS: 0-0 Gd: 0-2 GF: - Fm: 0-0
Distance: 2m/2m3: 0-2 2m4-2m7: 0-0 3m+: 0-0
Track: LH: 0-2 RH: 0-0 Tight: 0-2 Gall: 0-0
Aids: Bl: 0-0 Vi: 0-0 Tstrap: 0-0
Best Rating: 92 10/01 Kels 2m110y gd-sft Hdl

Freecom Net (IRE)
71 38
5-y-o b g Zieten (USA)-Radiance (IRE) (Thatching)
A Crook (A P Jarvis 21/9) The Black Swan (Middleham) Racing Club

Placings:00P (4433)
2002/03: 16^6G, 16^6S, 16^6PG

	Starts	1st	2nd	3rd	Win & Pl
Hurdles	3	0	0	0	0
Career Total	3	0	0	0	0

Going: Sf: 0-1 GS: 0-1 Gd: 0-1 GF: - Fm: 0-0
Distance: 2m/2m3: 0-3 2m4-2m7: 0-0 3m+: 0-0
Track: LH: 0-3 RH: 0-0 Tight: 0-1 Gall: 0-2
Aids: Bl: 0-0 Vi: 0-0 Tstrap: 0-0
Best Rating: 38 3/03 Catt 2m soft Hdl

Freedom Fighter

12-y-o b g Fearless Action (USA)-Zuleika Hill (Yellow River)
Mrs Rosemary Gasson Mrs Rosemary Gasson

Placings:1PF2P/P303P/52PP43C-PPP (3952)
2002/03: 26^6GF, 24^5PGF, 23^8GS

	Starts	1st	2nd	3rd	Win & Pl
Chases	3	0	0	0	
Career Total	20	1	2	3	5792

90 5/99 Strf 3m H Ch G-S £3184
Total win prize-money £3184

Going: Sf: 0-0 GS: 0-1 Gd: 0-0 GF: - Fm: 0-2
Distance: 2m/2m3: 0-0 2m4-2m7: 0-0 3m+: 0-3
Track: LH: 0-1 RH: 0-2 Tight: 0-0 Gall: 0-2
Aids: Bl: 0-0 Vi: 0-0 Tstrap: 0-0
Best Rating: 97 5/00 Strf 3m gd-fm Ch

Winning pointer, prefers a sound surface.

Freedom Quest (IRE)

8-y-o b g Polish Patriot (USA)-Recherchee (Rainbow Quest (USA))
Mrs P Robeson T E Short

Placings:0/P (1890)
2002/03: 16^5PGS,

	Starts	1st	2nd	3rd	Win & Pl
Hurdles	1	0	0	0	
Career Total	2	0	0	0	

Going: Sf: 0-0 GS: 0-1 Gd: 0-0 GF: - Fm: 0-0
Distance: 2m/2m3: 0-1 2m4-2m7: 0-0 3m+: 0-0
Track: LH: 0-0 RH: 0-1 Tight: 0-0 Gall: 0-1
Aids: Bl: 0-0 Vi: 0-0 Tstrap: 0-0
Best Rating: 82 2/01 Ludl 2m gd-sft Hdl

Freeline Fantasy (IRE)
102 95
6-y-o ch g Shernazar-Lollia Paulina (IRE) (Phardante (FR))
P R Webber Irving Struel & Geoffrey Thomas

Placings:3-44 (2713)
2002/03: 20^4S, 20^4HY,

	Starts	1st	2nd	3rd	Win & Pl
Hurdles	2	0	0	0	311
Career Total	3	0	0	1	558

Going: Sf: 0-2 GS: 0-0 Gd: 0-0 GF: - Fm: 0-0
Distance: 2m/2m3: 0-0 2m4-2m7: 0-2 3m+: 0-0
Track: LH: 0-2 RH: 0-0 Tight: 0-0 Gall: 0-0
Aids: Bl: 0-0 Vi: 0-0 Tstrap: 0-0
Best Rating: 101 4/02 Towc 2m good NHF

Out of a mare who placed in a fast-ground bumper, ran a promising race on his racecourse bow in a Towcester bumper April 2002. Showed up well in novice hurdles at Chepstow in December on testing ground.

Freetown (IRE)
90 (101c) (120c) 154
7-y-o b g Shirley Heights-Pageantry (Welsh Pageant)
L Lungo Miss S Blumberg & R Nairn

Placings:32/111123/34113-0 (0070)
2002/03: 23^0G,

	Starts	1st	2nd	3rd	Win & Pl
Hurdles	1	0	0	0	
Career Total	14	6	2	4	64843

154 3/02 Chel 3m1f110yA HHdl G-S £32500
113 2/02 Ayr 2m4f C Ch HVY £8807
136 12/00 Weth 2m7f D Hdl SFT £3250
114 11/00 Carl 3m110y E Hdl HVY £2396
121 10/00 Carl 3m110y E Hdl SFT £2475
120 6/00 Prth 3m110y E Hdl SFT £2933
Total win prize-money £52363

Going: Sf: 0-0 GS: 0-0 Gd: 0-1 GF: - Fm: 0-0
Distance: 2m/2m3: 0-0 2m4-2m7: 0-0 3m+: 0-1
Track: LH: 0-1 RH: 0-0 Tight: 0-0 Gall: 0-0
Aids: Bl: 0-0 Vi: 0-0 Tstrap: 0-0
Best Rating: 154 4/02 Aint 3m110y good Hdl

His big pay day came when successful in the Pertemps Final at the Cheltenham Festival in March 2002. As effective over hurdles as fences, he stays beyond three miles and acts well with cut in the ground.

French Connection
102 (106h) (79h) 64
8-y-o b g Tirol-Heaven-Liegh-Grey (Grey Desire)
B D Leavy S H Riley

Placings:4/5410631/50000005-4004P24604P20 (3161)
2002/03: 16^4GS, 17^0HY, 16^9GF, 17^4S, 21^0GF, 17^2G, 17^4G, 16^6G, 16^9G, 16^4G, 16^6G, 17^2GS, 16^9G,

	Starts	1st	2nd	3rd	Win & Pl
Hurdles	3	0	1	0	693
Chases	10	0	1	0	2391
Career Total	30	2	2	1	7022

81 4/01 MRas 2m1f110yG(0-95)HHdl HVY £1820
81 8/00 Uttx 2m G(0-95)HHdl G-F £1904
Total win prize-money £3724

Going: Sf: 0-2 GS: 0-2 Gd: 0-7 GF: - Fm: 0-2
Distance: 2m/2m3: 0-12 2m4-2m7: 0-1 3m+: 0-0
Track: LH: 0-10 RH: 0-3 Tight: 0-7 Gall: 0-0
Aids: Bl: 0-10 Vi: 0-0 Tstrap: 0-6
Best Rating: 81 4/01 MRas 2m1f110y heavy Hdl

Plating-class hurdler/chaser, best at around two miles, acts on any ground.

French Executive (IRE)
105 (102h) (109h) 122
8-y-o br g Beau Sher-Executive Move (IRE) (Executive Perk)
P F Nicholls T Chappell,R Eddy,Mrs Jackson,Mrs Solman

Placings:43/223216332-143P322 (4758)
2002/03: 26^1GS, 29^4S, 24^3HY, 26^8HY, 26^3GF, 26^2GF, 22^8GF,

	Starts	1st	2nd	3rd	Win & Pl
Chases	7	1	2	2	12069
Career Total	18	2	6	6	20678

122 11/02 Plum 3m2f D(0-110)HCh G-S £5443
109 1/02 Tntn 2m3f110yE(0-105)HHdl SFT £2870
Total win prize-money £8314

Going: Sf: 0-3 GS: 1-1 Gd: 0-7 GF: - Fm: 0-3
Distance: 2m/2m3: 0-0 2m4-2m7: 0-0 3m+: 1-6
Track: LH: 1-5 RH: 0-0 Tight: 1-5 Gall: 0-0
Aids: Bl: 0-0 Vi: 0-0 Tstrap: 0-0
Best Rating: 122 3/03 Plum 3m2f gd-fm Ch

Modest chaser; stays well; lacks a turn of foot; acts on fast and soft ground.

French Guest
67 54
4-y-o ch g Most Welcome-Laleston (Junius (USA))
P J Hobbs (M A Jarvis 21/10) Yusof Sepiuddin

Placings:P0R00 (4693)
2002/03: 17^5S, 17^0S, 17^8HY, 17^9G, 17^0G,

	Starts	1st	2nd	3rd	Win & Pl
Hurdles	5	0	0	0	
Career Total	5	0	0	0	

Going: Sf: 0-3 GS: 0-0 Gd: 0-2 GF: - Fm: 0-0
Distance: 2m/2m3: 0-5 2m4-2m7: 0-0 3m+: 0-0
Track: LH: 0-1 RH: 0-4 Tight: 0-3 Gall: 0-0
Aids: Bl: 0-0 Vi: 0-0 Tstrap: 0-0
Best Rating: 54 3/03 Extr 2m1f good Hdl

French Mannequin (IRE)

105   **100**

4-y-o b/br f Key Of Luck (USA)-Paris Model (IRE) (Thatching)
Mrs A J Hamilton-Fairley (R M Beckett 23/9) Runs In The Family

Placings:63110   (4573)
2002/03: 16⁶GS, 16³S, 17¹G, 16¹GF, 16⁹GF,

	Starts	1st	2nd	3rd	Win & Pl
Hurdles	5	2	0	1	7219
Career Total	5	2	0	1	7219
91	3/03	Plum	2m	E Hdl	G-F	£3513
91	3/03	Folk	2m1f110yF Hdl	GD	£3083

Total win prize-money £6597

Going:	Sf: 0-1 GS: 0-1 Gd: 1-1 GF: - Fm: 1-2
Distance:	2m/2m3: 2-5 2m4-2m7: 0-0 3m+: 0-0
Track:	LH: 1-2 RH: 1-3 Tight: 2-3 Gall: 0-0
Aids:	Bl: 0-0 Vi: 0-0 Tstrap: 0-0
Best Rating:	91 4/03 Strf 2m110y gd-fm Hdl

Modest hurdler; front-runner; acts on both fast and soft ground; suited by a sharp track.

French Master (IRE)

78   **59**

6-y-o b g Petardia-Reasonably French (Reasonable (FR))
Miss T M Ide Miss Tracey Ide

Placings:400/00-0PP   (0510)
2002/03: 16⁹G, 22⁹GS, 20⁹G,

	Starts	1st	2nd	3rd	Win & Pl
Hurdles	3	0	0	0	
Career Total	8	0	0	0	268

Going:	Sf: 0-0 GS: 0-1 Gd: 0-2 GF: - Fm: 0-0
Distance:	2m/2m3: 0-1 2m4-2m7: 0-2 3m+: 0-0
Track:	LH: 0-3 RH: 0-0 Tight: 0-2 Gall: 0-0
Aids:	Bl: 0-0 Vi: 0-0 Tstrap: 0-0
Best Rating:	60 5/02 Sthl 2m good Hdl

French Tune (FR)

94   **66**

5-y-o ch g Green Tune (USA)-Guerre De Troie (Risk Me (FR))
Miss S E Hall C Platts

Placings:40   (3965)
2002/03: 20⁴GS, 16⁰S,

	Starts	1st	2nd	3rd	Win & Pl
Hurdles	2	0	0	0	263
Career Total	2	0	0	0	263

Going:	Sf: 0-1 GS: 0-1 Gd: 0-0 GF: - Fm: 0-0
Distance:	2m/2m3: 0-1 2m4-2m7: 0-1 3m+: 0-0
Track:	LH: 0-1 RH: 0-1 Tight: 0-1 Gall: 0-0
Aids:	Bl: 0-0 Vi: 0-0 Tstrap: 0-0
Best Rating:	66 3/03 Catt 2m soft Hdl

Frentzen

102(100h)   (84h)**89+**

6-y-o b g Golden Heights-Milly Black (IRE) (Double Schwartz)
Miss E C Lavelle J Spence

Placings:FP63U2   (4759)
2002/03: 22ᶠG, 24ᴾGS, 26⁶G, 26³GF, 25ᵁGF, 27²GF,

	Starts	1st	2nd	3rd	Win & Pl
Hurdles	6	0	1	1	2645
Career Total	6	0	1	1	2645

Going:	Sf: 0-0 GS: 0-1 Gd: 0-2 GF: - Fm: 0-3
Distance:	2m/2m3: 0-0 2m4-2m7: 0-1 3m+: 0-5
Track:	LH: 0-1 RH: 0-3 Tight: 0-3 Gall: 0-2
Aids:	Bl: 0-0 Vi: 0-0 Tstrap: 0-1
Best Rating:	84 4/03 Font 3m3f gd-fm Hdl

Plating-class maiden hurdler; good second to Maidstone Monument on chasing debut in 3m Worcester handicap July 2003; normal improvement should see him go one better; stays 3m 3f; acts on fast ground.

Freteval (FR)

6-y-o b g Valanjou (FR)-La Beaumont (FR) (Hellios (USA))
Mrs K J Gilmore S N Wilshire

Placings:064FFP/P26-1   (3954)
2002/03: 20¹GS,

	Starts	1st	2nd	3rd	Win & Pl
Chases	1	1	0	0	2171
Career Total	10	1	1	0	6476
106	3/03	Leic	2m4f110y	H Ch	G-S	£2171

Total win prize-money £2171

Going:	Sf: 0-0 GS: 1-1 Gd: 0-0 GF: - Fm: 0-0
Distance:	2m/2m3: 0-0 2m4-2m7: 1-1 3m+: 0-0
Track:	LH: 0-0 RH: 1-1 Tight: 0-0 Gall: 0-0
Aids:	Bl: 0-0 Vi: 0-0 Tstrap: 0-0
Best Rating:	106 3/03 Leic 2m4f110y gd-sft Ch

Freydis (IRE)

97f   **84f**

5-y-o b m Supreme Leader-Lulu Buck (Buckskin (FR))
S Gollings The Highfield House Partnership

Placings:0   (4162)
2002/03: 17⁹G,

	Starts	1st	2nd	3rd	Win & Pl
NH Flat	1	0	0	0	
Career Total	1	0	0	0	

Going:	Sf: 0-0 GS: 0-0 Gd: 0-1 GF: - Fm: 0-0
Distance:	2m/2m3: 0-1 2m4-2m7: 0-0 3m+: 0-0
Track:	LH: 0-0 RH: 0-1 Tight: 0-1 Gall: 0-0
Aids:	Bl: 0-0 Vi: 0-0 Tstrap: 0-0
Best Rating:	84 3/03 MRas 2m1f110y good NHF

Finished midfield on debut in a modest bumper.

Friar Waddon

10-y-o b g Pablond-Looking Swell (Simbir)
K Cumings P J Clarke

Placings:F6P3-3FP   (4443)
2002/03: 21³GF, 22ᶠG, 19⁷G,

	Starts	1st	2nd	3rd	Win & Pl
Chases	3	0	0	1	434
Career Total	7	0	0	2	705

Going:	Sf: 0-0 GS: 0-0 Gd: 0-2 GF: - Fm: 0-1
Distance:	2m/2m3: 0-0 2m4-2m7: 0-0 3m+: 0-3 3m-: 0-0

Track:	LH: 0-2 RH: 0-1 Tight: 0-0 Gall: 0-2
Aids:	Bl: 0-0 Vi: 0-0 Tstrap: 0-0
Best Rating:	101 5/02 Chel 2m5f gd-fm Ch

Fair pointer/hunter; handles any ground.

Friedhelmo (GER)

106(82h)   (95+h)**120d**

7-y-o ch g Dashing Blade-Fox For Gold (Glint Of Gold)
Miss Venetia Williams G H Leatham

Placings:03/1/0-0041UP55   (4342)
2002/03: 16⁹G, 17⁹GS, 16⁴G, 16¹GS, 16ᵁGS, 20⁹GS, 19⁵G, 16⁵GF,

	Starts	1st	2nd	3rd	Win & Pl
Hurdles	2	0	0	0	0
Chases	6	1	0	0	3984
Career Total	12	2	0	1	6757
125	12/02	Sthl	2m	E(0-110)HCh	G-S	£3571
109	5/00	Worc	2m	E Hdl	G-F	£2401

Total win prize-money £5973

Going:	Sf: 0-0 GS: 1-4 Gd: 0-3 GF: - Fm: 0-1
Distance:	2m/2m3: 1-7 2m4-2m7: 0-1 3m+: 0-0
Track:	LH: 1-5 RH: 0-3 Tight: 1-4 Gall: 0-2
Aids:	Bl: 0-0 Vi: 0-0 Tstrap: 1-6
Best Rating:	125 12/02 Sthl 2m gd-sft Ch

Won over hurdles at Worcester in May 2000 but was then off the track nearly two years; smooth winner over fences at Southwell in December jumping well but held when departing three out next time; most disapointing latest start.

Friend's Amigo (IRE)

106   **131**

6-y-o b g Accordion-Lady Sipash (Erin s Hope)
P M J Doyle Absent Friends Syndicate

Placings:1-1616   (4462)
2002/03: 16¹S, 16⁶SH, 16¹HY, 20⁶G,

	Starts	1st	2nd	3rd	Win & Pl
Hurdles	4	2	0	0	12526
Career Total	5	3	0	0	17256
130	3/03	Naas	2m	Hdl	HVY	£6272
131	11/02	Punc	2m	Hdl	SFT	£5503
116	10/01	Naas	2m	NHF	Y-S	£4729

Total win prize-money £16506

Going:	Sf: 2-2 GS: 0-0 Gd: 0-1 GF: - Fm: 0-0
Distance:	2m/2m3: 2-3 2m4-2m7: 0-1 3m+: 0-0
Track:	LH: 1-2 RH: 1-2 Tight: 0-1 Gall: 0-0
Aids:	Bl: 0-0 Vi: 0-0 Tstrap: 0-0
Best Rating:	131 12/02 Fair 2m sft-hvy Hdl

Useful Irish-trained novice hurdler; has only ever raced over two miles; acts well on a soft surface.

Friendly Request

47

4-y-o b/br f Environment Friend-Who Tells Jan (Royal Fountain)
Mrs P Ford W E Donohue

Placings:00   (3138)
2002/03: 16⁶S, 21⁹S,

	Starts	1st	2nd	3rd	Win & Pl
Hurdles	2	0	0	0	
Career Total	2	0	0	0	

Going:	Sf: 0-2 GS: 0-0 Gd: 0-0 GF: - Fm: 0-0

Distance:	2m/2m3: 0-1 2m4-2m7: 0-1 3m+: 0-0
Track:	LH: 0-1 RH: 0-1 Tight: 0-0 Gall: 0-0
Aids:	Bl: 0-0 Vi: 0-0 Tstrap: 0-0
Best Rating:	0 1/03 Ludl 2m5f soft Hdl

Frileux Royal (FR)

(109h)

10-y-o br g Sarpedon (FR)-La Frileuse (FR) (El Toro (FR))
T R George Nelson Morrison Underwriting Agency

Placings:F/12411PU0/443RPP/2R0RR0120P-0   (0147)
2002/03: 24⁰GF,

	Starts	1st	2nd	3rd	Win & Pl
Hurdles	1	0	0	0	
Career Total	26	4	3	1	23621
96	2/02	Ludl	3m2f110yE(0-110)HHdl	G-S	£3688
	12/99	Seic	3m110y Ch	SFT	£6459
	11/99	Agtn	2m6f110y Ch	HVY	£3445
	9/99	Chag	2m6f110y Ch	SFT	£2153

Total win prize-money £15746

Going:	Sf: 0-0 GS: 0-0 Gd: 0-0 GF: - Fm: 0-1
Distance:	2m/2m3: 0-0 2m4-2m7: 0-0 3m+: 0-1
Track:	LH: 0-1 RH: 0-0 Tight: 0-0 Gall: 0-0
Aids:	Bl: 0-0 Vi: 0-0 Tstrap: 0-0
Best Rating:	129 11/00 Chel 3m7f soft Ch

From Little Acorns (IRE)

100   104

7-y-o b g Denel (FR)-Mount Gawn (Harwell)
Ferdy Murphy Mrs A T B Kearney

Placings:00/2005-311   (0399)
2002/03: 21³GF, 20¹G, 20¹GF,

	Starts	1st	2nd	3rd	Win & Pl
Hurdles	3	2	0	1	5008
Career Total	9	2	1	1	6579
104	6/02	Hexm	2m4f110yE(0-110)HHdl	G-F	£2236
104	5/02	Hexm	2m4f110yF Hdl	GD	£2404

Total win prize-money £4642

Going:	Sf: 0-0 GS: 0-0 Gd: 1-1 GF: - Fm: 1-2
Distance:	2m/2m3: 0-0 2m4-2m7: 2-3 3m+: 0-0
Track:	LH: 2-3 RH: 0-0 Tight: 0-1 Gall: 0-0
Aids:	Bl: 0-0 Vi: 0-0 Tstrap: 0-0
Best Rating:	104 6/02 Hexm 2m4f110y gd-fm Hdl

Ex-Irish, has shown ability over hurdles on fast ground and got off the mark under those conditions at Hexham in May 2002.

Frosty Canyon

119(100h)   (144+h)143

10-y-o b g Arctic Lord-Rose Ravine (Deep Run)
P R Webber Mrs P Sherwood

Placings:1210/1564/P041144/122114-4042624   (4791)
2002/03: 25⁴GS, 26⁹GS, 29⁴HY, 24²HY, 28⁶G, 24²G, 29⁴G,

	Starts	1st	2nd	3rd	Win & Pl
Hurdles	2	0	1	0	10300
Chases	5	0	1	0	23900
Career Total	28	8	5	0	96508
149	2/02	Newb	3m	C Ch	SFT	£7150
136	1/02	Newb	2m6f110yD Ch	GD	£5525
136	10/01	Strf	3m	D Ch	G-S	£4127
151	1/01	Wwck	3m1f	B HHdl	SFT	£8632
136	12/00	Kemp	3m110y	C(0-135)HHdl	G-S	£7410
115	11/99	Hayd	2m	D Hdl	GD	£3403
123	2/99	Sand	2m110y	H NHF	G-S	£1588

| 118 | 11/98 | Chep | 2m110y H NHF | G-S | £1660 |

Total win prize-money £39447

Going:	Sf: 0-2 GS: 0-2 Gd: 0-3 GF: - Fm: 0-0
Distance:	2m/2m3: 0-0 2m4-2m7: 0-0 3m+: 0-7
Track:	LH: 0-4 RH: 0-3 Tight: 0-0 Gall: 0-1
Aids:	Bl: 0-0 Vi: 0-5 Tstrap: 0-0
Best Rating:	151 2/01 Sand 2m6f heavy Hdl

Very useful handicap chaser/hurdler; stays three and a half miles; usually wears a visor; acts on good and soft ground; a consistent sort.

Frosty Run (IRE)

83f

5-y-o b g Commanche Run-Here To-Day (King's Equity)
Mrs H Dalton C B Compton

Placings:6   (4090)
2002/03: 16⁶GS,

	Starts	1st	2nd	3rd	Win & Pl
NH Flat	1	0	0	0	0
Career Total	1	0	0	0	0

Going:	Sf: 0-0 GS: 0-1 Gd: 0-0 GF: - Fm: 0-0
Distance:	2m/2m3: 0-1 2m4-2m7: 0-0 3m+: 0-0
Track:	LH: 0-0 RH: 0-0 Tight: 0-0 Gall: 0-0
Aids:	Bl: 0-0 Vi: 0-0 Tstrap: 0-0
Best Rating:	85 3/03 Strf 2m110y gd-sft NHF

Fryup Booster

6-y-o ch g Bollin William-Comedy Imp (Import)
P D Niven John Lees

Placings:PP0   (3262)
2002/03: 17⁵PS, 20⁵GS, 16⁹GS,

	Starts	1st	2nd	3rd	Win & Pl
Hurdles	3	0	0	0	0
Career Total	3	0	0	0	0

Going:	Sf: 0-1 GS: 0-2 Gd: 0-0 GF: - Fm: 0-0
Distance:	2m/2m3: 0-2 2m4-2m7: 0-1 3m+: 0-0
Track:	LH: 0-1 RH: 0-2 Tight: 0-2 Gall: 0-1
Aids:	Bl: 0-0 Vi: 0-0 Tstrap: 0-1
Best Rating:	0 1/03 Donc 2m110y gd-sft Hdl

Fryup Satellite

12-y-o br g Leading Star-Comedy Imp (Import)
Miss Freya Hartley Miss Freya Hartley

Placings:002050556/61033225/322432/005603/2   (0166)
2002/03: 25²GF,

	Starts	1st	2nd	3rd	Win & Pl
Chases	1	0	1	0	442
Career Total	30	1	7	5	9744
84	12/96	Catt	2m3f	F(0-100)HHdl	GD	£2120

Total win prize-money £2120

Going:	Sf: 0-0 GS: 0-0 Gd: 0-0 GF: - Fm: 0-1
Distance:	2m/2m3: 0-0 2m4-2m7: 0-0 3m+: 0-1
Track:	LH: 0-1 RH: 0-0 Tight: 0-0 Gall: 0-0
Aids:	Bl: 0-0 Vi: 0-0 Tstrap: 0-0
Best Rating:	103 11/97 Catt 2m good Ch

Pointer/hunter chaser; one-time fair handicap hurdler; on the downgrade now.

Fuero Real (FR)

90   55

8-y-o b g Highest Honor (FR)-Highest Pleasure (USA) (Foolish Pleasure (USA))
S T Lewis Simon T Lewis

Placings:0P2P/0UP0/0P/006U0P-PPP0PP   (1931)
2002/03: 24⁶G, 23⁶G, 24⁶F, 25⁶GF, 26⁶G, 24⁶GS,

	Starts	1st	2nd	3rd	Win & Pl
Hurdles	5	0	0	0	0
Chases	1	0	0	0	0
Career Total	22	0	1	0	704

Going:	Sf: 0-0 GS: 0-1 Gd: 0-3 GF: - Fm: 0-2
Distance:	2m/2m3: 0-0 2m4-2m7: 0-0 3m+: 0-6
Track:	LH: 0-2 RH: 0-4 Tight: 0-3 Gall: 0-1
Aids:	Bl: 0-0 Vi: 0-0 Tstrap: 0-0
Best Rating:	81 4/99 Tntn 2m1f firm Hdl

Full Egalite

93   63

7-y-o gr g Ezzoud (IRE)-Milva (Jellaby)
B A Pearce Miss J Webster

Placings:U5-060P   (4116)
2002/03: 16⁹GS, 16⁶G, 16⁹GF, 21⁶G,

	Starts	1st	2nd	3rd	Win & Pl
Hurdles	4	0	0	0	0
Career Total	6	0	0	0	0

Going:	Sf: 0-0 GS: 0-1 Gd: 0-2 GF: - Fm: 0-1
Distance:	2m/2m3: 0-3 2m4-2m7: 0-1 3m+: 0-0
Track:	LH: 0-1 RH: 0-3 Tight: 0-1 Gall: 0-2
Aids:	Bl: 0-4 Vi: 0-0 Tstrap: 0-0
Best Rating:	69 2/02 Folk 2m1f110y soft Hdl

Full Irish (IRE)

114   139

7-y-o ch g Rashar (USA)-Ross Gale (Strong Gale)
L Lungo D Stronach

Placings:2/11F111-1200   (4476)
2002/03: 21¹S, 16²S, 17⁹G, 16⁹G,

	Starts	1st	2nd	3rd	Win & Pl
Hurdles	4	1	1	0	11405
Career Total	11	6	2	0	28949
139	11/02	Sedg	2m5f110yB HHdl	SFT	£8897
127	4/02	Prth	2m110y D Hdl	GD	£3874
137	3/02	Donc	2m4f	C Hdl	G-S	£5648
115	1/02	Sedg	2m1f	D Hdl	HVY	£3464
121	11/01	Hayd	2m	H NHF	SFT	£2170
120	10/01	Sedg	2m1f	H NHF	GD	£1575

Total win prize-money £25630

Going:	Sf: 1-2 GS: 0-0 Gd: 0-2 GF: - Fm: 0-0
Distance:	2m/2m3: 0-3 2m4-2m7: 1-1 3m+: 0-0
Track:	LH: 1-4 RH: 0-0 Tight: 1-2 Gall: 0-2
Aids:	Bl: 0-0 Vi: 0-0 Tstrap: 0-0
Best Rating:	139 11/02 Sedg 2m5f110y soft Hdl

Very useful handicap hurdler; winning four times from five starts in 2002; stays two miles five furlongs; acts on ground ranging from good to heavy.

Full Minty

101   (121h)108

8-y-o br g Phardante (FR)-Jouvencelle (Rusticaro (FR))
N A Twiston-Davies H R Mould

Placings:30/F1P1/P2   (3516)
2002/03: 24PS, 22QGS,

	Starts	1st	2nd	3rd	Win & Pl
Chases	2	0	1	0	1708
Career Total	8	2	1	1	8914
121 4/01	Kemp 2m5f	D(0-115)HHdl		GD	£3822
120 1/01	Ludl 2m5f	E Hdl		SFT	£2912
			Total win prize-money £6734		

Going: Sf: 0-1 GS: 0-1 Gd: 0-0 GF: - Fm: 0-0
Distance: 2m/2m3: 0-0 2m4-2m7: 0-1 3m+: 0-1
Track: LH: 0-2 RH: 0-0 Tight: 0-1 Gall: 0-0
Aids: Bl: 0-0 Vi: 0-0 Tstrap: 0-0
Best Rating: 121 4/01 Kemp 2m5f   good   Hdl

Fair novice chaser; stays two miles six; effective with cut in the ground.

Full On
102   96
6-y-o b g Le Moss-Flighty Dove (Cruise Missile)
A M Hales Andrew L Cohen

Placings:0-42PP   (4173)
2002/03: 184S, 212S, 25PHY, 20PS,

	Starts	1st	2nd	3rd	Win & Pl
NH Flat	1	0	0	0	0
Hurdles	3	0	1	0	929
Career Total	5	0	1	0	929

Going: Sf: 0-4 GS: 0-0 Gd: 0-0 GF: - Fm: 0-0
Distance: 2m/2m3: 0-1 2m4-2m7: 0-2 3m+: 0-1
Track: LH: 0-3 RH: 0-0 Tight: 0-1 Gall: 0-0
Aids: Bl: 0-0 Vi: 0-0 Tstrap: 0-0
Best Rating: 96 11/02 Plum 2m5f   soft   Hdl

Lightly-raced staying hurdler; acts on soft ground.

Full Suit
7-y-o b m Local Suitor (USA)-Dereks Daughter (Derek H)
C E N Smith Mrs J Smith

Placings:00-PP   (0581)
2002/03: 16PG, 16PG,

	Starts	1st	2nd	3rd	Win & Pl
Hurdles	2	0	0	0	
Career Total	4	0	0	0	

Going: Sf: 0-0 GS: 0-0 Gd: 0-2 GF: - Fm: 0-0
Distance: 2m/2m3: 0-2 2m4-2m7: 0-0 3m+: 0-0
Track: LH: 0-2 RH: 0-0 Tight: 0-0 Gall: 0-0
Aids: Bl: 0-0 Vi: 0-0 Tstrap: 0-0
Best Rating: 0 6/02 Hexm 2m110y   good   Hdl

Fullards
95   71
5-y-o b g Alderbrook-Milly Kelly (Murrayfield)
Mrs P Sly M S Smith

Placings:0P   (3938)
2002/03: 19QGS, 21PGS,

	Starts	1st	2nd	3rd	Win & Pl
Hurdles	2	0	0	0	
Career Total	2	0	0	0	

Going: Sf: 0-0 GS: 0-2 Gd: 0-0 GF: - Fm: 0-0
Distance: 2m/2m3: 0-0 2m4-2m7: 0-2 3m+: 0-0
Track: LH: 0-1 RH: 0-1 Tight: 0-1 Gall: 0-0

Fullopep
9-y-o b g Dunbeath (USA)-Suggia (Alzao (USA))
Mrs M Reveley Mr & Mrs W J Williams

Placings:112/1155/PP/113350-P   (0413)
2002/03: 17PGF,

	Starts	1st	2nd	3rd	Win & Pl
Chases	1	0	0		
Career Total	16	6	1	2	27515
134 5/01	Newc 2m110y	D(0-125)HCh	G-F	£4696
125 5/01	Weth 2m	E(0-115)HCh	GD	£3346
125 11/99	Sedg 2m5f	C Ch	GD	£6937
122 10/99	Sedg 2m5f	E Ch	GD	£3436
118 9/98	Sedg 2m1f	E Hdl	GD	£2687
104 9/98	Sedg 2m1f	E Hdl	GD	£2337
			Total win prize-money £23442		

Going: Sf: 0-0 GS: 0-0 Gd: 0-0 GF: - Fm: 0-1
Distance: 2m/2m3: 0-1 2m4-2m7: 0-0 3m+: 0-1
Track: LH: 0-1 RH: 0-0 Tight: 0-1 Gall: 0-0
Aids: Bl: 0-0 Vi: 0-0 Tstrap: 0-0
Best Rating: 134 10/01 Weth 2m4f110y   good   Ch

Fair hunter chaser; formerly useful hurdler; stays three miles; likes good to firm.

Fulwell Hill
93f   85f
5-y-o b m Anshan-Finkin (Fine Blue)
Ian Williams J Tredwell

Placings:0   (3930)
2002/03: 16QG,

	Starts	1st	2nd	3rd	Win & Pl
NH Flat	1	0	0	0	
Career Total	1	0	0	0	

Going: Sf: 0-0 GS: 0-0 Gd: 0-1 GF: - Fm: 0-0
Distance: 2m/2m3: 0-1 2m4-2m7: 0-0 3m+: 0-0
Track: LH: 0-0 RH: 0-1 Tight: 0-0 Gall: 0-1
Aids: Bl: 0-0 Vi: 0-0 Tstrap: 0-0
Best Rating: 72 3/03 Hntg 2m110y   good   NHF

Fundamental
106   103
4-y-o ch g Rudimentary (USA)-I LI Try (Try My Best (USA))
T P Tate D N Green

Placings:3214   (4033)
2002/03: 16QGS, 16QS, 16QGS, 16QS,

	Starts	1st	2nd	3rd	Win & Pl
Hurdles	4	1	1	1	5551
Career Total	4	1	1	1	5551
103 2/03	Ayr 2m	E Hdl	G-S	£3610
			Total win prize-money £3611		

Going: Sf: 0-2 GS: 1-2 Gd: 0-0 GF: - Fm: 0-0
Distance: 2m/2m3: 1-4 2m4-2m7: 0-0 3m+: 0-0
Track: LH: 1-4 RH: 0-0 Tight: 0-1 Gall: 0-0
Aids: Bl: 0-0 Vi: 0-0 Tstrap: 0-0
Best Rating: 103 2/03 Ayr 2m   gd-sft Hdl

Some ability on the Flat; fair efforts in ordinary company over hurdles so far; acts on easy ground.

Funny Farm
13-y-o ch g Funny Man-Ba Ba Belle (Petit Instant)
Alan Walter Mrs Jane Walter

Placings:3/P-6   (3548)
2002/03: 25QG,

	Starts	1st	2nd	3rd	Win & Pl
Chases	1	0	0	0	0
Career Total	3	0	0	1	413

Going: Sf: 0-0 GS: 0-0 Gd: 0-1 GF: - Fm: 0-0
Distance: 2m/2m3: 0-0 2m4-2m7: 0-0 3m+: 0-1
Track: LH: 0-0 RH: 0-1 Tight: 0-0 Gall: 0-0
Aids: Bl: 0-0 Vi: 0-0 Tstrap: 0-0
Best Rating: 81 4/00 Trntn 3m   gd-sft Ch

Funny Genie (FR)
(87c)
10-y-o b g Genereux Genie-Sauteuse De Retz (FR) (Funny Hobby)
Miss H M Irving Miss H M Irving

Placings:P/P0PP11/P62331P/P/5U4-P   (4678)
2002/03: 19PGF,

	Starts	1st	2nd	3rd	Win & Pl
Chases	1	0	0	0	
Career Total	19	3	1	2	9148
93 3/00	Folk 2m	F(0-90)HCh	G-F	£2452
88 2/98	Folk 2m1f110yF(0-95)HHdl		G-F	£2136
90 2/98	Hrfd 2m1f	F(0-90)HHdl	GD	£2570
			Total win prize-money £7159		

Going: Sf: 0-0 GS: 0-0 Gd: 0-0 GF: - Fm: 0-1
Distance: 2m/2m3: 0-1 2m4-2m7: 0-0 3m+: 0-0
Track: LH: 0-0 RH: 0-1 Tight: 0-0 Gall: 0-0
Aids: Bl: 0-0 Vi: 0-0 Tstrap: 0-0
Best Rating: 93 3/00 Folk 2m   gd-fm   Ch

Futona
87(83h)   (58h)59
11-y-o ch m Fearless Action (USA)-Chaise Longue (Full Of Hope)
A J Wilson Mrs T D Pilkington

Placings:00/006/06P20661P/40PP/02-P0   (0382)
2002/03: 21PGF, 20QG,

	Starts	1st	2nd	3rd	Win & Pl
Chases	2	0	0	0	
Career Total	22	1	2	0	4843
105 3/00	Winc 2m6f	E Hdl	GD	£2751
			Total win prize-money £2751		

Going: Sf: 0-0 GS: 0-0 Gd: 0-1 GF: - Fm: 0-0
Distance: 2m/2m3: 0-0 2m4-2m7: 0-2 3m+: 0-3m+: 0-0
Track: LH: 0-0 RH: 0-2 Tight: 0-0 Gall: 0-1
Aids: Bl: 0-0 Vi: 0-0 Tstrap: 0-0
Best Rating: 105 3/00 Winc 2m6f   good   Hdl

Gabidia

77

6-y-o br m Bin Ajwaad (IRE)-Diabaig (Precocious)
A J Martin J H Lowry

Placings:00/0   (4762)
2002/03: 16⁰G,

	Starts	1st	2nd	3rd	Win & Pl
Hurdles	1	0	0	0	
Career Total	3	0	0	0	

Going: Sf: 0-0 GS: 0-0 Gd: 0-1 GF: - Fm: 0-0
Distance: 2m/2m3: 0-1 2m4-2m7: 0-0 3m+: 0-0
Track: LH: 0-0 RH: 0-1 Tight: 0-0 Gall: 0-0
Aids: Bl: 0-0 Vi: 0-0 Tstrap: 0-0
Best Rating: 52 11/00 Clon 2m   heavy   Hdl

Gabor

102   **106d**

4-y-o b g Danzig Connection (USA)-Kiomi (Niniski (USA))
G L Moore Leydens Farm Stud

Placings:122P   (4460)
2002/03: 16¹G, 16²GF, 16²GF, 16⁶PG,

	Starts	1st	2nd	3rd	Win & Pl
Hurdles	4	1	2	0	8917
Career Total	4	1	2	0	8917
106 9/02 Plum 2m		D Hdl		GD	£5073

Total win prize-money £5073

Going: Sf: 0-0 GS: 0-0 Gd: 1-2 GF: - Fm: 0-2
Distance: 2m/2m3: 1-4 2m4-2m7: 0-0 3m+: 0-0
Track: LH: 1-4 RH: 0-0 Tight: 1-2 Gall: 0-0
Aids: Bl: 0-0 Vi: 0-0 Tstrap: 0-0
Best Rating: 106 10/02 Chel 2m10y   gd-fm   Hdl

Fair middle-distance handicapper on the Flat; took well to
hurdles when winning a typical early-season juvenile hurdle
at Plumpton; runner-up in better races in October; acts on a
sound surface.

Gadz'Art (FR)

97   **136**

9-y-o b g Art Bleu-Naftane (FR) (Trac)
A King Michael Gates

Placings:11313/144264/531P2245/0PP45/623FP02U-4
                                                (0054)
2002/03: 20⁴G,

	Starts	1st	2nd	3rd	Win & Pl
Chases	1	0	0	0	518
Career Total	33	5	5	4	192932
10/99 Autl	2m7f110y HCh		VS	£53821
6/98 Autl	2m1f110y Ch		VS	£12121
3/98 Pau	2m2f110y Ch		GD	£7071
1/98 Pau	2m2f110y Ch		HVY	£4803
1/98 Pau	2m110y Hdl		HVY	£5050

Total win prize-money £82866

Going: Sf: 0-0 GS: 0-0 Gd: 0-1 GF: - Fm: 0-0
Distance: 2m/2m3: 0-0 2m4-2m7: 0-1 3m+: 0-0
Track: LH: 0-1 RH: 0-0 Tight: 0-1 Gall: 0-0
Aids: Bl: 0-1 Vi: 0-0 Tstrap: 0-0
Best Rating: 136 12/01 Sand 2m4f110y gd-sft   Ch

Formerly a useful chaser in France, he showed little in two
runs for Kim Bailey in December 2000 and is now with Alan
King. Fair efforts without winning and seems best when fitted with blinkers. Looks best over two and a half miles with
plenty of cut in the ground.

Gaia Grey

101   **97**

7-y-o gr m Environment Friend-Princess David (USA) (Irish
River (FR))
R Ford (T P Tate 17/7) Mrs J M Russell

Placings:1/300-P22P1   (0771)
2002/03: 20⁵GF, 23²G, 25²GS, 24²G, 24¹GF,

	Starts	1st	2nd	3rd	Win & Pl
Hurdles	5	1	2	0	4804
Career Total	9	2	2	1	6686
97 7/02 Worc 3m		E Hdl		G-F	£2842
105 2/01 Donc	2m110y	H NHF		GD	£1659

Total win prize-money £4501

Going: Sf: 0-0 GS: 0-1 Gd: 0-2 GF: - Fm: 1-2
Distance: 2m/2m3: 0-0 2m4-2m7: 0-2 3m+: 1-3
Track: LH: 1-5 RH: 0-0 Tight: 0-0 Gall: 0-0
Aids: Bl: 0-0 Vi: 0-0 Tstrap: 0-0
Best Rating: 105 11/01 Wwck 2m   good   NHF

Runaway bumper winner on her debut but has taken time to
find her feet over hurdles. Eventually got off the mark over
timber in three mile novice hurdle at Worcester July 2002.
Has given problems at the start.

Gainful

87   **11**

4-y-o ch f Elmaamul (USA)-Regain (Relko)
G F H Charles-Jones Miss Helen Wynne

Placings:40F0P0   (4693)
2002/03: 16⁴GF, 16⁰G, 17⁵HY, 17⁰GS, 17⁰GS, 17⁰G,

	Starts	1st	2nd	3rd	Win & Pl
Hurdles	6	0	0	0	314
Career Total	6	0	0	0	314

Going: Sf: 0-1 GS: 0-2 Gd: 0-2 GF: - Fm: 0-1
Distance: 2m/2m3: 0-6 2m4-2m7: 0-0 3m+: 0-0
Track: LH: 0-3 RH: 0-3 Tight: 0-0 Gall: 0-1
Aids: Bl: 0-0 Vi: 0-0 Tstrap: 0-0
Best Rating: 70 10/02 Chep 2m110y gd-fm   Hdl

Gala Du Moulin Mas (FR)

91(96h)   (66h)**80**

9-y-o b g Le Riverain (FR)-Soiree D Ex (FR) (Kashtan (FR))
M E D Francis Mrs Merrick Francis Iii

Placings:12/344P/PP43-20U044PP   (3431)
2002/03: 16²GF, 16⁰G, 17⁰GF, 16⁹S, 19⁴GS, 22⁴HY, 20⁰S, 22⁰S,

	Starts	1st	2nd	3rd	Win & Pl
Hurdles	1	0	0	0	0
Chases	7	0	1	0	1236
Career Total	18	1	2	2	10959
7/98 Diep	2m1f110y Ch		SFT	£3535

Total win prize-money £3535

Going: Sf: 0-4 GS: 0-1 Gd: 0-1 GF: - Fm: 0-2
Distance: 2m/2m3: 0-5 2m4-2m7: 0-3 3m+: 0-0
Track: LH: 0-4 RH: 0-2 Tight: 0-5 Gall: 0-1
Aids: Bl: 0-0 Vi: 0-0 Tstrap: 0-0
Best Rating: 84 5/02 Worc 2m   gd-fm   Ch

Ex-French chaser, returned from an absence in 2002.
Showed his best form on fast ground in the spring.

Gala Performance (USA)

97   **101**

5-y-o b g Theatrical-Claxton s Slew (USA) (Seattle Slew
(USA))
Jonjo O Neill Russell McAllister

Placings:30554   (3619)
2002/03: 17⁵HY, 16⁰HY, 16⁵S, 17⁵S, 16⁴HY,

	Starts	1st	2nd	3rd	Win & Pl
NH Flat	2	0	0	1	317
Hurdles	3	0	0	0	401
Career Total	5	0	0	1	718

Going: Sf: 0-4 GS: 0-0 Gd: 0-1 GF: - Fm: 0-0
Distance: 2m/2m3: 0-5 2m4-2m7: 0-0 3m+: 0-0
Track: LH: 0-3 RH: 0-0 Tight: 0-2 Gall: 0-0
Aids: Bl: 0-0 Vi: 0-0 Tstrap: 0-2
Best Rating: 101 12/02 Hayd 2m   good   Hdl

Formerly trained by Aidan O Brien; has shown just fair form
in novice hurdles; banned for 30-days for schooling in public
at Haydock on his third start.

Galadhrim (IRE)

86f   **86f**

6-y-o b g Glacial Storm (USA)-La Mode Lady (Mandalus)
Edward Butler Mrs S C Butler

Placings:06   (3563)
2002/03: 16⁰GS, 17⁶HY,

	Starts	1st	2nd	3rd	Win & Pl
NH Flat	2	0	0	0	0
Career Total	2	0	0	0	0

Going: Sf: 0-1 GS: 0-1 Gd: 0-0 GF: - Fm: 0-0
Distance: 2m/2m3: 0-2 2m4-2m7: 0-0 3m+: 0-0
Track: LH: 0-0 RH: 0-2 Tight: 0-1 Gall: 0-0
Aids: Bl: 0-0 Vi: 0-0 Tstrap: 0-0
Best Rating: 86 2/03 Folk 2m1f110y heavy   NHF

Galant Eye (IRE)

85   **86**

4-y-o ch g Eagle Eyed (USA)-Galandria (Sharpo)
F Jordan Graham Brown

Placings:343365P   (3557)
2002/03: 18³G, 16⁴GF, 18³GF, 16³GF, 18⁶G, 16⁵HY, 22⁰HY,

	Starts	1st	2nd	3rd	Win & Pl
Hurdles	7	0	0	3	2469
Career Total	7	0	0	3	2469

Going: Sf: 0-2 GS: 0-0 Gd: 0-2 GF: - Fm: 0-3
Distance: 2m/2m3: 0-6 2m4-2m7: 0-1 3m+: 0-0
Track: LH: 0-6 RH: 0-1 Tight: 0-5 Gall: 0-0
Aids: Bl: 0-0 Vi: 0-0 Tstrap: 0-0
Best Rating: 86 10/02 Chel 2m110y gd-fm   Hdl

Moderate maiden hurdler.

Galant Moss (FR)

99(107c)   (124c)**120**

9-y-o b/br g Tip Moss (FR)-Tchela (FR) (Le Nain Jaune
(FR))
M C Pipe C M , B J & R F Batterham Ii

Placings:213222323311/6P2400/01P414P3/12F65030401-
2352536PP0P00   (4367)

2002/03: 20²S, 25³VS, 19⁵S, 20²VS, 20⁵HY, 19³GS, 24⁶S, 20ᴾG, 24ᴾGS, 23⁰GS, 18ᴾHO, 21⁰G, 20⁰G,

	Starts	1st	2nd	3rd	Win & Pl
Hurdles	9	0	2	1	52883
Chases	4	0	0	1	2826
Career Total	50	7	9	8	243864

133	4/02	Autl	2m2f		Hdl	VS	£14723
	6/01	Autl	2m2f		Hdl	VS	£12124
142	12/00	Asct	2m3f110yA Ch			SFT	£13200
120	10/00	Sedg	2m5f	E Ch		G-S	£3282
151	5/99	Hayd	2m7f110yB Hdl			GD	£6905
144	4/99	Asct	3m	A Hdl		G-F	£18750
	6/98	Autl	2m2f		HHdl	VS	£19192
					Total win prize-money £88177		

Going: Sf: 0-4 GS: 0-3 Gd: 0-3 GF: - Fm: 0-0
Distance: 2m/2m3: 0-1 2m4-2m7: 0-8 3m+: 0-4
Track: LH: 0-8 RH: 0-4 Tight: 0-1 Gall: 0-1
Aids: Bl: 0-0 Vi: 0-2 Tstrap: 0-0
Best Rating: 151 2/00 Kemp 3m110y soft Hdl

Decent hurdler/chaser; winner of some competitive races over both hurdles and fences; probably best at distances short of three miles although he stays that trip; does not want the ground too fast; loves Auteuil, and regularly in action there in 2002, has not jumped well over fences in 2002/03.

Galapiat Du Mesnil (FR)
101(95h) (106h)**140d**
9-y-o b g Sarpedon (FR)-Polka De Montrin (FR) (Danoso)
P F Nicholls Mel Fordham B Fulton S Fisher T Hayward

Placings:3210/4131513/31F25/102412210-1600P (4172)
2002/03: 24¹GF, 25⁶G, 31⁰GS, 20ᴴHY, 34ᴾS,

	Starts	1st	2nd	3rd	Win & Pl
Hurdles	1	0	0	0	0
Chases	4	1	0	0	10121
Career Total	30	9	5	4	91210

140	5/02	Chep	3m	B(0-145)HCh	G-F	£10120
136	3/02	Chep	3m3f110yC(0-135)HCh		G-S	£10029
136	10/01	Chep	2m7f110yC(0-130)HCh		SFT	£9150
130	5/01	Strf	3m	C(0-135)HCh	G-F	£6942
130	9/00	Worc	2m7f110yC(0-135)HCh		G-F	£8127
130	11/99	Asct	3m110y C HCh		GD	£6840
123	10/99	Worc	2m7f110yD Ch		G-F	£4109
112	1/99	Plum	2m4f	E Hdl	HVY	£2215
				Total win prize-money £61441		

Going: Sf: 0-2 GS: 0-1 Gd: 0-1 GF: - Fm: 1-1
Distance: 2m/2m3: 0-0 2m4-2m7: 0-1 3m+: 1-4
Track: LH: 1-5 RH: 0-0 Tight: 0-0 Gall: 0-0
Aids: Bl: 0-0 Vi: 0-0 Tstrap: 0-0
Best Rating: 140 5/02 Chep 3m gd-fm Ch

Very useful chaser; versatile when it comes to trip, stays 3m 7f; especially suited by soft ground.

Galaxy Sam (USA)
91 **71**
4-y-o ch g Royal Academy (USA)-Istiska (FR) (Irish River (FR))
S Dow (W J Haggas 19/9) S Munir

Placings:00P0 (4371)
2002/03: 16⁰S, 16⁰HY, 16ᴾHY, 16⁰G,

	Starts	1st	2nd	3rd	Win & Pl
Hurdles	4	0	0	0	
Career Total	4	0	0	0	

Going: Sf: 0-3 GS: 0-0 Gd: 0-1 GF: - Fm: 0-0
Distance: 2m/2m3: 0-4 2m4-2m7: 0-0 3m+: 0-0
Track: LH: 0-0 RH: 0-4 Tight: 0-0 Gall: 0-0
Aids: Bl: 0-0 Vi: 0-0 Tstrap: 0-0
Best Rating: 71 12/02 Kemp 2m soft Hdl

Very moderate performer on the Flat and over hurdles.

Galeaway (IRE)
105 **84**
9-y-o b g Strong Gale-Geeaway (Gala Performance (USA))
M J Roberts Mike Roberts

Placings:0/415/PF4-PP43 (4761)
2002/03: 25⁶GS, 25ᴾGS, 24⁴G, 26³GF,

	Starts	1st	2nd	3rd	Win & Pl
Chases	4	0	0	1	732
Career Total	11	1	0	1	2628

85	5/00	Folk	3m2f	H Ch	GD	£1456
				Total win prize-money £1456		

Going: Sf: 0-0 GS: 0-2 Gd: 0-1 GF: - Fm: 0-1
Distance: 2m/2m3: 0-0 2m4-2m7: 0-0 3m+: 0-4
Track: LH: 0-1 RH: 0-2 Tight: 0-2 Gall: 0-0
Aids: Bl: 0-1 Vi: 0-0 Tstrap: 0-0
Best Rating: 85 5/00 Folk 3m2f good Ch

Plating-class chaser; stays three miles-two; acts on a sound surface.

Galeshan (IRE)
110 **98**
11-y-o b g Strong Gale-Shan s Pal (Pals Passage)
Mrs H Dalton Miss L Hales

Placings:3/55F5/5/P5/16/50132P (1593)
2002/03: 22⁵G, 21⁰GF, 20¹G, 19³GF, 26²GF, 23ᴾG,

	Starts	1st	2nd	3rd	Win & Pl
Chases	6	1	1	1	5343
Career Total	15	2	1	2	8049

98	8/02	Worc	2m4f110yF(0-100)HCh		GD	£3475
98	5/00	Newc	2m4f	F(0-95)Ch	G-F	£2495
				Total win prize-money £5972		

Going: Sf: 0-0 GS: 0-0 Gd: 1-3 GF: - Fm: 0-3
Distance: 2m/2m3: 0-1 2m4-2m7: 1-3 3m+: 0-2
Track: LH: 1-3 RH: 0-3 Tight: 0-1 Gall: 0-0
Aids: Bl: 0-0 Vi: 0-0 Tstrap: 1-6
Best Rating: 98 8/02 Worc 2m4f110y good Ch

Well backed when narrow winner of Class F handicap at Worcester in August. Acts on good or faster ground. Best at around two and a half miles and a confirmed front runner.

Galileo (POL)
98 **135**
7-y-o b g Jape (USA)-Goldika (POL) (Dakota)
T R George Mrs S Nelson,Allan Stennett,Terry Warner

Placings:11-06 (4439)
2002/03: 24⁰G, 24⁶G,

	Starts	1st	2nd	3rd	Win & Pl
Hurdles	2	0	0	0	600
Career Total	4	2	0	0	60470

154	3/02	Chel	2m5f	A Hdl	G-S	£52200
142	2/02	Kemp	2m5f	C Hdl	GD	£7670
				Total win prize-money £59870		

Going: Sf: 0-0 GS: 0-0 Gd: 0-2 GF: - Fm: 0-0
Distance: 2m/2m3: 0-0 2m4-2m7: 0-0 3m+: 0-0
Track: LH: 0-1 RH: 0-1 Tight: 0-0 Gall: 0-1
Aids: Bl: 0-0 Vi: 0-0 Tstrap: 0-0
Best Rating: 154 3/02 Chel 2m5f gd-sft Hdl

High-class hurdler; winner of the Polish St Leger and Listed placed on the Flat in Germany; bolted up on his hurdling debut at Kempton in February 2002 and followed up with a brilliant win in the Royal & SunAlliance Hurdle the following month, despite not getting the best of runs and appearing green in front; stays 2m 5f and gives the impression he will get much farther, although held on first run for a year in 2003 Stayers Hurdle; disappointing next time; seems to act on any ground.

Gallant Glen (IRE)
10-y-o b g Zaffaran (USA)-Furmore (Furry Glen)
Perry Harding-Jones (John J Costello 9/6) Derek J Harding-Jones

Placings:F112/006/2100U4-40P6 (4459)
2002/03: 20⁴S, 20⁰YS, 22ᴾS, 21⁶G,

	Starts	1st	2nd	3rd	Win & Pl
Chases	4	0	0	0	429
Career Total	17	3	2	0	15498

113	5/01	Baln	2m1f	(0-109)HCh	G-Y	£5286
105	4/00	Cork	3m	Ch	YLD	£3864
97	3/00	Clon	3m	Ch	G-Y	£2980
				Total win prize-money £12131		

Going: Sf: 0-2 GS: 0-0 Gd: 0-1 GF: - Fm: 0-0
Distance: 2m/2m3: 0-0 2m4-2m7: 0-4 3m+: 0-0
Track: LH: 0-1 RH: 0-2 Tight: 0-1 Gall: 0-0
Aids: Bl: 0-0 Vi: 0-0 Tstrap: 0-0
Best Rating: 113 3/02 Cork 2m4f yld-sft Ch

Ex-Irish chaser; winning pointer in 2003.

Gallik Dawn
83 **37**
5-y-o ch g Anshan-Sticky Money (Relkino)
A Hollingsworth Perry Adams

Placings:0 (4090)
2002/03: 16⁰GS,

	Starts	1st	2nd	3rd	Win & Pl
NH Flat	1	0	0	0	
Career Total	1	0	0	0	

Going: Sf: 0-0 GS: 0-1 Gd: 0-0 GF: - Fm: 0-0
Distance: 2m/2m3: 0-1 2m4-2m7: 0-0 3m+: 0-0
Track: LH: 0-0 RH: 0-0 Tight: 0-0 Gall: 0-0
Aids: Bl: 0-0 Vi: 0-0 Tstrap: 0-0
Best Rating: 44 3/03 Strf 2m110y gd-sft NHF

Gallileo Strike (IRE)
103 **92**
7-y-o b g Magical Strike (USA)-Dame Daffodil (IRE) (Petorius)
Thomas Cooper Thornbirds Syndicate

Placings:000/1100-000400 (1943)
2002/03: 19⁰S, 16⁰YS, 17⁰G, 16⁴G, 16⁶G, 21⁰G,

	Starts	1st	2nd	3rd	Win & Pl
Hurdles	6	0	0	0	270
Career Total	13	2	0	0	11677

99	9/01	List	2m	(0-109)HHdl	G-F	£6399
99	9/01	Tral	2m	(0-109)HHdl	GD	£5008
				Total win prize-money £11407		

Going: Sf: 0-1 GS: 0-0 Gd: 0-4 GF: - Fm: 0-0
Distance: 2m/2m3: 0-5 2m4-2m7: 0-1 3m+: 0-0
Track: LH: 0-1 RH: 0-0 Tight: 0-2 Gall: 0-1
Aids: Bl: 0-0 Vi: 0-0 Tstrap: 0-0
Best Rating: 99 9/01 List 2m gd-fm Hdl

An Irish-trained dual purpose gelding. He won on the Flat before scoring twice over hurdles in September 2001. Suited by a good/fast surface.

Gallion's Reach (IRE)

108   (87h)**81+**

8-y-o b g Good Thyne (USA)-Raise Our Hopes (IRE) (Salluceva)
M F Harris (N A Twiston-Davies 6/5) Let s Live Racing II

Placings:3505/62P1003/42PP2P-2U2F14U3P3P402 (4349)
2002/03: 24⁴GF, 21¹¹GF, 24²GF, 24⁴G, 25⁴GS, 25⁴UGS, 25³S, 29⁹GS, 21³GS, 24⁴PS, 21⁴S, 25⁰S, 24⁴GF,

	Starts	1st	2nd	3rd	Win & Pl
Hurdles	1	0	0	0	
Chases	13	1	3	2	10658
Career Total	31	2	6	4	19637
89	8/02	Strf	3m	E(0-105)HCh	SFT	£4095
94	2/01	Hayd	2m	C(0-125)HHdl	HVY	£5083
				Total win prize-money £9178

Going: Sf: 1-5 GS: 0-4 Gd: 0-1 GF: - Fm: 0-4
Distance: 2m/2m3: 0-2 2m4-2m7: 0-3 3m+: 1-11
Track: LH: 1-9 RH: 0-5 Tight: 1-8 Gall: 0-1
Aids: Bl: 0-1 Vi: 0-0 Tstrap: 1-12
Best Rating: 100 12/99 Uttx   2m   soft   NHF

Plating-class chaser; stays three miles; acts on soft ground.

Gallium

66   **49**

6-y-o gr m Terimon-Genie Spirit (Nishapour (FR))
D J Caro The Swinging Richards

Placings:654   (3546)
2002/03: 16⁶G, 16⁵GS, 19⁴G,

	Starts	1st	2nd	3rd	Win & Pl
NH Flat	1	0	0	0	0
Hurdles	2	0	0	0	394
Career Total	3	0	0	0	394

Going: Sf: 0-0 GS: 0-1 Gd: 0-2 GF: - Fm: 0-0
Distance: 2m/2m3: 0-2 2m4-2m7: 0-1 3m+: 0-0
Track: LH: 0-1 RH: 0-2 Tight: 0-1 Gall: 0-0
Aids: Bl: 0-0 Vi: 0-0 Tstrap: 0-0
Best Rating: 65 12/02 Ludl   2m   good   NHF

Gallop Rhythm (IRE)

(88h)   (94h)

7-y-o ch g Mister Lord (USA)-Kiltannon (Dalsaan)
R J Baker St Bartholomews & The Royal London Turf

Placings:0/002-PP   (4485)
2002/03: 19³GS, 19²GF,

	Starts	1st	2nd	3rd	Win & Pl
Hurdles	1	0	0	0	0
Chases	1	0	0	0	0
Career Total	6	0	1	0	766

Going: Sf: 0-0 GS: 0-1 Gd: 0-0 GF: - Fm: 0-1
Distance: 2m/2m3: 0-2 2m4-2m7: 0-0 3m+: 0-0
Track: LH: 0-0 RH: 0-2 Tight: 0-0 Gall: 0-0
Aids: Bl: 0-0 Vi: 0-0 Tstrap: 0-0
Best Rating: 94 4/02 Chep   2m4f   gd-fm Hdl

Novice hurdler, stays two and a half miles.

Galway (IRE)

10-y-o b g Jurado (USA)-Solanum (Green Shoon)
Mrs Marilyn Scudamore The Yes - No - Wait   Sorries

Placings:00/605F60/0P003/152U/0-P   (4133)
2002/03: 26⁶PG,

	Starts	1st	2nd	3rd	Win & Pl
Chases	1	0	0	0	
Career Total	19	1	1	1	3450
117	2/01	Muss	3m	H Ch	GD	£2352
				Total win prize-money £2352

Going: Sf: 0-0 GS: 0-0 Gd: 0-1 GF: - Fm: 0-0
Distance: 2m/2m3: 0-0 2m4-2m7: 0-0 3m+: 0-1
Track: LH: 0-1 RH: 0-0 Tight: 0-0 Gall: 0-1
Aids: Bl: 0-0 Vi: 0-0 Tstrap: 0-0
Best Rating: 117 2/01 Muss   3m   good   Ch

Galwaybay Stan (IRE)

5-y-o b g Safety Catch (USA)-Crook Lady (Croghan Hill)
L Wells Paul Zetter

Placings:34   (3782)
2002/03: 18³HY, 17⁴GS,

	Starts	1st	2nd	3rd	Win & Pl
NH Flat	2	0	0	1	556
Career Total	2	0	0	1	556

Going: Sf: 0-1 GS: 0-1 Gd: 0-0 GF: - Fm: 0-0
Distance: 2m/2m3: 0-2 2m4-2m7: 0-0 3m+: 0-0
Track: LH: 0-1 RH: 0-1 Tight: 0-0 Gall: 0-0
Aids: Bl: 0-0 Vi: 0-0 Tstrap: 0-0
Best Rating: 99 2/03 Extr   2m1f   gd-sft NHF

Winner of a four-year-old point in Ireland in 2002, staying on third on debut at Plumpton in a bumper, far to sharp a test. Chaser in the making; who has potential for improvement.

Game Gunner

11-y-o b g Gunner B-The Waiting Game (Cruise Missile)
Miss B Lewis Miss B Lewis

Placings:14U4P2-P   (3548)
2002/03: 25⁶PG,

	Starts	1st	2nd	3rd	Win & Pl
Chases	1	0	0	0	
Career Total	7	1	1	0	5227
95	6/01	Strf	3m	H Ch	G-F	£3705
				Total win prize-money £3705

Going: Sf: 0-0 GS: 0-0 Gd: 0-1 GF: - Fm: 0-0
Distance: 2m/2m3: 0-0 2m4-2m7: 0-0 3m+: 0-1
Track: LH: 0-0 RH: 0-1 Tight: 0-0 Gall: 0-0
Aids: Bl: 0-0 Vi: 0-0 Tstrap: 0-0
Best Rating: 95 3/02 Donc   2m3f110y   soft   Ch

Winning hunter chaser; likes fast ground.

Game On (IRE)

106(99h)   (90h)**98**

7-y-o b g Terimon-Nun So Game (The Parson)
B N Pollock (Mrs Nicola Pollock 14/3) Mrs S Platt

Placings:2P24P-U6   (4523)
2002/03: 21⁴UG, 16⁶G,

	Starts	1st	2nd	3rd	Win & Pl
Chases	2	0	0	0	0
Career Total	7	0	2	0	1358

Going: Sf: 0-0 GS: 0-0 Gd: 0-2 GF: - Fm: 0-0
Distance: 2m/2m3: 0-1 2m4-2m7: 0-1 3m+: 0-0
Track: LH: 0-2 RH: 0-0 Tight: 0-1 Gall: 0-0
Aids: Bl: 0-0 Vi: 0-0 Tstrap: 0-0
Best Rating: 109 5/01 Folk   2m1f110y   gd-sft NHF

Poor novice chaser; former pointer; yet to get off the mark in either sphere.

Gandon

103   **83**

6-y-o ch g Hernando (FR)-Severine (USA) (Trempolino (USA))
P G Murphy On The Move

Placings:00000-0650004   (3937)
2002/03: 20⁰G, 18⁵GF, 19⁵F, 22⁰G, 19⁰GS, 22⁰GS, 18⁴S,

	Starts	1st	2nd	3rd	Win & Pl
Hurdles	7	0	0	0	0
Career Total	12	0	0	0	0

Going: Sf: 0-1 GS: 0-2 Gd: 0-2 GF: - Fm: 0-2
Distance: 2m/2m3: 0-3 2m4-2m7: 0-4 3m+: 0-0
Track: LH: 0-3 RH: 0-4 Tight: 0-3 Gall: 0-0
Aids: Bl: 0-0 Vi: 0-1 Tstrap: 0-1
Best Rating: 83 3/03 Font   2m2f110y   soft   Hdl

Gangsters R Us (IRE)

101(96c)   (75c)**102+**

7-y-o br g Treasure Hunter-Our Mare Mick (Choral Society)
A Parker J B Purefoy

Placings:P/536-6310   (4016)
2002/03: 16⁶S, 21³GS, 20¹HY, 22⁰S,

	Starts	1st	2nd	3rd	Win & Pl
Hurdles	2	1	0	0	3150
Chases	2	0	0	1	716
Career Total	8	1	0	2	4235
102	2/03	Ayr	2m4f	F(0-95)HHdl	HVY	£3150
				Total win prize-money £3150

Going: Sf: 1-3 GS: 0-1 Gd: 0-0 GF: - Fm: 0-0
Distance: 2m/2m3: 0-0 2m4-2m7: 1-3 3m+: 0-0
Track: LH: 1-3 RH: 0-1 Tight: 0-0 Gall: 0-0
Aids: Bl: 0-0 Vi: 0-0 Tstrap: 0-0
Best Rating: 102 2/03 Ayr   2m4f   heavy Hdl

Modest hurdler/chaser, appreciates patient tactics.

Garden Feature

66   **36**

5-y-o b m Minster Son-Super Fountain (Royal Fountain)
J B Walton Messrs F T Walton

Placings:5650   (4590)
2002/03: 16⁵GS, 16⁶HY, 16⁵G, 20⁰G,

	Starts	1st	2nd	3rd	Win & Pl
NH Flat	3	0	0	0	0
Hurdles	1	0	0	0	0
Career Total	4	0	0	0	0

Going: Sf: 0-1 GS: 0-1 Gd: 0-2 GF: - Fm: 0-0
Distance: 2m/2m3: 0-3 2m4-2m7: 0-1 3m+: 0-0

Track: LH: 0-3 RH: 0-1 Tight: 0-1 Gall: 0-0
Aids: Bl: 0-0 Vi: 0-0 Tstrap: 0-0
Best Rating: 80 3/03 Hexm 2m110y good NHF

Lightly-raced individual. Moderate form over hurdles. Unseated on chasing debut in spring of 2001. Improved to score a couple of times at up to three and a quarter miles. Acts on any ground.

moderate Towcester hunter chase in March 2002, having won two earlier points. A winning pointer this year; suited by good ground or slightly easier.

Garden Party Ii (FR)
98   88
9-y-o br g Argument (FR)-Betty Royale (FR) (Royal Charter (FR))
Mrs J C McGregor Discounted Cashflow

Placings: 2604/0060F0/0P62F50/30032454-33456443
                                               (4163)
2002/03: 17³G, 17³S, 16⁴GS, 20⁵GF, 16⁶G, 20⁴HY, 16⁴S, 16³GS,

	Starts	1st	2nd	3rd	Win & Pl
Chases	8	0	0	3	3374
Career Total	33	0	3	5	7583

Going: Sf: 0-3 GS: 0-2 Gd: 0-2 GF: - Fm: 0-1
Distance: 2m/2m3: 0-6 2m4-2m7: 0-2 3m+: 0-0
Track: LH: 0-6 RH: 0-2 Tight: 0-5 Gall: 0-1
Aids: Bl: 0-0 Vi: 0-0 Tstrap: 0-0
Best Rating: 104 3/99 Ludl 2m good NHF

Plating-class maiden chaser; has run well on varying ground; lacks a turn of foot.

Gardor (FR)
101   97
5-y-o b g Kendor (FR)-Garboesque (Priolo (USA))
T J Fitzgerald (J G Fitzgerald 13/12) Mrs Anne M Halewood

Placings: 452-0500   (4591)
2002/03: 16⁶G, 16⁵GS, 16⁶G, 16⁶G,

	Starts	1st	2nd	3rd	Win & Pl
Hurdles	4	0	0	0	0
Career Total	7	0	1	0	1130

Going: Sf: 0-0 GS: 0-1 Gd: 0-3 GF: - Fm: 0-0
Distance: 2m/2m3: 0-4 2m4-2m7: 0-0 3m+: 0-0
Track: LH: 0-4 RH: 0-0 Tight: 0-0 Gall: 0-1
Aids: Bl: 0-0 Vi: 0-0 Tstrap: 0-0
Best Rating: 99 3/02 MRas 2m1f110y gd-sft Hdl

Moderate maiden hurdler; narrowly beaten in seller at Kelso in May and would have finished runner-up in a better race at Wetherby a week later but for falling at the last; best at two miles; aats on any ground; has worn a tongue tie.

Gare Hill (IRE)
92   98
9-y-o ch g Aristocracy-Morning Jane (IRE) (Over The River (FR))
J T Gifford Michael S Wilson

Placings: 500/P/U/5F1413P-3   (2312)
2002/03: 26³HY,

	Starts	1st	2nd	3rd	Win & Pl
Chases	1	0	0	1	626
Career Total	13	2	0	2	7255
98 1/02	Plum	3m2f		F(0-90)HCh	SFT £3150
81 12/01	Folk	2m5f		F(0-95)HCh	GD £2814

Total win prize-money £5965

Going: Sf: 0-1 GS: 0-0 Gd: 0-0 GF: - Fm: 0-0
Distance: 2m/2m3: 0-0 2m4-2m7: 0-0 3m+: 0-1
Track: LH: 0-1 RH: 0-0 Tight: 0-0 Gall: 0-0
Aids: Bl: 0-0 Vi: 0-0 Tstrap: 0-0
Best Rating: 98 1/02 Plum 3m2f soft Ch

Garethson (IRE)
12-y-o b g Cataldi-Tartan Sash (Crofter (USA))
O W King A King

Placings: 3233/30613/1U40FP5/2U/133-3P   (4443)
2002/03: 20³G, 19³G,

	Starts	1st	2nd	3rd	Win & Pl
Chases	2	0	0	1	262
Career Total	23	3	2	8	14930
98 2/02	Donc	2m3f110yH Ch			SFT £1596
128 5/98	Towc	2m6f	E Ch		GD £3065
127 3/98	Extr	2m3f110yD Ch			SFT £3906

Total win prize-money £8568

Going: Sf: 0-0 GS: 0-0 Gd: 0-0 GF: - Fm: 0-0
Distance: 2m/2m3: 0-0 2m4-2m7: 0-0 3m+: 0-0
Track: LH: 0-0 RH: 0-0 Tight: 0-1 Gall: 0-0
Aids: Bl: 0-0 Vi: 0-0 Tstrap: 0-0
Best Rating: 128 5/98 Towc 2m6f good Ch

Gargoyle Girl
101   84+
6-y-o b m Be My Chief (USA)-May Hills Legacy (IRE) (Be My Guest (USA))
J S Goldie Mrs C Brown

Placings: 0502-214   (1559)
2002/03: 16²GF, 16¹GS, 16⁴G,

	Starts	1st	2nd	3rd	Win & Pl
Hurdles	3	1	1	0	4115
Career Total	7	1	2	0	5251
95 6/02	Prth	2m110y	F(0-90)HHdl	G-S	£2957

Total win prize-money £2958

Going: Sf: 0-0 GS: 1-1 Gd: 0-1 GF: - Fm: 0-1
Distance: 2m/2m3: 1-3 2m4-2m7: 0-0 3m+: 0-0
Track: LH: 0-1 RH: 1-2 Tight: 0-1 Gall: 0-0
Aids: Bl: 0-0 Vi: 0-0 Tstrap: 0-0
Best Rating: 95 6/02 Prth 2m110y gd-sft Hdl

Moderate hurdler, seems suited by a sound surface.

Garolo (FR)
13-y-o b g Garde Royale-Valgoya (FR) (Valdingran (FR))
Mrs F Browne Miss S L Samworth

Placings: F25/13020/3121022PF/3P453/3323655/P/P15-P   (4133)
2002/03: 26⁶PG,

	Starts	1st	2nd	3rd	Win & Pl
Chases	1	0	0	0	
Career Total	34	4	6	7	29029
98 3/02	Towc	3m1f	H Ch	SFT	£2173
117 12/96	Uttx	2m	D Ch	G-S	£3598
1/96	Cagn	2m55y	Hdl	SFT	£7905

Total win prize-money £13678

Going: Sf: 0-0 GS: 0-0 Gd: 0-1 GF: - Fm: 0-0
Distance: 2m/2m3: 0-0 2m4-2m7: 0-0 3m+: 0-1
Track: LH: 0-1 RH: 0-0 Tight: 0-0 Gall: 0-1
Aids: Bl: 0-1 Vi: 0-0 Tstrap: 0-0
Best Rating: 134 2/96 Kemp 2m soft Hdl

A formerly decent hurdler/chaser, improved for the re-application of blinkers last season and completed a hat-trick in a

Garolsa (FR)
106   85
9-y-o b g Rivelago (FR)-Rols Du Chatelier (FR) (Diaghilev)
C Tizzard R G And C L Tizzard

Placings: 02/1/2P4/P2P/026PP-22U4U4P   (1850)
2002/03: 21²GF, 26²GF, 26ᴜGF, 26⁴G, 25ᴜF, 25⁴G, 25ᴾG,

	Starts	1st	2nd	3rd	Win & Pl
Chases	7	0	2	0	4083
Career Total	21	1	6	0	17210
105 3/99	Chep	2m4f110yD Hdl		SFT	£2996

Total win prize-money £2996

Going: Sf: 0-0 GS: 0-0 Gd: 0-3 GF: - Fm: 0-4
Distance: 2m/2m3: 0-0 2m4-2m7: 0-1 3m+: 0-6
Track: LH: 0-4 RH: 0-3 Tight: 0-1 Gall: 0-0
Aids: Bl: 0-4 Vi: 0-1 Tstrap: 0-0
Best Rating: 111 4/00 Asct 3m110y soft Ch

Mainly disappointing over fences, and does not always look keen. Acts on fast ground. Stays three miles.

Garraheen Lucy (IRE)
63
7-y-o b/br m Alphabatim (USA)-Ravaleen (IRE) (Executive Perk)
B J Llewellyn (P A Fahy 17/3) B J Llewellyn

Placings: 00045P   (4693)
2002/03: 16⁶S, 20⁰SH, 16⁰Y, 16⁴Y, 16⁵S, 17⁵G,

	Starts	1st	2nd	3rd	Win & Pl
NH Flat	2	0	0	0	208
Hurdles	4	0	0	0	0
Career Total	6	0	0	0	208

Going: Sf: 0-2 GS: 0-0 Gd: 0-0 GF: - Fm: 0-0
Distance: 2m/2m3: 0-5 2m4-2m7: 0-1 3m+: 0-0
Track: LH: 0-1 RH: 0-1 Tight: 0-1 Gall: 0-0
Aids: Bl: 0-0 Vi: 0-0 Tstrap: 0-0
Best Rating: 89 2/03 Thur 2m yield NHF

Garrison Friendly (IRE)
10-y-o b g Buckskin (FR)-Ikeathy (Be Friendly)
Mrs S J Hickman Noel Wilson

Placings: 562/2142F45/5   (0314)
2002/03: 31⁵G,

	Starts	1st	2nd	3rd	Win & Pl
Chases	1	0	0	0	
Career Total	13	1	3	0	7263
115 11/98	Wind	3m	E(0-100)HCh	GD	£3293

Total win prize-money £3293

Going: Sf: 0-0 GS: 0-0 Gd: 0-1 GF: - Fm: 0-0
Distance: 2m/2m3: 0-0 2m4-2m7: 0-0 3m+: 0-1
Track: LH: 0-0 RH: 0-1 Tight: 0-1 Gall: 0-0
Aids: Bl: 0-1 Vi: 0-0 Tstrap: 0-0
Best Rating: 115 2/99 Font 3m2f110y soft Ch

Garruth (IRE)

103(99h)   (135dh)126

9-y-o gr g Good Thyne (USA)-Lady Sipash (Erin s Hope)
P F Nicholls   A Bloom

Placings:6/405331/00113221141/14363251-5P02P (3946)
2002/03: 28⁵GS, 26⁵GS, 24⁰S, 24²S, 30⁵S,

	Starts	1st	2nd	3rd	Win & Pl
Hurdles	1	0	0	0	0
Chases	4	0	1	0	1774
Career Total	31	8	4	5	81505
102	4/02	Sedg	3m3f	D Ch		G-F	£4378
108	11/01	Plum	3m2f	D Ch		GD	£4322
150	4/01	Aint	3m110y	A Hdl		SFT	£29000
135	1/01	Uttx	3m110y	C(0-135)HHdl		HVY	£5239
127	12/00	Chel	3m	A Hdl		SFT	£12000
126	10/00	Kels	2m6f110yE Hdl			G-S	£2422
104	9/00	Sedg	2m5f110yE Hdl			SFT	£2716
91	4/00	List	2m4f	NHF		SH	£3588

Total win prize-money £63667

Going:	Sf: 0-3 GS: 0-2 Gd: 0-0 GF: - Fm: 0-0
Distance:	2m/2m3: 0-0 2m4-2m7: 0-0 3m+: 0-5
Track:	LH: 0-2 RH: 0-2 Tight: 0-3 Gall: 0-1
Aids:	Bl: 0-2 Vi: 0-0 Tstrap: 0-0
Best Rating:	150 4/01 Aint 3m110y soft Hdl

A bumper winner in Ireland, he has won at up to three miles over hurdles and handled the bottomless conditions really well when winning the 2001 Sefton Novices Hurdle at Aintree by a distance. Made a workmanlike start to his career over fences at Plumpton, but subsequently went backwards. Disappointing when returning after a wind operation in late 2002. Stays really well, but does not always look an easy ride.

Garsington (IRE)

(66c)94

6-y-o ch g Over The River (FR)-Apicat (Buckskin (FR))
Michael Hourigan   W Neville

Placings:4P040F00P04 (4646a)
2002/03: 17⁴G, 22²HY, 22⁰S, 18⁴Y, 24⁰S, 17⁴S, 18⁰YS, 22⁰S, 20⁰HY, 20⁰GY, 19⁴GF,

	Starts	1st	2nd	3rd	Win & Pl
NH Flat	2	0	0	0	260
Hurdles	4	0	0	0	294
Chases	5	0	0	0	0
Career Total	11	0	0	0	554

Going:	Sf: 0-6 GS: 0-0 Gd: 0-1 GF: - Fm: 0-1
Distance:	2m/2m3: 0-5 2m4-2m7: 0-5 3m+: 0-1
Track:	LH: 0-2 RH: 0-2 Tight: 0-1 Gall: 0-0
Aids:	Bl: 0-0 Vi: 0-0 Tstrap: 0-0
Best Rating:	95 4/03 Cork 2m3f gd-fm NHF

Garth Pool (IRE)

6-y-o b g Sri Pekan (USA)-Millionetta (IRE) (Danehill (USA))
G F Edwards (I A Wood 2/5)   G F Edwards

Placings:P5 (0925)
2002/03: 17⁰GF, 17⁵GF,

	Starts	1st	2nd	3rd	Win & Pl
Hurdles	2	0	0	0	0
Career Total	2	0	0	0	0

Going:	Sf: 0-0 GS: 0-0 Gd: 0-0 GF: - Fm: 0-2
Distance:	2m/2m3: 0-2 2m4-2m7: 0-0 3m+: 0-0
Track:	LH: 0-2 RH: 0-0 Tight: 0-2 Gall: 0-0

Gary's Pimpernel

106f   97f

4-y-o b g Shaddad (USA)-Pennine Star (IRE) (Pennine Walk)
M W Easterby   M W Easterby

Placings:12 (4357)
2002/03: 16¹S, 16²GF,

	Starts	1st	2nd	3rd	Win & Pl
NH Flat	2	1	1	0	2521
Career Total	2	1	1	0	2521
90	3/03	Catt	2m	H NHF		SFT	£1939

Total win prize-money £1939

Going:	Sf: 1-1 GS: 0-0 Gd: 0-0 GF: - Fm: 0-1
Distance:	2m/2m3: 1-2 2m4-2m7: 0-0 3m+: 0-0
Track:	LH: 1-2 RH: 0-0 Tight: 1-1 Gall: 0-0
Aids:	Bl: 0-0 Vi: 0-0 Tstrap: 0-0
Best Rating:	99 3/03 Weth 2m gd-fm NHF

Made a successfull bow in low-grade bumper at Catterick in March; ran well when runner-up under a penalty at Wetherby two weeks later.

Gastornis

104   113+

5-y-o ch g Primitive Rising (USA)-Meggies Dene (Apollo Eight)
M W Easterby   Lord Daresbury

Placings:5-212121 (4715)
2002/03: 16²GF, 16¹GF, 17²G, 20¹GF, 16²G, 20¹GF,

	Starts	1st	2nd	3rd	Win & Pl
NH Flat	3	1	2	0	3310
Hurdles	3	2	1	0	7992
Career Total	7	3	3	0	11302
116	4/03	Weth	2m4f110yE Hdl		G-F	£3724
104	3/03	Weth	2m4f110yF Hdl		G-F	£3167
98	10/02	Hexm	2m110y H NHF		G-F	£1827

Total win prize-money £8719

Going:	Sf: 0-0 GS: 0-0 Gd: 0-2 GF: - Fm: 3-4
Distance:	2m/2m3: 1-4 2m4-2m7: 2-2 3m+: 0-0
Track:	LH: 3-5 RH: 0-0 Tight: 0-1 Gall: 0-0
Aids:	Bl: 0-0 Vi: 0-0 Tstrap: 2-4
Best Rating:	116 4/03 Weth 2m4f110y gd-fm Hdl

Fair novice hurdler; showed useful form in bumpers; got off the mark over hurdles at the first attempt and touched off next time when dropped in trip; won again at Wetherby; effective up to two miles four furlongs; acts on decent ground; usually wears a tongue tie.

Gate Expectations

82   58

5-y-o b m Alflora (IRE)-Dorazine (Kalaglow)
R J Price   Englands Gate Limited

Placings:0-060600 (3152)
2002/03: 16⁰G, 17⁶GF, 16⁰G, 16⁶G, 16⁰G, 16⁰HY,

	Starts	1st	2nd	3rd	Win & Pl
NH Flat	2	0	0	0	0
Hurdles	4	0	0	0	0
Career Total	7	0	0	0	0

Going:	Sf: 0-1 GS: 0-0 Gd: 0-4 GF: - Fm: 0-1
Distance:	2m/2m3: 0-6 2m4-2m7: 0-0 3m+: 0-0
Track:	LH: 0-3 RH: 0-5 Tight: 0-1 Gall: 0-0

Gatejumper (IRE)

74f   71f

5-y-o b g Zaffaran (USA)-Nelly Don (Shackleton)
R H Alner   Pell-Mell Partners

Placings:0 (3782)
2002/03: 17⁰GS,

	Starts	1st	2nd	3rd	Win & Pl
NH Flat	1	0	0	0	
Career Total	1	0	0	0	

Going:	Sf: 0-0 GS: 0-1 Gd: 0-0 GF: - Fm: 0-0
Distance:	2m/2m3: 0-1 2m4-2m7: 0-0 3m+: 0-0
Track:	LH: 0-0 RH: 0-1 Tight: 0-0 Gall: 0-0
Aids:	Bl: 0-0 Vi: 0-0 Tstrap: 0-0
Best Rating:	71 2/03 Extr 2m1f gd-sft NHF

Gatflax (IRE)

106(82h)   (98h)96

11-y-o b g Supreme Leader-Polly s Slipper (Pollerton)
Andrew Turnell   Dr John Hollowood

Placings:1/ f6312135/030P/552RP/PP24564/51352133065-P51P2B (1949)
2002/03: 16⁶G, 17⁵GF, 17¹S, 20⁶GF, 17²G, 16⁸S,

	Starts	1st	2nd	3rd	Win & Pl
Chases	6	1	1	0	6020
Career Total	42	7	5	6	37691
96	8/02	Strf	2m1f110yE(0-105)HCh		SFT	£4777
96	12/01	Sthl	2m	F(0-110)HCh		SFT	£2884
94	6/01	Worc	2m	F(0-95)HCh		GD	£2782
129	2/98	Chep	2m110y	E Hdl		G-S	£2612
135	1/98	Asct	2m110y	D Hdl		SFT	£3728
115	10/97	Hntg	2m110y	H NHF		GD	£1381
116	3/97	Asct	2m110y	H NHF		GD	£1955

Total win prize-money £20123

Going:	Sf: 1-2 GS: 0-0 Gd: 0-2 GF: - Fm: 0-2
Distance:	2m/2m3: 1-5 2m4-2m7: 0-1 3m+: 0-0
Track:	LH: 1-5 RH: 0-0 Tight: 1-3 Gall: 0-1
Aids:	Bl: 0-0 Vi: 0-0 Tstrap: 0-0
Best Rating:	146 3/98 Chel 2m110y good Hdl

A smart novice hurdler in the 1997/1998 campaign, he cost his current connections a massive 200,000 guineas. Landed low grade soft ground handicap chases as Southwell in December 2001 and Stratford August 2002. Best at around two miles.

Gatorade (NZ)

113(102h)   (107h)110+

11-y-o ch g Dahar (USA)-Ribena (NZ) (Battle-Waggon)
N H Oliver (Ian Williams 5/10)   The Cider Sauce Partnership

Placings:046/0112201212P/421245P-1245202P (4678)
2002/03: 20¹G, 20²GF, 20⁴GF, 20⁵GF, 22²GF, 20⁰GF, 24²G, 19²GF,

	Starts	1st	2nd	3rd	Win & Pl
Hurdles	2	1	0	0	1589
Chases	6	1	2	0	9639
Career Total	29	6	9	0	39410
115	6/02	Worc	2m4f110yC(0-130)HCh		GD	£6760
112	7/01	Strf	2m1f110yE Ch		GD	£3055
121	9/00	Uttx	2m4f110yB(0-140)HHdl		G-S	£6721
104	8/00	NAbb	2m1f	D Hdl		GD	£2879
113	6/00	Worc	2m4f	F(0-110)HHdl		G-F	£2348

105 6/00 Uttx 2m4f110yD Hdl   G-F £3237
Total win prize-money £25002

Going:	Sf: 0-0 GS: 0-0 Gd: 1-2 GF: - Fm: 0-6
Distance:	2m/2m3: 0-1 **2m4-2m7: 1-6** 3m+: 0-1
Track:	**LH: 1-5** RH: 0-3 Tight: 0-3 Gall: 0-0
Aids:	Bl: 0-0 Vi: 0-0 Tstrap: 0-0
Best Rating:	**121** 10/00 Chel 2m5f good Hdl

Fair chaser/hurdler in his time; runner-up in hunter chase at Stratford April; 2003; won extended 2m5f handicap chase at Southwell July 2003 on first outing for Richard Guest; followed up in facile fashion at Sedgefield a week later; acts on most types of ground.

Gaudi Parc
86   66
5-y-o ch g King s Signet (USA)-Witch (Risk Me (FR))
Mrs S J Smith Mrs S Watkinson

Placings:PO06   (4616)
2002/03: 16²G, 16⁰G, 16⁰G, 17⁶GF,

	Starts	1st	2nd	3rd	Win & Pl
Hurdles	4	0	0	0	0
Career Total	4	0	0	0	0

Going:	Sf: 0-0 GS: 0-0 Gd: 0-3 GF: - Fm: 0-1
Distance:	2m/2m3: 0-4 2m4-2m7: 0-0 3m+: 0-0
Track:	LH: 0-3 RH: 0-1 Tight: 0-0 Gall: 0-1
Aids:	Bl: 0-0 Vi: 0-0 Tstrap: 0-0
Best Rating:	**66** 4/03 Uttx 2m good Hdl

Plating-class hurdler; poor form so far.

Gaultier Gale (IRE)
94
9-y-o b g Ajraas (USA)-David s Pleasure (Welsh Saint)
Mrs L B Normile Steve Whiting,John Beaton,Alison Kendall

Placings:15060/500/00B0351206P44/342014144F0/10P50
PPP-6U   (0356)
2002/03: 20⁶GF, 24ᵁGS,

	Starts	1st	2nd	3rd	Win & Pl
Chases	2	0	0	0	0
Career Total	42	5	2	2	19111
94 5/01	Fknm	2m5f110yF(0-90)HCh		G-F	£2536
94 8/00	Sthl	2m4f110yF(0-105)HCh		GD	£3406
85 7/00	Sthl	2m4f110yF(0-95)HCh		G-F	£2808
79 9/99	Dpat	2m2f	(0-95)HCh	GD	£2464
113 12/97	Clon	2m	Hdl	HVY	£2712

Total win prize-money £13928

Going:	Sf: 0-0 GS: 0-1 Gd: 0-0 GF: - Fm: 0-1
Distance:	2m/2m3: 0-0 2m4-2m7: 0-0 3m+: 0-1
Track:	LH: 0-1 RH: 0-1 Tight: 0-1 Gall: 0-0
Aids:	Bl: 0-0 Vi: 0-0 Tstrap: 0-0
Best Rating:	**113** 12/97 Clon 2m heavy Hdl

Moderate handicap chaser. Stays two and a half miles. Acts on a sound surface.

Gay Abandon

8-y-o ch m Risk Me (FR)-School Dinners (Sharpo)
C R Johnson C R Johnson

Placings:P   (4288)
2002/03: 20⁰GF,

	Starts	1st	2nd	3rd	Win & Pl
Chases	1	0	0	0	
Career Total	1	0	0	0	

Going:	Sf: 0-0 GS: 0-0 Gd: 0-0 GF: - Fm: 0-1
Distance:	2m/2m3: 0-0 2m4-2m7: 0-1 3m+: 0-0
Track:	LH: 0-0 RH: 0-1 Tight: 0-1 Gall: 0-0
Aids:	Bl: 0-0 Vi: 0-0 Tstrap: 0-0
Best Rating:	**0** 3/03 Ludl 2m4f gd-fm Ch

Gayble
91f   70f
5-y-o b g Good Times (ITY)-High Kabour (Kabour)
P F Nicholls R G Gay

Placings:4   (1398)
2002/03: 16⁴GF,

	Starts	1st	2nd	3rd	Win & Pl
NH Flat	1	0	0	0	0
Career Total	1	0	0	0	0

Going:	Sf: 0-0 GS: 0-0 Gd: 0-0 GF: - Fm: 0-1
Distance:	2m/2m3: 0-1 2m4-2m7: 0-0 3m+: 0-0
Track:	LH: 0-1 RH: 0-0 Tight: 0-0 Gall: 0-0
Aids:	Bl: 0-0 Vi: 0-0 Tstrap: 0-0
Best Rating:	**70** 10/02 Chep 2m110y gd-fm NHF

Gaye Dream
93f   102f
5-y-o b g Gildoran-Gaye Fame (Ardross)
D J Caro Mrs S Tainton

Placings:50   (3174)
2002/03: 16⁵S, 16⁰GS,

	Starts	1st	2nd	3rd	Win & Pl
NH Flat	2	0	0	0	0
Career Total	2	0	0	0	0

Going:	Sf: 0-1 GS: 0-1 Gd: 0-0 GF: - Fm: 0-0
Distance:	2m/2m3: 0-2 2m4-2m7: 0-0 3m+: 0-0
Track:	LH: 0-2 RH: 0-0 Tight: 0-0 Gall: 0-0
Aids:	Bl: 0-0 Vi: 0-0 Tstrap: 0-0
Best Rating:	**102** 12/02 Wwck 2m soft NHF

Modest form in bumpers on soft ground.

Gayles And Showers (IRE)
107   100
9-y-o b g Lord Americo-Decent Shower (Decent Fellow)
Mrs S C Bradburne Copland, Hardie And Steel

Placings:/0364/305046F50P/51416141520U3/50560P124P-
3242634P   (4017)
2002/03: 24³GF, 20²G, 22⁴S, 16²S, 25⁶S, 20⁵G, 16⁴HY, 20⁵S,

	Starts	1st	2nd	3rd	Win & Pl
Chases	8	0	2	2	6091
Career Total	45	5	4	5	33464
101 3/02	Ayr	2m4f	E(0-110)HCh	HVY	£3851
112 1/01	Ayr	2m4f	C(0-130)HCh	SFT	£6103
107 11/00	Newc	2m110y	E(0-115)HCh	SFT	£2938
102 10/00	Hexm	2m110y	F(0-90)Ch	HVY	£2716
102 5/00	Prth	2m	D Ch	G-S	£4108

Total win prize-money £19717

Going:	Sf: 0-6 GS: 0-0 Gd: 0-1 GF: - Fm: 0-1
Distance:	2m/2m3: 0-2 2m4-2m7: 0-4 3m+: 0-2
Track:	LH: 0-7 RH: 0-1 Tight: 0-2 Gall: 0-1
Aids:	Bl: 0-0 Vi: 0-0 Tstrap: 0-0
Best Rating:	**112** 2/01 Newc 2m4f heavy Ch

Moderate chaser, winner several times over fences in both novice and handicap company, he acts on a soft surface and stays three miles, but is effective over shorter.

Gayling
(80h)   (56h)
8-y-o ch m Carlingford Castle-Gay Ticket (New Member)
P J Hobbs A L Hobbs

Placings:0/000/0P   (2780)
2002/03: 19⁰GF, 19ᴾS,

	Starts	1st	2nd	3rd	Win & Pl
Hurdles	1	0	0	0	0
Chases	1	0	0	0	0
Career Total	6	0	0	0	0

Going:	Sf: 0-1 GS: 0-0 Gd: 0-0 GF: - Fm: 0-1
Distance:	2m/2m3: 0-1 2m4-2m7: 0-1 3m+: 0-0
Track:	LH: 0-0 RH: 0-2 Tight: 0-2 Gall: 0-0
Aids:	Bl: 0-0 Vi: 0-0 Tstrap: 0-0
Best Rating:	**68** 5/00 Extr 2m1f good Hdl

Gaynor
89(100h)   (83h)76
7-y-o b m Almoojid-High Kabour (Kabour)
P F Nicholls R G Gay

Placings:41/55-65   (0772)
2002/03: 17⁶GF, 16⁵GF,

	Starts	1st	2nd	3rd	Win & Pl
Hurdles	1	0	0	0	0
Chases	1	0	0	0	0
Career Total	6	1	0	0	3523
89 9/00	Chep	2m110y D Hdl		GD	£3523

Total win prize-money £3523

Going:	Sf: 0-0 GS: 0-0 Gd: 0-0 GF: - Fm: 0-2
Distance:	2m/2m3: 0-2 2m4-2m7: 0-0 3m+: 0-0
Track:	LH: 0-2 RH: 0-0 Tight: 0-1 Gall: 0-0
Aids:	Bl: 0-0 Vi: 0-0 Tstrap: 0-0
Best Rating:	**89** 9/00 Chep 2m110y good Hdl

Gaysun
109(98h)   (107h)118
11-y-o b g Lir-Indomitable (FR) (Indian King (USA))
P F Nicholls R G Gay

Placings:54/110221F33/43212354/211163222-312230
(1396)
2002/03: 26³GF, 26¹GF, 24²G, 24²GF, 26³G, 24⁰GF,

	Starts	1st	2nd	3rd	Win & Pl
Hurdles	1	0	1	0	1822
Chases	5	1	2	1	11696
Career Total	34	8	10	7	58118
118 7/02	NAbb	3m2f110yC(0-135)HCh		G-F	£7669
107 8/01	Strf	2m6f110yE Hdl		G-F	£2957
107 7/01	Worc	3m	E Hdl	SFT	£2408
118 6/01	Strf	3m	D(0-125)HCh	G-F	£4403
118 8/00	Uttx	2m4f	D(0-125)HCh	G-F	£4030
105 10/99	Winc	2m5f	E(0-115)HCh	GD	£5225
92 8/99	NAbb	2m5f110yD(0-125)HCh		G-S	£3710
98 5/99	Extr	2m3f	H Ch	FRM	£1567

Total win prize-money £31973

Going:	Sf: 0-0 GS: 0-0 Gd: 0-2 GF: - Fm: 1-4
Distance:	2m/2m3: 0-0 2m4-2m7: 0-0 **3m+: 1-6**
Track:	**LH: 1-6** RH: 0-0 **Tight: 1-4** Gall: 0-0
Aids:	Bl: 0-0 Vi: 0-0 Tstrap: 0-0
Best Rating:	**118** 9/02 Strf 3m gd-fm Ch

A former hunter chaser, he is a useful summer jumper over

both hurdles and fences. Stays three miles and acts on fast ground.

Gazeila

86   **59**

4-y-o b f Makbul-Liberatrice (FR) (Assert)
J J Bridger The Hop-Pickers Partnership

Placings:006   (4755)
2002/03: 16⁰GS, 17⁰F, 18⁶GF,

	Starts	1st	2nd	3rd	Win & Pl
Hurdles	3	0	0	0	0
Career Total	3	0	0	0	0

Going:	Sf: 0-0 GS: 0-1 Gd: 0-0 GF: - Fm: 0-2
Distance:	2m/2m3: 0-3 2m4-2m7: 0-0 3m+: 0-0
Track:	LH: 0-1 RH: 0-2 Tight: 0-2 Gall: 0-0
Aids:	Bl: 0-0 Vi: 0-0 Tstrap: 0-0
Best Rating:	59 12/02 Winc 2m gd-sft Hdl

Gazump (FR)

78f   **95f**

5-y-o b g Iris Noir (FR)-Viva Sacree (FR) (Maiymad)
N A Twiston-Davies H R Mould

Placings:300   (3528)
2002/03: 17³G, 12⁰G, 16⁶G,

	Starts	1st	2nd	3rd	Win & Pl
NH Flat	3	0	0	1	480
Career Total	3	0	0	1	480

Going:	Sf: 0-0 GS: 0-0 Gd: 0-3 GF: - Fm: 0-0
Distance:	2m/2m3: 0-2 2m4-2m7: 0-0 3m+: 0-0
Track:	LH: 0-2 RH: 0-0 Tight: 0-0 Gall: 0-1
Aids:	Bl: 0-0 Vi: 0-0 Tstrap: 0-0
Best Rating:	95 11/02 Aint 2m1f good NHF

Promising debut in a bumper. Held subsequently.

Gebora (FR)

102   **100**

4-y-o ch g Villez (USA)-Sitapanoki (FR) (Houston (FR))
M C Pipe Neil J Edwards

Placings:162   (4431)
2002/03: 17¹HY, 17⁵GS, 18²GF,

	Starts	1st	2nd	3rd	Win & Pl
NH Flat	3	1	1	0	3189
Career Total	3	1	1	0	3189
91 2/03 Folk 2m1f110yH NHF				HVY	£2093
				Total win prize-money £2093

Going:	Sf: 1-1 GS: 0-1 Gd: 0-0 GF: - Fm: 0-1
Distance:	2m/2m3: 1-3 2m4-2m7: 0-0 3m+: 0-0
Track:	LH: 0-1 RH: 1-2 Tight: 1-1 Gall: 0-0
Aids:	Bl: 0-0 Vi: 0-0 Tstrap: 0-0
Best Rating:	106 3/03 Plum 2m2f gd-fm NHF

Won heavy ground bumper on debut at Folkestone; disappointing next time and hung right on third start at Plumpton; easy winner on hurdling debut at Exeter May 2003; seems to act on all types of ground.

Gee A Two (IRE)

74   **36**

6-y-o gr h Roselier (FR)-Miss Doogles (Beau Charmeur (FR))
Ferdy Murphy S L & M A Hubbard Rodwell

                                                         (3801)
2002/03: 16⁰HY, 24⁰S,

	Starts	1st	2nd	3rd	Win & Pl
NH Flat	1	0	0	0	0
Hurdles	1	0	0	0	0
Career Total	3	0	0	0	0

Going:	Sf: 0-2 GS: 0-0 Gd: 0-0 GF: - Fm: 0-0
Distance:	2m/2m3: 0-1 2m4-2m7: 0-0 3m+: 0-1
Track:	LH: 0-2 RH: 0-0 Tight: 0-0 Gall: 0-1
Aids:	Bl: 0-0 Vi: 0-0 Tstrap: 0-0
Best Rating:	66 1/03 Newc 2m heavy NHF

Gee Bee Boy

87(92c)   (73c)**55**

9-y-o ch g Beveled (USA)-Blue And White (Busted)
G F Bridgwater (D G Bridgwater 9/8) Woodnorton Hall - Evesham

Placings:23/361U4PP020/323413106/0U045034600040-00000   (2168)
2002/03: 17⁰G, 21⁰G, 16⁰GS, 16⁰G, 19⁰GS,

	Starts	1st	2nd	3rd	Win & Pl
Hurdles	5	0	0	0	
Career Total	40	3	3	6	12620
100 10/00 Strf 2m110y F(0-100)HHdl				SFT	£2310
100 8/00 Worc 2m G Hdl				G-F	£1498
105 6/99 Uttx 2m D Hdl				G-S	£3793
				Total win prize-money £7602

Going:	Sf: 0-0 GS: 0-2 Gd: 0-3 GF: - Fm: 0-0
Distance:	2m/2m3: 0-4 2m4-2m7: 0-1 3m+: 0-0
Track:	LH: 0-3 RH: 0-2 Tight: 0-2 Gall: 0-0
Aids:	Bl: 0-0 Vi: 0-0 Tstrap: 0-1
Best Rating:	105 6/99 Uttx 2m gd-sft Hdl

Gem Of Holly

68

10-y-o b m Holly Buoy-Stuart s Gem (Meldrum)
R S Wood R S Wood

Placings:0/003/00P/54006F1P6/06/0300660-P   (0359)
2002/03: 24⁰GS,

	Starts	1st	2nd	3rd	Win & Pl
Hurdles	1	0	0	0	
Career Total	26	1	0	2	2122
76 1/00 Sedg 2m5f110yG(0-90)Hdl			SFT	£1736
			Total win prize-money £1736

Going:	Sf: 0-0 GS: 0-1 Gd: 0-0 GF: - Fm: 0-0
Distance:	2m/2m3: 0-0 2m4-2m7: 0-0 3m+: 0-1
Track:	LH: 0-1 RH: 0-0 Tight: 0-1 Gall: 0-0
Aids:	Bl: 0-0 Vi: 0-0 Tstrap: 0-1
Best Rating:	76 1/00 Sedg 2m5f110y soft Hdl

Gemi Bed (FR)

99   **85**

8-y-o b g Double Bed (FR)-Gemia (FR) (King Of Macedon)
G L Moore B Lennard

Placings:6-2003   (4631)
2002/03: 16²GF, 17⁰G, 16⁶S, 16³GF,

	Starts	1st	2nd	3rd	Win & Pl
Hurdles	4	0	1	1	1068
Career Total	5	0	1	1	1068

Going:	Sf: 0-1 GS: 0-0 Gd: 0-0 GF: - Fm: 0-0
Distance:	2m/2m3: 0-4 2m4-2m7: 0-0 3m+: 0-0

Gemineye Lord (IRE)

Track: LH: 0-3 RH: 0-1 Tight: 0-2 Gall: 0-1
Aids: Bl: 0-4 Vi: 0-0 Tstrap: 0-0
Best Rating: 98 5/02 Hntg 2m110y gd-fm Hdl

Moderate hurdler; French import, lightly raced over hurdles, but has shown ability; wears blinkers.

Gemineye Lord (IRE)

6-y-o b g Mister Lord (USA)-Mum s Eyes (Al Sirat (USA))
Mrs S J Smith The Kalleys

Placings:00P   (4715)
2002/03: 16⁰GS, 17⁰GS, 20⁰GF,

	Starts	1st	2nd	3rd	Win & Pl
NH Flat	2	0	0	0	0
Hurdles	1	0	0	0	0
Career Total	3	0	0	0	0

Going:	Sf: 0-0 GS: 0-2 Gd: 0-0 GF: - Fm: 0-1
Distance:	2m/2m3: 0-2 2m4-2m7: 0-1 3m+: 0-0
Track:	LH: 0-2 RH: 0-1 Tight: 0-0 Gall: 0-0
Aids:	Bl: 0-0 Vi: 0-0 Tstrap: 0-0
Best Rating:	73 3/03 Carl 2m1f gd-sft NHF

Gemolly (IRE)

95(87h)   **11**

10-y-o b m Be My Native (USA)-Hayhurst (Sandhurst Prince)
T Needham T Needham

Placings:P00P4/35P4P0UP/P6466/04P0-P5P3040 (4627)
2002/03: 25⁵GS, 23⁵G, 25⁵GF, 21³G, 19⁰G, 25⁴S, 21⁰GF,

	Starts	1st	2nd	3rd	Win & Pl
Chases	7	0	0	1	623
Career Total	29	0	0	2	1393

Going:	Sf: 0-1 GS: 0-1 Gd: 0-3 GF: - Fm: 0-2
Distance:	2m/2m3: 0-0 2m4-2m7: 0-3 3m+: 0-4
Track:	LH: 0-4 RH: 0-3 Tight: 0-2 Gall: 0-0
Aids:	Bl: 0-2 Vi: 0-0 Tstrap: 0-0
Best Rating:	71 10/98 MRas 3m gd-sft Hdl

General

113   **116**

6-y-o b g Cadeaux Genereux-Bareilly (USA) (Lyphard (USA))
Mrs N Smith Tony Hayward

Placings:05/301151-501505   (3829)
2002/03: 16⁵S, 16⁶S, 16¹HY, 17⁵HY, 20⁰HY, 16⁵GS,

	Starts	1st	2nd	3rd	Win & Pl
Hurdles	6	1	0	0	4446
Career Total	14	4	0	1	13851
123 12/02 Chep 2m110y D(0-120)HHdl			HVY	£3786
123 3/02 Plum 2m E Hdl			G-S	£2457
120 1/02 Leic 2m E Hdl			SFT	£3451
115 12/01 Towc 2m E Hdl			HVY	£3073
			Total win prize-money £12767

Going:	Sf: 1-5 GS: 0-1 Gd: 0-0 GF: - Fm: 0-0
Distance:	2m/2m3: 1-5 2m4-2m7: 0-1 3m+: 0-0
Track:	LH: 1-4 RH: 0-2 Tight: 0-0 Gall: 0-2
Aids:	Bl: 0-0 Vi: 0-0 Tstrap: 0-0
Best Rating:	123 12/02 Chep 2m110y heavy Hdl

Fair handicap hurdler; acts well in testing ground; won

novice hurdles at Towcester, Leicester and Plumpton in 2001/02; returned to form at Chepstow in December 2002; suited by two miles and soft/heavy ground.

General Assembly (IRE)

11-y-o b g Pharly (FR)-Hastening (Shirley Heights)
Mrs Peter Hall P P Hall

Placings:3P3304/5446/F   (0154)
2002/03: 24FG,

	Starts	1st	2nd	3rd	Win & Pl
Chases	1	0	0	0	
Career Total	11	0	0	3	1270

Going:	Sf: 0-0 GS: 0-0 Gd: 0-1 GF: - Fm: 0-0
Distance:	2m/2m3: 0-0 2m4-2m7: 0-0 3m+: 0-1
Track:	LH: 0-1 RH: 0-0 Tight: 0-1 Gall: 0-0
Aids:	Bl: 0-0 Vi: 0-0 Tstrap: 0-0
Best Rating:	114 3/98 Chel 2m110y good Hdl

General Claremont (IRE)

108   **128**

10-y-o gr g Strong Gale-Kasam (General Ironside)
P F Nicholls K G Manley

Placings:0/300305/2F1F0/51243/P1224U4-22165U4U
    (4796)
2002/03: 28²G, 32²GF, 23¹S, 24⁶F, 24⁵GF, 31¹G, 31⁴GS, 28⁴UGF,

	Starts	1st	2nd	3rd	Win & Pl
Chases	8	1	2	0	22575
Career Total	32	4	6	3	43669
128	8/02	Worc	2m7f110yC(0-130)HCh	SFT	£8855
126	6/01	NAbb	3m2f110yD(0-120)HCh	GD	£4124
120	11/00	Tntn	3m	F(0-105)HCh	GD	£2925
112	1/00	Leic	2m4f110yE Ch	GD	£3042

Total win prize-money £18946

Going:	Sf: 1-1 GS: 0-2 Gd: 0-1 GF: - Fm: 0-4
Distance:	2m/2m3: 0-0 2m4-2m7: 0-0 3m+: 1-8
Track:	LH: 1-7 RH: 0-0 Tight: 0-2 Gall: 0-0
Aids:	Bl: 0-1 Vi: 0-0 Tstrap: 0-0
Best Rating:	128 9/02 List 3m firm Ch

Fair staying chaser on good ground or faster; also handles cut in the ground; often let down by his jumping; stays extreme distances.

General Dominion

88

6-y-o b g Governor General-Innocent Princess (NZ) (Full On Aces (AUS))
Mrs A M Thorpe Three A s Caravans

Placings:50-P   (0217)
2002/03: 17PG,

	Starts	1st	2nd	3rd	Win & Pl
Hurdles	1	0	0	0	
Career Total	3	0	0	0	0

Going:	Sf: 0-0 GS: 0-0 Gd: 0-1 GF: - Fm: 0-0
Distance:	2m/2m3: 0-1 2m4-2m7: 0-0 3m+: 0-0
Track:	LH: 0-0 RH: 0-1 Tight: 0-0 Gall: 0-0
Aids:	Bl: 0-0 Vi: 0-0 Tstrap: 0-0
Best Rating:	88 4/02 MRas 2m1f110y gd-fm Hdl

General Duroc (IRE)

105   **122**

7-y-o ch g Un Desperado (FR)-Satula (Deep Run)
R T Phillips Graeme Love

Placings:26-604111   (4304)
2002/03: 16⁶G, 16⁹GS, 20⁴HY, 24¹S, 24¹S, 22¹G,

	Starts	1st	2nd	3rd	Win & Pl
NH Flat	1	0	0	0	
Hurdles	5	3	0	0	13306
Career Total	8	3	1	0	14338
122	3/03	Kels	2m6f110yE Hdl	GD	£4368
109	3/03	Ayr	3m110y D(0-115)HHdl	SFT	£5492
109	2/03	Newc	3m	E Hdl	SFT	£3445

Total win prize-money £13306

Going:	Sf: 2-3 GS: 0-1 Gd: 1-2 GF: - Fm: 0-0
Distance:	2m/2m3: 0-2 2m4-2m7: 1-2 3m+: 2-2
Track:	LH: 3-3 RH: 0-3 Tight: 1-2 Gall: 1-1
Aids:	Bl: 0-0 Vi: 0-0 Tstrap: 0-0
Best Rating:	122 3/03 Kels 2m6f110y good Hdl

Progressive novice hurdler; stays three miles; completed a hat-trick at the start of 2003; acts on any ground.

General Gossip (IRE)

95

7-y-o b/br g Supreme Leader-Sno-Sleigh (Bargello)
Miss H C Knight (J A B Old 24/5) The Early Birds

Placings:052-FPP   (2134)
2002/03: 16⁶G, 21⁹S, 21⁰G,

	Starts	1st	2nd	3rd	Win & Pl
Hurdles	3	0	0	0	
Career Total	6	0	1	0	1392

Going:	Sf: 0-1 GS: 0-0 Gd: 0-2 GF: - Fm: 0-0
Distance:	2m/2m3: 0-1 2m4-2m7: 0-0 3m+: 0-0
Track:	LH: 0-0 RH: 0-3 Tight: 0-0 Gall: 0-0
Aids:	Bl: 0-0 Vi: 0-0 Tstrap: 0-1
Best Rating:	113 2/02 Asct 2m110y soft NHF

General Jackson

6-y-o ch g Cadeaux Genereux-Moidart (Electric)
Jane Southcombe Vivant & V R V Partnership

Placings:0PP   (4196)
2002/03: 22²G, 24PS, 24PG,

	Starts	1st	2nd	3rd	Win & Pl
Hurdles	3	0	0	0	
Career Total	3	0	0	0	

Going:	Sf: 0-1 GS: 0-0 Gd: 0-2 GF: - Fm: 0-0
Distance:	2m/2m3: 0-0 2m4-2m7: 0-0 3m+: 0-2
Track:	LH: 0-1 RH: 0-2 Tight: 0-0 Gall: 0-0
Aids:	Bl: 0-0 Vi: 0-0 Tstrap: 0-0
Best Rating:	0 3/03 Ludl 3m good Hdl

General O'Keeffe

6-y-o b g Alflora (IRE)-Rosie O Keeffe (IRE) (Royal Fountain)
J D Frost Mrs B C Willcocks

Placings:0P   (3140)

2002/03: 16⁰S, 19PS,

	Starts	1st	2nd	3rd	Win & Pl
NH Flat	1	0	0	0	
Hurdles	1	0	0	0	0
Career Total	2	0	0	0	

Going:	Sf: 0-2 GS: 0-0 Gd: 0-0 GF: - Fm: 0-0
Distance:	2m/2m3: 0-1 2m4-2m7: 0-1 3m+: 0-0
Track:	LH: 0-1 RH: 0-1 Tight: 0-1 Gall: 0-0
Aids:	Bl: 0-0 Vi: 0-0 Tstrap: 0-0
Best Rating:	79 12/02 Wwck 2m soft NHF

General Seymour

83(82h)   (50h)**40**

8-y-o ch g Seymour Hicks (FR)-Madge Hill (Spartan General)
R Ford L A E Hopkins

Placings:0/0000   (3561)
2002/03: 17⁰HY, 20⁰G, 20⁰S, 25⁰S,

	Starts	1st	2nd	3rd	Win & Pl
Hurdles	2	0	0	0	0
Chases	2	0	0	0	
Career Total	5	0	0	0	

Going:	Sf: 0-3 GS: 0-0 Gd: 0-1 GF: - Fm: 0-0
Distance:	2m/2m3: 0-1 2m4-2m7: 0-2 3m+: 0-1
Track:	LH: 0-1 RH: 0-3 Tight: 0-1 Gall: 0-0
Aids:	Bl: 0-0 Vi: 0-0 Tstrap: 0-0
Best Rating:	50 11/02 Carl 2m1f heavy Hdl

General Tantrum (IRE)

81   **67**

6-y-o b g Ilium-Barna Havna (Crash Course)
A Ennis A T A Wates

Placings:P00P   (3549)
2002/03: 21PS, 19⁰GS, 17PG,

	Starts	1st	2nd	3rd	Win & Pl
Hurdles	4	0	0	0	
Career Total	4	0	0	0	

Going:	Sf: 0-1 GS: 0-1 Gd: 0-2 GF: - Fm: 0-0
Distance:	2m/2m3: 0-2 2m4-2m7: 0-2 3m+: 0-0
Track:	LH: 0-3 RH: 0-1 Tight: 0-1 Gall: 0-1
Aids:	Bl: 0-0 Vi: 0-0 Tstrap: 0-0
Best Rating:	67 12/02 Newb 2m110y good Hdl

General Typhoon

12-y-o ch g Nearly A Hand-Steel Typhoon (General Ironside)
Mrs H M Tory R J Tory

Placings:U   (0218)
2002/03: 25UG,

	Starts	1st	2nd	3rd	Win & Pl
Chases	1	0	0	0	
Career Total	1	0	0	0	

Going:	Sf: 0-0 GS: 0-0 Gd: 0-1 GF: - Fm: 0-0
Distance:	2m/2m3: 0-0 2m4-2m7: 0-0 3m+: 0-1
Track:	LH: 0-0 RH: 0-1 Tight: 0-0 Gall: 0-0
Aids:	Bl: 0-0 Vi: 0-0 Tstrap: 0-0

Best Rating: 0   5/02   Hrfd   3m1f110y   good   Ch

General Wolfe

14-y-o ch g Rolfe (USA)-Pillbox (Spartan General)
T W Dennis Mark Gichero

Placings:6/4141/U411/211F2/140/261/1F60P/24B5/521-2
(4459)
2002/03: 21²G,

	Starts	1st	2nd	3rd	Win & Pl
Chases	1	0	1	0	7500
Career Total	33	10	6	0	129500
125 4/02	Prth	3m7f	H Ch		GD	£4186
166 1/99	Hayd	3m	A HCh		SFT	£25300
152 1/98	Hayd	3m	A HCh		SFT	£25408
152 3/97	Hayd	3m	C(0-135)HCh		G-S	£4531
147 2/96	Hayd	3m	C(0-135)HCh		G-S	£4508
127 1/96	Carl	3m	B(0-140)HCh		G-S	£7185
118 3/95	Worc	2m7f	F(0-100)HCh		G-S	£3315
120 1/95	Leic	3m	C(0-110)HCh		G-S	£3522
126 2/94	Folk	2m6f110y	Hdl		HVY	£1896
106 12/93	Towc	2m5f	Hdl		SFT	£2041
			Total win prize-money £81895

Going: Sf: 0-0 GS: 0-0 Gd: 0-1 GF: - Fm: 0-0
Distance: 2m2m3: 0-0 2m4-2m7: 0-0 3m+: 0-0
Track: LH: 0-1 RH: 0-0 Tight: 0-1 Gall: 0-0
Aids: Bl: 0-0 Vi: 0-0 Tstrap: 0-0
Best Rating: 166 1/99 Hayd 3m   soft   Ch

Very useful staying chaser at his best but now in the veteran
stage; very lightly raced in recent years and now competes
in hunter chases, runner-up in the Foxhunters at Aintree in
April 2003; best when fresh; stays extreme distances; suited
by an easy surface.

Generals Laststand (IRE)

87f   90f

5-y-o b g Little Bighorn-Our Dorcet (Condorcet (FR))
Miss G Browne Mrs Rhona Alexander

Placings:10
(3174)
2002/03: 18¹S, 16⁰GS,

	Starts	1st	2nd	3rd	Win & Pl
NH Flat	2	1	0	0	2226
Career Total	2	1	0	0	2226
95 12/02	Font	2m2f110yH NHF		SFT	£2226
		Total win prize-money £2226

Going: Sf: 1-1 GS: 0-1 Gd: 0-0 GF: - Fm: 0-0
Distance: 2m2/m3: 1-2 2m4-2m7: 0-0 3m+: 0-0
Track: LH: 1-2 RH: 0-0 Tight: 1-1 Gall: 0-0
Aids: Bl: 0-0 Vi: 0-0 Tstrap: 0-0
Best Rating: 95 12/02 Font 2m2f110y soft   NHF

Well backed when giving his trainer her first winner in a
bumper at Fontwell in December 2002. Should improve.

Generation Power

7-y-o gr m Arzanni-Hallowed (Wolver Hollow)
P A Pritchard Woodlands (worcestershire) Ltd

Placings:00
(2450)
2002/03: 16⁰GF, 16⁰G,

	Starts	1st	2nd	3rd	Win & Pl
NH Flat	2	0	0	0	
Career Total	2	0	0	0	

Going: Sf: 0-0 GS: 0-0 Gd: 0-1 GF: - Fm: 0-1
Distance: 2m/2m3: 0-2 2m4-2m7: 0-0 3m+: 0-0
Track: LH: 0-0 RH: 0-1 Tight: 0-0 Gall: 0-0
Aids: Bl: 0-0 Vi: 0-0 Tstrap: 0-0
Best Rating: 0   12/02 Ludl   2m   good   NHF

Genereux

10-y-o ch g Generous (IRE)-Flo Russell (USA) (Round
Table)
Mrs A Price Mrs A Price

Placings:P43/33334/0PPP-64
(4541)
2002/03: 25⁶S, 24⁴G,

	Starts	1st	2nd	3rd	Win & Pl
Chases	2	0	0	0	0
Career Total	14	0	0	5	1570

Going: Sf: 0-1 GS: 0-0 Gd: 0-1 GF: - Fm: 0-0
Distance: 2m/2m3: 0-0 2m4-2m7: 0-0 3m+: 0-2
Track: LH: 0-0 RH: 0-2 Tight: 0-1 Gall: 0-0
Aids: Bl: 0-0 Vi: 0-0 Tstrap: 0-0
Best Rating: 81 5/97 Extr   2m3f110y good   Hdl

Generous Ways

104   93

8-y-o ch g Generous (IRE)-Clara Bow (USA) (Coastal
(USA))
R Lee George Brookes & Family

Placings:PP021
(4597)
2002/03: 20⁵S, 21⁵S, 16⁰S, 16²GF, 17¹GF,

	Starts	1st	2nd	3rd	Win & Pl
Hurdles	5	1	1	0	5238
Career Total	5	1	1	0	5238
93 4/03	Extr	2m1f	E(0-105)HHdl	G-F	£3718
		Total win prize-money £3718

Going: Sf: 0-3 GS: 0-0 Gd: 0-0 GF: - Fm: 1-2
Distance: 2m/2m3: 1-3 2m4-2m7: 0-2 3m+: 0-0
Track: LH: 0-2 RH: 1-3 Tight: 0-1 Gall: 0-0
Aids: Bl: 0-0 Vi: 0-0 Tstrap: 1-4
Best Rating: 93 4/03 Extr   2m1f   gd-fm   Hdl

Staying handicapper on the Flat; improved form to win
extended two mile novices handicap on fast ground at
Exeter April 2003; looks well treated and can score again.

Genetic

97

8-y-o b g Syrtos-Abdera (Ahonoora)
D G Bridgwater Mrs S A Macechern

Placings:00430/20/P1P-P
(0075)
2002/03: 25⁰GF,

	Starts	1st	2nd	3rd	Win & Pl
Chases	1	0	0	0	
Career Total	11	1	1	1	6070
97 11/01	Ludl	3m	D Ch		G-F	£4979
		Total win prize-money £4979

Going: Sf: 0-0 GS: 0-0 Gd: 0-0 GF: - Fm: 0-1
Distance: 2m/2m3: 0-0 2m4-2m7: 0-1 3m+: 0-1
Track: LH: 0-0 RH: 0-1 Tight: 0-0 Gall: 0-0
Aids: Bl: 0-0 Vi: 0-0 Tstrap: 0-0
Best Rating: 103 11/00 Wwck 2m5f   heavy   Hdl

Effective at three miles, he acts on good to firm ground.

Genetic George (IRE)

91

11-y-o b g King s Ride-Ballyea Jacki (Straight Lad)
Dr P Pritchard A J Whiting

Placings:513/B06/3U/3-5F
(0355)
2002/03: 17⁵GF, 20⁴GS,

	Starts	1st	2nd	3rd	Win & Pl
Chases	2	0	0	0	0
Career Total	11	1	0	3	5157
99 4/99	Cork	2m4f		Hdl	SFT	£3683
		Total win prize-money £3683

Going: Sf: 0-0 GS: 0-1 Gd: 0-0 GF: - Fm: 0-1
Distance: 2m/2m3: 0-1 2m4-2m7: 0-1 3m+: 0-0
Track: LH: 0-2 RH: 0-0 Tight: 0-2 Gall: 0-0
Aids: Bl: 0-0 Vi: 0-0 Tstrap: 0-0
Best Rating: 99 4/99 Cork 2m4f   sft-hvy Hdl

Won a maiden hurdle in Ireland in 1999 but held since over
hurdles. Better efforts in novice chases at around two miles.
Has won on soft, handles faster ground.

Gentle Beau

93f   111f

5-y-o b g Homo Sapien-Tapua Taranata (IRE) (Mandalus)
P J Hobbs Rod Hamilton

Placings:2
(3782)
2002/03: 17²GS,

	Starts	1st	2nd	3rd	Win & Pl
NH Flat	1	0	1	0	588
Career Total	1	0	1	0	588

Going: Sf: 0-0 GS: 0-1 Gd: 0-0 GF: - Fm: 0-0
Distance: 2m/2m3: 0-1 2m4-2m7: 0-0 3m+: 0-0
Track: LH: 0-0 RH: 0-0 Tight: 0-0 Gall: 0-0
Aids: Bl: 0-0 Vi: 0-0 Tstrap: 0-0
Best Rating: 111 2/03 Extr   2m1f   gd-sft NHF

Placed in all three starts in bumpers on ground varying from
soft to good to firm.

Gentle Rivage (FR)

106   113

9-y-o b g Rose Laurel-Silverado Trail (USA) (Greinton)
N A Twiston-Davies Geoffrey & Donna Keeys

Placings:3212422341/112213234/2U2FF4-3343
(2373)
2002/03: 20³GS, 20⁵S, 19⁴S, 26³GS,

	Starts	1st	2nd	3rd	Win & Pl
Chases	4	0	0	3	4035
Career Total	29	5	9	7	56118
140 11/99	Uttx	2m4f110yA Hdl		SFT	£9525
123 9/99	Prth	3m110y	E Hdl		SFT	£2775
116 9/99	Worc	2m4f	E Hdl		G-F	£2407
114 5/99	Uttx	2m6f110yE Hdl		GD	£2599
110 11/98	Hayd	2m	H NHF		SFT	£1215
		Total win prize-money £18523

Going: Sf: 0-2 GS: 0-2 Gd: 0-0 GF: - Fm: 0-0
Distance: 2m/2m3: 0-0 2m4-2m7: 0-0 3m+: 0-1
Track: LH: 0-3 RH: 0-1 Tight: 0-1 Gall: 0-0
Aids: Bl: 0-0 Vi: 0-0 Tstrap: 0-0
Best Rating: 149 4/00 Aint   3m110y   good   Hdl

He was a very useful novice hurdler in 1999/2000, finishing
third to Monsignor at the Festival. He missed the following
season and though he has run well over fences since returning, he has also paid the penalty for some poor jumping.

Geomar

96   **86**

10-y-o ch g Lord Bud-Pretty Soon (Tina s Pet)
P Beaumont Queens Head Racing Club

Placings: *0/00006P/330P42* (0981)
2002/03: 17³S, 20³GF, 22⁰GF, 20⁰G, 16⁴GF, 17²GF,

	Starts	1st	2nd	3rd	Win & Pl
Chases	6	0	1	2	2564
Career Total	13	0	1	2	2564

Going:	Sf: 0-1 GS: 0-0 Gd: 0-1 GF: - Fm: 0-4
Distance:	2m/2m3: 0-0 2m4-2m7: 0-0 3m+: 0-0
Track:	LH: 0-3 RH: 0-3 Tight: 0-5 Gall: 0-0
Aids:	Bl: 0-0 Vi: 0-0 Tstrap: 0-0
Best Rating:	86 8/02 Sthl 2m1f gd-fm Ch

Moderate maiden over hurdles and fences.

Geordies Express

11-y-o b g Tina s Pet-Maestroes Beauty (Music Maestro)
G T Bewley G T Bewley

Placings: 5/33U261-5PU1 (4508)
2002/03: 25⁵GS, 24⁰G, 25⁰G, 25¹G,

	Starts	1st	2nd	3rd	Win & Pl
Chases	4	1	0	0	3038
Career Total	11	2	1	2	6604
113	4/03	Kels	3m1f	H Ch	GD	£3038
99	4/02	Kels	3m1f	H Ch	G-F	£2587
				Total win prize-money £5625

Going:	Sf: 0-0 GS: 0-1 Gd: 1-3 GF: - Fm: 0-0
Distance:	2m/2m3: 0-0 2m4-2m7: 0-0 3m+: 1-4
Track:	LH: 1-3 RH: 0-1 Tight: 1-4 Gall: 0-0
Aids:	Bl: 0-0 Vi: 0-0 Tstrap: 0-0
Best Rating:	113 4/03 Kels 3m1f good Ch

Decent hunter chaser/pointer; suited by a sound surface, but acts on softer; stays three miles one; has been blighted by jumping errors, but jumped well to win at Kelso in April 2003.

George Street (IRE)

5-y-o b g Danehill (USA)-Sweet Justice (Law Society (USA))
M C Pipe W F Frewen & M C Pipe

Placings: 0P0P (3445)
2002/03: 17⁰F, 22⁰G, 19⁰GS, 16⁰HY,

	Starts	1st	2nd	3rd	Win & Pl
Hurdles	4	0	0	0	0
Career Total	4	0	0	0	0

Going:	Sf: 0-1 GS: 0-1 Gd: 0-1 GF: - Fm: 0-1
Distance:	2m/2m3: 0-3 2m4-2m7: 0-1 3m+: 0-0
Track:	LH: 0-1 RH: 0-3 Tight: 0-1 Gall: 0-0
Aids:	Bl: 0-0 Vi: 0-0 Tstrap: 0-0
Best Rating:	0 2/03 Chep 2m110y heavy Hdl

Georgia Peach (IRE)

96   **84**

5-y-o b g Pennekamp (USA)-Across The Ice (USA) (General Holme (USA))
L Lungo Miss S Blumberg

Placings: 50-4 (0483)
2002/03: 16⁴GS,

	Starts	1st	2nd	3rd	Win & Pl
Hurdles	1	0	0	0	0

Career Total	3	0	0	0	0

Going:	Sf: 0-0 GS: 0-1 Gd: 0-0 GF: - Fm: 0-0
Distance:	2m/2m3: 0-1 2m4-2m7: 0-0 3m+: 0-0
Track:	LH: 0-0 RH: 0-1 Tight: 0-0 Gall: 0-0
Aids:	Bl: 0-0 Vi: 0-0 Tstrap: 0-0
Best Rating:	84 6/02 Prth 2m110y gd-sft Hdl

Georgias Gift

8-y-o b g Genuine Gift (CAN)-Georgias Fancy (Montreal Boy)
A M Crow A M Crow

Placings: P (4590)
2002/03: 20PG,

	Starts	1st	2nd	3rd	Win & Pl
Hurdles	1	0	0	0	0
Career Total	1	0	0	0	0

Going:	Sf: 0-0 GS: 0-0 Gd: 0-1 GF: - Fm: 0-0
Distance:	2m/2m3: 0-0 2m4-2m7: 0-1 3m+: 0-0
Track:	LH: 0-1 RH: 0-0 Tight: 0-0 Gall: 0-0
Aids:	Bl: 0-0 Vi: 0-0 Tstrap: 0-0
Best Rating:	0 4/03 Hexm 2m4f110y good Hdl

Georgic Blaze

95   **69**

9-y-o b g Petoski-Pooka (Dominion)
G A Ham E Simmons

Placings: 60P/000/P1PU0U0F-U000U3 (4693)
2002/03: 19ᵁS, 19⁰GS, 16⁰HY, 17⁰GS, 19ᵁG, 17³G,

	Starts	1st	2nd	3rd	Win & Pl
Hurdles	4	0	0	1	440
Chases	2	0	0	0	0
Career Total	20	1	0	1	2729
91	11/01	NAbb	2m1f	G Hdl	SFT	£2289
				Total win prize-money £2289

Going:	Sf: 0-2 GS: 0-2 Gd: 0-2 GF: - Fm: 0-0
Distance:	2m/2m3: 0-4 2m4-2m7: 0-2 3m+: 0-0
Track:	LH: 0-4 RH: 0-2 Tight: 0-1 Gall: 0-0
Aids:	Bl: 0-0 Vi: 0-0 Tstrap: 0-0
Best Rating:	91 11/01 NAbb 2m1f soft Hdl

Plating-class hurdler; runner-up in the mud at Uttoxeter in April 2003; ran well on ground faster than he prefers at Chepstow next time.

Geos (FR)

112(121h)   (162h)**157**

8-y-o b/br g Pistolet Bleu (IRE)-Kaprika (FR) (Cadoudal (FR))
N J Henderson Thurloe Finsbury

Placings: 12111/063132102/31132/264P-3312405 (4790)
2002/03: 20³GS, 17³G, 16¹HY, 19⁴GS, 16⁴G, 20⁵G, 16⁵G,

	Starts	1st	2nd	3rd	Win & Pl
Hurdles	2	0	0	1	8250
Chases	5	1	1	1	69850
Career Total	30	9	6	6	301412
153	12/02	Weth	2m	A Ch	HVY	£26800
154	12/00	Kemp	2m	A Hdl	G-S	£29000
167	12/00	Chel	2m1f	A Hdl	SFT	£24000
164	2/00	Newb	2m110y	A HHdl	G-S	£58000
135	11/99	Leic	2m	C(0-130)HHdl	G-S	£7200
	3/99	Lyrh	2m1f	Ch	HLD	£4306
	12/98	Engh	2m1f110y	Hdl	HLD	£11111

	12/98	Engh	2m1f110y	Hdl	VS	£10101
	6/98	Vitr	1m7f	Hdl	SFT	£2626
				Total win prize-money £173144

Going:	Sf: 1-1 GS: 0-2 Gd: 0-4 GF: - Fm: 0-0
Distance:	2m/2m3: 1-4 2m4-2m7: 0-3 3m+: 0-0
Track:	LH: 1-4 RH: 0-3 Tight: 0-1 Gall: 0-3
Aids:	Bl: 0-0 Vi: 0-0 Tstrap: 0-0
Best Rating:	167 4/01 Sand 2m110y soft Hdl

High-class hurdler/chaser; winner of the Bula and Christmas Hurdles in 2000; landed the Castleford Chase at Wetherby on Boxing Day 2002, but tends to find a few to beat him at the top level; good fourth in the 2003 Champion Chase; has good form on heavy ground, but reportedly prefers a sound surface.

Get Real (IRE)

114(85h)   (85h)**148**

12-y-o br g Executive Perk-Lisa s Music (Abwah)
N J Henderson Pioneer Heat-Treatment

Placings: 42/654/1112/212/11P15/1224224/206P-45F (2615)
2002/03: 16⁴HY, 16⁵S, 16⁵S,

	Starts	1st	2nd	3rd	Win & Pl
Chases	3	0	0	0	3346
Career Total	31	8	9	0	124448
155	5/00	Punc	2m	Ch	YLD	£29920
160	12/99	Asct	2m	B HCh	G-S	£9403
150	11/99	Asct	2m	B HCh	GD	£10756
147	10/99	Asct	2m	B HCh	GD	£16758
143	12/98	Asct	2m	B HCh	G-S	£9339
134	4/98	Ludl	2m	D Ch	GD	£3582
127	12/97	Hntg	2m110y	E(0-105)HCh	GD	£3731
123	11/97	Ludl	2m	E Ch	GD	£2918
				Total win prize-money £86411

Going:	Sf: 0-3 GS: 0-0 Gd: 0-0 GF: - Fm: 0-0
Distance:	2m/2m3: 0-3 2m4-2m7: 0-0 3m+: 0-0
Track:	LH: 0-0 RH: 0-3 Tight: 0-0 Gall: 0-0
Aids:	Bl: 0-0 Vi: 0-0 Tstrap: 0-0
Best Rating:	160 2/01 Kemp 2m good Ch

Fine front-running two-mile chaser on his day who was at his best going right-handed. Tragically lost in action at his beloved Ascot in December 2002. Gained eight wins over fences, the pick of which came in the valuable B.M.W Chase at Punchestown in May 2000. He will be sadly missed. (DEAD)

Get The Point

100   **86**

9-y-o b g Sadler s Wells (USA)-Tolmi (Great Nephew)
R M Stronge Berkshire Commercial Components Ltd

Placings: 631P01335/6610016664/046/2056 (4189)
2002/03: 16²S, 19⁰G, 17⁵S, 16⁶G,

	Starts	1st	2nd	3rd	Win & Pl
Chases	4	0	1	0	1220
Career Total	26	4	1	3	18647
125	2/00	Donc	2m110y	C(0-135)HHdl	GD	£6955
120	1/00	Leic	2m	F(0-110)HHdl	SFT	£2422
122	3/99	Towc	2m	D(0-120)HHdl	SFT	£2784
118	2/99	Towc	2m	E Hdl	SFT	£2512
				Total win prize-money £14675

Going:	Sf: 0-2 GS: 0-0 Gd: 0-2 GF: - Fm: 0-0
Distance:	2m/2m3: 0-4 2m4-2m7: 0-0 3m+: 0-0
Track:	LH: 0-2 RH: 0-2 Tight: 0-2 Gall: 0-0
Aids:	Bl: 0-0 Vi: 0-0 Tstrap: 0-0
Best Rating:	125 2/00 Donc 2m110y good Hdl

Get Up And Go Go (IRE)

65f   35f

6-y-o ch g Mister Lord (USA)-Monadante (IRE) (Phardante (FR))
K C Bailey Graham And Alison Jelley

Placings:0   (1598)
2002/03: 17⁰G,

	Starts	1st	2nd	3rd	Win & Pl
NH Flat	1	0	0	0	
Career Total	1	0	0	0	

Going: Sf: 0-0 GS: 0-0 Gd: 0-1 GF: - Fm: 0-0
Distance: 2m/2m3: 0-1 2m4-2m7: 0-0 3m+: 0-0
Track: LH: 0-0 RH: 0-1 Tight: 0-0 Gall: 0-0
Aids: Bl: 0-0 Vi: 0-0 Tstrap: 0-0
Best Rating: 35 10/02 Extr 2m1f   good NHF

Get Wise (USA)

76   37

7-y-o b g Silver Hawk (USA)-Wising Up (USA) (Smarten (USA))
R Allan R McCulloch

Placings:106/0   (0697)
2002/03: 19⁰G,

	Starts	1st	2nd	3rd	Win & Pl
Hurdles	1	0	0	0	
Career Total	4	1	0	0	2219
94	9/00	Prth	2m110y	H NHF	HVY £2219

Total win prize-money £2219

Going: Sf: 0-0 GS: 0-0 Gd: 0-1 GF: - Fm: 0-0
Distance: 2m/2m3: 0-0 2m4-2m7: 0-1 3m+: 0-0
Track: LH: 0-0 RH: 0-1 Tight: 0-1 Gall: 0-0
Aids: Bl: 0-0 Vi: 0-0 Tstrap: 0-0
Best Rating: 94 1/01 Catt 2m   gd-sft NHF

Ghaazi

95(102h)   (94h)78

7-y-o ch g Lahib (USA)-Shurooq (USA) (Affirmed (USA))
M Hill Fun In The Sun Partnership

Placings:4233405/34043-000024   (0995)
2002/03: 19⁰GF, 17⁰GF, 16⁰GF, 16⁰GF, 21²GF, 21⁴GF,

	Starts	1st	2nd	3rd	Win & Pl
Hurdles	2	0	0	0	0
Chases	4	0	1	0	1206
Career Total	18	0	2	4	5001

Going: Sf: 0-0 GS: 0-0 Gd: 0-0 GF: - Fm: 0-6
Distance: 2m/2m3: 0-4 2m4-2m7: 0-2 3m+: 0-0
Track: LH: 0-6 RH: 0-0 Tight: 0-6 Gall: 0-0
Aids: Bl: 0-2 Vi: 0-3 Tstrap: 0-0
Best Rating: 94 12/01 Tntn 2m3f110y gd-sft Hdl

Maiden over hurdles and fences, best suited by good or fast ground and a good gallop. Has worn headgear.

Ghadames (FR)

102   120+

9-y-o b g Synefos (USA)-Ouargla (FR) (Armos)
W M Brisbourne (M Todhunter 26/5) T G K Construction Ltd

Placings:50/0P12/6152/11-1F0P   (1112)

2002/03: 20¹GS, 20²GF, 22⁰Y, 21⁸GF,

	Starts	1st	2nd	3rd	Win & Pl
Chases	4	1	0	0	4202
Career Total	16	5	2	0	18615
120	5/02	Sthl	2m4f110yE(0-110)HCh	G-S	£4202
120	8/01	Bang	2m4f110yF(0-95)HCh	GD	£2996
108	5/01	Hexm	2m4f110yF(0-105)HCh	FRM	£2814
112	10/00	Ludl	2m5f	E(0-105)HHdl	G-F	£2695
92	3/00	Bang	2m1f110yD Ch	GD	£3867

Total win prize-money £16576

Going: Sf: 0-0 GS: 1-1 Gd: 0-0 GF: - Fm: 0-2
Distance: 2m/2m3: 0-0 2m4-2m7: 1-4 3m+: 0-0
Track: LH: 1-3 RH: 0-1 Tight: 1-1 Gall: 0-0
Aids: Bl: 0-0 Vi: 0-0 Tstrap: 0-0
Best Rating: 120 5/02 Sthl 2m4f110y gd-sft Ch

Modest chaser; effective at two and a half miles; appears to act on most types of ground; needs a decent pace.

Ghali (USA)

76

8-y-o b g Alleged (USA)-Kareema (USA) (Coastal (USA))
J F Coupland J F Coupland

Placings:0054/P45400P400/0P000/P0-PP0 (0331)
2002/03: 23⁰G, 24⁰G, 20⁰G,

	Starts	1st	2nd	3rd	Win & Pl
Hurdles	3	0	0	0	
Career Total	24	0	0	0	382

Going: Sf: 0-0 GS: 0-0 Gd: 0-3 GF: - Fm: 0-0
Distance: 2m/2m3: 0-0 2m4-2m7: 0-1 3m+: 0-2
Track: LH: 0-3 RH: 0-0 Tight: 0-0 Gall: 0-0
Aids: Bl: 0-0 Vi: 0-0 Tstrap: 0-3
Best Rating: 90 3/00 Sedg 2m5f110y gd-fm Hdl

Ghost Moon

98   55

8-y-o b g Cadeaux Genereux-Sickle Moon (Shirley Heights)
R J Hodges Mrs J B Jenkins

Placings:30/F02/PP00/0-0525FU00   (4359)
2002/03: 19⁰S, 16⁵S, 19²S, 17⁵HY, 19⁷G, 18⁰GS, 24⁰F,

	Starts	1st	2nd	3rd	Win & Pl
Hurdles	1	0	0	0	0
Chases	7	0	1	0	1360
Career Total	18	0	2	1	2296

Going: Sf: 0-5 GS: 0-1 Gd: 0-1 GF: - Fm: 0-0
Distance: 2m/2m3: 0-6 2m4-2m7: 0-1 3m+: 0-0
Track: LH: 0-2 RH: 0-5 Tight: 0-5 Gall: 0-0
Aids: Bl: 0-0 Vi: 0-0 Tstrap: 0-0
Best Rating: 79 1/99 MRas 1m5f110y soft NHF

Very moderate novice chaser.

Ghutah

107(105h)   (69h)94

9-y-o ch g Lycius (USA)-Barada (USA) (Damascus (USA))
Mrs A M Thorpe Three A s Caravans

Placings:0F0PP/U23046P/6F1115450433-515P46F0134F
                                       (1699)
2002/03: 16⁵G, 16¹GF, 17⁵GF, 16⁸GF, 16⁴GF, 16⁰G, 20⁰GF, 16⁰G,
17¹F, 19³F, 16⁴G, 17⁶GF,

	Starts	1st	2nd	3rd	Win & Pl
Hurdles	7	1	0	1	2650
Chases	5	1	0	0	3612
Career Total	36	5	1	4	14936

95	10/02	Extr	2m1f	G(0-95)HHdl	FRM	£2324
100	6/02	Hntg	2m110y	E(0-105)HCh	G-F	£3248
88	8/01	Sedg	2m1f	G(0-95)HHdl	G-F	£2033
83	8/01	Uttx	2m	G(0-95)HHdl	G-F	£2009
83	8/01	Sedg	2m1f	G(0-90)HHdl	G-F	£1981

Total win prize-money £11596

Going: Sf: 0-0 GS: 0-0 Gd: 0-4 GF: - Fm: 2-8
Distance: 2m/2m3: 2-11 2m4-2m7: 0-1 3m+: 0-0
Track: LH: 0-6 RH: 2-6 Tight: 0-6 Gall: 1-2
Aids: Bl: 0-0 Vi: 0-0 Tstrap: 0-0
Best Rating: 100 6/02 Hntg 2m110y gd-fm Ch

Easily won handicap chase at Huntingdon June 2002. Useful selling plater over hurdles. At his best when held up. Acts on fast ground.

Gianluca (IRE)

95   101

9-y-o br g Un Desperado (FR)-Belwood Girl (Ballymore)
C R Egerton M E T Davies

Placings:1/1-0   (0919)
2002/03: 16⁰GS,

	Starts	1st	2nd	3rd	Win & Pl
Hurdles	1	0	0	0	
Career Total	3	2	0	0	4868
101	11/01	Leic	2m	E Hdl	G-S	£3230
115	12/99	Ludl	2m	H NHF	GD	£1637

Total win prize-money £4868

Going: Sf: 0-0 GS: 0-1 Gd: 0-0 GF: - Fm: 0-0
Distance: 2m/2m3: 0-1 2m4-2m7: 0-0 3m+: 0-0
Track: LH: 0-0 RH: 0-1 Tight: 0-0 Gall: 0-0
Aids: Bl: 0-0 Vi: 0-0 Tstrap: 0-0
Best Rating: 115 12/99 Ludl 2m   good NHF

Fairly promising hurdler; easy winner of a bumper at Ludlow on his racecourse debut in December 1999; absent until winning on hurdling bow in modest company at Leicester in November 2001 and seemingly exposed when stepped up in class subsequently after another long layoff; has raced only over 2m; acts on good and good to soft ground; likely to be suited by strongly run races.

Gielgud

103   98

6-y-o b g Faustus (USA)-Shirl (Shirley Heights)
P R Webber Mrs J K Powell

Placings:20632-0002   (4677)
2002/03: 24⁰S, 20⁰S, 20⁰G, 19²GF,

	Starts	1st	2nd	3rd	Win & Pl
Hurdles	4	0	1	0	1112
Career Total	9	0	3	1	3262

Going: Sf: 0-2 GS: 0-0 Gd: 0-1 GF: - Fm: 0-1
Distance: 2m/2m3: 0-0 2m4-2m7: 0-3 3m+: 0-1
Track: LH: 0-0 RH: 0-4 Tight: 0-0 Gall: 0-0
Aids: Bl: 0-0 Vi: 0-0 Tstrap: 0-2
Best Rating: 98 4/03 Hrld 2m3f110y gd-fm Hdl

Modest hurdler; runner-up at Hereford in April; took a weak event on firm ground at Wetherby the following month; stays 2m 4f; acts on fast ground; has worn a tongue strap.

Giftneyev (FR)

71   85

4-y-o b/br g Goldneyev (USA)-Girl s Gift (FR) (Gairloch)
C P Morlock Pell-Mell Partners

Placings:5   (4567)

2002/03: 20⁵GF,

	Starts	1st	2nd	3rd	Win & Pl
Hurdles	1	0	0	0	0
Career Total	1	0	0	0	0

Going:	Sf: 0-0 GS: 0-0 Gd: 0-0 GF: - Fm: 0-1
Distance:	2m/2m3: 0-0 2m4-2m7: 0-1 3m+: 0-0
Track:	LH: 0-1 RH: 0-0 Tight: 0-1 Gall: 0-0
Aids:	Bl: 0-0 Vi: 0-0 Tstrap: 0-0
Best Rating:	66 4/03 Bang 2m4f gd-fm Hdl

Gig Harbor
80   55

4-y-o b c Efisio-Petonica (IRE) (Petoski)
Miss E C Lavelle (B W Hills 14/10) Fraser Miller Racing

Placings:0   (2720)
2002/03: 16⁰S,

	Starts	1st	2nd	3rd	Win & Pl
Hurdles	1	0	0	0	
Career Total	1	0	0	0	

Going:	Sf: 0-1 GS: 0-0 Gd: 0-0 GF: - Fm: 0-0
Distance:	2m/2m3: 0-1 2m4-2m7: 0-0 3m+: 0-0
Track:	LH: 0-0 RH: 0-1 Tight: 0-0 Gall: 0-0
Aids:	Bl: 0-0 Vi: 0-0 Tstrap: 0-0
Best Rating:	53 12/02 Kemp 2m soft Hdl

Gigha

4-y-o b f Never So Bold-Racing Brenda (Faustus (USA))
Simon Earle Mrs J K Powell

Placings:P   (4675)
2002/03: 17PGF,

	Starts	1st	2nd	3rd	Win & Pl
Hurdles	1	0	0	0	
Career Total	1	0	0	0	

Going:	Sf: 0-0 GS: 0-0 Gd: 0-0 GF: - Fm: 0-1
Distance:	2m/2m3: 0-1 2m4-2m7: 0-0 3m+: 0-0
Track:	LH: 0-0 RH: 0-1 Tight: 0-0 Gall: 0-0
Aids:	Bl: 0-0 Vi: 0-0 Tstrap: 0-0
Best Rating:	0 4/03 Hrfd 2m1f gd-fm Hdl

Gigi Beach (IRE)
     (105h)**113**

12-y-o ch g Roselier (FR)-Cranagh Lady (Le Bavard (FR))
Ian Williams Mrs Rosemary Paterson

Placings:54U11/23P4121/25223F0/F2P2340/P6P2535-6
     (0035)
2002/03: 22⁶G,

	Starts	1st	2nd	3rd	Win & Pl
Hurdles	1	0	0	0	0
Career Total	34	4	8	4	45516
125	4/99	Chel	3m2f110yC(0-135)HCh	GD	£8247
120	3/99	Extr	3m6f	D(0-125)HCh	SFT £7415
123	4/98	Font	3m2f110yE Ch	SFT	£3353
94	3/98	Font	3m2f110yE Ch	G-F	£2768

Total win prize-money £21783

Going:	Sf: 0-0 GS: 0-0 Gd: 0-1 GF: - Fm: 0-0
Distance:	2m/2m3: 0-0 2m4-2m7: 0-0 3m+: 0-0
Track:	LH: 0-0 RH: 0-1 Tight: 0-0 Gall: 0-0
Aids:	Bl: 0-0 Vi: 0-0 Tstrap: 0-0
Best Rating:	125 5/99 Wwck 3m2f good Ch

He lacks pace and is most effective forcing the issue over extreme distances. Disappointing in 2000/2001 and has changed stables since. Seems best on good ground. Has worn blinkers unsuccessfully but ran better in a visor.

Gigs Bounty
94f   90f

5-y-o ch g Weld-City s Sister (Maystreak)
M Pitman J Barson

Placings:44   (4542)
2002/03: 14⁴GF, 16⁴G,

	Starts	1st	2nd	3rd	Win & Pl
NH Flat	2	0	0	0	0
Career Total	2	0	0	0	0

Going:	Sf: 0-0 GS: 0-0 Gd: 0-1 GF: - Fm: 0-0
Distance:	2m/2m3: 0-1 2m4-2m7: 0-0 3m+: 0-0
Track:	LH: 0-0 RH: 0-1 Tight: 0-0 Gall: 0-0
Aids:	Bl: 0-0 Vi: 0-0 Tstrap: 0-0
Best Rating:	90 3/03 Hrfd 1m6f gd-fm NHF

Half-brother to Better Times Ahead; signs of ability in modest bumpers.

Gigs Gambit (IRE)
   (94h)   (92h)

6-y-o ch g Hubbly Bubbly (USA)-Music Slipper (Orchestra)
M Pitman J Barson

Placings:350-255F   (2604)
2002/03: 16²G, 16⁵G, 24⁵GS, 16FGS,

	Starts	1st	2nd	3rd	Win & Pl
Hurdles	3	0	1	0	1216
Chases	1	0	0	0	0
Career Total	7	0	1	1	1502

Going:	Sf: 0-0 GS: 0-2 Gd: 0-2 GF: - Fm: 0-0
Distance:	2m/2m3: 0-3 2m4-2m7: 0-0 3m+: 0-1
Track:	LH: 0-3 RH: 0-1 Tight: 0-1 Gall: 0-0
Aids:	Bl: 0-0 Vi: 0-0 Tstrap: 0-0
Best Rating:	99 2/02 Sand 2m110y soft NHF

Showed ability in bumpers and novice hurdles; fell on chase debut; should stay two and a half miles.

Gilbert White
98   73

10-y-o b g Little Wolf-Caribs Love (Caliban)
R Lee Mrs G Rowan-Hamilton

Placings:4P/P3/0/00F-4P5   (4679)
2002/03: 16⁴HY, 19PS, 16⁵GF,

	Starts	1st	2nd	3rd	Win & Pl
Hurdles	3	0	0	0	270
Career Total	11	0	0	1	772

Going:	Sf: 0-2 GS: 0-0 Gd: 0-0 GF: - Fm: 0-1
Distance:	2m/2m3: 0-3 2m4-2m7: 0-0 3m+: 0-0
Track:	LH: 0-1 RH: 0-2 Tight: 0-1 Gall: 0-1
Aids:	Bl: 0-0 Vi: 0-0 Tstrap: 0-0
Best Rating:	99 3/99 Chep 2m110y gd-sft NHF

Poor selling hurdler; lightly raced in recent seasons.

Gilden Magic
89   84

5-y-o b g Magic Ring (IRE)-Have Form (Haveroid)

P W Hiatt (M Blanshard 29/8) Mrs Jane Gillett

Placings:0   (2166)
2002/03: 16⁹GS,

	Starts	1st	2nd	3rd	Win & Pl
Hurdles	1	0	0	0	
Career Total	1	0	0	0	

Going:	Sf: 0-0 GS: 0-1 Gd: 0-0 GF: - Fm: 0-0
Distance:	2m/2m3: 0-1 2m4-2m7: 0-0 3m+: 0-0
Track:	LH: 0-1 RH: 0-0 Tight: 0-0 Gall: 0-0
Aids:	Bl: 0-0 Vi: 0-0 Tstrap: 0-0
Best Rating:	84 11/02 Wvck 2m gd-sft Hdl

Gildorans Spice

5-y-o gr m Gildoran-Sea Spice (Precipice Wood)
G Brown Ellis Davies

Placings:0P   (3269)
2002/03: 17⁰HY, 17PHY,

	Starts	1st	2nd	3rd	Win & Pl
NH Flat	1	0	0	0	0
Hurdles	1	0	0	0	0
Career Total	2	0	0	0	0

Going:	Sf: 0-2 GS: 0-0 Gd: 0-0 GF: - Fm: 0-0
Distance:	2m/2m3: 0-2 2m4-2m7: 0-0 3m+: 0-0
Track:	LH: 0-0 RH: 0-2 Tight: 0-2 Gall: 0-0
Aids:	Bl: 0-0 Vi: 0-0 Tstrap: 0-0
Best Rating:	31 12/02 Folk 2m1f110y heavy NHF

Gilfoot Breeze (IRE)
97   83

6-y-o b g Forest Wind (USA)-Ma Bella Luna (Jalmood (USA))
A Robson A Robson

Placings:3006/0600-454   (4507)
2002/03: 16⁴S, 20⁵G, 16⁴G,

	Starts	1st	2nd	3rd	Win & Pl
Hurdles	3	0	0	0	728
Career Total	11	0	0	1	1090

Going:	Sf: 0-1 GS: 0-0 Gd: 0-2 GF: - Fm: 0-0
Distance:	2m/2m3: 0-2 2m4-2m7: 0-1 3m+: 0-0
Track:	LH: 0-3 RH: 0-0 Tight: 0-1 Gall: 0-0
Aids:	Bl: 0-0 Vi: 0-0 Tstrap: 0-0
Best Rating:	86 11/00 MRas 2m1f110y soft Hdl

Plating-class hurdler; yet to prove he stays two and a half miles.

Gill The Till (IRE)
88   49

4-y-o ch f Anshan-Bilander (High Line)
R J Baker Graham Brown

Placings:5F500   (4568)
2002/03: 17⁵G, 17FGF, 18⁵GF, 17⁰G, 22⁰GF,

	Starts	1st	2nd	3rd	Win & Pl
Hurdles	5	0	0	0	0
Career Total	5	0	0	0	0

Going:	Sf: 0-0 GS: 0-0 Gd: 0-2 GF: - Fm: 0-3
Distance:	2m/2m3: 0-4 2m4-2m7: 0-1 3m+: 0-0
Track:	LH: 0-3 RH: 0-2 Tight: 0-3 Gall: 0-0

Aids: Bl: 0-0 Vi: 0-0 Tstrap: 0-0
Best Rating: 49 3/03 Extr 2m1f   good Hdl

Gill'Mar (FR)

9-y-o b g Le Nain Jaune (FR)-Lolomar (FR) (Midnight Sun)
G C Evans Mr & Mrs M P Wiggin

Placings:424/61/PP1P/4   (3548)
2002/03: 25⁴G,

	Starts	1st	2nd	3rd	Win & Pl
Chases	1	0	0	0	0
Career Total	10	2	1	0	11928
108	1/00	Uttx	2m7f	E(0-115)HCh	SFT £4540
106	1/99	Leic	2m4f110yE Ch	G-S	£3348

Total win prize-money £7888

Going: Sf: 0-0 GS: 0-0 Gd: 0-1 GF: - Fm: 0-0
Distance: 2m2/m3: 0-0 2m4-2m7: 0-0 3m+: 0-1
Track: LH: 0-0 RH: 0-1 Tight: 0-0 Gall: 0-0
Aids: Bl: 0-0 Vi: 0-0 Tstrap: 0-0
Best Rating: 108 1/00 Uttx 2m7f soft Ch

Gilleen Lad

11-y-o ch g Gildoran-Miss Colleen (Joshua)
Mrs K J Gilmore G Bodily

Placings:6P/00F/540/FP   (0187)
2002/03: 16⁴GF, 20ᴾGF,

	Starts	1st	2nd	3rd	Win & Pl
Chases	2	0	0	0	
Career Total	10	0	0	0	149

Going: Sf: 0-0 GS: 0-0 Gd: 0-0 GF: - Fm: 0-2
Distance: 2m2/m3: 0-1 2m4-2m7: 0-1 3m+: 0-0
Track: LH: 0-1 RH: 0-1 Tight: 0-0 Gall: 0-2
Aids: Bl: 0-0 Vi: 0-0 Tstrap: 0-0
Best Rating: 64 5/98 Towc 2m   gd-fm Hdl

Gillman's Point (IRE)

7-y-o ch g Persian Mews-Davidmoss (IRE) (Le Moss)
Mrs L B Normile John Findlay

Placings:0P   (4304)
2002/03: 16⁰GF, 22ᴾG,

	Starts	1st	2nd	3rd	Win & Pl
NH Flat	1	0	0	0	0
Hurdles	1	0	0	0	0
Career Total	2	0	0	0	

Going: Sf: 0-0 GS: 0-0 Gd: 0-0 GF: - Fm: 0-1
Distance: 2m2/m3: 0-1 2m4-2m7: 0-1 3m+: 0-0
Track: LH: 0-1 RH: 0-1 Tight: 0-2 Gall: 0-0
Aids: Bl: 0-0 Vi: 0-0 Tstrap: 0-0
Best Rating: 67 12/02 Muss 2m   gd-fm NHF

Gillymoss

70

9-y-o b/br m Gildoran-Mossy Morning (Le Moss)
J C Tuck Mrs J M F Dibben

Placings:0PP/6P3-0PPP   (4252)

2002/03: 22⁰GS, 24ᴾS, 21ᴾS, 22ᴾG,

	Starts	1st	2nd	3rd	Win & Pl
Hurdles	4	0	0	0	
Career Total	10	0	0	1	341

Going: Sf: 0-2 GS: 0-1 Gd: 0-1 GF: - Fm: 0-0
Distance: 2m2/m3: 0-0 2m4-2m7: 0-3 3m+: 0-1
Track: LH: 0-1 RH: 0-3 Tight: 0-1 Gall: 0-1
Aids: Bl: 0-0 Vi: 0-0 Tstrap: 0-0
Best Rating: 71 12/01 Extr 2m6f110y good Hdl

Gilou

96   **79**

7-y-o b m Midyan (USA)-Lunagraphe (USA) (Time For A Change (USA))
C W Fairhurst P Richmond & Partners

Placings:05/32/220   (0789)
2002/03: 16²GF, 22²GF, 26⁰GF,

	Starts	1st	2nd	3rd	Win & Pl
Hurdles	3	0	2	0	1474
Career Total	7	0	3	1	2554

Going: Sf: 0-0 GS: 0-0 Gd: 0-0 GF: - Fm: 0-3
Distance: 2m2/m3: 0-1 2m4-2m7: 0-1 3m+: 0-1
Track: LH: 0-3 RH: 0-0 Tight: 0-1 Gall: 0-0
Aids: Bl: 0-0 Vi: 0-0 Tstrap: 0-0
Best Rating: 91 6/00 MRas 3m   gd-sft Hdl

Poor hurdler; well beaten third after over a year off at Sedgefield in July.

Gilston Lad

10-y-o b g Broadsword (USA)-Cannes Beach (Canadel Ii)
J M Dun Mrs G R Dun

Placings:P   (0158)
2002/03: 16ᴾG,

	Starts	1st	2nd	3rd	Win & Pl
Hurdles	1	0	0	0	
Career Total	1	0	0	0	

Going: Sf: 0-0 GS: 0-0 Gd: 0-0 GF: - Fm: 0-0
Distance: 2m2/m3: 0-1 2m4-2m7: 0-0 3m+: 0-0
Track: LH: 0-1 RH: 0-0 Tight: 0-1 Gall: 0-0
Aids: Bl: 0-0 Vi: 0-0 Tstrap: 0-0
Best Rating: 0 5/02 Kels 2m110y good Hdl

Gilzine

91   **66**

7-y-o b g Gildoran-Sherzine (Gorytus (USA))
M Hill Martin Hill

Placings:34/6U-406   (0959)
2002/03: 22⁴GS, 22⁰G, 20⁶S,

	Starts	1st	2nd	3rd	Win & Pl
Hurdles	3	0	0	0	0
Career Total	7	0	0	1	253

Going: Sf: 0-1 GS: 0-1 Gd: 0-1 GF: - Fm: 0-0
Distance: 2m2/m3: 0-0 2m4-2m7: 0-3 3m+: 0-3
Track: LH: 0-3 RH: 0-0 Tight: 0-2 Gall: 0-0
Aids: Bl: 0-0 Vi: 0-0 Tstrap: 0-0
Best Rating: 89 5/00 Extr 2m1f   gd-fm NHF

Gimme Shelter (IRE)

101(104h)   (82 h)**104**

9-y-o ch m Glacial Storm (USA)-Glen Dieu (Furry Glen)
S J Marshall S J Marshall

Placings:004042P/4/F-P3140P44212   (4765)
2002/03: 20ᴾS, 22³S, 27¹S, 22⁴HY, 27⁰S, 27ᴾHY, 25⁴G, 24⁴G, 24²S, 32¹S, 31²G,

	Starts	1st	2nd	3rd	Win & Pl
Hurdles	8	1	0	1	6531
Chases	3	1	2	0	10772
Career Total	20	2	3	1	17917
100	3/03	Hexm	4m	F(0-100)HCh	SFT £3805
82	11/02	Kels	3m3f	J(0-110)HHdl	SFT £5096

Total win prize-money £8902

Going: Sf: 2-8 GS: 0-0 Gd: 0-3 GF: - Fm: 0-0
Distance: 2m2/m3: 0-0 2m4-2m7: 0-3 3m+: 2-8
Track: LH: 2-7 RH: 0-3 Tight: 1-7 Gall: 0-0
Aids: Bl: 0-0 Vi: 0-0 Tstrap: 0-0
Best Rating: 104 4/03 Prth 3m7f   good Ch

Modest form over hurdles and fences; runaway winner of a long distance handicap chase run in bad ground at Hexham in March 2003; best on soft ground.

Gimmick (FR)

101(104c)   (114+c)**112**

9-y-o b g Chamberlin (FR)-Jaida (FR) (Alfaro)
Jonjo O Neill The Risky Partnership

Placings:12/111/0F26F20P2   (4571)
2002/03: 21⁰G, 22⁴S, 16²GS, 16⁶G, 16ᶠS, 16²HY, 16⁰S, 16ᴾS, 16²GF,

	Starts	1st	2nd	3rd	Win & Pl
Hurdles	5	0	1	0	1696
Chases	4	0	2	0	2952
Career Total	14	4	4	0	17052
125	8/00	MRas	2m3f110yE Hdl	G-F	£2834
116	7/00	MRas	2m3f110yD Hdl	GD	£3721
111	6/00	Worc	2m	E Hdl	G-F	£2642
111	4/00	Tntn	2m1f	E Hdl	G-S	£2478

Total win prize-money £11676

Going: Sf: 0-6 GS: 0-0 Gd: 0-2 GF: - Fm: 0-1
Distance: 2m2/m3: 0-7 2m4-2m7: 0-2 3m+: 0-0
Track: LH: 0-5 RH: 0-4 Tight: 0-4 Gall: 0-0
Aids: Bl: 0-1 Vi: 0-0 Tstrap: 0-0
Best Rating: 125 8/00 MRas 2m3f110y gd-fm Hdl

Fair hurdler; has shown ability in novice chases in 2002/3; stays two miles three; acts on ground ranging from good to firm to heavy.

Gin And Terimonic

95f   **73f**

5-y-o gr m Terimon-Genie Spirit (Nishapour (FR))
P Winkworth Katie Powell, Jessica Winkworth

Placings:4   (4672)
2002/03: 16⁴G,

	Starts	1st	2nd	3rd	Win & Pl
NH Flat	1	0	0	0	0
Career Total	1	0	0	0	0

Going: Sf: 0-0 GS: 0-0 Gd: 0-1 GF: - Fm: 0-0
Distance: 2m2/m3: 0-1 2m4-2m7: 0-0 3m+: 0-0
Track: LH: 0-1 RH: 0-0 Tight: 0-1 Gall: 0-0
Aids: Bl: 0-0 Vi: 0-0 Tstrap: 0-0
Best Rating: 73 4/03 Fknm 2m   good NHF

Some promise in a bumper on debut.

Gin N Ice (IRE)

103(83h)   (54h)**63**

10-y-o gr g Glacial Storm (USA)-Theo s Gin (Teofane)
J R Cornwall J R Cornwall

Placings:026010050/4P03F0/000**P40PP4PU42-34PFF**P
                                            (1504)
2002/03: 24³GF, 21⁴GS, 16³G, 21³G, 24⁴G, 17³G,

	Starts	1st	2nd	3rd	Win & Pl
Hurdles	1	0	0	0	0
Chases	5	0	0	0	789
Career Total	34	1	2	2	5841
79 8/99 Kbgn 2m3f		Hdl		G-Y	£2464

Total win prize-money £2464

Going:	Sf: 0-0 GS: 0-1 Gd: 0-4 GF: - Fm: 0-1
Distance:	2m/2m3: 0-2 2m4-2m7: 0-2 3m+: 0-2
Track:	LH: 0-5 RH: 0-1 Tight: 0-1 Gall: 0-1
Aids:	Bl: 0-6 Vi: 0-0 Tstrap: 0-0
Best Rating:	91 9/00 Gowr 2m good Hdl

Poor novice chaser, usually wears blinkers, does not want the ground too soft.

Gin Palace (IRE)

107   **123**

5-y-o gr g King s Theatre (IRE)-Ikala (Lashkari)
G L Moore Mrs Patricia Gilmore

Placings:42-26511   (4323)
2002/03: 17²GS, 16⁶G, 17⁵GS, 16¹S, 16¹G,

	Starts	1st	2nd	3rd	Win & Pl
Hurdles	5	2	1	0	24137
Career Total	7	2	2	0	25880
122 3/03 Newb 2m110y B(0-140)HHdl				GD	£18513
113 2/03 Plum 2m		F Hdl		SFT	£3094

Total win prize-money £21608

Going:	Sf: 1-1 GS: 0-2 Gd: 1-2 GF: - Fm: 0-0
Distance:	2m/2m3: 2-5 2m4-2m7: 0-0 3m+: 0-0
Track:	LH: 2-3 RH: 0-2 Tight: 1-2 Gall: 1-2
Aids:	Bl: 0-0 Vi: 0-0 Tstrap: 0-0
Best Rating:	123 1/03 Chel 2m1f gd-sft Hdl

Decent hurdler; acts on good ground, but may be better on soft ground; suited by two miles.

Gingembre (FR)

119   **163**

9-y-o ch g Le Nain Jaune (FR)-Teuphaine (FR) (Barbotan (FR))
Mrs L C Taylor Mrs L C Taylor

Placings:45F51U2111/UBF2P41/323P   (4479)
2002/03: 25³GS, 26²GS, 25³GS, 36PG,

	Starts	1st	2nd	3rd	Win & Pl
Chases	4	0	1	2	37400
Career Total	21	5	3	2	154237
160 4/01 Ayr 4m1f		A HCh		G-F	£60000
137 4/00 Ayr 2m4f		A Ch		GD	£17030
146 3/00 Strf 2m4f		D Ch		GD	£4828
125 2/00 Donc 3m		E Ch		GD	£3445
99 12/99 Donc 2m110y		D Ch		G-F	£3876

Total win prize-money £89180

Going:	Sf: 0-0 GS: 0-3 Gd: 0-1 GF: - Fm: 0-0
Distance:	2m/2m3: 0-0 2m4-2m7: 0-0 3m+: 0-4
Track:	LH: 0-4 RH: 0-0 Tight: 0-1 Gall: 0-0
Aids:	Bl: 0-0 Vi: 0-0 Tstrap: 0-0
Best Rating:	163 11/02 Newb 3m2f110y gd-sft Ch

Gingerbread Man

High-class chaser; gained his biggest victory to date in the 2001 Scottish National; missed the following season due to injury; has run well in very decent company in 2002/3; effective on good ground or faster; all his wins have been on fairly flat, left-handed tracks.

8-y-o ch g Derrylin-Red Rambler (Rymer)
J A Moore Mrs J M Moore

Placings:000/PP-P   (4339)
2002/03: 24PGF,

	Starts	1st	2nd	3rd	Win & Pl
Chases	1	0	0	0	
Career Total	6	0	0	0	

Going:	Sf: 0-0 GS: 0-0 Gd: 0-0 GF: - Fm: 0-1
Distance:	2m/2m3: 0-0 2m4-2m7: 0-0 3m+: 0-1
Track:	LH: 0-0 RH: 0-1 Tight: 0-0 Gall: 0-1
Aids:	Bl: 0-0 Vi: 0-0 Tstrap: 0-0
Best Rating:	68 7/00 Worc 2m good NHF

Gingko

102   **92**

6-y-o b g Pursuit Of Love-Arboretum (IRE) (Green Desert (USA))
P R Webber Olympic Group Of Partners

Placings:0P34   (4522)
2002/03: 16⁰S, 16PS, 17³G, 16⁴G,

	Starts	1st	2nd	3rd	Win & Pl
Hurdles	4	0	0	1	603
Career Total	4	0	0	1	603

Going:	Sf: 0-2 GS: 0-0 Gd: 0-2 GF: - Fm: 0-0
Distance:	2m/2m3: 0-4 2m4-2m7: 0-0 3m+: 0-0
Track:	LH: 0-4 RH: 0-0 Tight: 0-1 Gall: 0-1
Aids:	Bl: 0-0 Vi: 0-0 Tstrap: 0-0
Best Rating:	92 4/03 Uttx 2m good Hdl

Novice hurdler; acts on a sound surface.

Ginner Morris

96   **80**

8-y-o b g Emarati (USA)-Just Run (IRE) (Runnett)
J Hetherton Formulated Polymer Products Ltd

Placings:UP5F/33/P256F   (3799)
2002/03: 17PS, 16²GS, 16⁵S, 16⁶G, 16⁶S,

	Starts	1st	2nd	3rd	Win & Pl
Hurdles	5	0	1	0	1115
Career Total	11	0	1	2	1818

Going:	Sf: 0-3 GS: 0-1 Gd: 0-1 GF: - Fm: 0-0
Distance:	2m/2m3: 0-5 2m4-2m7: 0-0 3m+: 0-0
Track:	LH: 0-5 RH: 0-0 Tight: 0-3 Gall: 0-2
Aids:	Bl: 0-0 Vi: 0-0 Tstrap: 0-0
Best Rating:	86 5/00 Ctml 2m1f110y gd-fm Hdl

Selling hurdler, runner-up at Catterick in December.

Ginski

81   **55**

7-y-o b g Petoski-Upham Lass (Sula Bula)
C J Drewe C J Drewe

Placings:0/0000-0006   (4568)
2002/03: 17⁰G, 18⁰S, 16⁹GF, 22⁶GF,

	Starts	1st	2nd	3rd	Win & Pl
Hurdles	4	0	0	0	0
Career Total	9	0	0	0	0

Giocomo (IRE)

107   **132d**

5-y-o ch g Indian Ridge-Karri Valley (USA) (Storm Bird (CAN))
P Monteith (Jonjo O Neill 8/2) Euan & Bernardine Roger

Placings:4311P0-061P00   (4308)
2002/03: 20⁰S, 16⁶S, 20¹S, 16PHY, 16⁹G, 18⁰G,

	Starts	1st	2nd	3rd	Win & Pl
Hurdles	6	1	0	0	15649
Career Total	12	3	0	1	37033
132 12/02 Chep 2m4f		B(0-140)HHdl		SFT	£15274
127 2/02 Kemp 2m		A Hdl		GD	£12000
117 2/02 Hntg 2m110y		B Hdl		SFT	£8671

Total win prize-money £35945

Going:	Sf: 1-4 GS: 0-0 Gd: 0-2 GF: - Fm: 0-0
Distance:	2m/2m3: 0-4 2m4-2m7: 1-2 3m+: 0-0
Track:	LH: 1-5 RH: 0-1 Tight: 0-1 Gall: 0-2
Aids:	Bl: 0-0 Vi: 0-0 Tstrap: 0-0
Best Rating:	132 12/02 Chep 2m4f soft Hdl

Very useful hurdler; stays two miles four, but effective over shorter; acts on good ground but prefers softer.

Giolla Valley (IRE)

74   (59h)**98**

9-y-o b g Boyne Valley-Bean Giolla (Giolla Mear)
Mrs M Reveley The Mary Reveley Racing Club

Placings:06F640/2PU242-0   (1638)
2002/03: 16⁹S,

	Starts	1st	2nd	3rd	Win & Pl
Chases	1	0	0	0	
Career Total	13	0	3	0	3403

Going:	Sf: 0-1 GS: 0-0 Gd: 0-0 GF: - Fm: 0-0
Distance:	2m/2m3: 0-1 2m4-2m7: 0-0 3m+: 0-0
Track:	LH: 0-0 RH: 0-1 Tight: 0-0 Gall: 0-0
Aids:	Bl: 0-0 Vi: 0-0 Tstrap: 0-0
Best Rating:	98 1/02 Newc 2m110y soft Ch

He failed to trouble the judges when tried over hurdles, but is running better over fences.

Gipsy Cricketer

98(77h)   (51h)**80**

7-y-o b g Anshan-Tinkers Fairy (Myjinski (USA))
D J Caro (Mrs Marilyn Scudamore 11/5) The Yes - No - Wait Sorries

Placings:006P/53003600/0P-6421PP   (1199)
2002/03: 16⁶GF, 20⁴F, 16²GF, 16¹GF, 17⁶S, 19⁹GF,

	Starts	1st	2nd	3rd	Win & Pl
Chases	6	1	1	0	3721
Career Total	20	1	1	2	4410
86 7/02 Worc 2m		F(0-95)HCh		G-F	£2736

Total win prize-money £2737

Going: Sf: 0-1 GS: 0-0 Gd: 0-0 GF: - Fm: 1-5
Distance: 2m/2m3: 1-5 2m4-2m7: 0-1 3m+: 0-0
Track: LH: 1-5 RH: 0-1 Tight: 0-1 Gall: 0-1
Aids: Bl: 0-0 Vi: 0-0 Tstrap: 0-0
Best Rating: 86 7/02 Worc 2m   gd-fm Ch

A useful pointer; made all when winning 2m handicap at Worcester July 2002; pulled up on unsuitable soft ground next time; bolted before start when suffering the same fate next outing.

Gipsy Geof (IRE)

109(104h)   (107h)99

12-y-o b g Miners Lamp-Princess Menelek (Menelek)
Ferdy Murphy Exors Of The Late G A Hubbard

Placings: 605/43/FP3152**P**1/34F25/P6F/452FU/42P43112O
-1   (0058)
2002/03: 16¹G,

	Starts	1st	2nd	3rd	Win & Pl
Chases	1	1	0	0	3276
Career Total	36	5	5	4	21870
99	5/02	Folk	2m	F(0-90)Ch	GD	£3276
107	4/02	Weth	2m	F(0-100)HHdl	GD	£2345
107	3/02	MRas	2m1f110y(0-95)HHdl	G-S	£1722
109	3/98	Sand	2m	D Ch	GD	£3692
108	11/97	Leic	2m	E Hdl	G-S	£2616
			Total win prize-money £13652

Going: Sf: 0-0 GS: 0-0 Gd: 1-1 GF: - Fm: 0-0
Distance: 2m/2m3: 1-1 2m4-2m7: 0-0 3m+: 0-0
Track: LH: 0-0 RH: 1-1 Tight: 1-1 Gall: 0-0
Aids: Bl: 0-0 Vi: 0-0 Tstrap: 0-0
Best Rating: 118 2/98 Ling 2m   gd-sft Ch

A half-brother to Imperial Call, he can make mistakes. Effective at the lowest level these days, he stays two and a half miles and acts in soft ground.

Gipsy Girl

68

8-y-o b m Motivate-Young Gipsy (The Brianstan)
L J Williams Mrs C M Marles

Placings: 0P   (3147)
2002/03: 21⁰S, 24³HY,

	Starts	1st	2nd	3rd	Win & Pl
Hurdles	2	0	0	0	
Career Total	2	0	0	0	

Going: Sf: 0-2 GS: 0-0 Gd: 0-0 GF: - Fm: 0-0
Distance: 2m/2m3: 0-0 2m4-2m7: 0-0 3m+: 0-1
Track: LH: 0-1 RH: 0-1 Tight: 0-0 Gall: 0-0
Aids: Bl: 0-0 Vi: 0-0 Tstrap: 0-0
Best Rating: 68 1/03 Ludl 2m5f   soft Hdl

Gipsy Wood

75   52

7-y-o gr m Rakaposhi King-Silva Linda (Precipice Wood)
P Beaumont Mrs Sue Plowright

Placings: 6   (3996)
2002/03: 20⁶G,

	Starts	1st	2nd	3rd	Win & Pl
Hurdles	1	0	0	0	0
Career Total	1	0	0	0	0

Going: Sf: 0-0 GS: 0-0 Gd: 0-1 GF: - Fm: 0-0
Distance: 2m/2m3: 0-0 2m4-2m7: 0-0 3m+: 0-0
Track: LH: 0-1 RH: 0-0 Tight: 0-0 Gall: 0-0

Aids: Bl: 0-0 Vi: 0-0 Tstrap: 0-0
Best Rating: 53 3/03 Weth 2m4f110y good Hdl

Girl Band (IRE)

5-y-o b m Bluebird (USA)-Bandit Girl (Robellino (USA))
E A Elliott Mrs Anne E Elliott

Placings: P-0   (3911)
2002/03: 17⁰GS,

	Starts	1st	2nd	3rd	Win & Pl
Hurdles	1	0	0	0	
Career Total	2	0	0	0	

Going: Sf: 0-0 GS: 0-1 Gd: 0-0 GF: - Fm: 0-0
Distance: 2m/2m3: 0-1 2m4-2m7: 0-0 3m+: 0-0
Track: LH: 0-0 RH: 0-1 Tight: 0-0 Gall: 0-0
Aids: Bl: 0-0 Vi: 0-0 Tstrap: 0-0
Best Rating: 0 3/03 Carl 2m1f   gd-sft Hdl

Girl Of Pleasure (IRE)

100   82

4-y-o b f Namaqualand (USA)-Shrewd Girl (USA) (Sagace (FR))
Mrs P N Dutfield Darren C Mercer

Placings: 12F0   (1729)
2002/03: 16¹GF, 16²GS, 16⁶GF, 16⁰GS,

	Starts	1st	2nd	3rd	Win & Pl
Hurdles	4	1	1	0	5650
Career Total	4	1	1	0	5650
73	7/02	Strf	2m110y	D Hdl	G-F	£4095
			Total win prize-money £4095

Going: Sf: 0-0 GS: 0-2 Gd: 0-0 GF: - Fm: 1-2
Distance: 2m/2m3: 1-4 2m4-2m7: 0-0 3m+: 0-0
Track: LH: 1-3 RH: 0-1 Tight: 1-3 Gall: 0-0
Aids: Bl: 0-0 Vi: 0-0 Tstrap: 0-0
Best Rating: 82 8/02 Strf 2m110y gd-sft Hdl

Overcame jumping errors when winning on juvenile hurdle debut in weak Stratford contest in July 2002 and ran second to a decent sort next time. Suited by a sound surface.

Girl's Best Friend

79   24

6-y-o b m Nicolotte-Diamond Princess (Horage)
D W P Arbuthnot (N J Henderson 29/4) Stephen Crown

Placings: 5/P6-   (0008)
2002/03: 16⁶G,

	Starts	1st	2nd	3rd	Win & Pl
Hurdles	1	0	0	0	0
Career Total	3	0	0	0	0

Going: Sf: 0-0 GS: 0-0 Gd: 0-0 GF: - Fm: 0-0
Distance: 2m/2m3: 0-1 2m4-2m7: 0-0 3m+: 0-0
Track: LH: 0-1 RH: 0-0 Tight: 0-1 Gall: 0-0
Aids: Bl: 0-0 Vi: 0-0 Tstrap: 0-0
Best Rating: 34 4/02 Plum 2m   good Hdl

Girson Girl (IRE)

55f

4-y-o b f Kadeed (IRE)-Hill s Proposal (IRE) (Posen (USA))
Mrs H O Graham Mrs H O Graham

Placings: 0   (4665)
2002/03: 17⁰GF,

	Starts	1st	2nd	3rd	Win & Pl
NH Flat	1	0	0	0	
Career Total	1	0	0	0	

Going: Sf: 0-0 GS: 0-0 Gd: 0-0 GF: - Fm: 0-1
Distance: 2m/2m3: 0-1 2m4-2m7: 0-0 3m+: 0-0
Track: LH: 0-0 RH: 0-1 Tight: 0-0 Gall: 0-0
Aids: Bl: 0-0 Vi: 0-0 Tstrap: 0-0
Best Rating: 0

Gismo

79   88

6-y-o ch g Arazi (USA)-Gisarne (USA) (Diesis)
Miss Jacqueline S Doyle Tom Ford

Placings: 00/10-600F   (4641)
2002/03: 16⁶S, 16⁰S, 19⁶GF,

	Starts	1st	2nd	3rd	Win & Pl
Hurdles	4	0	0	0	0
Career Total	8	1	0	0	1572
87	5/01	Folk	2m1f110yH NHF	G-F	£1571
			Total win prize-money £1572

Going: Sf: 0-2 GS: 0-1 Gd: 0-0 GF: - Fm: 0-1
Distance: 2m/2m3: 0-2 2m4-2m7: 0-0 3m+: 0-0
Track: LH: 0-1 RH: 0-3 Tight: 0-1 Gall: 0-1
Aids: Bl: 0-0 Vi: 0-0 Tstrap: 0-0
Best Rating: 91 4/03 Strf 2m3f   gd-fm Hdl

A bumper winner, he was sixth on his hurdles bow in December 2002 after a lengthy lay-off; four lengths clear when falling at the last in 2m 3f maiden hurdle at Stratford April 2003; best on a sound surface.

Give An Inch (IRE)

8-y-o b m Inchinor-Top Heights (High Top)
W Storey Alan Osborne

Placings: PP   (3769)
2002/03: 16⁵S, 20⁶PGS,

	Starts	1st	2nd	3rd	Win & Pl
Hurdles	2	0	0	0	
Career Total	2	0	0	0	

Going: Sf: 0-1 GS: 0-1 Gd: 0-0 GF: - Fm: 0-0
Distance: 2m/2m3: 0-1 2m4-2m7: 0-0 3m+: 0-0
Track: LH: 0-2 RH: 0-0 Tight: 0-0 Gall: 0-0
Aids: Bl: 0-0 Vi: 0-0 Tstrap: 0-0
Best Rating: 0 2/03 Ayr 2m4f   gd-sft Hdl

Give Over (IRE)

97(107c)   (141c)131

10-y-o b g Lord Americo-Romany River (Over The River (FR))
Edward U Hales Mrs E Queally

Placings: 06/2632312500/030131010/05211UB6P2-23020
                                          (3087a)

2002/03: 20²S, 24³S, 26⁶GS, 24²HY, 24⁰S,

	Starts	1st	2nd	3rd	Win & Pl
Hurdles	3	0	2	0	7460
Chases	2	0	1	0	7730
Career Total	36	6	7	5	90165
131	12/01	Leop	3m	Ch	YLD	£15725
119	12/01	Fair	3m1f	Ch	YLD	£6677
131	4/01	Cork	2m4f	(0-130)HHdl	Y-S	£13104

124	2/01	Naas	3m	(0-116)HHdl	SH	£5008
138	11/00	Clon	3m	(0-116)HHdl	SH	£3312
118	1/00	Punc	3m	Hdl	Y-S	£4416
				Total win prize-money £48244		

Going:	Sf: 0-4 GS: 0-1 Gd: 0-0 GF: - Fm: 0-0
Distance:	2m/2m3: 0-0 2m4-2m7: 0-1 3m+: 0-4
Track:	LH: 0-3 RH: 0-0 Tight: 0-0 Gall: 0-1
Aids:	Bl: 0-0 Vi: 0-0 Tstrap: 0-0
Best Rating:	141 11/02 DRoy 3m soft Ch

He took well to fences and scored twice in December 2001. An early casualty on his next two starts, he was well beaten in the Sun Alliance at Cheltenham. Running well in the autumn of 2002. Stays well.

Give Us A Price

8-y-o b m Silly Prices-Give Us A Treat (Cree Song)
John A Harris   I R Bennett

Placings:P0-0P	(0418)

2002/03: 16⁰GF, 22ᴾHY,

	Starts	1st	2nd	3rd	Win & Pl
Hurdles	2	0	0		0
Career Total	4	0	0		0

Going:	Sf: 0-1 GS: 0-0 Gd: 0-0 GF: - Fm: 0-1
Distance:	2m/2m3: 0-1 2m4-2m7: 0-0 3m+: 0-0
Track:	LH: 0-2 RH: 0-0 Tight: 0-0 Gall: 0-0
Aids:	Bl: 0-0 Vi: 0-0 Tstrap: 0-0
Best Rating:	0 6/02 Ctml 2m6f heavy Hdl

Giveaway
93

8-y-o ch g Generous (IRE)-Radiant Bride (USA) (Blushing Groom (FR))
D J Wintle   The Lavender Hill Mob

Placings:6/1600/000/P3400430-50PP	(2453)

2002/03: 19⁵GF, 19⁰G, 24ᴾG, 19ᴾGS,

	Starts	1st	2nd	3rd	Win & Pl
Hurdles	2	0	0	0	0
Chases	2	0	0	0	0
Career Total	20	1	0	2	3695
101	5/99	Gowr	2m	Hdl	GD	£2700
				Total win prize-money £2701		

Going:	Sf: 0-0 GS: 0-1 Gd: 0-2 GF: - Fm: 0-1
Distance:	2m/2m3: 0-2 2m4-2m7: 0-1 3m+: 0-1
Track:	LH: 0-0 RH: 0-4 Tight: 0-1 Gall: 0-0
Aids:	Bl: 0-0 Vi: 0-0 Tstrap: 0-3
Best Rating:	109 5/00 Punc 2m good Hdl

Ex-Irish, best at two miles; acts on soft ground but suited by good; has worn a tongue tie.

Givendale
61f   29f

5-y-o b g Perpendicular-Knocksharry (Palm Track)
J R Turner   J R Turner

Placings:00	(3998)

2002/03: 16⁰G, 16⁰G,

	Starts	1st	2nd	3rd	Win & Pl
NH Flat	2	0	0		0
Career Total	2	0	0		0

Going:	Sf: 0-0 GS: 0-0 Gd: 0-2 GF: - Fm: 0-0
Distance:	2m/2m3: 0-2 2m4-2m7: 0-0 3m+: 0-0

Glacial Enterprise (IRE)

10-y-o ch g Glacial Storm (USA)-Miss Shamrock (Saritamer (USA))
Mrs H J Cobb (P J Hobbs 10/6)   D B Evatt

Placings:22/1520/32P10-3P	(3674)

2002/03: 26³G, 26ᴾGS,

	Starts	1st	2nd	3rd	Win & Pl
Chases	2	0	0	1	615
Career Total	13	2	4	2	14612
111	2/02	Font	3m2f110yD Ch		HVY	£3965
110	11/00	Tntn	3m110y C Hdl		GD	£5284
			Total win prize-money £9250			

Going:	Sf: 0-0 GS: 0-1 Gd: 0-1 GF: - Fm: 0-0
Distance:	2m/2m3: 0-0 2m4-2m7: 0-0 3m+: 0-2
Track:	LH: 0-1 RH: 0-0 Tight: 0-2 Gall: 0-0
Aids:	Bl: 0-1 Vi: 0-0 Tstrap: 0-0
Best Rating:	117 1/01 Font 3m2f110y soft Ch

Winner of an Irish point to point. Has mixed chasing and hurdling. Stays three miles. Has won on good ground.

Glacial Evening (IRE)

7-y-o b/br g Glacial Storm (USA)-Cold Evening (IRE) (Strong Gale)
R H Buckler   The Deadly Sins Partnership

Placings:5/00P	(3319)

2002/03: 16⁰G, 16⁰G, 21ᴾGS,

	Starts	1st	2nd	3rd	Win & Pl
NH Flat	2	0	0	0	0
Hurdles	1	0	0	0	0
Career Total	4	0	0	0	0

Going:	Sf: 0-0 GS: 0-1 Gd: 0-2 GF: - Fm: 0-0
Distance:	2m/2m3: 0-2 2m4-2m7: 0-1 3m+: 0-0
Track:	LH: 0-1 RH: 0-0 Tight: 0-0 Gall: 0-0
Aids:	Bl: 0-0 Vi: 0-0 Tstrap: 0-0
Best Rating:	87 12/00 Hntg 2m110y soft NHF

Glacial Missile (IRE)
102(100c)   (107c)95

10-y-o ch m Glacial Storm (USA)-Trident Missile (Vulgan Slave)
P Bowen   R Owen

Placings:2233P3332P/05P1111344P/P3UP/1F-PP313	
	(1131)

2002/03: 23ᴾGF, 23ᴾG, 20³GF, 21¹GF, 19³GF,

	Starts	1st	2nd	3rd	Win & Pl
Hurdles	3	1	0	2	4831
Chases	2	0	0	0	0
Career Total	32	6	3	9	25088
95	8/02	Sthl	2m5f110yD(0-115)HHdl	G-F	£3581
107	8/01	Worc	2m4f110yD Ch	G-F	£3848
109	8/99	MRas	2m3f110yE Hdl	G-F	£2705
99	7/99	MRas	2m3f110yD Hdl	G-F	£3857
97	7/99	Worc	2m4f E Hdl	G-F	£2318
96	6/99	Worc	2m4f E Hdl	G-F	£2652
			Total win prize-money £18963		

Going:	Sf: 0-0 GS: 0-0 Gd: 0-1 GF: - Fm: 1-4
Distance:	2m/2m3: 0-0 2m4-2m7: 1-3 3m+: 0-2
Track:	LH: 1-4 RH: 0-1 Tight: 0-1 Gall: 0-0
Aids:	Bl: 1-2 Vi: 0-0 Tstrap: 0-0
Best Rating:	109 8/99 MRas 2m3f110y gd-fm Hdl

Moderate hurdler/chaser; likes fast ground; effective at two and a half miles.

Glacial River (IRE)
103(96h)   (85h)100

10-y-o ch g Glacial Storm (USA)-Lucky Trout (Beau Charmeur (FR))
D J Caro   D J Caro

Placings:60/603U/6350/3/22-P223P	(2667)

2002/03: 21ᴾGS, 21²S, 25²G, 29³GS, 26ᴾS,

	Starts	1st	2nd	3rd	Win & Pl
Chases	5	0	2	1	6179
Career Total	18	0	4	4	8562

Going:	Sf: 0-2 GS: 0-2 Gd: 0-1 GF: - Fm: 0-0
Distance:	2m/2m3: 0-0 2m4-2m7: 0-2 3m+: 0-3
Track:	LH: 0-4 RH: 0-0 Tight: 0-4 Gall: 0-0
Aids:	Bl: 0-0 Vi: 0-0 Tstrap: 0-0
Best Rating:	98 12/02 Wwck 3m5f gd-sft Ch

Modest performer, placed over hurdles and on his second run over fences in November 2002. Stays well.

Glacial Sunset (IRE)
104   123+

8-y-o ch g Glacial Storm (USA)-Twinkle Sunset (Deep Run)
A J Lidderdale   George Ward

Placings:4/10/34-12114	(4789)

2002/03: 22¹GF, 20²G, 26¹GF, 24¹G, 24⁴GF,

	Starts	1st	2nd	3rd	Win & Pl
Hurdles	5	3	1	0	18828
Career Total	10	4	1	1	21032
123	12/02	Chel	3m	B HHdl	GD	£9448
123	6/02	Hrfd	3m2f	E Hdl	G-F	£2968
116	5/02	Winc	2m6f	F(0-100)HHdl	G-F	£3150
111	5/00	Font	2m2f110yH NHF		GD	£1736
			Total win prize-money £17302			

Going:	Sf: 0-0 GS: 0-0 Gd: 1-2 GF: - Fm: 2-3
Distance:	2m/2m3: 0-0 2m4-2m7: 1-2 3m+: 2-3
Track:	LH: 1-2 RH: 2-2 Tight: 0-0 Gall: 1-1
Aids:	Bl: 0-0 Vi: 0-0 Tstrap: 0-0
Best Rating:	123 12/02 Chel 3m good Hdl

Decent hurdler; a lightly-raced bumper winner; he has improved with being stepped up in trip, recording his best result when winning a three-mile handicap at Cheltenham in December 2002; well held in Grade Two event four months later; appreciates a sound surface.

Glacial Tabhairne (IRE)
93   73

9-y-o ch g Glacial Storm (USA)-Taberna Lady (Paddy s Stream)
K C Bailey   J Perriss

Placings:F0-0506	(0562)

2002/03: 16⁰G, 26⁵G, 24⁰G, 19⁶GF,

	Starts	1st	2nd	3rd	Win & Pl
Hurdles	4	0	0	0	0
Career Total	6	0	0	0	0

Going: Sf: 0-0 GS: 0-0 Gd: 0-2 GF: - Fm: 0-2
Distance: 2m/2m3: 0-1 2m4-2m7: 0-1 3m+: 0-2
Track: LH: 0-1 RH: 0-3 Tight: 0-1 Gall: 0-2
Aids: Bl: 0-2 Vi: 0-0 Tstrap: 0-0
Best Rating: 76 4/02 Prth 2m4f110y good Hdl

Glacial Trial (IRE)

10-y-o b m Glacial Storm (USA)-Protrial (Proverb)
P Jones M J Parr

Placings:0/1 (0392)
2002/03: 24¹G,

	Starts	1st	2nd	3rd	Win & Pl
Chases	1	1	0	0	3042
Career Total	2	1	0	0	3042
99 5/02 Strf 3m	H Ch			GD	£3041

Total win prize-money £3042

Going: Sf: 0-0 GS: 0-0 Gd: 1-1 GF: - Fm: 0-0
Distance: 2m/2m3: 0-0 2m4-2m7: 0-0 3m+: 1-1
Track: LH: 1-1 RH: 0-0 Tight: 1-1 Gall: 0-0
Aids: Bl: 0-0 Vi: 0-0 Tstrap: 0-0
Best Rating: 99 5/02 Strf 3m good Ch

Fair pointer/hunter chaser; needs to go left-handed.

Gladiateur Iv (FR)
112(98h) (97h)145
9-y-o b g Useful (FR)-Friga (FR) (Montevideo (ZIM))
P J Hobbs The Cobra Partnership

Placings:3315/323P01313/15125231P/431013-112F
(1311a)
2002/03: 20¹GF, 24¹GF, 20²GF, 24F F,

	Starts	1st	2nd	3rd	Win & Pl
Hurdles	1	0	1	0	752
Chases	3	2	0	0	18902
Career Total	32	10	4	9	72203
145 5/02 Strf	3m	C(0-135)HCh		G-F	£8502
145 5/02 Worc	2m4f110yB(0-145)HCh			G-F	£10400
131 8/01 NAbb	2m5f110yD(0-120)HCh			G-F	£3997
132 7/01 Strf	2m4f	C(0-135)HCh		G-F	£5902
129 10/00 Tntn	3m	D(0-120)HCh		GD	£5694
123 6/00 Worc	2m4f110yD(0-120)HCh			G-F	£3721
130 5/00 Worc	2m4f110yD(0-125)HCh			GD	£3835
116 3/00 Ludl	2m4f	D Ch		GD	£4127
116 2/00 Ludl	2m4f	E Ch		GD	£3250
110 1/99 Ling	2m110y	E Hdl		HVY	£2256

Total win prize-money £51687

Going: Sf: 0-0 GS: 0-0 Gd: 0-0 GF: - Fm: 2-4
Distance: 2m/2m3: 0-0 2m4-2m7: 1-2 3m+: 1-2
Track: LH: 2-4 RH: 0-0 Tight: 1-1 Gall: 0-0
Aids: Bl: 0-0 Vi: 0-0 Tstrap: 0-0
Best Rating: 145 5/02 Strf 3m gd-fm Ch

A respectable fast ground chaser, he is effective from two and a half to three miles and is usually held up.

Gladtoknowyou (IRE)
104 104
10-y-o ch g Over The River (FR)-Jonsemma (IRE) (Denel (FR))
R Rowe W Packham

Placings:34/2/15 (3622)
2002/03: 20¹GS, 24⁵S,

	Starts	1st	2nd	3rd	Win & Pl
Chases	2	1	0	0	5798
Career Total	5	1	1	1	7169
104 1/03 Kemp	2m4f110yD(0-115)HCh			G-S	£5798

Total win prize-money £5798

Going: Sf: 0-1 GS: 1-1 Gd: 0-0 GF: - Fm: 0-0
Distance: 2m/2m3: 0-0 2m4-2m7: 1-1 3m+: 0-1
Track: LH: 0-0 RH: 1-2 Tight: 0-0 Gall: 0-0
Aids: Bl: 0-0 Vi: 0-0 Tstrap: 0-0
Best Rating: 104 1/03 Kemp 2m4f110y gd-sft Ch

Gladys May (IRE)

6-y-o b m Moscow Society (USA)-Cashla (IRE) (Duky)
P J Hobbs R J B Partners

Placings:03-06P (0631)
2002/03: 16⁰G, 17⁵G, 17⁸GF,

	Starts	1st	2nd	3rd	Win & Pl
NH Flat	2	0	0	0	0
Hurdles	1	0	0	0	0
Career Total	5	0	0	1	318

Going: Sf: 0-0 GS: 0-0 Gd: 0-2 GF: - Fm: 0-1
Distance: 2m/2m3: 0-3 2m4-2m7: 0-0 3m+: 0-1
Track: LH: 0-3 RH: 0-0 Tight: 0-2 Gall: 0-0
Aids: Bl: 0-0 Vi: 0-0 Tstrap: 0-0
Best Rating: 90 4/02 Ludl 2m gd-fm NHF

Glamanglitz
94 113
13-y-o ch g Town And Country-Pretty Useful (Firestreak)
P T Dalton Mrs Julie Martin

Placings:20065/PFU433F3U/12135214P1/10212454/00P4
3133523032/U14021225/342P300-50543 (1403)
2002/03: 20⁵GF, 20⁹GF, 21⁵G, 16⁴G, 21³GF,

	Starts	1st	2nd	3rd	Win & Pl
Chases	5	0	0	1	1752
Career Total	67	9	11	12	72530
118 9/00 Worc	2m	C(0-135)HCh		G-F	£6745
105 5/00 Aint	2m	C(0-130)HCh		G-F	£4498
105 10/99 Worc	2m	D(0-135)HCh		G-F	£3744
122 9/98 Uttx	2m	D(0-130)HCh		G-F	£5105
123 5/98 Uttx	2m4f	D(0-125)HCh		GD	£3501
119 2/98 Donc	2m3f110yE(0-105)HCh			G-F	£3496
119 11/97 Uttx	2m5f	E(0-105)HCh		GD	£2963
104 6/97 Uttx	2m5f	C Ch		GD	£5363
106 5/97 Uttx	2m7f	E Ch		GD	£2914

Total win prize-money £38334

Going: Sf: 0-0 GS: 0-0 Gd: 0-2 GF: - Fm: 0-3
Distance: 2m/2m3: 0-1 2m4-2m7: 0-4 3m+: 0-2
Track: LH: 0-5 RH: 0-0 Tight: 0-0 Gall: 0-0
Aids: Bl: 0-0 Vi: 0-0 Tstrap: 0-0
Best Rating: 125 11/00 Chel 2m gd-sft Ch

Successful over fences, he is best when racing prominently on good ground or faster. Most effective at up to two and a half miles but has been out of form for some time.

Glamorous Leader (IRE)
87 103d
7-y-o b m Supreme Leader-Glamorous Gale (Strong Gale)
C Weedon (C Roche 23/8) Colin Weedon

Placings:3200/5000-6130 (2445)

2002/03: 17⁵G, 16¹YS, 19³GF, 16⁰G,

	Starts	1st	2nd	3rd	Win & Pl
NH Flat	2	1	0	0	3810
Hurdles	2	0	0	1	515
Career Total	12	1	1	2	5329
92 8/02 Kbgn 2m	NHF			Y-S	£3809

Total win prize-money £3810

Going: Sf: 0-0 GS: 0-0 Gd: 0-2 GF: - Fm: 0-1
Distance: 2m/2m3: 1-2 2m4-2m7: 0-0 3m+: 0-0
Track: LH: 0-0 RH: 0-1 Tight: 0-0 Gall: 0-0
Aids: Bl: 0-0 Vi: 0-0 Tstrap: 0-1
Best Rating: 103 9/01 Tral 2m good Hdl

Glamour Girl
89 49
7-y-o b m Lord Americo-Money Galore (IRE) (Monksfield)
F Jordan (M J Wilkinson 24/5) Mrs S G Davies

Placings:0/000-0040P6 (4020)
2002/03: 16⁵G, 19⁵S, 21⁴G, 20⁴GS, 25⁸G, 26⁸S,

	Starts	1st	2nd	3rd	Win & Pl
Hurdles	6	0	0	0	268
Career Total	10	0	0	0	268

Going: Sf: 0-2 GS: 0-1 Gd: 0-3 GF: - Fm: 0-0
Distance: 2m/2m3: 0-1 2m4-2m7: 0-3 3m+: 0-2
Track: LH: 0-2 RH: 0-4 Tight: 0-2 Gall: 0-0
Aids: Bl: 0-0 Vi: 0-0 Tstrap: 0-0
Best Rating: 74 2/02 Hntg 2m110y soft Hdl

Glanamana (IRE)
105(100h) (95h)104+
7-y-o b g Be My Native (USA)-Brides Choice (Cheval)
B G Powell Mrs Marygold O Kelly

Placings:31/0300PP-63U1 (3622)
2002/03: 25⁸GF, 26³G, 24⁰S, 24¹S,

	Starts	1st	2nd	3rd	Win & Pl
Chases	4	1	0	1	6291
Career Total	12	2	0	3	9713
105 2/03 Sand	3m110y	D(0-115)HCh		SFT	£5850
111 3/01 Newb	2m110y H NHF			HVY	£2646

Total win prize-money £8496

Going: Sf: 1-2 GS: 0-0 Gd: 0-1 GF: - Fm: 0-1
Distance: 2m/2m3: 0-0 2m4-2m7: 0-0 3m+: 1-4
Track: LH: 0-2 RH: 1-2 Tight: 0-1 Gall: 0-0
Aids: Bl: 0-0 Vi: 0-0 Tstrap: 0-0
Best Rating: 111 3/01 Newb 2m110y heavy NHF

Modest novice chaser; stays really well; acts on a soft surface.

Glanmerin (IRE)
104 100
12-y-o b g Lomond (USA)-Abalvina (FR) (Abdos)
R Lee Rex Norton

Placings:113/0/5024/02P/U2114/503/U624P01-P30P262 (4192)
2002/03: 16⁸PGS, 20³G, 20⁰GS, 20⁵S, 20²S, 20⁶GS, 20⁰G,

	Starts	1st	2nd	3rd	Win & Pl
Chases	7	0	2	1	3825
Career Total	33	5	6	3	28163
102 3/02 Sthl	2m4f110yF(0-90)HCh			HVY	£3119
123 3/00 Hntg	2m110y	D(0-125)HCh		SFT	£4396
123 2/00 Hntg	2m110y	D(0-125)HCh		SFT	£4420
113 3/95 Worc	2m	E Hdl		G-S	£2320
106 2/95 Nott	2m	D Hdl		G-S	£3662

Total win prize-money £17918

Going:	Sf: 0-2 GS: 0-3 Gd: 0-2 GF: - Fm: 0-0
Distance:	2m/2m3: 0-1 2m4-2m7: 0-6 3m+: 0-0
Track:	LH: 0-1 RH: 0-6 Tight: 0-2 Gall: 0-1
Aids:	Bl: 0-0 Vi: 0-0 Tstrap: 0-0
Best Rating:	124 2/97 Hntg 2m110y good Hdl

Modest chaser; effective at around two and a half miles in the mud.

Glashedy Rock (IRE)

97   **91**

6-y-o b g Shemazar-Classical Lady (IRE) (Orchestra)
Miss H C Knight Flora Lane & Gwen meacham

Placings:4F64   (4595)
2002/03: 16⁴GS, 22⁵GS, 19⁶GS, 22⁴GF,

	Starts	1st	2nd	3rd	Win & Pl
Hurdles	4	0	0	0	624
Career Total	4	0	0	0	624

Going:	Sf: 0-0 GS: 0-3 Gd: 0-0 GF: - Fm: 0-1
Distance:	2m/2m3: 0-0 2m4-2m7: 0-3 3m+: 0-0
Track:	LH: 0-2 RH: 0-2 Tight: 0-0 Gall: 0-1
Aids:	Bl: 0-0 Vi: 0-0 Tstrap: 0-0
Best Rating:	91 4/03 Extr 2m6f110y gd-fm Hdl

Moderate hurdler; Irish point winner; showed some promise on hurdling bow at Doncaster in January 2003 but disappointing since; stays at least two and a half miles; may do better when switching to fences.

Glass Breaker

9-y-o b g Infantry-Bottle Basher (Le Soleil)
T D Bryce C J Hays

Placings:P   (0272)
2002/03: 20ᴾGF,

	Starts	1st	2nd	3rd	Win & Pl
Chases	1	0	0	0	
Career Total	1	0	0	0	

Going:	Sf: 0-0 GS: 0-0 Gd: 0-0 GF: - Fm: 0-1
Distance:	2m/2m3: 0-0 2m4-2m7: 0-1 3m+: 0-0
Track:	LH: 0-1 RH: 0-0 Tight: 0-1 Gall: 0-0
Aids:	Bl: 0-1 Vi: 0-0 Tstrap: 0-0
Best Rating:	0 5/02 Strf 2m4f gd-fm Ch

Glebe Beauty (IRE)

81(67h)   (32h)**42**

7-y-o b m Good Thyne (USA)-Le Bavellen (Le Bavard (FR))
Mrs L B Normile The Friday Agreement

Placings:000P-06   (2557)
2002/03: 22ᴴHY, 20ᴾGF,

	Starts	1st	2nd	3rd	Win & Pl
Hurdles	1	0	0	0	0
Chases	1	0	0	0	0
Career Total	6	0	0	0	0

Going:	Sf: 0-1 GS: 0-0 Gd: 0-0 GF: - Fm: 0-1
Distance:	2m/2m3: 0-0 2m4-2m7: 0-2 3m+: 0-0
Track:	LH: 0-1 RH: 0-1 Tight: 0-2 Gall: 0-0
Aids:	Bl: 0-0 Vi: 0-0 Tstrap: 0-0
Best Rating:	83 5/01 Thur 2m2f gd-fm NHF

Glen Canyon (IRE)

57f   **57f**

6-y-o b g Tidaro (USA)-Glenadore (Furry Glen)
T Needham T Needham

Placings:00   (0523)
2002/03: 16⁰G, 17⁰G,

	Starts	1st	2nd	3rd	Win & Pl
NH Flat	2	0	0	0	
Career Total	2	0	0	0	

Going:	Sf: 0-0 GS: 0-0 Gd: 0-0 GF: - Fm: 0-0
Distance:	2m/2m3: 0-2 2m4-2m7: 0-0 3m+: 0-0
Track:	LH: 0-2 RH: 0-0 Tight: 0-1 Gall: 0-0
Aids:	Bl: 0-0 Vi: 0-0 Tstrap: 0-0
Best Rating:	57 5/02 Worc 2m good NHF

Glen Warrior

111   **111**

7-y-o b g Michelozzo (USA)-Mascara Vii (Damsire Unregistered)
J S Smith Donald Smith

Placings:0U-302213   (3778)
2002/03: 16³G, 22⁰HY, 19²S, 19²S, 24¹S, 24³GS,

	Starts	1st	2nd	3rd	Win & Pl
Hurdles	6	1	2	2	6986
Career Total	8	1	2	2	6986
97 1/03	Tntn		3m110y	E(0-110)HHdl	SFT £3770

Total win prize-money £3770

Going:	Sf: 1-4 GS: 0-1 Gd: 0-1 GF: - Fm: 0-0
Distance:	2m/2m3: 0-2 2m4-2m7: 0-2 3m+: 1-2
Track:	LH: 0-1 RH: 1-5 Tight: 1-2 Gall: 0-0
Aids:	Bl: 0-0 Vi: 0-0 Tstrap: 0-0
Best Rating:	102 12/02 Extr 2m3f soft Hdl

Modest hurdler; acts on a soft surface; stays three miles.

Glenahary Rose (IRE)

10-y-o b g Roselier (FR)-Ara Go On (Sandalay)
Mrs T White (Michael McCullagh 27/5) Captain Edward Martin

Placings:040P052FU/00PP4/30020B-46P   (4031)
2002/03: 24⁴S, 25⁶YS, 24ᴾS,

	Starts	1st	2nd	3rd	Win & Pl
Chases	3	0	0	0	245
Career Total	23	0	2	1	3682

Going:	Sf: 0-2 GS: 0-0 Gd: 0-0 GF: - Fm: 0-0
Distance:	2m/2m3: 0-0 2m4-2m7: 0-0 3m+: 0-3
Track:	LH: 0-1 RH: 0-1 Tight: 0-0 Gall: 0-0
Aids:	Bl: 0-0 Vi: 0-0 Tstrap: 0-0
Best Rating:	80 5/02 Navn 3m soft Ch

Glenalla Braes (IRE)

(79h)   (29h)

10-y-o b g Roi Guillaume (FR)-Willowho Pride (Arapaho)
M J Gingell Robert Barr

Placings:P/04-PP000   (4339)
2002/03: 20ᴾGS, 21ᴾS, 26ᴾG, 16⁰G, 24⁰GF,

	Starts	1st	2nd	3rd	Win & Pl
Hurdles	3	0	0	0	0

| Chases | 2 | 0 | 0 | 0 | 0 |
| Career Total | 8 | 0 | 0 | 0 | 0 |

Going:	Sf: 0-1 GS: 0-1 Gd: 0-2 GF: - Fm: 0-1
Distance:	2m/2m3: 0-1 2m4-2m7: 0-2 3m+: 0-2
Track:	LH: 0-3 RH: 0-2 Tight: 0-3 Gall: 0-2
Aids:	Bl: 0-0 Vi: 0-3 Tstrap: 0-0
Best Rating:	62 5/01 Weth 3m1f firm Hdl

Glenburn (IRE)

88   **72**

5-y-o br g Dr Devious (IRE)-Edwina (IRE) (Caerleon (USA))
Miss Lucinda V Russell (I Semple 3/6) Mrs Ann Rutherford

Placings:PP0P   (4762)
2002/03: 16ᴾGF, 16ᴾS, 16⁰GF, 16ᴾG,

	Starts	1st	2nd	3rd	Win & Pl
Hurdles	4	0	0	0	
Career Total	4	0	0	0	

Going:	Sf: 0-1 GS: 0-0 Gd: 0-1 GF: - Fm: 0-2
Distance:	2m/2m3: 0-4 2m4-2m7: 0-0 3m+: 0-0
Track:	LH: 0-2 RH: 0-2 Tight: 0-2 Gall: 0-0
Aids:	Bl: 0-0 Vi: 0-0 Tstrap: 0-3
Best Rating:	0 4/03 Prth 2m110y good Hdl

Glendamah (IRE)

101   **87**

6-y-o b g Mukaddamah (USA)-Sea Glen (IRE) (Glenstal (USA))
J R Weymes White Rose Poultry Ltd

Placings:650026-1124   (0620)
2002/03: 16¹GS, 16¹G, 16²G, 16⁴GF,

	Starts	1st	2nd	3rd	Win & Pl
Hurdles	4	2	1	0	4882
Career Total	10	2	2	0	5440
87 5/02	Hexm	2m110y	G(0-95)HHdl	GD	£2478
85 5/02	Hexm	2m110y	G Hdl		G-S	£1841

Total win prize-money £4319

Going:	Sf: 0-0 GS: 1-1 Gd: 1-2 GF: - Fm: 0-1
Distance:	2m/2m3: 2-4 2m4-2m7: 0-0 3m+: 0-0
Track:	LH: 2-4 RH: 0-0 Tight: 0-0 Gall: 0-0
Aids:	Bl: 0-0 Vi: 0-0 Tstrap: 0-0
Best Rating:	87 6/02 Hexm 2m110y good Hdl

Plating-class hurdler, winner of two sellers at Hexham in May 2002. Suited by a sound surface.

Glenelly Gale (IRE)

98   **133**

9-y-o b/br g Strong Gale-Smart Fashion (Carlburg)
A L T Moore F Bradley

Placings:0/2F140/5124U13/5035103-4F3104   (4654a)
2002/03: 20⁴YS, 16ᶠG, 16³G, 17¹S, 16⁹G, 17⁴GF,

	Starts	1st	2nd	3rd	Win & Pl
Chases	6	1	0	1	16806
Career Total	26	5	2	4	66518
132 3/03	Limk	2m1f	HCh	SFT	£12662
119 1/02	Thur	2m	Ch	Y-S	£7831
122 2/01	Fair	2m100y	Ch	HVY	£18346
119 10/00	Gowr	2m1f	Ch	SFT	£4692
123 1/00	Punc	2m	Hdl	SFT	£3312

Total win prize-money £46844

| Going: | Sf: 1-1 GS: 0-0 Gd: 0-3 GF: - Fm: 0-1 |

Distance: 2m/2m3: **1-5** 2m4-2m7: 0-1 3m+: 0-0
Track: LH: 0-3 RH: 0-1 Tight: 0-1 Gall: 0-1
Aids: BI: 0-0 Vi: 0-0 Tstrap: 0-0
Best Rating: **132** 4/03 Fair 2m1f   gd-fm Ch

Fair Irish handicap chaser; best at around two miles; acts on soft/heavy ground.

Glenfarclas Boy (IRE)

103(100h)   (78h)112

7-y-o b g Montelimar (USA)-Fairy Blaze (IRE) (Good Thyne (USA))
Miss Lucinda V Russell Mrs Ishbel Grant

Placings:600F/0F4P46-U1PP2F5233P   (4751)
2002/03: 22^UGF, 16^1GS, 20^PGS, 16^PS, 16^2GS, 16^FGF, 16^5G, 21^2GS, 16^9S, 20^3G, 20^PG,

	Starts	1st	2nd	3rd	Win & Pl
Chases	11	1	2	2	10408
Career Total	21	1	2	2	10408
108 6/02 Prth	2m		D Ch		G-S £5012

Total win prize-money £5012

Going: Sf: 0-2 GS: 1-4 Gd: 0-3 GF: - Fm: 0-2
Distance: 2m/2m3: **1-6** 2m4-2m7: 0-5 3m+: 0-0
Track: LH: 0-6 **RH: 1-5** Tight: 0-4 Gall: 0-0
Aids: BI: 0-0 Vi: 0-0 Tstrap: 0-0
Best Rating: **112** 4/03 Ayr 2m4f   good Ch

Moderate novice chaser; stays 2m 5f; races prominently.

Glengolden (IRE)

99   77

10-y-o ch m Glenstal (USA)-Talk Is Cheap (Le Bavard (FR))
Mrs S C Bradburne Timothy Hardie

Placings:50/54-45   (0250)
2002/03: 25^4GS, 24^5GF,

	Starts	1st	2nd	3rd	Win & Pl
Chases	2	0	0	0	245
Career Total	6	0	0	0	802

Going: Sf: 0-0 GS: 0-1 Gd: 0-0 GF: - Fm: 0-1
Distance: 2m/2m3: 0-0 2m4-2m7: 0-0 3m+: 0-2
Track: LH: 0-1 RH: 0-1 Tight: 0-0 Gall: 0-0
Aids: BI: 0-0 Vi: 0-0 Tstrap: 0-0
Best Rating: **80** 5/02 Hexm 3m1f   gd-sft Ch

Glengooley Flyer (IRE)

11-y-o b g Ore-Trim Hen (Trimmingham)
Mrs Lynne Ward D R Obank

Placings:0/43/0   (0402)
2002/03: 20^0GF,

	Starts	1st	2nd	3rd	Win & Pl
Chases	1	0	0	0	
Career Total	4	0	0	1	270

Going: Sf: 0-0 GS: 0-0 Gd: 0-0 GF: - Fm: 0-1
Distance: 2m/2m3: 0-0 2m4-2m7: 0-1 3m+: 0-0
Track: LH: 0-1 RH: 0-0 Tight: 0-0 Gall: 0-0
Aids: BI: 0-0 Vi: 0-0 Tstrap: 0-0
Best Rating: **81** 12/99 Plum 2m5f   heavy Hdl

Glenhaven Nugget (IRE)

107   130

7-y-o br g Supreme Leader-Jasmine Melody (Jasmine Star)
E J O Grady David Cahill

Placings:20211-143151   (4726a)
2002/03: 18^1YS, 16^4YS, 16^3S, 16^1Y, 16^5G, 16^1GF,

	Starts	1st	2nd	3rd	Win & Pl
Hurdles	6	3	0	1	36105
Career Total	11	5	2	1	48588
130 4/03 Fair	2m	Hdl		G-F	£23214
123 2/03 Thur	2m	Hdl		YLD	£5376
118 10/02 Thur	2m2f	Hdl		Y-S	£4868
120 4/02 Punc	2m	NHF		G-Y	£6984
109 4/02 Gowr	2m1f	NHF		YLD	£3809

Total win prize-money £44254

Going: Sf: 0-1 GS: 0-0 Gd: 0-1 GF: - Fm: 1-1
Distance: 2m/2m3: **3-6** 2m4-2m7: 0-0 3m+: 0-0
Track: LH: 0-2 **RH: 2-2** Tight: 0-1 Gall: 0-0
Aids: BI: 0-0 Vi: 0-0 Tstrap: 0-0
Best Rating: **130** 4/03 Fair 2m   gd-fm Hdl

Decent Irish-trained novice hurdler; most disappointing in Grade Two at Aintree, fading badly after looking a real danger; stays 2m 2f; acts on soft ground.

Glenmoss Tara (IRE)

107   122+

5-y-o b m Zaffaran (USA)-Majestic Run (Deep Run)
N G Richards West Coast Fiddlers

Placings:112-1112   (4326)
2002/03: 19^1G, 20^1S, 20^1G, 21^2G,

	Starts	1st	2nd	3rd	Win & Pl
Hurdles	4	3	1	0	22524
Career Total	7	5	2	0	30101
104 1/03 Muss	2m4f	D Hdl		GD	£6077
115 12/02 Ayr	2m4f	E Hdl		SFT	£3052
105 11/02 Catt	2m3f	F Hdl		GD	£2394
98 2/02 Donc	2m110y	H NHF		SFT	£2002

Total win prize-money £13526

Going: Sf: 1-1 GS: 0-0 Gd: 2-3 GF: - Fm: 0-0
Distance: 2m/2m3: 1-1 **2m4-2m7: 2-3** 3m+: 0-0
Track: **LH: 2-3** RH: 1-1 Tight: 2-2 Gall: 0-1
Aids: BI: 0-0 Vi: 0-0 Tstrap: 0-0
Best Rating: **127** 3/03 Newb 2m5f   good Hdl

Fair novice hurdler; stays two miles four and acts on good ground or softer.

Glensan (IRE)

83   54

6-y-o b g Insan (USA)-Strikes Glen (Le Moss)
Mrs H Dalton A J Brazier

Placings:4P-60   (2232)
2002/03: 16^6GS, 20^0S,

	Starts	1st	2nd	3rd	Win & Pl
Hurdles	2	0	0	0	0
Career Total	4	0	0	0	0

Going: Sf: 0-1 GS: 0-1 Gd: 0-0 GF: - Fm: 0-0
Distance: 2m/2m3: 0-1 2m4-2m7: 0-1 3m+: 0-0
Track: LH: 0-1 RH: 0-0 Tight: 0-0 Gall: 0-1
Aids: BI: 0-0 Vi: 0-0 Tstrap: 0-0
Best Rating: **92** 12/01 Hntg 2m110y   gd-sft NHF

Glentrust

5-y-o ch g Eastern Whisper (USA)-Esprit De Femme (FR) (Esprit Du Nord (USA))
D M Grissell Mrs L R Browning

Placings:0P   (4077)
2002/03: 18^0S, 18^0HY, 21^PHY,

	Starts	1st	2nd	3rd	Win & Pl
NH Flat	2	0	0	0	0
Hurdles	1	0	0	0	0
Career Total	3	0	0	0	

Going: Sf: 0-3 GS: 0-0 Gd: 0-0 GF: - Fm: 0-0
Distance: 2m/2m3: 0-2 2m4-2m7: 0-1 3m+: 0-0
Track: LH: 0-3 RH: 0-0 Tight: 0-1 Gall: 0-0
Aids: BI: 0-0 Vi: 0-0 Tstrap: 0-0
Best Rating: **54** 2/03 Plum 2m2f   heavy NHF

Glinger (IRE)

106(96h)   (91h)112+

10-y-o b g Remainder Man-Harilla (Sir Herbert)
N G Richards James Westoll

Placings:6650/FP/4422-3113   (1690)
2002/03: 20^3G, 20^1GF, 20^1GF, 20^3G,

	Starts	1st	2nd	3rd	Win & Pl
Chases	4	2	0	2	13657
Career Total	14	2	2	2	16928
112 10/02 Carl	2m4f	D Ch		G-F	£5668
99 8/02 MRas	2m4f	D(0-120)HCh		G-F	£5109

Total win prize-money £10777

Going: Sf: 0-0 GS: 0-0 Gd: 0-2 GF: - Fm: 2-2
Distance: 2m/2m3: 0-0 **2m4-2m7: 2-4** 3m+: 0-0
Track: LH: 0-1 **RH: 2-3** Tight: 1-1 Gall: 0-1
Aids: BI: 0-0 Vi: 0-0 Tstrap: 0-0
Best Rating: **112** 10/02 Chel 2m4f110y good Ch

Moderate chaser; won two fast-ground events over two and a half miles in the autumn of 2002; runner-up twice over hurdles in July; should continue to win his share of modest events over fences.

Globe Beauty (IRE)

37f

5-y-o b m Shalford (IRE)-Pen Bal Duchess (Chaparly (FR))
A Parker G & P Barker Ltd/globe Engineering

Placings:0   (4411)
2002/03: 16^0G,

	Starts	1st	2nd	3rd	Win & Pl
NH Flat	1	0	0	0	
Career Total	1	0	0	0	

Going: Sf: 0-0 GS: 0-0 Gd: 0-1 GF: - Fm: 0-0
Distance: 2m/2m3: 0-1 2m4-2m7: 0-0 3m+: 0-0
Track: LH: 0-1 RH: 0-0 Tight: 0-0 Gall: 0-0
Aids: BI: 0-0 Vi: 0-0 Tstrap: 0-0
Best Rating: **37** 3/03 Hexm 2m110y   good NHF

Globe Queen (IRE)

73   62

6-y-o ch m River Falls-Kristar (Kris)
D McCain G & P Barker Ltd/globe Engineering

Placings:5PP0   (3508)
2002/03: 16^5GF, 17^PG, 16^PG, 16^0G,

	Starts	1st	2nd	3rd	Win & Pl
Hurdles	4	0	0	0	0
Career Total	4	0	0	0	0

Going: Sf: 0-0 GS: 0-0 Gd: 0-3 GF: - Fm: 0-1
Distance: 2m/2m3: 0-4 2m4-2m7: 0-0 3m+: 0-0
Track: LH: 0-4 RH: 0-0 Tight: 0-3 Gall: 0-0
Aids: Bl: 0-0 Vi: 0-0 Tstrap: 0-0
Best Rating: 62 7/02 Strf 2m110y gd-fm Hdl

Glorious Welcome
82   38
5-y-o b g Past Glories-Rest And Welcome (Town And Country)
Jane Southcombe Mrs V H Nicholas

Placings:004P-P06P   (4020)
2002/03: 19PGS, 24OGS, 24OGS, 26PS,

	Starts	1st	2nd	3rd	Win & Pl
Hurdles	4	0	0	0	0
Career Total	8	0	0	0	0

Going: Sf: 0-1 GS: 0-3 Gd: 0-0 GF: - Fm: 0-0
Distance: 2m/2m3: 0-1 2m4-2m7: 0-0 3m+: 0-3
Track: LH: 0-0 RH: 0-3 Tight: 0-1 Gall: 0-0
Aids: Bl: 0-0 Vi: 0-0 Tstrap: 0-4
Best Rating: 53 12/01 Plum 2m good Hdl

Glory Storey (IRE)
112   (82h)104
9-y-o b g Tremblant-Boule De Soie (The Parson)
K C Bailey I M S Racing

Placings:403/0U455213-1P   (1566)
2002/03: 241GF, 25PGS,

	Starts	1st	2nd	3rd	Win & Pl
Chases	2	1	0	0	3301
Career Total	13	2	1	2	10547
104 6/02	Hntg	3m	F(0-100)HCh	G-F	£3300
104 4/02	Ludl	3m	D(0-110)HCh	G-F	£4498
			Total win prize-money £7799		

Going: Sf: 0-0 GS: 0-1 Gd: 0-0 GF: - Fm: 1-1
Distance: 2m/2m3: 0-0 2m4-2m7: 0-0 3m+: 1-2
Track: LH: 0-0 RH: 1-2 Tight: 0-1 Gall: 1-1
Aids: Bl: 0-0 Vi: 0-0 Tstrap: 0-0
Best Rating: 104 6/02 Hntg 3m gd-fm Ch

Moderate chaser; stays three miles; handles a sound surface.

Glory Trail (IRE)

9-y-o b g Supreme Leader-Death Or Glory (Hasdrubal)
Mrs D M Grissell Richard Griffiths

Placings:00/6-4   (0208)
2002/03: 224G,

	Starts	1st	2nd	3rd	Win & Pl
Chases	1	0	0	0	219
Career Total	4	0	0	0	219

Going: Sf: 0-0 GS: 0-0 Gd: 0-1 GF: - Fm: 0-0
Distance: 2m/2m3: 0-0 2m4-2m7: 0-1 3m+: 0-0
Track: LH: 0-0 RH: 0-1 Tight: 0-0 Gall: 0-0
Aids: Bl: 0-0 Vi: 0-0 Tstrap: 0-0
Best Rating: 76 6/01 Strf 2m6f110y gd-fm Hdl

Gloves Off (IRE)
84   (57h)69
6-y-o br g Naheez (USA)-River Dance View (IRE) (Orchestra)
Mrs A J Hamilton-Fairley (John Joseph Murphy 10/5)
Mrs A Hamilton-Fairley

Placings:0/0000000-36P   (3552)
2002/03: 16OG, 20OS, 26PS,

	Starts	1st	2nd	3rd	Win & Pl
Chases	3	0	0	1	687
Career Total	11	0	0	1	687

Going: Sf: 0-2 GS: 0-0 Gd: 0-1 GF: - Fm: 0-0
Distance: 2m/2m3: 0-1 2m4-2m7: 0-1 3m+: 0-1
Track: LH: 0-1 RH: 0-1 Tight: 0-2 Gall: 0-0
Aids: Bl: 0-0 Vi: 0-0 Tstrap: 0-0
Best Rating: 74 5/01 Klny 2m1f gd-fm NHF

Glynn Dingle (IRE)
101   (43h)117
10-y-o b g Millfontaine-Banner Lady (Milan)
A J Martin Patrick McCaughey

Placings:0/FF0602P51   (4773)
2002/03: 24FS, 24FY, 24OY, 17OGF, 17OGF, 16²S, 18PS, 20OGS, 201G,

	Starts	1st	2nd	3rd	Win & Pl
Hurdles	1	0	0	0	0
Chases	8	1	1	0	10708
Career Total	10	1	1	0	10708
106 4/03	Prth	2m4f110yD(0-115)HCh	GD	£8287	
		Total win prize-money £8288			

Going: Sf: 0-3 GS: 0-1 Gd: 1-1 GF: - Fm: 0-2
Distance: 2m/2m3: 0-4 2m4-2m7: 1-2 3m+: 0-3
Track: LH: 0-2 RH: 1-2 Tight: 0-0 Gall: 0-1
Aids: Bl: 0-0 Vi: 0-0 Tstrap: 0-0
Best Rating: 106 4/03 Prth 2m4f110y good Ch

Moderate chaser; ex-Irish; acts on good and soft ground; stays two and a half miles.

Go Ballistic
102   146
14-y-o br g Celtic Cone-National Clover (National Trust)
R T Phillips Mrs B J Lockhart

Placings:1232/50313P41P/124F42BF461/4121F4P/P54U4 10B/5P224/222P/102/03P0-6P   (4100)
2002/03: 25OG, 24FG,

	Starts	1st	2nd	3rd	Win & Pl
Chases	2	0	0	0	662
Career Total	57	9	11	4	246505
140 12/00	Chel	3m	B HHdl	SFT	£8923
171 2/98	Winc	3m1f110yB Ch	G-F	£11925	
146 12/96	Asct	3m110y B HCh	G-F	£24378	
133 11/96	Asct	3m110y B HCh	GF	£8013	
128 4/96	Asct	3m110y C Ch	G-F	£11464	
121 10/95	Worc	2m4f	C(0-130)HHdl	GD	£3416
116 3/95	Donc	2m4f	E HHdl	GD	£2845
112 12/94	Leic	2m	Hdl	HVY	£2249
118 2/94	Sand	2m110y	NHF	G-S	£1926
		Total win prize-money £75142			

Going: Sf: 0-0 GS: 0-0 Gd: 0-2 GF: - Fm: 0-0
Distance: 2m/2m3: 0-0 2m4-2m7: 0-0 3m+: 0-2
Track: LH: 0-2 RH: 0-0 Tight: 0-0 Gall: 0-2
Aids: Bl: 0-0 Vi: 0-0 Tstrap: 0-0
Best Rating: 171 3/99 Chel 3m2f110y gd-sft Ch

Formerly top-class chaser; durable and versatile; runner-up to See More Business in the Gold Cup of 1999; best on soft ground; goes well fresh; has a history of wind problems. He has now been honourably retired.

Go Boy
58   19
5-y-o b g Sovereign Water (FR)-Tinkle (Petoski)
R D E Woodhouse Go Racing

Placings:00-6   (1133)
2002/03: 19OGF,

	Starts	1st	2nd	3rd	Win & Pl
Hurdles	1	0	0	0	0
Career Total	3	0	0	0	0

Going: Sf: 0-0 GS: 0-0 Gd: 0-0 GF: - Fm: 0-1
Distance: 2m/2m3: 0-0 2m4-2m7: 0-1 3m+: 0-0
Track: LH: 0-0 RH: 0-1 Tight: 0-1 Gall: 0-0
Aids: Bl: 0-0 Vi: 0-0 Tstrap: 0-0
Best Rating: 65 2/02 Sand 2m110y soft NHF

Go Go Barney

8-y-o gr g Sylvan Express-Elegant Mary (Grey Ghost)
G A Harker P I Harker

Placings:0/0/FP   (1375)
2002/03: 16FGF, 17PGF,

	Starts	1st	2nd	3rd	Win & Pl
Hurdles	1	0	0	0	0
Chases	1	0	0	0	0
Career Total	4	0	0	0	0

Going: Sf: 0-0 GS: 0-0 Gd: 0-0 GF: - Fm: 0-2
Distance: 2m/2m3: 0-2 2m4-2m7: 0-0 3m+: 0-0
Track: LH: 0-1 RH: 0-1 Tight: 0-1 Gall: 0-0
Aids: Bl: 0-0 Vi: 0-0 Tstrap: 0-0
Best Rating: 64 1/00 Ayr 2m soft NHF

Go Man (IRE)

9-y-o b g Mandalus-Cherry Park (Netherkelly)
Colin Staley Colin Staley

Placings:00/P/06-0   (4487)
2002/03: 16OGF,

	Starts	1st	2nd	3rd	Win & Pl
Chases	1	0	0	0	0
Career Total	6	0	0	0	0

Going: Sf: 0-0 GS: 0-0 Gd: 0-0 GF: - Fm: 0-1
Distance: 2m/2m3: 0-1 2m4-2m7: 0-0 3m+: 0-0
Track: LH: 0-0 RH: 0-0 Tight: 0-0 Gall: 0-0
Aids: Bl: 0-0 Vi: 0-0 Tstrap: 0-0
Best Rating: 83 4/02 Uttx 2m good Hdl

Go Nomadic

9-y-o br g Nomadic Way (USA)-Dreamago (Sir Mago)
D G Atkinson D G Atkinson

Placings:210-332321   (4777)
2002/03: 28OG, 24³S, 27²S, 25³G, 25²G, 311G,

	Starts	1st	2nd	3rd	Win & Pl
Chases	6	1	2	3	6363

Career Total	9	2	3	3	9509
105 4/03 Prth	3m7f	H Ch		GD	£4069
105 3/02 Kels	3m1f	H Ch		HVY	£2691
			Total win prize-money		£6761

Going: Sf: 0-2 GS: 0-0 Gd: 1-4 GF: - Fm: -
Distance: 2m/2m3: 0-0 2m4-2m7: 0-0 **3m+: 1-6**
Track: LH: 0-5 RH: 0-0 Tight: 0-5 Gall: 0-0
Aids: Bl: 0-0 Vi: 0-0 **Tstrap: 1-6**
Best Rating: 105 4/03 Prth 3m7f good Ch

Fair hunter chaser; acts on a good and soft surface; stays three miles-seven; usually wears a tongue strap.

Go Roger Go (IRE)
113 (112h)**151+**
11-y-o b g Phardante (FR)-Tonto s Girl (Strong Gale)
E J O Grady J P McManus

Placings:20/241120/FF4F/11121R2U/221/323U6 (4334a)
2002/03: 17^3HY, 17^2S, 16^3Y, 20^UG, 20^8GY,

	Starts	1st	2nd	3rd	Win & Pl
Chases	5	0	1	2	9076
Career Total	28	7	8	2	119158
142 12/00 Chel	2m5f	A HCh		SFT	£46400
133 11/99 Punc	2m	Ch		YLD	£11607
123 9/99 List	2m	Ch		HVY	£5285
126 8/99 Tral	2m	Ch		YLD	£4312
110 7/99 Gway	2m1f	Ch		G-F	£6138
114 11/97 Navn	2m	Hdl		G-Y	£6782
126 10/97 Tipp	2m	Hdl		SH	£12772
			Total win prize-money		£93298

Going: Sf: 0-2 GS: 0-0 Gd: 0-1 GF: - Fm: 0-0
Distance: 2m/2m3: 0-3 2m4-2m7: 0-2 3m+: 0-0
Track: LH: 0-4 RH: 0-1 Tight: 0-0 Gall: 0-1
Aids: Bl: 0-0 Vi: 0-0 Tstrap: 0-0
Best Rating: 145 1/03 Fair 2m1f soft Ch

Very useful Irish chaser; won the Tripleprint Gold Cup at Cheltenham in December 2000, but lightly raced since; suited by soft ground; best at around two and a half miles.

Go To Shul
4-y-o b g Runnett-Kopjes (Bay Express)
M W Easterby Winton Bloodstock Ltd

Placings:00 (3998)
2002/03: 16^0GS, 16^9G,

	Starts	1st	2nd	3rd	Win & Pl
NH Flat	2	0	0	0	
Career Total	2	0	0	0	

Going: Sf: 0-0 GS: 0-1 Gd: 0-1 GF: - Fm: 0-0
Distance: 2m/2m3: 0-2 2m4-2m7: 0-0 3m+: 0-0
Track: LH: 0-2 RH: 0-0 Tight: 0-0 Gall: 0-1
Aids: Bl: 0-0 Vi: 0-0 Tstrap: 0-0
Best Rating: 0 3/03 Weth 2m good NHF

Go White Lightning (IRE)
106(95h) (91h)**115**
8-y-o gr g Zaffaran (USA)-Rosy Posy (IRE) (Roselier (FR))
M Bradstock Fishtank Racing

Placings:U1/1/0U-3P234 (3516)
2002/03: 19^3GS, 24^PS, 24^2G, 23^3S, 22^4GS,

	Starts	1st	2nd	3rd	Win & Pl
Chases	5	0	1	2	3149

Career Total	10	2	1	2	6572
107 5/00 Hrfd	2m1f	H NHF		GD	£1841
107 4/00 MRas	2m1f10yH	NHF		SFT	£1582
			Total win prize-money		£3423

Going: Sf: 0-2 GS: 0-2 Gd: 0-1 GF: - Fm: 0-0
Distance: 2m/2m3: 0-1 2m4-2m7: 0-0 3m+: 0-3
Track: LH: 0-3 RH: 0-2 Tight: 0-0 Gall: 0-1
Aids: Bl: 0-0 Vi: 0-0 Tstrap: 0-0
Best Rating: 115 1/03 Donc 3m good Ch

Bumper winner; decent novice chaser; stays three miles.

Go-Onmyson
110
10-y-o b g Primitive Rising (USA)-Ice Lass (Heroic Air)
Mrs A C Tate J A Simpson

Placings:5/40360F1/1PP64346460/31304350/0231P0-P (0837)
2002/03: 22^PGF,

	Starts	1st	2nd	3rd	Win & Pl
Hurdles	1	0	0	0	
Career Total	34	4	1	6	16724
110 10/01 Ludl	3m	E(0-115)HHdl		G-F	£4420
104 6/00 Worc	2m4f	F(0-100)HHdl		G-F	£2093
99 5/99 Chep	2m110y	E(0-105)HHdl		GF	£2528
73 3/99 Chep	2m110y	G Hdl		G-S	£1604
			Total win prize-money		£10645

Going: Sf: 0-0 GS: 0-0 Gd: 0-0 GF: - Fm: 0-1
Distance: 2m/2m3: 0-0 2m4-2m7: 0-1 3m+: 0-0
Track: LH: 0-1 RH: 0-0 Tight: 0-0 Gall: 0-0
Aids: Bl: 0-0 Vi: 0-0 Tstrap: 0-0
Best Rating: 110 10/01 Ludl 3m gd-fm Hdl

Modest hurdler; goes well between two and three miles; acts on most types of ground.

Godfather (IRE)
57f **8f**
5-y-o ch g Insan (USA)-Lady Letitia (Le Bavard (FR))
M Pitman Malcolm C Denmark

Placings:00 (4053)
2002/03: 16^6HY, 16^0HY,

	Starts	1st	2nd	3rd	Win & Pl
NH Flat	2	0	0	0	
Career Total	2	0	0	0	

Going: Sf: 0-1 GS: 0-1 Gd: 0-0 GF: - Fm: 0-0
Distance: 2m/2m3: 0-2 2m4-2m7: 0-0 3m+: 0-0
Track: LH: 0-0 RH: 0-2 Tight: 0-0 Gall: 0-0
Aids: Bl: 0-0 Vi: 0-0 Tstrap: 0-0
Best Rating: 8 1/03 Kemp 2m gd-sft NHF

Gods Token
97f **100f**
5-y-o gr g Gods Solution-Pro-Token (Proverb)
G P Kelly C I Ratcliffe

Placings:612 (1326)
2002/03: 17^6GF, 17^1GF, 17^2GF,

	Starts	1st	2nd	3rd	Win & Pl
NH Flat	3	1	1	0	2129
Career Total	3	1	1	0	2129
95 6/02 MRas	2m1f110y	H NHF		G-F	£1561
			Total win prize-money		£1561

Going: Sf: 0-0 GS: 0-0 Gd: 0-0 GF: - Fm: 1-3

Distance: 2m/2m3: 1-3 2m4-2m7: 0-0 3m+: 0-0
Track: LH: 0-0 RH: 1-3 Tight: 1-3 Gall: 0-0
Aids: Bl: 0-0 Vi: 0-0 Tstrap: 0-0
Best Rating: 100 9/02 MRas 2m1f110y gd-fm NHF

Landed a fast-ground bumper in June 2002.

Gofagold
89(102h) (88h)**88+**
8-y-o ch g Tina s Pet-Golden Della (Glint Of Gold)
A C Whillans Mrs L M Whillans

Placings:40/53/0432-222F (3503)
2002/03: 16^2G, 18^2G, 16^2HY, 20^0HY,

	Starts	1st	2nd	3rd	Win & Pl
Hurdles	2	0	2	0	1800
Chases	2	0	1	0	1678
Career Total	12	0	4	2	5417

Going: Sf: 0-2 GS: 0-0 Gd: 0-2 GF: - Fm: 0-0
Distance: 2m/2m3: 0-3 2m4-2m7: 0-1 3m+: 0-0
Track: LH: 0-4 RH: 0-0 Tight: 0-1 Gall: 0-0
Aids: Bl: 0-0 Vi: 0-0 Tstrap: 0-0
Best Rating: 88 1/03 Ayr 2m heavy Ch

Placed at a low level in novices hurdles.

Goguenard (FR)
118 **149**
9-y-o b g Gaspard De La Nuit (FR)-Laika Iii (FR) (El Toro (FR))
Mrs S J Smith (N J Henderson 23/5) Trevor Hemmings

Placings:012113/3214/0412F331500/415421/00P0F6-241U5131UU (4479)
2002/03: 20^0GF, 25^4G, 20^1GS, 27^4GS, 20^5GS, 20^1HY, 24^3GS, 20^1G, 20^UG, 36^0UG,

	Starts	1st	2nd	3rd	Win & Pl
Chases	10	3	1	1	54715
Career Total	43	11	5	5	153148
149 3/03 Hayd	2m4f	B HCh		GD	£17039
144 12/02 Weth	2m4f110yB	HCh		HVY	£15099
137 11/02 Weth	2m4f110yB(0-150)HCh			G-S	£11190
144 4/01 Sand	2m4f110yB(0-150)HCh			SFT	£19500
11/00 Toul	2m5f110y	Hdl		SFT	£6244
1/00 Pau	2m4f110y	HCh		SFT	£9606
9/99 Nior	2m3f	Hdl		VS	£3229
4/99 Toul	2m1f110y	Ch			£3767
3/98 Engh	2m1f110y	Ch		SFT	£10101
1/98 Pau	2m1f	Ch		HVY	£5051
			Total win prize-money		£104755

Going: Sf: 1-1 GS: 1-4 Gd: 1-4 GF: - Fm: 0-1
Distance: 2m/2m3: 0-0 2m4-2m7: 3-6 3m+: 0-4
Track: LH: 3-10 RH: 0-0 Tight: 0-0 Gall: 0-2
Aids: Bl: 0-0 Vi: 0-0 Tstrap: 0-0
Best Rating: 149 3/03 Chel 2m4f110y good Ch

Smart chaser; ex-French; best over two and a half miles, but does get further; still going well when falling in the Mildmay Of Flete at the 2003 Cheltenham Festival; fell fatally in the Grand National. (DEAD)

Gohh
98(101h) (97h)**102**
7-y-o ch g Alflora (USA)-Lavenham s Last (Rymer)
M W Easterby Mrs P A H Hartley

Placings:45/1021P-0303F (4227)
2002/03: 20^0GS, 16^3HY, 20^0G, 16^3G, 25^2GF,

	Starts	1st	2nd	3rd	Win & Pl
Hurdles	3	0	0	1	603

Chases	2	0	0	1	633
Career Total	**12**	**2**	**1**	**2**	**7117**
97	12/01 MRas	2m1f110yD Hdl		SFT	£3444
97	10/01 MRas	2m1f110yH NHF		G-S	£1582
		Total win prize-money £5026			

Going:	Sf: 0-1 GS: 0-1 Gd: 0-2 GF: - Fm: 0-1
Distance:	2m2/2m3: 0-2 2m4-2m7: 0-2 3m+: 0-1
Track:	LH: 0-5 RH: 0-0 Tight: 0-1 Gall: 0-1
Aids:	Bl: 0-0 Vi: 0-0 Tstrap: 0-5
Best Rating:	102 2/03 Weth 2m good Ch

A bumper winner at Market Rasen, he won a novice hurdle over the same course and distance in December 2001; made mistakes but shaped well when third on chasing debut at Wetherby in February.

Going Global (IRE)
100　　　　　　　　112
6-y-o ch g Bob Back (USA)-Ukraine Girl (Targowice (USA))
G L Moore　Allen House Partnership

Placings:000/3310-66　　　　　　　　(2199)
2002/03: 19⁶GS, 19⁶GF,

	Starts	1st	2nd	3rd	Win & Pl
Hurdles	2	0	0	0	0
Career Total	**9**	**1**	**0**	**2**	**4196**
112	2/02 Plum	2m5f	E Hdl	HVY	£2604
		Total win prize-money £2604			

Going:	Sf: 0-0 GS: 0-2 Gd: 0-0 GF: - Fm: 0-0
Distance:	2m2/2m3: 0-1 2m4-2m7: 0-1 3m+: 0-0
Track:	LH: 0-1 RH: 0-1 Tight: 0-1 Gall: 0-1
Aids:	Bl: 0-0 Vi: 0-0 Tstrap: 0-1
Best Rating:	112 2/02 Plum 2m5f heavy Hdl

Useful on the Flat, he has not looked a natural over hurdles and has undergone a soft palate operation. Landed a novice hurdle in bad ground in February 2002.

Going Solo

7-y-o ch m Sula Bula-Little Beaver (Privy Seal)
Mrs S Gardner　D V Gardner

Placings:00-0P6　　　　　　　　(0631)
2002/03: 17⁰G, 16⁰S, 17⁶GF,

	Starts	1st	2nd	3rd	Win & Pl
NH Flat	1	0	0	0	0
Hurdles	2	0	0	0	0
Career Total	**5**	**0**	**0**	**0**	**0**

Going:	Sf: 0-1 GS: 0-0 Gd: 0-1 GF: - Fm: 0-1
Distance:	2m2/2m3: 0-3 2m4-2m7: 0-0 3m+: 0-0
Track:	LH: 0-2 RH: 0-1 Tight: 0-1 Gall: 0-0
Aids:	Bl: 0-0 Vi: 0-0 Tstrap: 0-0
Best Rating:	73 5/02 Extr 2m1f good NHF

Gola Cher (IRE)
112　　　　　　　　140
9-y-o b g Beau Sher-Owen Money (Master Owen)
A King　Mr & Mrs F C Welch

Placings:11212/1210-2F3　　　　　　　　(4050)
2002/03: 25²G, 26³GS, 24²S,

	Starts	1st	2nd	3rd	Win & Pl
Chases	3	0	1	0	12248
Career Total	**12**	**5**	**4**	**1**	**60110**
118	1/02 Kemp	3m	D Ch	SFT	£4114
131	11/01 Chep	2m3f110yA Ch	G-S	£15000
126	2/01 Sand	2m6f	B Hdl	HVY	£7182

132	11/00 Asct	3m	C Hdl	SFT	£4836
113	10/00 Strf	2m6f110yE Hdl	G-S	£2681
		Total win prize-money £33815			

Going:	Sf: 0-1 GS: 0-1 Gd: 0-1 GF: - Fm: 0-0
Distance:	2m2/2m3: 0-0 2m4-2m7: 0-0 3m+: 0-3
Track:	LH: 0-1 RH: 0-2 Tight: 0-0 Gall: 0-1
Aids:	Bl: 0-1 Vi: 0-0 Tstrap: 0-0
Best Rating:	140 11/02 Winc 3m1f110y good Ch

Very useful handicap chaser; stays three miles two; effective in soft ground.

Gola Supreme (IRE)
103(98h)　　　　(103h)116
8-y-o gr g Supreme Leader-Coal Burn (King Sitric)
A King　Jerry Wright & Peter Smith

Placings:1P-2UP　　　　　　　　(3116)
2002/03: 24²HY, 24ᵁS, 24ᴾS,

	Starts	1st	2nd	3rd	Win & Pl
Chases	3	0	1	0	1500
Career Total	**5**	**1**	**1**	**0**	**6388**
103	11/01 Asct	3m	C Hdl	GD	£4888
		Total win prize-money £4888			

Going:	Sf: 0-3 GS: 0-0 Gd: 0-0 GF: - Fm: 0-0
Distance:	2m2/2m3: 0-0 2m4-2m7: 0-0 3m+: 0-3
Track:	LH: 0-2 RH: 0-1 Tight: 0-1 Gall: 0-0
Aids:	Bl: 0-0 Vi: 0-0 Tstrap: 0-0
Best Rating:	116 11/02 Bang 3m110y heavy Ch

A winner of a point to point in Ireland, he scored on his hurdles debut at Ascot, but was disappointing after that at Warwick in January 2002. Runner-up on his chase debut in November and unseated when in contention next time out. Stays three miles. Acts on an easy surface.

Gold Menelek (IRE)
81f　　　　　　　　56f
4-y-o ch g Goldmark (USA)-Newlands Cross (Mandalus)
T P McGovern　Lewes Racing

Placings:0　　　　　　　　(4122)
2002/03: 16⁰G,

	Starts	1st	2nd	3rd	Win & Pl
NH Flat	1	0	0	0	
Career Total	**1**	**0**	**0**	**0**	

Going:	Sf: 0-0 GS: 0-0 Gd: 0-0 GF: - Fm: 0-0
Distance:	2m2/2m3: 0-0 2m4-2m7: 0-0 3m+: 0-0
Track:	LH: 0-0 RH: 0-1 Tight: 0-0 Gall: 0-0
Aids:	Bl: 0-0 Vi: 0-0 Tstrap: 0-0
Best Rating:	45 3/03 Hntg 2m110y good NHF

Gold Merit (NZ)
72　　　　　　　　46
12-y-o ch g Gold Blend (USA)-Teresavari (NZ) (Godavari)
P T Dalton　Mrs Lucia Farmer

Placings:0/521142/6　　　　　　　　(3518)
2002/03: 20⁶GS,

	Starts	1st	2nd	3rd	Win & Pl
Hurdles	1	0	0	0	0
Career Total	**8**	**2**	**2**	**0**	**14698**
121	11/99 Uttx	2m	E Hdl	G-S	£2515
116	11/99 Uttx	2m	E Hdl	G-S	£2739
		Total win prize-money £5256			

| **Going:** | Sf: 0-0 GS: 0-1 Gd: 0-0 GF: - Fm: 0-0 |
| **Distance:** | 2m2/2m3: 0-0 2m4-2m7: 0-1 3m+: 0-0 |

Track:	LH: 0-1 RH: 0-0 Tight: 0-0 Gall: 0-0
Aids:	Bl: 0-0 Vi: 0-0 Tstrap: 0-0
Best Rating:	141 4/00 Aint 2m110y good Hdl

Gold Native (IRE)
101f　　　　　　　　95f
5-y-o br g Be My Native (USA)-Goldiyana (FR) (Glint Of Gold)
B Ellison　K M Everitt

Placings:43　　　　　　　　(3160)
2002/03: 16⁴GF, 16³G,

	Starts	1st	2nd	3rd	Win & Pl
NH Flat	2	0	0	1	425
Career Total	**2**	**0**	**0**	**1**	**425**

Going:	Sf: 0-0 GS: 0-0 Gd: 0-1 GF: - Fm: 0-1
Distance:	2m2/2m3: 0-2 2m4-2m7: 0-0 3m+: 0-0
Track:	LH: 0-0 RH: 0-2 Tight: 0-2 Gall: 0-0
Aids:	Bl: 0-0 Vi: 0-0 Tstrap: 0-0
Best Rating:	95 1/03 Muss 2m good NHF

Improved on initial effort when third in a bumper at Musselburgh in January.

Gold Quest (IRE)
89　　　　　　　　114
6-y-o ch g Rainbow Quest (USA)-My Potters (USA) (Irish River (FR))
C J Mann　The Tramp Partnership

Placings:0P105P-00P　　　　　　　　(3317)
2002/03: 21³G, 19⁰GS, 24³GS,

	Starts	1st	2nd	3rd	Win & Pl
Hurdles	3	0	0	0	
Career Total	**9**	**1**	**0**	**0**	**3035**
114	2/02 Ludl	2m5f	E Hdl	SFT	£3034
		Total win prize-money £3035			

Going:	Sf: 0-0 GS: 0-2 Gd: 0-1 GF: - Fm: 0-0
Distance:	2m2/2m3: 0-0 2m4-2m7: 0-2 3m+: 0-1
Track:	LH: 0-1 RH: 0-2 Tight: 0-1 Gall: 0-1
Aids:	Bl: 0-0 Vi: 0-0 Tstrap: 0-3
Best Rating:	114 4/02 Asct 2m4f gd-fm Hdl

Formerly decent on the Flat, he showed nothing on his first two runs over hurdles but, following a soft palate operation, he sprung a 50/1 surprise at Ludlow in January 2002. Stays two miles five furlongs, acts on soft ground.

Goldanzig (IRE)
　　　　　　　　124
8-y-o b g Posen (USA)-Sharp Invite (Sharpo)
T P McGovern　N Abbott and Wellpool Ltd

Placings:22211/6P/50U2/0-P　　　　　　　　(1640)
2002/03: 21ᴾG,

	Starts	1st	2nd	3rd	Win & Pl
Hurdles	1	0	0	0	
Career Total	**13**	**2**	**4**	**0**	**10754**
114	10/98 Navn	2m	Hdl	SH	£3586
112	10/98 Gowr	2m	Hdl	SFT	£3586
		Total win prize-money £7174			

Going:	Sf: 0-0 GS: 0-0 Gd: 0-1 GF: - Fm: 0-0
Distance:	2m2/2m3: 0-0 2m4-2m7: 0-1 3m+: 0-0
Track:	LH: 0-0 RH: 0-1 Tight: 0-0 Gall: 0-0
Aids:	Bl: 0-0 Vi: 0-0 Tstrap: 0-1
Best Rating:	124 4/01 Newb 2m3f soft Hdl

Goldbridge (IRE)
102   96
8-y-o b g Distinctly North (USA)-Bold Kate (Bold Lad (IRE))
T P McGovern Alan W Clarke

Placings:413000/255034/622112124/**3P233-3**   (0391)
2002/03: 20³GS, 21³G,

	Starts	1st	2nd	3rd	Win & Pl
Chases	2	0	0	2	1579
Career Total	27	4	6	6	19633
120 8/00	Sthl	2m4f110yE(0-115)HHdl	G-F	£2352
115 7/00	Strf	2m6f110yF(0-110)HHdl	G-F	£2310
118 6/00	MRas	2m3f110yF(0-105)HHdl	G-F	£2747
95 8/98	Tram	2m	Hdl	G-F	£2391

Total win prize-money £9801

Going: Sf: 0-0 GS: 0-1 Gd: 0-1 GF: - Fm: 0-0
Distance: 2m/2m3: 0-0 2m4-2m7: 0-2 3m+: 0-0
Track: LH: 0-1 RH: 0-0 Tight: 0-1 Gall: 0-0
Aids: Bl: 0-0 Vi: 0-0 Tstrap: 0-0
Best Rating: 120 9/00 Hntg 2m4f110y gd-fm Hdl

Fast ground staying hurdler. In the frame over fences.

Goldbrook
98   101
5-y-o b g Alderbrook-Miss Marigold (Norwick (USA))
R J Hodges S J Norman

Placings:23342   (3931)
2002/03: 17²GS, 17³GS, 17³S, 17⁴S, 20²S,

	Starts	1st	2nd	3rd	Win & Pl
Hurdles	5	0	2	2	3817
Career Total	5	0	2	2	3817

Going: Sf: 0-3 GS: 0-2 Gd: 0-0 GF: - Fm: 0-0
Distance: 2m/2m3: 0-4 2m4-2m7: 0-1 3m+: 0-0
Track: LH: 0-0 RH: 0-4 Tight: 0-5 Gall: 0-0
Aids: Bl: 0-0 Vi: 0-0 Tstrap: 0-0
Best Rating: 101 3/03 Font 2m4f   soft   Hdl

Modest novice hurdler; suited by racing prominently; stays two and a half miles; suited by fast ground, but acts on softer.

Golden (FR)
101   77+
5-y-o ch m Sanglamore (USA)-Golden Sea (FR) (Saint Cyrien (FR))
N A Gaselee K V Stenborg

Placings:0014-50   (0633)
2002/03: 16⁴G, 17⁵G, 17⁰GF,

	Starts	1st	2nd	3rd	Win & Pl
Hurdles	3	0	0	0	
Career Total	6	1	0	0	2800
70 4/02	Tntn	2m1f	E Hdl	G-S	£2800

Total win prize-money £2800

Going: Sf: 0-0 GS: 0-0 Gd: 0-2 GF: - Fm: 0-1
Distance: 2m/2m3: 0-3 2m4-2m7: 0-0 3m+: 0-0
Track: LH: 0-2 RH: 0-1 Tight: 0-2 Gall: 0-0
Aids: Bl: 0-0 Vi: 0-0 Tstrap: 0-0
Best Rating: 80 4/02 Plum 2m   good   Hdl

Shrewdly placed to land very modest hurdle at Taunton in April 2002. Handles good or softer.

Golden Alpha (IRE)
113(109h)   (137h) 156+
9-y-o b g Alphabatim (USA)-Gina s Love (Golden Love)

M C Pipe D A Johnson

Placings:1/120/131064-11112U24F1   (4458)
2002/03: 16¹F, 16¹S, 16¹GF, 16¹G, 16²GS, 16ᵁG, 16²S, 16⁴G, 16ᶠG, 16¹G,

	Starts	1st	2nd	3rd	Win & Pl
Chases	10	5	2	0	67136
Career Total	20	9	3	1	91056
156 4/03	Aint	2m	A HCh	GD	£40600
120 7/02	Wolv	2m	E Ch	GD	£3497
133 6/02	NAbb	2m110y	D Ch	G-F	£3991
146 5/02	NAbb	2m110y	E Ch	SFT	£3435
115 5/02	Wwck	2m110y	E Ch	FRM	£3094
120 1/02	Winc	2m	E Hdl	G-S	£3136
128 12/01	Chep	2m110y	D Hdl	SFT	£3412
128 2/99	Newb	2m110y	H NHF	GD	£2931
121 4/98	Punc	2m	NHF	HVY	£5956

Total win prize-money £70055

Going: Sf: 1-2 GS: 0-1 Gd: 2-5 GF: - Fm: 2-2
Distance: 2m/2m3: 5-10 2m4-2m7: 0-0 3m+: 0-0
Track: LH: 5-9 RH: 0-1 Tight: 4-4 Gall: 0-4
Aids: Bl: 0-0 Vi: 0-0 Tstrap: 0-0
Best Rating: 156 4/03 Aint 2m   good   Ch

Very useful novice chaser; every chance when fell in Grand Annual Handicap at Cheltenham; ran away with competitive handicap at Aintree; all form around 2m; acts on any ground; very much suited by forcing tactics; has worn a visor.

Golden Arms
80f   55f
4-y-o ch g Blushing Flame (USA)-Beacon Hill (Bustino)
M W Easterby Lord Daresbury

Placings:00   (3412)
2002/03: 16⁹G, 16⁰GS,

	Starts	1st	2nd	3rd	Win & Pl
NH Flat	2	0	0	0	
Career Total	2	0	0	0	

Going: Sf: 0-0 GS: 0-1 Gd: 0-1 GF: - Fm: 0-0
Distance: 2m/2m3: 0-2 2m4-2m7: 0-0 3m+: 0-0
Track: LH: 0-2 RH: 0-0 Tight: 0-1 Gall: 0-0
Aids: Bl: 0-0 Vi: 0-0 Tstrap: 0-2
Best Rating: 56 2/03 Weth 2m   gd-sft NHF

Golden Chance (IRE)
82   51
6-y-o b g Unfuwain (USA)-Golden Digger (USA) (Mr Prospector (USA))
M W Easterby The Shooting Syndicate

Placings:5-P0   (3816)
2002/03: 20ᴾHG, 19⁰G,

	Starts	1st	2nd	3rd	Win & Pl
Hurdles	2	0	0	0	
Career Total	3	0	0	0	0

Going: Sf: 0-1 GS: 0-0 Gd: 0-1 GF: - Fm: 0-0
Distance: 2m/2m3: 0-1 2m4-2m7: 0-1 3m+: 0-0
Track: LH: 0-2 RH: 0-0 Tight: 0-1 Gall: 0-0
Aids: Bl: 0-0 Vi: 0-0 Tstrap: 0-0
Best Rating: 56 2/03 Catt 2m3f   good   Hdl

Golden Chimes (USA)

8-y-o ch g Woodman (USA)-Russian Ballet (USA) (Nijinsky (CAN))
G Tuer G Tuer

Placings:P222/1000/14-4   (3968)
2002/03: 25⁴S,

	Starts	1st	2nd	3rd	Win & Pl
Chases	1	0	0	0	110
Career Total	11	2	3	0	8142
116 7/01	Sedg	2m5f110yD(0-120)HHdl	G-F	£3255
114 5/00	Sedg	2m5f110yE Hdl	G-F	£2646

Total win prize-money £5901

Going: Sf: 0-1 GS: 0-0 Gd: 0-0 GF: - Fm: 0-0
Distance: 2m/2m3: 0-0 2m4-2m7: 0-0 3m+: 0-0
Track: LH: 0-1 RH: 0-0 Tight: 0-1 Gall: 0-0
Aids: Bl: 0-0 Vi: 0-0 Tstrap: 0-1
Best Rating: 116 7/01 Sedg 2m5f110y gd-fm Hdl

Golden Coin
97   84
7-y-o ch g St Ninian-Legal Coin (Official)
W M Brisbourne Bob Moseley

Placings:6-114533U   (3845)
2002/03: 16¹G, 16¹GS, 16⁴S, 20⁵G, 20³GS, 17³GS, 21ᵁG,

	Starts	1st	2nd	3rd	Win & Pl
NH Flat	3	2	0	0	3875
Hurdles	4	0	0	2	1368
Career Total	8	2	0	2	5243
116 5/02	Sthl	2m	H NHF	G-S	£1677
105 5/02	Uttx	2m	H NHF	GD	£2198

Total win prize-money £3875

Going: Sf: 0-1 GS: 1-3 Gd: 1-3 GF: - Fm: 0-0
Distance: 2m/2m3: 2-4 2m4-2m7: 0-3 3m+: 0-0
Track: LH: 2-6 RH: 0-0 Tight: 1-3 Gall: 0-0
Aids: Bl: 0-0 Vi: 0-0 Tstrap: 0-0
Best Rating: 116 5/02 Sthl 2m   gd-sft NHF

Dual bumper winner but has struggled so far over hurdles.

Golden Cross (IRE)
117   136
4-y-o b g Goldmark (USA)-Fordes Cross (Ya Zaman (USA))
M Halford Mrs H Johnson

Placings:16213   (4130)
2002/03: 16¹S, 16⁶HY, 16²S, 16¹YS, 17³G,

	Starts	1st	2nd	3rd	Win & Pl
Hurdles	5	2	1	1	44632
Career Total	5	2	1	1	44632
136 2/03	Fair	2m	Hdl	Y-S	£13506
121 11/02	Fair	2m	Hdl	SFT	£13957

Total win prize-money £27463

Going: Sf: 1-3 GS: 0-0 Gd: 0-1 GF: - Fm: 0-0
Distance: 2m/2m3: 2-5 2m4-2m7: 0-0 3m+: 0-0
Track: LH: 0-3 RH: 2-2 Tight: 0-0 Gall: 0-1
Aids: Bl: 0-0 Vi: 0-0 Tstrap: 0-0
Best Rating: 136 2/03 Fair 2m   yld-sft Hdl

Very useful juvenile hurdler; third in the Triumph Hurdle; effective on soft ground; goes well over two miles.

Golden Crusader
106   108

6-y-o b g Gildoran-Pusey Street (Native Bazaar)
J W Mullins First Impressions Racing Group

Placings:00/305P00-0O4343   (4093)
2002/03: 16⁶S, 16⁰G, 16⁶HY, 17³HY, 17⁴GS, 17⁹HY,

	Starts	1st	2nd	3rd	Win & Pl
Hurdles	6	0	0	2	1454
Career Total	14	0	0	3	1996

Going: Sf: 0-4 GS: 0-1 Gd: 0-1 GF: - Fm: 0-0
Distance: 2m/2m3: 0-6 2m4-2m7: 0-0 3m+: 0-0
Track: LH: 0-1 RH: 0-5 Tight: 0-2 Gall: 0-0
Aids: Bl: 0-0 Vi: 0-0 Tstrap: 0-0
Best Rating: 91   11/01   Winc   2m   good   NHF

Modest novice hurdler; inclined to be headstrong and often makes the running; let down by his jumping when fourth in a handicap at Exeter February 2003.

Golden Dawn
90(77h)   (69h)54

6-y-o gr g Gran Alba (USA)-Golden Curd (FR) (Nice Havrais (USA))
G M Moore Mrs Alurie O Sullivan

Placings:00P40-06   (0420)
2002/03: 20⁰G, 16⁰G, 17⁶HY,

	Starts	1st	2nd	3rd	Win & Pl
Hurdles	1	0	0	0	0
Chases	2	0	0	0	0
Career Total	7	0	0	0	0

Going: Sf: 0-1 GS: 0-0 Gd: 0-2 GF: - Fm: 0-0
Distance: 2m/2m3: 0-2 2m4-2m7: 0-1 3m+: 0-0
Track: LH: 0-3 RH: 0-0 Tight: 0-2 Gall: 0-1
Aids: Bl: 0-0 Vi: 0-0 Tstrap: 0-0
Best Rating: 69   4/02   Hexm   2m110y   gd-fm   Hdl

Golden Fact (USA)
82   71

9-y-o b g Known Fact (USA)-Cosmic Sea Queen (USA) (Determined Cosmic (USA))
B A McMahon (R McGlinchey 10/11) T Cassidy

Placings:00-0   (4446)
2002/03: 16⁶G,

	Starts	1st	2nd	3rd	Win & Pl
Hurdles	1	0	0	0	
Career Total	3	0	0	0	

Going: Sf: 0-0 GS: 0-0 Gd: 0-1 GF: - Fm: 0-0
Distance: 2m/2m3: 0-1 2m4-2m7: 0-0 3m+: 0-0
Track: LH: 0-0 RH: 0-1 Tight: 0-0 Gall: 0-0
Aids: Bl: 0-0 Vi: 0-0 Tstrap: 0-0
Best Rating: 94   12/01   Fair   2m   yield   Hdl

Golden Flight (FR)
104   114

4-y-o b g Saint Cyrien (FR)-Sunday Flight (FR) (Johnny O Day (USA))
G Macaire J D Cotton

Placings:2-1523   (4084)
2002/03: 17¹VS, 16⁵S, 16²GS, 18³VS,

	Starts	1st	2nd	3rd	Win & Pl
Hurdles	4	1	1	1	18040

Career Total   5   1   2   1   24813
104 5/02 Autl   2m1f110y Hdl   VS   £11779
                 Total win prize-money £11779

Going: Sf: 0-1 GS: 0-1 Gd: 0-0 GF: - Fm: 0-0
Distance: 2m/2m3: 1-4 2m4-2m7: 0-0 3m+: 0-0
Track: LH: 0-2 RH: 0-0 Tight: 0-1 Gall: 0-1
Aids: Bl: 0-0 Vi: 0-0 Tstrap: 0-0
Best Rating: 114   3/03   Strf   2m110y   gd-sft   Hdl

Winning French hurdler at two miles one and a half furlongs in the mud.

Golden Gent (IRE)

8-y-o ch g Ikdam-Golden Seekers (Manado)
T D Walford (L J Archdeacon 23/6) Neil Watson

Placings:06P   (4592)
2002/03: 20⁰G, 16⁶G, 25⁶G,

	Starts	1st	2nd	3rd	Win & Pl
NH Flat	1	0	0	0	0
Chases	2	0	0	0	0
Career Total	3	0	0	0	0

Going: Sf: 0-0 GS: 0-0 Gd: 0-3 GF: - Fm: 0-0
Distance: 2m/2m3: 0-1 2m4-2m7: 0-1 3m+: 0-1
Track: LH: 0-2 RH: 0-0 Tight: 0-0 Gall: 0-1
Aids: Bl: 0-0 Vi: 0-0 Tstrap: 0-1
Best Rating: 61   4/03   Newc   2m110y   good   Ch

Golden Goal (GER)
109(107h)   (132h)142

7-y-o br g Nebos (GER)-Goralin (GER) (La Tour (GER))
Miss Venetia Williams Favourites Racing

Placings:3102202/032P/6131114-26   (2489)
2002/03: 21²GS, 21⁶G,

	Starts	1st	2nd	3rd	Win & Pl
Chases	2	0	1	0	8298
Career Total	20	5	5	3	77200
142	2/02	Kemp	2m4f110yA Ch	GD	£16375
142	2/02	Sand	2m4f110yA Ch	G-S	£24000
135	1/02	Plum	2m4f	E Ch	SFT	£3250
125	11/01	Hayd	2m6f	C Ch	GD	£8855
122	12/99	Fknm	2m	D Hdl	GD	£2777
			Total win prize-money £55257

Going: Sf: 0-0 GS: 0-1 Gd: 0-1 GF: - Fm: 0-0
Distance: 2m/2m3: 0-0 2m4-2m7: 0-2 3m+: 0-0
Track: LH: 0-1 RH: 0-1 Tight: 0-0 Gall: 0-1
Aids: Bl: 0-0 Vi: 0-0 Tstrap: 0-0
Best Rating: 142   12/02   Winc   2m5f   gd-sft   Ch

Very useful chaser; did well as a novice over fences in 2001/2002, winning four times including decent events at Sandown and Kempton before finishing fourth in the Cathcart at Cheltenham; good efforts after though his jumping sometimes let him down; Suited by good ground or softer and a flat track; stayed two miles six. (DEAD)

Golden Gravel (IRE)
85   70

10-y-o ch g Domynsky-Whimbrel (Dara Monarch)
S T Lewis Simon T Lewis

Placings:0P/05/0RP-015PPP   (4020)
2002/03: 17⁰S, 20¹HY, 19⁶S, 26⁶S, 16⁶HY, 26⁶S,

	Starts	1st	2nd	3rd	Win & Pl
Hurdles	6	1	0	0	2268
Career Total	13	1	0	0	2268

---

70   12/02 Leic   2m4f110yG(0-90)HHdl   HVY   £2268
              Total win prize-money £2268

Going: Sf: 1-6 GS: 0-0 Gd: 0-0 GF: - Fm: 0-0
Distance: 2m/2m3: 0-3 2m4-2m7: 1-1 3m+: 0-2
Track: LH: 0-1 RH: 1-5 Tight: 0-0 Gall: 0-0
Aids: Bl: 1-2 Vi: 0-0 Tstrap: 0-0
Best Rating: 70   12/02   Leic   2m4f110y   heavy   Hdl

Won a seller at Leicester in December, liking the soft ground.

Golden Hawk (USA)
99   81

8-y-o ch g Silver Hawk (USA)-Crockadore (USA) (Nijinsky (CAN))
Mrs D M Ewart Mrs J A Niven

Placings:40/1/60/055-3   (0251)
2002/03: 16³GF,

	Starts	1st	2nd	3rd	Win & Pl
Hurdles	1	0	0	1	422
Career Total	9	1	0	1	2795
100	9/99	Hntg	2m110y E Hdl	G-F	£2372
			Total win prize-money £2373

Going: Sf: 0-0 GS: 0-0 Gd: 0-0 GF: - Fm: 0-1
Distance: 2m/2m3: 0-1 2m4-2m7: 0-0 3m+: 0-0
Track: LH: 0-0 RH: 0-1 Tight: 0-0 Gall: 0-0
Aids: Bl: 0-0 Vi: 0-0 Tstrap: 0-0
Best Rating: 103   12/98   Leic   2m   gd-sft   Hdl

Moderate hurdler, may benefit from further than the minimum trip.

Golden Haze
84   29

6-y-o ch m Safawan-Hazel Hill (Abednego)
J K Cresswell J K S Cresswell

Placings:00   (0823)
2002/03: 17⁰S, 16⁰GF,

	Starts	1st	2nd	3rd	Win & Pl
NH Flat	2	0	0	0	
Career Total	2	0	0	0	

Going: Sf: 0-1 GS: 0-0 Gd: 0-0 GF: - Fm: 0-1
Distance: 2m/2m3: 0-2 2m4-2m7: 0-0 3m+: 0-0
Track: LH: 0-2 RH: 0-0 Tight: 0-1 Gall: 0-0
Aids: Bl: 0-0 Vi: 0-0 Tstrap: 0-0
Best Rating: 37   5/02   Bang   2m1f   soft   NHF

Golden Legend (IRE)

6-y-o b g Last Tycoon-Adjalisa (IRE) (Darshaan)
R J Price E G Bevan

Placings:PP/PP   (1713)
2002/03: 16²F, 16⁶G,

	Starts	1st	2nd	3rd	Win & Pl
Hurdles	2	0	0	0	
Career Total	4	0	0	0	

Going: Sf: 0-0 GS: 0-0 Gd: 0-1 GF: - Fm: 0-1
Distance: 2m/2m3: 0-2 2m4-2m7: 0-0 3m+: 0-0
Track: LH: 0-1 RH: 0-1 Tight: 0-1 Gall: 0-0
Aids: Bl: 0-0 Vi: 0-0 Tstrap: 0-0
Best Rating: 0   10/02   Strf   2m110y   good   Hdl

Golden Nougat (IRE)

87f   **99+f**

5-y-o ch g Montelimar (USA)-Serenade Run (Deep Run)
L Wells Paul Zetter

Placings:*14*   (4601)
2002/03: 16^{1}GF, 17^{4}GF,

	Starts	1st	2nd	3rd	Win & Pl
NH Flat	2	1	0	0	2569
Career Total	2	1	0	0	2569

99 3/03 Ludl 2m   H NHF   G-F £2569
Total win prize-money £2569

Going:	Sf: 0-0 GS: 0-0 Gd: 0-0 GF: – Fm: 1-2
Distance:	2m/2m3: 1-2 2m4-2m7: 0-0 3m+: 0-0
Track:	LH: 0-0 RH: 1-2 Tight: 0-0 Gall: 0-0
Aids:	Bl: 0-0 Vi: 0-0 Tstrap: 0-0
Best Rating:	99 3/03 Ludl 2m gd-fm NHF

Did not achieve much when winning four-runner bumper at Ludlow March 2003.

Golden Orion (IRE)

93+

8-y-o ch g Phardante (FR)-Raise The Bells (Belfalas)
Mrs J C McGregor Discounted Cashflow

Placings:*65606233550-P*   (1294)
2002/03: 24^{P}GF,

	Starts	1st	2nd	3rd	Win & Pl
Hurdles	1	0	0	0	
Career Total	12	0	1	2	1752

Going:	Sf: 0-0 GS: 0-0 Gd: 0-0 GF: – Fm: 0-1
Distance:	2m/2m3: 0-0 2m4-2m7: 0-0 3m+: 0-1
Track:	LH: 0-0 RH: 0-1 Tight: 0-0 Gall: 0-0
Aids:	Bl: 0-0 Vi: 0-0 Tstrap: 0-0
Best Rating:	93 9/02 Prth 3m110y gd-fm Hdl

Modest novice hurdler, stays two and a half miles.

Golden Rivet

74f   **54f**

6-y-o b g Weld-Golden Valley (Hotfoot)
T D Walford Anthony Preston

Placings:*0*   (1569)
2002/03: 17^{0}G,

	Starts	1st	2nd	3rd	Win & Pl
NH Flat	1	0	0	0	
Career Total	1	0	0	0	

Going:	Sf: 0-0 GS: 0-0 Gd: 0-0 GF: 0-1 Fm: 0-0
Distance:	2m/2m3: 0-1 2m4-2m7: 0-0 3m+: 0-0
Track:	LH: 0-0 RH: 0-1 Tight: 0-1 Gall: 0-0
Aids:	Bl: 0-0 Vi: 0-0 Tstrap: 0-0
Best Rating:	54 10/02 MRas 2m1f110y good NHF

Golden Rod

105   **86**

6-y-o ch g Rainbows For Life (CAN)-Noble Form (Double Form)
K C Bailey (P W Harris 21/9) Neil Rodway & Carol Cope

Placings:*5000051*   (4704)
2002/03: 16^{5}GS, 16^{0}S, 16^{0}S, 24^{0}G, 20^{4}GF, 20^{5}GF, 20^{1}G,

	Starts	1st	2nd	3rd	Win & Pl
Hurdles	7	1	0	0	3367

Career Total	7	1	0	0	3367
86 4/03 Uttx	2m4f110y			F(0-100)HHdl	
GD £3367					

Total win prize-money £3367

Going:	Sf: 0-2 GS: 0-1 Gd: 1-2 GF: – Fm: 0-2
Distance:	2m/2m3: 0-3 2m4-2m7: 1-3 3m+: 0-1
Track:	LH: 1-3 RH: 0-4 Tight: 0-1 Gall: 0-3
Aids:	Bl: 0-0 Vi: 0-0 Tstrap: 0-0
Best Rating:	86 4/03 Uttx 2m4f110y good Hdl

Plating-class; effective at around two and a half miles; acts well on good ground.

Golden Rose (IRE)

104(95h)   (91h)**98d**

11-y-o br m Roselier (FR)-Lady Nethertown (Windjammer (USA))
T P McGovern Ahmed Abdel-Khaleq

Placings:*25/P1/F350FP42U3/P15114P/5023U0-U20P5P*
(3108)
2002/03: 20^{U}GF, 20^{2}GS, 20^{0}GS, 20^{P}G, 20^{5}S, 21^{P}S,

	Starts	1st	2nd	3rd	Win & Pl
Chases	6	0	1	0	1700
Career Total	33	4	4	3	14708
115 1/01 Font	2m4f	E Hdl		SFT	£3178
110 12/00 Hntg	2m5f110yF(0-100)HHdl			HVY	£2095
113 11/00 Plum	2m5f	E(0-115)HHdl		HVY	£2317
99 3/99 Towc	2m	H NHF		SFT	£1451

Total win prize-money £9043

Going:	Sf: 0-2 GS: 0-2 Gd: 0-1 GF: – Fm: 0-1
Distance:	2m/2m3: 0-0 2m4-2m7: 0-6 3m+: 0-0
Track:	LH: 0-1 RH: 0-2 Tight: 0-5 Gall: 0-1
Aids:	Bl: 0-0 Vi: 0-0 Tstrap: 0-0
Best Rating:	115 1/01 Font 2m4f soft Hdl

A game handicap hurdler who loves cut in the ground, the majority of her successes have come over two miles five furlongs. Made a creditable start over fences in January 2002 but has not really gone on from that. Acts on a soft surface.

Golden Thunderbolt (FR)

100(90c)   (105c)**86**

10-y-o b g Persian Bold-Carmita (Caerleon (USA))
H Alexander Phil Lever & Mrs S Dallas

Placings:*2205/34523232/35244533/3624226P2415/5520P
PP0123144-40352600336*
(4795)
2002/03: 20^{4}GS, 20^{0}GF, 22^{3}GS, 19^{5}GS, 17^{2}S, 20^{6}HY, 20^{0}S, 19^{0}S, 21^{3}G, 16^{3}GF, 21^{6}GF,

	Starts	1st	2nd	3rd	Win & Pl
Hurdles	11	0	1	3	2260
Career Total	57	3	13	11	22591
103 4/02 Fknm	2m4f	E(0-105)HHdl		GD	£3003
105 1/02 Catt	2m3f	G(0-90)HHdl		SFT	£1904
100 2/01 Fknm	2m	G(0-90)HHdl		SFT	£1877

Total win prize-money £6784

Going:	Sf: 0-4 GS: 0-3 Gd: 0-1 GF: – Fm: 0-3
Distance:	2m/2m3: 0-4 2m4-2m7: 0-7 3m+: 0-0
Track:	LH: 0-10 RH: 0-1 Tight: 0-6 Gall: 0-1
Aids:	Bl: 0-0 Vi: 0-0 Tstrap: 0-0
Best Rating:	103 4/02 Fknm 2m4f good Hdl

Plating-class front-running hurdler; acts on good and soft ground; effective at up to two miles three furlongs and likes a sharp track, particularly Fakenham.

Golden Thyne (IRE)

76   **53**

9-y-o ch g Alphabatim (USA)-Droichidin (Good Thyne (USA))
Ms A E Embiricos Ms A E Embiricos

Placings:*6/0*   (0337)
2002/03: 16^{0}G,

	Starts	1st	2nd	3rd	Win & Pl
Hurdles	1	0	0	0	
Career Total	2	0	0	0	0

Going:	Sf: 0-0 GS: 0-0 Gd: 0-1 GF: – Fm: 0-0
Distance:	2m/2m3: 0-1 2m4-2m7: 0-0 3m+: 0-0
Track:	LH: 0-0 RH: 0-1 Tight: 0-0 Gall: 0-0
Aids:	Bl: 0-0 Vi: 0-0 Tstrap: 0-0
Best Rating:	79 5/00 Folk 2m1f110y good NHF

Goldoak

69

8-y-o ch g Sunley Builds-Indian Election (Sula Bula)
R E Pocock T E Pocock

Placings:*006U6P-P*   (0035)
2002/03: 22^{P}G,

	Starts	1st	2nd	3rd	Win & Pl
Hurdles	1	0	0	0	
Career Total	7	0	0	0	0

Going:	Sf: 0-0 GS: 0-0 Gd: 0-0 GF: – Fm: 0-0
Distance:	2m/2m3: 0-0 2m4-2m7: 0-0 3m+: 0-0
Track:	LH: 0-0 RH: 0-0 Tight: 0-0 Gall: 0-0
Aids:	Bl: 0-1 Vi: 0-0 Tstrap: 0-0
Best Rating:	91 10/01 Chep 2m110y good NHF

Goldstone

11-y-o b g Precious Metal-Moon Chant (Humdoleila)
S Flook Mrs S E Vaughan

Placings:*P-5*   (0145)
2002/03: 24^{5}GF,

	Starts	1st	2nd	3rd	Win & Pl
Chases	1	0	0	0	0
Career Total	2	0	0	0	0

Going:	Sf: 0-0 GS: 0-0 Gd: 0-0 GF: – Fm: 0-1
Distance:	2m/2m3: 0-0 2m4-2m7: 0-0 3m+: 0-1
Track:	LH: 0-1 RH: 0-0 Tight: 0-0 Gall: 0-0
Aids:	Bl: 0-0 Vi: 0-0 Tstrap: 0-0
Best Rating:	50 5/02 Chep 3m gd-fm Ch

Golf Land (IRE)

11-y-o ch g Be My Native (USA)-Just Clara (Camden Town)
W M Aitchison W M Aitchison

Placings:*030/236500/64/60/P*   (0083)
2002/03: 25^{P}GS,

	Starts	1st	2nd	3rd	Win & Pl
Chases	1	0	0	0	0
Career Total	14	0	1	2	1053

Going:	Sf: 0-0 GS: 0-1 Gd: 0-0 GF: – Fm: 0-0
Distance:	2m/2m3: 0-0 2m4-2m7: 0-0 3m+: 0-1

Track:	LH: 0-1 RH: 0-0 Tight: 0-0 Gall: 0-0
Aids:	Bl: 0-0 Vi: 0-0 Tstrap: 0-0
Best Rating:	90 9/96 Prth 2m110y gd-fm NHF

Golfagent

102   102

5-y-o b g Kris-Alusha (Soviet Star (USA))
Miss K Marks (P D Evans 13/11) Nick Shutts

Placings:PF212325002633L1   (4709)
2002/03: 16PS, 16FGF, 16²GF, 19¹S, 20²G, 18³GF, 19²GS, 21⁵G, 17⁰S, 17⁰GS, 20²GS, 19⁶S, 19³S, 22³G, 24¹G, 24¹G,

	Starts	1st	2nd	3rd	Win & Pl
Hurdles	16	2	4	3	15900
Career Total	16	2	4	3	15900
102	4/03	Uttx	3m110y	E(0-100)HHdl	GD	£3689
81	8/02	Strf	2m3f	D Hdl	SFT	£4225

Total win prize-money £7914

Going:	Sf: 1-5 GS: 0-3 Gd: 1-5 GF: - Fm: 0-3
Distance:	2m/2m3: 1-8 2m4-2m7: 0-6 3m+: 1-2
Track:	LH: 2-12 RH: 0-4 Tight: 1-9 Gall: 0-3
Aids:	Bl: 0-0 Vi: 0-0 Tstrap: 2-16
Best Rating:	102 4/03 Uttx 3m110y good Hdl

Moderate hurdler; returned to form when just denied at Bangor in February 2003, and won a novice event at Uttoxeter in April; stays three miles; acts on most types of ground; wears a tongue tie.

Golly (IRE)

7-y-o b g Toulon-Tor-Na-Grena (Torus)
M Pitman Gollyhott Trading Ltd

Placings:U   (0063)
2002/03: 17UG,

	Starts	1st	2nd	3rd	Win & Pl
NH Flat	1	0	0	0	
Career Total	1	0	0	0	

Going:	Sf: 0-0 GS: 0-0 Gd: 0-1 GF: - Fm: 0-0
Distance:	2m/2m3: 0-1 2m4-2m7: 0-0 3m+: 0-0
Track:	LH: 0-0 RH: 0-0 Tight: 0-1 Gall: 0-0
Aids:	Bl: 0-0 Vi: 0-0 Tstrap: 0-0
Best Rating:	

Gone Bonkers (IRE)

8-y-o b g Lord Americo-Lady Harrier (Some Hawk)
Mark Campion (J T R Dreaper 9/8) The Gone Bonkers Partnership

Placings:000   (4408)
2002/03: 16⁰GS, 17⁰GS, 16⁰G,

	Starts	1st	2nd	3rd	Win & Pl
Hurdles	3	0	0	0	
Career Total	3	0	0	0	

Going:	Sf: 0-0 GS: 0-2 Gd: 0-1 GF: - Fm: 0-0
Distance:	2m/2m3: 0-3 2m4-2m7: 0-0 3m+: 0-0
Track:	LH: 0-2 RH: 0-1 Tight: 0-1 Gall: 0-0
Aids:	Bl: 0-0 Vi: 0-0 Tstrap: 0-0
Best Rating:	0 3/03 Hexm 2m110y good Hdl

Gone Far (USA)

104   125

6-y-o b g Gone West (USA)-Vallee Dansante (USA)

(Lyphard (USA))
M C Pipe Matt Archer & Miss Jean Broadhurst

Placings:134-5   (3288)
2002/03: 17⁵GS,

	Starts	1st	2nd	3rd	Win & Pl
Hurdles	1	0	0	0	565
Career Total	4	1	0	1	5508
119	1/02	Tntn	2m1f	E Hdl	SFT	£2643

Total win prize-money £2643

Going:	Sf: 0-0 GS: 0-1 Gd: 0-0 GF: - Fm: 0-0
Distance:	2m/2m3: 0-1 2m4-2m7: 0-0 3m+: 0-0
Track:	LH: 0-1 RH: 0-0 Tight: 0-0 Gall: 0-1
Aids:	Bl: 0-0 Vi: 0-0 Tstrap: 0-0
Best Rating:	125 1/03 Chel 2m1f gd-sft Hdl

A useful stayer on the Flat in France. Made a winning debut over hurdle for new connections at Taunton in January 2002 and may have been unlucky not to follow-up in a Grade Two at Kempton before flopping in a weak race next time. Fair run on return in January 2003.

Good Good (IRE)

9-y-o ch m Good Thyne (USA)-Pinata (Deep Run)
F J Brennan F J Brennan

Placings:260/0/2-6   (4480)
2002/03: 25⁶G,

	Starts	1st	2nd	3rd	Win & Pl
Chases	1	0	0	0	
Career Total	6	0	2	0	1114

Going:	Sf: 0-0 GS: 0-0 Gd: 0-1 GF: - Fm: 0-0
Distance:	2m/2m3: 0-0 2m4-2m7: 0-0 3m+: 0-1
Track:	LH: 0-1 RH: 0-0 Tight: 0-1 Gall: 0-0
Aids:	Bl: 0-0 Vi: 0-0 Tstrap: 0-1
Best Rating:	100 3/00 Towc 2m soft NHF

Winning pointer at a minor level, ran a sound race on her hunter chase debut at Towcester in April.

Good Heart (IRE)

88(86c)   (75c)70

8-y-o ch g Be My Native (USA)-Johnstown Love (IRE) (Golden Love)
T H Caldwell M J Caldwell

Placings:1/06/43/06-0F4   (4403)
2002/03: 19⁰G, 20FG, 22⁴GF,

	Starts	1st	2nd	3rd	Win & Pl
Hurdles	1	0	0	0	387
Chases	2	0	0	0	
Career Total	10	1	0	1	2588
119	2/99	Hayd	2m	H NHF	SFT	£1495

Total win prize-money £1495

Going:	Sf: 0-0 GS: 0-0 Gd: 0-2 GF: - Fm: 0-1
Distance:	2m/2m3: 0-1 2m4-2m7: 0-2 3m+: 0-0
Track:	LH: 0-2 RH: 0-1 Tight: 0-0 Gall: 0-0
Aids:	Bl: 0-0 Vi: 0-0 Tstrap: 0-0
Best Rating:	119 2/99 Hayd 2m soft NHF

Took a bumper on his debut in 1999 but has gone the wrong way since.

Good Looking Guy

89

14-y-o ch g Cruise Missile-Saxon Belle (Deep Run)
Mrs J A Young Mrs Judy Young

Placings:00P/U/3/334F4P/3P40U2P/0553P0-P   (0243)
2002/03: 23PG,

	Starts	1st	2nd	3rd	Win & Pl
Chases	1	0	0	0	
Career Total	25	0	1	5	4292

Going:	Sf: 0-0 GS: 0-0 Gd: 0-1 GF: - Fm: 0-0
Distance:	2m/2m3: 0-0 2m4-2m7: 0-0 3m+: 0-1
Track:	LH: 0-0 RH: 0-1 Tight: 0-0 Gall: 0-0
Aids:	Bl: 0-0 Vi: 0-0 Tstrap: 0-0
Best Rating:	95 5/98 Strf 3m4f good Ch

Good Lord Murphy (IRE)

97(108c)   (99c)99

11-y-o br g Montelimar (USA)-Semiwild (USA) (Rumbo (USA))
Dr P Pritchard The Breakfast Set

Placings:2/0211214/P50P/1212/10P/30-06F06R4   (4623)
2002/03: 21⁰G, 21⁶G, 21FG, 24⁰GS, 22⁶S, 21RG, 27⁴GF,

	Starts	1st	2nd	3rd	Win & Pl
Hurdles	4	0	0	0	0
Chases	3	0	0	0	0
Career Total	28	6	5	1	45351
140	11/00	Asct	3m110y	B(0-150)HCh	SFT	£10296
135	12/99	Hrfd	3m1f110yE Ch		HVY	£4340
128	11/99	Towc	3m1f	D Ch	GD	£4086
127	3/98	Sand	2m6f	D Hdl	SFT	£3663
127	2/98	Sand	2m6f	D Hdl	GD	£3598
108	1/98	Wwck	2m4f110yE Hdl		SFT	£3352

Total win prize-money £29338

Going:	Sf: 0-1 GS: 0-1 Gd: 0-4 GF: - Fm: 0-1
Distance:	2m/2m3: 0-0 2m4-2m7: 0-5 3m+: 0-2
Track:	LH: 0-5 RH: 0-2 Tight: 0-4 Gall: 0-0
Aids:	Bl: 0-0 Vi: 0-0 Tstrap: 0-0
Best Rating:	140 11/00 Asct 3m110y soft Ch

Moderate hurdler/decent chaser; very useful in his time, but on the way down at a fair rate these days; has shown only modest in 2002/2003; his attitude is also in question; best on easy ground; stays well.

Good Potential (IRE)

98   (64c)95+

7-y-o b g Petardia-Steel Duchess (IRE) (Yashgan)
D J Wintle Brigadier Racing 2000

Placings:00400446/5246126P0/P331-P40P00   (4004)
2002/03: 21PS, 17⁴HY, 19⁰GS, 21PHY, 19⁰GS, 22⁰S,

	Starts	1st	2nd	3rd	Win & Pl
Hurdles	4	0	0	0	0
Chases	2	0	0	0	326
Career Total	27	2	2	2	8553
90	3/02	Font	2m6f110yF(0-100)HHdl	SFT	£2509
96	1/01	Sthl	2m	F(0-95)HHdl	HVY	£2443

Total win prize-money £4953

Going:	Sf: 0-4 GS: 0-2 Gd: 0-0 GF: - Fm: 0-0
Distance:	2m/2m3: 0-2 2m4-2m7: 0-4 3m+: 0-0
Track:	LH: 0-4 RH: 0-2 Tight: 0-2 Gall: 0-0
Aids:	Bl: 0-0 Vi: 0-0 Tstrap: 0-5
Best Rating:	96 2/01 Carl 2m1f heavy Hdl

Moderate handicap hurdler; raised 11lb after easy win in 2m 6f Class E handicap at Newton Abbot June 2003; disappointing next time and is inconsistent; stays at least 2m 6f; acts on soft and fast ground.

Good Shuil (IRE)

114(86h)   (136h)**138**

8-y-o b g Good Thyne (USA)-Shuil Run (Deep Run)
C J Mann (T J Taaffe 22/3) Richard Newsholme & Fergus Wilson

Placings:0002114/3F43U132PP-054300P   (4479)
2002/03: 16⁶S, 20⁵G, 20⁴YS, 27³GS, 25⁰G, 20⁰GY, 36⁰G,

	Starts	1st	2nd	3rd	Win & Pl
Hurdles	1	0	0	0	
Chases	6	0	0	1	6968
Career Total	24	3	2	4	47941

122	1/02	Punc	2m5f		Ch		SH	£7831
130	2/01	Fair	3m		HHdl		Y-S	£15725
109	1/01	DRoy	2m4f		Hdl		YLD	£6120

Total win prize-money £29678

Going: Sf: 0-1 GS: 0-1 Gd: 0-3 GF: - Fm: 0-0
Distance: 2m/2m3: 0-1 2m4-2m7: 0-3 3m+: 0-3
Track: LH: 0-4 RH: 0-3 Tight: 0-1 Gall: 0-2
Aids: Bl: 0-0 Vi: 0-0 Tstrap: 0-0
Best Rating: 138 11/02 Chel 3m3f110y gd-sft Ch

Useful Irish-trained chaser; stays three miles three; acts on a soft surface.

Good Thyne Johnny (IRE)

104   **96**

9-y-o b g Good Thyne (USA)-Wiasma (Ashmore (FR))
L A Dace New World Racing

Placings:00014034/P003PP/00-0120P2U25P   (1245)
2002/03: 20⁰GF, 24¹G, 21²G, 22⁰GF, 24⁰G, 25²G, 27ᵁGF, 24²S, 26⁵GF, 24⁰G,

	Starts	1st	2nd	3rd	Win & Pl
Hurdles	10	1	3	0	4611
Career Total	26	2	3	2	9091

96	5/02	Uttx	3m110y	E(0-105)HHdl	GD	£2786
90	3/00	Dpat	2m1f172y	Hdl	SFT	£2760

Total win prize-money £5546

Going: Sf: 0-1 GS: 0-0 Gd: 1-5 GF: - Fm: 0-4
Distance: 2m/2m3: 0-0 2m4-2m7: 0-3 3m+: 1-7
Track: LH: 1-7 RH: 0-3 Tight: 0-5 Gall: 0-2
Aids: Bl: 0-0 Vi: 0-0 Tstrap: 0-0
Best Rating: 96 8/02 Bang 3m soft Hdl

Ex-Irish hurdler, surprise winner at Uttoxeter in May 2002 under a positive ride and those look the ideal tactics for him. Suited by fast ground and stays well.

Good Time Bobby

84   **61**

6-y-o b g Primitive Rising (USA)-Goodreda (Good Times (ITY))
G A Swinbank Mrs K Morrell

Placings:0/00PU3-0   (4504)
2002/03: 16⁰G,

	Starts	1st	2nd	3rd	Win & Pl
Hurdles	1	0	0	0	
Career Total	7	0	0	1	386

Going: Sf: 0-0 GS: 0-0 Gd: 0-1 GF: 0-0
Distance: 2m/2m3: 0-0 2m4-2m7: 0-0 3m+: 0-0
Track: LH: 0-1 RH: 0-0 Tight: 0-1 Gall: 0-0
Aids: Bl: 0-0 Vi: 0-0 Tstrap: 0-0
Best Rating: 87 4/01 MRas 1m5f110y gd-sft NHF

Modest hurdler, seems better on a sound surface.

Good Timing

72   **31**

5-y-o bl g Timeless Times (USA)-Fort Vally (Belfort (FR))
J J Quinn Mrs M Lingwood

Placings:0   (3965)
2002/03: 16⁰S,

	Starts	1st	2nd	3rd	Win & Pl
Hurdles	1	0	0	0	
Career Total	1	0	0	0	

Going: Sf: 0-1 GS: 0-0 Gd: 0-0 GF: - Fm: 0-0
Distance: 2m/2m3: 0-1 2m4-2m7: 0-0 3m+: 0-0
Track: LH: 0-1 RH: 0-0 Tight: 0-1 Gall: 0-0
Aids: Bl: 0-0 Vi: 0-0 Tstrap: 0-0
Best Rating: 31 3/03 Catt 2m soft Hdl

Goodbye Goldstone

86   **69**

7-y-o b g Mtoto-Shareehan (Dancing Brave (USA))
T P McGovern Ashley Carr

Placings:04-00   (3248)
2002/03: 16⁰GS, 16⁰HY,

	Starts	1st	2nd	3rd	Win & Pl
Hurdles	2	0	0	0	
Career Total	4	0	0	0	0

Going: Sf: 0-1 GS: 0-1 Gd: 0-0 GF: - Fm: 0-0
Distance: 2m/2m3: 0-2 2m4-2m7: 0-0 3m+: 0-0
Track: LH: 0-1 RH: 0-1 Tight: 0-1 Gall: 0-1
Aids: Bl: 0-0 Vi: 0-0 Tstrap: 0-0
Best Rating: 69 1/03 Plum 2m heavy Hdl

Goodbye Mrs Chips

4-y-o ch f Zilzal (USA)-Happydrome (Ahonoora)
Mrs L B Normile (J D Bethell 26/11) Robert Gibbons

Placings:PP   (4762)
2002/03: 16⁰S, 16⁰G,

	Starts	1st	2nd	3rd	Win & Pl
Hurdles	2	0	0	0	
Career Total	2	0	0	0	

Going: Sf: 0-1 GS: 0-0 Gd: 0-1 GF: - Fm: 0-0
Distance: 2m/2m3: 0-2 2m4-2m7: 0-0 3m+: 0-0
Track: LH: 0-1 RH: 0-1 Tight: 0-0 Gall: 0-0
Aids: Bl: 0-0 Vi: 0-0 Tstrap: 0-2
Best Rating: 0 4/03 Prth 2m110y good Hdl

Goodtime George (IRE)

82

10-y-o b g Strong Gale-Game Sunset (Menelek)
M Pitman Mrs M J Bone

Placings:32550/22110/13/F/6   (3289)
2002/03: 19⁶G,

	Starts	1st	2nd	3rd	Win & Pl
Chases	1	0	0	0	
Career Total	14	3	3	2	12634

137	5/99	Uttx	3m110y	E Hdl	G-F	£2442
131	1/99	Donc	3m110y	D Hdl	GD	£3330
135	12/98	Strf	2m6f110yE Hdl	SFT	£2250

Gordi (USA)

86   **76**

10-y-o ch g Theatrical-Royal Alydar (USA) (Alydar (USA))
Miss L Bower Miss Lindsay Bower

Placings:0/01/050F-000   (0628)
2002/03: 17⁰G, 22⁰GF, 22⁰GF,

	Starts	1st	2nd	3rd	Win & Pl
Hurdles	3	0	0	0	
Career Total	10	1	0	0	2002

118	10/99	Dpat	2m1f87y	Hdl	Y-S	£2002

Total win prize-money £2002

Going: Sf: 0-0 GS: 0-0 Gd: 0-1 GF: - Fm: 0-2
Distance: 2m/2m3: 0-1 2m4-2m7: 0-2 3m+: 0-0
Track: LH: 0-1 RH: 0-2 Tight: 0-2 Gall: 0-0
Aids: Bl: 0-0 Vi: 0-0 Tstrap: 0-0
Best Rating: 118 10/99 Dpat 2m1f87y yld-sft Hdl

Gordon Highlander

102f   **82f**

4-y-o b f Master Willie-No Chili (Glint Of Gold)
Mrs P Robeson M S Anderson

Placings:060   (4444)
2002/03: 16⁰G, 17⁰G, 16⁰G,

	Starts	1st	2nd	3rd	Win & Pl
NH Flat	3	0	0	0	
Career Total	3	0	0	0	

Going: Sf: 0-0 GS: 0-0 Gd: 0-3 GF: - Fm: 0-0
Distance: 2m/2m3: 0-3 2m4-2m7: 0-0 3m+: 0-0
Track: LH: 0-0 RH: 0-3 Tight: 0-1 Gall: 0-1
Aids: Bl: 0-0 Vi: 0-0 Tstrap: 0-0
Best Rating: 82 4/03 Asct 2m110y good NHF

Gorsey Bank (IRE)

11-y-o b g Lancastrian-Yankee s Princess (Yankee Gold)
E A Thomas E A Thomas

Placings:PP/4P40-P   (4255)
2002/03: 25⁰G,

	Starts	1st	2nd	3rd	Win & Pl
Chases	1	0	0	0	
Career Total	7	0	0	0	287

Going: Sf: 0-0 GS: 0-0 Gd: 0-1 GF: - Fm: 0-0
Distance: 2m/2m3: 0-0 2m4-2m7: 0-0 3m+: 0-1
Track: LH: 0-0 RH: 0-1 Tight: 0-0 Gall: 0-0
Aids: Bl: 0-0 Vi: 0-0 Tstrap: 0-0
Best Rating: 66 3/02 Strf 3m gd-sft Ch

Gort Na Gcappill

10-y-o b g Presidium-Ranipa (Raga Navarro (ITY))
O O Neill Owen O Neill

Going: Sf: 0-0 GS: 0-0 Gd: 0-1 GF: - Fm: 0-0
Distance: 2m/2m3: 0-1 2m4-2m7: 0-0 3m+: 0-0
Track: LH: 0-1 RH: 0-0 Tight: 0-0 Gall: 0-0
Aids: Bl: 0-0 Vi: 0-0 Tstrap: 0-0
Best Rating: 137 5/99 Uttx 3m110y gd-fm Hdl

Placings:P   (0902)
2002/03: 20^0G,

	Starts	1st	2nd	3rd	Win & Pl
Hurdles	1	0	0	0	
Career Total	1	0	0	0	

Going: Sf: 0-0 GS: 0-0 Gd: 0-1 GF: - Fm: 0-0
Distance: 2m/2m3: 0-0 2m4-2m7: 0-1 3m+: 0-0
Track: LH: 0-1 RH: 0-0 Tight: 0-0 Gall: 0-0
Aids: Bl: 0-0 Vi: 0-0 Tstrap: 0-0
Best Rating: 0   8/02 Worc 2m4f   good   Hdl

Gortmore Mews (IRE)
70(103h)   (113h)111
9-y-o b g Persian Mews-Flat Out (Random Shot)
Ferdy Murphy   John McMullen W F-Clennell Susan Sample

Placings:51/152010/02103/U550143P-0   (2293)
2002/03: 19^0G,

	Starts	1st	2nd	3rd	Win & Pl
Chases	1	0	0	0	
Career Total	22	5	2	2	19103
111 12/01 Hrfd	2m3f	F(0-105)HCh		GD	£3349
6/00 Tral	2m	Ch		Y-S	£3312
99 3/00 Leop	2m	Hdl		GD	£3588
119 5/99 Gowr	2m	NHF		YLD	£3069
106 3/99 Wxfd	2m2f	NHF		Y-S	£2608
		Total win prize-money £15928			

Going: Sf: 0-0 GS: 0-0 Gd: 0-1 GF: - Fm: 0-0
Distance: 2m/2m3: 0-1 2m4-2m7: 0-0 3m+: 0-0
Track: LH: 0-0 RH: 0-1 Tight: 0-0 Gall: 0-0
Aids: Bl: 0-0 Vi: 0-0 Tstrap: 0-0
Best Rating: 119 5/99 Gowr 2m   yield   NHF

Formerly trained in Ireland, he won three times over hurdles and on his chasing debut at Tralee in June 2000. Went missing after July of that year until joining Ferdy Murphy in the autumn of 2001. Suited by two miles to two miles-three and good or softer ground.

Gortroe Guy (IRE)
83   68
11-y-o b g Carlingford Castle-Calfstown Night (Bargello)
J F Panvert   J F Panvert

Placings:06030206626/00F/00F6FP/400UPPU6-000   (0559)
2002/03: 25^6G, 27^0GF, 21^0G, 26^6GF,

	Starts	1st	2nd	3rd	Win & Pl
Hurdles	4	0	0	0	0
Career Total	31	0	2	1	2129

Going: Sf: 0-0 GS: 0-0 Gd: 0-2 GF: - Fm: 0-2
Distance: 2m/2m3: 0-0 2m4-2m7: 0-1 3m+: 0-3
Track: LH: 0-1 RH: 0-2 Tight: 0-1 Gall: 0-1
Aids: Bl: 0-1 Vi: 0-0 Tstrap: 0-2
Best Rating: 101 1/99 Punc 3m   heavy   Hdl

Gosh Josh (IRE)
5-y-o b g Blues Traveller (IRE)-Freedom s Flame (IRE) (Caerleon (USA))
R A Fahey   R A Fahey

Placings:0   (0261)
2002/03: 16^0GF,

	Starts	1st	2nd	3rd	Win & Pl
NH Flat	1	0	0	0	
Career Total	1	0	0	0	

Going: Sf: 0-0 GS: 0-0 Gd: 0-0 GF: - Fm: 0-1
Distance: 2m/2m3: 0-0 2m4-2m7: 0-0 3m+: 0-0
Track: LH: 0-0 RH: 0-1 Tight: 0-0 Gall: 0-0
Aids: Bl: 0-0 Vi: 0-0 Tstrap: 0-0
Best Rating: 0   5/02 Prth 2m110y   gd-fm   NHF

Gospel Song
102   85
11-y-o ch g King Among Kings-Market Blues (Porto Bello)
A C Whillans   Chas N Whillans

Placings:432/023/416415/2453415/6025/02620005/P0003-131P550   (4260)
2002/03: 17^1HY, 24^3GS, 16^1G, 20^PHY, 16^5S, 22^5S, 21^0G,

	Starts	1st	2nd	3rd	Win & Pl
Hurdles	7	2	0	1	6271
Career Total	43	5	6	5	21814
92 6/02 Hexm	2m110y	E(0-105)HHdl		GD	£2562
92 6/02 Ctml	2m1f110yG(0-90)HHdl			HVY	£3290
114 3/99 Ayr	2m4f	C(0-130)HHdl		SFT	£2804
111 3/98 Ayr	2m	D(0-110)HHdl		SFT	£2910
109 1/98 Muss	2m	F Hdl		G-S	£2185
		Total win prize-money £13751			

Going: Sf: 1-4 GS: 0-1 Gd: 1-2 GF: - Fm: 0-0
Distance: 2m/2m3: 2-3 2m4-2m7: 0-3 3m+: 0-1
Track: LH: 2-6 RH: 0-1 Tight: 1-2 Gall: 0-2
Aids: Bl: 0-0 Vi: 0-0 Tstrap: 0-0
Best Rating: 114 11/00 Newc 2m   soft   Hdl

Plating-class hurdler; best at two miles but stays further.

Got Alot On (USA)
95   80
5-y-o b/br g Charnwood Forest (IRE)-Fleety Belle (GER) (Assert)
Miss M Bragg   Mrs Anne Standing & Gordon Gout

Placings:0-0450   (3781)
2002/03: 19^0GS, 17^4S, 17^5S, 17^0GS,

	Starts	1st	2nd	3rd	Win & Pl
Hurdles	4	0	0	0	383
Career Total	5	0	0	0	383

Going: Sf: 0-2 GS: 0-2 Gd: 0-0 GF: - Fm: 0-0
Distance: 2m/2m3: 0-3 2m4-2m7: 0-1 3m+: 0-0
Track: LH: 0-0 RH: 0-4 Tight: 0-3 Gall: 0-0
Aids: Bl: 0-0 Vi: 0-0 Tstrap: 0-0
Best Rating: 80 12/02 Tntn 2m1f   soft   Hdl

Got News For You
(107h)   (98h)110
9-y-o gr g Positive Statement (USA)-Madame Ruby (FR) (Homing)
N J Hawke   Mrs D A Wetherall

Placings:56/6/F010020/F1PP6-630   (3189)
2002/03: 25^6GS, 24^3GS, 22^0GS,

	Starts	1st	2nd	3rd	Win & Pl
Hurdles	2	0	0	1	658
Chases	3	0	0	0	
Career Total	18	2	1	1	7343
110 10/01 Sthl	2m4f110yE Ch			GD	£3073
109 11/00 Hrfd	2m3f110yE Hdl			SFT	£2870
		Total win prize-money £5943			

Going: Sf: 0-0 GS: 0-2 Gd: 0-0 GF: - Fm: 0-1
Distance: 2m/2m3: 0-0 2m4-2m7: 0-1 3m+: 0-2
Track: LH: 0-0 RH: 0-3 Tight: 0-1 Gall: 0-0
Aids: Bl: 0-0 Vi: 0-1 Tstrap: 0-0
Best Rating: 110 10/01 Sthl 2m4f110y   good   Ch

A fair hurdler, he made amends for falling on his chasing debut at Market Rasen in September 2001 by making a quick winning reappearance at Southwell ten days later. Suited by two and a half miles and especially suited by soft ground.

Got One Too (FR)
109(115h)   (148h)143
6-y-o ch g Green Tune (USA)-Gloria Mundi (FR) (Saint Cyrien (FR))
N J Henderson   Sir Eric Parker & Mary Anne Parker

Placings:202/1115140-12U10   (4134)
2002/03: 16^1G, 16^2S, 16^4UGS, 18^1S, 16^0G,

	Starts	1st	2nd	3rd	Win & Pl
Chases	5	2	1	0	18316
Career Total	15	6	3	0	61746
142 3/03 Newb	2m2f110yC Ch			SFT	£8890
140 11/02 Leic	2m	D Ch		GD	£4784
148 1/02 Asct	2m110y	B HHdl		G-S	£10179
147 12/01 Newb	2m110y	A(0-145)HHdl		SFT	£15500
120 11/01 Newb	2m3f	D Hdl		GD	£3952
125 5/01 Hrfd	2m1f	E Hdl		GD	£3272
		Total win prize-money £46578			

Going: Sf: 1-2 GS: 0-1 Gd: 1-2 GF: - Fm: 0-0
Distance: 2m/2m3: 2-5 2m4-2m7: 0-0 3m+: 0-0
Track: LH: 1-2 RH: 1-3 Tight: 0-0 Gall: 1-2
Aids: Bl: 0-0 Vi: 0-0 Tstrap: 0-0
Best Rating: 148 1/02 Asct 2m110y   gd-sft   Hdl

Useful novice chaser; formerly very useful novice hurdler; best effort over fences 3 1/2l 2nd to Epervier D Or (rec 7lb) in Wayward Lad Novices Chase at Kempton, subsequently well beaten when fell behind Azertyuiop at Wincanton; won at Newbury in March; suited by 2m, probably stays 2m 3f; acts on ground good or softer; suited by forcing tactics.

Gotham (IRE)
101   106+
6-y-o gr g Gothland (FR)-Inchriver (IRE) (Over The River (FR))
R H Alner   Pell-Mell Partners

Placings:00-12   (1658)
2002/03: 16^1GF, 16^2G,

	Starts	1st	2nd	3rd	Win & Pl
Hurdles	2	1	1	0	4194
Career Total	4	1	1	0	4194
106 10/02 Plum	2m	E Hdl		G-F	£2989
		Total win prize-money £2989			

Going: Sf: 0-0 GS: 0-0 Gd: 0-1 GF: - Fm: 1-1
Distance: 2m/2m3: 1-2 2m4-2m7: 0-0 3m+: 0-0
Track: LH: 1-1 RH: 0-1 Tight: 1-1 Gall: 0-0
Aids: Bl: 0-0 Vi: 0-0 Tstrap: 0-0
Best Rating: 106 10/02 Plum 2m   gd-fm   Hdl

Gotham Abbey (IRE)
94   70
6-y-o gr m Gothland (FR)-Abbeyside (Paddy s Stream)
B Llewellyn (A J Kennedy 28/7)   Mrs M Llewellyn

Placings:00-00PPF   (4283)
2002/03: 16^6S, 20^0GF, 20^PHY, 19^PGS, 16^FGF,

	Starts	1st	2nd	3rd	Win & Pl
Hurdles	5	0	0	0	
Career Total	7	0	0	0	

Going: Sf: 0-2 GS: 0-1 Gd: 0-0 GF: - Fm: 0-2
Distance: 2m/2m3: 0-2 2m4-2m7: 0-3 3m+: 0-0
Track: LH: 0-1 RH: 0-2 Tight: 0-1 Gall: 0-0
Aids: Bl: 0-0 Vi: 0-0 Tstrap: 0-0
Best Rating: 70 3/03 Ludl 2m   gd-fm Hdl

Gottabe
108(107h)   (115h)124d
10-y-o ch g Gunner B-Topsy Bee (Be Friendly)
Mrs S J Smith Keith Nicholson

Placings:02U46134/2600153430-1211345F4   (4353)
2002/03: 20¹GF, 20²G, 23¹G, 25¹HY, 25³G, 26⁴GS, 25⁵GS, 24ᶠGS, 23⁴GF,

	Starts	1st	2nd	3rd	Win & Pl
Chases	9	3	1	1	21294
Career Total	27	5	3	4	31833
124	11/02 Weth	3m1f	D(0-120)HCh	HVY	£7294
115	6/02 Worc	2m7f110yD Ch		GD	£4153
102	5/02 Weth	2m4f110yD(0-110)HCh		G-F	£4108
115	12/01 Sthl	2m4f110yD(0-125)HHdl		SFT	£3464
108	2/01 Sedg	2m5f110yE Hdl		SFT	£2548

Total win prize-money £21569

Going: Sf: 1-1 GS: 0-3 Gd: 1-3 GF: - Fm: 0-0
Distance: 2m/2m3: 0-0 2m4-2m7: 1-2 3m+: 2-7
Track: LH: 3-8 RH: 0-0 Tight: 0-0 Gall: 0-2
Aids: Bl: 0-0 Vi: 0-0 Tstrap: 0-0
Best Rating: 124 11/02 Weth 3m1f   heavy Ch

Fair chaser; stays three miles plus and acts on any ground; likes to race prominently.

Govamix
118f   132f
5-y-o gr g Linamix (FR)-Segovia (Groom Dancer (USA))
D K Weld S Mulryan

Placings:43-10   (4115)
2002/03: 16¹HY, 16⁰G,

	Starts	1st	2nd	3rd	Win & Pl
NH Flat	2	1	0	0	5503
Career Total	4	1	0	1	6632
126	12/02 Leop	2m	NHF	HVY	£5503

Total win prize-money £5503

Going: Sf: 1-1 GS: 0-0 Gd: 0-1 GF: - Fm: 0-0
Distance: 2m/2m3: 1-2 2m4-2m7: 0-0 3m+: 0-0
Track: LH: 0-1 RH: 0-0 Tight: 0-0 Gall: 0-0
Aids: Bl: 0-0 Vi: 0-0 Tstrap: 0-0
Best Rating: 132 3/03 Chel 2m110y good NHF

Governor Daniel
108(102c)   (108c)112
12-y-o g g Governor General-Princess Semele (Imperial Fling (USA))
Ian Williams Dsm Demolition Limited

Placings:2/0306/1U44/4P50/42131/11PF111P/P5P0-31114113312   (4686)
2002/03: 22³GF, 20¹GF, 17¹GF, 20¹GF, 21⁴GF, 16¹GS, 16¹G, 20³G, 21³GS, 21¹GF, 17²GF,

	Starts	1st	2nd	3rd	Win & Pl
Hurdles	8	4	1	3	11136
Chases	3	2	0	0	7517
Career Total	41	14	3	5	50656

108	4/03 NAbb	2m5f110yG(0-95)HCh	G-F	£3024
112	11/02 Ludl	2m G Hdl	GD	£2765
105	11/02 Ludl	2m G Hdl	G-S	£2712
99	9/02 Font	2m4f E(0-105)HCh	G-F	£4134
99	8/02 MRas	2m1f110yG Hdl	G-F	£2058
101	8/02 Hntg	2m4f110yG Hdl	G-F	£1903
115	9/00 Plum	2m5f D(0-125)HHdl	G-F	£3103
115	9/00 Hrfd	2m3f110yF(0-100)HHdl	G-F	£2877
115	8/00 Sthl	2m4f110yF(0-110)HHdl	GD	£2891
112	6/00 MRas	2m4f C(0-135)HCh	G-F	£10481
115	6/00 NAbb	2m110y F(0-105)HCh	G-F	£3454
102	9/99 Sedg	2m5f E Ch		£3254
95	8/99 MRas	2m1f110yG(0-95)HHdl	G-F	£1679
105	5/96 Sthl	2m2f E Hdl	G-F	£2658

Total win prize-money £46996

Going: Sf: 0-0 GS: 1-2 Gd: 1-2 GF: - Fm: 4-7
Distance: 2m/2m3: 3-4 2m4-2m7: 3-7 3m+: 0-0
Track: LH: 1-4 RH: 4-6 Tight: 3-6 Gall: 1-2
Aids: Bl: 0-0 Vi: 0-0 Tstrap: 0-1
Best Rating: 115 9/00 Plum 2m5f   gd-fm Hdl

Modest chaser/hurdler; has a superb record in selling grade; likes fast ground, best at around two miles, but stays two and a half.

Graceful Dancer
108   96
6-y-o b m Old Vic-Its My Turn (Palm Track)
C P Morlock The Fairway Connection

Placings:20-55601212   (4188)
2002/03: 17⁵S, 20⁵S, 20⁶HY, 21⁰GS, 24¹S, 21²S, 26¹S, 28²G,

	Starts	1st	2nd	3rd	Win & Pl
NH Flat	1	0	0	0	0
Hurdles	7	2	2	0	8638
Career Total	10	2	3	0	9114
92	3/03 Hrfd	2m2f F(0-95)HHdl	SFT	£3045
92	2/03 Tntn	3m110y F(0-100)HHdl	SFT	£3454

Total win prize-money £6500

Going: Sf: 2-6 GS: 0-1 Gd: 0-1 GF: - Fm: 0-0
Distance: 2m/2m3: 0-1 2m4-2m7: 0-4 3m+: 2-3
Track: LH: 0-5 RH: 2-3 Tight: 1-5 Gall: 0-0
Aids: Bl: 0-1 Vi: 2-4 Tstrap: 0-0
Best Rating: 98 3/02 Donc 2m110y soft NHF

Moderate handicap hurdler; improved since being fitted with a visor and stepped up in distance; loves the mud and stamina is her forte.

Grady
4-y-o ch c Bluegrass Prince (IRE)-Lady Sabina (Bairn (USA))
Miss Jacqueline S Doyle B L C Partnership

Placings:P   (2329)
2002/03: 16ᴾGS,

	Starts	1st	2nd	3rd	Win & Pl
Hurdles	1	0	0	0	
Career Total	1	0	0	0	

Going: Sf: 0-0 GS: 0-1 Gd: 0-0 GF: - Fm: 0-0
Distance: 2m/2m3: 0-1 2m4-2m7: 0-0 3m+: 0-0
Track: LH: 0-1 RH: 0-0 Tight: 0-0 Gall: 0-0
Aids: Bl: 0-0 Vi: 0-0 Tstrap: 0-0
Best Rating: 0 12/02 Winc 2m   gd-sft Hdl

Gralmano (IRE)
115(101c)   (117+c)137
8-y-o b g Scenic-Llangollen (IRE) (Caerleon (USA))

K A Ryan Coleorton Moor Racing

Placings:111-2P1102   (4475)
2002/03: 16²G, 17ᴾGS, 16¹G, 20¹GF, 16⁹G, 20²G,

	Starts	1st	2nd	3rd	Win & Pl
Hurdles	4	0	2	0	20900
Chases	2	2	0	0	10225
Career Total	9	5	2	0	42043
106	12/02 Muss	2m4f D Ch	G-F	£5434
117	11/02 Catt	2m D Ch	GD	£4790
130	12/01 Weth	2m C(0-135)HHdl	SFT	£5343
126	11/01 Kels	2m110y E Hdl	G-S	£3125
122	10/01 Kels	2m110y E Hdl	GD	£2450

Total win prize-money £21144

Going: Sf: 0-0 GS: 0-1 Gd: 1-4 GF: - Fm: 1-1
Distance: 2m/2m3: 1-4 2m4-2m7: 1-2 3m+: 0-0
Track: LH: 1-4 RH: 1-2 Tight: 2-4 Gall: 0-1
Aids: Bl: 0-0 Vi: 0-0 Tstrap: 0-0
Best Rating: 137 4/03 Aint 2m4f   good Hdl

A useful handicapper on the Flat, he took to hurdles well in 2001/02, winning all his three starts; good second when just out of the handicap in the Swinton Hurdle; won his first two starts over fences at the end of 2002 but well beaten in the Tote Gold Trophy; runner-up in Listed race at Aintree; stays two and a half miles and goes very well on fast ground.

Gran Clicquot
77   53
8-y-o gr m Gran Alba (USA)-Tina s Beauty (Tina s Pet)
G P Enright Frederick Gray

Placings:P/P5   (1426)
2002/03: 16ᴾG, 16⁵GF,

	Starts	1st	2nd	3rd	Win & Pl
Hurdles	2	0	0	0	0
Career Total	3	0	0	0	0

Going: Sf: 0-0 GS: 0-0 Gd: 0-1 GF: - Fm: 0-1
Distance: 2m/2m3: 0-2 2m4-2m7: 0-0 3m+: 0-0
Track: LH: 0-2 RH: 0-0 Tight: 0-2 Gall: 0-0
Aids: Bl: 0-0 Vi: 0-0 Tstrap: 0-0
Best Rating: 53 10/02 Plum 2m   gd-fm Hdl

Gran Statement
66   38
6-y-o b g Gran Alba (USA)-State Lady (IRE) (Strong Statement (USA))
Ferdy Murphy C W Cooper

Placings:0-0   (2166)
2002/03: 16⁰GS,

	Starts	1st	2nd	3rd	Win & Pl
Hurdles	1	0	0	0	
Career Total	2	0	0	0	

Going: Sf: 0-0 GS: 0-1 Gd: 0-0 GF: - Fm: 0-0
Distance: 2m/2m3: 0-1 2m4-2m7: 0-0 3m+: 0-0
Track: LH: 0-1 RH: 0-0 Tight: 0-0 Gall: 0-0
Aids: Bl: 0-0 Vi: 0-0 Tstrap: 0-0
Best Rating: 52 5/01 Hntg 2m110y gd-fm NHF

Granby Bell
106   117d
12-y-o b g Ballacashtal (CAN)-Betbellof (Averof)
Miss E C Lavelle H A Watton

Placings:00P230/04133260/0B434121P/6F10P/P30P2P41
241-4152PU6P   (4430)
2002/03: 20¹G, 20⁴S, 19¹GF, 20⁵GF, 19²G, 20ᴾGS, 19ᵁG, 19⁴GS,
20ᴾGF,

	Starts	1st	2nd	3rd	Win & Pl
Chases	9	2	1	0	9507
Career Total	47	7	6	5	40344
117 6/02 Hrfd	2m3f	E(0-110)HCh		G-F	£3454
116 4/02 Plum	2m4f	E(0-110)HCh		GD	£3430
117 3/02 Plum	2m4f	E(0-110)HCh		G-S	£3234
113 11/00 Hrfd	2m3f	E(0-115)HCh		G-S	£4114
110 3/00 Newb	2m2f110yD(0-110)HCh			G-F	£5564
113 2/00 Kemp	2m4f110yD(0-110)HCh			GD	£5118
94 12/98 Hrfd	2m4f110yF(0-100)HHdl			G-S	£2206

Total win prize-money £27123

Going: Sf: 0-1 GS: 0-2 Gd: 1-3 GF: - Fm: 1-3
Distance: 2m/2m3: 1-2 2m4-2m7: 1-7 3m+: 0-0
Track: LH: 1-7 RH: 1-2 Tight: 1-4 Gall: 0-1
Aids: Bl: 0-0 Vi: 2-6 Tstrap: 0-0
Best Rating: 117 10/02 Chep 2m3f110y good   Ch

A modest front-running chaser, he stays two and a half
miles, but does not want the ground too soft. Often wears a
visor and has broken blood-vessels. (DEAD)

Grand Ambition (USA)

90(91c)   (77c)94
7-y-o b g Lear Fan (USA)-Longing To Dance (USA)
(Nureyev (USA))
Mrs P Sly (Michael Hourigan 9/8) Thorney Racing Club

Placings:0/30063P0P3-4F00001   (4667)
2002/03: 16⁴GY, 21ᶠS, 20⁵SH, 17ᵁGF, 22ᵁGY, 24ᴼYS, 21¹G,

	Starts	1st	2nd	3rd	Win & Pl
Hurdles	2	0	0	0	
Chases	5	1	0	0	2356
Career Total	17	1	0	3	3730
77 4/03 Fknm	2m5f110yH Ch		GD	£2048

Total win prize-money £2049

Going: Sf: 0-1 GS: 0-0 Gd: 1-1 GF: - Fm: 0-1
Distance: 2m/2m3: 0-2 2m4-2m7: 1-4 3m+: 0-1
Track: LH: 1-1 RH: 0-1 Tight: 1-1 Gall: 0-0
Aids: Bl: 0-1 Vi: 0-0 Tstrap: 0-0
Best Rating: 94 5/01 Hntg 2m110y   gd-fm Hdl

Ex-Irish hunter chaser; won at Fakenham in April; suited by
fast ground.

Grand Finale (IRE)

104   108+
6-y-o b h Sadler s Wells (USA)-Final Figure (USA) (Super
Concorde (USA))
Miss Venetia Williams Leinster Bar

Placings:P4   (3643)
2002/03: 16ᴾS, 16⁴GS,

	Starts	1st	2nd	3rd	Win & Pl
Hurdles	2	0	0	0	438
Career Total	2	0	0	0	438

Going: Sf: 0-1 GS: 0-1 Gd: 0-0 GF: - Fm: 0-0
Distance: 2m/2m3: 0-2 2m4-2m7: 0-0 3m+: 0-0
Track: LH: 0-0 RH: 0-2 Tight: 0-0 Gall: 0-0
Aids: Bl: 0-0 Vi: 0-0 Tstrap: 0-0
Best Rating: 95 2/03 Winc 2m   gd-sft Hdl

Modest hurdler; ex-Irish; very useful on the Flat; ready winner of 2m maiden hurdle at Worcester May 2003; possibly
found the ground on the fast side next time; acts on good
and soft ground; has breathing problems.

Grand Fougeray (FR)

(81h)   (56h)90
9-y-o b g Port Etienne (FR)-Poupee Du Fougeray (FR)
(Rigolo Iv)
A W Carroll R T C Racing

Placings:134/1F10/PFPP2FPP-U40P   (0736)
2002/03: 16ᴾGS, 21ᵁG, 20⁴G, 16⁸GF, 16ᴾGF,

	Starts	1st	2nd	3rd	Win & Pl
Hurdles	3	0	0	0	0
Chases	2	0	0	0	
Career Total	19	3	1	1	9856
9/00 PLOR	2m4f	Ch	GD	£2305
8/00 Blng	2m4f	Ch	GD	£2498
5/99	2m2f	Ch	GD	£2368

Total win prize-money £7171

Going: Sf: 0-0 GS: 0-1 Gd: 0-2 GF: - Fm: 0-2
Distance: 2m/2m3: 0-3 2m4-2m7: 0-2 3m+: 0-0
Track: LH: 0-4 RH: 0-1 Tight: 0-2 Gall: 0-0
Aids: Bl: 0-0 Vi: 0-0 Tstrap: 0-0
Best Rating: 90 12/01 Ludl 2m   good   Ch

Three times a winner over fences in the French Provinces,
he has shown little since moving to Britain.

Grand Gousier (FR)

100   106
9-y-o b g Perrault-Tartifume Ii (FR) (Mistigri)
H D Daly Mrs M Wiggin

Placings:22/P0/P25P421P/01214/2435   (3348)
2002/03: 17²G, 20⁴GS, 20³G, 20⁵S,

	Starts	1st	2nd	3rd	Win & Pl
Chases	4	0	1	1	3235
Career Total	21	3	6	1	20710
112 1/01 Sthl	2m4f110yE(0-115)HCh	HVY	£3469
109 11/00 Leic	2m4f110yE(0-115)HCh	G-S	£3510
105 3/00 Wwck	2m4f	D(0-110)HCh	SFT	£5668

Total win prize-money £12647

Going: Sf: 0-1 GS: 0-1 Gd: 0-2 GF: - Fm: 0-0
Distance: 2m/2m3: 0-1 2m4-2m7: 0-3 3m+: 0-0
Track: LH: 0-2 RH: 0-2 Tight: 0-2 Gall: 0-1
Aids: Bl: 0-0 Vi: 0-0 Tstrap: 0-0
Best Rating: 112 1/01 Sthl 2m4f110y heavy Ch

Fair chaser at up to two and a half miles. Ran well when
second in October 2002, his first run for more than eighteen
months.

Grand Jury (IRE)

75   55
6-y-o ch g Grand Lodge (USA)-Scales Of Justice (Final
Straw)
J S Smith Grand Jury Partnership

Placings:00P   (2453)
2002/03: 19ᴼGS, 16ᴼGS, 19ᴾGS,

	Starts	1st	2nd	3rd	Win & Pl
Hurdles	3	0	0	0	
Career Total	3	0	0	0	

Going: Sf: 0-0 GS: 0-3 Gd: 0-0 GF: - Fm: 0-0
Distance: 2m/2m3: 0-2 2m4-2m7: 0-1 3m+: 0-0
Track: LH: 0-1 RH: 0-2 Tight: 0-1 Gall: 0-0
Aids: Bl: 0-0 Vi: 0-0 Tstrap: 0-0
Best Rating: 55 11/02 Wwck 2m   gd-sft Hdl

Grand Prairie (SWE)

71
7-y-o b g Prairie-Platonica (ITY) (Primo Dominie)
R C Guest (N B Mason 17/11) N J Jones

Placings:5U-P   (3753)
2002/03: 21ᴾG,

	Starts	1st	2nd	3rd	Win & Pl
Hurdles	1	0	0	0	
Career Total	3	0	0	0	0

Going: Sf: 0-0 GS: 0-0 Gd: 0-1 GF: - Fm: 0-0
Distance: 2m/2m3: 0-0 2m4-2m7: 0-1 3m+: 0-0
Track: LH: 0-0 RH: 0-1 Tight: 0-0 Gall: 0-0
Aids: Bl: 0-0 Vi: 0-0 Tstrap: 0-0
Best Rating: 71 3/02 Carl 2m1f   gd-sft Hdl

Grand Prompt

102   90
4-y-o ch g Grand Lodge (USA)-Prompting (Primo Dominie)
Mrs L Wadham (R Gibson 20/10) P A Philipps, T S
Redman, P Coe

Placings:3P06   (4561)
2002/03: 16³GS, 17ᴾS, 16⁹G, 20⁶GF,

	Starts	1st	2nd	3rd	Win & Pl
Hurdles	4	0	0	1	696
Career Total	4	0	0	1	696

Going: Sf: 0-1 GS: 0-1 Gd: 0-1 GF: - Fm: 0-1
Distance: 2m/2m3: 0-3 2m4-2m7: 0-1 3m+: 0-0
Track: LH: 0-3 RH: 0-1 Tight: 0-3 Gall: 0-1
Aids: Bl: 0-1 Vi: 0-2 Tstrap: 0-0
Best Rating: 95 12/02 Newb 2m110y   good Hdl

Relished fast ground and sharp track when winning modest
2m 4f novice hurdle at Fakenham May 2003; disappointing
next two starts; better effort when staying on third over and
adequate 2m 3f at Stratford in July.

Grand Slam (IRE)

102(96h)   (104h)91
8-y-o b g Second Set (IRE)-Lady In The Park (IRE) (Last
Tycoon)
A C Whillans (L Lungo 31/7) 7 Up Partnership

Placings:00/312/120045P0-P0025   (1472)
2002/03: 16ᴾG, 16⁸GF, 17⁹GF, 16²GF, 20⁵GF,

	Starts	1st	2nd	3rd	Win & Pl
Hurdles	3	0	0	0	
Chases	2	0	1	0	1033
Career Total	18	2	3	1	8635
98 5/01 Ayr	2m	E Hdl	G-F	£2999
88 1/01 Muss	2m	E Hdl	G-S	£2254

Total win prize-money £5254

Going: Sf: 0-0 GS: 0-0 Gd: 0-1 GF: - Fm: 0-4
Distance: 2m/2m3: 0-4 2m4-2m7: 0-1 3m+: 0-0
Track: LH: 0-2 RH: 0-3 Tight: 0-2 Gall: 0-0
Aids: Bl: 0-0 Vi: 0-0 Tstrap: 0-0
Best Rating: 104 5/01 MRas 2m1f110y good Hdl

Some ability over fences, but is not the most reliable of
sorts.

Grandmere

71   52
8-y-o gr m Gran Alba (USA)-Cuckmere Grange (Floriana)
P Beaumont Queens Head Racing Club

Placings:0P0   (3996)
2002/03: 16⁰G, 20⁰G, 20⁰G,

	Starts	1st	2nd	3rd	Win & Pl
Hurdles	3	0	0	0	
Career Total	3	0	0	0	

Going: Sf: 0-0 GS: 0-0 Gd: 0-3 GF: - Fm: 0-0
Distance: 2m/2m3: 0-1 2m4-2m7: 0-2 3m+: 0-0
Track: LH: 0-3 RH: 0-0 Tight: 0-1 Gall: 0-0
Aids: Bl: 0-0 Vi: 0-0 Tstrap: 0-0
Best Rating: 52 2/03 Catt 2m good Hdl

Grangewick Flight
106   **109**
9-y-o b g Lighter-Feathery (Le Coq D Or)
N Wilson Mrs H D Marks

Placings:F4463-POP222F01UU233   (4773)
2002/03: 24⁸GS, 23⁰GF, 21⁸G, 20⁹HY, 24²GS, 21²GS, 20⁴S, 27⁰HY, 20¹S, 22⁴US, 20⁴S, 20²GS, 24³G, 20³G,

	Starts	1st	2nd	3rd	Win & Pl
Chases	14	1	4	2	11131
Career Total	19	1	4	3	12280

99 2/03 Newc 2m4f F(0-100)HCh SFT £3399
Total win prize-money £3400

Going: Sf: 1-6 GS: 0-4 Gd: 0-3 GF: - Fm: 0-1
Distance: 2m/2m3: 0-0 2m4-2m7: 1-9 3m+: 0-5
Track: LH: 1-8 RH: 0-5 Tight: 0-5 Gall: 1-2
Aids: Bl: 0-0 Vi: 0-0 Tstrap: 0-0
Best Rating: 109 4/03 Prth 2m4f110y good Ch

Modest chaser; stays three miles, but effective at shorter; acts on soft ground; not the most fluent jumper.

Granit D'Estruval (FR)
(107h)   (120h)**143d**
9-y-o b g Quart De Vin (FR)-Jalousie (FR) (Blockhaus)
Ferdy Murphy W J Gott

Placings:5/2/211F/12P1-P   (4050)
2002/03: 24⁰S,

	Starts	1st	2nd	3rd	Win & Pl
Chases	1	0	0	0	
Career Total	11	4	3	0	21000

120 2/02 Uttx 3m110y D Hdl HVY £3649
143 1/02 Carl 3m2f C(0-130)HCh SFT £6922
120 12/00 Newc 3m E Ch SFT £3120
104 11/00 Carl 3m2f F Ch SFT £2353
Total win prize-money £16046

Going: Sf: 0-1 GS: 0-0 Gd: 0-0 GF: - Fm: 0-0
Distance: 2m/2m3: 0-0 2m4-2m7: 0-0 3m+: 0-1
Track: LH: 0-0 RH: 0-1 Tight: 0-0 Gall: 0-0
Aids: Bl: 0-0 Vi: 0-0 Tstrap: 0-0
Best Rating: 143 11/01 Carl 3m2f soft Ch

Useful chaser; winner over hurdles at Uttoxeter in February 2002; absent for over a year subsequently and was pulled up on his return; stays very well; effective in soft and heavy conditions.

Granite Steps
92(107h)   (108h)97
7-y-o gr g Gran Alba (USA)-Pablena (Pablond)
Ferdy Murphy Mrs T H Barclay/Mrs F D McInnes Skinner

Placings:0/22231-FU3P   (3770)
2002/03: 25⁶GS, 24⁰GS, 24³S, 25⁰GS,

	Starts	1st	2nd	3rd	Win & Pl
Chases	4	0	0	1	826
Career Total	10	1	3	2	5793

103 3/02 Towc 2m5f F Hdl G-S £1953
Total win prize-money £1953

Going: Sf: 0-1 GS: 0-3 Gd: 0-0 GF: - Fm: 0-0
Distance: 2m/2m3: 0-0 2m4-2m7: 0-0 3m+: 0-4
Track: LH: 0-4 RH: 0-0 Tight: 0-2 Gall: 0-0
Aids: Bl: 0-0 Vi: 0-0 Tstrap: 0-0
Best Rating: 108 2/02 Newc 2m4f soft Hdl

Granny Dick
90
8-y-o ch m Broadsword (USA)-Penny s Colours (Hornet)
J L Spearing B Dowling

Placings:35354/P0F0P44-   (0015)
2002/03: 21⁴GS,

	Starts	1st	2nd	3rd	Win & Pl
Hurdles	1	0	0	0	0
Career Total	12	0	0	2	998

Going: Sf: 0-0 GS: 0-1 Gd: 0-0 GF: - Fm: 0-0
Distance: 2m/2m3: 0-0 2m4-2m7: 0-1 3m+: 0-0
Track: LH: 0-0 RH: 0-1 Tight: 0-0 Gall: 0-0
Aids: Bl: 0-0 Vi: 0-0 Tstrap: 0-0
Best Rating: 90 4/01 Asct 2m4f heavy Hdl

Granny Rich
90   **102d**
9-y-o ch m Ardross-Weareagrandmother (Prince Tenderfoot (USA))
P M Rich P M Rich

Placings:30/0P0/411115F/4FP4/0015F21-P50   (1815)
2002/03: 27⁸PS, 20⁵GS, 19⁰G,

	Starts	1st	2nd	3rd	Win & Pl
Hurdles	3	0	0	0	
Career Total	26	6	1	1	17928

102 4/02 Chep 2m4f D(0-125)HHdl G-S £3465
94 11/01 Chep 2m110y F(0-90)Hdl SFT £2324
118 1/00 Hrfd 2m4f F(0-110)HHdl G-S £3331
115 12/99 Wwck 2m2f110yE(0-105)HHdl SFT £2402
96 12/99 Hrfd 2m1f E(0-105)HHdl GD £2640
99 11/99 Uttx 2m G(0-90)HHdl G-S £1647
Total win prize-money £15810

Going: Sf: 0-1 GS: 0-1 Gd: 0-0 GF: - Fm: 0-0
Distance: 2m/2m3: 0-2 2m4-2m7: 0-4 3m+: 0-1
Track: LH: 0-2 RH: 0-1 Tight: 0-0 Gall: 0-0
Aids: Bl: 0-0 Vi: 0-0 Tstrap: 0-0
Best Rating: 118 1/00 Hrfd 2m3f110y gd-sft Hdl

Modest handicap hurdler, suited by soft ground. Stays two and a half miles, has won over two, tends to come from behind.

Grate Deel (IRE)
107   **108**
13-y-o ch g The Parson-Cahernane Girl (Bargello)
Mrs S J Smith Mrs M Ashby

Placings:6/05014/5632/4224P/3P0P11622P/36550/343514 10/0P5-114141P (1566)
2002/03: 25¹GS, 30¹G, 24⁴GF, 25¹GS, 26⁴G, 26¹GF, 25⁴GS,

	Starts	1st	2nd	3rd	Win & Pl
Chases	7	4	0	0	20266
Career Total	48	9	5	5	50364

108 10/02 Uttx 3m2f E(0-110)HCh G-F £4230
108 8/02 MRas 3m1f E(0-110)HCh G-S £4891
98 6/02 Ctml 3m6f D(0-130)HCh GD £6825
95 5/02 Weth 3m1f E(0-110)HCh G-S £3388
104 10/00 MRas 3m4f110yF(0-100)HCh GD £3667
104 8/00 MRas 3m1f F(0-100)HCh G-F £7377
108 11/98 Hayd 2m4f D Ch SFT £4335
108 10/98 Weth 3m1f E(0-105)HCh GD £3493
93 2/96 Sedg 2m5f110yE Hdl GD £2407
Total win prize-money £40615

Going: Sf: 0-0 GS: 2-3 Gd: 1-2 GF: - Fm: 1-2
Distance: 2m/2m3: 0-0 2m4-2m7: 0-0 3m+: 4-7
Track: LH: 2-4 RH: 1-2 Tight: 1-3 Gall: 0-0
Aids: Bl: 0-0 Vi: 0-0 Tstrap: 0-0
Best Rating: 108 10/02 Uttx 3m2f gd-fm Ch

Modest handicap chaser, effective at three miles. In good form in the summer of 2002.

Grattan Lodge (IRE)
106   **118+**
6-y-o gr g Roselier (FR)-Shallow Run (Deep Run)
J Howard Johnson W M G Black

Placings:P0P-601111   (3915)
2002/03: 20⁶PG, 23⁰G, 20¹S, 20¹HY, 27¹HY, 24¹GS,

	Starts	1st	2nd	3rd	Win & Pl
Hurdles	6	4	0	0	14445
Career Total	9	4	0	0	14445

118 3/03 Carl 3m110y D(0-125)HHdl G-S £5460
105 1/03 Sedg 3m3f110yE(0-105)HHdl HVY £3412
90 11/02 Carl 2m4f E(0-105)HHdl HVY £2919
90 11/02 Newc 2m4f F(0-90)HHdl SFT £2653
Total win prize-money £14445

Going: Sf: 3-3 GS: 1-1 Gd: 0-1 GF: - Fm: 0-1
Distance: 2m/2m3: 0-0 2m4-2m7: 2-4 3m+: 2-2
Track: LH: 2-4 RH: 2-2 Tight: 1-1 Gall: 1-1
Aids: Bl: 0-0 Vi: 0-0 Tstrap: 0-0
Best Rating: 118 3/03 Carl 3m110y gd-sft Hdl

Showed much improved form when taking a low-grade handicap hurdle at Newcastle in November and followed up in a poor amateurs' event at Carlisle; clear-cut winner over three and a half miles in heavy ground at Sedgefield in January and won again at Carlisle in March and is clearly improving fast.

Grave Doubts
114   **132**
7-y-o ch g Karinga Bay-Redgrave Girl (Deep Run)
K Bishop Bill Davies & Bernard Tottle

Placings:1302-03061111PF   (4608)
2002/03: 16⁵GF, 17³GF, 17⁰GF, 17⁶G, 16¹G, 17¹F, 17¹G, 16¹G, 16⁵G, 17⁶G,

	Starts	1st	2nd	3rd	Win & Pl
Hurdles	10	4	0	1	21756
Career Total	14	5	1	2	24890

129 10/02 Chel 2m110y B HHdl GD £10938
116 10/02 Hrfd 2m1f E Hdl GD £3633
110 10/02 Extr 2m1f E Hdl FRM £3430
103 9/02 Plum 2m E Hdl GD £3220
110 6/01 NAbb 2m1f H NHF GD £2282
Total win prize-money £23505

Going: Sf: 0-0 GS: 0-0 Gd: 3-6 GF: - Fm: 1-4
Distance: 2m/2m3: 4-10 2m4-2m7: 0-0 3m+: 0-0
Track: LH: 2-7 RH: 2-3 Tight: 1-5 Gall: 0-1
Aids: Bl: 0-0 Vi: 0-0 Tstrap: 4-7
Best Rating: 129 10/02 Chel 2m110y good Hdl

Fair bumper performer who progressed with experience over hurdles and completed a fine four-timer in the autumn of 2002; likes a sound surface.

Gray Knight (IRE)
87   **86d**

6-y-o gr g Insan (USA)-Moohono (IRE) (Roselier (FR))
Miss H C Knight Ramp Partnership

Placings:5/40-6P40   (3120)
2002/03: 17⁵G, 22⁴GS, 20⁴S, 20⁰S,

	Starts	1st	2nd	3rd	Win & Pl
Hurdles	4	0	0	0	265
Career Total	7	0	0	0	265

Going: Sf: 0-2 GS: 0-1 Gd: 0-1 GF: - Fm: 0-0
Distance: 2m/2m3: 0-1 2m4-2m7: 0-3 3m+: 0-0
Track: LH: 0-0 RH: 0-3 Tight: 0-1 Gall: 0-1
Aids: Bl: 0-0 Vi: 0-0 Tstrap: 0-0
Best Rating: 86   11/01 NAbb 2m1f   good   Hdl

Gray's Eulogy
92   **85**

5-y-o b g Presenting-Gray s Ellergy (Oats)
D R Gandolfo M A Dore

Placings:0   (2111)
2002/03: 16⁰G,

	Starts	1st	2nd	3rd	Win & Pl
Hurdles	1	0	0	0	
Career Total	1	0	0	0	

Going: Sf: 0-0 GS: 0-0 Gd: 0-1 GF: - Fm: 0-0
Distance: 2m/2m3: 0-1 2m4-2m7: 0-0 3m+: 0-0
Track: LH: 0-0 RH: 0-0 Tight: 0-1 Gall: 0-0
Aids: Bl: 0-0 Vi: 0-0 Tstrap: 0-0
Best Rating: 85   11/02 Aint   2m110y   good   Hdl

Grayslake (IRE)
101   **92**

7-y-o b g King s Ride-Castlegrace (IRE) (Kemal (FR))
Miss H C Knight Prof D B A & Mrs H E Silk, D J Coldman

Placings:003   (4196)
2002/03: 21⁰S, 22⁰GS, 24³G,

	Starts	1st	2nd	3rd	Win & Pl
Hurdles	3	0	0	1	526
Career Total	3	0	0	1	526

Going: Sf: 0-1 GS: 0-1 Gd: 0-1 GF: - Fm: 0-0
Distance: 2m/2m3: 0-0 2m4-2m7: 0-2 3m+: 0-1
Track: LH: 0-2 RH: 0-1 Tight: 0-1 Gall: 0-0
Aids: Bl: 0-0 Vi: 0-0 Tstrap: 0-0
Best Rating: 92   3/03 Ludl   3m   good   Hdl

Great As Gold (IRE)
102   **98**

4-y-o b g Goldmark (USA)-Great Land (USA) (Friend s Choice (USA))
B Ellison (Miss V Haigh 29/5) Mrs Andrea M Mallinson

Placings:523   (3940)
2002/03: 16⁵GS, 16²S, 17³GS,

	Starts	1st	2nd	3rd	Win & Pl
Hurdles	3	0	1	1	1476
Career Total	3	0	1	1	1476

Going: Sf: 0-1 GS: 0-2 Gd: 0-0 GF: - Fm: 0-0
Distance: 2m/2m3: 0-3 2m4-2m7: 0-0 3m+: 0-0

Track: LH: 0-2 RH: 0-1 Tight: 0-1 Gall: 0-1
Aids: Bl: 0-0 Vi: 0-0 Tstrap: 0-0
Best Rating: 93   11/02 Newc 2m   soft   Hdl

A moderate stayer on the Flat, he won on Fibresand in March 2002; not disgraced on hurdling debut in valuable event at Wetherby in November and runner-up at Newcastle two week later.

Great Chaos (IRE)
96f   **98f**

4-y-o b g Great Commotion (USA)-Hassosi (IRE) (High Estate)
Michael Cunningham Mrs Michael Cunningham

Placings:25   (3976a)
2002/03: 16²HY, 16⁵HY,

	Starts	1st	2nd	3rd	Win & Pl
NH Flat	2	0	1	0	540
Career Total	2	0	1	0	540

Going: Sf: 0-2 GS: 0-0 Gd: 0-0 GF: - Fm: 0-0
Distance: 2m/2m3: 0-2 2m4-2m7: 0-0 3m+: 0-0
Track: LH: 0-1 RH: 0-0 Tight: 0-0 Gall: 0-0
Aids: Bl: 0-0 Vi: 0-0 Tstrap: 0-0
Best Rating: 90   1/03 Ayr   2m   heavy   NHF

Moderate Irish bumper performer; handles any ground.

Great Crusader
108(88c)   **(94c)117**

11-y-o ch g Deploy-Shannon Princess (Connaught)
M J Hogan Mrs Barbara Hogan

Placings:32/44P3FP-3114516114   (4774)
2002/03: 22³HY, 17¹HY, 24¹S, 24⁴S, 21⁵HY, 22¹HY, 22⁶HY, 28¹G, 24¹G, 27⁴G,

	Starts	1st	2nd	3rd	Win & Pl
Hurdles	10	5	0	1	18555
Career Total	18	5	1	3	22873
117 4/03 Prth	3m110y	E(0-105)HHdl		GD	£5876
106 3/03 Folk	3m4f	F(0-100)HHdl		GD	£3425
106 2/03 Folk	2m6f110yF(0-95)HHdl			HVY	£3129
92 12/02 Tntn	3m110y	G(0-90)HHdl		SFT	£2058
88 12/02 Folk	2m1f110yG(0-95)HHdl			HVY	£2268
				Total win prize-money £16757	

Going: Sf: 3-7 GS: 0-0 Gd: 2-3 GF: - Fm: 0-0
Distance: 2m/2m3: 1-1 2m4-2m7: 1-4 3m+: 3-5
Track: LH: 0-1 RH: 5-8 Tight: 4-5 Gall: 0-0
Aids: Bl: 0-0 Vi: 0-0 Tstrap: 0-0
Best Rating: 133   1/99 Sand   2m110y   soft   Hdl

Moderate staying hurdler; stays 3m 4f; acts best on soft ground, but handles faster; yet to win on a left-handed course.

Great News
84   **73**

8-y-o b g Elmaamul (USA)-Amina (Brigadier Gerard)
N Tinkler A J and B Sawbridge

Placings:P0   (2507)
2002/03: 20⁵S, 16⁰G,

	Starts	1st	2nd	3rd	Win & Pl
Hurdles	2	0	0	0	
Career Total	2	0	0	0	

Going: Sf: 0-1 GS: 0-0 Gd: 0-1 GF: - Fm: 0-0
Distance: 2m/2m3: 0-1 2m4-2m7: 0-1 3m+: 0-0
Track: LH: 0-2 RH: 0-0 Tight: 0-0 Gall: 0-0

Aids: Bl: 0-0 Vi: 0-0 Tstrap: 0-0
Best Rating: 73   12/02 Hayd   2m   good   Hdl

Great Oaks
85(96h)   **(84h)77**

9-y-o b g Sylvan Express-Springdale Hall (USA) (Bates Motel (USA))
J M Jefferson P Gaffney & J N Stevenson

Placings:043/3/446   (3327)
2002/03: 22⁴S, 20⁴GF, 20⁶G,

	Starts	1st	2nd	3rd	Win & Pl
Hurdles	3	0	0	0	599
Career Total	7	0	0	2	1457

Going: Sf: 0-1 GS: 0-0 Gd: 0-1 GF: - Fm: 0-0
Distance: 2m/2m3: 0-0 2m4-2m7: 0-3 3m+: 0-0
Track: LH: 0-1 RH: 0-2 Tight: 0-3 Gall: 0-0
Aids: Bl: 0-0 Vi: 0-0 Tstrap: 0-0
Best Rating: 84   12/02 Muss   2m4f   gd-fm   Hdl

Plating-class hurdler; effective on good ground; stays two miles four and should stay further.

Great Ovation (FR)
85   **75**

4-y-o ch f Boston Two Step (USA)-Baldiloa (No Lute (FR))
R T Phillips (T Trapenard 2/7) Mrs Claire Smith

Placings:050   (4328)
2002/03: 16⁰G, 17⁵GS, 16⁶G,

	Starts	1st	2nd	3rd	Win & Pl
Hurdles	3	0	0	0	0
Career Total	3	0	0	0	0

Going: Sf: 0-0 GS: 0-1 Gd: 0-2 GF: - Fm: 0-0
Distance: 2m/2m3: 0-3 2m4-2m7: 0-0 3m+: 0-0
Track: LH: 0-2 RH: 0-1 Tight: 0-0 Gall: 0-1
Aids: Bl: 0-0 Vi: 0-0 Tstrap: 0-1
Best Rating: 75   1/03 Extr   2m1f   gd-sft   Hdl

Ex-French middle-distance/stayer; some signs of promise second start over hurdles; effective on an easy surface, will stay beyond 2m over hurdles.

Grecian Star

11-y-o b g Crested Lark-Grecian Lace (Spartan General)
G J Tarry R John White

Placings:512-32P6   (3952)
2002/03: 33³GF, 25²S, 26⁶P, 23⁶GS,

	Starts	1st	2nd	3rd	Win & Pl
Chases	4	0	1	1	2972
Career Total	7	1	2	1	6044
105 3/02 Towc	2m6f	H Ch		G-S	£2226
				Total win prize-money £2226	

Going: Sf: 0-1 GS: 0-1 Gd: 0-1 GF: - Fm: 0-1
Distance: 2m/2m3: 0-0 2m4-2m7: 0-0 3m+: 0-4
Track: LH: 0-2 RH: 0-2 Tight: 0-0 Gall: 0-1
Aids: Bl: 0-0 Vi: 0-0 Tstrap: 0-0
Best Rating: 105   5/02   Towc   3m1f   soft   Ch

Hunter chaser; headstrong sort; good jumper; stays very well; appears to act on all types of ground.

Green Admiral
87f   **82f**

4-y-o b g Slip Anchor-Jade Mistress (Damister (USA))

J J Quinn Mrs C T Bletsoe

Placings:60   (3570)
2002/03: 16⁶GS, 17⁹HY,

	Starts	1st	2nd	3rd	Win & Pl
NH Flat	2	0	0	0	0
Career Total	2	0	0	0	0

Going: Sf: 0-1 GS: 0-1 Gd: 0-0 GF: - Fm: 0-0
Distance: 2m/2m3: 0-2 2m4-2m7: 0-0 3m+: 0-0
Track: LH: 0-2 RH: 0-0 Tight: 0-0 Gall: 0-0
Aids: Bl: 0-0 Vi: 0-0 Tstrap: 0-0
Best Rating: 82 1/03   Hayd   2m   gd-sft NHF

Green Go (GER)
98   99
5-y-o ch g Secret n Classy (CAN)-Green Fee (GER)
(Windwurf (GER))
A Sadik A Sadik

Placings:51364P   (1330)
2002/03: 16⁵GF, 20¹GF, 21³GF, 18⁶G, 21⁴G, 17⁶G,

	Starts	1st	2nd	3rd	Win & Pl
Hurdles	5	1	0	1	4476
Chases	1	0	0	0	0
Career Total	6	1	0	1	4476
91 7/02 Uttx 2m4f110yD Hdl				G-F	£4056

Total win prize-money £4056

Going: Sf: 0-0 GS: 0-0 Gd: 0-3 GF: - Fm: 1-3
Distance: 2m/2m3: 0-3 **2m4-2m7: 1-3** 3m+: 0-0
Track: **LH: 1-6** RH: 0-0 Tight: 0-4 Gall: 0-0
Aids: Bl: 0-0 Vi: 0-0 Tstrap: 0-0
Best Rating: 93 9/02   Sthl   2m5f110y   good   Hdl

Winner on the Flat in the Czech Republic; moderate hurdler;
stays 2m 4f; acts on fast ground.

Green Iceni
96f   82f
4-y-o br g Greensmith-Boadicea s Chariot (Commanche
Run)
J R Best P E Hudson

Placings:04   (4190)
2002/03: 16⁹G, 17⁴G,

	Starts	1st	2nd	3rd	Win & Pl
NH Flat	2	0	0	0	0
Career Total	2	0	0	0	0

Going: Sf: 0-0 GS: 0-0 Gd: 0-2 GF: - Fm: 0-0
Distance: 2m/2m3: 0-2 2m4-2m7: 0-0 3m+: 0-0
Track: LH: 0-0 RH: 0-2 Tight: 0-0 Gall: 0-0
Aids: Bl: 0-0 Vi: 0-0 Tstrap: 0-0
Best Rating: 82 3/03   Folk   2m1f110y   good   NHF

Half-brother to Aggrippina out of a winning middle
distance/hurdles performer; showed ability in bumpers.

Green Ideal
111   129
5-y-o b g Mark Of Esteem (IRE)-Emerald (USA) (El Gran
Senor (USA))
N J Henderson Thurloe Thoroughbreds Viii

Placings:1P0-024   (4449)
2002/03: 16⁹G, 16²GS, 16⁴G,

	Starts	1st	2nd	3rd	Win & Pl
Hurdles	3	0	1	0	2011
Career Total	6	1	1	0	6438

---

121 12/01 Newb 2m110y D Hdl   G-S £4426
Total win prize-money £4427

Going: Sf: 0-0 GS: 0-1 Gd: 0-2 GF: - Fm: 0-0
Distance: 2m/2m3: 0-3 2m4-2m7: 0-0 3m+: 0-0
Track: LH: 0-0 RH: 0-3 Tight: 0-0 Gall: 0-0
Aids: Bl: 0-0 Vi: 0-0 Tstrap: 0-0
Best Rating: 129 2/03   Winc   2m   gd-sft Hdl

Useful hurdler; effective at around two miles and acts on any
ground bar extremes.

Green Jacket
29
8-y-o b g Green Desert (USA)-Select Sale (Auction Ring
(USA))
J Joseph Jack Joseph

Placings:000P2/00/05PBP/60-P   (0789)
2002/03: 26⁵GF,

	Starts	1st	2nd	3rd	Win & Pl
Hurdles	1	0	0		
Career Total	15	0	1	0	660

Going: Sf: 0-0 GS: 0-0 Gd: 0-0 GF: - Fm: 0-1
Distance: 2m/2m3: 0-0 2m4-2m7: 0-0 3m+: 0-1
Track: LH: 0-1 RH: 0-0 Tight: 0-0 Gall: 0-0
Aids: Bl: 0-1 Vi: 0-0 Tstrap: 0-0
Best Rating: 74 5/99   Extr   2m1f   firm   Hdl

Green Pursuit
7-y-o b g Green Desert (USA)-Vayavaig (Damister (USA))
W M Brisbourne K Bennett

Placings:0/P-P   (1571)
2002/03: 16⁶G,

	Starts	1st	2nd	3rd	Win & Pl
Hurdles	1	0	0	0	
Career Total	3	0	0	0	

Going: Sf: 0-0 GS: 0-0 Gd: 0-1 GF: - Fm: 0-0
Distance: 2m/2m3: 0-1 2m4-2m7: 0-0 3m+: 0-0
Track: LH: 0-1 RH: 0-0 Tight: 0-1 Gall: 0-0
Aids: Bl: 0-0 Vi: 0-0 Tstrap: 0-0
Best Rating: 0 10/02   Strf   2m110y   good   Hdl

Green Smoke
100(105h)   (82h)90
7-y-o gr g Green Adventure (USA)-Smoke (Rusticaro (FR))
J M Jefferson Mrs J U Hales

Placings:U/000/20325-332   (3802)
2002/03: 16³G, 16³HY, 20²S,

	Starts	1st	2nd	3rd	Win & Pl
Chases	3	0	1	2	2251
Career Total	12	0	3	3	4487

Going: Sf: 0-2 GS: 0-0 Gd: 0-1 GF: - Fm: 0-0
Distance: 2m/2m3: 0-2 2m4-2m7: 0-1 3m+: 0-0
Track: LH: 0-3 RH: 0-0 Tight: 0-1 Gall: 0-2
Aids: Bl: 0-0 Vi: 0-0 Tstrap: 0-0
Best Rating: 90 2/03   Newc   2m4f   soft   Ch

Moderate maiden over hurdles and fences.

Greenacres Boy
78   41
8-y-o b g Roscoe Blake-Deep Goddess (Deep Run)
C N Kellett Geoffrey Arthur Probin

Placings:6   (0567)
2002/03: 16⁶GS,

	Starts	1st	2nd	3rd	Win & Pl
Hurdles	1	0	0	0	0
Career Total	1	0	0	0	0

Going: Sf: 0-0 GS: 0-1 Gd: 0-0 GF: - Fm: 0-0
Distance: 2m/2m3: 0-1 2m4-2m7: 0-0 3m+: 0-0
Track: LH: 0-1 RH: 0-0 Tight: 0-0 Gall: 0-0
Aids: Bl: 0-0 Vi: 0-0 Tstrap: 0-0
Best Rating: 41 6/02   Uttx   2m   gd-sft Hdl

Greenacres Miss
6-y-o b m Michelozzo (USA)-Royal Cause (Le Bavard (FR))
M Mullineaux Geoffrey Arthur Probin

Placings:00-P   (4320)
2002/03: 17⁶G,

	Starts	1st	2nd	3rd	Win & Pl
Hurdles	1	0	0	0	
Career Total	3	0	0	0	

Going: Sf: 0-0 GS: 0-0 Gd: 0-1 GF: - Fm: 0-0
Distance: 2m/2m3: 0-1 2m4-2m7: 0-0 3m+: 0-0
Track: LH: 0-1 RH: 0-0 Tight: 0-1 Gall: 0-0
Aids: Bl: 0-0 Vi: 0-0 Tstrap: 0-0
Best Rating: 30 9/01   Hrfd   2m1f   gd-fm   NHF

Greenback (BEL)
106   106
12-y-o b g Absalom-Batalya (BEL) (Boulou)
J D Frost Jack Joseph

Placings:U2112122111100/1/**23F1113313**/504005443/233
110-1340   (2438)
2002/03: 19¹G, 19³GS, 17⁴F, 21⁹GS,

	Starts	1st	2nd	3rd	Win & Pl
Hurdles	4	1	0	1	3384
Career Total	44	15	6	8	71511
102 6/02 Hrfd 2m3f110yG Hdl				GD	£2128
100 11/01 Ludl 2m G Hdl				G-F	£2107
90 11/01 Ludl 2m G Hdl				G-F	£2096
130 4/97 Asct 2m3f110yC Ch				G-F	£5654
130 12/96 Kemp 2m4f110yB Ch				G-F	£10308
121 12/96 Folk 2m E Ch				G-S	£3305
115 11/96 Tntn 2m3f C Ch				G-F	£4531
124 5/95 Towc 2m D(0-125)HHdl				G-F	£2883
124 2/95 Kemp 2m A Hdl				HVY	£9780
104 12/94 Sand 2m110y Hdl				GD	£3129
118 11/94 Kemp 2m Hdl				GD	£2448
112 11/94 Sand 2m110y Hdl				SFT	£3192
104 9/94 Tntn 2m1f Hdl				G-F	£1733
81 8/94 Extr 2m1f110y Hdl				FRM	
£2263					
91 8/94 NAbb 2m1f Hdl				G-S	£1818

Total win prize-money £57382

Going: Sf: 0-0 GS: 0-2 Gd: 1-1 GF: - Fm: 0-1
Distance: 2m/2m3: 0-1 **2m4-2m7: 1-3** 3m+: 0-1
Track: LH: 0-0 **RH: 1-4** Tight: 0-1 Gall: 0-1
Aids: Bl: 0-0 Vi: 0-0 Tstrap: 0-0
Best Rating: 130 4/97   Asct   2m3f110y   gd-fm   Ch

Moderate hurdler nowadays; likes fast ground and stays 2m 4f; front-runner; genuine sort.

Greenborough (IRE)
60   18
5-y-o b g Dr Devious (IRE)-Port Isaac (USA) (Seattle Song (USA))
Mrs P Ford W E Donohue

Placings:0   (0323)
2002/03: 16⁰G,

	Starts	1st	2nd	3rd	Win & Pl
Hurdles	1	0	0	0	
Career Total	1	0	0	0	

Going: Sf: 0-0 GS: 0-0 Gd: 0-1 GF: - Fm: 0-0
Distance: 2m/2m3: 0-1 2m4-2m7: 0-0 3m+: 0-0
Track: LH: 0-1 RH: 0-0 Tight: 0-0 Gall: 0-0
Aids: Bl: 0-0 Vi: 0-0 Tstrap: 0-0
Best Rating: 18 5/02 Worc 2m   good   Hdl

Greenfield (IRE)
101   114+
5-y-o ch g Pleasant Tap (USA)-No Review (USA) (Nodouble (USA))
R T Phillips (J R Fanshawe 9/11) Mrs S J Harvey

Placings:33   (3515)
2002/03: 16³S, 16³GS,

	Starts	1st	2nd	3rd	Win & Pl
Hurdles	2	0	0	2	1327
Career Total	2	0	0	2	1327

Going: Sf: 0-1 GS: 0-1 Gd: 0-0 GF: - Fm: 0-0
Distance: 2m/2m3: 0-2 2m4-2m7: 0-0 3m+: 0-0
Track: LH: 0-1 RH: 0-1 Tight: 0-0 Gall: 0-1
Aids: Bl: 0-0 Vi: 0-0 Tstrap: 0-0
Best Rating: 114 1/03 Hntg 2m110y   soft   Hdl

Decent middle-distance handicapper on the Flat; has shown signs of promise both starts over hurdles and looks as though he ll improve once stepped up to distances beyond 2m.

Greenfire (FR)
93f   97f
5-y-o ch g Ashkalani (IRE)-Greenvera (USA) (Riverman (USA))
Mrs Dianne Sayer Andrew Sayer

Placings:0-00   (1477)
2002/03: 17⁹GF, 17⁰GF,

	Starts	1st	2nd	3rd	Win & Pl
NH Flat	2	0	0	0	
Career Total	3	0	0	0	

Going: Sf: 0-0 GS: 0-0 Gd: 0-0 GF: - Fm: 0-0
Distance: 2m/2m3: 0-2 2m4-2m7: 0-0 3m+: 0-0
Track: LH: 0-0 RH: 0-2 Tight: 0-1 Gall: 0-0
Aids: Bl: 0-0 Vi: 0-0 Tstrap: 0-1
Best Rating: 27 9/02 MRas 2m1f110y gd-fm NHF

Greenhope (IRE)
101   124
5-y-o b g Definite Article-Unbidden Melody (USA) (Chieftain li)

N J Henderson Lynn Wilson Giles Wilson Martin Landau

Placings:1110-0   (3727)
2002/03: 16⁹G,

	Starts	1st	2nd	3rd	Win & Pl
Hurdles	1	0	0	0	
Career Total	5	3	0	0	20547
118 12/01 Kemp 2m		B Hdl		GD	£7052
118 11/01 Chel 2m110y B Hdl				GD	£8619
118 11/01 Asct 2m110y C Hdl				GD	£4875

Total win prize-money £20547

Going: Sf: 0-0 GS: 0-0 Gd: 0-1 GF: - Fm: 0-0
Distance: 2m/2m3: 0-1 2m4-2m7: 0-0 3m+: 0-0
Track: LH: 0-0 RH: 0-1 Tight: 0-0 Gall: 0-0
Aids: Bl: 0-0 Vi: 0-0 Tstrap: 0-0
Best Rating: 118 12/01 Kemp 2m   good   Hdl

Useful hurdler; does not want the ground too soft and is seen to best effect when making the running; effect over two miles.

Greenkeys (AUS)
88(75c)   (64c)67
9-y-o b g Bonhomie (USA)-Cindy Doll (AUS) (Cindy s Son)
R C Guest N B Mason

Placings:6000/0-5   (3745)
2002/03: 16⁵G,

	Starts	1st	2nd	3rd	Win & Pl
Chases	1	0	0	0	0
Career Total	6	0	0	0	0

Going: Sf: 0-0 GS: 0-0 Gd: 0-1 GF: - Fm: 0-0
Distance: 2m/2m3: 0-1 2m4-2m7: 0-0 3m+: 0-0
Track: LH: 0-0 RH: 0-1 Tight: 0-0 Gall: 0-1
Aids: Bl: 0-0 Vi: 0-0 Tstrap: 0-0
Best Rating: 71 3/00 Uttx   2m4f110y good   Hdl

Greensmith Lane
86   79
7-y-o br g Greensmith-Handy Lane (Nearly A Hand)
N J Hawke M L Stoddart

Placings:26F-465P020   (4486)
2002/03: 17⁴S, 17⁶G, 17⁵GF, 19⁸S, 17⁹GS, 17²G, 17⁹GF,

	Starts	1st	2nd	3rd	Win & Pl
Hurdles	7	0	1	0	1231
Career Total	10	0	2	0	1912

Going: Sf: 0-2 GS: 0-1 Gd: 0-2 GF: - Fm: 0-2
Distance: 2m/2m3: 0-6 2m4-2m7: 0-1 3m+: 0-0
Track: LH: 0-3 RH: 0-4 Tight: 0-4 Gall: 0-0
Aids: Bl: 0-0 Vi: 0-0 Tstrap: 0-0
Best Rating: 91 11/01 Tntn 2m1f   good   NHF

Improved effort when second on drop into a seller at Exeter March 2003; capable of taking a similar event.

Gregs Way
105(110h)   (88h)105+
9-y-o br g Nomadic Way (USA)-Gregory s Lady (Meldrum)
Mrs S J Smith Keith Nicholson

Placings:4/050/F3360-54014121   (1476)
2002/03: 17⁵GS, 20⁴GF, 24⁸G, 19⁴GF, 20⁴GS, 16¹G, 20²G, 16¹GF,

	Starts	1st	2nd	3rd	Win & Pl
Hurdles	3	1	0	0	3614
Chases	5	2	1	0	12759
Career Total	17	3	1	2	17432

105 10/02 Carl   2m   D(0-125)HCh   G-F   £4845
100 8/02 Prth   2m   D Ch   GD   £5343
88 7/02 Strf   2m3f   E(0-105)HHdl G-F   £3614
Total win prize-money £13803

Going: Sf: 0-0 GS: 0-1 Gd: 1-3 GF: - Fm: 2-4
Distance: 2m/2m3: 3-4 2m4-2m7: 0-3 3m+: 0-1
Track: LH: 1-4 RH: 2-4 Tight: 1-3 Gall: 0-0
Aids: Bl: 0-0 Vi: 0-0 Tstrap: 0-0
Best Rating: 105 10/02 Carl 2m   gd-fm Ch

A winner over hurdles, he has been in good form over fences in the summer and autumn of 2002, winning three times. Effective from two to two and a half miles and best on fast ground.

Gretton
90f   91f
6-y-o b m Terimon-Gulsha (Glint Of Gold)
Noel T Chance (N A Twiston-Davies 11/5) Danny O Sullivan

Placings:0-0   (3322)
2002/03: 16⁹GS,

	Starts	1st	2nd	3rd	Win & Pl
NH Flat	1	0	0	0	
Career Total	2	0	0	0	

Going: Sf: 0-0 GS: 0-1 Gd: 0-0 GF: - Fm: 0-0
Distance: 2m/2m3: 0-1 2m4-2m7: 0-0 3m+: 0-0
Track: LH: 0-0 RH: 0-1 Tight: 0-0 Gall: 0-0
Aids: Bl: 0-0 Vi: 0-0 Tstrap: 0-0
Best Rating: 91 4/02 Aint 2m1f   good   NHF

Grey Abbey (IRE)
116   155
9-y-o gr g Nestor-Tacovaon (Avocat)
F P Murtagh Ken Roper,Elinor M Roper,Norman Furness

Placings:50/P0P11153/4F62F11121/51F4P0314-453P   (3407)
2002/03: 25⁴GS, 24⁵S, 21³HY, 20⁸GS,

	Starts	1st	2nd	3rd	Win & Pl
Chases	4	0	1		6900
Career Total	33	9	2	3	72226

155 4/02 Weth   3m1f   B(0-150)HCh   GD   £10962
144 11/01 Ayr   3m1f   C(0-135)HCh   G-S   £6812
135 4/01 Ayr   2m4f   A Ch   G-F   £15600
133 2/01 Kels   3m1f   D Ch   SFT   £3867
125 1/01 Ayr   2m   D Ch   G-S   £4134
129 1/01 Ayr   2m5f110y D Ch   SFT   £4108
116 2/00 Newc   2m4f   F(0-90)HHdl   SFT   £1974
108 2/00 Newc   2m   F(0-100)HHdl SFT   £1939
85 12/99 Ayr   2m   E(0-105)HHdl HVY   £2654
Total win prize-money £52051

Going: Sf: 0-2 GS: 0-2 Gd: 0-0 GF: - Fm: 0-0
Distance: 2m/2m3: 0-0 2m4-2m7: 0-2 3m+: 0-0
Track: LH: 0-4 RH: 0-0 Tight: 0-0 Gall: 0-1
Aids: Bl: 0-0 Vi: 0-0 Tstrap: 0-4
Best Rating: 155 4/02 Weth 3m1f   good   Ch

Very useful chaser; bold jumper; at his best when forcing the pace, seems to act on any ground; stays beyond four miles; goes very well at Ayr.

Grey Badger
56f   28f
6-y-o gr g Terimon-Tsarella (Mummy s Pet)
J Howard Johnson J Howard Johnson

Placings:00 (3570)
2002/03: 16⁰G, 17⁰HY,

	Starts	1st	2nd	3rd	Win & Pl
NH Flat	2	0	0	0	
Career Total	2	0	0	0	

Going: Sf: 0-1 GS: 0-0 Gd: 0-1 GF: - Fm: 0-0
Distance: 2m/2m3: 0-2 2m4-2m7: 0-0 3m+: 0-0
Track: LH: 0-1 RH: 0-1 Tight: 0-2 Gall: 0-0
Aids: Bl: 0-0 Vi: 0-0 Tstrap: 0-0
Best Rating: 28 2/03 Sedg 2m1f   heavy NHF

Grey Brother
96   110+
5-y-o gr g Morpeth-Pigeon Loft (IRE) (Bellypha)
J D Frost Christine And Aubrey Loze

Placings:03231 (3780)
2002/03: 17⁰G, 17³G, 17²HY, 19³GS, 22¹GS,

	Starts	1st	2nd	3rd	Win & Pl
NH Flat	3	0	1	1	946
Hurdles	2	1	0	1	4252
Career Total	5	1	1	2	5197
110 2/03 Extr 2m6f110yE Hdl				G-S	£3737

Total win prize-money £3738

Going: Sf: 0-1 GS: 1-2 Gd: 0-2 GF: - Fm: 0-0
Distance: 2m/2m3: 0-4 2m4-2m7: 1-1 3m+: 0-0
Track: LH: 0-1 RH: 1-4 Tight: 0-1 Gall: 0-0
Aids: Bl: 0-0 Vi: 0-0 Tstrap: 0-0
Best Rating: 110 2/03 Extr 2m6f110y gd-sft Hdl

Got off the mark over hurdles when winning over two miles six on good to soft ground; looks a real stayer.

Grey Ciseaux (IRE)
100(96h)   (80+h)80
8-y-o gr g Mujtahid (USA)-Inisfail (Persian Bold)
A E Jones (Mrs S Gardner 29/6) Miss Sophie Parmentier

Placings:P030/51P63326/5/3656PP (4467)
2002/03: 25³G, 24⁶GF, 26⁵GF, 25⁶G, 24⁶F, 24⁵F,

	Starts	1st	2nd	3rd	Win & Pl
Chases	6	0	0	1	544
Career Total	19	1	1	4	4220
84 6/99 Kbgn 2m			Hdl	GD	£2455

Total win prize-money £2455

Going: Sf: 0-0 GS: 0-0 Gd: 0-2 GF: - Fm: 0-4
Distance: 2m/2m3: 0-0 2m4-2m7: 0-0 3m+: 0-6
Track: LH: 0-2 RH: 0-4 Tight: 0-4 Gall: 0-0
Aids: Bl: 0-0 Vi: 0-0 Tstrap: 0-0
Best Rating: 91 5/02 Extr 3m1f110y good Ch

Moderate chaser; winning pointer, suited by a sound surface.

Greycoat
87   83
5-y-o ch g Lion Cavern (USA)-It s Academic (Royal Academy (USA))
Jean-Rene Auvray Lambourn Racing

Placings:350U-4PP (1091)
2002/03: 16⁴GF, 16⁶GF, 17⁷GF,

	Starts	1st	2nd	3rd	Win & Pl
Hurdles	3	0	0	0	272
Career Total	7	0	0	1	626

Going: Sf: 0-0 GS: 0-0 Gd: 0-0 GF: - Fm: 0-3

Distance: 2m/2m3: 0-3 2m4-2m7: 0-0 3m+: 0-0
Track: LH: 0-2 RH: 0-1 Tight: 0-2 Gall: 0-0
Aids: Bl: 0-1 Vi: 0-0 Tstrap: 0-0
Best Rating: 83 9/01 Plum 2m   gd-fm Hdl

Greyfield (IRE)
95(85h)   (100h)108
7-y-o b g Persian Bold-Noble Dust (USA) (Dust Commander (USA))
K Bishop Slabs And Lucan

Placings:531F5/354/024-34 (3336)
2002/03: 16³GS, 16⁴S,

	Starts	1st	2nd	3rd	Win & Pl
Chases	2	0	0	1	1148
Career Total	13	1	1	3	12591
120 3/00 Winc 2m			E Hdl	G-S	£2247

Total win prize-money £2247

Going: Sf: 0-1 GS: 0-1 Gd: 0-0 GF: - Fm: 0-0
Distance: 2m/2m3: 0-2 2m4-2m7: 0-0 3m+: 0-0
Track: LH: 0-0 RH: 0-2 Tight: 0-2 Gall: 0-0
Aids: Bl: 0-0 Vi: 0-0 Tstrap: 0-0
Best Rating: 136 9/00 Chep 2m110y good Hdl

He was a useful juvenile in 1999-2000 and ran creditably in the face of stiff tasks last season. Raced around two miles, he has been running creditably back on the Flat and ran well when runner-up on his chasing debut. Lightly-raced since.

Greyton (IRE)
10-y-o gr g Zaffaran (USA)-Rosy Posy (IRE) (Roselier (FR))
R Rowe Tim Clowes

Placings:352045/34154/2-4 (3828)
2002/03: 19⁴GS,

	Starts	1st	2nd	3rd	Win & Pl
Chases	1	0	0	0	
Career Total	13	1	2	2	7541
98 1/01 Winc 3m1f110y			E(0-115)HCh		
SFT £4173					

Total win prize-money £4173

Going: Sf: 0-0 GS: 0-1 Gd: 0-0 GF: - Fm: 0-0
Distance: 2m/2m3: 0-0 2m4-2m7: 0-1 3m+: 0-0
Track: LH: 0-1 RH: 0-0 Tight: 0-0 Gall: 0-0
Aids: Bl: 0-0 Vi: 0-0 Tstrap: 0-0
Best Rating: 98 5/01 Hntg 3m   gd-fm Ch

Grimaldi Lass
5-y-o b m Factual (USA)-Carousel Zingira (Reesh)
M D Hammond A Saccomando

Placings:0 (1569)
2002/03: 17⁰G,

	Starts	1st	2nd	3rd	Win & Pl
NH Flat	1	0	0	0	
Career Total	1	0	0	0	

Going: Sf: 0-0 GS: 0-0 Gd: 0-1 GF: - Fm: 0-0
Distance: 2m/2m3: 0-1 2m4-2m7: 0-0 3m+: 0-0
Track: LH: 0-0 RH: 0-1 Tight: 0-0 Gall: 0-0
Aids: Bl: 0-0 Vi: 0-0 Tstrap: 0-0
Best Rating: 0 10/02 MRas 2m1f110y good NHF

Grizzly Golfwear (IRE)
9-y-o b g Commanche Run-Dunwellan (Tekoah)
Mrs S E Hughes Mrs S E Hughes

Placings:FP/5P500/P06-23F (4736)
2002/03: 24²GS, 24³GF, 24⁶GF,

	Starts	1st	2nd	3rd	Win & Pl
Chases	3	0	1	1	1429
Career Total	13	0	1	1	1429

Going: Sf: 0-0 GS: 0-1 Gd: 0-0 GF: - Fm: 0-2
Distance: 2m/2m3: 0-0 2m4-2m7: 0-0 3m+: 0-3
Track: LH: 0-3 RH: 0-0 Tight: 0-2 Gall: 0-0
Aids: Bl: 0-0 Vi: 0-0 Tstrap: 0-0
Best Rating: 85 4/03 Chep 3m   gd-fm Ch

Hunter chaser; dual winning pointer; effective on good.

Groovejet
4-y-o b g Emperor Jones (USA)-Sir Hollow (USA) (Sir Ivor)
J R Jenkins R M Ellis

Placings:P (1729)
2002/03: 16⁶GS,

	Starts	1st	2nd	3rd	Win & Pl
Hurdles	1	0	0	0	
Career Total	1	0	0	0	

Going: Sf: 0-0 GS: 0-1 Gd: 0-0 GF: - Fm: 0-0
Distance: 2m/2m3: 0-1 2m4-2m7: 0-0 3m+: 0-0
Track: LH: 0-0 RH: 0-1 Tight: 0-0 Gall: 0-0
Aids: Bl: 0-0 Vi: 0-0 Tstrap: 0-0
Best Rating: 0 11/02 Asct 2m110y gd-sft Hdl

Ground Ball (IRE)
116(110h)   (113h)137
6-y-o b/br g Bob s Return (IRE)-Bettyhill (Ardross)
C F Swan J P McManus

Placings:1/42105-F2123F2 (4208a)
2002/03: 16⁵S, 16²G, 20¹S, 21²S, 20³HY, 24⁶YS, 20²Y,

	Starts	1st	2nd	3rd	Win & Pl
Hurdles	1	0	1	0	1662
Chases	6	1	2	0	19232
Career Total	13	3	4	1	35206
135 12/02 Navn 2m4f			Ch	SFT	£6773
121 1/02 Navn 2m			Hdl	Y-S	£8009
123 4/01 Cork 2m			NHF	Y-S	£4173

Total win prize-money £18955

Going: Sf: 1-3 GS: 0-0 Gd: 0-1 GF: - Fm: 0-0
Distance: 2m/2m3: 0-2 2m4-2m7: 1-4 3m+: 0-1
Track: LH: 1-4 RH: 0-2 Tight: 0-1 Gall: 0-0
Aids: Bl: 0-0 Vi: 0-0 Tstrap: 0-0
Best Rating: 137 2/03 Sand 2m4f110y heavy Ch

Fair Irish novice chaser; stays two and a half miles; ran with credit in graded events in early in 2003; acts on soft ground.

Group One's Hope
(73h)   (10h)
7-y-o b m Absalom-Hopeful Waters (Forlorn River)
A W Carroll Group 1 Racing (1994) Ltd

Placings:0/0-P0FP (2060)

2002/03: 19^PGF, 16^9G, 16^FG, 16^PS,

	Starts	1st	2nd	3rd	Win & PI
Hurdles	2	0	0	0	0
Chases	2	0	0	0	0
Career Total	6	0	0	0	

Going: Sf: 0-1 GS: 0-0 Gd: 0-2 GF: - Fm: 0-1
Distance: 2m/2m3: 0-3 2m4-2m7: 0-1 3m+: 0-0
Track: LH: 0-2 RH: 0-2 Tight: 0-2 Gall: 0-0
Aids: BI: 0-0 Vi: 0-0 Tstrap: 0-0
Best Rating: 14 10/02 Strf 2m110y good Hdl

Grouse Hall
107   96+
9-y-o ch g Primitive Rising (USA)-Em-Kay-Em (Slim Jim)
M Todhunter P E Sowerby

Placings: 10/6U0026/4/4-32   (2100)
2002/03: 20^3GS, 19^2G,

	Starts	1st	2nd	3rd	Win & PI
Chases	2	0	1	1	2299
Career Total	12	1	2	1	4720

103 3/99 Ayr 2m H NHF SFT £1346
Total win prize-money £1347

Going: Sf: 0-0 GS: 0-1 Gd: 0-1 GF: - Fm: 0-0
Distance: 2m/2m3: 0-1 2m4-2m7: 0-1 3m+: 0-0
Track: LH: 0-2 RH: 0-0 Tight: 0-1 Gall: 0-0
Aids: BI: 0-0 Vi: 0-0 Tstrap: 0-0
Best Rating: 103 3/99 Ayr 2m soft NHF

Won a bumper in the soft, has had problems since but showed promise when third over fences at Wetherby in November. Suffered a hind leg injury when runner-up at Catterick the following month.

Grouse Moor (USA)
85f   86f
4-y-o b g Distant View (USA)-Caithness (USA) (Roberto (USA))
P Winkworth Tweenhills Racing (Cleeve Hill)

Placings: 40   (3754)
2002/03: 18^4HY, 16^9G,

	Starts	1st	2nd	3rd	Win & PI
NH Flat	2	0	0	0	0
Career Total	2	0	0	0	0

Going: Sf: 0-1 GS: 0-0 Gd: 0-1 GF: - Fm: 0-0
Distance: 2m/2m3: 0-2 2m4-2m7: 0-0 3m+: 0-0
Track: LH: 0-1 RH: 0-1 Tight: 0-1 Gall: 0-0
Aids: BI: 0-0 Vi: 0-0 Tstrap: 0-0
Best Rating: 86 2/03 Kemp 2m good NHF

Grove House
90   81
7-y-o b g Hatim (USA)-Camden Grove (Uncle Pokey)
Miss Victoria Scott (A Scott 16/5) A Rice

Placings: 3420-20   (4762)
2002/03: 24^2GF, 16^9G,

	Starts	1st	2nd	3rd	Win & PI
Hurdles	2	0	1	0	866
Career Total	6	0	2	1	1890

Going: Sf: 0-0 GS: 0-0 Gd: 0-1 GF: - Fm: 0-1
Distance: 2m/2m3: 0-1 2m4-2m7: 0-0 3m+: 0-0
Track: LH: 0-0 RH: 0-2 Tight: 0-0 Gall: 0-0

Aids: BI: 0-0 Vi: 0-0 Tstrap: 0-0
Best Rating: 103 4/02 Hexm 2m110y gd-fm NHF

Fair form in bumpers and hurdles, stays three miles and acts on a fast surface.

Grumpy Stumpy
(91h)   (81h)96
8-y-o ch g Gunner B-Moaning Jenny (Privy Seal)
N A Twiston-Davies The Yes - No - Wait Sorries

Placings: 23/36F33-4   (1921)
2002/03: 24^4GS,

	Starts	1st	2nd	3rd	Win & PI
Chases	1	0	0	0	438
Career Total	8	0	1	4	2878

Going: Sf: 0-0 GS: 0-1 Gd: 0-0 GF: - Fm: 0-0
Distance: 2m/2m3: 0-0 2m4-2m7: 0-0 3m+: 0-1
Track: LH: 0-1 RH: 0-0 Tight: 0-0 Gall: 0-1
Aids: BI: 0-0 Vi: 0-0 Tstrap: 0-0
Best Rating: 112 3/01 Newb 2m110y heavy NHF

Guard Duty
107   128
6-y-o b g Deploy-Hymne D Amour (USA) (Dixieland Band (USA))
M C Pipe Neil Edwards And Malcolm Jones

Placings: 211114/2000-50F350   (4456)
2002/03: 25^5GS, 24^0HY, 24^FG, 23^3GS, 25^5G, 24^0G,

	Starts	1st	2nd	3rd	Win & PI
Hurdles	6	0	0	1	4790
Career Total	16	4	2	1	19544

131 2/01 Wwck 2m5f E(0-115)HHdl SFT £3818
125 2/01 Tntn 2m3f110yF(0-110)HHdl HVY £3540
134 1/01 Tntn 2m3f110yF(0-100)HHdl HVY £2381
112 1/01 Tntn 2m1f G Hdl SFT £1631
Total win prize-money £11372

Going: Sf: 0-1 GS: 0-2 Gd: 0-3 GF: - Fm: 0-0
Distance: 2m/2m3: 0-0 2m4-2m7: 0-0 3m+: 0-6
Track: LH: 0-6 RH: 0-0 Tight: 0-1 Gall: 0-3
Aids: BI: 0-0 Vi: 0-0 Tstrap: 0-6
Best Rating: 134 1/01 Tntn 2m3f110y heavy Hdl

Fair hurdler; acts well on a soft surface; suited by trips around two miles five furlongs, but just stays three; usually tongue tied these days.

Gudlage (USA)
96(92c)   (111c)109+
7-y-o b g Gulch (USA)-Triple Kiss (Shareef Dancer (USA))
M W Easterby Lord Daresbury

Placings: 0/1P3003-12   (4415)
2002/03: 16^1GS, 17^2G,

	Starts	1st	2nd	3rd	Win & PI
Hurdles	2	1	1	0	5855
Career Total	9	2	1	2	10546

109 11/02 Newc 2m E(0-110)HHdl G-S £3259
96 10/01 Aint 2m110y E Hdl GD £3248
Total win prize-money £6507

Going: Sf: 0-0 GS: 1-1 Gd: 0-1 GF: - Fm: 0-0
Distance: 2m/2m3: 1-2 2m4-2m7: 0-0 3m+: 0-0
Track: LH: 1-1 RH: 0-1 Tight: 0-1 Gall: 1-1
Aids: BI: 0-0 Vi: 0-0 Tstrap: 1-2
Best Rating: 109 3/03 MRas 2m1f110y good Hdl

Fair hurdler; best over two miles; winner at Newcastle in

November and runner-up at Market Rasen in March; goes well fresh; usually tongue tied.

Gue Au Loup (FR)
99   99
9-y-o gr g Royal Charter (FR)-Arche D Alliance (FR) (Pamponi (FR))
H D Daly Mr & Mrs M P Wiggin

Placings: 2552/F5/2/12-05U346   (4192)
2002/03: 21^0G, 16^5S, 16^UGS, 20^3S, 20^4S, 20^6G,

	Starts	1st	2nd	3rd	Win & PI
Chases	6	0	0	1	1437
Career Total	15	1	4	1	15595

109 5/01 Bang 2m1f110yF(0-100)HCh G-S £4485
Total win prize-money £4485

Going: Sf: 0-3 GS: 0-1 Gd: 0-2 GF: - Fm: 0-0
Distance: 2m/2m3: 0-2 2m4-2m7: 0-3 3m+: 0-0
Track: LH: 0-3 RH: 0-3 Tight: 0-4 Gall: 0-0
Aids: BI: 0-0 Vi: 0-0 Tstrap: 0-0
Best Rating: 120 5/01 Bang 2m4f110y good Ch

Ex-French; moderate chaser; effective at around two and a half miles; acts on fast ground.

Guernsey Bob
5-y-o ch g Beveled (USA)-Martian Melody (Enchantment (ZIM))
R J Hodges Footsteps Flyers

Placings: 0   (1937)
2002/03: 17^0GS,

	Starts	1st	2nd	3rd	Win & PI
NH Flat	1	0	0	0	
Career Total	1	0	0	0	

Going: Sf: 0-0 GS: 0-1 Gd: 0-0 GF: - Fm: 0-0
Distance: 2m/2m3: 0-1 2m4-2m7: 0-0 3m+: 0-0
Track: LH: 0-0 RH: 0-0 Tight: 0-0 Gall: 0-0
Aids: BI: 0-0 Vi: 0-0 Tstrap: 0-0
Best Rating: 0 11/02 Tntn 2m1f gd-sft NHF

Guest Line (FR)
85   70
4-y-o ch g Ashkalani (IRE)-Double Line (FR) (What A Guest)
C J Mann (B J Meehan 24/7) Mrs L G Turner

Placings: 3   (1174)
2002/03: 16^9GF,

	Starts	1st	2nd	3rd	Win & PI
Hurdles	1	0	0	1	652
Career Total	1	0	0	1	652

Going: Sf: 0-0 GS: 0-0 Gd: 0-0 GF: - Fm: 0-1
Distance: 2m/2m3: 0-1 2m4-2m7: 0-0 3m+: 0-0
Track: LH: 0-1 RH: 0-0 Tight: 0-1 Gall: 0-0
Aids: BI: 0-0 Vi: 0-0 Tstrap: 0-0
Best Rating: 70 9/02 Strf 2m110y gd-fm Hdl

Guid Willie Waught (IRE)
109(103h)   (85h)102+
8-y-o ch g Montelimar (USA)-Drumdeels Star (IRE) (Le Bavard (FR))
J R Adam J W Hazeldean

Placings:5506/32604654-1125   (0915)
2002/03: 21¹G, 22¹GF, 20²GF, 20⁵GS,

	Starts	1st	2nd	3rd	Win & Pl
Chases	4	2	1	0	11198
Career Total	16	2	2	1	13256
102 6/02 MRas 2m6f110yE(0-105)HCh G-F £3786
91 5/02 Strf 2m5f110yD(0-110)HCh GD £4891
Total win prize-money £8677

Going:	Sf: 0-0 GS: 0-1 Gd: 1-1 GF: - Fm: 1-2
Distance:	2m/2m3: 0-0 2m4-2m7: 2-4 3m+: 0-0
Track:	LH: 1-2 RH: 1-2 Tight: 2-3 Gall: 0-0
Aids:	Bl: 0-0 Vi: 0-0 Tstrap: 0-0
Best Rating:	102 6/02 MRas 2m6f110y gd-fm Ch

Fair novice chaser, suited by fast ground and two and a half miles.

Guignol Du Cochet (FR)
104   95
9-y-o ch g Secret Of Success-Pasquita (FR) (Bourbon (FR))
Mrs L Richards The Guignol Partnership

Placings:P14P4P0/4403251322240/221340/0224F (3743)
2002/03: 16⁵G, 16²GS, 16²GS, 16⁴HY, 16⁶G,

	Starts	1st	2nd	3rd	Win & Pl
Chases	5	0	2	0	2892
Career Total	31	3	8	3	21913
102 12/00 Folk 2m F(0-100)HCh SFT £2359
99 11/99 Worc 2m F(0-100)HCh GD £2530
5/98 Fntb 2m3f Ch GD £3232
Total win prize-money £8121

Going:	Sf: 0-1 GS: 0-2 Gd: 0-2 GF: - Fm: 0-0
Distance:	2m/2m3: 0-5 2m4-2m7: 0-0 3m+: 0-0
Track:	LH: 0-2 RH: 0-3 Tight: 0-2 Gall: 0-1
Aids:	Bl: 0-0 Vi: 0-0 Tstrap: 0-0
Best Rating:	102 1/01 Folk 2m heavy Ch

Came back after a year and a half off to run well on second start finishing runner-up at Southwell in December.

Guilsborough Gorse
108   100
8-y-o b g Past Glories-Buckby Folly (Netherkelly)
T D Walford Mrs E C York

Placings:32P3/525F31-22P105334   (4787)
2002/03: 20²GF, 17²GF, 20⁵GF, 20¹G, 24⁵GS, 23⁵GF, 17³G, 20³G, 20⁴G,

	Starts	1st	2nd	3rd	Win & Pl
Chases	9	1	2	2	8225
Career Total	19	2	4	5	15251
100 10/02 Hexm 2m4f110yD(0-115)HCh GD £4550
96 4/02 Weth 2m4f110yE Ch £3503
Total win prize-money £8054

Going:	Sf: 0-0 GS: 0-1 Gd: 1-4 GF: - Fm: 0-4
Distance:	2m/2m3: 0-0 2m4-2m7: 1-5 3m+: 0-2
Track:	LH: 1-4 RH: 0-4 Tight: 0-4 Gall: 0-1
Aids:	Bl: 0-1 Vi: 0-0 Tstrap: 0-0
Best Rating:	100 10/02 Hexm 2m4f110y good Ch

Won a point-to-point in Febuary 2000, he has shown moderate form over fences and eventually broke his duck in a modest event at Wetherby in April 2002; scored at Hexham in October.

Gulch King (USA)
88   62
5-y-o b g Gulch (USA)-Crockadore (USA) (Nijinsky (CAN))

G L Moore Paul Chapman

Placings:0P0-0   (2058)
2002/03: 16⁵G,

	Starts	1st	2nd	3rd	Win & Pl
Hurdles	1	0	0	0	
Career Total	4	0	0	0	

Going:	Sf: 0-0 GS: 0-0 Gd: 0-1 GF: - Fm: 0-0
Distance:	2m/2m3: 0-1 2m4-2m7: 0-0 3m+: 0-0
Track:	LH: 0-0 RH: 0-0 Tight: 0-0 Gall: 0-0
Aids:	Bl: 0-0 Vi: 0-0 Tstrap: 0-0
Best Rating:	62 11/02 Kemp 2m good Hdl

Gumley Gale
114   121d
8-y-o b g Greensmith-Clodaigh Gale (Strong Gale)
K Bishop Portcullis Racing

Placings:34/0/2631F512-14065   (2630)
2002/03: 20¹G, 20⁴G, 19⁴G, 22⁶S, 20⁵S,

	Starts	1st	2nd	3rd	Win & Pl
Hurdles	5	1	0		11005
Career Total	16	3	2	2	21454
121 5/02 Uttx 2m4f110yB(0-140)HHdl GD £10478
121 11/01 NAbb 2m6f D(0-125)HHdl GD £3267
110 7/01 Worc 2m4f E(0-115)HHdl SFT £3510
Total win prize-money £17256

Going:	Sf: 0-2 GS: 0-0 Gd: 1-3 GF: - Fm: 0-0
Distance:	2m/2m3: 0-0 2m4-2m7: 1-5 3m+: 0-0
Track:	LH: 1-3 RH: 0-2 Tight: 0-0 Gall: 0-0
Aids:	Bl: 0-0 Vi: 0-0 Tstrap: 0-0
Best Rating:	121 5/02 Uttx 2m4f110y good Hdl

Fair handicap hurdler, handles any ground and stays two miles six.

Gumption
104   105
5-y-o b g Muhtarram (USA)-Dancing Spirit (IRE) (Ahonoora)
K C Bailey (J L Dunlop 6/6) Sir David Sieff

Placings:2   (3852)
2002/03: 24²GS,

	Starts	1st	2nd	3rd	Win & Pl
Hurdles	1	0	1	0	1370
Career Total	1	0	1	0	1370

Going:	Sf: 0-0 GS: 0-1 Gd: 0-0 GF: - Fm: 0-0
Distance:	2m/2m3: 0-0 2m4-2m7: 0-0 3m+: 0-1
Track:	LH: 0-0 RH: 0-1 Tight: 0-1 Gall: 0-0
Aids:	Bl: 0-0 Vi: 0-0 Tstrap: 0-0
Best Rating:	105 2/03 Tntn 3m110y gd-sft Hdl

Fair maiden on the Flat; promising over hurdles.

Gun Shot
84(105h)   (99h)30
8-y-o ch m Gunner B-Real Beauty (Kinglet)
N M Babbage B & M Babbage & Co Ltd

Placings:002/6P0/006113102-6060   (2944)
2002/03: 21⁵GF, 24³GS, 24⁵HY, 24⁰GS,

	Starts	1st	2nd	3rd	Win & Pl
Hurdles	3	0	0	0	241
Chases	1	0	0	0	0
Career Total	19	3	2	1	15735
99 11/01 Towc 2m5f D(0-125)HHdl SFT £6994
99 8/01 MRas 3m D Hdl G-F £4241

| 89 7/01 Sthl 3m110y F(0-90)HHdl G-F £2296 |
| Total win prize-money £13531 |

Going:	Sf: 0-1 GS: 0-2 Gd: 0-0 GF: - Fm: 0-1
Distance:	2m/2m3: 0-0 2m4-2m7: 0-1 3m+: 0-3
Track:	LH: 0-3 RH: 0-1 Tight: 0-2 Gall: 0-1
Aids:	Bl: 0-0 Vi: 0-0 Tstrap: 0-0
Best Rating:	99 3/02 Towc 3m soft Hdl

Fair handicap hurdler. She stays well and landed a brace of novice hurdles in the summer.

Gun'n Roses II (FR)
104   143
9-y-o gr g Royal Charter (FR)-Offenbach li (FR) (Ermitage (FR))
T D Easterby Lady Clarke

Placings:11P32/12P0/3P/1P11P/3F516F-P1P6 (3885)
2002/03: 21⁶GS, 20¹GS, 24⁶G, 20⁶G,

	Starts	1st	2nd	3rd	Win & Pl
Hurdles	1	0	0	0	
Chases	3	1	0	0	10907
Career Total	26	8	2	3	62862
143 12/02 Weth 2m4f110yB(0-145)HCh G-S £10907
145 1/02 Donc 2m3f110yC(0-130)HCh SFT £6376
134 3/01 Hayd 2m6f D Ch HVY £5671
145 2/01 Wwck 2m4f110yC(0-130)HCh SFT £6695
138 12/00 Chep 2m3f110yD(0-125)HCh SFT £6776
116 5/98 Uttx 2m E Hdl G-S £2263
1/98 Pau 2m2f Hdl SFT £6061
12/97 Pau 2m110y Hdl VS £6734
Total win prize-money £51485

Going:	Sf: 0-0 GS: 1-2 Gd: 0-2 GF: - Fm: 0-0
Distance:	2m/2m3: 0-0 2m4-2m7: 1-3 3m+: 0-1
Track:	LH: 1-3 RH: 0-1 Tight: 0-1 Gall: 0-1
Aids:	Bl: 0-1 Vi: 0-0 Tstrap: 0-0
Best Rating:	145 1/02 Donc 2m3f110y soft Ch

Very useful chaser; has been around a few yards; has won at up to two miles six; suited by cut in the ground.

Gung Ho (IRE)
60   72
6-y-o b g Mister Lord (USA)-Deruma Lady (IRE) (Black Minstrel)
M C Pipe (M Pitman 26/8) G-Force Partnership

Placings:052   (4386)
2002/03: 16⁰G, 22⁵GF, 19²F,

	Starts	1st	2nd	3rd	Win & Pl
NH Flat	1	0	0	0	
Hurdles	2	0	1	0	1542
Career Total	3	0	1	0	1542

Going:	Sf: 0-0 GS: 0-0 Gd: 0-0 GF: - Fm: 0-3
Distance:	2m/2m3: 0-2 2m4-2m7: 0-1 3m+: 0-0
Track:	LH: 0-2 RH: 0-1 Tight: 0-1 Gall: 0-0
Aids:	Bl: 0-0 Vi: 0-0 Tstrap: 0-0
Best Rating:	72 3/03 Extr 2m3f firm Hdl

Showed nothing in a bumper and a hurdle for Mark Pitman; fortunate to finish second in weak 19 furlong novice hurdle on firm ground at Exeter on first start for Martin Pipe March 2003.

Gunner B Special
96   76
10-y-o ch g Gunner B-Sola Mia (Tolomeo)
R Lee The Eagle Racing Partnership

Placings:04P/0400/P/0102566-5   (0039)
2002/03: 19⁵G,

	Starts	1st	2nd	3rd	Win & Pl
Chases	1	0	0	0	0
Career Total	16	1	1	0	3721
73 7/01 Worc 2m			F(0-95)HCh	SFT	£2756
			Total win prize-money £2756		

Going:	Sf: 0-0 GS: 0-0 Gd: 0-0 GF: - Fm: 0-0
Distance:	2m/2m3: 0-0 2m4-2m7: 0-1 3m+: 0-0
Track:	LH: 0-0 RH: 0-1 Tight: 0-0 Gall: 0-0
Aids:	Bl: 0-0 Vi: 0-0 Tstrap: 0-0
Best Rating:	76 5/02 Extr 2m3f110y good Ch

Fair novice chaser, suited by easy ground and two miles. Good efforts given those conditions in the summer of 2001. Lightly raced since.

Gunner Dream

89   75

7-y-o b g Gunner B-Star Route (Owen Dudley)
C Grant The Hon Mrs M Faulkner

Placings:543   (3831)
2002/03: 24⁵G, 20⁴HY, 25³G,

	Starts	1st	2nd	3rd	Win & Pl
Chases	3	0	0	1	1573
Career Total	3	0	0	1	1573

Going:	Sf: 0-1 GS: 0-0 Gd: 0-2 GF: - Fm: 0-0
Distance:	2m/2m3: 0-0 2m4-2m7: 0-1 3m+: 0-2
Track:	LH: 0-3 RH: 0-0 Tight: 0-0 Gall: 0-2
Aids:	Bl: 0-0 Vi: 0-0 Tstrap: 0-0
Best Rating:	75 1/03 Newc 2m4f heavy Ch

Runner-up in maiden points but struggling under Rules.

Gunner Sid

96   57

12-y-o ch g Gunner B-At Long Last (John French)
W Jenks W Jenks

Placings:653/2/00OFU0/20F0661/10010P1/111/3-6055
              (4735)
2002/03: 20⁶GS, 24⁰S, 20⁵G, 19⁵GF,

	Starts	1st	2nd	3rd	Win & Pl
Chases	4	0	0	0	0
Career Total	32	7	2	2	12433
7/00 LES 2m1f			Hdl	G-S	£1500
6/00 LES 2m2f			HHdl	G-F	£1050
5/00 LES 2m			HHdl	GD	£1050
4/00 LES 2m			HHdl	GD	£1050
93 12/99 Ludl 2m			E(0-115)HHdl	G-S	£3225
7/99 LES 2m1f			Hdl	G-F	£1200
91 3/99 Hrfd 2m1f			G Hdl	G-S	£1870
			Total win prize-money £10945		

Going:	Sf: 0-1 GS: 0-1 Gd: 0-1 GF: - Fm: 0-1
Distance:	2m/2m3: 0-0 2m4-2m7: 0-3 3m+: 0-1
Track:	LH: 0-1 RH: 0-3 Tight: 0-3 Gall: 0-0
Aids:	Bl: 0-0 Vi: 0-0 Tstrap: 0-0
Best Rating:	98 1/96 Hayd 2m soft NHF

Gunner Welburn

119   144

11-y-o ch g Gunner B-Vedra (IRE) (Carlingford Castle)
A M Balding (I A Balding 27/12) W A Ritson/D H Hall

Placings:1/111/F121/5122-13014   (4479)
2002/03: 24¹S, 29³HY, 24⁹G, 24¹S, 36⁴G,

	Starts	1st	2nd	3rd	Win & Pl
Chases	5	2	0	1	56101

		Career Total	17	9	3	1	114580
144	3/03	Newb 3m		C(0-130)HCh	SFT	£9966
138	12/02	Chep 3m		C(0-130)HCh	SFT	£7884
119	2/02	Hayd 2m6f		H Ch	HVY	£6890
144	4/01	Aint 2m5f110yB Ch			SFT	£18460
140	2/01	Hayd 3m		H Ch	HVY	£6857
128	4/00	Bang 3m110y		H Ch	G-S	£1715
128	2/00	Font 3m2f110yH Ch			SFT	£3591
110	2/00	Wwck 3m1f110yH Ch			GD	£1270
105	4/99	Chel 3m1f110yH Ch			G-S	£2775
		Total win prize-money £59411				

Going:	Sf: 2-3 GS: 0-0 Gd: 0-2 GF: - Fm: 0-0
Distance:	2m/2m3: 0-0 2m4-2m7: 0-0 **3m+: 2-5**
Track:	**LH: 2-5** RH: 0-0 Tight: 0-1 **Gall: 1-2**
Aids:	Bl: 0-0 Vi: 0-0 Tstrap: 0-0
Best Rating:	**144** 3/03 Newb 3m soft Ch

Useful staying handicap chaser; formerly a top hunter chaser; highly impressive when winning at Chepstow in December 2002 on his first run for his new stable; held in better races subsequently before an easy win at Newbury; made much of the running when fourth in the Grand National; revels in the mud; stays well; jumps well.

Gunnerbe Posh

95(92h)   (84h)66

9-y-o ch g Rakaposhi King-Triggered (Gunner B)
Noel T Chance Mrs S Maxse & J Maxse

Placings:23/P00240-00   (3316)
2002/03: 20⁰S, 19⁰G,

	Starts	1st	2nd	3rd	Win & Pl
Hurdles	2	0	0	0	
Career Total	10	0	2	1	1407

Going:	Sf: 0-1 GS: 0-1 Gd: 0-0 GF: - Fm: 0-0
Distance:	2m/2m3: 0-1 2m4-2m7: 0-1 3m+: 0-0
Track:	LH: 0-0 RH: 0-2 Tight: 0-0 Gall: 0-1
Aids:	Bl: 0-0 Vi: 0-0 Tstrap: 0-0
Best Rating:	105 3/99 Newb 2m110y soft NHF

Gunsmoke

5-y-o gr g Thethingaboutitis (USA)-Fairy Princess (USA) (Fairy King (USA))
D McCain Mrs S K Maan

Placings:0P   (4316)
2002/03: 16⁰G, 17⁷G,

	Starts	1st	2nd	3rd	Win & Pl
NH Flat	1	0	0	0	0
Hurdles	1	0	0	0	0
Career Total	2	0	0	0	

Going:	Sf: 0-0 GS: 0-0 Gd: 0-2 GF: - Fm: 0-0
Distance:	2m/2m3: 0-2 2m4-2m7: 0-0 3m+: 0-0
Track:	LH: 0-2 RH: 0-0 Tight: 0-2 Gall: 0-0
Aids:	Bl: 0-0 Vi: 0-0 Tstrap: 0-0
Best Rating:	38 1/03 Sthl 2m good NHF

Gunson Hight

6-y-o b g Be My Chief (USA)-Glas Y Dorlan (Sexton Blake)
M Todhunter Lord Cavendish And Bill Parkinson

Placings:00   (3095)
2002/03: 16⁹GS, 16⁹GS,

	Starts	1st	2nd	3rd	Win & Pl
NH Flat	1	0	0	0	0

Hurdles	1	0	0	0	0
Career Total	2	0	0	0	

Gunther McBride (IRE)

112(115h)   (117h)146

8-y-o b g Glacial Storm (USA)-What Side (General Ironside)
P J Hobbs M J Tuckey

Placings:1/3P1/12221163-1052U3   (4791)
2002/03: 25¹HY, 26⁹GS, 24⁵HY, 24²G, 33⁹G, 29³G,

	Starts	1st	2nd	3rd	Win & Pl
Hurdles	1	1	0	0	4310
Chases	5	0	1	1	39750
Career Total	18	6	4	3	134348
120	11/02 Kemp 3m1f	D(0-120)HHdl	HVY	£4309
146	2/02 Kemp 3m	A HCh	GD	£52200
125	1/02 Kemp 3m	D(0-125)HCh	SFT	£7215
117	10/01 Extr 2m6f110yE Hdl		GD	£2716
106	4/01 Leop 3m	Ch	SH	£5564
78	4/00 Cork 3m	Ch	Y-S	£3588
		Total win prize-money £75594		

Going:	Sf: 1-2 GS: 0-1 Gd: 0-3 GF: - Fm: 0-0
Distance:	2m/2m3: 0-0 2m4-2m7: 0-0 **3m+: 1-6**
Track:	LH: 0-2 **RH: 1-4** Tight: 0-0 Gall: 0-1
Aids:	Bl: 0-0 Vi: 0-0 Tstrap: 0-0
Best Rating:	**146** 2/03 Kemp 3m good Ch

Very useful handicap chaser; keen sort; won the Racing Post Chase at Kempton in 2002 and runner-up in 2003; winner over hurdles first time out in 2002/3; acts on good and soft ground; effective at three miles, stays four; likes a right-handed track and goes well at Kempton.

Guru

109   108

5-y-o b g Slip Anchor-Ower (IRE) (Lomond (USA))
G L Moore (S Dow 6/1) Will Bennett

Placings:164-3P0011   (4214)
2002/03: 17⁹G, 21⁷G, 16⁹HY, 16⁰S, 16¹S, 18¹G,

	Starts	1st	2nd	3rd	Win & Pl
Hurdles	6	2	0	1	10327
Career Total	9	3	0	1	13539
108	3/03 Font 2m2f110yD(0-115)HHdl	GD	£5079
108	2/03 Plum 2m D(0-115)HHdl	SFT	£4823
101	12/01 Folk 2m1f110yE Hdl	SFT	£2894
		Total win prize-money £12798		

Going:	Sf: 1-3 GS: 0-0 Gd: 1-3 GF: - Fm: 0-0
Distance:	**2m/2m3: 2-5** 2m4-2m7: 0-1 3m+: 0-0
Track:	**LH: 2-3** RH: 0-3 **Tight: 2-3** Gall: 0-0
Aids:	Bl: 0-0 Vi: 0-0 Tstrap: 0-0
Best Rating:	108 3/03 Font 2m2f110y good Hdl

Modest hurdler; acts on good and soft ground; is effective at around two miles.

Gus Berry (IRE)

10-y-o ch g Montelimar (USA)-Eurolink Sea Baby (Deep Run)
P England P England

Placings: 10P/P2520/FPP145/6P11P/U4240-35   (4261)
2002/03: 27³S, 27⁵G,

	Starts	1st	2nd	3rd	Win & Pl
Chases	2	0	0	1	219
Career Total	26	4	3	1	17929
96	2/01	Sedg	3m3f		F(0-110)HCh	G-S	£4026
103	12/00	Sedg	3m3f		F(0-95)HCh	SFT	£3978
106	2/00	Sedg	3m3f110yF(0-110)HHdl			G-S	£5239
84	12/97	Catt	2m		H NHF		G-S	£1213

Total win prize-money £14458

Going: Sf: 0-1 GS: 0-0 Gd: 0-1 GF: - Fm: 0-0
Distance: 2m/2m3: 0-0 2m4-2m7: 0-0 3m+: 0-2
Track: LH: 0-2 RH: 0-0 Tight: 0-2 Gall: 0-0
Aids: Bl: 0-0 Vi: 0-0 Tstrap: 0-0
Best Rating: 106   2/00   Sedg   3m3f110y   gd-sft   Hdl

Hunter chaser; likes Sedgefield; stays well; best with give in the ground.

Gus Des Bois (FR)
105   118
9-y-o ch g Lampon (FR)-Fiacina (FR) (Fiasco)
R H Alner The Cd Partnership

Placings: F61/53512/F0F2010/254/F4-UP4213P   (4175)
2002/03: 27ᵁGS, 24ᴾS, 16⁴G, 20²GS, 20¹HY, 19³GS, 21ᴾS,

	Starts	1st	2nd	3rd	Win & Pl
Chases	7	1	1	1	10047
Career Total	27	4	4	2	36748
118	1/03	Plum	2m4f		D(0-125)HCh	HVY	£5395
	4/00	Drtl	2m6f110y	Ch		SFT	£3074
	8/98	LE L	2m4f		Ch		SFT	£7071
	4/98	Ange	2m2f110y	Ch		HVY	£3030

Total win prize-money £18570

Going: Sf: 1-3 GS: 0-3 Gd: 0-1 GF: - Fm: 0-0
Distance: 2m/2m3: 0-1 2m4-2m7: 1-4 3m+: 0-2
Track: LH: 1-5 RH: 0-2 Tight: 1-2 Gall: 0-0
Aids: Bl: 1-3 Vi: 0-0 Tstrap: 0-0
Best Rating: 118   2/03   Chep   2m3f110y   gd-sft   Ch

Winning chaser in France at up to two miles six furlongs; won at Plumpton in January 2003 when fitted with blinkers; acts on a soft surface; best going left-handed.

Gwen

4-y-o ch f Beveled (USA)-Taffidale (Welsh Pageant)
B L Lay B L Lay

Placings: 0   (3747)
2002/03: 16⁰G,

	Starts	1st	2nd	3rd	Win & Pl
NH Flat	1	0	0	0	
Career Total	1	0	0	0	

Going: Sf: 0-0 GS: 0-0 Gd: 0-1 GF: - Fm: 0-0
Distance: 2m/2m3: 0-1 2m4-2m7: 0-0 3m+: 0-0
Track: LH: 0-0 RH: 0-0 Tight: 0-0 Gall: 0-1
Aids: Bl: 0-0 Vi: 0-0 Tstrap: 0-0
Best Rating: 0   2/03   Hntg   2m110y   good   NHF

Gypsy (IRE)
107   101
7-y-o b g Distinctly North (USA)-Winscarlet North (Garland Knight)
Ian Williams (Miss Venetia Williams 3/6) Favourites Racing

Placings: 5333015-463314020   (1805)

2002/03: 24⁴GF, 20⁶GS, 20³G, 22³GF, 20¹GS, 20⁴G, 20⁰G, 21²G, 20⁰G,

	Starts	1st	2nd	3rd	Win & Pl
Hurdles	9	1	1	2	6567
Career Total	16	2	1	5	11812
101	7/02	Wolv	2m4f110yE(0-110)HHdl			G-S	£3284
97	3/02	Strf	2m3f		G Hdl		G-S	£2912

Total win prize-money £6196

Going: Sf: 0-0 GS: 1-2 Gd: 0-0 GF: - Fm: 0-2
Distance: 2m/2m3: 0-0 2m4-2m7: 1-8 3m+: 0-1
Track: LH: 1-8 RH: 0-1 Tight: 1-5 Gall: 0-0
Aids: Bl: 0-0 Vi: 0-0 Tstrap: 0-0
Best Rating: 101   10/02   Sedg   2m5f110y   good   Hdl

Had to be dropped into a seller to get off the mark at Stratford in March 2002. Added a modest handicap hurdle at Wolverhampton in July. Suited by two miles and easy ground.

Gypsy Music (IRE)
63   8
7-y-o b m Treasure Kay-Mighty Special (IRE) (Head For Heights)
I W McInnes Robert E Cook

Placings: 0   (1471)
2002/03: 17⁰GF,

	Starts	1st	2nd	3rd	Win & Pl
Hurdles	1	0	0	0	
Career Total	1	0	0	0	

Going: Sf: 0-0 GS: 0-0 Gd: 0-0 GF: - Fm: 0-1
Distance: 2m/2m3: 0-0 2m4-2m7: 0-0 3m+: 0-0
Track: LH: 0-0 RH: 0-1 Tight: 0-0 Gall: 0-0
Aids: Bl: 0-0 Vi: 0-0 Tstrap: 0-0
Best Rating: 14   10/02   Carl   2m1f   gd-fm   Hdl

Haafel (USA)
96 (98h)   (104h) 104
6-y-o ch g Diesis-Dish Dash (Bustino)
G L Moore D R Hunnisett

Placings: 0/1P66P-U2   (4429)
2002/03: 21ᴾG, 18ᵁGS, 21²GF,

	Starts	1st	2nd	3rd	Win & Pl
Hurdles	3	0	1	0	1096
Career Total	8	1	1	0	3483
111	11/01	Font	2m4f		E Hdl		G-S	£2387

Total win prize-money £2387

Going: Sf: 0-0 GS: 0-1 Gd: 0-1 GF: - Fm: 0-1
Distance: 2m/2m3: 0-1 2m4-2m7: 0-0 3m+: 0-0
Track: LH: 0-3 RH: 0-0 Tight: 0-3 Gall: 0-0
Aids: Bl: 0-1 Vi: 0-0 Tstrap: 0-0
Best Rating: 111   11/01   Font   2m4f   gd-sft   Hdl

Plating-class hurdler; acts in soft and fast ground; stays 2m 5f; has worn blinkers.

Hachty Boy (FR)
(104h) 111
7-y-o br g Cadoudal (FR)-Hachty Girl (FR) (Ashtar)
Miss H C Knight David Zeffman

Placings: 55606/015344/32324-0P   (0508)
2002/03: 23⁰G, 23ᴾG,

	Starts	1st	2nd	3rd	Win & Pl
Chases	2	0	0	0	
Career Total	18	1	2	3	7658
111	11/00	Hrfd	2m3f110yF(0-100)HHdl			G-S	£2733

Total win prize-money £2734

Going: Sf: 0-0 GS: 0-0 Gd: 0-2 GF: - Fm: 0-0
Distance: 2m/2m3: 0-0 2m4-2m7: 0-0 3m+: 0-2
Track: LH: 0-1 RH: 0-0 Tight: 0-0 Gall: 0-0
Aids: Bl: 0-0 Vi: 0-0 Tstrap: 0-0
Best Rating: 111   11/01   Strf   2m4f   soft   Ch

He showed fair form in novice hurdles and was placed on his first three starts over fences and appreciated the step up to three miles when opening his account at Wetherby in May 2003.

Hadaway Lad

11-y-o ch g Meadowbrook-Little Swinburn (Apollo Eight)
R A Ross (Trainer Unknown 26/5) S A Sinclair

Placings: 0/65P0/0   (0402)
2002/03: 20⁰GF,

	Starts	1st	2nd	3rd	Win & Pl
Chases	1	0	0	0	0
Career Total	6	0	0	0	0

Going: Sf: 0-0 GS: 0-0 Gd: 0-0 GF: - Fm: 0-1
Distance: 2m/2m3: 0-0 2m4-2m7: 0-1 3m+: 0-0
Track: LH: 0-1 RH: 0-0 Tight: 0-0 Gall: 0-0
Aids: Bl: 0-1 Vi: 0-0 Tstrap: 0-0
Best Rating: 50   12/96   Catt   2m3f   good   Hdl

Hades De Sienne (FR)
103 (96h)   (76h) 105
8-y-o g Concorde Jr (USA)-Aube De Sienne (FR) (Cupids Dew)
A Parker Mr & Mrs Raymond Anderson Green

Placings: PF454/22P13/4232F2-6P022   (3986)
2002/03: 25⁶S, 28ᴾS, 27⁰HY, 24²S, 26²S,

	Starts	1st	2nd	3rd	Win & Pl
Hurdles	1	0	0	0	
Chases	4	0	2	0	2764
Career Total	21	1	7	2	23457
94	1/01	Ayr	3m1f		E(0-105)HCh	SFT	£3256

Total win prize-money £3257

Going: Sf: 0-5 GS: 0-0 Gd: 0-0 GF: - Fm: 0-0
Distance: 2m/2m3: 0-0 2m4-2m7: 0-0 3m+: 0-5
Track: LH: 0-4 RH: 0-1 Tight: 0-2 Gall: 0-1
Aids: Bl: 0-0 Vi: 0-0 Tstrap: 0-0
Best Rating: 105   3/03   Carl   3m2f   soft   Ch

Modest, consistent handicap chaser; stays three miles; acts on soft ground.

Hadith
96   78
8-y-o h h Nashwan (USA)-Azyaa (Kris)
Ferdy Murphy Dennis Crozier

Placings: 063P   (3940)
2002/03: 16⁶S, 19⁶GS, 16³G, 17ᴾGS,

	Starts	1st	2nd	3rd	Win & Pl
Hurdles	4	0	0	1	624
Career Total	4	0	0	1	624

Going: Sf: 0-1 GS: 0-2 Gd: 0-1 GF: - Fm: 0-0
Distance: 2m/2m3: 0-3 2m4-2m7: 0-1 3m+: 0-0
Track: LH: 0-2 RH: 0-2 Tight: 0-2 Gall: 0-1

Aids: Bl: 0-0 Vi: 0-0 Tstrap: 0-0
Best Rating: 78 1/03 Muss 2m   good   Hdl

Winner twice in Dubai but little signs of ability over hurdles here so far.

Haditovski

114   **131**

7-y-o b g Hatim (USA)-Grand Occasion (Great Nephew)
J Mackie   Mrs Sue Adams

Placings: U641005662/20111140303126/220153206-52405
                                   (3899)
2002/03: 16^5HY, 16^2S, 16^4S, 16^9G, 16^5S,

	Starts	1st	2nd	3rd	Win & Pl
Hurdles	5	0	1	0	4450
Career Total	38	7	7	3	47351
131	12/01	Uttx	2m	C(0-130)HHdl	SFT	£4992
122	3/01	Newb	2m110y	C(0-130)HHdl	HVY	£5902
129	11/00	Hntg	2m110y	D(0-120)HHdl	G-S	£7117
120	11/00	Weth	2m	D(0-125)HHdl	HVY	£3601
110	11/00	Uttx	2m	F(0-100)HHdl	HVY	£2324
115	10/00	Sthl	2m	F(0-105)HHdl	SFT	£1808
111	11/99	Uttx	2m	E Hdl	SFT	£2337

Total win prize-money £28083

Going: Sf: 0-4 GS: 0-0 Gd: 0-1 GF: - Fm: 0-0
Distance: 2m/2m3: 0-5 2m4-2m7: 0-0 3m+: 0-0
Track: LH: 0-5 RH: 0-0 Tight: 0-0 Gall: 0-3
Aids: Bl: 0-0 Vi: 0-5 Tstrap: 0-0
Best Rating: 131 11/02 Newb 2m110y soft Hdl

Useful handicap hurdler; suited by around two miles and a soft surface; usually races prominently; regularly visored.

Haikal

94   **84**

6-y-o b g Owington-Magic Milly (Simply Great (FR))
E W Tuer   E Tuer

Placings: P45/52430021P-44600   (4434)
2002/03: 21^4GF, 21^4S, 16^6G, 22^9G, 20^9G,

	Starts	1st	2nd	3rd	Win & Pl
Hurdles	5	0	0	0	
Career Total	17	1	2	1	5354
88	4/02	Carl	2m4f	E(0-110)HHdl	GD	£2982

Total win prize-money £2982

Going: Sf: 0-1 GS: 0-0 Gd: 0-3 GF: - Fm: 0-1
Distance: 2m/2m3: 0-1 2m4-2m7: 0-4 3m+: 0-0
Track: LH: 0-3 RH: 0-1 Tight: 0-0 Gall: 0-1
Aids: Bl: 0-1 Vi: 0-0 Tstrap: 0-0
Best Rating: 93 2/01 Muss 2m   good   Hdl

Modest hurdler; stays two miles-four; acts on any ground.

Hailstorm (IRE)

102   **73**

10-y-o ch g Glacial Storm (USA)-Sindys Gale (Strong Gale)
Miss Lucinda V Russell   Peter K Dale Ltd

Placings: 064222100/4/6422/6P02143/1UFPP60-03232C6P06
                                 (4588)
2002/03: 20^0G, 20^3G, 24^2S, 24^3GF, 25^2GF, 20^CHY, 24^6GS, 20^9S, 20^6S, 20^6G,

	Starts	1st	2nd	3rd	Win & Pl
Chases	10	0	2	2	3263
Career Total	38	3	8	2	20547
95	9/01	MRas	2m4f	D(0-120)HCh	G-F	£4478
98	12/00	Ayr	2m5f110yD(0-110)HCh	SFT	£4046
111	2/98	Ludl	2m5f110yE Hdl	GD	£2500

Total win prize-money £11025

Going: Sf: 0-4 GS: 0-1 Gd: 0-3 GF: - Fm: 0-2
Distance: 2m/2m3: 0-0 2m4-2m7: 0-6 3m+: 0-4
Track: LH: 0-10 RH: 0-0 Tight: 0-1 Gall: 0-2
Aids: Bl: 0-0 Vi: 0-0 Tstrap: 0-0
Best Rating: 119 12/97 Strf   2m110y   soft   Hdl

Plating-class chaser; suited by a sound surface; probably needs further than two and a half miles.

Haithem (IRE)

6-y-o b g Mtoto-Wukk (IRE) (Glow (USA))
D Shaw   Century Racing

Placings: 0-P   (1207)
2002/03: 16^PG,

	Starts	1st	2nd	3rd	Win & Pl
Hurdles	1	0	0	0	
Career Total	2	0	0	0	

Going: Sf: 0-0 GS: 0-0 Gd: 0-1 GF: - Fm: 0-0
Distance: 2m/2m3: 0-1 2m4-2m7: 0-0 3m+: 0-0
Track: LH: 0-1 RH: 0-0 Tight: 0-0 Gall: 0-0
Aids: Bl: 0-0 Vi: 0-0 Tstrap: 0-0
Best Rating: 0   9/02 Uttx   2m   good   Hdl

Hakim (NZ)

107   **98**

9-y-o ch g Half Iced (USA)-Topitup (NZ) (Little Brown Jug (NZ))
J L Spearing   T N Siviter

Placings: 2-P350235   (3882)
2002/03: 16^PGS, 16^3S, 19^5GS, 17^9GS, 16^2GS, 17^3G, 16^5GS,

	Starts	1st	2nd	3rd	Win & Pl
Hurdles	7	0	1	2	1997
Career Total	8	0	2	2	3044

Going: Sf: 0-1 GS: 0-5 Gd: 0-1 GF: - Fm: 0-0
Distance: 2m/2m3: 0-6 2m4-2m7: 0-1 3m+: 0-0
Track: LH: 0-5 RH: 0-2 Tight: 0-1 Gall: 0-4
Aids: Bl: 0-0 Vi: 0-0 Tstrap: 0-0
Best Rating: 98 2/03 Hrfd   2m1f   good   Hdl

Modest hurdler; keen sort; effective at two miles.

Hale Bopp (GER)

108   **117+**

6-y-o b b h Monsun (GER)-Heatherland (FR) (Be My Guest (USA))
Frau E Mader   G K Stadtwald

Placings: F412   (4081)
2002/03: 18^FHY, 17^4HY, 17^1HY, 16^2HY,

	Starts	1st	2nd	3rd	Win & Pl
Hurdles	4	1	0	0	5276
Career Total	4	1	0	0	5276
117	2/03	Folk	2m1f110yE Hdl	HVY	£3612

Total win prize-money £3612

Going: Sf: 1-4 GS: 0-0 Gd: 0-0 GF: - Fm: 0-0
Distance: 2m/2m3: 1-4 2m4-2m7: 0-0 3m+: 0-0
Track: LH: 0-1 RH: 1-2 Tight: 1-3 Gall: 0-0
Aids: Bl: 0-0 Vi: 0-0 Tstrap: 0-0
Best Rating: 117 3/03 Plum   2m   heavy   Hdl

German-trained horse; fair novice hurdler; acts in heavy ground; effective at around two miles.

Halexy (FR)

113   **139**

8-y-o b g Iron Duke (FR)-Tartifume Ii (FR) (Mistigri)
Miss Venetia Williams   Sir Robert Ogden

Placings: 10116/4144/P-11U0   (3286)
2002/03: 19^1G, 20^1GS, 21^UHY, 21^9GS,

	Starts	1st	2nd	3rd	Win & Pl
Chases	4	2	0	0	19587
Career Total	14	6	0	0	33041
133	11/02	Chel	2m4f110yD(0-125)HCh	G-S	£12876
129	10/02	Chep	2m3f110yD(0-125)HCh	GD	£6711
128	12/00	Sthl	3m110y E Ch	SFT	£2866
119	2/00	MRas	2m3f110yD Hdl	G-S	£3282
128	1/00	Hayd	2m	D Hdl	SFT	£3266
110	11/99	NAbb	2m1f	H NHF	SFT	£1565

Total win prize-money £30568

Going: Sf: 0-1 GS: 1-2 Gd: 1-1 GF: - Fm: 0-0
Distance: 2m/2m3: 0-0 2m4-2m7: 2-4 3m+: 0-0
Track: LH: 2-4 RH: 0-0 Tight: 0-0 Gall: 1-3
Aids: Bl: 0-0 Vi: 0-0 Tstrap: 0-0
Best Rating: 133 11/02 Chel   2m4f110y   gd-sft   Ch

Useful handicap chaser; bounced back from injury with an easy win at Chepstow in October 2002; followed up at Cheltenham, but unable to supplement those wins since; acts well on soft but handles good; stays three miles but better at shorter.

Half A Calf

6-y-o ch g Jupiter Island-Chief Lady Nicola (Nicholas Bill)
R H Buckler   D R Fear

Placings: 400   (3476)
2002/03: 18^4S, 16^9S, 22^9GS,

	Starts	1st	2nd	3rd	Win & Pl
NH Flat	2	0	0	0	0
Hurdles	1	0	0	0	0
Career Total	3	0	0	0	0

Going: Sf: 0-2 GS: 0-1 Gd: 0-0 GF: - Fm: 0-0
Distance: 2m/2m3: 0-2 2m4-2m7: 0-1 3m+: 0-0
Track: LH: 0-1 RH: 0-2 Tight: 0-1 Gall: 0-0
Aids: Bl: 0-0 Vi: 0-0 Tstrap: 0-0
Best Rating: 85 12/02 Font   2m2f110y   soft   NHF

Half An Hour

103   **109**

6-y-o b g Alflora (IRE)-Country Mistress (Town And Country)
A King   C W Lane

Placings: 136-04410   (4602)
2002/03: 16^0G, 22^4GS, 24^4GS, 22^1GF, 21^0G,

	Starts	1st	2nd	3rd	Win & Pl
Hurdles	5	1	0	0	6172
Career Total	8	2	0	0	9788
106	3/03	Hayd	2m6f	D Hdl	G-F	£5031
114	1/02	Hayd	2m	H NHF	SFT	£2338

Total win prize-money £7369

Going: Sf: 0-0 GS: 0-2 Gd: 0-2 GF: - Fm: 1-0
Distance: 2m/2m3: 0-1 2m4-2m7: 1-3 3m+: 0-1
Track: LH: 1-2 RH: 0-3 Tight: 0-1 Gall: 0-1
Aids: Bl: 0-0 Vi: 0-0 Tstrap: 0-0
Best Rating: 114 2/02 Wwck   2m   soft   NHF

Modest novice hurdler; half-brother to winning pointer and novice chaser Libido; winner of a bumper and a novice hurdle, both at Haydock; stays two miles six; acts on fast and soft ground.

Half Each

11-y-o b m Weld-Golden Valley (Hotfoot)
Mrs C A Watson Mrs C A Watson

Placings:0/PP5U/LPP/P   (0083)
2002/03: 25PGS,

	Starts	1st	2nd	3rd	Win & Pl
Chases	1	0	0	0	
Career Total	9	0	0	0	0

Going: Sf: 0-0 GS: 0-1 Gd: 0-0 GF: - Fm: 0-0
Distance: 2m/2m3: 0-0 2m4-2m7: 0-0 3m+: 0-1
Track: LH: 0-1 RH: 0-0 Tight: 0-0 Gall: 0-0
Aids: Bl: 0-0 Vi: 0-0 Tstrap: 0-0
Best Rating: 45 3/99 Kels 2m6f110y good Hdl

Half Nelson
86   75

5-y-o br g Be My Chief (USA)-Petindia (Petong)
T R George Mrs Sharon C Nelson

Placings:0-4P   (0567)
2002/03: 16⁴G, 16PGS,

	Starts	1st	2nd	3rd	Win & Pl
Hurdles	2	0	0	0	0
Career Total	3	0	0	0	0

Going: Sf: 0-0 GS: 0-1 Gd: 0-1 GF: - Fm: 0-0
Distance: 2m/2m3: 0-2 2m4-2m7: 0-0 3m+: 0-0
Track: LH: 0-1 RH: 0-1 Tight: 0-0 Gall: 0-0
Aids: Bl: 0-0 Vi: 0-0 Tstrap: 0-0
Best Rating: 70 5/02 Towc 2m good Hdl

Half The Pot (IRE)
111   115

8-y-o b g Homo Sapien-Deep Green (Deep Run)
R Rowe Mrs P V Crocker

Placings:52P/46B0/B421111P-6654P1401F   (4214)
2002/03: 25⁶G, 25⁵HY, 22⁵S, 20⁴S, 20PHY, 17¹HY, 18⁴S, 20⁰S,
22¹S, 18FG,

	Starts	1st	2nd	3rd	Win & Pl
Hurdles	10	2	0	0	11089
Career Total	25	6	2	0	24320
113	3/03	Font	2m6f110yD(0-120)HHdl	SFT	£5460
108	1/03	Folk	2m1f110yD(0-115)HHdl	HVY	£4686
116	1/02	Font	2m2f110yD(0-125)HHdl	SFT	£4108
117	1/02	Plum	2m4f D(0-125)HHdl	SFT	£3444
96	12/01	Folk	2m6f110yF(0-105)HHdl	HVY	£2259
117	11/01	Folk	2m4f110yF(0-100)HHdl	SFT	£1897

Total win prize-money £21856

Going: Sf: 2-8 GS: 0-0 Gd: 0-2 GF: - Fm: 0-0
Distance: 2m/2m3: 1-3 2m4-2m7: 1-5 3m+: 0-2
Track: LH: 1-3 RH: 1-5 Tight: 2-5 Gall: 0-0
Aids: Bl: 0-0 Vi: 0-0 Tstrap: 0-0
Best Rating: 117 1/02 Plum 2m5f soft Hdl

Fair hurdler, seems suited by forcing tactics and used them
successfully to score four times in a row between November
2001 and January 2002, and to win at Folkestone in January
2003. Suited by soft ground. Stays two miles six.

Hall's Mill (IRE)

14-y-o ch g Buckskin (FR)-Grainne Geal (General Ironside)
Miss S Waugh Rupert C Irving

Placings:6/U/U23/456/1/F-3   (0032)
2002/03: 21³GF,

	Starts	1st	2nd	3rd	Win & Pl
Chases	1	0	0	1	558
Career Total	11	1	1	2	3532
101	5/00	Chel	2m5f	H Ch	GD	£2262

Total win prize-money £2262

Going: Sf: 0-0 GS: 0-0 Gd: 0-0 GF: - Fm: 0-1
Distance: 2m/2m3: 0-0 2m4-2m7: 0-1 3m+: 0-0
Track: LH: 0-1 RH: 0-0 Tight: 0-0 Gall: 0-1
Aids: Bl: 0-0 Vi: 0-0 Tstrap: 0-0
Best Rating: 109 5/98 Chep 3m good Ch

Winning pointer/hunter chaser, acted on most ground bar
extremes of going; reportedly retired.

Halland Park Lad (IRE)
89   88+

4-y-o ch g Danehill Dancer (IRE)-Lassalia (Sallust)
S Kirk S J McCay

Placings:4   (2417)
2002/03: 18⁴G,

	Starts	1st	2nd	3rd	Win & Pl
Hurdles	1	0	0	0	0
Career Total	1	0	0	0	0

Going: Sf: 0-0 GS: 0-0 Gd: 0-1 GF: - Fm: 0-0
Distance: 2m/2m3: 0-1 2m4-2m7: 0-0 3m+: 0-0
Track: LH: 0-1 RH: 0-0 Tight: 0-1 Gall: 0-0
Aids: Bl: 0-0 Vi: 0-0 Tstrap: 0-0
Best Rating: 88 12/02 Font 2m2f110y good Hdl

Hallyards Gael (IRE)
105(112h)   (115h)130

9-y-o br g Strong Gale-Secret Ocean (Most Secret)
L Lungo (Mrs M Reveley 26/12) G M Mair

Placings:4/411/32323-31P311   (4617)
2002/03: 17³G, 20¹GS, 20PGS, 21³GS, 20¹G, 24¹GF,

	Starts	1st	2nd	3rd	Win & Pl
Chases	6	3	0	2	23347
Career Total	15	5	2	5	34501
	4/03	Carl	3m	D Ch	G-F	£10800
124	3/03	Carl	2m4f	D Ch	GD	£7085
116	5/02	Weth	2m4f110yD Ch	G-S	£4256
116	10/00	Kels	2m110y	E Hdl	G-S	£2506
96	6/00	Prth	2m110y	D Hdl	GD	£3435

Total win prize-money £28082

Going: Sf: 0-0 GS: 1-3 Gd: 1-2 GF: - Fm: 1-1
Distance: 2m/2m3: 0-1 2m4-2m7: 2-4 3m+: 1-1
Track: LH: 1-4 RH: 2-2 Tight: 0-1 Gall: 0-0
Aids: Bl: 0-0 Vi: 0-0 Tstrap: 0-0
Best Rating: 124 3/03 Carl 2m4f good Ch

Fair novice chaser/hurdler; has had various problems but
sparkled on first outing for present trainer taking a novices
chase on fast ground at Carlisle in March; handed a
walkover at the same track the following month.

Hamadeenah
105   99

5-y-o ch m Alhijaz-Mahbob Dancer (FR) (Groom Dancer
(USA))
D McCain (K C Bailey 13/5) Mrs N L Spence

Placings:5416-55514152   (4798)

2002/03: 16⁵GF, 16⁵G, 17⁵G, 16¹G, 21⁴GF, 16¹GF, 16⁵G, 17²GF,

	Starts	1st	2nd	3rd	Win & Pl
Hurdles	8	2	1	0	7151
Career Total	12	3	1	0	9909
87	3/03	Ludl	2m	F Hdl	G-F	£3010
83	9/02	Uttx	2m	G Hdl	GD	£2058
93	3/02	Hntg	2m110y	E Hdl	G-F	£2758

Total win prize-money £7826

Going: Sf: 0-0 GS: 0-0 Gd: 1-4 GF: - Fm: 1-4
Distance: 2m/2m3: 2-7 2m4-2m7: 0-1 3m+: 0-0
Track: LH: 1-5 RH: 1-3 Tight: 0-3 Gall: 0-0
Aids: Bl: 0-0 Vi: 0-0 Tstrap: 0-0
Best Rating: 99 4/03 Sedg 2m1f gd-fm Hdl

Plating-class hurdler; effective at around two miles and acts
on a sound surface; likes to race prominently.

Hammock (IRE)
85   60

5-y-o b/br g Hamas (IRE)-Sure Victory (IRE) (Stalker)
P S McEntee Mr & Mrs Paul McEntee

Placings:P00   (4148)
2002/03: 21PGS, 20⁰G, 16⁰G,

	Starts	1st	2nd	3rd	Win & Pl
Hurdles	3	0	0	0	
Career Total	3	0	0	0	

Going: Sf: 0-0 GS: 0-1 Gd: 0-2 GF: - Fm: 0-0
Distance: 2m/2m3: 0-1 2m4-2m7: 0-2 3m+: 0-0
Track: LH: 0-1 RH: 0-2 Tight: 0-1 Gall: 0-2
Aids: Bl: 0-0 Vi: 0-0 Tstrap: 0-0
Best Rating: 60 3/03 Fknm 2m good Hdl

Hamunaptra
70   53

4-y-o ch g Alhijaz-Princess Dancer (Alzao (USA))
M Wigham (P L Gilligan 19/10) Michael Wigham

Placings:5PP   (4337)
2002/03: 16⁵GS, 16PS, 16PGF,

	Starts	1st	2nd	3rd	Win & Pl
Hurdles	3	0	0	0	
Career Total	3	0	0	0	

Going: Sf: 0-1 GS: 0-1 Gd: 0-0 GF: - Fm: 0-1
Distance: 2m/2m3: 0-3 2m4-2m7: 0-0 3m+: 0-0
Track: LH: 0-0 RH: 0-3 Tight: 0-0 Gall: 0-2
Aids: Bl: 0-0 Vi: 0-0 Tstrap: 0-0
Best Rating: 53 11/02 Hntg 2m110y gd-sft Hdl

Hanakham (IRE)

14-y-o b g Phardante (FR)-Evas Charm (Carlburg)
D McCain Jnr (D McCain 5/6) D A Malam

Placings:1U31/3/1/F0F/2604-3F511   (4565)
2002/03: 20³G, 25FG, 26⁵GS, 24¹S, 24¹GF,

	Starts	1st	2nd	3rd	Win & Pl
Hurdles	1	0	0	0	0
Chases	4	2	0	1	5740
Career Total	18	5	1	3	81274
95	4/03	Bang	3m110y	H Ch	G-F	£2373
107	3/03	Bang	3m110y	H Ch	SFT	£2331
153	11/99	Chel	3m3f110yB HCh	GD	£10250
159	3/97	Chel	3m110y	A Ch	G-F	£57282
140	10/96	Winc	3m1f110yD Ch	G-F	£3658

Total win prize-money £75895

Going:	Sf: 1-1 GS: 0-1 Gd: 0-2 Gf: - Fm: 1-1
Distance:	2m/2m3: 0-0 2m4-2m7: 0-1 3m+: 2-4
Track:	LH: 2-5 RH: 0-0 Tight: 2-5 Gall: 0-0
Aids:	Bl: 0-0 Vi: 0-0 Tstrap: 0-0
Best Rating:	160 2/99 Sand 3m110y good Ch

Modest hunter chaser these days; won the Sun Alliance Chase in 1997 but injury blighted his career; stays three and a quarter miles; acts on good and soft ground.

Hanbrin Rose
99   80

6-y-o gr m Lancastrian-Rymolbreese (Rymer)
R Dickin John Hanley

Placings:03   (4635)
2002/03: 16[0]GS, 19[3]GF,

	Starts	1st	2nd	3rd	Win & Pl
NH Flat	1	0	0	0	0
Hurdles	1	0	0	1	430
Career Total	**2**	**0**	**0**	**1**	**430**

Going:	Sf: 0-0 GS: 0-1 Gd: 0-0 GF: - Fm: 0-1
Distance:	2m/2m3: 0-2 2m4-2m7: 0-0 3m+: 0-0
Track:	LH: 0-1 RH: 0-1 Tight: 0-1 Gall: 0-0
Aids:	Bl: 0-0 Vi: 0-0 Tstrap: 0-0
Best Rating:	80 4/03 Strf 2m3f gd-fm Hdl

Modest third in low grade 2m 3f maiden on hurdling debut at Stratford April 2003.

Hancock
92   43

11-y-o b g Jester-Fresh Line (High Line)
J Hetherton L Turnbull,T Hornby,Mrs C Brown

Placings:54/60F23421/P/PU/50002U0F/0PPP00   (2688)
2002/03: 16[0]GS, 21[P]S, 17[P]S, 19[P]S, 16[0]S, 17[0]GS,

	Starts	1st	2nd	3rd	Win & Pl
Hurdles	6	0	0	0	
Career Total	**27**	**1**	**3**	**1**	**5281**
92 4/97 MRas 2m5f110y(0-105)HHdl			GD	£2272	

Total win prize-money £2273

Going:	Sf: 0-4 GS: 0-2 Gd: 0-0 GF: - Fm: 0-0
Distance:	2m/2m3: 0-4 2m4-2m7: 0-2 3m+: 0-0
Track:	LH: 0-3 RH: 0-3 Tight: 0-4 Gall: 0-1
Aids:	Bl: 0-0 Vi: 0-0 Tstrap: 0-0
Best Rating:	92 4/97 MRas 2m5f110y good Hdl

Hand Inn Hand
117(105h)   (133h)148+

7-y-o b g Alflora (IRE)-Deep Line (Deep Run)
H D Daly Patrick Burling Developments Ltd

Placings:141/015-311115   (4098)
2002/03: 19[3]S, 19[1]S, 20[1]S, 16[1]HY, 20[1]G, 16[5]G,

	Starts	1st	2nd	3rd	Win & Pl
Chases	6	4	0	1	49967
Career Total	**12**	**7**	**0**	**1**	**62941**
148 2/03 Kemp 2m4f110yA Ch			GD	£20300	
148 2/03 Uttx 2m C Ch			HVY	£10251	
141 12/02 Hayd 2m4f C Ch			SFT	£7722	
133 12/02 Chep 2m3f110yD Ch			SFT	£4784	
133 2/02 Asct 2m110y D(0-120)HHdl			SFT	£4836	
124 3/01 MRas 2m1f110yD Hdl			G-S	£3822	
118 1/01 Tntn 2m3f110yD Hdl			SFT	£3626	

Total win prize-money £55341

Going:	Sf: 3-4 GS: 0-0 Gd: 1-2 GF: - Fm: 0-0
Distance:	2m/2m3: 1-2 2m4-2m7: 3-4 3m+: 0-0
Track:	LH: 3-5 RH: 1-1 Tight: 0-0 Gall: 0-1
Aids:	Bl: 0-0 Vi: 0-0 Tstrap: 0-0
Best Rating:	148 3/03 Chel 2m good Ch

Smart novice chaser; easy winner of three modest events before decisively taking a Grade Two at Kempton in February 2003; a little disappointing when fifth in the Arkle; effective from 2m to 2m 4f; suited by cut in the ground, but handles good; regularly held up.

Handover

6-y-o b g Nearly A Hand-Keylu (Sula Bula)
M Madgwick S R Cobden

Placings:40P   (2984)
2002/03: 17[4]F, 16[0]HY, 18[0]HY,

	Starts	1st	2nd	3rd	Win & Pl
NH Flat	2	0	0	0	0
Hurdles	1	0	0	0	0
Career Total	**3**	**0**	**0**	**0**	**0**

Going:	Sf: 0-2 GS: 0-0 Gd: 0-0 GF: - Fm: 0-1
Distance:	2m/2m3: 0-3 2m4-2m7: 0-0 3m+: 0-0
Track:	LH: 0-2 RH: 0-0 Tight: 0-1 Gall: 0-0
Aids:	Bl: 0-0 Vi: 0-0 Tstrap: 0-0
Best Rating:	88 10/02 Tntn 2m1f firm NHF

Handsome Lad (IRE)

5-y-o b g Inzar (USA)-Elite Exhibition (Exhibitioner)
A Scott Andy Scott

Placings:P00P-P06   (4521)
2002/03: 22[P]GS, 20[0]G, 17[6]G,

	Starts	1st	2nd	3rd	Win & Pl
Hurdles	3	0	0	0	0
Career Total	**7**	**0**	**0**	**0**	**0**

Going:	Sf: 0-0 GS: 0-1 Gd: 0-2 GF: - Fm: 0-0
Distance:	2m/2m3: 0-1 2m4-2m7: 0-2 3m+: 0-0
Track:	LH: 0-3 RH: 0-0 Tight: 0-2 Gall: 0-0
Aids:	Bl: 0-0 Vi: 0-0 Tstrap: 0-0
Best Rating:	34 4/02 Sedg 2m1f gd-fm Hdl

Handy Money
105   122+

6-y-o b g Imperial Frontier (USA)-Cryptic Gold (Glint Of Gold)
M J Ryan William Dixon

Placings:000-4325214   (4048)
2002/03: 17[4]G, 16[3]G, 17[2]S, 16[5]S, 16[3]HY, 19[1]GS, 20[4]HY,

	Starts	1st	2nd	3rd	Win & Pl
NH Flat	1	0	0	0	0
Hurdles	6	1	2	1	9738
Career Total	**10**	**1**	**2**	**1**	**9738**
103 2/03 Donc 2m3f110yE Hdl			G-S	£3718	

Total win prize-money £3718

Going:	Sf: 0-4 GS: 1-1 Gd: 0-2 GF: - Fm: 0-0
Distance:	2m/2m3: 0-5 2m4-2m7: 1-2 3m+: 0-0
Track:	LH: 1-1 RH: 0-6 Tight: 0-2 Gall: 0-1
Aids:	Bl: 0-0 Vi: 0-0 Tstrap: 0-0
Best Rating:	109 2/03 Sand 2m110y heavy Hdl

Fair novice hurdler; finally got off the mark at Doncaster in February; acts on soft; stays nearly two and a half miles.

Handyman (IRE)
111   128

9-y-o b g Hollow Hand-Shady Ahan (Mon Capitaine)
P J Hobbs Elizabeth Hodgson And Denise Winton

Placings:2/2421/U12P36/126U22-12F3P3   (4603)
2002/03: 23[1]G, 23[2]G, 25[5]GS, 24[3]S, 24[P]HY, 26[3]G,

	Starts	1st	2nd	3rd	Win & Pl
Chases	6	1	1	2	17057
Career Total	**23**	**4**	**8**	**3**	**35716**
123 5/02 Extr 2m7f110yC(0-135)HCh			GD	£6916	
127 10/01 Extr 3m1f110yF(0-105)HCh			G-S	£3024	
127 11/00 Uttx 3m D Ch			HVY	£3740	
106 3/00 NAbb 2m6f E Hdl			GD	£2359	

Total win prize-money £16040

Going:	Sf: 0-2 GS: 0-1 Gd: 1-3 GF: - Fm: 0-0
Distance:	2m/2m3: 0-0 2m4-2m7: 0-0 3m+: 1-6
Track:	LH: 0-1 RH: 1-5 Tight: 0-0 Gall: 0-1
Aids:	Bl: 0-0 Vi: 0-0 Tstrap: 0-0
Best Rating:	128 12/02 Kemp 3m soft Ch

Useful handicap chaser; suited by three miles plus; acts on good and soft ground.

Hang'Em High
96   (114h)80+

9-y-o b g Supreme Leader-Culinary (Tower Walk)
Seamus O Farrell Seamus O Farrell

Placings:0/123/04/513P00/5343-0000000F   (2869a)
2002/03: 24[0]YS, 21[0]HY, 21[0]G, 16[6]S, 17[0]S, 16[0]S, 16[0]G, 20[0]HY,

	Starts	1st	2nd	3rd	Win & Pl
Hurdles	3	0	0	0	
Chases	5	0	0	0	
Career Total	**24**	**2**	**1**	**4**	**12129**
101 6/00 Cork 2m1f Hdl			G-F	£4140	
81 5/98 Tipp 2m4f NHF			G-F	£2382	

Total win prize-money £6523

Going:	Sf: 0-5 GS: 0-0 Gd: 0-2 GF: - Fm: 0-0
Distance:	2m/2m3: 0-4 2m4-2m7: 0-3 3m+: 0-1
Track:	LH: 0-3 RH: 0-2 Tight: 0-0 Gall: 0-0
Aids:	Bl: 0-1 Vi: 0-0 Tstrap: 0-0
Best Rating:	114 6/01 Gowr 2m gd-fm Hdl

Hang'Em Out To Dry (IRE)
106

12-y-o b g Executive Perk-Obsession (Wolver Hollow)
B De Haan Mrs S M Russell & Aidan Walls

Placings:60P/P/42113P/12/FP50P/16P0-P   (1490)
2002/03: 17[P]GS,

	Starts	1st	2nd	3rd	Win & Pl
Chases	1	0	0	0	
Career Total	**22**	**4**	**2**	**1**	**20341**
106 10/01 Bang 2m1f110yF(0-110)HCh			GD	£4845	
108 11/99 Kemp 2m D(0-120)HCh			GD	£4674	
99 1/99 Donc 2m110y E(0-105)HCh			G-S	£3935	
95 1/99 Leic 2m1f E(0-105)HCh			G-S	£3496	

Total win prize-money £16951

Going:	Sf: 0-0 GS: 0-1 Gd: 0-0 GF: - Fm: 0-0
Distance:	2m/2m3: 0-0 2m4-2m7: 0-0 3m+: 0-0
Track:	LH: 0-1 RH: 0-0 Tight: 0-1 Gall: 0-0
Aids:	Bl: 0-0 Vi: 0-0 Tstrap: 0-0
Best Rating:	115 11/99 Wwck 2m good Ch

Modest chaser; best around two miles; acts on good ground.

Hannah Park (IRE)
72   104
7-y-o b m Lycius (USA)-Wassl This Then (IRE) (Wassl)
P Monteith The Dregs Of Humanity

Placings:5/P1451-5   (0486)
2002/03: 20⁵GS,

	Starts	1st	2nd	3rd	Win & Pl
Hurdles	1	0	0	0	0
Career Total	7	2	0	0	7647
104	4/02	Prth	2m4f110yD(0-110)HHdl	GD	£4602
97	8/01	Ctml	2m1f110yE Hdl	GD	£3045
				Total win prize-money	£7647

Going:	Sf: 0-0 GS: 0-1 Gd: 0-0 GF: - Fm: 0-0
Distance:	2m/2m3: 0-0 2m4-2m7: 0-1 3m+: 0-0
Track:	LH: 0-0 RH: 0-1 Tight: 0-0 Gall: 0-0
Aids:	Bl: 0-0 Vi: 0-0 Tstrap: 0-0
Best Rating:	104 4/02 Prth 2m4f110y good Hdl

Hannibal Two
54f   5f
6-y-o b g Rock City-Appealing (Star Appeal)
P D Evans P D Evans

Placings:0   (2947)
2002/03: 16⁰S,

	Starts	1st	2nd	3rd	Win & Pl
NH Flat	1	0	0	0	
Career Total	1	0	0	0	

Going:	Sf: 0-1 GS: 0-0 Gd: 0-0 GF: - Fm: 0-0
Distance:	2m/2m3: 0-1 2m4-2m7: 0-0 3m+: 0-0
Track:	LH: 0-0 RH: 0-1 Tight: 0-0 Gall: 0-0
Aids:	Bl: 0-0 Vi: 0-0 Tstrap: 0-0
Best Rating:	5 1/03 Ludl 2m soft NHF

Hanoi Hanna

7-y-o b m Lancastrian-Farm Track (Saxon Farm)
R Johnson Harry Humble

Placings:P-P0   (0451)
2002/03: 21ᴾGF, 16⁰G,

	Starts	1st	2nd	3rd	Win & Pl
Hurdles	2	0	0	0	
Career Total	3	0	0	0	

Going:	Sf: 0-0 GS: 0-0 Gd: 0-1 GF: - Fm: 0-1
Distance:	2m/2m3: 0-1 2m4-2m7: 0-1 3m+: 0-0
Track:	LH: 0-2 RH: 0-0 Tight: 0-1 Gall: 0-0
Aids:	Bl: 0-0 Vi: 0-0 Tstrap: 0-0
Best Rating:	0 6/02 Hexm 2m110y good Hdl

Hanover Square
104(104h)   108d
7-y-o b g Le Moss-Hilly-Down Lass (Deep Run)
N A Twiston-Davies The Oriental Partnership Iii

Placings:60/U20P-253P44   (3946)
2002/03: 28²GS, 26⁵S, 27³GS, 30ᴾS, 24⁴S, 30⁴S,

	Starts	1st	2nd	3rd	Win & Pl
Chases	6	0	1	1	4082
Career Total	12	0	2	1	5346

Going:	Sf: 0-4 GS: 0-2 Gd: 0-0 GF: - Fm: 0-0

Distance:	2m/2m3: 0-0 2m4-2m7: 0-0 3m+: 0-6
Track:	LH: 0-3 RH: 0-3 Tight: 0-5 Gall: 0-0
Aids:	Bl: 0-0 Vi: 0-0 Tstrap: 0-0
Best Rating:	106 11/02 Tntn 3m3f gd-sft Ch

Good form in novice hurdles; has struggled to make his mark over fences and has not been foot perfect.

Hansbury (IRE)
97   117+
7-y-o gr g Roselier (FR)-Ramble Bramble (Random Shot)
P F Nicholls R M Penny

Placings:2F   (3428)
2002/03: 25²G, 26ᶠS,

	Starts	1st	2nd	3rd	Win & Pl
Chases	2	0	1	0	1272
Career Total	2	0	1	0	1272

Going:	Sf: 0-1 GS: 0-0 Gd: 0-1 GF: - Fm: 0-0
Distance:	2m/2m3: 0-0 2m4-2m7: 0-0 3m+: 0-2
Track:	LH: 0-0 RH: 0-1 Tight: 0-0 Gall: 0-0
Aids:	Bl: 0-0 Vi: 0-0 Tstrap: 0-0
Best Rating:	117 12/02 Hrfd 3m1f110y good Ch

Novice chaser; showed promise on his chasing debut but was sadly destroyed next time. (DEAD)

Hanseat (GER)
77   71
6-y-o b g Goofalik (USA)-Hanseatin (GER) (Pentathlon)
Frau E Mader Stall Africa

Placings:56-1F0   (3101)
2002/03: 16¹S, 20ᶠHO, 16⁰S,

	Starts	1st	2nd	3rd	Win & Pl
Hurdles	3	1	0	0	1595
Career Total	5	1	0	0	1758
	10/02	Brem	2m	Hdl	SFT £1595
				Total win prize-money	£1595

Going:	Sf: 1-2 GS: 0-0 Gd: 0-0 GF: - Fm: 0-0
Distance:	2m/2m3: 1-2 2m4-2m7: 0-1 3m+: 0-0
Track:	LH: 0-1 RH: 0-0 Tight: 0-1 Gall: 0-0
Aids:	Bl: 0-0 Vi: 0-0 Tstrap: 0-0
Best Rating:	71 1/03 Plum 2m soft Hdl

Happicat (IRE)
81(109h)   (119h)81+
8-y-o g Cataldi-Gladonia (Godswalk (USA))
P R Webber D A Beaumont

Placings:O6/0P00/23552/122120-0660   (0682)
2002/03: 16⁰G, 16⁶S, 17⁶GF, 17⁰G,

	Starts	1st	2nd	3rd	Win & Pl
Hurdles	1	0	0	0	0
Chases	3	0	0	0	0
Career Total	21	2	5	1	12598
115	7/01	Strf	2m110y C(0-130)HHdl	G-F	£4888
99	5/01	Hrfd	2m1f D(0-110)HHdl	GD	£3150
				Total win prize-money	£8038

Going:	Sf: 0-1 GS: 0-0 Gd: 0-2 GF: - Fm: 0-1
Distance:	2m/2m3: 0-4 2m4-2m7: 0-1 3m+: 0-0
Track:	LH: 0-3 RH: 0-1 Tight: 0-2 Gall: 0-0
Aids:	Bl: 0-0 Vi: 0-0 Tstrap: 0-0
Best Rating:	119 5/02 Hayd 2m good Hdl

Fair hurdler who goes well on fast ground and a tight track. Has won on a right-handed track but apparently prefers to go in the other direction.

Happy Change (GER)
104(95h)   (86h)96
9-y-o ch g Surumu (GER)-Happy Gini (USA) (Ginistrelli (USA))
Ian Williams (Miss Venetia Williams 26/5) Favourites Racing

Placings:1/0/0-332PP   (2672)
2002/03: 20³G, 16³GS, 16²G, 20ᴾS, 19ᴾS,

	Starts	1st	2nd	3rd	Win & Pl
Chases	5	0	1	2	3146
Career Total	8	1	1	2	6777
117	10/99	Uttx	2m	D Hdl	G-S £3631
				Total win prize-money	£3631

Going:	Sf: 0-2 GS: 0-1 Gd: 0-2 GF: - Fm: 0-0
Distance:	2m/2m3: 0-3 2m4-2m7: 0-2 3m+: 0-0
Track:	LH: 0-4 RH: 0-1 Tight: 0-2 Gall: 0-0
Aids:	Bl: 0-0 Vi: 0-0 Tstrap: 0-0
Best Rating:	117 10/99 Uttx 2m gd-sft Hdl

Novice chaser; placed in a Group One on the Flat; has been a long way off that form in recent years; possibly unsuited by really soft ground.

Happy Days
93   83
8-y-o b g Primitive Rising (USA)-Miami Dolphin (Derrylin)
James Moffatt (D Moffatt 15/11) C Lewis

Placings:050F333/30/45/64005-40PB2   (4434)
2002/03: 20⁴G, 17⁰G, 20ᴾS, 19ᴮG, 20²G,

	Starts	1st	2nd	3rd	Win & Pl
Hurdles	5	0	1	0	722
Career Total	21	0	1	4	2164

Going:	Sf: 0-1 GS: 0-0 Gd: 0-4 GF: - Fm: 0-0
Distance:	2m/2m3: 0-2 2m4-2m7: 0-3 3m+: 0-0
Track:	LH: 0-5 RH: 0-0 Tight: 0-3 Gall: 0-2
Aids:	Bl: 0-0 Vi: 0-0 Tstrap: 0-0
Best Rating:	92 3/99 Kels 2m110y soft Hdl

Plating-class novice hurdler.

Happy Hussar (IRE)
104(104c)   (88c)94d
10-y-o b g Balinger-Merry Mirth (Menelek)
Dr P Pritchard Dr J J Kabler

Placings:130P/U03PBP/02P5U/2401343546604-33P22031254   (4606)
2002/03: 26³G, 24³GS, 23ᴾS, 26²GF, 22²F, 25⁰GF, 20³GS, 22¹GS, 17²GS, 23⁶G, 24⁴G,

	Starts	1st	2nd	3rd	Win & Pl
Hurdles	8	1	3	1	7923
Chases	3	0	0	5	1151
Career Total	39	3	5	7	19301
94	12/02	Extr	2m6f110yF(0-100)HHdl	G-S	£2828
88	10/01	Hrfd	3m1f110yE Ch	GD	£3100
101	12/98	Ludl	2m H NHF	G-S	£1350
				Total win prize-money	£7279

Going:	Sf: 0-1 GS: 1-4 Gd: 0-3 GF: - Fm: 0-3
Distance:	2m/2m3: 0-1 2m4-2m7: 1-3 3m+: 0-7
Track:	LH: 0-8 RH: 1-3 Tight: 0-2 Gall: 0-2
Aids:	Bl: 0-0 Vi: 0-0 Tstrap: 0-0
Best Rating:	101 12/98 Ludl 2m gd-sft NHF

Modest handicap chaser/hurdler; stays well; acts on most ground.

Happy Medium (IRE)

10-y-o b g Fairy King (USA)-Belle Origine (USA) (Exclusive Native (USA))
Mrs T H Hayward Mrs T H Hayward

Placings:0/24050/000P/U   (4147)
2002/03: 21ᵁG,

	Starts	1st	2nd	3rd	Win & Pl
Chases	1	0	0		
Career Total	11	0	1	0	786

Going: Sf: 0-0 GS: 0-0 Gd: 0-1 GF: - Fm: 0-0
Distance: 2m/2m3: 0-0 2m4-2m7: 0-1 3m+: 0-0
Track: LH: 0-1 RH: 0-0 Tight: 0-1 Gall: 0-0
Aids: Bl: 0-0 Vi: 0-0 Tstrap: 0-0
Best Rating: 86 10/98 Towc 2m   gd-fm Hdl

Harasarah (FR)
97

8-y-o b g Glaieul (USA)-Carasarah (FR) (Noir Et Or)
M C Pipe Phil Lake, Huw Lake

Placings:40331051/F50/12F11F/F4F   (1607)
2002/03: 16ᶠGF, 21⁴GF, 19ᶠG,

	Starts	1st	2nd	3rd	Win & Pl
Chases	3	0	0		600
Career Total	20	5	1	2	51234
133	11/00	Plum	2m1f	E Ch	HVY £3122
133	11/00	Chep	2m110y	E Ch	HVY £2860
	5/00	Autl	2m2f	Hdl	VS £6244
	4/99	Autl	2m3f110y Hdl		VS £21529
	1/99	Pau	2m2f	Hdl	GD £6459

Total win prize-money £40214

Going: Sf: 0-0 GS: 0-0 Gd: 0-0 GF: 0-1 GF: - Fm: 0-2
Distance: 2m/2m3: 0-0 2m4-2m7: 0-2 3m+: 0-0
Track: LH: 0-3 RH: 0-0 Tight: 0-1 Gall: 0-0
Aids: Bl: 0-0 Vi: 0-0 Tstrap: 0-0
Best Rating: 133 11/00 Plum 2m1f   heavy Ch

A winning hurdler in France, he revelled in the mud when winning twice in November 2000 soon after arriving here but has had problems with his jumping and shown little since.

Harbour Bell
76   58

4-y-o b g Bal Harbour-Bellara (Thowra (FR))
J White (B R Millman 26/6) Nick Quesnel

Placings:50   (2213)
2002/03: 16⁵GS, 16⁰S,

	Starts	1st	2nd	3rd	Win & Pl
Hurdles	2	0	0	0	0
Career Total	2	0	0	0	0

Going: Sf: 0-1 GS: 0-1 Gd: 0-0 GF: - Fm: 0-0
Distance: 2m/2m3: 0-2 2m4-2m7: 0-0 3m+: 0-0
Track: LH: 0-2 RH: 0-0 Tight: 0-0 Gall: 0-2
Aids: Bl: 0-0 Vi: 0-0 Tstrap: 0-0
Best Rating: 52 11/02 Newb 2m110y   gd-sft Hdl

Harbour Pilot (IRE)
117   (128h)166+

8-y-o b g Be My Native (USA)-Las-Cancellas (Monksfield)
Noel Meade Kays Syndicate

Placings:110/2S11534/1161U2-3333   (4132)
2002/03: 26³GS, 24³HY, 24³YS, 26³G,

	Starts	1st	2nd	3rd	Win & Pl
Chases	4	0	0	4	67748
Career Total	20	7	2	5	190308
154	2/02	Leop	2m5f	Ch	HVY £43865
141	12/01	Fair	2m4f	Ch	YLD £31451
144	10/01	Gway	2m6f	Ch	SH £8125
141	12/00	Navn	2m4f	Hdl	HVY £13000
127	11/00	Naas	2m3f	Hdl	SH £4416
111	3/00	Navn	2m	NHF	Y-S £3588
97	1/00	Naas	2m	NHF	SH £3312

Total win prize-money £107758

Going: Sf: 0-1 GS: 0-1 Gd: 0-1 GF: - Fm: 0-0
Distance: 2m/2m3: 0-0 2m4-2m7: 0-0 3m+: 0-4
Track: LH: 0-4 RH: 0-0 Tight: 0-0 Gall: 0-2
Aids: Bl: 0-2 Vi: 0-0 Tstrap: 0-0
Best Rating: 166 3/03 Chel 3m2f110y good Ch

Useful chaser; good form in novice company in 2001/2; let down by his jumping when a fine third in the Hennessy at Newbury in November 2002; creditable placed efforts behind Beef Or Salmon in the Ericsson and the Irish Hennessy at Leopardstown since, and when third to Best Mate in the Cheltenham Gold Cup; stays three miles; has won on soft, acts on heavy; still improving.

Harbour Point (IRE)
96   71

7-y-o b g Glacial Storm (USA)-Forest Jem (Croghan Hill)
D J Caro Eddie Moss

Placings:0-136B3   (4692)
2002/03: 16¹GS, 17³S, 19⁶S, 19⁸GF, 22³G,

	Starts	1st	2nd	3rd	Win & Pl
NH Flat	1	1	0	0	1777
Hurdles	4	0	0	2	1159
Career Total	6	1	0	2	2935
101	10/02	Fknm	2m	H NHF	G-S £1776

Total win prize-money £1777

Going: Sf: 0-2 GS: 1-1 Gd: 0-1 GF: - Fm: 0-1
Distance: 2m/2m3: 1-2 2m4-2m7: 0-3 3m+: 0-0
Track: LH: 1-2 RH: 0-3 Tight: 1-3 Gall: 0-0
Aids: Bl: 0-0 Vi: 0-0 Tstrap: 0-0
Best Rating: 101 10/02 Fknm 2m   gd-sft NHF

Moderate hurdler; got off the mark in a bumper at Fakenham in October 2002; well beaten over hurdles to date and appears to have stamina limitations.

Harcamone (FR)
86(78h)   90

8-y-o br g Passing Sale (FR)-Raise A Baby (FR) (Albert De Vongy)
A G Hobbs (M Sheppard 29/4) R W Guilding

Placings:F3/FF00/002P115P/0FU34404F-65PP   (2603)
2002/03: 16ᶠGS, 16ᶠG, 20⁵GF, 16ᴾG, 20ᴾS,

	Starts	1st	2nd	3rd	Win & Pl
Hurdles	2	0	0	0	0
Chases	3	0	0	0	0
Career Total	27	2	1	2	10336
110	2/01	Bang	2m1f	F(0-110)HHdl	HVY £3623
96	1/01	Wwck	2m	E(0-105)HHdl	SFT £3653

Total win prize-money £7277

Going: Sf: 0-1 GS: 0-1 Gd: 0-2 GF: - Fm: 0-1
Distance: 2m/2m3: 0-3 2m4-2m7: 0-2 3m+: 0-0
Track: LH: 0-1 RH: 0-4 Tight: 0-3 Gall: 0-0
Aids: Bl: 0-0 Vi: 0-0 Tstrap: 0-2
Best Rating: 110 2/01 Bang 2m1f   heavy Hdl

Picked up a couple of weak hurdle races in the mud last term and is described by his trainer as an unpredictable character. Two miles suits him well.

Harchibald (FR)
109   124

4-y-o b g Perugino (USA)-Dame D Harvard (USA) (Quest For Fame)
Noel Meade (B Goudot 23/9) D P Sharkey

Placings:1403252   (4724a)
2002/03: 16¹S, 16⁴HY, 16⁰YS, 16³YS, 16²GY, 16⁵G, 16²GF,

	Starts	1st	2nd	3rd	Win & Pl
Hurdles	7	1	2	1	15274
Career Total	7	1	2	1	15274
125	12/02	Fair	2m	Hdl	SFT £5503

Total win prize-money £5503

Going: Sf: 1-2 GS: 0-0 Gd: 0-1 GF: - Fm: 0-1
Distance: 2m/2m3: 0-0 2m4-2m7: 0-0 3m+: 0-0
Track: LH: 0-3 RH: 1-4 Tight: 0-1 Gall: 0-0
Aids: Bl: 0-0 Vi: 0-0 Tstrap: 0-4
Best Rating: 125 12/02 Leop 2m   heavy Hdl

Useful Irish juvenile hurdler; held in better company since winning debut; effective in soft ground; has worn a tongue tie.

Hard Lines (USA)
108(104h)   (94h)101

7-y-o b g Silver Hawk (USA)-Arctic Eclipse (USA) (Northern Dancer)
M D Hammond Turner Technology Ltd

Placings:4FPU/140P-421   (1822)
2002/03: 17⁴G, 16²S, 16¹HY,

	Starts	1st	2nd	3rd	Win & Pl
Hurdles	1	0	0	0	0
Chases	2	1	1	0	4114
Career Total	11	2	1	0	6746
104	11/02	Hexm	2m110y	F(0-95)HCh	HVY £2775
94	8/01	Ctml	2m1f110yE(0-105)HHdl		G-S £2632

Total win prize-money £5408

Going: Sf: 1-2 GS: 0-0 Gd: 0-1 GF: - Fm: 0-0
Distance: 2m/2m3: 1-3 2m4-2m7: 0-0 3m+: 0-0
Track: LH: 1-2 RH: 0-1 Tight: 0-0 Gall: 0-0
Aids: Bl: 0-0 Vi: 0-0 Tstrap: 0-0
Best Rating: 104 11/02 Hexm 2m110y   heavy Ch

A modest peformer on the Flat and over hurdles, he ran creditably on his chasing debut at Carlisle in October 2002.

Hard Pressed (IRE)
80   44

7-y-o b g Jurado (USA)-Valantonia (IRE) (Over The River (FR))
B J Llewellyn Peter Gent

Placings:400P   (3780)
2002/03: 16⁴GF, 17⁰HY, 17⁰GS, 22ᴾGS,

	Starts	1st	2nd	3rd	Win & Pl
NH Flat	2	0	0	0	
Hurdles	2	0	0	0	
Career Total	4	0	0	0	

Going: Sf: 0-1 GS: 0-2 Gd: 0-0 GF: - Fm: 0-1
Distance: 2m/2m3: 0-3 2m4-2m7: 0-1 3m+: 0-0
Track: LH: 0-3 RH: 0-1 Tight: 0-0 Gall: 0-0
Aids: Bl: 0-0 Vi: 0-0 Tstrap: 0-0
Best Rating: 84 6/02 Worc 2m   gd-fm NHF

Hard To Know (IRE)
94   103+
5-y-o b g Common Grounds-Lady Fern (Old Vic)
P J Hobbs   Ms C Hehir

Placings:0002-10U (0613)
2002/03: 16¹GF, 17⁹G, 16ᵁGF,

	Starts	1st	2nd	3rd	Win & Pl
Hurdles	3	1	0	0	3533
Career Total	7	1	1	0	4377
103 5/02 Ludl	2m	E(0-105)HHdl		G-F	£3532
			Total win prize-money		£3533

Going:	Sf: 0-0 GS: 0-0 Gd: 0-1 GF: - Fm: 1-2
Distance:	2m/2m3: 1-3 2m4-2m7: 0-0 3m+: 0-0
Track:	LH: 0-2 RH: 1-1 Tight: 0-1 Gall: 0-0
Aids:	Bl: 1-3 Vi: 0-0 Tstrap: 0-0
Best Rating:	103 5/02 Ludl 2m gd-fm Hdl

Showed improved form when runner-up on firm ground in novices handicap at Exeter April 2002. Scored at Ludlow the following month.

Hard To Lay (IRE)
88   82+
5-y-o br m Dolphin Street (FR)-Yavarro (Raga Navarro (ITY))
P J Hobbs   Ms C Hehir

Placings:410 (0872)
2002/03: 17⁴G, 16¹GF, 17⁹GF,

	Starts	1st	2nd	3rd	Win & Pl
Hurdles	3	1	0	0	2310
Career Total	3	1	0	0	2310
81 7/02 Strf	2m110y	G Hdl		G-F	£2310
			Total win prize-money		£2310

Going:	Sf: 0-0 GS: 0-0 Gd: 0-1 GF: - Fm: 1-2
Distance:	2m/2m3: 1-3 2m4-2m7: 0-0 3m+: 0-0
Track:	LH: 1-3 RH: 0-0 Tight: 1-3 Gall: 0-0
Aids:	Bl: 0-0 Vi: 0-0 Tstrap: 0-0
Best Rating:	91 6/02 NAbb 2m1f good Hdl

Won a fast-ground seller on her second start over hurdles.

Harden Glen

12-y-o b g Respect-Polly Peril (Politico (USA))
C Storey   M H Walton

Placings:63/2032054312/63SPP0P/52503UPP/050-0 (0045)
2002/03: 25⁹GS,

	Starts	1st	2nd	3rd	Win & Pl
Chases	1	0	0	0	
Career Total	31	1	4	5	10723
97 4/99 Kels	3m1f	D Ch		G-F	£3837
			Total win prize-money		£3838

Going:	Sf: 0-0 GS: 0-1 Gd: 0-0 GF: - Fm: 0-0
Distance:	2m/2m3: 0-0 2m4-2m7: 0-0 3m+: 0-1
Track:	LH: 0-1 RH: 0-0 Tight: 0-1 Gall: 0-0
Aids:	Bl: 0-0 Vi: 0-0 Tstrap: 0-0
Best Rating:	97 5/99 Weth 3m1f good Ch

Hardi De Chalamont (FR)
94(86c)   85
8-y-o gr g Royal Charter (FR)-Naita Ii (FR) (Dom Luc (FR))
A Parker   Mr & Mrs Raymond Anderson Green

Placings:14/1FP2/F3P-554234F0 (4591)
2002/03: 16⁵GF, 16⁵GF, 17⁴S, 18⁵S, 18³HY, 20⁴S, 16⁵S, 16⁹G,

	Starts	1st	2nd	3rd	Win & Pl
Hurdles	6	0	1	1	1884
Chases	2	0	0	0	0
Career Total	17	2	2	2	14035
5/00 Fntb	2m3f	Ch		GD	£3074
1/00 Pau	2m2f	Hdl		SFT	£5764
			Total win prize-money		£8838

Going:	Sf: 0-5 GS: 0-0 Gd: 0-1 GF: - Fm: 0-2
Distance:	2m/2m3: 0-7 2m4-2m7: 0-1 3m+: 0-0
Track:	LH: 0-6 RH: 0-2 Tight: 0-3 Gall: 0-0
Aids:	Bl: 0-0 Vi: 0-7 Tstrap: 0-0
Best Rating:	111 4/01 Ayr 2m good Ch

Hardy Breeze (IRE)
94   (55h)78
12-y-o b g Henbit (USA)-Chake-Chake (Goldhill)
Miss A M Newton-Smith   Mrs John Grist

Placings:P5606/5P656/02P30051/56P25/000552-33 (0339)
2002/03: 25³GS, 25³G,

	Starts	1st	2nd	3rd	Win & Pl
Chases	2	0	0	2	1009
Career Total	31	1	3	3	6638
83 4/00 Plum	3m2f	F(0-90)HCh		GD	£2898
			Total win prize-money		£2898

Going:	Sf: 0-0 GS: 0-1 Gd: 0-1 GF: - Fm: 0-0
Distance:	2m/2m3: 0-0 2m4-2m7: 0-0 3m+: 0-2
Track:	LH: 0-0 RH: 0-2 Tight: 0-0 Gall: 0-0
Aids:	Bl: 0-0 Vi: 0-0 Tstrap: 0-0
Best Rating:	85 12/96 Folk 2m6f110y gd-sft Hdl

Moderate staying chaser. Seems to handle any ground.

Hardy Eustace (IRE)
124   149
6-y-o b g Archway (IRE)-Sterna Star (Corvaro (USA))
D T Hughes   Laurence Byrne

Placings:516-111215 (4473)
2002/03: 16¹S, 16¹SH, 20¹HY, 18²S, 21¹G, 24⁵G,

	Starts	1st	2nd	3rd	Win & Pl
Hurdles	6	4	1	0	114634
Career Total	9	5	1	0	138775
149 3/03 Chel	2m5f	A Hdl		GD	£58000
144 12/02 Leop	2m4f	Hdl		HVY	£11963
144 12/02 Fair	2m	Hdl		SH	£27914
123 11/02 Punc	2m	Hdl		SFT	£5503
120 4/02 Fair	2m	NHF		YLD	£24141
			Total win prize-money		£127521

Going:	Sf: 2-3 GS: 0-0 Gd: 1-2 GF: - Fm: 0-0
Distance:	2m/2m3: 2-3 2m4-2m7: 2-2 3m+: 0-1
Track:	LH: 2-4 RH: 2-2 Tight: 0-1 Gall: 1-1
Aids:	Bl: 0-0 Vi: 0-0 Tstrap: 0-0
Best Rating:	149 3/03 Chel 2m5f good Hdl

Smart Irish novice hurdler; winner of a string of novice hurdles before famous victory in the Royal & SunAlliance Novices Hurdle at the 2003 Festival; stays 2m 5f and will get further; acts on testing ground; an exciting long term prospect but ran badly at Aintree.

Harebelle
96   68
6-y-o b m Almoojid-Velvet Heart (IRE) (Damister (USA))
A D Smith   David M Williams

Placings:00P/60-FU00 (3497)
2002/03: 17⁵GS, 24ᵁS, 16⁰HY, 21⁹GS,

	Starts	1st	2nd	3rd	Win & Pl
Hurdles	4	0	0	0	
Career Total	9	0	0	0	0

Going:	Sf: 0-2 GS: 0-2 Gd: 0-0 GF: - Fm: 0-0
Distance:	2m/2m3: 0-2 2m4-2m7: 0-1 3m+: 0-1
Track:	LH: 0-1 RH: 0-3 Tight: 0-1 Gall: 0-0
Aids:	Bl: 0-0 Vi: 0-0 Tstrap: 0-0
Best Rating:	67 2/03 Kemp 2m5f gd-sft Hdl

Harem Scarem (IRE)
95(95h)   (64h)86
12-y-o b g Lord Americo-River Rescue (Over The River (FR))
Mrs L Williamson   Halewood International Ltd

Placings:014/06PB30F6/O003410622120F2/0P535136P52-224 (2036)
2002/03: 21²G, 21²G, 17⁴HY,

	Starts	1st	2nd	3rd	Win & Pl
Chases	3	0	2	0	2082
Career Total	40	4	7	4	21151
86 2/02 Hrfd	2m	F(0-100)HCh		HVY	£3848
84 3/01 Ling	2m	F(0-95)HCh		HVY	£2947
83 1/01 Leic	2m	G(0-90)HHdl		HVY	£1932
102 8/97 Tral	2m1f	NHF		SFT	£3391
			Total win prize-money		£12118

Going:	Sf: 0-1 GS: 0-0 Gd: 0-2 GF: - Fm: 0-0
Distance:	2m/2m3: 0-1 2m4-2m7: 0-2 3m+: 0-0
Track:	LH: 0-3 RH: 0-0 Tight: 0-3 Gall: 0-0
Aids:	Bl: 0-0 Vi: 0-0 Tstrap: 0-0
Best Rating:	102 8/97 Tral 2m1f soft NHF

Modest two-mile chaser, although stays further, likes to front run and effective in testing ground.

Harfdecent
84   112
12-y-o b g Primitive Rising (USA)-Grand Queen (Grand Conde (FR))
Mrs M Reveley   A G Knowles

Placings:0/030P413/453112/F314P/332112P/P0/3P26F-66FU2 (1096)
2002/03: 22⁶G, 20⁶GS, 23⁶S, 23ᵁS, 21²GF,

	Starts	1st	2nd	3rd	Win & Pl
Chases	5	0	1	0	1160
Career Total	38	6	5	7	35048
124 1/00 Donc	2m3f110y	C(0-130)HCh		G-F	£5993
114 1/00 Muss	3m	E(0-115)HCh		SFT	£3575
113 2/99 Donc	2m3f110y	E(0-115)HCh		G-F	£2960
108 4/98 Sedg	2m5f	E(0-115)HCh		G-S	£4055
108 3/98 Catt	2m3f	D Ch		SFT	£3574
88 3/97 Sedg	2m5f110y	E Hdl		G-F	£2253
			Total win prize-money		£22410

Going:	Sf: 0-2 GS: 0-1 Gd: 0-1 GF: - Fm: 0-1
Distance:	2m/2m3: 0-2 2m4-2m7: 0-3 3m+: 0-2
Track:	LH: 0-5 RH: 0-0 Tight: 0-1 Gall: 0-0
Aids:	Bl: 0-0 Vi: 0-0 Tstrap: 0-0
Best Rating:	127 1/02 Catt 2m3f soft Ch

Fair chaser, stays three miles but possibly most effective at shorter. Handles soft ground but probably best on a sound surface.

Harik

108   **117**

9-y-o ch g Persian Bold-Yaqut (USA) (Northern Dancer)
G L Moore The Best Beech Partnership

Placings:P/32F36331/53436/21136/306212P23P-
23442114 (4570)
2002/03: 20²GF, 16³GF, 21⁴GS, 18⁴G, 18²GF, 19¹F, 20¹GF, 20⁴G,

	Starts	1st	2nd	3rd	Win & Pl
Chases	8	2	2	1	14392
Career Total	37	6	7	10	35221
117	3/03	Plum	2m4f	E(0-110)HCh	G-F	£5616
112	3/03	Tntn	2m3f	E(0-105)HCh	FRM	£3932
109	9/01	Font	2m4f	F(0-105)HCh	G-F	£3167
105	5/00	Font	2m4f	F Ch	GD	£2843
105	5/00	Hntg	2m110y	E Ch	G-F	£2880
113	4/99	Font	2m2f110yE Hdl		GD	£2215

Total win prize-money £20656

Going: Sf: 0-0 GS: 0-1 Gd: 0-2 GF: - Fm: 2-5
Distance: 2m/2m3: 1-4 2m4-2m7: 1-4 3m+: 0-0
Track: LH: 1-4 RH: 1-2 Tight: 2-6 Gall: 0-2
Aids: Bl: 2-5 Vi: 0-2 Tstrap: 2-8
Best Rating: 117 4/03 Strf 2m4f good Ch

Modest chaser; very versatile performer; splits his time between racing on sand and over fences and is successful under both codes; has found things tougher since being raised over a stone after winning two chases in March 2003; suited by fast ground over fences; stays 2m 4f; has worn a tongue tie, visor and blinkers.

Harleidalus (IRE)

93   **97**

9-y-o b g Mandalus-Spartan Park (Scorpio (FR))
Mrs L B Normile K J Fehilly

Placings:50/0/P31-P65 (1560)
2002/03: 24PGS, 25RGF, 25RG,

	Starts	1st	2nd	3rd	Win & Pl
Chases	3	0	0	0	0
Career Total	9	1	0	1	4727
97	6/01	Prth	3m	D Ch	G-F	£4095

Total win prize-money £4095

Going: Sf: 0-0 GS: 0-1 Gd: 0-1 GF: - Fm: 0-1
Distance: 2m/2m3: 0-0 2m4-2m7: 0-0 3m+: 0-3
Track: LH: 0-1 RH: 0-2 Tight: 0-2 Gall: 0-4
Aids: Bl: 0-0 Vi: 0-0 Tstrap: 0-0
Best Rating: 97 6/01 Prth 3m gd-fm Ch

Harlov (FR)

106(109h)   (104h)**104**

8-y-o ch g Garde Royale-Paulownia (FR) (Montevideo (ZIM))
A Parker Mr & Mrs Raymond Anderson Green

Placings:00/3030313/2F22/F26602131-12 (2190)
2002/03: 20¹HY, 26²HY,

	Starts	1st	2nd	3rd	Win & Pl
Chases	2	1	1	0	7006
Career Total	24	4	6	5	26686
103	11/02	Carl	2m4f	D(0-115)HCh	HVY	£4595
104	4/02	Hexm	3m1f	E Ch	GD	£3672
95	3/02	Carl	3m2f	D Ch	G-S	£4868
91	3/00	Ayr	3m110y	D(0-115)HHdl	HVY	£3614

Total win prize-money £16752

Going: Sf: 1-2 GS: 0-0 Gd: 0-0 GF: - Fm: 0-0
Distance: 2m/2m3: 0-0 2m4-2m7: 1-1 3m+: 0-1
Track: LH: 0-0 RH: 1-2 Tight: 0-0 Gall: 0-0
Aids: Bl: 0-0 Vi: 0-0 Tstrap: 0-0

Best Rating: 104 11/02 Carl 3m2f heavy Ch

Fair staying handicap chaser in the north; suited by soft ground.

Harmonic (USA)

107   **92**

6-y-o b m Shadeed (USA)-Running Melody (Rheingold)
H J Collingridge (G Prodromou 3/2) Alan Macalister

Placings:P224522-2551140P0 (2501)
2002/03: 16²GS, 16⁵G, 16⁵GF, 16¹S, 16¹G, 20⁴GS, 16⁹GS, 16PGS, 16⁹GS,

	Starts	1st	2nd	3rd	Win & Pl
Hurdles	9	2	1	0	8327
Career Total	16	2	5	0	11366
100	10/02	Fknm	2m	D Hdl	GD	£4075
93	8/02	Worc	2m	E Hdl	SFT	£3136

Total win prize-money £7212

Going: Sf: 1-1 GS: 0-5 Gd: 1-2 GF: - Fm: 0-1
Distance: 2m/2m3: 2-8 2m4-2m7: 0-1 3m+: 0-0
Track: LH: 2-9 RH: 0-0 Tight: 1-7 Gall: 0-0
Aids: Bl: 0-0 Vi: 0-0 Tstrap: 0-0
Best Rating: 100 10/02 Fknm 2m good Hdl

Modest hurdler, acts on any ground. Got off the mark at Worcester in August, followed up at Fakenham.

Harmony Hall

102   **106**

9-y-o ch g Music Boy-Fleeting Affair (Hotfoot)
J M Bradley E A Hayward

Placings:3F0/3/1154/5 (1618)
2002/03: 16⁵F,

	Starts	1st	2nd	3rd	Win & Pl
Hurdles	1	0	0	0	0
Career Total	9	2	0	2	9032
127	10/99	Asct	2m110y	C Hdl	GD	£5083
114	10/99	Strf	2m110y	E Hdl	G-F	£3002

Total win prize-money £8087

Going: Sf: 0-0 GS: 0-0 Gd: 0-0 GF: - Fm: 0-1
Distance: 2m/2m3: 0-1 2m4-2m7: 0-0 3m+: 0-0
Track: LH: 0-0 RH: 0-1 Tight: 0-0 Gall: 0-0
Aids: Bl: 0-0 Vi: 0-0 Tstrap: 0-0
Best Rating: 127 10/99 Asct 2m110y good Hdl

Very lightly raced over hurdles since back-to-back victories in October 1999; fit from the Flat when defying top weight in Class F handicap at Worcester July 2003; acts on ground good and faster; best at 2m.

Harpasgon De L'Ombre (FR)

95   **102**

8-y-o b g Mbaiki (FR)-Undress (FR) (Signani (FR))
O Sherwood It Wasn t Us

Placings:464F42-PF1440 (4414)
2002/03: 24PG, 18FGF, 20¹F, 22⁴S, 25⁴G, 22⁰G,

	Starts	1st	2nd	3rd	Win & Pl
Chases	6	1	0	0	5445
Career Total	12	1	1	0	7503
95	10/02	Ludl	2m4f	E Ch	FRM	£4704

Total win prize-money £4704

Going: Sf: 0-1 GS: 0-0 Gd: 0-3 GF: - Fm: 1-2
Distance: 2m/2m3: 0-1 2m4-2m7: 1-3 3m+: 0-2
Track: LH: 0-2 RH: 1-3 Tight: 1-4 Gall: 0-1
Aids: Bl: 0-1 Vi: 0-0 Tstrap: 0-0

Best Rating: 102 12/02 Newb 2m6f110y soft Ch

Modest novice chaser; had his task made easier by the early exit of the favourite when winning poor two and a half mile novice chase at Ludlow in October 2002; suited by fast ground.

Harpoon

7-y-o b g Kris-Jezebel Monroe (USA) (Lyphard (USA))
P R Webber P A Deal

Placings:3PP (3847)
2002/03: 22PHY, 16PG,

	Starts	1st	2nd	3rd	Win & Pl
Hurdles	2	0	0	0	
Career Total	3	0	0	1	473

Going: Sf: 0-1 GS: 0-0 Gd: 0-1 GF: - Fm: 0-0
Distance: 2m/2m3: 0-1 2m4-2m7: 0-1 3m+: 0-0
Track: LH: 0-0 RH: 0-2 Tight: 0-0 Gall: 0-0
Aids: Bl: 0-0 Vi: 0-0 Tstrap: 0-0
Best Rating: 97 4/01 Ayr 2m gd-fm NHF

Harrovian

100   **102**

6-y-o b g Deploy-Homeoftheclassics (Tate Gallery (USA))
Ferdy Murphy Major & Mrs Ivan Straker

Placings:2-54 (2189)
2002/03: 16⁵S, 20⁴HY,

	Starts	1st	2nd	3rd	Win & Pl
Hurdles	2	0	0	0	275
Career Total	3	0	1	0	3725

Going: Sf: 0-2 GS: 0-0 Gd: 0-0 GF: - Fm: 0-0
Distance: 2m/2m3: 0-1 2m4-2m7: 0-1 3m+: 0-0
Track: LH: 0-1 RH: 0-1 Tight: 0-1 Gall: 0-0
Aids: Bl: 0-0 Vi: 0-0 Tstrap: 0-0
Best Rating: 107 2/02 Newb 2m110y soft NHF

Promising debut in a Newbury bumper, when runner-up. Disappointing on hurdling debut when only fifth.

Harry B

98   **95**

4-y-o b g Midyan (USA)-Vilcabamba (USA) (Green Dancer (USA))
R J Price (G C Bravery 30/9) R J Price

Placings:33 (1756)
2002/03: 16⁹F, 16³G,

	Starts	1st	2nd	3rd	Win & Pl
Hurdles	2	0	0	2	1160
Career Total	2	0	0	2	1160

Going: Sf: 0-0 GS: 0-0 Gd: 0-1 GF: - Fm: 0-1
Distance: 2m/2m3: 0-2 2m4-2m7: 0-0 3m+: 0-0
Track: LH: 0-1 RH: 0-1 Tight: 0-0 Gall: 0-0
Aids: Bl: 0-0 Vi: 0-0 Tstrap: 0-0
Best Rating: 94 11/02 Wwck 2m good Hdl

Claimed out of Giles Bravery s stable after winning over a mile and a half at Wolverhampton September 2002. Satisfactory efforts over hurdles so far, but may need further than two miles.

Harry Collins

75   **35**

5-y-o ch g Sir Harry Lewis (USA)-Run Fast For Gold (Deep Run)
B I Case B I Case

Placings:*000*   (4117)
2002/03: 16⁰GS, 17⁰HY, 16⁰G,

	Starts	1st	2nd	3rd	Win & Pl
NH Flat	2	0	0	0	0
Hurdles	1	0	0	0	0
Career Total	3	0	0	0	

Going:	Sf: 0-1 GS: 0-1 Gd: 0-1 GF: - Fm: 0-0
Distance:	2m/2m3: 0-2 2m4-2m7: 0-0 3m+: 0-0
Track:	LH: 0-0 RH: 0-3 Tight: 0-1 Gall: 0-1
Aids:	Bl: 0-0 Vi: 0-0 Tstrap: 0-0
Best Rating:	80 2/03 Folk 2m1f110y heavy NHF

Harry Hooly

99   **101**

8-y-o b g Lithgie-Brig-Drummond Lass (Peacock (FR))
Mrs H O Graham Mrs H O Graham

Placings:*0030P4101U31-010646*   (2037)
2002/03: 22⁰GS, 20¹GS, 22⁰GF, 17⁶S, 27⁴G, 27⁶S,

	Starts	1st	2nd	3rd	Win & Pl
Hurdles	6	1	0	0	3395
Career Total	18	4	0	2	10860
101	5/02	Hexm	2m4f110yD(0-125)HHdl	G-S	£3395
93	3/02	Hexm	3m	F(0-100)HHdl	HVY £2044
88	1/02	Sedg	3m3f110yE(0-105)HHdl	HVY	£2450
88	12/01	Hexm	3m	F(0-105)HHdl	SFT £2138
			Total win prize-money £10028		

Going:	Sf: 0-2 GS: 1-2 Gd: 0-1 GF: - Fm: 0-1
Distance:	2m/2m3: 0-1 **2m4-2m7: 1-3** 3m+: 0-2
Track:	**LH: 1-5** RH: 0-1 Tight: 0-4 Gall: 0-0
Aids:	Bl: 0-0 Vi: 0-0 Tstrap: 0-0
Best Rating:	101 5/02 Hexm 2m4f110y gd-sft Hdl

Modest handicap hurdler. He is effective at around three miles and acts on soft ground.

Harry Junior

5-y-o b g River Falls-Badger Bay (IRE) (Salt Dome (USA))
J S Wainwright (B W Murray 7/7) B Murray

Placings:*P*   (1375)
2002/03: 17⁰GF,

	Starts	1st	2nd	3rd	Win & Pl
Hurdles	1	0	0	0	
Career Total	1	0	0	0	

Going:	Sf: 0-0 GS: 0-0 Gd: 0-0 GF: - Fm: 0-1
Distance:	2m/2m3: 0-1 2m4-2m7: 0-0 3m+: 0-0
Track:	LH: 0-1 RH: 0-0 Tight: 0-1 Gall: 0-0
Aids:	Bl: 0-0 Vi: 0-0 Tstrap: 0-0
Best Rating:	0 10/02 Sedg 2m1f gd-fm Hdl

Poor performer on the flat and pulled up on hurdling bow.

Harry The Horse

5-y-o b g Sir Harry Lewis (USA)-Miss Optimist (Relkino)
Miss E C Lavelle Club Ten

Placings:*P*   (3332)

2002/03: 17⁰S,

	Starts	1st	2nd	3rd	Win & Pl
Hurdles	1	0	0	0	
Career Total	1	0	0	0	

Harry's Ace

5-y-o b g Phountzi (USA)-Throw In Your Hand (Niniski (USA))
P D Williams Mrs D J Hughes

Placings:*00*   (4005)
2002/03: 17⁰G, 16⁰S,

	Starts	1st	2nd	3rd	Win & Pl
NH Flat	2	0	0	0	
Career Total	2	0	0	0	

Going:	Sf: 0-1 GS: 0-0 Gd: 0-0 GF: - Fm: 0-0
Distance:	2m/2m3: 0-2 2m4-2m7: 0-0 3m+: 0-0
Track:	LH: 0-0 RH: 0-2 Tight: 0-0 Gall: 0-0
Aids:	Bl: 0-0 Vi: 0-0 Tstrap: 0-0
Best Rating:	74 3/03 Winc 2m soft NHF

Showed improvement on faster ground third start in bumpers.

Harry's Dream

103   **98**

6-y-o b g Alflora (IRE)-Cheryls Pet (IRE) (General Ironside)
J W Mullins Peter Partridge

Placings:*P5P040*   (4622)
2002/03: 20⁰S, 19⁰G, 21⁰G, 19⁰GS, 19⁴GF, 22⁰GF,

	Starts	1st	2nd	3rd	Win & Pl
Hurdles	6	0	0	0	284
Career Total	6	0	0	0	284

Going:	Sf: 0-1 GS: 0-1 Gd: 0-2 GF: - Fm: 0-2
Distance:	2m/2m3: 0-1 2m4-2m7: 0-5 3m+: 0-0
Track:	LH: 0-3 RH: 0-3 Tight: 0-2 Gall: 0-1
Aids:	Bl: 0-0 Vi: 0-0 Tstrap: 0-0
Best Rating:	98 4/03 Hrfd 2m3f110y gd-fm Hdl

Moderate hurdler; brother to smart chaser Farmer Jack; winner of a point-to-point over three miles on a fast surface; improved form when encountering similar ground on fifth start over hurdles.

Harrycone Lewis

98   **91**

5-y-o b g Sir Harry Lewis (USA)-Rosie Cone (Celtic Cone)
Mrs P Sly The Craftsmen

Placings:*60*   (3558)
2002/03: 19⁰GS, 20⁴HY,

	Starts	1st	2nd	3rd	Win & Pl
Hurdles	2	0	0	0	0
Career Total	2	0	0	0	0

Going:	Sf: 0-1 GS: 0-1 Gd: 0-0 GF: - Fm: 0-0
Distance:	2m/2m3: 0-0 2m4-2m7: 0-2 3m+: 0-0
Track:	LH: 0-1 RH: 0-1 Tight: 0-1 Gall: 0-0

2002/03: 17⁰PS,

	Starts	1st	2nd	3rd	Win & Pl
Hurdles	1	0	0	0	
Career Total	1	0	0	0	

Aids:	Bl: 0-0 Vi: 0-0 Tstrap: 0-0
Best Rating:	91 1/03 Donc 2m3f110y gd-sft Hdl

Showed a glimmer of ability on racecourse bow in a novices hurdle at Doncaster in January.

Hartest Rose

4-y-o b f Komaite (USA)-Plough Hill (North Briton)
D E Cantillon J W Orbell

Placings:*01*   (4542)
2002/03: 16⁰G, 16¹G,

	Starts	1st	2nd	3rd	Win & Pl
NH Flat	2	1	0	0	2923
Career Total	2	1	0	0	2923
93	4/03	Ludl	2m	H NHF	GD £2922
			Total win prize-money £2923		

Going:	Sf: 0-0 GS: 0-0 Gd: 1-2 GF: - Fm: 0-0
Distance:	2m/2m3: **1-2** 2m4-2m7: 0-0 3m+: 0-0
Track:	LH: 0-1 **RH: 1-1** Tight: 0-1 Gall: 0-0
Aids:	Bl: 0-0 Vi: 0-0 Tstrap: 0-0
Best Rating:	93 4/03 Ludl 2m good NHF

Appreciated the fast ground when ready winner of modest bumper at Ludlow in April; poor efforts so far over hurdles.

Hartshead

94f   **77f**

4-y-o b g Machiavellian (USA)-Zalitzine (USA) (Zilzal (USA))
G A Swinbank C N Barnes

Placings:*0*   (4322)
2002/03: 17⁰G,

	Starts	1st	2nd	3rd	Win & Pl
NH Flat	1	0	0	0	
Career Total	1	0	0	0	

Going:	Sf: 0-0 GS: 0-0 Gd: 0-1 GF: - Fm: 0-0
Distance:	2m/2m3: 0-1 2m4-2m7: 0-0 3m+: 0-0
Track:	LH: 0-1 RH: 0-0 Tight: 0-1 Gall: 0-0
Aids:	Bl: 0-0 Vi: 0-0 Tstrap: 0-0
Best Rating:	77 3/03 Bang 2m1f good NHF

Harvey's Sister

75f   **58f**

7-y-o ch m Le Moss-Wings Ground (Murrayfield)
J M Jefferson J R Salter

Placings:*0*   (0280)
2002/03: 17⁰S,

	Starts	1st	2nd	3rd	Win & Pl
NH Flat	1	0	0	0	
Career Total	1	0	0	0	

Going:	Sf: 0-1 GS: 0-0 Gd: 0-0 GF: - Fm: 0-0
Distance:	2m/2m3: 0-1 2m4-2m7: 0-0 3m+: 0-0
Track:	LH: 0-1 RH: 0-0 Tight: 0-1 Gall: 0-0
Aids:	Bl: 0-0 Vi: 0-0 Tstrap: 0-0
Best Rating:	58 5/02 Bang 2m1f soft NHF

Harvis (FR)

109(103h)   (121h)**130**

8-y-o b g Djarvis (FR)-Tirana (FR) (Over)
Miss Venetia Williams Peter Richardson

Placings:6302233/4111FF0/**12422-F3226106**   **(4458)**
2002/03: 24FGF, 20³G, 24²GS, 19²HY, 20⁶GS, 16¹S, 16⁰G, 16⁶G,

	Starts	1st	2nd	3rd	Win & Pl
Hurdles	1	0	0		283
Chases	7	1	2	1	18400
Career Total	**27**	**5**	**7**	**4**	**75497**
130	2/03	Sand	2m	C(0-135)HCh	SFT £12209
129	12/01	Hayd	2m4f	C Ch	HVY £6435
136	12/00	Chep	2m110y	D(0-120)HHdl	SFT £10400
130	11/00	Leic	2m4f110yD Hdl		HVY £3367
110	11/00	Towc	2m	E Hdl	SFT £2324

Total win prize-money £34735

Going: Sf: 1-2 GS: 0-2 Gd: 0-3 GF: - Fm: 0-1
Distance: 2m/2m3: 1-3 2m4-2m7: 0-3 3m+: 0-2
Track: LH: 0-6 RH: 1-2 Tight: 0-2 Gall: 0-1
Aids: Bl: 0-0 Vi: 0-0 Tstrap: 0-0
Best Rating: 136 12/00 Chep 2m110y soft Hdl

Ex-French; decent handicap chaser; effective from two to three miles; acts on soft ground.

Harweld

11-y-o ch g Weld-Fruit Farm (Twiberry)
Mrs Edward Crow E H Crow

Placings:R   **(0029)**
2002/03: 21RGF,

	Starts	1st	2nd	3rd	Win & Pl
Chases	1	0	0	0	
Career Total	**1**	**0**	**0**	**0**	

Going: Sf: 0-0 GS: 0-0 Gd: 0-0 GF: - Fm: 0-1
Distance: 2m/2m3: 0-0 2m4-2m7: 0-1 3m+: 0-0
Track: LH: 0-1 RH: 0-0 Tight: 0-0 Gall: 0-1
Aids: Bl: 0-0 Vi: 0-0 Tstrap: 0-0
Best Rating:

Hasard Saisi (FR)
93   (89h)114d

7-y-o ch g Mill Pond (FR)-Askja (FR) (Jefferson (ZIM))
C Tizzard (P F Nicholls 11/11) Anthony Knott

Placings:PP3456/53163510124/**P305-3P0**   **(2550)**
2002/03: 16³GS, 18PGS, 17⁰HY,

	Starts	1st	2nd	3rd	Win & Pl
Hurdles	1	0	0	0	0
Chases	2	0	0	1	604
Career Total	**24**	**3**	**1**	**5**	**21281**
1/01	Pau	2m3f110y		Ch	HVY £6305
11/00	Seic	2m1f110y	Ch	HLD	£2882
6/00	Lrsy	2m1f		Ch	GD £2690

Total win prize-money £11877

Going: Sf: 0-0 GS: 0-2 Gd: 0-0 GF: - Fm: 0-0
Distance: 2m/2m3: 0-3 2m4-2m7: 0-0 3m+: 0-0
Track: LH: 0-1 RH: 0-1 Tight: 0-3 Gall: 0-0
Aids: Bl: 0-0 Vi: 0-0 Tstrap: 0-1
Best Rating: 114 11/01 Winc 2m gd-fm Ch

Good chaser in France, he made his debut in England in April of 2001, and ran with some promise, but was very disappointing after a break at Stratford in October, where he pulled up.

Hasary (FR)

8-y-o b g Marasali-Asterie L Ermitage (FR) (Hamster (FR))
G Macaire (J-M Robin 11/11) J-M Robin

Placings:3/4130/363-203PP   **(2714)**
2002/03: 21²GS, 21⁰G, 19³HO, 26PS, 19PHY,

	Starts	1st	2nd	3rd	Win & Pl
Chases	5	0	1	1	3166
Career Total	**13**	**1**	**1**	**5**	**13131**
6/00	Chat	2m1f	Hdl	GD	£2882

Total win prize-money £2882

Going: Sf: 0-2 GS: 0-1 Gd: 0-1 GF: - Fm: 0-0
Distance: 2m/2m3: 0-1 2m4-2m7: 0-3 3m+: 0-1
Track: LH: 0-2 RH: 0-0 Tight: 0-1 Gall: 0-0
Aids: Bl: 0-1 Vi: 0-0 Tstrap: 0-0
Best Rating: 0 12/02 Chep 2m3f110y heavy Ch

Haste Ye Back (IRE)
98(96c)   (78c)73

9-y-o b g All Haste (USA)-Less Pressure (IRE) (Torus)
D J Caro The Yes - No - Wait   Sorries

Placings:5P654F/U221P4430/**43PP4P04**   **(4340)**
2002/03: 24⁴G, 26³G, 29PGS, 24PS, 26⁴S, 24PS, 26⁰G, 26⁴GF,

	Starts	1st	2nd	3rd	Win & Pl
Hurdles	3	0	0	0	267
Chases	5	0	0	1	856
Career Total	**23**	**1**	**2**	**2**	**6072**
102	12/00	Towc	3m	E(0-115)HHdl	HVY £2443

Total win prize-money £2443

Going: Sf: 0-3 GS: 0-1 Gd: 0-3 GF: - Fm: 0-1
Distance: 2m/2m3: 0-2 2m4-2m7: 0-0 3m+: 0-8
Track: LH: 0-3 RH: 0-4 Tight: 0-2 Gall: 0-2
Aids: Bl: 0-4 Vi: 0-1 Tstrap: 0-0
Best Rating: 102 4/01 Newb 3m110y soft Hdl

A winner over hurdles, is yet to win over fences. Stays three miles and suited by soft ground.

Hasten Bak
85(98c)   (81c)82

10-y-o ch g Shaab-Kirstins Pride (Silly Prices)
Mrs S Gardner D V Gardner

Placings:032/4P13P5/323PFF5/00P0**F4F0040U0-00**   **(0343)**
2002/03: 22⁰GF, 22⁰GS,

	Starts	1st	2nd	3rd	Win & Pl
Hurdles	2	0	0	0	
Career Total	**31**	**1**	**2**	**4**	**7028**
98	1/00	Extr	2m1f110yE(0-105)HCh	HVY	£3298

Total win prize-money £3299

Going: Sf: 0-0 GS: 0-1 Gd: 0-0 GF: - Fm: 0-0
Distance: 2m/2m3: 0-0 2m4-2m7: 0-2 3m+: 0-0
Track: LH: 0-1 RH: 0-1 Tight: 0-1 Gall: 0-0
Aids: Bl: 0-0 Vi: 0-0 Tstrap: 0-0
Best Rating: 102 6/00 NAbb 2m6f gd-fm Hdl

Hasty Prince
102   134+

5-y-o ch g Halling (USA)-Sister Sophie (USA) (Effervescing (USA))
Jonjo O Neill (B Hanbury 21/9) F F Racing Services Partnership III

Placings:21B1   **(3877)**
2002/03: 16²S, 16¹S, 16BG, 19¹GS,

	Starts	1st	2nd	3rd	Win & Pl
Hurdles	4	2	1	0	11392
Career Total	**4**	**2**	**1**	**0**	**11392**

134	3/03	Donc	2m3f110yC Hdl	G-S	£6753
121	1/03	Hntg	2m110y E Hdl	SFT	£3668

Total win prize-money £10422

Going: Sf: 1-2 GS: 1-1 Gd: 0-1 GF: - Fm: 0-0
Distance: 2m/2m3: 1-3 2m4-2m7: 1-1 3m+: 0-0
Track: LH: 1-3 RH: 1-1 Tight: 0-0 **Gall: 1-2**
Aids: Bl: 0-0 Vi: 0-0 Tstrap: 0-0
Best Rating: 134 3/03 Donc 2m3f110y gd-sft Hdl

Fair middle-distance handicapper on the Flat; has looked quite useful over hurdles early in 2003, winning novice events at Huntingdon and Doncaster; acts on any ground; stays two miles three.

Hatch Gate

10-y-o gr g Lighter-Yankee Silver (Yankee Gold)
P York Mrs K H York

Placings:4   **(0312)**
2002/03: 21⁴G,

	Starts	1st	2nd	3rd	Win & Pl
Chases	1	0	0	0	164
Career Total	**1**	**0**	**0**	**0**	**164**

Going: Sf: 0-0 GS: 0-0 Gd: 0-1 GF: - Fm: 0-0
Distance: 2m/2m3: 0-0 2m4-2m7: 0-1 3m+: 0-0
Track: LH: 0-0 RH: 0-1 Tight: 0-1 Gall: 0-0
Aids: Bl: 0-0 Vi: 0-0 Tstrap: 0-0
Best Rating: 48 5/02 Folk 2m5f good Ch

Novice hunter chaser; prolific winner between the flags; likes fast ground; stays three miles well.

Hatcham Boy (IRE)

13-y-o br g Roselier (FR)-Auling (Tarqogan)
Mrs Ruth Hayter A Howland Jackson

Placings:20S12/1U2P2/23FUU02/3/21P2/232-23   **(0314)**
2002/03: 30²GF, 31³G,

	Starts	1st	2nd	3rd	Win & Pl
Chases	2	0	1	1	1166
Career Total	**27**	**3**	**11**	**4**	**21924**
106	5/00	Uttx	4m2f	H Ch	G-F £2912
128	11/96	Newb	3m	C Ch	G-S £4627
120	1/96	Hayd	2m6f	D Hdl	SFT £3035

Total win prize-money £10574

Going: Sf: 0-0 GS: 0-0 Gd: 0-1 GF: - Fm: 0-0
Distance: 2m/2m3: 0-0 2m4-2m7: 0-0 3m+: 0-2
Track: LH: 0-0 RH: 0-2 Tight: 0-1 Gall: 0-1
Aids: Bl: 0-0 Vi: 0-0 Tstrap: 0-0
Best Rating: 128 11/96 Newb 3m gd-sft Ch

Veteran hunter chaser, suited by marathon trips and a sound surface.

Hatsnall
100   (69c)87

5-y-o b g Mtoto-Anna Of Brunswick (Rainbow Quest (USA))
Miss C J E Caroe (F Flood 28/8) Miss C J E Caroe

Placings:460F0-P043504   **(4784)**
2002/03: 16PHY, 16⁰F, 16⁴GY, 16³GF, 16⁵G, 22⁵GF, 19⁴G,

	Starts	1st	2nd	3rd	Win & Pl
Hurdles	5	0	0	0	623
Chases	2	0	0	1	558
Career Total	**12**	**0**	**0**	**1**	**1464**

Going: Sf: 0-1 GS: 0-0 Gd: 0-2 GF: - Fm: 0-3
Distance: 2m/2m3: 0-5 2m4-2m7: 0-2 3m+: 0-0
Track: LH: 0-2 RH: 0-1 Tight: 0-2 Gall: 0-0
Aids: Bl: 0-0 Vi: 0-0 Tstrap: 0-0
Best Rating: 90 3/02 Navn 2m sft-hvy Hdl

Very moderate ex-French and ex-Irish novice chaser/hurdler.

Hatton Farm Babe

12-y-o b m Lochnager-Hatton Farm Girl (Humdoleila)
Mrs Susan Norbury Mrs Susan Norbury

Placings:P/F/3PP-F51P   (0414)
2002/03: 20FGF, 22SG, 26TG, 28PGF,

	Starts	1st	2nd	3rd	Win & Pl
Chases	4	1	0	0	1859
Career Total	9	1	0	1	2028
86	5/02	Uttx	3m2f	H Ch	GD	£1859

Total win prize-money £1859

Going: Sf: 0-0 GS: 0-0 Gd: 1-2 GF: - Fm: 0-2
Distance: 2m/2m3: 0-0 2m4-2m7: 0-2 3m+: 1-2
Track: LH: 1-2 RH: 0-2 Tight: 0-1 Gall: 0-1
Aids: Bl: 0-0 Vi: 0-0 Tstrap: 0-0
Best Rating: 86 5/02 Uttx 3m2f good Ch

Modest hunter chaser, stepped up on previous form when winning at Uttoxeter in May.

Haut Cercy (FR)
118   145

8-y-o b g Roi De Rome (USA)-Marnoussia (FR) (Laniste)
H D Daly The Wiggin Partnership

Placings:3/213221/2/3325F-143132   (4100)
2002/03: 24TG, 22AGS, 24SGS, 25TGS, 25SGS, 24AG,

	Starts	1st	2nd	3rd	Win & Pl
Chases	6	2	1	2	37137
Career Total	19	4	6	6	50337
135	1/03	Winc	3m1f110yC(0-135)HCh	G-S	£8775
127	10/02	Chep	3m	D Ch	GD	£4784
120	3/00	Tntn	3m110y	E Hdl	GD	£2459
119	12/99	Hrfd	2m3f110yE Hdl	SFT	£2206

Total win prize-money £18225

Going: Sf: 0-0 GS: 1-4 Gd: 1-2 GF: - Fm: 0-0
Distance: 2m/2m3: 0-0 2m4-2m7: 0-1 3m+: 2-5
Track: LH: 1-4 RH: 1-2 Tight: 0-0 Gall: 0-2
Aids: Bl: 0-0 Vi: 0-0 Tstrap: 0-0
Best Rating: 145 3/03 Chel 3m110y good Ch

Useful chaser; runner-up in William Hill National Hunt Handicap Chase at Cheltenham in 2003; stays as far as three miles one; effective on good and soft ground.

Havetwotaketwo (IRE)

9-y-o b g Phardante (FR)-Arctic Tartan (Deep Run)
Michael Smith Michael Smith

Placings:000/PU-   (0005)
2002/03: 20UG,

	Starts	1st	2nd	3rd	Win & Pl
Chases	1	0	0	0	
Career Total	5	0	0	0	

Going: Sf: 0-0 GS: 0-0 Gd: 0-1 GF: - Fm: 0-0
Distance: 2m/2m3: 0-0 2m4-2m7: 0-1 3m+: 0-0
Track: LH: 0-1 RH: 0-0 Tight: 0-0 Gall: 0-1

Aids: Bl: 0-0 Vi: 0-0 Tstrap: 0-0
Best Rating: 74 4/02 Newc 2m4f good Ch

Havoc

4-y-o b g Hurricane Sky (AUS)-Padelia (Thatching)
N Wilson Nigel Paul Sennett

Placings:P   (2325)
2002/03: 17PS,

	Starts	1st	2nd	3rd	Win & Pl
Hurdles	1	0	0	0	
Career Total	1	0	0	0	

Going: Sf: 0-0 GS: 0-0 Gd: 0-0 GF: - Fm: 0-0
Distance: 2m/2m3: 0-1 2m4-2m7: 0-0 3m+: 0-0
Track: LH: 0-0 RH: 0-1 Tight: 0-1 Gall: 0-0
Aids: Bl: 0-0 Vi: 0-0 Tstrap: 0-0
Best Rating: 0 12/02 MRas 2m1f110y soft Hdl

Hawadeth
115   132

8-y-o ch g Machiavellian (USA)-Ghzaalh (USA) (Northern Dancer)
V R A Dartnall Nick Viney

Placings:30234/24121612-325320B0   (4476)
2002/03: 16RG, 16PS, 16RHY, 16RS, 16PG, 16PHY, 17RG, 16UG,

	Starts	1st	2nd	3rd	Win & Pl
Hurdles	8	0	2	2	22056
Career Total	21	3	6	4	39852
121	3/02	NAbb	2m1f	D(0-115)HHdl	GD	£5720
119	1/02	Plum	2m	E Hdl	SFT	£2688
109	12/01	NAbb	2m1f	D Hdl	HVY	£3519

Total win prize-money £11928

Going: Sf: 0-4 GS: 0-0 Gd: 0-4 GF: - Fm: 0-0
Distance: 2m/2m3: 0-8 2m4-2m7: 0-0 3m+: 0-0
Track: LH: 0-4 RH: 0-5 Tight: 0-2 Gall: 0-1
Aids: Bl: 0-0 Vi: 0-0 Tstrap: 0-0
Best Rating: 132 1/03 Kemp 2m good Hdl

Decent handicap hurdler; effective at around two miles; acts on soft and good ground; consistent performer.

Hawick
100f   110f

6-y-o b g Toulon-Slave s Bangle (Prince Rheingold)
D W Whillans Chas N Whillans

Placings:23   (4039)
2002/03: 16²HY, 16³S,

	Starts	1st	2nd	3rd	Win & Pl
NH Flat	2	0	1	1	858
Career Total	2	0	1	1	858

Going: Sf: 0-2 GS: 0-0 Gd: 0-0 GF: - Fm: 0-0
Distance: 2m/2m3: 0-2 2m4-2m7: 0-0 3m+: 0-0
Track: LH: 0-2 RH: 0-0 Tight: 0-0 Gall: 0-0
Aids: Bl: 0-0 Vi: 0-0 Tstrap: 0-0
Best Rating: 110 2/03 Ayr 2m heavy NHF

Useful form in bumpers but is looking exposed; effective at two miles; acts on a sound surface.

Hawk's Landing (IRE)
106f   114f

6-y-o gr g Peacock (FR)-Lady Cheyenne (Stanford)

Jonjo O Neill (Miss F M Crowley 24/10) J P McManus

Placings:214   (3623)
2002/03: 16²YS, 16TGS, 16⁴HY,

	Starts	1st	2nd	3rd	Win & Pl
NH Flat	3	1	1	0	3169
Career Total	3	1	1	0	3169
111	1/03	Kemp	2m	H NHF	G-S	£2383

Total win prize-money £2384

Going: Sf: 0-1 GS: 1-1 Gd: 0-0 GF: - Fm: 0-0
Distance: 2m/2m3: 1-3 2m4-2m7: 0-0 3m+: 0-0
Track: LH: 0-0 RH: 1-2 Tight: 0-0 Gall: 0-0
Aids: Bl: 0-0 Vi: 0-0 Tstrap: 0-0
Best Rating: 114 2/03 Sand 2m110y heavy NHF

Modest bumper form on soft ground. Likely to progress over hurdles.

Hawkes Run
104   116

5-y-o b g Hernando (FR)-Wise Speculation (USA) (Mr Prospector (USA))
C J Mann The Baron Rouge Partnership

Placings:11213P0-5C5   (2563)
2002/03: 20⁵S, 22CS, 24⁵GS,

	Starts	1st	2nd	3rd	Win & Pl
Hurdles	3	0	0	0	875
Career Total	10	3	1	1	20689
116	11/01	Hntg	2m110y	B Hdl	GD	£8190
94	8/01	Strf	2m110y	E Hdl	GD	£2989
95	7/01	MRas	2m1f110y	D Hdl	G-S	£3835

Total win prize-money £15014

Going: Sf: 0-2 GS: 0-1 Gd: 0-0 GF: - Fm: 0-1
Distance: 2m/2m3: 0-0 2m4-2m7: 0-2 3m+: 0-1
Track: LH: 0-2 RH: 0-1 Tight: 0-1 Gall: 0-0
Aids: Bl: 0-0 Vi: 0-0 Tstrap: 0-0
Best Rating: 129 12/01 Chep 2m110y gd-sft Hdl

Useful juvenile hurdler in 2001/2 winning three times; lightly-raced and not as good since; acts on good ground or slightly softer; has been tried in blinkers and cheekpieces.

Hawthorn
21

7-y-o ch g Primo Dominie-Starr Danias (USA) (Sensitive Prince (USA))
M F Harris Vivamus Racing

Placings:36/0/0-5P   (1229)
2002/03: 17⁵GF, 17PG,

	Starts	1st	2nd	3rd	Win & Pl
Hurdles	2	0	0	0	0
Career Total	6	0	0	1	243

Going: Sf: 0-0 GS: 0-0 Gd: 0-1 GF: - Fm: 0-1
Distance: 2m/2m3: 0-2 2m4-2m7: 0-0 3m+: 0-0
Track: LH: 0-2 RH: 0-0 Tight: 0-2 Gall: 0-0
Aids: Bl: 0-0 Vi: 0-0 Tstrap: 0-0
Best Rating: 95 4/00 Ayr 2m good NHF

Hawthorn Prince (IRE)
96   114

8-y-o ch g Black Monday-Goose Loose (Dual)
Michael Hourigan Ms L Costelloe

Placings:00000-0PUU30 (1528)
2002/03: 16⁰G, 16ᴾGY, 17ᵁG, 20ᵁF, 20³F, 21⁰G,

	Starts	1st	2nd	3rd	Win & Pl
NH Flat	2	0	0	1	537
Hurdles	4	0	0	0	0
Career Total	11	0	0	1	537

Going: Sf: 0-0 GS: 0-0 Gd: 0-3 GF: - Fm: 0-2
Distance: 2m/2m3: 0-2 2m4-2m7: 0-3 3m+: 0-0
Track: LH: 0-2 RH: 0-1 Tight: 0-1 Gall: 0-0
Aids: Bl: 0-4 Vi: 0-0 Tstrap: 0-0
Best Rating: 96 9/02 List 2m4f firm NHF

Won back-to-back points spring 2002; completed four-timer
with two clear-cut victories in 3m novice hurdles at
Fakenham in May; acts on good to firm.

Hay Dance

12-y-o b g Shareef Dancer (USA)-Hay Reef (Mill Reef
(USA))
J Ibbott Mrs S J Ruddle

Placings:000/021431211531/F/F35/F/3P (4147)
2002/03: 20³GF, 21ᴾG,

	Starts	1st	2nd	3rd	Win & Pl
Chases	2	0	0	1	208
Career Total	22	5	2	4	18566
119	4/97	NAbb	2m1f	D(0-125)HHdl	FRM	£2735
121	1/97	Winc	2m	D(0-125)HHdl	G-F	£3183
109	12/96	Hrfd	2m1f	D(0-120)HHdl	G-S	£2857
96	11/96	Tntn	2m1f	C HHdl	G-F	£3533
87	7/96	Baln	2m	Hdl	GD	£2295
				Total win prize-money £14605

Going: Sf: 0-0 GS: 0-0 Gd: 0-1 GF: - Fm: 0-1
Distance: 2m/2m3: 0-0 2m4-2m7: 0-2 3m+: 0-0
Track: LH: 0-1 RH: 0-1 Tight: 0-1 Gall: 0-1
Aids: Bl: 0-0 Vi: 0-0 Tstrap: 0-0
Best Rating: 122 12/98 Tntn 2m1f good Hdl

Modest hunter chaser/pointer, suited by fast ground.

Hayaain
106   118
10-y-o b g Shirley Heights-Littlefield (Bay Express)
P G Murphy (J Barclay 31/5) Kinneston Racing

Placings:1451/1024400/0050B2112P0-0252 (1200)
2002/03: 18⁰GS, 24²GF, 27⁵GF, 26²GF,

	Starts	1st	2nd	3rd	Win & Pl
Hurdles	4	0	2	0	2346
Career Total	26	5	5	0	34907
110	12/01	Muss	3m	D(0-125)HHdl	GD	£8465
105	12/01	Muss	3m	D(0-125)HHdl	G-F	£4891
132	9/99	Hntg	2m4f110yD(0-125)HHdl	G-F	£7002
97	3/97	Uttx	2m4f110yE Hdl	G-F	£2200
108	2/97	Sand	2m110y C Hdl	G-F	£3517
				Total win prize-money £26078

Going: Sf: 0-0 GS: 0-1 Gd: 0-0 GF: - Fm: 0-3
Distance: 2m/2m3: 0-1 2m4-2m7: 0-0 3m+: 0-3
Track: LH: 0-2 RH: 0-2 Tight: 0-2 Gall: 0-0
Aids: Bl: 0-0 Vi: 0-0 Tstrap: 0-0
Best Rating: 132 11/99 Asct 3m good Hdl

A fair hurdler at one time, he lost his way until a change of
stable jolted him back to winning form for his new trainer Jim
Barclay, scoring twice at Musselburgh in December 2001.
He looks to need three miles and a sound surface.

Hayburn Vaults

5-y-o b m Bettergeton-Agdistis (Petoski)
Mrs S J Smith Mrs A E Astall

Placings:0 (3998)
2002/03: 16⁰G,

	Starts	1st	2nd	3rd	Win & Pl
NH Flat	1	0	0	0	
Career Total	1	0	0	0	

Going: Sf: 0-0 GS: 0-0 Gd: 0-1 GF: - Fm: 0-0
Distance: 2m/2m3: 0-1 2m4-2m7: 0-0 3m+: 0-0
Track: LH: 0-1 RH: 0-0 Tight: 0-0 Gall: 0-0
Aids: Bl: 0-0 Vi: 0-0 Tstrap: 0-0
Best Rating: 0 3/03 Weth 2m good NHF

Haydens Field
114   137
9-y-o b g Bedford (USA)-Releta (Relkino)
P M Rich Miss H Lewis

Placings:63623/21-111PP26 (4171)
2002/03: 24¹G, 22¹GS, 25¹GS, 20ᴾS, 23ᴾGS, 22²HY, 22⁶S,

	Starts	1st	2nd	3rd	Win & Pl
Hurdles	7	3	1	0	13338
Career Total	14	4	3	2	18872
137	5/02	Weth	3m1f	D Hdl	G-S	£3332
123	5/02	NAbb	2m6f	E Hdl	G-S	£3073
123	5/02	Bang	3m	E Hdl	GD	£3122
120	4/02	Chep	2m4f	E Hdl	G-S	£2961
				Total win prize-money £12488

Going: Sf: 0-3 GS: 2-3 Gd: 1-1 GF: - Fm: 0-0
Distance: 2m/2m3: 0-0 2m4-2m7: 0-1 3m+: 2-3
Track: LH: 3-6 RH: 0-1 Tight: 2-2 Gall: 0-0
Aids: Bl: 0-0 Vi: 0-0 Tstrap: 0-0
Best Rating: 137 5/02 Weth 3m1f gd-sft Hdl

Decent staying hurdler; completed a four-timer of front-running victories in the spring of 2002; back to that sort of form
when resuming his winning ways at Uttoxeter in April; stays
three miles and suited by soft ground.

Haydn James (USA)
107(101h)   (116h)125
9-y-o ch g Danzig Connection (USA)-Royal Fi Fi (USA)
(Conquistador Cielo (USA))
P J Hobbs Mrs Ann Painter

Placings:14102112/F1064065-141613440 (1548)
2002/03: 20¹GF, 20⁴GF, 20¹GF, 20⁶GF, 22¹GF, 21³GF, 24⁴GF,
22⁴G, 24⁰F,

	Starts	1st	2nd	3rd	Win & Pl
Hurdles	1	1	0	0	3847
Chases	8	2	1	0	13168
Career Total	25	8	2	1	35325
101	8/02	NAbb	2m6f	D(0-125)HHdl	G-F	£3847
125	6/02	Uttx	2m4f	C(0-135)HCh	G-F	£6665
125	5/02	Font	2m4f	D(0-115)HCh	G-F	£3945
116	8/01	Bang	2m4f	D(0-115)HHdl	GD	£4095
106	8/00	Font	2m2f	E Ch	G-F	£3580
108	8/00	Font	2m4f	E Ch	GD	£3097
98	6/00	NAbb	2m1f	F(0-100)HHdl	G-F	£2282
98	5/00	Hrfd	2m3f110yE Hdl	GD	£2600
				Total win prize-money £30114

Going: Sf: 0-0 GS: 0-0 Gd: 0-1 GF: - Fm: 3-8
Distance: 2m/2m3: 0-0 2m4-2m7: 3-7 3m+: 0-2
Track: LH: 2-6 RH: 0-1 Tight: 2-6 Gall: 0-0
Aids: Bl: 0-1 Vi: 0-0 Tstrap: 0-0

Best Rating: 125 6/02 Uttx 2m4f gd-fm Ch

Fair hurdler/chaser, suited by good or fast ground with his
best form in the last couple of seasons coming in the summer months. Best over two and a half miles. His jumping
has not been at its best on recent starts.

Hayton Boy

9-y-o ch g Gypsy Castle-Young Christine Vii (Damsire
Unregistered)
S G Chadwick S Chadwick

Placings:UPF (0916)
2002/03: 16ᵁGS, 26ᴾGS, 20ᶠGS,

	Starts	1st	2nd	3rd	Win & Pl
Hurdles	3	0	0	0	
Career Total	3	0	0	0	

Going: Sf: 0-0 GS: 0-3 Gd: 0-0 GF: - Fm: 0-0
Distance: 2m/2m3: 0-1 2m4-2m7: 0-1 3m+: 0-1
Track: LH: 0-2 RH: 0-1 Tight: 0-2 Gall: 0-0
Aids: Bl: 0-0 Vi: 0-0 Tstrap: 0-1
Best Rating: 0 8/02 Prth 2m4f110y gd-sft Hdl

Hazel Reilly (IRE)

12-y-o b m Mister Lord (USA)-Vickies Gold (Golden Love)
Mrs Sarah L Dent John Mackley

Placings:6243/3422-P11242 (4777)
2002/03: 25ᴾS, 28¹G, 25¹GS, 24²GS, 25⁴G, 31²G,

	Starts	1st	2nd	3rd	Win & Pl
Chases	6	2	2	0	6582
Career Total	14	2	5	2	9280
78	3/03	Kels	3m1f	H Ch	G-S	£2479
99	2/03	Catt	3m4f110yH Ch	GD	£1491
				Total win prize-money £3971

Going: Sf: 0-1 GS: 1-2 Gd: 1-3 GF: - Fm: 0-0
Distance: 2m/2m3: 0-0 2m4-2m7: 0-0 3m+: 2-6
Track: LH: 2-4 RH: 0-1 Tight: 2-3 Gall: 0-1
Aids: Bl: 0-0 Vi: 0-0 Tstrap: 0-0
Best Rating: 99 4/03 Prth 3m7f good Ch

Modest hunter chaser; out-and-out stayer; acts on any
ground.

He's A Rascal (IRE)
88(88h)   (97dh)45
5-y-o b g Fumo Di Londra (IRE)-Lovely Ali (IRE) (Dunbeath
(USA))
Jean-Rene Auvray Lambourn Racing

Placings:0405P0F (3921)
2002/03: 16⁰G, 16⁴G, 16⁶S, 16⁵GS, 22ᴾGS, 21⁰S, 26ᶠS,

	Starts	1st	2nd	3rd	Win & Pl
Hurdles	5	0	0	0	273
Chases	2	0	0	0	0
Career Total	7	0	0	0	273

Going: Sf: 0-3 GS: 0-2 Gd: 0-2 GF: - Fm: 0-0
Distance: 2m/2m3: 0-4 2m4-2m7: 0-0 3m+: 0-1
Track: LH: 0-3 RH: 0-3 Tight: 0-4 Gall: 0-0
Aids: Bl: 0-2 Vi: 0-0 Tstrap: 0-0
Best Rating: 86 10/02 Chep 2m110y good Hdl

He's My Uncle

8-y-o ch g Phardante (FR)-Red Dusk (Deep Run)
Mrs J K M Oliver Mrs J K M Oliver

Placings:0P-P   (4014)
2002/03: 16^{P}S,

	Starts	1st	2nd	3rd	Win & Pl
Hurdles	1	0	0	0	
Career Total	3	0	0	0	

Going:	Sf: 0-1 GS: 0-0 Gd: 0-0 GF: - Fm: 0-0
Distance:	2m/2m3: 0-1 2m4-2m7: 0-0 3m+: 0-0
Track:	LH: 0-1 RH: 0-0 Tight: 0-0 Gall: 0-0
Aids:	Bl: 0-0 Vi: 0-0 Tstrap: 0-0
Best Rating:	63 11/01 Carl 2m1f soft NHF

He's The Biz (FR)
92   77

4-y-o b g Nikos-Irun (FR) (Son Of Silver)
Nick Williams Mrs Jane Williams

Placings:0065P   (3549)
2002/03: 12^{D}GS, 16^{D}S, 16^{6}GS, 16^{5}HY, 17^{P}G,

	Starts	1st	2nd	3rd	Win & Pl
NH Flat	1	0	0	0	0
Hurdles	4	0	0	0	900
Career Total	5	0	0	0	900

Going:	Sf: 0-2 GS: 0-2 Gd: 0-1 GF: - Fm: 0-0
Distance:	2m/2m3: 0-4 2m4-2m7: 0-0 3m+: 0-0
Track:	LH: 0-3 RH: 0-2 Tight: 0-0 Gall: 0-1
Aids:	Bl: 0-0 Vi: 0-0 Tstrap: 0-0
Best Rating:	77 12/02 Winc 2m gd-sft Hdl

Only moderate abililty shown in outings to date.

He's The Boss (IRE)
116f   127f

6-y-o b g Supreme Leader-Attykee (IRE) (Le Moss)
R H Buckler M J Hallett

Placings:01-260   (4115)
2002/03: 16^{2}HY, 16^{6}G, 16^{0}G,

	Starts	1st	2nd	3rd	Win & Pl
NH Flat	3	0	1	0	3980
Career Total	5	1	1	0	7081
109 3/02 Strf	2m110y H NHF		G-S	£3101	
	Total win prize-money £3101				

Going:	Sf: 0-1 GS: 0-0 Gd: 0-2 GF: - Fm: 0-0
Distance:	2m/2m3: 0-3 2m4-2m7: 0-0 3m+: 0-0
Track:	LH: 0-3 RH: 0-0 Tight: 0-0 Gall: 0-1
Aids:	Bl: 0-0 Vi: 0-0 Tstrap: 0-0
Best Rating:	127 3/03 Chel 2m110y good NHF

Won a Stratford bumper in great style on his second start and came back to run a good second in a Chepstow Grade Two. Handles soft ground.

Head For Home (IRE)

6-y-o ch m Executive Perk-Lancastrian Rose (IRE) (Lancastrian)
Mrs Dianne Sayer Mrs Dianne Sayer

Placings:P00P-P   (1497)

2002/03: 16^{P}G,

	Starts	1st	2nd	3rd	Win & Pl
Hurdles	1	0	0	0	
Career Total	5	0	0	0	

Going:	Sf: 0-0 GS: 0-0 Gd: 0-1 GF: - Fm: 0-0
Distance:	2m/2m3: 0-1 2m4-2m7: 0-0 3m+: 0-0
Track:	LH: 0-1 RH: 0-0 Tight: 0-0 Gall: 0-0
Aids:	Bl: 0-0 Vi: 0-0 Tstrap: 0-1
Best Rating:	65 2/02 Muss 2m soft NHF

Hear My Song (IRE)
83(85h)   (72h)63

7-y-o b g Commanche Run-Pampered Finch Vii (Damsire Unregistered)
J S King Turville Racing Partnership

Placings:000PP-0   (0036)
2002/03: 17^{0}G,

	Starts	1st	2nd	3rd	Win & Pl
Chases	1	0	0	0	
Career Total	6	0	0	0	

Going:	Sf: 0-0 GS: 0-0 Gd: 0-0 GF: - Fm: 0-0
Distance:	2m/2m3: 0-1 2m4-2m7: 0-0 3m+: 0-0
Track:	LH: 0-0 RH: 0-1 Tight: 0-0 Gall: 0-0
Aids:	Bl: 0-0 Vi: 0-0 Tstrap: 0-0
Best Rating:	72 1/02 Winc 2m good Hdl

Heartache
83   70

6-y-o b g Jurado (USA)-Heresy (IRE) (Black Minstrel)
R Mathew Robin Mathew

Placings:P-3O0   (4733)
2002/03: 19^{3}F, 19^{0}GF, 16^{0}GF,

	Starts	1st	2nd	3rd	Win & Pl
Hurdles	3	0	0	1	771
Career Total	4	0	0	1	771

Going:	Sf: 0-0 GS: 0-0 Gd: 0-0 GF: - Fm: 0-3
Distance:	2m/2m3: 0-3 2m4-2m7: 0-0 3m+: 0-0
Track:	LH: 0-2 RH: 0-1 Tight: 0-1 Gall: 0-0
Aids:	Bl: 0-0 Vi: 0-0 Tstrap: 0-0
Best Rating:	70 3/03 Extr 2m3f firm Hdl

Heather Lad

10-y-o ch g Highlands-Ragged Rose (Scallywag)
C B Taylor C B Taylor

Placings:P   (0402)
2002/03: 20^{P}GF,

	Starts	1st	2nd	3rd	Win & Pl
Chases	1	0	0	0	
Career Total	1	0	0	0	

Going:	Sf: 0-0 GS: 0-0 Gd: 0-0 GF: - Fm: 0-1
Distance:	2m/2m3: 0-0 2m4-2m7: 0-0 3m+: 0-1
Track:	LH: 0-1 RH: 0-0 Tight: 0-0 Gall: 0-0
Aids:	Bl: 0-0 Vi: 0-0 Tstrap: 0-0
Best Rating:	0 6/02 Hexm 2m4f110y gd-fm Ch

Heatherjack
62   25

6-y-o b m Nalchik (USA)-Healaughs Pride (Healaugh Fox)
B Mactaggart J Jack

Placings:0   (4665)
2002/03: 17^{0}GF,

	Starts	1st	2nd	3rd	Win & Pl
NH Flat	1	0	0	0	
Career Total	1	0	0	0	

Going:	Sf: 0-0 GS: 0-0 Gd: 0-0 GF: - Fm: 0-1
Distance:	2m/2m3: 0-1 2m4-2m7: 0-0 3m+: 0-0
Track:	LH: 0-0 RH: 0-1 Tight: 0-0 Gall: 0-0
Aids:	Bl: 0-0 Vi: 0-0 Tstrap: 0-0
Best Rating:	6 4/03 Carl 2m1f gd-fm NHF

Heathyards Element
86   (73c)84

7-y-o ch g Henbit (USA)-Moment s Pleasure (USA) (What A Pleasure (USA))
D McCain L A Morgan

Placings:2043/0F005/25543530-P6   (0692)
2002/03: 20^{P}GF, 16^{6}S,

	Starts	1st	2nd	3rd	Win & Pl
Hurdles	2	0	0	0	0
Career Total	19	0	2	3	3128

Going:	Sf: 0-1 GS: 0-0 Gd: 0-0 GF: - Fm: 0-1
Distance:	2m/2m3: 0-1 2m4-2m7: 0-1 3m+: 0-0
Track:	LH: 0-2 RH: 0-0 Tight: 0-1 Gall: 0-0
Aids:	Bl: 0-1 Vi: 0-0 Tstrap: 0-0
Best Rating:	86 1/00 Ludl 2m good NHF

Heathyards Friend
91   75

4-y-o b g Forest Wind (USA)-Heathyards Lady (USA) (Mining (USA))
R Hollinshead L A Morgan

Placings:2100   (4522)
2002/03: 17^{2}S, 16^{1}G, 17^{0}G, 16^{0}G,

	Starts	1st	2nd	3rd	Win & Pl
Hurdles	4	1	1	0	3927
Career Total	4	1	1	0	3927
68 12/02 Donc	2m110y G Hdl		GD	£3026	
	Total win prize-money £3027				

Going:	Sf: 0-1 GS: 0-0 Gd: 1-3 GF: - Fm: 0-0
Distance:	2m/2m3: 1-4 2m4-2m7: 0-0 3m+: 0-0
Track:	LH: 1-3 RH: 0-1 Tight: 0-1 Gall: 1-1
Aids:	Bl: 0-0 Vi: 0-0 Tstrap: 0-0
Best Rating:	75 8/02 Bang 2m1f soft Hdl

Clear-cut winner of a selling hurdle at Doncaster in December.

Heathyards Guest (IRE)
92   80

5-y-o ch g Be My Guest (USA)-Noble Nadia (Thatching)
Mrs K Walton G M Marshall

Placings:04-3406   (4258)

2002/03: 16³GF, 16⁴G, 19⁹GS, 17⁶G,

	Starts	1st	2nd	3rd	Win & Pl
Hurdles	4	0	0	1	366
Career Total	6	0	0	1	366

Going:	Sf: 0-0 GS: 0-1 Gd: 0-2 GF: - Fm: 0-1
Distance:	2m/2m3: 0-3 2m4-2m7: 0-1 3m+: 0-0
Track:	LH: 0-4 RH: 0-0 Tight: 0-1 Gall: 0-0
Aids:	Bl: 0-0 Vi: 0-0 Tstrap: 0-0
Best Rating:	84 4/02 Sedg 2m1f gd-fm Hdl

Heathyards Mate

83   56

6-y-o b g Timeless Times (USA)-Quenlyn (Welsh Pageant)
R J Baker Churchgoers Anonymous

Placings:50P   (1603)
2002/03: 16⁵GF, 16⁰F, 16⁶G,

	Starts	1st	2nd	3rd	Win & Pl
Hurdles	3	0	0	0	0
Career Total	3	0	0	0	0

Going:	Sf: 0-0 GS: 0-0 Gd: 0-0 GF: - Fm: 0-2
Distance:	2m/2m3: 0-3 2m4-2m7: 0-0 3m+: 0-0
Track:	LH: 0-2 RH: 0-1 Tight: 0-0 Gall: 0-0
Aids:	Bl: 0-0 Vi: 0-0 Tstrap: 0-0
Best Rating:	47 8/02 Worc 2m gd-fm Hdl

Heathyards Tipple (IRE)

91

7-y-o b m Marju (IRE)-Nikki s Groom (Shy Groom (USA))
D McCain Mrs D McCain

Placings:114223P316/06/00355002400-13P   (0787)
2002/03: 16¹GF, 16³GF, 17⁶GF,

	Starts	1st	2nd	3rd	Win & Pl
Hurdles	3	1	0	1	2365
Career Total	26	4	3	4	14276
91	6/02	Hexm	2m110y	E(0-110)HHdl	G-F	£1886
91	3/00	Sedg	2m1f	E(0-105)HHdl	G-F	£2282
88	9/99	Sedg	2m1f	E Hdl	G-F	£2425
86	8/99	Ctml	2m1f110yE Hdl		GD	£2635
			Total win prize-money £9229

Going:	Sf: 0-0 GS: 0-0 Gd: 0-0 GF: - Fm: 1-3
Distance:	2m/2m3: 1-3 2m4-2m7: 0-0 3m+: 0-0
Track:	LH: 1-3 RH: 0-0 Tight: 0-0 Gall: 0-0
Aids:	Bl: 0-0 Vi: 0-0 Tstrap: 0-0
Best Rating:	91 6/02 Hexm 2m110y gd-fm Hdl

Moderate hurdler; suited by two miles and fast ground.

Heavenly Hill

72   27

6-y-o b m Nomadic Way (USA)-Tees Gazette Girl
(Kalaglow)
M J Gingell (Mrs M Reveley 12/2) Gentlemen Don t Work
On Mondays

Placings:0-30   (4672)
2002/03: 16³G, 16⁹G,

	Starts	1st	2nd	3rd	Win & Pl
NH Flat	2	0	0	1	425
Career Total	3	0	0	1	425

Going:	Sf: 0-0 GS: 0-0 Gd: 0-2 GF: - Fm: 0-0

Distance:	2m/2m3: 0-2 2m4-2m7: 0-0 3m+: 0-0
Track:	LH: 0-1 RH: 0-1 Tight: 0-2 Gall: 0-0
Aids:	Bl: 0-0 Vi: 0-0 Tstrap: 0-0
Best Rating:	94 2/03 Muss 2m good NHF

Moderate form in bumper company; acts on good ground;
effective over two miles.

Heavenly King

98   80

5-y-o b g Homo Sapien-Chapel Hill (IRE) (The Parson)
P Bowen Dr D & Mrs C & D & Ms A & J O Brien

Placings:6PPP   (3311)
2002/03: 17⁶GF, 20⁰PHY, 16⁶PS, 19⁰PGS,

	Starts	1st	2nd	3rd	Win & Pl
NH Flat	1	0	0	0	0
Hurdles	3	0	0	0	0
Career Total	4	0	0	0	0

Going:	Sf: 0-2 GS: 0-1 Gd: 0-0 GF: - Fm: 0-1
Distance:	2m/2m3: 0-3 2m4-2m7: 0-1 3m+: 0-0
Track:	LH: 0-1 RH: 0-3 Tight: 0-1 Gall: 0-1
Aids:	Bl: 0-0 Vi: 0-0 Tstrap: 0-0
Best Rating:	73 9/02 MRas 2m1f110y gd-fm NHF

Pulled up in soft ground on first three starts over hurdles;
second on fast ground to the progressive Anzal at Exeter
May 2003.

Heavenly Stride

82(88h)   (111h)115

7-y-o b g Karinga Bay-Chapel Hill (IRE) (The Parson)
D McCain Eamonn O Malley

Placings:121/2051-F31F   (4458)
2002/03: 16⁶HY, 20³S, 16¹S, 16⁶G,

	Starts	1st	2nd	3rd	Win & Pl
Chases	4	1	0	1	8727
Career Total	11	4	2	1	19488
115	3/03	Sand	2m	D(0-125)HCh	SFT	£6678
115	3/02	Bang	2m1f110yD Ch		SFT	£4134
111	4/00	Carl	2m1f	E Hdl	G-S	£2548
102	3/00	Ayr	2m	E Hdl	HVY	£2310
			Total win prize-money £15671

Going:	Sf: 1-3 GS: 0-0 Gd: 0-1 GF: - Fm: 0-0
Distance:	2m/2m3: 1-3 2m4-2m7: 0-1 3m+: 0-0
Track:	LH: 0-3 RH: 1-1 Tight: 0-1 Gall: 0-0
Aids:	Bl: 0-0 Vi: 0-0 Tstrap: 0-0
Best Rating:	115 3/03 Sand 2m soft Ch

Fair, lightly-raced hurdler/chaser; effective at two miles; acts
on soft ground.

Hedgehunter (IRE)

112(82h)   (126h)135+

7-y-o b g Montelimar (USA)-Aberedw (IRE) (Caerwent)
W P Mullins Trevor Hemmings

Placings:22/22242621-22310   (4113)
2002/03: 20²YS, 22²S, 20³SH, 28¹SH, 32⁰G,

	Starts	1st	2nd	3rd	Win & Pl
Chases	5	1	2	1	18596
Career Total	15	2	9	1	30797
130	2/03	Punc	3m4f	HCh	SH	£13506
125	2/02	Clon	3m	Hdl	HVY	£4868
			Total win prize-money £18374

Going:	Sf: 0-1 GS: 0-0 Gd: 0-1 GF: - Fm: 0-0
Distance:	2m/2m3: 0-0 2m4-2m7: 0-3 3m+: 1-2
Track:	LH: 0-1 RH: 0-2 Tight: 0-0 Gall: 0-1

Aids:	Bl: 0-0 Vi: 0-0 Tstrap: 0-0
Best Rating:	135 3/03 Chel 4m good Ch

Fair front-running Irish hurdler/chaser; has taken well to
fences in 2002/03, winning the Punchestown Grand National
Trial on his handicap debut; every chance when blundered
two out in National Hunt Challenge Cup at Cheltenham;
stays very well and acts on testing ground.

Heidi Iii (FR)

109(95h)   (89h)127

8-y-o b g Bayolidaan (FR)-Irlandaise (FR) (Or De Chine)
Mrs L Williamson Turner Technology Ltd

Placings:01/21/11222110/52PP2-602   (2383)
2002/03: 22⁶S, 27⁰GS, 25²GS,

	Starts	1st	2nd	3rd	Win & Pl
Hurdles	1	0	0	0	0
Chases	2	0	1	0	2300
Career Total	20	6	7	0	75573
138	2/01	Newc	2m4f	B(0-140)HCh	HVY	£8684
138	1/01	Donc	3m	B(0-145)HCh	GD	£31850
128	6/00	Prth	2m4f110yE Hdl		HVY	£2691
113	5/00	Weth	2m	E Hdl	G-F	£2772
117	4/00	Carl	2m1f	E Hdl	SFT	£2786
	1/99	Pau	2m1f	Ch		HLD	£5382
			Total win prize-money £54166

Going:	Sf: 0-1 GS: 0-2 Gd: 0-0 GF: - Fm: 0-0
Distance:	2m/2m3: 0-0 2m4-2m7: 0-1 3m+: 0-2
Track:	LH: 0-3 RH: 0-0 Tight: 0-2 Gall: 0-0
Aids:	Bl: 0-0 Vi: 0-0 Tstrap: 0-0
Best Rating:	138 2/01 Newc 2m4f heavy Ch

Tough and consistent, he enjoyed a cracking 2000/2001
season highlighted by a brave win in the Great Yorkshire
Chase at Doncaster in 2001. Had a light campaign the following season. Acts on soft/heavy. Has won at two and a
half and three miles.

Helical Girl

5-y-o b m Presidium-Oubeck (Mummy s Game)
P S McEntee (T T Clement 27/5) Keybeam Technology
Limited

Placings:P   (1085)
2002/03: 16⁰GF,

	Starts	1st	2nd	3rd	Win & Pl
Hurdles	1	0	0	0	
Career Total	1	0	0	0	

Going:	Sf: 0-0 GS: 0-0 Gd: 0-0 GF: - Fm: 0-1
Distance:	2m/2m3: 0-1 2m4-2m7: 0-0 3m+: 0-0
Track:	LH: 0-0 RH: 0-1 Tight: 0-0 Gall: 0-1
Aids:	Bl: 0-0 Vi: 0-0 Tstrap: 0-0
Best Rating:	0 8/02 Hntg 2m110y gd-fm Hdl

Helixir Du Theil (FR)

(106h)   (107h)88

8-y-o ch g Aelan Hapi (USA)-Manolette (FR) (Signani (FR))
R H Buckler The Manolettes

Placings:0/4P/0400222-4342   (1216)
2002/03: 24⁴G, 26³GF, 26⁴GF, 21²G,

	Starts	1st	2nd	3rd	Win & Pl
Hurdles	2	0	0	1	424
Chases	2	0	1	0	1439
Career Total	14	0	4	1	5822

Going: Sf: 0-0 GS: 0-0 Gd: 0-2 GF: - Fm: 0-2
Distance: 2m/2m3: 0-2 2m4-2m7: 0-1 3m+: 0-3
Track: LH: 0-3 RH: 0-1 Tight: 0-1 Gall: 0-0
Aids: Bl: 0-0 Vi: 0-0 Tstrap: 0-0
Best Rating: 111 4/02 Bang 3m   good   Hdl

Modest hurdler/chaser who often makes the frame without winning. Needs a stamina test and has looked less than keen under pressure.

Hell-Of-A-Shindy (IRE)

91(90h)   (78h)118

9-y-o b g Phardante (FR)-Tonto s Girl (Strong Gale)
Jonjo O Neill J P McManus

Placings:4F/F3/P15324-125PP   (4324)
2002/03: 21¹G, 24²HY, 24⁴GS, 21⁵GS, 24³G,

	Starts	1st	2nd	3rd	Win & Pl
Hurdles	1	0	0	0	0
Chases	4	1	1	0	9245
Career Total	15	2	2	2	18261
114 11/02 Winc	2m5f		D(0-115)HCh	GD	£7525
95 6/01 Clon	3m		Ch	FRM	£3895
			Total win prize-money £11420

Going: Sf: 0-1 GS: 0-2 Gd: 1-2 GF: - Fm: 0-0
Distance: 2m/2m3: 0-0 2m4-2m7: 1-2 3m+: 0-3
Track: LH: 1-4 RH: 1-4 Tight: 0-0 Gall: 0-0
Aids: Bl: 0-0 Vi: 0-0 Tstrap: 0-0
Best Rating: 118 11/02 Asct   3m110y   heavy   Ch

Fair handicap chaser; won a Wincanton handicap in November 2002; stays three miles; acts on a sound surface.

Hello De Vauxbuin (FR)

99(68h)   (24h)97

8-y-o b g Le Nain Jaune (FR)-Quadrille De Cuy (FR) (Baraban)
R Ford Mick Coulson

Placings:P0P/35/0P01-3FR0   (1528)
2002/03: 24¹G, 20³G, 24²FGS, 26⁸GF, 21⁰G,

	Starts	1st	2nd	3rd	Win & Pl
Hurdles	1	0	0	0	0
Chases	4	1	0	1	3648
Career Total	13	1	0	2	4073
100 4/02 Newc	3m		E(0-105)HCh	GD	£3248
			Total win prize-money £3248

Going: Sf: 0-0 GS: 0-1 Gd: 1-3 GF: - Fm: 0-1
Distance: 2m/2m3: 0-0 2m4-2m7: 0-2 3m+: 1-3
Track: LH: 3-1 RH: 0-1 Tight: 0-1 Gall: 1-1
Aids: Bl: 0-0 Vi: 0-0 Tstrap: 0-0
Best Rating: 100 4/02 Newc   3m   good   Ch

Lightly-raced gelding with modest form to date over hurdles and fences. Successful at Newcastle in April 2002. Suited by good ground.

Hello Dee

100f   92f

5-y-o b m Alflora (IRE)-Donna Farina (Little Buskins)
Jonjo O Neill Mrs R H Thompson

Placings:32   (4162)
2002/03: 16³G, 17²G,

	Starts	1st	2nd	3rd	Win & Pl
NH Flat	2	0	1	1	809
Career Total	2	0	1	1	809

Going: Sf: 0-0 GS: 0-0 Gd: 0-2 GF: - Fm: 0-0
Distance: 2m/2m3: 0-2 2m4-2m7: 0-1 3m+: 0-0
Track: LH: 0-2 RH: 0-2 Tight: 0-1 Gall: 0-1
Aids: Bl: 0-0 Vi: 0-0 Tstrap: 0-0
Best Rating: 92 3/03 MRas 2m1f110y good NHF

Third in a bumper on her debut at Huntingdon in February and runner-up in similar event at Market Rasen the following month.

Hello Stranger (IRE)

91   95

7-y-o gr g Roselier (FR)-Emily Bishop (IRE) (The Parson)
A M Hales Andrew L Cohen

Placings:0   (1601)
2002/03: 20⁰G,

	Starts	1st	2nd	3rd	Win & Pl
Hurdles	1	0	0	0	0
Career Total	1	0	0	0	0

Going: Sf: 0-0 GS: 0-0 Gd: 0-1 GF: - Fm: 0-0
Distance: 2m/2m3: 0-0 2m4-2m7: 0-1 3m+: 0-0
Track: LH: 0-1 RH: 0-0 Tight: 0-0 Gall: 0-0
Aids: Bl: 0-0 Vi: 0-0 Tstrap: 0-0
Best Rating: 95 10/02 Chep 2m4f   good   Hdl

Helmsley Flier

9-y-o ch g Sula Bula-Penair (Good Times (ITY))
Miss Jenny Garley Miss Jenny Garley

Placings:3/6556P6404/P53FPPP/5   (0187)
2002/03: 20⁵GF,

	Starts	1st	2nd	3rd	Win & Pl
Chases	1	0	0	0	0
Career Total	18	0	0	2	650

Going: Sf: 0-0 GS: 0-0 Gd: 0-0 GF: - Fm: 0-1
Distance: 2m/2m3: 0-0 2m4-2m7: 0-1 3m+: 0-0
Track: LH: 0-0 RH: 0-1 Tight: 0-0 Gall: 0-1
Aids: Bl: 0-0 Vi: 0-1 Tstrap: 0-1
Best Rating: 93 3/99 Donc   2m110y   gd-sft Hdl

Help Yourself (IRE)

99   67

7-y-o gr m Roselier (FR)-Sweet Run (Deep Run)
L Lungo Alistair Duncan

Placings:16-00500   (3814)
2002/03: 16⁰G, 20⁰HY, 19⁵S, 17⁰HY, 16⁰G,

	Starts	1st	2nd	3rd	Win & Pl
Hurdles	5	0	0	0	0
Career Total	7	1	0	0	1526
98 11/01 Weth	2m		H NHF	GD	£1526
			Total win prize-money £1526

Going: Sf: 0-3 GS: 0-0 Gd: 0-2 GF: - Fm: 0-0
Distance: 2m/2m3: 0-3 2m4-2m7: 0-2 3m+: 0-0
Track: LH: 0-4 RH: 0-1 Tight: 0-3 Gall: 0-0
Aids: Bl: 0-0 Vi: 0-0 Tstrap: 0-0
Best Rating: 98 11/01 Weth   2m   good   NHF

Won an ordinary Wetherby bumper on her debut but has achieved little over hurdles.

Helvetius

105(102h)   (99h)113

7-y-o b g In The Wings-Hejraan (USA) (Alydar (USA))
P C Ritchens John Pearl

Placings:0/44221324420-512542PP3   (4758)
2002/03: 20⁵GS, 21¹¹GF, 21²GF, 25⁵G, 20⁴G, 22²S, 24⁵HY, 22⁶S, 22³GF,

	Starts	1st	2nd	3rd	Win & Pl
Hurdles	1	0	0	0	0
Chases	8	1	2	1	9321
Career Total	21	2	6	2	16486
101 7/02 NAbb	2m5f110yD Ch			G-F	£4690
82 8/01 NAbb	2m6f		D Hdl	GD	£3210
			Total win prize-money £7901

Going: Sf: 0-3 GS: 0-1 Gd: 0-2 GF: - Fm: 1-3
Distance: 2m/2m3: 0-0 2m4-2m7: 1-7 3m+: 0-2
Track: LH: 1-7 RH: 0-1 Tight: 1-4 Gall: 0-3
Aids: Bl: 0-0 Vi: 0-0 Tstrap: 0-0
Best Rating: 113 4/03 Font   2m6f   gd-fm   Ch

Moderate novice chaser; suited by two and three-quarter miles and a sound surface.

Hemsworthy

99   94

8-y-o ch g North Col-Look Back (Country Retreat)
Miss M Bragg W H Whitley

Placings:035/0   (2173)
2002/03: 20⁰S,

	Starts	1st	2nd	3rd	Win & Pl
Hurdles	1	0	0	0	0
Career Total	4	0	0	1	227

Going: Sf: 0-1 GS: 0-0 Gd: 0-0 GF: - Fm: 0-0
Distance: 2m/2m3: 0-0 2m4-2m7: 0-1 3m+: 0-0
Track: LH: 0-1 RH: 0-0 Tight: 0-0 Gall: 0-0
Aids: Bl: 0-0 Vi: 0-0 Tstrap: 0-0
Best Rating: 92 10/00 Chep 2m110y   gd-sft NHF

Henbit's Party

6-y-o ch m Henbit (USA)-Bantel Bouquet (Red Regent)
B A McMahon T E Wardall

Placings:000-5P   (1928)
2002/03: 17⁵GF, 16⁶GS,

	Starts	1st	2nd	3rd	Win & Pl
NH Flat	1	0	0	0	0
Hurdles	4	0	0	0	0
Career Total	5	0	0	0	0

Going: Sf: 0-0 GS: 0-1 Gd: 0-0 GF: - Fm: 0-1
Distance: 2m/2m3: 0-2 2m4-2m7: 0-0 3m+: 0-0
Track: LH: 0-0 RH: 0-2 Tight: 0-1 Gall: 0-0
Aids: Bl: 0-0 Vi: 0-0 Tstrap: 0-0
Best Rating: 67 10/01 Hrfd   2m1f   good   NHF

Henbridge

108   68

7-y-o ch m Henbit (USA)-Celtic Bridge (Celtic Cone)
Mrs S M Johnson E J Praill

Placings:000/P500P0-6F   (0658)
2002/03: 16⁶GF, 16⁶GF,

	Starts	1st	2nd	3rd	Win & Pl
Hurdles	2	0	0	0	0

Career Total   11   0   0   0   0

Going:	Sf: 0-0 GS: 0-0 Gd: 0-0 GF: - Fm: 0-2				
Distance:	2m/2m3: 0-2 2m4-2m7: 0-0 3m+: 0-0				
Track:	LH: 0-2 RH: 0-0 Tight: 0-0 Gall: 0-0				
Aids:	Bl: 0-0 Vi: 0-0 Tstrap: 0-0				
Best Rating:	61 2/01 Ludl 2m good Hdl				

Selling hurdler; best effort to date when close third from 10lb wrong at Newton Abbot June 2003; acts on good to firm; yet to prove she can be effective at 2m 4f.

Henderson

4-y-o br g Wesaam (USA)-Akatombo (Ilium)
D E Cantillon   Bet Big Win Big Partnership

Placings:F   (1641)
2002/03: 16FG,

	Starts	1st	2nd	3rd	Win & Pl
Hurdles	1	0	0	0	
Career Total	1	0	0	0	

Going:	Sf: 0-0 GS: 0-0 Gd: 0-0 GF: - Fm: 0-0
Distance:	2m/2m3: 0-1 2m4-2m7: 0-0 3m+: 0-0
Track:	LH: 0-0 RH: 0-1 Tight: 0-0 Gall: 0-0
Aids:	Bl: 0-0 Vi: 0-0 Tstrap: 0-0
Best Rating:	0 10/02 Kemp 2m good Hdl

Henna

5-y-o ch m Henbit (USA)-Celtic Chimes (Celtic Cone)
G P Enright   Homebred Racing

Placings:00P   (4431)
2002/03: 17HY, 16PG, 18PGF,

	Starts	1st	2nd	3rd	Win & Pl
NH Flat	3	0	0	0	
Career Total	3	0	0	0	

Going:	Sf: 0-1 GS: 0-0 Gd: 0-1 GF: - Fm: 0-1
Distance:	2m/2m3: 0-3 2m4-2m7: 0-0 3m+: 0-0
Track:	LH: 0-1 RH: 0-2 Tight: 0-1 Gall: 0-1
Aids:	Bl: 0-0 Vi: 0-0 Tstrap: 0-0
Best Rating:	0 3/03 Plum 2m2f gd-fm NHF

Hennerwood Ivy

8-y-o b m Tina s Pet-Come On Clover (Oats)
R J Price   Cyril Thomas

Placings:0-FP   (1178)
2002/03: 16FGF, 16PGF,

	Starts	1st	2nd	3rd	Win & Pl
Hurdles	2	0	0	0	
Career Total	3	0	0	0	

Going:	Sf: 0-0 GS: 0-0 Gd: 0-0 GF: - Fm: 0-2
Distance:	2m/2m3: 0-2 2m4-2m7: 0-0 3m+: 0-0
Track:	LH: 0-2 RH: 0-0 Tight: 0-1 Gall: 0-0
Aids:	Bl: 0-0 Vi: 0-0 Tstrap: 0-0
Best Rating:	0 8/02 Worc 2m gd-fm Hdl

Henrianjames

106(92h)   (90+h)**115**
8-y-o b g Tina s Pet-Real Claire (Dreams To Reality (USA))

Mrs M Reveley   K Benson

Placings:0/00616-2F4003S123   (4687)
2002/03: 16FG, 16PGS, 16FS, 174GF, 17PGF, 17PG, 173G, 16SGF, 161GF, 162GF, 173G,

	Starts	1st	2nd	3rd	Win & Pl
Hurdles	1	0	1	0	724
Chases	10	1	1	2	9457
Career Total	16	2	2	2	13509

103	9/02	Prth	2m	D Ch		G-F	£6727
94	4/02	Newc	2m110y	E Ch	FRM		£3328

Total win prize-money £10057

Going:	Sf: 0-1 GS: 0-1 Gd: 0-4 GF: - Fm: 1-5
Distance:	2m/2m3: 1-11 2m4-2m7: 0-0 3m+: 0-0
Track:	LH: 0-7 RH: 1-4 Tight: 0-5 Gall: 0-1
Aids:	Bl: 0-0 Vi: 0-0 Tstrap: 0-0
Best Rating:	115 10/02 Hexm 2m110y gd-fm Ch

Modest chaser; comfortable winner at Wetherby in May; best on a sound surface, but handles good to soft; suited by around two miles.

Henry Bruce

11-y-o ch g Buckley-Booterstown (Master Owen)
Miss R S Reynolds   Bill Jackson

Placings:4P1/F4F/4PP/0   (3548)
2002/03: 25PG,

	Starts	1st	2nd	3rd	Win & Pl
Chases	1	0	0	0	
Career Total	10	1	0	0	2230

101	3/99	Extr	3m2f	H Ch	GD	£1954

Total win prize-money £1954

Going:	Sf: 0-0 GS: 0-0 Gd: 0-1 GF: - Fm: 0-0
Distance:	2m/2m3: 0-0 2m4-2m7: 0-0 3m+: 0-1
Track:	LH: 0-0 RH: 0-1 Tight: 0-0 Gall: 0-0
Aids:	Bl: 0-0 Vi: 0-0 Tstrap: 0-0
Best Rating:	108 2/00 Font 3m2f110y soft Ch

Henry Isaiah (IRE)

6-y-o b g Corrouge (USA)-Maid In The Mist (Pry)
C Tizzard   Alvin Trowbridge

Placings:PP0BP-PF   (2551)
2002/03: 17PGS, 16FS,

	Starts	1st	2nd	3rd	Win & Pl
Chases	2	0	0	0	
Career Total	7	0	0	0	

Going:	Sf: 0-1 GS: 0-1 Gd: 0-0 GF: - Fm: 0-0
Distance:	2m/2m3: 0-2 2m4-2m7: 0-0 3m+: 0-0
Track:	LH: 0-0 RH: 0-0 Tight: 0-1 Gall: 0-0
Aids:	Bl: 0-0 Vi: 0-0 Tstrap: 0-0
Best Rating:	0 12/02 Folk 2m soft Ch

Henry Pearson (USA)

96   **86+**
5-y-o ch g Distant View (USA)-Lady Ellen (USA) (Explosive Bid (USA))
H P Hogarth   Hogarth Racing

Placings:0-0   (2558)
2002/03: 16PGF,

	Starts	1st	2nd	3rd	Win & Pl
Hurdles	1	0	0	0	

Career Total   2   0   0   0

Going:	Sf: 0-0 GS: 0-0 Gd: 0-0 GF: - Fm: 0-1
Distance:	2m/2m3: 0-1 2m4-2m7: 0-0 3m+: 0-0
Track:	LH: 0-0 RH: 0-1 Tight: 0-1 Gall: 0-0
Aids:	Bl: 0-0 Vi: 0-0 Tstrap: 0-1
Best Rating:	86 12/02 Muss 2m gd-fm Hdl

Hera

60f   **17f**
6-y-o b m Thethingaboutitis (USA)-Zalina (Tyrnavos)
M Wellings   Mrs M A Powis

Placings:00   (4542)
2002/03: 17PG, 16PG,

	Starts	1st	2nd	3rd	Win & Pl
NH Flat	2	0	0	0	
Career Total	2	0	0	0	

Going:	Sf: 0-0 GS: 0-0 Gd: 0-0 GF: - Fm: 0-0
Distance:	2m/2m3: 0-2 2m4-2m7: 0-0 3m+: 0-0
Track:	LH: 0-0 RH: 0-2 Tight: 0-0 Gall: 0-0
Aids:	Bl: 0-0 Vi: 0-0 Tstrap: 0-0
Best Rating:	17 4/03 Ludl 2m good NHF

Heracles

110(108h)   (120h)**120**
7-y-o b g Unfuwain (USA)-La Masse (High Top)
B G Powell   Mrs D A La Trobe

Placings:022/1135/524P-31511334   (1640)
2002/03: 18SGF, 201GS, 20PG, 211GF, 231GF, 213GF, 213G, 214G,

	Starts	1st	2nd	3rd	Win & Pl
Hurdles	3	0	0	1	880
Chases	5	3	0	2	13460
Career Total	19	5	3	4	26484

120	7/02	Worc	2m7f110yE Ch	G-F	£3506
106	6/02	NAbb	2m5f110yD Ch	G-F	£4153
120	5/02	Sthl	2m4f110yE Ch	G-S	£3149
116	1/01	Kemp	2m5f D Hdl	SFT	£3851
125	1/01	Kemp	2m D Hdl	SFT	£4738

Total win prize-money £19400

Going:	Sf: 0-0 GS: 1-1 Gd: 0-3 GF: - Fm: 2-4
Distance:	2m/2m3: 0-1 2m4-2m7: 2-6 3m+: 1-1
Track:	LH: 3-7 RH: 0-1 Tight: 2-4 Gall: 0-0
Aids:	Bl: 0-0 Vi: 0-0 Tstrap: 0-0
Best Rating:	127 2/01 Kemp 2m5f gd-sft Hdl

Landed his first two starts over hurdles, both at Kempton, but beaten in better company afterwards. Won minor novice chase at Southwell May 2002. Stays two and a half miles plus, acts on soft ground, and is suited by a flat, right-handed track.

Heraclitean Fire (IRE)

103   **99**
6-y-o b g Norwich-Mazovia (FR) (Taufan (USA))
Seamus O Farrell   Seamus O Farrell

Placings:000065504   (2530a)
2002/03: 16PS, 19PYS, 16PS, 17PYS, 16PG, 16SGY, 16SGS, 16PS, 204S,

	Starts	1st	2nd	3rd	Win & Pl
NH Flat	2	0	0	0	0
Hurdles	7	0	0	0	769
Career Total	9	0	0	0	769

Going:	Sf: 0-4 GS: 0-1 Gd: 0-1 GF: - Fm: 0-0

Distance: 2m/2m3: 0-8 2m4-2m7: 0-1 3m+: 0-0
Track: LH: 0-1 RH: 0-2 Tight: 0-0 Gall: 0-0
Aids: Bl: 0-0 Vi: 0-0 Tstrap: 0-0
Best Rating: 102 11/02 Thur 2m gd-yld Hdl

Irish novice hurdler who has yet to get off the mark.

Here Comes Henry
96   107
9-y-o ch g Dortino-Epryana (English Prince)
R H Alner A D & Mrs S A Old

Placings:136/P-522U023P4 (4636)
2002/03: 23^5G, 24^2S, 20^2G, 21^UGS, 24^0GS, 26^2GS, 28^3G, 24^PG, 24^4G,

	Starts	1st	2nd	3rd	Win & Pl
Chases	9	0	3	1	4883
Career Total	13	1	3	2	8827
127 3/01 Strf 3m	H Ch			SFT	£2249

Total win prize-money £2249

Going: Sf: 0-1 GS: 0-3 Gd: 0-5 GF: - Fm: 0-0
Distance: 2m/2m3: 0-0 2m4-2m7: 0-2 3m+: 0-7
Track: LH: 0-3 RH: 0-5 Tight: 0-4 Gall: 0-0
Aids: Bl: 0-1 Vi: 0-0 Tstrap: 0-0
Best Rating: 127 3/01 Strf 3m soft Ch

Modest chaser; stays well; acts on a sound surface.

Here Comes Steve
111   93
6-y-o b g Primitive Rising (USA)-Keldholme (Derek H)
A Crook Dent,Byrne,Savage,Proctor & Colley

Placings:00-4362 (3353)
2002/03: 20^4S, 24^3GS, 16^6S, 24^2HY,

	Starts	1st	2nd	3rd	Win & Pl
Hurdles	4	0	1	1	1675
Career Total	6	0	1	1	1675

Going: Sf: 0-3 GS: 0-1 Gd: 0-0 GF: - Fm: 0-0
Distance: 2m/2m3: 0-2 2m4-2m7: 0-1 3m+: 0-2
Track: LH: 0-4 RH: 0-0 Tight: 0-0 Gall: 0-3
Aids: Bl: 0-0 Vi: 0-0 Tstrap: 0-0
Best Rating: 93 1/03 Newc 3m heavy Hdl

Easily best effort over hurdles when narrowly denied over three miles at Newcastle in January.

Herecomestanley
59f
4-y-o b g Missed Flight-Moonspell (Batshoof)
M F Harris The Paddysaurus Coming Partnership

Placings:0 (4090)
2002/03: 16^0GS,

	Starts	1st	2nd	3rd	Win & Pl
NH Flat	1	0	0	0	
Career Total	1	0	0	0	

Going: Sf: 0-0 GS: 0-1 Gd: 0-0 GF: - Fm: 0-0
Distance: 2m/2m3: 0-1 2m4-2m7: 0-0 3m+: 0-0
Track: LH: 0-0 RH: 0-0 Tight: 0-0 Gall: 0-0
Aids: Bl: 0-0 Vi: 0-0 Tstrap: 0-0
Best Rating: 61 3/03 Strf 2m110y gd-sft NHF

Heresthething
7-y-o b g Thethingaboutitis (USA)-Chocolate Ripple (Hasty Word)

J S King Mrs R M Hill

Placings:000/PUP (3947)
2002/03: 19^PG, 24^UGS, 19^PS,

	Starts	1st	2nd	3rd	Win & Pl
Hurdles	1	0	0	0	0
Chases	2	0	0	0	0
Career Total	6	0	0	0	

Going: Sf: 0-1 GS: 0-1 Gd: 0-1 GF: - Fm: 0-0
Distance: 2m/2m3: 0-0 2m4-2m7: 0-2 3m+: 0-1
Track: LH: 0-1 RH: 0-2 Tight: 0-0 Gall: 0-0
Aids: Bl: 0-0 Vi: 0-0 Tstrap: 0-0
Best Rating: 59 1/01 Kemp 2m soft NHF

Hermes Iii (FR)
109(110h)   (123+h)144
8-y-o b g Quart De Vin (FR)-Queenly (FR) (Pot D Or (FR))
N J Henderson Thurloe Thoroughbreds Iv

Placings:1/52-1113P (4114)
2002/03: 20^1GS, 20^1GS, 20^1S, 21^3GS, 20^PG,

	Starts	1st	2nd	3rd	Win & Pl
Hurdles	2	2	0	0	6244
Chases	3	1	0	1	14220
Career Total	8	4	1	1	24936
144 12/02 Sand 2m4f110yC(0-135)HCh				SFT	£9820
116 6/02 Prth 2m4f110yE Hdl				G-S	£2884
123 5/02 Weth 2m4f110yD Hdl				G-S	£3360
4/00 Fntb 2m1f110y Ch				SFT	£3074

Total win prize-money £19138

Going: Sf: 1-1 GS: 2-3 Gd: 0-1 GF: - Fm: 0-0
Distance: 2m/2m3: 0-0 2m4-2m7: 3-5 3m+: 0-0
Track: LH: 1-3 RH: 2-2 Tight: 0-0 Gall: 0-2
Aids: Bl: 0-0 Vi: 0-0 Tstrap: 0-0
Best Rating: 144 12/02 Sand 2m4f110y soft Ch

A winner in France over fences; he won twice over hurdles in 2002; decisive winner over fences at Sandown in December 2002 on handicap and chasing debut in this country; best at up to two and a half miles.

Hermit's Hideaway
6-y-o b g Rock City-Adriya (Vayrann)
Mrs A M Thorpe (T D Barron 26/7) Mrs A M Thorpe

Placings:P (1713)
2002/03: 16^PG,

	Starts	1st	2nd	3rd	Win & Pl
Hurdles	1	0	0	0	
Career Total	1	0	0	0	

Going: Sf: 0-0 GS: 0-0 Gd: 0-1 GF: - Fm: 0-0
Distance: 2m/2m3: 0-1 2m4-2m7: 0-0 3m+: 0-0
Track: LH: 0-1 RH: 0-0 Tight: 0-1 Gall: 0-0
Aids: Bl: 0-0 Vi: 0-0 Tstrap: 0-0
Best Rating: 0 10/02 Strf 2m110y good Hdl

Hernandita
96   92
5-y-o b m Hernando (FR)-Dara Dee (Dara Monarch)
M C Pipe P Clarke

Placings:1145-00P (3249)
2002/03: 19^0GS, 16^0S, 25^PHY,

	Starts	1st	2nd	3rd	Win & Pl
Hurdles	3	0	0	0	

	Career Total	7	2	0	0	5407
110 1/02 Sthl 2m	E Hdl				G-S	£2464
113 12/01 Winc 2m	E Hdl				GD	£2569

Total win prize-money £5033

Going: Sf: 0-2 GS: 0-1 Gd: 0-0 GF: - Fm: 0-0
Distance: 2m/2m3: 0-1 2m4-2m7: 0-1 3m+: 0-1
Track: LH: 0-1 RH: 0-2 Tight: 0-1 Gall: 0-0
Aids: Bl: 0-0 Vi: 0-0 Tstrap: 0-0
Best Rating: 113 12/01 Winc 2m good Hdl

Made a good start to her hurdling career with two wins in modest company, but jumped poorly when flopping on her third start. Held since. Suited by two miles and has won on good and heavy ground.

Heroicus (NZ)
87(80h)   (63h)45
6-y-o ch g Heroicity (AUS)-Glenford (NZ) (Sackford (USA))
F Kirby Fred Kirby

Placings:04FPPP-6PP000 (4408)
2002/03: 16^8GF, 17^PG, 16^PHY, 16^0S, 17^0G, 16^0G,

Hurdles	6	0	0	0
Career Total	12	0	0	0

Going: Sf: 0-2 GS: 0-0 Gd: 0-3 GF: - Fm: 0-1
Distance: 2m/2m3: 0-6 2m4-2m7: 0-0 3m+: 0-0
Track: LH: 0-6 RH: 0-0 Tight: 0-2 Gall: 0-1
Aids: Bl: 0-0 Vi: 0-0 Tstrap: 0-0
Best Rating: 76 11/01 Ludl 2m gd-fm NHF

Heron's Ghyll (IRE)
98f   101f
6-y-o b g Simply Great (FR)-Leisure Centre (IRE) (Tanfirion)
Miss Venetia Williams Mrs Vida Bingham

Placings:251 (3789)
2002/03: 17^2GS, 18^5S, 17^1G,

	Starts	1st	2nd	3rd	Win & Pl
NH Flat	3	1	1	0	2747
Career Total	3	1	1	0	2747
101 2/03 Hrfd 2m1f	H NHF			GD	£2051

Total win prize-money £2051

Going: Sf: 0-1 GS: 0-1 Gd: 1-1 GF: - Fm: 0-0
Distance: 2m/2m3: 1-3 2m4-2m7: 0-0 3m+: 0-0
Track: LH: 0-1 RH: 1-1 Tight: 0-1 Gall: 0-0
Aids: Bl: 0-0 Vi: 0-0 Tstrap: 0-0
Best Rating: 101 2/03 Hrfd 2m1f good NHF

Made it third time lucky in bumpers with a narow success at Hereford in February.

Heronstown (IRE)
105f
4-y-o b g Standiford (USA)-Eleckydo (Electric)
William Coleman O Brien Noel Monaghan

Placings:024 (3837a)
2002/03: 13^0S, 16^2S, 16^4YS,

	Starts	1st	2nd	3rd	Win & Pl
NH Flat	1	0	0	0	0
Hurdles	2	0	1	0	1455
Career Total	3	0	1	0	1455

Going: Sf: 0-2 GS: 0-0 Gd: 0-0 GF: - Fm: 0-0
Distance: 2m/2m3: 0-2 2m4-2m7: 0-0 3m+: 0-0
Track: LH: 0-0 RH: 0-1 Tight: 0-0 Gall: 0-0

Aids: Bl: 0-0 Vi: 0-0 Tstrap: 0-0
Best Rating: 114 1/03 Tram 2m   soft   Hdl

Modest irish hurdler; acts on soft.

Herself

92   **108**

6-y-o b m Hernando (FR)-Kirsten (Kris)
J Mackie Ms Caroline F Breay

Placings:352/446313252-5   (1827)
2002/03: 24⁴S,

	Starts	1st	2nd	3rd	Win & Pl
Hurdles	1	0	0	0	0
Career Total	13	1	3	3	7011

106 11/01 Leic   2m4f110yE(0-105)HHdl   G-S   £2989
Total win prize-money £2989

Going: Sf: 0-1 GS: 0-0 Gd: 0-0 GF: - Fm: 0-0
Distance: 2m/2m3: 0-0 2m4-2m7: 0-0 3m+: 0-1
Track: LH: 0-1 RH: 0-0 Tight: 0-0 Gall: 0-0
Aids: Bl: 0-0 Vi: 0-0 Tstrap: 0-0
Best Rating: 108 4/02 Uttx 2m4f110y   good   Hdl

A consistent performer. She relishes the mud, stays two miles six.

Hersilia (IRE)

100(102c)   (87+c)**92**

12-y-o br m Mandalus-Milan Pride (Northern Guest (USA))
R Ford L A E Hopkins

Placings:0/5564533214604/035064450212/F00F3620425/5-3236   (0764)
2002/03: 24³G, 24²GS, 27³GF, 27⁶GF,

	Starts	1st	2nd	3rd	Win & Pl
Hurdles	3	0	0	2	1174
Chases	1	0	1	0	2065
Career Total	42	2	6	6	12742

95 3/97 DRoy 2m   Ch   G-Y   £2373
102 1/96 Tram 2m4f   Hdl   YLD   £2648
Total win prize-money £5022

Going: Sf: 0-0 GS: 0-1 Gd: 0-1 GF: - Fm: 0-2
Distance: 2m/2m3: 0-0 2m4-2m7: 0-0 3m+: 0-4
Track: LH: 0-3 RH: 0-1 Tight: 0-2 Gall: 0-0
Aids: Bl: 0-0 Vi: 0-0 Tstrap: 0-0
Best Rating: 109 3/97 Dpat 3m   gd-yld   Ch

Hersov (IRE)

107(106h)   (123h)**124+**

7-y-o gr g Roselier (FR)-Higher Again (IRE) (Strong Gale)
N J Henderson Michael H Watt

Placings:352-114   (3522)
2002/03: 23¹G, 24¹GS, 24⁴G,

	Starts	1st	2nd	3rd	Win & Pl
Chases	3	2	0	0	12672
Career Total	6	2	1	1	15668

124 1/03 Kemp 3m   D Ch   G-S   £7910
124 12/02 Leic 2m7f110yE   Ch   GD   £4124
Total win prize-money £12034

Going: Sf: 0-0 GS: 1-1 Gd: 1-2 GF: - Fm: 0-0
Distance: 2m/2m3: 0-0 2m4-2m7: 0-0 **3m+: 2-3**
Track: LH: 0-1 **RH: 2-2** Tight: 0-0 Gall: 0-1
Aids: Bl: 0-0 Vi: 0-0 Tstrap: 0-0
Best Rating: 124 1/03 Kemp 3m   gd-sft   Ch

Decent novice chaser; shaped well in novice hurdles in 2001/02; won on chasing debut at Leicester in December

and followed up at kempton over Christmas; stays three miles and acts on good and soft ground.

Hesk (FR)

8-y-o b g Spoleto-Negrilla (FR) (Signani (FR))
M C Pipe C M , B J & R F Batterham Ii

Placings:F/04P5F10FU/1111F/P   (1176)
2002/03: 17⁵GF,

	Starts	1st	2nd	3rd	Win & Pl
Chases	1	0	0	0	
Career Total	16	5	0	0	20245

135 9/00 Worc 2m   D Ch   G-F   £4536
124 8/00 NAbb 2m110y   E Ch   GD   £3018
122 7/00 Worc 2m   E Ch   G-F   £2886
117 7/00 NAbb 2m110y   D Ch   G-F   £3672
    2/00 Pau 2m2f   Hdl   GD   £4803
Total win prize-money £18917

Going: Sf: 0-0 GS: 0-0 Gd: 0-0 GF: - Fm: 0-1
Distance: 2m/2m3: 0-1 2m4-2m7: 0-0 3m+: 0-0
Track: LH: 0-1 RH: 0-0 Tight: 0-1 Gall: 0-0
Aids: Bl: 0-0 Vi: 0-0 Tstrap: 0-0
Best Rating: 135 9/00 Worc 2m   gd-fm   Ch

Hetland Hill

7-y-o ch g Secret Appeal-Mohibbah (USA) (Conquistador Cielo (USA))
L Lungo Mrs Barbara Lungo

Placings:36   (2769)
2002/03: 17³G, 16⁶GS,

	Starts	1st	2nd	3rd	Win & Pl
NH Flat	2	0	0	1	324
Career Total	2	0	0	1	324

Going: Sf: 0-0 GS: 0-1 Gd: 0-1 GF: - Fm: 0-0
Distance: 2m/2m3: 0-0 2m4-2m7: 0-0 3m+: 0-0
Track: LH: 0-1 RH: 0-0 Tight: 0-2 Gall: 0-0
Aids: Bl: 0-0 Vi: 0-0 Tstrap: 0-0
Best Rating: 95 10/02 Sedg 2m1f   good   NHF

Hever Golf Glory

101   **75**

9-y-o b g Efisio-Zaius (Artaius (USA))
C N Kellett D H & Mrs R E Muir

Placings:600/05-0   (4666)
2002/03: 16⁶G,

	Starts	1st	2nd	3rd	Win & Pl
Hurdles	1	0	0	0	
Career Total	6	0	0	0	0

Going: Sf: 0-2 GS: 0-0 Gd: 0-1 GF: - Fm: 0-1
Distance: 2m/2m3: 0-1 2m4-2m7: 0-0 3m+: 0-0
Track: LH: 0-1 RH: 0-0 Tight: 0-1 Gall: 0-0
Aids: Bl: 0-0 Vi: 0-0 Tstrap: 0-0
Best Rating: 69 5/01 Hntg 2m110y   gd-fm   Hdl

Hey Ref (IRE)

102   **120+**

6-y-o b g King s Ride-Jeanarie (Reformed Character)
Jonjo O Neill J P McManus

Placings:0-141   (3515)

2002/03: 17¹S, 20⁴GS, 16¹GS,

	Starts	1st	2nd	3rd	Win & Pl
NH Flat	1	1	0	0	2050
Hurdles	2	1	0	0	5607
Career Total	4	2	0	0	7657

120 2/03 Hayd 2m   D Hdl   G-S   £5216
111 10/02 Carl 2m1f   H NHF   SFT   £2049
Total win prize-money £7266

Going: Sf: 1-1 GS: 1-2 Gd: 0-0 GF: - Fm: 0-0
Distance: 2m/2m3: 2-2 2m4-2m7: 0-1 3m+: 0-0
Track: LH: 1-2 RH: 1-1 Tight: 0-0 Gall: 0-0
Aids: Bl: 0-0 Vi: 0-0 Tstrap: 0-0
Best Rating: 120 2/03 Hayd 2m   gd-sft   Hdl

Novice hurdler; won at Haydock in February 2003; effective at two miles on soft ground.

Heynestown Pride (IRE)

91   **75**

6-y-o ch m Zaffaran (USA)-Mayobridge (Our Mirage)
N G Richards (Patrick Boyle 11/1) Mrs O E Matthews

Placings:0-000056   (4749)
2002/03: 16⁰S, 18⁰SH, 16⁰S, 16⁰S, 21⁵S, 20⁶G,

	Starts	1st	2nd	3rd	Win & Pl
NH Flat	4	0	0	0	0
Hurdles	2	0	0	0	0
Career Total	7	0	0	0	0

Going: Sf: 0-4 GS: 0-0 Gd: 0-1 GF: - Fm: 0-0
Distance: 2m/2m3: 0-4 2m4-2m7: 0-2 3m+: 0-0
Track: LH: 0-1 RH: 0-1 Tight: 0-1 Gall: 0-0
Aids: Bl: 0-0 Vi: 0-0 Tstrap: 0-0
Best Rating: 76 12/02 Navn 2m   soft   NHF

Hi Buddy

90   **90**

6-y-o br g High Kicker (USA)-Star Thyme (Point North)
J Mackie R M Mitchell

Placings:400-F4030   (0623)
2002/03: 16⁶FG, 20⁴S, 16⁶G, 16⁹HY, 17⁰GF,

	Starts	1st	2nd	3rd	Win & Pl
Hurdles	5	0	0	1	782
Career Total	8	0	0	1	1062

Going: Sf: 0-2 GS: 0-0 Gd: 0-2 GF: - Fm: 0-1
Distance: 2m/2m3: 0-4 2m4-2m7: 0-1 3m+: 0-0
Track: LH: 0-4 RH: 0-1 Tight: 0-4 Gall: 0-0
Aids: Bl: 0-2 Vi: 0-3 Tstrap: 0-0
Best Rating: 90 6/02 Uttx 2m   heavy   Hdl

Hi Cloy (IRE)

115   **135**

6-y-o b g Be My Native (USA)-Thomastown Girl (Tekoah)
Michael Hourigan Mrs S McCloy

Placings:0-231144F   (4109)
2002/03: 16²S, 18³SH, 16¹HY, 20¹S, 18⁴S, 20⁴Y, 21⁶FG,

	Starts	1st	2nd	3rd	Win & Pl
NH Flat	2	0	1	1	1417
Hurdles	5	2	0	0	17572
Career Total	8	2	1	1	18989

133 1/03 Leop 2m4f   Hdl   SFT   £8441
119 12/02 Leop 2m   Hdl   HVY   £6773
Total win prize-money £15215

Column 1

Going: Sf: 2-4 GS: 0-0 Gd: 0-1 GF: - Fm: 0-0
Distance: 2m/2m3: 1-4 2m4-2m7: 1-3 3m+: 0-0
Track: LH: 2-4 RH: 0-1 Tight: 0-0 Gall: 0-1
Aids: Bl: 0-0 Vi: 0-0 Tstrap: 0-0
Best Rating: 135 2/03 Leop 2m2f   soft   Hdl

Irish-trained novice hurdler; stays two and a half miles; acts in testing conditions.

Hi Fi

98   83d

5-y-o b g Homo Sapien-Baroness Orkzy (Baron Blakeney)
Ian Williams Mrs Rosemary Paterson

Placings:044065   (4677)
2002/03: 16⁰G, 17⁴S, 19⁴GS, 19⁰GS, 22⁶G, 19⁵GF,

	Starts	1st	2nd	3rd	Win & Pl
NH Flat	1	0	0	0	0
Hurdles	5	0	0	0	0
Career Total	6	0	0	0	0

Going: Sf: 0-1 GS: 0-2 Gd: 0-2 GF: - Fm: 0-1
Distance: 2m/2m3: 0-3 2m4-2m7: 0-3 3m+: 0-0
Track: LH: 0-0 RH: 0-6 Tight: 0-1 Gall: 0-0
Aids: Bl: 0-0 Vi: 0-0 Tstrap: 0-0
Best Rating: 93 11/02 Winc 2m   good   NHF

Moderate hurdler; effective up to two miles three with cut in the ground.

Hi Jamie (IRE)

(78h)   (62h)**79**

11-y-o b g Parliament-Lilo Lil (Dunphy)
F P Murtagh (J G Cromwell 28/9) F P Murtagh

Placings:00F/1003002/44450006/00210305/056026/4UF03
500-0060   (2161)
2002/03: 20⁰Y, 24⁰G, 19⁶F, 17⁰S,

	Starts	1st	2nd	3rd	Win & Pl
Hurdles	2	0	0	0	0
Chases	2	0	0	0	0
Career Total	44	2	3	3	10076
82	7/99	Baln	2m1f		(0-102)HCh	Y-S	£2915
106	7/97	Bell	2m1f		NHF	G-Y	£2712
Total win prize-money £5629

Going: Sf: 0-1 GS: 0-0 Gd: 0-1 GF: - Fm: 0-1
Distance: 2m/2m3: 0-2 2m4-2m7: 0-1 3m+: 0-1
Track: LH: 0-1 RH: 0-0 Tight: 0-1 Gall: 0-1
Aids: Bl: 0-0 Vi: 0-0 Tstrap: 0-0
Best Rating: 119 4/98 Fair 2m   good   Hdl

Hi Lily

100(100h)   (94h)**89**

7-y-o b m Jupiter Island-By Line (High Line)
C C Bealby Michael Hill

Placings:0/05-P223P22P01P2   (4633)
2002/03: 16⁶G, 16²G, 16²HY, 20³GF, 21⁶GS, 16²GS, 20²GS, 25⁵S,
20⁶GS, 20¹GF, 21⁶G, 20²GF,

	Starts	1st	2nd	3rd	Win & Pl
Hurdles	5	0	3	1	3755
Chases	7	1	2	0	5893
Career Total	15	1	5	1	9648
90	3/03	Sthl	2m4f110yF(0-90)HCh	G-F	£3513
Total win prize-money £3513

Going: Sf: 0-2 GS: 0-4 Gd: 0-3 GF: - Fm: 1-3
Distance: 2m/2m3: 0-4 2m4-2m7: 1-7 3m+: 0-1
Track: LH: 1-8 RH: 0-4 Tight: 1-7 Gall: 0-1

Column 2

Aids: Bl: 0-0 Vi: 0-0 Tstrap: 0-0
Best Rating: 94 12/02 Hntg 2m4f110y gd-sft Ch

Moderate chaser; suited by fast ground; effective at two and a half miles.

Hi Rudolf

96(78h)   (76h)**88**

8-y-o b g Ballet Royal (USA)-Hi Darlin (Prince De Galles)
H J Manners H J Manners

Placings:053P/0P/P/53P3-535FPP1F   (4273)
2002/03: 25⁵GF, 19³G, 22⁵S, 21⁵HY, 17⁵S, 20⁵GS, 20¹S, 19⁵G,

	Starts	1st	2nd	3rd	Win & Pl
Hurdles	1	0	0	0	0
Chases	7	1	0	1	4800
Career Total	19	1	0	4	5867
88	3/03	Font	2m4f		E Ch	SFT	£4357
Total win prize-money £4358

Going: Sf: 1-4 GS: 0-1 Gd: 0-2 GF: - Fm: 0-1
Distance: 2m/2m3: 0-2 2m4-2m7: 1-5 3m+: 0-1
Track: LH: 0-5 RH: 0-2 Tight: 1-5 Gall: 0-1
Aids: Bl: 0-0 Vi: 0-0 Tstrap: 0-0
Best Rating: 88 3/03 Font 2m4f   soft   Ch

Modest hunter/novice chaser; best at around two and a half miles; acts on soft ground.

Hi Tech

91   72

4-y-o b g Polar Falcon (USA)-Just Speculation (IRE)
(Ahonoora)
Dr P Pritchard (M A Jarvis 11/7) Mrs T Pritchard

Placings:0P654P   (4525)
2002/03: 16⁶GF, 16⁶GS, 17⁶HY, 16⁵HY, 17⁴HY, 16⁶G,

	Starts	1st	2nd	3rd	Win & Pl
Hurdles	6	0	0	0	246
Career Total	6	0	0	0	246

Going: Sf: 0-3 GS: 0-1 Gd: 0-1 GF: - Fm: 0-1
Distance: 2m/2m3: 0-6 2m4-2m7: 0-0 3m+: 0-0
Track: LH: 0-5 RH: 0-1 Tight: 0-0 Gall: 0-1
Aids: Bl: 0-0 Vi: 0-0 Tstrap: 0-0
Best Rating: 72 3/03 Tntn 2m1f   heavy   Hdl

Has shown little so far.

Hi Tek

76   61

8-y-o ch m Arzanni-Storm Foot (Import)
Mrs A C Tate Hi Tek Group

Placings:00000/40/P400400-6P   (0655)
2002/03: 26⁶GF, 24⁰GF,

	Starts	1st	2nd	3rd	Win & Pl
Hurdles	2	0	0	0	0
Career Total	16	0	0	0	233

Going: Sf: 0-0 GS: 0-0 Gd: 0-0 GF: - Fm: 0-2
Distance: 2m/2m3: 0-2 2m4-2m7: 0-0 3m+: 0-2
Track: LH: 0-1 RH: 0-1 Tight: 0-0 Gall: 0-2
Aids: Bl: 0-0 Vi: 0-0 Tstrap: 0-0
Best Rating: 71 1/00 Ludl 2m   good   NHF

Hickey's Gift (IRE)

91

7-y-o ch g Over The River (FR)-Chorabelle (Choral Society)

Column 3

Aids: Bl: 0-0 Vi: 0-0 Tstrap: 0-0
Best Rating: 94 12/02 Hntg 2m4f110y gd-sft Ch

Moderate chaser; suited by fast ground; effective at two and a half miles.

R H Alner R Alner

Placings:05P-10   (0578)
2002/03: 21¹F, 22⁰G,

	Starts	1st	2nd	3rd	Win & Pl
Hurdles	2	1	0	0	2688
Career Total	5	1	0	0	2688
91	5/02	Wwck	2m5f		E Hdl	FRM	£2688
Total win prize-money £2688

Going: Sf: 0-0 GS: 0-0 Gd: 0-1 GF: - Fm: 1-1
Distance: 2m/2m3: 0-0 2m4-2m7: 1-2 3m+: 0-0
Track: LH: 1-2 RH: 0-0 Tight: 0-1 Gall: 0-0
Aids: Bl: 0-0 Vi: 0-0 Tstrap: 0-0
Best Rating: 91 5/02 Wwck 2m5f   firm   Hdl

Showed little before landing a weak Warwick novice hurdle on firm ground in May 2002. A chasing type.

Hickleton Club

83f   59f

5-y-o b g Aragon-Honest Opinion (Free State)
G A Swinbank D Leech

Placings:0   (2769)
2002/03: 16⁰GS,

	Starts	1st	2nd	3rd	Win & Pl
NH Flat	1	0	0	0	
Career Total	1	0	0	0	

Going: Sf: 0-0 GS: 0-1 Gd: 0-0 GF: - Fm: 0-0
Distance: 2m/2m3: 0-1 2m4-2m7: 0-0 3m+: 0-0
Track: LH: 0-0 RH: 0-1 Tight: 0-1 Gall: 0-0
Aids: Bl: 0-0 Vi: 0-0 Tstrap: 0-0
Best Rating: 59 12/02 Muss 2m   gd-sft NHF

Hidden Affair (IRE)

86   83

7-y-o b g Mandalus-Lovely Affair (IRE) (Roselier (FR))
C J Mann Roger Maggs

Placings:46/PP64P   (3777)
2002/03: 22⁵GS, 20⁰G, 22⁶HY, 17⁴G, 17⁵PGS,

	Starts	1st	2nd	3rd	Win & Pl
Hurdles	4	0	0	0	0
Chases	1	0	0	0	0
Career Total	7	0	0	0	279

Going: Sf: 0-1 GS: 0-2 Gd: 0-2 GF: - Fm: 0-0
Distance: 2m/2m3: 0-2 2m4-2m7: 0-3 3m+: 0-0
Track: LH: 0-2 RH: 0-2 Tight: 0-3 Gall: 0-0
Aids: Bl: 0-3 Vi: 0-0 Tstrap: 0-0
Best Rating: 98 12/00 Newb 2m3f   soft   Hdl

Hidden Exit

98   75

7-y-o b m Landyap (USA)-Queen Of The Nile (Hittite Glory)
Mrs L Williamson R A Hughes

Placings:000-453456   (1668)
2002/03: 16⁴GF, 16⁵GF, 17³G, 16⁴GF, 17⁵GS, 17⁶S,

	Starts	1st	2nd	3rd	Win & Pl
NH Flat	1	0	0	0	0
Hurdles	5	0	0	1	588
Career Total	9	0	0	1	588

Going: Sf: 0-1 GS: 0-1 Gd: 0-1 GF: - Fm: 0-3
Distance: 2m/2m3: 0-6 2m4-2m7: 0-0 3m+: 0-0

Track: LH: 0-5 RH: 0-0 Tight: 0-4 Gall: 0-0
Aids: Bl: 0-0 Vi: 0-0 Tstrap: 0-0
Best Rating: 75 10/02 Bang 2m1f gd-sft Hdl

Poor novice hurdler.

Hidden Pearl (IRE)

92(91h)   (65h)**73**

7-y-o b g Posen (USA)-Cockney Miss (Camden Town)
J A Supple (Ferdy Murphy 26/12) Geoff Hubbard Racing

Placings:P0P05-56300   (4418)
2002/03: 21⁵GS, 23⁶G, 16⁶GS, 19³S, 17⁰GS, 22⁰G,

	Starts	1st	2nd	3rd	Win & Pl
Hurdles	6	0	0	1	318
Career Total	10	0	0	1	318

Going: Sf: 0-1 GS: 0-3 Gd: 0-2 GF: - Fm: 0-0
Distance: 2m/2m3: 0-2 2m4-2m7: 0-3 3m+: 0-1
Track: LH: 0-2 RH: 0-3 Tight: 0-4 Gall: 0-0
Aids: Bl: 0-0 Vi: 0-0 Tstrap: 0-0
Best Rating: 68 5/02 Fknm 2m7f110y good Hdl

First worthwhile form when well beaten third in a selling handicap hurdle at Market Rasen in December.

Hidden Smile (USA)

105   **71**

6-y-o b m Twilight Agenda (USA)-Smooth Edge (USA)
(Meadowlake (USA))
F Jordan The Bhiss Partnership

Placings:0P   (1891)
2002/03: 20⁰G, 16ᴾGS,

	Starts	1st	2nd	3rd	Win & Pl
Hurdles	2	0	0	0	
Career Total	2	0	0	0	

Going: Sf: 0-0 GS: 0-1 Gd: 0-1 GF: - Fm: 0-0
Distance: 2m/2m3: 0-1 2m4-2m7: 0-1 3m+: 0-0
Track: LH: 0-1 RH: 0-1 Tight: 0-0 Gall: 0-1
Aids: Bl: 0-0 Vi: 0-0 Tstrap: 0-0
Best Rating: 16 10/02 Hayd 2m4f good Hdl

Poor novice hurdler; just denied at Uttoxeter in July.

Hidden Valley

104   (127h)**113**

11-y-o b g St Columbus-Leven Valley (Ragstone)
J D Frost G G A Gregson

Placings:0/0/05112F62/011F11/544024-P622P   (3601)
2002/03: 23ᴾG, 23⁶G, 20²G, 19²S, 24ᴾS,

	Starts	1st	2nd	3rd	Win & Pl
Chases	5	2	0	2		3524
Career Total	27	6	5	4		31262
127	4/01	Extr	2m3f	D(0-125)HHdl	SFT	£3969
127	3/01	Extr	2m6f110yD(0-125)HHdl	HVY	£3656
109	1/01	Extr	2m1f110yF(0-100)HCh	HVY	£3132
103	11/00	NAbb	2m5f110yD(0-110)HCh	HVY	£5404
80	11/99	Extr	2m6f	E(0-105)HHdl	G-S	£2921
90	8/99	NAbb	2m1f	F(0-100)HHdl	G-F	£2862

Total win prize-money £21945

Going: Sf: 0-2 GS: 0-0 Gd: 0-3 GF: - Fm: 0-0
Distance: 2m/2m3: 0-1 2m4-2m7: 0-1 3m+: 0-3
Track: LH: 0-1 RH: 0-4 Tight: 0-2 Gall: 0-0
Aids: Bl: 0-0 Vi: 0-0 Tstrap: 0-0
Best Rating: 127 4/01 Extr 2m3f soft Hdl

Fair handicapper over both hurdles and fences who stays two miles-seven in the mud and loves Exeter.

Hiers De Brouage (FR)

105   **110**

8-y-o b g Neustrien (FR)-Thalandrezienne (FR) (Le Correzien (FR))
J G Portman Seddon - Brown Partnership

Placings:0300/PP16-310P1   (4254)
2002/03: 19³S, 21¹GS, 24⁰GS, 20ᴾS, 19¹G,

	Starts	1st	2nd	3rd	Win & Pl
Chases	5	2	0	1		11039
Career Total	13	3	0	2		16766
110	3/03	Extr	2m3f110yD(0-115)HCh	GD	£5739
107	12/02	Winc	2m5f	E(0-105)HCh	G-S	£4257
107	3/02	Chep	2m3f110yD Ch	G-S	£3997

Total win prize-money £13996

Going: Sf: 0-2 GS: 1-2 Gd: 1-1 GF: - Fm: 0-0
Distance: 2m/2m3: 0-1 **2m4-2m7: 2-3** 3m+: 0-1
Track: LH: 0-1 **RH: 2-4** Tight: 0-0 Gall: 0-1
Aids: Bl: 0-0 Vi: 0-0 Tstrap: 0-0
Best Rating: 110 3/03 Extr 2m3f110y good Ch

Modest ex-French chaser; had luck on his side when winning a Chepstow novice chase in March 2002; successful at Wincanton in December; stays two miles-four when winning at Exeter March 2003; inconsistent; unsuited by extremes of going.

Hifinanba

(102h)   (81 h)

7-y-o gr m Gran Alba (USA)-High Finesse (High Line)
J W Mullins Miss C A James

Placings:6/06ᴿ6P003-426R   (3145)
2002/03: 16³G, 19⁴G, 16²G, 19⁶S, 19ᴿS,

	Starts	1st	2nd	3rd	Win & Pl
Hurdles	4	0	1	1		1624
Chases	1	0	0	0		0
Career Total	13	0	1	1		1624

Going: Sf: 0-2 GS: 0-0 Gd: 0-3 GF: - Fm: 0-0
Distance: 2m/2m3: 0-3 2m4-2m7: 0-2 3m+: 0-0
Track: LH: 0-1 RH: 0-4 Tight: 0-3 Gall: 0-0
Aids: Bl: 0-0 Vi: 0-0 Tstrap: 0-0
Best Rating: 90 4/01 Tntn 2m1f gd-fm NHF

Modest hurdler, effective at two miles.

High And Mighty

97   **100**

8-y-o b g Shirley Heights-Air Distingue (USA) (Sir Ivor)
G Barnett J C Bradbury

Placings:3P   (3091)
2002/03: 16³G, 19ᴾGS,

	Starts	1st	2nd	3rd	Win & Pl
Hurdles	2	0	0	1		625
Career Total	2	0	0	1		625

Going: Sf: 0-0 GS: 0-1 Gd: 0-1 GF: - Fm: 0-0
Distance: 2m/2m3: 0-1 2m4-2m7: 0-1 3m+: 0-0
Track: LH: 0-2 RH: 0-0 Tight: 0-0 Gall: 0-0
Aids: Bl: 0-0 Vi: 0-0 Tstrap: 0-0
Best Rating: 100 12/02 Hayd 2m good Hdl

Winner of the 1999 Ascot Stakes on the flat, made a promising start over hurdles at Haydock (two miles) in December 2002. Should do better over further, suited by fast ground.

High Cheviot

99   **89d**

6-y-o b g Shirley Heights-Cutleaf (Kris)
Ferdy Murphy High Cheviot Racing Partnership

Placings:22-425035P0   (4148)
2002/03: 16⁴GF, 22²HY, 20⁵GF, 20⁰S, 20³GF, 19⁵HY, 19ᴾS, 16⁰G,

	Starts	1st	2nd	3rd	Win & Pl
Hurdles	8	0	1	1		2093
Career Total	10	0	3	1		3821

Going: Sf: 0-4 GS: 0-0 Gd: 0-1 GF: - Fm: 0-3
Distance: 2m/2m3: 0-4 2m4-2m7: 0-4 3m+: 0-0
Track: LH: 0-4 RH: 0-3 Tight: 0-4 Gall: 0-1
Aids: Bl: 0-2 Vi: 0-0 Tstrap: 0-0
Best Rating: 100 4/02 Uttx 2m good Hdl

In the frame in novice hurdles, but lacks pace.

High Cotton (IRE)

107(104h)   (114h)**124**

8-y-o gr g Ala Hounak-Planalife (Beau Charmeur (FR))
D R C Elsworth R Burrridge, H Burridge, J H W Lloyd

Placings:62522/243543-244244P   (4438)
2002/03: 19²GS, 24⁴S, 33⁴S, 24²G, 25⁴GS, 32⁴G, 24ᴾG,

	Starts	1st	2nd	3rd	Win & Pl
Chases	7	0	2	0		10568
Career Total	18	0	6	2		25206

Going: Sf: 0-2 GS: 0-2 Gd: 0-3 GF: - Fm: 0-0
Distance: 2m/2m3: 0-2 2m4-2m7: 0-1 3m+: 0-6
Track: LH: 0-4 RH: 0-3 Tight: 0-0 Gall: 0-3
Aids: Bl: 0-1 Vi: 0-0 Tstrap: 0-0
Best Rating: 132 12/01 Kemp 3m good Ch

Fair hurdler/decent chaser; acts on good ground but appreciates very soft ground; probably stays 4m; has worn sheepskin cheekpieces; is not easy to win with.

High Drama

110   **106**

6-y-o b/br g In The Wings-Maestrale (Top Ville)
P Bowen T W Raymond

Placings:332PP01   (4372)
2002/03: 22³F, 17³F, 22²G, 24ᴾGS, 20ᴾG, 22⁰G, 21¹G,

	Starts	1st	2nd	3rd	Win & Pl
Hurdles	7	1	1	2		5455
Career Total	7	1	1	2		5455
106	3/03	Sedg	2m5f110yE Hdl	GD	£3535

Total win prize-money £3535

Going: Sf: 0-0 GS: 0-1 Gd: 1-4 GF: - Fm: 0-2
Distance: 2m/2m3: 0-1 **2m4-2m7: 1-5** 3m+: 0-1
Track: **LH: 1-3** RH: 0-4 **Tight: 1-5** Gall: 0-0
Aids: Bl: 0-0 Vi: 0-0 Tstrap: 0-0
Best Rating: 106 3/03 Sedg 2m5f110y good Hdl

Modest novice hurdler; runaway winner at Sedgefield in March 2003; followed-up in 2m 6f handicap at Exeter the following month; needs the ground good or faster; reported to have schooled well over fences.

High Expectations (IRE)

8-y-o ch g Over The River (FR)-Andy s Fancy (IRE) (Andretti)

J S Haldane J S Haldane

Placings: *0/U-04*   (4506)
2002/03: 25⁰GS, 25⁴G,

	Starts	1st	2nd	3rd	Win & Pl
Chases	2	0	0	0	219
Career Total	4	0	0	0	219

Going: Sf: 0-0 GS: 0-1 Gd: 0-1 GF: - Fm: 0-0
Distance: 2m/2m3: 0-0 2m4-2m7: 0-0 3m+: 0-0
Track: LH: 0-2 RH: 0-0 Tight: 0-2 Gall: 0-0
Aids: Bl: 0-0 Vi: 0-0 Tstrap: 0-0
Best Rating: 84 4/99 Towc 2m   good NHF

Moderate pointer/hunter chaser; multiple winner between the flags in his time; stays three miles plus; suited by cut in the ground.

High Fields

103f   79f

4-y-o b g Sovereign Water (FR)-Once Bitten (Brave Invader (USA))
M W Easterby M W Easterby

Placings: *300*   (4665)
2002/03: 16³G, 16⁹GF, 17⁰GF,

	Starts	1st	2nd	3rd	Win & Pl
NH Flat	3	0	0	1	354
Career Total	3	0	0	1	354

Going: Sf: 0-0 GS: 0-0 Gd: 0-1 GF: - Fm: 0-2
Distance: 2m/2m3: 0-3 2m4-2m7: 0-0 3m+: 0-0
Track: LH: 0-2 RH: 0-1 Tight: 0-1 Gall: 0-0
Aids: Bl: 0-0 Vi: 0-0 Tstrap: 0-0
Best Rating: 79 3/03 Weth 2m   good NHF

Third first time in a bumper at Wetherby in March.

High Green

59

11-y-o b g Green Adventure (USA)-High Affair (High Line)
J L Spearing Mrs Peter Badger

Placings: *PP5-P*   (0431)
2002/03: 24⁰GF,

	Starts	1st	2nd	3rd	Win & Pl
Chases	1	0	0	0	0
Career Total	4	0	0	0	0

Going: Sf: 0-0 GS: 0-0 Gd: 0-0 GF: - Fm: 0-1
Distance: 2m/2m3: 0-0 2m4-2m7: 0-0 3m+: 0-1
Track: LH: 0-0 RH: 0-1 Tight: 0-0 Gall: 0-1
Aids: Bl: 0-0 Vi: 0-0 Tstrap: 0-0
Best Rating: 63 1/02 Winc 2m5f   good Ch

High Hope (FR)

101   109

5-y-o ch h Lomitas-Highness Lady (GER) (Cagliostro (GER))
G L Moore (R Gibson 12/8) Rdm Racing

Placings: *46*   (3527)
2002/03: 16⁴G, 16⁶G,

	Starts	1st	2nd	3rd	Win & Pl
Hurdles	2	0	0	0	365
Career Total	2	0	0	0	365

Going: Sf: 0-0 GS: 0-0 Gd: 0-2 GF: - Fm: 0-0

Distance: 2m/2m3: 0-2 2m4-2m7: 0-0 3m+: 0-0
Track: LH: 0-2 RH: 0-0 Tight: 0-0 Gall: 0-2
Aids: Bl: 0-0 Vi: 0-0 Tstrap: 0-0
Best Rating: 109 12/02 Newb 2m110y   good Hdl

Ex-French with form on Polytrack. Ran a fair race on hurdling debut.

High Learie

13-y-o b g Petoski-Lady Doubloon (Pieces Of Eight)
Mrs D M Grissell Major J R D Barnard

Placings: 44/16F46/**1222**/F414322B/3451P/FPP/5/3P0-5   (0313)
2002/03: 25⁵G,

	Starts	1st	2nd	3rd	Win & Pl
Chases	1	0	0	0	0
Career Total	32	4	5	3	21330
102	3/99	Hntg	3m	E(0-115)HCh	SFT £3782
95	2/97	Plum	3m1f110yE Ch		G-S £3290
106	12/95	Extr	2m2f	E Hdl	G-S £4111

Total win prize-money £14207

Going: Sf: 0-0 GS: 0-0 Gd: 0-1 GF: - Fm: 0-0
Distance: 2m/2m3: 0-0 2m4-2m7: 0-0 3m+: 0-1
Track: LH: 0-0 RH: 0-1 Tight: 0-1 Gall: 0-0
Aids: Bl: 0-1 Vi: 0-0 Tstrap: 0-0
Best Rating: 106 3/97 Folk 3m2f   good Ch

High Mood

13-y-o b g Jalmood (USA)-Copt Hall Princess (Crowned Prince (USA))
Mrs J A Wall D B Roberts

Placings: *00/UP/004U/141F6/235243F6/U312164/21644/4-P*   (3521)
2002/03: 22⁰GS,

	Starts	1st	2nd	3rd	Win & Pl
Chases	1	0	0	0	
Career Total	35	5	4	3	28561
124	11/00	Newb	2m6f110yE(0-115)HCh	G-S	£5200
107	2/00	Newc	2m4f	D(0-125)HCh	SFT £3721
94	12/99	Sedg	2m5f	F(0-105)HCh	SFT £2901
100	12/97	Uttx	2m5f	E(0-105)HCh	SFT £3522
100	11/97	Weth	2m	D(0-110)HCh	GD £3600

Total win prize-money £18945

Going: Sf: 0-0 GS: 0-1 Gd: 0-0 GF: - Fm: 0-0
Distance: 2m/2m3: 0-0 2m4-2m7: 0-1 3m+: 0-0
Track: LH: 0-1 RH: 0-0 Tight: 0-0 Gall: 0-0
Aids: Bl: 0-0 Vi: 0-0 Tstrap: 0-0
Best Rating: 124 11/00 Newb 2m6f110y gd-sft Ch

High Paddy

94   86

4-y-o b g Master Willie-Ivy Edith (Blakeney)
R Ingram Glen Antill

Placings: *4*   (4605)
2002/03: 17⁴G,

	Starts	1st	2nd	3rd	Win & Pl
Hurdles	1	0	0	0	840
Career Total	1	0	0	0	840

Going: Sf: 0-0 GS: 0-0 Gd: 0-1 GF: - Fm: 0-0
Distance: 2m/2m3: 0-1 2m4-2m7: 0-0 3m+: 0-0
Track: LH: 0-1 RH: 0-0 Tight: 0-0 Gall: 0-1

Aids: Bl: 0-0 Vi: 0-0 Tstrap: 0-0
Best Rating: 86 4/03 Chel 2m1f   good Hdl

Modest fourth in a moderate contest on his hurdling debut.

High Peak

102   89

6-y-o b g Afflora (IRE)-High Heels (IRE) (Supreme Leader)
C Grant Lord Daresbury

Placings: *00354-06030240*   (4418)
2002/03: 16⁰G, 17⁵G, 20⁵S, 16³G, 16⁰G, 20²G, 19⁴GS, 22⁹G,

	Starts	1st	2nd	3rd	Win & Pl
Hurdles	8	0	1	1	1732
Career Total	13	0	1	2	2252

Going: Sf: 0-1 GS: 0-1 Gd: 0-6 GF: - Fm: 0-0
Distance: 2m/2m3: 0-4 2m4-2m7: 0-4 3m+: 0-0
Track: LH: 0-6 RH: 0-1 Tight: 0-5 Gall: 0-1
Aids: Bl: 0-0 Vi: 0-3 Tstrap: 0-0
Best Rating: 89 2/03 Donc 2m3f110y gd-sft Hdl

Modest hurdling form, stays two and a half miles. Has worn a visor when not disgraced last two starts.

High Places

80f   52f

5-y-o b g Shirley Heights-Fajjoura (IRE) (Fairy King (USA))
G A Swinbank Derek Hyde

Placings: *2-00*   (4594)
2002/03: 16⁰G, 16⁰G,

	Starts	1st	2nd	3rd	Win & Pl
NH Flat	2	0	0	0	
Career Total	3	0	1	0	512

Going: Sf: 0-0 GS: 0-0 Gd: 0-2 GF: - Fm: 0-0
Distance: 2m/2m3: 0-2 2m4-2m7: 0-0 3m+: 0-0
Track: LH: 0-1 RH: 0-1 Tight: 0-0 Gall: 0-1
Aids: Bl: 0-0 Vi: 0-0 Tstrap: 0-0
Best Rating: 103 4/02 Hntg 2m110y gd-fm NHF

High Ratio (NZ)

96

7-y-o b g Classic Fame (USA)-Ginevra (NZ) (Alvaro)
A King Nigel Bunter

Placings: *0/040-P*   (0417)
2002/03: 16⁰GF,

	Starts	1st	2nd	3rd	Win & Pl
Hurdles	1	0	0	0	
Career Total	5	0	0	0	0

Going: Sf: 0-0 GS: 0-0 Gd: 0-0 GF: - Fm: 0-1
Distance: 2m/2m3: 0-1 2m4-2m7: 0-0 3m+: 0-0
Track: LH: 0-1 RH: 0-0 Tight: 0-1 Gall: 0-0
Aids: Bl: 0-0 Vi: 0-0 Tstrap: 0-0
Best Rating: 90 10/01 Chel 2m110y   good Hdl

High Rocker

86   46

5-y-o b g First Trump-Wild Abandon (USA) (Graustark)
M C Pipe Lucayan Stud

Placings: *00*   (4005)
2002/03: 16⁰GS, 16⁰S,

	Starts	1st	2nd	3rd	Win & Pl
NH Flat	2	0	0	0	
Career Total	2	0	0	0	

Going: Sf: 0-1 GS: 0-1 Gd: 0-0 GF: - Fm: 0-0
Distance: 2m/2m3: 0-2 2m4-2m7: 0-0 3m+: 0-0
Track: LH: 0-0 RH: 0-2 Tight: 0-0 Gall: 0-0
Aids: Bl: 0-0 Vi: 0-0 Tstrap: 0-1
Best Rating: 103 2/03 Winc 2m   gd-sft NHF

High Sturt

9-y-o b m Petoski-Barge Mistress (Bargello)
J W Dufosee J Myerscough-Walker

Placings: F (0312)
2002/03: 21FG,

	Starts	1st	2nd	3rd	Win & Pl
Chases	1	0	0	0	
Career Total	1	0	0	0	

Going: Sf: 0-0 GS: 0-0 Gd: 0-1 GF: - Fm: 0-0
Distance: 2m/2m3: 0-0 2m4-2m7: 0-1 3m+: 0-0
Track: LH: 0-0 RH: 0-1 Tight: 0-1 Gall: 0-0
Aids: Bl: 0-1 Vi: 0-0 Tstrap: 0-1
Best Rating: 0 5/02 Folk 2m5f   good Ch

High Sun
77   56

7-y-o b g High Estate-Clyde Goddess (IRE) (Scottish Reel)
Mrs A M Thorpe (P Monteith 23/7) M V Morgan

Placings: 00-P (1236)
2002/03: 20FG,

	Starts	1st	2nd	3rd	Win & Pl
Hurdles	1	0	0	0	
Career Total	3	0	0	0	

Going: Sf: 0-0 GS: 0-0 Gd: 0-1 GF: - Fm: 0-0
Distance: 2m/2m3: 0-0 2m4-2m7: 0-1 3m+: 0-0
Track: LH: 0-1 RH: 0-0 Tight: 0-0 Gall: 0-0
Aids: Bl: 0-0 Vi: 0-0 Tstrap: 0-0
Best Rating: 49 10/01 Kels 2m110y   good Hdl

High Thyne (IRE)

12-y-o b g Good Thyne (USA)-Annie Buskins (Little Buskins)
P C Shires P C Shires

Placings: 034FPP0P/4F443PP/P (0211)
2002/03: 25PS,

	Starts	1st	2nd	3rd	Win & Pl
Chases	1	0	0	0	
Career Total	16	0	0	2	2493

Going: Sf: 0-1 GS: 0-0 Gd: 0-0 GF: - Fm: 0-0
Distance: 2m/2m3: 0-0 2m4-2m7: 0-0 3m+: 0-1
Track: LH: 0-0 RH: 0-1 Tight: 0-0 Gall: 0-0
Aids: Bl: 0-1 Vi: 0-0 Tstrap: 0-0
Best Rating: 97 10/99 Chep 3m   gd-fm Ch

Highbank
105   94

11-y-o b g Puissance-Highland Daisy (He Loves Me)

Mrs M Reveley D H & C Thrower

Placings: 03114412/522/0P300/**010P**/0032301002212/2415
/04061040B30-000003103 (4686)
2002/03: 16QGF, 19QGS, 19QS, 17QGS, 16QG, 19QG, 171G, 20QG,
17QGF,

	Starts	1st	2nd	3rd	Win & Pl
Hurdles	9	1	0	2	3174
Career Total	57	9	8	7	31075
94	3/03	MRas	2m1f110yG(0-95)HHdl	GD	£2464
103	12/01	Donc	2m4f	E(0-115)HHdl	GD £3178
114	12/00	Newc	2m	F(0-105)HHdl	SFT £2380
93	12/99	Muss	2m	G(0-95)HHdl	G-S £2668
93	8/99	Hntg	2m4f110yG(0-90)HHdl	G-F £1618
80	5/98	Hexm	2m110y E Ch	G-F £2310
110	4/96	Weth	2m	F(0-100)HHdl	GD £2547
97	1/96	Newc	2m	G Hdl	GD £2099
99	12/95	Donc	2m110y G Hdl	G-F £2176

Total win prize-money £21442

Going: Sf: 0-1 GS: 0-2 Gd: 1-4 GF: - Fm: 0-2
Distance: **2m/2m3: 1-7** 2m4-2m7: 0-2 3m+: 0-0
Track: LH: 0-6 **RH: 1-3** Tight: 1-6 Gall: 0-1
Aids: Bl: 1-5 Vi: 0-2 Tstrap: 0-0
Best Rating: 114 12/00 Newc 2m   soft Hdl

Plating-class hurdler; has been around a bit, but is still effective in selling hurdle company and added another victory in that grade at Market Rasen in March 2003; best at up to two and a half miles on good to soft ground.

Highbeath
94   105

12-y-o b g Dunbeath (USA)-Singing High (Julio Mariner)
N Wilson Mrs K Jackson

Placings: 5/030450/13105**311**/12500/3212313/001254531/6
3P/0010F-000P (0982)
2002/03: 22QG, 21QGF, 16QGF, 21PGF,

	Starts	1st	2nd	3rd	Win & Pl
Chases	4	0	0	0	
Career Total	48	10	4	8	45678
105	6/01	MRas	2m6f110yE(0-100)HCh	G-F	£3766
119	12/99	Hntg	2m110y E(0-110)HCh	GD £2864
119	9/99	MRas	2m4f	D(0-120)HCh	G-F £4384
116	10/98	Ludl	2m4f	E(0-115)HCh	G-F £2762
116	8/98	MRas	2m6f110yE(0-115)HCh	G-F £3094
115	9/97	MRas	2m4f	E(0-110)HCh	GD £4042
97	4/97	MRas	2m4f	E(0-115)HCh	GD £3299
108	3/97	Donc	2m3f110yD(0-110)HCh	G-F £4305
96	10/96	Weth	2m7f	C Hdl	GD £3860
107	5/96	MRas	2m1f110yD Hdl	GD £3164

Total win prize-money £35542

Going: Sf: 0-0 GS: 0-0 Gd: 0-1 GF: - Fm: 0-3
Distance: 2m/2m3: 0-1 2m4-2m7: 0-3 3m+: 0-0
Track: LH: 0-3 RH: 0-1 Tight: 0-3 Gall: 0-0
Aids: Bl: 0-0 Vi: 0-0 Tstrap: 0-0
Best Rating: 132 9/98 MRas 2m4f   good Ch

Moderate chaser, stays two miles-six and suited by a sharp, right-handed track and a sound surface. Likes Market Rasen.

Highcroft Boy
95(93h)   (95 h)

8-y-o b gr g Silver Owl-Caroline Ranger (Pony Express)
P J Hobbs Mrs Ann Weston

Placings: 2-122 (4718)
2002/03: 221GF, 23QG, 22ZF,

	Starts	1st	2nd	3rd	Win & Pl
Hurdles	2	1	1	0	3660
Chases	1	0	1	0	1278

Career Total	4	1	3	0	5422
110	5/02	Winc	2m6f	E Hdl	G-F £2618

Total win prize-money £2618

Going: Sf: 0-0 GS: 0-0 Gd: 0-1 GF: - Fm: 1-2
Distance: 2m/2m3: 0-0 **2m4-2m7: 1-2** 3m+: 0-1
Track: LH: 0-1 **RH: 1-2** Tight: 0-0 Gall: 0-0
Aids: Bl: 0-0 Vi: 0-0 Tstrap: 0-0
Best Rating: 110 5/02 Winc 2m6f   gd-fm Hdl

Modest hurdler; lightly-raced over fences; stays two miles six; acts on decent ground.

Highland Dancer (IRE)

4-y-o b g Barathea (IRE)-Dancer Tully (USA) (Seattle Dancer (USA))
C N Kellett Mrs Helen Herrick

Placings: 0PP0P (4488)
2002/03: 12QGS, 16PS, 24PHY, 19QG, 26PGF,

	Starts	1st	2nd	3rd	Win & Pl
NH Flat	1	0	0	0	0
Hurdles	4	0	0	0	0
Career Total	5	0	0	0	0

Going: Sf: 0-2 GS: 0-1 Gd: 0-1 GF: - Fm: 0-1
Distance: 2m/2m3: 0-1 2m4-2m7: 0-1 3m+: 0-2
Track: LH: 0-3 RH: 0-2 Tight: 0-0 Gall: 0-0
Aids: Bl: 0-1 Vi: 0-0 Tstrap: 0-0
Best Rating: 26 11/02 Newb 1m4f110y gd-sft NHF

Highland Monarch

10-y-o b g Super Sunrise-Highland Chance (Bronze Hill)
C Storey Mrs A D Wauchope

Placings: P-FP (3895)
2002/03: 20FGF, 25PGS,

	Starts	1st	2nd	3rd	Win & Pl
Chases	2	0	0	0	
Career Total	3	0	0	0	

Going: Sf: 0-0 GS: 0-1 Gd: 0-0 GF: - Fm: 0-1
Distance: 2m/2m3: 0-0 2m4-2m7: 0-1 3m+: 0-1
Track: LH: 0-0 RH: 0-1 Tight: 0-1 Gall: 0-0
Aids: Bl: 0-0 Vi: 0-0 Tstrap: 0-2
Best Rating: 0 3/03 Kels 3m1f   gd-sft Ch

Highland Rose (IRE)
99   95d

7-y-o b m Roselier (FR)-Carrick Grinder (Sheer Grit)
Ms A E Embiricos S N J Embiricos

Placings: 0010-PF00 (3836)
2002/03: 16PGF, 19FGS, 22QHY, 16QG,

	Starts	1st	2nd	3rd	Win & Pl
Hurdles	3	0	0	0	0
Chases	1	0	0	0	0
Career Total	8	1	0	0	2646
90	3/02	Hntg	2m110y E Hdl	SFT £2646

Total win prize-money £2646

Going: Sf: 0-1 GS: 0-1 Gd: 0-1 GF: - Fm: 0-1
Distance: 2m/2m3: 0-3 2m4-2m7: 0-1 3m+: 0-0
Track: LH: 0-2 RH: 0-2 Tight: 0-1 Gall: 0-0
Aids: Bl: 0-0 Vi: 0-0 Tstrap: 0-0

Best Rating: 90 11/02 Wwck 2m3f gd-sft Hdl

Won 2m soft ground novice hurdle at Huntingdon March 2002; has since been tried over a variety of distances and is struggling to find her best trip.

Highpoint (GER)
90   **87**

5-y-o b m Acatenango (GER)-Holly (GER) (Cortez (GER))
Mrs L Wadham Mrs C Bailey

Placings:004   (3931)
2002/03: 19⁰GS, 20⁰HY, 20⁴S,

	Starts	1st	2nd	3rd	Win & Pl
Hurdles	3	0	0	0	0
Career Total	3	0	0	0	0

Going: Sf: 0-2 GS: 0-1 Gd: 0-0 GF: - Fm: 0-0
Distance: 2m/2m3: 0-0 2m4-2m7: 0-0 3m+: 0-0
Track: LH: 0-1 RH: 0-1 Tight: 0-2 Gall: 0-0
Aids: Bl: 0-0 Vi: 0-0 Tstrap: 0-0
Best Rating: 87 3/03 Font 2m4f soft Hdl

Highway Robbery

6-y-o b g Un Desperado (FR)-Drivers Bureau (Proverb)
Miss E C Lavelle R J Lavelle

Placings:6FP   (2572)
2002/03: 16⁶G, 16⁶S, 19ᴾG,

	Starts	1st	2nd	3rd	Win & Pl
NH Flat	1	0	0	0	0
Hurdles	2	0	0	0	0
Career Total	3	0	0	0	0

Going: Sf: 0-1 GS: 0-0 Gd: 0-2 GF: - Fm: 0-0
Distance: 2m/2m3: 0-3 2m4-2m7: 0-0 3m+: 0-0
Track: LH: 0-3 RH: 0-0 Tight: 0-0 Gall: 0-2
Aids: Bl: 0-0 Vi: 0-0 Tstrap: 0-0
Best Rating: 97 10/02 Chep 2m110y good NHF

Hijacked
96   **76**

9-y-o b g True Song-Scamper (Abwah)
A Hollingsworth Kombined Motor Services Ltd

Placings:PP60   (4151)
2002/03: 23³G, 26ᴾHY, 19⁶G, 29⁰G,

	Starts	1st	2nd	3rd	Win & Pl
Chases	4	0	0	0	0
Career Total	4	0	0	0	0

Going: Sf: 0-1 GS: 0-0 Gd: 0-3 GF: - Fm: 0-0
Distance: 2m/2m3: 0-1 2m4-2m7: 0-0 3m+: 0-3
Track: LH: 0-2 RH: 0-2 Tight: 0-0 Gall: 0-0
Aids: Bl: 0-0 Vi: 0-0 Tstrap: 0-0
Best Rating: 76 2/03 Hrfd 2m3f good Ch

Hill Charm

5-y-o ch m Minster Son-Snarry Hill (Vitiges (FR))
C Grant Roy Robinson

Placings:6-0P   (0581)
2002/03: 16⁰G, 16ᴾG,

	Starts	1st	2nd	3rd	Win & Pl
NH Flat	1	0	0	0	0
Hurdles	1	0	0	0	0
Career Total	3	0	0	0	0

Going: Sf: 0-0 GS: 0-0 Gd: 0-2 GF: - Fm: 0-0
Distance: 2m/2m3: 0-2 2m4-2m7: 0-0 3m+: 0-0
Track: LH: 0-2 RH: 0-0 Tight: 0-0 Gall: 0-0
Aids: Bl: 0-0 Vi: 0-0 Tstrap: 0-0
Best Rating: 61 4/02 Newc 2m firm NHF

Hill Forts Henry
90   **66**

5-y-o ch g Karinga Bay-Maggie Tee (Lepanto (GER))
J W Mullins R L Scorgie

Placings:50F0   (4001)
2002/03: 17⁵GS, 18⁰HY, 17ᶠS, 16⁰S,

	Starts	1st	2nd	3rd	Win & Pl
NH Flat	2	0	0	0	0
Hurdles	2	0	0	0	0
Career Total	4	0	0	0	0

Going: Sf: 0-3 GS: 0-1 Gd: 0-0 GF: - Fm: 0-0
Distance: 2m/2m3: 0-4 2m4-2m7: 0-0 3m+: 0-0
Track: LH: 0-1 RH: 0-2 Tight: 0-1 Gall: 0-0
Aids: Bl: 0-0 Vi: 0-0 Tstrap: 0-0
Best Rating: 79 11/02 Tntn 2m1f gd-sft NHF

Hill Magic
82   **65**

8-y-o br g Magic Ring (IRE)-Stock Hill Lass (Air Trooper)
L G Cottrell Eric Gadsden

Placings:0   (2193)
2002/03: 17⁰GS,

	Starts	1st	2nd	3rd	Win & Pl
Hurdles	1	0	0	0	0
Career Total	1	0	0	0	0

Going: Sf: 0-0 GS: 0-1 Gd: 0-0 GF: - Fm: 0-0
Distance: 2m/2m3: 0-1 2m4-2m7: 0-0 3m+: 0-0
Track: LH: 0-0 RH: 0-1 Tight: 0-1 Gall: 0-0
Aids: Bl: 0-0 Vi: 0-0 Tstrap: 0-0
Best Rating: 65 11/02 Tntn 2m1f gd-sft Hdl

Hilltop Harry (IRE)
100   **81**

6-y-o b g Commanche Run-What s In A Name (IRE) (Le Moss)
Lady Connell Sir Michael Connell

Placings:553   (4153)
2002/03: 16⁶S, 24⁵S, 25³G,

	Starts	1st	2nd	3rd	Win & Pl
NH Flat	1	0	0	0	0
Hurdles	2	0	0	1	534
Career Total	3	0	0	1	534

Going: Sf: 0-2 GS: 0-0 Gd: 0-1 GF: - Fm: 0-0
Distance: 2m/2m3: 0-1 2m4-2m7: 0-0 3m+: 0-2
Track: LH: 0-2 RH: 0-1 Tight: 0-1 Gall: 0-0
Aids: Bl: 0-0 Vi: 0-0 Tstrap: 0-0
Best Rating: 94 12/02 Uttx 2m soft NHF

Irish point winner; modest form in long distance novice hurdles.

Him Of Praise (IRE)

13-y-o b g Paean-Tamed (Rusticaro (FR))
Simon Bloss J G Phillips

Placings:1/331/111132R/502135/2/004536/6-4   (3674)
2002/03: 26⁴GS,

	Starts	1st	2nd	3rd	Win & Pl
Chases	1	0	0	0	256
Career Total	26	7	3	5	138379
146	2/99	Uttx	3m4f	B HCh	HVY £32455
135	1/98	Sand	3m5f110yB HCh		G-S £20734
131	12/97	Hayd	4m110y	B(0-145)HCh	SFT £6729
127	11/97	Hayd	3m4f110yB(0-140)HCh		SFT £10123
132	11/97	Towc	3m1f	C(0-135)HCh	GD £4289
106	3/97	Towc	2m6f	E Ch	G-S £3483
113	3/96	Sand	2m6f	D Hdl	G-S £2983

Total win prize-money £80799

Going: Sf: 0-0 GS: 0-1 Gd: 0-0 GF: - Fm: 0-0
Distance: 2m/2m3: 0-0 2m4-2m7: 0-0 3m+: 0-1
Track: LH: 0-0 RH: 0-0 Tight: 0-1 Gall: 0-0
Aids: Bl: 0-0 Vi: 0-0 Tstrap: 0-0
Best Rating: 148 2/98 Hayd 3m4f110y good Ch

A nightmare ride, he stays any trip but takes a deal of driving and is not one to trust.

Himalayan Blue
96   **96+**

11-y-o b g Hailgate-Orange Parade (Dara Monarch)
P Beaumont Mrs E H Heath

Placings:6/P5P/PFPU-2UPP   (0798)
2002/03: 20²GF, 20ᵁGF, 20ᴾG, 20ᴾGS,

	Starts	1st	2nd	3rd	Win & Pl
Chases	4	0	1	0	1284
Career Total	12	0	1	0	1284

Going: Sf: 0-0 GS: 0-1 Gd: 0-1 GF: - Fm: 0-2
Distance: 2m/2m3: 0-0 2m4-2m7: 0-4 3m+: 0-0
Track: LH: 0-0 RH: 0-4 Tight: 0-4 Gall: 0-0
Aids: Bl: 0-0 Vi: 0-0 Tstrap: 0-0
Best Rating: 96 6/02 MRas 2m4f gd-fm Ch

Hint Of Magic
82   **69**

6-y-o b g Magic Ring (IRE)-Thames Glow (Kalaglow)
H W Lavis Bob And Mrs Vicky Burks

Placings:P-P640   (4445)
2002/03: 19ᴾG, 17⁶S, 16⁴G, 16⁰G,

	Starts	1st	2nd	3rd	Win & Pl
Hurdles	4	0	0	0	0
Career Total	5	0	0	0	0

Going: Sf: 0-1 GS: 0-0 Gd: 0-3 GF: - Fm: 0-0
Distance: 2m/2m3: 0-3 2m4-2m7: 0-1 3m+: 0-0
Track: LH: 0-1 RH: 0-3 Tight: 0-0 Gall: 0-0
Aids: Bl: 0-0 Vi: 0-0 Tstrap: 0-0
Best Rating: 69 12/02 Hrfd 2m1f soft Hdl

Hip Pocket (IRE)
109   **111**

7-y-o b g Ela-Mana-Mou-Ebony And Ivory (IRE) (Bob Back (USA))
D K Weld Mrs Susan McCarthy

Placings:0/1/0-F35   (1943)

2002/03: 20FYS, 203S, 215G,

	Starts	1st	2nd	3rd	Win & Pl
Hurdles	3	0	0	1	2352
Career Total	6	1	0	1	4698
110 9/00 Dpat 2m1f172y Hdl			GD		£2345

Total win prize-money £2346

Going: Sf: 0-1 GS: 0-0 Gd: 0-1 GF: - Fm: 0-0
Distance: 2m/2m3: 0-0 2m4-2m7: 0-3 3m+: 0-0
Track: LH: 0-1 RH: 0-1 Tight: 0-0 Gall: 0-1
Aids: BI: 0-2 Vi: 0-0 Tstrap: 0-0
Best Rating: 111 11/02 Chel 2m5f　　good　Hdl

Irish handicap hurdler, effective with cut in the ground, stays two and a half miles.

Hirapour (IRE)
106　　　　　　　135+
7-y-o b g Kahyasi-Himaya (IRE) (Mouktar)
Ian Williams (Mrs A J Perrett 19/10) C N Barnes And M Murphy

Placings:423111　　　　　　　　　　(4767)
2002/03: 164GS, 192G, 203HY, 211G, 171GF, 201G,

	Starts	1st	2nd	3rd	Win & Pl
Hurdles	6	3	1	1	19067
Career Total	6	3	1	1	19067
135 4/03 Prth 2m4f110yD(0-130)HHdl			GD		£8401
139 4/03 Extr 2m1f F(0-100)HHdl			G-F		£3556
124 4/03 Ludl 2m5f E(0-105)HHdl			GD		£4875

Total win prize-money £16832

Going: Sf: 0-1 GS: 0-1 Gd: 2-3 GF: - Fm: 1-1
Distance: 2m/2m3: 1-2 2m4-2m7: 2-4 3m+: 0-0
Track: LH: 0-0 RH: 3-5 Tight: 0-0 Gall: 0-1
Aids: BI: 0-0 Vi: 0-0 Tstrap: 0-0
Best Rating: 139 4/03 Extr 2m1f　　gd-fm　Hdl

Useful hurdler; progressive this season, completing a five-timer in the spring of 2003; effective on good to soft and fast ground; stays at least 2m 6f and likely to get further.

Hirayna
99f　　　　　　　97+f
4-y-o b f Doyoun-Himaya (IRE) (Mouktar)
W M Brisbourne R Russell

Placings:0　　　　　　　　　　(2172)
2002/03: 140GS,

	Starts	1st	2nd	3rd	Win & Pl
NH Flat	1	0	0	0	
Career Total	1	0	0	0	

Going: Sf: 0-0 GS: 0-1 Gd: 0-0 GF: - Fm: 0-0
Distance: 2m/2m3: 0-0 2m4-2m7: 0-0 3m+: 0-0
Track: LH: 0-1 RH: 0-0 Tight: 0-0 Gall: 0-0
Aids: BI: 0-0 Vi: 0-0 Tstrap: 0-0
Best Rating: 67 11/02 Wwck 1m6f　　gd-sft　NHF

Has shown ability in bumpers, winning at Perth; acts on good ground.

Hirt Lodge
100　　　　　　　92d
12-y-o ch g Jumbo Hirt (USA)-Holly Lodge (Rubor)
J E Dixon Mrs S F Dixon

Placings:6026/30626/30416P0　　　　(3914)
2002/03: 223G, 220HY, 224G, 221S, 226HY, 24PHY, 20PGS,

	Starts	1st	2nd	3rd	Win & Pl
Hurdles	7	1	0	1	3857
Career Total	16	1	2	2	5511

---

92 11/02 Kels	2m6f110yF(0-100)HHdl		SFT	£3471

Total win prize-money £3471

Going: Sf: 1-4 GS: 0-1 Gd: 0-2 GF: - Fm: 0-0
Distance: 2m/2m3: 0-0 2m4-2m7: 1-6 3m+: 0-1
Track: LH: 1-6 RH: 0-1 Tight: 1-5 Gall: 0-0
Aids: BI: 0-0 Vi: 0-0 Tstrap: 0-0
Best Rating: 92 11/02 Kels 2m6f110y soft　Hdl

Took a while to get off the mark over hurdles and when he did it was in a weak race at Kelso. Stays three miles.

Hirvine (FR)
101　　　　　　　94
5-y-o ch g Snurge-Guadanella (FR) (Guadanini (FR))
T P Tate The Ivy Syndicate

Placings:3F　　　　　　　　　　(3504)
2002/03: 273S, 20FHY,

	Starts	1st	2nd	3rd	Win & Pl
Hurdles	2	0	0	1	476
Career Total	2	0	0	1	476

Going: Sf: 0-2 GS: 0-0 Gd: 0-0 GF: - Fm: 0-0
Distance: 2m/2m3: 0-0 2m4-2m7: 0-1 3m+: 0-1
Track: LH: 0-2 RH: 0-0 Tight: 0-1 Gall: 0-0
Aids: BI: 0-0 Vi: 0-0 Tstrap: 0-0
Best Rating: 81 12/02 Sedg 3m3f110y soft　Hdl

Big-type, will make a chaser in time; dropped in trip game winner of two mile novices' hurdle at Hexham in April; followed up in similar event at Sedgefield two weeks later.

His Nibs (IRE)
109　　　　　　　114
6-y-o b g Alflora (IRE)-Mrs Jennifer (River Knight (FR))
Miss Venetia Williams John Galvanoni

Placings:150-133P　　　　　　　　(4048)
2002/03: 171HY, 173S, 213S, 20PHY,

	Starts	1st	2nd	3rd	Win & Pl
Hurdles	4	1	0	2	5735
Career Total	7	2	0	2	7639
118 12/02 Folk 2m1f110yE Hdl			HVY		£3073
105 5/01 Folk 2m1f110yH NHF			G-S		£1904

Total win prize-money £4977

Going: Sf: 1-4 GS: 0-0 Gd: 0-0 GF: - Fm: 0-0
Distance: 2m/2m3: 1-2 2m4-2m7: 0-2 3m+: 0-0
Track: LH: 0-2 RH: 1-2 Tight: 1-1 Gall: 0-2
Aids: BI: 0-0 Vi: 0-0 Tstrap: 0-0
Best Rating: 118 12/02 Folk 2m1f110y heavy　Hdl

Fair novice hurdler, acts in soft ground; stays two and a half miles.

His Song (IRE)
108　　　　　　　131
10-y-o ch g Accordion-Pampered Finch VII (Damsire Unregistered)
N J Henderson David Lloyd

Placings:111221/112115U/32341P0/6P/4000-024　(3178)
2002/03: 170G, 242S, 214G,

	Starts	1st	2nd	3rd	Win & Pl
Hurdles	3	0	1	0	2985
Career Total	29	9	5	2	147934
133 2/00 Naas 2m		Ch	SFT	£15600
144 1/99 Leop 2m1f		Ch	HVY	£16187
145 12/98 Leop 2m1f		Ch	SFT	£22608
132 10/98 Punc 2m		Ch	SFT	£3586
126 10/98 Tipp 2m		Ch	SH	£3586

---

146 4/98 Punc 2m	Hdl		HVY £22826
136 12/97 Leop 2m	Hdl		HVY £9579
120 11/97 Fair 2m2f		Y-S	£3391
109 11/97 Naas 2m	Hdl		Y-S £3730

Total win prize-money £101097

Going: Sf: 0-1 GS: 0-0 Gd: 0-2 GF: - Fm: 0-0
Distance: 2m/2m3: 0-1 2m4-2m7: 0-1 3m+: 0-1
Track: LH: 0-1 RH: 0-2 Tight: 0-0 Gall: 0-1
Aids: BI: 0-0 Vi: 0-0 Tstrap: 0-0
Best Rating: 147 3/98 Chel 2m110y　good　Hdl

A big, imposing ex-Irish gelding, he has not reached the heights expected of him over fences and has reverted, unsuccessfully, to hurdling. Now with Nicky Henderson, he is gradually finding his form as he drops in the handicap. Lacks a turn of foot, suited by soft ground, and two and a half miles looks his best trip.

Hisar (IRE)
96(79h)　　　　　　　61
10-y-o br g Doyoun-Himaya (IRE) (Mouktar)
P C Ritchens R Catton

Placings:002/21U2/53P2301/3122226212/3600/422111115 40-33043　　　　　　　(4719)
2002/03: 173GF, 203GF, 163GS, 164GF, 163F,

	Starts	1st	2nd	3rd	Win & Pl
Chases	5	0	0	3	3803
Career Total	44	9	12	7	57195
124 9/01 Worc 2m	C(0-135)HCh	G-F	£6679
128 8/01 Strf	2m1f110yD(0-125)HCh	GD	£5434
128 8/01 NAbb	2m110y D(0-125)HCh	GD	£3721
117 7/01 Wolv 2m	C(0-135)HCh	G-S	£8080
114 6/01 NAbb 2m110y	F(0-105)HCh	G-F	£2947
122 11/99 Wwck 2m	D(0-125)HCh	GD	£3822
108 5/99 Hrfd 2m	E Ch	GD	£3257
112 4/99 Hrfd 2m1f	E(0-115)HHdl	G-F	£2931
103 10/97 Uttx 2m	E Hdl	GD	£2337

Total win prize-money £39212

Going: Sf: 0-0 GS: 0-1 Gd: 0-0 GF: - Fm: 0-4
Distance: 2m/2m3: 0-0 2m4-2m7: 0-1 3m+: 0-0
Track: LH: 0-3 RH: 0-2 Tight: 0-4 Gall: 0-0
Aids: BI: 0-0 Vi: 0-0 Tstrap: 0-0
Best Rating: 128 8/01 Strf 2m1f110y good　Ch

Likes forcing the pace which offsets his lack of a turn of foot; completed a fine five-timer over fences in the summer of 2001; best on fast ground.

Historg (FR)
114　　　　　　　134
8-y-o b g Cyborg (FR)-Kalliste (FR) (Calicot (FR))
Ferdy Murphy Jim McCarthy

Placings:40/4300/0212/P1F1P2-321366　　(4100)
2002/03: 253S, 252GS, 261S, 283HY, 246G, 246G,

	Starts	1st	2nd	3rd	Win & Pl
Chases	6	1	1	2	30700
Career Total	22	4	4	3	51553
134 12/02 Chel 3m2f110yB(0-145)HCh			SFT	£15877
124 2/02 Hayd 2m6f D Ch			HVY	£4611
103 12/01 MRas 2m1f110yE Ch			SFT	£3094
119 1/01 Newc 2m4f E Hdl			HVY	£2702

Total win prize-money £26285

Going: Sf: 1-3 GS: 0-1 Gd: 0-2 GF: - Fm: 0-0
Distance: 2m/2m3: 0-0 2m4-2m7: 0-0 3m+: 1-6
Track: LH: 1-5 RH: 0-1 Tight: 0-1 Gall: 1-2
Aids: BI: 0-0 Vi: 0-0 Tstrap: 0-0
Best Rating: 134 12/02 Chel 3m2f110y soft　Ch

Useful chaser; good winner at Cheltenham in December

2002, but held since; suited by soft ground; stays three and a quarter miles.

Hit And Run (FR)
103   135
8-y-o ch g River Mist (USA)-La Dunanerie (FR) (Guadanini (FR))
M C Pipe Gerry Scanlon & Miss J Kirk

Placings:11112351/5230/0243P/**1130-315**P   (1079)
2002/03: 16³F, 16¹G, 20⁵GF, 20⁶G,

	Starts	1st	2nd	3rd	Win & Pl
Hurdles	1	0	0	0	0
Chases	3	1	0	1	5097
Career Total	25	8	3	5	62352
125 6/02	Hrfd	2m	E Ch	GD	£3409
135 1/02	Donc	2m11y	D Ch	SFT	£4452
128 11/01	Plum	2m1f	F Ch	GD	£2990
143 4/99	Wwck	2m	C(0-135)HHdl	SFT	£4789
128 12/98	Sand	2m110y	D Hdl	GD	£2775
119 10/98	Chel	2m110y	C Hdl	GD	£4260
122 9/98	Sedg	2m1f	E Hdl	GF	£2390
100 9/98	NAbb	2m1f	E Hdl	G-F	£2130
			Total win prize-money £27196		

Going: Sf: 0-0 GS: 0-0 Gd: 1-2 GF: - Fm: 0-2
Distance: 2m/2m3: 1-2 2m4-2m7: 0-2 3m+: 0-0
Track: LH: 0-1 RH: 1-2 Tight: 0-2 Gall: 0-0
Aids: Bl: 0-1 Vi: 0-0 Tstrap: 0-0
Best Rating: 158 2/01 Newb 2m110y soft Hdl

A smart front-running handicap hurdler, he made a successful chasing debut at Plumpton, before following up Doncaster in January 2002. Held in better company before landing the odds in a small race at Hereford. He has won on fast ground but seems better on a yielding surface. Effective at around two miles. He is not the biggest to be running over fences. Pulled up in a claiming hurdle in August and looks to have his problems.

Hit Royal (FR)
112(105h)   (95h)110
8-y-o ch g Montorselli-Valse Royale (FR) (Cap Martin (FR))
P R Webber David Czarnetzki

Placings:066/515P/**241**F32F6-**1145**   (2571)
2002/03: 16¹GF, 17¹GF, 20⁴GS, 18⁶G,

	Starts	1st	2nd	3rd	Win & Pl
Chases	4	2	0	0	10419
Career Total	19	4	2	1	19981
110 9/02	MRas	2m1f110yD(0-120)HCh	G-F	£6857
102 8/02	Hntg	2m110y	F(0-100)HCh	GD	£2940
110 11/01	Ludl	2m	C(0-105)HCh	G-F	£3760
103 8/00	Worc	3m	F(0-95)HHdl	G-F	£1799
		Total win prize-money £15357		

Going: Sf: 0-0 GS: 0-1 Gd: 0-1 GF: - Fm: 2-2
Distance: 2m/2m3: 2-3 2m4-2m7: 0-1 3m+: 0-0
Track: LH: 0-1 RH: 2-3 Tight: 1-1 Gall: 1-3
Aids: Bl: 0-0 Vi: 0-0 Tstrap: 0-0
Best Rating: 110 9/02 MRas 2m1f110y gd-fm Ch

Fair chaser, effective at two miles and best on good ground.

Hitchhiker
96   46
9-y-o b g Picea-Lady Lax (Henbit (USA))
R Ford Miss J M Slater

Placings:0000000/6022144320/240**122**P1P/**F5**/UPF6-**P245**U0F   (4264)
2002/03: 20⁰GF, 21²S, 24⁴GS, 20⁵G, 24⁰G, 24⁰S, 20⁶GF,

	Starts	1st	2nd	3rd	Win & Pl
Chases	7	0	1	0	1778
Career Total	39	3	7	1	19495
108 3/00	Newc	3m	E(0-115)HCh	GD	£5421
102 12/99	Hntg	3m	E(0-105)HCh	GD	£3446
90 10/98	Weth	3m1f	E(0-105)HHdl	GD	£2903
			Total win prize-money £11771		

Going: Sf: 0-2 GS: 0-1 Gd: 0-2 GF: - Fm: 0-2
Distance: 2m/2m3: 0-2 2m4-2m7: 0-4 3m+: 0-3
Track: LH: 0-2 RH: 0-5 Tight: 0-4 Gall: 0-1
Aids: Bl: 0-1 Vi: 0-0 Tstrap: 0-0
Best Rating: 108 3/00 Newc 3m good Ch

Hitman (IRE)
103(115h)   (109h)130
8-y-o b g Contract Law (USA)-Loveville (USA) (Assert)
M Pitman The Paper Boys

Placings:P/46/401410P-**F13FP4**   (4555)
2002/03: 18⁵S, 16¹S, 16³HY, 16⁶G, 19⁹G, 16⁴G,

	Starts	1st	2nd	3rd	Win & Pl
Hurdles	1	0	0	0	2000
Chases	5	1	0	1	5119
Career Total	16	3	0	1	27919
128 1/03	Wwck	2m110y	E Ch	SFT	£4270
134 2/02	Kemp	2m	A Hdl	G-S	£12000
136 1/02	Asct	2m110y	C Hdl	G-S	£5200
		Total win prize-money £21470		

Going: Sf: 1-3 GS: 0-0 Gd: 0-3 GF: - Fm: 0-0
Distance: 2m/2m3: 1-5 2m4-2m7: 0-1 3m+: 0-0
Track: LH: 1-4 RH: 0-2 Tight: 0-0 Gall: 0-2
Aids: Bl: 0-1 Vi: 0-0 Tstrap: 0-0
Best Rating: 154 12/00 Chel 2m1f soft Hdl

Former smart performer on the Flat and over hurdles; very useful novice chaser; effective over two miles; acts on yielding and soft ground, but best on good; likes to dominate.

Hitman Herons (IRE)
85f   81f
7-y-o ch g Glacial Storm (USA)-Popular View (Torus)
J L Spearing Miss Julia Oakey

Placings:54   (1425)
2002/03: 16⁵G, 17⁴GF,

	Starts	1st	2nd	3rd	Win & Pl
NH Flat	2	0	0	0	0
Career Total	2	0	0	0	0

Going: Sf: 0-0 GS: 0-0 Gd: 0-1 GF: - Fm: 0-1
Distance: 2m/2m3: 0-2 2m4-2m7: 0-0 3m+: 0-0
Track: LH: 0-1 RH: 0-1 Tight: 0-1 Gall: 0-0
Aids: Bl: 0-0 Vi: 0-0 Tstrap: 0-0
Best Rating: 81 9/02 Worc 2m good NHF

Hiyah (IRE)
77   68
4-y-o ch g Petardia-Stairway To Heaven (IRE) (Godswalk (USA))
John R Upson The Three Horseshoes Sporting Club

Placings:P0001   (4698)
2002/03: 16⁸GF, 17⁰G, 16⁹G, 16⁸GS, 16¹GF,

	Starts	1st	2nd	3rd	Win & Pl
Hurdles	5	1	0	0	4300
Career Total	5	1	0	0	4300

---

68 4/03	Plum	2m	E Hdl	G-F	£4300
		Total win prize-money £4300				

Going: Sf: 0-0 GS: 0-1 Gd: 0-2 GF: - Fm: 1-2
Distance: 2m/2m3: 1-5 2m4-2m7: 0-0 3m+: 0-0
Track: LH: 1-3 RH: 0-2 Tight: 1-2 Gall: 0-1
Aids: Bl: 1-3 Vi: 0-0 Tstrap: 0-0
Best Rating: 68 4/03 Plum 2m gd-fm Hdl

Plating-class hurdler; gifted sole success at Plumpton in 2003; wears blinkers.

Hobart Junction (IRE)
92   74
8-y-o ch g Classic Secret (USA)-Art Duo (Artaius (USA))
J A T De Giles J A T De Giles

Placings:PU/002540/04325/14305065000-03P2U   (4465)
2002/03: 16⁰GF, 20³G, 22⁸PG, 19²F, 24⁰UF,

	Starts	1st	2nd	3rd	Win & Pl
Hurdles	5	0	1	1	975
Career Total	29	1	3	3	5403
84 6/01	NAbb	2m1f	G(0-95)HHdl	GD	£2380
		Total win prize-money £2380			

Going: Sf: 0-0 GS: 0-0 Gd: 0-2 GF: - Fm: 0-3
Distance: 2m/2m3: 0-2 2m4-2m7: 0-2 3m+: 0-1
Track: LH: 0-2 RH: 0-2 Tight: 0-3 Gall: 0-0
Aids: Bl: 0-0 Vi: 0-0 Tstrap: 0-0
Best Rating: 84 8/01 Strf 2m110y good Hdl

Selling hurdler. Won a two mile amateur riders event at Newton Abbot in June 2001. Disappointing until runner-up over 19 furlongs at Exeter October 2002.

Hobbycyr (FR)

8-y-o b g Saint Cyrien (FR)-Sauteuse De Retz (FR) (Funny Hobby)
R Kelvin-Hughes R Kelvin-Hughes

Placings:0/010/0/1-PP4   (0371)
2002/03: 16⁸GF, 25⁸G, 26⁴S,

	Starts	1st	2nd	3rd	Win & Pl
Chases	3	0	0	0	257
Career Total	9	2	0	0	5285
101 3/02	Strf	3m	H Ch	G-S	£2808
112 12/99	Hrfd	2m3f110yE Hdl	SFT	£2220
		Total win prize-money £5028			

Going: Sf: 0-1 GS: 0-0 Gd: 0-1 GF: - Fm: 0-1
Distance: 2m/2m3: 0-1 2m4-2m7: 0-0 3m+: 0-2
Track: LH: 0-2 RH: 0-1 Tight: 0-1 Gall: 0-2
Aids: Bl: 0-0 Vi: 0-0 Tstrap: 0-0
Best Rating: 112 12/99 Hrfd 2m3f110y soft Hdl

Landed a novice hunter chase at Stratford in March 2002.

Hoh Invader (IRE)
107(84c)   (85c)100d
11-y-o b g Accordion-Newgate Fairy (Flair Path)
Mrs A Duffield Exors Of The Late N Midgley

Placings:501/112142040/**1322**PP/**212**024/0P**1500**   (4434)
2002/03: 16⁰GF, 20⁸GS, 20¹G, 20⁵G, 19⁰GS, 20⁰G,

	Starts	1st	2nd	3rd	Win & Pl
Hurdles	5	1	0	0	2947
Chases	1	0	0	0	0
Career Total	30	7	7	1	42696
96 1/03	Muss	2m4f	G Hdl	GD	£2947
123 6/00	Strf	2m1f110yC(0-135)HCh	GD	£6142

108	8/99	Prth	2m	D Ch	G-F	£4104
128	11/98	Chel	2m110y	A Hdl	GD	£9002
108	9/98	Worc	2m	E Hdl	G-F	£2302
114	5/98	Worc	2m	H NHF	G-F	£1560
95	9/97	Gway	2m	NHF	Y-S	£3391

Total win prize-money £29450

Going: Sf: 0-0 GS: 0-2 Gd: 1-3 GF: - Fm: 0-1
Distance: 2m/2m3: 0-1 2m4-2m7: 1-5 3m+: 0-0
Track: LH: 0-4 RH: 1-2 Tight: 1-2 Gall: 0-2
Aids: Bl: 0-0 Vi: 0-0 Tstrap: 0-0
Best Rating: 134 12/98 Asct 2m110y soft Hdl

One-time useful chaser, but looks just modest these days, including over hurdles; acts on decent ground; effective at up to two and a half miles.

Hoh No

102(101h)   (91h)73

7-y-o b g Efisio-Primetta (Precocious)
R M Stronge Mrs Bernice Stronge

Placings:0/F0/3-4465U05632   (1427)
2002/03: 16⁴GS, 16⁴S, 21⁸GF, 17⁵GF, 17ᵁS, 16⁰S, 24⁵GF, 16⁶G, 17³G, 17²GF,

	Starts	1st	2nd	3rd	Win & Pl
Hurdles	5	0	0	0	0
Chases	5	0	1	1	1862
Career Total	14	0	1	2	2239

Going: Sf: 0-3 GS: 0-1 Gd: 0-2 GF: - Fm: 0-4
Distance: 2m/2m3: 0-8 2m4-2m7: 0-1 3m+: 0-1
Track: LH: 0-9 RH: 0-1 Tight: 0-6 Gall: 0-0
Aids: Bl: 0-1 Vi: 0-0 Tstrap: 0-3
Best Rating: 91 10/01 Plum 2m soft Hdl

A dual Flat winner, he is very moderate over hurdles and fences. Best on a sound surface.

Hoh Tel (IRE)

9-y-o ch g Montelimar (USA)-Party Dancer (Be My Guest (USA))
G F White (K C Bailey 19/5) F V White

Placings:0/230620/FU4U6P0/5   (4506)
2002/03: 25⁵G,

	Starts	1st	2nd	3rd	Win & Pl
Chases	1	0	0	0	0
Career Total	15	0	2	1	2253

Going: Sf: 0-0 GS: 0-0 Gd: 0-1 GF: - Fm: 0-0
Distance: 2m/2m3: 0-0 2m4-2m7: 0-1 3m+: 0-1
Track: LH: 0-1 RH: 0-0 Tight: 0-1 Gall: 0-0
Aids: Bl: 0-0 Vi: 0-1 Tstrap: 0-0
Best Rating: 112 5/99 Hrfd 2m1f gd-sft NHF

Moderate pointer/hunter chaser; dual winner between the flags; stays three miles one; usually wears a visor.

Holborn Hill (IRE)
107   111

11-y-o gr g Riberetto-Grey Tor (Ahonoora)
A King J E Brown

Placings:06/13P0434/12FF51/1/60-P0F   (4607)
2002/03: 22ᴾHY, 21⁰G, 21ᶠG,

	Starts	1st	2nd	3rd	Win & Pl
Hurdles	3	0	0	0	
Career Total	21	4	1	2	30193

| 138 | 5/00 | Uttx | 3m110y | B(0-140)HHdl | GD | £10757 |

136	4/00	Chel	2m5f110yB HHdl	SFT	£10036
120	5/99	Strf	2m6f110yD Hdl	G-S	£3486
100	11/98	Asct	3m	C Hdl	G-S	£3810

Total win prize-money £28091

Going: Sf: 0-1 GS: 0-0 Gd: 0-2 GF: - Fm: 0-0
Distance: 2m/2m3: 0-0 2m4-2m7: 0-3 3m+: 0-0
Track: LH: 0-2 RH: 0-1 Tight: 0-0 Gall: 0-1
Aids: Bl: 0-0 Vi: 0-0 Tstrap: 0-0
Best Rating: 138 5/00 Uttx 3m110y good Hdl

Decent hurdler; winner twice in the spring of 2000 but very lightly raced since; stays three miles; suited by good ground or softer.

Hold The Fort

12-y-o b g Baron Blakeney-Mizpah (Lochnager)
T Needham T Needham

Placings:UP/PP/U   (1329)
2002/03: 20ᵁG,

	Starts	1st	2nd	3rd	Win & Pl
Chases	1	0	0	0	
Career Total	5	0	0	0	

Going: Sf: 0-0 GS: 0-0 Gd: 0-1 GF: - Fm: 0-0
Distance: 2m/2m3: 0-0 2m4-2m7: 0-1 3m+: 0-0
Track: LH: 0-1 RH: 0-0 Tight: 0-0 Gall: 0-0
Aids: Bl: 0-0 Vi: 0-0 Tstrap: 0-0
Best Rating: 0 9/02 Plum 2m4f good Ch

Holland Park (IRE)
99   105

6-y-o gr g Roselier (FR)-Bluebell Avenue (Boreen Beag)
Mrs S D Williams B M Yin

Placings:323   (3780)
2002/03: 17³HY, 19²GS, 22³GS,

	Starts	1st	2nd	3rd	Win & Pl
Hurdles	3	0	1	2	2218
Career Total	3	0	1	2	2218

Going: Sf: 0-1 GS: 0-2 Gd: 0-0 GF: - Fm: 0-0
Distance: 2m/2m3: 0-2 2m4-2m7: 0-1 3m+: 0-0
Track: LH: 0-1 RH: 0-2 Tight: 0-0 Gall: 0-0
Aids: Bl: 0-0 Vi: 0-0 Tstrap: 0-0
Best Rating: 105 12/02 Extr 2m3f gd-sft Hdl

Fair maiden hurdler; stays two miles six; acts on a soft surface.

Holland's Nephew

6-y-o b g Nearly A Hand-Our Mrs P (Idiots Delight)
P R Chamings L R Attrill

Placings:000-PFRU   (3928)
2002/03: 20ᴾS, 21ᶠHY, 21ᴿS, 26ᵁG,

	Starts	1st	2nd	3rd	Win & Pl
Hurdles	1	0	0	0	
Chases	3	0	0	0	
Career Total	7	0	0	0	

Going: Sf: 0-3 GS: 0-0 Gd: 0-1 GF: - Fm: 0-0
Distance: 2m/2m3: 0-0 2m4-2m7: 0-3 3m+: 0-1
Track: LH: 0-1 RH: 0-3 Tight: 0-3 Gall: 0-1
Aids: Bl: 0-0 Vi: 0-0 Tstrap: 0-0
Best Rating: 0 3/03 Hntg 3m2f good Hdl

Holloa Away (IRE)
91   74

11-y-o b g Red Sunset-Lili Bengam (Welsh Saint)
J A T De Giles J A T De Giles

Placings:f40/354P/0/04163000-6   (0628)
2002/03: 22⁶GF,

	Starts	1st	2nd	3rd	Win & Pl
Hurdles	1	0	0	0	0
Career Total	17	2	2	2	4068

| 70 | 9/01 | Strf | 2m6f110yG(0-95)HHdl | G-F | £1946 |
| 101 | 5/97 | Worc | 2m | H NHF | G-S | £1402 |

Total win prize-money £3349

Going: Sf: 0-0 GS: 0-0 Gd: 0-0 GF: - Fm: 0-1
Distance: 2m/2m3: 0-0 2m4-2m7: 0-1 3m+: 0-0
Track: LH: 0-1 RH: 0-0 Tight: 0-1 Gall: 0-0
Aids: Bl: 0-0 Vi: 0-0 Tstrap: 0-0
Best Rating: 101 5/97 Worc 2m gd-sft NHF

Failed to fulfil the promise of his bumper win at Worcester May 1997; won extended 2m 6f conditional selling handicap at Stratford September 2001; lightly raced in recent years; acts on good to soft and good to firm.

Hollow Legs
         78

7-y-o ch m Alflora (IRE)-Sayshar (Sayfar)
Miss Z C Davison Auld Firm Partnership

Placings:006500/320-LP   (1788)
2002/03: 16ᴸG, 17ᴾGS,

	Starts	1st	2nd	3rd	Win & Pl
Hurdles	2	0	0	0	
Career Total	11	0	1	1	1218

Going: Sf: 0-0 GS: 0-1 Gd: 0-1 GF: - Fm: 0-0
Distance: 2m/2m3: 0-2 2m4-2m7: 0-0 3m+: 0-0
Track: LH: 0-1 RH: 0-1 Tight: 0-2 Gall: 0-0
Aids: Bl: 0-0 Vi: 0-0 Tstrap: 0-0
Best Rating: 79 1/01 Weth 2m heavy NHF

Hollows Mill
101   90

7-y-o b g Rudimentary (USA)-Strawberry Song (Final Straw)
F P Murtagh The Great Expectations Sporting Club

Placings:0004-4536551   (4661)
2002/03: 16⁴G, 16⁵G, 17³GF, 16⁶G, 17⁵G, 16⁵G, 17¹GF,

	Starts	1st	2nd	3rd	Win & Pl
Hurdles	7	1	0	1	3881
Career Total	11	1	0	1	4169

| 90 | 4/03 | Carl | 2m1f | E Hdl | G-F | £3458 |

Total win prize-money £3458

Going: Sf: 0-0 GS: 0-0 Gd: 0-5 GF: - Fm: 1-2
Distance: 2m/2m3: 1-7 2m4-2m7: 0-0 3m+: 0-0
Track: LH: 0-6 RH: 1-1 Tight: 0-5 Gall: 0-0
Aids: Bl: 0-0 Vi: 0-0 Tstrap: 0-0
Best Rating: 90 4/03 Carl 2m1f gd-fm Hdl

Moderate hurdler; clear cut winner at Carlisle in April; keen sort and is likely to be best at around two miles.

Hollybush Hybrid

7-y-o ch m Risk Me (FR)-Absent Lover (Nearly A Hand)
S E H Sherwood Hollybush Nurseries Ltd

Placings:0-FPP   (4021)

2002/03: 19FS, 19PG, 17PS,

	Starts	1st	2nd	3rd	Win & Pl
Hurdles	3	0	0	0	
Career Total	4	0	0	0	

Going:	Sf: 0-2 GS: 0-0 Gd: 0-1 GF: - Fm: 0-0
Distance:	2m/2m3: 0-1 2m4-2m7: 0-2 3m+: 0-0
Track:	LH: 0-0 RH: 0-3 Tight: 0-0 Gall: 0-0
Aids:	Bl: 0-2 Vi: 0-0 Tstrap: 0-0
Best Rating:	78 4/02 Uttx 2m good NHF

Holme Farm Boy (IRE)
90   72

7-y-o b g River Falls-Lady Conchita (IRE) (Whistling Deer)
G M Moore M K Roddis

Placings:4440P0/4P   (0789)
2002/03: 194G, 26PGF,

	Starts	1st	2nd	3rd	Win & Pl
Hurdles	2	0	0	0	319
Career Total	8	0	0	0	529

Going:	Sf: 0-0 GS: 0-0 Gd: 0-1 GF: - Fm: 0-1
Distance:	2m/2m3: 0-0 2m4-2m7: 0-1 3m+: 0-1
Track:	LH: 0-1 RH: 0-1 Tight: 0-1 Gall: 0-0
Aids:	Bl: 0-0 Vi: 0-0 Tstrap: 0-0
Best Rating:	88 12/99 Leic 2m good Hdl

Holmesdale (IRE)
84f   95f

5-y-o b g Norwich-Sister Cecelia (Trombone)
M J Ryan Extraman Ltd

Placings:04   (4053)
2002/03: 160S, 164HY,

	Starts	1st	2nd	3rd	Win & Pl
NH Flat	2	0	0	0	0
Career Total	2	0	0	0	0

Going:	Sf: 0-1 GS: 0-0 Gd: 0-1 GF: - Fm: 0-0
Distance:	2m/2m3: 0-2 2m4-2m7: 0-0 3m+: 0-0
Track:	LH: 0-0 RH: 0-2 Tight: 0-0 Gall: 0-0
Aids:	Bl: 0-0 Vi: 0-0 Tstrap: 0-0
Best Rating:	95 2/03 Kemp 2m good NHF

Holy Orders (IRE)
122   153

6-y-o b h Unblest-Shadowglow (Shaadi (USA))
W P Mullins A McLuckie

Placings:611/3-0000   (4099)
2002/03: 16DHY, 16DS, 16DG, 16DG,

	Starts	1st	2nd	3rd	Win & Pl
Hurdles	4	0	0	0	
Career Total	8	2	0	1	48960
133	4/01	Fair	2m	Hdl	Y-S £42500
121	2/01	Gowr	2m	Hdl	HVY £5008
					Total win prize-money £47508

Going:	Sf: 0-2 GS: 0-0 Gd: 0-2 GF: - Fm: 0-0
Distance:	2m/2m3: 0-4 2m4-2m7: 0-0 3m+: 0-0
Track:	LH: 0-3 RH: 0-1 Tight: 0-0 Gall: 0-1
Aids:	Bl: 0-4 Vi: 0-0 Tstrap: 0-0
Best Rating:	149 3/03 Chel 2m110y good Hdl

Useful handicap hurdler; decent juvenile in 2000/01, but has

shown little over hurdles since; appreciates cut in the ground; best at two miles; usually wears blinkers.

Holyrood Princess (IRE)
75   16

4-y-o b f Moshaajir (USA)-Kawarau Queen (Taufan (USA))
A R Dicken William Jardine

Placings:0   (2035)
2002/03: 160S,

	Starts	1st	2nd	3rd	Win & Pl
Hurdles	1	0	0	0	
Career Total	1	0	0	0	

Going:	Sf: 0-1 GS: 0-0 Gd: 0-0 GF: - Fm: 0-0
Distance:	2m/2m3: 0-1 2m4-2m7: 0-0 3m+: 0-0
Track:	LH: 0-1 RH: 0-0 Tight: 0-1 Gall: 0-0
Aids:	Bl: 0-0 Vi: 0-0 Tstrap: 0-0
Best Rating:	16 11/02 Kels 2m110y soft Hdl

Holywell Girl

6-y-o b m Alhaatmi-Merry Maggie (Stanford)
John A Harris Christopher Morris

Placings:000-P   (1568)
2002/03: 19PG,

	Starts	1st	2nd	3rd	Win & Pl
Hurdles	1	0	0	0	
Career Total	4	0	0	0	

Going:	Sf: 0-0 GS: 0-0 Gd: 0-1 GF: - Fm: 0-0
Distance:	2m/2m3: 0-0 2m4-2m7: 0-1 3m+: 0-0
Track:	LH: 0-0 RH: 0-1 Tight: 0-1 Gall: 0-0
Aids:	Bl: 0-0 Vi: 0-0 Tstrap: 0-0
Best Rating:	58 1/02 Catt 2m gd-sft NHF

Hombre
104   85

8-y-o ch g Shernazar-Delray Jet (USA) (Northjet)
M D Hammond R D Bickenson

Placings:F05P/245601P/0PP005-13243P   (4670)
2002/03: 211S, 243GS, 162HY, 204S, 213S, 21PG,

	Starts	1st	2nd	3rd	Win & Pl
Chases	6	1	1	2	7347
Career Total	23	2	2	2	11236
85	12/02	Sedg	2m5f	E(0-105)HCh	SFT £4075
95	1/01	Weth	2m4f110y		E(0-105)HCh
HVY £3133					
					Total win prize-money £7209

Going:	Sf: 1-4 GS: 0-1 Gd: 0-1 GF: - Fm: 0-0
Distance:	2m/2m3: 0-1 2m4-2m7: 1-4 3m+: 0-1
Track:	LH: 1-5 RH: 0-1 Tight: 1-5 Gall: 0-1
Aids:	Bl: 0-0 Vi: 0-0 Tstrap: 0-0
Best Rating:	103 5/00 Sedg 2m5f110y gd-fm Hdl

Plating-class handicap chaser; best around two and a half miles; suited by soft ground; may have found three miles just beyond him at Ludlow.

Home James (IRE)
98   120

6-y-o b g Commanche Run-Take Me Home (Amoristic (USA))

A King Mrs Stewart Catherwood

Placings:1-3211   (4784)
2002/03: 223S, 202S, 191G, 191G,

	Starts	1st	2nd	3rd	Win & Pl
Hurdles	4	2	1	1	10613
Career Total	5	3	1	1	12384
119	4/03	MRas	2m3f110yD Hdl	GD	£5232
120	2/03	Hrfd	2m3f110yE Hdl	GD	£3844
103	3/02	Sthl	2m	H NHF	HVY £1771
				Total win prize-money £10849

Going:	Sf: 0-2 GS: 0-0 Gd: 2-2 GF: - Fm: 0-0
Distance:	2m/2m3: 0-0 2m4-2m7: 2-4 3m+: 0-0
Track:	LH: 0-2 RH: 2-2 Tight: 1-1 Gall: 0-0
Aids:	Bl: 0-0 Vi: 0-0 Tstrap: 0-0
Best Rating:	120 2/03 Hrfd 2m3f110y good Hdl

Successful debut in a bumper; most decisive winner of a novices hurdle at Hereford in February; followed up at Market Rasen in April; should make an even better chaser.

Home Made

5-y-o b g Homo Sapien-Inch Maid (Le Moss)
S A Brookshaw Miss H Brookshaw

Placings:0-0   (0091)
2002/03: 160G,

	Starts	1st	2nd	3rd	Win & Pl
NH Flat	1	0	0	0	
Career Total	2	0	0	0	

Going:	Sf: 0-0 GS: 0-0 Gd: 0-1 GF: - Fm: 0-0
Distance:	2m/2m3: 0-1 2m4-2m7: 0-0 3m+: 0-0
Track:	LH: 0-1 RH: 0-0 Tight: 0-0 Gall: 0-0
Aids:	Bl: 0-0 Vi: 0-0 Tstrap: 0-0
Best Rating:	58 5/02 Uttx 2m good NHF

Home Tor
90f   76f

6-y-o b g Homo Sapien-Torus Queen (Torus)
S A Brookshaw S A Brookshaw

Placings:05   (1459)
2002/03: 170GF, 16PF,

	Starts	1st	2nd	3rd	Win & Pl
NH Flat	2	0	0	0	0
Career Total	2	0	0	0	0

Going:	Sf: 0-0 GS: 0-0 Gd: 0-0 GF: - Fm: 0-2
Distance:	2m/2m3: 0-2 2m4-2m7: 0-0 3m+: 0-0
Track:	LH: 0-0 RH: 0-2 Tight: 0-0 Gall: 0-0
Aids:	Bl: 0-0 Vi: 0-0 Tstrap: 0-0
Best Rating:	76 10/02 Ludl 2m firm NHF

Homeleigh Mooncoin
109   121+

8-y-o ch g Jamesmead-Super Sol (Rolfe (USA))
Mrs L Wadham Miss S Wilson

Placings:61114   (1758)
2002/03: 200GF, 201GF, 211G, 261G, 254G,

	Starts	1st	2nd	3rd	Win & Pl
Hurdles	5	3	0	0	9192
Career Total	5	3	0	0	9192
121	10/02	Sthl	3m2f	E Hdl	GD £2961

121	9/02	Sthl	2m5f110yE Hdl	GD	£2996
110	8/02	Worc	2m4f	E Hdl	G-F	£2940

Total win prize-money £8897

Going: Sf: 0-0 GS: 0-0 Gd: 2-3 GF: - Fm: 1-2
Distance: 2m/2m3: 0-0 **2m4-2m7: 2-3** 3m+: 1-2
Track: **LH: 3-5** RH: 0-0 Tight: 0-0 Gall: 0-0
Aids: Bl: 0-0 Vi: 0-0 Tstrap: 0-0
Best Rating: 121 10/02 Sthl 3m2f   good Hdl

Showed tremendous improvement on his debut when causing a 50/1 shock in two and a half mile maiden hurdle at Worcester August 2002. Followed up with two wide margin wins at Southwell.

Homely Sort (IRE)

4-y-o b f Petardia-Safe Home (Home Guard (USA))
Mrs S Lamyman R D Letby

Placings:PPP   (3236)
2002/03: 16PGS, 16PHY, 16PS,

	Starts	1st	2nd	3rd	Win & Pl
Hurdles	3	0	0	0	
Career Total	3	0	0	0	

Going: Sf: 0-2 GS: 0-1 Gd: 0-0 GF: - Fm: 0-0
Distance: 2m/2m3: 0-3 2m4-2m7: 0-0 3m+: 0-0
Track: LH: 0-3 RH: 0-0 Tight: 0-2 Gall: 0-1
Aids: Bl: 0-0 Vi: 0-0 Tstrap: 0-0
Best Rating: 0 1/03 Fknm 2m   soft Hdl

Homemaker

13-y-o b m Homeboy-Ganadora (Good Times (ITY))
A E Jones Miss Sophie Parmentier

Placings:41/0U0/PP   (2587)
2002/03: 16PS, 22PGS,

	Starts	1st	2nd	3rd	Win & Pl
Hurdles	2	0	0	0	
Career Total	7	1	0	0	1606
89	10/93 Ludl	2m		Hdl	GD £1605

Total win prize-money £1606

Going: Sf: 0-1 GS: 0-1 Gd: 0-0 GF: - Fm: 0-0
Distance: 2m/2m3: 0-1 2m4-2m7: 0-1 3m+: 0-0
Track: LH: 0-1 RH: 0-1 Tight: 0-1 Gall: 0-0
Aids: Bl: 0-0 Vi: 0-0 Tstrap: 0-0
Best Rating: 89 10/93 Ludl 2m   good Hdl

Homer (IRE)
102   108
6-y-o b g Sadler s Wells (USA)-Gravieres (FR) (Saint Estephe (FR))
M C Pipe (N M Babbage 28/6) V J Tickel

Placings:6001002220-P020   (1131)
2002/03: 19PGF, 16PGF, 20PGF, 19PGF,

	Starts	1st	2nd	3rd	Win & Pl
Hurdles	4	0	1	0	1165
Career Total	14	1	4	0	10545
114	7/01 Naas	2m3f		Hdl	GD £6677

Total win prize-money £6677

Going: Sf: 0-0 GS: 0-0 Gd: 0-0 GF: - Fm: 0-4
Distance: 2m/2m3: 0-1 2m4-2m7: 0-3 3m+: 0-0
Track: LH: 0-2 RH: 0-2 Tight: 0-4 Gall: 0-0
Aids: Bl: 0-0 Vi: 0-0 Tstrap: 0-3
Best Rating: 114 12/01 Donc 2m4f   good Hdl

A winning hurdler in Ireland who was trained by Aidan O Brien as a juvenile. Runner-up on his British debut in November 2001.

Homestead
85   105d
9-y-o ch g Indian Ridge-Bertrade (Homeboy)
E McNamara Dooradoyle Syndicate

Placings:0/340343020/0F460412320036-4500056S (1943)
2002/03: 24AGY, 205GY, 24PYS, 20PGY, 20PF, 205G, 206YS, 21SG,

	Starts	1st	2nd	3rd	Win & Pl
Hurdles	8	0	0	0	368
Career Total	32	1	3	5	15645
101	12/01 Punc	2m4f	(0-95)HHdl	Y-S	£5564

Total win prize-money £5565

Going: Sf: 0-0 GS: 0-0 Gd: 0-2 GF: - Fm: 0-1
Distance: 2m/2m3: 0-0 2m4-2m7: 0-6 3m+: 0-2
Track: LH: 0-2 RH: 0-2 Tight: 0-0 Gall: 0-1
Aids: Bl: 0-8 Vi: 0-0 Tstrap: 0-0
Best Rating: 105 3/02 Dpat 2m6f   soft Hdl

An All-Weather winner who has shown some form over hurdles at a modest level in Ireland.

Homme De Fer
105   117
11-y-o b g Arctic Lord-Florence May (Grange Melody)
K C Bailey The Hon C Leigh

Placings:66/623/1211045/2113/4022/01124P-516023
                                             (4682)
2002/03: 255G, 241G, 276G, 240G, 242GF, 243GF,

	Starts	1st	2nd	3rd	Win & Pl
Chases	6	1	1	1	7818
Career Total	32	8	7	3	41117
117	11/02 Ludl	3m	D(0-115)HCh	GD	£5736
114	11/01 Ludl	3m	F(0-110)HCh	G-F	£3672
107	11/01 Winc	2m5f	E(0-115)HCh	GD	£5323
111	7/99 NAbb	2m5f110yE Ch		G-F	£3403
111	6/99 NAbb	2m5f110yE Ch		GD	£3156
119	1/99 Font	2m2f110yD Hdl		SFT	£3062
121	12/98 Hrfd	2m3f110yE Hdl		SFT	£3060
118	10/98 Plum	2m4f	E Hdl	G-F	£2302

Total win prize-money £29719

Going: Sf: 0-0 GS: 0-0 Gd: 1-4 GF: - Fm: 0-2
Distance: 2m/2m3: 0-0 2m4-2m7: 0-0 **3m+: 1-6**
Track: LH: 0-1 **RH: 1-5** Tight: 1-4 Gall: 0-1
Aids: Bl: 0-0 Vi: 0-0 Tstrap: 0-0
Best Rating: 121 12/98 Hrfd 2m3f110y soft Hdl

Fair chaser; stays three miles; prefers a sound surface.

Honest Herbert (IRE)
55
10-y-o b g Salluceva-Bold And True (Sir Herbert)
K F Clutterbuck K F Clutterbuck

Placings:P030/P2-P   (1247)
2002/03: 23PG,

	Starts	1st	2nd	3rd	Win & Pl
Chases	1	0	0	0	
Career Total	7	0	1	1	1311

Going: Sf: 0-0 GS: 0-0 Gd: 0-1 GF: - Fm: 0-0
Distance: 2m/2m3: 0-0 2m4-2m7: 0-0 3m+: 0-1
Track: LH: 0-1 RH: 0-0 Tight: 0-0 Gall: 0-0
Aids: Bl: 0-0 Vi: 0-0 Tstrap: 0-0

Best Rating: 75 2/99 Muss 2m   firm Hdl

Honey Honey (FR)

8-y-o gr g Djarvis (FR)-Urta (FR) (Le Pontet (FR))
Ms Lisa Stock H R Neaves

Placings:1P/P3/1360/0-P   (4640)
2002/03: 21PG,

	Starts	1st	2nd	3rd	Win & Pl
Chases	1	0	0	0	
Career Total	10	2	0	2	7667
6/00	Vich	2m5f110y Ch		GD	£2882
4/99	Fntb	2m3f	Ch		VS	£3445

Total win prize-money £6327

Going: Sf: 0-0 GS: 0-0 Gd: 0-1 GF: - Fm: 0-0
Distance: 2m/2m3: 0-0 2m4-2m7: 0-1 3m+: 0-0
Track: LH: 0-1 RH: 0-0 Tight: 0-1 Gall: 0-0
Aids: Bl: 0-0 Vi: 0-0 Tstrap: 0-0
Best Rating: 81 9/00 Worc 2m4f   gd-fm Hdl

Honey Thyme

5-y-o ch m Palais De Danse-Forever Honey (Palm Track)
R Ford Trevor Barnes

Placings:0P-P   (4222)
2002/03: 17PGF,

	Starts	1st	2nd	3rd	Win & Pl
Hurdles	1	0	0	0	
Career Total	3	0	0	0	

Going: Sf: 0-0 GS: 0-0 Gd: 0-0 GF: - Fm: 0-1
Distance: 2m/2m3: 0-1 2m4-2m7: 0-0 3m+: 0-0
Track: LH: 0-0 RH: 0-1 Tight: 0-0 Gall: 0-0
Aids: Bl: 0-0 Vi: 0-0 Tstrap: 0-0
Best Rating: 0 3/03 Hrfd 2m1f   gd-fm Hdl

Honey Trader
92(98h)   (86h)80
11-y-o b g Beveled (USA)-Lizzie Bee (Kind Of Hush)
C L Popham T J Hawkins

Placings:3003400/24411604222022563200/15424422F431
0506/02411003122F5/362460PBPP/0P412060P43-056450
                                             (0853)
2002/03: 19PG, 16SG, 186GF, 164S, 16SGF, 17PGF,

	Starts	1st	2nd	3rd	Win & Pl
Hurdles	2	0	0	0	0
Chases	4	0	0	0	0
Career Total	83	8	15	7	49235
79	7/01 NAbb	2m1f	F(0-90)Hdl	GD	£2317
112	11/99 DRoy	2m	(0-116)HCh	SFT	£6160
112	7/99 Klny	2m1f	(0-123)HCh	GD	£4296
110	6/99 Tral	2m	Ch	GD	£2915
117	11/98 Clon	2m	(88-116)HHdl	SFT	£2690
115	5/98 Tral	2m	(0-116)Hdl	GD	£3573
94	6/97 Limk	2m	(0-102)HHdl	FRM	£3391
93	5/97 Baln	2m	Hdl	GD	£2015

Total win prize-money £27550

Going: Sf: 0-1 GS: 0-0 Gd: 0-2 GF: - Fm: 0-3
Distance: 2m/2m3: 0-5 2m4-2m7: 0-1 3m+: 0-0
Track: LH: 0-4 RH: 0-1 Tight: 0-4 Gall: 0-0
Aids: Bl: 0-0 Vi: 0-0 Tstrap: 0-0
Best Rating: 124 11/99 Newb 2m1f   gd-sft Ch

Modest hurdler/chaser. Suited by a sound surface and the minimum trip. Seems most effective when held up.

Honey's Gift
102   77

4-y-o f Terimon-Honeycroft (Crofter (USA))
G G Margarson Russell Evans

Placings:U0U35   (3924)
2002/03: 16UGS, 17OS, 16US, 16²S, 16⁵G,

	Starts	1st	2nd	3rd	Win & Pl
Hurdles	5	0	0	1	751
Career Total	5	0	0	1	751

Going: Sf: 0-3 GS: 0-1 Gd: 0-1 GF: - Fm: 0-0
Distance: 2m/2m3: 0-5 2m4-2m7: 0-0 3m+: 0-0
Track: LH: 0-2 RH: 0-3 Tight: 0-2 Gall: 0-2
Aids: BI: 0-0 Vi: 0-0 Tstrap: 0-0
Best Rating: 79 1/03 Fknm 2m   soft   Hdl

Honeybunch (IRE)
98f   87f

5-y-o b m Supreme Leader-Hunter s Pet (Cracksman)
C F Swan Malm Syndicate

Placings:44   (4424a)
2002/03: 16⁴G, 16⁴F,

	Starts	1st	2nd	3rd	Win & Pl
NH Flat	2	0	0	0	208
Career Total	2	0	0	0	208

Going: Sf: 0-0 GS: 0-0 Gd: 0-1 GF: - Fm: 0-1
Distance: 2m/2m3: 0-2 2m4-2m7: 0-0 3m+: 0-0
Track: LH: 0-0 RH: 0-1 Tight: 0-1 Gall: 0-0
Aids: BI: 0-0 Vi: 0-0 Tstrap: 0-0
Best Rating: 87 3/03 DRoy 2m   firm   NHF

Honneur Fontenail (FR)
80   44

4-y-o ch g Tel Quel (FR)-Fontanalia (FR) (Rex Magna (FR))
N J Hawke Wags To Riches Partnership

Placings:00   (3183)
2002/03: 12OGS, 16OGS,

	Starts	1st	2nd	3rd	Win & Pl
NH Flat	1	0	0	0	0
Hurdles	1	0	0	0	0
Career Total	2	0	0	0	

Going: Sf: 0-0 GS: 0-2 Gd: 0-0 GF: - Fm: 0-0
Distance: 2m/2m3: 0-1 2m4-2m7: 0-0 3m+: 0-0
Track: LH: 0-1 RH: 0-1 Tight: 0-0 Gall: 0-0
Aids: BI: 0-0 Vi: 0-0 Tstrap: 0-0
Best Rating: 68 11/02 Newb 1m4f110y gd-sft NHF

Honor's Lad
69   38

4-y-o ch g Sabrehill (USA)-Ackcontent (USA) (Key To Content (USA))
Mrs L C Jewell (C N Kellett 12/7) Mrs A Greengrow

Placings:PP0   (4184)
2002/03: 17PHY, 16PHY, 17OG,

	Starts	1st	2nd	3rd	Win & Pl
Hurdles	3	0	0	0	
Career Total	3	0	0	0	

Going: Sf: 0-2 GS: 0-0 Gd: 0-1 GF: - Fm: 0-0
Distance: 2m/2m3: 0-3 2m4-2m7: 0-0 3m+: 0-0
Track: LH: 0-1 RH: 0-2 Tight: 0-3 Gall: 0-0
Aids: BI: 0-0 Vi: 0-1 Tstrap: 0-0
Best Rating: 38 3/03 Folk 2m1f110y good   Hdl

Honourable Chief
85   74

6-y-o b g Be My Chief (USA)-Magic Orb (Primo Dominie)
J T Gifford (G Prodromou 8/5) J P Aston Evans

Placings:06050   (1869)
2002/03: 16OG, 18⁶G, 16OG, 16⁵S, 18OGS,

	Starts	1st	2nd	3rd	Win & Pl
Hurdles	5	0	0	0	0
Career Total	5	0	0	0	0

Going: Sf: 0-1 GS: 0-1 Gd: 0-3 GF: - Fm: 0-0
Distance: 2m/2m3: 0-5 2m4-2m7: 0-0 3m+: 0-0
Track: LH: 0-5 RH: 0-0 Tight: 0-4 Gall: 0-0
Aids: BI: 0-1 Vi: 0-0 Tstrap: 0-0
Best Rating: 63 10/02 Chep 2m110y good   Hdl

Hopbine
99   111

7-y-o ch m Gildoran-Haraka Sasa (Town And Country)
J L Spearing Miss S Howell

Placings:50/025511225-060020   (4441)
2002/03: 21OGS, 21⁶G, 20OHY, 19OG, 22²G, 20OG,

	Starts	1st	2nd	3rd	Win & Pl
Hurdles	6	0	1	0	1646
Career Total	17	2	4	0	27555
105 2/02 Wwck 2m5f D Hdl   HVY £4077
99 1/02 Sthl 2m4f110y   E(0-105)HHdl
G-S £2534

Total win prize-money £6612

Going: Sf: 0-1 GS: 0-1 Gd: 0-4 GF: - Fm: 0-0
Distance: 2m/2m3: 0-0 2m4-2m7: 0-6 3m+: 0-0
Track: LH: 0-2 RH: 0-3 Tight: 0-0 Gall: 0-1
Aids: BI: 0-0 Vi: 0-0 Tstrap: 0-0
Best Rating: 118 3/02 Newb 2m5f   gd-sft Hdl

A decent hurdler, winner of a Southwell handicap and a Warwick novices event at the start of 2002, she ran really well without winning in much tougher events after that; stays well and looks best on soft ground, though she does handle faster conditions.

Hope Value
84(76c)   (60c)76

8-y-o b g Rock City-Folle Idee (USA) (Foolish Pleasure (USA))
G F Edwards G F Edwards

Placings:02/614P4FP/U00-00   (4256)
2002/03: 18⁶S, 17OG,

	Starts	1st	2nd	3rd	Win & Pl
Hurdles	2	0	0	0	
Career Total	14	1	1	0	3502
99 8/00 NAbb 2m1f D Hdl   G-S £2848

Total win prize-money £2848

Going: Sf: 0-1 GS: 0-0 Gd: 0-1 GF: - Fm: 0-0
Distance: 2m/2m3: 0-2 2m4-2m7: 0-0 3m+: 0-0
Track: LH: 0-1 RH: 0-1 Tight: 0-1 Gall: 0-0
Aids: BI: 0-0 Vi: 0-0 Tstrap: 0-0
Best Rating: 99 11/00 Tntn 2m3f110y good   Hdl

Hoppertree

7-y-o b g Rock Hopper-Snow Tree (Welsh Pageant)
R S Brookhouse R S Brookhouse

Placings:5/04F-U   (3311)
2002/03: 19UGS,

	Starts	1st	2nd	3rd	Win & Pl
Hurdles	1	0	0	0	
Career Total	5	0	0	0	0

Going: Sf: 0-0 GS: 0-1 Gd: 0-0 GF: - Fm: 0-0
Distance: 2m/2m3: 0-1 2m4-2m7: 0-0 3m+: 0-0
Track: LH: 0-0 RH: 0-1 Tight: 0-0 Gall: 0-0
Aids: BI: 0-0 Vi: 0-0 Tstrap: 0-0
Best Rating: 105 1/02 Font 2m2f110y good   NHF

Hopping Mad

10-y-o b m Puget (USA)-Mapleline (Shy Groom (USA))
B G Duke B G Duke

Placings:0PP/5   (4417)
2002/03: 25⁵G,

	Starts	1st	2nd	3rd	Win & Pl
Chases	1	0	0	0	
Career Total	4	0	0	0	0

Going: Sf: 0-0 GS: 0-0 Gd: 0-1 GF: - Fm: 0-0
Distance: 2m/2m3: 0-0 2m4-2m7: 0-0 3m+: 0-1
Track: LH: 0-0 RH: 0-1 Tight: 0-1 Gall: 0-0
Aids: BI: 0-0 Vi: 0-0 Tstrap: 0-0
Best Rating: 65 3/03 MRas 3m1f   good   Ch

Horatio (IRE)
85   58

7-y-o b g Warcraft (USA)-Cool Russ Quay (Quayside)
R J Hodges Mrs Carol Taylor

Placings:4/005   (3920)
2002/03: 16OS, 17OS, 18⁵S,

	Starts	1st	2nd	3rd	Win & Pl
NH Flat	1	0	0	0	
Hurdles	2	0	0	0	
Career Total	4	0	0	0	

Going: Sf: 0-3 GS: 0-0 Gd: 0-0 GF: - Fm: 0-0
Distance: 2m/2m3: 0-3 2m4-2m7: 0-0 3m+: 0-0
Track: LH: 0-2 RH: 0-1 Tight: 0-2 Gall: 0-0
Aids: BI: 0-0 Vi: 0-0 Tstrap: 0-0
Best Rating: 76 5/00 Folk 2m1f110y good   NHF

Horizon (FR)

6-y-o ch g Arctic Tern (USA)-Furtchella (FR) (Dancing Spree (USA))
P C Ritchens R Catton

Placings:00042540/000151P0-4P   (2063)
2002/03: 21⁴G, 19PS,

	Starts	1st	2nd	3rd	Win & Pl
Hurdles	2	0	0	0	589
Career Total	18	2	1	0	20011
10/01 Saum 2m4f Ch   G-S £3104
10/01 LePe 2m2f110y Ch   HLD £2910

Total win prize-money £6014

Going: Sf: 0-1 GS: 0-0 Gd: 0-1 GF: - Fm: 0-0
Distance: 2m/2m3: 0-0 2m4-2m7: 0-2 3m+: 0-0
Track: LH: 0-1 RH: 0-1 Tight: 0-0 Gall: 0-1
Aids: Bl: 0-0 Vi: 0-0 Tstrap: 0-0
Best Rating: 0   11/02 Hrfd 2m3f110y soft Hdl

Hornbill
66   **16**
5-y-o b g Sir Harry Lewis (USA)-Tangara (Town Crier)
Mrs P Robeson   Mrs P Robeson

Placings:0P (3926)
2002/03: 17GS, 20PG,

	Starts	1st	2nd	3rd	Win & Pl
Hurdles	2	0	0	0	
Career Total	2	0	0	0	

Going: Sf: 0-0 GS: 0-1 Gd: 0-1 GF: - Fm: 0-0
Distance: 2m/2m3: 0-1 2m4-2m7: 0-0 3m+: 0-0
Track: LH: 0-1 RH: 0-1 Tight: 0-0 Gall: 0-1
Aids: Bl: 0-0 Vi: 0-0 Tstrap: 0-0
Best Rating: 16 2/03 Bang 2m1f gd-sft Hdl

Hors La Loi (FR)
115   **119**
7-y-o ch g Exit To Nowhere (USA)-Kernia (IRE) (Raise A Cup (USA))
Ian Williams   The Not So Risky Partnership

Placings:30/411430/0032 (4754)
2002/03: 16GS, 17GS, 16GF, 16G,

	Starts	1st	2nd	3rd	Win & Pl
Hurdles	4	0	1	1	2928
Career Total	12	2	1	3	11123
119 12/00 Tntn	2m1f	E(0-115)HHdl		SFT	£3883
107 12/00 Donc	2m110y	F(0-100)HHdl		HVY	£2457

Total win prize-money £6341

Going: Sf: 0-0 GS: 0-2 Gd: 0-1 GF: - Fm: 0-1
Distance: 2m/2m3: 0-4 2m4-2m7: 0-0 3m+: 0-0
Track: LH: 0-3 RH: 0-1 Tight: 0-1 Gall: 0-1
Aids: Bl: 0-0 Vi: 0-0 Tstrap: 0-0
Best Rating: 119 12/00 Tntn 2m1f soft Hdl

Modest hurdler; effective at around two miles; acts well on a soft surface, but effective on faster.

Hors La Loi Iii (FR)
117   **118**
8-y-o b g Cyborg (FR)-Quintessence Iii (FR) (El Condor (FR))
J R Fanshawe   Paul Green

Placings:11111/30124/PP2P/23311-F43L0 (4478)
2002/03: 17FG, 16FS, 16GS, 16LG, 20HG,

	Starts	1st	2nd	3rd	Win & Pl
Hurdles	5	0	0	1	9250
Career Total	24	8	3	4	399370
166 3/02 Chel	2m110y	A Hdl		G-S	£156600
164 2/02 Winc	2m	A Hdl		G-S	£21000
148 2/00 Winc	2m	A Hdl		GD	£21000
155 4/99 Aint	2m110y	A Hdl		G-S	£23750
159 3/99 Chel	2m110y	A Hdl		G-S	£45960
151 1/99 Chel	2m1f	A Hdl		SFT	£9645
137 12/98 Ling	2m110y	A Hdl		SFT	£9002
11/98 Autl	2m2f	Hdl		VS	£10101

Total win prize-money £297058

Going: Sf: 0-1 GS: 0-1 Gd: 0-3 GF: - Fm: 0-0
Distance: 2m/2m3: 0-4 2m4-2m7: 0-1 3m+: 0-0
Track: LH: 0-3 RH: 0-2 Tight: 0-1 Gall: 0-1
Aids: Bl: 0-0 Vi: 0-0 Tstrap: 0-5
Best Rating: 166 3/02 Chel 2m110y gd-sft Hdl

Former Champion Hurdler; brilliant winner of the 1999 Supreme Novices Hurdle and runner-up to Istabraq in the 2000 Champion Hurdle; struggled afterwards until returning to form in the spring of 2002, winning the Kingwell Hurdle at Wincanton and following up in the Champion Hurdle; yet to hit top form in 2002/2003, reportedly needing the race still when well beaten by Rhinestone Cowboy in the 2003 Kingwell; refused to take part in this years Champion; wears a tongue-tie and has broken blood vessels in the past; suited by 2m and the ground good or on the easy side of good, but doesn t want it soft.

Horton Dancer
95   **86**
6-y-o b g Rambo Dancer (CAN)-Horton Lady (Midyan (USA))
I W McInnes (D W Barker 7/7)   Robert E Cook

Placings:1603P-0 (4354)
2002/03: 20PGF,

	Starts	1st	2nd	3rd	Win & Pl
Hurdles	1	0	0	0	
Career Total	6	1	0	1	2911
86 10/01 Sedg	2m1f	E Hdl		G-S	£2576

Total win prize-money £2576

Going: Sf: 0-0 GS: 0-0 Gd: 0-0 GF: - Fm: 0-1
Distance: 2m/2m3: 0-0 2m4-2m7: 0-1 3m+: 0-0
Track: LH: 0-1 RH: 0-0 Tight: 0-0 Gall: 0-0
Aids: Bl: 0-0 Vi: 0-0 Tstrap: 0-0
Best Rating: 86 12/01 Muss 2m1f gd-fm Hdl

Acts on most types of ground and goes well at around two miles.

Horus (IRE)
107   **148d**
8-y-o b g Teenoso (USA)-Jennie s First (Idiots Delight)
M C Pipe (D Pipe 13/5)   B A Kilpatrick

Placings:1P-13111406P (4469)
2002/03: 26TGS, 25JS, 24TGF, 20TGS, 25TG, 26JS, 21HGS, 20HG, 25PG,

	Starts	1st	2nd	3rd	Win & Pl
Chases	9	4	0	1	65233
Career Total	11	5	0	1	66585
148 12/02 Chel	3m1f110yB	HCh		GD	£25589
143 11/02 Newb	2m4f	B(0-145)HCh		G-S	£20300
133 6/02 Strf	3m	D(0-125)HCh		G-F	£10400
120 5/02 Chel	3m2f110yH	Ch		G-F	£5395
132 2/02 Winc	3m1f110yH	Ch		SFT	£1352

Total win prize-money £63037

Going: Sf: 0-2 GS: 1-2 Gd: 1-3 GF: - Fm: 2-2
Distance: 2m/2m3: 0-0 2m4-2m7: 1-3 3m+: 3-6
Track: LH: 4-8 RH: 0-1 Tight: 1-2 Gall: 3-6
Aids: Bl: 0-0 Vi: 0-1 Tstrap: 0-0
Best Rating: 148 12/02 Chel 3m1f110y good Ch

Very useful chaser; Pipe and won five times in 2002 including in good handicaps at Newbury and Cheltenham in the autumn; stays further than three miles and acts on any ground.

Hot Bunny (IRE)
101   **(68c)94**
7-y-o b m Distinctly North (USA)-Debach Dust (Indian King (USA))
C F Swan   Bucket Syndicate

Placings:S00U02134/313550/006F-00000P (1016)
2002/03: 20HY, 19HGF, 18HY, 18HGY, 22HG, 20PG,

	Starts	1st	2nd	3rd	Win & Pl
Hurdles	6	0	0	0	
Career Total	25	2	1	3	9701
98 5/00 Leop	2m	(0-109)HHdl		GD	£4416
92 3/00 Muss	2m	E Hdl		G-F	£2618

Total win prize-money £7034

Going: Sf: 0-0 GS: 0-0 Gd: 0-2 GF: - Fm: 0-1
Distance: 2m/2m3: 0-3 2m4-2m7: 0-3 3m+: 0-0
Track: LH: 0-1 RH: 0-4 Tight: 0-0 Gall: 0-0
Aids: Bl: 0-0 Vi: 0-0 Tstrap: 0-0
Best Rating: 98 5/00 Leop 2m good Hdl

Hot Classic
4-y-o b f Classic Cliche (IRE)-White Heat (Last Tycoon)
J R Best   D S Nevison

Placings:0 (3849)
2002/03: 16HG,

	Starts	1st	2nd	3rd	Win & Pl
NH Flat	1	0	0	0	
Career Total	1	0	0	0	

Going: Sf: 0-0 GS: 0-0 Gd: 0-1 GF: - Fm: 0-0
Distance: 2m/2m3: 0-1 2m4-2m7: 0-0 3m+: 0-0
Track: LH: 0-0 RH: 0-1 Tight: 0-0 Gall: 0-0
Aids: Bl: 0-0 Vi: 0-0 Tstrap: 0-0
Best Rating: 0 2/03 Ludl 2m good NHF

Hot Produxion (USA)
110   **102**
4-y-o ch g Tabasco Cat (USA)-Princess Harriet (USA) (Mt. Livermore (USA))
J Mackie (Mrs A J Perrett 7/7)   A J Winterton

Placings:02332 (4325)
2002/03: 17HG, 16PG, 16HS, 16HG, 19PG,

	Starts	1st	2nd	3rd	Win & Pl
Hurdles	5	0	2	2	3674
Career Total	5	0	2	2	3674

Going: Sf: 0-1 GS: 0-0 Gd: 0-4 GF: - Fm: 0-0
Distance: 2m/2m3: 0-5 2m4-2m7: 0-0 3m+: 0-0
Track: LH: 0-4 RH: 0-1 Tight: 0-0 Gall: 0-2
Aids: Bl: 0-0 Vi: 0-3 Tstrap: 0-0
Best Rating: 102 3/03 Newb 2m3f good Hdl

Modest hurdler; stays two miles three; acts on decent ground.

Hot Shots (FR)
110(107c)   **(138c)125**
8-y-o b g Passing Sale (FR)-Uguette Iv (FR) (Chamberlin (FR))
M Pitman   Mrs Jill Eynon & Robin Eynon

Placings:343210/6300/213416220P-P50UU12P (4639)
2002/03: 16PF, 16FS, 16HG, 16UGS, 16US, 11GF, 16HG, 16PGF,

	Starts	1st	2nd	3rd	Win & Pl
Hurdles	7	1	1	0	6861
Chases	1	0	0	0	0
Career Total	28	4	5	4	29530
125 3/03 Winc	2m	D(0-125)HHdl		G-F	£4771

116	9/01	Worc	2m	D Ch	G-F	£3926
108	6/01	Baln	2m1f	Ch	GD	£5564
110	2/00	Punc	2m	Hdl	Y-S	£4140

Total win prize-money £18402

Going: Sf: 0-2 GS: 0-1 Gd: 0-2 GF: - Fm: 1-3
Distance: 2m/2m3: 1-8 2m4-2m7: 0-0 3m+: 0-0
Track: LH: 0-2 RH: 1-6 Tight: 0-1 Gall: 0-0
Aids: Bl: 0-0 Vi: 0-0 Tstrap: 0-0
Best Rating: 138 11/01 Sand 2m   gd-sft   Ch

Useful hurdler/chaser; winner over fences in Ireland; made a successful British debut at Worcester in September 2001; reverted to hurdles in 2002/2003 and was successful at Wincanton; suited by two miles and a sound surface.

Hot To Trot (IRE)
102   103

10-y-o b g Yashgan-La Tante (Bold Lad (IRE))
C J Gray (C J Mann 17/5) S C Botham

Placings:211P/P/0P0P0/3PF-23   (0923)
2002/03: 27²GF, 22³GF,

	Starts	1st	2nd	3rd	Win & Pl
Hurdles	2	0	1	1	1314
Career Total	15	2	2	2	9512
125	2/99	Folk	2m6f110yE Hdl		G-S	£2386
125	11/98	Newb	3m110y C Hdl		GD	£4032

Total win prize-money £6420

Going: Sf: 0-0 GS: 0-0 Gd: 0-0 GF: - Fm: 0-2
Distance: 2m/2m3: 0-0 2m4-2m7: 0-1 3m+: 0-1
Track: LH: 0-2 RH: 0-0 Tight: 0-2 Gall: 0-0
Aids: Bl: 0-0 Vi: 0-0 Tstrap: 0-0
Best Rating: 125 2/99 Folk 2m6f110y gd-sft Hdl

Staying hurdler. Acts on most types of ground. Finished lame in a claimer in August. (DEAD)

Hot Weld
67f   93f

4-y-o b g Weld-Deb s Ball (Glenstal (USA))
T P Tate T P Tate

Placings:2   (3917)
2002/03: 17²GS,

	Starts	1st	2nd	3rd	Win & Pl
NH Flat	1	0	1	0	574
Career Total	1	0	1	0	574

Going: Sf: 0-0 GS: 0-1 Gd: 0-0 GF: - Fm: 0-0
Distance: 2m/2m3: 0-1 2m4-2m7: 0-0 3m+: 0-0
Track: LH: 0-0 RH: 0-1 Tight: 0-0 Gall: 0-0
Aids: Bl: 0-0 Vi: 0-0 Tstrap: 0-0
Best Rating: 99 3/03 Carl 2m1f gd-sft NHF

Dam prolific winner over hurdles; just denied on racecourse bow in bumper at Carlisle in March.

Hoteliers' Dream
66   54

5-y-o b m Reprimand-Pride Of Britain (CAN) (Linkage (USA))
W S Kittow Reg Gifford

Placings:FP0   (4251)
2002/03: 17FS, 16PHY, 17ºG,

	Starts	1st	2nd	3rd	Win & Pl
Hurdles	3	0	0	0	
Career Total	3	0	0	0	

Going: Sf: 0-2 GS: 0-1 Gd: 0-1 GF: - Fm: 0-0
Distance: 2m/2m3: 0-3 2m4-2m7: 0-0 3m+: 0-0
Track: LH: 0-1 RH: 0-2 Tight: 0-1 Gall: 0-0
Aids: Bl: 0-0 Vi: 0-0 Tstrap: 0-0
Best Rating: 54 3/03 Extr 2m1f good Hdl

Hotspur Street
99   80

11-y-o b g Cadeaux Genereux-Excellent Alibi (USA) (Exceller (USA))
E L James Mrs D C Samworth

Placings:04/445U04/060406650056612/066433550/23535 6/025253P-50   (0180)
2002/03: 17³G, 22³GF,

	Starts	1st	2nd	3rd	Win & Pl
Hurdles	2	0	0	0	0
Career Total	47	1	4	5	6086
77	3/98	Towc	2m	G Hdl	G-S	£1576

Total win prize-money £1576

Going: Sf: 0-0 GS: 0-0 Gd: 0-0 GF: - Fm: 0-0
Distance: 2m/2m3: 0-0 2m4-2m7: 0-1 3m+: 0-0
Track: LH: 0-0 RH: 0-2 Tight: 0-1 Gall: 0-0
Aids: Bl: 0-2 Vi: 0-0 Tstrap: 0-0
Best Rating: 89 12/99 Leic 2m soft Hdl

Appears to act on most types of ground, but is best on a soft surface and effective at two miles. Has a poor strike rate.

Hotters (IRE)
93(104h)   (64h)91

8-y-o b g Be My Native (USA)-Siul Currach (Deep Run)
M Pitman Reddal Racing

Placings:0/100554-004UF505   (4280)
2002/03: 21³G, 23ºG, 25⁴G, 23ºG, 33FS, 26⁵HY, 26ºG, 275GF,

	Starts	1st	2nd	3rd	Win & Pl
Hurdles	4	0	0	0	0
Chases	4	0	0	0	323
Career Total	15	1	0	0	2175
82	10/01	Hntg	2m110y	H NHF	GD	£1452

Total win prize-money £1453

Going: Sf: 0-2 GS: 0-0 Gd: 0-5 GF: - Fm: 0-1
Distance: 2m/2m3: 0-0 2m4-2m7: 0-2 3m+: 0-6
Track: LH: 0-1 RH: 0-6 Tight: 0-5 Gall: 0-1
Aids: Bl: 0-1 Vi: 0-0 Tstrap: 0-0
Best Rating: 98 1/02 Font 2m2f110y good Hdl

Moderate hurdler; on the downgrade.

Houlihans Choice
83f   85f

6-y-o ch g Norton Challenger-Model Lady (Le Bavard (FR))
Ferdy Murphy Paddy O Donnell

Placings:0-0   (2444)
2002/03: 16ºGS,

	Starts	1st	2nd	3rd	Win & Pl
NH Flat	1	0	0	0	
Career Total	2	0	0	0	

Going: Sf: 0-0 GS: 0-1 Gd: 0-0 GF: - Fm: 0-0
Distance: 2m/2m3: 0-1 2m4-2m7: 0-0 3m+: 0-0
Track: LH: 0-0 RH: 0-1 Tight: 0-0 Gall: 0-1
Aids: Bl: 0-0 Vi: 0-0 Tstrap: 0-0
Best Rating: 85 3/02 Hayd 2m good NHF

Houselope Beck

13-y-o ch g Meadowbrook-Hallo Cheeky (Flatbush)
Miss C Osborne (G F White 26/5) F V White

Placings:4/0FU/5   (4107)
2002/03: 27⁵S,

	Starts	1st	2nd	3rd	Win & Pl
Chases	1	0	0	0	0
Career Total	5	0	0	0	136

Going: Sf: 0-1 GS: 0-0 Gd: 0-0 GF: - Fm: 0-0
Distance: 2m/2m3: 0-0 2m4-2m7: 0-0 3m+: 0-1
Track: LH: 0-1 RH: 0-0 Tight: 0-1 Gall: 0-0
Aids: Bl: 0-0 Vi: 0-0 Tstrap: 0-0
Best Rating: 73 5/96 Ctml 3m2f gd-fm Ch

Houseparty (IRE)

5-y-o b/br g Grand Lodge (USA)-Special Display (Welsh Pageant)
J A B Old W E Sturt

Placings:F   (4001)
2002/03: 16FS,

	Starts	1st	2nd	3rd	Win & Pl
Hurdles	1	0	0	0	
Career Total	1	0	0	0	

Going: Sf: 0-1 GS: 0-0 Gd: 0-0 GF: - Fm: 0-0
Distance: 2m/2m3: 0-1 2m4-2m7: 0-0 3m+: 0-0
Track: LH: 0-0 RH: 0-1 Tight: 0-0 Gall: 0-0
Aids: Bl: 0-0 Vi: 0-0 Tstrap: 0-0
Best Rating: 0 3/03 Winc 2m soft Hdl

How Great Thou Art
99   82

7-y-o b g Almoojid-Mamamere (Tres Gate)
R J Baker D R Walsh

Placings:0/03-66005   (4574)
2002/03: 17⁶G, 20⁶S, 19ºGS, 19ºGS, 22⁵GF,

	Starts	1st	2nd	3rd	Win & Pl
NH Flat	1	0	0	0	0
Hurdles	4	0	0	0	0
Career Total	8	0	0	1	214

Going: Sf: 0-1 GS: 0-2 Gd: 0-1 GF: - Fm: 0-1
Distance: 2m/2m3: 0-2 2m4-2m7: 0-3 3m+: 0-0
Track: LH: 0-2 RH: 0-3 Tight: 0-2 Gall: 0-0
Aids: Bl: 0-0 Vi: 0-0 Tstrap: 0-0
Best Rating: 92 10/02 Extr 2m1f good NHF

Modest novice hurdler; improved form since being stepped up in distance; no match for Dun An Doras in 2m 6f maiden hurdle at Newton Abbot June 2003.

How Ran On (IRE)
104   85d

12-y-o b/br g Mandalus-Kelly s Bridge (Netherkelly)
Mrs L Williamson Halewood International Ltd

Placings:41/20010/F0F0254P22/P115F3/0P0/0O51026523 400-42634521103   (2036)
2002/03: 16⁴S, 17²S, 16⁶GF, 17³G, 16⁴G, 16⁵GF, 16²G, 16¹F, 16¹G, 18ºGS, 17³HY,

	Starts	1st	2nd	3rd	Win & Pl
Chases	11	2	2	2	10226

Career Total	50	7	8	4	33127	
81	11/02	Wwck	2m110y	F(0-100)HCh	GD	£3038
80	10/02	Ludl	2m	G(0-95)HCh	FRM	£3406
99	6/01	NAbb	2m110y	F(0-100)HCh	GD	£2982
116	6/99	Gowr	2m5f	(0-109)HCh	GD	£4296
109	5/99	Wxfd	2m4f	(0-109)HCh	Y-S	£3376
99	4/98	Navn	2m	Hdl	SH	£2680
109	4/97	List	2m4f	NHF	G-Y	£3391

Total win prize-money £23170

Going: Sf: 0-3 GS: 0-1 Gd: 1-4 GF: - Fm: 1-3
Distance: 2m/2m3: 2-11 2m4-2m7: 0-0 3m+: 0-0
Track: LH: 1-8 RH: 1-2 Tight: 1-5 Gall: 0-1
Aids: Bl: 0-0 Vi: 0-0 Tstrap: 0-0
Best Rating: 116 6/99 Gowr 2m5f good Ch

Plating-class handicap chaser; best at around two miles; appears to act on all types of ground.

Howaboys Quest (USA)
98   78+

6-y-o b g Quest For Fame-Doctor Black (USA) (Family Doctor (USA))
Ferdy Murphy Winlow Brothers

Placings:0345044-640   (2102)
2002/03: 20^6G, 16^4G, 16^6G,

	Starts	1st	2nd	3rd	Win & Pl
Hurdles	2	0	0	0	0
Chases	1	0	0	0	0
Career Total	10	0	0	1	413

Going: Sf: 0-0 GS: 0-0 Gd: 0-3 GF: - Fm: 0-0
Distance: 2m/2m3: 0-2 2m4-2m7: 0-1 3m+: 0-0
Track: LH: 0-3 RH: 0-0 Tight: 0-1 Gall: 0-0
Aids: Bl: 0-0 Vi: 0-0 Tstrap: 0-0
Best Rating: 77 4/02 Hntg 2m110y gd-fm Hdl

Moderate hurdler; took a selling handicap hurdle in smooth style at Cartmel in July; stays two mile six.

Howdydoody (IRE)
108   110

7-y-o b g Hawkstone (IRE)-Larry s Law (IRE) (Law Society (USA))
P F Nicholls B L Blinman

Placings:0^f/33131   (4280)
2002/03: 22^3G, 24^3GS, 24^1S, 24^3G, 27^1GF,

	Starts	1st	2nd	3rd	Win & Pl
Hurdles	5	2	0	3	11664
Career Total	5	2	0	3	11664

110	3/03	Font	3m3f	D(0-120)HHdl	G-F £4920
103	1/03	Tntn	3m110y	E Hdl	SFT £4478

Total win prize-money £9400

Going: Sf: 1-1 GS: 0-1 Gd: 0-2 GF: - Fm: 1-1
Distance: 2m/2m3: 0-0 2m4-2m7: 0-1 3m+: 2-4
Track: LH: 0-0 RH: 1-4 Tight: 2-3 Gall: 0-0
Aids: Bl: 0-0 Vi: 0-0 Tstrap: 2-5
Best Rating: 110 3/03 Font 3m3f gd-fm Hdl

Fair hurdler; stays three miles three; acts on both fast and soft ground.

Howey In The Hills (IRE)
40

7-y-o b g Phardante (FR)-Tacova (Avocat)
D McCain D McCain

Placings:00-P   (0021)
2002/03: 20^P G,

	Starts	1st	2nd	3rd	Win & Pl
Hurdles	1	0	0	0	
Career Total	3	0	0	0	

Going: Sf: 0-0 GS: 0-0 Gd: 0-1 GF: - Fm: 0-0
Distance: 2m/2m3: 0-0 2m4-2m7: 0-1 3m+: 0-0
Track: LH: 0-1 RH: 0-0 Tight: 0-0 Gall: 0-0
Aids: Bl: 0-0 Vi: 0-0 Tstrap: 0-0
Best Rating: 66 1/02 Hayd 2m soft NHF

Howrwenow (IRE)
102   103

5-y-o b g Commanche Run-Maythefifth (Hard Boy)
Miss H C Knight Toby Cole

Placings:624   (4442)
2002/03: 16^6S, 19^2GS, 20^4G,

	Starts	1st	2nd	3rd	Win & Pl
Hurdles	3	0	1	0	1548
Career Total	3	0	1	0	1548

Going: Sf: 0-1 GS: 0-1 Gd: 0-1 GF: - Fm: 0-0
Distance: 2m/2m3: 0-2 2m4-2m7: 0-1 3m+: 0-0
Track: LH: 0-1 RH: 0-2 Tight: 0-1 Gall: 0-1
Aids: Bl: 0-0 Vi: 0-0 Tstrap: 0-0
Best Rating: 103 2/03 Extr 2m3f gd-sft Hdl

Won maiden Irish point on debut in 2002; promising effort when second to Vanormix over an inadequate 19 furlongs at Exeter February 2003; will appreciate a stiffer test of stamina; chaser in the making.

Hubbly Bubbly
85f   71f

5-y-o b g Gildoran-Spinayab (King Of Spain)
J W Mullins J H Mead

Placings:000-5   (4601)
2002/03: 17^5GF,

	Starts	1st	2nd	3rd	Win & Pl
NH Flat	1	0	0	0	0
Career Total	4	0	0	0	0

Going: Sf: 0-0 GS: 0-0 Gd: 0-0 GF: - Fm: 0-1
Distance: 2m/2m3: 0-1 2m4-2m7: 0-0 3m+: 0-0
Track: LH: 0-0 RH: 0-1 Tight: 0-0 Gall: 0-0
Aids: Bl: 0-0 Vi: 0-0 Tstrap: 0-0
Best Rating: 71 4/03 Extr 2m1f gd-fm NHF

Huge Heart (NZ)
(57h)   (73h)

7-y-o b g T V Heart Throb (USA)-Christmas Lady (NZ) (Palm Beach (FR))
R N Bevis Raymond McNeill

Placings:P0PU0   (4567)
2002/03: 19^P G, 17^0GS, 19^P S, 16^U S, 20^0GF,

	Starts	1st	2nd	3rd	Win & Pl
Hurdles	5	0	0	0	
Career Total	5	0	0	0	

Going: Sf: 0-2 GS: 0-1 Gd: 0-1 GF: - Fm: 0-1
Distance: 2m/2m3: 0-2 2m4-2m7: 0-3 3m+: 0-0
Track: LH: 0-2 RH: 0-3 Tight: 0-3 Gall: 0-1
Aids: Bl: 0-0 Vi: 0-0 Tstrap: 0-0
Best Rating: 73 1/03 Hntg 2m110y soft Hdl

Hugh Daniels

15-y-o b g Adonijah-Golden Realm (Red Regent)
C J Hemsley Brett Hemsley

Placings:6323360/6331000/05002403230/FU0222505P5/0
66PPP/364445444P/0U03P34556/P34606/0066/0-P0
  (0556)
2002/03: 16^P G, 16^0GF,

	Starts	1st	2nd	3rd	Win & Pl
Chases	2	0	0	0	
Career Total	75	1	6	11	12001

104	8/93	Wxfd	2m2f	Hdl	GD £2969

Total win prize-money £2970

Going: Sf: 0-0 GS: 0-0 Gd: 0-1 GF: - Fm: 0-1
Distance: 2m/2m3: 0-2 2m4-2m7: 0-0 3m+: 0-1
Track: LH: 0-1 RH: 0-1 Tight: 0-0 Gall: 0-1
Aids: Bl: 0-0 Vi: 0-0 Tstrap: 0-0
Best Rating: 104 8/93 Wxfd 2m2f good Hdl

Hugo De Grez (FR)
109(107h)   (96+h)141

8-y-o b g Useful (FR)-Piqua Des Gres (FR) (Waylay)
A Parker Mr & Mrs Raymond Anderson Green

Placings:01P0/223111/1240/21P5-U11205   (4164)
2002/03: 26^U S, 26^1HY, 25^1HY, 20^2S, 28^0G, 24^5GS,

	Starts	1st	2nd	3rd	Win & Pl
Hurdles	1	0	0	0	0
Chases	5	2	1	0	25221
Career Total	24	8	5	1	72472

138	12/02	Kels	3m1f	B(0-145)HCh	HVY £13325
134	11/02	Carl	3m2f	C(0-130)HCh	HVY £7800
127	11/01	Carl	3m2f	C(0-130)HCh	HVY £6890
127	11/00	Carl	3m2f	C(0-130)HCh	SFT £7020
112	4/00	Carl	3m2f	E Ch	SFT £3542
117	3/00	Carl	3m2f	D(0-115)HCh	G-S £14495
102	2/00	Carl	2m4f110yF(0-105)HCh		HVY £3558
72	2/99	Ayr	3m110y	E Hdl	SFT £2670

Total win prize-money £59302

Going: Sf: 2-4 GS: 0-1 Gd: 0-1 GF: - Fm: 0-0
Distance: 2m/2m3: 0-0 2m4-2m7: 0-1 3m+: 2-5
Track: LH: 1-4 RH: 1-2 Tight: 1-1 Gall: 0-1
Aids: Bl: 0-0 Vi: 0-0 Tstrap: 0-1
Best Rating: 141 2/03 Ayr 2m4f soft Ch

Very useful handicap chaser; stays 3m 2f; effective on heavy ground; goes well at Carlisle; has worn a tongue tie.

Hugo De Perro (FR)
113(106c)   (115c)131

8-y-o b g Perrault-Fontaine Aux Faons (FR) (Nadjar (FR))
P Monteith J W D Campbell

Placings:52501414/5304/1F36432-313R155P12   (4164)
2002/03: 18^3GS, 22^1GS, 21^3S, 20^P S, 21^2HY, 20^5GS, 20^5HY, 20^P S, 20^1S, 24^2GS,

	Starts	1st	2nd	3rd	Win & Pl
Hurdles	9	3	1	2	16741
Chases	1	0	0	0	0
Career Total	29	6	3	5	34083

110	3/03	Carl	2m4f	F Hdl	SFT £3066
129	12/02	Kels	2m6f110yD(0-125)HHdl		HVY £4069
131	6/02	Ctml	2m6f	D(0-120)HHdl	G-S £3796
113	5/01	MRas	2m6f	D Ch	SFT £5096
136	2/00	Wwck	2m4f110yE(0-115)HHdl		SFT £2632
124	1/00	Leic	2m	E Hdl	SFT £3042

Total win prize-money £21701

Going: Sf: 2-6 GS: 1-4 Gd: 0-0 GF: - Fm: 0-0
Distance: 2m/2m3: 0-1 **2m4-2m7:** 3-8 3m+: 0-1
Track: **LH: 2-9** RH: 1-1 **Tight: 2-4** Gall: 0-1
Aids: Bl: 0-0 Vi: 0-0 Tstrap: 0-0
Best Rating: **136** 2/00 Wwck 2m4f110y soft Hdl

Useful handicap hurdler; scored at Cartmel and Kelso in 2002 and won weak contest at Carlisle in March 2003; acts on soft and heavy ground; stays 2m 4f; refused to race on one occasion.

Huic Holloa (IRE)
97   **54**
7-y-o b g Denel (FR)-Buckalgo (IRE) (Buckskin (FR))
J A T De Giles   V W H Hunt Partnership

Placings: 0/036-05   (4347)
2002/03: 19⁰GS, 25⁵GF,

	Starts	1st	2nd	3rd	Win & Pl
Hurdles	2	0	0	0	0
Career Total	6	0	0	1	341

Going: Sf: 0-0 GS: 0-1 Gd: 0-0 GF: - Fm: 0-1
Distance: 2m/2m3: 0-1 2m4-2m7: 0-0 3m+: 0-1
Track: LH: 0-1 RH: 0-1 Tight: 0-0 Gall: 0-0
Aids: Bl: 0-0 Vi: 0-0 Tstrap: 0-0
Best Rating: 86 12/01 Wwck 2m soft NHF

Huish (IRE)

12-y-o br g Orchestra-Lysanders Lady (Saulingo)
Mrs N Macauley   W Murdoch

Placings: U/0/006P/06604/3-P   (4119)
2002/03: 16⁰G,

	Starts	1st	2nd	3rd	Win & Pl
Hurdles	1	0	0	0	
Career Total	13	0	0	1	319

Going: Sf: 0-0 GS: 0-0 Gd: 0-0 GF: 0-1 Fm: 0-0
Distance: 2m/2m3: 0-1 2m4-2m7: 0-0 3m+: 0-0
Track: LH: 0-0 RH: 0-1 Tight: 0-0 Gall: 0-0
Aids: Bl: 0-0 Vi: 0-0 Tstrap: 0-0
Best Rating: 81 3/97 Sand 2m110y good Hdl

Huka Lodge (IRE)
92   **73**
6-y-o ch g Roselier (FR)-Derrella (Derrylin)
L Lungo   R A Bartlett

Placings: 0530   (3914)
2002/03: 20⁰S, 20⁵S, 16³HY, 20⁰GS,

	Starts	1st	2nd	3rd	Win & Pl
Hurdles	4	0	0	1	531
Career Total	4	0	0	1	531

Going: Sf: 0-3 GS: 0-1 Gd: 0-0 GF: - Fm: 0-0
Distance: 2m/2m3: 0-1 2m4-2m7: 0-0 3m+: 0-0
Track: LH: 0-3 RH: 0-1 Tight: 0-0 Gall: 0-1
Aids: Bl: 0-0 Vi: 0-0 Tstrap: 0-0
Best Rating: 73 1/03 Ayr 2m heavy Hdl

Humming
92   **85+**
6-y-o b g Bluebird (USA)-Risanda (Kris)

Miss M E Rowland Miss M E Rowland

Placings: 0/50-P2   (4220)
2002/03: 19⁹GS, 19²GF,

	Starts	1st	2nd	3rd	Win & Pl
Hurdles	2	0	1	0	674
Career Total	5	0	1	0	674

Going: Sf: 0-0 GS: 0-1 Gd: 0-0 GF: - Fm: 0-1
Distance: 2m/2m3: 0-0 2m4-2m7: 0-2 3m+: 0-0
Track: LH: 0-1 RH: 0-1 Tight: 0-0 Gall: 0-0
Aids: Bl: 0-0 Vi: 0-0 Tstrap: 0-0
Best Rating: 85 3/03 Hrfd 2m3f110y gd-fm Hdl

Hunt In Pairs
86   **67**
4-y-o b g Pursuit Of Love-Emily-Mou (IRE) (Cadeaux Genereux)
R H York (Mrs J R Ramsden 3/6)   C Cheesman

Placings: P500   (2720)
2002/03: 16⁵S, 16⁵S, 16⁰S, 16⁰S,

	Starts	1st	2nd	3rd	Win & Pl
Hurdles	4	0	0	0	0
Career Total	4	0	0	0	0

Going: Sf: 0-4 GS: 0-0 Gd: 0-0 GF: - Fm: 0-0
Distance: 2m/2m3: 0-4 2m4-2m7: 0-0 3m+: 0-0
Track: LH: 0-1 RH: 0-3 Tight: 0-0 Gall: 0-0
Aids: Bl: 0-0 Vi: 0-0 Tstrap: 0-0
Best Rating: 65 12/02 Kemp 2m soft Hdl

Hunter Gold (FR)
101(96h)   (81h)**64**
8-y-o br g Chamberlin (FR)-Une de Mai IV (FR) (Ice Light (FR))
T R George   Sir Stanley Clarke

Placings: P5213/24P/3-P35   (4118)
2002/03: 21⁰GS, 16³S, 24⁵G,

	Starts	1st	2nd	3rd	Win & Pl
Chases	3	0	0	1	517
Career Total	12	1	2	3	8765
12/99 Ange 2m3f		Ch		HVY	£3842

Total win prize-money £3842

Going: Sf: 0-1 GS: 0-1 Gd: 0-1 GF: - Fm: 0-0
Distance: 2m/2m3: 0-1 2m4-2m7: 0-1 3m+: 0-1
Track: LH: 0-0 RH: 0-3 Tight: 0-0 Gall: 0-1
Aids: Bl: 0-0 Vi: 0-0 Tstrap: 0-1
Best Rating: 94 11/00 Hayd 2m4f soft Hdl

A winning chaser in France, he has shown promise over hurdles in this country.

Hunters Creek (IRE)
101(102h)   (101h)**110**
9-y-o b g Persian Mews-Creek s Sister (King s Ride)
Mrs M Reveley   Bewley s Hotels, Glasgow (bsh Ltd)

Placings: 20/33F1213F-532621   (4794)
2002/03: 19⁵G, 20³GS, 20⁰S, 20⁶HY, 20²GF, 21¹GF,

	Starts	1st	2nd	3rd	Win & Pl
Hurdles	4	0	2	1	2395
Chases	2	1	0	0	4391
Career Total	16	3	4	4	19216
110 4/03 Sedg 2m5f		E(0-110)HCh	G-F	£4390
120 1/02 Catt 2m3f		D Ch	SFT	£4179
116 12/01 Catt 2m3f		F Ch	GD	£2886

Total win prize-money £11457

Going: Sf: 0-2 GS: 0-1 Gd: 0-1 GF: - Fm: 1-2
Distance: 2m/2m3: 0-1 **2m4-2m7:** 1-5 3m+: 0-0
Track: **LH: 1-6** RH: 0-0 **Tight: 1-2** Gall: 0-0
Aids: Bl: 0-0 Vi: 0-0 Tstrap: 0-0
Best Rating: 120 1/02 Catt 2m3f soft Ch

Fair chaser/modest hurdler; effective at up to two miles five; goes well on a sharp track (likes Catterick); acts on any ground.

Hunters Tweed
114(109h)   (134h)**134**
7-y-o ch g Nashwan (USA)-Zorette (USA) (Zilzal (USA))
P Beaumont   Trevor Hemmings

Placings: 113022/03634000-1233321U1   (4751)
2002/03: 24¹GF, 25²G, 22³S, 24³GS, 20³S, 24²G, 22¹G, 20ᵁG, 20¹G,

	Starts	1st	2nd	3rd	Win & Pl
Chases	9	3	2	3	29692
Career Total	23	5	4	6	57810
133 4/03 Prth	2m4f110yD(0-125)HCh	GD	£12504
134 3/03 Hayd	2m6f	D(0-120)HCh	GD	£5395
117 5/02 Prth	3m	D Ch	G-F	£5499
134 2/01 Kels	2m110y	D Hdl	SFT	£4013
126 12/00 Weth	2m	D Hdl	SFT	£3679

Total win prize-money £31092

Going: Sf: 0-2 GS: 0-1 Gd: 2-5 GF: - Fm: 1-1
Distance: 2m/2m3: 0-0 **2m4-2m7:** 2-5 3m+: 1-4
Track: LH: 1-6 **RH: 2-3** Tight: 0-3 Gall: 0-0
Aids: Bl: 0-0 Vi: 0-0 Tstrap: 0-0
Best Rating: 134 3/03 Hayd 2m6f good Ch

Fair novice chaser; stays three miles; seems best on decent ground.

Hunters Wood (IRE)

8-y-o gr g Wood Chanter-Barnmeen Lass (IRE) (Floriferous)
R J Baker   David Heath

Placings: P/5-4   (4696)
2002/03: 26⁴G,

	Starts	1st	2nd	3rd	Win & Pl
Chases	1	0	0	0	317
Career Total	3	0	0	0	317

Going: Sf: 0-0 GS: 0-0 Gd: 0-1 GF: - Fm: 0-0
Distance: 2m/2m3: 0-0 2m4-2m7: 0-0 3m+: 0-1
Track: LH: 0-1 RH: 0-0 Tight: 0-1 Gall: 0-0
Aids: Bl: 0-0 Vi: 0-0 Tstrap: 0-0
Best Rating: 0 4/03 NAbb 3m2f110y good Ch

Huntersway (IRE)
71   **47**
6-y-o ch g Treasure Hunter-Dunmanway (Le Bavard (FR))
Mrs A Price   Mrs A Price

Placings: P5   (1376)
2002/03: 24⁰G, 19⁵GF,

	Starts	1st	2nd	3rd	Win & Pl
Hurdles	2	0	0	0	0
Career Total	2	0	0	0	0

Going: Sf: 0-0 GS: 0-0 Gd: 0-1 GF: - Fm: 0-1
Distance: 2m/2m3: 0-2 2m4-2m7: 0-1 3m+: 0-1
Track: LH: 0-1 RH: 0-1 Tight: 0-0 Gall: 0-1
Aids: Bl: 0-0 Vi: 0-0 Tstrap: 0-0
Best Rating: 50 10/02 Hrfd 2m3f110y gd-fm Hdl

Hurdante (IRE)

13-y-o ch g Phardante (FR)-Hurry (Deep Run)
Mrs L A Parker   D W Parker

Placings:24/1201603/2/5/P415UPP/P6-P0   (0209)
2002/03: 21PGF, 16OG,

	Starts	1st	2nd	3rd	Win & Pl
Chases	2	0	0	0	
Career Total	22	3	3	1	19657
121	12/00 Newb	2m3f		D(0-125)HHdl	SFT £5398
112	1/97 Leic	2m4f110yE Hdl			G-S £2329
112	5/96 Dund	2m135y NHF			YLD £2295

Total win prize-money £10022

Going:	Sf: 0-0 GS: 0-0 Gd: 0-1 GF: - Fm: 0-1
Distance:	2m/2m3: 0-1 2m4-2m7: 0-1 3m+: 0-0
Track:	LH: 0-1 RH: 0-1 Tight: 0-0 Gall: 0-1
Aids:	Bl: 0-0 Vi: 0-0 Tstrap: 0-0
Best Rating:	127 4/97 Aint 2m4f good Hdl

Hurlyburly (IRE)
90f   88f

6-y-o ch g Hubbly Bubbly (USA)-Swans Leap (Swan s Rock)
M Pitman   B R H Burrough

Placings:40-0   (3930)
2002/03: 16OG,

	Starts	1st	2nd	3rd	Win & Pl
NH Flat	1	0	0	0	
Career Total	3	0	0	0	0

Going:	Sf: 0-0 GS: 0-0 Gd: 0-0 GF: - Fm: 0-0
Distance:	2m/2m3: 0-1 2m4-2m7: 0-0 3m+: 0-0
Track:	LH: 0-0 RH: 0-1 Tight: 0-0 Gall: 0-1
Aids:	Bl: 0-0 Vi: 0-0 Tstrap: 0-0
Best Rating:	88 5/01 NAbb 2m1f gd-fm NHF

Hurricane Bay
109(96h)   (77h)82

7-y-o ch g Karinga Bay-Clodaigh Gale (Strong Gale)
Jonjo O Neill   Ian G M Dalgleish

Placings:5006-2530   (0774)
2002/03: 20OG, 26²G, 24⁵G, 22³GF, 23⁹GF,

	Starts	1st	2nd	3rd	Win & Pl
Hurdles	4	0	1	1	1162
Chases	1	0	0	0	0
Career Total	8	0	1	1	1162

Going:	Sf: 0-0 GS: 0-0 Gd: 0-3 GF: - Fm: 0-2
Distance:	2m/2m3: 0-0 2m4-2m7: 0-2 3m+: 0-3
Track:	LH: 0-4 RH: 0-1 Tight: 0-1 Gall: 0-2
Aids:	Bl: 0-2 Vi: 0-0 Tstrap: 0-2
Best Rating:	79 6/02 Strf 2m6f110y gd-fm Hdl

Moderate chaser; finally opened his account in a three mile handicap chase at Wetherby in May; stays well and handles quick ground.

Hurricane Coast

4-y-o b g Hurricane Sky (AUS)-Tread Carefully (Sharpo)
T D Easterby   Mrs Ian Wills

Placings:PP   (1806)
2002/03: 16PGF, 16PG,

	Starts	1st	2nd	3rd	Win & Pl
Hurdles	2	0	0	0	

Career Total   2   0   0   0

Going:	Sf: 0-0 GS: 0-0 Gd: 0-1 GF: - Fm: 0-1
Distance:	2m/2m3: 0-2 2m4-2m7: 0-0 3m+: 0-0
Track:	LH: 0-2 RH: 0-0 Tight: 0-1 Gall: 0-0
Aids:	Bl: 0-0 Vi: 0-0 Tstrap: 0-0
Best Rating:	0 11/02 Hayd 2m good Hdl

Hurricane Dipper (IRE)

5-y-o b g Glacial Storm (USA)-Minnies Dipper (Royal Captive)
Miss A M Newton-Smith   John Grist

Placings:00   (4442)
2002/03: 16OG, 20OG,

	Starts	1st	2nd	3rd	Win & Pl
NH Flat	1	0	0	0	0
Hurdles	1	0	0	0	0
Career Total	2	0	0	0	

Going:	Sf: 0-0 GS: 0-0 Gd: 0-2 GF: - Fm: 0-0
Distance:	2m/2m3: 0-1 2m4-2m7: 0-1 3m+: 0-0
Track:	LH: 0-1 RH: 0-1 Tight: 0-0 Gall: 0-1
Aids:	Bl: 0-0 Vi: 0-0 Tstrap: 0-0
Best Rating:	35 2/03 Newb 2m110y good NHF

Hurricane Georges

7-y-o b g Milieu-Miss Colonnette (Flatbush)
J N R Billinge   Fife Foxhounds Racing

Placings:040-P   (2923)
2002/03: 22PHY,

	Starts	1st	2nd	3rd	Win & Pl
Hurdles	1	0	0	0	
Career Total	4	0	0	0	0

Going:	Sf: 0-1 GS: 0-0 Gd: 0-0 GF: - Fm: 0-0
Distance:	2m/2m3: 0-0 2m4-2m7: 0-1 3m+: 0-0
Track:	LH: 0-1 RH: 0-0 Tight: 0-0 Gall: 0-0
Aids:	Bl: 0-0 Vi: 0-0 Tstrap: 0-0
Best Rating:	91 11/01 Sedg 2m1f good NHF

Hurricane Lamp
109   131

12-y-o b g Derrylin-Lampstone (Ragstone)
A King   Mr & Mrs F C Welch & Partners

Placings:16/112F/6U1230/126143F/12523/144F0/4133411 PP0-22212P042   (4603)
2002/03: 24²GF, 21²GF, 20²G, 20¹G, 19²GS, 20PG, 20OGS, 20⁴G, 26²G,

	Starts	1st	2nd	3rd	Win & Pl
Chases	9	1	5	0	29907
Career Total	48	12	10	5	120661
144	11/02 Kemp	2m4f110yB(0-140)HCh		GD £11128
144	12/01 Sand	2m4f110yC(0-135)HCh		G-S £6955
142	11/01 Hntg	2m4f110yC(0-130)HCh		GD £6776
144	5/01 Wwck	2m4f110yC(0-135)HCh		GD £8684
144	5/00 Wwck	2m	B Ch		G-F £8743
140	10/99 Weth	2m	C(0-135)HCh		GD £5735
134	1/99 Sand	2m	B HCh		G-S £8130
122	5/98 Uttx	2m	D Ch		G-S £3533
127	1/98 Ludl	2m	E Ch		SFT £3004

121	12/96 Sand	2m110y	D Hdl		GD £2970
110	11/96 Wwck	2m	E Hdl		GD £2721
114	2/96 Sand	2m110y	H NHF		SFT £2304

Total win prize-money £70685

Going:	Sf: 0-0 GS: 0-2 Gd: 1-5 GF: - Fm: 0-2
Distance:	2m/2m3: 0-1 2m4-2m7: 1-6 3m+: 0-2
Track:	LH: 0-6 RH: 1-3 Tight: 0-3 Gall: 0-2
Aids:	Bl: 0-0 Vi: 0-0 Tstrap: 0-0
Best Rating:	144 12/02 Donc 2m3f gd-sft Ch

Useful handicap chaser; acted on most types of ground; effective from two to three miles; at the veteran stage and reportedly retired after sustaining an injury at Cheltenham in April 2003.

Hussard Collonges (FR)
119   (122h)168

8-y-o b g Video Rock (FR)-Ariane Collonges (FR) (Quart De Vin (FR))
P Beaumont   N W A Bannister

Placings:00012/21F21-252P   (4132)
2002/03: 25²GS, 26⁵GS, 24²GS, 26PG,

	Starts	1st	2nd	3rd	Win & Pl
Chases	4	0	2	0	26825
Career Total	14	3	5	0	113570
156	3/02 Chel	3m110y A Ch		G-S £72500
141	12/01 Weth	2m4f110yD(0-110)HCh		G-S £4446
122	4/01 Weth	2m4f110yD Hdl		G-S £3395

Total win prize-money £80341

Going:	Sf: 0-0 GS: 0-3 Gd: 0-1 GF: - Fm: 0-0
Distance:	2m/2m3: 0-0 2m4-2m7: 0-0 3m+: 0-4
Track:	LH: 0-4 RH: 0-0 Tight: 0-0 Gall: 0-2
Aids:	Bl: 0-0 Vi: 0-0 Tstrap: 0-0
Best Rating:	168 1/03 Hayd 3m gd-sft Ch

High-class chaser; a leading novice in 2001/2, running much his best race when a game winner of the Royal & SunAlliance Chase at Cheltenham; running really well in defeat in top company this season, but found to have sore throat after pulling up in Cheltenham Gold Cup; jumps well; suited by forcing tactics; acts on yielding and soft ground; stays 3m 2f; tough.

Hussy
94   66

9-y-o b m Broadsword (USA)-Smart Chick (True Song)
Mrs Sarah Horner-Harker   Mrs Sarah Horner-Harker

Placings:0P/30P4/PP6P03/P540P-460   (0331)
2002/03: 21⁴GF, 20⁶G, 20OG,

	Starts	1st	2nd	3rd	Win & Pl
Hurdles	3	0	0	0	0
Career Total	20	0	0	2	835

Going:	Sf: 0-0 GS: 0-0 Gd: 0-2 GF: - Fm: 0-1
Distance:	2m/2m3: 0-0 2m4-2m7: 0-3 3m+: 0-0
Track:	LH: 0-3 RH: 0-0 Tight: 0-1 Gall: 0-0
Aids:	Bl: 0-0 Vi: 0-0 Tstrap: 0-0
Best Rating:	91 11/99 Wwck 2m good Hdl

Hydemilla

13-y-o b m Idiots Delight-Bellaloo (Privy Seal)
Mrs C J A Suthern (Mrs T D Pilkington 12/5) Mrs C J A Suthern

Placings:0/0603/405340/003P30/**U**004000/0353605/56/0
(0392)
2002/03: 24⁰G,

	Starts	1st	2nd	3rd	Win & Pl
Chases	1	0	0		
Career Total	34	0	0	6	2286

Going:	Sf: 0-0 GS: 0-0 Gd: 0-1 GF: - Fm: 0-0
Distance:	2m/2m3: 0-0 2m4-2m7: 0-0 3m+: 0-0
Track:	LH: 0-1 RH: 0-0 Tight: 0-0 Gall: 0-0
Aids:	Bl: 0-0 Vi: 0-0 Tstrap: 0-0
Best Rating:	83 3/96 Wwck 2m4f110y good Hdl

Hyperactive (IRE)
95   85
7-y-o b g Perugino (USA)-Hyannis (FR) (Esprit Du Nord (USA))
B Ellison Mrs Claire Ellison

Placings:560-1
(1072)
2002/03: 17¹G,

	Starts	1st	2nd	3rd	Win & Pl
Hurdles	1	1	0	0	3220
Career Total	4	1	0	0	3220
79 8/02 Ctml 2m1f110yG(0-90)HHdl GD £3220

Total win prize-money £3220

Going:	Sf: 0-0 GS: 0-0 Gd: 1-1 GF: - Fm: 0-0
Distance:	2m/2m3: 1-1 2m4-2m7: 0-0 3m+: 0-0
Track:	LH: 1-1 RH: 0-0 Tight: 1-1 Gall: 0-0
Aids:	Bl: 0-0 Vi: 0-0 Tstrap: 0-0
Best Rating:	85 8/01 Sedg 2m1f gd-fm Hdl

Showed his first worthwhile form when landing a selling hurdle at Cartmel in August 2002.

Hyperion Du Moulin II (FR)
97   90
8-y-o b g Kedellic (FR)-Mipour (FR) (Shakapour)
Lady Herries Lady Sarah Clutton

Placings:0/0/0-P1P
(0642)
2002/03: 20ᴾGF, 18¹GF, 22ᴾGF,

	Starts	1st	2nd	3rd	Win & Pl
Hurdles	3	1	0	0	2552
Career Total	6	1	0	0	2552
90 6/02 Font 2m2f110yE(0-105)HHdl G-F £2551

Total win prize-money £2552

Going:	Sf: 0-0 GS: 0-0 Gd: 0-0 GF: - Fm: 1-3
Distance:	2m/2m3: 1-1 2m4-2m7: 0-2 3m+: 0-0
Track:	LH: 1-2 RH: 0-0 Tight: 1-3 Gall: 0-0
Aids:	Bl: 0-0 Vi: 0-0 Tstrap: 0-0
Best Rating:	108 3/00 Sand 2m110y good NHF

Hypersonic
65
6-y-o b g Marju (IRE)-Hi-Li (High Top)
B R Millman H J W Davies

Placings:0FP/PF3P00-P
(1232)
2002/03: 16ᴾG,

	Starts	1st	2nd	3rd	Win & Pl
Hurdles	1	0	0	0	
Career Total	10	0	0	1	277

Going:	Sf: 0-0 GS: 0-0 Gd: 0-1 GF: - Fm: 0-0

Distance:	2m/2m3: 0-1 2m4-2m7: 0-0 3m+: 0-0
Track:	LH: 0-1 RH: 0-0 Tight: 0-0 Gall: 0-0
Aids:	Bl: 0-0 Vi: 0-0 Tstrap: 0-0
Best Rating:	65 1/02 Leic 2m soft Hdl

I Can't Remember
65   54
9-y-o gr g Petong-Glenfield Portion (Mummy s Pet)
Miss Lucinda V Russell The Gypsy King Partnership

Placings:0P5-P55
(1303)
2002/03: 16ᴾGF, 16⁵GS, 20⁵GF,

	Starts	1st	2nd	3rd	Win & Pl
Hurdles	3	0	0	0	0
Career Total	6	0	0	0	0

Going:	Sf: 0-0 GS: 0-1 Gd: 0-0 GF: - Fm: 0-2
Distance:	2m/2m3: 0-2 2m4-2m7: 0-1 3m+: 0-0
Track:	LH: 0-0 RH: 0-3 Tight: 0-0 Gall: 0-0
Aids:	Bl: 0-0 Vi: 0-0 Tstrap: 0-0
Best Rating:	54 4/02 Prth 2m110y good Hdl

I Cried For You (IRE)
97   96
8-y-o b g Statoblest-Fall Of The Hammer (IRE) (Auction Ring (USA))
J G Given One Stop Partnership

Placings:066
(3830)
2002/03: 16⁰G, 16⁶GS, 16⁶G,

	Starts	1st	2nd	3rd	Win & Pl
Hurdles	3	0	0	0	0
Career Total	3	0	0	0	0

Going:	Sf: 0-0 GS: 0-1 Gd: 0-2 GF: - Fm: 0-0
Distance:	2m/2m3: 0-3 2m4-2m7: 0-0 3m+: 0-0
Track:	LH: 0-3 RH: 0-0 Tight: 0-0 Gall: 0-1
Aids:	Bl: 0-0 Vi: 0-0 Tstrap: 0-0
Best Rating:	96 2/03 Weth 2m good Hdl

Prolific winner on the level but stamina looks strictly limited so far over hurdles.

I Got Rhythm
105   103
5-y-o gr m Lycius (USA)-Eurythmic (Pharly (FR))
Mrs M Reveley G Thomson

Placings:516-4F023
(3868)
2002/03: 16⁴GF, 20ᶠGS, 16⁰G, 16²G, 16³GS,

	Starts	1st	2nd	3rd	Win & Pl
Hurdles	5	1	1	1	3558
Career Total	8	1	1	1	7254
102 11/01 Weth 2m D Hdl GD £3696

Total win prize-money £3696

Going:	Sf: 0-0 GS: 0-2 Gd: 0-2 GF: - Fm: 0-1
Distance:	2m/2m3: 0-4 2m4-2m7: 0-1 3m+: 0-0
Track:	LH: 0-5 RH: 0-0 Tight: 0-2 Gall: 0-1
Aids:	Bl: 0-0 Vi: 0-0 Tstrap: 0-0
Best Rating:	104 2/03 Donc 2m110y gd-sft Hdl

Plating-class stayer on the Flat, she has already proved much better over hurdles; suited by good ground or faster.

I Hear Thunder (IRE)
74f   58f
5-y-o b g Montelimar (USA)-Carrigeen Gala (Strong Gale)
R H Buckler Nick Elliott

Placings:00
(3174)
2002/03: 16⁰HY, 16⁰GS,

	Starts	1st	2nd	3rd	Win & Pl
NH Flat	2	0	0	0	
Career Total	2	0	0	0	

Going:	Sf: 0-1 GS: 0-1 Gd: 0-0 GF: - Fm: 0-0
Distance:	2m/2m3: 0-2 2m4-2m7: 0-0 3m+: 0-0
Track:	LH: 0-2 RH: 0-0 Tight: 0-0 Gall: 0-1
Aids:	Bl: 0-0 Vi: 0-0 Tstrap: 0-0
Best Rating:	58 1/03 Hayd 2m gd-sft NHF

I Tina
95   73
7-y-o b m Lycius (USA)-Tintomara (IRE) (Niniski (USA))
A G Juckes (J G Portman 16/9) R Axford

Placings:004
(4626)
2002/03: 17⁰S, 19⁰S, 17⁴GF,

	Starts	1st	2nd	3rd	Win & Pl
Hurdles	3	0	0	0	277
Career Total	3	0	0	0	277

Going:	Sf: 0-2 GS: 0-0 Gd: 0-0 GF: - Fm: 0-1
Distance:	2m/2m3: 0-2 2m4-2m7: 0-1 3m+: 0-0
Track:	LH: 0-1 RH: 0-2 Tight: 0-2 Gall: 0-0
Aids:	Bl: 0-0 Vi: 0-0 Tstrap: 0-0
Best Rating:	52 4/03 NAbb 2m1f gd-fm Hdl

Poor maiden hurdler; modest form over hurdles so far.

I'Lleveit Tou (IRE)
89f
7-y-o b g King Luthier-Shady Jumbo (Callernish)
R Rowe Thomas Thompson

Placings:2-
(0013)
2002/03: 18²G,

	Starts	1st	2nd	3rd	Win & Pl
NH Flat	1	0	1	0	488
Career Total	1	0	1	0	488

Going:	Sf: 0-0 GS: 0-0 Gd: 0-1 GF: - Fm: 0-0
Distance:	2m/2m3: 0-1 2m4-2m7: 0-0 3m+: 0-0
Track:	LH: 0-1 RH: 0-0 Tight: 0-0 Gall: 0-0
Aids:	Bl: 0-0 Vi: 0-0 Tstrap: 0-0
Best Rating:	89 4/02 Plum 2m2f good NHF

I'm Dreaming (IRE)
9-y-o ch g White Christmas-Suffolk Bells (London Bells (CAN))
Andrew J Martin Andrew J Martin

Placings:0240/P00PP/0P-3P546
(4615)
2002/03: 20³S, 24ᴾS, 20⁵GF, 24⁴G, 26⁶G,

	Starts	1st	2nd	3rd	Win & Pl
Chases	5	0	0	1	339
Career Total	16	0	1	1	1363

Going:	Sf: 0-2 GS: 0-0 Gd: 0-2 GF: - Fm: 0-1
Distance:	2m/2m3: 0-0 2m4-2m7: 0-2 3m+: 0-3
Track:	LH: 0-3 RH: 0-2 Tight: 0-2 Gall: 0-2
Aids:	Bl: 0-0 Vi: 0-0 Tstrap: 0-0
Best Rating:	77 3/03 Ludl 2m4f gd-fm Ch

Modest hunter chaser; third at Sandown in February.

I'm For Waiting
88   80

7-y-o ch g Democratic (USA)-Faustelerie (Faustus (USA))
John Allen Hobson s Choice Partnership

Placings:0550006P6/060145/430-2   (4149)
2002/03: 21³G,

	Starts	1st	2nd	3rd	Win & Pl
Hurdles	1	0	1	0	772
Career Total	19	1	1	1	2590

76 11/00 MRas 2m3f110yG(0-90)HHdl   G-S   £1498
                    Total win prize-money £1498

Going:	Sf: 0-0 GS: 0-0 Gd: 0-1 GF: - Fm: 0-0
Distance:	2m/2m3: 0-0 2m4-2m7: 0-1 3m+: 0-0
Track:	LH: 0-1 RH: 0-0 Tight: 0-0 Gall: 0-0
Aids:	Bl: 0-0 Vi: 0-0 Tstrap: 0-0
Best Rating:	80 3/03 Wwck 2m5f good Hdl

Won extended 19 furlong seller at Market Rasen November 2000; returned after a 16 month absence to finish second at 40/1 in Warwick claimer March 2003; still capable of winning that sort of grade.

I'm The Man

12-y-o ro g Say Primula-Vinovia (Ribston)
Mrs S H Shirley-Beavan Marco Syndicate

Placings:60/05403/434143/1220U21F5053130/PP01311/4
313F/45P0P3P63F01-23   (4459)
2002/03: 28²G, 21³G,

	Starts	1st	2nd	3rd	Win & Pl
Chases	2	0	1	1	4176
Career Total	54	9	4	11	47787

96	2/02	Muss	3m	F(0-95)HCh	SFT	£3220
111	5/00	Ctml	3m6f	C(0-130)HCh	G-S	£7117
110	4/00	Carl	3m2f	F(0-95)HCh	SFT	£3851
103	4/00	Carl	2m4f110yF(0-110)HCh		SFT	£3328
111	3/00	Muss	3m	E(0-115)HCh	G-F	£3657
97	2/99	Muss	3m	E(0-115)HHdl	GD	£2827
104	10/98	Sedg	3m3f	E(0-110)HCh	G-S	£4320
87	5/98	Hexm	3m1f	E(0-115)HCh	G-F	£2490
90	3/98	Hexm	2m4f110yF(0-110)HCh		SFT	£3288
			Total win prize-money £34101			

Going:	Sf: 0-0 GS: 0-0 Gd: 0-2 GF: - Fm: 0-0
Distance:	2m/2m3: 0-0 2m4-2m7: 0-1 3m+: 0-1
Track:	LH: 0-2 RH: 0-0 Tight: 0-0 Gall: 0-0
Aids:	Bl: 0-0 Vi: 0-0 Tstrap: 0-0
Best Rating:	111 6/00 Prth 3m good Ch

Hunter chaser; stays 3m 4f; effective in soft ground; races prominently; excellent third in the Foxhunters at Aintree in April.

I'm Willie's Girl

7-y-o br m Royal Fountain-Milton Lass (Scallywag)
F P Murtagh William Armour

Placings:P   (0021)
2002/03: 20³G,

	Starts	1st	2nd	3rd	Win & Pl
Hurdles	1	0	0	0	

Career Total   1   0   0   0

Going:	Sf: 0-0 GS: 0-0 Gd: 0-1 GF: - Fm: 0-0
Distance:	2m/2m3: 0-0 2m4-2m7: 0-0 3m+: 0-0
Track:	LH: 0-1 RH: 0-0 Tight: 0-0 Gall: 0-0
Aids:	Bl: 0-0 Vi: 0-0 Tstrap: 0-0
Best Rating:	

Iacacia (FR)
91(97h)   (91h)102+

7-y-o b/br g Silver Rainbow-Palencia (FR) (Taj Dewan)
Miss Venetia Williams James Williams

Placings:B4/U54/2-0   (4173)
2002/03: 20⁰S,

	Starts	1st	2nd	3rd	Win & Pl
Hurdles	1	0	0	0	
Career Total	7	0	1	0	8481

Going:	Sf: 0-1 GS: 0-0 Gd: 0-0 GF: - Fm: 0-0
Distance:	2m/2m3: 0-0 2m4-2m7: 0-1 3m+: 0-0
Track:	LH: 0-1 RH: 0-0 Tight: 0-0 Gall: 0-0
Aids:	Bl: 0-0 Vi: 0-0 Tstrap: 0-0
Best Rating:	101 5/01 Extr 2m6f110y gd-sft Hdl

Ex-French hurdler/chaser; just touched off on British debut at Exeter in May 2001; not seen again until March 2003; did not impress with his attitude when well beaten runner-up back over fences at Uttoxeter in July; effective in soft ground; stays two miles six.

Iadora
94(90h)   (89h)74

8-y-o br m Gildoran-Combe Hill (Crozier)
J A B Old Mrs J A Fowler/the Kentish Men

Placings:20/U330-0P4   (4024)
2002/03: 22⁰GS, 19⁰GS, 25⁴S,

	Starts	1st	2nd	3rd	Win & Pl
Hurdles	1	0	0	0	0
Chases	2	0	0	0	309
Career Total	9	0	1	2	1667

Going:	Sf: 0-1 GS: 0-2 Gd: 0-0 GF: - Fm: 0-0
Distance:	2m/2m3: 0-0 2m4-2m7: 0-2 3m+: 0-1
Track:	LH: 0-0 RH: 0-3 Tight: 0-0 Gall: 0-1
Aids:	Bl: 0-0 Vi: 0-0 Tstrap: 0-0
Best Rating:	100 11/00 Folk 2m1f110y heavy NHF

Moderate hurdler/chaser; suited by easy ground.

Ibal (FR)
110(81h)   (144h)145+

7-y-o b g Balsamo (FR)-Quart D Hekla (FR) (Quart De Vin (FR))
Mrs N Smith Tony Hayward And Barry Fulton

Placings:3335/0F21312/24020P-31111   (4047)
2002/03: 16³GS, 20¹HY, 19¹HY, 26¹HY, 16¹S,

	Starts	1st	2nd	3rd	Win & Pl
Chases	5	4	0	1	24875
Career Total	22	6	4	5	72976

145	3/03	Sand	2m	D Ch	SFT	£7157
128	1/03	Plum	3m2f	D Ch	HVY	£7245
133	12/02	Chep	2m3f110yD Ch		HVY	£5215
124	12/02	Plum	2m4f	E Ch	HVY	£4522
144	3/01	Sand	2m110y	B HHdl	HVY	£23200
125	1/01	Leic	2m	E Hdl	HVY	£3209
			Total win prize-money £50550			

Going:	Sf: 4-4 GS: 0-1 Gd: 0-0 GF: - Fm: 0-0
Distance:	2m/2m3: 1-2 2m4-2m7: 2-2 3m+: 1-1
Track:	LH: 3-3 RH: 1-2 Tight: 2-2 Gall: 0-0
Aids:	Bl: 0-0 Vi: 0-0 Tstrap: 0-0
Best Rating:	145 3/03 Sand 2m soft Ch

Smart hurdler/novice chaser; very much at home on bottomless ground, so conditions were ideal when he landed the 2001 Imperial Cup in good style and when runner-up in a valuable handicap at Aintree; improved with experience over fences to win four times on testing ground in the winter of 2002/03; stays three miles plus, but effective at shorter.

Iberus (GER)
98   113+

5-y-o b g Monsun (GER)-Iberica (GER) (Green Dancer (USA))
M C Pipe (P Schiergen 29/6) D A Johnson

Placings:3F6   (4412)
2002/03: 16³S, 16⁵G, 17⁶G,

	Starts	1st	2nd	3rd	Win & Pl
Hurdles	3	0	0	1	442
Career Total	3	0	0	1	442

Going:	Sf: 0-1 GS: 0-0 Gd: 0-2 GF: - Fm: 0-0
Distance:	2m/2m3: 0-3 2m4-2m7: 0-0 3m+: 0-0
Track:	LH: 0-2 RH: 0-1 Tight: 0-2 Gall: 0-0
Aids:	Bl: 0-0 Vi: 0-1 Tstrap: 0-0
Best Rating:	113 2/03 Plum 2m soft Hdl

Listed-class miler/middle-distance performer on the Flat in Germany; not suited by slow pace and hurdled poorly when producing modest effort on debut over hurdles in moderate company at Plumpton in February 2003; badly outclassed before falling in the Champion Hurdle next time; ran poorly in novice company at Market Rasen two weeks later; suited by ground good or softer; has worn a visor.

Ibin St James
101(88h)   (90h)103+

9-y-o b g Salse (USA)-St James s Antigua (IRE) (Law Society (USA))
M Bradstock Dave Breakspear

Placings:04/P11301001/P0P0P/P04P-4101   (3746)
2002/03: 25⁴GS, 29¹GS, 32⁰GS, 24¹G,

	Starts	1st	2nd	3rd	Win & Pl
Chases	4	2	0	0	8454
Career Total	24	6	0	1	19755

103	2/03	Hntg	3m	F(0-90)HCh	GD	£3469
103	11/02	Fknm	3m5f110yF(0-100)HCh		G-S	£4706
117	3/00	Hntg	3m2f	E(0-115)HHdl	SFT	£2887
115	12/99	Towc	3m	E(0-115)HHdl	GD	£2547
109	9/99	Hrfd	3m2f	E(0-115)HHdl	SFT	£3113
93	8/99	Worc	3m	F(0-95)HHdl	SFT	£2045
			Total win prize-money £18769			

Going:	Sf: 0-0 GS: 1-3 Gd: 1-1 GF: - Fm: 0-0
Distance:	2m/2m3: 0-0 2m4-2m7: 0-0 3m+: 2-4
Track:	LH: 0-0 RH: 1-3 Tight: 0-0 Gall: 1-1
Aids:	Bl: 2-3 Vi: 0-0 Tstrap: 0-0
Best Rating:	117 3/00 Hntg 3m2f soft Hdl

Moderate chaser; stays very well; acts on good and soft ground.

Ibis Rochelais (FR)
109(108h)   (115h)129

7-y-o b g Passing Sale (FR)-Ta Rochelaise (FR) (Carmont (FR))
A Ennis A T A Wates

Placings:F2/3P/134252F-232212P (4474)
2002/03: 20^2G, 24^3G, 20^2S, 21^2GS, 24^1S, 24^2G, 25^PG,

	Starts	1st	2nd	3rd	Win & Pl
Chases	7	1	4	1	35582
Career Total	18	2	7	3	44675

129 2/03 Sand 3m110y B(0-140)HCh SFT £12678
115 5/01 Folk 2m1f110yE Hdl G-S £3080
Total win prize-money £15759

Going: Sf: 1-2 GS: 0-1 Gd: 0-4 GF: - Fm: 0-0
Distance: 2m/2m3: 0-0 2m4-2m7: 0-3 3m+: 1-4
Track: LH: 0-3 RH: 1-4 Tight: 0-1 Gall: 0-2
Aids: Bl: 0-0 Vi: 0-0 Tstrap: 0-0
Best Rating: 129 2/03 Sand 3m110y soft Ch

Decent chaser; stays three miles; acts on good and soft ground; progressive.

Icare D'Oudairies (FR)
83 108
7-y-o ch g Port Etienne (FR)-Vellea (FR) (Cap Martin (FR))
C Tizzard Anthony Knott

Placings:100/2400/1500-0 (1702)
2002/03: 19^0GF,

	Starts	1st	2nd	3rd	Win & Pl
Hurdles	1	0	0	0	
Career Total	12	2	1	0	5715

108 12/01 Weth 2m4f110yE(0-105)HHdl SFT £2926
102 1/00 Hayd 2m H NHF SFT £1771
Total win prize-money £4697

Going: Sf: 0-0 GS: 0-0 Gd: 0-0 GF: - Fm: 0-1
Distance: 2m/2m3: 0-0 2m4-2m7: 0-1 3m+: 0-0
Track: LH: 0-0 RH: 0-1 Tight: 0-1 Gall: 0-0
Aids: Bl: 0-0 Vi: 0-0 Tstrap: 0-0
Best Rating: 108 12/01 Weth 2m4f110y soft Hdl

Best caught fresh. He has been successful in a bumper and over hurdles. Acts on a soft surface and stays two miles four furlongs.

Ice Cool Lad (IRE)
98 82
9-y-o b g Glacial Storm (USA)-My Serena (No Argument)
R Rowe Mrs J A C Lundgren

Placings:0/065PP/15PP/032FP10-635P015 (4761)
2002/03: 20^6GF, 21^3GF, 22^2S, 20^PS, 20^5S, 28^1G, 26^5GF,

	Starts	1st	2nd	3rd	Win & Pl
Chases	7	1	0	1	4993
Career Total	24	3	1	2	12783

82 3/03 Font 3m4f E(0-105)HCh GD £4361
94 2/02 Font 2m2f E(0-105)HCh HVY £3234
94 12/00 Font 2m4f F(0-100)HCh SFT £3172
Total win prize-money £10768

Going: Sf: 0-3 GS: 0-0 Gd: 1-1 GF: - Fm: 0-3
Distance: 2m/2m3: 0-0 2m4-2m7: 0-5 3m+: 1-2
Track: LH: 0-1 RH: 0-2 Tight: 0-0 Gall: 0-0
Aids: Bl: 0-1 Vi: 0-0 Tstrap: 0-0
Best Rating: 94 2/02 Font 2m2f heavy Ch

Plating-class chaser; stays three miles four, but effective at shorter; acts on both good and soft ground.

Ice Crystal
104 115
6-y-o b g Slip Anchor-Crystal Fountain (Great Nephew)
S Woodman Fortune Racing

Placings:0-0000 (2301)
2002/03: 16^0GS, 17^0S, 17^0GS, 16^0GS,

	Starts	1st	2nd	3rd	Win & Pl

Placings:R42411/2PP-P1 (2982)
2002/03: 22^PGS, 20^1HY,

	Starts	1st	2nd	3rd	Win & Pl
Hurdles	2	1	0	0	6078
Career Total	11	3	2	0	15152

113 1/03 Font 2m4f D(0-125)HHdl HVY £6078
109 4/01 Font 2m6f110yE Hdl GD £2639
96 4/01 Plum 2m5f E Hdl HVY £3528
Total win prize-money £12245

Going: Sf: 1-1 GS: 0-1 Gd: 0-0 GF: - Fm: 0-0
Distance: 2m/2m3: 0-0 2m4-2m7: 1-2 3m+: 0-0
Track: LH: 0-1 RH: 0-0 Tight: 1-2 Gall: 0-0
Aids: Bl: 0-0 Vi: 0-0 Tstrap: 0-0
Best Rating: 115 10/01 Kemp 2m5f gd-sft Hdl

A modest hurdler who is effective at the minor venues in the south. Suited by a tight track, he has a good record at Fontwell and needs trips of at least two and a half miles.

Ice Cube
99(92c) (32c)67
7-y-o b g Rakaposhi King-Arctic Rymes (Rymer)
Mrs L Williamson Miss Judy Eaton

Placings:F000302003250/300530P/00350100-00406500 (4711)
2002/03: 16^0G, 22^0G, 19^4S, 16^0HY, 16^6HY, 20^5GF, 19^0GF, 16^0GF,

	Starts	1st	2nd	3rd	Win & Pl
Hurdles	6	0	0	0	289
Chases	2	0	0	0	
Career Total	36	1	2	5	6769

76 2/02 Tntn 2m110y E(0-100)HCh SFT £3428
Total win prize-money £3429

Going: Sf: 0-3 GS: 0-0 Gd: 0-2 GF: - Fm: 0-3
Distance: 2m/2m3: 0-5 2m4-2m7: 0-3 3m+: 0-0
Track: LH: 0-6 RH: 0-2 Tight: 0-4 Gall: 0-1
Aids: Bl: 0-1 Vi: 0-0 Tstrap: 0-1
Best Rating: 86 4/01 Plum 2m5f heavy Hdl

Ice Saint
102 91
8-y-o gr g Ballacashtal (CAN)-Sylvan Song (Song)
M J Gingell C N & Mrs A V Roberts & T J Bater

Placings:0566P/3402/1014300 (3668)
2002/03: 22^1GF, 24^0G, 22^1GF, 19^4GF, 22^3S, 26^0GF, 22^0GS,

	Starts	1st	2nd	3rd	Win & Pl
Hurdles	7	2	0	1	9031
Career Total	16	2	1	2	10221

91 7/02 Strf 2m6f110yD Hdl G-F £4858
86 6/02 Strf 2m6f110yF(0-95)HHdl G-F £3272
Total win prize-money £8132

Going: Sf: 0-1 GS: 0-1 Gd: 0-1 GF: - Fm: 2-4
Distance: 2m/2m3: 0-1 2m4-2m7: 2-4 3m+: 0-2
Track: LH: 2-6 RH: 0-1 Tight: 2-5 Gall: 0-1
Aids: Bl: 0-0 Vi: 0-0 Tstrap: 0-0
Best Rating: 91 7/02 Strf 2m6f110y gd-fm Hdl

Modest pointer, winner twice over hurdles at Stratford in the summer of 2002.

Icealion
85 53
5-y-o b g Lion Cavern (USA)-Icecapped (Caerleon (USA))
M W Easterby J W P Curtis

Placings:0-0000 (2301)
2002/03: 16^0GS, 17^0S, 17^0GS, 16^0GS,

	Starts	1st	2nd	3rd	Win & Pl

		Starts	1st	2nd	3rd
Hurdles	4	0	0	0	
Career Total	5	0	0	0	

Going: Sf: 0-1 GS: 0-3 Gd: 0-0 GF: - Fm: 0-0
Distance: 2m/2m3: 0-4 2m4-2m7: 0-0 3m+: 0-0
Track: LH: 0-3 RH: 0-1 Tight: 0-3 Gall: 0-0
Aids: Bl: 0-0 Vi: 0-0 Tstrap: 0-2
Best Rating: 61 11/02 MRas 2m1f110y gd-sft Hdl

Iceberge (IRE)
103 101+
7-y-o b g Glacial Storm (USA)-Laura Daisy (Buckskin (FR))
Ian Williams Mcmahon (contractors Services) Ltd

Placings:622-235311 (4196)
2002/03: 20^2GF, 21^3S, 20^5S, 24^3S, 26^1G, 24^1G,

	Starts	1st	2nd	3rd	Win & Pl
Hurdles	6	2	1	2	8631
Career Total	9	2	3	2	9749

101 3/03 Ludl 3m E Hdl GD £3415
101 3/03 Hntg 3m2f F Hdl GD £2733
Total win prize-money £6150

Going: Sf: 0-3 GS: 0-0 Gd: 2-2 GF: - Fm: 0-1
Distance: 2m/2m3: 0-0 2m4-2m7: 0-3 3m+: 2-3
Track: LH: 0-3 RH: 2-3 Tight: 0-0 Gall: 1-1
Aids: Bl: 0-0 Vi: 0-0 Tstrap: 0-0
Best Rating: 105 12/02 Wwck 2m5f soft Hdl

Modest hurdler; stays three miles two; acts on good ground.

Icelandic Lord

10-y-o b g Arctic Lord-Arctic Ander (Leander)
Mrs L B Normile Mrs L Normile

Placings:FP/P/PP-P0 (1128)
2002/03: 16^PGS, 17^0GF,

	Starts	1st	2nd	3rd	Win & Pl
Hurdles	1	0	0	0	
Chases	1	0	0	0	
Career Total	7	0	0	0	

Going: Sf: 0-0 GS: 0-1 Gd: 0-0 GF: - Fm: 0-1
Distance: 2m/2m3: 0-2 2m4-2m7: 0-0 3m+: 0-0
Track: LH: 0-0 RH: 0-2 Tight: 0-0 Gall: 0-0
Aids: Bl: 0-0 Vi: 0-0 Tstrap: 0-0
Best Rating: 0 8/02 MRas 2m1f110y gd-fm Hdl

Icelandic Spring

11-y-o ch g Derrylin-Snow Time (Deep Run)
J E Brockbank J E Brockbank

Placings:P/0633 (4664)
2002/03: 25^0GS, 25^6GF, 25^3G, 24^3GF,

	Starts	1st	2nd	3rd	Win & Pl
Chases	4	0	0	2	660
Career Total	5	0	0	2	660

Going: Sf: 0-0 GS: 0-1 Gd: 0-1 GF: - Fm: 0-2
Distance: 2m/2m3: 0-0 2m4-2m7: 0-0 3m+: 0-4
Track: LH: 0-3 RH: 0-1 Tight: 0-2 Gall: 0-0
Aids: Bl: 0-2 Vi: 0-0 Tstrap: 0-0
Best Rating: 80 4/03 Kels 3m1f good Ch

Moderate pointer/hunter chaser; handles a sound surface; has won blinkers.

Iceni Queen

5-y-o b m Formidable (USA)-Queen Warrior (Daring March)
D J Minty D J Minty

Placings:P-P (0040)
2002/03: 17PG,

	Starts	1st	2nd	3rd	Win & Pl
Hurdles	1	0	0	0	
Career Total	2	0	0	0	

Going: Sf: 0-0 GS: 0-0 Gd: 0-1 GF: - Fm: 0-0
Distance: 2m/2m3: 0-1 2m4-2m7: 0-0 3m+: 0-0
Track: LH: 0-0 RH: 0-1 Tight: 0-0 Gall: 0-0
Aids: Bl: 0-0 Vi: 0-0 Tstrap: 0-0
Best Rating:

Ichi Beau (IRE)

107(105h) (113h)**133**
9-y-o b g Convinced-May As Well (Kemal (FR))
Ferdy Murphy Mrs Fiona Butterly

Placings:00000/504/11F52312/351233264-56P222 (4762)
2002/03: 165GF, 17PG, 16PG, 202G, 162G, 162G,

	Starts	1st	2nd	3rd	Win & Pl
Hurdles	1	0	1	0	1780
Chases	5	0	2	0	9261
Career Total	31	4	7	4	64213
144	12/01	Donc	2m110y	C(0-135)HCh	GD £6097
128	4/01	Ayr	2m	C Ch	GD £6301
121	11/00	Aint	2m	D(0-115)HCh	G-S £10383
118	10/00	Carl	2m	F(0-100)HCh	G-S £2886
				Total win prize-money £25669	

Going: Sf: 0-0 GS: 0-0 Gd: 0-0 GF: 0-5 GF: - Fm: 0-1
Distance: 2m/2m3: 0-5 2m4-2m7: 0-1 3m+: 0-0
Track: LH: 0-3 RH: 0-3 Tight: 0-1 Gall: 0-0
Aids: Bl: 0-0 Vi: 0-0 Tstrap: 0-6
Best Rating: 144 2/02 Kemp 2m good Ch

Useful chaser/modest hurdler; consistent sort; best over two miles; effective on a sound surface; suited by a flat, left-handed track; regularly tongue tied; made the most of simple opportunities in novices hurdles in the summer of 2003.

Ickford Okey

11-y-o b g Broadsword (USA)-Running Kiss (Deep Run)
Mrs S S Harbour P J Morgan

Placings:00/50U/2P6-52U (4003)
2002/03: 255GF, 242GF, 25US,

	Starts	1st	2nd	3rd	Win & Pl
Chases	3	0	1	0	426
Career Total	11	0	2	0	1290

Going: Sf: 0-1 GS: 0-0 Gd: 0-0 GF: - Fm: 0-2
Distance: 2m/2m3: 0-0 2m4-2m7: 0-0 3m+: 0-3
Track: LH: 0-0 RH: 0-3 Tight: 0-0 Gall: 0-1
Aids: Bl: 0-1 Vi: 0-0 Tstrap: 0-0
Best Rating: 101 3/02 Strf 3m gd-sft Ch

A winning pointer, he was narrowly beaten in a novice hunter chase at Stratford and huntingdon in the spring of 2002 and ought to have won on both occasions. One to be wary of.

Iconic

9-y-o b g Reprimand-Miami Melody (Miami Springs)

Darren Page Darren Page

Placings:0/64/0206P/4/P-5 (0315)
2002/03: 215G,

	Starts	1st	2nd	3rd	Win & Pl
Chases	1	0	0	0	0
Career Total	11	0	1	0	1068

Going: Sf: 0-0 GS: 0-0 Gd: 0-1 GF: - Fm: 0-0
Distance: 2m/2m3: 0-0 2m4-2m7: 0-1 3m+: 0-0
Track: LH: 0-0 RH: 0-1 Tight: 0-1 Gall: 0-0
Aids: Bl: 0-0 Vi: 0-0 Tstrap: 0-0
Best Rating: 79 7/99 Sedg 2m110y gd-fm Ch

Icy River (IRE)

92 **93**
6-y-o ch g Over The River (FR)-Icy Lou (Blue Rullah)
Mrs M Reveley Andy Peake & David Jackson

Placings:5606 (4435)
2002/03: 165HY, 165S, 169G, 206G,

	Starts	1st	2nd	3rd	Win & Pl
NH Flat	2	0	0	0	0
Hurdles	2	0	0	0	0
Career Total	4	0	0	0	0

Going: Sf: 0-2 GS: 0-0 Gd: 0-2 GF: - Fm: 0-0
Distance: 2m/2m3: 0-2 2m4-2m7: 0-1 3m+: 0-0
Track: LH: 0-3 RH: 0-1 Tight: 0-0 Gall: 0-1
Aids: Bl: 0-0 Vi: 0-0 Tstrap: 0-0
Best Rating: 93 1/03 Newc 2m heavy NHF

Jump-bred, showed some ability on first outing in a bumper at Newcastle in January; runner-up in a weak event at Wetherby in May on hurdling bow; should improve especially over further.

Idaho D'Ox (FR)

104(118h) (133h)**130+**
7-y-o b/br g Bad Conduct (USA)-Queseda (FR) (Quart De Vin (FR))
M C Pipe The Dionysius Partnership

Placings:4F00F462F66/O413123200120-P0020005 (4476)
2002/03: 17PG, 16HY, 165S, 162HY, 169G, 16PHY, 17PG, 165G,

	Starts	1st	2nd	3rd	Win & Pl
Hurdles	7	0	1	0	23000
Chases	1	0	0	0	0
Career Total	32	3	5	2	59164
125	4/02	Winc	2m	E Hdl	GD £2884
120	12/01	Sand	2m110y	D(0-110)HHdl	SFT £7117
93	10/01	Extr	2m6f110yE Hdl	G-F £2450
				Total win prize-money £12452	

Going: Sf: 0-4 GS: 0-0 Gd: 0-4 GF: - Fm: 0-0
Distance: 2m/2m3: 0-8 2m4-2m7: 0-0 3m+: 0-0
Track: LH: 0-2 RH: 0-6 Tight: 0-1 Gall: 0-1
Aids: Bl: 0-0 Vi: 0-8 Tstrap: 0-0
Best Rating: 138 4/02 Aint 2m110y good Hdl

Decent handicap hurdler; left in lead at the last when making it three out of three in novice chases at Newton Abbot in June; extended his winning run on handicap bow at Southwell two weeks later; stayed 2m 6f over hurdles but effective at shorter trips; seems to handle any ground; wears a visor.

Idbury (IRE)

83f **89f**
5-y-o b g Zaffaran (USA)-Delcarrow (Roi Guillaume (FR))

N A Twiston-Davies H R Mould

Placings:005 (3890)
2002/03: 16PHY, 17PS, 165G,

	Starts	1st	2nd	3rd	Win & Pl
NH Flat	3	0	0	0	0
Career Total	3	0	0	0	0

Going: Sf: 0-2 GS: 0-0 Gd: 0-1 GF: - Fm: 0-0
Distance: 2m/2m3: 0-3 2m4-2m7: 0-0 3m+: 0-0
Track: LH: 0-2 RH: 0-1 Tight: 0-0 Gall: 0-0
Aids: Bl: 0-0 Vi: 0-0 Tstrap: 0-0
Best Rating: 89 3/03 Hayd 2m good NHF

Ideal Du Bois Beury (FR)

107(102c) (110c)**112**
7-y-o b/br g Useful (FR)-Pampa Star (FR) (Pampabird)
M C Pipe D A Johnson

Placings:5/132110P-224P000 (4112)
2002/03: 162S, 19PGS, 164S, 21PGS, 22PHY, 21UG, 21UG,

	Starts	1st	2nd	3rd	Win & Pl
Hurdles	3	0	0	0	0
Chases	4	0	2	0	4291
Career Total	15	3	3	1	38550
134	2/02	Asct	2m4f	B(0-150)HHdl	SFT £18087
116	1/02	Leic	2m4f110yE(0-110)HHdl	SFT £5648
120	12/01	Newb	2m110y	B Hdl	SFT £7410
				Total win prize-money £31146	

Going: Sf: 0-3 GS: 0-2 Gd: 0-2 GF: - Fm: 0-0
Distance: 2m/2m3: 0-3 2m4-2m7: 0-4 3m+: 0-0
Track: LH: 0-3 RH: 0-4 Tight: 0-2 Gall: 0-2
Aids: Bl: 0-0 Vi: 0-2 Tstrap: 0-0
Best Rating: 134 2/02 Asct 2m4f soft Hdl

Decent hurdler; effective over two and a half miles; goes well in soft ground; disappointing over fences in 2002/3 and reverted to hurdles; has worn a visor.

Ideal Jack (FR)

104 **104**
7-y-o b g Agent Bleu (FR)-Nuit Des Fanges (FR) (Trac)
M C Pipe Peter R Masters

Placings:2/24F321U3/3P30 (4695)
2002/03: 193S, 17PS, 193G, 16PG,

	Starts	1st	2nd	3rd	Win & Pl
Chases	4	0	0	2	1743
Career Total	13	1	3	4	14683
96	7/00	Worc	2m4f	E Hdl	G-F £2401
				Total win prize-money £2401	

Going: Sf: 0-2 GS: 0-0 Gd: 0-2 GF: - Fm: 0-0
Distance: 2m/2m3: 0-3 2m4-2m7: 0-1 3m+: 0-0
Track: LH: 0-3 RH: 0-1 Tight: 0-3 Gall: 0-0
Aids: Bl: 0-0 Vi: 0-4 Tstrap: 0-0
Best Rating: 107 5/00 Autl 2m1f110y v soft Ch

Maiden hurdle-race winner, third over fences at Taunton in January but jumped poorly and was pulled up next time.

Idealko (FR)

103(97h) (100h)**112**
7-y-o b g Kadalko (FR)-Belfaster (FR) (Royal Charter (FR))
Ian Williams Mrs Maggie Bull

Placings:62/4/1111/0-42PU133 (4538)
2002/03: 204GS, 20PHY, 20PGS, 21UG, 201G, 203G, 203G,

	Starts	1st	2nd	3rd	Win & Pl
Hurdles	4	0	1	0	1844
Chases	3	1	0	2	5758
Career Total	15	5	2	2	20064

108 3/03 Ludl 2m4f F(0-100)HCh GD £3523
4/01 Lrsy 2m1f Ch GD £3201
6/00 Diep 2m1f110y Ch GD £2882
6/00 Roya 2m2f Ch GD £2690
6/00 Gemz 2m3f Ch GD £1537
Total win prize-money £13833

Going: Sf: 0-1 GS: 0-2 Gd: 1-4 GF: - Fm: 0-0
Distance: 2m/2m3: 0-0 **2m4-2m7: 1-7** 3m+: 0-0
Track: LH: 0-0 **RH: 1-5 Tight: 1-4** Gall: 0-0
Aids: Bl: 0-0 Vi: 0-0 Tstrap: 0-0
Best Rating: 108 3/03 Ludl 2m4f good Ch

Winner of four chases in France, he showed ability over hurdles in this country before winning a two and a half mile chase in March 2003; suited by good ground; has shown a tendency to jump left handed.

Ideas Man (IRE)
97(68h) (36h)**73**
7-y-o b g Executive Perk-Emmodee (Bowling Pin)
D McCain B Dunn

Placings:50-R544FP (4516)
2002/03: 17RS, 17SG, 16⁴GF, 16⁴G, 20FG, 21PG,

	Starts	1st	2nd	3rd	Win & Pl
Hurdles	2	0	0	0	0
Chases	4	0	0	0	891
Career Total	8	0	0	0	891

Going: Sf: 0-1 GS: 0-0 Gd: 0-4 GF: - Fm: 0-1
Distance: 2m/2m3: 0-4 2m4-2m7: 0-2 3m+: 0-0
Track: LH: 0-5 RH: 0-1 Tight: 0-4 Gall: 0-0
Aids: Bl: 0-1 Vi: 0-0 Tstrap: 0-0
Best Rating: 81 12/01 Ludl 2m good NHF

Has shown very little so far.

Idlewild (IRE)
89 **66**
8-y-o br g Phardante (FR)-Delia Murphy (Golden Love)
M J Polglase (Miss A Nolan 26/5) P J Parsons

Placings:P-5PP (4684)
2002/03: 20⁵GF, 20PG, 16PGF,

	Starts	1st	2nd	3rd	Win & Pl
Hurdles	2	0	0	0	0
Chases	1	0	0	0	0
Career Total	4	0	0	0	0

Going: Sf: 0-0 GS: 0-0 Gd: 0-1 GF: - Fm: 0-2
Distance: 2m/2m3: 0-1 2m4-2m7: 0-2 3m+: 0-0
Track: LH: 0-2 RH: 0-1 Tight: 0-1 Gall: 0-2
Aids: Bl: 0-1 Vi: 0-0 Tstrap: 0-0
Best Rating: 66 3/03 Sthl 2m4f110y gd-fm Hdl

Maiden pointer; no form so far under Rules.

Ifni Du Luc (FR)
111 (120h)**134d**
7-y-o b/br m Chamberlin (FR)-Acca Du Luc (FR) (Djarvis (FR))
N J Henderson Mary-Anne Parker,Sir Eric Parker,P White

Placings:1224/10200/**2121P-2F40U6** (4792)
2002/03: 20²G, 24FS, 24⁴HY, 24⁴G, 21UG, 20⁶G,

	Starts	1st	2nd	3rd	Win & Pl
Chases	6	0	1	0	5434

Career Total		20	4	6	0	41925
137	1/02	Hayd	2m6f	B Ch	SFT	£10185
104	12/01	Winc	2m	D Ch	GD	£4095
121	12/00	Font	2m2f110yC(0-130)HHdl	SFT		£7046
109	12/99	Sand	2m110y	D Hdl	G-S	£3046

Total win prize-money £24372

Going: Sf: 0-2 GS: 0-0 Gd: 0-4 GF: - Fm: 0-0
Distance: 2m/2m3: 0-0 2m4-2m7: 0-3 3m+: 0-3
Track: LH: 0-2 RH: 0-4 Tight: 0-1 Gall: 0-1
Aids: Bl: 0-0 Vi: 0-0 Tstrap: 0-0
Best Rating: 145 11/02 Leic 2m4f110y good Ch

Very useful handicap chaser; stays two miles six; acts on good and soft ground.

Ifrane Balima (FR)
105 **104d**
7-y-o ch g Video Rock (FR)-Balima Des Saccart (FR) (Quart De Vin (FR))
J C Tuck The Kermit Klub

Placings:000F00-3114600 (4256)
2002/03: 17³G, 16¹HY, 16¹HY, 16⁴GS, 16⁶HY, 18⁰S, 17⁰G,

	Starts	1st	2nd	3rd	Win & Pl
Hurdles	7	2	0	1	10654
Career Total	13	2	0	1	10654

104 11/02 Leic 2m D(0-120)HHdl HVY £6870
92 11/02 Uttx 2m F(0-100)HHdl HVY £2702
Total win prize-money £9573

Going: Sf: 2-4 GS: 0-1 Gd: 0-2 GF: - Fm: 0-0
Distance: 2m/2m3: **2-7** 2m4-2m7: 0-0 3m+: 0-0
Track: LH: 1-3 RH: 1-4 Tight: 0-1 Gall: 0-0
Aids: Bl: 0-0 Vi: 0-0 Tstrap: 0-0
Best Rating: 104 11/02 Leic 2m heavy Hdl

Ex-French, he showed little over hurdles in 2001/2 but ran a better race on his seasonal bow in October 2002 and scored at Uttoxeter next time, and then followed up at Leicester the time after. Suited by two miles and handles plenty of cut.

Iftikhar (USA)
100f **97f**
4-y-o ch g Storm Cat (USA)-Muhbubh (USA) (Blushing Groom (FR))
W M Brisbourne L R Owen

Placings:2 (4197)
2002/03: 16²G,

	Starts	1st	2nd	3rd	Win & Pl
NH Flat	1	0	1	0	560
Career Total	1	0	1	0	560

Going: Sf: 0-0 GS: 0-0 Gd: 0-1 GF: - Fm: 0-0
Distance: 2m/2m3: 0-1 2m4-2m7: 0-0 3m+: 0-0
Track: LH: 0-0 RH: 0-1 Tight: 0-0 Gall: 0-0
Aids: Bl: 0-0 Vi: 0-0 Tstrap: 0-0
Best Rating: 97 3/03 Ludl 2m good NHF

Ijika (FR)
69(108h) (55h)
7-y-o ch g Aelan Hapi (USA)-Belle Des Airs (FR) (Saumon (FR))
H D Daly Roy Van Gelder & Brian Luby

Placings:00/26033-0PPP (3520)
2002/03: 17⁰GS, 16⁶G, 19⁵S, 20PGS,

	Starts	1st	2nd	3rd	Win & Pl
Hurdles	1	0	0	0	0
Chases	3	0	0	0	0

Career Total		11	0	1	2	2383

Going: Sf: 0-1 GS: 0-2 Gd: 0-1 GF: - Fm: 0-0
Distance: 2m/2m3: 0-3 2m4-2m7: 0-1 3m+: 0-0
Track: LH: 0-2 RH: 0-0 Tight: 0-3 Gall: 0-0
Aids: Bl: 0-0 Vi: 0-0 Tstrap: 0-0
Best Rating: 100 4/02 Strf 2m110y good Hdl

From the family of Edmond, he showed nothing in the mud in bumpers, but made a much more pleasing effort in his debut over hurdles at Stratford in November. Held since, he is effective at up to an extended two miles six furlongs.

Ikrenel Royal (FR)
99 **126**
7-y-o b g Bricassar (USA)-Kreneldore (FR) (Trenel)
N J Henderson Lynn Wilson

Placings:630111/P6 (3181)
2002/03: 24PS, 20⁶G,

	Starts	1st	2nd	3rd	Win & Pl
Chases	2	0	0	0	414
Career Total	8	3	0	1	40982

146 4/01 Sand 2m4f110yB Ch G-S £17225
12/00 Autl 2m2f Hdl HVY £9606
11/00 Engh 2m3f Ch HLD £10567
Total win prize-money £37398

Going: Sf: 0-1 GS: 0-0 Gd: 0-1 GF: - Fm: 0-0
Distance: 2m/2m3: 0-2 2m4-2m7: 0-1 3m+: 0-1
Track: LH: 0-0 RH: 0-2 Tight: 0-0 Gall: 0-0
Aids: Bl: 0-0 Vi: 0-0 Tstrap: 0-0
Best Rating: 146 4/01 Sand 2m4f110y gd-sft Ch

Very useful ex-French chaser; looked a classy prospect when winning at Sandown in April of 2001 but subsequently injured and has not looked the same horse since; effective over two and a half miles; acts on soft ground.

Il Capitano
113(110h) (128h)**130**
6-y-o ch g Be My Chief (USA)-Taza (Persian Bold)
P F Nicholls Terry Evans

Placings:25/152363621-11311112131 (4779)
2002/03: 26¹GF, 20¹GF, 22³GF, 24¹F, 20¹GF, 19¹F, 19¹F, 24²G, 19¹F, 25³G, 20¹GF,

	Starts	1st	2nd	3rd	Win & Pl
Hurdles	3	3	0	0	13742
Chases	8	5	1	2	40805
Career Total	22	10	4	4	68622

129 4/03 Sand 2m4f110yB HCh G-F £15812
110 4/03 Tntn 2m3f D Ch FRM £5564
117 10/02 Tntn 2m3f D Ch FRM £5900
127 10/02 Extr 2m4f D(0-125)HHdl FRM £4602
123 10/02 Chep 2m4f D(0-120)HHdl G-F £4134
122 10/02 Extr 3m110y D(0-125)HHdl FRM £5005
106 5/02 Font 2m4f E Ch G-F £3081
117 5/02 Font 3m2f110yE Ch G-F £3071
116 4/02 Font 2m3f D(0-125)HHdl G-F £3482
95 10/01 Tntn 2m1f E Hdl FRM £3276
Total win prize-money £53473

Going: Sf: 0-0 GS: 0-0 Gd: 0-2 GF: - Fm: 8-9
Distance: 2m/2m3: 3-3 2m4-2m7: 3-4 3m+: 2-4
Track: LH: 1-3 **RH: 5-5 Tight: 4-5** Gall: 0-1
Aids: Bl: 0-0 Vi: 0-0 Tstrap: 0-0
Best Rating: 129 4/03 Sand 2m4f110y gd-fm Ch

Useful hurdler/chaser; in sparkling form in 2002/2003 with eight wins, five over fences; won at Ludlow on first run of 2003/4 season; stays two and a half miles; fast-ground specialist; suited by a right-handed track.

Il Cavaliere

110   **127**

8-y-o b g Mtoto-Kalmia (Miller s Mate)
Mrs M Reveley The Thoughtful Partnership

Placings: 15214/322-2211F   (3751)
2002/03: 20²S, 19²GS, 20¹GS, 21¹G, 21FG,

	Starts	1st	2nd	3rd	Win & Pl
Hurdles	5	2	2		12675
Career Total	13	4	5	1	20480
125 1/03 Kemp 2m5f	C(0-130)HHdl		GD		£6554
124 12/02 Muss 2m4f	D Hdl		G-S		£4202
117 10/99 Sedg 2m1f	H NHF		GD		£1647
115 6/99 MRas 1m5f110yH NHF			G-F		£1493

Total win prize-money £13898

Going:	Sf: 0-1 GS: 1-2 Gd: 1-2 GF: - Fm: 0-0
Distance:	2m/2m3: 0-0 2m4-2m7: 2-5 3m+: 0-0
Track:	LH: 0-2 RH: 2-3 Tight: 1-1 Gall: 0-1
Aids:	Bl: 0-0 Vi: 0-0 Tstrap: 0-0
Best Rating:	127 2/03 Kemp 2m5f good Hdl

Decent handicap hurdler; effective at around two and a half miles; acts on good and soft ground; suited by a flat track.

Il'Athou (FR)

115   (95h)**147**

7-y-o b g Lute Antique (FR)-Va Thou Line (FR) (El Badr)
S E H Sherwood Lady Thompson

Placings: 2/011P0/111P-F2P13   (3885)
2002/03: 20FGS, 20²GS, 20PGS, 20¹GS, 20³G,

	Starts	1st	2nd	3rd	Win & Pl
Chases	5	1	1	1	18587
Career Total	15	6	2	1	50460
147 2/03 Weth 2m4f110yB HCh		G-S			£13481
140 1/02 Asct 2m	A Ch	GD			£16750
133 11/01 Hntg 2m4f110yD Ch		GD			£4280
135 11/01 Bang 2m1f110yD Ch		SFT			£4134
116 1/01 Folk 2m1f110yF(0-105)HHdl		HVY			£2226
109 12/00 Folk 2m1f110yE Hdl		HVY			£3042

Total win prize-money £43913

Going:	Sf: 0-0 GS: 1-4 Gd: 0-1 GF: - Fm: 0-0
Distance:	2m/2m3: 0-0 2m4-2m7: 1-5 3m+: 0-0
Track:	LH: 1-4 RH: 0-1 Tight: 0-0 Gall: 0-2
Aids:	Bl: 0-0 Vi: 0-0 Tstrap: 0-0
Best Rating:	147 2/03 Weth 2m4f110y gd-sft Ch

Very useful handicap chaser at around two and a half miles; suited by soft ground; jumps well.

Ilabon (FR)

104   **113**

7-y-o ch g Secret Haunt (USA)-Ahuille (FR) (Haltea (FR))
M C Pipe (L Viel 28/9) Beau Girls

Placings: 4532   (4328)
2002/03: 19⁴G, 18⁵VS, 16³HY, 16²G,

	Starts	1st	2nd	3rd	Win & Pl
Hurdles	4	0	1	1	4364
Career Total	4	0	1	1	4364

Going:	Sf: 0-1 GS: 0-0 Gd: 0-2 GF: - Fm: 0-0
Distance:	2m/2m3: 0-4 2m4-2m7: 0-0 3m+: 0-0
Track:	LH: 0-2 RH: 0-0 Tight: 0-0 Gall: 0-1
Aids:	Bl: 0-0 Vi: 0-0 Tstrap: 0-0
Best Rating:	113 3/03 Newb 2m110y good Hdl

Decent novice hurdler; should stay two and a half miles; acts on good ground.

Ile De Librate

100(100h)   (69h)**101**

9-y-o b g Librate-Little Missile (Ile De Bourbon (USA))
R J O Sullivan Skampcargo Racing Partnership

Placings: 222F02214/4360/22/5/421212-000U   (4761)
2002/03: 22⁰GS, 22⁰S, 24⁰G, 26UGF,

	Starts	1st	2nd	3rd	Win & Pl
Hurdles	2	0	0	0	0
Chases	2	0	0	0	0
Career Total	26	3	10	1	19701
101 9/01 Worc 2m7f110yD Ch			G-F		£3900
101 7/01 Strf 3m	D Ch		GD		£4338
98 3/98 Plum 2m4f	E Hdl		GD		£2763

Total win prize-money £11002

Going:	Sf: 0-1 GS: 0-1 Gd: 0-1 GF: - Fm: 0-1
Distance:	2m/2m3: 0-0 2m4-2m7: 0-2 3m+: 0-1
Track:	LH: 0-3 RH: 0-0 Tight: 0-3 Gall: 0-0
Aids:	Bl: 0-0 Vi: 0-0 Tstrap: 0-2
Best Rating:	101 9/01 Font 3m2f110y gd-fm Ch

Moderate staying hurdler/chaser; acts on a sound surface.

Ile Distinct (IRE)

96(99h)   (41h)**79**

9-y-o b g Dancing Dissident (USA)-Golden Sunlight (Ile De Bourbon (USA))
K R Pearce Keith R Pearce

Placings: 2/40/FF0454-P6   (0730)
2002/03: 16PGF, 21RGF,

	Starts	1st	2nd	3rd	Win & Pl
Chases	2	0	0	0	0
Career Total	11	0	1	0	668

Going:	Sf: 0-0 GS: 0-0 Gd: 0-0 GF: - Fm: 0-2
Distance:	2m/2m3: 0-1 2m4-2m7: 0-1 3m+: 0-0
Track:	LH: 0-2 RH: 0-0 Tight: 0-1 Gall: 0-0
Aids:	Bl: 0-0 Vi: 0-0 Tstrap: 0-0
Best Rating:	96 9/99 Kels 2m2f gd-fm Hdl

Ilewin Janine (IRE)

74(97h)   (94h)**85**

12-y-o b m Soughaan (USA)-Mystery Queen (Martinmas)
G Brown Tom Segrue

Placings: 604/560F4P2/22/216/0PP/002111513/052P41P-03   (1874)
2002/03: 19⁰G, 18³GS,

	Starts	1st	2nd	3rd	Win & Pl
Chases	2	0	0	1	538
Career Total	36	6	6	2	19369
85 2/02 Folk 2m	F(0-90)HCh	SFT			£4065
99 1/01 Leic 2m	G(0-90)HHdl	HVY			£1981
83 9/00 Hrfd 2m3f	G(0-95)HCh	G-S			£2795
80 9/00 Font 2m2f110yG(0-95)HHdl		GD			£2352
79 9/00 Sedg 2m1f	G(0-95)HHdl	GD			£1547
99 5/98 Uttx 2m	G(0-95)HHdl	G-F			£1595

Total win prize-money £14336

Going:	Sf: 0-0 GS: 0-1 Gd: 0-1 GF: - Fm: 0-0
Distance:	2m/2m3: 0-1 2m4-2m7: 0-1 3m+: 0-0
Track:	LH: 0-1 RH: 0-0 Tight: 0-1 Gall: 0-0
Aids:	Bl: 0-0 Vi: 0-0 Tstrap: 0-0
Best Rating:	99 1/01 Leic 2m heavy Hdl

Moderate dual -purpose performer, she was in good heart in the 2000/2001 season winning four times on firm ground. She has since proved she can handle the mud, and showed a good attitude when winning with pricked ears over the minimum distance in a Folkestone hurdle in February.

Ill Swing By (IRE)

88(89h)   (55h)**72**

9-y-o b m Jurado (USA)-Big Sally (Salluceva)
Miss S E Forster D J Simpson

Placings: 2/4P0/4P60F05   (4138)
2002/03: 16⁴G, 21PGF, 20⁶S, 21⁰S, 16FGF, 16⁵S, 16⁵S,

	Starts	1st	2nd	3rd	Win & Pl
Hurdles	5	0	0	0	0
Chases	2	0	0	0	0
Career Total	11	0	1	0	454

Going:	Sf: 0-4 GS: 0-0 Gd: 0-1 GF: - Fm: 0-2
Distance:	2m/2m3: 0-4 2m4-2m7: 0-3 3m+: 0-0
Track:	LH: 0-5 RH: 0-2 Tight: 0-3 Gall: 0-1
Aids:	Bl: 0-0 Vi: 0-0 Tstrap: 0-0
Best Rating:	104 4/00 MRas 2m1f110y soft NHF

Maiden point winner; only selling class under Rules.

Illineylad (IRE)

101(91h)   (83h)**81**

9-y-o b g Whitehall Bridge-Illiney Girl (Lochnager)
Mrs N S Sharpe The Illiney Group

Placings: 064/60/PF03443P-P2P3   (1411)
2002/03: 24PGF, 23²G, 24PG, 22³G,

	Starts	1st	2nd	3rd	Win & Pl
Chases	4	0	1	1	1629
Career Total	17	0	1	3	2762

Going:	Sf: 0-0 GS: 0-0 Gd: 0-3 GF: - Fm: 0-1
Distance:	2m/2m3: 0-0 2m4-2m7: 0-1 3m+: 0-3
Track:	LH: 0-2 RH: 0-1 Tight: 0-3 Gall: 0-0
Aids:	Bl: 0-0 Vi: 0-0 Tstrap: 0-0
Best Rating:	83 9/01 Worc 3m gd-fm Hdl

Former point winner, he stays three miles and is better on a sounder surface.

Illuminate

95   **76**

10-y-o b g Marju (IRE)-Light Bee (USA) (Majestic Light (USA))
D C O Brien D C O Brien

Placings: 5P4/532240/50201432/606P/50   (4629)
2002/03: 18⁵S, 21⁰GF,

	Starts	1st	2nd	3rd	Win & Pl
Hurdles	2	0	0	0	0
Career Total	23	1	4	2	4869
91 2/99 Ling 2m3f110yF(0-100)HHdl		SFT			£1814

Total win prize-money £1815

Going:	Sf: 0-1 GS: 0-0 Gd: 0-0 GF: - Fm: 0-0
Distance:	2m/2m3: 0-1 2m4-2m7: 0-1 3m+: 0-0
Track:	LH: 0-2 RH: 0-0 Tight: 0-2 Gall: 0-0
Aids:	Bl: 0-0 Vi: 0-0 Tstrap: 0-0
Best Rating:	97 1/97 Folk 2m1f110y soft Hdl

Ilnamar (FR)

107(107c)   (149c)**160**

7-y-o b g Officiel (FR)-Quillemare (FR) (Le Pontet (FR))
M C Pipe Joe Moran

Placings: 22F1323/P0121/54U11-3   (3171)
2002/03: 16³GS,

	Starts	1st	2nd	3rd	Win & Pl
Hurdles	1	0	0	1	4400

Career Total		18	5	4	3	186903	
165 4/02	Aint	2m4f	A Hdl			GD	£69600
159 3/02	Chel	2m5f	A HHdl			G-S	£42000
12/00	Autl	2m2f	Hdl			HVY	£14409
10/00	Autl	2m1f110y	Ch			HVY	£10567
2/00	Pau	2m2f	Hdl			HVY	£4803
					Total win prize-money £141379		

Going: Sf: 0-0 GS: 0-1 Gd: 0-0 GF: - Fm: 0-0
Distance: 2m/2m3: 0-1 2m4-2m7: 0-0 3m+: 0-0
Track: LH: 0-1 RH: 0-0 Tight: 0-0 Gall: 0-0
Aids: Bl: 0-0 Vi: 0-0 Tstrap: 0-0
Best Rating: 165 4/02 Aint 2m4f good Hdl

High-class ex-French hurdler; he won twice over two miles in heavy ground at Auteuil over hurdles and fences; failed to develop over fences in this country and successfully returned to hurdles, gaining a sparkling victory in the Coral Cup at the 2002 Festival and followed up in the Aintree Hurdle; disappointing on his 2003 return; best over two and a half plus, he acts well on soft ground.

Ilton
97   78
4-y-o ch g Dr Devious (IRE)-Madame Crecy (USA) (Al Nasr (FR))
M E Sowersby (J D Bethell 26/8) R D Seldon

Placings:PF4530P   (4352)
2002/03: 16PGS, 16FG, 16AGS, 20SGS, 173HY, 16QG, 16PGF,

	Starts	1st	2nd	3rd	Win & Pl
Hurdles	7	0	0	1	2102
Career Total	7	0	0	1	2102

Going: Sf: 0-1 GS: 0-3 Gd: 0-0 GF: - Fm: 0-1
Distance: 2m/2m3: 0-6 2m4-2m7: 0-1 3m+: 0-0
Track: LH: 0-7 RH: 0-0 Tight: 0-1 Gall: 0-1
Aids: Bl: 0-0 Vi: 0-0 Tstrap: 0-0
Best Rating: 81 11/02 Weth 2m gd-sft Hdl

Moderate Flat performer, yet to show much over hurdles.

Image De Marque II (FR)
108   128
7-y-o b m Royal Charter (FR)-Tourbrune (FR) (Pamponi (FR))
M C Pipe D A Johnson

Placings:2F/210222FF/PP041111223-6F00   (4549)
2002/03: 22GGS, 20FG, 17QG, 16QG,

		Starts	1st	2nd	3rd	Win & Pl	
Hurdles		4	0	0	0	414	
Career Total		25	5	7	1	63619	
131 11/01	Newb	2m5f	D(0-110)HHdl	G-S		£3696	
128 11/01	Tntn	2m1f	D(0-120)HHdl	G-S		£4777	
116 11/01	Winc	2m	F(0-100)HHdl	G-F		£2527	
116 11/01	Chel	2m110y	D(0-110)HHdl	GD		£9204	
6/00	Autl	2m4f110y	Ch	VS		£11527	
				Total win prize-money £31732			

Going: Sf: 0-0 GS: 0-1 Gd: 0-3 GF: - Fm: 0-0
Distance: 2m/2m3: 0-2 2m4-2m7: 0-0 3m+: 0-0
Track: LH: 0-3 RH: 0-0 Tight: 0-0 Gall: 0-1
Aids: Bl: 0-0 Vi: 0-0 Tstrap: 0-4
Best Rating: 135 12/01 Sand 2m110y soft Hdl

Very useful hurdler; effective from two to two miles five; acts on soft ground, but has won on a sound surface; often tongue tied.

Imaginaire (USA)
98   125
8-y-o b g Quest For Fame-Hail The Dancer (USA) (Green Dancer (USA))
Miss Venetia Williams Miss J Davies,L Jakeman,W Fenn

Placings:P66/00243406P/02200125/33214F-43B34 (3136)
2002/03: 16AGF, 16QG, 21BG, 20QGS, 20AS,

		Starts	1st	2nd	3rd	Win & Pl	
Chases		5	0	0	2	3031	
Career Total		31	2	5		65959	
129 3/02	Strf	2m4f	D Ch	G-S		£5284	
120 1/01	Folk	2m6f110yE Hdl		HVY		£2744	
				Total win prize-money £8029			

Going: Sf: 0-1 GS: 0-1 Gd: 0-2 GF: - Fm: 0-1
Distance: 2m/2m3: 0-2 2m4-2m7: 0-3 3m+: 0-0
Track: LH: 0-2 RH: 0-3 Tight: 0-1 Gall: 0-1
Aids: Bl: 0-0 Vi: 0-0 Tstrap: 0-0
Best Rating: 129 3/02 Strf 2m4f gd-sft Ch

Fair ex-French chaser. Suited by two and a half miles and easy ground over fences. Unlucky when brought down at Cheltenham in December.

Imago Ii (FR)
87 (96h)   (102h) 98
7-y-o b g Chamberlin (FR)-Pensee D Amour (FR) (Porto Rafti (FR))
Jonjo O Neill Tony Eaves

Placings:1/340-P06   (2774)
2002/03: 22PGS, 24QGS, 22BS,

		Starts	1st	2nd	3rd	Win & Pl	
Chases		3	0	0	0	0	
Career Total		7	1	0	1	2754	
110 2/01	Hayd	2m	H NHF	SFT		£2159	
				Total win prize-money £2160			

Going: Sf: 0-1 GS: 0-2 Gd: 0-0 GF: - Fm: 0-0
Distance: 2m/2m3: 0-0 2m4-2m7: 0-2 3m+: 0-1
Track: LH: 0-1 RH: 0-2 Tight: 0-1 Gall: 0-2
Aids: Bl: 0-1 Vi: 0-0 Tstrap: 0-0
Best Rating: 110 2/01 Hayd 2m soft NHF

A Haydock bumper winner, he showed only moderate form over hurdles and has been let down by his jumping over fences so far.

Immola (FR)
93   100+
7-y-o b/br g Quart De Vin (FR)-Jessica (FR) (Laniste)
Miss E C Lavelle Mrs Sarah Stevens

Placings:0451   (4051)
2002/03: 16QHY, 16AHY, 16SHY, 16THY,

	Starts	1st	2nd	3rd	Win & Pl	
NH Flat	2	0	0	0		
Hurdles	2	1	0	0	4908	
Career Total	4	1	0	0	4908	
100 3/03	Sand	2m110y	D Hdl	HVY	£4907
			Total win prize-money £4908		

Going: Sf: 1-4 GS: 0-0 Gd: 0-0 GF: - Fm: 0-0
Distance: 2m/2m3: 1-4 2m4-2m7: 0-0 3m+: 0-0
Track: LH: 0-2 RH: 1-2 Tight: 0-1 Gall: 0-1
Aids: Bl: 0-0 Vi: 0-0 Tstrap: 0-0
Best Rating: 100 3/03 Sand 2m110y heavy Hdl

Moderate hurdler; acts on testing ground.

Imnotalady
5-y-o ch m Shalford (IRE)-Lissahane Lass (Daring March)
P R Hedger J J Whelan

Placings:4-65   (2662)
2002/03: 13GS, 18SS,

	Starts	1st	2nd	3rd	Win & Pl
NH Flat	1	0	0	0	0
Hurdles	1	0	0	0	0
Career Total	3	0	0	0	0

Going: Sf: 0-2 GS: 0-0 Gd: 0-0 GF: - Fm: 0-0
Distance: 2m/2m3: 0-1 2m4-2m7: 0-0 3m+: 0-0
Track: LH: 0-1 RH: 0-1 Tight: 0-1 Gall: 0-0
Aids: Bl: 0-0 Vi: 0-0 Tstrap: 0-0
Best Rating: 74 12/02 Extr 1m5f soft NHF

Impala
81   55
9-y-o ch g Interrex (CAN)-Raleigh Gazelle (Absalom)
W G M Turner Mrs Aileen Croft

Placings:50262/4000/2660/21313304/B0PPPP   (1158)
2002/03: 16BG, 16QGF, 16PGF, 17SGF, 17PGF, 17PG,

		Starts	1st	2nd	3rd	Win & Pl	
Hurdles		6	0	0	0		
Career Total		27	2	4	3	12240	
102 8/00	NAbb	2m1f	E Hdl	GD		£2749	
107 7/00	Strf	2m110y	F(0-110)HHdl	G-F		£2873	
				Total win prize-money £5623			

Going: Sf: 0-0 GS: 0-0 Gd: 0-0 GF: - Fm: 0-4
Distance: 2m/2m3: 0-6 2m4-2m7: 0-0 3m+: 0-0
Track: LH: 0-6 RH: 0-0 Tight: 0-5 Gall: 0-0
Aids: Bl: 0-0 Vi: 0-0 Tstrap: 0-1
Best Rating: 107 9/00 Plum 2m good Hdl

Impek (FR)
119 (122h)   (153h) 158
7-y-o b g Lute Antique (FR)-Attualita (FR) (Master Thatch)
Miss H C Knight Jim Lewis

Placings:2150/24423-11123   (4477)
2002/03: 16TG, 16TG, 16TS, 16QG, 16QG,

		Starts	1st	2nd	3rd	Win & Pl	
Chases		5	3	1		69154	
Career Total		14	4	4	2	98001	
158 12/02	Sand	2m	A Ch	SFT		£20100	
148 11/02	Hrfd	2m	E Ch	GD		£4199	
128 5/02	Hntg	2m110y	E Ch	GD		£3055	
131 2/01	Ludl	2m	E Hdl	G-S		£3006	
				Total win prize-money £30361			

Going: Sf: 1-1 GS: 0-0 Gd: 2-4 GF: - Fm: 0-0
Distance: 2m/2m3: 3-5 2m4-2m7: 0-0 3m+: 0-0
Track: LH: 0-2 RH: 3-3 Tight: 0-1 Gall: 1-2
Aids: Bl: 0-0 Vi: 0-0 Tstrap: 0-0
Best Rating: 158 12/02 Sand 2m soft Ch

Very useful novice chaser; formerly useful hurdler; winner of first three chases, including comprehensive defeat of Le Roi Miguel in Grade 2 novices chase at Sandown; creditable runner-up to Azertyuiop in Arkle at Cheltenham but below best when soundly beaten by Le Roi Miguel in Grade 1 novices chase at Aintree (possibly not as effective on faster ground and hung right); suited by a strongly run race over 2m and should appreciate farther; acts on good and soft ground; needs to be led in at the start and generally reported to be not that straightforward a horse who dislikes being crowded in big fields.

Imperial De Thaix (FR)

101(106h)   (95h)

7-y-o b g Roi De Rome (USA)-Soiree D Ete (FR) (Prove It Baby (USA))
M C Pipe J S Lammiman

Placings:16411PF/F1-032P000P   (4387)
2002/03: 23⁰G, 23³G, 26⁴HY, 25⁹GS, 21⁰S, 24⁰GS, 21⁹G, 22⁸F,

	Starts	1st	2nd	3rd	Win & Pl
Hurdles	5	0	0	0	
Chases	3	0	1	1	3339
Career Total	17	4	1	1	26257

125 4/02 Chel 2m5f110yB HHdl   G-F £10452
120 1/01 Chep 3m   E Ch   G-S £2960
141 12/00 Chep 2m3f110yD Ch   SFT £3838
   10/00 Nant 2m1f110y Hdl   HVY £3362
     Total win prize-money £20613

Going:	Sf: 0-2 GS: 0-2 Gd: 0-3 GF: - Fm: 0-1
Distance:	2m/2m3: 0-0 2m4-2m7: 0-3 3m+: 0-5
Track:	LH: 0-3 RH: 0-5 Tight: 0-1 Gall: 0-1
Aids:	Bl: 0-0 Vi: 0-0 Tstrap: 0-5
Best Rating:	141 12/00 Chep 2m3f110y soft Ch

A fair hurdler, he is quite useful over fences; stays beyond three miles; acts on any ground; often wears a tongue tie.

Imperial Dream (IRE)

101f   **95f**

5-y-o b g Roselier (FR)-Royal Nora (IRE) (Dromod Hill)
Miss H C Knight Hogarth Racing

Placings:22   (4322)
2002/03: 16²G, 17²G,

	Starts	1st	2nd	3rd	Win & Pl
NH Flat	2	0	2	0	1174
Career Total	2	0	2	0	1174

Going:	Sf: 0-0 GS: 0-0 Gd: 0-2 GF: - Fm: 0-0
Distance:	2m/2m3: 0-2 2m4-2m7: 0-0 3m+: 0-0
Track:	LH: 0-1 RH: 0-1 Tight: 0-1 Gall: 0-1
Aids:	Bl: 0-0 Vi: 0-0 Tstrap: 0-0
Best Rating:	95 3/03 Bang 2m1f good NHF

Moderate form in bumpers on good ground.

Imperial Eye (IRE)

5-y-o b m Eagle Eyed (USA)-Capellino (IRE) (Imperial Frontier (USA))
John R Upson Mrs Diane Upson

Placings:P   (0800)
2002/03: 17ᴾS,

	Starts	1st	2nd	3rd	Win & Pl
Hurdles	1	0	0	0	
Career Total	1	0	0	0	

Going:	Sf: 0-1 GS: 0-0 Gd: 0-0 GF: - Fm: 0-0
Distance:	2m/2m3: 0-1 2m4-2m7: 0-0 3m+: 0-0
Track:	LH: 0-0 RH: 0-1 Tight: 0-1 Gall: 0-0
Aids:	Bl: 0-0 Vi: 0-0 Tstrap: 0-0
Best Rating:	0 7/02 MRas 2m1f110y soft Hdl

Imperial Honors (IRE)

12-y-o ch g Crowning Honors (CAN)-Within A Whisper (Welsh Pageant)
N M Lampard Miss Z L Urquhart

Placings:00/04P05/6P/05   (4147)
2002/03: 16⁰GS, 21⁵G,

	Starts	1st	2nd	3rd	Win & Pl
Chases	2	0	0	0	0
Career Total	11	0	0	0	0

Going:	Sf: 0-0 GS: 0-1 Gd: 0-1 GF: - Fm: 0-0
Distance:	2m/2m3: 0-1 2m4-2m7: 0-1 3m+: 0-0
Track:	LH: 0-1 RH: 0-1 Tight: 0-1 Gall: 0-0
Aids:	Bl: 0-0 Vi: 0-0 Tstrap: 0-0
Best Rating:	73 2/96 Asct 2m110y soft NHF

Imperial Line (IRE)

9-y-o ch g Mac s Imp (USA)-Ellaline (Corvaro (USA))
Mrs P A Cowey Mrs P A Cowey

Placings:00/062   (0503)
2002/03: 25⁰GF, 20⁶GF, 26²G,

	Starts	1st	2nd	3rd	Win & Pl
Chases	3	0	1	0	708
Career Total	5	0	1	0	708

Going:	Sf: 0-0 GS: 0-0 Gd: 0-1 GF: - Fm: 0-2
Distance:	2m/2m3: 0-0 2m4-2m7: 0-1 3m+: 0-2
Track:	LH: 0-3 RH: 0-0 Tight: 0-1 Gall: 0-0
Aids:	Bl: 0-0 Vi: 0-0 Tstrap: 0-2
Best Rating:	77 6/02 Ctml 3m2f good Ch

Ex-pointer; runner-up in maiden hunter chase on good ground; stays three miles two.

Imperial Man (IRE)

(72c)   (70c)

8-y-o b g Mandalus-The Foalicule (Imperial Fling (USA))
P Spottiswood P Spottiswood

Placings:3/0000000450/060060F45F05P-0   (4616)
2002/03: 17⁰GF,

	Starts	1st	2nd	3rd	Win & Pl
Hurdles	1	0	0	0	
Career Total	25	0	0	1	440

Going:	Sf: 0-0 GS: 0-0 Gd: 0-0 GF: - Fm: 0-1
Distance:	2m/2m3: 0-1 2m4-2m7: 0-0 3m+: 0-0
Track:	LH: 0-0 RH: 0-1 Tight: 0-0 Gall: 0-0
Aids:	Bl: 0-0 Vi: 0-0 Tstrap: 0-0
Best Rating:	92 12/00 Clon 2m sft-hvy NHF

Imperial Mist (IRE)

                    67

9-y-o br g Royal Fountain-Mossy Mistress (IRE) (Le Moss)
K F Clutterbuck K F Clutterbuck

Placings:3   (0321)
2002/03: 26³G,

	Starts	1st	2nd	3rd	Win & Pl
Chases	1	0	0	1	485
Career Total	1	0	0	1	485

Going:	Sf: 0-0 GS: 0-0 Gd: 0-1 GF: - Fm: 0-0
Distance:	2m/2m3: 0-0 2m4-2m7: 0-0 3m+: 0-1
Track:	LH: 0-1 RH: 0-0 Tight: 0-0 Gall: 0-0
Aids:	Bl: 0-0 Vi: 0-0 Tstrap: 0-0
Best Rating:	67 5/02 Uttx 3m2f good Ch

Point winner, distant third in a novice chase in May 2002.

Imperial Sho

                    23f

4-y-o ch g Royal Abjar (USA)-Magnetic Point (USA) (Bering)
J R Weymes White Rose Poultry Ltd

Placings:0   (2142)
2002/03: 14⁰GS,

	Starts	1st	2nd	3rd	Win & Pl
NH Flat	1	0	0	0	
Career Total	1	0	0	0	

Going:	Sf: 0-0 GS: 0-1 Gd: 0-0 GF: - Fm: 0-0
Distance:	2m/2m3: 0-0 2m4-2m7: 0-0 3m+: 0-0
Track:	LH: 0-1 RH: 0-0 Tight: 0-0 Gall: 0-0
Aids:	Bl: 0-0 Vi: 0-0 Tstrap: 0-0
Best Rating:	23 11/02 Newc 1m6f gd-sft NHF

Impero

72   **33**

5-y-o b g Emperor Jones (USA)-Fight Right (FR) (Crystal Glitters (USA))
R J Armson R J Armson

Placings:565P0-PPP   (4525)
2002/03: 19ᴾGS, 19ᴾGS, 16ᴾG,

	Starts	1st	2nd	3rd	Win & Pl
Hurdles	3	0	0	0	
Career Total	8	0	0	0	0

Going:	Sf: 0-0 GS: 0-2 Gd: 0-1 GF: - Fm: 0-0
Distance:	2m/2m3: 0-0 2m4-2m7: 0-1 3m+: 0-0
Track:	LH: 0-3 RH: 0-0 Tight: 0-0 Gall: 0-0
Aids:	Bl: 0-0 Vi: 0-0 Tstrap: 0-0
Best Rating:	69 10/01 Weth 2m good Hdl

Impertio

102   **108**

9-y-o b g Primitive Rising (USA)-Silly Beggar (Silly Prices)
P Beaumont Mrs S Sunter

Placings:4542/36632633233/422F22331/0322U31U20P-4403323P   (4765)
2002/03: 26⁴S, 25⁴S, 27⁰GS, 24³HY, 24³S, 24²S, 24³GS, 31ᴾG,

	Starts	1st	2nd	3rd	Win & Pl
Chases	8	0	1	3	5823
Career Total	43	2	11	13	33116

114 2/02 Leic 2m7f110yD(0-125)HCh   SFT £7150
114 4/01 Prth 2m   D Ch   HVY £3698
     Total win prize-money £10849

Going:	Sf: 0-5 GS: 0-2 Gd: 0-1 GF: - Fm: 0-0
Distance:	2m/2m3: 0-0 2m4-2m7: 0-0 3m+: 0-8
Track:	LH: 0-6 RH: 0-1 Tight: 0-3 Gall: 0-3
Aids:	Bl: 0-0 Vi: 0-0 Tstrap: 0-0
Best Rating:	114 3/02 Sthl 3m110y heavy Ch

Modest chaser, stays three miles; suited by soft ground; does not win very often; likes to be held up.

Impetus (GER)

80   **79**

7-y-o b g Lomitas-Ile De Re (GER) (Readily (ARG))
P Wegmann P Wegmann

Placings:22P000/3-000   (1089)
2002/03: 16⁰S, 17⁰GF, 16⁰GF,

	Starts	1st	2nd	3rd	Win & Pl
Hurdles	3	0	0	0	
Career Total	10	0	2	1	1700

Going:	Sf: 0-1 GS: 0-0 Gd: 0-0 GF: - Fm: 0-2
Distance:	2m/2m3: 0-3 2m4-2m7: 0-0 3m+: 0-0
Track:	LH: 0-2 RH: 0-1 Tight: 0-1 Gall: 0-1
Aids:	Bl: 0-0 Vi: 0-0 Tstrap: 0-0
Best Rating:	79 5/01 Bang 2m1f gd-sft Hdl

Impinda (IRE)

92f   **79f**

4-y-o b f Idris (IRE)-Last Finale (USA) (Stop The Music
(USA))
P Monteith Mrs A F Tullie

Placings:300   (3775)
2002/03: 14³GS, 16⁰G, 16⁰GS,

	Starts	1st	2nd	3rd	Win & Pl
NH Flat	3	0	0	1	378
Career Total	3	0	0	1	378

Going:	Sf: 0-0 GS: 0-2 Gd: 0-1 GF: - Fm: 0-0
Distance:	2m/2m3: 0-2 2m4-2m7: 0-0 3m+: 0-0
Track:	LH: 0-2 RH: 0-1 Tight: 0-1 Gall: 0-0
Aids:	Bl: 0-0 Vi: 0-0 Tstrap: 0-2
Best Rating:	79 11/02 Newc 1m6f gd-sft NHF

Finished third to a good sort on debut.

Impish Jude

111   **100**

5-y-o b m Imp Society (USA)-Miss Nanna (Vayrann)
J Mackie P A Bartlett

Placings:031020   (3814)
2002/03: 16⁰GS, 16³HY, 17¹S, 16⁰GS, 17²G, 16⁰G,

	Starts	1st	2nd	3rd	Win & Pl
Hurdles	6	1	1	1	3437
Career Total	6	1	1	1	3437
100 12/02 Hrfd 2m1f   G Hdl   SFT £2065
Total win prize-money £2065

Going:	Sf: 1-2 GS: 0-2 Gd: 0-2 GF: - Fm: 0-0
Distance:	2m/2m3: 1-6 2m4-2m7: 0-0 3m+: 0-0
Track:	LH: 0-3 RH: 1-3 Tight: 0-1 Gall: 0-1
Aids:	Bl: 0-0 Vi: 0-0 Tstrap: 0-0
Best Rating:	100 2/03 Hrfd 2m1f good Hdl

Moderate hurdler; effective at two miles; handles good and
heavy ground.

Impish Lad

74   **66**

5-y-o b g Imp Society (USA)-Madonna Da Rossi (Mtoto)
D W Whillans Chas N Whillans

Placings:4F5PP-0   (0375)
2002/03: 16⁰G,

	Starts	1st	2nd	3rd	Win & Pl
Hurdles	1	0	0	0	
Career Total	6	0	0	0	0

| Going: | Sf: 0-0 GS: 0-1 Gd: 1-4 GF: - Fm: 0-1 |

Going:	Sf: 0-0 GS: 0-0 Gd: 0-1 GF: - Fm: 0-0
Distance:	2m/2m3: 0-1 2m4-2m7: 0-0 3m+: 0-0
Track:	LH: 0-1 RH: 0-0 Tight: 0-1 Gall: 0-0
Aids:	Bl: 0-0 Vi: 0-0 Tstrap: 0-0
Best Rating:	66 2/02 Muss 2m soft Hdl

Important Boy (ARG)

89   **74**

6-y-o ch g Equalize (USA)-Important Girl (ARG) (Candy
Stripes (USA))
J A B Old W E Sturt

Placings:0603P   (1620)
2002/03: 16⁰GF, 17⁵G, 16⁰GS, 16³F, 21⁰PF,

	Starts	1st	2nd	3rd	Win & Pl
Hurdles	5	0	0	1	434
Career Total	5	0	0	1	434

Going:	Sf: 0-0 GS: 0-1 Gd: 0-1 GF: - Fm: 0-3
Distance:	2m/2m3: 0-4 2m4-2m7: 0-1 3m+: 0-0
Track:	LH: 0-2 RH: 0-3 Tight: 0-1 Gall: 0-0
Aids:	Bl: 0-0 Vi: 0-0 Tstrap: 0-0
Best Rating:	77 10/02 Winc 2m firm Hdl

Imprevue (IRE)

102   **79+**

9-y-o ch m Priolo (USA)-Las Bela (Welsh Pageant)
R J O Sullivan P W Saunders

Placings:60/0-14   (1040)
2002/03: 20¹GF, 20⁴GF,

	Starts	1st	2nd	3rd	Win & Pl
Hurdles	2	1	0	0	1992
Career Total	5	1	0	0	1992
79 7/02 Worc 2m4f   G(0-90)HHdl   G-F £1991
Total win prize-money £1992

Going:	Sf: 0-0 GS: 0-0 Gd: 0-0 GF: - Fm: 1-2
Distance:	2m/2m3: 0-0 2m4-2m7: 1-2 3m+: 0-0
Track:	LH: 1-1 RH: 0-0 Tight: 0-0 Gall: 0-0
Aids:	Bl: 1-2 Vi: 0-0 Tstrap: 0-0
Best Rating:	79 8/02 Font 2m4f gd-fm Hdl

Appreciated a combination of a drop in class and fast
ground when winning a two and a half mile selling hurdle at
Worcester July 2002.

In Contrast (IRE)

(123h)   (154 h)

7-y-o b/br g Be My Native (USA)-Ballinamona Lady (IRE)
(Le Bavard (FR))
P J Hobbs Tony Staple

Placings:2/2110/211F311-3F3461   (4555)
2002/03: 16³GF, 16FGS, 21³G, 16⁴G, 16⁰G, 16¹G,

	Starts	1st	2nd	3rd	Win & Pl
Hurdles	6	1	2	2	42016
Career Total	18	7	3	3	128521
153 4/03 Ayr   2m   A HHdl   GD £24800
144 4/02 Chel 2m5f110yB Hdl   G-F £19500
151 4/02 Aint 2m110y A Hdl   GD £29000
137 12/01 Newb 2m110y D Hdl   GD £4914
117 12/01 Chel 2m1f   B Hdl   GD £8697
142 11/00 Chel 2m110y B NHF   G-S £7670
113 10/00 Chel 2m110y H NHF   GD £2964
Total win prize-money £97545

| Going: | Sf: 0-0 GS: 0-1 Gd: 1-4 GF: - Fm: 0-1 |

Distance:	2m/2m3: 1-5 2m4-2m7: 0-1 3m+: 0-0
Track:	LH: 1-5 RH: 0-0 Tight: 0-0 Gall: 0-2
Aids:	Bl: 0-0 Vi: 0-0 Tstrap: 0-0
Best Rating:	154 3/03 Chel 2m110y good Hdl

Very useful hurdler; won four times in the 2001/02 season
and finished third in the Supreme Novices Hurdle at
Cheltenham; creditable staying-on 4th in the 2003 Tote Gold
Trophy at Newbury and a most creditable 6th in the
Champion Hurdle; had conditions to suit when winning the
Scottish Champion Hurdle at Ayr; effective from 2m to 2m
5f; suffering from hip injury when pulled-up after the first on
his chasing debut at Stratford in May; does not want the
ground too soft; tends to hang left and needs a left-handed
track.

In Extremis Ii (FR)

95(105h)   (95h)**95**

7-y-o b g Useful (FR)-Princesa Real (FR) (Garde Royale)
G M Moore Mrs I I Plumb

Placings:25/540P/5P6P0F2-125323220   (1611)
2002/03: 21¹GF, 20²G, 22⁵G, 21³GF, 21²G, 21³GF, 21²G, 20²GF,
23⁰G,

	Starts	1st	2nd	3rd	Win & Pl
Hurdles	9	1	4	2	7069
Career Total	22	1	6	2	8550
95 5/02 Sedg 2m5f110yE(0-100)HHdl   G-F £2632
Total win prize-money £2632

Going:	Sf: 0-0 GS: 0-0 Gd: 0-5 GF: - Fm: 1-4
Distance:	2m/2m3: 0-0 2m4-2m7: 1-8 3m+: 0-1
Track:	LH: 1-8 RH: 0-1 Tight: 1-5 Gall: 0-0
Aids:	Bl: 0-1 Vi: 0-0 Tstrap: 0-0
Best Rating:	95 10/02 Carl 2m4f gd-fm Hdl

Modest hurdler, stays three miles; has achieved little over
fences so far despite finishing runner-up at Wetherby in
May; best on fast ground.

In Good Faith

101(98c)   (82c)**82**

11-y-o b g Beveled (USA)-Dulcidene (Behistoun)
R E Barr P Cartmell

Placings:02240/4F/41P5/4110/23236514331165256 4/4351
115125P0/055045440650   (2516)
2002/03: 16⁰GF, 16⁰G, 16⁵S, 17⁰GF, 16⁴GF, 16⁵GF, 21⁴GF, 16⁴G,
16⁰G, 16⁴HY, 16⁵GS, 16⁰S,

	Starts	1st	2nd	3rd	Win & Pl
Hurdles	8	0	0	0	278
Chases	4	0	0	0	544
Career Total	57	10	6	5	38655
129 8/00 Sthl 2m   C(0-130)HHdl   G-F £4793
125 7/00 Uttx 2m   C(0-130)HHdl   G-F £5044
119 6/00 Hexm 2m   F(0-115)HHdl   G-F £2363
117 6/00 Hexm 2m   F(0-105)HHdl   G-F £2187
110 12/99 Hexm 2m   D(0-125)HHdl   HVY £3106
110 11/99 Newc 2m   E(0-130)HHdl   GD £2872
110 10/99 Sthl 2m   F(0-110)HHdl   G-S £2284
104 4/99 Hexm 2m   E(0-115)HHdl   GD £2586
93 4/99 Sedg 2m1f   E(0-115)HHdl   FRM £2337
95 5/97 Ctml 2m1f110yE Hdl   G-F £2318
Total win prize-money £29896

Going:	Sf: 0-3 GS: 0-1 Gd: 0-3 GF: - Fm: 0-5
Distance:	2m/2m3: 0-11 2m4-2m7: 0-1 3m+: 0-0
Track:	LH: 0-10 RH: 0-2 Tight: 0-2 Gall: 0-2
Aids:	Bl: 0-0 Vi: 0-0 Tstrap: 0-0
Best Rating:	129 8/00 Uttx 2m gd-fm Hdl

Has won 11 times over hurdles, latest selling handicap at
Cartmel in May; moderate maiden over fences and time is
not on his side.

In Question

75(102h)   (121h)**128d**
9-y-o b g Deploy-Questionable (Rainbow Quest (USA))
Ian Williams   Favourites Racing & Mrs V Griffiths

Placings:116F/1F/1F2P/012P-23F0   **(2105)**
2002/03: 20²GF, 21³GF, 19²G, 20⁴GS,

	Starts	1st	2nd	3rd	Win & Pl
Hurdles	3	0	1	1	1151
Chases	1	0	0	0	
Career Total	**18**	**5**	**3**	**1**	**26323**
121	9/01	Hntg	2m4f110yC(0-135)HCh	GD	£6691
117	12/00	Ludl	2m4f	E(0-115)HCh	G-S	£5590
100	11/99	Leic	2m	E Ch	G-F	£3327
140	2/99	Ludl	2m	E Hdl	GD	£2052
99	10/98	Kels	2m2f	E Hdl	G-S	£2430

Total win prize-money £20090

Going:	Sf: 0-0 GS: 0-1 Gd: 0-1 GF: - Fm: 0-2
Distance:	2m/2m3: 0-0 2m4-2m7: 0-4 3m+: 0-0
Track:	LH: 0-4 RH: 0-3 Tight: 0-1 Gall: 0-2
Aids:	Bl: 0-0 Vi: 0-0 Tstrap: 0-0
Best Rating:	140 2/99 Ludl 2m good Hdl

Fair hurdler/chaser when fresh; he is best on good ground or faster; has had his jumping problems however, and they resurfaced at Huntingdon in November.

In The Flow (USA)

89   **106**
6-y-o b g Irish River (FR)-In The Mood (USA) (Lyphard (USA))
P J Hobbs   Aramis Racing Syndicate

Placings:000440/102103-00   **(1158)**
2002/03: 16⁶G, 17⁹G,

	Starts	1st	2nd	3rd	Win & Pl
Hurdles	2	0	0	0	
Career Total	**14**	**2**	**1**	**1**	**7198**
106	6/01	Strf	2m110y	D(0-120)HHdl	G-F	£3536
106	5/01	Sthl	2m	F(0-95)HHdl	FRM	£2380

Total win prize-money £5916

Going:	Sf: 0-0 GS: 0-0 Gd: 0-2 GF: - Fm: 0-0
Distance:	2m/2m3: 0-2 2m4-2m7: 0-0 3m+: 0-0
Track:	LH: 0-2 RH: 0-0 Tight: 0-1 Gall: 0-0
Aids:	Bl: 0-0 Vi: 0-0 Tstrap: 0-0
Best Rating:	106 6/01 Strf 2m110y gd-fm Hdl

Decent hurdler, suited by fast ground and two miles.

In The Rough (IRE)

104(103h)   **101**
12-y-o b g Strong Gale-Cherry Dawn (Pollerton)
J A B Old   Mrs L R Lovell

Placings:1/4/0U/214/1531F/13U62-20   **(3946)**
2002/03: 25²H, 30⁶S,

	Starts	1st	2nd	3rd	Win & Pl
Hurdles	1	0	1	0	1590
Chases	1	0	0	0	0
Career Total	**19**	**5**	**3**	**2**	**26970**
117	11/01	NAbb	3m2f110yC(0-130)HCh	GD	£5944
112	2/01	Weth	3m1f	C(0-130)HHdl	SFT	£5411
103	5/00	Towc	3m	D Hdl	SFT	£3009
124	3/00	Chep	2m3f110yD Ch	G-S	£3737
93	3/96	Ludl	2m	H NHF	GD	£1346

Total win prize-money £19451

Going:	Sf: 0-2 GS: 0-0 Gd: 0-0 GF: - Fm: 0-0
Distance:	2m/2m3: 0-0 2m4-2m7: 0-0 3m+: 0-2
Track:	LH: 0-1 RH: 0-1 Tight: 0-1 Gall: 0-0
Aids:	Bl: 0-0 Vi: 0-0 Tstrap: 0-0

Best Rating: 124 3/00   Chep   2m3f110y gd-sft   Ch

Fair chaser; stays three and a quarter miles; acts on soft ground, but handles good.

Inaki (FR)

106   **105**
6-y-o b g Dounba (FR)-Incredule (FR) (Concertino (FR))
P Winkworth   Robert Scott & Partners

Placings:P0P046F13F00F/005F43444-561522   **(4145)**
2002/03: 17⁵GS, 16⁶G, 20¹S, 20⁵HY, 20²GS, 21²G,

	Starts	1st	2nd	3rd	Win & Pl
Chases	6	1	2	0	7646
Career Total	**28**	**2**	**2**	**2**	**18724**
105	1/03	Plum	2m4f	E(0-105)HCh	SFT	£4065
	1/01	Pau	2m1f	Ch	HLD	£3880

Total win prize-money £7946

Going:	Sf: 1-2 GS: 0-2 Gd: 0-2 GF: - Fm: 0-0
Distance:	2m/2m3: 0-2 2m4-2m7: 1-0 3m+: 0-0
Track:	LH: 1-4 RH: 0-2 Tight: 1-5 Gall: 0-0
Aids:	Bl: 0-0 Vi: 0-2 Tstrap: 0-0
Best Rating:	105 3/03 Fknm 2m5f110y good Ch

Winning chaser in France; got off the mark in Britain over two and a half miles at Plumpton in January 2003; acts on soft ground; has worn visor.

Inca Trail (IRE)

107   **132**
7-y-o br g Un Desperado (FR)-Katday (FR) (Miller s Mate)
Miss H C Knight   Philip F Myerscough

Placings:1-3210P   **(4462)**
2002/03: 16³GS, 16²S, 21¹S, 16⁹G, 20⁹G,

	Starts	1st	2nd	3rd	Win & Pl
NH Flat	1	0	0	1	2005
Hurdles	4	1	0	0	5522
Career Total	**6**	**2**	**1**	**1**	**11336**
115	1/03	Ludl	2m5f	E Hdl	SFT	£3737
120	1/02	Naas	2m	NHF	YLD	£3809

Total win prize-money £7548

Going:	Sf: 1-2 GS: 0-1 Gd: 0-2 GF: - Fm: 0-0
Distance:	2m/2m3: 0-3 2m4-2m7: 1-2 3m+: 0-0
Track:	LH: 0-3 RH: 1-2 Tight: 0-1 Gall: 0-0
Aids:	Bl: 0-0 Vi: 0-0 Tstrap: 0-0
Best Rating:	132 3/03 Chel 2m110y good Hdl

Useful novice hurdler; brother to Best Mate; bumper winner and has shown plenty of promise in two starts over hurdles, latter a victory in moderate company at Ludlow; stays 2m 5f, but probably better over shorter; effective with some cut in the ground.

Inch Perfect

101(110c)   (105c)**97**
8-y-o b g Inchinor-Scarlet Veil (Tyrnavos)
R A Fahey   J J Staunton

Placings:PP/36/42123   **(4521)**
2002/03: 16⁴G, 16²HY, 16¹S, 16²GF, 17³G,

	Starts	1st	2nd	3rd	Win & Pl
Hurdles	3	0	1	1	1879
Chases	2	1	1	0	6631
Career Total	**9**	**1**	**2**	**2**	**9019**
105	3/03	Catt	2m	D Ch	SFT	£5395

Total win prize-money £5395

Going:	Sf: 1-2 GS: 0-0 Gd: 0-2 GF: - Fm: 0-1
Distance:	2m/2m3: 1-5 2m4-2m7: 0-0 3m+: 0-0
Track:	LH: 1-5 RH: 0-0 Tight: 1-3 Gall: 0-0

Aids: Bl: 0-0 Vi: 0-0 Tstrap: 0-0
Best Rating: 105 3/03   Weth   2m   gd-fm   Ch

Modest novice hurdler/chaser, prolific winner in the past on the Flat; made an impressive chasing bow in a weak event at Catterick in March and runner-up at Wetherby two weeks later; returned to hurdles to finish third at Sedgefield in April; suited by some cut.

Inch Way (IRE)

81   **67**
11-y-o br g Kambalda-Glenaveel (Furry Glen)
A J Lockwood   Highgreen Partnership

Placings:20/6052306/455531/2202P/PPU4-P6   **(3162)**
2002/03: 24²GS, 25⁶G,

	Starts	1st	2nd	3rd	Win & Pl
Chases	2	0	0	0	
Career Total	**26**	**1**	**5**	**2**	**6582**
85	4/00	Uttx	3m	G(0-90)HCh	HVY	£1946

Total win prize-money £1946

Going:	Sf: 0-0 GS: 0-1 Gd: 0-1 GF: - Fm: 0-0
Distance:	2m/2m3: 0-0 2m4-2m7: 0-0 3m+: 0-2
Track:	LH: 0-2 RH: 0-0 Tight: 0-1 Gall: 0-1
Aids:	Bl: 0-0 Vi: 0-0 Tstrap: 0-0
Best Rating:	89 3/99 Newc 3m good Ch

Moderate handicap chaser. Stays three miles, suited by soft ground.

Inching Closer

111   **149**
6-y-o b g Inchinor-Maiyaasah (Kris)
Jonjo O Neill   Mrs N L Spence

Placings:6/14010-110   **(4456)**
2002/03: 20¹GS, 25¹G, 24⁰G,

	Starts	1st	2nd	3rd	Win & Pl
Hurdles	3	2	0	0	41690
Career Total	**9**	**4**	**0**	**0**	**47609**
149	3/03	Chel	3m1f110yA HHdl	GD	£34860
140	2/03	Hayd	2m4f	C(0-130)HHdl	G-S	£6890
129	3/02	Sedg	3m3f110yD(0-120)HHdl	SFT	£3265
117	11/01	Uttx	2m6f110yE Hdl	SFT	£2653

Total win prize-money £47609

Going:	Sf: 0-0 GS: 1-1 Gd: 1-2 GF: - Fm: 0-0
Distance:	2m/2m3: 0-0 2m4-2m7: 1-1 3m+: 1-2
Track:	LH: 2-3 RH: 0-0 Tight: 0-1 Gall: 1-1
Aids:	Bl: 0-0 Vi: 0-0 Tstrap: 0-0
Best Rating:	149 3/03 Chel 3m1f110y good Hdl

Smart hurdler; effective from 2m 4f to 3m 1f; acts on good ground or softer; narrow winner of the Pertemps Final at the Cheltenham Festival in March 2003.

Incorporation

4-y-o b g In The Wings-Danishkada (Thatch (USA))
J K Price (R Charlton 6/8)   J K Price

Placings:P   **(2059)**
2002/03: 17⁶S,

	Starts	1st	2nd	3rd	Win & Pl
Hurdles	1	0	0	0	
Career Total	**1**	**0**	**0**	**0**	

Going:	Sf: 0-1 GS: 0-0 Gd: 0-0 GF: - Fm: 0-0
Distance:	2m/2m3: 0-1 2m4-2m7: 0-0 3m+: 0-0
Track:	LH: 0-0 RH: 0-1 Tight: 0-0 Gall: 0-0
Aids:	Bl: 0-0 Vi: 0-0 Tstrap: 0-0

Best Rating: 0   11/02 Hrfd 2m1f   soft   Hdl

Indalo (IRE)

109(111h)   (134h)126
8-y-o b g Lord Americo-Parsons Princess (The Parson)
Miss Venetia Williams Roa Arkle Partnership

Placings:301/523624544/3131135-124311533   (4792)
2002/03: 16¹G, 22²S, 17⁴GS, 20³S, 19¹S, 20¹GS, 21⁵S, 20³G, 20³G,

	Starts	1st	2nd	3rd	Win & Pl
Chases	9	3	1	3	33715
Career Total	28	7	3	8	57126

99	2/03	Plum	2m4f	D Ch		G-S	£6695
126	1/03	Tntn	2m3f	D(0-125)HCh	SFT	£6890
110	10/02	Hayd	2m	D Ch		GD	£6711
134	3/02	Hayd	2m6f	D Hdl		GD	£5096
127	3/02	Hrfd	2m3f110yE Hdl		GD	£2807
110	1/02	Leic	2m4f110yE Hdl		SFT	£3052
95	11/99	Fair	2m	NHF		SFT	£3850

Total win prize-money £35101

Going:	Sf: 1-4 GS: 1-2 Gd: 1-3 GF: - Fm: 0-0
Distance:	2m/2m3: 2-3 2m4-2m7: 1-6 3m+: 0-0
Track:	LH: 2-5 RH: 1-4 Tight: 2-3 Gall: 0-0
Aids:	Bl: 0-0 Vi: 0-0 Tstrap: 0-0
Best Rating:	134 3/02 Hayd 2m6f good Hdl

Decent hurdler/ novice chaser; keen sort, he stays two miles six and has a high cruising speed; won easily on chasing debut at Haydock in October 2002, but did not jump fluently; learning with experience, though; acts on good and soft ground.

Indecisive

55

8-y-o ch m Then Again-Nine Hans (Prince Hansel)
M J Coombe Mrs N M Coombe

Placings:0-0P   (3852)
2002/03: 22⁶S, 24ᴾGS,

	Starts	1st	2nd	3rd	Win & Pl
Hurdles	2	0	0	0	
Career Total	3	0	0	0	

Going:	Sf: 0-0 GS: 0-1 Gd: 0-0 GF: 0-0 Fm: 0-0
Distance:	2m/2m3: 0-0 2m4-2m7: 0-1 3m+: 0-1
Track:	LH: 0-1 RH: 0-1 Tight: 0-2 Gall: 0-0
Aids:	Bl: 0-0 Vi: 0-0 Tstrap: 0-0
Best Rating:	55 3/02 Extr 2m3f good Hdl

Indeed (IRE)

103(105h)   (109h)121+
8-y-o b g Camden Town-Pamrina (Pamroy)
J T Gifford Pell-Mell Partners

Placings:4F1-0F22   (4121)
2002/03: 18⁰G, 21ᶠGS, 20²GS, 20²G,

	Starts	1st	2nd	3rd	Win & Pl
Hurdles	1	0	0	0	0
Chases	3	1	2	0	3400
Career Total	7	1	2	0	8280
109	3/02	Sand	2m4f110yD Hdl		G-S	£4309

Total win prize-money £4310

Going:	Sf: 0-0 GS: 0-2 Gd: 0-2 GF: - Fm: 0-0
Distance:	2m/2m3: 0-1 2m4-2m7: 0-3 3m+: 0-0
Track:	LH: 0-1 RH: 0-3 Tight: 0-1 Gall: 0-1
Aids:	Bl: 0-0 Vi: 0-0 Tstrap: 0-0
Best Rating:	121 2/03 Kemp 2m4f110y gd-sft Ch

Showed ability before getting off the mark at Sandown in March 2002. Has shown fair form over fences. Suited by two and a half miles; acts on good or good to soft ground.

Indeed To Goodness (IRE)

109(104h)   (105h)115
8-y-o b m Welsh Term-Clare s Sheen (Choral Society)
J W Mullins Ian M McGready

Placings:0/433P43/013U3106-321UF3P   (3552)
2002/03: 19³G, 20²S, 26¹S, 19⁰GS, 20ᶠS, 26³HY, 26ᴾS,

	Starts	1st	2nd	3rd	Win & Pl
Hurdles	2	0	1	1	2162
Chases	5	1	0	1	6511
Career Total	22	3	1	7	20482

110	11/02	Plum	3m2f	D Ch		SFT	£5476
105	2/02	Kemp	2m5f	B HHdl		SFT	£6955
102	10/01	Font	2m6f110yE Hdl		G-S	£2513

Total win prize-money £14944

Going:	Sf: 1-5 GS: 0-1 Gd: 0-1 GF: - Fm: 0-0
Distance:	2m/2m3: 0-1 2m4-2m7: 0-3 3m+: 1-3
Track:	LH: 1-4 RH: 0-3 Tight: 1-5 Gall: 0-0
Aids:	Bl: 0-0 Vi: 0-0 Tstrap: 0-0
Best Rating:	115 1/03 Plum 3m2f heavy Ch

Fair hurdler/novice chase; stays well and acts on soft ground. Seemingly lost confidence over fences due to jumping errors.

Independence Hall (IRE)

98   87
6-y-o b g Sadler s Wells (USA)-Fruition (Rheingold)
J E Long Mick Robinson

Placings:60050   (3557)
2002/03: 17⁵GS, 22⁰HY, 22⁰HY, 22⁵HY, 22⁰HY,

	Starts	1st	2nd	3rd	Win & Pl
Hurdles	5	0	0	0	278
Career Total	5	0	0	0	278

Going:	Sf: 0-4 GS: 0-1 Gd: 0-0 GF: - Fm: 0-0
Distance:	2m/2m3: 0-1 2m4-2m7: 0-4 3m+: 0-0
Track:	LH: 0-1 RH: 0-4 Tight: 0-4 Gall: 0-0
Aids:	Bl: 0-0 Vi: 0-0 Tstrap: 0-0
Best Rating:	87 2/03 Sand 2m6f heavy Hdl

Indian Beat

105   75+
6-y-o ch g Indian Ridge-Rappa Tap Tap (FR) (Tap On Wood)
C L Popham Mrs C R Hayton

Placings:0-5P   (1154)
2002/03: 16⁵GF, 22ᴾG,

	Starts	1st	2nd	3rd	Win & Pl
Hurdles	2	0	0	0	0
Career Total	3	0	0	0	0

Going:	Sf: 0-0 GS: 0-0 Gd: 0-1 GF: - Fm: 0-0
Distance:	2m/2m3: 0-1 2m4-2m7: 0-1 3m+: 0-0
Track:	LH: 0-2 RH: 0-0 Tight: 0-1 Gall: 0-0
Aids:	Bl: 0-0 Vi: 0-0 Tstrap: 0-0
Best Rating:	71 2/02 Tntn 2m1f soft Hdl

Lightly raced selling hurdler.

Indian Chance

106   120
9-y-o b g Teenoso (USA)-Icy Miss (Random Shot)
Dr J R J Naylor Chris and Stella Watson And Jock Cullen

Placings:00/3F61311-P46   (3397)
2002/03: 25¹GS, 25ᴾGS, 25⁴GS, 24⁶HY,

	Starts	1st	2nd	3rd	Win & Pl
Chases	4	1	0	0	5647
Career Total	12	3	0	2	15558

120	4/02	Towc	3m1f	D(0-115)HCh	G-S	£4221
115	3/02	Winc	3m1f110yE(0-110)HCh	SFT	£5375
106	2/02	Leic	2m7f110yE(0-105)HCh	SFT	£3263

Total win prize-money £12861

Going:	Sf: 0-1 GS: 1-3 Gd: 0-0 GF: - Fm: 0-0
Distance:	2m/2m3: 0-0 2m4-2m7: 0-0 3m+: 1-4
Track:	LH: 0-0 RH: 1-4 Tight: 0-0 Gall: 0-0
Aids:	Bl: 0-0 Vi: 0-0 Tstrap: 0-0
Best Rating:	120 4/02 Towc 3m1f gd-sft Ch

Fair staying chaser; gets beyond three miles; acts on soft ground.

Indian Gunner

112   126
10-y-o b g Gunner B-Icy Miss (Random Shot)
Dr J R J Naylor Mrs S P Elphick

Placings:54/260P/21U-31P0110   (4472)
2002/03: 20³G, 16¹GS, 16ᴾS, 16⁰G, 21¹S, 25¹GF, 21⁰G,

	Starts	1st	2nd	3rd	Win & Pl
Chases	7	3	0	1	20781
Career Total	16	4	2	1	26812

126	3/03	Winc	3m1f110yE(0-110)HCh	G-F	£6760
123	3/03	Winc	2m5f	C(0-130)HCh	SFT	£8307
105	12/02	Winc	2m	D(0-115)HCh	G-S	£4982
86	12/01	Leic	2m	D(0-110)HCh	GD	£4127

Total win prize-money £24177

Going:	Sf: 1-2 GS: 1-1 Gd: 0-3 GF: - Fm: 1-1
Distance:	2m/2m3: 1-3 2m4-2m7: 1-3 3m+: 1-1
Track:	LH: 0-1 RH: 3-6 Tight: 0-1 Gall: 0-1
Aids:	Bl: 0-0 Vi: 0-0 Tstrap: 0-0
Best Rating:	126 3/03 Winc 3m1f110y gd-fm Ch

Fair handicap chaser; acts on good ground but is effective on soft; stays three miles one.

Indian Miss

11-y-o b m Idiots Delight-Icy Miss (Random Shot)
Dr J R J Naylor Dr J R J Naylor

Placings:00/12/4F4/0P-P   (0244)
2002/03: 25ᴾG,

	Starts	1st	2nd	3rd	Win & Pl
Chases	1	0	0	0	
Career Total	10	1	1	0	5968
101	12/98	Extr	2m3f	D Ch		SFT	£3622

Total win prize-money £3623

Going:	Sf: 0-0 GS: 0-0 Gd: 0-1 GF: - Fm: 0-0
Distance:	2m/2m3: 0-0 2m4-2m7: 0-0 3m+: 0-1
Track:	LH: 0-0 RH: 0-1 Tight: 0-0 Gall: 0-0
Aids:	Bl: 0-0 Vi: 0-0 Tstrap: 0-0
Best Rating:	114 2/99 Tntn 3m gd-sft Ch

Indian Scout (IRE)

109   136
8-y-o b g Phardante (FR)-Kemchee (Kemal (FR))

B De Haan Indian Scout Partnership

Placings:51U11P/**12F**   (3626)
2002/03: 20¹G, 21²S, 24FGS,

	Starts	1st	2nd	3rd	Win & Pl
Chases	3	1	1	0	17929
Career Total	9	4	1	0	35476
136 11/02 Hayd	2m4f	B Ch		GD	£16477
131 2/01 Uttx	2m4f110yA Hdl			HVY	£12000
131 1/01 Leic	2m4f110yE Hdl			HVY	£3272
109 12/00 Extr	2m1f	E Hdl		HVY	£2275

Total win prize-money £34026

Going:	Sf: 0-1 GS: 0-1 Gd: 1-1 GF: - Fm: 0-0
Distance:	2m/2m3: 0-0 **2m4-2m7: 1-2** 3m+: 0-1
Track:	**LH: 1-2** RH: 0-1 Tight: 0-0 Gall: 0-0
Aids:	Bl: 0-0 Vi: 0-0 Tstrap: 0-0
Best Rating:	**136** 11/02 Hayd 2m4f good Ch

Useful novice chaser; formerly very useful novice hurdler; best over two and a half miles; acts on good ground, but very much suited by testing conditions; likes to race prominently.

Indian Star (GER)

97   **84**

5-y-o br g Sternkoenig (IRE)-Indian Night (GER) (Windwurf (GER))
J C Tuck (P Schiergen 13/10) M Tuck

Placings:001   (4641)
2002/03: 16⁰G, 16⁰GF, 19¹GF,

	Starts	1st	2nd	3rd	Win & Pl
Hurdles	3	1	0	0	3010
Career Total	3	1	0	0	3010
87 4/03 Strf	2m3f	F Hdl		G-F	£3010

Total win prize-money £3010

Going:	Sf: 0-0 GS: 0-0 Gd: 0-1 GF: - Fm: 1-2
Distance:	**2m/2m3: 1-3** 2m4-2m7: 0-0 3m+: 0-0
Track:	**LH: 1-1** RH: 0-2 Tight: 1-1 Gall: 0-2
Aids:	Bl: 0-0 Vi: 0-0 Tstrap: 0-0
Best Rating:	**87** 4/03 Strf 2m3f gd-fm Hdl

Improved on first two efforts over hurdles when fortunate winner of 2m 3f maiden at Stratford April 2003.

Indian Sun

99   **83**

6-y-o ch g Indian Ridge-Star Tulip (Night Shift (USA))
R L Brown R L Brown

Placings:0-00P25F1   (4445)
2002/03: 16⁰G, 16⁰G, 17⁰G, 17²GS, 16⁵G, 16FHY, 16¹G,

	Starts	1st	2nd	3rd	Win & Pl
Hurdles	7	1	1	0	3834
Career Total	8	1	1	0	3834
77 4/03 Ludl	2m	G Hdl		GD	£3250

Total win prize-money £3250

Going:	Sf: 0-2 GS: 0-0 Gd: 1-5 GF: - Fm: 0-0
Distance:	**2m/2m3: 1-7** 2m4-2m7: 0-0 3m+: 0-0
Track:	LH: 0-3 **RH: 1-4** Tight: 0-1 Gall: 0-0
Aids:	Bl: 0-0 Vi: 0-0 **Tstrap: 1-6**
Best Rating:	**78** 2/03 Chep 2m1f10y heavy Hdl

Plating-class hurdler; won his first race for some time when scoring at Ludlow in early April.

Indian Temple

73(71h)   (42h)**72**

12-y-o g Minster Son-Indian Flower (Mansingh (USA))
K Bishop Derek Clarke

Placings:052F0204/2455/002643/421263PF2/221325451P4P5/4P5/0/00650-P0   (0555)
2002/03: 25PG, 25⁰GF,

	Starts	1st	2nd	3rd	Win & Pl
Chases	2	0	0	0	
Career Total	51	3	10	3	21378
89 10/98 Tntn	3m	D(0-120)HCh	FRM	£3857
93 9/98 Extr	3m3f110yE(0-110)HCh	FRM	£3178
81 10/97 Tntn	2m3f	F(0-95)HCh	FRM	£2595

Total win prize-money £9631

Going:	Sf: 0-0 GS: 0-0 Gd: 0-1 GF: - Fm: 0-1
Distance:	2m/2m3: 0-0 2m4-2m7: 0-0 3m+: 0-2
Track:	LH: 0-0 RH: 0-2 Tight: 0-0 Gall: 0-0
Aids:	Bl: 0-0 Vi: 0-0 Tstrap: 0-0
Best Rating:	**93** 5/98 Extr 2m3f110y firm Ch

Indian Venture (IRE)

102(109h)   (116h)**118**

9-y-o b g Commanche Run-Believe It Or Not (Quayside)
N G Richards Dr K S Fraser & Ashleybank Investments

Placings:10/0/31102321-4F42511   (4689)
2002/03: 16⁴G, 20FGF, 16⁴G, 16⁶G, 20⁵S, 16¹G, 17¹G,

	Starts	1st	2nd	3rd	Win & Pl
Chases	7	2	1	0	11627
Career Total	18	6	3	2	28033
110 4/03 MRas	2m1f110yD Ch		GD	£5414
104 3/03 Sedg	2m110y E Ch		GD	£4046
116 4/02 Prth	2m110y D(0-120)HHdl	GD	£5746
105 11/01 Kels	2m2f	F(0-110)HHdl	GD	£2257
96 10/01 Carl	2m	E Hdl	G-S	£2654
105 12/99 Muss	2m	H NHF	G-S	£1576

Total win prize-money £21695

Going:	Sf: 0-1 GS: 0-0 Gd: 2-5 GF: - Fm: 0-1
Distance:	**2m/2m3: 2-5** 2m4-2m7: 0-2 3m+: 0-0
Track:	LH: 1-1 RH: 1-6 Tight: **2-5** Gall: 0-0
Aids:	Bl: 0-0 Vi: 0-0 Tstrap: 0-0
Best Rating:	**116** 4/02 Prth 2m110y good Hdl

A bumper winner, he has done well in modest handicap hurdles in the north. Took a few attempts before scoring twice in the spring. Suited by two miles and the ground good or slightly softer.

Indian Viceroy

85

10-y-o b g Lord Bud-Poppadom (Rapid River)
P Winkworth Bill Naylor

Placings:0600000/04600/036/213/RU5-P0P   (3233)
2002/03: 19⁰G, 21⁰GF, 16PS,

	Starts	1st	2nd	3rd	Win & Pl
Chases	3	0	0	0	
Career Total	24	1	1	2	4759
90 11/00 Hntg	2m4f110yF(0-110)HCh	G-S	£2834

Total win prize-money £2834

Going:	Sf: 0-1 GS: 0-0 Gd: 0-1 GF: - Fm: 0-1
Distance:	2m/2m3: 0-1 2m4-2m7: 0-2 3m+: 0-0
Track:	LH: 0-2 RH: 0-1 Tight: 0-2 Gall: 0-0
Aids:	Bl: 0-0 Vi: 0-0 Tstrap: 0-0
Best Rating:	**90** 11/00 Hntg 2m4f110y gd-sft Ch

Indian Wings (IRE)

101(109h)   (117h)**86**

10-y-o b g Commanche Run-Got To Fly (IRE) (Kemal (FR))
A Scott Andy Scott

Placings:P62P0P/0P2112P5PP536-**2**   (1012)
2002/03: 16²G,

	Starts	1st	2nd	3rd	Win & Pl
Chases	1	0	1	0	1644
Career Total	20	2	4	1	10389
117 11/01 Carl	2m4f	F(0-100)HHdl	SFT	£2802
107 11/01 Kels	2m6f110yD(0-125)HHdl	GD	£3307

Total win prize-money £6111

Going:	Sf: 0-0 GS: 0-0 Gd: 0-1 GF: - Fm: 0-0
Distance:	2m/2m3: 0-1 2m4-2m7: 0-0 3m+: 0-0
Track:	LH: 0-0 RH: 0-1 Tight: 0-0 Gall: 0-0
Aids:	Bl: 0-0 Vi: 0-0 Tstrap: 0-0
Best Rating:	**117** 11/01 Carl 2m4f soft Hdl

An Irish point winner. Lightly-raced. Ran an encouraging race when reappearing at Carlisle in October 2002 and scored two back-to-back wins at Kelso and Carlisle in November 2001, making all both times. Rather lost his way afterwards but returned with a promising chasing debut at Perth in August. Acts on decent ground, handles soft. Should stay further.

Indiana Journey (IRE)

(97h)   (106h)**103**

8-y-o b m Eurobus-Indiana Dancer (Hallgate)
A J Martin J H Lowry

Placings:6314/032124003-3U641350   (2461a)
2002/03: 22³YS, 16UGS, 16⁶G, 20⁴GF, 18¹G, 16³F, 16⁵HY, 18⁰YS,

	Starts	1st	2nd	3rd	Win & Pl
Hurdles	2	0	0	1	387
Chases	6	1	0	4	5644
Career Total	21	3	2	5	16256
103 9/02 Dpat	Ch		GD	£4868
98 7/01 DRoy	2m	Hdl	FRM	£3895
102 8/00 Dpat	2m1f172y NHF	G-F	£2345

Total win prize-money £11109

Going:	Sf: 0-1 GS: 0-1 Gd: 1-2 GF: - Fm: 0-2
Distance:	**2m/2m3: 1-6** 2m4-2m7: 0-2 3m+: 0-0
Track:	LH: 0-0 RH: 0-1 Tight: 0-0 Gall: 0-0
Aids:	Bl: 0-0 Vi: 0-0 Tstrap: 0-0
Best Rating:	**106** 6/01 DRoy 2m gd-fm Hdl

Moderate irish chaser; acts on a sound surface.

Indien Du Boulay (FR)

110(100h)   (102h)**116**

7-y-o ch g Chef De Clan Ii (FR)-Radesgirl (FR) (Radetzky Marsch (USA))
P Monteith Major General C A Ramsay

Placings:6/21112F3-4F3410P   (3893)
2002/03: 22⁴G, 20FGF, 20³GS, 16⁴S, 24¹GS, 24⁰G, 22PGS,

	Starts	1st	2nd	3rd	Win & Pl
Hurdles	2	0	0	0	311
Chases	5	1	0	1	11590
Career Total	15	4	2	2	25169
116 12/02 Muss	3m	D(0-120)HCh	GD	£10036
114 11/01 Ayr	2m	D Ch	GD	£4127
102 5/01 Newc	2m4f	E Hdl	G-F	£2894
100 5/01 Prth	2m4f110yE Hdl	G-S	£3241

Total win prize-money £20300

Going:	Sf: 0-1 GS: 1-3 Gd: 0-2 GF: - Fm: 0-1
Distance:	2m/2m3: 0-1 2m4-2m7: 0-4 **3m+: 1-2**
Track:	LH: 0-3 **RH: 1-4** Tight: 1-5 Gall: 0-0
Aids:	Bl: 0-0 Vi: 0-1 Tstrap: 0-0
Best Rating:	**116** 12/02 Muss 3m gd-sft Ch

Fair hurdler/chaser, stays two and a half miles and is suited by a sound surface. Has worn blinkers.

Indien Royal (FR)
112   **116+**
4-y-o b g Dauphin Du Bourg (FR)-Royale Nabeysse (FR) (Beyssac (FR))
P F Nicholls (B Barbier 19/10) Mrs Kathy Stuart

Placings:500322221   (4608)
2002/03: 15²S, 16⁹VS, 18⁰VS, 18³VS, 16²S, 16²HY, 16²S, 16²G, 17¹G,

	Starts	1st	2nd	3rd	Win & Pl
Hurdles	9	1	4	1	26152
Career Total	9	1	4	1	26152
116 4/03 Chel	2m1f		B Hdl	GD	£9787

Total win prize-money £9787

Going: Sf: 0-4 GS: 0-0 Gd: 1-2 GF: - Fm: 0-0
Distance: 2m/2m3: 1-8 2m4-2m7: 0-0 3m+: 0-0
Track: LH: 1-5 RH: 0-1 Tight: 0-1 Gall: 1-2
Aids: Bl: 0-0 Vi: 0-0 Tstrap: 0-0
Best Rating: 116 4/03 Chel 2m1f   good   Hdl

Ex-French; fair juvenile hurdler; ended a frustrating run when winning at Cheltenham in April; effective in testing ground, but does act on a sound surface; should stay further than two miles.

Indigo Beach (IRE)
105   **93**
7-y-o b g Rainbows For Life (CAN)-Sandy Maid (Sandy Creek)
P S McEntee Mrs R L McEntee

Placings:P224/303004/0155-011   (0349)
2002/03: 17⁰G, 16¹G, 16¹G,

	Starts	1st	2nd	3rd	Win & Pl
Hurdles	3	2	0	0	3588
Career Total	17	3	2	2	7616
93 5/02 Fknm	2m	G(0-90)HHdl		GD	£1971
92 5/02 Fknm	2m	G Hdl		GD	£1615
70 4/02 Fknm	2m	G(0-90)HHdl		GD	£1887

Total win prize-money £5475

Going: Sf: 0-0 GS: 0-0 Gd: 2-3 GF: - Fm: 0-0
Distance: 2m/2m3: 2-2 2m4-2m7: 0-0 3m+: 0-0
Track: LH: 2-2 RH: 0-1 Tight: 2-3 Gall: 0-0
Aids: Bl: 2-3 Vi: 0-0 Tstrap: 2-2
Best Rating: 103 10/00 Font 2m4f   good   Hdl

Selling grade hurdler. Acts on a sound surface and is effective at around two miles.

Indiscret (FR)
88   **81**
7-y-o b g Garde Royale-Please (FR) (Le Pontet (FR))
F Jordan Tony Cocum, Mark Doyle, Stephen Green

Placings:60P4-F6FF3U01   (4349)
2002/03: 20⁴GS, 22⁻GS, 16⁻GF, 20⁻GS, 26⁻G, 22³G, 24⁰S, 22⁴HY, 24¹GF,

	Starts	1st	2nd	3rd	Win & Pl
Chases	9	1	0	1	4675
Career Total	12	1	0	1	4675
81 3/03 Wwck	3m110y	F(0-95)HCh		G-F	£3630

Total win prize-money £3630

Going: Sf: 0-2 GS: 0-3 Gd: 0-2 GF: - Fm: 1-2
Distance: 2m/2m3: 0-1 2m4-2m7: 0-5 3m+: 1-3
Track: LH: 1-4 RH: 0-2 Tight: 0-3 Gall: 0-0
Aids: Bl: 0-0 Vi: 0-0 Tstrap: 0-0

Best Rating: 81 3/03 Wwck 3m110y   gd-fm   Ch

Plating-class chaser; stays three miles; effective on good and fast ground.

Indium
106   **111+**
9-y-o b g Groom Dancer (USA)-Gold Bracelet (Golden Fleece (USA))
D E Cantillon Mrs Edward Cantillon

Placings:0-1P   (0393)
2002/03: 16¹GF, 16PGF,

	Starts	1st	2nd	3rd	Win & Pl
Hurdles	2	1	0	0	2429
Career Total	3	1	0	0	2429
111 5/02 Hntg	2m110y	E Hdl		G-F	£2429

Total win prize-money £2429

Going: Sf: 0-0 GS: 0-0 Gd: 0-0 GF: - Fm: 1-2
Distance: 2m/2m3: 1-2 2m4-2m7: 0-0 3m+: 0-0
Track: LH: 0-1 RH: 1-1 Tight: 0-1 Gall: 1-1
Aids: Bl: 0-0 Vi: 0-0 Tstrap: 0-0
Best Rating: 111 5/02 Hntg 2m110y   gd-fm   Hdl

Fair Flat handicapper, got off the mark over hurdles in May 2001. Lightly raced since. Suited by fast ground and a flat track.

Indoux (FR)
105   **94**
7-y-o b g Useful (FR)-Pin Hup (FR) (Signani (FR))
R J Hodges Frank E Crumpler

Placings:300/5-6010016P   (4252)
2002/03: 22⁶G, 24⁰GS, 19¹S, 17⁰GS, 19⁰GS, 20¹HY, 21⁶S, 22⁶G,

	Starts	1st	2nd	3rd	Win & Pl
Hurdles	8	2	0	0	8101
Career Total	12	2	0	1	8316
94 2/03 Sand	2m4f110yD(0-110)HHdl		HVY	£5346
94 12/02 Extr	2m3f	F(0-95)HHdl	SFT	£2754

Total win prize-money £8101

Going: Sf: 2-3 GS: 0-3 Gd: 0-2 GF: - Fm: 0-0
Distance: 2m/2m3: 1-3 2m4-2m7: 1-4 3m+: 0-1
Track: LH: 0-2 RH: 2-6 Tight: 0-2 Gall: 0-1
Aids: Bl: 0-0 Vi: 0-0 Tstrap: 0-0
Best Rating: 94 2/03 Sand 2m4f110y heavy Hdl

Modest handicapper; has twice won this season at double figure odds; stays two and a half miles; acts well in soft ground.

Inducement
109   **123**
7-y-o ch g Sabrehill (USA)-Verchinina (Star Appeal)
R M Stronge (Mrs A J Perrett 10/6) A P Holland

Placings:4/15641/P350P53-22303   (1061)
2002/03: 18²GF, 16²S, 16³G, 17⁰GS, 20³GF,

	Starts	1st	2nd	3rd	Win & Pl
Hurdles	5	0	2	2	3216
Career Total	18	2	2	4	13515
121 4/01 Extr	2m1f	E Hdl	G-S	£2153
117 12/00 Tntn	2m1f	C Hdl	SFT	£5573

Total win prize-money £7727

Going: Sf: 0-1 GS: 0-1 Gd: 0-1 GF: - Fm: 0-2
Distance: 2m/2m3: 0-4 2m4-2m7: 0-1 3m+: 0-2
Track: LH: 0-2 RH: 0-3 Tight: 0-2 Gall: 0-1
Aids: Bl: 0-0 Vi: 0-1 Tstrap: 0-0
Best Rating: 123 5/02 Font 2m2f110y gd-fm Hdl

A fair handicapper on the Flat, he has developed into a fair sort over hurdles, but currently looks held by the Handicapper. Acts on fast ground, but looks better with some cut.

Indulge (IRE)
(91h)   (70h)
10-y-o b g Mandalus-Phantom Thistle (Deep Run)
M Pitman Mrs T Brown

Placings:0/3/55212/00P   (4078)
2002/03: 20⁰HY, 20⁰GS, 20PS,

	Starts	1st	2nd	3rd	Win & Pl
Hurdles	0	0	0	0	0
Chases	2	0	0	0	0
Career Total	10	1	2	1	6904
105 3/00 Sand	2m4f110yD(0-115)HCh	G-F	£4578

Total win prize-money £4578

Going: Sf: 0-2 GS: 0-1 Gd: 0-0 GF: - Fm: 0-0
Distance: 2m/2m3: 0-0 2m4-2m7: 0-3 3m+: 0-0
Track: LH: 0-2 RH: 0-1 Tight: 0-1 Gall: 0-0
Aids: Bl: 0-0 Vi: 0-0 Tstrap: 0-0
Best Rating: 105 4/00 Hrfd 2m3f   good   Ch

Infamelia
84   **70**
7-y-o b m Infantry-Incamelia (St Columbus)
N J Henderson Mrs D A Henderson

Placings:0000P-0   (0505)
2002/03: 24⁰G,

	Starts	1st	2nd	3rd	Win & Pl
Hurdles	1	0	0	0	
Career Total	6	0	0	0	

Going: Sf: 0-0 GS: 0-0 Gd: 0-1 GF: - Fm: 0-0
Distance: 2m/2m3: 0-0 2m4-2m7: 0-0 3m+: 0-1
Track: LH: 0-1 RH: 0-0 Tight: 0-0 Gall: 0-0
Aids: Bl: 0-0 Vi: 0-0 Tstrap: 0-0
Best Rating: 88 5/01 Folk 2m1f110y gd-sft NHF

Infini (FR)
97(105c)   (108c)**112**
7-y-o gr g Le Nain Jaune (FR)-Contessina (FR) (Mistigri)
M C Pipe Roa Arkle Partnership

Placings:00/0PP01/541110P23-PF1005   (4027)
2002/03: 20PG, 16FS, 16¹GF, 18⁰G, 16⁰HY, 16⁵HY,

	Starts	1st	2nd	3rd	Win & Pl
Hurdles	4	1	0	0	2814
Chases	2	0	0	0	0
Career Total	22	5	1	1	17293
108 7/02 Worc	2m	E(0-110)HHdl	G-F	£2814
108 9/01 NAbb	2m110y	E Ch	G-F	£3368
108 7/01 MRas	2m1f110yD Hdl	G-S	£3997
4/01 Fntb	2m1f110y Ch	VS	£3880

Total win prize-money £14060

Going: Sf: 0-2 GS: 0-1 Gd: 0-2 GF: - Fm: 1-1
Distance: 2m/2m3: 1-5 2m4-2m7: 0-1 3m+: 0-0
Track: LH: 1-4 RH: 0-2 Tight: 0-3 Gall: 0-0
Aids: Bl: 0-0 Vi: 0-1 Tstrap: 0-0
Best Rating: 108 7/02 Worc 2m   gd-fm   Hdl

Fair hurdler/chaser who handles fast and soft ground and may be best at two miles, although has won over two and a half.

Infinite Risk

85   **71**

4-y-o gr g Vettori (IRE)-Dolly Bevan (Another Realm)
N J Hawke Mrs D Horton

Placings:0065P   (4693)
2002/03: 16⁰GS, 17⁰G, 16⁶G, 16⁵F, 17⁰G,

	Starts	1st	2nd	3rd	Win & Pl
Hurdles	5	0	0	0	0
Career Total	5	0	0	0	0

Going: Sf: 0-0 GS: 0-1 Gd: 0-3 GF: - Fm: 0-1
Distance: 2m/2m3: 0-5 2m4-2m7: 0-0 3m+: 0-0
Track: LH: 0-4 RH: 0-1 Tight: 0-0 Gall: 0-0
Aids: Bl: 0-0 Vi: 0-0 Tstrap: 0-0
Best Rating: 46   9/02   Uttx   2m   good   Hdl

Inflation (FR)

98   **91**

7-y-o b m Port Etienne (FR)-Ravenna Iii (FR) (Unoaprile)
G Prodromou Alan Macalister

Placings:1/200601-366P   (0987)
2002/03: 20³GS, 25⁶G, 19⁶GF, 21ᴾGF,

	Starts	1st	2nd	3rd	Win & Pl
Hurdles	4	0	0	1	469
Career Total	11	2	1	1	5949
68	4/02	Plum	2m5f	E Hdl	G-F £2796
108	2/01	Wwck	2m	H NHF	SFT £1935

Total win prize-money £4733

Going: Sf: 0-0 GS: 0-1 Gd: 0-1 GF: - Fm: 0-2
Distance: 2m/2m3: 0-1 2m4-2m7: 0-0 3m+: 0-1
Track: LH: 0-4 RH: 0-0 Tight: 0-3 Gall: 0-0
Aids: Bl: 0-1 Vi: 0-1 Tstrap: 0-0
Best Rating: 108   2/01   Wwck   2m   soft   NHF

Made a winning bumper debut in February 2001on soft ground, but is not a natural jumper over hurdles and had to be galvanised by McCoy to win a weak event at Plumpton in April 2002. Held since.

Influence Pedler

102   **91d**

10-y-o b g Keen-La Vie En Primrose (Henbit (USA))
Miss K M George The Entrepreneurs

Placings:61203/3253063/213P14411PP/033121242/P4052
223422P1-233346   (4796)
2002/03: 25²GF, 24³G, 24³GF, 24³G, 24⁴F, 28⁶GF,

	Starts	1st	2nd	3rd	Win & Pl
Chases	6	0	1	3	4960
Career Total	51	8	12	11	57187
99	4/02	Extr	3m1f110yD	(0-115)	HCh	FRM	£5193
105	9/99	Sedg	3m3f	E	(0-115)	HCh	G-F	£3470
105	8/99	Strf	3m	F	(0-105)	HCh	GD	£3018
109	12/98	Hrfd	2m3f	E	(0-110)	HCh	GD	£3430
108	11/98	Ludl	2m4f	D Ch		GD	£3972
91	8/98	MRas	2m4f	D Ch		GD	£3418
88	6/98	MRas	2m1f110yD Ch		G-F	£4176
114	2/97	Wwck	2m4f110yB Hdl		GD	£7100

Total win prize-money £33781

Going: Sf: 0-0 GS: 0-0 Gd: 0-2 GF: - Fm: 0-4
Distance: 2m/2m3: 0-0 2m4-2m7: 0-0 3m+: 0-6
Track: LH: 0-4 RH: 0-2 Tight: 0-4 Gall: 0-0
Aids: Bl: 0-0 Vi: 0-0 Tstrap: 0-0
Best Rating: 121   11/97   NAbb   2m6f   gd-fm   Hdl

Plating-class chaser; stays three miles-three; likes ground conditions good or faster, consistent and often makes the frame.

Infrasonique (FR)

113   **125**

7-y-o b g Teresio-Quatalina Iii (FR) (Chateau Du Diable (FR))
Mrs L C Taylor Miss M Talbot

Placings:43225/2412324204221-5206345   (4278)
2002/03: 20⁵GF, 24²GS, 26⁹GS, 26⁶GS, 24³S, 24⁴S, 26⁵GF,

	Starts	1st	2nd	3rd	Win & Pl
Chases	7	0	1	1	6342
Career Total	25	2	9	3	60679
133	4/02	Ayr	3m1f	B HCh	GD	£21450
6/01	Autl	2m4f110y	Ch	SFT	£12124

Total win prize-money £33574

Going: Sf: 0-2 GS: 0-3 Gd: 0-0 GF: - Fm: 0-2
Distance: 2m/2m3: 0-0 2m4-2m7: 0-1 3m+: 0-6
Track: LH: 0-3 RH: 0-3 Tight: 0-1 Gall: 0-2
Aids: Bl: 0-0 Vi: 0-0 Tstrap: 0-0
Best Rating: 133   11/02   Asct   3m110y   gd-sft   Ch

Decent handicap chaser; sound jumper, usually in the frame; acts on good and soft ground.

Ingenu (FR)

97(107h)   (109h)**95**

7-y-o b g Royal Charter (FR)-Una Volta (FR) (Artaius (USA))
R H Alner G L Porter

Placings:403/1423522/352P6-014405   (4568)
2002/03: 20⁰GS, 20¹S, 20⁴G, 20⁴GS, 24⁰GS, 22⁵GF,

	Starts	1st	2nd	3rd	Win & Pl
Hurdles	5	1	0	0	5295
Chases	1	0	0	0	0
Career Total	21	2	4	3	26773
108	11/02	Hayd	2m4f	D Hdl	SFT	£3913
8/00	Diep	2m1f110y	Ch	SFT	£3362

Total win prize-money £7275

Going: Sf: 1-1 GS: 0-3 Gd: 0-1 GF: - Fm: 0-1
Distance: 2m/2m3: 0-2 2m4-2m7: 0-0 3m+: 0-1
Track: LH: 1-4 RH: 0-2 Tight: 0-1 Gall: 0-1
Aids: Bl: 0-0 Vi: 0-0 Tstrap: 0-0
Best Rating: 115   12/01   Plum   2m4f   soft   Ch

Ex-French chaser; won over hurdles at Haydock in November 2002; likes soft ground; stays two and a half miles.

Inherit The Earth

9-y-o b m Silver Season-Balayer (Balidar)
Mary Meek Mrs Mary Meek

Placings:PPP   (4626)
2002/03: 16ᴾGF, 16ᴾGF, 17ᴾGF,

	Starts	1st	2nd	3rd	Win & Pl
Hurdles	3	0	0	0	0
Career Total	3	0	0	0	0

Going: Sf: 0-0 GS: 0-0 Gd: 0-0 GF: - Fm: 0-3
Distance: 2m/2m3: 0-3 2m4-2m7: 0-0 3m+: 0-0
Track: LH: 0-3 RH: 0-0 Tight: 0-3 Gall: 0-0
Aids: Bl: 0-0 Vi: 0-0 Tstrap: 0-1
Best Rating: 0   4/03   NAbb   2m1f   gd-fm   Hdl

Inigo Jones (IRE)

103   (82c)**108**

7-y-o b g Alzao (USA)-Kindjal (Kris)
G Brown Mrs Amanda Killick

Placings:3U15-4P34   (4287)
2002/03: 17⁴GF, 19ᴾGS, 18³S, 16⁴GF,

	Starts	1st	2nd	3rd	Win & Pl
Hurdles	2	0	0	1	861
Chases	2	0	0	0	308
Career Total	8	1	0	2	4240
120	4/02	Sedg	2m1f	E Hdl	G-F	£2702

Total win prize-money £2702

Going: Sf: 0-1 GS: 0-1 Gd: 0-0 GF: - Fm: 0-2
Distance: 2m/2m3: 0-4 2m4-2m7: 0-0 3m+: 0-0
Track: LH: 0-2 RH: 0-2 Tight: 0-3 Gall: 0-0
Aids: Bl: 0-4 Vi: 0-0 Tstrap: 0-0
Best Rating: 120   4/02   Sedg   2m1f   gd-fm   Hdl

Modest, free-running novice hurdler; got off the mark when blinkered at Sedgefield in April 2002; suited by fast ground; the type to need everything his own way.

Inigo Montoya

11-y-o b g Liberated-Darklands (Feelings (FR))
C P Dennis Mrs A W Scott-Harden

Placings:4-0   (0083)
2002/03: 25⁰GS,

	Starts	1st	2nd	3rd	Win & Pl
Chases	1	0	0	0	
Career Total	2	0	0	0	121

Going: Sf: 0-0 GS: 0-1 Gd: 0-0 GF: - Fm: 0-0
Distance: 2m/2m3: 0-0 2m4-2m7: 0-0 3m+: 0-1
Track: LH: 0-1 RH: 0-0 Tight: 0-0 Gall: 0-0
Aids: Bl: 0-0 Vi: 0-0 Tstrap: 0-0
Best Rating: 60   4/02   Hexm   3m1f   good   Ch

Inis Cara (IRE)

11-y-o b g Carlingford Castle-Good Sailing (Scorpio (FR))
G W Thomas (Miss Venetia Williams 8/5) G W Thomas

Placings:1/026051161106/113F1232264/023310664/34350
F/04P-55P   (3848)
2002/03: 24⁵GF, 25⁵G, 27ᴾG,

	Starts	1st	2nd	3rd	Win & Pl
Chases	3	0	0	0	0
Career Total	45	9	5	6	126593
132	12/99	Leop	3m	(0-140)	HCh	SFT	£63616
123	1/99	Tram	2m4f	Ch		HVY	£4296
127	11/98	Fair	2m5f110y	Ch		Y-S	£3586
132	10/98	Gowr	2m6f	Ch		SH	£4782
133	2/98	Clon	2m4f	(0-116)	HHdl	Y-S	£2680
122	12/98	Leop	2m6f	(0-130)	HHdl	Y-S	£3573
112	12/97	Thur	2m6f110y	Hdl		SFT	£2204
111	11/97	Dpat	2m6f	Hdl		SH	£2712
106	4/97	Slig	2m	NHF		HVY	£2204

Total win prize-money £89658

Going: Sf: 0-0 GS: 0-0 Gd: 0-2 GF: - Fm: 0-1
Distance: 2m/2m3: 0-2 2m4-2m7: 0-0 3m+: 0-3
Track: LH: 0-1 RH: 0-2 Tight: 0-1 Gall: 0-0
Aids: Bl: 0-0 Vi: 0-0 Tstrap: 0-0
Best Rating: 140   11/00   DRoy   3m   gd-yld   Ch

Formerly a useful hurdler and smart chaser in Ireland, where he landed the valuable Paddy Power Chase at Leopardstown in 1999. Has not seen much action since falling in the 2001 Grand National his first start for Venetia Williams. Best over three miles. Acts on soft ground.

Inis Eile (IRE)

99(80c)   (36c)85

8-y-o b g Peacock (FR)-Slippery Bell (No Argument)
Mrs S J Smith Mrs S Smith

Placings: 0/00003-400F0253   (1184)
2002/03: 20⁴GS, 24⁹G, 25⁵GF, 20⁶GF, 21⁰G, 24²GS, 22⁵G, 26³G,

	Starts	1st	2nd	3rd	Win & Pl
Hurdles	7	0	1	1	1598
Chases	1	0	0	0	0
Career Total	14	0	1	2	1948

Going:	Sf: 0-0 GS: 0-2 Gd: 0-4 GF: - Fm: 0-2
Distance:	2m/2m3: 0-0 2m4-2m7: 0-4 3m+: 0-4
Track:	LH: 0-7 RH: 0-1 Tight: 0-4 Gall: 0-0
Aids:	Bl: 0-1 Vi: 0-0 Tstrap: 0-0
Best Rating:	85 12/01 Hayd 2m4f soft Hdl

Placed form in bumpers and hurdles so far. Stays three miles.

Initiative

(105h)   (99h)

7-y-o ch g Arazi (USA)-Dance Quest (FR) (Green Dancer (USA))
J Hetherton Frank Reay

Placings: 0-451P23341500   (3564)
2002/03: 17⁴S, 17⁵G, 17¹GF, 16PGF, 17²GF, 16³G, 16³HY, 17⁴S, 17¹S, 17⁵S, 16⁰GS, 17⁰HY,

	Starts	1st	2nd	3rd	Win & Pl
Hurdles	12	2	1	2	7675
Career Total	13	2	1	2	7675
99	12/02	Sedg	2m1f	E(0-100)HHdl	SFT	£3304
95	9/02	Sedg	2m1f	G(0-95)HHdl	G-F	£2009

Total win prize-money £5313

Going:	Sf: 1-6 GS: 0-1 Gd: 0-2 GF: - Fm: 1-3
Distance:	2m/2m3: 2-12 2m4-2m7: 0-0 3m+: 0-0
Track:	LH: 2-11 RH: 0-1 Tight: 2-8 Gall: 0-1
Aids:	Bl: 0-0 Vi: 0-0 Tstrap: 0-0
Best Rating:	99 12/02 Sedg 2m1f soft Hdl

Moderate hurdler. Acts on any ground and is effective at around two miles.

Injun

90   83

4-y-o ch g Efisio-Lassoo (Caerleon (USA))
Miss A M Newton-Smith (C W Thornton 10/5) Julian Smith

Placings: 0000   (3924)
2002/03: 16⁹S, 16⁰S, 17⁰GS, 16⁹G,

	Starts	1st	2nd	3rd	Win & Pl
Hurdles	4	0	0	0	
Career Total	4	0	0	0	

Going:	Sf: 0-1 GS: 0-1 Gd: 0-2 GF: - Fm: 0-0
Distance:	2m/2m3: 0-4 2m4-2m7: 0-0 3m+: 0-0
Track:	LH: 0-0 RH: 0-0 Tight: 0-1 Gall: 0-1
Aids:	Bl: 0-0 Vi: 0-0 Tstrap: 0-2
Best Rating:	83 10/02 Kemp 2m good Hdl

Modest efforts on the Flat. Yet to show anything.

Inlet (IRE)

88   86

6-y-o ch g Insan (USA)-River Rescue (Over The River (FR))
J T Gifford Pell-Mell Partners

Placings: 0-6005   (4310)

2002/03: 16⁶S, 19⁰G, 19⁰S, 24⁵G,

	Starts	1st	2nd	3rd	Win & Pl
Hurdles	4	0	0	0	0
Career Total	5	0	0	0	0

Going:	Sf: 0-2 GS: 0-0 Gd: 0-2 GF: - Fm: 0-0
Distance:	2m/2m3: 0-3 2m4-2m7: 0-0 3m+: 0-1
Track:	LH: 0-4 RH: 0-0 Tight: 0-0 Gall: 0-4
Aids:	Bl: 0-0 Vi: 0-0 Tstrap: 0-0
Best Rating:	93 3/02 Sand 2m110y gd-sft NHF

Inn Antique (FR)

106   121

7-y-o b g Lute Antique (FR)-Taghera (FR) (Toujours Pret (USA))
Ferdy Murphy (P F Nicholls 29/6) W J Gott

Placings: 0P1P1FP/4P2F-1421210   (3727)
2002/03: 16¹GF, 16⁴S, 17²GF, 17¹S, 16²GS, 17¹HY, 16⁶G,

	Starts	1st	2nd	3rd	Win & Pl
Hurdles	7	3	2	0	14530
Career Total	18	5	3	0	31445
121	1/03	Sedg	2m1f	E Hdl	HVY	£4527
121	11/02	Sedg	2m1f	D Hdl	SFT	£4316
115	5/02	Winc	2m	E Hdl	G-F	£2688
116	1/01	Kemp	2m	D Ch	SFT	£4290
	9/00	Autl	2m2f		VS	£11527

Total win prize-money £27348

Going:	Sf: 2-3 GS: 0-1 Gd: 0-1 GF: - Fm: 1-2
Distance:	2m/2m3: 3-7 2m4-2m7: 0-0 3m+: 0-0
Track:	LH: 2-5 RH: 1-2 Tight: 2-3 Gall: 0-0
Aids:	Bl: 0-0 Vi: 0-0 Tstrap: 0-0
Best Rating:	121 1/03 Sedg 2m1f heavy Hdl

Useful hurdler; effective at around two miles; acts on any ground; goes well at Sedgefield.

Inn From The Cold (IRE)

94   59

7-y-o ch g Glacial Storm (USA)-Silver Apollo (General Ironside)
L Lungo Mrs Barbara Lungo

Placings: 0-P0P060   (4019)
2002/03: 24PGS, 22⁰G, 22PS, 20⁰GS, 16⁶HY, 16⁰S,

	Starts	1st	2nd	3rd	Win & Pl
Hurdles	6	0	0	0	0
Career Total	7	0	0	0	0

Going:	Sf: 0-3 GS: 0-2 Gd: 0-1 GF: - Fm: 0-0
Distance:	2m/2m3: 0-2 2m4-2m7: 0-3 3m+: 0-1
Track:	LH: 0-6 RH: 0-0 Tight: 0-0 Gall: 0-1
Aids:	Bl: 0-0 Vi: 0-0 Tstrap: 0-0
Best Rating:	59 1/03 Newc 2m heavy Hdl

Inner Sanctum (IRE)

75   85

6-y-o ch g Bob s Return (IRE)-Princess Wager (Pollerton)
Miss Venetia Williams P Ryan

Placings: 304   (4567)
2002/03: 18³HY, 16⁹G, 20⁴GF,

	Starts	1st	2nd	3rd	Win & Pl
NH Flat	2	0	0	1	278
Hurdles	1	0	0	0	286
Career Total	3	0	0	1	564

Going:	Sf: 0-1 GS: 0-0 Gd: 0-1 GF: - Fm: 0-1
Distance:	2m/2m3: 0-2 2m4-2m7: 0-1 3m+: 0-0
Track:	LH: 0-3 RH: 0-0 Tight: 0-2 Gall: 0-0
Aids:	Bl: 0-0 Vi: 0-0 Tstrap: 0-0
Best Rating:	93 1/03 Font 2m2f110y heavy NHF

Innovate (IRE)

101   73

11-y-o b m Posen (USA)-Innate (Be My Native (USA))
Miss Lucinda V Russell Peter K Dale

Placings: 00P350/5PPF02/5144P/6113P/P4-23P3   (4662)
2002/03: 24²GF, 26³GF, 24PG, 26³GF,

	Starts	1st	2nd	3rd	Win & Pl
Chases	4	0	1	2	2491
Career Total	28	3	2	4	14173
91	10/00	Towc	3m1f	F(0-90)HCh	G-F	£2821
91	8/00	Uttx	3m	F(0-100)HCh	G-F	£2710
92	6/99	Hexm	2m4f110y		F Ch	G-F	£2909

Total win prize-money £8442

Going:	Sf: 0-0 GS: 0-0 Gd: 0-1 GF: - Fm: 0-3
Distance:	2m/2m3: 0-0 2m4-2m7: 0-0 3m+: 0-4
Track:	LH: 0-3 RH: 0-1 Tight: 0-0 Gall: 0-4
Aids:	Bl: 0-0 Vi: 0-0 Tstrap: 0-4
Best Rating:	95 10/00 Aint 3m1f good Ch

Plating-class staying chaser; lightly raced since winning extended three miles handicap chase at Towcester October 2000; stays three miles-two; likes fast ground.

Innox (FR)

139d

7-y-o b g Lute Antique (FR)-Savane Iii (FR) (Quart De Vin (FR))
F Doumen Marquise De Moratalla

Placings: 0F/324F/62512F321P2-04344P50   (4587a)
2002/03: 21⁰VS, 23⁴VS, 27³HY, 24⁴S, 24PS, 22⁵VS, 22⁰VS,

	Starts	1st	2nd	3rd	Win & Pl
Chases	8	0	0	1	48798
Career Total	25	2	5	3	149724
134	2/02	Wwck	3m2f	C Ch	SFT	£6812
	9/01	Autl	2m5f110y	HCh	VS	£10699

Total win prize-money £17511

Going:	Sf: 0-4 GS: 0-0 Gd: 0-0 GF: - Fm: 0-0
Distance:	2m/2m3: 0-0 2m4-2m7: 0-4 3m+: 0-4
Track:	LH: 0-4 RH: 0-2 Tight: 0-0 Gall: 0-0
Aids:	Bl: 0-0 Vi: 0-0 Tstrap: 0-0
Best Rating:	139 12/01 Kemp 3m good Ch

Very useful French chaser; stays three miles; likes soft ground.

Ins And Outs (IRE)

105   122

9-y-o ch g Insan (USA)-My Dear Good Woman (Lucifer (USA))
J T Gifford Pell-Mell Partners

Placings: 244/10/4F142   (4368)
2002/03: 16⁴G, 16PGS, 16¹S, 21⁴S, 19²G,

	Starts	1st	2nd	3rd	Win & Pl
Chases	5	1	1	0	9590
Career Total	10	2	2	0	14854
120	1/03	Hntg	2m110y	D Ch	SFT	£7262
109	10/00	Chel	2m110y	D Hdl	GD	£4634

Total win prize-money £11898

Going:	Sf: 1-2 GS: 0-1 Gd: 0-2 GF: - Fm: 0-0

Distance:	**2m/2m3: 1-3** 2m4-2m7: 0-2 3m+: 0-0
Track:	LH: 0-0 **RH: 1-5** Tight: 0-1 **Gall: 1-1**
Aids:	Bl: 0-0 Vi: 0-0 Tstrap: 0-0
Best Rating:	**122** 3/03 Asct 2m3f110y good Ch

Decent novice chaser; won at Huntingdon in January 2003; effective at two miles; acts on soft ground.

Inshallah

8-y-o ch m Durgam (USA)-Kaliala (FR) (Pharly (FR))
Miss Lucinda V Russell Alight Bloodstock

Placings:P   (4616)
2002/03: 17PGF,

	Starts	1st	2nd	3rd	Win & Pl
Hurdles	1	0	0	0	
Career Total	1	0	0	0	

Going:	Sf: 0-0 GS: 0-0 Gd: 0-0 GF: - Fm: 0-1
Distance:	2m/2m3: 0-1 2m4-2m7: 0-0 3m+: 0-0
Track:	LH: 0-0 RH: 0-1 Tight: 0-0 Gall: 0-0
Aids:	Bl: 0-0 Vi: 0-0 Tstrap: 0-0
Best Rating:	**0** 4/03 Carl 2m1f gd-fm Hdl

Insharann (FR)

4-y-o b g Sheyrann-My Last Chance (FR) (Tiffauges)
N J Henderson W H Ponsonby

Placings:P   (4601)
2002/03: 17PGF,

	Starts	1st	2nd	3rd	Win & Pl
NH Flat	1	0	0	0	
Career Total	1	0	0	0	

Going:	Sf: 0-0 GS: 0-0 Gd: 0-0 GF: - Fm: 0-1
Distance:	2m/2m3: 0-1 2m4-2m7: 0-0 3m+: 0-0
Track:	LH: 0-0 RH: 0-1 Tight: 0-0 Gall: 0-0
Aids:	Bl: 0-0 Vi: 0-0 Tstrap: 0-0
Best Rating:	**0** 4/03 Extr 2m1f gd-fm NHF

Instant Appeal
95   99+

6-y-o gr g Terimon-Free Travel (Royalty)
P Winkworth G Clark, C Haycock, M Rogerson

Placings:60P2   (3926)
2002/03: 17RGS, 16PS, 22PHY, 20PG,

	Starts	1st	2nd	3rd	Win & Pl
NH Flat	1	0	0	0	
Hurdles	3	0	1	0	1159
Career Total	4	0	1	0	1159

Going:	Sf: 0-2 GS: 0-1 Gd: 0-1 GF: - Fm: 0-0
Distance:	2m/2m3: 0-1 2m4-2m7: 0-2 3m+: 0-0
Track:	LH: 0-1 RH: 0-3 Tight: 0-2 Gall: 0-1
Aids:	Bl: 0-0 Vi: 0-0 Tstrap: 0-0
Best Rating:	**99** 3/03 Hntg 2m4f110y good Hdl

Moderate hurdler; seems to appreciate a sound surface.

Instant Justice (IRE)

7-y-o gr g Roselier (FR)-Montekova (IRE) (Montekin)

D M Grissell Pepin Racing

Placings:0/5-PP0   (4573)
2002/03: 18PHY, 22PHY, 16PGF,

	Starts	1st	2nd	3rd	Win & Pl
Hurdles	3	0	0	0	
Career Total	5	0	0	0	0

Going:	Sf: 0-2 GS: 0-0 Gd: 0-0 GF: - Fm: 0-1
Distance:	2m/2m3: 0-2 2m4-2m7: 0-1 3m+: 0-0
Track:	LH: 0-2 RH: 0-1 Tight: 0-3 Gall: 0-0
Aids:	Bl: 0-0 Vi: 0-0 Tstrap: 0-0
Best Rating:	**86** 9/01 Font 2m2f110y gd-fm Hdl

Intelligent (IRE)
111(116h)   (127h)153+

7-y-o b g Religiously (USA)-Culkeem (Master Buck)
Mrs John Harrington Norman Moore

Placings:6/12/502313430-2P1216321   (4172)
2002/03: 24²YS, 17PYS, 20¹HY, 24²GS, 20¹S, 21⁶S, 21⁶S, 16⁵G, 34¹S,

	Starts	1st	2nd	3rd	Win & Pl
Hurdles	1	0	1	0	4080
Chases	8	3	2	1	93753
Career Total	21	5	5	4	110184
153	3/03	Uttx	4m2f	A HCh	SFT £58000
147	12/02	Limk	2m4f	Ch	SFT £17944
126	11/02	DRoy	2m4f	Ch	HVY £6984
117	2/02	Thur	2m6f	Hdl	HVY £3809
105	10/00	Punc	2m	NHF	G-Y £3588
					Total win prize-money £90328

Going:	Sf: 3-5 GS: 0-1 Gd: 0-0 GF: - Fm: 0-0
Distance:	2m/2m3: 0-0 **2m4-2m7: 2-3** 3m+: 1-5
Track:	LH: 1-5 RH: 1-2 Tight: 0-0 Gall: 0-0
Aids:	Bl: 0-0 Vi: 0-0 Tstrap: 0-0
Best Rating:	**153** 3/03 Uttx 4m2f soft Ch

Irish hurdler, stays 3m; suited by soft ground.

Inter Rock (FR)
81

7-y-o b g Video Rock (FR)-Aniste (FR) (Brezzo (FR))
R C Harper R C Harper

Placings:055/61043/P4P-P   (0215)
2002/03: 25PG,

	Starts	1st	2nd	3rd	Win & Pl
Chases	1	0	0	0	
Career Total	12	1	0	1	2904
108	12/00	Fknm	2m7f110yE Hdl	G-S	£2261
				Total win prize-money £2261	

Going:	Sf: 0-0 GS: 0-0 Gd: 0-1 GF: - Fm: 0-0
Distance:	2m/2m3: 0-0 2m4-2m7: 0-0 3m+: 0-1
Track:	LH: 0-0 RH: 0-1 Tight: 0-0 Gall: 0-0
Aids:	Bl: 0-0 Vi: 0-0 Tstrap: 0-0
Best Rating:	**108** 1/01 Donc 3m110y good Hdl

Interdit (FR)
111(106h)   (107h)114

7-y-o b/br g Shafoun (FR)-Solaine (FR) (Pot D Or (FR))
Mrs B K Thomson (P J Hobbs 10/10) Mrs B K Thomson

Placings:4120/F55426-212F233122245136225   (4558)
2002/03: 26²GF, 25¹G, 25²G, 24⁴GF, 24²GF, 23³G, 24³F, 24¹F, 25⁸S, 22²HY, 25²GS, 24⁴GS, 24⁵G, 25¹HY, 22³GS, 24⁶GS, 32²G, 24²G, 25⁴G,

	Starts	1st	2nd	3rd	Win & Pl
Hurdles	3	0	1	1	2030

Chases	16	3	7	2	42642
Career Total	29	4	10	3	49201
109	2/03	Ayr	3m1f	D(0-120)HCh	HVY £6890
114	10/02	Ludl	3m	D(0-110)HCh	FRM £5638
112	5/02	Extr	3m1f110yD(0-115)HCh	GD	£5018
100	12/00	Extr	2m1f	E Hdl	HVY £2275
				Total win prize-money £19822	

Going:	Sf: 1-3 GS: 0-4 Gd: 1-7 GF: - Fm: 1-5
Distance:	2m/2m3: 0-0 2m4-2m7: 0-2 **3m+: 3-17**
Track:	LH: 1-12 **RH: 2-6** Tight: 1-8 Gall: 0-2
Aids:	**Bl: 2-7** Vi: 0-0 Tstrap: 0-0
Best Rating:	**114** 3/03 Carl 3m good Ch

Fair chaser; stays three miles two; acts on any ground; has worn blinkers.

Intersky Falcon
128   164

6-y-o ch g Polar Falcon (USA)-I LI Try (Try My Best (USA))
Jonjo O Neill Interskyracing.com & Mrs Jonjo O Neill

Placings:32/2312111612-11115   (4099)
2002/03: 16¹G, 16¹GF, 16¹GS, 16¹S, 16⁵G,

	Starts	1st	2nd	3rd	Win & Pl
Hurdles	5	4	0	0	143802
Career Total	17	9	4	2	198328
164	12/02	Kemp	2m	A Hdl	SFT £43500
164	11/02	Newc	2m	A Hdl	G-S £29000
154	10/02	Tipp	2m	Hdl	G-F £31901
159	5/02	Hayd	2m	A HHdl	GD £31900
149	4/02	Aint	2m110y A HHdl	GD £23200
124	2/02	Donc	2m110y C(0-130)HHdl	SFT £5876
108	11/01	Sedg	2m1f	D Hdl	GD £3328
121	9/01	Sedg	2m1f	E Hdl	GD £2380
102	8/01	MRas	2m3f110yE Hdl	G-F £3104
				Total win prize-money £174192	

Going:	Sf: 1-1 GS: 1-1 Gd: 1-2 GF: - Fm: 1-1
Distance:	**2m/2m3: 4-5** 2m4-2m7: 0-0 3m+: 0-0
Track:	LH: **2-3** RH: 1-1 Tight: 0-0 **Gall: 1-1**
Aids:	**Bl: 4-5** Vi: 0-0 Tstrap: 0-0
Best Rating:	**164** 12/02 Kemp 2m soft Hdl

Top-class hurdler; scored five times in 2001/02 including defying a 30lb hike in the ratings when carrying top weight to a hard fought victory in the Swinton Hurdle; made a winning return at Tipperary in October and followed up in the Fighting Fifth at Newcastle and the Christmas Hurdle at Kempton; acts on good ground or faster, but has won on soft; has won over further, but best form around 2m; much improved since being fitted with blinkers; travels well and is suited by positive tactics; tough.

Intersky Native (IRE)
97(86c)   (40c)87

7-y-o ch g Be My Native (USA)-Creative Music (Creative Plan (USA))
N G Richards interskyracing.com

Placings:25-604   (4435)
2002/03: 16⁶G, 19⁰GS, 20⁴G,

	Starts	1st	2nd	3rd	Win & Pl
Hurdles	3	0	0	0	264
Career Total	5	0	1	0	763

Going:	Sf: 0-0 GS: 0-1 Gd: 0-2 GF: - Fm: 0-0
Distance:	2m/2m3: 0-1 2m4-2m7: 0-2 3m+: 0-0
Track:	LH: 0-3 RH: 0-0 Tight: 0-1 Gall: 0-1
Aids:	Bl: 0-0 Vi: 0-0 Tstrap: 0-0
Best Rating:	**106** 12/01 Bang 2m1f gd-sft NHF

Plating-class hurdler; yet to win a race and becoming disappointing; stays three miles; acts on fast ground.

Intersky Sovereign (IRE)

5-y-o b g Aristocracy-Queen s Prize (Random Shot)
J Howard Johnson interskyracing.com

Placings:0 (4167)
2002/03: 16⁰GS,

	Starts	1st	2nd	3rd	Win & Pl
Hurdles	1	0	0	0	
Career Total	1	0	0	0	

Going:	Sf: 0-0 GS: 0-1 Gd: 0-0 GF: - Fm: 0-0
Distance:	2m/2m3: 0-1 2m4-2m7: 0-0 3m+: 0-0
Track:	LH: 0-1 RH: 0-0 Tight: 0-0 Gall: 0-1
Aids:	Bl: 0-0 Vi: 0-0 Tstrap: 0-0
Best Rating:	0 3/03 Newc 2m gd-sft Hdl

Inthaar
69   30
6-y-o b g Nashwan (USA)-Twafeaj (USA) (Topsider (USA))
R Brotherton The Joiners Arms Racing Club Quarndon

Placings:0/00 (0323)
2002/03: 19⁰GF, 16⁰G,

	Starts	1st	2nd	3rd	Win & Pl
Hurdles	2	0	0	0	
Career Total	3	0	0	0	

Going:	Sf: 0-0 GS: 0-0 Gd: 0-1 GF: - Fm: 0-1
Distance:	2m/2m3: 0-1 2m4-2m7: 0-1 3m+: 0-0
Track:	LH: 0-1 RH: 0-1 Tight: 0-0 Gall: 0-0
Aids:	Bl: 0-0 Vi: 0-0 Tstrap: 0-0
Best Rating:	68 1/01 Newc 2m soft NHF

Intox III (FR)
100   112+
7-y-o ch g Garde Royale-Naftane (FR) (Trac)
M C Pipe Stef Stefanou

Placings:10/2156P0P/15611F3-54B04P00 (3809)
2002/03: 17⁵GS, 20⁴GF, 19⁸GS, 19⁹GS, 17⁴S, 17⁷S, 17⁹S, 16⁹S,

	Starts	1st	2nd	3rd	Win & Pl
Hurdles	8	0	0	0	697
Career Total	24	5	1	1	13940
120	9/01	NAbb	2m1f	E(0-110)HHdl	G-F	£2639
115	8/01	NAbb	2m1f	F(0-100)HHdl	G-F	£2667
108	5/01	MRas	2m1f110yF(0-105)HHdl	GD	£2138
108	7/00	NAbb	2m1f	D Hdl	G-F	£3088
99	1/00	Towc	2m	H NHF	HVY	£1641
				Total win prize-money £12176		

Going:	Sf: 0-4 GS: 0-2 Gd: 0-1 GF: - Fm: 0-1
Distance:	2m/2m3: 0-6 2m4-2m7: 0-2 3m+: 0-0
Track:	LH: 0-4 RH: 0-4 Tight: 0-6 Gall: 0-1
Aids:	Bl: 0-0 Vi: 0-3 Tstrap: 0-0
Best Rating:	125 1/02 Tntn 2m1f soft Hdl

Handicap hurdler, fitted with a tongue tie and got his own way out in front when scoring for the fourth time over the extended 2m at Newton Abbot June 2003; acts on most types of ground; effective over 2m.

Intrepid Mogal
102(99h)   (91h)101
6-y-o b g Terimon-Padrigal (Paddy s Stream)
N J Pomfret J N Cheatle

Placings:00P53-PP2226 (4786)
2002/03: 22⁸G, 16⁸GF, 20²S, 24²GS, 25²G, 22⁶G,

	Starts	1st	2nd	3rd	Win & Pl
Hurdles	6	0	3	0	2734
Career Total	11	0	3	1	3174

Going:	Sf: 0-1 GS: 0-1 Gd: 0-3 GF: - Fm: 0-1
Distance:	2m/2m3: 0-1 2m4-2m7: 0-3 3m+: 0-2
Track:	LH: 0-3 RH: 0-2 Tight: 0-0 Gall: 0-2
Aids:	Bl: 0-0 Vi: 0-0 Tstrap: 0-0
Best Rating:	91 2/03 Chep 3m gd-sft Hdl

Modest hurdler; just touched off on chasing bow at Uttoxeter in May; stays well; handles heavy ground.

Intymcginty (IRE)
104   101
6-y-o b g Port Lucaya-Mother Tongue (Montelimar (USA))
Noel T Chance Let s Get Ready to Rumble Partnership

Placings:56-5320 (4311)
2002/03: 16⁵S, 19³G, 19²S, 21⁰G,

	Starts	1st	2nd	3rd	Win & Pl
NH Flat	1	0	0	0	0
Hurdles	3	0	1	1	2476
Career Total	6	0	1	1	2476

Going:	Sf: 0-2 GS: 0-0 Gd: 0-2 GF: - Fm: 0-0
Distance:	2m/2m3: 0-3 2m4-2m7: 0-1 3m+: 0-0
Track:	LH: 0-3 RH: 0-1 Tight: 0-0 Gall: 0-3
Aids:	Bl: 0-0 Vi: 0-0 Tstrap: 0-0
Best Rating:	109 12/01 Newb 2m110y good NHF

Has shown ability in bumpers and over hurdles; stays two miles three.

Investor Relations (IRE)
101   91
5-y-o b g Goldmark (USA)-Debach Delight (Great Nephew)
N J Hawke N J McMullan

Placings:4453-03132520 (1158)
2002/03: 17⁰GF, 17³S, 17¹G, 17³GF, 16²GF, 17⁵GF, 17²GF, 17⁰G,

	Starts	1st	2nd	3rd	Win & Pl
Hurdles	8	1	2	2	4319
Career Total	12	1	2	3	4696
89	6/02	NAbb	2m1f	G(0-95)HHdl	GD	£2268
				Total win prize-money £2268		

Going:	Sf: 0-1 GS: 0-0 Gd: 1-2 GF: - Fm: 0-5
Distance:	2m/2m3: 1-8 2m4-2m7: 0-0 3m+: 0-0
Track:	LH: 1-7 RH: 0-0 Tight: 1-7 Gall: 0-0
Aids:	Bl: 0-0 Vi: 0-0 Tstrap: 0-0
Best Rating:	91 8/02 NAbb 2m1f gd-fm Hdl

Won amateur riders selling handicap over 17 furlongs on good ground June 2002.

Invitado (IRE)
84   74
4-y-o ch g Be My Guest (USA)-Lady Dulcinea (ARG) (General (FR))
T J Fitzgerald (J G Fitzgerald 4/12) A Huddlestone

Placings:5 (2300)
2002/03: 16⁵GS,

	Starts	1st	2nd	3rd	Win & Pl
Hurdles	1	0	0	0	0
Career Total	1	0	0	0	0

Going:	Sf: 0-0 GS: 0-1 Gd: 0-0 GF: - Fm: 0-0
Distance:	2m/2m3: 0-1 2m4-2m7: 0-0 3m+: 0-0
Track:	LH: 0-1 RH: 0-0 Tight: 0-1 Gall: 0-0
Aids:	Bl: 0-0 Vi: 0-0 Tstrap: 0-0
Best Rating:	45 12/02 Catt 2m gd-sft Hdl

Inzarmood (IRE)
102   69
5-y-o b m Inzar (USA)-Pepilin (Coquelin (USA))
K R Burke Mrs Elaine M Burke

Placings:340200 (4679)
2002/03: 17³GS, 16⁴GF, 16⁰G, 16²G, 16⁹G, 16⁹GF,

	Starts	1st	2nd	3rd	Win & Pl
Hurdles	6	0	1	1	1027
Career Total	6	0	1	1	1027

Going:	Sf: 0-0 GS: 0-1 Gd: 0-3 GF: - Fm: 0-2
Distance:	2m/2m3: 0-6 2m4-2m7: 0-0 3m+: 0-0
Track:	LH: 0-5 RH: 0-1 Tight: 0-3 Gall: 0-2
Aids:	Bl: 0-4 Vi: 0-1 Tstrap: 0-0
Best Rating:	69 3/03 Fknm 2m good Hdl

Ioga (FR)
97   87
7-y-o b/br g Video Rock (FR)-Valentia (FR) (Brezzo (FR))
Miss Venetia Williams Tony Eaves

Placings:P00/5-06 (0318)
2002/03: 24⁰G, 20⁶G,

	Starts	1st	2nd	3rd	Win & Pl
Hurdles	2	0	0	0	0
Career Total	6	0	0	0	0

Going:	Sf: 0-0 GS: 0-0 Gd: 0-2 GF: - Fm: 0-0
Distance:	2m/2m3: 0-0 2m4-2m7: 0-1 3m+: 0-1
Track:	LH: 0-2 RH: 0-0 Tight: 0-1 Gall: 0-0
Aids:	Bl: 0-0 Vi: 0-0 Tstrap: 0-0
Best Rating:	87 5/01 Aint 2m4f good Hdl

Iorana (FR)
106(108c)   (121c)115
7-y-o ch g Marignan (USA)-Fareham (FR) (Fast Topaze (USA))
M C Pipe Mrs Alison C Farrant

Placings:3/F111502/14121U5/PP4-33111143452 (4283)
2002/03: 16⁴G, 19³G, 19³G, 16¹G, 16¹GF, 16¹F, 16¹G, 16⁴S, 16³GS, 16⁴S, 17⁵S, 16²GF,

	Starts	1st	2nd	3rd	Win & Pl
Hurdles	8	3	1	2	10369
Chases	4	1	0	1	6022
Career Total	29	10	3	4	47892
121	10/02	Hrfd	2m	E(0-110)HCh	GD	£4030
103	10/02	Ludl	2m	G Hdl	FRM	£3062
99	10/02	Uttx	2m	G Hdl	G-F	£1820
108	8/02	Worc	2m	D(0-115)HHdl	GD	£4036
105	2/01	Uttx	2m	D Ch	SFT	£3718
130	9/00	Chep	2m110y	B HHdl	GD	£9821
130	8/00	Uttx	2m	2m4f110yD(0-125)HHdl	G-F	£3090
115	9/99	Font	2m	2m2f110yE Hdl	GD	£2232

105	8/99	Worc	2m	E Hdl	G-S	£2355
	6/99	Autl	1m7f	Hdl	VS	£6997

Total win prize-money £41166

Going: Sf: 0-3 GS: 0-1 Gd: 2-5 GF: - Fm: 2-3
Distance: 2m/2m3: 4-10 2m4-2m7: 0-2 3m+: 0-0
Track: LH: 2-5 RH: 2-7 Tight: 0-2 Gall: 0-0
Aids: Bl: 0-0 Vi: 0-0 Tstrap: 0-0
Best Rating: 130 9/00 Chep 2m10y good Hdl

Fair hurdler/chaser, career total stands at nine; effective at around two miles; has won in the soft but is probably better on a sounder surface; below par since being claimed out of Martin Pipe s yard.

Ipledgeallegiance (USA)

108   95

7-y-o b g Alleged (USA)-Yafill (USA) (Nureyev (USA))
K A Morgan Michael Hill

Placings:2U/43520125U403-400P   (2506)
2002/03: 20⁴GF, 16⁰G, 16⁹HY, 16⁶G,

	Starts	1st	2nd	3rd	Win & Pl
Hurdles	4	0	0	0	322
Career Total	18	1	3	2	6476
104 12/01 Hayd 2m	F(0-110)HHdl			SFT	£2702

Total win prize-money £2702

Going: Sf: 0-1 GS: 0-0 Gd: 0-2 GF: - Fm: 0-1
Distance: 2m/2m3: 0-3 2m4-2m7: 0-1 3m+: 0-0
Track: LH: 0-2 RH: 0-2 Tight: 0-0 Gall: 0-0
Aids: Bl: 0-0 Vi: 0-0 Tstrap: 0-2
Best Rating: 104 1/02 Fknm 2m soft Hdl

Suited by soft ground and two miles, he won at Haydock in December 2001 and has run well in defeat since. Regularly wears a tongue strap.

Ira Hayes (IRE)

(106h)   (115dh)112

8-y-o b g Commanche Run-Parsons Glen (IRE) (Glen Quaich)
John A Codd John J Brennan

Placings:400421402060-U242F3F0PPF   (4583a)
2002/03: 20ᵁYS, 21²S, 20⁴GF, 24²GY, 20⁸GS, 20³SH, 25ᶠS, 24ᴰYS, 25ᴾYS, 21ᴾHY, 20ᶠGF,

	Starts	1st	2nd	3rd	Win & Pl
Hurdles	1	0	0	0	417
Chases	10	0	2	1	3828
Career Total	23	1	4	1	17560
113 10/01 Fair 2m4f	Hdl			YLD	£6677

Total win prize-money £6677

Going: Sf: 0-3 GS: 0-1 Gd: 0-0 GF: - Fm: 0-2
Distance: 2m/2m3: 0-0 2m4-2m7: 0-7 3m+: 0-4
Track: LH: 0-4 RH: 0-5 Tight: 0-0 Gall: 0-1
Aids: Bl: 0-0 Vi: 0-0 Tstrap: 0-0
Best Rating: 116 12/02 Punc 2m4f sft-hvy Ch

Irbee

97(94h)   111

11-y-o b g Gunner B-Cupids Bower (Owen Dudley)
P F Nicholls Mrs Bunty Millard

Placings:5/11PF21123/2233115/1F/43523044-22134   (4459)
2002/03: 20²S, 24²GS, 26¹S, 25³G, 21⁴G,

	Starts	1st	2nd	3rd	Win & Pl
Chases	5	1	2	1	5603

	Career Total	32	8	7	6	90152
99	3/03 Plum 3m2f	H Ch			SFT	£1820
108	10/00 Chep 2m110y	D Hdl			G-S	£2996
148	2/00 Kemp 2m	B Ch			SFT	£10042
145	1/00 Hayd 2m	B(0-145)HCh			SFT	£8649
144	3/99 Uttx 2m5f	C(0-135)HCh			G-S	£7132
148	3/99 Chep 2m3f110yD Ch				SFT	£4030
134	11/98 Chep 2m3f110yA(0-115)Ch				G-S	£12680
130	10/98 Worc 2m4f110yD Ch				SFT	£3738

Total win prize-money £51091

Going: Sf: 1-2 GS: 0-1 Gd: 0-2 GF: - Fm: 0-0
Distance: 2m/2m3: 0-0 2m4-2m7: 0-3 3m+: 1-3
Track: LH: 1-2 RH: 0-3 Tight: 1-3 Gall: 0-0
Aids: Bl: 1-5 Vi: 0-0 Tstrap: 0-0
Best Rating: 148 2/00 Kemp 2m soft Ch

Formerly a useful chaser; now hunter chasing and has developed a questionable attitude; stays three miles two but effective at shorter, probably best on good ground or softer; usually wears blinkers.

Ireland's Eye (IRE)

102   101

8-y-o b g Shareef Dancer (USA)-So Romantic (IRE) (Teenoso (USA))
J R Norton Ejam Connection

Placings:1214/651431-4044   (4260)
2002/03: 20⁴GS, 20⁵S, 20⁴G, 21⁴G,

	Starts	1st	2nd	3rd	Win & Pl
Hurdles	4	0	0	0	767
Career Total	14	4	1	1	12040
113 3/02 Newc 2m4f	E Hdl			HVY	£2702
96 12/01 Hexm 2m	D Hdl			SFT	£3705
111 3/99 Newc 2m	H NHF			SFT	£1710
99 1/99 Catt 2m	H NHF			SFT	£1842

Total win prize-money £9960

Going: Sf: 0-1 GS: 0-1 Gd: 0-2 GF: - Fm: 0-0
Distance: 2m/2m3: 0-2 2m4-2m7: 0-4 3m+: 0-0
Track: LH: 0-4 RH: 0-0 Tight: 0-1 Gall: 0-1
Aids: Bl: 0-0 Vi: 0-0 Tstrap: 0-0
Best Rating: 118 4/99 Ayr 2m soft NHF

Moderate hurdler, stays two and a half miles and acts on soft ground.

Iris Bleu (FR)

115   162

7-y-o ch g Beyssac (FR)-Dear Blue (FR) (Cyborg (FR))
M C Pipe D A Johnson

Placings:011/12446/3222223PF5-1123P   (4479)
2002/03: 24¹G, 24¹HY, 25²GS, 28³G, 36ᴾG,

	Starts	1st	2nd	3rd	Win & Pl
Chases	5	2	1	1	59731
Career Total	23	5	7	3	120901
162 2/03 Sand 3m110y HCh				HVY	£29000
136 11/02 Chel 3m110y E(0-135)HCh				GD	£9831
131 5/00 Autl 2m1f110y Ch				VS	£11527
4/00 Autl 2m2f Hdl				HLD	£10567
4/00 Autl 2m1f110y Hdl				HLD	£9606

Total win prize-money £70531

Going: Sf: 1-1 GS: 0-1 Gd: 1-3 GF: - Fm: 0-0
Distance: 2m/2m3: 0-0 2m4-2m7: 0-0 3m+: 2-5
Track: LH: 1-3 RH: 1-2 Tight: 0-1 Gall: 1-1
Aids: Bl: 0-0 Vi: 0-0 Tstrap: 0-0
Best Rating: 162 3/03 Hayd 3m4f110y good Ch

Smart chaser; consistently placed over fences, but frustrating, before he finally got off the mark in Britain at Cheltenham on his seasonal reappearance in November

2002 and followed-up by routing his field in a better race at Sandown; well held in good race at Wincanton, before a good third in the Red Square Vodka Gold Cup at Haydock; injured and pulled up after one circuit in the Grand National; handles good or softer and stays three miles four.

Iris Collonges (FR)

103(103h)   (115h)114

7-y-o b g Luchiroverte (IRE)-Soubrette Collonge (FR) (Saumon (FR))
N J Henderson The Barrow Boys Ii

Placings:0/2312/6446-2P   (4368)
2002/03: 19²G, 19ᴾG,

	Starts	1st	2nd	3rd	Win & Pl
Chases	2	0	1	0	1287
Career Total	11	1	3	1	7245
113 1/01 Winc 2m	E Hdl			G-S	£2037

Total win prize-money £2037

Going: Sf: 0-0 GS: 0-0 Gd: 0-2 GF: - Fm: 0-0
Distance: 2m/2m3: 0-1 2m4-2m7: 0-1 3m+: 0-0
Track: LH: 0-0 RH: 0-2 Tight: 0-0 Gall: 0-0
Aids: Bl: 0-0 Vi: 0-0 Tstrap: 0-0
Best Rating: 120 3/01 Asct 2m110y heavy Hdl

A winner over hurdles on good to soft ground; has taken time to find his feet over fences but a good effort when runner-up to potentially useful sort at Hereford in February.

Iris D'Estruval (FR)

7-y-o b g Quart De Vin (FR)-Claire D Estruval (FR) (Mistigri)
E Retter (N J Henderson 12/5) Edward Retter

Placings:U   (0347)
2002/03: 26ᵁGS,

	Starts	1st	2nd	3rd	Win & Pl
Chases	1	0	0	0	
Career Total	1	0	0	0	

Going: Sf: 0-0 GS: 0-1 Gd: 0-0 GF: - Fm: 0-0
Distance: 2m/2m3: 0-0 2m4-2m7: 0-0 3m+: 0-1
Track: LH: 0-1 RH: 0-0 Tight: 0-1 Gall: 0-0
Aids: Bl: 0-0 Vi: 0-0 Tstrap: 0-0
Best Rating:

Iris Royal (FR)

112(117h)   (136h)131

7-y-o b g Garde Royale-Tchela (FR) (Le Nain Jaune (FR))
N J Henderson Sir Robert Ogden

Placings:41521/1PPP/231022-211PP2   (4779)
2002/03: 24²G, 24¹G, 24¹G, 24ᴾG, 20ᴾG, 20²GF,

	Starts	1st	2nd	3rd	Win & Pl
Chases	6	2	2	0	20613
Career Total	21	6	6	1	82274
131 2/03 Donc 3m	E Ch			GD	£4776
131 12/02 Newb 3m	C Ch			GD	£8450
131 2/03 Sand 2m6f	A HHdl			SFT	£29000
129 1/01 Font 2m4f	C(0-135)HHdl			SFT	£5382
121 4/00 Ayr 2m4f	C HHdl			GD	£4861
119 1/00 Wwck 2m	D Hdl			SFT	£4543

Total win prize-money £57034

Going: Sf: 0-0 GS: 0-0 Gd: 2-5 GF: - Fm: 0-1
Distance: 2m/2m3: 0-2 2m4-2m7: 0-2 3m+: 2-4
Track: LH: 2-4 RH: 0-2 Tight: 0-0 Gall: 2-3
Aids: Bl: 0-0 Vi: 0-0 Tstrap: 0-0
Best Rating: 136 4/02 Chel 3m good Hdl

Useful chaser; disappointing at Cheltenham and Aintree, but useful form otherwise; probably best over three miles and suited by fast ground.

Iris's Gift
118   173
6-y-o gr g Gunner B-Shirley s Gift (Scallywag)
Jonjo O Neill Robert Lester

Placings: *11152*-1111121   (4473)
2002/03: 20¹GS, 25¹GF, 24¹G, 20¹HY, 23¹G, 24²G, 24¹G,

	Starts	1st	2nd	3rd	Win & Pl
Hurdles	7	6	1	0	141398
Career Total	12	9	2	0	160308

169	4/03	Aint	3m110y	A Hdl		GD	£46400
160	3/03	Hayd	2m7f110yA Hdl		GD	£17850
160	2/03	Uttx	2m4f110yA Hdl		HVY	£20100
150	12/02	Chel	3m	A Hdl		GD	£14500
139	10/02	Chel	3m1f110yC Hdl		G-F	£7113
123	10/02	Bang	2m4f	E Hdl		G-S	£3094
116	2/02	Newb	2m110y	A NHF		SFT	£9000
102	9/01	Worc	2m	H NHF		G-F	£1515
95	8/01	Worc	2m	H NHF		G-F	£1494
				Total win prize-money £121069			

Going:	Sf: 1-1 GS: 1-1 Gd: 3-4 GF: - Fm: 1-1
Distance:	2m/2m3: 0-0 2m4-2m7: 2-2 3m+: 4-5
Track:	LH: 6-7 RH: 0-0 Tight: 2-2 Gall: 2-3
Aids:	Bl: 0-0 Vi: 0-0 Tstrap: 0-0
Best Rating:	173 3/03 Chel 3m good Hdl

Smart, progressive staying novice hurdler; a winner of three bumpers and unbeaten over hurdles until high-class second to Baracouda in Stayers Hurdle at Cheltenham; clear-cut winner of Grade One novices event at Aintree; acts on any ground, but better with cut; stays three miles one; excellent chase prospect.

Irish Blessing (USA)
90   53
6-y-o b g Ghazi (USA)-Win For Leah (USA) (His Majesty (USA))
F Jordan The Bhiss Partnership

Placings: 05P-0   (0380)
2002/03: 26⁰G,

	Starts	1st	2nd	3rd	Win & Pl
Hurdles	1	0	0	0	
Career Total	4	0	0	0	0

Going:	Sf: 0-0 GS: 0-0 Gd: 0-0 GF: - Fm: 0-0
Distance:	2m/2m3: 0-0 2m4-2m7: 0-0 3m+: 0-1
Track:	LH: 0-0 RH: 0-1 Tight: 0-0 Gall: 0-1
Aids:	Bl: 0-1 Vi: 0-0 Tstrap: 0-0
Best Rating:	30 8/01 Ctml 2m1f110y good Hdl

Irish Chapel (IRE)
68f   53f
7-y-o b g College Chapel-Heart Of Flame (Top Ville)
H E Haynes Miss Sally R Haynes

Placings: 00-0   (0523)
2002/03: 17⁰G,

	Starts	1st	2nd	3rd	Win & Pl
NH Flat	1	0	0	0	
Career Total	3	0	0	0	

Going:	Sf: 0-0 GS: 0-0 Gd: 0-1 GF: - Fm: 0-0
Distance:	2m/2m3: 0-1 2m4-2m7: 0-0 3m+: 0-0
Track:	LH: 0-1 RH: 0-0 Tight: 0-1 Gall: 0-0

Aids:	Bl: 0-0 Vi: 0-0 Tstrap: 0-0
Best Rating:	53 7/01 Worc 2m good NHF

Irish Distinction (IRE)
108   106
5-y-o b g Distinctly North (USA)-Shane s Girl (IRE) (Marktingo)
T R George (M C Pipe 21/11) Ryder Racing Ltd

Placings: F003   (4468)
2002/03: 16ᶠGF, 16⁰G, 16⁰G, 17³F,

	Starts	1st	2nd	3rd	Win & Pl
Hurdles	4	0	0	1	520
Career Total	4	0	0	1	520

Going:	Sf: 0-0 GS: 0-0 Gd: 0-2 GF: - Fm: 0-0
Distance:	2m/2m3: 0-4 2m4-2m7: 0-0 3m+: 0-0
Track:	LH: 0-2 RH: 0-2 Tight: 0-0 Gall: 0-0
Aids:	Bl: 0-0 Vi: 0-0 Tstrap: 0-0
Best Rating:	90 10/02 Chel 2m110y gd-fm Hdl

Moderate handicap hurdler; on the upgrade and completed a hat-trick with an ultimate wide margin success at Wetherby in May; may have been unsuited by the ground next time; likes a strong gallop; effective at around two miles; acts on fast ground.

Irish Fashion (USA)
90(104h)   (113h)77
8-y-o ch g Nashwan (USA)-L Irlandaise (USA) (Irish River (FR))
Dr P Pritchard A J Whiting

Placings: 4030531/000/60312120634-5   (1394)
2002/03: 19⁵GF,

	Starts	1st	2nd	3rd	Win & Pl
Chases	1	0	0	0	
Career Total	22	3	2	4	11979

106	12/01	Plum	2m	F(0-110)HHdl	GD	£3542
103	12/01	Wwck	2m	F(0-100)HHdl	SFT	£2000
113	4/00	Plum	2m	F(0-90)Hdl	HVY	£2394
				Total win prize-money £7938		

Going:	Sf: 0-0 GS: 0-0 Gd: 0-0 GF: - Fm: 0-1
Distance:	2m/2m3: 0-0 2m4-2m7: 0-1 3m+: 0-0
Track:	LH: 0-1 RH: 0-0 Tight: 0-0 Gall: 0-0
Aids:	Bl: 0-0 Vi: 0-0 Tstrap: 0-0
Best Rating:	113 2/02 Asct 2m110y soft Hdl

Fair hurdler, if slightly one-paced, he likes the mud and is suited by positive tactics. Made a return to form in December 2001, winning at Warwick and Plumpton, but was held off higher marks.

Irish Gold (IRE)
62   48
8-y-o b g Good Thyne (USA)-Ardfallon (IRE) (Supreme Leader)
P Winkworth R R A Eadie

Placings: 0/5   (4077)
2002/03: 21⁵HY,

	Starts	1st	2nd	3rd	Win & Pl
Hurdles	1	0	0	0	0
Career Total	2	0	0	0	0

Going:	Sf: 0-1 GS: 0-0 Gd: 0-0 GF: - Fm: 0-0
Distance:	2m/2m3: 0-0 2m4-2m7: 0-1 3m+: 0-0

Track:	LH: 0-1 RH: 0-0 Tight: 0-1 Gall: 0-0
Aids:	Bl: 0-0 Vi: 0-0 Tstrap: 0-0
Best Rating:	53 7/01 Worc 2m good NHF

Irish Hussar (IRE)
115(110h)   (141h)151
7-y-o b g Supreme Leader-Shuil Ard (Quayside)
N J Henderson Major Christopher Hanbury

Placings: 1/210-1F121   (4474)
2002/03: 21¹GS, 21ᶠGS, 23¹GS, 21²G, 25¹G,

	Starts	1st	2nd	3rd	Win & Pl
Chases	5	3	1	0	73377
Career Total	9	5	2	0	83085

143	4/03	Aint	3m1f	A Ch	GD	£44625
127	2/03	Leic	2m7f110yD Ch	G-S	£5590
134	12/02	Winc	2m5f	D Ch	G-S	£5561
125	3/02	Newb	2m3f	D Hdl	SFT	£4953
127	3/01	Sand	2m110y	H NHF	HVY	£2803
				Total win prize-money £63534		

Going:	Sf: 0-0 GS: 2-3 Gd: 1-2 GF: - Fm: 0-0
Distance:	2m/2m3: 0-0 2m4-2m7: 1-3 3m+: 2-2
Track:	LH: 1-3 RH: 2-2 Tight: 1-1 Gall: 0-2
Aids:	Bl: 0-0 Vi: 0-0 Tstrap: 0-0
Best Rating:	151 3/03 Chel 2m5f good Ch

Useful hurdler/smart novice chaser; won on chasing debut at Wincanton in December 2002, but held when falling next time; bounced back to win average contest at Leicester, and then excelled himself when runner-up in the Cathcart Chase at the Festival; comfortable winner of Grade Two at Aintree; stays three miles; acts on soft ground.

Irish Native (IRE)
6-y-o b g Be My Native (USA)-Thats Irish (Furry Glen)
Miss H C Knight Martin Broughton

Placings: 0P-P   (1712)
2002/03: 20ᴾGS,

	Starts	1st	2nd	3rd	Win & Pl
Chases	1	0	0	0	
Career Total	3	0	0	0	

Going:	Sf: 0-0 GS: 0-1 Gd: 0-0 GF: - Fm: 0-0
Distance:	2m/2m3: 0-0 2m4-2m7: 0-1 3m+: 0-0
Track:	LH: 0-1 RH: 0-0 Tight: 0-1 Gall: 0-0
Aids:	Bl: 0-0 Vi: 0-0 Tstrap: 0-0
Best Rating:	69 11/01 Winc 2m good NHF

Irish Option (IRE)
105   107
10-y-o ch g Executive Perk-Erins Treasure (Brave Invader (USA))
J T Gifford Mrs Jean Plackett

Placings: 3/4403/421332/53521/4324F2P   (4528)
2002/03: 20⁴GS, 20³GS, 21²S, 24⁴GS, 26ᶠGS, 26²S, 24ᴾG,

	Starts	1st	2nd	3rd	Win & Pl
Chases	7	0	4	4	4548
Career Total	23	2	5	6	15518

107	2/01	Plum	2m4f	E Ch	SFT	£3107
100	11/99	Plum	2m5f	E Hdl	GD	£2530
				Total win prize-money £5637		

Going:	Sf: 0-2 GS: 0-4 Gd: 0-1 GF: - Fm: 0-0
Distance:	2m/2m3: 0-0 2m4-2m7: 0-3 3m+: 0-4
Track:	LH: 0-3 RH: 0-3 Tight: 0-4 Gall: 0-1
Aids:	Bl: 0-0 Vi: 0-0 Tstrap: 0-0

Aids:	Bl: 0-0 Vi: 0-0 Tstrap: 0-0
Best Rating:	53 7/01 Worc 2m good NHF

Track: LH: 0-1 RH: 0-0 Tight: 0-1 Gall: 0-0
Aids: Bl: 0-0 Vi: 0-0 Tstrap: 0-0
Best Rating: 89 11/00 Extr 2m1f   gd-sft Hdl

Best Rating: 107   12/02 Folk   2m5f   soft   Ch

Modest handicap chaser; formerly useful; best at around two and a half miles; a soft surface suits best.

Irish Paddy (IRE)
79   46
4-y-o b g Idris (IRE)-Ceili Queen (IRE) (Shareef Dancer (USA))
I A Brown   I A Brown

Placings:00000PP   (4352)
2002/03: 17⁰GF, 16⁰GF, 16⁰G, 16⁰G, 16⁰G, 17ᴾHY, 16ᴾGF,

	Starts	1st	2nd	3rd	Win & Pl
Hurdles	7	0	0	0	
Career Total	7	0	0	0	

Going: Sf: 0-1 GS: 0-0 Gd: 0-3 GF: - Fm: 0-3
Distance: 2m/2m3: 0-2 2m4-2m7: 0-0 3m+: 0-0
Track: LH: 0-6 RH: 0-1 Tight: 0-4 Gall: 0-1
Aids: Bl: 0-0 Vi: 0-0 Tstrap: 0-0
Best Rating: 39   12/02 Donc   2m110y   good   Hdl

Irish Patriarch (IRE)
68f   53f
7-y-o b g Mister Lord (USA)-Moon Lock (Lock And Load (USA))
P G Murphy   T P Ronan

Placings:0   (2009)
2002/03: 17⁰S,

	Starts	1st	2nd	3rd	Win & Pl
NH Flat	1	0	0	0	
Career Total	1	0	0	0	

Going: Sf: 0-1 GS: 0-0 Gd: 0-0 GF: - Fm: 0-0
Distance: 2m/2m3: 0-1 2m4-2m7: 0-0 3m+: 0-0
Track: LH: 0-0 RH: 0-1 Tight: 0-1 Gall: 0-0
Aids: Bl: 0-0 Vi: 0-0 Tstrap: 0-0
Best Rating: 53   11/02 Folk   2m1f110y   soft   NHF

Irish Prince (IRE)
64   53
7-y-o b g Fresh Breeze (USA)-Kilivarig (Crozier)
D Shaw (J G M O Shea 14/5) Owen Lutchmaya

Placings:0P2P   (4173)
2002/03: 17⁰G, 19ᴾGS, 25ᴾS, 20ᴾS,

	Starts	1st	2nd	3rd	Win & Pl
NH Flat	1	0	0	0	0
Hurdles	3	0	1	0	1028
Career Total	4	0	1	0	1028

Going: Sf: 0-2 GS: 0-1 Gd: 0-1 GF: - Fm: 0-0
Distance: 2m/2m3: 0-1 2m4-2m7: 0-2 3m+: 0-1
Track: LH: 0-3 RH: 0-1 Tight: 0-0 Gall: 0-0
Aids: Bl: 0-0 Vi: 0-1 Tstrap: 0-0
Best Rating: 82   5/02 Hrfd   2m1f   good   NHF

Irish Sea (USA)
95(95h)   96
10-y-o b g Zilzal (USA)-Dunkellin (USA) (Irish River (FR))
S Flook   Glyn Byard

Placings:050P/6622F10U556011/B12/P/3P13-F33   (4443)

2002/03: 22ᶠGS, 16³GS, 19³G,

	Starts	1st	2nd	3rd	Win & Pl
Chases	3	0	0	2	795
Career Total	29	5	3	4	12356

90	4/02	Uttx	2m7f	H Ch	G-F	£1631
91	7/99	Worc	2m2f	E(0-115)HHdl	G-F	£2372
85	4/99	Folk	2m1f110yG(0-95)HHdl		G-F	£1660
74	4/99	Tntn	2m3f110yG(0-90)HHdl		G-S	£1509
84	10/98	MRas	2m1f110yG(0-95)HHdl		SFT	£1576
				Total win prize-money £8749		

Going: Sf: 0-0 GS: 0-2 Gd: 0-1 GF: - Fm: 0-0
Distance: 2m/2m3: 0-1 2m4-2m7: 0-2 3m+: 0-0
Track: LH: 0-6 RH: 0-2 Tight: 0-0 Gall: 0-0
Aids: Bl: 0-0 Vi: 0-0 Tstrap: 0-0
Best Rating: 96   4/03   Asct   2m3f110y   good   Ch

Took advantage of the misfortune of two rivals when springing a surprise in a 23-furlong hunters chase at Uttoxeter in April 2002. Fair efforts since.

Irishkawa Bellevue (FR)
92   72+
5-y-o b/br g Irish Prospector (FR)-Strakawa (FR) (Sukawa (FR))
Jean-Rene Auvray   The Magpie Partnership

Placings:64505   (4634)
2002/03: 18⁶S, 17⁴G, 16⁵G, 22⁹GF, 21⁵GF,

	Starts	1st	2nd	3rd	Win & Pl
NH Flat	3	0	0	0	0
Hurdles	2	0	0	0	0
Career Total	5	0	0	0	0

Going: Sf: 0-1 GS: 0-0 Gd: 0-2 GF: - Fm: 0-2
Distance: 2m/2m3: 0-3 2m4-2m7: 0-2 3m+: 0-0
Track: LH: 0-3 RH: 0-2 Tight: 0-3 Gall: 0-0
Aids: Bl: 0-0 Vi: 0-0 Tstrap: 0-0
Best Rating: 95   3/03   Ludl   2m   good   NHF

Improved on debut effort when respectable fourth in bumper at Hereford in February 2002; disappointing over hurdles so far.

Irishman (IRE)
(64h)   (29h)
9-y-o b g Bob Back (USA)-Future Tense (USA) (Pretense)
Miss I E Craig (Paul A Roche 29/9) Miss I E L Craig

Placings:0/0005003F00P/P/632044̸01F2P-031UF303P5   (4662)
2002/03: 16⁹G, 20³Y, 24¹GF, 22ᵁGY, 20ᶠG, 24³F, 20⁰S, 24³GF, 20ᴾG, 26⁵GF,

	Starts	1st	2nd	3rd	Win & Pl
Hurdles	3	0	0	1	429
Chases	7	1	0	2	6176
Career Total	34	2	2	5	17046
94	7/02	Wxfd	3m	(0-88)HCh	G-F	£4868
86	8/01	Tram	2m4f	(0-95)HCh	G-Y	£5842
				Total win prize-money £10711		

Going: Sf: 0-1 GS: 0-0 Gd: 0-3 GF: - Fm: 1-4
Distance: 2m/2m3: 0-1 2m4-2m7: 0-5 3m+: 1-4
Track: LH: 0-4 RH: 1-3 Tight: 0-1 Gall: 0-1
Aids: Bl: 0-2 Vi: 0-0 Tstrap: 0-0
Best Rating: 107   5/01   Dund   2m135y   firm   NHF

Moderate ex-Irish hurdler/chaser; showed little on British debut at Newcastle; stays 3m; acts on a sound surface; has worn blinkers.

Irlandais Ii (FR)
76(86h)   (56h)46
7-y-o ch g Moon Madness-Platine Iii (FR) (Iveday (FR))
G A Harker   Lord Bolton

Placings:0PP4/0654606P-P00PP   (3802)
2002/03: 16ᴾG, 16⁰G, 24⁰GS, 27ᴾS, 20ᴾS,

	Starts	1st	2nd	3rd	Win & Pl
Chases	5	0	0	0	
Career Total	17	0	0	0	790

Going: Sf: 0-2 GS: 0-1 Gd: 0-2 GF: - Fm: 0-0
Distance: 2m/2m3: 0-2 2m4-2m7: 0-1 3m+: 0-2
Track: LH: 0-4 RH: 0-1 Tight: 0-2 Gall: 0-2
Aids: Bl: 0-0 Vi: 0-0 Tstrap: 0-0
Best Rating: 100   4/01   Ayr   2m   good   Ch

Iro Origny (FR)
91(99h)   (88h)78
7-y-o b g Saint Cyrien (FR)-Coralline (FR) (Iron Duke (FR))
Miss Venetia Williams   M J Morris

Placings:6/6F205043/P6434RR   (2780)
2002/03: 22ᴾPP, 20⁶GF, 19⁴GF, 19³G, 19⁴G, 20ᴿG, 19ᴿS,

	Starts	1st	2nd	3rd	Win & Pl
Hurdles	2	0	0	0	0
Chases	5	0	0	1	1293
Career Total	16	0	1	2	4917

Going: Sf: 0-1 GS: 0-0 Gd: 0-3 GF: - Fm: 0-3
Distance: 2m/2m3: 0-4 2m4-2m7: 0-3 3m+: 0-0
Track: LH: 0-2 RH: 0-4 Tight: 0-4 Gall: 0-0
Aids: Bl: 0-0 Vi: 0-0 Tstrap: 0-6
Best Rating: 88   4/01   Tntn   2m3f110y   gd-fm   Hdl

A rather inconsistent character.

Iron Dragon (IRE)
5-y-o b g Royal Academy (USA)-Kerry Project (IRE) (Project Manager)
Mrs M Reveley   Lucayan Stud

Placings:U   (0199)
2002/03: 16ᵁGF,

	Starts	1st	2nd	3rd	Win & Pl
Hurdles	1	0	0	0	
Career Total	1	0	0	0	

Going: Sf: 0-0 GS: 0-0 Gd: 0-0 GF: - Fm: 0-1
Distance: 2m/2m3: 0-1 2m4-2m7: 0-0 3m+: 0-0
Track: LH: 0-1 RH: 0-0 Tight: 0-0 Gall: 0-0
Aids: Bl: 0-0 Vi: 0-0 Tstrap: 0-0
Best Rating: 0   5/02   Worc   2m   gd-fm   Hdl

Iron Express
108   (82h)102
7-y-o b g Teenoso (USA)-Sylvia Beach (The Parson)
G M Moore   David Parker

Placings:30/433210/P-3355343   (4589)
2002/03: 21³G, 21³S, 19⁵GS, 16⁵G, 25³G, 21⁴G, 25³G,

	Starts	1st	2nd	3rd	Win & Pl
Chases	7	0	0	4	2822
Career Total	16	1	1	7	6540
90	1/01	Donc	2m4f	E Hdl	GD	£2254
				Total win prize-money £2254		

Going:	Sf: 0-1 GS: 0-1 Gd: 0-5 GF: - Fm: 0-0
Distance:	2m/2m3: 0-2 2m4-2m7: 0-3 3m+: 0-2
Track:	LH: 0-7 RH: 0-0 Tight: 0-5 Gall: 0-0
Aids:	Bl: 0-0 Vi: 0-0 Tstrap: 0-0
Best Rating:	102 10/02 Sedg 2m5f good Ch

Moderate chaser; stays three miles one; suited by good or softer; finally off the mark over fences at Hexham in April; returned to form when runner-up at Cartmel in July.

Iron Mountain (IRE)
96   86
8-y-o b g Scenic-Merlannah (IRE) (Shy Groom (USA))
Mrs L C Jewell   A Emanuel, A Paterson, J Shannon

Placings:5/260/0F2   (2319)
2002/03: 16⁰GS, 16ᶠG, 16²HY,

	Starts	1st	2nd	3rd	Win & Pl
Hurdles	3	0	1	0	866
Career Total	7	0	2	0	1570

Going:	Sf: 0-1 GS: 0-1 Gd: 0-1 GF: - Fm: 0-0
Distance:	2m/2m3: 0-3 2m4-2m7: 0-0 3m+: 0-0
Track:	LH: 0-3 RH: 0-0 Tight: 0-0 Gall: 0-0
Aids:	Bl: 0-0 Vi: 0-0 Tstrap: 0-0
Best Rating:	101 11/00 Uttx 2m heavy Hdl

A modest handicapper over hurdles, he struggles to get the trip in testing conditions.

Iron N Gold
79   94+
11-y-o b g Heights Of Gold-Southern Dynasty (Gunner B)
B G Powell   D C T Partnership

Placings:023/12P03145/5/22235/2425311-P0P   (4735)
2002/03: 20ᴾS, 21⁰S, 19ᴾGF,

	Starts	1st	2nd	3rd	Win & Pl
Chases	3	0	0	0	0
Career Total	27	4	7	4	20606
103	11/01 Uttx	2m4f	F(0-110)HCh	HVY	£3400
93	11/01 Uttx	2m4f	E(0-105)HCh	SFT	£3120
99	3/97 Hntg	2m110y	E(0-110)HHdl	G-F	£2267
94	10/96 Strf	2m110y	E Hdl	GD	£2757
			Total win prize-money £11546		

Going:	Sf: 0-2 GS: 0-0 Gd: 0-0 GF: - Fm: 0-1
Distance:	2m/2m3: 0-0 2m4-2m7: 0-3 3m+: 0-0
Track:	LH: 0-2 RH: 0-1 Tight: 0-0 Gall: 0-0
Aids:	Bl: 0-0 Vi: 0-0 Tstrap: 0-0
Best Rating:	103 11/01 Uttx 2m4f heavy Ch

Dual winner at Uttoxeter in 2001; absent for a year when pulled up on return; also pulled up in selling handicap at Chepstow April 2003; has been breaking blood vessels and was promptly retired after landing 2m 5f handicap chase at Uttoxeter the following month.

Iron Princess (IRE)
7-y-o b m Insan (USA)-Mrs Cullen (Over The River (FR))
G M Moore   David Parker

Placings:0/P30PP-P   (0079)
2002/03: 25ᴾGS,

	Starts	1st	2nd	3rd	Win & Pl
Chases	1	0	0	0	0
Career Total	7	0	0	1	358

| Going: | Sf: 0-0 GS: 0-1 Gd: 0-0 GF: - Fm: 0-0 |
| Distance: | 2m/2m3: 0-0 2m4-2m7: 0-0 3m+: 0-1 |

Track:	LH: 0-1 RH: 0-0 Tight: 0-0 Gall: 0-0
Aids:	Bl: 0-1 Vi: 0-0 Tstrap: 0-0
Best Rating:	18 4/01 Fknm 2m gd-sft NHF

Iron Trooper (IRE)
5-y-o ch g Glacial Storm (USA)-Iron Star (General Ironside)
J Wade   John Wade

Placings:00   (3864)
2002/03: 21⁰HY, 19⁰GS,

	Starts	1st	2nd	3rd	Win & Pl
Hurdles	2	0	0	0	
Career Total	2	0	0	0	

Going:	Sf: 0-1 GS: 0-1 Gd: 0-0 GF: - Fm: 0-0
Distance:	2m/2m3: 0-0 2m4-2m7: 0-2 3m+: 0-0
Track:	LH: 0-2 RH: 0-0 Tight: 0-1 Gall: 0-0
Aids:	Bl: 0-0 Vi: 0-0 Tstrap: 0-0
Best Rating:	0 2/03 Donc 2m3f110y gd-sft Hdl

Isam Top (FR)
110(98c)   (95c)105
7-y-o b g Siam (USA)-Miss Sic Top (FR) (Mister Sic Top (FR))
M J Hogan   Mrs Barbara Hogan

Placings:60/P6022246P0/422300324-5FP0P01243 (1552)
2002/03: 16⁵G, 21ᶠGF, 18ᴾGF, 20⁰S, 16ᴾGF, 22⁰GF, 18¹G, 17²G, 18⁴G, 17³G,

	Starts	1st	2nd	3rd	Win & Pl
Hurdles	7	1	1	1	5724
Chases	3	0	0	0	0
Career Total	31	1	7	3	14929
105	8/02 Font	2m2f110y		D(0-115)HHdl	GD	£3786
			Total win prize-money £3786		

Going:	Sf: 0-1 GS: 0-0 Gd: 1-5 GF: - Fm: 0-4
Distance:	2m/2m3: 1-7 2m4-2m7: 0-3 3m+: 0-0
Track:	LH: 1-7 RH: 0-3 Tight: 1-6 Gall: 0-0
Aids:	Bl: 0-1 Vi: 0-0 Tstrap: 0-0
Best Rating:	106 10/00 Kemp 2m gd-sft Hdl

Modest hurdler/chaser, suited by a sound surface.

Isard III (FR)
110   132+
7-y-o gr g Royal Charter (FR)-Aurore D Ex (FR) (Mont Basile (FR))
M C Pipe   C M, B J & R F Batterham Ii

Placings:1/F1   (4442)
2002/03: 20ᶠGS, 20¹G,

	Starts	1st	2nd	3rd	Win & Pl
Hurdles	1	1	0	0	5174
Chases	1	0	0	0	0
Career Total	3	2	0	0	6924
132	4/03 Asct	2m4f	D Hdl	GD	£5174
111	4/01 Newb	2m110y	H NHF	SFT	£1750
			Total win prize-money £6924		

Going:	Sf: 0-0 GS: 0-1 Gd: 1-1 GF: - Fm: 0-0
Distance:	2m/2m3: 0-0 2m4-2m7: 1-2 3m+: 0-0
Track:	LH: 0-1 RH: 1-1 Tight: 0-0 Gall: 0-0
Aids:	Bl: 0-0 Vi: 0-0 Tstrap: 0-0
Best Rating:	132 4/03 Asct 2m4f good Hdl

Useful performer; landed a bumper at Newbury first time up, before winning a point-to-point in February 2002; fell on

---

chasing debut at Newbury; off track for a while after that until returning in hurdle to win at Ascot; acts on soft ground; stays three miles; not seen under rules since April 2001.

Isca Maiden
80(109h)   (69h)69
9-y-o b m Full Extent (USA)-Sharp N Easy (Swing Easy (USA))
G Brown   Mrs C A Davies

Placings:660P00/01B306/46565P/P100P-630P   (4258)
2002/03: 19⁶S, 17³HY, 16⁶GS, 17ᴾG,

	Starts	1st	2nd	3rd	Win & Pl
Hurdles	2	0	0	0	0
Chases	2	0	0	1	474
Career Total	27	2	0	2	6899
80	10/01 Towc	2m	F(0-100)HHdl	SFT	£4407
87	12/99 Towc	2m	G(0-95)HHdl	SFT	£1660
			Total win prize-money £6067		

Going:	Sf: 0-2 GS: 0-1 Gd: 0-1 GF: - Fm: 0-0
Distance:	2m/2m3: 0-3 2m4-2m7: 0-1 3m+: 0-0
Track:	LH: 0-2 RH: 0-2 Tight: 0-4 Gall: 0-0
Aids:	Bl: 0-0 Vi: 0-0 Tstrap: 0-0
Best Rating:	87 5/00 Towc 2m gd-fm Hdl

Moderate hurdler/chaser, a winner twice at Towcester over two miles on soft ground. She favours being ridden prominently.

Isefoul De Bellevue (FR)
86(69h)   (62 h)56
7-y-o b g Useful (FR)-Frika (FR) (Kashneb (FR))
R M Stronge   The Turf Tavern Partnership

Placings:000002/4050F060-PPU40   (4735)
2002/03: 21ᴾHY, 26ᴾG, 20⁰G, 16⁴GF, 19⁰GF,

	Starts	1st	2nd	3rd	Win & Pl
Hurdles	2	0	0	0	0
Chases	3	0	0	0	311
Career Total	19	0	1	0	1633

Going:	Sf: 0-1 GS: 0-0 Gd: 0-2 GF: - Fm: 0-2
Distance:	2m/2m3: 0-1 2m4-2m7: 0-3 3m+: 0-1
Track:	LH: 0-4 RH: 0-1 Tight: 0-0 Gall: 0-0
Aids:	Bl: 0-0 Vi: 0-0 Tstrap: 0-3
Best Rating:	97 5/01 Klny 2m1f gd-fm Hdl

Ishandraz (GER)
103   92
6-y-o gr g Mondrian (GER)-Isla Limpia (GER) (Limbo (GER))
M C Pipe   Roger Stanley & Yvonne Reynolds

Placings:50012   (4622)
2002/03: 17⁵S, 17⁰S, 16⁰S, 25¹GF, 22²GF,

	Starts	1st	2nd	3rd	Win & Pl
Hurdles	5	1	1	0	4726
Career Total	5	1	1	0	4726
90	3/03 Plum	3m1f110y		F(0-95)HHdl	G-F	£2901
			Total win prize-money £2902		

Going:	Sf: 0-3 GS: 0-0 Gd: 0-0 GF: - Fm: 1-2
Distance:	2m/2m3: 0-0 2m4-2m7: 0-1 3m+: 1-1
Track:	LH: 0-2 RH: 0-2 Tight: 0-4 Gall: 0-0
Aids:	Bl: 0-0 Vi: 0-0 Tstrap: 0-0
Best Rating:	92 4/03 NAbb 2m6f gd-fm Hdl

Plating-class hurdler; got off the mark over hurdles in Britain on handicap debut at Plumpton in March; acts well on a fast surface; stays three miles plus well.

Isio (FR)

110(117h)   (135h)**151**

7-y-o b g Silver Rainbow-Swifty (FR) (Le Riverain (FR))
N J Henderson   Sir Peter and Lady Gibbings

Placings:221211-1113   (4098)
2002/03: 16^{1}G, 16^{1}G, 16^{1}G, 16^{3}G,

	Starts	1st	2nd	3rd	Win & Pl
Chases	4	3	0	1	30031
Career Total	10	6	3	1	49701

141	2/03	Hntg	2m110y	D Ch	GD £5434
138	1/03	Donc	2m110y	E Ch	GD £4169
138	11/02	Kemp	2m	D Ch	GD £5027
135	4/02	Ayr	2m	C Hdl	GD £5183
133	3/02	Newb	2m110y	D Hdl	G-S £4504
123	2/02	Ludl	2m	E Hdl	SFT £3003

Total win prize-money £27323

Going: Sf: 0-0 GS: 0-0 Gd: 3-4 GF: - Fm: 0-0
Distance: 2m/2m3: 3-4 2m4-2m7: 0-0 3m+: 0-0
Track: LH: 1-2 RH: 2-2 Tight: 0-0 Gall: 2-3
Aids: Bl: 0-0 Vi: 0-0 Tstrap: 0-0
Best Rating: 151 3/03 Chel 2m   good   Ch

Smart novice chaser; formerly useful hurdler; easy winner of three minor novice chases to date; third in Arkle at Cheltenham, all form around 2m; acts on ground good or softer.

Iskan (GER)

8-y-o b g Perceive Arrogance (USA)-Ifakara (GER)
(Athenagoras (GER))
A Parker   H Henderson

Placings:31P/P000/304PPFPP-0PP   (2423)
2002/03: 17^{0}S, 16^{P}HY, 21^{P}S,

	Starts	1st	2nd	3rd	Win & Pl
Hurdles	3	0	0	0	
Career Total	18	1	0	2	3746
98	3/00 Carl	2m4f110y		E Hdl	HVY £2562

Total win prize-money £2562

Going: Sf: 0-3 GS: 0-0 Gd: 0-0 GF: - Fm: 0-0
Distance: 2m/2m3: 0-2 2m4-2m7: 0-1 3m+: 0-0
Track: LH: 0-2 RH: 0-1 Tight: 0-1 Gall: 0-0
Aids: Bl: 0-0 Vi: 0-0 Tstrap: 0-0
Best Rating: 98 3/00 Carl 2m4f110y heavy Hdl

Island Faith (IRE)

106   **106**

6-y-o b/br g Turtle Island (IRE)-Keep The Faith (Furry Glen)
Ferdy Murphy   K Lee

Placings:10-623102   (4019)
2002/03: 20^{6}S, 20^{2}GS, 22^{3}HY, 20^{1}HY, 21^{0}G, 16^{2}S,

	Starts	1st	2nd	3rd	Win & Pl
Hurdles	6	1	2	1	6363
Career Total	8	2	2	1	8197
100	1/03 Newc	2m4f		E Hdl	HVY £3445
119	4/02 Carl	2m1f		H NHF	GD £1834

Total win prize-money £5279

Going: Sf: 1-4 GS: 0-1 Gd: 0-1 GF: - Fm: 0-0
Distance: 2m/2m3: 0-1 2m4-2m7: 1-5 3m+: 0-0
Track: LH: 1-5 RH: 0-1 Tight: 0-0 Gall: 1-2
Aids: Bl: 0-0 Vi: 0-0 Tstrap: 0-0

Best Rating: 119 4/02 Carl 2m1f   good   NHF

Fair novice hurdler; winner over two and a half miles in heavy ground.

Island Fortress

85f   **81f**

4-y-o ch f Infantry-Misty Fort (Menelek)
H D Daly   J B Sumner

Placings:55   (3849)
2002/03: 17^{5}S, 16^{5}G,

	Starts	1st	2nd	3rd	Win & Pl
NH Flat	2	0	0	0	
Career Total	2	0	0	0	

Going: Sf: 0-1 GS: 0-0 Gd: 0-1 GF: - Fm: 0-0
Distance: 2m/2m3: 0-2 2m4-2m7: 0-0 3m+: 0-0
Track: LH: 0-0 RH: 0-1 Tight: 0-1 Gall: 0-0
Aids: Bl: 0-0 Vi: 0-0 Tstrap: 0-0
Best Rating: 83 1/03 Tntn   2m1f   soft   NHF

Island Sound

101(108h)   (126h)**114**

6-y-o b g Turtle Island (IRE)-Ballet (Sharrood (USA))
D R C Elsworth   Mrs Michael Meredith

Placings:412P5-U32U   (4346)
2002/03: 16^{U}S, 16^{3}GS, 16^{2}HY, 16^{U}GF,

	Starts	1st	2nd	3rd	Win & Pl
Chases	4	0	1	1	3056
Career Total	9	2	2	1	11089
125	12/01 Tntn	2m1f		C Hdl	G-S £5853

Total win prize-money £5853

Going: Sf: 0-2 GS: 0-1 Gd: 0-0 GF: - Fm: 0-1
Distance: 2m/2m3: 0-4 2m4-2m7: 0-0 3m+: 0-0
Track: LH: 0-1 RH: 0-3 Tight: 0-1 Gall: 0-0
Aids: Bl: 0-0 Vi: 0-0 Tstrap: 0-0
Best Rating: 126 12/01 Kemp 2m   good   Hdl

Useful front-running hurdler/chaser; won weakly contested extended 2m novice chase at Stratford May 2003; has been let down by his jumping; best suited by 2m and decent ground.

Island Stream (IRE)

103   **82**

4-y-o b g Turtle Island (IRE)-Tilbrook (IRE) (Don t Forget Me)
J R Jenkins   Mark Apps

Placings:0404   (4148)
2002/03: 16^{0}G, 16^{4}HY, 16^{0}S, 16^{4}G,

	Starts	1st	2nd	3rd	Win & Pl
Hurdles	4	0	0	0	411
Career Total	4	0	0	0	411

Going: Sf: 0-2 GS: 0-0 Gd: 0-2 GF: - Fm: 0-0
Distance: 2m/2m3: 0-4 2m4-2m7: 0-0 3m+: 0-0
Track: LH: 0-2 RH: 0-2 Tight: 0-1 Gall: 0-1
Aids: Bl: 0-0 Vi: 0-0 Tstrap: 0-0
Best Rating: 97 2/03 Sand 2m110y heavy Hdl

Has become disappointing after showing fair form in quite decent company on first two starts over hurdles.

Island Warrior (IRE)

(102h)   (78h)**45**

8-y-o b g Warcraft (USA)-Only Flower (Warpath)

Best Rating: **119** 4/02 Carl   2m1f   good   NHF

F Jordan   M N Dennis

Placings:00/006200/045PPP0P121F-3FP   (0772)
2002/03: 22^{3}GF, 22^{F}GF, 16^{P}GF,

	Starts	1st	2nd	3rd	Win & Pl
Hurdles	2	0	0	1	331
Chases	1	0	0	0	0
Career Total	23	2	2	1	5420
78	4/02 Sedg	2m5f110yG(0-100)HHdl	G-F	£1953
72	3/02 Hntg	2m5f110yG(0-90)HHdl	G-F	£1708

Total win prize-money £3661

Going: Sf: 0-0 GS: 0-0 Gd: 0-0 GF: - Fm: 0-3
Distance: 2m/2m3: 0-1 2m4-2m7: 0-2 3m+: 0-0
Track: LH: 0-3 RH: 0-0 Tight: 0-1 Gall: 0-0
Aids: Bl: 0-0 Vi: 0-0 Tstrap: 0-0
Best Rating: 84   11/00 Dpat   2m1f172y   soft   NHF

Plating-class hurdler; shock winner of a selling handicap hurdle at Huntingdon in March 2002, and added to that the following month. Suited by two miles-five, a sharp track and fast ground.

Ismene (FR)

105   **112**

7-y-o b m Bad Conduct (USA)-Athena De L Isle (FR) (Quart De Vin (FR))
Miss Venetia Williams   Alan Parker

Placings:263/31F5-1PF1   (4274)
2002/03: 20^{1}HY, 20^{P}GS, 20^{F}GS, 20^{1}G,

	Starts	1st	2nd	3rd	Win & Pl
Hurdles	3	2	0	0	8372
Chases	1	0	0	0	0
Career Total	13	3	1	2	12670
112	3/03 Chep	2m4f	D(0-125)HHdl	GD	£4956
108	6/02 Uttx	2m4f110yD(0-115)HHdl	HVY	£3415
103	1/02 Ludl	2m5f	E Hdl	GD	£2807

Total win prize-money £11179

Going: Sf: 1-1 GS: 0-2 Gd: 1-1 GF: - Fm: 0-0
Distance: 2m/2m3: 0-0 2m4-2m7: 2-4 3m+: 0-0
Track: LH: 2-3 RH: 0-0 Tight: 0-1 Gall: 0-1
Aids: Bl: 0-0 Vi: 0-0 Tstrap: 0-0
Best Rating: 112 3/03 Chep 2m4f   good   Hdl

Fair hurdler; let her supporters down on a few occasions before making amends at Ludlow in January 2002 and added another victory at Uttoxeter in June; fell early on chasing debut at Huntingdon in December; returned to hurdles successfully at Chepstow; acts on good and heavy ground; stays two and a half miles.

Ismeno

12-y-o b g Ela-Mana-Mou-Seattle Siren (USA) (Seattle Slew (USA))
S Dow   Mrs A M Upsdell

Placings:51P/12/110/PP   (3096)
2002/03: 16^{P}S, 21^{P}S,

	Starts	1st	2nd	3rd	Win & Pl
Hurdles	2	0	0	0	
Career Total	10	4	1	0	28507
139	2/99 Asct	2m4f	B(0-150)HHdl	G-S	£20656
135	2/99 Towc	2m	E(0-110)HHdl	SFT	£2302
109	12/96 Plum	2m4f	F(0-105)HHdl	G-S	£1974
102	12/95 Towc	2m	E Hdl	SFT	£2477

Total win prize-money £27413

Going: Sf: 0-2 GS: 0-0 Gd: 0-0 GF: - Fm: 0-0
Distance: 2m/2m3: 0-1 2m4-2m7: 0-1 3m+: 0-0
Track: LH: 0-1 RH: 0-1 Tight: 0-1 Gall: 0-0
Aids: Bl: 0-0 Vi: 0-0 Tstrap: 0-0

Iso Bald (FR)

Best Rating: 139 2/99 Asct 2m4f gd-sft Hdl

98(97h)   (39h)**84**

7-y-o ch g Cyborg (FR)-Renny (FR) (Diaghilev)
A M Crow The Ancrum Pointer

Placings:61502-36PP0   (4774)
2002/03: 16³GF, 20⁶HY, 16ᴾHY, 16ᴾG, 27ᵠG,

	Starts	1st	2nd	3rd	Win & Pl
Hurdles	1	0	0	0	0
Chases	4	0	0	1	517
Career Total	10	1	1	1	4671
98	6/01 Worc	2m4f	E Hdl	GD	£2492
			Total win prize-money £2492		

Going: Sf: 0-2 GS: 0-0 Gd: 0-2 GF: - Fm: 0-1
Distance: 2m/2m3: 0-3 2m4-2m7: 0-1 3m+: 0-1
Track: LH: 0-3 RH: 0-1 Tight: 0-0 Gall: 0-0
Aids: Bl: 0-0 Vi: 0-0 Tstrap: 0-0
Best Rating: 98 11/01 Extr 2m6f110y gd-fm Hdl

Made hard work of winning a weak maiden hurdle in June 2001 and looks to have been harshly rated on that. little impact over fences.

Isou (FR)

94(105h)   (114h)**90+**

7-y-o ch g Dom Alco (FR)-Aghate De Saisy (FR) (Rhapsodien)
V R A Dartnall The Isou Partnership

Placings:6505/212F0-642   (2674)
2002/03: 21⁸HG, 26⁴GS, 25²S,

	Starts	1st	2nd	3rd	Win & Pl
Chases	3	0	1	0	1784
Career Total	12	1	3	0	7165
114	12/01 NAbb	2m6f	E(0-105)HHdl	HVY	£2863
			Total win prize-money £2863		

Going: Sf: 0-2 GS: 0-1 Gd: 0-0 GF: - Fm: 0-0
Distance: 2m/2m3: 0-0 2m4-2m7: 0-1 3m+: 0-2
Track: LH: 0-2 RH: 0-1 Tight: 0-0 Gall: 0-0
Aids: Bl: 0-0 Vi: 0-0 Tstrap: 0-0
Best Rating: 114 12/01 NAbb 2m6f heavy Hdl

Fair novice hurdler, has shown ability on fast and heavy ground. Stays two miles six.

It Takes Time (IRE)

117(119h)   (163h)**154**

9-y-o b g Montelimar (USA)-Dysart Lady (King s Ride)
M C Pipe D A Johnson

Placings:2110/111/1113331-32162   (4474)
2002/03: 25³GS, 25²G, 21¹GS, 24⁶G, 25²G,

	Starts	1st	2nd	3rd	Win & Pl
Hurdles	1	0	0	1	5913
Chases	4	1	2	0	40740
Career Total	19	10	3	4	167872
154	1/03 Hayd	2m6f	B Ch	G-S	£16640
151	4/02 Sand	3m	B Hdl	GD	£29000
149	12/01 Chel	3m	B HHdl	GD	£8572
139	11/01 Chel	3m1f110yB HHdl	GD	£27716
138	11/01 NAbb	4m	C(0-130)HHdl	SFT	£4820
134	2/01 Font	2m6f110yD(0-125)HHdl	GS	£5489
123	1/01 Donc	3m110y	D Hdl	GD	£3752
104	10/00 Extr	2m3f	D Hdl	SFT	£3445
128	1/00 Leop	2m2f	NHF	YLD	£3588
120	12/99 Leop	2m	NHF	SH	£4312
			Total win prize-money £107335		

High-class chasing prospect; former high-class staying hurdler, a good third in both the Cheltenham Stayers and the Martell Aintree Hurdle in 2002; won decent novice chase at Haydock on second start over fences in impressive fashion; runner-up in Grade 2 at Aintree; stays at least 3m 1f; has won on good ground and soft.

It's All A Chance (IRE)

100(106h)   (93h)**81**

8-y-o ch g Eve s Error-Butlers Pier (Good Thyne (USA))
J Howard Johnson J Howard Johnson

Placings:060/050P62/4U522F431-02   (1241)
2002/03: 20⁰GS, 20²GF,

	Starts	1st	2nd	3rd	Win & Pl
Hurdles	1	0	0	0	0
Chases	1	0	1	0	1078
Career Total	20	1	4	1	7486
93	4/02 Hexm	2m4f110yD(0-125)HHdl	G-F	£3535
			Total win prize-money £3535		

Going: Sf: 0-0 GS: 0-1 Gd: 0-0 GF: - Fm: 0-1
Distance: 2m/2m3: 0-0 2m4-2m7: 0-2 3m+: 0-0
Track: LH: 0-2 RH: 0-0 Tight: 0-0 Gall: 0-0
Aids: Bl: 0-0 Vi: 0-0 Tstrap: 0-0
Best Rating: 93 4/02 Hexm 2m4f110y gd-fm Hdl

Handicap hurdler. Suited by two and a half miles and soft ground. Also effective on a fast surface.

It's Beyond Belief (IRE)

103   **120**

9-y-o b g Supreme Leader-Rossacurra (Deep Run)
P F Nicholls J G Crumpler

Placings:22-1   (4080)
2002/03: 26¹S,

	Starts	1st	2nd	3rd	Win & Pl
Chases	1	1	0	0	7189
Career Total	3	1	2	0	7189
120	3/03 Plum	3m2f	E Ch	SFT	£7189
			Total win prize-money £7189		

Going: Sf: 1-1 GS: 0-0 Gd: 0-0 GF: - Fm: 0-0
Distance: 2m/2m3: 0-0 2m4-2m7: 0-0 3m+: 1-1
Track: LH: 1-1 RH: 0-0 Tight: 1-1 Gall: 0-0
Aids: Bl: 0-0 Vi: 0-0 Tstrap: 0-0
Best Rating: 120 3/03 Plum 3m2f soft Ch

Winning pointer, fair novice chaser; returned from a 15-month break to win at Plumpton in March 2003; stays three miles two; acts on soft ground.

It's Harry

93f   **88f**

5-y-o b g Aragon-Andbracket (Import)
Mrs S J Smith Mrs S Smith

Placings:24   (0724)
2002/03: 17²G, 16⁴G,

	Starts	1st	2nd	3rd	Win & Pl
NH Flat	2	0	1	0	446
Career Total	2	0	1	0	446

Going: Sf: 0-0 GS: 1-2 Gd: 0-3 GF: - Fm: 0-0
Distance: 2m/2m3: 0-0 2m4-2m7: 1-1 3m+: 0-4
Track: LH: 1-5 RH: 0-0 Tight: 0-1 Gall: 0-3
Aids: Bl: 0-0 Vi: 0-0 Tstrap: 0-0
Best Rating: 163 11/02 Chel 3m1f110y gd-sft Hdl

Very moderate bumper performer.

It's Himself

95   **133**

11-y-o b g Rakaposhi King-Coole Pilate (Celtic Cone)
A J Martin P M Barrett

Placings:00P4/104/2F/025F21-F5   (3519)
2002/03: 29ᶠHY, 24⁵G,

	Starts	1st	2nd	3rd	Win & Pl
Chases	2	0	0	0	0
Career Total	17	2	3	0	62490
130	4/02 Punc	3m1f	HCh	G-Y	£36134
132	2/00 Hayd	3m	H Ch	HVY	£7475
			Total win prize-money £43610		

Going: Sf: 0-1 GS: 0-1 Gd: 0-0 GF: - Fm: 0-0
Distance: 2m/2m3: 0-0 2m4-2m7: 0-0 3m+: 0-2
Track: LH: 0-2 RH: 0-0 Tight: 0-0 Gall: 0-0
Aids: Bl: 0-0 Vi: 0-0 Tstrap: 0-2
Best Rating: 133 2/03 Hayd 3m gd-sft Ch

Useful hunter/handicap chaser; stays three and a half miles; acts on soft ground; not the best of jumpers.

It's Just Sally

86   **72+**

6-y-o b m Kylian (USA)-Hush It Up (Tina s Pet)
C R Egerton James Blackshaw

Placings:36-55   (1445)
2002/03: 16⁵S, 17⁵F,

	Starts	1st	2nd	3rd	Win & Pl
Hurdles	2	0	0	0	0
Career Total	4	0	0	1	230

Going: Sf: 0-1 GS: 0-0 Gd: 0-0 GF: - Fm: 0-1
Distance: 2m/2m3: 0-2 2m4-2m7: 0-0 3m+: 0-0
Track: LH: 0-1 RH: 0-0 Tight: 0-0 Gall: 0-0
Aids: Bl: 0-0 Vi: 0-0 Tstrap: 0-0
Best Rating: 86 1/02 Folk 2m1f110y soft NHF

A half-sister to Shadow Leader. Staying on third in a Folkestone bumper on her debut on soft ground but has not built on that. Looks like better ground will suit.

It'snotsimple (IRE)

11-y-o b m Homo Sapien-Perpetue (Proverb)
H Messer-Bennetts (Trainer Unknown 12/5) Mrs Sally Messer-Bennetts

Placings:00/PP0P/64P/P   (0371)
2002/03: 26ᴾS,

	Starts	1st	2nd	3rd	Win & Pl
Chases	1	0	0	0	0
Career Total	11	0	0	0	219

Going: Sf: 0-1 GS: 0-0 Gd: 0-0 GF: - Fm: 0-0
Distance: 2m/2m3: 0-0 2m4-2m7: 0-0 3m+: 0-1
Track: LH: 0-1 RH: 0-0 Tight: 0-1 Gall: 0-0
Aids: Bl: 0-0 Vi: 0-0 Tstrap: 0-0
Best Rating: 65 10/98 NAbb 2m5f110y good Ch

Italian Counsel (IRE)

116(97c)   (93c)115+

6-y-o b g Leading Counsel (USA)-Mullaghroe (Tarboosh (USA))
B J Llewellyn B V Ward

Placings:00000000-50123P03265P   (4670)
2002/03: 16⁵GF, 16⁰GF, 17¹GS, 18²G, 17³G, 17⁰GF, 16⁰G, 16³GS, 16²HY, 17⁶S, 16⁵GS, 21⁰G,

	Starts	1st	2nd	3rd	Win & Pl
Hurdles	6	1	1	1	3616
Chases	6	0	1	1	1688
Career Total	20	1	2	2	5304

83 8/02 MRas 2m1f110yG(0-95)HHdl   G-S £2023
Total win prize-money £2023

Going: Sf: 0-2 GS: 1-3 Gd: 0-4 GF: - Fm: 0-3
Distance: 2m/2m3: 1-11 2m4-2m7: 0-1 3m+: 0-0
Track: LH: 0-7 RH: 1-5 Tight: 1-9 Gall: 0-0
Aids: Bl: 0-0 Vi: 0-0 Tstrap: 0-0
Best Rating: 98 8/02 Font 2m2f110y good Hdl

Moderate but progressive hurdler/chaser; surprise winner of valuable handicap hurdle at Market Rasen in July; suited to two miles and acts on most types of ground, though probably best on a fast surface.

Itcanbedone Again (IRE)

103   90+

4-y-o b c Sri Pekan (USA)-Maradata (IRE) (Shardari)
Ian Williams (R Hollinshead 25/9) The Knavesmire Alliance

Placings:60   (2503)
2002/03: 16⁶S, 16⁰GS,

	Starts	1st	2nd	3rd	Win & Pl
Hurdles	2	0	0	0	0
Career Total	2	0	0	0	0

Going: Sf: 0-1 GS: 0-1 Gd: 0-0 GF: - Fm: 0-0
Distance: 2m/2m3: 0-2 2m4-2m7: 0-0 3m+: 0-0
Track: LH: 0-1 RH: 0-1 Tight: 0-1 Gall: 0-0
Aids: Bl: 0-0 Vi: 0-0 Tstrap: 0-0
Best Rating: 65 11/02 Sand 2m110y soft Hdl

Plating-class hurdler; unlikely to stay beyond two miles; acts on fast ground.

Itch

102   64

8-y-o b g Puissance-Panienka (POL) (Dom Racine (FR))
R Bastiman Mrs P Bastiman

Placings:P4P   (3830)
2002/03: 16⁵S, 16⁴HY, 16⁶G,

	Starts	1st	2nd	3rd	Win & Pl
Hurdles	3	0	0	0	0
Career Total	3	0	0	0	0

Going: Sf: 0-2 GS: 0-0 Gd: 0-1 GF: - Fm: 0-0
Distance: 2m/2m3: 0-3 2m4-2m7: 0-0 3m+: 0-0
Track: LH: 0-3 RH: 0-0 Tight: 0-0 Gall: 0-1
Aids: Bl: 0-0 Vi: 0-0 Tstrap: 0-0
Best Rating: 70 2/03 Uttx 2m heavy Hdl

Itchen Mill

86   66

6-y-o b m Afflora (IRE)-Treble Chance (Balinger)
R H Alner Roger and Victoria Harrison

Placings:5   (4600)
2002/03: 17⁵GF,

	Starts	1st	2nd	3rd	Win & Pl
NH Flat	1	0	0	0	0
Career Total	1	0	0	0	0

Going: Sf: 0-0 GS: 0-0 Gd: 0-0 GF: - Fm: 0-1
Distance: 2m/2m3: 0-1 2m4-2m7: 0-0 3m+: 0-0
Track: LH: 0-0 RH: 0-1 Tight: 0-0 Gall: 0-0
Aids: Bl: 0-0 Vi: 0-0 Tstrap: 0-0
Best Rating: 79 4/03 Extr 2m1f gd-fm NHF

Itchintogo (IRE)

5-y-o b g Namaqualand (USA)-Lamp Of Phoebus (USA) (Sunshine Forever (USA))
L A Dace Luke Dace

Placings:0   (2313)
2002/03: 18⁰HY,

	Starts	1st	2nd	3rd	Win & Pl
NH Flat	1	0	0	0	
Career Total	1	0	0	0	

Going: Sf: 0-1 GS: 0-0 Gd: 0-0 GF: - Fm: 0-0
Distance: 2m/2m3: 0-1 2m4-2m7: 0-0 3m+: 0-0
Track: LH: 0-1 RH: 0-0 Tight: 0-0 Gall: 0-0
Aids: Bl: 0-0 Vi: 0-0 Tstrap: 0-0
Best Rating: 0 12/02 Plum 2m2f heavy NHF

Its Only Polite (IRE)

82(104h)   (108h)94

7-y-o b g Roselier (FR)-Decent Debbie (Decent Fellow)
A J Lidderdale Bonusprint

Placings:0/4433-215   (3151)
2002/03: 24²S, 25¹S, 26⁵HY,

	Starts	1st	2nd	3rd	Win & Pl
Chases	3	1	1	0	6162
Career Total	8	1	1	2	7510

91 12/02 Hrfd 3m1f110yE Ch   SFT £4585
Total win prize-money £4586

Going: Sf: 1-3 GS: 0-0 Gd: 0-0 GF: - Fm: 0-0
Distance: 2m/2m3: 0-0 2m4-2m7: 0-0 **3m+: 1-3**
Track: LH: 0-2 RH: 1-1 Tight: 0-0 Gall: 0-0
Aids: Bl: 0-0 Vi: 0-0 Tstrap: 0-0
Best Rating: 108 3/02 Newb 3m110y soft Hdl

By Roselier, he showed ability over hurdles and was not given a hard time on his chasing debut. Scrambled home in a real slog next time.

Its Time For A Win (IRE)

105   149

11-y-o b g Lord Bud-Autumn Gift (Martinmas)
W P Mullins John Kenny

Placings:112263221301F/F11F0F242/6/5FF22131-5F
(1966)
2002/03: 16⁵YS, 20⁶GS,

Chases	Starts	1st	2nd	3rd	Win & Pl
	2	0	0	0	
Career Total	33	8	8	3	109932

149	4/02	Aint	2m5f110yyB(0-150)HCh	GD	£32500
139	2/02	Navn	2m4f	HCh	SFT	£11963
126	10/99	Tipp	2m6f	Ch	SH	£14508
126	10/99	Dund	2m11f	Ch	Y-S	£4937
119	2/99	Naas	2m	HHdl	SFT	£6138
112	12/98	Navn	2m2f	Hdl	HVY	£3586
113	6/98	Tipp	2m	NHF	Y-S	£2382
114	5/98	Navn	2m	NHF	Y-S	£2680

Total win prize-money £78698

Going: Sf: 0-0 GS: 0-1 Gd: 0-0 GF: - Fm: 0-0
Distance: 2m/2m3: 0-1 2m4-2m7: 0-1 3m+: 0-0
Track: LH: 0-2 RH: 0-0 Tight: 0-0 Gall: 0-1
Aids: Bl: 0-0 Vi: 0-0 Tstrap: 0-0
Best Rating: 149 4/02 Aint 2m5f110y good Ch

A tough individual, he lost his way after a couple of long absences, but bounced back well during the spring of 2002, including running a good third in the Mildmay of Flete. Jumped really when over the Grand National fences when landing the Topham. Possibly best at distances short of three miles. Needed to go left-handed. (DEAD)

Its Wallace Jnr

102   111

4-y-o b g Bedford (USA)-Built In Heaven (Sunley Builds)
Miss Sheena West Grand Day Out Partnership

Placings:1300   (4325)
2002/03: 16¹GS, 16³S, 17⁹G, 19⁹G,

	Starts	1st	2nd	3rd	Win & Pl
Hurdles	4	1	0	1	4052
Career Total	4	1	0	1	4052

96 12/02 Winc 2m E Hdl   G-S £3192
Total win prize-money £3192

Going: Sf: 0-1 GS: 1-1 Gd: 0-2 GF: - Fm: 0-0
Distance: 2m/2m3: 1-4 2m4-2m7: 0-0 3m+: 0-0
Track: LH: 0-3 RH: 1-1 Tight: 0-1 Gall: 0-2
Aids: Bl: 0-0 Vi: 0-0 Tstrap: 0-0
Best Rating: 111 3/03 Chel 2m1f good Hdl

Fair novice hurdler; acts on yielding ground; effective at around two miles.

Itsalf

90f   86f

5-y-o ch g Afzal-Sail On Sunday (Sunyboy)
R J Smith D H Morgan

Placings:066   (4542)
2002/03: 16⁰GS, 18⁶GF, 16⁶G,

	Starts	1st	2nd	3rd	Win & Pl
NH Flat	3	0	0	0	0
Career Total	3	0	0	0	0

Going: Sf: 0-0 GS: 0-1 Gd: 0-1 GF: - Fm: 0-1
Distance: 2m/2m3: 0-3 2m4-2m7: 0-0 3m+: 0-0
Track: LH: 0-1 RH: 0-2 Tight: 0-0 Gall: 0-0
Aids: Bl: 0-0 Vi: 0-0 Tstrap: 0-0
Best Rating: 86 2/03 Winc 2m gd-sft NHF

Itsanothergirl

89   74

7-y-o b m Reprimand-Tasmin (Be My Guest (USA))
M W Easterby M W Easterby

Placings:36550/0   (2700)

2002/03: 16⁰S,

	Starts	1st	2nd	3rd	Win & Pl
Hurdles	1	0	0	0	
Career Total	6	0	0	1	423

Going:	Sf: 0-1 GS: 0-0 Gd: 0-0 GF: - Fm: 0-0
Distance:	2m/2m3: 0-1 2m4-2m7: 0-0 3m+: 0-0
Track:	LH: 0-1 RH: 0-0 Tight: 0-0 Gall: 0-0
Aids:	Bl: 0-0 Vi: 0-0 Tstrap: 0-0
Best Rating:	88 1/00 Newc 2m soft Hdl

Itsdedfast (IRE)

7-y-o ch g Lashkari-Amazing Silks (Furry Glen)
L Lungo C Anderson

Placings: 1P   (2556)
2002/03: 17¹G, 20ᴾGF,

	Starts	1st	2nd	3rd	Win & Pl
NH Flat	1	1	0	0	2268
Hurdles	1	0	0	0	0
Career Total	2	1	0	0	2268
107 10/02 Sedg 2m1f		H NHF		GD	£2268

Total win prize-money £2268

Going:	Sf: 0-0 GS: 0-0 Gd: 1-1 GF: - Fm: 0-1
Distance:	2m/2m3: 1-1 2m4-2m7: 0-1 3m+: 0-0
Track:	LH: 1-1 RH: 0-1 Tight: 1-2 Gall: 0-0
Aids:	Bl: 0-0 Vi: 0-0 Tstrap: 0-0
Best Rating:	107 10/02 Sedg 2m1f good NHF

Moderate bumper winner in 2002.

Itsmyturnnow (IRE)
93   95

8-y-o b g Glacial Storm (USA)-Snuggle (Music Boy)
M J Roberts Mike Roberts

Placings: 65   (4758)
2002/03: 24⁸G, 22⁵GF,

	Starts	1st	2nd	3rd	Win & Pl
Chases	2	0	0	0	0
Career Total	2	0	0	0	0

Going:	Sf: 0-0 GS: 0-0 Gd: 0-1 GF: - Fm: 0-1
Distance:	2m/2m3: 0-0 2m4-2m7: 0-1 3m+: 0-1
Track:	LH: 0-0 RH: 0-1 Tight: 0-2 Gall: 0-0
Aids:	Bl: 0-0 Vi: 0-0 Tstrap: 0-0
Best Rating:	75 4/03 Ludl 3m good Ch

Hunter chaser; dual winning pointer; suited by good ground; stays three miles, but yet to prove he gets further.

Itsonlyme (IRE)
108   126

10-y-o b g Broken Hearted-Over The Arctic (Over The River (FR))
Miss Venetia Williams Mel Davies

Placings: 13110/11561/P/F21-13FP   (3591)
2002/03: 20¹GS, 22¹GS, 25³G, 24ᶠS, 24ᴾS,

	Starts	1st	2nd	3rd	Win & Pl
Chases	5	2	0	1	15614
Career Total	18	8	1	2	31326
126 5/02 Towc 2m6f	D Ch		G-S	£4745
126 4/02 Towc 2m4f	D Ch		G-S	£5369
126 4/00 Font	2m6f110yE Hdl		GD	£2702
126 11/99 Bang	2m1f E Hdl		SFT	£2752
118 11/99 Wwck	2m2f110yD Hdl		GD	£4198
116 3/99 Hntg	2m110y H NHF		G-S	£1462
116 1/99 Folk	2m1f110yH NHF		HVY	£1457

---

107 11/98 Aint   2m110y H NHF   G-S   £2029

Total win prize-money £24715

Going:	Sf: 0-2 GS: 2-2 Gd: 0-1 GF: - Fm: 0-0
Distance:	2m/2m3: 0-0 **2m4-2m7: 2-2** 3m+: 0-3
Track:	LH: 0-0 **RH: 1-4** Tight: 0-0 Gall: 0-0
Aids:	Bl: 0-0 Vi: 0-0 Tstrap: 0-0
Best Rating:	126 11/02 Winc 3m1f110y good Ch

Fair chaser; not the best of jumpers; acts on good and soft ground; stays three miles, possibly more effective over two and a half.

Ivanoph (FR)
111 (97h)   (111h) 131

7-y-o b g Roi De Rome (USA)-Veronique Iv (FR) (Mont Basile (FR))
P F Nicholls Neil Smith

Placings: 06F/62142/F132F3P-214022   (4781)
2002/03: 16²G, 16¹GS, 17⁴GS, 17⁹GS, 17²S, 16²GF,

	Starts	1st	2nd	3rd	Win & Pl
Hurdles	1	0	0	0	0
Chases	5	1	3	0	16327
Career Total	21	3	6	2	47399
125 11/02 Winc	2m	D(0-120)HCh	G-S	£4754
111 10/01 Chep	2m110y D Hdl		SFT	£3454
10/00 Autl	2m1f110y Ch		HLD	£11527

Total win prize-money £19737

Going:	Sf: 0-1 GS: 1-3 Gd: 0-1 GF: - Fm: 0-1
Distance:	2m/2m3: 1-6 2m4-2m7: 0-0 3m+: 0-0
Track:	LH: 0-3 **RH: 1-3** Tight: 0-1 Gall: 0-3
Aids:	Bl: 0-0 Vi: 0-0 Tstrap: 0-0
Best Rating:	131 2/03 Newb 2m1f soft Ch

Decent handicap chaser; effective over two miles and goes well with cut in the ground; has shown a tendency to jump to his left.

Iverain (FR)
110 (106h)   (136h) 126

7-y-o b g Le Riverain (FR)-Ursala (FR) (Toujours Pret (USA))
P F Nicholls C G Roach

Placings: 0004/11P-124341   (4732)
2002/03: 25¹G, 20²GS, 25⁴G, 19⁴HY, 21⁴GS, 24¹GF,

	Starts	1st	2nd	3rd	Win & Pl
Chases	6	2	1	1	16965
Career Total	13	4	1	1	31240
116 4/03 Chep	3m	E Ch	G-F	£5028
119 10/02 Winc	3m1f110yD Ch		GD	£4800
136 2/02 Winc	2m6f	C(0-135)HHdl	G-S	£8463
112 11/01 Chep	2m4f	D Hdl	SFT	£3484

Total win prize-money £21775

Going:	Sf: 0-1 GS: 0-2 Gd: 1-2 GF: - Fm: 1-1
Distance:	2m/2m3: 0-0 2m4-2m7: 0-3 **3m+: 2-3**
Track:	LH: 1-4 RH: 1-2 Tight: 0-0 Gall: 0-2
Aids:	Bl: 0-1 Vi: 0-0 Tstrap: 0-0
Best Rating:	136 2/02 Winc 2m6f gd-sft Hdl

Fair chaser; lightly raced in France, he won a Chepstow novice hurdle on his British debut; returned from a bout of coughing to score in a handicap at Wincanton early in 2002; won novice chase at Wincanton in October; successful in match at Chepstow April 2003; stays three miles; handles soft ground; has worn blinkers.

Ivorsagoodun
97   86

4-y-o b f Piccolo-Malibasta (Auction Ring (USA))

M C Pipe (Mrs P N Dutfield 18/11) W I M Perry

Placings: 544636   (4598)
2002/03: 17⁵HY, 17⁴S, 17⁴GS, 17⁶HY, 16³GF, 19⁶GF,

	Starts	1st	2nd	3rd	Win & Pl
Hurdles	6	0	0	1	1160
Career Total	6	0	0	1	1160

Going:	Sf: 0-3 GS: 0-1 Gd: 0-0 GF: - Fm: 0-2
Distance:	2m/2m3: 0-6 2m4-2m7: 0-0 3m+: 0-0
Track:	LH: 0-1 RH: 0-5 Tight: 0-4 Gall: 0-0
Aids:	Bl: 0-0 Vi: 0-1 Tstrap: 0-0
Best Rating:	86 2/03 Extr 2m1f gd-sft Hdl

Plating-class hurdler at up to 3m; acts on soft ground.

Iznogoud (FR)
109   (70h) 149

7-y-o b/br g Shafoun (FR)-Vancia (FR) (Top Dancer (FR))
M C Pipe County Stores-Avalon Surfacing

Placings: 21140/312F-P5U05   (4791)
2002/03: 26ᴾGS, 24⁵GS, 24ᵁG, 21⁹G, 29⁵G,

	Starts	1st	2nd	3rd	Win & Pl
Chases	5	0	0	0	5250
Career Total	14	3	2	1	61981
149 2/02 Asct	2m3f110yB Ch		G-S	£10808
144 1/01 Asct	2m110y A Hdl		SFT	£12000
117 12/00 Chep	2m110y D Hdl		HVY	£3383

Total win prize-money £26191

Going:	Sf: 0-0 GS: 0-2 Gd: 0-3 GF: - Fm: 0-0
Distance:	2m/2m3: 0-0 2m4-2m7: 0-1 3m+: 0-4
Track:	LH: 0-4 RH: 0-1 Tight: 0-0 Gall: 0-3
Aids:	Bl: 0-0 Vi: 0-1 Tstrap: 0-0
Best Rating:	154 3/02 Chel 3m110y gd-sft Ch

Very useful novice chaser in 2001/2; fine second to Hussard Collonges in the Royal & SunAlliance Chase at the Festival; best run of 2002/3 when fifth in attheraces Gold Cup, stays 3m 5f; effective in yielding ground.

J Dee
95   78

10-y-o ch g Rakaposhi King-Just Pam (Pamroy)
John Allen (J C McConnochie 26/5) J A Bianchi

Placings: 0/P000P/450321PP3P-PP3   (1451)
2002/03: 24ᴾG, 26ᴾGF, 24³G,

	Starts	1st	2nd	3rd	Win & Pl
Chases	3	0	0	1	617
Career Total	19	1	1	3	6579
78 8/01 Sthl	3m110y E Ch		G-F	£3555

Total win prize-money £3555

Going:	Sf: 0-0 GS: 0-0 Gd: 0-2 GF: - Fm: 0-1
Distance:	2m/2m3: 0-0 2m4-2m7: 0-0 3m+: 0-3
Track:	LH: 0-3 RH: 0-0 Tight: 0-3 Gall: 0-0
Aids:	Bl: 0-0 Vi: 0-0 Tstrap: 0-0
Best Rating:	78 8/01 Sthl 3m110y gd-fm Ch

J J Baboo (IRE)
105   85

10-y-o b g Be My Guest (USA)-Maricica (Ahonoora)
Jedd O Keeffe Roland Roper

Placings: 5442/622245302/43065/32131/2P03P/0031PP   (4765)
2002/03: 19⁰G, 25⁰G, 24³G, 25¹G, 24ᴾG, 31ᴾG,

	Starts	1st	2nd	3rd	Win & Pl
Chases	6	1	0	1	4801

Career Total	34	3	7	6	24137
85 3/03 Weth 3m1f	F(0-100)HCh			GD	£4160
99 4/00 Sedg 2m5f	D Ch			GD	£3984
96 3/00 Catt 2m	D Ch			G-F	£4290

Total win prize-money £12435

Going: Sf: 0-0 GS: 0-0 Gd: 1-6 GF: - Fm: 0-0
Distance: 2m/2m3: 0-1 2m4-2m7: 0-0 **3m+: 1-5**
Track: **LH: 1-4** RH: 0-1 Tight: 0-3 Gall: 0-0
Aids: Bl: 0-0 Vi: 0-0 Tstrap: 0-0
Best Rating: 105 11/00 Catt 2m3f good Ch

Plating-class chaser; stays three miles; off the track for nearly two years through injury after December 2000; emerged from the wilderness with a narrow win at Wetherby in March.

J'Ubio
72 **48**
4-y-o b f Bijou D Inde-Eternal Triangle (USA) (Barachois (CAN))
B A Pearce Patrick Barter

Placings:F00 (2195)
2002/03: 16⁶G, 16⁹GS, 17⁹GS,

	Starts	1st	2nd	3rd	Win & Pl
Hurdles	3	0	0	0	
Career Total	3	0	0	0	

Going: Sf: 0-0 GS: 0-0 Gd: 0-1 GF: - Fm: 0-0
Distance: 2m/2m3: 0-2 2m4-2m7: 0-0 3m+: 0-0
Track: LH: 0-1 RH: 0-2 Tight: 0-2 Gall: 0-0
Aids: Bl: 0-0 Vi: 0-0 Tstrap: 0-0
Best Rating: 53 11/02 Tntn 2m1f gd-sft Hdl

Jabiru (IRE)
10-y-o b/br g Lafontaine (USA)-Country Glen (Furry Glen)
Mrs K M Sanderson Mrs K M Sanderson

Placings:200/335F6/P/1-21230114 (4615)
2002/03: 21²GF, 26¹GS, 28²GF, 24³GS, 26⁶G, 24¹F, 24¹F, 26⁴G,

	Starts	1st	2nd	3rd	Win & Pl
Chases	8	3	2	1	15399
Career Total	18	4	3	3	18345
89 4/03 Tntn 3m	H Ch			FRM	£2681
99 3/03 Tntn 3m	H Ch			FRM	£3094
101 5/02 NAbb 3m2f110yH Ch				G-S	£2212
97 4/02 Extr 2m7f110yH Ch				FRM	£1761

Total win prize-money £9749

Going: Sf: 0-0 GS: 1-2 Gd: 0-2 GF: - Fm: 2-4
Distance: 2m/2m3: 0-0 2m4-2m7: 0-1 **3m+: 3-7**
Track: LH: 1-5 **RH: 2-3** Tight: 3-5 Gall: 0-3
Aids: Bl: 0-0 Vi: 0-0 Tstrap: 0-0
Best Rating: 123 6/02 Strf 3m4f gd-fm Ch

Useful pointer/hunter chaser; blinkered for the first time when making all under canny ride in restricted 3m 2f hunter chase at Newton Abbot May 2003; stays 3m; handles any ground; probably best going right-handed.

Jabo Origny (FR)
94 **105**
6-y-o gr g Royal Charter (FR)-Coralline (FR) (Iron Duke (FR))
Miss Venetia Williams B Moore & E C Stephens

Placings:5-F64 (4561)
2002/03: 20⁵S, 16⁶S, 20⁴GF,

	Starts	1st	2nd	3rd	Win & Pl
Hurdles	3	0	0	0	286
Career Total	4	0	0	0	286

Going: Sf: 0-2 GS: 0-0 Gd: 0-0 GF: - Fm: 0-1
Distance: 2m/2m3: 0-1 2m4-2m7: 0-2 3m+: 0-0
Track: LH: 0-3 RH: 0-0 Tight: 0-1 Gall: 0-0
Aids: Bl: 0-0 Vi: 0-0 Tstrap: 0-0
Best Rating: 105 3/03 Uttx 2m soft Hdl

Jaboune (FR)
103(117h)   (135h)**120+**
6-y-o ch g Johann Quatz (FR)-Seasonal Pleasure (USA) (Graustark)
A King Mrs R J Skan

Placings:2323-2111P122032050 (4470)
2002/03: 16²G, 17¹G, 17¹G, 17¹GF, 17⁹GS, 16¹GS, 16²G, 16²S, 16⁵S, 16³G, 16²G, 16⁹G, 17⁵G, 16⁶G,

	Starts	1st	2nd	3rd	Win & Pl
Hurdles	14	4	4	1	41325
Career Total	18	4	6	3	48040
123 11/02 Weth 2m	C Hdl			G-S	£6805
131 6/02 MRas 2m1f110yC(0-130)HHdl				G-F	£7150
119 6/02 NAbb 2m1f	D Hdl			GD	£3469
108 6/02 Hrfd 2m1f	E Hdl			GD	£2765

Total win prize-money £20191

Going: Sf: 0-2 GS: 1-2 Gd: 2-9 GF: - Fm: 1-1
Distance: **2m/2m3: 4-14** 2m4-2m7: 0-0 3m+: 0-0
Track: LH: 2-9 RH: 2-5 **Tight: 2-4** Gall: 0-3
Aids: Bl: 0-0 Vi: 0-0 **Tstrap: 3-5**
Best Rating: 135 3/03 Chel 2m1f good Hdl

Useful hurdler; successful in first two novice chases at Hereford and Fakenham May 2003; seemed unsuited to going left-handed when jumping right next time; stays at least 2m 3f; acts on most types of ground; has worn a tongue-tie; likes to race prominently.

Jac An Ree (IRE)
7-y-o b g Supreme Leader-Nic An Ree (IRE) (King s Ride)
D M Grissell C Newport, J Draper & T Edmonds

Placings:2-65 (3098)
2002/03: 16⁶S, 21⁵S,

	Starts	1st	2nd	3rd	Win & Pl
NH Flat	1	0	0	0	0
Hurdles	1	0	0	0	0
Career Total	3	0	1	0	415

Going: Sf: 0-2 GS: 0-0 Gd: 0-0 GF: - Fm: 0-0
Distance: 2m/2m3: 0-1 2m4-2m7: 0-1 3m+: 0-0
Track: LH: 0-2 RH: 0-0 Tight: 0-1 Gall: 0-0
Aids: Bl: 0-0 Vi: 0-0 Tstrap: 0-0
Best Rating: 101 12/02 Wwck 2m soft NHF

Poor form so far.

Jacdor (IRE)
115 **127**
9-y-o b g Be My Native (USA)-Bellalma (Belfalas)
R Dickin Jackie Matthews & Doreen Evans

Placings:45220/3016P/153FFP/PF41305414-12612 (4318)
2002/03: 16¹G, 16²HY, 17⁶G, 25¹HY, 24²G,

	Starts	1st	2nd	3rd	Win & Pl
Hurdles	5	2	2	0	16769
Career Total	31	6	4	3	36043
127 1/03 Wwck 3m1f	D(0-120)HHdl			HVY	£5167
117 10/02 Chel 2m110y	E(0-135)HHdl			GD	£6954
111 3/02 Towc 2m	E(0-110)HHdl			SFT	£2628
105 11/01 Bang 2m1f	F(0-110)HHdl			G-S	£3558
119 11/00 Wwck 2m110y	D(0-125)HCh			SFT	£4192
125 3/00 Bang 2m1f110yE Ch				SFT	£3412

Total win prize-money £25916

Going: Sf: 1-2 GS: 0-0 Gd: 1-3 GF: - Fm: 0-0
Distance: 2m/2m3: 1-3 2m4-2m7: 0-0 3m+: 1-2
Track: **LH: 2-4** RH: 0-1 Tight: 0-1 Gall: 0-1
Aids: Bl: 1-3 Vi: 1-2 Tstrap: 0-0
Best Rating: 127 1/03 Wwck 3m1f heavy Hdl

Fair hurdler/chaser; suited by three miles plus; suited by soft but is effective on good; has worn blinkers; won in first-time visor.

Jack (IRE)
93
11-y-o br g Be My Native (USA)-Martialette (Welsh Saint)
J C Tuck The Cat & Custard Pot

Placings:06/4U60/0452532P/0303P/0001232326-0 (1115)
2002/03: 16⁶GF,

	Starts	1st	2nd	3rd	Win & Pl
Hurdles	1	0	0	0	
Career Total	30	1	5	5	8717
73 8/01 Worc 2m	G(0-90)HHdl			G-F	£1608

Total win prize-money £1609

Going: Sf: 0-0 GS: 0-0 Gd: 0-0 GF: - Fm: 0-1
Distance: 2m/2m3: 0-1 2m4-2m7: 0-0 3m+: 0-0
Track: LH: 0-1 RH: 0-0 Tight: 0-0 Gall: 0-0
Aids: Bl: 0-0 Vi: 0-0 Tstrap: 0-0
Best Rating: 100 3/99 Ludl 2m4f good Ch

Got off the mark in a seller at Worcester in August of 2001 over two miles on good to firm, and has continued to run well since in handicap hurdles.

Jack Be Smart
61
8-y-o ch g Henbit (USA)-Trimar Gold (Goldhill)
J Howard Johnson (Ferdy Murphy 30/5) John Smart

Placings:250/360/04PFP53-PPP (3813)
2002/03: 26⁶G, 27⁶HY, 25⁶G,

	Starts	1st	2nd	3rd	Win & Pl
Hurdles	1	0	0	0	0
Chases	2	0	0	0	0
Career Total	16	0	1	2	1767

Going: Sf: 0-1 GS: 0-0 Gd: 0-2 GF: - Fm: 0-0
Distance: 2m/2m3: 0-0 2m4-2m7: 0-0 3m+: 0-3
Track: LH: 0-2 RH: 0-1 Tight: 0-2 Gall: 0-1
Aids: Bl: 0-0 Vi: 0-0 Tstrap: 0-0
Best Rating: 99 2/00 Sedg 2m1f gd-sft NHF

Poor form so far.

Jack Dawson (IRE)
99 **117+**
6-y-o b g Persian Bold-Dream Of Jenny (Caerleon (USA))
John Berry The Premier Cru

Placings:P-12 (1426)
2002/03: 17¹G, 16²GF,

	Starts	1st	2nd	3rd	Win & Pl
Hurdles	2	1	1	0	3815
Career Total	3	1	1	0	3815
117 9/02 Sthl 2m1f	E Hdl			GD	£2961

Total win prize-money £2961

Going: Sf: 0-0 GS: 0-0 Gd: 1-1 GF: - Fm: 0-1

Distance: 2m/2m3: 1-2 2m4-2m7: 0-0 3m+: 0-0
Track: LH: 1-2 RH: 0-0 Tight: 0-1 Gall: 0-0
Aids: Bl: 0-0 Vi: 0-0 Tstrap: 0-0
Best Rating: 117 9/02 Sthl 2m1f   good Hdl

Fair staying handicapper on the Flat who created a good impression when winning a weak novices hurdle at Southwell in September 2002. Beaten at long odds-on next time. Must have fast ground.

Jack Fry (IRE)
80   72

6-y-o gr g Lashkari-Most Of All (Absalom)
Noel T Chance Louisville Syndicate

Placings:0-006F04   (4668)
2002/03: 16⁰G, 16⁰G, 19⁶GS, 16⁶G, 16⁹GF, 20⁴G,

	Starts	1st	2nd	3rd	Win & Pl
NH Flat	1	0	0	0	0
Hurdles	5	0	0	0	0
Career Total	7	0	0	0	0

Going: Sf: 0-0 GS: 0-1 Gd: 0-4 GF: - Fm: 0-1
Distance: 2m/2m3: 0-5 2m4-2m7: 0-1 3m+: 0-0
Track: LH: 0-4 RH: 0-2 Tight: 0-1 Gall: 0-2
Aids: Bl: 0-0 Vi: 0-0 Tstrap: 0-0
Best Rating: 84 4/02 Asct 2m110y   gd-fm NHF

Plating-class novice hurdler; has disappointed since falling at Newbury in February 2003.

Jack Fuller (IRE)
98   87

6-y-o b g Be My Native (USA)-Jacks Sister (IRE) (Entitled)
D M Grissell The Brightling Club 1997

Placings:304003   (4186)
2002/03: 17³G, 16⁶S, 21⁴S, 22⁹HY, 19⁰GS, 17³G,

	Starts	1st	2nd	3rd	Win & Pl
NH Flat	2	0	0	1	252
Hurdles	4	0	0	1	535
Career Total	6	0	0	2	786

Going: Sf: 0-3 GS: 0-1 Gd: 0-2 GF: - Fm: 0-0
Distance: 2m/2m3: 0-3 2m4-2m7: 0-3 3m+: 0-0
Track: LH: 0-2 RH: 0-4 Tight: 0-3 Gall: 0-0
Aids: Bl: 0-0 Vi: 0-0 Tstrap: 0-0
Best Rating: 97 5/02 Folk 2m1f110y   good NHF

Jack Lynch
92f

7-y-o ch g Lancastrian-Troublewithjack (Sulaafah (USA))
Ferdy Murphy Mrs Helen Lynch

Placings:4   (0584)
2002/03: 16⁴G,

	Starts	1st	2nd	3rd	Win & Pl
NH Flat	1	0	0	0	0
Career Total	1	0	0	0	0

Going: Sf: 0-0 GS: 0-0 Gd: 0-1 GF: - Fm: 0-0
Distance: 2m/2m3: 0-1 2m4-2m7: 0-0 3m+: 0-0
Track: LH: 0-1 RH: 0-0 Tight: 0-0 Gall: 0-0
Aids: Bl: 0-0 Vi: 0-0 Tstrap: 0-0
Best Rating: 92 6/02 Hexm 2m110y   good NHF

Jack Martin (IRE)
102f   106+f

6-y-o ch g Erin s Isle-Rolling Penny (IRE) (Le Moss)
M Hill Edward Retter

Placings:34   (2718)
2002/03: 16⁹HY, 16⁴HY,

	Starts	1st	2nd	3rd	Win & Pl
NH Flat	2	0	0	1	1223
Career Total	2	0	0	1	1223

Going: Sf: 0-2 GS: 0-0 Gd: 0-0 GF: - Fm: 0-0
Distance: 2m/2m3: 0-2 2m4-2m7: 0-0 3m+: 0-0
Track: LH: 0-2 RH: 0-0 Tight: 0-0 Gall: 0-0
Aids: Bl: 0-0 Vi: 0-0 Tstrap: 0-0
Best Rating: 106 11/02 Chep 2m110y   heavy NHF

Third in a bumper in heavy ground on his debut and did not do badly in a Grade two next time.

Jack Pot II (FR)
98   90

6-y-o ch g Luchiroverte (IRE)-Roxane Ii (FR) (Signani (FR))
L Lungo Ashleybank Investments Limited

Placings:364   (4225)
2002/03: 16⁹HY, 16⁶HY, 20⁴GF,

	Starts	1st	2nd	3rd	Win & Pl
NH Flat	2	0	0	1	273
Hurdles	1	0	0	0	0
Career Total	3	0	0	1	273

Going: Sf: 0-2 GS: 0-0 Gd: 0-0 GF: - Fm: 0-1
Distance: 2m/2m3: 0-2 2m4-2m7: 0-1 3m+: 0-0
Track: LH: 0-3 RH: 0-0 Tight: 0-0 Gall: 0-0
Aids: Bl: 0-0 Vi: 0-0 Tstrap: 0-0
Best Rating: 107 1/03 Ayr 2m   heavy NHF

A half-brother to Acajou, ran with promise on his bumper debut at Ayr in January but pulled too hard and disappointed next time; showed some promise when fourth on hurdling debut at Wetherby in March but disapointing since.

Jack The Bear (IRE)
109   112+

9-y-o b/br g Un Desperado (FR)-Vale Of Peace (Wolver Hollow)
P F Nicholls Derek Millard

Placings:3/22F314/133   (2336)
2002/03: 26¹S, 26³HY, 32³GS,

	Starts	1st	2nd	3rd	Win & Pl
Chases	3	1	0	2	7763
Career Total	10	2	2	4	17577
112 11/02 NAbb 3m2f110yD(0-120)HCh				SFT	£5044
109 4/01 Extr 3m1f110yD Ch				G-S	£5070
Total win prize-money £10114					

Going: Sf: 1-2 GS: 0-1 Gd: 0-0 GF: - Fm: 0-0
Distance: 2m/2m3: 0-0 2m4-2m7: 0-0 3m+: 1-3
Track: LH: 1-2 RH: 0-1 Tight: 1-2 Gall: 0-1
Aids: Bl: 0-0 Vi: 0-0 Tstrap: 0-0
Best Rating: 120 11/00 NAbb 3m2f110y   heavy Ch

Fair front-running staying chaser. Suited by trips in excess of three miles and soft ground.

Jack Weighell
83f   50f

4-y-o b g Accordion-Magic Bloom (Full Of Hope)

J M Jefferson P Nelson

Placings:0   (3817)
2002/03: 16⁹G,

	Starts	1st	2nd	3rd	Win & Pl
NH Flat	1	0	0	0	0
Career Total	1	0	0	0	0

Going: Sf: 0-0 GS: 0-0 Gd: 0-1 GF: - Fm: 0-0
Distance: 2m/2m3: 0-1 2m4-2m7: 0-0 3m+: 0-0
Track: LH: 0-1 RH: 0-0 Tight: 0-1 Gall: 0-0
Aids: Bl: 0-0 Vi: 0-0 Tstrap: 0-0
Best Rating: 50 2/03 Catt 2m   good NHF

Jack Yeats (IRE)
(64h)   (23h)101

11-y-o b g Don t Forget Me-Petty Session (Blakeney)
Ferdy Murphy Leeds Plywood And Doors Ltd

Placings:0/20P04420/64F22315234/0P3FF/26300/21PPPP
P346-0   (1817)
2002/03: 26⁰G,

	Starts	1st	2nd	3rd	Win & Pl
Hurdles	1	0	0	0	0
Career Total	41	2	7	5	16031
91 5/01 Prth 3m2f110yF(0-95)HCh			G-F	£3770
108 10/97 Fair 2m2f (0-102)HCh			GD	£3051
Total win prize-money £6822				

Going: Sf: 0-0 GS: 0-0 Gd: 0-1 GF: - Fm: 0-0
Distance: 2m/2m3: 0-0 2m4-2m7: 0-0 3m+: 0-1
Track: LH: 0-0 RH: 0-1 Tight: 0-0 Gall: 0-0
Aids: Bl: 0-0 Vi: 0-0 Tstrap: 0-0
Best Rating: 111 12/96 Leop 2m   yield Hdl

Infrequent finisher and a light of other days.

Jackem (IRE)
98(103h)   (106 h)101

9-y-o b/br g Lord Americo-Laurence Lady (Laurence O)
Ian Williams The Duck Racing Partnership

Placings:U4 1BFP0/UF536350S0-134334022   (4690)
2002/03: 23¹G, 23³G, 25⁴GF, 24³GF, 25³G, 27⁴HY, 24⁰G, 24²GF, 25²G,

	Starts	1st	2nd	3rd	Win & Pl
Hurdles	5	1	0	3	3835
Chases	4	0	2	0	3014
Career Total	26	2	2	5	11008
106 5/02 Fknm 2m7f110yE Hdl			GD	£2373
108 11/00 Tram 2m NHF			HVY	£2760
Total win prize-money £5133				

Going: Sf: 0-1 GS: 0-1 Gd: 1-5 GF: - Fm: 0-2
Distance: 2m/2m3: 0-0 2m4-2m7: 0-1 3m+: 1-8
Track: LH: 1-5 RH: 0-4 Tight: 1-5 Gall: 0-1
Aids: Bl: 0-0 Vi: 0-0 Tstrap: 0-0
Best Rating: 108 11/00 Tram 2m   heavy NHF

Jackie C (IRE)
(106h)115

8-y-o b g Supreme Leader-Gloria St Julien (Duky)
T R George R J McAlpine

Placings:0440/210F23-U   (2566)
2002/03: 20ᵁS,

	Starts	1st	2nd	3rd	Win & Pl
Chases	1	0	0	0	
Career Total	11	1	2	1	8113
106 6/01 Slig 2m Hdl			GD	£4451

Total win prize-money £4452

Going:	Sf: 0-1 GS: 0-0 Gd: 0-0 GF: - Fm: 0-0
Distance:	2m/2m3: 0-0 2m4-2m7: 0-1 3m+: 0-0
Track:	LH: 0-1 RH: 0-0 Tight: 0-1 Gall: 0-0
Aids:	Bl: 0-0 Vi: 0-0 Tstrap: 0-0
Best Rating:	115 1/02 Leic 2m7f110y good Ch

Moderate Irish hurdler, he is now with Tom George. He is improving over fences but still has something to learn.

Jackie Jarvis (IRE)

6-y-o b m Alphabatim (USA)-Miss Brantridge (Riboboy (USA))
P York Miss Ellen Delaney

Placings:00/R-U1   (4147)
2002/03: 21UG, 211G,

	Starts	1st	2nd	3rd	Win & Pl
Chases	2	1	0	0	2085
Career Total	5	1	0	0	2085
107 3/03 Fknm 2m5f110yH Ch			GD		£2085

Total win prize-money £2085

Going:	Sf: 0-0 GS: 0-0 Gd: 1-2 GF: - Fm: 0-0
Distance:	2m/2m3: 0-0 2m4-2m7: 1-2 3m+: 0-0
Track:	LH: 1-1 RH: 0-1 Tight: 1-2 Gall: 0-0
Aids:	Bl: 0-0 Vi: 0-0 Tstrap: 0-0
Best Rating:	107 3/03 Fknm 2m5f110y good Ch

Jacklighte Bellevue (FR)

95(99h)   (114h)94
6-y-o b g Saint Cyrien (FR)-Kalighte (FR) (Light Butterfly)
Mrs H Dalton J Hales

Placings:033124-503   (3821)
2002/03: 205G, 190G, 233GS,

	Starts	1st	2nd	3rd	Win & Pl
Chases	3	0	0	1	860
Career Total	9	1	1	3	9973
114 1/02 Kemp 2m5f	D Hdl		SFT		£3965

Total win prize-money £3965

Going:	Sf: 0-0 GS: 0-1 Gd: 0-2 GF: - Fm: 0-0
Distance:	2m/2m3: 0-1 2m4-2m7: 0-1 3m+: 0-1
Track:	LH: 0-1 RH: 0-2 Tight: 0-0 Gall: 0-0
Aids:	Bl: 0-0 Vi: 0-0 Tstrap: 0-0
Best Rating:	114 2/02 Wwck 2m5f heavy Hdl

Ex-French; won a novice hurdle at Kempton in January 2002, but disappointing on his chasing debut; stays two miles five furlongs; acts on soft/heavy ground.

Jackofalltrades (IRE)

5-y-o b g Lord Americo-Wind Chimes (The Parson)
A C Whillans Robert Robinson

Placings:50P   (3987)
2002/03: 165HY, 160HY, 20PS,

	Starts	1st	2nd	3rd	Win & Pl
NH Flat	2	0	0	0	0
Hurdles	1	0	0	0	0
Career Total	3	0	0	0	0

| Going: | Sf: 0-3 GS: 0-0 Gd: 0-0 GF: - Fm: 0-0 |
| Distance: | 2m/2m3: 0-2 2m4-2m7: 0-1 3m+: 0-0 |

Track:	LH: 0-2 RH: 0-1 Tight: 0-0 Gall: 0-0
Aids:	Bl: 0-0 Vi: 0-0 Tstrap: 0-0
Best Rating:	53 2/03 Ayr 2m heavy NHF

Jacks Birthday (IRE)

81   60
5-y-o b g Mukaddamah (USA)-High Concept (IRE) (Thatching)
D J Caro Jack Joseph

Placings:53-0P0   (4486)
2002/03: 160S, 19PGF, 170GF,

	Starts	1st	2nd	3rd	Win & Pl
Hurdles	3	0	0	0	
Career Total	5	0	0	1	469

Going:	Sf: 0-1 GS: 0-0 Gd: 0-0 GF: - Fm: 0-2
Distance:	2m/2m3: 0-2 2m4-2m7: 0-1 3m+: 0-0
Track:	LH: 0-0 RH: 0-2 Tight: 0-0 Gall: 0-1
Aids:	Bl: 0-1 Vi: 0-0 Tstrap: 0-0
Best Rating:	81 10/01 Winc 2m gd-fm Hdl

Jacks Craic (IRE)

98f   78f
4-y-o b g Lord Americo-Boleree (IRE) (Mandalus)
C Weedon Bbb Computer Services

Placings:0   (4444)
2002/03: 160G,

	Starts	1st	2nd	3rd	Win & Pl
NH Flat	1	0	0	0	
Career Total	1	0	0	0	

Going:	Sf: 0-0 GS: 0-0 Gd: 0-1 GF: - Fm: 0-0
Distance:	2m/2m3: 0-1 2m4-2m7: 0-0 3m+: 0-0
Track:	LH: 0-0 RH: 0-1 Tight: 0-0 Gall: 0-0
Aids:	Bl: 0-0 Vi: 0-0 Tstrap: 0-0
Best Rating:	78 4/03 Asct 2m110y good NHF

Jacks Jewel (IRE)

66f   74f
6-y-o b g Welsh Term-September Daydream (IRE) (Phardante (FR))
M Hill Ken Field

Placings:40   (4628)
2002/03: 174F, 170GF,

	Starts	1st	2nd	3rd	Win & Pl
NH Flat	2	0	0	0	0
Career Total	2	0	0	0	0

Going:	Sf: 0-0 GS: 0-0 Gd: 0-0 GF: - Fm: 0-2
Distance:	2m/2m3: 0-2 2m4-2m7: 0-0 3m+: 0-0
Track:	LH: 0-1 RH: 0-0 Tight: 0-1 Gall: 0-0
Aids:	Bl: 0-0 Vi: 0-0 Tstrap: 0-0
Best Rating:	74 3/03 Tntn 2m1f firm NHF

Jackson (FR)

95   77+
6-y-o b g Passing Sale (FR)-Tynia (FR) (Djarvis (FR))
Mrs H Dalton C B Brookes

Placings:0/0-005   (3488)

2002/03: 179GS, 200GS, 175GS,

	Starts	1st	2nd	3rd	Win & Pl
NH Flat	1	0	0	0	0
Hurdles	2	0	0	0	0
Career Total	5	0	0	0	0

Going:	Sf: 0-0 GS: 0-3 Gd: 0-0 GF: - Fm: 0-0
Distance:	2m/2m3: 0-2 2m4-2m7: 0-1 3m+: 0-0
Track:	LH: 0-3 RH: 0-0 Tight: 0-3 Gall: 0-0
Aids:	Bl: 0-0 Vi: 0-0 Tstrap: 0-2
Best Rating:	77 2/03 Bang 2m1f gd-sft Hdl

Very limited ability over hurdles.

Jackson's Bay

5-y-o b m Primitive Rising (USA)-Crammond Brig (New Brig)
M W Easterby W H Jackson

Placings:1500P5   (4355)
2002/03: 171GF, 165HY, 170HY, 160G, 20PG, 205GF,

	Starts	1st	2nd	3rd	Win & Pl
NH Flat	4	1	0	0	1991
Hurdles	2	0	0	0	0
Career Total	6	1	0	0	1991
97 10/02 Carl 2m1f H NHF			G-F		£1990

Total win prize-money £1991

Going:	Sf: 0-2 GS: 0-0 Gd: 0-2 GF: - Fm: 1-2
Distance:	2m/2m3: 1-4 2m4-2m7: 0-2 3m+: 0-0
Track:	LH: 0-4 RH: 1-2 Tight: 0-1 Gall: 0-1
Aids:	Bl: 0-0 Vi: 0-0 Tstrap: 0-0
Best Rating:	97 10/02 Carl 2m1f gd-fm NHF

Made a winning debut in a bumper at Carlisle in October 2002 and should do well over hurdles granted a test of stamina.

Jackson's Hole

100(97h)   (101h)73
10-y-o b g Brush Aside (USA)-Jack s The Girl (IRE) (Supreme Leader)
M W Easterby Michael A Proudfoot

Placings:4/050U/0/F2P/35563-46F4P   (3802)
2002/03: 214G, 256HY, 24FHY, 274HY, 20PS,

	Starts	1st	2nd	3rd	Win & Pl
Chases	5	0	0	0	623
Career Total	19	0	1	2	2599

Going:	Sf: 0-4 GS: 0-0 Gd: 0-1 GF: - Fm: 0-0
Distance:	2m/2m3: 0-0 2m4-2m7: 0-2 3m+: 0-3
Track:	LH: 0-5 RH: 0-0 Tight: 0-2 Gall: 0-2
Aids:	Bl: 0-0 Vi: 0-0 Tstrap: 0-0
Best Rating:	101 12/01 Catt 2m3f soft Hdl

Scored four times out of five between the flags in 2000 but has yet to translate this form to hurdles or fences. Tends to fade badly in the closing stages.

Jacksonville (FR)

100(98h)   (102h)97+
6-y-o b g Petit Montmorency (USA)-Quinine Des Aulnes (FR) (Air Du Nord (USA))
A Parker Mr & Mrs Raymond Anderson Green

Placings:0/0223P-2   (1985)
2002/03: 212S,

	Starts	1st	2nd	3rd	Win & Pl
Chases	1	0	1	0	1556
Career Total	7	0	3	1	3702

Going: Sf: 0-1 GS: 0-0 Gd: 0-0 GF: - Fm: 0-0
Distance: 2m/2m3: 0-0 2m4-2m7: 0-1 3m+: 0-0
Track: LH: 0-1 RH: 0-0 Tight: 0-0 Gall: 0-0
Aids: Bl: 0-0 Vi: 0-0 Tstrap: 0-0
Best Rating: 102 2/02 Ayr   2m4f   heavy Hdl

Fair hurdler, stays three miles, suited by soft ground.

Jacob's Wife

13-y-o gr m Baron Blakeney-Vido (Vimadee)
G L Edwards (Mrs Edward Crow 12/5) Miss S Hopkins

Placings:003414/3115/FP4F/15PP34/P2/4/4   (0278)
2002/03: 24⁴S,
	Starts	1st	2nd	3rd	Win & Pl
Chases	1	0	0	0	273
Career Total	24	4	1	3	17723
117	5/97	Bang	2m4f110yD(0-120)HCh	GD	£4182
115	3/96	Wwck	2m	D Ch	GD	£3834
88	12/95	Uttx	2m	D Ch	G-F	£3623
104	4/95	Worc	2m	E Hdl	GD	£2757

Total win prize-money £14398

Going: Sf: 0-1 GS: 0-0 Gd: 0-0 GF: - Fm: 0-0
Distance: 2m/2m3: 0-0 2m4-2m7: 0-0 3m+: 0-1
Track: LH: 0-1 RH: 0-0 Tight: 0-0 Gall: 0-0
Aids: Bl: 0-0 Vi: 0-0 Tstrap: 0-0
Best Rating: 118 11/95 Chep 2m110y gd-sft Ch

Fair hunter chaser.

Jacopo (FR)
103   96

6-y-o b g Grand Tresor (FR)-Qolombine (FR) (Damsire Unregistered)
R Dickin Fairfield Flyers

Placings:0006-66422416   (4606)
2002/03: 16⁶GS, 16⁶G, 16⁴S, 19²HY, 20²GS, 21⁴S, 20¹GF, 24⁶G,
	Starts	1st	2nd	3rd	Win & Pl
Hurdles	8	1	2	0	7300
Career Total	12	1	2	0	7300
90	3/03	Sthl	2m4f110yE Hdl	G-F	£3633

Total win prize-money £3633

Going: Sf: 0-3 GS: 0-2 Gd: 0-2 GF: - Fm: 1-1
Distance: 2m/2m3: 0-4 2m4-2m7: 1-3 3m+: 0-1
Track: LH: 1-5 RH: 0-3 Tight: 1-2 Gall: 0-2
Aids: Bl: 0-0 Vi: 0-0 Tstrap: 0-0
Best Rating: 96 1/03 Sthl   2m4f110y gd-sft Hdl

Moderate handicap hurdler; stays two and a half miles; acts on most ground.

Jaffeg Storm (IRE)
**   39**

7-y-o b g Glacial Storm (USA)-She s A Monkey (Monksfield)
Miss Lucinda V Russell A A Bissett

Placings:0-P   (1820)
2002/03: 20⁰HY,
	Starts	1st	2nd	3rd	Win & Pl
Hurdles	1	0	0	0	
Career Total	2	0	0		

Going: Sf: 0-1 GS: 0-0 Gd: 0-0 GF: - Fm: 0-0
Distance: 2m/2m3: 0-0 2m4-2m7: 0-1 3m+: 0-0
Track: LH: 0-1 RH: 0-0 Tight: 0-0 Gall: 0-0
Aids: Bl: 0-0 Vi: 0-0 Tstrap: 0-0
Best Rating: 49 4/02 Kels   2m110y   gd-fm Hdl

Jaguar (NZ)
81(71c)   (76c)**100d**

10-y-o b g St Hilarion (USA)-Saab (NZ) (Three Legs)
J S Wainwright (P J Hobbs 11/5) Ms Julie French

Placings:12/1/53-5P0P6   (3124)
2002/03: 23⁵GF, 22ᴾGF, 20⁰GF, 22ᴾGF, 20⁶HY,
	Starts	1st	2nd	3rd	Win & Pl
Hurdles	3	0	0	0	
Chases	2	0	0	0	
Career Total	10	2	1	1	7083
118	10/00	Extr	3m110y E(0-115)HHdl	SFT	£3250
102	11/99	Newc	2m4f	E Hdl	GD	£2379

Total win prize-money £5629

Going: Sf: 0-1 GS: 0-0 Gd: 0-0 GF: - Fm: 0-4
Distance: 2m/2m3: 0-0 2m4-2m7: 0-4 3m+: 0-1
Track: LH: 0-4 RH: 0-1 Tight: 0-2 Gall: 0-1
Aids: Bl: 0-0 Vi: 0-0 Tstrap: 0-0
Best Rating: 118 10/00 Extr 3m110y   soft   Hdl

Selling hurdler nowadays.

Jaguar
**   105**

7-y-o b g Barathea (IRE)-Oasis (Valiyar)
J R Best (N A Twiston-Davies 14/5) F J Mills & W Mills

Placings:12442503/06P000/64F0UP-0   (0214)
2002/03: 19⁰G,
	Starts	1st	2nd	3rd	Win & Pl
Hurdles	1	0	0	0	
Career Total	21	1	2	1	7313
120	9/99	Extr	2m1f	E Hdl	G-S	£2373

Total win prize-money £2373

Going: Sf: 0-0 GS: 0-0 Gd: 0-0 GF: - Fm: 0-0
Distance: 2m/2m3: 0-0 2m4-2m7: 0-1 3m+: 0-0
Track: LH: 0-0 RH: 0-1 Tight: 0-0 Gall: 0-0
Aids: Bl: 0-0 Vi: 0-0 Tstrap: 0-0
Best Rating: 120 1/00 Wwck   2m   soft   Hdl

A winner over hurdles, he acts well on good to soft ground and goes well over two miles one furlong. Has not won since September 1999.

Jaguar (NZ)
81(71c)   (76c)**100d**

10-y-o b g St Hilarion (USA)-Saab (NZ) (Three Legs)
J S Wainwright (P J Hobbs 11/5) Ms Julie French

Placings:12/1/53-5P0P6   (3124)
2002/03: 23⁵GF, 22ᴾGF, 20⁰GF, 22ᴾGF, 20⁶HY,
	Starts	1st	2nd	3rd	Win & Pl
Hurdles	3	0	0	0	
Chases	2	0	0	0	
Career Total	10	2	1	1	7083
118	10/00	Extr	3m110y E(0-115)HHdl	SFT	£3250
102	11/99	Newc	2m4f	E Hdl	GD	£2379

Total win prize-money £5629

Going: Sf: 0-1 GS: 0-0 Gd: 0-0 GF: - Fm: 0-4
Distance: 2m/2m3: 0-0 2m4-2m7: 0-4 3m+: 0-1
Track: LH: 0-4 RH: 0-1 Tight: 0-2 Gall: 0-1
Aids: Bl: 0-0 Vi: 0-0 Tstrap: 0-0
Best Rating: 118 10/00 Extr 3m110y   soft   Hdl

Selling hurdler nowadays.

Jahash
112   123

5-y-o ch g Hernando (FR)-Jalsun (Jalmood (USA))

P J Hobbs (Sir Mark Prescott 18/10) J Hawkins

Placings:12231   (4536)
2002/03: 17¹GS, 19²GS, 17²GS, 16³G, 24¹G,
	Starts	1st	2nd	3rd	Win & Pl
Hurdles	5	2	2	1	13864
Career Total	5	2	2	1	13864
108	4/03	Ludl	3m	E Hdl	GD	£3770
97	11/02	Tntn	2m1f	D Hdl	G-S	£4316

Total win prize-money £8086

Going: Sf: 0-0 GS: 1-3 Gd: 1-2 GF: - Fm: 0-0
Distance: 2m/2m3: 1-4 2m4-2m7: 0-0 3m+: 1-1
Track: LH: 0-2 RH: 2-3 Tight: 1-1 Gall: 0-1
Aids: Bl: 0-0 Vi: 0-0 Tstrap: 0-0
Best Rating: 123 1/03 Chel   2m1f   gd-sft Hdl

Decent novice hurdler; won extended two mile maiden hurdle at Taunton November 2002; appreciated the step up to three miles when scrambling home at Ludlow April 2003; likes the top of the ground.

Jair Du Cochet (FR)
118(113h)   (165h)**155**

6-y-o b g Rahotep (FR)-Dilaure (FR) (Rose Laurel)
G Macaire Mrs F Montauban

Placings:C111211/41302-1111U2   (4110)
2002/03: 17¹S, 16¹GF, 20¹GS, 24¹S, 24⁴GS, 24²G,
	Starts	1st	2nd	3rd	Win & Pl
Chases	6	4	1	0	84389
Career Total	18	10	3	1	172399
155	12/02	Kemp	3m	A Ch	SFT	£29000
149	11/02	Newb	2m4f	A Ch	G-S	£10846
127	11/02	Folk	2m	E Ch	G-F	£3731
	5/02	LE L	2m1f	Ch	SFT	£10012
165	1/02	Hayd	2m7f110yA Hdl	SFT	£15080
165	1/01	Chel	2m1f	A Hdl	SFT	£12000
156	12/00	Chep	2m110y	A Hdl	SFT	£17400
	11/00	Engh	2m110y	Hdl	HVY	£9606
	10/00	Engh	2m110y	Hdl	HLD	£9606
	10/00	Comp	2m	Hdl	VS	£3362

Total win prize-money £120643

Going: Sf: 2-2 GS: 1-2 Gd: 0-1 GF: - Fm: 1-1
Distance: 2m/2m3: 2-2 2m4-2m7: 1-1 3m+: 1-3
Track: LH: 1-2 RH: 2-3 Tight: 1-1 Gall: 1-2
Aids: Bl: 0-0 Vi: 0-0 Tstrap: 0-0
Best Rating: 165 1/02 Hayd   2m7f110y soft   Hdl

High-class French-trained hurdler/chaser, winning several times at graded level over hurdles in Britain between 2000 and 2002; won his first four starts over fences including the Feltham at Kempton and finished good second in the 2003 Royal & SunAlliance Chase at the 2003 Festival; acts on any ground but it well suited by soft ground; stays three miles.

Jakari (FR)
105(109h)   (107h)**131**

6-y-o b g Apeldoorn (FR)-Tartifume Ii (FR) (Mistigri)
H D Daly The Earl Cadogan

Placings:5/1-32311P   (4474)
2002/03: 17³GS, 20²S, 19³G, 19¹G, 20¹GS, 25ᴾG,
	Starts	1st	2nd	3rd	Win & Pl
Hurdles	1	0	0	1	410
Chases	5	2	1	1	12458
Career Total	8	3	1	2	15556
131	3/03	Strf	2m4f	D Ch	G-S	£5512
119	2/03	Hrfd	2m3f	E Ch	GD	£4182
107	11/01	Uttx	2m	E Hdl	SFT	£2688

Total win prize-money £12383

Going: Sf: 0-1 GS: 1-2 Gd: 1-3 GF: - Fm: 0-0
Distance: 2m/2m3: 1-3 2m4-2m7: 1-2 3m+: 0-1
Track: LH: 1-4 RH: 1-2 Tight: 1-3 Gall: 0-0
Aids: Bl: 0-0 Vi: 0-0 Tstrap: 0-0
Best Rating: 131 3/03 Strf 2m4f gd-sft Ch

Decent novice chaser; lightly raced over hurdles; got off the mark over fences at Hereford in February and followed up at Stratford in March; effective on good and soft ground; stays two and a half miles.

Jake The Jumper (IRE)
90
6-y-o b g Jolly Jake (NZ)-Princess Tino (IRE) (Rontino)
Miss G Browne Mrs Rosalinde Elsbury

Placings:5045-2P (1711)
2002/03: 21²F, 22PG,

	Starts	1st	2nd	3rd	Win & Pl
Hurdles	2	0	1	0	768
Career Total	6	0	1	0	1127

Going: Sf: 0-0 GS: 0-0 Gd: 0-1 GF: - Fm: 0-1
Distance: 2m/2m3: 0-0 2m4-2m7: 0-2 3m+: 0-0
Track: LH: 0-2 RH: 0-0 Tight: 0-1 Gall: 0-0
Aids: Bl: 0-0 Vi: 0-0 Tstrap: 0-0
Best Rating: 90 5/02 Wwck 2m5f firm Hdl

Lightly-raced individual, with only moderate form to date on soft and firm ground.

Jalb (IRE)
111   95
9-y-o b g Robellino (USA)-Adjacent (IRE) (Doulab (USA))
P G Murphy Family And Friends

Placings:P/0042122/26200-22 (0426)
2002/03: 16²G, 22²GF,

	Starts	1st	2nd	3rd	Win & Pl
Hurdles	2	0	2	0	1884
Career Total	15	1	7	0	8809
90 4/99 Ludl 2m5f110yE(0-105)HHdl GD £3022					

Total win prize-money £3022

Going: Sf: 0-0 GS: 0-0 Gd: 0-1 GF: - Fm: 0-0
Distance: 2m/2m3: 0-1 2m4-2m7: 0-1 3m+: 0-0
Track: LH: 0-1 RH: 0-1 Tight: 0-1 Gall: 0-0
Aids: Bl: 0-2 Vi: 0-0 Tstrap: 0-2
Best Rating: 95 6/02 Font 2m6f110y gd-fm Hdl

Modest hurdler, acts on good or softer.

Jallastep (FR)
108   101+
6-y-o b g Boston Two Step (USA)-Balladine (FR) (Rivelago (FR))
J S Goldie Mr & Mrs Raymond Anderson Green

Placings:60P510-32101 (2389)
2002/03: 20⁰G, 20³GF, 22¹G, 21⁹G, 20¹GS,

	Starts	1st	2nd	3rd	Win & Pl
Hurdles	6	2	1	1	9001
Career Total	11	3	1	1	11773
101 12/02 Ayr 2m4f E(0-105)HHdl GD £3066					
85 10/02 Kels 2m6f110yF(0-100)HHdl GD £4199					
77 4/02 Hexm 2m110y E(0-105)HHdl G-F £2772					

Total win prize-money £10037

Going: Sf: 0-0 GS: 1-1 Gd: 1-3 GF: - Fm: 0-2
Distance: 2m/2m3: 0-0 2m4-2m7: 2-6 3m+: 0-0

Track: LH: 2-5 RH: 0-1 Tight: 1-2 Gall: 0-2
Aids: Bl: 0-0 Vi: 0-0 Tstrap: 0-0
Best Rating: 101 12/02 Ayr 2m4f gd-sft Hdl

Lightly-raced moderate hurdler, acts on a fast surface and stays two miles-six plus. Idles in front.

Jalons Star (IRE)
95(106h)   (92h)94
5-y-o b g Eagle Eyed (USA)-Regina St Cyr (IRE) (Doulab (USA))
M Quinn J G Dooley

Placings:4435204012-00605 (4780)
2002/03: 00²HY, 16⁰S, 21⁶S, 17⁰G, 16⁵GF,

	Starts	1st	2nd	3rd	Win & Pl
Hurdles	5	0	0	0	1500
Career Total	15	1	2	1	8809
107 3/02 Sedg 2m1f D(0-115)HHdl SFT £3297					

Total win prize-money £3297

Going: Sf: 0-3 GS: 0-0 Gd: 0-1 GF: - Fm: 0-1
Distance: 2m/2m3: 0-0 2m4-2m7: 0-2 3m+: 0-0
Track: LH: 0-2 RH: 0-3 Tight: 0-0 Gall: 0-1
Aids: Bl: 0-0 Vi: 0-0 Tstrap: 0-0
Best Rating: 107 3/02 Newb 2m10y gd-sft Hdl

Moderate hurdler; best effort over fences when runner-up in four horse race at Uttoxeter June 2003; stays 2m 4f, probably better over shorter; acts on soft ground.

Jaloux D'Estruval (FR)
102(86h)   (73h)122+
6-y-o b g Kadalko (FR)-Pommette Iii (FR) (Trac)
Mrs L C Taylor Mrs W Morrell

Placings:05/40P-1F3F (3522)
2002/03: 25¹G, 25FS, 24³G, 24FG,

	Starts	1st	2nd	3rd	Win & Pl
Chases	4	1	0	1	4794
Career Total	9	1	0	1	4794
122 12/02 Hrfd 3m1f110yE Ch GD £4134					

Total win prize-money £4134

Going: Sf: 0-1 GS: 0-0 Gd: 1-3 GF: - Fm: 0-0
Distance: 2m/2m3: 0-0 2m4-2m7: 0-0 3m+: 1-4
Track: LH: 0-2 RH: 1-2 Tight: 0-0 Gall: 0-2
Aids: Bl: 0-0 Vi: 0-0 Tstrap: 0-0
Best Rating: 122 2/03 Newb 3m good Ch

Useful novice; caused a 100-1 shock when successful on his second start over fences, but has had his jumping problems since.

Jalpreuil Malta (FR)
87   120
6-y-o gr g Saint Preuil (FR)-Alzira (FR) (Numbi (FR))
P F Nicholls (G Macaire 8/1) Mr & Mrs Ian Marshall

Placings:430220/3P3212 (4389)
2002/03: 21³G, 21PHY, 18³HO, 20²S, 20¹HY, 25²F,

	Starts	1st	2nd	3rd	Win & Pl
Chases	6	1	2	2	13666
Career Total	12	1	4	3	21115
1/03 Pau 2m4f110y Ch HVY £6234					

Total win prize-money £6234

Going: Sf: 1-3 GS: 0-0 Gd: 0-1 GF: - Fm: 0-1
Distance: 2m/2m3: 0-1 2m4-2m7: 1-4 3m+: 0-1
Track: LH: 0-0 RH: 0-4 Tight: 0-0 Gall: 0-0
Aids: Bl: 0-0 Vi: 0-0 Tstrap: 0-0

Best Rating: 120 3/03 Extr 3m1f110y firm Ch

French import; won two and a half mile cross-country race in the mud at Pau January 2003; well beaten in the end when runner-up to Chicuelo on firm ground over extended three miles at Exeter in March.

Jamaican Flight (USA)
102   116
10-y-o b h Sunshine Forever (USA)-Kalamona (USA) (Hawaii)
Mrs S Lamyman P Lamyman

Placings:UO52/11111326/31213400/62P24/50F/44604-41PP5 (2690)
2002/03: 19⁴GF, 19¹GF, 17PGF, 21PG, 19⁵GS,

	Starts	1st	2nd	3rd	Win & Pl
Hurdles	5	1	0	0	3835
Career Total	38	8	5	3	39300
116 9/02 MRas 2m3f110yE(0-110)HHdl G-F £3486					
132 11/98 MRas 2m5f110yB HHdl HVY £6716					
131 10/98 MRas 2m3f110yD(0-130)HHdl GD £4445					
128 9/97 MRas 2m3f110yD(0-120)HHdl GD £2745					
105 7/97 MRas 2m3f110yD Hdl GD £2882					
113 6/97 MRas 2m3f110yD Hdl GD £2872					
109 5/97 MRas 2m3f110yD(0-120)HHdl G-F £2951					
102 5/97 Towc 2m E Hdl GD £2407					

Total win prize-money £28508

Going: Sf: 0-0 GS: 0-1 Gd: 0-1 GF: - Fm: 1-3
Distance: 2m/2m3: 0-0 2m4-2m7: 1-4 3m+: 0-0
Track: LH: 0-0 RH: 1-5 Tight: 1-5 Gall: 0-0
Aids: Bl: 0-0 Vi: 0-0 Tstrap: 0-0
Best Rating: 132 12/99 MRas 2m3f110y good Hdl

A natural front-runner, this smashing dual-purpose horse has given his connections tremendous value for money on the Flat and over hurdles. Goes particularly well at Market Rasen. Unraced over fences, his last hurdle win was November 1998.

James Dee (IRE)
86   74
7-y-o b g Shalford (IRE)-Glendale Joy (IRE) (Glenstal (USA))
Mrs P Ford R S Herbert

Placings:060P040F (2941)
2002/03: 16⁰GF, 16⁶S, 16⁹GF, 24PG, 16⁰G, 16⁴G, 16⁰G, 16FS,

	Starts	1st	2nd	3rd	Win & Pl
Hurdles	8	0	0	0	0
Career Total	8	0	0	0	0

Going: Sf: 0-2 GS: 0-0 Gd: 0-4 GF: - Fm: 0-2
Distance: 2m/2m3: 0-7 2m4-2m7: 0-0 3m+: 0-1
Track: LH: 0-4 RH: 0-4 Tight: 0-1 Gall: 0-1
Aids: Bl: 0-0 Vi: 0-0 Tstrap: 0-1
Best Rating: 74 11/02 Ludl 2m good Hdl

James Victor (IRE)
75f   61f
5-y-o b g Be My Guest (USA)-Antakiya (IRE) (Ela-Mana-Mou)
C R Egerton J S Dale

Placings:5 (2987)
2002/03: 18⁵HY,

	Starts	1st	2nd	3rd	Win & Pl
NH Flat	1	0	0	0	0

Career Total	1	0	0	0	0

Going: Sf: 0-1 GS: 0-0 Gd: 0-0 GF: - Fm: 0-0
Distance: 2m/2m3: 0-1 2m4-2m7: 0-0 3m+: 0-0
Track: LH: 0-1 RH: 0-0 Tight: 0-1 Gall: 0-0
Aids: Bl: 0-0 Vi: 0-0 Tstrap: 0-0
Best Rating: 61 1/03 Font 2m2f110y heavy NHF

Jamies First (IRE)

10-y-o ch g Commanche Run-Avionne (Derrylin)
Mrs H J Cobb Mrs Felicity Ashfield

Placings:0P0/P   (3951)
2002/03: 16PGS,

	Starts	1st	2nd	3rd	Win & Pl
Chases	1	0	0	0	
Career Total	4	0	0	0	

Going: Sf: 0-0 GS: 0-1 Gd: 0-0 GF: - Fm: 0-0
Distance: 2m/2m3: 0-1 2m4-2m7: 0-0 3m+: 0-0
Track: LH: 0-0 RH: 0-1 Tight: 0-0 Gall: 0-0
Aids: Bl: 0-0 Vi: 0-0 Tstrap: 0-0
Best Rating: 40 3/97 Plum 2m4f gd-fm Hdl

Jamorin Dancer
104(98h)   (68h)89

8-y-o b g Charmer-Geryea (USA) (Desert Wine (USA))
R C Guest (N B Mason 25/10) Miss C Metcalfe

Placings:0P0V40/5/0003426005-033306036P00401 (4783)
2002/03: 16PG, 16PG, 16PGS, 16PG, 17PGF, 17PG, 17PGF, 16PG,
16PGF, 17PG, 16PGS, 16PG, 174G, 20PG, 171G,

	Starts	1st	2nd	3rd	Win & Pl
Hurdles	7	0	0	1	294
Chases	8	1	0	3	6436
Career Total	32	1	1	5	7711
89	4/03	MRas	2m1f110yE(0-105)HCh	GD	£4438

Total win prize-money £4438

Going: Sf: 0-0 GS: 0-2 Gd: 1-10 GF: - Fm: 0-3
Distance: 2m/2m3: 1-14 2m4-2m7: 0-1 3m+: 0-3
Track: LH: 0-11 RH: 1-4 Tight: 1-8 Gall: 0-2
Aids: Bl: 0-0 Vi: 0-0 Tstrap: 0-0
Best Rating: 89 4/03 MRas 2m1f110y good Ch

Modest novice chaser; runner-up four times on the trot in the summer of 2003; best at around 2m; effective on good ground; usually wears cheekpieces.

Jan's Dream (IRE)
106   100

9-y-o ch m Executive Perk-Aunty Babs (Sexton Blake)
P R Webber Mrs J A Chenery

Placings:46/01/300/4PUR225-P42   (4189)
2002/03: 16PS, 16AGS, 16²G,

	Starts	1st	2nd	3rd	Win & Pl
Chases	3	0	1	0	1590
Career Total	17	1	3	1	7120
100	4/00	NAbb	2m1f	E Hdl	HVY £2555

Total win prize-money £2555

Going: Sf: 0-1 GS: 0-1 Gd: 0-1 GF: - Fm: 0-0
Distance: 2m/2m3: 0-3 2m4-2m7: 0-0 3m+: 0-0
Track: LH: 0-0 RH: 0-3 Tight: 0-2 Gall: 0-0
Aids: Bl: 0-0 Vi: 0-0 Tstrap: 0-1
Best Rating: 100 3/03 Folk 2m good Ch

Winner of a maiden hurdle in the spring of 2000 in bottom-less ground. Well held since over hurdles. Has moderate form over fences. Stays two and a half miles. Acts on soft/heavy ground.

Jandal
96   80

9-y-o ch g Arazi (USA)-Littlefield (Bay Express)
Jane Southcombe Ray Bown

Placings:0054/60F/0/4P042-0   (0077)
2002/03: 17PGF,

	Starts	1st	2nd	3rd	Win & Pl
Hurdles	1	0	0	0	
Career Total	14	0	1	0	602

Going: Sf: 0-0 GS: 0-0 Gd: 0-0 GF: - Fm: 0-1
Distance: 2m/2m3: 0-1 2m4-2m7: 0-0 3m+: 0-0
Track: LH: 0-0 RH: 0-1 Tight: 0-0 Gall: 0-0
Aids: Bl: 0-0 Vi: 0-0 Tstrap: 0-0
Best Rating: 80 4/02 Hrfd 2m1f gd-fm Hdl

Improved form on fast ground including when narrowly beaten in a Hereford seller in April 2002.

Jane Corcoran (IRE)
75   51

7-y-o ch m Persian Mews-Back To Bahrain (Mandalus)
D Burchell Colm Kedney

Placings:00-0PP   (2127)
2002/03: 20PG, 16PS, 21PS,

	Starts	1st	2nd	3rd	Win & Pl
Hurdles	3	0	0	0	
Career Total	5	0	0	0	

Going: Sf: 0-2 GS: 0-0 Gd: 0-1 GF: - Fm: 0-0
Distance: 2m/2m3: 0-1 2m4-2m7: 0-2 3m+: 0-0
Track: LH: 0-3 RH: 0-0 Tight: 0-1 Gall: 0-0
Aids: Bl: 0-0 Vi: 0-0 Tstrap: 0-0
Best Rating: 75 6/01 Wxfd 2m4f gd-fm NHF

Janidou (FR)
(119h)   (123h)119

7-y-o b g Cadoudal (FR)-Majathen (FR) (Carmarthen (FR))
A L T Moore J P McManus

Placings:6/621/0P630-000300   (4742a)
2002/03: 17PGY, 16PS, 16PS, 16PHY, 23PGS, 22PGS,

	Starts	1st	2nd	3rd	Win & Pl
Hurdles	6	0	0	1	1461
Career Total	15	1	1	2	15882
130	1/01	Tram	2m	Hdl	SH £5564

Total win prize-money £5565

Going: Sf: 0-4 GS: 0-0 Gd: 0-1 GF: - Fm: 0-0
Distance: 2m/2m3: 0-6 2m4-2m7: 0-0 3m+: 0-0
Track: LH: 0-2 RH: 0-3 Tight: 0-0 Gall: 0-0
Aids: Bl: 0-0 Vi: 0-0 Tstrap: 0-0
Best Rating: 130 1/01 Tram 2m sft-hvy Hdl

Fair Irish hurdler; effective over two miles; acts on a soft surface.

Janiture (FR)
105(101h)   (112h)128

6-y-o gr m Turgeon (USA)-Majaway (FR) (Timmy s Way (FR))

P F Nicholls Malcolm Pearce & Gerry Mizel

Placings:46P111/P23-51F311   (4719)
2002/03: 17⁵G, 19¹GS, 21FGS, 21³GS, 17¹GF, 16¹F,

	Starts	1st	2nd	3rd	Win & Pl
Chases	6	3	0	1	17306
Career Total	15	6	1	2	28823
128	4/03	Winc	2m	D(0-115)HCh	FRM £5726
124	4/03	Plum	2m1f	E Ch	G-F £4410
128	11/02	Tntn	2m3f	E(0-125)HCh	G-S £5460
	4/01	Nant	2m1f110y	Hdl	VS £3492
	4/01	Loud	2m1f	Hdl	VS £2716
	3/01	Seno	1m7f	Hdl	HVY £2716

Total win prize-money £24520

Going: Sf: 0-0 GS: 1-3 Gd: 0-1 GF: - Fm: 2-2
Distance: 2m/2m3: 3-4 2m4-2m7: 0-2 3m+: 0-0
Track: LH: 1-1 RH: 2-5 Tight: 2-2 Gall: 0-0
Aids: Bl: 0-0 Vi: 0-0 Tstrap: 0-0
Best Rating: 128 4/03 Winc 2m firm Ch

Decent novice chaser; successful three times over hurdles in France; got off the mark over fences at Taunton in November 2002; won two three-runner races in quick succession in April 2003; stays two miles five; acts on soft and firm ground; improving.

Jansue Charlie
98   98

9-y-o ch g Ardar-Kincherinchee (Dunbeath (USA))
R Nixon G R S Nixon

Placings:50/0P06423P501/612140/020PP   (3896)
2002/03: 22PS, 22³HY, 20PHY, 23PGS, 22PGS,

	Starts	1st	2nd	3rd	Win & Pl
Hurdles	5	0	1	0	1252
Career Total	24	3	3	1	13188
107	11/00	Kels	2m6f110yD(0-125)HHdl	SFT	£3006
107	10/00	Kels	2m6f110yD(0-125)HHdl	SFT	£3120
99	3/00	Kels	2m6f110yE(0-115)HHdl	G-S	£2873

Total win prize-money £8999

Going: Sf: 0-3 GS: 0-2 Gd: 0-0 GF: - Fm: 0-0
Distance: 2m/2m3: 0-0 2m4-2m7: 0-5 3m+: 0-0
Track: LH: 0-5 RH: 0-0 Tight: 0-3 Gall: 0-0
Aids: Bl: 0-0 Vi: 0-0 Tstrap: 0-0
Best Rating: 107 11/00 Kels 2m6f110y soft Hdl

January Sixteenth
69   57

7-y-o b g Presidium-Espanita (Riboboy (USA))
D C O Brien D C O Brien

Placings:0/0500-0   (0059)
2002/03: 17PG,

	Starts	1st	2nd	3rd	Win & Pl
Hurdles	1	0	0	0	
Career Total	6	0	0	0	0

Going: Sf: 0-0 GS: 0-0 Gd: 0-1 GF: - Fm: 0-0
Distance: 2m/2m3: 0-1 2m4-2m7: 0-0 3m+: 0-0
Track: LH: 0-0 RH: 0-1 Tight: 0-0 Gall: 0-0
Aids: Bl: 0-0 Vi: 0-0 Tstrap: 0-0
Best Rating: 57 3/02 Font 2m2f110y soft Hdl

Jardin De Beaulieu (FR)
104   117

6-y-o ch g Rough Magic (FR)-Emblem (FR) (Siberian Express (USA))

Ian Williams Mr & Mrs John Poynton

Placings:2/2P3F-P245 (3788)
2002/03: 20^PGS, 20^2GS, 20^4S, 19^5G,

	Starts	1st	2nd	3rd	Win & Pl
Chases	4	0	1	0	2066
Career Total	9	0	3	1	7248

Going:	Sf: 0-1 GS: 0-2 Gd: 0-1 GF: - Fm: 0-0
Distance:	2m/2m3: 0-1 2m4-2m7: 0-3 3m+: 0-0
Track:	LH: 0-3 RH: 0-1 Tight: 0-0 Gall: 0-1
Aids:	Bl: 0-0 Vi: 0-0 Tstrap: 0-0
Best Rating:	117 12/02 Weth 2m4f110y gd-sft Ch

Fair front-running chaser; flattered when runner-up behind a potentially smart sort at Wetherby in December; well beaten since.

Jarro (FR)
107   128
7-y-o b g Pistolet Bleu (IRE)-Junta (FR) (Cariellor (FR))
Miss Venetia Williams Mrs P A H Hartley

Placings:1PF135/5/31513-F241P25 (4369)
2002/03: 16^FG, 16^2GS, 16^4GS, 16^1S, 16^PHY, 16^2S, 16^5G,

	Starts	1st	2nd	3rd	Win & Pl
Chases	7	1	2	0	17641
Career Total	19	5	2	3	61484
128 12/02 Uttx 2m	C(0-130)HCh		SFT		£11625
113 3/02 Plum 2m1f	E Ch		GD		£3120
123 1/02 Tntn 2m110y	D Ch		SFT		£4823
1/00 Pau 2m2f	Hdl		GD		£13449
10/99 Autl 1m7f	Hdl		HLD		£7535
				Total win prize-money	£40552

Going:	Sf: 1-3 GS: 0-2 Gd: 0-2 GF: - Fm: 0-0
Distance:	2m/2m3: 1-7 2m4-2m7: 0-0 3m+: 0-0
Track:	LH: 1-4 RH: 0-3 Tight: 0-1 Gall: 0-0
Aids:	Bl: 0-0 Vi: 0-0 Tstrap: 0-0
Best Rating:	128 3/03 Sand 2m soft Ch

Handicap chaser, very easy winner at Uttoxeter in December. Likes heavy ground and best at two miles.

Jaseur (USA)
108(87c)   (47c)113
10-y-o b g Lear Fan (USA)-Spur Wing (USA) (Storm Bird (CAN))
G Barnett J C Bradbury

Placings:2U220/2456-4605316513 (4606)
2002/03: 24^4G, 24^6GS, 21^6GF, 20^5G, 20^3G, 20^1GS, 20^6S, 19^5GS, 20^1GS, 24^3G,

	Starts	1st	2nd	3rd	Win & Pl
Hurdles	9	2	0	2	10721
Chases	1	0	0	0	0
Career Total	19	2	4	2	18376
110 2/03 Bang 2m4f	E(0-105)HHdl		G-S		£4855
110 12/02 Weth 2m4f110y	E(0-105)HHdl		G-S		£3178
				Total win prize-money	£8034

Going:	Sf: 0-1 GS: 2-4 Gd: 0-4 GF: - Fm: 0-1
Distance:	2m/2m3: 0-0 2m4-2m7: 2-7 3m+: 0-3
Track:	LH: 2-10 RH: 0-0 Tight: 1-4 Gall: 0-1
Aids:	Bl: 2-7 Vi: 0-2 Tstrap: 0-0
Best Rating:	125 12/00 Asct 2m110y heavy Hdl

Modest hurdler; likes the mud, but is effective on decent ground; stays two and a half miles; usually wears a visor or blinkers.

Jasmin Guichois (FR)
106(90h)   (90+h)104
6-y-o ch g Dom Alco (FR)-Lady Belle (FR) (Or De Chine)
Miss Venetia Williams Seasons Holidays

Placings:4/FP-01033F (3900)
2002/03: 16^6G, 20^1HY, 20^9HY, 25^3GS, 24^3GS, 20^FS,

	Starts	1st	2nd	3rd	Win & Pl
Hurdles	3	1	0	0	2261
Chases	3	0	0	2	1754
Career Total	9	1	0	2	5955
90 12/02 Folk 2m4f110yF Hdl			HVY		£2261
				Total win prize-money	£2261

Going:	Sf: 1-3 GS: 0-2 Gd: 0-1 GF: - Fm: 0-0
Distance:	2m/2m3: 0-1 2m4-2m7: 1-3 3m+: 0-2
Track:	LH: 0-2 RH: 1-3 Tight: 1-2 Gall: 0-1
Aids:	Bl: 0-0 Vi: 0-0 Tstrap: 0-0
Best Rating:	104 3/03 Newb 2m4f soft Ch

Moderate ex-French hurdler/chaser; modest form over hurdles and fences before winning a small hurdle at Folkestone in December 2002; every chance when fell at the last over fences in March 2003; stays three miles but effective at shorter; handles testing ground.

Jasper Lad
7-y-o ch g Fearless Action (USA)-Last Shower (Town And Country)
J Gallagher Horses Away Racing Club

Placings:0/0P- (0019)
2002/03: 16^PGS,

	Starts	1st	2nd	3rd	Win & Pl
Hurdles	1	0	0	0	
Career Total	3	0	0	0	

Going:	Sf: 0-0 GS: 0-0 Gd: 0-0 GF: - Fm: 0-0
Distance:	2m/2m3: 0-2 2m4-2m7: 0-0 3m+: 0-0
Track:	LH: 0-0 RH: 0-1 Tight: 0-0 Gall: 0-0
Aids:	Bl: 0-0 Vi: 0-0 Tstrap: 0-0
Best Rating:	45 6/01 Worc 2m good NHF

Jato Dancer (IRE)
88
8-y-o b m Mukaddamah (USA)-Que Tranquila (Dominion)
R Hollinshead Mrs Norman Hill

Placings:323F0-PP (0692)
2002/03: 19^PG, 16^PS,

	Starts	1st	2nd	3rd	Win & Pl
Hurdles	2	0	0	0	
Career Total	7	0	1	2	1151

Going:	Sf: 0-1 GS: 0-0 Gd: 0-1 GF: - Fm: 0-0
Distance:	2m/2m3: 0-1 2m4-2m7: 0-1 3m+: 0-0
Track:	LH: 0-1 RH: 0-1 Tight: 0-1 Gall: 0-0
Aids:	Bl: 0-0 Vi: 0-0 Tstrap: 0-0
Best Rating:	88 11/01 Strf 2m110y soft Hdl

She won twice on the Flat and ran well over hurdles in November when second at Stratford in a relatively competitive seller over two miles.

Javelot D'Or (FR)
6-y-o b/br g Useful (FR)-Flika D Or (FR) (Pot D Or (FR))

Miss Venetia Williams John Nicholls (banbury) Ltd

Placings:10/4111-P (4440)
2002/03: 19^PG,

	Starts	1st	2nd	3rd	Win & Pl
Chases	1	0	0	0	
Career Total	7	4	0	0	13386
6/01 Diep 2m1f110y Ch			GD		£3686
6/01 Sbri 2m2f Ch			G-S		£3104
5/01 LE L 2m1f Ch			GD		£3880
3/01 Seno 1m7f Hdl			HVY		£2716
				Total win prize-money	£13386

Going:	Sf: 0-0 GS: 0-0 Gd: 0-1 GF: - Fm: 0-0
Distance:	2m/2m3: 0-0 2m4-2m7: 0-1 3m+: 0-0
Track:	LH: 0-0 RH: 0-1 Tight: 0-0 Gall: 0-0
Aids:	Bl: 0-0 Vi: 0-0 Tstrap: 0-0
Best Rating:	0 4/03 Asct 2m3f110y good Ch

Ex-French chaser; pulled up on British debut after long absence; acts on good ground or softer.

Jawleyford Court
4-y-o b f Moshaajir (USA)-Mrs Jawleyford (USA) (Dixieland Band (USA))
C Smith C Smith

Placings:UP (4156)
2002/03: 16US, 17^PG,

	Starts	1st	2nd	3rd	Win & Pl
Hurdles	2	0	0	0	
Career Total	2	0	0	0	

Going:	Sf: 0-1 GS: 0-0 Gd: 0-1 GF: - Fm: 0-0
Distance:	2m/2m3: 0-2 2m4-2m7: 0-0 3m+: 0-0
Track:	LH: 0-1 RH: 0-1 Tight: 0-0 Gall: 0-0
Aids:	Bl: 0-0 Vi: 0-0 Tstrap: 0-0
Best Rating:	0 3/03 MRas 2m1f110y good Hdl

Jawwala (USA)
105   91
4-y-o b f Green Dancer (USA)-Fetch N Carry (USA) (Alleged (USA))
J R Jenkins (J W Payne 8/10) American Horse Racing Club Ltd

Placings:032P63 (3956)
2002/03: 16^6G, 17^3HY, 16^2S, 16^PHY, 17^6G, 17^3S,

	Starts	1st	2nd	3rd	Win & Pl
Hurdles	6	0	1	2	2541
Career Total	6	0	1	2	2541

Going:	Sf: 0-4 GS: 0-0 Gd: 0-2 GF: - Fm: 0-0
Distance:	2m/2m3: 0-6 2m4-2m7: 0-0 3m+: 0-0
Track:	LH: 0-4 RH: 0-2 Tight: 0-4 Gall: 0-1
Aids:	Bl: 0-0 Vi: 0-0 Tstrap: 0-0
Best Rating:	91 2/03 Hrfd 2m1f good Hdl

Modest form over hurdles so far; has shown plenty of temperament and virtually refused to race on one occasion.

Jay Bee Ell
106   91
6-y-o b g Pursuit Of Love-On Request (IRE) (Be My Guest (USA))
A King J M & A L Longman

Placings:405-14 (0410)
2002/03: 16^5GS, 22^1GF, 22^4GF,

	Starts	1st	2nd	3rd	Win & Pl
Hurdles	3	1	0	0	4483
Career Total	5	1	0	0	4483

90 5/02 Strf 2m6f110y D Hdl G-F £4147

Total win prize-money £4147

Going:	Sf: 0-0 GS: 0-1 Gd: 0-0 GF: - Fm: 1-2
Distance:	2m/2m3: 0-1 2m4-2m7: 1-2 3m+: 0-0
Track:	LH: 1-2 RH: 0-1 Tight: 1-2 Gall: 0-0
Aids:	Bl: 0-0 Vi: 0-0 Tstrap: 0-0
Best Rating:	110 12/01 Newb 2m110y good NHF

Novice hurdler. Won a slowly run 22 furlong novice hurdle at Stratford in May 2002. Acts on a sound surface.

Jayas (FR)
76

6-y-o b/br g Rasi Brasak-Rigolette (FR) (Lychee (FR))
M C Pipe Clive D Smith

Placings:021160/0P-PP4 (1101)
2002/03: 21^P GF, 16^P GF, 21^4 GF,

	Starts	1st	2nd	3rd	Win & Pl
Hurdles	1	0	0	0	0
Chases	2	0	0	0	0
Career Total	11	2	1	0	8227

92 2/01 Ludl 2m E Hdl GD £2222
8/00 Stma 2m Hdl VS £4323

Total win prize-money £6546

Going:	Sf: 0-0 GS: 0-0 Gd: 0-0 GF: - Fm: 0-3
Distance:	2m/2m3: 0-1 2m4-2m7: 0-2 3m+: 0-0
Track:	LH: 0-3 RH: 0-0 Tight: 0-1 Gall: 0-0
Aids:	Bl: 0-0 Vi: 0-3 Tstrap: 0-2
Best Rating:	92 2/01 Ludl 2m good Hdl

Jaybeedee
111

7-y-o b g Rudimentary (USA)-Meavy (Kalaglow)
K C Bailey Mrs C A T Swire & G D W Swire

Placings:36/3230514-4 (1792)
2002/03: 16^4 S,

	Starts	1st	2nd	3rd	Win & Pl
Hurdles	1	0	0	0	265
Career Total	10	1	1	3	6028

111 3/02 Uttx 2m D Hdl HVY £3552

Total win prize-money £3552

Going:	Sf: 0-1 GS: 0-0 Gd: 0-0 GF: - Fm: 0-0
Distance:	2m/2m3: 0-1 2m4-2m7: 0-0 3m+: 0-0
Track:	LH: 0-0 RH: 0-1 Tight: 0-0 Gall: 0-0
Aids:	Bl: 0-0 Vi: 0-0 Tstrap: 0-0
Best Rating:	111 3/02 Uttx 2m heavy Hdl

Placed in bumpers and on his hurdling debut in Ireland, he put up respectable efforts on first two runs in Britain and won well in very testing conditions at Uttoxeter in March 2002. Should have no problem staying two and a half miles.

Jaybejay (NZ)
107(103h)   (126h)126

8-y-o b g High Ice (USA)-Galaxy Light (NZ) (Balios)
M C Pipe Lady Clarke

Placings:310-0315P330 (4461)
2002/03: 20^0 G, 16^3 G, 21^1 GS, 20^5 GS, 20^P G, 21^3 S, 19^3 G, 20^0 G,

	Starts	1st	2nd	3rd	Win & Pl
Hurdles	1	0	0	0	0
Chases	7	1	0	3	8250
Career Total	11	2	0	4	12733

126 1/03 Winc 2m5f D Ch G-S £5928
116 2/02 Winc 2m D Hdl G-S £3990

Total win prize-money £9918

Going:	Sf: 0-1 GS: 1-2 Gd: 0-5 GF: - Fm: 0-0
Distance:	2m/2m3: 0-1 2m4-2m7: 1-7 3m+: 0-0
Track:	LH: 0-2 RH: 1-6 Tight: 0-2 Gall: 0-0
Aids:	Bl: 0-0 Vi: 0-0 Tstrap: 0-0
Best Rating:	126 3/03 Winc 2m5f soft Ch

Fair novice chaser; stays two miles five, could well get further; effective on good to soft ground; keen sort.

Jayed (IRE)
102   88

5-y-o b/br g Marju (IRE)-Taqreem (IRE) (Nashwan (USA))
M Bradstock Miss J C Blackwell

Placings:3540 (4573)
2002/03: 17^3 GF, 17^5 S, 16^4 G, 16^0 GF,

	Starts	1st	2nd	3rd	Win & Pl
Hurdles	4	0	0	1	860
Career Total	4	0	0	1	860

Going:	Sf: 0-1 GS: 0-0 Gd: 0-1 GF: - Fm: 0-2
Distance:	2m/2m3: 0-0 2m4-2m7: 0-0 3m+: 0-0
Track:	LH: 0-2 RH: 0-2 Tight: 0-2 Gall: 0-0
Aids:	Bl: 0-0 Vi: 0-0 Tstrap: 0-0
Best Rating:	88 3/03 Ludl 2m good Hdl

Best effort when narrowly beaten by Governor Daniel in Worcester seller June 2003; has been inclined to pull too hard in the past.

Jazz Band
67f   34f

5-y-o b g Alhijaz-Little Preston (IRE) (Pennine Walk)
Mrs L C Jewell Mrs Linda Jewell

Placings:0 (1425)
2002/03: 17^0 GF,

	Starts	1st	2nd	3rd	Win & Pl
NH Flat	1	0	0	0	
Career Total	1	0	0	0	

Going:	Sf: 0-0 GS: 0-0 Gd: 0-0 GF: - Fm: 0-1
Distance:	2m/2m3: 0-1 2m4-2m7: 0-0 3m+: 0-0
Track:	LH: 0-0 RH: 0-1 Tight: 0-1 Gall: 0-0
Aids:	Bl: 0-0 Vi: 0-0 Tstrap: 0-0
Best Rating:	34 10/02 MRas 2m1f110y gd-fm NHF

Jazz Du Forez (FR)
102(100h)   (65h)73

6-y-o b g Video Rock (FR)-Ophyr Du Forez (FR) (Fin Bon)
John Allen Avon Estates Ltd

Placings:00000-P3B23663 (4265)
2002/03: 20^P G, 19^3 G, 22^B G, 21^2 GS, 25^3 HY, 24^6 GS, 25^6 G, 24^3 GF,

	Starts	1st	2nd	3rd	Win & Pl
Hurdles	7	0	1	2	1354
Chases	1	0	0	0	591
Career Total	13	0	1	3	1945

Going:	Sf: 0-1 GS: 0-2 Gd: 0-4 GF: - Fm: 0-1
Distance:	2m/2m3: 0-0 2m4-2m7: 0-4 3m+: 0-4
Track:	LH: 0-5 RH: 0-2 Tight: 0-4 Gall: 0-0
Aids:	Bl: 0-2 Vi: 0-0 Tstrap: 0-0
Best Rating:	73 3/03 Sthl 3m110y gd-fm Ch

First worthwhile form when runner-up in poor selling hurdle at Market Rasen in November.

Jazz Duke
101   95

10-y-o ch g Rising-Gone (Whistling Wind)
M J Weeden M J Weeden

Placings:0/320PP/F16P04/3344230/2543U-230 (3314)
2002/03: 26^2 GS, 24^3 GS, 25^0 GS,

	Starts	1st	2nd	3rd	Win & Pl
Chases	3	0	1	1	2551
Career Total	27	1	4	6	14006

110 12/99 Tntn 3m110y D(0-120)HHdl G-S £3631

Total win prize-money £3631

Going:	Sf: 0-0 GS: 0-3 Gd: 0-0 GF: - Fm: 0-0
Distance:	2m/2m3: 0-0 2m4-2m7: 0-0 3m+: 0-3
Track:	LH: 0-2 RH: 0-1 Tight: 0-1 Gall: 0-1
Aids:	Bl: 0-0 Vi: 0-0 Tstrap: 0-0
Best Rating:	110 12/99 Tntn 3m110y gd-sft Hdl

An error-prone novice over hurdles, he showed better form over fences and was been repeatedly in the frame last term. He stays three miles and is suited to cut in the ground.

Jazz Night
95   75

6-y-o b g Alhijaz-Hen Night (Mummy s Game)
N A Twiston-Davies The Berryman Lycett Experience

Placings:6-200 (1967)
2002/03: 16^2 G, 16^0 GF, 16^0 GS,

	Starts	1st	2nd	3rd	Win & Pl
Hurdles	3	0	1	0	852
Career Total	4	0	1	0	852

Going:	Sf: 0-0 GS: 0-1 Gd: 0-0 GF: - Fm: 0-1
Distance:	2m/2m3: 0-0 2m4-2m7: 0-0 3m+: 0-0
Track:	LH: 0-0 RH: 0-0 Tight: 0-0 Gall: 0-0
Aids:	Bl: 0-0 Vi: 0-0 Tstrap: 0-0
Best Rating:	75 9/02 Worc 2m good Hdl

Runner-up in a maiden hurdle at Worcester September 2002. May have trouble lasting the trip.

Je Suis (IRE)
60

7-y-o b m Le Bavard (FR)-La Tortue (Lafontaine (USA))
B J Eckley Brian Eckley

Placings:0/00-0 (1812)
2002/03: 17^0 G,

	Starts	1st	2nd	3rd	Win & Pl
Hurdles	1	0	0	0	
Career Total	4	0	0	0	

Going:	Sf: 0-0 GS: 0-0 Gd: 0-1 GF: - Fm: 0-0
Distance:	2m/2m3: 0-1 2m4-2m7: 0-0 3m+: 0-0
Track:	LH: 0-0 RH: 0-1 Tight: 0-0 Gall: 0-0
Aids:	Bl: 0-0 Vi: 0-0 Tstrap: 0-0
Best Rating:	33 2/02 Ludl 2m good NHF

Jean D'Auteuil (FR)
123

7-y-o b g River Sand (FR)-Santa Marta (FR) (Cadmus li)
M C Pipe Terry Neill

Placings:164/233-PP (3315)
2002/03: 22^PS, 19^PGS,

	Starts	1st	2nd	3rd	Win & Pl
Chases	2	0	0	0	
Career Total	8	1	1	2	6575
103 11/00 Tntn	2m1f	E Hdl		GD	£3192
			Total win prize-money £3192		

Going:	Sf: 0-1 GS: 0-1 Gd: 0-0 GF: - Fm: 0-0
Distance:	2m/2m3: 0-0 2m4-2m7: 0-2 3m+: 0-0
Track:	LH: 0-0 RH: 0-1 Tight: 0-1 Gall: 0-0
Aids:	Bl: 0-0 Vi: 0-0 Tstrap: 0-1
Best Rating:	123 11/00 Tntn 2m3f gd-sft Ch

A French import, he made a winning British debut at Taunton in November 2000, but was off the track for ten months before an adequate effort on his chasing debut in November 2001, although he disappointed after that. Stays two and a half miles. Acts on a sound surface.

Jean Guy (FR)
91   90

6-y-o b g Passing Sale (FR)-Umea Iv (FR) (Maiymad)
G Pannier (P J Hobbs 5/12) G Petit

Placings:PP6/3214F45-60P (2330)
2002/03: 24^6HY, 25^6GS, 18^PHO,

	Starts	1st	2nd	3rd	Win & Pl
Chases	3	0	0	0	
Career Total	13	1	1	1	22798
6/01 Autl	2m4f110y Ch		SFT	£12124
		Total win prize-money £12124		

Going:	Sf: 0-1 GS: 0-1 Gd: 0-0 GF: - Fm: 0-0
Distance:	2m/2m3: 0-1 2m4-2m7: 0-0 3m+: 0-2
Track:	LH: 0-0 RH: 0-2 Tight: 0-0 Gall: 0-0
Aids:	Bl: 0-1 Vi: 0-0 Tstrap: 0-0
Best Rating:	102 11/01 Hntg 2m4f110y gd-sft Ch

A winning chaser in France over two and a half miles, he has yet to show much in Britain. Acts on soft ground.

Jeannot De Beauchene (FR)
113   130

6-y-o b g En Calcat (FR)-Chipie D Angron (FR) (Grand Tresor (FR))
R H Alner Martin Short

Placings:11P-2203P (2710)
2002/03: 21^2GF, 20^2S, 20^0S, 20^3G, 22^PGS,

	Starts	1st	2nd	3rd	Win & Pl
Hurdles	5	0	2	1	10357
Career Total	8	2	2	1	16459
118 12/01 Chep	2m4f	D Hdl	G-S	£3757
95 10/01 Folk	2m6f110yE Hdl		HVY	£2345
			Total win prize-money £6102	

Going:	Sf: 0-2 GS: 0-1 Gd: 0-1 GF: - Fm: 0-1
Distance:	2m/2m3: 0-0 2m4-2m7: 0-5 3m+: 0-0
Track:	LH: 0-4 RH: 0-1 Tight: 0-0 Gall: 0-1
Aids:	Bl: 0-0 Vi: 0-0 Tstrap: 0-0
Best Rating:	130 12/02 Hayd 2m4f good Hdl

Decent hurdler, put in an impressive performance to win in gruelling conditions on his hurdling debut over 2m6f at Folkestone. Followed up in a better race at Chepstow. Despite not appearing to be particularly well handicapped, ran well in handicaps on varying ground in the autumn of 2002.

Jefertiti (FR)
101(98h)   (100h)97

6-y-o ch g Le Nain Jaune (FR)-Nefertiti (FR) (Tourangeau (FR))
Miss H C Knight (M De Montfort 14/5) Jim Lewis

Placings:3526 (4608)
2002/03: 18^3VS, 16^5GS, 16^2S, 17^6G,

	Starts	1st	2nd	3rd	Win & Pl
Hurdles	2	0	0	0	253
Chases	2	0	1	1	5271
Career Total	4	0	1	1	5524

Going:	Sf: 0-1 GS: 0-1 Gd: 0-1 GF: - Fm: 0-0
Distance:	2m/2m3: 0-4 2m4-2m7: 0-0 3m+: 0-0
Track:	LH: 0-3 RH: 0-0 Tight: 0-0 Gall: 0-1
Aids:	Bl: 0-0 Vi: 0-0 Tstrap: 0-0
Best Rating:	100 11/02 Wwck 2m gd-sft Hdl

Showed ability over fences in France; placed in novice chases in this country; suited by fast ground; stays 2m 4f.

Jelali (IRE)
96(93h)   (83h)83+

10-y-o b g Last Tycoon-Lautreamont (Auction Ring (USA))
C Moore Mrs T Moore

Placings:1PP/355PF/6P/P (0278)
2002/03: 24^PS,

	Starts	1st	2nd	3rd	Win & Pl
Chases	1	0	0	0	
Career Total	11	1	0	1	2670
95 12/96 Font	2m2f110yE Hdl		GD	£2343
		Total win prize-money £2343		

Going:	Sf: 0-0 GS: 0-0 Gd: 0-0 GF: - Fm: 0-0
Distance:	2m/2m3: 0-0 2m4-2m7: 0-0 3m+: 0-1
Track:	LH: 0-1 RH: 0-0 Tight: 0-1 Gall: 0-0
Aids:	Bl: 0-0 Vi: 0-0 Tstrap: 0-0
Best Rating:	97 11/98 Uttx 2m4f110y soft Hdl

Keen maiden hurdler, shaped slightly better on chasing bow at Sedgefield in October, first outing for new stable.

Jemaro (IRE)
102   90

12-y-o b g Tidaro (USA)-Jeremique (Sunny Way)
Mrs C J Robinson Jeremy Beasley

Placings:00P/PPF5453F1/151U152FP/3114360/5UP606/3 31P (4640)
2002/03: 25^3G, 25^3S, 24^1G, 21^PG,

	Starts	1st	2nd	3rd	Win & Pl
Chases	4	1	0	2	3700
Career Total	38	7	1	5	31196
105 4/03 Ludl	3m	H Ch	GD	£3250
116 12/99 Hayd	3m	D(0-125)HCh	SFT	£6481
113 11/99 Hayd	3m	E(0-115)HCh	G-S	£3241
116 12/98 Ludl	2m4f	E(0-115)HCh	GD	£3126
115 11/98 Hayd	2m4f	E(0-115)HCh	HVY	£2879
95 5/98 Ludl	3m	E(0-100)HCh	G-F	£3412
87 4/98 Ludl	3m	D(0-110)HCh	GD	£3200
			Total win prize-money £25589	

Going:	Sf: 0-1 GS: 0-0 Gd: 1-3 GF: - Fm: 0-0
Distance:	2m/2m3: 0-0 2m4-2m7: 0-0 3m+: 1-3
Track:	LH: 0-1 RH: 1-3 Tight: 1-2 Gall: 0-0
Aids:	Bl: 0-0 Vi: 0-0 Tstrap: 0-0
Best Rating:	117 3/99 Ludl 3m good Ch

Fair hunter chaser these days; acts on good ground; stays three miles, but effective at shorter; goes well at Ludlow and Haydock.

Jenga
102   90+

6-y-o ro m Minster Son-Maybe Daisy (Nicholas Bill)
K C Bailey John Loudon

Placings:11 (3945)
2002/03: 21^1S, 19^1S,

	Starts	1st	2nd	3rd	Win & Pl
Hurdles	2	2	0	0	9142
Career Total	2	2	0	0	9142
90 3/03 Extr	2m3f	D Hdl	SFT	£5245
90 1/03 Ludl	2m5f	E Hdl	SFT	£3896
			Total win prize-money £9143	

Going:	Sf: 2-2 GS: 0-0 Gd: 0-0 GF: - Fm: 0-0
Distance:	2m/2m3: 1-1 2m4-2m7: 1-1 3m+: 0-0
Track:	LH: 0-0 RH: 2-2 Tight: 0-0 Gall: 0-0
Aids:	Bl: 0-0 Vi: 0-0 Tstrap: 0-0
Best Rating:	90 3/03 Extr 2m3f soft Hdl

Placed in a point before winning a mares maiden hurdle at Ludlow in January 2003; followed up in a similar event at Exeter March 2003; should stay three miles; likes soft ground.

Jenko (FR)
96(93h)   (83h)83+

6-y-o b g Cadoubel (FR)-Maika D Ores (FR) (Gaur)
M Todhunter Network Training Ii

Placings:4/605P-5 (1372)
2002/03: 21^5GF,

	Starts	1st	2nd	3rd	Win & Pl
Chases	1	0	0	0	0
Career Total	6	0	0	0	258

Going:	Sf: 0-0 GS: 0-0 Gd: 0-0 GF: - Fm: 0-1
Distance:	2m/2m3: 0-0 2m4-2m7: 0-1 3m+: 0-0
Track:	LH: 0-1 RH: 0-0 Tight: 0-1 Gall: 0-0
Aids:	Bl: 0-0 Vi: 0-0 Tstrap: 0-0
Best Rating:	87 1/02 Tntn 2m1f soft Hdl

Keen maiden hurdler, shaped slightly better on chasing bow at Sedgefield in October, first outing for new stable.

Jenny Rocket
102   90

7-y-o b m Minster Son-Jane s Affair (Alleging (USA))
Miss K Marks Nick Shutts

Placings:5222410PP/552P15-3021343P (1200)
2002/03: 16^3GF, 19^0GF, 16^2HY, 16^1S, 20^3GF, 16^4G, 24^3GF, 26^PGF,

	Starts	1st	2nd	3rd	Win & Pl
Hurdles	8	1	1	3	5724
Career Total	23	3	5	3	11952
86 6/02 Uttx	2m	F(0-95)HHdl	SFT	£1890
73 4/02 Hrfd	2m1f	G Hdl	GD	£1970
91 11/00 Catt	2m3f	F Hdl	GD	£1438
			Total win prize-money £5300	

Going:	Sf: 1-2 GS: 0-0 Gd: 0-1 GF: - Fm: 0-5
Distance:	2m/2m3: 1-5 2m4-2m7: 0-1 3m+: 0-2
Track:	LH: 1-6 RH: 0-2 Tight: 0-1 Gall: 0-0
Aids:	Bl: 0-0 Vi: 0-0 Tstrap: 0-0
Best Rating:	94 10/00 MRas 2m1f110y good NHF

Moderate hurdler, stays two and a quarter miles.

Jenski

99   **97**

8-y-o b g Petoski-Mrs Jennifer (River Knight (FR))
R J Hodges Mrs R Vickery

Placings:60/5-163   (4021)
2002/03: 21¹HY, 22⁶S, 17³S,

	Starts	1st	2nd	3rd	Win & Pl
Hurdles	3	1	0	1	3027
Career Total	**6**	**1**	**0**	**1**	**3027**
97	1/03	Plum	2m5f	G Hdl	HVY £2670

Total win prize-money £2671

Going: Sf: 1-3 GS: 0-0 Gd: 0-0 GF: - Fm: 0-0
Distance: 2m/2m3: 0-1 **2m4-2m7: 1-2** 3m+: 0-0
Track: LH: 1-2 RH: 0-1 Tight: 1-2 Gall: 0-0
Aids: Bl: 0-0 Vi: 0-0 Tstrap: 0-0
Best Rating: 97 1/03 Plum 2m5f   heavy Hdl

Modest hurdler; stays 2m 5f; effective in heavy ground.

Jeremy Spider

104   **124**

10-y-o b g Nearly A Hand-Lucibella (Comedy Star (USA))
C Tizzard R G Tizzard

Placings:4152U221/4/P22P1-310   (4472)
2002/03: 29³S, 23¹GS, 21⁰G,

	Starts	1st	2nd	3rd	Win & Pl
Chases	3	1	0	1	9933
Career Total	**17**	**4**	**5**	**1**	**23275**
124	2/03	Leic	2m7f110yD(0-115)HCh	G-S	£7007
115	2/02	Tntn	3m	E Ch	SFT £3656
110	4/00	Extr	2m7f	E Hdl	HVY £2254
110	12/99	Plum	2m5f	E Hdl	HVY £2040

Total win prize-money £14958

Going: Sf: 0-1 GS: 1-1 Gd: 0-1 GF: - Fm: 0-0
Distance: 2m/2m3: 0-0 2m4-2m7: 0-1 **3m+: 1-2**
Track: LH: 0-2 **RH: 1-1** Tight: 0-2 Gall: 0-0
Aids: Bl: 0-0 Vi: 0-0 Tstrap: 0-0
Best Rating: 124 2/03 Leic 2m7f110y gd-sft Ch

Staying novice chaser; winner of a point-to-point and has also been successful over hurdles; acts well with cut in the ground; front-runner; stays three miles.

Jericho III (FR)

101(104h)   **115d**

6-y-o b g Lute Antique (FR)-La Salamandre (Pot D Or (FR))
N J Henderson Sir Robert Ogden

Placings:141P-F1F4   (3818)
2002/03: 19⁴GS, 16¹S, 16⁴S, 16⁴GS,

	Starts	1st	2nd	3rd	Win & Pl
Chases	4	1	0	0	5136
Career Total	**8**	**3**	**0**	**0**	**11059**
114	1/03	Leic	2m	E Ch	SFT £4771
106	1/02	Hntg	2m110y	D Hdl	G-S £3643
97	11/01	Winc	2m	H NHF	GD £1610

Total win prize-money £10025

Going: Sf: 1-2 GS: 0-2 Gd: 0-0 GF: - Fm: 0-0
Distance: **2m/2m3: 1-4** 2m4-2m7: 0-0 3m+: 0-0
Track: LH: 0-0 **RH: 1-4** Tight: 0-1 Gall: 0-1
Aids: Bl: 0-0 Vi: 0-0 Tstrap: 0-0
Best Rating: 115 11/02 Tntn 2m3f   gd-sft Ch

useful novice chaser; formerly fair hurdler; best over two miles; suited by soft ground; does not look an easy ride; suited by forcing tactics, but his jumping has let him down

on more than one occasion and appears to have lost his confidence over fences.

Jerpahni

82   **58**

4-y-o b f Distant Relative-Oublier L Ennui (FR) (Bellman (FR))
P D Evans (T Wall 2/8) E A R Morgans

Placings:0P0P6P   (2610)
2002/03: 17⁰GS, 17⁵S, 16⁰F, 16⁴GS, 17⁶S, 16⁶S,

	Starts	1st	2nd	3rd	Win & Pl
Hurdles	6	0	0	0	0
Career Total	**6**	**0**	**0**	**0**	**0**

Going: Sf: 0-3 GS: 0-2 Gd: 0-0 GF: - Fm: 0-1
Distance: 2m/2m3: 0-6 2m4-2m7: 0-0 3m+: 0-0
Track: LH: 0-2 RH: 0-4 Tight: 0-2 Gall: 0-1
Aids: Bl: 0-1 Vi: 0-1 Tstrap: 0-0
Best Rating: 55 10/02 Ludl 2m   firm Hdl

Jerroboam (FR)

78   **47**

6-y-o b g Luchiroverte (IRE)-Banouda (FR) (Crin Noir Ii (FR))
S E H Sherwood The Hon Mrs S Sherwood

Placings:0-0P   (2376)
2002/03: 22⁰GS, 21⁴PS,

	Starts	1st	2nd	3rd	Win & Pl
Hurdles	2	0	0	0	
Career Total	**3**	**0**	**0**	**0**	

Going: Sf: 0-1 GS: 0-0 Gd: 0-0 GF: - Fm: 0-1
Distance: 2m/2m3: 0-0 2m4-2m7: 0-2 3m+: 0-0
Track: LH: 0-2 RH: 0-0 Tight: 0-1 Gall: 0-0
Aids: Bl: 0-0 Vi: 0-0 Tstrap: 0-0
Best Rating: 62 3/02 Wwck 2m   gd-sft NHF

Jeruflo (IRE)

91(102h)   (109h)**92**

8-y-o b m Glacial Storm (USA)-Martiness (Martinmas)
P R Webber Raymond Anderson Green

Placings:310/PP1/1-P53   (4170)
2002/03: 21⁴GS, 20⁵G, 21³S,

	Starts	1st	2nd	3rd	Win & Pl
Chases	3	0	0	1	3300
Career Total	**10**	**3**	**0**	**2**	**10572**
109	5/01	Hexm	2m4f110yE Hdl	G-F	£1900
97	4/01	Plum	2m	D Hdl	SFT £3500
103	3/00	Towc	2m	H NHF	SFT £1652

Total win prize-money £7053

Going: Sf: 0-1 GS: 0-1 Gd: 0-1 GF: - Fm: 0-0
Distance: 2m/2m3: 0-2 2m4-2m7: 0-3 3m+: 0-0
Track: LH: 0-1 RH: 0-2 Tight: 0-1 Gall: 0-0
Aids: Bl: 0-0 Vi: 0-0 Tstrap: 0-3
Best Rating: 109 5/01 Hexm 2m4f110y gd-fm Hdl

Decent hurdler; has shown ability over fences; stays 2m 5f; acts on fast and soft ground.

Jet Files (IRE)

109

12-y-o ro g Roselier (FR)-Deepdecending (Deep Run)
M Pitman Jet Uk Limited

Placings:450P/21020P/P21-2   (0244)
2002/03: 25²G,

	Starts	1st	2nd	3rd	Win & Pl
Chases	1	0	1	0	1544
Career Total	**14**	**2**	**4**	**0**	**20586**
109	4/02	Chel	2m5f	D(0-115)HCh	G-F £13013
91	12/97	Towc	2m5f	D Hdl	G-S £3008

Total win prize-money £16021

Going: Sf: 0-0 GS: 0-0 Gd: 0-1 GF: - Fm: 0-0
Distance: 2m/2m3: 0-0 2m4-2m7: 0-0 3m+: 0-1
Track: LH: 0-0 RH: 0-1 Tight: 0-0 Gall: 0-0
Aids: Bl: 0-0 Vi: 0-0 Tstrap: 0-0
Best Rating: 109 5/02 Extr 3m1f110y good Ch

Back to form when reappearing in 2002 after missing three seasons, and landed a competitive novices handicap at Cheltenham. Stays three miles. Acts on soft and fast ground.

Jetowa Du Bois Hue (FR)

110(98h)   (103h)**115**

6-y-o b g Kadrou (FR)-Vaika (FR) (Cosmopolitan (FR))
T R George B A Kilpatrick

Placings:260-3414   (4695)
2002/03: 16³G, 17⁴S, 16¹GF, 16⁴G,

	Starts	1st	2nd	3rd	Win & Pl
Chases	4	1	0	1	5703
Career Total	**7**	**1**	**1**	**1**	**6599**
102	3/03	Hrfd	2m	E(0-100)HCh	G-F £4410

Total win prize-money £4410

Going: Sf: 0-1 GS: 0-0 Gd: 0-2 GF: - Fm: 1-1
Distance: 2m/2m3: **1-4** 2m4-2m7: 0-0 3m+: 0-0
Track: LH: 0-2 **RH: 1-2** Tight: 0-2 Gall: 0-0
Aids: Bl: 0-0 Vi: 0-0 Tstrap: 0-0
Best Rating: 109 12/02 Hrfd 2m   good Ch

Jewel Fighter

85(97h)   (67h)**55**

9-y-o br m Good Times (ITY)-Duellist (Town Crier)
J L Spearing Fighting Chance Syndicate

Placings:0/0/P02F-P5   (0430)
2002/03: 21⁶G, 16⁵GF,

	Starts	1st	2nd	3rd	Win & Pl
Hurdles	2	0	0	0	0
Career Total	**8**	**0**	**1**	**0**	**495**

Going: Sf: 0-0 GS: 0-0 Gd: 0-1 GF: - Fm: 0-1
Distance: 2m/2m3: 0-1 2m4-2m7: 0-1 3m+: 0-0
Track: LH: 0-0 RH: 0-2 Tight: 0-1 Gall: 0-2
Aids: Bl: 0-0 Vi: 0-0 Tstrap: 0-0
Best Rating: 67 4/02 Hntg 2m110y gd-fm Hdl

Plating-class novice hurdler.

Jewel Of India

96   **84**

4-y-o ch g Bijou D Inde-Low Hill (Rousillon (USA))
P J Hobbs (Sir Mark Prescott 28/10) Richard Green (fine Paintings)

Placings:4   (2207)
2002/03: 17⁴S,

	Starts	1st	2nd	3rd	Win & Pl
Hurdles	1	0	0	0	0
Career Total	**1**	**0**	**0**	**0**	**0**

Going:	Sf: 0-1 GS: 0-0 Gd: 0-0 GF: - Fm: 0-0
Distance:	2m/2m3: 0-1 2m4-2m7: 0-0 3m+: 0-0
Track:	LH: 0-1 RH: 0-0 Tight: 0-1 Gall: 0-0
Aids:	Bl: 0-0 Vi: 0-0 Tstrap: 0-0
Best Rating:	84 11/02 Bang 2m1f soft Hdl

Jexel (FR)
105   106+
6-y-o b g Video Rock (FR)-Siesta (FR) (Prove It Baby (USA))
J S Goldie Mr & Mrs Raymond Anderson Green

Placings:*0/322-113*					(1987)
2002/03: 18¹G, 24¹GS, 20³S,					
	Starts	1st	2nd	3rd	Win & Pl
Hurdles	3	2	0	1	7415
Career Total	7	2	2		8679
106 6/02 Prth	3m110y E Hdl			G-S	£2877
94 5/02 Kels	2m2f		D Hdl	GD	£3484
			Total win prize-money £6361		

Going:	Sf: 0-1 GS: 1-1 Gd: 1-1 GF: - Fm: 0-0
Distance:	2m/2m3: 1-1 2m4-2m7: 0-1 3m+: 1-1
Track:	LH: 1-2 RH: 1-1 Tight: 1-1 Gall: 0-0
Aids:	Bl: 0-0 Vi: 0-0 Tstrap: 0-0
Best Rating:	106 6/02 Prth 3m110y gd-sft Hdl

Modest hurdler; stays three miles; acts on good ground or softer.

Jim (FR)
110   121
6-y-o b g Glaieul (USA)-Beautywal (FR) (Magwal (FR))
J T R Dreaper Mrs P J Conway

Placings:*06-0401*					(3907a)
2002/03: 16⁰S, 16⁴S, 16⁶GS, 16¹HY,					
	Starts	1st	2nd	3rd	Win & Pl
Hurdles	4	1	0	0	6214
Career Total	6	1	0	0	6214
121 3/03 Fair	2m	Hdl		HVY	£5824
		Total win prize-money £5825			

Going:	Sf: 1-3 GS: 0-1 Gd: 0-0 GF: - Fm: 0-0
Distance:	2m/2m3: 1-4 2m4-2m7: 0-0 3m+: 0-0
Track:	LH: 0-3 RH: 1-1 Tight: 0-0 Gall: 0-0
Aids:	Bl: 0-0 Vi: 0-0 Tstrap: 0-0
Best Rating:	121 3/03 Fair 2m heavy Hdl

Decent Irish-trained hurdler; acts well on heavy ground; effective over two miles.

Jim Bell (IRE)
108   109+
8-y-o br g Supreme Leader-Mightyatom (Black Minstrel)
J G M O Shea K W Bell

Placings:*4/0030P6-33121*					(4141)
2002/03: 20³S, 21³HY, 25¹G, 25²G, 24¹S,					
	Starts	1st	2nd	3rd	Win & Pl
Hurdles	5	2	1	2	8252
Career Total	12	2	1	3	8789
109 3/03 Hexm 3m	F(0-100)HHdl			SFT	£2646
107 2/03 Catt	3m1f110yE(0-105)HHdl			GD	£3454
			Total win prize-money £6101		

Going:	Sf: 1-3 GS: 0-0 Gd: 1-2 GF: - Fm: 0-0
Distance:	2m/2m3: 0-0 2m4-2m7: 0-2 3m+: 2-3
Track:	LH: 2-5 RH: 0-0 Tight: 1-2 Gall: 0-0
Aids:	Bl: 0-0 Vi: 0-0 Tstrap: 0-0
Best Rating:	109 3/03 Hexm 3m soft Hdl

Exposed novice hurdler, appreciated step up to three miles when off the mark in handicap company at Catterick in February; let down by his jumping when runner-up from a higher mark there two weeks later but jumped much better when returning to winning form at Hexham in March.

Jim Jam Joey (IRE)
106   91
10-y-o ch g Big Sink Hope (USA)-Ascot Princess (Prince Hansel)
Miss Suzy Smith Miss Suzy Smith

Placings:*2315226/6F123/3/4420-2000*					(3668)
2002/03: 24²S, 24⁰S, 25⁰HY, 22⁰GS,					
	Starts	1st	2nd	3rd	Win & Pl
Hurdles	4	0	1	0	1142
Career Total	21	2	6	3	15173
125 2/00 Folk	2m6f110yF(0-110)HHdl		SFT	£2395	
105 12/98 Font	2m6f110yE Hdl		SFT	£2775	
	Total win prize-money £5170				

Going:	Sf: 0-3 GS: 0-1 Gd: 0-0 GF: - Fm: 0-0
Distance:	2m/2m3: 0-0 2m4-2m7: 0-1 3m+: 0-3
Track:	LH: 0-2 RH: 0-0 Tight: 0-1 Gall: 0-0
Aids:	Bl: 0-0 Vi: 0-0 Tstrap: 0-0
Best Rating:	125 4/00 Chel 3m soft Hdl

Handicap hurdler, acts on soft ground and is effective at around two miles six furlongs.

Jimmy Blues
96(84h)   (86h)69
8-y-o b g Durgam (USA)-Tibbi Blues (Cure The Blues (USA))
Ferdy Murphy Miss Barbara Spittal

Placings:*4/00/46066-P0645*					(1241)
2002/03: 20⁰G, 16⁰GF, 20⁰GS, 26⁴G, 20⁵GF,					
	Starts	1st	2nd	3rd	Win & Pl
Hurdles	1	0	0	0	0
Chases	4	0	0	0	323
Career Total	13	0	0	0	323

Going:	Sf: 0-0 GS: 0-1 Gd: 0-2 GF: - Fm: 0-2
Distance:	2m/2m3: 0-0 2m4-2m7: 0-3 3m+: 0-1
Track:	LH: 0-4 RH: 0-1 Tight: 0-2 Gall: 0-0
Aids:	Bl: 0-0 Vi: 0-0 Tstrap: 0-0
Best Rating:	86 5/01 Ayr 2m gd-fm Hdl

Jimmy Jumbo (IRE)
10-y-o ch g Dragon Palace (USA)-Sail On Lady (New Member)
J S Swindells J S Swindells

Placings:*0/06P/P0*					(0503)
2002/03: 24²S, 26⁰G,					
	Starts	1st	2nd	3rd	Win & Pl
Chases	2	0	0	0	
Career Total	6	0	0	0	

Going:	Sf: 0-1 GS: 0-0 Gd: 0-1 GF: - Fm: 0-0
Distance:	2m/2m3: 0-0 2m4-2m7: 0-0 3m+: 0-2
Track:	LH: 0-2 RH: 0-0 Tight: 0-2 Gall: 0-0
Aids:	Bl: 0-0 Vi: 0-0 Tstrap: 0-0
Best Rating:	62 5/00 Dpat 3m gd-fm Ch

Jimmy Morse
69f   51f
5-y-o b g Chaddleworth (IRE)-Sea Crossing (FR) (Kala Shikari)
J White B C Allen

Placings:*0*					(0219)
2002/03: 17⁰G,					
	Starts	1st	2nd	3rd	Win & Pl
NH Flat	1	0	0	0	
Career Total	1	0	0	0	

Going:	Sf: 0-0 GS: 0-0 Gd: 0-1 GF: - Fm: 0-0
Distance:	2m/2m3: 0-0 2m4-2m7: 0-0 3m+: 0-0
Track:	LH: 0-0 RH: 0-1 Tight: 0-0 Gall: 0-0
Aids:	Bl: 0-0 Vi: 0-0 Tstrap: 0-0
Best Rating:	51 5/02 Hrfd 2m1f good NHF

Jimmy Tennis (FR)
131d
6-y-o b/br g Video Rock (FR)-Via Tennise (FR) (Brezzo (FR))
Miss Venetia Williams Derek And Jean Clee

Placings:*35/2131PP-U5*					(2363)
2002/03: 24ᵁS, 26⁵S,					
	Starts	1st	2nd	3rd	Win & Pl
Chases	2	0	0	0	1000
Career Total	10	2	1	2	47819
131 2/02 Asct	3m110y A ChG-S		£20825		
6/01 Autl	2m1f110y Ch		VS	£12124	
	Total win prize-money £32949				

Going:	Sf: 0-2 GS: 0-0 Gd: 0-0 GF: - Fm: 0-0
Distance:	2m/2m3: 0-0 2m4-2m7: 0-0 3m+: 0-2
Track:	LH: 0-2 RH: 0-0 Tight: 0-0 Gall: 0-0
Aids:	Bl: 0-0 Vi: 0-0 Tstrap: 0-0
Best Rating:	131 2/02 Asct 3m110y gd-sft Ch

Ex-French winning chaser, he is suited by soft ground and usually wears blinkers. Impressive winner of the Reynoldstown at Ascot in February 2002, but has been well held since.

Jimmy Wiskers (IRE)
90
8-y-o b g Insan (USA)-Jackson Miss (Condorcet (FR))
Ferdy Murphy The Ferdy Murphy Racing Club

Placings:*50/446023-004*					(2423)
2002/03: 20⁰GS, 19⁰S, 21⁴S,					
	Starts	1st	2nd	3rd	Win & Pl
Hurdles	3	0	0	0	0
Career Total	11	0	1	1	1870

Going:	Sf: 0-2 GS: 0-1 Gd: 0-0 GF: - Fm: 0-0
Distance:	2m/2m3: 0-0 2m4-2m7: 0-0 3m+: 0-0
Track:	LH: 0-1 RH: 0-2 Tight: 0-1 Gall: 0-0
Aids:	Bl: 0-1 Vi: 0-0 Tstrap: 0-0
Best Rating:	97 12/00 Donc 2m110y heavy NHF

Well held in moderate hurdle company.

Jimmy's Cross (IRE)
13-y-o ch g Phardante (FR)-Foredefine (Bonne Noel)
Mrs Sue Maude Mrs Sue Maude

Placings:131B21225/P/24U/44124P0/0433P4431444566P/

235F6-0   (0193)

2002/03: 20⁰F,

	Starts	1st	2nd	3rd	Win & Pl
Chases	1	0	0	0	
Career Total	42	5	6	5	27018
83	9/99	Hrfd	2m3f	G(0-95)HCh	GD	£2948
93	6/98	NAbb	2m5f110yD Ch		GD	£3485
109	3/96	Hntg	2m4f110yE Hdl		G-F	£2010
107	10/95	Font	2m2f	Hdl	GD	£2069
98	6/95	Worc	2m	H NHF	G-F	£1688

Total win prize-money £12201

Going: Sf: 0-0 GS: 0-0 Gd: 0-0 GF: - Fm: 0-1
Distance: 2m/2m3: 0-0 2m4-2m7: 0-1 3m+: 0-0
Track: LH: 0-1 RH: 0-0 Tight: 0-0 Gall: 0-0
Aids: Bl: 0-0 Vi: 0-0 Tstrap: 0-0
Best Rating: 122 4/96 Chel 2m5f110y gd-sft Hdl

Jineful (FR)

(89h)   (69h)**70**

6-y-o b g Useful (FR)-Finegrila (FR) (Fin Bon)
N J Henderson N J Henderson

Placings:4/05-6P4F   (1567)

2002/03: 20⁶GF, 20⁰G, 26⁴GF, 22⁴GF,

	Starts	1st	2nd	3rd	Win & Pl
Hurdles	2	0	0	0	0
Chases	2	0	0	0	276
Career Total	7	0	0	0	276

Going: Sf: 0-0 GS: 0-1 Gd: 0-1 GF: - Fm: 0-2
Distance: 2m/2m3: 0-0 2m4-2m7: 0-3 3m+: 0-1
Track: LH: 0-3 RH: 0-1 Tight: 0-1 Gall: 0-0
Aids: Bl: 0-0 Vi: 0-0 Tstrap: 0-0
Best Rating: 76 10/02 MRas 2m6f110y gd-sft Ch

Maiden over hurdles and fences.

Jivaros (FR)

105(92h)   (106h)**113+**

6-y-o br g Video Rock (FR)-Rives (FR) (Reasonable Choice (USA))
H D Daly Mrs G Leigh

Placings:001-6P1   (3927)

2002/03: 25⁶G, 24⁴G, 24¹G,

	Starts	1st	2nd	3rd	Win & Pl
Chases	3	1	0	0	5512
Career Total	6	2	0	0	8116
113	3/03	Hntg	3m	C(0-110)HCh	GD	£5512
106	3/02	Wwck	3m1f	E Hdl	G-S	£2604

Total win prize-money £8116

Going: Sf: 0-0 GS: 0-0 Gd: 1-3 GF: - Fm: 0-0
Distance: 2m/2m3: 0-0 2m4-2m7: 0-0 3m+: 1-3
Track: LH: 0-1 RH: 1-2 Tight: 0-0 Gall: 1-2
Aids: Bl: 0-0 Vi: 0-0 Tstrap: 0-0
Best Rating: 113 3/03 Hntg 3m good Ch

A winning hurdler, he scored on his third start over fences; stays three miles; acts on good ground.

Job Rage (IRE)

83(105h)   (94h)**66**

9-y-o b/br g Yashgan-Snatchingly (Thatch (USA))
A Bailey Mrs J Bailey

Placings:215/P5/U/4036-1053U423000B   (4341)

2002/03: 20¹G, 22⁰GS, 19⁵G, 22³GF, 20ᵁGF, 17⁴G, 17³GF,
19⁰GF, 20⁰S, 20⁸GF,

	Starts	1st	2nd	3rd	Win & Pl
Hurdles	9	1	1	2	3553
Chases	3	0	0	0	0
Career Total	22	2	2	3	7001
94	5/02	Uttx	2m4f110yG(0-100)HHdl	GD	£2142
102	3/98	Ayr	2m	E Hdl	G-S	£2259

Total win prize-money £4401

Going: Sf: 0-2 GS: 0-1 Gd: 1-3 GF: - Fm: 0-6
Distance: 2m/2m3: 0-2 2m4-2m7: 1-10 3m+: 0-0
Track: LH: 1-6 RH: 0-6 Tight: 0-5 Gall: 0-1
Aids: Bl: 0-0 Vi: 0-0 Tstrap: 0-0
Best Rating: 102 3/98 Ayr 2m gd-sft Hdl

Jockie Wells

82   62

5-y-o b g Primitive Rising (USA)-Princess Maxine (IRE) (Horage)
Miss Lucinda V Russell Miss G Joughin

Placings:600   (4772)

2002/03: 16⁶HY, 16⁰GS, 16⁰G,

	Starts	1st	2nd	3rd	Win & Pl
NH Flat	2	0	0	0	0
Hurdles	1	0	0	0	0
Career Total	3	0	0	0	0

Going: Sf: 0-1 GS: 0-1 Gd: 0-1 GF: - Fm: 0-0
Distance: 2m/2m3: 0-0 2m4-2m7: 0-0 3m+: 0-0
Track: LH: 0-2 RH: 0-1 Tight: 0-0 Gall: 0-0
Aids: Bl: 0-0 Vi: 0-0 Tstrap: 0-0
Best Rating: 64 2/03 Ayr 2m gd-sft NHF

Jocko Glasses

93   119d

6-y-o ch g Inchinor-Corinthia (USA) (Empery (USA))
Mrs M Reveley David J Jackson

Placings:4150/640P0-3P   (1539)

2002/03: 16³G, 16⁶PGF,

	Starts	1st	2nd	3rd	Win & Pl
Hurdles	2	0	0	1	621
Career Total	11	1	0	1	8966
121	12/00	Kemp	2m	B Hdl	G-S	£7377

Total win prize-money £7378

Going: Sf: 0-0 GS: 0-0 Gd: 0-1 GF: - Fm: 0-1
Distance: 2m/2m3: 0-2 2m4-2m7: 0-0 3m+: 0-0
Track: LH: 0-2 RH: 0-0 Tight: 0-0 Gall: 0-0
Aids: Bl: 0-0 Vi: 0-0 Tstrap: 0-0
Best Rating: 122 2/01 Kemp 2m gd-sft Hdl

Continues to disappoint and joined Mary Reveley in the summer of 2002. Suited by two miles and a sound surface.

Jocks Cross (IRE)

106   137

12-y-o ch g Riberetto-Shuil Le Dia (Kabale)
Miss Venetia Williams Mrs Gill Harrison

Placings:2215410/11400/15/2111F31/2252P1PU/421P2F/5
02F3-P5P   (4307)

2002/03: 27⁵PGS, 28⁵G, 32⁶PG,

	Starts	1st	2nd	3rd	Win & Pl
Chases	3	0	0	0	2750
Career Total	43	11	9	2	180799
149	12/00	Chep	3m5f110yA HCh	SFT	£43500
135	3/00	Chep	3m2f110yD(0-145)HCh	G-S	£10062
137	4/99	Punc	3m1f	HCh	GD	£33214
112	3/99	Strfl	2m4f	D Ch	HVY	£4524

134	2/99	Font	3m2f110yE Ch	GD	£2802
129	2/99	Font	3m2f110yD Ch	SFT	£4506
124	4/98	Carl	2m4f110yD(0-125)HHdl	SFT	£2829
125	11/96	Newc	3m	C(0-135)HHdl	GD	£3355
114	10/96	Carl	3m110y	E(0-115)HHdl	GD	£2290
118	3/96	Bang	2m1f	E Hdl	G-S	£2290
107	1/96	Carl	2m1f	E Hdl	G-S	£2598

Total win prize-money £111971

Going: Sf: 0-0 GS: 0-1 Gd: 0-2 GF: - Fm: 0-0
Distance: 2m/2m3: 0-0 2m4-2m7: 0-0 3m+: 0-3
Track: LH: 0-3 RH: 0-0 Tight: 0-1 Gall: 0-1
Aids: Bl: 0-0 Vi: 0-0 Tstrap: 0-0
Best Rating: 149 12/01 Chep 3m5f110y gd-sft Ch

Small but tough, he likes soft ground and goes well at Chepstow, where he won the Welsh National in 2000 and was runner-up in 2001. Stays very well and is effective in soft ground.

Jodante (IRE)

96   89

6-y-o ch g Phardante (FR)-Crashtown Lucy (Crash Course)
P Beaumont Trevor Hemmings

Placings:0-54   (2760)

2002/03: 16⁵G, 16⁴S,

	Starts	1st	2nd	3rd	Win & Pl
NH Flat	1	0	0	0	0
Hurdles	1	0	0	0	363
Career Total	3	0	0	0	363

Going: Sf: 0-1 GS: 0-0 Gd: 0-1 GF: - Fm: 0-0
Distance: 2m/2m3: 0-2 2m4-2m7: 0-0 3m+: 0-0
Track: LH: 0-2 RH: 0-0 Tight: 0-0 Gall: 0-0
Aids: Bl: 0-0 Vi: 0-0 Tstrap: 0-0
Best Rating: 92 12/02 Hayd 2m soft Hdl

Dam sister to Gold Cup winner Jodami. Looks a long term chasing prospect.

Joe Crump

94(94h)   (119h)**96**

9-y-o ch g Interrex (CAN)-Nellie O Dowd (USA) (Diesis)
J Mackie Pickering Properties Ltd

Placings:6/624P/P41111P50/30-54U   (3289)

2002/03: 20⁵GS, 24⁴G, 19ᵁG,

	Starts	1st	2nd	3rd	Win & Pl
Chases	3	0	0	0	377
Career Total	19	4	1	1	18812
123	12/00	Donc	2m4f	E(0-115)HHdl	GD	£3094
118	11/00	Uttx	2m6f110yD(0-125)HHdl	HVY	£2879
115	11/00	Chel	2m5f	E(0-115)HHdl	G-S	£8742
111	10/00	Towc	2m5f	F(0-100)HHdl	G-S	£1939

Total win prize-money £16656

Going: Sf: 0-0 GS: 0-1 Gd: 0-2 GF: - Fm: 0-0
Distance: 2m/2m3: 0-2 2m4-2m7: 0-1 3m+: 0-1
Track: LH: 0-2 RH: 0-1 Tight: 0-0 Gall: 0-2
Aids: Bl: 0-0 Vi: 0-3 Tstrap: 0-3
Best Rating: 123 12/00 Donc 2m4f gd-sft Hdl

Joe Cullen (IRE)

97(110h)   (123 h)**113**

8-y-o ch g River Falls-Moycullen (Le Moss)
Ian Williams (W P Mullins 3/10) Mark F Sheasby

Placings:11/13/42105000-300   (4136)

2002/03: 17³GY, 16⁰G, 17⁶G,

	Starts	1st	2nd	3rd	Win & Pl
Hurdles	3	0	0	1	2761

Career Total	15	4	1	2	44790
137 11/01	Punc 2m		Hdl	SFT	£7233
137 2/01	Fair 2m		Hdl	HVY	£5008
149 3/00	Chel 2m110y	A NHF		GD	£18000
118 6/99	Tral 2m		NHF	GD	£3222

Total win prize-money £33465

Going: Sf: 0-0 GS: 0-0 Gd: 0-2 GF: - Fm: 0-0
Distance: 2m/2m3: 0-3 2m4-2m7: 0-0 3m+: 0-0
Track: LH: 0-2 RH: 0-0 Tight: 0-0 Gall: 0-2
Aids: Bl: 0-0 Vi: 0-0 Tstrap: 0-0
Best Rating: 149 3/00 Chel 2m110y good NHF

Ex-Irish hurdler/chase; former Cheltenham Festival bumper winner; does not seem at as good these days; comfortably held on chasing debut; suited by soft ground.

Joe Deane (IRE)

103(93h)   (92+h)96

7-y-o ch g Alphabatim (USA)-Craic Go Leor (Deep Run)
T R George Mr & Mrs D A Gamble

Placings:632P   (4174)
2002/03: 24⁶HY, 16²S, 26²G, 26⁶S,

	Starts	1st	2nd	3rd	Win & Pl
Hurdles	2	0	1	0	1069
Chases	2	0	0	1	750
Career Total	4	0	1	1	1819

Going: Sf: 0-3 GS: 0-0 Gd: 0-1 GF: - Fm: 0-0
Distance: 2m/2m3: 0-1 2m4-2m7: 0-0 3m+: 0-3
Track: LH: 0-2 RH: 0-2 Tight: 0-0 Gall: 0-0
Aids: Bl: 0-0 Vi: 0-0 Tstrap: 0-0
Best Rating: 96 2/03 Leic 2m soft Ch

Chasing type; reverted to hurdles when runner-up over extended three miles at Hereford in February.

Joe Di Capo (IRE)

102(100h)   (94h)94

8-y-o b g Phardante (FR)-Supreme Glen (IRE) (Supreme Leader)
A Crook Joe Buzzeo

Placings:432F/01PP-422F2F244   (4396)
2002/03: 23⁴GF, 20²S, 24²GS, 25²S, 24²HY, 24²F, 22²G, 24⁴GS, 24⁴G,

	Starts	1st	2nd	3rd	Win & Pl
Chases	9	0	4	0	7909
Career Total	17	1	5	1	11689
94 11/01	Newc 2m4f	E Hdl		GD	£2618

Total win prize-money £2618

Going: Sf: 0-3 GS: 0-2 Gd: 0-3 GF: - Fm: 0-1
Distance: 2m/2m3: 0-0 2m4-2m7: 0-2 3m+: 0-7
Track: LH: 0-6 RH: 0-2 Tight: 0-1 Gall: 0-5
Aids: Bl: 0-4 Vi: 0-1 Tstrap: 0-0
Best Rating: 106 12/00 Newc 3m soft Hdl

Moderate chaser; stays three miles; likes to be ridden prominently; yet to win over fences; has worn blinkers and cheekpieces.

Joe Luke (IRE)

98(104c)   (131dc)101

11-y-o b g Satco (FR)-Garden County (Ragapan)
G M Moore A J Racehorses

Placings:5/000/66/11/P245/14FF2U-006PU (3406)
2002/03: 22⁶S, 24⁰S, 27⁶S, 27⁹HY, 23⁴GS,

	Starts	1st	2nd	3rd	Win & Pl
Hurdles	5	0	0	0	0

Career Total	23	3	2	0	15158
121 5/01	Prth 3m	D Ch		G-S	£4264
122 4/00	Uttx 3m110y	F(0-100)HHdl		SFT	£3146
110 3/00	Carl 3m110y	E(0-105)HHdl		G-S	£4680

Total win prize-money £12090

Going: Sf: 0-4 GS: 0-1 Gd: 0-0 GF: - Fm: 0-0
Distance: 2m/2m3: 0-0 2m4-2m7: 0-2 3m+: 0-3
Track: LH: 0-4 RH: 0-1 Tight: 0-3 Gall: 0-0
Aids: Bl: 0-0 Vi: 0-0 Tstrap: 0-0
Best Rating: 122 1/02 Newc 3m soft Hdl

A winner over hurdles and of a novice chase. He stays three miles and is effective on a soft surface.

Joely Green

103   98

6-y-o b g Binary Star (USA)-Comedy Lady (Comedy Star (USA))
N P Littmoden Paul J Dixon

Placings:0-1P   (1219)
2002/03: 16¹GF, 17⁷G,

	Starts	1st	2nd	3rd	Win & Pl
Hurdles	2	1	0	0	2218
Career Total	3	1	0	0	2218
98 8/02	Hntg 2m110y	F Hdl		G-F	£2217

Total win prize-money £2218

Going: Sf: 0-0 GS: 0-0 Gd: 0-1 GF: - Fm: 1-1
Distance: 2m/2m3: 1-2 2m4-2m7: 0-0 3m+: 0-0
Track: LH: 0-1 RH: 1-1 Tight: 0-0 Gall: 1-1
Aids: Bl: 0-0 Vi: 0-0 Tstrap: 0-0
Best Rating: 98 8/02 Hntg 2m110y gd-fm Hdl

Made a winning hurdles debut in August 2002; acts on fast ground.

Joey Dunlop (IRE)

                     (71c)

9-y-o br g Maelstrom Lake-Middle Verde (USA) (Sham (USA))
J J Lambe Grange And Yellow Ford Syndicate

Placings:0/4460P   (1071)
2002/03: 24⁴GF, 20⁴GF, 27⁶GF, 20⁰S, 22³G,

	Starts	1st	2nd	3rd	Win & Pl
Hurdles	2	0	0	0	0
Chases	3	0	0	0	479
Career Total	6	0	0	0	479

Going: Sf: 0-1 GS: 0-0 Gd: 0-1 GF: - Fm: 0-3
Distance: 2m/2m3: 0-0 2m4-2m7: 0-3 3m+: 0-2
Track: LH: 0-2 RH: 0-1 Tight: 0-2 Gall: 0-0
Aids: Bl: 0-0 Vi: 0-0 Tstrap: 0-0
Best Rating: 71 7/02 Wxfd 2m4f gd-fm Ch

Joey The Schnoze

92   94

5-y-o ch g Zilzal (USA)-Linda s Design (Persian Bold)
S J Magnier Fergus Jones

Placings:02604P-400   (2301)
2002/03: 17⁴G, 16⁰HY, 16⁰GS,

	Starts	1st	2nd	3rd	Win & Pl
Hurdles	3	0	0	0	0
Career Total	9	0	1	0	1042

Going: Sf: 0-1 GS: 0-1 Gd: 0-1 GF: - Fm: 0-0
Distance: 2m/2m3: 0-3 2m4-2m7: 0-0 3m+: 0-0

Track: LH: 0-3 RH: 0-0 Tight: 0-2 Gall: 0-0
Aids: Bl: 0-0 Vi: 0-3 Tstrap: 0-1
Best Rating: 94 10/02 Sedg 2m1f good Hdl

Joey Tribbiani (IRE)

112(94h)   (81h)110

6-y-o b g Foxhound (USA)-Mardi Gras Belle (USA) (Masked Dancer (USA))
Ian Williams newmarketconnections.com

Placings:PP/0-63356212312   (4684)
2002/03: 16⁰GS, 16⁶GF, 17³GF, 17³S, 16⁵GF, 16⁸G, 16²GS, 16¹G, 16²G, 16³S, 16¹GF, 16²GF,

	Starts	1st	2nd	3rd	Win & Pl
Hurdles	4	0	0	1	377
Chases	8	2	3	2	14884
Career Total	14	2	3	3	15261
105 3/03	Hntg 2m110y	D(0-115)HCh		G-F	£5356
95 2/03	Hrfd 2m	F(0-100)HCh		GD	£3360

Total win prize-money £8717

Going: Sf: 0-2 GS: 0-2 Gd: 1-3 GF: - Fm: 1-5
Distance: 2m/2m3: 2-12 2m4-2m7: 0-0 3m+: 0-0
Track: LH: 0-0 RH: 2-12 Tight: 0-2 Gall: 1-6
Aids: Bl: 0-0 Vi: 0-0 Tstrap: 0-0
Best Rating: 110 4/03 Hntg 2m110y gd-fm Ch

Modest chaser; on the upgrade; keen sort; effective on good ground; best at around two miles.

Johann De Vonnas (FR)

94f   100f

6-y-o b g Cadoudal (FR)-Diana De Vonnas (FR) (El Badr)
N J Henderson B T M Racing

Placings:0-3   (0128)
2002/03: 18³GF,

	Starts	1st	2nd	3rd	Win & Pl
NH Flat	1	0	0	1	250
Career Total	2	0	0	1	250

Going: Sf: 0-0 GS: 0-0 Gd: 0-0 GF: - Fm: 0-1
Distance: 2m/2m3: 0-1 2m4-2m7: 0-0 3m+: 0-0
Track: LH: 0-1 RH: 0-0 Tight: 0-1 Gall: 0-0
Aids: Bl: 0-0 Vi: 0-0 Tstrap: 0-0
Best Rating: 100 5/02 Font 2m2f110y gd-fm NHF

Fair form in bumpers on varying ground.

John Bush (IRE)

99   86+

9-y-o b g Asir-Philosophical (Welsh Chanter)
Ferdy Murphy Miss J V Morgan

Placings:014/154120/0P/4   (0831)
2002/03: 21⁴GF,

	Starts	1st	2nd	3rd	Win & Pl
Hurdles	1	0	0	0	283
Career Total	12	3	1	0	6448
101 12/98	Catt 2m3f	E Hdl		GD	£2640
105 5/98	Hrfd 2m1f	H NHF		GD	£1229
98 3/98	Hntg 2m110y	H NHF		GD	£1245

Total win prize-money £5114

Going: Sf: 0-0 GS: 0-0 Gd: 0-0 GF: - Fm: 0-1
Distance: 2m/2m3: 0-0 2m4-2m7: 0-1 3m+: 0-0
Track: LH: 0-1 RH: 0-0 Tight: 0-0 Gall: 0-0
Aids: Bl: 0-0 Vi: 0-0 Tstrap: 0-0
Best Rating: 105 1/99 Donc 2m4f gd-sft Hdl

John Foley (IRE)
92   99

5-y-o b g Petardia-Fast Bay (Bay Express)
Mrs H Dalton (P S Felgate 7/7) Foley Steelstock

Placings:4530-6   (0167)
2002/03: 16⁶GF,

	Starts	1st	2nd	3rd	Win & Pl
Hurdles	1	0	0	0	0
Career Total	5	0	0	1	1260

Going:	Sf: 0-0 GS: 0-0 Gd: 0-0 GF: - Fm: 0-1
Distance:	2m/2m3: 0-1 2m4-2m7: 0-0 3m+: 0-0
Track:	LH: 0-1 RH: 0-0 Tight: 0-0 Gall: 0-0
Aids:	Bl: 0-0 Vi: 0-0 Tstrap: 0-0
Best Rating:	99 11/01 Hntg 2m110y good Hdl

Fair form in juvenile hurdles in the autumn of 2001 at around two miles on a sound surface.

John Hunter (IRE)
97   100

6-y-o b g Unfuwain (USA)-Aigue (High Top)
M C Pipe Lucayan Stud

Placings:31-0064045   (4362)
2002/03: 16⁰G, 17⁰HY, 17⁴S, 18⁰S, 17⁴GS, 19⁵F,

	Starts	1st	2nd	3rd	Win & Pl
Hurdles	7	0	0	1	709
Career Total	9	1	0	1	3823
104 4/02 Plum 2m		E Hdl		G-F	£2719

Total win prize-money £2720

Going:	Sf: 0-4 GS: 0-1 Gd: 0-1 GF: - Fm: 0-1
Distance:	2m/2m3: 0-6 2m4-2m7: 0-1 3m+: 0-1
Track:	LH: 0-4 RH: 0-3 Tight: 0-5 Gall: 0-0
Aids:	Bl: 0-0 Vi: 0-0 Tstrap: 0-7
Best Rating:	106 11/02 Wwck 2m good Hdl

Modest hurdler; best over two miles and fast ground.

John Oliver (IRE)
123+f

5-y-o gr h Lure (USA)-Glitter Grey (Nishapour (FR))
E J O Grady P F Lehane

Placings:0-110   (4481)
2002/03: 16¹Y, 16¹HY, 17⁰G,

	Starts	1st	2nd	3rd	Win & Pl
NH Flat	3	2	0	0	10753
Career Total	4	2	0	0	10753
123 3/03 Navn 2m		NHF		HVY	£4928
110 2/03 Naas 2m		NHF		YLD	£5824

Total win prize-money £10754

Going:	Sf: 1-1 GS: 0-0 Gd: 0-1 GF: - Fm: 0-0
Distance:	2m/2m3: 2-3 2m4-2m7: 0-0 3m+: 0-0
Track:	LH: 0-0 RH: 0-0 Tight: 0-0 Gall: 0-0
Aids:	Bl: 0-0 Vi: 0-0 Tstrap: 0-0
Best Rating:	123 3/03 Navn 2m heavy NHF

Winner of bumpers at Naas in February and Navan the following month; sent off favourite for Grade 2 at Aintree but finished well beaten.

John Steed (IRE)
89   75

6-y-o b g Thatching-Trinity Hall (Hallgate)
Mrs A C Tate (J W Mullins 18/10) Richard Tate

Placings:P2004-0106P   (4677)

2002/03: 16⁰G, 19¹G, 19⁰GF, 19⁶S, 19⁰GF,

	Starts	1st	2nd	3rd	Win & Pl
Hurdles	5	1	0	0	1918
Career Total	10	1	1	0	2584
75 10/02 Hrfd	2m3f110y		G Hdl	GD	£1918

Total win prize-money £1918

Going:	Sf: 0-1 GS: 0-0 Gd: 1-2 GF: - Fm: 0-2
Distance:	2m/2m3: 0-1 2m4-2m7: 1-4 3m+: 0-0
Track:	LH: 0-1 RH: 1-4 Tight: 0-2 Gall: 0-0
Aids:	Bl: 0-0 Vi: 0-0 Tstrap: 0-0
Best Rating:	83 11/01 Plum 2m gd-sft Hdl

Appreciated a return to a lower grade when well backed winner of a Hereford seller over just short of two and a half miles. Subsequently bought for 3,400 guineas.

John The Mole (IRE)
92   86

5-y-o ch g Glacial Storm (USA)-City Dame (Golden Love)
M D Hammond The Adbrokes Partnership

Placings:430-3500300   (3896)
2002/03: 16⁵GF, 20⁵GF, 16⁰GS, 16⁰G, 20³HY, 24⁰G, 22⁰GS,

	Starts	1st	2nd	3rd	Win & Pl
NH Flat	1	0	0	1	262
Hurdles	6	0	0	1	663
Career Total	10	0	0	3	1174

Going:	Sf: 0-1 GS: 0-2 Gd: 0-2 GF: - Fm: 0-2
Distance:	2m/2m3: 0-3 2m4-2m7: 0-3 3m+: 0-1
Track:	LH: 0-6 RH: 0-1 Tight: 0-3 Gall: 0-0
Aids:	Bl: 0-0 Vi: 0-0 Tstrap: 0-0
Best Rating:	98 3/02 MRas 2m1f110y gd-sft NHF

Placed in bumpers but very moderate form over hurdles so far.

John Tufty

12-y-o ch g Vin St Benet-Raffles Virginia (Whistling Deer)
Miss C Wolstenholme Miss C Wolstenholme

Placings:1P00/3403/22/22464504264U5/0U60/0006306P6
65F/250/PP   (0383)
2002/03: 16⁶G, 24⁶G,

	Starts	1st	2nd	3rd	Win & Pl
Chases	2	0	0	0	
Career Total	44	1	6	3	7065
73 11/94 Hntg	2m110y	Hdl		GD	£1917

Total win prize-money £1918

Going:	Sf: 0-0 GS: 0-0 Gd: 0-2 GF: - Fm: 0-0
Distance:	2m/2m3: 0-1 2m4-2m7: 0-0 3m+: 0-1
Track:	LH: 0-0 RH: 0-2 Tight: 0-0 Gall: 0-1
Aids:	Bl: 0-1 Vi: 0-0 Tstrap: 0-0
Best Rating:	87 4/00 Towc 2m6f good Ch

Johnlegood
100(106h)   (112h)108

7-y-o ch g Karinga Bay-Dancing Years (USA) (Fred Astaire (USA))
G L Moore Bryan Pennick

Placings:004/4F43P13-24FR52520   (4614)
2002/03: 17²G, 16⁴G, 24⁵GF, 20⁵S, 20⁵HY, 19²G, 18⁵S, 20²GF, 21⁰G,

	Starts	1st	2nd	3rd	Win & Pl
Hurdles	1	0	1	0	848
Chases	8	0	2	0	3539

2002/03: 16⁰G, 19¹G, 19⁰GF, 19⁶S, 19⁰GF,

Career Total	19 1 3 2 9044
112   3/02   Font   2m2f110yD Hdl   SFT   £3528

Total win prize-money £3528

Going:	Sf: 0-3 GS: 0-1 Gd: 0-4 GF: - Fm: 0-1
Distance:	2m/2m3: 0-4 2m4-2m7: 0-4 3m+: 0-1
Track:	LH: 0-2 RH: 0-4 Tight: 0-5 Gall: 0-1
Aids:	Bl: -0-0 Vi: 0-0 Tstrap: 0-0
Best Rating:	113 5/02 Folk 2m1f110y good Hdl

Modest chaser; effective at around two and a half miles; acts on decent and soft ground.

Johnny Grand
72   66

6-y-o b g Kasakov-Richesse (FR) (Far Away Son (USA))
D P Keane Avon Thoroughbreds Ltd

Placings:U0P4   (4389)
2002/03: 20ᵁS, 21⁰GS, 20ᴾHY, 25⁴F,

	Starts	1st	2nd	3rd	Win & Pl
Hurdles	2	0	0	0	0
Chases	2	0	0	0	542
Career Total	4	0	0	0	542

Going:	Sf: 0-2 GS: 0-1 Gd: 0-0 GF: - Fm: 0-1
Distance:	2m/2m3: 0-0 2m4-2m7: 0-3 3m+: 0-1
Track:	LH: 0-2 RH: 0-2 Tight: 0-0 Gall: 0-2
Aids:	Bl: 0-1 Vi: 0-0 Tstrap: 0-0
Best Rating:	66 3/03 Extr 3m1f110y firm Ch

Johnson's Point
97   92

5-y-o ch m Sabrehill (USA)-Watership (USA) (Foolish Pleasure (USA))
M W Easterby J W P Curtis

Placings:1PF   (4366)
2002/03: 20¹G, 16⁵S, 20⁵G,

	Starts	1st	2nd	3rd	Win & Pl
Hurdles	3	1	0	0	3066
Career Total	3	1	0	0	3066
92 10/02 Hayd	2m4f		E Hdl	GD	£3066

Total win prize-money £3066

Going:	Sf: 0-1 GS: 0-0 Gd: 1-2 GF: - Fm: 0-0
Distance:	2m/2m3: 0-1 2m4-2m7: 1-2 3m+: 0-0
Track:	LH: 1-2 RH: 0-1 Tight: 0-0 Gall: 0-1
Aids:	Bl: 0-1 Vi: 0-0 Tstrap: 0-0
Best Rating:	92 10/02 Hayd 2m4f good Hdl

Johnston's Art (IRE)
107   105+

10-y-o b g Law Society (USA)-Mirror Of Flowers (Artaius (USA))
Mrs J C McGregor (Mrs D Thomson 7/6) The Coutts McGregor Clan

Placings:350/f3312/P3FPP5/100300/P45052061P40-
213120P44P0P00   (4774)
2002/03: 22²GS, 24¹GF, 27³G, 24¹GS, 24²GF, 22⁰GF, 22⁴HY, 24⁴GF, 24²G, 24⁰GS, 27⁶G, 22⁰G, 27⁰G,

	Starts	1st	2nd	3rd	Win & Pl
Hurdles	14	2	2	1	11120
Career Total	46	6	4	6	26059
105   6/02   Prth   3m1f110y   E(0-110)HHdl   G-S   £2933
103   5/02   Prth   3m(0-120)HHdl   G-F   £4124
103   1/02   Muss   3m   E(0-110)HHdl   SFT   £3388
116   10/00   Font   2m6f110yD(0-120)HHdl   GD   £3168
115   3/99   Plum   2m4f   E Hdl   SFT   £2285

114 1/99 Ling 2m110y H NHF HVY £1327
Total win prize-money £17226

Going: Sf: 0-2 GS: 1-3 Gd: 0-5 GF: - Fm: 1-4
Distance: 2m/2m3: 0-0 2m4-2m7: 0-4 **3m+: 2-10**
Track: LH: 0-7 **RH: 2-6** Tight: 0-8 Gall: 0-0
Aids: **Bl: 2-14** Vi: 0-0 Tstrap: 0-0
Best Rating: **120** 4/99 Plum 2m4f gd-sft Hdl

Modest hurdler; stays three miles plus; acts on any ground; not the most resolute.

Joint Account
110

13-y-o ch g Sayyaf-Dancing Clara (Billion (USA))
R Tate (Mrs F E Needham 15/3) K Needham

Placings:00/U/14221/132PF1/24/15U3FP11-125235P
(4526)
2002/03: 25¹G, 23²S, 20⁵GS, 23²S, 25³G, 25⁵GS, 24³G,

	Starts	1st	2nd	3rd	Win & Pl
Chases	7	1	2	1	15488
Career Total	31	8	6	3	35897
135 5/02	Weth	3m1f	B(0-145)HCh	GD	£9236
124 4/02	Weth	2m7f110yD(0-120)HCh	G-F	£5492
116 3/02	MRas	2m4f	E(0-110)HCh	G-S	£3388
115 5/01	Weth	3m1f	H Ch	GD	£2030
102 4/00	Sedg	3m3f	H Ch	GD	£1578
109 5/99	MRas	3m1f	H Ch	GD	£1062
116 4/99	Hntg	3m	H Ch	GD	£1623
105 5/98	Uttx	2m5f	H Ch	GD	£1127

Total win prize-money £25541

Going: Sf: 0-2 GS: 0-2 Gd: 1-3 GF: - Fm: 0-0
Distance: 2m/2m3: 0-0 2m4-2m7: 0-1 **3m+: 1-6**
Track: **LH: 1-5** RH: 0-2 Tight: 0-2 Gall: 0-0
Aids: Bl: 0-0 Vi: 0-0 Tstrap: 0-0
Best Rating: **135** 6/02 Worc 2m7f110y soft Ch

Modest hunter chaser these days; suited by three miles and a sound surface.

Joint Authority (IRE)
78(97h)   (87h)52+

8-y-o g Religiously (USA)-Highway s Last (Royal Highway)
L Lungo Mrs Barbara Lungo

Placings:P04423
(4661)
2002/03: 22⁸S, 16⁹GS, 20⁴GS, 16⁴G, 20²GS, 17³GF,

	Starts	1st	2nd	3rd	Win & Pl
Hurdles	6	0	1	1	2425
Career Total	6	0	1	1	2425

Going: Sf: 0-1 GS: 0-3 Gd: 0-1 GF: - Fm: 0-0
Distance: 2m/2m3: 0-3 2m4-2m7: 0-3 3m+: 0-0
Track: LH: 0-3 RH: 0-3 Tight: 0-2 Gall: 0-2
Aids: Bl: 0-0 Vi: 0-0 Tstrap: 0-0
Best Rating: **87** 3/03 Newc 2m4f gd-sft Hdl

Moderate novice hurdler; stays two and a half miles; acts on easy ground.

Jojo (FR)
90   51

6-y-o ch g Dadarissime (FR)-Belle Morne (FR) (Grand Tresor (FR))
N W Alexander Jamie Alexander

Placings:00024-503FP305
(4749)
2002/03: 21⁵G, 22⁰G, 20³G, 21⁵G, 21⁰G, 20³G, 20⁰G, 20⁵G,

	Starts	1st	2nd	3rd	Win & Pl
Hurdles	1	0	0	0	0
Chases	7	0	0	2	1310
Career Total	13	0	1	2	3334

Going: Sf: 0-0 GS: 0-0 Gd: 0-8 GF: - Fm: 0-0
Distance: 2m/2m3: 0-0 2m4-2m7: 0-8 3m+: 0-0
Track: LH: 0-0 RH: 0-0 Tight: 0-0 Gall: 0-0
Aids: Bl: 0-0 Vi: 0-0 Tstrap: 0-0
Best Rating: **76** 4/03 Prth 2m4f110y good Hdl

Ex-French; a bitter disappointment here.

Jokers Charm
95   100

12-y-o b g Idiots Delight-By The Lake (Tyrant (USA))
N B Mason N B Mason

Placings:50P/05303/5310004225330 1440/4136651130442
206/35245-P6P1
(1529)
2002/03: 20²⁰G, 21⁶G, 20⁸G, 16¹G,

	Starts	1st	2nd	3rd	Win & Pl
Hurdles	1	0	0	0	0
Chases	3	1	0	0	4979
Career Total	50	6	5	8	32582
100 10/02	Sedg	2m110y	D(0-115)HCh	GD	£4979
109 12/00	Muss	2m	F(0-95)HCh	GD	£2821
109 12/00	Fknm	2m110y	F(0-100)HCh	G-S	£4072
109 9/00	Sedg	2m5f	D(0-120)HCh	GD	£3851
103 11/99	Hexm	2m110y	F(0-95)HCh	GD	£2748
94 7/99	Sedg	2m110y	E Ch	G-F	£3285

Total win prize-money £21757

Going: Sf: 0-0 GS: 0-0 Gd: 1-4 GF: - Fm: 0-0
Distance: **2m/2m3: 1-1** 2m4-2m7: 0-3 3m+: 0-0
Track: **LH: 1-3** RH: 0-1 **Tight: 1-3** Gall: 0-0
Aids: **Bl: 1-4** Vi: 0-0 Tstrap: 1-4
Best Rating: **109** 2/01 Sedg 2m110y soft Ch

Jokesmith (IRE)
73

5-y-o b g Mujadil (USA)-Grinning (IRE) (Bellypha)
K A Ryan (B J Meehan 26/10) Uncle Jacks Pub

Placings:P
(3103)
2002/03: 16⁸HY,

	Starts	1st	2nd	3rd	Win & Pl
Hurdles	1	0	0	0	0
Career Total	1	0	0	0	0

Going: Sf: 0-1 GS: 0-0 Gd: 0-0 GF: - Fm: 0-0
Distance: 2m/2m3: 0-1 2m4-2m7: 0-0 3m+: 0-0
Track: LH: 0-1 RH: 0-0 Tight: 0-0 Gall: 0-0
Aids: Bl: 0-0 Vi: 0-0 Tstrap: 0-0
Best Rating: **73** 1/03 Ayr 2m heavy Hdl

Joli Posh
68   28

6-y-o ch m Rakaposhi King-Nunswalk (The Parson)
R J Hodges Joli Racing

Placings:00
(3146)
2002/03: 16⁶S, 17⁰S,

	Starts	1st	2nd	3rd	Win & Pl
NH Flat	2	0	0	0	
Career Total	2	0	0	0	

Going: Sf: 0-2 GS: 0-0 Gd: 0-0 GF: - Fm: 0-0

Distance: 2m/2m3: 0-2 2m4-2m7: 0-0 3m+: 0-0
Track: LH: 0-0 RH: 0-1 Tight: 0-0 Gall: 0-0
Aids: Bl: 0-0 Vi: 0-0 Tstrap: 0-0
Best Rating: **56** 1/03 Tntn 2m1f soft NHF

Jolika (FR)
83   79+

6-y-o b m Grand Tresor (FR)-Unika li (FR) (Rolling Bowl (FR))
L Lungo Dr Kenneth S Fraser

Placings:4/13-2
(3230)
2002/03: 17²HY,

	Starts	1st	2nd	3rd	Win & Pl
NH Flat	1	0	1	0	530
Career Total	4	1	1	1	3072
100 5/01	Prth	2m110y	H NHF	SFT	£2289

Total win prize-money £2289

Going: Sf: 0-1 GS: 0-0 Gd: 0-0 GF: - Fm: 0-0
Distance: 2m/2m3: 0-1 2m4-2m7: 0-0 3m+: 0-0
Track: LH: 0-1 RH: 0-0 Tight: 0-1 Gall: 0-0
Aids: Bl: 0-0 Vi: 0-0 Tstrap: 0-0
Best Rating: **102** 1/03 Sedg 2m1f heavy NHF

Jollands
84   64

5-y-o b g Ezzoud (IRE)-Rainbow Fleet (Nomination)
R Curtis D Marks

Placings:4P4
(1426)
2002/03: 17⁴G, 24²G, 16⁴GF,

	Starts	1st	2nd	3rd	Win & Pl
Hurdles	3	0	0	0	267
Career Total	3	0	0	0	267

Going: Sf: 0-0 GS: 0-0 Gd: 0-1 GF: - Fm: 0-2
Distance: 2m/2m3: 0-2 2m4-2m7: 0-0 3m+: 0-1
Track: LH: 0-3 RH: 0-0 Tight: 0-2 Gall: 0-0
Aids: Bl: 0-0 Vi: 0-0 Tstrap: 0-0
Best Rating: **79** 6/02 NAbb 2m1f gd-fm Hdl

Jollie Bollie (IRE)
112   128

8-y-o b m Husyan (USA)-Jet Travel (Deep Run)
Miss Venetia Williams Mrs Liz Cooper-Mitchell & Mrs Ann Hawke

Placings:632 1/2P210-1210000
(4610)
2002/03: 20¹S, 22²S, 22¹GS, 22⁰HY, 21⁹G, 20⁹G, 21⁹G,

	Starts	1st	2nd	3rd	Win & Pl
Hurdles	7	2	1	0	16230
Career Total	16	4	4	1	23711
141 12/02	Winc	2m6f	B HHdl	G-S	£8902
134 11/02	Folk	2m4f110yD(0-125)HHdl	SFT	£5037
114 1/02	Hrfd	2m3f110yE Hdl	SFT	£2838
119 4/01	Winc	2m	H NHF	SFT	£1673

Total win prize-money £18452

Going: Sf: 1-3 GS: 1-1 Gd: 0-3 GF: - Fm: 0-0
Distance: 2m/2m3: 0-0 **2m4-2m7: 2-7** 3m+: 0-0
Track: LH: 0-1 **RH: 2-6 Tight: 1-1** Gall: 0-1
Aids: Bl: 0-0 Vi: 0-0 Tstrap: 0-0
Best Rating: **141** 12/02 Winc 2m6f gd-sft Hdl

Useful hurdler; stays two miles six; best on soft ground.

Jolly Giant (IRE)

98   109

7-y-o b g Jolly Jake (NZ)-Reve Clair (Deep Run)
P F Nicholls Jeffrey Hordle

Placings:4P-F31PF1U   (4253)
2002/03: 26FG, 24JG, 241S, 26PHY, 25FGS, 251GS, 23UG,

	Starts	1st	2nd	3rd	Win & Pl
Chases	7	2	0	1	10655
Career Total	9	2	0	1	11081
109 1/03 Extr	3m1ff110yE(0-105)HCh			G-S	£5785
101 11/02 Chep	3m	E(0-110)HCh		SFT	£4134
			Total win prize-money £9919		

Going:	Sf: 1-2 GS: 1-2 Gd: 0-3 GF: - Fm: 0-0
Distance:	2m/2m3: 0-0 2m4-2m7: 0-0 3m+: 2-7
Track:	LH: 1-4 RH: 1-3 Tight: 0-1 Gall: 0-0
Aids:	Bl: 1-2 Vi: 0-0 Tstrap: 0-0
Best Rating:	109 1/03 Extr 3m1ff110y gd-sft Ch

Modest chaser; stays an extended three miles one; acts on soft ground; has worn blinkers.

Jolly Green Giant (IRE)

10-y-o b g Glacial Storm (USA)-Rambling Love (Golden Love)
P R Webber Paul Green

Placings:2010/1111P/PPP-P   (3479)
2002/03: 25PGS,

	Starts	1st	2nd	3rd	Win & Pl
Chases	1	0	0	0	
Career Total	13	5	1	0	28596
143 3/01 Wwck	3m110y C Ch			HVY	£7392
145 2/01 Hayd	2m6f	C Ch		HVY	£7150
149 1/01 Wwck	2m4f110yC Ch			SFT	£6968
123 12/00 Chep	2m3f110yD Ch			HVY	£3789
109 2/00 Sedg	2m5f110yE Hdl			G-S	£2534
			Total win prize-money £27834		

Going:	Sf: 0-0 GS: 0-1 Gd: 0-0 GF: - Fm: 0-0
Distance:	2m/2m3: 0-0 2m4-2m7: 0-0 3m+: 0-1
Track:	LH: 0-0 RH: 0-1 Tight: 0-0 Gall: 0-0
Aids:	Bl: 0-0 Vi: 0-0 Tstrap: 0-0
Best Rating:	149 1/01 Wwck 2m4f110y soft Ch

Formerly fair chaser; well named; took to fences well in 2000/01, winning four times; lightly raced and pulled up on each of his starts since; at his best effective between two and a half and three miles on soft/heavy ground; now hunter chasing.

Jolly Hopeful (IRE)

92

6-y-o b g Glacial Storm (USA)-Tudor Lady (Green Shoon)
C P Morlock Michael Padfield

Placings:03-P   (1786)
2002/03: 22PGS,

	Starts	1st	2nd	3rd	Win & Pl
Hurdles	1	0	0	0	
Career Total	3	0	0	1	383

Going:	Sf: 0-0 GS: 0-1 Gd: 0-0 GF: - Fm: 0-0
Distance:	2m/2m3: 0-0 2m4-2m7: 0-1 3m+: 0-0
Track:	LH: 0-0 RH: 0-1 Tight: 0-1 Gall: 0-0
Aids:	Bl: 0-0 Vi: 0-0 Tstrap: 0-0
Best Rating:	99 2/02 Kemp 2m good NHF

Jolly John (IRE)

96   (97c)94

12-y-o b g Jolly Jake (NZ)-Golden Seekers (Manado)
C J Mann E P F De Plumpton Hunter

Placings:00/440U/B50303/603042P6/0P1UF0/065365/443   (0820)
3235P-34234

2002/03: 223GF, 234GS, 242G, 243G, 244GF,

	Starts	1st	2nd	3rd	Win & Pl
Hurdles	5	0	1	2	1850
Career Total	45	1	3	9	10187
93 11/99 Thur	2m2f	Ch		Y-S	£3850
			Total win prize-money £3850		

Going:	Sf: 0-0 GS: 0-1 Gd: 0-2 GF: - Fm: 0-2
Distance:	2m/2m3: 0-0 2m4-2m7: 0-1 3m+: 0-4
Track:	LH: 0-4 RH: 0-1 Tight: 0-1 Gall: 0-0
Aids:	Bl: 0-0 Vi: 0-0 Tstrap: 0-0
Best Rating:	105 10/97 Gowr 2m2f gd-fm Ch

Ex-Irish dual-purpose individual, he has been extremely uninspiring over both hurdles and fences. He returned to hurdles after joining Charlie Mann's yard.

Jolly Side (IRE)

98(99h)   (96 h)100

10-y-o b g Jolly Jake (NZ)-South Quay Lady (Quayside)
C J Mann Rod & Mandy Bransgrove

Placings:410/4664522004P0/6212P22P236F14F/31/63P43   (4189)
0

2002/03: 16HHY, 163GS, 16PS, 164GS, 163GS, 16PG,

	Starts	1st	2nd	3rd	Win & Pl
Hurdles	1	0	0	0	
Chases	5	0	0	2	1185
Career Total	38	4	7	4	27128
121 5/00 Cork	2m	Ch		GD	£5032
121 3/00 Wxfd	2m	Ch		YLD	£5520
90 6/99 Cork	2m1f	Ch		G-F	£4296
113 1/98 Gowr	2m	NHF		YLD	£2382
			Total win prize-money £17232		

Going:	Sf: 0-2 GS: 0-3 Gd: 0-1 GF: - Fm: 0-0
Distance:	2m/2m3: 0-6 2m4-2m7: 0-0 3m+: 0-0
Track:	LH: 0-2 RH: 0-4 Tight: 0-3 Gall: 0-1
Aids:	Bl: 0-0 Vi: 0-0 Tstrap: 0-0
Best Rating:	123 4/00 Gowr 2m2f gd-yld Ch

Fair novice chaser in Ireland in the spring of 2000; shaped well after two and a half years off at Leicester in November 2002 and again at Huntingdon the following month; often pulls too hard for his own good.

Jollyolly

105   107+

4-y-o gr g Environment Friend-Off The Air (IRE) (Taufan (USA))
P Bowen Eamonn O'Malley

Placings:002   (4688)
2002/03: 18UGS, 16OS, 192GF,

	Starts	1st	2nd	3rd	Win & Pl
NH Flat	2	0	0	0	
Hurdles	1	0	1	0	1520
Career Total	3	0	1	0	1520

Going:	Sf: 0-1 GS: 0-1 Gd: 0-0 GF: - Fm: 0-1
Distance:	2m/2m3: 0-2 2m4-2m7: 0-1 3m+: 0-0
Track:	LH: 0-1 RH: 0-2 Tight: 0-2 Gall: 0-0
Aids:	Bl: 0-0 Vi: 0-0 Tstrap: 0-0
Best Rating:	95 4/03 MRas 2m3f110y gd-fm Hdl

Jollyshau (IRE)

93   77

5-y-o b g Jolly Jake (NZ)-Escheat (IRE) (Torus)
Miss A M Newton-Smith Michael Coates

Placings:040   (4442)
2002/03: 20OHY, 214HY, 20OG,

	Starts	1st	2nd	3rd	Win & Pl
Hurdles	3	0	0	0	267
Career Total	3	0	0	0	267

Going:	Sf: 0-2 GS: 0-0 Gd: 0-1 GF: - Fm: 0-0
Distance:	2m/2m3: 0-0 2m4-2m7: 0-3 3m+: 0-0
Track:	LH: 0-1 RH: 0-2 Tight: 0-2 Gall: 0-0
Aids:	Bl: 0-0 Vi: 0-0 Tstrap: 0-0
Best Rating:	77 4/03 Asct 2m4f good Hdl

Joly Bey (FR)

115(104h)   (116+h)146

6-y-o ch g Beyssac (FR)-Rivolie (FR) (Mistigri)
P F Nicholls (G Macaire 4/6) Million In Mind Partnership (12)

Placings:0532-15212311123   (4474)
2002/03: 201VS, 22PVS, 212GS, 211HY, 242S, 243G, 241S, 201S, 241GS, 202S, 253G,

	Starts	1st	2nd	3rd	Win & Pl
Hurdles	1	1	0	0	3552
Chases	10	4	3	2	56075
Career Total	15	5	4	3	68461
116 2/03 Chep	3m	E Hdl		G-S	£3552
146 2/03 Sand	2m4f110yD Ch			SFT	£7525
140 1/03 Fknm	3m110y D Ch			SFT	£5782
135 11/02 NAbb	2m5f110y C Ch			HVY	£7568
5/02 Autl	2m4f110y Ch			VS	£12368
			Total win prize-money £36796		

Going:	Sf: 3-5 GS: 1-2 Gd: 0-2 GF: - Fm: 0-0
Distance:	2m/2m3: 0-0 2m4-2m7: 3-6 3m+: 2-5
Track:	LH: 3-8 RH: 1-2 Tight: 2-4 Gall: 0-2
Aids:	Bl: 0-0 Vi: 0-0 Tstrap: 0-0
Best Rating:	146 2/03 Sand 2m4f110y soft Ch

Very useful novice chaser; won a novice hurdle in February 2003; suited by trips of up to three miles; acts on soft ground; handles a sharp track.

Joly Bois (FR)

96   81

6-y-o ch g Mister Sicy (FR)-Brindille Jolie (Lee (FR))
M C Pipe B A Kilpatrick

Placings:PP4-5000   (4311)
2002/03: 19US, 16OHY, 22OS, 21OG,

	Starts	1st	2nd	3rd	Win & Pl
Hurdles	4	0	0	0	0
Career Total	7	0	0	0	0

Going:	Sf: 0-3 GS: 0-0 Gd: 0-1 GF: - Fm: 0-0
Distance:	2m/2m3: 0-1 2m4-2m7: 0-3 3m+: 0-0
Track:	LH: 0-1 RH: 0-3 Tight: 0-1 Gall: 0-1
Aids:	Bl: 0-1 Vi: 0-3 Tstrap: 0-0
Best Rating:	81 1/03 Tntn 2m3f110y soft Hdl

French import who has been disappointing over hurdles to date.

Jonaem (IRE)

105(102c)   (59c)79

13-y-o b g Mazaad-Priors Mistress (Sallust)

Mrs Dianne Sayer (Mrs E Slack 26/11) Mrs Evelyn Slack

Placings:00P0/25000236/55412600063/F502/P11/F006/3/ P00-3300421P33041P5P104 **(4662)**
2002/03: 27³GF, 25³GF, 30⁰G, 20⁹GF, 27⁴GF, 17²G, 21¹G, 22⁶G, 20³GF, 25³GF, 22⁰G, 27⁴G, 27¹S, 27⁹S, 21⁵HY, 27⁹S, 27¹G, 21⁰G, 26⁴GF,

	Starts	1st	2nd	3rd	Win & Pl
Hurdles	11	3	1	0	7887
Chases	8	0	0	4	2627
Career Total	57	6	5	7	24538

79	3/03	Sedg	3m3f110yE(0-110)HHdl	GD	£3479
79	11/02	Sedg	3m3f110yE(0-90)HHdl	SFT	£1890
73	8/02	Sedg	2m5f110yG(0-95)HHdl	GD	£1960
98	4/99	Sedg	3m3f	F(0-110)HCh	G-F	£3852
93	4/99	Sedg	3m3f	D Ch	G-S	£3606
84	10/96	Carl	2m4f110yE(0-100)HHdl	FRM	£2332

Total win prize-money £17120

Going: Sf: 1-4 GS: 0-0 Gd: 2-8 GF: - Fm: 0-7
Distance: 2m/2m3: 0-2 2m4-2m7: 1-7 3m+: 2-11
Track: LH: 3-17 RH: 0-1 Tight: 3-13 Gall: 0-0
Aids: Bl: 0-0 Vi: 0-0 Tstrap: 0-0
Best Rating: 98 4/99 Sedg 3m3f gd-fm Ch

Plating-class hurdler/chaser, stays three miles plus, acts on any ground and has gained almost all his wins at Sedgefield.

Jonanaud

94f **82f**
4-y-o b g Ballet Royal (USA)-Margaret Modes (Thatching)
H J Manners H J Manners

Placings:002 **(4350)**
2002/03: 16⁶G, 16⁰G, 16²GF,

	Starts	1st	2nd	3rd	Win & Pl
NH Flat	3	0	1	0	582
Career Total	3	0	1	0	582

Going: Sf: 0-0 GS: 0-0 Gd: 0-2 GF: - Fm: 0-1
Distance: 2m/2m3: 0-3 2m4-2m7: 0-0 3m+: 0-0
Track: LH: 0-3 RH: 0-0 Tight: 0-0 Gall: 0-1
Aids: Bl: 0-0 Vi: 0-0 Tstrap: 0-0
Best Rating: 82 3/03 Wwck 2m good NHF

Modest bumper performer.

Jones Lad (IRE)

100(101h) (85h)**96**
8-y-o b g Posen (USA)-Dame s Folly (IRE) (King s Lake (USA))
R H Buckler The Crop Circle

Placings:0063/005010500/62P/0500520-6P**2223** **(0850)**
2002/03: 22⁶GF, 20⁷GS, 16²GF, 16⁷G, 16²GF, 16³GF,

	Starts	1st	2nd	3rd	Win & Pl
Hurdles	2	0	0	0	0
Chases	4	0	3	1	3958
Career Total	29	1	5	2	8003

85	9/99	Clon	2m4f	Hdl	G-F	£2217

Total win prize-money £2218

Going: Sf: 0-0 GS: 0-1 Gd: 0-1 GF: - Fm: 0-4
Distance: 2m/2m3: 0-4 2m4-2m7: 0-2 3m+: 0-0
Track: LH: 0-5 RH: 0-1 Tight: 0-4 Gall: 0-0
Aids: Bl: 0-1 Vi: 0-0 Tstrap: 0-0
Best Rating: 96 7/02 NAbb 2m110y gd-fm Ch

Moderate hurdler, suited to good/fast ground and is suited by being ridden positively. Respectable debut over fences at Newton Abbot June 2002 despite being no match for the useful Golden Alpha. Narrowly beaten on handicap debut over same course and distance the following month.

Jongleur Collonges (FR)

101 **104**
6-y-o gr g Royal Charter (FR)-Soubrette Collonge (FR) (Saumon (FR))
R H Alner Andrew Wiles

Placings:345-3465 **(4606)**
2002/03: 21³S, 21⁴S, 20⁶G, 24⁵G,

	Starts	1st	2nd	3rd	Win & Pl
Hurdles	4	0	0	1	1671
Career Total	7	0	0	2	1895

Going: Sf: 0-2 GS: 0-0 Gd: 0-2 GF: - Fm: 0-0
Distance: 2m/2m3: 0-0 2m4-2m7: 0-3 3m+: 0-1
Track: LH: 0-2 RH: 0-2 Tight: 0-0 Gall: 0-2
Aids: Bl: 0-0 Vi: 0-0 Tstrap: 0-0
Best Rating: 104 11/02 Newb 2m5f soft Hdl

Modest hurdler; some ability in bumpers and ran well on his hurdling debut over two miles-five; looks suited by soft ground.

Jonjo

5-y-o b g Charnwood Forest (IRE)-Katy-Q (IRE) (Taufan (USA))
B P J Baugh Mr & Mrs D J Smart

Placings:F **(3515)**
2002/03: 16²FGS,

	Starts	1st	2nd	3rd	Win & Pl
Hurdles	1	0	0	0	0
Career Total	1	0	0	0	

Going: Sf: 0-0 GS: 0-1 Gd: 0-0 GF: - Fm: 0-0
Distance: 2m/2m3: 0-1 2m4-2m7: 0-0 3m+: 0-0
Track: LH: 0-1 RH: 0-0 Tight: 0-0 Gall: 0-0
Aids: Bl: 0-0 Vi: 0-0 Tstrap: 0-0
Best Rating: 0 2/03 Hayd 2m gd-sft Hdl

Jordan's Ridge (IRE)

107(102h) **115**
7-y-o b/br g Indian Ridge-Sadie Jordan (USA) (Hail The Pirates (USA))
P Monteith Allan W Melville

Placings:0/05002442200/33525341-**41242** **(0696)**
2002/03: 22⁴G, 16¹G, 16²GS, 16⁴G, 20⁶G,

	Starts	1st	2nd	3rd	Win & Pl
Hurdles	1	0	0	0	0
Chases	4	1	2	0	6141
Career Total	25	2	6	3	12261

99	6/02	Hexm	2m110y E Ch	GD	£3055
102	4/02	Newc	2m4f	G(0-95)HHdl	FRM	£1792

Total win prize-money £4847

Going: Sf: 0-0 GS: 0-1 Gd: 1-4 GF: - Fm: 0-0
Distance: 2m/2m3: 1-3 2m4-2m7: 0-2 3m+: 0-0
Track: LH: 1-3 RH: 0-2 Tight: 0-2 Gall: 0-0
Aids: Bl: 0-0 Vi: 0-0 Tstrap: 0-0
Best Rating: 112 6/02 Prth 2m gd-sft Ch

Moderate chaser; stays two and a half miles; effective on good ground.

Jorn Du Soleil (FR)

102(88h) (95h)**101**
6-y-o ch g Murmure (FR)-Ina Du Soleil (FR) (Or De Chine)
M D Hammond D J & F A Jackson

Placings:200-B43 **(3966)**
2002/03: 20⁸GS, 16⁴G, 16³S,

	Starts	1st	2nd	3rd	Win & Pl
Chases	3	0	0	1	1146
Career Total	6	0	1	1	3085

Going: Sf: 0-1 GS: 0-1 Gd: 0-1 GF: - Fm: 0-0
Distance: 2m/2m3: 0-2 2m4-2m7: 0-1 3m+: 0-0
Track: LH: 0-3 RH: 0-0 Tight: 0-1 Gall: 0-0
Aids: Bl: 0-0 Vi: 0-0 Tstrap: 0-0
Best Rating: 101 2/03 Weth 2m good Ch

A winner on the Flat in the French Provinces, he was brought down on his chasing debut; faded badly when well beaten fourth there in February and again faded badly a week later.

Jorodama King

102 **82**
9-y-o b g Lighter-Princess Hecate (Autre Prince)
O Sherwood P Joe Davis

Placings:200U/56PF/P20U01-504033330PUP **(4702)**
2002/03: 26¹G, 24⁵GF, 25⁹GF, 24⁴GF, 20⁰G, 26³G, 24³F, 24³F, 24³GF, 27⁰G, 25⁹GF, 25⁰GF, 25⁰GF, 26⁹GF,

	Starts	1st	2nd	3rd	Win & Pl
Chases	13	1	0	4	6816
Career Total	26	1	2	4	8882

83	4/02	Plum	3m2f	E Ch	GD	£3640

Total win prize-money £3640

Going: Sf: 0-0 GS: 0-0 Gd: 1-4 GF: - Fm: 0-9
Distance: 2m/2m3: 0-0 2m4-2m7: 0-1 3m+: 1-12
Track: LH: 1-6 RH: 0-7 Tight: 1-7 Gall: 0-1
Aids: Bl: 0-4 Vi: 0-0 Tstrap: 0-0
Best Rating: 93 11/99 Ludl 2m good NHF

Wide-margin winner of a poor novices chase at Plumpton in April 2002; held since; acts on a sound surface.

Josanjamic

93(78h) (50h)**67**
6-y-o b m King Luthier-Ndita (Be My Native (USA))
W S Kittow Kenneth Heard

Placings:23-250603 **(4569)**
2002/03: 16²G, 17⁵G, 22⁰G, 24⁶HY, 22⁰GS, 24³G,

	Starts	1st	2nd	3rd	Win & Pl
NH Flat	2	0	1	0	569
Hurdles	3	0	0	0	0
Chases	1	0	1	0	870
Career Total	8	0	2	2	2103

Going: Sf: 0-1 GS: 0-1 Gd: 0-4 GF: - Fm: 0-0
Distance: 2m/2m3: 0-2 2m4-2m7: 0-2 3m+: 0-2
Track: LH: 0-3 RH: 0-3 Tight: 0-1 Gall: 0-0
Aids: Bl: 0-0 Vi: 0-0 Tstrap: 0-0
Best Rating: 89 10/02 Extr 2m1f good NHF

Joseph William (IRE)

91 **76**
4-y-o b g College Chapel-Murroe Star (Glenstal (USA))
C N Kellett Sean A Taylor

Placings:00045PP   (3148)
2002/03: 16⁰G, 17⁰G, 16⁹G, 16⁴HY, 17⁵G, 24ᴾS, 16ᴾHY,

	Starts	1st	2nd	3rd	Win & Pl
Hurdles	7	0	0	0	
Career Total	7	0	0	0	0

Going: Sf: 0-3 GS: 0-0 Gd: 0-4 GF: - Fm: 0-0
Distance: 2m/2m3: 0-6 2m4-2m7: 0-0 3m+: 0-1
Track: LH: 0-4 RH: 0-3 Tight: 0-0 Gall: 0-0
Aids: Bl: 0-0 Vi: 0-0 Tstrap: 0-0
Best Rating: 76 11/02 Leic 2m   heavy Hdl

Joshua's Bay
105   86
5-y-o b g Karinga Bay-Bonita Blakeney (Baron Blakeney)
J R Jenkins Mr & Mrs Leon Shack

Placings:2-000U60322414   (4573)
2002/03: 17⁰G, 17⁰GF, 16⁹GF, 20ᵁGF, 16⁶G, 16⁹G, 16³GS, 16²S,
16²HY, 18⁴S, 17¹S, 16⁴GF,

	Starts	1st	2nd	3rd	Win & Pl
NH Flat	2	0	0	0	
Hurdles	10	1	2	1	6463
Career Total	13	1	3	1	6917
86 3/03 Sedg 2m1f E(0-105)HHdl SFT £3486					

Total win prize-money £3486

Going: Sf: 1-4 GS: 0-1 Gd: 0-3 GF: - Fm: 0-4
Distance: 2m/2m3: 1-11 2m4-2m7: 0-1 3m+: 0-0
Track: LH: 1-8 RH: 0-4 Tight: 1-10 Gall: 0-1
Aids: Bl: 0-0 Vi: 0-0 Tstrap: 0-0
Best Rating: 90 3/02 Hntg 2m110y   gd-fm NHF

Plating-class hurdler; broke his duck at Sedgefield in March 2003; may have come up against a well handicapped rival when second at Worcester in May; effective at around two miles; has shown form on decent ground, but looks better on a soft surface.

Joshua's Vision (IRE)
12-y-o b g Vision (USA)-Perle s Fashion (Sallust)
Lady Susan Brooke Lady Susan Brooke

Placings:25/32P02/02/FF/0566P3/P404523F/5-PP (4026)
2002/03: 26ᴾHY, 25ᴾS,

	Starts	1st	2nd	3rd	Win & Pl
Chases	2	0	0	0	
Career Total	28	0	5	3	4249

Going: Sf: 0-2 GS: 0-0 Gd: 0-0 GF: - Fm: 0-0
Distance: 2m/2m3: 0-0 2m4-2m7: 0-0 3m+: 0-2
Track: LH: 0-1 RH: 0-1 Tight: 0-0 Gall: 0-0
Aids: Bl: 0-0 Vi: 0-0 Tstrap: 0-0
Best Rating: 102 4/96 Worc 2m   gd-fm Hdl

Joss Naylor (IRE)
106(115h)   (148h)151
8-y-o b g Be My Native (USA)-Sister Ida (Bustino)
Jonjo O Neill Darren C Mercer

Placings:15/1351125-1110   (4100)
2002/03: 24¹S, 20¹S, 21¹S, 24⁹G,

	Starts	1st	2nd	3rd	Win & Pl
Chases	4	3	0	0	24996
Career Total	13	7	1	1	60583
145 1/03 Chel 2m5f B Ch SFT £13206					

151	12/02	Bang	2m4f110yD Ch	SFT	£5486
124	11/02	Uttx	3m D Ch	SFT	£6304
148	2/02	Wwck	2m5f B Hdl	SFT	£10497
125	1/02	Donc	2m4f D Hdl	SFT	£3727
119	10/01	Carl	2m1f H NHF	G-S	£1687
117	10/00	Chep	2m110y H NHF	G-S	£1589

Total win prize-money £42498

Going: Sf: 3-3 GS: 0-0 Gd: 0-1 GF: - Fm: 0-0
Distance: 2m/2m3: 0-0 2m4-2m7: 2-2 3m+: 1-2
Track: LH: 3-4 RH: 0-0 Tight: 1-1 Gall: 1-2
Aids: Bl: 0-0 Vi: 0-0 Tstrap: 0-0
Best Rating: 151 12/02 Bang 2m4f110y soft Ch

A very useful novice hurdler in 2001/02; easy winner of his first two novice chases in 2002/3; just came out best in a thrilling battle with Tarxien at Cheltenham; disappointed in a hot handicap on fourth start; will be suited by three miles; effective in soft ground; looks a highly promising chasing recruit.

Joueur D'Estruval (FR)
107   121+
6-y-o gr g Perrault-Alrose (FR) (Kalyan (FR))
W P Mullins Mrs V O Leary

Placings:14-510   (4097)
2002/03: 16⁵HY, 16¹S, 16⁹G,

	Starts	1st	2nd	3rd	Win & Pl
Hurdles	3	1	0	0	4929
Career Total	5	2	0	0	10560
121	1/03	Navn	2m	Hdl	SFT	£4928
106	3/02	Fair	2m	NHF	G-Y	£5079

Total win prize-money £10009

Going: Sf: 1-2 GS: 0-0 Gd: 0-1 GF: - Fm: 0-0
Distance: 2m/2m3: 1-3 2m4-2m7: 0-0 3m+: 0-0
Track: LH: 1-3 RH: 0-0 Tight: 0-0 Gall: 0-0
Aids: Bl: 0-0 Vi: 0-0 Tstrap: 0-0
Best Rating: 121 1/03 Navn 2m   soft Hdl

Useful Irish-trained novice hurdler; showed very useful form in bumpers; suited by 2m and acts on soft ground; capable of further improvement.

Jour J (FR)
135d
6-y-o gr g Royal Charter (FR)-Ability (FR) (Olmeto)
M C Pipe Stef Stefanou

Placings:331F12P-P   (2635)
2002/03: 20ᴾGS,

	Starts	1st	2nd	3rd	Win & Pl
Chases	1	0	0	0	
Career Total	8	2	1	2	20990
135	1/02	Wwck	2m4f110yD Ch	SFT	£4426
	11/01	Nant	2m5f110y Ch	VS	£8244

Total win prize-money £12671

Going: Sf: 0-0 GS: 0-1 Gd: 0-0 GF: - Fm: 0-0
Distance: 2m/2m3: 0-0 2m4-2m7: 0-1 3m+: 0-0
Track: LH: 0-1 RH: 0-0 Tight: 0-0 Gall: 0-0
Aids: Bl: 0-0 Vi: 0-0 Tstrap: 0-0
Best Rating: 135 1/02 Wwck 2m4f110y soft Ch

A winner over fences in France, he fell at the first on his British debut but made all at Warwick next time over two miles four and a half furlongs. Just touched off at Fontwell. A keen sort, he likes soft ground. Not the safest of conveyances.

Journey
10-y-o ch g Tina s Pet-Lady Vynz (Whitstead)
Mrs Sarah Horner-Harker Mrs Sarah Horner-Harker

Placings:6000/00/0/6   (0068)
2002/03: 21⁶GF,

	Starts	1st	2nd	3rd	Win & Pl
Chases	1	0	0	0	0
Career Total	8	0	0	0	0

Going: Sf: 0-0 GS: 0-0 Gd: 0-0 GF: - Fm: 0-1
Distance: 2m/2m3: 0-0 2m4-2m7: 0-1 3m+: 0-0
Track: LH: 0-1 RH: 0-0 Tight: 0-1 Gall: 0-0
Aids: Bl: 0-0 Vi: 0-0 Tstrap: 0-0
Best Rating: 77 2/98 Naas 2m   soft Hdl

Jowoody
108(93h)   (101h)111
10-y-o ch m Gunner B-Maskwood (Precipice Wood)
E W Tuer Tagwood Syndicate

Placings:0/34322564/454111/463P/31UF3346-122 (0258)
2002/03: 25¹GS, 22²G, 24²GF,

	Starts	1st	2nd	3rd	Win & Pl
Chases	3	1	2	0	10968
Career Total	30	5	4	6	30032
106	5/02	Kels	3m1f	C(0-130)HCh	G-S	£6753
111	12/01	Ayr	3m5f	E(0-115)HCh	SFT	£3178
106	2/99	Newc	3m	F(0-105)HHdl	G-S	£2155
98	1/99	Ayr	3m110y	D(0-110)HHdl	HVY	£2862
93	1/99	MRas	3m	F(0-100)HHdl	SFT	£1821

Total win prize-money £16771

Going: Sf: 0-0 GS: 1-1 Gd: 0-1 GF: - Fm: 0-1
Distance: 2m/2m3: 0-0 2m4-2m7: 0-1 3m+: 1-2
Track: LH: 1-2 RH: 0-1 Tight: 1-2 Gall: 0-0
Aids: Bl: 0-0 Vi: 0-0 Tstrap: 0-0
Best Rating: 111 5/02 Prth 3m   gd-fm Ch

Fair staying chaser, suited by soft ground but handles faster.

Joy Again
78f   46f
5-y-o ch m Then Again-Silver Spring (Silver Season)
R Allan Mrs K Christie

Placings:0   (0261)
2002/03: 16⁹GF,

	Starts	1st	2nd	3rd	Win & Pl
NH Flat	1	0	0	0	
Career Total	1	0	0	0	

Going: Sf: 0-0 GS: 0-0 Gd: 0-0 GF: - Fm: 0-1
Distance: 2m/2m3: 0-1 2m4-2m7: 0-0 3m+: 0-0
Track: LH: 0-0 RH: 0-0 Tight: 0-0 Gall: 0-0
Aids: Bl: 0-0 Vi: 0-0 Tstrap: 0-0
Best Rating: 46 5/02 Prth 2m110y   gd-fm NHF

Joy De Disse (FR)
6-y-o b g Grand Tresor (FR)-Surprise De L Isle (FR) (Rubloff (USA))
N G Richards Ashleybank Investments Limited

Placings:0-0   (3160)
2002/03: 16⁰G,

	Starts	1st	2nd	3rd	Win & Pl
NH Flat	1	0	0	0	

Career Total   2   0   0   0

Going: Sf: 0-0 GS: 0-0 Gd: 0-1 GF: - Fm: 0-0
Distance: 2m/2m3: 0-1 2m4-2m7: 0-0 3m+: 0-0
Track: LH: 0-0 RH: 0-1 Tight: 0-1 Gall: 0-0
Aids: Bl: 0-0 Vi: 0-0 Tstrap: 0-0
Best Rating: **0**   1/03   Muss   2m   good   NHF

Joy For Life (IRE)
90d
12-y-o b m Satco (FR)-Joy s Toy (Wolverlife)
R M Stronge   Mrs Bernice Stronge

Placings:05U4/P20064/PP2213/5023/2P0P3F/3/P510-FPP4   (3808)
2002/03: 30^FS, 26^PS, 25^PGS, 26⁴GS,

	Starts	1st	2nd	3rd	Win & Pl
Chases	4	0	0		414
Career Total	35	2	5	4	14775
90	3/02	Sthl	3m110y	D(0-115)HCh	HVY £4108
110	4/98	Asct	3m110y	H Ch	G-S £2736

Total win prize-money £6844

Going: Sf: 0-2 GS: 0-2 Gd: 0-0 GF: - Fm: 0-0
Distance: 2m/2m3: 0-0 2m4-2m7: 0-0 3m+: 0-4
Track: LH: 0-2 RH: 0-1 Tight: 0-3 Gall: 0-0
Aids: Bl: 0-0 Vi: 0-0 Tstrap: 0-0
Best Rating: **110**   4/98   Asct   3m110y   gd-sft   Ch

Modest chaser, stays three miles plus and acts on soft ground.

Joyce Bel (FR)
84(86h)   (49h)97
10-y-o br g Rose Laurel-Jeanne De Laval (FR) (Gairloch)
Mrs H Dalton   Norton House Racing

Placings:0/P000600/00P02224004U/621F020/551F6-0PF246U   (1617)
2002/03: 17^QGF, 25^PGS, 20^FGF, 17²GF, 22⁴GF, 19⁶GF, 16^UF,

	Starts	1st	2nd	3rd	Win & Pl
Hurdles	1	0	0		0
Chases	6	0	1	0	1565
Career Total	38	2	5	0	13181
101	9/01	Dpat	2m2f	(0-95)HCh	G-F £4729
86	7/00	Wxfd	2m4f	Ch	FRM £3588

Total win prize-money £8318

Going: Sf: 0-0 GS: 0-1 Gd: 0-0 GF: - Fm: 0-6
Distance: 2m/2m3: 0-0 2m4-2m7: 0-2 3m+: 0-1
Track: LH: 0-3 RH: 0-3 Tight: 0-3 Gall: 0-0
Aids: Bl: 0-0 Vi: 0-0 Tstrap: 0-0
Best Rating: **101**   9/01   Dpat   2m2f   gd-fm   Ch

Joyeuse
97   96+
5-y-o b m Saddlers Hall (IRE)-Jouvencelle (Rusticaro (FR))
N A Twiston-Davies   H R Mould

Placings:12356F   (3546)
2002/03: 17¹G, 16²G, 16³GS, 19⁵S, 20⁶HY, 19^FG,

	Starts	1st	2nd	3rd	Win & Pl
NH Flat	3	1	1	1	2884
Hurdles	3	0	0	0	0
Career Total	6	1	1	1	2884
102	10/02	MRas	2m1f110yH NHF		GD £2009

Total win prize-money £2009

Going: Sf: 0-2 GS: 0-1 Gd: 1-3 GF: - Fm: 0-0
Distance: 2m/2m3: 1-3 2m4-2m7: 0-3 3m+: 0-0

Track: LH: 0-3 RH: 1-3 Tight: 1-1 Gall: 0-0
Aids: Bl: 0-0 Vi: 0-0 Tstrap: 0-0
Best Rating: **102**   11/02   Weth   2m   gd-sft   NHF

Bumper winner; modest novice hurdler; not a fluent jumper.

Joyeux Royal (FR)
104(102h)   (103h)121
6-y-o b g Cyborg (FR)-Samba Du Cochet (FR) (Tanlas (FR))
P F Nicholls   Barry Fulton, Liam Brady, Tony Hayward

Placings:40/02125-21FPP6   (3829)
2002/03: 17²G, 17¹GS, 21^FG, 20^PS, 16^PS, 16⁶GS,

	Starts	1st	2nd	3rd	Win & Pl
Hurdles	1	0	0		0
Chases	5	1	1	0	5698
Career Total	13	2	3	0	11451
121	11/02	Plum	2m1f	E(0-110)HCh	G-S £4043
103	12/01	Winc	2m	F(0-95)HHdl	GD £2709

Total win prize-money £6752

Going: Sf: 0-2 GS: 1-2 Gd: 0-2 GF: - Fm: 0-0
Distance: 2m/2m3: 1-4 2m4-2m7: 0-2 3m+: 0-0
Track: LH: 1-4 RH: 0-2 Tight: 1-3 Gall: 0-0
Aids: Bl: 0-1 Vi: 0-0 Tstrap: 0-0
Best Rating: **121**   11/02   Winc   2m5f   good   Ch

May have been unlucky not to win in a chase at Plumpton in October 2002 but gained compensation there next time. Held when falling when tackling further. Suited by two miles, a sound surface and a tongue tie.

Jubilee Gunner
8-y-o b g Gunner B-Smokey Baby (Sagaro)
A P Garland   A P Garland

Placings:0/P   (4487)
2002/03: 16^PGF,

	Starts	1st	2nd	3rd	Win & Pl
Chases	1	0	0	0	
Career Total	2	0	0		

Going: Sf: 0-0 GS: 0-0 Gd: 0-0 GF: - Fm: 0-0
Distance: 2m/2m3: 0-1 2m4-2m7: 0-0 3m+: 0-0
Track: LH: 0-0 RH: 0-1 Tight: 0-1 Gall: 0-0
Aids: Bl: 0-0 Vi: 0-0 Tstrap: 0-0
Best Rating: **23**   1/01   Donc   2m110y   good   NHF

Judaic Ways
108(99h)   (72h)106
9-y-o b g Rudimentary (USA)-Judeah (Great Nephew)
H D Daly   D Sandells & T Broderick

Placings:604/5004F0P0/6FF14/P1P12PP0-30133P   (4636)
2002/03: 24³GF, 19⁰G, 24¹GS, 24³G, 20³GF, 24^PG,

	Starts	1st	2nd	3rd	Win & Pl
Chases	6	1	0	3	10511
Career Total	30	4	1	3	26109
102	1/03	Ludl	3m	E(0-105)HCh	G-S £6812
105	11/01	Ludl	3m	E(0-115)HCh	G-F £4810
95	7/01	Worc	2m7f110yF(0-100)HCh		GD £3209
94	2/01	Ludl	3m	F(0-95)HCh	GD £4634

Total win prize-money £19467

Going: Sf: 0-0 GS: 1-1 Gd: 0-3 GF: - Fm: 0-2
Distance: 2m/2m3: 0-1 2m4-2m7: 0-1 3m+: 1-4
Track: LH: 0-1 RH: 1-5 Tight: 1-4 Gall: 0-1
Aids: Bl: 0-0 Vi: 0-0 Tstrap: 0-0
Best Rating: **106**   2/03   Ludl   3m   good   Ch

Modest handicap chaser; suited by fast ground but has won on good to soft; Ludlow specialist.

Judes Law
74f   45f
5-y-o gr m Contract Law (USA)-Linen Thread (Broxted)
P R Rodford   P R Rodford

Placings:0   (0907)
2002/03: 16⁶G,

	Starts	1st	2nd	3rd	Win & Pl
NH Flat	1	0	0		
Career Total	1	0	0		

Going: Sf: 0-0 GS: 0-0 Gd: 0-1 GF: - Fm: 0-0
Distance: 2m/2m3: 0-1 2m4-2m7: 0-0 3m+: 0-0
Track: LH: 0-1 RH: 0-0 Tight: 0-0 Gall: 0-0
Aids: Bl: 0-0 Vi: 0-0 Tstrap: 0-0
Best Rating:

Judicious (IRE)
65   16
6-y-o b g Fairy King (USA)-Kama Tashoof (Mtoto)
I Semple (C J Mann 3/5)   M & M Hunter

Placings:P-0   (0057)
2002/03: 17⁰G,

	Starts	1st	2nd	3rd	Win & Pl
Hurdles	1	0	0		
Career Total	2	0	0		

Going: Sf: 0-0 GS: 0-0 Gd: 0-1 GF: - Fm: 0-0
Distance: 2m/2m3: 0-1 2m4-2m7: 0-0 3m+: 0-0
Track: LH: 0-0 RH: 0-1 Tight: 0-1 Gall: 0-0
Aids: Bl: 0-0 Vi: 0-0 Tstrap: 0-0
Best Rating: **16**   5/02   Folk   2m1f110y   good   Hdl

Judy Gale (IRE)
5-y-o bl m Glacial Storm (USA)-Gale Choice (IRE) (Strong Gale)
B G Powell   D & J Newell

Placings:0P   (3672)
2002/03: 17⁰HY, 22^PGS,

	Starts	1st	2nd	3rd	Win & Pl
NH Flat	1	0	0	0	0
Hurdles	1	0	0	0	0
Career Total	2	0	0		

Going: Sf: 0-1 GS: 0-1 Gd: 0-0 GF: - Fm: 0-0
Distance: 2m/2m3: 0-1 2m4-2m7: 0-1 3m+: 0-0
Track: LH: 0-1 RH: 0-1 Tight: 0-2 Gall: 0-0
Aids: Bl: 0-0 Vi: 0-0 Tstrap: 0-0
Best Rating: **46**   12/02   Folk   2m1f110y   heavy   NHF

Juicy Lucy
76   47
6-y-o b m Bonny Scot (IRE)-Bijou Georgie (Rhodomantade)
J S King   Mrs Carrie Janaway

Placings:5PP0   (4426)
2002/03: 18⁵S, 19^PS, 22^PGF, 16⁰GF,

	Starts	1st	2nd	3rd	Win & Pl
NH Flat	1	0	0	0	0

| Hurdles | 3 | 0 | 0 | 0 | 0 |
| Career Total | 4 | 0 | 0 | 0 | 0 |

Going: Sf: 0-2 GS: 0-0 Gd: 0-0 GF: - Fm: 0-2
Distance: 2m/2m3: 0-3 2m4-2m7: 0-1 3m+: 0-0
Track: LH: 0-2 RH: 0-2 Tight: 0-2 Gall: 0-0
Aids: Bl: 0-0 Vi: 0-0 Tstrap: 0-0
Best Rating: 47 3/03 Plum 2m   gd-fm Hdl

Julia's Choice

90   73

4-y-o ch f Elmaamul (USA)-Daarat Alayaam (IRE)
(Reference Point)
J R Jenkins M Ng

Placings:05033   (4344)
2002/03: 12⁰G, 17⁵HY, 16⁹G, 17³S, 16³GF,

	Starts	1st	2nd	3rd	Win & Pl
NH Flat	3	0	0	0	0
Hurdles	2	0	0	2	960
Career Total	5	0	0	2	960

Going: Sf: 0-2 GS: 0-0 Gd: 0-2 GF: - Fm: 0-1
Distance: 2m/2m3: 0-4 2m4-2m7: 0-0 3m+: 0-0
Track: LH: 0-3 RH: 0-2 Tight: 0-2 Gall: 0-1
Aids: Bl: 0-0 Vi: 0-0 Tstrap: 0-0
Best Rating: 73 3/03 Bang 2m1f   soft Hdl

Modest novice hurdler; no form in bumpers.

Julie's Leader (IRE)

103(106h)   (113h)115+

9-y-o b g Supreme Leader-Parkavoureen (Deep Run)
P F Nicholls T Curry

Placings:0/U4F14/1U33/32041-F4PP11   (4623)
2002/03: 26⁶G, 24⁴HY, 22⁵G, 23⁶S, 20¹GF, 27¹GF,

	Starts	1st	2nd	3rd	Win & Pl
Hurdles	3	2	0	0	5780
Chases	3	0	0	0	0
Career Total	21	5	1	3	22080
103	4/03	NAbb	3m3f	F Hdl	G-F	£2947
92	3/03	Font	2m4f	G Hdl	G-F	£2359
87	4/02	Ludl	3m	D Ch	GD	£5200
125	1/01	Tntn	3m110y	F(0-110)HHdl	HVY	£3262
105	3/00	Tntn	3m110y	E Hdl	GD	£2472

Total win prize-money £16240

Going: Sf: 0-2 GS: 0-0 Gd: 0-2 GF: - Fm: 2-2
Distance: 2m/2m3: 0-0 2m4-2m7: 1-2 3m+: 1-4
Track: LH: 1-4 RH: 0-1 Tight: 2-3 Gall: 0-1
Aids: Bl: 0-0 Vi: 0-0 Tstrap: 0-0
Best Rating: 125 11/01 Chep 3m   gd-sft Hdl

Fair hurdler/chaser; in fine form over hurdles in the spring of 2003; effective at up to 3m 3f; acts on most types of ground; needs a break between his races.

Julies Boy (IRE)

83   106

6-y-o b g Toulon-Chickmo (IRE) (Seclude (USA))
T R George (John O Callaghan 22/12) R P Foden

Placings:02P0   (4602)
2002/03: 16⁰S, 16²Y, 20⁶G, 21⁰G,

	Starts	1st	2nd	3rd	Win & Pl
NH Flat	1	0	0	0	0
Hurdles	3	0	1	0	1129
Career Total	4	0	1	0	1129

Going: Sf: 0-1 GS: 0-0 Gd: 0-2 GF: - Fm: 0-0
Distance: 2m/2m3: 0-2 2m4-2m7: 0-2 3m+: 0-0
Track: LH: 0-2 RH: 0-1 Tight: 0-1 Gall: 0-1
Aids: Bl: 0-0 Vi: 0-0 Tstrap: 0-0
Best Rating: 106 12/02 Thur 2m   yield Hdl

Ex-Irish novice hurdler; pulled up in hot race on British debut.

Jumbo's Dream

101(99h)   (56h)87+

12-y-o b g Jumbo Hirt (USA)-Joyful Star (Rubor)
J E Dixon Mrs E M Dixon

Placings:00/23065/10000/421000/006336/000P0-6F (0378)
2002/03: 24⁶G, 27⁶G,

	Starts	1st	2nd	3rd	Win & Pl
Hurdles	2	0	0	0	0
Career Total	31	2	2	3	7450
88	6/99	Hexm	3m	F(0-105)HHdl	G-F	£2658
78	10/98	Hexm	3m	E Hdl	GD	£2238

Total win prize-money £4896

Going: Sf: 0-0 GS: 0-0 Gd: 0-2 GF: - Fm: 0-0
Distance: 2m/2m3: 0-0 2m4-2m7: 0-0 3m+: 0-2
Track: LH: 0-2 RH: 0-0 Tight: 0-1 Gall: 0-0
Aids: Bl: 0-0 Vi: 0-0 Tstrap: 0-0
Best Rating: 89 5/99 Ctml 3m2f   gd-fm Hdl

Poor handicap hurdler; well beaten over fences; stays three miles.

Jumbo's Flyer

27

6-y-o ch g Jumbo Hirt (USA)-Fragrant Princess (Germont)
F P Murtagh T H Littleton

Placings:0P0F-0   (0953)
2002/03: 17⁰G,

	Starts	1st	2nd	3rd	Win & Pl
Hurdles	1	0	0	0	0
Career Total	5	0	0	0	0

Going: Sf: 0-0 GS: 0-0 Gd: 0-1 GF: - Fm: 0-0
Distance: 2m/2m3: 0-1 2m4-2m7: 0-0 3m+: 0-0
Track: LH: 0-1 RH: 0-0 Tight: 0-1 Gall: 0-0
Aids: Bl: 0-0 Vi: 0-0 Tstrap: 0-0
Best Rating: 27 10/01 Aint 2m110y good Hdl

Jumpty Dumpty (FR)

96   90

6-y-o b/br g Chamberlin (FR)-Caryatide (FR) (Maiymad)
J C Tuck M Tuck

Placings:0/3323160P-144006   (4540)
2002/03: 22¹G, 26⁴G, 20⁴G, 22⁰GS, 19⁰S, 21⁶G,

	Starts	1st	2nd	3rd	Win & Pl
Hurdles	6	1	0	0	3654
Career Total	15	2	1	3	12139
90	5/02	Extr	2m6f110yE(0-100)HHdl	GD	£3255
	10/01	Pina	2m4f110y Ch	SFT	£3395

Total win prize-money £6650

Going: Sf: 0-1 GS: 0-1 Gd: 1-4 GF: - Fm: 0-0
Distance: 2m/2m3: 0-0 2m4-2m7: 1-5 3m+: 0-1
Track: LH: 0-1 RH: 1-5 Tight: 0-2 Gall: 0-1
Aids: Bl: 0-0 Vi: 0-0 Tstrap: 0-0
Best Rating: 90 9/02 Bang 2m4f   good Hdl

An ex-French gelding who has won over fences in his native country on soft ground. Appeared to appreciate sounder surface when winning 22 furlong novices handicap hurdle at Exeter May 2002.

June's River (IRE)

100   114

10-y-o ch g Over The River (FR)-June Bug (Welsh Saint)
Mrs M Reveley A Flannigan

Placings:002/444011/F/F251U210/U4-P23PP6   (3990)
2002/03: 17⁵S, 20²GS, 16³S, 16⁵HY, 24⁴PS, 16⁶S,

	Starts	1st	2nd	3rd	Win & Pl
Chases	6	0	1	1	4124
Career Total	26	4	4	1	19957
112	2/01	Carl	2m	F(0-105)HCh	HVY	£3477
106	12/00	Hntg	2m110y	F(0-105)HCh	SFT	£2616
110	3/99	Carl	2m	F(0-110)HCh	SFT	£2723
98	2/99	Carl	2m	E(0-105)HCh	HVY	£2931

Total win prize-money £11749

Going: Sf: 0-5 GS: 0-1 Gd: 0-0 GF: - Fm: 0-0
Distance: 2m/2m3: 0-4 2m4-2m7: 0-1 3m+: 0-1
Track: LH: 0-5 RH: 0-1 Tight: 0-1 Gall: 0-3
Aids: Bl: 0-0 Vi: 0-0 Tstrap: 0-0
Best Rating: 116 3/02 Newc 2m110y heavy Ch

Fair chaser; best over two miles; suited by soft ground; not always the best of jumpers; likes to be held up.

Jungle Jinks (IRE)

107(105h)   (120h)135

8-y-o b g Proud Panther (FR)-Three Ladies (Menelek)
G M Moore Mrs Mary And Miss Susan Hatfield

Placings:6114-11121   (3831)
2002/03: 25¹G, 21¹S, 25¹S, 25²GS, 25¹G,

	Starts	1st	2nd	3rd	Win & Pl
Chases	5	4	1	0	35761
Career Total	9	6	1	0	42390
135	2/03	Weth	3m1f	C Ch	GD	£8841
130	12/02	Weth	3m1f	D Ch	SFT	£6041
135	11/02	Sedg	2m5f	C Ch	SFT	£8375
122	11/02	Weth	3m1f	D Ch	GD	£4803
101	4/02	Carl	2m4f	E Hdl	GD	£3143
115	3/02	Ayr	3m110y	E Hdl	SFT	£2712

Total win prize-money £33917

Going: Sf: 2-2 GS: 0-1 Gd: 2-2 GF: - Fm: 0-0
Distance: 2m/2m3: 0-0 2m4-2m7: 1-1 3m+: 3-4
Track: LH: 4-5 RH: 0-0 Tight: 1-1 Gall: 0-0
Aids: Bl: 0-0 Vi: 0-0 Tstrap: 0-0
Best Rating: 135 2/03 Weth 3m1f   good Ch

A fair hurdler, took well to fences, winning four times; stays three miles, handles good or softer ground. Suited by forcing tactics.

Jungle Juice

92   89

7-y-o ch g Henbit (USA)-Deep In The Arctic (Deep Run)
Mrs L Wadham Mrs C M Cooke

Placings:6   (1568)
2002/03: 19⁶G,

	Starts	1st	2nd	3rd	Win & Pl
Hurdles	1	0	0	0	0
Career Total	1	0	0	0	0

Going: Sf: 0-0 GS: 0-0 Gd: 0-1 GF: - Fm: 0-0
Distance: 2m/2m3: 0-0 2m4-2m7: 0-1 3m+: 0-0
Track: LH: 0-0 RH: 0-1 Tight: 0-1 Gall: 0-0

Aids: Bl: 0-0 Vi: 0-0 Tstrap: 0-0
Best Rating: 89 10/02 MRas 2m3f110y good Hdl

Jungle Rumbler
87   51
4-y-o b f Charnwood Forest (IRE)-Blueberry Walk (Green Desert (USA))
P Winkworth (R Gibson 2/11) Mrs Tessa Winkworth

Placings:PF0   (4148)
2002/03: 16PS, 16FHY, 16RG,

	Starts	1st	2nd	3rd	Win & Pl
Hurdles	3	0	0	0	
Career Total	3	0	0	0	

Going: Sf: 0-2 GS: 0-0 Gd: 0-1 GF: - Fm: 0-0
Distance: 2m2m3: 0-3 2m4-2m7: 0-0 3m+: 0-0
Track: LH: 0-3 RH: 0-0 Tight: 0-3 Gall: 0-0
Aids: Bl: 0-0 Vi: 0-0 Tstrap: 0-0
Best Rating: 51 3/03 Fknm 2m good Hdl

Flat winner in France; no promise so far over hurdles.

Jungli (IRE)
(102h)   (132h)151
10-y-o b g Be My Native (USA)-Simple Mind (Decent Fellow)
P R Webber Mrs P Starkey

Placings:243/312410/1213311/1221U6/563324-F (1738)
2002/03: 20FGS,

	Starts	1st	2nd	3rd	Win & Pl
Chases	1	0	0	0	
Career Total	29	8	6	6	95865
151	1/01	Donc	2m110y	B(0-150)HCh	GD	£10413
140	10/00	Weth	2m	C(0-135)HCh	G-S	£6405
140	4/00	Aint	2m	A HCh	GD	£30000
140	3/00	Newb	2m1f	C(0-135)HCh	SFT	£6244
130	12/99	Wwck	2m	D Ch	SFT	£4816
116	10/99	Weth	2m	E Ch	GD	£2908
130	3/99	Uttx	2m4f110yC Hdl		G-S	£5537
130	12/98	Uttx	2m	E Hdl	SFT	£2431
			Total win prize-money £68756			

Going: Sf: 0-0 GS: 0-1 Gd: 0-0 GF: - Fm: 0-0
Distance: 2m2m3: 0-0 2m4-2m7: 0-1 3m+: 0-0
Track: LH: 0-1 RH: 0-0 Tight: 0-0 Gall: 0-0
Aids: Bl: 0-0 Vi: 0-0 Tstrap: 0-0
Best Rating: 151 12/01 Weth 2m gd-sft Ch

A game performer, he jumps well and is a credit to connections. He won four of his first seven races in his first season over fences and has continued to give a good account of himself in subsequent seasons. Best suited by two miles and good, good/soft ground but acts on soft. Races prominently.

Junkanoo
102   130
7-y-o ch g Generous (IRE)-Lupescu (Dixieland Band (USA))
Mrs M Reveley Lucayan Stud

Placings:51/110/1P3P-120P   (2703)
2002/03: 201S, 202GS, 20QG, 23PHY,

	Starts	1st	2nd	3rd	Win & Pl
Hurdles	4	1	1	0	15296
Career Total	13	5	1	1	25361
130	11/02	Hayd	2m4f	B(0-140)HHdl	SFT	£13747
111	12/01	Weth	2m7f	D Hdl	SFT	£3591
130	12/00	Newc	2m	H NHF	SFT	£1575
125	12/00	Hntg	2m110y	H NHF	SFT	£1694

---

110 4/00 MRas 2m1ff110y   H NHF SFT
£1589

Total win prize-money £22197

Going: Sf: 1-2 GS: 0-1 Gd: 0-1 GF: - Fm: 0-0
Distance: 2m2m3: 0-0 2m4-2m7: 1-4 3m+: 0-0
Track: LH: 1-4 RH: 0-0 Tight: 0-0 Gall: 0-1
Aids: Bl: 0-0 Vi: 0-0 Tstrap: 0-0
Best Rating: 130 11/02 Hayd 2m4f soft Hdl

Fair handicap hurdler. Acts on soft ground and stays two and a half miles. Occasionally runs very badly for no apparent reason.

Jupiter De Bussy (FR)
105   115
6-y-o b/br g Silver Rainbow-Tosca De Bussy (FR) (Le Riverain (FR))
L Lungo Ashleybank Investments Limited

Placings:65-5411P5   (4504)
2002/03: 175S, 164S, 161G, 161GS, 20PHY, 165G,

	Starts	1st	2nd	3rd	Win & Pl
NH Flat	1	0	0	0	
Hurdles	5	2	0	0	8362
Career Total	8	2	0	0	8362
115	12/02	Ayr	2m	E(0-105)HHdl	G-S	£3080
115	11/02	Aint	2m110y	D Hdl	GD	£4998
			Total win prize-money £8079			

Going: Sf: 0-3 GS: 1-1 Gd: 1-2 GF: - Fm: 0-0
Distance: 2m2m3: 2-5 2m4-2m7: 0-1 3m+: 0-0
Track: LH: 2-4 RH: 0-2 Tight: 1-3 Gall: 0-0
Aids: Bl: 0-0 Vi: 0-0 Tstrap: 0-0
Best Rating: 115 12/02 Ayr 2m gd-sft Hdl

Fair novice hurdler, effective over two miles on good and soft ground; won at Aintree and Ayr late 2002; has shown signs of temperament.

Jupiter Diamond
81
8-y-o b g Jupiter Island-Noire Small (USA) (Elocutionist (USA))
Ian Williams M Murphy

Placings:4/060003-P   (0322)
2002/03: 24PG,

	Starts	1st	2nd	3rd	Win & Pl
Hurdles	1	0	0	0	
Career Total	8	0	0	1	416

Going: Sf: 0-0 GS: 0-0 Gd: 0-1 GF: - Fm: 0-0
Distance: 2m2m3: 0-0 2m4-2m7: 0-0 3m+: 0-1
Track: LH: 0-1 RH: 0-0 Tight: 0-0 Gall: 0-0
Aids: Bl: 0-0 Vi: 0-0 Tstrap: 0-0
Best Rating: 81 4/02 Hrfd 3m2f gd-fm Hdl

Adopted front running tactics when third over an extended three miles in Novices handicap at Hereford April 2002.

Jupiter Jo
88   73
7-y-o b g Jupiter Island-Marejo (Creetown)
J B Walton Messrs F T Walton

Placings:00-4P   (0617)
2002/03: 164G, 20PGF,

	Starts	1st	2nd	3rd	Win & Pl
Chases	2	0	0	0	235

Career Total   4   0   0   0   235

Going: Sf: 0-0 GS: 0-0 Gd: 0-1 GF: - Fm: 0-1
Distance: 2m2m3: 0-1 2m4-2m7: 0-1 3m+: 0-0
Track: LH: 0-2 RH: 0-0 Tight: 0-0 Gall: 0-0
Aids: Bl: 0-0 Vi: 0-0 Tstrap: 0-0
Best Rating: 90 5/01 Newc 2m gd-fm NHF

Jupiter's Fancy
88(84h)   (52h)69
8-y-o ch m Jupiter Island-Joe s Fancy (Apollo Eight)
A Kirtley A Kirtley

Placings:4300P-P   (3968)
2002/03: 25PS,

	Starts	1st	2nd	3rd	Win & Pl
Chases	1	0	0	0	
Career Total	6	0	0	1	233

Going: Sf: 0-1 GS: 0-0 Gd: 0-0 GF: - Fm: 0-0
Distance: 2m2m3: 0-0 2m4-2m7: 0-0 3m+: 0-1
Track: LH: 0-1 RH: 0-0 Tight: 0-0 Gall: 0-0
Aids: Bl: 0-0 Vi: 0-0 Tstrap: 0-0
Best Rating: 82 12/01 Catt 2m good NHF

Modest hunter chaser; best on fast ground.

Jupon Vert (FR)
98(98h)   (101h)99
6-y-o b g Lights Out (FR)-Danse Verte (FR) (Brezzo (FR))
P F Nicholls Fear, White & Hawkins

Placings:P5/2P42-546120143F3   (4695)
2002/03: 215GF, 164G, 166S, 191GS, 192S, 190S, 161GS, 164S, 16RG, 19FF, 16RG,

	Starts	1st	2nd	3rd	Win & Pl
Hurdles	3	1	1	0	2852
Chases	8	1	0	2	5754
Career Total	17	2	3	2	12238
95	2/03	Tntn	2m110y	E(0-100)HCh	G-S	£4290
86	12/02	Tntn	2m3f110yG Hdl		G-S	£1988
			Total win prize-money £6278			

Going: Sf: 0-4 GS: 2-2 Gd: 0-3 GF: - Fm: 0-2
Distance: 2m2m3: 1-8 2m4-2m7: 1-3 3m+: 0-0
Track: LH: 0-4 RH: 2-7 Tight: 2-6 Gall: 0-0
Aids: Bl: 0-0 Vi: 0-0 Tstrap: 2-10
Best Rating: 101 12/02 Wwck 2m3f soft Hdl

Moderate hurdler/chaser; effective with cut in the ground; stays two and a half miles.

Juralan (IRE)
106(96h)   (93h)131
8-y-o b g Jurado (USA)-Boylan (Buckskin (FR))
Miss H C Knight Hogarth Racing

Placings:624/511P-PPP3   (4369)
2002/03: 21PGS, 20PG, 20PG, 16RG,

	Starts	1st	2nd	3rd	Win & Pl
Chases	4	0	0	1	2266
Career Total	11	2	1	1	14069
131	1/02	Winc	2m5f	D Ch	GD	£4602
124	11/01	Tntn	2m3f	C Ch	G-S	£6756
			Total win prize-money £11359			

Going: Sf: 0-0 GS: 0-1 Gd: 0-3 GF: - Fm: 0-0
Distance: 2m2m3: 0-1 2m4-2m7: 0-3 3m+: 0-0
Track: LH: 0-1 RH: 0-3 Tight: 0-0 Gall: 0-1
Aids: Bl: 0-0 Vi: 0-0 Tstrap: 0-0

Best Rating: 131 3/03 Asct 2m good Ch

Very useful chaser; jumps well; stays two miles five and acts on a sound surface; out of sorts so far in 2002/2003.

Jurancon II (FR)

103(112h)   (126+h)**133+**
6-y-o b g Scooter Bleu (IRE)-Volniste (FR) (Olmeto)
M C Pipe D A Johnson

Placings:456011P-1P13   (4172)
2002/03: 21¹G, 21ᴾGS, 21¹S, 34³S,

	Starts	1st	2nd	3rd	Win & Pl
Hurdles	2	1	0	0	11005
Chases	2	1	0	1	15716
Career Total	11	4	0	1	34694

126	12/02	Uttx	2m5f	D Ch		SFT	£4715
126	11/02	Chel	2m5f	E(0-115)HHdl	GD	£11005
109	2/02	Plum	2m5f	D(0-115)HHdl	HVY	£5330
112	2/02	MRas	2m5f110yE(0-110)HHdl	G-S	£2642

Total win prize-money £23694

Going: Sf: 1-2 GS: 0-1 Gd: 1-1 GF: - Fm: 0-0
Distance: 2m/2m3: 0-0 **2m4-2m7: 2-3** 3m+: 0-1
Track: LH: **2-3** RH: 0-1 Tight: 0-1 **Gall: 1-1**
Aids: Bl: 0-0 Vi: 0-0 Tstrap: 0-0
Best Rating: 126 12/02 Uttx 2m5f soft Ch

Useful, lightly raced chaser; won on chase debut in December 2002, before a good third in the Midlands National; returned after a break to win Summer National back at Uttoxeter; handles soft and fast ground; stays 4m 2f.

Jurassic Scratch (IRE)

100(100h)   (81h)**81**
7-y-o b g Jurado (USA)-On The Scratch (Le Bavard (FR))
R Rowe Tim Clowes

Placings:6462530P-FP0P20P   (3824)
2002/03: 23ᶠG, 26ᴾG, 23³GS, 26ᴾS, 26²HY, 25⁰S, 26ᴾGS,

	Starts	1st	2nd	3rd	Win & Pl
Chases	7	0	1	0	1036
Career Total	15	0	2	1	1888

Going: Sf: 0-3 GS: 0-2 Gd: 0-2 GF: - Fm: 0-0
Distance: 2m/2m3: 0-0 2m4-2m7: 0-0 3m+: 0-7
Track: LH: 0-3 RH: 0-4 Tight: 0-3 Gall: 0-0
Aids: Bl: 0-0 Vi: 0-0 Tstrap: 0-0
Best Rating: 81 1/03 Folk 3m2f heavy Ch

Unlucky not to win at Folkestone in December and looks to have a race in him.

Jurist

(99h)   (83h)**61**
9-y-o b g Then Again-Forest Frolic (Celtic Cone)
B S Rothwell J T Brown

Placings:2/60U5-F   (4227)
2002/03: 25ᶠGF,

	Starts	1st	2nd	3rd	Win & Pl
Chases	1	0	0	0	
Career Total	6	0	1	0	421

Going: Sf: 0-0 GS: 0-0 Gd: 0-0 GF: - Fm: 0-1
Distance: 2m/2m3: 0-0 2m4-2m7: 0-0 3m+: 0-1
Track: LH: 0-1 RH: 0-0 Tight: 0-0 Gall: 0-0
Aids: Bl: 0-0 Vi: 0-0 Tstrap: 0-0
Best Rating: 108 4/99 MRas 1m5f110y soft NHF

Jusful (FR)

69   **46**
6-y-o b g Useful (FR)-Contesty (FR) (Sicyos (USA))
M C Pipe Matt Archer & Miss Jean Broadhurst

Placings:0/PP0P   (0959)
2002/03: 20ᴾGF, 22ᴾGS, 22⁰G, 20ᴾS,

	Starts	1st	2nd	3rd	Win & Pl
Hurdles	4	0	0	0	
Career Total	5	0	0	0	

Going: Sf: 0-1 GS: 0-1 Gd: 0-1 GF: - Fm: 0-1
Distance: 2m/2m3: 0-0 2m4-2m7: 0-4 3m+: 0-0
Track: LH: 0-3 RH: 0-0 Tight: 0-3 Gall: 0-0
Aids: Bl: 0-4 Vi: 0-0 Tstrap: 0-0
Best Rating: 75 3/01 MRas 2m1f110y good NHF

Just A Minute (FR)

108(107h)   (106 h)**106+**
6-y-o b m Le Nain Jaune (FR)-Brave Again (FR) (Pot D Or (FR))
R H Alner H V Perry

Placings:00524-1303P21F   (3947)
2002/03: 17¹G, 20³G, 22⁰GF, 21³GF, 21ᴾG, 25²S, 19¹GS, 19ᶠS,

	Starts	1st	2nd	3rd	Win & Pl
Hurdles	5	1	0	2	3571
Chases	3	1	1	0	5233
Career Total	13	2	2	2	10146

106	12/02	Extr	2m3f110yE Ch		G-S	£4160
104	5/02	Extr	2m1f	E Hdl	GD	£2660

Total win prize-money £6820

Going: Sf: 0-2 GS: 1-1 Gd: 1-3 GF: - Fm: 0-2
Distance: 2m/2m3: 1-1 2m4-2m7: 1-6 3m+: 0-1
Track: LH: 0-3 **RH: 2-5** Tight: 0-3 Gall: 0-0
Aids: Bl: 0-0 Vi: 0-0 Tstrap: 0-0
Best Rating: 106 12/02 Extr 2m3f110y gd-sft Ch

Modest hurdler, stays two and a half miles; won mares only novices chase at Exeter December 2002; acts on any ground.

Just A Touch

106   **96**
7-y-o ch g Rakaposhi King-Minim (Rymer)
P Winkworth D Turnbull, R Robinson, R Scott

Placings:000/F014-P11524   (3809)
2002/03: 16ᴾHY, 19¹GS, 16¹S, 19⁵GS, 17²HY, 16⁴S,

	Starts	1st	2nd	3rd	Win & Pl
Hurdles	6	2	1	0	7315
Career Total	13	3	1	0	10003

96	12/02	Wwck	2m	E(0-110)HHdl	SFT	£3013
79	11/02	Wwck	2m3f	F(0-100)HHdl	G-S	£2488
82	2/02	Folk	2m1f110yF(0-90)HHdl	SFT	£2688

Total win prize-money £8191

Going: Sf: 1-4 GS: 1-2 Gd: 0-0 GF: - Fm: 0-0
Distance: **2m/2m3: 2-5** 2m4-2m7: 0-1 3m+: 0-0
Track: **LH: 2-5** RH: 0-1 Tight: 0-2 Gall: 0-0
Aids: Bl: 0-0 Vi: 0-0 Tstrap: 0-0
Best Rating: 96 2/03 Plum 2m soft Hdl

Moderate handicap hurdler, progressing judged by two victories at Warwick in late 2002; stays two miles three; acts in soft ground.

Just Barney Boy

85(83h)   (48h)**62**
6-y-o b g Past Glories-Pablena (Pablond)

R Nixon G R S Nixon

Placings:44005F-PPPC   (3895)
2002/03: 25ᴾGS, 24ᶠGF, 20ᴾGF, 25ᶜGS,

	Starts	1st	2nd	3rd	Win & Pl
Chases	4	0	0	0	
Career Total	10	0	0	0	0

Going: Sf: 0-0 GS: 0-2 Gd: 0-0 GF: - Fm: 0-2
Distance: 2m/2m3: 0-0 2m4-2m7: 0-1 3m+: 0-3
Track: LH: 0-3 RH: 0-1 Tight: 0-1 Gall: 0-0
Aids: Bl: 0-0 Vi: 0-0 Tstrap: 0-0
Best Rating: 48 12/01 Kels 2m110y gd-sft Hdl

Plating-class chaser; rattled up a hat-trick of points in spring 2003; has found life much tougher under Rules; stays three miles; effective on decent ground.

Just Beth

100   **81**
7-y-o ch m Carlingford Castle-One For The Road (Warpath)
G Fierro G Fierro

Placings:00440/05-P20   (3224)
2002/03: 21ᴾS, 24²S, 27⁰HY,

	Starts	1st	2nd	3rd	Win & Pl
Hurdles	3	0	1	0	758
Career Total	10	0	1	0	758

Going: Sf: 0-3 GS: 0-0 Gd: 0-0 GF: - Fm: 0-0
Distance: 2m/2m3: 0-0 2m4-2m7: 0-1 3m+: 0-2
Track: LH: 0-3 RH: 0-0 Tight: 0-1 Gall: 0-0
Aids: Bl: 0-0 Vi: 0-0 Tstrap: 0-0
Best Rating: 98 3/01 Hntg 2m110y soft NHF

Small mare, just denied in weak handicap hurdle at Uttoxeter in December; looked temperamental when taking a weak novices hurdle at Market Rasen in June; stays three miles.

Just Caramel

99
7-y-o b m Montelimar (USA)-Cream By Post (Torus)
A G Hobbs (P F Nicholls 26/8) Mrs Sue Head

Placings:2/02P2402-P2344PP0   (4149)
2002/03: 22ᴾG, 22²G, 24³GF, 22⁴GF, 22⁴GF, 22ᴾGS, 26ᴾG, 21⁰G,

	Starts	1st	2nd	3rd	Win & Pl
Hurdles	8	0	1	1	1252
Career Total	16	0	5	1	4896

Going: Sf: 0-0 GS: 0-1 Gd: 0-4 GF: - Fm: 0-3
Distance: 2m/2m3: 0-0 2m4-2m7: 0-6 3m+: 0-2
Track: LH: 0-5 RH: 0-3 Tight: 0-3 Gall: 0-1
Aids: Bl: 0-0 Vi: 0-0 Tstrap: 0-0
Best Rating: 100 4/01 Tntn 2m1f gd-fm NHF

Out of a useful point-to-pointer, she has a habit of coming second due to an apparent lack of toe at the business end. Acts on any ground. May do better over fences.

Just Ed

100   **76**
7-y-o ch g Greensmith-Sovereign Maiden (Nearly A Hand)
R Nixon G R S Nixon

Placings:00P50-64P   (1417)
2002/03: 16⁶G, 16⁴G, 22ᴾGF,

	Starts	1st	2nd	3rd	Win & Pl
Hurdles	3	0	0	0	0

Career Total	8	0	0	0	0

Going: Sf: 0-0 GS: 0-0 Gd: 0-2 GF: - Fm: 0-1
Distance: 2m/2m3: 0-2 2m4-2m7: 0-1 3m+: 0-0
Track: LH: 0-3 RH: 0-0 Tight: 0-2 Gall: 0-0
Aids: BI: 0-0 Vi: 0-0 Tstrap: 0-0
Best Rating: 81 5/02 Kels 2m110y good Hdl

Just For Fun (IRE)
82f   87f
5-y-o b g Kahyasi-Copper Breeze (IRE) (Strong Gale)
Ferdy Murphy Northumberland Jumpers

Placings:0   (3890)
2002/03: 16⁰G,

	Starts	1st	2nd	3rd	Win & Pl
NH Flat	1	0	0	0	
Career Total	1	0	0	0	

Going: Sf: 0-0 GS: 0-0 Gd: 0-1 GF: - Fm: 0-0
Distance: 2m/2m3: 0-1 2m4-2m7: 0-0 3m+: 0-0
Track: LH: 0-1 RH: 0-0 Tight: 0-0 Gall: 0-0
Aids: BI: 0-0 Vi: 0-0 Tstrap: 0-0
Best Rating: 87 3/03 Hayd 2m good NHF

Just For Ger (IRE)
101(97h)   (78h)103
9-y-o b g Beau Sher-Reasonar (Reasonable (FR))
J S Goldie Strathayr Publishing Ltd

Placings:000/100000/53U334132-00144   (4588)
2002/03: 20⁰GS, 19⁰G, 16¹S, 16⁴GS, 20⁴G,

	Starts	1st	2nd	3rd	Win & Pl
Hurdles	2	0	0	0	
Chases	3	1	0	0	4558
Career Total	23	3	1	4	15860
103 3/03 Ayr	F(0-95)HCh			SFT	£4225
103 1/02 Muss	2m4f		E(0-110)HCh	SFT	£4192
86 5/00 Dpat	2m1f172y Hdl			GD	£2345
			Total win prize-money £10764		

Going: Sf: 1-1 GS: 0-2 Gd: 0-2 GF: - Fm: 0-0
Distance: 2m/2m3: 1-3 2m4-2m7: 0-2 3m+: 0-0
Track: LH: 1-5 RH: 0-0 Tight: 0-1 Gall: 0-1
Aids: BI: 0-0 Vi: 0-0 Tstrap: 0-0
Best Rating: 103 3/03 Ayr 2m soft Ch

Moderate hurdler/chaser; returned to chasing with victory at Ayr in March; effective at 2m to 2m 4f; likes soft ground.

Just George
71
9-y-o b g Primitive Rising (USA)-Just Jessica (State Diplomacy (USA))
Ms Liz Harrison David Alan Harrison

Placings:PP66PF-PPP   (0785)
2002/03: 25⁰GF, 22⁰G, 26⁰GF,

	Starts	1st	2nd	3rd	Win & Pl
Hurdles	1	0	0	0	0
Chases	2	0	0	0	0
Career Total	9	0	0	0	0

Going: Sf: 0-0 GS: 0-0 Gd: 0-1 GF: - Fm: 0-2
Distance: 2m/2m3: 0-0 2m4-2m7: 0-1 3m+: 0-2
Track: LH: 0-3 RH: 0-0 Tight: 0-1 Gall: 0-0
Aids: BI: 0-1 Vi: 0-0 Tstrap: 0-0
Best Rating: 71 1/02 Carl 3m2f heavy Ch

Just Good Friends (IRE)
72   65
6-y-o b g Shalford (IRE)-Sinfonietta (Foolish Pleasure (USA))
Denys Smith B Batey

Placings:606/6PP05636-0P   (1371)
2002/03: 16⁰GF, 17⁰GF,

	Starts	1st	2nd	3rd	Win & Pl
Hurdles	2	0	0	0	
Career Total	13	0	0	1	368

Going: Sf: 0-0 GS: 0-0 Gd: 0-0 GF: - Fm: 0-2
Distance: 2m/2m3: 0-2 2m4-2m7: 0-0 3m+: 0-0
Track: LH: 0-2 RH: 0-0 Tight: 0-1 Gall: 0-0
Aids: BI: 0-0 Vi: 0-0 Tstrap: 0-0
Best Rating: 75 10/00 Kels 2m110y good Hdl

Poor performer.

Just Henry

6-y-o gr g Arzanni-Silk Touch (Lochnager)
A King Roger Allsop

Placings:0-00   (2073)
2002/03: 16⁰G, 22⁰GS,

	Starts	1st	2nd	3rd	Win & Pl
NH Flat	1	0	0	0	0
Hurdles	1	0	0	0	0
Career Total	3	0	0	0	0

Going: Sf: 0-0 GS: 0-1 Gd: 0-1 GF: - Fm: 0-0
Distance: 2m/2m3: 0-1 2m4-2m7: 0-1 3m+: 0-0
Track: LH: 0-1 RH: 0-1 Tight: 0-0 Gall: 0-0
Aids: BI: 0-0 Vi: 0-0 Tstrap: 0-0
Best Rating: 69 3/02 Hrfd 2m1f soft NHF

Just Hoping
107   96
10-y-o b g Primitive Rising (USA)-Happy Penny (Tower Joy)
Lady Susan Watson Lady Susan Watson

Placings:P4U10-P20P   (0659)
2002/03: 20⁰GF, 16²GS, 16⁰G, 16⁶GF,

	Starts	1st	2nd	3rd	Win & Pl
Chases	4	0	1	0	913
Career Total	9	1	1	0	4306
96 4/02 Weth	2m	E Ch		GD	£3071
			Total win prize-money £3071		

Going: Sf: 0-0 GS: 0-1 Gd: 0-1 GF: - Fm: 0-0
Distance: 2m/2m3: 0-3 2m4-2m7: 0-1 3m+: 0-0
Track: LH: 0-4 RH: 0-0 Tight: 0-1 Gall: 0-0
Aids: BI: 0-0 Vi: 0-0 Tstrap: 0-0
Best Rating: 96 5/02 Fknm 2m110y gd-sft Ch

Novice chaser. Effective with cut in the ground and also acts on good ground. Best at around two miles.

Just In Time
103(108h)   (134h)120
8-y-o b g Night Shift (USA)-Future Past (USA) (Super Concorde (USA))
P J Hobbs B K Peppiatt

Placings:130/113043-1113F   (2056)

2002/03: 17¹G, 17¹GF, 20¹GF, 19³GF, 20⁶G,

	Starts	1st	2nd	3rd	Win & Pl
Chases	5	3	0	1	16191
Career Total	14	6	0	4	34857
120 9/02 Prth	2m4f110yD Ch			G-F	£6760
116 5/02 Strf	2m1f110yD Ch			G-F	£4858
109 5/02 Extr	2m1f110yE Ch			GD	£3737
132 5/01 Prth	2m110y D Hdl			G-F	£3432
128 5/01 Extr	2m1f D Hdl			GD	£3836
118 12/00 Tntn	2m1f D Hdl			SFT	£5211
			Total win prize-money £27837		

Going: Sf: 0-0 GS: 0-0 Gd: 1-2 GF: - Fm: 2-3
Distance: 2m/2m3: 2-3 2m4-2m7: 1-2 3m+: 0-0
Track: LH: 1-1 RH: 2-4 Tight: 1-2 Gall: 0-0
Aids: BI: 0-0 Vi: 0-0 Tstrap: 0-0
Best Rating: 134 6/01 Worc 2m gd-fm Hdl

A one-time decent hurdler, he won his first three starts over fences in the middle of 2002, but built up penalties as a result and then started to struggle. Effective from two to two and a half miles, he will not be easy to place.

Just Jake

10-y-o b g Jendali (USA)-Dohty Baby (Hittite Glory)
Mrs C M Tinkler Mrs C M Tinkler

Placings:000P/P5301/0U01P24512F40/63P342U4434/5
                            (0154)
2002/03: 24⁸G,

	Starts	1st	2nd	3rd	Win & Pl
Chases	1	0	0	0	0
Career Total	34	3	3	4	12801
93 1/00 Sedg	2m5f	F(0-95)HCh		SFT	£2990
83 10/99 Hexm	2m110y F(0-95)HCh			GD	£2678
75 5/99 Hexm	2m	G(0-95)HHdl		GD	£2219
			Total win prize-money £7887		

Going: Sf: 0-0 GS: 0-0 Gd: 0-1 GF: - Fm: 0-0
Distance: 2m/2m3: 0-0 2m4-2m7: 0-0 3m+: 0-1
Track: LH: 0-1 RH: 0-0 Tight: 0-1 Gall: 0-0
Aids: BI: 0-0 Vi: 0-0 Tstrap: 0-0
Best Rating: 93 3/00 Sedg 2m5f gd-fm Ch

Just Jasmine
118   140
11-y-o ch m Nicholas Bill-Linguistic (Porto Bello)
K Bishop Mrs E K Ellis

Placings:64/354/3301F4334/35022111/162/5153P/543232
3-2120U   (3524)
2002/03: 16²GS, 16¹G, 16²HY, 21⁰GS, 17⁰G,

	Starts	1st	2nd	3rd	Win & Pl
Chases	5	1	2	0	24959
Career Total	42	7	7	10	101701
140 11/02 Chel	2m	B HCh		GD	£14811
140 1/01 Tntn	2m3f	D(0-125)HCh		HVY	£6987
130 1/00 Tntn	2m3f	D(0-125)HCh		HVY	£6987
121 4/99 Extr	2m1f110yD(0-120)HCh			SFT	£4138
119 3/99 Uttx	2m5f	C HCh		G-S	£18156
110 2/99 Uttx	2m4f	D Ch		HVY	£5558
94 12/97 Worc	2m	E Hdl		SFT	£2425
			Total win prize-money £59065		

Going: Sf: 0-1 GS: 0-2 Gd: 1-2 GF: - Fm: 0-0
Distance: 2m/2m3: 1-4 2m4-2m7: 0-1 3m+: 0-0
Track: LH: 1-3 RH: 0-2 Tight: 0-0 Gall: 1-3
Aids: BI: 0-0 Vi: 0-0 Tstrap: 0-0
Best Rating: 140 11/02 Asct 2m heavy Ch

A useful mare from two miles to two and a half. Goes well in testing conditions, and ran some good races in useful com-

pany during the 2001/2002 season, but looked in the grip of the Handicapper. Nothing looked to have changed when she finished runner-up on her reappearance, but she finally won a decent prize when beating Lady Cricket at Cheltenham at the Open meeting. She was then a good second at Ascot next time. Suited by the ground good or softer and is usually held up.

Distance: 2m/2m3: 0-0 2m4-2m7: 0-1 3m+: 3-7
Track: LH: 2-4 RH: 1-3 Tight: 2-4 Gall: 0-0
Aids: Bl: 3-5 Vi: 0-0 Tstrap: 0-0
Best Rating: 131 2/03 Uttx 3m2f heavy Ch

Fair staying chaser; stays three miles six; progressing well in 2002/3; best in blinkers; acts on soft ground.

Decent handicap hurdler; made a promising chase debut when winning at Kelso in May 2003; eventually a well beaten second under a penalty by Brother Joe at Worcester next time; narrow winner when faced with an easier task at the same venue the following month. acts on both fast and soft ground; effective over two miles.

Just Jimbo
99   75
7-y-o ch g Karinga Bay-Ruby Green Vii (Damsire Unregistered)
W G M Turner R J Hart

Placings:0/00020   (4358)
2002/03: 17QGS, 17QG, 16QG, 17²HY, 19QF,

	Starts	1st	2nd	3rd	Win & Pl
Hurdles	5	0	1	0	1345
Career Total	6	0	1	0	1345

Going: Sf: 0-1 GS: 0-1 Gd: 0-2 GF: - Fm: 0-1
Distance: 2m/2m3: 0-4 2m4-2m7: 0-1 3m+: 0-0
Track: LH: 0-1 RH: 0-4 Tight: 0-3 Gall: 0-0
Aids: Bl: 0-0 Vi: 0-0 Tstrap: 0-0
Best Rating: 75 3/03 Tntn 2m1f heavy Hdl

Moderate novice hurdler.

Just Lizzie
117
10-y-o b m Rakaposhi King-Kilglass (Fidel)
R Nixon G R S Nixon

Placings:66/061561341100/063/FF2305P010/600041244-F
(0070)
2002/03: 23FG,

	Starts	1st	2nd	3rd	Win & Pl
Hurdles	1	0	0	0	
Career Total	37	6	2	3	28766
112 3/02 Ayr	2m4f	D(0-125)HHdl	HVY	£3500	
117 4/01 Weth	2m4f110yB(0-145)HHdl	G-S	£5421		
101 2/99 Carl	2m1f	D(0-125)HHdl	HVY	£5706	
100 1/99 Catt	2m	F(0-110)HHdl	SFT	£2374	
97 11/98 Hexm	2m	F(0-100)HHdl	HVY	£2469	
83 6/98 Hexm	2m	E Hdl	HVY	£2469	
		Total win prize-money	£21663		

Going: Sf: 0-0 GS: 0-0 Gd: 0-1 GF: - Fm: 0-0
Distance: 2m/2m3: 0-0 2m4-2m7: 0-0 3m+: 0-1
Track: LH: 0-1 RH: 0-0 Tight: 0-0 Gall: 0-0
Aids: Bl: 0-0 Vi: 0-0 Tstrap: 0-0
Best Rating: 117 4/01 Weth 2m4f110y gd-sft Hdl

A useful handicap hurdler. Suited by two and a half miles and testing conditions. Does not want firm ground.

Just Maybe (IRE)
107(102h)   (97h)**131**
9-y-o b g Glacial Storm (USA)-Purlace (Realm)
Miss Venetia Williams W E Prichard

Placings:0/0U40P/5F022-4355111P   (4172)
2002/03: 25⁴G, 22³GS, 29⁵S, 32⁵GS, 30¹S, 27¹S, 26¹HY, 34PS,

	Starts	1st	2nd	3rd	Win & Pl
Chases	8	3	0	1	28003
Career Total	19	3	2	1	29915
131 2/03 Uttx	3m2f	B HCh	HVY	£12810	
125 1/03 Tntn	3m3f	C(0-130)HCh	SFT	£8151	
119 12/02 Bang	3m6f	D(0-120)HCh	SFT	£5434	
		Total win prize-money	£26395		

Going: Sf: 3-5 GS: 0-2 Gd: 0-1 GF: - Fm: 0-0

Just Midas
106   66+
5-y-o b g Merdon Melody-Thabeh (Shareef Dancer (USA))
N A Smith D G & D J Robinson

Placings:06-00   (4733)
2002/03: 16QG, 16QGF,

	Starts	1st	2nd	3rd	Win & Pl
Hurdles	2	0	0	0	
Career Total	4	0	0	0	0

Going: Sf: 0-0 GS: 0-0 Gd: 0-1 GF: - Fm: 0-1
Distance: 2m/2m3: 0-2 2m4-2m7: 0-0 3m+: 0-0
Track: LH: 0-2 RH: 0-0 Tight: 0-0 Gall: 0-0
Aids: Bl: 0-0 Vi: 0-0 Tstrap: 0-0
Best Rating: 70 11/01 Catt 2m gd-fm Hdl

Poor selling hurdler; narrow winner at Uttoxeter in July 2003 on first outing for Martin Pipe.

Just Muckin Around (IRE)
96(102h)   (70h)**84**
7-y-o gr g Celio Rufo-Cousin Muck (IRE) (Henbit (USA))
R H Buckler Twentyman

Placings:05PP-46BFP42   (4699)
2002/03: 22⁴G, 18⁶GF, 19⁸G, 20⁶GS, 22PHY, 22⁴S, 17²GF,

	Starts	1st	2nd	3rd	Win & Pl
Hurdles	4	0	0	0	0
Chases	3	0	1	0	739
Career Total	11	0	1	0	739

Going: Sf: 0-2 GS: 0-1 Gd: 0-2 GF: - Fm: 0-2
Distance: 2m/2m3: 0-2 2m4-2m7: 0-5 3m+: 0-0
Track: LH: 0-6 RH: 0-1 Tight: 0-6 Gall: 0-0
Aids: Bl: 0-0 Vi: 0-0 Tstrap: 0-0
Best Rating: 84 4/03 Plum 2m1f gd-fm Ch

Plating-class chaser/hurdler; yet to win a race; best effort when runner-up in a poor selling chase at Plumpton in April 2003; suited by decent ground; stays two miles six.

Just Murphy (IRE)
105(109h)   (126 h)**124**
5-y-o b g Namaqualand (USA)-Bui-Doi (IRE) (Dance Of Life (USA))
N J Henderson Raymond Tooth

Placings:4513-23350   (4441)
2002/03: 18²GF, 16⁹GS, 16³S, 20⁵G, 20⁹G,

	Starts	1st	2nd	3rd	Win & Pl
Hurdles	5	0	1	2	4349
Career Total	9	1	1	3	9238
126 3/02 Hrfd	2m1f	D Hdl	SFT	£3575	
		Total win prize-money	£3575		

Going: Sf: 0-1 GS: 0-1 Gd: 0-2 GF: - Fm: 0-1
Distance: 2m/2m3: 0-3 2m4-2m7: 0-2 3m+: 0-0
Track: LH: 0-1 RH: 0-4 Tight: 0-1 Gall: 0-0
Aids: Bl: 0-0 Vi: 0-0 Tstrap: 0-0
Best Rating: 126 1/03 Winc 2m gd-sft Hdl

Just Nobby
8-y-o b g Totem (USA)-Loving Doll (Godswalk (USA))
A E Jones Graham Brown

Placings:0/00/P   (0243)
2002/03: 23PG,

	Starts	1st	2nd	3rd	Win & Pl
Chases	1	0	0	0	
Career Total	4	0	0	0	

Going: Sf: 0-0 GS: 0-0 Gd: 0-1 GF: - Fm: 0-0
Distance: 2m/2m3: 0-0 2m4-2m7: 0-0 3m+: 0-1
Track: LH: 0-0 RH: 0-1 Tight: 0-0 Gall: 0-0
Aids: Bl: 0-0 Vi: 0-0 Tstrap: 0-0
Best Rating: 59 10/99 Ludl 2m gd-fm Hdl

Just Reuben (IRE)
108   58
8-y-o gr g Roselier (FR)-Sharp Mama Vii (Damsire Unregistered)
C Tizzard Alvin Trowbridge

Placings:F04P2345-F25453   (4717)
2002/03: 22FS, 20²GS, 23⁵G, 26⁴GF, 25⁵G, 25³F,

	Starts	1st	2nd	3rd	Win & Pl
Chases	6	0	1	1	3729
Career Total	14	0	2	2	5745

Going: Sf: 0-1 GS: 0-1 Gd: 0-2 GF: - Fm: 0-2
Distance: 2m/2m3: 0-2 2m4-2m7: 0-2 3m+: 0-4
Track: LH: 0-3 RH: 0-2 Tight: 0-3 Gall: 0-0
Aids: Bl: 0-0 Vi: 0-0 Tstrap: 0-0
Best Rating: 80 2/03 Plum 2m4f gd-sft Ch

Plating-class chaser; stays three miles plus; effective on good ground.

Just Sal
104   82
7-y-o b m Silly Prices-Hanim (IRE) (Hatim (USA))
R Nixon G R S Nixon

Placings:5030P00-64P0234501P6   (4750)
2002/03: 16⁶G, 20⁴GF, 24PGS, 22QS, 22²S, 23³HY, 21⁴HY, 20⁵HY, 17QHY, 16¹S, 20PG, 24⁶G,

	Starts	1st	2nd	3rd	Win & Pl
Hurdles	12	1	1	1	5007
Career Total	19	1	1	2	5231
82 3/03 Hexm	2m110y	E(0-110)HHdl	SFT	£3395	
		Total win prize-money	£3395		

Going: Sf: 1-7 GS: 0-1 Gd: 0-3 GF: - Fm: 0-1
Distance: 2m/2m3: 1-3 2m4-2m7: 0-7 3m+: 0-2
Track: LH: 1-9 RH: 0-3 Tight: 0-5 Gall: 0-0
Aids: Bl: 0-0 Vi: 0-0 Tstrap: 0-0
Best Rating: 88 11/01 Carl 2m1f soft NHF

Plating-class hurdler; best at around two miles; acts on soft ground.

Just Sally

80f   **47f**

5-y-o b m Afzal-Hatherley (Deep Run)
J D Frost Mrs G A Robarts

Placings:0-0   **(0248)**
2002/03: 17⁰G,

	Starts	1st	2nd	3rd	Win & Pl
NH Flat	1	0	0	0	
Career Total	2	0	0	0	

Going:	Sf: 0-0 GS: 0-0 Gd: 0-0 GF: - Fm: 0-0
Distance:	2m/2m3: 0-1 2m4-2m7: 0-0 3m+: 0-0
Track:	LH: 0-0 RH: 0-1 Tight: 0-0 Gall: 0-0
Aids:	Bl: 0-0 Vi: 0-0 Tstrap: 0-0
Best Rating:	62 5/02 Extr 2m1f good NHF

Just Serenade

92   **79+**

4-y-o ch f Factual (USA)-Thimbalina (Salmon Leap (USA))
M J Ryan William Dixon

Placings:1   **(1174)**
2002/03: 16¹GF,

	Starts	1st	2nd	3rd	Win & Pl
Hurdles	1	1	0	0	4238
Career Total	1	1	0	0	4238
79 9/02 Strf	2m110y	D Hdl		G-F	£4238

Total win prize-money £4238

Going:	Sf: 0-0 GS: 0-0 Gd: 0-0 GF: - Fm: 1-1
Distance:	2m/2m3: 1-1 2m4-2m7: 0-0 3m+: 0-0
Track:	LH: 1-1 RH: 0-0 Tight: 1-1 Gall: 0-0
Aids:	Bl: 0-0 Vi: 0-0 Tstrap: 0-0
Best Rating:	79 9/02 Strf 2m110y gd-fm Hdl

Just So Jolly

63   **16**

9-y-o b g Joligeneration-Military Star Vii (Damsire Unregistered)
Lady Susan Watson Lady Susan Watson

Placings:P0F00   **(4591)**
2002/03: 19²G, 16⁰G, 16⁵G, 17⁰G, 16⁰G,

	Starts	1st	2nd	3rd	Win & Pl
Hurdles	5	0	0	0	
Career Total	5	0	0	0	

Going:	Sf: 0-1 GS: 0-1 Gd: 0-3 GF: - Fm: 0-0
Distance:	2m/2m3: 0-4 2m4-2m7: 0-1 3m+: 0-0
Track:	LH: 0-5 RH: 0-0 Tight: 0-0 Gall: 0-0
Aids:	Bl: 0-0 Vi: 0-0 Tstrap: 0-0
Best Rating:	16 2/03 Catt 2m good Hdl

Just Sooty

95   **92**

8-y-o br g Be My Native (USA)-March Fly (Sousa)
N G Richards David Wesley Yates

Placings:0/3/62F5-5   **(1011)**
2002/03: 20⁵G,

	Starts	1st	2nd	3rd	Win & Pl
Hurdles	1	0	0	0	0
Career Total	7	0	1	1	1070

Going:	Sf: 0-0 GS: 0-0 Gd: 0-1 GF: - Fm: 0-0

Distance:	2m/2m3: 0-0 2m4-2m7: 0-1 3m+: 0-0
Track:	LH: 0-0 RH: 0-1 Tight: 0-0 Gall: 0-0
Aids:	Bl: 0-0 Vi: 0-0 Tstrap: 0-0
Best Rating:	92 11/01 Newc 2m4f good Hdl

Lightly-raced plating-class hurdler, he favours holding-up tactics.

Just Strong (IRE)

106   **89**

10-y-o b/br g Strong Gale-Just Dont Know (Buckskin (FR))
Mrs A M Naughton Miss J M Thompson

Placings:301/P/44PPP14-264535   **(4619)**
2002/03: 25²GS, 24⁶GS, 24⁴GF, 25⁵G, 20³G, 24⁵GF,

	Starts	1st	2nd	3rd	Win & Pl
Chases	6	0	1	1	2193
Career Total	17	2	1	2	11042
94 4/02 Carl	2m4f	E(0-110)HCh		G-F	£3542
78 4/00 MRas	3m1f	D Ch		G-F	£4371

Total win prize-money £7914

Going:	Sf: 0-0 GS: 0-2 Gd: 0-2 GF: - Fm: 0-2
Distance:	2m/2m3: 0-0 2m4-2m7: 0-1 3m+: 0-5
Track:	LH: 0-3 RH: 0-3 Tight: 0-2 Gall: 0-0
Aids:	Bl: 0-0 Vi: 0-0 Tstrap: 0-0
Best Rating:	97 5/02 Weth 3m1f gd-sft Ch

Modest and inconsistent chaser, stays three miles, best on fast ground in the spring.

Just Superb

4-y-o ch g Superlative-Just Greenwich (Chilibang)
P A Pritchard D R Pritchard

Placings:0P0   **(4641)**
2002/03: 16⁰HY, 16⁰HY, 19⁰GF,

	Starts	1st	2nd	3rd	Win & Pl
Hurdles	3	0	0	0	
Career Total	3	0	0	0	

Going:	Sf: 0-2 GS: 0-0 Gd: 0-0 GF: - Fm: 0-1
Distance:	2m/2m3: 0-3 2m4-2m7: 0-0 3m+: 0-0
Track:	LH: 0-2 RH: 0-1 Tight: 0-1 Gall: 0-0
Aids:	Bl: 0-0 Vi: 0-0 Tstrap: 0-0
Best Rating:	0 4/03 Strf 2m3f gd-fm Hdl

Just The Jobe

95f   **94f**

5-y-o gr g Roselier (FR)-Radical Lady (Radical)
N B Mason N B Mason

Placings:264   **(1709)**
2002/03: 16²GF, 16⁶GF, 17⁴G,

	Starts	1st	2nd	3rd	Win & Pl
NH Flat	3	0	1	0	539
Career Total	3	0	1	0	539

Going:	Sf: 0-0 GS: 0-0 Gd: 0-1 GF: - Fm: 0-2
Distance:	2m/2m3: 0-3 2m4-2m7: 0-0 3m+: 0-0
Track:	LH: 0-3 RH: 0-0 Tight: 0-0 Gall: 0-0
Aids:	Bl: 0-0 Vi: 0-0 Tstrap: 0-0
Best Rating:	94 10/02 Sedg 2m1f good NHF

A half-brother to Red Imp. Showed plenty of promise for the future when second to the useful Dusty Too in a Worcester bumper August 2002.

Just Tom

97(92h)   (97h)**72**

8-y-o ch g Primitive Rising (USA)-Edenburt (Bargello)
Jedd O Keeffe Mrs A J Findlay

Placings:630/006-3P   **(1985)**
2002/03: 25³GF, 21⁴PS,

	Starts	1st	2nd	3rd	Win & Pl
Chases	2	0	0	1	624
Career Total	8	0	0	2	804

Going:	Sf: 0-1 GS: 0-0 Gd: 0-0 GF: - Fm: 0-1
Distance:	2m/2m3: 0-0 2m4-2m7: 0-1 3m+: 0-1
Track:	LH: 0-2 RH: 0-0 Tight: 0-1 Gall: 0-0
Aids:	Bl: 0-0 Vi: 0-0 Tstrap: 0-0
Best Rating:	97 1/02 Weth 2m gd-sft Hdl

Just Whiskey (IRE)

10-y-o b g Satco (FR)-Illinois Belle (Le Bavard (FR))
N A Twiston-Davies Mrs R Vaughan

Placings:0/3/0P/44/21-PP   **(3500)**
2002/03: 20⁰PS, 24⁰PGS,

	Starts	1st	2nd	3rd	Win & Pl
Chases	2	0	0	0	
Career Total	10	1	1	1	5834
100 10/01 Plum	3m2f	D(0-110)HCh		SFT	£4095

Total win prize-money £4095

Going:	Sf: 0-1 GS: 0-1 Gd: 0-0 GF: - Fm: 0-0
Distance:	2m/2m3: 0-0 2m4-2m7: 0-1 3m+: 0-1
Track:	LH: 0-1 RH: 0-1 Tight: 0-0 Gall: 0-0
Aids:	Bl: 0-0 Vi: 0-0 Tstrap: 0-0
Best Rating:	115 4/99 Ayr 2m soft NHF

Justin Mac (IRE)

106   **77**

12-y-o br g Satco (FR)-Quantas (Roan Rocket)
Mrs H Dalton Mrs Caroline Shaw

Placings:121143/P14350P/512F4P0/1RP/6U1P-415205   **(4160)**
2002/03: 16⁴GF, 21¹S, 20⁵G, 20²GF, 20⁰GS, 20⁵GS,

	Starts	1st	2nd	3rd	Win & Pl
Chases	6	1	1	0	11412
Career Total	33	8	3	2	34321
110 5/02 NAbb	2m5f110yB HCh			SFT	£10067
105 3/02 Leic	2m	H Ch		SFT	£2198
100 2/01 Fknm	2m5f110yH Ch			SFT	£2256
118 11/99 Carl	2m1f	F(0-110)HHdl		SFT	£5281
132 11/98 Kels	2m110y	D(0-125)HHdl		SFT	£2731
114 12/97 Weth	2m	D Hdl		SFT	£3323
113 11/97 Aint	2m110y	H NHF		G-S	£1987
113 10/97 Sedg	2m1f	H NHF		G-F	£1213

Total win prize-money £29059

Going:	Sf: 1-1 GS: 0-2 Gd: 0-1 GF: - Fm: 0-2
Distance:	2m/2m3: 0-1 **2m4-2m7:** 1-5 3m+: 0-0
Track:	LH: 1-4 RH: 0-2 Tight: 1-3 Gall: 0-1
Aids:	Bl: 0-0 Vi: 0-0 Tstrap: 0-1
Best Rating:	132 11/98 Kels 2m110y soft Hdl

Appears to go on any ground; won the 21 furlong handicap hunter chase on soft ground at Newton Abbot May 2002; does not quite get three miles.

Justjim

103   **113**

11-y-o b g Derring Rose-Crystal Run Vii (Damsire Unregistered)
Mrs H Dalton E T Clarke

Placings:000/P0650/6/1411/62012B6PF2P/23P4PP-4PPP
(1245)
2002/03: 20⁴G, 24ᴾS, 23ᴾGF, 24ᴾG,

	Starts	1st	2nd	3rd	Win & Pl
Hurdles	1	0	0	0	0
Chases	3	0	0	0	313
Career Total	34	4	4	1	23123
110 8/00 Bang	3m110y	D(0-125)HCh		GD	£4914
106 8/99 Worc	2m7f110yE(0-125)HCh			SFT	£2966
85 8/99 Bang	2m4f110yF(0-100)HCh			GD	£4338
87 7/99 Worc	2m	F(0-100)HCh		G-F	£2672
				Total win prize-money	£14891

Going: Sf: 0-1 GS: 0-0 Gd: 0-2 GF: - Fm: 0-1
Distance: 2m2/m3: 0-0 2m4-2m7: 0-0 3m+: 0-3
Track: LH: 0-4 RH: 0-0 Tight: 0-0 Gall: 0-0
Aids: Bl: 0-0 Vi: 0-0 Tstrap: 0-0
Best Rating: 113 11/01 Newb 2m4f   good   Ch

He is not all that consistent, but shows fair form in modest staying chases. He has won on soft ground, but looks better on fast and shows his best form in the summer.

Kabeer

55f   **95f**

5-y-o ch g Unfuwain (USA)-Ta Rib (USA) (Mr Prospector (USA))
Julian Poulton Placida Racing

Placings:2
(4685)
2002/03: 16²GF,

	Starts	1st	2nd	3rd	Win & Pl
NH Flat	1	0	1	0	552
Career Total	1	0	1	0	552

Going: Sf: 0-0 GS: 0-0 Gd: 0-0 GF: - Fm: 0-1
Distance: 2m2/m3: 0-1 2m4-2m7: 0-0 3m+: 0-0
Track: LH: 0-0 RH: 0-1 Tight: 0-0 Gall: 0-1
Aids: Bl: 0-0 Vi: 0-0 Tstrap: 0-0
Best Rating: 95 4/03 Hntg 2m110y   gd-fm   NHF

Classically-bred but sold cheaply; runner-up behind clear cut winner in weak bumper on debut at Huntingdon in April.

Kadara (IRE)

110   **113+**

4-y-o b f Slip Anchor-Kadassa (IRE) (Shardari)
R H Alner (A De Royer-Dupre 8/9) Mrs Norma Kelly

Placings:16P
(3495)
2002/03: 16¹S, 17⁶GS, 16ᴾGS,

	Starts	1st	2nd	3rd	Win & Pl
Hurdles	3	1	0	0	7062
Career Total	3	1	0	0	7062
111 12/02 Kemp	2m	C Hdl		SFT	£6612
				Total win prize-money	£6612

Going: Sf: 1-1 GS: 0-2 Gd: 0-0 GF: - Fm: 0-0
Distance: 2m2/m3: 1-3 2m4-2m7: 0-0 3m+: 0-0
Track: LH: 0-1 RH: 1-2 Tight: 0-0 Gall: 0-1
Aids: Bl: 0-0 Vi: 0-0 Tstrap: 0-0
Best Rating: 111 12/02 Kemp 2m   soft   Hdl

Fair hurdler; won first time out; excuses since; effective in soft ground.

Kadarann (IRE)

113   **166**

6-y-o b g Bigstone (IRE)-Kadassa (IRE) (Shardari)
P F Nicholls Notalotterry

Placings:121P/1101211-U2110313
(4556)
2002/03: 16ᵁF, 18²S, 16¹G, 17¹G, 16⁹G, 20³G, 20¹G, 16³G,

	Starts	1st	2nd	3rd	Win & Pl
Chases	8	3	1	2	83161
Career Total	19	10	3	2	132683
145 4/03 Ayr	2m4f	B HCh		GD	£13491
166 2/03 Newb	2m1f	A Ch		GD	£31000
158 12/02 Chel	2m110y	B(0-145)HCh		GD	£14101
147 4/02 Prth	2m	C Ch		GD	£7124
145 4/02 Ayr	2m	B HCh		GD	£13403
145 3/02 Winc	2m	D Ch		SFT	£4134
136 2/02 Winc	2m	C Ch		G-S	£6288
132 11/01 Wwck	2m110y	C Ch		GD	£6753
128 12/00 Fknm	2m	E Hdl		G-S	£2257
120 10/00 Chel	2m110y	C Hdl		GD	£5486
				Total win prize-money	£104041

Going: Sf: 0-1 GS: 0-0 Gd: 3-6 GF: - Fm: 0-1
Distance: 2m2/m3: 2-6 2m4-2m7: 1-2 3m+: 0-0
Track: LH: 3-7 RH: 0-0 Tight: 0-1 Gall: 2-3
Aids: Bl: 0-0 Vi: 0-0 Tstrap: 0-0
Best Rating: 166 2/03 Newb 2m1f   good   Ch

Top-class chaser; very useful novice in 2001/2, but was well beaten in the Arkle at Cheltenham; gained his most notable success to date when accounting for stablemate Cenkos (giving 6lb) by 8l in the Game Spirit Chase at Newbury in February 2003, but was most disappointing in the 2003 Champion Chase; won handicap at Ayr in April but disappointing when turned out a day later; travels well; best form over 2m; ideally suited to a sound surface; reportedly much stronger horse this term and appears to have made significant improvement.

Kadito

99(103h)   (104 h)**115+**

7-y-o b g Petoski-Kadastra (FR) (Stradavinsky)
R Dickin A P Paton

Placings:4/02500U0450-1104133
(4150)
2002/03: 19¹S, 19¹S, 17⁶S, 20⁴HY, 19¹G, 19³G, 20³G,

	Starts	1st	2nd	3rd	Win & Pl
Hurdles	5	2	0	1	7909
Chases	2	1	0	1	5184
Career Total	18	3	1	2	14044
115 2/03 Hrfd	2m3f	E(0-100)HCh		GD	£4576
104 12/02 Wwck	2m3f	E(0-100)HHdl		SFT	£3024
104 11/02 Hrfd	2m3f110yE(0-100)HHdl			SFT	£3571
				Total win prize-money	£11172

Going: Sf: 2-4 GS: 0-0 Gd: 1-3 GF: - Fm: 0-0
Distance: 2m2/m3: 2-3 2m4-2m7: 1-4 3m+: 0-0
Track: LH: 1-3 RH: 2-4 Tight: 0-0 Gall: 0-1
Aids: Bl: 0-0 Vi: 0-0 Tstrap: 0-0
Best Rating: 115 2/03 Hrfd 2m3f   good   Ch

Modest winning hurdler; successful on chasing debut in February 2003; suited by cut in the ground; effective at up to two and a half miles.

Kadlass (FR)

105   **96**

8-y-o b g Kadounor (FR)-Brave Lass (Ridan)
Mrs D A Hamer J L Flint

Placings:6525/21
(4486)
2002/03: 17²S, 17¹GF,

	Starts	1st	2nd	3rd	Win & Pl
Hurdles	2	1	1	0	3337
Career Total	6	1	2	0	4057
89 4/03 Hrfd	2m1f	G Hdl		G-F	£2625
				Total win prize-money	£2625

Going: Sf: 0-1 GS: 0-0 Gd: 0-0 GF: - Fm: 1-1
Distance: 2m2/m3: 1-2 2m4-2m7: 0-0 3m+: 0-0
Track: LH: 0-0 RH: 1-2 Tight: 0-0 Gall: 0-0
Aids: Bl: 0-0 Vi: 0-0 Tstrap: 0-0
Best Rating: 105 12/99 Kemp 2m   soft   Hdl

Plating-class hurdler; ex-pointer; won extended two mile seller at Hereford on good to firm ground April 2003; acts in soft ground.

Kadou Nonantais (FR)

132

10-y-o b g Cadoudal (FR)-Belle Nonantaise (FR) (Charonville (FR))
O Sherwood D & G Mercer

Placings:11511/0111211F/PPP/PP54/33534P3F-F (1999)
2002/03: 24ᶠS,

	Starts	1st	2nd	3rd	Win & Pl
Chases	1	0	0	0	
Career Total	29	9	1	4	54778
151 2/99 Newb	3m	C Ch		G-S	£5995
148 1/99 Weth	3m1f	A Ch		HVY	£13720
143 12/98 Ling	2m4f110yC(0-135)HCh			SFT	£4889
119 11/98 Uttx	2m	D Ch		SFT	£3737
126 11/98 Uttx	2m	D Ch		SFT	£3566
132 4/98 Ayr	2m	C Hdl		GD	£4380
137 3/98 Bang	2m1f	E Hdl		G-S	£2285
116 12/97 Wwck	2m	E Hdl		SFT	£2962
108 12/97 Hrfd	2m1f	H NHF		GD	£1030
				Total win prize-money	£42568

Going: Sf: 0-1 GS: 0-0 Gd: 0-0 GF: - Fm: 0-0
Distance: 2m2/m3: 0-0 2m4-2m7: 0-0 3m+: 0-1
Track: LH: 0-1 RH: 0-0 Tight: 0-0 Gall: 0-0
Aids: Bl: 0-1 Vi: 0-0 Tstrap: 0-0
Best Rating: 151 2/99 Newb 3m   gd-sft   Ch

He has failed to recapture the promise of his early performances since taking a crashing fall in the William Hill Handicap Chase at the 1999 Cheltenham Festival. Best around three miles, he showed slight signs of a recovery in 2001 and ran his best race this year in the Peter Marsh Chase, but he remains one to treat with caution. Runs in blinkers or visor these days and suited by an easy surface.

Kadouko (FR)

107   **101**

10-y-o b g Cadoudal (FR)-Perle Bleue (FR) (Iron Duke (FR))
J Howard Johnson G F Bear

Placings:33/33160/26F25/11545/365453P-531
(3990)
2002/03: 17⁵HY, 16³HY, 16¹S,

	Starts	1st	2nd	3rd	Win & Pl
Chases	3	1	0	1	5179
Career Total	27	4	2	7	23172
102 3/03 Carl	2m	E(0-105)HCh		SFT	£4556
118 12/00 Thur	2m2f	(0-109)HCh		HVY	£5520
114 11/00 Thur	2m2f	Ch		HVY	£4140
104 1/99 Fair	2m2f	Hdl		HVY	£3069
				Total win prize-money	£17286

Going: Sf: 1-3 GS: 0-0 Gd: 0-0 GF: - Fm: 0-0
Distance: 2m2/m3: 1-3 2m4-2m7: 0-0 3m+: 0-0
Track: LH: 0-2 RH: 1-1 Tight: 0-0 Gall: 0-0
Aids: Bl: 0-0 Vi: 0-0 Tstrap: 0-0

Best Rating: 118 12/00 Thur 2m2f   heavy   Ch

A winner over hurdles and fences, he is suited by heavy ground and is possibly best going right-handed.

Kafri D'Airy (FR)

(90h)   (78h)
5-y-o b m Sheyrann-Afrika D Airy (FR) (Marasali)
R T Phillips (J Ortet 10/5) Mrs Claire Smith

Placings: 322P-466   (3934)
2002/03: 17⁴S, 19⁶GS, 20⁶S,

	Starts	1st	2nd	3rd	Win & Pl
Hurdles	2	0	0	0	
Chases	1	0	0	0	2448
Career Total	7	0	2	1	12060

Going: Sf: 0-2 GS: 0-1 Gd: 0-0 GF: - Fm: 0-0
Distance: 2m/2m3: 0-2 2m4-2m7: 0-1 3m+: 0-0
Track: LH: 0-0 RH: 0-1 Tight: 0-1 Gall: 0-0
Aids: Bl: 0-0 Vi: 0-0 Tstrap: 0-0
Best Rating: 78   3/03   Font   2m4f   soft   Hdl

Kagram (IRE)
77   36+
8-y-o ch g Roi Danzig (USA)-Mexican-Two-Step (Gay Fandango (USA))
Ferdy Murphy Mrs E A Kettlewell & F Murphy

Placings: 44/0/0   (4435)
2002/03: 20⁰G,

	Starts	1st	2nd	3rd	Win & Pl
Hurdles	1	0	0	0	
Career Total	4	0	0	0	342

Going: Sf: 0-0 GS: 0-0 Gd: 0-1 GF: - Fm: 0-0
Distance: 2m/2m3: 0-0 2m4-2m7: 0-1 3m+: 0-0
Track: LH: 0-1 RH: 0-0 Tight: 0-0 Gall: 0-1
Aids: Bl: 0-0 Vi: 0-0 Tstrap: 0-0
Best Rating: 104   3/00   Carl   2m1f   gd-sft   NHF

Kahuna (IRE)
107f   123f
6-y-o b g Mister Lord (USA)-My Baloo (On Your Mark)
E Sheehy Mrs Roisin Sheehy

Placings: 120   (4115)
2002/03: 16¹HY, 16²YS, 16⁰G,

	Starts	1st	2nd	3rd	Win & Pl
NH Flat	3	1	1	0	6854
Career Total	3	1	1	0	6854
118 12/02 Leop	2m		NHF		HVY £5503

Total win prize-money £5503

Going: Sf: 1-1 GS: 0-0 Gd: 0-1 GF: - Fm: 0-0
Distance: 2m/2m3: 1-3 2m4-2m7: 0-0 3m+: 0-0
Track: LH: 0-1 RH: 0-0 Tight: 0-0 Gall: 0-0
Aids: Bl: 0-0 Vi: 0-0 Tstrap: 0-0
Best Rating: 123   1/03   Leop   2m   yld-sft   NHF

Kaid (IRE)
109(101h)   (99 h)93
8-y-o b g Alzao (USA)-Very Charming (USA) (Vaguely Noble)
R Lee Richard Lee

Placings: 6/452/021264/004526P0-3022P160   (4194)
2002/03: 17³G, 20⁰GS, 21²GF, 20²G, 19⁰GF, 17¹S, 19⁶S, 21⁰G,

	Starts	1st	2nd	3rd	Win & Pl
Hurdles	4	1	0	0	2044
Chases	4	0	2	1	2979
Career Total	26	2	6	1	11692
99 11/02 Hrfd	2m1f	G(0-95)HHdl		SFT	£2044
106 11/00 Hrfd	2m1f	E(0-105)HHdl		SFT	£2607

Total win prize-money £4652

Going: Sf: 1-2 GS: 0-1 Gd: 0-3 GF: - Fm: 0-2
Distance: 2m/2m3: 1-3 2m4-2m7: 0-5 3m+: 0-0
Track: LH: 0-4 RH: 1-4 Tight: 0-3 Gall: 0-0
Aids: Bl: 0-0 Vi: 0-0 Tstrap: 0-0
Best Rating: 112 11/00 Weth 2m   heavy   Hdl

Plating-class hurdler/chaser; acts on soft and fast ground; best at 2m 4f.

Kaikovra (IRE)
106   105d
7-y-o ch g Toulon-Dreffiane Supreme (Rusticaro (FR))
Noel T Chance B Andrews,C Potter & D Archard

Placings: 02134/P6265F6-403222   (4721)
2002/03: 17⁴G, 16⁰G, 16³G, 16²G, 17²GF, 16⁶F,

	Starts	1st	2nd	3rd	Win & Pl
Hurdles	6	0	3	1	4905
Career Total	18	1	5	2	10689
103 10/00 Fknm	2m		H NHF		GD £1463

Total win prize-money £1463

Going: Sf: 0-0 GS: 0-0 Gd: 0-4 GF: - Fm: 0-2
Distance: 2m/2m3: 0-6 2m4-2m7: 0-0 3m+: 0-0
Track: LH: 0-3 RH: 0-3 Tight: 0-4 Gall: 0-0
Aids: Bl: 0-0 Vi: 0-0 Tstrap: 0-0
Best Rating: 105 4/03 Hrfd 2m1f   gd-fm Hdl

Won Fakenham bumper in October 2000; disappointing maiden hurdler; suited by fast ground; best over two miles.

Kaiserstolz (GER)
100   91
10-y-o b g Sure Blade (USA)-Kaisertreue (GER) (Luciano)
Ian Williams Favourites Racing

Placings: 351P13/1002F5UP/00-510   (0987)
2002/03: 16⁵GF, 20¹GF, 21⁰GF,

	Starts	1st	2nd	3rd	Win & Pl
Hurdles	3	1	0	0	2632
Career Total	19	4	1	2	16901
115 6/02 Worc	2m4f	E(0-110)HHdl		G-F	£2632
127 5/00 Aint	2m110y	B(0-145)HHdl		G-F	£7039
109 4/00 Sedg	2m1f	E Hdl		GD	£2492
116 2/00 Sedg	2m1f	E Hdl		G-S	£2537

Total win prize-money £14702

Going: Sf: 0-0 GS: 0-0 Gd: 0-0 GF: - Fm: 1-3
Distance: 2m/2m3: 0-1 2m4-2m7: 1-2 3m+: 0-0
Track: LH: 1-3 RH: 0-0 Tight: 0-1 Gall: 0-0
Aids: Bl: 0-0 Vi: 0-0 Tstrap: 1-3
Best Rating: 127 5/00 Aint 2m110y gd-fm Hdl

Formerly useful on the Flat in Germany, he won easily at Sedgefield but was out of his depth at the Festival.

Kaki Crazy (FR)
109(109h)   (128 h)133
8-y-o b g Passing Sale (FR)-Radiante Rose (FR) (Akarad (FR))
M C Pipe Archie Gooch

Placings: 15P311F1034P/V515526FP104/64P54F0/412PU
4503-P5   (3946)
2002/03: 30⁵PS, 30⁵S,

	Starts	1st	2nd	3rd	Win & Pl
Chases	2	0	0	0	469
Career Total	42	7	2	3	85397
127 5/01 Bang	3m6f	D(0-125)HCh		GD	£5551
2/00 Autl	2m5f	HCh		HVY	£14409
7/99 Claf	2m1f	HCh		GD	£5920
12/98 Autl	2m2f	Hdl		HVY	£6566
11/98 Autl	2m2f	Hdl		HVY	£6566
10/98 Autl	2m2f	Hdl		HLD	£6566
8/98 Claf	2m	Hdl		VS	£4040

Total win prize-money £49618

Going: Sf: 0-2 GS: 0-0 Gd: 0-0 GF: - Fm: 0-0
Distance: 2m/2m3: 0-2 2m4-2m7: 0-0 3m+: 0-2
Track: LH: 0-1 RH: 0-1 Tight: 0-1 Gall: 0-0
Aids: Bl: 0-0 Vi: 0-2 Tstrap: 0-0
Best Rating: 136 6/01 Strf 3m4f   gd-fm   Ch

Fair ex-French chaser; winner of four hurdles and two chases in France; picked up cheaply by present connections is one of the few to have improved since leaving Martin Pipe; ran away with a claiming hurdle at Wetherby in May 2003; followed up with easy win in 2m 5f chase at Newton Abbot next time; seems best on good ground or faster; usually wears a visor or blinkers.

Kalca Mome (FR)
109   130+
5-y-o b g En Calcat (FR)-Belle Mome (FR) (Grand Tresor (FR))
P J Hobbs Miss I D Du Pre

Placings: 210151   (3999)
2002/03: 16²G, 16¹G, 16⁰S, 17¹S, 16⁵S, 16¹S,

	Starts	1st	2nd	3rd	Win & Pl
Hurdles	6	3	1	0	22833
Career Total	6	3	1	0	22833
130 3/03 Winc	2m	D(0-125)HHdl		SFT	£12557
116 1/03 Tntn	2m1f	E Hdl		SFT	£4530
100 11/02 Hayd	2m	D Hdl		GD	£4381

Total win prize-money £21469

Going: Sf: 2-4 GS: 0-0 Gd: 1-2 GF: - Fm: 0-0
Distance: 2m/2m3: 3-6 2m4-2m7: 0-0 3m+: 0-0
Track: LH: 1-2 RH: 2-4 Tight: 1-2 Gall: 0-0
Aids: Bl: 0-0 Vi: 0-0 Tstrap: 0-0
Best Rating: 130 3/03 Winc 2m   soft   Hdl

Fair hurdler; effective at two miles; acts on good an soft ground.

Kali Des Obeaux (FR)
104   107
5-y-o b m Panoramic-Alpaga (FR) (Le Pontet (FR))
A King (G Macaire 25/6) Million In Mind Partnership (12)

Placings: 1131232002   (4536)
2002/03: 18¹G, 17¹G, 18³VS, 20¹VS, 16²GS, 16³GS, 19²GS, 21⁰GS, 16⁰GS, 24²G,

	Starts	1st	2nd	3rd	Win & Pl
Hurdles	6	0	3	1	3823
Chases	4	3	0	1	22454
Career Total	10	3	3	2	26277
6/02 Autl	2m4f110y	Ch		VS	£13252
5/02 Csma	2m1f	Ch		GD	£2650
5/02 Roya	2m2f	Ch		GD	£2945

Total win prize-money £18847

Going: Sf: 0-0 GS: 0-5 Gd: 2-3 GF: - Fm: 0-0
Distance: 2m/2m3: 2-6 2m4-2m7: 1-3 3m+: 0-1

Track: LH: 0-4 RH: 0-2 Tight: 0-1 Gall: 0-1
Aids: Bl: 0-0 Vi: 0-0 Tstrap: 0-0
Best Rating: 108 11/02 Wwck 2m   gd-sft Hdl

Winner three times over fences in France; best effort over hurdles when narrowly beaten by Jahash over three miles on good to firm at Ludlow April 2003.

Kalic D'Alm (FR)
79f   79f
5-y-o b g Passing Sale (FR)-Bekaa II (FR) (Djarvis (FR))
Miss Suzy Smith Miss Suzy Smith

Placings: 5P   (3337)
2002/03: 17⁵S, 17⁹S,

	Starts	1st	2nd	3rd	Win & Pl
NH Flat	2	0	0	0	0
Career Total	2	0	0	0	0

Going: Sf: 0-2 GS: 0-0 Gd: 0-0 GF: - Fm: 0-0
Distance: 2m/2m3: 0-2 2m4-2m7: 0-0 3m+: 0-0
Track: LH: 0-0 RH: 0-1 Tight: 0-1 Gall: 0-0
Aids: Bl: 0-0 Vi: 0-0 Tstrap: 0-0
Best Rating: 79 11/02 Folk 2m1f110y soft NHF

Kaliko Boy
80f   63f
7-y-o b g Perpendicular-Reddy Girl (Doctor Wall)
G J Smith Miss Sarah M Thomas

Placings: 0   (0409)
2002/03: 17⁰GF,

	Starts	1st	2nd	3rd	Win & Pl
NH Flat	1	0	0	0	
Career Total	1	0	0	0	

Going: Sf: 0-0 GS: 0-0 Gd: 0-0 GF: - Fm: 0-1
Distance: 2m/2m3: 0-1 2m4-2m7: 0-0 3m+: 0-0
Track: LH: 0-0 RH: 0-1 Tight: 0-1 Gall: 0-0
Aids: Bl: 0-0 Vi: 0-0 Tstrap: 0-0
Best Rating: 63 6/02 MRas 2m1f110y gd-fm NHF

Kalingalinga
56
6-y-o b g Zafonic (USA)-Bell Toll (High Line)
B J Curley Mrs B J Curley

Placings: P0-P   (0217)
2002/03: 17⁶G,

	Starts	1st	2nd	3rd	Win & Pl
Hurdles	1	0	0	0	
Career Total	3	0	0	0	

Going: Sf: 0-0 GS: 0-0 Gd: 0-1 GF: - Fm: 0-0
Distance: 2m/2m3: 0-1 2m4-2m7: 0-0 3m+: 0-0
Track: LH: 0-0 RH: 0-1 Tight: 0-0 Gall: 0-0
Aids: Bl: 0-0 Vi: 0-0 Tstrap: 0-0
Best Rating: 56 3/02 Hntg 2m110y gd-fm Hdl

Kalinnjar (FR)
97   109?
6-y-o b m Barathea (IRE)-Kalajana (USA) (Green Dancer (USA))
Graham John McKeever F Thompson

Placings: 060F02U123   (1691)
2002/03: 19⁰Ys, 17⁶GS, 17⁹G, 17⁷G, 16⁰G, 17²G, 20ᵁGF, 16¹GF, 17²GF, 16³G,

	Starts	1st	2nd	3rd	Win & Pl
Hurdles	10	1	2	1	5088
Career Total	10	1	2	1	5088
92 10/02 Hexm 2m110y G Hdl			G-F	£1988	
				Total win prize-money £1988		

Going: Sf: 0-0 GS: 0-1 Gd: 0-5 GF: - Fm: 1-3
Distance: 2m/2m3: 1-9 2m4-2m7: 0-1 3m+: 0-0
Track: LH: 1-5 RH: 0-3 Tight: 0-3 Gall: 0-0
Aids: Bl: 1-7 Vi: 0-0 Tstrap: 1-7
Best Rating: 95 10/02 Chel 2m110y good Hdl

Irish-trained, she showed some form in modest hurdles in the autumn of 2002. Suited by two miles and fast ground.

Kalivar
60f   79f
5-y-o ch m Gunner B-Promitto (Roaring Riva)
Miss K Marks Nick Shutts

Placings: 400-0   (1670)
2002/03: 17⁰S,

	Starts	1st	2nd	3rd	Win & Pl
NH Flat	1	0	0	0	
Career Total	4	0	0	0	

Going: Sf: 0-1 GS: 0-0 Gd: 0-0 GF: - Fm: 0-0
Distance: 2m/2m3: 0-1 2m4-2m7: 0-0 3m+: 0-0
Track: LH: 0-1 RH: 0-0 Tight: 0-1 Gall: 0-0
Aids: Bl: 0-0 Vi: 0-0 Tstrap: 0-0
Best Rating: 79 1/02 Tntn 2m1f soft NHF

Kalko Du Charmil (FR)
6-y-o b g Kadalko (FR)-Licada (FR) (A Tempo (FR))
Mrs M Reveley Mr And Mrs J D Cotton

Placings: 00F6-U6F   (1718)
2002/03: 16ᵁG, 19⁶G, 18⁸G,

	Starts	1st	2nd	3rd	Win & Pl
Chases	3	0	0	0	0
Career Total	7	0	0	0	0

Going: Sf: 0-0 GS: 0-0 Gd: 0-3 GF: - Fm: 0-0
Distance: 2m/2m3: 0-3 2m4-2m7: 0-0 3m+: 0-0
Track: LH: 0-1 RH: 0-0 Tight: 0-0 Gall: 0-0
Aids: Bl: 0-0 Vi: 0-0 Tstrap: 0-0
Best Rating: 96 10/01 Chel 2m110y good NHF

Kallassor (FR)
90   77
5-y-o b g Assessor (IRE)-Balladine (FR) (Rivelago (FR))
P C Ritchens Alan Kidd And Mr Andrew Johnson

Placings: 05-0U34P   (4116)
2002/03: 16⁰GF, 26ᵁG, 22³G, 25⁴S, 21⁸G,

	Starts	1st	2nd	3rd	Win & Pl
Hurdles	5	0	0	1	423
Career Total	7	0	0	1	423

Going: Sf: 0-1 GS: 0-0 Gd: 0-3 GF: - Fm: 0-1
Distance: 2m/2m3: 0-1 2m4-2m7: 0-2 3m+: 0-2
Track: LH: 0-3 RH: 0-2 Tight: 0-2 Gall: 0-2

Aids: Bl: 0-0 Vi: 0-4 Tstrap: 0-0
Best Rating: 77 6/02 NAbb 2m6f   good   Hdl

Moderate hurdler; winner on the Flat in France; stays three miles one over hurdles; acts on good and softer.

Kalou (GER)
84   78
5-y-o br g Law Society (USA)-Kompetenz (IRE) (Be My Guest (USA))
B J Curley (A Trybuhl 15/9) P Byrne

Placings: 600   (3367)
2002/03: 20⁶GS, 16⁰S, 20⁹GS,

	Starts	1st	2nd	3rd	Win & Pl
Hurdles	3	0	0	0	0
Career Total	3	0	0	0	0

Kaluga (IRE)
95   82
5-y-o ch m Tagula (IRE)-Another Baileys (Deploy)
P R Rodford Mrs Christine Priest

Placings: 600053-00   (2712)
2002/03: 19⁹GS, 16⁹GS,

	Starts	1st	2nd	3rd	Win & Pl
Hurdles	2	0	0	0	
Career Total	8	0	0	1	392

Going: Sf: 0-0 GS: 0-2 Gd: 0-0 GF: - Fm: 0-0
Distance: 2m/2m3: 0-1 2m4-2m7: 0-0 3m+: 0-0
Track: LH: 0-0 RH: 0-2 Tight: 0-1 Gall: 0-0
Aids: Bl: 0-1 Vi: 0-0 Tstrap: 0-0
Best Rating: 82 3/02 Winc 2m6f soft Hdl

Kamloops (IRE)
8-y-o b g Insan (USA)-Furry Lady (Furry Glen)
Ferdy Murphy Mrs M B Scholey

Placings: 006/3/P   (3266)
2002/03: 16⁶G,

	Starts	1st	2nd	3rd	Win & Pl
Chases	1	0	0	0	
Career Total	5	0	0	1	663

Going: Sf: 0-0 GS: 0-0 Gd: 0-1 GF: - Fm: 0-0
Distance: 2m/2m3: 0-1 2m4-2m7: 0-1 3m+: 0-0
Track: LH: 0-1 RH: 0-0 Tight: 0-0 Gall: 0-1
Aids: Bl: 0-0 Vi: 0-0 Tstrap: 0-0
Best Rating: 91 11/00 Aint 2m110y gd-sft Hdl

Small amounts of ability over hurdles.

Kandles-Korner
9-y-o b g Gold Dust-My Kizzy (The Ditton)
J W Tudor W Ralph Thomas

Placings: U   (0272)

2002/03: 20^U GF,

	Starts	1st	2nd	3rd	Win & Pl
Chases	1	0	0	0	
Career Total	1	0	0	0	

Going: Sf: 0-0 GS: 0-0 Gd: 0-0 GF: - Fm: 0-1
Distance: 2m/2m3: 0-0 2m4-2m7: 0-1 3m+: 0-0
Track: LH: 0-1 RH: 0-0 Tight: 0-1 Gall: 0-0
Aids: Bl: 0-0 Vi: 0-0 Tstrap: 0-0
Best Rating: 0 5/02 Strf 2m4f gd-fm Ch

Kandy Four (NZ)
105   109

8-y-o ch g Zeditave (AUS)-Executive Suite (NZ) (Western Symphony (USA))
P F Nicholls D J & F A Jackson

Placings:3/0324032/23P2362F-2211F2 (4773)
2002/03: 16^2GF, 21^2G, 20^1GS, 20^1GS, 21^FGF, 20^2G,

	Starts	1st	2nd	3rd	Win & Pl
Chases	6	2	3	0	16854
Career Total	22	2	8	5	25317
114 8/02 Prth 2m4f110yD(0-115)HCh				G-S	£8131
114 7/02 MRas 2m4f E Ch				G-S	£4375

Total win prize-money £12507

Going: Sf: 0-0 GS: 2-2 Gd: 0-2 GF: - Fm: 0-2
Distance: 2m/2m3: 0-1 2m4-2m7: 2-5 3m+: 0-0
Track: LH: 0-2 RH: 2-4 Tight: 1-3 Gall: 0-1
Aids: Bl: 0-0 Vi: 0-0 Tstrap: 0-0
Best Rating: 114 8/02 Prth 2m4f110y gd-sft Ch

Modest chaser; stays two miles-five; acts on good to firm and good to soft ground; lacks a turn of foot.

Kanona

12-y-o ch g Gunner B-Pugilistic (Hard Fought)
David F Smith J Michael Walker

Placings:0/0P/03/0 (0402)
2002/03: 20^0GF,

	Starts	1st	2nd	3rd	Win & Pl
Chases	1	0	0	0	
Career Total	6	0	0	1	298

Going: Sf: 0-0 GS: 0-0 Gd: 0-0 GF: - Fm: 0-1
Distance: 2m/2m3: 0-0 2m4-2m7: 0-1 3m+: 0-0
Track: LH: 0-1 RH: 0-0 Tight: 0-0 Gall: 0-0
Aids: Bl: 0-0 Vi: 0-0 Tstrap: 0-0
Best Rating: 64 10/96 Sedg 2m5f110y gd-fm Hdl

Kansas City (FR)
97   89

5-y-o b/br m Lute Antique (FR)-Tenacity (FR) (Prove It Baby (USA))
M F Harris (E Vagne 27/9) Let s Live Racing III

Placings:1056433F3PP (4687)
2002/03: 18^1G, 17^0VS, 18^5G, 18^6G, 16^4GF, 16^3G, 16^3G, 21^FS, 19^3S, 16^2GF, 17^6G,

	Starts	1st	2nd	3rd	Win & Pl
Hurdles	1	0	0	0	0
Chases	10	1	0	3	6532
Career Total	11	1	0	3	6532
5/02 Clun 2m2f Ch				GD	£2945

Total win prize-money £2945

Going: Sf: 0-2 GS: 0-0 Gd: 1-6 GF: - Fm: 0-2

Distance: 2m/2m3: 1-10 2m4-2m7: 0-1 3m+: 0-0
Track: LH: 0-5 RH: 0-2 Tight: 0-5 Gall: 0-1
Aids: Bl: 0-0 Vi: 0-0 Tstrap: 0-0
Best Rating: 89 11/02 Wwck 2m110y good Ch

Did not progress after winning a small race in the French Provinces on the first of her four starts over fences in her native country. Has made only a modest impact so far in Britain.

Kaolin De Perche (FR)
87+

5-y-o b g Luchiroverte (IRE)-Craven Ii (FR) (Rhapsodien)
C P Morlock Pell-Mell Partners

Placings:0F (4055)
2002/03: 19^0GS, 25^FS,

	Starts	1st	2nd	3rd	Win & Pl
Hurdles	2	0	0	0	
Career Total	2	0	0	0	

Going: Sf: 0-1 GS: 0-1 Gd: 0-0 GF: - Fm: 0-0
Distance: 2m/2m3: 0-0 2m4-2m7: 0-1 3m+: 0-1
Track: LH: 0-2 RH: 0-0 Tight: 0-0 Gall: 0-0
Aids: Bl: 0-0 Vi: 0-0 Tstrap: 0-0
Best Rating: 87 3/03 Wwck 3m1f soft Hdl

Kappelhoff (IRE)
87   70d

6-y-o b g Mukaddamah (USA)-Miss Penguin (General Assembly (USA))
Mrs L Richards Mrs Lydia Richards

Placings:000-U000U (4428)
2002/03: 20US, 18^0HY, 17^0HY, 22^0G, 25^UGF,

	Starts	1st	2nd	3rd	Win & Pl
Hurdles	5	0	0	0	
Career Total	8	0	0	0	

Going: Sf: 0-3 GS: 0-0 Gd: 0-1 GF: - Fm: 0-1
Distance: 2m/2m3: 0-2 2m4-2m7: 0-2 3m+: 0-1
Track: LH: 0-2 RH: 0-2 Tight: 0-3 Gall: 0-0
Aids: Bl: 0-0 Vi: 0-0 Tstrap: 0-0
Best Rating: 88 5/01 Font 2m2f110y gd-fm NHF

Kapska (FR)
59   26

5-y-o b g Silver Rainbow-Chapska (FR) (Le Pontet (FR))
M J Roberts Mike Roberts

Placings:P0 (4446)
2002/03: 18^PS, 16^0G,

	Starts	1st	2nd	3rd	Win & Pl
Hurdles	2	0	0	0	
Career Total	2	0	0	0	

Going: Sf: 0-1 GS: 0-0 Gd: 0-1 GF: - Fm: 0-0
Distance: 2m/2m3: 0-2 2m4-2m7: 0-0 3m+: 0-0
Track: LH: 0-1 RH: 0-1 Tight: 0-1 Gall: 0-0
Aids: Bl: 0-0 Vi: 0-0 Tstrap: 0-0
Best Rating: 26 4/03 Ludl 2m good Hdl

Karadin (FR)
105(100h)   (105h)112

9-y-o b g Akarad (FR)-In River (FR) (In Fijar (USA))

R H Buckler Mrs D A La Trobe

Placings:6004013212/4/0200-P24012 (4265)
2002/03: 17^PGF, 16^2S, 16^4GF, 21^0GF, 21^1GF, 24^2GF,

	Starts	1st	2nd	3rd	Win & Pl
Chases	6	1	2	0	7204
Career Total	21	3	5	1	17859
112 8/02 NAbb 2m5f110yD Ch				G-F	£4725
105 3/00 Winc 2m D(0-125)HHdl				G-S	£5213
105 1/00 Sthl 2m F(0-95)HHdl				G-S	£2509

Total win prize-money £12449

Going: Sf: 0-1 GS: 0-0 Gd: 0-0 GF: - Fm: 1-5
Distance: 2m/2m3: 0-3 2m4-2m7: 1-2 3m+: 0-1
Track: LH: 1-5 RH: 0-1 Tight: 1-5 Gall: 0-0
Aids: Bl: 0-0 Vi: 0-0 Tstrap: 0-0
Best Rating: 112 8/02 NAbb 2m5f110y gd-fm Ch

Successful hurdler over two miles, he landed a chase over two miles five at Newton Abbot in August. Acts on most type of ground.

Karahisar (IRE)

4-y-o b g Common Grounds-Karamiyna (IRE) (Shernazar)
N P McCormack Mrs D McCormack

Placings:0 (3357)
2002/03: 16^0HY,

	Starts	1st	2nd	3rd	Win & Pl
NH Flat	1	0	0	0	
Career Total	1	0	0	0	

Going: Sf: 0-1 GS: 0-0 Gd: 0-0 GF: - Fm: 0-0
Distance: 2m/2m3: 0-1 2m4-2m7: 0-0 3m+: 0-0
Track: LH: 0-1 RH: 0-0 Tight: 0-0 Gall: 0-0
Aids: Bl: 0-0 Vi: 0-0 Tstrap: 0-0
Best Rating: 0 1/03 Newc 2m heavy NHF

Karajan (IRE)
97(103h)   (102h)91

6-y-o b g Fairy King (USA)-Dernier Cri (Slip Anchor)
G M Moore J R F (management Consultants) Ltd

Placings:5434241222550-235 (2515)
2002/03: 16^2HY, 20^3HY, 20^5S,

	Starts	1st	2nd	3rd	Win & Pl
Chases	3	0	1	1	2419
Career Total	16	1	5	2	9504
102 9/01 Prth 2m4f110yE Hdl				GD	£3157

Total win prize-money £3157

Going: Sf: 0-3 GS: 0-0 Gd: 0-0 GF: - Fm: 0-0
Distance: 2m/2m3: 0-1 2m4-2m7: 0-2 3m+: 0-0
Track: LH: 0-1 RH: 0-2 Tight: 0-0 Gall: 0-1
Aids: Bl: 0-0 Vi: 0-0 Tstrap: 0-0
Best Rating: 102 2/02 MRas 2m5f110y gd-sft Hdl

Modest hurdler, he was well held when second on chasing debut in November 2002. Stays two and a half miles, suited by good ground but handles soft.

Karakum
91   65

4-y-o b g Mtoto-Magongo (Be My Chief (USA))
A J Chamberlain (M A Jarvis 1/6) A J Chamberlain

Placings:056 (1614)
2002/03: 16^0GS, 17^5GF, 16^6F,

	Starts	1st	2nd	3rd	Win & Pl
Hurdles	3	0	0	0	0

| Career Total | 3 | 0 | 0 | 0 | 0 |

Going: Sf: 0-0 GS: 0-1 Gd: 0-0 GF: - Fm: 0-2
Distance: 2m/2m3: 0-3 2m4-2m7: 0-0 3m+: 0-0
Track: LH: 0-1 RH: 0-2 Tight: 0-1 Gall: 0-0
Aids: Bl: 0-0 Vi: 0-0 Tstrap: 0-0
Best Rating: 62 10/02 Ludl 2m   firm   Hdl

Karency (FR)
95(80h)   (47h)76+
5-y-o ch g Video Rock (FR)-Reina Tennise (FR) (Quart De Vin (FR))
Miss H C Knight Mrs P Turner

Placings:04   (3925)
2002/03: 17OS, 16⁴G,

	Starts	1st	2nd	3rd	Win & Pl
Hurdles	1	0	0	0	0
Chases	1	0	0	0	312
Career Total	2	0	0	0	312

Going: Sf: 0-1 GS: 0-0 Gd: 0-1 GF: - Fm: 0-0
Distance: 2m/2m3: 0-2 2m4-2m7: 0-0 3m+: 0-0
Track: LH: 0-0 RH: 0-2 Tight: 0-1 Gall: 0-1
Aids: Bl: 0-0 Vi: 0-0 Tstrap: 0-0
Best Rating: 76 3/03 Hntg 2m110y   good   Ch

Karisaban

4-y-o b g Hatim (USA)-Swiss Beauty (Ballacashtal (CAN))
R Johnson K Eichler

Placings:00   (4437)
2002/03: 17OGS, 16OG,

	Starts	1st	2nd	3rd	Win & Pl
NH Flat	2	0	0	0	
Career Total	2	0	0	0	

Going: Sf: 0-0 GS: 0-1 Gd: 0-1 GF: - Fm: 0-0
Distance: 2m/2m3: 0-2 2m4-2m7: 0-0 3m+: 0-0
Track: LH: 0-1 RH: 0-1 Tight: 0-0 Gall: 0-0
Aids: Bl: 0-0 Vi: 0-0 Tstrap: 0-0
Best Rating: 30 3/03 Carl 2m1f   gd-sft   NHF

Karo De Vindecy (FR)
100(93h)   (72h)66
5-y-o b g Mollicone Junior (FR)-Preves Du Forez (FR) (Quart De Vin (FR))
M D Hammond Racing Management & Training Ltd

Placings:46000   (4406)
2002/03: 16⁴S, 17⁶GS, 17OHY, 16OS, 20OG,

	Starts	1st	2nd	3rd	Win & Pl
Hurdles	5	0	0	0	758
Career Total	5	0	0	0	758

Going: Sf: 0-3 GS: 0-1 Gd: 0-1 GF: - Fm: 0-0
Distance: 2m/2m3: 0-4 2m4-2m7: 0-1 3m+: 0-0
Track: LH: 0-2 RH: 0-2 Tight: 0-1 Gall: 0-1
Aids: Bl: 0-0 Vi: 0-0 Tstrap: 0-3
Best Rating: 72 11/02 Carl 2m1f   heavy   Hdl

Has shown ability in France but ran poorly over hurdles here; took a very modest event on his debut over fences at Cartmel in May; best at around two miles.

Karolena Bay
106   94+
6-y-o ch m Karinga Bay-Owena Deep (Deep Run)
N A Twiston-Davies The Yes - No - Wait Sorries

Placings:06-61PF15P   (2053)
2002/03: 16⁶GS, 16¹GF, 20PGS, 20FGF, 26¹GF, 23⁵G, 24PG,

	Starts	1st	2nd	3rd	Win & Pl
Hurdles	7	2	0	0	4557
Career Total	9	2	0	0	4557
94 7/02 Sthl 3m2f	F(0-90)HHdl			G-F	£2275
88 5/02 Strf 2m110y G Hdl				G-F	£2282
				Total win prize-money £4557

Going: Sf: 0-0 GS: 0-2 Gd: 0-2 GF: - Fm: 2-3
Distance: 2m/2m3: 1-2 2m4-2m7: 0-2 3m+: 1-3
Track: LH: 2-5 RH: 0-2 Tight: 1-2 Gall: 0-0
Aids: Bl: 0-0 Vi: 0-0 Tstrap: 0-0
Best Rating: 94 7/02 Sthl 3m2f   gd-fm   Hdl

Won two mile novices seller at Stratford in May 2002. Improved form when stepped up to three and a quarter miles to win Class F novices handicap at Southwell in July. Acts on the top of the ground.

Karzhang

11-y-o b g Rakaposhi King-Smokey Baby (Sagaro)
Mrs C J Robinson Jeremy Beasley

Placings:000/5P0/3040/24/F-6   (4288)
2002/03: 20⁶GF,

	Starts	1st	2nd	3rd	Win & Pl
Chases	1	0	0	0	0
Career Total	14	0	1	1	1474

Going: Sf: 0-0 GS: 0-0 Gd: 0-0 GF: - Fm: 0-1
Distance: 2m/2m3: 0-0 2m4-2m7: 0-1 3m+: 0-0
Track: LH: 0-0 RH: 0-1 Tight: 0-1 Gall: 0-0
Aids: Bl: 0-0 Vi: 0-0 Tstrap: 0-1
Best Rating: 88 5/00 Bang 2m1f   good   Hdl

Kasalan (IRE)
47f
5-y-o br m Hawkstone (IRE)-Larry s Law (IRE) (Law Society (USA))
K A Ryan Mrs K E Fletcher & Mrs J Ryan

Placings:0   (3167)
2002/03: 16OG,

	Starts	1st	2nd	3rd	Win & Pl
NH Flat	1	0	0	0	
Career Total	1	0	0	0	

Going: Sf: 0-0 GS: 0-0 Gd: 0-1 GF: - Fm: 0-0
Distance: 2m/2m3: 0-1 2m4-2m7: 0-0 3m+: 0-0
Track: LH: 0-1 RH: 0-0 Tight: 0-1 Gall: 0-0
Aids: Bl: 0-0 Vi: 0-0 Tstrap: 0-0
Best Rating: 0 1/03 Catt 2m   good   NHF

Kassala (FR)
106   119+
7-y-o b m Phantom Breeze-Tip Land (FR) (Tip Moss (FR))
A King Jules Sigler

Placings:301F2100/3FP/P44F162-P1P3332144   (1714)
2002/03: 16PGS, 17¹GF, 16PGS, 16³GF, 16³GF, 17³GF, 16²G, 16¹GF, 17⁴G, 17⁴GS,

Karolena Bay (continued — right column)

	Starts	1st	2nd	3rd	Win & Pl
Chases	10	2	1	3	17299
Career Total	28	5	3	5	58731
119 10/02 Hrfd 2m	D(0-115)HCh		G-F	£4615
114 6/02 Strf	2m1f110yC(0-135)HCh		G-F	£7308
111 11/01 Winc 2m	D(0-120)HCh		G-F	£4075
3/00 Engh 2m1f		Ch	HLD	£11527
10/99 Engh 2m110y Hdl			VS	£10764
				Total win prize-money £38290

Going: Sf: 0-0 GS: 0-3 Gd: 0-2 GF: - Fm: 2-5
Distance: 2m/2m3: 2-10 2m4-2m7: 0-0 3m+: 0-0
Track: LH: 1-9 RH: 1-1 Tight: 1-8 Gall: 0-0
Aids: Bl: 0-0 Vi: 0-0 Tstrap: 0-0
Best Rating: 119 10/02 Hrfd 2m   gd-fm   Ch

A winner over hurdles and fences in France, she is a fair handicap chaser at around two miles. Suited by fast ground and hold-up tactics.

Kataholic
64   37
4-y-o b c Bluegrass Prince (IRE)-Langton Herring (Nearly A Hand)
G A Ham (I A Wood 2/5) All For One

Placings:60   (4733)
2002/03: 17⁶F, 16OGF,

	Starts	1st	2nd	3rd	Win & Pl
Hurdles	2	0	0	0	0
Career Total	2	0	0	0	0

Going: Sf: 0-0 GS: 0-0 Gd: 0-0 GF: - Fm: 0-2
Distance: 2m/2m3: 0-2 2m4-2m7: 0-0 3m+: 0-0
Track: LH: 0-1 RH: 0-1 Tight: 0-1 Gall: 0-0
Aids: Bl: 0-0 Vi: 0-0 Tstrap: 0-0
Best Rating: 37 3/03 Tntn 2m1f   firm   Hdl

Katarino (FR)
115   145
8-y-o b g Pistolet Bleu (IRE)-Katevana (FR) (Cadoudal (FR))
N J Henderson Robert Waley-Cohen

Placings:4P311111/25400/4/13-255U   (4479)
2002/03: 21²HY, 21⁵GS, 24⁵G, 36UG,

	Starts	1st	2nd	3rd	Win & Pl
Chases	4	0	1	0	11050
Career Total	20	6	2	3	171133
146 12/01 Newb 2m4f	A Ch		SFT	£9390
144 4/99 Punc 2m	Hdl		YLD	£38750
155 3/99 Chel 2m1f	A Hdl		G-S	£45960
158 2/99 Kemp 2m	A Hdl		SFT	£9555
145 11/98 Chel 2m110y	B Hdl		GD	£7067
126 11/98 Newb 2m110y	C Hdl		G-S	£3847
				Total win prize-money £114570

Going: Sf: 0-1 GS: 0-1 Gd: 0-2 GF: - Fm: 0-0
Distance: 2m/2m3: 0-0 2m4-2m7: 0-2 3m+: 0-2
Track: LH: 0-4 RH: 0-0 Tight: 0-1 Gall: 0-3
Aids: Bl: 0-0 Vi: 0-0 Tstrap: 0-0
Best Rating: 158 3/00 Chel 2m110y   good   Hdl

Very useful chaser; he was also pretty good over hurdles, winning the Triumph Hurdle in 1999; lightly-raced in recent years; suited by soft ground; effective at around two and a half miles, although does appear to stay three.

Kate's Cottage
87f   79f
7-y-o b m Faustus (USA)-Try G S (Hotfoot)
R Ford Richard Ford

Placings:60-6   (1459)
2002/03: 16⁶F,

	Starts	1st	2nd	3rd	Win & Pl
NH Flat	1	0	0	0	0
Career Total	3	0	0	0	0

Going: Sf: 0-0 GS: 0-0 Gd: 0-0 GF: - Fm: 0-1
Distance: 2m/2m3: 0-1 2m4-2m7: 0-0 3m+: 0-0
Track: LH: 0-0 RH: 0-1 Tight: 0-0 Gall: 0-0
Aids: Bl: 0-0 Vi: 0-0 Tstrap: 0-0
Best Rating: 79   2/02   Donc   2m110y   soft   NHF

Kates Ivy Hill (IRE)

9-y-o b m King Of Shannon-Raj Kumari (Vitiges (FR))
Mark Doyle   M W Jones

Placings:0000/0005P-P   (4026)
2002/03: 25^PS,

	Starts	1st	2nd	3rd	Win & Pl
Chases	1	0	0	0	0
Career Total	10	0	0	0	0

Going: Sf: 0-1 GS: 0-0 Gd: 0-0 GF: - Fm: 0-0
Distance: 2m/2m3: 0-0 2m4-2m7: 0-0 3m+: 0-1
Track: LH: 0-0 RH: 0-1 Tight: 0-0 Gall: 0-0
Aids: Bl: 0-0 Vi: 0-0 Tstrap: 0-0
Best Rating: 50   8/01   Bang   2m4f110y   good   Ch

Kates Son (IRE)
71   22
6-y-o ch g Fayruz-Kates Choice (IRE) (Taufan (USA))
Noel T Chance   Fizzgigg Partnership

Placings:00P/0-0   (0613)
2002/03: 16⁹GF,

	Starts	1st	2nd	3rd	Win & Pl
Hurdles	1	0	0	0	0
Career Total	5	0	0	0	0

Going: Sf: 0-0 GS: 0-0 Gd: 0-0 GF: - Fm: 0-1
Distance: 2m/2m3: 0-1 2m4-2m7: 0-0 3m+: 0-0
Track: LH: 0-1 RH: 0-0 Tight: 0-0 Gall: 0-0
Aids: Bl: 0-0 Vi: 0-1 Tstrap: 0-0
Best Rating: 69   12/00   Folk   2m1f110y   heavy   Hdl

Kathakali (IRE)
104   103
6-y-o b g Dancing Dissident (USA)-She s A Dancer (IRE) (Alzao (USA))
C J Bennett (S Dow 31/5)   C J Bennett

Placings:000P   (4020)
2002/03: 16⁶S, 17⁰S, 16⁶S, 26⁶S,

	Starts	1st	2nd	3rd	Win & Pl
Hurdles	4	0	0	0	0
Career Total	4	0	0	0	0

Going: Sf: 0-4 GS: 0-0 Gd: 0-0 GF: - Fm: 0-0
Distance: 2m/2m3: 0-3 2m4-2m7: 0-0 3m+: 0-1
Track: LH: 0-1 RH: 0-3 Tight: 0-0 Gall: 0-0
Aids: Bl: 0-0 Vi: 0-0 Tstrap: 0-0
Best Rating: 45   12/02   Wwck   2m   soft   Hdl

Finally lived up to his Flat form when causing 66/1 shock when readily winning 2m maiden hurdle at Worcester July 2003; unsuited by soft ground.

Kathella (IRE)
83
6-y-o b m Fourstars Allstar (USA)-Niat Supreme (IRE) (Supreme Leader)
N G Ayliffe   R Allatt

Placings:00-0000PP   (4598)
2002/03: 17⁰G, 17⁰G, 16⁸GF, 19⁹GS, 19⁹GS, 19⁰GF,

	Starts	1st	2nd	3rd	Win & Pl
Hurdles	6	0	0	0	
Career Total	8	0	0	0	

Going: Sf: 0-0 GS: 0-2 Gd: 0-2 GF: - Fm: 0-2
Distance: 2m/2m3: 0-4 2m4-2m7: 0-2 3m+: 0-0
Track: LH: 0-2 RH: 0-4 Tight: 0-3 Gall: 0-0
Aids: Bl: 0-0 Vi: 0-0 Tstrap: 0-0
Best Rating: 72   6/02   NAbb   2m1f   good   Hdl

Katie Broon
48f   60f
6-y-o ch m Minster Son-Gale Storm (Midland Gayle)
Joseph Brown   Joseph Brown

Placings:00   (4411)
2002/03: 17⁰GS, 16⁰G,

	Starts	1st	2nd	3rd	Win & Pl
NH Flat	2	0	0	0	
Career Total	2	0	0	0	

Going: Sf: 0-0 GS: 0-1 Gd: 0-1 GF: - Fm: 0-0
Distance: 2m/2m3: 0-2 2m4-2m7: 0-0 3m+: 0-0
Track: LH: 0-1 RH: 0-1 Tight: 0-0 Gall: 0-0
Aids: Bl: 0-0 Vi: 0-0 Tstrap: 0-0
Best Rating: 60   3/03   Carl   2m1f   gd-sft   NHF

Katie Buckers (IRE)
109   58
9-y-o ch m Yashgan-Glenkins (Furry Glen)
K C Bailey   K C Bailey

Placings:103PP/43411-144P0P   (3572)
2002/03: 20¹G, 24⁴S, 24⁴S, 25^PS, 25⁰GS, 20⁰S,

	Starts	1st	2nd	3rd	Win & Pl				
Chases	6	1	0	0	4088				
Career Total	16	4	0	2	14774				
104	5/02	Uttx	2m4f	E(0-105)HCh	GD	£3328			
104	3/02	Uttx	3m2f	E(0-105)HCh	HVY	£4095			
96	3/02	Hrld	3m11f110y	Ch	GD	£3357			
100	11/00	Chep	2m110y H NHF		HVY	£1505			
				Total win prize-money		£12286			

Going: Sf: 0-4 GS: 0-1 Gd: 1-1 GF: - Fm: 0-0
Distance: 2m/2m3: 0-2 2m4-2m7: 1-2 3m+: 0-4
Track: LH: 1-3 RH: 0-3 Tight: 0-1 Gall: 0-0
Aids: Bl: 0-0 Vi: 0-0 Tstrap: 0-0
Best Rating: 104   5/02   Uttx   2m4f   good   Ch

Fair form in novice chases. completed a hat-trick in the spring of 2002; bang out of form of late; stays three and a quarter miles; acts on heavy ground.

Katies Dolphin (IRE)
84   82
5-y-o ch m Dolphin Street (FR)-Kuwah (IRE) (Be My Guest (USA))
R Johnson (A Berry 27/7)   Robert Johnson

Placings:600436   (4366)

2002/03: 16⁶S, 16⁹GS, 16⁹G, 16⁴G, 21³S, 20⁶G,

	Starts	1st	2nd	3rd	Win & Pl
Hurdles	6	0	0	1	504
Career Total	6	0	0	1	504

Going: Sf: 0-2 GS: 0-1 Gd: 0-3 GF: - Fm: 0-0
Distance: 2m/2m3: 0-4 2m4-2m7: 0-2 3m+: 0-0
Track: LH: 0-5 RH: 0-1 Tight: 0-4 Gall: 0-1
Aids: Bl: 0-0 Vi: 0-0 Tstrap: 0-3
Best Rating: 82   3/03   Sedg   2m5f110y   soft   Hdl

Plating-class hurdler; acts on soft; has worn tongue tie.

Katies Genie
46   14
5-y-o b m Syrtos-Reine De La Chasse (FR) (Ti King (FR))
M C Pipe   D G & D J Robinson

Placings:0   (4251)
2002/03: 17⁰G,

	Starts	1st	2nd	3rd	Win & Pl
Hurdles	1	0	0	0	
Career Total	1	0	0	0	

Going: Sf: 0-0 GS: 0-0 Gd: 0-1 GF: - Fm: 0-0
Distance: 2m/2m3: 0-1 2m4-2m7: 0-0 3m+: 0-0
Track: LH: 0-0 RH: 0-1 Tight: 0-0 Gall: 0-0
Aids: Bl: 0-0 Vi: 0-0 Tstrap: 0-0
Best Rating: 14   3/03   Extr   2m1f   good   Hdl

Katies Hero
80f   62f
5-y-o b g Pontevecchio Notte-Kindly Lady (Kind Of Hush)
J D Frost   D C & Mrs T M Fisher

Placings:00   (4628)
2002/03: 17⁰GS, 17⁰GF,

	Starts	1st	2nd	3rd	Win & Pl
NH Flat	2	0	0	0	
Career Total	2	0	0	0	

Going: Sf: 0-0 GS: 0-1 Gd: 0-0 GF: - Fm: 0-1
Distance: 2m/2m3: 0-2 2m4-2m7: 0-0 3m+: 0-0
Track: LH: 0-1 RH: 0-1 Tight: 0-1 Gall: 0-0
Aids: Bl: 0-0 Vi: 0-0 Tstrap: 0-0
Best Rating: 62   4/03   NAbb   2m1f   gd-fm   NHF

Katies Tight Jeans

9-y-o b m Green Adventure (USA)-Haraka Sasa (Town And Country)
R E Peacock   M F Harris

Placings:05/0/00/P6-PP   (2351)
2002/03: 16^PGS, 16^PGS,

	Starts	1st	2nd	3rd	Win & Pl
Hurdles	2	0	0	0	
Career Total	9	0	0	0	

Going: Sf: 0-0 GS: 0-2 Gd: 0-0 GF: - Fm: 0-0
Distance: 2m/2m3: 0-2 2m4-2m7: 0-0 3m+: 0-0
Track: LH: 0-2 RH: 0-0 Tight: 0-1 Gall: 0-0
Aids: Bl: 0-0 Vi: 0-0 Tstrap: 0-0
Best Rating: 65   5/00   Worc   2m   gd-fm   NHF

Katinka

91   **49**

10-y-o b m Rymer-Millymeeta (New Brig)
A M Thomson A M Thomson

Placings:F4/06P-   (0006)
2002/03: 20FG,

	Starts	1st	2nd	3rd	Win & Pl
Hurdles	1	0	0	0	
Career Total	5	0	0	0	450

Going: Sf: 0-0 GS: 0-0 Gd: 0-1 GF: - Fm: 0-0
Distance: 2m/2m3: 0-0 2m4-2m7: 0-1 3m+: 0-0
Track: LH: 0-1 RH: 0-0 Tight: 0-0 Gall: 0-1
Aids: Bl: 0-0 Vi: 0-0 Tstrap: 0-1
Best Rating:

Katiypour (IRE)

96   **94**

6-y-o ch g Be My Guest (USA)-Katiyfa (Auction Ring (USA))
T D Barron (P R Webber 21/9) Nigel Shields

Placings:66-5P   (0417)
2002/03: 16SGF, 16PGF,

	Starts	1st	2nd	3rd	Win & Pl
Hurdles	2	0	0	0	0
Career Total	4	0	0	0	0

Going: Sf: 0-0 GS: 0-0 Gd: 0-0 GF: - Fm: 0-2
Distance: 2m/2m3: 0-2 2m4-2m7: 0-0 3m+: 0-0
Track: LH: 0-1 RH: 0-0 Tight: 0-1 Gall: 0-0
Aids: Bl: 0-0 Vi: 0-1 Tstrap: 0-0
Best Rating: 94 5/02 Winc 2m   gd-fm Hdl

Yet to prove he stays two miles over hurdles.

Kattegat

103(89c)   (105c)**108d**

7-y-o b g Slip Anchor-Kirsten (Kris)
Mrs H M Bridges Mrs H M Bridges

Placings:220/04/100353P-33534F   (3843)
2002/03: 16RS, 19RGS, 20FS, 20GHY, 214HY, 24FG,

	Starts	1st	2nd	3rd	Win & Pl
Hurdles	6	0	0	3	2704
Career Total	18	1	2	5	13131
112 11/01 Leic 2m		C(0-130)HHdl	G-S	£5395	
			Total win prize-money £5395		

Going: Sf: 0-4 GS: 0-1 Gd: 0-1 GF: - Fm: 0-0
Distance: 2m/2m3: 0-1 2m4-2m7: 0-0 3m+: 0-1
Track: LH: 0-2 RH: 0-4 Tight: 0-3 Gall: 0-0
Aids: Bl: 0-0 Vi: 0-0 Tstrap: 0-0
Best Rating: 115 2/00 Hntg 2m4f110y soft Hdl

Fair hurdler; effective from two miles to two miles five furlongs; goes well on a soft surface.

Katy The Duck (IRE)

105   **78**

8-y-o br m Over The River (FR)-Zagliarelle (FR) (Rose Laurel)
R J Price R J Price

Placings:0P6/0U0-250106   (4706)
2002/03: 172GF, 21SG, 21QG, 17TG, 17QGF, 20RG,

	Starts	1st	2nd	3rd	Win & Pl
Hurdles	6	1	1	0	3318

Career Total   12   1   1   0   3318
78 3/03 Bang 2m1f   F Hdl   GD £2618
                          Total win prize-money £2618

Going: Sf: 0-0 GS: 0-0 Gd: 1-4 GF: - Fm: 0-2
Distance: 2m/2m3: 1-3 2m4-2m7: 0-3 3m+: 0-0
Track: LH: 1-2 RH: 0-4 Tight: 1-1 Gall: 0-2
Aids: Bl: 0-0 Vi: 0-0 Tstrap: 0-0
Best Rating: 78 3/03 Bang 2m1f   good Hdl

Kauroa Mail (NZ)

                                                    74

9-y-o b g First Norman (USA)-Penny Letter (NZ) (One Pound Sterling)
B P J Baugh Mrs C Norlander

Placings:54F/0/U03053000400-P   (4403)
2002/03: 22PGF,

	Starts	1st	2nd	3rd	Win & Pl
Hurdles	1	0	0	0	
Career Total	17	0	0	2	1249

Going: Sf: 0-0 GS: 0-0 Gd: 0-0 GF: - Fm: 0-1
Distance: 2m/2m3: 0-0 2m4-2m7: 0-1 3m+: 0-0
Track: LH: 0-1 RH: 0-0 Tight: 0-0 Gall: 0-0
Aids: Bl: 0-0 Vi: 0-0 Tstrap: 0-0
Best Rating: 105 12/99 Uttx 2m   soft Hdl

Kausse De Thaix (FR)

101f   **96f**

5-y-o ch g Iris Noir (FR)-Etoile De Thaix (FR) (Lute Antique (FR))
A M Hales Andrew L Cohen

Placings:40   (3528)
2002/03: 164GS, 16QG,

	Starts	1st	2nd	3rd	Win & Pl
NH Flat	2	0	0	0	0
Career Total	2	0	0	0	0

Going: Sf: 0-0 GS: 0-1 Gd: 0-1 GF: - Fm: 0-0
Distance: 2m/2m3: 0-2 2m4-2m7: 0-0 3m+: 0-0
Track: LH: 0-1 RH: 0-1 Tight: 0-0 Gall: 0-1
Aids: Bl: 0-0 Vi: 0-0 Tstrap: 0-0
Best Rating: 96 1/03 Kemp 2m   gd-sft NHF

Kaytash

83   **60**

4-y-o b f Silverdale Knight-Lady Swift (Jalmood (USA))
K W Hogg K W Hogg

Placings:5P0   (1304)
2002/03: 17SS, 17PG, 16QGF,

	Starts	1st	2nd	3rd	Win & Pl
Hurdles	3	0	0	0	0
Career Total	3	0	0	0	0

Going: Sf: 0-1 GS: 0-0 Gd: 0-1 GF: - Fm: 0-1
Distance: 2m/2m3: 0-3 2m4-2m7: 0-0 3m+: 0-0
Track: LH: 0-2 RH: 0-1 Tight: 0-2 Gall: 0-0
Aids: Bl: 0-0 Vi: 0-0 Tstrap: 0-0
Best Rating: 60 9/02 Prth 2m110y   gd-fm Hdl

Kaytee Diamond

7-y-o b m Afzal-Lasses Nightshade (Deadly Nightshade)
Dr P Pritchard T Teague

Placings:FFP   (4344)
2002/03: 22FGS, 18FS, 16PGF,

	Starts	1st	2nd	3rd	Win & Pl
Hurdles	3	0	0	0	
Career Total	3	0	0	0	

Going: Sf: 0-1 GS: 0-1 Gd: 0-0 GF: - Fm: 0-1
Distance: 2m/2m3: 0-2 2m4-2m7: 0-1 3m+: 0-0
Track: LH: 0-2 RH: 0-1 Tight: 0-1 Gall: 0-0
Aids: Bl: 0-0 Vi: 0-0 Tstrap: 0-0
Best Rating: 0 3/03 Wwck 2m   gd-fm Hdl

Keaneo (IRE)

100(98h)   (97h)**105+**

8-y-o b g Aristocracy-Nessa-Pride (IRE) (Balbo)
N A Twiston-Davies N A Twiston-Davies

Placings:4F00/1P02003-FU61211   (1906)
2002/03: 16FGS, 21UG, 19RGF, 191GF, 19PG, 261G, 201GS,

	Starts	1st	2nd	3rd	Win & Pl
Hurdles	2	1	0	0	3426
Chases	5	2	1	0	7750
Career Total	18	4	2	1	16362
105 11/02 Sthl		2m4f110yF(0-90)Ch	G-S	£4030	
100 11/02 Hrfd		3m2f F(0-90)Hdl	GD	£3425	
94 10/02 Hrfd		2m3f G(0-95)HCh	G-F	£2439	
97 9/01 Prth		2m4f110yF(0-100)HHdl	GD	£3484	
		Total win prize-money £13380			

Going: Sf: 0-0 GS: 1-2 Gd: 1-3 GF: - Fm: 1-2
Distance: 2m/2m3: 1-3 2m4-2m7: 1-3 3m+: 1-1
Track: LH: 1-2 RH: 2-5 Tight: 1-2 Gall: 0-0
Aids: Bl: 0-0 Vi: 0-0 Tstrap: 0-0
Best Rating: 105 11/02 Sthl   2m4f110y gd-sft   Ch

Equally effective over fences and hurdles, he won under both codes in the autumn of 2002. Stays beyond three miles.

Kedge Anchor Man

100   **96**

12-y-o b g Bustino-Jenny Mere (Brigadier Gerard)
N A Gaselee Anthony M Green

Placings:3/F/2265/6U2F4/02115-20355   (4120)
2002/03: 22FS, 22QS, 223GS, 20SHY, 26SG,

	Starts	1st	2nd	3rd	Win & Pl
Hurdles	5	0	1	1	1980
Career Total	21	2	5	2	12454
106 2/02 Sand		2m4f110y		D(0-110)HHdl	HVY	£4446
100 1/02 Hntg		2m4f110y		F(0-95)HHdl	G-S	£2024
		Total win prize-money £6470			

Going: Sf: 0-3 GS: 0-1 Gd: 0-1 GF: - Fm: 0-0
Distance: 2m/2m3: 0-0 2m4-2m7: 0-4 3m+: 0-1
Track: LH: 0-0 RH: 0-5 Tight: 0-0 Gall: 0-1
Aids: Bl: 0-0 Vi: 0-0 Tstrap: 0-0
Best Rating: 109 12/99 Extr   2m7f110y gd-sft   Ch

Landed two weak novices handicap hurdles early in 2002. Stays two and a half miles, effective on testing ground.

Kedon (CZE)

102   **86**

8-y-o gr g Mill Pond (FR)-Kelda (FR) (Northern Baby (CAN))
Josef Vana li Javor Stable

Placings:124/111/1U/112U11-321230   (1940)
2002/03: 21³G, 22²G, 23¹G, 29²S, 34³HY, 31⁰GS,

	Starts	1st	2nd	3rd	Win & Pl
Chases	6	1	2	2	14183
Career Total	20	10	4	2	19013

7/02	Svet	2m7f	Ch	GD	£966
10/01	Pard	2m6f110y	Ch	SFT	£1084
9/01	Olsy	3m	Ch	GD	£903
6/01	Most	2m3f	Ch	GD	£542
5/01	Pard	2m4f	Ch	GD	£271
9/00	Most	1m7f	Hdl	GD	£347
8/99	Svet	2m1f110y	Ch	GD	£306
7/99	Karl	2m1f	Ch	GD	£306
6/99	Pard	2m1f110y	Hdl	GD	£347
8/98	VelC	1m5f	Hdl	GD	£209

Total win prize-money £5281

Going: Sf: 0-2 GS: 0-1 Gd: 1-3 GF: - Fm: 0-0
Distance: 2m/2m3: 0-0 **2m4-2m7:** 1-3 3m+: 0-3
Track: LH: 0-2 RH: 0-0 Tight: 0-0 Gall: 0-0
Aids: Bl: 0-0 Vi: 0-0 Tstrap: 0-0
Best Rating: 89 11/02 Chel 3m7f   gd-sft   Ch

Czech-trained gelding. He finished third in the cross-country
Velka Pardubicka of 2002.

Keegan Bearnais (FR)

90   **69**

5-y-o b g Tropular-Sofyland (FR) (Kashneb (FR))
A M Hales Andrew L Cohen

Placings:553-4P3PP   (4706)
2002/03: 19⁴VS, 22²GS, 20³GF, 16²GF, 20²G,

	Starts	1st	2nd	3rd	Win & Pl
Hurdles	4	0	0	1	519
Chases	1	0	0	0	525
Career Total	8	0	0	2	4105

Going: Sf: 0-0 GS: 0-1 Gd: 0-1 GF: - Fm: 0-2
Distance: 2m/2m3: 0-1 2m4-2m7: 0-4 3m+: 0-0
Track: LH: 0-4 RH: 0-0 Tight: 0-3 Gall: 0-0
Aids: Bl: 0-1 Vi: 0-0 Tstrap: 0-0
Best Rating: 69 3/03 Sthl 2m4f110y gd-fm   Hdl

Keen Leader (IRE)

112(113h)   (154h)**157+**

7-y-o b g Supreme Leader-Keen Gale (IRE) (Strong Gale)
Jonjo O Neill Mrs Stewart Catherwood

Placings:1/111F-F1115   (4110)
2002/03: 24⁶G, 22¹S, 25¹GS, 24¹GS, 24⁵G,

	Starts	1st	2nd	3rd	Win & Pl
Chases	5	3	0	0	62510
Career Total	10	7	0	0	84597

157	2/03	Asct	3m110y	A Ch	G-S	£27300
154	2/03	Weth	3m1f	A Ch	G-S	£20825
150	11/02	Hayd	2m6f	C Ch	SFT	£10885
154	2/02	Uttx	2m4f110yA	Hdl	HVY	£12000
126	1/02	Leic	2m4f110yE	Hdl	SFT	£3052
114	12/01	Towc	2m5f	D Hdl	HVY	£4192
124	4/01	Prth	2m110y	H NHF	HVY	£2842

Total win prize-money £81097

Going: Sf: 1-1 GS: 2-2 Gd: 0-2 GF: - Fm: 0-0

Distance: 2m/2m3: 0-0 2m4-2m7: 1-1 **3m+:** 2-4
Track: **LH:** 2-4 RH: 1-1 Tight: 0-0 Gall: 0-2
Aids: Bl: 0-0 Vi: 0-0 Tstrap: 0-0
Best Rating: 157 2/03 Asct 3m110y   gd-sft   Ch

Very promising novice chaser; easy winner of his first three
completed starts over fences in 2002/2003 including facile
success in the Reynoldstown at Ascot in February; disappointing in the 2003 Royal & SunAlliance Chase at the 2003
Festival; handles soft conditions well, unproven on faster;
stays at least 3m 1f; suited by small fields.

Keen To The Last (FR)

109(103h)   (102h)**109**

11-y-o ch g Keen-Derniere Danse (Gay Mecene (USA))
Mrs S J Smith D E Allen & S Balmer

Placings:03223/13442/2122/P44514/22/12F22641P-12
                                                  (0376)
2002/03: 24¹G, 25²GF,

	Starts	1st	2nd	3rd	Win & Pl
Chases	2	1	1	0	5102
Career Total	33	6	12	3	37138

109	5/02	Sthl	3m110y	E(0-110)HCh	GD	£3718
106	3/02	Sedg	2m5f	D(0-115)HCh	SFT	£4284
102	10/01	Sthl	2m4f110yE	(0-115)HHdl	GD	£2562
107	3/00	MRas	2m4f	F(0-110)HCh	G-F	£3581
113	3/99	Newc	2m4f	E Ch	SFT	£4195
97	10/96	Weth	2m4f110yE	Hdl	GD	£2075

Total win prize-money £20416

Going: Sf: 0-0 GS: 0-0 Gd: 1-1 GF: - Fm: 0-1
Distance: 2m/2m3: 0-0 2m4-2m7: 0-0 **3m+:** 1-2
Track: **LH:** 1-2 RH: 0-0 Tight: 1-2 Gall: 0-0
Aids: Bl: 0-0 Vi: 0-0 Tstrap: 0-0
Best Rating: 113 4/99 Weth 2m4f110y good   Ch

Modest chaser, effective at around two and a half miles.
Needs the top of the ground to stay three miles but handles
all types of going.

Keep Ikis

96   **69**

9-y-o ch m Anshan-Santee Sioux (Dancing Brave (USA))
Mrs M Reveley T McGoran

Placings:3420/4060   (3578)
2002/03: 19⁴G, 19⁰GS, 25⁶G, 24⁰G,

	Starts	1st	2nd	3rd	Win & Pl
Hurdles	4	0	0	0	
Career Total	8	0	1	1	525

Going: Sf: 0-0 GS: 0-1 Gd: 0-3 GF: - Fm: 0-0
Distance: 2m/2m3: 0-1 2m4-2m7: 0-1 3m+: 0-2
Track: LH: 0-3 RH: 0-1 Tight: 0-3 Gall: 0-0
Aids: Bl: 0-1 Vi: 0-0 Tstrap: 0-0
Best Rating: 89 6/98 MRas 1m5f110y gd-fm NHF

Two mile handicapper on the Flat, very disapointing so far
over hurdles.

Keep On Running (FR)

(106h)   (116dh)

5-y-o ch g Beyssac (FR)-Kiruna V (a.Arab) (FR) (Thalian)
A King Paul Green

Placings:10P   (4310)
2002/03: 19¹S, 20⁰GS, 24⁰G,

	Starts	1st	2nd	3rd	Win & Pl
Hurdles	3	1	0	0	3605

| Career Total | 3 | 1 | 0 | 0 | 3605 |
| 116 | 12/02 Hrfd | 2m3f110y | | E Hdl | SFT |
| £3605 |

Total win prize-money £3605

Going: Sf: 1-1 GS: 0-1 Gd: 0-1 GF: - Fm: 0-0
Distance: 2m/2m3: 0-0 **2m4-2m7:** 1-2 3m+: 0-1
Track: LH: 0-2 **RH:** 1-1 Tight: 0-0 Gall: 0-1
Aids: Bl: 0-0 Vi: 0-0 Tstrap: 0-0
Best Rating: 116 12/02 Hrfd 2m3f110y soft   Hdl

Comfortable winner of a novice hurdle at Hereford on his
debut.

Keep On Ski

5-y-o b g Petoski-Keep On Dancing (Crooner)
Mrs J Candlish (A Streeter 28/10) Mrs Maxine Kavanagh

Placings:00PP   (4527)
2002/03: 17⁰G, 17⁰S, 20⁰GF, 20⁰G,

	Starts	1st	2nd	3rd	Win & Pl
NH Flat	2	0	0	0	0
Hurdles	2	0	0	0	0
Career Total	4	0	0	0	

Going: Sf: 0-1 GS: 0-0 Gd: 0-2 GF: - Fm: 0-1
Distance: 2m/2m3: 0-2 2m4-2m7: 0-2 3m+: 0-0
Track: LH: 0-3 RH: 0-1 Tight: 0-3 Gall: 0-0
Aids: Bl: 0-0 Vi: 0-1 Tstrap: 0-0
Best Rating: 54 10/02 Bang 2m1f   soft   NHF

Keep Out Of Debt

6-y-o b m Castle Keep-Deep In Debt (Deep Run)
E R Clough E R Clough

Placings:PP6P   (1812)
2002/03: 16⁰S, 16⁰GF, 17⁶F, 17⁰G,

	Starts	1st	2nd	3rd	Win & Pl
NH Flat	3	0	0	0	0
Hurdles	1	0	0	0	0
Career Total	4	0	0	0	

Going: Sf: 0-1 GS: 0-0 Gd: 0-1 GF: - Fm: 0-2
Distance: 2m/2m3: 0-0 2m4-2m7: 0-0 3m+: 0-0
Track: LH: 0-2 RH: 0-1 Tight: 0-0 Gall: 0-0
Aids: Bl: 0-0 Vi: 0-0 Tstrap: 0-0
Best Rating: 53 10/02 Tntn 2m1f   firm   NHF

Keep Right On (IRE)

89f   **75f**

5-y-o b g Be My Native (USA)-Mystery Woman (Tula
Rocket)
A M Hales Andrew L Cohen

Placings:0   (3322)
2002/03: 16⁰GS,

	Starts	1st	2nd	3rd	Win & Pl
NH Flat	1	0	0	0	
Career Total	1	0	0	0	

Going: Sf: 0-0 GS: 0-1 Gd: 0-0 GF: - Fm: 0-0
Distance: 2m/2m3: 0-1 2m4-2m7: 0-0 3m+: 0-0
Track: LH: 0-0 RH: 0-1 Tight: 0-0 Gall: 0-0
Aids: Bl: 0-0 Vi: 0-0 Tstrap: 0-0
Best Rating: 75 1/03 Kemp 2m   gd-sft NHF

Keep Smiling (IRE)
105(92h)   (85h)**124+**
7-y-o b g Broken Hearted-Laugh Away (Furry Glen)
Miss H C Knight Mrs R A Humphries

Placings:64P-F1UUP   (3927)
2002/03: 18FGF, 201GS, 20UGS, 20US, 24PG,

	Starts	1st	2nd	3rd	Win & Pl
Chases	5	1	0	0	5796
Career Total	8	1	0	0	6070
121 10/02 Bang	2m4f110yD Ch			G-S	£5796

Total win prize-money £5796

Going: Sf: 0-1 GS: 1-2 Gd: 0-1 GF: - Fm: 0-1
Distance: 2m/2m3: 0-1 **2m4-2m7: 1-3** 3m+: 0-1
Track: LH: 1-2 RH: 0-2 **Tight: 1-2** Gall: 0-2
Aids: Bl: 0-0 Vi: 0-0 Tstrap: 0-0
Best Rating: 121 10/02 Bang 2m4f110y gd-sft Ch

Fair chaser; placed in an Irish point; did not achieve much over hurdles; jumping has been far from fluent over fences so far; seemingly best over two and a half miles; may prefer decent ground.

Keepatem (IRE)
108   **130**
7-y-o ch g Be My Native (USA)-Ariannrun (Deep Run)
M F Morris J P McManus

Placings:0/0B1/00051413   (4456)
2002/03: 200S, 200S, 160YS, 225S, 241S, 194S, 241SH, 243G,

	Starts	1st	2nd	3rd	Win & Pl
Hurdles	8	2	0	1	34351
Career Total	12	3	0	1	38803
123 2/03 Punc	3m	HHdl		SH	£12678
113 1/03 Leop	3m	HHdl		SFT	£16883
114 2/01 Thur	2m	Hdl		Y-S	£4451

Total win prize-money £34014

Going: Sf: 1-5 GS: 0-0 Gd: 0-1 GF: - Fm: 0-0
Distance: 2m/2m3: 0-2 2m4-2m7: 0-3 **3m+: 2-3**
Track: LH: 1-4 RH: 1-2 Tight: 0-1 Gall: 0-0
Aids: Bl: 0-0 Vi: 0-0 Tstrap: 0-0
Best Rating: 130 4/03 Aint 3m110y good Hdl

Useful Irish hurdler; goes well in soft ground; effective at two miles but seemingly better suited by three.

Keeper's Call (IRE)

11-y-o ch g Mandalus-Thistletopper (Le Bavard (FR))
Mrs V J Makin R G Makin

Placings:12/4/P/56-5   (4777)
2002/03: 313G,

	Starts	1st	2nd	3rd	Win & Pl
Chases	1	0	0	0	0
Career Total	7	1	1	0	2433
102 4/99 Carl	3m2f	H Ch		GD	£1155

Total win prize-money £1155

Going: Sf: 0-0 GS: 0-0 Gd: 0-1 GF: - Fm: 0-0
Distance: 2m/2m3: 0-0 2m4-2m7: 0-0 3m+: 0-1
Track: LH: 0-0 RH: 0-0 Tight: 0-0 Gall: 0-0
Aids: Bl: 0-0 Vi: 0-0 Tstrap: 0-0
Best Rating: 107 4/99 Chel 3m1f110y gd-sft Ch

Keepers Mead (IRE)
76   **73**
5-y-o ch g Aahsaylad-Runaway Pilot (Cheval)
R H Alner J C Browne

Placings:6F6P   (4212)
2002/03: 186S, 20FS, 186S, 18PG,

	Starts	1st	2nd	3rd	Win & Pl
NH Flat	1	0	0	0	0
Hurdles	3	0	0	0	0
Career Total	4	0	0	0	0

Going: Sf: 0-3 GS: 0-0 Gd: 0-1 GF: - Fm: 0-0
Distance: 2m/2m3: 0-3 2m4-2m7: 0-1 3m+: 0-0
Track: LH: 0-4 RH: 0-0 Tight: 0-2 Gall: 0-0
Aids: Bl: 0-0 Vi: 0-0 Tstrap: 0-0
Best Rating: 87 11/02 Plum 2m2f soft NHF

Moderate hurdler; not disgraced in a Plumpton bumper November 2002; shown little over hurdles.

Keetchy (IRE)
93   **86**
4-y-o b g Darshaan-Ezana (Ela-Mana-Mou)
J D Frost (J L Dunlop 25/10) The Tuesday Syndicate

Placings:5   (4084)
2002/03: 165GS,

	Starts	1st	2nd	3rd	Win & Pl
Hurdles	1	0	0	0	0
Career Total	1	0	0	0	0

Going: Sf: 0-0 GS: 0-1 Gd: 0-0 GF: - Fm: 0-0
Distance: 2m/2m3: 0-1 2m4-2m7: 0-0 3m+: 0-0
Track: LH: 0-1 RH: 0-0 Tight: 0-1 Gall: 0-0
Aids: Bl: 0-0 Vi: 0-0 Tstrap: 0-0
Best Rating: 86 3/03 Strf 2m110y gd-sft Hdl

Kefir D'Angron (FR)
94   **113**
5-y-o b g Panoramic-Wagama (FR) (Rigolo lv (FR))
G Macaire J D Cotton

Placings:12F1116   (2239)
2002/03: 171G, 182VS, 17FVS, 171G, 191S, 171HY, 166S,

	Starts	1st	2nd	3rd	Win & Pl
Hurdles	7	4	1	0	52298
Career Total	7	4	1	0	52298
11/02 Engh	2m1f110y Hdl		HVY	£22086
113 9/02 Stra	2m3f	Hdl	SFT	£10601
9/02 Chol	2m1f	Hdl	GD	£10601
5/02 Chat	2m1f	Hdl	GD	£3534

Total win prize-money £46822

Going: Sf: 2-3 GS: 0-0 Gd: 2-2 GF: - Fm: 0-0
Distance: **2m/2m3: 4-7** 2m4-2m7: 0-0 3m+: 0-0
Track: LH: 0-1 RH: 0-0 Tight: 0-0 Gall: 0-1
Aids: Bl: 0-0 Vi: 0-0 Tstrap: 0-0
Best Rating: 113 11/02 Newb 2m110y soft Hdl

Decent novice hurdler, four-times winner in France, sixth at Newbury in December 2002.

Keiran (IRE)
110(107h)   (101h)**125**
9-y-o b g Be My Native (USA)-Myra Gaye (Buckskin (FR))
H P Hogarth (D M Forster 23/5) Hogarth Racing

Placings:60/241400-261213P412   (4558)
2002/03: 162GF, 166G, 211S, 212G, 241GS, 243GF, 24PG, 224G, 241GS, 25PG,

	Starts	1st	2nd	3rd	Win & Pl
Hurdles	2	0	1	0	1152
Chases	8	3	2	1	26747

Career Total	18	4	4	1	31652
124 3/03 Newc	3m	D(0-115)HCh	G-S	£6747
117 11/02 Newc	3m	D Ch	G-S	£6711
117 10/02 Sedg	2m5f	E Ch	GD	£4030
101 11/01 Catt	2m	F(0-100)HHdl	G-F	£2607

Total win prize-money £20096

Going: Sf: 0-0 GS: 2-2 Gd: 1-6 GF: - Fm: 0-2
Distance: 2m/2m3: 0-2 2m4-2m7: 1-3 **3m+: 2-5**
Track: **LH: 3-9** RH: 0-1 Tight: 1-3 Gall: 2-3
Aids: Bl: 0-1 Vi: 0-0 Tstrap: 0-0
Best Rating: 125 4/03 Ayr 3m1f good Ch

Fair novice chaser, stays three miles in soft ground.

Kelantan
85   **100**
6-y-o b g Kris-Surf Bird (Shareef Dancer (USA))
K C Bailey Have Fun Racing Partnership

Placings:0/6   (0328)
2002/03: 166G,

	Starts	1st	2nd	3rd	Win & Pl
NH Flat	1	0	0	0	0
Career Total	2	0	0	0	0

Going: Sf: 0-0 GS: 0-0 Gd: 0-1 GF: - Fm: 0-0
Distance: 2m/2m3: 0-1 2m4-2m7: 0-0 3m+: 0-0
Track: LH: 0-1 RH: 0-0 Tight: 0-0 Gall: 0-0
Aids: Bl: 0-0 Vi: 0-0 Tstrap: 0-0
Best Rating: 88 5/02 Worc 2m good NHF

No form in two bumpers; upset a long odds-on shot on second outing over hurdles at Wetherby in May; should stay well; handles quick ground.

Kelly Canyon

11-y-o ch g Good Thyne (USA)-Kitty Castle (Rubor)
A M Thomson A M Thomson

Placings:P/0-P   (4777)
2002/03: 31PG,

	Starts	1st	2nd	3rd	Win & Pl
Chases	1	0	0	0	
Career Total	3	0	0	0	

Going: Sf: 0-0 GS: 0-0 Gd: 0-1 GF: - Fm: 0-0
Distance: 2m/2m3: 0-0 2m4-2m7: 0-0 3m+: 0-1
Track: LH: 0-0 RH: 0-0 Tight: 0-0 Gall: 0-0
Aids: Bl: 0-0 Vi: 0-0 Tstrap: 0-0
Best Rating: 44 4/02 Kels 3m1f gd-fm Ch

Kelly Pride
99   **78**
6-y-o b g Alflora (IRE)-Pearly-B (IRE) (Gunner B)
Mrs S J Smith (J Howard Johnson 4/5) J Townson, A Thomason, P Chapman

Placings:000-P503   (3938)
2002/03: 24PGS, 166G, 250G, 213GS,

	Starts	1st	2nd	3rd	Win & Pl
Hurdles	4	0	0	1	520
Career Total	7	0	0	1	520

Going: Sf: 0-0 GS: 0-2 Gd: 0-2 GF: - Fm: 0-0
Distance: 2m/2m3: 0-1 2m4-2m7: 0-1 3m+: 0-2
Track: LH: 0-3 RH: 0-1 Tight: 0-2 Gall: 0-1
Aids: Bl: 0-0 Vi: 0-0 Tstrap: 0-0

Best Rating: 75 3/03 MRas 2m5f110y gd-sft Hdl

Very limited ability over hurdles to date.

Kelnik Glory

102   **75**

7-y-o b g Nalchik (USA)-Areal (IRE) (Roselier (FR))
Mrs S M Johnson G Button

Placings:000062/P-50   (2338)
2002/03: 19⁵S, 19⁰S,

	Starts	1st	2nd	3rd	Win & Pl
Hurdles	2	0	0	0	0
Career Total	9	0	1	0	623

Going: Sf: 0-2 GS: 0-0 Gd: 0-0 GF: - Fm: 0-0
Distance: 2m/2m3: 0-1 2m4-2m7: 0-1 3m+: 0-0
Track: LH: 0-0 RH: 0-2 Tight: 0-0 Gall: 0-0
Aids: Bl: 0-0 Vi: 0-0 Tstrap: 0-0
Best Rating: 75 4/01 Plum 2m5f   heavy Hdl

Modest maiden hurdler at up to 2m 6f.

Kelrev (FR)

95   **116**

5-y-o ch g Video Rock (FR)-Belliie II (FR) (Brezzo (FR))
Miss Venetia Williams Len Jakeman, Flintham, King & Roberts

Placings:21F111333   (3618)
2002/03: 16²S, 16¹G, 17⁵S, 17¹S, 18¹G, 19¹HY, 16³S, 16³HY, 20³S,

	Starts	1st	2nd	3rd	Win & Pl
Hurdles	2	1	1	0	5742
Chases	7	3	0	3	24115
Career Total	9	4	1	3	29857
	11/02 Engh	2m3f	Ch	HVY	£12368
	10/02 Pina	2m2f110y	Ch	GD	£3534
	9/02 Comp	2m1f110y	Ch	SFT	£4417
	8/02 Vich	2m110y	Hdl	GD	£3828
			Total win prize-money £24147		

Going: Sf: 2-7 GS: 0-0 Gd: 2-2 GF: - Fm: 0-0
Distance: 2m/2m3: 4-8 2m4-2m7: 0-1 3m+: 0-0
Track: LH: 0-1 RH: 0-2 Tight: 0-0 Gall: 0-1
Aids: Bl: 0-0 Vi: 0-0 Tstrap: 0-0
Best Rating: 116 1/03 Hntg 2m110y soft Ch

A winning hurdler/chaser in France; has won over two miles over hurdles and two miles three over fences; acts on good and and heavy ground.

Keltech Gold (IRE)

(84h)   (85h)**94**

6-y-o b g Petorius-Creggan Vale Lass (Simply Great (FR))
S J Treacy (B Palling 26/7) D Brennan Accountants Synd

Placings:0600000U4U4   (4645a)
2002/03: 17⁰G, 16⁶G, 17⁰G, 18⁰GY, 18⁰YS, 20⁰HY, 16⁰Y, 16⁰HY, 16⁶S, 16ᵁGF, 16⁴GF,

	Starts	1st	2nd	3rd	Win & Pl
Hurdles	5	0	0	0	0
Chases	6	0	0	0	701
Career Total	11	0	0	0	701

Going: Sf: 0-3 GS: 0-0 Gd: 0-3 GF: 0-2 Fm: 0-2
Distance: 2m/2m3: 0-10 2m4-2m7: 0-1 3m+: 0-0
Track: LH: 0-2 RH: 0-4 Tight: 0-0 Gall: 0-0
Aids: Bl: 0-0 Vi: 0-0 Tstrap: 0-2
Best Rating: 94 3/03 Wxfd 2m   soft Ch

Keltic Bard

108   **139+**

6-y-o b g Emperor Jones (USA)-Broughton Singer (IRE) (Common Grounds)
C J Mann M Rowland, M Collins & P Cox

Placings:4/63245-1021F4   (4097)
2002/03: 16¹S, 16⁰HY, 16²S, 17¹GS, 16⁶S, 16⁴G,

	Starts	1st	2nd	3rd	Win & Pl
Hurdles	6	2	1	0	23346
Career Total	12	2	2	1	25245
129 1/03 Chel	2m1f	D(0-120)HHdl	G-S	£10483
124 11/02 Newb	2m110y C Hdl	SFT	£6815
	Total win prize-money £17298		

Going: Sf: 1-4 GS: 1-1 Gd: 0-1 GF: - Fm: 0-0
Distance: 2m/2m3: 2-6 2m4-2m7: 0-0 3m+: 0-0
Track: LH: 2-4 RH: 0-2 Tight: 0-0 Gall: 2-4
Aids: Bl: 0-0 Vi: 0-0 Tstrap: 0-0
Best Rating: 139 3/03 Chel 2m110y good Hdl

Decent, progressive hurdler; suited by trips of around 2m; best with cut in the ground; suited by coming late off a strong pace.

Keltic Flute

85   **55**

4-y-o b g Piccolo-Nanny Doon (Dominion)
Mrs Lucinda Featherstone (D Morris 7/8) Largesse Racing

Placings:0   (1336)
2002/03: 16⁰GF,

	Starts	1st	2nd	3rd	Win & Pl
Hurdles	1	0	0	0	
Career Total	1	0	0	0	

Going: Sf: 0-0 GS: 0-0 Gd: 0-0 GF: - Fm: 0-1
Distance: 2m/2m3: 0-1 2m4-2m7: 0-0 3m+: 0-0
Track: LH: 0-0 RH: 0-1 Tight: 0-0 Gall: 0-1
Aids: Bl: 0-0 Vi: 0-0 Tstrap: 0-0
Best Rating: 56 9/02 Hntg 2m110y gd-fm Hdl

Keltic Heritage (IRE)

105(104h)   (97h)**120**

9-y-o gr g Roselier (FR)-Peek-A-Step (IRE) (Step Together (USA))
L A Dace Danny O Sullivan

Placings:5P0/06P/32311202-41F634211P   (4791)
2002/03: 22⁴G, 25¹G, 24ᶠGS, 24⁶S, 20³GS, 24⁴G, 24²GS, 25¹G, 25¹G, 29ᴾG,

	Starts	1st	2nd	3rd	Win & Pl
Hurdles	1	0	0	0	
Chases	9	3	1	1	29483
Career Total	24	5	4	3	37088
120 4/03 Chel	3m1f110y	B Ch	GD	£13030
120 3/03 MRas	3m1f	D Ch	GD	£6760
114 10/02 Hrfd	3m1f110y	E Ch	GD	£4134
91 1/02 Font	2m6f110yF(0-90)HHdl	SFT	£2324
83 1/02 Hntg	2m5f110yF(0-95)HHdl	G-S	£2058
	Total win prize-money £28307		

Going: Sf: 0-1 GS: 0-3 Gd: 3-5 GF: - Fm: 0-1
Distance: 2m/2m3: 0-0 2m4-2m7: 0-2 3m+: 3-8
Track: LH: 1-5 RH: 2-5 Tight: 1-5 Gall: 1-2
Aids: Bl: 0-0 Vi: 0-0 Tstrap: 3-10
Best Rating: 120 4/03 Chel 3m1f110y good Ch

Fair novice chaser; stays three miles one; off the mark at Hereford in October 2002 and scored again at Market Rasen in March 2003; had its task made easier when the favourite went lame when winning at Cheltenham in April; front-runner; jumps soundly and likes fast ground; wears a tongue tie.

Kemal's Council (IRE)

107(102h)   (113h)**121**

7-y-o gr g Leading Counsel (USA)-Kemal s Princess (Kemal (FR))
Jonjo O Neill Bateman, Gilruth, Milward & Singleton

Placings:4⅓3/1222P-11FP   (4172)
2002/03: 25¹GS, 24¹GS, 28ᶠHY, 34ᴾS,

	Starts	1st	2nd	3rd	Win & Pl
Chases	4	2	0	0	9169
Career Total	12	3	3	1	15340
120 12/02 Fknm	3m110y E Ch	G-S	£4424
121 11/02 Weth	3m1f	D Ch	G-S	£4745
113 5/01 Hexm	3m	E Hdl	SFT	£2688
	Total win prize-money £11857		

Going: Sf: 0-2 GS: 2-2 Gd: 0-0 GF: - Fm: 0-0
Distance: 2m/2m3: 0-0 2m4-2m7: 0-0 3m+: 2-4
Track: LH: 2-4 RH: 0-0 Tight: 1-1 Gall: 0-0
Aids: Bl: 0-0 Vi: 0-0 Tstrap: 0-0
Best Rating: 121 11/02 Weth 3m1f   gd-sft Ch

Fair handicap hurdler, made a good start over fences in late 2002; stays 3m 1f; acts well in soft ground.

Ken Scott (FR)

109   **112+**

5-y-o b g Kendor (FR)-Scottish Bride (FR) (Owen Dudley)
P Winkworth Help-Yourself

Placings:1642   (3427)
2002/03: 16¹GS, 16⁶GS, 17⁴S, 18²S,

	Starts	1st	2nd	3rd	Win & Pl
Hurdles	4	1	1	0	4991
Career Total	4	1	1	0	4991
108 11/02 Hntg	2m110y E Hdl	G-S	£3003
	Total win prize-money £3003		

Going: Sf: 0-2 GS: 1-2 Gd: 0-0 GF: - Fm: 0-0
Distance: 2m/2m3: 1-4 2m4-2m7: 0-0 3m+: 0-0
Track: LH: 0-2 RH: 1-2 Tight: 0-2 Gall: 1-1
Aids: Bl: 0-0 Vi: 0-0 Tstrap: 0-0
Best Rating: 112 2/03 Font 2m2f110y soft Hdl

A winner on the level in France, won on his debut over hurdles at Huntingdon in November 2002, fair efforts since. Acts on soft ground.

Ken's Dream

99   **115**

4-y-o b c Bin Ajwaad (IRE)-Shoag (USA) (Affirmed (USA))
Ms A E Embiricos Michael Underwood

Placings:25500   (4460)
2002/03: 16²GS, 16⁵S, 17⁵GS, 17⁰G, 16⁰G,

	Starts	1st	2nd	3rd	Win & Pl
Hurdles	5	0	1	0	4227
Career Total	5	0	1	0	4227

Going: Sf: 0-1 GS: 0-2 Gd: 0-2 GF: - Fm: 0-0
Distance: 2m/2m3: 0-5 2m4-2m7: 0-0 3m+: 0-0
Track: LH: 0-3 RH: 0-2 Tight: 0-1 Gall: 0-3
Aids: Bl: 0-0 Vi: 0-0 Tstrap: 0-0

Best Rating: 115 1/03　Chel　2m1f　gd-sft　Hdl

Decent hurdler; does not want the ground too soft; effective over two miles.

Ken'Tucky (FR)
103f　　　　　　　　　105f
5-y-o b g Video Rock (FR)-La Salamandre (FR) (Pot D Or (FR))
N J Henderson　Sir Robert Ogden

Placings:*343*　　　　　　　　　　(4560)
2002/03: 16³GS, 16⁴G, 16³G,

	Starts	1st	2nd	3rd	Win & Pl
NH Flat	3	0	0	2	891
Career Total	3	0	0	2	891

Going:　Sf: 0-0 GS: 0-1 Gd: 0-2 GF: - Fm: 0-0
Distance:　2m/2m3: 0-3 2m4-2m7: 0-0 3m+: 0-0
Track:　LH: 0-2 RH: 0-1 Tight: 0-0 Gall: 0-0
Aids:　Bl: 0-0 Vi: 0-0 Tstrap: 0-0
Best Rating: 105 3/03　Wwck 2m　good　NHF

A brother to the top French chaser El Paso III; ran well on all three starts in bumpers; does not look short of stamina.

Kenilworth (USA)
113　　　　　　　　　125
4-y-o b c Darshaan-Kerenza (Seattle Dancer (USA))
Patrick O Brady (John M Oxx 17/10)　Miss Rita Shah

Placings:0221301　　　　　　　　　(4330a)
2002/03: 16⁰S, 16²HY, 16²YS, 16¹S, 16³S, 17⁰G, 16¹GY,

	Starts	1st	2nd	3rd	Win & Pl
Hurdles	7	2	2	1	26140
Career Total	7	2	2	1	26140
124 3/03	Navn 2m	Hdl		G-Y	£6272
125 2/03	Punc 2m	Hdl		SFT	£7168

Total win prize-money £13442

Going:　Sf: 1-4 GS: 0-0 Gd: 0-1 GF: - Fm: 0-0
Distance:　**2m/2m3: 2-7** 2m4-2m7: 0-0 3m+: 0-0
Track:　LH: 1-4 RH: 1-3 Tight: 0-0 Gall: 0-1
Aids:　Bl: 0-0 Vi: 0-0 Tstrap: 0-0
Best Rating: 129 1/03　Punc 2m　yld-sft　Hdl

Useful Irish juvenile hurdler; effective in soft ground over two miles.

Kennythorpe Boppy (IRE)
60　　　　　　　　　36
5-y-o ch g Aragon-Spark (IRE) (Flash Of Steel)
J S Wainwright　J S Wainwright

Placings:U-0　　　　　　　　　(1743)
2002/03: 16⁰GS,

	Starts	1st	2nd	3rd	Win & Pl
Hurdles	1	0	0	0	
Career Total	2	0	0	0	

Going:　Sf: 0-0 GS: 0-1 Gd: 0-0 GF: - Fm: -
Distance:　2m/2m3: 0-1 2m4-2m7: 0-0 3m+: 0-0
Track:　LH: 0-1 RH: 0-0 Tight: 0-0 Gall: 0-0
Aids:　Bl: 0-0 Vi: 0-0 Tstrap: 0-0
Best Rating: 36 11/02　Weth 2m　gd-sft　Hdl

Kentford Busy B
9-y-o b m Petoski-Busy Mittens (Nearly A Hand)
M F Loggin　Miss S A Loggin

Placings:*3245/526P5/6P1350/6*　　　　(0187)
2002/03: 20⁶GF,

	Starts	1st	2nd	3rd	Win & Pl
Chases	1	0	0	0	0
Career Total	16	1	2	2	5182
100 10/00	Extr	2m6f110yE(0-105)HHdl	SFT	£3071

Total win prize-money £3071

Going:　Sf: 0-0 GS: 0-0 Gd: 0-0 GF: - Fm: 0-1
Distance:　2m/2m3: 0-0 2m4-2m7: 0-1 3m+: 0-0
Track:　LH: 0-0 RH: 0-1 Tight: 0-0 Gall: 0-1
Aids:　Bl: 0-0 Vi: 0-0 Tstrap: 0-0
Best Rating: 100 11/00　Extr　2m6f110y　gd-sft　Hdl

Kentford Fern
110　　　　　(95h)113
8-y-o b m El Conquistador-Busy Mittens (Nearly A Hand)
J W Mullins　D I Bare

Placings:*662P/1044/64-21P2P*　　　　(4674)
2002/03: 25²S, 20¹GS, 24²S, 25²PS, 25PGF,

	Starts	1st	2nd	3rd	Win & Pl
Chases	5	1	2	0	14536
Career Total	15	2	3	0	19280
113 1/03	Sthl	2m4f110yD Ch		G-S	£5421
114 1/01	Font	2m6f110yE Hdl		SFT	£2534

Total win prize-money £7955

Going:　Sf: 0-3 GS: 1-1 Gd: 0-0 GF: - Fm: 0-1
Distance:　2m/2m3: 0-0 **2m4-2m7: 1-2** 3m+: 0-3
Track:　**LH: 1-2** RH: 0-3 **Tight: 1-2** Gall: 0-0
Aids:　Bl: 0-0 Vi: 0-0 Tstrap: 0-0
Best Rating: 114 1/01　Font　2m6f110y　soft　Hdl

Fair chaser; absent for 14 months before running well at Folkestone on her return in January 2003; won a virtual match at Southwell next time; pulled up lame in April; stays 3m 2f; acts on good ground and softer.

Kentford Grebe
91　　　　　　　　　73+
4-y-o b f Teenoso (USA)-Notinhand (Nearly A Hand)
J W Mullins　D I Bare

Placings:*600U3*　　　　　　　　　(3934)
2002/03: 14⁶GS, 12⁰G, 19⁰GS, 22ᵁGS, 20³S,

	Starts	1st	2nd	3rd	Win & Pl
NH Flat	2	0	0	0	
Hurdles	3	0	0	1	521
Career Total	5	0	0	1	521

Going:　Sf: 0-1 GS: 0-3 Gd: 0-1 GF: - Fm: 0-0
Distance:　2m/2m3: 0-1 2m4-2m7: 0-2 3m+: 0-0
Track:　LH: 0-2 RH: 0-2 Tight: 0-1 Gall: 0-0
Aids:　Bl: 0-0 Vi: 0-0 Tstrap: 0-0
Best Rating: 73 3/03　Font　2m4f　soft　Hdl

Novice hurdler; better effort when third at Fontwell in February; stays two and a half miles.

Kentish Warrior (IRE)
81f　　　　　　　　　46f
5-y-o b g Warcraft (USA)-Garden County (Ragapan)

B I Case　Lady Jane Grosvenor

Placings:*0*　　　　　　　　　　(4329)
2002/03: 16⁰G,

	Starts	1st	2nd	3rd	Win & Pl
NH Flat	1	0	0	0	
Career Total	1	0	0	0	

Going:　Sf: 0-0 GS: 0-0 Gd: 0-1 GF: - Fm: 0-0
Distance:　2m/2m3: 0-1 2m4-2m7: 0-0 3m+: 0-0
Track:　LH: 0-1 RH: 0-0 Tight: 0-0 Gall: 0-1
Aids:　Bl: 0-0 Vi: 0-0 Tstrap: 0-0
Best Rating: 46 3/03　Newb　2m110y　good　NHF

Kercabellec (FR)
103　　　　　　　　　108
5-y-o b/br g Useful (FR)-Marie De Geneve (FR) (Nishapour (FR))
N J Henderson　Sir Peter & The Hon Lady Gibbings

Placings:2-5　　　　　　　　　(2770)
2002/03: 16⁵HY,

	Starts	1st	2nd	3rd	Win & Pl
Hurdles	1	0	0	0	0
Career Total	2	0	1	0	1914

Going:　Sf: 0-1 GS: 0-0 Gd: 0-0 GF: - Fm: 0-0
Distance:　2m/2m3: 0-1 2m4-2m7: 0-0 3m+: 0-0
Track:　LH: 0-1 RH: 0-0 Tight: 0-0 Gall: 0-1
Aids:　Bl: 0-0 Vi: 0-0 Tstrap: 0-0
Best Rating: 108 12/02　Newb　2m110y　heavy　Hdl

Runner-up over hurdles in France in March 2002, now with Nicky Henderson.

Kerrigand (FR)
105(110h)　　　　　(121h)135+
5-y-o gr g April Night (FR)-Gouerie (FR) (Cadoudal (FR))
M C Pipe (M Rolland 11/6)　Mrs Sarah Ling

Placings:52400-3521250　　　　(4102)
2002/03: 18⁰VS, 17⁰VS, 16²S, 17¹S, 22²HY, 23⁵GS, 25⁰G,

	Starts	1st	2nd	3rd	Win & Pl
Hurdles	6	1	2	1	15437
Chases	1	0	0	0	1160
Career Total	12	1	3	1	30177
116 12/02	Tntn	2m1f		D Hdl	SFT	£4972

Total win prize-money £4973

Going:　Sf: 1-3 GS: 0-1 Gd: 0-1 GF: - Fm: 0-0
Distance:　**2m/2m3: 1-4** 2m4-2m7: 0-1 3m+: 0-2
Track:　LH: 0-4 RH: 1-1 Tight: 1-1 Gall: 0-1
Aids:　Bl: 0-0 Vi: 0-1 Tstrap: 0-0
Best Rating: 121 2/03　Hayd　2m7f110y　gd-sft　Hdl

Ex-French; decent novice hurdler; won 3m novice chases at Worcester May 2003 on first two starts over fences; acts on most types of ground; has worn blinkers; looks the type to run up a sequence in novice chases and won a match by a wide margin at Uttoxeter in June.

Kerry Lads (IRE)
107(106h)　　　　　(106h)129
8-y-o ch g Mister Lord (USA)-Minstrel Top (Black Minstrel)
Miss Lucinda V Russell　Mrs C G Greig

Placings:*340/30F3312132-3F321F4*　　(4557)
2002/03: 26³S, 25⁵S, 25³GS, 25⁴HY, 25¹GS, 25⁵S, 33⁴G,

	Starts	1st	2nd	3rd	Win & Pl
Chases	7	1	1	2	17572

Career Total	20	3	3	7	41375
129 2/03 Ayr	3m1f	D(0-125)HCh		G-S	£6812
114 3/02 Ayr	3m1f	D Ch		HVY	£4452
101 1/02 Carl	3m2f	D Ch		HVY	£4959

Total win prize-money £16224

Going: Sf: 0-4 GS: 1-2 Gd: 0-1 GF: - Fm: 0-0
Distance: 2m2m3: 0-0 2m4-2m7: 0-0 3m+: 1-7
Track: LH: 1-6 RH: 0-1 Tight: 0-0 Gall: 0-0
Aids: Bl: 0-0 Vi: 0-0 Tstrap: 0-0
Best Rating: 129 4/03 Ayr 4m1f   good   Ch

Very useful handicap chaser; consistent sort; ran a cracker to finish fourth in the Scottish National; stays 3m 2f; effective in testing ground.

Kerry Soldier Blue

14-y-o gr g Fine Blue-Kerry Maid (Maestoso)
D O Stephens   D O Stephens

Placings:P3/P2/24P/62430F-0   (4736)
2002/03: 24⁰GF,

	Starts	1st	2nd	3rd	Win & Pl
Chases	1	0	0	0	
Career Total	14	0	3	2	3922

Going: Sf: 0-0 GS: 0-0 Gd: 0-0 GF: - Fm: 0-1
Distance: 2m/2m3: 0-0 2m4-2m7: 0-0 3m+: 0-1
Track: LH: 0-1 RH: 0-0 Tight: 0-0 Gall: 0-0
Aids: Bl: 0-0 Vi: 0-0 Tstrap: 0-0
Best Rating: 100 4/00 Chep 3m   soft   Ch

Kestle Mill (IRE)
73   87

7-y-o ch g Be My Guest (USA)-Tatisha (Habitat)
M J Coombe   Mr & Mrs D A Gamble

Placings:0060-60   (2332)
2002/03: 22⁶GS, 22⁹GS,

	Starts	1st	2nd	3rd	Win & Pl
Hurdles	2	0	0	0	0
Career Total	6	0	0	0	0

Going: Sf: 0-0 GS: 0-2 Gd: 0-0 GF: - Fm: 0-0
Distance: 2m/2m3: 0-0 2m4-2m7: 0-2 3m+: 0-0
Track: LH: 0-0 RH: 0-2 Tight: 0-0 Gall: 0-0
Aids: Bl: 0-0 Vi: 0-0 Tstrap: 0-0
Best Rating: 87 9/01 Clon 2m   gd-fm   Hdl

Kety Star (FR)
100(102h)   (94 h)104

5-y-o b g Bojador (FR)-Danystar (FR) (Alycos (FR))
Miss Venetia Williams   Mrs S A J Kinsella-Hurley

Placings:3F06   (3902)
2002/03: 16³GF, 19⁶GF, 19⁰GS, 16⁶S,

	Starts	1st	2nd	3rd	Win & Pl
Hurdles	4	0	0	1	380
Career Total	4	0	0	1	380

Going: Sf: 0-1 GS: 0-1 Gd: 0-0 GF: - Fm: 0-2
Distance: 2m/2m3: 0-2 2m4-2m7: 0-2 3m+: 0-0
Track: LH: 0-3 RH: 0-1 Tight: 0-0 Gall: 0-1
Aids: Bl: 0-0 Vi: 0-0 Tstrap: 0-0
Best Rating: 94 5/02 Worc 2m   gd-fm   Hdl

Keen sort; placed at up to 13f in the French provinces; disappointing on soft ground over hurdles and needs a sound surface; probably a lucky winner when landing 2m Class F handicap chase at Newton Abbot next time.

Kew
56   3

4-y-o b g Royal Applause-Cutleaf (Kris)
J J Bridger   Connaught Racing

Placings:P0F   (4698)
2002/03: 16⁸GS, 16⁰S, 16⁶GF,

	Starts	1st	2nd	3rd	Win & Pl
Hurdles	3	0	0	0	
Career Total	3	0	0	0	

Going: Sf: 0-1 GS: 0-1 Gd: 0-0 GF: - Fm: 0-1
Distance: 2m/2m3: 0-3 2m4-2m7: 0-0 3m+: 0-0
Track: LH: 0-2 RH: 0-1 Tight: 0-1 Gall: 0-1
Aids: Bl: 0-0 Vi: 0-0 Tstrap: 0-0
Best Rating: 5   11/02 Newb 2m110y   soft   Hdl

Keynote (IRE)
70

11-y-o ch g Orchestra-St Moritz (Linacre)
R Rowe   The Reality Partnership

Placings:0/604/51FU/0/43-B   (0643)
2002/03: 20⁸GF,

	Starts	1st	2nd	3rd	Win & Pl
Chases	1	0	0	0	
Career Total	12	1	0	1	2985
108 2/00 Folk	2m5f	F(0-90)HCh		GD	£2496

Total win prize-money £2496

Going: Sf: 0-0 GS: 0-0 Gd: 0-0 GF: - Fm: 0-1
Distance: 2m/2m3: 0-0 2m4-2m7: 0-0 3m+: 0-0
Track: LH: 0-1 RH: 0-0 Tight: 0-1 Gall: 0-0
Aids: Bl: 0-0 Vi: 0-0 Tstrap: 0-0
Best Rating: 108 2/00 Folk 2m5f   good   Ch

Lightly-raced dual-purpose handicapper, best at around two and a half miles on good to soft. Not the most reliable jumper.

Keyssac (FR)
28

5-y-o b g Beyssac (FR)-Dhop La (FR) (Son Of Silver)
A M Hales   Andrew L Cohen

Placings:0U-0   (0985)
2002/03: 17⁰GF,

	Starts	1st	2nd	3rd	Win & Pl
Hurdles	1	0	0	0	
Career Total	3	0	0	0	

Going: Sf: 0-0 GS: 0-0 Gd: 0-0 GF: - Fm: 0-0
Distance: 2m/2m3: 0-1 2m4-2m7: 0-0 3m+: 0-0
Track: LH: 0-1 RH: 0-0 Tight: 0-0 Gall: 0-0
Aids: Bl: 0-0 Vi: 0-0 Tstrap: 0-0
Best Rating: 28 12/01 Font 2m2f110y   good   Hdl

Kez
94   93

7-y-o b g Polar Falcon (USA)-Briggsmaid (Elegant Air)
P R Webber   Dennis Yardy

Placings:0/5   (1400)
2002/03: 16⁵GF,

	Starts	1st	2nd	3rd	Win & Pl
Hurdles	1	0	0	0	0
Career Total	2	0	0	0	0

Khaladjistan (IRE)
96   88+

5-y-o gr g Tirol-Khaladja (IRE) (Akarad (FR))
P F Nicholls (N J Henderson 11/5)   Notalotterry

Placings:4535-64   (1552)
2002/03: 16⁶GF, 17⁴G,

	Starts	1st	2nd	3rd	Win & Pl
Hurdles	2	0	0	0	280
Career Total	6	0	0	1	723

Going: Sf: 0-0 GS: 0-0 Gd: 0-1 GF: - Fm: 0-1
Distance: 2m/2m3: 0-2 2m4-2m7: 0-0 3m+: 0-0
Track: LH: 0-1 RH: 0-1 Tight: 0-0 Gall: 0-0
Aids: Bl: 0-0 Vi: 0-0 Tstrap: 0-0
Best Rating: 97 1/02 Hayd 2m   soft   NHF

Some ability in bumpers and is going to need a test of stamina over hurdles. Gelded since bought out of Nicky Henderson s yard was a disappointing beaten favourite at Hereford October 2002 on first start for Paul Nicholls.

Khan Kicker (IRE)
99   118

7-y-o b g Husyan (USA)-Orient Conquest (Dual)
Ferdy Murphy   E H Birkbeck,A Stewart,Sir David Landale

Placings:422/0F21412-0003   (3581)
2002/03: 20⁰GS, 20⁰GS, 16⁰G, 16³G,

	Starts	1st	2nd	3rd	Win & Pl
Hurdles	4	0	0	1	1032
Career Total	14	2	4	1	13011
116 4/02 Kels	2m110y	E Hdl		G-F	£3010
120 1/02 Muss	2m	E Hdl		SFT	£2814

Total win prize-money £5824

Going: Sf: 0-0 GS: 0-2 Gd: 0-2 GF: - Fm: 0-0
Distance: 2m/2m3: 0-2 2m4-2m7: 0-2 3m+: 0-0
Track: LH: 0-2 RH: 0-2 Tight: 0-3 Gall: 0-0
Aids: Bl: 0-0 Vi: 0-0 Tstrap: 0-0
Best Rating: 132 4/02 Ayr 2m   good   Hdl

Decent hurdler; effective at two miles; acts on most types of ground.

Kharak (FR)
101   98

4-y-o gr g Danehill (USA)-Khariyda (FR) (Shakapour)
Mrs S C Bradburne   Hardie, Robb, Copland & Steel

Placings:1324   (4762)
2002/03: 16¹S, 16³GF, 16²G, 16⁴G,

	Starts	1st	2nd	3rd	Win & Pl
Hurdles	4	1	1	1	6991
Career Total	4	1	1	1	6991
97 3/03 Ayr	2m	E Hdl		SFT	£3510

Total win prize-money £3510

Going: Sf: 1-1 GS: 0-0 Gd: 0-2 GF: - Fm: 0-1
Distance: 2m/2m3: 1-4 2m4-2m7: 0-0 3m+: 0-0
Track: LH: 1-3 RH: 0-1 Tight: 0-0 Gall: 0-0
Aids: Bl: 0-0 Vi: 0-0 Tstrap: 0-0

Best Rating: 98 4/03 Prth 2m110y good Hdl

Ex-French juvenile hurdler; took a modest contest on soft ground on debut and ran well on fast ground subsequently; looks likely to get further.

Khatani (IRE)
108   (100h)**105**
8-y-o b g Kahyasi-Khanata (USA) (Riverman (USA))
D R Gandolfo R E Brinkworth

Placings:35351/111144/13235-1346   (4440)
2002/03: 20¹G, 21³GF, 20⁴GF, 19⁶G,

	Starts	1st	2nd	3rd	Win & Pl
Hurdles	1	0	0	0	516
Chases	3	1	0	1	8289
Career Total	20	7	1	5	40346
126	5/02	Bang	2m4f110yC(0-130)HCh	GD	£6734
119	5/01	Hrfd	2m3f	D Ch	GD	£4875
126	7/00	Worc	2m4f	C(0-135)HHdl	GD	£5395
123	6/00	Worc	2m4f	C(0-135)HHdl	GD	£4875
120	5/00	Worc	2m	D(0-120)HHdl	GD	£3497
119	5/00	Bang	2m1f	D(0-120)HHdl	GD	£4348
115	4/00	Font	2m2f110yE Hdl	GD	£2240

Total win prize-money £31965

Going: Sf: 0-0 GS: 0-0 Gd: 1-2 GF: - Fm: 0-2
Distance: 2m/2m3: 0-0 2m4-2m7: 1-4 3m+: 0-0
Track: LH: 1-3 RH: 0-1 Tight: 1-2 Gall: 0-0
Aids: Bl: 0-0 Vi: 0-0 Tstrap: 0-0
Best Rating: 129 6/01 Strf 2m5f110y gd-fm Ch

Fair handicap chaser when the ground rides fast but has looked quirky on occasion; back to winning form at Bangor in May 2002 over an extended two and a half miles.

Khayal (USA)
(102c)   (82c)
9-y-o b g Green Dancer (USA)-Look Who s Dancing (USA) (Affirmed (USA))
P J Hobbs Gordon James Cossey

Placings:2P430/05/4403-6   (0106)
2002/03: 24⁶GF,

	Starts	1st	2nd	3rd	Win & Pl
Chases	1	0	0	0	0
Career Total	12	0	1	2	1434

Going: Sf: 0-0 GS: 0-0 Gd: 0-0 GF: - Fm: 0-1
Distance: 2m/2m3: 0-0 2m4-2m7: 0-0 3m+: 0-1
Track: LH: 0-0 RH: 0-1 Tight: 0-1 Gall: 0-0
Aids: Bl: 0-0 Vi: 0-0 Tstrap: 0-0
Best Rating: 84 8/97 NAbb 2m1f gd-fm Hdl

One-time decent pointer, his jumping lacks fluency under Rules.

Khayali (IRE)
100(88h)   (77h)**83+**
9-y-o b g Unfuwain (USA)-Coven (Sassafras (FR))
A R Dicken Mr & Mrs Raymond Anderson Green

Placings:005P554264-1   (1005)
2002/03: 20¹GF,

	Starts	1st	2nd	3rd	Win & Pl
Chases	1	1	0	0	4310
Career Total	11	1	0	0	5816
83	8/02	Bang	2m4f110yE(0-100)HCh	G-F	£4309

Total win prize-money £4310

Going: Sf: 0-0 GS: 0-0 Gd: 0-0 GF: - Fm: 1-1
Distance: 2m/2m3: 0-0 2m4-2m7: 1-1 3m+: 0-0

Track: LH: 1-1 RH: 0-0 Tight: 1-1 Gall: 0-0
Aids: Bl: 0-0 Vi: 0-0 Tstrap: 0-0
Best Rating: 83 8/02 Bang 2m4f110y gd-fm Ch

Plating-class hurdler; got off the mark over jumps on his chasing debut in August 2002, but broke down in doing so; stays two and a half miles; acts on any ground.

Khaysar (IRE)
76   **106**
5-y-o br g Pennekamp (USA)-Khaytada (IRE) (Doyoun)
Mrs L Wadham (D Morris 3/10) Dingley Dell Racing Ltd

Placings:2FP033214-0   (2413)
2002/03: 18⁴G,

	Starts	1st	2nd	3rd	Win & Pl
Hurdles	1	0	0	0	0
Career Total	10	1	2	2	7998
106	4/02	MRas	2m1f110yD(0-115)HHdl	GD	£5362

Total win prize-money £5363

Going: Sf: 0-0 GS: 0-0 Gd: 0-1 GF: - Fm: 0-0
Distance: 2m/2m3: 0-1 2m4-2m7: 0-0 3m+: 0-0
Track: LH: 0-1 RH: 0-0 Tight: 0-1 Gall: 0-0
Aids: Bl: 0-0 Vi: 0-0 Tstrap: 0-0
Best Rating: 106 4/02 MRas 2m1f110y good Hdl

Ex-Irish, has shown promise so far over hurdles and won a small handicap at Market Rasen in April 2002.

Khuzdar (IRE)
98   **84**
4-y-o ch g Definite Article-Mariyda (IRE) (Vayrann)
M R Channon Imperial Racing

Placings:50   (3776)
2002/03: 16⁵GS, 17⁰GS,

	Starts	1st	2nd	3rd	Win & Pl
Hurdles	2	0	0	0	0
Career Total	2	0	0	0	0

Going: Sf: 0-0 GS: 0-2 Gd: 0-0 GF: - Fm: 0-0
Distance: 2m/2m3: 0-2 2m4-2m7: 0-0 3m+: 0-0
Track: LH: 0-0 RH: 0-2 Tight: 0-0 Gall: 0-0
Aids: Bl: 0-0 Vi: 0-0 Tstrap: 0-0
Best Rating: 84 2/03 Winc 2m gd-sft Hdl

Kick For Touch (IRE)
110(92h)   (93h)**115+**
6-y-o ch g Insan (USA)-Anns Run (Deep Run)
Miss H C Knight Trevor Hemmings

Placings:64-F32211   (4569)
2002/03: 20⁶G, 21³GS, 20²S, 24²G, 24¹GF, 24¹G,

	Starts	1st	2nd	3rd	Win & Pl
Chases	6	2	2	1	13323
Career Total	8	2	2	1	13323
115	4/03	Strf	3m	D Ch	GD	£5655
100	3/03	Hntg	3m	E Ch	G-F	£4163

Total win prize-money £9818

Going: Sf: 0-1 GS: 0-1 Gd: 1-3 GF: - Fm: 1-1
Distance: 2m/2m3: 0-0 2m4-2m7: 0-3 3m+: 2-3
Track: LH: 1-2 RH: 1-4 Tight: 1-2 Gall: 1-2
Aids: Bl: 0-0 Vi: 0-0 Tstrap: 0-0
Best Rating: 115 4/03 Strf 3m good Ch

Fair novice chaser, successful over fences at Huntingdon in March 2003 and followed up at Stratford the following month; stays 3m; acts on fast and soft ground.

Kicking Bear (IRE)
72   **19**
5-y-o b g Little Bighorn-Rongo (IRE) (Tumble Gold)
D M Grissell The Brightling Club 1998

Placings:O50   (4032)
2002/03: 18⁰HY, 175HY, 20⁰HY,

	Starts	1st	2nd	3rd	Win & Pl
NH Flat	2	0	0	0	0
Hurdles	1	0	0	0	0
Career Total	3	0	0	0	0

Going: Sf: 0-3 GS: 0-0 Gd: 0-0 GF: - Fm: 0-0
Distance: 2m/2m3: 0-2 2m4-2m7: 0-1 3m+: 0-0
Track: LH: 0-1 RH: 0-2 Tight: 0-2 Gall: 0-0
Aids: Bl: 0-0 Vi: 0-0 Tstrap: 0-0
Best Rating: 87 2/03 Folk 2m1f110y heavy NHF

Kicking King (IRE)
122   **145**
5-y-o b g Old Vic-Fairy Blaze (IRE) (Good Thyne (USA))
T J Taaffe Conor Clarkson

Placings:13-12112   (4097)
2002/03: 16¹S, 20²YS, 18¹S, 16¹SH, 16²G,

	Starts	1st	2nd	3rd	Win & Pl
Hurdles	5	3	2	0	64417
Career Total	7	4	2	1	70203
142	2/03	Punc	2m	Hdl	SH	£21103
131	1/03	Cork	2m2f	Hdl	SFT	£8288
122	11/02	Naas	2m	Hdl	SFT	£7196
105	1/02	Leop	2m	NHF	Y-S	£5291

Total win prize-money £41880

Going: Sf: 2-2 GS: 0-0 Gd: 0-1 GF: - Fm: 0-0
Distance: 2m/2m3: 3-4 2m4-2m7: 0-1 3m+: 0-0
Track: LH: 1-3 RH: 1-1 Tight: 0-0 Gall: 0-0
Aids: Bl: 0-0 Vi: 0-0 Tstrap: 0-0
Best Rating: 145 3/03 Chel 2m110y good Hdl

Useful Irish-trained novice hurdler; runner-up in the Supreme Novices at Cheltenham in 2003; effective from 2m to 2m 4f; acts on good and soft ground; likes to race prominently.

Kid'Z'Play (IRE)
103   **113d**
7-y-o b g Rudimentary (USA)-Saka Saka (Camden Town)
J S Goldie Liam McGuigan

Placings:P/350   (3262)
2002/03: 16³GS, 16⁵HY, 16⁰GS,

	Starts	1st	2nd	3rd	Win & Pl
Hurdles	3	0	0	1	439
Career Total	4	0	0	1	439

Going: Sf: 0-1 GS: 0-2 Gd: 0-0 GF: - Fm: 0-0
Distance: 2m/2m3: 0-3 2m4-2m7: 0-0 3m+: 0-0
Track: LH: 0-3 RH: 0-0 Tight: 0-0 Gall: 0-1
Aids: Bl: 0-0 Vi: 0-0 Tstrap: 0-0
Best Rating: 113 12/02 Ayr 2m gd-sft Hdl

A winner on the Flat, he was third over hurdles at Ayr in December 2002 despite looking a tricky ride and was very unco-operative next time.

Kidithou (FR)
104   **120+**
5-y-o b g Royal Charter (FR)-De Thou (FR) (Trebrook (FR))

L Lungo Roman Wall Racing

Placings:23P46   (3769)
2002/03: 16²GF, 20³HY, 22PHY, 20⁴HY, 20⁶GS,

	Starts	1st	2nd	3rd	Win & Pl
NH Flat	1	0	1	0	670
Hurdles	4	0	0	1	842
Career Total	5	0	1	1	1512

Going: Sf: 0-3 GS: 0-1 Gd: 0-0 GF: - Fm: 0-1
Distance: 2m/2m3: 0-1 2m4-2m7: 0-4 3m+: 0-0
Track: LH: 0-3 RH: 0-2 Tight: 0-0 Gall: 0-0
Aids: Bl: 0-0 Vi: 0-0 Tstrap: 0-0
Best Rating: 101 1/03 Ayr 2m4f   heavy   Hdl

Moderate, but progressive hurdler; stays two and a half miles; best form on a sound surface.

Kids Inheritance (IRE)

95f   **102f**
5-y-o b g Presenting-Princess Tino (IRE) (Rontino)
J M Jefferson   Mr & Mrs J M Davenport

Placings:3520   (3357)
2002/03: 17³S, 16²GS, 16²S, 16⁹HY,

	Starts	1st	2nd	3rd	Win & Pl
NH Flat	4	0	1	1	865
Career Total	4	0	1	1	865

Going: Sf: 0-3 GS: 0-1 Gd: 0-0 GF: - Fm: 0-0
Distance: 2m/2m3: 0-4 2m4-2m7: 0-0 3m+: 0-0
Track: LH: 0-3 RH: 0-1 Tight: 0-1 Gall: 0-0
Aids: Bl: 0-0 Vi: 0-0 Tstrap: 0-0
Best Rating: 102 10/02 Carl 2m1f   soft   NHF

Showed promise in bumpers and should find races over hurdles.

Kilbragh Khan

7-y-o br g Rakaposhi King-Kilbragh Dreamer (IRE) (Decent Fellow)
A J Wilson   Mrs Elizabeth Allsop

Placings:0-P5P   (4569)
2002/03: 21PHY, 16⁵S, 24PG,

	Starts	1st	2nd	3rd	Win & Pl
Chases	3	0	0	0	0
Career Total	4	0	0	0	0

Going: Sf: 0-2 GS: 0-0 Gd: 0-1 GF: - Fm: 0-0
Distance: 2m/2m3: 0-1 2m4-2m7: 0-1 3m+: 0-1
Track: LH: 0-3 RH: 0-0 Tight: 0-2 Gall: 0-0
Aids: Bl: 0-0 Vi: 0-0 Tstrap: 0-0
Best Rating: 84 3/02 Hayd 2m   good   NHF

Kilcaroon (IRE)

(82h)   (54h)**93**
8-y-o b g Jurado (USA)-Alfuraat (Auction Ring (USA))
J Howard Johnson   W M G Black

Placings:50/00/63P-FU0   (2556)
2002/03: 23FGF, 25ᵁG, 20PGF,

	Starts	1st	2nd	3rd	Win & Pl
Hurdles	1	0	0	0	0
Chases	2	0	0	0	0
Career Total	10	0	0	1	641

Going: Sf: 0-0 GS: 0-0 Gd: 0-1 GF: - Fm: 0-2
Distance: 2m/2m3: 0-0 2m4-2m7: 0-1 3m+: 0-2
Track: LH: 0-1 RH: 0-1 Tight: 0-2 Gall: 0-0
Aids: Bl: 0-0 Vi: 0-0 Tstrap: 0-0
Best Rating: 93 4/02 Kels 3m1f   gd-fm   Ch

Irish point winner but yet to show much here.

Kilcaskin Gold (IRE)

8-y-o ch g Ore-Maypole Gayle (Strong Gale)
R A Ross   The Pavillion Syndicate

Placings:4U0-P   (4592)
2002/03: 25PG,

	Starts	1st	2nd	3rd	Win & Pl
Chases	1	0	0	0	
Career Total	4	0	0	0	270

Going: Sf: 0-0 GS: 0-0 Gd: 0-1 GF: - Fm: 0-0
Distance: 2m/2m3: 0-0 2m4-2m7: 0-0 3m+: 0-1
Track: LH: 0-0 RH: 0-0 Tight: 0-0 Gall: 0-0
Aids: Bl: 0-0 Vi: 0-0 Tstrap: 0-0
Best Rating: 0 4/03 Hexm 3m1f   good   Ch

Kildare Chiller (IRE)

103   **102**
9-y-o ch g Shahrastani (USA)-Ballycuirke (Taufan (USA))
P R Hedger   P R Hedger

Placings:0500/101000/210F55/65222361-6650350426   (4214)
2002/03: 17⁶G, 18⁶GF, 17⁵S, 22⁹GF, 18³G, 20⁵HY, 18⁰S, 19⁴S, 18²S, 18⁶G,

	Starts	1st	2nd	3rd	Win & Pl
Hurdles	10	0	1	1	3828
Career Total	34	4	5	2	21357

107 3/02 Font 2m2f110yD(0-115)HHdl SFT £5382
117 10/00 Font 2m2f110yD(0-120)HHdl G-S £3168
106 11/98 Thur 2m2f   (0-102)HHdl SFT £2301
    5/98 Dpat 2m1f172y Hdl   G-F £1489
              Total win prize-money £12342

Going: Sf: 0-5 GS: 0-0 Gd: 0-3 GF: - Fm: 0-2
Distance: 2m/2m3: 0-7 2m4-2m7: 0-3 3m+: 0-0
Track: LH: 0-7 RH: 0-2 Tight: 0-10 Gall: 0-0
Aids: Bl: 0-0 Vi: 0-0 Tstrap: 0-0
Best Rating: 117 1/01 Plum 2m   heavy   Hdl

Modest hurdler; best at around two and a quarter miles; suited by easy ground.

Kildee Lass

                      83f
4-y-o gr f Morpeth-Pigeon Loft (IRE) (Bellypha)
J D Frost   J F O Donovan

Placings:4000   (4224)
2002/03: 14⁴GS, 13⁰S, 17⁰S, 14⁰GF,

	Starts	1st	2nd	3rd	Win & Pl
NH Flat	4	0	0	0	0
Career Total	4	0	0	0	0

Going: Sf: 0-2 GS: 0-1 Gd: 0-0 GF: - Fm: 0-1
Distance: 2m/2m3: 0-1 2m4-2m7: 0-1 3m+: 0-0
Track: LH: 0-0 RH: 0-2 Tight: 0-1 Gall: 0-0
Aids: Bl: 0-0 Vi: 0-0 Tstrap: 0-0
Best Rating: 83 11/02 Wwck 1m6f   gd-sft   NHF

Kildorragh (IRE)

108   **123**
9-y-o b g Glacial Storm (USA)-Take A Dare (Pragmatic)
L Wells   Mrs Carrie Zetter-Wells

Placings:0002045/12/3PU1U1-P22P   (4172)
2002/03: 26PHY, 26²GS, 24²G, 34PS,

	Starts	1st	2nd	3rd	Win & Pl
Chases	4	0	2	0	8744
Career Total	19	3	4	1	36786

123 12/01 Chep 3m2f110yC(0-130)HCh SFT £10166
123 11/01 Font 3m2f110yD(0-125)HCh G-S £3818
121 2/01 Font 3m2f110yH Ch   G-S £7345
             Total win prize-money £21330

Going: Sf: 0-2 GS: 0-1 Gd: 0-1 GF: - Fm: 0-0
Distance: 2m/2m3: 0-0 2m4-2m7: 0-0 3m+: 0-4
Track: LH: 0-3 RH: 0-0 Tight: 0-1 Gall: 0-1
Aids: Bl: 0-0 Vi: 0-0 Tstrap: 0-0
Best Rating: 123 12/01 Chep 3m2f110y   soft   Ch

Decent handicap chaser; acts on soft ground; handles a fast surface; stays 3m2f.

Kildrummy Castle

96   **86+**
11-y-o b g Komaite (USA)-Khadine (Astec)
Ferdy Murphy   Major P H K Steveney

Placings:2/0000125/45122/2445/F/2/P062-16P   (0558)
2002/03: 24²G, 21¹G, 21⁶G, 19PGF,

	Starts	1st	2nd	3rd	Win & Pl
Chases	4	1	1	0	3434
Career Total	26	3	7	0	14042

86 5/02 Fknm 2m2f110yF(0-90)HCh GD £2506
94 2/98 Sedg 2m110y E(0-110)HCh GD £3254
81 3/97 Uttx 2m   E(0-100)HHdl G-F £2316
             Total win prize-money £8076

Going: Sf: 0-0 GS: 0-0 Gd: 1-3 GF: - Fm: 0-1
Distance: 2m/2m3: 0-1 2m4-2m7: 1-2 3m+: 0-1
Track: LH: 1-3 RH: 0-1 Tight: 1-2 Gall: 0-1
Aids: Bl: 0-0 Vi: 0-0 Tstrap: 0-0
Best Rating: 98 3/98 Newc 2m110y   good   Ch

Killala Bay (IRE)

8-y-o b m Executive Perk-Killinure Point (Smooth Stepper)
K C Bailey   Mrs J Way

Placings:40/6P   (3844)
2002/03: 16⁶S, 20PG,

	Starts	1st	2nd	3rd	Win & Pl
Chases	2	0	0	0	0
Career Total	4	0	0	0	0

Going: Sf: 0-1 GS: 0-0 Gd: 0-1 GF: - Fm: 0-0
Distance: 2m/2m3: 0-1 2m4-2m7: 0-1 3m+: 0-0
Track: LH: 0-0 RH: 0-2 Tight: 0-1 Gall: 0-0
Aids: Bl: 0-0 Vi: 0-0 Tstrap: 0-0
Best Rating: 88 10/00 Sthl 2m   soft   NHF

Killalongford (IRE)

101   **84**
6-y-o b g Tenby-Queen Crab (Private Walk)
Mrs S M Johnson   Mrs M E Mason

Placings:00630-00P02244   (4786)
2002/03: 21⁹G, 22⁰S, 26PS, 20⁰GS, 17²GS, 21²G, 20⁴GF, 22⁴G,

	Starts	1st	2nd	3rd	Win & Pl
Hurdles	8	0	2	0	2392
Career Total	13	0	2	1	2778

Going: Sf: 0-2 GS: 0-2 Gd: 0-3 GF: - Fm: 0-1
Distance: 2m/2m3: 0-1 2m4-2m7: 0-6 3m+: 0-1
Track: LH: 0-2 RH: 0-5 Tight: 0-2 Gall: 0-0
Aids: Bl: 0-0 Vi: 0-0 Tstrap: 0-0
Best Rating: 100 12/01 Navn 2m   yld-sft Hdl

Plating-class hurdler; effective over two miles, but needs further; acts on a soft surface.

Killarney
100   72

5-y-o gr m Pursuit Of Love-Laune (AUS) (Kenmare (FR))
Miss Kate Milligan E Whalley

Placings:0P0-30240   (1072)
2002/03: 16⁰GS, 16⁹G, 17²GF, 21⁴G, 17⁰G,

	Starts	1st	2nd	3rd	Win & Pl
Hurdles	5	0	1	1	763
Career Total	8	0	1	1	763

Going: Sf: 0-0 GS: 0-1 Gd: 0-3 GF: - Fm: 0-1
Distance: 2m/2m3: 0-4 2m4-2m7: 0-1 3m+: 0-0
Track: LH: 0-4 RH: 0-1 Tight: 0-3 Gall: 0-0
Aids: Bl: 0-0 Vi: 0-0 Tstrap: 0-0
Best Rating: 72 6/02 MRas 2m1f110y gd-fm Hdl

Selling hurdler, best at around two miles.

Killeaney (IRE)

6-y-o b g Classic Memory-Welsh Duchy (Welsh Saint)
John G Carr James Hepburn

Placings:060   (4182a)
2002/03: 19⁰S, 16⁶GS, 20⁰S,

	Starts	1st	2nd	3rd	Win & Pl
NH Flat	1	0	0	0	0
Hurdles	1	0	0	0	0
Chases	1	0	0	0	0
Career Total	3	0	0	0	0

Going: Sf: 0-2 GS: 0-1 Gd: 0-0 GF: - Fm: 0-0
Distance: 2m/2m3: 0-2 2m4-2m7: 0-1 3m+: 0-0
Track: LH: 0-0 RH: 0-1 Tight: 0-0 Gall: 0-0
Aids: Bl: 0-0 Vi: 0-0 Tstrap: 0-0
Best Rating: 58 3/03 Tram 2m4f   soft   Ch

Killer (FR)

5-y-o ch g Cupidon (FR)-Kaoutchka (FR) (Bakst (USA))
Jonjo O Neill Mrs M C Sweeney

Placings:P   (2214)
2002/03: 21⁰S,

	Starts	1st	2nd	3rd	Win & Pl
Hurdles	1	0	0	0	
Career Total	1	0	0	0	

Going: Sf: 0-1 GS: 0-0 Gd: 0-0 GF: - Fm: 0-0
Distance: 2m/2m3: 0-0 2m4-2m7: 0-1 3m+: 0-0
Track: LH: 0-1 RH: 0-0 Tight: 0-0 Gall: 0-1
Aids: Bl: 0-0 Vi: 0-0 Tstrap: 0-1
Best Rating: 0   11/02 Newb 2m5f   soft   Hdl

Killing Time

12-y-o b g Good Times (ITY)-Kelly s Bid (Pitskelly)
S T Lewis Simon T Lewis

Placings:0032000P54/15P01U051/0P0306/6533010/3P/00
6350/006-PP   (3853)
2002/03: 16ᴾHY, 19ᴾGS,

	Starts	1st	2nd	3rd	Win & Pl
Hurdles	2	0	0	0	
Career Total	45	4	1	6	9335
76	11/98	Tntn	2m1f		G(0-90)HHdl	GD	£1658
90	4/97	Extr	2m2f		G Hdl	G-F	£1767
80	2/97	Folk	2m1f110yG(0-90)Hdl	HVY	£1639
90	9/96	Extr	2m3f		E Hdl	FRM	£2347
Total win prize-money £7414

Going: Sf: 0-1 GS: 0-1 Gd: 0-0 GF: - Fm: 0-0
Distance: 2m/2m3: 0-1 2m4-2m7: 0-1 3m+: 0-0
Track: LH: 0-0 RH: 0-2 Tight: 0-1 Gall: 0-0
Aids: Bl: 0-0 Vi: 0-0 Tstrap: 0-0
Best Rating: 90 4/97 Extr 2m2f   gd-fm Hdl

Killough Hill (IRE)
70f   66f

6-y-o ch g Fourstars Allstar (USA)-Bristol Fairy (Smartset)
C J Bennett C J Bennett

Placings:0-0   (0205)
2002/03: 16⁰GF,

	Starts	1st	2nd	3rd	Win & Pl
NH Flat	1	0	0	0	
Career Total	2	0	0	0	

Going: Sf: 0-0 GS: 0-0 Gd: 0-0 GF: - Fm: 0-0
Distance: 2m/2m3: 0-1 2m4-2m7: 0-0 3m+: 0-0
Track: LH: 0-1 RH: 0-0 Tight: 0-0 Gall: 0-0
Aids: Bl: 0-0 Vi: 0-0 Tstrap: 0-0
Best Rating: 66 4/02 MRas 2m1f110y good NHF

Killultagh Storm (IRE)
108   (113h) 143

9-y-o b g Mandalus-Rostrevor Lady (Kemal (FR))
W P Mullins Mrs Rose Boyd

Placings:00/603330133221 1/133320124/2U130536622-
P5054641   (4654a)
2002/03: 16ᴾYS, 20⁵GS, 21⁰G, 17⁵S, 16⁴SH, 16⁶Y, 20⁴GY, 17¹GF,

	Starts	1st	2nd	3rd	Win & Pl
Chases	8	1	0		29188
Career Total	43	7	7	10	149256
143	4/03	Fair	2m1f		HCh	G-F	£25324
142	11/01	DRoy	2m2f	Ch	Y-S	£20967
124	2/01	Naas	2m	Ch	SH	£6120
135	5/00	Punc	2m	(0-135)HHdl	GD	£8320
130	4/00	Fair	2m	HHdl	SFT	£39000
123	3/00	Leop	2m	(0-116)HHdl	GD	£5520
105	11/99	Fair	2m	(0-109)HHdl	SFT	£5236
Total win prize-money £110491

Going: Sf: 0-1 GS: 0-1 Gd: 0-1 GF: - Fm: 1-1
Distance: 2m/2m3: 1-5 2m4-2m7: 0-3 3m+: 0-0
Track: LH: 0-2 RH: 1-3 Tight: 0-0 Gall: 0-2
Aids: Bl: 0-0 Vi: 0-0 Tstrap: 0-0
Best Rating: 143 4/03 Fair 2m1f   gd-fm Ch

Useful Irish chaser; acts on good and soft ground; effective from 2m to 2m 4f.

Killusty (IRE)
109   151

9-y-o b g Phardante (FR)-Lepida (Royal Match)
C R Egerton Lady Lloyd Webber

Placings:1121/0111/1FP   (4791)
2002/03: 24¹S, 36ᶠG, 29ᴾG,

	Starts	1st	2nd	3rd	Win & Pl
Chases	3	1	0	0	8112
Career Total	11	7	1	0	29894
151	3/03	Sand	3m110y	C(0-135)HCh	SFT	£8112
142	2/01	Kemp	3m	C Ch	GD	£7020
142	1/01	Fknm	3m110y	D Ch	SFT	£4630
133	12/00	Leic	2m4f110yE Ch	G-S	£3328
127	4/00	Bang	2m4f	E Hdl	G-S	£2534
116	12/99	Towc	2m	H NHF	GD	£1758
119	11/99	Worc	2m	H NHF	G-S	£1786
Total win prize-money £29168

Going: Sf: 1-1 GS: 0-0 Gd: 0-2 GF: - Fm: 0-0
Distance: 2m/2m3: 0-0 2m4-2m7: 0-0 3m+: 1-3
Track: LH: 0-1 RH: 1-2 Tight: 0-1 Gall: 0-0
Aids: Bl: 0-0 Vi: 0-0 Tstrap: 0-0
Best Rating: 151 3/03 Sand 3m110y soft Ch

Very useful chaser; showed decent form in novice chases in 2000/1 but absent for a long time afterwards; made a winning return when hacking up at Sandown in March 2003; didn t jump that well but making ground when coming down at Becher s on the final circuit in the Grand National; suffered a recurrence of ligament injury in attheraces Gold Cup; stays three miles plus; acts on good and soft ground.

Killy Beach
87   73

5-y-o b g Kuwait Beach (USA)-Spiritual Lily (Brianston Zipper)
J W Mullins J A G Meaden

Placings:000-44   (1660)
2002/03: 22⁴F, 22⁴G,

	Starts	1st	2nd	3rd	Win & Pl
Hurdles	2	0	0	0	0
Career Total	5	0	0	0	0

Going: Sf: 0-0 GS: 0-0 Gd: 0-0 GF: 0-1 Fm: -
Distance: 2m/2m3: 0-0 2m4-2m7: 0-2 3m+: 0-0
Track: LH: 0-0 RH: 0-2 Tight: 0-0 Gall: 0-0
Aids: Bl: 0-0 Vi: 0-0 Tstrap: 0-0
Best Rating: 73 10/02 Winc 2m6f   good   Hdl

Kilmeade Prince (IRE)

7-y-o ch g Satco (FR)-Snowy Gunner (Gunner B)
P M J Doyle Philip M Hickey

Placings:030060/0350-P   (1814)
2002/03: 17ᴾG,

	Starts	1st	2nd	3rd	Win & Pl
Hurdles	1	0	0	0	
Career Total	11	0	0	2	760

Going: Sf: 0-0 GS: 0-0 Gd: 0-1 GF: - Fm: 0-0
Distance: 2m/2m3: 0-1 2m4-2m7: 0-0 3m+: 0-0
Track: LH: 0-0 RH: 0-1 Tight: 0-0 Gall: 0-0
Aids: Bl: 0-0 Vi: 0-0 Tstrap: 0-0
Best Rating: 100 11/00 Clon 2m   heavy NHF

Kilmeena Star

5-y-o b h So Factual (USA)-Kilmeena Glen (Beveled (USA))
J C Fox Mrs J A Cleary

Placings:PO **(4001)**
2002/03: 16^{P}S, 16°S,

	Starts	1st	2nd	3rd	Win & Pl
Hurdles	2	0	0	0	
Career Total	**2**	**0**	**0**	**0**	

Going: Sf: 0-2 GS: 0-0 Gd: 0-0 GF: - Fm: 0-0
Distance: 2m/2m3: 0-2 2m4-2m7: 0-0 3m+: 0-0
Track: LH: 0-1 RH: 0-1 Tight: 0-0 Gall: 0-1
Aids: Bl: 0-0 Vi: 0-0 Tstrap: 0-0
Best Rating: **0** 3/03 Winc 2m soft Hdl

Kilmeny (IRE)

104 **101**
5-y-o b m Royal Abjar (USA)-Mouchez Le Nez (IRE) (Cyrano De Bergerac)
M C Pipe (H Morrison 16/9) Hush Hush Partnership

Placings:0232F **(4626)**
2002/03: 16^{0}G, 18^{2}S, 16^{3}GS, 17^{2}GF, 17^{F}GF,

	Starts	1st	2nd	3rd	Win & Pl
Hurdles	5	0	2	1	3226
Career Total	**5**	**0**	**2**	**1**	**3226**

Going: Sf: 0-1 GS: 0-1 Gd: 0-1 GF: - Fm: 0-2
Distance: 2m/2m3: 0-5 2m4-2m7: 0-0 3m+: 0-0
Track: LH: 0-4 RH: 0-1 Tight: 0-3 Gall: 0-0
Aids: Bl: 0-0 Vi: 0-1 Tstrap: 0-0
Best Rating: **101** 12/02 Font 2m2f110y soft Hdl

Moderate hurdler; would have broken her duck in first-time visor at Newton Abbot in April 2003, but was sadly killed in a fall at the second last. (DEAD)

Kilmore Quay (IRE)

8-y-o ch g Over The River (FR)-Sustenance (Torus)
D J Wintle Stan Miller,Max Aitken,Bill & John Craig

Placings:PP **(3404)**
2002/03: 16^{P}GS, 24^{P}HY,

	Starts	1st	2nd	3rd	Win & Pl
Hurdles	2	0	0	0	
Career Total	**2**	**0**	**0**	**0**	

Going: Sf: 0-1 GS: 0-1 Gd: 0-0 GF: - Fm: 0-0
Distance: 2m/2m3: 0-1 2m4-2m7: 0-0 3m+: 0-1
Track: LH: 0-1 RH: 0-1 Tight: 0-0 Gall: 0-0
Aids: Bl: 0-0 Vi: 0-0 Tstrap: 0-0
Best Rating: **0** 2/03 Uttx 3m110y heavy Hdl

Kilt (FR)

63 **45**
5-y-o ch g Luchiroverte (IRE)-Unite Ii (FR) (Toujours Pret (USA))
Mrs L Williamson Halewood International Ltd

Placings:0P0-00P **(2943)**
2002/03: 16^{0}S, 16^{P}S, 16^{P}S,

	Starts	1st	2nd	3rd	Win & Pl
Hurdles	3	0	0	0	
Career Total	**6**	**0**	**0**	**0**	

Going: Sf: 0-3 GS: 0-0 Gd: 0-0 GF: - Fm: 0-0
Distance: 2m/2m3: 0-3 2m4-2m7: 0-0 3m+: 0-0
Track: LH: 0-2 RH: 0-1 Tight: 0-0 Gall: 0-1
Aids: Bl: 0-0 Vi: 0-0 Tstrap: 0-0
Best Rating: **45** 10/01 Kels 2m110y good Hdl

Kim Fontaine (FR)

117f **131f**
5-y-o b/br g Silver Rainbow-Blanche Fontaine (FR) (Oakland)
W P Mullins B Doyle

Placings:*10* **(4115)**
2002/03: 16^{1}S, 16^{0}G,

	Starts	1st	2nd	3rd	Win & Pl
NH Flat	2	1	0	0	4032
Career Total	**2**	**1**	**0**	**0**	**4032**

112 1/03 Thur 2m NHF SFT £4032
Total win prize-money £4032

Going: Sf: 1-1 GS: 0-0 Gd: 0-1 GF: - Fm: 0-0
Distance: **2m/2m3: 1-2** 2m4-2m7: 0-0 3m+: 0-0
Track: LH: 0-1 RH: 0-0 Tight: 0-0 Gall: 0-0
Aids: Bl: 0-0 Vi: 0-0 Tstrap: 0-0
Best Rating: **131** 3/03 Chel 2m110y good NHF

Kimberley

111(108c) (125c)**120**
8-y-o b g Shareef Dancer (USA)-Willowbank (Gay Fandango (USA))
J G M O Shea K W Bell

Placings:433/22111U/505**0B00F05231250P**-06614 **(3880)**
2002/03: 24^{0}HY, 24^{6}GS, 25^{6}HY, 22^{1}HY, 24^{4}GS,

	Starts	1st	2nd	3rd	Win & Pl
Hurdles	5	1	0	0	9156
Career Total	**31**	**5**	**4**	**3**	**42867**

120 2/03 Uttx 2m6f110yC(0-135)HHdl HVY £8106
108 4/02 Fair 2m6f100y Ch G-Y £7831
131 10/00 Naas 2m4f HHdl YLD £7800
126 10/00 Cork 2m4f Hdl SFT £6072
117 9/00 List 2m4f Hdl HVY £4416
Total win prize-money £34226

Going: Sf: 1-3 GS: 0-2 Gd: 0-0 GF: - Fm: 0-0
Distance: 2m/2m3: 0-0 **2m4-2m7: 1-1** 3m+: 0-4
Track: **LH: 1-5** RH: 0-0 Tight: 0-1 Gall: 0-1
Aids: Bl: 0-0 **Vi: 1-3** Tstrap: 0-0
Best Rating: **135** 5/01 Fair 2m4f gd-yld Hdl

Useful hurdler; acts well on a soft surface; effective at up to two miles six; successful in a visor.

Kimdaloo (IRE)

110(86h) (56h)**98**
11-y-o b g Mandalus-Kimin (Kibenka)
M A Barnes J G Graham

Placings:*0*/560/5P/4560**F10/U25/33P22223566-253000PB411242500** **(4763)**
2002/03: 16^{2}GS, 16^{5}G, 16^{3}GS, 17^{0}GF, 21^{0}GF, 17^{0}G, 17^{P}G, 17^{B}G, 16^{4}GF, 16^{1}GF, 16^{1}G, 17^{2}S, 16^{4}S, 17^{2}HY, 16^{5}S, 20^{0}G, 16^{0}G,

	Starts	1st	2nd	3rd	Win & Pl
Hurdles	1	0	0	0	0
Chases	16	2	3	1	11457
Career Total	**44**	**3**	**8**	**4**	**22241**

98 10/02 Hexm 2m110y F(0-90)Ch GD £2863
98 10/02 Hexm 2m110y F(0-100)HCh G-F £3080
68 2/00 Newc 2m110y E(0-105)HCh SFT £3143
Total win prize-money £9086

Going: Sf: 0-4 GS: 0-2 Gd: 1-7 GF: - Fm: 1-4
Distance: **2m/2m3: 2-15** 2m4-2m7: 0-2 3m+: 0-0
Track: **LH: 2-13** RH: 0-4 Tight: 0-7 Gall: 0-1
Aids: Bl: 0-0 Vi: 0-0 **Tstrap: 2-13**
Best Rating: **98** 11/02 Kels 2m1f heavy Ch

Moderate chaser; suited by two miles; best with cut in the ground; goes well at Hexham; wears tongue tie.

Kimoe Warrior

106 **88**
5-y-o ch g Royal Abjar (USA)-Thewaari (USA) (Eskimo (USA))
M Mullineaux Michael Mullineaux

Placings:F004354PP6-P63053 **(4463)**
2002/03: 16^{P}GS, 16^{6}HY, 17^{3}HY, 17^{0}GS, 17^{5}HY, 17^{3}F,

	Starts	1st	2nd	3rd	Win & Pl
Hurdles	6	0	0	2	948
Career Total	**16**	**0**	**0**	**3**	**1635**

Going: Sf: 0-3 GS: 0-2 Gd: 0-0 GF: - Fm: 0-1
Distance: 2m/2m3: 0-6 2m4-2m7: 0-0 3m+: 0-0
Track: LH: 0-1 RH: 0-5 Tight: 0-3 Gall: 0-0
Aids: Bl: 0-0 Vi: 0-0 Tstrap: 0-0
Best Rating: **84** 4/03 Tntn 2m1f firm Hdl

Poor hurdler; acts on soft.

Kincora (IRE)

12-y-o b g King Persian-Miss Noora (Ahonoora)
Ms Lisa Stock Ms Lisa Stock

Placings:*000000*/454/454P/U66-3 **(0315)**
2002/03: 21^{3}G,

	Starts	1st	2nd	3rd	Win & Pl
Chases	1	0	0	1	220
Career Total	**17**	**0**	**0**	**1**	**782**

Going: Sf: 0-0 GS: 0-0 Gd: 0-1 GF: - Fm: 0-0
Distance: 2m/2m3: 0-0 2m4-2m7: 0-1 3m+: 0-0
Track: LH: 0-0 RH: 0-1 Tight: 0-1 Gall: 0-0
Aids: Bl: 0-0 Vi: 0-0 Tstrap: 0-0
Best Rating: **92** 5/99 Folk 2m5f gd-fm Ch

Kind Prince

96 **53**
11-y-o b g Kind Of Hush-Silent Princess (King Of Spain)
John A Harris The Norking Partnership

Placings:6000000/03/2160P00/0PP/0 **(0074)**
2002/03: 17^{0}GF,

	Starts	1st	2nd	3rd	Win & Pl
Hurdles	1	0	0	0	
Career Total	**20**	**1**	**1**	**1**	**2546**

90 10/98 Towc 2m G Hdl G-S £1744
Total win prize-money £1744

Going: Sf: 0-0 GS: 0-0 Gd: 0-0 GF: - Fm: 0-1
Distance: 2m/2m3: 0-1 2m4-2m7: 0-0 3m+: 0-0
Track: LH: 0-0 RH: 0-1 Tight: 0-0 Gall: 0-0
Aids: Bl: 0-0 Vi: 0-0 Tstrap: 0-0
Best Rating: **97** 11/98 Chel 2m110y gd-sft Hdl

Kind Sir

109(91h) (96h)**117**
7-y-o b g Generous (IRE)-Noble Conquest (USA) (Vaguely Noble)

A W Carroll Layton T Cheshire

Placings:23206/60P204/**0023**P3-P**4321F111U2P**   **(3815)**
2002/03: 19⁹GF, 19⁴G, 16³G, 16²S, 16¹G, 16FS, 19¹S, 16¹S, 16¹G, 20ᵁGS, 20²S, 16PG,

	Starts	1st	2nd	3rd	Win & Pl
Hurdles	1	0	0	0	0
Chases	11	4	2	1	21475
Career Total	29	4	6	4	26340
117 1/03	Catt	2m	E(0-105)HCh	GD	£3870
117 1/03	Leic	2m	F(0-90)Ch	SFT	£3357
117 12/02	Hrfd	2m3f	D(0-110)HCh	SFT	£5928
105 12/02	Hrfd	2m	F(0-95)HCh	GD	£3799

Total win prize-money £16955

Going: Sf: 2-5 GS: 0-1 Gd: 2-5 GF: - Fm: 0-1
Distance: 2m/2m3: 4-9 2m4-2m7: 0-3 3m+: 0-0
Track: LH: 1-2 RH: 3-10 Tight: 1-4 Gall: 0-0
Aids: Bl: 0-0 Vi: 0-0 Tstrap: 0-0
Best Rating: 117 1/03 Catt 2m   good   Ch

Modest two mile chaser; winner four times around turn of year but has shot up the ratings.

Kindle Ball (FR)
91   75
5-y-o gr m Kaldounevees (FR)-Scala Iv (FR) (Quart De Vin (FR))
Miss Venetia Williams Cheltenham Racing Ltd

Placings:3   **(4697)**
2002/03: 17³G,

	Starts	1st	2nd	3rd	Win & Pl
NH Flat	1	0	0	1	428
Career Total	1	0	0	1	428

Going: Sf: 0-0 GS: 0-0 Gd: 0-1 GF: - Fm: 0-0
Distance: 2m/2m3: 0-1 2m4-2m7: 0-0 3m+: 0-0
Track: LH: 0-1 RH: 0-0 Tight: 0-1 Gall: 0-0
Aids: Bl: 0-0 Vi: 0-0 Tstrap: 0-0
Best Rating: 40 4/03 NAbb 2m1f   good   NHF

Has shown ability in bumpers and novice hurdle company; acts on fast ground.

Kinfauns Lady (IRE)
105   85
8-y-o b m King s Ride-Dalkey Sound (Crash Course)
D W Whillans E J Jamieson

Placings:20/P60/344F3P-353F303   **(4376)**
2002/03: 21³G, 22⁵HY, 24³G, 24FG, 24³G, 25⁰G, 27³G,

	Starts	1st	2nd	3rd	Win & Pl
Hurdles	7	0	0	4	2234
Career Total	18	0	1	6	3665

Going: Sf: 0-1 GS: 0-0 Gd: 0-6 GF: - Fm: 0-0
Distance: 2m/2m3: 0-0 2m4-2m7: 0-2 3m+: 0-5
Track: LH: 0-4 RH: 0-3 Tight: 0-7 Gall: 0-0
Aids: Bl: 0-0 Vi: 0-0 Tstrap: 0-0
Best Rating: 89 2/00 Ayr 2m   heavy   NHF

Plating-class novice hurdler, stays three miles and handles any ground; tends to find one or two too good.

King Bavard (IRE)
86   83
9-y-o b g Jurado (USA)-Discerning Lady (Le Bavard (FR))
J I A Charlton Mr & Mrs Raymond Anderson Green

Placings:0223/1U04/6F425-0   **(0182)**

2002/03: 25⁰G,

	Starts	1st	2nd	3rd	Win & Pl
Chases	1	0	0	0	
Career Total	14	1	3	1	6719
103 5/00	Dpat	2m4f110y NHF		GD	£2760

Total win prize-money £2760

Going: Sf: 0-0 GS: 0-0 Gd: 0-1 GF: - Fm: 0-0
Distance: 2m/2m3: 0-0 2m4-2m7: 0-0 3m+: 0-1
Track: LH: 0-1 RH: 0-0 Tight: 0-0 Gall: 0-0
Aids: Bl: 0-0 Vi: 0-0 Tstrap: 0-0
Best Rating: 111 4/00 Ayr 2m   good   NHF

Modest chaser, stays three miles, does not want the ground too soft.

King Bee (IRE)
110   104+
6-y-o b g Supreme Leader-Honey Come Back (Master Owen)
H D Daly Trevor Hemmings

Placings:305-16645   **(3914)**
2002/03: 20¹GS, 20⁶S, 20⁶HY, 24⁴HY, 20⁵GS,

	Starts	1st	2nd	3rd	Win & Pl
Hurdles	5	1	0	0	4666
Career Total	8	1	0	1	5060
102 11/02	Asct	2m4f	E(0-105)Hdl	G-S	£4290

Total win prize-money £4290

Going: Sf: 0-3 GS: 1-2 Gd: 0-0 GF: - Fm: 0-0
Distance: 2m/2m3: 0-0 2m4-2m7: 1-4 3m+: 0-1
Track: LH: 0-3 RH: 1-2 Tight: 0-0 Gall: 0-0
Aids: Bl: 0-0 Vi: 0-0 Tstrap: 0-0
Best Rating: 104 11/02 Hayd 2m4f   soft   Hdl

Fair novice hurdler, a winner at Ascot in November 2002, but held subsequently. Acts on easy ground.

King Claudius (IRE)
104   90
7-y-o b g King s Ride-Lepida (Royal Match)
P R Webber M C Banks

Placings:13-0350   **(4608)**
2002/03: 21⁰GS, 16³G, 21⁵G, 17⁰G,

	Starts	1st	2nd	3rd	Win & Pl
Hurdles	4	0	0	1	819
Career Total	6	1	0	2	3217
108 1/02	Kemp	2m	H NHF	SFT	£2002

Total win prize-money £2002

Going: Sf: 0-0 GS: 0-1 Gd: 0-3 GF: - Fm: 0-0
Distance: 2m/2m3: 0-2 2m4-2m7: 0-2 3m+: 0-0
Track: LH: 0-2 RH: 0-2 Tight: 0-0 Gall: 0-3
Aids: Bl: 0-0 Vi: 0-0 Tstrap: 0-0
Best Rating: 117 3/02 Newb 2m110y   gd-sft NHF

A half-brother to useful chaser Killusty, moderate hurdler; acts on good and soft ground.

King Dante (IRE)
87   94
6-y-o b/br g King s Ride-Tulladante (IRE) (Phardante (FR))
P Beaumont Trevor Hemmings

Placings:0505   **(4772)**
2002/03: 16⁰GS, 16⁵GS, 16⁹G, 16⁵G,

	Starts	1st	2nd	3rd	Win & Pl
NH Flat	2	0	0	0	0
Hurdles	2	0	0	0	0
Career Total	4	0	0	0	0

Going: Sf: 0-3 GS: 0-1 Gd: 0-1 GF: - Fm: 0-0
Distance: 2m/2m3: 0-3 2m4-2m7: 0-2 3m+: 0-0
Track: LH: 0-5 RH: 0-0 Tight: 0-0 Gall: 0-0
Aids: Bl: 0-0 Vi: 0-0 Tstrap: 0-0
Best Rating: 56 1/03 Sedg 2m1f   heavy   Hdl

Going: Sf: 0-0 GS: 0-2 Gd: 0-2 GF: - Fm: 0-0
Distance: 2m/2m3: 0-4 2m4-2m7: 0-0 3m+: 0-0
Track: LH: 0-2 RH: 0-2 Tight: 0-1 Gall: 0-1
Aids: Bl: 0-0 Vi: 0-0 Tstrap: 0-0
Best Rating: 94 4/03 Prth 2m110y   good   Hdl

King Georges (FR)
100   96
5-y-o b g Kadalko (FR)-Djoumi (FR) (Brezzo (FR))
J C Tuck The Try-Line Partnership

Placings:F0-P015416   **(3944)**
2002/03: 19PGS, 16⁰HY, 16¹GS, 16²S, 19⁴GS, 17¹GS, 17⁶S,

	Starts	1st	2nd	3rd	Win & Pl
Hurdles	7	2	0	0	6461
Career Total	9	2	0	0	6461
96 2/03	Extr	2m1f	F(0-90)HHdl	G-S	£3059
82 12/02	Winc	2m	F(0-95)HHdl	G-S	£3402

Total win prize-money £6461

Going: Sf: 0-3 GS: 2-4 Gd: 0-0 GF: - Fm: 0-0
Distance: 2m/2m3: 2-7 2m4-2m7: 0-0 3m+: 0-0
Track: LH: 0-0 RH: 2-7 Tight: 0-0 Gall: 0-0
Aids: Bl: 0-0 Vi: 0-0 Tstrap: 0-0
Best Rating: 96 2/03 Extr 2m1f   gd-sft Hdl

Moderate hurdler; showed tremendous improvement when winning two mile novices handicap at Wincanton on Boxing Day 2002; disappointing next two starts; bounced back to form when winning at Exeter February 2003 off an 11lb higher mark; acts on good to soft ground; inconsistent.

King Harald (IRE)
97   124+
5-y-o b g King s Ride-Cuilin Bui (IRE) (Kemal (FR))
M Bradstock Piers Pottinger And P B-J Partnership

Placings:33341   **(3875)**
2002/03: 21³G, 19³GS, 19³GS, 19⁴GS, 21¹S,

	Starts	1st	2nd	3rd	Win & Pl
Hurdles	5	1	0	3	6244
Career Total	5	1	0	3	6244
124 2/03	Newb	2m5f	E(0-105)HHdl	SFT	£3952

Total win prize-money £3952

Going: Sf: 1-1 GS: 0-3 Gd: 0-1 GF: - Fm: 0-0
Distance: 2m/2m3: 0-0 2m4-2m7: 1-4 3m+: 0-0
Track: LH: 1-4 RH: 0-1 Tight: 0-0 Gall: 1-2
Aids: Bl: 0-0 Vi: 0-0 Tstrap: 0-0
Best Rating: 124 2/03 Newb 2m5f   soft   Hdl

Fair novice hurdler, stays two and a half miles; acts on soft ground.

King Of Arms
75   47
5-y-o b g Rakaposhi King-Herald The Dawn (Dubassoff (USA))
J Howard Johnson Dick Thackeray

Placings:00P0P   **(4304)**
2002/03: 17⁰HY, 21⁰HY, 18PGS, 17⁰S, 22PG,

	Starts	1st	2nd	3rd	Win & Pl
Hurdles	5	0	0	0	
Career Total	5	0	0	0	

Going: Sf: 0-3 GS: 0-1 Gd: 0-1 GF: - Fm: 0-0
Distance: 2m/2m3: 0-3 2m4-2m7: 0-2 3m+: 0-0
Track: LH: 0-5 RH: 0-0 Tight: 0-0 Gall: 0-0
Aids: Bl: 0-0 Vi: 0-0 Tstrap: 0-0
Best Rating: 56 1/03 Sedg 2m1f   heavy   Hdl

King Of Barbury (IRE)

91   **97+**

6-y-o b g Moscow Society (USA)-Aine s Alice (IRE) (Drumalis)
A King Miss J M Bodycote

Placings:42-343P   (4004)
2002/03: 16³S, 16⁴S, 19³GS, 22⁶S,

	Starts	1st	2nd	3rd	Win & Pl
Hurdles	4	0	0	2	1419
Career Total	6	0	1	2	2305

Going: Sf: 0-3 GS: 0-1 Gd: 0-0 GF: - Fm: 0-0
Distance: 2m/2m3: 0-2 2m4-2m7: 0-2 3m+: 0-0
Track: LH: 0-3 RH: 0-1 Tight: 0-0 Gall: 0-0
Aids: Bl: 0-0 Vi: 0-0 Tstrap: 0-0
Best Rating: 99 3/02 Strf 2m10y gd-sft NHF

He has shown ability in bumpers and novice hurdles.

King Of Mommur (IRE)

102(93h)   (98h)**105**

8-y-o b g Fairy King (USA)-Monoglow (Kalaglow)
B G Powell The Three Bears Racing

Placings:6135/0P0/1155-5114   (4682)
2002/03: 18⁵GF, 16¹GS, 18¹GF, 24⁴GF,

	Starts	1st	2nd	3rd	Win & Pl
Hurdles	1	0	0	0	0
Chases	3	2	0	0	10229
Career Total	15	5	0	1	19228
105	3/03	Font	2m2f	D(0-115)HCh	G-F	5655
102	2/03	Leic	2m	F(0-95)Ch	G-S	4153
105	5/01	Font	2m4f	F Ch	G-F	2973
109	5/01	Sthl	2m	F(0-110)HCh	G-F	2968
115	3/00	Extr	2m3f110yE Hdl		G-S	2556

Total win prize-money £18307

Going: Sf: 0-0 GS: 1-1 Gd: 0-0 GF: - Fm: 1-3
Distance: 2m/2m3: 2-3 2m4-2m7: 0-0 3m+: 0-1
Track: LH: 0-1 RH: 1-2 Tight: 1-2 Gall: 0-1
Aids: Bl: 0-0 Vi: 0-0 Tstrap: 0-0
Best Rating: 115 3/00 Chep 2m110y good Hdl

Fair chaser; well-placed to win third chase in five starts at Leicester in February; followed up at Fontwell in March; has worn blinkers and cheekpieces; stays two and a half miles; acts well on decent ground.

King Of Sparta

99   **120d**

10-y-o b g Kefaah (USA)-Khaizaraan (CAN) (Sham (USA))
J G Portman Mrs Richard Tice

Placings:P12/21102/112133111134324/41024/3252U0P/20
23-P051   (4414)
2002/03: 24⁵S, 24⁰GS, 24⁵GS, 22¹G,

	Starts	1st	2nd	3rd	Win & Pl
Chases	4	1	0	0	10452
Career Total	43	12	10	6	110645
106	3/03	MRas	2m6f110yD(0-120)HCh	GD	10452
133	2/00	Winc	2m5f	D(0-125)HCh	GD	6955
137	12/98	Chel	2m5f	C Ch	GD	6909
129	12/98	Winc	2m5f	E(0-105)HCh	G-S	4201
127	11/98	Winc	2m5f	E(0-105)HCh	GD	7392
137	11/98	Tntn	2m5f	E(0-105)HCh	GF	7392
107	7/98	NAbb	2m5f110yE(0-120)Ch	G-F	2762
104	6/98	Uttx	2m5f	C Ch	GD	5340
117	5/98	Uttx	2m5f	D Ch	G-F	3485

114	10/97	Plum	2m4f	D(0-120)HHdl	GD	3159
114	9/97	Extr	2m3f	D(0-120)HHdl	G-F	2697
91	4/97	Uttx	2m	E Hdl	G-F	2432

Total win prize-money £63182

Going: Sf: 0-1 GS: 0-2 Gd: 1-1 GF: - Fm: 0-0
Distance: 2m/2m3: 0-0 **2m4-2m7: 1-1** 3m+: 0-3
Track: LH: 0-4 **RH: 1-2** Tight: 1-2 Gall: 0-1
Aids: Bl: 0-0 Vi: 0-0 Tstrap: 0-0
Best Rating: 137 12/98 Chel 2m5f good Ch

Modest chaser who has lost his way; took advantage of a lenient mark to record his first win for over three years at Market Rasen in March; suited by trips short of three miles.

King Of The Blues

65

11-y-o b g Rakaposhi King-Colonial Princess (Roscoe Blake)
Graeme Roe Roe Racing Ltd

Placings:325/06402P/0/P00P02P0PP-PPP0   (1407)
2002/03: 20⁰G, 22⁶GS, 23⁰G, 20⁰G,

	Starts	1st	2nd	3rd	Win & Pl
Hurdles	3	0	0	0	0
Chases	1	0	0	0	0
Career Total	24	0	3	1	1812

Going: Sf: 0-0 GS: 0-1 Gd: 0-3 GF: - Fm: 0-0
Distance: 2m/2m3: 0-0 2m4-2m7: 0-3 3m+: 0-1
Track: LH: 0-3 RH: 0-0 Tight: 0-2 Gall: 0-0
Aids: Bl: 0-0 Vi: 0-2 Tstrap: 0-0
Best Rating: 90 1/97 Ludl 2m gd-fm NHF

Plating-class maiden hurdler.

King Of The Castle (IRE)

96   **109**

8-y-o b g Cataldi-Monashuna (Boreen (FR))
B Mactaggart The Potassium Partnership

Placings:11/F0PP1/2023100-3   (0160)
2002/03: 16³G,

	Starts	1st	2nd	3rd	Win & Pl
Hurdles	1	0	0	1	399
Career Total	15	4	2	2	23103
109	10/01	Extr	2m3f	E(0-115)HHdl	G-S	3290
103	4/01	Tntn	2m1f	F(0-95)HHdl	GD	2415
128	11/99	Aint	2m110y	A NHF	GD	13200
109	3/99	Folk	2m1f110yH NHF		G-S	1577

Total win prize-money £20483

Going: Sf: 0-0 GS: 0-0 Gd: 0-1 GF: - Fm: 0-0
Distance: 2m/2m3: 0-1 2m4-2m7: 0-0 3m+: 0-0
Track: LH: 0-1 RH: 0-0 Tight: 0-1 Gall: 0-0
Aids: Bl: 0-0 Vi: 0-0 Tstrap: 0-0
Best Rating: 128 4/99 Aint 2m110y good NHF

He was a useful bumper horse, but has been very disappointing over hurdles and has had problems including breathing problems. Does not want to be put under too much pressure. Has won from two miles to two miles three. Seems to handle most surfaces.

King Of The Dawn

100   **96**

12-y-o b/br g Rakaposhi King-Dawn Encounter (Rymer)
P R Hedger Mrs J Howell

Placings:14/11206/03/03424P/32P03/U6321360P0-12

(3108)
2002/03: 22¹HY, 21²S,

	Starts	1st	2nd	3rd	Win & Pl
Chases	2	1	1	0	4392
Career Total	32	5	5	6	24526
96	1/03	Font	2m6f	F(0-90)HCh	HVY	3339
103	10/01	Font	2m6f	F(0-95)HCh	SFT	2899
116	11/97	Extr	2m1f110yE Hdl		G-S	2679
109	8/97	Tram	2m	Hdl	GD	2712
100	9/96	Clon	2m	NHF	GD	2471

Total win prize-money £14102

Going: Sf: 1-2 GS: 0-0 Gd: 0-0 GF: - Fm: 0-0
Distance: 2m/2m3: 0-0 **2m4-2m7: 1-2** 3m+: 0-0
Track: LH: 0-0 RH: 0-1 **Tight: 1-2** Gall: 0-0
Aids: Bl: 0-0 Vi: 0-0 Tstrap: 0-0
Best Rating: 116 11/97 Extr 2m1f110y gd-sft Hdl

Moderate chaser; handles most types of ground; suited by trips at around two and a half miles.

King Of The Forest (IRE)

100   **98**

8-y-o b g Good Thyne (USA)-Coolbawn Lady (Laurence O)
Miss S E Forster A G & Mrs E J Bell

Placings:5/0-242   (3106)
2002/03: 25²HY, 24⁴GS, 25²S,

	Starts	1st	2nd	3rd	Win & Pl
Chases	3	0	2	0	2815
Career Total	5	0	2	0	2815

Going: Sf: 0-2 GS: 0-1 Gd: 0-0 GF: - Fm: 0-0
Distance: 2m/2m3: 0-0 2m4-2m7: 0-0 3m+: 0-3
Track: LH: 0-3 RH: 0-0 Tight: 0-0 Gall: 0-1
Aids: Bl: 0-0 Vi: 0-0 Tstrap: 0-0
Best Rating: 98 1/03 Ayr 3m1f soft Ch

Winner of three points. but struggling to make much of an impact under Rules.

King Of The Sea (IRE)

72f   **52f**

6-y-o b g Gone Fishin-Reign Of Swing (Star Appeal)
V R A Dartnall Fishermens Friends

Placings:00   (2675)
2002/03: 17⁰G, 17⁰S,

	Starts	1st	2nd	3rd	Win & Pl
NH Flat	2	0	0	0	
Career Total	2	0	0	0	

Going: Sf: 0-1 GS: 0-0 Gd: 0-1 GF: - Fm: 0-0
Distance: 2m/2m3: 0-2 2m4-2m7: 0-0 3m+: 0-0
Track: LH: 0-0 RH: 0-2 Tight: 0-0 Gall: 0-0
Aids: Bl: 0-0 Vi: 0-0 Tstrap: 0-0
Best Rating: 52 10/02 Extr 2m1f good NHF

King Plato (IRE)

108   **93+**

6-y-o b g King s Ride-You Are A Lady (IRE) (Lord Americo)
M D Hammond (A Crook 5/6) Jay Dee Bloodstock Limited

Placings:640-6501153   (1817)
2002/03: 20⁶G, 17⁵GS, 20⁰GF, 24¹S, 20¹S, 23⁵G, 26³G,

	Starts	1st	2nd	3rd	Win & Pl
Hurdles	7	2	0	1	6054

Career Total	10	2	0	1	6054
83	8/02	Worc	2m4f	E(0-100)HHdl	SFT £3122
93	8/02	Bang	3m	F(0-95)HHdl	SFT £2404

Total win prize-money £5527

Going:	Sf: 2-2 GS: 0-1 Gd: 0-3 GF: - Fm: 0-1
Distance:	2m/2m3: 0-1 2m4-2m7: 1-4 3m+: 1-2
Track:	LH: 2-6 RH: 0-1 Tight: 1-2 Gall: 0-0
Aids:	Bl: 0-0 Vi: 0-0 Tstrap: 0-0
Best Rating:	93 8/02 Bang 3m soft Hdl

Improved form when winning three-mile conditional jockeys handicap hurdle at Bangor August 2002 and followed up at Worcester. Has a high knee action and appreciated the rain-softened ground on both occasions.

King Player (IRE)
109f   110+f
6-y-o b g King s Ride-West Along (Crash Course)
N J Henderson Trevor Hemmings

Placings:2   (2776)
2002/03: 16²HY,

	Starts	1st	2nd	3rd	Win & Pl
NH Flat	1	0	1	0	756
Career Total	1	0	1	0	756

Going:	Sf: 0-1 GS: 0-0 Gd: 0-0 GF: - Fm: 0-0
Distance:	2m/2m3: 0-1 2m4-2m7: 0-0 3m+: 0-0
Track:	LH: 0-1 RH: 0-0 Tight: 0-0 Gall: 0-1
Aids:	Bl: 0-0 Vi: 0-0 Tstrap: 0-0
Best Rating:	110 12/02 Newb 2m110y heavy NHF

Runner-up in a heavy-ground Newbury bumper on debut.

King Solomon (FR)
106   117
4-y-o gr c Simon Du Desert (FR)-All Square (FR) (Holst (USA))
Miss Venetia Williams (P F I Cole 28/10) Seasons Holidays

Placings:200   (4460)
2002/03: 17²GS, 17⁹G, 16⁹G,

	Starts	1st	2nd	3rd	Win & Pl
Hurdles	3	0	1	0	1084
Career Total	3	0	1	0	1084

Going:	Sf: 0-0 GS: 0-1 Gd: 0-0 GF: 0-0
Distance:	2m/2m3: 0-3 2m4-2m7: 0-0 3m+: 0-0
Track:	LH: 0-2 RH: 0-1 Tight: 0-1 Gall: 0-1
Aids:	Bl: 0-0 Vi: 0-0 Tstrap: 0-0
Best Rating:	117 3/03 Chel 2m1f good Hdl

Smart middle-distance performer on the Flat for Paul Cole; runner up on hurdles bow, decent run in Triumph Hurdle; held subsequently.

King Torus (IRE)
92   90
13-y-o b g Torus-Kam A Dusk (Kambalda)
V R A Dartnall Nick Viney

Placings:00/1110/1630233/351/61233100/20166P-0325P (0867)
2002/03: 21⁹GF, 21³S, 21²GF, 21⁵GF, 21³GF,

	Starts	1st	2nd	3rd	Win & Pl
Chases	5	0	1	1	1447
Career Total	35	8	4	7	27278
109	8/01	Font	2m6f	F(0-110)HCh	G-F £3428
109	8/00	Font	2m6f	F(0-110)HCh	G-F £3692

106	5/00	Winc	2m5f	H Ch	FRM £1991
101	3/00	Font	2m4f	H Ch	G-F £2212
96	5/98	Winc	2m5f	H Ch	GD £2024
113	3/98	Tntn	3m	H Ch	G-S £1068
114	5/97	Uttx	2m5f	H Ch	G-F £1127
103	5/97	NAbb	2m5f110yH Ch		GD £1030

Total win prize-money £16576

Going:	Sf: 0-1 GS: 0-0 Gd: 0-0 GF: - Fm: 0-4
Distance:	2m/2m3: 0-0 2m4-2m7: 0-5 3m+: 0-0
Track:	LH: 0-5 RH: 0-0 Tight: 0-2 Gall: 0-1
Aids:	Bl: 0-5 Vi: 0-0 Tstrap: 0-0
Best Rating:	114 5/97 Uttx 2m5f gd-fm Ch

One time useful hunter but is on the decline now.

King Triton (IRE)
104   88
6-y-o br g Mister Lord (USA)-Deepwater Woman (The Parson)
L Wells Selsey Clubbers

Placings:3352-03221   (4083)
2002/03: 24⁸GS, 25³HY, 22²HY, 27²S, 25¹HY,

	Starts	1st	2nd	3rd	Win & Pl
Hurdles	5	1	2	1	5333
Career Total	9	1	3	3	6562
88	3/03	Plum	3m1f110yF(0-95)HHdl		HVY £2611

Total win prize-money £2611

Going:	Sf: 1-4 GS: 0-1 Gd: 0-0 GF: - Fm: 0-0
Distance:	2m/2m3: 0-0 2m4-2m7: 0-1 3m+: 1-4
Track:	LH: 0-0 RH: 0-2 Tight: 0-0 Gall: 0-0
Aids:	Bl: 0-0 Vi: 0-0 Tstrap: 0-0
Best Rating:	88 3/03 Plum 3m1f110y heavy Hdl

Modest hurdler; third in two bumpers; fair efforts in modest company early in 2003; stays three miles three; acts on testing ground.

King's Bank (IRE)
73   68
6-y-o b g King s Ride-Super Cailin (Brave Invader (USA))
P J Hobbs I L Shaw

Placings:0   (2218)
2002/03: 16⁵S,

	Starts	1st	2nd	3rd	Win & Pl
Hurdles	1	0	0	0	
Career Total	1	0	0	0	

Going:	Sf: 0-1 GS: 0-0 Gd: 0-0 GF: - Fm: 0-0
Distance:	2m/2m3: 0-1 2m4-2m7: 0-0 3m+: 0-0
Track:	LH: 0-1 RH: 0-0 Tight: 0-0 Gall: 0-1
Aids:	Bl: 0-0 Vi: 0-0 Tstrap: 0-0
Best Rating:	68 11/02 Newb 2m110y soft Hdl

King's Bounty
109(108h)   (112h)103
7-y-o b g Le Moss-Fit For A King (Royalty)
T D Easterby C H Stevens

Placings:003/542123-03F0B322114   (4714)
2002/03: 20⁵GS, 20³S, 25⁵GS, 21⁹G, 24⁸G, 24³G, 27²HY, 25²G, 20¹GF, 25¹G, 25⁴GF,

	Starts	1st	2nd	3rd	Win & Pl
Hurdles	1	0	0	0	0
Chases	10	2	2	2	14056
Career Total	20	3	4	4	18896
101	4/03	Kels	3m1f	D Ch	GD £5395
103	3/03	Weth	2m4f110yE Ch		G-F £4075

109	2/02	Newc	2m4f	E Hdl	SFT £2555

Total win prize-money £12026

Going:	Sf: 0-2 GS: 0-2 Gd: 1-5 GF: - Fm: 1-2
Distance:	2m/2m3: 0-0 2m4-2m7: 1-4 3m+: 1-7
Track:	LH: 2-11 RH: 0-0 Tight: 1-3 Gall: 0-4
Aids:	Bl: 0-0 Vi: 0-0 Tstrap: 0-0
Best Rating:	112 3/02 Donc 2m4f soft Hdl

Fair chaser; suited by three miles plus; jumps well; likes a sound surface; finally broke his duck over fences at Wetherby in March 2003 and followed up at Kelso in April.

King's Chambers
89   82
7-y-o ch g Sabrehill (USA)-Flower Girl (Pharly (FR))
N J Hawke C G Newman

Placings:F/0011F3/220P-5   (4693)
2002/03: 17⁵G,

	Starts	1st	2nd	3rd	Win & Pl
Hurdles	1	0	0	0	0
Career Total	12	2	2	1	4731
84	12/00	MRas	2m1f110yG(0-95)HHdl		G-S £1505
76	11/00	MRas	2m3f110yG(0-95)HHdl		SFT £1477

Total win prize-money £2982

Going:	Sf: 0-0 GS: 0-0 Gd: 0-1 GF: - Fm: 0-0
Distance:	2m/2m3: 0-1 2m4-2m7: 0-0 3m+: 0-0
Track:	LH: 0-1 RH: 0-0 Tight: 0-1 Gall: 0-0
Aids:	Bl: 0-0 Vi: 0-0 Tstrap: 0-0
Best Rating:	91 9/01 MRas 2m3f110y gd-fm Hdl

Plating-class performer; best with give at around two miles.

King's Country (IRE)
104(99h)   (92h)78
11-y-o b g King s Ride-Tatlock (Paico)
N B Mason N B Mason

Placings:005/4P2F5FP4/221/2001-25   (3577)
2002/03: 16²GF, 24⁵G,

	Starts	1st	2nd	3rd	Win & Pl
Chases	2	0	1	0	1236
Career Total	20	2	5	0	11209
92	12/01	Leic	2m4f110yF(0-105)HHdl		SFT £3705
92	4/01	Prth	2m4f110yG(0-90)HHdl		HVY £3465

Total win prize-money £7170

Going:	Sf: 0-0 GS: 0-0 Gd: 0-1 GF: - Fm: 0-1
Distance:	2m/2m3: 0-1 2m4-2m7: 0-0 3m+: 0-1
Track:	LH: 0-0 RH: 0-2 Tight: 0-2 Gall: 0-0
Aids:	Bl: 0-0 Vi: 0-0 Tstrap: 0-0
Best Rating:	99 10/98 Kels 2m2f gd-sft Hdl

Plating-class chaser/hurdler; stays two miles six; acts with cut in the ground.

King's Echo
91f   83f
5-y-o b g Rakaposhi King-Welgenco (Welsh Saint)
S Gollings J B Webb

Placings:44   (4350)
2002/03: 16⁴GS, 16⁴GF,

	Starts	1st	2nd	3rd	Win & Pl
NH Flat	2	0	0	0	
Career Total	2	0	0	0	

Going:	Sf: 0-0 GS: 0-1 Gd: 0-0 GF: - Fm: 0-1
Distance:	2m/2m3: 0-2 2m4-2m7: 0-0 3m+: 0-1
Track:	LH: 0-2 RH: 0-0 Tight: 0-0 Gall: 0-1

Aids: BI: 0-0 Vi: 0-0 Tstrap: 0-0
Best Rating: 83 3/03 Wwck 2m gd-fm NHF

Well beaten fourth in bumpers in March 2003 on varying ground.

King's Envoy (USA)
81   52
4-y-o b g Royal Academy (USA)-Island Of Silver (USA) (Forty Niner (USA))
Mrs J C McGregor (E A L Dunlop 10/5) Mrs Dorothy Thomson

Placings:0PP (4749)
2002/03: 16⁰S, 16⁸GS, 20⁰G,

	Starts	1st	2nd	3rd	Win & Pl
Hurdles	3	0	0	0	
Career Total	3	0	0	0	

Going: Sf: 0-1 GS: 0-1 Gd: 0-1 GF: - Fm: 0-0
Distance: 2m/2m3: 0-2 2m4-2m7: 0-1 3m+: 0-0
Track: LH: 0-2 RH: 0-1 Tight: 0-1 Gall: 0-0
Aids: BI: 0-0 Vi: 0-0 Tstrap: 0-0
Best Rating: 52 11/02 Ayr 2m soft Hdl

King's Hussar
(91c)   (66c)65
8-y-o b g Be My Chief (USA)-Croire (IRE) (Lomond (USA))
Mrs S Lamyman Miss D M Foley

Placings:420501/542215F1066/0432F04/00P003U-4 (1419)
2002/03: 24⁴GF,

	Starts	1st	2nd	3rd	Win & Pl
Hurdles	1	0	0	0	0
Career Total	32	3	4	2	12295
98 1/00 Sedg	3m3f110yF(0-105)HHdl		SFT		£2765
98 11/99 Sedg	3m3f110yG(0-95)HHdl		GD		£1490
91 4/99 Sedg	2m5f110yF(0-100)HHdl		G-S		£3715
				Total win prize-money	£7971

Going: Sf: 0-0 GS: 0-0 Gd: 0-0 GF: - Fm: 0-1
Distance: 2m/2m3: 0-0 2m4-2m7: 0-0 3m+: 0-1
Track: LH: 0-0 RH: 0-1 Tight: 0-1 Gall: 0-0
Aids: BI: 0-0 Vi: 0-0 Tstrap: 0-1
Best Rating: 98 1/00 Sedg 3m3f110y soft Hdl

Winner three times over hurdles but little impact over fences. A lazy sort, he needs plenty of driving, likes Sedgefield.

King's Mill (IRE)
102   111
6-y-o b g Doyoun-Adarika (King s Lake (USA))
N A Graham First Millennium Racing

Placings:520 (3114)
2002/03: 16⁵HY, 16²G, 16⁰S,

	Starts	1st	2nd	3rd	Win & Pl
Hurdles	3	0	1	0	1458
Career Total	3	0	1	0	1458

Going: Sf: 0-2 GS: 0-0 Gd: 0-1 GF: - Fm: 0-0
Distance: 2m/2m3: 0-2 2m4-2m7: 0-0 3m+: 0-0
Track: LH: 0-1 RH: 0-2 Tight: 0-0 Gall: 0-2
Aids: BI: 0-0 Vi: 0-0 Tstrap: 0-0
Best Rating: 111 12/02 Newb 2m110y good Hdl

Decent on the Flat, he was all but brought down on his hurdling debut but showed what he can do when runner-up at Newbury next time.

King's Reign (IRE)
100   86
7-y-o b g King s Ride-Lena s Reign (Quayside)
N A Twiston-Davies Mrs Lorna Berryman

Placings:00P-0000 (3595)
2002/03: 20⁰G, 19⁰GS, 22⁰GS, 20⁰HY,

	Starts	1st	2nd	3rd	Win & Pl
Hurdles	4	0	0	0	
Career Total	7	0	0	0	

Going: Sf: 0-1 GS: 0-2 Gd: 0-1 GF: - Fm: 0-0
Distance: 2m/2m3: 0-1 2m4-2m7: 0-3 3m+: 0-0
Track: LH: 0-2 RH: 0-2 Tight: 0-0 Gall: 0-1
Aids: BI: 0-0 Vi: 0-0 Tstrap: 0-0
Best Rating: 86 11/02 Newb 2m3f gd-sft Hdl

Plating-class hurdler; best at just short of three miles; acts on fast and soft ground.

King's Stride (IRE)
(53h)101
11-y-o b g King s Ride-Anavore (Darantus)
P Monteith Mrs Maud Monteith

Placings:0/3/4/12040U0/1P054104P0PPUP-0 (0452)
2002/03: 20⁰G,

	Starts	1st	2nd	3rd	Win & Pl
Chases	1	0	0	0	
Career Total	25	3	1	1	11250
101 8/01 Ctml	2m1f110yF(0-100)HCh		G-S		£2769
100 5/01 Hexm	2m110y F(0-105)HCh		SFT		£3346
96 9/00 Prth	2m4f110yE Hdl		HVY		£2795
				Total win prize-money	£8910

Going: Sf: 0-0 GS: 0-0 Gd: 0-1 GF: - Fm: 0-0
Distance: 2m/2m3: 0-0 2m4-2m7: 0-1 3m+: 0-0
Track: LH: 0-1 RH: 0-0 Tight: 0-0 Gall: 0-0
Aids: BI: 0-0 Vi: 0-0 Tstrap: 0-0
Best Rating: 101 8/01 Ctml 2m1f110y gd-sft Ch

King's Travel (FR)
99(82c)   (56c)87
7-y-o gr g Balleroy (USA)-Travel Free (Be My Guest (USA))
J D Frost C Johnston

Placings:P/0-50601 (4693)
2002/03: 17⁵S, 16⁰S, 16⁶S, 16⁰GS, 17¹G,

	Starts	1st	2nd	3rd	Win & Pl
Hurdles	4	1	0	0	3080
Chases	1	0	0	0	0
Career Total	7	1	0	0	3080
87 4/03 NAbb	2m1f G(0-95)HHdl		GD		£3080
				Total win prize-money	£3080

Going: Sf: 0-3 GS: 0-1 Gd: 1-1 GF: - Fm: 0-0
Distance: 2m/2m3: 1-5 2m4-2m7: 0-0 3m+: 0-0
Track: LH: 1-3 RH: 0-2 Tight: 1-3 Gall: 0-0
Aids: BI: 0-0 Vi: 0-0 Tstrap: 0-0
Best Rating: 87 4/03 NAbb 2m1f good Hdl

Plating-class hurdler, successful in weak event at Newton Abbot in April 2003.

King-For-Life (IRE)
5-y-o ch g Rainbows For Life (CAN)-Fair Song (Pitskelly)
J R Cornwall (G A Swinbank 5/3) J R Cornwall

Placings:0622P (4641)

2002/03: 17⁰S, 16⁶G, 16²G, 16²S, 19⁰GF,

	Starts	1st	2nd	3rd	Win & Pl
NH Flat	4	0	2	0	1142
Hurdles	1	0	0	0	
Career Total	5	0	2	0	1142

Going: Sf: 0-2 GS: 0-0 Gd: 0-2 GF: - Fm: 0-1
Distance: 2m/2m3: 0-5 2m4-2m7: 0-0 3m+: 0-0
Track: LH: 0-4 RH: 0-1 Tight: 0-4 Gall: 0-0
Aids: BI: 0-0 Vi: 0-0 Tstrap: 0-0
Best Rating: 86 2/03 Catt 2m good NHF

Much improved effort when runner-up in a bumper at Catterick in February (hung badly) and turned in an almost identical performance there a week later.

Kingfisher Flyer (IRE)
83   74
9-y-o b g King s Ride-Melarka (Dara Monarch)
P R Webber Mrs M Fisher

Placings:210/U4P (3319)
2002/03: 16⁵S, 16⁴S, 21⁰GS,

	Starts	1st	2nd	3rd	Win & Pl
Hurdles	3	0	0	0	446
Career Total	6	1	1	0	2289
110 1/99 Hayd	2m H NHF		SFT		£1362
				Total win prize-money	£1362

Going: Sf: 0-2 GS: 0-1 Gd: 0-0 GF: - Fm: 0-0
Distance: 2m/2m3: 0-2 2m4-2m7: 0-1 3m+: 0-0
Track: LH: 0-1 RH: 0-2 Tight: 0-0 Gall: 0-1
Aids: BI: 0-0 Vi: 0-0 Tstrap: 0-0
Best Rating: 110 1/99 Hayd 2m soft NHF

Kingfisher Star
8-y-o ch g Derrylin-Legata (IRE) (Orchestra)
S R Andrews D Morgan

Placings:63 (0312)
2002/03: 22⁶G, 21³G,

	Starts	1st	2nd	3rd	Win & Pl
Chases	2	0	0	1	327
Career Total	2	0	0	1	327

Going: Sf: 0-0 GS: 0-0 Gd: 0-2 GF: - Fm: 0-0
Distance: 2m/2m3: 0-0 2m4-2m7: 0-2 3m+: 0-0
Track: LH: 0-0 RH: 0-2 Tight: 0-1 Gall: 0-0
Aids: BI: 0-0 Vi: 0-0 Tstrap: 0-0
Best Rating: 49 5/02 Folk 2m5f good Ch

Kingfisher Sunset
89f   65f
7-y-o b g Alflora (IRE)-Jack It In (Derrilly)
J G M O Shea K A Ayres

Placings:0450 (1696)
2002/03: 16⁸G, 17⁴GF, 16⁵GF, 16⁰G,

	Starts	1st	2nd	3rd	Win & Pl
NH Flat	4	0	0	0	0
Career Total	4	0	0	0	0

Going: Sf: 0-0 GS: 0-0 Gd: 0-2 GF: - Fm: 0-2
Distance: 2m/2m3: 0-4 2m4-2m7: 0-0 3m+: 0-0
Track: LH: 0-4 RH: 0-0 Tight: 0-1 Gall: 0-0

Aids: BI: 0-0 Vi: 0-0 Tstrap: 0-0
Best Rating: 65 10/02 Chep 2m110y gd-fm NHF

Kingkohler (IRE)
96   91+

4-y-o b g King s Theatre (IRE)-Legit (IRE) (Runnett)
K A Morgan (Edward Lynam 16/10) Jo Champion, H Morgan, E Barlow

Placings:3   (4156)
2002/03: 17³G,

	Starts	1st	2nd	3rd	Win & Pl
Hurdles	1	0	0	1	744
Career Total	1	0	0	1	744

Going: Sf: 0-0 GS: 0-0 Gd: 0-1 GF: - Fm: 0-0
Distance: 2m/2m3: 0-1 2m4-2m7: 0-0 3m+: 0-0
Track: LH: 0-0 RH: 0-1 Tight: 0-1 Gall: 0-0
Aids: BI: 0-0 Vi: 0-0 Tstrap: 0-0
Best Rating: 91 3/03 MRas 2m1f110y good Hdl

All-Weather maiden winner on the Flat; keen when third in an ordinary juvenile hurdle at Market Rasen in March.

Kingley Vale
82

9-y-o br g Neltino-Altaghaderry Run (Deep Run)
Mrs L Richards B Seal

Placings:0/0/3F2/1432-0P0   (3746)
2002/03: 25⁰GF, 26⁸G, 24⁰G,

	Starts	1st	2nd	3rd	Win & Pl
Chases	3	0	0		
Career Total	12	1	2	2	8810
87 11/01 Folk 3m1f E Ch				GD	£3666

Total win prize-money £3666

Going: Sf: 0-0 GS: 0-0 Gd: 0-2 GF: - Fm: 0-1
Distance: 2m/2m3: 0-0 2m4-2m7: 0-0 3m+: 0-3
Track: LH: 0-1 RH: 0-2 Tight: 0-1 Gall: 0-0
Aids: BI: 0-0 Vi: 0-0 Tstrap: 0-0
Best Rating: 90 1/02 Folk 3m1f soft Ch

Poor chaser, stays three miles plus and acts on good ground.

Kings Avenue
90   71

6-y-o b g Gran Alba (USA)-G W Supermare (Rymer)
G B Balding Double Kings Partnership

Placings:0-P0   (3315)
2002/03: 21⁸S, 19⁰GS,

	Starts	1st	2nd	3rd	Win & Pl
Hurdles	1	0	0	0	0
Chases	1	0	0	0	0
Career Total	3	0	0	0	

Going: Sf: 0-1 GS: 0-1 Gd: 0-0 GF: - Fm: 0-0
Distance: 2m/2m3: 0-0 2m4-2m7: 0-2 3m+: 0-0
Track: LH: 0-1 RH: 0-1 Tight: 0-0 Gall: 0-1
Aids: BI: 0-0 Vi: 0-0 Tstrap: 0-0
Best Rating: 72 2/02 Sand 2m110y soft NHF

Well held in a bumper on his debut.

Kings Cherry (IRE)
84   90

15-y-o b g King s Ride-Another Cherry (Le Bavard (FR))

J A B Old Martin Lovatt

Placings:0/5O00/04051416/3UP1PF/502215F/5244/0P242/06PFF/300P-0   (0110)
2002/03: 16⁰GS,

	Starts	1st	2nd	3rd	Win & Pl
Chases	1	0	0	0	
Career Total	45	4	5	2	32736
120 2/97 Newb 2m1f C(0-135)HCh				G-S	£4429
114 2/96 Chep 2m3f110yB Ch				SFT	£6890
104 4/95 Tipp 2m4f (0-123)HCh				SFT	£2712
104 3/95 Limk 2m6f Ch				HVY	£2712

Total win prize-money £16745

Going: Sf: 0-0 GS: 0-1 Gd: 0-0 GF: - Fm: 0-0
Distance: 2m/2m3: 0-1 2m4-2m7: 0-0 3m+: 0-0
Track: LH: 0-0 RH: 0-0 Tight: 0-0 Gall: 0-0
Aids: BI: 0-0 Vi: 0-0 Tstrap: 0-0
Best Rating: 123 4/00 Aint 2m6f good Ch

Kings Command
72   63

6-y-o b g Henbit (USA)-Country Festival (Town And Country)
A King Miss Janet Menzies

Placings:04   (4122)
2002/03: 16⁰GS, 16⁴G,

	Starts	1st	2nd	3rd	Win & Pl
NH Flat	2	0	0	0	0
Career Total	2	0	0	0	0

Going: Sf: 0-0 GS: 0-1 Gd: 0-1 GF: - Fm: 0-0
Distance: 2m/2m3: 0-2 2m4-2m7: 0-0 3m+: 0-0
Track: LH: 0-0 RH: 0-2 Tight: 0-0 Gall: 0-0
Aids: BI: 0-0 Vi: 0-0 Tstrap: 0-0
Best Rating: 102 2/03 Winc 2m gd-sft NHF

Kings Delite (IRE)
55   66

5-y-o b m Rakaposhi King-Bella Delite (Uncle Pokey)
R D Tudor (H D Daly 4/2) R D Tudor

Placings:00-0P5P   (4677)
2002/03: 21⁰S, 20⁰HY, 16⁵GF, 19⁰GF,

	Starts	1st	2nd	3rd	Win & Pl
Hurdles	4	0	0	0	0
Career Total	6	0	0	0	0

Going: Sf: 0-2 GS: 0-0 Gd: 0-0 GF: - Fm: 0-2
Distance: 2m/2m3: 0-1 2m4-2m7: 0-3 3m+: 0-0
Track: LH: 0-2 RH: 0-2 Tight: 0-0 Gall: 0-0
Aids: BI: 0-0 Vi: 0-0 Tstrap: 0-0
Best Rating: 73 3/02 Towc 2m soft NHF

Kings Highway (IRE)
82   51

8-y-o b g King s Ride-Highways Daughter (IRE) (Phardante (FR))
Dr P Pritchard Mrs T Pritchard

Placings:3/0-OPP60   (1592)
2002/03: 16⁰GS, 17⁸GF, 17⁰GS, 17⁶F, 22⁰G,

	Starts	1st	2nd	3rd	Win & Pl
Hurdles	5	0	0	0	0
Career Total	7	0	0	1	280

Going: Sf: 0-0 GS: 0-2 Gd: 0-1 GF: - Fm: 0-2
Distance: 2m/2m3: 0-4 2m4-2m7: 0-1 3m+: 0-0
Track: LH: 0-1 RH: 0-4 Tight: 0-3 Gall: 0-0
Aids: BI: 0-0 Vi: 0-0 Tstrap: 0-1
Best Rating: 99 11/00 Thur 2m soft NHF

Kings Knight (IRE)
90   84

8-y-o b g King s Ride-Right Hand (Oats)
H M Kavanagh Mrs S Kavanagh

Placings:24P0   (0840)
2002/03: 16²G, 16⁴GS, 16⁸G, 19⁰GF,

	Starts	1st	2nd	3rd	Win & Pl
Hurdles	3	0	1	0	754
Chases	1	0	0	0	0
Career Total	4	0	1	0	754

Going: Sf: 0-0 GS: 0-1 Gd: 0-2 GF: - Fm: 0-1
Distance: 2m/2m3: 0-4 2m4-2m7: 0-0 3m+: 0-0
Track: LH: 0-4 RH: 0-0 Tight: 0-1 Gall: 0-0
Aids: BI: 0-0 Vi: 0-0 Tstrap: 0-0
Best Rating: 84 6/02 Uttx 2m good Hdl

Runner-up in a weak novices hurdle on his racecourse bow. Held subsequently.

Kings Linen (IRE)
89   81

7-y-o b g Persian Mews-Kings Princess (King s Ride)
B I Case Dudley C Moore

Placings:0/0-030F636   (4709)
2002/03: 19⁰GS, 20⁰HY, 20⁰GS, 21⁵GS, 22⁶G, 26⁵GF, 24⁶G,

	Starts	1st	2nd	3rd	Win & Pl
Hurdles	7	0	0	2	872
Career Total	9	0	0	2	872

Going: Sf: 0-1 GS: 0-3 Gd: 0-2 GF: - Fm: 0-1
Distance: 2m/2m3: 0-1 2m4-2m7: 0-4 3m+: 0-2
Track: LH: 0-3 RH: 0-3 Tight: 0-3 Gall: 0-1
Aids: BI: 0-0 Vi: 0-0 Tstrap: 0-0
Best Rating: 81 4/03 Hrfd 3m2f gd-fm Hdl

Plating-class hurdler; improved effort when third in three and a quarter mile Class E conditional jockeys handicap hurdle at Hereford April 2003; stays well; likes fast ground.

Kings Minstral (IRE)
93   68

13-y-o ch g Andretti-Tara Minstral Vii (Damsire Unregistered)
D A Lamb D A Lamb

Placings:000/4000P/2130P065/5LU2214P2/F230/P4P/4P0 41-005U0   (1708)
2002/03: 25⁰GF, 21⁰GF, 25⁵GF, 27⁴G, 27⁰G,

	Starts	1st	2nd	3rd	Win & Pl
Chases	5	0	0	0	
Career Total	42	3	5	2	14853
82 4/02 Hexm 3m1f G(0-90)HCh				G-F	£2534
90 11/97 Kels 3m1f E Ch				G-F	£3452
78 11/96 Hexm 2m4f110yE(0-100)HHdl				GD	£2595

Total win prize-money £8581

Going: Sf: 0-0 GS: 0-0 Gd: 0-2 GF: - Fm: 0-3
Distance: 2m/2m3: 0-0 2m4-2m7: 0-1 3m+: 0-4
Track: LH: 0-5 RH: 0-0 Tight: 0-3 Gall: 0-0
Aids: BI: 0-0 Vi: 0-0 Tstrap: 0-0

Best Rating: 100 5/98 Kels 2m6f110y gd-fm Ch

Poor handicap chaser. Stays beyond three miles and acts on a sound surface.

Kings Mistral (IRE)
112   127

10-y-o b g Strong Gale-Mrs Simpson (Kinglet)
P R Chamings R V Shaw

Placings:024/02/00/12/3P160-1141   (4029)
2002/03: 24¹HY, 24¹GS, 24⁴S, 24¹S,

	Starts	1st	2nd	3rd	Win & Pl
Chases	4	3	0	0	21822
Career Total	18	5	3	1	38138
117 3/03	Sand	3m110y	E Ch		SFT	£8151
127 12/02	Sand	3m110y	D(0-120)HCh	G-S	£6987
120 11/02	Asct	3m110y	D(0-115)HCh	HVY	£5590
112 2/02	Sand	3m110y	E Ch		SFT	£5564
116 3/01	Sand	3m110y	E Ch		SFT	£7117

Total win prize-money £33411

Going: Sf: 2-3 GS: 1-1 Gd: 0-0 GF: - Fm: 0-0
Distance: 2m/2m3: 0-0 2m4-2m7: 0-0 3m+: 3-4
Track: LH: 0-0 RH: 3-4 Tight: 0-0 Gall: 0-0
Aids: Bl: 0-0 Vi: 0-0 Tstrap: 0-0
Best Rating: 127 12/02 Sand 3m110y gd-sft Ch

Fair handicap chaser; dual winner of the Grand Military Gold Cup at Sandown; jumps well; stays three miles one; acts on soft ground.

Kings Rapid (IRE)
95d

9-y-o b g King s Ride-Smokey River (Over The River (FR))
Mrs S J Smith Trevor Hemmings

Placings:23/1/3PP-PP0   (2187)
2002/03: 21ᴾG, 20ᴾG, 17⁰HY,

	Starts	1st	2nd	3rd	Win & Pl
Hurdles	2	0	0	0	0
Chases	1	0	0	0	0
Career Total	9	1	1	2	3732
121 11/00	Wwck 2m	E Hdl	HVY	£2380

Total win prize-money £2380

Going: Sf: 0-1 GS: 0-0 Gd: 0-2 GF: - Fm: 0-0
Distance: 2m/2m3: 0-1 2m4-2m7: 0-2 3m+: 0-0
Track: LH: 0-2 RH: 0-1 Tight: 0-1 Gall: 0-0
Aids: Bl: 0-0 Vi: 0-0 Tstrap: 0-0
Best Rating: 121 11/00 Wwck 2m heavy Hdl

Kings To Open
92   61

6-y-o b g First Trump-Shadiyama (Nishapour (FR))
R Dickin Peter Burton

Placings:025-000   (4338)
2002/03: 17⁰G, 17⁰G, 20⁰GF,

	Starts	1st	2nd	3rd	Win & Pl
Hurdles	3	0	0	0	
Career Total	6	0	1	0	599

Going: Sf: 0-0 GS: 0-0 Gd: 0-1 GF: - Fm: 0-1
Distance: 2m/2m3: 0-2 2m4-2m7: 0-1 3m+: 0-0
Track: LH: 0-1 RH: 0-2 Tight: 0-0 Gall: 0-2
Aids: Bl: 0-0 Vi: 0-0 Tstrap: 0-0
Best Rating: 89 11/01 Wwck 2m good Hdl

Kingsbridge (IRE)
97(85h)   (68h)82

9-y-o b g Cataldi-Rockport Rosa (IRE) (Roselier (FR))
M C Pipe M C Pipe

Placings:0/P06304-P35   (0926)
2002/03: 22ᴾGF, 16³GF, 16⁵GF,

	Starts	1st	2nd	3rd	Win & Pl
Hurdles	1	0	0	0	0
Chases	2	0	0	1	469
Career Total	10	0	0	2	1170

Going: Sf: 0-0 GS: 0-0 Gd: 0-0 GF: - Fm: 0-3
Distance: 2m/2m3: 0-2 2m4-2m7: 0-1 3m+: 0-0
Track: LH: 0-3 RH: 0-0 Tight: 0-3 Gall: 0-0
Aids: Bl: 0-0 Vi: 0-0 Tstrap: 0-0
Best Rating: 82 7/02 NAbb 2m110y gd-fm Ch

Winning pointer; plating-class chaser under Rules; acts on fast ground.

Kingscliff (IRE)

6-y-o b g Toulon-Pixies Glen (Furry Glen)
Mrs S Alner A J Sendell

Placings:11   (4133)
2002/03: 25¹GS, 26¹G,

	Starts	1st	2nd	3rd	Win & Pl
Chases	2	2	0	0	24712
Career Total	2	2	0	0	24712
140 3/03	Chel	3m2f110yB Ch	GD	£23200
143 2/03	Winc	3m1f110yH Ch	G-S	£1512

Total win prize-money £24712

Going: Sf: 0-0 GS: 1-1 Gd: 1-1 GF: - Fm: 0-0
Distance: 2m/2m3: 0-0 2m4-2m7: 0-0 3m+: 2-2
Track: LH: 1-1 RH: 1-1 Tight: 0-0 Gall: 1-1
Aids: Bl: 0-0 Vi: 0-0 Tstrap: 0-0
Best Rating: 143 2/03 Winc 3m1f110y gd-sft Ch

Highly promising recruit from the pointing field; impressive winner on his hunter chase debut in February 2003 and added the Christie s Foxhunter Chase at Cheltenham; stays an extended 3m 2f; will join Robert Alner for a handicap campaign in 2003/4.

Kingscote Thunder (IRE)
103f   107f

6-y-o b g Montelimar (USA)-Sweet Thunder (Le Bavard (FR))
Noel T Chance Pulse Racing & Mrs S Rowley-Williams

Placings:0-01   (4737)
2002/03: 16⁰GS, 16¹GF,

	Starts	1st	2nd	3rd	Win & Pl
NH Flat	2	1	0	0	2016
Career Total	3	1	0	0	2016
105 4/03	Chep	2m110y	H NHF	G-F	£2016

Total win prize-money £2016

Going: Sf: 0-0 GS: 0-1 Gd: 0-0 GF: - Fm: 1-1
Distance: 2m/2m3: 1-2 2m4-2m7: 0-0 3m+: 0-0
Track: LH: 1-2 RH: 0-0 Tight: 0-0 Gall: 0-0
Aids: Bl: 0-0 Vi: 0-0 Tstrap: 0-0
Best Rating: 105 4/03 Chep 2m110y gd-fm NHF

Highly tried on good to soft ground in his first two bumpers; did not beat much when winning on a fast surface at Chepstow April 2003; fair run in defeat next time.

Kingsdon (IRE)
71

6-y-o b g Brief Truce (USA)-Richly Deserved (IRE) (King s Lake (USA))
J G Fitzgerald Mike Browne

Placings:00-4P   (2123)
2002/03: 17⁴S, 16ᴾGS,

	Starts	1st	2nd	3rd	Win & Pl
Hurdles	2	0	0	0	332
Career Total	4	0	0	0	332

Going: Sf: 0-1 GS: 0-1 Gd: 0-0 GF: - Fm: 0-0
Distance: 2m/2m3: 0-2 2m4-2m7: 0-0 3m+: 0-0
Track: LH: 0-2 RH: 0-0 Tight: 0-2 Gall: 0-0
Aids: Bl: 0-0 Vi: 0-2 Tstrap: 0-2
Best Rating: 71 11/02 Sedg 2m1f soft Hdl

Kingsdown Trix (IRE)
105(81c)   (45c)89

9-y-o b g Contract Law (USA)-Three Of Trumps (Tyrnavos)
R Dickin (R J Smith 12/8) The Invincibles

Placings:0414P000/545115/056/316/03020-5035P0040
          (4623)
2002/03: 24⁵GF, 20⁰S, 24³G, 23⁵GF, 23ᴾG, 26⁹GF, 19⁰GS, 26⁴GF, 27⁰GF,

	Starts	1st	2nd	3rd	Win & Pl
Hurdles	7	0	0	1	327
Chases	2	0	0	0	0
Career Total	34	4	0	3	14699
104 4/01	Fknm	2m4f	F(0-105)HHdl	G-S	£3108
97 4/99	Fknm	2m4f	F(0-110)HHdl	GD	£3310
98 3/99	Font	2m6f110yE(0-115)HHdl	G-F	£2477
93 12/97	Font	2m2f110yE Hdl	SFT	£2532

Total win prize-money £11428

Going: Sf: 0-1 GS: 0-1 Gd: 0-2 GF: - Fm: 0-5
Distance: 2m/2m3: 0-0 2m4-2m7: 0-2 3m+: 0-7
Track: LH: 0-7 RH: 0-2 Tight: 0-2 Gall: 0-0
Aids: Bl: 0-1 Vi: 0-0 Tstrap: 0-0
Best Rating: 104 4/02 Chep 2m4f gd-sft Hdl

Plating-class hurdler; stays two miles six furlongs; suited by good ground.

Kingsfold Freddie
98   79

5-y-o ch g Rock City-Kingsfold Flame (No Loiterer)
P R Webber Mrs Ann Shaw

Placings:03000   (4567)
2002/03: 14⁰GS, 16³S, 16⁰GS, 16⁰G, 20⁰GF,

	Starts	1st	2nd	3rd	Win & Pl
NH Flat	3	0	0	1	404
Hurdles	2	0	0	0	0
Career Total	5	0	0	1	404

Going: Sf: 0-1 GS: 0-2 Gd: 0-1 GF: - Fm: 0-1
Distance: 2m/2m3: 0-3 2m4-2m7: 0-1 3m+: 0-0
Track: LH: 0-2 RH: 0-3 Tight: 0-1 Gall: 0-1
Aids: Bl: 0-0 Vi: 0-0 Tstrap: 0-0
Best Rating: 94 2/03 Winc 2m gd-sft NHF

Has shown a little ability in bumpers.

Kingsland Taverner
97

12-y-o ch g True Song-Princess Hecate (Autre Prince)

M F Harris E O Steward

Placings:3/22/4PF5F/3/P6P44/0P/P3F   (0319)
2002/03: 25PGF, 24³GF, 26FG,

	Starts	1st	2nd	3rd	Win & Pl
Chases	3	0	0	1	213
Career Total	19	0	2	3	2446

Going:	Sf: 0-0 GS: 0-0 Gd: 0-1 GF: - Fm: 0-2
Distance:	2m/2m3: 0-0 2m4-2m7: 0-0 3m+: 0-3
Track:	LH: 0-1 RH: 0-2 Tight: 0-0 Gall: 0-1
Aids:	Bl: 0-0 Vi: 0-0 Tstrap: 0-0
Best Rating:	96 5/96 Hrfd 2m1f firm NHF

Moderate hunter chaser, suited by a sound surface.

Kingsmark (IRE)
123   166
10-y-o gr g Roselier (FR)-Gaye Le Moss (Le Moss)
M Todhunter Sir Robert Ogden

Placings:3/111120/51F1322/11160310/124-13   (2510)
2002/03: 24¹S, 24³G,

	Starts	1st	2nd	3rd	Win & Pl
Chases	2	1	0	1	35500
Career Total	27	12	4	4	200140

166	11/02	Hayd	3m	A HCh	SFT	£30000
166	11/01	Hayd	3m	A HCh	GD	£27000
158	4/01	Aint	3m1f	B HCh	SFT	£26000
158	11/00	Hayd	3m	A HCh	SFT	£25200
140	10/00	MRas	3m1f	C(0-130)HCh		£9178
141	10/00	Kels	3m1f	D(0-125)HCh	GD	£3887
131	1/00	Folk	3m2f	E Ch	SFT	£3510
137	11/99	Bang	3m4½y	D Ch	SFT	£4842
137	1/99	Kemp	2m5f	D Hdl	HVY	£3793
121	12/98	Folk	2m6f110yE Hdl		SFT	£2650
131	11/98	Folk	2m6f110yF Hdl		SFT	£2008
116	10/98	Strf	2m6f110yE Hdl		G-S	£2075

Total win prize-money £140146

Going:	Sf: 1-1 GS: 0-0 Gd: 0-1 GF: - Fm: 0-0
Distance:	2m/2m3: 0-0 2m4-2m7: 0-0 3m+: 1-2
Track:	LH: 1-2 RH: 0-0 Tight: 0-0 Gall: 0-0
Aids:	Bl: 0-0 Vi: 0-0 Tstrap: 0-0
Best Rating:	166 11/02 Hayd 3m soft Ch

High-class handicap chaser; well suited by a flat, left-handed track and three miles; suffered an over-reach when a distant fourth in the Grand National in 2002, but came back to complete a hat-trick in the Edward Hanmer at Haydock in November 2002; goes on good ground but is better with give.

Kingsmoor
(92h)   (88h)
7-y-o b g Regal Embers (IRE)-Cupids Bower (Owen Dudley)
K Bishop R D Cox

Placings:0/6-F   (3851)
2002/03: 24FGS,

	Starts	1st	2nd	3rd	Win & Pl
Chases	1	0	0	0	
Career Total	3	0	0	0	0

Going:	Sf: 0-0 GS: 0-1 Gd: 0-0 GF: - Fm: 0-0
Distance:	2m/2m3: 0-0 2m4-2m7: 0-0 3m+: 0-1
Track:	LH: 0-0 RH: 0-1 Tight: 0-1 Gall: 0-0
Aids:	Bl: 0-0 Vi: 0-0 Tstrap: 0-0
Best Rating:	88 5/01 Winc 2m6f gd-fm Hdl

Kingsthorpe
15-y-o ch g Brotherly (USA)-Miss Kewmill (Billion (USA))
M R Daniell Mervyn Jones

Placings:P/F00PF/0P/10/3-P   (0033)
2002/03: 25PGF,

	Starts	1st	2nd	3rd	Win & Pl
Chases	1	0	0	0	
Career Total	12	1	0	1	3158
94	5/98	Strf	3m	H Ch	GD	£2898

Total win prize-money £2898

Going:	Sf: 0-0 GS: 0-0 Gd: 0-0 GF: - Fm: 0-1
Distance:	2m/2m3: 0-0 2m4-2m7: 0-0 3m+: 0-1
Track:	LH: 0-1 RH: 0-0 Tight: 0-0 Gall: 0-1
Aids:	Bl: 0-0 Vi: 0-0 Tstrap: 0-0
Best Rating:	94 5/98 Strf 3m good Ch

Kingston Bill
96   103+
6-y-o b g Then Again-Tricata (Electric)
W G M Turner Miss Corinne J Overton

Placings:0/356P5   (3349)
2002/03: 16³G, 19⁵GS, 16⁶S, 16⁶PS, 16⁵HY,

	Starts	1st	2nd	3rd	Win & Pl
Hurdles	5	0	0	1	545
Career Total	6	0	0	1	545

Going:	Sf: 0-3 GS: 0-1 Gd: 0-1 GF: - Fm: 0-0
Distance:	2m/2m3: 0-1 2m4-2m7: 0-0 3m+: 0-0
Track:	LH: 0-2 RH: 0-3 Tight: 0-1 Gall: 0-0
Aids:	Bl: 0-0 Vi: 0-0 Tstrap: 0-0
Best Rating:	92 10/02 Chep 2m110y good Hdl

Novice hurdler, effective at around two miles.

Kingston Game
4-y-o b g Mind Games-Valmaranda (USA) (Sir Ivor)
Miss K M George Stableline

Placings:PPP   (1004)
2002/03: 17PGS, 16PGF, 17PGF,

	Starts	1st	2nd	3rd	Win & Pl
Hurdles	3	0	0	0	
Career Total	3	0	0	0	

Going:	Sf: 0-0 GS: 0-1 Gd: 0-0 GF: - Fm: 0-2
Distance:	2m/2m3: 0-3 2m4-2m7: 0-0 3m+: 0-0
Track:	LH: 0-0 RH: 0-1 Tight: 0-3 Gall: 0-0
Aids:	Bl: 0-0 Vi: 0-0 Tstrap: 0-0
Best Rating:	0 8/02 Bang 2m1f gd-fm Hdl

Kingston Venture
78(103h)   (107h)47
7-y-o b g Interrex (CAN)-Tricata (Electric)
W G M Turner Miss Corinne J Overton

Placings:23312/513/PP4-30244P   (2942)
2002/03: 20³G, 24⁰GS, 19²GS, 19⁴GS, 19⁴S, 20PGS,

	Starts	1st	2nd	3rd	Win & Pl
Hurdles	4	0	1	1	1568
Chases	2	0	0	0	456
Career Total	17	2	3	4	14380
118	6/00	Strf	2m110y	C(0-135)HHdl	GD	£5239
91	11/99	Hrfd	2m1f	D Hdl	GD	£2885

Total win prize-money £8124

Going:	Sf: 0-1 GS: 0-4 Gd: 0-1 GF: - Fm: 0-0
Distance:	2m/2m3: 0-2 2m4-2m7: 0-3 3m+: 0-1
Track:	LH: 0-2 RH: 0-4 Tight: 0-3 Gall: 0-0
Aids:	Bl: 0-1 Vi: 0-0 Tstrap: 0-0
Best Rating:	118 7/00 Wolv 2m4f110y good Hdl

Lightly raced hurdler, decent effort on his reappearance in 2002/3.

Kingston Wish (IRE)
67   37
4-y-o b g Mujadil (USA)-Well Wisher (USA) (Sanglamore (USA))
Ian Emmerson Ian Emmerson

Placings:0   (3579)
2002/03: 16⁰G,

	Starts	1st	2nd	3rd	Win & Pl
Hurdles	1	0	0	0	
Career Total	1	0	0	0	

Going:	Sf: 0-0 GS: 0-0 Gd: 0-0 GF: - Fm: 0-0
Distance:	2m/2m3: 0-1 2m4-2m7: 0-0 3m+: 0-0
Track:	LH: 0-0 RH: 0-1 Tight: 0-1 Gall: 0-0
Aids:	Bl: 0-0 Vi: 0-0 Tstrap: 0-0
Best Rating:	37 2/03 Muss 2m good Hdl

Kingston-Banker
100   117
7-y-o b g Teamster-Happy Manda (Mandamus)
R H Alner H Wellstead

Placings:60/332-523P2F   (4427)
2002/03: 24⁵G, 21²HY, 24³GS, 24PGS, 19²G, 26PGF,

	Starts	1st	2nd	3rd	Win & Pl
Chases	6	0	2	1	4851
Career Total	11	0	3	3	7314

Going:	Sf: 0-1 GS: 0-2 Gd: 0-0 GF: - Fm: 0-1
Distance:	2m/2m3: 0-0 2m4-2m7: 0-2 3m+: 0-4
Track:	LH: 0-6 RH: 0-0 Tight: 0-3 Gall: 0-0
Aids:	Bl: 0-0 Vi: 0-0 Tstrap: 0-0
Best Rating:	117 12/02 Sthl 3m10y gd-sft Ch

Fair chaser; acts on soft ground; stays three miles.

Kingtobee (IRE)
98f   83f
5-y-o b g King s Ride-Zephyrelle (IRE) (Celio Rufo)
J A B Old W E Sturt

Placings:0   (4329)
2002/03: 16⁰G,

	Starts	1st	2nd	3rd	Win & Pl
NH Flat	1	0	0	0	
Career Total	1	0	0	0	

Going:	Sf: 0-0 GS: 0-0 Gd: 0-0 GF: - Fm: 0-0
Distance:	2m/2m3: 0-1 2m4-2m7: 0-0 3m+: 0-0
Track:	LH: 0-1 RH: 0-0 Tight: 0-0 Gall: 0-1
Aids:	Bl: 0-0 Vi: 0-0 Tstrap: 0-0
Best Rating:	83 3/03 Newb 2m110y good NHF

Kinnino
93   76
9-y-o b g Polish Precedent (USA)-On Tiptoes (Shareef Dancer (USA))

G L Moore Exors Of The Late Mr A Moore

Placings:55/F0-050PP   (3937)
2002/03: 16⁰GF, 17⁵G, 16⁰S, 16ᴾHY, 18ᴾS,

	Starts	1st	2nd	3rd	Win & Pl
Hurdles	5	0	0		0
Career Total	9	0	0		0

Going: Sf: 0-3 GS: 0-0 Gd: 0-1 GF: - Fm: 0-1
Distance: 2m2/2m3: 0-5 2m4-2m7: 0-0 3m+: 0-0
Track: LH: 0-3 RH: 0-2 Tight: 0-3 Gall: 0-1
Aids: Bl: 0-0 Vi: 0-0 Tstrap: 0-0
Best Rating: 76   5/02   Hntg   2m110y   gd-fm   Hdl

Kino's Cross

80

14-y-o b g Relkino-Coral Delight (Idiots Delight)
A J Wilson   N V Harvey

Placings:6004012/B320100/**4PPF**606331/4500/003212143/
3262/0/F00002260-P   (0326)
2002/03: 16ᴾG,

	Starts	1st	2nd	3rd	Win & Pl
Hurdles	1	0	0		0
Career Total	52	5	8	6	35859
121	3/99	Winc	2m		D(0-125)HHdl	G-S	£5277
121	1/99	Winc	2m		D(0-125)HHdl	SFT	£5550
104	4/97	Worc	2m		D(0-125)HHdl	SFT	£3092
115	2/96	Weth	2m		B(0-140)HHdl	G-S	£7100
99	2/95	Winc	2m		F(0-105)HHdl	SFT	£2574

Total win prize-money £23593

Going: Sf: 0-0 GS: 0-0 Gd: 0-1 GF: - Fm: 0-0
Distance: 2m2/2m3: 0-1 2m4-2m7: 0-0 3m+: 0-0
Track: LH: 0-1 RH: 0-0 Tight: 0-0 Gall: 0-0
Aids: Bl: 0-0 Vi: 0-0 Tstrap: 0-0
Best Rating: 121   11/99   Worc   2m   gd-sft   Hdl

Fair hurdler now at the veteran stage, he has never won beyond two miles and looks best with some cut.

Kiora Bay

83f   65f

6-y-o b g Karinga Bay-Equasion (IRE) (Cyrano De Bergerac)
Jonjo O Neill   C D Carr

Placings:0   (2292)
2002/03: 17⁰G,

	Starts	1st	2nd	3rd	Win & Pl
NH Flat	1	0	0		0
Career Total	1	0	0		0

Going: Sf: 0-0 GS: 0-0 Gd: 0-1 GF: - Fm: 0-0
Distance: 2m2/2m3: 0-1 2m4-2m7: 0-0 3m+: 0-0
Track: LH: 0-0 RH: 0-1 Tight: 0-0 Gall: 0-0
Aids: Bl: 0-0 Vi: 0-0 Tstrap: 0-0
Best Rating: 65   12/02   Hrfd   2m1f   good   NHF

Kipling

99   85

7-y-o b g Rudimentary (USA)-Sharmood (USA) (Sharpen Up)
Miss Sheena West   Graham Flight

Placings:653P3   (3935)
2002/03: 17⁶S, 18⁵HY, 21³S, 24ᴾS, 27³S,

	Starts	1st	2nd	3rd	Win & Pl
NH Flat	2	0	0	0	0

Hurdles   3   0   0   2   1231
Career Total   5   0   0   2   1231

Hurdles	3	0	0	2	1231
Career Total	5	0	0	2	1231

Going: Sf: 0-5 GS: 0-0 Gd: 0-0 GF: - Fm: 0-0
Distance: 2m2/2m3: 0-2 2m4-2m7: 0-1 3m+: 0-2
Track: LH: 0-2 RH: 0-2 Tight: 0-3 Gall: 0-0
Aids: Bl: 0-0 Vi: 0-0 Tstrap: 0-0
Best Rating: 85   3/03   Font   3m3f   soft   Hdl

Modest novice hurdler; stays three miles three.

Kippanour (USA)

103(91c)   (68c)90

11-y-o b g Alleged (USA)-Innsbruck (General Assembly (USA))
A G Hobbs   Furnish With Abbey

Placings:12323/33020005/P6**5433**65P/P6/**16310P**214406/
56123016000-351P0633055   (3992)
2002/03: 27³GF, 27⁵GF, 27¹S, 24ᴾG, 25⁰G, 24⁶GS, 26³GS, 26³S,
25⁰HY, 26⁵G, 25⁴G,

	Starts	1st	2nd	3rd	Win & Pl
Hurdles	11	1	0	3	4013
Career Total	58	7	5	11	26283
96	5/02	NAbb	3m3f		E(0-110)HHdl	SFT	£2933
101	1/02	Hrfd	3m2f		F(0-90)Hdl	SFT	£2765
93	9/01	Hntg	3m2f		F(0-90)HHdl	GD	£2044
89	11/00	Hntg	3m2f		G(0-95)HHdl	GD	£1951
92	7/00	Worc	2m7f110y	F(0-100)HCh	G-F	£2970
92	5/00	Uttx	3m2f		F(0-90)HCh	GD	£2960
93	9/95	Slig	2m		Hdl	GD	£2204

Total win prize-money £17830

Going: Sf: 1-3 GS: 0-2 Gd: 0-4 GF: - Fm: 0-2
Distance: 2m2/2m3: 0-0 2m4-2m7: 0-0 **3m+:** 1-11
Track: **LH:** 1-5 RH: 0-4 **Tight:** 1-3 Gall: 0-2
Aids: **Bl:** 1-10 Vi: 0-1 Tstrap: 0-0
Best Rating: 120   12/95   Chel   2m1f   good   Hdl

Plating-class handicap hurdler; out-and-out stayer who finds soft ground helping bring his stamina into play.

Kippour (FR)

70

5-y-o b g Luchiroverte (IRE)-Obole Iii (FR) (Signani (FR))
H D Daly   Trevor Hemmings

Placings:2-50P   (3938)
2002/03: 17⁵G, 19⁰GS, 21ᴾGS,

	Starts	1st	2nd	3rd	Win & Pl
NH Flat	1	0	0	0	
Hurdles	2	0	0	0	
Career Total	4	0	1	0	615

Going: Sf: 0-0 GS: 0-2 Gd: 0-1 GF: - Fm: 0-0
Distance: 2m2/2m3: 0-1 2m4-2m7: 0-2 3m+: 0-0
Track: LH: 0-1 RH: 0-1 Tight: 0-1 Gall: 0-0
Aids: Bl: 0-0 Vi: 0-0 Tstrap: 0-0
Best Rating: 90   11/02   Aint   2m1f   good   NHF

Runner-up in a fast-ground Warwick bumper on his debut. Held over hurdles.

Kirdford (IRE)

83

9-y-o b/br g Miners Lamp-Somelli (Candy Cane)
R H Buckler   The Eight Optimists

Placings:056014/2/56-F   (1842)
2002/03: 22ᶠS,

	Starts	1st	2nd	3rd	Win & Pl
Hurdles	1	0	0	0	

Career Total	10	1	1	0	4050

83   4/00   Ludl   2m5f   E(0-105)HHdl   GD   £3250

Total win prize-money £3250

Going: Sf: 0-1 GS: 0-0 Gd: 0-0 GF: - Fm: 0-0
Distance: 2m2/2m3: 0-0 2m4-2m7: 0-1 3m+: 0-0
Track: LH: 0-0 RH: 0-1 Tight: 0-0 Gall: 0-0
Aids: Bl: 0-0 Vi: 0-0 Tstrap: 0-0
Best Rating: 83   10/01   Chep   2m4f   soft   Hdl

Kirisnippa

8-y-o b g Beveled (USA)-Kiri Te (Liboi (USA))
A P Jones   D A Drake

Placings:P/P-P   (0035)
2002/03: 22ᴾG,

	Starts	1st	2nd	3rd	Win & Pl
Hurdles	1	0	0		0
Career Total	3	0	0		0

Going: Sf: 0-0 GS: 0-0 Gd: 0-1 GF: - Fm: 0-0
Distance: 2m2/2m3: 0-0 2m4-2m7: 0-1 3m+: 0-0
Track: LH: 0-0 RH: 0-1 Tight: 0-0 Gall: 0-0
Aids: Bl: 0-0 Vi: 0-0 Tstrap: 0-0
Best Rating:

Kirkharle (IRE)

83(87h)   (60h)66

9-y-o b g Commanche Run-Dardy Daughter (Side Track)
K F Clutterbuck (Mrs A Hamilton 19/5)   K F Clutterbuck

Placings:0P/342-0P63P   (3746)
2002/03: 25⁰GS, 19ᴾGS, 24⁶GS, 24³GS, 24ᴾG,

	Starts	1st	2nd	3rd	Win & Pl
Hurdles	2	0	0	0	0
Chases	3	0	0	1	632
Career Total	10	0	1	2	1836

Going: Sf: 0-0 GS: 0-4 Gd: 0-1 GF: - Fm: 0-0
Distance: 2m2/2m3: 0-1 2m4-2m7: 0-0 3m+: 0-4
Track: LH: 0-4 RH: 0-1 Tight: 0-2 Gall: 0-2
Aids: Bl: 0-0 Vi: 0-0 Tstrap: 0-0
Best Rating: 66   4/02   Hexm   3m1f   good   Ch

Modest pointer/hunter chaser, handles any ground.

Kirsty Lea

4-y-o b f Presidium-Adder Howe (Amboise)
I W McInnes   Mrs Susan Johnson

Placings:0   (2142)
2002/03: 14⁰GS,

	Starts	1st	2nd	3rd	Win & Pl
NH Flat	1	0	0		0
Career Total	1	0	0		0

Going: Sf: 0-0 GS: 0-1 Gd: 0-0 GF: - Fm: 0-0
Distance: 2m2/2m3: 0-0 2m4-2m7: 0-0 3m+: 0-0
Track: LH: 0-1 RH: 0-0 Tight: 0-0 Gall: 0-0
Aids: Bl: 0-0 Vi: 0-0 Tstrap: 0-0
Best Rating: 0   11/02   Newc   1m6f   gd-sft   NHF

Kiss Me Kate

105   78

7-y-o b m Aragon-Ingerence (FR) (Akarad (FR))

Mrs P Robeson The Royal George Racing Partnership

Placings:44115F/4005/2 (2168)
2002/03: 19²GS,

	Starts	1st	2nd	3rd	Win & Pl
Hurdles	1	0	1	0	711
Career Total	11	2	1	0	5935

109 3/00 Plum 2m F(0-110)HHdl GD £2226
111 2/00 Hntg 2m110y E Hdl SFT £2730
Total win prize-money £4956

Going: Sf: 0-0 GS: 0-1 Gd: 0-0 GF: - Fm: 0-0
Distance: 2m/2m3: 0-1 2m4-2m7: 0-0 3m+: 0-0
Track: LH: 0-1 RH: 0-0 Tight: 0-0 Gall: 0-0
Aids: Bl: 0-0 Vi: 0-0 Tstrap: 0-0
Best Rating: 111 6/00 Uttx 2m4f110y gd-fm Hdl

Poor, lightly-raced hurdler; acts on good ground or softer.

Kissed By Moonlite

7-y-o gr m Petong-Rose Bouquet (General Assembly (USA))
J W Unett A Fairfield

Placings:P (0614)
2002/03: 20³GF,

	Starts	1st	2nd	3rd	Win & Pl
Hurdles	1	0	0	0	
Career Total	1	0	0	0	

Going: Sf: 0-0 GS: 0-0 Gd: 0-0 GF: - Fm: 0-1
Distance: 2m/2m3: 0-0 2m4-2m7: 0-1 3m+: 0-0
Track: LH: 0-1 RH: 0-0 Tight: 0-0 Gall: 0-0
Aids: Bl: 0-0 Vi: 0-0 Tstrap: 0-0
Best Rating: 0 6/02 Worc 2m4f gd-fm Hdl

Kit Smartie (IRE)
103   132
11-y-o b g Be My Native (USA)-Smart Cookie (Lord Gayle (USA))
D M Forster D M Forster

Placings:63/30513111/12/0302PP-214P0 (4557)
2002/03: 25²S, 28¹S, 25⁴G, 28⁶G, 33⁹G,

	Starts	1st	2nd	3rd	Win & Pl
Chases	5	1	1	0	17243
Career Total	23	6	3	4	55272

132 11/02 Hayd 3m4f110y(0-135)HCh SFT £12156
126 11/00 Sedg 2m5f C Ch SFT £6968
132 4/98 Prth 3m110y B Hdl G-S £6193
126 4/98 Ayr 2m6f C Hdl GD £4510
120 3/98 Sedg 2m5f110yE Hdl G-S £2530
101 1/98 Hntg 2m5f110yF(0-105)HHdl G-S £1982
Total win prize-money £34340

Going: Sf: 1-2 GS: 0-0 Gd: 0-3 GF: - Fm: 0-0
Distance: 2m/2m3: 0-0 2m4-2m7: 0-0 3m+: 1-5
Track: LH: 1-5 RH: 0-0 Tight: 0-0 Gall: 0-1
Aids: Bl: 0-1 Vi: 0-0 Tstrap: 0-1
Best Rating: 132 11/02 Hayd 3m4f110y soft Ch

Useful staying handicap chaser; sometimes wears a tongue-strap and/or sheepskin cheekpieces; gets three and a half miles; acts on soft ground.

Kitimat
93(85h)   (89h)63
6-y-o b g Then Again-Quago (New Member)
R H Buckler The Eight Optimists

Placings:06-P40560P46 (4327)
2002/03: 22⁶GF, 19⁴GF, 17⁰G, 22⁵G, 20⁶S, 19⁰S, 25⁰GS, 18⁴S, 18⁶G,

	Starts	1st	2nd	3rd	Win & Pl
Hurdles	5	0	0	0	0
Chases	4	0	0	0	317
Career Total	11	0	0	0	317

Going: Sf: 0-3 GS: 0-1 Gd: 0-3 GF: - Fm: 0-2
Distance: 2m/2m3: 0-4 2m4-2m7: 0-4 3m+: 0-1
Track: LH: 0-1 RH: 0-6 Tight: 0-3 Gall: 0-1
Aids: Bl: 0-0 Vi: 0-0 Tstrap: 0-0
Best Rating: 89 6/02 Hrfd 2m3f110y gd-fm Hdl

Kitley Creek
85
8-y-o b g Michelozzo (USA)-May Reef (IRE) (Simply Great (FR))
M Hill Fun In The Sun Partnership

Placings:105/55-PP (1595)
2002/03: 22⁶GF, 17⁵G,

	Starts	1st	2nd	3rd	Win & Pl
Hurdles	2	0	0	0	
Career Total	7	1	0	0	1540

91 6/00 NAbb 2m1f H NHF G-F £1540
Total win prize-money £1540

Going: Sf: 0-0 GS: 0-0 Gd: 0-1 GF: - Fm: 0-1
Distance: 2m/2m3: 0-2 2m4-2m7: 0-1 3m+: 0-0
Track: LH: 0-1 RH: 0-1 Tight: 0-1 Gall: 0-0
Aids: Bl: 0-0 Vi: 0-0 Tstrap: 0-0
Best Rating: 91 6/00 NAbb 2m1f gd-fm NHF

Kittenkat
101(109h)   (111h)95
9-y-o b m Riverwise (USA)-Cut Above The Rest (Indiaro)
N R Mitchell Piers Butler

Placings:60/02033P3P1/462411003P3P/34450460-3533F5U54206 (4438)
2002/03: 23³GF, 19⁵S, 26³S, 26³G, 26⁶FY, 24⁵GS, 26⁵S, 24⁵S, 24⁴GS, 26⁵S, 32⁰G, 24⁶G,

	Starts	1st	2nd	3rd	Win & Pl
Chases	12	0	1	3	4954
Career Total	43	3	3	9	31820

123 12/00 Winc 2m6f B HHdl G-S £8424
106 12/00 Folk 2m4f110yC(0-130)HHdl HVY £6773
95 4/00 Extr 2m7f E Hdl HVY £2254
Total win prize-money £17452

Going: Sf: 0-6 GS: 0-2 Gd: 0-3 GF: - Fm: 0-1
Distance: 2m/2m3: 0-0 2m4-2m7: 0-3 3m+: 0-11
Track: LH: 0-5 RH: 0-3 Tight: 0-6 Gall: 0-1
Aids: Bl: 0-0 Vi: 0-0 Tstrap: 0-0
Best Rating: 123 4/01 Extr 2m6f110y gd-sft Hdl

Moderate chaser; stays well; acts in the mud; has only ever won going right-handed.

Kivotos (USA)
106   109+
5-y-o gr g Trempolino (USA)-Authorized Staff (USA) (Relaunch (USA))
A C Whillans C Bird

Placings:01P32 (4776)
2002/03: 16⁰S, 16¹HY, 18⁵GS, 20³S, 20²G,

	Starts	1st	2nd	3rd	Win & Pl
Hurdles	5	1	1	1	5794
Career Total	5	1	1	1	5794

102 1/03 Ayr 2m E Hdl HVY £3451
Total win prize-money £3452

Going: Sf: 1-3 GS: 0-1 Gd: 0-1 GF: - Fm: 0-0
Distance: 2m/2m3: 1-3 2m4-2m7: 0-2 3m+: 0-0
Track: LH: 1-3 RH: 0-2 Tight: 0-2 Gall: 0-0
Aids: Bl: 0-0 Vi: 0-0 Tstrap: 0-0
Best Rating: 102 1/03 Ayr 2m heavy Hdl

Modest hurdler; stays two and a half miles; acts on any ground.

Klondike Charger (USA)
108   111
9-y-o b g Crafty Prospector (USA)-Forever Waving (USA) (Hoist The Flag (USA))
Dr P Pritchard (P F Nicholls 3/6) David & Lesley Byrne

Placings:0333/1P26/1212/5PP-3PP2P522520 (2448)
2002/03: 25³G, 26⁶G, 23⁵GF, 24²G, 26⁶GF, 27⁵G, 22²G, 24²F, 24⁵G, 24²G, 27⁰G,

	Starts	1st	2nd	3rd	Win & Pl
Chases	11	0	4	1	7772
Career Total	26	3	7	4	22421

114 9/00 NAbb 3m2f110yE Ch G-F £3234
114 5/00 Font 3m2f110yE Ch GD £3580
100 10/99 Weth 3m1f E(0-105)HHdl G-F £2304
Total win prize-money £9118

Going: Sf: 0-0 GS: 0-0 Gd: 0-8 GF: - Fm: 0-3
Distance: 2m/2m3: 0-0 2m4-2m7: 0-1 3m+: 0-10
Track: LH: 0-5 RH: 0-5 Tight: 0-6 Gall: 0-0
Aids: Bl: 0-0 Vi: 0-0 Tstrap: 0-0
Best Rating: 114 9/00 NAbb 3m2f110y gd-fm Ch

Modest, inconsistent staying chaser; best on fast ground; not one to trust.

Knight Of Kilcash (IRE)
8-y-o ch g Buckskin (FR)-Lady Pauper (IRE) (Le Moss)
Mrs O Bush J H Burbidge

Placings:P (0316)
2002/03: 21⁰G,

	Starts	1st	2nd	3rd	Win & Pl
Chases	1	0	0	0	
Career Total	1	0	0	0	

Going: Sf: 0-0 GS: 0-0 Gd: 0-1 GF: - Fm: 0-0
Distance: 2m/2m3: 0-0 2m4-2m7: 0-1 3m+: 0-0
Track: LH: 0-0 RH: 0-1 Tight: 0-0 Gall: 0-0
Aids: Bl: 0-0 Vi: 0-0 Tstrap: 0-0
Best Rating: 0 5/02 Folk 2m5f good Ch

Knight Of Passion
11-y-o b g Arctic Lord-Lovelek (Golden Love)
Miss S E Robinson R K Crabb

Placings:13/F20/02055-P (4031)
2002/03: 24⁰PS,

	Starts	1st	2nd	3rd	Win & Pl
Chases	1	0	0	0	
Career Total	11	1	2	1	6621

127 4/99 Towc 3m1f H Ch SFT £4123
Total win prize-money £4124

Going: Sf: 0-1 GS: 0-0 Gd: 0-0 GF: - Fm: 0-0
Distance: 2m/2m3: 0-0 2m4-2m7: 0-0 3m+: 0-1
Track: LH: 0-0 RH: 0-1 Tight: 0-0 Gall: 0-0
Aids: Bl: 0-1 Vi: 0-0 Tstrap: 0-0
Best Rating: 129 3/00 Chel 3m2f110y gd-fm Ch

Knight Of Silver

101   **70**

6-y-o g g Presidium-Misty Rocket (Roan Rocket)
R Williams (M J Gingell 17/12) R Williams

Placings: P00P/U-00402PP323P02   (4675)
2002/03: 16⁹G, 16⁹GF, 19⁴GF, 20⁹GF, 22²S, 22ᴾGS, 24ᴾGF, 21³G, 20²G, 16³GS, 20ᴾGS, 17⁹HY, 17²GF,

	Starts	1st	2nd	3rd	Win & Pl
Hurdles	13	0	3	2	3173
Career Total	**18**	**0**	**3**	**2**	**3173**

Going: Sf: 0-2 GS: 0-3 Gd: 0-3 GF: - Fm: 0-5
Distance: 2m/2m3: 0-6 2m4-2m7: 0-6 3m+: 0-1
Track: LH: 0-11 RH: 0-2 Tight: 0-9 Gall: 0-0
Aids: Bl: 0-3 Vi: 0-1 Tstrap: 0-0
Best Rating: 74 10/02 Fknm 2m4f good Hdl

Poor hurdler; ideally suited by sharp tracks.

Knight Templar (IRE)

10-y-o b g Roselier (FR)-Rathsallagh Tartan (Strong Gale)
C P Dennis Mrs C Orton

Placings: 013/121P1/2F341/23P0/PP4315-4   (4520)
2002/03: 27⁴G,

	Starts	1st	2nd	3rd	Win & Pl
Chases	1	0	0	0	0
Career Total	**24**	**6**	**3**	**4**	**31631**
101 4/02	Sedg	3m3f	H Ch		G-F	£1512
122 3/00	Donc	3m2f	B(0-145)HCh		GD	£10481
126 4/99	Winc	3m1f110yE Ch			GD	£3498
126 12/98	Font	3m2f110yE Ch			G-S	£3037
123 12/98	Font	3m2f110yE Ch			G-S	£2770
91 4/98	Font	3m3f	E Hdl		G-S	£2469
			Total win prize-money £23768			

Going: Sf: 0-0 GS: 0-0 Gd: 0-0 GF: - Fm: 0-0
Distance: 2m/2m3: 0-0 2m4-2m7: 0-0 3m+: 0-1
Track: LH: 0-1 RH: 0-0 Tight: 0-1 Gall: 0-0
Aids: Bl: 0-0 Vi: 0-0 Tstrap: 0-0
Best Rating: 126 4/99 Winc 3m1f110y good Ch

Modest pointer/hunter chaser; suited by three miles-two plus; handles cut in the ground but well suited by a sound surface.

Knight's Crest (IRE)

99

13-y-o ch g The Parson-Sno-Cat (Arctic Slave)
R Dickin G Hutsby

Placings: 040/042FP2/131P22/P/524645P-   (0014)
2002/03: 25ᴾGS,

	Starts	1st	2nd	3rd	Win & Pl
Chases	1	0	0	0	
Career Total	**23**	**2**	**5**	**1**	**14953**
116 12/98	Wwck	3m2f	D Ch		G-S	£3964
108 11/98	Ludl	3m	E(0-115)HCh		GD	£3322
			Total win prize-money £7287			

Going: Sf: 0-0 GS: 0-1 Gd: 0-0 GF: - Fm: 0-0

Distance: 2m/2m3: 0-0 2m4-2m7: 0-0 3m+: 0-1
Track: LH: 0-0 RH: 0-1 Tight: 0-0 Gall: 0-0
Aids: Bl: 0-0 Vi: 0-0 Tstrap: 0-0
Best Rating: 119 3/99 Sand 3m110y gd-sft Ch

Lightly-raced, modest staying chaser who has won on good to soft. Has gone well at Warwick.

Knight's Emperor (IRE)

(104h)   **(103h)103**

6-y-o b g Grand Lodge (USA)-So Kind (Kind Of Hush)
J L Spearing M Olden

Placings: F6/F12140-35321F   (1235)
2002/03: 16³GF, 16⁵GF, 16³G, 17¹G, 16⁶G,

	Starts	1st	2nd	3rd	Win & Pl
Hurdles	4	0	1	2	2696
Chases	2	1	0	0	4007
Career Total	**14**	**3**	**2**	**2**	**13031**
103 9/02	Sthl	2m1f	E Ch		GD	£4007
102 11/01	Hntg	2m110y	E Hdl		GD	£2429
101 9/01	Worc	2m	E Hdl		G-F	£2443
			Total win prize-money £8879			

Going: Sf: 0-0 GS: 0-0 Gd: 1-3 GF: - Fm: 0-3
Distance: 2m/2m3: 1-6 2m4-2m7: 0-0 3m+: 0-3
Track: LH: 1-6 RH: 0-0 Tight: 0-2 Gall: 0-0
Aids: Bl: 0-0 Vi: 0-0 Tstrap: 0-0
Best Rating: 103 9/02 Sthl 2m1f good Ch

Fair chaser, odds-on winner of extended two mile novice chase at Southwell September 2002. Unlucky not to defy a penalty when falling at Worcester next time. Suited by a sound surface.

Knighton Star

73   **96+**

7-y-o b m Gildoran-Barrica (Main Reef)
R T Phillips R Argles

Placings: 0/0-2   (0554)
2002/03: 19²GF,

	Starts	1st	2nd	3rd	Win & Pl
Hurdles	1	0	1	0	763
Career Total	**3**	**0**	**1**	**0**	**763**

Going: Sf: 0-0 GS: 0-0 Gd: 0-0 GF: - Fm: 0-1
Distance: 2m/2m3: 0-0 2m4-2m7: 0-1 3m+: 0-0
Track: LH: 0-0 RH: 0-1 Tight: 0-0 Gall: 0-0
Aids: Bl: 0-0 Vi: 0-0 Tstrap: 0-0
Best Rating: 96 6/02 Hrfd 2m3f110y gd-fm Hdl

Knightsbridge King

105   **101**

7-y-o ch g Michelozzo (USA)-Shahdjat (IRE) (Vayrann)
A King Knightsbridge Bc

Placings: 20040-20345212   (4486)
2002/03: 19²GF, 21⁰G, 16³G, 16⁴G, 19⁵S, 19²G, 17¹S, 17²GF,

	Starts	1st	2nd	3rd	Win & Pl
Hurdles	8	1	3	1	5720
Career Total	**13**	**1**	**4**	**1**	**6220**
96 3/03	Hrfd	2m1f	G Hdl		SFT	£2492
			Total win prize-money £2492			

Going: Sf: 1-2 GS: 0-0 Gd: 0-4 GF: - Fm: 0-2
Distance: 2m/2m3: 1-5 2m4-2m7: 0-3 3m+: 0-0
Track: LH: 0-4 RH: 1-6 Tight: 0-2 Gall: 0-0
Aids: Bl: 0-4 Vi: 1-1 Tstrap: 0-0

Selling hurdler; effective at two miles; acts in soft ground; unreliable.

Knockaun Wood (IRE)

9-y-o ch g Be My Native (USA)-Misty Venture (Foggy Bell)
C A Fuller C A Fuller

Placings: 0/0/P/0-P   (3950)
2002/03: 23ᴾGS,

	Starts	1st	2nd	3rd	Win & Pl
Chases	1	0	0	0	
Career Total	**4**	**0**	**0**	**0**	

Going: Sf: 0-0 GS: 0-1 Gd: 0-0 GF: - Fm: 0-0
Distance: 2m/2m3: 0-0 2m4-2m7: 0-0 3m+: 0-1
Track: LH: 0-0 RH: 0-1 Tight: 0-0 Gall: 0-0
Aids: Bl: 0-0 Vi: 0-0 Tstrap: 0-0
Best Rating: 109 4/99 Chel 2m1f good Hdl

Knockdoo (IRE)

108(96c)   (84c)**112**

10-y-o ch g Be My Native (USA)-Ashken (Artaius (USA))
J S Goldie (George Goldie 7/3) Mrs D I Goldie

Placings: 00/0000/241562/00515/3031016023/352U54-3042   (4752)
2002/03: 24³GS, 24⁰GS, 21⁴S, 24²G,

	Starts	1st	2nd	3rd	Win & Pl
Hurdles	3	0	1	1	2761
Chases	1	0	0	0	
Career Total	**37**	**4**	**5**	**5**	**22603**
116 11/00	Carl	2m1f	F(0-110)HHdl		HVY	£2588
98 9/00	Gway	2m	(0-102)HHdl		YLD	£4416
81 9/99	Gway	2m	(0-102)HHdl		HVY	£3696
80 9/98	List	2m	(0-102)HHdl		Y-S	£4184
			Total win prize-money £14886			

Going: Sf: 0-1 GS: 0-2 Gd: 0-1 GF: - Fm: 0-0
Distance: 2m/2m3: 0-0 2m4-2m7: 0-1 3m+: 0-3
Track: LH: 0-2 RH: 0-2 Tight: 0-1 Gall: 0-0
Aids: Bl: 0-0 Vi: 0-0 Tstrap: 0-0
Best Rating: 116 11/00 Carl 2m1f heavy Hdl

Modest hurdler; best around two miles; acts on testing ground.

Knockfiarne Magic (IRE)

11-y-o b g Buzzard s Bay-Daisy Star (Star Appeal)
B P J Baugh D Williams

Placings: P   (0667)
2002/03: 20ᴾGF,

	Starts	1st	2nd	3rd	Win & Pl
Hurdles	1	0	0	0	
Career Total	**1**	**0**	**0**	**0**	

Going: Sf: 0-0 GS: 0-0 Gd: 0-0 GF: - Fm: 0-1
Distance: 2m/2m3: 0-0 2m4-2m7: 0-1 3m+: 0-0
Track: LH: 0-1 RH: 0-0 Tight: 0-0 Gall: 0-0
Aids: Bl: 0-0 Vi: 0-0 Tstrap: 0-0
Best Rating: 0 6/02 Uttx 2m4f110y gd-fm Hdl

Knockholt
107 **100**

7-y-o b g Be My Chief (USA)-Saffron Crocus (Shareef Dancer (USA))
L Lungo Roman Wall Racing

Placings:0-2242 (1015)
2002/03: 24⁴GS, 20²GF, 21⁴GF, 24²G,

	Starts	1st	2nd	3rd	Win & Pl
Hurdles	4	0	3	0	2805
Career Total	5	0	3	0	2805

Going:	Sf: 0-0 GS: 0-1 Gd: 0-1 GF: - Fm: 0-2
Distance:	2m/2m3: 0-0 2m4-2m7: 0-2 3m+: 0-2
Track:	LH: 0-2 RH: 0-2 Tight: 0-1 Gall: 0-0
Aids:	Bl: 0-0 Vi: 0-1 Tstrap: 0-0
Best Rating:	100 8/02 Prth 3m110y good Hdl

Fair handicapper on the Flat, placed in novice hurdles in the North in the summer of 2002, but appears to be regressing.

Knockout (IRE)
93

7-y-o b g Persian Mews-Knockaville (Crozier)
Miss K Marks Nick Shutts

Placings:030055-PPP (1231)
2002/03: 16^PG, 20^PG, 16^PG,

	Starts	1st	2nd	3rd	Win & Pl
Hurdles	3	0	0	0	
Career Total	9	0	0	1	508

Going:	Sf: 0-0 GS: 0-0 Gd: 0-2 GF: - Fm: 0-1
Distance:	2m/2m3: 0-2 2m4-2m7: 0-1 3m+: 0-0
Track:	LH: 0-3 RH: 0-0 Tight: 0-1 Gall: 0-0
Aids:	Bl: 0-0 Vi: 0-1 Tstrap: 0-0
Best Rating:	96 6/01 Gowr 2m4f gd-fm NHF

Knockrigg (IRE)
98(107c) (98c)**88**

9-y-o ch g Commanche Run-Gaiety Lass (Le Moss)
Dr P Pritchard Norwester Racing Club

Placings:000/0632201/254342136/4223F5200-666022552 (4693)
2002/03: 20⁶S, 22⁶GF, 17⁶GF, 16⁹G, 17²HY, 17²HY, 16⁵HY, 17⁵GS, 17²G,

	Starts	1st	2nd	3rd	Win & Pl
Hurdles	8	0	3	0	2354
Chases	1	0	0	0	0
Career Total	37	2	10	4	19444
96 2/01 Leic 2m	F(0-110)HCh			SFT	£3370
85 4/00 Cork 2m	(0-102)HHdl			G-Y	£4140
				Total win prize-money	£7511

Going:	Sf: 0-4 GS: 0-1 Gd: 0-2 GF: - Fm: 0-2
Distance:	2m/2m3: 0-7 2m4-2m7: 0-2 3m+: 0-0
Track:	LH: 0-7 RH: 0-2 Tight: 0-5 Gall: 0-0
Aids:	Bl: 0-0 Vi: 0-0 Tstrap: 0-0
Best Rating:	98 7/01 Worc 2m4f110y soft Ch

Plating-class hurdler; lost his way over fences, and is a frustrating type, finishing in the frame quite often but rarely winning; suited by two miles on soft ground.

Knocktopher Abbey
100 **102**

6-y-o ch g Pursuit Of Love-Kukri (Kris)
Miss Venetia Williams (B R Millman 29/10) Seasons Holidays

Placings:3-341 (4733)
2002/03: 16³GF, 16⁴G, 16¹GF,

	Starts	1st	2nd	3rd	Win & Pl
Hurdles	3	1	0	1	5323
Career Total	4	1	0	2	5775
102 4/03 Chep 2m110y E Hdl				G-F	£3549
				Total win prize-money	£3549

Going:	Sf: 0-0 GS: 0-0 Gd: 0-1 GF: - Fm: 1-2
Distance:	2m/2m3: 1-3 2m4-2m7: 0-0 3m+: 0-0
Track:	LH: 1-2 RH: 0-1 Tight: 0-0 Gall: 0-0
Aids:	Bl: 0-1 Vi: 0-0 Tstrap: 0-0
Best Rating:	105 11/01 Tntn 2m1f good Hdl

Moderate hurdler; won strongly-run 2m maiden hurdle at Chepstow April 2003; disappointing over 2m 4f at the same course next time; blinkered second start; acts on fast ground; likely to prove best at 2m.

Know Thyne (IRE)
70 **78**

9-y-o ch g Good Thyne (USA)-Bail Out (Quayside)
P T Dalton (H D Daly 17/7) Mrs R Gabb & The Hon Mrs A H Todd

Placings:1P-P00P (4561)
2002/03: 22^PGF, 16^9GF, 20^0GF, 20^PGF,

	Starts	1st	2nd	3rd	Win & Pl
Hurdles	4	0	0	0	
Career Total	6	1	0	0	3895
122 5/01 Tipp 2m4f NHF				G-F	£3895
				Total win prize-money	£3895

Going:	Sf: 0-0 GS: 0-0 Gd: 0-0 GF: - Fm: 0-4
Distance:	2m/2m3: 0-1 2m4-2m7: 0-3 3m+: 0-0
Track:	LH: 0-4 RH: 0-0 Tight: 0-2 Gall: 0-0
Aids:	Bl: 0-0 Vi: 0-0 Tstrap: 0-0
Best Rating:	122 5/01 Tipp 2m4f gd-fm NHF

Knowhow (IRE)
84 **68**

6-y-o br g Mister Lord (USA)-Mossy Mistress (IRE) (Le Moss)
M Pitman Malcolm C Denmark

Placings:3-064 (3901)
2002/03: 16^0S, 19^6GS, 24⁴S,

	Starts	1st	2nd	3rd	Win & Pl
Hurdles	3	0	0	0	406
Career Total	4	0	0	1	772

Going:	Sf: 0-2 GS: 0-1 Gd: 0-0 GF: - Fm: 0-0
Distance:	2m/2m3: 0-1 2m4-2m7: 0-1 3m+: 0-1
Track:	LH: 0-2 RH: 0-1 Tight: 0-1 Gall: 0-2
Aids:	Bl: 0-0 Vi: 0-0 Tstrap: 0-0
Best Rating:	104 2/02 Kemp 2m good NHF

Kock De La Vesvre (FR)
102 **128**

5-y-o b g Sassanian (USA)-Csardas (FR) (Maiymad)
Miss Venetia Williams (T Civel 25/6) O P Dakin

Placings:42252622-610231F21 (4766)
2002/03: 17⁶S, 17¹VS, 20⁰VS, 20²S, 16³S, 17¹S, 20⁷G, 17²GF, 16¹G,

	Starts	1st	2nd	3rd	Win & Pl
Chases	9	3	2	1	30504
Career Total	17	3	7	1	52669
120 4/03 Prth 2m C Ch				GD	£8268
128 3/03 Bang 2m1f110yD Ch				SFT	£5343
5/02 Autl 2m1f110y Ch				VS	£12368
				Total win prize-money	£25979

Going:	Sf: 1-4 GS: 0-0 Gd: 1-2 GF: - Fm: 0-1
Distance:	2m/2m3: 3-6 2m4-2m7: 0-3 3m+: 0-0
Track:	LH: 1-4 RH: 1-2 Tight: 1-5 Gall: 0-0
Aids:	Bl: 1-1 Vi: 0-0 Tstrap: 0-0
Best Rating:	128 3/03 Bang 2m1f110y soft Ch

Fair novice chaser; ex-French; effective from two to two and a half miles; best on soft ground but handles faster.

Kolpatcheva (FR)
80 (63c)**46**

6-y-o b m Cricket Ball (USA)-Tosca De Bellouet (FR) (Olmeto)
G Brown Tom Segrue

Placings:325/5P-FUF0F0 (4373)
2002/03: 19^FGS, 16US, 16^FS, 17^0S, 16^FHY, 17^9G,

	Starts	1st	2nd	3rd	Win & Pl
Hurdles	4	0	0	0	
Chases	2	0	0	0	
Career Total	11	0	1	1	3143

Going:	Sf: 0-4 GS: 0-1 Gd: 0-1 GF: - Fm: 0-0
Distance:	2m/2m3: 0-6 2m4-2m7: 0-0 3m+: 0-0
Track:	LH: 0-2 RH: 0-4 Tight: 0-3 Gall: 0-0
Aids:	Bl: 0-0 Vi: 0-0 Tstrap: 0-0
Best Rating:	63 1/02 Leic 2m4f110y good Ch

Kombinacja (POL)
108 **112+**

5-y-o ch m Jape (USA)-Komancza (POL) (Dakota)
T R George C Davies,S Nelson,A Stennett,T Warner

Placings:04 (3753)
2002/03: 16^0HY, 21⁴G,

	Starts	1st	2nd	3rd	Win & Pl
Hurdles	2	0	0	0	590
Career Total	2	0	0	0	590

Going:	Sf: 0-1 GS: 0-0 Gd: 0-1 GF: - Fm: 0-0
Distance:	2m/2m3: 0-1 2m4-2m7: 0-1 3m+: 0-0
Track:	LH: 0-1 RH: 0-1 Tight: 0-0 Gall: 0-1
Aids:	Bl: 0-0 Vi: 0-0 Tstrap: 0-0
Best Rating:	89 2/03 Kemp 2m5f good Hdl

High-class mare on the Flat in Poland; very disppointing on her hurdles debut, but ran much better on good ground at Kempton in February 2003; shown true colours in winning both starts in summer of 2003; needs a sound surface.

Komori (IRE)
97 **68**

13-y-o b/br g Rising-Pandos Pet (Dusky Boy)
A M Crow Mrs H G Peplinski

Placings:B/0023P33-60P (1899)
2002/03: 25⁶G, 20⁵S, 27⁵S,

	Starts	1st	2nd	3rd	Win & Pl
Chases	3	0	0	0	
Career Total	11	0	1	3	3224

Going:	Sf: 0-2 GS: 0-0 Gd: 0-1 GF: - Fm: 0-0
Distance:	2m/2m3: 0-0 2m4-2m7: 0-1 3m+: 0-2

Track: LH: 0-2 RH: 0-1 Tight: 0-1 Gall: 0-0
Aids: Bl: 0-0 Vi: 0-0 Tstrap: 0-0
Best Rating: 93   4/02   Carl   2m4f   gd-fm   Ch

Kompliment

5-y-o ch g Komaite (USA)-Eladale (IRE) (Ela-Mana-Mou)
Mrs H Dalton   Ray Bailey

Placings: P   (1110)
2002/03: 16PGF,

	Starts	1st	2nd	3rd	Win & Pl
Hurdles	1	0	0	0	
Career Total	1	0	0	0	

Going: Sf: 0-0 GS: 0-0 Gd: 0-0 GF: - Fm: 0-1
Distance: 2m/2m3: 0-1 2m4-2m7: 0-0 3m+: 0-0
Track: LH: 0-1 RH: 0-0 Tight: 0-0 Gall: 0-0
Aids: Bl: 0-0 Vi: 0-0 Tstrap: 0-0
Best Rating: 0   8/02   Uttx   2m   gd-fm   Hdl

Konfuzius (GER)
95   67

5-y-o b g Motley (USA)-Katrina (GER) (Windwurf (GER))
P Monteith   Oriental Mist Partnership

Placings: 60F604P   (4434)
2002/03: 16SHY, 16DGF, 24FHY, 176HY, 16DS, 174G, 20PG,

	Starts	1st	2nd	3rd	Win & Pl
Hurdles	7	0	0	0	
Career Total	7	0	0	0	0

Going: Sf: 0-4 GS: 0-0 Gd: 0-2 GF: - Fm: 0-1
Distance: 2m/2m3: 0-5 2m4-2m7: 0-1 3m+: 0-1
Track: LH: 0-6 RH: 0-1 Tight: 0-4 Gall: 0-2
Aids: Bl: 0-0 Vi: 0-0 Tstrap: 0-0
Best Rating: 68   12/02   Kels   2m110y   heavy   Hdl

Konker
102   130

8-y-o ch g Selkirk (USA)-Helens Dreamgirl (Caerleon (USA))
Mrs M Reveley   J & M Leisure / Unos Restaurant

Placings: 5040/11315/66405004-2   (1868)
2002/03: 172GS,

	Starts	1st	2nd	3rd	Win & Pl
Hurdles	1	0	1	0	820
Career Total	18	3	1	1	12636
133 1/01 Weth 2m		C(0-130)HHdl	G-S		£5382
122 11/00 Newc 2m		E(0-115)HHdl	SFT		£2541
122 11/00 Weth 2m		E(0-105)HHdl	HVY		£2925
		Total win prize-money £10848			

Going: Sf: 0-0 GS: 0-1 Gd: 0-0 GF: - Fm: 0-0
Distance: 2m/2m3: 0-1 2m4-2m7: 0-0 3m+: 0-0
Track: LH: 0-0 RH: 0-1 Tight: 0-0 Gall: 0-0
Aids: Bl: 0-0 Vi: 0-0 Tstrap: 0-0
Best Rating: 133   1/01   Weth   2m   gd-sft   Hdl

Fair handicap hurdler, suited by two miles and soft ground.

Kopeck (IRE)
108   146+

5-y-o ch g Moscow Society (USA)-Cashla (IRE) (Duky)
J T Gifford   P H Betts

Placings: 2-15   (3187)

2002/03: 161S, 165GS,

	Starts	1st	2nd	3rd	Win & Pl
Hurdles	2	1	0	0	15500
Career Total	3	1	1	0	16274
146 12/02 Asct 2m110y A Hdl			SFT £14500		
		Total win prize-money £14500			

Going: Sf: 1-1 GS: 0-1 Gd: 0-0 GF: - Fm: 0-0
Distance: 2m/2m3: 1-2 2m4-2m7: 0-0 3m+: 0-0
Track: LH: 0-0 RH: 1-2 Tight: 0-0 Gall: 0-0
Aids: Bl: 0-0 Vi: 0-0 Tstrap: 0-0
Best Rating: 146   12/02   Asct   2m110y   soft   Hdl

Useful novice hurdler; runner-up in an Ascot bumper on his debut: he scored at 33/1 in a Grade Two novice event on his hurdling debut at the same track; possibly under the weather when disappointing next time.

Korakor (FR)
114   143

9-y-o ch g Nikos-Aniflore (FR) (Satingo)
Ian Williams   Mr And Mrs J D Cotton

Placings: 1/31/331P/516434/PP4P1/051232-PP203012   (4612)
2002/03: 20PGF, 20PGS, 20²GS, 20⁰GS, 19³GS, 16⁰G, 16¹G, 16²G,

	Starts	1st	2nd	3rd	Win & Pl
Chases	8	1	2	1	25209
Career Total	32	7	4	6	147902
143 4/03 Ayr 2m	HCh	GD	£15680		
139 12/01 Donc 2m3f110yC(0-135)HCh		GD	£7130		
141 4/01 Ayr 2m4f	HCh	GD	£10787		
11/99 Autl 2m4f110y Ch		HVY	£21529		
11/98 Autl 2m4f110y Ch		VS	£12121		
9/97 Autl 2m2f	Hdl	SFT	£22447		
4/97 Autl 1m7f	Hdl	VS	£13468		
		Total win prize-money £103163			

Going: Sf: 0-0 GS: 0-4 Gd: 1-3 GF: - Fm: 0-1
Distance: 2m/2m3: 1-4 2m4-2m7: 0-4 3m+: 0-0
Track: LH: 1-6 RH: 0-2 Tight: 0-2 Gall: 0-3
Aids: Bl: 0-0 Vi: 0-0 Tstrap: 0-0
Best Rating: 143   4/03   Ayr   2m   good   Ch

Very useful chaser; had the run of the race when successful at Ayr in April 2003; runner-up under a penalty at Cheltenham five days later; may now be in the grip of the Handicapper; stays two miles four furlongs; effective on good ground; goes well fresh.

Korelo (FR)
114   146

5-y-o b g Cadoudal (FR)-Lora Du Charmil (FR) (Panoramic)
M C Pipe (G Cherel 3/11)   D A Johnson

Placings: 63325-2505314115P   (4462)
2002/03: 20²S, 17⁵S, 20⁰VS, 22⁵HY, 17³G, 17¹S, 16⁴GS, 20¹S, 16¹HY, 21⁵G, 20PG,

	Starts	1st	2nd	3rd	Win & Pl
Hurdles	8	3	0	1	67298
Chases	3	0	1	0	13804
Career Total	16	3	2	3	92687
146 3/03 Sand 2m110y B(0-150)HHdl		HVY £29000			
136 2/03 Asct 2m4f B(0-140)HHdl		SFT £29000			
107 12/02 Tntn 2m1f D Hdl		SFT £4972			
		Total win prize-money £62973			

Going: Sf: 3-6 GS: 0-1 Gd: 0-3 GF: - Fm: 0-0
Distance: 2m/2m3: 2-5 2m4-2m7: 1-6 3m+: 0-0
Track: LH: 0-4 RH: 3-4 Tight: 1-2 Gall: 0-2
Aids: Bl: 0-0 Vi: 0-0 Tstrap: 0-0
Best Rating: 146   3/03   Sand   2m110y   heavy   Hdl

Useful hurdler; ex-French; handles good ground, but prefers softer; stays two miles five very well and was well supported when successful at Ascot in February and when following up in the Imperial Cup; ran well in defeat at Cheltenham.

Kosamet (IRE)
100   96

6-y-o b g Jurado (USA)-Liffey s Choice (Little Buskins)
M J Gingell (G M McCourt 19/7)   Mrs J M Penney And Andy Middleton

Placings: 0-255206204   (2004)
2002/03: 16²GF, 21⁵GF, 19⁵S, 16²S, 16⁰GF, 16⁶G, 20²GF, 16⁰G, 17⁴S,

	Starts	1st	2nd	3rd	Win & Pl
NH Flat	1	0	1	0	632
Hurdles	8	0	2	0	2019
Career Total	10	0	3	0	2651

Going: Sf: 0-3 GS: 0-0 Gd: 0-2 GF: - Fm: 0-4
Distance: 2m/2m3: 0-7 2m4-2m7: 0-2 3m+: 0-0
Track: LH: 0-5 RH: 0-3 Tight: 0-2 Gall: 0-2
Aids: Bl: 0-0 Vi: 0-0 Tstrap: 0-0
Best Rating: 96   10/02   Hntg   2m4f110y   gd-fm   Hdl

Has shown form at a modest level in bumpers and hurdles.

Kosmic Lady
93   70

6-y-o b m Cosmonaut-Ktolo (Tolomeo)
P W Hiatt   P J Morgan

Placings: 040-640   (3135)
2002/03: 17⁵S, 17⁴G, 16⁰S,

	Starts	1st	2nd	3rd	Win & Pl
Hurdles	3	0	0	0	0
Career Total	6	0	0	0	0

Going: Sf: 0-2 GS: 0-0 Gd: 0-1 GF: - Fm: 0-0
Distance: 2m/2m3: 0-3 2m4-2m7: 0-3 3m+: 0-0
Track: LH: 0-0 RH: 0-3 Tight: 0-0 Gall: 0-0
Aids: Bl: 0-0 Vi: 0-0 Tstrap: 0-3
Best Rating: 70   12/02   Hrfd   2m1f   good   Hdl

Kosovko (FR)

4-y-o b g Kadalko (FR)-Brumelli (FR) (Tip Moss (FR))
M C Pipe   B Boutboul

Placings: 00P   (3780)
2002/03: 12⁰G, 16⁰GS, 22PGS,

	Starts	1st	2nd	3rd	Win & Pl
NH Flat	2	0	0	0	0
Hurdles	1	0	0	0	0
Career Total	3	0	0	0	0

Going: Sf: 0-0 GS: 0-2 Gd: 0-1 GF: - Fm: 0-0
Distance: 2m/2m3: 0-1 2m4-2m7: 0-1 3m+: 0-0
Track: LH: 0-1 RH: 0-2 Tight: 0-0 Gall: 0-0
Aids: Bl: 0-0 Vi: 0-0 Tstrap: 0-0
Best Rating: 75   12/02   Newb   1m4f110y   good   NHF

Koumba (FR)
94   77

5-y-o b g Luchiroverte (IRE)-Agenore (FR) (Le Riverain (FR))

B N Pollock Mrs Nicola Pollock

Placings:50   (4527)
2002/03: 16⁵GF, 20⁰G,

	Starts	1st	2nd	3rd	Win & Pl
NH Flat	1	0	0	0	0
Hurdles	1	0	0	0	0
Career Total	2	0	0	0	0

Going: Sf: 0-0 GS: 0-0 Gd: 0-1 GF: - Fm: 0-1
Distance: 2m/2m3: 0-1 2m4-2m7: 0-1 3m+: 0-0
Track: LH: 0-2 RH: 0-0 Tight: 0-1 Gall: 0-0
Aids: Bl: 0-0 Vi: 0-0 Tstrap: 0-0
Best Rating: 76 3/03 Sthl 2m   gd-fm NHF

Krabloonik (FR)
106(88h)   (92h)**111**
9-y-o b g Bering-Key Role (Be My Guest (USA))
A King Mrs Deborah Potter

Placings:550/33212U33/1P32342341/53650424/523P4440
-264P0   (3267)
2002/03: 16²GS, 20⁶GS, 16⁴G, 20⁵S, 19⁹G,

	Starts	1st	2nd	3rd	Win & Pl
Chases	5	0	1	0	1785
Career Total	42	3	7	9	39947
131 3/00 Newb	2m110y	C(0-130)HHdl		G-F	£5761
100 5/99 Weth	2m	D Hdl		GD	£2867
115 1/99 Winc	2m	F(0-110)HHdl		G-S	£2374

Total win prize-money £11004

Going: Sf: 0-1 GS: 0-2 Gd: 0-2 GF: - Fm: 0-0
Distance: 2m/2m3: 0-3 2m4-2m7: 0-2 3m+: 0-0
Track: LH: 0-1 RH: 0-4 Tight: 0-2 Gall: 0-1
Aids: Bl: 0-0 Vi: 0-0 Tstrap: 0-1
Best Rating: 133 12/01 Sand 2m _   gd-sft   Ch

Useful hurdler and novice chaser at two miles. Acts on most types of ground.

Krach (FR)
94   **118+**
5-y-o b g Lute Antique (FR)-Voilette (FR) (Brezzo (FR))
F Doumen J P McManus

Placings:2-2   (2079)
2002/03: 24²HY,

	Starts	1st	2nd	3rd	Win & Pl
Hurdles	1	0	1	0	1572
Career Total	2	0	2	0	6907

Going: Sf: 0-1 GS: 0-0 Gd: 0-0 GF: - Fm: 0-0
Distance: 2m/2m3: 0-0 2m4-2m7: 0-0 3m+: 0-1
Track: LH: 0-0 RH: 0-1 Tight: 0-0 Gall: 0-0
Aids: Bl: 0-0 Vi: 0-0 Tstrap: 0-0
Best Rating: 118 11/02 Asct 3m   heavy Hdl

Frech-trained hurdler; stays three miles; acts on heavy ground.

Krack De L'Isle (FR)
103   **116**
5-y-o b g Kadalko (FR)-Ceres De L Isle (FR) (Bad Conduct (USA))
A C Whillans John J Elliot

Placings:44-5413U   (3502)
2002/03: 16⁵S, 16⁴S, 22¹HY, 20⁹HY, 24ᵁS,

	Starts	1st	2nd	3rd	Win & Pl
NH Flat	2	0	0	0	0

Hurdles	3	1	0	1	4126
Career Total	7	1	0	1	4126
116 1/03 Ayr	2m6f	E Hdl		HVY	£3542

Total win prize-money £3542

Going: Sf: 1-5 GS: 0-0 Gd: 0-0 GF: - Fm: 0-0
Distance: 2m/2m3: 0-2 2m4-2m7: 1-2 3m+: 0-1
Track: LH: 1-5 RH: 0-0 Tight: 0-0 Gall: 0-0
Aids: Bl: 0-0 Vi: 0-0 Tstrap: 0-0
Best Rating: 116 1/03 Ayr 2m6f   heavy Hdl

Modest bumper performer; looked much improved for the switch to hurdles and step up in trip in early 2003; stays two miles six; acts on soft ground.

Kristineau
70   **63+**
5-y-o ch m Cadeaux Genereux-Kantikoy (Alzao (USA))
Mrs E Slack A Slack

Placings:6   (1417)
2002/03: 22⁶GF,

	Starts	1st	2nd	3rd	Win & Pl
Hurdles	1	0	0	0	0
Career Total	1	0	0	0	0

Going: Sf: 0-0 GS: 0-0 Gd: 0-0 GF: - Fm: 0-0
Distance: 2m/2m3: 0-0 2m4-2m7: 0-1 3m+: 0-0
Track: LH: 0-1 RH: 0-0 Tight: 0-1 Gall: 0-0
Aids: Bl: 0-0 Vi: 0-0 Tstrap: 0-0
Best Rating: 63 10/02 Kels 2m6f110y gd-fm Hdl

Kroisos (IRE)
100   **76**
5-y-o b g Kris-Lydia Maria (Dancing Brave (USA))
R Curtis Mrs R A Smith

Placings:60642   (4083)
2002/03: 22⁶S, 16⁰S, 22⁶HY, 25⁴HY, 25²HY,

	Starts	1st	2nd	3rd	Win & Pl
Hurdles	5	0	1	0	1167
Career Total	5	0	1	0	1167

Going: Sf: 0-4 GS: 0-1 Gd: 0-0 GF: - Fm: 0-0
Distance: 2m/2m3: 0-1 2m4-2m7: 0-2 3m+: 0-2
Track: LH: 0-1 RH: 0-2 Tight: 0-3 Gall: 0-0
Aids: Bl: 0-0 Vi: 0-0 Tstrap: 0-0
Best Rating: 76 3/03 Plum 3m1f110y heavy Hdl

Maiden staying hurdler.

Krzyszkowiak (IRE)
104f   **98f**
5-y-o b g Polish Precedent (USA)-Overdrive (Shirley Heights)
C R Egerton Chris Brasher

Placings:022   (3789)
2002/03: 17⁰G, 18²GS, 17²G,

	Starts	1st	2nd	3rd	Win & Pl
NH Flat	3	0	2	0	1140
Career Total	3	0	2	0	1140

Going: Sf: 0-0 GS: 0-1 Gd: 0-2 GF: - Fm: 0-0
Distance: 2m/2m3: 0-3 2m4-2m7: 0-0 3m+: 0-0
Track: LH: 0-1 RH: 0-2 Tight: 0-1 Gall: 0-0
Aids: Bl: 0-0 Vi: 0-0 Tstrap: 0-0
Best Rating: 101 2/03 Hrfd 2m1f   good NHF

Runner-up in bumpers on second and third start; beaten a whisker at Hereford in February, latest start.

Kung Hei Fat Choi (IRE)
106   **105**
8-y-o b g Roselier (FR)-Gallant Blade (Fine Blade (USA))
J S Goldie Strathayr Publishing Ltd

Placings:0506/34140-43631422P   (4690)
2002/03: 25⁴G, 20³S, 25⁶GS, 25³S, 25¹G, 25⁴HY, 20²S, 24²GS, 25ᴾG,

	Starts	1st	2nd	3rd	Win & Pl
Chases	9	1	2	2	8679
Career Total	18	2	2	3	11083
93 1/03 Catt	3m1f110yF(0-100)HCh		GD	£3474
98 3/02 Ayr	2m5f110yH Ch		HVY	£1589

Total win prize-money £5063

Going: Sf: 0-4 GS: 0-2 Gd: 1-3 GF: - Fm: 0-0
Distance: 2m/2m3: 0-0 2m4-2m7: 0-2 3m+: 1-7
Track: LH: 1-8 RH: 0-1 Tight: 1-2 Gall: 0-1
Aids: Bl: 0-0 Vi: 0-0 Tstrap: 0-0
Best Rating: 98 3/02 Kels 3m1f   heavy Ch

Moderate staying chaser; former hunter chaser; acts on heavy; stays 3m plus.

Kustom Kit Kevin

7-y-o b g Local Suitor (USA)-Sweet Revival (Claude Monet (USA))
Miss L V Davis Miss Louise Davis

Placings:P-P   (0690)
2002/03: 16ᴾGS,

	Starts	1st	2nd	3rd	Win & Pl
Hurdles	1	0	0	0	
Career Total	2	0	0	0	

Going: Sf: 0-0 GS: 0-1 Gd: 0-0 GF: - Fm: 0-0
Distance: 2m/2m3: 0-1 2m4-2m7: 0-0 3m+: 0-0
Track: LH: 0-1 RH: 0-0 Tight: 0-1 Gall: 0-0
Aids: Bl: 0-0 Vi: 0-0 Tstrap: 0-0
Best Rating: 0 7/02 Wolv 2m   gd-sft Hdl

Kuwait Millennium
106   **98**
6-y-o b g Salse (USA)-Lypharitissima (FR) (Lightning (FR))
Mrs A M Thorpe (J Neville 8/5) Miss Derien Edwards

Placings:2/342325512002-05012   (4218)
2002/03: 22⁰G, 17⁵G, 22⁰GS, 22¹S, 26²GF,

	Starts	1st	2nd	3rd	Win & Pl
Hurdles	5	1	1	0	3458
Career Total	18	2	6	2	11471
97 3/03 Font	2m6f110yG(0-95)HHdl		SFT	£2450
95 1/02 Hrfd	2m1f	F Hdl		SFT	£2586

Total win prize-money £5037

Going: Sf: 1-1 GS: 0-1 Gd: 0-2 GF: - Fm: 0-1
Distance: 2m/2m3: 0-1 2m4-2m7: 1-3 3m+: 0-1
Track: LH: 1-2 RH: 0-3 Tight: 1-2 Gall: 0-0
Aids: Bl: 0-0 Vi: 0-0 Tstrap: 0-1
Best Rating: 104 5/01 Font 2m2f110y gd-fm Hdl

Moderate hurdler; acts on soft and fast ground; stays two and three-quarter miles.

Kuwait Thunder (IRE)

95   82

7-y-o ch g Mac s Imp (USA)-Romangoddess (IRE) (Rhoman Rule (USA))
D Carroll (J L Eyre 14/8) The Flowerpot Men

Placings:0/40000   (4711)
2002/03: 16⁴S, 19⁰GS, 17⁰GS, 17⁰G, 16⁰GF,

	Starts	1st	2nd	3rd	Win & Pl
Hurdles	5	0	0	0	0
Career Total	6	0	0	0	0

Going: Sf: 0-1 GS: 0-2 Gd: 0-1 GF: - Fm: 0-1
Distance: 2m/2m3: 0-4 2m4-2m7: 0-1 3m+: 0-0
Track: LH: 0-5 RH: 0-0 Tight: 0-1 Gall: 0-2
Aids: Bl: 0-0 Vi: 0-0 Tstrap: 0-5
Best Rating: 90   12/02 Donc 2m110y   soft   Hdl

Plater on the Flat, seemed to run well when fourth in a novices hurdle at Doncaster in December.

Kway De La Foret (FR)

69f   40f

5-y-o b/br g Bobinski-Rose De La Foret (FR) (Ice Light (FR))
R J Hodges Bob Andrews

Placings:0   (1696)
2002/03: 16⁰G,

	Starts	1st	2nd	3rd	Win & Pl
NH Flat	1	0	0	0	0
Career Total	1	0	0	0	0

Going: Sf: 0-0 GS: 0-0 Gd: 0-1 GF: - Fm: 0-0
Distance: 2m/2m3: 0-1 2m4-2m7: 0-0 3m+: 0-0
Track: LH: 0-1 RH: 0-0 Tight: 0-0 Gall: 0-0
Aids: Bl: 0-0 Vi: 0-0 Tstrap: 0-0
Best Rating: 40   10/02 Chel 2m110y   good   NHF

Kylie Time (IRE)

6-y-o ch g Good Thyne (USA)-Miss Kylogue (IRE) (Lancastrian)
P Beaumont Mr & Mrs Raymond Anderson Green

Placings:000P   (4749)
2002/03: 16⁰GS, 16⁰GS, 16⁰G, 20⁰G,

	Starts	1st	2nd	3rd	Win & Pl
NH Flat	3	0	0	0	0
Hurdles	1	0	0	0	0
Career Total	4	0	0	0	0

Going: Sf: 0-0 GS: 0-2 Gd: 0-2 GF: - Fm: 0-0
Distance: 2m/2m3: 0-3 2m4-2m7: 0-1 3m+: 0-0
Track: LH: 0-3 RH: 0-1 Tight: 0-0 Gall: 0-0
Aids: Bl: 0-0 Vi: 0-0 Tstrap: 0-0
Best Rating: 90   1/03 Hayd 2m   gd-sft   NHF

Kylkenny

67   37

8-y-o b g Kylian (USA)-Fashion Flow (Balidar)
H Morrison H Morrison

Placings:56/0   (2570)

2002/03: 16⁰G,

	Starts	1st	2nd	3rd	Win & Pl
Hurdles	1	0	0	0	0
Career Total	3	0	0	0	0

Going: Sf: 0-0 GS: 0-0 Gd: 0-1 GF: - Fm: 0-0
Distance: 2m/2m3: 0-1 2m4-2m7: 0-0 3m+: 0-0
Track: LH: 0-1 RH: 0-0 Tight: 0-0 Gall: 0-1
Aids: Bl: 0-0 Vi: 0-0 Tstrap: 0-0
Best Rating: 86   11/00 Wwck 2m   heavy   Hdl

Winning handicapper on the Flat; yet to show much over hurdles.

Kylmax

4-y-o b g Classic Cliche (IRE)-Dame Lorraine (Damister (USA))
H A McWilliams J J Wright

Placings:P   (1537)
2002/03: 16⁰GF,

	Starts	1st	2nd	3rd	Win & Pl
Hurdles	1	0	0	0	0
Career Total	1	0	0	0	0

Going: Sf: 0-0 GS: 0-0 Gd: 0-0 GF: - Fm: 0-1
Distance: 2m/2m3: 0-1 2m4-2m7: 0-0 3m+: 0-0
Track: LH: 0-1 RH: 0-0 Tight: 0-0 Gall: 0-0
Aids: Bl: 0-0 Vi: 0-0 Tstrap: 0-0
Best Rating: 0   10/02 Weth 2m   gd-fm   Hdl

Kymani Prince (IRE)

90   101+

7-y-o b g Shemazar-Best Of British (Young Generation)
L Lungo D Stronach & R Buck

Placings:3-2   (4772)
2002/03: 16²G,

	Starts	1st	2nd	3rd	Win & Pl
Hurdles	1	0	1	0	1724
Career Total	2	0	1	1	2036

Going: Sf: 0-0 GS: 0-0 Gd: 0-1 GF: - Fm: 0-0
Distance: 2m/2m3: 0-1 2m4-2m7: 0-0 3m+: 0-0
Track: LH: 0-0 RH: 0-1 Tight: 0-0 Gall: 0-0
Aids: Bl: 0-0 Vi: 0-0 Tstrap: 0-0
Best Rating: 102 3/02 Donc 2m110y   gd-sft   NHF

Lightly- raced individual; modest form in a bumper and hurdle races; possibly best on a sound surface.

Kymberlya (FR)

108   105

5-y-o ch g Esteem Ball (FR)-Catty Douce (FR) (Cadoudal (FR))
M C Pipe (Jack Barbe 12/8) P A Deal

Placings:FP3   (4446)
2002/03: 20⁰GF, 20⁰G, 16³G,

	Starts	1st	2nd	3rd	Win & Pl
Hurdles	3	0	0	1	750
Career Total	3	0	0	1	750

Going: Sf: 0-0 GS: 0-0 Gd: 0-2 GF: - Fm: 0-1
Distance: 2m/2m3: 0-1 2m4-2m7: 0-2 3m+: 0-0
Track: LH: 0-1 RH: 0-2 Tight: 0-0 Gall: 0-0
Aids: Bl: 0-0 Vi: 0-0 Tstrap: 0-0

2002/03: 16⁰G,

	Starts	1st	2nd	3rd	Win & Pl
Hurdles	1	0	0	0	0
Career Total	3	0	0	0	0

Going: Sf: 0-0 GS: 0-0 Gd: 0-1 GF: - Fm: 0-0
Distance: 2m/2m3: 0-1 2m4-2m7: 0-0 3m+: 0-0
Track: LH: 0-1 RH: 0-0 Tight: 0-0 Gall: 0-1
Aids: Bl: 0-0 Vi: 0-0 Tstrap: 0-0
Best Rating: 86   11/00 Wwck 2m   heavy   Hdl

Moderate hurdler; acted on fast ground; stayed 2m 4f; (DEAD).

Kyper Disco (FR)

103   110

5-y-o b g Epervier Bleu-Disconea (FR) (Bayolidaan (FR))
N J Henderson Newbury Racehorse Owners Group

Placings:25-325   (3558)
2002/03: 16³S, 18²HY, 20⁵HY,

	Starts	1st	2nd	3rd	Win & Pl
Hurdles	3	0	1	1	1698
Career Total	5	0	2	1	2490

Going: Sf: 0-3 GS: 0-0 Gd: 0-0 GF: - Fm: 0-0
Distance: 2m/2m3: 0-2 2m4-2m7: 0-1 3m+: 0-0
Track: LH: 0-2 RH: 0-1 Tight: 0-2 Gall: 0-1
Aids: Bl: 0-0 Vi: 0-0 Tstrap: 0-0
Best Rating: 110 1/03 Font 2m2f110y heavy   Hdl

A French-bred, he is out of a middle-distance winner; showed promise when runner-up on his debut in a Newbury bumper; held subsequently.

L'Epicurien (FR)

106   (142h)133d

7-y-o ch g Chef De Clan Ii (FR)-L Epicurienne (FR) (Rex Magna (FR))
M C Pipe David L Estrange

Placings:11314/463214/12321F6-114225P0   (4694)
2002/03: 17¹S, 21¹GS, 21⁴GF, 16²S, 20²HY, 20⁵G, 21⁸S, 21⁹G,

	Starts	1st	2nd	3rd	Win & Pl
Chases	8	2	2	0	14215
Career Total	26	8	5	3	61440
133	5/02	NAbb	2m5f110yD(0-125)HCh	G-S	£4075
124	5/02	Bang	2m1f110yE Ch	SFT	£3575
133	12/01	Kemp	2m4f110yC(0-130)HCh	GD	£14625
112	5/01	Extr	2m1f110yE Ch	G-S	£3428
142	4/01	Asct	2m4f C(0-130)HHdl	HVY	£6353
128	2/00	Kemp	2m D Hdl	GD	£3688
	8/99	Vich	2m110y Hdl	VS	£4306
	7/99	Pomp	1m2f110y Hdl	GD	£3229

Total win prize-money £43283

Going: Sf: 1-4 GS: 1-1 Gd: 0-2 GF: - Fm: 0-1
Distance: 2m/2m3: 1-2 2m4-2m7: 1-6 3m+: 0-0
Track: LH: 2-7 RH: 0-1 Tight: 2-5 Gall: 0-0
Aids: Bl: 2-8 Vi: 0-0 Tstrap: 0-0
Best Rating: 142 4/01 Hayd 2m   soft   Hdl

A French import; he was a decent hurdler and has developed into a chaser of similar quality; suited by a right-handed track; acts on any ground; stays two and a half miles; usually blinkered.

L'Etang Bleu (FR)

97(101h)   (99 h)99

5-y-o gr g Graveron (FR)-Strawberry Jam (FR) (Fill My Hopes (FR))
M C Pipe M C Pipe

Placings:P4/632222332-35600020S1   (4525)
2002/03: 22³GF, 19⁵GF, 16⁶GF, 19⁰G, 19⁰GF, 19⁰S, 17²GS, 16⁶HY, 17⁸GS, 16¹G,

	Starts	1st	2nd	3rd	Win & Pl
Hurdles	10	1	1	1	3881
Career Total	21	1	6	4	14534
99	4/03	Uttx	2m	G(0-90)HHdl	GD	£2471

Total win prize-money £2471

Going:	Sf: 0-2 GS: 0-2 Gd: 1-2 GF: - Fm: 0-4
Distance:	2m/2m3: 1-7 2m4-2m7: 0-3 3m+: 0-0
Track:	LH: 1-2 RH: 0-8 Tight: 0-1 Gall: 0-0
Aids:	Bl: 0-0 Vi: 0-0 Tstrap: 0-0
Best Rating:	99 4/03 Uttx 2m good Hdl

Plating-class hurdler; got off the mark in his 16th hurdle race in a poor seller at Uttoxeter in April 2003; looked unlucky not to make a winning debut over fences when falling at the last at Worcester next time; disappointing since; handles any ground.

L'Idefix (IRE)

92

11-y-o ch g Buckskin (FR)-Katty London (Camden Town)
T R George Mrs Patrick Stevenson

Placings: 321/2654014/U102/4   (1566)
2002/03: 25⁴GS,

	Starts	1st	2nd	3rd	Win & Pl
Chases	1	0	0	0	795
Career Total	15	3	3	1	14940
110 10/00 Towc	3m1f	D(0-120)HCh		GD	£6909
106 3/99 NAbb	2m6f	E Hdl		SFT	£2274
106 2/98 Wwck	2m	H NHF		GD	£1413

Total win prize-money £10597

Going:	Sf: 0-0 GS: 0-1 Gd: 0-0 GF: - Fm: 0-0
Distance:	2m/2m3: 0-0 2m4-2m7: 0-0 3m+: 0-1
Track:	LH: 0-0 RH: 0-1 Tight: 0-1 Gall: 0-0
Aids:	Bl: 0-0 Vi: 0-0 Tstrap: 0-0
Best Rating:	110 1/01 Donc 3m good Ch

Moderate chaser; acts on good ground or softer.

L'Orphelin

(93h)   (78h)

8-y-o ch g Gildoran-Balula (Balinger)
C Tizzard Mrs John Pope And Friends

Placings: 310/P04   (4292)
2002/03: 24⁵PS, 24⁰GS, 16⁴GF,

	Starts	1st	2nd	3rd	Win & Pl
Hurdles	3	0	0	0	0
Career Total	6	1	0	1	1924
107 12/00 Ludl	2m	H NHF	SFT	£1680

Total win prize-money £1680

Going:	Sf: 0-1 GS: 0-1 Gd: 0-0 GF: - Fm: 0-1
Distance:	2m/2m3: 0-1 2m4-2m7: 0-0 3m+: 0-2
Track:	LH: 0-1 RH: 0-2 Tight: 0-1 Gall: 0-0
Aids:	Bl: 0-0 Vi: 0-0 Tstrap: 0-0
Best Rating:	107 12/00 Ludl 2m soft NHF

La Colina (IRE)

102   80

8-y-o ch g Be My Native (USA)-Deep Stream (Deep Run)
C J Mann J E Brown,N Edgley,R Lucas & S Dix

Placings: 0/004/0055031500F/0-16F54   (3866)
2002/03: 17¹GS, 19⁶GS, 20⁵HY, 16⁵G, 16⁴G,

	Starts	1st	2nd	3rd	Win & Pl
Chases	5	1	0	0	5213
Career Total	21	2	0	1	9095
96 11/02 MRas	2m1f110yE(0-110)HCh	G-S	£4793
89 9/00 Baln	2m4f	Hdl	G-Y	£3312

Total win prize-money £8106

Going:	Sf: 0-1 GS: 1-2 Gd: 0-2 GF: - Fm: 0-0
Distance:	2m/2m3: 1-4 2m4-2m7: 0-1 3m+: 0-0
Track:	LH: 0-1 RH: 1-3 Tight: 1-3 Gall: 0-1

Aids:	Bl: 0-0 Vi: 0-0 Tstrap: 0-0
Best Rating:	96 11/02 MRas 2m1f110y gd-sft Ch

Moderate chaser; stays two and a half miles.

La Femme En Rouge

82f   42f

4-y-o b f Slip Anchor-Bayrouge (IRE) (Gorytus (USA))
Mrs M Reveley D Jackson, A Peake & M Reveley

Placings: 00   (3817)
2002/03: 14⁴GS, 16⁰G,

	Starts	1st	2nd	3rd	Win & Pl
NH Flat	2	0	0	0	
Career Total	2	0	0	0	

Going:	Sf: 0-0 GS: 0-1 Gd: 0-1 GF: - Fm: 0-0
Distance:	2m/2m3: 0-1 2m4-2m7: 0-0 3m+: 0-0
Track:	LH: 0-2 RH: 0-0 Tight: 0-1 Gall: 0-0
Aids:	Bl: 0-0 Vi: 0-0 Tstrap: 0-0
Best Rating:	42 2/03 Catt 2m good NHF

La Landiere (FR)

114(105h)   (122h)161+

8-y-o b m Synefos (USA)-As You Are (FR) (Saint Estephe (FR))
R T Phillips Mrs R J Skan

Placings: 42112104/0200/5400-21111111   (4135)
2002/03: 16²G, 20¹GF, 19¹GF, 21¹GS, 20¹S, 21¹GS, 24¹G, 21¹G,

	Starts	1st	2nd	3rd	Win & Pl
Chases	8	7	1	0	151056
Career Total	24	10	4	0	168502
151 3/03 Chel	2m5f	A Ch	GD	£46400
161 2/03 Kemp	3m	A HCh	GD	£58000
157 1/03 Chel	2m5f	B HCh	G-S	£12818
153 12/02 Kemp	2m4f110yC(0-130)HCh	SFT	£13392
140 11/02 Winc	2m5f	D Ch	G-S	£5218
127 10/02 Chep	2m3f110yC Ch	G-F	£10114
97 6/02 MRas	2m4f	D Ch	G-F	£4173
120 2/00 Sand	2m110y	D Hdl	SFT	£3753
129 12/99 Uttx	2m	E Hdl	SFT	£2473
126 12/99 Tntn	2m1f	C Hdl	G-S	£5158

Total win prize-money £161503

Going:	Sf: 1-1 GS: 2-2 Gd: 2-3 GF: - Fm: 2-2
Distance:	2m/2m3: 0-1 2m4-2m7: 6-6 3m+: 1-1
Track:	LH: 3-3 RH: 4-5 Tight: 1-1 Gall: 2-3
Aids:	Bl: 0-0 Vi: 0-0 Tstrap: 0-0
Best Rating:	161 2/03 Kemp 3m good Ch

Fair hurdler; has progressed into a very useful novice chaser in 2002/3, rattling up a seven-timer, culminating in the Racing Post Chase and Cathcart Chase; stays three miles but very effective at shorter; acts on soft and fast ground.

La Luna (IRE)

98f   84f

6-y-o b m Gothland (FR)-Diane s Glen (Furry Glen)
Noel T Chance Mrs S Rowley-Williams

Placings: 0/6-2   (1095)
2002/03: 17²GF,

	Starts	1st	2nd	3rd	Win & Pl
NH Flat	1	0	1	0	626
Career Total	3	0	1	0	626

Going:	Sf: 0-0 GS: 0-0 Gd: 0-0 GF: - Fm: 0-1

Well beaten second on racecourse debut in Newton Abbot bumper August 2002; just held on when next seen in similar event at Market Rasen June 2003; acts on a sound surface.

La Maestra (FR)

92   88

5-y-o b m Zayyani-Ginestra (USA) (L Emigrant (USA))
Miss S J Wilton John Pointon And Sons

Placings: 664/0231100-050   (1083)
2002/03: 17⁰G, 16⁵S, 20⁰GF,

	Starts	1st	2nd	3rd	Win & Pl
Hurdles	3	0	0	0	
Career Total	13	2	1	1	9377
86 11/01 Leic	2m	G Hdl	G-S	£1981
79 10/01 Tntn	2m1f	F Hdl	FRM	£2639

Total win prize-money £4620

Going:	Sf: 0-1 GS: 0-0 Gd: 0-1 GF: - Fm: 0-1
Distance:	2m/2m3: 0-2 2m4-2m7: 0-1 3m+: 0-0
Track:	LH: 0-2 RH: 0-1 Tight: 0-2 Gall: 0-1
Aids:	Bl: 0-0 Vi: 0-0 Tstrap: 0-0
Best Rating:	88 9/01 Font 2m2f110y gd-fm Hdl

A French import, she was dropped in class to land a modest claimer at Taunton and followed up in a seller at Leicester in 2001. Held since.

La Marette

100   80

5-y-o ch m Karinga Bay-Persistent Gunner (Gunner B)
R J Hodges Miss R Dobson

Placings: 0006-5555P5413   (4718)
2002/03: 17⁵GS, 16³GS, 16⁵S, 21⁵GS, 20⁵S, 17⁵HY, 17⁴G, 17¹GF, 22³F,

	Starts	1st	2nd	3rd	Win & Pl
Hurdles	9	1	0	1	4396
Career Total	13	1	0	1	4396
73 4/03 NAbb	2m1f	E Hdl	G-F	£3596

Total win prize-money £3596

Going:	Sf: 0-3 GS: 0-3 Gd: 0-1 GF: - Fm: 1-2
Distance:	2m/2m3: 1-6 2m4-2m7: 0-3 3m+: 0-0
Track:	LH: 1-1 RH: 0-7 Tight: 1-4 Gall: 0-0
Aids:	Bl: 0-0 Vi: 0-0 Tstrap: 0-1
Best Rating:	80 4/03 Winc 2m6f firm Hdl

Novice hurdler; no promise in two starts before lucky winner of maiden hurdle at Newton Abbot in April 2003; stays two miles five; seems to go on most types of ground.

La Minera

74f   61f

5-y-o b m Miners Lamp-Bignor Girl (Torus)
R J Armson R J Armson

Placings: 0-0   (0091)
2002/03: 16⁰G,

	Starts	1st	2nd	3rd	Win & Pl
NH Flat	1	0	0	0	
Career Total	2	0	0	0	

Going:	Sf: 0-0 GS: 0-0 Gd: 0-1 GF: - Fm: 0-0
Distance:	2m/2m3: 0-1 2m4-2m7: 0-0 3m+: 0-0
Track:	LH: 0-1 RH: 0-0 Tight: 0-0 Gall: 0-0
Aids:	Bl: 0-0 Vi: 0-0 Tstrap: 0-0

Best Rating: 61 5/02 Uttx 2m   good NHF

La Mola Sun

98   **98**

9-y-o b g Henbit (USA)-Moheli (Ardross)
Mrs J C McGregor Mrs Dorothy Thomson

Placings:2065/1/33   (1561)
2002/03: 22³GF, 22³G,

	Starts	1st	2nd	3rd	Win & Pl
Hurdles	2	0	0	2	1192
Career Total	7	1	1	2	4464

107 5/00 Winc 2m6f   E Hdl   FRM £2779
                        Total win prize-money £2779

Going: Sf: 0-0 GS: 0-0 Gd: 0-1 GF: - Fm: 0-1
Distance: 2m/2m3: 0-0 2m4-2m7: 0-2 3m+: 0-0
Track: LH: 0-2 RH: 0-0 Tight: 0-2 Gall: 0-0
Aids: Bl: 0-0 Vi: 0-0 Tstrap: 0-0
Best Rating: 107 5/00 Winc 2m6f   firm   Hdl

Modest staying handicap hurdler who goes well on fast ground. Returned from spell pointing to make the frame twice at Kelso in October 2002. Stays two miles-six, acts on fast ground.

La Yolam

96   **99**

5-y-o ch m Unfuwain (USA)-Massorah (FR) (Habitat)
N J Henderson Roa Dawn Run Partnership

Placings:64-43   (0417)
2002/03: 17⁴G, 16³GF,

	Starts	1st	2nd	3rd	Win & Pl
Hurdles	2	0	0	1	556
Career Total	4	0	0	1	556

Going: Sf: 0-0 GS: 0-0 Gd: 0-1 GF: - Fm: 0-1
Distance: 2m/2m3: 0-2 2m4-2m7: 0-0 3m+: 0-0
Track: LH: 0-1 RH: 0-1 Tight: 0-0 Gall: 0-0
Aids: Bl: 0-0 Vi: 0-0 Tstrap: 0-0
Best Rating: 99 6/02 Strf 2m110y   gd-fm Hdl

Bought for 30,000gns off the Flat, has shown modest form over hurdles so far.

Laazim Afooz

107(99h)   (91h)**92**

10-y-o b g Mtoto-Balwa (USA) (Danzig (USA))
R T Phillips Nut Club Partnership

Placings:023/0003121/002/01112F4P/4333433564-
332231560   (4218)
2002/03: 23³G, 23³GF, 26²GF, 26²GF, 26³GF, 27¹G, 27⁵G, 22⁶GS,
26⁶GF,

	Starts	1st	2nd	3rd	Win & Pl
Hurdles	2	0	0	0	0
Chases	7	1	2	3	6356
Career Total	40	6	6	10	27617

92	10/02	Sedg	3m3f	F(0-100)HCh	GD	£3367
115	8/00	Strf	3m	F(0-105)HCh	G-F	£2941
110	6/00	Worc	2m7f110yE Ch		G-F	£2938
120	6/00	Folk	3m2f	F(0-95)HCh	GD	£2486
104	9/98	NAbb	2m6f	E Hdl		G-F	£2088
99	8/98	NAbb	2m6f	D Hdl		G-F	£2805

                        Total win prize-money £16627

Going: Sf: 0-0 GS: 0-0 GS: 0-1 Gd: 1-3 GF: - Fm: 0-5
Distance: 2m/2m3: 0-0 2m4-2m7: 0-1 3m+: 1-8
Track: LH: 1-7 RH: 0-1 Tight: 1-6 Gall: 0-0
Aids: Bl: 0-1 Vi: 0-0 Tstrap: 1-8

Best Rating: 120 6/00 Folk 3m2f   good   Ch

Fairly consistent chaser at a low level. Suited by three miles and fast ground.

Labula Bay

9-y-o b g Sula Bula-Lady Barunbe (Deep Run)
Miss C F Elliott H R Cook

Placings:00PP0/16-3   (0311)
2002/03: 26³G,

	Starts	1st	2nd	3rd	Win & Pl
Chases	1	0	0	1	221
Career Total	8	1	0	1	2244

112 3/02 Fknm 2m5f110yH Ch   GD   £2022
                        Total win prize-money £2023

Going: Sf: 0-0 GS: 0-0 Gd: 0-1 GF: - Fm: 0-0
Distance: 2m/2m3: 0-0 2m4-2m7: 0-0 3m+: 0-1
Track: LH: 0-0 RH: 0-1 Tight: 0-1 Gall: 0-0
Aids: Bl: 0-0 Vi: 0-0 Tstrap: 0-0
Best Rating: 112 3/02 Fknm 2m5f110y good   Ch

Modest hunter chaser; acts on good ground.

Lady Anglesby

75f   **53f**

6-y-o b m Then Again-Moy Ran Lady (Black Minstrel)
C J Drewe E J Saunders

Placings:0   (0149)
2002/03: 16⁰GF,

	Starts	1st	2nd	3rd	Win & Pl
NH Flat	1	0	0	0	
Career Total	1	0	0	0	

Going: Sf: 0-0 GS: 0-0 Gd: 0-0 GF: - Fm: 0-1
Distance: 2m/2m3: 0-1 2m4-2m7: 0-0 3m+: 0-0
Track: LH: 0-1 RH: 0-0 Tight: 0-0 Gall: 0-0
Aids: Bl: 0-0 Vi: 0-0 Tstrap: 0-0
Best Rating: 53 5/02 Chep 2m110y   gd-fm NHF

Lady Arnica

90   **75**

4-y-o b f Ezzoud (IRE)-Brand (Shareef Dancer (USA))
A W Carroll Roger Clarke

Placings:3002   (4708)
2002/03: 16³GS, 16⁶S, 16⁶S, 20²G,

	Starts	1st	2nd	3rd	Win & Pl
Hurdles	4	0	1	1	1641
Career Total	4	0	1	1	1641

Going: Sf: 0-2 GS: 0-1 Gd: 0-1 GF: - Fm: 0-0
Distance: 2m/2m3: 0-3 2m4-2m7: 0-1 3m+: 0-0
Track: LH: 0-3 RH: 0-1 Tight: 0-0 Gall: 0-2
Aids: Bl: 0-0 Vi: 0-0 Tstrap: 0-0
Best Rating: 75 4/03 Uttx 2m4f110y good   Hdl

Plating-class hurdler; placed on a couple of occasions; stays two and a half miles; acts on good ground.

Lady B Warned (IRE)

56

6-y-o b m Zaffaran (USA)-Frostbite (Prince Tenderfoot (USA))
N A Twiston-Davies The Yes - No - Wait Sorries

Placings:40P20-P   (0115)
2002/03: 24⁸GS,

	Starts	1st	2nd	3rd	Win & Pl
Hurdles	1	0	0	0	
Career Total	6	0	1	0	892

Going: Sf: 0-0 GS: 0-1 Gd: 0-0 GF: - Fm: 0-0
Distance: 2m/2m3: 0-0 2m4-2m7: 0-0 3m+: 0-1
Track: LH: 0-0 RH: 0-1 Tight: 0-0 Gall: 0-0
Aids: Bl: 0-0 Vi: 0-0 Tstrap: 0-0
Best Rating: 76 12/01 Hrfd 2m1f   soft   NHF

Very modest form in novice hurdles.

Lady Blackthorn

5-y-o br m Seymour Hicks (FR)-Myblackthorn (IRE)
(Mandalus)
B J M Ryall Hunt & Co (bournemouth) Ltd

Placings:00P   (4595)
2002/03: 18⁰GS, 16⁰S, 22⁸GF,

	Starts	1st	2nd	3rd	Win & Pl
NH Flat	2	0	0	0	0
Hurdles	1	0	0	0	0
Career Total	3	0	0	0	

Going: Sf: 0-1 GS: 0-1 Gd: 0-0 GF: - Fm: 0-1
Distance: 2m/2m3: 0-2 2m4-2m7: 0-1 3m+: 0-0
Track: LH: 0-1 RH: 0-2 Tight: 0-1 Gall: 0-0
Aids: Bl: 0-0 Vi: 0-0 Tstrap: 0-0
Best Rating: 39 2/03 Font 2m2f110y gd-sft NHF

Lady Bob Back

96   **83**

6-y-o br m Bob Back (USA)-Whimbrel (Dara Monarch)
M A Barnes (Mrs M Reveley 2/3) John Wills

Placings:60540-5P25603   (4621)
2002/03: 23⁵G, 25⁸GS, 20²HY, 21⁵HY, 24⁶S, 20⁰GS, 20³GF,

	Starts	1st	2nd	3rd	Win & Pl
Hurdles	7	0	1	1	1887
Career Total	12	0	1	1	1887

Going: Sf: 0-3 GS: 0-2 Gd: 0-1 GF: - Fm: 0-1
Distance: 2m/2m3: 0-2 2m4-2m7: 0-5 3m+: 0-2
Track: LH: 0-5 RH: 0-2 Tight: 0-1 Gall: 0-0
Aids: Bl: 0-0 Vi: 0-0 Tstrap: 0-0
Best Rating: 87 3/02 Donc 2m110y   soft   NHF

Moderate hurdler; inconsistent; first worthwhile form when runner-up in a moderate novices handicap hurdle at Wetherby on Boxing Day. mixed efforts since.

Lady Cricket (FR)

112   **163**

9-y-o ch m Cricket Ball (USA)-Lady Mariza (Dunbeath (USA))
M C Pipe D A Johnson

Placings:1/110651/11044/12120/1402/212-21352 (4457)
2002/03: 16²G, 21¹GS, 17³G, 20⁵G, 25²G,

	Starts	1st	2nd	3rd	Win & Pl
Chases	5	1	2	1	68831
Career Total	29	11	7	1	320987

163	1/03	Chel	2m5f	A HCh		G-S	£23200
163	3/02	Newb	2m1f	A Ch		SFT	£20880
162	11/00	Chel	2m4f110yA HCh		G-S	£46400
155	12/99	Chel	2m5f	B Ch		G-S	£9940

137	11/99	Chep	2m3f110yA Ch		SFT	£14310
146	2/99	Font	2m2f110yB Hdl		GD	£7265
157	2/99	Newb	2m5f	B HHdl	G-S	£5965
	4/98	Autl	2m3f110y Hdl		VS	£35354
	11/97	Autl	2m2f	HHdl	HLD	£24691
	11/97	Autl	1m7f	Hdl	SFT	£13468
	4/97	Autl	1m7f	Hdl	SFT	£13468

Total win prize-money £214941

Going: Sf: 0-0 GS: 1-1 Gd: 0-4 GF: - Fm: 0-0
Distance: 2m/2m3: 0-2 **2m4-2m7: 1-2** 3m+: 0-1
Track: LH: **1-5** RH: 0-0 Tight: 0-1 **Gall: 1-4**
Aids: Bl: **1-5** Vi: 0-0 Tstrap: 0-0
Best Rating: 163 4/03 Aint 3m1f good Ch

High-class chaser; in good form this term landing the Ladbroke Trophy Chase at Cheltenham; runner-up in the Martell Cup at Aintree; effective on good ground, but prefers some cut, especially over 2m; probably better over 2m 4f than 2m and stays 3m 1f; makes the odd mistake; regularly blinkered but game mare; has now been retired to stud.

Lady Domitor
84   **77**
8-y-o b m Domitor (USA)-Dawn O Er Kells (IRE) (Pitskelly)
Mrs D A Hamer   A J Cook

Placings:P/0/50600-4P   (1156)
2002/03: 20⁴GF, 22⁵G,

	Starts	1st	2nd	3rd	Win & Pl
Hurdles	2	0	0	0	0
Career Total	9	0	0	0	

Going: Sf: 0-0 GS: 0-0 Gd: 0-1 GF: - Fm: 0-1
Distance: 2m/2m3: 0-0 2m4-2m7: 0-2 3m+: 0-0
Track: LH: 0-2 RH: 0-0 Tight: 0-2 Gall: 0-0
Aids: Bl: 0-0 Vi: 0-0 Tstrap: 0-0
Best Rating: 77 8/01 Kbgn 2m good Hdl

Lady Faustus
107f   **104f**
6-y-o b m Faustus (USA)-Princess Lucy (Local Suitor (USA))
Jonjo O Neill   D J Deer

Placings:10-20   (2718)
2002/03: 16²GS, 16⁰HY,

	Starts	1st	2nd	3rd	Win & Pl
NH Flat	2	0	1	0	730
Career Total	4	1	1	0	2291
103	3/02 Uttx	2m	H NHF	HVY	£1561

Total win prize-money £1561

Going: Sf: 0-1 GS: 0-1 Gd: 0-0 GF: - Fm: 0-0
Distance: 2m/2m3: 0-2 2m4-2m7: 0-0 3m+: 0-0
Track: LH: 0-2 RH: 0-0 Tight: 0-0 Gall: 0-0
Aids: Bl: 0-0 Vi: 0-0 Tstrap: 0-0
Best Rating: 104 11/02 Weth 2m gd-sft NHF

Big mare. Won a bumper in bad ground at Uttoxeter in March 2002 on her debut. When going hurdling she will appreciate two and a half miles.

Lady Felix
103(93h)   (120h)**97**
8-y-o br m Batshoof-Volcalmeh (Lidhame)
R H Alner   J P M & J W Cook

Placings:455B41/1132201/42   (4569)
2002/03: 24⁴G, 24²G,

	Starts	1st	2nd	3rd	Win & Pl
Hurdles	1	0	0	0	410

Chases	1	0	1	0	1740
Career Total	15	4	3	1	21888
157	4/01 Kemp	3m110y	C(0-130)HHdl	GD	£7441
120	4/01 Kemp	3m110y	C(0-130)HHdl	GD	£7441
112	6/00 MRas	3m	E Hdl	G-S	£2455
110	5/00 MRas	3m	D Hdl	G-F	£3096
99	4/00 Ludl	3m	E Hdl	G-S	£2796

Total win prize-money £15791

Going: Sf: 0-0 GS: 0-0 Gd: 0-2 GF: - Fm: 0-0
Distance: 2m/2m3: 0-0 2m4-2m7: 0-0 3m+: 0-0
Track: LH: 0-1 RH: 0-1 Tight: 0-1 Gall: 0-0
Aids: Bl: 0-0 Vi: 0-0 Tstrap: 0-0
Best Rating: 120 4/01 Kemp 3m110y good Hdl

Fair hurdler/novice chaser; runner-up on chase debut at Stratford in April 2003; stays well; seems to go on all types of ground.

Lady Inch
37
5-y-o b m Inchinor-Head Turner (My Dad Tom (USA))
S L Keightley   The Dyball Partnership

Placings:60-PPP   (2438)
2002/03: 16⁰GS, 21⁰GS, 21⁰GS,

	Starts	1st	2nd	3rd	Win & Pl
Hurdles	3	0	0	0	
Career Total	5	0	0	0	0

Going: Sf: 0-0 GS: 0-0 Gd: 0-1 GF: - Fm: 0-0
Distance: 2m/2m3: 0-0 2m4-2m7: 0-2 3m+: 0-0
Track: LH: 0-1 RH: 0-2 Tight: 0-2 Gall: 0-1
Aids: Bl: 0-0 Vi: 0-2 Tstrap: 0-0
Best Rating: 37 8/01 Strf 2m110y good Hdl

Lady Jeannie
94   **92**
6-y-o b m Emarati (USA)-Cottonwood (Teenoso (USA))
M J Haynes   G R Sanford & Partners

Placings:15P   (3101)
2002/03: 16¹HY, 17⁵HY, 16⁶S,

	Starts	1st	2nd	3rd	Win & Pl
Hurdles	3	1	0	0	3052
Career Total	3	1	0	0	3052
82	12/02 Plum	2m	E Hdl	HVY	£3052

Total win prize-money £3052

Going: Sf: 1-3 GS: 0-0 Gd: 0-0 GF: - Fm: 0-0
Distance: 2m/2m3: 1-3 2m4-2m7: 0-0 3m+: 0-0
Track: LH: 1-2 RH: 0-1 Tight: 1-3 Gall: 0-0
Aids: Bl: 0-0 Vi: 0-0 Tstrap: 0-0
Best Rating: 92 12/02 Folk 2m1f110y heavy Hdl

Moderate hurdler; acts on heavy ground.

Lady Jones
6-y-o b/br m Emperor Jones (USA)-So Beguiling (USA) (Woodman (USA))
P L Gilligan   Mrs Jean Routledge

Placings:055-PFF   (3812)
2002/03: 19⁰S, 16⁰HY, 19⁰G,

	Starts	1st	2nd	3rd	Win & Pl
Hurdles	3	0	0	0	
Career Total	6	0	0	0	0

Going: Sf: 0-2 GS: 0-0 Gd: 0-1 GF: - Fm: 0-0
Distance: 2m/2m3: 0-3 2m4-2m7: 0-0 3m+: 0-0
Track: LH: 0-3 RH: 0-0 Tight: 0-1 Gall: 0-0

Aids: Bl: 0-0 Vi: 0-0 Tstrap: 0-0
Best Rating: 92 2/02 Hntg 2m110y soft Hdl

Lady Lap Dancer
103   **90+**
5-y-o b m Shareef Dancer (USA)-Jelabna (Jalmood (USA))
Mrs M Reveley   Mrs C Strang Steel

Placings:4361P23   (4509)
2002/03: 16⁴G, 16³S, 16⁶S, 16¹S, 16⁶HY, 20²G, 22³G,

	Starts	1st	2nd	3rd	Win & Pl
Hurdles	7	1	1	2	4526
Career Total	7	1	1	2	4526
90	11/02 Kels	2m110y	G Hdl	SFT	£2257

Total win prize-money £2258

Going: Sf: 1-4 GS: 0-0 Gd: 0-3 GF: - Fm: 0-0
Distance: **2m/2m3: 1-5** 2m4-2m7: 0-2 3m+: 0-0
Track: LH: **1-6** RH: 0-1 Tight: **1-4** Gall: 0-0
Aids: Bl: 0-0 Vi: 0-0 Tstrap: 0-0
Best Rating: 90 4/03 Kels 2m6f110y good Hdl

Moderate hurdler; got off the mark in a seller over two miles at Kelso; showed improved form over further when placed at Hexham and Kelso; acts on good and soft.

Lady Laureate
104   **108**
5-y-o b m Sir Harry Lewis (USA)-Cyrillic (Rock City)
G C Bravery   Blackfoot Bloodstock

Placings:64-043PP   (3868)
2002/03: 16⁰G, 20⁴S, 21³HY, 23⁰S, 16⁰GS,

	Starts	1st	2nd	3rd	Win & Pl
Hurdles	5	0	0	1	5100
Career Total	7	0	0	1	10100

Going: Sf: 0-3 GS: 0-1 Gd: 0-1 GF: - Fm: 0-0
Distance: 2m/2m3: 0-2 2m4-2m7: 0-2 3m+: 0-1
Track: LH: 0-4 RH: 0-1 Tight: 0-1 Gall: 0-2
Aids: Bl: 0-0 Vi: 0-0 Tstrap: 0-0
Best Rating: 120 4/02 Aint 2m110y good Hdl

Fair hurdler; four times a winner on the level; highly tried over hurdles and is still looking for her first win; dropped in class, but bandaged all round, was pulled up at Fakenham; seems best suited by a sound surface; stays 2m 5f.

Lady Lewis
92   **70**
7-y-o b m Sir Harry Lewis (USA)-Gaygo Lady (Gay Fandango (USA))
C J Down   Mike Rowe

Placings:3-66   (4595)
2002/03: 19⁶G, 22⁶GF,

	Starts	1st	2nd	3rd	Win & Pl
Hurdles	2	0	0	0	0
Career Total	3	0	0	1	214

Going: Sf: 0-0 GS: 0-0 Gd: 0-1 GF: - Fm: 0-1
Distance: 2m/2m3: 0-0 2m4-2m7: 0-2 3m+: 0-0
Track: LH: 0-0 RH: 0-2 Tight: 0-0 Gall: 0-0
Aids: Bl: 0-0 Vi: 0-0 Tstrap: 0-0
Best Rating: 84 8/01 Worc 2m gd-fm NHF

Lady Lighthouse
64f   **36f**
5-y-o b m Alhijaz-Fairfields Breeze (Buckskin (FR))

R J Price Derek & Cheryl Holder

Placings:*0* (0907)
2002/03: 16⁰G,

	Starts	1st	2nd	3rd	Win & Pl
NH Flat	1	0	0	0	
Career Total	1	0	0	0	

Going: Sf: 0-0 GS: 0-0 Gd: 0-1 GF: - Fm: 0-0
Distance: 2m/2m3: 0-1 2m4-2m7: 0-0 3m+: 0-0
Track: LH: 0-1 RH: 0-0 Tight: 0-0 Gall: 0-0
Aids: Bl: 0-0 Vi: 0-0 Tstrap: 0-0
Best Rating: 36　8/02　Worc　2m　good　NHF

Lady Mercury
96　　　　　　　　　　10
5-y-o b m Rock Hopper-Bellezza (Ardross)
Miss K M George Allen And Bowler

Placings:PPP0P (4798)
2002/03: 17ᴾGS, 17ᴾGS, 24ᴾS, 16⁰G, 17ᴾGF,

	Starts	1st	2nd	3rd	Win & Pl
Hurdles	5	0	0	0	
Career Total	5	0	0	0	

Going: Sf: 0-1 GS: 0-2 Gd: 0-1 GF: - Fm: 0-1
Distance: 2m/2m3: 0-4 2m4-2m7: 0-0 3m+: 0-1
Track: LH: 0-1 RH: 0-4 Tight: 0-4 Gall: 0-0
Aids: Bl: 0-0 Vi: 0-1 Tstrap: 0-0
Best Rating: 10　4/03　Ludl　2m　good　Hdl

Lady Netbetsports (IRE)
90　　　　　　　　　　61
4-y-o b f In The Wings-Auntie Maureen (IRE) (Roi Danzig (USA))
B S Rothwell Paul Moorhouse

Placings:6F (3891)
2002/03: 16⁶S, 16ᶠGS,

	Starts	1st	2nd	3rd	Win & Pl
Hurdles	2	0	0	0	0
Career Total	2	0	0	0	0

Going: Sf: 0-1 GS: 0-1 Gd: 0-0 GF: - Fm: 0-0
Distance: 2m/2m3: 0-2 2m4-2m7: 0-0 3m+: 0-0
Track: LH: 0-2 RH: 0-0 Tight: 0-1 Gall: 0-0
Aids: Bl: 0-0 Vi: 0-0 Tstrap: 0-0
Best Rating: 61　1/03　Ayr　2m　soft　Hdl

Lady Of Lisle
81　　　　　　　　　　42
5-y-o ch m Afzal-Holy Times (IRE) (The Parson)
C P Morlock J Wild

Placings:00P0 (4366)
2002/03: 16⁰G, 22⁰GS, 19ᴾS, 20⁰G,

	Starts	1st	2nd	3rd	Win & Pl
NH Flat	1	0	0	0	0
Hurdles	3	0	0	0	0
Career Total	4	0	0	0	0

Going: Sf: 0-1 GS: 0-1 Gd: 0-2 GF: - Fm: 0-0
Distance: 2m/2m3: 0-2 2m4-2m7: 0-2 3m+: 0-0
Track: LH: 0-1 RH: 0-3 Tight: 0-0 Gall: 0-0

Aids: Bl: 0-0 Vi: 0-0 Tstrap: 0-0
Best Rating: 48　3/03　Asct　2m4f　good　Hdl

Lady Of Ta'Pinu
79　　　　　　　　　　52
4-y-o ch f Greensmith-Pitcairn Princess (Capricorn Line)
C N Kellett Willwewontwe Club

Placings:0004 (1323)
2002/03: 16⁰GS, 17⁰G, 16⁰G, 17⁴GF,

	Starts	1st	2nd	3rd	Win & Pl
Hurdles	4	0	0	0	0
Career Total	4	0	0	0	0

Going: Sf: 0-0 GS: 0-1 Gd: 0-2 GF: - Fm: 0-1
Distance: 2m/2m3: 0-4 2m4-2m7: 0-0 3m+: 0-0
Track: LH: 0-3 RH: 0-1 Tight: 0-3 Gall: 0-0
Aids: Bl: 0-0 Vi: 0-1 Tstrap: 0-0
Best Rating: 52　9/02　MRas　2m1f110y　gd-fm　Hdl

Very moderate over hurdles.

Lady Of The Inn (IRE)
106　　　　　　　　　　90
4-y-o ch f Hamas (IRE)-Faakirah (Dragonara Palace (USA))
M C Pipe (D Nicholls 7/8) Eugene O Connell

Placings:213 (2586)
2002/03: 17²GF, 17¹F, 17³GS,

	Starts	1st	2nd	3rd	Win & Pl
Hurdles	3	1	1	1	3782
Career Total	3	1	1	1	3782
78	10/02	Tntn	2m1f	F Hdl	FRM £2676

Total win prize-money £2677

Going: Sf: 0-0 GS: 0-1 Gd: 0-0 GF: - Fm: 1-2
Distance: **2m/2m3:** 1-3 2m4-2m7: 0-0 3m+: 0-0
Track: LH: 0-0 RH: 1-3 Tight: 1-1 Gall: 0-0
Aids: Bl: 0-0 Vi: 0-0 Tstrap: 0-0
Best Rating: 91　12/02　Extr　2m1f　gd-sft　Hdl

Made a promising debut when runner-up in a decent juvenile hurdle at Hereford. Should stay a two miles four in future.

Lady Of The Lamp
79　　　　　　　　　　78
8-y-o b m Miners Lamp-Lady Westgate (Welsh Chanter)
P J Jones P J Jones

Placings:*0004/P00036/122P1P0/P6143P0-0P0* (3600)
2002/03: 20⁰S, 23ᴾS, 24⁰S,

	Starts	1st	2nd	3rd	Win & Pl
Hurdles	3	0	0	0	
Career Total	27	3	2	2	11347
92	11/01	Hayd	2m7f110yE(0-115)HHdl	GD	£3737
87	2/01	Tntn	3m110y F(0-100)HHdl	HVY	£3003
78	5/00	Towc	3m F(0-100)HHdl	SFT	£1856

Total win prize-money £8597

Going: Sf: 0-3 GS: 0-0 Gd: 0-0 GF: - Fm: 0-0
Distance: 2m/2m3: 0-0 2m4-2m7: 0-0 3m+: 1-3
Track: LH: 0-1 RH: 0-2 Tight: 0-1 Gall: 0-0
Aids: Bl: 0-0 Vi: 0-0 Tstrap: 0-0
Best Rating: 92　11/01　Hayd　2m7f110y　good　Hdl

Poor staying hurdler, suited by three miles and soft ground, although has won on faster.

Lady Qc (IRE)
77　　　　　　　　　　90
7-y-o b m Leading Counsel (USA)-Tuesdaynightmare (Celtic Cone)
L Lungo Mrs Sheila Macleod

Placings:43/2400-P0 (0615)
2002/03: 24⁰G, 20⁰GF,

	Starts	1st	2nd	3rd	Win & Pl
Hurdles	2	0	0	0	
Career Total	8	0	1	1	883

Going: Sf: 0-0 GS: 0-0 Gd: 0-1 GF: - Fm: 0-1
Distance: 2m/2m3: 0-0 2m4-2m7: 0-1 3m+: 0-1
Track: LH: 0-2 RH: 0-0 Tight: 0-0 Gall: 0-0
Aids: Bl: 0-1 Vi: 0-0 Tstrap: 0-0
Best Rating: 90　11/01　Catt　2m3f　gd-fm　Hdl

Lady Racquet (IRE)
84f　　　　　　　　　62f
4-y-o b f Glacial Storm (USA)-Kindly Light (IRE) (Supreme Leader)
Mrs A J Bowlby The Norman Partnership

Placings:*0* (3747)
2002/03: 16⁰G,

	Starts	1st	2nd	3rd	Win & Pl
NH Flat	1	0	0	0	
Career Total	1	0	0	0	

Going: Sf: 0-0 GS: 0-0 Gd: 0-1 GF: - Fm: 0-0
Distance: 2m/2m3: 0-1 2m4-2m7: 0-0 3m+: 0-0
Track: LH: 0-0 RH: 0-1 Tight: 0-0 Gall: 0-1
Aids: Bl: 0-0 Vi: 0-0 Tstrap: 0-0
Best Rating: 62　2/03　Hntg　2m110y　good　NHF

Lady Santana (IRE)
6-y-o b m Doyoun-Santana Lady (IRE) (Blakeney)
R S Brookhouse Mrs S J Brookhouse

Placings:P-P4 (3810)
2002/03: 16ᴾGS, 16⁴S,

	Starts	1st	2nd	3rd	Win & Pl
Hurdles	2	0	0	0	0
Career Total	3	0	0	0	0

Going: Sf: 0-1 GS: 0-1 Gd: 0-0 GF: - Fm: 0-0
Distance: 2m/2m3: 0-2 2m4-2m7: 0-0 3m+: 0-0
Track: LH: 0-2 RH: 0-0 Tight: 0-2 Gall: 0-0
Aids: Bl: 0-0 Vi: 0-0 Tstrap: 0-0
Best Rating: 0　2/03　Plum　2m　soft　Hdl

Lady Shrek
5-y-o b m King s Signet (USA)-Come To Good (Swing Easy (USA))
G A Ham P A Dales

Placings:*0* (2339)
2002/03: 13⁰S,

	Starts	1st	2nd	3rd	Win & Pl
NH Flat	1	0	0	0	
Career Total	1	0	0	0	

Going: Sf: 0-1 GS: 0-0 Gd: 0-0 GF: - Fm: 0-0
Distance: 2m/2m3: 0-0 2m4-2m7: 0-0 3m+: 0-0
Track: LH: 0-0 RH: 0-1 Tight: 0-0 Gall: 0-0
Aids: Bl: 0-0 Vi: 0-0 Tstrap: 0-0
Best Rating: 0 12/02 Extr 1m5f soft NHF

Lady Solrski

(19h)

6-y-o b m Petoski-Flaxen Tina (Beau Tudor)
A C Whillans Solway Racing Syndicate

Placings:600-PPP (3502)
2002/03: 20^PHY, 20^PG, 24^PS,

	Starts	1st	2nd	3rd	Win & Pl
Hurdles	3	0	0	0	
Career Total	6	0	0	0	0

Going: Sf: 0-2 GS: 0-0 Gd: 0-1 GF: - Fm: 0-0
Distance: 2m/2m3: 0-0 2m4-2m7: 0-2 3m+: 0-1
Track: LH: 0-1 RH: 0-2 Tight: 0-1 Gall: 0-0
Aids: Bl: 0-0 Vi: 0-0 Tstrap: 0-0
Best Rating: 88 3/02 Ayr 2m heavy NHF

Lady Stratagem

87   39

4-y-o gr f Mark Of Esteem (IRE)-Grey Angel (Kenmare (FR))
E W Tuer (R Hannon 26/6) E Tuer

Placings:1P00P (4262)
2002/03: 16^1GF, 16^PGS, 16^2GS, 16^6G, 17^PG,

	Starts	1st	2nd	3rd	Win & Pl
Hurdles	5	1	0	0	3874
Career Total	5	1	0	0	3874

82 10/02 Kels 2m110y D Hdl G-F £3874
Total win prize-money £3874

Going: Sf: 0-0 GS: 0-2 Gd: 0-2 GF: - Fm: 1-1
Distance: 2m/2m3: 1-5 2m4-2m7: 0-0 3m+: 0-0
Track: LH: 1-5 RH: 0-1 Tight: 1-4 Gall: 0-0
Aids: Bl: 0-0 Vi: 0-0 Tstrap: 0-0
Best Rating: 82 10/02 Kels 2m110y gd-fm Hdl

Made a winning debut in a weak juvenile hurdle at Kelso in October. Well beaten after.

Lady Tearaway

58f   29f

4-y-o b f Arrasas (USA)-Manageress (Mandamus)
J E Long John Nicholson

Placings:0 (3754)
2002/03: 16^6G,

	Starts	1st	2nd	3rd	Win & Pl
NH Flat	1	0	0	0	
Career Total	1	0	0	0	

Going: Sf: 0-0 GS: 0-0 Gd: 0-1 GF: - Fm: 0-0
Distance: 2m/2m3: 0-1 2m4-2m7: 0-0 3m+: 0-0
Track: LH: 0-0 RH: 0-1 Tight: 0-0 Gall: 0-0
Aids: Bl: 0-0 Vi: 0-0 Tstrap: 0-0
Best Rating: 29 2/03 Kemp 2m good NHF

Lady Terimond

98f   99f

6-y-o br m Terimon-Kitty Come Home (Monsanto (FR))
N J Henderson Raymond Parish & Miss Terri Griffiths

Placings:222 (2064)
2002/03: 17^2G, 16^2S, 17^2S,

	Starts	1st	2nd	3rd	Win & Pl
NH Flat	3	0	3	0	1486
Career Total	3	0	3	0	1486

Going: Sf: 0-2 GS: 0-0 Gd: 0-1 GF: - Fm: 0-0
Distance: 2m/2m3: 0-3 2m4-2m7: 0-0 3m+: 0-0
Track: LH: 0-1 RH: 0-2 Tight: 0-0 Gall: 0-0
Aids: Bl: 0-0 Vi: 0-0 Tstrap: 0-0
Best Rating: 99 6/02 Worc 2m soft NHF

Runner-up on her first three starts in bumpers.

Lady Tilly

87   50

6-y-o b m Puissance-Lady Of Itatiba (BEL) (King Of Macedon)
B Mactaggart Miss E Johnston

Placings:5/5 (1497)
2002/03: 16^5G,

	Starts	1st	2nd	3rd	Win & Pl
Hurdles	1	0	0	0	0
Career Total	2	0	0	0	0

Going: Sf: 0-0 GS: 0-0 Gd: 0-1 GF: - Fm: 0-0
Distance: 2m/2m3: 0-1 2m4-2m7: 0-0 3m+: 0-0
Track: LH: 0-1 RH: 0-0 Tight: 0-0 Gall: 0-0
Aids: Bl: 0-0 Vi: 0-0 Tstrap: 0-1
Best Rating: 50 10/02 Hexm 2m110y good Hdl

Lady Turk (FR)

97(106h)   (99 h)103

6-y-o b m Baby Turk-Alyda (FR) (Dalal (FR))
C Tizzard R G Tizzard

Placings:44/P540P0P0P20/P541132P11P-U3P06F30132 (4674)
2002/03: 23^UG, 24^3GF, 26^PHY, 16^5GS, 20^6HY, 24^FS, 24^3S, 21^0S, 22^1G, 25^2GF,

	Starts	1st	2nd	3rd	Win & Pl
Hurdles	5	0	0	1	651
Chases	6	1	1	2	6920
Career Total	35	5	3	4	32007

97 3/03 Font 2m6f E Ch GD £3997
112 2/02 Tntn 2m1f G Hdl SFT £1775
125 2/02 Font 2m6f110yG Hdl HVY £1932
107 8/01 Font 2m2f110yE Hdl G-F £2408
102 7/01 Worc 2m4f E Hdl GD £2436
Total win prize-money £12549

Going: Sf: 0-5 GS: 0-1 Gd: 1-2 GF: - Fm: 0-3
Distance: 2m/2m3: 0-1 2m4-2m7: 1-4 3m+: 0-6
Track: LH: 0-3 RH: 0-6 Tight: 1-8 Gall: 0-0
Aids: Bl: 0-3 Vi: 0-1 Tstrap: 1-7
Best Rating: 125 2/02 Font 2m6f110y heavy Hdl

Modest hurdler/chaser; stays two miles six; acts on most types of ground.

Lady Ward (IRE)

109   81

5-y-o b m Mujadil (USA)-Sans Ceriph (IRE) (Thatching)
S C Burrough (P R Rodford 27/1) Les Trott

Placings:51-322332206040 (3781)
2002/03: 17^3G, 16^2GF, 16^2GF, 16^3GF, 20^3GF, 17^2GF, 20^2S, 16^5S, 16^6HY, 19^0GS, 17^4S, 17^0GS,

	Starts	1st	2nd	3rd	Win & Pl
Hurdles	12	0	4	3	4216

Career Total 14 1 4 3 6323
71 4/02 Hrfd 2m1f G Hdl G-F £2107
Total win prize-money £2107

Going: Sf: 0-4 GS: 0-2 Gd: 0-1 GF: - Fm: 0-5
Distance: 2m/2m3: 0-10 2m4-2m7: 0-2 3m+: 0-0
Track: LH: 0-8 RH: 0-4 Tight: 0-4 Gall: 0-0
Aids: Bl: 0-0 Vi: 0-0 Tstrap: 0-0
Best Rating: 81 2/03 Tntn 2m1f soft Hdl

Plating class hurdler; won amateur riders seller at Newton Abbot June 2003; suited to waiting tactics; best at around 2m; likes good to firm ground.

Lady Widd (IRE)

85   56

5-y-o ch m Commanche Run-Lady Geeno (IRE) (Cheval)
S J Marshall S J Marshall

Placings:000-U4P0 (3803)
2002/03: 16^UG, 24^4S, 24^PGS, 20^5S,

	Starts	1st	2nd	3rd	Win & Pl
Hurdles	4	0	0	0	0
Career Total	7	0	0	0	0

Going: Sf: 0-2 GS: 0-1 Gd: 0-1 GF: - Fm: 0-0
Distance: 2m/2m3: 0-1 2m4-2m7: 0-1 3m+: 0-2
Track: LH: 0-2 RH: 0-2 Tight: 0-1 Gall: 0-1
Aids: Bl: 0-0 Vi: 0-0 Tstrap: 0-0
Best Rating: 65 2/02 Muss 2m soft NHF

Laganside (IRE)

10-y-o b g Montelimar (USA)-Ruby Girl (Crash Course)
J F W Muir J F W Muir

Placings:106313/1P4/266451P-P (4459)
2002/03: 21^PG,

	Starts	1st	2nd	3rd	Win & Pl
Chases	1	0	0	0	
Career Total	17	4	1	2	20090

112 12/01 Muss 3m D(0-120)HCh GD £6126
120 5/00 Prth 2m4f110yE(0-115)HCh GD £4940
109 12/99 Muss 2m4f E Ch G-S £4221
82 5/99 Dpat 2m1f172y Hdl G-F £1994
Total win prize-money £17282

Going: Sf: 0-0 GS: 0-0 Gd: 0-1 GF: - Fm: 0-0
Distance: 2m/2m3: 0-0 2m4-2m7: 0-1 3m+: 0-0
Track: LH: 0-1 RH: 0-0 Tight: 0-1 Gall: 0-0
Aids: Bl: 0-0 Vi: 0-0 Tstrap: 0-0
Best Rating: 120 5/01 Prth 2m4f110y gd-sft Ch

Former fair chaser, winning pointer in 2003; stays three miles and seems to handle most ground; suited by a sharp, right-handed track.

Lager Dash

5-y-o b g Suave Dancer (USA)-Padelia (Thatching)
R J Price E G Bevan

Placings:P (2064)
2002/03: 17^PS,

	Starts	1st	2nd	3rd	Win & Pl
NH Flat	1	0	0	0	
Career Total	1	0	0	0	

Going: Sf: 0-1 GS: 0-0 Gd: 0-0 GF: - Fm: 0-0
Distance: 2m/2m3: 0-1 2m4-2m7: 0-0 3m+: 0-0
Track: LH: 0-0 RH: 0-1 Tight: 0-0 Gall: 0-0

Aids: Bl: 0-0 Vi: 0-0 Tstrap: 0-0
Best Rating: 0   11/02 Hrfd 2m1f   soft   NHF

Lago Di Levico
107   100+
6-y-o ch g Pelder (IRE)-Langton Herring (Nearly A Hand)
C J Down   M R Lavis

Placings:FUP/0R00-210   (1943)
2002/03: 19²GF, 22¹G, 21⁰G,

	Starts	1st	2nd	3rd	Win & Pl
Hurdles	3	1	1	0	5355
Career Total	10	1	1	0	5355
102	10/02	Strf	2m6f110yD Hdl	GD	£4441

Total win prize-money £4442

Going: Sf: 0-0 GS: 0-0 Gd: 1-2 GF: - Fm: 0-1
Distance: 2m/2m3: 0-0 **2m4-2m7: 1-3** 3m+: 0-0
Track: **LH: 1-2** RH: 0-1 **Tight: 1-1** Gall: 0-1
Aids: Bl: 0-0 Vi: 0-0 Tstrap: 0-0
Best Rating: 102 10/02 Strf 2m6f110y good Hdl

First signs of form when a narrowly beaten 100/1 shot at Hereford September 2002. Showed that effort was no fluke when a wide margin winner of a 22 furlong maiden hurdle at Stratford the following month. Appears to be on the upgrade.

Lakefield Leader (IRE)
101(88c)   (91c)112
12-y-o b g Supreme Leader-Debonair Dolly (Cidrax (FR))
C Tizzard   I R Snowden

Placings:0/425/12/51320/**216P/P35**-3440   (0731)
2002/03: 21⁵G, 24³GF, 27⁴S, 17⁴GF, 22⁰GF,

	Starts	1st	2nd	3rd	Win & Pl
Hurdles	5	0	0	1	383
Career Total	22	3	4	3	17617
109	11/00	Towc	2m6f	E Ch	SFT £2925
134	3/00	Newb	2m5f	D(0-125)HHdl	SFT £5297
113	5/98	Uttx	3m110y	E Hdl	GD £2400

Total win prize-money £10623

Going: Sf: 0-1 GS: 0-0 Gd: 0-1 GF: - Fm: 0-3
Distance: 2m/2m3: 0-1 2m4-2m7: 0-2 3m+: 0-2
Track: LH: 0-5 RH: 0-0 Tight: 0-4 Gall: 0-0
Aids: Bl: 0-3 Vi: 0-2 Tstrap: 0-0
Best Rating: 134 4/00 Asct 3m   soft   Hdl

A one-time useful staying hurdler, he lost his way when put over fences. Handles soft and fast ground.

Lakeside Lad
104   98
11-y-o b g St Columbus-Beyond The Trimm (Trimmingham)
R Wilman   Mrs Joanna Hughes

Placings:0L/PB24/UU322PUF33/U4P/5F400P2-12P (0781)
2002/03: 24¹G, 26²G, 26⁶GF,

	Starts	1st	2nd	3rd	Win & Pl
Chases	3	1	1	0	4586
Career Total	29	1	5	3	10320
98	5/02	Fknm	3m110y	E Ch	GD £3616

Total win prize-money £3617

Going: Sf: 0-0 GS: 0-0 Gd: 1-2 GF: - Fm: 0-1
Distance: 2m/2m3: 0-0 2m4-2m7: 0-0 **3m+: 1-3**
Track: **LH: 1-3** RH: 0-0 **Tight: 1-1** Gall: 0-0
Aids: Bl: 0-0 Vi: 0-0 Tstrap: 0-0
Best Rating: 98 5/02 Uttx 3m2f   good   Ch

Moderate chaser; stays 3m 2f; acts on a sound surface.

Lambadora
103   86
5-y-o ch m Suave Dancer (USA)-Lust (Pursuit Of Love)
Miss K Marks (J G M O Shea 6/5) Nick Shutts

Placings:4001-1PPP   (0904)
2002/03: 16¹G, 16¹GF, 22²G, 19⁰G, 16⁰G,

	Starts	1st	2nd	3rd	Win & Pl
Hurdles	5	2	0	0	4774
Career Total	8	2	0	0	4774
86	5/02	Ludl	2m	G Hdl	G-F £2145
78	4/02	Plum	2m	E Hdl	GD £2628

Total win prize-money £4775

Going: Sf: 0-0 GS: 0-0 Gd: 1-4 GF: - Fm: 1-1
Distance: **2m/2m3: 2-3** 2m4-2m7: 0-2 3m+: 0-0
Track: LH: 1-2 RH: 1-3 **Tight: 1-1** Gall: 0-0
Aids: Bl: 0-0 Vi: 0-0 Tstrap: 0-0
Best Rating: 86 5/02 Ludl 2m   gd-fm   Hdl

Winning plater over hurdles, acts on fast ground.

Lambhill Stakes (IRE)
99   91+
5-y-o gr g King s Ride-Summerhill Express (IRE) (Roselier (FR))
J M Jefferson   Ashleybank Investments Limited

Placings:0-4225   (3801)
2002/03: 17⁴GF, 23²GS, 25²G, 24⁵S,

	Starts	1st	2nd	3rd	Win & Pl
NH Flat	1	0	0	0	0
Hurdles	3	0	2	0	2251
Career Total	5	0	2	0	2251

Going: Sf: 0-1 GS: 0-1 Gd: 0-1 GF: - Fm: 0-1
Distance: 2m/2m3: 0-1 2m4-2m7: 0-1 3m+: 0-2
Track: LH: 0-3 RH: 0-1 Tight: 0-2 Gall: 0-1
Aids: Bl: 0-0 Vi: 0-0 Tstrap: 0-0
Best Rating: 91 1/03 Catt 3m1f110y good Hdl

Well beaten when runner-up behind useful sorts at Wetherby in December and Catterick the following month.

Lambrini Bianco (IRE)
103f   91f
5-y-o br g Roselier (FR)-Darjoy (Darantus)
Mrs L Williamson   Halewood International Ltd

Placings:10-00   (4122)
2002/03: 16⁰G, 16⁰G,

	Starts	1st	2nd	3rd	Win & Pl
NH Flat	2	0	0	0	
Career Total	4	1	0	0	1729
89	3/02	Bang	2m1f	H NHF	SFT £1729

Total win prize-money £1729

Going: Sf: 0-0 GS: 0-0 Gd: 0-2 GF: - Fm: 0-0
Distance: 2m/2m3: 0-2 2m4-2m7: 0-0 3m+: 0-0
Track: LH: 0-1 RH: 0-1 Tight: 0-0 Gall: 0-1
Aids: Bl: 0-0 Vi: 0-0 Tstrap: 0-0
Best Rating: 91 11/02 Hayd 2m   good   NHF

Half-brother to some smart staying chasers, including 1995 Grand National winner Royal Athlete. Won a soft-ground bumper in March 2002. Held subsequently.

Lambrini Gold
81   105
9-y-o b g Gildoran-Fille De Soleil (Sunyboy)
D McCain   Halewood International Ltd

Placings:443211/1P/4P2P   (4472)
2002/03: 20⁴HY, 19²GS, 20²S, 21PG,

	Starts	1st	2nd	3rd	Win & Pl
Chases	4	0	1	0	1867
Career Total	12	3	2	1	16383
122	11/00	Hayd	2m	D(0-125)HCh	HVY £5983
110	4/00	Hexm	2m4f110yE Ch	GD	£3373
110	3/00	Hexm	2m110y	E Ch	SFT £3003

Total win prize-money £12360

Going: Sf: 0-2 GS: 0-1 Gd: 0-1 GF: - Fm: 0-0
Distance: 2m/2m3: 0-0 2m4-2m7: 0-4 3m+: 0-0
Track: LH: 0-4 RH: 0-0 Tight: 0-1 Gall: 0-0
Aids: Bl: 0-0 Vi: 0-0 Tstrap: 0-1
Best Rating: 122 11/00 Hayd 2m   heavy   Ch

Fair chaser; won three chases in 2000; off the course for more than two years after November of that year and has broken blood vessels and suffered breathing problems; effective at 2m to 2m 4f.

Lambrini Mist
5-y-o gr g Terimon-Miss Fern (Cruise Missile)
Mrs L Williamson   Halewood International Ltd

Placings:3-00   (2609)
2002/03: 17⁰S, 20⁰S,

	Starts	1st	2nd	3rd	Win & Pl
NH Flat	1	0	0	0	0
Hurdles	1	0	0	0	0
Career Total	3	0	0	1	245

Going: Sf: 0-2 GS: 0-0 Gd: 0-0 GF: - Fm: 0-0
Distance: 2m/2m3: 0-1 2m4-2m7: 0-1 3m+: 0-0
Track: LH: 0-1 RH: 0-1 Tight: 0-0 Gall: 0-0
Aids: Bl: 0-0 Vi: 0-0 Tstrap: 0-0
Best Rating: 69 4/02 Plum 2m2f   gd-fm   NHF

Shaped with promise on his bumper debut. Held since.

Lancashire Lass
99   70+
7-y-o b m Lancastrian-Chanelle (The Parson)
J S King   T L Morshead

Placings:00600/6-200P036   (4629)
2002/03: 22²G, 19⁰S, 19⁰S, 20PHY, 22⁰GF, 24³F, 21⁶GF,

	Starts	1st	2nd	3rd	Win & Pl
Hurdles	7	0	1	1	1624
Career Total	13	0	1	1	1624

Going: Sf: 0-3 GS: 0-0 Gd: 0-1 GF: - Fm: 0-3
Distance: 2m/2m3: 0-1 2m4-2m7: 0-5 3m+: 0-1
Track: LH: 0-2 RH: 0-5 Tight: 0-3 Gall: 0-0
Aids: Bl: 0-0 Vi: 0-0 Tstrap: 0-0
Best Rating: 70 11/00 Tntn 2m1f   good   NHF

Modest novice hurdler at up 2m 6f; best effort when narrowly beaten after pecking at the last in 2m 6f mares only event at Newton Abbot July 2003; acts on fast ground.

Lancastrian Island
76f   57f
5-y-o b m Lancastrian-Kelly s Island (Jupiter Island)

John A Harris G Copley

Placings:0   (2477)
2002/03: 16⁰GS,

	Starts	1st	2nd	3rd	Win & Pl
NH Flat	1	0	0	0	
Career Total	1	0	0	0	

Going: Sf: 0-0 GS: 0-1 Gd: 0-0 GF: - Fm: 0-0
Distance: 2m2/m3: 0-1 2m4-2m7: 0-0 3m+: 0-0
Track: LH: 0-1 RH: 0-0 Tight: 0-0 Gall: 0-1
Aids: Bl: 0-0 Vi: 0-0 Tstrap: 0-0
Best Rating: 60 12/02 Donc 2m110y gd-sft NHF

Lancastrian Jet (IRE)
106   128

12-y-o b g Lancastrian-Kilmurray Jet (Le Bavard (FR))
H D Daly The Hon Mrs A E Heber-Percy

Placings:0/P2211/41252/121U5P/5535P/2133-2206 (3946)
2002/03: 26⁰HY, 32²GS, 24⁰HY, 30⁶S,

	Starts	1st	2nd	3rd	Win & Pl
Chases	4	0	2	0	5851
Career Total	30	6	8	3	61412
127	12/01 Extr	4m	D(0-125)HCh	G-S	£8255
131	1/00 Sand	3m5f110yB HCh		SFT	£20800
131	10/99 Towc	3m1f	E(0-115)HCh	GD	£3142
130	12/98 Towc	3m1f	C(0-130)HCh	SFT	£4926
127	4/98 Uttx	3m2f	E Ch	SFT	£3801
124	3/98 Tntn	3m	E Ch	G-S	£2918

Total win prize-money £43842

Going: Sf: 0-3 GS: 0-1 Gd: 0-0 GF: - Fm: 0-0
Distance: 2m2/m3: 0-0 2m4-2m7: 0-0 3m+: 0-4
Track: LH: 0-0 RH: 0-4 Tight: 0-0 Gall: 0-0
Aids: Bl: 0-0 Vi: 0-0 Tstrap: 0-0
Best Rating: 131 1/00 Sand 3m5f110y soft Ch

Veteran staying chaser, best going right-handed on soft ground and likes stiff tracks like Towcester; stays four miles.

Land Girl
99   65

5-y-o b m General Monash (USA)-Charming Madam (General Holme (USA))
J G M O Shea Bill Tyler

Placings:0-35P   (1441)
2002/03: 16³GS, 16⁵HY, 19⁷F,

	Starts	1st	2nd	3rd	Win & Pl
Hurdles	3	0	0	1	326
Career Total	4	0	0	1	326

Going: Sf: 0-1 GS: 0-0 Gd: 0-0 GF: - Fm: 0-2
Distance: 2m2/m3: 0-3 2m4-2m7: 0-0 3m+: 0-0
Track: LH: 0-2 RH: 0-1 Tight: 0-1 Gall: 0-0
Aids: Bl: 0-0 Vi: 0-0 Tstrap: 0-0
Best Rating: 71 6/02 Uttx 2m heavy Hdl

Landing Light (IRE)
121   162

8-y-o b g In The Wings-Gay Hellene (Ela-Mana-Mou)
N J Henderson Mr & Mrs John Poynton

Placings:1/311P1/1156-4204   (4439)
2002/03: 20⁴HY, 17²G, 16⁶G, 24⁴G,

	Starts	1st	2nd	3rd	Win & Pl
Hurdles	4	0	1	0	20000

Career Total   14   6   1   1   202792

164	12/01 Kemp	2m	A Hdl	GD	£29750
161	12/01 Newc	2m	A Hdl	G-S	£22200
170	4/01 Sand	2m110y	A Hdl	SFT	£49300
154	2/01 Newb	2m110y	A HHdl	SFT	£58000
147	1/01 Chel	2m1f	B(0-145)HHdl	SFT	£11095
134	2/00 Winc	2m	D Hdl	GD	£3623

Total win prize-money £173970

Going: Sf: 0-1 GS: 0-1 Gd: 0-3 GF: - Fm: 0-0
Distance: 2m2/m3: 0-2 2m4-2m7: 0-1 3m+: 0-1
Track: LH: 0-2 RH: 0-2 Tight: 0-0 Gall: 0-1
Aids: Bl: 0-2 Vi: 0-0 Tstrap: 0-0
Best Rating: 170 4/01 Sand 2m110y soft Hdl

A high-class hurdler who won five times from six starts during 2001 including the Tote Gold Trophy, the Coral Eurobet Championship Hurdle, the Fighting Fifth and the Christmas Hurdle; 4 1/4l fifth in the 2002 Champion Hurdle and returned to that level of form when fitted with blinkers to finish 2 1/2l runner-up to Rooster Booster in Bula Hurdle at Cheltenham in December; well beaten by that rival in the 2003 Champion Hurdle; tends to need plenty of driving; seemingly going downhill these days; effective on good and soft ground, but not heavy.

Landings
105   82

4-y-o ch f Deploy-Sandblaster (Most Welcome)
N G Richards Hale Racing Limited

Placings:36062   (4433)
2002/03: 16³S, 16⁸GS, 16⁵HY, 16⁶G, 16²G,

	Starts	1st	2nd	3rd	Win & Pl
Hurdles	5	0	1	1	1225
Career Total	5	0	1	1	1225

Going: Sf: 0-2 GS: 0-1 Gd: 0-2 GF: - Fm: 0-0
Distance: 2m2/m3: 0-5 2m4-2m7: 0-0 3m+: 0-0
Track: LH: 0-4 RH: 0-1 Tight: 0-2 Gall: 0-2
Aids: Bl: 0-0 Vi: 0-0 Tstrap: 0-0
Best Rating: 82 11/02 Ayr 2m soft Hdl

Third on debut over hurdles at Ayr in November 2002; disappointing since.

Langcourt Jester
75f   64f

5-y-o ch m Royal Vulcan-Singing Clown (True Song)
S J Gilmore R A Jeffery

Placings:00   (2136)
2002/03: 16⁰GS, 16⁰G,

	Starts	1st	2nd	3rd	Win & Pl
NH Flat	2	0	0	0	
Career Total	2	0	0	0	

Going: Sf: 0-0 GS: 0-1 Gd: 0-1 GF: - Fm: 0-0
Distance: 2m2/m3: 0-2 2m4-2m7: 0-0 3m+: 0-0
Track: LH: 0-1 RH: 0-1 Tight: 0-1 Gall: 0-0
Aids: Bl: 0-0 Vi: 0-0 Tstrap: 0-0
Best Rating: 64 11/02 Sthl 2m gd-sft NHF

Lanmire Glen (IRE)
104   (98h)102

6-y-o b g Jurado (USA)-Cool Glen (Furry Glen)
E Bolger Edward O Connell

Placings:0/22036021-23P   (4113)
2002/03: 16²SH, 20³S, 32²G,

Chases	3	0	1	1	2240
Career Total	12	1	4	2	10276
100	4/02 Punc	3m1f	Ch	YLD	£4656

Total win prize-money £4656

Going: Sf: 0-1 GS: 0-0 Gd: 0-1 GF: - Fm: 0-0
Distance: 2m2/m3: 0-1 2m4-2m7: 0-1 3m+: 0-1
Track: LH: 0-1 RH: 0-2 Tight: 0-0 Gall: 0-1
Aids: Bl: 0-1 Vi: 0-0 Tstrap: 0-0
Best Rating: 102 2/03 Limk 2m4f soft Ch

Moderate Irish chaser; stays 3m 1f; acts on soft.

Lanmire Leader (IRE)
102(95h)   (83h)85

8-y-o b g Supreme Leader-Dark Fluff (Mandalus)
A Ennis Equine America (UK) Ltd

Placings:062P5225-233P0P6   (3111)
2002/03: 26²G, 21³F, 21³S, 22²G, 22⁰HY, 20²S, 22⁶HY,

	Starts	1st	2nd	3rd	Win & Pl
Hurdles	3	0	0	1	384
Chases	4	0	1	1	1578
Career Total	15	0	4	2	4871

Going: Sf: 0-4 GS: 0-0 Gd: 0-2 GF: - Fm: 0-0
Distance: 2m2/m3: 0-0 2m4-2m7: 0-6 3m+: 0-1
Track: LH: 0-1 RH: 0-4 Tight: 0-6 Gall: 0-0
Aids: Bl: 0-0 Vi: 0-0 Tstrap: 0-0
Best Rating: 92 10/01 Folk 2m6f110y heavy Hdl

He is a modest sort over hurdles and fences at around two and a half miles, although he has recently been tried over further. Acts on soft ground.

Lanmire Tower (IRE)
107   126

9-y-o b g Celio Rufo-Lanigans Tower (The Parson)
S Gollings (A King 12/12) Rowfield Racing

Placings:00/F050R/501134/2035/12P1F13-431440542
                                              (4796)
2002/03: 24⁴GF, 28³GS, 25¹GS, 27⁴G, 24⁴G, 24⁰G, 32²G, 24⁴GF, 28²GF,

	Starts	1st	2nd	3rd	Win & Pl
Chases	9	1	1	1	9532
Career Total	33	6	3	4	43985
129	4/02 Chel	3m1f110yB Ch		GD	£15008
129	2/02 Ludl	3m	E Ch	GD	£3425
85	10/01 Hntg	3m	E Ch	GD	£3626
107	10/99 Weth	3m1f	F(0-100)HHdl	GD	£1835
100	10/99 Carl	2m4f110yE(0-105)HHdl		GD	£2332

Total win prize-money £26227

Going: Sf: 0-0 GS: 1-2 Gd: 0-4 GF: - Fm: 0-3
Distance: 2m2/m3: 0-0 2m4-2m7: 0-0 **3m+: 1-9**
Track: LH: 0-4 **RH: 1-2** Tight: 0-5 Gall: 0-2
Aids: **Bl: 1-7** Vi: 0-1 Tstrap: 0-0
Best Rating: 129 12/02 Ludl 3m3f110y good Ch

Fair handicap chaser; stays 4m; best on a sound surface; goes well in headgear.

Lannkaran (IRE)
91   125

10-y-o b g Shardari-Lankarana (Auction Ring (USA))
H D Daly The Hon Simon Sainsbury

Placings:0211/05/313411/643P1/P3FP0214-6   (4175)
2002/03: 21⁶S,

	Starts	1st	2nd	3rd	Win & Pl
Chases	1	0	0	0	0
Career Total	26	7	2	4	34359

125	4/02	Towc	2m6f	D(0-125)HCh	GD	£5252
117	4/01	Hntg	3m	D(0-120)HCh	SFT	£4855
134	4/00	Strf	3m	D Ch	GD	£4374
124	3/00	Towc	2m6f	E Ch	SFT	£3198
115	12/99	Towc	2m6f	D Ch	SFT	£4574
131	4/98	Chel	2m1f	D Hdl	HVY	£3680
124	3/98	Chep	2m110y	E Hdl	GD	£2444

Total win prize-money £28380

Going: Sf: 0-1 GS: 0-0 Gd: 0-0 GF: - Fm: 0-0
Distance: 2m/2m3: 0-0 2m4-2m7: 0-1 3m+: 0-0
Track: LH: 0-1 RH: 0-0 Tight: 0-0 Gall: 0-0
Aids: Bl: 0-0 Vi: 0-0 Tstrap: 0-0
Best Rating: 134 4/00 Strf 3m good Ch

Fair handicap chaser; effective at two and a half to three miles; best on soft ground; appreciates positive tactics.

Lanos (POL)
90   89

5-y-o ch g Special Power-Lubeka (POL) (Milione (FR))
R Ford (T R George 31/10) D W Watson

Placings:03-406   (1713)
2002/03: 16⁴GF, 16⁰G, 16⁶G,

	Starts	1st	2nd	3rd	Win & Pl
Hurdles	3	0	0	0	250
Career Total	5	0	0	1	815

Going: Sf: 0-0 GS: 0-0 Gd: 0-2 GF: - Fm: 0-1
Distance: 2m/2m3: 0-3 2m4-2m7: 0-0 3m+: 0-0
Track: LH: 0-3 RH: 0-0 Tight: 0-0 Gall: 0-0
Aids: Bl: 0-1 Vi: 0-0 Tstrap: 0-0
Best Rating: 89 10/02 Uttx 2m gd-fm Hdl

Prolific winner on the Flat in his native Poland but struggling to make his mark over hurdles here.

Lanoso (IRE)

5-y-o b g Charnwood Forest (IRE)-Silver Spark (USA) (Silver Hawk (USA))
H M Kavanagh Mrs S Kavanagh

Placings:P-P   (0199)
2002/03: 16ᴾGF,

	Starts	1st	2nd	3rd	Win & Pl
Hurdles	1	0	0	0	
Career Total	2	0	0	0	

Going: Sf: 0-0 GS: 0-0 Gd: 0-0 GF: - Fm: 0-1
Distance: 2m/2m3: 0-0 2m4-2m7: 0-0 3m+: 0-0
Track: LH: 0-1 RH: 0-0 Tight: 0-0 Gall: 0-0
Aids: Bl: 0-0 Vi: 0-0 Tstrap: 0-0
Best Rating: 0 5/02 Worc 2m gd-fm Hdl

Lanzlo (FR)
107   96

6-y-o b/br g Le Balafre (FR)-L Eternite (FR) (Cariellor (FR))
James Moffatt (P J Hobbs 26/8) The Sheroot Partnership

Placings:120F23/115500-2203P454   (4663)
2002/03: 16²GF, 19²GF, 20⁵GF, 18³G, 16ᴾHY, 24⁴G, 16⁵G, 17⁴GF,

	Starts	1st	2nd	3rd	Win & Pl
Hurdles	8	0	2	1	3479

		Starts	1st	2nd	3rd	Win & Pl
Career Total		20	3	4	2	15449

113	9/01	Strf	2m110y	D(0-125)HHdl	G-F	£3458
115	7/01	Strf	2m110y	F(0-110)HHdl	GD	£3020
115	9/00	Chep	2m110y	D Hdl	GD	£3347

Total win prize-money £9827

Going: Sf: 0-1 GS: 0-0 Gd: 0-3 GF: - Fm: 0-4
Distance: 2m/2m3: 0-5 2m4-2m7: 0-2 3m+: 0-1
Track: LH: 0-5 RH: 0-3 Tight: 0-4 Gall: 0-0
Aids: Bl: 0-0 Vi: 0-0 Tstrap: 0-0
Best Rating: 115 7/01 Strf 2m110y good Hdl

Moderate handicap hurdler; stays two and a half miles; effective on a sound surface; suited by a sharp track.

Laouen (FR)
109   134

5-y-o br g Funny Baby (FR)-Olive Noire (FR) (Cadoudal (FR))
L Lungo Ashley Bank Investments & Dr K Fraser

Placings:12-21111   (4762)
2002/03: 16²S, 16¹S, 16¹G, 16¹G,

	Starts	1st	2nd	3rd	Win & Pl
NH Flat	1	0	1	0	575
Hurdles	4	4	0	0	23472
Career Total	7	5	2	0	26790

134	4/03	Prth	2m110y	D Hdl	GD	£5785
126	4/03	Ayr	2m	C Hdl	GD	£7410
122	1/03	Muss	2m	C Hdl	GD	£7182
112	12/02	Donc	2m110y	E Hdl	SFT	£3094
106	3/02	Ayr	2m	H NHF	HVY	£1788

Total win prize-money £25261

Going: Sf: 1-2 GS: 0-0 Gd: 3-3 GF: - Fm: 0-0
Distance: 2m/2m3: 4-5 2m4-2m7: 0-0 3m+: 0-0
Track: LH: 2-3 RH: 2-2 Tight: 1-1 Gall: 1-1
Aids: Bl: 0-0 Vi: 0-0 Tstrap: 0-0
Best Rating: 134 4/03 Prth 2m110y good Hdl

Useful hurdler; has a tremendous strike rate; best over two miles; acts on good ground or softer; likes to be held up; progressive.

Lapland (IRE)
98   84

6-y-o b g Arctic Lord-Ride Of Honour (King s Ride)
N A Callaghan G C Hartigan

Placings:P25-505   (2613)
2002/03: 16⁵GS, 19⁹GS, 24⁵S,

	Starts	1st	2nd	3rd	Win & Pl
Hurdles	3	0	0	0	0
Career Total	6	0	1	0	1096

Going: Sf: 0-1 GS: 0-2 Gd: 0-0 GF: - Fm: 0-0
Distance: 2m/2m3: 0-2 2m4-2m7: 0-0 3m+: 0-1
Track: LH: 0-2 RH: 0-1 Tight: 0-0 Gall: 0-1
Aids: Bl: 0-0 Vi: 0-0 Tstrap: 0-0
Best Rating: 84 12/01 Leic 2m4f110y soft Hdl

Plating-class hurdler; acts on soft ground and is effective at two miles four furlongs.

Lara's Delight
75   48

8-y-o b m Then Again-Sarah Dream (IRE) (Strong Gale)
M J Weeden Mrs S Frost

Placings:00/P06   (0649)
2002/03: 17ᴾG, 16⁰GF, 17⁶GF,

	Starts	1st	2nd	3rd	Win & Pl
Hurdles	3	0	0	0	0

	Starts	1st	2nd	3rd	Win & Pl
Career Total	5	0	0	0	0

Going: Sf: 0-0 GS: 0-0 Gd: 0-1 GF: - Fm: 0-2
Distance: 2m/2m3: 0-3 2m4-2m7: 0-0 3m+: 0-0
Track: LH: 0-1 RH: 0-2 Tight: 0-1 Gall: 0-0
Aids: Bl: 0-0 Vi: 0-0 Tstrap: 0-0
Best Rating: 48 5/02 Winc 2m gd-fm Hdl

Laras Grey (IRE)

10-y-o gr g Celio Rufo-Persian Winter (Persian Bold)
S Flook Mrs S E Vaughan

Placings:220/14121003/3PP/30/005   (4615)
2002/03: 25⁰G, 27⁰G, 26⁵G,

	Starts	1st	2nd	3rd	Win & Pl
Chases	3	0	0	0	0
Career Total	19	3	3	3	10194

91	9/98	Rosc	2m5f	Ch	Y-S	£2690
95	8/98	Kbgn	3m	Hdl	G-Y	£1942
98	7/98	Klny	2m1f	NHF	G-Y	£2690

Total win prize-money £7323

Going: Sf: 0-0 GS: 0-0 Gd: 0-3 GF: - Fm: 0-0
Distance: 2m/2m3: 0-0 2m4-2m7: 0-0 3m+: 0-3
Track: LH: 0-1 RH: 0-2 Tight: 0-1 Gall: 0-1
Aids: Bl: 0-0 Vi: 0-0 Tstrap: 0-0
Best Rating: 98 7/98 Klny 2m1f gd-yld NHF

Last Gesture
86   51

4-y-o b g Jester-Suile Mor (Satin Wood)
Jean-Rene Auvray Jean-Rene Auvray

Placings:44   (0971)
2002/03: 16⁴GF, 16⁴GS,

	Starts	1st	2nd	3rd	Win & Pl
Hurdles	2	0	0	0	704
Career Total	2	0	0	0	704

Going: Sf: 0-0 GS: 0-1 Gd: 0-0 GF: - Fm: 0-1
Distance: 2m/2m3: 0-2 2m4-2m7: 0-0 3m+: 0-0
Track: LH: 0-2 RH: 0-0 Tight: 0-2 Gall: 0-0
Aids: Bl: 0-1 Vi: 0-0 Tstrap: 0-0
Best Rating: 51 8/02 Strf 2m110y gd-sft Hdl

Last Option
106   132

11-y-o br g Primitive Rising (USA)-Saint Motunde (Tyrant (USA))
R Tate R Tate

Placings:12/21O3231/121F2/33P4/431U6-433323P   (4557)
2002/03: 24⁴GF, 28³GF, 25³GS, 22³GS, 24²G, 26³G, 33ᴾG,

	Starts	1st	2nd	3rd	Win & Pl
Chases	7	0	1	4	10170
Career Total	30	6	6	9	71720

131	3/02	Chel	3m2f110yB Ch		GD	£26000
108	4/00	Towc	2m6f	H Ch	GD	£1610
126	5/99	Strf	3m	H Ch	G-S	£2136
129	4/99	Chel	3m2f110yH Ch		GD	£3598
112	5/98	Strf	3m4f	H Ch	GD	£5507
104	4/98	Weth	3m1f	H Ch	G-S	£1067

Total win prize-money £39920

Going: Sf: 0-0 GS: 0-2 Gd: 0-3 GF: - Fm: 0-2
Distance: 2m/2m3: 0-0 2m4-2m7: 0-1 3m+: 0-6
Track: LH: 0-6 RH: 0-1 Tight: 0-3 Gall: 0-1

Aids: Bl: 0-0 Vi: 0-0 Tstrap: 0-0
Best Rating: 132 3/03 Chel 3m2f110y good Ch

Fair chaser; leading hunter; won the Cheltenham Foxhunters in 2002, third in that event in 2003; stays marathon distances; appreciates decent ground, but does acts with cut.

Last Rebel (IRE)
83   **73**
4-y-o b g Danehill (USA)-La Curamalal (IRE) (Rainbow Quest (USA))
R T Phillips (P Schiergen 23/6) Coral & Graham Russell

Placings:60   (3177)
2002/03: 17⁶S, 16⁹G,

	Starts	1st	2nd	3rd	Win & Pl
Hurdles	2	0	0	0	0
Career Total	2	0	0	0	0

Going: Sf: 0-1 GS: 0-0 Gd: 0-0 GF: - Fm: 0-0
Distance: 2m/2m3: 0-2 2m4-2m7: 0-0 3m+: 0-0
Track: LH: 0-0 RH: 0-2 Tight: 0-1 Gall: 0-0
Aids: Bl: 0-0 Vi: 0-0 Tstrap: 0-0
Best Rating: 73 1/03 Kemp 2m good Hdl

Last Symphony
75   **66**
6-y-o b g Last Tycoon-Dancing Heights (IRE) (High Estate)
W J Reed W J Reed

Placings:FP-00F   (3598)
2002/03: 17⁰S, 17⁰S, 17⁷S,

	Starts	1st	2nd	3rd	Win & Pl
Hurdles	3	0	0	0	
Career Total	5	0	0	0	

Going: Sf: 0-3 GS: 0-0 Gd: 0-0 GF: - Fm: 0-0
Distance: 2m/2m3: 0-3 2m4-2m7: 0-0 3m+: 0-0
Track: LH: 0-0 RH: 0-3 Tight: 0-3 Gall: 0-0
Aids: Bl: 0-0 Vi: 0-0 Tstrap: 0-0
Best Rating: 66 1/03 Tntn 2m1f soft Hdl

Last Theatre (IRE)
104   **115+**
5-y-o b m King s Theatre (IRE)-Last Flair (Busted)
Jonjo O Neill (J S Bolger 25/8) J P McManus

Placings:4P3P1   (3868)
2002/03: 16⁴G, 16⁶S, 16³G, 20⁶GS, 16¹GS,

	Starts	1st	2nd	3rd	Win & Pl
Hurdles	5	1	0	1	14590
Career Total	5	1	0	1	14590
116 2/03 Donc 2m110y D(0-120)HHdl G-S £13520

Total win prize-money £13520

Going: Sf: 0-1 GS: 1-2 Gd: 0-2 GF: - Fm: 0-0
Distance: 2m/2m3: 1-4 2m4-2m7: 0-1 3m+: 0-0
Track: LH: 1-4 RH: 0-1 Tight: 0-0 Gall: 1-2
Aids: Bl: 0-0 Vi: 0-0 Tstrap: 0-0
Best Rating: 116 2/03 Donc 2m110y gd-sft Hdl

Useful middle-distance performer on the Flat in Ireland; .a little disappointing on her hurdles bow and finished distressed next time, but ran with more promise at Newbury and broke her duck at Doncaster in February.

Last Try (IRE)
89   **104**
12-y-o ch g Try My Best (USA)-Alpenwind (Tumble Wind (USA))
B S Rothwell H J Harenberg

Placings:555/60611430/42631/4412522446/313322121236 /302U42223/04356000-P544   (0786)
2002/03: 21⁸G, 20⁵GS, 23⁴G, 17⁴GF,

	Starts	1st	2nd	3rd	Win & Pl
Chases	4	0	0		312
Career Total	59	7	12	9	52148
109	10/99	Bang	2m4f110yD(0-125)HCh	SFT	£6175
106	9/99	Sedg	2m5f	E(0-115)HCh	GD	£4146
108	6/99	Uttx	2m	D(0-120)HCh	GD	£3712
97	6/98	Uttx	2m	D(0-120)HCh	GD	£4084
110	3/98	Sedg	2m110y	C Ch	G-S	£5670
101	12/96	Catt	2m	F(0-95)HHdl	GD	£2138
96	11/96	Catt	2m	E(0-100)HHdl	G-F	£1830

Total win prize-money £27758

Going: Sf: 0-0 GS: 0-1 Gd: 0-2 GF: - Fm: 0-1
Distance: 2m/2m3: 0-1 2m4-2m7: 0-2 3m+: 0-1
Track: LH: 0-4 RH: 0-0 Tight: 0-2 Gall: 0-0
Aids: Bl: 0-2 Vi: 0-0 Tstrap: 0-4
Best Rating: 113 11/98 Sedg 2m110y gd-sft Ch

Fair handicap chaser. Best suited by two/two and a half miles. Has run well at Sedgefield. Last won back in 1999. Acts on soft ground.

Latalomne (USA)
107(113h)   (128h)**165**
9-y-o ch g Zilzal (USA)-Sanctuary (Welsh Pageant)
B Ellison Alderclad Roofing/k M Everitt

Placings:13/0111/15F6-550F   (4111)
2002/03: 17⁵G, 16⁵GS, 17⁰G, 16⁴G,

	Starts	1st	2nd	3rd	Win & Pl
Hurdles	2	0	0	0	1250
Chases	2	0	0	0	1050
Career Total	14	5	0	1	38215
158	11/01	Chel	2m	B(0-145)HCh	GD	£14218
133	2/01	Sedg	2m5f	E Ch	G-S	£3103
125	1/01	Muss	2m	E Ch	G-S	£3393
124	1/01	Muss	2m	D Ch	GD	£4270
119	2/00	Catt	2m	E Hdl	GD	£3103

Total win prize-money £28091

Going: Sf: 0-0 GS: 0-1 Gd: 0-3 GF: - Fm: 0-0
Distance: 2m/2m3: 0-4 2m4-2m7: 0-0 3m+: 0-0
Track: LH: 0-3 RH: 0-1 Tight: 0-0 Gall: 0-2
Aids: Bl: 0-0 Vi: 0-0 Tstrap: 0-0
Best Rating: 165 3/03 Chel 2m good Ch

Very useful chaser; suited by two miles and a sound surface, though he does stay further; capable of top-class form on his day.

Late Harvest (NZ)
(95h)   (83h)**84**
11-y-o b g Tarrago (ITY)-Pamira (AUS) (Nassau (AUS))
A J Deakin A J Deakin

Placings:5/P05/203233FP05/65063FP0-P   (0074)
2002/03: 17⁰GF,

	Starts	1st	2nd	3rd	Win & Pl
Hurdles	1	0	0	0	
Career Total	23	0	2	4	3091

Going: Sf: 0-0 GS: 0-0 Gd: 0-0 GF: - Fm: 0-0
Distance: 2m/2m3: 0-1 2m4-2m7: 0-0 3m+: 0-0

Track: LH: 0-0 RH: 0-1 Tight: 0-0 Gall: 0-0
Aids: Bl: 0-0 Vi: 0-1 Tstrap: 0-0
Best Rating: 91 9/00 Hrfd 2m3f110y gd-sft Hdl

Modest dual-purpose handicapper over the minimum trip.

Late Night Out
101   **88**
8-y-o b g Lahib (USA)-Chain Dance (Shareef Dancer (USA))
W Jarvis J M Greetham

Placings:5   (1448)
2002/03: 16⁵G,

	Starts	1st	2nd	3rd	Win & Pl
Hurdles	1	0	0	0	0
Career Total	1	0	0	0	0

Going: Sf: 0-0 GS: 0-0 Gd: 0-0 GF: - Fm: 0-0
Distance: 2m/2m3: 0-1 2m4-2m7: 0-0 3m+: 0-0
Track: LH: 0-1 RH: 0-0 Tight: 0-0 Gall: 0-0
Aids: Bl: 0-0 Vi: 0-0 Tstrap: 0-0
Best Rating: 88 10/02 Fknm 2m good Hdl

Very useful Flat performer at seven furlongs or a mile, but did not stay on his hurdling debut.

Latensaani
101(97h)   (120+h)**97**
5-y-o b g Shaamit (IRE)-Intoxication (Great Nephew)
G M Moore (W J Haggas 15/8) Keith Nicholson

Placings:U1112P   (2114)
2002/03: 21⁰G, 20¹GF, 21¹GF, 20¹GF, 21²G, 20⁹G,

	Starts	1st	2nd	3rd	Win & Pl
Hurdles	6	3	1	0	12340
Career Total	6	3	1	0	12340
120	10/02	Weth	2m4f110yD Hdl	G-F	£3916
113	10/02	Sedg	2m5f110yE Hdl	G-F	£2884
100	9/02	Hexm	2m4f110yE Hdl	G-F	£2950

Total win prize-money £9751

Going: Sf: 0-0 GS: 0-0 Gd: 0-3 GF: - Fm: 3-3
Distance: 2m/2m3: 0-0 **2m4-2m7: 3-6** 3m+: 0-0
Track: LH: 3-6 RH: 0-0 Tight: 1-3 Gall: 0-1
Aids: Bl: 0-0 Vi: 0-0 Tstrap: 0-0
Best Rating: 120 10/02 Weth 2m4f110y gd-fm Hdl

Moderate novice hurdler, unlucky on his debut before completing a hat-trick. Second of four in a better race at Cheltenham. Acts well on fast ground.

Latimer's Place
99(113h)   (110h)**93**
7-y-o b g Teenoso (USA)-Pennethorne Place (Deep Run)
G B Balding Sir Christopher Wates

Placings:01641-50   (3315)
2002/03: 21⁵GS, 19⁰GS,

	Starts	1st	2nd	3rd	Win & Pl
Chases	2	0	0	0	0
Career Total	9	2	1	0	24987
110	3/02	Sand	2m4f110yA HHdl	G-S	£21460
103	12/01	Extr	2m1f	E Hdl	G-S	£3185

Total win prize-money £24645

Going: Sf: 0-0 GS: 0-2 Gd: 0-0 GF: - Fm: 0-0
Distance: 2m/2m3: 0-0 2m4-2m7: 0-2 3m+: 0-0
Track: LH: 0-0 RH: 0-2 Tight: 0-0 Gall: 0-0
Aids: Bl: 0-0 Vi: 0-0 Tstrap: 0-0
Best Rating: 110 3/02 Sand 2m4f110y gd-sft Hdl

Surprise winner of a novices hurdle at Exeter in December

2001, he went on to land the EBF Final at Sandown in March 2002. Held over fences. Stays two and a half miles and looks best on good to soft ground.

Lauderdale

111(98h)   (81h)**114**

7-y-o b g Sula Bula-Miss Tullulah (Hubble Bubble)
Miss Lucinda V Russell Kelso Members Lowflyers Club

Placings:206P5P/550001P60-16FFPF21253305   (4505)
2002/03: 17¹GS, 16⁶GF, 20⁴GF, 21²GF, 24²GF, 17⁶G, 17²S, 17¹HY, 16²GS, 20⁵S, 16³HY, 17³GS, 20⁴G, 17⁵G,

	Starts	1st	2nd	3rd	Win & Pl
Hurdles	1	0	0	0	0
Chases	13	2	2		13140
Career Total	29	3	3	2	16854
110 11/02 Kels	2m1f		E(0-105)HCh	HVY	£3978
99 5/02 Kels	2m1f		D Ch	G-S	£4387
81 2/02 Ayr	3m110y		E Hdl	HVY	£3080

Total win prize-money £11446

Going: Sf: 1-4 GS: 1-3 Gd: 0-3 GF: - Fm: 0-4
Distance: 2m/2m3: 2-9 2m4-2m7: 0-4 3m+: 0-1
Track: LH: 2-12 RH: 0-2 Tight: 2-7 Gall: 0-1
Aids: Bl: 0-0 Vi: 0-0 Tstrap: 0-0
Best Rating: 114 3/03   Kels   2m1f   gd-sft   Ch

Modest chaser; likes to race prominently; effective at two miles; suited by give in the ground.

Laundmower

93   **85**

7-y-o br g Perpendicular-Sound Work (Workboy)
Mrs S J Smith John Endersby

Placings:3-5   (4715)
2002/03: 20⁵GF,

	Starts	1st	2nd	3rd	Win & Pl
Hurdles	1	0	0	0	0
Career Total	2	0	0	1	246

Going: Sf: 0-0 GS: 0-0 Gd: 0-0 GF: - Fm: 0-1
Distance: 2m/2m3: 0-0 2m4-2m7: 0-1 3m+: 0-0
Track: LH: 0-1 RH: 0-0 Tight: 0-0 Gall: 0-0
Aids: Bl: 0-0 Vi: 0-0 Tstrap: 0-0
Best Rating: 96 3/02   Catt   2m   gd-sft   NHF

Plating-class maiden hurdler; effective at around two and a half miles.

Lauras Theme (IRE)

86   **69+**

5-y-o ch m Nucleon (USA)-Lovely Leitrim (IRE) (Erin s Hope)
L Lungo Mrs Ann Fortune

Placings:050P   (0498)
2002/03: 16⁰GS, 16⁵GF, 20⁰G, 16P GS,

	Starts	1st	2nd	3rd	Win & Pl
Hurdles	4	0	0	0	0
Career Total	4	0	0	0	0

Going: Sf: 0-0 GS: 0-2 Gd: 0-1 GF: - Fm: 0-1
Distance: 2m/2m3: 0-3 2m4-2m7: 0-1 3m+: 0-0
Track: LH: 0-3 RH: 0-1 Tight: 0-1 Gall: 0-0
Aids: Bl: 0-0 Vi: 0-0 Tstrap: 0-0
Best Rating: 69 5/02   Weth   2m   gd-fm   Hdl

Has shown little over hurdles to date.

Laurel Prince

105   **97**

7-y-o b g Reprimand-Laurel Queen (IRE) (Viking (USA))
Mrs A M Thorpe (B D Leavy 26/2) Don Jones

Placings:456342/0433624120/640033F06U5P55-4500PU0114   (4256)
2002/03: 16⁴GF, 16⁵G, 16⁹G, 17⁹GS, 20P S, 16U G, 16⁹S, 16¹HY, 16¹GS, 17⁴G,

	Starts	1st	2nd	3rd	Win & Pl
Hurdles	10	2	0	0	5530
Career Total	40	3	3	5	13548
97 2/03 Chep	2m110y		G(0-90)HHdl	G-S	£2478
79 1/03 Leic	2m		G(0-90)HHdl	HVY	£2681
98 1/01 Donc	2m110y		F(0-100)HHdl	GD	£2159

Total win prize-money £7319

Going: Sf: 1-3 GS: 1-2 Gd: 0-4 GF: - Fm: 0-1
Distance: 2m/2m3: 2-9 2m4-2m7: 0-1 3m+: 0-0
Track: LH: 1-7 RH: 1-3 Tight: 0-2 Gall: 0-0
Aids: Bl: 0-1 Vi: 2-2 Tstrap: 0-0
Best Rating: 98 5/01   Weth   2m   good   Hdl

Plating-class hurdler; in good form in February 2003; effective at around two miles on any ground; usually wears a visor or blinkers.

Laurier Rose (FR)

98(91h)   (61h)**108**

6-y-o b g Subotica (FR)-Light Of Realm (Realm)
Lindsay Woods (E J O Grady 15/9) Patrick Doherty

Placings:1/420215000-5352100   (4037)
2002/03: 17⁵S, 17³GF, 17⁵GY, 20¹F, 20⁰GF, 20⁰S,

	Starts	1st	2nd	3rd	Win & Pl
Hurdles	2	0	0	0	0
Chases	5	1	1	1	7549
Career Total	17	3	3	1	18218
108 8/02 Tipp	2m4f		Ch	FRM	£5714
103 9/01 Tral	2m1f		Hdl	GD	£4451
113 2/01 Thur	2m		NHF	SFT	£3895

Total win prize-money £14062

Going: Sf: 0-2 GS: 0-0 Gd: 0-0 GF: - Fm: 1-3
Distance: 2m/2m3: 0-3 2m4-2m7: 1-4 3m+: 0-0
Track: LH: 0-1 RH: 0-0 Tight: 0-0 Gall: 0-0
Aids: Bl: 0-0 Vi: 0-0 Tstrap: 0-1
Best Rating: 113 2/01   Thur   2m   soft   NHF

Lavender Lady (IRE)

98   **77**

7-y-o b/br m Lord Americo-Polarogan (Targogan)
M J Gingell (G M Moore 12/10) Andy Middleton

Placings:0/044P-34054664FP   (2349)
2002/03: 20³G, 20⁴G, 22⁰HY, 16⁵G, 20⁴GF, 16⁶G, 16⁶GS, 16⁴GS, 21F GS, 24P GS,

	Starts	1st	2nd	3rd	Win & Pl
Hurdles	9	0	0	1	669
Chases	1	0	0	0	0
Career Total	15	0	0	1	669

Going: Sf: 0-1 GS: 0-4 Gd: 0-4 GF: - Fm: 0-1
Distance: 2m/2m3: 0-4 2m4-2m7: 0-5 3m+: 0-1
Track: LH: 0-10 RH: 0-0 Tight: 0-5 Gall: 0-1
Aids: Bl: 0-0 Vi: 0-0 Tstrap: 0-0
Best Rating: 88 5/02   Hexm   2m4f110y   good   Hdl

Law Unto Himself

70   **42**

5-y-o b g Contract Law (USA)-Malacanang (Riboboy (USA))
N J Hawke The Fairway Boys

Placings:50-P00   (2588)
2002/03: 20⁰G, 17⁰GS, 19⁰GS,

	Starts	1st	2nd	3rd	Win & Pl
Hurdles	3	0	0	0	0
Career Total	5	0	0	0	0

Going: Sf: 0-0 GS: 0-2 Gd: 0-1 GF: - Fm: 0-0
Distance: 2m/2m3: 0-2 2m4-2m7: 0-1 3m+: 0-0
Track: LH: 0-1 RH: 0-2 Tight: 0-1 Gall: 0-0
Aids: Bl: 0-0 Vi: 0-0 Tstrap: 0-0
Best Rating: 77 3/02   Winc   2m   soft   NHF

Lawahik

9-y-o b g Lahib (USA)-Lightning Legacy (USA) (Super Concorde (USA))
T H Caldwell T H Caldwell

Placings:14323134/25/50/PP   (3369)
2002/03: 19P S, 16P GS,

	Starts	1st	2nd	3rd	Win & Pl
Hurdles	2	0	0	0	
Career Total	14	2	2	3	12187
119 3/99 Bang	2m1f		E Hdl	G-S	£3004
122 12/98 Hayd	2m		D Hdl	SFT	£2871

Total win prize-money £5875

Going: Sf: 0-1 GS: 0-1 Gd: 0-0 GF: - Fm: 0-0
Distance: 2m/2m3: 0-1 2m4-2m7: 0-1 3m+: 0-0
Track: LH: 0-2 RH: 0-0 Tight: 0-1 Gall: 0-0
Aids: Bl: 0-0 Vi: 0-0 Tstrap: 0-0
Best Rating: 134 11/99   Chel   2m110y   good   Hdl

Lawn

5-y-o b m Contract Law (USA)-Pastures Green (Monksfield)
P Bowen Homebred Racing

Placings:P0   (3789)
2002/03: 17P HY, 17⁰G,

	Starts	1st	2nd	3rd	Win & Pl
NH Flat	2	0	0	0	
Career Total	2	0	0	0	

Going: Sf: 0-1 GS: 0-0 Gd: 0-1 GF: - Fm: 0-0
Distance: 2m/2m3: 0-2 2m4-2m7: 0-0 3m+: 0-0
Track: LH: 0-0 RH: 0-2 Tight: 0-1 Gall: 0-0
Aids: Bl: 0-0 Vi: 0-0 Tstrap: 0-0
Best Rating: 0 2/03   Hrfd   2m1f   good   NHF

Lawz (IRE)

110   **128**

9-y-o br g Lahib (USA)-Sea Port (Averof)
C J Mann (P Hughes 10/5) A L R Morton

Placings:531542/0262402/01F0032400-03313   (4049)
2002/03: 18⁰G, 16³HY, 17³S, 18¹S, 16³HY,

	Starts	1st	2nd	3rd	Win & Pl
Hurdles	5	1	0	3	12094
Career Total	28	3	5	5	39156
128 2/03 Font	2m2f110yD(0-115)HHdl			SFT	£5216
127 10/01 Punc	2m2f		Hdl	SFT	£6677

116 1/00 Fair 2m Hdl SFT £3588
Total win prize-money £15481

Going: Sf: 1-4 GS: 0-0 Gd: 0-1 GF: - Fm: 0-0
Distance: 2m/2m3: 1-5 2m4-2m7: 0-0 3m+: 0-0
Track: LH: 1-3 RH: 0-2 Tight: 1-3 Gall: 0-0
Aids: Bl: 0-0 Vi: 0-0 Tstrap: 0-0
Best Rating: 129 2/01 Leop 2m heavy Hdl

Decent handicap hurdler; ex-Irish; suited by two to two and a quarter miles on soft ground; usually makes the running.

Lazy But Lively (IRE)
105   **125**
7-y-o b g Supreme Leader-Oriel Dream (Oats)
R F Fisher   S P Marsh

Placings:00662/53FF10115-23P   (4164)
2002/03: 22²S, 24³S, 24PGS,

	Starts	1st	2nd	3rd	Win & Pl
Hurdles	3	0	1	1	2022
Career Total	17	3	2	2	12180
118 3/02 Hexm	3m	E Hdl	HVY		£2551
118 3/02 Ayr	3m110y	D(0-115)HHdl	HVY		£3601
108 11/01 Carl	2m4f	E Hdl	HVY		£3094

Total win prize-money £9247

Going: Sf: 0-2 GS: 0-1 Gd: 0-0 GF: - Fm: 0-0
Distance: 2m/2m3: 0-0 2m4-2m7: 0-1 3m+: 0-2
Track: LH: 0-3 RH: 0-0 Tight: 0-2 Gall: 0-1
Aids: Bl: 0-0 Vi: 0-0 Tstrap: 0-0
Best Rating: 125 11/02 Kels 2m6f110y soft Hdl

Decent hurdler; effective at 3m; goes well in testing ground.

Lazzaz
105   **90**
5-y-o b g Muhtarram (USA)-Astern (USA) (Polish Navy (USA))
P W Hiatt   Phil Kelly

Placings:4-036F6   (2290)
2002/03: 16⁹G, 16³GF, 17⁶G, 17FGS, 17⁶G,

	Starts	1st	2nd	3rd	Win & Pl
Hurdles	5	0	0	1	665
Career Total	6	0	0	1	665

Going: Sf: 0-0 GS: 0-1 Gd: 0-3 GF: - Fm: 0-1
Distance: 2m/2m3: 0-5 2m4-2m7: 0-0 3m+: 0-0
Track: LH: 0-2 RH: 0-3 Tight: 0-3 Gall: 0-0
Aids: Bl: 0-0 Vi: 0-0 Tstrap: 0-0
Best Rating: 92 11/02 Tntn 2m1f gd-sft Hdl

Le Cabro D'Or
107   **132**
9-y-o b g Gildoran-Deirdre s Choice (Golden Love)
John R Upson   Mrs Sheree Tucker

Placings:12U2P3-1P   (2584)
2002/03: 26¹HY, 25PGS,

	Starts	1st	2nd	3rd	Win & Pl
Chases	2	1	0	0	7833
Career Total	8	2	2	1	16482
132 11/02 Carl	3m2f	C(0-130)HCh	HVY		£7832
132 11/01 Uttx	3m	D Ch	SFT		£4483

Total win prize-money £12317

Going: Sf: 1-1 GS: 0-1 Gd: 0-0 GF: - Fm: 0-0
Distance: 2m/2m3: 0-0 2m4-2m7: 0-0 3m+: 1-2

Track: LH: 0-0 RH: 1-2 Tight: 0-0 Gall: 0-0
Aids: Bl: 0-0 Vi: 0-0 Tstrap: 0-0
Best Rating: 132 11/02 Carl 3m2f heavy Ch

Fair chaser; has developed into an effective front-running staying chaser, but makes too many jumping errors; suited by soft ground and a test of stamina.

Le Coudray (FR)
115   **151**
9-y-o b g Phantom Breeze-Mos Lie (FR) (Tip Moss (FR))
C Roche   J P McManus

Placings:13/111112P/12/F111F4   (4135)
2002/03: 22FS, 16¹S, 20¹SH, 17¹HY, 21FYS, 21⁴G,

	Starts	1st	2nd	3rd	Win & Pl
Chases	6	3	0	0	80558
Career Total	17	10	2	1	333571
151 12/02 Leop	2m1f	Ch	HVY		£39877
151 12/02 Fair	2m4f	Ch	SH		£29907
137 11/02 Naas	2m	Ch	SFT		£6773
173 10/99 Navn	2m4f	Hdl	Y-S		£13058
169 1/99 Naas	2m4f	Hdl	HVY		£4910
11/98 Autl	2m4f110y	Hdl	HLD		£60606
10/98 Autl	2m3f110y	Hdl	SFT		£30303
10/98 Autl	2m2f	Hdl	VS		£30303
6/98 Autl	2m3f110y	Hdl	VS		£50505
11/97 Autl	2m2f	HHdl	HVY		£39282

Total win prize-money £305526

Going: Sf: 2-3 GS: 0-0 Gd: 0-1 GF: - Fm: 0-0
Distance: 2m/2m3: 2-2 2m4-2m7: 1-4 3m+: 0-0
Track: LH: 2-4 RH: 1-1 Tight: 0-0 Gall: 0-1
Aids: Bl: 0-0 Vi: 0-0 Tstrap: 1-3
Best Rating: 173 10/99 Navn 2m4f yld-sft Hdl

Ex-French gelding; formerly a high-class hurdler, runner-up to Anzum in the Stayers at Cheltenham in 1999; injured later that year and absent for three years; high-class novice chaser in 2002/3, successful in Grade Ones at Fairyhouse and Leopardstown in December before taking terrible fall at latter track when travelling best five out in February; held in the Cathcart; stays 3m, effective at shorter; promising chasing prospect.

Le Diamont (FR)
81   **80**
4-y-o ch g Broadway Flyer (USA)-Lady Diamond (FR) (Diamond Prospect (USA))
C P Morlock   Pell-Mell Partners

Placings:500   (4635)
2002/03: 16⁵GS, 16⁹G, 19⁰GF,

	Starts	1st	2nd	3rd	Win & Pl
NH Flat	2	0	0	0	0
Hurdles	1	0	0	0	0
Career Total	3	0	0	0	0

Going: Sf: 0-0 GS: 0-1 Gd: 0-1 GF: - Fm: 0-1
Distance: 2m/2m3: 0-3 2m4-2m7: 0-0 3m+: 0-0
Track: LH: 0-1 RH: 0-2 Tight: 0-1 Gall: 0-0
Aids: Bl: 0-0 Vi: 0-0 Tstrap: 0-0
Best Rating: 82 1/03 Kemp 2m gd-sft NHF

Le Duc (FR)
114   **132**
4-y-o ch g Villez (USA)-Beberova (FR) (Synefos (USA))
P F Nicholls   J-P Pelat 31/5) Mrs J Stewart

Placings:2224F461   (4460)
2002/03: 15²S, 17²G, 16²GS, 16⁴GS, 16FHY, 17⁴GS, 17⁶G, 16¹G,

	Starts	1st	2nd	3rd	Win & Pl
Hurdles	8	1	3	0	78987
Career Total	8	1	3	0	78987
132 4/03 Aint	2m110y	A Hdl	GD		£63800

Total win prize-money £63800

Going: Sf: 0-2 GS: 0-3 Gd: 1-3 GF: - Fm: 0-0
Distance: 2m/2m3: 1-7 2m4-2m7: 0-0 3m+: 0-0
Track: LH: 1-5 RH: 0-2 Tight: 1-1 Gall: 0-3
Aids: Bl: 0-2 Vi: 0-0 Tstrap: 0-0
Best Rating: 132 4/03 Aint 2m110y good Hdl

Very useful juvenile hurdler; ex-French; surprise winner of Grade Two race at Aintree in April; best over 2m and acts on ground good or softer; sometimes blinkered;

Le Grand Gousier (USA)
9-y-o ch g Strawberry Road (AUS)-Sandy Baby (USA) (Al Hattab (USA))
R J Price   R J Price

Placings:142F150/P00563160330/00P6400250P/PP   (0628)
2002/03: 24PG, 22PGF,

	Starts	1st	2nd	3rd	Win & Pl
Hurdles	1	0	0	0	0
Chases	1	0	0	0	0
Career Total	32	3	2	3	9610
82 7/98 Bang	2m1f	G(0-95)HHdl	GD		£2326
80 10/97 Winc	2m	F Hdl	FRM		£2174
80 8/97 MRas	2m1f110yD Hdl		G-F		£2938

Total win prize-money £7439

Going: Sf: 0-0 GS: 0-0 Gd: 0-1 GF: - Fm: 0-0
Distance: 2m/2m3: 0-0 2m4-2m7: 0-1 3m+: 0-1
Track: LH: 0-1 RH: 0-1 Tight: 0-1 Gall: 0-1
Aids: Bl: 0-0 Vi: 0-2 Tstrap: 0-0
Best Rating: 82 9/98 Extr 2m1f good Hdl

Le Grand Rocher
85f   **94f**
6-y-o ch g Factual (USA)-Honey Bridge (Crepello)
D J Caro   The Swinging Richards

Placings:2   (0517)
2002/03: 16²S,

	Starts	1st	2nd	3rd	Win & Pl
NH Flat	1	0	1	0	434
Career Total	1	0	1	0	434

Going: Sf: 0-1 GS: 0-0 Gd: 0-0 GF: - Fm: 0-0
Distance: 2m/2m3: 0-1 2m4-2m7: 0-0 3m+: 0-0
Track: LH: 0-1 RH: 0-0 Tight: 0-0 Gall: 0-0
Aids: Bl: 0-0 Vi: 0-0 Tstrap: 0-0
Best Rating: 94 6/02 Worc 2m soft NHF

Le Grand Vizier
4-y-o br g Doyoun-Just Visiting (Superlative)
J R Jenkins   H R Moszkowicz

Placings:P   (2317)
2002/03: 16PHY,

	Starts	1st	2nd	3rd	Win & Pl
Hurdles	1	0	0	0	
Career Total	1	0	0	0	

Going: Sf: 0-1 GS: 0-0 Gd: 0-0 GF: - Fm: 0-0
Distance: 2m/2m3: 0-1 2m4-2m7: 0-0 3m+: 0-0
Track: LH: 0-0 RH: 0-1 Tight: 0-0 Gall: 0-0
Aids: Bl: 0-0 Vi: 0-0 Tstrap: 0-0
Best Rating: 0   12/02 Leic 2m   heavy Hdl

Le Guvnor

44   **23**

8-y-o br g Le Moss-High Heels (IRE) (Supreme Leader)
G J Smith Mrs A D Aldred

Placings:PPP0PP   (4104)
2002/03: 21PF, 20PGS, 20PG, 16OHY, 21PGS, 27PS,

	Starts	1st	2nd	3rd	Win & Pl
Hurdles	6	0	0	0	
Career Total	6	0	0	0	

Going: Sf: 0-2 GS: 0-2 Gd: 0-1 GF: - Fm: 0-1
Distance: 2m/2m3: 0-1 2m4-2m7: 0-4 3m+: 0-1
Track: LH: 0-4 RH: 0-2 Tight: 0-3 Gall: 0-0
Aids: Bl: 0-0 Vi: 0-0 Tstrap: 0-0
Best Rating: 23   2/03 Leic 2m   heavy Hdl

Le Millenaire (FR)

60f   **67f**

4-y-o b/br g Ragmar (FR)-Ezaia (FR) (Iron Duke (FR))
S H Shirley-Beavan S H Shirley-Beavan

Placings:0   (3775)
2002/03: 16OGS,

	Starts	1st	2nd	3rd	Win & Pl
NH Flat	1	0	0	0	
Career Total	1	0	0	0	

Going: Sf: 0-0 GS: 0-1 Gd: 0-0 GF: - Fm: 0-0
Distance: 2m/2m3: 0-1 2m4-2m7: 0-0 3m+: 0-0
Track: LH: 0-1 RH: 0-0 Tight: 0-0 Gall: 0-0
Aids: Bl: 0-0 Vi: 0-0 Tstrap: 0-0
Best Rating: 67   2/03 Ayr 2m   gd-sft NHF

Le Pero (FR)

5-y-o b g Perrault-Nuit D Ecajeul (FR) (Matahawk)
G Macaire Mme M Bryant

Placings:3261   (3623)
2002/03: 16³HY, 17²HO, 18⁶VS, 19¹VS,

	Starts	1st	2nd	3rd	Win & Pl
NH Flat	1	0	0	1	380
Hurdles	3	1	1	0	20260
Career Total	4	1	1	1	20640
	4/03 Autl	2m3f110y Hdl		VS	£12468
			Total win prize-money £12468		

Going: Sf: 0-1 GS: 0-0 Gd: 0-0 GF: - Fm: 0-0
Distance: 2m/2m3: 0-3 2m4-2m7: 1-1 3m+: 0-0
Track: LH: 1-1 RH: 0-1 Tight: 0-0 Gall: 0-0
Aids: Bl: 0-0 Vi: 0-0 Tstrap: 0-0
Best Rating: 108   2/03 Sand 2m110y   heavy NHF

Dam a winning stayer; good third on his debut in a Sandown
bumper. progressed to win a soft-ground hurdle at Aintree.

Le Roi Miguel (FR)

122(100h)   (121h)**159+**

5-y-o b g Point Of No Return (FR)-Loumir (USA) (Bob s
Dusty (USA))

P F Nicholls Mrs J Stewart

Placings:6212-22F1   (4477)
2002/03: 19²S, 16²S, 16FG, 16¹G,

	Starts	1st	2nd	3rd	Win & Pl
Chases	4	1	2	0	80420
Career Total	8	2	4	0	97320
159 4/03 Aint	2m	A Ch		GD	£67000
116 11/01 Newb	2m110y	C Hdl		GD	£5447
			Total win prize-money £72447		

Going: Sf: 0-2 GS: 0-0 Gd: 1-2 GF: - Fm: 0-0
Distance: 2m/2m3: 1-3 2m4-2m7: 0-1 3m+: 0-0
Track: LH: 1-3 RH: 0-1 Tight: 1-1 Gall: 0-1
Aids: Bl: 0-0 Vi: 0-0 Tstrap: 0-0
Best Rating: 159 4/03 Aint 2m   good Ch

Top-class ex-French novice chaser; runner-up first two
starts over fences in good company including 1 1/2l 2nd to
Impek in Grade Two event at Sandown in December 2002;
brilliant winner of Grade One novices chase at Aintree subsequently; suited by 2m; acts on good and soft ground;
races enthusiastically and capable of further improvement.

Le Sauvage (IRE)

98   **85**

8-y-o b g Tirol-Cistus (Sun Prince)
D W Barker The Ebor Partnership

Placings:00/5534/1126/0P0-0P23540   (4795)
2002/03: 24⁰G, 21PS, 20²HY, 20³S, 19⁵S, 20⁴G, 21⁰GF,

	Starts	1st	2nd	3rd	Win & Pl
Hurdles	7	0	1	1	1055
Career Total	20	2	2	2	7031
105 10/00 Carl	2m4f110yE(0-105)HHdl		SFT	£2497	
102 10/00 Carl	2m4f110yF(0-100)HHdl		G-S	£2289	
		Total win prize-money £4787			

Going: Sf: 0-4 GS: 0-0 Gd: 0-2 GF: - Fm: 0-1
Distance: 2m/2m3: 0-1 2m4-2m7: 0-5 3m+: 0-1
Track: LH: 0-7 RH: 0-0 Tight: 0-3 Gall: 0-3
Aids: Bl: 0-0 Vi: 0-0 Tstrap: 0-0
Best Rating: 110 11/00 Carl 2m4f110y   heavy Hdl

Moderate hurdler; best over 2m 4f on soft ground.

Le Sauvignon (FR)

116   **145**

9-y-o b g Morespeed-Tarde (FR) (Kashtan (FR))
P F Nicholls D J & F A Jackson

Placings:11/61/21520/11111/11-12   (2683)
2002/03: 25¹S, 24²S,

	Starts	1st	2nd	3rd	Win & Pl
Chases	2	1	1	0	16285
Career Total	18	12	3	0	478317
135 12/02 Folk	3m1f	D Ch	SFT	£5285	
165 6/01 Autl	3m1f110y Hdl		VS	£77595	
141 5/01 Autl	2m5f110y Hdl		SFT	£38797	
151 4/01 Autl	2m4f110y Hdl		HVY	£38797	
11/00 Autl	3m	Hdl	HVY	£67243	
9/00 Autl	2m3f110y Hdl		VS	£28818	
6/00 Autl	2m3f110y Hdl		VS	£76849	
5/00 Autl	2m5f110y Hdl		VS	£38425	
6/99 Autl	2m2f	HHdl		VS	£29064
7/98 Autl	2m3f110y Hdl		VS	£22020	
12/97 Engh	2m1f110y Hdl		HLD	£12346	
11/97 Engh	2m110y Hdl		VS	£11223	
		Total win prize-money £444644			

Going: Sf: 1-2 GS: 0-0 Gd: 0-0 GF: - Fm: 0-0
Distance: 2m/2m3: 0-0 2m4-2m7: 0-0 3m+: 1-2
Track: LH: 0-0 RH: 1-2 Tight: 1-1 Gall: 0-0
Aids: Bl: 0-0 Vi: 0-0 Tstrap: 0-0

Best Rating: 165 6/01 Autl   3m1f110y v soft Hdl

An oustanding hurdler in France, he was sidelined for 18
months with leg problems. Easy winner at Folkestone on his
chase debut and his first start for Nicholls, but tragically collapsed and died after finishing second at Kempton on
Boxing Day. (DEAD)

Le Ski D'Or

80   **65**

7-y-o b g Petoski-Page Of Gold (Goldhill)
D R Gandolfo A W F Clapperton

Placings:60-0   (1873)
2002/03: 20⁰GS,

	Starts	1st	2nd	3rd	Win & Pl
Hurdles	1	0	0	0	
Career Total	3	0	0	0	0

Going: Sf: 0-0 GS: 0-1 Gd: 0-0 GF: - Fm: 0-0
Distance: 2m/2m3: 0-0 2m4-2m7: 0-1 3m+: 0-0
Track: LH: 0-0 RH: 0-0 Tight: 0-1 Gall: 0-0
Aids: Bl: 0-0 Vi: 0-0 Tstrap: 0-0
Best Rating: 75 10/01 Bang 2m1f   soft NHF

Lead Story (IRE)

10-y-o br g Lead On Time (USA)-Mashmoon (USA)
(Habitat)
G Chambers Mrs M Trueman

Placings:P000/P/21P50/6106-FP   (4467)
2002/03: 25FS, 24PF,

	Starts	1st	2nd	3rd	Win & Pl
Chases	2	0	0	0	
Career Total	16	2	1	0	4811
100 5/01 NAbb	3m2f110yH Ch		G-F	£2177	
112 6/00 NAbb	3m2f110yH Ch		GD	£2177	
		Total win prize-money £4354			

Going: Sf: 0-1 GS: 0-0 Gd: 0-0 GF: - Fm: 0-1
Distance: 2m/2m3: 0-0 2m4-2m7: 0-0 3m+: 0-2
Track: LH: 0-0 RH: 0-2 Tight: 0-1 Gall: 0-0
Aids: Bl: 0-0 Vi: 0-0 Tstrap: 0-0
Best Rating: 112 6/00 NAbb 3m2f110y   good Ch

Lead Vocalist (IRE)

14-y-o ch g Orchestra-Eternal Youth (Continuation)
Miss Lucy Brack Miss Lucy Brack

Placings:1200/13350100/3143311/3/062460/2/P-P (0033)
2002/03: 25PGF,

	Starts	1st	2nd	3rd	Win & Pl
Chases	1	0	0	0	
Career Total	29	6	3	6	24459
119 4/96 Chep	2m4f110yD(0-125)HHdl		G-F	£3090	
116 3/96 Sand	2m6f	D(0-125)HHdl		G-S	£3629
108 10/95 Worc	2m4f	B(0-140)HHdl		GD	£4987
102 2/95 Fknm	2m4f	D Hdl		G-S	£2650
112 11/94 Leic	2m	Hdl	SFT	£2105	
109 12/93 Hntg	2m110y	NHF		G-S	£1951
		Total win prize-money £18415			

Going: Sf: 0-0 GS: 0-0 Gd: 0-0 GF: - Fm: 0-1
Distance: 2m/2m3: 0-0 2m4-2m7: 0-0 3m+: 0-1
Track: LH: 0-1 RH: 0-0 Tight: 0-0 Gall: 0-1
Aids: Bl: 0-0 Vi: 0-0 Tstrap: 0-0
Best Rating: 124 5/96 Worc 3m   gd-fm Hdl

Leader Supreme (IRE)

83(90h)   (36h)60

8-y-o b m Supreme Leader-Country Daisy Vii (Damsire Unregistered)
J R Jenkins Humphrey Solomons

Placings:0/F6-00P034F4   (4213)
2002/03: 16⁰HY, 21⁰GS, 25ᴾHY, 20⁰GS, 20³GS, 27⁴G, 22⁴G,

	Starts	1st	2nd	3rd	Win & Pl
Hurdles	5	0	0	0	0
Chases	3	0	0	1	1142
Career Total	11	0	0	1	1142

Going: Sf: 0-3 GS: 0-3 Gd: 0-2 GF: - Fm: 0-0
Distance: 2m/2m3: 0-1 2m4-2m7: 0-4 3m+: 0-3
Track: LH: 0-3 RH: 0-2 Tight: 0-4 Gall: 0-1
Aids: Bl: 0-0 Vi: 0-0 Tstrap: 0-0
Best Rating: 92 4/01 Kemp 2m   good NHF

Leagues (NZ)

105(101h)   (96h)103d

8-y-o b g Kenfair (NZ)-Hidden Depths (NZ) (Beaufort Sea (USA))
Mrs L C Taylor Mrs W Morrell

Placings:5000-P4P60   (4327)
2002/03: 16ᴾG, 16⁴G, 16ᴾS, 16⁶G, 18⁰G,

	Starts	1st	2nd	3rd	Win & Pl
Chases	5	0	0	0	365
Career Total	9	0	0	0	365

Going: Sf: 0-1 GS: 0-0 Gd: 0-4 GF: - Fm: 0-0
Distance: 2m/2m3: 0-5 2m4-2m7: 0-0 3m+: 0-0
Track: LH: 0-3 RH: 0-2 Tight: 0-0 Gall: 0-3
Aids: Bl: 0-0 Vi: 0-0 Tstrap: 0-0
Best Rating: 103 12/02 Donc 2m110y   good   Ch

Big sort, very limited ability over hurdles and fences so far.

Learn The Lingo

87f

7-y-o b g Teenoso (USA)-Charlotte Gray (Rolfe (USA))
Mrs H Dalton David M Hughes

Placings:40-P   (1095)
2002/03: 17ᴾGF,

	Starts	1st	2nd	3rd	Win & Pl
NH Flat	1	0	0	0	0
Career Total	3	0	0	0	0

Going: Sf: 0-0 GS: 0-0 Gd: 0-0 GF: - Fm: 0-1
Distance: 2m/2m3: 0-1 2m4-2m7: 0-0 3m+: 0-0
Track: LH: 0-1 RH: 0-0 Tight: 0-1 Gall: 0-0
Aids: Bl: 0-0 Vi: 0-0 Tstrap: 0-0
Best Rating: 87 12/01 Ludl 2m   good   NHF

Showed ability on first start in bumper company but disappointing since.

Learned Lad (FR)

5-y-o ch g Royal Academy (USA)-Blushing Storm (USA) (Blushing Groom (FR))
Jamie Poulton J Wotherspoon

Placings:P   (1723)

2002/03: 16ᴾGS,

	Starts	1st	2nd	3rd	Win & Pl
Hurdles	1	0	0	0	
Career Total	1	0	0	0	

Going: Sf: 0-0 GS: 0-1 Gd: 0-0 GF: - Fm: 0-0
Distance: 2m/2m3: 0-1 2m4-2m7: 0-0 3m+: 0-0
Track: LH: 0-0 RH: 0-1 Tight: 0-0 Gall: 0-0
Aids: Bl: 0-0 Vi: 0-0 Tstrap: 0-0
Best Rating: 0   11/02 Asct 2m110y   gd-sft Hdl

Leatherback (IRE)

98   102

5-y-o b g Turtle Island (IRE)-Phyllode (Pharly (FR))
N A Callaghan M Tabor

Placings:3361-000   (2723)
2002/03: 16⁰GS, 16⁹GS, 16⁸S,

	Starts	1st	2nd	3rd	Win & Pl
Hurdles	3	0	0	0	
Career Total	7	1	0	2	4263
109 3/02 Fknm 2m		E Hdl		GD	£2618
			Total win prize-money £2618		

Going: Sf: 0-1 GS: 0-2 Gd: 0-0 GF: - Fm: 0-0
Distance: 2m/2m3: 0-3 2m4-2m7: 0-0 3m+: 0-0
Track: LH: 0-0 RH: 0-3 Tight: 0-0 Gall: 0-2
Aids: Bl: 0-0 Vi: 0-0 Tstrap: 0-0
Best Rating: 109 3/02 Fknm 2m   good   Hdl

Moderate hurdler; preferred soft ground on the Flat but has won on good ground over hurdles. Mainly campaigned at around two miles.

Leckampton

77   28

7-y-o b m Bedford (USA)-I m Unforgettable (Dublin Taxi)
S E H Sherwood I W Thompson

Placings:0-6   (4222)
2002/03: 17⁶GF,

	Starts	1st	2nd	3rd	Win & Pl
Hurdles	1	0	0	0	0
Career Total	2	0	0	0	0

Going: Sf: 0-0 GS: 0-0 Gd: 0-0 GF: - Fm: 0-1
Distance: 2m/2m3: 0-1 2m4-2m7: 0-0 3m+: 0-0
Track: LH: 0-0 RH: 0-1 Tight: 0-0 Gall: 0-0
Aids: Bl: 0-0 Vi: 0-0 Tstrap: 0-0
Best Rating: 74 8/01 Worc 2m   gd-fm NHF

Lee's Rosie (IRE)

8-y-o b m Zaffaran (USA)-Muse Of Fire (Laurence O)
Miss Bianca Dunk (N A Twiston-Davies 3/5) Miss Bianca Dunk

Placings:05/0PP-01   (4592)
2002/03: 20⁰G, 25¹G,

	Starts	1st	2nd	3rd	Win & Pl
Hurdles	1	0	0	0	0
Chases	1	1	0	0	1456
Career Total	7	1	0	0	1456
73 4/03 Hexm 3m1f		H Ch		GD	£1456
			Total win prize-money £1456		

Going: Sf: 0-0 GS: 0-0 Gd: 1-2 GF: - Fm: 0-0
Distance: 2m/2m3: 0-0 2m4-2m7: 0-0 3m+: 1-1
Track: LH: 1-2 RH: 0-0 Tight: 0-1 Gall: 0-1

Aids: Bl: 0-0 Vi: 0-0 Tstrap: 0-0
Best Rating: 79 1/01 Ludl 2m   soft   NHF

Fair hunter chaser; stays beyond three miles and acts on good ground.

Leefen Queen (IRE)

89f   91f

6-y-o b m King s Ride-Splendid Run (Deep Run)
N J Henderson Michael J Lee

Placings:36   (4672)
2002/03: 16³GF, 16⁶G,

	Starts	1st	2nd	3rd	Win & Pl
NH Flat	2	0	0	1	367
Career Total	2	0	0	1	367

Going: Sf: 0-0 GS: 0-0 Gd: 0-1 GF: - Fm: 0-1
Distance: 2m/2m3: 0-2 2m4-2m7: 0-0 3m+: 0-0
Track: LH: 0-1 RH: 0-1 Tight: 0-1 Gall: 0-0
Aids: Bl: 0-0 Vi: 0-0 Tstrap: 0-0
Best Rating: 91 3/03 Ludl 2m   gd-fm NHF

Half-sister to Sigma Run; close third in a bumper on debut but well beaten subsequently.

Leet Brig

12-y-o b g Pitpan-Gilzie Bank (New Brig)
Miss Charlotte Mooney Miss Charlotte Mooney

Placings:664PP/P   (4506)
2002/03: 25ᴾG,

	Starts	1st	2nd	3rd	Win & Pl
Chases	1	0	0	0	0
Career Total	6	0	0	0	198

Going: Sf: 0-0 GS: 0-0 Gd: 0-1 GF: - Fm: 0-0
Distance: 2m/2m3: 0-0 2m4-2m7: 0-0 3m+: 0-1
Track: LH: 0-1 RH: 0-0 Tight: 0-1 Gall: 0-0
Aids: Bl: 0-0 Vi: 0-0 Tstrap: 0-0
Best Rating: 79 1/98 Kels 2m2f   heavy   Hdl

Left Bank (IRE)

102(100h)   (77h)71

7-y-o ch g Over The River (FR)-My Friend Fashion (Laurence O)
Mrs M Reveley C C Buckley

Placings:00/400260633-3P164U30130   (4614)
2002/03: 20³GF, 21ᴾS, 23¹GF, 20⁶G, 24⁴GS, 21ᵁS, 25³G, 24⁰G, 25¹GF, 24³G, 21⁰G,

	Starts	1st	2nd	3rd	Win & Pl
Chases	11	2	0	3	10217
Career Total	22	2	1	5	11789
84 3/03 Weth 3m1f		E(0-105)HCh		G-F	£4173
80 10/02 Weth 2m7f110y		E(0-105)HCh		G-F	£3786
			Total win prize-money £7959		

Going: Sf: 0-2 GS: 0-1 Gd: 0-5 GF: - Fm: 2-3
Distance: 2m/2m3: 0-0 2m4-2m7: 0-5 3m+: 2-6
Track: LH: 1-8 RH: 0-2 Tight: 0-3 Gall: 0-3
Aids: Bl: 0-2 Vi: 0-1 Tstrap: 0-0
Best Rating: 84 3/03 Weth 3m1f   gd-fm Ch

Modest chaser, stays three miles, wears headgear; suited by a sound surface and had conditions in his favour when a fortuitous winner at Wetherby in March.

Leg Beforum (IRE)

9-y-o b g Distinctly North (USA)-Paulines Girl (Hello Gorgeous (USA))
Mrs Sarah L Dent John Mackley

Placings:04/PU0P/U (0402)
2002/03: 20^UGF,

	Starts	1st	2nd	3rd	Win & Pl
Chases	1	0	0	0	
Career Total	7	0	0	0	0

Going: Sf: 0-0 GS: 0-0 Gd: 0-0 GF: - Fm: 0-1
Distance: 2m/2m3: 0-0 2m4-2m7: 0-1 3m+: 0-0
Track: LH: 0-0 RH: 0-1 Tight: 0-0 Gall: 0-0
Aids: Bl: 0-0 Vi: 0-0 Tstrap: 0-0
Best Rating: 80 12/98 Muss 2m4f gd-fm Hdl

Legal Lunch (USA)
103 104

8-y-o b g Alleged (USA)-Dinner Surprise (USA) (Lyphard (USA))
R M Stronge Berkshire Commercial Components Ltd

Placings:02120/124-05P0 (4441)
2002/03: 23⁰GS, 24⁵GS, 22^FS, 20⁰G,

	Starts	1st	2nd	3rd	Win & Pl
Hurdles	4	0	0	0	0
Career Total	12	2	3	0	22617
132	10/01	Sthl	2m4f110yC(0-130)HHdl	GD	£6890
126	2/01	Font	2m6f110yE Hdl	G-S	£3167

Total win prize-money £10058

Going: Sf: 0-1 GS: 0-2 Gd: 0-1 GF: - Fm: 0-0
Distance: 2m/2m3: 0-0 2m4-2m7: 0-2 3m+: 0-2
Track: LH: 0-3 RH: 0-1 Tight: 0-1 Gall: 0-1
Aids: Bl: 0-0 Vi: 0-0 Tstrap: 0-0
Best Rating: 132 10/01 Sthl 2m4f110y good Hdl

Modest dual-purpose performer; travels well in his races, but does not always find too much; stays two and a half miles and acts on a sound surface; has worn a visor.

Legal Perk (IRE)

9-y-o b m Executive Perk-Running Valley (Buckskin (FR))
J L Needham J L Needham

Placings:0/06-P (1908)
2002/03: 16^PGS,

	Starts	1st	2nd	3rd	Win & Pl
Hurdles	1	0	0	0	
Career Total	4	0	0	0	0

Going: Sf: 0-0 GS: 0-1 Gd: 0-0 GF: - Fm: 0-0
Distance: 2m/2m3: 0-0 2m4-2m7: 0-0 3m+: 0-0
Track: LH: 0-1 RH: 0-0 Tight: 0-0 Gall: 0-0
Aids: Bl: 0-0 Vi: 0-0 Tstrap: 0-0
Best Rating: 51 2/01 Ludl 2m gd-sft Hdl

Legal Tender

6-y-o b g Contract Law (USA)-Slip A Coin (Slip Anchor)
Mrs D A Hamer Tycroes Five Star Racing

Placings:0/P (0214)
2002/03: 19^PG,

	Starts	1st	2nd	3rd	Win & Pl
Hurdles	1	0	0	0	

Leggies Legacy
106 91d

12-y-o b g Jupiter Island-Hit The Line (Saulingo)
J Gallagher (L Wells 6/5) A Russell & P B Davis Insurance

Placings:0/P/U143/205-000130 (3922)
2002/03: 22⁰GF, 21⁰G, 22⁰HY, 21¹S, 21³HY, 22⁰S,

	Starts	1st	2nd	3rd	Win & Pl
Hurdles	6	1	0	1	6575
Career Total	15	2	1	2	11177
91	1/03	Plum	2m5f	D(0-125)HHdl	SFT	£5512
86	3/01	Plum	2m5f	E Hdl	HVY	£2618

Total win prize-money £8130

Going: Sf: 1-4 GS: 0-0 Gd: 0-1 GF: - Fm: 0-1
Distance: 2m/2m3: 0-0 2m4-2m7: 1-6 3m+: 0-0
Track: LH: 1-5 RH: 0-1 Tight: 1-5 Gall: 0-1
Aids: Bl: 0-0 Vi: 0-0 Tstrap: 0-0
Best Rating: 94 2/02 Plum 2m5f heavy Hdl

Moderate hurdler; looks best suited by around two miles five furlongs; acts well on soft and heavy ground.

Legolas
96f 76f

4-y-o b c Primitive Rising (USA)-Teddy s Bow (IRE) (Archway (IRE))
M W Easterby Lord Daresbury

Placings:44 (3817)
2002/03: 17⁴HY, 16⁴G,

	Starts	1st	2nd	3rd	Win & Pl
NH Flat	2	0	0	0	0
Career Total	2	0	0	0	0

Going: Sf: 0-1 GS: 0-0 Gd: 0-1 GF: - Fm: 0-0
Distance: 2m/2m3: 0-2 2m4-2m7: 0-0 3m+: 0-0
Track: LH: 0-2 RH: 0-0 Tight: 0-2 Gall: 0-0
Aids: Bl: 0-0 Vi: 0-0 Tstrap: 0-0
Best Rating: 76 2/03 Catt 2m good NHF

Has shown limited ability in bumpers.

Leinster (IRE)
108 138

6-y-o br g Supreme Leader-Jennycomequick (Furry Glen)
D T Hughes Cathal M Ryan

Placings:1-24421 (4462)
2002/03: 18²SH, 16⁴HY, 16⁴YS, 16²HY, 20¹G,

	Starts	1st	2nd	3rd	Win & Pl
Hurdles	5	1	2	2	32706
Career Total	6	2	2	2	39691
138	4/03	Aint	2m4f	A Hdl	GD	£29000
118	4/02	Punc	2m	NHF	GD	£6984

Total win prize-money £35985

Going: Sf: 0-2 GS: 0-0 Gd: 1-1 GF: - Fm: 0-0
Distance: 2m/2m3: 0-4 2m4-2m7: 1-1 3m+: 0-0
Track: LH: 1-3 RH: 0-2 Tight: 1-1 Gall: 0-1
Aids: Bl: 0-0 Vi: 0-0 Tstrap: 0-0
Best Rating: 138 4/03 Aint 2m4f good Hdl

Very useful Irish-trained novice hurdler; smart bumper winner; made the most of a good opportunity in Grade Two race at Aintree in April; stays two miles four; best on good ground, but handles softer.

Leith Hill Star
101 85

7-y-o ch m Comme L Etoile-Sunnyday (Sunley Builds)
R Rowe Mrs N F Maltby

Placings:40/0404-4F6542 (4700)
2002/03: 16⁴HY, 22^FS, 21⁵S, 25⁵HY, 25⁴GF, 21²GF,

	Starts	1st	2nd	3rd	Win & Pl
Hurdles	5	0	1	0	1078
Chases	1	0	0	0	0
Career Total	12	0	1	0	1078

Going: Sf: 0-4 GS: 0-0 Gd: 0-0 GF: - Fm: 0-2
Distance: 2m/2m3: 0-1 2m4-2m7: 0-2 3m+: 0-2
Track: LH: 0-3 RH: 0-0 Tight: 0-3 Gall: 0-0
Aids: Bl: 0-0 Vi: 0-0 Tstrap: 0-0
Best Rating: 91 1/01 Folk 2m1f110y heavy NHF

Plating-class hurdler; stays three miles one; seems to act on any ground.

Leith Lynx
96 48

6-y-o ch m Minster Son-Pinkie Hill (Le Coq D Or)
P Monteith Mrs Maud Monteith

Placings:0/00P-00P5P (1015)
2002/03: 18⁰G, 16⁰G, 21^PGF, 21⁵G, 24^PG,

	Starts	1st	2nd	3rd	Win & Pl
Hurdles	5	0	0	0	0
Career Total	9	0	0	0	0

Going: Sf: 0-0 GS: 0-0 Gd: 0-4 GF: - Fm: 0-1
Distance: 2m/2m3: 0-2 2m4-2m7: 0-2 3m+: 0-1
Track: LH: 0-4 RH: 0-1 Tight: 0-3 Gall: 0-0
Aids: Bl: 0-0 Vi: 0-0 Tstrap: 0-0
Best Rating: 82 4/01 Ayr 2m gd-fm NHF

Leixlip (IRE)
89f 87f

5-y-o b g Jurado (USA)-The Parson s Filly (IRE) (The Parson)
Mrs K B Mactaggart Mrs Jean Sole

Placings:6 (2560)
2002/03: 16⁶GF,

	Starts	1st	2nd	3rd	Win & Pl
NH Flat	1	0	0	0	0
Career Total	1	0	0	0	0

Going: Sf: 0-0 GS: 0-0 Gd: 0-0 GF: - Fm: 0-1
Distance: 2m/2m3: 0-1 2m4-2m7: 0-0 3m+: 0-0
Track: LH: 0-0 RH: 0-1 Tight: 0-1 Gall: 0-0
Aids: Bl: 0-0 Vi: 0-0 Tstrap: 0-0
Best Rating: 87 12/02 Muss 2m gd-fm NHF

Lemon Bridge (IRE)
99 98

8-y-o b g Shalford (IRE)-Sharply (Sharpman)
Ian Williams Lemon Connections

Placings:3/260/15   **(1131)**
2002/03: 19¹GF, 19⁵GF,

	Starts	1st	2nd	3rd	Win & Pl
Hurdles	2	1	0	0	3094
Career Total	6	1	1	1	4260
98 6/02 Strf	2m3f	E(0-110)HHdl		G-F	£3094

Total win prize-money £3094

Going:	Sf: 0-0 GS: 0-0 Gd: 0-0 GF: - Fm: 1-2
Distance:	2m/2m3: 1-1 2m4-2m7: 0-1 3m+: 0-0
Track:	LH: 1-1 RH: 0-1 Tight: 1-2 Gall: 0-0
Aids:	Bl: 1-1 Vi: 0-0 Tstrap: 1-1
Best Rating:	107 2/00 Folk 2m1f110y gd-sft Hdl

Blinkered for the first time when winning 19 furlong amateur riders handicap hurdle at Stratford June 2002.

Leopard Spot (IRE)
103   106
5-y-o b g Sadler s Wells (USA)-Savoureuse Lady (Caerleon (USA))
Jonjo O Neill Russell McAllister

Placings:0563-P2   **(1635)**
2002/03: 20⁵S, 20²S,

	Starts	1st	2nd	3rd	Win & Pl
Hurdles	2	0	1	0	916
Career Total	6	0	1	1	1664

Going:	Sf: 0-2 GS: 0-0 Gd: 0-0 GF: - Fm: 0-0
Distance:	2m/2m3: 0-0 2m4-2m7: 0-2 3m+: 0-0
Track:	LH: 0-1 RH: 0-1 Tight: 0-1 Gall: 0-0
Aids:	Bl: 0-0 Vi: 0-0 Tstrap: 0-0
Best Rating:	106 10/02 Carl 2m4f soft Hdl

Some form in modest events over hurdles; acts on soft.

Leophin Dancer (USA)
96   76
5-y-o b g Green Dancer (USA)-Happy Gal (FR) (Habitat)
P W Hiatt Clive Roberts

Placings:P60   **(2941)**
2002/03: 17ᴾGS, 16⁶G, 16⁹S,

	Starts	1st	2nd	3rd	Win & Pl
Hurdles	3	0	0	0	0
Career Total	3	0	0	0	0

Going:	Sf: 0-1 GS: 0-1 Gd: 0-1 GF: - Fm: 0-0
Distance:	2m/2m3: 0-3 2m4-2m7: 0-0 3m+: 0-0
Track:	LH: 0-0 RH: 0-3 Tight: 0-1 Gall: 0-0
Aids:	Bl: 0-0 Vi: 0-0 Tstrap: 0-1
Best Rating:	76 12/02 Ludl 2m good Hdl

Lescer's Lad
79f   96f
6-y-o b g Perpendicular-Grange Gracie (Oats)
J Hetherton (B Ellison 16/5) L Turnbull

Placings:0-03   **(4594)**
2002/03: 16⁰GS, 16³G,

	Starts	1st	2nd	3rd	Win & Pl
NH Flat	2	0	0	1	272
Career Total	3	0	0	1	272

Going:	Sf: 0-0 GS: 0-0 Gd: 0-1 GF: - Fm: 0-1
Distance:	2m/2m3: 0-2 2m4-2m7: 0-0 3m+: 0-0

Track: LH: 0-1 RH: 0-1 Tight: 0-0 Gall: 0-0
Aids: Bl: 0-0 Vi: 0-0 Tstrap: 0-0
Best Rating: 96 4/03 Hexm 2m110y good NHF

Lesdream
102   96
6-y-o b g Morpeth-Lesbet (Hotfoot)
J D Frost Mrs L W Carlson

Placings:4/0P-00211   **(3777)**
2002/03: 19⁰GS, 20⁰S, 20²S, 17¹G, 17¹GS,

	Starts	1st	2nd	3rd	Win & Pl
Hurdles	5	2	1	0	8830
Career Total	8	2	1	0	8830
96 2/03 Extr	2m1f	D(0-110)HHdl		G-S	£4823
92 2/03 Hrfd	2m1f	F(0-95)HHdl		GD	£2947

Total win prize-money £7770

Going:	Sf: 0-2 GS: 1-2 Gd: 1-1 GF: - Fm: 0-0
Distance:	2m/2m3: 2-3 2m4-2m7: 0-2 3m+: 0-0
Track:	LH: 0-1 RH: 2-3 Tight: 0-1 Gall: 0-0
Aids:	Bl: 0-0 Vi: 0-0 Tstrap: 0-0
Best Rating:	96 2/03 Extr 2m1f gd-sft Hdl

Moderate handicap hurdler; effective over two miles, but stays further; acts on good and good to soft ground.

Lester Longfellow
7-y-o b/br g Riverwise (USA)-Cut Above The Rest (Indiaro)
N R Mitchell N R Mitchell

Placings:0-P   **(2127)**
2002/03: 21ᴾS,

	Starts	1st	2nd	3rd	Win & Pl
Hurdles	1	0	0	0	
Career Total	2	0	0	0	

Going:	Sf: 0-1 GS: 0-0 Gd: 0-0 GF: - Fm: 0-0
Distance:	2m/2m3: 0-0 2m4-2m7: 0-1 3m+: 0-0
Track:	LH: 0-1 RH: 0-0 Tight: 0-1 Gall: 0-0
Aids:	Bl: 0-0 Vi: 0-0 Tstrap: 0-0
Best Rating:	59 2/02 Winc 2m gd-sft NHF

Let's Dance
36f   82f
4-y-o b f Master Willie-Quick Quick Sloe (Scallywag)
C J Down Dr S G F Cave

Placings:4   **(4600)**
2002/03: 17⁴GF,

	Starts	1st	2nd	3rd	Win & Pl
NH Flat	1	0	0	0	0
Career Total	1	0	0	0	0

Going:	Sf: 0-0 GS: 0-0 Gd: 0-0 GF: - Fm: 0-1
Distance:	2m/2m3: 0-1 2m4-2m7: 0-0 3m+: 0-0
Track:	LH: 0-0 RH: 0-1 Tight: 0-0 Gall: 0-0
Aids:	Bl: 0-0 Vi: 0-0 Tstrap: 0-0
Best Rating:	82 4/03 Extr 2m1f gd-fm NHF

Out of a winning pointer; unsuited by slowly-run race on bumper debut at Exeter.

Let's Fly (FR)
97(100h)   (110h)83
8-y-o b g Rose Laurel-Harpyes (FR) (Quart De Vin (FR))
Mrs M Reveley Sir Robert Ogden

Track: LH: 0-1 RH: 0-1 Tight: 0-0 Gall: 0-0
Aids: Bl: 0-0 Vi: 0-0 Tstrap: 0-0
Best Rating: 96 4/03 Hexm 2m110y good NHF

Placings:110/1P2-1P3   **(0912)**
2002/03: 16¹GS, 17ᴾGS, 20³GS,

	Starts	1st	2nd	3rd	Win & Pl
Hurdles	2	1	0	0	2534
Chases	1	0	0	1	739
Career Total	9	4	1	1	11701
103 5/02 Sthl	2m	E Hdl		G-S	£2534
103 10/01 Uttx	2m	E Hdl		G-S	£3250
112 12/00 Hntg	2m110y	H NHF		HVY	£1554
114 11/00 Weth	2m	H NHF		HVY	£2530

Total win prize-money £9869

Going:	Sf: 0-0 GS: 1-3 Gd: 0-0 GF: - Fm: 0-0
Distance:	2m/2m3: 1-2 2m4-2m7: 0-1 3m+: 0-0
Track:	LH: 1-1 RH: 0-2 Tight: 1-3 Gall: 0-0
Aids:	Bl: 0-0 Vi: 0-0 Tstrap: 0-0
Best Rating:	114 11/00 Weth 2m heavy NHF

Plating-class hurdler; dual heavy ground bumper winner at the end of 2000, he has been lightly raced since, but did manage to win over hurdles at Uttoxeter in October 2001 and at Southwell in May 2002. Disappointing on his chasing debut. Very much suited by soft ground.

Lets Go Dutch
107   112
7-y-o b m Nicholas Bill-Dutch Majesty (Homing)
K Bishop Mrs E K Ellis

Placings:U2/4351F-6213   **(4030)**
2002/03: 24⁶GS, 24²S, 24¹GS, 22³HY,

	Starts	1st	2nd	3rd	Win & Pl
Hurdles	4	1	1	1	8493
Career Total	11	2	2	2	13134
112 2/03 Extr	3m110y	D(0-125)HHdl		G-S	£5720
100 3/02 Tntn	2m3f110yD Hdl		SFT		£3649

Total win prize-money £9369

Going:	Sf: 0-2 GS: 1-2 Gd: 0-0 GF: - Fm: 0-0
Distance:	2m/2m3: 0-0 2m4-2m7: 0-1 3m+: 1-3
Track:	LH: 0-0 RH: 1-4 Tight: 0-1 Gall: 0-0
Aids:	Bl: 0-0 Vi: 0-0 Tstrap: 0-0
Best Rating:	112 3/03 Sand 2m6f heavy Hdl

Modest hurdler; stays well; acts in soft ground.

Letz Bee On
59f   35f
5-y-o b g Flying Tyke-Jacques Point (Jester)
P R Wood Hampston Hillbillies

Placings:00   **(3817)**
2002/03: 17⁰HY, 16⁰G,

	Starts	1st	2nd	3rd	Win & Pl
NH Flat	2	0	0	0	
Career Total	2	0	0	0	

Going:	Sf: 0-0 GS: 0-0 Gd: 0-1 GF: - Fm: 0-0
Distance:	2m/2m3: 0-2 2m4-2m7: 0-0 3m+: 0-0
Track:	LH: 0-2 RH: 0-0 Tight: 0-2 Gall: 0-0
Aids:	Bl: 0-0 Vi: 0-0 Tstrap: 0-0
Best Rating:	35 2/03 Sedg 2m1f heavy NHF

Levallois (IRE)
87   92
7-y-o b g Trempolino (USA)-Broken Wave (Bustino)
P J Hobbs (J-P Gallorini 12/11) Tweenhills Racing (Cleeve Hill)

Placings:22/26114424/010051055-FP33400   **(4171)**
2002/03: 18ᶠVS, 18ᴾVS, 21³S, 19³HO, 18⁴HY, 22⁰GS, 22⁰S,

	Starts	1st	2nd	3rd	Win & Pl
Hurdles	6	0	0	1	0
Chases	1	0	0	1	2920
Career Total	26	4	4	2	97613

9/01 Engh 2m3f	Ch	HLD	£11639
5/01 Autl 2m3f110y	HHdl	SFT	£26188
9/00 Engh 2m1f	Ch	VS	£11527
7/00 Diep 2m1f	Hdl	VS	£10567
		Total win prize-money	£59921

Going: Sf: 0-3 GS: 0-1 Gd: 0-0 GF: - Fm: 0-0
Distance: 2m/2m3: 0-4 2m4-2m7: 0-3 3m+: 0-0
Track: LH: 0-1 RH: 0-1 Tight: 0-0 Gall: 0-0
Aids: Bl: 0-0 Vi: 0-0 Tstrap: 0-0
Best Rating: 117 6/01 Autl 3m1f110y v soft Hdl

Modest ex-French hurdler/chaser; successful twice over hurdles and twice over fences in his home country; best between two miles and two miles three; acts on soft ground.

Lewis Island (IRE)
112   **127d**
4-y-o b c Turtle Island (IRE)-Phyllode (Pharly (FR))
N A Twiston-Davies (T G Mills 14/10) Mr & Mrs Peter Orton

Placings:512320   (4460)
2002/03: 16^5GS, 16^1HY, 16^2HY, 16^3HY, 16^2HY, 16^0G,

	Starts	1st	2nd	3rd	Win & Pl
Hurdles	6	1	2	1	15277
Career Total	6	1	2	1	15277

124 12/02 Leic 2m	D Hdl	HVY	£4836
		Total win prize-money	£4836

Going: Sf: 1-4 GS: 0-1 Gd: 0-1 GF: - Fm: 0-0
Distance: 2m/2m3: 1-6 2m4-2m7: 0-0 3m+: 0-0
Track: LH: 0-4 RH: 1-2 Tight: 0-1 Gall: 0-0
Aids: Bl: 0-0 Vi: 0-0 Tstrap: 0-0
Best Rating: 124 12/02 Chep 2m110y heavy Hdl

Useful juvenile hurdler; suited by heavy ground and forcing tactics.

Lewis Mead
71f   **62f**
4-y-o b g Sir Harry Lewis (USA)-Normead Lass (Norwick (USA))
Mrs S A Liddiard Mrs Felicity Ashfield

Placings:06   (4350)
2002/03: 14^0GF, 16^6GF,

	Starts	1st	2nd	3rd	Win & Pl
NH Flat	2	0	0	0	0
Career Total	2	0	0	0	0

Going: Sf: 0-0 GS: 0-0 Gd: 0-0 GF: - Fm: 0-2
Distance: 2m/2m3: 0-1 2m4-2m7: 0-0 3m+: 0-0
Track: LH: 0-1 RH: 0-0 Tight: 0-0 Gall: 0-0
Aids: Bl: 0-0 Vi: 0-0 Tstrap: 0-0
Best Rating: 66 3/03 Hrfd 1m6f gd-fm NHF

Liberdal (FR)
92   **99+**
5-y-o b g Cadoudal (FR)-Libertina (FR) (Balsamo (FR))
G Macaire Mme B Gabeur

Placings:4P2-233   (2713)
2002/03: 17^2S, 18^3HY, 20^3HY,

	Starts	1st	2nd	3rd	Win & Pl
Hurdles	3	0	1	2	3971
Career Total	6	0	2	2	6745

Going: Sf: 0-2 GS: 0-0 Gd: 0-1 GF: - Fm: 0-0
Distance: 2m/2m3: 0-0 2m4-2m7: 0-0 3m+: 0-3
Track: LH: 0-1 RH: 0-2 Tight: 0-1 Gall: 0-0
Aids: Bl: 0-0 Vi: 0-0 Tstrap: 0-0

Going: Sf: 0-3 GS: 0-0 Gd: 0-0 GF: - Fm: 0-0
Distance: 2m/2m3: 0-2 2m4-2m7: 0-1 3m+: 0-0
Track: LH: 0-1 RH: 0-0 Tight: 0-0 Gall: 0-0
Aids: Bl: 0-0 Vi: 0-0 Tstrap: 0-0
Best Rating: 99 12/02 Chep 2m4f heavy Hdl

Fair French-trained novice hurdler, stays two and a half miles, acts on soft ground.

Liberman (IRE)
123f   **142f**
5-y-o b g Standiford (USA)-Hail To You (USA) (Kirtling)
M C Pipe (P Mullins 5/7) D A Johnson

Placings:21-121   (4115)
2002/03: 17^1Y, 16^2GS, 16^1G,

	Starts	1st	2nd	3rd	Win & Pl
NH Flat	3	2	1	0	31231
Career Total	5	3	2	0	41501

142 3/03 Chel 2m110y A NHF	GD	£23200
93 7/02 Bell 2m1f NHF	YLD	£4021
111 4/02 Punc 2m NHF	YLD	£6773
	Total win prize-money	£33994

Going: Sf: 0-0 GS: 0-1 Gd: 1-1 GF: - Fm: 0-0
Distance: 2m/2m3: 2-3 2m4-2m7: 0-0 3m+: 0-0
Track: LH: 1-2 RH: 0-0 Tight: 0-0 Gall: 0-0
Aids: Bl: 0-0 Vi: 0-0 Tstrap: 0-0
Best Rating: 142 3/03 Chel 2m110y good NHF

Winner of two bumpers in Ireland, and runner-up on his British debut at Cheltenham before landing the Champion Bumper at the Cheltenham Festival; effective at around two miles and acts on a soft surface; high-class hurdles prospect.

Liberty's Melody
65f   **50f**
6-y-o ch m Gildoran-Music Interpreter (Kampala)
Mrs S M Johnson Alastair McCubbing

Placings:0   (0517)
2002/03: 16^0S,

	Starts	1st	2nd	3rd	Win & Pl
NH Flat	1	0	0	0	
Career Total	1	0	0	0	

Going: Sf: 0-1 GS: 0-0 Gd: 0-0 GF: - Fm: 0-0
Distance: 2m/2m3: 0-1 2m4-2m7: 0-0 3m+: 0-0
Track: LH: 0-1 RH: 0-0 Tight: 0-0 Gall: 0-0
Aids: Bl: 0-0 Vi: 0-0 Tstrap: 0-0
Best Rating: 50 6/02 Worc 2m soft NHF

Libido
114
8-y-o b g Good Thyne (USA)-Country Mistress (Town And Country)
H D Daly The Hopeful Partnership

Placings:3024/25U-P00   (3787)
2002/03: 24^4S, 24^0HY, 26^0G,

	Starts	1st	2nd	3rd	Win & Pl
Hurdles	2	0	0	0	0
Chases	1	0	0	0	0
Career Total	10	0	2	1	4312

Going: Sf: 0-2 GS: 0-0 Gd: 0-1 GF: - Fm: 0-0
Distance: 2m/2m3: 0-0 2m4-2m7: 0-0 3m+: 0-3
Track: LH: 0-1 RH: 0-2 Tight: 0-1 Gall: 0-0
Aids: Bl: 0-0 Vi: 0-0 Tstrap: 0-0

Best Rating: 114 9/01 Bang 2m4f110y good Ch

Light Hearted Lily
96f   **77f**
4-y-o b f Deploy-Darling Splodge (Elegant Air)
R M Beckett The Foxons Fillies Partnership

Placings:0   (4122)
2002/03: 16^0G,

	Starts	1st	2nd	3rd	Win & Pl
NH Flat	1	0	0	0	
Career Total	1	0	0	0	

Going: Sf: 0-0 GS: 0-0 Gd: 0-1 GF: - Fm: 0-0
Distance: 2m/2m3: 0-1 2m4-2m7: 0-0 3m+: 0-0
Track: LH: 0-0 RH: 0-1 Tight: 0-0 Gall: 0-1
Aids: Bl: 0-0 Vi: 0-0 Tstrap: 0-0
Best Rating: 40 3/03 Hntg 2m110y good NHF

Has gradually been improving in modest bumpers and finished third at Worcester July 2003.

Light Programme
98   **76**
9-y-o b g El Gran Senor (USA)-Nashmeel (USA) (Blushing Groom (FR))
A L Forbes Tony Forbes

Placings:5/0/5P0-10P   (1172)
2002/03: 16^1G, 19^4GF, 22^PGF,

	Starts	1st	2nd	3rd	Win & Pl
Hurdles	3	1	0	0	2947
Career Total	8	1	0	0	2947

76 7/02 Wolv 2m E(0-105)HHdl	GD	£2947
	Total win prize-money	£2947

Going: Sf: 0-0 GS: 0-0 Gd: 0-0 GF: - Fm: 0-2
Distance: 2m/2m3: 1-2 2m4-2m7: 0-1 3m+: 0-0
Track: LH: 1-3 RH: 0-0 Tight: 1-3 Gall: 0-0
Aids: Bl: 0-0 Vi: 0-0 Tstrap: 0-0
Best Rating: 76 7/02 Wolv 2m good Hdl

A disappointing performer, he hinted at some ability over hurdles in 2001, but improved a lot to win a moderate novices handicap at Wolverhampton in July 2002.

Light Reflections
(79h)   **(47h)88**
10-y-o b g Rainbow Quest (USA)-Tajfah (USA) (Shadeed (USA))
P G Murphy Miss J Collison

Placings:000/0F3F461/26PPP/5352P453-F   (0127)
2002/03: 26^PGF,

	Starts	1st	2nd	3rd	Win & Pl
Chases	1	0	0	0	
Career Total	24	1	2	3	7795

88 4/00 Plum 3m2f F(0-95)HCh	SFT	£2678
	Total win prize-money	£2678

Going: Sf: 0-0 GS: 0-0 Gd: 0-0 GF: - Fm: 0-1
Distance: 2m/2m3: 0-0 2m4-2m7: 0-0 3m+: 0-1
Track: LH: 0-0 RH: 0-0 Tight: 0-1 Gall: 0-0
Aids: Bl: 0-0 Vi: 0-0 Tstrap: 0-0
Best Rating: 88 4/02 Font 3m2f110y gd-fm Ch

Fair staying chaser, a regular at the south coast tracks. Has won on soft, acts on good.

Light Scent (USA)
85   **74**

4-y-o ch g Silver Hawk (USA)-Music Lane (USA) (Miswaki (USA))
J Akehurst (Sir Michael Stoute 14/10) A D Spence

Placings:005   (4184)
2002/03: 16⁰HY, 16⁰S, 17⁵G,

	Starts	1st	2nd	3rd	Win & Pl
Hurdles	3	0	0		0
Career Total	3	0	0		0

Going: Sf: 0-2 GS: 0-0 Gd: 0-1 GF: - Fm: 0-0
Distance: 2m/2m3: 0-3 2m4-2m7: 0-0 3m+: 0-0
Track: LH: 0-1 RH: 0-2 Tight: 0-1 Gall: 0-1
Aids: Bl: 0-0 Vi: 0-0 Tstrap: 0-0
Best Rating: 74 3/03 Folk 2m1f110y good Hdl

Light The Fuse (IRE)
94   **74**

11-y-o b g Electric-Celtic Bombshell (Celtic Cone)
B G Powell A F Lousada

Placings:21/0/6O4446422/2/023F-05P0P30P   (2367)
2002/03: 22⁰GF, 22⁵GS, 24⁰G, 22⁰GF, 24⁰G, 22³S, 24⁰G, 16⁰FS,

	Starts	1st	2nd	3rd	Win & Pl
Hurdles	8	0	0	1	570
Career Total	25	1	5	2	8171
112 4/97	Prth	2m110y	H NHF		GD £2052
				Total win prize-money £2052	

Going: Sf: 0-2 GS: 0-1 Gd: 0-3 GF: - Fm: 0-0
Distance: 2m/2m3: 0-1 2m4-2m7: 0-4 3m+: 0-3
Track: LH: 0-5 RH: 0-3 Tight: 0-3 Gall: 0-0
Aids: Bl: 0-0 Vi: 0-0 Tstrap: 0-0
Best Rating: 112 4/97 Prth 2m110y good NHF

Plating-class hurdler; landed a bumper in April 1997, but has not won since. Placed over hurdles, but is very one-paced at the end of his races. Probably best over two and a half miles.

Light The Sky

10-y-o b g Lighter-Saleander (Leander)
Ms A E Embiricos Mrs Emma Littmoden

Placings:0/4P4-PP   (0317)
2002/03: 22ᴾG, 34ᴾG,

	Starts	1st	2nd	3rd	Win & Pl
Chases	2	0	0	0	
Career Total	6	0	0	0	85

Going: Sf: 0-0 GS: 0-0 Gd: 0-2 GF: - Fm: 0-0
Distance: 2m/2m3: 0-0 2m4-2m7: 0-0 3m+: 0-1
Track: LH: 0-1 RH: 0-1 Tight: 0-0 Gall: 0-0
Aids: Bl: 0-0 Vi: 0-0 Tstrap: 0-0
Best Rating: 69 5/01 Hntg 2m4f110y gd-fm Ch

Light-O-Day

10-y-o gr g Gods Solution-Brampton Lyn (Derrylin)
C Grant Chris Grant

Placings:P   (0765)
2002/03: 21ᴾGF,

	Starts	1st	2nd	3rd	Win & Pl
Hurdles	1	0	0		0
Career Total	1	0	0		0

Going: Sf: 0-0 GS: 0-0 Gd: 0-0 GF: - Fm: 0-1
Distance: 2m/2m3: 0-0 2m4-2m7: 0-1 3m+: 0-0
Track: LH: 0-1 RH: 0-0 Tight: 0-1 Gall: 0-0
Aids: Bl: 0-0 Vi: 0-0 Tstrap: 0-0
Best Rating: 0 7/02 Sedg 2m5f110y gd-fm Hdl

Lightmoor Lady
63f   **10f**

5-y-o b m Puget (USA)-Dragon Fire (Dragonara Palace (USA))
Mrs L Williamson R A Hughes

Placings:0   (4672)
2002/03: 16⁰G,

	Starts	1st	2nd	3rd	Win & Pl
NH Flat	1	0	0	0	
Career Total	1	0	0	0	

Going: Sf: 0-0 GS: 0-0 Gd: 0-1 GF: - Fm: 0-0
Distance: 2m/2m3: 0-0 2m4-2m7: 0-0 3m+: 0-0
Track: LH: 0-1 RH: 0-0 Tight: 0-1 Gall: 0-0
Aids: Bl: 0-0 Vi: 0-0 Tstrap: 0-0
Best Rating: 10 4/03 Fknm 2m good NHF

Lightning Gale (IRE)
87   (48h)**67**

10-y-o br m Strong Gale-Laurie Belle (Boreen (FR))
J McCaghy J McCaghy

Placings:0/000000/U0/0P06060F/PPS4034-F0306   (1631a)
2002/03: 20⁴YS, 17⁰GF, 20³F, 16⁰G, 18⁶YS,

	Starts	1st	2nd	3rd	Win & Pl
Chases	5	0	0	1	494
Career Total	29	0	0	2	1562

Going: Sf: 0-0 GS: 0-0 Gd: 0-1 GF: - Fm: 0-2
Distance: 2m/2m3: 0-3 2m4-2m7: 0-2 3m+: 0-0
Track: LH: 0-0 RH: 0-3 Tight: 0-0 Gall: 0-5
Aids: Bl: 0-0 Vi: 0-0 Tstrap: 0-5
Best Rating: 77 8/00 Tram 2m gd-fm Ch

Lightning Quest (IRE)
106(105h)   (99h)**112**

12-y-o b g Rainbow Quest (USA)-Rare Roberta (USA) (Roberto (USA))
Mrs S J Smith Mrs S Smith

Placings:0/33530/1025161/6/35014541/4F242FF   (1503)
2002/03: 17⁴GF, 20⁴GF, 23²GF, 19⁴GS, 20²G, 21³GF, 21⁶FG,

	Starts	1st	2nd	3rd	Win & Pl
Hurdles	2	0	0	0	1022
Chases	5	2	0	0	3177
Career Total	29	5	3	4	20264
112 3/00	Donc	2m3f110yD Ch		GD	£3789
112 11/99	Hayd	2m4f	E(0-115)HHdl	GD	£2582
116 3/98	Kels	2m2f	D(0-120)HHdl	GD	£2801
108 8/97	MRas	2m5f110yF(0-95)HHdl		GD	£2108
90 6/97	Strf	2m3f	E Hdl	GD	£2276
				Total win prize-money £13558	

Going: Sf: 0-0 GS: 0-1 Gd: 0-2 GF: - Fm: 0-4

Distance: 2m/2m3: 0-1 2m4-2m7: 0-5 3m+: 0-1
Track: LH: 0-4 RH: 0-3 Tight: 0-2 Gall: 0-0
Aids: Bl: 0-0 Vi: 0-0 Tstrap: 0-0
Best Rating: 116 3/98 Kels 2m2f good Hdl

Returned from a long break in 2002, running well over both hurdles and fences. Ran an excellent race when just losing out to an in-form rival at Perth in August.

Lightning Star (USA)
98   **97**

8-y-o b g El Gran Senor (USA)-Cuz s Star (USA) (Galaxy Libra)
T P McGovern Phil Collins

Placings:535/02303121233/403321310/P-0P620   (4116)
2002/03: 25⁰G, 22ᴾGS, 16⁶S, 16²GS, 21⁰G,

	Starts	1st	2nd	3rd	Win & Pl
Hurdles	5	0	1	0	708
Career Total	29	4	5	8	14852
112 2/01	Towc	2m	F(0-110)HHdl	HVY	£1876
114 1/01	Folk	2m1f110yG Hdl		HVY	£1554
101 1/00	Folk	2m1f110yG Hdl		SFT	£1519
100 12/99	Chep	2m4f	G Hdl	G-S	£1679
				Total win prize-money £6628	

Going: Sf: 0-1 GS: 0-2 Gd: 0-2 GF: - Fm: 0-0
Distance: 2m/2m3: 0-2 2m4-2m7: 0-2 3m+: 0-1
Track: LH: 0-3 RH: 0-1 Tight: 0-2 Gall: 0-1
Aids: Bl: 0-5 Vi: 0-0 Tstrap: 0-0
Best Rating: 114 1/01 Folk 2m1f110y heavy Hdl

Plating-class hurdler; effective at two miles.

Lightning Strikes (IRE)
98   **108**

9-y-o b g Zaffaran (USA)-Nimbi (Orchestra)
Mrs L Wadham R B Holt

Placings:231/1/P-01   (4691)
2002/03: 20⁰G, 19¹GF,

	Starts	1st	2nd	3rd	Win & Pl
Hurdles	2	1	0	0	4826
Career Total	7	3	1	1	9673
110 4/03	MRas	2m3f110yD(0-120)HHdl		G-F	£4826
110 10/99	Bang	2m1f	E Hdl	G-S	£2305
100 5/99	Uttx	2m	H NHF	GD	£1899
				Total win prize-money £9032	

Going: Sf: 0-0 GS: 0-0 Gd: 0-1 GF: - Fm: 1-1
Distance: 2m/2m3: 0-0 2m4-2m7: 1-2 3m+: 0-0
Track: LH: 0-0 RH: 1-2 Tight: 1-1 Gall: 0-0
Aids: Bl: 0-0 Vi: 0-0 Tstrap: 0-0
Best Rating: 110 4/03 MRas 2m3f110y gd-fm Hdl

Modest hurdler; has been very lightly raced in recent seasons, but retains his ability; suited by two and a half miles and acts on any ground; still has scope.

Like-A-Butterfly (IRE)
112   **158**

9-y-o b m Montelimar (USA)-Swifts Butterfly (Furry Glen)
C Roche J P McManus

Placings:111/111113-103   (4478)
2002/03: 16¹YS, 16⁰G, 20³G,

	Starts	1st	2nd	3rd	Win & Pl
Hurdles	3	1	0	1	72994

Career Total		12	9	0	2	222859
158	1/03	Leop	2m	Hdl		Y-S	£56493
147	3/02	Chel	2m110y	A Hdl		G-S	£52200
156	2/02	Leop	2m2f	Hdl		HVY	£23926
139	12/01	Leop	2m4f	Hdl		YLD	£8911
142	12/01	Fair	2m	Hdl		YLD	£28830
110	11/01	Navn	2m	Hdl		Y-S	£5842
142	4/01	Leop	2m	NHF		SH	£15725
141	1/01	Leop	2m2f	NHF		SFT	£5564
133	1/01	Naas	2m	NHF		SFT	£3895

Total win prize-money £201391

Going:	Sf: 0-0 GS: 0-0 Gd: 0-2 GF: - Fm: 0-0
Distance:	2m/2m3: 1-2 2m4-2m7: 0-1 3m+: 0-0
Track:	LH: 1-3 RH: 0-0 Tight: 0-1 Gall: 0-0
Aids:	Bl: 0-0 Vi: 0-0 Tstrap: 0-0
Best Rating:	158 1/03 Leop 2m yld-sft Hdl

High-class hurdler, won the Supreme Novices Hurdle at the 2002 Cheltenham Festival; below form on fastish ground over 2m 4f when beaten 9l by Davenport Milenium at Punchestown subsequently and produced best effort to date when just touching off Limestone Lad in 2003 Irish Champion Hurdle, but found ground too fast in the Champion Hurdle; best form up to 2m 4f; hurdles very well and will make a smart chaser; suited by cut in the ground; game and genuine.

Lilac Lady

6-y-o b m Weld-Lilac Wood (Precipice Wood)
F Jordan G L Edwards

Placings:P0   (0361)
2002/03: 17PS, 16QGS,

	Starts	1st	2nd	3rd	Win & Pl
NH Flat	2	0	0	0	
Career Total	2	0	0	0	

Going:	Sf: 0-1 GS: 0-1 Gd: 0-0 GF: - Fm: 0-0
Distance:	2m/2m3: 0-2 2m4-2m7: 0-0 3m+: 0-0
Track:	LH: 0-2 RH: 0-0 Tight: 0-2 Gall: 0-0
Aids:	Bl: 0-0 Vi: 0-0 Tstrap: 0-0
Best Rating:	0 5/02 Sthl 2m gd-sft NHF

Lilardo
100   70

6-y-o b/br m Son Pardo-Jimlil (Nicholas Bill)
B Palling Mrs M M Palling

Placings:3554/0P0-P53   (4220)
2002/03: 20PGF, 20SG, 19³GF,

	Starts	1st	2nd	3rd	Win & Pl
Hurdles	3	0	0	1	337
Career Total	10	0	0	2	776

Going:	Sf: 0-0 GS: 0-0 Gd: 0-1 GF: - Fm: 0-2
Distance:	2m/2m3: 0-0 2m4-2m7: 0-3 3m+: 0-0
Track:	LH: 0-2 RH: 0-1 Tight: 0-0 Gall: 0-0
Aids:	Bl: 0-0 Vi: 0-0 Tstrap: 0-2
Best Rating:	73 5/01 Hrfd 2m1f good Hdl

Lilium De Cotte (FR)
112   131

4-y-o b g Ragmar (FR)-Vanille De Cotte (FR) (Italic (FR))
G Macaire R Fougedoire

Placings:3122414   (4130)
2002/03: 15³S, 16¹G, 16²G, 17²G, 16⁴HY, 16¹HY, 17⁴G,

	Starts	1st	2nd	3rd	Win & Pl
Hurdles	7	2	2	1	23459
Career Total	7	2	2	1	23459
110	2/03	Sand	2m110y	D Hdl		HVY	£5346
	8/02	Vich	2m110y	Hdl		GD	£4417

Total win prize-money £9763

Going:	Sf: 1-3 GS: 0-0 Gd: 1-4 GF: - Fm: 0-0
Distance:	2m/2m3: 2-6 2m4-2m7: 0-0 3m+: 0-0
Track:	LH: 0-3 RH: 1-1 Tight: 0-0 Gall: 0-2
Aids:	Bl: 0-0 Vi: 0-0 Tstrap: 0-0
Best Rating:	131 3/03 Chel 2m1f good Hdl

Useful French-trained juvenile hurdler; fourth in the Triumph Hurdle, staying on from the rear; acts on good and heavy ground.

Lillieplant (IRE)

11-y-o b m Aristocracy-Canute Princess (Torenaga)
E J Ford E J Ford

Placings:6040/000-F   (0032)
2002/03: 21FGF,

	Starts	1st	2nd	3rd	Win & Pl
Chases	1	0	0	0	
Career Total	8	0	0	0	0

Going:	Sf: 0-0 GS: 0-0 Gd: 0-0 GF: - Fm: 0-1
Distance:	2m/2m3: 0-0 2m4-2m7: 0-1 3m+: 0-0
Track:	LH: 0-1 RH: 0-0 Tight: 0-0 Gall: 0-1
Aids:	Bl: 0-0 Vi: 0-0 Tstrap: 0-0
Best Rating:	69 4/01 Hntg 2m10y soft Hdl

Lily Brown
93 (92h)   (84h) 85

8-y-o br m Sula Bula-Lily Mab (FR) (Prince Mab (FR))
D P Keane Proverbial Optimists

Placings:4FPP04   (4078)
2002/03: 16⁴S, 19FGS, 19PHY, 19PG, 18⁰S, 20⁴S,

	Starts	1st	2nd	3rd	Win & Pl
Hurdles	2	0	0	0	0
Chases	4	0	0	0	626
Career Total	6	0	0	0	626

Going:	Sf: 0-4 GS: 0-0 Gd: 0-1 GF: - Fm: 0-0
Distance:	2m/2m3: 0-2 2m4-2m7: 0-4 3m+: 0-0
Track:	LH: 0-4 RH: 0-2 Tight: 0-0 Gall: 0-0
Aids:	Bl: 0-0 Vi: 0-0 Tstrap: 0-0
Best Rating:	85 11/02 Chep 2m110y soft Ch

Lily Pads

5-y-o b m Barrish-Ballyorney Girl (New Member)
P R Rodford P R Rodford

Placings:PP   (1156)
2002/03: 20PG, 22PG,

	Starts	1st	2nd	3rd	Win & Pl
Hurdles	2	0	0	0	
Career Total	2	0	0	0	

Going:	Sf: 0-0 GS: 0-0 Gd: 0-2 GF: - Fm: 0-0
Distance:	2m/2m3: 0-0 2m4-2m7: 0-2 3m+: 0-0
Track:	LH: 0-2 RH: 0-0 Tight: 0-0 Gall: 0-0
Aids:	Bl: 0-0 Vi: 0-0 Tstrap: 0-0
Best Rating:	0 9/02 NAbb 2m6f good Hdl

Limbo Lad
91   77+

4-y-o b g Millkom-Bumble Boogie (IRE) (Bluebird (USA))
P C Haslam Mrs B M Hawkins

Placings:2P44P   (1705)
2002/03: 16²GF, 17PGF, 16⁴G, 17⁴F, 17PG,

	Starts	1st	2nd	3rd	Win & Pl
Hurdles	5	0	1	0	1577
Career Total	5	0	1	0	1577

Going:	Sf: 0-0 GS: 0-0 Gd: 0-2 GF: - Fm: 0-3
Distance:	2m/2m3: 0-5 2m4-2m7: 0-0 3m+: 0-0
Track:	LH: 0-4 RH: 0-1 Tight: 0-4 Gall: 0-0
Aids:	Bl: 0-0 Vi: 0-0 Tstrap: 0-0
Best Rating:	77 9/02 Uttx 2m good Hdl

Made a satisfactory hurdle debut when finishing runner-up in weak juvenile event at Stratford min July 2002. Held since.

Limerick Boy (GER)
117   141+

5-y-o b h Alwuhush (USA)-Limoges (GER) (Konigsstuhl (GER))
Miss Venetia Williams (A Schutz 3/10) Favourites Racing

Placings:161   (4470)
2002/03: 16¹S, 16⁶G, 16¹G,

		Starts	1st	2nd	3rd	Win & Pl
Hurdles		3	2	0	0	34546
Career Total		3	2	0	0	34546
135	4/03	Aint	2m110y	A Hdl		GD	£29000
114	3/03	Winc	2m	E Hdl		SFT	£4046

Total win prize-money £33046

Going:	Sf: 1-1 GS: 0-0 Gd: 1-2 GF: - Fm: 0-0
Distance:	2m/2m3: 2-3 2m4-2m7: 0-0 3m+: 0-0
Track:	LH: 1-2 RH: 1-1 Tight: 1-1 Gall: 0-0
Aids:	Bl: 0-0 Vi: 0-0 Tstrap: 0-0
Best Rating:	135 4/03 Aint 2m110y good Hdl

Group-class performer on the Flat in Germany; made a winning debut over hurdles at Wincanton in March 2003, before running very well to be sixth in the Supreme Novices ; improved on that effort when taking a Grade Two at Aintree; acts on soft ground; effective over two miles.

Limerick Leader (IRE)
102f   106+f

5-y-o b g Supreme Leader-View Of The Hills (Croghan Hill)
P J Hobbs D R Peppiatt

Placings:002   (4155)
2002/03: 16⁰GS, 16⁰G, 16²G,

	Starts	1st	2nd	3rd	Win & Pl
NH Flat	3	0	1	0	606
Career Total	3	0	1	0	606

Going:	Sf: 0-0 GS: 0-1 Gd: 0-2 GF: - Fm: 0-0
Distance:	2m/2m3: 0-3 2m4-2m7: 0-0 3m+: 0-0
Track:	LH: 0-3 RH: 0-0 Tight: 0-0 Gall: 0-1
Aids:	Bl: 0-0 Vi: 0-0 Tstrap: 0-0
Best Rating:	106 3/03 Wwck 2m good NHF

Has shown plenty of ability in bumpers; looks the type who is going to need at least two and a half miles over hurdles.

Limestone Lad (IRE)

120   (148c)**174**

11-y-o b g Aristocracy-Limestone Miss (Raise You Ten)
James Bowe James Bowe

Placings:0/545136152251/41112121113/122111114112/21
1114113/221111211-1111123   (4131)
2002/03: 20¹YS, 16¹S, 20¹SH, 20¹YS, 24¹HY, 16²YS, 24³G,

	Starts	1st	2nd	3rd	Win & Pl
Hurdles	7	5	1	1	129019
Career Total	61	35	12	4	542573

174	12/02	Leop	3m	Hdl		HVY	£19938
171	12/02	Navn	2m4f	Hdl		Y-S	£7975
170	12/02	Fair	2m4f	Hdl		SH	£29907
163	11/02	Navn	2m	Hdl		SFT	£19049
167	11/02	Navn	2m4f	Hdl		Y-S	£19938
157	4/02	Punc	3m	Hdl		GD	£30429
166	1/02	Naas	2m4f	Hdl		SH	£8773
162	12/01	Navn	2m4f	Hdl		YLD	£10483
170	12/01	Fair	2m4f	Hdl		YLD	£31451
163	11/01	Punc	2m	Hdl		SFT	£18346
174	11/01	Navn	2m4f	Hdl		Y-S	£15725
159	2/01	Navn	3m	Hdl		SFT	£20967
154	1/01	Naas	2m4f	Hdl		SFT	£8911
147	11/00	Punc	2m	Ch		SFT	£11040
120	11/00	Navn	2m	Ch		HVY	£11088
147	10/00	Cork	2m6f	Ch		YLD	£13000
125	10/00	Cork	2m5f	Ch		Y-S	£5796
176	2/00	Navn	3m	Hdl		SH	£13000
172	1/00	Naas	2m4f	Hdl		SH	£5328
174	12/99	Leop	3m	Hdl		SFT	£14508
176	12/99	Navn	2m4f	Hdl		HVY	£8705
171	11/99	Fair	2m4f	Hdl		SFT	£26116
154	11/99	Punc	2m4f	Hdl		YLD	£11607
166	11/99	Navn	2m4f	Hdl		Y-S	£8705
149	10/99	Dund	2m4f153y	Hdl		Y-S	£4928
159	3/99	Leop	2m4f	HHdl		YLD	£6138
169	3/99	Naas	2m3f	HHdl		Y-S	£6138
152	3/99	Leop	2m	(0-144)HHdl		SFT	£4910
146	2/99	Leop	2m	HHdl		SH	£8671
144	12/98	Leop	2m	HHdl		SH	£5978
132	12/98	Navn	2m	HHdl		HVY	£5978
128	11/98	Naas	2m	(0-132)HHdl		Y-S	£4782
123	4/98	Clon	2m4f	Hdl		HVY	£1935
118	2/98	Naas	2m	NHF		SFT	£2680
107	12/97	Limk	2m	NHF		HVY	£3391

Total win prize-money £426328

Going: Sf: 2-2 GS: 0-0 Gd: 0-1 GF: - Fm: 0-0
Distance: 2m/2m3: 1-2 **2m4-2m7:** 3-3 3m+: 1-2
Track: LH: 4-6 RH: 1-1 Tight: 0-0 Gall: 0-1
Aids: Bl: 0-0 Vi: 0-0 Tstrap: 0-0
Best Rating: 176 2/00 Navn 3m   sft-hvy Hdl

Top-class front-running Irish-trained hurdler, winner of a remarkable 35 races; stays three miles, but effective over shorter as he showed when creditable second to Like-A-Butterfly over two miles in the AIG Champion Hurdle; ideally suited by an easy surface; famously tough and genuine, never goes down without a fight.

Limited Edition (IRE)

92   **84**

5-y-o b g Parthian Springs-Rosemount Rose (Ashmore (FR))
M Pitman Malcolm C Denmark

Placings:2F50   (4470)
2002/03: 16²S, 16FGS, 19⁵S, 16⁰G,

	Starts	1st	2nd	3rd	Win & Pl
NH Flat	1	0	1	0	572
Hurdles	3	0	0	0	0
Career Total	4	0	1	0	572

Going: Sf: 0-2 GS: 0-1 Gd: 0-1 GF: - Fm: 0-0
Distance: 2m/2m3: 0-4 2m4-2m7: 0-0 3m+: 0-0
Track: LH: 0-3 RH: 0-1 Tight: 0-0 Gall: 0-1
Aids: Bl: 0-0 Vi: 0-0 Tstrap: 0-0
Best Rating: 106 12/02 Wwck 2m   soft NHF

A half-brother to Choisty; he looks to have more speed than his relation judged on his debut in a Warwick bumper; fell on his hurdling debut; showed promise next time; stays 2m 3f.

Lincoln Cross (IRE)

101   **86**

8-y-o b g Lord Americo-Keen Cross (IRE) (Black Minstrel)
O Sherwood I W Harfitt & Partners

Placings:02-0053   (4622)
2002/03: 20⁰GS, 16⁰GS, 17⁵GS, 22³GF,

	Starts	1st	2nd	3rd	Win & Pl
Hurdles	4	0	0	1	912
Career Total	6	0	1	1	1327

Going: Sf: 0-0 GS: 0-3 Gd: 0-0 GF: - Fm: 0-1
Distance: 2m/2m3: 0-2 2m4-2m7: 0-2 3m+: 0-0
Track: LH: 0-2 RH: 0-2 Tight: 0-3 Gall: 0-0
Aids: Bl: 0-0 Vi: 0-0 Tstrap: 0-0
Best Rating: 100 10/01 Hntg 2m110y   good NHF

Moderate novice hurdler; runner-up in a Huntingdon bumper on second start; improved form when stepped up to two miles six to finish third at Newton Abbot.

Lincoln Dean

7-y-o b g Mtoto-Play With Me (IRE) (Alzao (USA))
F P Murtagh Clayton Bigley Partnership Ltd

Placings:P0-PB   (1163)
2002/03: 16²G, 17⁸GF,

	Starts	1st	2nd	3rd	Win & Pl
Hurdles	2	0	0	0	
Career Total	4	0	0	0	

Going: Sf: 0-0 GS: 0-0 Gd: 0-1 GF: - Fm: 0-0
Distance: 2m/2m3: 0-2 2m4-2m7: 0-0 3m+: 0-0
Track: LH: 0-1 RH: 0-1 Tight: 0-1 Gall: 0-0
Aids: Bl: 0-0 Vi: 0-0 Tstrap: 0-0
Best Rating: 0 9/02 Sedg 2m1f   gd-fm Hdl

Lincoln Place (IRE)

112(101h)   (95 h)**112**

8-y-o ch g Be My Native (USA)-Miss Lou (Levanter)
P J Hobbs A J Scrimgeour

Placings:0000/00P/11F423   (4676)
2002/03: 16¹GF, 20¹G, 21FGF, 17⁴G, 20²GF, 19³GF,

	Starts	1st	2nd	3rd	Win & Pl
Hurdles	1	0	0	0	0
Chases	5	2	1	1	10164
Career Total	13	2	1	1	10164

103	8/02	Worc	2m4f110yE(0-105)HCh		GD	£3818
97	6/02	Worc	2m	F(0-95)HCh	G-F	£3198

Total win prize-money £7017

Going: Sf: 0-0 GS: 0-0 Gd: 1-2 GF: - Fm: 1-4
Distance: 2m/2m3: 1-3 2m4-2m7: 1-3 3m+: 0-0
Track: LH: 2-4 RH: 0-2 Tight: 0-2 Gall: 0-1

Aids: Bl: 0-0 Vi: 0-0 Tstrap: 0-0
Best Rating: 112 9/02 Hntg 2m4f110y gd-fm   Ch

Fair handicap chaser; effective at up to two miles four; acts on a sound surface.

Lincoln Star

5-y-o b g Lugana Beach-Esilam (Frimley Park)
A G Hobbs J Parfitt

Placings:00-0PP   (0512)
2002/03: 16⁰G, 16PG, 16PS,

	Starts	1st	2nd	3rd	Win & Pl
NH Flat	1	0	0	0	0
Hurdles	2	0	0	0	0
Career Total	5	0	0	0	

Going: Sf: 0-1 GS: 0-0 Gd: 0-2 GF: - Fm: 0-0
Distance: 2m/2m3: 0-3 2m4-2m7: 0-0 3m+: 0-0
Track: LH: 0-3 RH: 0-0 Tight: 0-0 Gall: 0-0
Aids: Bl: 0-0 Vi: 0-0 Tstrap: 0-0
Best Rating: 60 4/02 Ludl 2m   gd-fm NHF

Lindajane (IRE)

106   (67h)**80**

11-y-o b m Erin s Hope-Tempo Rose (Crash Course)
D W Whillans Mrs H M Whillans

Placings:33/6/331040/14030/0054/F312O30P   (4765)
2002/03: 25FG, 22³GF, 20¹G, 20²G, 20⁰HY, 21³S, 20⁰G, 31³PG,

	Starts	1st	2nd	3rd	Win & Pl
Chases	8	1	2	2	6039
Career Total	26	3	1	7	13386

77	6/02	Hexm	2m4f110yE(0-105)HCh		GD	£3388
89	5/99	Prth	2m110y E(0-105)HHdl		HVY	£2970
89	2/99	Ayr	2m	E Hdl		SFT	£2705

Total win prize-money £9063

Going: Sf: 0-2 GS: 0-0 Gd: 1-5 GF: - Fm: 0-1
Distance: 2m/2m3: 0-0 **2m4-2m7:** 1-6 3m+: 0-2
Track: LH: 1-7 RH: 0-0 Tight: 0-1 Gall: 0-0
Aids: Bl: 0-0 Vi: 0-0 Tstrap: 0-0
Best Rating: 89 5/99 Prth 2m110y   heavy Hdl

Plating-class chaser, effective at up to three miles; acts on a sound surface.

Lindiwe (IRE)

80f   **68f**

6-y-o gr m Roselier (FR)-Sacajawea (Tanfirion)
N J Henderson Mrs E Roberts

Placings:0   (0280)
2002/03: 17⁰S,

	Starts	1st	2nd	3rd	Win & Pl
NH Flat	1	0	0	0	
Career Total	1	0	0	0	

Going: Sf: 0-1 GS: 0-0 Gd: 0-0 GF: - Fm: 0-0
Distance: 2m/2m3: 0-1 2m4-2m7: 0-0 3m+: 0-0
Track: LH: 0-1 RH: 0-0 Tight: 0-1 Gall: 0-0
Aids: Bl: 0-0 Vi: 0-0 Tstrap: 0-0
Best Rating: 68 5/02 Bang 2m1f   soft NHF

Lindon Run

14-y-o b g Cruise Missile-Trial Run (Deep Run)

K Robson Mrs O Donaldson

Placings:UF/00/P/4/03/0-P   (0085)
2002/03: 20ºG, 25ºGS,

	Starts	1st	2nd	3rd	Win & Pl
Chases	2	0	0	0	
Career Total	10	0	0	1	177

Going:	Sf: 0-0 GS: 0-1 Gd: 0-1 GF: - Fm: 0-0
Distance:	2m/2m3: 0-0 2m4-2m7: 0-1 3m+: 0-1
Track:	LH: 0-2 RH: 0-0 Tight: 0-0 Gall: 0-1
Aids:	Bl: 0-0 Vi: 0-0 Tstrap: 0-2
Best Rating:	63 5/00 Hexm 2m4f110y good Ch

Line Apple (FR)
95   94

6-y-o ch m Apple Tree (FR)-Cackle (USA) (Crow (FR))
J J Boulter (J Ortet 29/9) J J Boulter

Placings:4F1/150P1-211140F5F   (4508)
2002/03: 21², 17¹S, 21¹G, 21¹G, 19⁴VS, 21⁰S, 20²S, 24⁵GS, 25⁵FG,

	Starts	1st	2nd	3rd	Win & Pl
Chases	9	3	1	0	22349
Career Total	17	6	1	0	47297
8/02	Vitt	2m5f		Ch	GD	£7656
7/02	Vitt	2m5f		Ch	GD	£3534
7/02	Claf	2m1f		HCh	SFT	£6184
10/01	Nime	2m1f		Ch	G-S	£3395
5/01	Autl	2m2f		Hdl	G-S	£14549
4/01	Pau	2m110y		Hdl	VS	£4365
			Total win prize-money £39683

Going:	Sf: 1-3 GS: 0-1 Gd: 2-3 GF: - Fm: 0-0
Distance:	2m/2m3: 1-2 2m4-2m7: 2-5 3m+: 0-2
Track:	LH: 0-2 RH: 0-1 Tight: 0-3 Gall: 0-0
Aids:	Bl: 0-0 Vi: 0-0 Tstrap: 0-0
Best Rating:	74 2/03 Tntn 3m gd-sft Ch

Prolific winner of minor chases in France. Well beaten when falling late on in hunter chase at Bangor in February.

Lingering Fog (IRE)
83   43

9-y-o br g Over The River (FR)-Mandasari (Mandalus)
J D Frost (M Higgins 6/6) R G Frost

Placings:0000/P000P-00   (1592)
2002/03: 20ºYS, 22ºG,

	Starts	1st	2nd	3rd	Win & Pl
Hurdles	1	0	0	0	0
Chases	1	0	0	0	0
Career Total	11	0	0	0	

Going:	Sf: 0-0 GS: 0-0 Gd: 0-1 GF: - Fm: 0-0
Distance:	2m/2m3: 0-0 2m4-2m7: 0-2 3m+: 0-0
Track:	LH: 0-0 RH: 0-2 Tight: 0-0 Gall: 0-0
Aids:	Bl: 0-0 Vi: 0-0 Tstrap: 0-0
Best Rating:	59 3/00 Navn 2m2f yld-sft Hdl

Lingham Bridesmaid
100   83

7-y-o b m Minster Son-Lingham Bride (Deep Run)
Mrs J C McGregor (Mrs D Thomson 7/6) Tillyrie Racing Club

Placings:6/630003P6PP3-22334024030   (4750)
2002/03: 16²GF, 16²GS, 20³GF, 20³GF, 20⁴S, 16⁰GS, 20²G, 20⁴G, 20⁰GS, 16³G, 24⁰G,

---

	Starts	1st	2nd	3rd	Win & Pl
Hurdles	11	0	3	3	5452
Career Total	23	0	3	6	6879

Going:	Sf: 0-1 GS: 0-3 Gd: 0-4 GF: - Fm: 0-3
Distance:	2m/2m3: 0-4 2m4-2m7: 0-6 3m+: 0-1
Track:	LH: 0-2 RH: 0-9 Tight: 0-3 Gall: 0-0
Aids:	Bl: 0-0 Vi: 0-0 Tstrap: 0-0
Best Rating:	85 1/03 Muss 2m4f good Hdl

Moderate hurdler, has been well beaten in ordinary company; placed nine times but yet to get off the mark; stays two miles four.

Liniyan (IRE)
110

8-y-o b g Kahyasi-Linnga (IRE) (Shardari)
Miss Venetia Williams Mrs P A H Hartley

Placings:210/13P1P/UFP/61PP-   (0014)
2002/03: 25ᴾGS,

	Starts	1st	2nd	3rd	Win & Pl
Chases	1	0	0	0	
Career Total	13	3	1	1	9033
95	12/01	Font	3m2f110yE Ch		GD	£3776
113	10/99	Strf	2m6f110yE Hdl		G-S	£2040
98	3/99	Strf	2m110y H NHF		HVY	£2305
			Total win prize-money £8122

Going:	Sf: 0-0 GS: 0-1 Gd: 0-0 GF: - Fm: 0-0
Distance:	2m/2m3: 0-0 2m4-2m7: 0-0 3m+: 0-1
Track:	LH: 0-0 RH: 0-1 Tight: 0-0 Gall: 0-0
Aids:	Bl: 0-0 Vi: 0-0 Tstrap: 0-0
Best Rating:	113 10/99 Strf 2m6f110y gd-sft Hdl

Modest chaser; lightly raced; has had breathing problems; stays three and a quarter miles; acts on soft ground.

Link Copper

14-y-o ch g Whistlefield-Letitica (Deep Run)
Mrs E J Taplin Mrs E J Taplin

Placings:5P/PP/2P/4-3   (4467)
2002/03: 24³F,

	Starts	1st	2nd	3rd	Win & Pl
Chases	1	0	0	1	383
Career Total	8	0	1	1	1029

Going:	Sf: 0-0 GS: 0-0 Gd: 0-0 GF: - Fm: 0-0
Distance:	2m/2m3: 0-0 2m4-2m7: 0-0 3m+: 0-1
Track:	LH: 0-0 RH: 0-1 Tight: 0-1 Gall: 0-0
Aids:	Bl: 0-0 Vi: 0-0 Tstrap: 0-0
Best Rating:	93 5/97 Winc 2m5f firm Ch

Modest hunter chaser.

Linning Wine (IRE)
70

7-y-o b g Scenic-Zallaka (IRE) (Shardari)
B G Powell Favourites Racing

Placings:103/0-P   (0263)
2002/03: 16ᴾG,

	Starts	1st	2nd	3rd	Win & Pl
Hurdles	1	0	0	0	
Career Total	5	1	0	1	1940
107	1/01	Kemp	2m	H NHF	SFT	£1673
			Total win prize-money £1673

Going:	Sf: 0-0 GS: 0-0 Gd: 0-1 GF: - Fm: 0-0

Distance:	2m/2m3: 0-1 2m4-2m7: 0-0 3m+: 0-0
Track:	LH: 0-1 RH: 0-0 Tight: 0-1 Gall: 0-0
Aids:	Bl: 0-0 Vi: 0-0 Tstrap: 0-0
Best Rating:	107 4/01 MRas 1m5f110y gd-sft NHF

Linus
103   94

5-y-o b g Bin Ajwaad (IRE)-Land Line (High Line)
M C Pipe (G A Ham 19/12) G Doel

Placings:R00116   (4391)
2002/03: 16ᴿGF, 19ᴿG, 19⁴GS, 19¹GS, 17¹S, 17⁶F,

	Starts	1st	2nd	3rd	Win & Pl
Hurdles	6	2	0	0	5712
Career Total	6	2	0	0	5712
91	3/03	Extr	2m1f	F(0-95)HHdl	SFT	£3192
94	2/03	Tntn	2m3f110yG(0-95)HHdl	G-S	£2520
			Total win prize-money £5712

Going:	Sf: 1-1 GS: 1-2 Gd: 0-0 GF: - Fm: 0-3
Distance:	2m/2m3: 1-4 2m4-2m7: 1-2 3m+: 0-0
Track:	LH: 0-1 RH: 2-5 Tight: 1-2 Gall: 0-0
Aids:	Bl: 0-0 Vi: 0-0 Tstrap: 0-0
Best Rating:	94 2/03 Tntn 2m3f110y gd-sft Hdl

Plating-class hurdler; bolted up when dropped into selling company on his first start for Pipe; followed up under a penalty in Class F amateur riders handicap at Exeter five days later; let down by sloppy jumping off 21lb higher mark on firm ground at Exeter March 2003; changed stables since; effective at two miles, may be better over further; acts on soft ground.

Lion Guest (IRE)
99   87+

6-y-o ch g Lion Cavern (USA)-Decrescendo (IRE) (Polish Precedent (USA))
Mrs S C Bradburne Cornelius Lysaght

Placings:0P6004   (4591)
2002/03: 16ᴾGF, 20ᴾGS, 16ᴿG, 16⁰GS, 16⁰G, 16⁴G,

	Starts	1st	2nd	3rd	Win & Pl
Hurdles	6	0	0	0	
Career Total	6	0	0	0	

Going:	Sf: 0-0 GS: 0-2 Gd: 0-3 GF: - Fm: 0-1
Distance:	2m/2m3: 0-5 2m4-2m7: 0-1 3m+: 0-0
Track:	LH: 0-3 RH: 0-3 Tight: 0-4 Gall: 0-0
Aids:	Bl: 0-0 Vi: 0-0 Tstrap: 0-0
Best Rating:	82 4/03 Hexm 2m110y good Hdl

Moderate novice hurdler; winner at Perth in July 2003; does not stay two miles six.

Lirfox (FR)
106(109h)   (127 h)123+

6-y-o ch m Foxhound (USA)-Lirfa (USA) (Lear Fan (USA))
M C Pipe (C Aubert 16/1) D A Johnson

Placings:11032   (4547)
2002/03: 17¹S, 19¹VS, 16⁰G, 16³G, 16²G,

	Starts	1st	2nd	3rd	Win & Pl
Hurdles	5	2	1	1	27315
Career Total	5	2	1	1	27315
1/03	Pau	2m3f	Hdl		VS	£12468
12/02	Pau	2m1f110y	Hdl		SFT	£7067
			Total win prize-money £19535

Going:	Sf: 1-1 GS: 0-0 Gd: 0-3 GF: - Fm: 0-0
Distance:	2m/2m3: 2-5 2m4-2m7: 0-0 3m+: 0-0
Track:	LH: 0-3 RH: 0-0 Tight: 0-1 Gall: 0-0

Aids: Bl: 0-0 Vi: 0-0 Tstrap: 0-0
Best Rating: 127 3/03 Chel 2m110y good Hdl

A winner on the Flat and over hurdles in France; creditable efforts to make the frame in warm novice hurdles at Aintree and Ayr; easy winner of three novice chases at Hereford May and June 2003; keen sort, best at 2m, acts on most types of ground.

Lirsleftover

92　　　　　　　　　　80

11-y-o ch g Lir-Full Tan (Dairialatan)
Miss S Young B R J Young

Placings:605F56-050　　　　　　　　　　(0867)
2002/03: 17⁰G, 21⁵GF, 21⁰GF,

	Starts	1st	2nd	3rd	Win & Pl
Chases	3	0	0	0	0
Career Total	9	0	0	0	0

Going: Sf: 0-0 GS: 0-0 Gd: 0-1 GF: - Fm: 0-2
Distance: 2m/2m3: 0-1 2m4-2m7: 0-2 3m+: 0-0
Track: LH: 0-2 RH: 0-1 Tight: 0-2 Gall: 0-0
Aids: Bl: 0-0 Vi: 0-0 Tstrap: 0-0
Best Rating: 80 5/01 Chel 2m5f good Ch

Lisa Du Chenet (FR)

102f　　　　　　　　　89f

4-y-o b f Garde Royale-Tchela (FR) (Le Nain Jaune (FR))
Mrs Susan Nock The Siblings

Placings:460　　　　　　　　　　(4611)
2002/03: 16⁴S, 16⁶G, 17⁰G,

	Starts	1st	2nd	3rd	Win & Pl
NH Flat	3	0	0	0	0
Career Total	3	0	0	0	0

Going: Sf: 0-1 GS: 0-0 Gd: 0-2 GF: - Fm: 0-0
Distance: 2m/2m3: 0-3 2m4-2m7: 0-0 3m+: 0-0
Track: LH: 0-3 RH: 0-0 Tight: 0-0 Gall: 0-3
Aids: Bl: 0-0 Vi: 0-0 Tstrap: 0-0
Best Rating: 82 3/03 Newb 2m110y soft NHF

Fair form in a couple of decent bumpers at Newbury.

Lisa-B (IRE)

(97h)　　　　　　　　(64h)

6-y-o b m Case Law-Nishiki (USA) (Brogan (USA))
D L Williams Thrush Golf Club

Placings:55060-P260P430P02P　　　　　(4710)
2002/03: 27⁸GF, 16²G, 17⁶GS, 16⁶GF, 22⁵GF, 20⁴G, 21³GS,
20⁵GF, 26⁶GF, 19⁰F, 19²G, 23⁵GF,

	Starts	1st	2nd	3rd	Win & Pl
Hurdles	12	0	2	1	1355
Career Total	17	0	2	1	1355

Going: Sf: 0-0 GS: 0-1 Gd: 0-3 GF: - Fm: 0-8
Distance: 2m/2m3: 0-3 2m4-2m7: 0-7 3m+: 0-2
Track: LH: 0-6 RH: 0-4 Tight: 0-5 Gall: 0-1
Aids: Bl: 0-0 Vi: 0-6 Tstrap: 0-0
Best Rating: 76 5/02 Towc 2m good Hdl

Selling hurdler.

Lisaan (IRE)

105(107h)　　　　　　117

6-y-o ch g Bigstone (IRE)-Linnga (IRE) (Shardari)

William Durkan Mrs Beatrice Durkan

Placings:00116/50B4031200-6054005P442　(4085)
2002/03: 16⁶S, 16⁹HY, 18⁵S, 16⁴S, 18⁰HY, 16⁰S, 20⁵SH, 16⁸S,
18⁴YS, 16⁴Y, 20²GS,

	Starts	1st	2nd	3rd	Win & Pl
Hurdles	4	0	0	0	0
Chases	7	0	1	0	2731
Career Total	26	3	2	1	41740
129 1/02	Cork 2m		(0-123)HHdl	SFT	£9969
134 2/01	Leop 2m		Hdl	HVY	£18346
119 1/01	Gowr 2m		Hdl	SFT	£5564
		Total win prize-money £33881			

Going: Sf: 0-7 GS: 0-1 Gd: 0-0 GF: - Fm: 0-0
Distance: 2m/2m3: 0-9 2m4-2m7: 0-2 3m+: 0-0
Track: LH: 0-4 RH: 0-4 Tight: 0-1 Gall: 0-0
Aids: Bl: 0-0 Vi: 0-0 Tstrap: 0-0
Best Rating: 134 2/01 Leop 2m heavy Hdl

Fair Irish novice chaser; acts very well with cut in the ground; best over two miles; has worn blinkers.

Liscombe

7-y-o b m Petoski-Take The Veil (Monksfield)
D R Stoddart D R Stoddart

Placings:0/P　　　　　　　　　　(0269)
2002/03: 16⁵⁰GF,

	Starts	1st	2nd	3rd	Win & Pl
Hurdles	1	0	0	0	0
Career Total	2	0	0	0	0

Going: Sf: 0-0 GS: 0-0 Gd: 0-0 GF: - Fm: 0-1
Distance: 2m/2m3: 0-1 2m4-2m7: 0-0 3m+: 0-0
Track: LH: 0-1 RH: 0-0 Tight: 0-1 Gall: 0-0
Aids: Bl: 0-0 Vi: 0-0 Tstrap: 0-0
Best Rating: 0 5/02 Strf 2m110y gd-fm Hdl

Lisdante (IRE)

112　　　　　　　123

10-y-o b g Phardante (FR)-Shuil Eile (Deep Run)
Mrs S J Smith Keith Nicholson

Placings:004F3F4/200042P23P231/1P15P/52-
11PP42163P　　　　　　　　　　(3365)
2002/03: 25¹G, 28¹G, 32⁸GF, 24⁰G, 23⁴G, 26²GF, 26¹S, 24⁶S,
28³S, 24⁸GS,

	Starts	1st	2nd	3rd	Win & Pl
Chases	10	3	1	1	28499
Career Total	37	6	6	4	55135
123 10/02	Carl 3m2f	D(0-120)HCh	SFT	£13617
117 5/03	Strf 3m4f	D(0-120)HCh	GD	£4793
123 5/02	Aint 3m1f	D(0-120)HCh	GD	£5304
104 11/00	Weth 3m1f	D(0-120)HCh	HVY	£6608
105 6/00	MRas 2m6f110yE(0-105)HCh	G-F	£4290
99 4/00	Weth 3m5f	C HCh	SFT	£5980
		Total win prize-money £40594		

Going: Sf: 1-3 GS: 0-1 Gd: 2-4 GF: - Fm: 0-2
Distance: 2m/2m3: 0-0 2m4-2m7: 0-0 3m+: 3-10
Track: LH: 2-7 RH: 1-2 Tight: 2-4 Gall: 0-0
Aids: Bl: 0-0 Vi: 0-0 Tstrap: 0-0
Best Rating: 123 10/02 Carl 3m2f soft Ch

Fair chaser, in good form over fences in the early summer of 2002 with wins at Aintree and Stratford and regained winning form at Carlisle in October; out of sorts so far in 2003; stays three and a half miles; acts on any ground.

Lislaughtin Abbey

108(94h)　　　　　　(77h)109+

11-y-o ch g Nicholas Bill-Kates Fling (USA) (Quiet Fling (USA))
O Brennan T W R Bayley

Placings:0/P00P/244U53231344/1FP21243121/U225P/P24
4P316-P02551　　　　　　　　　　(4670)
2002/03: 24⁸PG, 16⁰G, 16²S, 16⁵S, 16⁵GS, 21¹G,

	Starts	1st	2nd	3rd	Win & Pl
Hurdles	1	0	0	0	0
Chases	5	1	1	0	6856
Career Total	47	7	9	5	40601
99 4/03	Fknm 2m5f110yE(0-110)HCh	GD	£5607
99 4/02	Sedg 2m5f D(0-115)HCh	G-F	£3874
116 4/00	Fknm 2m5f110yF(0-110)HCh	GD	£4621
116 3/00	Fknm 2m5f110yE(0-110)HCh	GD	£3974
109 12/99	Fknm 2m110y F(0-100)HCh	GD	£2263
92 5/99	Fknm 2m5f110yE(0-110)HCh	G-F	£3989
86 10/98	Sthl 2m4f110yE(0-110)HCh	GD	£2997
	Total win prize-money £27329		

Going: Sf: 0-2 GS: 0-1 Gd: 1-3 GF: - Fm: 0-0
Distance: 2m/2m3: 0-4 2m4-2m7: 1-1 3m+: 0-1
Track: LH: 1-6 RH: 0-0 Tight: 1-4 Gall: 0-1
Aids: Bl: 0-0 Vi: 0-0 Tstrap: 0-0
Best Rating: 116 12/00 Fknm 3m110y gd-sft Ch

Moderate handicap chaser; a Fakenham specialist; has won five times at the Norfolk track; in good form when registering back-to-back wins in April and June 2003; best on good ground or faster; stays 3m, but is probably better over shorter.

Lismeenan (IRE)

101(103h)　　　　　　(94h)92

9-y-o ch g Be My Native (USA)-Sakanda (IRE) (Vayrann)
C P Morlock Mrs Z S Clark

Placings:63405/315F25414/P003-00544　(2291)
2002/03: 17⁰G, 16⁰GF, 19⁵GF, 20⁴GF, 16⁴G,

	Starts	1st	2nd	3rd	Win & Pl
Hurdles	4	0	0	0	0
Chases	1	0	0	0	292
Career Total	23	2	1	3	10540
109 11/99	Naas 2m	(0-132)HHdl	Y-S	£5236
99 6/99	Rosc 2m	Hdl	G-F	£2516
	Total win prize-money £7754		

Going: Sf: 0-0 GS: 0-0 Gd: 0-2 GF: - Fm: 0-3
Distance: 2m/2m3: 0-4 2m4-2m7: 0-1 3m+: 0-0
Track: LH: 0-3 RH: 0-2 Tight: 0-2 Gall: 0-0
Aids: Bl: 0-0 Vi: 0-0 Tstrap: 0-0
Best Rating: 109 11/99 Fair 2m yld-sft Hdl

Won a maiden hurdle in Ireland before winning a handicap hurdle in 1999. Returned from nearly two years off when making his British debut at Exeter in November 2001, but was pulled up. Looks suited by two miles and most types of ground, bar extremes of going. Showed definite signs of a return to form when running well from out of the handicap at Stratford April 2002.

Liss A Paoraigh (IRE)

125　　　　　　　160

8-y-o b m Husyan (USA)-Shuil Liss (Deep Run)
John E Kiely Mrs N Flynn

Placings:31/11112/312F20-222125　　(4131)
2002/03: 20²YS, 16²S, 20²YS, 16¹HY, 16²Y, 24⁵G,

	Starts	1st	2nd	3rd	Win & Pl
Hurdles	6	1	4	0	53774
Career Total	19	7	7	2	158237

160	12/02	Leop	2m	Hdl	HVY £29907
160	11/01	Navn	2m4f	Hdl	YLD £19657
137	12/00	Fair	2m	Hdl	Y-S £23400
116	11/00	Naas	2m3f	Hdl	Y-S £4692
128	10/00	Gowr	2m1f	Hdl	SFT £4416
123	5/00	Punc	2m	NHF	GD £13000
99	3/00	Clon	2m2f	NHF	G-Y £3036

Total win prize-money £98109

Going: Sf: 1-2 GS: 0-0 Gd: 0-1 GF: - Fm: 0-0
Distance: 2m2m3: 1-3 2m4-2m7: 0-2 3m+: 0-1
Track: LH: 1-5 RH: 0-0 Tight: 0-0 Gall: 0-1
Aids: Bl: 0-0 Vi: 0-0 Tstrap: 0-0
Best Rating: 160 12/02 Leop 2m heavy Hdl

A high-class Irish hurdler, she ran up a sequence of five wins in bumpers and hurdles in Ireland in 2002 and has run well at the highest level since, including winning a Grade One at Leopardstown at the end of 2002; effective at two miles, but at her best over two and a half miles on ground with give; she is a very tough, game mare.

Listen Up

100   **108+**

8-y-o b m Good Thyne (USA)-Inbisat (Beldale Flutter (USA))
R T Phillips The Listeners

Placings:110/032P-1 (1903)
2002/03: 21¹S,

	Starts	1st	2nd	3rd	Win & Pl
Hurdles	1	1	0	0	3308
Career Total	8	3	1	1	8098

108	11/02	Sedg	2m5f110yE(0-105)HHdl	SFT	£3307
102	3/01	MRas	2m1f110yH NHF	GD	£1736
110	1/01	Folk	2m1f110yH NHF	HVY	£1498

Total win prize-money £6542

Going: Sf: 1-1 GS: 0-0 Gd: 0-0 GF: - Fm: 0-0
Distance: 2m2m3: 0-0 2m4-2m7: 1-1 3m+: 0-0
Track: LH: 1-1 RH: 0-0 Tight: 1-1 Gall: 0-0
Aids: Bl: 0-0 Vi: 0-0 Tstrap: 0-0
Best Rating: 110 1/01 Folk 2m1f110y heavy NHF

Twice a winner in bumpers, she has been placed in novice hurdles at around two and a half miles. Won her only start over hurdles of the 2002/2003 season. Suited by soft ground.

Lite The Way

76f   **54f**

6-y-o b m Miners Lamp-Polly Tix (Politico) (USA))
P D Williams Mrs D J Hughes

Placings:0 (4275)
2002/03: 16⁰G,

	Starts	1st	2nd	3rd	Win & Pl
NH Flat	1	0	0	0	
Career Total	1	0	0	0	

Going: Sf: 0-0 GS: 0-0 Gd: 0-1 GF: - Fm: 0-0
Distance: 2m2m3: 0-1 2m4-2m7: 0-0 3m+: 0-0
Track: LH: 0-1 RH: 0-0 Tight: 0-0 Gall: 0-0
Aids: Bl: 0-0 Vi: 0-0 Tstrap: 0-0
Best Rating: 54 3/03 Chep 2m110y good NHF

Little Alfie (IRE)

98   **76**

6-y-o b g Shahanndeh-Debbies Scud (IRE) (Roselier (FR))

B S Rothwell John H Price

Placings:00-P40404 (1473)
2002/03: 16⁶GS, 16⁴G, 17⁰GF, 16⁴GF, 17⁰GF, 20⁴GF,

	Starts	1st	2nd	3rd	Win & Pl
Hurdles	6	0	0	0	0
Career Total	8	0	0	0	0

Going: Sf: 0-0 GS: 0-1 Gd: 0-1 GF: - Fm: 0-4
Distance: 2m2m3: 0-5 2m4-2m7: 0-1 3m+: 0-0
Track: LH: 0-4 RH: 0-2 Tight: 0-3 Gall: 0-0
Aids: Bl: 0-0 Vi: 0-0 Tstrap: 0-0
Best Rating: 76 6/02 Uttx 2m good Hdl

Little Big Horse (IRE)

105   **99**

7-y-o b g Little Bighorn-Little Gort (Roselier (FR))
Mrs S J Smith Paul J Dixon

Placings:2660P-22424523 (4602)
2002/03: 20²GF, 16²G, 20⁴GS, 19²GS, 16⁴GS, 24⁵G, 20²GS, 21³G,

	Starts	1st	2nd	3rd	Win & Pl
Hurdles	8	0	4	1	7516
Career Total	13	0	5	1	8190

Going: Sf: 0-0 GS: 0-4 Gd: 0-3 GF: - Fm: 0-1
Distance: 2m2m3: 0-2 2m4-2m7: 0-5 3m+: 0-1
Track: LH: 0-5 RH: 0-3 Tight: 0-4 Gall: 0-1
Aids: Bl: 0-0 Vi: 0-0 Tstrap: 0-0
Best Rating: 103 11/01 Weth 2m good NHF

Moderate maiden hurdler; handles most types of ground; stays two and a half miles; yet to win a race.

Little Blackie

59   **12**

6-y-o br m Royal Fountain-Mother Machree (Bing Ii)
F P Murtagh S J Marshall

Placings:P (4750)
2002/03: 24⁰G,

	Starts	1st	2nd	3rd	Win & Pl
Hurdles	1	0	0	0	
Career Total	1	0	0	0	

Going: Sf: 0-0 GS: 0-0 Gd: 0-1 GF: - Fm: 0-0
Distance: 2m2m3: 0-0 2m4-2m7: 0-0 3m+: 0-1
Track: LH: 0-0 RH: 0-1 Tight: 0-0 Gall: 0-0
Aids: Bl: 0-0 Vi: 0-0 Tstrap: 0-0
Best Rating: 0 4/03 Prth 3m110y good Hdl

Little Brown Bear (IRE)

112(93h)   (81+h)**106**

9-y-o br g Strong Gale-Gladtogetit (Green Shoon)
R Ford G B Barlow

Placings:P/3F3142-13323223 (4796)
2002/03: 27¹GF, 25³G, 28³G, 27²G, 28³GF, 27²G, 28²G, 28³GF,

	Starts	1st	2nd	3rd	Win & Pl
Chases	8	1	3	4	13238
Career Total	15	2	4	6	20181

105	5/02	Sedg	3m3f	E(0-110)HCh	G-F £3668
90	2/02	Muss	3m	E(0-105)HCh	G-S £5096

Total win prize-money £8764

Going: Sf: 0-0 GS: 0-0 Gd: 0-5 GF: - Fm: 1-3
Distance: 2m/2m3: 0-0 2m4-2m7: 0-0 3m+: 1-8
Track: LH: 1-7 RH: 0-1 Tight: 1-8 Gall: 0-0
Aids: Bl: 0-0 Vi: 0-0 Tstrap: 0-0
Best Rating: 106 3/03 Sedg 3m3f good Ch

Moderate chaser/hurdler; suited by positive tactics; acts on a sound surface, stays three and a half miles.

Little Bud

105   **100**

9-y-o br m Lord Bud-Sindur (Rolfe (USA))
Miss A M Newton-Smith Mrs John Grist

Placings:6/0660P/6020/P030144/154011FP54-633P511 (4700)
2002/03: 21⁶GF, 16³S, 16³HY, 21⁸HY, 16⁵G, 21¹GF, 21¹GF,

	Starts	1st	2nd	3rd	Win & Pl
Hurdles	7	2	0	2	8130
Career Total	34	6	1	3	19064

100	4/03	Plum	2m5f	E(0-105)HHdl	G-F £3503
95	3/03	Plum	2m5f	F(0-110)HHdl	G-F £3562
95	11/01	Plum	2m	F(0-110)HHdl	GD £3178
95	11/01	Plum	2m5f	F(0-90)HHdl	G-S £2352
89	5/01	Folk	2m1f110y	G(0-95)HHdl	G-S £1666
80	11/00	Plum	2m	F Hdl	HVY £2278

Total win prize-money £16541

Going: Sf: 0-3 GS: 0-0 Gd: 0-1 GF: - Fm: 2-3
Distance: 2m/2m3: 0-3 2m4-2m7: 2-4 3m+: 0-0
Track: LH: 2-6 RH: 0-1 Tight: 2-6 Gall: 0-0
Aids: Bl: 0-0 Vi: 0-0 Tstrap: 0-0
Best Rating: 100 4/03 Plum 2m5f gd-fm Hdl

Moderate hurdler; stays 2m 5f, effective at shorter; acts on fast ground; goes well at Plumpton.

Little Em

59   **12**

8-y-o ch m Rock City-Sleepline Princess (Royal Palace)
R Johnson (R J Hodges 19/5) Miss Tina Hammond

Placings:0FP (1165)
2002/03: 17⁰GF, 17⁵G, 21⁸G,

	Starts	1st	2nd	3rd	Win & Pl
Hurdles	3	0	0	0	
Career Total	3	0	0	0	

Going: Sf: 0-0 GS: 0-0 Gd: 0-2 GF: - Fm: 0-1
Distance: 2m/2m3: 0-2 2m4-2m7: 0-1 3m+: 0-0
Track: LH: 0-3 RH: 0-0 Tight: 0-3 Gall: 0-0
Aids: Bl: 0-0 Vi: 0-0 Tstrap: 0-0
Best Rating: 14 7/02 Sedg 2m1f gd-fm Hdl

Little Enam (IRE)

82   **49**

7-y-o gr g Un Desperado (FR)-Black Pheasant (IRE) (Sexton Blake)
C R Egerton R K Carvill

Placings:66 (3140)
2002/03: 16⁶HY, 19⁶S,

	Starts	1st	2nd	3rd	Win & Pl
NH Flat	1	0	0	0	0
Hurdles	1	0	0	0	0
Career Total	2	0	0	0	0

Going: Sf: 0-2 GS: 0-0 Gd: 0-0 GF: - Fm: 0-0
Distance: 2m/2m3: 0-1 2m4-2m7: 0-1 3m+: 0-0

Track: LH: 0-1 RH: 0-1 Tight: 0-1 Gall: 0-1
Aids: Bl: 0-0 Vi: 0-0 Tstrap: 0-0
Best Rating: 81 12/02 Newb 2m110y   heavy NHF

Little Flora

106   **103**

7-y-o ch m Alflora (IRE)-Sister s Choice (Lepanto (GER))
A Scott Mrs A Scott

Placings:0/00P35003/02334312355046101-5535   (0722)
2002/03: 16⁵G, 20⁵GF, 16³GF, 16⁶G,

	Starts	1st	2nd	3rd	Win & Pl
Hurdles	4	0	0	1	270
Career Total	30	3	2	7	12261
103 4/02 Sedg	2m5f110yE(0-105)HHdl			G-F	£2618
90 4/02 Hexm	2m110y E Hdl			G-F	£2835
91 7/01 Sedg	2m5f110yE Hdl			G-F	£2471
			Total win prize-money		£7924

Going: Sf: 0-0 GS: 0-0 Gd: 0-2 GF: - Fm: 0-2
Distance: 2m/2m3: 0-3 2m4-2m7: 0-1 3m+: 0-0
Track: LH: 0-3 RH: 0-1 Tight: 0-1 Gall: 0-0
Aids: Bl: 0-0 Vi: 0-0 Tstrap: 0-0
Best Rating: 103 4/02 Sedg 2m5f110y gd-fm Hdl

Moderate hurdler, best on a sound surface and sharp tracks.
Was winning for the third time when successful at
Sedgefield in April. Appreciates fast ground.

Little Heck (IRE)

6-y-o b g Executive Perk-Princess Andromeda (Corvaro
(USA))
T D Easterby The Rumpole Partnership

Placings:0   (3817)
2002/03: 16⁶G,

	Starts	1st	2nd	3rd	Win & Pl
NH Flat	1	0	0	0	
Career Total	1	0	0	0	

Going: Sf: 0-0 GS: 0-0 Gd: 0-1 GF: - Fm: 0-0
Distance: 2m/2m3: 0-1 2m4-2m7: 0-0 3m+: 0-0
Track: LH: 0-1 RH: 0-0 Tight: 0-1 Gall: 0-0
Aids: Bl: 0-0 Vi: 0-0 Tstrap: 0-0
Best Rating: 0 2/03 Catt 2m   good NHF

Little Herman (IRE)

90(79h)   (90h)**66+**

7-y-o b g Mandalus-Kilbricken Bay (Salluceva)
J A B Old W E Sturt

Placings:060-00   (3253)
2002/03: 20⁰S, 20⁶S,

	Starts	1st	2nd	3rd	Win & Pl
Hurdles	1	0	0	0	0
Chases	1	0	0	0	0
Career Total	5	0	0	0	0

Going: Sf: 0-2 GS: 0-0 Gd: 0-0 GF: - Fm: 0-0
Distance: 2m/2m3: 0-0 2m4-2m7: 0-2 3m+: 0-0
Track: LH: 0-2 RH: 0-0 Tight: 0-0 Gall: 0-0
Aids: Bl: 0-0 Vi: 0-0 Tstrap: 0-0
Best Rating: 90 1/02 Asct 2m4f   gd-sft Hdl

Well held all starts to date.

Little John

63   **68**

7-y-o b g Warrshan (USA)-Silver Venture (USA) (Silver
Hawk (USA))
Miss L A Perratt McCloskey Partnership

Placings:5/56/5   (1475)
2002/03: 17⁵GF,

	Starts	1st	2nd	3rd	Win & Pl
Hurdles	1	0	0	0	0
Career Total	4	0	0	0	0

Going: Sf: 0-0 GS: 0-0 Gd: 0-0 GF: - Fm: 0-1
Distance: 2m/2m3: 0-1 2m4-2m7: 0-0 3m+: 0-0
Track: LH: 0-0 RH: 0-1 Tight: 0-0 Gall: 0-0
Aids: Bl: 0-0 Vi: 0-0 Tstrap: 0-0
Best Rating: 85 12/00 Muss 2m   good Hdl

Little Knowledge

58f   **49f**

5-y-o b m Terimon-Madam-M (Tina s Pet)
N A Twiston-Davies H R Mould

Placings:0   (0328)
2002/03: 16⁰G,

	Starts	1st	2nd	3rd	Win & Pl
NH Flat	1	0	0	0	
Career Total	1	0	0	0	

Going: Sf: 0-0 GS: 0-0 Gd: 0-1 GF: - Fm: 0-0
Distance: 2m/2m3: 0-1 2m4-2m7: 0-0 3m+: 0-0
Track: LH: 0-1 RH: 0-0 Tight: 0-0 Gall: 0-0
Aids: Bl: 0-0 Vi: 0-0 Tstrap: 0-0
Best Rating: 49 5/02 Worc 2m   good NHF

Little Laura

79f   **79f**

7-y-o ch m Casteddu-At First Sight (He Loves Me)
K W Hogg K W Hogg

Placings:5/00   (1309)
2002/03: 16⁰GF, 16⁰GF,

	Starts	1st	2nd	3rd	Win & Pl
NH Flat	2	0	0	0	
Career Total	3	0	0	0	0

Going: Sf: 0-0 GS: 0-0 Gd: 0-0 GF: - Fm: 0-2
Distance: 2m/2m3: 0-2 2m4-2m7: 0-0 3m+: 0-0
Track: LH: 0-1 RH: 0-1 Tight: 0-0 Gall: 0-0
Aids: Bl: 0-0 Vi: 0-0 Tstrap: 0-0
Best Rating: 79 9/00 Prth 2m110y   heavy NHF

Little Les

95   **83**

7-y-o b g Jumbo Hirt (USA)-Hand On Heart (IRE) (Taufan
(USA))
F P Murtagh L Irving

Placings:P/50P05SP-6323P   (0828)
2002/03: 16⁸GF, 16²G, 16²G, 20³GF, 17⁰GF,

	Starts	1st	2nd	3rd	Win & Pl
Hurdles	5	0	1	2	1374
Career Total	13	0	1	2	1374

Going: Sf: 0-0 GS: 0-0 Gd: 0-2 GF: - Fm: 0-3

Little Madame

87   **58**

4-y-o b f Faustus (USA)-Sprig Muslin (Ra Nova)
D R Gandolfo M A Dore

Placings:P3P   (2610)
2002/03: 17⁶S, 17³GF, 16⁶S,

	Starts	1st	2nd	3rd	Win & Pl
Hurdles	3	0	0	1	565
Career Total	3	0	0	1	565

Going: Sf: 0-2 GS: 0-0 Gd: 0-0 GF: - Fm: 0-1
Distance: 2m/2m3: 0-3 2m4-2m7: 0-0 3m+: 0-0
Track: LH: 0-3 RH: 0-0 Tight: 0-2 Gall: 0-0
Aids: Bl: 0-2 Vi: 0-0 Tstrap: 0-0
Best Rating: 58 8/02 Bang 2m1f   gd-fm Hdl

Little Mick (IRE)

73   **36**

6-y-o br g Mister Lord (USA)-Strong Trump (IRE) (Strong
Gale)
J A B Old Mrs J A Fowler/M Lovatt

Placings:0P   (2602)
2002/03: 17⁰GS, 20⁵S,

	Starts	1st	2nd	3rd	Win & Pl
NH Flat	1	0	0	0	0
Hurdles	1	0	0	0	0
Career Total	2	0	0	0	

Going: Sf: 0-1 GS: 0-1 Gd: 0-0 GF: - Fm: 0-0
Distance: 2m/2m3: 0-1 2m4-2m7: 0-1 3m+: 0-0
Track: LH: 0-0 RH: 0-1 Tight: 0-0 Gall: 0-0
Aids: Bl: 0-0 Vi: 0-0 Tstrap: 0-0
Best Rating: 56 11/02 Tntn 2m1f   gd-sft NHF

Little Mickey

89   **83**

5-y-o ch g Rock Hopper-Sixslip (USA) (Diesis)
N A Twiston-Davies S P Tindall

Placings:43UP3   (3928)
2002/03: 18⁴HY, 18³S, 21ᵁGS, 24⁴S, 26³G,

	Starts	1st	2nd	3rd	Win & Pl
NH Flat	2	0	0	1	318
Hurdles	3	0	0	1	391
Career Total	5	0	0	2	709

Going: Sf: 0-3 GS: 0-1 Gd: 0-1 GF: - Fm: 0-0
Distance: 2m/2m3: 0-2 2m4-2m7: 0-1 3m+: 0-2
Track: LH: 0-2 RH: 0-3 Tight: 0-1 Gall: 0-1
Aids: Bl: 0-0 Vi: 0-0 Tstrap: 0-0
Best Rating: 87 12/02 Font 2m2f110y   soft NHF

Little Mister

7-y-o ch g Gran Alba (USA)-Chrissytino (Baron Blakeney)
N R Mitchell N J Powell

Placings:00-PP (3334)
2002/03: 18^{P}HY, 24^{P}S,

	Starts	1st	2nd	3rd	Win & Pl
Hurdles	2	0	0	0	
Career Total	**4**	**0**	**0**	**0**	

Going: Sf: 0-2 GS: 0-0 Gd: 0-0 GF: - Fm: 0-0
Distance: 2m/2m3: 0-1 2m4-2m7: 0-0 3m+: 0-1
Track: LH: 0-1 RH: 0-1 Tight: 0-2 Gall: 0-0
Aids: Bl: 0-0 Vi: 0-0 Tstrap: 0-0
Best Rating: **0** 1/03 Tntn 3m110y soft Hdl

Little Nobby

71 **41**

4-y-o b g Makbul-Simply Style (Bairn (USA))
R Hollinshead R Hollinshead

Placings:0 (1209)
2002/03: 16^{0}G,

	Starts	1st	2nd	3rd	Win & Pl
Hurdles	1	0	0	0	
Career Total	**1**	**0**	**0**	**0**	

Going: Sf: 0-0 GS: 0-0 Gd: 0-1 GF: - Fm: 0-0
Distance: 2m/2m3: 0-1 2m4-2m7: 0-0 3m+: 0-0
Track: LH: 0-1 RH: 0-0 Tight: 0-0 Gall: 0-0
Aids: Bl: 0-0 Vi: 0-0 Tstrap: 0-0
Best Rating: **41** 9/02 Uttx 2m good Hdl

Little Rock

92 **90**

7-y-o b h Warning-Much Too Risky (Bustino)
F Doumen J M Greetham

Placings:0 (2570)
2002/03: 16^{0}G,

	Starts	1st	2nd	3rd	Win & Pl
Hurdles	1	0	0	0	
Career Total	**1**	**0**	**0**	**0**	

Going: Sf: 0-0 GS: 0-0 Gd: 0-1 GF: - Fm: 0-0
Distance: 2m/2m3: 0-1 2m4-2m7: 0-0 3m+: 0-0
Track: LH: 0-1 RH: 0-0 Tight: 0-0 Gall: 0-1
Aids: Bl: 0-0 Vi: 0-0 Tstrap: 0-0
Best Rating: **90** 12/02 Newb 2m110y good Hdl

Group-class performer on the Flat; did not sparkle on his hurdling debut.

Little Rort (IRE)

103 **122**

4-y-o b g Ali-Royal (IRE)-Florinda (CAN) (Vice Regent (CAN))
M J Grassick Mrs C Grassick

Placings:25150 (4130)
2002/03: 16^{2}HY, 16^{5}S, 16^{1}HY, 16^{5}YS, 17^{0}G,

	Starts	1st	2nd	3rd	Win & Pl
Hurdles	5	1	1	0	7399
Career Total	**5**	**1**	**1**	**0**	**7399**

108	12/02	Limk	2m	Hdl	HVY	£5926

Total win prize-money £5926

Going: Sf: 1-3 GS: 0-0 Gd: 0-1 GF: - Fm: 0-0
Distance: **2m/2m3: 1-5** 2m4-2m7: 0-0 3m+: 0-0
Track: LH: 0-1 RH: 0-2 Tight: 0-0 Gall: 0-1
Aids: Bl: 0-0 Vi: 0-0 Tstrap: 0-2
Best Rating: **122** 2/03 Fair 2m yld-sft Hdl

Fair juvenile hurdler; effective on heavy ground.

Little Ross

101(96h) (91h)**87**

8-y-o b g St Ninian-Little Katrina (Little Buskins)
D M Grissell Barry & Baroness Noakes

Placings:*0/5/*06-3**U345P** (4430)
2002/03: 21^{3}HY, 20^{U}S, 16^{3}S, 18^{4}S, 16^{5}G, 20^{P}GF,

	Starts	1st	2nd	3rd	Win & Pl
Hurdles	1	0	0	1	426
Chases	5	0	0	1	938
Career Total	**10**	**0**	**0**	**2**	**1364**

Going: Sf: 0-4 GS: 0-0 Gd: 0-1 GF: - Fm: 0-1
Distance: 2m/2m3: 0-3 2m4-2m7: 0-3 3m+: 0-0
Track: LH: 0-2 RH: 0-2 Tight: 0-6 Gall: 0-0
Aids: Bl: 0-0 Vi: 0-0 Tstrap: 0-6
Best Rating: **96** 4/00 Hntg 2m110y good NHF

Moderate hurdler, suited by two miles five furlongs and soft ground.

Little Sky

89 **52**

6-y-o gr m Terimon-Brown Coast (Oats)
D Mullarkey Dune Racing

Placings:*0-0*UP (4426)
2002/03: 16^{0}G, 16^{U}GF, 16^{P}GF,

	Starts	1st	2nd	3rd	Win & Pl
NH Flat	1	0	0	0	0
Hurdles	2	0	0	0	0
Career Total	**4**	**0**	**0**	**0**	

Going: Sf: 0-0 GS: 0-0 Gd: 0-1 GF: - Fm: 0-2
Distance: 2m/2m3: 0-3 2m4-2m7: 0-0 3m+: 0-0
Track: LH: 0-2 RH: 0-1 Tight: 0-2 Gall: 0-1
Aids: Bl: 0-0 Vi: 0-0 Tstrap: 0-0
Best Rating: **42** 1/03 Sthl 2m good NHF

Little Sport (IRE)

109 **134**

6-y-o ch g Moscow Society (USA)-Ath Dara (Duky)
A Scott Andy Scott

Placings:*206*-2311232100 (4456)
2002/03: 17^{2}S, 20^{3}HY, 20^{1}S, 20^{1}GS, 23^{2}HY, 20^{3}GS, 20^{2}HY, 24^{1}S, 21^{0}G, 24^{0}G,

	Starts	1st	2nd	3rd	Win & Pl
NH Flat	1	0	1	0	586
Hurdles	9	3	2	2	16785
Career Total	**13**	**3**	**4**	**2**	**17890**

134	2/03	Newc	3m	D(0-125)HHdl	SFT	£5040
125	11/02	Newc	2m4f	D Hdl	G-S	£3731
105	11/02	Newc	2m4f	E Hdl	SFT	£3538

Total win prize-money £12311

Going: Sf: 2-6 GS: 1-2 Gd: 0-2 GF: - Fm: 0-0
Distance: 2m/2m3: 0-1 **2m4-2m7: 2-7** 3m+: 1-2
Track: **LH: 3-9** RH: 0-1 Tight: 0-1 **Gall: 3-4**
Aids: Bl: 0-0 Vi: 0-0 Tstrap: 0-0
Best Rating: **134** 3/03 Chel 2m5f good Hdl

Useful hurdler; stays three miles, effective over shorter; acts on a soft surface; tough and genuine.

Little Task

103(102h) (89h)**101**

5-y-o b g Environment Friend-Lucky Thing (Green Desert (USA))
J S Wainwright Keith Jackson

Placings:14340-16056200600 (4711)
2002/03: 16^{1}G, 17^{6}G, 20^{0}GF, 16^{5}GF, 16^{6}GF, 17^{2}GF, 16^{0}G, 16^{0}G, 16^{6}G, 17^{0}G, 16^{0}GF,

	Starts	1st	2nd	3rd	Win & Pl
Hurdles	10	1	1	0	7206
Chases	1	0	0	0	0
Career Total	**16**	**2**	**1**	**1**	**10592**

96	5/02	Weth	2m	D(0-115)HHdl	GD	£6449
83	9/01	Strf	2m110y	E Hdl	G-F	£3041

Total win prize-money £9492

Going: Sf: 0-0 GS: 0-0 Gd: 1-6 GF: - Fm: 0-5
Distance: **2m/2m3: 1-10** 2m4-2m7: 0-1 3m+: 0-0
Track: **LH: 1-10** RH: 0-1 Tight: 0-5 Gall: 0-1
Aids: Bl: 0-0 Vi: 0-1 Tstrap: 0-0
Best Rating: **96** 5/02 Weth 2m good Hdl

Modest hurdler, suited by fast ground and is effective at around two miles.

Little Tobias (IRE)

103 **93**

4-y-o ch g Millkom-Barbara Frietchie (IRE) (Try My Best (USA))
Andrew Turnell Mrs Claire Hollowood

Placings:1 (1366)
2002/03: 17^{1}F,

	Starts	1st	2nd	3rd	Win & Pl
Hurdles	1	1	0	0	4017
Career Total	**1**	**1**	**0**	**0**	**4017**

93	10/02	Extr	2m1f	D Hdl	FRM	£4017

Total win prize-money £4017

Going: Sf: 0-0 GS: 0-0 Gd: 0-0 GF: - Fm: 1-1
Distance: **2m/2m3: 1-1** 2m4-2m7: 0-0 3m+: 0-0
Track: LH: 0-0 **RH: 1-1** Tight: 0-0 Gall: 0-0
Aids: Bl: 0-0 Vi: 0-0 Tstrap: 0-0
Best Rating: **93** 10/02 Extr 2m1f firm Hdl

Made a winning debut when winning a poor event at Exeter October 2002; acts on fast ground.

Little Tuska (IRE)

108(89h) (82h)**60**

13-y-o gr g Step Together (USA)-Peek-A-Boo (Bustino)
M J M Evans (N B Mason 15/9) M J M Evans

Placings:06/**P041/6P651/231130630230F0F555/24212/PP 43F026353-6346P4554** (4735)
2002/03: 16^{6}GS, 17^{3}GF, 17^{4}GF, 21^{6}GF, 20^{P}G, 21^{4}G, 16^{5}HY, 16^{5}G, 19^{4}GF,

	Starts	1st	2nd	3rd	Win & Pl
Hurdles	2	0	0	0	0
Chases	7	0	0	1	750
Career Total	**54**	**5**	**6**	**8**	**29637**

85	9/00	Plum	2m1f	F(0-110)HCh	G-F	£2908
98	6/99	Hrfd	2m3f	E(0-115)HCh	GD	£4201
102	6/99	Prth	2m	E(0-115)HCh	SFT	£3387
84	5/99	Hexm	2m110y	F(0-100)HCh	GD	£2945
102	4/98	Prth	2m	D Ch	G-S	£4500

Total win prize-money £17945

Going: Sf: 0-1 GS: 0-1 Gd: 0-3 GF: - Fm: 0-4
Distance: 2m/2m3: 0-5 2m4-2m7: 0-4 3m+: 0-0
Track: LH: 0-8 RH: 0-1 Tight: 0-2 Gall: 0-0
Aids: Bl: 0-6 Vi: 0-0 Tstrap: 0-9
Best Rating: **102** 6/99 Prth 2m soft Ch

Modest chaser who has had just the one win since the summer of 1999, he is getting on now and is best at around two miles one these days. Acts on most surfaces.

Little Worsall (IRE)

10-y-o ch g Broadsword (USA)-In My View (King s Ride)
Mrs K J Tutty N D Tutty

Placings: 40P/6P/P32U0/PF330P-05   (4592)
2002/03: 25⁰S, 25⁵G,

	Starts	1st	2nd	3rd	Win & Pl
Chases	2	0	0	0	0
Career Total	18	0	1	3	2318

Going: Sf: 0-1 GS: 0-0 Gd: 0-1 GF: - Fm: 0-0
Distance: 2m/2m3: 0-0 2m4-2m7: 0-0 3m+: 0-2
Track: LH: 0-2 RH: 0-0 Tight: 0-1 Gall: 0-0
Aids: Bl: 0-0 Vi: 0-0 Tstrap: 0-0
Best Rating: 89 3/99 Muss 2m   good NHF

Littleton Boreas (USA)

4-y-o b/br c Foxhound (USA)-Susita Song (USA) (Seattle Song (USA))
T J Naughton (R J White 7/8) Littleton Manor Racing

Placings: P   (2120)
2002/03: 16ᴾGS,

	Starts	1st	2nd	3rd	Win & Pl
Hurdles	1	0	0	0	
Career Total	1	0	0	0	

Going: Sf: 0-0 GS: 0-1 Gd: 0-0 GF: - Fm: 0-0
Distance: 2m/2m3: 0-1 2m4-2m7: 0-0 3m+: 0-0
Track: LH: 0-1 RH: 0-0 Tight: 0-1 Gall: 0-0
Aids: Bl: 0-0 Vi: 0-0 Tstrap: 0-0
Best Rating: 0 11/02 Fknm 2m   gd-sft Hdl

Littleton Zeus (IRE)
79   60

4-y-o ch g Woodborough (USA)-La Fandango (IRE) (Taufan (USA))
W S Cunningham (R J White 2/5) J D T Smith

Placings: 00   (4156)
2002/03: 16⁰G, 17⁰G,

	Starts	1st	2nd	3rd	Win & Pl
Hurdles	2	0	0	0	
Career Total	2	0	0	0	

Going: Sf: 0-0 GS: 0-0 Gd: 0-2 GF: - Fm: 0-0
Distance: 2m/2m3: 0-2 2m4-2m7: 0-0 3m+: 0-0
Track: LH: 0-0 RH: 0-2 Tight: 0-2 Gall: 0-0
Aids: Bl: 0-0 Vi: 0-0 Tstrap: 0-0
Best Rating: 60 2/03 Muss 2m   good Hdl

Lituus (USA)

10-y-o gr g El Gran Senor (USA)-Liturgism (USA) (Native Charger)
Miss Gay Kelleway (A Chaille-Chaille 3/6) E Oertel

Placings: P-33PP   (1449)
2002/03: 17³G, 18³GS, 16ᴾGF, 16ᴾG,

	Starts	1st	2nd	3rd	Win & Pl
Hurdles	3	0	0	2	1718
Chases	1	0	0	0	0

Career Total   5   0   0   2   1718

Going: Sf: 0-0 GS: 0-1 Gd: 0-2 GF: - Fm: 0-1
Distance: 2m/2m3: 0-4 2m4-2m7: 0-0 3m+: 0-0
Track: LH: 0-1 RH: 0-0 Tight: 0-1 Gall: 0-0
Aids: Bl: 0-0 Vi: 0-0 Tstrap: 0-0
Best Rating: 0 10/02 Fknm 2m110y   good Ch

Live The Dream
114   124+

5-y-o b m Exit To Nowhere (USA)-Inveraven (Alias Smith (USA))
M C Pipe The Reims Partnership

Placings: 1122060-600341   (2848)
2002/03: 16⁵GF, 20⁰G, 20⁰S, 21³GS, 24⁴G, 21¹S,

	Starts	1st	2nd	3rd	Win & Pl
Hurdles	6	1	0	1	19358
Career Total	13	3	2	1	41029
124 12/02 Chel	2m5f110yB HHdl		SFT	£15326	
127 11/01 Asct	2m110y B Hdl		GD	£8209	
97 11/01 Wwck	2m D Hdl		GD	£3423	

Total win prize-money £26959

Going: Sf: 1-2 GS: 0-1 Gd: 0-2 GF: - Fm: 0-1
Distance: 2m/2m3: 0-1 2m4-2m7: 1-4 3m+: 0-1
Track: LH: 1-6 RH: 0-0 Tight: 0-0 Gall: 1-3
Aids: Bl: 0-0 Vi: 0-0 Tstrap: 0-0
Best Rating: 127 11/01 Asct 2m110y   good Hdl

Fair hurdler; winning plater on the Flat, she developed into a decent juvenile hurdler in 2001/02. A tough sort, she took time to find her form in 2002/3, but improved when upped in trip and won at Cheltenham in December.

Lively Dessert (IRE)
107(86h)   (53h)

10-y-o b g Be My Native (USA)-Liffey Travel (Le Bavard (FR))
F P Murtagh Mrs M E James

Placings: 000/000025632/0F000004P06/01131201/PPP33-2PF4PPP5P   (4765)
2002/03: 25²GS, 25⁵PGS, 28⁴S, 27⁴S, 24²HY, 24⁴S, 32⁴S, 24⁴G, 31⁴G,

	Starts	1st	2nd	3rd	Win & Pl
Hurdles	1	0	0	0	
Chases	8	0	1	0	2386
Career Total	45	4	4	4	36355
119 11/01 Prth	3m	C Ch	HVY	£7702	
119 12/00 Ayr	3m1f	D(0-125)HCh	SFT	£7231	
103 10/00 Aint	3m1f	F(0-105)HCh	GD	£5213	
108 10/00 Sthl	3m110y	F(0-100)HCh	HVY	£2723	

Total win prize-money £22871

Going: Sf: 0-5 GS: 0-2 Gd: 0-2 GF: - Fm: 0-0
Distance: 2m/2m3: 0-0 2m4-2m7: 0-0 3m+: 0-9
Track: LH: 0-6 RH: 0-2 Tight: 0-3 Gall: 0-1
Aids: Bl: 0-0 Vi: 0-0 Tstrap: 0-0
Best Rating: 119 4/01 Prth 3m   heavy Ch

Livenlearnlad
80f   67f

7-y-o b g Norton Challenger-Welcoming Arms (Free State)
B De Haan Miss Victoria Scott Jnr

Placings: 0   (1627)
2002/03: 16⁰GS,

	Starts	1st	2nd	3rd	Win & Pl
NH Flat	1	0	0	0	

Career Total   1   0   0   0

Going: Sf: 0-0 GS: 0-1 Gd: 0-2 GF: - Fm: 0-0
Distance: 2m/2m3: 0-1 2m4-2m7: 0-0 3m+: 0-0
Track: LH: 0-1 RH: 0-0 Tight: 0-1 Gall: 0-0
Aids: Bl: 0-0 Vi: 0-0 Tstrap: 0-0
Best Rating: 67 10/02 Fknm 2m   gd-sft NHF

Lizzy Lamb
90f   75f

5-y-o gr m Bustino-Caroline Lamb (Hotfoot)
Miss S E Hall Miss S E Hall

Placings: 3   (0834)
2002/03: 17³GF,

	Starts	1st	2nd	3rd	Win & Pl
NH Flat	1	0	0	1	263
Career Total	1	0	0	1	263

Going: Sf: 0-0 GS: 0-0 Gd: 0-0 GF: - Fm: 0-1
Distance: 2m/2m3: 0-1 2m4-2m7: 0-0 3m+: 0-0
Track: LH: 0-1 RH: 0-0 Tight: 0-1 Gall: 0-0
Aids: Bl: 0-0 Vi: 0-0 Tstrap: 0-0
Best Rating: 75 7/02 Sedg 2m1f   gd-fm NHF

Related to Lord Lamb and Mr Lamb, made a fair debut to finish third in a Sedgefield bumper.

Lizzys First
102   101

11-y-o b g Town And Country-Lizzy Longstocking (Jimsun)
C J Down Stephen Goss

Placings: 0P/FU21311455/55264/0UFPP0P0/030-34162015   (4599)
2002/03: 19³GS, 22⁴S, 19¹S, 19⁶S, 19²GS, 21⁰G, 24¹F, 24⁵GF,

	Starts	1st	2nd	3rd	Win & Pl
Hurdles	8	2	1	1	8014
Career Total	36	5	3	3	18225
101 4/03 Tntn	3m110y G(0-95)HHdl	FRM	£2483	
101 12/02 Hrfd	2m3f110yE(0-105)HHdl	SFT	£4033	
107 2/99 Tntn	2m3f110yE(0-115)HHdl	G-S	£2775	
107 2/99 Tntn	2m3f110yE(0-105)HHdl	G-S	£2309	
92 12/98 Extr	2m1f110yE(0-100)HHdl	SFT	£2532	

Total win prize-money £14133

Going: Sf: 1-3 GS: 0-2 Gd: 0-1 GF: - Fm: 1-2
Distance: 2m/2m3: 0-0 2m4-2m7: 1-6 3m+: 1-2
Track: LH: 0-0 RH: 2-8 Tight: 1-4 Gall: 0-0
Aids: Bl: 0-0 Vi: 0-0 Tstrap: 0-0
Best Rating: 109 11/00 NAbb 2m5f110y   heavy Ch

Moderate hurdler, ended a long losing run in December 2002; won again in April 2003; stays two and a half miles and suited by soft ground, but has won on fast.

Loblite Leader (IRE)
99   92

6-y-o b g Tirol-Cyrano Beauty (IRE) (Cyrano De Bergerac)
G A Swinbank Montagu Bloodstock Ltd

Placings: 53   (3816)
2002/03: 16⁵G, 19³G,

	Starts	1st	2nd	3rd	Win & Pl
Hurdles	2	0	0	1	569
Career Total	2	0	0	1	569

Going: Sf: 0-0 GS: 0-0 Gd: 0-2 GF: - Fm: 0-0
Distance: 2m/2m3: 0-2 2m4-2m7: 0-0 3m+: 0-0

Track: LH: 0-1 RH: 0-1 Tight: 0-2 Gall: 0-0
Aids: Bl: 0-0 Vi: 0-0 Tstrap: 0-0
Best Rating: 97 2/03 Catt 2m3f   good   Hdl

Multiple winner on the Flat; improved effort when third over hurdles at Catterick in February 2003.

Lobuche (IRE)

77(105h)   (62h)52
8-y-o b g Petardia-Lhotse (IRE) (Shernazar)
M C Chapman   K D Blanch

Placings:21/360366540240055/16233230/04100521200P0
354P-66   (2324)
2002/03: 17⁶HY, 17⁶S,

	Starts	1st	2nd	3rd	Win & Pl
Hurdles	1	0	0	0	0
Chases	1	0	0	0	0
Career Total	44	4	6	6	20508
97	9/01	MRas	2m3f110yE(0-115)HHdl	G-F	£3332
97	6/01	MRas	2m3f110yE(0-105)HHdl	G-F	£2949
91	5/00	Ctml	2m1f110yG(0-90)HHdl	GD	£3582
99	3/99	MRas	2m1f110yD Hdl	G-S	£3367
				Total win prize-money £13233	

Going: Sf: 0-2 GS: 0-0 Gd: 0-0 GF: - Fm: 0-0
Distance: 2m/2m3: 0-2 2m4-2m7: 0-0 3m+: 0-0
Track: LH: 0-1 RH: 0-1 Tight: 0-0 Gall: 0-0
Aids: Bl: 0-0 Vi: 0-0 Tstrap: 0-2
Best Rating: 104 3/00 Chel 2m1f   gd-fm   Hdl

Loch Na Bpeisc (IRE)

74   58
6-y-o b g Over The River (FR)-Ballyhire Lady (IRE) (Callernish)
P G Murphy   Mrs John Spielman

Placings:00P   (3147)
2002/03: 21⁰GS, 20⁶S, 24PHY,

	Starts	1st	2nd	3rd	Win & Pl
Hurdles	3	0	0	0	
Career Total	3	0	0	0	

Going: Sf: 0-2 GS: 0-1 Gd: 0-0 GF: - Fm: 0-0
Distance: 2m/2m3: 0-0 2m4-2m7: 0-2 3m+: 0-1
Track: LH: 0-3 RH: 0-0 Tight: 0-0 Gall: 0-1
Aids: Bl: 0-0 Vi: 0-0 Tstrap: 0-0
Best Rating: 58 11/02 Catt 2m5f   gd-sft   Hdl

Loch Torridon

66f   40f
4-y-o b g Syrtos-Loch Scavaig (IRE) (The Parson)
James Moffatt   Mrs G A Turnbull

Placings:0   (3969)
2002/03: 16⁶S,

	Starts	1st	2nd	3rd	Win & Pl
NH Flat	1	0	0	0	
Career Total	1	0	0	0	

Going: Sf: 0-1 GS: 0-0 Gd: 0-0 GF: - Fm: 0-0
Distance: 2m/2m3: 0-1 2m4-2m7: 0-0 3m+: 0-0
Track: LH: 0-1 RH: 0-0 Tight: 0-1 Gall: 0-0
Aids: Bl: 0-0 Vi: 0-0 Tstrap: 0-0
Best Rating: 40 3/03 Catt 2m   soft   NHF

Lochbuy Junior (FR)

107   113
8-y-o b g Saumarez-Chalabiah (Akarad (FR))
M Todhunter   The G-Guck Group

Placings:F2/4415P2P5/2PP-1   (4037)
2002/03: 20¹S,

	Starts	1st	2nd	3rd	Win & Pl
Hurdles	1	1	0	0	4843
Career Total	14	2	3	0	11525
104	3/03	Ayr	2m4f	D(0-125)HHdl	SFT	£4842
115	11/00	Catt	2m3f	F(0-110)HHdl	G-S	£1911
				Total win prize-money £6754		

Going: Sf: 1-1 GS: 0-0 Gd: 0-0 GF: - Fm: 0-0
Distance: 2m/2m3: 0-0 2m4-2m7: 1-1 3m+: 0-0
Track: LH: 1-1 RH: 0-0 Tight: 0-0 Gall: 0-0
Aids: Bl: 0-0 Vi: 0-0 Tstrap: 1-1
Best Rating: 115 11/00 Catt 2m3f   gd-sft   Hdl

Modest hurdler. Had his first run for new connections and his first outing since April when runner-up at Market Rasen in October 2001. Best at around a mile and a half on an easy surface.

Lochiedubs

90   89
8-y-o br g Cragador-Linn Falls (Royal Fountain)
Mrs L B Normile   Mrs L Normile

Placings:3/535034-30   (3811)
2002/03: 20³HY, 25⁶G,

	Starts	1st	2nd	3rd	Win & Pl
Hurdles	2	0	0	1	417
Career Total	9	0	0	4	1780

Going: Sf: 0-1 GS: 0-0 Gd: 0-0 GF: - Fm: 0-0
Distance: 2m/2m3: 0-0 2m4-2m7: 0-1 3m+: 0-1
Track: LH: 0-1 RH: 0-1 Tight: 0-1 Gall: 0-0
Aids: Bl: 0-0 Vi: 0-0 Tstrap: 0-0
Best Rating: 100 10/01 Carl 2m1f   gd-sft   NHF

Lochnagen

9-y-o b g Lochnager-Broken Paws (Busted)
S E H Sherwood   Rosemary Viscountess Boyne

Placings:P   (0143)
2002/03: 20PGF,

	Starts	1st	2nd	3rd	Win & Pl
Hurdles	1	0	0	0	
Career Total	1	0	0	0	

Going: Sf: 0-0 GS: 0-0 Gd: 0-0 GF: - Fm: 0-1
Distance: 2m/2m3: 0-0 2m4-2m7: 0-1 3m+: 0-0
Track: LH: 0-1 RH: 0-0 Tight: 0-0 Gall: 0-0
Aids: Bl: 0-0 Vi: 0-0 Tstrap: 0-0
Best Rating: 0 5/02 Chep 2m4f   gd-fm   Hdl

Lodestar (IRE)

102(107h)   (114+h)107
6-y-o br g Good Thyne (USA)-Lets Compromise (No Argument)
Ian Williams   Sir Robert Ogden

Placings:0-P4F5212   (4673)
2002/03: 19PG, 25⁴S, 24FG, 23⁵GS, 20²G, 22¹GF, 26²GF,

	Starts	1st	2nd	3rd	Win & Pl
Hurdles	2	1	1	0	5319

Chases   5   0   1   0   1584
Career Total   8   1   2   0   6903
93   4/03   Strf   2m6f110y   E Hdl   G-F £4260
            Total win prize-money £4261

Going: Sf: 0-1 GS: 0-1 Gd: 0-3 GF: - Fm: 1-2
Distance: 2m/2m3: 0-0 2m4-2m7: 1-3 3m+: 0-4
Track: LH: 1-3 RH: 0-4 Tight: 1-2 Gall: 0-1
Aids: Bl: 0-0 Vi: 0-0 Tstrap: 0-0
Best Rating: 110 4/03 Hrfd 3m2f   gd-fm   Hdl

Modest novice chaser/hurdler; got off the mark over hurdles at Stratford in April 2003 after an unsuccessful spell chasing; followed-up in Class C handicap hurdle at Worcester the next month; seems best on a sound surface; stays 3m 2f.

Log On Intersky (IRE)

107(111h)   (93h)131
7-y-o ch g Insan (USA)-Arctic Mo (IRE) (Mandalus)
J Howard Johnson   interskyracing.com

Placings:00/030FP32-315211414   (4458)
2002/03: 21³GF, 21¹G, 20⁵GF, 21²G, 16¹S, 16¹GS, 19⁴G, 16¹G, 16⁴G,

	Starts	1st	2nd	3rd	Win & Pl
Hurdles	3	1	0	1	3267
Chases	6	3	1	0	19022
Career Total	18	4	2	3	24573
129	2/03	Catt	2m	D Ch	GD	£5476
129	12/02	Catt	2m	E(0-105)HCh	G-S	£3818
116	10/02	Carl	2m	E(0-100)HCh	SFT	£4348
93	9/02	Sedg	2m5f110yE Hdl		GD	£2891
				Total win prize-money £16535		

Going: Sf: 1-1 GS: 1-1 Gd: 2-5 GF: - Fm: 0-2
Distance: 2m/2m3: 3-5 2m4-2m7: 1-4 3m+: 0-0
Track: LH: 3-7 RH: 1-2 Tight: 3-6 Gall: 0-0
Aids: Bl: 0-0 Vi: 0-0 Tstrap: 1-3
Best Rating: 131 4/03 Aint 2m   good   Ch

Moderate hurdler/decent chaser; stays trips of around two and a half miles; acts on good or softer; has worn a tongue tie.

Logician (NZ)

116   149
12-y-o b g Lord Ballina (AUS)-Thornton Lady (NZ) (Sound Reason (CAN))
I A Balding   Robert Roulston

Placings:3/2/1021143/140F64B2-132   (2240)
2002/03: 16¹GS, 20³GS, 17²GS,

	Starts	1st	2nd	3rd	Win & Pl
Chases	3	1	1	1	17422
Career Total	20	5	4	3	81043
145	7/02	Wolv	2m	C(0-135)HCh	G-S	£6734
144	5/01	Bang	2m1f110yE Ch		G-S	£3607
	9/00	Moon	2m	Ch	FRM	£5743
	7/00	Moon	2m2f110y	Ch	SFT	£26807
	6/00	Sann	1m6f	Hdl	SFT	£5743
				Total win prize-money £48635		

Going: Sf: 0-0 GS: 1-3 Gd: 0-0 GF: - Fm: 0-0
Distance: 2m/2m3: 1-2 2m4-2m7: 0-1 3m+: 0-0
Track: LH: 1-2 RH: 0-1 Tight: 1-2 Gall: 0-1
Aids: Bl: 0-0 Vi: 0-0 Tstrap: 0-0
Best Rating: 149 11/02 Newb 2m1f   gd-sft   Ch

Useful ex-Australian-trained handicap chaser, best suited to a sound surface; he is effective at two miles but has been tried over further with little success. Reportedly retired.

Loi De Martiale (IRE)

102f   96f

5-y-o br g Presenting-Thresa-Anita (IRE) (Over The River (FR))
J M Jefferson R G Marshall

Placings:20   (3160)
2002/03: 16²GS, 16⁰G,

	Starts	1st	2nd	3rd	Win & Pl
NH Flat	2	0	1	0	1272
Career Total	2	0	1	0	1272

Going: Sf: 0-0 GS: 0-1 Gd: 0-1 GF: - Fm: 0-0
Distance: 2m/2m3: 0-2 2m4-2m7: 0-0 3m+: 0-0
Track: LH: 0-0 RH: 0-2 Tight: 0-2 Gall: 0-0
Aids: Bl: 0-0 Vi: 0-0 Tstrap: 0-0
Best Rating: 96 12/02 Muss 2m   gd-sft NHF

Showed promise when runner-up on debut in bumper at Musselburgh in December but ran poorly there next time.

Lolly Copse

66f   24f

5-y-o b m Lancastrian-Game Spinney (Precipice Wood)
S J Gilmore Michael Moss And Lyn Appleton

Placings:00   (3747)
2002/03: 16⁰GS, 16⁰G,

	Starts	1st	2nd	3rd	Win & Pl
NH Flat	2	0	0	0	0
Career Total	2	0	0	0	0

Going: Sf: 0-0 GS: 0-1 Gd: 0-1 GF: - Fm: 0-0
Distance: 2m/2m3: 0-2 2m4-2m7: 0-0 3m+: 0-0
Track: LH: 0-0 RH: 0-2 Tight: 0-0 Gall: 0-1
Aids: Bl: 0-0 Vi: 0-0 Tstrap: 0-0
Best Rating: 24 1/03 Kemp 2m   gd-sft NHF

Londolozi Lad (IRE)

97   79+

4-y-o b g Ali-Royal (IRE)-Ashdown (Pharly (FR))
P C Haslam David H Morgan & Northern Lights Racing

Placings:F10   (1716)
2002/03: 16ᶠGF, 16¹G, 16⁰G,

	Starts	1st	2nd	3rd	Win & Pl
Hurdles	3	1	0	0	4121
Career Total	3	1	0	0	4121
79	9/02 Uttx	2m	D Hdl	GD	£4121
			Total win prize-money £4121		

Going: Sf: 0-0 GS: 0-0 Gd: 1-2 GF: - Fm: 0-1
Distance: 2m/2m3: 1-3 2m4-2m7: 0-0 3m+: 0-0
Track: LH: 1-3 RH: 0-0 Tight: 0-2 Gall: 0-0
Aids: Bl: 0-0 Vi: 0-0 Tstrap: 0-0
Best Rating: 79 9/02 Uttx 2m   good Hdl

Plating-class hurdler; acts on good ground.

Lone Soldier (FR)

93(100c)   (118c)103

7-y-o ch g Songlines (FR)-Caring Society (Caerleon (USA))
S B Clark S B Clark

Placings:22P431/54020/401440-600   (0694)
2002/03: 16⁶GS, 16⁰G, 24⁰G,

	Starts	1st	2nd	3rd	Win & Pl
Hurdles	3	0	0	0	0

Career Total   20   2   3   1   9805
108 6/01 Worc 2m   E Ch   G-F £3260
102 3/00 Tntn 2m1f   F(0-100)HHdl GD £2107
                    Total win prize-money £5367

Going: Sf: 0-0 GS: 0-1 Gd: 0-2 GF: - Fm: 0-0
Distance: 2m/2m3: 0-2 2m4-2m7: 0-0 3m+: 0-1
Track: LH: 0-2 RH: 0-1 Tight: 0-1 Gall: 0-0
Aids: Bl: 0-0 Vi: 0-0 Tstrap: 0-3
Best Rating: 108 6/01 Worc 2m   gd-fm Ch

Winning hurdle/chaser; best on a sound surface.

Lone Star (IRE)

11-y-o b g Satco (FR)-Masterstown Lucy (Bargello)
A M Hales Andrew L Cohen

Placings:P/PP3/360/PUF/P-4   (0099)
2002/03: 16⁰GS, 20⁴GF,

	Starts	1st	2nd	3rd	Win & Pl
Hurdles	2	0	0	0	0
Career Total	12	0	0	2	980

Going: Sf: 0-0 GS: 0-1 Gd: 0-0 GF: - Fm: 0-1
Distance: 2m/2m3: 0-1 2m4-2m7: 0-1 3m+: 0-0
Track: LH: 0-0 RH: 0-1 Tight: 0-1 Gall: 0-0
Aids: Bl: 0-0 Vi: 0-0 Tstrap: 0-0
Best Rating: 97 5/99 Hrfd 2m3f   good Ch

Loner

80   60

5-y-o b g Magic Ring (IRE)-Jolis Absent (Primo Dominie)
M Wigham Michael Wigham

Placings:6   (1934)
2002/03: 17⁶GS,

	Starts	1st	2nd	3rd	Win & Pl
Hurdles	1	0	0	0	0
Career Total	1	0	0	0	0

Going: Sf: 0-0 GS: 0-1 Gd: 0-0 GF: - Fm: 0-0
Distance: 2m/2m3: 0-1 2m4-2m7: 0-0 3m+: 0-0
Track: LH: 0-0 RH: 0-1 Tight: 0-1 Gall: 0-0
Aids: Bl: 0-0 Vi: 0-0 Tstrap: 0-0
Best Rating: 60 11/02 Tntn 2m1f   gd-sft Hdl

Lonesome Dealer (IRE)

(87h)   (81h)85

7-y-o b/br g Supreme Leader-Slievenaree (IRE) (Lancastrian)
B G Powell (P M J Doyle 24/10) Tweenhills Racing (Cleeve Hill)

Placings:60415000-04P40   (4563)
2002/03: 16⁰GF, 17⁴GF, 22ᴾG, 18⁴YS, 24⁰GF,

	Starts	1st	2nd	3rd	Win & Pl
Hurdles	1	0	0	0	0
Chases	4	0	0	0	626
Career Total	13	1	0	0	7094
108	12/01 Limk	2m	Hdl	SFT	£6129
			Total win prize-money £6129		

Going: Sf: 0-0 GS: 0-0 Gd: 0-1 GF: - Fm: 0-3
Distance: 2m/2m3: 0-3 2m4-2m7: 0-1 3m+: 0-0
Track: LH: 0-0 RH: 0-1 Tight: 0-1 Gall: 0-0
Aids: Bl: 0-0 Vi: 0-0 Tstrap: 0-0
Best Rating: 108 12/01 Limk 2m   soft Hdl

Long Journey (IRE)

107

4-y-o b c Blues Traveller (IRE)-Pudgy Poppet (Danehill (USA))
Edward Butler M O Brien

Placings:F   (1968)
2002/03: 16ᶠGS,

	Starts	1st	2nd	3rd	Win & Pl
Hurdles	1	0	0	0	0
Career Total	1	0	0	0	0

Going: Sf: 0-0 GS: 0-1 Gd: 0-0 GF: - Fm: 0-0
Distance: 2m/2m3: 0-1 2m4-2m7: 0-0 3m+: 0-0
Track: LH: 0-1 RH: 0-0 Tight: 0-0 Gall: 0-0
Aids: Bl: 0-1 Vi: 0-0 Tstrap: 0-1
Best Rating: 104 11/02 Chel 2m110y   gd-sft Hdl

Long Shot

104   98

6-y-o b m Sir Harry Lewis (USA)-Kovalevskia (Ardross)
N J Henderson W H Ponsonby

Placings:4210-0143F2   (4750)
2002/03: 17⁰GS, 22¹G, 21⁴GS, 22³GS, 21ᶠG, 24²G,

	Starts	1st	2nd	3rd	Win & Pl
Hurdles	6	1	1	1	6911
Career Total	10	2	2	1	9055
98	11/02 Winc	2m6f	D Hdl	GD	£4309
93	4/02 Fknm	2m	H NHF	GD	£1540
			Total win prize-money £5850		

Going: Sf: 0-0 GS: 0-2 Gd: 1-4 GF: - Fm: 0-0
Distance: 2m/2m3: 0-1 **2m4-2m7:** 1-4 3m+: 0-1
Track: LH: 0-2 RH: 1-4 Tight: 0-0 Gall: 0-1
Aids: Bl: 0-0 Vi: 0-0 Tstrap: 0-0
Best Rating: 98 4/03 Prth 3m110y   good Hdl

Bumper winner; modest hurdler; acts on good and soft ground; stays two and three-quarter miles.

Longshanks

107(97c)   (99c)104

6-y-o b g Broadsword (USA)-Brass Castle (IRE) (Carlingford Castle)
K C Bailey D A Halsall

Placings:402P2   (4173)
2002/03: 20⁴S, 21⁰G, 20²S, 20ᴾGS, 20²S,

	Starts	1st	2nd	3rd	Win & Pl
Hurdles	4	0	2	0	2977
Chases	1	0	0	0	0
Career Total	5	0	2	0	2977

Going: Sf: 0-3 GS: 0-1 Gd: 0-1 GF: - Fm: 0-0
Distance: 2m/2m3: 0-0 2m4-2m7: 0-5 3m+: 0-0
Track: LH: 0-5 RH: 0-0 Tight: 0-0 Gall: 0-1
Aids: Bl: 0-0 Vi: 0-0 Tstrap: 0-0
Best Rating: 104 12/02 Hayd 2m4f   soft Hdl

Irish point winner; opened his account over hurdles here with a narrow victory at Uttoxeter in April; stays well; suited by soft ground; should make a chaser.

Longstone Boy (IRE)

108   91

11-y-o br g Mazaad-Inger-Lea (Record Run)

E R Clough E R Clough

Placings:*0*/P26/23 (4736)
2002/03: 23²GS, 24³GF,

	Starts	1st	2nd	3rd	Win & Pl
Chases	2	0	1	1	1190
Career Total	6	0	2	1	2094

Going: Sf: 0-0 GS: 0-1 Gd: 0-0 GF: - Fm: 0-1
Distance: 2m/2m3: 0-0 2m4-2m7: 0-0 3m+: 0-2
Track: LH: 0-1 RH: 0-1 Tight: 0-0 Gall: 0-0
Aids: Bl: 0-0 Vi: 0-0 Tstrap: 0-0
Best Rating: 91 3/03 Leic 2m7f110y gd-sft Ch

Modest chaser; acts on fast and easy ground.

Longstone Lad

11-y-o b g Pittacus (USA)-Fatu Hiva (GER) (Marduk (GER))
R Rawle R Rawle

Placings:*65*/3P3U24/50/U/2UP (3855)
2002/03: 26²GS, 26ᵁHY, 24ᴾGS,

	Starts	1st	2nd	3rd	Win & Pl
Chases	3	0	1	0	632
Career Total	14	0	2	2	2238

Going: Sf: 0-1 GS: 0-2 Gd: 0-0 GF: - Fm: 0-0
Distance: 2m/2m3: 0-0 2m4-2m7: 0-0 3m+: 0-3
Track: LH: 0-2 RH: 0-1 Tight: 0-0 Gall: 0-0
Aids: Bl: 0-0 Vi: 0-0 Tstrap: 0-0
Best Rating: 98 4/99 NAbb 2m6f soft Hdl

Longstone Lady (IRE)
78f   50f

6-y-o b m Mister Lord (USA)-Monamandy (IRE) (Mandalus)
J D Frost Mrs J R Bastard

Placings:*0* (0737)
2002/03: 17⁰GF,

	Starts	1st	2nd	3rd	Win & Pl
NH Flat	1	0	0	0	
Career Total	1	0	0	0	

Going: Sf: 0-0 GS: 0-0 Gd: 0-0 GF: - Fm: 0-1
Distance: 2m/2m3: 0-1 2m4-2m7: 0-0 3m+: 0-0
Track: LH: 0-1 RH: 0-0 Tight: 0-1 Gall: 0-0
Aids: Bl: 0-0 Vi: 0-0 Tstrap: 0-0
Best Rating: 50 7/02 NAbb 2m1f gd-fm NHF

Longstone Loch (IRE)

6-y-o b g Executive Perk-Lyre-Na-Gcloc (Le Moss)
D J Caro (T Keddy 18/1) Ady Boughen

Placings:0P (4561)
2002/03: 25⁰G, 20ᴾGF,

	Starts	1st	2nd	3rd	Win & Pl
Hurdles	2	0	0	0	
Career Total	2	0	0	0	

Going: Sf: 0-0 GS: 0-0 Gd: 0-1 GF: - Fm: 0-1
Distance: 2m/2m3: 0-0 2m4-2m7: 0-0 3m+: 0-1
Track: LH: 0-2 RH: 0-0 Tight: 0-2 Gall: 0-0

Aids: Bl: 0-0 Vi: 0-0 Tstrap: 0-0
Best Rating: 0 4/03 Bang 2m4f gd-fm Hdl

Longterm (IRE)
106   123+

6-y-o b g Welsh Term-Sahob (Roselier (FR))
Jonjo O Neill J P McManus

Placings:*2-12* (2000)
2002/03: 17¹G, 20²S,

	Starts	1st	2nd	3rd	Win & Pl
NH Flat	1	0	0	0	2181
Hurdles	1	0	1	0	1180
Career Total	3	1	2	0	4328
122	10/02	Extr	2m1f	H NHF	GD	£2180

Total win prize-money £2181

Going: Sf: 0-0 GS: 0-0 Gd: 1-1 GF: - Fm: 0-0
Distance: 2m/2m3: 1-1 2m4-2m7: 0-1 3m+: 0-0
Track: LH: 0-1 RH: 1-1 Tight: 0-0 Gall: 0-0
Aids: Bl: 0-0 Vi: 0-0 Tstrap: 0-0
Best Rating: 123 11/02 Hayd 2m4f soft Hdl

Ex-Irish, he stayed on well to land an Exeter bumper in October 2002. acts on good ground or softer.

Look In The Mirror

12-y-o b g Rakaposhi King-Moaning Jenny (Privy Seal)
Fergal O Brien Chris Hammett

Placings:*0006*P/42P025/21PPP/2/1241/4105-0U (0414)
2002/03: 25⁰G, 28ᵁGF,

	Starts	1st	2nd	3rd	Win & Pl
Chases	2	0	0	0	
Career Total	27	4	5	0	26574
123	6/01	Strf	3m4f	B Ch	G-F	£17355
108	4/01	Extr	2m7f110yH Ch		SFT	£2282
108	5/00	Hrfd	3m1f110yH Ch		GD	£2100
93	5/98	Hrfd	3m2f	G(0-95)HHdl	GD	£1593

Total win prize-money £23330

Going: Sf: 0-0 GS: 0-0 Gd: 0-1 GF: - Fm: 0-1
Distance: 2m/2m3: 0-0 2m4-2m7: 0-0 3m+: 0-2
Track: LH: 0-1 RH: 0-1 Tight: 0-1 Gall: 0-0
Aids: Bl: 0-0 Vi: 0-0 Tstrap: 0-0
Best Rating: 123 6/01 Strf 3m4f gd-fm Ch

Useful point-to-pointer/hunter chaser. Stays three and a half miles. Has won on most types of ground but does not want it too sticky.

Look Sharp (FR)

6-y-o b g Keen-Hunt The Thimble (FR) (Relkino)
T Wall V And J Properties

Placings:*21*-P (1642)
2002/03: 16ᴾG,

	Starts	1st	2nd	3rd	Win & Pl
Hurdles	1	0	0	0	
Career Total	3	1	1	0	5723
	7/01	Comp	2m1f110y Hdl	SFT	£3880

Total win prize-money £3880

Going: Sf: 0-0 GS: 0-0 Gd: 0-0 GF: - Fm: 0-0
Distance: 2m/2m3: 0-1 2m4-2m7: 0-0 3m+: 0-0
Track: LH: 0-0 RH: 0-1 Tight: 0-0 Gall: 0-0
Aids: Bl: 0-0 Vi: 0-0 Tstrap: 0-0
Best Rating: 0 10/02 Kemp 2m good Hdl

Look Sharpe

12-y-o b g Looking Glass-Washburn Flyer (Owen Dudley)
T S Sharpe T S Sharpe

Placings:*20*/P/U5-040 (4592)
2002/03: 25⁰GF, 20⁴GF, 25⁰G,

	Starts	1st	2nd	3rd	Win & Pl
Chases	3	0	0	0	211
Career Total	8	0	1	0	667

Going: Sf: 0-0 GS: 0-0 Gd: 0-1 GF: - Fm: 0-2
Distance: 2m/2m3: 0-0 2m4-2m7: 0-1 3m+: 0-2
Track: LH: 0-2 RH: 0-0 Tight: 0-0 Gall: 0-0
Aids: Bl: 0-0 Vi: 0-0 Tstrap: 0-0
Best Rating: 76 5/01 Weth 2m4f110y firm Ch

Look To The Future (IRE)
103   101

9-y-o b g Roselier (FR)-Toevarro (Raga Navarro (ITY))
C J Mann The Whitcoombe Partnership

Placings:*50*/0002240/0006/P2PP36P3 (4514)
2002/03: 19ᴾGS, 20²G, 22ᴾGS, 19ᴾS, 20³HY, 21⁶G, 25ᴾG, 22³GF,

	Starts	1st	2nd	3rd	Win & Pl
Hurdles	6	0	1	2	2657
Chases	2	0	0	0	
Career Total	21	0	3	2	4548

Going: Sf: 0-2 GS: 0-2 Gd: 0-3 GF: - Fm: 0-1
Distance: 2m/2m3: 0-2 2m4-2m7: 0-5 3m+: 0-1
Track: LH: 0-2 RH: 0-6 Tight: 0-3 Gall: 0-1
Aids: Bl: 0-0 Vi: 0-0 Tstrap: 0-0
Best Rating: 104 11/02 Aint 2m4f good Hdl

Maiden over both hurdles and fences at up to three miles.

Looking Deadly
102(88c)   (49c)33

9-y-o b m Neltino-Princess Constanza (Relkino)
F P Murtagh Teddy Bears & Big Bear Syndicate

Placings:*00000*/2P/0500PP-2045U55P (2264)
2002/03: 17²GS, 16⁰G, 17⁴G, 17⁵G, 25ᵁGF, 27⁵G, 17⁵HY, 18ᴾHY,

	Starts	1st	2nd	3rd	Win & Pl
Hurdles	4	0	1	0	693
Chases	4	0	0	0	268
Career Total	21	0	2	0	1637

Going: Sf: 0-2 GS: 0-1 Gd: 0-4 GF: - Fm: 0-2
Distance: 2m/2m3: 0-6 2m4-2m7: 0-0 3m+: 0-2
Track: LH: 0-8 RH: 0-0 Tight: 0-6 Gall: 0-0
Aids: Bl: 0-0 Vi: 0-0 Tstrap: 0-0
Best Rating: 85 5/00 Kels 2m110y good Hdl

Looking Forward
103   95+

7-y-o b g Primitive Rising (USA)-Gilzie Bank (New Brig)
Ferdy Murphy Mrs G Handley

Placings:P53-4PFU1 (4519)
2002/03: 22⁴HY, 24ᴾS, 16ᶠS, 21ᵁG, 21¹G,

	Starts	1st	2nd	3rd	Win & Pl
Chases	5	1	0	0	5350
Career Total	8	1	0	1	5823

95 4/03 Sedg 2m5f   E(0-110)HCh   GD   £5031
Total win prize-money £5031

Going:	Sf: 0-3 GS: 0-0 Gd: 1-2 GF: - Fm: 0-0
Distance:	2m/2m3: 0-1 **2m4-2m7: 1-3** 3m+: 0-1
Track:	LH: **1-4** RH: 0-1 Tight: **1-3** Gall: 0-0
Aids:	Bl: 0-0 Vi: 0-0 Tstrap: 0-0
Best Rating:	95 4/03 Sedg 2m5f good Ch

Moderate chaser; former pointer; put jumping problems behind him when successful at Sedgefield in April 2003; stays two miles five.

Looks Like Mine
56f

6-y-o b g Miners Lamp-Glenisla (Sunyboy)
A P Jones Miss Sue Morris

Placings:*0*   (0687)
2002/03: 16⁰GF,

	Starts	1st	2nd	3rd	Win & Pl
NH Flat	1	0	0	0	
Career Total	1	0	0	0	

Going:	Sf: 0-0 GS: 0-0 Gd: 0-0 GF: - Fm: 0-1
Distance:	2m/2m3: 0-1 2m4-2m7: 0-0 3m+: 0-0
Track:	LH: 0-0 RH: 0-0 Tight: 0-0 Gall: 0-0
Aids:	Bl: 0-0 Vi: 0-0 Tstrap: 0-0
Best Rating:	56 7/02 Strf 2m110y gd-fm NHF

Looks Like Value (IRE)

7-y-o gr g Euphemism-Crossdrumrosie (IRE) (Roselier (FR))
K C Bailey Have Fun Racing Partnership

Placings:*0*PP5   (4339)
2002/03: 16⁰GS, 20⁰S, 25ᴾGS, 24⁵GF,

	Starts	1st	2nd	3rd	Win & Pl
NH Flat	1	0	0	0	0
Chases	3	0	0	0	0
Career Total	4	0	0	0	0

Going:	Sf: 0-1 GS: 0-2 Gd: 0-0 GF: - Fm: 0-1
Distance:	2m/2m3: 0-1 2m4-2m7: 0-1 3m+: 0-2
Track:	LH: 0-2 RH: 0-2 Tight: 0-0 Gall: 0-1
Aids:	Bl: 0-0 Vi: 0-0 Tstrap: 0-0
Best Rating:	51 11/02 Chel 2m110y gd-sft NHF

Looksharp Lad (IRE)
69f   56f

5-y-o b g Simply Great (FR)-Merry Madness (Raise You Ten)
Mrs A J Bowlby J Shaw

Placings:*6*   (4053)
2002/03: 16⁶HY,

	Starts	1st	2nd	3rd	Win & Pl
NH Flat	1	0	0	0	0
Career Total	1	0	0	0	0

Going:	Sf: 0-1 GS: 0-0 Gd: 0-0 GF: - Fm: 0-0
Distance:	2m/2m3: 0-1 2m4-2m7: 0-0 3m+: 0-0
Track:	LH: 0-0 RH: 0-0 Tight: 0-0 Gall: 0-0
Aids:	Bl: 0-0 Vi: 0-0 Tstrap: 0-0
Best Rating:	65 3/03 Sand 2m110y heavy NHF

Loop The Loup
109   130

7-y-o b g Petit Loup (USA)-Mithi Al Gamar (USA) (Blushing Groom (FR))
Mrs M Reveley Mr And Mrs J D Cotton

Placings:*0/102/3-332B31*   (4713)
2002/03: 20³G, 20³G, 17²GS, 16ᴮGS, 22³G, 20¹GF,

	Starts	1st	2nd	3rd	Win & Pl
Hurdles	6	1	1	3	21725
Career Total	11	2	2	4	27833
130 4/03 Weth	2m4f110yB(0-145)HHdl		G-F	£9516	
130 12/00 Muss	2m4f	E Hdl		GD	£2840

Total win prize-money £12357

Going:	Sf: 0-0 GS: 0-2 Gd: 0-3 GF: - Fm: 1-1
Distance:	2m/2m3: 0-2 **2m4-2m7: 1-4** 3m+: 0-0
Track:	LH: **1-5** RH: 0-1 Tight: 0-1 Gall: 0-0
Aids:	Bl: 0-2 Vi: 0-0 Tstrap: 0-0
Best Rating:	130 4/03 Weth 2m4f110y gd-fm Hdl

Useful hurdler; fair stayer on the Flat; best over two and a half miles on fast ground; needs a strong pace and a galloping track; sometimes wears blinkers.

Loopy Linda (IRE)

5-y-o b g Simply Great (FR)-Albane (Shirley Heights)
T D Easterby Ron George

Placings:*01124*   (3350)
2002/03: 16⁰HY, 16¹GS, 16¹GS, 16²G, 20⁴HY,

	Starts	1st	2nd	3rd	Win & Pl
NH Flat	4	2	1	0	7683
Hurdles	1	0	0	0	422
Career Total	5	2	1	0	8105
107 12/02 Muss	2m	H NHF		G-S	£4134
110 12/02 Donc	2m110y	H NHF		G-S	£2698

Total win prize-money £6833

Going:	Sf: 0-2 GS: 2-2 Gd: 0-1 GF: - Fm: 0-0
Distance:	**2m/2m3: 2-4** 2m4-2m7: 0-1 3m+: 0-0
Track:	LH: 1-2 RH: 1-3 Tight: 1-2 Gall: 1-1
Aids:	Bl: 0-0 Vi: 0-0 Tstrap: 0-0
Best Rating:	110 1/03 Muss 2m good NHF

Fair bumper performer; acts on fast and easy ground.

Loramore

6-y-o ch m Afflora (IRE)-Apsimore (Touching Wood (USA))
J C Tuck Mrs Erica Griffiths

Placings:*0P*   (2706)
2002/03: 17⁰G, 16ᴾGS,

	Starts	1st	2nd	3rd	Win & Pl
NH Flat	1	0	0	0	0
Hurdles	1	0	0	0	0
Career Total	2	0	0	0	0

Going:	Sf: 0-0 GS: 0-1 Gd: 0-1 GF: - Fm: 0-0
Distance:	2m/2m3: 0-2 2m4-2m7: 0-0 3m+: 0-0
Track:	LH: 0-0 RH: 0-2 Tight: 0-0 Gall: 0-0
Aids:	Bl: 0-0 Vi: 0-0 Tstrap: 0-0
Best Rating:	80 5/02 Extr 2m1f good NHF

Lord 'N' Master (IRE)
110(105h)   (96h)120

7-y-o b g Lord Americo-Miss Good Night (Buckskin (FR))

R Rowe Dr B Alexander

Placings:*565-613413P1P5*   (4779)
2002/03: 22⁶GF, 19¹G, 22³GS, 24⁴G, 20¹GS, 22³S, 20ᴾS, 24¹S, 26ᴾS, 20⁵GF,

	Starts	1st	2nd	3rd	Win & Pl
Hurdles	4	1	0	1	4779
Chases	6	2	0	1	15334
Career Total	13	3	0	2	20113
120 3/03 Sand	3m110y D(0-115)HCh		SFT	£6841	
115 12/02 Sand	2m4f110yD(0-110)HCh		G-S	£6994	
96 10/02 Extr	2m3f	D(0-115)HHdl	GD	£3978	

Total win prize-money £17813

Going:	Sf: 1-4 GS: 1-2 Gd: 1-2 GF: - Fm: 0-2
Distance:	2m/2m3: 1-1 2m4-2m7: 1-6 3m+: 1-3
Track:	LH: 0-5 RH: **3-5** Tight: 0-3 Gall: 0-1
Aids:	Bl: 0-0 Vi: 0-0 Tstrap: 0-0
Best Rating:	120 3/03 Sand 3m110y soft Ch

Modest hurdler/chaser. Stays two and a half miles.

Lord Alvinru (IRE)
99   87

6-y-o b g Lord Americo-Alvinru (Sandalay)
G A Swinbank Arnie Flower

Placings:*04032-5P6U*   (1375)
2002/03: 20⁰G, 16ᴾGF, 20⁶GF, 17ᵁGF,

	Starts	1st	2nd	3rd	Win & Pl
Hurdles	4	0	0	0	0
Career Total	9	0	1	1	1350

Going:	Sf: 0-0 GS: 0-0 Gd: 0-1 GF: - Fm: 0-3
Distance:	2m/2m3: 0-2 2m4-2m7: 0-2 3m+: 0-0
Track:	LH: 0-4 RH: 0-0 Tight: 0-2 Gall: 0-0
Aids:	Bl: 0-0 Vi: 0-0 Tstrap: 0-0
Best Rating:	87 4/02 Hexm 2m110y gd-fm Hdl

Lord Alyn (IRE)
100f   91f

5-y-o b g Topanoora-Glenstal Priory (Glenstal (USA))
C R Egerton Alan & Linda Bird

Placings:*P*   (3630)
2002/03: 16ᴾS,

	Starts	1st	2nd	3rd	Win & Pl
NH Flat	1	0	0	0	0
Career Total	1	0	0	0	0

Going:	Sf: 0-1 GS: 0-0 Gd: 0-0 GF: - Fm: 0-0
Distance:	2m/2m3: 0-1 2m4-2m7: 0-0 3m+: 0-0
Track:	LH: 0-0 RH: 0-1 Tight: 0-0 Gall: 0-0
Aids:	Bl: 0-0 Vi: 0-0 Tstrap: 0-0
Best Rating:	0 2/03 Asct 2m110y soft NHF

Had shown gradual improvement in bumpers prior to winning modest Worcester event July 2003.

Lord Atterbury (IRE)

7-y-o ch g Mister Lord (USA)-Tammyiris (Arapahos (FR))
D Pipe P J Finn

Placings:*11*   (4480)
2002/03: 23¹GS, 25¹G,

	Starts	1st	2nd	3rd	Win & Pl
Chases	2	2	0	0	14190
Career Total	2	2	0	0	14190
143 4/03 Aint	3m1f	B Ch		GD	£12025

121 3/03 Leic 2m7f110y   H Ch G-S
£2164

Total win prize-money £14190

Going: Sf: 0-0 GS: 1-1 Gd: 1-1 GF: - Fm: 0-0
Distance: 2m/2m3: 0-0 2m4-2m7: 0-0 3m+: 2-2
Track: LH: 1-1 RH: 1-1 Tight: 1-1 Gall: 0-0
Aids: Bl: 0-0 Vi: 0-0 Tstrap: 0-0
Best Rating: 143 4/03 Aint 3m1f   good Ch

Smart pointer, very promising hunter chaser; runaway winner of valuable novices event at Aintree in April; followed up at Cheltenham; jumps soundly and stays really well; should continue to do well.

Lord Belfry

7-y-o ch g Baron Blakeney-Capricious Lady (IRE)
(Capricorn Line)
A Charlton Miss Juliet E Reed

Placings:00/PP   (2307)
2002/03: 20PGS, 21PHY,

	Starts	1st	2nd	3rd	Win & Pl
Hurdles	2	0	0	0	
Career Total	4	0	0	0	

Going: Sf: 0-1 GS: 0-1 Gd: 0-0 GF: - Fm: 0-0
Distance: 2m/2m3: 0-0 2m4-2m7: 0-2 3m+: 0-0
Track: LH: 0-1 RH: 0-0 Tight: 0-2 Gall: 0-0
Aids: Bl: 0-0 Vi: 0-0 Tstrap: 0-0
Best Rating: 47 1/01 Kemp 2m   soft NHF

Lord Brex (FR)

99(100h)   (95h)**95**
7-y-o gr g Saint Estephe (FR)-Light Moon (FR) (Mendez (FR))
J G M O Shea Gary Roberts

Placings:31451/2/000P-1623   (4272)
2002/03: 17¹S, 19⁶GS, 20²S, 16³G,

	Starts	1st	2nd	3rd	Win & Pl
Hurdles	4	1	1	1	3727
Career Total	14	3	2	2	49018
95	2/03	Tntn	2m1f	G Hdl	SFT £2513
136	4/00	Aint	2m110y	A Hdl	GD £24000
126	1/00	Sand	2m110y	D Hdl	SFT £4400

Total win prize-money £30914

Going: Sf: 1-2 GS: 0-1 Gd: 0-1 GF: - Fm: 0-0
Distance: 2m/2m3: 1-2 2m4-2m7: 0-2 3m+: 0-0
Track: LH: 0-2 RH: 1-2 Tight: 1-1 Gall: 0-0
Aids: Bl: 0-2 Vi: 0-1 Tstrap: 0-0
Best Rating: 137 5/00 Punc 2m   good Hdl

Useful hurdler at his best; suited by two miles and acts on ground good or softer; very good form as a juvenile in 2000, but has had problems since and is now down to contesting sellers.

Lord Broadway (IRE)

109(90h)   (46h)**86**
7-y-o b g Shardari-Country Course (IRE) (Crash Course)
N M Babbage D G & D J Robinson

Placings:50/0PP25-0P4F32224   (4613)
2002/03: 25⁰GF, 23PGF, 21⁴G, 23⁷G, 24⁵S, 24²G, 24²G, 24²G, 25⁴G,

	Starts	1st	2nd	3rd	Win & Pl
Chases	9	0	3	1	5607

Career Total   **16**   **0**   **4**   **1**   **6723**

Going: Sf: 0-1 GS: 0-0 Gd: 0-6 GF: - Fm: 0-2
Distance: 2m/2m3: 0-0 2m4-2m7: 0-1 3m+: 0-8
Track: LH: 0-5 RH: 0-4 Tight: 0-2 Gall: 0-3
Aids: Bl: 0-0 Vi: 0-0 Tstrap: 0-0
Best Rating: 97 3/01 Strf 2m10y soft NHF

Plating-class chaser; stays three miles.

Lord Buckingham

91f   **100f**
5-y-o ch g Carroll House-Lady Buck (Pollerton)
N J Henderson Mrs Hugh Maitland-Jones

Placings:50   (4329)
2002/03: 16⁵S, 16⁹G,

	Starts	1st	2nd	3rd	Win & Pl
NH Flat	2	0	0	0	0
Career Total	2	0	0	0	0

Going: Sf: 0-1 GS: 0-0 Gd: 0-1 GF: - Fm: 0-0
Distance: 2m/2m3: 0-2 2m4-2m7: 0-0 3m+: 0-0
Track: LH: 0-2 RH: 0-0 Tight: 0-0 Gall: 0-2
Aids: Bl: 0-0 Vi: 0-0 Tstrap: 0-1
Best Rating: 93 3/03 Newb 2m110y soft NHF

Lord Capitaine (IRE)

104   **113**
9-y-o b/br g Mister Lord (USA)-Salvation Sue (Mon Capitaine)
J Howard Johnson The Scottish Steeplechasing Partnership

Placings:P311P/645635P/U511-P3411   (4375)
2002/03: 25PGS, 24³S, 26⁴S, 27¹G, 28¹G,

	Starts	1st	2nd	3rd	Win & Pl
Chases	5	2	0	1	10331
Career Total	21	6	0	3	24273
111	3/03	Sedg	3m4f	E(0-110)HCh	GD £5021
110	3/03	Sedg	3m3f	E(0-105)HCh	GD £4342
113	11/01	Sedg	3m3f	F(0-100)HCh	SFT £2569
105	10/01	Sedg	3m3f	F(0-100)HCh	GD £2905
116	2/00	Sedg	3m3f	D Ch	G-S £3575
106	1/00	Muss	3m4f	E Ch	SFT £3282

Total win prize-money £21695

Going: Sf: 0-2 GS: 0-1 Gd: 2-2 GF: - Fm: 0-0
Distance: 2m/2m3: 0-0 2m4-2m7: 0-0 3m+: 2-5
Track: LH: 2-4 RH: 0-1 Tight: 2-3 Gall: 0-1
Aids: Bl: 0-0 Vi: 0-0 Tstrap: 0-0
Best Rating: 116 2/00 Sedg 3m3f gd-sft Ch

Modest chaser; steadily improving, he was unbeaten in his first three outings over fences over the three mile three furlong trip at Sedgefield; pulled up on his return to action at Catterick in December but bounced back to win twice at Sedgefield in March (unbeaten in five outings there); just stays and handles fast ground.

Lord Conyers (IRE)

78   **49**
4-y-o b f Inzar (USA)-Primelta (Primo Dominie)
B Ellison The Lord Conyers Racing Partnership

Placings:5   (1323)
2002/03: 17⁵GF,

	Starts	1st	2nd	3rd	Win & Pl
Hurdles	1	0	0	0	0
Career Total	1	0	0	0	0

Going: Sf: 0-0 GS: 0-0 Gd: 0-0 GF: - Fm: 0-1
Distance: 2m/2m3: 0-1 2m4-2m7: 0-0 3m+: 0-0
Track: LH: 0-0 RH: 0-1 Tight: 0-1 Gall: 0-0
Aids: Bl: 0-0 Vi: 0-0 Tstrap: 0-0
Best Rating: 49 9/02 MRas 2m1f110y gd-fm Hdl

Lord Dal (FR)

91   **69**
10-y-o b g Cadoudal (FR)-Lady Corteira (FR) (Carvin)
A J Whitehead A J Whitehead

Placings:1235/140124/2624/4/UP-000P   (4566)
2002/03: 24⁰S, 19⁰S, 19⁰S, 0-000P

	Starts	1st	2nd	3rd	Win & Pl
Hurdles	4	0	0	0	
Career Total	21	3	4	1	28461
120	1/99	Tram	2m4f	Ch	SH £3376
124	11/98	Naas	2m4f	HHdl	YLD £8445
103	12/97	Leop	2m	Hdl	HVY £4069

Total win prize-money £15891

Going: Sf: 0-3 GS: 0-0 Gd: 0-0 GF: - Fm: 0-1
Distance: 2m/2m3: 0-1 2m4-2m7: 0-2 3m+: 0-1
Track: LH: 0-2 RH: 0-2 Tight: 0-3 Gall: 0-0
Aids: Bl: 0-0 Vi: 0-0 Tstrap: 0-0
Best Rating: 129 11/99 Naas 2m4f yld-sft Hdl

Lord Dilrock (IRE)

89   **68**
7-y-o ch g Lord Americo-Dilrock Damsel (Over The River (FR))
Miss G Browne Mrs Rosalinde Elsbury

Placings:P   (0273)
2002/03: 22PGF,

	Starts	1st	2nd	3rd	Win & Pl
Hurdles	1	0	0	0	
Career Total	1	0	0	0	

Going: Sf: 0-0 GS: 0-0 Gd: 0-0 GF: - Fm: 0-1
Distance: 2m/2m3: 0-0 2m4-2m7: 0-1 3m+: 0-0
Track: LH: 0-1 RH: 0-0 Tight: 0-1 Gall: 0-0
Aids: Bl: 0-0 Vi: 0-0 Tstrap: 0-0
Best Rating: 0 5/02 Strf 2m6f110y gd-fm Hdl

Lord Dixon (IRE)

(86h)   (51h)
7-y-o b/br g Lord Americo-Dixons Dutchess (IRE) (Over The River (FR))
C J Gray A G Fear

Placings:2/300-F   (4080)
2002/03: 26FS,

	Starts	1st	2nd	3rd	Win & Pl
Chases	1	0	0	0	
Career Total	5	0	1	1	313

Going: Sf: 0-1 GS: 0-0 Gd: 0-0 GF: - Fm: 0-0
Distance: 2m/2m3: 0-0 2m4-2m7: 0-0 3m+: 0-1
Track: LH: 0-1 RH: 0-0 Tight: 0-1 Gall: 0-0
Aids: Bl: 0-0 Vi: 0-0 Tstrap: 0-0
Best Rating: 109 4/01 Tntn 2m1f gd-fm NHF

Lord Dundaniel (IRE)

95   **88**
6-y-o b/br g Arctic Lord-Killoskehan Queen (Bustineto)

B De Haan Willsford Racing Incorporated

Placings:064   (3779)
2002/03: 16⁰S, 16⁶S, 19⁴GS,

	Starts	1st	2nd	3rd	Win & Pl
NH Flat	1	0	0	0	0
Hurdles	2	0	0	0	288
Career Total	3	0	0	0	288

Going: Sf: 0-2 GS: 0-1 Gd: 0-0 GF: - Fm: 0-0
Distance: 2m/2m3: 0-3 2m4-2m7: 0-0 3m+: 0-0
Track: LH: 0-1 RH: 0-2 Tight: 0-0 Gall: 0-0
Aids: Bl: 0-0 Vi: 0-0 Tstrap: 0-0
Best Rating: 88 2/03 Extr 2m3f   gd-sft Hdl

Has shown some ability in points and novice hurdles but looks more of a chasing-type.

Lord Ector

7-y-o b g Mon Tresor-Lady Ector (USA) (King Pellinore (USA))
G F Bridgwater Michael Appleby

Placings:P   (0516)
2002/03: 16PS,

	Starts	1st	2nd	3rd	Win & Pl
NH Flat	1	0	0	0	
Career Total	1	0	0	0	

Going: Sf: 0-1 GS: 0-0 Gd: 0-0 GF: - Fm: 0-0
Distance: 2m/2m3: 0-1 2m4-2m7: 0-0 3m+: 0-0
Track: LH: 0-1 RH: 0-0 Tight: 0-0 Gall: 0-0
Aids: Bl: 0-0 Vi: 0-0 Tstrap: 0-1
Best Rating: 0 6/02 Worc 2m   soft NHF

Lord Edwards Army (IRE)

93(108h)   (100h)100
8-y-o b g Warcraft (USA)-Celtic Bombshell (Celtic Cone)
P Mullins P M Brady

Placings:630/00.0/4116/54102205-0050002064053 (4655a)
2002/03: 25⁰G, 19⁰YS, 24⁵G, 22⁰G, 19⁹GF, 21⁰GY, 20²F, 21⁰G, 24⁶HY, 20⁴SH, 16⁰S, 18⁵YS, 22³GF,

	Starts	1st	2nd	3rd	Win & Pl
Hurdles	9	0	1	0	1080
Chases	4	0	0	1	1208
Career Total	31	3	3	2	23777
115	9/01	List	2m4f		Hdl	G-F	£7862
107	7/01	Bell	2m1f		NHF	G-F	£3895
97	6/01	Kbgn	2m3f		NHF	GD	£3338

Total win prize-money £15097

Going: Sf: 0-2 GS: 0-0 Gd: 0-4 GF: - Fm: 0-3
Distance: 2m/2m3: 0-4 2m4-2m7: 0-6 3m+: 0-3
Track: LH: 0-3 RH: 0-2 Tight: 0-0 Gall: 0-1
Aids: Bl: 0-0 Vi: 0-0 Tstrap: 0-0
Best Rating: 120 11/01 Navn 2m   yield Hdl

Moderate novice hurdler. Stays two and a half miles. Acts on a sound surface.

Lord Fernando

106   81
4-y-o ch g Forzando-Lady Lacey (Kampala)
G B Balding The P J Partnership

Placings:040303414   (4193)

2002/03: 16⁰G, 17⁴S, 16⁰GS, 16³GS, 16⁰HY, 16³HY, 17⁴G, 16¹G, 16⁴G,

	Starts	1st	2nd	3rd	Win & Pl
Hurdles	9	1	0	2	4934
Career Total	9	1	0	2	4934
81	3/03	Hntg	2m110y	E(0-105)HHdl	GD	£3406

Total win prize-money £3406

Going: Sf: 0-3 GS: 0-2 Gd: 1-4 GF: - Fm: 0-0
Distance: 2m/2m3: 0-2 2m4-2m7: 0-0 3m+: 0-0
Track: LH: 0-3 RH: 1-6 Tight: 0-1 Gall: 1-1
Aids: Bl: 0-0 Vi: 1-6 Tstrap: 0-0
Best Rating: 81 3/03 Ludl 2m   good Hdl

Plating-class maiden hurdler; has shown form at around two miles; acts on a soft surface.

Lord Fleet (IRE)

100   72
9-y-o b g Aristocracy-Sweet And Fleet (Whistling Deer)
J R Cornwall J R Cornwall

Placings:P/P1F4PP-62P2406P02   (4264)
2002/03: 17⁶GF, 20²GF, 22PGF, 22²GF, 20⁴GF, 20⁰G, 16⁶GS, 24PGS, 20⁰GS, 20²GF,

	Starts	1st	2nd	3rd	Win & Pl
Chases	10	0	3	0	5293
Career Total	17	1	3	0	9095
103	6/01	Dpat	2m1f172y	Hdl	FRM	£3477

Total win prize-money £3478

Going: Sf: 0-0 GS: 0-3 Gd: 0-1 GF: - Fm: 0-6
Distance: 2m/2m3: 0-2 2m4-2m7: 0-7 3m+: 0-1
Track: LH: 0-3 RH: 0-7 Tight: 0-5 Gall: 0-4
Aids: Bl: 0-0 Vi: 0-0 Tstrap: 0-0
Best Rating: 103 6/01 Dpat 2m1f172y firm Hdl

Ex-Irish hurdler/chaser. Modest form over fences in this country.

Lord George

11-y-o ch g Lord Bud-Mini Gazette (London Gazette)
G C Evans (D G Atkinson 3/5) N Morgan

Placings:0F0   (4288)
2002/03: 21⁰GF, 24FGS, 20⁰GF,

	Starts	1st	2nd	3rd	Win & Pl
Chases	3	0	0	0	
Career Total	3	0	0	0	

Going: Sf: 0-0 GS: 0-1 Gd: 0-0 GF: - Fm: 0-2
Distance: 2m/2m3: 0-0 2m4-2m7: 0-2 3m+: 0-1
Track: LH: 0-2 RH: 0-1 Tight: 0-3 Gall: 0-0
Aids: Bl: 0-0 Vi: 0-0 Tstrap: 0-0
Best Rating: 48 3/03 Ludl 2m4f   gd-fm Ch

Lord Gizzmo

96   60
6-y-o ch g Democratic (USA)-Figrant (USA) (L Emigrant (USA))
J Cullinan The Paddy Pipers

Placings:5000   (4622)
2002/03: 16⁵HY, 20⁰HY, 16⁰G, 22⁰GF,

	Starts	1st	2nd	3rd	Win & Pl
Hurdles	4	0	0	0	0
Career Total	4	0	0	0	0

Going: Sf: 0-2 GS: 0-0 Gd: 0-1 GF: - Fm: 0-1

Lord Grey (IRE)

100(105h)   (107h)125
10-y-o gr g Celio Rufo-Clooragh Rose (IRE) (Boreen (FR))
D P Kelly Mrs Barbara Marchant

Placings:34/00001/00316500/10122U-61211400   (4458)
2002/03: 17⁶G, 16¹F, 16²G, 16¹F, 16¹GF, 16⁴Y, 16⁰G, 16⁰G,

	Starts	1st	2nd	3rd	Win & Pl
Hurdles	3	1	0	0	8764
Chases	5	2	1	0	15552
Career Total	29	7	3	2	45674
105	10/02	Tipp	2m	(74-116)HHdl	G-F	£8374
125	9/02	List	2m	(0-130)HCh	FRM	£7975
117	8/02	Tipp	2m	(0-123)HCh	FRM	£6349
113	8/01	Tral	2m	(0-109)HCh	G-F	£6120
99	5/01	Tipp	2m	( )Ch	G-F	£5286
102	7/00	Bell	2m1f	(0-109)HHdl	GD	£3174
90	4/00	Clon	2m	(0-95)HHdl	GD	£2760

Total win prize-money £40040

Going: Sf: 0-0 GS: 0-0 Gd: 0-4 GF: - Fm: 3-3
Distance: 2m/2m3: 3-8 2m4-2m7: 0-0 3m+: 0-0
Track: LH: 2-5 RH: 0-0 Tight: 0-1 Gall: 0-1
Aids: Bl: 0-0 Vi: 0-0 Tstrap: 0-0
Best Rating: 125 9/02 List 2m   firm Ch

Modest hurdler/fair chaser; effective on a sound surface; best at two miles.

Lord Harry (IRE)

11-y-o b g Mister Lord (USA)-Vickies Gold (Golden Love)
Mrs Edward Crow M J Parr

Placings:2/3/1126/1PF-31P   (0414)
2002/03: 26³GF, 24¹S, 28PGF,

	Starts	1st	2nd	3rd	Win & Pl
Chases	3	1	0	1	4373
Career Total	12	4	2	2	19637
103	5/02	Bang	3m110y	H Ch	SFT	£3542
107	5/01	Bang	3m110y	H Ch	G-S	£2940
121	6/01	Strf	3m4f	H Ch	GD	£7410
106	5/00	Bang	3m110y	H Ch	GD	£3461

Total win prize-money £17354

Going: Sf: 1-1 GS: 0-0 Gd: 0-0 GF: - Fm: 0-2
Distance: 2m/2m3: 0-0 2m4-2m7: 0-0 3m+: 1-3
Track: LH: 1-3 RH: 0-0 Tight: 1-2 Gall: 0-0
Aids: Bl: 0-0 Vi: 0-0 Tstrap: 0-0
Best Rating: 121 6/00 Strf 3m4f   good Ch

A smart hunter chaser/point-to-pointer, he stays long distances and goes well on decent ground. Basically a sound jumper.

Lord Jack (IRE)

107(103h)   (107h)140
7-y-o ch g Mister Lord (USA)-Gentle Gill (Pollerton)
N G Richards Trevor Hemmings

Placings:0561120-121130   (4101)
2002/03: 21¹S, 21²S, 21¹S, 20¹S, 24³HY, 24⁰G,

	Starts	1st	2nd	3rd	Win & Pl
Chases	6	3	1	1	22692
Career Total	13	5	2	1	29738

140	1/03	Ayr	2m4f	D(0-125)HCh	SFT	£6747
111	12/02	Sedg	2m5f	E Ch	SFT	£3799
124	11/02	Sedg	2m5f	E Ch	SFT	£4069
109	2/02	Muss	3m	D(0-110)HHdl	SFT	£3526
107	1/02	Muss	2m4f	E(0-100)HHdl	SFT	£2744
				Total win prize-money £20885		

Going: Sf: 3-5 GS: 0-0 Gd: 0-1 GF: - Fm: 0-0
Distance: 2m/2m3: 0-0 **2m4-2m7: 3-4** 3m+: 0-2
Track: LH: 3-5 RH: 0-1 Tight: 2-3 Gall: 0-1
Aids: Bl: 0-0 Vi: 0-0 Tstrap: 3-6
Best Rating: 140 1/03 Ayr 2m4f soft Ch

Useful novice chaser; acts on soft and heavy ground and gets three miles; wears a tongue tie.

Lord Jurado (IRE)
67   29
7-y-o b g Jurado (USA)-Via Del Tabacco (Ballymoss)
T P McGovern M J O Riordan

Placings:000-60   (1285)
2002/03: 21⁶G, 18⁰GF,

	Starts	1st	2nd	3rd	Win & Pl
Hurdles	2	0	0	0	0
Career Total	5	0	0	0	0

Going: Sf: 0-0 GS: 0-0 Gd: 0-1 GF: - Fm: 0-1
Distance: 2m/2m3: 0-1 2m4-2m7: 0-1 3m+: 0-0
Track: LH: 0-2 RH: 0-0 Tight: 0-1 Gall: 0-0
Aids: Bl: 0-0 Vi: 0-0 Tstrap: 0-1
Best Rating: 75 5/01 Tram 2m gd-fm NHF

Lord Khalice (IRE)
(90h)   (74h)113
12-y-o b g King s Ride-Khalice (Khalkis)
Ferdy Murphy Geoff Hubbard Racing

Placings:24022/1/1P56FUP/P2423203134/3/34113-P0
(2104)
2002/03: 28ᴾGS, 26⁰GS,

	Starts	1st	2nd	3rd	Win & Pl
Hurdles	1	0	0	0	0
Chases	1	0	0	0	0
Career Total	32	5	6	6	27913
113	2/02	Fknm	3m110y	F(0-100)HCh	G-S	£4143
113	1/02	Fknk	3m2f	F(0-100)HCh	SFT	£3318
101	3/00	Hntg	3m	C(0-115)HCh	SFT	£3061
113	10/98	MRas	3m	D(0-125)HHdl	SFT	£3096
96	10/97	Uttx	2m6f110yC Hdl		GD	£4086
			Total win prize-money £17707			

Going: Sf: 0-0 GS: 0-2 Gd: 0-0 GF: - Fm: 0-0
Distance: 2m/2m3: 0-0 2m4-2m7: 0-0 3m+: 0-2
Track: LH: 0-1 RH: 0-0 Tight: 0-1 Gall: 0-1
Aids: Bl: 0-0 Vi: 0-0 Tstrap: 0-0
Best Rating: 113 2/02 Fknm 3m110y gd-sft Ch

Fair chaser. Acts on a soft surface, effective at two miles six plus. Goes well at Huntingdon.

Lord Kilpatrick (IRE)
9-y-o ch g Mister Lord (USA)-Running Frau (Deep Run)
Mrs Laura J Young T W C Edwards

Placings:2P4   (4314)
2002/03: 24²S, 24ᴾS, 22⁴G,

	Starts	1st	2nd	3rd	Win & Pl
Chases	3	0	1	0	2136

Career Total	3	0	1	0	2136

Going: Sf: 0-2 GS: 0-0 Gd: 0-1 GF: - Fm: 0-0
Distance: 2m/2m3: 0-0 2m4-2m7: 0-1 3m+: 0-2
Track: LH: 0-1 RH: 0-2 Tight: 0-0 Gall: 0-1
Aids: Bl: 0-0 Vi: 0-0 Tstrap: 3-6

Fair performer; runner-up in 2003 Royal Artillery Gold Cup; acts well on soft ground; stays three miles.

Lord Knox (IRE)
13-y-o ch g Tale Quale-Lady Knox (Dalsaan)
Ms K Clark Ms K Clark

Placings:P/6/2/3-4   (0154)
2002/03: 24⁴G,

	Starts	1st	2nd	3rd	Win & Pl
Chases	1	0	0	0	0
Career Total	5	0	1	1	764

Going: Sf: 0-0 GS: 0-0 Gd: 0-1 GF: - Fm: 0-0
Distance: 2m/2m3: 0-0 2m4-2m7: 0-0 3m+: 0-1
Track: LH: 0-1 RH: 0-0 Tight: 0-1 Gall: 0-0
Aids: Bl: 0-0 Vi: 0-0 Tstrap: 0-0
Best Rating: 85 5/00 Folk 2m5f good Ch

Moderate pointer/hunter chaser.

Lord Lupin (IRE)
101   87
7-y-o b g Sadler s Wells (USA)-Penza (Soviet Star (USA))
T H Caldwell T H Caldwell

Placings:2/00-0P40442   (4392)
2002/03: 20⁰G, 20ᴾGS, 20⁴GS, 20⁰GS, 26⁴G, 24⁴S, 24²G,

	Starts	1st	2nd	3rd	Win & Pl
Hurdles	7	0	1	0	1705
Career Total	10	0	2	0	2431

Going: Sf: 0-1 GS: 0-3 Gd: 0-3 GF: - Fm: 0-0
Distance: 2m/2m3: 0-2 2m4-2m7: 0-4 3m+: 0-3
Track: LH: 0-4 RH: 0-3 Tight: 0-0 Gall: 0-0
Aids: Bl: 0-0 Vi: 0-0 Tstrap: 0-0
Best Rating: 116 2/01 Kemp 2m gd-sft NHF

Moderate novice hurdler; stays three miles.

Lord Maizey (IRE)
109   106+
6-y-o b g Mister Lord (USA)-My Maizey (Buckskin (FR))
N A Twiston-Davies (J A Berry 23/11) Mr & Mrs Peter Orton

Placings:741   (3575)
2002/03: 16¹S, 26⁴HY, 16¹S,

	Starts	1st	2nd	3rd	Win & Pl
NH Flat	1	1	0	0	3810
Chases	2	1	0	0	5196
Career Total	3	2	0	0	9006
106	2/03	Leic	2m	E Ch	SFT	£4875
109	11/02	Naas	2m	NHF	SFT	£3809
			Total win prize-money £8685			

Going: Sf: 2-3 GS: 0-0 Gd: 0-0 GF: - Fm: 0-0
Distance: **2m/2m3: 2-2** 2m4-2m7: 0-0 3m+: 0-1
Track: LH: 0-1 RH: 1-1 Tight: 0-0 Gall: 0-0
Aids: Bl: 0-0 Vi: 0-0 Tstrap: 0-0
Best Rating: 109 11/02 Naas 2m soft NHF

Career Total	3	0	1	0	2136

Irish bumper winner; stays two miles; won maiden chase at Leicester in February 2003.

Lord Mistral
91   78
4-y-o b g Makbul-South Wind (Tina s Pet)
Mrs N S Sharpe (B R Millman 29/4) B Owen

Placings:0F04065   (4539)
2002/03: 16⁰GS, 17ᶠG, 17⁰G, 16⁴GS, 16⁰GS, 16⁶G, 16⁵G,

	Starts	1st	2nd	3rd	Win & Pl
Hurdles	7	0	0	0	323
Career Total	7	0	0	0	323

Going: Sf: 0-0 GS: 0-3 Gd: 0-4 GF: - Fm: 0-0
Distance: 2m/2m3: 0-7 2m4-2m7: 0-0 3m+: 0-0
Track: LH: 0-2 RH: 0-5 Tight: 0-2 Gall: 0-1
Aids: Bl: 0-0 Vi: 0-0 Tstrap: 0-0
Best Rating: 75 12/02 Winc 2m gd-sft Hdl

Very limited ability so far.

Lord Moose (IRE)
105   122
9-y-o b g Mister Lord (USA)-Moose (IRE) (Royal Fountain)
H D Daly The Hon Simon Sainsbury

Placings:PF1/P01-13432   (4050)
2002/03: 20¹GS, 22³S, 22⁴G, 24³GS, 24²S,

	Starts	1st	2nd	3rd	Win & Pl
Chases	5	1	2	2	14289
Career Total	11	3	1	2	28433
122	11/02	Sand	2m4f110yC(0-135)HCh	G-S	£8463
119	3/02	Newb	2m6f110yD(0-120)HCh	SFT	£9009
116	4/00	Asct	2m4f	C Hdl	SFT	£5135
			Total win prize-money £22607		

Going: Sf: 0-2 GS: 1-2 Gd: 0-1 GF: - Fm: 0-0
Distance: 2m/2m3: 0-0 **2m4-2m7: 1-3** 3m+: 0-2
Track: LH: 0-2 RH: **1-3** Tight: 0-0 Gall: 0-2
Aids: Bl: 0-0 Vi: 0-0 Tstrap: 0-0
Best Rating: 122 3/03 Sand 3m110y soft Ch

Fair handicap chaser; stays three miles; acts on a soft surface.

Lord Native (IRE)
59   57
8-y-o b g Be My Native (USA)-Whakapohane (Kampala)
N J Henderson Lady Annabel Goldsmith

Placings:106/02/1-P6   (4027)
2002/03: 16ᴾGS, 16⁶HY,

	Starts	1st	2nd	3rd	Win & Pl
Hurdles	2	0	0	0	0
Career Total	8	2	1	0	5950
96	6/01	MRas	2m1f110yE Hdl		G-F	£2509
92	7/99	Klny	2m1f	NHF	G-F	£2915
			Total win prize-money £5426		

Going: Sf: 0-1 GS: 0-1 Gd: 0-0 GF: - Fm: 0-0
Distance: 2m/2m3: 0-2 2m4-2m7: 0-0 3m+: 0-0
Track: LH: 0-0 RH: 0-2 Tight: 0-0 Gall: 0-0
Aids: Bl: 0-0 Vi: 0-0 Tstrap: 0-0
Best Rating: 110 1/01 Fknm 2m soft Hdl

Modest ex-Irish hurdler; effective around two miles; acts on fast ground; absent for 20 months after winning at Market Rasen in June 2001.

Lord Nellsson

108　　　　　　　　　　**96**

7-y-o b g Arctic Lord-Miss Petronella (Petoski)
J S King　Dajam Ltd

Placings:3600-2032P0　　　　　　　　**(4450)**
2002/03: 16²G, 16⁰GS, 17³S, 21²G, 20⁰HY, 21⁰G,

	Starts	1st	2nd	3rd	Win & Pl
Hurdles	6	0	2	1	3765
Career Total	10	0	2	2	4290

Going:	Sf: 0-2 GS: 0-1 Gd: 0-3 GF: - Fm: 0-0
Distance:	2m/2m3: 0-3 2m4-2m7: 0-3 3m+: 0-0
Track:	LH: 0-0 RH: 0-6 Tight: 0-0 Gall: 0-1
Aids:	Bl: 0-0 Vi: 0-0 Tstrap: 0-0
Best Rating:	98　2/03　Ludl　2m5f　good　Hdl

Moderate novice hurdler; stays two miles five.

Lord Noelie (IRE)

97　　　　　　　　　　**170d**

10-y-o b g Lord Americo-Leallen (Le Bavard (FR))
Miss H C Knight　Executive Racing

Placings:4/16F14/2121/4U2/F4503-U0P　　**(2685)**
2002/03: 25⁰⁰GS, 26⁰GS, 24³S,

	Starts	1st	2nd	3rd	Win & Pl
Chases	3	0	0		
Career Total	21	4	3	1	139095
154 3/00	Chel	3m110y A Ch		GD	£66700
142 11/99	Newb	3m	C Ch	GD	£6440
130 2/99	Winc	2m6f	B Hdl	G-S	£10755
112 10/98	Strf	2m6f110yD Hdl		GD	£3183
		Total win prize-money £87078			

Going:	Sf: 0-1 GS: 0-2 Gd: 0-0 GF: - Fm: 0-0
Distance:	2m/2m3: 0-0 2m4-2m7: 0-0 3m+: 0-3
Track:	LH: 0-2 RH: 0-1 Tight: 0-0 Gall: 0-1
Aids:	Bl: 0-0 Vi: 0-0 Tstrap: 0-0
Best Rating:	170　12/01　Newb　3m2f110y　soft　Ch

Top-class chaser; winner of the Royal & SunAlliance Chase in 2000; things have not really gone his way since, but capable of high-class form when conditions are right; best on fast ground.

Lord North (IRE)

107　　　　　　　　　　**131**

8-y-o b g Mister Lord (USA)-Mrs Hegarty (Decent Fellow)
P R Webber　Jerry Wright

Placings:4P/3150-21P1P4FP　　　　　　**(4319)**
2002/03: 20²G, 20¹S, 21PGF, 20¹GS, 24PGS, 23⁴S, 21FS, 20PG,

	Starts	1st	2nd	3rd	Win & Pl
Chases	8	2	1	0	20571
Career Total	14	3	1	1	24429
131 12/02	Leic	2m4f110yD(0-125)HCh	G-S	£10595
117 5/02	Bang	2m4f110yD(0-120)HCh	SFT	£7247
95 11/01	Leic	2m	E Ch	G-F	£3307
		Total win prize-money £21151			

Going:	Sf: 1-3 GS: 1-2 Gd: 0-2 GF: - Fm: 0-1
Distance:	2m/2m3: 0-0 **2m4-2m7: 2-6** 3m+: 0-2
Track:	LH: 1-4 RH: 1-4 **Tight: 1-4** Gall: 0-0
Aids:	Bl: 0-0 Vi: 0-0 **Tstrap: 1-5**
Best Rating:	131　12/02　Leic　2m4f110y　gd-sft　Ch

Decent handicap chaser; acts on fast and soft ground; stays two and a half miles; has worn a tongue strap.

Lord O'All Seasons (IRE)

120

10-y-o b/br g Mister Lord (USA)-Autumn News (Giolla Mear)
N J Henderson　S Keeling

Placings:01/P223P-　　　　　　　　**(0014)**
2002/03: 25PGS,

	Starts	1st	2nd	3rd	Win & Pl
Chases	1	0	0	0	
Career Total	7	1	2	1	10526
100 2/01	Leic	2m7f110yD Ch	SFT	£4466
		Total win prize-money £4466			

Going:	Sf: 0-0 GS: 0-1 Gd: 0-0 GF: - Fm: 0-0
Distance:	2m/2m3: 0-0 2m4-2m7: 0-0 3m+: 0-1
Track:	LH: 0-0 RH: 0-1 Tight: 0-0 Gall: 0-0
Aids:	Bl: 0-0 Vi: 0-0 Tstrap: 0-0
Best Rating:	120　2/02　Ludl　3m　gd-sft　Ch

Lightly raced, fair chaser, he is effective at three miles and acts on soft ground.

Lord Of Illusion (IRE)

104　　　　　　　　　　**108**

6-y-o b g Mister Lord (USA)-Jellaride (IRE) (King s Ride)
T R George　P J Kennedy

Placings:00120　　　　　　　　　　**(4774)**
2002/03: 20⁰HY, 16⁰GS, 17¹GS, 22²G, 27⁰G,

	Starts	1st	2nd	3rd	Win & Pl
Hurdles	5	1	1	0	5137
Career Total	5	1	1	0	5137
98 2/03	Bang	2m1f	E Hdl	G-S	£3822
		Total win prize-money £3822			

Going:	Sf: 0-1 GS: 1-2 Gd: 0-2 GF: - Fm: 0-0
Distance:	**2m/2m3: 1-2** 2m4-2m7: 0-2 3m+: 0-1
Track:	**LH: 1-2** RH: 0-2 **Tight: 1-1** Gall: 0-0
Aids:	Bl: 0-0 Vi: 0-0 Tstrap: 0-0
Best Rating:	108　3/03　Extr　2m6f110y　good　Hdl

Fair novice hurdler; took advantage of the favourite s departure to take a weak contest at Bangor in February 2003; good effort under top weight in two and three quarter mile novices handicap at Exeter next time.

Lord Of Love

96　　　　　　　　　　**93**

8-y-o b g Noble Patriarch-Gymcrak Lovebird (Taufan (USA))
D Burchell　Mouse Racing

Placings:2360410221246/64052130F423F06255/216005P
00/322000-462U　　　　　　　　　　**(1556)**
2002/03: 24⁴GF, 24⁶G, 19²GF, 17⁰G,

	Starts	1st	2nd	3rd	Win & Pl
Hurdles	4	0	1	0	961
Career Total	50	4	11	4	27815
122 5/00	Strf	3m3f	E(0-115)HHdl	G-F	£2898
112 12/99	Hrfd	2m3f110yF(0-105)HHdl	HVY	£3137
120 2/99	Ling	2m3f110yE Hdl	SFT	£2108
107 12/98	Font	2m2f110yE Hdl	G-S	£1935
		Total win prize-money £10078			

Going:	Sf: 0-0 GS: 0-0 Gd: 0-2 GF: - Fm: 0-2
Distance:	2m/2m3: 0-1 2m4-2m7: 0-1 3m+: 0-2
Track:	LH: 0-2 RH: 0-2 Tight: 0-0 Gall: 0-0
Aids:	Bl: 0-0 Vi: 0-0 Tstrap: 0-0
Best Rating:	124　2/99　Font　2m2f110y　good　Hdl

Moderate chaser; appreciates give in the ground, and stays two miles six, but does not seem to stay three miles plus unless the ground rides fast.

Lord Of The Hill (IRE)

89　　　　　　　　　　**62**

8-y-o b g Dromod Hill-Telegram Mear (Giolla Mear)
G Brown　Middx Packaging Ltd

Placings:0P0U/F4　　　　　　　　　　**(0382)**
2002/03: 18FGF, 20⁴G,

	Starts	1st	2nd	3rd	Win & Pl
Chases	2	0	0	0	243
Career Total	6	0	0	0	243

Going:	Sf: 0-0 GS: 0-0 Gd: 0-1 GF: - Fm: 0-1
Distance:	2m/2m3: 0-1 2m4-2m7: 0-1 3m+: 0-0
Track:	LH: 0-0 RH: 0-1 Tight: 0-1 Gall: 0-1
Aids:	Bl: 0-0 Vi: 0-0 Tstrap: 0-0
Best Rating:	62　5/02　Hntg　2m4f110y　good　Ch

Lord Of The Land

108(104c)　　　　　　　(104c)**94**

10-y-o b g Lord Bud-Saint Motunde (Tyrant (USA))
Mrs E Slack　A Slack

Placings:650/000/61110431130/044UFP0/621-00　**(4795)**
2002/03: 20⁰G, 21⁰GF,

	Starts	1st	2nd	3rd	Win & Pl
Hurdles	2	0	0		
Career Total	29	6	1	2	17037
94 5/01	Hexm	3m1f	F(0-95)HCh	G-F	£2716
119 9/99	Sedg	2m5f110yD(0-125)HHdl	GD	£2914
107 9/99	Kels	2m6f110yF(0-105)HHdl	G-F	£2276
119 6/99	Hexm	2m4f110yE(0-105)HHdl	G-F	£2607
104 5/99	Hexm	2m4f110yE Hdl	G-F	£1716
96 5/99	Kels	2m2f	E Hdl	G-F	£1955
		Total win prize-money £14186			

Going:	Sf: 0-0 GS: 0-0 Gd: 0-1 GF: - Fm: 0-1
Distance:	2m/2m3: 0-0 2m4-2m7: 0-2 3m+: 0-0
Track:	LH: 0-1 RH: 0-1 Tight: 0-1 Gall: 0-0
Aids:	Bl: 0-0 Vi: 0-0 Tstrap: 0-0
Best Rating:	119　9/99　Sedg　2m5f110y　good　Hdl

Moderate hurdler/chaser; showed a return to form when runner-up at Cartmel in May; effective over two miles but stays really well; best on decent ground.

Lord Of The Loch (IRE)

102　　　　　　　　　　**99**

12-y-o b/br g Lord Americo-Loughamaire (Brave Invader (USA))
W G Young　W G Young

Placings:U243/4/1333/1/5401536320-46446U06　**(3159)**
2002/03: 18⁴GS, 20⁶GS, 20⁴S, 20⁴HY, 20⁶GS, 24⁰GF, 20⁰GS,
24⁶G,

	Starts	1st	2nd	3rd	Win & Pl
Hurdles	8	0	0	0	1004
Career Total	26	4	6	6	13335
112 2/02	Muss	2m4f	F(0-100)HHdl	SFT	£3038
107 2/01	Carl	2m1f	F(0-105)HHdl	HVY	£2702
101 5/99	Prth	2m4f110yE Hdl	SFT	£2409
		Total win prize-money £8150			

Going:	Sf: 0-2 GS: 0-4 Gd: 0-1 GF: - Fm: 0-1
Distance:	2m/2m3: 0-1 2m4-2m7: 0-5 3m+: 0-2
Track:	LH: 0-4 RH: 0-4 Tight: 0-4 Gall: 0-1

Aids: Bl: 0-0 Vi: 0-0 Tstrap: 0-0
Best Rating: 112 2/02 Muss 2m4f   soft   Hdl

Fair hurdler, lightly raced due to leg trouble, he likes the mud and stays two and a half miles.

Lord Of The Manor (SWE)

(95h)   (70 h)
6-y-o b g Spectacular Tide (USA)-Sobhiato (AUS) (Motavato (USA))
D W P Arbuthnot   East Wind Racing Ltd

Placings:0606-00P   (0659)
2002/03: 22⁰GF, 20⁰G, 16ᴾGF,

	Starts	1st	2nd	3rd	Win & Pl
Hurdles	2	0	0	0	0
Chases	1	0	0	0	0
Career Total	7	0	0	0	0

Going: Sf: 0-0 GS: 0-0 Gd: 0-1 GF: - Fm: 0-2
Distance: 2m/2m3: 0-1 2m4-2m7: 0-2 3m+: 0-0
Track: LH: 0-2 RH: 0-1 Tight: 0-0 Gall: 0-0
Aids: Bl: 0-1 Vi: 0-0 Tstrap: 0-3
Best Rating: 71 5/02 Winc 2m6f   gd-fm Hdl

Lord Of The North (IRE)

99   74
6-y-o br g Arctic Lord-Ballyfin Maid (IRE) (Boreen (FR))
M R Hoad   Mrs J E Taylor

Placings:0-5P300   (4629)
2002/03: 17⁵HY, 22ᴾS, 20³GF, 25⁰GF, 21⁰GF,

	Starts	1st	2nd	3rd	Win & Pl
Hurdles	5	0	0	1	337
Career Total	6	0	0	1	337

Going: Sf: 0-2 GS: 0-0 Gd: 0-0 GF: - Fm: 0-3
Distance: 2m/2m3: 0-1 2m4-2m7: 0-3 3m+: 0-1
Track: LH: 0-2 RH: 0-1 Tight: 0-4 Gall: 0-0
Aids: Bl: 0-0 Vi: 0-0 Tstrap: 0-0
Best Rating: 74 3/03 Font 2m4f   gd-fm Hdl

Lord Of The River (IRE)

99   113
11-y-o br g Lord Americo-Well Over (Over The River (FR))
N J Henderson   B T Stewart-Brown

Placings:5/11415/1F2112/5U2-65   (3898)
2002/03: 24⁶S, 24⁵S,

	Starts	1st	2nd	3rd	Win & Pl
Chases	2	0	0	0	747
Career Total	17	6	3	0	89868
154 2/99 Asct	3m110y A Ch			GD	£19050
154 12/98 Kemp	3m A Ch			G-S	£22715
123 11/98 Extr	2m3f C Ch			SFT	£5433
123 3/98 Newb	2m5f D Hdl			HVY	£3038
120 12/97 Uttx	2m4f110yE Hdl			G-S	£1945
107 11/97 Wind	2m4f D Hdl			GD	£2810
				Total win prize-money £54992	

Going: Sf: 0-2 GS: 0-0 Gd: 0-0 GF: - Fm: 0-0
Distance: 2m/2m3: 0-0 2m4-2m7: 0-0 3m+: 0-2
Track: LH: 0-1 RH: 0-1 Tight: 0-0 Gall: 0-1
Aids: Bl: 0-0 Vi: 0-0 Tstrap: 0-0

Best Rating: 154 2/99 Asct   3m110y   good   Ch

Decent chaser; high-class novice in 1998/9, but off the track for a long time afterwards and not as good these days; stays three miles; acts on good and soft ground.

Lord Pat (IRE)

89(104h)   (79h)79
12-y-o ch g Mister Lord (USA)-Arianrhod (L Homme Arme)
Miss Kate Milligan   The L P Club

Placings:05/05000/321P1033P/62P00/432/0124666-60F31P3   (4264)
2002/03: 21⁶G, 21⁰G, 20⁵S, 21³GS, 19¹S, 20ᴾS, 20³GF,

	Starts	1st	2nd	3rd	Win & Pl
Hurdles	6	1	0	1	2555
Chases	1	0	0	1	541
Career Total	38	4	4	6	15355
79 12/02 MRas	2m3f110yG(0-95)HHdl			SFT	£2226
90 11/01 Newc	2m4f F(0-90)HHdl			GD	£2009
91 1/99 Muss	2m4f F(0-100)HHdl			SFT	£4533
81 11/98 Sedg	2m1f G(0-95)HHdl			G-S	£1626
				Total win prize-money £10395	

Going: Sf: 1-3 GS: 0-1 Gd: 0-2 GF: - Fm: 0-1
Distance: 2m/2m3: 0-0 2m4-2m7: 1-7 3m+: 0-0
Track: LH: 0-5 RH: 1-2 Tight: 1-5 Gall: 0-2
Aids: Bl: 0-0 Vi: 0-0 Tstrap: 0-0
Best Rating: 91 11/99 Kels   2m110y   good   Hdl

Selling hurdler, getting on in age. Retired after recording career win number four at Market Rasen in December.

Lord Perseus (IRE)

90   69
6-y-o ch g Mister Lord (USA)-Greek Empress (Royal Buck)
M Pitman   J F Garrett

Placings:30-1   (4685)
2002/03: 16¹GF,

	Starts	1st	2nd	3rd	Win & Pl
NH Flat	1	1	0	0	1932
Career Total	3	1	0	1	2220
103 4/03 Hntg	2m110y H NHF			G-F	£1932
				Total win prize-money £1932	

Going: Sf: 0-0 GS: 0-0 Gd: 0-0 GF: - Fm: 1-1
Distance: 2m/2m3: 1-1 2m4-2m7: 0-0 3m+: 0-0
Track: LH: 0-0 RH: 1-1 Tight: 0-0 Gall: 1-1
Aids: Bl: 0-0 Vi: 0-0 Tstrap: 0-0
Best Rating: 103 4/03 Hntg   2m110y   gd-fm NHF

Promising third in a Kempton bumper on his debut; returned after a year off to make all on third career start in a weak bumper on fast ground at Huntingdon in April; well beaten on hurdling bow.

Lord Pierce

86   73
5-y-o b g Tragic Role (USA)-Mirkan Honey (Ballymore)
J Howard Johnson   Hertford Offset Limited

Placings:24-3660   (4591)
2002/03: 17³S, 20⁶GS, 17⁶HY, 16⁰G,

	Starts	1st	2nd	3rd	Win & Pl
Hurdles	4	0	0	1	664
Career Total	6	0	1	1	1779

Going: Sf: 0-2 GS: 0-1 Gd: 0-1 GF: - Fm: 0-0
Distance: 2m/2m3: 0-3 2m4-2m7: 0-1 3m+: 0-0
Track: LH: 0-3 RH: 0-1 Tight: 0-3 Gall: 0-1
Aids: Bl: 0-0 Vi: 0-0 Tstrap: 0-2

Best Rating: 80 2/02 Muss 2m   soft   Hdl

A winner on heavy ground on the Flat, he has disapointed so far over hurdles.

Lord Rapier

113(86h)   (121h)121
10-y-o b g Broadsword (USA)-Doddycross (Deep Run)
D J Caro   J A S Hardcastle

Placings:322/61/1-42PF2132P   (4564)
2002/03: 21⁴GS, 25²S, 28ᴾS, 24ᶠHY, 30²S, 25¹S, 26³S, 24²GF, 24ᴾGF,

	Starts	1st	2nd	3rd	Win & Pl
Chases	9	1	3	1	14154
Career Total	15	3	5	2	21365
118 3/03 MRas	3m1f D Ch			SFT	£5330
121 5/01 Bang	3m E Hdl			GD	£3416
104 4/01 Hntg	2m5f110yE Hdl			SFT	£2478
				Total win prize-money £11224	

Going: Sf: 1-6 GS: 0-1 Gd: 0-0 GF: - Fm: 0-2
Distance: 2m/2m3: 0-0 2m4-2m7: 0-1 3m+: 1-8
Track: LH: 0-7 RH: 1-2 Tight: 1-5 Gall: 0-0
Aids: Bl: 0-3 Vi: 0-0 Tstrap: 0-0
Best Rating: 121 3/03 Hayd   3m   gd-fm   Ch

Decent performer over hurdles and more recently fences, getting off the mark at Market Rasen in March 2003; acts on good and soft ground; stays well; has worn blinkers.

Lord Richfield (NZ)

89(97c)   (111c)90
12-y-o b g Kirmann-Lady Grange (NZ) (Sir Bart (NZ))
B P J Baugh   Dave Arrowsmith

Placings:22502/21513144353/P5F02U4UPP/22002P5/303 60-040P4   (0895)
2002/03: 20⁰G, 24⁴S, 22⁰GF, 24ᴾG, 24⁴S,

	Starts	1st	2nd	3rd	Win & Pl
Hurdles	5	0	0	0	0
Career Total	43	3	8	5	23477
115 12/98 Uttx	2m C(0-130)HHdl			G-S	£5225
114 11/98 Uttx	2m D(0-125)HHdl			SFT	£2843
102 10/98 Strf	2m6f110yE Hdl			G-S	£2075
				Total win prize-money £10143	

Going: Sf: 0-2 GS: 0-0 Gd: 0-2 GF: - Fm: 0-1
Distance: 2m/2m3: 0-0 2m4-2m7: 0-2 3m+: 0-3
Track: LH: 0-4 RH: 0-1 Tight: 0-2 Gall: 0-0
Aids: Bl: 0-0 Vi: 0-1 Tstrap: 0-0
Best Rating: 115 11/00 Hayd   2m   heavy   Hdl

Lord Rochester

89(96c)   (62c)72
7-y-o b g Distant Relative-Kentfield (Busted)
K F Clutterbuck (C J Mann 24/8) K F Clutterbuck

Placings:523/12132314/03F053114-44F3P66   (1505)
2002/03: 23⁴G, 20⁴GF, 24ᶠGF, 24³GF, 23ᴾG, 20⁶GF, 21⁶G,

	Starts	1st	2nd	3rd	Win & Pl
Hurdles	2	0	0	0	0
Chases	5	0	0	1	1442
Career Total	27	3	6	3	20769
121 10/01 Chep	2m D(0-125)HHdl			GD	£3474
117 9/01 Plum	2m5f D(0-125)HHdl			G-F	£3342
123 10/00 Folk	2m1f110yF(0-110)HHdl			G-F	£1757
110 5/00 Font	2m2f110yE Hdl			GD	£2285
104 5/00 Folk	2m1f110yE Hdl			GD	£2432
				Total win prize-money £13293	

Going: Sf: 0-0 GS: 0-0 Gd: 0-3 GF: - Fm: 0-4

Distance: 2m/2m3: 0-0 2m4-2m7: 0-3 3m+: 0-4
Track: LH: 0-5 RH: 0-2 Tight: 0-3 Gall: 0-0
Aids: Bl: 0-7 Vi: 0-0 Tstrap: 0-0
Best Rating: 124 10/01 Chel 2m5f   good   Hdl

Fair hurdler at his best but looks on the downgrade.. Effective over two and a half miles, he is suited by good to firm ground. Usually wears blinkers. Yet to convince over fences.

Lord Sam (IRE)
111   150+
7-y-o b/br g Supreme Leader-Russian Gale (IRE) (Strong Gale)
V R A Dartnall   Plain Peeps

Placings:*11*-1113   (4109)
2002/03: 16¹S, 16¹S, 21¹G, 21³G,

	Starts	1st	2nd	3rd	Win & Pl
Hurdles	4	3	0	1	35839
Career Total	6	5	0	1	40690
141	1/03	Kemp 2m5f	B Hdl	GD	£12458
137	12/02	Kemp 2m	C Hdl	SFT	£6583
121	12/02	Sand 2m110y	D Hdl	SFT	£5798
123	3/02	Newb 2m110y	H NHF	G-S	£2576
121	2/02	Sand 2m110y	H NHF	SFT	£2275

Total win prize-money £29690

Going: Sf: 2-2 GS: 0-0 Gd: 1-2 GF: - Fm: 0-0
Distance: 2m/2m3: 2-2 2m4-2m7: 1-2 3m+: 0-0
Track: LH: 0-1 RH: 3-3 Tight: 0-0 Gall: 0-1
Aids: Bl: 0-0 Vi: 0-0 Tstrap: 0-0
Best Rating: 146 3/03 Chel 2m5f   good   Hdl

Smart novice; unbeaten in two bumpers and three starts over hurdles in his first five starts; finished a good third in the Royal & SunAlliance Novices Hurdle at the 2003 Festival; stays 2m 5f; has won on good and soft ground; has room for improvement in his jumping.

Lord Sandrovitch (IRE)
97(95h)
8-y-o b g Be My Native (USA)-Killiney Side (General Ironside)
M W Easterby   Harold Winton & Gordon Winton

Placings:*20/35*211/P/21FUP-635P   (3741)
2002/03: 16⁶G, 24³S, 21⁵GS, 20ᴾG,

	Starts	1st	2nd	3rd	Win & Pl
Hurdles	2	0	0	0	0
Chases	2	0	0	1	880
Career Total	17	3	3	2	13926
114	1/02	Newc 2m4f	E Ch	SFT	£3071
125	1/00	Asct 2m4f	C Hdl	G-S	£5096
114	1/00	Font	2m2f110yE Hdl	G-S	£2607

Total win prize-money £10775

Going: Sf: 0-1 GS: 0-1 Gd: 0-2 GF: - Fm: 0-0
Distance: 2m/2m3: 0-1 2m4-2m7: 0-2 3m+: 0-1
Track: LH: 0-2 RH: 0-2 Tight: 0-0 Gall: 0-3
Aids: Bl: 0-1 Vi: 0-0 Tstrap: 0-0
Best Rating: 125 1/00 Asct 2m4f   gd-sft   Hdl

Moderate chaser/hurdler; fair novice hurdler in 2000; lightly raced over fences since and is not a natural jumper; suited by soft ground.

Lord Scroop (IRE)

9-y-o br g Supreme Leader-Henry Woman (IRE) (Mandalus)
Mrs K Walton   The White Liners

Placings:*0/54*432/PU03P/P5U34P2PP4P-   (0002)
2002/03: 24ᴾG,

	Starts	1st	2nd	3rd	Win & Pl
Chases	1	0	0	0	
Career Total	22	0	2	3	3975

Going: Sf: 0-0 GS: 0-0 Gd: 0-1 GF: - Fm: 0-0
Distance: 2m/2m3: 0-0 2m4-2m7: 0-0 3m+: 0-1
Track: LH: 0-1 RH: 0-0 Tight: 0-0 Gall: 0-1
Aids: Bl: 0-1 Vi: 0-0 Tstrap: 0-1
Best Rating: 106 11/99 Chel 2m110y   good   NHF

Maiden over flights. Stays three miles.

Lord Seamus
100(96h)   (88h)112
8-y-o b g Arctic Lord-Erica Superba (Langton Heath)
K C Bailey   I F W Buchan

Placings:*0/40/*0434F231-5F303   (4619)
2002/03: 23⁵G, 30ᶠGS, 24³S, 32⁰G, 24³GF,

	Starts	1st	2nd	3rd	Win & Pl
Chases	5	0	2	3404	
Career Total	16	1	1	4	17347
135	4/02	Asct	3m110y B Ch	G-F	£10998

Total win prize-money £10998

Going: Sf: 0-1 GS: 0-1 Gd: 0-2 GF: - Fm: 0-1
Distance: 2m/2m3: 0-0 2m4-2m7: 0-0 3m+: 0-5
Track: LH: 0-1 RH: 0-4 Tight: 0-1 Gall: 0-1
Aids: Bl: 0-0 Vi: 0-0 Tstrap: 0-0
Best Rating: 135 4/02 Asct 3m110y   gd-fm   Ch

Fair staying chaser; moderate form in novice chases until bolting up over three miles on fast ground at Ascot in April 2002; seems to need at least 3m.

Lord Strickland
111(106h)   (109h)116
10-y-o b g Strong Gale-Lady Rag (Ragapan)
P J Hobbs   Miss H L Cope

Placings:*0660/*41450306/1113214/401321454-03331F   (0997)
2002/03: 22⁰GF, 20³G, 22³G, 23³GF, 21¹GF, 21ᶠGF,

	Starts	1st	2nd	3rd	Win & Pl
Hurdles	2	0	0	1	473
Chases	4	1	0	2	6160
Career Total	34	8	2	6	32209
115	7/02	NAbb	2m5f110yD(0-120)HCh	G-F	£4541
117	8/01	NAbb	2m5f110yF(0-105)HCh	G-F	£3654
110	7/01	Strf	2m6f110yF(0-110)HHdl	G-F	£2572
108	8/00	Hntg	2m4f110yE Ch	G-F	£3445
119	6/00	NAbb	2m6f	F(0-105)HHdl	G-F	£2988
116	5/00	Font	2m6f	E(0-115)HHdl	GD	£2411
115	5/00	Winc	2m6f	F(0-100)HHdl	FRM	£3133
85	5/99	Kbgn	2m3f	Hdl	GD	£2455

Total win prize-money £25204

Going: Sf: 0-0 GS: 0-0 Gd: 0-2 GF: - Fm: 1-4
Distance: 2m/2m3: 0-0 2m4-2m7: 1-5 3m+: 0-0
Track: LH: 1-6 RH: 0-0 Tight: 1-4 Gall: 0-0
Aids: Bl: 0-0 Vi: 0-0 Tstrap: 0-0
Best Rating: 119 7/00 Worc 3m   gd-fm   Hdl

Fair staying hurdler/chaser, suited by fast ground; has front run but suited by a sharp track and waiting tactics.

Lord Thomas (IRE)

5-y-o b g Grand Lodge (USA)-Noble Rocket (Reprimand)
A J Wilson   Tim Leadbeater

Placings:*0*   (3412)
2002/03: 16⁰GS,

	Starts	1st	2nd	3rd	Win & Pl
NH Flat	1	0	0	0	
Career Total	1	0	0	0	

Going: Sf: 0-0 GS: 0-1 Gd: 0-0 GF: - Fm: 0-0
Distance: 2m/2m3: 0-1 2m4-2m7: 0-0 3m+: 0-0
Track: LH: 0-1 RH: 0-0 Tight: 0-0 Gall: 0-0
Aids: Bl: 0-0 Vi: 0-0 Tstrap: 0-0
Best Rating: 0 2/03 Weth 2m   gd-sft   NHF

Lord Token
28
9-y-o b g Lighter-Lady Token (Roscoe Blake)
Mrs S J Smith   Mrs S Smith

Placings:*P*0PP-P0   (0331)
2002/03: 25ᴾGS, 20⁰G,

	Starts	1st	2nd	3rd	Win & Pl
Hurdles	1	0	0	0	0
Chases	1	0	0	0	
Career Total	6	0	0	0	

Going: Sf: 0-0 GS: 0-1 Gd: 0-1 GF: - Fm: 0-0
Distance: 2m/2m3: 0-0 2m4-2m7: 0-1 3m+: 0-1
Track: LH: 0-2 RH: 0-0 Tight: 0-0 Gall: 0-0
Aids: Bl: 0-0 Vi: 0-0 Tstrap: 0-0
Best Rating: 28 10/01 Weth 2m4f110y   good   Hdl

Lord Transcend (IRE)
107   160
6-y-o gr g Aristocracy-Capincur Lady (Over The River (FR))
J Howard Johnson   Transcend (Hair And Beauty) Limited

Placings:*1*-1115   (4478)
2002/03: 16¹HY, 16¹GS, 23¹GS, 20⁵G,

	Starts	1st	2nd	3rd	Win & Pl
Hurdles	4	3	0	0	32864
Career Total	5	4	0	0	35524
160	1/03	Hayd	2m7f110yA Hdl	G-S	£23200
145	11/02	Newc	2m	D(0-115)HHdl	G-S	£3701
120	11/02	Hexm	2m110y	F(0-100)HHdl	HVY	£2212
99	3/02	Newc	2m	E Hdl	HVY	£2660

Total win prize-money £31774

Going: Sf: 1-1 GS: 2-2 Gd: 0-1 GF: - Fm: 0-0
Distance: 2m/2m3: 2-2 2m4-2m7: 0-1 3m+: 1-1
Track: LH: 3-4 RH: 0-0 Tight: 0-1 Gall: 1-1
Aids: Bl: 0-0 Vi: 0-0 Tstrap: 0-0
Best Rating: 160 1/03 Hayd 2m7f110y   gd-sft   Hdl

Smart hurdler; progressing really well and won a Grade Two at Haydock over nearly three miles on his fourth run; unbeaten three times over two miles prior to that; ran with credit in Grade One at Aintree; acts well on a soft surface and looks an exciting chasing prospect.

Lord Ville (FR)
104   92
4-y-o b g Useful (FR)-Triaina (Lancastrian)

P J Hobbs Rod Hamilton

Placings:656051 (4721)
2002/03: 16⁶S, 16⁵S, 17⁶GS, 17⁰HY, 17⁵F, 16¹F,

	Starts	1st	2nd	3rd	Win & Pl
Hurdles	6	1	0	0	3416
Career Total	6	1	0	0	3416
92	4/03	Winc	2m		E(0-110)HHdl FRM £3416
					Total win prize-money £3416

Going:	Sf: 0-3 GS: 0-1 Gd: 0-0 GF: - Fm: 1-2
Distance:	2m/2m3: 1-6 2m4-2m7: 0-0 3m+: 0-0
Track:	LH: 0-1 RH: 1-5 Tight: 0-1 Gall: 0-2
Aids:	Bl: 0-0 Vi: 0-0 Tstrap: 0-0
Best Rating:	92 4/03 Winc 2m firm Hdl

Plating-class; suited by two miles; acts on fast ground.

Lord Warford

102(98h) (90h)83
8-y-o b g Bustino-Jupiter s Message (Jupiter Island)
C L Popham H J W Davies, Rodney Peacock

Placings:03/0432/160/605-55P44 (4339)
2002/03: 21⁵GF, 16⁵S, 19⁶GS, 21⁴S, 24⁴GF,

	Starts	1st	2nd	3rd	Win & Pl
Chases	5	0	0	0	754
Career Total	17	1	1	2	7166
114	5/00	NAbb	2m6f		C Hdl G-F £4810
					Total win prize-money £4810

Going:	Sf: 0-2 GS: 0-1 Gd: 0-0 GF: - Fm: 0-2
Distance:	2m/2m3: 0-2 2m4-2m7: 0-2 3m+: 0-1
Track:	LH: 0-2 RH: 0-3 Tight: 0-3 Gall: 0-1
Aids:	Bl: 0-0 Vi: 0-0 Tstrap: 0-0
Best Rating:	114 5/00 NAbb 2m6f gd-fm Hdl

Lord York (IRE)

108(106h) (112h)137
11-y-o b/br g Strong Gale-Bunkilla (Arctic Slave)
Ian Williams (M Todhunter 16/10) David J Dunne

Placings:2013/4560/14112221011/2060/113133323-45P34103 (4781)
2002/03: 16⁴G, 21⁵GF, 20⁶GS, 17³GF, 21⁴G, 16¹G, 16⁶G, 16³GF,

	Starts	1st	2nd	3rd	Win & Pl
Hurdles	2	0	0	1	1215
Chases	6	1	0	1	15698
Career Total	40	11	6	8	117292
137	3/03	Asct	2m	C(0-135)HCh	GD £11948
138	11/01	Asct	2m	A(0-150)HCh	GD £18119
138	5/01	Hntg	2m110y	C(0-135)HCh	G-F £6668
138	5/01	Extr	2m1f110yD(0-125)HCh	GD £4826
138	4/00	Ayr	2m	B HCh	GD £13312
122	4/00	Ayr	2m	C Ch	GD £5752
138	3/00	Newb	2m2f110yD(0-125)HCh	G-F £7247
133	10/99	Towc	2m110y	E(0-115)HCh	GD £3142
122	10/99	Extr	2m1f	D(0-110)HCh	GD £3837
107	9/99	MRas	2m6f110yE Ch	G-F £3286
110	3/98	Donc	2m4f	E Hdl	GD £2658
					Total win prize-money £80799

Going:	Sf: 0-0 GS: 0-1 Gd: 1-4 GF: - Fm: 0-3
Distance:	2m/2m3: 1-5 2m4-2m7: 0-3 3m+: 0-0
Track:	LH: 0-4 RH: 1-4 Tight: 0-4 Gall: 0-0
Aids:	Bl: 1-4 Vi: 0-3 Tstrap: 0-1
Best Rating:	141 4/02 Aint 2m good Ch

Useful handicap chaser; best at two miles, stays 2m 5f; likes to front-run; effective on a sound surface; has worn blinkers/visor/tongue tie.

Lordberniebouffant (IRE)

(102h) (132h)131
10-y-o b g Denel (FR)-Noon Hunting (Green Shoon)
J T Gifford The Marvellous Partnership

Placings:5324212/33F004/413124/3051F0-5 (2466)
2002/03: 24⁵G,

	Starts	1st	2nd	3rd	Win & Pl
Hurdles	1	0	0	0	407
Career Total	26	4	4	5	60433
121	3/02	Newb	3m	C(0-130)HCh	G-S £9552
121	1/01	Font	3m4f	D(0-125)HCh	SFT £13650
107	9/00	Hntg	3m	E Ch	G-F £3607
125	3/99	Sand	2m4f110yA HHdl	SFT £16299
					Total win prize-money £43111

Going:	Sf: 0-0 GS: 0-0 Gd: 0-1 GF: - Fm: 0-0
Distance:	2m/2m3: 0-0 2m4-2m7: 0-0 3m+: 0-1
Track:	LH: 0-1 RH: 0-0 Tight: 0-0 Gall: 0-0
Aids:	Bl: 0-0 Vi: 0-0 Tstrap: 0-0
Best Rating:	132 12/02 Chel 3m good Hdl

A decent staying handicap chaser, he acts on most types of ground, but does not like it heavy. Stays three and a half miles.

Lords Best (IRE)

107 129+
7-y-o b g Mister Lord (USA)-Ballinlonig Star (Black Minstrel)
A King Jerry Wright, Peter Smith & Jules Sigler

Placings:34224-11431 (4318)
2002/03: 21¹S, 22¹GS, 24⁴G, 24³GS, 24¹G,

	Starts	1st	2nd	3rd	Win & Pl
Hurdles	5	3	0	1	19958
Career Total	10	3	2	4	24812
129	3/03	Bang	3m	C(0-135)HHdl	GD £6812
121	11/02	Winc	2m6f	C HHdl	G-S £6610
114	11/02	Kemp	2m5f	D Hdl	SFT £4504
					Total win prize-money £17928

Going:	Sf: 1-1 GS: 1-2 Gd: 1-2 GF: - Fm: 0-0
Distance:	2m/2m3: 0-0 2m4-2m7: 2-2 3m+: 1-3
Track:	LH: 1-2 RH: 2-3 Tight: 1-1 Gall: 0-1
Aids:	Bl: 0-0 Vi: 0-0 Tstrap: 0-0
Best Rating:	129 3/03 Bang 3m good Hdl

Decent hurdler; has hung right-handed before; best at around three miles; needs a sound surface.

Lorenzino (IRE)

104 119
6-y-o ch g Thunder Gulch (USA)-Russian Ballet (USA) (Nijinsky (CAN))
Jonjo O Neill P Piller

Placings:12/152110-6F060UP (4171)
2002/03: 23⁶G, 19⁷G, 24⁵G, 22⁶HY, 22⁰GS, 20⁰G, 22⁵S,

	Starts	1st	2nd	3rd	Win & Pl
Hurdles	7	0	0	0	1217
Career Total	15	4	2	0	32033
130	2/02	Kemp	2m5f	C(0-130)HHdl	GD £13942
125	11/01	Weth	2m4f110yC(0-130)HHdl	GD £7020
120	5/01	Bang	2m1f	D(0-120)HHdl	G-S £4485
120	2/01	Weth	2m	E HHdl	SFT £2628
					Total win prize-money £28077

Going:	Sf: 0-2 GS: 0-1 Gd: 0-4 GF: - Fm: 0-0
Distance:	2m/2m3: 0-1 2m4-2m7: 0-4 3m+: 0-2
Track:	LH: 0-5 RH: 0-2 Tight: 0-1 Gall: 0-1
Aids:	Bl: 0-0 Vi: 0-0 Tstrap: 0-2

Best Rating: 130 2/02 Kemp 2m5f good Hdl

Useful hurdler; suited by two and a half miles plus and a sound surface; best racing just off the pace.

Lorgnette

102(101c) (104c)108
9-y-o b m Emperor Fountain-Speckyfoureyes (Blue Cashmere)
R H Alner Alvin Trowbridge

Placings:316453/513514-40224025323 (4720)
2002/03: 22⁴G, 24⁰G, 24²GF, 19²GS, 24⁴G, 24⁰GS, 22²GS, 22⁵S, 22³S, 22²F, 22³F,

	Starts	1st	2nd	3rd	Win & Pl
Hurdles	7	0	2	2	4656
Chases	4	0	2	0	3751
Career Total	23	3	4	5	16725
108	11/01	Plum	2m5f	E Hdl	GD £2460
96	10/01	Winc	2m6f	F(0-105)HHdl	G-F £3052
95	10/00	Tntn	2m1f	H NHF	GD £1536
					Total win prize-money £7050

Going:	Sf: 0-2 GS: 0-3 Gd: 0-3 GF: - Fm: 0-3
Distance:	2m/2m3: 0-1 2m4-2m7: 0-6 3m+: 0-4
Track:	LH: 0-3 RH: 0-8 Tight: 0-6 Gall: 0-0
Aids:	Bl: 0-0 Vi: 0-0 Tstrap: 0-0
Best Rating:	108 1/03 Winc 2m6f gd-sft Hdl

Fair staying handicap hurdler; needs to come late; likes fast ground.

Los Vados (GER)

98 89
4-y-o b g Dashing Blade-La Vega (GER) (Turfkonig (GER))
Ian Williams Allwood-Vaughan-Harris

Placings:64U (4698)
2002/03: 16⁶G, 16⁴G, 16ᵁGF,

	Starts	1st	2nd	3rd	Win & Pl
Hurdles	3	0	0	0	322
Career Total	3	0	0	0	322

Going:	Sf: 0-0 GS: 0-0 Gd: 0-2 GF: - Fm: 0-1
Distance:	2m/2m3: 0-3 2m4-2m7: 0-0 3m+: 0-0
Track:	LH: 0-1 RH: 0-2 Tight: 0-1 Gall: 0-0
Aids:	Bl: 0-0 Vi: 0-0 Tstrap: 0-0
Best Rating:	69 4/03 Ludl 2m good Hdl

Modest novice hurdler.

Lost Direction

8-y-o b m Heading North-Precis (Pitpan)
O J Carter O J Carter

Placings:PP5 (0655)
2002/03: 20⁰GF, 26⁶G, 24⁵GF,

	Starts	1st	2nd	3rd	Win & Pl
Hurdles	1	0	0	0	0
Chases	2	0	0	0	0
Career Total	3	0	0	0	0

Going:	Sf: 0-0 GS: 0-0 Gd: 0-1 GF: - Fm: 0-2
Distance:	2m/2m3: 0-0 2m4-2m7: 0-1 3m+: 0-2
Track:	LH: 0-3 RH: 0-0 Tight: 0-1 Gall: 0-0
Aids:	Bl: 0-0 Vi: 0-0 Tstrap: 0-0
Best Rating:	0 8/02 NAbb 3m2f110y gd-fm Ch

Lost In Normandy (IRE)

73   **57**

6-y-o b g Treasure Hunter-Auntie Honnie (IRE) (Radical)
Mrs L Williamson (G M McCourt 14/5) Blush Syndicate

Placings:500P5   (3566)
2002/03: 17⁵G, 17⁰G, 16⁰S, 17ᴾGS, 21⁵HY,

	Starts	1st	2nd	3rd	Win & Pl
NH Flat	2	0	0	0	0
Hurdles	3	0	0	0	0
Career Total	5	0	0	0	0

Going: Sf: 0-2 GS: 0-1 Gd: 0-2 GF: - Fm: 0-0
Distance: 2m/2m3: 0-4 2m4-2m7: 0-1 3m+: 0-0
Track: LH: 0-3 RH: 0-1 Tight: 0-2 Gall: 0-0
Aids: Bl: 0-0 Vi: 0-0 Tstrap: 0-0
Best Rating: 96   5/02   Hrfd   2m1f   good   NHF

Lost The Plot

99(106h)   (104h)**107+**

8-y-o b m Lyphento (USA)-La Comedienne (Comedy Star (USA))
D W P Arbuthnot The Kennet Partnership

Placings: 11/3000/226/430542-3112   (1505)
2002/03: 20³GS, 21¹G, 22¹GF, 21²G,

	Starts	1st	2nd	3rd	Win & Pl
Hurdles	4	2	1	1	8553
Career Total	19	4	4	3	27525
101 9/02	Font	2m6f110yE(0-110)HHdl		G-F	£3052
97 9/02	Sthl	2m5f110yE Hdl		GD	£3001
107 4/99	Chel	2m1f H NHF		GD	£14070
97 2/99	Font	2m2f110yH NHF		GD	£1556

Total win prize-money £21681

Going: Sf: 0-0 GS: 0-0 Gd: 1-2 GF: - Fm: 1-2
Distance: 2m/2m3: 0-0 **2m4-2m7: 2-4** 3m+: 0-0
Track: **LH: 2-4** RH: 0-0 Tight: **1-1** Gall: 0-0
Aids: Bl: 0-0 Vi: 0-0 Tstrap: 0-0
Best Rating: 107   4/99   Chel   2m1f   good   NHF

Modest hurdler; winner of her two bumpers in the spring of 1999, won a poor race at Southwell in September 2002 and followed up later that month at Fontwell. Stays two miles six and acts on decent ground.

Lothian Emerald

6-y-o ch m Greensmith-Lothian Rose (Roscoe Blake)
D McCain Champ Chicken Co Ltd

Placings:0P   (0474)
2002/03: 17⁰S, 17ᴾGS,

	Starts	1st	2nd	3rd	Win & Pl
NH Flat	1	0	0	0	0
Hurdles	1	0	0	0	0
Career Total	2	0	0	0	0

Going: Sf: 0-1 GS: 0-1 Gd: 0-0 GF: - Fm: 0-0
Distance: 2m/2m3: 0-2 2m4-2m7: 0-0 3m+: 0-0
Track: LH: 0-0 RH: 0-0 Tight: 0-2 Gall: 0-0
Aids: Bl: 0-0 Vi: 0-0 Tstrap: 0-0
Best Rating: 0   6/02   Ctml   2m1f110y gd-sft   Hdl

Lottery Lil

8-y-o ch m Petoski-Quarry Machine (Laurence O)

I Hudson I Hudson

Placings:0/P   (0392)
2002/03: 24ᴾG,

	Starts	1st	2nd	3rd	Win & Pl
Chases	1	0	0	0	
Career Total	2	0	0	0	

Going: Sf: 0-0 GS: 0-0 Gd: 0-1 GF: - Fm: 0-0
Distance: 2m/2m3: 0-0 2m4-2m7: 0-0 3m+: 0-1
Track: LH: 0-1 RH: 0-0 Tight: 0-1 Gall: 0-0
Aids: Bl: 0-0 Vi: 0-0 Tstrap: 0-0
Best Rating: 37   11/99   Wwck   2m   good   NHF

Lottery Ticket (IRE)

14-y-o b g The Parson-Beauty Run (Deep Run)
S J Robinson S J Robinson

Placings:2021/3220PB/2UP5/324FFP125/P4PP/U/56-U   (0477)
2002/03: 26ᵁGS,

	Starts	1st	2nd	3rd	Win & Pl
Chases	1	0	0	0	
Career Total	31	2	7	2	10664
110 3/98	Uttx	3m2f	E(0-110)HCh	GD	£2934
109 4/95	Hexm	2m	H NHF	SFT	£1465

Total win prize-money £4400

Going: Sf: 0-0 GS: 0-1 Gd: 0-0 GF: - Fm: 0-0
Distance: 2m/2m3: 0-0 2m4-2m7: 0-0 3m+: 0-1
Track: LH: 0-1 RH: 0-0 Tight: 0-1 Gall: 0-0
Aids: Bl: 0-0 Vi: 0-0 Tstrap: 0-0
Best Rating: 122   3/96   Chel   2m5f   gd-sft   Hdl

Loudy Rowdy (IRE)

91(92h)   (77h)**49**

12-y-o br g Strong Gale-Express Film (Ashmore (FR))
Mrs J K M Oliver The British Beef Partnership

Placings:14/F0/P0/044P5P-5P3   (4659)
2002/03: 22⁵G, 21ᴾG, 20³GF,

	Starts	1st	2nd	3rd	Win & Pl
Hurdles	2	0	0	1	500
Chases	1	0	0	0	
Career Total	15	1	0	1	4115
108 10/97	Wxfd	2m	NHF	G-F	£3221

Total win prize-money £3222

Going: Sf: 0-0 GS: 0-0 Gd: 0-2 GF: - Fm: 0-1
Distance: 2m/2m3: 0-0 2m4-2m7: 0-3 3m+: 0-0
Track: LH: 0-2 RH: 0-0 Tight: 0-2 Gall: 0-0
Aids: Bl: 0-0 Vi: 0-0 Tstrap: 0-0
Best Rating: 108   10/97   Wxfd   2m   gd-fm   NHF

Plating-class hurdler/chaser, suited by a sound surface; also handles soft ground.

Lougaroo (FR)

101   **105**

4-y-o ch c Snurge-Titian Queen (Sicyos (USA))
G Macaire (Y Fouin 15/11) F-X Chaussonniere

Placings:F12130   (3287)
2002/03: 15ᶠS, 16¹S, 17²HY, 18¹HY, 16³HY, 17⁰GS,

	Starts	1st	2nd	3rd	Win & Pl
Hurdles	6	2	1	1	21187
Career Total	6	2	1	1	21187
12/02	Autl	2m2f	Hdl	HVY	£10601
10/02	Bord	2m110y	Hdl	SFT	£4417

Total win prize-money £15018

Going: Sf: 2-5 GS: 0-1 Gd: 0-0 GF: - Fm: 0-0
Distance: 2m/2m3: 2-5 2m4-2m7: 0-0 3m+: 0-0
Track: LH: 0-2 RH: 0-0 Tight: 0-0 Gall: 0-1
Aids: Bl: 0-0 Vi: 0-0 Tstrap: 0-0
Best Rating: 105   12/02   Chep   2m110y   heavy   Hdl

Fair juvenile hurdler; dual winner in France; well held in warm company in Britain; effective on heavy ground.

Lough Lein Lady (IRE)

(73h)   (22h)

8-y-o ch m Alphabatim (USA)-Cap Reform (IRE) (Phardante (FR))
A W Carroll Roger Clarke And Adam Simpson

Placings:0/U0PPP-   (0016)
2002/03: 20ᴾGS,

	Starts	1st	2nd	3rd	Win & Pl
Chases	1	0	0	0	
Career Total	6	0	0	0	

Going: Sf: 0-0 GS: 0-1 Gd: 0-0 GF: - Fm: 0-0
Distance: 2m/2m3: 0-0 2m4-2m7: 0-1 3m+: 0-0
Track: LH: 0-0 RH: 0-0 Tight: 0-0 Gall: 0-0
Aids: Bl: 0-0 Vi: 0-0 Tstrap: 0-1
Best Rating: 48   5/00   Tipp   2m2f   gd-fm   NHF

Lough Rynn (IRE)

84   **64**

5-y-o b g Beneficial-Liffey Lady (Camden Town)
Miss H C Knight Carfield/Baxter

Placings:650   (3871)
2002/03: 16⁶GS, 17⁵S, 19⁰S,

	Starts	1st	2nd	3rd	Win & Pl
NH Flat	2	0	0	0	0
Hurdles	1	0	0	0	0
Career Total	3	0	0	0	0

Going: Sf: 0-2 GS: 0-1 Gd: 0-0 GF: - Fm: 0-0
Distance: 2m/2m3: 0-3 2m4-2m7: 0-0 3m+: 0-0
Track: LH: 0-1 RH: 0-2 Tight: 0-0 Gall: 0-2
Aids: Bl: 0-0 Vi: 0-0 Tstrap: 0-0
Best Rating: 90   12/02   Hrfd   2m1f   soft   NHF

Loughbeg Rambler

106   (91h)**94**

8-y-o ch g Weld-Rose Rambler (Scallywag)
Donal Hassett M McGrogan

Placings:0000/6F6-02112234   (1994)
2002/03: 24⁰S, 16²GF, 16¹G, 16¹G, 19²F, 24²G, 22³G, 20⁴GS,

	Starts	1st	2nd	3rd	Win & Pl
Hurdles	2	0	1	1	1951
Chases	6	2	2	0	15174
Career Total	15	2	3	1	17125
88 8/02	Tral	2m	(0-116)HCh	GD	£5291
81 8/02	Tral	2m	(0-95)HCh	GD	£5926

Total win prize-money £11217

Going: Sf: 0-1 GS: 0-1 Gd: 2-4 GF: - Fm: 0-2
Distance: 2m/2m3: 2-4 2m4-2m7: 0-2 3m+: 0-2
Track: LH: 0-1 RH: 0-2 Tight: 0-0 Gall: 0-1
Aids: Bl: 0-0 Vi: 0-0 Tstrap: 2-7
Best Rating: 93   9/02   List   2m3f   firm   Ch

Modest chaser/hurdler; winner over fences in Ireland over two miles on good ground. Has been a beaten favourite over hurdles twice in October 2002.

Loughcrew (IRE)
99
7-y-o ch g Good Thyne (USA)-Marys Course (Crash Course)
L Lungo Mrs Barbara Lungo

Placings:00000/0110P00-P   (3353)
2002/03: 24PHY,

	Starts	1st	2nd	3rd	Win & Pl
Hurdles	1	0	0	0	
Career Total	13	2	0	0	8625
99 9/01	Gowr	3m		(0-109)HHdl	G-F £4729
95 9/01	Clon	2m4f		(0-109)HHdl	G-F £3895
				Total win prize-money	£8625

Going:	Sf: 0-1 GS: 0-0 Gd: 0-0 GF: - Fm: 0-0
Distance:	2m/2m3: 0-0 2m4-2m7: 0-0 3m+: 0-1
Track:	LH: 0-1 RH: 0-0 Tight: 0-0 Gall: 0-1
Aids:	Bl: 0-0 Vi: 0-0 Tstrap: 0-0
Best Rating:	99 9/01 Gowr 3m gd-fm Hdl

Louises Glory (IRE)
(99h) (93h) 101
8-y-o ch g Executive Perk-Ring-Em-All (Decent Fellow)
D J Wintle Mrs Sara Bacon

Placings:040242O/4005100635-60   (2168)
2002/03: 18PGS, 19OGS,

	Starts	1st	2nd	3rd	Win & Pl
Hurdles	2	0	0	0	
Career Total	19	1	2	1	8410
93 1/02	Punc	2m	(0-102)HHdl	Y-S	£5503
			Total win prize-money		£5503

Going:	Sf: 0-0 GS: 0-2 Gd: 0-0 GF: - Fm: 0-0
Distance:	2m/2m3: 0-2 2m4-2m7: 0-0 3m+: 0-0
Track:	LH: 0-2 RH: 0-0 Tight: 0-1 Gall: 0-0
Aids:	Bl: 0-0 Vi: 0-0 Tstrap: 0-1
Best Rating:	104 11/00 Clon 2m sft-hvy NHF

Loup Bleu (USA)
100 112+
5-y-o b g Nureyev (USA)-Louve Bleue (USA) (Irish River (FR))
P J Hobbs (J-P Gallorini 16/10) Richard Green (fine Paintings)

Placings:22430-442   (2777)
2002/03: 19⁴S, 17⁴G, 17²S,

	Starts	1st	2nd	3rd	Win & Pl
Hurdles	3	0	1	0	5726
Career Total	8	0	3	1	39117

Going:	Sf: 0-2 GS: 0-0 Gd: 0-1 GF: - Fm: 0-0
Distance:	2m/2m3: 0-3 2m4-2m7: 0-0 3m+: 0-0
Track:	LH: 0-0 RH: 0-1 Tight: 0-0 Gall: 0-0
Aids:	Bl: 0-0 Vi: 0-0 Tstrap: 0-0
Best Rating:	112 12/02 Tntn 2m1f soft Hdl

Fair novice hurdler; ex-French; suited by two miles, but stays further and best on soft ground; yet to win a race

Love Diamonds (IRE)
92 81

7-y-o b g Royal Academy (USA)-Baby Diamonds (Habitat)
Miss C Dyson Miss C Dyson

Placings:004454P-0R04P4   (0743)
2002/03: 17OGF, 16RGF, 16OG, 16⁴G, 16PGF, 16⁴G,

	Starts	1st	2nd	3rd	Win & Pl
Hurdles	6	0	0	0	0
Career Total	13	0	0	0	521

Going:	Sf: 0-0 GS: 0-0 Gd: 0-3 GF: - Fm: 0-3
Distance:	2m/2m3: 0-6 2m4-2m7: 0-0 3m+: 0-0
Track:	LH: 0-4 RH: 0-3 Tight: 0-1 Gall: 0-2
Aids:	Bl: 0-0 Vi: 0-0 Tstrap: 0-1
Best Rating:	81 9/01 Worc 2m gd-fm Hdl

Love Kiss (IRE)
91 82
8-y-o b g Brief Truce (USA)-Pendulina (Prince Tenderfoot (USA))
M Dods (W Storey 15/6) K Knox

Placings:256501P-34P4P   (4157)
2002/03: 16³GS, 20⁴GS, 16PG, 16⁴S, 17PG,

	Starts	1st	2nd	3rd	Win & Pl
Hurdles	5	0	0	1	534
Career Total	12	1	1	1	3916
89 1/02	Newc	2m	E(0-105)HHdl	SFT	£2646
			Total win prize-money		£2646

Going:	Sf: 0-1 GS: 0-2 Gd: 0-2 GF: - Fm: 0-0
Distance:	2m/2m3: 0-4 2m4-2m7: 0-1 3m+: 0-0
Track:	LH: 0-3 RH: 0-2 Tight: 0-2 Gall: 0-0
Aids:	Bl: 0-0 Vi: 0-0 Tstrap: 0-4
Best Rating:	89 1/02 Newc 2m soft Hdl

Modest hurdler, best a two miles on very soft ground although acts on faster. Has broken blood-vessels. Suited by hold-up tactics.

Love Potion
94
8-y-o br m Neltino-Celtic Honey (Celtic Cone)
E L James Mrs J N Humphreys

Placings:2/030/0053-P   (0269)
2002/03: 21³GS, 16PGF,

	Starts	1st	2nd	3rd	Win & Pl
Hurdles	2	0	0	1	283
Career Total	9	0	1	2	1010

Going:	Sf: 0-0 GS: 0-1 Gd: 0-0 GF: - Fm: 0-1
Distance:	2m/2m3: 0-1 2m4-2m7: 0-1 3m+: 0-0
Track:	LH: 0-1 RH: 0-1 Tight: 0-1 Gall: 0-0
Aids:	Bl: 0-0 Vi: 0-0 Tstrap: 0-0
Best Rating:	90 10/00 Wwck 2m soft NHF

Love Venture

9-y-o b m Pursuit Of Love-Our Shirley (Shirley Heights)
Miss M E Rowland Miss M E Rowland

Placings:06560/4P/P   (2471)
2002/03: 16PG,

	Starts	1st	2nd	3rd	Win & Pl
Hurdles	1	0	0	0	
Career Total	8	0	0	0	0

Going:	Sf: 0-0 GS: 0-0 Gd: 0-1 GF: - Fm: 0-0

Distance:	2m/2m3: 0-1 2m4-2m7: 0-0 3m+: 0-0
Track:	LH: 0-1 RH: 0-0 Tight: 0-0 Gall: 0-1
Aids:	Bl: 0-0 Vi: 0-0 Tstrap: 0-0
Best Rating:	76 6/99 MRas 2m1f110y gd-fm Hdl

Lovers Tale
90 65
5-y-o b g Pursuit Of Love-Kintail (Kris)
H M Kavanagh Mrs S Kavanagh

Placings:0-000   (4191)
2002/03: 17OS, 17OS, 16OG,

	Starts	1st	2nd	3rd	Win & Pl
NH Flat	1	0	0	0	0
Hurdles	2	0	0	0	0
Career Total	4	0	0	0	

Going:	Sf: 0-2 GS: 0-0 Gd: 0-1 GF: - Fm: 0-0
Distance:	2m/2m3: 0-3 2m4-2m7: 0-0 3m+: 0-0
Track:	LH: 0-0 RH: 0-3 Tight: 0-0 Gall: 0-0
Aids:	Bl: 0-0 Vi: 0-0 Tstrap: 0-0
Best Rating:	65 3/03 Ludl 2m good Hdl

Lowena

5-y-o ch m Carlingford Castle-Walnut Way (Gambling Debt)
M R Hoad Mr & Mrs D A Gamble

Placings:0P   (4187)
2002/03: 18OS, 20PG,

	Starts	1st	2nd	3rd	Win & Pl
NH Flat	1	0	0	0	0
Hurdles	1	0	0	0	0
Career Total	2	0	0	0	

Going:	Sf: 0-1 GS: 0-0 Gd: 0-1 GF: - Fm: 0-0
Distance:	2m/2m3: 0-1 2m4-2m7: 0-1 3m+: 0-0
Track:	LH: 0-1 RH: 0-0 Tight: 0-2 Gall: 0-0
Aids:	Bl: 0-0 Vi: 0-0 Tstrap: 0-0
Best Rating:	0 3/03 Folk 2m4f110y good Hdl

Lowry (USA)

5-y-o b/br g Gulch (USA)-Aviara (USA) (Cox s Ridge (USA))
J S King D Goodenough Removals & Transport

Placings:P   (1891)
2002/03: 16PGS,

	Starts	1st	2nd	3rd	Win & Pl
Hurdles	1	0	0	0	
Career Total	1	0	0	0	

Going:	Sf: 0-0 GS: 0-1 Gd: 0-0 GF: - Fm: 0-0
Distance:	2m/2m3: 0-1 2m4-2m7: 0-0 3m+: 0-0
Track:	LH: 0-0 RH: 0-1 Tight: 0-0 Gall: 0-1
Aids:	Bl: 0-0 Vi: 0-0 Tstrap: 0-0
Best Rating:	0 11/02 Hntg 2m110y gd-sft Hdl

Loxley
86 59
4-y-o b g Ezzoud (IRE)-Shewillifshewants (IRE) (Alzao (USA))
Mrs S J Smith Mrs D J Buckley

Placings:P06 (1051)
2002/03: 17PGS, 17OG, 17RG,

	Starts	1st	2nd	3rd	Win & Pl
Hurdles	3	0	0	0	0
Career Total	3	0	0	0	0

Going: Sf: 0-0 GS: 0-1 Gd: 0-2 GF: - Fm: 0-0
Distance: 2m/2m3: 0-3 2m4-2m7: 0-0 3m+: 0-0
Track: LH: 0-2 RH: 0-1 Tight: 0-3 Gall: 0-0
Aids: Bl: 0-0 Vi: 0-0 Tstrap: 0-0
Best Rating: 59 8/02 Sedg 2m1f good Hdl

Lozzy Lee (IRE)
94f   102+f
5-y-o b g Zaffaran (USA)-Amazing Lee (IRE) (Amazing Bust)
D J Caro Mrs S Tainton

Placings:024 (2675)
2002/03: 12OGS, 18?HY, 17?S,

	Starts	1st	2nd	3rd	Win & Pl
NH Flat	3	0	1	0	678
Career Total	3	0	1	0	678

Going: Sf: 0-2 GS: 0-1 Gd: 0-0 GF: - Fm: 0-0
Distance: 2m/2m3: 0-2 2m4-2m7: 0-0 3m+: 0-0
Track: LH: 0-2 RH: 0-1 Tight: 0-0 Gall: 0-0
Aids: Bl: 0-0 Vi: 0-0 Tstrap: 0-0
Best Rating: 102 12/02 Plum 2m2f heavy NHF

Modest bumper performer; acts on a soft surface.

Lucien (IRE)
86   21
5-y-o ch g Catrail (USA)-What A Candy (USA) (Key To The Mint (USA))
M F Harris (N J Henderson 16/5) Jennie Hall & Jean Webb

Placings:00-30P000P00 (4513)
2002/03: 16RGF, 17OGF, 16PG, 17OG, 16OGS, 16OS, 16PS, 16OS, 19RGF,

	Starts	1st	2nd	3rd	Win & Pl
NH Flat	2	0	0	1	335
Hurdles	7	0	0	0	0
Career Total	11	0	0	1	335

Going: Sf: 0-3 GS: 0-1 Gd: 0-2 GF: - Fm: 0-3
Distance: 2m/2m3: 0-9 2m4-2m7: 0-0 3m+: 0-0
Track: LH: 0-5 RH: 0-4 Tight: 0-4 Gall: 0-1
Aids: Bl: 0-0 Vi: 0-0 Tstrap: 0-0
Best Rating: 83 3/02 Newb 2m110y gd-sft NHF

Well beaten in soft ground bumpers, but did better on faster ground at Perth in May.

Lucky Bay (IRE)
114(102h)   (119h)139
7-y-o b g Convinced-Current Liability (Caribo)
Miss H C Knight Executive Racing II

Placings:6/512P-F22156P (4474)
2002/03: 23RG, 25?G, 24?G, 24?S, 24?S, 32RG, 25PG,

	Starts	1st	2nd	3rd	Win & Pl
Chases	7	1	2	0	25686
Career Total	12	2	3	0	31846
139 11/02 Newb 3m	A Ch			SFT	£17400
114 11/01 Winc 2m6f	C Hdl			G-F	£5343

Total win prize-money £22743

Going: Sf: 1-2 GS: 0-0 Gd: 0-5 GF: - Fm: 0-0
Distance: 2m/2m3: 0-0 2m4-2m7: 0-0 3m+: 1-7
Track: LH: 1-4 RH: 0-3 Tight: 0-1 Gall: 1-3
Aids: Bl: 0-0 Vi: 0-0 Tstrap: 0-0
Best Rating: 139 11/02 Newb 3m soft Ch

Very useful novice chaser; unlucky at Cheltenham in November 2002, won a Grade Two event at Newbury next time; stays three miles; acts on any ground.

Lucky Brush (IRE)
9-y-o b g Brush Aside (USA)-Luck Daughter (Lucky Brief)
N W Alexander (Miss Caroline Barclay 22/5) Jamie Alexander

Placings:3-635 (4309)
2002/03: 26RG, 25?GS, 25?G,

	Starts	1st	2nd	3rd	Win & Pl
Chases	3	0	0	1	382
Career Total	4	0	0	2	713

Going: Sf: 0-0 GS: 0-1 Gd: 0-2 GF: - Fm: 0-0
Distance: 2m/2m3: 0-0 2m4-2m7: 0-0 3m+: 0-3
Track: LH: 0-3 RH: 0-0 Tight: 0-2 Gall: 0-0
Aids: Bl: 0-0 Vi: 0-0 Tstrap: 0-0
Best Rating: 78 3/03 Kels 3m1f gd-sft Ch

Lucky Catch (IRE)
58f   81f
5-y-o b g Safety Catch (USA)-Lucky Monday (Lucky Wednesday)
R C Guest N B Mason

Placings:0 (3917)
2002/03: 17OGS,

	Starts	1st	2nd	3rd	Win & Pl
NH Flat	1	0	0	0	
Career Total	1	0	0	0	

Going: Sf: 0-0 GS: 0-1 Gd: 0-0 GF: - Fm: 0-0
Distance: 2m/2m3: 0-1 2m4-2m7: 0-0 3m+: 0-0
Track: LH: 0-0 RH: 0-1 Tight: 0-0 Gall: 0-0
Aids: Bl: 0-0 Vi: 0-0 Tstrap: 0-0
Best Rating: 87 3/03 Carl 2m1f gd-sft NHF

Lucky Clover
106   87
11-y-o ch g Push On-Winning Clover (Winden)
C Tizzard Mrs P O Perry

Placings:F0P0P/1P2211221P-P40400 (2467)
2002/03: 27RGF, 26RG, 24OGF, 24?F, 31OGS, 31OGS,

	Starts	1st	2nd	3rd	Win & Pl
Hurdles	1	0	0	0	0
Chases	5	0	0	0	781
Career Total	21	4	4	0	39103
127 11/01 Chel 3m7f	B Ch			GD	£21157
116 8/01 NAbb 3m2f110yE(0-105)HCh				G-F	£3410
120 8/01 NAbb 3m2f110yE Ch				GD	£3376
90 5/01 Extr 2m7f110yE Ch				FRM	£4166

Total win prize-money £32113

Going: Sf: 0-0 GS: 0-2 Gd: 0-1 GF: - Fm: 0-3
Distance: 2m/2m3: 0-0 2m4-2m7: 0-0 3m+: 0-6
Track: LH: 0-5 RH: 0-0 Tight: 0-3 Gall: 0-0
Aids: Bl: 0-1 Vi: 0-0 Tstrap: 0-0
Best Rating: 127 11/01 Chel 3m7f good Ch

Fair staying chaser on fast ground. In good form in the summer of 2001, but put in his place by Southern Star at Cheltenham in October 2001. Put in a brave performance to win the Sporting Index Cross Country Chase at Cheltenham in November before losing his way. Again ran well in the Cross Country Chase the following year when seventh.

Lucky Do (IRE)
98   83
6-y-o b g Camden Town-Lane Baloo (Lucky Brief)
R Dickin D A N Ross

Placings:60-020 (3742)
2002/03: 21OS, 17?GS, 16OG,

	Starts	1st	2nd	3rd	Win & Pl
Hurdles	3	0	1	0	1176
Career Total	5	0	1	0	1176

Going: Sf: 0-1 GS: 0-1 Gd: 0-1 GF: - Fm: 0-0
Distance: 2m/2m3: 0-2 2m4-2m7: 0-1 3m+: 0-0
Track: LH: 0-2 RH: 0-1 Tight: 0-0 Gall: 0-1
Aids: Bl: 0-0 Vi: 0-0 Tstrap: 0-0
Best Rating: 85 4/02 Asct 2m110y gd-fm NHF

Runner-up in a weak novices hurdle at Bangor in February.

Lucky Duck
84f   85f
6-y-o ch g Minster Son-Petroc Concert (Tina s Pet)
Mrs A Hamilton Ian Hamilton

Placings:0-0 (1639)
2002/03: 17OS,

	Starts	1st	2nd	3rd	Win & Pl
NH Flat	1	0	0	0	
Career Total	2	0	0	0	

Going: Sf: 0-1 GS: 0-0 Gd: 0-0 GF: - Fm: 0-0
Distance: 2m/2m3: 0-1 2m4-2m7: 0-0 3m+: 0-0
Track: LH: 0-0 RH: 0-1 Tight: 0-0 Gall: 0-0
Aids: Bl: 0-0 Vi: 0-0 Tstrap: 0-0
Best Rating: 85 10/02 Carl 2m1f soft NHF

Lucky Heather (IRE)
96   62
6-y-o b m Soviet Lad (USA)-Idrak (Young Generation)
R J Baker Graham Brown

Placings:650P-40540 (2941)
2002/03: 16RGF, 16OGF, 16RG, 16RG, 16OS,

	Starts	1st	2nd	3rd	Win & Pl
Hurdles	5	0	0	0	0
Career Total	9	0	0	0	0

Going: Sf: 0-1 GS: 0-0 Gd: 0-2 GF: - Fm: 0-2
Distance: 2m/2m3: 0-5 2m4-2m7: 0-0 3m+: 0-0
Track: LH: 0-4 RH: 0-1 Tight: 0-3 Gall: 0-0
Aids: Bl: 0-0 Vi: 0-0 Tstrap: 0-0
Best Rating: 82 11/01 Ludl 2m gd-fm Hdl

Moderate maiden over hurdles.

Lucky Joe (IRE)
92(83c)   (73c)73
10-y-o br g Denel (FR)-Breezy Dawn (Kemal (FR))
J White Nick Quesnel

Placings:P/PP4-36   (0418)
2002/03: 26³G, 226⁴HY,

	Starts	1st	2nd	3rd	Win & Pl
Hurdles	1	0	0	0	0
Chases	1	0	0	1	520
Career Total	6	0	0	1	520

Going: Sf: 0-1 GS: 0-0 Gd: 0-1 GF: - Fm: 0-0
Distance: 2m/2m3: 0-2 2m4-2m7: 0-1 3m+: 0-0
Track: LH: 0-1 RH: 0-1 Tight: 0-2 Gall: 0-0
Aids: Bl: 0-0 Vi: 0-0 Tstrap: 0-0
Best Rating: 73 6/02 Ctml 2m6f   heavy   Hdl

Won twice between the flags in 2001. Modest form under Rules.

Lucky Leader (IRE)
94   91
8-y-o b g Supreme Leader-Lucky House (Pollerton)
N R Mitchell (John Brassil 10/6) Michael Green

Placings:60/PP23F   (4438)
2002/03: 17⁶SH, 24⁴S, 24²GS, 26³S, 24ᶠG,

	Starts	1st	2nd	3rd	Win & Pl
Chases	5	0	1	1	2785
Career Total	7	0	1	1	2785

Going: Sf: 0-2 GS: 0-1 Gd: 0-1 GF: - Fm: 0-0
Distance: 2m/2m3: 0-1 2m4-2m7: 0-0 3m+: 0-4
Track: LH: 0-2 RH: 0-2 Tight: 0-2 Gall: 0-0
Aids: Bl: 0-0 Vi: 0-0 Tstrap: 0-0
Best Rating: 91 2/03 Chep 3m   gd-sft   Ch

Moderate novice chaser; stays three miles; acts on soft ground.

Lucky Lucky Bob (USA)
85   79
6-y-o b g Alleged (USA)-Alloy (FR) (Pharly (FR))
P R Chamings Highfield Partnership

Placings:00-360   (3101)
2002/03: 16³HY, 17⁶S, 16⁹S,

	Starts	1st	2nd	3rd	Win & Pl
Hurdles	3	0	0	1	436
Career Total	5	0	0	1	436

Going: Sf: 0-3 GS: 0-0 Gd: 0-0 GF: - Fm: 0-0
Distance: 2m/2m3: 0-3 2m4-2m7: 0-0 3m+: 0-0
Track: LH: 0-2 RH: 0-1 Tight: 0-3 Gall: 0-0
Aids: Bl: 0-0 Vi: 0-0 Tstrap: 0-0
Best Rating: 79 12/02 Tntn 2m1f   soft   Hdl

Lucky Master (IRE)
100(101h)   (100h)82
11-y-o b g Roselier (FR)-Golden Chestnut (Green Shoon)
John R Upson Mrs Ann Key

Placings:005/26426421/22013363/5/46PP240-033 (2564)
2002/03: 24⁶GS, 29³GS, 30³S,

	Starts	1st	2nd	3rd	Win & Pl
Hurdles	1	0	0	0	0
Chases	2	0	0	2	1560
Career Total	30	2	6	5	19860
118	11/99	Uttx	3m	E Ch	G-S £3501
91	4/99	Sedg	2m5f110yE Hdl		G-F £2582

Total win prize-money £6084

Lucky Mick (IRE)
99   93
8-y-o b g Husyan (USA)-Kindly Go (IRE) (Buckley)
J I A Charlton H Proud

Placings:02/00/32451-460P   (3985)
2002/03: 20⁴GF, 25⁶GF, 17⁹HY, 20⁴S,

	Starts	1st	2nd	3rd	Win & Pl
Hurdles	3	0	0	0	0
Chases	1	0	0	0	0
Career Total	13	1	2	1	4556
93	4/02	Newc	2m4f	E Hdl	FRM £2779

Total win prize-money £2779

Going: Sf: 0-2 GS: 0-0 Gd: 0-0 GF: - Fm: 0-2
Distance: 2m/2m3: 0-1 2m4-2m7: 0-2 3m+: 0-1
Track: LH: 0-3 RH: 0-1 Tight: 0-2 Gall: 0-0
Aids: Bl: 0-0 Vi: 0-0 Tstrap: 0-4
Best Rating: 110 4/00 Carl 2m1f   gd-sft NHF

Moderate novice hurdler, handles firm ground and stays two and a half miles. Has worn a tongue-strap.

Lucky Nomad
80   51
7-y-o br g Nomadic Way (USA)-Daleena (Dalesa)
I W McInnes Peter Mee

Placings:P446P   (1568)
2002/03: 20⁸GF, 19⁴GF, 174⁴GS, 19⁶GF, 19⁹G,

	Starts	1st	2nd	3rd	Win & Pl
Hurdles	5	0	0	0	615
Career Total	5	0	0	0	615

Going: Sf: 0-0 GS: 0-1 Gd: 0-1 GF: - Fm: 0-3
Distance: 2m/2m3: 0-1 2m4-2m7: 0-0 3m+: 0-0
Track: LH: 0-1 RH: 0-4 Tight: 0-4 Gall: 0-0
Aids: Bl: 0-0 Vi: 0-0 Tstrap: 0-0
Best Rating: 47 7/02 MRas 2m3f110y gd-fm Hdl

Lucky Penny
82   68
7-y-o ch m Karinga Bay-Redgrave Rose (Tug Of War)
K Bishop D J Bridger & D M Bell

Placings:450-06   (1849)
2002/03: 16⁶G, 22⁶G,

	Starts	1st	2nd	3rd	Win & Pl
NH Flat	1	0	0	0	0
Hurdles	1	0	0	0	0
Career Total	5	0	0	0	0

Going: Sf: 0-0 GS: 0-0 Gd: 0-2 GF: - Fm: 0-0
Distance: 2m/2m3: 0-1 2m4-2m7: 0-1 3m+: 0-0
Track: LH: 0-1 RH: 0-1 Tight: 0-0 Gall: 0-0
Aids: Bl: 0-0 Vi: 0-0 Tstrap: 0-0
Best Rating: 95 4/02 Uttx 2m   good NHF

Glimmer of promise in bumpers.

Going: Sf: 0-1 GS: 0-2 Gd: 0-0 GF: - Fm: 0-0
Distance: 2m/2m3: 0-0 2m4-2m7: 0-0 3m+: 0-3
Track: LH: 0-1 RH: 0-1 Tight: 0-1 Gall: 0-0
Aids: Bl: 0-0 Vi: 0-0 Tstrap: 0-0
Best Rating: 118 1/00 Folk 3m2f   soft   Ch

Plating-class chaser/hurdler; out of sorts over fences but returned to form when reverting to hurdling. Stays very well and likes fast ground.

Lucky Shamrock
9-y-o b m Muqadar (USA)-Bonnie Wednesday (Lucky Wednesday)
W G M Turner L T Woodhouse

Placings:0/P   (2671)
2002/03: 17⁸S,

	Starts	1st	2nd	3rd	Win & Pl
Hurdles	1	0	0	0	
Career Total	2	0	0	0	

Going: Sf: 0-1 GS: 0-0 Gd: 0-0 GF: - Fm: 0-0
Distance: 2m/2m3: 0-1 2m4-2m7: 0-0 3m+: 0-0
Track: LH: 0-0 RH: 0-1 Tight: 0-0 Gall: 0-0
Aids: Bl: 0-0 Vi: 0-0 Tstrap: 0-0
Best Rating: 32 6/99 Worc 2m   gd-fm NHF

Lucky Sinna (IRE)
89   119
7-y-o b/br g Insan (USA)-Bit Of A Chance (Lord Ha Ha)
J T Gifford John Plackett

Placings:3/444/2343F-2   (0174)
2002/03: 22²GF,

	Starts	1st	2nd	3rd	Win & Pl
Hurdles	1	0	1	0	748
Career Total	10	0	2	3	6627

Going: Sf: 0-0 GS: 0-0 Gd: 0-0 GF: - Fm: 0-1
Distance: 2m/2m3: 0-0 2m4-2m7: 0-1 3m+: 0-0
Track: LH: 0-0 RH: 0-1 Tight: 0-0 Gall: 0-0
Aids: Bl: 0-0 Vi: 0-0 Tstrap: 0-1
Best Rating: 126 4/00 Asct 2m110y soft NHF

Lightly-raced novice hurdler, appears not to find much off the bridle and has become rather disappointing. Does not want heavy ground.

Lucky Teeny (IRE)
6-y-o ch m Phardante (FR)-Rusty Iron (General Ironside)
D G Bridgwater Mrs C Kelly

Placings:346-PF0   (1812)
2002/03: 22⁸PS, 20⁴S, 17⁰G,

	Starts	1st	2nd	3rd	Win & Pl
Hurdles	3	0	0	0	
Career Total	6	0	0	1	228

Going: Sf: 0-2 GS: 0-0 Gd: 0-1 GF: - Fm: 0-0
Distance: 2m/2m3: 0-1 2m4-2m7: 0-2 3m+: 0-0
Track: LH: 0-2 RH: 0-1 Tight: 0-2 Gall: 0-0
Aids: Bl: 0-0 Vi: 0-0 Tstrap: 0-0
Best Rating: 81 3/02 Towc 2m   soft NHF

Lucky Time (IRE)
102   99
11-y-o b g Phardante (FR)-Rock Ellie (Random Shot)
Ferdy Murphy K Lee

Placings:5/224/02-1P33P4   (0830)
2002/03: 16²G, 19¹G, 25⁸G, 25³GF, 25³GF, 21⁶GF, 27⁴GF,

	Starts	1st	2nd	3rd	Win & Pl
Hurdles	1	0	0	0	0
Chases	6	1	1	2	5080
Career Total	12	1	3	2	7330

99	5/02 Hrfd	2m3f	F Ch		GD	£2873

Total win prize-money £2873

Going: Sf: 0-0 GS: 0-0 Gd: 1-3 GF: - Fm: 0-4
Distance: 2m/2m3: 1-2 2m4-2m7: 0-1 3m+: 0-4
Track: LH: 0-4 **RH: 1-3** Tight: 0-1 Gall: 0-1
Aids: Bl: 0-0 Vi: 0-0 Tstrap: 0-0
Best Rating: 99 6/02 Hrfd 3m1f110y gd-fm Ch

Moderate novice chaser, stays two miles three furlongs and acts on good and fast ground.

Lucky Tyrol (IRE)

5-y-o ch g Midhish-Tirol s Luck (IRE) (Tirol)
N B Mason N B Mason

Placings:P   (2302)
2002/03: 19PGS,

	Starts	1st	2nd	3rd	Win & Pl
Hurdles	1	0	0	0	
Career Total	1	0	0	0	

Going: Sf: 0-0 GS: 0-1 Gd: 0-0 GF: - Fm: 0-0
Distance: 2m/2m3: 0-1 2m4-2m7: 0-0 3m+: 0-0
Track: LH: 0-1 RH: 0-0 Tight: 0-1 Gall: 0-0
Aids: Bl: 0-0 Vi: 0-0 Tstrap: 0-1
Best Rating: 0 12/02 Catt 2m3f gd-sft Hdl

Lucy Lancaster
72   58

8-y-o b m Elegant Monarch-Lancaster Rose (Canadel Ii)
Miss G Browne Brian Hurst

Placings:B   (4574)
2002/03: 22BGF,

	Starts	1st	2nd	3rd	Win & Pl
Hurdles	1	0	0	0	
Career Total	1	0	0	0	

Going: Sf: 0-0 GS: 0-0 Gd: 0-0 GF: - Fm: 0-1
Distance: 2m/2m3: 0-0 2m4-2m7: 0-1 3m+: 0-0
Track: LH: 0-1 RH: 0-0 Tight: 0-1 Gall: 0-0
Aids: Bl: 0-0 Vi: 0-0 Tstrap: 0-0
Best Rating: 0 4/03 Strf 2m6f110y gd-fm Hdl

Lucys Lad
109(84h)   (14h)101

9-y-o b g Le Moss-Lucy Lastic (Tycoon Ii)
Miss Venetia Williams Ali Bar Bar

Placings:03P4P/021P6/0P-15F2P11UU4PP   (3946)
2002/03: 251GS, 255G, 24FS, 242G, 25PG, 261S, 231S, 25US, 24UGS, 244GS, 26PGS, 30PS,

	Starts	1st	2nd	3rd	Win & Pl
Chases	12	3	1	0	16996
Career Total	24	4	2	1	23216
111	1/03 Leic	2m7f110yD(0-125)HCh	SFT	£6870	
111	12/02 Font	3m2f110yF(0-90)Ch	SFT	£4784	
93	5/02 Towc	3m1f F(0-90)HCh	G-S	£3630	
93	12/00 Ludl	3m F(0-100)HCh	G-S	£4745	

Total win prize-money £20030

Going: Sf: 2-5 GS: 1-4 Gd: 0-3 GF: - Fm: 0-0
Distance: 2m/2m3: 0-0 2m4-2m7: 0-0 3m+: 3-12
Track: LH: 0-4 **RH: 2-6** Tight: 1-6 Gall: 0-0
Aids: Bl: 0-0 Vi: 0-0 Tstrap: 0-0
Best Rating: 111 1/03 Leic 2m7f110y soft Ch

Moderate staying handicap chaser who is prone to mistakes; returned from a five-month break to score at Fontwell in December and won again at Leicester; has won on good and soft ground; stays three miles plus.

Ludere (IRE)
101   98

8-y-o ch g Desse Zenny (USA)-White Jasmin (Jalmood (USA))
B J Llewellyn B W Parren

Placings:65/16406/430132/2143-056610342P   (4120)
2002/03: 20VG, 19SG, 226HY, 216GS, 201HY, 240S, 223S, 244GS, 242S, 26PG,

	Starts	1st	2nd	3rd	Win & Pl
Hurdles	10	1	1	1	5727
Career Total	27	4	3	4	13831
98	12/02 Leic	2m4f110yE(0-105)HHdl	HVY	£3474	
98	12/01 Tntn	2m3f110yG Hdl	G-S	£1596	
97	12/00 Tntn	2m3f110yG Hdl	SFT	£1533	
89	7/99 Sedg	2m1f E Hdl	G-F	£2302	

Total win prize-money £8906

Going: Sf: 1-5 GS: 0-2 Gd: 0-3 GF: - Fm: 0-0
Distance: 2m/2m3: 0-0 2m4-2m7: 1-6 3m+: 0-4
Track: LH: 0-4 RH: 1-6 Tight: 0-4 Gall: 0-2
Aids: Bl: 0-0 Vi: 0-0 Tstrap: 0-0
Best Rating: 98 3/03 Bang 3m soft Hdl

Modest hurdler, stays three miles; acts in soft ground.

Luftikus (GER)
97   70

6-y-o ch g Formidable (USA)-La Paz (GER) (Roi Dagobert)
A G Hobbs (C Von Der Recke 25/10) Furnish With Abbey

Placings:300   (4117)
2002/03: 16AGS, 20OS, 16QG,

	Starts	1st	2nd	3rd	Win & Pl
Hurdles	3	0	0	1	428
Career Total	3	0	0	1	428

Going: Sf: 0-1 GS: 0-1 Gd: 0-1 GF: - Fm: 0-0
Distance: 2m/2m3: 0-2 2m4-2m7: 0-1 3m+: 0-0
Track: LH: 0-1 RH: 0-0 Tight: 0-0 Gall: 0-2
Aids: Bl: 0-0 Vi: 0-0 Tstrap: 0-0
Best Rating: 77 11/02 Hntg 2m110y gd-sft Hdl

Multiple winner on the level in Germany. Well beaten on hurdling bow when third at Huntingdon in November. Held subsequently.

Luke Warm
104   82

13-y-o ch g Nearly A Hand-Hot n Scopey (Hot Brandy)
D R Gandolfo Mrs John Lee

Placings:4660/52433/2131P2/12100/0F32646/21442135/3 3415F56-P54355344   (4738)
2002/03: 25PG, 245GS, 244GS, 243S, 265S, 245GS, 265S, 244G, 244GF,

	Starts	1st	2nd	3rd	Win & Pl
Chases	9	0	0	2	2182
Career Total	52	7	7	9	63350
113	12/01 Towc	2m6f C(0-130)HCh	HVY	£16680	
111	11/00 Towc	2m6f C(0-130)HCh	HVY	£10374	
110	10/00 Font	2m6f D(0-120)HCh	GD	£4231	
109	2/99 MRas	2m4f C(0-135)HCh	SFT	£6872	
99	1/99 Wwck	2m4f110yE(0-115)HCh	SFT	£3301	
93	12/97 Tntn	2m3f F(0-95)HCh	GD	£2836	
103	11/97 NAbb	2m5f110yE(0-100)HCh	SFT	£2818	

Total win prize-money £47115

Going: Sf: 0-3 GS: 0-3 Gd: 0-2 GF: - Fm: 0-1
Distance: 2m/2m3: 0-0 2m4-2m7: 0-0 3m+: 0-9
Track: LH: 0-6 RH: 0-2 Tight: 0-6 Gall: 0-0
Aids: Bl: 0-0 Vi: 0-0 Tstrap: 0-0
Best Rating: 113 2/02 Kemp 3m soft Ch

Moderate chaser nowadays; suited by soft ground; stays 3m 2f.

Lumaca (IRE)
95(103h)   (88h)70

8-y-o b g Riberetto-Broken Mirror (Push On)
C Roberts (J Neville 12/3) C G Bolton

Placings:046/5602/15P0-6P63   (3785)
2002/03: 266S, 25PGS, 256S, 256G,

	Starts	1st	2nd	3rd	Win & Pl
Hurdles	1	0	0	0	0
Chases	3	0	0	1	648
Career Total	15	1	1	1	4231
88	1/02 Tntn	3m110y E(0-110)HHdl	SFT	£2593	

Total win prize-money £2594

Going: Sf: 0-2 GS: 0-1 Gd: 0-1 GF: - Fm: 0-0
Distance: 2m/2m3: 0-0 2m4-2m7: 0-0 3m+: 0-4
Track: LH: 0-0 RH: 0-4 Tight: 0-1 Gall: 0-0
Aids: Bl: 0-0 Vi: 0-0 Tstrap: 0-0
Best Rating: 103 2/00 Kemp 2m soft NHF

Plating-class novice chaser; stays well.

Lumback (IRE)

4-y-o b g Desert Style (IRE)-Bellingham Jester (Jester)
N Wilson J McKinnon

Placings:0   (2142)
2002/03: 14OGS,

	Starts	1st	2nd	3rd	Win & Pl
NH Flat	1	0	0	0	
Career Total	1	0	0	0	

Going: Sf: 0-0 GS: 0-1 Gd: 0-0 GF: - Fm: 0-0
Distance: 2m/2m3: 0-0 2m4-2m7: 0-0 3m+: 0-0
Track: LH: 0-1 RH: 0-0 Tight: 0-0 Gall: 0-0
Aids: Bl: 0-0 Vi: 0-0 Tstrap: 0-0
Best Rating: 0 11/02 Newc 1m6f gd-sft NHF

Luna Nova
92   53

5-y-o b g Aragon-Lucidity (Vision (USA))
D Moffatt The Sheroot Partnership

Placings:0PP-P60P   (1163)
2002/03: 17PS, 176G, 22QG, 17PGF,

	Starts	1st	2nd	3rd	Win & Pl
Hurdles	4	0	0	0	0
Career Total	7	0	0	0	0

Going: Sf: 0-1 GS: 0-0 Gd: 0-2 GF: - Fm: 0-1
Distance: 2m/2m3: 0-3 2m4-2m7: 0-1 3m+: 0-0
Track: LH: 0-4 RH: 0-0 Tight: 0-4 Gall: 0-0
Aids: Bl: 0-0 Vi: 0-0 Tstrap: 0-0
Best Rating: 53 8/02 Sedg 2m1f good Hdl

Lunar Crystal (IRE)
110   123

5-y-o b g Shirley Heights-Solar Crystal (IRE) (Alzao (USA))

M C Pipe Teddington Racing Club

Placings:25-21111156 (3727)
2002/03: 16²GF, 18¹GF, 16¹GF, 17¹S, 17¹S, 17¹GF, 16⁵GF, 16⁶G,

	Starts	1st	2nd	3rd	Win & Pl
Hurdles	8	5	1	0	24662
Career Total	10	5	2	0	25802

122	8/02	NAbb	2m1f	B HHdl	G-F	£8723
123	8/02	Bang	2m1f	D Hdl	SFT	£4578
123	7/02	MRas	2m1f110y	D Hdl	SFT	£4225
121	6/02	Strf	2m110y	D Hdl	G-F	£3679
107	6/02	Font	2m2f110y	E Hdl	G-F	£2436

Total win prize-money £23641

Going: Sf: 2-2 GS: 0-0 Gd: 0-1 GF: - Fm: 3-5
Distance: 2m/2m3: 5-8 2m4-2m7: 0-0 3m+: 0-0
Track: LH: 4-6 RH: 1-2 Tight: 5-5 Gall: 0-0
Aids: BI: 0-0 Vi: 0-1 Tstrap: 0-0
Best Rating: 123 8/02 Bang 2m1f soft Hdl

Fair novice hurdler; completed a five-timer in the summer of 2002; suited by two miles and acts on any ground; suited by forcing tactics.

Lunar Dram
75f   71f

5-y-o ch g Cosmonaut-Moonshine Malt (Superlative)
M Dods Les Waugh

Placings:00 (2518)
2002/03: 16⁰HY, 16⁹S,

	Starts	1st	2nd	3rd	Win & Pl
NH Flat	2	0	0	0	
Career Total	2	0	0	0	

Going: Sf: 0-2 GS: 0-0 Gd: 0-0 GF: - Fm: 0-0
Distance: 2m/2m3: 0-2 2m4-2m7: 0-0 3m+: 0-0
Track: LH: 0-2 RH: 0-0 Tight: 0-0 Gall: 0-0
Aids: BI: 0-0 Vi: 0-1 Tstrap: 0-0
Best Rating: 71 11/02 Weth 2m heavy NHF

Lunar Lord
81   101

7-y-o b g Elmaamul (USA)-Cache (Bustino)
D Burchell Brian Williams

Placings:2515/54-0 (3369)
2002/03: 16⁰GS,

	Starts	1st	2nd	3rd	Win & Pl
Hurdles	1	0	0	0	
Career Total	7	1	1	0	3118

105	1/01	Chep	2m110y	E Hdl	G-S	£2555

Total win prize-money £2555

Going: Sf: 0-0 GS: 0-1 Gd: 0-0 GF: - Fm: 0-0
Distance: 2m/2m3: 0-1 2m4-2m7: 0-0 3m+: 0-0
Track: LH: 0-1 RH: 0-0 Tight: 0-0 Gall: 0-0
Aids: BI: 0-0 Vi: 0-0 Tstrap: 0-0
Best Rating: 105 1/01 Chep 2m110y gd-sft Hdl

Lunar Maxwell
99(106h)   (99h)106+

8-y-o b g Dancing High-Pauper Moon (Pauper)
J I A Charlton J W Robson

Placings:4443/62400/62132-3245 (3511)
2002/03: 25³G, 25²GS, 25⁴S, 30⁵G,

	Starts	1st	2nd	3rd	Win & Pl
Chases	4	0	1	1	2563
Career Total	18	1	4	3	7906

93	11/01	Weth	2m7f	F(0-100)HHdl	GD	£2506

Total win prize-money £2506

Going: Sf: 0-1 GS: 0-1 Gd: 0-2 GF: - Fm: 0-0
Distance: 2m/2m3: 0-0 2m4-2m7: 0-0 3m+: 0-4
Track: LH: 0-4 RH: 0-0 Tight: 0-1 Gall: 0-0
Aids: BI: 0-0 Vi: 0-0 Tstrap: 0-0
Best Rating: 106 11/02 Weth 3m1f gd-sft Ch

Modest staying novice, appreciated the step up to three miles in the autumn of 2001. Suited by good ground.

Lunardi (IRE)
94(101h)   75

5-y-o b g Indian Ridge-Gold Tear (USA) (Tejano (USA))
D L Williams D L Williams

Placings:5421565046-30 (4711)
2002/03: 25³G, 16⁹GF,

	Starts	1st	2nd	3rd	Win & Pl
Hurdles	1	0	0	0	0
Chases	1	0	0	1	191
Career Total	12	1	1	1	4555

102	11/01	Hrfd	2m1f	E Hdl	GD	£2471

Total win prize-money £2471

Going: Sf: 0-0 GS: 0-0 Gd: 0-1 GF: - Fm: 0-1
Distance: 2m/2m3: 0-1 2m4-2m7: 0-0 3m+: 0-1
Track: LH: 0-1 RH: 0-1 Tight: 0-0 Gall: 0-0
Aids: BI: 0-0 Vi: 0-0 Tstrap: 0-0
Best Rating: 102 11/01 Hrfd 2m1f good Hdl

Moderate hunter chaser/hurdler; best on a sound surface; yet to prove he stays three miles.

Lupin (FR)
86f   90f

4-y-o b c Luchiroverte (IRE)-Amarante Ii (FR) (Brezzo (FR))
F Doumen E Puerari

Placings:5 (3754)
2002/03: 16⁵G,

	Starts	1st	2nd	3rd	Win & Pl
NH Flat	1	0	0	0	0
Career Total	1	0	0	0	0

Going: Sf: 0-0 GS: 0-0 Gd: 0-1 GF: - Fm: 0-0
Distance: 2m/2m3: 0-1 2m4-2m7: 0-0 3m+: 0-0
Track: LH: 0-0 RH: 0-1 Tight: 0-0 Gall: 0-0
Aids: BI: 0-0 Vi: 0-0 Tstrap: 0-0
Best Rating: 90 2/03 Kemp 2m good NHF

French-trained half-brother to an Irish maiden hurdler. Some promise on his Kempton debut.

Lurpak Legend (IRE)
99(102h)   (92h)75

9-y-o br g Castle Keep-Welsh Tan (Welsh Saint)
Mrs M Reveley The Mary Reveley Racing Club

Placings:000000/352152U013/22F060406/6014500-03062 (0906)
2002/03: 16⁰G, 20⁰GS, 19³GF, 24⁰G, 21⁶S, 20²G,

	Starts	1st	2nd	3rd	Win & Pl
Hurdles	5	0	0	1	241
Chases	1	0	1	0	1175
Career Total	37	3	5	3	12102

92	12/01	Catt	2m	G(0-95)HHdl	SFT	£1932
93	3/00	Catt	2m3f	F(0-100)HHdl	G-F	£1918
76	10/99	Carl	2m4f110y	F(0-100)HHdl	GD	£2290

Total win prize-money £6140

Going: Sf: 0-1 GS: 0-1 Gd: 0-3 GF: - Fm: 0-1
Distance: 2m/2m3: 0-1 2m4-2m7: 0-4 3m+: 0-1
Track: LH: 0-3 RH: 0-3 Tight: 0-4 Gall: 0-1
Aids: BI: 0-0 Vi: 0-0 Tstrap: 0-0
Best Rating: 93 5/00 MRas 2m4f gd-sft Ch

Plating-class hurdler; acts on any ground.

Luxembourg
50   4

4-y-o b g Bigstone (IRE)-Princess Borghese (USA) (Nijinsky (CAN))
N A Twiston-Davies Mrs Lorna Berryman

Placings:0U0 (2637)
2002/03: 12⁰GS, 16⁰GS, 16⁹S,

	Starts	1st	2nd	3rd	Win & Pl
NH Flat	1	0	0	0	0
Hurdles	2	0	0	0	0
Career Total	3	0	0	0	

Going: Sf: 0-1 GS: 0-2 Gd: 0-0 GF: - Fm: 0-0
Distance: 2m/2m3: 0-2 2m4-2m7: 0-0 3m+: 0-0
Track: LH: 0-2 RH: 0-1 Tight: 0-0 Gall: 0-0
Aids: BI: 0-0 Vi: 0-1 Tstrap: 0-0
Best Rating: 67 11/02 Newb 1m4f110y gd-sft NHF

Luzcadou (FR)
110   134

10-y-o b g Cadoudal (FR)-Luzenia (FR) (Armos)
Ferdy Murphy A G Chappell

Placings:FF461P40123/36531/F5110P/066P1P/0042UF00-1 (1957)
2002/03: 20¹S,

	Starts	1st	2nd	3rd	Win & Pl
Chases	1	1	0	0	5425
Career Total	37	7	2	3	156251

133	11/02	Ayr	2m4f	D(0-120)HCh	SFT	£5425
119	12/00	Newc	2m4f	C(0-135)HHdl	SFT	£5187
148	2/00	Ayr	2m4f	B(0-145)HCh	HVY	£13065
141	1/00	Ayr	2m4f	B(0-140)HCh	SFT	£9197
111	12/97	Carl	2m4f110y	E Hdl	SFT	£22038
	3/97	Autl	1m7f110y			£35671

Total win prize-money £86394

Going: Sf: 1-1 GS: 0-0 Gd: 0-0 GF: - Fm: 0-0
Distance: 2m/2m3: 0-0 2m4-2m7: 1-1 3m+: 0-0
Track: LH: 1-1 RH: 0-0 Tight: 0-0 Gall: 0-0
Aids: BI: 1-1 Vi: 0-0 Tstrap: 0-0
Best Rating: 148 2/00 Ayr 2m4f heavy Ch

Useful chaser; has scored over hurdles and fences, he is suited by soft ground and two and a half miles, but has yet to prove he stays three miles. Well beaten in useful company in 2002, but won an uncompetitive race at Ayr in November 2002.

Lydia's Echo

7-y-o b m Backchat (USA)-Lydia s Well (Current Magic)
J W Mullins Richard Bailey

Placings:00-P0 (0367)
2002/03: 16⁹GS, 22²GF, 17⁹S,

	Starts	1st	2nd	3rd	Win & Pl
NH Flat	1	0	0	0	0
Hurdles	2	0	0	0	0
Career Total	4	0	0	0	

Going: Sf: 0-1 GS: 0-1 Gd: 0-0 GF: - Fm: 0-1
Distance: 2m/2m3: 0-2 2m4-2m7: 0-1 3m+: 0-0
Track: LH: 0-1 RH: 0-2 Tight: 0-1 Gall: 0-0
Aids: Bl: 0-1 Vi: 0-0 Tstrap: 0-0
Best Rating: 72 2/02 Winc 2m gd-sft NHF

Lynchahaun (IRE)
90   84
7-y-o b/br g Good Thyne (USA)-Smart Decision (IRE) (Le Moss)
P Monteith P Monteith

Placings:0   (4749)
2002/03: 20⁰G,

	Starts	1st	2nd	3rd	Win & Pl
Hurdles	1	0	0	0	
Career Total	1	0	0	0	

Going: Sf: 0-0 GS: 0-0 Gd: 0-1 GF: - Fm: 0-0
Distance: 2m/2m3: 0-0 2m4-2m7: 0-1 3m+: 0-0
Track: LH: 0-0 RH: 0-1 Tight: 0-0 Gall: 0-0
Aids: Bl: 0-0 Vi: 0-0 Tstrap: 0-0
Best Rating: 42 4/03 Prth 2m4f110y good Hdl

Novide hurdler; limited promise so far; may do better in handicaps.

Lynphord Girl
98   95?
12-y-o ch m Lyphento (USA)-Woodlands Angel (Levanter)
Dr J R J Naylor The Cayford Partnership

Placings:0/0/2F024   (1086)
2002/03: 20²GF, 21ᶠGS, 20⁰G, 20²GS, 20⁴GF,

	Starts	1st	2nd	3rd	Win & Pl
Chases	5	0	2	0	2985
Career Total	7	0	2	0	2985

Going: Sf: 0-0 GS: 0-2 Gd: 0-1 GF: - Fm: 0-2
Distance: 2m/2m3: 0-0 2m4-2m7: 0-5 3m+: 0-0
Track: LH: 0-1 RH: 0-4 Tight: 0-4 Gall: 0-1
Aids: Bl: 0-0 Vi: 0-0 Tstrap: 0-0
Best Rating: 95 5/02 NAbb 2m5f110y gd-sft Ch

Winning pointer, runner-up in modest novice chases after two years off the track.

Lynrick Lady (IRE)
101   98
7-y-o b m Un Desperado (FR)-Decent Lady (Decent Fellow)
J G Portman Milady Partnership

Placings:0/0-P5140   (4326)
2002/03: 24ᴾS, 22⁵HY, 20¹HY, 20⁴G, 21⁰G,

	Starts	1st	2nd	3rd	Win & Pl
Hurdles	5	1	0	0	4351
Career Total	7	1	0	0	4351
98	2/03	Chep	2m4f	E Hdl	HVY £3922

Total win prize-money £3923

Going: Sf: 1-3 GS: 0-0 Gd: 0-2 GF: - Fm: 0-0
Distance: 2m/2m3: 0-0 **2m4-2m7:** 1-4 3m+: 0-1
Track: LH: 1-4 RH: 0-1 Tight: 0-1 Gall: 0-1
Aids: Bl: 0-0 Vi: 0-0 Tstrap: 0-1
Best Rating: 98 2/03 Weth 2m4f110y good Hdl

Modest novice hurdler; got off the mark over hurdles when winning at Chepstow in February; stays two miles six; acts on soft ground.

Lynwood Legend
66f   65f
5-y-o ch g Gold Dust-Beths Wish (Rustingo)
B J Llewellyn Colin M Price

Placings:00   (4628)
2002/03: 14⁰GF, 17⁰GF,

	Starts	1st	2nd	3rd	Win & Pl
NH Flat	2	0	0	0	
Career Total	2	0	0	0	

Going: Sf: 0-0 GS: 0-0 Gd: 0-0 GF: - Fm: 0-2
Distance: 2m/2m3: 0-1 2m4-2m7: 0-0 3m+: 0-0
Track: LH: 0-1 RH: 0-0 Tight: 0-1 Gall: 0-0
Aids: Bl: 0-0 Vi: 0-0 Tstrap: 0-0
Best Rating: 65 3/03 Hrfd 1m6f gd-fm NHF

Lyphard's Fable (USA)
12-y-o b g Al Nasr (FR)-Affirmative Fable (USA) (Affirmed (USA))
Mrs David Plunkett (T R George 26/5) Miss E A Plunkett

Placings:0P04/40004233F6F/F064/2FF126263/2423325/50 50/0/6-P   (0416)
2002/03: 24ᴾGF,

	Starts	1st	2nd	3rd	Win & Pl
Chases	1	0	0	0	
Career Total	42	1	7	5	9500
74	12/97	Chep	2m4f110yG Hdl	SFT	£1898

Total win prize-money £1898

Going: Sf: 0-0 GS: 0-0 Gd: 0-0 GF: - Fm: 0-1
Distance: 2m/2m3: 0-0 2m4-2m7: 0-0 3m+: 0-1
Track: LH: 0-1 RH: 0-0 Tight: 0-1 Gall: 0-0
Aids: Bl: 0-0 Vi: 0-0 Tstrap: 0-0
Best Rating: 89 11/98 Plum 2m4f soft Hdl

Lyringo
75
9-y-o b m Rustingo-Lyricist (Averof)
B J Llewellyn Glyn Tarrel Stud

Placings:05/54P41/00-P00P   (4429)
2002/03: 16⁰G, 24⁰S, 18⁰S, 21ᴾGF,

	Starts	1st	2nd	3rd	Win & Pl
Hurdles	4	0	0	0	
Career Total	13	1	0	0	2016
82	10/00	Strf	2m110y G Hdl	SFT	£2016

Total win prize-money £2016

Going: Sf: 0-2 GS: 0-0 Gd: 0-1 GF: - Fm: 0-1
Distance: 2m/2m3: 0-2 2m4-2m7: 0-1 3m+: 0-1
Track: LH: 0-2 RH: 0-2 Tight: 0-3 Gall: 0-0
Aids: Bl: 0-0 Vi: 0-0 Tstrap: 0-0
Best Rating: 88 8/00 Worc 2m gd-fm NHF

Lysander's Quest (IRE)
92   89
5-y-o br g King's Theatre (IRE)-Haramayda (FR) (Doyoun)
L Montague Hall Mrs E N Nield

Placings:00   (4117)
2002/03: 16⁰G, 16⁰G,

	Starts	1st	2nd	3rd	Win & Pl
Hurdles	2	0	0	0	
Career Total	2	0	0	0	

Going: Sf: 0-0 GS: 0-0 Gd: 0-2 GF: - Fm: 0-0
Distance: 2m/2m3: 0-2 2m4-2m7: 0-0 3m+: 0-0
Track: LH: 0-1 RH: 0-1 Tight: 0-0 Gall: 0-2
Aids: Bl: 0-0 Vi: 0-0 Tstrap: 0-0
Best Rating: 89 12/02 Newb 2m110y good Hdl

Ma Barnicle (IRE)
95   84
10-y-o ch m Al Hareb (USA)-Soltina (Sun Prince)
T D McCarthy Mrs D H McCarthy

Placings:0P0/520220000/12231225/04P/4-0562PP (4189)
2002/03: 16⁰G, 16⁵G, 21⁶G, 18²GF, 16ᴾG, 16ᴾG,

	Starts	1st	2nd	3rd	Win & Pl
Chases	6	0	0	0	648
Career Total	30	2	8	1	11737
98	10/99	Worc	2m	F(0-100)HCh	GD £2350
98	6/99	NAbb	2m1f	F(0-100)HHdl	GD £2759

Total win prize-money £5110

Going: Sf: 0-0 GS: 0-0 Gd: 0-5 GF: - Fm: 0-1
Distance: 2m/2m3: 0-5 2m4-2m7: 0-0 3m+: 0-0
Track: LH: 0-0 RH: 0-5 Tight: 0-5 Gall: 0-0
Aids: Bl: 0-0 Vi: 0-0 Tstrap: 0-5
Best Rating: 98 11/99 Worc 2m good Ch

Ma's Confusion
5-y-o b m Mr Confusion (IRE)-Spirited Lady Vii (Damsire Unregistered)
N Tinkler The Listowel Racers

Placings:P   (0516)
2002/03: 16ᴾS,

	Starts	1st	2nd	3rd	Win & Pl
NH Flat	1	0	0	0	
Career Total	1	0	0	0	

Going: Sf: 0-1 GS: 0-0 Gd: 0-0 GF: - Fm: 0-0
Distance: 2m/2m3: 0-1 2m4-2m7: 0-0 3m+: 0-0
Track: LH: 0-1 RH: 0-0 Tight: 0-0 Gall: 0-0
Aids: Bl: 0-0 Vi: 0-0 Tstrap: 0-0
Best Rating: 0 6/02 Worc 2m soft NHF

Maas (IRE)
87   82
8-y-o br h Elbio-Payne s Grey (Godswalk (USA))
N B Mason N B Mason

Placings:P036P-60   (0375)
2002/03: 16⁶G, 16⁰G,

	Starts	1st	2nd	3rd	Win & Pl
Hurdles	2	0	0	0	0
Career Total	7	0	0	1	269

Going: Sf: 0-0 GS: 0-0 Gd: 0-0 GF: - Fm: 0-0
Distance: 2m/2m3: 0-2 2m4-2m7: 0-0 3m+: 0-0
Track: LH: 0-2 RH: 0-0 Tight: 0-2 Gall: 0-0
Aids: Bl: 0-0 Vi: 0-0 Tstrap: 0-1
Best Rating: 82 12/01 Leic 2m gd-sft Hdl

Mac Five (IRE) 63

8-y-o gr g Sharp Victor (USA)-Fine Flame (Le Prince)
C L Popham M H Holland

Placings:0/PP-F3 (0848)
2002/03: 24FGF, 26³GF,

	Starts	1st	2nd	3rd	Win & Pl
Chases	2	0	0	1	575
Career Total	5	0	0	1	575

Going: Sf: 0-0 GS: 0-0 Gd: 0-0 GF: - Fm: 0-2
Distance: 2m/2m3: 0-0 2m4-2m7: 0-0 3m+: 0-2
Track: LH: 0-2 RH: 0-0 Tight: 0-2 Gall: 0-0
Aids: Bl: 0-0 Vi: 0-0 Tstrap: 0-0
Best Rating: 63 7/02 NAbb 3m2f110y gd-fm Ch

Mac Hine (IRE)
100 106

6-y-o b g Eurobus-Zoe Baird (Aragon)
Jonjo O Neill J P McManus

Placings:142000 (4415)
2002/03: 16¹S, 20⁴S, 16²GS, 16⁹GS, 21⁰G, 17⁰G,

	Starts	1st	2nd	3rd	Win & Pl
NH Flat	1	1	0	0	2457
Hurdles	5	0	1	0	1419
Career Total	6	1	1	0	3876

106 11/02 Sand 2m110y H NHF SFT £2457
Total win prize-money £2457

Going: Sf: 1-2 GS: 0-2 Gd: 0-2 GF: - Fm: 0-0
Distance: 2m/2m3: 1-4 2m4-2m7: 0-2 3m+: 0-0
Track: LH: 0-2 RH: 1-4 Tight: 0-1 Gall: 0-1
Aids: Bl: 0-0 Vi: 0-0 Tstrap: 0-0
Best Rating: 106 1/03 Donc 2m110y gd-sft Hdl

Modest novice hurdler; got up on the line to make winning debut in a bumper at Sandown in November; hung badly when runner-up over hurdles at Doncaster two months later; held subsequently.

Mac's Diamond (IRE)
77 60

7-y-o b m Mac s Imp (USA)-Plunkets Choice (Home Guard (USA))
D J Wintle (Michael Vaughan 22/8) D Shorey

Placings:0/00/60 (1571)
2002/03: 20⁶GF, 16⁹G,

	Starts	1st	2nd	3rd	Win & Pl
Hurdles	2	0	0	0	
Career Total	5	0	0	0	

Going: Sf: 0-0 GS: 0-0 Gd: 0-1 GF: - Fm: 0-1
Distance: 2m/2m3: 0-1 2m4-2m7: 0-1 3m+: 0-0
Track: LH: 0-1 RH: 0-0 Tight: 0-1 Gall: 0-0
Aids: Bl: 0-0 Vi: 0-0 Tstrap: 0-0
Best Rating: 77 4/00 Cork 2m gd-yld NHF

Macanillo (GER)

5-y-o gr g Acatenango (GER)-Midday Girl (GER) (Black Tie Affair)
Ian Williams G P Services (UK) Ltd

Placings:PP (2492)
2002/03: 16PG, 16PS,

	Starts	1st	2nd	3rd	Win & Pl
Hurdles	2	0	0	0	
Career Total	2	0	0	0	

Going: Sf: 0-1 GS: 0-0 Gd: 0-1 GF: - Fm: 0-0
Distance: 2m/2m3: 0-2 2m4-2m7: 0-0 3m+: 0-0
Track: LH: 0-2 RH: 0-0 Tight: 0-0 Gall: 0-1
Aids: Bl: 0-0 Vi: 0-0 Tstrap: 0-0
Best Rating: 0 12/02 Donc 2m110y soft Hdl

Maceo (GER)
103(113h) (112h)90

9-y-o ch g Acatenango (GER)-Metropolitan Star (USA) (Lyphard (USA))
Mrs M Reveley Les De La Haye

Placings:030/4/02241F-1443436 (4226)
2002/03: 16¹G, 19⁴GS, 16⁴S, 16²S, 16⁴GS, 20³G, 16⁸GF,

	Starts	1st	2nd	3rd	Win & Pl
Hurdles	7	1	0	2	10186
Career Total	17	2	2	3	17707

117 11/02 Weth 2m C(0-135)HHdl GD £6259
112 3/02 Newb 2m110y D(0-110)HHdl G-S £4582
Total win prize-money £10843

Going: Sf: 0-2 GS: 0-2 Gd: 1-2 GF: - Fm: 0-1
Distance: 2m/2m3: 1-6 2m4-2m7: 0-1 3m+: 0-0
Track: LH: 1-7 RH: 0-0 Tight: 0-0 Gall: 0-3
Aids: Bl: 0-0 Vi: 0-0 Tstrap: 0-0
Best Rating: 118 11/02 Newb 2m110y soft Hdl

Fair handicap hurdler; runner-up in chase latest; effective at around two miles but stays two and a half miles; acts on good and soft ground.

Macgeorge (IRE)

13-y-o b g Mandalus-Colleen Donn (Le Moss)
R Lee Mr & Mrs J H Watson

Placings:443/3215/U5F1122/1U44111/126441/4PU2F/4/43 5163-PP11U2 (4615)
2002/03: 25PG, 26PHY, 25¹G, 26¹GS, 25UG, 26²G,

	Starts	1st	2nd	3rd	Win & Pl
Chases	6	2	1	0	5155
Career Total	45	12	6	4	131662

118 3/03 Wwck 3m2f H Ch G-S £1470
128 2/03 Hrfd 3m1f110yH Ch GD £1624
141 2/02 Wwck 3m2f C(0-130)HCh SFT £7020
164 4/99 Aint 3m1f A Ch G-S £38275
151 11/98 Wwck 3m2f B(0-140)HCh GD £7236
145 3/98 Newb 3m B HCh G-S £7726
143 3/98 Newb 3m C(0-135)HCh HVY £7600
136 2/98 Leic 2m7f110yC(0-130)HCh GD £5390
127 5/97 Worc 2m7f110yE Ch G-S £3455
135 2/97 Leic 2m4f110yE(0-115)HCh G-F £3179
130 1/97 Weth 2m4f110yD(0-110)HCh GD £3480
120 2/96 Hayd 2m6f D Hdl HVY £3263
Total win prize-money £89721

Going: Sf: 0-1 GS: 1-1 Gd: 1-4 GF: - Fm: 0-0
Distance: 2m/2m3: 0-0 2m4-2m7: 0-0 3m+: 2-6
Track: LH: 1-4 RH: 1-2 Tight: 0-0 Gall: 0-0
Aids: Bl: 0-0 Vi: 0-0 Tstrap: 0-0
Best Rating: 164 4/99 Aint 3m1f gd-sft Ch

Very useful chaser in his prime; won Aintree s Martell Cup in 1999; winning hunter chaser in 2003; stays three and a quarter miles; acts on good and soft ground; sometimes let down by his jumping.

Macgyver (NZ)
111(84h) (92h)90

7-y-o b g Jahafil-Corazon (NZ) (Pag-Asa (AUS))
Mrs L C Taylor Mrs L C Taylor

Placings:210450P32552 (4223)
2002/03: 14²F, 14¹S, 13⁹HY, 17⁴G, 16⁵G, 16⁰S, 16PG, 16³S, 16²GS, 16⁵S, 16⁵G, 16²GF,

	Starts	1st	2nd	3rd	Win & Pl
Hurdles	7	1	1	0	1207
Chases	5	0	2	1	3376
Career Total	12	1	3	1	4583

6/02 Wang 1m6f SFT £893
Total win prize-money £893

Going: Sf: 1-5 GS: 0-1 Gd: 0-4 GF: - Fm: 0-2
Distance: 2m/2m3: 0-9 2m4-2m7: 0-0 3m+: 0-0
Track: LH: 0-4 RH: 0-5 Tight: 0-3 Gall: 0-1
Aids: Bl: 0-0 Vi: 0-0 Tstrap: 0-0
Best Rating: 90 3/03 Hrfd 2m gd-fm Ch

Moderate ex-New Zealand horse, he has ability but is somewhat headstrong.

Mach Four (IRE)
100f 94f

5-y-o b g Bob Back (USA)-Tasmania Star (Captain James)
N A Twiston-Davies A M Armitage

Placings:000 (3754)
2002/03: 16⁰S, 16⁰GS, 16⁰G,

	Starts	1st	2nd	3rd	Win & Pl
NH Flat	3	0	0	0	
Career Total	3	0	0	0	

Going: Sf: 0-1 GS: 0-1 Gd: 0-1 GF: - Fm: 0-0
Distance: 2m/2m3: 0-3 2m4-2m7: 0-0 3m+: 0-0
Track: LH: 0-0 RH: 0-3 Tight: 0-0 Gall: 0-0
Aids: Bl: 0-0 Vi: 0-0 Tstrap: 0-0
Best Rating: 94 2/03 Kemp 2m good NHF

Machete Man

8-y-o b g Broadsword (USA)-Ribo Melody (Riboboy (USA))
P R Webber J G Phillips

Placings:45/F-P (1787)
2002/03: 16PGF,

	Starts	1st	2nd	3rd	Win & Pl
Chases	1	0	0	0	
Career Total	4	0	0	0	0

Going: Sf: 0-0 GS: 0-0 Gd: 0-0 GF: - Fm: 0-1
Distance: 2m/2m3: 0-1 2m4-2m7: 0-0 3m+: 0-0
Track: LH: 0-0 RH: 0-1 Tight: 0-0 Gall: 0-0
Aids: Bl: 0-0 Vi: 0-0 Tstrap: 0-0
Best Rating: 93 11/00 Towc 2m soft NHF

Mackinus (IRE)
106 (80h)88

7-y-o b g Tidaro (USA)-Tepukei River (Tepuki)
P A Fahy P J McGrath

Placings:6060/0F0463043-520642324U2410 (4113)
2002/03: 22⁵YS, 20²YS, 22⁹GY, 16⁶G, 24⁴YS, 17²S, 26³SH, 18²YS, 16⁴YS, 22⁴HY, 24²S, 20⁴SH, 24¹S, 32⁰G,

	Starts	1st	2nd	3rd	Win & Pl
NH Flat	1	0	0	0	0
Chases	13	1	4	1	13786

Career Total	27	1	4	3	15522
88 2/03 Clon 3m	(0-109)HCh	SFT	£6720		

Total win prize-money £6721

Going: Sf: 1-4 GS: 0-0 Gd: 0-2 GF: - Fm: 0-0
Distance: 2m/2m3: 0-4 2m4-2m7: 0-5 3m+: 1-5
Track: LH: 0-1 RH: 1-6 Tight: 0-0 Gall: 0-1
Aids: Bl: 0-0 Vi: 0-0 Tstrap: 0-4
Best Rating: 106 12/00 Leop 2m   sft-hvy NHF

Plating-class Irish-trained chaser; stays three miles; acts on soft ground.

Mackoy (IRE)

10-y-o b g Riverhead (USA)-Urdite (FR) (Concertino (FR))
M J Gingell R T Sturgis

Placings:0   (4029)
2002/03: 24[0]S,

	Starts	1st	2nd	3rd	Win & Pl
Chases	1	0	0	0	
Career Total	1	0	0	0	

Going: Sf: 0-1 GS: 0-0 Gd: 0-0 GF: - Fm: 0-0
Distance: 2m/2m3: 0-0 2m4-2m7: 0-0 3m+: 0-1
Track: LH: 0-0 RH: 0-1 Tight: 0-0 Gall: 0-0
Aids: Bl: 0-0 Vi: 0-0 Tstrap: 0-0
Best Rating: 0 3/03 Sand 3m110y soft Ch

Macnance (IRE)   105 ... 110

7-y-o b m Mandalus-Colleen Donn (Le Moss)
R Lee Mrs Keith Lowry

Placings:26-2212U2   (4561)
2002/03: 17[2]G, 17[2]G, 16[1]S, 19[2]G, 21[U]G, 20[2]GF,

	Starts	1st	2nd	3rd	Win & Pl
Hurdles	6	1	4	0	8408
Career Total	8	1	5	0	9316

111 11/02 Leic 2m D Hdl SFT £3867
Total win prize-money £3868

Going: Sf: 1-1 GS: 0-0 Gd: 0-4 GF: - Fm: 0-1
Distance: 2m/2m3: 1-3 2m4-2m7: 0-3 3m+: 0-0
Track: LH: 0-2 RH: 1-4 Tight: 0-1 Gall: 0-0
Aids: Bl: 0-0 Vi: 0-0 Tstrap: 0-0
Best Rating: 111 11/02 Leic 2m soft Hdl

Half-sister to Macgeorge; fair winning novice hurdler; acts on good ground, but does handle the soft; stays two and a half miles.

Maconnor (IRE)   102 ... 111

6-y-o b g Religiously (USA)-Door Belle (Fidel)
H D Daly Daniel O Connor

Placings:0-F4023   (4176)
2002/03: 25[2]G, 16[4]S, 16[0]S, 16[2]HY, 16[3]S,

	Starts	1st	2nd	3rd	Win & Pl
Hurdles	5	0	1	1	2640
Career Total	6	0	1	1	2640

Going: Sf: 0-4 GS: 0-0 Gd: 0-1 GF: - Fm: 0-0
Distance: 2m/2m3: 0-4 2m4-2m7: 0-0 3m+: 0-1
Track: LH: 0-5 RH: 0-0 Tight: 0-0 Gall: 0-0
Aids: Bl: 0-0 Vi: 0-0 Tstrap: 0-0
Best Rating: 111 2/03 Chep 2m110y heavy Hdl

Modest novice hurdler; acts in soft ground; sure to win races when tackling two and a half miles.

Macreater   81 ... 49

5-y-o b m Mazaad-Gold Caste (USA) (Singh (USA))
K A Morgan Nigel Stokes

Placings:04350   (4611)
2002/03: 16[0]GS, 16[4]G, 17[3]HY, 16[5]GS, 17[0]G,

	Starts	1st	2nd	3rd	Win & Pl
NH Flat	5	0	0	1	265
Career Total	5	0	0	1	265

Going: Sf: 0-1 GS: 0-2 Gd: 0-2 GF: - Fm: 0-0
Distance: 2m/2m3: 0-5 2m4-2m7: 0-0 3m+: 0-0
Track: LH: 0-4 RH: 0-1 Tight: 0-2 Gall: 0-2
Aids: Bl: 0-0 Vi: 0-0 Tstrap: 0-0
Best Rating: 81 1/03 Sedg 2m1f heavy NHF

Modest form in bumpers.

Macs Gildoran   111 ... 149

9-y-o b g Gildoran-Shamrock Bridge (Golden Love)
W P Mullins Mrs Margaret McManus

Placings:21241/13O5-1P32   (4472)
2002/03: 17[1]SH, 24[2]S, 21[3]G, 21[2]G,

	Starts	1st	2nd	3rd	Win & Pl
Chases	4	1	1	1	32175
Career Total	13	4	3	2	66654

137 12/02 Fair 2m1f (0-135)HCh SH £7975
126 11/01 Navn 2m4f Ch Y-S £5842
136 2/01 Naas 2m4f Hdl Y-S £15725
130 12/00 Leop 2m4f NHF HVY £5520
Total win prize-money £35064

Going: Sf: 0-1 GS: 0-0 Gd: 0-2 GF: - Fm: 0-0
Distance: 2m/2m3: 1-1 2m4-2m7: 0-2 3m+: 0-1
Track: LH: 0-3 RH: 1-1 Tight: 0-1 Gall: 0-1
Aids: Bl: 0-0 Vi: 0-0 Tstrap: 0-0
Best Rating: 149 4/03 Aint 2m5f110y good Ch

Very useful Irish-trained chaser; ran well to be third in the Cathcart Chase at Cheltenham in 2003; runner-up in the Topham at Aintree; suited by softish ground; effective up to two miles five, unproven over further.

Mad Genius   55 ... 9

4-y-o b g Makbul-Rinca (Unfuwain (USA))
Miss A M Newton-Smith Julian Smith

Placings:06   (1284)
2002/03: 16[0]G, 18[6]GF,

	Starts	1st	2nd	3rd	Win & Pl
Hurdles	2	0	0	0	0
Career Total	2	0	0	0	0

Going: Sf: 0-0 GS: 0-0 Gd: 0-1 GF: - Fm: 0-1
Distance: 2m/2m3: 0-2 2m4-2m7: 0-0 3m+: 0-0
Track: LH: 0-2 RH: 0-0 Tight: 0-1 Gall: 0-0
Aids: Bl: 0-0 Vi: 0-0 Tstrap: 0-0
Best Rating: 9 9/02 Uttx 2m good Hdl

Mad Jack

8-y-o b g Mazaad-Glazepta Final (Final Straw)

M J Ryan P Picton-Warlow

Placings:00[1]P-PPP   (3235)
2002/03: 24[0]GS, 24[0]S, 24[0]S,

	Starts	1st	2nd	3rd	Win & Pl
Chases	3	0	0	0	
Career Total	6	0	0	0	

Going: Sf: 0-2 GS: 0-1 Gd: 0-0 GF: - Fm: 0-0
Distance: 2m/2m3: 0-0 2m4-2m7: 0-0 3m+: 0-3
Track: LH: 0-2 RH: 0-1 Tight: 0-2 Gall: 0-1
Aids: Bl: 0-0 Vi: 0-0 Tstrap: 0-1
Best Rating: 65 1/00 Donc 2m110y gd-fm NHF

Madalyar (IRE)   97 ... 93+

4-y-o b g Darshaan-Madaniyya (USA) (Shahrastani (USA))
Jonjo O Neill (John M Oxx 26/9) Albert Reynolds

Placings:55F   (3312)
2002/03: 16[5]GS, 16[5]GS, 17[F]GS,

	Starts	1st	2nd	3rd	Win & Pl
Hurdles	3	0	0	0	0
Career Total	3	0	0	0	0

Going: Sf: 0-0 GS: 0-3 Gd: 0-0 GF: - Fm: 0-0
Distance: 2m/2m3: 0-3 2m4-2m7: 0-0 3m+: 0-0
Track: LH: 0-1 RH: 0-2 Tight: 0-1 Gall: 0-0
Aids: Bl: 0-0 Vi: 0-0 Tstrap: 0-0
Best Rating: 93 12/02 Fknm 2m gd-sft Hdl

Middle-distance winner on the Flat in Ireland; yet to show much over hurdles, banned under non-triers Rule second start; ran badly latest and was reported to have a breathing problem.

Madam Flora   110 ... 110

6-y-o b m Alflora (IRE)-Madam s Choice (New Member)
M J Weeden T J Swaffield

Placings:30/36230-0231321   (4290)
2002/03: 16[0]G, 16[2]GS, 22[3]GS, 16[1]GS, 16[3]GS, 22[2]GS, 22[1]GF,

	Starts	1st	2nd	3rd	Win & Pl
Hurdles	7	2	2	2	10292
Career Total	14	2	3	5	12232

102 3/03 Winc 2m6f E Hdl G-F £3510
110 12/02 Winc 2m E Hdl G-S £3010
Total win prize-money £6521

Going: Sf: 0-0 GS: 1-5 Gd: 0-1 GF: - Fm: 1-1
Distance: 2m/2m3: 1-4 2m4-2m7: 1-3 3m+: 0-0
Track: LH: 0-0 RH: 2-7 Tight: 0-0 Gall: 0-0
Aids: Bl: 0-0 Vi: 0-0 Tstrap: 0-0
Best Rating: 110 2/03 Winc 2m6f gd-sft Hdl

Fair novice, placed in bumpers and running well over hurdles in 2002/3; acts on soft ground; stays two miles six.

Madam Mosso   104(105h) ... (101h)109+

7-y-o b m Le Moss-Rochestown Lass (Deep Run)
Mrs A M Thorpe Aled R Evans

Placings:0-52144414521   (4024)
2002/03: 22[5]GF, 22[0]GS, 24[1]HY, 22[4]GF, 26[4]GF, 25[4]GF, 22[1]S, 23[4]S, 21[5]HY, 26[2]G, 25[1]S,

	Starts	1st	2nd	3rd	Win & Pl
Hurdles	10	2	2	0	9885
Chases	1	1	0	0	4017

Career Total	12	3	2	0	13902
109	3/03	Hrfd	3m1f110yE Ch	SFT	£4017
101	12/02	Extr	2m6f110yD(0-115)HHdl	SFT	£4013
95	6/02	Uttx	3m110y E Hdl	HVY	£2569

Total win prize-money £10600

Going: Sf: 3-5 GS: 0-1 Gd: 0-1 GF: - Fm: 0-4
Distance: 2m/2m3: 0-0 2m4-2m7: 1-5 3m+: 2-6
Track: LH: 1-7 RH: 2-4 Tight: 0-4 Gall: 0-3
Aids: Bl: 0-0 Vi: 0-0 Tstrap: 0-0
Best Rating: 109 3/03 Hrfd 3m1f110y soft Ch

Modest hurdler; showed her liking for soft ground and a test of stamina when making a successful chasing debut in mares only event at Hereford March 2003; stays beyond three miles; acts well on a soft surface.

Madam's Man

(111h) (106h)**111**
7-y-o b g Sir Harry Lewis (USA)-Madam-M (Tina s Pet)
N A Twiston-Davies H R Mould

Placings:000223-30134 (2071)
2002/03: 24³G, 24⁰GS, 24¹G, 26³GF, 22⁴S,

	Starts	1st	2nd	3rd	Win & Pl
Hurdles	4	1	0	2	3330
Chases	1	0	0	0	424
Career Total	11	1	2	3	6072
100	6/02	Worc	3m	F(0-100)HHdl	GD	£2345

Total win prize-money £2345

Going: Sf: 0-1 GS: 0-1 Gd: 1-2 GF: - Fm: 0-1
Distance: 2m/2m3: 0-0 2m4-2m7: 0-0 3m+: 1-4
Track: LH: 1-3 RH: 0-2 Tight: 0-3 Gall: 0-0
Aids: Bl: 0-0 Vi: 0-0 Tstrap: 0-0
Best Rating: 111 11/02 MRas 2m6f110y soft Ch

Defied top weight to win a three mile novices' handicap hurdle at Worcester June 2002. Would have finished respectable runner-up but for falling on last on chasing bow at Market Rasen in November.

Madame Derry

11-y-o ch m Derrylin-Teletex (Pollerton)
Mrs K Lundberg-Young Mrs Kin Lundberg-Young

Placings:0-0P (0174)
2002/03: 22⁰G, 22ᴾGF,

	Starts	1st	2nd	3rd	Win & Pl
Hurdles	2	0	0	0	
Career Total	3	0	0	0	

Going: Sf: 0-0 GS: 0-0 Gd: 0-1 GF: - Fm: 0-1
Distance: 2m/2m3: 0-0 2m4-2m7: 0-2 3m+: 0-0
Track: LH: 0-0 RH: 0-2 Tight: 0-0 Gall: 0-0
Aids: Bl: 0-0 Vi: 0-0 Tstrap: 0-0
Best Rating: 0 5/02 Winc 2m6f gd-fm Hdl

Madame Poulet

7-y-o gr m Gold Dust-Came Cottage (Nearly A Hand)
N R Mitchell Mrs E Mitchell

Placings:0-0PP (4755)
2002/03: 16⁰HY, 24ᴾS, 18ᴾGF,

	Starts	1st	2nd	3rd	Win & Pl
NH Flat	1	0	0	0	0
Hurdles	2	0	0	0	0
Career Total	4	0	0	0	0

Going: Sf: 0-2 GS: 0-0 Gd: 0-0 GF: - Fm: 0-1
Distance: 2m/2m3: 0-2 2m4-2m7: 0-0 3m+: 0-1
Track: LH: 0-2 RH: 0-0 Tight: 0-2 Gall: 0-1
Aids: Bl: 0-0 Vi: 0-0 Tstrap: 0-0
Best Rating: 70 5/01 Extr 2m1f good NHF

Maddy's Supreme (IRE)

98 92
7-y-o b m Supreme Leader-Shannon Lough (IRE) (Deep Run)
T D Easterby J Henderson (co Durham)

Placings:05223-643F (2705)
2002/03: 23⁶G, 21⁴S, 19³G, 20ᶠHY,

	Starts	1st	2nd	3rd	Win & Pl
Hurdles	4	0	0	1	342
Career Total	9	0	2	2	2277

Going: Sf: 0-2 GS: 0-0 Gd: 0-2 GF: - Fm: 0-0
Distance: 2m/2m3: 0-1 2m4-2m7: 0-3 3m+: 0-0
Track: LH: 0-4 RH: 0-0 Tight: 0-2 Gall: 0-0
Aids: Bl: 0-0 Vi: 0-0 Tstrap: 0-0
Best Rating: 92 11/02 Catt 2m3f good Hdl

Placed in modest company in novice hurdles. Stays two and a half miles plus, handles good and soft ground.

Mademist Sam

94 86
11-y-o b g Lord Bud-Mademist Susie (French Vine)
P Beaumont Mrs C M Clarke

Placings:00/066/000F3255/625/14335032P1/3 (2001)
2002/03: 22³S,

	Starts	1st	2nd	3rd	Win & Pl
Chases	1	0	0	1	556
Career Total	27	2	3	5	14166
100	9/00	Sedg	2m5f	E Ch	SFT	£3250
100	5/00	Weth	2m4f110yD Ch	G-F	£4160

Total win prize-money £7410

Going: Sf: 0-1 GS: 0-0 Gd: 0-0 GF: - Fm: 0-0
Distance: 2m/2m3: 0-0 2m4-2m7: 0-1 3m+: 0-0
Track: LH: 0-1 RH: 0-0 Tight: 0-0 Gall: 0-0
Aids: Bl: 0-0 Vi: 0-0 Tstrap: 0-0
Best Rating: 102 3/99 MRas 2m4f gd-sft Ch

Madforit

57 23
5-y-o b g Prince Sabo-Elusive (Little Current (USA))
M J Roberts Mike Roberts

Placings:4-0P0 (4446)
2002/03: 12⁰GS, 18ᴾHY, 16⁰G,

	Starts	1st	2nd	3rd	Win & Pl
NH Flat	1	0	0	0	0
Hurdles	2	0	0	0	0
Career Total	4	0	0	0	0

Going: Sf: 0-1 GS: 0-1 Gd: 0-1 GF: - Fm: 0-0
Distance: 2m/2m3: 0-2 2m4-2m7: 0-0 3m+: 0-0
Track: LH: 0-2 RH: 0-1 Tight: 0-1 Gall: 0-0
Aids: Bl: 0-0 Vi: 0-0 Tstrap: 0-0
Best Rating: 46 11/02 Newb 1m4f110y gd-sft NHF

Madge Carroll (IRE)

110 93
6-y-o b m Hollow Hand-Spindle Tree (Laurence O)
T R George Madge At Slad Partnership

Placings:2160 (3497)
2002/03: 21²GS, 20¹GS, 19⁶GS, 21⁰GS,

	Starts	1st	2nd	3rd	Win & Pl
Hurdles	4	1	1	0	4951
Career Total	4	1	1	0	4951
93	12/02	Hntg	2m4f110yD Hdl	G-S	£3747

Total win prize-money £3747

Going: Sf: 0-0 GS: 1-4 Gd: 0-0 GF: - Fm: 0-0
Distance: 2m/2m3: 0-0 2m4-2m7: 1-4 3m+: 0-0
Track: LH: 0-2 RH: 1-2 Tight: 0-0 Gall: 1-1
Aids: Bl: 0-0 Vi: 0-0 Tstrap: 0-0
Best Rating: 93 12/02 Hntg 2m4f110y gd-sft Hdl

Got off the mark over two and a half miles over hurdles on good to soft ground at Huntingdon in December. acts on easy ground.

Madhaze (IRE)

85 50
12-y-o ch g Zaffaran (USA)-Canhaar (Sparkler)
A E Jones (Miss Sophie Parmentier 21/3) Miss Sophie Parmentier

Placings:2/0P4P-PF4 (4699)
2002/03: 23ᴾG, 22ᶠG, 17⁴GF,

	Starts	1st	2nd	3rd	Win & Pl
Chases	3	0	0	0	0
Career Total	8	0	1	0	582

Going: Sf: 0-0 GS: 0-0 Gd: 0-2 GF: - Fm: 0-1
Distance: 2m/2m3: 0-1 2m4-2m7: 0-1 3m+: 0-1
Track: LH: 0-2 RH: 0-1 Tight: 0-1 Gall: 0-1
Aids: Bl: 0-0 Vi: 0-0 Tstrap: 0-0
Best Rating: 102 9/96 Worc 2m gd-fm NHF

Poor chaser; very lightly raced for one in the veteran stage; seems best on fast ground.

Madiba

95 92
4-y-o b g Emperor Jones (USA)-Priluki (Lycius (USA))
S Dow (R Guest 18/5) Eastwell Manor Racing Ltd

Placings:30 (1968)
2002/03: 16³GS, 16⁰GS,

	Starts	1st	2nd	3rd	Win & Pl
Hurdles	2	0	0	1	682
Career Total	2	0	0	1	682

Going: Sf: 0-0 GS: 0-2 Gd: 0-0 GF: - Fm: 0-0
Distance: 2m/2m3: 0-2 2m4-2m7: 0-0 3m+: 0-0
Track: LH: 0-1 RH: 0-1 Tight: 0-0 Gall: 0-0
Aids: Bl: 0-0 Vi: 0-0 Tstrap: 0-0
Best Rating: 100 11/02 Asct 2m110y gd-sft Hdl

Moderate maiden on the Flat; fair run on hurdles debut.

Madison Avenue (GER)

98   **92**

6-y-o b g Mondrian (GER)-Madly Noble (GER) (Irish River (FR))
T M Jones (C Von Der Recke 4/12) Richard L Page

Placings:1P452   (4086)
2002/03: 21¹HY, 24²S, 174⁴HY, 165²HY, 192⁶GS,

	Starts	1st	2nd	3rd	Win & Pl
Hurdles	5	1	1	0	4181
Career Total	5	1	1	0	4181
108 12/02 Plum	2m5f		F Hdl	HVY	£2978

Total win prize-money £2979

Going: Sf: 1-4 GS: 0-1 Gd: 0-0 GF: - Fm: 0-0
Distance: 2m/2m3: 0-3 **2m4-2m7: 1-1** 3m+: 0-1
Track: LH: 1-2 RH: 0-3 Tight: 1-3 Gall: 0-0
Aids: Bl: 0-1 Vi: 0-0 Tstrap: 0-0
Best Rating: 108 12/02 Plum 2m5f   heavy   Hdl

Modest hurdler; trained in Germany when successful on hurdles debut at Plumpton in December 2002; subsequently disappointing until second in a Stratford seller; stays two miles five; has worn blinkers.

Magenko (IRE)

90   **88**

6-y-o ch g Forest Wind (USA)-Bebe Auction (IRE) (Auction Ring (USA))
F P Murtagh R & J Wharton

Placings:604440/3030340401-P0   (1561)
2002/03: 24²PG, 22⁰G,

	Starts	1st	2nd	3rd	Win & Pl
Hurdles	2	0	0	0	
Career Total	18	1	0	3	10006
88 4/02 Sedg	2m5f110yG HHdl		G-F	£8209	

Total win prize-money £8210

Going: Sf: 0-0 GS: 0-0 Gd: 0-2 GF: - Fm: 0-0
Distance: 2m/2m3: 0-0 2m4-2m7: 0-1 3m+: 0-1
Track: LH: 0-2 RH: 0-0 Tight: 0-1 Gall: 0-0
Aids: Bl: 0-0 Vi: 0-0 Tstrap: 0-0
Best Rating: 88 4/02 Sedg 2m5f110y   gd-fm   Hdl

Broke his duck at the 16th attempt when landing a valuable selling handicap hurdle at Sedgefield in April 2002.

Maggie's Pet

78   **63**

6-y-o b m Minshaanshu Amad (USA)-Run Fast For Gold (Deep Run)
K Bell (G M McCourt 25/7) Len Purdy

Placings:500P-6   (0487)
2002/03: 16⁵HY,

	Starts	1st	2nd	3rd	Win & Pl
Hurdles	1	0	0	0	0
Career Total	5	0	0	0	0

Going: Sf: 0-1 GS: 0-0 Gd: 0-0 GF: - Fm: 0-0
Distance: 2m/2m3: 0-1 2m4-2m7: 0-0 3m+: 0-0
Track: LH: 0-1 RH: 0-0 Tight: 0-0 Gall: 0-0
Aids: Bl: 0-0 Vi: 0-0 Tstrap: 0-0
Best Rating: 84 11/01 Extr 2m1f   gd-fm   NHF

Maggies Brother

10-y-o b g Brotherly (USA)-Sallisses (Pamroy)

R Shail (Mrs G M Shail 31/5) Mrs G M Shail

Placings:PF/52-1125P6FP   (4615)
2002/03: 25¹GF, 24¹GF, 25²G, 28⁵G, 26⁵HY, 27⁶G, 25⁵S, 26⁶G,

	Starts	1st	2nd	3rd	Win & Pl
Chases	8	2	1	0	5861
Career Total	12	2	2	0	6327
86 5/02 Hntg	3m	H Ch		G-F	£1384
88 5/02 Chel	3m1f110yH Ch		G-F	£3926	

Total win prize-money £5311

Going: Sf: 0-2 GS: 0-0 Gd: 0-4 GF: - Fm: 2-2
Distance: 2m/2m3: 0-0 2m4-2m7: 0-0 **3m+: 2-8**
Track: LH: 1-4 RH: 1-4 Tight: 0-3 **Gall: 2-3**
Aids: Bl: 0-0 Vi: 0-0 Tstrap: 0-0
Best Rating: 96 5/02 Strf 3m4f   good   Ch

Winning pointer/hunter chaser; stays extreme distances; acts on most types of ground.

Maggies Well

102   **82**

5-y-o b m Royal Fountain-Ragged Rose (Scallywag)
C Grant C B Taylor

Placings:5P20PP   (4355)
2002/03: 21⁵S, 27⁴S, 21²HY, 21⁰HY, 16⁵S, 20⁰GF,

	Starts	1st	2nd	3rd	Win & Pl
Hurdles	6	0	1	0	990
Career Total	6	0	1	0	990

Going: Sf: 0-5 GS: 0-0 Gd: 0-0 GF: - Fm: 0-1
Distance: 2m/2m3: 0-1 2m4-2m7: 0-4 3m+: 0-1
Track: LH: 0-6 RH: 0-0 Tight: 0-4 Gall: 0-0
Aids: Bl: 0-0 Vi: 0-0 Tstrap: 0-0
Best Rating: 82 1/03 Sedg 2m5f110y   heavy   Hdl

Much improved effort when runner-up in a poor mares only novices hurdle at Sedgefield in January.

Magic Arrow (USA)

78   **49**

7-y-o b g Defensive Play (USA)-Magic Blue (USA) (Cure The Blues (USA))
Ian Emmerson Ian Emmerson

Placings:P00/0F   (4518)
2002/03: 17⁰G, 21⁵G,

	Starts	1st	2nd	3rd	Win & Pl
Hurdles	2	0	0	0	
Career Total	5	0	0	0	

Going: Sf: 0-0 GS: 0-0 Gd: 0-0 GF: - Fm: 0-0
Distance: 2m/2m3: 0-1 2m4-2m7: 0-1 3m+: 0-0
Track: LH: 0-2 RH: 0-0 Tight: 0-0 Gall: 0-0
Aids: Bl: 0-0 Vi: 0-0 Tstrap: 0-0
Best Rating: 71 1/01 Muss 2m   gd-sft   Hdl

Magic Bengie

4-y-o b g Magic Ring (IRE)-Zinzi (Song)
F Kirby Fred Kirby

Placings:PF   (2304)
2002/03: 16⁰G, 16⁶GS,

	Starts	1st	2nd	3rd	Win & Pl
Hurdles	2	0	0	0	
Career Total	2	0	0	0	

Going: Sf: 0-0 GS: 0-1 Gd: 0-1 GF: - Fm: 0-0
Distance: 2m/2m3: 0-2 2m4-2m7: 0-0 3m+: 0-0
Track: LH: 0-2 RH: 0-0 Tight: 0-2 Gall: 0-0
Aids: Bl: 0-0 Vi: 0-0 Tstrap: 0-0
Best Rating: 0 12/02 Catt 2m   gd-sft   Hdl

Magic Box

98   **85**

5-y-o b g Magic Ring (IRE)-Princess Poquito (Hard Fought)
Miss Kate Milligan R A W Racing

Placings:40304-001550F   (1608)
2002/03: 16⁴G, 17⁰GF, 16⁰GF, 17¹GF, 17⁵S, 17⁵GF, 16⁶G,

	Starts	1st	2nd	3rd	Win & Pl
Hurdles	8	1	0	0	2898
Career Total	12	1	0	1	3231
88 7/02 Sedg	2m1f	E(0-105)HHdl	G-F	£2898	

Total win prize-money £2898

Going: Sf: 0-0 GS: 0-0 Gd: 0-4 GF: - Fm: 1-4
Distance: **2m/2m3: 1-8** 2m4-2m7: 0-0 3m+: 0-0
Track: LH: 1-7 RH: 0-1 Tight: 1-4 Gall: 0-1
Aids: Bl: 0-0 Vi: 0-0 Tstrap: 0-0
Best Rating: 88 7/02 Sedg 2m1f   gd-fm   Hdl

Plating-class hurdler; suited by two miles and fast ground.

Magic Charm

71   **29**

5-y-o b m Magic Ring (IRE)-Loch Clair (IRE) (Lomond (USA))
A G Newcombe Wetherby Racing Bureau 46

Placings:00   (2194)
2002/03: 16⁰G, 17⁰GS,

	Starts	1st	2nd	3rd	Win & Pl
Hurdles	2	0	0	0	
Career Total	2	0	0	0	

Going: Sf: 0-0 GS: 0-0 Gd: 0-0 GF: - Fm: 0-0
Distance: 2m/2m3: 0-2 2m4-2m7: 0-0 3m+: 0-0
Track: LH: 0-1 RH: 0-1 Tight: 0-2 Gall: 0-0
Aids: Bl: 0-0 Vi: 0-0 Tstrap: 0-0
Best Rating: 29 10/02 Strf 2m110y   good   Hdl

Magic Combination (IRE)

105   **138d**

10-y-o b g Scenic-Etage (Ile De Bourbon (USA))
L Lungo Sw Transport (swindon) Ltd & R J Gilbert

Placings:630/P/1U1/P10/0500/01102005-60001   (1016)
2002/03: 20⁶G, 20⁰G, 17⁰GF, 17⁰GS, 20¹G,

	Starts	1st	2nd	3rd	Win & Pl
Hurdles	5	1	0	0	5369
Career Total	27	6	1	1	67000
125 8/02 Prth	2m4f110yD(0-115)HHdl	GD	£5369	
138 7/01 MRas	2m1f110yD(0-140)HHdl	G-S	£20065	
135 5/01 MRas	2m3f110yC(0-130)HHdl	GF	£5772	
129 3/00 Sand	2m110y B HHdl	GD	£21450	
130 2/99 Asct	2m4f E(0-120)HHdl	G-S	£3550	
113 1/99 Kemp	2m5f E(0-110)HHdl	SFT	£2766	

Total win prize-money £58973

Going: Sf: 0-0 GS: 0-1 Gd: 1-3 GF: - Fm: 0-1
Distance: 2m/2m3: 0-2 **2m4-2m7: 1-3** 3m+: 0-0
Track: LH: 0-2 **RH: 1-3** Tight: 0-2 Gall: 0-0
Aids: Bl: 0-0 Vi: 0-0 Tstrap: 0-0
Best Rating: 138 11/01 DRoy 2m   soft   Hdl

Fair hurdler; winner of the Imperial Cup in 2000; nowhere near as good these days, but still capable of winning races; stays two and a half miles; best on a sound surface.

Magic Dancer (IRE)
95   66

10-y-o b g Carefree Dancer (USA)-Giveushope (Whistling Deer)
Capt J A George   Capt J A George

Placings: 20206046/66/62110621/222P60/4B53456-02P0P04   (4221)
2002/03: 25⁶GS, 24⁰GF, 25²S, 26⁰HY, 31⁰GS, 25⁰S, 25⁴GF,

	Starts	1st	2nd	3rd	Win & Pl
Chases	8	0	1	0	1334
Career Total	38	3	8	1	28998
118	4/00	Asct	3m110y	B Ch	SFT £10946
119	1/00	Hntg	2m5f110yD(0-120)HHdl	G-S	£3178
118	12/99	Extr	2m3f110yD(0-110)HHdl	G-S	£3168

Total win prize-money £17293

Going:	Sf: 0-4 GS: 0-2 Gd: 0-0 GF: - Fm: 0-2
Distance:	2m/2m3: 0-0 2m4-2m7: 0-0 3m+: 0-8
Track:	LH: 0-3 RH: 0-5 Tight: 0-2 Gall: 0-1
Aids:	Bl: 0-0 Vi: 0-0 Tstrap: 0-0
Best Rating:	127 11/00 Kemp 3m soft Ch

He is difficult to win with and a rather quirky sort. He stays three miles but is not one to place much faith in.

Magic Dragon (FR)
93f   91f

5-y-o ch g Cyborg (FR)-Dix Huit Brumaire (FR) (General Assembly (USA))
Mrs M Reveley   Sir Robert Ogden

Placings: 4   (4560)
2002/03: 16⁴G,

	Starts	1st	2nd	3rd	Win & Pl
NH Flat	1	0	0	0	275
Career Total	1	0	0	0	275

Going:	Sf: 0-0 GS: 0-0 Gd: 0-1 GF: - Fm: 0-0
Distance:	2m/2m3: 0-1 2m4-2m7: 0-0 3m+: 0-0
Track:	LH: 0-1 RH: 0-0 Tight: 0-0 Gall: 0-0
Aids:	Bl: 0-0 Vi: 0-0 Tstrap: 0-0
Best Rating:	91 4/03 Ayr 2m good NHF

Bumper performer; showed ability in sole start; looks sure to do better in time.

Magic Maid

4-y-o f Presidium-Mrs Magic (Magic Mirror)
H S Howe   R J Parish

Placings: P   (1153)
2002/03: 17⁰G,

	Starts	1st	2nd	3rd	Win & Pl
Hurdles	1	0	0	0	
Career Total	1	0	0	0	

Going:	Sf: 0-0 GS: 0-0 Gd: 0-1 GF: - Fm: 0-0
Distance:	2m/2m3: 0-1 2m4-2m7: 0-0 3m+: 0-0
Track:	LH: 0-1 RH: 0-0 Tight: 0-1 Gall: 0-0
Aids:	Bl: 0-0 Vi: 0-0 Tstrap: 0-0
Best Rating:	0 9/02 NAbb 2m1f good Hdl

Magic Of Sydney (IRE)
100   126

7-y-o b g Broken Hearted-Chat Her Up (Proverb)
R Rowe   Ann & John Symes

Placings: 06-1F2   (2549)
2002/03: 21¹G, 21⁶GS, 25²S,

	Starts	1st	2nd	3rd	Win & Pl
Chases	3	1	1	0	6203
Career Total	5	1	1	0	6203
126	11/02	Folk	2m5f	D Ch	GD £4693

Total win prize-money £4693

Going:	Sf: 0-1 GS: 0-1 Gd: 1-1 GF: - Fm: 0-0
Distance:	2m/2m3: 0-0 2m4-2m7: 1-2 3m+: 0-1
Track:	LH: 0-0 RH: 1-3 Tight: 1-2 Gall: 0-0
Aids:	Bl: 0-0 Vi: 0-0 Tstrap: 0-0
Best Rating:	126 12/02 Folk 3m1f soft Ch

Fair front-running novice chaser; scored on his first attempt over fences at Folkestone in November 2002; limitations exposed subsequently; stays two miles five; acts on good ground or softer.

Magic Route (IRE)
96(93c)   (63c)85

6-y-o b g Mr Confusion (IRE)-Another Chapter (Respect)
J Howard Johnson   Michael Thompson

Placings: 0P-20P5P   (4228)
2002/03: 16²GF, 16⁸GF, 16⁶HY, 16⁵GS, 25⁰GF,

	Starts	1st	2nd	3rd	Win & Pl
Hurdles	4	0	1	0	822
Chases	1	0	0	0	0
Career Total	7	0	1	0	822

Going:	Sf: 0-2 GS: 0-0 Gd: 0-0 GF: - Fm: 0-3
Distance:	2m/2m3: 0-4 2m4-2m7: 0-0 3m+: 0-1
Track:	LH: 0-4 RH: 0-1 Tight: 0-2 Gall: 0-1
Aids:	Bl: 0-0 Vi: 0-0 Tstrap: 0-0
Best Rating:	85 12/02 Muss 2m gd-fm Hdl

Magic Sound
80   47

5-y-o ch g Savahra Sound-Ace Girl (Stanford)
Mrs S J Smith (M J Polglase 5/7)   Paul J Dixon

Placings: 0F0PP   (3864)
2002/03: 17⁰HY, 16⁶G, 17⁰HY, 19⁰G, 19⁰GS,

	Starts	1st	2nd	3rd	Win & Pl
Hurdles	5	0	0	0	
Career Total	5	0	0	0	

Going:	Sf: 0-2 GS: 0-1 Gd: 0-2 GF: - Fm: 0-0
Distance:	2m/2m3: 0-4 2m4-2m7: 0-1 3m+: 0-0
Track:	LH: 0-4 RH: 0-1 Tight: 0-2 Gall: 0-1
Aids:	Bl: 0-0 Vi: 0-0 Tstrap: 0-0
Best Rating:	47 1/03 Sedg 2m1f heavy Hdl

Magic To Do (IRE)
102   87

5-y-o b g Spectrum (IRE)-Smouldering (IRE) (Caerleon (USA))
O Sherwood   Antony Sofroniou

Placings: 0040-13   (0616)

2002/03: 17¹G, 20³GF,

	Starts	1st	2nd	3rd	Win & Pl
Hurdles	2	1	0	1	2630
Career Total	6	1	0	1	2630
87	5/02	Folk	2m1f110yG(0-95)HHdl	GD £2261

Total win prize-money £2261

Going:	Sf: 0-0 GS: 0-0 Gd: 1-1 GF: - Fm: 0-1
Distance:	2m/2m3: 1-1 2m4-2m7: 0-1 3m+: 0-0
Track:	LH: 0-1 RH: 1-1 Tight: 1-1 Gall: 0-0
Aids:	Bl: 1-2 Vi: 0-0 Tstrap: 0-0
Best Rating:	87 5/02 Folk 2m1f110y good Hdl

Won a selling hurdle at Folkestone in May 2002: acts on good.

Magic Waters
101   92

5-y-o b g Ezzoud (IRE)-Paradise Waters (Celestial Storm (USA))
T D Easterby   D F Sills

Placings: 251224P-5P063   (4120)
2002/03: 16⁵GS, 23⁸HY, 19⁰GS, 20⁶G, 26³G,

	Starts	1st	2nd	3rd	Win & Pl
Hurdles	5	0	0	1	494
Career Total	12	1	3	1	6517
102	11/01	Newc	2m	E Hdl	GD £2639

Total win prize-money £2639

Going:	Sf: 0-1 GS: 0-2 Gd: 0-2 GF: - Fm: 0-0
Distance:	2m/2m3: 0-1 2m4-2m7: 0-3 3m+: 0-1
Track:	LH: 0-4 RH: 0-1 Tight: 0-2 Gall: 0-1
Aids:	Bl: 0-4 Vi: 0-0 Tstrap: 0-0
Best Rating:	109 12/02 Weth 2m gd-sft Hdl

Moderate hurdler, winning at Newcastle in November 2001; not the easiest of rides, has been placed since; Best at around two miles but stays further; eggfective on good and soft ground; has worn blinkers.

Magical Approach (IRE)

13-y-o ch g Callernish-Farm Approach (Tug Of War)
Giles Smyly   Major B D A Ridge

Placings: 2FFB/F3231135/303023/03P010/0-6O   (4031)
2002/03: 24⁶S, 24⁰S,

	Starts	1st	2nd	3rd	Win & Pl
Chases	2	0	0	0	0
Career Total	27	3	3	7	30329
114	2/01	Fair	2m4f	(0-116)HCh	HVY £5564
118	2/99	Punc	3m2f	HCh	HVY £8671
115	1/99	Gowr	2m4f	(0-116)HCh	SFT £3683

Total win prize-money £17920

Going:	Sf: 0-2 GS: 0-0 Gd: 0-0 GF: - Fm: 0-0
Distance:	2m/2m3: 0-0 2m4-2m7: 0-0 3m+: 0-2
Track:	LH: 0-0 RH: 0-2 Tight: 0-0 Gall: 0-0
Aids:	Bl: 0-0 Vi: 0-0 Tstrap: 0-0
Best Rating:	118 2/99 Punc 3m2f heavy Ch

Magical Attraction (USA)

6-y-o b/br g Exbourne (USA)-Abeer (USA) (Dewan (USA))
Mrs A Price   Mrs A Price

Placings: 0   (1552)
2002/03: 17⁰G,

	Starts	1st	2nd	3rd	Win & Pl
Hurdles	1	0	0	0	
Career Total	1	0	0	0	

Going:	Sf: 0-0 GS: 0-0 Gd: 0-1 GF: - Fm: 0-0
Distance:	2m/2m3: 0-1 2m4-2m7: 0-0 3m+: 0-0
Track:	LH: 0-0 RH: 0-1 Tight: 0-0 Gall: 0-0
Aids:	Bl: 0-0 Vi: 0-0 Tstrap: 0-0
Best Rating:	0 10/02 Hrfd 2m1f good Hdl

Magical Bailiwick (IRE)

(109h)   (105h)
7-y-o g Magical Wonder (USA)-Alpine Dance (USA) (Apalachee (USA))
R J Baker Islands Racing Connection

Placings:0530P/15P362505-P   (1094)
2002/03: 21PGF,

	Starts	1st	2nd	3rd	Win & Pl
Chases	1	0	0	0	
Career Total	15	1	1	2	4778
104 11/01 NAbb 2m1f E Hdl SFT £2968					
Total win prize-money £2968					

Going:	Sf: 0-0 GS: 0-0 Gd: 0-0 GF: - Fm: 0-1
Distance:	2m/2m3: 0-0 2m4-2m7: 0-1 3m+: 0-0
Track:	LH: 0-1 RH: 0-0 Tight: 0-1 Gall: 0-0
Aids:	Bl: 0-0 Vi: 0-0 Tstrap: 0-0
Best Rating:	108 1/01 Leic 2m heavy Hdl

Moderate hurdler. Effective over 17 furlongs. Acts on soft ground.

Magical Day

97   83
4-y-o ch f Halling (USA)-Ahla (Unfuwain (USA))
W G M Turner (Mrs J R Ramsden 4/6) M J B Racing

Placings:45222422103   (4079)
2002/03: 17⁴S, 17⁵GF, 17²F, 17²G, 16²HY, 17⁴S, 16²S, 16²S, 19¹G, 21⁰S, 16³HY,

	Starts	1st	2nd	3rd	Win & Pl
Hurdles	11	1	5	1	6684
Career Total	11	1	5	1	6684
83 2/03 Hrfd 2m3f110yF Hdl GD £2786					
Total win prize-money £2786					

Going:	Sf: 0-7 GS: 0-0 Gd: 1-2 GF: - Fm: 0-2
Distance:	2m/2m3: 0-9 2m4-2m7: 1-2 3m+: 0-0
Track:	LH: 1-4 RH: 1-4 Tight: 0-7 Gall: 0-0
Aids:	Bl: 0-3 Vi: 0-1 Tstrap: 0-0
Best Rating:	83 2/03 Hrfd 2m3f110y good Hdl

Moderate hurdler; acts on any ground; has worn headgear; stays two miles three; string of placed efforts in 2002/3 before winning Hereford claimer.

Magical Field

98   94
5-y-o ch m Deploy-Ash Glade (Nashwan (USA))
Mrs M Reveley Lightbody Celebration Cakes Ltd

Placings:4F4   (4167)
2002/03: 16⁴GS, 16⁶G, 16⁴GS,

	Starts	1st	2nd	3rd	Win & Pl
Hurdles	3	0	0	0	570
Career Total	3	0	0	0	570

Going:	Sf: 0-0 GS: 0-2 Gd: 0-1 GF: - Fm: 0-0
Distance:	2m/2m3: 0-3 2m4-2m7: 0-0 3m+: 0-0
Track:	LH: 0-3 RH: 0-0 Tight: 0-1 Gall: 0-2
Aids:	Bl: 0-0 Vi: 0-0 Tstrap: 0-0
Best Rating:	94 11/02 Newc 2m gd-sft Hdl

Ex-French, in front when coming to grief at the last in mares only novices hurdle at Catterick in February.

Magical Knight

                             71
5-y-o b g Sir Harry Lewis (USA)-Formal Affair (Rousillon (USA))
R T Phillips The Old Foresters Partnership

Placings:0-F   (0566)
2002/03: 17FGF,

	Starts	1st	2nd	3rd	Win & Pl
Hurdles	1	0	0	0	
Career Total	2	0	0	0	

Going:	Sf: 0-0 GS: 0-0 Gd: 0-0 GF: - Fm: 0-1
Distance:	2m/2m3: 0-1 2m4-2m7: 0-0 3m+: 0-0
Track:	LH: 0-0 RH: 0-1 Tight: 0-0 Gall: 0-0
Aids:	Bl: 0-0 Vi: 0-0 Tstrap: 0-0
Best Rating:	77 1/02 Wwck 2m heavy Hdl

Magical Liaison (IRE)

96f   90f
5-y-o b g Mujtahid (USA)-Instant Affair (USA) (Lyphard (USA))
W Jenks The Glazeley Partnership 2

Placings:5226   (4322)
2002/03: 16⁵G, 16²GS, 16²S, 17⁶G,

	Starts	1st	2nd	3rd	Win & Pl
NH Flat	4	0	2	0	1480
Career Total	4	0	2	0	1480

Going:	Sf: 0-1 GS: 0-1 Gd: 0-2 GF: - Fm: 0-0
Distance:	2m/2m3: 0-4 2m4-2m7: 0-0 3m+: 0-0
Track:	LH: 0-2 RH: 0-2 Tight: 0-1 Gall: 0-0
Aids:	Bl: 0-0 Vi: 0-0 Tstrap: 0-0
Best Rating:	90 1/03 Ludl 2m soft NHF

Narrowly beaten in a couple of Ludlow bumpers.

Magical Poitin (IRE)

10-y-o ch m Magical Strike (USA)-Poitin Still (Royal Match)
Ms Emma Anderson (Mrs S A Duffie 19/5) Mrs S A Duffie

Placings:00/PFP/P   (4506)
2002/03: 25PG,

	Starts	1st	2nd	3rd	Win & Pl
Chases	1	0	0	0	
Career Total	6	0	0	0	

Going:	Sf: 0-0 GS: 0-0 Gd: 0-1 GF: - Fm: 0-0
Distance:	2m/2m3: 0-0 2m4-2m7: 0-0 3m+: 0-1
Track:	LH: 0-1 RH: 0-0 Tight: 0-0 Gall: 0-0
Aids:	Bl: 0-0 Vi: 0-0 Tstrap: 0-0
Best Rating:	66 4/98 Fair 2m yield NHF

Magicien (FR)

                            (12h)
7-y-o b g Muroto-French Look (FR) (Green River (FR))
Miss K Marks Nick Shutts

Placings:0P/40/P   (0446)
2002/03: 19PG,

	Starts	1st	2nd	3rd	Win & Pl
Chases	1	0	0	0	
Career Total	5	0	0	0	243

Going:	Sf: 0-0 GS: 0-0 Gd: 0-1 GF: - Fm: 0-0
Distance:	2m/2m3: 0-1 2m4-2m7: 0-0 3m+: 0-0
Track:	LH: 0-0 RH: 0-1 Tight: 0-0 Gall: 0-0
Aids:	Bl: 0-0 Vi: 0-0 Tstrap: 0-1
Best Rating:	40 5/00 Ctml 2m1f110y good Hdl

Magique Etoile (IRE)

96   72
7-y-o b m Magical Wonder (USA)-She s A Dancer (IRE) (Alzao (USA))
Dr J R J Naylor Gallery Racing

Placings:05/30/500-040R6P   (1038)
2002/03: 17⁰G, 16⁴GF, 20⁶GF, 17⁶G, 16⁶GS, 20⁵GF,

	Starts	1st	2nd	3rd	Win & Pl
Hurdles	4	0	0	0	
Chases	2	0	0	0	
Career Total	13	0	1	344	

Going:	Sf: 0-0 GS: 0-1 Gd: 0-2 GF: - Fm: 0-3
Distance:	2m/2m3: 0-4 2m4-2m7: 0-2 3m+: 0-0
Track:	LH: 0-4 RH: 0-1 Tight: 0-3 Gall: 0-0
Aids:	Bl: 0-0 Vi: 0-0 Tstrap: 0-5
Best Rating:	77 9/00 Plum 2m gd-fm Hdl

Magnatism

85f   73f
6-y-o b g Charmer-Bright-One (Electric)
C W Thornton Exors of the late Peter Rawson

Placings:400   (1569)
2002/03: 17⁴GF, 16⁰GF, 17⁰G,

	Starts	1st	2nd	3rd	Win & Pl
NH Flat	3	0	0	0	0
Career Total	3	0	0	0	0

Going:	Sf: 0-0 GS: 0-0 Gd: 0-1 GF: - Fm: 0-2
Distance:	2m/2m3: 0-3 2m4-2m7: 0-0 3m+: 0-0
Track:	LH: 0-1 RH: 0-2 Tight: 0-2 Gall: 0-0
Aids:	Bl: 0-0 Vi: 0-0 Tstrap: 0-0
Best Rating:	76 9/02 Prth 2m110y gd-fm NHF

Magnus (FR)

97(89h)   (101h)112+
7-y-o b g Roakarad-Volcania (FR) (Neustrien (FR))
M C Pipe D A Johnson

Placings:F11336/111150-36   (2511)
2002/03: 21³HY, 16⁶G,

	Starts	1st	2nd	3rd	Win & Pl
Chases	2	0	0	1	1402
Career Total	14	6	0	3	201062
11/01 Autl 2m4f110y Hdl HLD £48497					

11/01	Autl	3m	Hdl	VS	£67895
10/01	Autl	2m4f110y	Hdl	VS	£31038
9/01	Autl	2m2f	HHdl	VS	£26188
2/01	Pau	2m3f	Hdl	SFT	£8729
1/01	Pau	2m3f	Hdl	HVY	£5820

Total win prize-money £188167

Going: Sf: 0-1 GS: 0-0 Gd: 0-1 GF: - Fm: 0-0
Distance: 2m/2m3: 0-1 2m4-2m7: 0-1 3m+: 0-0
Track: LH: 0-3 RH: 0-0 Tight: 0-1 Gall: 0-0
Aids: Bl: 0-0 Vi: 0-0 Tstrap: 0-0
Best Rating: 112 11/02 NAbb 2m5f110y heavy Ch

A French import bought by David Johnson for FF3,500,000, he was a multiple Graded race winner in France and was bidding for a five-timer over hurdles when disappointing on his British debut at Newbury. He was subsequently found to have burst a blood-vessel. Down the field at Cheltenham next time. Did not seem to stay 21 furlongs in heavy ground on chasing debut at Newton Abbot November 2002, but found two miles too short subsequently.

Mags Two

80   60

6-y-o b g Jumbo Hirt (USA)-Welsh Diamond (High Top)
Ms Liz Harrison David Alan Harrison

Placings:00006   (2661)
2002/03: 16⁵GF, 17⁰S, 20⁰S, 20⁰GS, 20⁶S,

	Starts	1st	2nd	3rd	Win & Pl
NH Flat	2	0	0	0	0
Hurdles	3	0	0	0	0
Career Total	5	0	0	0	0

Going: Sf: 0-3 GS: 0-1 Gd: 0-0 GF: - Fm: 0-1
Distance: 2m/2m3: 0-2 2m4-2m7: 0-3 3m+: 0-0
Track: LH: 0-3 RH: 0-2 Tight: 0-0 Gall: 0-0
Aids: Bl: 0-0 Vi: 0-0 Tstrap: 0-0
Best Rating: 71 10/02 Carl 2m1f soft NHF

Mai Point

10-y-o b m Blakeney-Quilpee Mai (Pee Mai)
Mrs P A Twinn D L Claydon

Placings:F   (0392)
2002/03: 24⁰G,

	Starts	1st	2nd	3rd	Win & Pl
Chases	1	0	0	0	
Career Total	1	0	0	0	

Going: Sf: 0-0 GS: 0-0 Gd: 0-1 GF: - Fm: 0-0
Distance: 2m/2m3: 0-0 2m4-2m7: 0-0 3m+: 0-1
Track: LH: 0-1 RH: 0-0 Tight: 0-1 Gall: 0-0
Aids: Bl: 0-0 Vi: 0-0 Tstrap: 0-0
Best Rating: 0 5/02 Strf 3m good Ch

Maid To Talk

91(96h)   (62h)63

9-y-o b m Arctic Lord-Chatty Lass (Le Bavard (FR))
W S Coltherd S Coltherd

Placings:00⁰0P0/0P600P5-5PPP34   (1472)
2002/03: 16⁵G, 17⁵G, 20⁴GS, 16ᴾGF, 20ᴾGF, 20³GF, 20⁴GF,

	Starts	1st	2nd	3rd	Win & Pl
Hurdles	1	0	0	0	0
Chases	6	0	0	1	1476
Career Total	18	0	0	1	1476

Maiden Flight (IRE)

91   88

7-y-o b m Jurado (USA)-Dream Of Money (IRE) (Good Thyne (USA))
P R Webber W S Watt

Placings:6/04-P40   (0789)
2002/03: 20ᴾG, 20⁴GF, 26⁰GF,

	Starts	1st	2nd	3rd	Win & Pl
Hurdles	3	0	0	0	278
Career Total	6	0	0	0	278

Going: Sf: 0-0 GS: 0-0 Gd: 0-0 GF: - Fm: 0-2
Distance: 2m/2m3: 0-0 2m4-2m7: 0-2 3m+: 0-1
Track: LH: 0-0 RH: 0-0 Tight: 0-0 Gall: 0-0
Aids: Bl: 0-0 Vi: 0-0 Tstrap: 0-0
Best Rating: 93 4/01 Font 2m2f110y good NHF

Maiden Voyage

108   105+

5-y-o b m Slip Anchor-Elaine Tully (IRE) (Persian Bold)
P R Webber (Mrs J R Ramsden 19/6) R J McAlpine

Placings:F02323   (4561)
2002/03: 16⁵S, 17⁰GS, 21²S, 19³HY, 20²G, 20³GF,

	Starts	1st	2nd	3rd	Win & Pl
Hurdles	6	0	2	2	3921
Career Total	6	0	2	2	3921

Going: Sf: 0-3 GS: 0-1 Gd: 0-1 GF: - Fm: 0-1
Distance: 2m/2m3: 0-2 2m4-2m7: 0-4 3m+: 0-0
Track: LH: 0-2 RH: 0-4 Tight: 0-0 Gall: 0-0
Aids: Bl: 0-0 Vi: 0-0 Tstrap: 0-0
Best Rating: 102 4/03 Bang 2m4f gd-fm Hdl

Modest hurdler; improved for the step up in trip to two miles five when runner-up at Ludlow in January 2003; confirmed his liking for the longer trip when placed next three starts; has now won two in a row and is progressing nicely; stays two and a half miles; appears to act on any ground.

Maidstone Magic (IRE)

96   59+

8-y-o b g Balinger-Anyone s Fancy (Callernish)
M C Pipe F G Wilson

Placings:U5U-5   (0922)
2002/03: 26⁵GF,

	Starts	1st	2nd	3rd	Win & Pl
Chases	1	0	0	0	0
Career Total	4	0	0	0	0

Going: Sf: 0-0 GS: 0-0 Gd: 0-0 GF: - Fm: 0-1
Distance: 2m/2m3: 0-0 2m4-2m7: 0-0 3m+: 0-1
Track: LH: 0-0 RH: 0-0 Tight: 0-1 Gall: 0-0
Aids: Bl: 0-0 Vi: 0-0 Tstrap: 0-0
Best Rating: 59 8/02 NAbb 3m2f110y gd-fm Ch

Maidstone Monarch (IRE)

10-y-o b/br g King s Ride-Curragh Breeze (Furry Glen)
Miss A M Newton-Smith F G Wilson

Placings:3/00P6/P30455P3/0P-UPP   (3552)
2002/03: 26ᵁS, 26ᴾHY, 26ᴾS,

	Starts	1st	2nd	3rd	Win & Pl
Chases	3	0	0	0	
Career Total	18	0	0	3	2173

Going: Sf: 0-3 GS: 0-0 Gd: 0-0 GF: - Fm: 0-0
Distance: 2m/2m3: 0-0 2m4-2m7: 0-0 3m+: 0-3
Track: LH: 0-3 RH: 0-0 Tight: 0-3 Gall: 0-0
Aids: Bl: 0-0 Vi: 0-0 Tstrap: 0-0
Best Rating: 94 1/98 Font 2m2f soft NHF

Poor chaser, stays three miles two and seems best on soft ground.

Maidstone Monument (IRE)

111(86h)   (53h)108+

8-y-o b g Jurado (USA)-Loreto Lady (Brave Invader (USA))
Mrs A M Thorpe Don Jenkins

Placings:50/P24153PP0P/06053432P-3P41241P2U4PP   (2231)
2002/03: 24³GF, 24ᴾGS, 24⁴GF, 26¹GF, 26²GF, 26⁴GF, 26¹G, 23ᴾG, 26²G, 26ᵁGF, 24⁴GS, 27ᴾGS, 24ᴾS,

	Starts	1st	2nd	3rd	Win & Pl
Chases	13	2	2	1	13077
Career Total	34	3	4	4	19856
108 9/02	NAbb	3m2f110yD(0-120)		HCh	GD	£4655
106 6/02	NAbb	3m2f110yE(0-110)		HCh	G-F	£3309
85 6/00	Hexm	2m	D Hdl		G-F	£3143

Total win prize-money £11108

Going: Sf: 0-1 GS: 0-3 Gd: 1-3 GF: - Fm: 1-6
Distance: 2m/2m3: 0-0 2m4-2m7: 0-0 3m+: 2-13
Track: LH: 2-11 RH: 0-2 Tight: 2-8 Gall: 0-2
Aids: Bl: 0-0 Vi: 0-0 Tstrap: 0-0
Best Rating: 108 9/02 Plum 3m2f good Ch

Modest handicap chaser; bounced back to form having been given a chance by the Handicapper when landing 3m Worcester handicap July 2003; well beaten second under penalty at the same venue next time; acts on a sound surface; stays 3m 2f.

Maidstone Mountie

7-y-o b g Royal Fountain-Millie Duffer (Furry Glen)
M C Pipe F G Wilson

Placings:0PP   (3334)
2002/03: 18⁰S, 25ᴾHY, 24ᴾS,

	Starts	1st	2nd	3rd	Win & Pl
NH Flat	1	0	0	0	0
Hurdles	2	0	0	0	0
Career Total	3	0	0	0	0

Going: Sf: 0-3 GS: 0-0 Gd: 0-0 GF: - Fm: 0-0
Distance: 2m/2m3: 0-1 2m4-2m7: 0-0 3m+: 0-2
Track: LH: 0-1 RH: 0-1 Tight: 0-2 Gall: 0-0
Aids: Bl: 0-0 Vi: 0-2 Tstrap: 0-0
Best Rating: 29 12/02 Font 2m2f110y soft NHF

Maisey Down

77f   **54f**

6-y-o b m Rakaposhi King-Win Green Hill (National Trust)
J A B Old Www.Theracingforum.Co.Uk

Placings:0   (2259)
2002/03: 17⁰HY,

	Starts	1st	2nd	3rd	Win & Pl
NH Flat	1	0	0	0	
Career Total	1	0	0	0	

Going: Sf: 0-1 GS: 0-0 Gd: 0-0 GF: - Fm: 0-0
Distance: 2m/2m3: 0-1 2m4-2m7: 0-0 3m+: 0-0
Track: LH: 0-0 RH: 0-1 Tight: 0-1 Gall: 0-0
Aids: Bl: 0-0 Vi: 0-0 Tstrap: 0-0
Best Rating: 0   12/02 Folk   2m1f110y   heavy   NHF

Maisiebel

83f   **56f**

5-y-o ch m Be My Native (USA)-High B (Gunner B)
R N Bevis Ewson Contractors

Placings:00   (3583)
2002/03: 17⁰GS, 16⁰G,

	Starts	1st	2nd	3rd	Win & Pl
NH Flat	2	0	0	0	
Career Total	2	0	0	0	

Going: Sf: 0-0 GS: 0-1 Gd: 0-1 GF: - Fm: 0-0
Distance: 2m/2m3: 0-2 2m4-2m7: 0-0 3m+: 0-0
Track: LH: 0-1 RH: 0-1 Tight: 0-2 Gall: 0-0
Aids: Bl: 0-0 Vi: 0-0 Tstrap: 0-0
Best Rating: 56   2/03 Muss   2m   good   NHF

Maitre De Musique (FR)

12-y-o ch g Quai Voltaire (USA)-Mativa (FR) (Satingo)
Mrs F E Needham (T D Walford 29/5) Dr M P Tate

Placings:10/003430/55420/1/422P23/P13P664/53/63-435
                                                  (3962)
2002/03: 25⁴S, 25³GF, 24⁵S,

	Starts	1st	2nd	3rd	Win & Pl
Chases	3	0	0	1	429
Career Total	34	3	4	7	23263
123 11/99 Newc	2m4f	D(0-125)HCh		GD	£3793
120 12/97 Weth	2m4f110yD Ch			GD	£3756
113 2/95 Kemp	2m	H NHF		HVY	£1996
			Total win prize-money £9546

Going: Sf: 0-2 GS: 0-0 Gd: 0-0 GF: - Fm: 0-1
Distance: 2m/2m3: 0-2 2m4-2m7: 0-0 3m+: 0-3
Track: LH: 0-2 RH: 0-1 Tight: 0-2 Gall: 0-0
Aids: Bl: 0-0 Vi: 0-0 Tstrap: 0-3
Best Rating: 126 4/99 Aint   2m6f   good   Ch

Majadou (FR)

120

9-y-o b g Cadoudal (FR)-Majathen (FR) (Carmarthen (FR))
M C Pipe C M , B J & R F Batterham li

Placings:13/0011115/014334/55P/0-P   (0734)
2002/03: 26⁶GF,

	Starts	1st	2nd	3rd	Win & Pl
Chases	1	0	0	0	

Career Total	20	6	0	3	98718
156 12/99 Chel	2m110y B HCh		G-S	£9918
160 3/99 Chel	2m4f110yB HCh		G-S	£35400
129 2/99 Ling	2m D Ch		SFT	£4298
144 1/99 Ling	2m E Ch		HVY	£3276
147 1/99 Chel	2m5f C Ch		G-S	£7002
3/98 Autl	2m1f110y Hdl		VS	£10101
			Total win prize-money £69998

Going: Sf: 0-0 GS: 0-0 Gd: 0-0 GF: - Fm: 0-1
Distance: 2m/2m3: 0-0 2m4-2m7: 0-0 3m+: 0-1
Track: LH: 0-1 RH: 0-1 Tight: 0-1 Gall: 0-0
Aids: Bl: 0-0 Vi: 0-0 Tstrap: 0-0
Best Rating: 160 3/99 Chel 2m4f110y gd-sft Ch

A ready winner of the 1999 Mildmay of Flete Chase, he was
punished by the Handicapper for that. Lightly raced of late.
Appreciates an easy surface.

Majed (FR)

91(114h)   (150h)**60**

7-y-o b g Fijar Tango (FR)-Full Of Passion (USA) (Blushing
Groom (FR))
M C Pipe Sandicroft Stud II

Placings:46PP050/62042321111/1210F0-00   (4479)
2002/03: 32⁰G, 36⁰G,

	Starts	1st	2nd	3rd	Win & Pl
Chases	2	0	0	0	
Career Total	26	6	4	1	66092
150 12/01 Winc	2m6f B HHdl		GD	£8430
139 11/01 Chep	2m4f B Hdl		G-S	£22750
128 4/01 Ayr	3m110y B HHdl		GD	£7228
127 4/01 Extr	2m1f E Hdl		G-S	£2153
133 3/01 Strf	2m6f110yD Hdl		SFT	£3965
115 2/01 Plum	2m E Hdl		SFT	£2075
			Total win prize-money £46603

Going: Sf: 0-0 GS: 0-0 Gd: 0-2 GF: - Fm: 0-0
Distance: 2m/2m3: 0-0 2m4-2m7: 0-0 3m+: 0-2
Track: LH: 0-2 RH: 0-0 Tight: 0-1 Gall: 0-1
Aids: Bl: 0-0 Vi: 0-2 Tstrap: 0-0
Best Rating: 150 12/01 Winc 2m6f   good   Hdl

Useful Ex-French hurdler/chaser; stiff tasks so far over
fences; completed the course in his own time in the Grand
National; seems to cope with all types of ground; stays really well; usually wears headgear.

Majestic (IRE)

113   (137c)**140**

8-y-o b g Belmez (USA)-Noble Lily (USA) (Vaguely Noble)
Ian Williams Patrick Kelly

Placings:111P/112/6F555-3F0F2   (4607)
2002/03: 24³GF, 21⁶GF, 21⁰G, 24⁶G, 21²G,

	Starts	1st	2nd	3rd	Win & Pl
Hurdles	5	0	1	1	5513
Career Total	17	5	2	1	27501
126 1/01 Fknm	3m110y D Ch		SFT	£4067
114 11/00 Newc	2m4f E Ch		G-S	£2918
138 11/99 Chel	2m5f B Hdl		GD	£7370
138 10/99 Chel	2m5f D Hdl		GD	£3876
119 10/99 Plum	2m5f E Hdl		G-F	£2600
			Total win prize-money £20833

Going: Sf: 0-0 GS: 0-0 Gd: 0-3 GF: - Fm: 0-0
Distance: 2m/2m3: 0-0 2m4-2m7: 0-3 3m+: 0-2
Track: LH: 0-4 RH: 0-1 Tight: 0-2 Gall: 0-3
Aids: Bl: 0-5 Vi: 0-0 Tstrap: 0-5
Best Rating: 140 4/03 Chel 2m5f110y good   Hdl

Useful hurdler/chaser; successful over fences twice in the
2000/2001 season, but off the track for ten months before

---

reappearing in February 2002 and has raced over hurdles
since; ran a blinder in the Coral Cup at the Festival in 2002;
not in same form since; stays three miles and handles any
ground; usually wears blinkers and a tongue tie.

Majestic Bay (IRE)

110(105h)   (110h)**127+**

7-y-o b g Unfuwain (USA)-That LI Be The Day (IRE)
(Thatching)
J A B Old W J Smith And M D Dudley

Placings:0654-4334231   (4438)
2002/03: 19⁴GS, 22³GS, 22³S, 24⁴S, 21²HY, 24³S, 24¹G,

	Starts	1st	2nd	3rd	Win & Pl
Hurdles	4	0	0	2	3005
Chases	3	1	1	1	12351
Career Total	11	1	1	3	15841
127 4/03 Asct	3m110y C Ch		GD	£10159
			Total win prize-money £10160

Going: Sf: 0-4 GS: 0-2 Gd: 1-1 GF: - Fm: 0-0
Distance: 2m/2m3: 0-1 2m4-2m7: 0-0 3m+: 1-3
Track: LH: 0-1 RH: 1-6 Tight: 0-2 Gall: 0-1
Aids: Bl: 0-0 Vi: 0-0 Tstrap: 0-0
Best Rating: 127 4/03 Asct 3m110y good   Ch

Fair hurdler/chaser; got off the mark over jumps when winning a novice chase at Ascot in early April; stays 3m; acts
on any ground, but better on a sound surface.

Majestic Moonbeam (IRE)

103f   **107f**

5-y-o b g Supreme Leader-Magic Moonbeam (IRE) (Decent
Fellow)
Jonjo O Neill Mrs T F Cusack

Placings:1   (4155)
2002/03: 16¹G,

	Starts	1st	2nd	3rd	Win & Pl
NH Flat	1	1	0	0	2121
Career Total	1	1	0	0	2121
107 3/03 Wwck	2m H NHF		GD	£2121
			Total win prize-money £2121

Going: Sf: 0-0 GS: 0-0 Gd: 1-1 GF: - Fm: 0-0
Distance: 2m/2m3: 1-1 2m4-2m7: 0-0 3m+: 0-0
Track: LH: 1-1 RH: 0-0 Tight: 0-0 Gall: 0-0
Aids: Bl: 0-0 Vi: 0-0 Tstrap: 0-0
Best Rating: 107 3/03 Wwck 2m   good   NHF

Out of an Irish bumper winner; well backed when making a
hard fought winning debut in Warwick bumper March 2003.

Majestic Storm (IRE)

85   **53**

10-y-o b/br g Glacial Storm (USA)-Grin And Bear It (Deep
Run)
Mrs L B Normile Mrs L Maben

Placings:F3RP0/P0/UPU-OO   (0255)
2002/03: 22⁰G, 24⁰GF,

	Starts	1st	2nd	3rd	Win & Pl
Hurdles	2	0	0	0	
Career Total	12	0	0	1	404

Going: Sf: 0-0 GS: 0-0 Gd: 0-1 GF: - Fm: 0-1
Distance: 2m/2m3: 0-0 2m4-2m7: 0-1 3m+: 0-1
Track: LH: 0-1 RH: 0-1 Tight: 0-1 Gall: 0-0
Aids: Bl: 0-0 Vi: 0-0 Tstrap: 0-0

Best Rating: 78   12/98   Wwck 3m2f   gd-sft   Ch

Majlis (IRE)
105   104

6-y-o b g Caerleon (USA)-Ploy (Posse (USA))
T R George   Terry Warner

Placings:623P/2041110P-F0600P   (4571)
2002/03: 16^{F}G, 16^{9}HY, 17^{8}HY, 16^{9}G, 16^{9}G, 16^{P}GF,

	Starts	1st	2nd	3rd	Win & Pl
Hurdles	5	0	0	0	396
Chases	1	0	0	0	0
Career Total	18	3	2	1	35026
128 1/02	Kemp	2m		B(0-145)HHdl	G-S £23200
122 1/02	Winc	2m		E Hdl	GD £2940
120 12/01	Tntn	2m1f		E(0-115)HHdl	G-S £3948

Total win prize-money £30089

Going: Sf: 0-2 GS: 0-0 Gd: 0-3 GF: - Fm: 0-1
Distance: 2m/2m3: 0-6 2m4-2m7: 0-0 3m+: 0-0
Track: LH: 0-4 RH: 0-2 Tight: 0-1 Gall: 0-2
Aids: Bl: 0-6 Vi: 0-0 Tstrap: 0-0
Best Rating: 128   1/02   Kemp   2m   gd-sft   Hdl

Moderate handicap hurdler; acts on good and good to soft ground; effective over two miles; wears blinkers.

Major Adventure (IRE)
109(101h)   (96h)108

10-y-o b g Glacial Storm (USA)-Dual Adventure (Deep Run)
Ian Williams   Allan Stennett

Placings:1410/2PP/553U3U-1F425   (1321)
2002/03: 24^{1}GF, 25^{F}G, 25^{4}GF, 25^{2}GF, 24^{5}GF,

	Starts	1st	2nd	3rd	Win & Pl
Hurdles	1	0	0	0	0
Chases	4	1	1	0	6401
Career Total	18	3	2	2	23932
108 5/02	Ludl	3m		E(0-105)HCh	G-F £4836
116 2/00	Uttx	2m6f110y	C(0-135)HHdl	SFT £12866
107 11/99	Worc	2m4f		E Hdl	G-S £2687

Total win prize-money £20391

Going: Sf: 0-0 GS: 0-0 Gd: 0-1 GF: - Fm: 1-4
Distance: 2m/2m3: 0-0 2m4-2m7: 0-0 3m+: 1-5
Track: LH: 0-4 RH: 1-5 Tight: 1-3 Gall: 0-0
Aids: Bl: 0-0 Vi: 0-0 Tstrap: 0-0
Best Rating: 116   2/00   Uttx   2m6f110y   soft   Hdl

An Irish point-to-point winner, he was a useful hurdler but he has yet to reach that level of form over fences. Effective in soft ground. Stays three miles.

Major Benefit (IRE)

6-y-o b g Executive Perk-Merendas Sister (Pauper)
Mrs P Grainger   Nick Shutts

Placings:3   (3446)
2002/03: 26^{3}HY,

	Starts	1st	2nd	3rd	Win & Pl
Chases	1	0	0	1	223
Career Total	1	0	0	1	223

Going: Sf: 0-1 GS: 0-0 Gd: 0-0 GF: - Fm: 0-0
Distance: 2m/2m3: 0-0 2m4-2m7: 0-0 3m+: 0-1
Track: LH: 0-1 RH: 0-0 Tight: 0-0 Gall: 0-0
Aids: Bl: 0-0 Vi: 0-0 Tstrap: 0-0
Best Rating: 0   3/03   Leic   2m4f110y   gd-sft   Ch

Major Bit
92(77h)   (79h)68

7-y-o b g Henbit (USA)-Cute Pam (Pamroy)
S A Brookshaw   Steven Brookshaw Racing Partnership I

Placings:00/206PP05-0P3   (1196)
2002/03: 24^{0}GF, 26^{P}G, 25^{3}GF,

	Starts	1st	2nd	3rd	Win & Pl
Chases	3	0	0	1	612
Career Total	12	0	1	1	1112

Going: Sf: 0-0 GS: 0-0 Gd: 0-1 GF: - Fm: 0-2
Distance: 2m/2m3: 0-0 2m4-2m7: 0-3 3m+: 0-3
Track: LH: 0-1 RH: 0-2 Tight: 0-1 Gall: 0-0
Aids: Bl: 0-0 Vi: 0-0 Tstrap: 0-3
Best Rating: 81   10/01   Ludl   2m   gd-fm   NHF

Inconsistent character so far over jumps.

Major Blade (GER)
91   84

5-y-o b g Dashing Blade-Misniniski (Niniski (USA))
B G Powell   G Lloyd

Placings:P55   (4328)
2002/03: 16^{P}S, 16^{5}S, 16^{5}G,

	Starts	1st	2nd	3rd	Win & Pl
Hurdles	3	0	0	0	0
Career Total	3	0	0	0	0

Going: Sf: 0-2 GS: 0-0 Gd: 0-1 GF: - Fm: 0-0
Distance: 2m/2m3: 0-3 2m4-2m7: 0-0 3m+: 0-0
Track: LH: 0-1 RH: 0-1 Tight: 0-0 Gall: 0-1
Aids: Bl: 0-0 Vi: 0-0 Tstrap: 0-0
Best Rating: 84   3/03   Newb   2m110y   good   Hdl

Major Blue
97   90

8-y-o ch g Scallywag-Town Blues (Charlottown)
J G M O Shea   H G Llewellyn

Placings:34-0362P   (4606)
2002/03: 20^{0}S, 24^{3}HY, 26^{6}G, 26^{2}GF, 24^{P}G,

	Starts	1st	2nd	3rd	Win & Pl
Hurdles	5	0	1	1	1889
Career Total	7	0	1	2	2135

Going: Sf: 0-2 GS: 0-0 Gd: 0-2 GF: - Fm: 0-1
Distance: 2m/2m3: 0-0 2m4-2m7: 0-1 3m+: 0-4
Track: LH: 0-3 RH: 0-2 Tight: 0-0 Gall: 0-1
Aids: Bl: 0-0 Vi: 0-0 Tstrap: 0-0
Best Rating: 97   10/01   Bang   2m1f   soft   NHF

Signs of ability in bumpers; improved form when encountering fast ground over hurdles; stays three miles.

Major Drive (IRE)
107   111+

5-y-o b g Sadler s Wells (USA)-Puck s Castle (Shirley Heights)
J Howard Johnson   Dick Thackeray

Placings:0650-21001   (3578)
2002/03: 17^{2}GF, 20^{1}GF, 20^{0}G, 19^{0}GS, 24^{1}G,

	Starts	1st	2nd	3rd	Win & Pl
Hurdles	5	2	1	0	8479
Career Total	9	2	1	0	8479
111 2/03	Muss	3m		D(0-110)HHdl	GD £4715

95   10/02   Hexm   2m4f110yE Hdl   G-F £2915

Total win prize-money £7632

Going: Sf: 0-0 GS: 0-1 Gd: 1-2 GF: - Fm: 1-2
Distance: 2m/2m3: 0-1 2m4-2m7: 1-3 3m+: 1-1
Track: LH: 1-4 RH: 1-1 Tight: 1-3 Gall: 0-0
Aids: Bl: 0-0 Vi: 0-0 Tstrap: 0-0
Best Rating: 111   2/03   Muss   3m   good   Hdl

Modest hurdler; stays three miles and acts on ground good or faster.

Major Euro (IRE)
95   95

6-y-o b g Lord Americo-Gold Bank (Over The River (FR))
S J Gilmore   Miss Jumbo Frost

Placings:00   (4444)
2002/03: 16^{9}G, 16^{9}G,

	Starts	1st	2nd	3rd	Win & Pl
NH Flat	2	0	0	0	
Career Total	2	0	0	0	

Going: Sf: 0-0 GS: 0-0 Gd: 0-2 GF: - Fm: 0-0
Distance: 2m/2m3: 0-2 2m4-2m7: 0-0 3m+: 0-0
Track: LH: 0-1 RH: 0-1 Tight: 0-0 Gall: 0-0
Aids: Bl: 0-0 Vi: 0-0 Tstrap: 0-0
Best Rating: 96   3/03   Wwck   2m   good   NHF

Won his last four Irish points; runner-up in 2m 4f events in 2003; acts on fast ground.

Major Option (IRE)
96f   107f

7-y-o b g Doubletour (USA)-Dainty Dancer (Prince Tenderfoot (USA))
M C Pipe   David L Estrange

Placings:2/10   (0907)
2002/03: 18^{1}GF, 16^{0}G,

	Starts	1st	2nd	3rd	Win & Pl
NH Flat	2	1	0	0	1750
Career Total	3	1	1	0	2524
105 5/02	Font	2m2f110yH NHF			G-F £1750

Total win prize-money £1750

Going: Sf: 0-0 GS: 0-0 Gd: 0-1 GF: - Fm: 1-1
Distance: 2m/2m3: 0-2 2m4-2m7: 0-0 3m+: 0-0
Track: LH: 1-2 RH: 0-0 Tight: 1-1 Gall: 0-0
Aids: Bl: 0-0 Vi: 0-0 Tstrap: 0-0
Best Rating: 107   4/01   Slig   2m   heavy   NHF

Ex-Irish, won a bumper at Fontwell on debut for Martin Pipe. Seems to handle any ground.

Major Shark (FR)
97   91

5-y-o b g Saint Preuil (FR)-Cindy Cad (FR) (Cadoudal (FR))
L A Dace   Luke Dace

Placings:035051P   (4083)
2002/03: 18^{0}S, 17^{3}S, 20^{5}S, 20^{0}HY, 22^{5}GS, 20^{1}S, 25^{P}HY,

	Starts	1st	2nd	3rd	Win & Pl
NH Flat	2	0	0	1	277
Hurdles	5	1	0	0	2695
Career Total	7	1	0	1	2972
91 3/03	Font	2m4f		F(0-90)HHdl	SFT £2695

Total win prize-money £2695

Going: Sf: 1-6 GS: 0-1 Gd: 0-0 GF: - Fm: 0-0
Distance: 2m/2m3: 0-2 2m4-2m7: 1-4 3m+: 0-1
Track: LH: 0-3 RH: 0-2 Tight: 1-4 Gall: 0-0

Aids: Bl: 0-0 Vi: 0-0 Tstrap: 0-0
Best Rating: 91 3/03 Font 2m4f   soft   Hdl

Plating-class hurdler; best at two and a half miles; acts on soft ground; has worn cheekpieces.

Major Sharpe (IRE)
104(98h)   (102h)105+

11-y-o b g Phardante (FR)-Winsome Doe (Buckskin (FR))
B J M Ryall B J M Ryall

Placings:2/32/F/2PPPP3-41F   (0652)
2002/03: 25³G, 254G, 251G, 26FGF,

	Starts	1st	2nd	3rd	Win & Pl
Hurdles	1	0	0	1	365
Chases	3	1	0	0	4235
Career Total	13	1	3	2	8236
105 6/02 Hrfd		3m1f110yD(0-115)HCh		GD	£3932

Total win prize-money £3933

Going: Sf: 0-0 GS: 0-0 Gd: 1-3 GF: - Fm: 0-1
Distance: 2m/2m3: 0-0 2m4-2m7: 0-0 3m+: 1-4
Track: LH: 0-1 RH: 1-2 Tight: 0-1 Gall: 0-0
Aids: Bl: 0-0 Vi: 0-0 Tstrap: 0-0
Best Rating: 109 10/98 Winc 3m1f110y gd-sft Ch

A maiden over jumps until making all in a handicap chase in June 2002. Stays three miles plus, effective on good ground.

Major Sponsor (IRE)
131

11-y-o b g Strong Gale-Hue N Cry (IRE) (Denel (FR))
G M Moore S P Graham Ltd

Placings:0/0356113/121123/32132355/1122P/4F3440-P
                    (0165)
2002/03: 16PGF,

	Starts	1st	2nd	3rd	Win & Pl
Chases	1	0	0	0	
Career Total	34	8	6	7	48919
142 8/00 Sedg	2m5f	D(0-125)HCh	GD	£4212
142 7/00 Sedg	2m110y	E(0-115)HCh	G-F	£3432
117 11/99 Newc	2m110y	D Ch	GD	£4143
138 1/99 Newc	2m	B Hdl	SFT	£7555
131 1/99 Catt	2m3f	E Hdl	GD	£2500
121 10/98 Sthl	2m	E Hdl	GD	£2290
130 3/98 Dpat	2m1f172y	NHF	YLD	£2978
116 3/98 DRoy	2m	NHF	GD	£1489

Total win prize-money £28599

Going: Sf: 0-0 GS: 0-0 Gd: 0-0 GF: - Fm: 0-1
Distance: 2m/2m3: 0-1 2m4-2m7: 0-0 3m+: 0-0
Track: LH: 0-1 RH: 0-0 Tight: 0-0 Gall: 0-0
Aids: Bl: 0-0 Vi: 0-0 Tstrap: 0-0
Best Rating: 142 8/00 Sedg 2m5f   good   Ch

A free-running individual, who was a decent hurdler, he has not quite lived up to expectations over fences. He is best on good or fast ground, although he has won on softer and is probably best around two and a half miles has something to prove these days.

Majority Verdict
106   112

7-y-o b g Leading Counsel (USA)-Culm Valley (Port Corsair)
H D Daly Gibson, Goddard, Hamer & Hawkes

Placings:21/2-2   (4176)
2002/03: 16²S,

	Starts	1st	2nd	3rd	Win & Pl
Hurdles	1	0	1	0	1578
Career Total	4	1	3	0	6565

---

124 3/01 Strf   2m110y H NHF   SFT   £3241
Total win prize-money £3241

Going: Sf: 0-1 GS: 0-0 Gd: 0-0 GF: - Fm: 0-0
Distance: 2m/2m3: 0-1 2m4-2m7: 0-0 3m+: 0-0
Track: LH: 0-1 RH: 0-0 Tight: 0-0 Gall: 0-0
Aids: Bl: 0-0 Vi: 0-0 Tstrap: 0-0
Best Rating: 124 3/01 Strf   2m110y   soft   NHF

Bumper winner; lightly raced; runner-up in novice hurdles; convincing winner at Uttoxeter in May; stays well; effective in soft ground.

Make Haste Slowly
95   101

6-y-o b g Terimon-Henry s True Love (Random Shot)
H D Daly T F F Nixon

Placings:2   (1928)
2002/03: 16²GS,

	Starts	1st	2nd	3rd	Win & Pl
Hurdles	1	0	1	0	1448
Career Total	1	0	1	0	1448

Going: Sf: 0-0 GS: 0-1 Gd: 0-0 GF: - Fm: 0-0
Distance: 2m/2m3: 0-1 2m4-2m7: 0-0 3m+: 0-0
Track: LH: 0-0 RH: 0-1 Tight: 0-0 Gall: 0-0
Aids: Bl: 0-0 Vi: 0-0 Tstrap: 0-0
Best Rating: 101 11/02 Ludl 2m   gd-sft Hdl

Runner-up in an easy ground novice hurdle on debut.

Makhpiya Patahn (IRE)

11-y-o r g Nestor-Our Mare Mick (Choral Society)
J H Young J H Young

Placings:0P0/55/4425P5/4-0F   (0311)
2002/03: 33QGF, 26FG,

	Starts	1st	2nd	3rd	Win & Pl
Chases	2	0	0	0	
Career Total	14	0	1	0	2739

Going: Sf: 0-0 GS: 0-0 Gd: 0-0 GF: - Fm: 0-1
Distance: 2m/2m3: 0-0 2m4-2m7: 0-0 3m+: 0-0
Track: LH: 0-1 RH: 0-1 Tight: 0-1 Gall: 0-1
Aids: Bl: 0-0 Vi: 0-0 Tstrap: 0-0
Best Rating: 88 11/99 Winc 3m1f110y good Ch

Makin' Doo (IRE)

13-y-o ch g Black Minstrel-Ariannrun (Deep Run)
Mrs V J Makin R G Makin

Placings:0P50/33P4/5P44/0P53P-P   (0208)
2002/03: 22PG,

	Starts	1st	2nd	3rd	Win & Pl
Chases	1	0	0	0	
Career Total	18	0	0	3	1849

Going: Sf: 0-0 GS: 0-0 Gd: 0-1 GF: - Fm: 0-0
Distance: 2m/2m3: 0-0 2m4-2m7: 0-1 3m+: 0-0
Track: LH: 0-0 RH: 0-1 Tight: 0-0 Gall: 0-0
Aids: Bl: 0-0 Vi: 0-0 Tstrap: 0-0
Best Rating: 89 3/01 MRas 3m1f   gd-sft Ch

Malaga Boy (IRE)
95f   90f

6-y-o b g Nordic Brave-Ardglass Mist (Black Minstrel)
C Tizzard Alvin Trowbridge

Placings:362   (3630)
2002/03: 173GF, 176S, 16²S,

	Starts	1st	2nd	3rd	Win & Pl
NH Flat	3	0	1	1	1019
Career Total	3	0	1	1	1019

Going: Sf: 0-2 GS: 0-0 Gd: 0-0 GF: - Fm: 0-1
Distance: 2m/2m3: 0-3 2m4-2m7: 0-0 3m+: 0-0
Track: LH: 0-1 RH: 0-1 Tight: 0-1 Gall: 0-0
Aids: Bl: 0-0 Vi: 0-0 Tstrap: 0-0
Best Rating: 90 2/03 Asct 2m110y soft NHF

A half-brother to a winning pointer. Made a satisfactory debut when third in a Newton Abbot bumper and finished runner-up at Ascot in February.

Malakal (IRE)
104   90+

7-y-o b g Shernazar-Malmada (USA) (Fappiano (USA))
B J Curley Mrs B J Curley

Placings:PP/64PP-12   (1380)
2002/03: 171GF, 17²GF,

	Starts	1st	2nd	3rd	Win & Pl
Hurdles	2	1	1	0	4343
Career Total	8	1	1	0	4343
90 9/02 MRas	2m1f110y		E(0-100)HHdl	

G-F £3475
Total win prize-money £3476

Going: Sf: 0-0 GS: 0-0 Gd: 0-0 GF: - Fm: 1-2
Distance: 2m/2m3: 1-2 2m4-2m7: 0-0 3m+: 0-0
Track: LH: 0-0 RH: 1-2 Tight: 1-1 Gall: 0-0
Aids: Bl: 0-0 Vi: 0-0 Tstrap: 0-0
Best Rating: 90 10/02 Hrfd 2m1f   gd-fm Hdl

Showed vastly improved form when impressive winner of 17 furlong handicap at Market Rasen September 2002. Disappointing at Hereford five days later when the race may have come too soon.

Malakand (IRE)
97   83

5-y-o b g Dolphin Street (FR)-Malmada (USA) (Fappiano (USA))
D Carroll L Ibbotson

Placings:00-26P   (2514)
2002/03: 23²HY, 246GS, 20PS,

	Starts	1st	2nd	3rd	Win & Pl
Hurdles	3	0	1	0	633
Career Total	5	0	1	0	633

Going: Sf: 0-2 GS: 0-1 Gd: 0-0 GF: - Fm: 0-0
Distance: 2m/2m3: 0-0 2m4-2m7: 0-3 3m+: 0-1
Track: LH: 0-3 RH: 0-0 Tight: 0-0 Gall: 0-2
Aids: Bl: 0-0 Vi: 0-0 Tstrap: 0-0
Best Rating: 83 11/02 Weth 2m7f   heavy Hdl

Malandra
87f   52f

4-y-o b f Mtoto-Nibabu (FR) (Nishapour (FR))
G L Moore Leydens Farm Stud

Placings:0 (3323)
2002/03: 16⁰GS,

	Starts	1st	2nd	3rd	Win & Pl
NH Flat	1	0	0	0	
Career Total	1	0	0	0	

Going: Sf: 0-0 GS: 0-1 Gd: 0-0 GF: - Fm: 0-0
Distance: 2m/2m3: 0-1 2m4-2m7: 0-0 3m+: 0-0
Track: LH: 0-0 RH: 0-1 Tight: 0-0 Gall: 0-0
Aids: Bl: 0-0 Vi: 0-0 Tstrap: 0-0
Best Rating: 51 1/03 Kemp 2m   gd-sft NHF

Malarkey
96   87

6-y-o b g Mukaddamah (USA)-Malwiya (USA) (Shahrastani (USA))
P R Hedger Jay Dee Bloodstock Limited

Placings:0435-45006 (2058)
2002/03: 16⁴GS, 20⁵S, 17⁹GF, 20⁹GS, 16⁶G,

	Starts	1st	2nd	3rd	Win & Pl
Hurdles	5	0	0	0	
Career Total	9	0	0	1	384

Going: Sf: 0-1 GS: 0-1 Gd: 0-1 GF: - Fm: 0-2
Distance: 2m/2m3: 0-3 2m4-2m7: 0-2 3m+: 0-0
Track: LH: 0-3 RH: 0-2 Tight: 0-2 Gall: 0-0
Aids: Bl: 0-0 Vi: 0-0 Tstrap: 0-0
Best Rating: 99 3/02 Newb 2m110y gd-sft Hdl

Moderate novice hurdler, but a winner on the Flat.

Malbec (IRE)

6-y-o b g Lord Americo-Key Door (IRE) (Beau Charmeur (FR))
Miss A M Newton-Smith Julian Smith

Placings:P-P4P (1931)
2002/03: 26⁹G, 21⁴S, 24⁹GS,

	Starts	1st	2nd	3rd	Win & Pl
Hurdles	3	0	0	0	0
Career Total	4	0	0	0	0

Going: Sf: 0-1 GS: 0-1 Gd: 0-1 GF: - Fm: 0-0
Distance: 2m/2m3: 0-0 2m4-2m7: 0-0 3m+: 0-2
Track: LH: 0-2 RH: 0-1 Tight: 0-2 Gall: 0-0
Aids: Bl: 0-1 Vi: 0-0 Tstrap: 0-0
Best Rating: 0 11/02 Tntn 3m110y gd-sft Hdl

Malek (IRE)
105(106c)   (110c)118

7-y-o b g Tremblant-Any Offers (Paddy s Stream)
Mrs M Reveley Mrs J W Furness & Lord Zetland

Placings:3U1-15 (3520)
2002/03: 20¹S, 20⁵GS,

	Starts	1st	2nd	3rd	Win & Pl
Hurdles	2	1	0	0	4370
Career Total	5	2	0	1	7778
118 11/02 Hayd 2m4f	D Hdl			SFT	£3835
100 3/02 Sthl 3m110y	E Ch			HVY	£3159
				Total win prize-money	£6994

Going: Sf: 1-1 GS: 0-1 Gd: 0-0 GF: - Fm: 0-0
Distance: 2m/2m3: 0-0 2m4-2m7: 1-2 3m+: 0-0
Track: LH: 1-2 RH: 0-0 Tight: 0-0 Gall: 0-0
Aids: Bl: 0-0 Vi: 0-0 Tstrap: 0-0

Best Rating: 118 11/02 Hayd 2m4f   soft Hdl

Winning hurdler/chaser; effective in soft ground; stays three miles.

Mallory
101   104

9-y-o b g North Col-Veritate (Roman Warrior)
M J Wilkinson D J Price

Placings:120/0P/4P32-P (0173)
2002/03: 24⁰G,

	Starts	1st	2nd	3rd	Win & Pl
Hurdles	1	0	0	0	
Career Total	10	1	2	1	3244
115 12/99 Hntg 2m110y H NHF				GD	£1800
				Total win prize-money	£1800

Going: Sf: 0-0 GS: 0-0 Gd: 0-1 GF: - Fm: 0-0
Distance: 2m/2m3: 0-0 2m4-2m7: 0-0 3m+: 0-1
Track: LH: 0-1 RH: 0-0 Tight: 0-1 Gall: 0-0
Aids: Bl: 0-0 Vi: 0-0 Tstrap: 0-0
Best Rating: 115 2/00 Folk 2m1f110y soft NHF

Plating-class hurdler; Huntingdon bumper winner December 1999; lightly raced until winning two novice handicap hurdles in spring 2003; just failed to make it a hat-trick of stone higher mark; stays 2m 6f; handles fast ground, but probably best on soft.

Mamboesque (USA)
106   85

5-y-o b g Miesque s Son (USA)-Brawl (USA) (Fit To Fight (USA))
J Mackie (W Clay 13/12) F E And Mrs J J Brindley

Placings:333-003300016 (4119)
2002/03: 16⁹GF, 20⁹GS, 16³G, 19³GF, 16⁰HY, 16⁰S, 16⁹G, 19¹S, 16⁶G,

	Starts	1st	2nd	3rd	Win & Pl
Hurdles	9	1	0	2	3440
Career Total	12	1	0	5	5405
85 3/03 Catt 2m3f	F(0-100)HHdl			SFT	£2681
				Total win prize-money	£2681

Going: Sf: 1-3 GS: 0-1 Gd: 0-3 GF: - Fm: 0-2
Distance: 2m/2m3: 1-7 2m4-2m7: 0-2 3m+: 0-0
Track: LH: 1-7 RH: 0-2 Tight: 1-2 Gall: 0-2
Aids: Bl: 1-2 Vi: 0-4 Tstrap: 0-0
Best Rating: 85 3/03 Catt 2m3f   soft Hdl

Plating-class hurdler; improved effort when finally getting off the mark at Catterick in March.

Mamideos (IRE)
109   105+

6-y-o br g Good Thyne (USA)-Heavenly Artist (IRE) (Heavenly Manna)
T R George Silkword Racing Partnership

Placings:41-103 (3845)
2002/03: 24¹GF, 20⁰HY, 21³G,

	Starts	1st	2nd	3rd	Win & Pl
Hurdles	3	1	0	1	5012
Career Total	5	2	0	1	6653
99 10/02 MRas 3m	D Hdl			G-F	£4143
110 3/02 Chep 2m110y H NHF				SFT	£1640
				Total win prize-money	£5785

Going: Sf: 0-1 GS: 0-0 Gd: 0-1 GF: - Fm: 1-1
Distance: 2m/2m3: 0-0 2m4-2m7: 0-2 3m+: 1-1
Track: LH: 0-0 RH: 1-3 Tight: 1-1 Gall: 0-0
Aids: Bl: 0-0 Vi: 0-0 Tstrap: 0-0

Best Rating: 110 3/02 Chep 2m110y soft NHF

Modest novice hurdler; bumper winner on soft ground; made a winning hurdling debut over three miles on fast ground.

Mamma's Boy
45

8-y-o b g Rock City-Henpot (IRE) (Alzao (USA))
A Berry Mrs J M Berry

Placings:0 (1076)
2002/03: 17⁹G,

	Starts	1st	2nd	3rd	Win & Pl
Hurdles	1	0	0	0	
Career Total	1	0	0	0	

Going: Sf: 0-0 GS: 0-0 Gd: 0-1 GF: - Fm: 0-0
Distance: 2m/2m3: 0-1 2m4-2m7: 0-0 3m+: 0-0
Track: LH: 0-1 RH: 0-0 Tight: 0-1 Gall: 0-0
Aids: Bl: 0-0 Vi: 0-0 Tstrap: 0-0
Best Rating: 0 8/02 Ctml 2m1f110y good Hdl

Man At The Top

7-y-o b g Northern Park (USA)-Kotsina (Top Ville)
R Wilman Mrs J Conway

Placings:P (0400)
2002/03: 20⁰GF,

	Starts	1st	2nd	3rd	Win & Pl
Hurdles	1	0	0	0	
Career Total	1	0	0	0	

Going: Sf: 0-0 GS: 0-0 Gd: 0-0 GF: - Fm: 0-1
Distance: 2m/2m3: 0-0 2m4-2m7: 0-1 3m+: 0-0
Track: LH: 0-1 RH: 0-0 Tight: 0-0 Gall: 0-0
Aids: Bl: 0-0 Vi: 0-0 Tstrap: 0-0
Best Rating: 0 6/02 Hexm 2m4f110y gd-fm Hdl

Man From Delcarrow (IRE)

6-y-o b g Zaffaran (USA)-Delcarrow (Roi Guillaume (FR))
O Sherwood Ledwidge Best Fforde

Placings:60 (4628)
2002/03: 16⁶GS, 17⁰GF,

	Starts	1st	2nd	3rd	Win & Pl
NH Flat	2	0	0	0	0
Career Total	2	0	0	0	0

Going: Sf: 0-0 GS: 0-1 Gd: 0-0 GF: - Fm: 0-1
Distance: 2m/2m3: 0-2 2m4-2m7: 0-0 3m+: 0-0
Track: LH: 0-2 RH: 0-0 Tight: 0-1 Gall: 0-1
Aids: Bl: 0-0 Vi: 0-0 Tstrap: 0-0
Best Rating: 104 12/02 Donc 2m110y gd-sft NHF

Disappointing in two starts in bumpers; beaten a long way on hurdling bow.

Man From Havana (USA)
99   94

4-y-o b g Green Dancer (USA)-Charmie Carmie (USA) (Lyphard (USA))

S Dow (P F I Cole 20/5) G Brain

Placings:20U   (2341)
2002/03: 16²G, 16⁰G, 16ᵁS,

	Starts	1st	2nd	3rd	Win & Pl
Hurdles	3	0	1	0	1561
Career Total	3	0	1	0	1561

Going:	Sf: 0-1 GS: 0-0 Gd: 0-2 GF: - Fm: 0-0
Distance:	2m/2m3: 0-3 2m4-2m7: 0-0 3m+: 0-0
Track:	LH: 0-1 RH: 0-2 Tight: 0-1 Gall: 0-0
Aids:	Bl: 0-0 Vi: 0-0 Tstrap: 0-0
Best Rating:	94 9/02 Plum 2m good Hdl

Maiden handicapper on the Flat who shaped encouragingly in an early-season juvenile hurdle at Plumpton. held subsequently.

Man From Highworth
85f   78f

4-y-o b g Ballet Royal (USA)-Cavisoir (Afzal)
H J Manners   H J Manners

Placings:5   (4737)
2002/03: 16⁵GF,

	Starts	1st	2nd	3rd	Win & Pl
NH Flat	1	0	0	0	0
Career Total	1	0	0	0	0

Going:	Sf: 0-0 GS: 0-0 Gd: 0-0 GF: - Fm: 0-1
Distance:	2m/2m3: 0-1 2m4-2m7: 0-0 3m+: 0-0
Track:	LH: 0-1 RH: 0-0 Tight: 0-0 Gall: 0-0
Aids:	Bl: 0-0 Vi: 0-0 Tstrap: 0-0
Best Rating:	78 4/03 Chep 2m110y gd-fm NHF

Man Murphy (IRE)
103(110h)   (121h)137

7-y-o b g Euphemism-Been About (IRE) (Remainder Man)
Mrs M Reveley   W Manners

Placings:1/3311165P-1111413   (3988)
2002/03: 17¹S, 20¹S, 20¹GS, 20¹S, 22⁴GS, 20¹HY, 20³S,

	Starts	1st	2nd	3rd	Win & Pl
Chases	7	5	0	1	29108
Career Total	16	9	0	3	43258
106	2/03	Ayr	2m4f	C Ch	HVY	9685
135	12/02	Newc	2m4f	D Ch	SFT	£5018
137	11/02	Newc	2m4f	E Ch	G-S	£3692
108	11/02	Newc	2m4f	E Ch	SFT	£3770
98	11/02	Kels	2m1f	E Ch	SFT	£4368
121	1/02	Catt	2m3f	D Hdl	SFT	£3377
121	1/02	Catt	2m1f	D Hdl	HVY	£3526
102	11/01	Newc	2m	D Hdl	G-S	£3570
106	1/01	Catt	2m	H NHF	G-S	£1659

Total win prize-money £38666

Going:	Sf: 4-5 GS: 1-2 Gd: 0-0 GF: - Fm: 0-0
Distance:	2m/2m3: 1-1 2m4-2m7: 4-6 3m+: 0-0
Track:	LH: 5-6 RH: 0-1 Tight: 1-1 Gall: 3-3
Aids:	Bl: 0-0 Vi: 0-0 Tstrap: 0-0
Best Rating:	137 11/02 Newc 2m4f gd-sft Ch

Useful novice chaser, being unbeaten til finishing last of four at Haydock in a really good race. Acts well on a soft surface and is effective from two miles to two miles four.

Man O'Mystery (USA)
115   131

6-y-o b g Diesis-Eurostorm (USA) (Storm Bird (CAN))

P R Webber (J Noseda 23/11) Ecurie Pharos

Placings:212   (4470)
2002/03: 17²S, 17¹GS, 16²G,

	Starts	1st	2nd	3rd	Win & Pl
Hurdles	3	1	2	0	16096
Career Total	3	1	2	0	16096
120	3/03	MRas	2m1f110y		E Hdl	G-S	£3486

Total win prize-money £3486

Going:	Sf: 0-0 GS: 1-1 Gd: 0-1 GF: - Fm: 0-0
Distance:	2m/2m3: 1-3 2m4-2m7: 0-0 3m+: 0-0
Track:	LH: 0-1 RH: 1-2 Tight: 1-3 Gall: 0-0
Aids:	Bl: 0-0 Vi: 0-0 Tstrap: 0-0
Best Rating:	131 4/03 Aint 2m110y good Hdl

Decent novice hurdler; useful on the Flat; cheeky winner on second start at Market Rasen in March 2003; runner-up in Grade Two at Aintree; probably best on good ground.

Mana-Mou Bay (IRE)
102   108

6-y-o b g Ela-Mana-Mou-Summerhill (Habitat)
B Ellison (D Nicholls 2/8) R Wagner

Placings:40051   (4793)
2002/03: 16⁴GF, 16⁰G, 16⁰GF, 17⁵G, 17¹GF,

	Starts	1st	2nd	3rd	Win & Pl
Hurdles	5	1	0	0	3783
Career Total	5	1	0	0	3783
108	4/03	Sedg	2m1f		E Hdl	G-F	£3451

Total win prize-money £3452

Going:	Sf: 0-0 GS: 0-0 Gd: 0-2 GF: - Fm: 1-3
Distance:	2m/2m3: 1-5 2m4-2m7: 0-0 3m+: 0-0
Track:	LH: 1-3 RH: 0-2 Tight: 1-3 Gall: 0-0
Aids:	Bl: 0-0 Vi: 0-0 Tstrap: 0-0
Best Rating:	108 4/03 Sedg 2m1f gd-fm Hdl

Moderate hurdler; effective at two miles; suited by a sound surface; has worn cheekpieces, but left off for only win.

Manawanui
82   65

5-y-o b g Karinga Bay-Kiwi Velocity (NZ) (Veloso (NZ))
R H Alner   J M Dare, T Hamlin, J W Snook

Placings:600   (3780)
2002/03: 16⁶NH, 19⁰GS, 22⁰GS,

	Starts	1st	2nd	3rd	Win & Pl
NH Flat	1	0	0	0	0
Hurdles	2	0	0	0	0
Career Total	3	0	0	0	0

Going:	Sf: 0-1 GS: 0-2 Gd: 0-0 GF: - Fm: 0-0
Distance:	2m/2m3: 0-2 2m4-2m7: 0-1 3m+: 0-0
Track:	LH: 0-1 RH: 0-2 Tight: 0-0 Gall: 0-0
Aids:	Bl: 0-0 Vi: 0-0 Tstrap: 0-0
Best Rating:	95 11/02 Chep 2m110y heavy NHF

Manbow (IRE)
30f   57f

5-y-o ch g Mandalus-Treble Base (IRE) (Orchestra)
M D Hammond   Hope Springs Eternal

Placings:0   (4397)
2002/03: 17⁰G,

	Starts	1st	2nd	3rd	Win & Pl
NH Flat	1	0	0	0	
Career Total	1	0	0	0	

Going:	Sf: 0-0 GS: 0-0 Gd: 0-1 GF: - Fm: 0-0
Distance:	2m/2m3: 0-1 2m4-2m7: 0-0 3m+: 0-0
Track:	LH: 0-0 RH: 0-0 Tight: 0-0 Gall: 0-0
Aids:	Bl: 0-0 Vi: 0-0 Tstrap: 0-0
Best Rating:	57 3/03 Carl 2m1f good NHF

Looked somewhat temperamental when beaten long way on first outing in bumper at Carlisle in March.

Manchester (IRE)
89   75d

4-y-o b g Danehill Dancer (IRE)-Lils Fairy (Fairy King (USA))
Miss A M Newton-Smith (Michael Croke 1/2) Julian Smith

Placings:P0PP   (4631)
2002/03: 16ᴾS, 16⁰S, 16ᴾG, 16ᴾGF,

	Starts	1st	2nd	3rd	Win & Pl
Hurdles	4	0	0	0	
Career Total	4	0	0	0	

Going:	Sf: 0-2 GS: 0-0 Gd: 0-1 GF: - Fm: 0-1
Distance:	2m/2m3: 0-4 2m4-2m7: 0-0 3m+: 0-0
Track:	LH: 0-2 RH: 0-1 Tight: 0-1 Gall: 0-1
Aids:	Bl: 0-0 Vi: 0-0 Tstrap: 0-0
Best Rating:	75 2/03 Punc 2m soft Hdl

Ex-Irish; placed on the Flat, but poor form over hurdles so far in this country.

Mandalias Boy

7-y-o b g Henbit (USA)-Mandalia (Mansingh (USA))
Mrs L Williamson   F E Phillips

Placings:PP   (4316)
2002/03: 17ᴾGS, 17ᴾG,

	Starts	1st	2nd	3rd	Win & Pl
Hurdles	2	0	0	0	
Career Total	2	0	0	0	

Going:	Sf: 0-0 GS: 0-1 Gd: 0-1 GF: - Fm: 0-0
Distance:	2m/2m3: 0-2 2m4-2m7: 0-0 3m+: 0-0
Track:	LH: 0-2 RH: 0-0 Tight: 0-2 Gall: 0-0
Aids:	Bl: 0-0 Vi: 0-0 Tstrap: 0-0
Best Rating:	0 3/03 Bang 2m1f good Hdl

Mandate Man (IRE)

9-y-o b g Mandalus-Atalaya Park (King Of Spain)
Miss J B W Monteith   David Johnson

Placings:050050/5/4-   (0005)
2002/03: 20⁴G,

	Starts	1st	2nd	3rd	Win & Pl
Chases	1	0	0	0	127
Career Total	8	0	0	0	127

Going:	Sf: 0-0 GS: 0-0 Gd: 0-1 GF: - Fm: 0-0
Distance:	2m/2m3: 0-0 2m4-2m7: 0-1 3m+: 0-0
Track:	LH: 0-1 RH: 0-0 Tight: 0-0 Gall: 0-1
Aids:	Bl: 0-0 Vi: 0-0 Tstrap: 0-0
Best Rating:	90 1/01 DRoy 3m gd-yld Ch

Mandoob
105

6-y-o b g Zafonic (USA)-Thaidah (CAN) (Vice Regent (CAN))

B R Johnson Kevin Nolan

Placings:63-3   (1642)
2002/03: 16³G,

	Starts	1st	2nd	3rd	Win & Pl
Hurdles	1	0	0	1	1254
Career Total	3	0	0	2	1610

Going:	Sf: 0-0 GS: 0-0 Gd: 0-1 GF: - Fm: 0-0
Distance:	2m/2m3: 0-1 2m4-2m7: 0-0 3m+: 0-0
Track:	LH: 0-0 RH: 0-1 Tight: 0-0 Gall: 0-0
Aids:	Bl: 0-0 Vi: 0-0 Tstrap: 0-1
Best Rating:	98 10/02 Kemp 2m good Hdl

A modest winner on the Flat, he has shown a little ability over hurdles. Handles soft ground.

Mandown
55   35
4-y-o b g Danehill Dancer (IRE)-Golden Decoy (Decoy Boy)
J S Moore Dead Loss Racing

Placings:0   (4001)
2002/03: 16⁰S,

	Starts	1st	2nd	3rd	Win & Pl
Hurdles	1	0	0	0	
Career Total	1	0	0	0	

Going:	Sf: 0-1 GS: 0-0 Gd: 0-0 GF: - Fm: 0-0
Distance:	2m/2m3: 0-1 2m4-2m7: 0-0 3m+: 0-0
Track:	LH: 0-0 RH: 0-1 Tight: 0-0 Gall: 0-0
Aids:	Bl: 0-0 Vi: 0-0 Tstrap: 0-0
Best Rating:	37 3/03 Winc 2m soft Hdl

Mandy Chat (IRE)
81(72h)   (55h)71
10-y-o m Mandalus-Double Talk (Dublin Taxi)
P T Dalton Mrs Julie Martin

Placings:50/P/P600P44PP2-P0P6052PU   (1502)
2002/03: 21PG, 17⁰GF, 16PGF, 16⁶GF, 17⁰G, 17⁵G, 17²G, 16PGF, 17UG,

	Starts	1st	2nd	3rd	Win & Pl
Chases	9	0	1	0	938
Career Total	22	0	2	0	1956

Going:	Sf: 0-0 GS: 0-0 Gd: 0-5 GF: - Fm: 0-4
Distance:	2m/2m3: 0-8 2m4-2m7: 0-1 3m+: 0-0
Track:	LH: 0-8 RH: 0-1 Tight: 0-3 Gall: 0-0
Aids:	Bl: 0-0 Vi: 0-0 Tstrap: 0-2
Best Rating:	85 5/99 Clon 2m soft NHF

Poor chaser who has made the frame in hunter chases and weak handicaps around two miles.

Mandy's Rose (IRE)
105(82h)   (67h)77
7-y-o b/br m Mandalus-Rookery Lady (IRE) (Callernish)
T R George Mr & Mrs D A Gamble

Placings:30P4F   (4418)
2002/03: 17³GG, 20⁰G, 20PHY, 174S, 22FG,

	Starts	1st	2nd	3rd	Win & Pl
NH Flat	1	0	0	1	290
Hurdles	4	0	0	0	264
Career Total	5	0	0	1	554

Going:	Sf: 0-2 GS: 0-0 Gd: 0-2 GF: - Fm: 0-1

Distance:	2m/2m3: 0-2 2m4-2m7: 0-3 3m+: 0-0
Track:	LH: 0-3 RH: 0-1 Tight: 0-2 Gall: 0-0
Aids:	Bl: 0-0 Vi: 0-0 Tstrap: 0-0
Best Rating:	76 10/02 MRas 2m1f110y gd-fm NHF

Dual point winner; modest novice hurdler off the mark at Huntingdon in May; well beaten on debut over regulation fences at Wetherby next time; suited by three miles plus.

Mane Frame
92   63
8-y-o b g Unfuwain (USA)-Moviegoer (Pharly (FR))
H Morrison Zycko Ltd

Placings:233/1PP-00P   (3874)
2002/03: 22⁰HY, 22⁰GS, 21PS,

	Starts	1st	2nd	3rd	Win & Pl
Hurdles	3	0	0	0	
Career Total	9	1	1	2	7644
110	3/02 Newb 2m5f		D(0-125)HHdl	G-S	£5720

Total win prize-money £5720

Going:	Sf: 0-2 GS: 0-1 Gd: 0-0 GF: - Fm: 0-0
Distance:	2m/2m3: 0-2 2m4-2m7: 0-3 3m+: 0-0
Track:	LH: 0-1 RH: 0-2 Tight: 0-0 Gall: 0-1
Aids:	Bl: 0-0 Vi: 0-0 Tstrap: 0-1
Best Rating:	113 2/01 Ludl 2m gd-sft Hdl

A useful stayer on the Flat. Fair form over hurdles so far, and a good winner on his handicap debut at Newbury in March 2002. Has struggled to complete since. Looks best suited by two and a half miles on soft ground.

Manful

11-y-o b g Efisio-Mandrian (Mandamus)
M J M Evans M J M Evans

Placings:32426/23440/P0   (3543)
2002/03: 20PHY, 17³G,

	Starts	1st	2nd	3rd	Win & Pl
Hurdles	2	0	0	0	
Career Total	12	0	3	2	2650

Going:	Sf: 0-1 GS: 0-0 Gd: 0-1 GF: - Fm: 0-0
Distance:	2m/2m3: 0-1 2m4-2m7: 0-1 3m+: 0-0
Track:	LH: 0-1 RH: 0-1 Tight: 0-0 Gall: 0-0
Aids:	Bl: 0-2 Vi: 0-0 Tstrap: 0-0
Best Rating:	108 1/98 Muss 2m gd-sft Hdl

Moderate hurdler, usually wears blinkers.

Mango Chutney

9-y-o b g Safawan-Malacanang (Riboboy (USA))
T Wall D B Roberts

Placings:P   (0217)
2002/03: 17PG,

	Starts	1st	2nd	3rd	Win & Pl
Hurdles	1	0	0	0	
Career Total	1	0	0	0	

Going:	Sf: 0-0 GS: 0-0 Gd: 0-1 GF: - Fm: 0-0
Distance:	2m/2m3: 0-1 2m4-2m7: 0-0 3m+: 0-0
Track:	LH: 0-0 RH: 0-1 Tight: 0-0 Gall: 0-0
Aids:	Bl: 0-0 Vi: 0-0 Tstrap: 0-0
Best Rating:	0 5/02 Hrfd 2m1f good Hdl

Manhattan Castle (IRE)

14-y-o br g Strong Gale-Allamanda (FR) (Versailles Ii)
Miss S E Cook Ms Barbara Ashby-Jones

Placings:543/1221311P3/1F41U44/01P13/2015135/44P23/3232/413506UPF/3U3PP-3P   (0414)
2002/03: 20³F, 28PGF,

	Starts	1st	2nd	3rd	Win & Pl
Chases	2	0	0	1	180
Career Total	56	11	6	12	113322
132	7/00	Strf	2m4f	D(0-125)HCh	G-F	£6987
110	2/98	Thur	2m4f	Ch	SFT	£11217
144	1/98	Naas	2m3f	HCh	HVY	£4765
146	4/97	Fair	2m4f	HCh	G-F	£9579
139	1/97	Leop	2m3f	HCh	G-Y	£5425
143	1/96	Leop	2m1f	Ch	SFT	£9974
128	11/95	Tipp	2m	Ch	GD	£5425
136	2/95	Leop	2m	HHdl	SH	£6782
122	1/95	Punc	2m4f	Hdl	HVY	£3730
129	12/94	Leop	2m2f	(0-120)HHdl	SFT	£6523
108	10/94	Tipp	2m	Hdl	SFT	£3261

Total win prize-money £73673

Going:	Sf: 0-0 GS: 0-0 Gd: 0-0 GF: - Fm: 0-2
Distance:	2m/2m3: 0-0 2m4-2m7: 0-1 3m+: 0-1
Track:	LH: 0-2 RH: 0-0 Tight: 0-1 Gall: 0-0
Aids:	Bl: 0-0 Vi: 0-0 Tstrap: 0-0
Best Rating:	146 4/97 Fair 2m4f gd-fm Ch

A smart chaser in his prime, he has deteriorated and tends to make mistakes nowadays.

Manhattan Rainbow (IRE)

12-y-o b g Mandalus-Clara Girl (Fine Blade (USA))
Mrs J M Hollands Mrs C J Kerr

Placings:0/P/3S23P32405/P1201/1PP0/P-244   (4508)
2002/03: 25²G, 254G, 254G,

	Starts	1st	2nd	3rd	Win & Pl
Chases	3	0	0	0	636
Career Total	25	3	4	3	11734
107	5/00	Kels	3m1f	H Ch	G-S	£1918
110	4/00	Kels	3m1f	H Ch	SFT	£2247
86	2/00	Kels	3m1f	H Ch	G-S	£2352

Total win prize-money £6517

Going:	Sf: 0-0 GS: 0-0 Gd: 0-3 GF: - Fm: 0-0
Distance:	2m/2m3: 0-0 2m4-2m7: 0-0 3m+: 0-3
Track:	LH: 0-3 RH: 0-0 Tight: 0-2 Gall: 0-0
Aids:	Bl: 0-0 Vi: 0-0 Tstrap: 0-0
Best Rating:	110 4/00 Kels 3m1f soft Ch

One time useful hunter chaser but a sad sight nowadays.

Maniatis
100   111
6-y-o b h Slip Anchor-Tamassos (Dance In Time (CAN))
M D Hammond (Mrs A J Perrett 26/10) Andy Peake

Placings:20   (3894)
2002/03: 16²GS, 18⁰GS,

	Starts	1st	2nd	3rd	Win & Pl
Hurdles	2	0	1	0	1605
Career Total	2	0	1	0	1605

Going:	Sf: 0-0 GS: 0-2 Gd: 0-0 GF: - Fm: 0-0
Distance:	2m/2m3: 0-2 2m4-2m7: 0-0 3m+: 0-0

Track: LH: 0-2 RH: 0-0 Tight: 0-1 Gall: 0-0
Aids: Bl: 0-0 Vi: 0-0 Tstrap: 0-0
Best Rating: 111 2/03 Hayd 2m   gd-sft Hdl

Formerly useful stayer on the Flat; has shown form over hurdles, but has looked like one to treat with caution; suited by two miles and acts on soft ground; suited by forcing tactics.

Manikato (USA)
91   70
9-y-o b g Clever Trick (USA)-Pasampsi (USA) (Crow (FR))
R Curtis Mrs K M Curtis

Placings:P/P5/6-0   (1231)
2002/03: 16⁰G,

	Starts	1st	2nd	3rd	Win & Pl
Hurdles	1	0	0	0	
Career Total	5	0	0	0	0

Going: Sf: 0-0 GS: 0-0 Gd: 0-1 GF: - Fm: 0-0
Distance: 2m/2m3: 0-1 2m4-2m7: 0-0 3m+: 0-0
Track: LH: 0-1 RH: 0-0 Tight: 0-0 Gall: 0-0
Aids: Bl: 0-0 Vi: 0-0 Tstrap: 0-0
Best Rating: 74 9/00 Worc 2m   gd-fm Hdl

Maninga
105   108
7-y-o ch m Karinga Bay-Amberush (No Rush)
Mrs L Richards The Maninga Partnership

Placings:5/04411P-500404   (3807)
2002/03: 22⁵S, 24⁰HY, 20⁰S, 21⁴S, 25⁰HY, 21⁴S,

	Starts	1st	2nd	3rd	Win & Pl
Hurdles	6	0	0	0	695
Career Total	13	2	0	0	8168
116 3/02	Towc	2m5f	E Hdl		SFT £3136
108 2/02	Winc	2m6f	D Hdl		SFT £3640

Total win prize-money £6776

Going: Sf: 0-6 GS: 0-0 Gd: 0-0 GF: - Fm: 0-0
Distance: 2m/2m3: 0-0 2m4-2m7: 0-4 3m+: 0-2
Track: LH: 0-5 RH: 0-1 Tight: 0-3 Gall: 0-0
Aids: Bl: 0-0 Vi: 0-0 Tstrap: 0-0
Best Rating: 116 3/02 Towc 2m5f   soft Hdl

A fair staying hurdler. Needs trips beyond two and a half miles and a stiff track.

Mankind
(107h)   (98h)
12-y-o b g Rakaposhi King-Mandarling (Mandalus)
J A T De Giles J A T De Giles

Placings:00/1/P6PP0/3P0230/10P/1-0R   (1593)
2002/03: 22⁰GF, 23⁰G,

	Starts	1st	2nd	3rd	Win & Pl
Hurdles	1	0	0	0	0
Chases	1	0	0	0	0
Career Total	20	3	1	2	7371
98 6/01	NAbb	2m6f	G(0-95)HHdl	G-F	£2415
98 5/99	Hrfd	2m3f110yG Hdl		GD	£1857
100 4/97	Strf	2m5f110yH Ch		GD	£2038

Total win prize-money £6311

Going: Sf: 0-0 GS: 0-0 Gd: 0-0 GF: - Fm: 0-1
Distance: 2m/2m3: 0-0 2m4-2m7: 0-1 3m+: 0-1
Track: LH: 0-1 RH: 0-1 Tight: 0-1 Gall: 0-0
Aids: Bl: 0-0 Vi: 0-0 Tstrap: 0-0
Best Rating: 100 4/97 Strf 2m5f110y good Ch

Manodee (IRE)
103   88
9-y-o b g Mandalus-Emmodee (Bowling Pin)
Miss Venetia Williams (A L T Moore 23/8) Frank Clarke

Placings:050/5/PP5/15FP0-P016F3   (2132)
2002/03: 20⁵S, 25⁰GF, 24¹GF, 23⁶G, 25⁵GF, 24³G,

	Starts	1st	2nd	3rd	Win & Pl
Chases	6	1	0	1	4446
Career Total	18	2	0	1	12237
88 9/02	Hntg	3m	E(0-110)HCh	G-F	£3604
88 5/01	Fair	2m4f	(0-109)HCh	GD	£7790

Total win prize-money £11394

Going: Sf: 0-1 GS: 0-0 Gd: 0-0 GF: - Fm: 1-3
Distance: 2m/2m3: 0-0 2m4-2m7: 0-1 3m+: 1-5
Track: LH: 0-0 RH: 1-5 Tight: 0-2 Gall: 1-1
Aids: Bl: 0-0 Vi: 0-0 Tstrap: 0-0
Best Rating: 88 11/02 Ludl 3m   good Ch

Handicap chaser, stays well and acts on a sound surface.

Manolito (IRE)
101   82
9-y-o b g Mandalus-Las-Cancellas (Monksfield)
B I Case (M J Wilkinson 17/8) Jeremy Hancock

Placings:0540/F236/0P/3P6F23F   (4636)
2002/03: 20³GS, 22⁸GF, 20⁶GF, 24⁶G, 24²G, 21³GS, 24⁶G,

	Starts	1st	2nd	3rd	Win & Pl
Chases	7	0	1	2	2299
Career Total	17	0	2	3	3681

Going: Sf: 0-0 GS: 0-2 Gd: 0-3 GF: - Fm: 0-2
Distance: 2m/2m3: 0-0 2m4-2m7: 0-4 3m+: 0-3
Track: LH: 0-6 RH: 0-1 Tight: 0-7 Gall: 0-0
Aids: Bl: 0-0 Vi: 0-0 Tstrap: 0-0
Best Rating: 94 11/99 Kemp 2m   gd-fm Hdl

Point winner; finally got off the mark under Rules when landing weak novice 2m 6f handicap chase at Market Rasen June 2003; acts on fast ground.

Manor Down (IRE)
5-y-o b g Moscow Society (USA)-Scalp Hunter (IRE) (Commanche Run)
P J Hobbs Colin W Poore

Placings:00P   (4311)
2002/03: 16⁰S, 16⁰S, 21ᴾG,

	Starts	1st	2nd	3rd	Win & Pl
NH Flat	2	0	0	0	0
Hurdles	1	0	0	0	0
Career Total	3	0	0	0	

Going: Sf: 0-1 GS: 0-1 Gd: 0-1 GF: - Fm: 0-0
Distance: 2m/2m3: 0-2 2m4-2m7: 0-1 3m+: 0-0
Track: LH: 0-1 RH: 0-2 Tight: 0-0 Gall: 0-1
Aids: Bl: 0-1 Vi: 0-0 Tstrap: 0-0
Best Rating: 36 3/03 Winc 2m   soft NHF

Manor From Heaven
5-y-o ch m Most Welcome-Manor Adventure (Smackover)
P T Dalton Mrs Julie Martin

Placings:PPP   (4320)
2002/03: 16ᴾGS, 16ᴾGS, 17ᴾG,

	Starts	1st	2nd	3rd	Win & Pl
Hurdles	3	0	0	0	
Career Total	3	0	0	0	

Going: Sf: 0-0 GS: 0-2 Gd: 0-1 GF: - Fm: 0-0
Distance: 2m/2m3: 0-3 2m4-2m7: 0-0 3m+: 0-0
Track: LH: 0-2 RH: 0-1 Tight: 0-0 Gall: 0-1
Aids: Bl: 0-0 Vi: 0-0 Tstrap: 0-0
Best Rating: 0 3/03 Bang 2m1f   good Hdl

Manor Star
79f   64f
4-y-o b f Weld-Call Coup (IRE) (Callernish)
B D Leavy Manor Racing Club

Placings:0   (3849)
2002/03: 16⁰G,

	Starts	1st	2nd	3rd	Win & Pl
NH Flat	1	0	0	0	
Career Total	1	0	0	0	

Going: Sf: 0-0 GS: 0-0 Gd: 0-1 GF: - Fm: 0-0
Distance: 2m/2m3: 0-1 2m4-2m7: 0-0 3m+: 0-0
Track: LH: 0-0 RH: 0-1 Tight: 0-0 Gall: 0-0
Aids: Bl: 0-0 Vi: 0-0 Tstrap: 0-0
Best Rating: 64 2/03 Ludl 2m   good NHF

Manoram (GER)
102   89
4-y-o ch g Zinaad-Mayada (USA) (The Minstrel (CAN))
Ian Williams Willsford Racing Incorporated

Placings:03   (4219)
2002/03: 16⁰GS, 17³GF,

	Starts	1st	2nd	3rd	Win & Pl
Hurdles	2	0	0	1	519
Career Total	2	0	0	1	519

Going: Sf: 0-0 GS: 0-1 Gd: 0-0 GF: - Fm: 0-1
Distance: 2m/2m3: 0-2 2m4-2m7: 0-0 3m+: 0-0
Track: LH: 0-0 RH: 0-2 Tight: 0-0 Gall: 0-0
Aids: Bl: 0-0 Vi: 0-0 Tstrap: 0-0
Best Rating: 69 3/03 Hrfd 2m1f   gd-fm Hdl

Eleven furlong soft ground winner in Germany; needed every yard of longer trip when winning 2m 4f novices handicap hurdle at Worcester May 2003; disappointing having been raised 9lb at Newton Abbot next time.

Manque Neuf
94   53
4-y-o b g Cadeaux Genereux-Flying Squaw (Be My Chief (USA))
Mrs L Richards (J D Bethell 7/8) B Seal

Placings:0   (4733)
2002/03: 16⁰GF,

	Starts	1st	2nd	3rd	Win & Pl
Hurdles	1	0	0	0	
Career Total	1	0	0	0	

Going: Sf: 0-0 GS: 0-0 Gd: 0-0 GF: - Fm: 0-1
Distance: 2m/2m3: 0-1 2m4-2m7: 0-0 3m+: 0-0
Track: LH: 0-1 RH: 0-0 Tight: 0-0 Gall: 0-0
Aids: Bl: 0-0 Vi: 0-0 Tstrap: 0-0
Best Rating: 53 4/03 Chep 2m110y   gd-fm Hdl

Showed an improvement in his jumping third start but seemed not to stay the 2m 4f.

Mantel Mini

4-y-o b f Reprimand-Foretell (Tirol)
B A Pearce   Miss J Webster

Placings:00   (3782)
2002/03: 16⁰G, 17⁰GS,

	Starts	1st	2nd	3rd	Win & Pl
NH Flat	2	0	0	0	
Career Total	2	0	0	0	

Going: Sf: 0-0 GS: 0-1 Gd: 0-1 GF: - Fm: 0-0
Distance: 2m/2m3: 0-2 2m4-2m7: 0-0 3m+: 0-0
Track: LH: 0-1 RH: 0-1 Tight: 0-0 Gall: 0-1
Aids: Bl: 0-0 Vi: 0-0 Tstrap: 0-0
Best Rating: 0   2/03   Extr   2m1f   gd-sft   NHF

Mantello

(72h)   (34h)
8-y-o ch g Mon Tresor-Laena (Roman Warrior)
B G Powell   Major Ian Thompson

Placings:P3304/P-P0P   (0555)
2002/03: 16ᴾGS, 20ᴾG, 18⁰GF, 25ᴾGF,

	Starts	1st	2nd	3rd	Win & Pl
Hurdles	3	0	0	0	0
Chases	1	0	0	0	0
Career Total	9	0	0	2	802

Going: Sf: 0-0 GS: 0-1 Gd: 0-1 GF: - Fm: 0-2
Distance: 2m/2m3: 0-2 2m4-2m7: 0-1 3m+: 0-1
Track: LH: 0-2 RH: 0-2 Tight: 0-1 Gall: 0-0
Aids: Bl: 0-1 Vi: 0-3 Tstrap: 0-2
Best Rating: 90   5/99   Hrfd   2m1f   good   Hdl

Mantilla

100   77
6-y-o b m Son Pardo-Well Tried (IRE) (Thatching)
J D Frost   R G Frost

Placings:2F6-0340303   (4513)
2002/03: 17⁰G, 17³F, 17⁴GS, 24⁰S, 17³G, 17⁰F, 19³GF,

	Starts	1st	2nd	3rd	Win & Pl
Hurdles	7	0	0	3	1564
Career Total	10	0	1	3	2166

Going: Sf: 0-1 GS: 0-1 Gd: 0-2 GF: - Fm: 0-3
Distance: 2m/2m3: 0-6 2m4-2m7: 0-0 3m+: 0-1
Track: LH: 0-0 RH: 0-7 Tight: 0-3 Gall: 0-0
Aids: Bl: 0-1 Vi: 0-0 Tstrap: 0-0
Best Rating: 96   11/01   Ludl   2m   gd-fm   Hdl

Plating-class hurdler; stays two miles three; best on a sound surface.

Mantles Prince

(115h)
9-y-o ch g Emarati (USA)-Miami Mouse (Miami Springs)
A G Juckes (P Hughes 4/6)   Emlyn Hughes Cleobury Golfers

Placings:52/123/5121132/55432643/46621312-2U6 (4780)
2002/03: 20²YS, 36ᵁG, 16⁶GF,

	Starts	1st	2nd	3rd	Win & Pl
Hurdles	1	0	0	0	900
Chases	2	0	1	0	2331
Career Total	31	6	8	5	163666
124	3/02	Naas	2m	Ch	HVY	£7975
134	1/02	Punc	2m	Ch	Y-S	£6561
155	1/00	Leop	2m	HHdl	SFT	£52240
139	1/00	Fair	2m	HHdl	SFT	£5920
127	11/99	Fair	2m	HHdl	Y-S	£11607
102	5/98	Limk	2m1f	Hdl	Y-S	£2978

Total win prize-money £87281

Going: Sf: 0-0 GS: 0-0 Gd: 0-1 GF: - Fm: 0-1
Distance: 2m/2m3: 0-1 2m4-2m7: 0-1 3m+: 0-1
Track: LH: 2-2 RH: 0-1 Tight: 0-1 Gall: 0-0
Aids: Bl: 0-0 Vi: 0-0 Tstrap: 0-0
Best Rating: 166   4/00   Aint   2m4f   good   Hdl

Very useful ex-Irish hurdler/chaser; he is best on soft ground over two miles; has four successes to his name over hurdles, including beating subsequent Tote Gold Trophy winner Geos in the 2000 Ladbroke; took well to fences in the early part of 2002, winning twice over two miles on soft/heavy ground; unseated rider in Grand National on debut for current yard.

Maousse Honor (FR)

95(107c)   (117+c)101
8-y-o b m Hero s Honor (USA)-Maousse (FR) (Labus (FR))
M C Pipe   Sean Lucey

Placings:22/111/5PP-112P1143P   (2455)
2002/03: 16¹S, 16¹GF, 16²GF, 17ᴾG, 16¹G, 17¹S, 17⁴HY, 16³S, 24ᴾGS,

	Starts	1st	2nd	3rd	Win & Pl
Hurdles	5	2	0	1	4911
Chases	4	2	1	0	10525
Career Total	17	7	3	1	49032
102	11/02	NAbb	2m1f	G Hdl	SFT	£2205
80	10/02	Strf	2m110y	G Hdl	GD	£2380
117	7/02	NAbb	2m110y	D Ch	G-F	£5009
113	6/02	Worc	2m	E Ch	SFT	£3445
114	8/99	NAbb	2m1f	E Hdl	GD	£2459
130	7/99	Worc	2m	D Hdl	G-F	£3150
	5/99	Autl	2m2f	Hdl	VS	£16146

Total win prize-money £34795

Going: Sf: 2-4 GS: 0-1 Gd: 1-2 GF: - Fm: 1-2
Distance: 2m/2m3: 4-8 2m4-2m7: 0-0 3m+: 0-1
Track: LH: 4-7 RH: 0-2 Tight: 3-5 Gall: 0-0
Aids: Bl: 0-0 Vi: 0-0 Tstrap: 0-0
Best Rating: 130   7/99   Worc   2m   gd-fm   Hdl

Selling class hurdler. Acts on fast and soft ground, suited by trips around two miles, likes to front-run.

Mapleton

105(81h)   (66h)108+
10-y-o br g Skyliner-Maple Syrup (Charlottown)
Mrs S J Smith   Keith Middleton

Placings:606605P/23420/503340323/2221P/422402PP5-311410 (1132)
2002/03: 24³G, 24¹GS, 20¹G, 23⁴GF, 21¹G, 25⁰GF,

	Starts	1st	2nd	3rd	Win & Pl
Chases	6	3	0	1	13224
Career Total	41	4	9	6	27546
108	8/02	Sedg	2m5f	D(0-125)HCh	GD	£4680
101	6/02	Hexm	2m4f110yD(0-115)HCh	GD	£3997
92	5/02	Sthl	3m110y F(0-90)HCh	G-S	£3685
90	7/00	Sthl	3m110y E Ch	G-F	£2921

Total win prize-money £15286

Going: Sf: 0-0 GS: 1-1 Gd: 2-3 GF: - Fm: 0-2

Distance: 2m/2m3: 0-0 2m4-2m7: 2-2 3m+: 1-4
Track: LH: 3-5 RH: 0-1 Tight: 2-4 Gall: 0-0
Aids: Bl: 0-0 Vi: 0-0 Tstrap: 0-0
Best Rating: 108   8/02   Sedg   2m5f   good   Ch

Consistent chaser at a low level, he seems to handle all types of ground and stays three miles.

Marabout (FR)

(82h)   (50h)
6-y-o b g Baby Turk-Maria Bethania (FR) (Pharly (FR))
Sir John Barlow Bt   Sir John & Lady Barlow

Placings:006/402353-0   (3911)
2002/03: 17⁰GS,

	Starts	1st	2nd	3rd	Win & Pl
Hurdles	1	0	0	0	
Career Total	10	0	1	2	16732

Going: Sf: 0-0 GS: 0-1 Gd: 0-0 GF: - Fm: 0-0
Distance: 2m/2m3: 0-1 2m4-2m7: 0-0 3m+: 0-0
Track: LH: 0-0 RH: 0-1 Tight: 0-0 Gall: 0-0
Aids: Bl: 0-0 Vi: 0-0 Tstrap: 0-0
Best Rating: 50   3/03   Carl   2m1f   gd-sft   Hdl

Maradan (IRE)

7-y-o b g Shernazar-Marmana (USA) (Blushing Groom (FR))
Mrs J C McGregor (T J O Mara 24/9)   Capt Ben Coutts

Placings:0/012060/0FP-UPU00P   (4394)
2002/03: 16ᵁS, 21ᴾS, 22ᵁYS, 24⁹G, 21⁹G, 20ᴾG,

	Starts	1st	2nd	3rd	Win & Pl
Hurdles	3	0	0	0	0
Chases	3	0	0	0	0
Career Total	16	1	1	0	3528
95	6/00	Tral	2m4f	Hdl	Y-S	£2760

Total win prize-money £2760

Going: Sf: 0-2 GS: 0-0 Gd: 0-3 GF: - Fm: 0-0
Distance: 2m/2m3: 0-1 2m4-2m7: 0-4 3m+: 0-1
Track: LH: 0-0 RH: 0-2 Tight: 0-0 Gall: 0-0
Aids: Bl: 0-0 Vi: 0-0 Tstrap: 0-0
Best Rating: 107   11/00   Chel   2m110y   gd-sft   Hdl

Maragun (GER)

103(107h)   (123h)112
7-y-o b g General Assembly (USA)-Marcelia (GER) (Priamos (GER))
M C Pipe   Stuart Mercer & Emlyn Hughes

Placings:3P/311261304-P26202B05   (4734)
2002/03: 16ᴾGF, 16²S, 21⁶G, 19²F, 16⁶S, 17²S, 17⁶G, 16⁰G, 16⁶GF,

	Starts	1st	2nd	3rd	Win & Pl
Hurdles	8	0	3	0	4350
Chases	1	0	0	0	0
Career Total	20	3	4	3	15683
120	11/01	Hntg	2m110y	E Hdl	GD	£2429
119	8/01	Uttx	2m	D Hdl	G-F	£3360
123	6/01	MRas	2m1f110yF(0-100)HHdl	G-F	£2902

Total win prize-money £8691

Going: Sf: 0-3 GS: 0-0 Gd: 0-3 GF: - Fm: 0-3
Distance: 2m/2m3: 0-8 2m4-2m7: 0-1 3m+: 0-0
Track: LH: 0-6 RH: 0-3 Tight: 0-3 Gall: 0-2
Aids: Bl: 0-0 Vi: 0-1 Tstrap: 0-3
Best Rating: 126   1/03   Tntn   2m1f   soft   Hdl

Decent handicap hurdler; suited by fast ground; effective over two miles to two miles three; has worn a visor.

Maraschino

10-y-o ch m Lycius (USA)-Mystery Ship (Decoy Boy)
K W Hogg K W Hogg

Placings:P   (0911)
2002/03: 17PGS,

	Starts	1st	2nd	3rd	Win & Pl
Hurdles	1	0	0	0	
Career Total	1	0	0	0	

Going: Sf: 0-0 GS: 0-1 Gd: 0-0 GF: - Fm: 0-0
Distance: 2m/2m3: 0-0 2m4-2m7: 0-0 3m+: 0-0
Track: LH: 0-0 RH: 0-1 Tight: 0-1 Gall: 0-0
Aids: Bl: 0-0 Vi: 0-0 Tstrap: 0-0
Best Rating: 0   8/02   MRas 2m1f110y gd-sft Hdl

Maraud

109   91

9-y-o ch g Midyan (USA)-Peak Squaw (USA) (Icecapade (USA))
M E Sowersby David Dyer

Placings:1313/0560060/513/33F56-4U30512O21446F
                                                       (4374)
2002/03: 244G, 27UG, 243G, 222GF, 245G, 271GF, 242G, 270G, 242GS, 251G, 274S, 254G, 246GF, 27FG,

	Starts	1st	2nd	3rd	Win & Pl
Hurdles	14	2	1	1	9623
Career Total	33	5	2	6	19637
99	11/02	Catt	3m1f110yD(0-115)HHdl	GD	£3672
92	7/02	Sedg	3m3f110yE(0-110)HHdl	G-F	£2926
97	7/99	Sedg	3m3f110yE(0-115)HHdl	G-F	£2745
110	2/98	Muss	2m	E Hdl	G-F	£2735
98	12/97	Catt	2m	E Hdl	GD	£1912

Total win prize-money £13992

Going: Sf: 0-1 GS: 0-1 Gd: 1-9 GF: - Fm: 1-3
Distance: 2m/2m3: 0-0 2m4-2m7: 0-0 3m+: 2-13
Track: LH: 2-13 RH: 0-0 Tight: 2-9 Gall: 0-0
Aids: Bl: 0-0 Vi: 0-0 Tstrap: 0-0
Best Rating: 110 3/98   Kels 2m110y good Hdl

Moderate hurdler; stays really well; suited by fast ground.

Marble Arch

120   152

7-y-o b g Rock Hopper-Mayfair Minx (St Columbus)
H Morrison M S Wilson, R Sweet, Mrs Mary Wilson

Placings:653/534223411/011P2-3450   (4099)
2002/03: 163GG, 174G, 165S, 160G,

	Starts	1st	2nd	3rd	Win & Pl
Hurdles	4	0	0	1	11125
Career Total	21	4	3	4	152344
155	12/01	Asct	2m110y	B(0-155)HHdl	GD	£58000
141	11/01	Newb	2m110y	C(0-130)HHdl	G-S	£9750
118	4/01	Ayr	2m	C Hdl	GD	£5443
118	3/01	Asct	2m110y	D(0-120)HHdl	HVY	£5213

Total win prize-money £78407

Going: Sf: 0-1 GS: 0-1 Gd: 0-2 GF: - Fm: 0-0
Distance: 2m/2m3: 0-4 2m4-2m7: 0-0 3m+: 0-0
Track: LH: 0-3 RH: 0-1 Tight: 0-0 Gall: 0-2
Aids: Bl: 0-0 Vi: 0-0 Tstrap: 0-0
Best Rating: 162 3/02   Chel 2m110y gd-sft Hdl

Top-class hurdler; won the Ladbroke Hurdle at Ascot in 2001 and 3l second in 2002 Champion Hurdle at Cheltenham; creditable 5 1/4l fourth to Rooster Booster in Bula Hurdle at Cheltenham and the ground was unsuitable when well beaten in the Christmas Hurdle at Kempton;

warmed up for his Champion Hurdle bid by winning a maiden on the Lingfield Polytrack; only twelfth at Cheltenham; suited by 2m and does not want the ground too soft; difficult ride who does not always find as much off the bridle as looks likely; may be capable of better than bare form.

March North

101(107h)   (92 h)103

8-y-o b g Petoski-Coral Delight (Idiots Delight)
Mrs P Robeson Ron Collins

Placings:435/5631/56164F6-0000623   (4528)
2002/03: 166G, 160HY, 163GS, 179G, 226S, 202GF, 243G,

	Starts	1st	2nd	3rd	Win & Pl
Hurdles	5	0	0	0	0
Chases	2	0	1	1	1788
Career Total	21	2	1	3	11162
113	11/01	Hntg	2m110y	D(0-120)HHdl	GD	£6873
106	1/01	Fknm	2m	F(0-110)HHdl	SFT	£1838

Total win prize-money £8712

Going: Sf: 0-2 GS: 0-1 Gd: 0-3 GF: - Fm: 0-1
Distance: 2m/2m3: 0-4 2m4-2m7: 0-2 3m+: 0-1
Track: LH: 0-2 RH: 0-5 Tight: 0-0 Gall: 0-1
Aids: Bl: 0-0 Vi: 0-0 Tstrap: 0-0
Best Rating: 113 11/01 Hntg 2m110y good Hdl

Fair handicap hurdler/novice chaser; effective at two miles, stays three; suited by a sharp track; effective on good ground or softer.

Marcus Maximus (USA)

109(104h)   (118h)115

8-y-o ch g Woodman (USA)-Star Pastures (Northfields (USA))
H D Daly Ludlow Racing Partnership

Placings:3/1210PP1-122F2   (3745)
2002/03: 161GF, 202F, 162G, 163GS, 162G,

	Starts	1st	2nd	3rd	Win & Pl
Hurdles	1	1	0	0	3150
Chases	4	0	3	0	4196
Career Total	13	4	4	1	16512
118	5/02	Ludl	2m	D Hdl	G-F	£3150
98	4/02	Ludl	2m	H Hdl	GD	£3250
106	11/01	Kemp	2m	F(0-100)HHdl	GD	£2926
103	11/01	Strf	2m110y	G Hdl	SFT	£2044

Total win prize-money £11370

Going: Sf: 0-0 GS: 0-1 Gd: 0-2 GF: - Fm: 1-2
Distance: 2m/2m3: 1-4 2m4-2m7: 0-1 3m+: 0-0
Track: LH: 0-0 RH: 1-5 Tight: 0-3 Gall: 0-1
Aids: Bl: 0-0 Vi: 0-0 Tstrap: 0-0
Best Rating: 118 5/02   Ludl 2m   gd-fm Hdl

Decent enough hurdler; running well over fences in novice company; acts on decent ground; effective at around two miles.

Marcus William (IRE)

104   97

6-y-o ch g Roselier (FR)-River Swell (IRE) (Over The River (FR))
B G Powell P H Betts

Placings:6U-56153   (4277)
2002/03: 165GS, 179S, 181HY, 205GS, 203GF,

	Starts	1st	2nd	3rd	Win & Pl
NH Flat	1	0	0	0	0
Hurdles	4	1	0	1	5184

Career Total	7	1	0	1	5184
109	1/03	Font	2m2f110yE Hdl	HVY	£3640

Total win prize-money £3640

Going: Sf: 1-2 GS: 0-2 Gd: 0-0 GF: - Fm: 0-1
Distance: 2m/2m3: 1-3 2m4-2m7: 0-2 3m+: 0-0
Track: LH: 1-2 RH: 0-1 Tight: 1-5 Gall: 0-0
Aids: Bl: 0-0 Vi: 0-0 Tstrap: 0-0
Best Rating: 122 2/03   Font 2m4f   gd-sft Hdl

Decent hurdler; stays two and a quarter miles plus; acts on testing and decent ground.

Mardani (IRE)

(103h)   (122h)

8-y-o b g Fairy King (USA)-Marmana (USA) (Blushing Groom (FR))
R S Brookhouse R S Brookhouse

Placings:2/3121P46-11P   (0995)
2002/03: 241GF, 211GF, 21PGF,

	Starts	1st	2nd	3rd	Win & Pl
Hurdles	2	2	0	0	8669
Chases	1	0	0	0	0
Career Total	11	4	2	1	16535
122	6/02	Hntg	2m5f110yD(0-125)HHdl	G-F	£3286
118	5/02	Worc	3m	C(0-130)HHdl	G-F	£5382
103	7/01	Worc	2m4f	E Hdl	GD	£2464
111	5/01	Extr	2m1f	E Hdl	FRM	£3130

Total win prize-money £14263

Going: Sf: 0-0 GS: 0-0 Gd: 0-0 GF: - Fm: 2-3
Distance: 2m/2m3: 0-0 2m4-2m7: 1-2 3m+: 1-1
Track: LH: 1-2 RH: 1-1 Tight: 0-1 Gall: 1-1
Aids: Bl: 2-3 Vi: 0-0 Tstrap: 0-0
Best Rating: 122 6/02   Hntg 2m5f110y gd-fm Hdl

A staying Handicapper on the Flat, he did well over hurdles on a sound surface in the summer of 2001 and returned to form when upped to three miles and fitted with a visor in May 2002.

Mardello

84f   70f

5-y-o b m Supreme Leader-Clonmello (Le Bavard (FR))
N J Henderson R D Chugg

Placings:0   (3747)
2002/03: 160G,

	Starts	1st	2nd	3rd	Win & Pl
NH Flat	1	0	0	0	
Career Total	1	0	0	0	

Going: Sf: 0-0 GS: 0-0 Gd: 0-0 GF: - Fm: 0-0
Distance: 2m/2m3: 0-1 2m4-2m7: 0-0 3m+: 0-0
Track: LH: 0-0 RH: 0-1 Tight: 0-0 Gall: 0-1
Aids: Bl: 0-0 Vi: 0-0 Tstrap: 0-0
Best Rating: 70   2/03   Hntg 2m110y good NHF

Mare Of Wetwang

71   50

5-y-o ch m River Falls-Kudos Blue (Elmaamul (USA))
J D Bethell Richard Whiteley

Placings:0P0   (3514)
2002/03: 169S, 16PHY, 160G,

	Starts	1st	2nd	3rd	Win & Pl
Hurdles	3	0	0	0	
Career Total	3	0	0	0	

Going: Sf: 0-2 GS: 0-0 Gd: 0-1 GF: - Fm: 0-0
Distance: 2m/2m3: 0-3 2m4-2m7: 0-0 3m+: 0-0
Track: LH: 0-3 RH: 0-0 Tight: 0-1 Gall: 0-1
Aids: Bl: 0-0 Vi: 0-0 Tstrap: 0-0
Best Rating: 50 2/03 Catt 2m good Hdl

Margoulin (FR)
98   90
8-y-o gr g Royal Charter (FR)-Marsaude (FR) (Tourangeau (FR))
Mrs H Dalton (A L T Moore 22/3) John Sheehan

Placings:500/414P/3F140-050F606   (4787)
2002/03: 16DSH, 205HY, 19DS, 16FS, 176HY, 17DGY, 20RG,

	Starts	1st	2nd	3rd	Win & Pl
Chases	7	0	0	0	
Career Total	19	2	0	1	13735
109 1/02 Fair	2m10y	Ch		Y-S	£6773
101 12/00 Gowr	2m2f	Hdl		HVY	£4692
				Total win prize-money	£11465

Going: Sf: 0-4 GS: 0-0 Gd: 0-1 GF: - Fm: 0-0
Distance: 2m/2m3: 0-5 2m4-2m7: 0-2 3m+: 0-0
Track: LH: 0-2 RH: 0-4 Tight: 0-1 Gall: 0-0
Aids: Bl: 0-0 Vi: 0-0 Tstrap: 0-3
Best Rating: 116 12/00 Fair 2m2f yld-sft Hdl

Ex-Irish; modest handicap chaser; best at two miles.

Marico (IRE)
91   83
10-y-o b g Lord Americo-Gilt Course (Crash Course)
D Brace (W Power 19/5) David Brace

Placings:00/05000/5/562P   (1898)
2002/03: 205GS, 226G, 192GF, 27PS,

	Starts	1st	2nd	3rd	Win & Pl
Hurdles	4	0	1	0	669
Career Total	12	0	1	0	669

Going: Sf: 0-1 GS: 0-1 Gd: 0-1 GF: - Fm: 0-1
Distance: 2m/2m3: 0-0 2m4-2m7: 0-3 3m+: 0-1
Track: LH: 0-2 RH: 0-2 Tight: 0-3 Gall: 0-0
Aids: Bl: 0-0 Vi: 0-0 Tstrap: 0-0
Best Rating: 92 1/00 Tram 2m sft-hvy NHF

Marigliano (USA)
102(110h)   (103h)109
10-y-o b g Riverman (USA)-Mount Holyoke (Golden Fleece (USA))
K A Morgan G S Alcock & B R Jones

Placings:P0/L034/F2113313/11042312/31022U/P0563P-3012   (3233)
2002/03: 163G, 169GS, 161GS, 162S,

	Starts	1st	2nd	3rd	Win & Pl
Hurdles	3	1	0	1	5671
Chases	1	0	1	0	2257
Career Total	38	8	6	8	50719
103 12/02 Fknm	2m	D(0-120)HHdl		G-S	£5096
114 1/01 Fknm	2m110y	F(0-110)HCh		SFT	£2525
111 3/00 MRas	2m1f110yD Ch			G-F	£5124
128 11/99 Hntg	2m110y	C(0-130)HHdl		G-S	£10365
116 11/99 Worc	2m	C(0-130)HHdl		G-S	£4744
111 2/99 Catt	2m	C(0-130)HHdl		GD	£4770
109 1/99 Catt	2m	D(0-120)HHdl		GD	£2775
119 12/98 Hayd	2m	C(0-120)HHdl		SFT	£2232
				Total win prize-money	£37632

Going: Sf: 0-1 GS: 1-2 Gd: 0-1 GF: - Fm: 0-0
Distance: 2m/2m3: 1-4 2m4-2m7: 0-0 3m+: 0-0
Track: LH: 1-3 RH: 0-1 Tight: 1-2 Gall: 0-1
Aids: Bl: 0-0 Vi: 0-0 Tstrap: 0-0
Best Rating: 128 11/99 Hntg 2m110y gd-fm Hdl

Versatile gelding who has won under all codes and goes particularly well on a tight track; handles anything but extremes of ground; effective at around two miles; has worn sheepskin cheekpieces.

Marino West (IRE)
(97h)   (104h)
8-y-o ch g Phardante (FR)-Seanaphobal Lady (Kambalda)
N M Babbage Provex Products Ltd

Placings:61P-0U   (0646)
2002/03: 20DGF, 24UGF,

	Starts	1st	2nd	3rd	Win & Pl
Hurdles	1	0	0	0	
Chases	1	0	0	0	
Career Total	5	1	0	0	5369
104 4/02 Asct	2m4f	C Hdl		G-F	£5369
				Total win prize-money	£5369

Going: Sf: 0-0 GS: 0-0 Gd: 0-0 GF: - Fm: 0-2
Distance: 2m/2m3: 0-0 2m4-2m7: 0-1 3m+: 0-1
Track: LH: 0-2 RH: 0-0 Tight: 0-1 Gall: 0-0
Aids: Bl: 0-0 Vi: 0-0 Tstrap: 0-0
Best Rating: 104 4/02 Asct 2m4f gd-fm Hdl

He showed nothing on his hurdling debut, but won a weak novice event at Ascot on his second start. Suited by two and a half miles and fast ground.

Marino Wood (IRE)
50   14
4-y-o ch f Woodpas (USA)-Forgren (IRE) (Thatching)
C N Kellett (R Wilman 14/6) Sean A Taylor

Placings:0   (1756)
2002/03: 16DG,

	Starts	1st	2nd	3rd	Win & Pl
Hurdles	1	0	0	0	
Career Total	1	0	0	0	

Going: Sf: 0-0 GS: 0-0 Gd: 0-0 GF: - Fm: 0-0
Distance: 2m/2m3: 0-1 2m4-2m7: 0-0 3m+: 0-0
Track: LH: 0-1 RH: 0-0 Tight: 0-0 Gall: 0-0
Aids: Bl: 0-0 Vi: 0-0 Tstrap: 0-0
Best Rating: 14 11/02 Wwck 2m good Hdl

Mark Equal
(106h)   108
7-y-o b g Nicholas Bill-Dissolution (Henbit (USA))
M C Pipe Heeru Kirpalani Racing

Placings:5/3104-30PP   (4624)
2002/03: 163S, 19DGS, 24PG, 26PGF,

	Starts	1st	2nd	3rd	Win & Pl
Chases	4	0	0	1	610
Career Total	9	1	0	2	5407
110 1/02 Tntn	2m3f110yD Hdl			SFT	£4130
				Total win prize-money	£4130

Going: Sf: 0-1 GS: 0-1 Gd: 0-1 GF: - Fm: 0-1
Distance: 2m/2m3: 0-1 2m4-2m7: 0-1 3m+: 0-2
Track: LH: 0-4 RH: 0-0 Tight: 0-0 Gall: 0-0
Aids: Bl: 0-0 Vi: 0-1 Tstrap: 0-0
Best Rating: 110 1/02 Tntn 2m3f110y soft Hdl

Modest hurdler/chaser; showed ability in bumpers before getting off the mark on his hurdling debut; held in handicaps in the spring of 2002; had jumping problems in chases; acts on soft ground and is effective at up to two miles three.

Mark It
101   93
4-y-o b g Botanic (USA)-Everdene (Bustino)
D E Cantillon (Mrs A J Perrett 6/7) Mrs E M Clarke

Placings:44113   (2325)
2002/03: 164G, 164G, 161GS, 161GS, 173S,

	Starts	1st	2nd	3rd	Win & Pl
Hurdles	5	2	0	1	9802
Career Total	5	2	0	1	9802
99 11/02 Fknm	2m	D Hdl		G-S	£4524
87 11/02 Hntg	2m110y	D Hdl		G-S	£4192
				Total win prize-money	£8717

Going: Sf: 0-1 GS: 2-2 Gd: 0-2 GF: - Fm: 0-0
Distance: 2m/2m3: 2-5 2m4-2m7: 0-0 3m+: 0-0
Track: LH: 1-2 RH: 1-3 Tight: 1-2 Gall: 1-1
Aids: Bl: 0-0 Vi: 0-0 Tstrap: 0-0
Best Rating: 99 12/02 MRas 2m1f110y soft Hdl

Off the mark at the third attempt in modest company at Huntingdon in November 2002, he followed up at Fakenham next time.

Mark-Antony (IRE)
(75c)   (93c)
9-y-o ch g Phardante (FR)-Judysway (Deep Run)
A D Smith David M Williams

Placings:0/F0FP-PU   (0663)
2002/03: 22PGF, 16UGF,

	Starts	1st	2nd	3rd	Win & Pl
Hurdles	2	0	0	0	
Career Total	7	0	0	0	

Going: Sf: 0-0 GS: 0-0 Gd: 0-0 GF: - Fm: 0-2
Distance: 2m/2m3: 0-1 2m4-2m7: 0-1 3m+: 0-0
Track: LH: 0-2 RH: 0-0 Tight: 0-1 Gall: 0-0
Aids: Bl: 0-0 Vi: 0-0 Tstrap: 0-0
Best Rating: 88 5/01 Hrfd 2m3f good Ch

Marked Man (IRE)
113   113+
7-y-o b g Grand Plaisir (IRE)-Teazle (Quayside)
R Lee Mr & Mrs C R Elliott

Placings:03040-6155   (4602)
2002/03: 176S, 201G, 215G, 215G,

	Starts	1st	2nd	3rd	Win & Pl
Hurdles	4	1	0	0	5294
Career Total	9	1	0	1	6135
95 11/02 Aint	2m4f	E(0-100)HHdl		GD	£4543
				Total win prize-money	£4544

Going: Sf: 0-1 GS: 0-0 Gd: 1-3 GF: - Fm: 0-0
Distance: 2m/2m3: 0-1 2m4-2m7: 1-3 3m+: 0-0
Track: LH: 1-3 RH: 0-1 Tight: 1-2 Gall: 0-1
Aids: Bl: 0-0 Vi: 0-0 Tstrap: 0-0
Best Rating: 104 4/03 Chel 2m5f110y good Hdl

Modest hurdler; suited by good ground; stays two and a half miles.

Markskeepingfaith (IRE)
95

8-y-o b m Ajraas (USA)-Felicitas (Mr Fluorocarbon)
N B Mason N B Mason

Placings:5/06/50-P   (0390)
2002/03: 16PGS,

	Starts	1st	2nd	3rd	Win & Pl
Hurdles	1	0	0	0	
Career Total	6	0	0	0	

Going: Sf: 0-0 GS: 0-1 Gd: 0-0 GF: - Fm: 0-0
Distance: 2m/2m3: 0-0 2m4-2m7: 0-0 3m+: 0-0
Track: LH: 0-1 RH: 0-0 Tight: 0-0 Gall: 0-0
Aids: Bl: 0-0 Vi: 0-0 Tstrap: 0-0
Best Rating: 95 6/01 Clon 2m   gd-fm Hdl

Marlborough (IRE)
120   160

11-y-o br g Strong Gale-Wrekenogan (Tarqogan)
N J Henderson Sir Robert Ogden

Placings:5213/U111FF/PU1216/111/34F0-102F05 (4457)
2002/03: 251GS, 263GS, 242GS, 24FG, 260G, 255G,

	Starts	1st	2nd	3rd	Win & Pl
Chases	6	1	1	0	66500
Career Total	29	10	3	2	271384
160	11/02	Weth	3m1f	A Ch	G-S	£29750
165	4/01	Sand	3m110y	A Ch	G-S	£58000
165	2/01	Winc	3m1f110yB Ch		GD	£16932
166	12/00	Chel	3m1f110yB HCh		SFT	£28678
158	3/00	Chel	3m110y	B HCh	GD	£39000
151	1/00	Kemp	3m	C(0-135)HCh		GD	£6955
135	1/99	Kemp	3m	D Ch	SFT	£4924
132	12/98	Ling	3m	E Ch	SFT	£3326
135	11/98	Worc	2m4f110yE Ch		HVY	£3600
126	3/98	Newb	2m5f	D Hdl	G-S	£3793

Total win prize-money £194961

Going: Sf: 0-1 GS: 1-2 Gd: 0-3 GF: - Fm: 0-0
Distance: 2m/2m3: 0-0 2m4-2m7: 0-0 3m+: 1-6
Track: LH: 1-5 RH: 0-1 Tight: 0-1 Gall: 0-3
Aids: Bl: 0-0 Vi: 0-0 Tstrap: 0-0
Best Rating: 170 12/02 Kemp 3m   soft Ch

Top-class staying chaser; produced best ever display when just failing to overcome Best Mate in King George at Kempton (mistake at last cost momentum); previously won Charlie Hall Chase at Wetherby despite being badly hampered; ran a bit free and beaten when falling behind Valley Henry in Aon Chase at Newbury in February; well beaten in Cheltenham Gold Cup; stays at least 3m 1f; effective on good and soft ground; has returned as good as ever after wind operation; ideally suited by being held up off a fast pace.

Marmaduke (IRE)
98   116

7-y-o ch g Perugino (USA)-Sympathy (Precocious)
M Pitman Martin Butler

Placings:201220/341646-22   (0787)
2002/03: 172GF, 172GF,

	Starts	1st	2nd	3rd	Win & Pl
Hurdles	2	0	2	0	2624
Career Total	14	2	5	1	13853
116	10/01	Hntg	2m110y	C(0-130)HHdl	GD	£5432
116	12/00	Ludl	2m	F Hdl	SFT	£2436

Total win prize-money £7868

Marrel
106   110

5-y-o b g Shareef Dancer (USA)-Upper Caen (High Top)
S L Keightley (B Hanbury 6/8) Miss H J Flower

Placings:645   (4784)
2002/03: 206G, 194GS, 195G,

	Starts	1st	2nd	3rd	Win & Pl
Hurdles	3	0	0	0	0
Career Total	3	0	0	0	0

Going: Sf: 0-0 GS: 0-1 Gd: 0-2 GF: - Fm: 0-0
Distance: 2m/2m3: 0-3 2m4-2m7: 0-0 3m+: 0-0
Track: LH: 0-1 RH: 0-2 Tight: 0-2 Gall: 0-1
Aids: Bl: 0-0 Vi: 0-0 Tstrap: 0-0
Best Rating: 74 3/03 Strf 2m3f   gd-sft Hdl

Modest hurdler; completed a hat-trick since being claimed after finishing runner-up at Hereford May 2003; not disgraced in much better company next time; acts on good ground; seems best at around 2m; appears to be improving.

Marsh Marigold
93   72

9-y-o br m Tina s Pet-Pulga (Blakeney)
G Fierro G Fierro

Placings:0/0031440054635/25003300000/1113561644360
1055P/00P-040   (2506)
2002/03: 17QGF, 164S, 169G,

	Starts	1st	2nd	3rd	Win & Pl
Hurdles	3	0	0	0	0
Career Total	49	6	1	6	18508
99	11/00	Chep	2m110y	F(0-90)Hdl	HVY	£1883
99	7/00	Worc	2m2f	E(0-115)HHdl	G-F	£4160
97	5/00	Hexm	2m	E(0-115)HHdl	GD	£1831
90	5/00	Worc	2m	F(0-105)HHdl	G-F	£2604
90	5/00	Towc	2m	F(0-105)HHdl	G-F	£2007
85	11/98	Leic	2m	G Hdl	SFT	£2616

Total win prize-money £15102

Going: Sf: 0-1 GS: 0-0 Gd: 0-1 GF: - Fm: 0-1
Distance: 2m/2m3: 0-3 2m4-2m7: 0-0 3m+: 0-0
Track: LH: 0-2 RH: 0-1 Tight: 0-1 Gall: 0-0
Aids: Bl: 0-0 Vi: 0-0 Tstrap: 0-2
Best Rating: 99 11/00 Chep 2m110y   heavy Hdl

Marshal Murat (IRE)
69f   50f

7-y-o ch g Executive Perk-Magneeto (IRE) (Brush Aside (USA))
C R Egerton Mrs Evelyn Hankinson

Placings:4/0   (1995)
2002/03: 16QGS,

	Starts	1st	2nd	3rd	Win & Pl
NH Flat	1	0	0	0	
Career Total	2	0	0	0	226

Going: Sf: 0-0 GS: 0-1 Gd: 0-0 GF: - Fm: 0-0

Going: Sf: 0-0 GS: 0-0 Gd: 0-0 GF: - Fm: 0-2
Distance: 2m/2m3: 0-2 2m4-2m7: 0-0 3m+: 0-0
Track: LH: 0-1 RH: 0-1 Tight: 0-0 Gall: 0-0
Aids: Bl: 0-0 Vi: 0-0 Tstrap: 0-0
Best Rating: 117 7/02 Sthl 2m1f   gd-fm Hdl

Fair hurdler; best around two miles; acts on good and good to soft ground.

Distance: 2m/2m3: 0-1 2m4-2m7: 0-0 3m+: 0-0
Track: LH: 0-1 RH: 0-0 Tight: 0-0 Gall: 0-0
Aids: Bl: 0-0 Vi: 0-0 Tstrap: 0-0
Best Rating: 101 2/01 Navn 2m   soft NHF

Martha Reilly (IRE)
106   91

7-y-o ch m Rainbows For Life (CAN)-Debach Delight (Great Nephew)
Mrs Barbara Waring P Haggerty, H Shapter

Placings:522215-35F43F   (4267)
2002/03: 243S, 225S, 23FS, 234GS, 213S, 24FGF,

	Starts	1st	2nd	3rd	Win & Pl
Hurdles	6	0	0	2	2006
Career Total	12	1	3	2	7277
89	11/01	Strf	2m6f110yE Hdl		SFT	£2628

Total win prize-money £2629

Going: Sf: 0-4 GS: 0-1 Gd: 0-0 GF: - Fm: 0-1
Distance: 2m/2m3: 0-0 2m4-2m7: 0-3 3m+: 0-3
Track: LH: 0-6 RH: 0-0 Tight: 0-1 Gall: 0-0
Aids: Bl: 0-0 Vi: 0-0 Tstrap: 0-0
Best Rating: 92 3/03 Sthl 3m110y   gd-fm Hdl

Moderate hurdler; stays three miles; acts on soft ground.

Martin Ossie
87   60

6-y-o b g Bonny Scot (IRE)-So We Know (Daring March)
Dr P Pritchard D Smith (saul)

Placings:000600   (4522)
2002/03: 16QGS, 16QS, 18QHY, 18FS, 16QG, 16QG,

	Starts	1st	2nd	3rd	Win & Pl
NH Flat	3	0	0	0	0
Hurdles	3	0	0	0	0
Career Total	6	0	0	0	0

Going: Sf: 0-3 GS: 0-1 Gd: 0-2 GF: - Fm: 0-0
Distance: 2m/2m3: 0-6 2m4-2m7: 0-0 3m+: 0-0
Track: LH: 0-4 RH: 0-2 Tight: 0-1 Gall: 0-1
Aids: Bl: 0-0 Vi: 0-0 Tstrap: 0-0
Best Rating: 63 1/03 Ludl 2m   soft NHF

Martinez (IRE)
(82h)   (69h)

7-y-o b g Tirol-Elka (USA) (Val De L Orne (FR))
K F Clutterbuck K F Clutterbuck

Placings:030/0P-50P   (1216)
2002/03: 165S, 20QGF, 21FQ,

	Starts	1st	2nd	3rd	Win & Pl
Hurdles	2	0	0	0	0
Chases	1	0	0	0	0
Career Total	8	0	0	1	294

Going: Sf: 0-1 GS: 0-0 Gd: 0-1 GF: - Fm: 0-1
Distance: 2m/2m3: 0-1 2m4-2m7: 0-2 3m+: 0-0
Track: LH: 0-3 RH: 0-0 Tight: 0-0 Gall: 0-0
Aids: Bl: 0-0 Vi: 0-0 Tstrap: 0-0
Best Rating: 83 2/01 Sedg 2m1f   gd-sft Hdl

Maryland (IRE)
103f   89f

6-y-o b m Executive Perk-Raven Night (IRE) (Mandalus)

O Brennan O Brennan

Placings:02   (4672)
2002/03: 17⁰G, 16²G,

	Starts	1st	2nd	3rd	Win & Pl
NH Flat	2	0	1	0	544
Career Total	2	0	1	0	544

Going: Sf: 0-0 GS: 0-0 Gd: 0-2 GF: - Fm: 0-0
Distance: 2m/2m3: 0-2 2m4-2m7: 0-0 3m+: 0-0
Track: LH: 0-1 RH: 0-1 Tight: 0-2 Gall: 0-0
Aids: Bl: 0-0 Vi: 0-0 Tstrap: 0-0
Best Rating: 89   4/03   Fknm   2m   good   NHF

Runner-up in a Fakenham bumper on her second start.

Marzelle (FR)
78   46
5-y-o b m Sillery (USA)-Marzipan (IRE) (Green Desert (USA))
S Dow S Dow

Placings:6   (1332)
2002/03: 16⁶G,

	Starts	1st	2nd	3rd	Win & Pl
Hurdles	1	0	0	0	0
Career Total	1	0	0	0	0

Going: Sf: 0-0 GS: 0-0 Gd: 0 GF: - Fm: 0-0
Distance: 2m/2m3: 0-1 2m4-2m7: 0-0 3m+: 0-0
Track: LH: 0-1 RH: 0-0 Tight: 0-1 Gall: 0-0
Aids: Bl: 0-0 Vi: 0-0 Tstrap: 0-0
Best Rating: 49   9/02   Plum   2m   good   Hdl

Mashhoor (USA)
91   56
5-y-o b g Thunder Gulch (USA)-Memorive (USA) (Riverman (USA))
Mrs Barbara Waring (B J Llewellyn 13/5) E S Chivers

Placings:600-036566   (4086)
2002/03: 16⁰GS, 16³S, 16⁶S, 16⁶S, 16⁶S, 19⁶GS,

	Starts	1st	2nd	3rd	Win & Pl
Hurdles	6	0	0	1	280
Career Total	9	0	0	1	280

Going: Sf: 0-4 GS: 0-2 Gd: 0-0 GF: - Fm: 0-0
Distance: 2m/2m3: 0-6 2m4-2m7: 0-0 3m+: 0-0
Track: LH: 0-5 RH: 0-1 Tight: 0-2 Gall: 0-0
Aids: Bl: 0-6 Vi: 0-0 Tstrap: 0-0
Best Rating: 72   11/02   Uttx   2m   soft   Hdl

Masouri Sana (IRE)

6-y-o br m Broken Hearted-Say Thanks (Thatching)
Miss M E Rowland Paul Mayo

Placings:0   (1494)
2002/03: 17⁰GS,

	Starts	1st	2nd	3rd	Win & Pl
NH Flat	1	0	0	0	
Career Total	1	0	0	0	

Going: Sf: 0-0 GS: 0-1 Gd: 0-0 GF: - Fm: 0-0
Distance: 2m/2m3: 0-1 2m4-2m7: 0-0 3m+: 0-0
Track: LH: 0-1 RH: 0-0 Tight: 0-1 Gall: 0-0
Aids: Bl: 0-0 Vi: 0-0 Tstrap: 0-0

Best Rating: 0   10/02   Bang   2m1f   gd-sft   NHF

Massenet (IRE)
98
8-y-o b g Caerleon (USA)-Massawippi (Be My Native (USA))
D J Wintle Hugh M Duffy

Placings:3030/1-U   (3853)
2002/03: 19⁰GS,

	Starts	1st	2nd	3rd	Win & Pl
Hurdles	1	0	0	0	
Career Total	6	1	0	2	3582
91	5/01	Bang	2m4f		G(0-95)HHdl GD £2604

Total win prize-money £2604

Going: Sf: 0-0 GS: 0-1 Gd: 0-0 GF: - Fm: 0-0
Distance: 2m/2m3: 0-0 2m4-2m7: 0-1 3m+: 0-0
Track: LH: 0-0 RH: 0-1 Tight: 0-1 Gall: 0-0
Aids: Bl: 0-0 Vi: 0-0 Tstrap: 0-0
Best Rating: 91   5/01   Bang   2m4f   good   Hdl

Massimo (CAN)
71   85
5-y-o b g Numerous (USA)-Qui Bid (USA) (Spectacular Bid (USA))
Jonjo O Neill Mrs Jonjo O Neill

Placings:PF20-0P   (0324)
2002/03: 16⁰G, 20⁰G,

	Starts	1st	2nd	3rd	Win & Pl
Hurdles	2	0	0	0	
Career Total	6	0	1	0	1060

Going: Sf: 0-0 GS: 0-0 Gd: 0-2 GF: - Fm: 0-0
Distance: 2m/2m3: 0-1 2m4-2m7: 0-0 3m+: 0-0
Track: LH: 0-2 RH: 0-0 Tight: 0-1 Gall: 0-0
Aids: Bl: 0-0 Vi: 0-0 Tstrap: 0-0
Best Rating: 85   3/02   Uttx   2m   heavy   Hdl

Master Billyboy (IRE)
109   109+
5-y-o b g Old Vic-Clonodfoy (Strong Gale)
Mrs S D Williams William Peto

Placings:0-50122   (3874)
2002/03: 16⁵G, 17⁰GS, 19¹GS, 19²GS, 21²S,

	Starts	1st	2nd	3rd	Win & Pl
Hurdles	5	1	2	0	6478
Career Total	6	1	2	0	6478
105	12/02	Extr	2m3f		E Hdl G-S £3584

Total win prize-money £3584

Going: Sf: 0-1 GS: 1-3 Gd: 0-1 GF: - Fm: 0-0
Distance: 2m/2m3: 1-4 2m4-2m7: 0-1 3m+: 0-0
Track: LH: 0-1 RH: 1-4 Tight: 0-1 Gall: 0-1
Aids: Bl: 0-0 Vi: 0-0 Tstrap: 0-0
Best Rating: 109   2/03   Newb   2m5f   soft   Hdl

Fair hurdler; best at around two and a half miles with ease in the ground.

Master Brew
86f   76f
5-y-o b g Homo Sapien-Edithmead (IRE) (Shardari)
J R Best P E Hudson

Placings:00   (2313)
2002/03: 17⁰S, 18⁰HY,

	Starts	1st	2nd	3rd	Win & Pl
NH Flat	2	0	0	0	
Career Total	2	0	0	0	

Going: Sf: 0-2 GS: 0-0 Gd: 0-0 GF: - Fm: 0-0
Distance: 2m/2m3: 0-2 2m4-2m7: 0-0 3m+: 0-0
Track: LH: 0-1 RH: 0-1 Tight: 0-0 Gall: 0-0
Aids: Bl: 0-0 Vi: 0-0 Tstrap: 0-0
Best Rating: 76   11/02   Hrfd   2m1f   soft   NHF

Master Chet (IRE)
(94c)   (86c) 81
13-y-o b g Callernish-C C Meade (Paddy s Stream)
Miss Z C Davison Barry Ward

Placings:1P/12/PU/FPP/33F0U4PP0U40-P   (0380)
2002/03: 26⁰G,

	Starts	1st	2nd	3rd	Win & Pl
Hurdles	1	0	0	0	
Career Total	22	2	1	2	8704
113	10/98	Towc	3m1f		E(0-115)HCh G-S £2804
113	12/97	Wwck	3m2f		E Ch G-S £3362

Total win prize-money £6167

Going: Sf: 0-0 GS: 0-0 Gd: 0-1 GF: - Fm: 0-0
Distance: 2m/2m3: 0-0 2m4-2m7: 0-0 3m+: 0-1
Track: LH: 0-0 RH: 0-1 Tight: 0-0 Gall: 0-1
Aids: Bl: 0-1 Vi: 0-0 Tstrap: 0-1
Best Rating: 113   12/98   Towc   3m1f   soft   Ch

Master Club Royal
108   91d
8-y-o b g Teenoso (USA)-Miss Club Royal (Avocat)
D McCain Halewood International Ltd

Placings:6P/53F4335/303P32244-331P464   (4259)
2002/03: 21³HY, 24³S, 27¹S, 26⁶HY, 24⁴S, 22⁶G, 27⁴G,

	Starts	1st	2nd	3rd	Win & Pl
Chases	7	1	0	2	5844
Career Total	25	1	2	8	13391
91	11/02	Sedg	3m3f		E(0-105)HCh SFT £3997

Total win prize-money £3998

Going: Sf: 1-5 GS: 0-0 Gd: 0-2 GF: - Fm: 0-0
Distance: 2m/2m3: 0-0 2m4-2m7: 0-2 3m+: 1-5
Track: LH: 1-7 RH: 0-0 Tight: 1-5 Gall: 0-0
Aids: Bl: 1-6 Vi: 0-0 Tstrap: 0-0
Best Rating: 91   11/02   Sedg   3m3f   soft   Ch

Finally broke his duck over fences at Sedgefield in November but is moody and hard to predict.

Master Cruise
7-y-o b g Zambrano-Miss Cruise (Cruise Missile)
N M Babbage C Bowkett

Placings:P   (3672)
2002/03: 22⁰PGS,

	Starts	1st	2nd	3rd	Win & Pl
Hurdles	1	0	0	0	
Career Total	1	0	0	0	

Going: Sf: 0-0 GS: 0-1 Gd: 0-0 GF: - Fm: 0-0
Distance: 2m/2m3: 0-0 2m4-2m7: 0-1 3m+: 0-0
Track: LH: 0-1 RH: 0-0 Tight: 0-1 Gall: 0-0
Aids: Bl: 0-0 Vi: 0-0 Tstrap: 0-0

Best Rating: 0   2/03   Font   2m6f110y   gd-sft   Hdl

Master Elect (IRE)
87f   88f
6-y-o ch g Phardante (FR)-Proud Polly (IRE) (Pollerton)
M Pitman   G C Stevens

Placings:5   (0907)
2002/03: 16⁵G,

	Starts	1st	2nd	3rd	Win & Pl
NH Flat	1	0	0	0	0
Career Total	1	0	0	0	0

Going: Sf: 0-0 GS: 0-0 Gd: 0-1 GF: - Fm: 0-0
Distance: 2m/2m3: 0-1 2m4-2m7: 0-0 3m+: 0-0
Track: LH: 0-1 RH: 0-0 Tight: 0-0 Gall: 0-0
Aids: Bl: 0-0 Vi: 0-0 Tstrap: 0-0
Best Rating: 88   8/02   Worc   2m   good   NHF

Some promise on his bumper debut.

Master Ellis (IRE)
89   70
4-y-o b g Turtle Island (IRE)-Take No Chances (IRE)
(Thatching)
P D Evans   P D Evans

Placings:P042   (4445)
2002/03: 17^PS, 16⁹GS, 174⁵S, 16²G,

	Starts	1st	2nd	3rd	Win & Pl
Hurdles	4	0	1	0	1000
Career Total	4	0	1	0	1000

Going: Sf: 0-2 GS: 0-1 Gd: 0-1 GF: - Fm: 0-0
Distance: 2m/2m3: 0-4 2m4-2m7: 0-0 3m+: 0-0
Track: LH: 0-0 RH: 0-4 Tight: 0-0 Gall: 0-0
Aids: Bl: 0-0 Vi: 0-0 Tstrap: 0-0
Best Rating: 70   4/03   Ludl   2m   good   Hdl

Very modest form over hurdles so far.

Master Florian (IRE)
103   101+
6-y-o gr g Roselier (FR)-Paddy s Well (Paddy s Stream)
P F Nicholls   K G Manley

Placings:114   (3335)
2002/03: 21¹S, 20¹S, 244⁴S,

	Starts	1st	2nd	3rd	Win & Pl
Hurdles	3	2	0	0	6987
Career Total	3	2	0	0	6987
102 12/02 Font	2m4f	E(0-105)HHdl	SFT	£3445
95 11/02 Plum	2m5f	E Hdl	SFT	£3251

Total win prize-money £6697

Going: Sf: 2-3 GS: 0-0 Gd: 0-0 GF: - Fm: 0-0
Distance: 2m/2m3: 0-0 **2m4-2m7: 2-2** 3m+: 0-1
Track: **LH: 1-1** RH: 0-1 **Tight: 2-3** Gall: 0-0
Aids: Bl: 0-0 Vi: 0-0 Tstrap: 0-0
Best Rating: 102   12/02   Font   2m4f   soft   Hdl

Winner of a point and his first two races over hurdles at
Plumpton and Fontwell. Looks to need a test of stamina.
Acts on soft.

Master Gatemaker
93   42
5-y-o b g Tragic Role (USA)-Girl At The Gate (Formidable
(USA))

R C Guest (N B Mason 16/12) George and Doris Racing

Placings:F0P00   (4679)
2002/03: 17^FG, 16⁰GS, 17^PG, 17⁰S, 16⁰GF,

	Starts	1st	2nd	3rd	Win & Pl
Hurdles	5	0	0	0	
Career Total	5	0	0	0	

Going: Sf: 0-1 GS: 0-1 Gd: 0-2 GF: - Fm: 0-1
Distance: 2m/2m3: 0-5 2m4-2m7: 0-0 3m+: 0-0
Track: LH: 0-3 RH: 0-2 Tight: 0-3 Gall: 0-1
Aids: Bl: 0-0 Vi: 0-0 Tstrap: 0-1
Best Rating: 35   4/03   Hntg   2m110y   gd-fm   Hdl

Master George
111   119d
6-y-o b g Mtoto-Topwinder (USA) (Topsider (USA))
P J Hobbs   David R Watson & Duncan Lofts

Placings:02P-1F0604   (4310)
2002/03: 20¹HY, 20^FS, 19⁰GS, 206⁶HY, 22⁰GS, 244⁴G,

	Starts	1st	2nd	3rd	Win & Pl
Hurdles	6	1	0	0	5561
Career Total	9	1	1	0	7921
126 11/02 Asct	2m4f	D Hdl	HVY	£5161

Total win prize-money £5161

Going: Sf: 1-3 GS: 0-2 Gd: 0-1 GF: - Fm: 0-0
Distance: 2m/2m3: 0-1 **2m4-2m7: 1-4** 3m+: 0-1
Track: LH: 0-2 RH: **1-4** Tight: 0-0 Gall: 0-1
Aids: Bl: 0-1 Vi: 0-0 Tstrap: 0-0
Best Rating: 126   11/02   Asct   2m4f   heavy   Hdl

Fair staying novice hurdler; stays 2m 4f, handles fast
ground, but is well suited by heavy; has been disappointing
since falling at Sandown in December 2002.

Master Ginger Pop
104(77h)   (85h)98
7-y-o b g Supreme Leader-Ruckinge Girl (Eborneezer)
Mrs S D Williams   William Peto

Placings:0/FP005P-444PP22   (4696)
2002/03: 234⁴G, 234⁴GS, 234⁴GS, 26⁵HY, 26²GS, 23²G, 26²G,

	Starts	1st	2nd	3rd	Win & Pl
Chases	7	0	2	0	4251
Career Total	14	0	2	0	4251

Going: Sf: 0-1 GS: 0-3 Gd: 0-3 GF: - Fm: 0-0
Distance: 2m/2m3: 0-0 2m4-2m7: 0-0 3m+: 0-7
Track: LH: 0-3 RH: 0-4 Tight: 0-1 Gall: 0-0
Aids: Bl: 0-5 Vi: 0-0 Tstrap: 0-0
Best Rating: 98   4/03   NAbb   3m2f110y   good   Ch

Plating-class chaser; acts on a sound surface; stays three
miles; has worn blinkers.

Master Jed (IRE)
91f   84f
6-y-o br g Bob s Return (IRE)-Evan s Love (Master Owen)
J A B Old   W E Sturt

Placings:06   (4296)
2002/03: 16⁰G, 16⁶GF,

	Starts	1st	2nd	3rd	Win & Pl
NH Flat	2	0	0	0	0
Career Total	2	0	0	0	0

Going: Sf: 0-0 GS: 0-0 Gd: 0-0 GF: - Fm: 0-1

Distance: 2m/2m3: 0-2 2m4-2m7: 0-0 3m+: 0-0
Track: LH: 0-1 RH: 0-1 Tight: 0-0 Gall: 0-0
Aids: Bl: 0-0 Vi: 0-0 Tstrap: 0-0
Best Rating: 84   3/03   Winc   2m   gd-fm   NHF

Master Jock
9-y-o ch g Scottish Reel-Mistress Corrado (New Member)
P Jones   P S Burke

Placings:4   (0503)
2002/03: 264⁴G,

	Starts	1st	2nd	3rd	Win & Pl
Chases	1	0	0	0	177
Career Total	1	0	0	0	177

Going: Sf: 0-0 GS: 0-0 Gd: 0-1 GF: - Fm: 0-0
Distance: 2m/2m3: 0-0 2m4-2m7: 0-0 3m+: 0-1
Track: LH: 0-1 RH: 0-0 Tight: 0-1 Gall: 0-0
Aids: Bl: 0-0 Vi: 0-0 Tstrap: 0-0
Best Rating: 62   6/02   Ctml   3m2f   good   Ch

Master Jones
34
6-y-o b g Emperor Jones (USA)-Tight Spin (High Top)
Mrs H L Walton   R Rayner

Placings:0-6   (0655)
2002/03: 246⁶GF,

	Starts	1st	2nd	3rd	Win & Pl
Hurdles	1	0	0	0	0
Career Total	2	0	0	0	0

Going: Sf: 0-0 GS: 0-0 Gd: 0-0 GF: - Fm: 0-1
Distance: 2m/2m3: 0-0 2m4-2m7: 0-0 3m+: 0-1
Track: LH: 0-1 RH: 0-0 Tight: 0-0 Gall: 0-0
Aids: Bl: 0-0 Vi: 0-0 Tstrap: 0-0
Best Rating: 34   4/02   MRas   2m3f110y   good   Hdl

Master McGrath (IRE)
105   115+
5-y-o b g Common Grounds-Darabaka (IRE) (Doyoun)
M C Pipe   Mrs Nicky Chambers & David Metcalf

Placings:413   (3499)
2002/03: 254⁴S, 24¹HY, 243⁴GS,

	Starts	1st	2nd	3rd	Win & Pl
Hurdles	3	1	0	1	3574
Career Total	3	1	0	1	3574
115 1/03 Chep	3m	F Hdl	HVY	£2765

Total win prize-money £2765

Going: Sf: 1-2 GS: 0-1 Gd: 0-0 GF: - Fm: 0-0
Distance: 2m/2m3: 0-0 2m4-2m7: 0-0 **3m+: 1-3**
Track: **LH: 1-2** RH: 0-1 Tight: 0-0 Gall: 0-0
Aids: Bl: 0-0 Vi: 0-0 Tstrap: 0-0
Best Rating: 115   1/03   Chep   3m   heavy   Hdl

Improving over hurdles and landed a maiden hurdle at
Chepstow in January 2003. Stays three miles and is suited
by testing conditions.

Master Millfield (IRE)
11-y-o b g Prince Rupert (FR)-Calash (Indian King (USA))

Stephen Richard Griffiths (R J Baker 6/5) R D Griffiths

Placings:444P/463123114/P60/103/P-PP   (4678)
2002/03: 16PGF, 19PGF,

	Starts	1st	2nd	3rd	Win & Pl
Hurdles	1	0	0	0	0
Chases	1	0	0	0	0
Career Total	22	4	1	3	12793
114	8/00	NAbb	2m1f	E(0-115)HHdl	G-F £2555
125	8/98	Worc	2m	D(0-125)HHdl	G-F £2859
113	8/98	NAbb	2m1f	E(0-100)HHdl	G-F £2911
107	6/98	NAbb	2m1f	E(0-100)HHdl	FRM £2183

Total win prize-money £10510

Going:	Sf: 0-0 GS: 0-0 Gd: 0-0 GF: - Fm: 0-2
Distance:	2m/2m3: 0-2 2m4-2m7: 0-0 3m+: 0-0
Track:	LH: 0-0 RH: 0-2 Tight: 0-0 Gall: 0-0
Aids:	Bl: 0-0 Vi: 0-0 Tstrap: 0-0
Best Rating:	125 8/98 Worc 2m gd-fm Hdl

Master Of Illusion (IRE)

107   **115**

10-y-o ch g Castle Keep-Galloping Gold Vii (Damsire Unregistered)
R Lee   Mrs G Goddard,Ben Hinchliff & Des Murray

Placings:40/03P210320P20P/23524102/2433211/63PP3P-32U201   (4087)
2002/03: 26³S, 25²HY, 24US, 30²S, 24UGS, 241GS,

	Starts	1st	2nd	3rd	Win & Pl
Chases	6	1	2	1	14802
Career Total	42	5	10	8	47365
115	3/03	Strf	3m	D(0-120)HCh	G-S £10270
115	4/01	NAbb	3m2f110yE(0-115)HCh	SFT £5538
115	3/01	Strf	3m	D(0-120)HCh	SFT £7150
115	3/00	Folk	3m2f	E Ch	G-F £3645
99	11/98	Clon	3m	Hdl	SFT £3288

Total win prize-money £29892

Going:	Sf: 0-4 GS: 1-2 Gd: 0-0 GF: - Fm: 0-0
Distance:	2m/2m3: 0-0 2m4-2m7: 0-0 3m+: 1-6
Track:	LH: 1-6 RH: 0-0 Tight: 1-4 Gall: 0-0
Aids:	Bl: 0-0 Vi: 1-4 Tstrap: 0-0
Best Rating:	115 3/03 Strf 3m gd-sft Ch

Fair staying chaser; suited by soft ground and a sharp track; stays in excess of three miles; regularly fitted with a visor.

Master Papa (IRE)

108   **118**

4-y-o br g Key Of Luck (USA)-Beguine (USA) (Green Dancer (USA))
N A Twiston-Davies (Kevin Prendergast 28/11) The Alchemists 2

Placings:413563   (4605)
2002/03: 164S, 161S, 173S, 165HY, 166G, 173G,

	Starts	1st	2nd	3rd	Win & Pl
Hurdles	6	1	0	2	7137
Career Total	6	1	0	2	7137
107	11/02	Thur	2m	Hdl	SFT £3809

Total win prize-money £3810

Going:	Sf: 1-4 GS: 0-0 Gd: 0-2 GF: - Fm: 0-0
Distance:	2m/2m3: 1-6 2m4-2m7: 0-0 3m+: 0-0
Track:	LH: 0-2 RH: 1-4 Tight: 0-1 Gall: 0-1
Aids:	Bl: 0-0 Vi: 0-0 Tstrap: 0-0
Best Rating:	107 2/03 Kemp 2m good Hdl

Ex-Irish; fair juvenile hurdler; shapes as though two and a half miles will suit; acts on good and soft ground.

Master Ride (IRE)

102(83h)   (114h)**99**

8-y-o b g King s Ride-Cahore (Quayside)
A J Lidderdale   Doubleprint

Placings:4/1P/0-223   (3826)
2002/03: 22²G, 23²GS, 24³GS,

	Starts	1st	2nd	3rd	Win & Pl
Hurdles	1	0	1	0	1054
Chases	2	0	1	1	2371
Career Total	7	1	2	1	6421
114	3/01	Font	2m2f110yD Hdl	HVY	£2996

Total win prize-money £2996

Going:	Sf: 0-0 GS: 0-2 Gd: 0-1 GF: - Fm: 0-0
Distance:	2m/2m3: 0-2 2m4-2m7: 0-1 3m+: 0-2
Track:	LH: 0-1 RH: 0-2 Tight: 0-0 Gall: 0-0
Aids:	Bl: 0-0 Vi: 0-0 Tstrap: 0-0
Best Rating:	114 5/02 Extr 2m6f110y good Hdl

Moderate novice chaser; stays three miles.

Master Russell (IRE)

89   **93d**

9-y-o b g Supreme Leader-Quality Suite (Prince Hansel)
P A Pritchard   P A Pritchard

Placings:400/05540/FU250/030-304F   (2634)
2002/03: 22³G, 22⁰S, 214GS, 19FS,

	Starts	1st	2nd	3rd	Win & Pl
Hurdles	4	0	0	1	635
Career Total	20	0	1	2	2064

Going:	Sf: 0-2 GS: 0-1 Gd: 0-1 GF: - Fm: 0-0
Distance:	2m/2m3: 0-1 2m4-2m7: 0-3 3m+: 0-0
Track:	LH: 0-3 RH: 0-1 Tight: 0-2 Gall: 0-0
Aids:	Bl: 0-0 Vi: 0-1 Tstrap: 0-0
Best Rating:	105 1/00 Font 2m2f110y gd-sft Hdl

Selling hurdler; stays well and suited by the mud but has yet to win a race.

Master T (USA)

109   **109**

4-y-o g Trempolino (USA)-Our Little C (USA) (Marquetry (USA))
G L Moore   Lancing Racing Syndicate

Placings:12   (4573)
2002/03: 171F, 162GF,

	Starts	1st	2nd	3rd	Win & Pl
Hurdles	2	1	1	0	5934
Career Total	2	1	1	0	5934
76	3/03	Tntn	2m1f	E Hdl	FRM £4134

Total win prize-money £4134

Going:	Sf: 0-0 GS: 0-0 Gd: 0-0 GF: - Fm: 1-2
Distance:	2m/2m3: 1-2 2m4-2m7: 0-0 3m+: 0-0
Track:	LH: 0-0 RH: 1-1 Tight: 1-2 Gall: 0-0
Aids:	Bl: 0-0 Vi: 0-0 Tstrap: 0-0
Best Rating:	100 4/03 Strf 2m110y gd-fm Hdl

Moderate hurdler; could have been a shade fortunate when making successful debut at Taunton March 2003; acts on fast ground.

Master Tern (USA)

117(114h)   (144h)**146+**

8-y-o ch g Generous (IRE)-Young Hostess (FR) (Arctic Tern (USA)

Jonjo O Neill   J P McManus

Placings:232/040111/260/3F113-4P421   (4469)
2002/03: 20⁴S, 20PGS, 164G, 20²G, 251G,

	Starts	1st	2nd	3rd	Win & Pl
Chases	5	1	1	0	33780
Career Total	22	6	4	3	107100
146	4/03	Aint	3m1f	B HCh	GD £26000
108	3/02	Hntg	2m110y	E Ch	SFT £2992
127	1/02	Leic	2m	E Ch	GD £3536
140	3/00	Chel	2m1f	A HHdl	G-F £30000
143	3/00	Kels	2m2f	B Hdl	G-S £14365
134	1/00	Chel	2m1f	D(0-120)HHdl	G-S £7442

Total win prize-money £84337

Going:	Sf: 0-1 GS: 0-1 Gd: 1-3 GF: - Fm: 0-0
Distance:	2m/2m3: 0-1 2m4-2m7: 0-0 3m+: 0-0
Track:	LH: 1-4 RH: 0-1 Tight: 1-2 Gall: 0-2
Aids:	Bl: 0-0 Vi: 0-0 Tstrap: 0-0
Best Rating:	149 12/00 Hayd 2m4f heavy Hdl

Very useful hurdler/useful chaser; winner of the County Hurdle at Cheltenham in March 2000; right back to best chase form when runner-up at Kempton in January 2003; took valuable handicap at Aintree in April despite at least one bad mistake; appreciates good ground, but acts on softer; stays three miles, but effective at shorter.

Master Trix (IRE)

108   **118**

6-y-o b g Lord Americo-Bannow Drive (IRE) (Miners Lamp)
M Pitman   Patrick Bancroft

Placings:16-1232PU   (4473)
2002/03: 171S, 212S, 203S, 222HY, 20PHY, 24UG,

	Starts	1st	2nd	3rd	Win & Pl
Hurdles	6	1	2	1	7101
Career Total	8	2	2	1	8739
125	11/02	Folk	2m1f110yE Hdl	SFT	£2905
118	2/02	Font	2m2f110yH NHF	SFT	£1638

Total win prize-money £4543

Going:	Sf: 1-5 GS: 0-0 Gd: 0-1 GF: - Fm: 0-0
Distance:	2m/2m3: 1-1 2m4-2m7: 0-4 3m+: 0-1
Track:	LH: 0-2 RH: 1-4 Tight: 1-3 Gall: 0-1
Aids:	Bl: 0-0 Vi: 0-0 Tstrap: 0-0
Best Rating:	125 11/02 Folk 2m1f110y soft Hdl

Decent novice hurdler; acts on soft ground; stays two miles six.

Master Tumnus (IRE)

51   **14**

7-y-o b g Bob Back (USA)-Implicit View (Persian Bold)
A Dickman   Mrs B M Bennett

Placings:1/0/0FP   (3963)
2002/03: 16⁰GS, 16FG, 16PS,

	Starts	1st	2nd	3rd	Win & Pl
Hurdles	3	0	0	0	
Career Total	5	1	0	0	2834
82	3/00	Strf	2m10y	H NHF	GD £2834

Total win prize-money £2834

Going:	Sf: 0-1 GS: 0-1 Gd: 0-0 GF: - Fm: 0-0
Distance:	2m/2m3: 0-3 2m4-2m7: 0-0 3m+: 0-0
Track:	LH: 0-3 RH: 0-0 Tight: 0-2 Gall: 0-1
Aids:	Bl: 0-0 Vi: 0-0 Tstrap: 0-0
Best Rating:	82 3/00 Strf 2m10y good NHF

Master Wood

12-y-o b g Wonderful Surprise-Miss Wood (Precipice Wood)
C Grant Chris Grant

Placings:5600/PP4111FPP326/P1P15104/1F31/PPP-44211UP (4714)
2002/03: 25⁴GS, 30⁴G, 25²GS, 22¹GS, 25¹G, 21^UG, 25^PGF,

	Starts	1st	2nd	3rd	Win & Pl
Chases	7	2	1	0	12027
Career Total	38	10	2	2	63187

126	3/03	Weth	3m1f	H Ch	GD	£2226
123	2/03	Hayd	2m6f	H Ch	G-S	£8840
132	12/00	Weth	2m4f110yB	HCh	SFT	£15008
131	10/00	Kels	2m6f110yD(0-120)HCh		SFT	£4654
130	3/00	Weth	2m4f110yC(0-135)HCh		G-S	£7182
111	1/00	Weth	2m4f110yD(0-125)HCh		SFT	£4177
107	11/99	Weth	3m1f	D(0-125)HCh	GD	£4090
118	11/98	Weth	3m1f	D Ch	GD	£4248
107	10/98	Weth	2m4f110yC	HCh	GD	£4739
118	10/98	Carl	2m4f110yE	Ch	HVY	£2918

Total win prize-money £58083

Going: Sf: 0-0 GS: 1-3 Gd: 1-3 GF: - Fm: 0-1
Distance: 2m2m3: 0-0 2m4-2m7: 1-2 3m+: 1-5
Track: LH: 2-6 RH: 0-0 Tight: 0-1 Gall: 0-0
Aids: Bl: 0-0 Vi: 0-0 Tstrap: 0-0
Best Rating: 132 12/00 Weth 2m4f110y soft Ch

Decent hunter chaser; beat Torduff Express at Haydock in February 2003 and followed up at Wetherby the following month; best at short of three miles; goes well on soft or heavy ground.

Material World
104f   110+f

5-y-o b m Karinga Bay-Material Girl (Busted)
Miss Suzy Smith Southern Bloodstock

Placings:1 (4788)
2002/03: 17¹G,

	Starts	1st	2nd	3rd	Win & Pl
NH Flat	1	1	0	0	2030
Career Total	1	1	0	0	2030

110	4/03	MRas	2m1f110yH NHF	GD	£2030

Total win prize-money £2030

Going: Sf: 0-0 GS: 0-0 Gd: 1-1 GF: - Fm: 0-0
Distance: 2m2m3: 1-1 2m4-2m7: 0-0 3m+: 0-0
Track: LH: 0-0 RH: 1-1 Tight: 1-1 Gall: 0-0
Aids: Bl: 0-0 Vi: 0-0 Tstrap: 0-0
Best Rating: 110 4/03 MRas 2m1f110y good NHF

Blind in her left eye, and needs to go right-handed; made a successful bow in modest bumper at Market Rasen in April; followed up at Hereford.

Matrix (AUS)
94   83

6-y-o b g Centaine (AUS)-Iced Lass (NZ) (Half Iced (USA))
K C Bailey Mrs M C Sweeney

Placings:00-0506 (4340)
2002/03: 19⁰G, 21⁵S, 16⁰S, 26⁶GF,

	Starts	1st	2nd	3rd	Win & Pl
Hurdles	4	0	0	0	0
Career Total	6	0	0	0	0

Going: Sf: 0-2 GS: 0-0 Gd: 0-1 GF: - Fm: 0-1
Distance: 2m2m3: 0-1 2m4-2m7: 0-2 3m+: 0-1
Track: LH: 0-0 RH: 0-4 Tight: 0-0 Gall: 0-2
Aids: Bl: 0-0 Vi: 0-0 Tstrap: 0-0

Best Rating: 98 2/02 Kemp 2m good NHF

Well held in two bumpers in early 2002.

Matt Holland
(100h)   (104h)

10-y-o b g Makbul-Shirley Grove (Vulgan Slave)
Mrs L Wadham Waterhall Racing

Placings:10/342/3-F0P (3995)
2002/03: 21^FS, 23⁹GS, 23^PG,

	Starts	1st	2nd	3rd	Win & Pl
Chases	3	0	0	0	
Career Total	9	1	1	2	3382

122	11/98	Worc	2m	H NHF	HVY	£1329

Total win prize-money £1329

Going: Sf: 0-1 GS: 0-1 Gd: 0-1 GF: - Fm: 0-0
Distance: 2m2m3: 0-0 2m4-2m7: 0-1 3m+: 0-0
Track: LH: 0-0 RH: 0-2 Tight: 0-1 Gall: 0-0
Aids: Bl: 0-0 Vi: 0-0 Tstrap: 0-0
Best Rating: 122 11/98 Worc 2m heavy NHF

Maunby Roller (IRE)

4-y-o b g Flying Spur (AUS)-Brown Foam (Horage)
P A Blockley (R Wilman 15/2) D S Cooper

Placings:PP (4372)
2002/03: 16⁶GS, 21^PG,

	Starts	1st	2nd	3rd	Win & Pl
Hurdles	2	0	0	0	
Career Total	2	0	0	0	

Going: Sf: 0-0 GS: 0-1 Gd: 0-1 GF: - Fm: 0-0
Distance: 2m2m3: 0-1 2m4-2m7: 0-1 3m+: 0-0
Track: LH: 0-2 RH: 0-0 Tight: 0-1 Gall: 0-0
Aids: Bl: 0-1 Vi: 0-0 Tstrap: 0-0
Best Rating: 0 3/03 Sedg 2m5f110y good Hdl

Maunsell's Road (IRE)
79   91

4-y-o b g Desert Style (IRE)-Zara s Birthday (IRE) (Waajib)
L Lungo (S Kirk 10/10) Clarke Boon

Placings:03 (4306)
2002/03: 17⁹GS, 18³G,

	Starts	1st	2nd	3rd	Win & Pl
Hurdles	2	0	0	1	644
Career Total	2	0	0	1	644

Going: Sf: 0-0 GS: 0-1 Gd: 0-1 GF: - Fm: 0-0
Distance: 2m2m3: 0-2 2m4-2m7: 0-0 3m+: 0-0
Track: LH: 0-1 RH: 0-1 Tight: 0-1 Gall: 0-0
Aids: Bl: 0-0 Vi: 0-0 Tstrap: 0-0
Best Rating: 91 3/03 Kels 2m2f good Hdl

Winner on the Flat; modest form over hurdles; best on fast ground.

Mawthook (USA)
10f

5-y-o ch g Silver Hawk (USA)-Zakiyya (USA) (Dayjur (USA))
J R Turner Oliver J Turner

Placings:0-0 (0361)

2002/03: 16⁰GS,

	Starts	1st	2nd	3rd	Win & Pl
NH Flat	1	0	0	0	
Career Total	2	0	0	0	

Max Pride
112(104h)   (98h)121

8-y-o br g Good Thyne (USA)-An Bothar Dubh (Strong Gale)
R Dickin Mrs J Cumiskey, M Doocey & K Doocey

Placings:05P/241UP/211F344P-14112 (4057)
2002/03: 22¹GS, 22⁴S, 29¹GS, 30¹S, 29²GS,

	Starts	1st	2nd	3rd	Win & Pl
Hurdles	1	1	0	0	3325
Chases	4	2	1	0	12928
Career Total	21	6	3	1	37758

121	2/03	Bang	3m6f	D(0-120)HCh	SFT	£5629
117	12/02	Wwck	3m5f	D(0-120)HCh	G-S	£4680
98	11/02	Extr	2m6f110yE(0-105)HHdl		G-S	£3325
112	11/01	Newb	2m6f110yE(0-115)HCh		GD	£5850
95	10/01	Towc	3m1f	D(0-120)HCh	SFT	£8437
100	2/01	Leic	2m4f110yF(0-95)HCh		SFT	£2931

Total win prize-money £30853

Going: Sf: 1-2 GS: 2-3 Gd: 0-0 GF: - Fm: 0-0
Distance: 2m2m3: 0-0 2m4-2m7: 1-2 3m+: 2-3
Track: LH: 2-4 RH: 1-1 Tight: 1-1 Gall: 0-1
Aids: Bl: 0-0 Vi: 0-0 Tstrap: 0-0
Best Rating: 121 3/03 Wwck 3m5f gd-sft Ch

Fair handicap hurdler/chaser; stays really well and was winning for the third time in his last four starts when scoring in most decisive fashion at Bangor in February 2003; jumps well.

Max's Micro (IRE)
97   78

4-y-o b g Inzar (USA)-Guess Who (Be My Guest (USA))
John Allen Dingley Dell Racing Ltd

Placings:06S50213 (3573)
2002/03: 17⁰G, 16⁶GS, 16⁵GS, 16⁵HY, 17⁰GS, 16²HY, 16¹HY, 16³HY,

	Starts	1st	2nd	3rd	Win & Pl
Hurdles	8	1	1	1	4801
Career Total	8	1	1	1	4801

78	1/03	Leic	2m	F Hdl	HVY	£3493

Total win prize-money £3494

Going: Sf: 1-4 GS: 0-3 Gd: 0-1 GF: - Fm: 0-0
Distance: 2m2m3: 1-8 2m4-2m7: 0-0 3m+: 0-0
Track: LH: 0-1 RH: 1-7 Tight: 0-1 Gall: 0-1
Aids: Bl: 0-0 Vi: 0-2 Tstrap: 0-0
Best Rating: 78 2/03 Leic 2m heavy Hdl

Moderate hurdler at around two miles on a soft surface.

Maxie McDonald (IRE)
103   108

10-y-o b g Homo Sapien-Lovely Sanara (Proverb)
N A Twiston-Davies Mrs J E Meek

Placings:000/4P/B122121F-3U42U (3320)

2002/03: 24³GF, 24ᵁGS, 23⁴G, 20²G, 24ᵁGS,

	Starts	1st	2nd	3rd	Win & Pl
Chases	5	0	1	1	4008
Career Total	18	3	4	1	24203
95 11/01 Asct	3m110y C(0-130)HCh		G-F		£8180
97 7/01 Worc	2m7f110yF(0-110)HCh		GD		£2429
96 5/01 Bang	2m4f110yF(0-105)HCh		GD		£3626

Total win prize-money £14235

Going:	Sf: 0-0 GS: 0-2 Gd: 0-2 GF: - Fm: 0-1
Distance:	2m/2m3: 0-0 2m4-2m7: 0-1 3m+: 0-4
Track:	LH: 0-3 RH: 0-2 Tight: 0-3 Gall: 0-0
Aids:	Bl: 0-0 Vi: 0-0 Tstrap: 0-0
Best Rating:	110 10/01 Chel 2m4f110y good Ch

He has taken well to chasing, winning three times in 2001, but his form appears to have plateaued. Suited by good ground and stays three miles.

Maximize (IRE)
115   (88h)144

9-y-o b g Mandalus-Lone Run (Kemal (FR))
Miss H C Knight Lady Vestey

Placings:322446/2121162-4404F   (4479)
2002/03: 25⁴G, 24⁴GS, 24⁰G, 24⁴G, 36⁴G,

	Starts	1st	2nd	3rd	Win & Pl
Chases	5	0	0	0	7344
Career Total	18	3	5	1	58905
141 12/01 Kemp	3m A Ch		GD		£29750
124 11/01 Kemp	3m D Ch		GD		£4153
121 10/01 Winc	3m1f110y D Ch		GD		£4407

Total win prize-money £38311

Going:	Sf: 0-0 GS: 0-1 Gd: 0-4 GF: - Fm: 0-0
Distance:	2m/2m3: 0-0 2m4-2m7: 0-0 3m+: 0-5
Track:	LH: 0-2 RH: 0-3 Tight: 0-1 Gall: 0-1
Aids:	Bl: 0-0 Vi: 0-0 Tstrap: 0-0
Best Rating:	144 12/02 Sand 3m110y gd-sft Ch

Useful handicap chaser; jumps well; effective on good ground; stays three miles.

Maximus (IRE)
100   97

8-y-o br g Un Desperado (FR)-Fais Vite (USA) (Sharpen Up)
C P Morlock (D M Grissell 3/6) Cockerell Cowing Racing

Placings:110/4U000-000230   (4030)
2002/03: 16⁰S, 22⁰GF, 17⁰S, 22²S, 22³GS, 22⁰HY,

	Starts	1st	2nd	3rd	Win & Pl
Hurdles	6	0	1	1	1348
Career Total	14	2	1	1	9735
123 2/01 Newb	2m110y C Hdl		SFT		£6045
116 1/01 Plum	2m E Hdl		SFT		£1918

Total win prize-money £7963

Going:	Sf: 0-4 GS: 0-1 Gd: 0-0 GF: - Fm: 0-1
Distance:	2m/2m3: 0-2 2m4-2m7: 0-4 3m+: 0-0
Track:	LH: 0-3 RH: 0-3 Tight: 0-4 Gall: 0-0
Aids:	Bl: 0-0 Vi: 0-0 Tstrap: 0-1
Best Rating:	123 10/01 Strf 2m3f gd-sft Hdl

Modest hurdler these days; best on soft ground; stays three miles.

Mayb-Mayb

13-y-o ch g Gunner B-Mayotte (Little Buskins)
J Neville Ian Muir

Placings:03/040/51F111/P2P310223P/4501P0P/000PP-0   (0343)

2002/03: 22⁰GS,

	Starts	1st	2nd	3rd	Win & Pl
Hurdles	1	0	0	0	
Career Total	34	6	3	3	21605
115 1/01 Winc	2m6f	E(0-115)HHdl	SFT	£3332
115 1/00 Plum	2m5f	D(0-125)HHdl	SFT	£3136
110 4/97 Worc	3m	E(0-100)HHdl	SFT	£2775
99 3/97 Plum	2m4f	F(0-100)HHdl	G-S	£2012
91 2/97 Plum	2m4f	F(0-100)HHdl	SFT	£1941
79 2/97 Plum	2m4f	F(0-105)HHdl	G-S	£2194

Total win prize-money £15391

Going:	Sf: 0-0 GS: 0-1 Gd: 0-0 GF: - Fm: 0-0
Distance:	2m/2m3: 0-0 2m4-2m7: 0-3 3m+: 0-0
Track:	LH: 0-1 RH: 0-0 Tight: 0-1 Gall: 0-0
Aids:	Bl: 0-1 Vi: 0-0 Tstrap: 0-1
Best Rating:	115 1/01 Winc 2m6f soft Hdl

Winning hurdler; placed in points; stays extreme distances.

Maybe Just Maybe (IRE)

6-y-o b g Tirol-Templemore (IRE) (Alzao (USA))
Mrs A M Thorpe Just Maybe Club

Placings:0/0-P   (0214)
2002/03: 19⁰G,

	Starts	1st	2nd	3rd	Win & Pl
Hurdles	1	0	0	0	
Career Total	3	0	0	0	

Going:	Sf: 0-0 GS: 0-0 Gd: 0-1 GF: - Fm: 0-0
Distance:	2m/2m3: 0-0 2m4-2m7: 0-1 3m+: 0-0
Track:	LH: 0-0 RH: 0-1 Tight: 0-0 Gall: 0-0
Aids:	Bl: 0-0 Vi: 0-0 Tstrap: 0-0
Best Rating:	41 1/02 Ludl 2m good NHF

Maybe The Business
110   134+

7-y-o ch g Karinga Bay-Music Interpreter (Kampala)
P F Nicholls D J & F A Jackson

Placings:11-F2144   (3291)
2002/03: 20⁴S, 16²GS, 22¹HY, 21⁴HY, 24⁴GS,

	Starts	1st	2nd	3rd	Win & Pl
Hurdles	5	1	1	0	6750
Career Total	7	3	1	0	12042
121 12/02 Folk	2m6f110yF Hdl		HVY		£2275
136 4/02 Ayr	2m	H NHF	GD		£3342
118 3/02 Winc	2m	H NHF	SFT		£1949

Total win prize-money £7568

Going:	Sf: 1-3 GS: 0-2 Gd: 0-0 GF: - Fm: 0-0
Distance:	2m/2m3: 0-1 2m4-2m7: 1-3 3m+: 0-1
Track:	LH: 0-4 RH: 1-1 Tight: 1-1 Gall: 0-2
Aids:	Bl: 0-0 Vi: 0-0 Tstrap: 0-0
Best Rating:	136 4/02 Ayr 2m good NHF

Winning pointer and fair novice hurdler but died after finishing fourth in a Grade Two at Doncaster in January 2003. (DEAD)

Maybe'N

6-y-o ch g Deploy-Travel Mystery (Godswalk (USA))
M Ranger P J Turner

Placings:4P60/P-4   (0247)

2002/03: 19⁴G,

	Starts	1st	2nd	3rd	Win & Pl
Chases	1	0	0	0	122
Career Total	6	0	0	0	122

Going:	Sf: 0-0 GS: 0-0 Gd: 0-1 GF: - Fm: 0-0
Distance:	2m/2m3: 0-0 2m4-2m7: 0-1 3m+: 0-0
Track:	LH: 0-0 RH: 0-0 Tight: 0-0 Gall: 0-0
Aids:	Bl: 0-0 Vi: 0-0 Tstrap: 0-0
Best Rating:	88 1/01 Folk 2m1f110y heavy Hdl

Maybelle
85   50

8-y-o b m Royal Vulcan-Full Of Love (Full Of Hope)
J S King W J Lee

Placings:00/0P-06   (4268)
2002/03: 21⁰GS, 16⁰G, 20⁶GF,

	Starts	1st	2nd	3rd	Win & Pl
Hurdles	3	0	0	0	0
Career Total	6	0	0	0	0

Going:	Sf: 0-0 GS: 0-1 Gd: 0-1 GF: - Fm: 0-1
Distance:	2m/2m3: 0-0 2m4-2m7: 0-2 3m+: 0-0
Track:	LH: 0-1 RH: 0-2 Tight: 0-1 Gall: 0-1
Aids:	Bl: 0-0 Vi: 0-0 Tstrap: 0-0
Best Rating:	50 3/03 Sthl 2m4f110y gd-fm Hdl

Maybeseven
93   70

9-y-o gr g Baron Blakeney-Ninth Of May (Comedy Star (USA))
T R George The Diamond Seven Partnership

Placings:00/44613/P04P/**P13P6PPP**-43PP   (3824)
2002/03: 26⁴HY, 20³S, 22²S, 26⁰GS,

	Starts	1st	2nd	3rd	Win & Pl
Chases	4	0	0	1	852
Career Total	23	2	0	3	7718
88 10/01 Folk	3m1f	F(0-100)HCh	GD	£3347
96 2/00 Hntg	3m2f	F(0-110)HHdl	SFT	£2296

Total win prize-money £5644

Going:	Sf: 0-3 GS: 0-1 Gd: 0-0 GF: - Fm: 0-0
Distance:	2m/2m3: 0-0 2m4-2m7: 0-2 3m+: 0-2
Track:	LH: 0-2 RH: 0-1 Tight: 0-2 Gall: 0-0
Aids:	Bl: 0-1 Vi: 0-0 Tstrap: 0-0
Best Rating:	96 2/00 Hntg 3m2f soft Hdl

A selling-class stayer, has been successful in modest races over hurdles and fences. Won a weak contest on his second start over fences at Folkestone in October 2001. Suited by cut in the ground and goes well on a right-handed track.

Mayerling
75   49

6-y-o b m Old Vic-Manon Lescaut (Then Again)
Miss E C Lavelle Mrs R J Lavelle

Placings:0-0F   (4366)
2002/03: 20⁰GS, 20⁴G,

	Starts	1st	2nd	3rd	Win & Pl
Hurdles	2	0	0	0	
Career Total	3	0	0	0	

Going:	Sf: 0-0 GS: 0-1 Gd: 0-1 GF: - Fm: 0-0
Distance:	2m/2m3: 0-0 2m4-2m7: 0-2 3m+: 0-0
Track:	LH: 0-0 RH: 0-2 Tight: 0-0 Gall: 0-1

Aids: Bl: 0-0 Vi: 0-0 Tstrap: 0-0
Best Rating: 63 3/02 Towc 2m soft NHF

Maylane

9-y-o b g Mtoto-Possessive Dancer (Shareef Dancer (USA))
B G Powell Jebel Ali Racing Stables

Placings:RR   (0775)
2002/03: 16RGF, 16RGF,

	Starts	1st	2nd	3rd	Win & Pl
Hurdles	2	0	0	0	
Career Total	2	0	0	0	

Going: Sf: 0-0 GS: 0-0 Gd: 0-0 GF: - Fm: 0-2
Distance: 2m/2m3: 0-2 2m4-2m7: 0-0 3m+: 0-0
Track: LH: 0-2 RH: 0-0 Tight: 0-1 Gall: 0-0
Aids: Bl: 0-0 Vi: 0-0 Tstrap: 0-0
Best Rating: 0 7/02 Worc 2m gd-fm Hdl

Mazeed (IRE)

96   84

10-y-o ch g Lycius (USA)-Maraatib (IRE) (Green Desert (USA))
Miss K M George Roland John Hair Studio Ii

Placings:P0P3250/6261330400/032155000-06064P (1172)
2002/03: 22OGF, 22RGF, 20OGF, 27RGF, 22AGF, 22PGF,

	Starts	1st	2nd	3rd	Win & Pl
Hurdles	6	0	0	0	0
Career Total	32	2	3	4	8927
84	7/01	Strf	2m3f	F(0-95)HHdl	GD	£2744
86	7/00	Sedg	2m5f110yE Hdl		FRM	£2296

Total win prize-money £5040

Going: Sf: 0-0 GS: 0-0 Gd: 0-0 GF: - Fm: 0-6
Distance: 2m/2m3: 0-0 2m4-2m7: 0-0 3m+: 0-1
Track: LH: 0-6 RH: 0-0 Tight: 0-5 Gall: 0-0
Aids: Bl: 0-3 Vi: 0-3 Tstrap: 0-0
Best Rating: 86 7/00 Sedg 2m5f110y firm Hdl

Mazileo

109(97h)   (91h)132+

10-y-o b g Mazilier (USA)-Embroglio (USA) (Empery (USA))
Ian Williams T J & Mrs H Parrott

Placings:41/5P052/1101621/31U31F15F/400/06033F414P-5U1   (1845)
2002/03: 24AGS, 24UGg, 241GS,

	Starts	1st	2nd	3rd	Win & Pl
Hurdles	1	0	0	0	0
Chases	2	1	0	0	8307
Career Total	39	10	3	4	55262
132	11/02	Sand	3m110y	C(0-130)HCh	G-S	£8307
121	4/02	Hrfd	3m1f110yE(0-110)HCh		G-F	£7577
123	11/99	Hayd	2m4f	B Ch	G-S	£11265
121	11/99	Ludl	2m4f	E Ch	GD	£3533
122	9/99	Hntg	2m110y	E Ch	G-F	£3441
124	4/99	Towc	2m	D(0-125)HHdl	GD	£3829
110	11/98	Ludl	2m	E Hdl	GD	£2948
122	10/98	Hrfd	2m1f	E Hdl	G-F	£2829
116	10/98	NAbb	2m1f	E Hdl	GD	£2583
92	3/97	NAbb	2m1f	H NHF	G-F	£1299

Total win prize-money £47613

Going: Sf: 0-0 GS: 1-1 Gd: 0-2 GF: - Fm: 0-0
Distance: 2m/2m3: 0-0 2m4-2m7: 0-0 3m+: 1-3
Track: LH: 0-0 RH: 1-2 Tight: 0-0 Gall: 0-0
Aids: Bl: 0-0 Vi: 0-0 Tstrap: 0-0

Best Rating: 132 11/02 Sand 3m110y gd-sft Ch

Mixes hurdling and chasing these days and jumped very well when winning at Sandown in November 2002. Stays three miles and acts on soft ground.

Mazram

78f   30f

4-y-o b f Muhtarram (USA)-Royal Mazi (King s Lake (USA))
G P Kelly A M McArdle

Placings:00   (4357)
2002/03: 17OG, 16OGF,

	Starts	1st	2nd	3rd	Win & Pl
NH Flat	2	0	0	0	
Career Total	2	0	0	0	

Going: Sf: 0-0 GS: 0-0 Gd: 0-1 GF: - Fm: 0-1
Distance: 2m/2m3: 0-2 2m4-2m7: 0-0 3m+: 0-0
Track: LH: 0-1 RH: 0-1 Tight: 0-1 Gall: 0-0
Aids: Bl: 0-0 Vi: 0-0 Tstrap: 0-0
Best Rating: 32 3/03 Weth 2m gd-fm NHF

Mazury (USA)

92   62

4-y-o b g Langfuhr (CAN)-Assurgent (USA) (Damascus (USA))
Miss J S Davis (M C Chapman 17/9) Miss J Davis

Placings:005P5   (4597)
2002/03: 17OGS, 16OG, 17SF, 16PF, 17SGF,

	Starts	1st	2nd	3rd	Win & Pl
Hurdles	5	0	0	0	0
Career Total	5	0	0	0	0

Going: Sf: 0-0 GS: 0-1 Gd: 0-2 GF: - Fm: 0-2
Distance: 2m/2m3: 0-5 2m4-2m7: 0-0 3m+: 0-0
Track: LH: 0-1 RH: 0-4 Tight: 0-1 Gall: 0-0
Aids: Bl: 0-0 Vi: 0-0 Tstrap: 0-0
Best Rating: 62 3/03 Tntn 2m1f firm Hdl

A mile winner on Fibresand; appears to be struggling to get the trip.

Mazzini (IRE)

103   99

12-y-o b g Celio Rufo-Dontellvi (The Parson)
R Rowe Richard Rowe

Placings:04/01210344/43FP/0/254/P3551016   (4759)
2002/03: 16PG, 22AGF, 22SGF, 26SGS, 221G, 20HY, 221G, 27SGF,

	Starts	1st	2nd	3rd	Win & Pl
Hurdles	8	2	0	1	6217
Career Total	26	4	2	3	14007
99	3/03	Font	2m6f110yF(0-100)HHdl		GD	£2765
99	12/02	Font	2m6f110yE(0-105)HHdl		GD	£3010
103	11/96	Winc	2m	E Hdl	GD	£2600
91	10/96	Kemp	2m	D Hdl	G-F	£2840

Total win prize-money £11215

Going: Sf: 0-1 GS: 0-1 Gd: 2-3 GF: - Fm: 0-3
Distance: 2m/2m3: 0-1 2m4-2m7: 2-5 3m+: 0-2
Track: LH: 2-5 RH: 0-2 Tight: 2-5 Gall: 0-1
Aids: Bl: 0-0 Vi: 0-0 Tstrap: 0-0
Best Rating: 104 11/97 Wind 2m good Hdl

Modest hurdler, stays two and three-quarter miles. Returned to action in the summer of 2002 after three years absence.

Mccrinkle (IRE)

6-y-o br g Mandalus-Crinkle Lady (Buckskin (FR))
Mrs C J Kerr Mrs C J Kerr

Placings:0   (4778)
2002/03: 16OG,

	Starts	1st	2nd	3rd	Win & Pl
NH Flat	1	0	0	0	
Career Total	1	0	0	0	

Going: Sf: 0-0 GS: 0-0 Gd: 0-1 GF: - Fm: 0-0
Distance: 2m/2m3: 0-1 2m4-2m7: 0-0 3m+: 0-0
Track: LH: 0-0 RH: 0-1 Tight: 0-0 Gall: 0-0
Aids: Bl: 0-0 Vi: 0-0 Tstrap: 0-0
Best Rating: 0 4/03 Prth 2m110y good NHF

Mcfarline (IRE)

7-y-o b g Ela-Mana-Mou-Highland Ball (Bold Lad (IRE))
N J Hawke N J Hawke

Placings:0001/03/F0PP   (4485)
2002/03: 19FS, 16OGS, 17PS, 19PGF,

	Starts	1st	2nd	3rd	Win & Pl
Hurdles	3	0	0	0	
Chases	1	0	0	0	
Career Total	10	1	0	1	2579
84	4/00	Plum	2m	E(0-105)HHdl	G-S	£2240

Total win prize-money £2240

Going: Sf: 0-2 GS: 0-1 Gd: 0-0 GF: - Fm: 0-1
Distance: 2m/2m3: 0-3 2m4-2m7: 0-1 3m+: 0-0
Track: LH: 0-1 RH: 0-3 Tight: 0-1 Gall: 0-0
Aids: Bl: 0-0 Vi: 0-0 Tstrap: 0-0
Best Rating: 84 5/00 Towc 2m gd-fm Hdl

Mcginty All Stars (IRE)

64f   38f

5-y-o b m Fourstars Allstar (USA)-Dowdstown Miss (Wolver Hollow)
R J Price R J Price

Placings:0   (2450)
2002/03: 16OG,

	Starts	1st	2nd	3rd	Win & Pl
NH Flat	1	0	0	0	
Career Total	1	0	0	0	

Going: Sf: 0-0 GS: 0-0 Gd: 0-1 GF: - Fm: 0-0
Distance: 2m/2m3: 0-1 2m4-2m7: 0-0 3m+: 0-0
Track: LH: 0-0 RH: 0-1 Tight: 0-0 Gall: 0-0
Aids: Bl: 0-0 Vi: 0-0 Tstrap: 0-0
Best Rating: 38 12/02 Ludl 2m good NHF

Mcgruders Cross (IRE)

113f   127f

5-y-o b g Toulon-Kayanna (Torenaga)
Anthony Mullins Leonard Kinsella & Mrs John Magnier

Placings:110   (4115)
2002/03: 16¹S, 16¹YS, 16OG,

	Starts	1st	2nd	3rd	Win & Pl
NH Flat	3	2	0	0	11649

Career Total	3	2	0	0	11649
126 2/03 Navn 2m	NHF		Y-S	£7168
127 1/03 Fair 2m	NHF		SFT	£4480
			Total win prize-money £11650

Going: Sf: 1-1 GS: 0-0 Gd: 0-1 GF: - Fm: 0-0
Distance: 2m/2m3: 2-3 2m4-2m7: 0-0 3m+: 0-0
Track: LH: 0-1 RH: 1-1 Tight: 0-0 Gall: 0-0
Aids: Bl: 0-0 Vi: 0-0 Tstrap: 0-0
Best Rating: 127 1/03 Fair 2m soft NHF

Useful Irish bumper performer.

Mcsnappy

97   **104**

6-y-o ch g Risk Me (FR)-Nannie Annie (Persian Bold)
J W Mullins Cum-Lake Racing

Placings: 22/3403-23   (2079)
2002/03: 24²S, 24³HY,

	Starts	1st	2nd	3rd	Win & Pl
Hurdles	2	0	1	1	1542
Career Total	8	0	3	3	4566

Going: Sf: 0-2 GS: 0-0 Gd: 0-0 GF: - Fm: 0-0
Distance: 2m/2m3: 0-0 2m4-2m7: 0-0 3m+: 0-2
Track: LH: 0-1 RH: 0-1 Tight: 0-0 Gall: 0-0
Aids: Bl: 0-0 Vi: 0-0 Tstrap: 0-0
Best Rating: 104 11/02 Chep 3m soft Hdl

Ran with promise in bumpers. Appreciated a step up to three miles when second in maiden hurdle at Chepstow November 2002. Seems capable of taking a similar event. Well suited to give in the ground.

Meadows Boy

106   **113**

11-y-o gr g Derrylin-What A Coup (Malicious)
R Lee Richard Edwards

Placings: 0040540/36RU00/53UP0F/R4RR104R-0F210   (2758)
2002/03: 20⁰G, 19F G, 19²G, 20¹G, 23⁰S,

	Starts	1st	2nd	3rd	Win & Pl
Hurdles	5	1	1	0	4408
Career Total	32	2	1	2	7845
113 11/02 Hayd 2m4f	F Hdl		GD	£2257
100 1/02 Wwck 2m5f	F(0-90)Hdl		HVY	£2212
			Total win prize-money £4470

Going: Sf: 0-1 GS: 0-0 Gd: 0-1 GF: - Fm: 0-0
Distance: 2m/2m3: 0-0 **2m4-2m7: 1-4** 3m+: 0-1
Track: **LH: 1-3** RH: 0-2 Tight: 0-1 Gall: 0-0
Aids: Bl: 0-0 Vi: 0-0 Tstrap: 0-0
Best Rating: 116 11/00 Winc 2m6f soft Hdl

Plating-class hurdler, but unreliable, often refusing to start. Beat a big field at Warwick in January 2002 and jumped well when scoring in good style at Haydock in November. Stays well.

Meal Ticket

72   **31**

10-y-o b g Henbit (USA)-Padykin (Bustino)
John G Carr Morgan J Ferris

Placings: 00/0F02/0P4005/24/P-46P   (1073)
2002/03: 16⁴GS, 16⁶G, 17⁰G,

	Starts	1st	2nd	3rd	Win & Pl
Chases	3	0	0	0	515
Career Total	18	0	0	0	1993

Going: Sf: 0-0 GS: 0-1 Gd: 0-2 GF: - Fm: 0-0

Distance: 2m/2m3: 0-3 2m4-2m7: 0-0 3m+: 0-0
Track: LH: 0-1 RH: 0-2 Tight: 0-1 Gall: 0-0
Aids: Bl: 0-3 Vi: 0-0 Tstrap: 0-3
Best Rating: 89 9/98 List 2m good Hdl

Meander (IRE)

91   **71**

8-y-o br g Mandalus-Lady Rerico (Pamroy)
Mrs K B Mactaggart (Miss H C Knight 7/12) Mrs Jean Sole

Placings: 46/40/2210-504   (4375)
2002/03: 24⁵G, 29⁰GS, 28⁴G,

	Starts	1st	2nd	3rd	Win & Pl
Chases	3	0	0	0	386
Career Total	11	1	2	0	6824
98 12/01 Sthl	3m110y E Ch		GD	£3846
			Total win prize-money £3847

Going: Sf: 0-0 GS: 0-1 Gd: 0-2 GF: - Fm: 0-0
Distance: 2m/2m3: 0-0 2m4-2m7: 0-0 3m+: 0-3
Track: LH: 0-2 RH: 0-1 Tight: 0-2 Gall: 0-0
Aids: Bl: 0-0 Vi: 0-0 Tstrap: 0-0
Best Rating: 103 11/01 Winc 2m5f gd-fm Ch

Winning chaser in 2001 but has changed stable and has a lot to prove now.

Measure Of The Man

(104h)   (98h) **100**

5-y-o b g Dr Devious (IRE)-Run Faster (IRE) (Commanche Run)
C Roche J P McManus

Placings: 005-0610   (2114)
2002/03: 16⁰YS, 17⁶G, 16¹G, 20⁰G,

	Starts	1st	2nd	3rd	Win & Pl
NH Flat	1	0	0	0	0
Hurdles	3	1	0	0	6350
Career Total	7	1	0	0	6350
91 10/02 Cork 2m	(67-109)HHdl		GD	£6349
			Total win prize-money £6350

Going: Sf: 0-0 GS: 0-0 Gd: 0-0 GF: - Fm: 0-0
Distance: **2m/2m3: 1-3** 2m4-2m7: 0-0 3m+: 0-0
Track: LH: 0-2 RH: 0-0 Tight: 0-1 Gall: 0-0
Aids: Bl: 0-0 Vi: 0-0 **Tstrap: 1-2**
Best Rating: 91 10/02 Cork 2m good Hdl

Moderate Irish-trained hurdler; suited by two miles; probably best on good ground.

Medallist

100   **73**

4-y-o b g Danehill (USA)-Obsessive (USA) (Seeking The Gold (USA))
B Ellison (Sir Michael Stoute 18/10) Ashley Young

Placings: 0504   (4262)
2002/03: 16⁰GS, 16⁵GS, 16⁰S, 17⁴G,

	Starts	1st	2nd	3rd	Win & Pl
Hurdles	4	0	0	0	0
Career Total	4	0	0	0	0

Going: Sf: 0-0 GS: 0-2 Gd: 0-1 GF: - Fm: 0-0
Distance: 2m/2m3: 0-4 2m4-2m7: 0-0 3m+: 0-0
Track: LH: 0-3 RH: 0-1 Tight: 0-4 Gall: 0-0
Aids: Bl: 0-0 Vi: 0-0 Tstrap: 0-0
Best Rating: 73 3/03 Sedg 2m1f good Hdl

Disappointing novice hurdler.

Medelai

100   **63**

7-y-o b m Marju (IRE)-No Islands (Lomond (USA))
A G Juckes Mrs K C Price

Placings: U/UP-4P5P3306   (2728)
2002/03: 17⁴GF, 16P GF, 17⁵GS, 16P S, 16³S, 17³GF, 16⁰G, 16P HY,

	Starts	1st	2nd	3rd	Win & Pl
Hurdles	8	0	0	2	640
Career Total	11	0	0	2	640

Going: Sf: 0-3 GS: 0-1 Gd: 0-1 GF: - Fm: 0-3
Distance: 2m/2m3: 0-8 2m4-2m7: 0-0 3m+: 0-0
Track: LH: 0-5 RH: 0-3 Tight: 0-3 Gall: 0-1
Aids: Bl: 0-8 Vi: 0-0 Tstrap: 0-0
Best Rating: 63 8/02 Sthl 2m1f gd-fm Hdl

Plating-class hurdler, suited by cut in the ground.

Medici (FR)

92f   **104+f**

5-y-o b/br g Cadoudal (FR)-Marie De Valois (FR) (Moulin)
Jonjo O Neill Sir Robert Ogden

Placings: 4   (3174)
2002/03: 16⁴GS,

	Starts	1st	2nd	3rd	Win & Pl
NH Flat	1	0	0	0	0
Career Total	1	0	0	0	0

Going: Sf: 0-0 GS: 0-1 Gd: 0-0 GF: - Fm: 0-0
Distance: 2m/2m3: 0-1 2m4-2m7: 0-0 3m+: 0-0
Track: LH: 0-1 RH: 0-0 Tight: 0-0 Gall: 0-0
Aids: Bl: 0-0 Vi: 0-0 Tstrap: 0-0
Best Rating: 104 1/03 Hayd 2m gd-sft NHF

Fair fourth on debut in a Haydock bumper.

Medium Wave

97(96h)   (77h)**102**

11-y-o b g Domynsky-Alumia (Great Nephew)
S E H Sherwood The Perseverance Mob

Placings: 33/354F4/0133U3/226P3541/442350P-44P   (0558)
2002/03: 19⁴GF, 16⁴GF, 19P GF,

	Starts	1st	2nd	3rd	Win & Pl
Chases	3	0	0	0	0
Career Total	31	2	3	8	13928
102 4/01 Hrfd 2m	F(0-110)HCh		GD	£4202
108 12/99 Ludl 2m	F(0-110)HHdl		GD	£2775
			Total win prize-money £6977

Going: Sf: 0-0 GS: 0-0 Gd: 0-1 GF: - Fm: 0-2
Distance: 2m/2m3: 0-2 2m4-2m7: 0-1 3m+: 0-0
Track: LH: 0-0 RH: 0-3 Tight: 0-0 Gall: 0-1
Aids: Bl: 0-2 Vi: 0-1 Tstrap: 0-2
Best Rating: 111 3/98 Chep 2m110y gd-sft NHF

Won over hurdles in December 1999, but had to wait nearly two years too follow up and he did that at Hereford in April 2001, although he has looked held since. Does not find much under pressure.

Medkhan (IRE)

92   **76**

6-y-o ch g Lahib (USA)-Safayn (USA) (Lyphard (USA))

F Jordan Miss L M Rochford

Placings:00   (0647)
2002/03: 16⁵S, 16⁹GF,

	Starts	1st	2nd	3rd	Win & Pl
Hurdles	2	0	0	0	
Career Total	2	0	0	0	

Going: Sf: 0-1 GS: 0-0 Gd: 0-0 GF: - Fm: 0-1
Distance: 2m/2m3: 0-2 2m4-2m7: 0-0 3m+: 0-0
Track: LH: 0-2 RH: 0-0 Tight: 0-1 Gall: 0-0
Aids: Bl: 0-0 Vi: 0-0 Tstrap: 0-0
Best Rating: 32 6/02 Strf 2m110y gd-fm Hdl

Mega (IRE)
71   83
7-y-o b m Petardia-Gobolino (Don)
M H Tompkins Mystic Meg Limited

Placings:0/55-0P   (0571)
2002/03: 16⁹G, 24⁹S,

	Starts	1st	2nd	3rd	Win & Pl
Hurdles	2	0	0	0	
Career Total	5	0	0	0	0

Going: Sf: 0-1 GS: 0-0 Gd: 0-1 GF: - Fm: 0-0
Distance: 2m/2m3: 0-1 2m4-2m7: 0-0 3m+: 0-1
Track: LH: 0-2 RH: 0-0 Tight: 0-1 Gall: 0-0
Aids: Bl: 0-0 Vi: 0-0 Tstrap: 0-0
Best Rating: 83 1/02 Hntg 2m110y gd-sft Hdl

Megabyte (IRE)

9-y-o b m Glacial Storm (USA)-Panalpina (Petorius)
Miss Lucinda V Russell The Gypsy King Partnership

Placings:04420/10F0500/54010PF4F33/040/F   (0692)
2002/03: 16⁶S,

	Starts	1st	2nd	3rd	Win & Pl
Hurdles	1	0	0	0	
Career Total	27	2	1	2	7657
77	10/99	Baln	2m1f	Ch		SFT	£2464
98	5/98	Slig	2m		Hdl	GD	£2382

Total win prize-money £4847

Going: Sf: 0-1 GS: 0-0 Gd: 0-0 GF: - Fm: 0-0
Distance: 2m/2m3: 0-1 2m4-2m7: 0-0 3m+: 0-0
Track: LH: 0-1 RH: 0-0 Tight: 0-1 Gall: 0-0
Aids: Bl: 0-0 Vi: 0-0 Tstrap: 0-0
Best Rating: 98 5/98 Slig 2m good Hdl

Megalex
95   85+
5-y-o ch m Karinga Bay-Flaming Rose (IRE) (Roselier (FR))
G L Moore (Miss G Browne 26/12) Darrell Hinds

Placings:3P41   (3934)
2002/03: 17⁷GF, 20⁸GS, 18⁴S, 20¹S,

	Starts	1st	2nd	3rd	Win & Pl
NH Flat	1	0	0	1	233
Hurdles	3	1	0	0	3781
Career Total	4	1	0	1	4014
85	3/03	Font	2m4f	E Hdl		SFT	£3386

Total win prize-money £3387

Going: Sf: 1-2 GS: 0-1 Gd: 0-0 GF: - Fm: 0-1
Distance: 2m/2m3: 0-2 2m4-2m7: 1-2 3m+: 0-0
Track: LH: 0-1 RH: 0-0 Tight: 1-2 Gall: 0-1

Aids: Bl: 0-0 Vi: 0-0 Tstrap: 0-0
Best Rating: 85 3/03 Font 2m4f soft Hdl

Novice hurdler; won mares' race at Fontwell in January 2003; stays two and a half miles; acts on soft ground.

Megazine
109   98
9-y-o b g Shaab-Sherzine (Gorytus (USA))
M Hill Singing In The Rain

Placings:0/0005053/4/0P0-235541551   (2783)
2002/03: 22²GS, 22³G, 17⁵G, 19⁵G, 22⁴S, 17¹HY, 19⁵GS, 17⁵GS, 17¹S,

	Starts	1st	2nd	3rd	Win & Pl
Hurdles	9	2	1	1	8880
Career Total	21	2	1	2	9298
98	12/02	Tntn	2m1f	D(0-115)HHdl	SFT	£4923
98	11/02	NAbb	2m1f	E(0-110)HHdl	HVY	£2891

Total win prize-money £7815

Going: Sf: 2-3 GS: 0-3 Gd: 0-3 GF: - Fm: 0-0
Distance: 2m/2m3: 2-5 2m4-2m7: 0-4 3m+: 0-0
Track: LH: 1-5 RH: 1-4 Tight: 2-7 Gall: 0-0
Aids: Bl: 0-0 Vi: 0-0 Tstrap: 0-0
Best Rating: 98 12/02 Tntn 2m1f soft Hdl

Moderate hurdler. Finally got off the mark when quite impressive winner of extended two mile Class E handicap in heavy ground at Newton Abbot November 2002. Scored again at Taunton. Likes soft ground, stays 22 furlongs.

Meggie's Beau (IRE)
111   112
7-y-o ch g Good Thyne (USA)-Romantic Rose (IRE) (Strong Gale)
Miss Venetia Williams T England

Placings:44/502P   (4749)
2002/03: 24⁵GS, 20⁰HY, 19²GS, 20⁶G,

	Starts	1st	2nd	3rd	Win & Pl
Hurdles	4	0	1	0	1652
Career Total	6	0	1	0	1652

Going: Sf: 0-1 GS: 0-2 Gd: 0-1 GF: - Fm: 0-0
Distance: 2m/2m3: 0-0 2m4-2m7: 0-3 3m+: 0-1
Track: LH: 0-0 RH: 0-4 Tight: 0-3 Gall: 0-0
Aids: Bl: 0-0 Vi: 0-0 Tstrap: 0-0
Best Rating: 112 2/03 Tntn 2m3f110y gd-sft Hdl

Meggie's Lad (IRE)
93f   105f
6-y-o b g Beau Sher-Kambaya (IRE) (Kambalda)
Miss Venetia Williams T England

Placings:15   (4053)
2002/03: 16¹GS, 16⁵HY,

	Starts	1st	2nd	3rd	Win & Pl
NH Flat	2	1	0	0	2384
Career Total	2	1	0	0	2384
105	11/02	Sthl	2m	H NHF	G-S	£2383

Total win prize-money £2384

Going: Sf: 0-1 GS: 1-1 Gd: 0-0 GF: - Fm: 0-0
Distance: 2m/2m3: 1-2 2m4-2m7: 0-0 3m+: 0-0
Track: LH: 1-1 RH: 0-1 Tight: 1-1 Gall: 0-0
Aids: Bl: 0-0 Vi: 0-0 Tstrap: 0-0
Best Rating: 105 11/02 Sthl 2m gd-sft NHF

Made a winning debut in a bumper at Southwell in November 2002.

Meggies Gamble (IRE)
104f   94f
6-y-o b g Zaffaran (USA)-Glaskerbeg Lady (IRE) (Radical)
Miss Venetia Williams T England

Placings:3   (3673)
2002/03: 18³GS,

	Starts	1st	2nd	3rd	Win & Pl
NH Flat	1	0	0	1	277
Career Total	1	0	0	1	277

Going: Sf: 0-1 GS: 0-1 Gd: 0-0 GF: - Fm: 0-0
Distance: 2m/2m3: 0-2 2m4-2m7: 0-0 3m+: 0-0
Track: LH: 0-1 RH: 0-0 Tight: 0-1 Gall: 0-0
Aids: Bl: 0-0 Vi: 0-0 Tstrap: 0-0
Best Rating: 97 2/03 Font 2m2f110y gd-sft NHF

Third in bumper on debut; bred to stay.

Meilleur (NZ)
90f   80f
5-y-o ch g Mellifont (USA)-Petite Cheval (NZ) (Engagement (USA))
A J Whitehead A J Whitehead

Placings:50   (3930)
2002/03: 16⁵S, 16⁹G,

	Starts	1st	2nd	3rd	Win & Pl
NH Flat	2	0	0	0	0
Career Total	2	0	0	0	0

Going: Sf: 0-1 GS: 0-0 Gd: 0-0 GF: - Fm: 0-0
Distance: 2m/2m3: 0-2 2m4-2m7: 0-0 3m+: 0-0
Track: LH: 0-0 RH: 0-2 Tight: 0-0 Gall: 0-1
Aids: Bl: 0-0 Vi: 0-0 Tstrap: 0-0
Best Rating: 80 1/03 Ludl 2m soft NHF

Meldrum Star (IRE)
94   94+
6-y-o ch g Fourstars Allstar (USA)-Meldrum Lass (Buckskin (FR))
Mrs S J Smith T Hannon

Placings:61P   (1907)
2002/03: 16⁶G, 16¹G, 20⁹GS,

	Starts	1st	2nd	3rd	Win & Pl
NH Flat	1	0	0	0	0
Hurdles	2	1	0	0	3952
Career Total	3	1	0	0	3952
94	10/02	Hayd	2m	D Hdl	GD	£3952

Total win prize-money £3952

Going: Sf: 0-0 GS: 0-1 Gd: 1-2 GF: - Fm: 0-0
Distance: 2m/2m3: 1-2 2m4-2m7: 0-1 3m+: 0-0
Track: LH: 1-3 RH: 0-0 Tight: 0-1 Gall: 0-0
Aids: Bl: 0-0 Vi: 0-0 Tstrap: 0-0
Best Rating: 94 10/02 Hayd 2m good Hdl

Moderate hurdler; probably stays 2m 6f; lightly raced; tough sort.

Melford (IRE)
72   67
5-y-o br g Presenting-Echo Creek (IRE) (Strong Gale)
Miss H C Knight John Melville

Placings:60   (2218)

2002/03: 16⁶S, 16⁹S,

	Starts	1st	2nd	3rd	Win & Pl
NH Flat	1	0	0	0	0
Hurdles	1	0	0	0	0
Career Total	2	0	0	0	0

Going: Sf: 0-2 GS: 0-0 Gd: 0-0 GF: - Fm: 0-0
Distance: 2m/2m3: 0-2 2m4-2m7: 0-0 3m+: 0-0
Track: LH: 0-1 RH: 0-1 Tight: 0-0 Gall: 0-1
Aids: Bl: 0-0 Vi: 0-0 Tstrap: 0-0
Best Rating: 96   11/02   Sand   2m110y   soft   NHF

Melstair

95   **71**

8-y-o b g Terimon-Kevins Lady (Alzao (USA))
A R Dicken Got To Be In It To Win It Partnership

Placings: 00U00/055F53403/PP004P0-UPP50P   (4434)
2002/03: 17⁰U GS, 20⁵G, 20⁶S, 20⁵GS, 20⁶PG,

	Starts	1st	2nd	3rd	Win & Pl
Hurdles	5	0	0	0	0
Chases	1	0	0	0	0
Career Total	27	0	0	2	843

Going: Sf: 0-1 GS: 0-2 Gd: 0-3 GF: - Fm: 0-0
Distance: 2m/2m3: 0-1 2m4-2m7: 0-5 3m+: 0-0
Track: LH: 0-4 RH: 0-2 Tight: 0-3 Gall: 0-2
Aids: Bl: 0-0 Vi: 0-0 Tstrap: 0-0
Best Rating: 79   1/01   Muss   2m4f   gd-sft   Hdl

Moderate hurdler, does not want the ground too soft.

Meltonian

91   **91**

6-y-o ch g Past Glories-Meltonby (Sayf El Arab (USA))
K F Clutterbuck (K C Bailey 26/5) K F Clutterbuck

Placings: 4O4P-4056323P   (1568)
2002/03: 19⁴GF, 17⁹G, 23⁵GS, 24⁶GF, 20³G, 21²G, 20³G, 19⁶G,

	Starts	1st	2nd	3rd	Win & Pl
Hurdles	8	0	1	2	1958
Career Total	12	0	1	2	1958

Going: Sf: 0-0 GS: 0-1 Gd: 0-5 GF: - Fm: 0-2
Distance: 2m/2m3: 0-1 2m4-2m7: 0-5 3m+: 0-2
Track: LH: 0-5 RH: 0-3 Tight: 0-3 Gall: 0-4
Aids: Bl: 0-0 Vi: 0-1 Tstrap: 0-0
Best Rating: 97   4/02   Hntg   2m110y   gd-fm   NHF

Modest hurdler at around two and a half miles.

Memorial Arch

92f   **85f**

5-y-o b g Meadowbrook-Sheer Luck (Shergar)
I A Balding Tunnel Vision

Placings: 033   (1326)
2002/03: 16⁰G, 16³GF, 17⁹GF,

	Starts	1st	2nd	3rd	Win & Pl
NH Flat	3	0	0	2	554
Career Total	3	0	0	2	554

Going: Sf: 0-0 GS: 0-1 Gd: 0-1 GF: - Fm: 0-2
Distance: 2m/2m3: 0-3 2m4-2m7: 0-0 3m+: 0-0
Track: LH: 0-2 RH: 0-1 Tight: 0-1 Gall: 0-0
Aids: Bl: 0-0 Vi: 0-0 Tstrap: 0-0
Best Rating: 85   9/02   MRas   2m1f110y   gd-fm   NHF

A half-brother to the two mile Flat winner Golden Arrow who went on to score at up to 22 furlongs over hurdles. Stepped up on debut when third in a Worcester bumper August 2002.

Memory Lane

8-y-o ro m Baron Blakeney-Raise Memories (Skyliner)
J C Tuck J C Tuck

Placings: 0/5/P   (0520)
2002/03: 17⁶PG,

	Starts	1st	2nd	3rd	Win & Pl
Hurdles	1	0	0	0	
Career Total	3	0	0	0	0

Going: Sf: 0-0 GS: 0-0 Gd: 0-1 GF: - Fm: 0-0
Distance: 2m/2m3: 0-1 2m4-2m7: 0-0 3m+: 0-0
Track: LH: 0-1 RH: 0-0 Tight: 0-1 Gall: 0-0
Aids: Bl: 0-0 Vi: 0-0 Tstrap: 0-0
Best Rating: 70   4/00   Hntg   2m110y   good   NHF

Memsahib Ofesteem

105   **99**

12-y-o gr m Neltino-Occatillo (Maris Piper)
S Gollings Tony French & Robert Jones

Placings: 130/302024/2P45215124/001/65P62435/0342416 5336-P304   (4610)
2002/03: 20⁰PS, 19³S, 20⁶S, 21⁴G,

	Starts	1st	2nd	3rd	Win & Pl
Hurdles	4	0	0	1	1994
Career Total	45	5	7	7	31525
111	1/02	Donc	2m4f	C(0-135)HHdl	SFT	£5616
120	3/00	Chep	2m4f	D(0-125)HHdl	GD	£3575
114	2/99	Fknm	2m	E(0-115)HHdl	G-S	£2978
106	1/99	Donc	2m4f	E(0-115)HHdl	G-S	£3055
102	2/97	Donc	2m110y	H NHF	GD	£1035

Total win prize-money £16260

Going: Sf: 0-3 GS: 0-0 Gd: 0-1 GF: - Fm: 0-0
Distance: 2m/2m3: 0-0 2m4-2m7: 0-4 3m+: 0-0
Track: LH: 0-3 RH: 0-1 Tight: 0-1 Gall: 0-1
Aids: Bl: 0-0 Vi: 0-0 Tstrap: 0-0
Best Rating: 120   3/00   Chep   2m4f   good   Hdl

Fair hurdler, best over two and a half miles; appreciates good ground or easy ground, but has won on heavy.

Mendip Manor

5-y-o b g Rakaposhi King-Broughton Manor (Dubassoff (USA))
S C Burrough Rob Croker

Placings: U0   (4444)
2002/03: 16⁰U GS, 16⁰G,

	Starts	1st	2nd	3rd	Win & Pl
NH Flat	2	0	0	0	0
Career Total	2	0	0	0	0

Going: Sf: 0-0 GS: 0-0 Gd: 0-1 GF: - Fm: 0-1
Distance: 2m/2m3: 0-2 2m4-2m7: 0-0 3m+: 0-0
Track: LH: 0-0 RH: 0-2 Tight: 0-0 Gall: 0-0
Aids: Bl: 0-0 Vi: 0-0 Tstrap: 0-0
Best Rating: 0   4/03   Asct   2m110y   good   NHF

Menelek Lord (IRE)

104(97c)   **92**

9-y-o b g Yashgan-Higcham (Le Moss)
R Ford (A Streeter 4/5) Dantom Production Solutions Ltd

Placings: 44625F64/03214FU2/P44-PPP325   (4141)
2002/03: 24⁶G, 24⁸S, 30⁸S, 25³G, 25⁴S, 24⁴S,

	Starts	1st	2nd	3rd	Win & Pl
Hurdles	3	0	1	1	2238
Chases	3	0	0	0	0
Career Total	25	1	4	2	10598
102	12/00	MRas	3m1f	E(0-105)HCh	SFT	£3607

Total win prize-money £3608

Going: Sf: 0-4 GS: 0-0 Gd: 0-2 GF: - Fm: 0-0
Distance: 2m/2m3: 0-0 2m4-2m7: 0-0 3m+: 0-6
Track: LH: 0-6 RH: 0-0 Tight: 0-2 Gall: 0-0
Aids: Bl: 0-3 Vi: 0-2 Tstrap: 0-0
Best Rating: 102   4/01   Hayd   3m   soft   Ch

Failed chaser; best effort back over hurdles when just held at Ayr in March; stays well.

Menesonic (IRE)

99   **128**

13-y-o b g Meneval (USA)-Kandy Kate (Pry)
R H Alner Mrs W H Walter

Placings: 20402525/3423513/1F15532/122223/6133230/P1 35/1446-5   (0038)
2002/03: 23⁵G,

	Starts	1st	2nd	3rd	Win & Pl
Chases	1	0	0	0	0
Career Total	44	7	10	9	70566
128	11/01	Sand	3m110y	C(0-135)HCh	G-S	£8697
128	11/00	Winc	3m1f110yC(0-135)HCh	SFT	£8417
128	11/99	Font	3m2f110yD(0-125)HCh	GD	£4634
134	10/98	Winc	3m1f110yE(0-110)HCh	G-S	£4240
117	11/97	Kemp	3m	D Ch	G-S	£3371
103	10/97	Winc	3m1f110yD Ch	GD	£3743
111	3/97	Extr	3m2f	E Hdl	G-S	£2452

Total win prize-money £35557

Going: Sf: 0-0 GS: 0-0 Gd: 0-1 GF: - Fm: 0-0
Distance: 2m/2m3: 0-0 2m4-2m7: 0-0 3m+: 0-1
Track: LH: 0-0 RH: 0-1 Tight: 0-0 Gall: 0-0
Aids: Bl: 0-0 Vi: 0-0 Tstrap: 0-0
Best Rating: 134   10/98   Winc   3m1f110y   gd-sft   Ch

He is devoid of pace, but stays forever and tries hard. He goes best when fresh. acts on soft ground.

Mensch (IRE)

95(88h)   (75h)**62**

7-y-o ch g Husyan (USA)-Floating Dollar (Master Owen)
Paul Morgan Paul Morgan

Placings: U0/600-24   (4736)
2002/03: 24²F, 24⁴GF,

	Starts	1st	2nd	3rd	Win & Pl
Chases	2	0	1	0	1028
Career Total	7	0	1	0	1028

Going: Sf: 0-0 GS: 0-0 Gd: 0-0 GF: - Fm: 0-2
Distance: 2m/2m3: 0-0 2m4-2m7: 0-0 3m+: 0-2
Track: LH: 0-1 RH: 0-1 Tight: 0-1 Gall: 0-0
Aids: Bl: 0-0 Vi: 0-0 Tstrap: 0-0
Best Rating: 70   3/02   MRas   2m1f110y   gd-sft   Hdl

Lightly-raced individual with modest form to date.

Mercato (FR)

108(101c)   (125c)**125**

7-y-o b g Mansonnien (FR)-Royal Lie (FR) (Garde Royale)
J R Best D S Nevison

Placings:43/21525611F/0P056-43U521055   (4214)
2002/03: 19⁴S, 16³S, 16⁰S, 16⁵G, 16²HY, 21¹HY, 20⁰S, 16⁵HY, 18⁵G,

	Starts	1st	2nd	3rd	Win & Pl
Hurdles	4	1	0	0	8156
Chases	5	0	1	1	7975
Career Total	25	4	3	2	27099
125	2/03	Plum	2m5f	D(0-115)HHdl	HVY £6906
117	3/01	MRas	2m1f110yF(0-105)HHdl	G-S £5356
113	3/01	Font	2m2f1110yE(0-115)HHdl	SFT £2628
100	10/00	Hntg	2m110y H NHF	G-F £1561

Total win prize-money £16452

Going:	Sf: 1-7 GS: 0-0 Gd: 0-2 GF: - Fm: 0-0
Distance:	2m/2m3: 0-6 2m4-2m7: 1-3 3m+: 0-0
Track:	LH: 1-4 RH: 0-5 Tight: 1-2 Gall: 0-2
Aids:	Bl: 0-0 Vi: 0-0 Tstrap: 0-1
Best Rating:	125 2/03 Plum 2m5f heavy Hdl

Fair hurdler/chaser; best effort to date was when finishing fifth in the Imperial Cup; stays beyond 2m 4f; acts on any ground.

Mercede (IRE)

104   **75**

6-y-o b m Perugino (USA)-Miss Busybody (IRE) (Phardante (FR))
N Wilson Josef Fusenich

Placings:0560-013   (0581)
2002/03: 16⁰GF, 17¹GS, 16³G,

	Starts	1st	2nd	3rd	Win & Pl
Hurdles	3	1	0	1	2789
Career Total	7	1	0	1	2789
76	6/02	Ctml	2m1f110yG Hdl	G-S £2425

Total win prize-money £2426

Going:	Sf: 0-0 GS: 1-1 Gd: 0-1 GF: - Fm: 0-1
Distance:	2m/2m3: 1-3 2m4-2m7: 0-0 3m+: 0-0
Track:	LH: 1-2 RH: 0-1 Tight: 1-1 Gall: 0-0
Aids:	Bl: 0-0 Vi: 0-0 Tstrap: 0-0
Best Rating:	78 4/02 Newc 2m firm Hdl

Winning plater over hurdles.

Merchants Friend (IRE)

111(106h)   (108h)**132**

8-y-o b g Lord Americo-Buck Maid (Buckskin (FR))
C J Mann (T J Taaffe 24/6) Magic Moments

Placings:/002021/014F1P/34PUP365-0301112422 (3574)
2002/03: 20⁵GY, 16³S, 19⁰S, 20¹S, 20¹GS, 20¹GS, 20²GS, 24⁴S, 24²GS, 23²S,

	Starts	1st	2nd	3rd	Win & Pl
Hurdles	4	1	0	1	3429
Chases	6	2	3	0	28779
Career Total	31	6	5	3	51333
125	11/02	Newb	2m4f	D(0-125)HCh	G-S £7085
122	11/02	Plum	2m4f	D(0-120)HCh	G-S £5525
	10/02	Pard	2m4f110y Hdl		SFT £2957
112	4/01	List	2m	(0-116)HCh	HVY £6955
95	11/00	Clon	2m1f	Ch	SFT £4416
97	4/00	List	3m	Hdl	SH £3864

Total win prize-money £30803

Going: Sf: 1-5 GS: 2-4 Gd: 0-0 GF: - Fm: 0-0

Distance:	2m/2m3: 0-2 2m4-2m7: 3-5 3m+: 0-3
Track:	LH: 2-4 RH: 0-3 Tight: 1-1 Gall: 1-2
Aids:	Bl: 0-0 Vi: 0-0 Tstrap: 0-0
Best Rating:	126 2/03 Leic 2m7f110y soft Ch

Fair handicap chaser; stays three miles; effective on soft ground.

Meritocracy (IRE)

88   **66**

5-y-o b g Lahib (USA)-Merry Devil (IRE) (Sadler s Wells (USA))
Miss A E Broyd (J C Hayden 6/7) Miss Alison Broyd

Placings:006   (4270)
2002/03: 17⁰S, 16⁰G, 16⁶G,

	Starts	1st	2nd	3rd	Win & Pl
Hurdles	3	0	0	0	0
Career Total	3	0	0	0	0

Going:	Sf: 0-1 GS: 0-0 Gd: 0-2 GF: - Fm: 0-0
Distance:	2m/2m3: 0-3 2m4-2m7: 0-0 3m+: 0-0
Track:	LH: 0-1 RH: 0-2 Tight: 0-1 Gall: 0-0
Aids:	Bl: 0-0 Vi: 0-0 Tstrap: 0-0
Best Rating:	66 3/03 Chep 2m110y good Hdl

Merlins Bay (IRE)

9-y-o b g Nearly A Nose (USA)-Kabarda (Relkino)
J F Panvert J F Panvert

Placings:0/0PF0PP/4U/04P/P0   (0957)
2002/03: 20⁰G, 16⁰GS,

	Starts	1st	2nd	3rd	Win & Pl
Hurdles	2	0	0	0	0
Career Total	14	0	0	0	313

Going:	Sf: 0-0 GS: 0-1 Gd: 0-1 GF: - Fm: 0-0
Distance:	2m/2m3: 0-1 2m4-2m7: 0-1 3m+: 0-0
Track:	LH: 0-2 RH: 0-0 Tight: 0-0 Gall: 0-0
Aids:	Bl: 0-0 Vi: 0-0 Tstrap: 0-0
Best Rating:	85 3/98 Sand 2m110y soft NHF

Merry Major

10-y-o br g K-Battery-Merry Missus (Bargello)
J B Walton J B Walton

Placings:0/0/FF/4/0   (0503)
2002/03: 26⁰G,

	Starts	1st	2nd	3rd	Win & Pl
Chases	1	0	0	0	0
Career Total	6	0	0	0	0

Going:	Sf: 0-0 GS: 0-0 Gd: 0-1 GF: - Fm: 0-0
Distance:	2m/2m3: 0-0 2m4-2m7: 0-0 3m+: 0-1
Track:	LH: 0-1 RH: 0-0 Tight: 0-1 Gall: 0-0
Aids:	Bl: 0-0 Vi: 0-0 Tstrap: 0-0
Best Rating:	82 3/97 Newc 2m gd-fm NHF

Merry Masquerade (IRE)

101(101h)   (131h)**111**

12-y-o b g King s Ride-Merry Madness (Raise You Ten)
Mrs M Reveley G S Brown

Placings:341/02111/31010/1212/00135/6425FP02-42
(0090)
2002/03: 25⁴GS, 26²G,

	Starts	1st	2nd	3rd	Win & Pl
Chases	2	0	1	0	1768
Career Total	32	9	6	3	80928
155	2/01	Kemp	3m110y A HHdl	G-S £13200
158	2/00	Hayd	2m7f110yB HHdl	HVY £7498
157	1/00	Uttx	3m110y C(0-135)HHdl	SFT £14495
132	4/99	Ayr	2m6f	B(0-145)HHdl	HVY £5936
129	3/99	Newc	3m	C(0-130)HHdl	SFT £6937
128	4/98	Uttx	3m110y E(0-100)HHdl	SFT £2431
120	3/98	Ayr	3m110y D(0-115)HHdl	G-S £3652
96	2/98	Ayr	2m6f E Hdl	HVY £2374
107	2/97	Ayr	H NHF	SFT £1380

Total win prize-money £57906

Going:	Sf: 0-0 GS: 0-1 Gd: 0-1 GF: - Fm: 0-0
Distance:	2m/2m3: 0-0 2m4-2m7: 0-0 3m+: 0-2
Track:	LH: 0-2 RH: 0-0 Tight: 0-1 Gall: 0-0
Aids:	Bl: 0-0 Vi: 0-0 Tstrap: 0-0
Best Rating:	159 2/00 Kemp 3m110y soft Hdl

An out-and-out stayer, he relishes testing conditions. Successful over hurdles, he now runs over fences, but has proved nowhere near as good over the larger obstacles so far. Stays three miles plus.

Merry Minstrel (IRE)

106   **105**

10-y-o b g Black Minstrel-Merry Lesa (Dalesa)
C J Mann Hugh Villiers

Placings:060/266F/U01311-2P23   (4763)
2002/03: 21²G, 19⁰G, 20²G, 16³G,

	Starts	1st	2nd	3rd	Win & Pl
Chases	4	0	2	1	6888
Career Total	17	3	3	2	21240
94	9/01	Plum	2m1f	E(0-105)HCh	G-S £3136
78	7/01	Wxfd	2m	(0-95)HCh	G-Y £5564
80	6/01	Dpat	2m2f	(0-95)HCh	FRM £4326

Total win prize-money £13028

Going:	Sf: 0-0 GS: 0-0 Gd: 0-4 GF: - Fm: 0-0
Distance:	2m/2m3: 0-2 2m4-2m7: 0-2 3m+: 0-0
Track:	LH: 0-2 RH: 0-2 Tight: 0-1 Gall: 0-1
Aids:	Bl: 0-0 Vi: 0-0 Tstrap: 0-0
Best Rating:	106 4/03 Ludl 2m4f good Ch

Moderate chaser; half-brother to Merry Gale; won two races in Ireland before coming to Britain; seemingly best on good ground; stays two and a half miles.

Merry Mole (IRE)

45

9-y-o b g Good Thyne (USA)-Merry Miss (Deep Run)
J A B Old R P Fry

Placings:0P/P-05P   (2167)
2002/03: 20⁰G, 20⁵GS, 26⁰G,

	Starts	1st	2nd	3rd	Win & Pl
Hurdles	1	0	0	0	0
Chases	2	0	0	0	0
Career Total	6	0	0	0	0

Going:	Sf: 0-0 GS: 0-1 Gd: 0-2 GF: - Fm: 0-0
Distance:	2m/2m3: 0-0 2m4-2m7: 0-2 3m+: 0-1
Track:	LH: 0-3 RH: 0-0 Tight: 0-0 Gall: 0-0
Aids:	Bl: 0-0 Vi: 0-0 Tstrap: 0-0
Best Rating:	45 8/02 Worc 2m4f110y gd-sft Ch

Merry Shot (IRE)

11-y-o b g Cataldi-Borgina (Boreen (FR))
C A Green C A Green

Placings:*10*PP/52PP22/P0/P/0   (0179)
2002/03: 21⁰GF,

	Starts	1st	2nd	3rd	Win & Pl
Chases	1	0	0	0	
Career Total	14	1	3	0	3898
105 12/97 Folk	2m1f110yH NHF			GD	£1255
		Total win prize-money £1256			

Going:	Sf: 0-0 GS: 0-0 Gd: 0-0 GF: - Fm: 0-1
Distance:	2m/2m3: 0-0 2m4-2m7: 0-1 3m+: 0-0
Track:	LH: 0-0 RH: 0-1 Tight: 0-0 Gall: 0-0
Aids:	Bl: 0-0 Vi: 0-0 Tstrap: 0-0
Best Rating:	105 12/97 Folk 2m1f110y good NHF

Merry Tina
99   (44h)70

8-y-o b m Tina s Pet-Merry Missus (Bargello)
J B Walton Messrs F T Walton

Placings:*000*/04605P26   (4753)
2002/03: 20⁰GF, 16⁴HY, 21⁶S, 16⁹HY, 21⁵HY, 25⁸G, 25²G, 24⁶G,

	Starts	1st	2nd	3rd	Win & Pl
Chases	8	0	1	0	1401
Career Total	11	0	1	0	1401

Going:	Sf: 0-4 GS: 0-0 Gd: 0-3 GF: - Fm: 0-1
Distance:	2m/2m3: 0-2 2m4-2m7: 0-3 3m+: 0-3
Track:	LH: 0-6 RH: 0-2 Tight: 0-3 Gall: 0-1
Aids:	Bl: 0-0 Vi: 0-0 Tstrap: 0-0
Best Rating:	62 2/01 Catt 2m soft NHF

Mersey Beat
108(91h)   (115h)115

9-y-o ch g Rock Hopper-Handy Dancer (Green God)
G L Moore Mrs J Moore

Placings:U26/124112/0025/010242/6P0P5U2-1212 (1329)
2002/03: 16²GS, 18¹GF, 20²GF, 16¹G, 20²G,

	Starts	1st	2nd	3rd	Win & Pl
Chases	5	2	3	0	11040
Career Total	30	6	9	0	31995
115 6/02 NAbb	2m110y	E(0-105)HCh		GD	£3334
113 5/02 Font	2m2f	E Ch		G-F	£3888
127 5/00 Towc	2m	D(0-120)HHdl		G-F	£2996
138 11/98 Tntn	2m1f	C HHdl		GD	£3940
126 11/98 Wind	2m	E Hdl		G-S	£2530
104 8/98 Strf	2m110y	E Hdl		G-F	£2010
		Total win prize-money £18700			

Going:	Sf: 0-0 GS: 0-1 Gd: 1-2 GF: - Fm: 1-2
Distance:	2m/2m3: 2-3 2m4-2m7: 0-2 3m+: 0-0
Track:	LH: 1-2 RH: 0-1 Tight: 2-4 Gall: 0-0
Aids:	Bl: 0-0 Vi: 0-0 Tstrap: 0-0
Best Rating:	138 11/98 Tntn 2m1f good Hdl

A fair two-mile plus handicap hurdler/chaser. Suited by fast ground. In good form in the summer of 2002, winning a couple of modest events.

Mersey Sound (IRE)
94   91

5-y-o b g Ela-Mana-Mou-Coral Sound (IRE) (Glow (USA))
D R C Elsworth Terry Neill

Placings:60   (2770)
2002/03: 16⁶G, 16⁹HY,

	Starts	1st	2nd	3rd	Win & Pl
Hurdles	2	0	0	0	0
Career Total	2	0	0	0	0

Going:	Sf: 0-1 GS: 0-0 Gd: 0-1 GF: - Fm: 0-0
Distance:	2m/2m3: 0-2 2m4-2m7: 0-0 3m+: 0-0
Track:	LH: 0-2 RH: 0-0 Tight: 0-0 Gall: 0-2
Aids:	Bl: 0-0 Vi: 0-0 Tstrap: 0-0
Best Rating:	91 12/02 Newb 2m110y good Hdl

Fair middle-distance handicapper on the Flat, well beaten so far over hurdles.

Metal Detector (IRE)
111   122

6-y-o b g Treasure Hunter-Las-Cancellas (Monksfield)
K C Bailey D Allen

Placings:0230-121015   (4563)
2002/03: 22¹G, 20²S, 24¹GS, 19⁰S, 21¹S, 24⁵GF,

	Starts	1st	2nd	3rd	Win & Pl
Hurdles	6	3	1	0	15168
Career Total	10	3	2	1	16486
120 3/03 Wwck	2m5f	D(0-115)HHdl		SFT	£5115
122 11/02 Tntn	3m110y	D Hdl		G-S	£5931
106 5/02 Uttx	2m6f110yE Hdl			GD	£2849
		Total win prize-money £13896			

Going:	Sf: 1-3 GS: 1-1 Gd: 1-1 GF: - Fm: 0-1
Distance:	2m/2m3: 0-0 2m4-2m7: 2-4 3m+: 1-2
Track:	LH: 2-4 RH: 1-2 Tight: 1-3 Gall: 0-0
Aids:	Bl: 0-0 Vi: 0-0 Tstrap: 0-0
Best Rating:	122 11/02 Tntn 3m110y gd-sft Hdl

Fair hurdler; consistent and tough; stays three miles and acts on most ground.

Meticulous (USA)
70   28

5-y-o b g Theatrical-Sha Tha (USA) (Mr Prospector (USA))
M D Hammond Million In Mind Partnership (12)

Placings:00   (2492)
2002/03: 16⁹GS, 16⁹S,

	Starts	1st	2nd	3rd	Win & Pl
Hurdles	2	0	0	0	
Career Total	2	0	0	0	

Going:	Sf: 0-1 GS: 0-1 Gd: 0-0 GF: - Fm: 0-0
Distance:	2m/2m3: 0-2 2m4-2m7: 0-0 3m+: 0-0
Track:	LH: 0-2 RH: 0-0 Tight: 0-0 Gall: 0-2
Aids:	Bl: 0-0 Vi: 0-0 Tstrap: 0-0
Best Rating:	28 12/02 Donc 2m110y soft Hdl

Mexican (USA)
97   88

4-y-o b c Pine Bluff (USA)-Cuando Quiere (USA) (Affirmed (USA))
M D Hammond (C E Brittain 22/10) L Ibbotson And M McCarthy

Placings:440   (4399)
2002/03: 16⁴GS, 16⁴S, 16⁰GF,

	Starts	1st	2nd	3rd	Win & Pl
Hurdles	3	0	0	0	705
Career Total	3	0	0	0	705

Going:	Sf: 0-1 GS: 0-0 Gd: 0-0 GF: - Fm: 0-0
Distance:	2m/2m3: 0-3 2m4-2m7: 0-0 3m+: 0-0
Track:	LH: 0-2 RH: 0-1 Tight: 0-0 Gall: 0-2
Aids:	Bl: 0-0 Vi: 0-0 Tstrap: 0-0
Best Rating:	91 12/02 Muss 2m gd-sft Hdl

Disappointing maiden on the Flat and well beaten so far over hurdles.

Mezzo Princess

11-y-o b m Remezzo-Kam Tsin Princess (Prince Regent (FR))
Mike Lurcock (Miss Katie Thory 19/5) Mike Lurcock

Placings:P0/PP4PF-640645   (4572)
2002/03: 26⁶GF, 24⁴GF, 20⁰GS, 21⁶G, 25⁴G, 24⁵G,

	Starts	1st	2nd	3rd	Win & Pl
Chases	6	0	0	0	202
Career Total	13	0	0	0	202

Going:	Sf: 0-0 GS: 0-1 Gd: 0-3 GF: - Fm: 0-2
Distance:	2m/2m3: 0-2 2m4-2m7: 0-2 3m+: 0-4
Track:	LH: 0-3 RH: 0-3 Tight: 0-3 Gall: 0-0
Aids:	Bl: 0-0 Vi: 0-0 Tstrap: 0-0
Best Rating:	70 3/03 MRas 3m1f good Ch

Poor pointer and bad hunter chaser.

Mi Favorita
84   51

5-y-o b m Piccolo-Mistook (USA) (Phone Trick (USA))
Miss Kate Milligan (Don Enrico Incisa 27/9) S Ward

Placings:0006P   (4782)
2002/03: 16⁰G, 16⁸G, 16⁰S, 17⁶G, 17⁰G,

	Starts	1st	2nd	3rd	Win & Pl
Hurdles	5	0	0	0	
Career Total	5	0	0	0	

Going:	Sf: 0-1 GS: 0-0 Gd: 0-4 GF: - Fm: 0-0
Distance:	2m/2m3: 0-5 2m4-2m7: 0-0 3m+: 0-0
Track:	LH: 0-4 RH: 0-1 Tight: 0-4 Gall: 0-1
Aids:	Bl: 0-0 Vi: 0-0 Tstrap: 0-0
Best Rating:	51 3/03 Sedg 2m1f good Hdl

Mi Odds
96   89+

7-y-o b g Sure Blade (USA)-Vado Via (Ardross)
Mrs N Macauley (Ian Williams 19/8) G Wiltshire

Placings:10-632   (0658)
2002/03: 16⁸HY, 16³GF, 16²GF,

	Starts	1st	2nd	3rd	Win & Pl
Hurdles	3	0	1	1	928
Career Total	5	1	1	1	3014
89 3/02 Hrfd	2m1f	G Hdl		GD	£2086
		Total win prize-money £2086			

Going:	Sf: 0-1 GS: 0-0 Gd: 0-0 GF: - Fm: 0-2
Distance:	2m/2m3: 0-3 2m4-2m7: 0-0 3m+: 0-0
Track:	LH: 0-3 RH: 0-0 Tight: 0-0 Gall: 0-0
Aids:	Bl: 0-0 Vi: 0-0 Tstrap: 0-0
Best Rating:	89 6/02 Worc 2m gd-fm Hdl

A useful performer on the All-Weather, he won a seller on his hurdling debut. fair efforts since. Acts on fast ground.

Mice Design (IRE)
70
6-y-o b g Presidium-Diplomatist (Dominion)
S B Clark S B Clark

Placings:51320-P6   (4782)
2002/03: 17⁶G, 17⁶G,

	Starts	1st	2nd	3rd	Win & Pl
Hurdles	2	0	0	0	0
Career Total	7	1	1	1	3675
86 10/01 Hntg	2m4f110yE Hdl			GD	£2590

Total win prize-money £2590

Going:	Sf: 0-0 GS: 0-0 Gd: 0-2 GF: - Fm: 0-0
Distance:	2m/2m3: 0-2 2m4-2m7: 0-0 3m+: 0-0
Track:	LH: 0-0 RH: 0-2 Tight: 0-2 Gall: 0-0
Aids:	Bl: 0-1 Vi: 0-0 Tstrap: 0-0
Best Rating:	100 1/02 Hrfd 2m1f soft Hdl

Moderate hurdler at his best; acts on good ground and is effective over two miles four.

Michael Finnegan (IRE)
98(109h)   (60h)90
10-y-o b/br g Phardante (FR)-Decent Slave (Decent Fellow)
Miss L C Siddall Mrs D J Morris

Placings:040/0360F2140/4313P6663/P056124-00202
                                                 (4138)
2002/03: 16⁹G, 16⁰HY, 16²HdI, 16⁶G, 16²S,

	Starts	1st	2nd	3rd	Win & Pl
Hurdles	2	0	0	0	0
Chases	3	0	2	0	2406
Career Total	33	3	4	4	13626
101 12/01 Leic	2m	F(0-110)HHdl	HVY	£2261
107 12/00 Hayd	2m	F(0-110)HHdl	HVY	£2576
85 2/00 Muss	2m	E(0-105)HHdl	GD	£2769

Total win prize-money £7606

Going:	Sf: 0-3 GS: 0-0 Gd: 0-2 GF: - Fm: 0-0
Distance:	2m/2m3: 0-5 2m4-2m7: 0-0 3m+: 0-0
Track:	LH: 0-4 RH: 0-1 Tight: 0-0 Gall: 0-1
Aids:	Bl: 0-0 Vi: 0-0 Tstrap: 0-0
Best Rating:	107 12/00 Newc 2m soft Hdl

Modest handicap hurdler/ novice chaser; goes well over two miles and suited by heavy ground; probably did not achieve a great deal when runner-up over fences at Newcastle in January and Hexham two months later.

Michael's Princess
106(103c)   (80+c)88
8-y-o b m King s Ride-Kathy Cook (Glenstal (USA))
M J Gingell Gentlemen Don t Work On Mondays

Placings:645530/U62605F01-2620643P36   (3254)
2002/03: 25¹G, 24²GF, 21⁶GF, 24²G, 24⁶GF, 25⁶GF, 24⁴S, 21³GS, 25⁵PHY, 23³S, 21⁶HY,

	Starts	1st	2nd	3rd	Win & Pl
Hurdles	10	1	2	1	5213
Chases	1	0	0	1	529
Career Total	25	1	3	3	7897
88 4/02 Plum	3m1f110yE(0-105)HHdl GD £2551

Total win prize-money £2552

Going:	Sf: 0-4 GS: 0-2 Gd: 1-2 GF: - Fm: 0-3
Distance:	2m/2m3: 0-0 2m4-2m7: 0-3 3m+: 1-8
Track:	LH: 0-5 RH: 0-4 Tight: 0-1 Gall: 0-0
Aids:	Bl: 0-0 Vi: 0-0 Tstrap: 0-0
Best Rating:	88 11/02 Wwck 2m5f gd-sft Hdl

Improved form since being stepped up to three miles and won a novices handicap at Plumpton April 2002. Got tired in soft ground on her chasing debut.

Michaelmas Daizy
95   89
8-y-o b m Michelozzo (USA)-Hals Lass (Halsall)
S E H Sherwood Netherley Racing

Placings:53004/300/5-U30   (2104)
2002/03: 27⁴G, 24³GS, 26⁰GS,

	Starts	1st	2nd	3rd	Win & Pl
Hurdles	3	0	0	1	865
Career Total	12	0	0	3	1756

Going:	Sf: 0-0 GS: 0-2 Gd: 0-1 GF: - Fm: 0-0
Distance:	2m/2m3: 0-0 2m4-2m7: 0-0 3m+: 0-3
Track:	LH: 0-2 RH: 0-1 Tight: 0-0 Gall: 0-1
Aids:	Bl: 0-0 Vi: 0-0 Tstrap: 0-0
Best Rating:	89 11/02 Sthl 3m110y gd-sft Hdl

Some ability in staying handicap hurdles.

Michaels Joy (IRE)
67f   93f
4-y-o br g Presenting-Scarteen Lower (IRE) (Royal Fountain)
G M Moore John Robson

Placings:4   (3917)
2002/03: 17⁴GS,

	Starts	1st	2nd	3rd	Win & Pl
NH Flat	1	0	0	0	0
Career Total	1	0	0	0	0

Going:	Sf: 0-0 GS: 0-1 Gd: 0-0 GF: - Fm: 0-0
Distance:	2m/2m3: 0-1 2m4-2m7: 0-0 3m+: 0-0
Track:	LH: 0-0 RH: 0-1 Tight: 0-0 Gall: 0-0
Aids:	Bl: 0-0 Vi: 0-0 Tstrap: 0-0
Best Rating:	100 3/03 Carl 2m1f gd-sft NHF

Somewhat unlucky close fourth on debut in bumper at Carlisle in March.

Michigan Blue
89   120d
11-y-o b g Rakaposhi King-Starquin (IRE) (Strong Gale)
M J M Evans Mrs J Z Munday

Placings:0/040622/PU/5304562/056/F11112P-6P4 (2375)
2002/03: 16⁶G, 19²S, 16⁴GS,

	Starts	1st	2nd	3rd	Win & Pl
Chases	3	0	0	0	565
Career Total	29	4	4	1	19372
108 12/01 Hrfd	2m	E(0-105)HCh	SFT	£3251
108 11/01 Hrfd	2m	E(0-105)HCh	GD	£3178
104 10/01 Hrfd	2m	F(0-110)HCh	G-S	£3307
99 10/01 Hrfd	2m3f	G(0-95)HCh	GD	£3062

Total win prize-money £12801

Going:	Sf: 0-1 GS: 0-1 Gd: 0-1 GF: - Fm: 0-0
Distance:	2m/2m3: 0-3 2m4-2m7: 0-0 3m+: 0-0
Track:	LH: 0-1 RH: 0-2 Tight: 0-2 Gall: 0-0
Aids:	Bl: 0-0 Vi: 0-0 Tstrap: 0-0
Best Rating:	108 12/01 Asct 2m good Ch

He rattled up a four-timer at his favourite track Hereford last season despite being raised a total of 36lb along the way. He stays two miles three and jumps well.

Mick Murphy (IRE)
38
6-y-o b g Jurado (USA)-Lee Ford Lady (Kemal (FR))
Mrs E Slack A Slack

Placings:00-0   (0181)
2002/03: 16⁰G,

	Starts	1st	2nd	3rd	Win & Pl
Hurdles	1	0	0	0	0
Career Total	3	0	0	0	0

Going:	Sf: 0-0 GS: 0-0 Gd: 0-1 GF: - Fm: 0-0
Distance:	2m/2m3: 0-1 2m4-2m7: 0-0 3m+: 0-0
Track:	LH: 0-1 RH: 0-0 Tight: 0-0 Gall: 0-0
Aids:	Bl: 0-0 Vi: 0-0 Tstrap: 0-0
Best Rating:	57 4/02 Carl 2m1f good NHF

Mickey Croke
102f   108f
6-y-o b g Alflora (IRE)-Praise The Lord (Lord Gayle (USA))
C R Egerton Lady Lloyd Webber

Placings:61   (2675)
2002/03: 17⁶G, 17¹S,

	Starts	1st	2nd	3rd	Win & Pl
NH Flat	2	1	0	0	2058
Career Total	2	1	0	0	2058
108 12/02 Hrfd	2m1f	H NHF	SFT	£2058

Total win prize-money £2058

Going:	Sf: 1-1 GS: 0-0 Gd: 0-1 GF: - Fm: 0-0
Distance:	2m/2m3: 1-2 2m4-2m7: 0-0 3m+: 0-0
Track:	LH: 0-0 RH: 1-2 Tight: 0-0 Gall: 0-0
Aids:	Bl: 0-0 Vi: 0-0 Tstrap: 0-0
Best Rating:	108 12/02 Hrfd 2m1f soft NHF

Brave winner of a bumper on his second start.

Mickley (IRE)
102   88
6-y-o b g Ezzoud (IRE)-Dawsha (IRE) (Slip Anchor)
P R Hedger Jay Dee Bloodstock Limited

Placings:000/02   (1431)
2002/03: 17⁰G, 21²GF,

	Starts	1st	2nd	3rd	Win & Pl
Hurdles	2	0	1	0	1060
Career Total	5	0	1	0	1060

Going:	Sf: 0-0 GS: 0-0 Gd: 0-1 GF: - Fm: 0-1
Distance:	2m/2m3: 0-1 2m4-2m7: 0-1 3m+: 0-0
Track:	LH: 0-2 RH: 0-0 Tight: 0-2 Gall: 0-0
Aids:	Bl: 0-0 Vi: 0-0 Tstrap: 0-0
Best Rating:	88 10/02 Plum 2m5f gd-fm Hdl

Best known as an All-Weather stayer, has shown ability over hurdles on fast ground. Usually wears sheepskin cheek-pieces.

Micklow Minster
97(103h)   85
9-y-o ch g Minster Son-Scotto s Regret (Celtic Cone)
C Grant W Raw

Placings:00/0624163150/53P0/5-0   (4710)
2002/03: 23⁰GS,

	Starts	1st	2nd	3rd	
Hurdles	1	0	0		

	Starts	1st	2nd	3rd	Win & Pl
Career Total	18	2	1	2	7871

112 1/00 Catt 3m1f110y E Hdl GD £2786

108 11/99 Newc 2m4f D Hdl G-S £2944

Total win prize-money £5730

Going: Sf: 0-0 GS: 0-0 Gd: 0-0 GF: - Fm: 0-1
Distance: 2m/2m3: 0-0 2m4-2m7: 0-1 3m+: 0-0
Track: LH: 0-1 RH: 0-0 Tight: 0-0 Gall: 0-0
Aids: Bl: 0-0 Vi: 0-0 Tstrap: 0-0
Best Rating: 112 1/00 Catt 3m1f110y good Hdl

Moderate novice chaser; stays 3m 3f.

Mickthecutaway (IRE)
126d

11-y-o b g Rontino-Le-Mu-Co (Varano)
Mrs H Dalton J N Dalton

Placings:U/3260/3/1/UU1120/212611-4FP (4564)
2002/03: 24⁴S, 25⁵S, 24⁸GF,

	Starts	1st	2nd	3rd	Win & Pl
Chases	3	0	0		607
Career Total	22	6	4	2	31347

126 3/02 Bang 2m4f110yC(0-135)HCh SFT £6955
126 3/02 Bang 3m110y D(0-120)HCh SFT £5169
118 12/01 Towc 3m1f E(0-115)HCh HVY £3445
112 2/01 Sand 3m110y D(0-115)HCh SFT £5164
107 1/01 Leic 2m7f110yF(0-95)HCh SFT £3251
101 3/00 Leic 2m7f110yH Ch G-S £2249

Total win prize-money £26235

Going: Sf: 0-2 GS: 0-0 Gd: 0-0 GF: - Fm: 0-1
Distance: 2m/2m3: 0-0 2m4-2m7: 0-0 3m+: 0-3
Track: LH: 0-3 RH: 0-0 Tight: 0-1 Gall: 0-0
Aids: Bl: 0-0 Vi: 0-0 Tstrap: 0-0
Best Rating: 126 3/02 Bang 2m4f110y soft Ch

Fair front-running chaser; stays three miles one but is effective over two and a half miles; jumps well; effective in soft ground.

Mickthetrick
77   52

7-y-o b g Henbit (USA)-Catherine Tudor (Tudor Wood)
Ian Emmerson Ian Emmerson

Placings:00-0F (4590)
2002/03: 21⁹G, 20⁵G,

	Starts	1st	2nd	3rd	Win & Pl
Hurdles	2	0	0	0	
Career Total	4	0	0	0	

Going: Sf: 0-0 GS: 0-0 Gd: 0-2 GF: - Fm: 0-0
Distance: 2m/2m3: 0-0 2m4-2m7: 0-2 3m+: 0-0
Track: LH: 0-2 RH: 0-0 Tight: 0-1 Gall: 0-0
Aids: Bl: 0-0 Vi: 0-0 Tstrap: 0-0
Best Rating: 56 3/03 Sedg 2m5f110y good Hdl

Micky Mansions (IRE)

9-y-o gr g Phardante (FR)-Reneagh (Prince Regent (FR))
W M Aitchison W M Aitchison

Placings:P (0083)
2002/03: 25⁵GS,

	Starts	1st	2nd	3rd	Win & Pl
Chases	1	0	0	0	
Career Total	1	0	0	0	

Going: Sf: 0-0 GS: 0-1 Gd: 0-0 GF: - Fm: 0-0
Distance: 2m/2m3: 0-0 2m4-2m7: 0-0 3m+: 0-1
Track: LH: 0-1 RH: 0-0 Tight: 0-0 Gall: 0-0
Aids: Bl: 0-0 Vi: 0-0 Tstrap: 0-0
Best Rating:

Micmac

5-y-o br g Be My Native (USA)-Padykin (Bustino)
P Winkworth Giles Dixon, John Winkworth

Placings:0PP (2257)
2002/03: 17⁰G, 16⁵S, 17⁸HY,

	Starts	1st	2nd	3rd	Win & Pl
NH Flat	1	0	0	0	0
Hurdles	2	0	0	0	0
Career Total	3	0	0	0	

Going: Sf: 0-2 GS: 0-0 Gd: 0-1 GF: - Fm: 0-0
Distance: 2m/2m3: 0-3 2m4-2m7: 0-0 3m+: 0-0
Track: LH: 0-1 RH: 0-2 Tight: 0-2 Gall: 0-0
Aids: Bl: 0-0 Vi: 0-0 Tstrap: 0-0
Best Rating: 26 5/02 Folk 2m1f110y good NHF

Middlethorpe
107   114

6-y-o b g Noble Patriarch-Prime Property (IRE) (Tirol)
M W Easterby J H Quickfall & A G Black

Placings:4224211 (3965)
2002/03: 20⁴HY, 16²GS, 16²G, 16⁴S, 17²HY, 16¹G, 16¹S,

	Starts	1st	2nd	3rd	Win & Pl
Hurdles	7	2	3	0	11930
Career Total	7	2	3	0	11930

108 3/03 Catt 2m E Hdl SFT £3630
114 2/03 Weth 2m E Hdl GD £4088

Total win prize-money £7718

Going: Sf: 1-4 GS: 0-1 Gd: 1-2 GF: - Fm: 0-0
Distance: 2m/2m3: 2-6 2m4-2m7: 0-1 3m+: 0-0
Track: LH: 2-7 RH: 0-0 Tight: 1-2 Gall: 0-1
Aids: Bl: 2-4 Vi: 0-0 Tstrap: 0-0
Best Rating: 114 2/03 Weth 2m good Hdl

Modest novice hurdler; formerly useful handicapper on the Flat; off the mark at the sixth attempt with an improved performance at Wetherby in February and followed up all out at Catterick a week later; suited by two miles; handles ground good or softer.

Middleway
95   72

7-y-o b g Milieu-Galway Gal (Proverb)
Miss Kate Milligan Mrs J M L Milligan

Placings:00P0-P20P460 (4786)
2002/03: 21⁸G, 22²G, 20⁴G, 25⁵G, 20⁴G, 22⁰G,

	Starts	1st	2nd	3rd	Win & Pl
Hurdles	7	0	1	0	1172
Career Total	11	0	1	0	1172

Going: Sf: 0-0 GS: 0-0 Gd: 0-6 GF: - Fm: 0-1
Distance: 2m/2m3: 0-0 2m4-2m7: 0-5 3m+: 0-2
Track: LH: 0-5 RH: 0-1 Tight: 0-3 Gall: 0-0
Aids: Bl: 0-0 Vi: 0-0 Tstrap: 0-0
Best Rating: 77 10/02 Kels 2m6f110y good Hdl

Novice hurdler, first sign of ability when runner-up at Kelso in October 2002.

Midland Flame (IRE)
110(105h)   (118h)134+

8-y-o b g Un Desperado (FR)-Lathanona (Reformed Character)
Miss H C Knight Trevor Hemmings

Placings:23/1123P43-2P231 (4461)
2002/03: 17²G, 19⁸GS, 16²G, 16³G, 20¹G,

	Starts	1st	2nd	3rd	Win & Pl
Chases	5	1	2	1	28158
Career Total	14	3	4	4	48038

134 4/03 Aint 2m4f B HCh GD £24895
109 10/01 Winc 2m D Hdl GD £3250
116 10/01 Bang 2m1f E Hdl GD £3136

Total win prize-money £31281

Going: Sf: 0-0 GS: 0-1 Gd: 1-4 GF: - Fm: 0-0
Distance: 2m/2m3: 0-3 2m4-2m7: 1-2 3m+: 0-0
Track: LH: 1-2 RH: 0-3 Tight: 1-1 Gall: 0-1
Aids: Bl: 0-0 Vi: 0-0 Tstrap: 0-0
Best Rating: 134 4/03 Aint 2m4f good Ch

Useful hurdler/novice chaser; broke his duck over fences on fifth start in valuable novices handicap at Aintree in April; best suited by good ground, a strong pace and trips in excess of two miles.

Midlem Melody
92(94h)   (69h)71

7-y-o b m Syrtos-Singing Hills (Crash Course)
W S Coltherd S Coltherd

Placings:060U64-41504605 (4407)
2002/03: 18⁴HY, 16¹S, 16⁵HY, 17⁰HY, 16⁴G, 16⁶S, 16⁹G, 16⁵G,

	Starts	1st	2nd	3rd	Win & Pl
Hurdles	5	1	0	0	2513
Chases	3	0	0	0	
Career Total	14	1	0	0	2513

70 12/02 Newc 2m G(0-95)HHdl SFT £2247

Total win prize-money £2247

Going: Sf: 1-5 GS: 0-0 Gd: 0-3 GF: - Fm: 0-0
Distance: 2m/2m3: 1-8 2m4-2m7: 0-0 3m+: 0-0
Track: LH: 1-8 RH: 0-0 Tight: 0-4 Gall: 1-2
Aids: Bl: 0-0 Vi: 0-0 Tstrap: 0-0
Best Rating: 80 11/01 Ayr 2m gd-sft NHF

Moderate hurdler, winner of a seller at Newcastle in December 2002. Acts with cut.

Midnight Coup
104(90c)   (74c)74d

7-y-o br g First Trump-Anhaar (Ela-Mana-Mou)
B G Powell Mark Barrett Racing

Placings:400/0P0/006-50435501
2002/03: 26⁵G, 20⁰G, 18⁴GF, 22³GF, 21⁵F, 19⁵G, 22⁰S, 16¹F,

	Starts	1st	2nd	3rd	Win & Pl
Hurdles	5	1	0	1	1811
Chases	3	0	0	0	
Career Total	17	1	0	1	1940

4/03 LES 2m Hdl FRM £1260

Total win prize-money £1260

Going: Sf: 0-1 GS: 0-0 Gd: 0-2 GF: - Fm: 1-5
Distance: 2m/2m3: 1-2 2m4-2m7: 0-5 3m+: 0-1
Track: LH: 1-3 RH: 0-3 Tight: 0-4 Gall: 0-1
Aids: Bl: 0-2 Vi: 0-0 Tstrap: 0-0
Best Rating: 84 7/02 NAbb 2m6f gd-fm Hdl

Midnight Creek
104   106
5-y-o br g Tragic Role (USA)-Greek Night Out (IRE) (Ela-Mana-Mou)
G A Swinbank (Mrs A J Perrett 16/10) M B Luong

Placings:153633   (3896)
2002/03: 16¹HY, 16⁵S, 20³HY, 20⁶GS, 20³GS, 22³GS,

	Starts	1st	2nd	3rd	Win & Pl
Hurdles	6	1	0	3	5474
Career Total	6	1	0	3	5474
103 12/02 Kels	2m110y	E Hdl		HVY	£3653
				Total win prize-money £3653	

Going: Sf: 1-3 GS: 0-3 Gd: 0-0 GF: - Fm: 0-0
Distance: 2m/2m3: 1-2 2m4-2m7: 0-4 3m+: 0-0
Track: LH: 1-6 RH: 0-0 Tight: 1-3 Gall: 0-1
Aids: Bl: 0-0 Vi: 0-0 Tstrap: 0-0
Best Rating: 106 1/03 Newc 2m4f   heavy Hdl

Stayer on the Flat; modest hurdler; acts in heavy ground; stays two and a half miles; not a straightforward individual.

Midnight Express (IRE)

8-y-o b/br g Orchestra-Loaker Lady (Furry Glen)
G J Morgan G J Morgan

Placings:U   (3592)
2002/03: 24ᵁS,

	Starts	1st	2nd	3rd	Win & Pl
Chases	1	0	0	0	
Career Total	1	0	0	0	

Going: Sf: 0-1 GS: 0-0 Gd: 0-0 GF: - Fm: 0-0
Distance: 2m/2m3: 0-0 2m4-2m7: 0-0 3m+: 0-1
Track: LH: 0-0 RH: 0-1 Tight: 0-0 Gall: 0-0
Aids: Bl: 0-0 Vi: 0-0 Tstrap: 0-0
Best Rating: 0 2/03 Sand 3m110y   soft   Ch

Midnight Gunner
110(110h)   (94h)120
9-y-o b g Gunner B-Light Tonight (Lighter)
A E Price (C J Price 27/2) M G Racing

Placings:000P06/226C363/41P2612P-2212141   (4603)
2002/03: 25²GF, 24²G, 27¹G, 24²S, 24¹G, 24⁴G, 26¹G,

	Starts	1st	2nd	3rd	Win & Pl
Chases	7	3	3	0	44556
Career Total	28	5	7	2	56615
120 4/03 Chel	3m2f110yC(0-135)HCh	GD	£13166		
116 2/03 Ludl	3m	D(0-125)HCh	GD	£13728	
106 12/02 Ludl	3m3f110yD(0-125)HCh	GD	£10003		
93 2/02 Ludl	3m	E(0-105)HHdl	GD	£4576	
92 5/01 Hrfd	2m3f	F Ch	GD	£2990	
				Total win prize-money £44464	

Going: Sf: 0-1 GS: 0-0 Gd: 3-5 GF: - Fm: 0-1
Distance: 2m/2m3: 0-0 2m4-2m7: 0-0 3m+: 3-7
Track: LH: 1-3 RH: 2-4 Tight: 2-3 Gall: 1-3
Aids: Bl: 0-0 Vi: 0-0 Tstrap: 0-0
Best Rating: 120 4/03 Chel 3m2f110y good   Ch

Fair chaser; in good form in 2002 winning at Cheltenham and at Ludlow twice; stays 3m 3f; likes good ground; good record at Ludlow.

Midnight Jazz (IRE)
92   73
13-y-o b g Shardari-Round Midnight (Star Appeal)
J Harriman John Harriman

Placings:030/000051306P2/P5/0U22/0P/0P626-PP3
                                               (4283)
2002/03: 17⁵GF, 19⁹GS, 16³GF,

	Starts	1st	2nd	3rd	Win & Pl
Hurdles	3	0	0	1	430
Career Total	30	1	4	3	6150
111 1/97 Tram	2m	Hdl		Y-S	£2204	
				Total win prize-money £2204	

Going: Sf: 0-0 GS: 0-1 Gd: 0-0 GF: - Fm: 0-2
Distance: 2m/2m3: 0-2 2m4-2m7: 0-1 3m+: 0-0
Track: LH: 0-0 RH: 0-3 Tight: 0-1 Gall: 0-0
Aids: Bl: 0-0 Vi: 0-0 Tstrap: 0-0
Best Rating: 111 1/97 Tram 2m   yld-sft Hdl

Midnight Missile

6-y-o b g Arms And The Man-Rewbell (Andy Rew)
Mrs D A Hamer D J Phillips

Placings:00-00   (0849)
2002/03: 20⁰G, 17⁰GF,

	Starts	1st	2nd	3rd	Win & Pl
Hurdles	2	0	0	0	
Career Total	4	0	0	0	

Going: Sf: 0-0 GS: 0-0 Gd: 0-1 GF: - Fm: 0-1
Distance: 2m/2m3: 0-1 2m4-2m7: 0-0 3m+: 0-0
Track: LH: 0-2 RH: 0-0 Tight: 0-0 Gall: 0-0
Aids: Bl: 0-0 Vi: 0-0 Tstrap: 0-0
Best Rating: 33 9/01 Hrfd 2m1f   gd-fm NHF

Midnight Moon
88   73
8-y-o b g Jupiter Island-Nunswalk (The Parson)
B D Leavy Mrs Alurie O Sullivan

Placings:0000/4P-0   (0439)
2002/03: 20⁰G,

	Starts	1st	2nd	3rd	Win & Pl
Hurdles	1	0	0	0	
Career Total	7	0	0	0	0

Going: Sf: 0-0 GS: 0-0 Gd: 0-1 GF: - Fm: 0-0
Distance: 2m/2m3: 0-0 2m4-2m7: 0-1 3m+: 0-0
Track: LH: 0-1 RH: 0-0 Tight: 0-0 Gall: 0-0
Aids: Bl: 0-0 Vi: 0-0 Tstrap: 0-0
Best Rating: 73 3/02 Hexm 3m   heavy Hdl

Modest hurdler, stays three miles.

Midnight Tango

6-y-o ch m Milieu-Whistle Binkie (Slim Jim)
Mrs H O Graham R D Graham

Placings:00P   (1633)
2002/03: 16⁰GF, 22⁰GF, 24⁴PS,

	Starts	1st	2nd	3rd	Win & Pl
NH Flat	1	0	0	0	0
Hurdles	2	0	0	0	0
Career Total	3	0	0	0	0

Going: Sf: 0-1 GS: 0-0 Gd: 0-0 GF: - Fm: 0-2

Distance: 2m/2m3: 0-1 2m4-2m7: 0-1 3m+: 0-1

Track: LH: 0-2 RH: 0-1 Tight: 0-1 Gall: 0-0
Aids: Bl: 0-0 Vi: 0-0 Tstrap: 0-0
Best Rating: 21 9/02 Hexm 2m110y   gd-fm NHF

Midnight Watch (USA)

9-y-o b g Capote (USA)-Midnight Air (USA) (Green Dancer (USA))
M A Allen B M Wallace

Placings:P/U05460P/P   (0192)
2002/03: 21ᴾGF,

	Starts	1st	2nd	3rd	Win & Pl
Hurdles	1	0	0	0	
Career Total	9	0	0	0	0

Going: Sf: 0-0 GS: 0-0 Gd: 0-0 GF: - Fm: 0-1
Distance: 2m/2m3: 0-0 2m4-2m7: 0-1 3m+: 0-0
Track: LH: 0-0 RH: 0-1 Tight: 0-0 Gall: 0-1
Aids: Bl: 0-0 Vi: 0-0 Tstrap: 0-1
Best Rating: 82 10/99 Winc 2m   good   Hdl

Midy's Risk (FR)
95(103h)   (108h)104
6-y-o gr g Take Risks (FR)-Martine Midy (FR) (Lashkari)
Mrs N Smith Tony Hayward And Barry Fulton

Placings:00/235134-442464   (4758)
2002/03: 21⁴G, 16⁴GS, 17⁴S, 20²HY, 17⁴S, 16⁶S, 22⁴GF,

	Starts	1st	2nd	3rd	Win & Pl
Hurdles	3	0	0	0	519
Chases	4	0	1	0	2402
Career Total	14	1	2	2	9113
113 2/02 Plum	2m	E Hdl		HVY	£2761	
				Total win prize-money £2762	

Going: Sf: 0-4 GS: 0-1 Gd: 0-1 GF: - Fm: 0-1
Distance: 2m/2m3: 0-4 2m4-2m7: 0-3 3m+: 0-0
Track: LH: 0-4 RH: 0-1 Tight: 0-6 Gall: 0-0
Aids: Bl: 0-1 Vi: 0-0 Tstrap: 0-0
Best Rating: 113 2/02 Plum 2m   heavy Hdl

Ex-French, he showed his first sign of ability over hurdles at Taunton in December 2001 and continued to run well before getting off the mark in a maiden hurdle in very testing ground at Plumpton in February. Suited by two miles and easy ground.

Mighty Fine
104(109h)   (87h)105
9-y-o gr g Arzanni-Kate Kimberley (Sparkler)
Mrs E Slack A Slack

Placings:0/2S40/0/0-304321U1U13   (4519)
2002/03: 16⁹GF, 17⁰GF, 25⁴GF, 16³S, 16²HY, 16¹S, 21ᵁS, 16¹S, 16ᵁGS, 21¹G, 21³G,

	Starts	1st	2nd	3rd	Win & Pl
Hurdles	2	0	0	1	425
Chases	9	3	1	2	13438
Career Total	18	3	2	3	14323
105 3/03 Sedg	2m5f	F(0-95)HCh	GD	£3386	
101 12/02 Sedg	2m110y	E(0-105)HCh	SFT	£4056	
87 11/02 Sedg	2m110y	F(0-100)HCh	SFT	£3386	
				Total win prize-money £10830	

Going: Sf: 2-5 GS: 0-1 Gd: 1-2 GF: - Fm: 0-3
Distance: 2m/2m3: 2-7 2m4-2m7: 1-3 3m+: 0-1

Track: LH: 3-9 RH: 0-2 **Tight:** 3-7 Gall: 0-1
Aids: Bl: 0-0 Vi: 0-0 Tstrap: 0-0
Best Rating: 105 4/03 Sedg 2m5f   good   Ch

Lightly-raced modest chaser, goes well at Sedgefield winning three times there in 2002/2003; stays two miles five; handles any ground.

Mighty Kilcash (IRE)

(97h)   (94h)
10-y-o ch g Black Minstrel-Any Wonder (Hard Boy)
K C Bailey Mrs M C Sweeney

Placings: 0/010/52131/3   (2984)
2002/03: 18³HY,

	Starts	1st	2nd	3rd	Win & Pl
Hurdles	1	0	0	1	520
Career Total	10	3	1	2	16351
114	2/01	Uttx	3m2f	D Ch	SFT	£4014
120	1/01	Donc	3m	D(0-115)HCh	GD	£4225
112	2/99	Thur	2m	NHF	HVY	£2455
			Total win prize-money £10695		

Going: Sf: 0-1 GS: 0-0 Gd: 0-0 GF: - Fm: 0-0
Distance: 2m/2m3: 0-1 2m4-2m7: 0-3 3m+: 0-0
Track: LH: 0-1 RH: 0-0 Tight: 0-1 Gall: 0-0
Aids: Bl: 0-0 Vi: 0-0 Tstrap: 0-0
Best Rating: 120 1/01 Donc 3m   good   Ch

Decent handicap chaser; jumps soundly; effective in soft ground; stays beyond three miles.

Mighty Man (IRE)

8-y-o b g Mandalus-Mossy Mistress (IRE) (Le Moss)
O Brennan Lady Anne Bentinck

Placings: 0/PP-P   (0330)
2002/03: 23ᴾG,

	Starts	1st	2nd	3rd	Win & Pl
Chases	1	0	0	0	
Career Total	4	0	0	0	

Going: Sf: 0-0 GS: 0-0 Gd: 0-1 GF: - Fm: 0-0
Distance: 2m/2m3: 0-0 2m4-2m7: 0-0 3m+: 0-1
Track: LH: 0-0 RH: 0-0 Tight: 0-0 Gall: 0-0
Aids: Bl: 0-0 Vi: 0-1 Tstrap: 0-0
Best Rating: 0   5/02 Weth 2m7f110y good   Ch

Mighty Max
83   71
5-y-o b g Well Beloved-Jokers High (USA) (Vaguely Noble)
G A Ham Max Pro Bets

Placings: 0P6   (2194)
2002/03: 16⁰G, 17ᴾS, 17⁶GS,

	Starts	1st	2nd	3rd	Win & Pl
Hurdles	3	0	0	0	0
Career Total	3	0	0	0	0

Going: Sf: 0-1 GS: 0-1 Gd: 0-1 GF: - Fm: 0-0
Distance: 2m/2m3: 0-3 2m4-2m7: 0-0 3m+: 0-0
Track: LH: 0-2 RH: 0-1 Tight: 0-3 Gall: 0-0
Aids: Bl: 0-0 Vi: 0-0 Tstrap: 0-0
Best Rating: 71 11/02 Tntn 2m1f   gd-sft Hdl

Plating-class hurdler; well beaten over hurdles so far; has worn tongue tie.

Mighty Minster
101   82
6-y-o ch m Minster Son-Mighty Fly (Comedy Star (USA))
R C Guest (N B Mason 29/1) N B Mason

Placings: 4455440   (3803)
2002/03: 16⁴GF, 17⁴GF, 19⁵G, 19⁵GS, 16⁴S, 16⁴HY, 20⁰S,

	Starts	1st	2nd	3rd	Win & Pl
NH Flat	2	0	0	0	0
Hurdles	5	0	0	0	534
Career Total	7	0	0	0	534

Going: Sf: 0-3 GS: 0-1 Gd: 0-1 GF: - Fm: 0-2
Distance: 2m/2m3: 0-6 2m4-2m7: 0-1 3m+: 0-0
Track: LH: 0-6 RH: 0-1 Tight: 0-2 Gall: 0-3
Aids: Bl: 0-0 Vi: 0-0 Tstrap: 0-0
Best Rating: 83 12/02 Catt 2m3f   gd-sft Hdl

Plating-class hurdler; half-sister to several winners, is out of a mare who won both the Lincoln and the Royal Hunt Cup; limited ability so far.

Mighty Montefalco
99(106h)   (116h)122+
7-y-o b g Mtoto-Glendera (Glenstal (USA))
Jonjo O Neill Mr & Mrs Peter S Thompson

Placings: 3661-211114   (4558)
2002/03: 22²GF, 22¹GS, 24¹GF, 24¹G, 24¹G, 25⁴G,

	Starts	1st	2nd	3rd	Win & Pl
Hurdles	3	2	1	0	9519
Chases	3	2	0	0	17534
Career Total	10	5	1	1	30491
121	10/02	Chel	3m110y	C Ch	GD	£9858
120	10/02	Strf	3m	D Ch	GD	£6041
116	8/02	Uttx	3m110y	E(0-110)HHdl	G-F	£3465
113	8/02	Strf	2m6f110yD Hdl		G-S	£4777
116	4/02	Strf	2m6f110y	E Hdl	GD	£3230
			Total win prize-money £27373		

Going: Sf: 0-0 GS: 1-1 Gd: 2-3 GF: - Fm: 1-2
Distance: 2m/2m3: 0-0 2m4-2m7: 1-2 3m+: 3-4
Track: LH: 4-6 RH: 0-0 Tight: 2-3 Gall: 1-1
Aids: Bl: 0-0 Vi: 0-0 Tstrap: 0-0
Best Rating: 122 4/03 Ayr 3m1f   good   Ch

Useful novice chaser; stays three miles; landed first two chases in style in October 2002; disappointing on handicap debut when returning from a break at Ayr in April 2003; does not want the ground too soft.

Mighty Moss (IRE)

12-y-o b g Moscow Society (USA)-Derry Girl (Rarity)
K Hutsby K Hutsby

Placings: 11233/112222/2134/1151/4P/U225-2   (4082)
2002/03: 26²S,

	Starts	1st	2nd	3rd	Win & Pl
Chases	1	0	1	0	520
Career Total	26	8	9	3	66264
130	4/00	Ayr	3m3f110yH Ch		GD	£2795
123	2/00	Hntg	3m	H Ch	SFT	£1260
110	2/00	Hntg	3m	H Ch	SFT	£1144
149	1/98	Chel	3m	B Hdl	G-S	£6156
135	11/96	Chep	2m4f110yC Hdl		SFT	£3965
119	11/96	Worc	2m4f	E Hdl	GD	£2722
122	1/96	Nott	2m	H NHF	G-S	£1721
112	12/95	Hntg	2m110y	H NHF	G-S	£1722
			Total win prize-money £21487		

Going: Sf: 0-1 GS: 0-0 Gd: 0-0 GF: - Fm: 0-0
Distance: 2m/2m3: 0-0 2m4-2m7: 0-0 3m+: 0-1
Track: LH: 0-0 RH: 0-0 Tight: 0-0 Gall: 0-0
Aids: Bl: 0-0 Vi: 0-1 Tstrap: 0-0
Best Rating: 155 3/98 Chel 3m   good   Hdl

Once a decent hurdler/chaser; now an iffy hunter chaser.

Mighty Mouse (IRE)

7-y-o b g Roi Guillaume (FR)-By Golly (IRE) (Mandalus)
Colin S McKeever Four Square Syndicate

Placings: 0P0   (1253a)
2002/03: 17⁰YS, 16ᴾG, 20⁰G,

	Starts	1st	2nd	3rd	Win & Pl
NH Flat	1	0	0	0	0
Hurdles	1	0	0	0	0
Chases	1	0	0	0	0
Career Total	3	0	0	0	

Going: Sf: 0-0 GS: 0-0 Gd: 0-2 GF: - Fm: 0-0
Distance: 2m/2m3: 0-2 2m4-2m7: 0-1 3m+: 0-0
Track: LH: 0-1 RH: 0-0 Tight: 0-1 Gall: 0-0
Aids: Bl: 0-0 Vi: 0-0 Tstrap: 0-0
Best Rating: 35 5/02 Dpat 2m1f172y yld-sft NHF

Mighty Strong
111   115
9-y-o b g Strong Gale-Muffet s Spider (Rymer)
N J Henderson J R Henderson

Placings: 44/510/PP102-F21FF43P   (3900)
2002/03: 19¹GF, 17²GF, 21¹G, 21²FG, 20⁵GS, 21⁴G, 20³GS, 20ᴾS,

	Starts	1st	2nd	3rd	Win & Pl
Chases	8	1	1	1	11524
Career Total	18	3	2	1	22948
120	10/02	Sthl	2m5f110yD(0-120)HCh		GD	£6776
111	1/02	Newb	2m1f	D(0-120)HCh	GD	£5590
108	12/00	Donc	2m110y	D Ch	HVY	£3867
			Total win prize-money £16234		

Going: Sf: 0-1 GS: 0-2 Gd: 1-3 GF: - Fm: 0-2
Distance: 2m/2m3: 0-2 2m4-2m7: 0-0 3m+: 1-6
Track: LH: 1-5 RH: 0-3 Tight: 0-2 Gall: 0-3
Aids: Bl: 0-0 Vi: 0-0 Tstrap: 0-0
Best Rating: 125 11/02 Newb 2m4f   gd-sft Ch

Fair front-running handicap chaser; he is effective from two to two miles five on ground ranging from good to heavy; would have won but for falling at the last at Newbury in November 2002; does suffer from jumping problems.

Mighty Surprise
86   88
7-y-o b m Sure Blade (USA)-Flash-By (Ilium)
P J Hobbs P J Hobbs

Placings: 0/344155/3-0   (0412)
2002/03: 19⁰GF,

	Starts	1st	2nd	3rd	Win & Pl
Hurdles	1	0	0	0	
Career Total	9	1	0	2	3319
			Total win prize-money £2698		
92	8/00	NAbb	2m6f	E Hdl	G-F	£2697

Going: Sf: 0-0 GS: 0-0 Gd: 0-0 GF: - Fm: 0-1
Distance: 2m/2m3: 0-1 2m4-2m7: 0-0 3m+: 0-0
Track: LH: 0-1 RH: 0-0 Tight: 0-0 Gall: 0-0
Aids: Bl: 0-0 Vi: 0-0 Tstrap: 0-0
Best Rating: 92 8/00 NAbb 2m6f   gd-fm Hdl

Mike Simmons

104　　　　　　　　**77**

7-y-o b g Ballacashtal (CAN)-Lady Crusty (Golden Dipper)
L P Grassick L P Grassick

Placings:0014/033531/006-P34P0　　　(4194)
2002/03: 24^{P}G, 19^{3}GS, 19^{4}GS, 19^{P}S, 21^{0}G,

	Starts	1st	2nd	3rd	Win & Pl
Hurdles	5	0	0	1	690
Career Total	18	2	0	4	8172
104 4/01 Font	2m4f			F(0-100)HHdl	GD £2761
83 2/00 Tntn	2m1f			E Hdl	SFT £2472

Total win prize-money £5234

Going:　Sf: 0-1 GS: 0-2 Gd: 0-2 GF: - Fm: 0-0
Distance:　2m/2m3: 0-2 2m4-2m7: 0-3 3m+: 0-1
Track:　LH: 0-2 RH: 0-3 Tight: 0-1 Gall: 0-0
Aids:　Bl: 0-0 Vi: 0-0 Tstrap: 0-0
Best Rating:　104 4/01 Font 2m4f　good Hdl

Moderate handicap hurdler; best at around 2m 4f; has won on good and soft ground.

Mike Stan (IRE)

95　　　　　　　　**106**

12-y-o b g Rontino-Fair Pirouette (Fair Turn)
L Lungo J M Crichton

Placings:540/14110U2/4223111/62F11/33F0/P-P　(4751)
2002/03: 20^{P}G,

	Starts	1st	2nd	3rd	Win & Pl
Chases	1	0	0	0	
Career Total	28	8	4	3	58473
139 4/00 Carl	3m2f		D(0-125)HCh	SFT £4426	
124 2/00 Muss	2m4f		D(0-120)HCh	G-S £4891	
143 4/99 Ayr	3m1f		C HCh	SFT £25532	
122 3/99 Ayr	3m1f		D Ch	SFT £4570	
128 2/99 Muss	3m		E(0-105)HCh	FRM £3192	
116 1/98 Ayr	2m4f		D Hdl	G-S £3345	
107 12/97 Uttx	3m110y		E(0-100)HHdl	G-S £2515	
96 11/97 Carl	2m4f110yE(0-100)HHdl		FRM £2388		

Total win prize-money £50863

Going:　Sf: 0-0 GS: 0-0 Gd: 0-1 GF: - Fm: 0-0
Distance:　2m/2m3: 0-0 2m4-2m7: 0-1 3m+: 0-0
Track:　LH: 0-0 RH: 0-1 Tight: 0-0 Gall: 0-0
Aids:　Bl: 0-0 Vi: 0-0 Tstrap: 0-0
Best Rating:　143 4/99 Ayr 3m1f　soft Ch

Modest chaser; best effort for some time when runner-up at Sedgefield in May.

Mikhail (USA)

71　　　　　　　　**64**

6-y-o ch g Nureyev (USA)-Rythmical (USA) (Fappiano (USA))
N J Hawke R J & Mrs J A Peake

Placings:0000-F0　　　　　　(0576)
2002/03: 19^{7}GF, 17^{P}G,

	Starts	1st	2nd	3rd	Win & Pl
Hurdles	2	0	0	0	0
Career Total	6	0	0	0	0

Going:　Sf: 0-0 GS: 0-0 Gd: 0-1 GF: - Fm: 0-1
Distance:　2m/2m3: 0-1 2m4-2m7: 0-1 3m+: 0-0
Track:　LH: 0-1 RH: 0-1 Tight: 0-1 Gall: 0-0
Aids:　Bl: 0-0 Vi: 0-0 Tstrap: 0-0
Best Rating:　64 1/02 Winc 2m　gd-sft Hdl

Milan King (IRE)

102(89c)　　　　　　(90c)**69**

10-y-o b g King s Ride-Milan Moss (Le Moss)
A J Lockwood Chester Bosomworth

Placings:5P00F000/P040F05F/041051P6P2/20110000/030
P40-50P5303P06P0U　　　　　　(4795)
2002/03: 17^{5}GF, 16^{0}G, 24^{F}G, 17^{5}G, 17^{3}GF, 20^{0}GF, 17^{3}GF, 17^{P}G,
16^{0}G, 17^{6}HY, 19^{P}G, 17^{0}G, 21^{U}GF,

	Starts	1st	2nd	3rd	Win & Pl
Hurdles	13	0	0	2	672
Career Total	53	4	2	3	9380
101 5/00 Sedg	2m1f		F(0-105)HHdl	GD £1855	
101 7/00 Sedg	2m1f		F(0-105)HHdl	G-F £1918	
83 2/00 Sedg	2m1f		F(0-100)HHdl	G-S £1991	
77 12/99 MRas	2m1f110yG(0-95)HHdl		GD £1584		

Total win prize-money £7350

Going:　Sf: 0-1 GS: 0-0 Gd: 0-7 GF: - Fm: 0-5
Distance:　2m/2m3: 0-0 2m4-2m7: 0-2 3m+: 0-1
Track:　LH: 0-9 RH: 0-4 Tight: 0-11 Gall: 0-0
Aids:　Bl: 0-0 Vi: 0-0 Tstrap: 0-0
Best Rating:　101 9/00 Sedg 2m1f　good Hdl

Selling handicap hurdler; scored three times over the extended two miles at Sedgefield in 2000; returned to form when winning there again in July; has broken blood vessels.

Milbrig

84　　　　　　　　**45**

7-y-o b m Milieu-Meadow Brig (Meadowbrook)
A C Whillans Mrs Anne Taylor

Placings:P0P　　　　　　(4750)
2002/03: 20^{P}HY, 22^{0}G, 24^{P}G,

	Starts	1st	2nd	3rd	Win & Pl
Hurdles	3	0	0	0	
Career Total	3	0	0	0	

Going:　Sf: 0-1 GS: 0-0 Gd: 0-2 GF: - Fm: 0-0
Distance:　2m/2m3: 0-0 2m4-2m7: 0-2 3m+: 0-1
Track:　LH: 0-2 RH: 0-1 Tight: 0-1 Gall: 0-0
Aids:　Bl: 0-0 Vi: 0-0 Tstrap: 0-0
Best Rating:　45 3/03 Kels 2m6f110y good Hdl

Mildon (IRE)

82　　　　　　　　**54**

7-y-o ch g Dolphin Street (FR)-Lycia (Targowice (USA))
J R Weymes Don Raper

Placings:050/0P-66　　　　　　(1056)
2002/03: 21^{5}G, 17^{6}G,

	Starts	1st	2nd	3rd	Win & Pl
Hurdles	2	0	0	0	0
Career Total	7	0	0	0	0

Going:　Sf: 0-0 GS: 0-0 Gd: 0-2 GF: - Fm: 0-0
Distance:　2m/2m3: 0-1 2m4-2m7: 0-1 3m+: 0-0
Track:　LH: 0-2 RH: 0-0 Tight: 0-2 Gall: 0-0
Aids:　Bl: 0-0 Vi: 0-0 Tstrap: 0-0
Best Rating:　79 2/01 Sedg 2m5f110y soft Hdl

Well held in modest company over hurdles. Suited to an easy surface. Has worn blinkers and a visor.

Militaire (FR)

102(78c)　　　　　　(71+c)**110**

5-y-o ch g Bering-Moon Review (USA) (Irish River (FR))
M D Hammond (J Bertran De Balanda 5/5) David J Jackson

Milan King (IRE) / right column

Placings:3526-05251PP　　　　　　(4226)
2002/03: 18^{0}VS, 16^{5}GS, 20^{2}HY, 16^{5}G, 16^{1}GS, 20^{P}G, 16^{P}GF,

	Starts	1st	2nd	3rd	Win & Pl
Hurdles	6	1	1	0	7858
Chases	1	0	0	0	
Career Total	11	1	2	1	19234
110 2/03 Weth	2m		C(0-135)HHdl	G-S £6942	

Total win prize-money £6942

Going:　Sf: 0-1 GS: 1-2 Gd: 0-2 GF: - Fm: 0-1
Distance:　2m/2m3: 1-5 2m4-2m7: 0-2 3m+: 0-0
Track:　LH: 1-5 RH: 0-1 Tight: 0-1 Gall: 0-0
Aids:　Bl: 0-0 Vi: 0-0 Tstrap: 0-0
Best Rating:　110 2/03 Weth 2m　gd-sft Hdl

Modest hurdler; effective from two to two and a half miles; best with cut in the ground

Milkat (IRE)

107　　　　　　　　**121**

5-y-o b h Machiavellian (USA)-Desert Victory (Green Desert (USA))
W P Mullins (Paul Nolan 12/7) J Comerford

Placings:000-001551200P　　　　　　(4729a)
2002/03: 16^{9}GY, 16^{0}G, 16^{1}GY, 16^{5}G, 16^{5}F, 16^{1}G, 16^{2}HY, 16^{0}HY,
16^{5}S, 22^{P}G,

	Starts	1st	2nd	3rd	Win & Pl
Hurdles	10	2	1	0	20359
Career Total	13	2	1	0	20359
108 10/02 Limk	2m		Hdl	GD £8972	
101 8/02 Wxfd	2m		Hdl	G-Y £3809	

Total win prize-money £12782

Going:　Sf: 0-3 GS: 0-0 Gd: 1-4 GF: - Fm: 0-1
Distance:　2m/2m3: 2-9 2m4-2m7: 0-1 3m+: 0-0
Track:　LH: 0-2 RH: 0-2 Tight: 0-0 Gall: 0-0
Aids:　Bl: 0-0 Vi: 0-0 Tstrap: 0-0
Best Rating:　121 1/03 Leop 2m　soft Hdl

Fair Irish-trained hurdler; acts on a sound surface, but effective with cut; goes well around two miles.

Mill Emerald

108(64c)　　　　　　(70c)**106**

6-y-o b m Old Vic-Milinetta (Milford)
Mrs M Reveley R Meredith

Placings:04001503-113434　　　　　　(4410)
2002/03: 20^{1}G, 20^{1}G, 20^{3}GS, 20^{4}GS, 20^{3}S, 20^{6}G,

	Starts	1st	2nd	3rd	Win & Pl
Hurdles	4	2	0	1	13383
Chases	2	0	0	1	1127
Career Total	14	3	0	3	16698
108 6/02 Uttx	2m4f110yG(0-100)HHdl		GD £10582		
105 5/02 Weth	2m4f110yF Hdl		GD £1995		
79 1/02 Newc	2m4f		G(0-95)HHdl	SFT £1932	

Total win prize-money £14509

Going:　Sf: 0-1 GS: 0-2 Gd: 2-3 GF: - Fm: 0-0
Distance:　2m/2m3: 0-0 2m4-2m7: 2-6 3m+: 0-0
Track:　LH: 2-4 RH: 0-2 Tight: 0-1 Gall: 0-1
Aids:　Bl: 0-0 Vi: 0-0 Tstrap: 0-0
Best Rating:　108 6/02 Uttx 2m4f110y good Hdl

Selling hurdler; changed hands for 6,400 gns after winning valuable 2m 4f seller at Uttoxeter for the second year in succession; acts on ground good and softer.

Mill Lord (IRE)

95　　　　　　　　**56**

10-y-o b g Aristocracy-Millflower (Millfontaine)

C J Drewe   W P Long

Placings:000/04/05PFPP/P3434500P-3P450PP53   (4699)
2002/03: 16PGS, 21³GF, 24PGF, 21⁴GF, 23⁵G, 22⁰G, 16PG, 20PS, 16⁵GF, 17³GF,

	Starts	1st	2nd	3rd	Win & Pl
Hurdles	1	0	0	0	0
Chases	9	0	0	2	1339
Career Total	29	0	0	4	2384

Going: Sf: 0-1 GS: 0-1 Gd: 0-3 GF: - Fm: 0-5
Distance: 2m/2m3: 0-4 2m4-2m7: 0-4 3m+: 0-2
Track: LH: 0-2 RH: 0-6 Tight: 0-4 Gall: 0-1
Aids: Bl: 0-8 Vi: 0 Tstrap: 0-0
Best Rating: 76   11/01   Extr   2m3f110y   gd-fm   Ch

Poor chaser; yet to win a race of any description; effective at two miles; suited by a sound surface; has worn blinkers.

Mill O'The Rags (IRE)

14-y-o b g Strong Gale-Lady Rag (Ragapan)
Neil King   Mrs E M Clarke

Placings:065P5/1514/144121152/22PP4P2/21P5P/43P/46 3-5   (0383)
2002/03: 24⁵G,

	Starts	1st	2nd	3rd	Win & Pl
Chases	1	0	0	0	0
Career Total	37	7	6	2	24341
101	5/98	Weth	2m4f110yH Ch		G-F £1308
109	10/96	Hntg	2m4f110yF(0-95)HCh		GD £2940
103	10/96	Towc	2m110y	E Ch	G-F £2877
97	9/96	Plum	2m5f	E Ch	G-F £2976
92	5/96	Hrfd	2m1f	E(0-100)HHdl	FRM £2070
84	11/95	Towc	2m	F(0-100)HHdl	FRM £2180
77	5/95	Towc	2m	D Hdl	G-F £2903
				Total win prize-money £17255

Going: Sf: 0-0 GS: 0-0 Gd: 0-1 GF: - Fm: 0-0
Distance: 2m/2m3: 0-0 2m4-2m7: 0-0 3m+: 0-1
Track: LH: 0-0 RH: 0-1 Tight: 0-0 Gall: 0-1
Aids: Bl: 0-0 Vi: 0-0 Tstrap: 0-0
Best Rating: 112   5/97   Hntg   2m4f110y   gd-fm   Ch

Moderate hunter chaser.

Millcroft Regatta (IRE)

11-y-o br g Miners Lamp-Stradbally Bay (Shackleton)
Mrs A L Tory   Mrs R E Gatland

Placings:0P0/2P2P/3052P/3P   (0395)
2002/03: 21³GF, 28PG,

	Starts	1st	2nd	3rd	Win & Pl
Chases	2	0	0	1	550
Career Total	14	0	3	2	4107

Going: Sf: 0-0 GS: 0-0 Gd: 0-1 GF: - Fm: 0-1
Distance: 2m/2m3: 0-0 2m4-2m7: 0-1 3m+: 0-1
Track: LH: 0-1 RH: 0-1 Tight: 0-1 Gall: 0-0
Aids: Bl: 0-0 Vi: 0-0 Tstrap: 0-0
Best Rating: 99   5/02   Winc   2m5f   gd-fm   Ch

Won two points in the spring of 2002. May have found 21 furlongs on the short side when third at Wincanton.

Millcroft Seaspray (IRE)

104(101c)   (110c)118
7-y-o br g Good Thyne (USA)-Bucks Gift (IRE) (Buckley)
R H Alner   John Carter

Placings:40/3122-233   (4274)
2002/03: 22⁰HY, 24³GS, 20³G,

	Starts	1st	2nd	3rd	Win & Pl
Hurdles	2	0	1	1	1899
Chases	1	0	0	1	750
Career Total	9	1	3	3	9200
110	1/02	Tntn	3m110y	D Hdl	SFT £4139
				Total win prize-money £4139

Going: Sf: 0-1 GS: 0-1 Gd: 0-1 GF: - Fm: 0-0
Distance: 2m/2m3: 0-0 2m4-2m7: 0-2 3m+: 0-1
Track: LH: 0-2 RH: 0-1 Tight: 0-0 Gall: 0-0
Aids: Bl: 0-0 Vi: 0-0 Tstrap: 0-0
Best Rating: 121   11/02   NAbb   2m6f   heavy   Hdl

Fair, lightly-raced hurdler/chaser. Stepped up to three miles to get off the mark at Taunton in January 2002, and ran well subsequently. Fair form over hurdles and fences last season. Acts on a soft surface.

Mille Et Une Nuits (FR)

73f   67f
4-y-o b f Ecologist-Migre (FR) (Le Gregol (FR))
Miss K Marks   Nick Shutts

Placings:6   (4600)
2002/03: 17⁶GF,

	Starts	1st	2nd	3rd	Win & Pl
NH Flat	1	0	0	0	0
Career Total	1	0	0	0	0

Going: Sf: 0-0 GS: 0-0 Gd: 0-0 GF: - Fm: 0-1
Distance: 2m/2m3: 0-1 2m4-2m7: 0-0 3m+: 0-0
Track: LH: 0-0 RH: 0-1 Tight: 0-0 Gall: 0-0
Aids: Bl: 0-0 Vi: 0-0 Tstrap: 0-0
Best Rating: 67   4/03   Extr   2m1f   gd-fm   NHF

Millenium Moonbeam (USA)

72   37
6-y-o ch g Phone Trick (USA)-Shywing (USA) (Wing Out (USA))
G G Margarson   Mr & Mrs John Harris

Placings:00   (1230)
2002/03: 16⁰GF, 16⁰G,

	Starts	1st	2nd	3rd	Win & Pl
Hurdles	2	0	0	0	0
Career Total	2	0	0	0	0

Going: Sf: 0-0 GS: 0-0 Gd: 0-1 GF: - Fm: 0-1
Distance: 2m/2m3: 0-0 2m4-2m7: 0-0 3m+: 0-0
Track: LH: 0-2 RH: 0-0 Tight: 0-0 Gall: 0-0
Aids: Bl: 0-0 Vi: 0-0 Tstrap: 0-0
Best Rating: 37   9/02   Worc   2m   good   Hdl

Millenium Way (IRE)

9-y-o ch g Ikdam-Fine Drapes (Le Bavard (FR))

J M Turner   J M Turner

Placings:2242330/33P33/PP-4   (4671)
2002/03: 24⁴G,

	Starts	1st	2nd	3rd	Win & Pl
Chases	1	0	0	0	0
Career Total	15	0	3	6	6782

Going: Sf: 0-0 GS: 0-0 Gd: 0-1 GF: - Fm: 0-0
Distance: 2m/2m3: 0-0 2m4-2m7: 0-0 3m+: 0-1
Track: LH: 0-1 RH: 0-0 Tight: 0-1 Gall: 0-0
Aids: Bl: 0-0 Vi: 0-0 Tstrap: 0-0
Best Rating: 106   1/00   Folk   2m6f110y   heavy   Hdl

Millennium Gold

88   (92h)77
8-y-o ch g Be My Chief (USA)-Forbearance (Bairn (USA))
C C Pimlott   David Ward

Placings:0060000/0030-3   (0402)
2002/03: 20³GF,

	Starts	1st	2nd	3rd	Win & Pl
Chases	1	0	0	1	225
Career Total	12	0	0	2	705

Going: Sf: 0-0 GS: 0-0 Gd: 0-0 GF: - Fm: 0-1
Distance: 2m/2m3: 0-0 2m4-2m7: 0-1 3m+: 0-0
Track: LH: 0-1 RH: 0-0 Tight: 0-0 Gall: 0-0
Aids: Bl: 0-0 Vi: 0-0 Tstrap: 0-0
Best Rating: 92   9/01   Tral   2m4f   good   Hdl

Winning pointer; modest novice chaser; stays well; acts on fast ground.

Millennium Summit (IRE)

(97h)   (75dh)
6-y-o b h Apple Tree (FR)-Word Of Honor (FR) (Highest Honor (FR))
T G McCourt   Gareth Bennett

Placings:550000-30004050000   (3982a)
2002/03: 16³S, 20⁰S, 20³G, 20³G, 24⁴YS, 18⁰GY, 23⁵F, 20⁰YS, 22⁰HY, 24⁰G, 18⁰S,

	Starts	1st	2nd	3rd	Win & Pl
Hurdles	9	0	0	1	638
Chases	2	0	0	0	0
Career Total	17	0	0	1	638

Going: Sf: 0-4 GS: 0-0 Gd: 0-3 GF: - Fm: 0-1
Distance: 2m/2m3: 0-3 2m4-2m7: 0-6 3m+: 0-2
Track: LH: 0-0 RH: 0-1 Tight: 0-1 Gall: 0-0
Aids: Bl: 0-1 Vi: 0-0 Tstrap: 0-0
Best Rating: 88   7/01   Gway   2m   yield   Hdl

Miller's Bay

119f   135f
5-y-o ch g Karinga Bay-Millers Action (Fearless Action (USA))
Miss H C Knight   Carfield Partners

Placings:215   (4115)
2002/03: 16²G, 17¹S, 16⁵G,

	Starts	1st	2nd	3rd	Win & Pl
NH Flat	3	1	1	0	4146
Career Total	3	1	1	0	4146
113	11/02	Hrfd	2m1f	H NHF	SFT £1876
				Total win prize-money £1876

Going: Sf: 1-1 GS: 0-0 Gd: 0-2 GF: - Fm: 0-0
Distance: 2m/2m3: 1-3 2m4-2m7: 0-0 3m+: 0-0
Track: LH: 0-2 RH: 1-1 Tight: 0-0 Gall: 0-0
Aids: Bl: 0-0 Vi: 0-0 Tstrap: 0-0
Best Rating: 135 3/03 Chel 2m110y good NHF

Useful bumper horse; narrowly beaten on his debut in Cheltenham bumper, comfortable winner next time; fifth in the Champion Bumper at Cheltenham.

Millers Way
65   18
5-y-o b m Nomadic Way (USA)-Keldholme (Derek H)
A Crook Minster Commercials

Placings:060P   (3834)
2002/03: 17⁰S, 16⁶GS, 20⁰GS, 20⁶G,

	Starts	1st	2nd	3rd	Win & Pl
NH Flat	2	0	0	0	0
Hurdles	2	0	0	0	0
Career Total	4	0	0	0	0

Going: Sf: 0-1 GS: 0-2 Gd: 0-1 GF: - Fm: 0-0
Distance: 2m/2m3: 0-2 2m4-2m7: 0-2 3m+: 0-0
Track: LH: 0-2 RH: 0-2 Tight: 0-0 Gall: 0-1
Aids: Bl: 0-1 Vi: 0-0 Tstrap: 0-0
Best Rating: 88 11/02 Weth 2m gd-sft NHF

Millersford
90(107c)   (75c)95
12-y-o b g Meadowbrook-My Seer (Menelek)
N A Gaselee Mrs Derek Fletcher

Placings:0240/14552/33235U/3531F2345/PF503/611P4P3/
20605-12P523PP   (4528)
2002/03: 20¹G, 24²S, 24⁶G, 24⁵GF, 22²G, 23⁹G, 23⁰G, 24⁰G,

	Starts	1st	2nd	3rd	Win & Pl
Chases	8	1	2	1	5943
Career Total	49	5	7	8	30647
101	5/02	Towc	2m4f	F(0-90)Ch	GD	2800
109	6/00	Uttx	3m	D(0-120)HCh	G-F	4176
109	5/00	Towc	2m6f	F(0-90)Ch	SFT	2415
104	11/98	Wind	3m	E Ch	G-S	3549
101	11/96	Kemp	2m5f	E Hdl	GD	2360
				Total win prize-money £15301

Going: Sf: 0-1 GS: 0-0 Gd: 1-6 GF: - Fm: 0-1
Distance: 2m/2m3: 0-0 2m4-2m7: 1-2 3m+: 0-6
Track: LH: 0-4 RH: 0-2 Tight: 0-2 Gall: 0-0
Aids: Bl: 0-0 Vi: 0-0 Tstrap: 0-0
Best Rating: 115 3/97 Sand 2m6f good Hdl

Modest chaser these days; landed three-mile handicap hurdle in bad ground at Uttoxeter in May, first success over hurdles for over six years.

Milliesome
39f   90f
5-y-o b m Milieu-Some Shiela (Remainder Man)
J P Dodds J R Jeffreys

Placings:0   (4437)
2002/03: 16⁰G,

	Starts	1st	2nd	3rd	Win & Pl
NH Flat	1	0	0	0	0
Career Total	1	0	0	0	0

Going: Sf: 0-0 GS: 0-0 Gd: 0-1 GF: - Fm: 0-0
Distance: 2m/2m3: 0-1 2m4-2m7: 0-0 3m+: 0-0
Track: LH: 0-1 RH: 0-0 Tight: 0-0 Gall: 0-0
Aids: Bl: 0-0 Vi: 0-0 Tstrap: 0-0

Best Rating: 0 4/03 Newc 2m good NHF

Milligan (FR)
99   146d
8-y-o b g Exit To Nowhere (USA)-Madigan Mill (Mill Reef (USA))
Miss Venetia Williams G H Leatham

Placings:01/3103360/12044031-0450   (4323)
2002/03: 16⁶G, 20⁴GS, 20⁵G, 16⁶G,

	Starts	1st	2nd	3rd	Win & Pl
Hurdles	4	0	0	0	0
Career Total	21	4	1	4	84750
146	4/02	Ayr	2m	A HHdl	GD	£15600
156	5/01	Hayd	2m	A HHdl	GD	£27000
133	10/00	Weth	2m	C(0-135)HHdl	G-S	£4888
119	3/00	Catt	2m	E Hdl	G-F	£3152
				Total win prize-money £50641

Going: Sf: 0-0 GS: 0-1 Gd: 0-3 GF: - Fm: 0-0
Distance: 2m/2m3: 0-2 2m4-2m7: 0-2 3m+: 0-0
Track: LH: 0-3 RH: 0-0 Tight: 0-1 Gall: 0-1
Aids: Bl: 0-0 Vi: 0-0 Tstrap: 0-0
Best Rating: 156 12/01 Kemp 2m good Hdl

Very useful handicap hurdler who landed the Scottish Champion Hurdle in April 2002; suited by two miles, decent ground and a flat track; jumps soundly.

Millions
90   86
6-y-o b g Bering-Miznah (IRE) (Sadler s Wells (USA))
Mrs H Dalton Hon J Borwick

Placings:U04150-P0   (1042)
2002/03: 17⁵GS, 22⁰GF,

	Starts	1st	2nd	3rd	Win & Pl
Hurdles	2	0	0	0	0
Career Total	8	1	0	0	2649
86	9/01	Sedg	2m5f110yE Hdl	G-F	£2772
			Total win prize-money £2772

Going: Sf: 0-0 GS: 0-1 Gd: 0-0 GF: - Fm: 0-1
Distance: 2m/2m3: 0-1 2m4-2m7: 0-1 3m+: 0-0
Track: LH: 0-1 RH: 0-1 Tight: 0-2 Gall: 0-0
Aids: Bl: 0-1 Vi: 0-0 Tstrap: 0-0
Best Rating: 86 9/01 Sedg 2m5f110y gd-fm Hdl

Millkom Elegance
82   54
4-y-o b f Millkom-Premier Princess (Hard Fought)
K A Ryan Yorkshire Racing Club lv

Placings:0   (2300)
2002/03: 16⁰GS,

	Starts	1st	2nd	3rd	Win & Pl
Hurdles	1	0	0	0	
Career Total	1	0	0	0	

Going: Sf: 0-0 GS: 0-1 Gd: 0-0 GF: - Fm: 0-0
Distance: 2m/2m3: 0-1 2m4-2m7: 0-0 3m+: 0-0
Track: LH: 0-1 RH: 0-0 Tight: 0-1 Gall: 0-0
Aids: Bl: 0-0 Vi: 0-0 Tstrap: 0-0
Best Rating: 33 12/02 Catt 2m gd-sft Hdl

Millys Filly
84   68
5-y-o b m Polish Precedent (USA)-Lemon s Mill (USA)

(Roberto (USA))
O Sherwood R Waters

Placings:005P   (4720)
2002/03: 17⁰S, 16⁰G, 20⁵G, 22²F,

	Starts	1st	2nd	3rd	Win & Pl
Hurdles	4	0	0	0	0
Career Total	4	0	0	0	0

Going: Sf: 0-1 GS: 0-0 Gd: 0-2 GF: - Fm: 0-1
Distance: 2m/2m3: 0-2 2m4-2m7: 0-2 3m+: 0-0
Track: LH: 0-1 RH: 0-3 Tight: 0-2 Gall: 0-1
Aids: Bl: 0-0 Vi: 0-0 Tstrap: 0-0
Best Rating: 68 3/03 Folk 2m4f110y good Hdl

Modest form over hurdles.

Miman James (FR)
80f   74f
5-y-o b g Montorselli-Kimolia (FR) (Prince Baladin)
P F Nicholls Langley Wellingtons

Placings:00   (1606)
2002/03: 17⁰G, 16⁰G,

	Starts	1st	2nd	3rd	Win & Pl
NH Flat	2	0	0	0	
Career Total	2	0	0	0	

Going: Sf: 0-0 GS: 0-0 Gd: 0-2 GF: - Fm: 0-0
Distance: 2m/2m3: 0-2 2m4-2m7: 0-0 3m+: 0-0
Track: LH: 0-1 RH: 0-1 Tight: 0-0 Gall: 0-0
Aids: Bl: 0-0 Vi: 0-0 Tstrap: 0-0
Best Rating: 74 5/02 Hrld 2m1f good NHF

Mincarlo
97   85
7-y-o ch m Karinga Bay-Atlantic View (Crash Course)
G B Balding G B Balding And Tony Geake

Placings:010-33F   (3474)
2002/03: 16³GS, 21³S, 22²GS,

	Starts	1st	2nd	3rd	Win & Pl
Hurdles	3	0	0	2	1030
Career Total	6	1	0	2	3329
105	3/02	Towc	2m	H NHF	SFT	£2299
			Total win prize-money £2300

Going: Sf: 0-1 GS: 0-2 Gd: 0-0 GF: - Fm: 0-0
Distance: 2m/2m3: 0-1 2m4-2m7: 0-2 3m+: 0-0
Track: LH: 0-0 RH: 0-3 Tight: 0-0 Gall: 0-0
Aids: Bl: 0-0 Vi: 0-0 Tstrap: 0-3
Best Rating: 105 3/02 Towc 2m soft NHF

Got off the mark at the second attempt in a Towcester bumper; showed promise over hurdles before being killed at Wincanton in February 2003. (DEAD)

Mind How You Go (FR)
112   120
5-y-o b g Hemando (FR)-Cos I Do (IRE) (Double Schwartz)
J R Best A Fiver In Mind Partnership

Placings:110-1320   (4602)
2002/03: 16¹GS, 18⁵S, 17²G, 21⁰G,

	Starts	1st	2nd	3rd	Win & Pl
Hurdles	4	1	1	1	6621
Career Total	7	3	1	1	16657
118	1/03	Winc	2m	E Hdl	G-S	£3920

108	2/02	Wwck	2m	A NHF		SFT	£8307
92	1/02	Catt	2m	H NHF		G-S	£1729
				Total win prize-money £13956			

Going:	Sf: 0-1 GS: 1-1 Gd: 0-2 GF: - Fm: 0-0
Distance:	2m/2m3: 1-3 2m4-2m7: 0-1 3m+: 0-0
Track:	LH: 0-2 RH: 1-2 Tight: 0-2 Gall: 0-1
Aids:	Bl: 0-0 Vi: 0-0 Tstrap: 0-0
Best Rating:	120 3/03 MRas 2m1f110y good Hdl

Fair novice hurdler; formerly useful bumper performer; won on his debut over hurdles at Wincanton in January but has had his limitations exposed since; best on soft ground.

Mind Of My Own
16f   40f
4-y-o ch f Master Willie-Come Dance With Me (IRE) (Rising)
J D Frost Miss H S Robarts

Placings:0   (4600)
2002/03: 17⁰GF,

	Starts	1st	2nd	3rd	Win & Pl
NH Flat	1	0	0	0	
Career Total	1	0	0	0	

Going:	Sf: 0-0 GS: 0-0 Gd: 0-0 GF: - Fm: 0-0
Distance:	2m/2m3: 0-1 2m4-2m7: 0-0 3m+: 0-0
Track:	LH: 0-0 RH: 0-1 Tight: 0-0 Gall: 0-0
Aids:	Bl: 0-0 Vi: 0-0 Tstrap: 0-0
Best Rating:	40 4/03 Extr 2m1f gd-fm NHF

Mindanao
105   126+
7-y-o b m Most Welcome-Salala (Connaught)
L Lungo (I Semple 17/1) Bob Slee Toby Noble & J B

Placings:10F023-21   (4410)
2002/03: 16²GS, 20¹G,

	Starts	1st	2nd	3rd	Win & Pl
Hurdles	2	1	1	0	5923
Career Total	8	2	2	1	10433
130	3/03	Hexm	2m4f110yD(0-125)HHdl	GD	£4784
103	1/02	Newc	2m	GD	£3052
			Total win prize-money £7836		

Going:	Sf: 0-0 GS: 0-1 Gd: 1-1 GF: - Fm: 0-0
Distance:	2m/2m3: 0-1 2m4-2m7: 1-1 3m+: 0-0
Track:	LH: 1-2 RH: 0-0 Tight: 0-0 Gall: 0-1
Aids:	Bl: 0-0 Vi: 0-0 Tstrap: 0-0
Best Rating:	130 3/03 Hexm 2m4f110y good Hdl

Fair handicap hurdler. Acts on a soft surface and effective at around two miles.

Minden Rose
10-y-o b m Lord Bud-Two Travellers (Deep Run)
Peter Maddison Peter Maddison

Placings:FP1-P   (0187)
2002/03: 20¹G, 20ᴾGF,

	Starts	1st	2nd	3rd	Win & Pl
Chases	2	1	0	0	1651
Career Total	4	1	0	0	1651
80	4/02	Newc	2m4f	H Ch	GD	£1651
			Total win prize-money £1651			

Going:	Sf: 0-0 GS: 0-0 Gd: 1-1 GF: - Fm: 0-1
Distance:	2m/2m3: 0-0 2m4-2m7: 1-2 3m+: 0-0
Track:	LH: 1-1 RH: 0-1 Tight: 0-0 Gall: 1-2
Aids:	Bl: 0-0 Vi: 0-0 Tstrap: 0-0

Mindyer Millions
7-y-o b g Milieu-Mindyer Manners (Faustus (USA))
George R Moscrop George R Moscrop

Placings:P   (0260)
2002/03: 20ᴾGF,

	Starts	1st	2nd	3rd	Win & Pl
Chases	1	0	0	0	
Career Total	1	0	0	0	

Going:	Sf: 0-0 GS: 0-0 Gd: 0-0 GF: - Fm: 0-1
Distance:	2m/2m3: 0-0 2m4-2m7: 0-1 3m+: 0-0
Track:	LH: 0-0 RH: 0-1 Tight: 0-0 Gall: 0-0
Aids:	Bl: 0-0 Vi: 0-0 Tstrap: 0-0
Best Rating:	0 5/02 Prth 2m4f110y gd-fm Ch

Mine Forever
4-y-o br g Royal Academy (USA)-Overseas Romance (USA) (Assert)
D McCain D McCain

Placings:PP0   (1209)
2002/03: 17ᴾS, 17ᴾG, 16⁰G,

	Starts	1st	2nd	3rd	Win & Pl
Hurdles	3	0	0	0	
Career Total	3	0	0	0	

Going:	Sf: 0-1 GS: 0-0 Gd: 0-2 GF: - Fm: 0-0
Distance:	2m/2m3: 0-3 2m4-2m7: 0-0 3m+: 0-0
Track:	LH: 0-3 RH: 0-0 Tight: 0-2 Gall: 0-0
Aids:	Bl: 0-1 Vi: 0-0 Tstrap: 0-2
Best Rating:	0 9/02 Uttx 2m good Hdl

Minella Gold (IRE)
14-y-o b g The Parson-Slieveglagh Queen (Proverb)
Alistair M Brown Mrs June Brown

Placings:312/2U1131203/3F/F556UP/66P2336/34/0U6-2345   (0477)
2002/03: 25²GS, 25³G, 25⁴GF, 26⁵GS,

	Starts	1st	2nd	3rd	Win & Pl
Chases	4	0	1	1	816
Career Total	36	4	5	8	29302
141	1/96	Navn	2m4f	Hdl	HVY	£3177
133	12/95	Fair	3m	Hdl	G-Y	£6782
123	11/95	Tipp	2m4f	Hdl	GD	£2712
119	4/95	Fair	2m	NHF	GD	£4747
				Total win prize-money £17421		

Going:	Sf: 0-0 GS: 0-2 Gd: 0-1 GF: - Fm: 0-1
Distance:	2m/2m3: 0-0 2m4-2m7: 0-0 3m+: 0-4
Track:	LH: 0-4 RH: 0-0 Tight: 0-4 Gall: 0-0
Aids:	Bl: 0-0 Vi: 0-0 Tstrap: 0-4
Best Rating:	143 4/96 Punc 3m soft Hdl

Minella Leisure (IRE)
98(99h)   (108h)118
9-y-o b g Phardante (FR)-Mrs Minella (Deep Run)
Michael Hourigan John J Nallen

Best Rating: 80 4/02 Newc 2m4f good Ch

Placings:2/005333-113P611243FF   (3538a)
2002/03: 20¹YS, 20¹G, 24³G, 20ᴾHY, 20⁶G, 17¹GF, 19¹F, 21²GF, 17⁴G, 20³GS, 21ᶠS, 21ᶠYS,

	Starts	1st	2nd	3rd	Win & Pl
Hurdles	5	2	0	1	12451
Chases	7	2	1	1	22441
Career Total	19	4	2	5	37227
113	9/02	List	2m3f	(0-123)HCh	FRM	£8466
105	9/02	Klny	2m1f	Ch	G-F	£5926
97	6/02	Limk	2m4f	(67-102)HHdl	GD	£6138
93	6/02	Cork	2m4f	Hdl	Y-S	£5926
				Total win prize-money £26456		

Going:	Sf: 0-2 GS: 0-1 Gd: 1-4 GF: - Fm: 2-3
Distance:	2m/2m3: 2-3 2m4-2m7: 2-8 3m+: 0-1
Track:	LH: 0-4 RH: 1-1 Tight: 0-0 Gall: 0-1
Aids:	Bl: 0-0 Vi: 0-0 Tstrap: 0-0
Best Rating:	121 11/02 Chel 2m4f110y gd-sft Ch

Irish-trained novice chaser, effective from two miles to two miles four. Acts on a sound surface.

Minella Silver (IRE)
110   114+
10-y-o gr g Roselier (FR)-Mrs Minella (Deep Run)
Mrs H Dalton Miss H J Hinckley

Placings:0/1/1P-344   (4028)
2002/03: 24³S, 24⁴HY, 24⁴S,

	Starts	1st	2nd	3rd	Win & Pl
Chases	3	0	0	1	1639
Career Total	7	2	0	1	6189
97	5/01	Bang	3m110y	H Ch	G-S	£1527
114	3/01	Asct	3m110y	H Ch	SFT	£3022
				Total win prize-money £4551		

Going:	Sf: 0-3 GS: 0-0 Gd: 0-0 GF: - Fm: 0-0
Distance:	2m/2m3: 0-0 2m4-2m7: 0-0 3m+: 0-3
Track:	LH: 0-2 RH: 0-1 Tight: 0-0 Gall: 0-1
Aids:	Bl: 0-0 Vi: 0-0 Tstrap: 0-0
Best Rating:	114 11/02 Hayd 3m soft Ch

A multiple winner in hunter chases and points, he is suited by three miles and soft ground.

Minella Storm (IRE)
94   (86h)95
11-y-o b g Strong Gale-Maul-More (Deep Run)
D J Wintle D Bishop, L Nash, J Reilly

Placings:12462120/F60/20263/243444/0241-4440 (3601)
2002/03: 20⁴G, 23⁴S, 26⁴HY, 24⁰S,

	Starts	1st	2nd	3rd	Win & Pl
Hurdles	1	0	0	0	0
Chases	3	0	0	0	788
Career Total	30	3	7	2	23734
95	8/01	Uttx	3m	E Ch	G-F	£3584
121	2/98	Navn	2m2f	Hdl	SFT	£2680
115	5/97	Klny	2m1f	NHF	Y-S	£3391
				Total win prize-money £9655		

Going:	Sf: 0-3 GS: 0-0 Gd: 0-1 GF: - Fm: 0-0
Distance:	2m/2m3: 0-0 2m4-2m7: 0-1 3m+: 0-3
Track:	LH: 0-1 RH: 0-3 Tight: 0-2 Gall: 0-0
Aids:	Bl: 0-0 Vi: 0-0 Tstrap: 0-0
Best Rating:	124 1/00 Leic 2m4f110y soft Hdl

Moderate ex-Irish hurdler/chaser, on the downgrade; has worn blinkers; acts on fast ground and with cut.

Miner's Gamble
(89h)   (79h)
6-y-o b g Miners Lamp-Just Rosie (Sula Bula)

A P Jones Aldbourne Racing Group

Placings:*0/3*PPP-4F   (1581)
2002/03: 20⁴G, 17⁶G,

	Starts	1st	2nd	3rd	Win & Pl
Hurdles	1	0	0	0	0
Chases	1	0	0	0	0
Career Total	7	0	0	1	321

Going:	Sf: 0-0 GS: 0-0 Gd: 0-2 GF: - Fm: 0-0
Distance:	2m/2m3: 0-1 2m4-2m7: 0-1 3m+: 0-0
Track:	LH: 0-2 RH: 0-0 Tight: 0-1 Gall: 0-0
Aids:	Bl: 0-0 Vi: 0-0 Tstrap: 0-0
Best Rating:	79 10/01 Sthl 2m good Hdl

Miners Dance (IRE)

10-y-o b g Miners Lamp-Prudent Birdie (Lucifer (USA))
J W Dufosee John Studd

Placings:*2B/U4UF*5045P/21114P5/4   (0031)
2002/03: 33⁴GF,

	Starts	1st	2nd	3rd	Win & Pl
Chases	1	0	0	0	431
Career Total	19	3	2		13147
120 1/01	Folk	3m1f	E Ch		SFT £3536
116 12/00	Folk	3m2f	F(0-110)HCh		SFT £3744
117 11/00	Plum	3m1f110yE(0-105)HHdl		HVY £2296
				Total win prize-money £9576

Going:	Sf: 0-0 GS: 0-0 Gd: 0-0 GF: - Fm: 0-1
Distance:	2m/2m3: 0-0 2m4-2m7: 0-0 3m+: 0-1
Track:	LH: 0-1 RH: 0-0 Tight: 0-0 Gall: 0-1
Aids:	Bl: 0-0 Vi: 0-0 Tstrap: 0-0
Best Rating:	120 1/01 Folk 3m1f soft Ch

Mini Dare

102   **91**
6-y-o b g Derrylin-Minim (Rymer)
O Sherwood Furrows Ltd

Placings:*63-*46625   (4218)
2002/03: 18³G, 16⁴GS, 19⁶G, 19⁶S, 24²G, 26⁵GF,

	Starts	1st	2nd	3rd	Win & Pl
NH Flat	1	0	0	1	244
Hurdles	5	0	1	0	2102
Career Total	7	0	1	1	2346

Going:	Sf: 0-1 GS: 0-1 Gd: 0-3 GF: - Fm: 0-1
Distance:	2m/2m3: 0-2 2m4-2m7: 0-0 3m+: 0-2
Track:	LH: 0-1 RH: 0-5 Tight: 0-0 Gall: 0-0
Aids:	Bl: 0-0 Vi: 0-0 Tstrap: 0-0
Best Rating:	93 2/03 Ludl 3m good Hdl

Moderate novice hurdler; improved run when stepped up to three miles in a handicap in February 2003; acts on good ground.

Mini Mandy

94   **89**
7-y-o b m Petoski-Cindie Girl (Orchestra)
R H Buckler R H Buckler

Placings:*4/*13-04440   (4326)
2002/03: 16⁰HY, 22⁴GS, 16⁴HY, 22⁴GS, 21⁰G,

	Starts	1st	2nd	3rd	Win & Pl
NH Flat	1	0	0	0	0
Hurdles	4	0	0	0	972
Career Total	8	1	0	1	5527

---

105 11/01 Extr   2m1f   H NHF   G-F £1767
           Total win prize-money £1768

Going:	Sf: 0-2 GS: 0-2 Gd: 0-1 GF: - Fm: 0-0
Distance:	2m/2m3: 0-2 2m4-2m7: 0-3 3m+: 0-0
Track:	LH: 0-3 RH: 0-0 Tight: 0-1 Gall: 0-1
Aids:	Bl: 0-1 Vi: 0-0 Tstrap: 0-0
Best Rating:	116 4/02 Chel 2m1f good NHF

Moderate novice hurdler; landed a bumper on fast ground; has yet to show that level of form over the sticks.

Mini Sensation (IRE)

125   **155**
10-y-o b g Be My Native (USA)-Minorettes Girl (Strong Gale)
Jonjo O Neill J P McManus

Placings:*361P/0*210/11/*11203*P2-411PP   (4172)
2002/03: 20⁴GS, 29¹HY, 28¹HY, 28²G, 34⁴S,

	Starts	1st	2nd	3rd	Win & Pl
Chases	5	2	0		91939
Career Total	22	8	3	2	151671
155 2/03	Uttx	3m4f	A HCh		HVY £47600
148 12/02	Chep	3m5f110yA HCh		HVY £43500
148 11/01	Bang	3m110y D Ch		G-S £5537
113 11/01	Weth	3m1f	D Ch		GD £4134
140 11/00	Hayd	2m4f	B(0-140)HHdl	SFT £10257
140 10/00	Weth	2m4f110yC(0-130)HHdl		SFT £7085
116 2/00	Gowr	2m4f	(0-130)HHdl	Y-S £5520
105 2/99	Gowr	2m	Hdl		SH £3683
			Total win prize-money £127316

Going:	Sf: 2-3 GS: 0-1 Gd: 0-1 GF: - Fm: 0-0
Distance:	2m/2m3: 0-0 2m4-2m7: 0-1 **3m+: 2-4**
Track:	**LH: 2-5** RH: 0-0 Tight: 0-0 Gall: 0-0
Aids:	Bl: 0-0 Vi: 0-0 Tstrap: 0-0
Best Rating:	**155 2/03 Uttx 3m4f heavy Ch**

Smart staying handicap chaser; landed a gamble in the Welsh National in December; followed up in the National Trial at Uttoxeter in February; stays extreme distances; suited by soft and heavy ground.

Miniature Rose

89f   **97f**
5-y-o ch m Anshan-Rose Ravine (Deep Run)
H Morrison Mrs Nicholas Jones

Placings:*510*   (4611)
2002/03: 12⁵G, 16¹G, 17⁰G,

	Starts	1st	2nd	3rd	Win & Pl
NH Flat	3	1	0	0	3126
Career Total	3	1	0	0	3126
92 2/03	Ludl	2m	H NHF		GD £3125
				Total win prize-money £3126

Going:	Sf: 0-0 GS: 0-0 Gd: 1-3 GF: - Fm: 0-0
Distance:	**2m/2m3: 1-2** 2m4-2m7: 0-0 3m+: 0-0
Track:	LH: 0-2 **RH: 1-1** Tight: 0-0 Gall: 0-0
Aids:	Bl: 0-0 Vi: 0-0 Tstrap: 0-0
Best Rating:	97 12/02 Newb 1m4f110y good NHF

Out of a top-class staying hurdler; won a bumper on her second start; looks a useful prospect.

Miniballist (IRE)

5-y-o b m Tragic Role (USA)-Herballistic (Rolfe (USA))
Jonjo O Neill Mrs B J Lockhart

Placings:PU   (0719)
2002/03: 22⁶GF, 20⁰⁰G,

	Starts	1st	2nd	3rd	Win & Pl
Hurdles	2	0	0	0	
Career Total	2	0	0	0	

Going:	Sf: 0-0 GS: 0-0 Gd: 0-1 GF: - Fm: 0-1
Distance:	2m/2m3: 0-0 2m4-2m7: 0-2 3m+: 0-0
Track:	LH: 0-2 RH: 0-0 Tight: 0-1 Gall: 0-0
Aids:	Bl: 0-0 Vi: 0-0 Tstrap: 0-0
Best Rating:	0 7/02 Worc 2m4f good Hdl

Minivet

107   (111c) **114**
8-y-o b g Midyan (USA)-Bronzewing (Beldale Flutter (USA))
T D Easterby Oakhill Wood Stud

Placings:21211101/PC0/P56F3-0113316   (4774)
2002/03: 19⁰GS, 16¹G, 16¹G, 20³S, 20³G, 22¹G, 27⁶G,

	Starts	1st	2nd	3rd	Win & Pl
Hurdles	7	3	0	2	11766
Career Total	23	8	2	3	32919
114 4/03	Kels	2m6f110yE(0-110)HHdl	GD £4225
109 2/03	Weth	2m	E(0-110)HHdl	GD £3752
104 2/03	Catt	2m	G Hdl	GD £2492
132 4/00	Ayr	2m	C Hdl	GD £5135
134 1/00	Donc	2m110y C(0-135)HHdl	GD £5850
118 1/00	Kels	2m110y D Hdl	GD £3201
118 1/00	Muss	2m	E Hdl	GD £2415
123 12/99	Donc	2m110y E Hdl	G-S £1976
			Total win prize-money £29047

Going:	Sf: 0-1 GS: 0-1 Gd: 3-5 GF: - Fm: 0-0
Distance:	**2m/2m3: 2-2** 2m4-2m7: 1-4 3m+: 0-1
Track:	**LH: 3-5** RH: 0-1 **Tight: 2-2** Gall: 0-0
Aids:	Bl: 0-0 Vi: 0-0 Tstrap: 0-0
Best Rating:	134 1/00 Donc 2m110y good Hdl

Fair handicap hurdler; winner of eight hurdle races; in good heart in 2003 winning three times, including when upped in trip to two miles six at Kelso; game and consistent; best on good ground, but acts on most going.

Minsgill Glen

91   **76**
7-y-o b m Minster Son-Gilmanscleuch (IRE) (Mandalus)
Mrs J K M Oliver Miss J S Peat

Placings:*000-*PP   (4590)
2002/03: 20⁶S, 20⁶G,

	Starts	1st	2nd	3rd	Win & Pl
Hurdles	1	0	0	0	0
Chases	1	0	0	0	0
Career Total	5	0	0	0	0

Going:	Sf: 0-1 GS: 0-0 Gd: 0-1 GF: - Fm: 0-0
Distance:	2m/2m3: 0-0 2m4-2m7: 0-2 3m+: 0-0
Track:	LH: 0-2 RH: 0-0 Tight: 0-0 Gall: 0-0
Aids:	Bl: 0-0 Vi: 0-0 Tstrap: 0-0
Best Rating:	79 4/02 Carl 2m1f good NHF

Minsgill Mans

91   **93**
5-y-o b g Minster Son-Gilmanscleuch (IRE) (Mandalus)
P D Williams Mrs D J Hughes

Placings:*00043*P4   (4020)
2002/03: 17⁰G, 17⁰GS, 19⁰G, 21⁴S, 24³HY, 26⁶G, 26⁴S,

	Starts	1st	2nd	3rd	Win & Pl
NH Flat	2	0	0	0	0

Hurdles	5	0 0 1	684
Career Total	7	0 0 1	684

Going: Sf: 0-3 GS: 0-1 Gd: 0-3 GF: - Fm: 0-0
Distance: 2m/2m3: 0-2 2m4-2m7: 0-2 3m+: 0-3
Track: LH: 0-1 RH: 0-5 Tight: 0-0 Gall: 0-0
Aids: Bl: 0-0 Vi: 0-0 Tstrap: 0-1
Best Rating: 93 1/03 Chep 3m heavy Hdl

Minster Bay
97f   98f
5-y-o b g Minster Son-Melaura Belle (Meldrum)
W Storey J S Simpson

Placings:220 (2117)
2002/03: 17²G, 17²G, 17⁹G,

	Starts	1st	2nd	3rd	Win & Pl
NH Flat	3	0	2	0	1214
Career Total	3	0	2	0	1214

Going: Sf: 0-0 GS: 0-0 Gd: 0-3 GF: - Fm: 0-0
Distance: 2m/2m3: 0-3 2m4-2m7: 0-0 3m+: 0-0
Track: LH: 0-2 RH: 0-0 Tight: 0-2 Gall: 0-0
Aids: Bl: 0-0 Vi: 0-0 Tstrap: 0-0
Best Rating: 98 10/02 Sedg 2m1f good NHF

Minster Fair
97   88
5-y-o b m Minster Son-Fair Echo (Quality Fair)
A C Whillans E Waugh

Placings:04-434555 (4304)
2002/03: 17⁴S, 22³S, 16⁴HY, 20⁵HY, 20⁵GS, 22⁵G,

	Starts	1st	2nd	3rd	Win & Pl
NH Flat	1	0	0	0	0
Hurdles	5	0	0	1	884
Career Total	8	0	0	1	884

Going: Sf: 0-4 GS: 0-1 Gd: 0-1 GF: - Fm: 0-0
Distance: 2m/2m3: 0-2 2m4-2m7: 0-4 3m+: 0-0
Track: LH: 0-5 RH: 0-1 Tight: 0-2 Gall: 0-1
Aids: Bl: 0-0 Vi: 0-0 Tstrap: 0-0
Best Rating: 96 10/02 Carl 2m1f soft NHF

Limited ability in bumpers and hurdles.

Minster Glory
101   116
12-y-o b g Minster Son-Rapid Glory (Hittite Glory)
M W Easterby Mrs P A H Hartley

Placings:002F/1/331U554/12223232/311F211/20106/4211
2-P42030 (4505)
2002/03: 16⁹G, 20⁴GS, 16²G, 17⁹S, 16³GF, 17⁰G,

	Starts	1st	2nd	3rd	Win & Pl
Chases	6	0	1	1	3509
Career Total	43	10	11	6	53183

135	11/01	MRas	2m1f110yD(0-120)HCh	G-S	£4498
121	11/01	Kels	2m1f E(0-115)HCh	GD	£3770
125	12/00	Muss	2m E(0-115)HCh	GD	£2866
119	3/00	Newc	2m110y E(0-115)HCh	GD	£3074
115	2/00	Catt	2m E(0-115)HCh	GD	£3503
112	1/00	Newc	2m110y E(0-115)HCh	SFT	£2983
111	12/99	Catt	2m F(0-105)HCh	G-F	£2862
99	11/98	Newc	2m110y E(0-115)HCh	GD	£2762
95	12/97	Catt	2m E Ch	GD	£3113
87	5/95	Weth	2m E Hdl	G-F	£2635
			Total win prize-money		£32071

Going: Sf: 0-1 GS: 0-1 Gd: 0-3 GF: - Fm: 0-1
Distance: 2m/2m3: 0-5 2m4-2m7: 0-1 3m+: 0-0
Track: LH: 0-5 RH: 0-1 Tight: 0-3 Gall: 0-1
Aids: Bl: 0-0 Vi: 0-0 Tstrap: 0-0
Best Rating: 139 12/01 Weth 2m gd-sft Ch

Fair handicap chaser, he won consecutive races at Kelso and Market Rasen in November 2001 before running a good second in the Grade Two Castleford Chase at Wetherby; has struggled since but as a result has come down the ratings; best around two miles on good ground.

Minster Sunshine
99
9-y-o ch g Minster Son-Own Free Will (Nicholas Bill)
K C Bailey J H King & Mrs S C Renshaw

Placings:35/0/63542-PP3 (2899)
2002/03: 24⁸S, 20⁸GS, 20³S,

	Starts	1st	2nd	3rd	Win & Pl
Chases	3	0	0	1	758
Career Total	11	0	1	3	3013

Going: Sf: 0-2 GS: 0-1 Gd: 0-0 GF: - Fm: 0-0
Distance: 2m/2m3: 0-0 2m4-2m7: 0-2 3m+: 0-1
Track: LH: 0-1 RH: 0-2 Tight: 0-0 Gall: 0-1
Aids: Bl: 0-0 Vi: 0-0 Tstrap: 0-0
Best Rating: 106 12/01 Folk 2m5f good Ch

Modest placed form in novice chases. Possibly best at short of three miles.

Minster York
107(93h)   (82h)124
9-y-o ch g Minster Son-Another Treat (Derring Do)
M D Hammond (A Crook 15/6) The Adbrokes Partnership

Placings:0035000P/45PP/32614343043-21211123456 (4763)
2002/03: 20²G, 16¹G, 20²GF, 17¹GF, 16¹GF, 20¹GF, 21²GF, 16³G, 16⁴GF, 16⁵GF, 16⁶G,

	Starts	1st	2nd	3rd	Win & Pl
Chases	11	3	1	2	25322
Career Total	34	5	4	6	32855

124	8/02	Bang	2m4f110yD(0-125)HCh	G-F	£6890
115	7/02	Sedg	2m110y D(0-115)HCh	G-F	£4732
114	7/02	MRas	2m1f110yE(0-110)HCh	G-F	£4257
103	5/02	Hexm	2m110y F(0-95)HCh	GD	£2754
90	9/01	Sedg	2m110y E Ch	GD	£3435
			Total win prize-money		£22070

Going: Sf: 0-0 GS: 0-0 Gd: 1-4 GF: - Fm: 3-7
Distance: 2m/2m3: 3-7 2m4-2m7: 1-4 3m+: 0-0
Track: LH: 3-7 RH: 1-4 Tight: 3-3 Gall: 0-1
Aids: Bl: 0-0 Vi: 0-0 Tstrap: 0-0
Best Rating: 124 8/02 Uttx 2m5f gd-fm Ch

Fair chaser who did well summer jumping in 2002, winning four times; stays two and a half miles; suited by ground good or faster.

Minstrel Fair (IRE)

6-y-o b g Roselier (FR)-Minstrel Park (Black Minstrel)
Mrs S J Smith Trevor Hemmings

Placings:065-P (2137)
2002/03: 20⁰GS,

	Starts	1st	2nd	3rd	Win & Pl
Hurdles	1	0	0	0	
Career Total	4	0	0	0	

Going: Sf: 0-0 GS: 0-1 Gd: 0-0 GF: - Fm: 0-0
Distance: 2m/2m3: 0-0 2m4-2m7: 0-0 3m+: 0-0
Track: LH: 0-1 RH: 0-0 Tight: 0-0 Gall: 0-1
Aids: Bl: 0-0 Vi: 0-0 Tstrap: 0-0
Best Rating: 87 4/02 Carl 2m1f good NHF

Minstrel Hall
102   84
4-y-o b f Saddlers Hall (IRE)-Mindomica (Dominion)
P Monteith (C W Thornton 12/6) Bill And Rachel Stewart

Placings:044304 (4433)
2002/03: 16⁰S, 16⁴HY, 17⁴GS, 16³S, 17⁰G, 16⁴G,

	Starts	1st	2nd	3rd	Win & Pl
Hurdles	6	0	0	1	806
Career Total	6	0	0	1	806

Going: Sf: 0-3 GS: 0-1 Gd: 0-2 GF: - Fm: 0-0
Distance: 2m/2m3: 0-6 2m4-2m7: 0-0 3m+: 0-0
Track: LH: 0-5 RH: 0-1 Tight: 0-1 Gall: 0-1
Aids: Bl: 0-0 Vi: 0-0 Tstrap: 0-4
Best Rating: 84 4/03 Newc 2m good Hdl

Plating-class hurdler.

Miracle Island
90   122
8-y-o b g Jupiter Island-Running Game (Run The Gantlet (USA))
K R Burke Champagne Racing

Placings:F3116F312414P0/00PP/411352-0 (0331)
2002/03: 16²G, 20⁴G,

	Starts	1st	2nd	3rd	Win & Pl
Hurdles	2	0	0	1	548
Career Total	25	6	2	3	22635

122	5/01	Newc	2m D(0-120)HHdl	G-F	£3978
116	5/01	Font	2m2f110yF Hdl	G-F	£2572
124	2/00	Font	2m1f110yE(0-115)HHdl	SFT	£5395
124	12/99	Folk	2m1f110yF(0-110)HHdl	SFT	£1759
109	9/99	NAbb	2m1f E Hdl	G-F	£2305
106	8/99	Worc	2m F Hdl	SFT	£2087
			Total win prize-money		£18098

Going: Sf: 0-0 GS: 0-0 Gd: 0-2 GF: - Fm: 0-0
Distance: 2m/2m3: 0-1 2m4-2m7: 0-1 3m+: 0-0
Track: LH: 0-2 RH: 0-0 Tight: 0-1 Gall: 0-0
Aids: Bl: 0-0 Vi: 0-0 Tstrap: 0-0
Best Rating: 124 2/00 Font 2m2f110y soft Hdl

Miracle Kid (USA)
98   111
9-y-o ch g Red Ransom (USA)-Fan Mail (USA) (Zen (USA))
N J Henderson Elite Racing Club

Placings:333/234/04P21310-00 (1754)
2002/03: 16⁹G, 16⁹G,

	Starts	1st	2nd	3rd	Win & Pl
Hurdles	2	0	0	0	
Career Total	16	2	2	5	11041

111	11/01	Wwck	2m D(0-125)HHdl	GD	£3339
102	10/01	Extr	2m1f E Hdl	G-F	£2765
			Total win prize-money		£6104

Going: Sf: 0-0 GS: 0-0 Gd: 0-1 GF: - Fm: 0-0
Distance: 2m/2m3: 0-2 2m4-2m7: 0-0 3m+: 0-0
Track: LH: 0-2 RH: 0-0 Tight: 0-0 Gall: 0-0
Aids: Bl: 0-0 Vi: 0-0 Tstrap: 0-0
Best Rating: 111 11/01 Wwck 2m good Hdl

Modest hurdler; has had his problems, but returned to form in the autumn of 2001 on fast ground with wins at Exeter and Warwick. Suited by positive tactics.

Mirant

109				118

4-y-o b c Danzig Connection (USA)-Ingerence (FR) (Akarad (FR))
M C Pipe (E A L Dunlop 4/7) Lucayan Stud

Placings:F23   (3887)
2002/03: 16²GS, 16²GS, 16³G,

	Starts	1st	2nd	3rd	Win & Pl
Hurdles	3	0	1	1	3786
Career Total	3	0	1	1	3786

Going: Sf: 0-0 GS: 0-2 Gd: 0-1 GF: - Fm: 0-0
Distance: 2m/2m3: 0-3 2m4-2m7: 0-0 3m+: 0-0
Track: LH: 0-2 RH: 0-1 Tight: 0-0 Gall: 0-1
Aids: Bl: 0-0 Vi: 0-0 Tstrap: 0-0
Best Rating: 112 3/03 Hayd 2m   good   Hdl

Fair hurdler; took advantage of a drop in class when twice making all at odds of 4/11 in extended 2m hurdles at Bangor and Fontwell May 2003.

Mirjan (IRE)

108				128

7-y-o b g Tenby-Mirana (IRE) (Ela-Mana-Mou)
L Lungo Mrs Barbara Lungo

Placings:63101/1406500/03100102-54P6012   (4713)
2002/03: 21⁵GS, 16⁴GS, 16²GS, 16⁶GS, 25⁰G, 22¹G, 20²GF,

	Starts	1st	2nd	3rd	Win & Pl
Hurdles	7	1	1	0	13607
Career Total	27	6	2	2	59512
127 4/03 Ayr	2m6f	B(0-150)HHdl	GD	£10197
135 11/01 Newc	2m4f	D(0-125)HHdl	G-S	£5018
131 5/01 Weth	2m4f110yD(0-120)HHdl	FRM	£3620
133 5/00 Hayd	2m	A HHdl	GD	£24000
128 4/00 Chel	2m1f	B Hdl	SFT	£6760
109 3/00 Kels	2m110y E Hdl	G-S	£2478

Total win prize-money £52074

Going: Sf: 0-0 GS: 0-4 Gd: 1-2 GF: - Fm: 0-1
Distance: 2m/2m3: 0-3 2m4-2m7: 1-3 3m+: 0-1
Track: LH: 1-6 RH: 0-1 Tight: 0-1 Gall: 0-2
Aids: Bl: 1-2 Vi: 0-0 Tstrap: 0-0
Best Rating: 135 11/01 Newc 2m4f   gd-sft Hdl

Useful handicap hurdler; suited by hold-up tactics; best around two miles four nowadays; has won on fast and soft ground; his last two wins have been in blinkers; has been tried in a visor.

Misbehaviour

102				78

4-y-o b g Tragic Role (USA)-Exotic Forest (Dominion)
P Butler (J G Portman 10/3) Homewoodgate Racing Club

Placings:0U1052535   (4629)
2002/03: 16⁰G, 17⁰US, 17¹GS, 16⁰S, 17⁵G, 16²HY, 16⁵G, 16³GF, 21⁵GF,

	Starts	1st	2nd	3rd	Win & Pl
Hurdles	9	1	1	1	3062
Career Total	9	1	1	1	3062
85 11/02 Tntn	2m1f	G Hdl	G-S	£1939

Total win prize-money £1939

Going: Sf: 0-3 GS: 1-1 Gd: 0-3 GF: - Fm: 0-2
Distance: 2m/2m3: 1-8 2m4-2m7: 0-1 3m+: 0-0

Track: LH: 0-4 RH: 1-5 Tight: 1-4 Gall: 0-0
Aids: Bl: 0-0 Vi: 0-0 Tstrap: 0-0
Best Rating: 87 2/03 Hrfd 2m1f   good   Hdl

Plating-class hurdler; suited by easy ground.

Misconduct

98				88

9-y-o gr m Risk Me (FR)-Grey Cree (Creetown)
J G Portman The Playmates

Placings:0061110/2164/00512354P164/43155-500U (4441)
2002/03: 16⁵HY, 16⁰S, 19⁴G, 20¹UG,

	Starts	1st	2nd	3rd	Win & Pl
Hurdles	4	0	0	0	525
Career Total	32	7	2	2	36234
117 11/01 Sand	2m110y C(0-130)HHdl	G-S	£8463
117 2/01 Asct	2m110y D(0-120)HHdl	HVY	£4212
112 11/00 Kemp	2m F(0-110)HHdl	SFT	£2863
116 2/00 Asct	2m110y D(0-120)HHdl	SFT	£3386
110 3/99 Fknm	2m D(0-120)HHdl	GD	£5279
106 3/99 Catt	2m F(0-95)HHdl	SFT	£2374
103 2/99 Folk	2m1f110yF(0-95)HHdl	G-S	£2107

Total win prize-money £28686

Going: Sf: 0-2 GS: 0-0 Gd: 0-2 GF: - Fm: 0-0
Distance: 2m/2m3: 0-2 2m4-2m7: 0-2 3m+: 0-0
Track: LH: 0-0 RH: 0-4 Tight: 0-0 Gall: 0-0
Aids: Bl: 0-0 Vi: 0-0 Tstrap: 0-0
Best Rating: 118 12/01 Chel 2m1f   good   Hdl

Fair hurdler, suited by two miles and cut in the ground.

Mise Rafturai (IRE)

107				121

5-y-o b/br g Erin s Isle-Nordic Union (IRE) (Nordico (USA))
Paul Nolan Donal Patrick O Gorman

Placings:0000-11110P0   (4742a)
2002/03: 17¹YS, 16¹G, 17¹G, 16¹S, 16⁰HY, 17⁵G, 16⁰G,

	Starts	1st	2nd	3rd	Win & Pl
Hurdles	7	4	0	0	41043
Career Total	11	4	0	0	41043
121 10/02 Gowr	2m	(0-135)HHdl	SFT	£11963
109 7/02 Klny	2m1f	(0-137)HHdl	GD	£14754
104 6/02 Gowr	2m	(0-140)HHdl	GD	£7975
89 6/02 Cork	2m1f	(67-109)HHdl	Y-S	£6349

Total win prize-money £41043

Going: Sf: 1-2 GS: 0-0 Gd: 2-4 GF: - Fm: 0-0
Distance: 2m/2m3: 4-7 2m4-2m7: 0-0 3m+: 0-0
Track: LH: 0-1 RH: 0-1 Tight: 0-0 Gall: 0-1
Aids: Bl: 0-0 Vi: 0-0 Tstrap: 0-0
Best Rating: 121 10/02 Gowr 2m   soft   Hdl

Decent Irish handicap hurdler; won four times at around two miles in the autumn of 2002; acts on good ground or softer.

Mishead

100				68

5-y-o ch g Unfuwain (USA)-Green Jannat (USA) (Alydar (USA))
M C Chapman N Malbon

Placings:30446-3P4   (0623)
2002/03: 17³GF, 17⁰GF, 17⁴GF,

	Starts	1st	2nd	3rd	Win & Pl
Hurdles	3	0	0	1	389
Career Total	8	0	0	2	1051

Going: Sf: 0-0 GS: 0-0 Gd: 0-0 GF: - Fm: 0-3

Distance: 2m/2m3: 0-3 2m4-2m7: 0-0 3m+: 0-0
Track: LH: 0-0 RH: 0-3 Tight: 0-3 Gall: 0-0
Aids: Bl: 0-0 Vi: 0-0 Tstrap: 0-0
Best Rating: 83 6/02 MRas 2m1f110y gd-fm Hdl

Plating-class hurdler.

Miss Aragont

4-y-o b f Aragon-Uninvited (Be My Guest (USA))
S G Chadwick S Chadwick

Placings:0   (4357)
2002/03: 16⁰GF,

	Starts	1st	2nd	3rd	Win & Pl
NH Flat	1	0	0	0	
Career Total	1	0	0	0	

Going: Sf: 0-0 GS: 0-0 Gd: 0-0 GF: - Fm: 0-1
Distance: 2m/2m3: 0-1 2m4-2m7: 0-0 3m+: 0-0
Track: LH: 0-1 RH: 0-0 Tight: 0-0 Gall: 0-0
Aids: Bl: 0-0 Vi: 0-0 Tstrap: 0-0
Best Rating: 23 3/03 Weth 2m   gd-fm NHF

Miss Blue Ice

5-y-o b m Michelozzo (USA)-Miss Vaigly Blue (Vaigly Great)
P Wegmann Mrs P J Campbell

Placings:P-0   (0091)
2002/03: 16⁰G,

	Starts	1st	2nd	3rd	Win & Pl
NH Flat	1	0	0	0	
Career Total	2	0	0	0	

Going: Sf: 0-0 GS: 0-0 Gd: 0-1 GF: - Fm: 0-0
Distance: 2m/2m3: 0-1 2m4-2m7: 0-0 3m+: 0-0
Track: LH: 0-1 RH: 0-0 Tight: 0-0 Gall: 0-0
Aids: Bl: 0-0 Vi: 0-0 Tstrap: 0-0
Best Rating:

Miss Cash

86				24

6-y-o b m Rock Hopper-Miss Cashtal (IRE) (Ballacashtal (CAN))
M E Sowersby R D Seldon

Placings:4PP/PP-0   (0764)
2002/03: 27⁰GF,

	Starts	1st	2nd	3rd	Win & Pl
Hurdles	1	0	0	0	
Career Total	6	0	0	0	244

Going: Sf: 0-0 GS: 0-0 Gd: 0-0 GF: - Fm: 0-1
Distance: 2m/2m3: 0-0 2m4-2m7: 0-0 3m+: 0-1
Track: LH: 0-1 RH: 0-0 Tight: 0-1 Gall: 0-0
Aids: Bl: 0-0 Vi: 0-0 Tstrap: 0-0
Best Rating: 70 9/00 Bang 2m1f   gd-fm Hdl

Miss Cool

88(110h)			(133 h)102+

7-y-o b m Jupiter Island-Laurel Diver (Celtic Cone)
M C Pipe N G Mills

Placings:103/13-334013   (4610)

2002/03: 16³GF, 16³G, 16⁴S, 17⁰G, 22¹GF, 21³G,

	Starts	1st	2nd	3rd	Win & Pl
Hurdles	6	1	0	3	20423
Career Total	11	3	0	5	27342
133	3/03	Hayd	2m6f	C(0-135)HHdl	G-F £10335
126	2/02	Ludl	2m	E Hdl	G-S £2688
107	9/00	Chep	2m110y	H NHF	GD £1617

Total win prize-money £14640

Going: Sf: 0-1 GS: 0-0 Gd: 0-3 GF: - Fm: 1-2
Distance: 2m/2m3: 0-4 **2m4-2m7:** 1-2 3m+: 0-0
Track: LH: 1-4 RH: 0-2 Tight: 0-0 Gall: 0-3
Aids: Bl: 0-0 Vi: 1-5 Tstrap: 0-0
Best Rating: 133 3/03 Hayd 2m6f   gd-fm   Hdl

Useful handicap hurdler; a sister to Mr Cool; lightly-raced; acts well on a sound surface, but yet to prove herself on really soft ground; effective at around 2m, but looked improved for a step up to 2m 6f when scoring at Haydock March 2003; fell on chasing debut; eventually well held by Quiet Water next time; has worn a visor of late.

Miss Cospector
88f   61f
4-y-o b f Emperor Fountain-Gypsy Race (IRE) (Good Thyne (USA))
T H Caldwell R Cabrera-Vargas

Placings:0   (4665)
2002/03: 17⁰GF,

	Starts	1st	2nd	3rd	Win & Pl
NH Flat	1	0	0	0	
Career Total	1	0	0	0	

Going: Sf: 0-0 GS: 0-0 Gd: 0-0 GF: - Fm: 0-1
Distance: 2m/2m3: 0-1 2m4-2m7: 0-0 3m+: 0-0
Track: LH: 0-0 RH: 0-1 Tight: 0-0 Gall: 0-0
Aids: Bl: 0-0 Vi: 0-0 Tstrap: 0-0
Best Rating: 61 4/03 Carl 2m1f   gd-fm   NHF

Miss Ellie
76(105h)   41
7-y-o b m Elmaamul (USA)-Jussoli (Don)
Mrs C J Kerr Mrs C J Kerr

Placings:560/3P511PU/45P603-PPP   (4137)
2002/03: 16⁶G, 22⁴S, 16⁶S,

	Starts	1st	2nd	3rd	Win & Pl
Hurdles	3	0	0	0	
Career Total	19	2	0	2	8149
105	1/01	Muss	2m4f	F(0-100)HHdl	G-S £3164
95	1/01	Muss	2m4f	F(0-100)HHdl	GD £3780

Total win prize-money £6944

Going: Sf: 0-2 GS: 0-0 Gd: 0-1 GF: - Fm: 0-0
Distance: 2m/2m3: 0-2 2m4-2m7: 0-1 3m+: 0-0
Track: LH: 0-2 RH: 0-0 Tight: 0-1 Gall: 0-0
Aids: Bl: 0-0 Vi: 0-0 Tstrap: 0-0
Best Rating: 105 1/01 Muss 2m4f   gd-sft   Hdl

Moderate handicapper over hurdles, best at around two and a half miles with cut in the ground.

Miss Fara (FR)
96   90
8-y-o ch m Galetto (FR)-Faracha (FR) (Kenmare (FR))
M C Pipe Mrs Christine Painting

Placings:200U/11211300F/4P/413P5060-P00   (4456)
2002/03: 21ᴾGS, 25⁰G, 24⁰G,

	Starts	1st	2nd	3rd	Win & Pl
Hurdles	3	0	0	0	

Career Total   26   5   2   2   31542

142	10/01	Strf	2m3f	C(0-135)HHdl	G-S	£5512
135	12/99	Chel	2m1f	C(0-135)HHdl	GD	£6905
133	11/99	Tntn	2m1f	C HHdl	GD	£4765
113	10/99	Towc	2m	D Hdl	GD	£3129
100	9/99	Tntn	2m3f110yD Hdl		G-F	£2640

Total win prize-money £22951

Going: Sf: 0-0 GS: 0-1 Gd: 0-2 GF: - Fm: 0-0
Distance: 2m/2m3: 0-0 2m4-2m7: 0-1 3m+: 0-2
Track: LH: 0-2 RH: 0-1 Tight: 0-2 Gall: 0-1
Aids: Bl: 0-0 Vi: 0-0 Tstrap: 0-0
Best Rating: 142 10/01 Chel 2m5f   good   Hdl

Useful hurdler and Cesarewitch winner on the Flat; stays two and a half miles over hurdles; does not want the ground too soft.

Miss Fencote
94   80
7-y-o b m Phardante (FR)-Jack s The Girl (IRE) (Supreme Leader)
P Beaumont Mrs H M Richardson

Placings:06/0B6535-564   (0418)
2002/03: 20⁵GF, 23⁶G, 22⁴HY,

	Starts	1st	2nd	3rd	Win & Pl
Hurdles	3	0	0	0	270
Career Total	11	0	0	1	768

Going: Sf: 0-1 GS: 0-0 Gd: 0-1 GF: - Fm: 0-1
Distance: 2m/2m3: 0-0 2m4-2m7: 0-3 3m+: 0-0
Track: LH: 0-3 RH: 0-0 Tight: 0-1 Gall: 0-0
Aids: Bl: 0-0 Vi: 0-0 Tstrap: 0-0
Best Rating: 80 3/02 Carl 2m4f   gd-sft   Hdl

Glimmer of ability in novices hurdles. Best effort came over two and a half miles on good to soft ground.

Miss Green
8-y-o b m Greensmith-Miss Comedy (Comedy Star (USA))
Miss L Bower Miss J Wilkinson

Placings:P-PPP   (0633)
2002/03: 17⁶G, 16⁰GF, 17ᴾGF,

	Starts	1st	2nd	3rd	Win & Pl
Hurdles	3	0	0	0	
Career Total	4	0	0	0	

Going: Sf: 0-0 GS: 0-0 Gd: 0-1 GF: - Fm: 0-2
Distance: 2m/2m3: 0-3 2m4-2m7: 0-0 3m+: 0-0
Track: LH: 0-1 RH: 0-2 Tight: 0-2 Gall: 0-0
Aids: Bl: 0-0 Vi: 0-0 Tstrap: 0-1
Best Rating: 0 6/02 NAbb 2m1f   gd-fm   Hdl

Miss Honeypenny (IRE)
98f   90f
5-y-o b m Old Vic-Honey Dream (Orchestra)
B G Powell D & J Newell

Placings:2   (4343)
2002/03: 16²GF,

	Starts	1st	2nd	3rd	Win & Pl
NH Flat	1	0	1	0	560
Career Total	1	0	1	0	560

Going: Sf: 0-0 GS: 0-0 Gd: 0-0 GF: - Fm: 0-1
Distance: 2m/2m3: 0-1 2m4-2m7: 0-0 3m+: 0-0
Track: LH: 0-0 RH: 0-1 Tight: 0-0 Gall: 0-1
Aids: Bl: 0-0 Vi: 0-0 Tstrap: 0-0
Best Rating: 90 3/03 Hntg 2m110y   gd-fm   NHF

Runner-up in weak bumper on debut.

Miss Janica
100   72
5-y-o b m Sir Harry Lewis (USA)-Supreme Wonder (IRE) (Supreme Leader)
Miss Venetia Williams B Moore & E C Stephens

Placings:6-00U23   (1008)
2002/03: 16⁹GS, 17⁰GF, 20ᵁGF, 19²S, 20³GF,

	Starts	1st	2nd	3rd	Win & Pl
NH Flat	2	0	0	0	0
Hurdles	3	0	1	1	1738
Career Total	6	0	1	1	1738

Going: Sf: 0-1 GS: 0-1 Gd: 0-0 GF: - Fm: 0-3
Distance: 2m/2m3: 0-3 2m4-2m7: 0-2 3m+: 0-0
Track: LH: 0-4 RH: 0-1 Tight: 0-0 Gall: 0-0
Aids: Bl: 0-0 Vi: 0-0 Tstrap: 0-0
Best Rating: 88 4/02 Uttx 2m   good   NHF

Unseated her rider at the start after being unruly in the paddock on her hurdling debut. Also looked a tricky customer next time. Is one to be wary of.

Miss Jeff (FR)
90   87+
5-y-o ch m Mansonnien (FR)-Miss Jefferson (FR) (Jefferson (ZIM))
M C Pipe Matt Archer & Miss Jean Broadhurst

Placings:60130-B5   (0782)
2002/03: 19ᴿG, 16⁵GF,

	Starts	1st	2nd	3rd	Win & Pl
Hurdles	2	0	0	0	
Career Total	7	1	0	1	6731
	6/01	Autl	1m7f	Hdl	VS £6305

Total win prize-money £6305

Going: Sf: 0-0 GS: 0-0 Gd: 0-1 GF: - Fm: 0-1
Distance: 2m/2m3: 0-1 2m4-2m7: 0-1 3m+: 0-0
Track: LH: 0-1 RH: 0-1 Tight: 0-0 Gall: 0-0
Aids: Bl: 0-0 Vi: 0-0 Tstrap: 0-0
Best Rating: 87 7/02 Uttx 2m   gd-fm   Hdl

Winner over hurdles in France but has cut little ice here so far.

Miss Kitz
(66h)   (26h)
7-y-o b m Cruise Missile-Frau Kitz (Master Buck)
Dr J R J Naylor The Villagers

Placings:00000-PP   (2608)
2002/03: 21ᴾS, 24ᴾS,

	Starts	1st	2nd	3rd	Win & Pl
Hurdles	1	0	0	0	0
Chases	1	0	0	0	0
Career Total	7	0	0	0	

Going: Sf: 0-2 GS: 0-0 Gd: 0-0 GF: - Fm: 0-0
Distance: 2m/2m3: 0-0 2m4-2m7: 0-1 3m+: 0-1
Track: LH: 0-2 RH: 0-0 Tight: 0-1 Gall: 0-0
Aids: Bl: 0-0 Vi: 0-1 Tstrap: 0-0
Best Rating: 60 6/01 NAbb 2m1f   good   NHF

Miss Koen (IRE)
98   79
4-y-o b f Barathea (IRE)-Fanny Blankers (IRE) (Persian Heights)
D L Williams (Kevin Prendergast 16/10) D L Williams

Placings:0PP00P   (4104)
2002/03: 16⁰GS, 16ᴾHY, 16ᴾHY, 16⁰G, 16⁰G, 27ᴾS,

	Starts	1st	2nd	3rd	Win & Pl
Hurdles	6	0	0	0	
Career Total	6	0	0	0	

Going:	Sf: 0-3 GS: 0-1 Gd: 0-2 GF: - Fm: 0-0
Distance:	2m/2m3: 0-5 2m4-2m7: 0-0 3m+: 0-1
Track:	LH: 0-2 RH: 0-4 Tight: 0-1 Gall: 0-2
Aids:	Bl: 0-0 Vi: 0-0 Tstrap: 0-0
Best Rating:	79 2/03 Kemp 2m good Hdl

Ex-Irish filly; has shown nothing over hurdles.

Miss Lacroix
105   76
8-y-o b m Picea-Smartie Lee (Dominion)
R Hollinshead Mrs Norma Harris

Placings:0656/6001/5010041336/02263U04630-03016630000   (4194)
2002/03: 16⁰G, 19³G, 16⁰GF, 22¹GF, 22⁶GF, 22⁶S, 16³G, 19⁰S, 17⁰G, 24⁰G, 21⁰G,

	Starts	1st	2nd	3rd	Win & Pl
Hurdles	11	1	0	2	4213
Career Total	40	4	2	6	16927
75	8/02	Font	2m6f110yF(0-110)HHdl		G-F	£3094
87	12/00	Ludl	2m	F(0-110)HHdl	SFT	£3178
84	5/00	MRas	2m1f110yF(0-105)HHdl		G-S	£2074
71	8/99	Bang	2m1f	E(0-105)HHdl	GD	£2931

Total win prize-money £11279

Going:	Sf: 0-2 GS: 0-0 Gd: 0-6 GF: - Fm: 1-3
Distance:	2m/2m3: 0-4 2m4-2m7: 1-6 3m+: 0-1
Track:	LH: 1-4 RH: 0-7 Tight: 1-4 Gall: 0-0
Aids:	Bl: 0-0 Vi: 0-0 Tstrap: 0-0
Best Rating:	87 2/01 Ludl 2m gd-sft Hdl

Plating-class hurdler; best when able to dominate; has run well on fast ground, but is better suited by cut; stays two and three-quarter miles.

Miss Lewis
94f   98f
5-y-o b m Sir Harry Lewis (USA)-Teelyna (Teenoso (USA))
C J Down May & Edwards

Placings:42   (4737)
2002/03: 16⁴G, 16²GF,

	Starts	1st	2nd	3rd	Win & Pl
NH Flat	2	0	1	0	576
Career Total	2	0	1	0	576

Going:	Sf: 0-0 GS: 0-0 Gd: 0-1 GF: - Fm: 0-1
Distance:	2m/2m3: 0-2 2m4-2m7: 0-0 3m+: 0-0
Track:	LH: 0-1 RH: 0-1 Tight: 0-0 Gall: 0-0
Aids:	Bl: 0-0 Vi: 0-0 Tstrap: 0-0
Best Rating:	98 4/03 Chep 2m110y gd-fm NHF

Signs of ability in first bumper; runner-up in uncompetitive affair next time.

Miss Mailmit
86f   72f
6-y-o b m Rakaposhi King-Flora Louisa (Rymer)

J A B Old Peter Guntrip

Placings:6   (4060)
2002/03: 16⁶S,

	Starts	1st	2nd	3rd	Win & Pl
NH Flat	1	0	0	0	0
Career Total	1	0	0	0	0

Going:	Sf: 0-1 GS: 0-0 Gd: 0-0 GF: - Fm: 0-0
Distance:	2m/2m3: 0-1 2m4-2m7: 0-0 3m+: 0-0
Track:	LH: 0-1 RH: 0-0 Tight: 0-0 Gall: 0-0
Aids:	Bl: 0-0 Vi: 0-0 Tstrap: 0-0
Best Rating:	80 3/03 Wwck 2m soft NHF

Miss Mattie Ross
91   61
7-y-o b m Milieu-Mother Machree (Bing Ii)
S J Marshall S J Marshall

Placings:PP-500P   (4752)
2002/03: 16⁵GS, 16⁰G, 21⁰G, 24ᴾG,

	Starts	1st	2nd	3rd	Win & Pl
Hurdles	4	0	0	0	
Career Total	6	0	0	0	

Going:	Sf: 0-0 GS: 0-1 Gd: 0-3 GF: - Fm: 0-0
Distance:	2m/2m3: 0-2 2m4-2m7: 0-1 3m+: 0-1
Track:	LH: 0-3 RH: 0-1 Tight: 0-2 Gall: 0-0
Aids:	Bl: 0-0 Vi: 0-0 Tstrap: 0-0
Best Rating:	75 5/02 Kels 2m110y gd-sft Hdl

Miss Melrose
85   51
6-y-o ch m Bob Back (USA)-Whatagale (Strong Gale)
L Lungo Mrs C Coxen

Placings:06-50   (0474)
2002/03: 16⁵GF, 17⁰GS,

	Starts	1st	2nd	3rd	Win & Pl
Hurdles	2	0	0	0	0
Career Total	4	0	0	0	0

Going:	Sf: 0-0 GS: 0-1 Gd: 0-0 GF: - Fm: 0-1
Distance:	2m/2m3: 0-2 2m4-2m7: 0-0 3m+: 0-0
Track:	LH: 0-1 RH: 0-1 Tight: 0-1 Gall: 0-0
Aids:	Bl: 0-0 Vi: 0-0 Tstrap: 0-0
Best Rating:	70 12/01 Muss 2m1f gd-fm NHF

Miss Nel
23
8-y-o b m Denel (FR)-Ice Lass (Heroic Air)
R H Goldie Robert H Goldie

Placings:P0-P   (0084)
2002/03: 24ᴾGS,

	Starts	1st	2nd	3rd	Win & Pl
Hurdles	1	0	0	0	
Career Total	3	0	0	0	

Going:	Sf: 0-0 GS: 0-1 Gd: 0-0 GF: - Fm: 0-0
Distance:	2m/2m3: 0-0 2m4-2m7: 0-0 3m+: 0-0
Track:	LH: 0-1 RH: 0-0 Tight: 0-0 Gall: 0-0
Aids:	Bl: 0-0 Vi: 0-0 Tstrap: 0-0
Best Rating:	23 4/02 Prth 2m110y good Hdl

Miss O'Grady (IRE)
11-y-o ch m Over The River (FR)-Polar Mistress (IRE) (Strong Gale)
Mrs S Alner (Miss L Alner 1/5) Mrs J M Miller

Placings:1/U/P/P2U-4212P   (4640)
2002/03: 26⁴GF, 25²S, 20¹G, 19²G, 21ᴾG,

	Starts	1st	2nd	3rd	Win & Pl
Chases	5	1	2	0	3509
Career Total	11	2	3	0	6471
92	3/03	Font	2m4f	H Ch	GD	£1834
101	4/99	Chel	2m5f	H Ch	G-S	£2078

Total win prize-money £3912

Going:	Sf: 0-1 GS: 0-0 Gd: 1-3 GF: - Fm: 0-1
Distance:	2m/2m3: 0-0 2m4-2m7: 1-3 3m+: 0-2
Track:	LH: 0-2 RH: 0-2 Tight: 1-2 Gall: 0-1
Aids:	Bl: 0-0 Vi: 0-0 Tstrap: 0-0
Best Rating:	101 4/99 Chel 2m5f gd-sft Ch

Useful pointer/hunter chaser; suited by 3m; acts on any ground.

Miss Opulence (IRE)
99   85+
4-y-o f Kylian (USA)-Oriental Splendour (Runnett)
B Ellison (Miss V Haigh 18/5) Gallant Denco Wallace Whittle

Placings:324   (2921)
2002/03: 16³G, 17²S, 16⁴S,

	Starts	1st	2nd	3rd	Win & Pl
Hurdles	3	0	1	1	1787
Career Total	3	0	1	1	1787

Going:	Sf: 0-2 GS: 0-0 Gd: 0-1 GF: - Fm: 0-0
Distance:	2m/2m3: 0-3 2m4-2m7: 0-0 3m+: 0-0
Track:	LH: 0-2 RH: 0-1 Tight: 0-1 Gall: 0-0
Aids:	Bl: 0-0 Vi: 0-0 Tstrap: 0-0
Best Rating:	85 12/02 MRas 2m1f110y soft Hdl

A nine-furlong winner on the Flat, has shown ability over hurdles but her stamina looks strictly limited.

Miss Portcello
10-y-o b m Bybicello-Port Mallaig (Royal Fountain)
Mrs J M Hollands W F Jeffrey

Placings:3U-33531   (4664)
2002/03: 25³GS, 20³GF, 24⁵G, 25³S, 24¹GF,

	Starts	1st	2nd	3rd	Win & Pl
Chases	5	1	0	3	2512
Career Total	7	1	0	4	2739
89	4/03	Carl	3m	H Ch	G-F	£1443

Total win prize-money £1443

Going:	Sf: 0-1 GS: 0-1 Gd: 0-1 GF: - Fm: 1-2
Distance:	2m/2m3: 0-0 2m4-2m7: 0-1 3m+: 1-4
Track:	LH: 0-3 RH: 1-2 Tight: 0-2 Gall: 0-0
Aids:	Bl: 0-0 Vi: 0-0 Tstrap: 0-0
Best Rating:	89 4/03 Carl 3m gd-fm Ch

Modest form in ladies points and hunter chases; scored at Carlisle in April; acts on any ground.

Miss Rennenski
102   84
7-y-o b m Petoski-Miss Wrensborough (Buckskin (FR))
D R Gandolfo D R Gandolfo Ltd

Placings:0/063P-2   (1052)
2002/03: 22[2]G,

	Starts	1st	2nd	3rd	Win & Pl
Hurdles	1	0	1	0	792
Career Total	6	0	1	1	1076

Going: Sf: 0-0 GS: 0-0 Gd: 0-0 GF: - Fm: 0-0
Distance: 2m/2m3: 0-0 2m4-2m7: 0-1 3m+: 0-0
Track: LH: 0-1 RH: 0-0 Tight: 0-1 Gall: 0-0
Aids: Bl: 0-0 Vi: 0-0 Tstrap: 0-0
Best Rating: 92 4/01 Font 2m2f110y good NHF

Modest plating hurdler who stays well.

Miss Sutton
98   60
5-y-o b m Formidable (USA)-Saysana (Sayf El Arab (USA))
G F H Charles-Jones Mrs Jessica Charles-Jones

Placings:0   (0269)
2002/03: 16[0]GF,

	Starts	1st	2nd	3rd	Win & Pl
Hurdles	1	0	0	0	
Career Total	1	0	0	0	

Going: Sf: 0-0 GS: 0-0 Gd: 0-0 GF: - Fm: 0-1
Distance: 2m/2m3: 0-1 2m4-2m7: 0-0 3m+: 0-0
Track: LH: 0-1 RH: 0-0 Tight: 0-1 Gall: 0-0
Aids: Bl: 0-0 Vi: 0-1 Tstrap: 0-0
Best Rating: 0 5/02 Strf 2m110y gd-fm Hdl

Miss Tango
84   81
6-y-o b m Batshoof-Spring Flyer (IRE) (Waajib)
M C Pipe Codan Trust Company Limited

Placings:21252/231P1-00PP   (4512)
2002/03: 17[0]S, 18[0]S, 24[P]GF, 24[P]GF,

	Starts	1st	2nd	3rd	Win & Pl
Hurdles	4	0	0	0	
Career Total	14	3	4	1	12219
119 10/01 Tntn	3m110y	F(0-110)HHdl		FRM	£3455
117 9/01 NAbb	2m6f	G Hdl		G-F	£2198
100 10/00 Ludl	2m	E Hdl		G-F	£2569

Total win prize-money £8223

Going: Sf: 0-2 GS: 0-1 Gd: 0-0 GF: - Fm: 0-0
Distance: 2m/2m3: 0-2 2m4-2m7: 0-0 3m+: 0-2
Track: LH: 0-1 RH: 0-3 Tight: 0-2 Gall: 0-0
Aids: Bl: 0-0 Vi: 0-0 Tstrap: 0-0
Best Rating: 119 10/01 Tntn 3m110y firm Hdl

Moderate staying hurdler; has run her best races with McCoy aboard and has shown a marked preference for top of the ground; stays three miles.

Miss Woodpecker
76f   46f
6-y-o b m Morpeth-Pigeon Loft (IRE) (Bellypha)
J D Frost R G Frost

Placings:6   (1095)
2002/03: 17[5]GF,

	Starts	1st	2nd	3rd	Win & Pl
NH Flat	1	0	0	0	0
Career Total	1	0	0	0	0

Going: Sf: 0-0 GS: 0-0 Gd: 0-0 GF: - Fm: 0-1
Distance: 2m/2m3: 0-1 2m4-2m7: 0-0 3m+: 0-0

Track: LH: 0-1 RH: 0-0 Tight: 0-1 Gall: 0-0
Aids: Bl: 0-0 Vi: 0-0 Tstrap: 0-0
Best Rating: 50 8/02 NAbb 2m1f gd-fm NHF

Miss Woodstick
103(103h)   (97h)89
7-y-o b m Teenoso (USA)-Born Bossy (Ebonneezer)
M J Gingell (J L Spearing 5/11) Going Grey Partnership

Placings:0/300032/25UPP1-0P034F   (4670)
2002/03: 24[0]GF, 24[P]GS, 24[0]G, 24[3]G, 28[4]G, 21[F]G,

	Starts	1st	2nd	3rd	Win & Pl
Hurdles	3	0	0	0	264
Chases	3	0	0	1	848
Career Total	19	1	2	3	6008
97 4/02 Hrfd	3m2f	E Hdl		GD	£2912

Total win prize-money £2912

Going: Sf: 0-0 GS: 0-1 Gd: 0-0 GF: - Fm: 0-1
Distance: 2m/2m3: 0-0 2m4-2m7: 0-0 3m+: 0-1
Track: LH: 0-2 RH: 0-4 Tight: 0-2 Gall: 0-2
Aids: Bl: 0-0 Vi: 0-0 Tstrap: 0-0
Best Rating: 97 4/02 Hrfd 3m2f good Hdl

Moderate hurdler/chaser; acts on a sound surface and has plenty of stamina.

Miss Woody
4-y-o b f Bin Ajwaad (IRE)-Miss Doody (Gorytus (USA))
P Butler Homewoodgate Racing Club

Placings:6   (1327)
2002/03: 16[6]G,

	Starts	1st	2nd	3rd	Win & Pl
Hurdles	1	0	0	0	0
Career Total	1	0	0	0	0

Going: Sf: 0-0 GS: 0-0 Gd: 0-1 GF: - Fm: 0-0
Distance: 2m/2m3: 0-1 2m4-2m7: 0-0 3m+: 0-0
Track: LH: 0-1 RH: 0-0 Tight: 0-1 Gall: 0-0
Aids: Bl: 0-0 Vi: 0-0 Tstrap: 0-0
Best Rating: 0 9/02 Plum 2m good Hdl

Poor maiden on the Flat.

Missdmena
98f   62f
4-y-o br f Carlton (GER)-Menas Gold (Heights Of Gold)
G P Enright Mrs Anne Gurney

Placings:05   (4760)
2002/03: 18[0]HY, 18[5]GF,

	Starts	1st	2nd	3rd	Win & Pl
NH Flat	2	0	0	0	
Career Total	2	0	0	0	

Going: Sf: 0-1 GS: 0-0 Gd: 0-0 GF: - Fm: 0-1
Distance: 2m/2m3: 0-2 2m4-2m7: 0-0 3m+: 0-0
Track: LH: 0-2 RH: 0-0 Tight: 0-1 Gall: 0-0
Aids: Bl: 0-0 Vi: 0-0 Tstrap: 0-0
Best Rating: 62 4/03 Font 2m2f110y gd-fm NHF

Mistanoora
107   123
4-y-o b g Topanoora-Mistinguett (IRE) (Doyoun)
N A Twiston-Davies A M J Duggan

Going: Sf: 0-2 GS: 0-1 Gd: 0-1 GF: - Fm: 0-0
Distance: 2m/2m3: 0-0 2m4-2m7: 0-0 3m+: 0-4
Track: LH: 0-3 RH: 0-1 Tight: 0-0 Gall: 0-1

Placings:463215102   (4605)
2002/03: 16[4]GF, 16[6]GF, 17[3]G, 16[2]S, 16[1]GS, 16[5]G, 16[1]HY, 16[0]G, 17[2]G,

	Starts	1st	2nd	3rd	Win & Pl
Hurdles	9	2	2	1	16129
Career Total	9	2	2	1	16129
123 2/03 Sand	2m110y	C Hdl		HVY	£6467
112 11/02 Weth	2m	D Hdl		G-S	£3835

Total win prize-money £10302

Going: Sf: 1-2 GS: 1-1 Gd: 0-4 GF: - Fm: 0-2
Distance: 2m/2m3: 2-9 2m4-2m7: 0-0 3m+: 0-0
Track: LH: 1-4 RH: 1-5 Tight: 0-1 Gall: 0-1
Aids: Bl: 2-7 Vi: 0-0 Tstrap: 0-0
Best Rating: 123 4/03 Chel 2m1f good Hdl

Useful novice hurdler; effective at around two miles; well suited by a soft surface; often wears blinkers.

Mistaway
72f   25f
5-y-o b m Nomadic Way (USA)-Miss Puck (Tepukei)
I A Brown W Brown

Placings:00   (4357)
2002/03: 17[0]HY, 16[0]GF,

	Starts	1st	2nd	3rd	Win & Pl
NH Flat	2	0	0	0	
Career Total	2	0	0	0	

Going: Sf: 0-1 GS: 0-0 Gd: 0-0 GF: - Fm: 0-1
Distance: 2m/2m3: 0-2 2m4-2m7: 0-0 3m+: 0-0
Track: LH: 0-2 RH: 0-0 Tight: 0-1 Gall: 0-0
Aids: Bl: 0-0 Vi: 0-0 Tstrap: 0-0
Best Rating: 27 3/03 Weth 2m gd-fm NHF

Mistella
7-y-o ch m Milieu-Streakella (Firestreak)
Mrs J C McGregor The Border Terriers

Placings:0PP   (2302)
2002/03: 17[0]GF, 22[P]S, 19[P]GS,

	Starts	1st	2nd	3rd	Win & Pl
NH Flat	1	0	0	0	0
Hurdles	2	0	0	0	0
Career Total	3	0	0	0	

Going: Sf: 0-1 GS: 0-1 Gd: 0-0 GF: - Fm: 0-1
Distance: 2m/2m3: 0-2 2m4-2m7: 0-1 3m+: 0-0
Track: LH: 0-2 RH: 0-1 Tight: 0-1 Gall: 0-0
Aids: Bl: 0-0 Vi: 0-0 Tstrap: 0-0
Best Rating: 36 10/02 Carl 2m1f gd-fm NHF

Mister Bigtime (IRE)
104   113
9-y-o br g Roselier (FR)-Cnoc An Oir (Goldhill)
B G Powell Mrs Jean R Bishop

Placings:452320/33220-4P3P   (3898)
2002/03: 25[4]G, 24[P]S, 25[3]GS, 24[P]S,

	Starts	1st	2nd	3rd	Win & Pl
Chases	4	0	0	1	1238
Career Total	15	0	4	4	11718

Going: Sf: 0-2 GS: 0-1 Gd: 0-1 GF: - Fm: 0-0
Distance: 2m/2m3: 0-0 2m4-2m7: 0-0 3m+: 0-4
Track: LH: 0-3 RH: 0-1 Tight: 0-0 Gall: 0-1

Aids: Bl: 0-0 Vi: 0-0 Tstrap: 0-0
Best Rating: 121 1/02 Newb 3m   good   Ch

Decent hurdler/chaser; he acts on good ground but handles softer; stays three miles.

Mister Brock

8-y-o b g Petoski-Romantic Run (Deep Run)
Miss E J Baker Michael J Arnold

Placings:00/P   (0029)
2002/03: 21PGF,

	Starts	1st	2nd	3rd	Win & Pl
Chases	1	0	0	0	
Career Total	3	0	0	0	

Going: Sf: 0-0 GS: 0-0 Gd: 0-0 GF: - Fm: 0-1
Distance: 2m/2m3: 0-0 2m4-2m7: 0-1 3m+: 0-0
Track: LH: 0-1 RH: 0-0 Tight: 0-0 Gall: 0-1
Aids: Bl: 0-0 Vi: 0-0 Tstrap: 0-0
Best Rating: 24 3/01 Sand 2m110y   heavy NHF

Mister Chisum
109   106

7-y-o b g Sabrehill (USA)-Anchor Inn (Be My Guest (USA))
R Allan (Miss Kariana Key 11/2) Mrs Jean Key

Placings:0063020/0/23022U440P111   (4507)
2002/03: 16²GS, 17³G, 17⁰GF, 17²G, 16²S, 16ᵁGS, 16⁴S, 16⁴HY, 16⁰GS, 17PHY, 16¹S, 16¹G, 16¹G,

	Starts	1st	2nd	3rd	Win & Pl
Hurdles	13	3	3	1	15015
Career Total	21	3	4	2	16077
104 4/03	Kels	2m110y	E(0-105)HHdl	GD	£4459
100 4/03	Newc	2m	F Hdl	GD	£2793
89 3/03	Ayr	2m	D(0-110)HHdl	SFT	£5005

Total win prize-money £12257

Going: Sf: 1-5 GS: 0-3 Gd: 2-4 GF: - Fm: 0-1
Distance: 2m/2m3: 3-13 2m4-2m7: 0-0 3m+: 0-0
Track: LH: 3-13 RH: 0-0 Tight: 1-6 Gall: 1-4
Aids: Bl: 0-0 Vi: 0-0 Tstrap: 0-0
Best Rating: 104 4/03 Kels 2m110y   good Hdl

Modest hurdler, in good heart to land a hat-trick of wins in the spring of 2003; likes to set the pace; suited by good ground but acts on softer; suited by two miles.

Mister Club Royal
99(82h)   (63h)78

7-y-o b g Alflora (IRE)-Miss Club Royal (Avocat)
D McCain John Singleton

Placings:0003F-P024   (4317)
2002/03: 17PG, 16⁰S, 20²S, 17⁴G,

	Starts	1st	2nd	3rd	Win & Pl
Chases	4	0	1	0	1909
Career Total	9	0	1	1	2644

Going: Sf: 0-2 GS: 0-0 Gd: 0-2 GF: - Fm: 0-0
Distance: 2m/2m3: 0-3 2m4-2m7: 0-1 3m+: 0-0
Track: LH: 0-3 RH: 0-1 Tight: 0-3 Gall: 0-0
Aids: Bl: 0-0 Vi: 0-0 Tstrap: 0-0
Best Rating: 78 3/03 Bang 2m4f110y   soft   Ch

Plating-class chaser; stays two and a half miles.

Mister Dave's (IRE)
105(104h)   (103 h)116

8-y-o ch g Bluffer-Tacovaon (Avocat)
Mrs S J Smith David Campbell

Placings:0605P01-00F22   (4374)
2002/03: 24⁰G, 25⁰G, 20FGS, 25²S, 27²G,

	Starts	1st	2nd	3rd	Win & Pl
Hurdles	3	0	1	0	994
Chases	2	0	1	0	1726
Career Total	12	1	2	0	5163
94 4/02	Weth	3m1f	F(0-95)HHdl	G-F	£2443

Total win prize-money £2443

Going: Sf: 0-1 GS: 0-1 Gd: 0-3 GF: - Fm: 0-0
Distance: 2m/2m3: 0-0 2m4-2m7: 0-1 3m+: 0-4
Track: LH: 0-5 RH: 0-0 Tight: 0-3 Gall: 0-0
Aids: Bl: 0-0 Vi: 0-0 Tstrap: 0-0
Best Rating: 116 12/02 Weth 3m1f   soft   Ch

Modest hurdler/chaser; opened his account in a modest novices handicap at Wetherby in April 2002; fell on his chasing debut but ran well next time when runner-up at an above average sort at Wetherby in December.

Mister Ermyn
(84h)   (49h)

10-y-o ch g Minster Son-Rosana Park (Music Boy)
L Montague Hall J Daniels

Placings:310/625/P/O60/1011PUS2UPP/P5P-P46   (2550)
2002/03: 16PGS, 20PGF, 22⁴HY, 17⁶HY,

	Starts	1st	2nd	3rd	Win & Pl
Hurdles	4	0	0	0	320
Career Total	27	4	2	1	12273
100 8/00	Worc	2m4f	F(0-100)HHdl	G-F	£1904
92 7/00	Strf	2m3f	E(0-105)HHdl	G-F	£2744
83 5/00	Folk	2m1f110yG(0-95)HHdl	GD	£1645
97 2/97	Asct	2m110y	H NHF	G-F	£2274

Total win prize-money £8567

Going: Sf: 0-2 GS: 0-1 Gd: 0-0 GF: - Fm: 0-1
Distance: 2m/2m3: 0-2 2m4-2m7: 0-2 3m+: 0-0
Track: LH: 0-1 RH: 0-3 Tight: 0-2 Gall: 0-0
Aids: Bl: 0-4 Vi: 0-0 Tstrap: 0-0
Best Rating: 101 11/00 Chel 2m110y   gd-sft Hdl

Mister Falcon (FR)
92   106

6-y-o b g Passing Sale (FR)-Falcon Crest (FR) (Cadoudal (FR))
M C Pipe Telefocus Ltd

Placings:363/122113655P-5P   (0927)
2002/03: 22⁵G, 22PGF,

	Starts	1st	2nd	3rd	Win & Pl
Hurdles	2	0	0	0	0
Career Total	15	3	2	3	11935
99 7/01	Strf	2m6f110yD Hdl	G-F	£3666
101 6/01	NAbb	2m6f	D Hdl	G-F	£3241
103 5/01	Sthl	2m4f110yE Hdl	FRM	£2233

Total win prize-money £9141

Going: Sf: 0-0 GS: 0-0 Gd: 0-1 GF: - Fm: 0-1
Distance: 2m/2m3: 0-0 2m4-2m7: 0-0 3m+: 0-0
Track: LH: 0-2 RH: 0-0 Tight: 0-2 Gall: 0-0
Aids: Bl: 0-0 Vi: 0-2 Tstrap: 0-0
Best Rating: 106 6/01 NAbb 2m6f   gd-sft Hdl

Mister Felix (IRE)
88   74

7-y-o b g Ore-Pixies Glen (Furry Glen)
Mrs Susan Nock (I A Gault 9/11) Gerard Nock

Placings:10   (3319)
2002/03: 16¹HY, 21⁰GS,

	Starts	1st	2nd	3rd	Win & Pl
NH Flat	1	1	0	0	4445
Hurdles	1	0	0	0	0
Career Total	2	1	0	0	4445
110 11/02	DRoy	2m		NHF	HVY £4444

Total win prize-money £4445

Going: Sf: 1-1 GS: 0-1 Gd: 0-0 GF: - Fm: 0-0
Distance: 2m/2m3: 1-1 2m4-2m7: 0-1 3m+: 0-0
Track: LH: 0-0 RH: 0-1 Tight: 0-0 Gall: 0-0
Aids: Bl: 0-0 Vi: 0-0 Tstrap: 0-0
Best Rating: 110 11/02 DRoy 2m   heavy NHF

Moderate irish bumper winner; acts on heavy ground.

Mister Flint
96f   111+f

5-y-o b g Petoski-National Clover (National Trust)
P J Hobbs Alan Peterson

Placings:22   (4053)
2002/03: 16²GS, 16²HY,

	Starts	1st	2nd	3rd	Win & Pl
NH Flat	2	0	2	0	1386
Career Total	2	0	2	0	1386

Going: Sf: 0-1 GS: 0-1 Gd: 0-0 GF: - Fm: 0-0
Distance: 2m/2m3: 0-2 2m4-2m7: 0-0 3m+: 0-0
Track: LH: 0-0 RH: 0-2 Tight: 0-0 Gall: 0-0
Aids: Bl: 0-0 Vi: 0-0 Tstrap: 0-0
Best Rating: 108 2/03 Winc 2m   gd-sft NHF

A half-brother to Go Ballistic; runner-up in first three starts prior to winning Worcester bumper May 2003; will now go hurdling.

Mister Friday (IRE)
107   110+

6-y-o b/br g Mister Lord (USA)-Rebecca s Storm (IRE) (Strong Gale)
P D Niven R A Bartlett

Placings:F213F2   (4774)
2002/03: 20FHY, 24²S, 20¹GS, 24³S, 20FG, 27²G,

	Starts	1st	2nd	3rd	Win & Pl
Hurdles	6	1	2	1	7664
Career Total	6	1	2	1	7664
103 2/03	Ayr	2m4f	E Hdl	G-S	£3591

Total win prize-money £3591

Going: Sf: 0-3 GS: 1-1 Gd: 0-2 GF: - Fm: 0-0
Distance: 2m/2m3: 0-0 2m4-2m7: 1-3 3m+: 0-3
Track: LH: 1-5 RH: 0-0 Tight: 0-0 Gall: 0-0
Aids: Bl: 0-0 Vi: 0-0 Tstrap: 0-0
Best Rating: 110 4/03 Prth 3m3f   good Hdl

Moderate hurdler; irish point winner; stays three miles well; acts on yielding ground.

Mister Graham
95(101c)   (57c)67

8-y-o b g Rock Hopper-Celestial Air (Rheingold)
K F Clutterbuck (Mrs S J Smith 13/9) K F Clutterbuck

Placings:*203*/650050/3325/3005P650-245P040500 (4666)
2002/03: 20²GF, 21⁴GF, 21⁵G, 21ᴾGS, 20⁰GS, 16⁴S, 20⁰G, 16⁵G, 16⁵GF, 16⁹G,

	Starts	1st	2nd	3rd	Win & Pl
Hurdles	6	0	0	0	0
Chases	4	0	1	0	1616
Career Total	31	0	3	4	4943

Going: Sf: 0-1 GS: 0-2 Gd: 0-4 GF: - Fm: 0-3
Distance: 2m/2m3: 0-4 2m4-2m7: 0-6 3m+: 0-0
Track: LH: 0-9 RH: 0-1 Tight: 0-7 Gall: 0-1
Aids: Bl: 0-0 Vi: 0-0 Tstrap: 0-0
Best Rating: 97 11/99 Weth 2m good Hdl

Mister Knight (IRE)
86f **63f**
4-y-o ch g Mister Lord (USA)-Knights Bounty (IRE) (Henbit (USA))
T P Tate T P Tate

Placings:*6* (3883)
2002/03: 16⁶GS,

	Starts	1st	2nd	3rd	Win & Pl
NH Flat	1	0	0	0	0
Career Total	1	0	0	0	0

Going: Sf: 0-0 GS: 0-1 Gd: 0-0 GF: - Fm: 0-0
Distance: 2m/2m3: 0-0 2m4-2m7: 0-0 3m+: 0-0
Track: LH: 0-1 RH: 0-0 Tight: 0-0 Gall: 0-1
Aids: Bl: 0-0 Vi: 0-0 Tstrap: 0-0
Best Rating: 63 3/03 Donc 2m110y gd-sft NHF

Mister Magnum (IRE)
100 **86**
5-y-o b g Be My Native (USA)-Miss Henrietta (IRE) (Step Together (USA))
M C Pipe D A Johnson

Placings:*044* (3850)
2002/03: 17⁰S, 17⁴S, 19⁴GS,

	Starts	1st	2nd	3rd	Win & Pl
NH Flat	1	0	0	0	0
Hurdles	2	0	0	0	816
Career Total	3	0	0	0	816

Going: Sf: 0-2 GS: 0-1 Gd: 0-0 GF: - Fm: 0-0
Distance: 2m/2m3: 0-2 2m4-2m7: 0-1 3m+: 0-0
Track: LH: 0-0 RH: 0-2 Tight: 0-2 Gall: 0-0
Aids: Bl: 0-0 Vi: 0-0 Tstrap: 0-0
Best Rating: 86 2/03 Tntn 2m1f soft Hdl

Mister Magpie
(96h) **(95h)**
7-y-o gr g Neltino-Magic (Sweet Revenge)
T R George Timothy N Chick

Placings:*035001-PUPP* (3823)
2002/03: 16ᴾG, 16ᵁGS, 16ᴾG, 16ᴾGS,

	Starts	1st	2nd	3rd	Win & Pl
Chases	4	0	0	0	
Career Total	10	1	0	1	3973

95 4/02 Prth 2m110y D Hdl GD £3744
Total win prize-money £3744

Going: Sf: 0-0 GS: 0-2 Gd: 0-2 GF: - Fm: 0-0
Distance: 2m/2m3: 0-4 2m4-2m7: 0-0 3m+: 0-0
Track: LH: 0-1 RH: 0-3 Tight: 0-1 Gall: 0-1
Aids: Bl: 0-1 Vi: 0-0 Tstrap: 0-0
Best Rating: 100 2/02 Winc 2m gd-sft NHF

Modest form in hurdles, but has failed to make an impact over fences so far; suited by a sound surface.

Mister McGoldrick
108 **138**
6-y-o b g Sabrehill (USA)-Anchor Inn (Be My Guest (USA))
Mrs S J Smith Richard Longley

Placings:00/6001104-10143004 (4713)
2002/03: 16¹HY, 16⁰S, 16¹GS, 16⁴GS, 20³G, 16⁰HY, 16⁰G, 20⁴GF,

	Starts	1st	2nd	3rd	Win & Pl
Hurdles	8	2	0	1	15772
Career Total	17	4	0	1	23538

138 12/02 Weth 2m C(0-135)HHdl G-S £6266
134 11/02 Weth 2m D(0-125)HHdl HVY £3916
115 3/02 Bang 2m1f E Hdl SFT £3262
112 3/02 Donc 2m110y E(0-105)HHdl G-S £4062
Total win prize-money £17507

Going: Sf: 1-3 GS: 1-2 Gd: 0-2 GF: - Fm: 0-1
Distance: 2m/2m3: 2-6 2m4-2m7: 0-2 3m+: 0-0
Track: LH: 2-7 RH: 0-1 Tight: 0-1 Gall: 0-1
Aids: Bl: 0-0 Vi: 0-0 Tstrap: 0-0
Best Rating: 138 3/03 Hayd 2m4f good Hdl

Very useful hurdler; well suited by soft ground; effective at around two miles.

Mister Mims (IRE)
98 **100**
7-y-o b g Scenic-Miss Bagatelle (Mummy s Pet)
C J Mann Mrs L G Turner

Placings:32 (0735)
2002/03: 20³GF, 17²GF,

	Starts	1st	2nd	3rd	Win & Pl
Hurdles	2	0	1	1	1538
Career Total	2	0	1	1	1538

Going: Sf: 0-0 GS: 0-0 Gd: 0-0 GF: - Fm: 0-2
Distance: 2m/2m3: 0-1 2m4-2m7: 0-1 3m+: 0-0
Track: LH: 0-2 RH: 0-0 Tight: 0-1 Gall: 0-0
Aids: Bl: 0-0 Vi: 0-0 Tstrap: 0-0
Best Rating: 100 7/02 NAbb 2m1f gd-fm Hdl

Moderate hurdler; maiden on the Flat in Ireland. Plenty of promise on first two starts over hurdles in the summer of 2002.

Mister Moss (IRE)
10-y-o b g Don Tristan (USA)-Lindas Statement (IRE) (Strong Statement (USA))
G D Hanmer D A Malam

Placings:P (0029)
2002/03: 21ᴾGF,

	Starts	1st	2nd	3rd	Win & Pl
Chases	1	0	0	0	
Career Total	1	0	0	0	

Going: Sf: 0-0 GS: 0-0 Gd: 0-0 GF: - Fm: 0-1
Distance: 2m/2m3: 0-0 2m4-2m7: 0-1 3m+: 0-0
Track: LH: 0-1 RH: 0-0 Tight: 0-0 Gall: 0-1
Aids: Bl: 0-0 Vi: 0-0 Tstrap: 0-0
Best Rating:

Mister Muddypaws
13-y-o b g Celtic Cone-Jane s Daughter (Pitpan)
C P Dennis T W Ellwood

Placings:2346/4121/P4P4/U3452231/FF433P1P/105P/P1P-4 (4552)
2002/03: 27⁴G,

	Starts	1st	2nd	3rd	Win & Pl
Chases	1	0	0	0	275
Career Total	36	6	4	5	48300

115 4/02 Newc 3m D(0-120)HCh FRM £5872
121 5/02 Sedg 3m4f D(0-125)HCh G-F £10822
116 3/00 Sedg 3m4f D(0-120)HCh G-F £4212
125 4/99 Sedg 3m4f C(0-130)HCh G-S £11422
104 11/95 Carl 3m110y E Hdl G-F £2136
93 5/95 Hexm 2m4f110y Hdl G-F £2469
Total win prize-money £36935

Going: Sf: 0-0 GS: 0-0 Gd: 0-1 GF: - Fm: 0-0
Distance: 2m/2m3: 0-0 2m4-2m7: 0-0 3m+: 0-1
Track: LH: 0-1 RH: 0-0 Tight: 0-0 Gall: 0-0
Aids: Bl: 0-0 Vi: 0-0 Tstrap: 0-0
Best Rating: 125 4/99 Sedg 3m4f gd-sft Ch

A dour stayer, suited by fast ground.

Mister Mustard (IRE)
106f **106f**
6-y-o b g Norwich-Monalma (IRE) (Montekin)
Ian Williams Favourites Racing

Placings:*13* (4329)
2002/03: 16¹S, 16³G,

	Starts	1st	2nd	3rd	Win & Pl
NH Flat	2	1	0	1	2931
Career Total	2	1	0	1	2931

95 2/03 Asct 2m110y H NHF SFT £2443
Total win prize-money £2443

Going: Sf: 1-1 GS: 0-0 Gd: 0-1 GF: - Fm: 0-0
Distance: 2m/2m3: 1-2 2m4-2m7: 0-0 3m+: 0-0
Track: LH: 1-1 RH: 1-1 Tight: 0-1 Gall: 0-1
Aids: Bl: 0-0 Vi: 0-0 Tstrap: 0-0
Best Rating: 106 3/03 Newb 2m110y good NHF

Decent form in bumpers; acts on good and soft ground.

Mister One
138
12-y-o b/br g Buckley-Miss Redlands (Dubassoff (USA))
C Tizzard C L Tizzard

Placings:4/113FP33/35012U0/10512-5 (0662)
2002/03: 32⁵GF,

	Starts	1st	2nd	3rd	Win & Pl
Chases	1	0	0	0	0
Career Total	21	5	2	4	53316

138 3/02 Extr 3m6f110yD(0-125)HCh GD £8417
133 1/02 Winc 3m1f110yD(0-125)HCh GD £5580
119 2/01 Sand 3m110y E Ch SFT £5486
133 12/99 Chel 3m1f110yC Ch GD £6905
132 11/99 Chel 3m110y B Ch GD £9530
Total win prize-money £35920

Going: Sf: 0-0 GS: 0-0 Gd: 0-0 GF: - Fm: 0-1
Distance: 2m/2m3: 0-0 2m4-2m7: 0-0 3m+: 0-1
Track: LH: 0-0 RH: 0-0 Tight: 0-0 Gall: 0-1
Aids: Bl: 0-0 Vi: 0-0 Tstrap: 0-0
Best Rating: 138 4/02 Chel 3m2f110y gd-fm Ch

A thorough stayer, has been in good heart in 2002. Best on decent ground and when fresh.

Mister Party

8-y-o b g Henbit (USA)-Sally s Dove (Celtic Cone)
Andrew J Martin Andrew J Martin

Placings:00/PF-P   (3951)
2002/03: 16PGS,

	Starts	1st	2nd	3rd	Win & Pl
Chases	1	0	0	0	
Career Total	5	0	0	0	

Going:	Sf: 0-0 GS: 0-1 Gd: 0-0 GF: - Fm: 0-0
Distance:	2m/2m3: 0-1 2m4-2m7: 0-0 3m+: 0-0
Track:	LH: 0-0 RH: 0-1 Tight: 0-0 Gall: 0-0
Aids:	Bl: 0-0 Vi: 0-0 Tstrap: 0-0
Best Rating:	71 2/00 Towc 2m heavy NHF

Mister Pickwick (IRE)

99(102c)   (78c)97+
8-y-o b g Commanche Run-Buckfast Lass (Buckskin (FR))
G L Moore Barry Prichard & Wayne Russell

Placings:3036001F/4P02FPP/P46P0304-5151   (1331)
2002/03: 21SGF, 221GF, 26SGF, 21IG,

	Starts	1st	2nd	3rd	Win & Pl
Hurdles	3	2	0	0	5670
Chases	1	0	0	0	0
Career Total	27	3	1	3	9922
97 9/02 Plum	2m5f	G(0-95)HHdl	GD	£2226	
85 6/02 Font	2m6f110yD(0-115)HHdl	G-F	£3444		
102 4/00 Plum	3m1f110y(0-105)HHdl	G-S	£2660		

Total win prize-money £8330

Going:	Sf: 0-0 GS: 0-0 Gd: 1-1 GF: - Fm: 1-3
Distance:	2m/2m3: 0-0 2m4-2m7: 2-3 3m+: 0-1
Track:	LH: 2-2 RH: 0-1 Tight: 2-3 Gall: 0-1
Aids:	Bl: 2-4 Vi: 0-0 Tstrap: 0-0
Best Rating:	102 4/00 Plum 3m1f110y gd-sft Hdl

Moderate, quirky hurdler/chaser, well suited by Fontwell/Plumpton. Stays well and seems to handle any ground.

Mister Putt (USA)

105   122+
5-y-o b/br g Mister Baileys-Theresita (GER) (Surumu (GER))
Mrs N Smith Tony Hayward And Barry Fulton

Placings:0432P-00131   (4081)
2002/03: 20OGS, 17OHY, 16THY, 163HY, 16THY,

	Starts	1st	2nd	3rd	Win & Pl
Hurdles	5	2	0	1	9638
Career Total	10	2	1	2	11427
122 3/03 Plum	2m	D Hdl	HVY	£5408	
103 1/03 Plum	2m	E(0-110)HHdl	HVY	£3474	

Total win prize-money £8882

Going:	Sf: 2-4 GS: 0-1 Gd: 0-0 GF: - Fm: 0-0
Distance:	2m/2m3: 2-4 2m4-2m7: 0-1 3m+: 0-0
Track:	LH: 2-2 RH: 0-1 Tight: 2-4 Gall: 0-0
Aids:	Bl: 2-3 Vi: 0-0 Tstrap: 1-2
Best Rating:	122 3/03 Plum 2m heavy Hdl

Fair novice hurdler; best over 2m; goes well at Plumpton and acts on good ground or softer.

Mister Sooty

5-y-o b g Dilum (USA)-Spring Flyer (IRE) (Waajib)
M C Pipe Codan Trust Company Limited

Placings:0P   (3780)
2002/03: 16OS, 22PGS,

	Starts	1st	2nd	3rd	Win & Pl
NH Flat	1	0	0	0	0
Hurdles	1	0	0	0	0
Career Total	2	0	0	0	

Going:	Sf: 0-1 GS: 0-1 Gd: 0-0 GF: - Fm: 0-0
Distance:	2m/2m3: 0-1 2m4-2m7: 0-1 3m+: 0-0
Track:	LH: 0-1 RH: 0-2 Tight: 0-0 Gall: 0-0
Aids:	Bl: 0-0 Vi: 0-0 Tstrap: 0-0
Best Rating:	32 1/03 Ludl 2m soft NHF

Mister Webb

104(87c)   (52c)89+
6-y-o b g Whittingham (IRE)-Ruda (FR) (Free Round (USA))
Dr J R J Naylor Norman E Webb

Placings:34-006P04   (4677)
2002/03: 21OS, 19OGS, 20SGS, 24PG, 20OGF, 194GF,

	Starts	1st	2nd	3rd	Win & Pl
Hurdles	4	0	0	0	278
Chases	2	0	0	0	0
Career Total	8	0	0	1	701

Going:	Sf: 0-1 GS: 0-2 Gd: 0-1 GF: - Fm: 0-2
Distance:	2m/2m3: 0-1 2m4-2m7: 0-4 3m+: 0-1
Track:	LH: 0-1 RH: 0-5 Tight: 0-0 Gall: 0-1
Aids:	Bl: 0-0 Vi: 0-0 Tstrap: 0-0
Best Rating:	91 11/01 Wwck 2m good Hdl

Moderate hurdler/chaser; maiden stayer on the Flat; easy winner of 2m 6f handicap hurdle at Newton Abbot June 2003; usually wears a visor.

Mister Wellard

118+
6-y-o b g Sir Harry Lewis (USA)-Cream By Post (Torus)
P F Nicholls T C Frost

Placings:1-15P   (2333)
2002/03: 17TF, 17SHY, 17PS,

	Starts	1st	2nd	3rd	Win & Pl
NH Flat	1	1	0	0	2226
Hurdles	2	0	0	0	0
Career Total	4	2	0	0	5782
116 10/02 Tntn	2m1f	H NHF	FRM	£2226	
116 4/02 Prth	2m110y	H NHF	GD	£3556	

Total win prize-money £5782

Going:	Sf: 0-2 GS: 0-0 Gd: 0-0 GF: - Fm: 1-1
Distance:	2m/2m3: 1-3 2m4-2m7: 0-0 3m+: 0-0
Track:	LH: 0-1 RH: 0-1 Tight: 0-1 Gall: 0-0
Aids:	Bl: 0-0 Vi: 0-0 Tstrap: 0-0
Best Rating:	118 11/02 NAbb 2m1f heavy Hdl

Winner of his first two starts in bumpers, he was killed over hurdles in December. (DEAD)

Misti Hunter (IRE)

14-y-o gr g Roselier (FR)-Lovely Stranger (Le Bavard (FR))
Mrs Carrie Ford (Miss L C Siddall 19/5) Miss Caroline Hurley

Placings:600P0000/032323141/P/240/030-50F   (4059)
2002/03: 28SG, 27OG, 26FGS,

	Starts	1st	2nd	3rd	Win & Pl
Chases	3	0	0	0	
Career Total	27	2	3	4	9554
90 4/96 MRas	3m1f	E(0-100)HCh	G-F	£2999	
87 11/95 Hexm	3m1f	F Ch	G-F	£2707	

Total win prize-money £5706

Going:	Sf: 0-0 GS: 0-1 Gd: 0-2 GF: - Fm: 0-0
Distance:	2m/2m3: 0-0 2m4-2m7: 0-0 3m+: 0-3
Track:	LH: 0-2 RH: 0-1 Tight: 0-2 Gall: 0-0
Aids:	Bl: 0-0 Vi: 0-0 Tstrap: 0-0
Best Rating:	95 5/00 MRas 2m6f110y gd-sft Ch

Mistletoe (IRE)

96   126
9-y-o gr m Montelimar (USA)-Nancy s Sister (The Parson)
K C Bailey Mrs John Loudon

Placings:2235/252/23211-F043P   (3774)
2002/03: 24FG, 24OS, 244HY, 243GS, 25PGS,

	Starts	1st	2nd	3rd	Win & Pl
Chases	5	0	0	1	2232
Career Total	17	2	6	3	31746
134 3/02 Uttx	2m5f	A HCh	HVY	£18760	
122 2/02 Ludl	2m4f	D Ch	G-S	£4680	

Total win prize-money £23440

Going:	Sf: 0-2 GS: 0-2 Gd: 0-1 GF: - Fm: 0-0
Distance:	2m/2m3: 0-0 2m4-2m7: 0-0 3m+: 0-5
Track:	LH: 0-4 RH: 0-1 Tight: 0-0 Gall: 0-1
Aids:	Bl: 0-0 Vi: 0-0 Tstrap: 0-0
Best Rating:	134 3/02 Uttx 2m5f heavy Ch

Decent handicap chaser; jumps well; probably stays three miles; acts on good to soft/soft ground.

Mistrato (GER)

9-y-o b/br g Surumu (GER)-Midnight Society (USA) (Imp Society (USA))
P Wegmann P Wegmann

Placings:30000/00/P0   (1232)
2002/03: 16PS, 16OG,

	Starts	1st	2nd	3rd	Win & Pl
Hurdles	2	0	0	0	
Career Total	9	0	0	1	574

Going:	Sf: 0-1 GS: 0-0 Gd: 0-1 GF: - Fm: 0-0
Distance:	2m/2m3: 0-2 2m4-2m7: 0-0 3m+: 0-0
Track:	LH: 0-2 RH: 0-0 Tight: 0-0 Gall: 0-0
Aids:	Bl: 0-0 Vi: 0-0 Tstrap: 0-0
Best Rating:	79 4/99 Ludl 2m good Hdl

Mistress Millie (IRE)

90   78
7-y-o ch m St Ninian-Nearly Married (Nearly A Hand)
A W Carroll Miss E J Marley

Placings:5-35P0624   (2112)
2002/03: 16OG, 16SGS, 20PGF, 16OGF, 19OGF, 20OG, 204G,

	Starts	1st	2nd	3rd	Win & Pl
NH Flat	2	0	0	1	314
Hurdles	5	0	1	0	1492
Career Total	8	0	1	1	1806

Going:	Sf: 0-0 GS: 0-1 Gd: 0-3 GF: - Fm: 0-3

Distance:	2m/2m3: 0-4 2m4-2m7: 0-3 3m+: 0-0
Track:	LH: 0-7 RH: 0-0 Tight: 0-5 Gall: 0-0
Aids:	Bl: 0-2 Vi: 0-0 Tstrap: 0-0
Best Rating:	90 5/02 Uttx 2m good NHF

Very modest hurdler, touched off at Fakenham in October 2002. Stays two and a half miles.

Mistress Ofthehall

5-y-o b m Son Pardo-Covent Garden Girl (Sizzling Melody)
Mrs N S Sharpe   J R B Williams

Placings:P					(3596)
2002/03: 17PS,					

	Starts	1st	2nd	3rd	Win & Pl
Hurdles	1	0	0	0	
Career Total	1	0	0	0	

Going:	Sf: 0-1 GS: 0-0 Gd: 0-0 GF: - Fm: 0-0
Distance:	2m/2m3: 0-1 2m4-2m7: 0-0 3m+: 0-0
Track:	LH: 0-0 RH: 0-1 Tight: 0-1 Gall: 0-0
Aids:	Bl: 0-0 Vi: 0-0 Tstrap: 0-0
Best Rating:	0 2/03 Tntn 2m1f soft Hdl

Misty Future
104   94

5-y-o b g Sanglamore (USA)-Star Of The Future (USA) (El Gran Senor (USA))
Miss Venetia Williams   The Mystics

Placings:0642					(4054)
2002/03: 16OGS, 17PS, 16PS, 16PS,					

	Starts	1st	2nd	3rd	Win & Pl
Hurdles	4	0	1	0	811
Career Total	4	0	1	0	811

Going:	Sf: 0-3 GS: 0-1 Gd: 0-0 GF: - Fm: 0-0
Distance:	2m/2m3: 0-4 2m4-2m7: 0-0 3m+: 0-0
Track:	LH: 0-3 RH: 0-1 Tight: 0-2 Gall: 0-1
Aids:	Bl: 0-0 Vi: 0-0 Tstrap: 0-0
Best Rating:	87 3/03 Wwck 2m soft Hdl

Plating-class performer; stays two miles; effective on good ground.

Misty Memory
83f   72f

4-y-o b f Alderbrook-Misty Sunset (Le Bavard (FR))
R F Knipe   Mrs R F Knipe

Placings:0					(3849)
2002/03: 16OG,					

	Starts	1st	2nd	3rd	Win & Pl
NH Flat	1	0	0	0	
Career Total	1	0	0	0	

Going:	Sf: 0-0 GS: 0-0 Gd: 0-1 GF: - Fm: 0-0
Distance:	2m/2m3: 0-1 2m4-2m7: 0-0 3m+: 0-0
Track:	LH: 0-0 RH: 0-1 Tight: 0-0 Gall: 0-0
Aids:	Bl: 0-0 Vi: 0-0 Tstrap: 0-0
Best Rating:	72 2/03 Ludl 2m good NHF

Misty Ramble (IRE)
102   95

8-y-o b g Roselier (FR)-Ramble Bramble (Random Shot)

Ferdy Murphy   Mrs M B Scholey

Placings:0/0420/34352-U52234					(3916)
2002/03: 28US, 25SS, 27²S, 27²S, 27³HY, 24⁴S,					

	Starts	1st	2nd	3rd	Win & Pl
Chases	6	0	2	1	3258
Career Total	16	0	4	3	7239

Going:	Sf: 0-6 GS: 0-0 Gd: 0-0 GF: - Fm: 0-0
Distance:	2m/2m3: 0-0 2m4-2m7: 0-0 3m+: 0-6
Track:	LH: 0-4 RH: 0-2 Tight: 0-4 Gall: 0-0
Aids:	Bl: 0-0 Vi: 0-0 Tstrap: 0-4
Best Rating:	102 11/01 Kels 3m1f gd-sft Ch

Plating-class chaser; often placed, but yet to get off the mark; stays well; best in soft ground; usually wears tongue tie; has worn blinkers.

Misty Ridge (IRE)
103(103h)   (96h)97

8-y-o b g Moscow Society (USA)-Abigail s Dream (Kalaglow)
Mrs S J Smith   Widdop Wanderers

Placings:0/05/030265U-50213321P					(1567)
2002/03: 16⁶G, 23⁹G, 20²GF, 19¹GF, 26³GF, 20³G, 22²GF, 22¹GF, 22⁶GS,					

	Starts	1st	2nd	3rd	Win & Pl
Hurdles	6	1	1	2	5948
Chases	3	1	1	0	5395
Career Total	19	2	3	3	12808
91 10/02 MRas	2m6f110y	E Ch		G-F	£4130
96 6/02 MRas	2m3f110y	D(0-120)HHdl		G-F	£4134
		Total win prize-money £8264			

Going:	Sf: 0-0 GS: 0-1 Gd: 0-3 GF: - Fm: 2-5
Distance:	2m/2m3: 0-1 2m4-2m7: 2-7 3m+: 0-1
Track:	LH: 0-4 RH: 2-5 Tight: 2-4 Gall: 0-0
Aids:	Bl: 2-5 Vi: 0-0 Tstrap: 0-0
Best Rating:	97 8/02 MRas 2m6f110y gd-fm Hdl

Very moderate chaser; effective over two and a half miles; acts well on a fast surface, although has gone in soft ground; out of form of late.

Mitcheldean (IRE)
90   (119h)125

7-y-o b g Be My Native (USA)-Pil Eagle (FR) (Piling (USA))
M Pitman   Ray Pascoe

Placings:35/P3112/3132U3-P5P					(2603)
2002/03: 25PGS, 20⁵G, 20PS,					

	Starts	1st	2nd	3rd	Win & Pl
Hurdles	1	0	0	0	
Chases	2	0	0	0	
Career Total	16	3	2	5	19321
128 12/01 Towc	2m6f	D Ch		HVY	£5798
119 4/01 Asct	2m4f	D Hdl		HVY	£5096
106 2/01 Fknm	2m4f	D Hdl		SFT	£3214
		Total win prize-money £14108			

Going:	Sf: 0-1 GS: 0-1 Gd: 0-1 GF: - Fm: 0-0
Distance:	2m/2m3: 0-0 2m4-2m7: 0-2 3m+: 0-1
Track:	LH: 0-1 RH: 0-2 Tight: 0-1 Gall: 0-0
Aids:	Bl: 0-1 Vi: 0-0 Tstrap: 0-0
Best Rating:	128 3/02 Chep 2m3f110y gd-sft Ch

Fair chaser. Acts well with cut in the ground, and stays two and three-quarter miles.

Mithak (USA)
107   114

9-y-o b g Silver Hawk (USA)-Kapalua Butterfly (USA) (Stagedoor Johnny)

R T Phillips   T Milson C Merson P Nichols R Stokes

Placings:3133/12/065/P40U03-22F112					(3317)
2002/03: 20²G, 26²GS, 22²G, 23¹S, 24¹S, 24²GS,					

	Starts	1st	2nd	3rd	Win & Pl
Hurdles	6	2	3	0	11908
Career Total	21	4	4	4	20487
114 1/03 Ludl	3m	D(0-115)HHdl		SFT	£4966
112 12/02 Hayd	2m7f110y	E(0-110)HHdl		SFT	£3627
124 5/99 Strf	2m6f110y	E Hdl		G-S	£2738
114 1/99 Ludl	2m5f110y	F Hdl		SFT	£2255
		Total win prize-money £13586			

Going:	Sf: 2-2 GS: 0-2 Gd: 0-2 GF: - Fm: 0-0
Distance:	2m/2m3: 0-0 2m4-2m7: 0-2 3m+: 2-4
Track:	LH: 1-3 RH: 1-3 Tight: 0-1 Gall: 0-1
Aids:	Bl: 0-0 Vi: 0-0 Tstrap: 0-0
Best Rating:	131 10/99 Chep 2m4f soft Hdl

Fair handicap hurdler. Not the best of jumpers. Was winning for the first time in over three years when successful at Haydock in December. Followed up at Ludlow. Effective from two miles to three miles two.

Mithraic (IRE)
91   96

11-y-o b g Kefaah (USA)-Persian s Glory (Prince Tenderfoot (USA))
W S Cunningham   Mrs Vicky Cunningham

Placings:5000/1233034/233P1P/124P00/313F/S/240-					(0004)
2002/03: 16⁰G,					

	Starts	1st	2nd	3rd	Win & Pl
Hurdles	1	0	0	0	
Career Total	31	4	4	7	12995
106 8/99 Sthl	2m	G Hdl		G-F	£1537
87 5/98 Sthl	2m	G Hdl		GD	£1758
115 2/98 Newc	2m	G(0-95)HHdl		GD	£1700
104 9/96 Prth	2m110y	E Hdl		G-F	£2780
		Total win prize-money £7775			

Going:	Sf: 0-0 GS: 0-0 Gd: 0-1 GF: - Fm: 0-0
Distance:	2m/2m3: 0-1 2m4-2m7: 0-0 3m+: 0-0
Track:	LH: 0-1 RH: 0-0 Tight: 0-0 Gall: 0-1
Aids:	Bl: 0-0 Vi: 0-0 Tstrap: 0-0
Best Rating:	115 2/98 Newc 2m good Hdl

Mixed Marriage (IRE)
98   115

5-y-o ch g Indian Ridge-Marie De Flandre (FR) (Crystal Palace (FR))
G L Moore   Straight Forward Racing

Placings:146					(4371)
2002/03: 16¹S, 16⁴HY, 16⁶G,					

	Starts	1st	2nd	3rd	Win & Pl
Hurdles	3	1	0	0	3510
Career Total	3	1	0	0	3510
115 2/03 Plum	2m	F Hdl		SFT	£3094
		Total win prize-money £3094			

Going:	Sf: 1-2 GS: 0-0 Gd: 0-1 GF: - Fm: 0-0
Distance:	2m/2m3: 1-3 2m4-2m7: 0-0 3m+: 0-0
Track:	LH: 1-2 RH: 0-1 Tight: 1-2 Gall: 0-0
Aids:	Bl: 0-0 Vi: 0-0 Tstrap: 0-0
Best Rating:	115 2/03 Plum 2m soft Hdl

Fair novice hurdler; best over two miles and soft ground.

Mixed Opinion (IRE)
62

10-y-o b g Be My Guest (USA)-Outside Pressure (Shernazar)
H M Kavanagh (C F C Jackson 27/7) Mrs S Kavanagh

Placings:04/F54550/63430/500/PP0   (0985)
2002/03: 22PGF, 19PGF, 17PGF,

	Starts	1st	2nd	3rd	Win & Pl
Hurdles	3	0	0	0	
Career Total	19	0	0	2	958

Going: Sf: 0-0 GS: 0-0 Gd: 0-0 GF: - Fm: 0-3
Distance: 2m/2m3: 0-2 2m4-2m7: 0-1 3m+: 0-0
Track: LH: 0-3 RH: 0-0 Tight: 0-2 Gall: 0-0
Aids: Bl: 0-1 Vi: 0-0 Tstrap: 0-0
Best Rating: 87 9/99 Worc 2m   gd-fm   Hdl

Mixsterthetrixster (USA)
111   134d

7-y-o b g Alleged (USA)-Parliament House (USA) (General Assembly (USA))
Miss T M Ide   Miss Tracey Ide

Placings:U12132120/50210F5   (4524)
2002/03: 16SG, 16BGS, 19ZS, 16SGS, 16BG, 17FG, 16SG,

	Starts	1st	2nd	3rd	Win & Pl
Hurdles	7	1	1	0	8292
Career Total	16	4	1	1	36938
134 1/03 Donc	2m110y	C(0-130)HHdl		G-S	£7104
123 2/00 Kels	2m2f	C Hdl		G-S	£5609
121 11/99 Newc	2m	D Hdl		GD	£3028
122 10/99 Weth	2m	A Hdl		GD	£9525

Total win prize-money £25269

Going: Sf: 0-1 GS: 1-2 Gd: 0-4 GF: - Fm: 0-0
Distance: 2m/2m3: 1-6 2m4-2m7: 0-1 3m+: 0-0
Track: LH: 1-5 RH: 0-2 Tight: 0-0 Gall: 1-3
Aids: Bl: 0-0 Vi: 0-0 Tstrap: 0-0
Best Rating: 134 1/03 Donc 2m110y   gd-sft   Hdl

Useful hurdler; has won from two to two and a quarter miles; acts on good/good to soft ground.

Mo's Keliro

11-y-o b m Lir-Bossy Cleo (Proud Challenge)
Mrs J Marsh   Clive Fowlie

Placings:6/5/F-P   (0145)
2002/03: 24PGF,

	Starts	1st	2nd	3rd	Win & Pl
Chases	1	0	0	0	
Career Total	4	0	0	0	0

Going: Sf: 0-0 GS: 0-0 Gd: 0-0 GF: - Fm: 0-1
Distance: 2m/2m3: 0-0 2m4-2m7: 0-0 3m+: 0-1
Track: LH: 0-1 RH: 0-0 Tight: 0-0 Gall: 0-0
Aids: Bl: 0-0 Vi: 0-0 Tstrap: 0-0
Best Rating: 61 5/99 Chep 3m   good   Ch

Mocho Wood

5-y-o ch g Husyan (USA)-Dawn Call (Rymer)
John Allen   T D Galer

Placings:0   (3998)
2002/03: 16DG,

	Starts	1st	2nd	3rd	Win & Pl
NH Flat	1	0	0	0	
Career Total	1	0	0	0	

Going: Sf: 0-0 GS: 0-0 Gd: 0-1 GF: - Fm: 0-0
Distance: 2m/2m3: 0-1 2m4-2m7: 0-0 3m+: 0-0
Track: LH: 0-1 RH: 0-0 Tight: 0-0 Gall: 0-0
Aids: Bl: 0-0 Vi: 0-0 Tstrap: 0-0
Best Rating: 0 3/03 Weth 2m   good   NHF

Model County (IRE)
62f   29f

6-y-o b g Montelimar (USA)-Sedan Lady (IRE) (Sandalay)
Mrs H Dalton   Mrs Heather Dalton

Placings:0   (2178)
2002/03: 16DHY,

	Starts	1st	2nd	3rd	Win & Pl
NH Flat	1	0	0	0	
Career Total	1	0	0	0	

Going: Sf: 0-1 GS: 0-0 Gd: 0-0 GF: - Fm: 0-0
Distance: 2m/2m3: 0-1 2m4-2m7: 0-0 3m+: 0-0
Track: LH: 0-1 RH: 0-0 Tight: 0-0 Gall: 0-0
Aids: Bl: 0-0 Vi: 0-0 Tstrap: 0-0
Best Rating: 29 11/02 Chep 2m110y   heavy   NHF

Modem (NZ)
120+

9-y-o br g Omnicorp (NZ)-Replica (NZ) (Creag-An-Sgor)
S E H Sherwood   T N Siviter

Placings:121/115-PP   (2496)
2002/03: 20PGS, 19PGS,

	Starts	1st	2nd	3rd	Win & Pl
Chases	2	0	0	0	
Career Total	8	4	1	0	17638
133 5/01 Aint	2m110y	B(0-145)HHdl		GD	£6929
125 5/01 Bang	2m1f	E(0-115)HHdl		GD	£4602
114 10/00 Chel	2m110y	E(0-135)HHdl		GD	£3445
107 9/00 Worc	2m	E Hdl		G-F	£1897

Total win prize-money £16873

Going: Sf: 0-0 GS: 0-2 Gd: 0-0 GF: - Fm: 0-0
Distance: 2m/2m3: 0-0 2m4-2m7: 0-0 3m+: 0-0
Track: LH: 0-1 RH: 0-0 Tight: 0-0 Gall: 0-1
Aids: Bl: 0-0 Vi: 0-0 Tstrap: 0-0
Best Rating: 133 5/01 Aint 2m110y   good   Hdl

Four times a winner over hurdles in 2000/01, he has clearly had his training problems as he has been very lightly raced since; pulled up on both starts over fences, he broke a blood vessel on the second occasion; bounced back with very impressive win in handicap hurdle at Southwell in June; stays two mile six.

Modulor (FR)
96(100c)   (106c)82

11-y-o gr g Less Ice-Chaumontaise (FR) (Armos)
M C Pipe (Y Fertillet 11/1)   F G Wilson

Placings:06FF3512102/0132F3P3/064422/14113/21354F4 511/3063610/00541301421F-0046P22453B60F   (4472)
2002/03: 18DG, 21DG, 21AS, 23DGS, 21PS, 172, 192, 174, 195, 18DHO, 18BVS, 17BVS, 26DG, 21FG,

	Starts	1st	2nd	3rd	Win & Pl
Chases	14	0	2	1	10530

Mohera King (IRE)
103   113

11-y-o b g King s Ride-Kilbrien Star (Goldhill)
Ferdy Murphy   Maurice J Barry

Placings:15340/0636153031/25336242/5F0345446P-4436313   (4395)
2002/03: 254S, 254GS, 213S, 20BG, 253GS, 201S, 203G,

	Starts	1st	2nd	3rd	Win & Pl
Chases	7	1	0	3	7723
Career Total	40	4	3	10	33908
113 3/03 Ayr	2m4f	E(0-110)HCh		SFT	£4127
113 4/00 Fair	2m6f	HHdl		G-Y	£8320
113 1/00 Naas	2m3f	Hdl		SH	£4416
113 11/98 Cork	2m4f	NHF		SFT	£2391

Total win prize-money £19255

Going: Sf: 1-3 GS: 0-2 Gd: 0-2 GF: - Fm: 0-0
Distance: 2m/2m3: 0-0 2m4-2m7: 1-4 3m+: 0-3
Track: LH: 1-5 RH: 0-2 Tight: 0-3 Gall: 0-0
Aids: Bl: 1-2 Vi: 0-0 Tstrap: 0-0
Best Rating: 113 3/03 Ayr 2m4f   soft   Ch

Modest novice chaser; took a weak event in the mud at Ayr in March. Best around two and a half miles.

Career Total

		73	13	9	10	194534
12/01 Cagn	2m3f	HCh		G-S	£9056
12/01 Cagn	2m2f110y	Ch		VS	£4382
8/01 Mesl	2m5f	Ch		FRM	£2424
10/00 Toul	2m1f110y	Ch		SFT	£2881
4/00 Nant	2m3f110y	Hdl		HVY	£4323
3/00 Toul	2m5f	HCh		SFT	£12488
10/99 Autl	2m2f110y	Ch		VS	£10764
6/98 Toul	2m4f	Hdl		G-S	£3030
6/98 Autl	2m4f	Ch		VS	£12121
5/98 Chol	2m3f	Hdl		SFT	£3030
10/96 Autl	2m1f110y	Ch		VS	£10540
3/96 Toul	2m1f110y	Hdl		SFT	£14456
1/96 Pau	2m110y	Hdl		VS	£6588

Total win prize-money £96084

Going: Sf: 0-2 GS: 0-1 Gd: 0-4 GF: - Fm: 0-0
Distance: 2m/2m3: 0-8 2m4-2m7: 0-5 3m+: 0-1
Track: LH: 0-3 RH: 0-1 Tight: 0-1 Gall: 0-1
Aids: Bl: 0-7 Vi: 0-2 Tstrap: 0-0
Best Rating: 106 3/03 Chel 3m2f110y   good   Ch

Decent chaser in France; best at around two and a half miles; finished last in Cheltenham Gold Cup on British debut; beaten in selling hurdle since; has worn blinkers and visor.

Mohawk Brave (IRE)
92f   99f

5-y-o b g Be My Native (USA)-Aunty Dawn (IRE) (Strong Gale)
K C Bailey   Mrs E A Kellar

Placings:04   (3139)
2002/03: 16DGS, 16AS,

	Starts	1st	2nd	3rd	Win & Pl
NH Flat	2	0	0	0	0
Career Total	2	0	0	0	0

Going: Sf: 0-1 GS: 0-1 Gd: 0-0 GF: - Fm: 0-0
Distance: 2m/2m3: 0-2 2m4-2m7: 0-0 3m+: 0-0
Track: LH: 0-1 RH: 0-1 Tight: 0-0 Gall: 0-0
Aids: Bl: 0-0 Vi: 0-0 Tstrap: 0-0
Best Rating: 99 11/02 Chel 2m110y   gd-sft   NHF

Moderate form in bumpers.

Mollycarrs Gambul

76   **25**

4-y-o b f General Gambul-Emma s Vision (IRE) (Vision (USA))
W G M Turner Mrs J Carr-Evans

Placings:06P   (1198)
2002/03: 17⁰S, 16⁶GS, 17P GF,

	Starts	1st	2nd	3rd	Win & Pl
Hurdles	3	0	0	0	0
Career Total	3	0	0	0	0

Going: Sf: 0-1 GS: 0-1 Gd: 0-0 GF: - Fm: 0-1
Distance: 2m/2m3: 0-3 2m4-2m7: 0-0 3m+: 0-0
Track: LH: 0-2 RH: 0-1 Tight: 0-2 Gall: 0-0
Aids: Bl: 0-0 Vi: 0-0 Tstrap: 0-0
Best Rating: 25   8/02   Strf   2m110y   gd-sft   Hdl

Mollycarrs Vision

6-y-o b g Yaheeb (USA)-Emma s Vision (IRE) (Vision (USA))
P R Rodford Mrs J Carr-Evans

Placings:0P   (0367)
2002/03: 16⁰GF, 17P S,

	Starts	1st	2nd	3rd	Win & Pl
NH Flat	1	0	0	0	0
Hurdles	1	0	0	0	0
Career Total	2	0	0	0	0

Going: Sf: 0-1 GS: 0-0 Gd: 0-0 GF: - Fm: 0-1
Distance: 2m/2m3: 0-2 2m4-2m7: 0-0 3m+: 0-0
Track: LH: 0-2 RH: 0-0 Tight: 0-1 Gall: 0-0
Aids: Bl: 0-0 Vi: 0-0 Tstrap: 0-0
Best Rating: 29   5/02   Chep   2m110y   gd-fm   NHF

Mollycarrsbrekfast

99   **89**

8-y-o b g Presidium-Imperial Flame (Imperial Lantern)
Miss S E Robinson (K Bishop 8/6) Mrs E M Davis

Placings:50/P46   (4678)
2002/03: 23P G, 24⁴F, 19⁶GF,

	Starts	1st	2nd	3rd	Win & Pl
Chases	3	0	0	0	0
Career Total	5	0	0	0	0

Going: Sf: 0-0 GS: 0-0 Gd: 0-0 GF: - Fm: 0-2
Distance: 2m/2m3: 0-1 2m4-2m7: 0-0 3m+: 0-2
Track: LH: 0-1 RH: 0-2 Tight: 0-1 Gall: 0-0
Aids: Bl: 0-0 Vi: 0-0 Tstrap: 0-0
Best Rating: 44   4/03   Hrfd   2m3f   gd-fm   Ch

Winner of four points; made mistakes when forcing a strong pace in ladies hunter chase at Stratford May 2003; suited by a return to front-running tactics when winning Class F 3m handicap at Worcester in July.

Moment Of Madness (IRE)

80f   **65f**

5-y-o ch g Treasure Hunter-Sip Of Orange (Celtic Cone)
J G Fitzgerald Mrs R A G Haggie

Placings:0   (3412)

2002/03: 16⁰GS,

	Starts	1st	2nd	3rd	Win & Pl
NH Flat	1	0	0	0	
Career Total	1	0	0	0	

Going: Sf: 0-0 GS: 0-1 Gd: 0-0 GF: - Fm: 0-0
Distance: 2m/2m3: 0-1 2m4-2m7: 0-0 3m+: 0-0
Track: LH: 0-1 RH: 0-0 Tight: 0-0 Gall: 0-0
Aids: Bl: 0-0 Vi: 0-0 Tstrap: 0-0
Best Rating: 66   2/03   Weth   2m   gd-sft   NHF

Momentous Jones

103   **86**

6-y-o b g Emperor Jones (USA)-Ivory Moment (USA) (Sir Ivor)
M Madgwick Peter Taplin

Placings:35F515105/F5454P6-05026P0   (4214)
2002/03: 22⁰GS, 16⁵GS, 20⁰S, 20²HY, 24⁶GS, 18P S, 18⁰G,

	Starts	1st	2nd	3rd	Win & Pl
Hurdles	6	0	1	0	2306
Chases	1	0	0	0	
Career Total	23	2	1	1	8405
110	1/01	Font	2m2f110yE Hdl		SFT £2502
110	12/00	Font	2m2f110yE Hdl		SFT £2317

Total win prize-money £4820

Going: Sf: 0-3 GS: 0-3 Gd: 0-1 GF: - Fm: 0-0
Distance: 2m/2m3: 0-3 2m4-2m7: 0-3 3m+: 0-1
Track: LH: 0-2 RH: 0-3 Tight: 0-4 Gall: 0-0
Aids: Bl: 0-0 Vi: 0-0 Tstrap: 0-0
Best Rating: 110   12/01   Font   2m2f110y   good   Hdl

He scored twice at Fontwell in the bottomless conditions he enjoys last season, but looks handicapped up to the hilt now.

Mon Esprit

88f   **77f**

6-y-o b m Terimon-Spartan Sprite (Country Retreat)
Ferdy Murphy Lord Somerleyton

Placings:04   (3230)
2002/03: 16⁰GS, 17⁴HY,

	Starts	1st	2nd	3rd	Win & Pl
NH Flat	2	0	0	0	0
Career Total	2	0	0	0	0

Going: Sf: 0-1 GS: 0-1 Gd: 0-0 GF: - Fm: 0-0
Distance: 2m/2m3: 0-2 2m4-2m7: 0-0 3m+: 0-0
Track: LH: 0-1 RH: 0-1 Tight: 0-1 Gall: 0-1
Aids: Bl: 0-0 Vi: 0-0 Tstrap: 0-0
Best Rating: 77   12/02   Hntg   2m110y   gd-sft   NHF

Mon Performer

97   **72d**

9-y-o ch g Mon Tresor-Hot Performer (Hotfoot)
D W Barker Anthony Neil McGilligan

Placings:044/6030PP   (4373)
2002/03: 17⁶GF, 17⁹G, 17³G, 17⁰S, 16P GS, 17P G,

	Starts	1st	2nd	3rd	Win & Pl
Hurdles	6	0	0	1	327
Career Total	9	0	0	1	327

Going: Sf: 0-1 GS: 0-1 Gd: 0-3 GF: - Fm: 0-1
Distance: 2m/2m3: 0-6 2m4-2m7: 0-0 3m+: 0-0
Track: LH: 0-5 RH: 0-1 Tight: 0-6 Gall: 0-0

Aids: Bl: 0-0 Vi: 0-0 Tstrap: 0-0
Best Rating: 75   11/97   Newc   2m   gd-fm   Hdl

Poor front-running novice hurdler, lightly-raced in recent seasons.

Monarch's Pursuit

112   **125**

9-y-o b g Pursuit Of Love-Last Detail (Dara Monarch)
T D Easterby Mrs Jean P Connew

Placings:115/0/F/3253U162/2201F504-3F326   (2508)
2002/03: 16³G, 20⁴GS, 16³GS, 20²GS, 16⁶G,

	Starts	1st	2nd	3rd	Win & Pl
Chases	5	0	1	2	6206
Career Total	26	4	5	4	36171
126	12/01	Uttx	2m	C(0-135)HCh	SFT £6727
117	2/01	Catt	2m3f	D Ch	SFT £4212
120	11/97	Weth	2m	A Hdl	G-F £8955
108	10/97	Weth	2m	D Hdl	G-F £2810

Total win prize-money £22705

Going: Sf: 0-0 GS: 0-3 Gd: 0-2 GF: - Fm: 0-0
Distance: 2m/2m3: 0-3 2m4-2m7: 0-2 3m+: 0-0
Track: LH: 0-4 RH: 0-1 Tight: 0-0 Gall: 0-1
Aids: Bl: 0-5 Vi: 0-0 Tstrap: 0-0
Best Rating: 126   12/01   Uttx   2m   soft   Ch

He is an effective sort in modest handicap chases. Stays two and a half miles, but better suited by shorter. Acts on soft ground. Usually wears blinkers, has worn a tongue tie.

Monash Freeway (IRE)

53   **95**

5-y-o ch h General Monash (USA)-Pennine Pearl (IRE) (Pennine Walk)
Miss Jacqueline S Doyle A W Regan

Placings:23-00   (3311)
2002/03: 16⁰HY, 19⁰GS,

	Starts	1st	2nd	3rd	Win & Pl
Hurdles	2	0	0	0	
Career Total	4	0	1	1	1179

Going: Sf: 0-1 GS: 0-1 Gd: 0-0 GF: - Fm: 0-0
Distance: 2m/2m3: 0-2 2m4-2m7: 0-0 3m+: 0-0
Track: LH: 0-1 RH: 0-1 Tight: 0-0 Gall: 0-1
Aids: Bl: 0-0 Vi: 0-0 Tstrap: 0-0
Best Rating: 95   11/01   Wwck   2m   good   Hdl

Moderate hurdler; has shown ability over hurdles and looks sure to find a race.

Monduru

69   **38**

6-y-o b g Lion Cavern (USA)-Bint Albadou (IRE) (Green Desert (USA))
Miss G Browne Pleasure Palace Racing

Placings:0P   (1891)
2002/03: 17⁰G, 16P GS,

	Starts	1st	2nd	3rd	Win & Pl
Hurdles	2	0	0	0	
Career Total	2	0	0	0	

Going: Sf: 0-0 GS: 0-1 Gd: 0-0 GF: - Fm: 0-0
Distance: 2m/2m3: 0-2 2m4-2m7: 0-0 3m+: 0-0
Track: LH: 0-0 RH: 0-2 Tight: 0-0 Gall: 0-1
Aids: Bl: 0-1 Vi: 0-0 Tstrap: 0-0

Best Rating: 56 10/02 Extr 2m1f   good Hdl

Monet's Garden (IRE)

77f   109+f

5-y-o gr g Roselier (FR)-Royal Remainder (IRE) (Remainder Man)
N G Richards David Wesley Yates

Placings:1				(3775)
2002/03: 16¹GS,				

	Starts	1st	2nd	3rd	Win & Pl
NH Flat	1	1	0	0	2016
Career Total	**1**	**1**	**0**	**0**	**2016**
109 2/03 Ayr	2m	H NHF		G-S	£2016

Total win prize-money £2016

Going:	Sf: 0-0 GS: 1-1 Gd: 0-0 GF: - Fm: 0-0
Distance:	2m/2m3: 1-1 2m4-2m7: 0-0 3m+: 0-0
Track:	LH: 1-1 RH: 0-0 Tight: 0-0 Gall: 0-0
Aids:	Bl: 0-0 Vi: 0-0 Tstrap: 0-0
Best Rating:	109 2/03 Ayr 2m gd-sft NHF

Bred to stay well, he won an Ayr bumper on his debut.

Money Magic

7-y-o ch m Weld-Susie s Money (Seymour Hicks (FR))
Miss S E Broadhurst J R Parrott

Placings:P				(4520)
2002/03: 27⁶G,				

	Starts	1st	2nd	3rd	Win & Pl
Chases	1	0	0	0	
Career Total	**1**	**0**	**0**	**0**	

Going:	Sf: 0-0 GS: 0-0 Gd: 0-1 GF: - Fm: 0-0
Distance:	2m/2m3: 0-0 2m4-2m7: 0-0 3m+: 0-1
Track:	LH: 0-1 RH: 0-0 Tight: 0-1 Gall: 0-0
Aids:	Bl: 0-0 Vi: 0-0 Tstrap: 0-0
Best Rating:	0 4/03 Sedg 3m3f good Ch

Money Mountain

68f   36f

6-y-o ch g Rakaposhi King-Black H Penny (Town And Country)
J A B Old A J Britten

Placings:0				(3528)
2002/03: 16⁶G,				

	Starts	1st	2nd	3rd	Win & Pl
NH Flat	1	0	0	0	
Career Total	**1**	**0**	**0**	**0**	

Going:	Sf: 0-0 GS: 0-0 Gd: 0-0 GF: - Fm: 0-0
Distance:	2m/2m3: 0-0 2m4-2m7: 0-0 3m+: 0-0
Track:	LH: 0-1 RH: 0-0 Tight: 0-0 Gall: 0-1
Aids:	Bl: 0-0 Vi: 0-0 Tstrap: 0-0
Best Rating:	36 2/03 Newb 2m110y good NHF

Moneytrain (GER)

104   125

4-y-o br g Platini (GER)-Miss Esther (GER) (Alkalde (GER))
C Von Der Recke Mrs T Hamann

Placings:421B0   (4460)

2002/03: 16⁴G, 16²HY, 17¹GS, 17⁸G, 16⁹G,

	Starts	1st	2nd	3rd	Win & Pl
Hurdles	5	1	1	0	19204
Career Total	**5**	**1**	**1**	**0**	**19204**
125 1/03 Chel	2m1f	A Hdl		G-S	£17400

Total win prize-money £17400

Going:	Sf: 0-1 GS: 1-1 Gd: 0-3 GF: - Fm: 0-0
Distance:	2m/2m3: 1-5 2m4-2m7: 0-0 3m+: 0-0
Track:	LH: 1-4 RH: 0-1 Tight: 0-1 Gall: 1-2
Aids:	Bl: 0-0 Vi: 0-0 Tstrap: 0-0
Best Rating:	125 1/03 Chel 2m1f gd-sft Hdl

German-trained; very useful juvenile hurdler; surprise winner of good event at Cheltenham in January; acts in good and heavy ground.

Monger Lane

112   120

7-y-o b m Karinga Bay-Grace Moore (Deep Run)
K Bishop Slabs And Lucan

Placings:03/4/0503011-0204				(4171)
2002/03: 21⁹GS, 21²S, 24⁰G, 22⁴S,				

	Starts	1st	2nd	3rd	Win & Pl
Hurdles	4	0	1	0	6609
Career Total	**14**	**2**	**1**	**2**	**52108**
120 4/02 Chel	2m5f110yA HHdl		GD	£19604
109 3/02 Newb	2m5f	A HHdl	G-S	£23200

Total win prize-money £42804

Going:	Sf: 0-2 GS: 0-1 Gd: 0-1 GF: - Fm: 0-0
Distance:	2m/2m3: 0-0 2m4-2m7: 0-3 3m+: 0-1
Track:	LH: 0-4 RH: 0-0 Tight: 0-0 Gall: 0-3
Aids:	Bl: 0-0 Vi: 0-0 Tstrap: 0-0
Best Rating:	120 3/03 Uttx 2m6f110y soft Hdl

Fair hurdler; caused a surprise by winning the valuable mares final at Newbury in March 2002; suited by a strong pace; stays 2m 5f; acts in soft ground, although does look best on decent going.

Monica Geller

91   62

5-y-o b m Komaite (USA)-Rion River (IRE) (Taufan (USA))
J W Payne newmarketconnections.com

Placings:000				(4337)
2002/03: 26⁰G, 16⁹G, 16⁰GF,				

	Starts	1st	2nd	3rd	Win & Pl
Hurdles	3	0	0	0	
Career Total	**3**	**0**	**0**	**0**	

Going:	Sf: 0-0 GS: 0-0 Gd: 0-2 GF: - Fm: 0-1
Distance:	2m/2m3: 0-2 2m4-2m7: 0-0 3m+: 0-1
Track:	LH: 0-0 RH: 0-3 Tight: 0-0 Gall: 0-3
Aids:	Bl: 0-0 Vi: 0-0 Tstrap: 0-0
Best Rating:	67 3/03 Hntg 2m110y gd-fm Hdl

Monicasman (IRE)

13-y-o br g Callernish-Sengirrefcha (Reformed Character)
Miss Caroline Barclay Jamie Alexander

Placings:115/12106/066233/21F125/3F23/3F3PP/605-60				(0377)
2002/03: 34⁶G, 25⁰GF,				

	Starts	1st	2nd	3rd	Win & Pl
Chases	2	0	0	0	
Career Total	**34**	**6**	**5**	**6**	**27580**
118 2/99 Fknm	3m110y	F(0-100)HCh	G-S	£4005
114 12/98 MRas	3m1f	E(0-105)HCh	HVY	£3860

120	3/96	Newb	2m110y	C Hdl	G-S	£4302
101	10/95	Chel	2m110y	D Hdl	G-F	£2850
119	3/95	Donc	2m110y	H NHF	GD	£1444
114	2/95	Nott	2m	H NHF	G-S	£1560

Total win prize-money £18023

Going:	Sf: 0-0 GS: 0-0 Gd: 0-1 GF: - Fm: 0-1
Distance:	2m/2m3: 0-0 2m4-2m7: 0-0 3m+: 0-0
Track:	LH: 0-2 RH: 0-0 Tight: 0-1 Gall: 0-0
Aids:	Bl: 0-0 Vi: 0-0 Tstrap: 0-0
Best Rating:	120 3/96 Newb 2m110y gd-sft Hdl

Monitor

(104h)125

9-y-o ch g Machiavellian (USA)-Instant Desire (USA) (Northern Dancer)
G M Lyons Trio Syndicate

Placings:0/42P0/011300/0344P-01PP26				(1145a)
2002/03: 20⁰G, 20¹GF, 20⁵GS, 22⁵Y, 22⁵GF, 20⁵GF,				

	Starts	1st	2nd	3rd	Win & Pl
Hurdles	1	0	0	0	0
Chases	5	1	1	0	8258
Career Total	**22**	**3**	**2**	**2**	**23317**
118 7/02 Wxfd	2m4f	(0-116)HCh	G-F	£5926
120 8/00 Kbgn	2m3f	(0-116)HHdl	G-F	£6072
120 8/00 Cork	2m4f	Hdl	Y-S	£4416

Total win prize-money £16414

Going:	Sf: 0-0 GS: 0-1 Gd: 0-1 GF: - Fm: 1-3
Distance:	2m/2m3: 0-0 2m4-2m7: 1-6 3m+: 0-0
Track:	LH: 0-0 RH: 1-4 Tight: 0-1 Gall: 0-0
Aids:	Bl: 0-0 Vi: 0-0 Tstrap: 1-6
Best Rating:	125 8/02 Tram 2m6f gd-fm Ch

Three time winner on the Flat, he has scored over hurdles and fences. Acts on most types of ground, and is effective at two and a half miles.

Monkerhostin (FR)

113(110c)   (127c)137

6-y-o b g Shining Steel-Ladoun (FR) (Kaldoun (FR))
O Sherwood M G St Quinton

Placings:3/1235221501-52F13546050				(4475)
2002/03: 16⁵G, 16²G, 16²FG, 16¹G, 16³G, 16⁵HY, 16⁴G, 16⁶G, 17⁹G, 16⁵G, 20⁰G,				

	Starts	1st	2nd	3rd	Win & Pl
Hurdles	8	0	1	0	11533
Chases	3	1	0	1	5429
Career Total	**22**	**4**	**4**	**3**	**41422**
127 11/02 Wwck	2m110y	D Ch	GD	£4693
132 4/02 Strf	2m110y	D(0-120)HHdl	GD	£3679
122 2/02 Sedg	2m1f	E Hdl	SFT	£2583
5/01 Pari	2m1f	Hdl	G-S	£4850

Total win prize-money £15805

Going:	Sf: 0-1 GS: 0-0 Gd: 1-10 GF: - Fm: 0-0
Distance:	2m/2m3: 1-10 2m4-2m7: 0-1 3m+: 0-0
Track:	LH: 1-8 RH: 0-3 Tight: 0-2 Gall: 0-3
Aids:	Bl: 0-0 Vi: 0-1 Tstrap: 0-0
Best Rating:	137 2/03 Newb 2m110y good Hdl

Very useful hurdler, also pretty decent, but lightly-raced over fences; acts on both good and soft ground; effective at around two miles; has worn cheekpieces.

Monkey Island

103

8-y-o b g Jupiter Island-Mikey s Monkey (Monksfield)
Ferdy Murphy The Monkey Island Partnership

Placings:00/554/30PFP340-155UPP   (4393)
2002/03: 20¹G, 20⁵GS, 20⁵G, 24ᵁGF, 24ᴾGS, 20ᴾG,

	Starts	1st	2nd	3rd	Win & Pl
Chases	6	1	0		3357
Career Total	19	1	0	2	4518

100 4/02 Hexm 2m4f110yE Ch   GD   £3357
Total win prize-money £3357

Going: Sf: 0-0 GS: 0-2 Gd: 1-3 GF: - Fm: 0-1
Distance: 2m/2m3: 0-0 2m4-2m7: 1-4 3m+: 0-2
Track: LH: 1-2 RH: 0-4 Tight: 0-3 Gall: 0-0
Aids: Bl: 1-5 Vi: 0-0 Tstrap: 0-0
Best Rating: 105 12/01 Muss 3m   good   Ch

Moderate front-running chaser, improved for the application of blinkers getting off the mark at Hexham in April 2002.

Monksford
85   64

4-y-o b g Minster Son-Mortify (Prince Sabo)
B J Llewellyn (Denys Smith 30/9) B W Parren

Placings:3   (3148)
2002/03: 16³HY,

	Starts	1st	2nd	3rd	Win & Pl
Hurdles	1	0	0	1	384
Career Total	1	0	0	1	384

Going: Sf: 0-1 GS: 0-0 Gd: 0-0 GF: - Fm: 0-0
Distance: 2m/2m3: 0-1 2m4-2m7: 0-0 3m+: 0-0
Track: LH: 0-1 RH: 0-0 Tight: 0-0 Gall: 0-0
Aids: Bl: 0-0 Vi: 0-0 Tstrap: 0-0
Best Rating: 64 1/03 Chep 2m110y heavy Hdl

Monolith
104   106+

5-y-o b g Bigstone (IRE)-Ancara (Dancing Brave (USA))
L Lungo Elite Racing Club

Placings:006   (3911)
2002/03: 17⁰S, 18⁰G, 17⁶GS,

	Starts	1st	2nd	3rd	Win & Pl
Hurdles	3	0	0	0	0
Career Total	3	0	0	0	0

Going: Sf: 0-1 GS: 0-1 Gd: 0-1 GF: - Fm: 0-0
Distance: 2m/2m3: 0-3 2m4-2m7: 0-0 3m+: 0-0
Track: LH: 0-2 RH: 0-1 Tight: 0-2 Gall: 0-0
Aids: Bl: 0-0 Vi: 0-0 Tstrap: 0-0
Best Rating: 67 3/03 Carl 2m1f gd-sft Hdl

Moderate hurdler; improved to win twice in May 2003; stays two miles four; effective on good and softer.

Monsieur De Rien (FR)
(88h)   (78h)74

8-y-o b/br g Vorias (USA)-Inmemoriam (IRE) (Buckskin (FR))
M Mullineaux Mrs C S Wilson

Placings:06/0045/0000P4-PUP   (3137)
2002/03: 20ᴾS, 24ᵁS, 24ᴾS,

	Starts	1st	2nd	3rd	Win & Pl
Hurdles	1	0	0	0	0
Chases	2	0	0	0	0
Career Total	15	0	0	0	264

Going: Sf: 0-3 GS: 0-0 Gd: 0-0 GF: - Fm: 0-0
Distance: 2m/2m3: 0-0 2m4-2m7: 0-1 3m+: 0-2
Track: LH: 0-2 RH: 0-1 Tight: 0-1 Gall: 0-0
Aids: Bl: 0-0 Vi: 0-0 Tstrap: 0-0
Best Rating: 100 2/00 Asct 2m110y soft NHF

Monsieur Poirot (IRE)
98   83

6-y-o b g Lapierre-Mallia Miss (IRE) (Executive Perk)
Mrs S C Bradburne The Hon Thomas Cochrane

Placings:0-34600   (3914)
2002/03: 16³HY, 20⁴S, 16⁶HY, 24⁰G, 20⁰GS,

	Starts	1st	2nd	3rd	Win & Pl
Hurdles	5	0	0	1	562
Career Total	6	0	0	1	562

Going: Sf: 0-3 GS: 0-1 Gd: 0-1 GF: - Fm: 0-0
Distance: 2m/2m3: 0-2 2m4-2m7: 0-2 3m+: 0-1
Track: LH: 0-3 RH: 0-2 Tight: 0-2 Gall: 0-0
Aids: Bl: 0-0 Vi: 0-0 Tstrap: 0-0
Best Rating: 90 4/02 Prth 2m110y good NHF

Monsieur Tagel (FR)
101(100h)   (110h)118

7-y-o b g Tagel (USA)-Miss Zonissa (FR) (Zino)
Ian Williams J Cullen Thermals Ltd

Placings:10442622/511F134F0/501033UF-302FPP (4570)
2002/03: 21³GF, 20⁰G, 20²G, 24⁴G, 24ᴾGS, 20ᴾG,

	Starts	1st	2nd	3rd	Win & Pl
Hurdles	2	0	0	1	1768
Chases	4	0	1	0	2060
Career Total	31	5	4	4	25573

118 11/01 Ludl 2m4f E Ch   G-F   £3770
127 10/00 Strf 2m6f110yD(0-120)HHdl G-S £3068
123 9/00 Chep 2m4f D(0-125)HHdl GD £3415
124 9/00 Hntg 2m4f110yD(0-120)HHdl G-F £4348
97 10/99 Worc 2m E Hdl GD £2215
Total win prize-money £16818

Going: Sf: 0-0 GS: 0-1 Gd: 0-4 GF: - Fm: 0-1
Distance: 2m/2m3: 0-0 2m4-2m7: 0-4 3m+: 0-2
Track: LH: 0-4 RH: 0-2 Tight: 0-5 Gall: 0-1
Aids: Bl: 0-0 Vi: 0-0 Tstrap: 0-0
Best Rating: 127 12/00 MRas 2m3f110y gd-sft Hdl

Fair hurdler/chaser; has won on good and soft; best at trips around two and a half miles.

Mont Aca (FR)

8-y-o b g Phantom Breeze-Azuzuama (FR) (Cadoudal (FR))
Miss Polly Curling The Notre Cheval Partnership

Placings:1242004/213P1/3FF-5   (4216)
2002/03: 20⁵G,

	Starts	1st	2nd	3rd	Win & Pl
Chases	1	0	0	0	0
Career Total	16	3	3	2	15071

118 4/01 Extr 2m3f110yE Ch   SFT   £3952
118 12/00 Tntn 2m3f F(0-110)HCh SFT £3198
111 10/99 Extr 2m1f E Hdl GD £2514
Total win prize-money £9664

Going: Sf: 0-0 GS: 0-0 Gd: 0-1 GF: - Fm: 0-0
Distance: 2m/2m3: 0-0 2m4-2m7: 0-1 3m+: 0-0
Track: LH: 0-0 RH: 0-0 Tight: 0-1 Gall: 0-0

Aids: Bl: 0-0 Vi: 0-0 Tstrap: 0-0
Best Rating: 118 4/01 Extr 2m3f110y soft Ch

Montagnette
101   81d

9-y-o ch m Gildoran-Deep Crevasse (Rolfe (USA))
M R Bosley Girls On Top Racing 2000

Placings:4000/454220/205PF126/06-24PP   (3600)
2002/03: 26²G, 24⁴S, 26ᴾS, 24ᴾS,

	Starts	1st	2nd	3rd	Win & Pl
Hurdles	4	0	1	0	1340
Career Total	24	1	5	0	5473

74 2/01 Towc 2m5f G(0-90)HHdl HVY £1694
Total win prize-money £1694

Going: Sf: 0-3 GS: 0-0 Gd: 0-1 GF: - Fm: 0-0
Distance: 2m/2m3: 0-0 2m4-2m7: 0-0 3m+: 0-4
Track: LH: 0-0 RH: 0-4 Tight: 0-1 Gall: 0-0
Aids: Bl: 0-0 Vi: 0-0 Tstrap: 0-0
Best Rating: 85 11/98 Wwck 2m soft NHF

Modest handicap hurdler. Lightly raced in recent years. Stays well and acts in the mud.

Montalcino (IRE)
113(120h)   (156h)143

7-y-o b g Robellino (USA)-Only Gossip (USA) (Trempolino (USA))
M C Pipe Favourites Racing

Placings:11P/3522400-1P   (3250)
2002/03: 18¹S, 16ᴾS,

	Starts	1st	2nd	3rd	Win & Pl
Chases	2	1	0	0	6909
Career Total	9	3	2	1	57512

143 12/02 Newb 2m2f110yD Ch SFT £6909
145 4/01 Aint 2m4f A Hdl SFT £29000
126 3/01 Hntg 2m110y E Hdl SFT £2723
Total win prize-money £38632

Going: Sf: 1-2 GS: 0-0 Gd: 0-0 GF: - Fm: 0-0
Distance: 2m/2m3: 1-2 2m4-2m7: 0-0 3m+: 0-0
Track: LH: 1-2 RH: 0-0 Tight: 0-0 Gall: 1-1
Aids: Bl: 0-0 Vi: 0-0 Tstrap: 0-0
Best Rating: 156 2/02 Font 2m4f soft Hdl

Useful novice chaser; formerly smart hurdler; effective from trips of around two and a half miles; suited by cut in the ground; an impressive winner on his chasing debut, but fatally injured next time. (DEAD)

Montana Moon (IRE)
77   59

4-y-o b g Ajraas (USA)-Batilde (IRE) (Victory Piper (USA))
R A Fahey Mrs Una Towell

Placings:0   (2098)
2002/03: 16⁰G,

	Starts	1st	2nd	3rd	Win & Pl
Hurdles	1	0	0	0	0
Career Total	1	0	0	0	0

Going: Sf: 0-0 GS: 0-0 Gd: 0-1 GF: - Fm: 0-0
Distance: 2m/2m3: 0-1 2m4-2m7: 0-0 3m+: 0-0
Track: LH: 0-1 RH: 0-0 Tight: 0-1 Gall: 0-0
Aids: Bl: 0-0 Vi: 0-0 Tstrap: 0-0
Best Rating: 59 11/02 Catt 2m good Hdl

Monte Cristo (FR)
103(109h)   (106h)114
5-y-o ch g Bigstone (IRE)-El Quahirah (FR) (Cadoudal (FR))
Mrs L C Taylor Mrs L C Taylor

Placings:435531P-24U122643223   (4680)
2002/03: 16²GF, 19⁴G, 19⁰S, 17¹S, 16²GS, 16²GS, 20⁶G, 16⁴HY, 16³GF, 18²G, 16²G, 20³GF,

	Starts	1st	2nd	3rd	Win & Pl
Hurdles	3	0	1	0	3376
Chases	9	1	4	2	13280
Career Total	19	2	5	4	28799
96 11/02 Plum	2m1f	E Ch		SFT	£3666
106 3/02 Hayd	2m	D Hdl		GD	£4862
			Total win prize-money		£8528

Going: Sf: 1-3 GS: 0-2 Gd: 0-4 GF: - Fm: 0-3
Distance: 2m2/2m3: 1-9 2m4-2m7: 0-3 3m+: 0-3
Track: LH: 1-5 RH: 0-7 Tight: 1-2 Gall: 0-3
Aids: Bl: 0-3 Vi: 1-5 Tstrap: 0-0
Best Rating: 114 3/03 Newb 2m2f110y good Ch

Fair chaser; acts on good and soft ground; effective at around two miles two, but should stay further; wears headgear.

Monte Rouge (IRE)
88   72
6-y-o ch g Montelimar (USA)-Drumdeels Star (IRE) (Le Bavard (FR))
Miss L C Siddall The Full Monte

Placings:2/55-6   (2512)
2002/03: 20⁶G,

	Starts	1st	2nd	3rd	Win & Pl
Hurdles	1	0	0	0	0
Career Total	4	0	1	0	560

Going: Sf: 0-0 GS: 0-0 Gd: 0-1 GF: - Fm: 0-0
Distance: 2m2/2m3: 0-0 2m4-2m7: 0-1 3m+: 0-0
Track: LH: 0-1 RH: 0-0 Tight: 0-0 Gall: 0-0
Aids: Bl: 0-0 Vi: 0-0 Tstrap: 0-0
Best Rating: 105 1/02 Hayd 2m soft NHF

Montel Girl (IRE)
96   89
7-y-o ch m Montelimar (USA)-Grassed (Busted)
T P McGovern (C Roche 6/9) The Walking Tall Partnership

Placings:060-63500   (3807)
2002/03: 16⁶G, 24³GF, 22⁵HY, 21⁰GS, 21⁰S,

	Starts	1st	2nd	3rd	Win & Pl
NH Flat	1	0	0	0	0
Hurdles	4	0	0	1	387
Career Total	8	0	0	1	387

Going: Sf: 0-2 GS: 0-1 Gd: 0-1 GF: - Fm: 0-1
Distance: 2m2/2m3: 0-1 2m4-2m7: 0-3 3m+: 0-1
Track: LH: 0-2 RH: 0-1 Tight: 0-2 Gall: 0-0
Aids: Bl: 0-0 Vi: 0-0 Tstrap: 0-0
Best Rating: 86 8/02 Tral 2m good NHF

Plating-class performer; stays three miles; acts on fast ground.

Montemoss (IRE)
99   86
6-y-o ch g Montelimar (USA)-Gaye Le Moss (Le Moss)
M G Rimell Mark Rimell

Placings:054   (4196)
2002/03: 16⁶GS, 23⁵S, 24⁴G,

	Starts	1st	2nd	3rd	Win & Pl
NH Flat	1	0	0	0	0
Hurdles	2	0	0	0	263
Career Total	3	0	0	0	263

Going: Sf: 0-1 GS: 0-1 Gd: 0-1 GF: - Fm: 0-0
Distance: 2m2/2m3: 0-1 2m4-2m7: 0-0 3m+: 0-2
Track: LH: 0-2 RH: 0-1 Tight: 0-1 Gall: 0-1
Aids: Bl: 0-0 Vi: 0-0 Tstrap: 0-0
Best Rating: 86 3/03 Ludl 3m good Hdl

Montesino
84   51
4-y-o b g Bishop Of Cashel-Sutosky (Great Nephew)
R C Guest Rae Guest

Placings:4   (3969)
2002/03: 16⁴S,

	Starts	1st	2nd	3rd	Win & Pl
NH Flat	1	0	0	0	0
Career Total	1	0	0	0	0

Going: Sf: 0-1 GS: 0-0 Gd: 0-0 GF: - Fm: 0-0
Distance: 2m2/2m3: 0-1 2m4-2m7: 0-0 3m+: 0-0
Track: LH: 0-1 RH: 0-0 Tight: 0-1 Gall: 0-0
Aids: Bl: 0-0 Vi: 0-0 Tstrap: 0-0
Best Rating: 86 3/03 Catt 2m soft NHF

Flat-bred; fourth in modest bumper on debut at Catterick in March.

Montessori Mio (FR)
103   100
4-y-o b g Robellino (USA)-Child s Play (USA) (Sharpen Up)
Mrs M Reveley (M Johnston 21/5) P D Savill

Placings:534530411   (4616)
2002/03: 16⁵GF, 16³GF, 16⁴GS, 16⁵S, 17³GS, 20⁰GS, 16⁴GF, 17¹G, 17¹GF,

	Starts	1st	2nd	3rd	Win & Pl
Hurdles	9	2	0	2	9387
Career Total	9	2	0	2	9387
100 4/03 Carl	2m1f	E Hdl		G-F	£3794
100 4/03 Sedg	2m1f	E Hdl		GD	£3542
			Total win prize-money		£7336

Going: Sf: 0-1 GS: 0-3 Gd: 1-1 GF: - Fm: 1-4
Distance: 2m2/2m3: 2-8 2m4-2m7: 0-1 3m+: 0-0
Track: LH: 1-7 RH: 1-2 Tight: 1-1 Gall: 0-2
Aids: Bl: 0-1 Vi: 0-0 Tstrap: 0-0
Best Rating: 100 4/03 Carl 2m1f gd-fm Hdl

Fair hurdler; broke his duck on his eighth start over hurdles at Sedgefield in April and followed up at Carlisle the same month; yet to prove he stays further than two miles; usually wears cheekpieces, but has worn blinkers; no great battler.

Montezuma
91   69
10-y-o br m Beveled (USA)-Miss Kuwait (The Brianstan)
N A Twiston-Davies A W M Priestley

Placings:0PP/4P3UU0   (3549)
2002/03: 20⁴G, 21²PG, 16³GF, 24⁰S, 21⁰GF, 17⁰G,

	Starts	1st	2nd	3rd	Win & Pl
Hurdles	1	0	0	0	0
Chases	5	0	0	1	735
Career Total	9	0	0	1	735

Monticello (IRE)
(96h)   (76h)
11-y-o ch g Accordion-Erck (Sun Prince)
G F Bridgwater Aubrey Ellis

Placings:002/524/P3115F0/30-PPP   (0446)
2002/03: 17⁵GF, 17⁵GF, 19⁵G,

	Starts	1st	2nd	3rd	Win & Pl
Hurdles	1	0	0	0	0
Chases	2	0	0	0	0
Career Total	18	2	2	2	4789
76 10/00 Extr	2m1f	G(0-95)HHdl		GD	£1696
76 10/00 Extr	2m3f	G(0-95)HHdl		GD	£1687
			Total win prize-money		£3384

Going: Sf: 0-0 GS: 0-0 Gd: 0-1 GF: - Fm: 0-2
Distance: 2m2/2m3: 0-3 2m4-2m7: 0-0 3m+: 0-0
Track: LH: 0-1 RH: 0-2 Tight: 0-1 Gall: 0-0
Aids: Bl: 0-0 Vi: 0-0 Tstrap: 0-0
Best Rating: 82 4/98 Extr 2m2f soft Hdl

Montifault (FR)
107   145
8-y-o ch g Morespeed-Tarde (FR) (Kashtan (FR))
P F Nicholls Mrs A E Fulton

Placings:056/1P13/233121/1P1P-P25P   (4791)
2002/03: 25⁵G, 24²G, 36⁵S, 29⁵G,

	Starts	1st	2nd	3rd	Win & Pl
Chases	4	0	1	0	21129
Career Total	21	6	3	3	94171
134 12/01 Winc	2m5f	B Ch		GD	£11060
152 11/01 Winc	3m1f110yA(0-150)HCh			GD	£26000
127 4/01 Font	2m6f	C Ch		GD	£7410
137 4/01 Asct	3m110y	B Ch		SFT	£10764
115 4/00 Plum	2m5f	E Hdl		HVY	£2674
127 11/99 Worc	2m4f	E Hdl		GD	£2495
			Total win prize-money		£60403

Going: Sf: 0-0 GS: 0-0 Gd: 0-4 GF: - Fm: 0-0
Distance: 2m2/2m3: 0-2 2m4-2m7: 0-0 3m+: 0-4
Track: LH: 0-2 RH: 0-2 Tight: 0-1 Gall: 0-1
Aids: Bl: 0-0 Vi: 0-0 Tstrap: 0-0
Best Rating: 152 11/01 Winc 3m1f110y good Ch

Very useful chaser; can be a bit in and out; ran well for a long way when fifth in the Grand National; acts on any ground; stays three miles plus.

Montoya (IRE)
105   100
4-y-o b g Kylian (USA)-Saborinie (Prince Sabo)
P D Cundell Peter Dimmock

Placings:5043   (4325)
2002/03: 18⁵S, 16⁰G, 16⁴GS, 19³G,

	Starts	1st	2nd	3rd	Win & Pl
Hurdles	4	0	0	1	1127
Career Total	4	0	0	1	1127

Going: Sf: 0-0 GS: 0-1 Gd: 0-3 GF: - Fm: 0-0

Distance: 2m/2m3: 0-4 2m4-2m7: 0-0 3m+: 0-0
Track: LH: 0-2 RH: 0-2 Tight: 0-1 Gall: 0-1
Aids: Bl: 0-0 Vi: 0-0 Tstrap: 0-0
Best Rating: 92   3/03   Newb 2m3f   good   Hdl

Moderate novice hurdler; probably found 2m 3f too far for him on handicap debut; runner-up to long odds-on chance at Worcester next time.

Montpelier (IRE)
93   132

10-y-o b g Montelimar (USA)-Liscarton (Le Bavard (FR))
N J Henderson The 2020 Droxford Partnership

Placings: 40/2F5003/11P0/3112-3   (4313)
2002/03: 18³G,

	Starts	1st	2nd	3rd	Win & Pl
Chases	1	0	0	1	1090
Career Total	17	4	2	3	26719
137	12/01	Chel	2m5f		E(0-125)HCh	GD	£8502
130	12/01	Hrfd	2m3f		E(0-115)HCh	SFT	£3523
124	10/00	Chel	2m4f110yD(0-110)HCh	GD	£5642
111	10/00	Hrfd	2m3f		E(0-105)HCh	GD	£3435
			Total win prize-money £21102

Going: Sf: 0-0 GS: 0-0 Gd: 0-1 GF: - Fm: 0-0
Distance: 2m/2m3: 0-1 2m4-2m7: 0-0 3m+: 0-0
Track: LH: 0-1 RH: 0-0 Tight: 0-0 Gall: 0-1
Aids: Bl: 0-0 Vi: 0-0 Tstrap: 0-0
Best Rating: 137   12/01   Kemp 2m4f110y   good   Ch

Useful chaser; suited by trips of around 2m 4f and acts on any ground; suited by good.

Montreal (FR)
107(109h)   (140h)135

6-y-o b/br g Chamberlin (FR)-Massada (FR) (Kashtan (FR))
M C Pipe D A Johnson

Placings: 3/2123P/611035-1225414U3   (4779)
2002/03: 19¹G, 19²GF, 20²S, 24⁵G, 24⁴G, 22¹GF, 20⁴G, 16ᵁG, 20³GF,

	Starts	1st	2nd	3rd	Win & Pl
Chases	9	2	2	1	28454
Career Total	21	5	4	4	67717
135	3/03	Hayd	2m6f	D Ch	G-F	£9440
135	11/02	Extr	2m3f110yD Ch	GD	£6162
134	12/01	Sand	2m6f	C(0-130)HHdl	SFT	£7410
128	11/01	Asct	3m	B(0-150)HHdl	GD	£8814
115	11/00	Chel	2m110y B Hdl	G-S	£7052
			Total win prize-money £38879

Going: Sf: 0-2 GS: 0-0 Gd: 1-5 GF: - Fm: 1-2
Distance: 2m/2m3: 0-3 **2m4-2m7: 2-6** 3m+: 0-2
Track: LH: 1-5 RH: 1-4 Tight: 0-2 Gall: 0-1
Aids: Bl: 0-0 Vi: 0-2 Tstrap: 0-0
Best Rating: 140   3/02   Chel 3m1f110y   gd-sft   Hdl

Useful staying hurdler/chaser; formerly trained in France; won on his chasing debut at Exeter and at Haydock in March 2003, but beaten in softer ground before running well in the Racing Post Chase and Kim Muir; won two-horse chase at Haydock late in March; effective from two and a half to three miles; acts on most ground.

Montu

6-y-o ch g Gunner B-Promitto (Roaring Riva)
Miss K M George Exterior Profiles Ltd

Placings: 0-00P   (4442)
2002/03: 16⁰G, 16⁰GS, 20ᴾG,

	Starts	1st	2nd	3rd	Win & Pl
NH Flat	2	0	0	0	0
Hurdles	1	0	0	0	0
Career Total	4	0	0		0

Going: Sf: 0-0 GS: 0-1 Gd: 0-2 GF: - Fm: 0-0
Distance: 2m/2m3: 0-2 2m4-2m7: 0-1 3m+: 0-0
Track: LH: 0-1 RH: 0-0 Tight: 0-0 Gall: 0-0
Aids: Bl: 0-0 Vi: 0-0 Tstrap: 0-0
Best Rating: 95   10/02   Chep 2m110y   good   NHF

Monty Be Quick
87   69

7-y-o ch g Mon Tresor-Spartiquick (Spartan General)
J M Castle J M Castle

Placings: 600-0003F3   (4716)
2002/03: 16⁰G, 16⁰G, 16⁰G, 19³F, 19ᶠGF, 16³F,

	Starts	1st	2nd	3rd	Win & Pl
NH Flat	1	0	0	0	0
Hurdles	5	0	0	2	1172
Career Total	9	0	0	2	1172

Going: Sf: 0-0 GS: 0-1 Gd: 0-2 GF: - Fm: 0-3
Distance: 2m/2m3: 0-2 2m4-2m7: 0-2 3m+: 0-1
Track: LH: 0-1 RH: 0-5 Tight: 0-2 Gall: 0-1
Aids: Bl: 0-0 Vi: 0-0 Tstrap: 0-4
Best Rating: 87   4/02   Hntg 2m110y   gd-fm   NHF

Some improvement when stepped up to two and a half miles; may be suited by even further.

Monty Flood (IRE)
78   56

6-y-o b g Camden Town-Clonroche Artic (Pauper)
Ferdy Murphy J Taqvi

Placings: 60   (3771)
2002/03: 16⁶S, 16⁰GS,

	Starts	1st	2nd	3rd	Win & Pl
Hurdles	2	0	0	0	0
Career Total	2	0	0	0	0

Going: Sf: 0-1 GS: 0-1 Gd: 0-0 GF: - Fm: 0-0
Distance: 2m/2m3: 0-2 2m4-2m7: 0-0 3m+: 0-0
Track: LH: 0-2 RH: 0-0 Tight: 0-0 Gall: 0-0
Aids: Bl: 0-0 Vi: 0-0 Tstrap: 0-0
Best Rating: 56   12/02   Hayd 2m   soft   Hdl

Monty Wolley (IRE)
40

5-y-o b g Turtle Island (IRE)-Sakanda (IRE) (Vayrann)
C Grant (Noel Meade 17/10) Mrs M J B Cookson

Placings: 0:00F   (4167)
2002/03: 16⁰YS, 16⁰GS, 16ᶠGS,

	Starts	1st	2nd	3rd	Win & Pl
Hurdles	3	0	0	0	0
Career Total	4	0	0		0

Going: Sf: 0-0 GS: 0-2 Gd: 0-0 GF: - Fm: 0-0
Distance: 2m/2m3: 0-3 2m4-2m7: 0-0 3m+: 0-0
Track: LH: 0-2 RH: 0-0 Tight: 0-0 Gall: 0-1
Aids: Bl: 0-0 Vi: 0-0 Tstrap: 0-0
Best Rating: 40   8/02   Kbgn 2m   yld-sft   Hdl

Monty's Double (IRE)
100   99

6-y-o b g Montelimar (USA)-Macamore Rose (Torus)
O Sherwood W S Watt

Placings: 5-4   (1924)
2002/03: 21⁴GS,

	Starts	1st	2nd	3rd	Win & Pl
Hurdles	1	0	0	0	273
Career Total	2	0	0		273

Going: Sf: 0-0 GS: 0-1 Gd: 0-0 GF: - Fm: 0-0
Distance: 2m/2m3: 0-0 2m4-2m7: 0-1 3m+: 0-0
Track: LH: 0-0 RH: 0-1 Tight: 0-0 Gall: 0-0
Aids: Bl: 0-0 Vi: 0-0 Tstrap: 0-0
Best Rating: 100   11/02   Ludl   2m5f   gd-sft   Hdl

Monty's Pass (IRE)
113(89h)   (112h)159+

10-y-o b g Montelimar (USA)-Friars Pass (Monksfield)
James Joseph Mangan Dee Racing Syndicate

Placings: 21/22460212421/4531323PF03/1326212336552-23P6313641   (4479)
2002/03: 20²G, 20³S, 20ᴾGF, 22⁶Y, 20³GF, 24¹F, 24³G, 16⁶HY, 16⁴Y, 36¹G,

	Starts	1st	2nd	3rd	Win & Pl
Hurdles	4	0	1	1	2077
Chases	6	2	0	2	406696
Career Total	47	8	12	10	511881
159	4/03	Aint	4m4f	A HCh	GD	£348000
142	9/02	List	3m	HCh	FRM	£51748
133	8/01	Tral	2m4f	HCh	GD	£18346
122	5/01	Tipp	2m4f	(0-130)HCh	G-F	£7233
108	6/00	Gowr	2m4f	(0-102)HCh	G-Y	£3588
102	4/00	List	2m4f	(0-95)HCh	SH	£4416
97	12/99	DRoy	2m4f	(0-102)HCh	HVY	£2464
101	4/99	Cork	3m	Ch	SH	£3069
			Total win prize-money £438866

Going: Sf: 0-2 GS: 0-0 Gd: 1-3 GF: - Fm: 1-3
Distance: 2m/2m3: 0-2 2m4-2m7: 0-5 **3m+: 2-3**
Track: **LH: 2-3** RH: 0-3 **Tight: 1-1** Gall: 0-0
Aids: Bl: 0-0 Vi: 0-0 Tstrap: 0-0
Best Rating: 159   4/03   Aint 4m4f   good   Ch

Smart Irish chaser; runner-up in the 2002 Topham; returned to land the 2003 Grand National, never putting a foot wrong and coming right away at the end; stays exceptionally well; acts on most types of ground.

Monty's Quest (IRE)
106(100h)   (89h)102

8-y-o b g Montelimar (USA)-A Bit Of Luck (IRE) (Good Thyne (USA))
P Beaumont Graham Frankland

Placings: 06/232/0-54F14   (4753)
2002/03: 20⁵G, 21⁴GS, 25ᶠS, 25¹G, 24⁴G,

	Starts	1st	2nd	3rd	Win & Pl
Hurdles	1	0	0	0	
Chases	4	1	0	0	5128
Career Total	11	1	2	1	6842
91	4/03	Hexm	3m1f	E Ch	GD	£4030
			Total win prize-money £4030

Going: Sf: 0-1 GS: 0-1 Gd: 1-3 GF: - Fm: 0-0
Distance: 2m/2m3: 0-0 2m4-2m7: 0-2 **3m+: 1-3**
Track: LH: 1-3 RH: 0-2 Tight: 0-2 Gall: 0-0

Aids: Bl: 0-0 Vi: 0-0 Tstrap: 0-0
Best Rating: 98 9/00 Uttx 2m6f110y gd-sft Hdl

Plating-class chaser; stays beyond three miles and acts on any ground.

Monty's Theme (IRE)
79   54

9-y-o b/br g Montelimar (USA)-Theme Music (Tudor Music)
P Wegmann P Wegmann

Placings:3/3F1145P-45650P   (3746)
2002/03: 17⁴G, 16⁵G, 16⁶GF, 22⁵G, 20⁰S, 24⁰G,

	Starts	1st	2nd	3rd	Win & Pl
Chases	6	0	0	0	311
Career Total	14	2	0	2	8530
106	8/01	Font	2m6f	E(0-105)HCh	G-F	£3201
101	7/01	NAbb	2m5f110yE Ch		GD	£3444

Total win prize-money £6645

Going: Sf: 0-1 GS: 0-0 Gd: 0-4 GF: - Fm: 0-1
Distance: 2m/2m3: 0-3 2m4-2m7: 0-2 3m+: 0-1
Track: LH: 0-3 RH: 0-2 Tight: 0-1 Gall: 0-1
Aids: Bl: 0-0 Vi: 0-1 Tstrap: 0-0
Best Rating: 106 8/01 Font 2m6f   gd-fm Ch

Very moderate chaser; won his first three starts in point to points. Acts on a sound surface. Won a maiden chase and a novice event when with Paul Nicholls. Stays three miles.

Montys Tag (IRE)

10-y-o b g Montelimar (USA)-Herbal Lady (Good Thyne (USA))
S R Andrews R Andrews

Placings:3/132-21114   (4443)
2002/03: 24²G, 25¹S, 28¹G, 22¹G, 19⁴G,

	Starts	1st	2nd	3rd	Win & Pl
Chases	5	3	1	0	15895
Career Total	9	4	2	2	18009
118	3/03	Newb	2m6f110yH Ch		GD	£1985
107	5/02	Strf	3m4f	H Ch	GD	£10452
104	5/02	Towc	3m1f	H Ch	SFT	£2996
104	2/02	Folk	2m5f	H Ch	SFT	£1079

Total win prize-money £16512

Going: Sf: 1-1 GS: 0-0 Gd: 2-4 GF: - Fm: 0-0
Distance: 2m/2m3: 0-0 2m4-2m7: 1-2 3m+: 2-3
Track: LH: 2-3 RH: 1-2 Tight: 1-2 Gall: 1-1
Aids: Bl: 0-0 Vi: 0-0 Tstrap: 0-0
Best Rating: 118 3/03 Newb 2m6f110y good Ch

Smart hunter chaser; stays 3m 4f and is effective on good ground; landed the prestigious John Corbet Cup at Stratford in May 2002.

Moody Blues (IRE)
87(89h)   (79h)68

9-y-o ch g Orchestra-Blue Rainbow (Balinger)
A M Hales Andrew L Cohen

Placings:3PF-5U6PP   (3561)
2002/03: 24⁵S, 25⁴S, 24⁶GS, 33⁵S, 25⁶S,

	Starts	1st	2nd	3rd	Win & Pl
Hurdles	1	0	0	0	0
Chases	4	0	0	0	0
Career Total	8	0	0	1	487

Going: Sf: 0-4 GS: 0-1 Gd: 0-0 GF: - Fm: 0-0

Distance: 2m/2m3: 0-0 2m4-2m7: 0-0 3m+: 0-5
Track: LH: 0-1 RH: 0-4 Tight: 0-3 Gall: 0-1
Aids: Bl: 0-1 Vi: 0-0 Tstrap: 0-0
Best Rating: 105 1/02 Hntg 3m   gd-sft Ch

A winning pointer in Ireland, he has shown only a little over fences so far. Stays well.

Moody Style (IRE)

6-y-o b m Desert Style (IRE)-Elle Meme (Ela-Mana-Mou)
Mrs J Scrivens Mrs J Scrivens

Placings:P   (0248)
2002/03: 17⁵G,

	Starts	1st	2nd	3rd	Win & Pl
NH Flat	1	0	0	0	
Career Total	1	0	0	0	

Going: Sf: 0-0 GS: 0-0 Gd: 0-1 GF: - Fm: 0-0
Distance: 2m/2m3: 0-1 2m4-2m7: 0-0 3m+: 0-0
Track: LH: 0-0 RH: 0-1 Tight: 0-0 Gall: 0-0
Aids: Bl: 0-0 Vi: 0-0 Tstrap: 0-0
Best Rating: 0 5/02 Extr 2m1f   good NHF

Moon At Night

8-y-o gr g Pursuit Of Love-La Nureyeva (USA) (Nureyev (USA))
Mrs P Ford (W S Kittow 5/9) Trevor Grist

Placings:P   (2374)
2002/03: 16⁵S,

	Starts	1st	2nd	3rd	Win & Pl
Hurdles	1	0	0	0	
Career Total	1	0	0	0	

Going: Sf: 0-1 GS: 0-0 Gd: 0-0 GF: - Fm: 0-0
Distance: 2m/2m3: 0-1 2m4-2m7: 0-0 3m+: 0-0
Track: LH: 0-1 RH: 0-0 Tight: 0-0 Gall: 0-0
Aids: Bl: 0-0 Vi: 0-0 Tstrap: 0-0
Best Rating: 0 12/02 Wwck 2m   soft Hdl

Moon Colony
103   93

10-y-o b g Top Ville-Honeymooning (USA) (Blushing Groom (FR))
A L Forbes Tony Forbes

Placings:0/00235/235-6245U3   (1456)
2002/03: 16⁶GF, 20²G, 16⁴GF, 21⁵G, 20⁰G, 24³F,

	Starts	1st	2nd	3rd	Win & Pl
Hurdles	6	0	1	1	1630
Career Total	15	0	3	3	3896

Going: Sf: 0-0 GS: 0-0 Gd: 0-3 GF: - Fm: 0-3
Distance: 2m/2m3: 0-2 2m4-2m7: 0-0 3m+: 0-1
Track: LH: 0-5 RH: 0-1 Tight: 0-3 Gall: 0-0
Aids: Bl: 0-0 Vi: 0-0 Tstrap: 0-0
Best Rating: 93 9/02 Sthl 2m5f110y good Hdl

Moderate handicap hurdler; finally broke his duck when making all in 2m handicap hurdle on heavy ground at Uttoxeter May 2003; acts on ground good and softer; stays 2m 4f.

Moon Glow (IRE)
102(100h)   (100h)117

7-y-o b g Fayruz-Jarmar Moon (Unfuwain (USA))

J Gallagher Mrs V W Jones

Placings:150/4P/0543FP620500-42332P14143   (4523)
2002/03: 17⁴G, 16²F, 16³G, 16³GF, 16²GF, 16⁶GF, 16¹GF, 17⁴GF, 17¹G, 16⁴GF, 16³G,

	Starts	1st	2nd	3rd	Win & Pl
Chases	11	2	2	3	13843
Career Total	28	3	3	4	18345
110	9/02	Plum	2m1f	E(0-105)HCh	GD	£4095
102	8/02	NAbb	2m110y	D(0-125)HCh	G-F	£4867
94	10/99	Weth	2m	D Hdl	G-F	£3129

Total win prize-money £12091

Going: Sf: 0-0 GS: 0-0 Gd: 1-4 GF: - Fm: 1-7
Distance: 2m/2m3: 2-11 2m4-2m7: 0-0 3m+: 0-0
Track: LH: 2-8 RH: 0-3 Tight: 2-6 Gall: 0-1
Aids: Bl: 0-7 Vi: 0-0 Tstrap: 0-0
Best Rating: 110 4/03 Uttx 2m   good Ch

Fair chaser; won at Plumpton and Newton Abbot in 2002; pulled up after being kicked in running at Worcester May 2003; bounced back when winning 2m handicap at Newton Abbot next time; likes fast ground; yet to win when wearing blinkers.

Moon Island
89   48

9-y-o b m Jupiter Island-Wild Moon (Belfalas)
S J Gilmore Mrs Vera Steggles

Placings:00/0P006-000   (0444)
2002/03: 16⁶GS, 21⁰GF, 20⁰G, 19⁰G,

	Starts	1st	2nd	3rd	Win & Pl
Hurdles	4	0	0	0	0
Career Total	10	0	0	0	0

Going: Sf: 0-0 GS: 0-1 Gd: 0-2 GF: - Fm: 0-1
Distance: 2m/2m3: 0-1 2m4-2m7: 0-3 3m+: 0-0
Track: LH: 0-1 RH: 0-3 Tight: 0-0 Gall: 0-1
Aids: Bl: 0-3 Vi: 0-1 Tstrap: 0-0
Best Rating: 48 6/02 Hrfd 2m3f110y good Hdl

Moon Rising

11-y-o b g Primitive Rising (USA)-Saucy Moon (Saucy Kit)
R Dench R Dench

Placings:P   (0315)
2002/03: 21⁰G,

	Starts	1st	2nd	3rd	Win & Pl
Chases	1	0	0	0	
Career Total	1	0	0	0	

Going: Sf: 0-0 GS: 0-0 Gd: 0-1 GF: - Fm: 0-0
Distance: 2m/2m3: 0-0 2m4-2m7: 0-1 3m+: 0-0
Track: LH: 0-0 RH: 0-1 Tight: 0-1 Gall: 0-0
Aids: Bl: 0-1 Vi: 0-0 Tstrap: 0-0
Best Rating: 0 5/02 Folk 2m5f   good Ch

Moon Royale
91   62

5-y-o ch m Royal Abjar (USA)-Ragged Moon (Raga Navarro (ITY))
Mrs N Macauley (Denys Smith 15/10) B Batey

Placings:0-0   (1162)
2002/03: 17⁰GF,

	Starts	1st	2nd	3rd	Win & Pl
Hurdles	1	0	0	0	

Career Total   **2**   **0**   **0**   **0**

Going:	Sf: 0-0 GS: 0-0 Gd: 0-0 GF: - Fm: 0-1
Distance:	2m/2m3: 0-1 2m4-2m7: 0-0 3m+: 0-0
Track:	LH: 0-1 RH: 0-0 Tight: 0-1 Gall: 0-0
Aids:	Bl: 0-0 Vi: 0-0 Tstrap: 0-0
Best Rating:	62 9/02 Sedg 2m1f gd-fm Hdl

Moon Spinner
106   **91**

6-y-o b m Elmaamul (USA)-Lunabelle (Idiots Delight)
J M Bradley (J Neville 21/11) Miss Derien Edwards

Placings:51224-003202300402064   (4597)
2002/03: 20⁹GF, 16⁹GF, 16⁹S, 16²GF, 17⁹G, 16²GF, 24³G, 19⁹S,
19⁹S, 17⁴G, 19⁹S, 17²GS, 21⁹G, 19⁶GF, 17⁴GF,

	Starts	1st	2nd	3rd	Win & Pl
Hurdles	15	0	3	2	4470
Career Total	20	1	5	2	7891
90	7/01	Worc	2m	H NHF	GD	£1477

Total win prize-money £1477

Going:	Sf: 0-4 GS: 0-1 Gd: 0-4 GF: - Fm: 0-6
Distance:	2m/2m3: 0-9 2m4-2m7: 0-5 3m+: 0-1
Track:	LH: 0-6 RH: 0-9 Tight: 0-4 Gall: 0-1
Aids:	Bl: 0-0 Vi: 0-0 Tstrap: 0-7
Best Rating:	96 2/02 Hntg 2m110y soft Hdl

Bumper winner; placed a number of times over hurdles; has become rather disappointing; took advantage of a drop in grade when winning 2m mares only novices seller at Stratford May 2003; stays 2m 4f; seems to act on most types of ground.

Mooning (IRE)
67f   **39f**

4-y-o ch f Moonax (IRE)-Miss Ming (Tender King)
S Gollings Michael Lowe

Placings:0   (4788)
2002/03: 17⁰G,

	Starts	1st	2nd	3rd	Win & Pl
NH Flat	1	0	0	0	
Career Total	1	0	0	0	

Going:	Sf: 0-0 GS: 0-0 Gd: 0-1 GF: - Fm: 0-0
Distance:	2m/2m3: 0-1 2m4-2m7: 0-0 3m+: 0-0
Track:	LH: 0-0 RH: 0-1 Tight: 0-1 Gall: 0-0
Aids:	Bl: 0-0 Vi: 0-0 Tstrap: 0-0
Best Rating:	39 4/03 MRas 2m1f110y good NHF

Moonlighting
94   (80c)**63**

6-y-o b m Lugana Beach-White Flash (Sure Blade (USA))
Mrs N S Sharpe (B R Johnson 15/5) B Owen

Placings:6UP-P4043   (4675)
2002/03: 16⁶G, 16⁶S, 17⁴G, 17⁰S, 19⁴GF, 17³GF,

	Starts	1st	2nd	3rd	Win & Pl
Hurdles	6	0	0	1	334
Career Total	8	0	0	1	334

Going:	Sf: 0-2 GS: 0-0 Gd: 0-2 GF: - Fm: 0-2
Distance:	2m/2m3: 0-5 2m4-2m7: 0-3 3m+: 0-0
Track:	LH: 0-2 RH: 0-4 Tight: 0-2 Gall: 0-0
Aids:	Bl: 0-0 Vi: 0-0 Tstrap: 0-1
Best Rating:	70 4/02 Plum 2m1f gd-fm Ch

Plating-class hurdler; often wears cheekpieces.

Moonlit Harbour
108f   **88f**

4-y-o b g Bal Harbour-Nuit De Lune (FR) (Crystal Palace (FR))
M W Easterby Steve Hull

Placings:133   (4437)
2002/03: 16¹G, 16³GF, 16³G,

	Starts	1st	2nd	3rd	Win & Pl
NH Flat	3	1	0	2	3049
Career Total	3	1	0	2	3049
88	3/03	Weth	2m	H NHF	GD	£2478

Total win prize-money £2478

Going:	Sf: 0-0 GS: 0-0 Gd: 1-2 GF: - Fm: 0-1
Distance:	2m/2m3: 1-3 2m4-2m7: 0-0 3m+: 0-0
Track:	LH: 1-3 RH: 0-0 Tight: 0-0 Gall: 0-0
Aids:	Bl: 0-0 Vi: 0-0 Tstrap: 0-0
Best Rating:	88 4/03 Newc 2m good NHF

Moderate bmper performer; took a bumper on debut at Wetherby in March and third under a penalty there two weeks later; well beaten third at Newcastle next time.

Moonlite Magic (IRE)
95(101h)   **75**

9-y-o br g Phardante (FR)-Lucey Allen (Strong Gale)
Ferdy Murphy John Duddy

Placings:3500/F02251U04-U6040   (2164)
2002/03: 25⁰G, 21⁶G, 27⁰G, 27⁴S, 27⁰S,

	Starts	1st	2nd	3rd	Win & Pl
Chases	5	0	0	0	262
Career Total	18	1	2	1	3359
93	11/01	Sedg	3m3f110yG(0-90)HHdl	SFT	£1547

Total win prize-money £1547

Going:	Sf: 0-2 GS: 0-0 Gd: 0-3 GF: - Fm: 0-0
Distance:	2m/2m3: 0-0 2m4-2m7: 0-1 3m+: 0-4
Track:	LH: 0-5 RH: 0-0 Tight: 0-4 Gall: 0-0
Aids:	Bl: 0-4 Vi: 0-0 Tstrap: 0-0
Best Rating:	97 10/00 Sthl 2m soft NHF

He is suited by marathon trips and soft ground. Has run well in blinkers.

Moonshine Bay (IRE)
(109h)   (105h)**131**

9-y-o b g Executive Perk-Sister Of Slane (The Parson)
J T Gifford Mrs Timothy Pilkington

Placings:06/30114/125040/3R23113F-F6   (3751)
2002/03: 20⁶GS, 21⁶G,

	Starts	1st	2nd	3rd	Win & Pl
Hurdles	1	0	0	0	345
Chases	1	0	0	0	0
Career Total	23	5	2	4	27091
131	3/02	Font	2m4f	D Ch	SFT	£4010
131	1/02	Font	2m4f	E Ch	GD	£3276
122	11/00	Winc	2m	D(0-120)HHdl	SFT	£5265
114	3/99	Sand	2m110y	D Hdl	G-S	£2905
100	11/98	Folk	2m1f110yE Hdl	SFT	£2264

Total win prize-money £17722

Going:	Sf: 0-0 GS: 0-1 Gd: 0-1 GF: - Fm: 0-0
Distance:	2m/2m3: 0-0 2m4-2m7: 0-3 3m+: 0-0
Track:	LH: 0-0 RH: 0-2 Tight: 0-0 Gall: 0-0
Aids:	Bl: 0-0 Vi: 0-0 Tstrap: 0-0
Best Rating:	131 3/02 Font 2m4f soft Ch

Useful chaser; fair hurdler; suited by two and a half miles on good/good to soft ground.

Moonzie Laird (IRE)
91f   **99f**

5-y-o b/br g Good Thyne (USA)-Sweet Roselier (IRE) (Roselier (FR))
J N R Billinge Sceptre House Golf Society

Placings:10   (4778)
2002/03: 16¹S, 16⁰G,

	Starts	1st	2nd	3rd	Win & Pl
NH Flat	2	1	0	0	2215
Career Total	2	1	0	0	2215
99	3/03	Ayr	2m	H NHF	SFT	£2214

Total win prize-money £2215

Going:	Sf: 1-1 GS: 0-0 Gd: 0-1 GF: - Fm: 0-0
Distance:	2m/2m3: 1-2 2m4-2m7: 0-0 3m+: 0-0
Track:	LH: 1-1 RH: 0-1 Tight: 0-0 Gall: 0-0
Aids:	Bl: 0-0 Vi: 0-0 Tstrap: 0-0
Best Rating:	99 3/03 Ayr 2m soft NHF

Moor Hall Hopper
61f   **46f**

7-y-o gr g Rock Hopper-Forgiving (Jellaby)
R S Brookhouse R S Brookhouse

Placings:0/00   (0823)
2002/03: 16⁰S, 16⁰GF,

	Starts	1st	2nd	3rd	Win & Pl
NH Flat	2	0	0	0	
Career Total	3	0	0	0	

Going:	Sf: 0-1 GS: 0-0 Gd: 0-0 GF: - Fm: 0-1
Distance:	2m/2m3: 0-2 2m4-2m7: 0-0 3m+: 0-0
Track:	LH: 0-2 RH: 0-0 Tight: 0-0 Gall: 0-0
Aids:	Bl: 0-0 Vi: 0-0 Tstrap: 0-0
Best Rating:	64 11/00 Ludl 2m good NHF

Moor Hall Lady
97   **59**

12-y-o gr m Rambo Dancer (CAN)-Forgiving (Jellaby)
R S Brookhouse R S Brookhouse

Placings:00/452604/6/3F/F61F4150/6533050/236P560-
0056P0P5P   (4786)
2002/03: 20⁰GF, 20⁰GF, 20⁵GF, 22⁶GF, 26⁰GF, 19⁰GF, 19⁰GS,
24⁵F, 22⁰G,

	Starts	1st	2nd	3rd	Win & Pl
Hurdles	9	0	0	0	0
Career Total	42	2	2	4	9707
106	9/99	Bang	2m1f	D Hdl	G-F	£3095
98	7/99	Strf	2m110y	E Hdl	GD	£2999

Total win prize-money £6094

Going:	Sf: 0-0 GS: 0-1 Gd: 0-1 GF: - Fm: 0-7
Distance:	2m/2m3: 0-0 2m4-2m7: 0-7 3m+: 0-2
Track:	LH: 0-3 RH: 0-5 Tight: 0-5 Gall: 0-2
Aids:	Bl: 0-0 Vi: 0-0 Tstrap: 0-0
Best Rating:	106 9/99 Bang 2m1f gd-fm Hdl

Moor Hall Rock
(101h)   (85h)**50**

8-y-o b g Rock Hopper-Forgiving (Jellaby)
R S Brookhouse R S Brookhouse

Placings:P/0000/34060-03SF (1216)
2002/03: 16^{6}G, 20^{3}GF, 20^{5}GF, 21^{6}G,

	Starts	1st	2nd	3rd	Win & Pl
Hurdles	2	0	0	1	357
Chases	2	0	0	0	0
Career Total	14	0	0	2	807

Going: Sf: 0-0 GS: 0-0 Gd: 0-2 GF: - Fm: 0-2
Distance: 2m/2m3: 0-1 2m4-2m7: 0-3 3m+: 0-0
Track: LH: 0-3 RH: 0-1 Tight: 0-1 Gall: 0-1
Aids: Bl: 0-3 Vi: 0-0 Tstrap: 0-0
Best Rating: 91 10/00 Chel 2m110y good NHF

Modest maiden hurdler, has shown a little ability on good ground.

Moor Lane
104   130
11-y-o b g Primitive Rising (USA)-Navos (Tyrnavos)
A M Balding (I A Balding 31/12) R P B Michaelson

Placings:2/311F/12/51120-4FP61U0 (4324)
2002/03: 24^{4}GS, 27^{F}GS, 26^{6}GS, 26^{6}S, 24^{1}G, 24^{U}G, 24^{0}G,

	Starts	1st	2nd	3rd	Win & Pl
Chases	7	1	0	0	8193
Career Total	19	6	3	1	83428

130 2/03 Kemp 3m D(0-125)HCh GD £6955
138 1/02 Donc 3m A(0-145)HCh SFT £39871
122 1/02 Newb 3m C(0-135)HCh GD £8931
134 9/99 Extr 2m6f110yE(0-115)HCh G-S £4279
124 1/99 Donc 2m3f110yD Ch GD £4211
127 11/98 Newb 2m4f C Ch SFT £7108
Total win prize-money £71356

Going: Sf: 0-1 GS: 0-3 Gd: 1-3 GF: - Fm: 0-0
Distance: 2m/2m3: 0-0 2m4-2m7: 0-0 3m+: 1-7
Track: LH: 0-5 RH: 1-2 Tight: 0-1 Gall: 0-4
Aids: Bl: 0-0 Vi: 0-2 Tstrap: 0-0
Best Rating: 138 3/02 Newb 3m gd-sft Ch

Useful handicap chaser; back to form with a win at Kempton in February 2003; effective at three miles; acts on good ground and faster; usually jumps well.

Moor Spirit
102f   85f
6-y-o b g Nomadic Way (USA)-Navos (Tyrnavos)
R D E Woodhouse J W Walmsley

Placings:4 (3998)
2002/03: 16^{4}G,

	Starts	1st	2nd	3rd	Win & Pl
NH Flat	1	0	0	0	0
Career Total	1	0	0	0	0

Going: Sf: 0-0 GS: 0-0 Gd: 0-1 GF: - Fm: 0-0
Distance: 2m/2m3: 0-1 2m4-2m7: 0-0 3m+: 0-0
Track: LH: 0-1 RH: 0-0 Tight: 0-0 Gall: 0-0
Aids: Bl: 0-0 Vi: 0-0 Tstrap: 0-0
Best Rating: 85 3/03 Weth 2m good NHF

Half-brother to Moor Lane; showed some ability on debut in bumper at Wetherby in March.

Moore's Law (USA)
110   126
5-y-o b g Technology (USA)-Brass Needles (USA) (Twice Worthy)
M J Grassick R Sanz

Placings:226-231202 (4725a)

2002/03: 16^{2}G, 21^{3}GS, 20^{1}GF, 20^{2}YS, 21^{0}G, 18^{2}GF,

	Starts	1st	2nd	3rd	Win & Pl
Hurdles	6	1	3	1	13131
Career Total	9	1	5	1	20809

115 12/02 Muss 2m4f E Hdl G-F £3737
Total win prize-money £3738

Going: Sf: 0-0 GS: 0-1 Gd: 0-2 GF: - Fm: 1-2
Distance: 2m/2m3: 0-2 2m4-2m7: 1-4 3m+: 0-0
Track: LH: 0-3 RH: 1-2 Tight: 1-1 Gall: 0-2
Aids: Bl: 0-0 Vi: 0-0 Tstrap: 0-0
Best Rating: 126 4/03 Fair 2m2f gd-fm Hdl

Irish novice hurdler; got off the mark over timber with an easy victory in a maiden hurdle at Musselburgh in December 2002; stays two miles five furlongs; acts on good ground but handles softer.

Moorhall (IRE)
79   81
4-y-o b g Persian Bold-Never Told (IRE) (Classic Secret (USA))
J G Cosgrave (Graham John McKeever 28/12) F Thompson

Placings:004 (4489a)
2002/03: 16^{0}G, 16^{0}GS, 16^{4}GF,

	Starts	1st	2nd	3rd	Win & Pl
Hurdles	3	0	0	0	260
Career Total	3	0	0	0	260

Going: Sf: 0-0 GS: 0-1 Gd: 0-1 GF: - Fm: 0-1
Distance: 2m/2m3: 0-3 2m4-2m7: 0-0 3m+: 0-0
Track: LH: 0-1 RH: 0-1 Tight: 0-1 Gall: 0-1
Aids: Bl: 0-0 Vi: 0-0 Tstrap: 0-1
Best Rating: 81 4/03 Tram 2m gd-fm Hdl

Moorland Highflyer
12-y-o b/br g Karlinsky (USA)-Moorland Heath Vii (Damsire Unregistered)
T Long Unity Farm Holiday Centre Ltd

Placings:F4U/U241F43122125/PUPP/U3F5P2PP3/0P0-P (0317)
2002/03: 34^{6}PG,

	Starts	1st	2nd	3rd	Win & Pl
Chases	1	0	0	0	
Career Total	33	3	5	3	19762

108 4/99 Chep 3m2f110yD(0-120)HCh SFT £4162
102 1/99 Ludl 3m E(0-115)HCh G-S £3582
96 6/98 NAbb 3m2f110yE(0-110)HCh GD £3550
Total win prize-money £11296

Going: Sf: 0-0 GS: 0-0 Gd: 0-1 GF: - Fm: 0-0
Distance: 2m/2m3: 0-0 2m4-2m7: 0-0 3m+: 0-1
Track: LH: 0-1 RH: 0-0 Tight: 0-0 Gall: 0-0
Aids: Bl: 0-0 Vi: 0-0 Tstrap: 0-1
Best Rating: 115 4/99 Chel 3m2f110y good Ch

Moorland Rose
8-y-o br m Lir-Moorland Heath Vii (Damsire Unregistered)
Miss P D Mitchell Miss P D Mitchell

Placings:5 (0347)
2002/03: 26^{5}GS,

	Starts	1st	2nd	3rd	Win & Pl
Chases	1	0	0	0	0
Career Total	1	0	0	0	0

Going: Sf: 0-0 GS: 0-0 Gd: 1-4 GF: - Fm: 1-4
Distance: 2m/2m3: 0-2 2m4-2m7: 2-5 3m+: 0-1
Track: LH: 2-5 RH: 0-3 Tight: 1-3 Gall: 0-1

Going: Sf: 0-0 GS: 0-1 Gd: 0-0 GF: - Fm: 0-0
Distance: 2m/2m3: 0-0 2m4-2m7: 0-0 3m+: 0-1
Track: LH: 0-1 RH: 0-0 Tight: 0-1 Gall: 0-0
Aids: Bl: 0-0 Vi: 0-0 Tstrap: 0-0
Best Rating: 38 5/02 NAbb 3m2f110y gd-sft Ch

Moorlands Again
109(104h)   (85h)122
8-y-o b g Then Again-Sandford Springs (USA) (Robellino (USA))
C Tizzard Mrs Lynda M Williams

Placings:55/0-212F5 (4113)
2002/03: 25^{2}HY, 26^{1}S, 26^{2}S, 24^{5}GS, 32^{5}G,

	Starts	1st	2nd	3rd	Win & Pl
Hurdles	1	0	1	0	1684
Chases	4	1	1	0	7593
Career Total	8	1	2	0	9277

110 2/03 Font 3m2f110yE Ch SFT £4368
Total win prize-money £4368

Going: Sf: 1-3 GS: 0-1 Gd: 0-1 GF: - Fm: 0-0
Distance: 2m/2m3: 0-0 2m4-2m7: 0-0 3m+: 1-5
Track: LH: 0-3 RH: 0-0 Tight: 1-2 Gall: 0-0
Aids: Bl: 0-0 Vi: 0-0 Tstrap: 0-0
Best Rating: 122 3/03 Chel 4m good Ch

Modest hurdler but much better over fences from what we've seen so far; winner at Fontwell, he went down fighting at Plumpton next time to a useful rival; gets three miles plus; jumps fluently; acts on heavy ground.

Moqui Marble (GER)
88   57
7-y-o b g Petit Loup (USA)-Margo s New Hope (USA) (Cannonade (USA))
B J Curley (D E Cantillon 11/1) Mrs B J Curley

Placings:00/0-0 (4143)
2002/03: 16^{0}G,

	Starts	1st	2nd	3rd	Win & Pl
Hurdles	1	0	0	0	
Career Total	4	0	0	0	

Going: Sf: 0-0 GS: 0-0 Gd: 0-1 GF: - Fm: 0-0
Distance: 2m/2m3: 0-2 2m4-2m7: 0-0 3m+: 0-0
Track: LH: 0-1 RH: 0-0 Tight: 0-1 Gall: 0-0
Aids: Bl: 0-0 Vi: 0-0 Tstrap: 0-0
Best Rating: 57 3/03 Fknm 2m good Hdl

Moral Justice (IRE)
107   100
10-y-o b g Lafontaine (USA)-Proven Right (IRE) (Kemal (FR))
S J Gilmore Miss Jumbo Frost

Placings:0f52122PP-32112PPP (4676)
2002/03: 19^{3}GD, 20^{4}G, 21^{1}G, 21^{1}GF, 25^{2}G, 21^{8}GF, 20^{8}G, 19^{8}GF,

	Starts	1st	2nd	3rd	Win & Pl
Chases	8	2	2	1	14457
Career Total	17	4	5	1	27509

102 6/02 Uttx 2m5f C Ch G-F £6968
102 6/02 NAbb 2m5f110yD Ch GD £4357
109 9/01 Fair 2m Hdl FRM £5564
105 8/01 Kbgn 2m NHF GD £3616
Total win prize-money £20508

Aids: Bl: 0-0 Vi: 0-1 Tstrap: 0-0
Best Rating: 122 10/01 Gowr 2m6f   good   Ch

Moderate chaser, winner twice in June 2002; took advantage of having dropped 15lb in the handicap when all out to win a handicap at Newton Abbot June 2003; best on fast ground; effective at up to an extended 2m 5f; suited by forcing tactics.

Moral Support (IRE)
106(99h)   (118h)118
11-y-o ch g Zaffaran (USA)-Marians Pride (Pry)
J S Moore Tom & Evelyn Yates

Placings:4010/42F/345150P6/1111236B/23PP-0P02P
                                                        (4307)
2002/03: 26⁰GS, 24PHY, 26⁹HY, 24²S, 32PG,

	Starts	1st	2nd	3rd	Win & Pl
Chases	5	0	1	0	3685
Career Total	32	6	4	3	74646
143 12/00 Chep	3m	A HCh		HVY	£21000
125 11/00 Hntg	3m6f110yC(0-130)HCh		G-S		£6955
129 11/00 Newb	3m	D(0-110)HCh		SFT	£4368
125 11/00 Kemp	3m	D(0-110)HCh		SFT	£4777
104 2/00 Thur	3m	(0-95)HHdl		HVY	£3588
102 3/97 Tipp	2m4f	Hdl		G-Y	£3391
		Total win prize-money £44080			

Going: Sf: 0-3 GS: 0-1 Gd: 0-1 GF: - Fm: 0-0
Distance: 2m/2m3: 0-0 2m4-2m7: 0-0 3m+: 0-5
Track: LH: 0-5 RH: 0-0 Tight: 0-1 Gall: 0-2
Aids: Bl: 0-0 Vi: 0-0 Tstrap: 0-0
Best Rating: 143 2/01 Hayd 3m   heavy   Ch

Decent staying chaser in 2000; on the decline since, but better run at Newbury in March 2003; stays marathon trips; acts on soft ground.

Mordon Boy (IRE)

11-y-o ch g Persian Mews-Kindly (Tarqogan)
David Pearson David Pearson

Placings:50/40/2265064/013U/P1P04-4P   (4288)
2002/03: 24⁴GF, 20PGF,

	Starts	1st	2nd	3rd	Win & Pl
Chases	2	0	0	0	800
Career Total	22	2	2	1	11415
109 5/01 Weth	3m1f	F(0-110)HCh	FRM	£3167
106 9/00 Bang	3m110y	F(0-100)HCh	G-F	£4290
		Total win prize-money £7458		

Going: Sf: 0-0 GS: 0-0 Gd: 0-0 GF: - Fm: 0-2
Distance: 2m/2m3: 0-0 2m4-2m7: 0-0 3m+: 0-1
Track: LH: 0-1 RH: 0-1 Tight: 0-2 Gall: 0-0
Aids: Bl: 0-0 Vi: 0-0 Tstrap: 0-0
Best Rating: 113 1/01 Catt 3m1f110y gd-sft Ch

Modest chaser; suited by three miles, he tends to struggle when the going gets soft.

More Tears (IRE)
97(94h)   (61h)92
7-y-o b g Witness Box (USA)-Anyone s Fancy (Callernish)
N J Hawke M J Disney

Placings:FF0/PF35-UF3F   (2608)
2002/03: 23⁴⁰G, 21FS, 23³GS, 24FS,

	Starts	1st	2nd	3rd	Win & Pl
Chases	4	0	0	1	687
Career Total	11	0	0	2	1039

Going: Sf: 0-2 GS: 0-1 Gd: 0-1 GF: - Fm: 0-0
Distance: 2m/2m3: 0-0 2m4-2m7: 0-1 3m+: 0-3
Track: LH: 0-2 RH: 0-1 Tight: 0-1 Gall: 0-0
Aids: Bl: 0-0 Vi: 0-0 Tstrap: 0-0
Best Rating: 92 12/02 Extr 2m7f110y gd-sft Ch

Has shown ability over fences, although he is not the best of jumpers.

More Than A Stroll (IRE)
97   152
11-y-o ch g Pennine Walk-Jenny s Child (Crash Course)
A L T Moore Mrs D Grehan

Placings:6433/0330F10/113212/2620313/040414360F-11421P   (4457)
2002/03: 24¹G, 24¹S, 20⁴SH, 22²HY, 20¹YS, 25PG,

	Starts	1st	2nd	3rd	Win & Pl
Chases	6	3	1	0	97121
Career Total	40	9	5	8	203193
147 2/03 Gowr	2m4f	Ch	Y-S	£14772
152 11/02 DRoy	3m	Ch	SFT	£53680
139 10/02 Limk	3m	HCh	GD	£23926
140 9/01 List	3m	HCh	G-F	£48588
131 2/01 Navn	2m4f	HCh	SFT	£12056
118 2/00 Navn	2m4f	HCh	SH	£7800
118 9/99 Gway	2m1f	Ch	SFT	£4312
113 8/99 Tral	2m	Ch	G-Y	£3696
99 4/99 Navn	2m	Hdl	HVY	£3069
		Total win prize-money £171903		

Going: Sf: 1-2 GS: 0-0 Gd: 1-2 GF: - Fm: 0-0
Distance: 2m/2m3: 0-0 2m4-2m7: 1-3 3m+: 2-3
Track: LH: 0-1 RH: 2-4 Tight: 0-1 Gall: 0-0
Aids: Bl: 0-0 Vi: 0-0 Tstrap: 3-6
Best Rating: 152 11/02 DRoy 3m   soft   Ch

Smart Irish-trained chaser; goes well on soft ground as he showed when winning a Grade One at Down Royal and a Grade Three at Gowran, but won the Kerry National at Listowel on good to firm; effective at 2m 4f to 3m; wears a tongue tie.

Morless
83
4-y-o b f Morpeth-Bush Radio (Hot Grove)
J D Frost P Tosh

Placings:P   (2195)
2002/03: 17PGS,

	Starts	1st	2nd	3rd	Win & Pl
Hurdles	1	0	0	0	
Career Total	1	0	0	0	

Going: Sf: 0-0 GS: 0-1 Gd: 0-0 GF: - Fm: 0-0
Distance: 2m/2m3: 0-0 2m4-2m7: 0-0 3m+: 0-0
Track: LH: 0-0 RH: 0-1 Tight: 0-1 Gall: 0-0
Aids: Bl: 0-0 Vi: 0-0 Tstrap: 0-0
Best Rating: 0 11/02 Tntn 2m1f gd-sft Hdl

Morning Flight (IRE)
86   76
7-y-o b m Supreme Leader-Morning Jane (IRE) (Over The River (FR))
Noel T Chance Top Flight Racing (2)

Placings:0P-5   (1232)
2002/03: 16⁵G,

	Starts	1st	2nd	3rd	Win & Pl
Hurdles	1	0	0	0	0

Career Total   3   0   0   0   0

Going: Sf: 0-0 GS: 0-0 Gd: 0-1 GF: - Fm: 0-0
Distance: 2m/2m3: 0-0 2m4-2m7: 0-0 3m+: 0-0
Track: LH: 0-1 RH: 0-0 Tight: 0-0 Gall: 0-0
Aids: Bl: 0-0 Vi: 0-0 Tstrap: 0-0
Best Rating: 76 1/02 Font 2m2f110y good Hdl

Morning Melody
71f   29f
5-y-o b m Afzal-Pacific Overture (Southern Music)
Mrs N S Sharpe Graham Richards

Placings:0   (4628)
2002/03: 17⁰GF,

	Starts	1st	2nd	3rd	Win & Pl
NH Flat	1	0	0	0	
Career Total	1	0	0	0	

Going: Sf: 0-0 GS: 0-0 Gd: 0-0 GF: - Fm: 0-1
Distance: 2m/2m3: 0-1 2m4-2m7: 0-0 3m+: 0-0
Track: LH: 0-1 RH: 0-0 Tight: 0-1 Gall: 0-0
Aids: Bl: 0-0 Vi: 0-0 Tstrap: 0-0
Best Rating: 0 4/03 NAbb 2m1f gd-fm NHF

Morning Mover (IRE)
87   33
10-y-o b g White Christmas-More Tabs (Cantab)
John R Upson A Hartgrove

Placings:6F0006/0   (1172)
2002/03: 22⁰GF,

	Starts	1st	2nd	3rd	Win & Pl
Hurdles	1	0	0	0	
Career Total	7	0	0	0	

Going: Sf: 0-0 GS: 0-0 Gd: 0-0 GF: - Fm: 0-1
Distance: 2m/2m3: 0-0 2m4-2m7: 0-0 3m+: 0-0
Track: LH: 0-1 RH: 0-0 Tight: 0-1 Gall: 0-0
Aids: Bl: 0-0 Vi: 0-0 Tstrap: 0-0
Best Rating: 78 10/99 Navn 2m yld-sft NHF

Morph
91   78
9-y-o gr g Baron Blakeney-Amber Marsh (Arctic Kanda)
R H York R H York

Placings:P0/00-2P   (1338)
2002/03: 24²G, 26PGF,

	Starts	1st	2nd	3rd	Win & Pl
Hurdles	2	0	1	0	636
Career Total	6	0	1	0	636

Going: Sf: 0-0 GS: 0-0 Gd: 0-1 GF: - Fm: 0-1
Distance: 2m/2m3: 0-0 2m4-2m7: 0-0 3m+: 0-2
Track: LH: 0-1 RH: 0-1 Tight: 0-0 Gall: 0-1
Aids: Bl: 0-0 Vi: 0-0 Tstrap: 0-0
Best Rating: 78 9/02 Worc 3m   good   Hdl

Lightly-raced hurdler; runner-up in his only completed point. Showed tremendous improvement when runner-up to a 50/1 shock winner in a three mile maiden hurdle at Worcester September 2002.

Morstock

105   **103**

13-y-o gr g Beveled (USA)-Miss Melmore (Nishapour (FR))
R J Hodges Mrs M Fairbairn

Placings:04335411446/2230340/4U221232636/322146343
U/33F223/45210634003/633F0441/23540603544U-116P
                                                    (0736)
2002/03: 19¹G, 16¹S, 16⁶G, 16ᴾGF,

	Starts	1st	2nd	3rd	Win & Pl
Chases	4	2	0	0	6573
Career Total	80	8	12	18	58465
101	5/02	NAbb	2m110y	F(0-100)HCh	SFT	£2933
96	5/02	Extr	2m3f110yF(0-95)HCh	GD	£3640
110	4/01	Font	2m2f	E(0-115)HCh	GD	£3797
118	12/99	Winc	2m	D(0-120)HCh	SFT	£4143
118	1/98	Kemp	2m	C(0-135)HCh	SFT	£4765
117	11/96	Winc	2m	C(0-135)HHdl	SFT	£3470
107	1/95	Winc	2m	E(0-110)HHdl	GD	£2574
98	12/94	Winc	2m	(0-100)HHdl	GD	£2267

Total win prize-money £27591

Going: Sf: 1-1 GS: 0-0 Gd: 1-2 GF: - Fm: 0-1
Distance: 2m/2m3: 1-3 2m4-2m7: 1-1 3m+: 0-0
Track: LH: 1-3 RH: 1-1 Tight: 1-3 Gall: 0-0
Aids: Bl: 0-0 Vi: 0-0 Tstrap: 0-0
Best Rating: 125 3/97 Chel 2m1f   good   Hdl

Moderate chaser; has always been best around two miles and acts on all types of ground. Took advantage of being dropped in the ratings with back-to-back victories at Exeter and Newton Abbot in May 2002.

Morticia

5-y-o b m Rudimentary (USA)-Valkyrie (Bold Lad (IRE))
M A Barnes J M Crichton

Placings:0-0   (2769)
2002/03: 16⁰GS,

	Starts	1st	2nd	3rd	Win & Pl
NH Flat	1	0	0	0	
Career Total	2	0	0	0	

Going: Sf: 0-0 GS: 0-1 Gd: 0-0 GF: - Fm: 0-0
Distance: 2m/2m3: 0-1 2m4-2m7: 0-0 3m+: 0-0
Track: LH: 0-0 RH: 0-1 Tight: 0-0 Gall: 0-0
Aids: Bl: 0-0 Vi: 0-0 Tstrap: 0-1
Best Rating: 0 12/02 Muss 2m   gd-sft NHF

Moscow Dancer (IRE)

                                                    58

6-y-o ch g Moscow Society (USA)-Cromhill Lady (Miners Lamp)
K Bishop J Stephenson

Placings:000-PP   (3777)
2002/03: 19ᴾGS, 17ᴾGS,

	Starts	1st	2nd	3rd	Win & Pl
Hurdles	2	0	0	0	
Career Total	5	0	0	0	

Going: Sf: 0-0 GS: 0-2 Gd: 0-0 GF: - Fm: 0-0
Distance: 2m/2m3: 0-2 2m4-2m7: 0-0 3m+: 0-0
Track: LH: 0-0 RH: 0-2 Tight: 0-0 Gall: 0-0
Aids: Bl: 0-0 Vi: 0-0 Tstrap: 0-0
Best Rating: 74 1/02 Hayd 2m   soft   NHF

Moscow Express (IRE)

106   **155**

11-y-o ch g Moscow Society (USA)-Corrielek (Menelek)
Miss F M Crowley John Corr

Placings:1//2121111/1433322/0161111425F0U5/11113FF/2
151F433141/3102512P1014-PP4353P   (4499a)
2002/03: 20ᴾG, 25ᴾGS, 20⁴HY, 20³S, 20⁸YS, 20³GY, 24ᴾGY,

	Starts	1st	2nd	3rd	Win & Pl
Chases	7	0	0	2	5688
Career Total	66	24	8	9	302273
140	3/02	Navn	2m4f	Ch		SH	£8889
155	2/02	Gowr	3m	Ch		SFT	£11963
160	11/01	Clon	2m4f	Ch		SFT	£23588
152	7/01	Klny	2m4f	Ch		GD	£8911
160	4/01	Fair	3m1f	Ch		SFT	£66524
152	2/01	Naas	2m	Ch		Y-S	£23588
153	10/00	Thur	2m1f	Ch		G-Y	£4968
130	7/00	Klny	2m4f	Ch		G-F	£5520
142	7/99	Gway	2m6f	HCh		G-F	£35859
144	7/99	Tipp	2m4f	HCh		G-Y	£7366
114	5/99	Cork	2m5f	Ch		G-Y	£4603
120	5/99	Tipp	2m4f	Ch		GD	£3683
136	9/98	List	2m	Ch		G-F	£4184
133	8/98	Tram	2m6f	HCh		G-F	£5978
133	7/98	Gway	2m6f	Ch		YLD	£5679
111	7/98	Klny	2m4f	Ch		GD	£2989
113	6/98	Cork	2m1f	Ch		GD	£3276
144	10/97	Towc	2m	C(0-135)HHdl		G-F	£3387
133	4/97	Fair	2m4f	Hdl		G-F	£6782
122	3/97	Leop	2m4f	Hdl		GD	£3051
122	2/97	Fair	2m4f	Hdl		G-Y	£4069
108	11/96	Punc	2m	Hdl		YLD	£3177
107	10/96	Navn	2m	NHF		GD	£3177
104	4/96	List	2m	NHF		SFT	£3530

Total win prize-money £253751

Going: Sf: 0-2 GS: 0-1 Gd: 0-1 GF: - Fm: 0-0
Distance: 2m/2m3: 0-0 2m4-2m7: 0-5 3m+: 0-2
Track: LH: 0-2 RH: 0-4 Tight: 0-0 Gall: 0-0
Aids: Bl: 0-0 Vi: 0-0 Tstrap: 0-0
Best Rating: 160 11/01 Clon 2m4f   soft   Ch

Smart Irish chaser; not at his best in 2002/3; rather inconsistent; acts on most types of ground; effective between 2m 4f and 3m; tends to make mistakes.

Moscow Fields (IRE)

95f   **109f**

5-y-o ch g Moscow Society (USA)-Cloverlady (Decent Fellow)
Miss H C Knight J D N Tillyard

Placings:2   (3903)
2002/03: 16²S,

	Starts	1st	2nd	3rd	Win & Pl
NH Flat	1	0	1	0	928
Career Total	1	0	1	0	928

Going: Sf: 0-1 GS: 0-0 Gd: 0-0 GF: - Fm: 0-0
Distance: 2m/2m3: 0-1 2m4-2m7: 0-0 3m+: 0-0
Track: LH: 0-1 RH: 0-0 Tight: 0-0 Gall: 0-1
Aids: Bl: 0-0 Vi: 0-0 Tstrap: 0-0
Best Rating: 102 3/03 Newb 2m110y   soft   NHF

Runner-up in soft-ground bumper.

Moscow Flyer (IRE)

118   (170h)**174+**

9-y-o b g Moscow Society (USA)-Meelick Lady (IRE) (Duky)

Mrs John Harrington Brian Kearney

Placings:6343/1110/13121F21/F111F11-1U111   (4111)
2002/03: 18¹S, 16ᵁS, 17¹HY, 16¹SH, 16¹G,

	Starts	1st	2nd	3rd	Win & Pl
Chases	5	4	0	0	200994
Career Total	28	16	2	3	525189
174	3/03	Chel	2m	A Ch		GD	£145000
163	2/03	Punc	2m	Ch		SH	£16683
162	12/02	Leop	2m1f	Ch		HVY	£17944
168	11/02	DRoy	2m2f	Ch		SFT	£21165
155	4/02	Punc	2m	Ch		GD	£32331
167	3/02	Chel	2m	A Ch		G-S	£72500
151	12/01	Leop	2m1f	Ch		YLD	£39314
151	11/01	Punc	2m	Ch		SFT	£13104
123	11/01	DRoy	2m	Ch		YLD	£7233
170	4/01	Leop	2m	Hdl		SH	£55645
165	12/00	Leop	2m	Hdl		HVY	£15600
151	11/00	Punc	2m	Hdl		SFT	£10400
150	5/00	Punc	2m	Hdl		YLD	£24800
133	11/99	Fair	2m	Hdl		SFT	£26116
121	11/99	DRoy	2m	Hdl		SFT	£8705
117	10/99	Punc	2m	Hdl		SFT	£3696

Total win prize-money £510441

Going: Sf: 2-3 GS: 0-0 Gd: 1-1 GF: - Fm: 0-0
Distance: 2m/2m3: 4-5 2m4-2m7: 0-0 3m+: 0-0
Track: LH: 2-2 RH: 1-2 Tight: 0-0 Gall: 1-1
Aids: Bl: 0-0 Vi: 0-0 Tstrap: 0-0
Best Rating: 174 3/03 Chel 2m   good   Ch

The best two-mile chaser in the British Isles; former high-class hurdler; developed into the top two-mile novice chaser in 2001/2, landing the Arkle Trophy at Cheltenham and following up at Punchestown; successful three times in 2002/2003 before brilliant win in the Queen Mother Champion Chase at the Festival; best at around 2m on good or soft ground; usually jumps well.

Moscow Gold (IRE)

80   **59**

6-y-o ch g Moscow Society (USA)-Vesper Time (The Parson)
A J Wilson (R J Smith 1/6) Janet Baker, David Smyth, Barrie Hughes

Placings:00-0005   (4196)
2002/03: 16⁰G, 22⁰GF, 17⁰S, 24⁵G,

	Starts	1st	2nd	3rd	Win & Pl
Hurdles	4	0	0	0	0
Career Total	6	0	0	0	0

Going: Sf: 0-1 GS: 0-0 Gd: 0-2 GF: - Fm: 0-1
Distance: 2m/2m3: 0-2 2m4-2m7: 0-1 3m+: 0-1
Track: LH: 0-1 RH: 0-3 Tight: 0-2 Gall: 0-0
Aids: Bl: 0-1 Vi: 0-0 Tstrap: 0-1
Best Rating: 77 4/02 Weth 2m   gd-fm NHF

Moscow Leader (IRE)

89f   **90f**

5-y-o ch g Moscow Society (USA)-Catrionas Castle (IRE) (Orchestra)
R C Guest (N B Mason 24/11) Miss P Overy

Placings:053   (4397)
2002/03: 17⁰G, 17⁵G, 17³G,

	Starts	1st	2nd	3rd	Win & Pl
NH Flat	3	0	0	1	317
Career Total	3	0	0	1	317

Going: Sf: 0-0 GS: 0-0 Gd: 0-3 GF: - Fm: 0-0
Distance: 2m/2m3: 0-3 2m4-2m7: 0-0 3m+: 0-0
Track: LH: 0-0 RH: 0-2 Tight: 0-0 Gall: 0-0
Aids: Bl: 0-0 Vi: 0-0 Tstrap: 0-0
Best Rating: 90 3/03 Carl 2m1f   good NHF

Some signs of ability in bumpers but looks basically slow.

Moscow Tradition (IRE)

103   99

5-y-o b g Moscow Society (USA)-Bucks Grove (IRE) (Buckskin (FR))
Jonjo O Neill Mr & Mrs John Poynton

Placings:0265   (3443)
2002/03: 21⁰GS, 20²S, 21⁶GS, 16⁵HY,

	Starts	1st	2nd	3rd	Win & Pl
Hurdles	4	0	1	0	834
Career Total	4	0	1	0	834

Going: Sf: 0-2 GS: 0-2 Gd: 0-0 GF: - Fm: 0-0
Distance: 2m/2m3: 0-3 2m4-2m7: 0-3 3m+: 0-0
Track: LH: 0-3 RH: 0-1 Tight: 0-0 Gall: 0-1
Aids: Bl: 0-0 Vi: 0-0 Tstrap: 0-0
Best Rating: 99 12/02 Chep 2m4f   soft Hdl

Ex-Irish hurdler; won his only point in Ireland as a four-year-old; showed his best form over hurdles when narrowly beaten over two and a half miles at Chepstow December 2002; acts on soft ground.

Moscow Whisper (IRE)

103   102

6-y-o b g Moscow Society (USA)-Native Woodfire (IRE) (Mister Majestic)
P J Hobbs Yusof Sepiuddin

Placings:331   (4749)
2002/03: 17³G, 22³GF, 20¹G,

	Starts	1st	2nd	3rd	Win & Pl
NH Flat	1	0	0	1	280
Hurdles	2	1	0	1	6522
Career Total	3	1	0	2	6802
102 4/03 Prth	2m4f110yD Hdl		GD		£5824
		Total win prize-money £5824			

Going: Sf: 0-0 GS: 0-0 Gd: 1-2 GF: - Fm: 0-1
Distance: 2m/2m3: 0-1 2m4-2m7: 1-2 3m+: 0-0
Track: LH: 0-0 RH: 1-3 Tight: 0-0 Gall: 0-0
Aids: Bl: 0-0 Vi: 0-0 Tstrap: 0-0
Best Rating: 102 4/03 Prth 2m4f110y good Hdl

Moderate hurdler; got off the mark over hurdles when winning over 2m 4f at Perth in April 2003; followed up over 2m 6f at Stratford in May but he is better going right-handed; stays well; likes decent ground.

Mose Harper (IRE)

93   (98h)66

11-y-o b g Supreme Leader-Miss Rockaway (Le Moss)
Thomas O Neill B P Beggan

Placings:63FF40⁰/3P43P22055/5105UP0U-
0C45P00060664   (4744a)
2002/03: 20⁹G, 22ᶜYS, 174⁵SH, 205⁵G, 20ᴾGF, 170⁵SH, 180⁵YS, 200⁵S, 24⁵S, 28⁹S, 20⁶HY, 16⁸Y, 174⁵G,

	Starts	1st	2nd	3rd	Win & Pl
Hurdles	2	0	0	0	0
Chases	11	0	0	0	782

Career Total 38 1 2 3 8608
100 10/01 Dpat 2m2f   (0-109)HCh   Y-S £4451
                        Total win prize-money £4452

Going: Sf: 0-4 GS: 0-0 Gd: 0-3 GF: - Fm: 0-1
Distance: 2m/2m3: 0-5 2m4-2m7: 0-5 3m+: 0-2
Track: LH: 0-5 RH: 0-2 Tight: 0-1 Gall: 0-0
Aids: Bl: 0-12 Vi: 0-0 Tstrap: 0-0
Best Rating: 100 10/01 Dpat 2m2f   yld-sft Ch

Moss Cottage

73f   31f

7-y-o b m Le Moss-Rodney s Sister (Leading Man)
T P Walshe Mrs Penny Walshe

Placings:00   (1606)
2002/03: 17⁹GF, 16⁶G,

	Starts	1st	2nd	3rd	Win & Pl
NH Flat	2	0	0	0	
Career Total	2	0	0	0	

Going: Sf: 0-0 GS: 0-0 Gd: 0-1 GF: - Fm: 0-1
Distance: 2m/2m3: 0-2 2m4-2m7: 0-0 3m+: 0-0
Track: LH: 0-1 RH: 0-1 Tight: 0-1 Gall: 0-0
Aids: Bl: 0-0 Vi: 0-0 Tstrap: 0-0
Best Rating: 31 10/02 Chep 2m110y good NHF

Moss Deeping

89   53

11-y-o ch g Le Moss-Lady Run (Deep Run)
R N Bevis R J Bevis

Placings:P50PU-4PP   (2670)
2002/03: 21ᵁGS, 20⁴GS, 27ᴾS, 26ᴾS,

	Starts	1st	2nd	3rd	Win & Pl
Hurdles	4	0	0	0	0
Career Total	8	0	0	0	0

Going: Sf: 0-2 GS: 0-2 Gd: 0-0 GF: - Fm: 0-0
Distance: 2m/2m3: 0-0 2m4-2m7: 0-2 3m+: 0-2
Track: LH: 0-1 RH: 0-3 Tight: 0-1 Gall: 0-0
Aids: Bl: 0-0 Vi: 0-0 Tstrap: 0-4
Best Rating: 65 12/01 Bang 2m1f   gd-sft Hdl

Moss Harvey

107(108h)   (136h)128+

8-y-o ch g Le Moss-Wings Ground (Murrayfield)
J M Jefferson J R Salter

Placings:53/1111226P-11534P   (4102)
2002/03: 21¹GS, 25¹S, 24⁵S, 25³S, 234⁵S, 25ᴾG,

	Starts	1st	2nd	3rd	Win & Pl
Hurdles	2	0	0	0	973
Chases	4	2	0	1	16420
Career Total	16	6	2	2	39925
128 11/02 Kels	3m1f	D Ch		SFT	£6734
128 10/02 Fknm	2m5f110yC Ch			G-S	£8073
140 12/01 Bang	3m	C(0-135)HHdl		G-S	£6929
131 12/01 Newc	3m	D Hdl		G-S	£3454
108 11/01 Kels	2m6f110yE Hdl			GD	£3136
104 10/01 Kels	2m6f110yE Hdl			G-S	£2544
		Total win prize-money £30872			

Going: Sf: 1-3 GS: 1-2 Gd: 0-1 GF: - Fm: 0-0
Distance: 2m/2m3: 0-0 2m4-2m7: 1-1 3m+: 1-5
Track: LH: 2-6 RH: 0-0 Tight: 2-2 Gall: 0-2
Aids: Bl: 0-0 Vi: 0-0 Tstrap: 0-0
Best Rating: 140 2/02 Hayd 2m7f110y heavy Hdl

Very smart novice hurdler in 2001/2; winning chaser in 2002/3; later lost his way and better effort back over hurdles; stays three miles; handles soft, although may prefer better ground.

Moss Pageant

95   80

13-y-o b g Then Again-Water Pageant (Welsh Pageant)
J B Walton Messrs F T Walton

Placings:PP0/0/PF224/54P324312/433P41F333P/04452P
P0P/2/5063-524066   (1014)
2002/03: 16⁵GS, 16²G, 164⁵GS, 16⁹G, 16⁸GF, 20⁶G,

	Starts	1st	2nd	3rd	Win & Pl
Chases	6	0	1	0	1201
Career Total	49	2	7	8	18789
98 12/98 Newc	2m110y D(0-125)HCh		SFT	£3468
96 3/98 Newc	2m110y E(0-115)HCh		GD	£2710
		Total win prize-money £6179			

Going: Sf: 0-0 GS: 0-2 Gd: 0-3 GF: - Fm: 0-1
Distance: 2m/2m3: 0-5 2m4-2m7: 0-1 3m+: 0-0
Track: LH: 0-4 RH: 0-2 Tight: 0-1 Gall: 0-0
Aids: Bl: 0-0 Vi: 0-0 Tstrap: 0-6
Best Rating: 102 1/98 Muss 2m   gd-sft Ch

A modest chaser with a liking for Newcastle; likes give in the ground; best at two miles.

Mosspat

84   62

4-y-o b g Reprimand-Queen And Country (Town And Country)
W G M Turner Mossie O Connell

Placings:P60   (2195)
2002/03: 17ᶠG, 16⁸HY, 17⁹GS,

	Starts	1st	2nd	3rd	Win & Pl
Hurdles	3	0	0	0	0
Career Total	3	0	0	0	0

Going: Sf: 0-1 GS: 0-1 Gd: 0-1 GF: - Fm: 0-0
Distance: 2m/2m3: 0-3 2m4-2m7: 0-0 3m+: 0-0
Track: LH: 0-0 RH: 0-3 Tight: 0-1 Gall: 0-0
Aids: Bl: 0-0 Vi: 0-0 Tstrap: 0-0
Best Rating: 62 11/02 Leic 2m   heavy Hdl

Mosstowie

7-y-o b m Le Moss-Rowan Ville (Sexton Blake)
G J Smith Ibra Racing Co

Placings:0-P   (0164)
2002/03: 16⁰GS, 20ᴾGF,

	Starts	1st	2nd	3rd	Win & Pl
NH Flat	1	0	0	0	0
Hurdles	1	0	0	0	0
Career Total	2	0	0	0	

Going: Sf: 0-0 GS: 0-1 Gd: 0-0 GF: - Fm: 0-1
Distance: 2m/2m3: 0-1 2m4-2m7: 0-1 3m+: 0-0
Track: LH: 0-1 RH: 0-1 Tight: 0-0 Gall: 0-0
Aids: Bl: 0-0 Vi: 0-0 Tstrap: 0-0
Best Rating: 37 4/02 Towc 2m   gd-sft NHF

Mossy Green (IRE)

106   146

9-y-o b g Moscow Society (USA)-Green Ajo (Green Shoon)

W P Mullins Greenstar Syndicate

Placings:2321/2120 (4109)
2002/03: 20²YS, 19¹S, 20²Y, 21⁰G,

	Starts	1st	2nd	3rd	Win & Pl
Hurdles	4	1	2	0	13476
Career Total	8	2	4	1	20391
137 1/03 Naas 2m3f		Hdl		SFT	£6720
127 4/01 Baln 2m		NHF		SFT	£4173

Total win prize-money £10894

Going: Sf: 1-1 GS: 0-0 Gd: 0-1 GF: - Fm: 0-0
Distance: 2m/2m3: 1-1 2m4-2m7: 0-3 3m+: 0-0
Track: LH: 1-2 RH: 0-0 Tight: 0-0 Gall: 0-1
Aids: Bl: 0-0 Vi: 0-0 Tstrap: 0-0
Best Rating: 146 2/03 Naas 2m4f   yield   Hdl

Very useful Irish-trained hurdler; stays 2m 4f; suited by cut in the ground; progressive.

Mostarsil (USA)
93   87
5-y-o ch g Kingmambo (USA)-Naazeq (Nashwan (USA))
G L Moore (J G M O Shea 22/11) G A Jackman

Placings:403-430 (1198)
2002/03: 20⁴GF, 17³GF, 17⁰GF,

	Starts	1st	2nd	3rd	Win & Pl
Hurdles	3	0	0	1	730
Career Total	6	0	0	2	1074

Going: Sf: 0-0 GS: 0-0 Gd: 0-0 GF: - Fm: 0-3
Distance: 2m/2m3: 0-2 2m4-2m7: 0-1 3m+: 0-0
Track: LH: 0-2 RH: 0-1 Tight: 0-1 Gall: 0-0
Aids: Bl: 0-0 Vi: 0-1 Tstrap: 0-0
Best Rating: 87 1/02 Catt 2m   soft   Hdl

Mostyn
12-y-o ch g Astral Master-Temple Rock (Melody Rock)
J E Tuck R Weaver

Placings:6P/0/P1-P (0245)
2002/03: 25⁰G,

	Starts	1st	2nd	3rd	Win & Pl
Chases	1	0	0	0	
Career Total	6	1	0	0	1661
86 5/01 Extr 2m3f110y		H Ch		FRM	£1660

Total win prize-money £1661

Going: Sf: 0-0 GS: 0-0 Gd: 0-1 GF: - Fm: 0-0
Distance: 2m/2m3: 0-0 2m4-2m7: 0-1 3m+: 0-1
Track: LH: 0-0 RH: 0-1 Tight: 0-0 Gall: 0-0
Aids: Bl: 0-0 Vi: 0-0 Tstrap: 0-0
Best Rating: 86 5/01 Extr 2m3f110y firm   Ch

Motafayel
99   103
5-y-o b g Unfuwain (USA)-Hamaya (USA) (Mr Prospector (USA))
Mrs S J Smith M Keightley

Placings:520-0B0300 (3882)
2002/03: 16⁰G, 16⁸GS, 16⁰S, 16³S, 16⁰HY, 16⁰GS,

	Starts	1st	2nd	3rd	Win & Pl
NH Flat	1	0	0	0	0
Hurdles	5	0	0	1	726
Career Total	9	0	1	1	1259

Going: Sf: 0-3 GS: 0-2 Gd: 0-1 GF: - Fm: 0-0
Distance: 2m/2m3: 0-6 2m4-2m7: 0-0 3m+: 0-0
Track: LH: 0-6 RH: 0-0 Tight: 0-0 Gall: 0-3
Aids: Bl: 0-0 Vi: 0-0 Tstrap: 0-0
Best Rating: 103 11/02 Weth 2m   gd-sft   Hdl

Best race over hurdles so far when modest third at Haydock in December. Most disapointing next time.

Motcomb Jam (IRE)
100   114
6-y-o b g Frimaire-Flying Flo Jo (USA) (Aloma s Ruler (USA))
C J Mann Bix Racers

Placings:40-B0134 (4527)
2002/03: 16⁸GS, 16⁰G, 16¹GS, 19³GS, 20⁴G,

	Starts	1st	2nd	3rd	Win & Pl
Hurdles	5	1	0	1	4124
Career Total	7	1	0	1	4124
114 1/03 Donc 2m110y E Hdl				G-S	£3552

Total win prize-money £3552

Going: Sf: 0-0 GS: 1-3 Gd: 0-2 GF: - Fm: 0-0
Distance: 2m/2m3: 1-3 2m4-2m7: 0-2 3m+: 0-0
Track: LH: 1-5 RH: 0-0 Tight: 0-0 Gall: 1-2
Aids: Bl: 0-0 Vi: 0-0 Tstrap: 0-0
Best Rating: 114 1/03 Donc 2m110y   gd-sft   Hdl

Showed ability in bumper company; cheeky winner over hurdles at Doncaster in January 2003; finished good third under a penalty at the same track the following month; stays 2m 4f.

Motellino (IRE)
9-y-o ch g Montelimar (USA)-Macamore Rose (Torus)
P J Millington P J Millington

Placings:P/4P5P-0 (3951)
2002/03: 16⁰GS,

	Starts	1st	2nd	3rd	Win & Pl
Chases	1	0	0	0	
Career Total	6	0	0	0	271

Going: Sf: 0-0 GS: 0-1 Gd: 0-0 GF: - Fm: 0-0
Distance: 2m/2m3: 0-0 2m4-2m7: 0-0 3m+: 0-0
Track: LH: 0-0 RH: 0-1 Tight: 0-0 Gall: 0-0
Aids: Bl: 0-0 Vi: 0-0 Tstrap: 0-0
Best Rating: 74 11/01 Uttx 3m   soft   Ch

Mother Says
91f   78f
7-y-o b g Landyap (USA)-Miami Blues (Palm Track)
Jean-Rene Auvray Jean-Rene Auvray

Placings:33 (1382)
2002/03: 17³GF, 17³GF,

	Starts	1st	2nd	3rd	Win & Pl
NH Flat	2	0	0	2	580
Career Total	2	0	0	2	580

Going: Sf: 0-0 GS: 0-0 Gd: 0-0 GF: - Fm: 0-2
Distance: 2m/2m3: 0-2 2m4-2m7: 0-0 3m+: 0-0
Track: LH: 0-1 RH: 0-1 Tight: 0-1 Gall: 0-0
Aids: Bl: 0-0 Vi: 0-0 Tstrap: 0-0
Best Rating: 78 10/02 Hrfd 2m1f   gd-fm   NHF

Third in both his bumpers. Much better effort second start.

Mothers Help
106   123d
8-y-o b m Relief Pitcher-Laundry Maid (Forzando)
D L Williams Berkshire Commercial Components Ltd

Placings:13362442/32433425546/111530F/PPP-5460541341130P44 (4293)
2002/03: 20⁵GF, 17⁴GF, 24⁶GF, 21⁰G, 25⁵GF, 24⁴GF, 28¹GF, 24³F, 28⁴GS, 25¹GF, 24¹GS, 24³S, 24⁴HY, 24⁶G, 25⁴GF,

	Starts	1st	2nd	3rd	Win & Pl
Chases	16	3	0	2	14985
Career Total	45	4	7	8	38644
123 11/02 Hntg	3m	E(0-105)HCh		G-S	£3604
114 11/02 Folk	3m1f	F(0-100)HCh		G-F	£4095
105 10/02 MRas	3m4f110yF(0-100)HCh			G-F	£3432
123 6/00 MRas	2m6f110yE(0-115)HCh			G-S	£3543
123 5/00 Hntg	2m4f110yE Ch			G-S	£2921
97 5/00 MRas	2m4f	D Ch		G-S	£4729
109 11/98 Wind	2m	E Hdl		G-S	£2460

Total win prize-money £24784

Going: Sf: 0-3 GS: 1-2 Gd: 0-2 GF: - Fm: 2-9
Distance: 2m/2m3: 0-0 2m4-2m7: 0-4 3m+: 3-13
Track: LH: 0-4 RH: 3-12 Tight: 2-8 Gall: 1-3
Aids: Bl: 0-0 Vi: 0-0 Tstrap: 0-4
Best Rating: 123 11/02 Hntg 3m   gd-sft   Ch

Fair handicap chaser; stays extreme distances; suited by a sound surface, but handles cut.

Motown Man (IRE)
60   6
6-y-o b g Detroit Sam (FR)-Hands Off (Nearly A Hand)
G B Balding Baldings (training) Ltd

Placings:000 (3850)
2002/03: 16⁰S, 19⁰G, 19⁰GS,

	Starts	1st	2nd	3rd	Win & Pl
NH Flat	1	0	0	0	0
Hurdles	2	0	0	0	0
Career Total	3	0	0	0	

Going: Sf: 0-1 GS: 0-1 Gd: 0-1 GF: - Fm: 0-0
Distance: 2m/2m3: 0-1 2m4-2m7: 0-2 3m+: 0-0
Track: LH: 0-0 RH: 0-3 Tight: 0-1 Gall: 0-0
Aids: Bl: 0-0 Vi: 0-0 Tstrap: 0-0
Best Rating: 38 1/03 Ludl 2m   soft   NHF

Moulouya (FR)
(98h)   (95h)101
8-y-o gr m Turgeon (USA)-Charabia (FR) (Bazin)
J R Best Mercato 1

Placings:2220/1301/03555F-F (0153)
2002/03: 24⁶G,

	Starts	1st	2nd	3rd	Win & Pl
Chases	1	0	0	0	
Career Total	15	2	3	2	8289
114 10/00 Hntg	2m4f110yE Hdl			G-F	£2481
112 5/00 Folk	2m1f110yE(0-115)HHdl			GD	£2453

Total win prize-money £4936

Going: Sf: 0-0 GS: 0-0 Gd: 0-1 GF: - Fm: 0-0
Distance: 2m/2m3: 0-0 2m4-2m7: 0-0 3m+: 0-1
Track: LH: 0-1 RH: 0-0 Tight: 0-1 Gall: 0-0
Aids: Bl: 0-0 Vi: 0-0 Tstrap: 0-0
Best Rating: 114 10/00 Hntg 2m4f110y   gd-fm   Hdl

A winner on the Flat in France, she is effective in moderate company over hurdles. She stays an extended two miles four furlongs, appreciates positive tactics and seems to act

on any ground, although best served by a fast surface. Showed ability over fences in the spring of 2002.

Mounsey Castle

108   110

6-y-o ch g Carlingford Castle-Gay Ticket (New Member)
P J Hobbs Alan Peterson

Placings:*46-*12211   (4574)
2002/03: 16¹GF, 20⁴GF, 21²G, 19¹GF, 22¹GF,

	Starts	1st	2nd	3rd	Win & Pl
NH Flat	1	1	0	0	1967
Hurdles	4	2	2	0	11858
Career Total	7	3	2	0	13825
104 4/03 Strf	2m6f110yE Hdl		G-F	£4260
102 4/03 Hrfd	2m3f110yE Hdl		G-F	£3692
100 5/02 Chep	2m110y H NHF		G-F	£1967
			Total win prize-money £9920

Going:	Sf: 0-0 GS: 0-0 Gd: 0-1 GF: - Fm: 3-4
Distance:	2m/2m3: 1-1 **2m4-2m7: 2-4** 3m+: 0-0
Track:	LH: **2-3** RH: 1-2 Tight: **1-1** Gall: 0-1
Aids:	Bl: 0-0 Vi: 0-0 Tstrap: 0-0
Best Rating:	104 4/03 Strf 2m6f110y gd-fm Hdl

Fair novice hurdler; bumper winner; landed the odds in minor events at Hereford and Stratford; likes fast ground; set to go chasing next term; should stay 3m.

Mount Alpha (IRE)

7-y-o ch g Alphabatim (USA)-Youthful Capitana (Hard Boy)
D McCain D McCain

Placings:*0*PP   (3225)
2002/03: 17⁵S, 20⁵S, 27⁵HY,

	Starts	1st	2nd	3rd	Win & Pl
NH Flat	1	0	0	0	0
Hurdles	1	0	0	0	0
Chases	1	0	0	0	0
Career Total	3	0	0	0	

Going:	Sf: 0-3 GS: 0-0 Gd: 0-0 GF: - Fm: 0-0
Distance:	2m/2m3: 0-1 2m4-2m7: 0-1 3m+: 0-1
Track:	LH: 0-2 RH: 0-1 Tight: 0-1 Gall: 0-0
Aids:	Bl: 0-0 Vi: 0-0 Tstrap: 0-0
Best Rating:	63 10/02 Carl 2m1f soft NHF

Mount Gay

102(104h)   (82h)99

10-y-o b g Montelimar (USA)-Candlebright (Lighter)
Mrs L B Normile Mrs D A Whitaker

Placings:21P   (1225)
2002/03: 20²GS, 22¹GF, 20⁰G,

	Starts	1st	2nd	3rd	Win & Pl
Hurdles	1	0	1	0	1051
Chases	2	1	0	0	4111
Career Total	3	1	1	0	5162
99 8/02 MRas	2m6f110yE Ch		G-F	£4111
			Total win prize-money £4111

Going:	Sf: 0-0 GS: 0-1 Gd: 0-1 GF: - Fm: 1-1
Distance:	2m/2m3: 0-0 **2m4-2m7: 1-3** 3m+: 0-0
Track:	LH: 0-1 **RH: 1-2** Tight: 1-2 Gall: 0-0
Aids:	Bl: 0-0 Vi: 0-0 Tstrap: 0-0
Best Rating:	99 8/02 MRas 2m6f110y gd-fm Ch

Point winner who finished runner-up in a poor novices hurdle at Perth. Successful chasing debut in an uncompetitive extended 22 furlong novice event at Market Rasen August 2002, but pulled up lame next time.

Mount Karinga

97f   103f

5-y-o b g Karinga Bay-Candarela (Damister (USA))
P F Nicholls Jeffrey Hordle

Placings:*1*   (4275)
2002/03: 16¹G,

	Starts	1st	2nd	3rd	Win & Pl
NH Flat	1	1	0	0	1988
Career Total	1	1	0	0	1988
103 3/03 Chep	2m110y H NHF		GD	£1988
			Total win prize-money £1988

Going:	Sf: 0-0 GS: 0-0 Gd: 1-1 GF: - Fm: 0-0
Distance:	**2m/2m3: 1-1** 2m4-2m7: 0-0 3m+: 0-0
Track:	**LH: 1-1** RH: 0-0 Tight: 0-0 Gall: 0-0
Aids:	Bl: 0-0 Vi: 0-0 Tstrap: 0-0
Best Rating:	103 3/03 Chep 2m110y good NHF

Mount Prague (IRE)

111   121

9-y-o br g Lord Americo-Celtic Duchess (Ya Zaman (USA))
K C Bailey W J Ives

Placings:*4/1*30546*1/0*F31F23/13453P-136P5   (4751)
2002/03: 20¹GS, 20³S, 20⁶G, 22⁴G, 20⁵G,

	Starts	1st	2nd	3rd	Win & Pl
Chases	5	1	0	1	8091
Career Total	26	5	1	6	27662
124 11/02 Hntg	2m4f110yD(0-115)HCh	G-S	£5473
128 1/02 Ludl	2m4f D(0-115)HCh	GD	£4537
123 12/00 Hntg	2m110y F(0-105)HCh	HVY	£2699
112 3/00 DRoy	2m Hdl	G-Y	£2760
111 10/99 Gway	2m NHF	SFT	£4004
			Total win prize-money £19474

Going:	Sf: 0-1 GS: 1-1 Gd: 0-3 GF: - Fm: 0-0
Distance:	2m/2m3: 0-0 **2m4-2m7: 1-5** 3m+: 0-0
Track:	LH: 0-0 **RH: 1-5** Tight: 0-1 **Gall: 1-1**
Aids:	Bl: 0-0 Vi: 0-0 Tstrap: 0-0
Best Rating:	128 1/02 Ludl 2m4f good Ch

Fair chaser; suited by soft ground and two and a half miles these days, all his wins have been on right-handed tracks; goes well fresh.

Mount Vernon (IRE)

91   68

7-y-o b g Darshaan-Chellita (Habitat)
P Wegmann P Wegmann

Placings:6P/0/5-P56   (4635)
2002/03: 17⁵PS, 17⁵F, 19⁶GF,

	Starts	1st	2nd	3rd	Win & Pl
Hurdles	3	0	0	0	0
Career Total	7	0	0	0	0

Going:	Sf: 0-1 GS: 0-0 Gd: 0-0 GF: - Fm: 0-2
Distance:	2m/2m3: 0-3 2m4-2m7: 0-0 3m+: 0-0
Track:	LH: 0-1 RH: 0-2 Tight: 0-3 Gall: 0-0
Aids:	Bl: 0-0 Vi: 0-0 Tstrap: 0-0
Best Rating:	72 5/01 Bang 2m1f gd-sft Hdl

Mountain Dream

91   39

10-y-o b g Batshoof-Echoing (Formidable (USA))
Miss S E Forster The Border Hotel

Placings:60/0040/546456P4P0/044314/03P0/00P   (1239)

2002/03: 20⁰GF, 27⁰GF, 20⁰GF,

	Starts	1st	2nd	3rd	Win & Pl
Hurdles	3	0	0	0	
Career Total	29	1	0	2	2506
79 11/99 Sedg	2m1f G(0-95)HHdl	GD	£1616
			Total win prize-money £1616

Going:	Sf: 0-0 GS: 0-0 Gd: 0-0 GF: - Fm: 0-3
Distance:	2m/2m3: 0-0 2m4-2m7: 0-2 3m+: 0-1
Track:	LH: 0-3 RH: 0-0 Tight: 0-1 Gall: 0-0
Aids:	Bl: 0-0 Vi: 0-0 Tstrap: 0-0
Best Rating:	79 11/99 Kels 2m110y good Hdl

Mountain Man (FR)

99   94

5-y-o b g Cadoudal (FR)-Montagne Bleue (Legend Of France (USA))
S E H Sherwood The Hon Mrs S Sherwood

Placings:*0*-54   (2492)
2002/03: 16⁵GS, 16⁴S,

	Starts	1st	2nd	3rd	Win & Pl
NH Flat	1	0	0	0	0
Hurdles	1	0	0	0	0
Career Total	3	0	0	0	

Going:	Sf: 0-1 GS: 0-1 Gd: 0-0 GF: - Fm: 0-0
Distance:	2m/2m3: 0-2 2m4-2m7: 0-0 3m+: 0-1
Track:	LH: 0-1 RH: 0-1 Tight: 0-1 Gall: 0-1
Aids:	Bl: 0-0 Vi: 0-0 Tstrap: 0-0
Best Rating:	90 12/02 Donc 2m110y soft Hdl

Best effort so far when creditable fourth in novices hurdle at Doncaster in December.

Mountain Native (IRE)

7-y-o ch g Be My Native (USA)-Mountain Beauty (IRE) (Executive Perk)
P J Hobbs Ellway Racing & P A Deal

Placings:*0*-PF   (0410)
2002/03: 20⁰GF, 22⁶GF,

	Starts	1st	2nd	3rd	Win & Pl
Hurdles	2	0	0	0	
Career Total	3	0	0	0	

Going:	Sf: 0-0 GS: 0-0 Gd: 0-0 GF: - Fm: 0-2
Distance:	2m/2m3: 0-0 2m4-2m7: 0-2 3m+: 0-0
Track:	LH: 0-2 RH: 0-0 Tight: 0-1 Gall: 0-0
Aids:	Bl: 0-0 Vi: 0-0 Tstrap: 0-0
Best Rating:	95 3/02 Newb 2m110y gd-sft NHF

Mountain Thyne (IRE)

10-y-o br g Good Thyne (USA)-Vanhalensdarling (Green Shoon)
Mrs R L Elliot J P Elliot

Placings:32-1F6   (4508)
2002/03: 25¹GS, 25⁵F, 25⁶G,

	Starts	1st	2nd	3rd	Win & Pl
Chases	3	1	0	0	2782
Career Total	5	1	1	1	3963
89 5/02 Hexm	3m1f H Ch	G-S	£2782
			Total win prize-money £2782

Going: Sf: 0-0 GS: 1-1 Gd: 0-2 GF: - Fm: 0-0
Distance: 2m/2m3: 0-0 2m4-2m7: 0-0 3m+: 1-3
Track: LH: 1-3 RH: 0-0 Tight: 0-2 Gall: 0-0
Aids: Bl: 0-0 Vi: 0-0 Tstrap: 0-0
Best Rating: 94 4/02 Kels 3m1f   gd-fm Ch

Mountrath Rock

97   83

6-y-o b m Rock Hopper-Point Of Law (Law Society (USA))
Miss B Sanders Mark L Champion

Placings:4/3-4001   (4629)
2002/03: 18⁴G, 17⁰GS, 16⁰G, 21¹GF,

	Starts	1st	2nd	3rd	Win & Pl
Hurdles	4	1	0	0	2450
Career Total	6	1	0	1	2903
83	4/03	Plum	2m5f	G(0-90)HHdl	G-F £2450

Total win prize-money £2450

Going: Sf: 0-0 GS: 0-1 Gd: 0-2 GF: - Fm: 1-1
Distance: 2m/2m3: 0-3 2m4-2m7: 1-1 3m+: 0-0
Track: LH: 1-2 RH: 0-2 Tight: 1-3 Gall: 0-0
Aids: Bl: 1-1 Vi: 0-0 Tstrap: 1-4
Best Rating: 83 4/03 Plum 2m5f   gd-fm Hdl

Plating-class hurdler; appreciated the drop in class when winning a Plumpton seller in April 2003; suited by fast ground; stays two miles five; wears tongue tie; has worn blinkers.

Mountsorrel (IRE)

67   30

4-y-o b g Charnwood Forest (IRE)-Play The Queen (IRE) (King Of Clubs)
T Wall (J R Best 7/9) D Pugh

Placings:00   (1614)
2002/03: 17⁰G, 16⁰F,

	Starts	1st	2nd	3rd	Win & Pl
Hurdles	2	0	0	0	
Career Total	2	0	0	0	

Going: Sf: 0-0 GS: 0-0 Gd: 0-1 GF: - Fm: 0-1
Distance: 2m/2m3: 0-2 2m4-2m7: 0-0 3m+: 0-0
Track: LH: 0-1 RH: 0-1 Tight: 0-1 Gall: 0-0
Aids: Bl: 0-0 Vi: 0-0 Tstrap: 0-0
Best Rating: 30 9/02 Bang 2m1f   good Hdl

Moving Earth (IRE)

109(108h)   (117 h)130

10-y-o b g Brush Aside (USA)-Park Breeze (IRE) (Strong Gale)
A W Carroll (P F Nicholls 11/11) P J Wilmott

Placings:2/F/F1/31L6351-PR11P   (4791)
2002/03: 20⁰GF, 24⁶GF, 18¹GS, 19¹GS, 29⁹GF,

	Starts	1st	2nd	3rd	Win & Pl
Hurdles	3	2	0	0	5415
Chases	2	0	0	0	
Career Total	16	5	1	2	34288
111	2/03	Donc	2m3f110yF Hdl		G-S £2702
104	11/02	Font	2m2f110yF Hdl		G-S £2712
130	4/02	Sand	2m4f(0-145)HCh		GD £17400
128	1/02	Winc	2m5f	D(0-120)HCh	GD £5027
115	3/01	Font	2m2f	F Ch	SFT £2873

Total win prize-money £30716

Going: Sf: 0-0 GS: 2-2 Gd: 0-1 GF: - Fm: 0-2
Distance: 2m/2m3: 1-1 2m4-2m7: 1-2 3m+: 0-2
Track: LH: 2-3 RH: 0-2 Tight: 1-2 Gall: 0-0

Aids: Bl: 0-0 Vi: 0-0 Tstrap: 0-0
Best Rating: 130 4/02 Sand 2m4f110y good Ch

Useful chaser; point winner in the past; had become very unreliable at the start, but has improved in that respect latterly; stays three miles; effective on good and soft ground.

Moving On Up

113(99c)   (103c)126

9-y-o b g Salse (USA)-Thundercloud (Electric)
C J Mann Hugh Villiers

Placings:134/1500/0210/0P35F0305P-332P0056 (4112)
2002/03: 16³S, 16²S, 16²S, 16⁵HY, 16⁹G, 24⁵G, 21⁵G,

	Starts	1st	2nd	3rd	Win & Pl
Hurdles	6	0	1	0	17525
Chases	2	0	0	3	1338
Career Total	29	3	2	5	46542
134	12/00	Leop	2m	HHdl	HVY £7176
127	8/99	Tral	2m1f	HHdl	YLD £8705
111	12/98	Leop	2m	Hdl	HVY £4184

Total win prize-money £20066

Going: Sf: 0-4 GS: 0-0 Gd: 0-4 GF: - Fm: 0-0
Distance: 2m/2m3: 0-6 2m4-2m7: 0-1 3m+: 0-1
Track: LH: 0-4 RH: 0-4 Tight: 0-1 Gall: 0-2
Aids: Bl: 0-8 Vi: 0-0 Tstrap: 0-0
Best Rating: 134 12/00 Leop 2m   heavy Hdl

Useful hurdler, but has yet to win in this country; stays two miles five but effective at shorter; acts on soft ground; wears blinkers.

Mowbray (USA)

95   112+

8-y-o b/br g Opening Verse (USA)-Peppy Raja (USA) (Raja Baba (USA))
G L Moore Graham Parker

Placings:430/223-1   (1873)
2002/03: 20¹GS,

	Starts	1st	2nd	3rd	Win & Pl
Hurdles	1	1	0	0	3297
Career Total	7	1	2	2	7320
114	11/02	Font	2m4f	E Hdl	G-S £3297

Total win prize-money £3297

Going: Sf: 0-0 GS: 1-1 Gd: 0-0 GF: - Fm: 0-0
Distance: 2m/2m3: 0-0 2m4-2m7: 1-1 3m+: 0-0
Track: LH: 0-0 RH: 0-0 Tight: 1-1 Gall: 0-0
Aids: Bl: 0-0 Vi: 0-0 Tstrap: 0-0
Best Rating: 114 11/02 Font 2m4f   gd-sft Hdl

Modest hurdler; stays two miles four; acts on easy ground.

Moykon (IRE)

66   14

6-y-o b g Gothland (FR)-Yawa Prince (IRE) (Yawa)
Miss H C Knight Mrs J K Peutherer

Placings:60-0   (0076)
2002/03: 19⁰GF,

	Starts	1st	2nd	3rd	Win & Pl
Hurdles	1	0	0	0	
Career Total	3	0	0	0	

Going: Sf: 0-0 GS: 0-0 Gd: 0-0 GF: - Fm: 0-1
Distance: 2m/2m3: 0-0 2m4-2m7: 0-1 3m+: 0-0
Track: LH: 0-0 RH: 0-1 Tight: 0-0 Gall: 0-0
Aids: Bl: 0-0 Vi: 0-0 Tstrap: 0-0
Best Rating: 82 12/01 Ludl 2m   good NHF

Aids: Bl: 0-0 Vi: 0-0 Tstrap: 0-0
Best Rating: 130 4/02 Sand 2m4f110y good Ch

Mploy (IRE)

79   64

6-y-o ch g Deploy-Sweet Quest (Rainbow Quest (USA))
Ferdy Murphy Mrs Marlene Kynaston

Placings:00-0   (1613)
2002/03: 16⁰G,

	Starts	1st	2nd	3rd	Win & Pl
Hurdles	1	0	0	0	
Career Total	3	0	0	0	

Going: Sf: 0-0 GS: 0-0 Gd: 0-1 GF: - Fm: 0-0
Distance: 2m/2m3: 0-0 2m4-2m7: 0-0 3m+: 0-0
Track: LH: 0-1 RH: 0-0 Tight: 0-0 Gall: 0-0
Aids: Bl: 0-0 Vi: 0-0 Tstrap: 0-0
Best Rating: 77 5/01 Hntg 2m110y   gd-fm NHF

Mr Babbage (IRE)

112f   119f

5-y-o b g Carroll House-Winsome Doe (Buckskin (FR))
W P Mullins George Creighton

Placings:10   (4115)
2002/03: 18¹S, 16⁰G,

	Starts	1st	2nd	3rd	Win & Pl
NH Flat	2	1	0	0	3584
Career Total	2	1	0	0	3584
111	2/03	Clon	2m2f	NHF	SFT £3584

Total win prize-money £3584

Going: Sf: 1-1 GS: 0-0 Gd: 0-1 GF: - Fm: 0-0
Distance: 2m/2m3: 0-0 2m4-2m7: 0-0 3m+: 0-0
Track: LH: 0-1 RH: 0-0 Tight: 0-0 Gall: 0-0
Aids: Bl: 0-0 Vi: 0-0 Tstrap: 0-0
Best Rating: 119 3/03 Chel 2m110y   good NHF

Mr Baxter Basics

111   138

12-y-o b g Lighter-Phyll-Tarquin (Tarqogan)
Miss Venetia Williams P Ryan

Placings:0/661242/F512F21U/111/P041431/U0364/253P-622U2F2   (4775)
2002/03: 20⁶GS, 20²S, 19²GS, 24⁰G, 20²G, 21⁶G, 24²G,

	Starts	1st	2nd	3rd	Win & Pl
Chases	7	0	4	0	18338
Career Total	41	8	9	3	80969
141	4/00	Fair	2m100y	HCh	G-Y £10400
137	1/00	Fair	2m100y	Ch	SFT £6624
136	7/98	Klny	2m4f	Ch	G-Y £8445
120	5/98	Cork	2m5f	Ch	GD £0
136	5/98	Navn	2m2f	HCh	Y-S £5956
130	3/98	Leop	2m2f	(0-130)HCh	G-Y £2978
	12/97	Cork	2m		HVY £3391

Total win prize-money £37796

Going: Sf: 0-1 GS: 0-2 Gd: 0-4 GF: - Fm: 0-0
Distance: 2m/2m3: 0-0 2m4-2m7: 0-5 3m+: 0-2
Track: LH: 0-4 RH: 0-3 Tight: 0-2 Gall: 0-2
Aids: Bl: 0-0 Vi: 0-0 Tstrap: 0-0
Best Rating: 141 4/00 Fair 2m100y   gd-yld Ch

Useful handicap chaser; formerly trained in Ireland; now at veteran; best at around two and a half miles; effective on soft ground.

Mr Ben Gunn

101(100h)   (99h)98

11-y-o ch g Newski (USA)-Long John Silvia (Celtic Cone)

J D Frost P A Tylor

Placings:64/5003F0-PP01333P   (1803)
2002/03: 22^PGS, 19^PG, 17⁰G, 20¹GS, 19³F, 20³GF, 23³G, 21^PS,

	Starts	1st	2nd	3rd	Win & Pl
Hurdles	3	0	0	1	438
Chases	5	1	0	2	6479
Career Total	16	1	0	4	7562
99 8/02 MRas 2m4f	D Ch		G-S	£5172	

Total win prize-money £5172

Going: Sf: 0-1 GS: 1-2 Gd: 0-3 GF: - Fm: 0-2
Distance: 2m/2m3: 0-3 2m4-2m7: 1-4 3m+: 0-1
Track: LH: 0-3 RH: 1-5 Tight: 1-4 Gall: 0-1
Aids: Bl: 0-0 Vi: 0-0 Tstrap: 0-0
Best Rating: 99 10/02 Hntg 2m4f110y gd-fm Ch

Looked a bit quirky in points but did win a maiden (good). Has shown limited promise over hurdles and seems to need a sound surface. Won a weak novice chase at Market Rasen in August 2002.

Mr Bossman (IRE)
113   129

10-y-o b g Jolly Jake (NZ)-Imperial Greeting (Be My Guest (USA))
R C Guest (N B Mason 24/1) T N Siviter

Placings:0/0/0000/1PP5/52211133-P56612144   (4612)
2002/03: 22^PS, 16⁵GS, 16⁶S, 19⁶G, 20¹G, 19²G, 21¹G, 21⁴G, 16⁴G,

	Starts	1st	2nd	3rd	Win & Pl
Chases	9	2	1	0	27150
Career Total	27	6	3	2	50528
127 3/03 Fknm	2m5f110yD(0-120)HCh		GD	£6682	
127 2/03 Kemp	2m4f110yC(0-130)HCh		GD	£12760	
121 3/02 Fknm	2m5f110yD(0-120)HCh		GD	£4347	
115 2/02 Muss	2m	D(0-110)HCh	SFT	£7150	
121 1/02 Muss	2m4f	E(0-110)HCh	GD	£3640	
103 2/01 Sedg	2m5f	H Ch	G-S	£1543	

Total win prize-money £36123

Going: Sf: 0-2 GS: 0-1 Gd: 2-6 GF: - Fm: 0-0
Distance: 2m/2m3: 0-5 2m4-2m7: 2-4 3m+: 0-0
Track: LH: 1-8 RH: 1-1 Tight: 1-4 Gall: 0-2
Aids: Bl: 0-0 Vi: 0-0 Tstrap: 0-2
Best Rating: 129 4/03 Aint 2m5f110y good Ch

Fair handicap chaser; stays two and a half miles plus; effective on good and soft ground; seems best on a sharp track; wears tongue tie and cheekpieces.

Mr Busby
96

10-y-o b g La Grange Music-Top-Anna (IRE) (Ela-Mana-Mou)
John A Harris D Wilcox

Placings:100/21242130/4F/60P666P/023633403-0 (0405)
2002/03: 17⁰GF,

	Starts	1st	2nd	3rd	Win & Pl
Hurdles	1	0	0	0	
Career Total	30	4	5	5	13190
110 2/99 Hayd	2m	C HHdl	SFT	£4485	
97 11/98 MRas	2m1f110yE Hdl		HVY	£2477	
111 1/98 Newc	2m	H NHF	G-S	£1392	

Total win prize-money £8356

Going: Sf: 0-1 GS: 0-0 Gd: 0-0 GF: - Fm: 0-1
Distance: 2m/2m3: 0-4 2m4-2m7: 0-0 3m+: 0-0
Track: LH: 0-0 RH: 0-1 Tight: 0-1 Gall: 0-0
Aids: Bl: 0-0 Vi: 0-0 Tstrap: 0-0
Best Rating: 113 3/99 Ayr 2m soft Hdl

Moderate handicap hurdler; has not won a race for a long time; best at two miles on soft ground.

Mr Cavallo (IRE)
107(103c)   (93c)86

11-y-o b g The Bart (USA)-Mrs Guru (Le Bavard (FR))
Miss Lucinda V Russell Peter J S Russell

Placings:000S/2.22.30/P1211416140364450/033313204023 540/00324125006/023PS2140-00264254200 (4752)
2002/03: 22⁰GS, 24⁰G, 20²GF, 24⁶G, 20⁴GS, 27²GF, 21⁵GF, 26⁴GF, 26²GF, 20⁰G, 24⁰G,

	Starts	1st	2nd	3rd	Win & Pl
Hurdles	11	0	3	0	2113
Career Total	72	8	13	9	38415
100 8/01 Sedg	3m3f110yF(0-110)HHdl	G-F	£2674		
105 8/00 Prth	2m4f110yE(0-115)HHdl	GD	£3351		
102 7/99 Wolv	2m4f110yF(0-110)HHdl	G-S	£2686		
107 10/98 Carl	2m4f110yF(0-100)HHdl	GD	£2388		
105 8/98 Ctml	2m6f	E(0-100)HHdl	GD	£2215	
94 8/98 Bang	2m4f110yE(0-100)HCh	GD	£3631		
99 7/98 Sedg	2m5f110yE(0-110)HHdl	G-S	£2250		
86 7/98 Sedg	2m5f110yF Hdl		G-F	£1954	

Total win prize-money £21149

Going: Sf: 0-0 GS: 0-2 Gd: 0-4 GF: - Fm: 0-5
Distance: 2m/2m3: 0-0 2m4-2m7: 0-5 3m+: 0-6
Track: LH: 0-7 RH: 0-4 Tight: 0-3 Gall: 0-2
Aids: Bl: 0-0 Vi: 0-0 Tstrap: 0-0
Best Rating: 107 10/98 Carl 2m4f110y good Hdl

Moderate hurdler/chaser; stays well; acts on most ground.

Mr Chataway (IRE)

12-y-o b g Le Bavard (FR)-Swift Invader (Brave Invader (USA))
Mrs D M Grissell Mrs A Bailey

Placings:0/00/22452/342P/456/0U-P (0312)
2002/03: 21^PG,

	Starts	1st	2nd	3rd	Win & Pl
Chases	1	0	0	0	
Career Total	18	0	4	1	4102

Going: Sf: 0-0 GS: 0-0 Gd: 0-1 GF: - Fm: 0-0
Distance: 2m/2m3: 0-0 2m4-2m7: 0-1 3m+: 0-0
Track: LH: 0-0 RH: 0-1 Tight: 0-0 Gall: 0-0
Aids: Bl: 0-0 Vi: 0-0 Tstrap: 0-0
Best Rating: 104 4/98 Font 2m6f110y gd-sft Hdl

Mr Christie
99   91d

11-y-o b g Doulab (USA)-Hi There (High Top)
Miss L C Siddall Lynn Siddall Racing

Placings:000/3P0455325146502/124060501005/4P506PU 00305424/3020023354/026051131000/6361001062-05620000 (4141)
2002/03: 23⁰G, 27⁵S, 24⁶S, 23²S, 27⁰HY, 24⁰HY, 25⁰G, 24⁰S,

	Starts	1st	2nd	3rd	Win & Pl
Hurdles	8	0	0	1	1116
Career Total	85	8	9	8	31502
92 1/02 Newc	3m	F(0-100)HHdl	SFT	£2212	
92 12/01 Hayd	2m7f110yF(0-110)HHdl	HVY	£3705		
92 12/00 Hrfd	3m	F(0-100)HHdl	HVY	£3227	
88 10/00 Sedg	3m3f110yF(0-100)HHdl	G-S	£2289		
82 10/00 Hexm	3m	F(0-100)HHdl	HVY	£2107	
103 3/98 Hntg	3m2f	E(0-110)HHdl	SFT	£2495	
105 5/97 Uttx	3m110y E Hdl		G-S	£2410	
95 2/97 Muss	3m	E(0-100)HHdl	G-S	£2807	

Total win prize-money £21253

Going: Sf: 0-6 GS: 0-0 Gd: 0-2 GF: - Fm: 0-0
Distance: 2m/2m3: 0-0 2m4-2m7: 0-0 3m+: 0-8
Track: LH: 0-7 RH: 0-1 Tight: 0-2 Gall: 0-1
Aids: Bl: 0-0 Vi: 0-0 Tstrap: 0-7
Best Rating: 105 5/97 Uttx 3m110y gd-sft Hdl

Moderate staying hurdler, well suited by soft ground. Usually tongue tied. Often gets well behind and is far from reliable.

Mr Collins
97   86

9-y-o b g Brush Aside (USA)-Music Interpreter (Kampala)
R Tate R Tate

Placings:1P2/P/5-1FFP (0508)
2002/03: 21¹GF, 20^FGF, 28^FG, 23^PG,

	Starts	1st	2nd	3rd	Win & Pl
Chases	4	1	0	0	1526
Career Total	9	2	1	0	4939
94 5/02 Sedg	2m5f	H Ch	G-F	£1526	
114 10/99 Chel	2m110y H NHF		GD	£2710	

Total win prize-money £4236

Going: Sf: 0-0 GS: 0-0 Gd: 0-2 GF: - Fm: 1-2
Distance: 2m/2m3: 0-0 2m4-2m7: 1-2 3m+: 0-2
Track: LH: 1-4 RH: 0-0 Tight: 1-3 Gall: 0-0
Aids: Bl: 0-0 Vi: 0-0 Tstrap: 0-0
Best Rating: 114 3/00 Tntn 3m110y good Hdl

very moderate hunter chaser/pointer. Stays three miles but effective at shorter. Appreciates a sound surface.

Mr Cool
112(112c)   (148c)153

9-y-o b g Jupiter Island-Laurel Diver (Celtic Cone)
M C Pipe N G Mills

Placings:10/111111/121023/120114-22562000 (4478)
2002/03: 16²G, 20²HY, 16⁵S, 16⁶HY, 21²GS, 16⁶G, 21⁰G, 20⁰G,

	Starts	1st	2nd	3rd	Win & Pl
Hurdles	8	0	3	0	28858
Career Total	28	12	6	1	105048
136 4/02 Chep	2m110y E Ch		G-F	£4204	
133 4/02 Tntn	2m3f	D Ch	G-S	£4702	
138 11/01 NAbb	2m110y D Ch		SFT	£3812	
156 12/00 Newb	2m110y B Hdl		SFT	£7020	
155 11/00 Newb	2m3f	C(0-135)HHdl	SFT	£5954	
136 3/00 Uttx	2m Hdl		GD	£3688	
119 2/00 Sand	2m110y D Hdl		SFT	£3770	
127 2/00 Folk	2m1f110yF Hdl		G-S	£2068	
136 12/99 Chep	2m110y A NHF		HVY	£7450	
126 11/99 Aint	2m110y H NHF		GD	£2008	
119 11/99 Winc	2m	H NHF	GD	£1621	
104 6/98 Sthl	2m	H NHF	GD	£1208	

Total win prize-money £47509

Going: Sf: 0-3 GS: 0-1 Gd: 0-4 GF: - Fm: 0-0
Distance: 2m/2m3: 0-4 2m4-2m7: 0-4 3m+: 0-0
Track: LH: 0-4 RH: 0-4 Tight: 0-1 Gall: 0-3
Aids: Bl: 0-0 Vi: 0-0 Tstrap: 0-0
Best Rating: 160 11/00 Newb 2m110y heavy Hdl

Smart hurdler/chaser; has won on good and soft, but would not want it too testing; nearly stole a race at Ascot in November 2002, just caught by Baracouda, and again caught late on by Classified at Cheltenham; well beaten twice since; effective at up to two miles five, but better at two; suited by front-running tactics.

Mr Cospector
105(105h)   (124h)122+

6-y-o b g Cosmonaut-L Ancressaan (Dalsaan)

D L Williams   D L Williams

Placings:653F22143-O41F   (2569)
2002/03: 20⁰GS, 21⁴S, 26¹GS, 24⁴G,

	Starts	1st	2nd	3rd	Win & Pl
Chases	4	1	0	0	5487
Career Total	13	2	2	2	18029
122	12/02 Wwck 3m2f	D Ch		G-S	£4842
124	2/02 Hayd 2m4f	B HHdl		HVY	£8885

Total win prize-money £13729

Going:	Sf: 0-1 GS: 1-2 Gd: 0-1 GF: - Fm: 0-0
Distance:	2m/2m3: 0-0 2m4-2m7: 0-2 3m+: 1-2
Track:	LH: 1-4 RH: 0-0 Tight: 0-1 Gall: 0-2
Aids:	Bl: 0-0 Vi: 0-0 Tstrap: 0-0
Best Rating:	124 2/02 Hayd 2m4f heavy Hdl

Useful novice hurdler, he has proved himself suited to three miles plus over fences. Acts on soft ground.

Mr Custard

11-y-o b g Newski (USA)-May Owen (Master Owen)
Miss L J C Sweeting Miss L J C Sweeting

Placings:332P/50003-4   (0245)
2002/03: 25⁴G,

	Starts	1st	2nd	3rd	Win & Pl
Chases	1	0	0	0	272
Career Total	10	0	1	3	2167

Going:	Sf: 0-0 GS: 0-0 Gd: 0-1 GF: - Fm: 0-0
Distance:	2m/2m3: 0-0 2m4-2m7: 0-0 3m+: 0-1
Track:	LH: 0-0 RH: 0-1 Tight: 0-0 Gall: 0-0
Aids:	Bl: 0-0 Vi: 0-0 Tstrap: 0-0
Best Rating:	98 5/00 Strf 3m gd-fm Ch

Held under Rules, he is a three-mile Ladies Open specialist. Has not run on extremes of ground and recent wins have come on the easy side of good ground.

Mr Dow Jones (IRE)

11-y-o b g The Bart (USA)-Roseowen (Derring Rose)
K Goldsworthy Mrs L A Goldsworthy

Placings:0F1/2P30/331U310/330011431-P5320   (4133)
2002/03: 25⁴G, 22⁵GS, 26³GS, 24²S, 26⁸G,

	Starts	1st	2nd	3rd	Win & Pl
Chases	5	0	1	1	1076
Career Total	28	6	2	8	24171
120	4/02 Chel	3m2f110yH Ch		GD	£5798
120	3/02 Hrfd	3m1f110yH Ch		GD	£1928
111	2/02 Hrfd	3m1f110yH Ch		HVY	£1865
104	4/01 Hrfd	2m3f	H Ch	GD	£2719
104	2/01 Ludl	3m	H Ch	G-S	£2628
108	4/99 Chep	3m	H Ch	HVY	£3598

Total win prize-money £18541

Going:	Sf: 0-1 GS: 0-2 Gd: 0-2 GF: - Fm: 0-0
Distance:	2m/2m3: 0-0 2m4-2m7: 0-1 3m+: 0-4
Track:	LH: 0-3 RH: 0-1 Tight: 0-0 Gall: 0-0
Aids:	Bl: 0-0 Vi: 0-0 Tstrap: 0-0
Best Rating:	120 4/02 Chel 3m2f110y good Ch

Useful hunter chaser; pays his way each season; scored back-to-back victories at Hereford and Uttoxeter spring 2003; possibly just failed to stay 3m 4f when third in Horse and Hound Cup ; likes cut in the ground.

Mr Ed (IRE)

99   96

5-y-o ch g In The Wings-Center Moriches (IRE) (Magical

Wonder (USA))
P Bowen Gwilym J Morris

Placings:424   (2669)
2002/03: 17⁴GS, 17²GS, 19⁴S,

	Starts	1st	2nd	3rd	Win & Pl
Hurdles	3	0	1	0	2512
Career Total	3	0	1	0	2512

Going:	Sf: 0-1 GS: 0-2 Gd: 0-0 GF: - Fm: 0-0
Distance:	2m/2m3: 0-2 2m4-2m7: 0-1 3m+: 0-0
Track:	LH: 0-0 RH: 0-3 Tight: 0-2 Gall: 0-0
Aids:	Bl: 0-0 Vi: 0-0 Tstrap: 0-0
Best Rating:	99 12/02 Tntn 2m1f gd-sft Hdl

Mr Evans

84   108+

8-y-o ch g Current Edition (IRE)-Manor Park Crumpet (True Song)
Miss E C Lavelle John Jones

Placings:100-2PU   (2585)
2002/03: 22²GS, 20²GS, 23¹UGS,

	Starts	1st	2nd	3rd	Win & Pl
Chases	3	0	1	0	1250
Career Total	6	1	1	0	2829
99	10/01 Sthl	2m	H NHF	GD	£1578

Total win prize-money £1579

Going:	Sf: 0-0 GS: 0-3 Gd: 0-0 GF: - Fm: 0-0
Distance:	2m/2m3: 0-0 2m4-2m7: 0-2 3m+: 0-1
Track:	LH: 0-0 RH: 0-2 Tight: 0-1 Gall: 0-1
Aids:	Bl: 0-0 Vi: 0-0 Tstrap: 0-0
Best Rating:	108 11/02 Font 2m6f gd-sft Ch

Mr Fluffy

107   130+

6-y-o br g Charmer-Hinton Bairn (Balinger)
P J Hobbs The Cockpit Crew

Placings:25/3504-F2111   (1156)
2002/03: 20⁶GF, 20²G, 20¹GF, 20¹G, 22¹G,

	Starts	1st	2nd	3rd	Win & Pl
Hurdles	5	3	1	0	11902
Career Total	11	3	2	1	13049
129	9/02 NAbb 2m6f	E Hdl		GD	£3267
120	8/02 Worc 2m4f	E Hdl		GD	£3451
111	6/02 Uttx	2m4f110yD Hdl		G-F	£3610

Total win prize-money £10331

Going:	Sf: 0-0 GS: 0-0 Gd: 2-3 GF: - Fm: 1-2
Distance:	2m/2m3: 0-0 2m4-2m7: 3-5 3m+: 0-0
Track:	LH: 3-4 RH: 0-0 Tight: 1-2 Gall: 0-0
Aids:	Bl: 0-0 Vi: 0-0 Tstrap: 0-0
Best Rating:	129 9/02 NAbb 2m6f good Hdl

Useful hurdler; has shown some ability in bumpers. Won three novice hurdles in the summer of 2002. Stays 18 furlongs. Considered a chaser in the making.

Mr Gisby (USA)

86   103

5-y-o b g Chief's Crown (USA)-Double Lock (Home Guard (USA)
Mrs L Wadham (S C Williams 3/3) Nightmare Partnership

Placings:3P55-5   (4482)
2002/03: 19⁵GF,

	Starts	1st	2nd	3rd	Win & Pl
Hurdles	1	0	0	0	0

| Career Total | 5 | 0 | 0 | 1 | 553 |

Going:	Sf: 0-0 GS: 0-0 Gd: 0-0 GF: - Fm: 0-1
Distance:	2m/2m3: 0-0 2m4-2m7: 0-1 3m+: 0-0
Track:	LH: 0-0 RH: 0-0 Tight: 0-0 Gall: 0-0
Aids:	Bl: 0-0 Vi: 0-0 Tstrap: 0-0
Best Rating:	103 12/01 Kemp 2m good Hdl

Very modest on the Flat, he has shown ability over hurdles at a moderate level; may need cut in the ground.

Mr Grimsdale (IRE)

11-y-o ch g Grimesgill (USA)-Lady Rose Walk (Sir Herbert)
Mrs A C Tate Mrs A C Tate

Placings:0/U21/0/P65-PP0   (4487)
2002/03: 19⁰G, 25⁵G, 16⁵GF,

	Starts	1st	2nd	3rd	Win & Pl
Chases	3	0	0	0	
Career Total	11	1	1	0	2115
98	4/00 Uttx 2m7f	H Ch		HVY	£1540

Total win prize-money £1540

Going:	Sf: 0-0 GS: 0-0 Gd: 0-2 GF: - Fm: 0-1
Distance:	2m/2m3: 0-1 2m4-2m7: 0-1 3m+: 0-1
Track:	LH: 0-0 RH: 0-3 Tight: 0-0 Gall: 0-0
Aids:	Bl: 0-0 Vi: 0-0 Tstrap: 0-0
Best Rating:	98 4/00 Uttx 2m7f heavy Ch

Mr Half Sharp

10-y-o ch g Mr Fluorocarbon-Star Shell (Queens Hussar)
Sidney J Smith Sidney J Smith

Placings:0P/4F050/13-P   (0208)
2002/03: 22⁵G,

	Starts	1st	2nd	3rd	Win & Pl
Chases	1	0	0	0	
Career Total	10	1	0	1	2790
95	4/02 Towc 2m6f	D Ch		GD	£2086

Total win prize-money £2087

Going:	Sf: 0-0 GS: 0-0 Gd: 0-1 GF: - Fm: 0-0
Distance:	2m/2m3: 0-0 2m4-2m7: 0-1 3m+: 0-0
Track:	LH: 0-0 RH: 0-1 Tight: 0-0 Gall: 0-0
Aids:	Bl: 0-0 Vi: 0-0 Tstrap: 0-0
Best Rating:	95 4/02 Towc 2m6f good Ch

Hunter chaser. Won easily at Towcester in April 2002 over two miles six furlongs. Suited by good to soft ground or faster.

Mr Hawkeye (USA)

4-y-o ch g Royal Academy (USA)-Port Plaisance (USA) (Woodman (USA))
Ms A E Embiricos (W J Haggas 17/9) Ms A E Embiricos

Placings:P   (3590)
2002/03: 16⁵HY,

	Starts	1st	2nd	3rd	Win & Pl
Hurdles	1	0	0	0	
Career Total	1	0	0	0	

Going:	Sf: 0-1 GS: 0-0 Gd: 0-0 GF: - Fm: 0-0
Distance:	2m/2m3: 0-1 2m4-2m7: 0-0 3m+: 0-0
Track:	LH: 0-0 RH: 0-1 Tight: 0-0 Gall: 0-0
Aids:	Bl: 0-0 Vi: 0-0 Tstrap: 0-0
Best Rating:	0 2/03 Sand 2m110y heavy Hdl

Mr Laggan

102(95h)   (74h)78
8-y-o b g Tina s Pet-Galway Gal (Proverb)
Miss Kate Milligan   Mrs J M L Milligan

Placings:56P4/30600P-240PPP5   (4787)
2002/03: 25²G, 25⁴GF, 25⁰GF, 27⁶G, 25ᴾHY, 25ᴾG, 20⁵G,

	Starts	1st	2nd	3rd	Win & Pl
Hurdles	1	0	0	0	
Chases	6	0	1	0	1130
Career Total	17	0	1	1	1556

Going: Sf: 0-1 GS: 0-0 Gd: 0-4 GF: - Fm: 0-2
Distance: 2m/2m3: 0-0 2m4-2m7: 0-1 3m+: 0-6
Track: LH: 0-6 RH: 0-1 Tight: 0-2 Gall: 0-0
Aids: Bl: 0-0 Vi: 0-0 Tstrap: 0-0
Best Rating: 96 9/00 MRas 1m5f110y gd-fm NHF

Plating-class hurdler/chaser; has not lived up to his second at Market Rasen June 2003; stays three miles.

Mr Lamb

(82h)   (80h)
8-y-o gr g Deploy-Caroline Lamb (Hotfoot)
S Dow Zero 3 Racing

Placings:1/1F2F/F0005/00-F   (1173)
2002/03: 21ᶠGF,

	Starts	1st	2nd	3rd	Win & Pl
Chases	1	0	0	0	
Career Total	13	2	1	0	9775

119 10/99 Chel 2m110y D Hdl GD £4071
99 1/99 Muss 2m H NHF G-S £1563
Total win prize-money £5636

Going: Sf: 0-0 GS: 0-0 Gd: 0-0 GF: - Fm: 0-1
Distance: 2m/2m3: 0-0 2m4-2m7: 0-1 3m+: 0-0
Track: LH: 0-1 RH: 0-0 Tight: 0-1 Gall: 0-0
Aids: Bl: 0-0 Vi: 0-0 Tstrap: 0-0
Best Rating: 137 3/00 Chel 2m110y good Hdl

Sold for big money after winning a bumper, he started off promisingly over hurdles but has disappointed and thus dropped down the handicap since. Not the best of jumpers.

Mr Lehman

99f   92f
6-y-o ch g Presidium-Lehmans Lot (Oats)
Mrs M Reveley D C Renton

Placings:430   (4437)
2002/03: 16⁴G, 16³GS, 16⁰G,

	Starts	1st	2nd	3rd	Win & Pl
NH Flat	3	0	0	1	286
Career Total	3	0	0	1	286

Going: Sf: 0-0 GS: 0-1 Gd: 0-2 GF: - Fm: 0-0
Distance: 2m/2m3: 0-3 2m4-2m7: 0-0 3m+: 0-0
Track: LH: 0-2 RH: 0-1 Tight: 0-1 Gall: 0-1
Aids: Bl: 0-0 Vi: 0-0 Tstrap: 0-0
Best Rating: 92 1/03 Muss 2m good NHF

Modest form in bumpers.

Mr Leroi (IRE)

10-y-o b g Camden Town-Black Tulip (Pals Passage)
R A Gadd   R A Gadd

Placings:F6/P43/5   (0312)

2002/03: 21⁵G,

	Starts	1st	2nd	3rd	Win & Pl
Chases	1	0	0	0	0
Career Total	6	0	0	1	363

Going: Sf: 0-0 GS: 0-0 Gd: 0-1 GF: - Fm: 0-0
Distance: 2m/2m3: 0-0 2m4-2m7: 0-1 3m+: 0-0
Track: LH: 0-0 RH: 0-1 Tight: 0-1 Gall: 0-0
Aids: Bl: 0-0 Vi: 0-0 Tstrap: 0-0
Best Rating: 79 3/99 Tntn 2m1f soft Hdl

Mr Magnetic (IRE)

12-y-o b g Point North-Miss Ironside (General Ironside)
Dominic Harvey   Dominic Harvey

Placings:505/041235F1/3FP340/0/1-5P   (3479)
2002/03: 26⁵GF, 25ᴾGS,

	Starts	1st	2nd	3rd	Win & Pl
Chases	2	0	0	0	0
Career Total	21	3	1	3	11050

103 4/02 Tntn 3m H Ch GD £2664
114 4/98 Hrfd 3m1f110yE Ch G-S £3130
104 6/97 Gowr 2m4f NHF G-Y £2712
Total win prize-money £8507

Going: Sf: 0-0 GS: 0-1 Gd: 0-0 GF: - Fm: 0-1
Distance: 2m/2m3: 0-0 2m4-2m7: 0-0 3m+: 0-2
Track: LH: 0-1 RH: 0-1 Tight: 0-0 Gall: 0-1
Aids: Bl: 0-0 Vi: 0-0 Tstrap: 0-0
Best Rating: 114 4/98 Hrfd 3m1f110y gd-sft Ch

Ex-Irish, he stays three miles and handles testing ground well but is not a natural jumper of fences.

Mr Mahdlo

111   103
9-y-o b g Rakaposhi King-Fedelm (Celtic Cone)
R D E Woodhouse (Jonjo O Neill 12/10) M K Oldham

Placings:000/335F25212PP/42P21PPP/P4P22PP/PPP-31PP13P3P   (3993)
2002/03: 25³GS, 24¹S, 24ᴾG, 26ᴾG, 27¹S, 30³GS, 24ᴾHY, 30⁸S, 25ᴾG,

	Starts	1st	2nd	3rd	Win & Pl
Chases	9	2	0	3	9729
Career Total	41	4	7	5	24952

100 11/02 Sedg 3m3f F(0-100)HCh SFT £3406
103 6/02 Uttx 3m D(0-120)HCh SFT £4095
117 1/00 Weth 3m1f D(0-125)HCh SFT £3825
96 1/99 Ayr 3m110y F(0-110)HHdl HVY £2851
Total win prize-money £14177

Going: Sf: 2-4 GS: 0-2 Gd: 0-3 GF: - Fm: 0-0
Distance: 2m/2m3: 0-0 2m4-2m7: 0-0 3m+: 2-9
Track: LH: 2-9 RH: 0-0 Tight: 1-4 Gall: 0-2
Aids: Bl: 0-0 Vi: 0-0 Tstrap: 0-0
Best Rating: 117 1/00 Weth 3m1f soft Ch

Modest staying chaser who is frequently pulled up; has ability, winning at Uttoxeter in June 2002 and at Sedgefield in November; well suited by soft ground; has worn sheepskin cheekpieces of late.

Mr Mann (IRE)

10-y-o ch g Duky-Slan Abhaile (Trimmingham)
Mrs M A Kendall   Mrs M A Kendall

Placings:F2/3F4P2-U   (3895)
2002/03: 25ᵁGS,

	Starts	1st	2nd	3rd	Win & Pl
Chases	1	0	0	0	
Career Total	8	0	2	1	2142

Going: Sf: 0-0 GS: 0-1 Gd: 0-0 GF: - Fm: 0-0
Distance: 2m/2m3: 0-0 2m4-2m7: 0-0 3m+: 0-1
Track: LH: 0-1 RH: 0-0 Tight: 0-1 Gall: 0-0
Aids: Bl: 0-0 Vi: 0-0 Tstrap: 0-0
Best Rating: 92 5/01 Strf 3m gd-fm Ch

Moderate chaser, stays three miles, acts on any ground.

Mr Markham (IRE)

97(113h)   (102h)129
11-y-o b g Naheez (USA)-Brighter Gail (Bustineto)
J T Gifford   Felix Rosenstiel s Widow & Son

Placings:115/221303/13441P210/400F/305015500-4U15F0   (4367)
2002/03: 21⁴G, 24ᵁGS, 29¹S, 25⁵GS, 27ᶠS, 20⁰G,

	Starts	1st	2nd	3rd	Win & Pl
Hurdles	1	0	0	0	0
Chases	5	1	0	0	16238
Career Total	37	8	3	4	73437

129 11/02 Plum 3m5f C(0-130)HCh SFT £15428
145 1/02 Kemp 2m5f C(0-130)HHdl G-S £7442
124 3/00 Font 2m4f D Ch G-S £3753
130 1/00 Plum 2m1f E Ch SFT £3006
140 10/99 Asct 2m110y B(0-150)HHdl GD £6097
143 12/97 Asct 2m110y B Hdl G-S £8091
119 2/97 Newb 2m110y H NHF GF £7006
107 11/96 Sand 2m110y H NHF GD £1997
Total win prize-money £52824

Going: Sf: 1-2 GS: 0-2 Gd: 0-2 GF: - Fm: 0-0
Distance: 2m/2m3: 0-0 2m4-2m7: 0-2 3m+: 1-4
Track: LH: 1-2 RH: 0-4 Tight: 1-3 Gall: 0-0
Aids: Bl: 1-3 Vi: 0-0 Tstrap: 0-0
Best Rating: 145 1/02 Kemp 2m5f gd-sft Hdl

Useful chaser; stays extreme distances and suited by cut in the ground; sometimes wears headgear.

Mr McDuck (IRE)

11-y-o ch g Denel (FR)-Coldwater Morning (Laurence O)
Ms S Duell   J A V Duell

Placings:0F0/0/PP/0046/4   (0068)
2002/03: 21⁴GF,

	Starts	1st	2nd	3rd	Win & Pl
Chases	1	0	0	0	0
Career Total	11	0	0	0	0

Going: Sf: 0-0 GS: 0-0 Gd: 0-0 GF: - Fm: 0-1
Distance: 2m/2m3: 0-0 2m4-2m7: 0-1 3m+: 0-0
Track: LH: 0-1 RH: 0-0 Tight: 0-1 Gall: 0-0
Aids: Bl: 0-0 Vi: 0-0 Tstrap: 0-0
Best Rating: 68 5/00 Hexm 2m4f110y good Hdl

Mr McDuff (IRE)

97(94h)   (65h)79
7-y-o b g Mandalus-Le Glen (Le Bavard (FR))
M J Gingell   The Duffers X

Placings:5P55U36-25431450000   (4573)
2002/03: 19²G, 24⁴GF, 20⁴G, 20³GF, 16¹G, 20⁴G, 20⁵GF, 16⁶G, 20⁵S, 16⁰G, 16⁰GF,

	Starts	1st	2nd	3rd	Win & Pl
Hurdles	10	1	1	0	4815

| Chases | 1 | 0 | 0 | 1 | 537 |
| Career Total | 18 | 1 | 1 | 2 | 5828 |

90 9/02 Worc 2m E Hdl GD £2989
Total win prize-money £2989

Going: Sf: 0-1 GS: 0-0 Gd: 1-6 GF: - Fm: 0-4
Distance: 2m/2m3: 1-4 2m4-2m7: 0-6 3m+: 0-1
Track: LH: 1-7 RH: 0-3 Tight: 0-5 Gall: 0-2
Aids: Bl: 0-0 Vi: 0-0 Tstrap: 0-0
Best Rating: 90 9/02 Worc 2m good Hdl

Plating-class hurdler; has had difficulty finding the right trip and appreciated a drop back to two miles when winning a moderate maiden hurdle at Worcester September 2002.

Mr Micky (IRE)
88   96
5-y-o b g Rudimentary (USA)-Top Berry (High Top)
T D Easterby David & Steven Dudley

Placings:00-0130   (3564)
2002/03: 16⁰GS, 16¹HY, 16³HY, 17⁰HY,

	Starts	1st	2nd	3rd	Win & Pl
Hurdles	4	1	0	1	3632
Career Total	6	1	0	1	3632

96 11/02 Weth 2m E(0-100)HHdl HVY £3094
Total win prize-money £3094

Going: Sf: 1-3 GS: 0-1 Gd: 0-0 GF: - Fm: 0-0
Distance: 2m/2m3: 1-4 2m4-2m7: 0-0 3m+: 0-0
Track: LH: 1-3 RH: 0-1 Tight: 0-1 Gall: 0-0
Aids: Bl: 0-0 Vi: 0-0 Tstrap: 0-0
Best Rating: 96 11/02 Weth 2m heavy Hdl

Moderate hurdler at around two miles and acts on a soft surface.

Mr Midaz
105   83
4-y-o ch g Danzig Connection (USA)-Marmy (Midyan (USA))
D W Whillans (Jedd O Keeffe 8/10) S C Carter

Placings:6450410   (4507)
2002/03: 16⁶GS, 17⁴G, 16⁵GF, 16⁰GS, 16⁴GS, 17¹G, 16⁰G,

	Starts	1st	2nd	3rd	Win & Pl
Hurdles	7	1	0	0	4052
Career Total	7	1	0	0	4052

83 3/03 Sedg 2m1f E(0-105)HHdl GD £3465
Total win prize-money £3465

Going: Sf: 0-0 GS: 0-2 Gd: 1-3 GF: - Fm: 0-2
Distance: 2m/2m3: 1-7 2m4-2m7: 0-0 3m+: 0-0
Track: LH: 1-6 RH: 0-1 Tight: 1-5 Gall: 0-0
Aids: Bl: 0-0 Vi: 0-0 Tstrap: 0-0
Best Rating: 83 3/03 Sedg 2m1f good Hdl

Plating-class hurdler; acts on good.

Mr Mighty (IRE)
7-y-o br g Montelimar (USA)-Laurie Belle (Boreen (FR))
N J Pewter N J Pewter

Placings:000-O   (4671)
2002/03: 24⁰G,

	Starts	1st	2nd	3rd	Win & Pl
Chases	1	0	0	0	
Career Total	4	0	0	0	

Going: Sf: 0-0 GS: 0-0 Gd: 0-1 GF: - Fm: 0-0
Distance: 2m/2m3: 0-0 2m4-2m7: 0-0 3m+: 0-1
Track: LH: 0-1 RH: 0-1 Tight: 0-1 Gall: 0-0

Aids: Bl: 0-0 Vi: 0-0 Tstrap: 0-0
Best Rating: 73 4/02 Fair 2m yield NHF

Mr Miller (IRE)
97   63d
11-y-o b g The Bart (USA)-Celtic Connection (Martinmas)
O Sherwood Pat & Peter Flaherty

Placings:P243/PPB434P64/P-644UFP   (4696)
2002/03: 23⁶GS, 26⁴S, 25⁴S, 26⁰GS, 25⁴G, 26⁰G,

	Starts	1st	2nd	3rd	Win & Pl
Chases	6	0	0	0	639
Career Total	20	0	1	2	2732

Going: Sf: 0-2 GS: 0-2 Gd: 0-2 GF: - Fm: 0-0
Distance: 2m/2m3: 0-0 2m4-2m7: 0-0 3m+: 0-6
Track: LH: 0-2 RH: 0-3 Tight: 0-4 Gall: 0-0
Aids: Bl: 0-2 Vi: 0-0 Tstrap: 0-0
Best Rating: 86 2/99 Plum 3m1f110y soft Ch

Poor staying chaser.

Mr Morris
88   68
7-y-o ch g Current Edition (IRE)-Manor Park Crumpet (True Song)
Miss E C Lavelle John Jones

Placings:P0   (4514)
2002/03: 22⁶GS, 22⁰GF,

	Starts	1st	2nd	3rd	Win & Pl
Hurdles	2	0	0	0	
Career Total	2	0	0	0	

Going: Sf: 0-0 GS: 0-1 Gd: 0-0 GF: - Fm: 0-1
Distance: 2m/2m3: 0-0 2m4-2m7: 0-2 3m+: 0-0
Track: LH: 0-1 RH: 0-1 Tight: 0-1 Gall: 0-0
Aids: Bl: 0-0 Vi: 0-0 Tstrap: 0-0
Best Rating: 68 4/03 Extr 2m6f110y gd-fm Hdl

Mr Music Man (IRE)
(91h)   (49h)52
10-y-o b g Accordion-A New Rose (IRE) (Saher)
Miss G Browne Brig C K Price

Placings:1300/P/2P0P/P/0P5004P   (2663)
2002/03: 16⁰GF, 16⁶G, 20⁵G, 20⁴GF, 17⁰GF, 20⁴GS, 22⁴S,

	Starts	1st	2nd	3rd	Win & Pl
Hurdles	5	0	0	0	0
Chases	2	0	0	0	275
Career Total	17	1	1	1	3383

115 1/98 Kemp 2m H NHF G-S £1507
Total win prize-money £1508

Going: Sf: 0-1 GS: 0-1 Gd: 0-2 GF: - Fm: 0-3
Distance: 2m/2m3: 0-3 2m4-2m7: 0-4 3m+: 0-0
Track: LH: 0-4 RH: 0-2 Tight: 0-2 Gall: 0-0
Aids: Bl: 0-4 Vi: 0-0 Tstrap: 0-0
Best Rating: 115 2/98 Newb 2m110y good NHF

Mr No Man
75   47
7-y-o b g Cosmonaut-Christmas Show (Petorius)
T J Fitzgerald (J G Fitzgerald 26/2) The No Man Partnership

Going: Sf: 0-3 GS: 0-0 Gd: 0-1 GF: - Fm: 0-0

Placings:5233/4/1-PP0   (4507)
2002/03: 23⁵GS, 20⁶G, 16⁰G,

	Starts	1st	2nd	3rd	Win & Pl
Hurdles	3	0	0	0	
Career Total	9	1	1	2	3787

91 5/01 Weth 2m E Hdl GD £2856
Total win prize-money £2856

Going: Sf: 0-0 GS: 0-1 Gd: 0-2 GF: - Fm: 0-0
Distance: 2m/2m3: 0-1 2m4-2m7: 0-2 3m+: 0-0
Track: LH: 0-3 RH: 0-0 Tight: 0-1 Gall: 0-0
Aids: Bl: 0-0 Vi: 0-0 Tstrap: 0-2
Best Rating: 97 3/01 MRas 2m1f110y gd-sft Hdl

Mr Pendleberry
(91c)   (89c)93
9-y-o ch g Symbolic-Antonoua (Anton Lad)
A Dickman Mike Smallman

Placings:000/1P5/4264-P   (0088)
2002/03: 20⁰G,

	Starts	1st	2nd	3rd	Win & Pl
Hurdles	1	0	0	0	
Career Total	11	1	1	0	3477

104 5/99 Prth 2m4f110yE Hdl SFT £2409
Total win prize-money £2410

Going: Sf: 0-0 GS: 0-0 Gd: 0-1 GF: - Fm: 0-0
Distance: 2m/2m3: 0-0 2m4-2m7: 0-1 3m+: 0-0
Track: LH: 0-1 RH: 0-0 Tight: 0-0 Gall: 0-0
Aids: Bl: 0-0 Vi: 0-0 Tstrap: 0-0
Best Rating: 104 5/99 Prth 2m4f110y soft Hdl

Modest hurdler, has shown fair form in modest company since returning from in excess of two years off in late 2001. Has achieved little over fences so far.

Mr Perry (IRE)
(103h)   (89h)73
7-y-o br g Perugino (USA)-Elegant Tune (USA) (Alysheba (USA))
Mrs P Ford R Champken & A Petrie

Placings:F33/P4F00/PP3343201-00P   (2133)
2002/03: 20⁰GF, 16⁰HY, 20⁶G,

	Starts	1st	2nd	3rd	Win & Pl
Hurdles	2	0	0	0	0
Chases	1	0	0	0	0
Career Total	20	1	1	5	4325

89 10/01 Uttx 2m G Hdl G-S £1750
Total win prize-money £1750

Going: Sf: 0-1 GS: 0-0 Gd: 0-1 GF: - Fm: 0-1
Distance: 2m/2m3: 0-1 2m4-2m7: 0-2 3m+: 0-0
Track: LH: 0-2 RH: 0-1 Tight: 0-2 Gall: 0-0
Aids: Bl: 0-0 Vi: 0-0 Tstrap: 0-0
Best Rating: 91 1/01 Catt 2m gd-sft Hdl

Mr Phipps
91   80
7-y-o b g Shareef Dancer (USA)-Frost In Summer (Busted)
P Winkworth Bill Naylor

Placings:F060   (4212)
2002/03: 18⁴HY, 18⁰S, 19⁶S, 16⁰G,

	Starts	1st	2nd	3rd	Win & Pl
Hurdles	4	0	0	0	0
Career Total	4	0	0	0	0

Going: Sf: 0-3 GS: 0-0 Gd: 0-1 GF: - Fm: 0-0

Distance: 2m/2m3: 0-4 2m4-2m7: 0-0 3m+: 0-0
Track: LH: 0-4 RH: 0-0 Tight: 0-3 Gall: 0-1
Aids: Bl: 0-0 Vi: 0-0 Tstrap: 0-0
Best Rating: 80 2/03 Newb 2m3f   soft   Hdl

Mr Pistachio (IRE)

8-y-o b g Royal Fountain-Knockananig (Pitpan)
Miss K Marks Nick Shutts

Placings:P/22P-55   (3950)
2002/03: 26⁵GF, 23⁵GS,

	Starts	1st	2nd	3rd	Win & Pl
Hurdles	1	0	0	0	0
Chases	1	0	0	0	0
Career Total	6	0	2	0	1051

Going: Sf: 0-0 GS: 0-1 Gd: 0-0 GF: - Fm: 0-1
Distance: 2m/2m3: 0-0 2m4-2m7: 0-0 3m+: 0-2
Track: LH: 0-0 RH: 0-2 Tight: 0-2 Gall: 0-0
Aids: Bl: 0-1 Vi: 0-0 Tstrap: 0-0
Best Rating: 86 5/01 Aint 3m1f   good   Ch

Mr Playfull

13-y-o br g Teamwork-Blue Nursery (Bluerullah)
Mrs L C Jewell Mrs Linda Jewell

Placings:0403/202432331/2241422U3/21F1FP13/2P425F3
43/13F455440015/F0P1/PPP-PP   (0555)
2002/03: 26ᴾGF, 25ᴾGF,

	Starts	1st	2nd	3rd	Win & Pl
Chases	2	0	0	0	
Career Total	60	8	10	9	45113
110	9/00	NAbb	2m5f110yD(0-125)HCh	G-F	£4036
110	3/00	NAbb	2m5f110yE(0-115)HCh	GD	£3057
117	5/99	Extr	2m7f110yD(0-120)HCh	G-F	£4684
119	4/98	Tntn	3m	D(0-120)Ch	SFT	£3615
107	9/97	NAbb	2m5f110yD(0-120)HCh	GD	£3441
109	5/97	Extr	2m3f110yF(0-105)HCh	GD	£3249
99	10/96	Extr	2m6f110yD Ch	G-F	£4140
93	4/96	NAbb	2m1f	E(0-100)HHdl	G-S	£2410
			Total win prize-money £28636		

Going: Sf: 0-0 GS: 0-0 Gd: 0-0 GF: - Fm: 0-2
Distance: 2m/2m3: 0-0 2m4-2m7: 0-0 3m+: 0-2
Track: LH: 0-0 RH: 0-0 Tight: 0-1 Gall: 0-0
Aids: Bl: 0-0 Vi: 0-0 Tstrap: 0-0
Best Rating: 119 4/98 Tntn 3m   soft   Ch

Mr Rathmore (IRE)

(100h)   (84h)
9-y-o gr g Valville (FR)-Lady Grasp (Ballad Rock)
N A Twiston-Davies Geoffrey & Donna Keeys

Placings:00/4353P6/5-PP   (2133)
2002/03: 21ᴾS, 20ᴾG,

	Starts	1st	2nd	3rd	Win & Pl
Chases	2	0	0	0	
Career Total	11	0	0	2	1099

Going: Sf: 0-1 GS: 0-0 Gd: 0-1 GF: - Fm: 0-0
Distance: 2m/2m3: 0-0 2m4-2m7: 0-0 3m+: 0-2
Track: LH: 0-1 RH: 0-1 Tight: 0-2 Gall: 0-0
Aids: Bl: 0-0 Vi: 0-0 Tstrap: 0-0
Best Rating: 89 1/01 Ludl 2m   soft   Hdl

Mr Smudge

11-y-o ch g Fearless Action (USA)-Amerian County
(Amerian (USA))
Mrs F J Marriott C Marriott

Placings:3PPP/P1-25PP   (4133)
2002/03: 25²GF, 25⁵S, 24ᴾS, 26ᴾG,

	Starts	1st	2nd	3rd	Win & Pl
Chases	4	0	1	0	1208
Career Total	10	1	1	1	5545
92	5/01	Chel	3m1f110yH Ch	GD	£3688
			Total win prize-money £3689		

Going: Sf: 0-2 GS: 0-0 Gd: 0-1 GF: - Fm: 0-1
Distance: 2m/2m3: 0-0 2m4-2m7: 0-0 3m+: 0-4
Track: LH: 0-2 RH: 0-2 Tight: 0-0 Gall: 0-2
Aids: Bl: 0-0 Vi: 0-0 Tstrap: 0-0
Best Rating: 92 5/01 Chel 3m1f110y   good   Ch

A winning pointer this season; suited by a sound surface; stays three miles one.

Mr Stitch

6-y-o br g Lancastrian-Hovian (Hotfoot)
Mrs L B Normile The Heatheryfour

Placings:0PUP   (4305)
2002/03: 17ᴾG, 20ᴾGF, 25ᵁS, 25ᴾG,

	Starts	1st	2nd	3rd	Win & Pl
NH Flat	1	0	0	0	0
Hurdles	1	0	0	0	0
Chases	2	0	0	0	0
Career Total	4	0	0	0	

Going: Sf: 0-1 GS: 0-0 Gd: 0-2 GF: - Fm: 0-1
Distance: 2m/2m3: 0-1 2m4-2m7: 0-1 3m+: 0-1
Track: LH: 0-2 RH: 0-1 Tight: 0-2 Gall: 0-0
Aids: Bl: 0-0 Vi: 0-0 Tstrap: 0-0
Best Rating: 17 11/02 Aint 2m1f   good   NHF

Mr Timbrology (IRE)
100   108

9-y-o b g Insan (USA)-Mary Kate (Callernish)
R H Alner P M De Wilde

Placings:0/2415/33/P41-2UP   (2775)
2002/03: 19²S, 25ᵁGS, 24ᴾS,

	Starts	1st	2nd	3rd	Win & Pl
Chases	3	0	1	0	2084
Career Total	13	2	2	2	10386
108	4/02	Chep	3m	E(0-110)HCh	G-F	£3610
102	1/00	Towc	2m	E Hdl	HVY	£2695
			Total win prize-money £6306		

Going: Sf: 0-2 GS: 0-1 Gd: 0-0 GF: - Fm: 0-0
Distance: 2m/2m3: 0-1 2m4-2m7: 0-0 3m+: 0-2
Track: LH: 0-1 RH: 0-2 Tight: 0-0 Gall: 0-1
Aids: Bl: 0-0 Vi: 0-0 Tstrap: 0-0
Best Rating: 108 11/02 Hrfd 2m3f   soft   Ch

Modest chaser, stays three miles and acts on fast ground.

Mr Woodentop (IRE)
106(106h)   (133 h)122

7-y-o b g Roselier (FR)-Una s Polly (Pollerton)
L Lungo Ashleybank Investments Limited

Placings:4/211S1-11P   (3988)

2002/03: 24¹S, 25¹S, 20ᴾS,

	Starts	1st	2nd	3rd	Win & Pl
Hurdles	1	1	0	0	4729
Chases	2	1	0	0	4726
Career Total	9	5	1	0	23348
122	1/03	Ayr	3m1f	E Ch	SFT	£4725
127	11/02	Ayr	3m110y	D(0-125)HHdl	SFT	£4728
122	4/02	Ayr	3m110y	B HHdl	GD	£7250
127	12/01	Ayr	2m4f	E Hdl	SFT	£2492
114	12/01	Hayd	2m4f	D Hdl	SFT	£3640
			Total win prize-money £22838		

Going: Sf: 2-3 GS: 0-0 Gd: 0-0 GF: - Fm: 0-0
Distance: 2m/2m3: 0-0 2m4-2m7: 0-1 3m+: 2-2
Track: LH: 2-2 RH: 0-1 Tight: 0-0 Gall: 0-0
Aids: Bl: 0-0 Vi: 0-0 Tstrap: 0-0
Best Rating: 127 11/02 Ayr 3m110y   soft   Hdl

A decent staying hurdler with a good strike rate, he made a successful chasing debut at Ayr in January 2003; pulled up next time when stable were out of sorts; stays three miles plus and is suited by soft ground.

Mr Woodland
105(103h)   (116h)116

9-y-o br g Landyap (USA)-Wood Corner (Sit In The Corner (USA))
J D Frost P A Tylor

Placings:4322150F3-12110   (2040)
2002/03: 21¹GF, 21²GF, 23¹S, 24¹GF, 21⁰HY,

	Starts	1st	2nd	3rd	Win & Pl
Chases	5	3	1	0	17789
Career Total	14	4	3	2	23920
111	10/02	Hntg	3m	D Ch	G-F	£4563
116	9/02	Worc	2m7f110yD Ch	GD	£4836
112	7/02	NAbb	2m5f110yD Ch	G-F	£4754
116	1/02	Winc	2m6f	E Hdl	GD	£2859
			Total win prize-money £17014		

Going: Sf: 0-1 GS: 0-0 Gd: 1-1 GF: - Fm: 2-3
Distance: 2m/2m3: 0-0 2m4-2m7: 1-3 3m+: 2-2
Track: LH: 2-4 RH: 1-1 Tight: 1-3 Gall: 1-1
Aids: Bl: 0-0 Vi: 0-0 Tstrap: 0-0
Best Rating: 116 9/02 Worc 2m7f110y   good   Ch

Fair chaser; gradually improved over hurdles and got off the mark at Wincanton in January 2002. In good form over fences in the second half of 2002 with wins at Newton Abbot, Worcester and Huntingdon. Suited by two and a half to three miles and fast ground.

Mrs Duf
96(86c)   (63+c)97

9-y-o b m Teenoso (USA)-Hatherley (Deep Run)
R H Alner R Alner

Placings:2350/12-4000   (4004)
2002/03: 25⁴S, 25⁰HY, 21⁰HY, 22⁰S,

	Starts	1st	2nd	3rd	Win & Pl
Hurdles	3	0	0	0	0
Chases	1	0	0	0	268
Career Total	10	1	2	1	4601
98	11/01	Plum	2m5f	E Hdl	GD	£2450
			Total win prize-money £2450		

Going: Sf: 0-4 GS: 0-0 Gd: 0-0 GF: - Fm: 0-0
Distance: 2m/2m3: 0-0 2m4-2m7: 0-2 3m+: 0-2
Track: LH: 0-2 RH: 0-2 Tight: 0-2 Gall: 0-0
Aids: Bl: 0-0 Vi: 0-0 Tstrap: 0-0
Best Rating: 102 12/00 Tntn 2m1f   soft   NHF

She showed some ability in bumpers before making a successful hurdling debut at Plumpton. Held since. Stays well.

Mrs I Know (IRE)

5-y-o b m Presenting-Minerstown (IRE) (Miners Lamp)
Ferdy Murphy Geoff Hubbard Racing

Placings:0P   (3926)
2002/03: 16⁰GS, 20ᴾG,

	Starts	1st	2nd	3rd	Win & Pl
NH Flat	1	0	0	0	0
Hurdles	1	0	0	0	0
Career Total	2	0	0		

Going:	Sf: 0-0 GS: 0-1 Gd: 0-1 GF: - Fm: 0-0
Distance:	2m/2m3: 0-1 2m4-2m7: 0-1 3m+: 0-0
Track:	LH: 0-1 RH: 0-1 Tight: 0-1 Gall: 0-1
Aids:	Bl: 0-0 Vi: 0-0 Tstrap: 0-0
Best Rating:	54 12/02 Fknm 2m gd-sft NHF

Mrs Jodi

98(90c)   (70+c)**116**
7-y-o b m Yaheeb (USA)-Knayton Lass (Presidium)
J M Jefferson Mr & Mrs J M Davenport

Placings:231161/0500/4256F1032P-4405   (1913)
2002/03: 16⁴GF, 16⁴G, 16⁰GF, 16⁵S,

	Starts	1st	2nd	3rd	Win & Pl
Hurdles	2	0	0	0	0
Chases	2	0	0	0	983
Career Total	24	4	3	2	19756
116	1/02	Carl	2m1f	D(0-120)HHdl	SFT	£3510
109	2/00	Hayd	2m	C HHdl	SFT	£5408
98	12/99	MRas	2m1f110yE Hdl		G-S	£2495
86	11/99	Newc	2m	E Hdl	GD	£2316

Total win prize-money £13729

Going:	Sf: 0-1 GS: 0-0 Gd: 0-1 GF: - Fm: 0-2
Distance:	2m/2m3: 0-4 2m4-2m7: 0-0 3m+: 0-0
Track:	LH: 0-3 RH: 0-1 Tight: 0-2 Gall: 0-0
Aids:	Bl: 0-0 Vi: 0-0 Tstrap: 0-0
Best Rating:	116 4/02 Kels 2m110y gd-fm Hdl

Fair handicap hurdler, she acts on good and soft ground and she seems suited by a test of stamina. Best at around two miles.

Mrs Philip

87   **57+**
4-y-o b f Puissance-Lightning Legacy (USA) (Super Concorde (USA))
P J Hobbs Jack Joseph & Mrs Philip Hobbs

Placings:22   (4600)
2002/03: 16²G, 17²GF,

	Starts	1st	2nd	3rd	Win & Pl
NH Flat	2	0	2	0	1757
Career Total	2	0	2	0	1757

Going:	Sf: 0-0 GS: 0-0 Gd: 0-1 GF: - Fm: 0-1
Distance:	2m/2m3: 0-2 2m4-2m7: 0-0 3m+: 0-0
Track:	LH: 0-0 RH: 0-2 Tight: 0-0 Gall: 0-0
Aids:	Bl: 0-0 Vi: 0-0 Tstrap: 0-0
Best Rating:	86 4/03 Extr 2m1f gd-fm NHF

Half-sister to the useful jumper Cabochon; runner-up in bumper on her debut; disqualified after narrow victory at Exeter next time; disappointing fourth on hurdling debut at the same course May 2003.

Mrs Pickles

104   **102**
8-y-o gr m Northern Park (USA)-Able Mabel (Absalom)

M D I Usher (G Brown 19/12) Midweek Racing

Placings:060/000P5/4/F22215F-5422134P   (3807)
2002/03: 22⁵S, 26⁴GS, 22²G, 22²GS, 16¹HY, 20³HY, 24⁴S, 21ᴾS,

	Starts	1st	2nd	3rd	Win & Pl
Hurdles	8	1	2	1	5220
Career Total	24	2	5	1	9585
102	1/03	Chep	2m110y	F(0-95)HHdl	HVY	£2779
96	2/02	Plum	2m5f	E(0-105)HHdl	HVY	£2457

Total win prize-money £5236

Going:	Sf: 1-5 GS: 0-2 Gd: 0-1 GF: - Fm: 0-0
Distance:	2m/2m3: 1-1 2m4-2m7: 0-5 3m+: 0-2
Track:	LH: 1-4 RH: 0-4 Tight: 0-3 Gall: 0-1
Aids:	Bl: 0-0 Vi: 0-0 Tstrap: 0-0
Best Rating:	102 1/03 Chep 2m110y heavy Hdl

Moderate hurdler; does not have the best strike rate, but tries her best. Stays well, but relished the testing conditions when winning a mares only event over two miles at Chepstow in January 2003.

Mrs Poppyford

79f   **66f**
5-y-o b m Mistertopogigo (IRE)-Mrs Jawleyford (USA) (Dixieland Band (USA))
C Smith C Smith

Placings:0   (0907)
2002/03: 16⁰G,

	Starts	1st	2nd	3rd	Win & Pl
NH Flat	1	0	0	0	
Career Total	1	0	0	0	

Going:	Sf: 0-0 GS: 0-0 Gd: 0-1 GF: - Fm: 0-0
Distance:	2m/2m3: 0-1 2m4-2m7: 0-0 3m+: 0-0
Track:	LH: 0-1 RH: 0-0 Tight: 0-0 Gall: 0-0
Aids:	Bl: 0-0 Vi: 0-0 Tstrap: 0-0
Best Rating:	66 8/02 Worc 2m good NHF

Mrs Ritchie

90f   **86f**
6-y-o b m Teenoso (USA)-Material Girl (Busted)
M Pitman Just Good Fun Club

Placings:53-   (0020)
2002/03: 16³GS,

	Starts	1st	2nd	3rd	Win & Pl
NH Flat	1	0	0	1	248
Career Total	2	0	0	1	248

Going:	Sf: 0-0 GS: 0-1 Gd: 0-0 GF: - Fm: 0-0
Distance:	2m/2m3: 0-1 2m4-2m7: 0-0 3m+: 0-0
Track:	LH: 0-0 RH: 0-1 Tight: 0-0 Gall: 0-0
Aids:	Bl: 0-0 Vi: 0-0 Tstrap: 0-0
Best Rating:	86 4/02 Towc 2m gd-sft NHF

Mrs Sherman

99(86h)   (59h)**59**
8-y-o b m Derrylin-Temporary Affair (Mandalus)
Mrs L Williamson M Williamson

Placings:3064060/603U463453-FP2   (0502)
2002/03: 26³G, 25ᶠG, 26ᴾG, 26²G,

	Starts	1st	2nd	3rd	Win & Pl
Chases	4	0	1	1	1488
Career Total	20	0	1	4	3304

Going:	Sf: 0-0 GS: 0-0 Gd: 0-4 GF: - Fm: 0-0

Distance:	2m/2m3: 0-0 2m4-2m7: 0-0 3m+: 0-4
Track:	LH: 0-4 RH: 0-0 Tight: 0-2 Gall: 0-0
Aids:	Bl: 0-4 Vi: 0-0 Tstrap: 0-0
Best Rating:	98 10/00 Bang 2m1f soft NHF

Ms Trude (IRE)

99(85h)   (61h)**78**
6-y-o b m Montelimar (USA)-Pencil (Crash Course)
A W Carroll Gary J Roberts

Placings:200-R66PP   (4020)
2002/03: 22ᴿS, 19ᴿGS, 22⁶HY, 21ᴾS, 26ᴾS,

	Starts	1st	2nd	3rd	Win & Pl
Hurdles	5	0	0	0	167
Career Total	8	0	1	0	824

Going:	Sf: 0-4 GS: 0-1 Gd: 0-0 GF: - Fm: 0-0
Distance:	2m/2m3: 0-0 2m4-2m7: 0-4 3m+: 0-1
Track:	LH: 0-2 RH: 0-3 Tight: 0-2 Gall: 0-1
Aids:	Bl: 0-0 Vi: 0-0 Tstrap: 0-0
Best Rating:	101 4/02 Chel 2m1f good NHF

Muallaf (IRE)

11-y-o b g Unfuwain (USA)-Honourable Sheba (USA) (Roberto (USA))
Mrs A M Woodrow Mrs Ann Woodrow

Placings:002/0P0P0/PS-PP   (2058)
2002/03: 16ᴾS, 16ᴾG,

	Starts	1st	2nd	3rd	Win & Pl
Hurdles	2	0	0	0	
Career Total	12	0	1	0	471

Going:	Sf: 0-1 GS: 0-0 Gd: 0-1 GF: - Fm: 0-0
Distance:	2m/2m3: 0-2 2m4-2m7: 0-0 3m+: 0-0
Track:	LH: 0-0 RH: 0-2 Tight: 0-0 Gall: 0-0
Aids:	Bl: 0-0 Vi: 0-0 Tstrap: 0-0
Best Rating:	79 4/97 Chep 2m110y firm NHF

Muck Savage

107   **118**
6-y-o b g Homo Sapien-Rare Luck (Rare One)
C J Mann (Anthony Mullins 24/6) Granville J Harper

Placings:3015600-06032U2P2   (3880)
2002/03: 16⁰YS, 20⁶YS, 19⁰S, 20³G, 24²GS, 21ᵁS, 21²S, 22ᴾHY, 24²GS,

	Starts	1st	2nd	3rd	Win & Pl
Hurdles	9	0	3	1	9409
Career Total	16	1	3	2	13953
106	11/01	Tram	2m	Hdl	YLD	£4173

Total win prize-money £4173

Going:	Sf: 0-4 GS: 0-2 Gd: 0-1 GF: - Fm: 0-0
Distance:	2m/2m3: 0-2 2m4-2m7: 0-5 3m+: 0-2
Track:	LH: 0-5 RH: 0-1 Tight: 0-3 Gall: 0-2
Aids:	Bl: 0-0 Vi: 0-0 Tstrap: 0-0
Best Rating:	118 3/03 Donc 3m110y gd-sft Hdl

Fair hurdler; stays three miles; acts on a soft surface; only win to date came in Ireland.

Muckle Mavis

(98h)   (81h)
7-y-o b m Nomadic Way (USA)-The Muckle Quine (Hubbly Bubbly (USA))

Miss Lucinda V Russell Miss G Joughin

Placings:00/505P2P-P300F5PF   (3772)
2002/03: 24PGS, 203G, 200G, 200GS, 21FGS, 165HY, 24PHY, 21FGS,

	Starts	1st	2nd	3rd	Win & Pl
Hurdles	6	0	0	1	353
Chases	2	0	0	0	
Career Total	16	0	1	1	1128

Going: Sf: 0-2 GS: 0-4 Gd: 0-2 GF: - Fm: 0-0
Distance: 2m/2m3: 0-1 2m4-2m7: 0-5 3m+: 0-2
Track: LH: 0-8 RH: 0-0 Tight: 0-0 Gall: 0-0
Aids: Bl: 0-0 Vi: 0-0 Tstrap: 0-0
Best Rating: 85 3/02 Ayr   3m110y   soft   Hdl

Mudlark
68(84c)   (82c)42
11-y-o b g Salse (USA)-Mortal Sin (USA) (Green Forest (USA))
J R Norton J Norton

Placings:00460/203/3F/420646/050/0F6P6P-0   (0088)
2002/03: 200G,

	Starts	1st	2nd	3rd	Win & Pl
Hurdles	1	0	0	0	
Career Total	25	0	2	2	1742

Going: Sf: 0-0 GS: 0-0 Gd: 0-1 GF: - Fm: 0-0
Distance: 2m/2m3: 0-0 2m4-2m7: 0-1 3m+: 0-0
Track: LH: 0-1 RH: 0-0 Tight: 0-0 Gall: 0-0
Aids: Bl: 0-0 Vi: 0-1 Tstrap: 0-0
Best Rating: 90 5/97 Uttx   2m   gd-sft Hdl

Mughas (IRE)
111   129
4-y-o b g Sadler s Wells (USA)-Quest Of Passion (FR) (Saumarez)
A King (Kevin Prendergast 16/10) B Winfield,A Longman,C Fenton & P McAdam

Placings:11256   (4460)
2002/03: 161HY, 161HY, 162G, 175G, 166G,

	Starts	1st	2nd	3rd	Win & Pl
Hurdles	5	2	1	0	18022
Career Total	5	2	1	0	18022
107 2/03 Plum 2m			E Hdl	HVY	£3562
110 1/03 Wwck 2m			E Hdl	HVY	£3710

Total win prize-money £7272

Going: Sf: 2-2 GS: 0-0 Gd: 0-3 GF: - Fm: 0-0
Distance: 2m/2m3: 2-5 2m4-2m7: 0-0 3m+: 0-0
Track: LH: 2-4 RH: 0-1 Tight: 1-2 Gall: 0-1
Aids: Bl: 0-0 Vi: 0-0 Tstrap: 0-0
Best Rating: 129 3/03 Chel   2m1f   good   Hdl

Fair hurdler; useful maiden on the level in Ireland; has improved for the change of codes and won two juvenile hurdles in heavy ground before running second in a Grade Two on good; not disgraced at either Cheltenham or Aintree.

Muhami (IRE)
92   85
6-y-o b g Phardante (FR)-The Vicarette (IRE) (The Parson)
Ferdy Murphy The Poppet Partnership

Placings:05066-P440   (2764)
2002/03: 20PS, 23AG, 204S, 200GS,

	Starts	1st	2nd	3rd	Win & Pl
Hurdles	4	0	0	0	0

Career Total   9   0   0   0   0

Going: Sf: 0-2 GS: 0-1 Gd: 0-1 GF: - Fm: 0-0
Distance: 2m/2m3: 0-0 2m4-2m7: 0-4 3m+: 0-0
Track: LH: 0-3 RH: 0-1 Tight: 0-2 Gall: 0-1
Aids: Bl: 0-0 Vi: 0-0 Tstrap: 0-0
Best Rating: 91 10/01 Carl   2m1f   gd-sft NHF

Modest novice hurdler; stays two miles seven.

Muharib Lady (IRE)
102(100c)   (90+c)90
8-y-o b m Muharib (USA)-Brickhill Lady (Le Bavard (FR))
P G Murphy P G Murphy

Placings:0/0030/30342303556-3321300621   (4759)
2002/03: 223GS, 233G, 262GF, 261GF, 263GS, 250G, 250HY, 246S, 252GF, 271GF,

	Starts	1st	2nd	3rd	Win & Pl
Hurdles	5	1	1	1	8132
Chases	5	1	1	2	7162
Career Total	26	2	3	8	17537
90 4/03 Plum 3m3f			E(0-110)HHdl	G-F	£6864
90 10/02 Plum 3m2f			E(0-110)HCh	G-F	£4326

Total win prize-money £11190

Going: Sf: 0-2 GS: 0-2 Gd: 0-2 GF: - Fm: 2-4
Distance: 2m/2m3: 0-0 2m4-2m7: 0-1 **3m+:** 2-9
Track: **LH: 1-4** RH: 0-2 Tight: 2-7 Gall: 0-0
Aids: Bl: 0-0 Vi: 0-0 Tstrap: 0-0
Best Rating: 90 4/03 Font   3m3f   gd-fm   Hdl

Plating-class hurdler; stays 3m 3f: suited by a sound surface.

Muhtadi (IRE)
91   69
10-y-o br g Marju (IRE)-Moon Parade (Welsh Pageant)
S B Clark S B Clark

Placings:0156/001/0000350/00/10P0/100-000   (3799)
2002/03: 160G, 160GS, 160G, 160S,

	Starts	1st	2nd	3rd	Win & Pl
Hurdles	4	0	0	0	
Career Total	26	4	0	1	8698
83 3/02 Sedg 2m1f			G(0-90)HHdl	SFT	£1946
79 1/01 Catt 2m			G(0-90)HHdl	G-S	£1666
85 3/98 Plum 2m			E Ch	SFT	£2956
92 3/97 Winc 2m			F Hdl	GD	£1900

Total win prize-money £8468

Going: Sf: 0-1 GS: 0-1 Gd: 0-2 GF: - Fm: 0-0
Distance: 2m/2m3: 0-0 2m4-2m7: 0-0 3m+: 0-0
Track: LH: 0-4 RH: 0-0 Tight: 0-1 Gall: 0-2
Aids: Bl: 0-4 Vi: 0-0 Tstrap: 0-0
Best Rating: 92 3/97 Bang   2m1f   good   Hdl

Mujalia (IRE)
5-y-o b g Mujtahid (USA)-Danalia (IRE) (Danehill (USA))
Jamie Poulton Ormonde Racing

Placings:R-   (0007)
2002/03: 16RG,

	Starts	1st	2nd	3rd	Win & Pl
Hurdles	1	0	0	0	
Career Total	1	0	0	0	

Going: Sf: 0-0 GS: 0-0 Gd: 0-1 GF: - Fm: 0-0
Distance: 2m/2m3: 0-1 2m4-2m7: 0-0 3m+: 0-0

Track: LH: 0-1 RH: 0-0 Tight: 0-1 Gall: 0-0
Aids: Bl: 0-1 Vi: 0-0 Tstrap: 0-0
Best Rating:

Mukdar (USA)
102   90
9-y-o b/br g Gulch (USA)-Give Thanks (Relko)
K C Bailey K C Bailey

Placings:6331142U155150/100/PP0P/0-0P260 (4256)
2002/03: 16RS, 16PHY, 162HY, 166GS, 179G,

	Starts	1st	2nd	3rd	Win & Pl
Hurdles	5	0	1	0	1512
Career Total	27	5	2	2	18379
124 5/99 Ludl 2m			D(0-120)HHdl	G-F	£2801
130 12/98 Hntg 2m110y			D(0-125)HHdl	SFT	£5407
116 11/98 Kemp 2m			E(0-110)HHdl	G-S	£2263
110 9/98 Hntg 2m110y			E Hdl	G-F	£2652
105 8/98 NAbb 2m1f			E Hdl	G-F	£2414

Total win prize-money £15539

Going: Sf: 0-3 GS: 0-1 Gd: 0-1 GF: - Fm: 0-0
Distance: 2m/2m3: 0-5 2m4-2m7: 0-0 3m+: 0-0
Track: LH: 0-1 RH: 0-4 Tight: 0-0 Gall: 0-0
Aids: Bl: 0-0 Vi: 0-0 Tstrap: 0-0
Best Rating: 130 12/98 Hntg   2m110y   soft   Hdl

Moderate hurdler; showed signs of coming back to best when runner-up at Leicester in February; handles very soft ground well.

Mulhacen (IRE)
100   94
7-y-o br m Supreme Leader-Lancaster Lady (IRE) (Lancastrian)
Ian Williams The Mulhacen Partnership

Placings:05/2B2   (4755)
2002/03: 192GF, 21BGF, 182GF,

	Starts	1st	2nd	3rd	Win & Pl
Hurdles	3	0	2	0	2160
Career Total	5	0	2	0	2160

Going: Sf: 0-0 GS: 0-0 Gd: 0-0 GF: - Fm: 0-3
Distance: 2m/2m3: 0-1 2m4-2m7: 0-2 3m+: 0-0
Track: LH: 0-1 RH: 0-2 Tight: 0-1 Gall: 0-1
Aids: Bl: 0-0 Vi: 0-0 Tstrap: 0-0
Best Rating: 94 4/03 Hrfd   2m3f110y gd-fm Hdl

Moderate novice hurdler; stays two and ahalf miles; acts on any ground.

Mulkev Prince (IRE)
105(77h)   (73h)121
12-y-o b g Lancastrian-Waltzing Shoon (Green Shoon)
David Pearson David Pearson

Placings:6/30O1O2/33OFP24P/6122102/F545P2/625304/5411U3F/05F126-004P21U20110   (4472)
2002/03: 16RG, 200GF, 204GF, 17PGF, 202G, 201GF, 20UG, 202S, 19AG, 201GS, 201GF, 210G,

	Starts	1st	2nd	3rd	Win & Pl
Chases	12	3	2	0	17880
Career Total	59	9	10	5	64650
121 3/03 Ludl 2m4f			D(0-115)HCh	G-F	£7224
115 3/03 Leic 2m4f110yE(0-110)HCh				G-S	£4069
115 11/02 Leic 2m4f110yF(0-100)HCh				G-F	£3464
110 3/02 Leic 2m4f110y H Ch				SFT	£2219
131 10/00 Carl 2m			D(0-125)HCh	GD	£4095
131 9/00 Prth 2m			E(0-115)HCh	HVY	£5408
139 2/98 Fair 2m			Ch	Y-S	£11217

115 11/97 Thur 2m Ch Y-S £2204
112 2/96 Fair 2m2f Hdl G-Y £3177
Total win prize-money £43079

Going: Sf: 0-1 GS: 1-1 Gd: 0-5 GF: - Fm: 2-5
Distance: 2m/2m3: 0-3 **2m4-2m7: 3-9** 3m+: 0-0
Track: LH: 0-7 **RH: 3-5 Tight: 1-6** Gall: 0-0
Aids: Bl: 0-0 Vi: 0-0 Tstrap: 0-1
Best Rating: 139 2/98 Fair 2m yld-sft Ch

Fair front-running handicap chaser at around two and a half miles; jumps well; acts on any ground, possibly best on fast though.

Mull's Nag (IRE)
96   95
9-y-o b m Lord Americo-Sue s A Lady (Le Moss)
Mrs S J Smith   Mrs A E Astall

Placings:00/0400000-30530   (0986)
2002/03: 16³GS, 17⁰GS, 20⁵G, 25³S, 26⁰GF,

	Starts	1st	2nd	3rd	Win & Pl
Hurdles	5	0	0	2	775
Career Total	14	0	0	2	1033

Going: Sf: 0-1 GS: 0-2 Gd: 0-1 GF: - Fm: 0-1
Distance: 2m/2m3: 0-2 2m4-2m7: 0-1 3m+: 0-0
Track: LH: 0-5 RH: 0-0 Tight: 0-3 Gall: 0-0
Aids: Bl: 0-0 Vi: 0-0 Tstrap: 0-0
Best Rating: 95 5/01 Tipp 2m gd-fm Hdl

Modest form in Ireland. Joined Sue Smith in the spring of 2002.

Mullensgrove

9-y-o b g Derrylin-Wedding Song (True Song)
D Lowe   D Lowe

Placings:0/PP/2-1P62F0   (4565)
2002/03: 24¹G, 27⁰G, 24⁶S, 25²GS, 21⁴G, 24⁰GF,

	Starts	1st	2nd	3rd	Win & Pl
Chases	6	1	1	0	1924
Career Total	11	1	2	0	2306
97	5/02	Bang	3m110y	H Ch	GD	£1501
Total win prize-money £1502

Going: Sf: 0-1 GS: 0-1 Gd: 1-3 GF: - Fm: 0-1
Distance: 2m/2m3: 0-0 2m4-2m7: 0-1 3m+: 1-5
Track: LH: 1-4 RH: 0-2 Tight: 1-6 Gall: 0-0
Aids: Bl: 0-0 Vi: 0-0 Tstrap: 0-0
Best Rating: 97 3/03 MRas 3m1f gd-sft Ch

Progressive hunter at a modest level, in great heart between the flags in 2002 and duly landed his first hunter chase at Bangor; just denied this time at Market Rasen in March; well suited by a sound surface.

Mulligan Express
95
9-y-o ch g Phardante (FR)-Tsarella (Mummy s Pet)
Ferdy Murphy   Peter Mulligan

Placings:0/511/3-U6   (3913)
2002/03: 21ᵁGS, 20⁶S,

	Starts	1st	2nd	3rd	Win & Pl
Chases	2	0	0	0	0
Career Total	7	2	0	1	5468
117	2/01	Carl	2m4f110yE Hdl		SFT	£1975
100	2/01	Carl	2m4f110yE Hdl		HVY	£2790
Total win prize-money £4765

Going: Sf: 0-1 GS: 0-1 Gd: 0-0 GF: - Fm: 0-0
Distance: 2m/2m3: 0-0 2m4-2m7: 0-2 3m+: 0-0
Track: LH: 0-1 RH: 0-1 Tight: 0-0 Gall: 0-0
Aids: Bl: 0-0 Vi: 0-0 Tstrap: 0-0
Best Rating: 117 2/01 Carl 2m4f110y soft Hdl

Mulligatawny (IRE)
105   113
9-y-o b g Abednego-Mullangale (Strong Gale)
J T Gifford   Pell-Mell Partners

Placings:2F32/4/0134   (3922)
2002/03: 16⁰S, 20¹S, 20³HY, 22⁴S,

	Starts	1st	2nd	3rd	Win & Pl
Hurdles	4	1	0	1	8230
Career Total	9	1	2	2	10765
113	12/02	Asct	2m4f	D(0-115)HHdl	SFT	£7036
Total win prize-money £7036

Going: Sf: 1-4 GS: 0-0 Gd: 0-0 GF: - Fm: 0-0
Distance: 2m/2m3: 0-1 **2m4-2m7: 1-3** 3m+: 0-0
Track: LH: 0-2 **RH: 1-2** Tight: 0-1 Gall: 0-1
Aids: Bl: 0-0 Vi: 0-0 Tstrap: 0-0
Best Rating: 113 2/03 Sand 2m4f110y heavy Hdl

Fair handicap hurdler; best at around two and a half miles; acts well on soft ground.

Mullintor (IRE)

12-y-o b g King Luthier-Latin Verses (Appiani Ii)
R Rowe   Thomas Thompson

Placings:400/3402P2221/44212453/011F141/0PU/P (0723)
2002/03: 23ᴾG,

	Starts	1st	2nd	3rd	Win & Pl
Chases	1	0	0	0	
Career Total	31	6	6	2	33419
112	12/99	Font	3m4f	D(0-125)HCh	G-S	£14603
103	11/99	Folk	3m2f	E(0-115)HCh	G-F	£3005
102	10/99	Font	2m6f	F(0-95)HCh	GD	£2542
90	9/99	Font	3m2f110yF(0-100)HCh	GD	£3030
93	12/98	Font	2m2f110yG Hdl	GD	£2753
95	4/97	Font	2m2f110yE Hdl	G-F	£2485
Total win prize-money £28421

Going: Sf: 0-0 GS: 0-0 Gd: 0-1 GF: - Fm: 0-0
Distance: 2m/2m3: 0-0 2m4-2m7: 0-0 3m+: 0-1
Track: LH: 0-1 RH: 0-0 Tight: 0-0 Gall: 0-0
Aids: Bl: 0-0 Vi: 0-0 Tstrap: 0-0
Best Rating: 112 12/99 Font 3m4f gd-sft Ch

Mulsanne
(51h)
5-y-o b g Clantime-Prim Lass (Reprimand)
P A Pritchard   P A Pritchard

Placings:00P-P   (0658)
2002/03: 16ᴾGF,

	Starts	1st	2nd	3rd	Win & Pl
Hurdles	1	0	0	0	
Career Total	4	0	0		

Going: Sf: 0-0 GS: 0-0 Gd: 0-0 GF: - Fm: 0-1
Distance: 2m/2m3: 0-1 2m4-2m7: 0-0 3m+: 0-0
Track: LH: 0-1 RH: 0-0 Tight: 0-0 Gall: 0-0
Aids: Bl: 0-0 Vi: 0-0 Tstrap: 0-0
Best Rating: 0 6/02 Worc 2m gd-fm Hdl

Multeen River (IRE)
99   115+
7-y-o b g Supreme Leader-Blackwater Mist (IRE) (King s Ride)
Jonjo O Neill   J P McManus

Placings:03124-21   (2565)
2002/03: 16²GS, 17¹GS,

	Starts	1st	2nd	3rd	Win & Pl
Hurdles	2	1	1	0	5468
Career Total	7	2	2	1	10827
115	12/02	Bang	2m1f	E Hdl	G-S	£3374
109	3/02	Thur	2m	NHF	SFT	£3386
Total win prize-money £6761

Going: Sf: 0-0 GS: 1-2 Gd: 0-0 GF: - Fm: 0-0
Distance: 2m/2m3: 1-2 2m4-2m7: 0-0 3m+: 0-0
Track: LH: 1-2 RH: 0-0 Tight: 1-1 Gall: 0-0
Aids: Bl: 0-0 Vi: 0-0 Tstrap: 0-0
Best Rating: 115 12/02 Bang 2m1f gd-sft Hdl

Fair hurdler; Irish bumper winner, narrowly denied on hurdling bow here at Wetherby in November. Travelled strongly but had little left at the finish when going one better at Bangor the following month.

Multi Talented (IRE)
109   113
7-y-o b g Montelimar (USA)-Boro Glen (Furry Glen)
L Wells   David Cox

Placings:321P   (4427)
2002/03: 22³S, 26²HY, 25¹G, 26ᴾGF,

	Starts	1st	2nd	3rd	Win & Pl
Chases	4	1	1	1	7550
Career Total	4	1	1	1	7550
113	3/03	Folk	3m1f	E Ch	GD	£4424
Total win prize-money £4424

Going: Sf: 0-2 GS: 0-0 Gd: 1-1 GF: - Fm: 0-1
Distance: 2m/2m3: 0-0 2m4-2m7: 0-1 **3m+: 1-3**
Track: LH: 0-2 **RH: 1-1** Tight: 1-4 Gall: 0-0
Aids: Bl: 0-0 Vi: 0-0 Tstrap: 0-0
Best Rating: 113 3/03 Folk 3m1f good Ch

Fair chaser; stays three and a quarter miles; acts on both good and soft ground.

Mumaris (USA)
106(108h)   (126h)115
9-y-o b/br g Capote (USA)-Barakat (Bustino)
Mark Campion   Faulkner West

Placings:31613/04043400/44405F5202231-2P51152P (4519)
2002/03: 16¹G, 16²G, 16ᴾG, 16⁵GF, 16¹G, 16¹G, 16⁵GS, 20²GF, 21ᴾG,

	Starts	1st	2nd	3rd	Win & Pl
Chases	9	3	2	0	13713
Career Total	34	5	5	4	27592
115	8/02	Sedg	2m110y	E Ch	GD	£3731
109	8/02	Sedg	2m110y	E Ch	GD	£3662
92	4/02	Newc	2m110y	E Ch	GD	£2957
107	8/98	Cork	2m	Hdl	FRM	£3586
119	7/98	Bell	2m1f	Hdl	G-F	£2391
Total win prize-money £16330

Going: Sf: 0-0 GS: 0-1 Gd: 3-6 GF: - Fm: 0-2
Distance: 2m/2m3: 3-7 2m4-2m7: 0-2 3m+: 0-0
Track: LH: 3-8 RH: 0-1 Tight: 2-5 Gall: 1-2
Aids: Bl: 0-0 Vi: 0-0 Tstrap: 0-0

Best Rating: 126 10/01 Gway 2m   sft-hvy Hdl

Fair chaser; ex-Irish; suited by two miles and good ground.

Mumbai

101(87h)   (60h)52

7-y-o b g Theatrical Charmer-Lehzen (Posse (USA))
M A Barnes The Purple Patch Racing Club

Placings:05PFP05U2/UB052U24U30-603543206P0P
                         (4589)
2002/03: 25⁶GS, 20⁰G, 17³HY, 17⁵G, 16⁴HY, 16³HY, 16²S, 16⁶G, 16⁶S, 17⁶G, 16⁶G, 25⁶G,

	Starts	1st	2nd	3rd	Win & Pl
Hurdles	2	0	0	0	
Chases	10	0	1	2	3009
Career Total	32	0	4	3	8143

Going: Sf: 0-5 GS: 0-1 Gd: 0-6 GF: - Fm: 0-0
Distance: 2m/2m3: 0-9 2m4-2m7: 0-1 3m+: 0-2
Track: LH: 0-10 RH: 0-2 Tight: 0-4 Gall: 0-0
Aids: Bl: 0-4 Vi: 0-0 Tstrap: 0-4
Best Rating: 86 11/02 Ayr 2m   soft   Ch

A strong-travelling type, he has been placed a number of times in minor chase company.

Mumuqa (IRE)

11-y-o ch g Noalto-Princess Isabella (Divine Gift)
Mrs A L Blanchard (B S Rothwell 8/5) J T Brown

Placings:42/11/F/03245P34P604-3P   (4443)
2002/03: 16³GF, 19P G,

	Starts	1st	2nd	3rd	Win & Pl
Chases	2	0	0	1	626
Career Total	19	2	2	3	10744
113	9/99	Sedg	2m110y	E Ch	G-F £3650
106	9/99	NAbb	2m110y	E Ch	G-F £2766

Total win prize-money £6418

Going: Sf: 0-0 GS: 0-0 Gd: 0-1 GF: - Fm: 0-1
Distance: 2m/2m3: 0-1 2m4-2m7: 0-1 3m+: 0-1
Track: LH: 0-1 RH: 0-1 Tight: 0-0 Gall: 0-0
Aids: Bl: 0-0 Vi: 0-0 Tstrap: 0-0
Best Rating: 113 7/01 Wolv 2m   gd-sft   Ch

Munadil

101   90

5-y-o ch g Nashwan (USA)-Bintalshaati (Kris)
P R Webber Lady Duff Gordon

Placings:633   (1230)
2002/03: 16⁶G, 16³GF, 16³G,

	Starts	1st	2nd	3rd	Win & Pl
Hurdles	3	0	0	2	744
Career Total	3	0	0	2	744

Going: Sf: 0-0 GS: 0-0 Gd: 0-1 GF: - Fm: 0-2
Distance: 2m/2m3: 0-3 2m4-2m7: 0-0 3m+: 0-0
Track: LH: 0-2 RH: 0-1 Tight: 0-0 Gall: 0-1
Aids: Bl: 0-0 Vi: 0-0 Tstrap: 0-3
Best Rating: 90 8/02 Hntg 2m110y   gd-fm   Hdl

Fair ten-furlong handicapper on the Flat. Gives the impression he may struggle to get the trip over hurdles.

Mundo Raro

95   90d

8-y-ob gZafonic(USA)-StarSpectacle(SpectacularBid (USA))

Going: Sf: 0-3 GS: 0-0 Gd: 0-0 GF: - Fm: 0-1

R M Stronge (J G Fitzgerald 6/5) David Waters

Placings:30500   (3349)
2002/03: 16³S, 17⁰GS, 16⁵HY, 17⁰GS, 16⁶HY,

	Starts	1st	2nd	3rd	Win & Pl
Hurdles	5	0	0	1	424
Career Total	5	0	0	1	424

Plating-class maiden hurdler.

Muqarrar (IRE)

89f   82f

4-y-o ch c Alhaarth (IRE)-Narjis (USA) (Blushing Groom (FR))
T J Fitzgerald N H T Wrigley

Placings:0   (3883)
2002/03: 16⁰GS,

	Starts	1st	2nd	3rd	Win & Pl
NH Flat	1	0	0	0	
Career Total	1	0	0	0	

Going: Sf: 0-0 GS: 0-1 Gd: 0-0 GF: - Fm: 0-0
Distance: 2m/2m3: 0-1 2m4-2m7: 0-0 3m+: 0-0
Track: LH: 0-1 RH: 0-0 Tight: 0-0 Gall: 0-1
Aids: Bl: 0-0 Vi: 0-0 Tstrap: 0-0
Best Rating: 57 3/03 Donc 2m110y   gd-sft NHF

Murawa Bellevue (FR)

6-y-o b m Murmure (FR)-Strakawa (FR) (Sukawa (FR))
Jean-Rene Auvray Jean-Rene Auvray

Placings:0P   (2553)
2002/03: 16⁰S, 22P HY,

	Starts	1st	2nd	3rd	Win & Pl
NH Flat	1	0	0	0	0
Hurdles	1	0	0	0	0
Career Total	2	0	0	0	

Going: Sf: 0-2 GS: 0-0 Gd: 0-0 GF: - Fm: 0-0
Distance: 2m/2m3: 0-1 2m4-2m7: 0-0 3m+: 0-0
Track: LH: 0-1 RH: 0-1 Tight: 0-1 Gall: 0-0
Aids: Bl: 0-0 Vi: 0-0 Tstrap: 0-0
Best Rating: 11 12/02 Wwck 2m   soft   NHF

Murchan Benwood (IRE)

100   82+

6-y-o b m Ridgewood Ben-Ardnamurchan (Ardross)
J Mackie The Mwm Racing Syndicate

Placings:006/506544F-4450   (4566)
2002/03: 16⁴HY, 20⁴S, 16⁵S, 20⁰GF,

	Starts	1st	2nd	3rd	Win & Pl
Hurdles	4	0	0	0	378
Career Total	14	0	0	0	378

Going: Sf: 0-3 GS: 0-0 Gd: 0-0 GF: - Fm: 0-1

Distance: 2m/2m3: 0-2 2m4-2m7: 0-2 3m+: 0-0
Track: LH: 0-3 RH: 0-1 Tight: 0-1 Gall: 0-1
Aids: Bl: 0-0 Vi: 0-0 Tstrap: 0-0
Best Rating: 82 2/03 Newc 2m4f   soft   Hdl

Murder Moss (IRE)

92(79h)   (23h)72

13-y-o ch g Doulab (USA)-Northern Wind (Northfields (USA))
W S Coltherd S Coltherd

Placings:P/PP/2/4/4PPU041/23/0/20-PUR4365   (1916)
2002/03: 16P G, 24U GS, 20R GF, 24⁴GF, 24³GF, 27⁶G, 28⁵S,

	Starts	1st	2nd	3rd	Win & Pl
Hurdles	2	0	0	1	723
Chases	5	0	0	0	0
Career Total	24	1	3	2	6001
94	5/99	Hexm	3m1f	H Ch	GD £2641

Total win prize-money £2642

Going: Sf: 0-1 GS: 0-1 Gd: 0-2 GF: - Fm: 0-3
Distance: 2m/2m3: 0-1 2m4-2m7: 0-1 3m+: 0-5
Track: LH: 0-6 RH: 0-1 Tight: 0-3 Gall: 0-0
Aids: Bl: 0-0 Vi: 0-2 Tstrap: 0-1
Best Rating: 102 2/97 Muss 3m   gd-sft   Ch

Moderate chaser. Stays three miles and acts on a sound surface.

Murphy's Cardinal (IRE)

103   140+

7-y-o b g Shernazar-Lady Swinford (Ardross)
Noel T Chance T Conway & Mrs Conway

Placings:1111   (3629)
2002/03: 17¹S, 22¹HY, 22¹HY, 24¹S,

	Starts	1st	2nd	3rd	Win & Pl
NH Flat	1	1	0	0	1939
Hurdles	3	3	0	0	10934
Career Total	4	4	0	0	12873
140	2/03	Asct	3m	D Hdl	SFT £5187
140	1/03	Folk	2m6f110yE Hdl		HVY £3472
117	12/02	Folk	2m6f110yF Hdl		HVY £2275
99	11/02	Folk	2m1f110yH NHF		SFT £1939

Total win prize-money £12873

Going: Sf: 4-4 GS: 0-0 Gd: 0-0 GF: - Fm: 0-0
Distance: 2m/2m3: 1-1 2m4-2m7: 2-2 3m+: 1-1
Track: LH: 0-0 RH: 4-4 Tight: 3-3 Gall: 0-0
Aids: Bl: 0-0 Vi: 0-0 Tstrap: 0-0
Best Rating: 140 2/03 Asct 3m   soft   Hdl

Decent novice hurdler; made a winning debut in a Folkestone bumper in November 2002, and has twice scored there over hurdles; took a better event over three miles at Ascot in February; a chaser in the making, he looks a promising sort; acts in testing ground.

Murphy's Nails (IRE)

92   109+

6-y-o b g Bob s Return (IRE)-Southern Run (Deep Run)
C R Egerton R K Carvill

Placings: (2378)
2002/03: 16⁰S,

	Starts	1st	2nd	3rd	Win & Pl
NH Flat	1	0	0	0	
Career Total	1	0	0	0	

Going: Sf: 0-1 GS: 0-0 Gd: 0-0 GF: - Fm: 0-0
Distance: 2m/2m3: 0-1 2m4-2m7: 0-0 3m+: 0-0
Track: LH: 0-1 RH: 0-0 Tight: 0-0 Gall: 0-0
Aids: Bl: 0-0 Vi: 0-0 Tstrap: 0-0
Best Rating: 85 12/02 Wwck 2m   soft   NHF

Novice hurdler; showed promise on hurdles debut; may do better when handicapped.

Murray River (FR)
95(106h)   (126h)85+
7-y-o b g Esprit Du Nord (USA)-Mulika (FR) (Procida (USA))
M C Pipe D A Johnson

Placings:22/5310/202   (4734)
2002/03: 16²G, 20⁰G, 16²GF,

	Starts	1st	2nd	3rd	Win & Pl
Hurdles	3	0	2	0	9247
Career Total	9	1	4	1	15933
130 11/00 Tntn	2m1f	D(0-125)HHdl	G-S	£4800	

Total win prize-money £4800

Going: Sf: 0-0 GS: 0-0 Gd: 0-2 GF: - Fm: 0-1
Distance: 2m/2m3: 0-2 2m4-2m7: 0-1 3m+: 0-0
Track: LH: 0-3 RH: 0-0 Tight: 0-1 Gall: 0-1
Aids: Bl: 0-0 Vi: 0-3 Tstrap: 0-2
Best Rating: 130 11/00 Tntn 2m1f   gd-sft   Hdl

Decent ex-French hurdler; won over hurdles in November 2000 but off for a long time following his next run; returned with good efforts in the spring of 2003; disappointed on chase debut; suited by two miles and acts on any ground; has worn headgear.

Murrendi (IRE)
96   90
5-y-o b g Ashkalani (IRE)-Formaestre (IRE) (Formidable (USA))
R J O Sullivan Jack Joseph

Placings:F5-044   (0644)
2002/03: 18⁰GF, 16⁴GF, 16⁴GF,

	Starts	1st	2nd	3rd	Win & Pl
Hurdles	3	0	0	0	552
Career Total	5	0	0	0	552

Going: Sf: 0-0 GS: 0-0 Gd: 0-0 GF: 0-3
Distance: 2m/2m3: 0-0 2m4-2m7: 0-0 3m+: 0-0
Track: LH: 0-3 RH: 0-0 Tight: 0-3 Gall: 0-0
Aids: Bl: 0-0 Vi: 0-0 Tstrap: 0-0
Best Rating: 90 12/01 Plum 2m   good   Hdl

Murt's Man (IRE)
116(86h)   (52h)145d
9-y-o b g Be My Native (USA)-Autumn Queen (Menelek)
P F Nicholls Derek Millard

Placings:3F1B/2F21PU/262P21PP-650   (3591)
2002/03: 27³GS, 29⁵HY, 24⁰S,

	Starts	1st	2nd	3rd	Win & Pl
Chases	3	0	0	0	2775
Career Total	21	3	5	1	39693
145 3/02 Chep	3m2f110yB(0-145)HCh	G-S	£10773	
135 1/01 Winc	3m1f110yC(0-135)HCh	SFT	£8307	
111 3/00 Donc	3m	E Ch	G-S	£3006	

Total win prize-money £22086

Going: Sf: 0-2 GS: 0-1 Gd: 0-0 GF: - Fm: 0-0
Distance: 2m/2m3: 0-0 2m4-2m7: 0-0 3m+: 0-3
Track: LH: 0-2 RH: 0-1 Tight: 0-0 Gall: 0-1
Aids: Bl: 0-0 Vi: 0-0 Tstrap: 0-0

Best Rating: 145 3/02 Chep 3m2f110y gd-sft   Ch

Useful handicap chaser; not the most fluent of jumpers; stays 3m 4f; acts on most types of ground; has worn blinkers.

Musally
109(79c)   (44c)89+
6-y-o ch g Muhtarram (USA)-Flourishing (IRE) (Trojan Fen)
W Jenks The Glazeley Partnership

Placings:P0/06F0-36353   (4677)
2002/03: 21³GF, 20⁶G, 16³GF, 17⁵GF, 19³GF,

	Starts	1st	2nd	3rd	Win & Pl
Hurdles	4	0	0	3	1766
Chases	1	0	0	0	0
Career Total	11	0	0	3	1766

Going: Sf: 0-0 GS: 0-0 Gd: 0-1 GF: - Fm: 0-4
Distance: 2m/2m3: 0-2 2m4-2m7: 0-3 3m+: 0-0
Track: LH: 0-0 RH: 0-5 Tight: 0-1 Gall: 0-0
Aids: Bl: 0-0 Vi: 0-0 Tstrap: 0-0
Best Rating: 83 3/03 Ludl 2m   gd-fm   Hdl

Modest hurdler; raised a total of 17lb after wins at Ludlow and Southwell in May and June 2003; suited by fast ground; stays 2m 5f.

Musalse
94
8-y-o b g Salse (USA)-Musical Sally (USA) (The Minstrel (CAN))
John R Upson K Hancock & P M Haslam

Placings:42/2/2-PP   (0354)
2002/03: 24⁰PG, 23⁰GS,

	Starts	1st	2nd	3rd	Win & Pl
Hurdles	2	0	0	0	
Career Total	6	0	3	0	2501

Going: Sf: 0-0 GS: 0-1 Gd: 0-1 GF: - Fm: 0-0
Distance: 2m/2m3: 0-0 2m4-2m7: 0-0 3m+: 0-2
Track: LH: 0-2 RH: 0-0 Tight: 0-2 Gall: 0-0
Aids: Bl: 0-0 Vi: 0-0 Tstrap: 0-0
Best Rating: 95 8/99 Ctml 2m6f   good   Hdl

Muscadin
85   70
5-y-o br g Shaamit (IRE)-As Mustard (Keen)
A C Whillans (N G Richards 6/10) D Payne

Placings:P-2P   (3771)
2002/03: 17²GF, 16⁶PGS,

	Starts	1st	2nd	3rd	Win & Pl
NH Flat	1	0	1	0	580
Hurdles	1	0	0	0	0
Career Total	3	0	1	0	580

Going: Sf: 0-0 GS: 0-1 Gd: 0-0 GF: - Fm: 0-1
Distance: 2m/2m3: 0-2 2m4-2m7: 0-0 3m+: 0-0
Track: LH: 0-1 RH: 0-0 Tight: 0-0 Gall: 0-0
Aids: Bl: 0-0 Vi: 0-0 Tstrap: 0-0
Best Rating: 89 10/02 MRas 2m1f110y gd-fm NHF

Has shown ability in ordinary bumpers.

Music Therapy (IRE)
13-y-o b g Roselier (FR)-Suny Salome (Sunyboy)

Best Rating: 145 3/02 Chep 3m2f110y gd-sft   Ch

Mrs Polly Stockton C J Stockton

Placings:0/003/2111/1/U54-P   (3962)
2002/03: 24⁸S,

	Starts	1st	2nd	3rd	Win & Pl
Chases	1	0	0	0	
Career Total	13	4	1	1	12409
123 3/01 Plum	3m2f	H Ch	HVY	£1302
133 3/98 Newb	3m	D Ch	G-S	£3574
122 3/98 Ling	3m	E Ch	G-S	£3184
122 12/97 Hntg	2m4f110yE Ch	G-S	£2698

Total win prize-money £10758

Going: Sf: 0-1 GS: 0-0 Gd: 0-0 GF: - Fm: 0-0
Distance: 2m/2m3: 0-0 2m4-2m7: 0-0 3m+: 0-1
Track: LH: 0-1 RH: 0-0 Tight: 0-1 Gall: 0-0
Aids: Bl: 0-0 Vi: 0-0 Tstrap: 0-0
Best Rating: 133 3/98 Newb 3m   gd-sft   Ch

Music To My Ears (IRE)
100f   107f
5-y-o ch g Phardante (FR)-Evas Charm (Carlburg)
Jonjo O Neill J P McManus

Placings:12   (3883)
2002/03: 16¹G, 16²GS,

	Starts	1st	2nd	3rd	Win & Pl
NH Flat	2	1	1	0	2595
Career Total	2	1	1	0	2595
100 1/03 Sthl	2m	H NHF	GD	£2023

Total win prize-money £2023

Going: Sf: 0-0 GS: 0-1 Gd: 1-1 GF: - Fm: 0-0
Distance: 2m/2m3: 1-2 2m4-2m7: 0-0 3m+: 0-0
Track: LH: 1-2 RH: 0-0 Tight: 1-1 Gall: 0-1
Aids: Bl: 0-0 Vi: 0-0 Tstrap: 0-0
Best Rating: 107 3/03 Donc 2m110y gd-sft NHF

A full-brother to Hanakham, he ran green under pressure but hung on to win a bumper at Southwell in January on his debut; runner-up at Doncaster two months later; chasing will ultimately be his game.

Musical Mayhem (IRE)
106   115
10-y-o b g Shernazar-Minstrels Folly (USA) (The Minstrel (CAN))
D J Wintle A A Wintle

Placings:10/122/142/01/1-212   (0961)
2002/03: 22²GF, 25¹G, 20²S,

	Starts	1st	2nd	3rd	Win & Pl
Hurdles	3	1	2	0	3560
Career Total	14	6	5	0	22790
100 7/02 Wolv	3m1f	F Hdl	GD	£2262
115 8/01 Strf	2m6f110yF Hdl	GD	£2310
115 9/99 List	2m	Hdl	Y-S	£4312
119 7/98 Gway	2m4f	Hdl	YLD	£3586
113 7/97 Tipp	2m	NHF	GD	£2882
102 2/97 Fair	2m	NHF	G-Y	£3051

Total win prize-money £18406

Going: Sf: 0-1 GS: 0-0 Gd: 1-1 GF: - Fm: 0-1
Distance: 2m/2m3: 0-0 2m4-2m7: 0-2 3m+: 1-1
Track: LH: 1-3 RH: 0-0 Tight: 1-2 Gall: 0-0
Aids: Bl: 0-0 Vi: 0-0 Tstrap: 0-0
Best Rating: 119 7/98 Gway 2m4f   yield   Hdl

An effective hurdler at a modest level, he stays well and likes fast ground.

Musical Sling (IRE)
87(83h)   (64h)**65**
10-y-o b g Orchestra-Coctail Bid (Mandalus)
Dr P Pritchard   Mrs T Pritchard

Placings:311330/P31PP1/PPP-P04034FP   (2119)
2002/03: 22⁶GS, 16⁰S, 20⁴GF, 16⁹GF, 22³GF, 17⁴S, 24²G, 29³GFS,

	Starts	1st	2nd	3rd	Win & Pl
Hurdles	4	0	0	1	904
Chases	4	0	0	0	1039
Career Total	23	4	0	5	17039
121 4/00 Winc	3m1f110yE Ch			G-S	£3815
127 1/00 Towc	3m1f E Ch			HVY	£3380
105 12/98 Extr	2m1f110yD Hdl			GD	£3676
112 11/98 Worc	2m4f E Hdl			HVY	£2547
	Total win prize-money £13420				

Going:	Sf: 0-2 GS: 0-2 Gd: 0-1 GF: - Fm: 0-3
Distance:	2m/2m3: 0-3 2m4-2m7: 0-3 3m+: 0-2
Track:	LH: 0-7 RH: 0-0 Tight: 0-4 Gall: 0-1
Aids:	Bl: 0-0 Vi: 0-0 Tstrap: 0-0
Best Rating:	127 1/00 Towc 3m1f heavy Ch

Plating-class hurdler/chaser, he acts on a soft surface and stays three miles.

Musimaro (FR)
103   **82**
5-y-o b g Solid Illusion (USA)-Musimara (FR) (Margouillat (FR))
O Sherwood   P Joe Davis

Placings:3103   (3920)
2002/03: 18³S, 16¹G, 21⁰S, 18³S,

	Starts	1st	2nd	3rd	Win & Pl
NH Flat	2	1	0	1	2843
Hurdles	2	0	0	1	554
Career Total	4	1	0	2	3397
101 11/02 Ludl	2m	H NHF		GD	£2499
	Total win prize-money £2499				

Going:	Sf: 0-3 GS: 0-0 Gd: 1-1 GF: - Fm: 0-0
Distance:	2m/2m3: 1-3 2m4-2m7: 0-1 3m+: 0-0
Track:	LH: 0-2 RH: 1-2 Tight: 0-1 Gall: 0-0
Aids:	Bl: 0-0 Vi: 0-0 Tstrap: 0-0
Best Rating:	101 11/02 Ludl 2m good NHF

Won Ludlow bumper November 2002; does not appear to stay 2m 4f over hurdles.

Muskatsturm (GER)
91   **78**
4-y-o b g Lecroix (GER)-Myrthe (GER) (Konigstuhl (GER))
B J Curley (Mario Hofer 4/11) Mrs B J Curley

Placings:264   (3926)
2002/03: 16²HY, 16⁶HY, 20⁴G,

	Starts	1st	2nd	3rd	Win & Pl
Hurdles	3	0	1	0	1350
Career Total	3	0	1	0	1350

Going:	Sf: 0-2 GS: 0-0 Gd: 0-1 GF: - Fm: 0-0
Distance:	2m/2m3: 0-2 2m4-2m7: 0-1 3m+: 0-0
Track:	LH: 0-1 RH: 0-2 Tight: 0-0 Gall: 0-1
Aids:	Bl: 0-2 Vi: 0-0 Tstrap: 0-0
Best Rating:	78 3/03 Hntg 2m4f110y good Hdl

Must Bite
    93
7-y-o b g Bustino-Once Bitten (Brave Invader (USA))

Jonjo O Neill   J P McManus
Placings:UU000/030-3   (4418)
2002/03: 22³G,

	Starts	1st	2nd	3rd	Win & Pl
Hurdles	1	0	0	1	463
Career Total	9	0	0	2	1084

Going:	Sf: 0-0 GS: 0-0 Gd: 0-1 GF: - Fm: 0-0
Distance:	2m/2m3: 0-0 2m4-2m7: 0-1 3m+: 0-0
Track:	LH: 0-0 RH: 0-0 Tight: 0-0 Gall: 0-0
Aids:	Bl: 0-0 Vi: 0-0 Tstrap: 0-0
Best Rating:	93 3/03 MRas 2m6f good Hdl

Modest form in bumpers and novices hurdles in Ireland; heavily backed to defy topweight in novices handicap at Market Rasen on first outing here in March but finished only third; will stay well.

Mustang Molly

11-y-o br m Soldier Rose-Little N Game (Convolvulus)
Andrew J Martin (P W Hiatt 7/9) Andrew J Martin

Placings:P5/2P0P-P442234P   (4640)
2002/03: 21PGF, 17⁴G, 20⁴GF, 20²GF, 21²GF, 21³G, 24⁴F, 21PG,

	Starts	1st	2nd	3rd	Win & Pl
Chases	8	0	2	1	3743
Career Total	14	0	3	1	4651

Going:	Sf: 0-0 GS: 0-0 Gd: 0-3 GF: - Fm: 0-5
Distance:	2m/2m3: 0-1 2m4-2m7: 0-6 3m+: 0-1
Track:	LH: 0-6 RH: 0-2 Tight: 0-6 Gall: 0-2
Aids:	Bl: 0-0 Vi: 0-0 Tstrap: 0-0
Best Rating:	90 5/01 Chel 2m110y good Ch

Hunter chaser; placed in novice chases in the summer of 2002; does not seem to stay three miles.

Mutabari (USA)
96   **70**
9-y-o ch g Seeking The Gold (USA)-Cagey Exuberance (USA) (Exuberant (USA))
J L Spearing   J Spearing

Placings:040/4   (1455)
2002/03: 16⁴F,

	Starts	1st	2nd	3rd	Win & Pl
Hurdles	1	0	0	0	0
Career Total	4	0	0	0	0

Going:	Sf: 0-0 GS: 0-0 Gd: 0-0 GF: - Fm: 0-1
Distance:	2m/2m3: 0-1 2m4-2m7: 0-0 3m+: 0-0
Track:	LH: 0-0 RH: 0-1 Tight: 0-0 Gall: 0-0
Aids:	Bl: 0-0 Vi: 0-0 Tstrap: 0-0
Best Rating:	70 10/02 Ludl 2m firm Hdl

Mutadarra (IRE)
106(93c)   (79c)**91**
10-y-o ch g Mujtahid (USA)-Silver Echo (Caerleon (USA))
J W Mullins   M S Green

Placings:014/634/310454300P-2250051140   (1935)
2002/03: 22²GF, 19²GF, 17⁵G, 17⁹GF, 22⁰GF, 27⁵GF, 16¹F, 16¹G, 16⁴G, 19⁰GS,

	Starts	1st	2nd	3rd	Win & Pl
Hurdles	10	2	2	0	8512
Career Total	26	4	2	3	14498
93 10/02 Strf	2m110y F(0-100)HHdl			GD	£3010

---

93 10/02 Winc	2m	E(0-105)HHdl	FRM	£3445
86 8/01 Worc	2m	G Hdl	G-F	£1591
97 3/00 Hntg	2m110y E Hdl		G-F	£2870
	Total win prize-money £10917			

Going:	Sf: 0-0 GS: 0-1 Gd: 1-3 GF: - Fm: 1-6
Distance:	2m/2m3: 2-6 2m4-2m7: 0-3 3m+: 0-1
Track:	LH: 1-6 RH: 1-4 Tight: 1-7 Gall: 0-0
Aids:	Bl: 0-0 Vi: 0-0 Tstrap: 0-0
Best Rating:	97 10/00 Hrfd 2m3f110y good Hdl

Moderate handicap hurdler; acts on a sound surface; yet to prove he can be effective beyond 2m.

Mutakarrim
116   **138**
6-y-o ch g Mujtahid (USA)-Alyakkh (IRE) (Sadler s Wells (USA))
D K Weld   Michael W J Smurfit

Placings:030-121402   (4726a)
2002/03: 16¹S, 16²YS, 16¹G, 16⁴SH, 16⁹G, 16²GF,

	Starts	1st	2nd	3rd	Win & Pl
Hurdles	6	2	2	0	45792
Career Total	9	2	2	1	46543
138 11/02 Chel	2m110y A Hdl		GD	£14500
117 7/02 Gway	2m	Hdl	SFT	£5503
	Total win prize-money £20003			

Going:	Sf: 1-1 GS: 0-0 Gd: 1-2 GF: - Fm: 0-1
Distance:	2m/2m3: 2-6 2m4-2m7: 0-0 3m+: 0-0
Track:	LH: 1-2 RH: 1-4 Tight: 0-0 Gall: 0-0
Aids:	Bl: 2-6 Vi: 0-0 Tstrap: 0-0
Best Rating:	138 11/02 Chel 2m110y good Hdl

Useful Irish-trained novice hurdler; Listed class on the Flat; best over two miles and acts on ground good or softer; usually blinkered.

Mutanassib (IRE)
75   **19**
10-y-o b g Mtoto-Lightning Legacy (USA) (Super Concorde (USA))
M C Pipe   Malcolm B Jones

Placings:2030/P/00056/133441/0PF   (3143)
2002/03: 21⁰G, 20PS, 19FS,

	Starts	1st	2nd	3rd	Win & Pl
Hurdles	3	0	0	0	
Career Total	19	2	1	3	10337
119 1/00 Donc	2m4f	C(0-135)HHdl	GD	£5073
123 8/99 NAbb	2m1f	F Hdl	G-S	£1822
	Total win prize-money £6896			

Going:	Sf: 0-2 GS: 0-0 Gd: 0-1 GF: - Fm: 0-0
Distance:	2m/2m3: 0-0 2m4-2m7: 0-3 3m+: 0-0
Track:	LH: 0-1 RH: 0-2 Tight: 0-1 Gall: 0-1
Aids:	Bl: 0-0 Vi: 0-0 Tstrap: 0-3
Best Rating:	123 11/99 Chep 3m soft Hdl

Mutasarrif (IRE)
113(88h)   (63h)**85**
10-y-o b g Polish Patriot (USA)-Bouffant (High Top)
Miss L V Davis (G F White 25/7) Miss Louise Davis

Placings:550/130015F0/3400F43F/53PF60-P0P525F   (1617)
2002/03: 16PGS, 20⁹GF, 22PGF, 17⁵GF, 16²G, 17⁵GS, 16⁶F,

	Starts	1st	2nd	3rd	Win & Pl
Hurdles	3	0	0	0	0
Chases	4	0	1	0	1042
Career Total	32	2	1	4	9275

107 2/99 Sedg 2m1f   F(0-100)HHdl   GD £2635
103 5/98 Cmtl 2m1f110yD Hdl   G-F £2944
Total win prize-money £5579

Going:	Sf: 0-0 GS: 0-2 Gd: 0-1 GF: - Fm: 0-4
Distance:	2m/2m3: 0-5 2m4-2m7: 0-2 3m+: 0-0
Track:	LH: 0-6 RH: 0-1 Tight: 0-3 Gall: 0-0
Aids:	Bl: 0-0 Vi: 0-0 Tstrap: 0-1
Best Rating:	**107** 2/99 Sedg 2m1f good Hdl

Poor chaser, fatally injured at Ludlow in October 2002. (DEAD)

Muted Gift

69   **35**

5-y-o ch m King s Signet (USA)-Ballet On Ice (FR) (Fijar Tango (FR))
W G M Turner Darren Coombes

Placings:0600-600   (2550)
2002/03: 16⁶S, 16⁹GS, 17⁰HY,

	Starts	1st	2nd	3rd	Win & Pl
Hurdles	3	0	0	0	0
Career Total	7	0	0	0	0

Going:	Sf: 0-2 GS: 0-1 Gd: 0-0 GF: - Fm: 0-0
Distance:	2m/2m3: 0-3 2m4-2m7: 0-0 3m+: 0-0
Track:	LH: 0-2 RH: 0-1 Tight: 0-2 Gall: 0-0
Aids:	Bl: 0-0 Vi: 0-0 Tstrap: 0-0
Best Rating:	**35** 11/02 Uttx 2m soft Hdl

Mutineer (IRE)

116   **136**

4-y-o gr g Highest Honor (FR)-Miss Amy R (USA) (Deputy Minister (CAN))
D T Hughes (Kevin Prendergast 15/5) Seven To Eleven Syndicate

Placings:33331110   (4130)
2002/03: 16⁹HY, 16²S, 16⁹S, 16²S, 16¹HY, 16¹YS, 16¹S, 17⁰G,

	Starts	1st	2nd	3rd	Win & Pl
Hurdles	8	3	0	4	44733
Career Total	8	3	0	4	44733
136 2/03	Leop	2m	Hdl	SFT	£21103
129 1/03	Punc	2m	Hdl	Y-S	£13506
123 12/02	Leop	2m	Hdl	HVY	£7975
					Total win prize-money £42585

Going:	Sf: 2-6 GS: 0-0 Gd: 0-1 GF: - Fm: 0-0
Distance:	2m/2m3: 3-8 2m4-2m7: 0-0 3m+: 0-0
Track:	LH: 2-4 RH: 1-3 Tight: 0-0 Gall: 0-1
Aids:	Bl: 3-4 Vi: 0-0 Tstrap: 2-7
Best Rating:	**136** 2/03 Leop 2m soft Hdl

Very useful, progressive juvenile hurdler; front-runner; suited by testing ground.

Mutiny

93   **61**

5-y-o ch g Selkirk (USA)-Indian Love Song (Be My Guest (USA))
B W Duke Miss A C Telling

Placings:P000   (2713)
2002/03: 22⁶G, 21⁰S, 25⁰S, 20⁰HY,

	Starts	1st	2nd	3rd	Win & Pl
Hurdles	4	0	0	0	0
Career Total	4	0	0	0	0

Going:	Sf: 0-3 GS: 0-0 Gd: 0-1 GF: - Fm: 0-0

Distance: 2m/2m3: 0-0 2m4-2m7: 0-3 3m+: 0-1
Track: LH: 0-4 RH: 0-0 Tight: 0-1 Gall: 0-0
Aids: Bl: 0-0 Vi: 0-0 Tstrap: 0-0
Best Rating: **65** 12/02 Wwck 2m5f   soft   Hdl

My Ace

71   **32**

5-y-o b m Definite Article-Miss Springtime (Bluebird (USA))
Mrs H Dalton R L Burrows

Placings:3-24204   (4266)
2002/03: 17²S, 16⁴S, 17²F, 17⁰G, 16⁴GF,

	Starts	1st	2nd	3rd	Win & Pl
NH Flat	3	0	2	0	1142
Hurdles	2	0	0	0	0
Career Total	6	0	2	1	1419

Going:	Sf: 0-2 GS: 0-0 Gd: 0-1 GF: - Fm: 0-2
Distance:	2m/2m3: 0-5 2m4-2m7: 0-0 3m+: 0-0
Track:	LH: 0-3 RH: 0-1 Tight: 0-2 Gall: 0-0
Aids:	Bl: 0-0 Vi: 0-0 Tstrap: 0-0
Best Rating:	**93** 10/02 Tntn 2m1f firm NHF

Has shown form in bumpers.

My Baton

106

8-y-o ch g Orchestra-Laurello (Bargello)
P Beaumont Trevor Hemmings

Placings:2102/1362P6/P42222-U   (1634)
2002/03: 20⁰S,

	Starts	1st	2nd	3rd	Win & Pl
Chases	1	0	0	0	0
Career Total	17	2	7	1	15193
102 11/00	Hayd	2m4f	D Hdl	SFT	£3510
116 2/00	Hayd	2m	H NHF	SFT	£2102
					Total win prize-money £5613

Going:	Sf: 0-1 GS: 0-0 Gd: 0-0 GF: - Fm: 0-0
Distance:	2m/2m3: 0-0 2m4-2m7: 0-1 3m+: 0-0
Track:	LH: 0-0 RH: 0-1 Tight: 0-0 Gall: 0-0
Aids:	Bl: 0-0 Vi: 0-0 Tstrap: 0-0
Best Rating:	**138** 4/00 Ayr 2m good NHF

Fair chaser, stayed three miles plus, acted on any ground. (DEAD)

My Bold Boyo

103(80c)   (68c) **103**

8-y-o b g Never So Bold-My Rosie (Forzando)
K Bishop E T Roberts

Placings:3006P511-00110600F2   (4596)
2002/03: 16⁶GF, 20⁶GF, 17¹F, 17¹F, 19⁰G, 19⁶GS, 19⁰GS, 19⁰F, 17⁶GF, 19²GF,

	Starts	1st	2nd	3rd	Win & Pl
Hurdles	9	2	1	0	9566
Chases	1	0	0	0	0
Career Total	18	4	1	4	15785
103 10/02	Extr	2m1f	E(0-110)HHdl	FRM	£4017
100 10/02	Extr	2m1f	D(0-120)HHdl	FRM	£4069
94 4/02	Extr	2m1f	E(0-105)HHdl	FRM	£2954
82 4/02	Extr	2m1f	F(0-100)HHdl	FRM	£2870
					Total win prize-money £13910

Going:	Sf: 0-0 GS: 0-2 Gd: 0-1 GF: - Fm: 2-7
Distance:	2m/2m3: 2-7 2m4-2m7: 0-3 3m+: 0-0
Track:	LH: 0-2 RH: 2-8 Tight: 0-3 Gall: 0-0
Aids:	Bl: 0-0 Vi: 0-0 Tstrap: 0-0
Best Rating:	**103** 4/03 Extr 2m3f gd-fm Hdl

Modest handicap hurdler; four times a winner over 17 furlongs at Exeter in 2002; suited by a stiff track; acts on fast ground.

My Galliano (IRE)

100(110h)   (101+h)**96**

7-y-o b g Muharib (USA)-Hogan Stand (Buckskin (FR))
B G Powell L Gilbert

Placings:00/0452125/U60FP31425-454235   (2291)
2002/03: 17⁴G, 16⁵G, 16⁴F, 16²G, 19³GS, 16⁵G,

	Starts	1st	2nd	3rd	Win & Pl
Hurdles	3	0	1	0	1355
Chases	3	0	0	1	840
Career Total	25	2	4	2	12727
99 11/00	Winc	2m	E(0-115)HHdl	G-F	£3523
94 11/00	Kemp	2m	F(0-100)HHdl	SFT	£2756
					Total win prize-money £6279

Going:	Sf: 0-0 GS: 0-1 Gd: 0-4 GF: - Fm: 0-1
Distance:	2m/2m3: 0-6 2m4-2m7: 0-0 3m+: 0-0
Track:	LH: 0-0 RH: 0-6 Tight: 0-2 Gall: 0-1
Aids:	Bl: 0-0 Vi: 0-0 Tstrap: 0-0
Best Rating:	**103** 10/02 Winc 2m good Hdl

Moderate hurdler at around two miles, he is effective on any ground.

My Good Son (NZ)

109(104c)   (100c)**98+**

8-y-o b g The Son (NZ)-Meadow Hall (NZ) (Pikehall (USA))
Ian Williams Men Behaving Sadly Partnership

Placings:4003210/010P/U0P650P1F1-FPPP31223U   (1328)
2002/03: 24⁶FG, 20⁶GS, 20⁶G, 27⁶GF, 22³GF, 24¹GF, 26²GF, 24²GF, 26³GF, 26⁰G,

	Starts	1st	2nd	3rd	Win & Pl
Hurdles	7	1	2	1	6190
Chases	3	0	0	1	627
Career Total	31	5	3	3	22369
91 7/02	Worc	3m	D(0-125)HHdl	G-F	£4095
100 4/02	Sedg	2m5f	D(0-120)HCh	G-F	£4075
100 4/02	Plum	3m2f	D(0-90)HCh	G-F	£2828
103 2/01	Hayd	2m4f	D(0-120)HHdl	HVY	£3552
99 3/00	Ludl	2m5f	E Hdl	GD	£2899
					Total win prize-money £17451

Going:	Sf: 0-0 GS: 0-1 Gd: 0-3 GF: - Fm: 1-6
Distance:	2m/2m3: 0-0 2m4-2m7: 0-0 3m+: 1-7
Track:	LH: 1-8 RH: 0-1 Tight: 0-6 Gall: 0-1
Aids:	Bl: 0-4 Vi: 0-0 Tstrap: 0-0
Best Rating:	**103** 2/01 Hayd 2m4f heavy Hdl

Moderate hurdler/chaser; handles heavy ground but prefers faster; stays three miles.

My Junes Moon

5-y-o b m Petoski-Peristyle (Tolomeo)
A D Smith Pertemps Group Limited

Placings:0   (0823)
2002/03: 16⁰GF,

	Starts	1st	2nd	3rd	Win & Pl
NH Flat	1	0	0	0	
Career Total	1	0	0	0	

Going:	Sf: 0-0 GS: 0-0 Gd: 0-0 GF: - Fm: 0-1
Distance:	2m/2m3: 0-1 2m4-2m7: 0-0 3m+: 0-0
Track:	LH: 0-1 RH: 0-0 Tight: 0-0 Gall: 0-0
Aids:	Bl: 0-0 Vi: 0-0 Tstrap: 0-0

Best Rating: **0**   7/02   Worc   2m   gd-fm   NHF

My Legal Eagle (IRE)
106   **103**

9-y-o b g Law Society (USA)-Majestic Nurse (On Your Mark)
R J Price   E G Bevan

Placings:420/6/5P06-4122   (0417)
2002/03: 17⁴GF, 16¹GF, 17²S, 16²GF,

	Starts	1st	2nd	3rd	Win & Pl
Hurdles	4	1	2	0	5093
Career Total	12	1	3	0	5812
103 5/02 Worc 2m E(0-105)HHdl				G-F	£2625
				Total win prize-money	£2625

Going: Sf: 0-1 GS: 0-0 Gd: 0-0 GF: - Fm: 1-3
Distance: **2m/2m3: 1-4** 2m4-2m7: 0-0 3m+: 0-0
Track: **LH: 1-3** RH: 0-0 Tight: 0-2 Gall: 0-0
Aids: Bl: 0-0 Vi: 0-0 Tstrap: 0-0
Best Rating: **103** 6/02 Strf 2m110y   gd-fm   Hdl

Moderate handicap hurdler. Effective at around two miles and acts on most types of ground.

My Line
105   **98**

6-y-o b g Perpendicular-My Desire (Grey Desire)
Mrs M Reveley   Mrs M Hoey

Placings:0-30F6   (3156)
2002/03: 17³HY, 16⁴G, 16⁶S, 16⁶G,

	Starts	1st	2nd	3rd	Win & Pl
Hurdles	4	0	0	1	432
Career Total	5	0	0	1	432

Going: Sf: 0-2 GS: 0-0 Gd: 0-2 GF: - Fm: 0-0
Distance: 2m/2m3: 0-4 2m4-2m7: 0-0 3m+: 0-0
Track: LH: 0-2 RH: 0-2 Tight: 0-1 Gall: 0-0
Aids: Bl: 0-0 Vi: 0-0 Tstrap: 0-0
Best Rating: **98** 12/02 Hayd 2m   good   Hdl

Moderate hurdler; winner on the Flat, but yet to score over obstacles; best on soft ground.

My Mate Whitey (IRE)
56   **11**

4-y-o ch g Millkom-Imagery (Vision (USA))
M A Allen (K Bell 12/6)   Brendan Laverty

Placings:P0   (2417)
2002/03: 16⁶G, 18⁹G,

	Starts	1st	2nd	3rd	Win & Pl
Hurdles	2	0	0	0	
Career Total	2	0	0	0	

Going: Sf: 0-0 GS: 0-1 Gd: 0-1 GF: - Fm: 0-0
Distance: 2m/2m3: 0-2 2m4-2m7: 0-0 3m+: 0-0
Track: LH: 0-1 RH: 0-1 Tight: 0-1 Gall: 0-0
Aids: Bl: 0-0 Vi: 0-0 Tstrap: 0-0
Best Rating: **11** 12/02 Font 2m2f110y   good   Hdl

My Native Land (IRE)
100   **86**

8-y-o b g Be My Native (USA)-Papukeena (Simbir)

Miss T M Ide   Miss Tracey Ide

Placings:60/6523000204-P04P40   (4083)
2002/03: 24⁵S, 24⁰G, 25⁴HY, 26⁸S, 22⁴HY, 25⁰HY,

	Starts	1st	2nd	3rd	Win & Pl
Hurdles	6	0	0	0	
Career Total	18	0	2	1	2363

Going: Sf: 0-5 GS: 0-0 Gd: 0-1 GF: - Fm: 0-0
Distance: 2m/2m3: 0-0 2m4-2m7: 0-1 3m+: 0-5
Track: LH: 0-1 RH: 0-3 Tight: 0-1 Gall: 0-0
Aids: Bl: 0-0 Vi: 0-0 Tstrap: 0-0
Best Rating: **101** 8/01 Slig 2m4f   sft-hvy   Hdl

My Native Miss (IRE)
82f   **66f**

5-y-o b m Be My Native (USA)-Explosive Missile (IRE) (Supreme Leader)
Mrs L C Jewell   The Red White And Blues

Placings:00   (4672)
2002/03: 16⁹GS, 16⁰G,

	Starts	1st	2nd	3rd	Win & Pl
NH Flat	2	0	0	0	
Career Total	2	0	0	0	

Going: Sf: 0-0 GS: 0-1 Gd: 0-1 GF: - Fm: 0-0
Distance: 2m/2m3: 0-2 2m4-2m7: 0-0 3m+: 0-0
Track: LH: 0-2 RH: 0-0 Tight: 0-1 Gall: 0-0
Aids: Bl: 0-0 Vi: 0-0 Tstrap: 0-0
Best Rating: **66** 12/02 Fknm 2m   gd-sft   NHF

My Shenandoah (IRE)
102   **123**

12-y-o br g Derrylin-Edwina s Dawn (Space King)
J Howard Johnson   Gordon Brown/bert Watson

Placings:60060U/O311216/35U2653/660115/5553012-41F4   (3154)
2002/03: 21⁴GS, 21¹GS, 20⁷GS, 20⁴G,

	Starts	1st	2nd	3rd	Win & Pl
Hurdles	4	1	0	0	3085
Career Total	37	7	3	4	28382
118 12/02 Hntg 2m5f110yF Hdl				G-S	£2310
116 3/02 MRas 2m5f110yD(0-115)HHdl				G-S	£3445
113 4/01 Muss 2m4f D(0-120)HHdl				G-F	£4355
104 3/01 MRas 2m5f110yE(0-115)HHdl				GD	£2604
108 2/98 Muss 2m4f E(0-115)HHdl				GD	£2895
104 1/98 Muss 2m4f E(0-100)HHdl				GD	£2696
93 12/97 Muss 2m4f E(0-100)HHdl				GD	£2724
				Total win prize-money	£21029

Going: Sf: 0-0 GS: 1-3 Gd: 0-1 GF: - Fm: 0-0
Distance: 2m/2m3: 0-0 **2m4-2m7: 1-4** 3m+: 0-0
Track: LH: 0-0 **RH: 1-4** Tight: 0-3 **Gall: 1-1**
Aids: Bl: 0-0 Vi: 0-0 Tstrap: 0-0
Best Rating: **123** 4/02 Prth 2m4f110y   good   Hdl

Fair hurdler; broke down at Musselburgh in January and retires winner of seven races from 35 starts.

My True Love (IRE)
93f   **85f**

4-y-o b g Beneficial-Elfi (IRE) (Le Moss)
R J Baker   Surerak Ins Cons (Racing)/Mrs S Rowe

Placings:5   (4628)
2002/03: 17⁵GF,

	Starts	1st	2nd	3rd	Win & Pl
NH Flat	1	0	0	0	0
Career Total	1	0	0	0	0

Going: Sf: 0-0 GS: 0-0 Gd: 0-0 GF: - Fm: 0-1
Distance: 2m/2m3: 0-1 2m4-2m7: 0-0 3m+: 0-0
Track: LH: 0-1 RH: 0-0 Tight: 0-1 Gall: 0-0
Aids: Bl: 0-0 Vi: 0-0 Tstrap: 0-0
Best Rating: **84** 4/03 NAbb 2m1f   gd-fm   NHF

My Very Own (IRE)
89   **88**

5-y-o ch g Persian Bold-Cossack Princess (IRE) (Lomond (USA))
K C Bailey   Mrs Gillian Curley

Placings:0-3   (0576)
2002/03: 17³G,

	Starts	1st	2nd	3rd	Win & Pl
Hurdles	1	0	0	1	427
Career Total	2	0	0	1	427

Going: Sf: 0-0 GS: 0-0 Gd: 0-0 GF: - Fm: 0-0
Distance: 2m/2m3: 0-1 2m4-2m7: 0-0 3m+: 0-0
Track: LH: 0-1 RH: 0-0 Tight: 0-1 Gall: 0-0
Aids: Bl: 0-0 Vi: 0-0 Tstrap: 0-0
Best Rating: **97** 6/02 NAbb 2m1f   good   Hdl

My Wakashan (IRE)
81(70h)   (41h)**43**

8-y-o b m Wakashan-My Wings (Erin s Hope)
J J Lambe   H Muldoon

Placings:0/00P/0-06   (1238)
2002/03: 17⁰G, 16⁶GF,

	Starts	1st	2nd	3rd	Win & Pl
Hurdles	1	0	0	0	0
Chases	1	0	0	0	0
Career Total	7	0	0	0	0

Going: Sf: 0-0 GS: 0-0 Gd: 0-0 GF: - Fm: 0-1
Distance: 2m/2m3: 0-2 2m4-2m7: 0-0 3m+: 0-0
Track: LH: 0-2 RH: 0-0 Tight: 0-1 Gall: 0-0
Aids: Bl: 0-0 Vi: 0-0 Tstrap: 0-0
Best Rating: **94** 5/00 Cork 2m   gd-yld   NHF

My Whisper (IRE)
81f   **62f**

4-y-o b f Zaffaran (USA)-Floreamus (Quayside)
A King   Mrs M C Sweeney

Placings:0   (4788)
2002/03: 17⁰G,

	Starts	1st	2nd	3rd	Win & Pl
NH Flat	1	0	0	0	
Career Total	1	0	0	0	

Going: Sf: 0-0 GS: 0-0 Gd: 0-1 GF: - Fm: 0-0
Distance: 2m/2m3: 0-1 2m4-2m7: 0-0 3m+: 0-0
Track: LH: 0-0 RH: 0-1 Tight: 0-1 Gall: 0-0
Aids: Bl: 0-0 Vi: 0-0 Tstrap: 0-0
Best Rating: **62** 4/03 MRas 2m1f110y   good   NHF

Well beaten on first ever outing in bumper at Market Rasen in April.

Mydante (IRE)

110   116

8-y-o b m Phardante (FR)-Carminda (Proverb)
J S Moore Ernie Houghton

Placings:340/310366433/505142/1260243354310-12
                                                    (0396)

2002/03: 24¹GS, 27²GF,

	Starts	1st	2nd	3rd	Win & Pl
Hurdles	2	1	1	0	7461
Career Total	33	5	4	8	44680
111 5/02	Towc	3m	C(0-130)HHdl	G-S	£6191
116 4/02	Uttx	3m110y	D(0-125)HHdl	G-F	£4329
111 5/01	Extr	3m110y	C(0-135)HHdl	GD	£5664
99 4/01	Newb	3m110y	F(0-100)HHdl	SFT	£3461
91 10/99	Navn	2m2f		Y-S	£13258

Total win prize-money £32905

Going: Sf: 0-0 GS: 1-1 Gd: 0-0 GF: - Fm: 0-1
Distance: 2m/2m3: 0-0 2m4-2m7: 0-0 3m+: 1-2
Track: LH: 0-1 RH: 1-1 Tight: 0-1 Gall: 0-0
Aids: Bl: 0-0 Vi: 0-0 Tstrap: 0-0
Best Rating: 116 4/02 Uttx 3m110y gd-fm Hdl

Fair hurdler; took advantage of the Handicapper s leniency
when easy winner of uncompetitive fast-ground three-mile
handicap hurdle at Uttoxeter in April 2002. Stays well.

Myheartisbroken (IRE)

9-y-o b g Broken Hearted-Lady Mearlane (Giolla Mear)
V R A Dartnall (David Wachman 9/5) Tom Casagranda

Placings:1/131/F3/PPP
                                                    (4625)
2002/03: 20ᴾYS, 20ᴾS, 17ᶠGF,

	Starts	1st	2nd	3rd	Win & Pl
Hurdles	3	0	0	0	
Career Total	9	3	0	2	14413
125 2/00	Thur	2m6f	Hdl	HVY	£4416
125 11/99	DRoy	2m	Hdl	SFT	£6160
120 3/99	Limk	2m1f	NHF	SH	£2608

Total win prize-money £13186

Going: Sf: 0-1 GS: 0-0 Gd: 0-0 GF: - Fm: 0-1
Distance: 2m/2m3: 0-1 2m4-2m7: 0-2 3m+: 0-0
Track: LH: 0-1 RH: 0-1 Tight: 0-1 Gall: 0-0
Aids: Bl: 0-0 Vi: 0-0 Tstrap: 0-1
Best Rating: 125 2/00 Thur 2m6f heavy Hdl

Mylo

103   96d

5-y-o gr g Faustus (USA)-Bellifontaine (FR) (Bellypha)
Jonjo O Neill J P McManus

Placings:2-2224065
                                                    (3595)
2002/03: 16²G, 16²G, 17²G, 19⁴G, 19⁶S, 17⁶HY, 20⁵HY,

	Starts	1st	2nd	3rd	Win & Pl
NH Flat	2	0	2	0	1084
Hurdles	5	0	1	0	1124
Career Total	8	0	4	0	2696

Going: Sf: 0-3 GS: 0-0 Gd: 0-4 GF: - Fm: 0-0
Distance: 2m/2m3: 0-5 2m4-2m7: 0-2 3m+: 0-0
Track: LH: 0-4 RH: 0-3 Tight: 0-3 Gall: 0-0
Aids: Bl: 0-0 Vi: 0-0 Tstrap: 0-0
Best Rating: 101 5/02 Worc 2m good NHF

Modest frustrating novice hurdler; stays two and a half
miles; seems best on good ground; no improvement when
tried in blinkers.

Mysie

8-y-o ch m Weld-Saucy Eater (Saucy Kit)
T R Greathead Mrs S Greathead

Placings:50/000516/P
                                                    (2670)
2002/03: 26ᴾS,

	Starts	1st	2nd	3rd	Win & Pl
Hurdles	1	0	0	0	
Career Total	9	1	0	0	2247
84 2/01	Plum	2m5f	F(0-105)HHdl	SFT	£2247

Total win prize-money £2247

Going: Sf: 0-1 GS: 0-0 Gd: 0-0 GF: - Fm: 0-0
Distance: 2m/2m3: 0-0 2m4-2m7: 0-0 3m+: 0-1
Track: LH: 0-0 RH: 0-1 Tight: 0-0 Gall: 0-0
Aids: Bl: 0-0 Vi: 0-0 Tstrap: 0-0
Best Rating: 84 2/01 Plum 2m5f soft Hdl

Myson (IRE)

85

4-y-o ch g Accordion-Ah Suzie (IRE) (King s Ride)
D M Grissell R Winchester & Son

Placings:4F
                                                    (4184)
2002/03: 17⁴HY, 17ᶠG,

	Starts	1st	2nd	3rd	Win & Pl
NH Flat	1	0	0	0	0
Hurdles	1	0	0	0	0
Career Total	2	0	0	0	0

Going: Sf: 0-1 GS: 0-0 Gd: 0-1 GF: - Fm: 0-0
Distance: 2m/2m3: 0-2 2m4-2m7: 0-0 3m+: 0-0
Track: LH: 0-0 RH: 0-2 Tight: 0-2 Gall: 0-0
Aids: Bl: 0-0 Vi: 0-0 Tstrap: 0-0
Best Rating: 85 3/03 Folk 2m1f110y good Hdl

Mysteri Dancer

87   86

5-y-o b g Rudimentary (USA)-Mystery Ship (Decoy Boy)
R J O Sullivan Jack Joseph

Placings:244
                                                    (0780)
2002/03: 16²G, 16⁴GF, 16⁴GF,

	Starts	1st	2nd	3rd	Win & Pl
Hurdles	3	0	1	0	1258
Career Total	3	0	1	0	1258

Going: Sf: 0-0 GS: 0-0 Gd: 0-1 GF: - Fm: 0-2
Distance: 2m/2m3: 0-3 2m4-2m7: 0-0 3m+: 0-0
Track: LH: 0-2 RH: 0-1 Tight: 0-1 Gall: 0-1
Aids: Bl: 0-0 Vi: 0-0 Tstrap: 0-0
Best Rating: 86 6/02 Strf 2m110y gd-fm Hdl

Plating-class hurdler; handles fast ground.

Mystic Glen

82f   51f

4-y-o b f Vettori (IRE)-Mystic Memory (Ela-Mana-Mou)
P D Niven Mrs J A Niven

Placings:0
                                                    (4404)
2002/03: 16⁰GF,

	Starts	1st	2nd	3rd	Win & Pl
NH Flat	1	0	0	0	
Career Total	1	0	0	0	

Going: Sf: 0-0 GS: 0-0 Gd: 0-1 GF: - Fm: 0-0
Distance: 2m/2m3: 0-1 2m4-2m7: 0-0 3m+: 0-0
Track: LH: 0-1 RH: 0-0 Tight: 0-0 Gall: 0-0
Aids: Bl: 0-0 Vi: 0-0 Tstrap: 0-0
Best Rating: 51 3/03 Hayd 2m gd-fm NHF

Subject of market support when well beaten on bumper
debut.

Mystic Hill

103   73

12-y-o b g Shirley Heights-Nuryana (Nureyev (USA))
J Joseph Jack Joseph

Placings:044121/4363031/212240/6/0/P06000-15003
                                                    (3933)
2002/03: 22¹GF, 21⁵G, 26⁰GS, 22⁰GS, 22³S,

	Starts	1st	2nd	3rd	Win & Pl
Hurdles	5	1	0	1	2688
Career Total	32	5	4	4	16970
77 9/02	Strf	2m6f110yG(0-95)HHdl	G-F	£2338
114 6/98	NAbb	2m6f	D(0-120)HHdl	GD	£2775
94 3/98	NAbb	2m1f	F(0-100)HHdl	SFT	£1827
96 4/97	Extr	2m3f110yE(0-110)HHdl	G-F	£2528
79 4/97	Tntn	2m1f	F Hdl	FRM	£2039

Total win prize-money £11509

Going: Sf: 0-1 GS: 0-2 Gd: 0-1 GF: - Fm: 1-1
Distance: 2m/2m3: 0-0 2m4-2m7: 1-4 3m+: 0-1
Track: LH: 1-3 RH: 0-2 Tight: 1-3 Gall: 0-1
Aids: Bl: 0-0 Vi: 0-0 Tstrap: 0-0
Best Rating: 114 6/98 NAbb 2m6f good Hdl

Plating-class hurdler; stays two and three-quarter miles;
suited by fast ground.

Mystic Isle (IRE)

13-y-o b g Callernish-Sleemana (Prince Hansel)
T R George S G B Morrison

Placings:24U61F0/2022/1P6P2143/15P0/354214/P (1583)
2002/03: 26ᴾG,

	Starts	1st	2nd	3rd	Win & Pl
Chases	1	0	0	0	
Career Total	30	5	6	2	23929
120 3/00	Folk	3m2f	F(0-105)HCh	G-F	£2520
124 1/99	Folk	3m2f	E(0-115)HCh	SFT	£3068
112 3/98	Folk	3m2f	D Ch	GD	£3927
116 11/97	Hrfd	3m1f110yE Ch	SFT	£3312
104 1/96	Wind	2m6f110yE Hdl	SFT	£2740

Total win prize-money £15568

Going: Sf: 0-0 GS: 0-0 Gd: 0-1 GF: - Fm: 0-0
Distance: 2m/2m3: 0-0 2m4-2m7: 0-0 3m+: 0-1
Track: LH: 0-1 RH: 0-0 Tight: 0-1 Gall: 0-0
Aids: Bl: 0-0 Vi: 0-0 Tstrap: 0-0
Best Rating: 124 1/99 Folk 3m2f soft Ch

Mystic Major

11-y-o b g Wace (USA)-Mystic Mintet (King Log)
Mrs I Hughes E R Hughes

Placings:F-P
                                                    (0055)
2002/03: 24ᴾG,

	Starts	1st	2nd	3rd	Win & Pl
Chases	1	0	0	0	
Career Total	2	0	0	0	

Going: Sf: 0-0 GS: 0-0 Gd: 0-1 GF: - Fm: 0-0

Distance: 2m/2m3: 0-0 2m4-2m7: 0-0 3m+: 0-1
Track: LH: 0-1 RH: 0-0 Tight: 0-1 Gall: 0-0
Aids: Bl: 0-0 Vi: 0-0 Tstrap: 0-0

Mystic Ridge

92(83h)   (71 h)**79**

9-y-o ch g Mystiko (USA)-Vallauris (Faustus (USA))
R Lee Osborne House Limited

Placings:P000/0/63-004   (4562)
2002/03: 16⁵S, 16⁹GF, 17⁴GF,

	Starts	1st	2nd	3rd	Win & Pl
Hurdles	2	0	0	0	0
Chases	1	0	0	0	433
Career Total	10	0	0	1	931

Going: Sf: 0-1 GS: 0-0 Gd: 0-0 GF: - Fm: 0-2
Distance: 2m/2m3: 0-3 2m4-2m7: 0-0 3m+: 0-0
Track: LH: 0-2 RH: 0-1 Tight: 0-1 Gall: 0-0
Aids: Bl: 0-0 Vi: 0-0 Tstrap: 0-0
Best Rating: 85   5/01   Bang   2m1f110y   good   Ch

Plating-class maiden chaser. (DEAD)

Mythical Charm

89   **66**

4-y-o f Charnwood Forest (IRE)-Triple Tricks (IRE) (Royal Academy (USA))
B R Johnson (J H M Gosden 31/8) Tann Racing

Placings:40   (4425)
2002/03: 16⁴HY, 16⁰GF,

	Starts	1st	2nd	3rd	Win & Pl
Hurdles	2	0	0	0	0
Career Total	2	0	0	0	0

Going: Sf: 0-1 GS: 0-0 Gd: 0-0 GF: - Fm: 0-1
Distance: 2m/2m3: 0-2 2m4-2m7: 0-0 3m+: 0-0
Track: LH: 0-2 RH: 0-0 Tight: 0-2 Gall: 0-0
Aids: Bl: 0-0 Vi: 0-0 Tstrap: 0-0
Best Rating: 66   3/03   Plum   2m   heavy   Hdl

Mythical King (IRE)

111   **125**

6-y-o b g Fairy King (USA)-Whatcombe (USA) (Alleged (USA))
R Lee (B Palling 24/10) Richard Edwards

Placings:312510   (4476)
2002/03: 16³S, 16¹S, 16²GS, 16⁵GS, 16¹GS, 16⁹G,

	Starts	1st	2nd	3rd	Win & Pl
Hurdles	6	2	1	1	13539
Career Total	6	2	1	1	13539
125	3/03	Strf	2m110y	D(0-125)HHdl	G-S	£8443
114	12/02	Uttx	2m	E Hdl	SFT	£3395
				Total win prize-money £11839		

Going: Sf: 1-2 GS: 1-3 Gd: 0-1 GF: - Fm: 0-0
Distance: 2m/2m3: 2-6 2m4-2m7: 0-0 3m+: 0-0
Track: LH: 2-6 RH: 0-0 Tight: 1-2 Gall: 0-1
Aids: Bl: 0-0 Vi: 0-0 Tstrap: 0-0
Best Rating: 125   3/03   Strf   2m110y   gd-sft   Hdl

Decent novice hurdler; effective at two miles; acts on soft and possibly capable of further improvement.

Mytimie (IRE)

105(104h)   (111h)**113**

8-y-o b g Be My Native (USA)-Snoqualmie (Warpath)

J M Jefferson Mr & Mrs Raymond Anderson Green

Placings:134/260/P13222P-21332   (3798)
2002/03: 20²S, 16¹HY, 16³GS, 16³G, 20²S,

	Starts	1st	2nd	3rd	Win & Pl
Chases	5	1	2	2	9831
Career Total	18	3	6	4	22825
113	11/02	Carl	2m	D Ch	HVY	£5206
104	10/01	Kels	2m110y	E Hdl	G-S	£2439
114	11/99	Carl	2m1f	H NHF	SFT	£1658
				Total win prize-money £9305		

Going: Sf: 1-3 GS: 0-1 Gd: 0-1 GF: - Fm: 0-0
Distance: 2m/2m3: 1-3 2m4-2m7: 0-2 3m+: 0-0
Track: LH: 0-2 RH: 1-3 Tight: 0-1 Gall: 0-1
Aids: Bl: 0-0 Vi: 0-0 Tstrap: 0-0
Best Rating: 114   11/99   Carl   2m1f   soft   NHF

Fair chaser; appreciates cut in the ground; stays two and a half miles.

Nagara Sound

12-y-o b g Lochnager-Safe 'n Sound (Good Investment (USA))
Mrs S Warren G L Edwards

Placings:402466630/F00600/P/0/05   (0247)
2002/03: 19⁵G,

	Starts	1st	2nd	3rd	Win & Pl
Chases	1	0	0	0	0
Career Total	18	0	1	1	823

Going: Sf: 0-0 GS: 0-0 Gd: 0-1 GF: - Fm: 0-0
Distance: 2m/2m3: 0-0 2m4-2m7: 0-1 3m+: 0-0
Track: LH: 0-0 RH: 0-1 Tight: 0-0 Gall: 0-0
Aids: Bl: 0-0 Vi: 0-0 Tstrap: 0-0
Best Rating: 97   11/95   MRas   1m5f110y   gd-sft   NHF

Nahthen Lad (IRE)

14-y-o b g Good Thyne (USA)-Current Call (Electrify)
J A Danahar J A Danahar

Placings:4/1P311606/121121/6P2P0/33P6F4/52P30P/13/P320-P0   (4133)
2002/03: 25⁵G, 26⁹G,

	Starts	1st	2nd	3rd	Win & Pl
Chases	2	0	0	0	
Career Total	40	8	5	6	122505
139	10/99	Asct	3m110y	B HCh	GD	£8486
157	3/96	Chel	3m110y	A Ch	G-S	£54672
139	1/96	Hayd	2m4f	D Ch	SFT	£3779
127	1/96	Wwck	2m4f110yD Ch		G-S	£4074
124	11/95	Chel	2m5f	C(0-130)HHdl	GD	£2827
113	2/95	Hntg	2m5f110yC Hdl		G-S	£7230
113	1/95	Hayd	2m4f	E Hdl	HVY	£2472
103	10/94	Towc	2m	Hdl	GD	£2075
				Total win prize-money £85617		

Going: Sf: 0-0 GS: 0-0 Gd: 0-2 GF: - Fm: 0-0
Distance: 2m/2m3: 0-0 2m4-2m7: 0-0 3m+: 0-2
Track: LH: 0-1 RH: 0-1 Tight: 0-0 Gall: 0-1
Aids: Bl: 0-1 Vi: 0-1 Tstrap: 0-0
Best Rating: 157   3/96   Chel   3m110y   gd-sft   Ch

A former high-class chaser but a modest hunter drawing his pension now.

Nailbiter

98   **84**

4-y-o b g Night Shift (USA)-Scylla (Rock City)

Mrs A Duffield Middleham Park Racing Xvi

Placings:503F5325   (4782)
2002/03: 14⁵GS, 14⁰GS, 16³G, 16⁶HY, 16⁵HY, 20³GF, 16²GF, 17⁵G,

	Starts	1st	2nd	3rd	Win & Pl
NH Flat	3	0	0	0	294
Hurdles	5	0	1	1	1519
Career Total	8	0	1	2	1813

Going: Sf: 0-2 GS: 0-2 Gd: 0-2 GF: - Fm: 0-2
Distance: 2m/2m3: 0-5 2m4-2m7: 0-1 3m+: 0-0
Track: LH: 0-6 RH: 0-2 Tight: 0-2 Gall: 0-0
Aids: Bl: 0-0 Vi: 0-0 Tstrap: 0-1
Best Rating: 84   3/03   Weth   2m   gd-fm   Hdl

Very moderate hurdler; finished fifth in bumper on debut; seemed to show much improved form when third in a modest novices hurdle run on fast ground at Wetherby in March; runner-up in a weak event there six days later.

Naj-De

82   **83+**

5-y-o ch g Zafonic (USA)-River Jig (USA) (Irish River (FR))
S Dow postcodeplumbers.co.uk

Placings:0-5P   (0613)
2002/03: 18⁵GF, 16⁰GF,

	Starts	1st	2nd	3rd	Win & Pl
Hurdles	2	0	0	0	0
Career Total	3	0	0	0	0

Going: Sf: 0-0 GS: 0-0 Gd: 0-0 GF: - Fm: 0-2
Distance: 2m/2m3: 0-2 2m4-2m7: 0-0 3m+: 0-0
Track: LH: 0-2 RH: 0-0 Tight: 0-1 Gall: 0-0
Aids: Bl: 0-0 Vi: 0-0 Tstrap: 0-0
Best Rating: 83   6/02   Font   2m2f110y   gd-fm   Hdl

Nameless Wonder (IRE)

101   **96**

7-y-o b g Supreme Leader-Miss Kylogue (IRE) (Lancastrian)
N J Henderson Major Christopher Hanbury

Placings:600-0043   (3120)
2002/03: 20⁰G, 16⁰GS, 22⁴GS, 20³S,

	Starts	1st	2nd	3rd	Win & Pl
Hurdles	4	0	0	1	386
Career Total	7	0	0	1	386

Going: Sf: 0-1 GS: 0-2 Gd: 0-1 GF: - Fm: 0-0
Distance: 2m/2m3: 0-1 2m4-2m7: 0-3 3m+: 0-0
Track: LH: 0-2 RH: 0-2 Tight: 0-0 Gall: 0-1
Aids: Bl: 0-3 Vi: 0-0 Tstrap: 0-0
Best Rating: 102   3/02   Newb   2m5f   soft   Hdl

Fair novice hurdler; suited by distances of around two and a half miles; has worn blinkers.

Nampara Cove

8-y-o b/br g Roscoe Blake-Lothian Lily (Alias Smith (USA))
R G Russ R G Russ

Placings:P-0   (0503)
2002/03: 26⁰G,

	Starts	1st	2nd	3rd	Win & Pl
Chases	1	0	0	0	

Career Total   2   0   0   0

Going:	Sf: 0-0 GS: 0-0 Gd: 0-1 GF: - Fm: 0-0
Distance:	2m/2m3: 0-0 2m4-2m7: 0-0 3m+: 0-1
Track:	LH: 0-1 RH: 0-0 Tight: 0-1 Gall: 0-0
Aids:	Bl: 0-0 Vi: 0-0 Tstrap: 0-0
Best Rating:	0 6/02 Ctml 3m2f good Ch

Namron (IRE)

10-y-o br g Strong Gale-Rigton Angle (Sit In The Corner (USA))
W R Hacking Mrs A Beney

Placings:600/P6/6P0/P   (0315)
2002/03: 21PG,

	Starts	1st	2nd	3rd	Win & Pl
Chases	1	0	0	0	
Career Total	9	0	0	0	

Going:	Sf: 0-0 GS: 0-0 Gd: 0-1 GF: - Fm: 0-0
Distance:	2m/2m3: 0-0 2m4-2m7: 0-1 3m+: 0-0
Track:	LH: 0-0 RH: 0-1 Tight: 0-1 Gall: 0-0
Aids:	Bl: 0-1 Vi: 0-0 Tstrap: 0-0
Best Rating:	61 8/99 Tram 2m gd-fm Ch

Naomh Padraig (IRE)

(99h)   (107h)**98**
7-y-o b g Be My Native (USA)-Shirley s Dream (IRE) (Mister Majestic)
C C Bealby (Noel Meade 6/5) R S Hunnisett

Placings:1040/03250420-1P   (0730)
2002/03: 201GF, 21PGF,

	Starts	1st	2nd	3rd	Win & Pl
Chases	2	1	0	0	4868
Career Total	14	2	2	1	12127
98	5/02	DRoy	2m4f	Ch	G-F	£4868
100	11/00	DRoy	2m	NHF	Y-S	£4140
				Total win prize-money £9008		

Going:	Sf: 0-0 GS: 0-0 Gd: 0-0 GF: - Fm: 1-2
Distance:	2m/2m3: 0-0 2m4-2m7: 1-2 3m+: 0-0
Track:	LH: 0-1 RH: 0-0 Tight: 0-1 Gall: 0-0
Aids:	Bl: 0-1 Vi: 0-0 Tstrap: 0-0
Best Rating:	107 10/01 Dpat 2m6f yld-sft Hdl

Moderate irish chaser; stays two miles four furlongs; acts on any ground.

Napoleon Bonaparte (IRE)

81   **52**
6-y-o b g Insan (USA)-Chiminee Fly (Proverb)
W J Musson H Spooner,I Weaver,E Benson,T Fearey

Placings:00-0F6   (4641)
2002/03: 160S, 22FGF, 196GF,

	Starts	1st	2nd	3rd	Win & Pl
Hurdles	3	0	0	0	0
Career Total	5	0	0	0	0

Going:	Sf: 0-1 GS: 0-0 Gd: 0-0 GF: - Fm: 0-2
Distance:	2m/2m3: 0-2 2m4-2m7: 0-1 3m+: 0-0
Track:	LH: 0-2 RH: 0-1 Tight: 0-2 Gall: 0-1
Aids:	Bl: 0-0 Vi: 0-0 Tstrap: 0-0

Best Rating: 100   2/02   Kemp   2m   good   NHF

Narrow Water (IRE)

99   **115**
10-y-o b g Mazaad-Miss Doogles (Beau Charmeur (FR))
Jonjo O Neill Getjar Limited

Placings:21211/PPPF6P-36   (2361)
2002/03: 203G, 246S,

	Starts	1st	2nd	3rd	Win & Pl
Chases	2	0	0	1	702
Career Total	13	3	2	1	46272
142	2/01	Newc	4m1f	B(0-150)HCh	HVY	£34800
139	2/01	Carl	3m2f	D Ch	HVY	£4114
141	11/00	Weth	3m1f	D Ch	SFT	£4123
				Total win prize-money £43038		

Going:	Sf: 0-1 GS: 0-0 Gd: 0-1 GF: - Fm: 0-0
Distance:	2m/2m3: 0-0 2m4-2m7: 0-1 3m+: 0-1
Track:	LH: 0-2 RH: 0-0 Tight: 0-0 Gall: 0-0
Aids:	Bl: 0-0 Vi: 0-0 Tstrap: 0-0
Best Rating:	142 2/01 Newc 4m1f heavy Ch

Fair chaser; disappointing after a fine season in 2000/1; stays four miles plus; effective on soft/heavy ground.

Narwhal (IRE)

103   **103**
5-y-o b/br g Naheez (USA)-Well Why (IRE) (The Parson)
J T Gifford Mrs S N J Embiricos

Placings:2-3   (2212)
2002/03: 163S,

	Starts	1st	2nd	3rd	Win & Pl
Hurdles	1	0	0	1	660
Career Total	2	0	1	1	1396

Going:	Sf: 0-1 GS: 0-0 Gd: 0-0 GF: - Fm: 0-0
Distance:	2m/2m3: 0-1 2m4-2m7: 0-0 3m+: 0-0
Track:	LH: 0-1 RH: 0-0 Tight: 0-0 Gall: 0-1
Aids:	Bl: 0-0 Vi: 0-0 Tstrap: 0-0
Best Rating:	103 11/02 Newb 2m110y soft Hdl

Fair efforts in a bumper and over hurdles.

Nas Na Riogh (IRE)

116   **131**
4-y-o b f King s Theatre (IRE)-Abstraite (Groom Dancer (USA))
N J Henderson Brian Twojohns Partnership

Placings:212211F   (4130)
2002/03: 162G, 161S, 162S, 172G, 161HY, 181S, 17FG,

	Starts	1st	2nd	3rd	Win & Pl
Hurdles	7	3	3	0	32440
Career Total	7	3	3	0	32440
112	3/03	Font	2m2f110yE Hdl		SFT	£3367
131	12/02	Chep	2m110y A Hdl		HVY	£21420
115	11/02	Sand	2m110y D Hdl		SFT	£4251
			Total win prize-money £29038			

Going:	Sf: 3-4 GS: 0-0 Gd: 0-3 GF: - Fm: 0-0
Distance:	2m/2m3: 3-7 2m4-2m7: 0-0 3m+: 0-0
Track:	LH: 2-4 RH: 1-2 Tight: 1-1 Gall: 0-3
Aids:	Bl: 0-0 Vi: 0-0 Tstrap: 0-0
Best Rating:	131 12/02 Chep 2m110y heavy Hdl

Very useful juvenile hurdler; won the Finale Hurdle at Chepstow in December 2002; suited by forcing tactics; effective in testing ground.

Nashville Star (USA)

12-y-o ch g Star De Naskra (USA)-Mary Davies (Tyrnavos)
R Mathew Robin Mathew

Placings:211340P10/6P5/4054010660/34331424363/5023
045/P00/0P6/650-PP   (0193)
2002/03: 21PGF, 20PF,

	Starts	1st	2nd	3rd	Win & Pl
Chases	2	0	0	0	
Career Total	51	5	3	7	28585
95	12/97	Wind	2m	D(0-125)HCh	GD	£4232
102	2/97	Bang	2m1f	E(0-110)HHdl	GD	£3517
104	3/95	Newb	2m110y	B HHdl	GD	£5994
91	10/94	Newc	2m110y	Hdl	FRM	£2232
90	10/94	Carl	2m1f	Hdl	GD	£1927
				Total win prize-money £17905		

Going:	Sf: 0-0 GS: 0-0 Gd: 0-0 GF: - Fm: 0-2
Distance:	2m/2m3: 0-0 2m4-2m7: 0-2 3m+: 0-0
Track:	LH: 0-2 RH: 0-0 Tight: 0-0 Gall: 0-1
Aids:	Bl: 0-0 Vi: 0-2 Tstrap: 0-0
Best Rating:	122 3/98 Chel 2m110y good Ch

Nasone (IRE)

12-y-o b g Nearly A Nose (USA)-Skateaway (Condorcet (FR))
Miss M P Bryant Miss M Bryant

Placings:10/42500/2/0/03252352/035/2P-PUP   (2003)
2002/03: 26PGF, 26UG, 25PG,

	Starts	1st	2nd	3rd	Win & Pl
Chases	3	0	0	0	
Career Total	25	1	6	3	11968
103	3/96	Newb	2m110y	H NHF	G-S	£1521
				Total win prize-money £1522		

Going:	Sf: 0-0 GS: 0-0 Gd: 0-2 GF: - Fm: 0-1
Distance:	2m/2m3: 0-0 2m4-2m7: 0-0 3m+: 0-3
Track:	LH: 0-1 RH: 0-1 Tight: 0-3 Gall: 0-0
Aids:	Bl: 0-0 Vi: 0-0 Tstrap: 0-0
Best Rating:	121 11/97 Winc 2m5f good Ch

Nat Gold

98   **95**
7-y-o b g Push On-April Airs (Grey Mirage)
Mrs D A Hamer E L Harries

Placings:4P   (3334)
2002/03: 244HY, 24PS,

	Starts	1st	2nd	3rd	Win & Pl
Hurdles	2	0	0	0	0
Career Total	2	0	0	0	0

Going:	Sf: 0-2 GS: 0-0 Gd: 0-0 GF: - Fm: 0-0
Distance:	2m/2m3: 0-0 2m4-2m7: 0-0 3m+: 0-2
Track:	LH: 0-1 RH: 0-1 Tight: 0-1 Gall: 0-0
Aids:	Bl: 0-0 Vi: 0-0 Tstrap: 0-0
Best Rating:	89 1/03 Chep 3m heavy Hdl

Runner-up in two points; wide margin winner of a poor novices hurdle at Uttoxeter in June but looked to finish lame; stays well.

Nativa Negra (IRE)

6-y-o br m Be My Native (USA)-Jayells Dream (Space King)

A King All The King s Men

Placings:*20*-RP   (1220)
2002/03: 19RGF, 21PG,

	Starts	1st	2nd	3rd	Win & Pl
Hurdles	2	0	0	0	
Career Total	4	0	1	0	456

Going:	Sf: 0-0 GS: 0-0 Gd: 0-1 GF: - Fm: 0-1
Distance:	2m/2m3: 0-0 2m4-2m7: 0-2 3m+: 0-0
Track:	LH: 0-1 RH: 0-1 Tight: 0-0 Gall: 0-0
Aids:	Bl: 0-0 Vi: 0-0 Tstrap: 0-0
Best Rating:	82 12/01 Hrfd 2m1f soft NHF

Native Affair (IRE)
107
9-y-o ch g Be My Native (USA)-Queens Romance (Imperial Fling (USA))
L Lungo Strathayr Publishing Ltd

Placings:*03110*/UP00/503/23220-F   (0249)
2002/03: 20FGF,

	Starts	1st	2nd	3rd	Win & Pl
Hurdles	1	0	0	0	
Career Total	18	2	3	3	6118
116 12/98 Muss	2m	H NHF		GD	£1521
111 12/98 Catt	2m	H NHF		GD	£1276
			Total win prize-money £2799

Going:	Sf: 0-0 GS: 0-0 Gd: 0-0 GF: - Fm: 0-1
Distance:	2m/2m3: 0-0 2m4-2m7: 0-1 3m+: 0-0
Track:	LH: 0-0 RH: 0-1 Tight: 0-0 Gall: 0-0
Aids:	Bl: 0-0 Vi: 0-0 Tstrap: 0-0
Best Rating:	118 4/99 Aint 2m110y good NHF

Fair form in novice hurdles befoore breaking a leg at Perth in May 2002. (DEAD)

Native Alibi (IRE)
95   82
6-y-o b g Be My Native (USA)-Perfect Excuse (Certingo)
S H Shirley-Beavan Mrs S H Shirley-Beavan

Placings:*5U5*   (3565)
2002/03: 24SGS, 20UHY, 27SHY,

	Starts	1st	2nd	3rd	Win & Pl
Chases	3	0	0	0	
Career Total	3	0	0	0	0

Going:	Sf: 0-2 GS: 0-1 Gd: 0-0 GF: - Fm: 0-0
Distance:	2m/2m3: 0-0 2m4-2m7: 0-1 3m+: 0-2
Track:	LH: 0-2 RH: 0-1 Tight: 0-2 Gall: 0-0
Aids:	Bl: 0-0 Vi: 0-0 Tstrap: 0-0
Best Rating:	82 2/03 Sedg 3m3f heavy Ch

Native Approach (IRE)
99   97
6-y-o b m Be My Native (USA)-Castle Stream (Paddy s Stream)
N J Henderson J Hanson

Placings:*3136320*   (4326)
2002/03: 17RG, 16IG, 19RGS, 21RS, 19RG, 20RG, 21RG,

	Starts	1st	2nd	3rd	Win & Pl
NH Flat	2	1	0	1	2126
Hurdles	5	0	1	2	3442
Career Total	7	1	1	3	5567

92 7/02 Worc 2m   H NHF   GD   £1801
                 Total win prize-money £1802

Going:	Sf: 0-1 GS: 0-1 Gd: 1-5 GF: - Fm: 0-0
Distance:	2m/2m3: 1-2 2m4-2m7: 0-5 3m+: 0-0
Track:	LH: 1-4 RH: 0-3 Tight: 0-2 Gall: 0-1
Aids:	Bl: 0-0 Vi: 0-0 Tstrap: 0-0
Best Rating:	97 2/03 Hrfd 2m3f110y good Hdl

Modest novice hurdler; stays two and a half miles.

Native Beat (IRE)
109(98h)   (113h)113
8-y-o b g Be My Native (USA)-Deeprunonthepound (IRE) (Deep Run)
J R H Fowler Miss Daisy Duggan

Placings:*06/00231640/640044610-05546603* (4657a)
2002/03: 20RS, 20RSH, 20RS, 19RS, 20RYS, 24RFY, 21RG, 25RGF,

	Starts	1st	2nd	3rd	Win & Pl
Chases	8	0	0	1	1753
Career Total	27	2	1	2	19959
113 3/02 Fair	2m4f	Ch		G-Y	£9312
109 2/01 Gowr	2m	Hdl		HVY	£5564
			Total win prize-money £14878

Going:	Sf: 0-3 GS: 0-0 Gd: 0-1 GF: - Fm: 0-1
Distance:	2m/2m3: 0-1 2m4-2m7: 0-5 3m+: 0-2
Track:	LH: 0-3 RH: 0-5 Tight: 0-1 Gall: 0-0
Aids:	Bl: 0-0 Vi: 0-0 Tstrap: 0-0
Best Rating:	117 12/02 Punc 2m4f sft-hvy Ch

Fair Irish chaser; best at two and a half miles; likes soft ground.

Native Buck (IRE)
95   123
10-y-o ch g Be My Native (USA)-Buckskins Chat (Buckskin (FR))
T R George The One Over Par Partnership

Placings:*00/063212/22P/1411P-2P16*   (4172)
2002/03: 28RS, 29RHY, 30IG, 34RS,

	Starts	1st	2nd	3rd	Win & Pl
Chases	4	1	1	0	16388
Career Total	20	5	5	1	41817
123 2/03 Catt	3m6f	C(0-130)HCh	GD	£10276
123 2/02 Uttx	3m2f	B HCh	HVY	£10976
116 12/01 Hayd	3m	D(0-110)HCh	HVY	£4114
109 11/01 Uttx	2m5f	F(0-110)HCh	SFT	£3532
91 12/98 Uttx	3m110y	E(0-100)HHdl	SFT	£2431
			Total win prize-money £31333

Going:	Sf: 0-3 GS: 0-0 Gd: 1-1 GF: - Fm: 0-0
Distance:	2m/2m3: 0-0 2m4-2m7: 0-0 3m+: 1-4
Track:	LH: 1-4 RH: 0-0 Tight: 1-1 Gall: 0-0
Aids:	Bl: 0-0 Vi: 0-0 Tstrap: 0-0
Best Rating:	123 2/03 Catt 3m6f good Ch

Fair staying chaser, gets three and a quarter miles and is especially suited by testing conditions.

Native Commander (IRE)
107(65h)   (114h)114
8-y-o b g Be My Native (USA)-The Better Half (IRE) (Deep Run)
S J Mahon (Patrick Morris 1/3) C P Byrne

Placings:*0/004000/0102640-30344210531* (4744a)
2002/03: 16RS, 16RG, 16RS, 17RSH, 18RYS, 16RHY, 16IYS, 19RS, 16RHY, 17RHY, 17RG,

---

	Starts	1st	2nd	3rd	Win & Pl
Chases	11	2	1	3	19218
Career Total	25	3	2	3	28648
114 4/03 Fair	2m1f	(0-116)HCh	GD	£8441
102 1/03 Punc	2m	(0-95)HCh	Y-S	£5600
105 11/01 Naas	2m	Ch	YLD	£6955
			Total win prize-money £20999

Going:	Sf: 0-6 GS: 0-0 Gd: 1-2 GF: - Fm: 0-0
Distance:	2m/2m3: 2-11 2m4-2m7: 0-0 3m+: 0-0
Track:	LH: 0-3 RH: 2-5 Tight: 0-1 Gall: 0-0
Aids:	Bl: 0-0 Vi: 0-0 Tstrap: 0-0
Best Rating:	114 4/03 Fair 2m1f good Ch

Native Cove (IRE)
11-y-o b g Be My Native (USA)-Down All The Coves (Athenius)
E Haddock Miss H M Newell

Placings:*P/2/F0PP/P3025-P2*   (4031)
2002/03: 24PGF, 24RS,

	Starts	1st	2nd	3rd	Win & Pl
Chases	2	0	1	0	1254
Career Total	13	0	3	1	2952

Going:	Sf: 0-1 GS: 0-0 Gd: 0-0 GF: - Fm: 0-1
Distance:	2m/2m3: 0-0 2m4-2m7: 0-0 3m+: 0-2
Track:	LH: 0-0 RH: 0-2 Tight: 0-1 Gall: 0-0
Aids:	Bl: 0-0 Vi: 0-0 Tstrap: 0-0
Best Rating:	101 4/00 Ludl 3m good Ch

Modest hunter chaser, stays well.

Native Cunning
84f   87f
5-y-o b g Be My Native (USA)-Icy Miss (Random Shot)
R H Buckler Anthony Jones and Nick Elliott

Placings:*000*   (4329)
2002/03: 13RS, 16RG, 16RG,

	Starts	1st	2nd	3rd	Win & Pl
NH Flat	3	0	0	0	
Career Total	3	0	0	0	

Going:	Sf: 0-1 GS: 0-0 Gd: 0-2 GF: - Fm: 0-0
Distance:	2m/2m3: 0-2 2m4-2m7: 0-0 3m+: 0-0
Track:	LH: 0-1 RH: 0-2 Tight: 0-0 Gall: 0-1
Aids:	Bl: 0-0 Vi: 0-0 Tstrap: 0-0
Best Rating:	87 2/03 Kemp 2m good NHF

Native Daisy (IRE)
89   75
8-y-o b m Be My Native (USA)-Castleblagh (General Ironside)
K J Burke (Mrs H Dalton 25/11) E O Brien

Placings:*00/0*U   (3521)
2002/03: 22UGS,

	Starts	1st	2nd	3rd	Win & Pl
Chases	1	0	0	0	
Career Total	4	0	0	0	

Going:	Sf: 0-0 GS: 0-1 Gd: 0-0 GF: - Fm: 0-0
Distance:	2m/2m3: 0-0 2m4-2m7: 0-1 3m+: 0-0
Track:	LH: 0-1 RH: 0-0 Tight: 0-0 Gall: 0-0
Aids:	Bl: 0-0 Vi: 0-0 Tstrap: 0-0
Best Rating:	98 4/00 Asct 2m110y soft NHF

Native Design (IRE)

93   **110**

6-y-o br m Be My Native (USA)-Artist s Design (Precipice Wood)
Michael J O Connor Mrs Fiona O Connor

Placings:3-15542.00   **(4462)**
2002/03: 16¹S, 16⁵S, 20⁵S, 16⁴S, 16²S, 16⁶GY, 20⁰G,

	Starts	1st	2nd	3rd	Win & Pl
NH Flat	2	1	0	0	4233
Hurdles	5	0	1	0	1899
Career Total	8	1	1	1	6583
107 5/02 Navn 2m		NHF		SFT	£4233

Total win prize-money £4233

Going:	Sf: 1-5 GS: 0-0 Gd: 0-1 GF: - Fm: 0-0
Distance:	2m/2m3: 1-5 2m4-2m7: 0-2 3m+: 0-0
Track:	LH: 1-3 RH: 0-1 Tight: 0-1 Gall: 0-0
Aids:	Bl: 0-0 Vi: 0-0 Tstrap: 0-4
Best Rating:	110 1/03 Navn 2m soft Hdl

Native Drum (IRE)

(85h)   (58h)

8-y-o b g Be My Native (USA)-Lantern Lass (Monksfield)
M W Easterby I Bray

Placings:006/0-5PP   **(3746)**
2002/03: 20⁵HY, 27⁶HY, 24⁵G,

	Starts	1st	2nd	3rd	Win & Pl
Hurdles	2	0	0	0	0
Chases	1	0	0	0	0
Career Total	7	0	0	0	0

Going:	Sf: 0-2 GS: 0-0 Gd: 0-1 GF: - Fm: 0-0
Distance:	2m/2m3: 0-2 2m4-2m7: 0-1 3m+: 0-2
Track:	LH: 0-2 RH: 0-1 Tight: 0-1 Gall: 0-1
Aids:	Bl: 0-2 Vi: 0-0 Tstrap: 0-0
Best Rating:	82 10/00 Gway 2m heavy NHF

Native Eire (IRE)

97(95h)   **73**

9-y-o b g Be My Native (USA)-Ballyline Dancer (Giolla Mear)
N Wilson Mrs N C Wilson

Placings:0/065B/0F5051-0B3   **(4785)**
2002/03: 20⁰GS, 20⁸G, 20³G,

	Starts	1st	2nd	3rd	Win & Pl
Chases	3	0	0	1	830
Career Total	14	1	0	1	3399
98 3/02 Sedg 2m5f110yE Hdl				SFT	£2569

Total win prize-money £2569

Going:	Sf: 0-0 GS: 0-1 Gd: 0-2 GF: - Fm: 0-0
Distance:	2m/2m3: 0-0 2m4-2m7: 0-3 3m+: 0-0
Track:	LH: 0-1 RH: 0-2 Tight: 0-1 Gall: 0-0
Aids:	Bl: 0-0 Vi: 0-0 Tstrap: 0-0
Best Rating:	98 3/02 Sedg 2m5f110y soft Hdl

Moderate chaser; off the mark at the third time of asking over hurdles in a Sedgefield amateur event in March 2002; handles soft.

Native Emperor

112   **158**

7-y-o br g Be My Native (USA)-Fiona s Blue (Crash Course)
Jonjo O Neill R & E H Investments Ltd

Placings:55/13145P/012114-123P   **(4131)**
2002/03: 25¹GS, 24²S, 25³S, 24⁴G,

	Starts	1st	2nd	3rd	Win & Pl
Hurdles	4	1	1	1	44375
Career Total	18	6	2	2	77685
143 11/02 Chel	3m1f110yA HHdl		G-S	£31175
139 2/02 Uttx	2m6f110yC(0-135)HHdl		HVY	£10504
132 1/02 Wwck	3m1f	D(0-125)HHdl	HVY	£3688
114 12/01 NAbb	2m6f	D(0-125)HHdl	HVY	£5382
123 11/00 Asct	2m4f	C Hdl	SFT	£4862
100 10/00 Strf	2m6f110yD Hdl		SFT	£3289

Total win prize-money £58901

Going:	Sf: 0-2 GS: 1-1 Gd: 0-1 GF: - Fm: 0-0
Distance:	2m/2m3: 0-0 2m4-2m7: 0-0 3m+: 1-4
Track:	LH: 1-3 RH: 0-1 Tight: 0-0 Gall: 1-3
Aids:	Bl: 0-0 Vi: 0-0 Tstrap: 0-0
Best Rating:	157 11/02 Newb 3m110y soft Hdl

Smart, progressive hurdler; creditable form in defeat in top-class staying company at Newbury and Ascot; needs distances in excess of 2m 6f and prefers testing conditions.

Native Field (IRE)

95   **91**

14-y-o b g Be My Native (USA)-Broomfield Ceili (Northfields (USA))
D J Wintle John W Egan

Placings:111/0013/2022300/6116/1105/132056/33011000/030245-2P   **(0379)**
2002/03: 27²GF, 21²PG,

	Starts	1st	2nd	3rd	Win & Pl
Hurdles	2	0	1	0	554
Career Total	44	11	6	6	38969
104 1/01 Leic	2m4f110yF Hdl		HVY	£2723
113 1/01 Folk	2m6f110yG(0-90)HHdl		HVY	£1568
113 11/99 Hayd	2m4f	F Hdl	G-S	£1987
125 12/98 Hayd	2m7f110yC(0-130)HHdl		SFT	£3896
116 11/98 NAbb	2m6f	D(0-125)HHdl	SFT	£2739
122 12/97 Towc	2m5f	F Hdl	SFT	£2104
111 11/97 Hayd	2m4f	F Hdl	SFT	£2120
94 3/94 Strf	2m110y	Hdl	G-S	£2070
4/93 Aint	2m110y	NHF	G-F	£7400
3/93 Donc	2m110y	NHF	FRM	£1772
2/93 Donc	2m110y	NHF	FRM	£1574

Total win prize-money £29954

Going:	Sf: 0-0 GS: 0-0 Gd: 0-1 GF: - Fm: 0-1
Distance:	2m/2m3: 0-0 2m4-2m7: 0-1 3m+: 0-1
Track:	LH: 0-0 RH: 0-1 Tight: 0-1 Gall: 0-1
Aids:	Bl: 0-0 Vi: 0-0 Tstrap: 0-0
Best Rating:	125 12/98 Hayd 2m7f110y soft Hdl

Veteran hurdler, suited by two and a half miles.

Native Fling (IRE)

111   **122**

11-y-o b g Be My Native (USA)-Queens Romance (Imperial Fling (USA))
P J Hobbs Christine And Aubrey Loze

Placings:30/100635/5/131122221/11/4050/1P2543-P3061344   **(4694)**
2002/03: 20⁰G, 17³GS, 20⁰GS, 16⁶GS, 16¹HY, 19³G, 20⁴G, 21⁴G,

	Starts	1st	2nd	3rd	Win & Pl
Chases	8	1	0	2	11262
Career Total	38	9	5	6	52663
122 1/03 Chep	2m110y C(0-135)HCh		HVY	£8320
128 11/01 Strf	2m1f110yD(0-125)HCh		SFT	£6077
121 10/99 Strf	2m1f110yC(0-135)HCh		G-S	£6419
120 10/99 Extr	2m1f	D(0-125)HHdl	GD	£3436
120 4/99 Punc	2m2f	Ch	YLD	£6138
114 1/99 Extr	2m1f110yF(0-100)HCh		HVY	£2377
128 12/98 Hrfd	2m	E(0-100)HCh	G-S	£2801
109 11/98 NAbb	2m1f	E Hdl	SFT	£2200

---

100 10/96 Dpat	2m1f172y NHF G-Y £1412

Total win prize-money £39182

Going:	Sf: 1-1 GS: 0-3 Gd: 0-4 GF: - Fm: 0-0
Distance:	2m/2m3: 1-3 2m4-2m7: 0-5 3m+: 0-0
Track:	LH: 1-5 RH: 0-3 Tight: 0-3 Gall: 0-1
Aids:	Bl: 0-0 Vi: 1-4 Tstrap: 0-0
Best Rating:	128 1/02 Uttx 2m heavy Ch

Fair handicap chaser; effective up to two and a quarter miles, he likes to get his toe in; has worn blinkers and visor.

Native Fox

105   **101**

8-y-o br m Be My Native (USA)-Leinthall Fox (Deep Run)
J L Needham Miss Joanna Needham

Placings:01242/2P4-321   **(0554)**
2002/03: 20³GF, 19²G, 19¹GF,

	Starts	1st	2nd	3rd	Win & Pl
Hurdles	3	1	1	1	4031
Career Total	11	2	4	1	7605
96 6/02 Hrfd	2m3f110yE Hdl		G-F	£2670
113 6/00 Uttx	2m	H HNHF	GD	£1575

Total win prize-money £4246

Going:	Sf: 0-0 GS: 0-0 Gd: 0-1 GF: - Fm: 1-2
Distance:	2m/2m3: 0-0 2m4-2m7: 1-3 3m+: 0-0
Track:	LH: 0-0 RH: 1-2 Tight: 0-1 Gall: 0-0
Aids:	Bl: 0-0 Vi: 0-0 Tstrap: 0-0
Best Rating:	113 6/00 Uttx 2m good NHF

Modest hurdler; stays two and three-quarter miles; best on fast ground.

Native Glen (IRE)

9-y-o b g Be My Native (USA)-The Gargle Monster (Furry Glen)
S Lloyd J Huckle

Placings:000550/0140P/000P/00PP-U   **(3951)**
2002/03: 16ᵁGS,

	Starts	1st	2nd	3rd	Win & Pl
Chases	1	0	0	0	
Career Total	20	1	0	0	3295
90 9/99 Gowr 2m		Hdl		Y-S	£3080

Total win prize-money £3080

Going:	Sf: 0-0 GS: 0-1 Gd: 0-0 GF: - Fm: 0-0
Distance:	2m/2m3: 0-1 2m4-2m7: 0-0 3m+: 0-0
Track:	LH: 0-0 RH: 0-1 Tight: 0-0 Gall: 0-0
Aids:	Bl: 0-0 Vi: 0-0 Tstrap: 0-1
Best Rating:	90 9/99 Gowr 2m yld-sft Hdl

Native Heather (IRE)

10-y-o b m Be My Native (USA)-Pisa (IRE) (Carlingford Castle)
N Wilson Mrs N C Wilson

Placings:0/00/665/0/00-PP   **(4590)**
2002/03: 16⁰HY, 20⁰PG,

	Starts	1st	2nd	3rd	Win & Pl
Hurdles	2	0	0	0	
Career Total	11	0	0	0	

Going:	Sf: 0-1 GS: 0-0 Gd: 0-1 GF: - Fm: 0-0
Distance:	2m/2m3: 0-1 2m4-2m7: 0-1 3m+: 0-0

Track: LH: 0-2 RH: 0-0 Tight: 0-0 Gall: 0-1
Aids: Bl: 0-0 Vi: 0-0 Tstrap: 0-1
Best Rating: 79   2/00   Thur   2m   sft-hvy NHF

Native Lady

7-y-o b m Distinct Native-Ladyville (Lord Nelson (FR))
F P Murtagh   Sam Hamilton

Placings:PP   (4589)
2002/03: 21PG, 25PG,

	Starts	1st	2nd	3rd	Win & Pl
Hurdles	1	0	0	0	0
Chases	1	0	0	0	0
Career Total	2	0	0	0	

Going: Sf: 0-0 GS: 0-0 Gd: 0-2 GF: - Fm: 0-0
Distance: 2m/2m3: 0-0 2m4-2m7: 0-1 3m+: 0-1
Track: LH: 0-2 RH: 0-0 Tight: 0-1 Gall: 0-0
Aids: Bl: 0-0 Vi: 0-0 Tstrap: 0-0
Best Rating: 0   3/03   Sedg   2m5f110y   good   Hdl

Native Legend (IRE)
104   108+

8-y-o b g Be My Native (USA)-Tickhill (General Assembly (USA))
Ferdy Murphy   J D Gordon

Placings:0/35041/4/F21   (2927)
2002/03: 24FG, 20GS, 24HY,

	Starts	1st	2nd	3rd	Win & Pl
Hurdles	3	1	1	0	3872
Career Total	10	2	1	1	7942
108 1/03	Ayr	3m110y	F(0-100)HHdl	HVY	£2996
93 2/00	Muss	2m4f	D Hdl	GD	£2925
			Total win prize-money £5921		

Going: Sf: 1-1 GS: 0-1 Gd: 0-1 GF: - Fm: 0-0
Distance: 2m/2m3: 0-0 2m4-2m7: 0-1 3m+: 1-2
Track: LH: 1-2 RH: 0-1 Tight: 0-0 Gall: 0-0
Aids: Bl: 0-0 Vi: 0-0 Tstrap: 0-0
Best Rating: 108   1/03   Ayr   3m110y   heavy   Hdl

Lodest, lightly-raced hurdler, off the track for a long time after October 2000. Good second at Ayr in December 2002 and scored at the same track in January 2003. Stays three miles plus, acts on a soft surface.

Native Man (IRE)

9-y-o b g Be My Native (USA)-Try Your Case (Proverb)
Jonjo O Neill   Anne Duchess Of Westminster

Placings:5143/1213050/220124/4PPU41211P-00PP (4263)
2002/03: 24GS, 23QS, 24FG, 24PGF,

	Starts	1st	2nd	3rd	Win & Pl
Chases	4	0	0	0	
Career Total	31	7	5	2	39129
126 2/02	Ludl	3m	D(0-125)HCh	G-S	£10192
117 2/02	Ludl	3m	E(0-105)HCh	G-S	£4953
106 1/02	Hntg	2m4f110yF(0-100)HCh		G-S	£2758
116 8/00	Bang	2m4f110yD HCh		GD	£3786
111 7/99	Tipp	2m4f	Hdl	G-Y	£3683
97 5/99	Tipp	2m	Hdl	G-F	£3069
104 12/98	Thur	2m	NHF	HVY	£2391
			Total win prize-money £30832		

Going: Sf: 0-1 GS: 0-1 Gd: 0-1 GF: - Fm: 0-0
Distance: 2m/2m3: 0-0 2m4-2m7: 0-0 3m+: 0-4
Track: LH: 0-1 RH: 0-3 Tight: 0-2 Gall: 0-0

Aids: Bl: 0-0 Vi: 0-0 Tstrap: 0-3
Best Rating: 126 2/02   Ludl   3m   gd-sft   Ch

Fair chaser; stays three miles; usually wears a tongue strap; suited by good ground.

Native New Yorker (IRE)
114   134+

8-y-o b g Be My Native (USA)-Sunbath (Krayyan)
R Rowe   Ann & John Symes

Placings:f200/1-F1F01P   (4136)
2002/03: 18FGF, 19¹G, 20FS, 16QS, 17¹GS, 17PG,

	Starts	1st	2nd	3rd	Win & Pl
Hurdles	6	2	0	0	20128
Career Total	11	4	1	0	23511
134 1/03	Chel	2m1f	B(0-145)HHdl	G-S	£13108
128 10/02	Strf	2m3f	C(0-135)HHdl	GD	£7020
112 10/01	Font	2m2f110yE Hdl		SFT	£2460
			Total win prize-money £22589		

Going: Sf: 0-2 GS: 1-1 Gd: 1-2 GF: - Fm: 0-1
Distance: 2m/2m3: 2-5 2m4-2m7: 0-1 3m+: 0-0
Track: LH: 2-6 RH: 0-0 Tight: 1-2 Gall: 1-3
Aids: Bl: 0-0 Vi: 0-0 Tstrap: 0-0
Best Rating: 134 1/03   Chel   2m1f   gd-sft   Hdl

Very useful handicap hurdler; stays two miles three and acts on most types of ground.

Native Peach (IRE)
84(115h)   (117h)43

8-y-o ch g Be My Native (USA)-Larry s Peach (Laurence O)
J A B Old   W E Sturt

Placings:0/1366-5   (4370)
2002/03: 24SG,

	Starts	1st	2nd	3rd	Win & Pl
Chases	1	0	0	0	
Career Total	6	1	0	1	3920
96 5/01	Wwck	3m1f	E Hdl	GD	£2824
			Total win prize-money £2825		

Going: Sf: 0-0 GS: 0-0 Gd: 0-1 GF: - Fm: 0-0
Distance: 2m/2m3: 0-0 2m4-2m7: 0-0 3m+: 0-1
Track: LH: 0-0 RH: 0-1 Tight: 0-0 Gall: 0-0
Aids: Bl: 0-0 Vi: 0-0 Tstrap: 0-0
Best Rating: 117 10/01   Chel   3m1f110y   good   Hdl

Out of a mare who won over three miles over hurdles and two and a half miles over fences. Winner over hurdles. Suited by a sound surface.

Native Performance (IRE)
106   (105h)115

8-y-o b g Be My Native (USA)-Noon Performance (Strong Gale)
Michael Hourigan   Donal O Connor

Placings:305/000030P65/6P142F2452P1-56063236 (1938)
2002/03: 20⁵S, 21⁶S, 20⁶S, 22⁶GY, 22³GF, 22²GF, 24³F, 24⁶G,

	Starts	1st	2nd	3rd	Win & Pl
Chases	8	0	1	2	10481
Career Total	32	2	4	4	35579
110 4/02	Cork	2m4f	(0-116)HCh	Y-S	£9969
97 6/01	Dpat	2m6f	Ch	FRM	£4451
			Total win prize-money £14421		

Going: Sf: 0-3 GS: 0-0 Gd: 0-1 GF: - Fm: 0-3
Distance: 2m/2m3: 0-0 2m4-2m7: 0-6 3m+: 0-2

Track: LH: 0-2 RH: 0-4 Tight: 0-0 Gall: 0-1
Aids: Bl: 0-0 Vi: 0-0 Tstrap: 0-0
Best Rating: 114   9/02   List   3m   firm   Ch

Modest handicap chaser. Successful between two and a half miles and two miles six, but stays three miles.

Native Scout (IRE)
112(120h)   (146h)143

7-y-o b g Be My Native (USA)-Carmels Castle (Deep Run)
Donal Hassett   Mark F Sheasby

Placings:32002/ f301121264-1FP120   (4134)
2002/03: 16¹YS, 16FSH, 20PSH, 16¹S, 17²S, 16⁶G,

	Starts	1st	2nd	3rd	Win & Pl
Chases	6	2	1	0	19529
Career Total	21	6	5	2	66480
141 12/02	Uttx	2m	D Ch	SFT	£5408
132 10/02	Wxfd	2m	Ch	Y-S	£4868
130 12/01	Limk	2m	Hdl	SFT	£8346
120 11/01	Clon	2m	Hdl	YLD	£5120
120 10/01	Gway	2m	Hdl	SH	£5286
113 5/01	Klny	2m1f	NHF	GD	£4173
			Total win prize-money £34203		

Going: Sf: 1-2 GS: 0-0 Gd: 0-1 GF: - Fm: 0-0
Distance: 2m/2m3: 2-5 2m4-2m7: 0-1 3m+: 0-0
Track: LH: 1-3 RH: 0-1 Tight: 0-0 Gall: 0-0
Aids: Bl: 0-0 Vi: 0-0 Tstrap: 1-5
Best Rating: 146 3/02   Chel   2m110y   gd-sft   Hdl

Useful novice chaser; acts on soft ground; effective at around two miles; wears a tongue tie.

Native Sparkle (IRE)
111   123

6-y-o br m Be My Native (USA)-Star With A Glimer (Montekin)
T Hogan   Liam O Regan

Placings:0404f0150-FU2f21150F1306605P   (4656a)
2002/03: 24FGY, 21FS, 19¹S, 20¹GY, 20¹GY, 21PS, 18⁵GY, 24FYS, 20FYS, 16¹YS, 20³S, 16⁶SH, 18⁶S, 20⁶Y, 21⁰G, 22⁵GY, 20PGF,

	Starts	1st	2nd	3rd	Win & Pl
NH Flat	1	0	0	0	4025
Hurdles	17	3	2	1	34055
Career Total	26	5	2	1	41248
123 11/02	Navn	2m	Hdl	Y-S	£13957
108 8/02	Gway	2m4f	Hdl	Y-S	£7831
107 7/02	Klny	2m4f	Hdl	G-Y	£4233
100 6/02	Kbgn	2m3f	NHF	SFT	£4024
95 3/02	Dpat	2m1f172y	NHF	SFT	£2751
			Total win prize-money £32798		

Going: Sf: 1-5 GS: 0-0 Gd: 0-1 GF: - Fm: 0-0
Distance: 2m/2m3: 2-5 2m4-2m7: 2-11 3m+: 0-2
Track: LH: 1-5 RH: 1-7 Tight: 0-0 Gall: 0-1
Aids: Bl: 0-0 Vi: 0-0 Tstrap: 0-2
Best Rating: 123 2/03   Naas   2m4f   yield   Hdl

Fair Irish-trained hurdler; best at two and a half miles in soft ground, but effective at shorter; has worn a tongue tie.

Native Speaker (IRE)
100   124

10-y-o ch g Be My Native (USA)-My Wonder (Deep Run)
P R Webber   J Dougall

Placings:13/35/13P53/1PP-3   (1847)

2002/03: 20³GS,

	Starts	1st	2nd	3rd	Win & Pl
Chases	1	0	0	1	1302
Career Total	13	3	0	5	16218
124 2/02 Winc	2m5f	D(0-120)HCh		G-S	£7215
126 11/99 MRas	2m4f	D Ch		G-S	£4221
109 3/98 Newb	2m110y	H NHF		G-S	£1411

Total win prize-money £12847

Going: Sf: 0-0 GS: 0-1 Gd: 0-0 GF: - Fm: 0-0
Distance: 2m/2m3: 0-0 2m4-2m7: 0-1 3m+: 0-0
Track: LH: 0-0 RH: 0-1 Tight: 0-0 Gall: 0-0
Aids: Bl: 0-0 Vi: 0-0 Tstrap: 0-0
Best Rating: 126 12/99 Sand 2m4f110y good Ch

Fair chaser; had been off the track for two years before winning a Wincanton handicap at the start of 2002. Best over two and a half miles on an good or a slightly easy surface.

Native Star (IRE)
96f   **96f**

5-y-o b g Be My Native (USA)-Star Chamber (FR) (Tower Walk)
P J Hobbs M J Tuckey

Placings:461   (4560)
2002/03: 17⁴G, 16⁶G, 16¹G,

	Starts	1st	2nd	3rd	Win & Pl
NH Flat	3	1	0	0	3575
Career Total	3	1	0	0	3575
96 4/03 Ayr	2m	H NHF		GD	£3575

Total win prize-money £3575

Going: Sf: 0-0 GS: 0-0 Gd: 1-3 GF: - Fm: 0-0
Distance: 2m/2m3: 1-3 2m4-2m7: 0-0 3m+: 0-0
Track: LH: 1-1 RH: 0-1 Tight: 0-0 Gall: 0-1
Aids: Bl: 0-0 Vi: 0-0 Tstrap: 0-0
Best Rating: 96 4/03 Ayr 2m good NHF

Modest bumper performer; got his head in front on his third start in an ordinary event at Ayr; effective on good ground.

Native Tash (IRE)
71   **82**

7-y-o b g Be My Native (USA)-Pallastown Gale (IRE) (Strong Gale)
D G McArdle D G McArdle

Placings:0/00F530P0050-U00   (1072)
2002/03: 16⁰HY, 17^UGF, 20⁰GF, 17⁰G,

	Starts	1st	2nd	3rd	Win & Pl
Hurdles	4	0	0	0	
Career Total	15	0	0	1	593

Going: Sf: 0-1 GS: 0-0 Gd: 0-1 GF: - Fm: 0-2
Distance: 2m/2m3: 0-2 2m4-2m7: 0-1 3m+: 0-0
Track: LH: 0-1 RH: 0-1 Tight: 0-0 Gall: 0-0
Aids: Bl: 0-0 Vi: 0-0 Tstrap: 0-4
Best Rating: 82 4/02 Gowr 2m4f yield Hdl

Native Upmanship (IRE)
121   **170**

10-y-o ch g Be My Native (USA)-Hi Upham (Deep Run)
A L T Moore Mrs John Magnier

Placings:31/4012221/11141/114P4/2221212-215121   (4471)
2002/03: 16²S, 20¹SH, 24⁵S, 20¹S, 16²G, 20¹G,

	Starts	1st	2nd	3rd	Win & Pl
Chases	6	3	2	0	205658
Career Total	32	14	10	1	583394
170 4/03 Aint	2m4f	A Ch		GD	£87000
152 1/03 Thur	2m4f	Ch		SFT	£21103
166 12/02 Punc	2m4f	Ch		SH	£35889
164 4/02 Aint	2m4f	A Ch		GD	£69600
167 1/02 Thur	2m4f	Ch		HVY	£19938
166 12/00 Punc	2m4f	Ch		SH	£26000
150 11/00 Navn	2m	Ch		HVY	£10880
160 4/00 Fair	2m4f	Ch		SFT	£31880
142 2/00 Leop	2m5f	Ch		YLD	£26000
150 12/99 Leop	2m1f	Ch		SH	£29017
127 11/99 Navn	2m4f	Ch		YLD	£4312
138 4/99 Punc	2m4f	Hdl		YLD	£27678
114 12/98 Leop	2m2f	Hdl		SFT	£4184
114 4/98 Punc	2m	NHF		HVY	£5956

Total win prize-money £399445

Going: Sf: 1-3 GS: 0-0 Gd: 1-2 GF: - Fm: 0-0
Distance: 2m/2m3: 0-0 2m4-2m7: 3-3 3m+: 0-1
Track: LH: 1-3 RH: 2-3 Tight: 1-1 Gall: 0-1
Aids: Bl: 0-0 Vi: 0-0 Tstrap: 0-0
Best Rating: 170 4/03 Aint 2m4f good Ch

Top-class chaser; seems best at 2m 4f these days and landed both the 2002 and 03 Martell Chase at Aintree, but can go well over 2m and finished runner-up in the Queen Mother Champion Chase in both 2002 and 2003; appeared not to stay when tried over 3m; suited by soft ground.

Nativetrial (IRE)
105   **(42h) 115**

8-y-o ch g Be My Native (USA)-Protrial (Proverb)
C J Mann Mrs P Dodd, Mr & Mrs Mark Hunter

Placings:00241P0/4033350/0-42112P   (3808)
2002/03: 26⁴G, 26²G, 33¹S, 26¹HY, 26²HY, 26PGS,

	Starts	1st	2nd	3rd	Win & Pl
Chases	6	2	2	0	18601
Career Total	21	3	3	3	24873
115 1/03 Font	3m2f110yE(0-110)HCh			HVY	£4007
110 12/02 MRas	4m1f	D(0-120)HCh		SFT	£10800
100 2/00 Clon	2m4f	Hdl		SH	£3036

Total win prize-money £17843

Going: Sf: 2-3 GS: 0-1 Gd: 0-2 GF: - Fm: 0-0
Distance: 2m/2m3: 0-0 2m4-2m7: 0-0 3m+: 2-6
Track: LH: 0-3 RH: 1-1 Tight: 2-4 Gall: 0-1
Aids: Bl: 0-0 Vi: 0-0 Tstrap: 0-0
Best Rating: 115 1/03 Font 3m2f110y heavy Ch

Fair ex-Irish chaser, stays very well and handles testing ground; finished alone when taking the Lincolnshire National in December 2002 and followed up at Fontwell just over a week later.

Natural (IRE)
105   **99d**

6-y-o b g Bigstone (IRE)-You Make Me Real (USA) (Give Me Strength (USA))
F P Murtagh G & P Barker Ltd/globe Engineering

Placings:450P2P-21F2000P   (4776)
2002/03: 17²GF, 17¹S, 17FGS, 17²HY, 16⁹G, 16⁹HY, 20⁰G, 20PG,

	Starts	1st	2nd	3rd	Win & Pl
Hurdles	8	1	2	0	5229
Career Total	14	1	3	0	6104
98 10/02 Bang	2m1f	E(0-105)HHdl		SFT	£3445

Total win prize-money £3445

Going: Sf: 1-3 GS: 0-1 Gd: 0-3 GF: - Fm: 0-1
Distance: 2m/2m3: 1-6 2m4-2m7: 0-2 3m+: 0-0
Track: LH: 1-4 RH: 0-4 Tight: 1-1 Gall: 0-1
Aids: Bl: 0-0 Vi: 0-0 Tstrap: 0-0
Best Rating: 99 11/02 Carl 2m1f heavy Hdl

Modest hurdler, suited by soft ground.

Naughty Dandy (IRE)
87(86h)   **(65h)73**

10-y-o gr g Celio Rufo-Annie Will Run (Deep Run)
N A Twiston-Davies N A Twiston-Davies

Placings:006P/666PF4-5040   (0694)
2002/03: 19³G, 23⁹GS, 25⁴GF, 24⁰G,

	Starts	1st	2nd	3rd	Win & Pl
Hurdles	2	0	0	0	0
Chases	2	0	0	0	0
Career Total	14	0	0	0	0

Going: Sf: 0-0 GS: 0-1 Gd: 0-2 GF: - Fm: 0-1
Distance: 2m/2m3: 0-1 2m4-2m7: 0-0 3m+: 0-3
Track: LH: 0-1 RH: 0-3 Tight: 0-2 Gall: 0-0
Aids: Bl: 0-0 Vi: 0-0 Tstrap: 0-0
Best Rating: 93 3/00 Chep 2m4f gd-sft Hdl

Naunton Downs
78   **48**

9-y-o b g Teenoso (USA)-Kitty Come Home (Monsanto (FR))
R J Smith Dick Hibberd

Placings:0/065/P-P6P0   (2359)
2002/03: 20PGF, 22PGF, 20PS, 20⁰S,

	Starts	1st	2nd	3rd	Win & Pl
Hurdles	4	0	0	0	0
Career Total	9	0	0	0	0

Going: Sf: 0-2 GS: 0-0 Gd: 0-0 GF: - Fm: 0-2
Distance: 2m/2m3: 0-0 2m4-2m7: 0-0 3m+: 0-0
Track: LH: 0-4 RH: 0-0 Tight: 0-1 Gall: 0-0
Aids: Bl: 0-1 Vi: 0-0 Tstrap: 0-0
Best Rating: 89 12/99 Wwck 2m soft NHF

Nautical
95   **88**

5-y-o gr h Lion Cavern (USA)-Russian Royal (USA) (Nureyev (USA))
M C Pipe Gary J Roberts

Placings:P03   (4733)
2002/03: 16PS, 16⁹G, 16³GF,

	Starts	1st	2nd	3rd	Win & Pl
Hurdles	3	0	0	1	546
Career Total	3	0	0	1	546

Going: Sf: 0-1 GS: 0-0 Gd: 0-1 GF: - Fm: 0-1
Distance: 2m/2m3: 0-3 2m4-2m7: 0-0 3m+: 0-0
Track: LH: 0-2 RH: 0-1 Tight: 0-0 Gall: 0-1
Aids: Bl: 0-0 Vi: 0-0 Tstrap: 0-0
Best Rating: 88 4/03 Chep 2m110y gd-fm Hdl

Winner on the Flat at up to ten furlongs in Dubai; seemed better suited to fast ground when third after forcing a strong pace at Chepstow April 2003.

Nautical Star
70   **38**

8-y-o b g Slip Anchor-Comic Talent (Pharly (FR))

A C Whillans Mrs Helen Greggan

Placings:005P41-00P   (2389)
2002/03: 18⁰S, 17⁰S, 20ᴾGS,

	Starts	1st	2nd	3rd	Win & Pl
Hurdles	3	0	0	0	
Career Total	9	1	0	0	3692
86	4/02	Prth	2m110y	G(0-90)HHdl	GD £3692

Total win prize-money £3692

Going: Sf: 0-2 GS: 0-1 Gd: 0-0 GF: - Fm: 0-0
Distance: 2m/2m3: 0-2 2m4-2m7: 0-1 3m+: 0-0
Track: LH: 0-3 RH: 0-0 Tight: 0-2 Gall: 0-0
Aids: Bl: 0-0 Vi: 0-0 Tstrap: 0-0
Best Rating: 86 4/02 Prth 2m110y good Hdl

Poor hurdler; got off the mark at the fifth attempt over hurdles at Perth in April 2002. Acts well on decent ground.

Navale (FR)
104   108
4-y-o gr f Baryshnikov (AUS)-Nabita (FR) (Akarad (FR))
A King (J H M Gosden 10/9) D Hearson

Placings:342245   (4605)
2002/03: 16³S, 17⁴HY, 16²GS, 17²G, 21⁴G, 17⁵G,

	Starts	1st	2nd	3rd	Win & Pl
Hurdles	6	0	2	1	4467
Career Total	6	0	2	1	4467

Going: Sf: 0-2 GS: 0-1 Gd: 0-3 GF: - Fm: 0-0
Distance: 2m/2m3: 0-5 2m4-2m7: 0-1 3m+: 0-0
Track: LH: 0-3 RH: 0-3 Tight: 0-1 Gall: 0-2
Aids: Bl: 0-0 Vi: 0-1 Tstrap: 0-0
Best Rating: 108 2/03 Kemp 2m gd-sft Hdl

Modest novice hurdler; stays 2m 5f, but lacks pace and keeps on finding one or two too good.

Navan Project (IRE)
80   61+
9-y-o gr g Project Manager-Just Possible (Kalaglow)
A R Dicken Got To Be In It To Win It Partnership

Placings:0/0P033400310/05554400260/6   (0450)
2002/03: 16⁶G,

	Starts	1st	2nd	3rd	Win & Pl
Chases	1	0	0	0	0
Career Total	24	1	1	3	3029
72	3/00	Sedg	2m1f	G(0-90)HHdl	G-F £1547

Total win prize-money £1547

Going: Sf: 0-0 GS: 0-0 Gd: 0-0 GF: - Fm: 0-0
Distance: 2m/2m3: 0-1 2m4-2m7: 0-0 3m+: 0-0
Track: LH: 0-1 RH: 0-0 Tight: 0-0 Gall: 0-0
Aids: Bl: 0-0 Vi: 0-0 Tstrap: 0-0
Best Rating: 94 5/98 Strf 2m110y good Hdl

Navarone
113   127
9-y-o b g Gunner B-Anamasi (Idiots Delight)
Ian Williams (N A Twiston-Davies 8/2) A J Cresser

Placings:554/4224315/33PP110-4221P11 (4775)
2002/03: 20⁴GF, 21²G, 20²GS, 22¹G, 24⁵GS, 24¹GF, 24¹G,

	Starts	1st	2nd	3rd	Win & Pl
Chases	7	3	2	0	44105
Career Total	24	6	4	3	58395
127	4/03	Prth	3m	B HCh	GD £18677
117	4/03	Bang	3m110y	C(0-135)HCh	G-F £10660
116	12/02	Newb	2m6f110yC(0-130)HCh	GD £8547
115	4/02	Uttx	2m4f	E(0-100)HCh	G-F £3373
109	4/02	Wwck	2m4f110yF(0-90)HCh	G-F £3220
104	3/00	Ling	2m7f	D Hdl	GD £3373

Total win prize-money £47853

Going: Sf: 0-0 GS: 0-2 Gd: 2-3 GF: - Fm: 1-2
Distance: 2m/2m3: 0-0 2m4-2m7: 1-4 3m+: 2-3
Track: LH: 2-6 RH: 1-1 Tight: 1-2 Gall: 1-2
Aids: Bl: 0-0 Vi: 0-0 Tstrap: 0-1
Best Rating: 127 4/03 Prth 3m good Ch

Fair chaser; stays three miles; suited by positive tactics and a sound surface; has worn a tongue tie; progressive.

Navarre Samson (FR)
96   114
8-y-o b/br g Ganges (USA)-L Eternite (FR) (Cariellor (FR))
P J Hobbs Winton Bloodstock Ltd

Placings:1111122360/204012/1/22-24212 (1154)
2002/03: 19²G, 22⁴GF, 22²GF, 26¹GF, 22²G,

	Starts	1st	2nd	3rd	Win & Pl
Hurdles	5	1	3	0	4228
Career Total	24	8	9	1	34887
97	8/02	Sthl	3m2f	G Hdl	G-F £2212
125	8/00	Strf	2m6f110yF Hdl	G-F £2492
120	7/99	Strf	2m6f110yD(0-125)HHdl	GD £3231
118	11/98	Sand	2m110y D Hdl	GD £2736
120	10/98	Weth	2m A Hdl	GD £8819
120	9/98	Extr	2m1f	E Hdl	GD £2242
120	8/98	Worc	2m E Hdl	GD £2285
111	8/98	Worc	2m E Hdl	GD £2355

Total win prize-money £26374

Going: Sf: 0-0 GS: 0-0 Gd: 0-2 GF: - Fm: 1-3
Distance: 2m/2m3: 0-0 2m4-2m7: 0-1 3m+: 1-1
Track: LH: 1-4 RH: 0-1 Tight: 0-3 Gall: 0-0
Aids: Bl: 0-0 Vi: 0-0 Tstrap: 1-5
Best Rating: 125 8/00 Strf 2m6f110y gd-fm Hdl

Modest hurdler, suited by fast ground. Pays his way in sellers.

Nawamees (IRE)
103   110
5-y-o b h Darshaan-Truly Generous (IRE) (Generous (IRE))
G L Moore (J E Hammond 18/9) Paul Stamp

Placings:543   (4328)
2002/03: 20⁵GS, 16⁴S, 16³G,

	Starts	1st	2nd	3rd	Win & Pl
Hurdles	3	0	0	1	1382
Career Total	3	0	0	1	1382

Going: Sf: 0-1 GS: 0-1 Gd: 0-1 GF: - Fm: 0-0
Distance: 2m/2m3: 0-2 2m4-2m7: 0-1 3m+: 0-0
Track: LH: 0-2 RH: 0-1 Tight: 0-1 Gall: 0-1
Aids: Bl: 0-0 Vi: 0-0 Tstrap: 0-0
Best Rating: 110 3/03 Newb 2m110y good Hdl

Ex-French; fair novice hurdler; acts on good ground; effective at around two miles.

Ndr's Cash For Fun
84   26
10-y-o b g Ballacashtal (CAN)-Basic Fun (Teenoso (USA))
A W Carroll Group 1 Racing (1994) Ltd

Placings:00/0P/0P1P1430-000F0   (4083)
2002/03: 17⁰GS, 24⁰S, 16⁰HY, 19ᶠGS, 25⁰HY,

	Starts	1st	2nd	3rd	Win & Pl

	Starts	1st	2nd	3rd	Win & Pl
	5	0	0	0	
Hurdles					

	Starts	1st	2nd	3rd	Win & Pl
Hurdles	5	0	0	0	
Career Total	17	2	0	1	3939
73	2/02	Tntn	2m3f110yG(0-95)HHdl	SFT £1750
73	1/02	Leic	2m	G(0-90)HHdl	SFT £1939

Total win prize-money £3689

Going: Sf: 0-3 GS: 0-2 Gd: 0-0 GF: - Fm: 0-0
Distance: 2m/2m3: 0-2 2m4-2m7: 0-1 3m+: 0-2
Track: LH: 0-1 RH: 0-3 Tight: 0-3 Gall: 0-0
Aids: Bl: 0-0 Vi: 0-0 Tstrap: 0-1
Best Rating: 82 4/98 Asct 2m110y good NHF

Lightly raced selling-class hurdler, who had a habit of pulling up early in his career. Needs humouring.

Ne M'Oublie Pas (FR)
95
7-y-o b/br g Shining Steel-Irish Lullaby (FR) (Prince Tenderfoot (USA))
P J Hobbs Triple Two

Placings:10436/P23003P4/0404021-P (0993)
2002/03: 26ᴾGF,

	Starts	1st	2nd	3rd	Win & Pl
Chases	1	0	0	0	
Career Total	21	2	2	3	13235
95	8/01	NAbb	3m2f110yF(0-90)HCh	GD £2513
	8/99	Claf	2m	Hdl	HLD £4306

Total win prize-money £6819

Going: Sf: 0-0 GS: 0-0 Gd: 0-0 GF: - Fm: 0-1
Distance: 2m/2m3: 0-0 2m4-2m7: 0-0 3m+: 0-1
Track: LH: 0-1 RH: 0-0 Tight: 0-1 Gall: 0-0
Aids: Bl: 0-0 Vi: 0-0 Tstrap: 0-0
Best Rating: 95 8/01 NAbb 3m2f110y good Ch

Nearly A Gimme (IRE)
98   100
7-y-o gr g Roselier (FR)-Cosmicechoexpress (Deep Run)
C F Swan G McManus

Placings:000/41-054405   (3159)
2002/03: 24⁰YS, 21⁵HY, 24⁴YS, 25⁴G, 24⁰SH, 24⁵G,

	Starts	1st	2nd	3rd	Win & Pl
Hurdles	6	0	0	0	700
Career Total	11	1	0	0	5212
100	11/01	Clon	3m	(0-116)HHdl	SFT £4173

Total win prize-money £4173

Going: Sf: 0-1 GS: 0-0 Gd: 0-2 GF: - Fm: 0-0
Distance: 2m/2m3: 0-2 2m4-2m7: 0-1 3m+: 0-5
Track: LH: 0-2 RH: 0-2 Tight: 0-2 Gall: 0-0
Aids: Bl: 0-0 Vi: 0-0 Tstrap: 0-0
Best Rating: 100 11/01 Clon 3m soft Hdl

Irish-trained staying handicap hurdler, acts in soft ground.

Nearly A Score
(89h)   (73h) 114
11-y-o b m Nearly A Hand-Boherash (Boreen (FR))
J D Frost T R Watts

Placings:00/5/2354F45/252035/U3F543-5 (0628)
2002/03: 22⁵GF,

	Starts	1st	2nd	3rd	Win & Pl
Hurdles	1	0	0	0	0
Career Total	23	0	3	4	14203

Going: Sf: 0-0 GS: 0-0 Gd: 0-0 GF: - Fm: 0-1
Distance: 2m/2m3: 0-0 2m4-2m7: 0-1 3m+: 0-0
Track: LH: 0-1 RH: 0-0 Tight: 0-1 Gall: 0-0
Aids: Bl: 0-0 Vi: 0-0 Tstrap: 0-0
Best Rating: 104 11/01 Chep 2m3f110y gd-sft Ch

Modest chaser; winning pointer, is somewhat inconsistent and has yet to get his head in front under rules, often jumping less than fluently. Looks best at around two and a half miles. Acts on soft ground.

Nearly Noble (IRE)
15

10-y-o b g The Bart (USA)-Crofter s Law (Furry Glen)
K R Pearce Keith R Pearce

Placings:0UF/040/0-4 (0646)
2002/03: 24⁴GF,

	Starts	1st	2nd	3rd	Win & Pl
Chases	1	0	0	0	275
Career Total	8	0	0	0	451

Going: Sf: 0-0 GS: 0-0 Gd: 0-0 GF: - Fm: 0-1
Distance: 2m/2m3: 0-0 2m4-2m7: 0-0 3m+: 0-1
Track: LH: 0-1 RH: 0-0 Tight: 0-1 Gall: 0-0
Aids: Bl: 0-0 Vi: 0-0 Tstrap: 0-0
Best Rating: 92 6/00 Dund 2m135y firm NHF

Ned Divine
97

8-y-o br g Primitive Rising (USA)-Coral Princess (Imperial Fling (USA))
Mrs L B Normile L B N Racing Club

Placings:PP/3P (2188)
2002/03: 20³S, 20²HY,

	Starts	1st	2nd	3rd	Win & Pl
Chases	2	0	0	1	773
Career Total	4	0	0	1	773

Going: Sf: 0-2 GS: 0-0 Gd: 0-0 GF: - Fm: 0-0
Distance: 2m/2m3: 0-0 2m4-2m7: 0-0 3m+: 0-2
Track: LH: 0-1 RH: 0-1 Tight: 0-0 Gall: 0-0
Aids: Bl: 0-0 Vi: 0-0 Tstrap: 0-0
Best Rating: 0 11/02 Carl 2m4f heavy Ch

Needwood Legend

(73h) (60h)
10-y-o b/br g Rolfe (USA)-Enchanting Kate (Enchantment)
A J Wilson Mrs M J Wilson

Placings:2000/00P424004/06053505/PP-6 (0384)
2002/03: 16⁶G,

	Starts	1st	2nd	3rd	Win & Pl
Hurdles	1	0	0	0	
Career Total	24	0	2	1	1881

Going: Sf: 0-0 GS: 0-0 Gd: 0-1 GF: - Fm: 0-0
Distance: 2m/2m3: 0-1 2m4-2m7: 0-0 3m+: 0-0
Track: LH: 0-0 RH: 0-1 Tight: 0-0 Gall: 0-1
Aids: Bl: 0-0 Vi: 0-0 Tstrap: 0-0
Best Rating: 90 9/98 Worc 2m gd-fm Hdl

Needwood Lion
107(102h) (107h)125

10-y-o b g Rolfe (USA)-Arctic Lion (Arctic Slave)

Miss Venetia Williams Tweenhills Racing (Gadbury Syndicate)

Placings:26/606511/021FF46/305352-641213403 (4145)
2002/03: 20⁶S, 19⁴S, 19¹G, 19²GS, 20¹S, 16³S, 20⁴S, 20⁰G, 21³G,

	Starts	1st	2nd	3rd	Win & Pl
Chases	9	2	1	2	20482
Career Total	30	5	4	4	35700
125 12/02 Kemp	2m4f110yD(0-120)HCh			SFT	£10653
120 12/02 Hrfd	2m3f	(0-115)HCh		GD	£5031
130 1/01 Uttx	2m	D Ch		HVY	£4143
104 4/00 Hrfd	2m3f110yE(0-105)HHdl			SFT	£2970
96 3/00 Tntn	2m1f	F(0-105)HHdl		SFT	£2524
			Total win prize-money £25323		

Going: Sf: 1-5 GS: 0-1 Gd: 1-3 GF: - Fm: 0-0
Distance: 2m/2m3: 1-4 2m4-2m7: 1-5 3m+: 0-0
Track: LH: 0-4 RH: 2-5 Tight: 0-4 Gall: 0-0
Aids: Bl: 0-0 Vi: 0-0 Tstrap: 0-0
Best Rating: 130 1/01 Winc 2m5f soft Ch

Fair handicap chaser; headstrong individual; he stays two and a half miles and likes to have his own way in front; effective on good ground or softer.

Needwood Merlin

7-y-o b g Sizzling Melody-Enchanting Kate (Enchantment)
K W Hogg K W Hogg

Placings:PP (0909)
2002/03: 21⁶GF, 24⁶GS,

	Starts	1st	2nd	3rd	Win & Pl
Hurdles	2	0	0	0	
Career Total	2	0	0	0	

Going: Sf: 0-0 GS: 0-1 Gd: 0-0 GF: - Fm: 0-1
Distance: 2m/2m3: 0-0 2m4-2m7: 0-1 3m+: 0-1
Track: LH: 0-1 RH: 0-1 Tight: 0-2 Gall: 0-0
Aids: Bl: 0-0 Vi: 0-0 Tstrap: 0-0
Best Rating: 0 8/02 MRas 3m gd-sft Hdl

Needwood Missile
75 37

7-y-o b g Sizzling Melody-Sea Dart (Air Trooper)
J L Spearing Bryan Mathieson

Placings:0/5-0 (1089)
2002/03: 16⁶GF,

	Starts	1st	2nd	3rd	Win & Pl
Hurdles	1	0	0	0	
Career Total	3	0	0	0	0

Going: Sf: 0-0 GS: 0-0 Gd: 0-0 GF: - Fm: 0-1
Distance: 2m/2m3: 0-1 2m4-2m7: 0-0 3m+: 0-0
Track: LH: 0-0 RH: 0-1 Tight: 0-0 Gall: 0-1
Aids: Bl: 0-0 Vi: 0-0 Tstrap: 0-0
Best Rating: 86 5/01 Sthl 2m gd-fm NHF

Needwood Spirit
106 109

8-y-o b g Rolfe (USA)-Needwood Nymph (Bold Owl)
Mrs A M Naughton Famous Five Racing

Placings:45/00P01/5611146-4620 (3294)
2002/03: 17⁴GS, 17⁶HY, 16²G, 16⁶GS,

	Starts	1st	2nd	3rd	Win & Pl
Hurdles	4	0	1	0	912
Career Total	18	4	1	0	15552

95	12/01 Hexm	2m	D(0-125)HHdl	SFT	£7020
110	11/01 Carl	2m4f	F(0-105)HHdl	HVY	£2299
110	11/01 Carl	2m1f	F(0-110)HHdl	SFT	£2664
87	4/01 Fknm	2m	G(0-90)HHdl	G-S	£1926
			Total win prize-money £13910		

Going: Sf: 0-1 GS: 0-2 Gd: 0-1 GF: - Fm: 0-0
Distance: 2m/2m3: 0-4 2m4-2m7: 0-0 3m+: 0-0
Track: LH: 0-2 RH: 0-2 Tight: 0-0 Gall: 0-1
Aids: Bl: 0-0 Vi: 0-0 Tstrap: 0-0
Best Rating: 110 11/01 Carl 2m4f heavy Hdl

Front-running handicap hurdler. Ideally suited by a stiff track and testing ground, goes well at Carlisle and has a good attitude. Stays two and a half miles.

Negresko (FR)
108 118

4-y-o gr g Great Palm (USA)-Negra (FR) (Tropular)
M C Pipe (J Bertran De Balanda 29/11) J Bertran De Balanda

Placings:00-0P3111113553 (4608)
2002/03: 15⁰VS, 17⁰VS, 15³G, 16¹G, 16¹GS, 15¹HO, 17¹S, 17¹S, 17³HO, 16⁵G, 20⁵G, 17³G,

	Starts	1st	2nd	3rd	Win & Pl
Hurdles	11	5	0	2	24923
Chases	1	0	0	1	1460
Career Total	14	5	0	3	26383
10/02 Pari	2m1f	Hdl		SFT	£5890
10/02 MARS	2m1f110y	Hdl		SFT	£4417
9/02 Lyrh	1m7f110y	Hdl		HLD	£4712
8/02 Divo	2m	Hdl		G-S	£2945
7/02 Divo	2m	Hdl		GD	£2650
			Total win prize-money £20614		

Going: Sf: 2-2 GS: 1-1 Gd: 1-5 GF: - Fm: 0-0
Distance: 2m/2m3: 4-8 2m4-2m7: 0-1 3m+: 0-0
Track: LH: 0-3 RH: 0-0 Tight: 0-1 Gall: 0-1
Aids: Bl: 3-4 Vi: 0-2 Tstrap: 0-0
Best Rating: 118 4/03 Chel 2m1f good Hdl

Fair chaser/hurdler; won five times over hurdles in France in 2002; third on chase debut; has looked reluctant; handles soft ground; often blinkered.

Neilstoneside (IRE)

5-y-o b m General Monash (USA)-Lady Counsel (IRE) (Law Society (USA))
M J Ryan Charles Alan McKechnie

Placings:00UPP-P (0379)
2002/03: 21⁵G,

	Starts	1st	2nd	3rd	Win & Pl
Hurdles	1	0	0	0	
Career Total	6	0	0	0	

Going: Sf: 0-0 GS: 0-0 Gd: 0-1 GF: - Fm: 0-0
Distance: 2m/2m3: 0-0 2m4-2m7: 0-1 3m+: 0-0
Track: LH: 0-0 RH: 0-1 Tight: 0-0 Gall: 0-1
Aids: Bl: 0-0 Vi: 0-0 Tstrap: 0-1
Best Rating: 69 3/02 Hntg 2m110y gd-fm NHF

Nelly Moser
91 74

6-y-o gr m Neltino-Boreen s Glory (Boreen (FR))
Mrs A J Hamilton-Fairley (Mrs D Haine 7/5) Mrs A Hamilton-Fairley

Placings:0-40 (4190)

2002/03: 18⁴GF, 17⁰G,

	Starts	1st	2nd	3rd	Win & Pl
NH Flat	3	0	0	0	0
Career Total	3	0	0	0	0

Going: Sf: 0-0 GS: 0-0 Gd: 0-1 GF: - Fm: 0-1
Distance: 2m/2m3: 0-2 2m4-2m7: 0-0 3m+: 0-0
Track: LH: 0-1 RH: 0-1 Tight: 0-2 Gall: 0-0
Aids: Bl: 0-0 Vi: 0-0 Tstrap: 0-0
Best Rating: 89 5/02 Font 2m2f110y gd-fm NHF

Modest form in bumpers.

Neltina
104   105

7-y-o gr m Neltino-Mimizan (IRE) (Pennine Walk)
Mrs J E Scrase Mrs J E Scrase

Placings:2141431 (4366)
2002/03: 18²GF, 16¹GF, 16⁴GF, 16¹G, 16⁴S, 18³S, 20¹G,

	Starts	1st	2nd	3rd	Win & Pl
NH Flat	4	2	1	0	4497
Hurdles	3	1	0	1	5940
Career Total	7	3	1	1	10437
109 3/03	Asct 2m4f	D Hdl		GD	£4823
114 11/02	Wwck 2m	H NHF		GD	£1785
96 7/02	Strf 2m110y	H NHF		G-F	£2212

Total win prize-money £8820

Going: Sf: 0-2 GS: 0-0 Gd: 2-2 GF: - Fm: 1-3
Distance: 2m/2m3: 2-6 2m4-2m7: 1-1 3m+: 0-0
Track: LH: 1-5 RH: 1-1 Tight: 0-2 Gall: 0-1
Aids: Bl: 0-0 Vi: 0-0 Tstrap: 0-0
Best Rating: 114 11/02 Wwck 2m good NHF

Modest hurdler; twice a bumper winner at Stratford and Warwick; off the mark over hurdles at Ascot; suited by a sound surface and forcing tactics.

Nemisto
102(104c) (119c)101

9-y-o gr g Mystiko (USA)-Nemesia (Mill Reef (USA))
R Lee R L C Hartley

Placings:62P/5330201/51252201/0056F/33355PP-
42230P46 (4599)
2002/03: 16⁴G, 16²HY, 17²HY, 20³S, 19⁹G, 17⁶G, 24⁴GF, 24⁶GF,

	Starts	1st	2nd	3rd	Win & Pl
Hurdles	8	0	2	1	4220
Career Total	38	3	7	6	23501
128 3/00	Chep 2m110y	D Hdl		GD	£3256
124 12/99	Hrfd 2m1f	D(0-115)HHdl		SFT	£2762
114 5/99	Hrfd 2m1f	D(0-110)HHdl		GD	£2560

Total win prize-money £8579

Going: Sf: 0-3 GS: 0-0 Gd: 0-3 GF: - Fm: 0-2
Distance: 2m/2m3: 0-4 2m4-2m7: 0-2 3m+: 0-2
Track: LH: 0-2 RH: 0-6 Tight: 0-0 Gall: 0-0
Aids: Bl: 0-0 Vi: 0-0 Tstrap: 0-0
Best Rating: 128 3/00 Chep 2m110y good Hdl

Modest hurdler/chaser; had not won since March 2000 until defying top weight in competitive 2m 6f selling handicap at Newton Abbot May 2003; acts on soft, but handles a sound surface; stays 2m 4f.

Nephite (NZ)
95(113c) (105c)75

9-y-o b g Star Way-Te Akau Charmer (NZ) (Sir Tristram)
R C Guest (N B Mason 21/1) Miss C Metcalfe

Placings:56633233005/441365131231P-064P4352161
(4413)

2002/03: 16⁶GS, 16⁶G, 17⁴G, 21⁸GS, 17⁴S, 16³S, 16⁵HY, 16²S, 16¹GS, 16⁶GF, 17¹G,

	Starts	1st	2nd	3rd	Win & Pl
Hurdles	1	0	0	0	0
Chases	10	2	1	1	11235
Career Total	35	6	3	8	30770
105 3/03	MRas 2m1f110y	E(0-105)HCh		GD	£4075
100 3/03	Newc 2m110y	G(0-105)HCh		G-S	£4332
98 4/02	MRas 2m1f110y	E(0-105)HCh		GD	£3570
98 1/02	Newc 2m110y	E(0-105)HCh		SFT	£3032
87 1/02	Fknm 2m110y	F(0-100)HCh		SFT	£4342
82 10/01	Carl 2m	F(0-100)HCh		SFT	£2938

Total win prize-money £22290

Going: Sf: 0-4 GS: 1-2 Gd: 1-4 GF: - Fm: 0-1
Distance: 2m/2m3: 2-10 2m4-2m7: 0-3 3m+: 0-0
Track: LH: 1-8 RH: 1-3 Tight: 1-8 Gall: 1-2
Aids: Bl: 0-0 Vi: 0-0 Tstrap: 0-5
Best Rating: 105 3/03 MRas 2m1f110y good Ch

Moderate chaser; suited by 2m on both soft and good ground, usually wears tongue tie and cheekpieces.

Neptune
92   80

7-y-o b g Dolphin Street (FR)-Seal Indigo (IRE) (Glenstal (USA))
J C Fox S J V Construction

Placings:00041 (4251)
2002/03: 16⁶S, 16⁹S, 16⁰G, 17⁴HY, 17¹G,

	Starts	1st	2nd	3rd	Win & Pl
Hurdles	5	1	0	0	3724
Career Total	5	1	0	0	3724
80 3/03	Extr 2m1f	G Hdl		GD	£3388

Total win prize-money £3388

Going: Sf: 0-3 GS: 0-0 Gd: 1-2 GF: - Fm: 0-0
Distance: 2m/2m3: 1-5 2m4-2m7: 0-0 3m+: 0-0
Track: LH: 0-3 RH: 1-2 Tight: 0-1 Gall: 0-2
Aids: Bl: 0-0 Vi: 0-0 Tstrap: 0-0
Best Rating: 80 3/03 Extr 2m1f good Hdl

Appreciated the combination of a drop in class and better ground when winning extended two mile selling hurdle at Exeter March 2003.

Nerina Princess (IRE)
79   48+

4-y-o b/br f Key Of Luck (USA)-Finessing (Indian King (USA))
J S Moore Tom & Evelyn Yates

Placings:04P (2098)
2002/03: 16⁹G, 16⁴GS, 16⁶G,

	Starts	1st	2nd	3rd	Win & Pl
Hurdles	3	0	0	0	316
Career Total	3	0	0	0	316

Going: Sf: 0-0 GS: 0-1 Gd: 0-2 GF: - Fm: 0-0
Distance: 2m/2m3: 0-3 2m4-2m7: 0-0 3m+: 0-0
Track: LH: 0-3 RH: 0-0 Tight: 0-1 Gall: 0-1
Aids: Bl: 0-0 Vi: 0-0 Tstrap: 0-0
Best Rating: 58 11/02 Newb 2m110y gd-sft Hdl

Nero's Palace
95   77

6-y-o b g Emperor Jones (USA)-Sayulita (Habitat)
M Todhunter Peter Boddy

Placings:456-65P (1015)
2002/03: 20⁶GF, 21⁵GF, 24⁶FG,

	Starts	1st	2nd	3rd	Win & Pl
Hurdles	3	0	0	0	0
Career Total	6	0	0	0	0

Going: Sf: 0-0 GS: 0-0 Gd: 0-1 GF: - Fm: 0-2
Distance: 2m/2m3: 0-0 2m4-2m7: 0-2 3m+: 0-1
Track: LH: 0-0 RH: 0-1 Tight: 0-1 Gall: 0-0
Aids: Bl: 0-0 Vi: 0-0 Tstrap: 0-0
Best Rating: 77 4/02 MRas 2m3f110y good Hdl

Nether Another
73   40

6-y-o b m Another Sam-Poppy Kelly (Netherkelly)
M J Gingell Miss S Wilson

Placings:0-FP0 (2124)
2002/03: 16⁶G, 20⁰GS, 16⁹S,

	Starts	1st	2nd	3rd	Win & Pl
Hurdles	3	0	0	0	
Career Total	4	0	0	0	

Going: Sf: 0-1 GS: 0-1 Gd: 0-1 GF: - Fm: 0-0
Distance: 2m/2m3: 0-0 2m4-2m7: 0-1 3m+: 0-0
Track: LH: 0-3 RH: 0-0 Tight: 0-3 Gall: 0-0
Aids: Bl: 0-0 Vi: 0-0 Tstrap: 0-0
Best Rating: 38 11/02 Plum 2m soft Hdl

Neutron (IRE)
112   128+

6-y-o ch g Nucleon (USA)-Balistic Princess (Lomond (USA))
M C Pipe Matt Archer & Miss Jean Broadhurst

Placings:2212200/4600-1412F (3727)
2002/03: 16¹G, 16⁴HY, 16¹GS, 21²S, 16⁶G,

	Starts	1st	2nd	3rd	Win & Pl
Hurdles	5	2	1	0	11911
Career Total	16	3	5	0	20125
123 12/02	Winc 2m	D(0-120)HHdl		G-S	£5398
115 10/02	Winc 2m	E(0-110)HHdl		GD	£3542
110 9/00	Cork 2m	Hdl		GD	£3864

Total win prize-money £12805

Going: Sf: 0-2 GS: 1-1 Gd: 1-2 GF: - Fm: 0-0
Distance: 2m/2m3: 2-4 2m4-2m7: 0-1 3m+: 0-0
Track: LH: 0-0 RH: 2-5 Tight: 0-0 Gall: 0-0
Aids: Bl: 0-0 Vi: 1-3 Tstrap: 0-0
Best Rating: 128 12/02 Kemp 2m5f soft Hdl

Useful handicap hurdler; ex-Irish; acts on a sound surface and with give; has never won beyond two miles, but does stay two five; wears a visor; has shown a questionable attitude.

Neva-Agree
11-y-o ch g St Columbus-Nee-Agree (Rymer)
Mrs P J Ikin Mrs P J Ikin

Placings:2/P43P/P33P02-P (3950)
2002/03: 23²⁰GS,

	Starts	1st	2nd	3rd	Win & Pl
Chases	1	0	0	0	
Career Total	12	0	2	3	3373

Going: Sf: 0-0 GS: 0-1 Gd: 0-0 GF: - Fm: 0-0
Distance: 2m/2m3: 0-0 2m4-2m7: 0-0 3m+: 0-1

Track: LH: 0-0 RH: 0-1 Tight: 0-0 Gall: 0-0
Aids: Bl: 0-1 Vi: 0-0 Tstrap: 0-0
Best Rating: 71 4/00 MRas 3m1f   gd-fm Ch

A winner of two point-to-points, has shown bits of form under rules. Acts on good ground.

Never (FR)

119   153

6-y-o b g Vettori (IRE)-Neraida (USA) (Giboulee (CAN))
F Doumen Sir Peter O Sullevan

Placings:411000-1500   (4476)
2002/03: 16[1]S, 17[5]G, 17[9]G, 16[6]G,

	Starts	1st	2nd	3rd	Win & Pl
Hurdles	4	1	0	0	16375
Career Total	10	3	0	0	39174
148	11/02	Newb	2m110y A(0-145)Hdl	SFT	£14500
140	12/01	Asct	2m110y A Hdl	GD	£13100
	11/01	Engh	2m1f110y Hdl	HVY	£9699

Total win prize-money £37299

Going: Sf: 1-1 GS: 0-0 Gd: 0-3 GF: - Fm: 0-0
Distance: 2m/2m3: 1-4 2m4-2m7: 0-0 3m+: 0-0
Track: LH: 1-4 RH: 0-0 Tight: 0-1 **Gall:** 1-3
Aids: Bl: 0-0 Vi: 0-0 Tstrap: 0-0
Best Rating: 153 12/02 Chel 2m1f   good Hdl

French-trained hurdler; won nicely on his British debut at Ascot in December 2001, but well held after until scoring on the Flat at Enghien in October 2002; returned to hurdling with a win in the Gerry Feilden at Newbury in 2002 and put up a reasonable effort when fifth in the Bula; suited by two miles; acts on a good and easy surface.

Never Can Tell

100   90

7-y-o ch g Emarati (USA)-Farmer s Pet (Sharrood (USA))
M Mullineaux Mrs Renee Farrington-Kirkham

Placings:P22050024F0/0020514/402644403-5P62 (4468)
2002/03: 16[5]HY, 17[6]GS, 19[6]F, 17[2]F,

	Starts	1st	2nd	3rd	Win & Pl
Hurdles	4	0	1	0	1040
Career Total	31	1	6	1	7904
92	1/01	Winc	2m	F Hdl	G-S	£1949

Total win prize-money £1950

Going: Sf: 0-1 GS: 0-1 Gd: 0-0 GF: - Fm: 0-2
Distance: 2m/2m3: 0-3 2m4-2m7: 0-1 3m+: 0-0
Track: LH: 0-0 RH: 0-4 Tight: 0-2 Gall: 0-0
Aids: Bl: 0-0 Vi: 0-0 Tstrap: 0-0
Best Rating: 94 2/00 MRas 2m1f110y gd-sft Hdl

Modest handicap hurdler with a poor wins to runs ratio.

Never Forget Bowie

78   62

7-y-o b g Superpower-Heldigvis (Hot Grove)
R Allan Robert Miller-Bakewell

Placings:0/00000-00   (0620)
2002/03: 16[9]GS, 16[9]G,

	Starts	1st	2nd	3rd	Win & Pl
Hurdles	2	0	0	0	
Career Total	8	0	0	0	

Going: Sf: 0-0 GS: 0-1 Gd: 0-0 GF: - Fm: 0-1
Distance: 2m/2m3: 0-2 2m4-2m7: 0-0 3m+: 0-0
Track: LH: 0-2 RH: 0-0 Tight: 0-0 Gall: 0-0
Aids: Bl: 0-0 Vi: 0-0 Tstrap: 0-0
Best Rating: 65 12/01 Muss 2m   good NHF

Never In Debt

85   63

11-y-o ch g Nicholas Bill-Deep In Debt (Deep Run)
E R Clough E R Clough

Placings:120/341104/2P/P524F425/4P/FPP-0P (0343)
2002/03: 24[0]GF, 22[P]GS,

	Starts	1st	2nd	3rd	Win & Pl
Hurdles	2	0	0	0	
Career Total	26	3	4	1	13020
110	2/98	Tntn	2m3f110yD(0-120)HHdl	G-F	£2814
108	1/98	Tntn	2m3f110yD Hdl	SFT	£2913
101	9/96	Worc	2m	H NHF	G-F	£1385

Total win prize-money £7112

Going: Sf: 0-0 GS: 0-1 Gd: 0-0 GF: - Fm: 0-1
Distance: 2m/2m3: 0-0 2m4-2m7: 0-1 3m+: 0-1
Track: LH: 0-2 RH: 0-0 Tight: 0-1 Gall: 0-0
Aids: Bl: 0-0 Vi: 0-0 Tstrap: 0-0
Best Rating: 115 11/98 Chel 2m5f   gd-sft Hdl

Never Wonder (IRE)

100   (112h)108

8-y-o b g John French-Mistress Anna (Arapaho)
M Bradstock Ever The Optimists

Placings:01/4123-P1606   (4151)
2002/03: 25[P]G, 23[1]G, 24[6]GS, 24[6]S, 29[6]G,

	Starts	1st	2nd	3rd	Win & Pl
Chases	5	1	0	0	4505
Career Total	11	3	1	1	13878
108	10/02	Extr	2m7f110yE(0-105)HCh	GD	£4504
108	12/01	Donc	3m	D Ch	GD	£5267
112	4/01	Extr	2m6f110yE Hdl	SFT	£2304

Total win prize-money £12077

Going: Sf: 0-1 GS: 0-1 Gd: 1-3 GF: - Fm: 0-0
Distance: 2m/2m3: 0-0 2m4-2m7: 0-0 **3m+:** 1-5
Track: LH: 0-1 **RH:** 1-4 Tight: 0-1 Gall: 0-0
Aids: Bl: 0-0 Vi: 0-0 Tstrap: 0-0
Best Rating: 112 4/01 Extr 2m6f110y soft Hdl

Modest chaser; winning pointer, he won at Doncaster on his second start over fences; won a handicap at Exeter in October 2002; stays well; likes to make the running.

New Bird (GER)

103   116

8-y-o b g Bluebird (USA)-Nouvelle Amour (GER) (Esclavo (FR))
Mrs H Dalton David M Hughes

Placings:3124012/3060/31/216F302-P356 (4612)
2002/03: 16[P]GF, 16[3]G, 16[5]GF, 16[6]G,

	Starts	1st	2nd	3rd	Win & Pl
Chases	4	0	0	1	1125
Career Total	24	4	4	9	29269
125	5/01	Aint	2m	D(0-125)HCh	GD	£5502
117	4/01	Weth	2m	E Ch	G-S	£3233
122	4/99	Hrfd	2m1f	D Hdl	G-F	£3009
117	12/98	Kemp	2m	C Hdl	SFT	£5083

Total win prize-money £16829

Going: Sf: 0-0 GS: 0-0 Gd: 0-2 GF: - Fm: 0-2
Distance: 2m/2m3: 0-4 2m4-2m7: 0-0 3m+: 0-0
Track: LH: 0-3 RH: 0-1 Tight: 0-1 Gall: 0-1
Aids: Bl: 0-0 Vi: 0-0 Tstrap: 0-0
Best Rating: 130 3/00 Chel 2m1f   gd-fm Hdl

Fair handicap chaser, best at 2m and likes to make the running; just touched off when trying to concede 16lb to the in

form The Staggery Boy at Newton Abbot June 2003; does not want the ground too soft.

New Era (IRE)

95   113

9-y-o b g Distinctly North (USA)-Vaguely Deesse (USA) (Vaguely Noble)
B De Haan Sidtenga Syndicate

Placings:363/21201/6   (4050)
2002/03: 24[6]S,

	Starts	1st	2nd	3rd	Win & Pl
Chases	1	0	0	0	
Career Total	9	2	2	2	11558
113	4/01	Kemp	3m	D Ch	GD	£5265
113	1/01	Wwck	2m4f110yF(0-90)HCh	HVY	£2695

Total win prize-money £7960

Going: Sf: 0-1 GS: 0-0 Gd: 0-0 GF: - Fm: 0-0
Distance: 2m/2m3: 0-0 2m4-2m7: 0-0 3m+: 0-1
Track: LH: 0-0 RH: 0-1 Tight: 0-0 Gall: 0-0
Aids: Bl: 0-0 Vi: 0-0 Tstrap: 0-0
Best Rating: 118 2/01 Sand 2m4f110y soft Ch

Winning novice chaser in 2000/1; absent for a long time subsequently; stays three miles; acts on good ground.

New Horizon (IRE)

72   75

5-y-o b g General Monash (USA)-Gulf Craft (IRE) (Petorius)
D Brace David Brace

Placings:06-0P   (1713)
2002/03: 17[0]G, 16[P]G,

	Starts	1st	2nd	3rd	Win & Pl
Hurdles	2	0	0	0	
Career Total	4	0	0	0	

Going: Sf: 0-0 GS: 0-0 Gd: 0-2 GF: - Fm: 0-0
Distance: 2m/2m3: 0-2 2m4-2m7: 0-0 3m+: 0-0
Track: LH: 0-1 RH: 0-1 Tight: 0-1 Gall: 0-0
Aids: Bl: 0-1 Vi: 0-0 Tstrap: 0-0
Best Rating: 75 10/01 Chep 2m110y   good Hdl

New Leader (IRE)

107   88

6-y-o b g Supreme Leader-Two Spots (Deep Run)
Mrs L Richards E T Wright

Placings:00020   (4595)
2002/03: 17[0]S, 18[0]S, 21[0]G, 25[2]GF, 22[0]GF,

	Starts	1st	2nd	3rd	Win & Pl
NH Flat	2	0	0	0	
Hurdles	3	0	1	0	1099
Career Total	5	0	1	0	1099

Going: Sf: 0-2 GS: 0-0 Gd: 0-1 GF: - Fm: 0-2
Distance: 2m/2m3: 0-2 2m4-2m7: 0-2 3m+: 0-1
Track: LH: 0-2 RH: 0-3 Tight: 0-2 Gall: 0-0
Aids: Bl: 0-0 Vi: 0-0 Tstrap: 0-0
Best Rating: 88 3/03 Wwck 3m1f   gd-fm Hdl

Novice hurdler; stays three miles; acts on fast ground.

New Leaf (IRE)

11-y-o b g Brush Aside (USA)-Page Of Gold (Goldhill)
J S Papworth (D R Gandolfo 12/5) J S Papworth

Placings:0261/254504/332313/2/3300/0-P   (3876)
2002/03: 24PS,

	Starts	1st	2nd	3rd	Win & Pl
Chases	1	0	0	0	
Career Total	23	2	4	6	16276
101 11/98 Asct	3m110y CHCh			GD	£6807
97 3/97 Carl	2m1f	E Hdl		G-S	£2122
		Total win prize-money £8930			

Going: Sf: 0-1 GS: 0-0 Gd: 0-0 GF: - Fm: 0-0
Distance: 2m/2m3: 0-0 2m4-2m7: 0-0 3m+: 0-1
Track: LH: 0-1 RH: 0-0 Tight: 0-0 Gall: 0-1
Aids: Bl: 0-0 Vi: 0-0 Tstrap: 0-0
Best Rating: 104 2/97 Newb 2m110y   good   NHF

New Mischief (IRE)
86f   84f

5-y-o b g Accordion-Alone Party (IRE) (Phardante (FR))
Noel T Chance W B Stawell

Placings:4   (2045)
2002/03: 17⁴HY,

	Starts	1st	2nd	3rd	Win & Pl
NH Flat	1	0	0	0	0
Career Total	1	0	0	0	0

Going: Sf: 0-1 GS: 0-0 Gd: 0-0 GF: - Fm: 0-0
Distance: 2m/2m3: 0-1 2m4-2m7: 0-0 3m+: 0-0
Track: LH: 0-1 RH: 0-0 Tight: 0-0 Gall: 0-0
Aids: Bl: 0-0 Vi: 0-0 Tstrap: 0-1
Best Rating: 84 11/02 NAbb 2m1f   heavy NHF

New Openings

4-y-o b c Puissance-Moushka (Song)
I W McInnes P T Midgley

Placings:P   (1205)
2002/03: 16PG,

	Starts	1st	2nd	3rd	Win & Pl
Hurdles	1	0	0	0	
Career Total	1	0	0	0	

Going: Sf: 0-0 GS: 0-0 Gd: 0-1 GF: - Fm: 0-0
Distance: 2m/2m3: 0-1 2m4-2m7: 0-0 3m+: 0-0
Track: LH: 0-1 RH: 0-0 Tight: 0-0 Gall: 0-0
Aids: Bl: 0-0 Vi: 0-0 Tstrap: 0-0
Best Rating: 0 9/02 Uttx 2m   good   Hdl

New Perk (IRE)
106   90

5-y-o b g Executive Perk-New Cello (IRE) (Orchestra)
M J Gingell A White

Placings:55026   (4631)
2002/03: 18⁵G, 20⁵GS, 16⁰S, 18²S, 16⁶GF,

	Starts	1st	2nd	3rd	Win & Pl
Hurdles	5	0	1	0	1108
Career Total	5	0	1	0	1108

Going: Sf: 0-2 GS: 0-1 Gd: 0-1 GF: - Fm: 0-1
Distance: 2m/2m3: 0-4 2m4-2m7: 0-1 3m+: 0-0
Track: LH: 0-5 RH: 0-0 Tight: 0-5 Gall: 0-0
Aids: Bl: 0-0 Vi: 0-0 Tstrap: 0-0
Best Rating: 90 3/03 Font 2m2f110y soft   Hdl

Plating-class hurdler; stays two and a half miles; suited by
soft ground.

New Rising
101   101

11-y-o b g Primitive Rising (USA)-Saucy (Muhtarram (USA))
P Winkworth Bill Naylor

Placings:5F43/0F/433254454/42412/FPP04P-P342FP   (3946)
2002/03: 23PG, 25³GF, 29⁴GS, 26²HY, 26FGS, 30PS,

	Starts	1st	2nd	3rd	Win & Pl
Chases	6	0	1	1	2225
Career Total	32	1	4	4	20978
116 1/01 Fknm	3m5f110yC(0-130)HCh			SFT	£6630
		Total win prize-money £6630			

Going: Sf: 0-2 GS: 0-2 Gd: 0-1 GF: - Fm: 0-1
Distance: 2m/2m3: 0-0 2m4-2m7: 0-0 3m+: 0-6
Track: LH: 0-0 RH: 0-3 Tight: 0-3 Gall: 0-0
Aids: Bl: 0-0 Vi: 0-5 Tstrap: 0-0
Best Rating: 116 3/01 Ling 3m4f110y heavy Ch

Moderate handicap chaser; rather slow, he requires a real
test of stamina; suited by heavy ground; usually visored.

New Ross (IRE)

11-y-o gr g Roselier (FR)-Miss Lucille (Fine Blade (USA))
Mrs A W K Merriam A W K Merriam

Placings:0/50/6U3U/P   (0311)
2002/03: 26PG,

	Starts	1st	2nd	3rd	Win & Pl
Chases	1	0	0	0	
Career Total	8	0	0	1	270

Going: Sf: 0-0 GS: 0-0 Gd: 0-1 GF: - Fm: 0-0
Distance: 2m/2m3: 0-0 2m4-2m7: 0-0 3m+: 0-1
Track: LH: 0-0 RH: 0-1 Tight: 0-1 Gall: 0-0
Aids: Bl: 0-0 Vi: 0-0 Tstrap: 0-0
Best Rating: 71 5/97 Ludl 2m   gd-fm Hdl

Newby End (IRE)
100   81

9-y-o br g Over The River (FR)-Comeallye (Kambalda)
M Madgwick J D Brownrigg

Placings:4/20/P6322P4/00/204/P52P30   (3824)
2002/03: 20PGS, 16⁵S, 22²G, 24PS, 25³S, 26⁹GS,

	Starts	1st	2nd	3rd	Win & Pl
Hurdles	1	0	0	0	
Chases	5	0	1	1	1805
Career Total	21	0	5	2	5203

Going: Sf: 0-3 GS: 0-2 Gd: 0-1 GF: - Fm: 0-0
Distance: 2m/2m3: 0-1 2m4-2m7: 0-2 3m+: 0-3
Track: LH: 0-2 RH: 0-2 Tight: 0-4 Gall: 0-0
Aids: Bl: 0-0 Vi: 0-2 Tstrap: 0-0
Best Rating: 107 12/98 Towc 2m5f   soft   Hdl

Modest pointer/novice chaser; best at around two miles six.

Newhall (IRE)
117   134

5-y-o b m Shernazar-Graffogue (IRE) (Red Sunset)
F Flood Mrs H McParland

Placings:3121232-06F4260   (4742a)
2002/03: 16⁰S, 16⁶HY, 16²S, 20⁴HY, 16²HY, 16⁶G, 16⁰G,

	Starts	1st	2nd	3rd	Win & Pl
Hurdles	7	0	1	0	12042

Career Total   14   2   4   2   97566
135 2/02 Leop 2m   Hdl   HVY £16748
117 12/01 Leop 2m   Hdl   YLD £20967
              Total win prize-money £37716

Going: Sf: 0-5 GS: 0-0 Gd: 0-2 GF: - Fm: 0-0
Distance: 2m/2m3: 0-6 2m4-2m7: 0-1 3m+: 0-0
Track: LH: 0-3 RH: 0-4 Tight: 0-1 Gall: 0-0
Aids: Bl: 0-0 Vi: 0-0 Tstrap: 0-0
Best Rating: 135 2/02 Leop 2m   heavy Hdl

Useful Irish-trained hurdler; runner-up in the 2002 Triumph
Hurdle, but has not won since; acts on ground ranging from
fast to heavy; effective over two miles.

Newick Park
95   99

8-y-o gr g Chilibang-Quilpee Mai (Pee Mai)
D M Grissell Newick Park Partnership

Placings:151P/1616P-534PP   (4282)
2002/03: 20⁵GS, 21³G, 24⁴S, 21PGS, 18PGF,

	Starts	1st	2nd	3rd	Win & Pl
Chases	5	0	0	1	2599
Career Total	14	4	0	1	16038
110 12/01 Sand	2m4f110yD(0-115)HCh			G-S	£5694
95 10/01 Folk	2m	E Ch		GD	£3406
100 11/00 Folk	2m1f110yE Hdl			HVY	£2390
105 6/00 Folk	2m1f110yF Hdl			GD	£1948
		Total win prize-money £13440			

Going: Sf: 0-1 GS: 0-2 Gd: 0-1 GF: - Fm: 0-1
Distance: 2m/2m3: 0-1 2m4-2m7: 0-3 3m+: 0-1
Track: LH: 0-2 RH: 0-2 Tight: 0-1 Gall: 0-2
Aids: Bl: 0-0 Vi: 0-0 Tstrap: 0-0
Best Rating: 110 12/01 Sand 2m4f110y gd-sft Ch

Moderate chaser; suited by two to two and a half miles and
cut in the ground.

Newkidontheblock (IRE)
94   80

8-y-o b g Be My Native (USA)-Jenny s Child (Crash Course)
J R Jenkins R M Ellis

Placings:106/65/5-2   (0510)
2002/03: 20²G,

	Starts	1st	2nd	3rd	Win & Pl
Hurdles	1	0	1	0	772
Career Total	7	1	1	0	2466
99 3/00 Hntg	2m110y H NHF			G-F	£1694
		Total win prize-money £1694			

Going: Sf: 0-0 GS: 0-0 Gd: 0-1 GF: - Fm: 0-0
Distance: 2m/2m3: 0-0 2m4-2m7: 0-1 3m+: 0-0
Track: LH: 0-1 RH: 0-0 Tight: 0-0 Gall: 0-0
Aids: Bl: 0-0 Vi: 0-0 Tstrap: 0-0
Best Rating: 107 4/00 Font 2m2f110y good NHF

Newlands Gold (IRE)
109   123

4-y-o ch c Goldmark (USA)-Persian Polly (Persian Bold)
M J P O Brien S Mulryan

Placings:12160   (4130)
2002/03: 16¹S, 16²HY, 16¹S, 16⁵S, 17⁰G,

	Starts	1st	2nd	3rd	Win & Pl
Hurdles	5	2	1	0	16276
Career Total	5	2	1	0	16276

116 1/03 Naas 2m Hdl SFT £8441
115 11/02 Navn 2m Hdl SFT £5503
Total win prize-money £13945

Going:	Sf: 2-4 GS: 0-0 Gd: 0-1 GF: - Fm: 0-0
Distance:	**2m/2m3: 2-5** 2m4-2m7: 0-0 3m+: 0-0
Track:	LH: **2-5** RH: 0-0 Tight: 0-0 Gall: 0-1
Aids:	Bl: **2-4** Vi: 0-0 Tstrap: 0-0
Best Rating:	**123** 3/03 Chel 2m1f good Hdl

Useful Irish juvenile hurdler; effective in soft ground; usually blinkered.

Newryman

94   (22c)**61**

8-y-o ch g Statoblest-With Love (Be My Guest (USA))
G P Kelly G P Kelly

Placings: 0/000P/0P/000-06P05   (1384)
2002/03: 17⁹GF, 17⁵G, 17⁸GF, 17⁰GF, 16⁵GF,

	Starts	1st	2nd	3rd	Win & Pl
Hurdles	4	0	0	0	0
Chases	1	0	0	0	0
Career Total	15	0	0	0	0

Going:	Sf: 0-0 GS: 0-0 Gd: 0-1 GF: - Fm: 0-4
Distance:	2m/2m3: 0-5 2m4-2m7: 0-0 3m+: 0-0
Track:	LH: 0-3 RH: 0-2 Tight: 0-3 Gall: 0-0
Aids:	Bl: 0-0 Vi: 0-0 Tstrap: 0-4
Best Rating:	64 11/99 Weth 2m good NHF

News Flash (IRE)

96   (84c)**81**

11-y-o b g Strong Gale-Gale Flash (News Item)
E R Clough E R Clough

Placings: 0/0F6/P/455FU   (1906)
2002/03: 20⁴GF, 24⁵G, 16⁵GF, 19⁸G, 20⁰GS,

	Starts	1st	2nd	3rd	Win & Pl
Hurdles	3	0	0	0	0
Chases	2	0	0	0	0
Career Total	10	0	0	0	0

Going:	Sf: 0-0 GS: 0-1 Gd: 0-2 GF: - Fm: 0-2
Distance:	2m/2m3: 0-1 2m4-2m7: 0-3 3m+: 0-1
Track:	LH: 0-5 RH: 0-0 Tight: 0-1 Gall: 0-0
Aids:	Bl: 0-0 Vi: 0-0 Tstrap: 0-0
Best Rating:	86 11/97 Newb 2m110y good Hdl

News Maker (IRE)

106(105h)   (107h)**129+**

7-y-o b g Good Thyne (USA)-Announcement (Laurence O)
Mrs H Dalton Mrs Caroline Shaw

Placings: 301334-2121P   (4174)
2002/03: 24²G, 24¹S, 26²HY, 23¹G, 26⁸S,

	Starts	1st	2nd	3rd	Win & Pl
Chases	5	2	2	0	17358
Career Total	11	3	2	3	21038
129	3/03	Weth	2m7f110yD Ch		GD £6624
126	12/02	Hayd	3m	D(0-110)HCh	SFT £5018
100	12/01	Uttx	2m4f110yE Hdl		SFT £2681
				Total win prize-money	£14323

Going:	Sf: 1-3 GS: 0-0 Gd: 1-2 GF: - Fm: 0-0
Distance:	2m/2m3: 0-0 2m4-2m7: 0-0 **3m+: 2-5**
Track:	LH: **1-4** RH: 0-0 Tight: 0-0 Gall: 0-1
Aids:	Bl: 0-0 Vi: 0-0 Tstrap: 0-0
Best Rating:	**129** 3/03 Weth 2m7f110y good Ch

Modest hurdler/decent chaser; acts on soft ground; stays three miles.

Newsplayer (IRE)

104(100h)   (91h)**96+**

7-y-o br g Alphabatim (USA)-Another Tycoon (IRE) (Phardante (FR))
R T Phillips Bradley, Dale, Deal, Hirschfeld

Placings: 0/30-5003   (4014)
2002/03: 16⁵G, 20⁹GS, 16⁹GS, 16³S,

	Starts	1st	2nd	3rd	Win & Pl
Hurdles	4	0	0	1	382
Career Total	7	0	0	2	674

Going:	Sf: 0-1 GS: 0-2 Gd: 0-1 GF: - Fm: 0-0
Distance:	2m/2m3: 0-3 2m4-2m7: 0-1 3m+: 0-0
Track:	LH: 0-3 RH: 0-1 Tight: 0-1 Gall: 0-0
Aids:	Bl: 0-0 Vi: 0-0 Tstrap: 0-0
Best Rating:	102 3/02 Ludl 2m soft NHF

Has shown ability in bumpers and novice hurdles; jumped right on chasing debut July 2003; does not appear to stay 2m4f.

Newton Commanche (IRE)

95   85

6-y-o b m Commanche Run-Ravens Way (Niels)
K C Bailey J H And N J Foxon

Placings: 6630-34   (1609)
2002/03: 16³GF, 20⁴G,

	Starts	1st	2nd	3rd	Win & Pl
Hurdles	2	0	0	1	427
Career Total	6	0	0	2	647

Going:	Sf: 0-0 GS: 0-0 Gd: 0-1 GF: - Fm: 0-1
Distance:	2m/2m3: 0-1 2m4-2m7: 0-1 3m+: 0-0
Track:	LH: 0-2 RH: 0-0 Tight: 0-1 Gall: 0-0
Aids:	Bl: 0-0 Vi: 0-0 Tstrap: 0-0
Best Rating:	91 4/02 Fknm 2m good NHF

Modest form in bumpers and over hurdles.

Newtown Dancer (IRE)

100   **109+**

4-y-o b f Danehill Dancer (IRE)-Patience Of Angels (IRE) (Distinctly North (USA))
T Hogan Mrs Josephine Hogan

Placings: 21   (1739)
2002/03: 16²G, 16¹GS,

	Starts	1st	2nd	3rd	Win & Pl
Hurdles	2	1	1	0	12154
Career Total	2	1	1	0	12154
104	11/02	Weth	2m	A Hdl	G-S £10387
				Total win prize-money	£10387

Going:	Sf: 0-0 GS: 1-1 Gd: 0-0 GF: - Fm: 0-1
Distance:	**2m/2m3: 1-2** 2m4-2m7: 0-0 3m+: 0-0
Track:	**LH: 1-2** RH: 0-0 Tight: 0-0 Gall: 0-0
Aids:	Bl: 0-0 Vi: 0-0 Tstrap: 0-0
Best Rating:	109 9/02 List 2m firm Hdl

Middle-distance winner on the Flat in Ireland, runner-up on his hurdling debut before winning at Wetherby in November 2002 on easy ground.

Newtownhen (IRE)

8-y-o b m Peacock (FR)-Cutty Sark (Strong Gale)
A C Whillans Stephen Gilchrist

Placings: PPP-PP   (1634)
2002/03: 25⁸GF, 20⁸S,

	Starts	1st	2nd	3rd	Win & Pl
Chases	2	0	0	0	
Career Total	5	0	0	0	

Going:	Sf: 0-1 GS: 0-0 Gd: 0-0 GF: - Fm: 0-1
Distance:	2m/2m3: 0-0 2m4-2m7: 0-1 3m+: 0-1
Track:	LH: 0-1 RH: 0-1 Tight: 0-1 Gall: 0-0
Aids:	Bl: 0-0 Vi: 0-0 Tstrap: 0-0
Best Rating:	0 10/02 Carl 2m4f soft Ch

Next To Nothing (IRE)

6-y-o b g Bob s Return (IRE)-Shuil Abhaile (Quayside)
N G Richards Ashleybank Investments Limited

Placings: 5P   (4304)
2002/03: 17⁵S, 22⁷G,

	Starts	1st	2nd	3rd	Win & Pl
NH Flat	1	0	0	0	0
Hurdles	1	0	0	0	0
Career Total	2	0	0	0	0

Going:	Sf: 0-1 GS: 0-0 Gd: 0-1 GF: - Fm: 0-0
Distance:	2m/2m3: 0-1 2m4-2m7: 0-1 3m+: 0-0
Track:	LH: 0-1 RH: 0-1 Tight: 0-1 Gall: 0-0
Aids:	Bl: 0-0 Vi: 0-0 Tstrap: 0-0
Best Rating:	94 3/03 Carl 2m1f soft NHF

Niagara (IRE)

106   104

6-y-o b g Rainbows For Life (CAN)-Highbrook (USA) (Alphabatim (USA))
M H Tompkins Pollards Stables

Placings: 2-2P40   (4608)
2002/03: 16²G, 16⁸PGS, 16⁴G, 17⁰G,

	Starts	1st	2nd	3rd	Win & Pl
Hurdles	4	0	1	0	1422
Career Total	5	0	2	0	2238

Going:	Sf: 0-0 GS: 0-1 Gd: 0-3 GF: - Fm: 0-0
Distance:	2m/2m3: 0-4 2m4-2m7: 0-0 3m+: 0-0
Track:	LH: 0-2 RH: 0-2 Tight: 0-1 Gall: 0-2
Aids:	Bl: 0-0 Vi: 0-0 Tstrap: 0-0
Best Rating:	104 3/03 Asct 2m110y good Hdl

Moderate hurdler; acts on fast ground; best at two miles; front runner.

Nice Approach (IRE)

10-y-o ch g Over The River (FR)-Gayles Approach (Strong Gale)
J W Dufosee Nice Approach Partnership

Placings: 2P0/3U5P3P0/50205P00P/40P/P2P-P   (0179)

2002/03: 21PGF,

	Starts	1st	2nd	3rd	Win & Pl
Chases	1	0	0		
Career Total	26	0	3	2	3391

Going:	Sf: 0-0 GS: 0-0 Gd: 0-0 GF: - Fm: 0-1
Distance:	2m/2m3: 0-0 2m4-2m7: 0-1 3m+: 0-0
Track:	LH: 0-0 RH: 0-1 Tight: 0-0 Gall: 0-0
Aids:	Bl: 0-0 Vi: 0-0 Tstrap: 0-0
Best Rating:	87 12/97 NAbb 2m1f heavy NHF

Nice One Ted (IRE)

7-y-o b g Posen (USA)-Arburie (Exbury)
Mrs Pippa Bickerton David Bickerton

Placings: 400P   (4641)
2002/03: 174GF, 160GS, 170S, 19PGF,

	Starts	1st	2nd	3rd	Win & Pl
NH Flat	3	0	0	0	0
Hurdles	1	0	0	0	0
Career Total	4	0	0	0	0

Going:	Sf: 0-1 GS: 0-1 Gd: 0-0 GF: - Fm: 0-2
Distance:	2m/2m3: 0-4 2m4-2m7: 0-0 3m+: 0-0
Track:	LH: 0-1 RH: 0-3 Tight: 0-1 Gall: 0-0
Aids:	Bl: 0-0 Vi: 0-0 Tstrap: 0-0
Best Rating:	77 10/02 Hrfd 2m1f gd-fm NHF

Nicely Presented (IRE)

100f   **100f**

6-y-o b g Executive Perk-Minimum Choice (IRE) (Miners Lamp)
Jonjo O Neill J P McManus

Placings: 433   (3337)
2002/03: 174G, 179GS, 173S,

	Starts	1st	2nd	3rd	Win & Pl
NH Flat	3	0	0	2	643
Career Total	3	0	0	2	643

Going:	Sf: 0-1 GS: 0-0 Gd: 0-1 GF: - Fm: 0-0
Distance:	2m/2m3: 0-3 2m4-2m7: 0-0 3m+: 0-0
Track:	LH: 0-1 RH: 0-1 Tight: 0-1 Gall: 0-0
Aids:	Bl: 0-0 Vi: 0-0 Tstrap: 0-0
Best Rating:	100 1/03 Tntn 2m1f soft NHF

Has struggled to see out the trip in bumpers and should do better over hurdles.

Nichol Fifty

93   **90**

9-y-o b g Old Vic-Jawaher (IRE) (Dancing Brave (USA))
N Wilson (D Nicholls 11/5) E J Govan and Mrs N C Wilson

Placings: 41P/00/P-305   (2067)
2002/03: 213GF, 170G, 215GS,

	Starts	1st	2nd	3rd	Win & Pl
Hurdles	3	0	0	1	567
Career Total	9	1	0	1	3758
114	3/98	MRas	2m1f110yD Hdl		G-S	£2979

Total win prize-money £2980

Going:	Sf: 0-0 GS: 0-1 Gd: 0-1 GF: - Fm: 0-1
Distance:	2m/2m3: 0-1 2m4-2m7: 0-2 3m+: 0-0
Track:	LH: 0-2 RH: 0-1 Tight: 0-3 Gall: 0-0
Aids:	Bl: 0-0 Vi: 0-0 Tstrap: 0-0

Best Rating: 114   3/98   MRas   2m1f110y   gd-sft   Hdl

Selling hurdler, largely out of form.

Nicholas Plant

97 (100h)   (64h) **84**

14-y-o ch g Nicholas Bill-Bustilly (Busted)
J S Goldie Miss M F Callaghan

Placings: 30/6P400/64414100 1/3000U05563/012613355U1 22222/13UFF21U5U/053/PP0PF/P340P0P/6PP524U65-45
                              (0452)
2002/03: 24SG, 274G, 20SG,

	Starts	1st	2nd	3rd	Win & Pl
Hurdles	1	0	0	0	271
Chases	2	0	0	0	0
Career Total	78	8	8	8	36668
117	3/98	Ayr	2m4f	D(0-120)HCh	SFT	£3880
112	5/97	Weth	2m4f110yC(0-130)HCh		G-S	£4532
109	2/97	Ayr	2m4f	D(0-125)HCh	SFT	£3522
100	10/96	Kels	2m6f110yD(0-120)HHdl		FRM	£2528
104	5/96	Hexm	2m4f110yE(0-110)HHdl		G-F	£2005
108	5/95	Hexm	2m4f110yD(0-110)HHdl		G-S	£3027
89	2/95	Ayr	2m	F(0-105)HHdl	HVY	£2696
74	1/95	Ayr	2m	G(0-90)HHdl	SFT	£2379

Total win prize-money £24571

Going:	Sf: 0-0 GS: 0-0 Gd: 0-3 GF: - Fm: 0-0
Distance:	2m/2m3: 0-0 2m4-2m7: 0-1 3m+: 0-2
Track:	LH: 0-3 RH: 0-0 Tight: 0-1 Gall: 0-1
Aids:	Bl: 0-0 Vi: 0-0 Tstrap: 0-0
Best Rating:	117 3/98 Ayr 2m4f soft Ch

Veteran handicap chaser who is on the downgrade. All his wins have been gained on left-handed tracks and he is indifferent to the state of the ground.

Nicholls Cross (IRE)

11-y-o b g Mandalus-Milan Pride (Northern Guest (USA))
S Wynne (E J O Grady 6/9) D A Malam

Placings: 4/40224/F31F21/3633F611U33F3/0533F526424/ 030004300-B651506   (3955)
2002/03: 24BGF, 23BYS, 24SGF, 251YS, 225GF, 259GF, 26SGS,

	Starts	1st	2nd	3rd	Win & Pl
Chases	7	1	0	0	5503
Career Total	52	5	5	11	54153
110	8/02	Kbgn	3m1f	(0-109)HCh	Y-S	£5503
128	10/99	Gowr	2m	(0-116)HCh	G-Y	£6776
135	9/99	List	2m3f	(0-123)HCh	HVY	£5544
119	9/98	Bang	2m1f	Ch	G-Y	£5978
112	7/98	Klny	2m1f	(0-109)HHdl	G-F	£2690

Total win prize-money £26493

Going:	Sf: 0-0 GS: 0-0 Gd: 0-0 GF: - Fm: 0-4
Distance:	2m/2m3: 0-0 2m4-2m7: 0-0 3m+: 1-4
Track:	LH: 0-0 RH: 0-3 Tight: 0-0 Gall: 0-0
Aids:	Bl: 0-0 Vi: 0-0 Tstrap: 0-0
Best Rating:	135 9/99 List 2m3f heavy Ch

Moderate ex-Irish chaser; stays three miles; acts on any ground.

Nick The Jewel

109 (66h)   (36h) **110**

8-y-o b g Nicholas Bill-Bijou Georgie (Rhodomantade)
J S King Marlborough Racing Partnership

Placings: 0F004-P111FP03   (4342)
2002/03: 19PGF, 161G, 161S, 161GS, 16FGS, 19PS, 169G, 163GF,

	Starts	1st	2nd	3rd	Win & Pl
Chases	8	3	0	1	13249

	Career Total		13	3	0	1	13515
108	12/02	Hntg	2m110y	E(0-105)HCh	G-S	£3545
110	11/02	Hrfd	2m	E(0-105)HCh	SFT	£4446
110	11/02	Ludl	2m	E(0-105)HCh	GD	£4433

Total win prize-money £12425

Going:	Sf: 1-2 GS: 1-2 Gd: 1-2 GF: - Fm: 0-2
Distance:	2m/2m3: 3-8 2m4-2m7: 0-0 3m+: 0-0
Track:	LH: 0-0 RH: 3-8 Tight: 1-3 Gall: 1-3
Aids:	Bl: 0-0 Vi: 0-0 Tstrap: 0-0
Best Rating:	110 3/03 Hntg 2m110y gd-fm Ch

Modest novice chaser at around two miles; acts on good and soft ground.

Nick's Choice

102   **110**

7-y-o b g Sula Bula-Clare s Choice (Pragmatic)
D Burchell Don Gould

Placings: 343005263/P0134/421P00611F-50601   (4194)
2002/03: 16SHY, 16AGS, 16BG, 22OS, 21TG,

	Starts	1st	2nd	3rd	Win & Pl
Hurdles	5	1	0	0	3552
Career Total	29	5	2	4	18495
99	3/03	Ludl	2m5f	E(0-105)HHdl	GD	£3552
110	3/02	Hrfd	2m3f110yF(0-100)HHdl		SFT	£3653
94	2/02	Tntn	2m1f	E(0-105)HHdl	SFT	£2782
101	5/01	Bang	2m4f	F(0-100)HHdl	GD	£2530
92	3/01	Extr	2m1f	F(0-100)HHdl	HVY	£2506

Total win prize-money £15025

Going:	Sf: 0-3 GS: 0-1 Gd: 1-1 GF: - Fm: 0-0
Distance:	2m/2m3: 0-2 2m4-2m7: 1-2 3m+: 0-0
Track:	LH: 0-2 RH: 1-3 Tight: 0-1 Gall: 0-0
Aids:	Bl: 0-0 Vi: 0-0 Tstrap: 0-0
Best Rating:	115 3/02 NAbb 2m1f good Hdl

Modest hurdler; stays two and a half miles and acts on good and heavy ground. Comes good in the spring.

Nickel Sun (IRE)

115   **124**

7-y-o b g Phardante (FR)-Deep Green (Deep Run)
Mrs S J Smith Keith Nicholson

Placings: 22153512-11010433   (4607)
2002/03: 201GF, 201G, 22OS, 201G, 19OGS, 204G, 223GF, 213G,

	Starts	1st	2nd	3rd	Win & Pl
Hurdles	8	3	0	2	32306
Career Total	16	5	3	3	39005
120	12/02	Hayd	2m4f	B HHdl	GD	£16835
120	5/02	Uttx	2m4f110yB(0-140)HHdl		GD	£6854
111	5/02	Weth	2m4f110yD Hdl		G-F	£3605
103	4/02	Carl	2m1f	E Hdl	GD	£2973
96	9/01	MRas	2m1f110yH NHF		SFT	£1596

Total win prize-money £31865

Going:	Sf: 0-1 GS: 0-1 Gd: 2-4 GF: - Fm: 1-2
Distance:	2m/2m3: 0-0 2m4-2m7: 3-8 3m+: 0-0
Track:	LH: 3-8 RH: 0-0 Tight: 0-0 Gall: 0-1
Aids:	Bl: 0-0 Vi: 0-0 Tstrap: 0-0
Best Rating:	122 4/03 Chel 2m5f110y good Hdl

Decent hurdler; stays two miles four; acts on most types of ground.

Nickel Sundancer

99   **70**

7-y-o b g Alflora (IRE)-Gunna Be Precious (Gunner B)
Mrs S J Smith Keith Nicholson

Placings: 03P-00556   (4621)

2002/03: 19⁰GS, 16⁰HY, 25⁵G, 27⁵G, 20⁶GF,

	Starts	1st	2nd	3rd	Win & Pl
Hurdles	5	0	0	0	0
Career Total	8	0	0	1	428

Going: Sf: 0-1 GS: 0-1 Gd: 0-2 GF: - Fm: 0-1
Distance: 2m/2m3: 0-1 2m4-2m7: 0-2 3m+: 0-2
Track: LH: 0-3 RH: 0-2 Tight: 0-3 Gall: 0-1
Aids: Bl: 0-0 Vi: 0-0 Tstrap: 0-0
Best Rating: 84 11/01 MRas 2m1f110y gd-sft Hdl

Poor novice hurdler; connections seem to be having trouble finding his trip.

Nickel Suntoo (IRE)
94   82+
6-y-o b g Convinced-The Scarlet Dragon (Oats)
Mrs S J Smith Keith Nicholson

Placings:200   (3167)
2002/03: 16²GS, 16⁹GS, 16⁹G,

	Starts	1st	2nd	3rd	Win & Pl
NH Flat	3	0	1	0	681
Career Total	3	0	1	0	681

Going: Sf: 0-0 GS: 0-2 Gd: 0-1 GF: - Fm: 0-0
Distance: 2m/2m3: 0-3 2m4-2m7: 0-0 3m+: 0-0
Track: LH: 0-3 RH: 0-0 Tight: 0-2 Gall: 0-1
Aids: Bl: 0-0 Vi: 0-0 Tstrap: 0-0
Best Rating: 97 11/02 Sthl 2m gd-sft NHF

Modest form in bumpers; runner-up to very easy winner in weak novices hurdle at Market Rasen in June.

Nickit (IRE)
106(89h)   (84h)85
7-y-o gr g Roselier (FR)-Run Trix (Deep Run)
Miss Venetia Williams John Nicholls (banbury) Ltd

Placings:4060-2F43F3   (4252)
2002/03: 23²GS, 23⁵F, 26⁴S, 22³S, 25⁵FS, 22³G,

	Starts	1st	2nd	3rd	Win & Pl
Hurdles	1	0	0	1	658
Chases	5	0	1	1	1857
Career Total	10	0	1	2	2515

Going: Sf: 0-4 GS: 0-1 Gd: 0-1 GF: - Fm: 0-0
Distance: 2m/2m3: 0-0 2m4-2m7: 0-2 3m+: 0-4
Track: LH: 0-1 RH: 0-4 Tight: 0-3 Gall: 0-0
Aids: Bl: 0-1 Vi: 0-0 Tstrap: 0-0
Best Rating: 88 2/03 Font 2m6f soft Ch

Plating-class chaser; acts on soft ground; not the best of jumpers; made mistakes when reverting to hurdles at Exeter March 2003.

Nicodemus
9-y-o br g St Ninian-Qurrat Al Ain (Wolver Hollow)
K F Clutterbuck K F Clutterbuck

Placings:500/005/PP   (1244)
2002/03: 23³PG, 24⁷G,

	Starts	1st	2nd	3rd	Win & Pl
Hurdles	1	0	0	0	0
Chases	1	0	0	0	0
Career Total	8	0	0	0	0

Going: Sf: 0-0 GS: 0-0 Gd: 0-2 GF: - Fm: 0-0

Nigel's Boy
11-y-o b g Bold Fort-Furnace Lass Vii (Damsire Unregistered)
Miss Victoria Scott Miss Victoria Scott

Placings:06/0001000/2   (0245)
2002/03: 25²G,

	Starts	1st	2nd	3rd	Win & Pl
Chases	1	0	1	0	1088
Career Total	10	1	1	0	1088
75 12/99 Tntn 3m110y G(0-90)HHdl SFT £1616

Total win prize-money £1616

Going: Sf: 0-0 GS: 0-0 Gd: 0-1 GF: - Fm: 0-0
Distance: 2m/2m3: 0-0 2m4-2m7: 0-0 3m+: 0-1
Track: LH: 0-0 RH: 0-1 Tight: 0-0 Gall: 0-0
Aids: Bl: 0-0 Vi: 0-0 Tstrap: 0-0
Best Rating: 92 5/02 Extr 3m1f110y good Ch

Lightly raced pointer, acts on any ground.

Night Diamond
78   64
6-y-o b g Night Shift (USA)-Dashing Water (Dashing Blade)
M C Pipe Tweenhills Racing (foscombe Syndicate)

Placings:P6   (1400)
2002/03: 16⁵GF, 16⁶GF,

	Starts	1st	2nd	3rd	Win & Pl
Hurdles	2	0	0	0	0
Career Total	2	0	0	0	0

Going: Sf: 0-0 GS: 0-0 Gd: 0-0 GF: - Fm: 0-2
Distance: 2m/2m3: 0-2 2m4-2m7: 0-0 3m+: 0-0
Track: LH: 0-1 RH: 0-1 Tight: 0-0 Gall: 0-0
Aids: Bl: 0-0 Vi: 0-0 Tstrap: 0-1
Best Rating: 64 10/02 Uttx 2m gd-fm Hdl

Winner on the Flat but has shown no aptitude for hurdling.

Night Driver (IRE)
95   91
4-y-o b g Night Shift (USA)-Highshaan (Pistolet Bleu (IRE))
P J Hobbs (B W Hills 21/10) Colin Brown Racing Ii

Placings:44   (4001)
2002/03: 17⁴S, 16⁴S,

	Starts	1st	2nd	3rd	Win & Pl
Hurdles	2	0	0	0	714
Career Total	2	0	0	0	714

Going: Sf: 0-2 GS: 0-0 Gd: 0-0 GF: - Fm: 0-0
Distance: 2m/2m3: 0-2 2m4-2m7: 0-0 3m+: 0-0
Track: LH: 0-0 RH: 0-2 Tight: 0-1 Gall: 0-0
Aids: Bl: 0-0 Vi: 0-0 Tstrap: 0-0
Best Rating: 82 3/03 Winc 2m soft Hdl

Night Fighter (GER)
105(104h)   (114+h)114
8-y-o b g Dashing Blade-Nouvelle (GER) (Nandino (GER))
R C Guest (N B Mason 12/2) N B Mason

Placings:060/2240056/P/121F44305-301P222314F0U
                                  (4763)
2002/03: 20³GS, 17⁰GF, 17¹G, 20⁸GF, 16²GF, 17²GS, 16²GS, 16³G, 16¹G, 20⁴S, 20⁷G, 16⁶G, 16⁰G,

	Starts	1st	2nd	3rd	Win & Pl
Hurdles	4	1	1	1	6306
Chases	9	1	2	1	9433
Career Total	33	4	6	3	22521
114 2/03 Donc 2m110y D(0-110)HCh GD £5443
114 8/02 Ctml 2m1f110yD(0-120)HHdl GD £4533
106 10/01 Towc 2m F(0-100)HHdl GD £2723
98 9/01 Worc 2m G(0-90)HHdl G-F £1671

Total win prize-money £14373

Going: Sf: 0-1 GS: 0-3 Gd: 2-6 GF: - Fm: 0-3
Distance: 2m/2m3: 2-9 2m4-2m7: 0-4 3m+: 0-0
Track: LH: 2-8 RH: 0-5 Tight: 1-6 Gall: 1-2
Aids: Bl: 0-0 Vi: 0-0 Tstrap: 1-7
Best Rating: 114 2/03 Donc 2m110y good Ch

Modest chaser; suited by trips of around two miles and good ground; usually tongue tied and wears cheekpieces; pulled up lame July 2003.

Night Music
97   74
6-y-o b/br m Piccolo-Oribi (Top Ville)
G F Edwards G F Edwards

Placings:00F4-F3P0   (4622)
2002/03: 17⁵S, 19³GS, 17⁹F, 22⁹GF,

	Starts	1st	2nd	3rd	Win & Pl
Hurdles	4	0	0	1	360
Career Total	8	0	0	1	360

Going: Sf: 0-1 GS: 0-1 Gd: 0-0 GF: - Fm: 0-2
Distance: 2m/2m3: 0-2 2m4-2m7: 0-2 3m+: 0-0
Track: LH: 0-1 RH: 0-3 Tight: 0-4 Gall: 0-0
Aids: Bl: 0-0 Vi: 0-0 Tstrap: 0-0
Best Rating: 74 2/03 Tntn 2m3f110y gd-sft Hdl

Plating-class hurdler.

Nightglade (IRE)
7-y-o b g Night Shift (USA)-Woodland Garden (Godswalk (USA))
B W Murray O R Dukes

Placings:P0P   (0700)
2002/03: 16²PGS, 16⁶G, 19⁹GF,

	Starts	1st	2nd	3rd	Win & Pl
Hurdles	3	0	0	0	0
Career Total	3	0	0	0	0

Going: Sf: 0-0 GS: 0-1 Gd: 0-1 GF: - Fm: 0-1
Distance: 2m/2m3: 0-2 2m4-2m7: 0-1 3m+: 0-0
Track: LH: 0-2 RH: 0-1 Tight: 0-2 Gall: 0-0
Aids: Bl: 0-0 Vi: 0-0 Tstrap: 0-2
Best Rating: 0 7/02 MRas 2m3f110y gd-fm Hdl

Nijway
75   40
13-y-o b g Nijin (USA)-Runaway Girl (FR) (Homeric)
M A Barnes M Barnes

Placings:00P40/P2R044241/33F06U4FU31U12P1/312405
2P13P/PUP44/1400P/S00P6060-PP   (4393)
2002/03: 24⁷PG, 20⁶PG,

	Starts	1st	2nd	3rd	Win & Pl
Hurdles	1	0	0	0	0

Chases	1	0	0	0	0
Career Total	61	7	5	5	32509
100	5/00	Sedg	3m3f	F(0-110)HCh	G-F £3955
104	3/99	Ayr	2m4f	D(0-120)HCh	SFT £3736
95	5/97	Hexm	3m1f	E(0-115)HCh	G-F £2406
98	4/97	Kels	3m1f	D(0-120)HCh	G-F £3986
90	3/97	Carl	3m	F(0-105)HCh	GD £3355
90	3/97	Sedg	2m5f	E Ch	GD £3023
86	4/96	Prth	2m110y	D(0-110)HHdl	SFT £3941

Total win prize-money £24405

Going: Sf: 0-0 GS: 0-0 Gd: 0-2 GF: - Fm: 0-0
Distance: 2m/2m3: 0-0 2m4-2m7: 0-1 3m+: 0-1
Track: LH: 0-1 RH: 0-1 Tight: 0-0 Gall: 0-0
Aids: Bl: 0-0 Vi: 0-0 Tstrap: 0-2
Best Rating: 104 3/99 Newc 3m   soft   Ch

Nikita's Gift (IRE)
29f

4-y-o ch g Topanoora-Little Nikita (Lafontaine (USA))
C F Swan Modreeny Syndicate

Placings:0   (4437)
2002/03: 16⁶G,

	Starts	1st	2nd	3rd	Win & Pl
NH Flat	1	0	0	0	0
Career Total	1	0	0	0	0

Going: Sf: 0-0 GS: 0-0 Gd: 0-1 GF: - Fm: 0-0
Distance: 2m/2m3: 0-1 2m4-2m7: 0-0 3m+: 0-0
Track: LH: 0-1 RH: 0-0 Tight: 0-0 Gall: 0-0
Aids: Bl: 0-0 Vi: 0-0 Tstrap: 0-0
Best Rating: 0 4/03 Newc 2m   good   NHF

Nikson (IRE)
85   50

7-y-o b g Elbio-Goldkrone (GER) (Wildschutz (GER))
M Pitman The Cristel Partnership

Placings:000   (3742)
2002/03: 16⁰S, 18⁰S, 16⁰G,

	Starts	1st	2nd	3rd	Win & Pl
NH Flat	1	0	0	0	0
Hurdles	2	0	0	0	0
Career Total	3	0	0	0	0

Going: Sf: 0-2 GS: 0-0 Gd: 0-1 GF: - Fm: 0-0
Distance: 2m/2m3: 0-3 2m4-2m7: 0-0 3m+: 0-0
Track: LH: 0-2 RH: 0-1 Tight: 0-1 Gall: 0-1
Aids: Bl: 0-0 Vi: 0-0 Tstrap: 0-0
Best Rating: 60 12/02 Uttx 2m   soft   NHF

Nil Desperandum (IRE)
123   145

6-y-o b g Un Desperado (FR)-Still Hoping (Kambalda)
Miss F M Crowley M L Shone

Placings:16121361   (4332a)
2002/03: 16¹G, 16⁶GS, 16¹SH, 20⁹HY, 16¹S, 18³S, 21⁶G, 22¹GY,

	Starts	1st	2nd	3rd	Win & Pl
NH Flat	2	1	0	0	3660
Hurdles	6	3	1	1	31614
Career Total	8	4	1	1	35274
122	3/03	Navn	2m6f	Hdl	G-Y £8288
137	1/03	Navn	2m	Hdl	SFT £8441
118	12/02	Punc	2m	Hdl	SH £5503

106	10/02	Rosc	2m	NHF	GD £3386

Total win prize-money £25621

Going: Sf: 1-3 GS: 0-1 Gd: 1-2 GF: - Fm: 0-0
Distance: 2m/2m3: 3-5 2m4-2m7: 1-3 3m+: 0-0
Track: LH: 2-6 RH: 1-1 Tight: 0-0 Gall: 0-1
Aids: Bl: 0-0 Vi: 0-0 Tstrap: 0-0
Best Rating: 141 3/03 Chel 2m5f   good   Hdl

Fair irish novice hurdler; best at two miles; acts on soft ground; also effective on good.

Niloufer

12-y-o br m Nader-Latanett (Dairialatan)
Mrs C Hobbs Mrs C Hobbs

Placings:2   (0392)
2002/03: 24²G,

	Starts	1st	2nd	3rd	Win & Pl
Chases	1	0	1	0	869
Career Total	1	0	1	0	869

Going: Sf: 0-0 GS: 0-0 Gd: 0-1 GF: - Fm: 0-0
Distance: 2m/2m3: 0-0 2m4-2m7: 0-0 3m+: 0-1
Track: LH: 0-1 RH: 0-0 Tight: 0-1 Gall: 0-0
Aids: Bl: 0-0 Vi: 0-0 Tstrap: 0-0
Best Rating: 90 5/02 Strf 3m   good   Ch

Nimbus Stratus
76   43

10-y-o br g Welsh Captain-Touching Clouds (Touching Wood (USA))
J D Frost Miss M McCarthy

Placings:53436P/06/0-60   (1592)
2002/03: 19⁶F, 22⁰G,

	Starts	1st	2nd	3rd	Win & Pl
Hurdles	2	0	0	0	0
Career Total	11	0	0	2	821

Going: Sf: 0-0 GS: 0-0 Gd: 0-1 GF: - Fm: 0-1
Distance: 2m/2m3: 0-1 2m4-2m7: 0-1 3m+: 0-0
Track: LH: 0-0 RH: 0-2 Tight: 0-0 Gall: 0-0
Aids: Bl: 0-1 Vi: 0-0 Tstrap: 0-0
Best Rating: 86 10/99 Chep 2m110y   soft   Hdl

Nine O Three (IRE)
98   88

14-y-o b g Supreme Leader-Grenache (Menelek)
Mrs S D Williams Bideford Tool Ltd

Placings:0/630000 f33040/3F2005343/350001/61226/1006/405/03F1114/2000/6143F-4322   (0851)
2002/03: 24⁴GF, 27³GF, 27²GF, 22²GF,

	Starts	1st	2nd	3rd	Win & Pl
Hurdles	4	0	2	1	4408
Career Total	60	8	6	10	45693
122	6/01	NAbb	3m3f	C(0-130)HHdl	G-F £4867
117	10/99	Worc	2m4f	C(0-130)HHdl	GD £6840
110	9/99	NAbb	3m3f	D(0-125)HHdl	G-F £2859
99	7/99	Worc	3m	C(0-135)HHdl	G-F £4796
115	12/97	Tntn	2m1f	D(0-125)HHdl	G-F £2794
106	6/96	Worc	2m4f	C(0-130)HHdl	G-F £3965
107	2/96	Tntn	2m1f	F(0-105)HHdl	G-S £2244
	2/94	Thur	2m	NHF	SFT £2628

Total win prize-money £31036

Going: Sf: 0-0 GS: 0-0 Gd: 0-0 GF: - Fm: 0-4

Distance: 2m/2m3: 0-0 2m4-2m7: 0-1 3m+: 0-3
Track: LH: 0-4 RH: 0-0 Tight: 0-3 Gall: 0-0
Aids: Bl: 0-0 Vi: 0-0 Tstrap: 0-0
Best Rating: 124 9/00 MRas 3m   gd-fm   Hdl

Veteran fast-ground staying hurdler.

Nip On
91(102h)   (95h)51

9-y-o b g Dunbeath (USA)-Popping On (Sonnen Gold)
J R Turner Robin Ellerbeck

Placings:0001/053P53F10/0/20-P3234   (4374)
2002/03: 24⁸GS, 25³G, 21²S, 24³HY, 27⁴G,

	Starts	1st	2nd	3rd	Win & Pl
Hurdles	5	0	1	2	1749
Career Total	21	2	2	4	9087
102	3/00	Sedg	3m3f110yD(0-120)HHdl	G-F £2938
95	4/99	Hexm	2m4f110yE Hdl	GD £2196

Total win prize-money £5134

Going: Sf: 0-2 GS: 0-1 Gd: 0-2 GF: - Fm: 0-0
Distance: 2m/2m3: 0-0 2m4-2m7: 0-1 3m+: 0-4
Track: LH: 0-5 RH: 0-0 Tight: 0-4 Gall: 0-0
Aids: Bl: 0-0 Vi: 0-0 Tstrap: 0-0
Best Rating: 102 3/00 Sedg 3m3f110y   gd-fm   Hdl

Modest hurdler; stays three miles plus but effective over much shorter.

Nipper Reed

(84h)   (57h)
13-y-o b g Celestial Storm (USA)-Figrant (USA) (L Emigrant (USA))
Miss K M George Roland John Hair Studio Ii

Placings:P613111/6132/1156005/1153/F2R5P/0-   (0017)
2002/03: 16⁶GS,

	Starts	1st	2nd	3rd	Win & Pl
Hurdles	1	0	0	0	0
Career Total	28	9	2	3	46983
139	1/99	Newb	2m1f	D Ch	HVY £4279
138	12/98	Uttx	2m	D Ch	SFT £3485
125	1/98	Asct	2m110y	B HHdl	SFT £10474
118	12/97	Uttx	2m	C(0-130)HHdl	G-S £3355
109	2/97	Ling	2m	E(0-110)HHdl	HVY £2201
113	1/95	Uttx	2m	F(0-100)HHdl	HVY £2120
105	12/94	Nott	2m	(0-100)HHdl	G-S £2302
98	12/94	Uttx	2m	HHdl	SFT £2242
87	11/94	Leic	2m	Hdl	G-S £1478

Total win prize-money £31940

Going: Sf: 0-0 GS: 0-1 Gd: 0-0 GF: - Fm: 0-0
Distance: 2m/2m3: 0-1 2m4-2m7: 0-0 3m+: 0-0
Track: LH: 0-0 RH: 0-1 Tight: 0-0 Gall: 0-0
Aids: Bl: 0-0 Vi: 0-0 Tstrap: 0-0
Best Rating: 149 3/99 Chel 2m   gd-sft   Ch

Nisbet
102(97h)   (80dh)85

9-y-o b g Lithgie-Brig-Drummond Lass (Peacock (FR))
Miss Lucinda V Russell Mrs Ann Rutherford

Placings:4455P33P4526   (4765)
2002/03: 24⁴GS, 24⁴GF, 22⁵S, 22⁵S, 22⁵HY, 20³GF, 24³GS, 20P G, 24⁵G, 24⁵G, 25²G, 31⁶G,

	Starts	1st	2nd	3rd	Win & Pl
Hurdles	5	0	0	0	0
Chases	7	0	1	2	4243
Career Total	12	0	1	2	4243

Going: Sf: 0-3 GS: 0-2 Gd: 0-5 GF: - Fm: 0-2
Distance: 2m/2m3: 0-0 2m4-2m7: 0-5 3m+: 0-7
Track: LH: 0-5 RH: 0-6 Tight: 0-8 Gall: 0-0
Aids: Bl: 0-0 Vi: 0-0 Tstrap: 0-0
Best Rating: 85 4/03 Kels 3m1f   good   Ch

Plating-class chaser; winning pointer, but yet to score under Rules; stays three miles; acts on any ground.

Nizaal (USA)

82   85

12-y-o ch g Diesis-Shicklah (USA) (The Minstrel (CAN))
T A K Cuthbert J J H Walker

Placings:03/03/P/043/0/PP5-4000   (0450)
2002/03: 20⁴G, 16⁰G, 16⁰GF, 16⁰G,

	Starts	1st	2nd	3rd	Win & Pl
Chases	4	0	0	0	258
Career Total	16	0	0	3	2146

Going: Sf: 0-0 GS: 0-0 Gd: 0-3 GF: - Fm: 0-1
Distance: 2m/2m3: 0-3 2m4-2m7: 0-1 3m+: 0-0
Track: LH: 0-3 RH: 0-1 Tight: 0-0 Gall: 0-0
Aids: Bl: 0-3 Vi: 0-0 Tstrap: 0-0
Best Rating: 90 4/00 Ayr 2m   good   Ch

Lightly-raced dual-purpose maiden. Likes cut in the ground.

No Collusion (IRE)

109   128

7-y-o b g Buckskin (FR)-Miss Ironside (General Ironside)
Noel T Chance T Collins

Placings:10-51P21324   (4607)
2002/03: 20⁵G, 19¹G, 21³HY, 19²GS, 18¹S, 18³GS, 20²G, 21⁴G,

	Starts	1st	2nd	3rd	Win & Pl
Hurdles	8	2	2	1	14485
Career Total	10	3	2	1	17162
124	2/03	Font	2m2f110yE Hdl	SFT	£3484
120	12/02	Hrfd	2m3f110yE Hdl	GD	£3503
117	12/01	Newb	2m110y H NHF	GD	£2677

Total win prize-money £9666

Going: Sf: 1-2 GS: 0-2 Gd: 1-4 GF: - Fm: 0-0
Distance: 2m/2m3: 1-2 2m4-2m7: 1-6 3m+: 0-0
Track: LH: 1-6 RH: 1-2 Tight: 1-2 Gall: 0-2
Aids: Bl: 0-0 Vi: 0-0 Tstrap: 0-0
Best Rating: 128 3/03 Asct 2m4f   good   Hdl

Decent hurdler; stays two miles three; scored at Fontwell in February despite the soft ground, beaten in a better race next time; seems to prefer a decent surface.

No Discount (IRE)

111(109c)   (120c)138

9-y-o b g Be My Native (USA)-Flameing Run (Deep Run)
T M Walsh Seamus Ross/edward Cawley/thomas Bailey

Placings:0452321/3121122/P/P462B413FF-P00300 (4102)
2002/03: 24⁵HY, 24⁰S, 24⁰SH, 24⁰YS, 20⁰YS, 25⁰G,

	Starts	1st	2nd	3rd	Win & Pl
Hurdles	6	0	1	0	2922
Career Total	31	5	6	4	70832
120	2/02	Navn	3m	Ch	SFT	£7831
137	2/00	Naas	2m4f	Hdl	YLD	£10400
127	1/00	Naas	2m3f	Hdl	SFT	£4416
126	12/99	Punc	2m4f	Hdl	SFT	£4312
103	3/99	Dpat	2m1f172y NHF	YLD	£3069

Total win prize-money £30029

Going: Sf: 0-2 GS: 0-0 Gd: 0-1 GF: - Fm: 0-0
Distance: 2m/2m3: 0-0 2m4-2m7: 0-1 3m+: 0-5

Track: LH: 0-4 RH: 0-2 Tight: 0-0 Gall: 0-1
Aids: Bl: 0-0 Vi: 0-0 Tstrap: 0-0
Best Rating: 154 4/00 Aint   3m110y   good   Hdl

Decent hurdler/fair chaser; a very good novice hurdler in 1999/2000; has only won once over fences; stays three miles; acts on soft ground.

No Forecast (IRE)

110   121+

9-y-o b g Executive Perk-Guess Twice (Deep Run)
A M Hales Andrew L Cohen

Placings:5120/0F6/4/1-3   (1994)
2002/03: 20³GS,

	Starts	1st	2nd	3rd	Win & Pl
Chases	1	0	0	1	2442
Career Total	10	2	1	1	10904
121	12/01	Newb	2m6f110yD(0-110)HCh	GD	£5996
108	12/98	Folk	2m1f110yH NHF	SFT	£1234

Total win prize-money £7231

Going: Sf: 0-0 GS: 0-1 Gd: 0-0 GF: - Fm: 0-0
Distance: 2m/2m3: 0-0 2m4-2m7: 0-1 3m+: 0-0
Track: LH: 0-1 RH: 0-0 Tight: 0-0 Gall: 0-1
Aids: Bl: 0-0 Vi: 0-0 Tstrap: 0-0
Best Rating: 123 2/99 Newb 2m110y   good   NHF

Fair chaser; stays two miles-six, and handles cut in the ground. Made most in a novices handicap chase at Newbury in December 2001. Good effort on his next run eleven months later.

No Gimmicks (IRE)

90   94

11-y-o b g Lord Americo-Catspaw (Laurence O)
J G Fitzgerald J G Fitzgerald

Placings:33/12565/P3FF/0/01420U2230-0   (1704)
2002/03: 27⁰G,

	Starts	1st	2nd	3rd	Win & Pl
Hurdles	1	0	0	0	
Career Total	23	2	4	4	9111
94	12/01	Catt	3m1f110yE(0-115)HHdl	GD	£2450
100	11/97	MRas	2m5f110yE Hdl	G-S	£2705

Total win prize-money £5155

Going: Sf: 0-0 GS: 0-0 Gd: 0-1 GF: - Fm: 0-0
Distance: 2m/2m3: 0-0 2m4-2m7: 0-0 3m+: 0-1
Track: LH: 0-1 RH: 0-0 Tight: 0-1 Gall: 0-0
Aids: Bl: 0-0 Vi: 0-0 Tstrap: 0-0
Best Rating: 108 12/97 Weth 2m7f   good   Hdl

Plating-class hurdler best on a sound surface.

No If's Or But's

76f   61f

5-y-o b g Perpendicular-Tommys Dream (Le Bavard (FR))
J Wade John Wade

Placings:60   (1709)
2002/03: 17⁵G, 17⁰G,

	Starts	1st	2nd	3rd	Win & Pl
NH Flat	2	0	0	0	
Career Total	2	0	0	0	

Going: Sf: 0-0 GS: 0-0 Gd: 0-2 GF: - Fm: 0-0
Distance: 2m/2m3: 0-2 2m4-2m7: 0-0 3m+: 0-0
Track: LH: 0-2 RH: 0-0 Tight: 0-0 Gall: 0-0
Aids: Bl: 0-0 Vi: 0-0 Tstrap: 0-0
Best Rating: 61 10/02 Sedg 2m1f   good   NHF

No Kidding

105   (98h)108

9-y-o b g Teenoso (USA)-Vaigly Fine (Vaigly Great)
J I A Charlton Miss J Palmer

Placings:0200P/214F5020/42561F403452-PPP1P610
                                                    (4763)
2002/03: 16⁵GF, 25⁵GF, 19⁰G, 16¹GF, 20⁰G, 17⁶G, 20¹G, 16⁰G,

	Starts	1st	2nd	3rd	Win & Pl
Chases	8	2	0	0	7472
Career Total	33	4	5	1	20644
108	4/03	Hexm	2m4f110yF(0-95)HCh	GD	£3454
104	12/02	Muss	2m	F(0-95)HCh	G-F	£4017
98	11/01	Catt	2m		G-F	£4153
84	5/00	Kels	2m2f	D Hdl	G-F	£3035

Total win prize-money £14662

Going: Sf: 0-0 GS: 0-0 Gd: 1-5 GF: - Fm: 1-3
Distance: 2m/2m3: 1-5 2m4-2m7: 1-2 3m+: 0-1
Track: LH: 1-5 RH: 1-3 Tight: 1-4 Gall: 0-0
Aids: Bl: 0-0 Vi: 0-0 Tstrap: 0-0
Best Rating: 108 4/03 Hexm 2m4f110y   good   Ch

Modest chaser; effective from two to two and a half miles on fast ground; not totally reliable.

No Language Please (IRE)

91   74

9-y-o ch g Arapahos (FR)-Strong Language (Formidable (USA))
R Curtis Mrs G Fletcher

Placings:2PP3/PP64P/36PP-0   (0147)
2002/03: 24⁰GF,

	Starts	1st	2nd	3rd	Win & Pl
Hurdles	1	0	0	0	
Career Total	14	0	1	2	1776

Going: Sf: 0-0 GS: 0-0 Gd: 0-0 GF: - Fm: 0-0
Distance: 2m/2m3: 0-0 2m4-2m7: 0-0 3m+: 0-1
Track: LH: 0-1 RH: 0-0 Tight: 0-0 Gall: 0-0
Aids: Bl: 0-0 Vi: 0-0 Tstrap: 0-0
Best Rating: 80 4/00 Plum 2m4f   gd-sft   Ch

No Merci (GER)

5-y-o ch m General Assembly (USA)-Non Plus Ultra (GER) (Lord Udo (GER))
C Von Der Recke (P Remmert 10/11) Stall Hosepe

Placings:P   (2548)
2002/03: 17⁵HY,

	Starts	1st	2nd	3rd	Win & Pl
Hurdles	1	0	0	0	
Career Total	1	0	0	0	

Going: Sf: 0-1 GS: 0-0 Gd: 0-0 GF: - Fm: 0-0
Distance: 2m/2m3: 0-1 2m4-2m7: 0-0 3m+: 0-0
Track: LH: 0-0 RH: 0-1 Tight: 0-1 Gall: 0-0
Aids: Bl: 0-0 Vi: 0-0 Tstrap: 0-0
Best Rating: 0 12/02 Folk 2m1f110y   heavy   Hdl

No Mercy

96   83

7-y-o ch g Faustus (USA)-Nashville Blues (IRE) (Try My Best (USA))

B A Pearce Richard J Gray

Placings:*6550/P0P-200*   (3445)
2002/03: 16²HY, 16⁰S, 16⁰HY,

	Starts	1st	2nd	3rd	Win & Pl
Hurdles	3	0	1	0	872
Career Total	10	0	1	0	872

Going:	Sf: 0-3 GS: 0-0 Gd: 0-0 GF: - Fm: 0-0
Distance:	2m/2m3: 0-3 2m4-2m7: 0-0 3m+: 0-0
Track:	LH: 0-3 RH: 0-0 Tight: 0-1 Gall: 0-0
Aids:	Bl: 0-0 Vi: 0-0 Tstrap: 0-0
Best Rating:	86 9/00 Worc 2m gd-fm Hdl

Poor novice hurdler.

No Moore Bills
91   81
8-y-o b m Nicholas Bill-Grace Moore (Deep Run)
K Bishop Slabs And Lucan

Placings:*4/4000/20P6/40PP-6P*   (0770)
2002/03: 22⁶GS, 20⁷GF,

	Starts	1st	2nd	3rd	Win & Pl
Hurdles	2	0	0	0	0
Career Total	15	0	1	0	588

Going:	Sf: 0-0 GS: 0-1 Gd: 0-0 GF: - Fm: 0-1
Distance:	2m/2m3: 0-0 2m4-2m7: 0-2 3m+: 0-0
Track:	LH: 0-2 RH: 0-0 Tight: 0-1 Gall: 0-0
Aids:	Bl: 0-0 Vi: 0-0 Tstrap: 0-0
Best Rating:	86 10/99 Bang 2m1f soft NHF

No More Hassle (IRE)
103   119
10-y-o ch g Magical Wonder (USA)-Friendly Ann (Artaius (USA))
J Akehurst The No Hassle Partnership

Placings:*01110/3303535/22212F22/1201U3201/P50/01445 P2-20444445*   (4682)
2002/03: 26²G, 32⁰GF, 24⁴G, 24⁴G, 24⁴HY, 21⁴S, 26⁴GF, 24⁵GF,

	Starts	1st	2nd	3rd	Win & Pl
Chases	8	0	1	0	3598
Career Total	47	8	10	5	50742
117	6/01	Worc	2m7f110yC(0-135)HCh	G-F	£7117
132	4/00	Hntg	3m	D(0-120)HCh	GD	£4189
126	12/99	MRas	2m6f110y(0-120)HCh	G-S	£3821
107	5/99	MRas	2m4f	D Ch	G-F	£3977
103	11/98	Hntg	2m4f110yE Ch	GD	£3311
122	2/97	Hayd	2m	C HHdl	GD	£5015
92	1/97	Towc	2m	E(0-110)HHdl	G-S	£2477
100	12/96	MRas	2m1f110yE Hdl	GD	£2758
			Total win prize-money £32668		

Going:	Sf: 0-2 GS: 0-0 Gd: 0-3 GF: - Fm: 0-3
Distance:	2m/2m3: 0-0 2m4-2m7: 0-1 3m+: 0-7
Track:	LH: 0-2 RH: 0-4 Tight: 0-3 Gall: 0-1
Aids:	Bl: 0-0 Vi: 0-0 Tstrap: 0-0
Best Rating:	132 4/00 Hntg 3m good Ch

Modest staying chaser; stays well and acts on any ground but does not look in love with the game.

No Nay Never (IRE)
(90h)   (70h)
8-y-o b g Tremblant-Monread (Le Tricolore)
J W Mullins Ian M McGready

Placings:*034/6/60B0-4*   (4693)
2002/03: 17⁴G,

	Starts	1st	2nd	3rd	Win & Pl
Hurdles	1	0	0	0	0
Career Total	9	0	0	1	232

Going:	Sf: 0-0 GS: 0-0 Gd: 0-1 GF: - Fm: 0-0
Distance:	2m/2m3: 0-1 2m4-2m7: 0-0 3m+: 0-0
Track:	LH: 0-1 RH: 0-0 Tight: 0-1 Gall: 0-0
Aids:	Bl: 0-0 Vi: 0-0 Tstrap: 0-0
Best Rating:	83 3/00 Ludl 2m good NHF

Plating-class performer; extremely lightly-raced for his age and has clearly had his problems.

No Need For Alarm
106(117h)   (131h)144
8-y-o ch m Romany Rye-Sunley Words (Sunley Builds)
P F Nicholls Tony Fear & Patrick Quinn

Placings:*22U1110-11F1FF1*   (4638)
2002/03: 16¹S, 16¹S, 16⁵S, 16¹HY, 17⁵FS, 16⁵G, 17¹G,

	Starts	1st	2nd	3rd	Win & Pl
Chases	7	4	0	0	22886
Career Total	14	7	2	0	35398
130	4/03	Strf	2m1f110yC Ch	GD	£8673
144	3/03	Chep	2m110y D Ch	HVY	£5518
124	11/02	Chep	2m110y E Ch	SFT	£4075
138	11/02	NAbb	2m110y D Ch	SFT	£4618
131	4/02	Uttx	2m	C(0-135)HHdl	GD	£5486
125	3/02	Sthl	2m	E Hdl	HVY	£2604
120	3/02	Bang	2m1f	E Hdl	SFT	£3122
			Total win prize-money £34099		

Going:	Sf: 3-5 GS: 0-0 Gd: 1-2 GF: - Fm: 0-0
Distance:	2m/2m3: 4-7 2m4-2m7: 0-0 3m+: 0-0
Track:	LH: 4-7 RH: 0-0 Tight: 2-3 Gall: 0-0
Aids:	Bl: 0-0 Vi: 0-0 Tstrap: 0-0
Best Rating:	144 2/03 Chep 2m110y heavy Ch

Smart novice chaser; best over two miles; suited by soft ground; very much suited by forcing tactics and has made all to win three times, but her jumping has also let her down on more than one occasion; fortunate winner at Stratford April 2003.

No Picnic (IRE)
104   98
5-y-o ch g Be My Native (USA)-Emmagreen (Green Shoon)
Mrs S C Bradburne Broad and Cochrane

Placings:*50240*   (4406)
2002/03: 16⁵GF, 16⁰S, 20²GF, 17⁴GS, 20⁰G,

	Starts	1st	2nd	3rd	Win & Pl
NH Flat	1	0	0	0	0
Hurdles	4	0	1	0	1430
Career Total	5	0	1	0	1430

Going:	Sf: 0-1 GS: 0-1 Gd: 0-1 GF: - Fm: 0-2
Distance:	2m/2m3: 0-3 2m4-2m7: 0-2 3m+: 0-0
Track:	LH: 0-2 RH: 0-3 Tight: 0-1 Gall: 0-0
Aids:	Bl: 0-0 Vi: 0-0 Tstrap: 0-0
Best Rating:	98 3/03 Carl 2m1f gd-sft Hdl

Moderate hurdler; put in a much-improved effort to finish-runner up to a smart sort in a maiden hurdle at Musselburgh on his second start over hurdles.

No Quarter (IRE)
(98h)   (103h)
10-y-o ch g Persian Mews-Back To Bahrain (Mandalus)

K C Bailey Mrs C A Waters

Placings:*31P0/43341-P*   (1921)
2002/03: 24⁹GS,

	Starts	1st	2nd	3rd	Win & Pl
Chases	1	0	0	0	
Career Total	10	2	0	3	4341
103	3/02	Towc	2m5f	F Hdl	G-S	£1953
107	12/98	Towc	2m	H NHF	SFT	£1287
			Total win prize-money £3240		

Going:	Sf: 0-0 GS: 0-1 Gd: 0-0 GF: - Fm: 0-0
Distance:	2m/2m3: 0-0 2m4-2m7: 0-0 3m+: 0-1
Track:	LH: 0-1 RH: 0-0 Tight: 0-0 Gall: 0-1
Aids:	Bl: 0-0 Vi: 0-0 Tstrap: 0-0
Best Rating:	110 4/99 Ayr 2m soft NHF

No Sam No
103(100h)   (81h)76
5-y-o b m Reprimand-Samjamalifran (Blakeney)
Mrs K Walton Percy Vere Partnership

Placings:*40006-34P240P204*   (4797)
2002/03: 22³HY, 20⁴GF, 24⁴PG, 21²G, 22⁴G, 22⁰G, 19⁰G, 21²G, 21⁰G, 27⁴GF,

	Starts	1st	2nd	3rd	Win & Pl
Hurdles	8	0	2	1	2110
Chases	2	0	0	0	334
Career Total	15	0	2	1	2444

Going:	Sf: 0-1 GS: 0-0 Gd: 0-7 GF: - Fm: 0-2
Distance:	2m/2m3: 0-1 2m4-2m7: 0-7 3m+: 0-2
Track:	LH: 0-9 RH: 0-1 Tight: 0-9 Gall: 0-0
Aids:	Bl: 0-0 Vi: 0-0 Tstrap: 0-0
Best Rating:	81 8/02 Ctml 2m6f good Hdl

Selling-class hurdler; running in chases in spring 2003; runner-up at Sedgefield on a couple of occasions in 2002/03; stays well; acts on good ground.

No Visibility (IRE)
103(101h)   (104h)137+
8-y-o b g Glacial Storm (USA)-Duhallow Lady (IRE) (Torus)
R H Alner David O Moon

Placings:*60/43000P/0005U-0311F*   (4638)
2002/03: 22⁰S, 17³S, 16¹S, 16¹HY, 17⁰FG,

	Starts	1st	2nd	3rd	Win & Pl
Hurdles	2	0	0	1	758
Chases	3	2	0	0	10955
Career Total	18	2	0	2	12461
131	3/03	Tntn	2m110y D Ch	HVY	£6223
117	1/03	Tntn	2m110y E Ch	SFT	£4732
			Total win prize-money £10955		

Going:	Sf: 2-4 GS: 0-0 Gd: 0-1 GF: - Fm: 0-0
Distance:	2m/2m3: 2-4 2m4-2m7: 0-1 3m+: 0-0
Track:	LH: 0-1 RH: 2-4 Tight: 2-4 Gall: 0-0
Aids:	Bl: 0-0 Vi: 0-0 Tstrap: 0-0
Best Rating:	137 4/03 Strf 2m1f110y good Ch

Ex-Irish hurdler/chaser; surprised his trainer by the improvement he showed when winning over two miles in soft ground on his first British fencing debut at Taunton January 2003; followed up over same course and distance next time; unlucky not to complete a hat-trick when falling at Stratford in April; acts on soft ground.

No Win No Fee
8-y-o gr g St Ninian-Nellie Bly (Dragonara Palace (USA))

K D Giles K D Giles

Placings: *0/0/F*   (4443)
2002/03: 19^FG,

	Starts	1st	2nd	3rd	Win & Pl
Chases	1	0	0	0	
Career Total	3	0	0	0	

Going: Sf: 0-0 GS: 0-0 Gd: 0-1 GF: - Fm: 0-0
Distance: 2m/2m3: 0-0 2m4-2m7: 0-1 3m+: 0-0
Track: LH: 0-0 RH: 0-1 Tight: 0-0 Gall: 0-0
Aids: Bl: 0-0 Vi: 0-0 Tstrap: 0-0
Best Rating: 67 12/99 Hntg 2m110y good NHF

Noaff (IRE)

9-y-o b g Mandalus-Good Sailing (Scorpio (FR))
John Moore (John F Gleeson 19/7) Iwan Thomas

Placings: *000500/0-0P2*   (4736)
2002/03: 24⁹GF, 20^PYS, 24²GF,

	Starts	1st	2nd	3rd	Win & Pl
Chases	3	0	1	0	1048
Career Total	10	0	1	0	1048

Going: Sf: 0-0 GS: 0-0 Gd: 0-0 GF: - Fm: 0-2
Distance: 2m/2m3: 0-0 2m4-2m7: 0-1 3m+: 0-2
Track: LH: 0-1 RH: 0-1 Tight: 0-0 Gall: 0-0
Aids: Bl: 0-0 Vi: 0-0 Tstrap: 0-0
Best Rating: 85 4/03 Chep 3m gd-fm Ch

Nobigsuprise (IRE)

4-y-o b f Courtship-Pennine Sue (IRE) (Pennine Walk)
W G M Turner (Patrick Martin 3/7) Michael Kelly

Placings: PP   (4094)
2002/03: 17^PS, 17^PHY,

	Starts	1st	2nd	3rd	Win & Pl
Hurdles	2	0	0	0	
Career Total	2	0	0	0	

Going: Sf: 0-2 GS: 0-0 Gd: 0-0 GF: - Fm: 0-0
Distance: 2m/2m3: 0-2 2m4-2m7: 0-0 3m+: 0-0
Track: LH: 0-0 RH: 0-2 Tight: 0-0 Gall: 0-0
Aids: Bl: 0-0 Vi: 0-0 Tstrap: 0-0
Best Rating: 0 3/03 Tntn 2m1f heavy Hdl

Noble Baron
88   78

7-y-o gr g Karinga Bay-Grey Baroness (Baron Blakeney)
C G Cox T Y Bissett

Placings: *01-003*   (4403)
2002/03: 16⁹GS, 19⁰S, 22³GF,

	Starts	1st	2nd	3rd	Win & Pl
NH Flat	1	0	0	0	0
Hurdles	2	0	0	1	774
Career Total	5	1	0	1	2787
104	1/02	Kemp	2m	H NHF	SFT £2012
			Total win prize-money £2013		

Going: Sf: 0-0 GS: 0-1 Gd: 0-0 GF: - Fm: 0-1
Distance: 2m/2m3: 0-2 2m4-2m7: 0-1 3m+: 0-0
Track: LH: 0-2 RH: 0-1 Tight: 0-0 Gall: 0-2
Aids: Bl: 0-0 Vi: 0-0 Tstrap: 0-0
Best Rating: 104 1/02 Kemp 2m soft NHF

Moderate novice hurdler; surprise winner of a Kempton bumper in January 2002; acts on soft ground.

Noble Caesar (IRE)

5-y-o b/br g Montelimar (USA)-Timely Run (IRE) (Deep Run)
J R Adam J W Hazeldean

Placings: PP   (3769)
2002/03: 20^PS, 20^PGS,

	Starts	1st	2nd	3rd	Win & Pl
Hurdles	2	0	0	0	
Career Total	2	0	0	0	

Going: Sf: 0-1 GS: 0-1 Gd: 0-0 GF: - Fm: 0-0
Distance: 2m/2m3: 0-0 2m4-2m7: 0-2 3m+: 0-0
Track: LH: 0-2 RH: 0-0 Tight: 0-0 Gall: 0-0
Aids: Bl: 0-0 Vi: 0-0 Tstrap: 0-0
Best Rating: 0 2/03 Ayr 2m4f gd-sft Hdl

Noble Comic
108   109

12-y-o b g Silly Prices-Barony (Ribston)
C Tizzard R E Dimond

Placings: *0P/6FP/413152P5/0211504-2321352614* (1662)
2002/03: 16²GS, 16²S, 16²G, 16¹GF, 20³GF, 16⁵GF, 16²GF, 17⁶GF, 21¹F, 25⁴G,

	Starts	1st	2nd	3rd	Win & Pl
Chases	10	2	3	2	14673
Career Total	30	6	5	3	33514
109	10/02	Winc	2m5f	E(0-110)HCh	FRM £5964
109	6/02	NAbb	2m110y	E(0-105)HCh	G-F £3360
108	8/01	NAbb	2m110y	F(0-110)HCh	GD £4315
104	7/01	NAbb	2m5f110yD(0-120)HCh	GD £3776
109	6/00	NAbb	2m110y	D Ch	G-F £3711
105	6/00	NAbb	2m5f110yD Ch	GD £3779
			Total win prize-money £24909		

Going: Sf: 0-1 GS: 0-1 Gd: 0-2 GF: - Fm: 2-6
Distance: 2m/2m3: 1-7 2m4-2m7: 1-2 3m+: 0-1
Track: LH: 1-8 RH: 1-2 Tight: 1-8 Gall: 0-0
Aids: Bl: 0-0 Vi: 0-0 Tstrap: 0-0
Best Rating: 109 10/02 Winc 2m5f firm Ch

Fair handicap chaser, successful five times at Newton Abbot. Likes good/fast ground, effective at up to 21 furlongs.

Noble Deed (IRE)
81   76

6-y-o b g Lord Americo-Legal Statement (IRE) (Strong Statement (USA))
Miss H C Knight Winter Madness

Placings: *0-P40*   (3140)
2002/03: 20^PGS, 16⁴HY, 19⁰S,

	Starts	1st	2nd	3rd	Win & Pl
Hurdles	3	0	0	0	0
Career Total	4	0	0	0	0

Going: Sf: 0-2 GS: 0-1 Gd: 0-0 GF: - Fm: 0-0
Distance: 2m/2m3: 0-1 2m4-2m7: 0-2 3m+: 0-0
Track: LH: 0-1 RH: 0-1 Tight: 0-3 Gall: 0-0
Aids: Bl: 0-0 Vi: 0-0 Tstrap: 0-0
Best Rating: 74 12/02 Plum 2m heavy Hdl

Noble Hymn

10-y-o br g Arctic Lord-Soraway (Choral Society)

Mrs C M Mulhall Mrs C M Mulhall

Placings: *3000/5P/F-62*   (4592)
2002/03: 25⁶GS, 25²G,

	Starts	1st	2nd	3rd	Win & Pl
Chases	2	0	1	0	448
Career Total	9	0	1	1	601

Going: Sf: 0-0 GS: 0-1 Gd: 0-1 GF: - Fm: 0-0
Distance: 2m/2m3: 0-0 2m4-2m7: 0-0 3m+: 0-2
Track: LH: 0-2 RH: 0-0 Tight: 0-0 Gall: 0-0
Aids: Bl: 0-0 Vi: 0-0 Tstrap: 0-1
Best Rating: 80 10/98 Sedg 2m1f good NHF

Hunter chaser; stays three miles; acts well with cut in the ground.

Noble Justice (IRE)
106

(93h)
7-y-o b g Jurado (USA)-Furry Hope (Furry Glen)
R J Hodges Fieldspring Racing

Placings: *03212-PP*   (3845)
2002/03: 20^PGS, 21^PG,

	Starts	1st	2nd	3rd	Win & Pl
Hurdles	1	0	0	0	0
Chases	1	0	0	0	0
Career Total	7	1	2	1	8059
106	11/01	Winc	2m5f	D Ch	G-F £4290
			Total win prize-money £4290		

Going: Sf: 0-0 GS: 0-1 Gd: 0-1 GF: - Fm: 0-0
Distance: 2m/2m3: 0-0 2m4-2m7: 0-2 3m+: 0-0
Track: LH: 0-0 RH: 0-2 Tight: 0-0 Gall: 0-0
Aids: Bl: 0-0 Vi: 0-0 Tstrap: 0-0
Best Rating: 106 12/01 Winc 2m5f good Ch

Lightly-raced hurdler/chaser; suited by a sound surface.

Noble Lord
119

10-y-o ch g Lord Bud-Chasers Bar (Oats)
R T Phillips G Lansbury

Placings: 11122340/223002/102104/2324032/16PF0/0 (1965)
2002/03: 27⁰GS,

	Starts	1st	2nd	3rd	Win & Pl
Chases	1	0	0	0	
Career Total	33	6	9	4	64160
143	1/01	Hayd	3m	B(0-140)HCh	SFT £9586
133	11/98	Aint	3m	D(0-115)HCh	G-S £10406
122	5/98	Strf	2m110y	D(0-120)HHdl	FRM £3183
117	11/96	Chel	2m110y	D Hdl	GD £2829
97	9/96	Extr	2m1f110yE Hdl	FRM £2211
97	9/96	NAbb	2m1f	D Hdl	GD £2725
			Total win prize-money £30941		

Going: Sf: 0-0 GS: 0-1 Gd: 0-0 GF: - Fm: 0-0
Distance: 2m/2m3: 0-0 2m4-2m7: 0-0 3m+: 0-1
Track: LH: 0-1 RH: 0-0 Tight: 0-0 Gall: 0-1
Aids: Bl: 0-0 Vi: 0-0 Tstrap: 0-0
Best Rating: 143 1/01 Hayd 3m soft Ch

Useful chaser; cracking second in the 2000 Scottish National from 9lb out of the handicap, he won in bad ground at Haydock on his reappearance the following season, but struggled on two subsequent starts. Got as far as the 13th at Aintree, but failed to get home in the Ayr equivalent. Off the track with injury for a long time afterwards. He stays well but is not very big and may not enjoy lumping big weights around in soft ground.

Noble Spy (IRE)

97   **81**

9-y-o b g Lord Americo-Flashey Blond (Buckskin (FR))
Mrs D A Hamer   J M B Pugh

Placings:*405/F00/1334F232-0P0*   (4563)
2002/03: 25⁰HY, 24PGS, 24⁰GF,

	Starts	1st	2nd	3rd	Win & Pl
Hurdles	2	0	0	0	0
Chases	1	0	0	0	0
Career Total	17	1	2	3	6386
84 8/01 Worc 2m4f	F Hdl		G-F	£1981	

Total win prize-money £1981

Going: Sf: 0-1 GS: 0-1 Gd: 0-0 GF: - Fm: 0-1
Distance: 2m/2m3: 0-0 2m4-2m7: 0-0 3m+: 0-3
Track: LH: 0-2 RH: 0-1 Tight: 0-2 Gall: 0-0
Aids: Bl: 0-0 Vi: 0-0 Tstrap: 0-0
Best Rating: **105** 2/02 Wwck 3m1f   soft   Hdl

Modest handicap hurdler, has won on a sound surface over two and a half miles but is effective in heavy ground too.

Noble Star

11-y-o b g Jester-Mickley Spacetrail (Space King)
Mrs J M Bush   Mrs J M Bush

Placings:*0-P*   (0034)
2002/03: 16PGF,

	Starts	1st	2nd	3rd	Win & Pl
Chases	1	0	0	0	
Career Total	2	0	0	0	

Going: Sf: 0-0 GS: 0-0 Gd: 0-0 GF: - Fm: 0-1
Distance: 2m/2m3: 0-1 2m4-2m7: 0-0 3m+: 0-0
Track: LH: 0-1 RH: 0-0 Tight: 0-0 Gall: 0-1
Aids: Bl: 0-0 Vi: 0-0 Tstrap: 0-0
Best Rating:

Noblefir (IRE)

101f   **98f**

5-y-o b g Shernazar-Chrisali (IRE) (Strong Gale)
L Lungo   P Gaffney & J N Stevenson

Placings:*023*   (4665)
2002/03: 16⁰GS, 16²G, 17³GF,

	Starts	1st	2nd	3rd	Win & Pl
NH Flat	3	0	1	1	1403
Career Total	3	0	1	1	1403

Going: Sf: 0-0 GS: 0-1 Gd: 0-1 GF: - Fm: 0-1
Distance: 2m/2m3: 0-3 2m4-2m7: 0-0 3m+: 0-0
Track: LH: 0-2 RH: 0-1 Tight: 0-0 Gall: 0-0
Aids: Bl: 0-0 Vi: 0-0 Tstrap: 0-0
Best Rating: **98** 4/03 Carl 2m1f   gd-fm NHF

Bumper performer; Irish point winner; has shown promise under Rules; acts on good ground.

Nobratinetta (FR)

105f   **97f**

4-y-o b f Celtic Swing-Bustinetta (Bustino)
Mrs M Reveley   P D Savill

Placings:*32114*   (4611)
2002/03: 12³GS, 14²GS, 16¹HY, 16¹G, 17⁴G,

	Starts	1st	2nd	3rd	Win & Pl
NH Flat	5	2	1	1	7302

Career Total	5	2	1	1	7302
97 2/03 Muss 2m	H NHF		GD	£2975	
95 1/03 Newc 2m	H NHF		HVY	£1897	

Total win prize-money £4872

Going: Sf: 1-1 GS: 0-2 Gd: 1-2 GF: - Fm: 0-0
Distance: **2m/2m3: 2-3** 2m4-2m7: 0-0 3m+: 0-0
Track: LH: 1-4 RH: 1-1 **Tight: 1-1** Gall: 0-1
Aids: Bl: 0-0 Vi: 0-0 Tstrap: 0-0
Best Rating: **97** 4/03 Chel 2m1f   good   NHF

Fair bumper performer; has won on good ground, but looks more at home on a soft surface; effective at around two miles.

Nod Ya Head

89   **49**

7-y-o m Minster Son-Little Mittens (Little Buskins)
R E Barr   R E Barr

Placings:*0*   (1242)
2002/03: 16⁰G,

	Starts	1st	2nd	3rd	Win & Pl
NH Flat	1	0	0	0	
Career Total	1	0	0	0	

Going: Sf: 0-0 GS: 0-0 Gd: 0-0 GF: - Fm: 0-1
Distance: 2m/2m3: 0-1 2m4-2m7: 0-0 3m+: 0-0
Track: LH: 0-1 RH: 0-0 Tight: 0-0 Gall: 0-0
Aids: Bl: 0-0 Vi: 0-0 Tstrap: 0-0
Best Rating: **54** 9/02 Hexm 2m110y   gd-fm NHF

Nod's Nephew

94   **73**

6-y-o b g Efisio-Nordan Raider (Domynsky)
D E Cantillon   Mrs E M Clarke

Placings:*0*   (1448)
2002/03: 16⁰G,

	Starts	1st	2nd	3rd	Win & Pl
Hurdles	1	0	0	0	
Career Total	1	0	0	0	

Going: Sf: 0-0 GS: 0-0 Gd: 0-0 GF: - Fm: 0-0
Distance: 2m/2m3: 0-1 2m4-2m7: 0-0 3m+: 0-0
Track: LH: 0-1 RH: 0-0 Tight: 0-0 Gall: 0-0
Aids: Bl: 0-0 Vi: 0-0 Tstrap: 0-1
Best Rating: **73** 10/02 Fknm 2m   good   Hdl

Nodform Returns

5-y-o ch m Minster Son-Gale Storm (Midland Gayle)
D Eddy   David Carr

Placings:*000P*   (4750)
2002/03: 17⁰G, 16⁰G, 16⁰G, 24PG,

	Starts	1st	2nd	3rd	Win & Pl
NH Flat	3	0	0	0	0
Hurdles	1	0	0	0	0
Career Total	4	0	0	0	0

Going: Sf: 0-0 GS: 0-0 Gd: 0-0 GF: - Fm: 0-0
Distance: 2m/2m3: 0-3 2m4-2m7: 0-0 3m+: 0-1
Track: LH: 0-2 RH: 0-2 Tight: 0-1 Gall: 0-0
Aids: Bl: 0-0 Vi: 0-0 Tstrap: 0-0
Best Rating: **69** 3/03 MRas 2m1f110y good   NHF

Noel's Pride

111(100c)   (99c)**128**

7-y-o b g Good Thyne (USA)-Kavali (Blakeney)
J M Jefferson   Pride Of Yorkshire Racing Club

Placings:*032/24/121211352-23041112523P*   (3832)
2002/03: 20²GS, 20³GF, 20⁹G, 21⁴GF, 21¹G, 20¹GF, 24¹G, 24²GF, 21⁵GF, 21²S, 20³GS, 20PG,

	Starts	1st	2nd	3rd	Win & Pl
Hurdles	10	3	3	1	21097
Chases	2	0	0	1	498
Career Total	26	7	8	4	39631
128 9/02 Uttx	3m110y D(0-125)HHdl	GD	£4199		
128 8/02 Worc	2m4f	D(0-120)HHdl	G-F	£4124	
120 8/02 Sedg	2m5f110yD(0-120)HHdl	G-F	£3721		
113 8/01 Uttx	3m110y E(0-115)HHdl	G-F	£3465		
105 7/01 Sedg	2m5f110yD(0-125)HHdl	G-F	£3276		
95 5/01 Hexm 2m	E Hdl		G-S	£2534	
90 5/01 Hexm 2m	E Hdl		G-F	£2716	

Total win prize-money £24035

Going: Sf: 0-1 GS: 0-2 Gd: 2-4 GF: - Fm: 1-5
Distance: 2m/2m3: 0-0 **2m4-2m7: 2-10** 3m+: 1-2
Track: **LH: 3-9** RH: 0-3 **Tight: 1-6** Gall: 0-1
Aids: Bl: 0-0 Vi: 0-0 Tstrap: 0-0
Best Rating: **128** 11/02 Sedg 2m5f110y soft   Hdl

Useful hurdler; showed the benefit of a soft-palate operation when winning four times in the summer of 2001; he stays three miles and has tried his hand unsuccessfully so far over fences; reverted to hurdling when successful three times in the autumn of 2002; suited by fast ground, although he has won no easier.

Noisetine (FR)

104   **107**

5-y-o ch m Mansonnien (FR)-Notabilite (FR) (No Pass No Sale)
Miss Venetia Williams   Mrs Jean F P Yeomans

Placings:*303/1511-063062*   (4566)
2002/03: 21⁰GS, 20⁶S, 20³S, 20⁰HY, 16⁶GS, 20²GF,

	Starts	1st	2nd	3rd	Win & Pl
Hurdles	6	0	1	1	3133
Career Total	13	3	1	3	17166
99 4/02 Uttx	2m4f110yE Hdl	GD	£3045		
105 3/02 Winc	2m6f	E Hdl	SFT	£2744	
5/01 Fntb	1m7f	Hdl	GD	£3880	

Total win prize-money £9669

Going: Sf: 0-3 GS: 0-2 Gd: 0-0 GF: - Fm: 0-1
Distance: 2m/2m3: 0-1 2m4-2m7: 0-5 3m+: 0-0
Track: LH: 0-5 RH: 0-1 Tight: 0-1 Gall: 0-2
Aids: Bl: 0-0 Vi: 0-0 Tstrap: 0-0
Best Rating: **107** 4/03 Bang 2m4f   gd-fm Hdl

Modest handicap hurdler; acts on soft ground and is effective over two miles six furlongs; expected to do better over fences in time.

Nokimover

98(103c)   (108dc)**97**

9-y-o ch g Scallywag-Town Blues (Charlottown)
J G M O Shea   H G Llewellyn

Placings:*400/113551/05-U13FU03P554*   (4599)
2002/03: 26UG, 23¹G, 26³G, 24FGF, 26UGF, 24⁰HY, 26³HY, 25PG, 19⁵HY, 21⁵G, 24⁴GF,

	Starts	1st	2nd	3rd	Win & Pl
Hurdles	4	0	0	0	370
Chases	7	1	0	2	5831
Career Total	22	4	0	3	14075
104 6/02 Uttx	2m7f	E Ch	GD	£3110	

108	4/01	Hrfd	3m2f	E Hdl	GD	£2296
101	12/00	Hrfd	2m3f110yE Hdl		HVY	£2954
101	11/00	Aint	2m1f	H NHF	G-S	£2275
				Total win prize-money £10635		

Going: Sf: 0-3 GS: 0-0 Gd: 1-5 GF: - Fm: 0-3
Distance: 2m/2m3: 0-0 2m4-2m7: 1-3 3m+: 0-8
Track: LH: 1-7 RH: 0-4 Tight: 0-3 Gall: 0-0
Aids: Bl: 0-0 Vi: 0-0 Tstrap: 0-0
Best Rating: 108 6/02 NAbb 3m2f110y good Ch

Able but quirky hurdler/chaser, was getting round for the first time over fences when successful at Uttoxeter in June 2002; seems best on good ground.

Nolife (IRE)
97   **70**

7-y-o b g Religiously (USA)-Gamerstown Lady (Pitpan)
Miss Lucinda V Russell Peter J S Russell

Placings:04   (1986)
2002/03: 20⁰GS, 22⁴S,

	Starts	1st	2nd	3rd	Win & Pl
Hurdles	2	0	0	0	0
Career Total	2	0	0	0	0

Going: Sf: 0-1 GS: 0-1 Gd: 0-0 GF: - Fm: 0-0
Distance: 2m/2m3: 0-0 2m4-2m7: 0-2 3m+: 0-0
Track: LH: 0-2 RH: 0-0 Tight: 0-1 Gall: 0-0
Aids: Bl: 0-0 Vi: 0-0 Tstrap: 0-0
Best Rating: 30 10/02 Bang 2m4f gd-sft Hdl

Nomadic Star

8-y-o br g Nomadic Way (USA)-Dreamago (Sir Mago)
D G Atkinson D G Atkinson

Placings:5   (3895)
2002/03: 25⁵GS,

	Starts	1st	2nd	3rd	Win & Pl
Chases	1	0	0	0	0
Career Total	1	0	0	0	0

Going: Sf: 0-0 GS: 0-1 Gd: 0-0 GF: - Fm: 0-0
Distance: 2m/2m3: 0-0 2m4-2m7: 0-0 3m+: 0-1
Track: LH: 0-1 RH: 0-0 Tight: 0-1 Gall: 0-0
Aids: Bl: 0-0 Vi: 0-0 Tstrap: 0-1
Best Rating: 66 3/03 Kels 3m1f gd-sft Ch

Non So (FR)
117   **146**

5-y-o b g Definite Article-Irish Woman (FR) (Assert)
N J Henderson Roa Dawn Run Partnership

Placings:0211P-511240   (4476)
2002/03: 18⁵G, 16¹S, 16¹G, 16²G, 17⁴G, 16⁰G,

	Starts	1st	2nd	3rd	Win & Pl
Hurdles	6	2	1	0	65899
Career Total	11	4	2	0	71881
139	1/03	Kemp 2m	B(0-145)HHdl	GD	29000
131	12/02	Kemp 2m	D(0-125)HHdl	SFT	£6728
107	1/02	Font	2m2f110yE Hdl	SFT	£2653
115	1/02	Folk	2m1f110yE Hdl	SFT	£2632
			Total win prize-money £41013		

Going: Sf: 1-1 GS: 0-0 Gd: 1-5 GF: - Fm: 0-0
Distance: 2m/2m3: 2-6 2m4-2m7: 0-0 3m+: 0-0
Track: LH: 0-4 RH: 2-2 Tight: 0-2 Gall: 0-2
Aids: Bl: 0-0 Vi: 0-0 Tstrap: 0-0

Best Rating: 146 3/03 Chel 2m1f good Hdl

Very useful handicap hurdler; won the Lanzarote at Kempton in January 2003 and runner-up in the Tote Gold Trophy next time; finished a very good fourth in the County Hurdle; suited by good ground or softer; stays two and a quarter miles; progressive.

Non Vintage (IRE)
93(102h)   (68h)**29**

12-y-o ch g Shy Groom (USA)-Great Alexandra (Runnett)
M C Chapman P T O Connell

Placings:34231/21300364356/024144FO6650010/4533040
5243P2003/34635432133436230405/55053065/65400/041-
66P4044   (2011)
2002/03: 24⁶G, 26⁶GF, 25⁵GF, 28⁴GF, 17⁰G, 16⁴GS, 23⁴GF,

	Starts	1st	2nd	3rd	Win & Pl
Hurdles	4	0	0	0	0
Chases	3	0	0	0	577
Career Total	90	6	7	17	66347
76	7/01	Uttx	3m2f	F(0-90)HCh	G-F	£3575
107	8/98	Ctml	2m1f110yD(0-120)HCh	G-S	£3418
130	2/97	MRas	2m1f110yD(0-120)HHdl	GD	£2796
132	10/96	MRas	2m1f110yC(0-135)HHdl	GD	£3355
123	11/95	Asct	2m110y B(0-145)HHdl	GD	£6691
94	3/95	Ludl	2m	E Hdl	G-S	£2528
			Total win prize-money £22364		

Going: Sf: 0-0 GS: 0-1 Gd: 0-2 GF: - Fm: 0-4
Distance: 2m/2m3: 0-2 2m4-2m7: 0-0 3m+: 0-5
Track: LH: 0-2 RH: 0-5 Tight: 0-5 Gall: 0-0
Aids: Bl: 0-1 Vi: 0-0 Tstrap: 0-0
Best Rating: 137 11/95 Newc 2m good Hdl

Veteran chaser/hurdler; his strike rate is very moderate despite several placings. He tends to drop himself out and has become unreliable.

Nonantais (FR)
112   **120+**

6-y-o b g Nikos-Sanhia (FR) (Sanhedrin (USA))
M Bradstock The Frankly Intolerable

Placings:363112   (4048)
2002/03: 17³G, 19⁶GS, 19³S, 17¹S, 19¹GS, 20²HY,

	Starts	1st	2nd	3rd	Win & Pl
NH Flat	1	0	0	1	258
Hurdles	5	2	1	1	22437
Career Total	6	2	1	2	22694
120	2/03	Tntn	2m3f110yD Hdl	G-S	£5369
108	2/03	Tntn	2m1f	D Hdl	SFT	£5232
			Total win prize-money £10602		

Going: Sf: 1-3 GS: 1-2 Gd: 0-1 GF: - Fm: 0-0
Distance: 2m/2m3: 1-3 2m4-2m7: 1-3 3m+: 0-0
Track: LH: 0-0 RH: 2-6 Tight: 2-3 Gall: 0-0
Aids: Bl: 0-0 Vi: 0-0 Tstrap: 0-0
Best Rating: 120 3/03 Sand 2m4f110y heavy Hdl

Decent novice hurdler; effective over two miles, but probably better over further; acts well on soft ground; progressive.

Norbert (IRE)
69   **24**

5-y-o ch g Imperial Frontier (USA)-Glowing Reeds (Kalaglow)
M F Harris M Harris

Placings:00   (4628)
2002/03: 16⁰G, 17⁰GF,

	Starts	1st	2nd	3rd	Win & Pl
NH Flat	2	0	0		

Career Total 2   0   0   0

Going: Sf: 0-0 GS: 0-0 Gd: 0-1 GF: - Fm: 0-1
Distance: 2m/2m3: 0-2 2m4-2m7: 0-0 3m+: 0-0
Track: LH: 0-1 RH: 0-1 Tight: 0-1 Gall: 0-0
Aids: Bl: 0-0 Vi: 0-0 Tstrap: 0-0
Best Rating: 66 4/03 Ludl 2m good NHF

Nordance Prince (IRE)
106   **144**

12-y-o b g Nordance (USA)-Shirleys Princess (Sandhurst Prince)
Miss Venetia Williams Pinks Gym & Leisure Wear Ltd

Placings:3/335534/112211001/11/1211FFF4/053-3F (3498)
2002/03: 20³G, 20⁷GS,

	Starts	1st	2nd	3rd	Win & Pl
Chases	2	0	0	1	3039
Career Total	31	10	3	6	134283
151	1/00	Asct	2m	A HCh	G-S	£30000
151	12/99	Weth	2m	A HCh	GD	£19300
151	11/99	Asct	2m3f110yA HCh	GD	£29775
140	10/98	Chel	2m	C Ch	GD	£4719
131	10/98	Towc	2m110y	E(0-120)Ch	GD	£2815
128	4/98	Prth	2m110y	D Hdl	GD	£3499
128	2/98	Donc	2m110y	B(0-140)HHdl	G-F	£5234
130	2/98	Asct	2m110y	C(0-115)HHdl	GD	£2840
101	5/97	Hntg	2m110y	E Hdl	G-F	£2355
115	5/97	NAbb	2m1f	E Hdl	G-F	£2505
			Total win prize-money £103045		

Going: Sf: 0-0 GS: 0-1 Gd: 0-1 GF: - Fm: 0-0
Distance: 2m/2m3: 0-0 2m4-2m7: 0-2 3m+: 0-0
Track: LH: 0-0 RH: 0-2 Tight: 0-0 Gall: 0-0
Aids: Bl: 0-0 Vi: 0-0 Tstrap: 0-0
Best Rating: 151 1/00 Asct 2m gd-sft Ch

Formerly a high-class handicap chaser; including when beating Flagship Uberalles in the 2000 Victor Chandler; then fell in three consecutive races and was off the track for almost two years; ran with credit without firing in 2002/3; best at two to two and a half miles; likes decent ground.

Nordic Crest (IRE)

9-y-o b g Danehill (USA)-Feather Glen (Glenstal (USA))
P R Webber The Silver Cod Partnership

Placings:04251/3/14P3/P22-4   (1695)
2002/03: 20⁴G,

	Starts	1st	2nd	3rd	Win & Pl
Chases	1	0	0	0	1080
Career Total	14	2	3	2	17673
102	10/00	Towc	2m110y	E Ch	GD	£3504
102	4/98	Ayr	2m	C HHdl	GD	£3817
			Total win prize-money £7322		

Going: Sf: 0-0 GS: 0-0 Gd: 0-0 GF: - Fm: 0-0
Distance: 2m/2m3: 0-0 2m4-2m7: 0-1 3m+: 0-0
Track: LH: 0-1 RH: 0-0 Tight: 0-0 Gall: 0-1
Aids: Bl: 0-0 Vi: 0-0 Tstrap: 0-0
Best Rating: 118 6/01 Strf 3m gd-fm Ch

Nordic Prince (IRE)
113(106h)   (114h)**118**

12-y-o b g Nordance (USA)-Royal Desire (Royal Match)
J G M O Shea Blue Shirts

Placings: *11*/03/133123P/1P/R3440/423231111231PP230/4
6264-32B141P3P   **(4564)**
2002/03: 24³HY, 24²GS, 24ᴮHY, 24¹GS, 30⁴S, 20¹G, 24ᴾG, 21³G,
24ᴾGF,

	Starts	1st	2nd	3rd	Win & Pl
Hurdles	4	1	1	2	6198
Chases	5	1	0	0	5932
Career Total	**49**	**12**	**7**	**11**	**62151**
99	2/03	Hntg	2m4f110yG Hdl		GD	£2548
118	1/03	Sthl	3m110y	D(0-125)HCh	G-S	£5499
118	11/00	Wwck	3m2f	D(0-125)HCh	HVY	£4020
115	10/00	Strf	3m	D(0-125)HCh	G-S	£3757
108	10/00	Bang	3m110y	D(0-120)HCh	SFT	£6857
82	8/00	Sthl	3m110y	E Ch		GD	£2815
92	8/00	Sthl	3m110y	G Hdl		G-F	£1501
126	10/98	Worc	2m4f	C(0-130)HHdl		GD	£3769
108	2/98	Tntn	2m6f110yE Hdl		GD	£2553
101	8/97	Uttx	2m4f110yD Hdl		GD	£2773
	11/95	Hexm	2m	H NHF		GD	£1371
	11/95	Worc	2m	H NHF		G-F	£2052

Total win prize-money £39518

Going: Sf: 0-3 GS: 1-2 Gd: 1-3 GF: - Fm: 0-1
Distance: 2m/2m3: 0-0 2m4-2m7: 1-2 3m+: 1-7
Track: LH: 1-8 RH: 1-1 Tight: 1-4 Gall: 1-2
Aids: Bl: 0-0 Vi: 0-0 Tstrap: 0-0
Best Rating: 126 10/98 Worc 2m4f   good   Hdl

Fair hurdler/chaser; now at the veteran stage; stays beyond three miles, but effective at shorter.

Norlandic (NZ)
98   108
11-y-o ch g First Norman (USA)-April Snow (NZ) (Icelandic)
P J Hobbs The Till House Partnership

Placings: 06/3/5521511/2122/154UP3/33-3FP3   **(3959)**
2002/03: 25³GS, 24ᶠS, 24ᴾGS, 24³S,

	Starts	1st	2nd	3rd	Win & Pl
Chases	4	0	0	2	2114
Career Total	**26**	**5**	**4**	**6**	**33878**
129	10/00	Extr	2m7f110yD(0-125)HCh	SFT	£5096
129	12/99	Winc	3m1f110yD(0-120)HCh	GD	£4143
124	4/99	Extr	2m7f110yE(0-105)HCh	G-S	£4079
115	3/99	Extr	2m7f110yE(0-105)HCh	GD	£5054
103	2/99	Tntn	3m110y	F(0-110)HHdl	G-F	£2246

Total win prize-money £20619

Going: Sf: 0-2 GS: 0-2 Gd: 0-0 GF: - Fm: 0-0
Distance: 2m/2m3: 0-0 2m4-2m7: 0-0 3m+: 0-4
Track: LH: 0-1 RH: 0-3 Tight: 0-2 Gall: 0-0
Aids: Bl: 0-0 Vi: 0-0 Tstrap: 0-0
Best Rating: 129 10/00 Extr 2m7f110y   soft   Ch

Modest staying chaser on good ground or softer; has won all his races on right-handed courses and goes well at Exeter; has been hindered by a tendency to make mistakes.

Normanby Road (NZ)
(96h)   (79h)67
12-y-o br g First Norman (USA)-Gladstone Lass (NZ) (Silver
Blaze (USA))
J L Spearing Miss S Howell

Placings: 5505/1141134B3400/3533604P/P0-P34F   **(3544)**
2002/03: 17ᴾS, 17³S, 16⁴S, 19ᶠG,

	Starts	1st	2nd	3rd	Win & Pl
Hurdles	3	0	0	1	300
Chases	1	0	0	0	0
Career Total	**30**	**4**	**0**	**6**	**15603**
113	7/99	NAbb	2m1f	D(0-120)HHdl	G-F	£2723
104	7/99	Worc	2m	E(0-115)HHdl	G-F	£2582
108	5/99	Strf	2m110y	E(0-105)HHdl	GD	£3272

---

95   5/99   Hrfd   2m1f   E(0-105)HHdl   G-S   £2598
Total win prize-money £11176

Going: Sf: 0-3 GS: 0-0 Gd: 0-1 GF: - Fm: 0-0
Distance: 2m/2m3: 0-4 2m4-2m7: 0-0 3m+: 0-0
Track: LH: 0-1 RH: 0-3 Tight: 0-1 Gall: 0-0
Aids: Bl: 0-0 Vi: 0-0 Tstrap: 0-0
Best Rating: 114 7/99 MRas 2m1f110y gd-fm Hdl

Veteran plater, acts on any ground. Lightly raced of late, has worn sheepskin cheekpieces.

Normandy Sands (IRE)
92   76
5-y-o b/br g Namaqualand (USA)-Buzz Along (Prince Bee)
L A Dace Luke Dace

Placings: 0665   **(4527)**
2002/03: 16⁶GS, 18⁶GS, 16⁶G, 20⁵G,

	Starts	1st	2nd	3rd	Win & Pl
NH Flat	3	0	0	0	0
Hurdles	1	0	0	0	0
Career Total	**4**	**0**	**0**	**0**	**0**

Going: Sf: 0-0 GS: 0-2 Gd: 0-2 GF: - Fm: 0-0
Distance: 2m/2m3: 0-3 2m4-2m7: 0-1 3m+: 0-0
Track: LH: 0-2 RH: 0-2 Tight: 0-1 Gall: 0-0
Aids: Bl: 0-0 Vi: 0-0 Tstrap: 0-0
Best Rating: 76 3/03 Hntg 2m110y good NHF

No form in bumpers; placed in weak novice hurdles in June; stays well.

Normania (NZ)
11-y-o b g First Norman (USA)-Brigania (NZ) (Brigand
(USA))
Miss Sarah West Pete Frayne

Placings: 20/0430214/3P3F/FP3/FF/5-42F   **(0403)**
2002/03: 21⁴GF, 21²GF, 22ᶠGF,

	Starts	1st	2nd	3rd	Win & Pl
Chases	3	0	1	0	2091
Career Total	**22**	**3**	**4**	**3**	**7932**
89	2/98	Hntg	2m4f110yE(0-105)HHdl	GD	£2897

Total win prize-money £2898

Going: Sf: 0-0 GS: 0-0 Gd: 0-0 GF: - Fm: 0-3
Distance: 2m/2m3: 0-0 2m4-2m7: 0-3 3m+: 0-0
Track: LH: 0-0 RH: 0-2 Tight: 0-1 Gall: 0-1
Aids: Bl: 0-0 Vi: 0-0 Tstrap: 0-0
Best Rating: 97 3/97 Winc 2m gd-fm NHF

A progressive hurdler, some promise in hunter chases in the spring of 2002.

Normanton Turville
7-y-o b g Lancastrian-Royal Pocket (True Song)
Miss L V Davis Miss Louise Davis

Placings: P   **(2000)**
2002/03: 20ᴾS,

	Starts	1st	2nd	3rd	Win & Pl
Hurdles	1	0	0	0	
Career Total	**1**	**0**	**0**	**0**	

Going: Sf: 0-1 GS: 0-0 Gd: 0-0 GF: - Fm: 0-0
Distance: 2m/2m3: 0-0 2m4-2m7: 0-1 3m+: 0-0

Track: LH: 0-1 RH: 0-0 Tight: 0-0 Gall: 0-0
Aids: Bl: 0-0 Vi: 0-0 Tstrap: 0-0
Best Rating: 0 11/02 Hayd 2m4f   soft   Hdl

Normarange (IRE)
103   94
13-y-o ch g Lancastrian-Perdeal (Perspex)
S C Burrough (P R Rodford 27/1) Mrs B Curtis

Placings: 3/3221U/211/4431/05446/424/005432-136505P   **(3601)**
2002/03: 25²GS, 25¹G, 25³G, 23⁶GF, 23⁵G, 31⁰GS, 25⁵GS, 24ᴾS,

	Starts	1st	2nd	3rd	Win & Pl
Chases	8	1	1	1	5054
Career Total	**34**	**5**	**5**	**5**	**28067**
98	5/02	Towc	3m1f	E(0-105)HCh	GD	£3150
109	4/99	Extr	2m3f	D(0-125)HCh	G-S	£4562
101	11/97	Wind	2m5f	D(0-120)HCh	G-F	£4150
98	11/97	Plum	2m5f	D(0-120)HCh	G-F	£3460
88	3/97	Plum	2m2f	F Ch		G-F	£2678

Total win prize-money £18001

Going: Sf: 0-1 GS: 0-3 Gd: 1-3 GF: - Fm: 0-1
Distance: 2m/2m3: 0-0 2m4-2m7: 0-0 3m+: 1-8
Track: LH: 0-2 RH: 1-6 Tight: 0-1 Gall: 0-0
Aids: Bl: 0-0 Vi: 0-0 Tstrap: 0-0
Best Rating: 110 1/97 Folk 2m5f   good   Ch

Veteran chaser, best suited by a sound surface, stays three miles. Has gone well at Plumpton in the past.

Normins Hussar (IRE)
11-y-o b g Glacial Storm (USA)-Little Slip (Super Slip)
C Grant Mrs M Dodgson

Placings: 00650/P6/P   **(0579)**
2002/03: 20ᴾG,

	Starts	1st	2nd	3rd	Win & Pl
Hurdles	1	0	0	0	
Career Total	**8**	**0**	**0**	**0**	**0**

Going: Sf: 0-0 GS: 0-0 Gd: 0-1 GF: - Fm: 0-0
Distance: 2m/2m3: 0-0 2m4-2m7: 0-1 3m+: 0-0
Track: LH: 0-1 RH: 0-0 Tight: 0-1 Gall: 0-0
Aids: Bl: 0-0 Vi: 0-0 Tstrap: 0-0
Best Rating: 69 4/97 Navn 2m2f   good   Hdl

Norse
81   52
10-y-o ch g Risk Me (FR)-Absent Lover (Nearly A Hand)
S E H Sherwood Jack Moody Limited

Placings: P-54   **(0446)**
2002/03: 17⁵S, 19⁴G,

	Starts	1st	2nd	3rd	Win & Pl
Chases	2	0	0	0	234
Career Total	**3**	**0**	**0**	**0**	**234**

Going: Sf: 0-1 GS: 0-0 Gd: 0-1 GF: - Fm: 0-0
Distance: 2m/2m3: 0-2 2m4-2m7: 0-0 3m+: 0-0
Track: LH: 0-1 RH: 0-1 Tight: 0-1 Gall: 0-0
Aids: Bl: 0-0 Vi: 0-0 Tstrap: 0-0
Best Rating: 55 5/02 Bang 2m1f110y soft Ch

North (IRE)

62   **35**

5-y-o br g Mukaddamah (USA)-Flamenco (USA) (Dance Spell (USA))
A C Wilson (D W Chapman 27/9) Cooper Wilson

Placings:0P   (3352)
2002/03: 16⁰G, 20ᴾHY,

	Starts	1st	2nd	3rd	Win & Pl
Hurdles	2	0	0	0	
Career Total	2	0	0	0	

Going:	Sf: 0-1 GS: 0-0 Gd: 0-1 GF: - Fm: 0-0
Distance:	2m/2m3: 0-1 2m4-2m7: 0-1 3m+: 0-0
Track:	LH: 0-1 RH: 0-1 Tight: 0-1 Gall: 0-1
Aids:	Bl: 0-0 Vi: 0-0 Tstrap: 0-0
Best Rating:	35 1/03 Muss 2m good Hdl

North Croft

7-y-o b g North Street-Sock Jinks (New Member)
C J Gray Mrs T Frampton

Placings:00-54P   (1057)
2002/03: 16⁵G, 17⁴GF, 20ᴾGF,

	Starts	1st	2nd	3rd	Win & Pl
NH Flat	1	0	0	0	0
Hurdles	2	0	0	0	290
Career Total	5	0	0	0	290

Going:	Sf: 0-0 GS: 0-0 Gd: 0-0 GF: - Fm: 0-3
Distance:	2m/2m3: 0-2 2m4-2m7: 0-1 3m+: 0-0
Track:	LH: 0-3 RH: 0-0 Tight: 0-1 Gall: 0-0
Aids:	Bl: 0-0 Vi: 0-0 Tstrap: 0-0
Best Rating:	51 9/01 Hrfd 2m1f gd-fm NHF

North Face

89(76c)   (49c)**65**

6-y-o ch g Factual (USA)-Northgate Dancer (Ile De Bourbon (USA))
Miss Lucinda V Russell Mrs L R Joughin

Placings:060/41F2P-0   (0157)
2002/03: 17⁰G,

	Starts	1st	2nd	3rd	Win & Pl
Chases	1	0	0	0	
Career Total	9	1	1	0	3960
80 6/01 Prth   2m110y E Hdl   G-F £3003
				Total win prize-money £3003

Going:	Sf: 0-0 GS: 0-0 Gd: 0-0 GF: - Fm: 0-0
Distance:	2m/2m3: 0-1 2m4-2m7: 0-0 3m+: 0-0
Track:	LH: 0-1 RH: 0-0 Tight: 0-0 Gall: 0-0
Aids:	Bl: 0-0 Vi: 0-0 Tstrap: 0-0
Best Rating:	80 12/01 Donc 2m110y good Hdl

North Gold (IRE)

92   **92**

5-y-o b g Distinctly North (USA)-Miss Goldie Locks (Dara Monarch)
M F Morris Mrs Sharon C Nelson

Placings:00034   (4749)
2002/03: 16⁶S, 16⁰HY, 18⁰S, 20³Y, 20⁴G,

	Starts	1st	2nd	3rd	Win & Pl
Hurdles	5	0	0	1	993
Career Total	5	0	0	1	993

Going:	Sf: 0-3 GS: 0-0 Gd: 0-1 GF: - Fm: 0-0
Distance:	2m/2m3: 0-3 2m4-2m7: 0-2 3m+: 0-0
Track:	LH: 0-1 RH: 0-4 Tight: 0-0 Gall: 0-0
Aids:	Bl: 0-0 Vi: 0-0 Tstrap: 0-0
Best Rating:	92 3/03 Punc 2m4f yield Hdl

Modest form in Ireland; decent enough fourth on only start in England.

North Point (IRE)

103   **115**

5-y-o b g Definite Article-Friendly Song (Song)
R Curtis (A P Jarvis 26/7) Heart Of The South Racing

Placings:1041   (4703)
2002/03: 16¹G, 16⁰G, 16⁴G, 16¹GF,

	Starts	1st	2nd	3rd	Win & Pl
Hurdles	4	2	0	0	8110
Career Total	4	2	0	0	8110
108 4/03 Plum 2m   E Hdl   G-F £3376
116 2/03 Ludl 2m   E Hdl   GD   £4358
			Total win prize-money £7735

Going:	Sf: 0-0 GS: 0-0 Gd: 1-3 GF: - Fm: 1-1
Distance:	2m/2m3: 2-4 2m4-2m7: 0-0 3m+: 0-0
Track:	LH: 1-2 RH: 1-2 Tight: 1-1 Gall: 0-0
Aids:	Bl: 0-0 Vi: 0-0 Tstrap: 0-0
Best Rating:	116 2/03 Ludl 2m good Hdl

Fair hurdler; made winning debut over hurdles; struggled in better races, but won again at Plumpton; suited by fast ground; effective at two miles.

Northaw Lad (IRE)

104f   **96f**

5-y-o ch g Executive Perk-Black Tulip (Pals Passage)
A J Lidderdale J Fishpool

Placings:5   (4444)
2002/03: 16⁵G,

	Starts	1st	2nd	3rd	Win & Pl
NH Flat	1	0	0	0	0
Career Total	1	0	0	0	0

Going:	Sf: 0-0 GS: 0-0 Gd: 0-1 GF: - Fm: 0-0
Distance:	2m/2m3: 0-1 2m4-2m7: 0-0 3m+: 0-0
Track:	LH: 0-0 RH: 0-1 Tight: 0-0 Gall: 0-0
Aids:	Bl: 0-0 Vi: 0-0 Tstrap: 0-0
Best Rating:	96 4/03 Asct 2m110y good NHF

Made a promising debut when fifth in an Ascot bumper in early April.

Northern Breeze

5-y-o ch m Lancastrian-The Mount (Le Moss)
N J Pomfret I P Crane

Placings:0P   (4574)
2002/03: 16⁰G, 22ᴾGF,

	Starts	1st	2nd	3rd	Win & Pl
NH Flat	1	0	0	0	0
Hurdles	1	0	0	0	0
Career Total	2	0	0	0	

Going:	Sf: 0-0 GS: 0-0 Gd: 0-1 GF: - Fm: 0-1
Distance:	2m/2m3: 0-1 2m4-2m7: 0-1 3m+: 0-0
Track:	LH: 0-1 RH: 0-1 Tight: 0-1 Gall: 0-1
Aids:	Bl: 0-0 Vi: 0-0 Tstrap: 0-0
Best Rating:	0 4/03 Strf 2m6f110y gd-fm Hdl

Northern Echo

98   **74**

6-y-o b g Pursuit Of Love-Stop Press (USA) (Sharpen Up)
Keith Thomas Keith Thomas

Placings:643FP2P0R-60P036004P0   (4711)
2002/03: 16⁶GS, 20⁰GF, 19ᴾG, 17⁰GF, 17³G, 17⁶G, 17⁰G, 17⁹GF, 17⁴GF, 17⁶G, 16⁹GF,

	Starts	1st	2nd	3rd	Win & Pl
Hurdles	11	0	0	1	279
Career Total	20	0	1	2	1033

Going:	Sf: 0-0 GS: 0-0 Gd: 0-5 GF: - Fm: 0-5
Distance:	2m/2m3: 0-9 2m4-2m7: 0-2 3m+: 0-0
Track:	LH: 0-10 RH: 0-1 Tight: 0-8 Gall: 0-0
Aids:	Bl: 0-0 Vi: 0-0 Tstrap: 0-0
Best Rating:	79 9/01 Hrfd 2m1f gd-fm Hdl

A poor performer on the level and over hurdles.

Northern Flash

89(67h)   (12h)**56**

9-y-o b g Rambo Dancer (CAN)-Spinster (Grundy)
J C Haynes J C Haynes

Placings:5064P0P00/603006000PP/0344P44404365/6232/PP604   (4378)
2002/03: 16ᴾHY, 20ᴾG, 16⁶G, 16⁹G, 21⁴G,

	Starts	1st	2nd	3rd	Win & Pl
Hurdles	3	0	0	0	0
Chases	3	0	0	0	261
Career Total	42	0	2	4	6394

Going:	Sf: 0-1 GS: 0-0 Gd: 0-4 GF: - Fm: 0-0
Distance:	2m/2m3: 0-3 2m4-2m7: 0-2 3m+: 0-0
Track:	LH: 0-5 RH: 0-0 Tight: 0-3 Gall: 0-0
Aids:	Bl: 0-0 Vi: 0-0 Tstrap: 0-0
Best Rating:	95 5/00 Ctml 2m1f110y good Ch

Plating-class maiden chaser.

Northern Fleet

98(101c)   (91c)**84**

10-y-o b g Slip Anchor-Kamkova (USA) (Northern Dancer)
P R Hedger Mrs J Howell

Placings:24244/212/0/0502460/35/0446PPP-32P   (1088)
2002/03: 21³G, 21²S, 26ᴾGF,

	Starts	1st	2nd	3rd	Win & Pl
Hurdles	3	0	1	1	882
Career Total	28	1	6	2	8886
103 8/97 Hntg   2m4f110yE Hdl   GD   £2232
			Total win prize-money £2233

Going:	Sf: 0-1 GS: 0-0 Gd: 0-1 GF: - Fm: 0-1
Distance:	2m/2m3: 0-2 2m4-2m7: 0-2 3m+: 0-1
Track:	LH: 0-0 RH: 0-3 Tight: 0-1 Gall: 0-2
Aids:	Bl: 0-3 Vi: 0-0 Tstrap: 0-0
Best Rating:	110 10/97 Hntg 2m4f110y good Hdl

Formerly a useful stayer on the Flat, but now a plating class performer over hurdles following several poor efforts over fences.

Northern Minster

66   **25**

4-y-o b g Minster Son-Hand On Heart (IRE) (Taufan (USA))
F P Murtagh L Irving & T Littleton

Placings:500   (4616)

2002/03: 16⁵S, 16⁰G, 17⁰GF,

	Starts	1st	2nd	3rd	Win & Pl
NH Flat	2	0	0	0	0
Hurdles	1	0	0	0	0
Career Total	3	0	0	0	0

Going: Sf: 0-1 GS: 0-0 Gd: 0-1 GF: - Fm: 0-1
Distance: 2m/2m3: 0-3 2m4-2m7: 0-0 3m+: 0-0
Track: LH: 0-2 RH: 0-1 Tight: 0-1 Gall: 0-0
Aids: Bl: 0-0 Vi: 0-0 Tstrap: 0-0
Best Rating: 84 3/03 Catt 2m soft NHF

Northern Motto

10-y-o b g Mtoto-Soulful (FR) (Zino)
C Weedon Alf Chadwick

Placings:U/025U3/2543/30/55343/00P4F0-50   (0681)
2002/03: 22⁵GF, 22⁰GF,

	Starts	1st	2nd	3rd	Win & Pl
Hurdles	2	0	0	0	0
Career Total	25	0	2	5	4282

Going: Sf: 0-0 GS: 0-0 Gd: 0-0 GF: - Fm: 0-2
Distance: 2m/2m3: 0-0 2m4-2m7: 0-2 3m+: 0-0
Track: LH: 0-2 RH: 0-0 Tight: 0-2 Gall: 0-0
Aids: Bl: 0-0 Vi: 0-0 Tstrap: 0-0
Best Rating: 104 10/99 Weth 3m1f gd-fm Hdl

A winning middle-distance handicapper on the Flat, he has not shown much over hurdles of late.

Northern Native (IRE)

92   **90+**

7-y-o br m Be My Native (USA)-Charming Mo (IRE) (Callernish)
Mrs M Reveley W J Smith M D Dudley C Raines M J Hutton

Placings:2/12-16   (3834)
2002/03: 16¹GS, 20⁶G,

	Starts	1st	2nd	3rd	Win & Pl
NH Flat	1	1	0	0	2555
Hurdles	1	0	0	0	0
Career Total	5	2	2	0	4997
109	11/02	Weth	2m	H NHF		G-S	£2555
92	11/01	Sedg	2m1f	H NHF		GD	£1568

Total win prize-money £4123

Going: Sf: 0-0 GS: 1-1 Gd: 0-1 GF: - Fm: 0-0
Distance: 2m/2m3: 1-1 2m4-2m7: 0-1 3m+: 0-0
Track: LH: 1-2 RH: 0-0 Tight: 0-0 Gall: 0-0
Aids: Bl: 0-0 Vi: 0-0 Tstrap: 0-0
Best Rating: 113 11/00 Hrfd 2m1f soft NHF

Related to Supreme Novices Hurdle winner Tourist Attraction, she won a Sedgefield bumper in November 2001 and another at Wetherby in November 2002; jumped poorly and well beaten on first try over hurdles.

Northern Raider (IRE)

5-y-o b g College Chapel-Pepper And Salt (IRE) (Double Schwartz)
Miss T Jackson H L Thompson

Placings:0100P-5   (3968)

2002/03: 25⁵S,

	Starts	1st	2nd	3rd	Win & Pl
Chases	1	0	0	0	0
Career Total	6	1	0	0	1897
57	12/01	Uttx	2m	G Hdl	SFT	£1897

Total win prize-money £1897

Going: Sf: 0-1 GS: 0-0 Gd: 0-0 GF: - Fm: 0-0
Distance: 2m/2m3: 0-0 2m4-2m7: 0-0 3m+: 0-1
Track: LH: 0-1 RH: 0-0 Tight: 0-1 Gall: 0-0
Aids:
Best Rating: 66 3/03 Catt 3m1f110y soft Ch

Northern Rambler (IRE)

87   **69**

6-y-o gr g Roselier (FR)-Ramble Bramble (Random Shot)
Mrs M Reveley W J Smith And M D Dudley

Placings:05060   (4435)
2002/03: 16⁵S, 16⁵HY, 16⁰GS, 16⁶S, 20⁰G,

	Starts	1st	2nd	3rd	Win & Pl
NH Flat	2	0	0	0	0
Hurdles	3	0	0	0	0
Career Total	5	0	0	0	0

Going: Sf: 0-3 GS: 0-1 Gd: 0-1 GF: - Fm: 0-0
Distance: 2m/2m3: 0-4 2m4-2m7: 0-1 3m+: 0-0
Track: LH: 0-5 RH: 0-0 Tight: 0-0 Gall: 0-1
Aids: Bl: 0-0 Vi: 0-0 Tstrap: 0-0
Best Rating: 88 1/03 Ayr 2m heavy NHF

Only moderate form so far in bumpers and over hurdles.

Northern Sound (IRE)

97   **125**

10-y-o b m Montelimar (USA)-Castle Felda (Le Moss)
Paul A Roche James Treacy

Placings:R/R/15032452115/P051610/PPPP45U2403P-043P   (4101)
2002/03: 24⁰SH, 20⁴YS, 25³YS, 24⁰G,

	Starts	1st	2nd	3rd	Win & Pl
Chases	4	0	0	1	2727
Career Total	36	5	3	3	60730
127	2/01	Fair	3m1f	HCh	HVY	£13104
129	1/01	Fair	3m1f	(0-116)HCh	HVY	£5564
108	4/00	Cork	3m	HCh	YLD	£7800
110	3/00	Gowr	3m	HCh	YLD	£10400
79	5/99	Dund	3m	Ch	GD	£2148

Total win prize-money £39018

Going: Sf: 0-0 GS: 0-0 Gd: 0-1 GF: - Fm: 0-0
Distance: 2m/2m3: 0-0 2m4-2m7: 0-1 3m+: 0-3
Track: LH: 0-1 RH: 0-3 Tight: 0-0 Gall: 0-1
Aids: Bl: 0-0 Vi: 0-0 Tstrap: 0-0
Best Rating: 137 4/02 Fair 3m5f gd-yld Ch

Useful soft-ground staying handicap chaser; seems to go well at Fairyhouse.

Northern Starlight

89   **124**

12-y-o b g Northern State (USA)-Ganadora (Good Times (ITY))
M C Pipe Arthur Souch

Placings:623023/411214/11111/F121112122/31U022/4534011/UP/0U-03   (4002)

2002/03: 20⁰G, 21³S,

	Starts	1st	2nd	3rd	Win & Pl
Chases	2	0	0	1	1278
Career Total	46	16	9	5	172139
143	4/00	Aint	2m6f	B(0-150)HCh	GD	£26000
144	4/00	Asct	2m3f110yB HCh	GD	£10072
144	12/98	Chel	2m5f	A HCh	GD	£47144
148	12/97	Chel	2m5f	B Ch	GD	£7335
143	11/97	Chep	2m3f110yA Ch	G-S	£12800
138	10/97	Worc	2m4f110yD Ch	GD	£3782
117	10/97	Ludl	2m4f	E Ch	G-F	£2827
134	5/97	Uttx	2m	C(0-135)HHdl	GD	£3436
138	4/97	Extr	2m3f110yC(0-130)HHdl	FRM	£4448
123	3/97	NAbb	2m1f	D(0-125)Hdl	G-F	£2849
137	3/97	Winc	2m	D(0-120)HHdl	G-F	£2805
121	3/97	Winc	2m	C(0-130)HHdl	G-F	£3415
119	2/97	Winc	2m	D(0-125)HHdl	G-F	£2826
108	11/95	Tntn	2m1f	B HHdl	G-F	£4719
100	10/95	Tntn	2m1f	G(0-90)HHdl	G-F	£2176
87	9/95	Tntn	2m1f	G Hdl	G-F	£1886

Total win prize-money £138522

Going: Sf: 0-1 GS: 0-0 Gd: 0-1 GF: - Fm: 0-0
Distance: 2m/2m3: 0-0 2m4-2m7: 0-2 3m+: 0-0
Track: LH: 0-2 RH: 0-2 Tight: 0-0 Gall: 0-0
Aids: Bl: 0-0 Vi: 0-0 Tstrap: 0-0
Best Rating: 152 12/97 Winc 2m5f gd-sft Ch

Very useful chaser at his best, but looks on the downgrade.

Northern Tennessee (IRE)

82   **110**

8-y-o ch g Muharib (USA)-Corun Girl (Apollo Eight)
B G Powell Tony Head

Placings:6/3/10251-32   (1218)
2002/03: 20³G, 17²G,

	Starts	1st	2nd	3rd	Win & Pl
Hurdles	2	0	1	1	1632
Career Total	9	2	2	2	8615
110	4/02	MRas	2m3f110yD Hdl	GD	£4046
103	5/01	Hntg	2m110y H NHF	GD	£1799

Total win prize-money £5845

Going: Sf: 0-0 GS: 0-0 Gd: 0-0 GF: - Fm: 0-0
Distance: 2m/2m3: 0-1 2m4-2m7: 0-1 3m+: 0-0
Track: LH: 0-2 RH: 0-0 Tight: 0-1 Gall: 0-0
Aids: Bl: 0-0 Vi: 0-0 Tstrap: 0-0
Best Rating: 110 9/02 Sthl 2m1f good Hdl

Modest hurdler; showed plenty of ability in bumpers, winning at Huntingdon. Won novice hurdle over just short of two and a half miles at Market Rasen April 2002. Appears to prefer a sound surface. Respectable runner-up over two miles on handicap bow. Capable of winning over further.

Norton Wood (IRE)

71   **35**

7-y-o ch g Shardari-Colligan Forest (Strong Gale)
Mrs A Price Mrs A Price

Placings:F0   (1552)
2002/03: 17⁶GS, 17⁰G,

	Starts	1st	2nd	3rd	Win & Pl
Hurdles	2	0	0	0	0
Career Total	2	0	0	0	0

Going: Sf: 0-0 GS: 0-1 Gd: 0-1 GF: - Fm: 0-0
Distance: 2m/2m3: 0-2 2m4-2m7: 0-0 3m+: 0-0
Track: LH: 0-1 RH: 0-1 Tight: 0-1 Gall: 0-0
Aids: Bl: 0-0 Vi: 0-0 Tstrap: 0-0
Best Rating: 36 10/02 Hrfd 2m1f good Hdl

Norvin (IRE)

102   **87**

6-y-o b g Nashwan (USA)-Percy s Lass (Blakeney)
Ian Williams Ian Williams

Placings:04U13   (4347)
2002/03: 16⁰G, 17⁴GS, 26³G, 25¹S, 25³GF,

	Starts	1st	2nd	3rd	Win & Pl
NH Flat	2	0	0	0	0
Hurdles	3	1	0	1	4148
Career Total	5	1	0	1	4148
87 3/03	Wwck	3m1f		E Hdl	SFT £3598

Total win prize-money £3598

Going: Sf: 1-1 GS: 0-1 Gd: 0-2 GF: - Fm: 0-1
Distance: 2m/2m3: 0-2 2m4-2m7: 0-0 **3m+: 1-3**
Track: **LH: 1-4** RH: 0-1 Tight: 0-1 Gall: 0-1
Aids: Bl: 0-0 Vi: 0-0 Tstrap: 0-0
Best Rating: 94 12/02 Bang 2m1f   gd-sft NHF

Top-class Flat pedigree but very limited ability in bumpers.

Norwood Park (NZ)

6-y-o b g Centaine (AUS)-Janine (NZ) (Wharf (USA))
Mrs M Reveley Mrs M Reveley

Placings:0-0P   (4433)
2002/03: 17⁰GF, 16ᴾG,

	Starts	1st	2nd	3rd	Win & Pl
NH Flat	1	0	0	0	0
Hurdles	1	0	0	0	0
Career Total	3	0	0	0	

Going: Sf: 0-0 GS: 0-0 Gd: 0-1 GF: - Fm: 0-1
Distance: 2m/2m3: 0-2 2m4-2m7: 0-0 3m+: 0-0
Track: LH: 0-2 RH: 0-0 Tight: 0-1 Gall: 0-1
Aids: Bl: 0-0 Vi: 0-0 Tstrap: 0-0
Best Rating: 47 12/01 Catt 2m   good NHF

Nosam

112   (79+h)**122**

13-y-o b g Idiots Delight-Socher (Anax)
R C Guest (N B Mason 26/12) N B Mason

Placings:0/6/1120/406U5113313423P3/23343114112200/0
6254622F1/3120352105-FP52463310   (4472)
2002/03: 25ᶠGS, 24ᴾGS, 20⁵G, 21²G, 21⁴G, 20⁶GF, 20³GS, 20³GS,
20¹G, 21⁰G,

	Starts	1st	2nd	3rd	Win & Pl
Hurdles	1	0	0	0	530
Chases	9	1	1	0	10600
Career Total	66	13	11	12	100052
122 2/03	Weth	2m4f110yD(0-125)HCh	GD	£5629
119 3/02	Donc	2m3f110yE(0-110)HCh	SFT	£3514
122 9/01	List	2m3f	(0-123)HCh	G-F	£7862
115 4/01	Prth	2m3f110yD(0-125)HCh	HVY	£7962
125 1/00	Donc	2m3f110yD(0-130)HCh	GD	£7020
124 1/00	Leic	2m4f110yD(0-120)HCh	GD	£5785
118 11/99	Catt	3m1f	E(0-115)HCh	G-F	£5572
114 11/99	Ayr	2m4f	D(0-120)HCh	GD	£3821
111 1/99	Donc	2m3f110yC(0-130)HCh	G-S	£5930
101 11/98	Sedg	2m5f	E Ch	G-S	£2940
97 10/98	Sedg	2m5f	E Ch	G-S	£3065
103 8/97	Ctml	2m6f	E Hdl	G-F	£2250
105 5/97	Ctml	2m6f	E Hdl	G-F	£2447

Total win prize-money £63803

Going: Sf: 0-0 GS: 0-4 Gd: 1-5 GF: - Fm: 0-1
Distance: 2m/2m3: 0-4 **2m4-2m7: 1-8** 3m+: 0-2
Track: **LH: 1-8** RH: 0-2 Tight: 0-2 Gall: 0-1

Aids: Bl: 0-0 Vi: 0-0 **Tstrap: 1-10**
Best Rating: **125** 9/00 Uttx 2m5f   gd-sft Ch

Modest chaser; he is as tough as old boots and is effective on any ground; best around two and a half miles; usually races with his tongue tied.

Noshinannikin

104(110c)   (129dc)**117**

9-y-o ch g Anshan-Preziosa (Homing)
M W Easterby Lord Daresbury

Placings:202/41045/14F1UR2/PP3P/P4412241P0C-
400006064211   (4711)
2002/03: 16⁴G, 16⁰HF, 20⁰G, 19⁰GS, 16⁰GS, 16⁶GS, 16⁰G, 16⁶G,
20⁴GF, 16²G, 16¹G, 16¹GF,

	Starts	1st	2nd	3rd	Win & Pl
Hurdles	11	2	1	0	8131
Chases	1	0	0	0	398
Career Total	42	7	6	1	34856
117 4/03	Weth	2m	F(0-100)HHdl	G-F	£2688
104 4/03	Hexm	2m110y	E(0-110)HHdl	GD	£3647
129 2/02	Hntg	2m110y	D(0-120)HCh	G-S	£3864
128 12/01	Newc	2m	E(0-115)HHdl	G-S	£3396
129 1/00	Weth	2m	E Ch	SFT	£3003
98 11/99	Hexm	2m110y	E Ch	GD	£3152
107 11/98	Newc	2m4f	E Hdl	G-S	£2410

Total win prize-money £22161

Going: Sf: 0-1 GS: 0-3 Gd: 1-6 GF: - Fm: 1-2
Distance: **2m/2m3: 2-9** 2m4-2m7: 0-3 3m+: 0-0
Track: **LH: 2-11** RH: 0-1 Tight: 0-5 Gall: 0-1
Aids: Bl: 0-1 Vi: 0-0 **Tstrap: 2-12**
Best Rating: **133** 4/00 Aint 2m4f   good Ch

Fair handicap hurdler at his best; decent chaser in his time, but on the downgrade these days; looked rejuvenated when winning over hurdles at Hexham and Wetherby in April 2003; effective over two miles; usually wears tongue strap.

Not Atall Atall

6-y-o b g Atall Atall-Paisley Park (Moor House)
M A Barnes Pointerfarm Racing Partnership

Placings:P   (1243)
2002/03: 16ᴾGF,

	Starts	1st	2nd	3rd	Win & Pl
NH Flat	1	0	0	0	
Career Total	1	0	0	0	

Going: Sf: 0-0 GS: 0-0 Gd: 0-0 GF: - Fm: 0-1
Distance: 2m/2m3: 0-1 2m4-2m7: 0-0 3m+: 0-0
Track: LH: 0-1 RH: 0-0 Tight: 0-0 Gall: 0-0
Aids: Bl: 0-0 Vi: 0-0 Tstrap: 0-0
Best Rating: 0 9/02 Hexm 2m110y   gd-fm NHF

Not Fade Away

66

5-y-o b g Ezzoud (IRE)-Green Flower (USA) (Fappiano (USA))
Miss E C Lavelle Mr & Mrs J R Lavelle

Placings:600-P   (0037)
2002/03: 22ᴾG,

	Starts	1st	2nd	3rd	Win & Pl
Hurdles	1	0	0	0	0
Career Total	4	0	0	0	0

Going: Sf: 0-0 GS: 0-0 Gd: 0-1 GF: - Fm: 0-0

Not For Parrot (IRE)

11-y-o ch g Be My Native (USA)-Sugar Quay (Quayside)
Gilbert Martin Gilbert Martin

Placings:0/234/21642/65506/3/P56004P-P   (4678)
2002/03: 19ᴾGF,

	Starts	1st	2nd	3rd	Win & Pl
Chases	1	0	0	0	
Career Total	23	1	3	2	5823
98 11/98	Winc	2m	E Hdl	G-S	£2430

Total win prize-money £2430

Going: Sf: 0-0 GS: 0-0 Gd: 0-0 GF: - Fm: 0-0
Distance: 2m/2m3: 0-1 2m4-2m7: 0-0 3m+: 0-0
Track: LH: 0-0 RH: 0-1 Tight: 0-0 Gall: 0-0
Aids: Bl: 0-0 Vi: 0-0 Tstrap: 0-0
Best Rating: 104 4/99 Worc 2m   gd-sft Hdl

Not Forgotten (USA)

67

9-y-o b g St Jovite (USA)-Past Remembered (USA) (Solford (USA))
M R Hoad Jay Byrds Partnership

Placings:3333/302012/05P5/0P53-P   (0123)
2002/03: 27ᴾGF,

	Starts	1st	2nd	3rd	Win & Pl
Hurdles	1	0	0	0	
Career Total	19	1	2	6	5259
77 11/98	Hntg	3m2f	G(0-95)HHdl	GD	£2430

Total win prize-money £2430

Going: Sf: 0-0 GS: 0-0 Gd: 0-0 GF: - Fm: 0-1
Distance: 2m/2m3: 0-0 2m4-2m7: 0-0 3m+: 0-1
Track: LH: 0-0 RH: 0-0 Tight: 0-1 Gall: 0-0
Aids: Bl: 0-0 Vi: 0-0 Tstrap: 0-0
Best Rating: 77 12/98 Towc 2m5f   soft Hdl

Not Now George

72f   **70f**

4-y-o b g Sovereign Water (FR)-Threads (Bedford (USA))
T H Caldwell Mrs S J Wall

Placings:00   (3174)
2002/03: 14⁰GS, 16⁰GS,

	Starts	1st	2nd	3rd	Win & Pl
NH Flat	2	0	0	0	
Career Total	2	0	0	0	

Going: Sf: 0-0 GS: 0-2 Gd: 0-0 GF: - Fm: 0-0
Distance: 2m/2m3: 0-1 2m4-2m7: 0-0 3m+: 0-0
Track: LH: 0-2 RH: 0-0 Tight: 0-0 Gall: 0-0
Aids: Bl: 0-0 Vi: 0-0 Tstrap: 0-0
Best Rating: 71 11/02 Wwck 1m6f   gd-sft NHF

Not Proven

74   **44**

4-y-o br g Mark Of Esteem (IRE)-Free City (USA) (Danzig (USA))

J G Fitzgerald Marquesa De Moratalla

Placings:0   (1944)
2002/03: 16⁰S,

	Starts	1st	2nd	3rd	Win & Pl
Hurdles	1	0	0	0	
Career Total	1	0	0	0	

Going:	Sf: 0-1 GS: 0-0 Gd: 0-0 GF: - Fm: 0-0
Distance:	2m/2m3: 0-1 2m4-2m7: 0-0 3m+: 0-0
Track:	LH: 0-1 RH: 0-0 Tight: 0-0 Gall: 0-1
Aids:	Bl: 0-0 Vi: 0-0 Tstrap: 0-0
Best Rating:	39 11/02 Newc 2m soft Hdl

Not To Be Missed
98   85
5-y-o gr m Missed Flight-Petinata (Petong)
R Dickin Only Horses And Fools

Placings:0005   (4522)
2002/03: 12⁰GS, 16⁰G, 17⁰S, 16⁵G,

	Starts	1st	2nd	3rd	Win & Pl
NH Flat	3	0	0	0	0
Hurdles	1	0	0	0	0
Career Total	4	0	0	0	0

Going:	Sf: 0-1 GS: 0-1 Gd: 0-2 GF: - Fm: 0-0
Distance:	2m/2m3: 0-3 2m4-2m7: 0-0 3m+: 0-0
Track:	LH: 0-2 RH: 0-2 Tight: 0-0 Gall: 0-0
Aids:	Bl: 0-0 Vi: 0-0 Tstrap: 0-0
Best Rating:	85 4/03 Uttx 2m good Hdl

Novice hurdler; can pull hard.

Not Yet Decent (IRE)
10-y-o gr g Decent Fellow-Yet (Last Fandango)
Mark Gillard T J C Seegar

Placings:544P5PP   (4417)
2002/03: 21⁵GF, 26⁴G, 24⁴G, 26ᴾHY, 25⁵S, 23ᴾGS, 25ᴾG,

	Starts	1st	2nd	3rd	Win & Pl
Chases	7	0	0	0	143
Career Total	7	0	0	0	143

Going:	Sf: 0-2 GS: 0-1 Gd: 0-3 GF: - Fm: 0-1
Distance:	2m/2m3: 0-0 2m4-2m7: 0-1 3m+: 0-6
Track:	LH: 0-2 RH: 0-5 Tight: 0-2 Gall: 0-1
Aids:	Bl: 0-0 Vi: 0-0 Tstrap: 0-0
Best Rating:	75 5/02 Uttx 3m2f good Ch

Notable Exception
14-y-o b g Top Ville-Shorthouse (Habitat)
R Dickin Mrs C M Dickin

Placings:01012/23212210423F3/6111F112460UP/3445026
43/11213/60454P/0FP/60P00/P   (0511)
2002/03: 20ᴾS,

	Starts	1st	2nd	3rd	Win & Pl
Hurdles	1	0	0	0	
Career Total	60	12	9	6	41368
107	10/96	Sedg	2m5f	E Ch		G-F £3150
103	10/96	Sedg	2m5f	E Ch		G-F £2877
92	7/96	Sthl	3m110y	D Ch		FRM £4354
123	10/94	Sedg	2m5f110y (0-125)HHdl			G-F £2108

120	9/94	Sedg	2m5f110y (0-115)HHdl		GD	£2178
111	9/94	Sedg	2m5f110y (0-115)HHdl		FRM	£2206
101	5/94	Weth	2m	Hdl	GD	£2425
106	5/94	Sedg	2m1f110y	Hdl	FRM	£1892
107	11/93	Newc	2m110y (0-130)HHdl		G-S	£2406
105	10/93	Sedg	2m1f110y (0-125)HHdl		G-F	£2532
90	2/93	Newc	2m110y	Hdl	GD	£1779
86	11/92	Catt	2m	Hdl	G-S	£1470
				Total win prize-money £29379		

Going:	Sf: 0-1 GS: 0-0 Gd: 0-0 GF: - Fm: 0-0
Distance:	2m/2m3: 0-0 2m4-2m7: 0-1 3m+: 0-0
Track:	LH: 0-1 RH: 0-0 Tight: 0-0 Gall: 0-0
Aids:	Bl: 0-0 Vi: 0-0 Tstrap: 0-0
Best Rating:	123 11/94 Sedg 2m5f110y good Hdl

Nothing Daunted
67   43
6-y-o ch g Selkirk (USA)-Khubza (Green Desert (USA))
J A Osborne (P Monteith 17/1) A Irvine

Placings:000   (3156)
2002/03: 16⁰GS, 16⁰GF, 16⁰G,

	Starts	1st	2nd	3rd	Win & Pl
Hurdles	3	0	0	0	
Career Total	3	0	0	0	

Going:	Sf: 0-0 GS: 0-1 Gd: 0-1 GF: - Fm: 0-1
Distance:	2m/2m3: 0-3 2m4-2m7: 0-0 3m+: 0-0
Track:	LH: 0-1 RH: 0-2 Tight: 0-2 Gall: 0-0
Aids:	Bl: 0-0 Vi: 0-0 Tstrap: 0-0
Best Rating:	43 1/03 Muss 2m good Hdl

Notty
(90h)   (65h)
8-y-o ch m Nicholas Bill-Silver Empress (Octavo (USA))
J C Fox P Hayward

Placings:6/0P/P/PPP-0440P0P   (1933)
2002/03: 17⁰G, 24⁴GF, 22⁴GF, 20⁰GF, 22ᴾGF, 16⁰G, 19ᴾGS,

	Starts	1st	2nd	3rd	Win & Pl
Hurdles	6	0	0	0	276
Chases	1	0	0	0	0
Career Total	14	0	0	0	276

Going:	Sf: 0-0 GS: 0-1 Gd: 0-2 GF: - Fm: 0-4
Distance:	2m/2m3: 0-3 2m4-2m7: 0-3 3m+: 0-1
Track:	LH: 0-6 RH: 0-1 Tight: 0-5 Gall: 0-0
Aids:	Bl: 0-0 Vi: 0-0 Tstrap: 0-0
Best Rating:	74 6/02 NAbb 2m1f good Hdl

Notwhatshewanted (IRE)
77   57
6-y-o b g Supreme Leader-Wise Nellie (IRE) (Brush Aside (USA))
J W Mullins Mrs M M Rayner

Placings:000P   (4673)
2002/03: 16⁰GS, 18⁰GS, 17⁰G, 26ᴾGF,

	Starts	1st	2nd	3rd	Win & Pl
NH Flat	3	0	0	0	0
Hurdles	1	0	0	0	0
Career Total	4	0	0	0	0

Going: Sf: 0-0 GS: 0-2 Gd: 0-1 GF: - Fm: 0-1

Nouf
103   115+
7-y-o b m Efisio-Miss Witch (High Line)
K C Bailey Mrs N L Spence

Placings:02314-532   (2441)
2002/03: 17⁵G, 16³GS, 16²GS,

	Starts	1st	2nd	3rd	Win & Pl
Hurdles	3	0	1	1	3177
Career Total	8	1	2	2	7499
110	2/02	Hntg	2m110y E Hdl		SFT	£2583
				Total win prize-money £2583		

Going:	Sf: 0-0 GS: 0-2 Gd: 0-1 GF: - Fm: 0-0
Distance:	2m/2m3: 0-3 2m4-2m7: 0-0 3m+: 0-0
Track:	LH: 0-1 RH: 0-2 Tight: 0-1 Gall: 0-2
Aids:	Bl: 0-0 Vi: 0-0 Tstrap: 0-0
Best Rating:	117 12/02 Hntg 2m110y gd-sft Hdl

Fair hurdler; winner on the Flat, she made the frame in ordinary novice hurdles before winning at Huntingdon in February 2002. Ran well there in a handicap in December, going down by only half a length. Suited by two miles and soft ground, used to handle good to firm on the Flat.

Noughtynova
67f   79f
6-y-o b m Petoski-Nova Spirit (Electric)
M S Saunders M S Saunders

Placings:25-05   (4296)
2002/03: 18⁰HY, 16⁵GF,

	Starts	1st	2nd	3rd	Win & Pl
NH Flat	2	0	0	0	0
Career Total	4	0	1	0	557

Going:	Sf: 0-1 GS: 0-0 Gd: 0-0 GF: - Fm: 0-1
Distance:	2m/2m3: 0-2 2m4-2m7: 0-0 3m+: 0-0
Track:	LH: 0-1 RH: 0-1 Tight: 0-1 Gall: 0-0
Aids:	Bl: 0-0 Vi: 0-0 Tstrap: 0-0
Best Rating:	102 3/02 Winc 2m soft NHF

Nousayri (IRE)
8-y-o b g Slip Anchor-Noufiyla (Top Ville)
Neil King (R Hollinshead 24/10) A R Humphrey

Placings:6/132/232666/320-405525F   (4147)
2002/03: 21⁴GF, 24⁰G, 24⁵GF, 16⁵GF, 20²F, 16⁵F, 21²G,

	Starts	1st	2nd	3rd	Win & Pl
Hurdles	3	0	0	0	
Chases	4	0	1	3	1344
Career Total	20	1	5	3	7314
103	5/99	Prth	2m110y H NHF		HVY	£1987
				Total win prize-money £1987		

Going:	Sf: 0-0 GS: 0-0 Gd: 0-2 GF: - Fm: 0-5
Distance:	2m/2m3: 0-2 2m4-2m7: 0-3 3m+: 0-1
Track:	LH: 0-4 RH: 0-3 Tight: 0-3 Gall: 0-1
Aids:	Bl: 0-0 Vi: 0-0 Tstrap: 0-3
Best Rating:	122 12/99 Hntg 2m110y good NHF

Hunter chaser; poor form recently.

Nouveau Cheval

101   **119**

8-y-o b m Picea-Freeracer (Free State)
S Woodman (M C Pipe 6/5) Fortune Racing

Placings:541015/1/3111U23-12   (1079)
2002/03: 16³G, 20¹GF, 20²G,

	Starts	1st	2nd	3rd	Win & Pl
Hurdles	3	1	1	1	3303
Career Total	16	7	2	2	19345

119	5/02	Font	2m4f	F Hdl	G-F £2383
119	3/02	Donc	2m4f	F Hdl	SFT £2415
110	2/02	Folk	2m1f110y	G Hdl	SFT £2282
94	2/02	Ludl	2m	G Hdl	SFT £2061
115	6/99	Worc	2m4f	D(0-120)HHdl	G-F £3116
109	4/99	Plum	2m4f	E Hdl	G-S £2460
104	2/99	Hntg	2m110y	E Hdl	G-S £2724
				Total win prize-money	£17443

Going: Sf: 0-0 GS: 0-0 Gd: 0-2 GF: - Fm: 1-1
Distance: 2m/2m3: 0-1 2m4-2m7: 1-2 3m+: 0-0
Track: LH: 0-1 RH: 0-0 **Tight: 1-3** Gall: 0-0
Aids: Bl: 0-0 Vi: 0-0 Tstrap: 1-2
Best Rating: 119   5/02   Font   2m4f   gd-fm   Hdl

Fair hurdler; came back better than ever after a year and a half absence and made hay in sellers and claimers over hurdles earlier this year. Stays two miles four furlongs. Well suited by plenty of give under foot.

Nova Girl

98(104h)   (84h)**84**

8-y-o b m Vital Season-Sols Joker (Comedy Star (USA))
P R Rodford P R Rodford

Placings:P/4504-P5542331U6   (2583)
2002/03: 22PGF, 20⁵G, 20⁶G, 26⁴G, 21²G, 20³G, 24³F, 21¹S, 21UGS, 19⁶GS,

	Starts	1st	2nd	3rd	Win & Pl
Hurdles	7	0	1	2	1792
Chases	3	1	0	0	3795
Career Total	15	1	1	2	5586
84	11/02 NAbb	2m5f110y E(0-105)HCh		SFT	£3794
		Total win prize-money			£3795

Going: Sf: 1-1 GS: 0-2 Gd: 0-5 GF: - Fm: 0-2
Distance: 2m/2m3: 0-0 2m4-2m7: 1-8 3m+: 0-2
Track: LH: 1-6 RH: 0-3 Tight: 1-5 Gall: 0-0
Aids: Bl: 0-0 Vi: 0-0 Tstrap: 0-2
Best Rating: 84   11/02   NAbb   2m5f110y   soft   Ch

Exposed plating hurdler. In the frame in weak mares maiden hurdle at Southwell in September. Fortunate winner on her chasing debut in November.

Novi Sad (IRE)

103   **96**

5-y-o b g Norwich-Shuil Na Gale (Strong Gale)
L Wells Mrs Carrie Zetter-Wells

Placings:02-510P53134   (4700)
2002/03: 17⁵GF, 18¹S, 17⁰GS, 21PGS, 21⁵S, 18³G, 16¹G, 16³GF, 21⁴GF,

	Starts	1st	2nd	3rd	Win & Pl
NH Flat	2	1	0	0	2405
Hurdles	7	1	0	2	7254
Career Total	11	2	1	2	10248
96	3/03	Asct	2m110y D(0-110)HHdl	GD	£5603
97	11/02	Plum	2m2f	H NHF	SFT £2404
			Total win prize-money		£8008

Going: Sf: 1-2 GS: 0-2 Gd: 1-2 GF: - Fm: 0-3
Distance: 2m/2m3: 2-6 2m4-2m7: 0-3 3m+: 0-0

Track: LH: 1-5 RH: 1-4 Tight: 0-6 Gall: 0-0
Aids: Bl: 0-0 Vi: 0-0 Tstrap: 0-0
Best Rating: 97   3/03   Font   2m2f110y good   Hdl

Modest hurdler; collared the reluctant favourite to land first hurdles success in March 2003; acts on soft and good ground; suited by further than two miles but effective at shorter.

Now Then Sid

97   **88**

4-y-o ch g Presidium-Callace (Royal Palace)
Mrs S A Watt Major E J Watt

Placings:4056   (4167)
2002/03: 14⁴GS, 16⁰G, 16⁵G, 16⁶GS,

	Starts	1st	2nd	3rd	Win & Pl
NH Flat	2	0	0	0	0
Hurdles	2	0	0	0	0
Career Total	4	0	0	0	0

Going: Sf: 0-0 GS: 0-2 Gd: 0-2 GF: - Fm: 0-0
Distance: 2m/2m3: 0-3 2m4-2m7: 0-0 3m+: 0-0
Track: LH: 0-4 RH: 0-0 Tight: 0-1 Gall: 0-1
Aids: Bl: 0-0 Vi: 0-0 Tstrap: 0-0
Best Rating: 88   2/03   Weth   2m   good   Hdl

Finished fourth on debut in bumper; showed ability on debut over hurdles at Wetherby in February.

Nowator (POL)

109   **107+**

6-y-o ch g Jape (USA)-Naradka (POL) (Dakota)
T R George Mrs S Nelson,Allan Stennett,Terry Warner

Placings:040   (4311)
2002/03: 16⁰G, 16⁴G, 21⁰G,

	Starts	1st	2nd	3rd	Win & Pl
Hurdles	3	0	0	0	0
Career Total	3	0	0	0	0

Going: Sf: 0-0 GS: 0-0 Gd: 0-3 GF: - Fm: 0-0
Distance: 2m/2m3: 0-2 2m4-2m7: 0-1 3m+: 0-0
Track: LH: 0-1 RH: 0-2 Tight: 0-0 Gall: 0-2
Aids: Bl: 0-0 Vi: 0-0 Tstrap: 0-0
Best Rating: 89   3/03   Hntg   2m110y   good   Hdl

Decent on the flat in Poland; off the mark in novice handicap hurdle at Hereford in May; lost chance at Wetherby next time when blundering two out; open to further improvement.

Nowell House

103   **110**

7-y-o ch g Polar Falcon (USA)-Langtry Lady (Pas De Seul)
M W Easterby Tony Swain & John Walsh

Placings:214/406-2515   (3408)
2002/03: 17²S, 16⁵G, 16¹HY, 16⁵GS,

	Starts	1st	2nd	3rd	Win & Pl
Hurdles	4	1	1	0	4721
Career Total	10	2	2	0	8135
110	1/03	Newc	2m	E(0-105)HHdl	HVY £3479
101	2/01	Sedg	2m1f	E Hdl	G-S £2044
			Total win prize-money		£5523

Going: Sf: 1-2 GS: 0-1 Gd: 0-1 GF: - Fm: 0-0
Distance: 2m/2m3: 1-4 2m4-2m7: 0-0 3m+: 0-0
Track: LH: 1-4 RH: 0-0 Tight: 0-1 Gall: 1-1
Aids: Bl: 0-0 Vi: 0-0 Tstrap: 0-0
Best Rating: 110   2/03   Weth   2m   gd-sft   Hdl

Modest, lightly raced hurdler, better known as a Flat per-

---

former. Suited by cut in the ground and scored with something in hand at Newcastle in January 2003.

Nowornever (IRE)

10-y-o b g Tidaro (USA)-China Blake (Private Walk)
M A Kemp M A Kemp

Placings:0/P   (0189)
2002/03: 30PGF,

	Starts	1st	2nd	3rd	Win & Pl
Chases	1	0	0	0	
Career Total	2	0	0	0	

Going: Sf: 0-0 GS: 0-0 Gd: 0-0 GF: - Fm: 0-1
Distance: 2m/2m3: 0-0 2m4-2m7: 0-0 3m+: 0-1
Track: LH: 0-0 RH: 0-1 Tight: 0-0 Gall: 0-1
Aids: Bl: 0-0 Vi: 0-0 Tstrap: 0-0
Best Rating: 0   5/02   Hntg   3m6f110y   gd-fm   Ch

Nowt

92   **67**

6-y-o b m Derrylin-Jolejester (Relkino)
D McCain Champ Chicken Co Ltd

Placings:P   (3958)
2002/03: 17PS,

	Starts	1st	2nd	3rd	Win & Pl
Hurdles	1	0	0	0	
Career Total	1	0	0	0	

Going: Sf: 0-1 GS: 0-0 Gd: 0-0 GF: - Fm: 0-0
Distance: 2m/2m3: 0-1 2m4-2m7: 0-0 3m+: 0-0
Track: LH: 0-1 RH: 0-0 Tight: 0-1 Gall: 0-0
Aids: Bl: 0-0 Vi: 0-0 Tstrap: 0-0
Best Rating: 0   3/03   Bang   2m1f   soft   Hdl

Noyan

13-y-o ch g Northern Baby (CAN)-Istiska (FR) (Irish River (FR))
D L Williams D L Williams

Placings:50121212F25/302000/1F12141/5065PP/P211/21 060/21P651-11PP12P   (4615)
2002/03: 26¹G, 24¹GF, 25⁵G, 25PG, 24¹G, 24²GF, 26PG,

	Starts	1st	2nd	3rd	Win & Pl
Chases	7	3	1	0	6058
Career Total	52	15	10	1	87983
116	5/02	Hntg	3m	H Ch	GD £1197
112	5/02	Ludl	3m	H Ch	GD £2607
108	5/02	Folk	3m2f	H Ch	GD £1157
116	4/02	Extr	2m7f110yH Ch		FRM £2250
108	5/01	Fknm	3m110y	H Ch	G-F £1579
108	5/00	Folk	3m2f	H Ch	G-F £1859
109	3/00	Sand	3m110y	H Ch	G-F £4212
102	3/00	Extr	3m1f	H Ch	G-F £2052
146	4/97	Punc	3m1f	Ch	GD £36831
135	2/97	Donc	2m3f110yD(0-115)HCh		GD £3600
120	1/97	Catt	2m	E Ch	GD £3336
113	12/96	Muss	3m4f	E Ch	GF £2953
118	12/94	Newc	2m4f	Hdl	GD £3243
124	12/94	Muss	3m4f	(0-100)HHdl	G-F £2253
100	11/94	Ayr	2m	Hdl	GD £1924
			Total win prize-money		£71059

Going: Sf: 0-0 GS: 0-0 Gd: 2-5 GF: - Fm: 1-2
Distance: 2m/2m3: 0-0 2m4-2m7: 0-0 3m+: 3-7
Track: LH: 0-3 RH: 3-4 Tight: 2-5 Gall: 1-2
Aids: Bl: 0-0 Vi: 0-0 Tstrap: 0-0
Best Rating: 146   4/97   Punc   3m1f   good   Ch

A cracking novice chaser in the 1997/1998 campaign, he had his fair share of training problems and did not return to winning form until 2000/2001 when dropped in class to hunter chases and points. Needs a sound surface and three miles plus. Won a point and hunter chases on a sound surface in 2002. Often front runs.

Nucleon Count (IRE)
84   74

7-y-o b g Nucleon (USA)-Clare s Hope (IRE) (Erin s Hope)
T D Easterby The G-Guck Group

Placings:000/3   (0700)
2002/03: 19³GF,

	Starts	1st	2nd	3rd	Win & Pl
Hurdles	1	0	0	1	638
Career Total	4	0	0	1	638

Going: Sf: 0-0 GS: 0-0 Gd: 0-0 GF: - Fm: 0-1
Distance: 2m/2m3: 0-0 2m4-2m7: 0-1 3m+: 0-0
Track: LH: 0-0 RH: 0-1 Tight: 0-1 Gall: 0-0
Aids: Bl: 0-0 Vi: 0-0 Tstrap: 0-0
Best Rating: 90 9/00 MRas 1m5f110y gd-fm NHF

Nurseryman (IRE)
81f   48f

6-y-o b g Mandalus-The Mighty Midge (Hardgreen (USA))
P Winkworth P Winkworth

Placings:0   (4444)
2002/03: 16⁰G,

	Starts	1st	2nd	3rd	Win & Pl
NH Flat	1	0	0	0	
Career Total	1	0	0	0	

Going: Sf: 0-0 GS: 0-0 Gd: 0-1 GF: - Fm: 0-0
Distance: 2m/2m3: 0-1 2m4-2m7: 0-0 3m+: 0-0
Track: LH: 0-0 RH: 0-1 Tight: 0-0 Gall: 0-0
Aids: Bl: 0-0 Vi: 0-0 Tstrap: 0-0
Best Rating: 48 4/03 Asct 2m110y good NHF

Nurzyk (POL)
103   81+

6-y-o ch g Freedom s Choice (USA)-Numeria (POL) (Dakota)
T R George C Davies,S Nelson,A Stennett,T Warner

Placings:P00   (4310)
2002/03: 22ᴾHY, 19⁰GS, 24⁰G,

	Starts	1st	2nd	3rd	Win & Pl
Hurdles	3	0	0	0	
Career Total	3	0	0	0	

Going: Sf: 0-1 GS: 0-1 Gd: 0-1 GF: - Fm: 0-0
Distance: 2m/2m3: 0-0 2m4-2m7: 0-2 3m+: 0-1
Track: LH: 0-2 RH: 0-1 Tight: 0-1 Gall: 0-1
Aids: Bl: 0-0 Vi: 0-0 Tstrap: 0-0
Best Rating: 0 3/03 Newb 3m110y good Hdl

Flat winner in Poland; winner over an extreme distance at Sedgefield in May; acts well in soft ground.

Nutcracker Lad (IRE)
55

5-y-o ch g Duky-Allercashin Moon (IRE) (Callernish)

M J Gingell C N & Mrs A V Roberts

Placings:0   (4685)
2002/03: 16⁰GF,

	Starts	1st	2nd	3rd	Win & Pl
NH Flat	1	0	0	0	
Career Total	1	0	0	0	

Going: Sf: 0-0 GS: 0-0 Gd: 0-0 GF: - Fm: 0-1
Distance: 2m/2m3: 0-1 2m4-2m7: 0-0 3m+: 0-0
Track: LH: 0-0 RH: 0-1 Tight: 0-0 Gall: 0-1
Aids: Bl: 0-0 Vi: 0-0 Tstrap: 0-0
Best Rating: 66 4/03 Hntg 2m110y gd-fm NHF

Nutley King (IRE)
101   99+

4-y-o b g Night Shift (USA)-Quintellina (Robellino (USA))
M C Pipe (J T Gorman 10/11) T A Jones

Placings:365   (3494)
2002/03: 16³S, 16⁶S, 16⁵GS,

	Starts	1st	2nd	3rd	Win & Pl
Hurdles	3	0	0	1	1254
Career Total	3	0	0	1	1254

Going: Sf: 0-2 GS: 0-1 Gd: 0-0 GF: - Fm: 0-0
Distance: 2m/2m3: 0-3 2m4-2m7: 0-0 3m+: 0-0
Track: LH: 0-0 RH: 0-3 Tight: 0-0 Gall: 0-1
Aids: Bl: 0-0 Vi: 0-0 Tstrap: 0-0
Best Rating: 97 2/03 Kemp 2m gd-sft Hdl

O J Selym (IRE)
98   (92h)103

9-y-o b g Be My Native (USA)-Myle Avenue (Push On)
H D Daly Michael Opperman

Placings:00/5405/46P1-633P   (0906)
2002/03: 16¹GS, 16⁶GS, 23³G, 23⁹GF, 20ᴾG,

	Starts	1st	2nd	3rd	Win & Pl
Chases	5	1	0	2	5324
Career Total	14	1	0	2	5795

103 4/02 Towc 2m110y E(0-105)HCh G-S £4357
Total win prize-money £4358

Going: Sf: 0-0 GS: 1-2 Gd: 0-2 GF: - Fm: 0-1
Distance: 2m/2m3: 1-2 2m4-2m7: 0-1 3m+: 0-2
Track: LH: 0-3 RH: 1-2 Tight: 0-0 Gall: 0-0
Aids: Bl: 0-0 Vi: 0-0 Tstrap: 0-0
Best Rating: 103 4/02 Towc 2m110y gd-sft Ch

Lightly raced, he got off the mark in a weak novices handicap chase at Towcester in 2002.

O So Bossy

13-y-o ch g Sousa-Bubbling Spirit (Hubble Bubble)
A W Congdon A W Congdon

Placings:F/4/U-3   (0371)
2002/03: 26³S,

	Starts	1st	2nd	3rd	Win & Pl
Chases	1	0	0	1	513
Career Total	4	0	0	1	513

Going: Sf: 0-1 GS: 0-0 Gd: 0-0 GF: - Fm: 0-0
Distance: 2m/2m3: 0-0 2m4-2m7: 0-0 3m+: 0-1
Track: LH: 0-1 RH: 0-0 Tight: 0-1 Gall: 0-0
Aids: Bl: 0-0 Vi: 0-0 Tstrap: 0-0
Best Rating: 87 5/02 NAbb 3m2f110y soft Ch

O'Flaherty'S (IRE)

11-y-o ch g Balinger-Deise Lady (Le Bavard (FR))
G D Blagbrough G D Blagbrough

Placings:0/30U   (4147)
2002/03: 20³GF, 24⁰G, 21ᵁG,

	Starts	1st	2nd	3rd	Win & Pl
Chases	3	0	0	1	315
Career Total	4	0	0	1	315

Going: Sf: 0-0 GS: 0-0 Gd: 0-2 GF: - Fm: 0-1
Distance: 2m/2m3: 0-0 2m4-2m7: 0-2 3m+: 0-1
Track: LH: 0-2 RH: 0-1 Tight: 0-2 Gall: 0-1
Aids: Bl: 0-0 Vi: 0-0 Tstrap: 0-0
Best Rating: 68 5/02 Strf 2m4f gd-fm Ch

Oakfords Lad
76   45

9-y-o b g Syrtos-Dame Nellie (Dominion)
R H Alner R Alner

Placings:0P   (4386)
2002/03: 19⁰GS, 19ᴾF,

	Starts	1st	2nd	3rd	Win & Pl
Hurdles	2	0	0	0	
Career Total	2	0	0	0	

Going: Sf: 0-0 GS: 0-1 Gd: 0-0 GF: - Fm: 0-1
Distance: 2m/2m3: 0-2 2m4-2m7: 0-0 3m+: 0-0
Track: LH: 0-0 RH: 0-2 Tight: 0-0 Gall: 0-0
Aids: Bl: 0-0 Vi: 0-0 Tstrap: 0-0
Best Rating: 45 2/03 Extr 2m3f gd-sft Hdl

Oaklands Millie (IRE)
93   49

10-y-o b m Millfontaine-Milpe (Milan)
I Park Ian Park

Placings:065PP-6660   (1704)
2002/03: 16⁶G, 20⁶G, 17⁶GF, 27⁰G,

	Starts	1st	2nd	3rd	Win & Pl
Hurdles	4	0	0	0	0
Career Total	9	0	0	0	0

Going: Sf: 0-0 GS: 0-0 Gd: 0-3 GF: - Fm: 0-1
Distance: 2m/2m3: 0-2 2m4-2m7: 0-1 3m+: 0-1
Track: LH: 0-3 RH: 0-1 Tight: 0-2 Gall: 0-0
Aids: Bl: 0-0 Vi: 0-0 Tstrap: 0-0
Best Rating: 65 5/01 Hexm 2m firm Hdl

Oakley Cello

7-y-o ch g Michelozzo (USA)-Susie Oakley Vii (Damsire Unregistered)
M Madgwick Brian C Oakley

Placings:0   (0328)
2002/03: 16⁰G,

	Starts	1st	2nd	3rd	Win & Pl
NH Flat	1	0	0	0	
Career Total	1	0	0	0	

Going: Sf: 0-0 GS: 0-0 Gd: 0-1 GF: - Fm: 0-0
Distance: 2m/2m3: 0-1 2m4-2m7: 0-0 3m+: 0-0
Track: LH: 0-1 RH: 0-0 Tight: 0-0 Gall: 0-0
Aids: Bl: 0-0 Vi: 0-0 Tstrap: 0-0

Oboedire (IRE)

102   83

10-y-o br g Royal Fountain-Another Pride (Golden Love)
Sir John Barlow Bt T D B Barlow

Placings:21P3P-P4   (4401)
2002/03: 25PG, 24AGF,

	Starts	1st	2nd	3rd	Win & Pl
Chases	2	0	0	0	664
Career Total	**7**	**1**	**1**	**1**	**13901**
101 11/01 Hayd	3m	B Ch		SFT	£9597
			Total win prize-money £9598

Going:	Sf: 0-0 GS: 0-0 Gd: 0-1 GF: - Fm: 0-1
Distance:	2m/2m3: 0-0 2m4-2m7: 0-0 3m+: 0-2
Track:	LH: 0-2 RH: 0-0 Tight: 0-0 Gall: 0-0
Aids:	Bl: 0-0 Vi: 0-0 Tstrap: 0-0
Best Rating:	101 11/01 Hayd 3m soft Ch

Modest chaser; winning point-to-pointer; likes soft ground;
stays three miles plus.

Occam (IRE)

97(105h)   (80 h)89

9-y-o ch g Sharp Victor (USA)-Monterana (Sallust)
A Bailey Mrs J Bailey

Placings:00/0-304130304440P023   (4783)
2002/03: 16³GF, 16⁹GF, 16⁴GF, 17¹GF, 17³G, 16⁹GF, 17³G, 16⁹G,
17⁴GF, 16⁴S, 16⁶S, 17⁷S, 17⁹G, 16²GF, 17³G,

	Starts	1st	2nd	3rd	Win & Pl
Hurdles	12	1	0	3	5221
Chases	4	0	1	1	2292
Career Total	**20**	**1**	**1**	**4**	**7513**
94 8/02 Bang	2m1f	E(0-105)HHdl	GF	£3770
			Total win prize-money £3770

Going:	Sf: 0-4 GS: 0-0 Gd: 0-5 GF: - Fm: 1-7
Distance:	2m/2m3: 1-16 2m4-2m7: 0-0 3m+: 0-0
Track:	LH: 1-12 RH: 0-4 Tight: 1-7 Gall: 0-0
Aids:	Bl: 0-0 Vi: 0-0 Tstrap: 0-0
Best Rating:	94 8/02 Bang 2m1f gd-fm Hdl

Winning hurdler; plating-class chaser; best at around two
miles.

Occold (IRE)

110   139

12-y-o b g Over The River (FR)-My Puttens (David Jack)
Ferdy Murphy Exors Of The Late G A Hubbard

Placings:3/12311F2/3P1P12-44   (0917)
2002/03: 23⁴YS, 24⁴GS,

	Starts	1st	2nd	3rd	Win & Pl
Chases	2	0	0	0	2225
Career Total	**16**	**5**	**3**	**3**	**44073**
139 3/02 Carl	3m2f	D(0-125)HCh	G-S	£5538
132 1/02 Towc	3m1f	C(0-130)HCh	HVY	£8365
143 1/98 Kemp	3m	D Ch	G-S	£4375
137 12/97 Hntg	2m4f110yE Ch	G-S	£2675
99 10/97 Strf	2m6f110yD Hdl	GD	£3213
			Total win prize-money £24169

Going:	Sf: 0-0 GS: 0-1 Gd: 0-0 GF: - Fm: 0-0
Distance:	2m/2m3: 0-0 2m4-2m7: 0-1 3m+: 0-1
Track:	LH: 0-0 RH: 0-1 Tight: 0-0 Gall: 0-0
Aids:	Bl: 0-0 Vi: 0-0 Tstrap: 0-0
Best Rating:	151 4/98 Aint 3m1f soft Ch

Very useful chaser; handles heavy ground, has won on
good,and stays three miles. Sustained muscle damage
when rearing over before disappointing at Kempton in
February 2002 but has won since.

Ocean Dancer

87   93+

6-y-o b g Primitive Rising (USA)-Bally Small (Sunyboy)
P Beaumont Mrs S Sunter

Placings:60062   (3095)
2002/03: 17⁶G, 17⁹G, 16⁹GS, 19⁶GS, 16²GS,

	Starts	1st	2nd	3rd	Win & Pl
NH Flat	2	0	0	0	0
Hurdles	3	0	1	0	1102
Career Total	**5**	**0**	**1**	**0**	**1102**

Going:	Sf: 0-0 GS: 0-3 Gd: 0-2 GF: - Fm: 0-0
Distance:	2m/2m3: 0-4 2m4-2m7: 0-1 3m+: 0-0
Track:	LH: 0-4 RH: 0-1 Tight: 0-2 Gall: 0-2
Aids:	Bl: 0-0 Vi: 0-0 Tstrap: 0-0
Best Rating:	93 1/03 Donc 2m110y gd-sft Hdl

Much improved form when game runner-up behind a useful
sort at Doncaster in January.

Ocean Line (IRE)

82   111

8-y-o b g Kefaah (USA)-Tropic Sea (IRE) (Sure Blade
(USA))
Jonjo O Neill The Cartmel Syndicate

Placings:3003P11/10540213-F61P   (1182)
2002/03: 16⁵S, 17⁶GF, 20¹G, 21⁶G,

	Starts	1st	2nd	3rd	Win & Pl
Hurdles	4	1	0	0	2258
Career Total	**19**	**5**	**1**	**3**	**22710**
111 8/02 Font	2m4f	F Hdl	GD	£2257
108 10/01 Ludl	2m	D(0-120)HHdl	G-F	£5057
110 5/01 Ayr	2m	D(0-125)HHdl	G-F	£5183
109 10/00 Ludl	2m	D(0-120)HHdl	G-F	£5057
99 10/00 Ludl	2m	G Hdl	G-F	£1960
			Total win prize-money £19516

Going:	Sf: 0-1 GS: 0-0 Gd: 1-2 GF: - Fm: 0-1
Distance:	2m/2m3: 0-2 2m4-2m7: 1-2 3m+: 0-0
Track:	LH: 0-3 RH: 0-0 Tight: 1-2 Gall: 0-0
Aids:	Bl: 0-0 Vi: 0-0 Tstrap: 0-0
Best Rating:	111 8/02 Font 2m4f good Hdl

He is an effective sort in minor handicap hurdles. Best on
fast ground.

Ocean Love (IRE)

71   66

5-y-o b m Dolphin Street (FR)-Scuba Diver (King s Lake
(USA))
C Weedon Alf Chadwick

Placings:0560P-0   (0417)
2002/03: 16⁹GF,

	Starts	1st	2nd	3rd	Win & Pl
Hurdles	1	0	0	0	0
Career Total	**6**	**0**	**0**	**0**	**0**

Going:	Sf: 0-0 GS: 0-0 Gd: 0-0 GF: - Fm: 0-0
Distance:	2m/2m3: 0-1 2m4-2m7: 0-0 3m+: 0-0
Track:	LH: 0-1 RH: 0-0 Tight: 0-1 Gall: 0-0
Aids:	Bl: 0-0 Vi: 0-0 Tstrap: 0-0
Best Rating:	66 1/02 Kemp 2m gd-sft Hdl

Modest middle-distance maiden on the Flat.

Ocean Peak (NZ)

94   74

10-y-o b g Gay Apollo-Red Sea (NZ) (Noble Bijou (USA))

B P J Baugh M W & A N Harris

Placings:1/P1U00/00P0-0P55040   (4706)
2002/03: 19⁹GS, 23PGS, 17⁵GS, 16⁵S, 16⁹GF, 16⁴GF, 20⁰G,

	Starts	1st	2nd	3rd	Win & Pl
Hurdles	7	0	0	0	0
Career Total	**17**	**2**	**0**	**0**	**5764**
114 12/00 Ludl	2m	D Ch	G-S	£3779
5/99 Trap	1m4f	Hdl	G-S	£1984
			Total win prize-money £5764

Going:	Sf: 0-1 GS: 0-3 Gd: 0-1 GF: - Fm: 0-2
Distance:	2m/2m3: 0-4 2m4-2m7: 0-3 3m+: 0-0
Track:	LH: 0-5 RH: 0-2 Tight: 0-2 Gall: 0-0
Aids:	Bl: 0-0 Vi: 0-0 Tstrap: 0-0
Best Rating:	114 12/00 Ludl 2m gd-sft Ch

Ocean Tide

105   110

6-y-o b g Deploy-Dancing Tide (Pharly (FR))
R Ford A Eyres & D F Price

Placings:5030/2133-14352U0   (3843)
2002/03: 22¹G, 22⁴S, 24³GS, 23⁵S, 24²G, 23⁴GS, 24⁰G,

	Starts	1st	2nd	3rd	Win & Pl
Hurdles	7	1	1	1	5917
Career Total	**15**	**2**	**2**	**4**	**13032**
110 5/02 Kels	2m6f110yE Hdl	GD	£2702
105 2/02 Muss	3m4f	D(0-115)HHdl	G-S	£4212
			Total win prize-money £6914

Going:	Sf: 0-2 GS: 0-2 Gd: 1-3 GF: - Fm: 0-0
Distance:	2m/2m3: 0-0 2m4-2m7: 1-3 3m+: 0-4
Track:	LH: 1-5 RH: 0-0 Tight: 1-3 Gall: 0-0
Aids:	Bl: 0-0 Vi: 1-7 Tstrap: 0-0
Best Rating:	110 1/03 Muss 3m good Hdl

Modest hurdler; had shown ability over hurdles before scoring at Musselburgh in February 2002 and added to that at
Kelso in May. Decent efforts since. Stays three miles. Acts
on most ground.

Ocean Trout

7-y-o b m Sea Raven (IRE)-Rosa Trout (Goldhill)
R D E Woodhouse R D E Woodhouse

Placings:30/0-P   (0335)
2002/03: 23⁹G,

	Starts	1st	2nd	3rd	Win & Pl
Hurdles	1	0	0	0	0
Career Total	**4**	**0**	**0**	**1**	**280**

Going:	Sf: 0-0 GS: 0-0 Gd: 0-1 GF: - Fm: 0-0
Distance:	2m/2m3: 0-0 2m4-2m7: 0-1 3m+: 0-0
Track:	LH: 0-1 RH: 0-0 Tight: 0-0 Gall: 0-0
Aids:	Bl: 0-0 Vi: 0-0 Tstrap: 0-0
Best Rating:	15 2/01 Weth 2m soft NHF

Ockley Flyer

90   74

4-y-o b g Sir Harry Lewis (USA)-Bewails (IRE) (Caerleon
(USA))
A Ennis Alan Walder

Placings:06300   (4292)
2002/03: 18⁰G, 17⁶HY, 16³HY, 20⁵S, 16⁹GF,

	Starts	1st	2nd	3rd	Win & Pl
Hurdles	5	0	0	1	548
Career Total	**5**	**0**	**0**	**1**	**548**

Going: Sf: 0-3 GS: 0-0 Gd: 0-1 GF: - Fm: 0-1
Distance: 2m/2m3: 0-4 2m4-2m7: 0-1 3m+: 0-0
Track: LH: 0-2 RH: 0-2 Tight: 0-4 Gall: 0-0
Aids: Bl: 0-0 Vi: 0-0 Tstrap: 0-4
Best Rating: 74 3/03 Winc 2m gd-fm Hdl

No better than plating class based on what we've seen so far. Best run came when third at Plumpton on heavy ground in a juvenile hurdle.

Octagonal (IRE)
98

6-y-o b g Woods Of Windsor (USA)-Strawberry Belle (IRE) (Vision (USA))
Miss K Marks (Miss F M Crowley 5/9) Nick Shutts

Placings:46600/3FP-403011P (3843)
2002/03: 20⁵HY, 16⁴S, 24⁰S, 17³Y, 24⁰YS, 20¹G, 20¹F, 24⁵G,

	Starts	1st	2nd	3rd	Win & Pl
Hurdles	8	2	0	1	8270
Career Total	15	2	0	2	9234
98	9/02	Clon	2m4f	(67-102)HHdl	FRM	£3809
97	9/02	Rosc	2m4f	Hdl	GD	£3809

Total win prize-money £7620

Going: Sf: 0-3 GS: 0-0 Gd: 1-2 GF: - Fm: 1-1
Distance: 2m/2m3: 0-2 **2m4-2m7: 2-3** 3m+: 0-3
Track: LH: 0-0 RH: 0-1 Tight: 0-0 Gall: 0-0
Aids: Bl: 2-5 Vi: 0-0 Tstrap: 0-0
Best Rating: 98 9/02 Clon 2m4f firm Hdl

Ex-Irish hurdler; stays two miles four; best on a sound surface although handles cut; wears blinkers.

October Mist (IRE)
113(103c)   (144c)134

9-y-o gr g Roselier (FR)-Bonny Joe (Derring Rose)
Mrs M Reveley Mrs E A Murray

Placings:2/3311116/1163/**121FP5**-44204 (3730)
2002/03: 16⁴GS, 20⁴G, 16²GS, 16⁹G, 24⁴G,

	Starts	1st	2nd	3rd	Win & Pl
Hurdles	5	0	1	0	14595
Career Total	23	8	3	3	54112
123	12/01	Weth	2m4f110y		D Ch	SFT	£4576
134	11/01	Weth	2m	E Ch	GD	£3857
159	11/00	Hayd	2m6f	B(0-140)HHdl	HVY	£6683
150	11/00	Ayr	2m4f	C(0-130)HHdl	SFT	£5018
148	2/00	Hayd	2m	C HHdl	HVY	£4914
122	1/00	Kels	2m2f	E Hdl	GD	£2394
119	12/99	Weth	2m4f110yD(0-110)HHdl	G-S	£3577
96	12/99	MRas	2m1f110yD Hdl	G-S	£3051

Total win prize-money £34073

Going: Sf: 0-0 GS: 0-2 Gd: 0-3 GF: - Fm: 0-0
Distance: 2m/2m3: 0-3 2m4-2m7: 0-1 3m+: 0-1
Track: LH: 0-4 RH: 0-1 Tight: 0-0 Gall: 0-2
Aids: Bl: 0-0 Vi: 0-0 Tstrap: 0-0
Best Rating: 159 11/00 Hayd 2m6f heavy Hdl

Useful hurdler, he is not as good over fences, but still quite decent; suited by a flat, left-handed track; best on easy ground; stays two miles four.

Odagh Odyssey (IRE)
102   137

9-y-o ch g Ikdam-Riverside Willow (Callernish)
Miss E C Lavelle R J Lavelle

Placings:40004/F111/3P11-5F (4050)

2002/03: 20⁵GS, 24⁶S,

	Starts	1st	2nd	3rd	Win & Pl
Chases	2	0	0	0	416
Career Total	15	5	0	1	34495
137	12/01	Asct	2m3f110yB(0-145)HCh	GD	£17342
134	12/01	Leic	2m4f110yE(0-115)HCh	GD	£4403
134	4/01	Hntg	2m110y E Ch	SFT	£3777
120	1/01	Tntn	2m3f	D(0-110)HCh	SFT	£4407
116	12/00	Tntn	2m3f	F(0-95)HCh	SFT	£3224

Total win prize-money £33155

Going: Sf: 0-1 GS: 0-1 Gd: 0-0 GF: - Fm: 0-0
Distance: 2m/2m3: 0-0 2m4-2m7: 0-1 3m+: 0-1
Track: LH: 0-0 RH: 0-2 Tight: 0-0 Gall: 0-0
Aids: Bl: 0-0 Vi: 0-0 Tstrap: 0-0
Best Rating: 137 12/01 Asct 2m3f110y good Ch

Useful chaser; satisfactory return to action in February 2003 after lengthy absence; suited by two and a half miles and good ground or softer; needs to race right-handed.

Odd Job (IRE)
83f   87f

5-y-o b/br g Jolly Jake (NZ)-Kristellita (FR) (Crystal Palace (FR))
Jonjo O Neill (D T Hughes 12/5) Mr & Mrs Peter S Thompson/Mrs J O Neill

Placings:04 (4788)
2002/03: 17⁰YS, 17⁴G,

	Starts	1st	2nd	3rd	Win & Pl
NH Flat	2	0	0	0	0
Career Total	2	0	0	0	0

Going: Sf: 0-0 GS: 0-0 Gd: 0-1 GF: - Fm: 0-0
Distance: 2m/2m3: 0-2 2m4-2m7: 0-0 3m+: 0-0
Track: LH: 0-0 RH: 0-1 Tight: 0-1 Gall: 0-0
Aids: Bl: 0-0 Vi: 0-0 Tstrap: 0-0
Best Rating: 84 4/03 MRas 2m1f110y good NHF

Well beaten fourth on first run here in modest bumper at Market Rasen in April.

Oddlydodd (IRE)
102   101

7-y-o b g Tremblant-Poor Times (IRE) (Roselier (FR))
T Keddy Mrs H Keddy

Placings:00PP410-P6PP03603 (4683)
2002/03: 20⁰GS, 24⁶GS, 24⁶GS, 19⁵GS, 16⁶HY, 20³G, 22⁶G, 17⁹G, 21³GF,

	Starts	1st	2nd	3rd	Win & Pl
Hurdles	6	0	0	2	870
Chases	3	0	0	0	0
Career Total	16	1	0	2	4440
101	3/02	Wwck	2m5f	D(0-115)HHdl	G-S	£3570

Total win prize-money £3570

Going: Sf: 0-1 GS: 0-4 Gd: 0-3 GF: - Fm: 0-1
Distance: 2m/2m3: 0-2 2m4-2m7: 0-5 3m+: 0-2
Track: LH: 0-2 RH: 0-6 Tight: 0-1 Gall: 0-4
Aids: Bl: 0-1 Vi: 0-0 Tstrap: 0-0
Best Rating: 101 3/03 MRas 2m6f good Hdl

Modest hurdler; acts on a soft surface; stays two miles five.

Odell (IRE)

13-y-o br g Torus-Indian Isle (Warpath)
Miss A E Broyd Miss Alison Broyd

Placings:P/61/5F/F0P/2PP3306/PFPP/6PP (0656)

2002/03: 20⁶F, 21⁸GF, 23⁸GF,

	Starts	1st	2nd	3rd	Win & Pl
Chases	3	0	0	0	0
Career Total	22	1	1	2	5235
89	3/97	Hntg	2m110y E Ch	G-F	£3258

Total win prize-money £3259

Going: Sf: 0-0 GS: 0-0 Gd: 0-0 GF: - Fm: 0-3
Distance: 2m/2m3: 0-0 2m4-2m7: 0-2 3m+: 0-1
Track: LH: 0-3 RH: 0-0 Tight: 0-1 Gall: 0-0
Aids: Bl: 0-0 Vi: 0-0 Tstrap: 0-0
Best Rating: 99 10/98 Font 2m3f gd-sft Ch

Off Broadway (IRE)
102f   106f

5-y-o b g Presenting-Mona Curra Gale (IRE) (Strong Gale)
A King The Presenters

Placings:2 (4005)
2002/03: 16²S,

	Starts	1st	2nd	3rd	Win & Pl
NH Flat	1	0	1	0	570
Career Total	1	0	1	0	570

Going: Sf: 0-1 GS: 0-0 Gd: 0-0 GF: - Fm: 0-0
Distance: 2m/2m3: 0-1 2m4-2m7: 0-0 3m+: 0-0
Track: LH: 0-0 RH: 0-1 Tight: 0-0 Gall: 0-0
Aids: Bl: 0-0 Vi: 0-0 Tstrap: 0-0
Best Rating: 106 3/03 Winc 2m soft NHF

Placed in a bumper on soft ground.

Off The Wood
67   25

7-y-o gr m Baron Blakeney-Rocquelle (Coquelin (USA))
Mrs Barbara Waring J Thow Wood

Placings:00P-P0 (0443)
2002/03: 16⁶GS, 17⁰G,

	Starts	1st	2nd	3rd	Win & Pl
Hurdles	2	0	0	0	
Career Total	5	0	0	0	

Going: Sf: 0-0 GS: 0-1 Gd: 0-1 GF: - Fm: 0-0
Distance: 2m/2m3: 0-2 2m4-2m7: 0-0 3m+: 0-0
Track: LH: 0-1 RH: 0-1 Tight: 0-1 Gall: 0-0
Aids: Bl: 0-0 Vi: 0-0 Tstrap: 0-0
Best Rating: 46 12/01 Ludl 2m good NHF

Offley Lucielastic

10-y-o b m Tromeros-Village Pride (Quality Fair)
R Hollinshead Miss Lynne Hartley

Placings:P (0055)
2002/03: 24⁷G,

	Starts	1st	2nd	3rd	Win & Pl
Chases	1	0	0	0	
Career Total	1	0	0	0	

Going: Sf: 0-0 GS: 0-0 Gd: 0-1 GF: - Fm: 0-0
Distance: 2m/2m3: 0-0 2m4-2m7: 0-0 3m+: 0-1
Track: LH: 0-1 RH: 0-0 Tight: 0-1 Gall: 0-0
Aids: Bl: 0-0 Vi: 0-0 Tstrap: 0-0
Best Rating:

Offshore (IRE)

10-y-o b g Over The River (FR)-Parsons Princess (The Parson)
T D McCarthy F R Jackson

Placings:344/P-P2PP   (4185)
2002/03: 26PS, 262S, 26PS, 25PG,

	Starts	1st	2nd	3rd	Win & Pl
Chases	4	0	1	0	1248
Career Total	8	0	1	1	1441

Going:	Sf: 0-3 GS: 0-0 Gd: 0-1 GF: - Fm: 0-0
Distance:	2m/2m3: 0-0 2m4-2m7: 0-0 3m+: 0-4
Track:	LH: 0-1 RH: 0-1 Tight: 0-4 Gall: 0-0
Aids:	Bl: 0-2 Vi: 0-0 Tstrap: 0-0
Best Rating:	103 4/98 Chel 2m1f heavy NHF

Very moderate pointer, distant second in a novice chase in February 2003.

Oh No Not Him

85   50

7-y-o b g Reprimand-Lucky Mill (Midyan (USA))
W M Brisbourne Mugs Inc

Placings:00/0P   (1498)
2002/03: 16PGF, 20PG,

	Starts	1st	2nd	3rd	Win & Pl
Hurdles	2	0	0	0	
Career Total	4	0	0	0	

Going:	Sf: 0-0 GS: 0-0 Gd: 0-1 GF: - Fm: 0-1
Distance:	2m/2m3: 0-1 2m4-2m7: 0-1 3m+: 0-0
Track:	LH: 0-2 RH: 0-0 Tight: 0-0 Gall: 0-0
Aids:	Bl: 0-0 Vi: 0-0 Tstrap: 0-0
Best Rating:	50 10/02 Uttx 2m gd-fm Hdl

Oh So Posh

73f   36f

4-y-o b f Overbury (IRE)-Sally Ho (Gildoran)
J R Bewley R Bewley

Placings:000   (3817)
2002/03: 14QGS, 17QHY, 16QG,

	Starts	1st	2nd	3rd	Win & Pl
NH Flat	3	0	0	0	
Career Total	3	0	0	0	

Going:	Sf: 0-1 GS: 0-1 Gd: 0-1 GF: - Fm: 0-0
Distance:	2m/2m3: 0-2 2m4-2m7: 0-0 3m+: 0-0
Track:	LH: 0-3 RH: 0-0 Tight: 0-2 Gall: 0-0
Aids:	Bl: 0-0 Vi: 0-0 Tstrap: 0-1
Best Rating:	36 12/02 Ayr 1m6f gd-sft NHF

Oh So Wisley

101(103h)   (103h)105+

8-y-o b g Teenoso (USA)-Easy Horse (FR) (Carmarthen (FR))
N A Twiston-Davies The Wisley Golf Partnership

Placings:0006/3213164/1-P230   (3523)
2002/03: 26PHY, 242QGS, 243S, 24QG,

	Starts	1st	2nd	3rd	Win & Pl
Hurdles	1	0	0	0	0
Chases	3	0	1	1	2466
Career Total	16	3	2	3	11942

103	9/01	Worc	3m	F(0-100)HHdl	G-F	£2838
105	1/01	Tntn	3m110y	F(0-110)HHdl	HVY	£2271
98	11/00	Wwck	2m5f	D(0-110)HHdl	HVY	£2850

Total win prize-money £7961

Going:	Sf: 0-2 GS: 0-1 Gd: 0-1 GF: - Fm: 0-0
Distance:	2m/2m3: 0-0 2m4-2m7: 0-0 3m+: 0-4
Track:	LH: 0-4 RH: 0-0 Tight: 0-1 Gall: 0-1
Aids:	Bl: 0-0 Vi: 0-0 Tstrap: 0-0
Best Rating:	105 12/02 Uttx 3m soft Ch

Progressive stayer over hurdles. Ran better on second start over fences when well beaten runner-up at Southwell in December 2002. Won on heavy and fast ground over hurdles.

Oh To Be

76   51

7-y-o b g Weld-At Long Last (John French)
G B Balding (Miss S Sharratt 12/5) Lady G Wates

Placings:P0   (3593)
2002/03: 19PGS, 16QHY,

	Starts	1st	2nd	3rd	Win & Pl
Hurdles	2	0	0	0	
Career Total	2	0	0	0	

Going:	Sf: 0-1 GS: 0-1 Gd: 0-0 GF: - Fm: 0-0
Distance:	2m/2m3: 0-2 2m4-2m7: 0-0 3m+: 0-0
Track:	LH: 0-0 RH: 0-2 Tight: 0-0 Gall: 0-0
Aids:	Bl: 0-0 Vi: 0-0 Tstrap: 0-0
Best Rating:	55 2/03 Sand 2m110y heavy Hdl

Oh Wise One

39f

6-y-o b g Homo Sapien-Bean Alainn (Candy Cane)
Miss K Marks Nick Shutts

Placings:0   (0907)
2002/03: 16QG,

	Starts	1st	2nd	3rd	Win & Pl
NH Flat	1	0	0	0	
Career Total	1	0	0	0	

Going:	Sf: 0-0 GS: 0-0 Gd: 0-1 GF: - Fm: 0-0
Distance:	2m/2m3: 0-1 2m4-2m7: 0-0 3m+: 0-0
Track:	LH: 0-1 RH: 0-0 Tight: 0-0 Gall: 0-0
Aids:	Bl: 0-0 Vi: 0-0 Tstrap: 0-0
Best Rating:	

Ojays Alibi (IRE)

103   97

7-y-o b g Witness Box (USA)-Tinkers Lady (Sheer Grit)
J D Frost Mrs C Irish

Placings:63   (3596)
2002/03: 18PS, 173S,

	Starts	1st	2nd	3rd	Win & Pl
NH Flat	1	0	0	0	0
Hurdles	1	0	0	1	805
Career Total	2	0	0	1	805

Going:	Sf: 0-2 GS: 0-0 Gd: 0-0 GF: - Fm: 0-0
Distance:	2m/2m3: 0-2 2m4-2m7: 0-0 3m+: 0-0
Track:	LH: 0-1 RH: 0-1 Tight: 0-2 Gall: 0-0
Aids:	Bl: 0-0 Vi: 0-0 Tstrap: 0-0
Best Rating:	97 2/03 Tntn 2m1f soft Hdl

Fair novice hurdler; acts on soft ground; will probably appreciate a test of stamina.

Ok So (IRE)

10-y-o ch g Naheez (USA)-Flowering Moss (IRE) (Le Moss)
K A Nelmes K A Nelmes

Placings:600/0F0P/3/62335-3   (0062)
2002/03: 26QG,

	Starts	1st	2nd	3rd	Win & Pl
Chases	1	0	0	1	165
Career Total	14	0	1	4	1995

Going:	Sf: 0-0 GS: 0-0 Gd: 0-1 GF: - Fm: 0-0
Distance:	2m/2m3: 0-0 2m4-2m7: 0-0 3m+: 0-1
Track:	LH: 0-0 RH: 0-1 Tight: 0-1 Gall: 0-0
Aids:	Bl: 0-0 Vi: 0-0 Tstrap: 0-0
Best Rating:	97 3/02 Tntn 3m soft Ch

Point winner and maiden hunter chaser, jumps well.

Olabud

86d

11-y-o ch g Lord Bud-Nugola (Derrylin)
P Winkworth Bill Naylor

Placings:P0P054/113/F6/53-PP   (2196)
2002/03: 16PGF, 19PGS,

	Starts	1st	2nd	3rd	Win & Pl
Chases	2	0	0	0	
Career Total	15	2	0	2	6161
113	10/99	Font	2m2f110yD(0-120)HHdl	GD	£3109
108	10/99	Font	2m2f110yE Hdl	GD	£1987

Total win prize-money £5098

Going:	Sf: 0-0 GS: 0-1 Gd: 0-0 GF: - Fm: 0-1
Distance:	2m/2m3: 0-2 2m4-2m7: 0-0 3m+: 0-0
Track:	LH: 0-0 RH: 0-2 Tight: 0-2 Gall: 0-0
Aids:	Bl: 0-0 Vi: 0-0 Tstrap: 0-0
Best Rating:	113 10/99 Font 2m2f110y good Hdl

Old Bean (IRE)

68   35

7-y-o b g Eurobus-Princess Petara (IRE) (Petorius)
N J Henderson Wrestlers Racing

Placings:151-0   (4328)
2002/03: 16QG,

	Starts	1st	2nd	3rd	Win & Pl
Hurdles	1	0	0	0	
Career Total	4	2	0	0	4256
104	3/02	Ludl	2m	H NHF	SFT	£2044
114	1/02	Ludl	2m	H NHF	GD	£2212

Total win prize-money £4256

Going:	Sf: 0-0 GS: 0-0 Gd: 0-0 GF: - Fm: 0-0
Distance:	2m/2m3: 0-1 2m4-2m7: 0-0 3m+: 0-0
Track:	LH: 0-1 RH: 0-0 Tight: 0-0 Gall: 0-1
Aids:	Bl: 0-0 Vi: 0-0 Tstrap: 0-0
Best Rating:	114 1/02 Ludl 2m good NHF

Dual Ludlow bumper winner; acts on good and soft ground.

Old California (IRE)

102   125

4-y-o b c Sadler s Wells (USA)-Turban (Glint Of Gold)
M C Pipe (J L Dunlop 19/9) Matt Archer & Miss Jean Broadhurst

Placings:1F (4130)
2002/03: 18¹G, 17²G,

	Starts	1st	2nd	3rd	Win & Pl
Hurdles	2	1	0	0	2954
Career Total	2	1	0	0	2954
125 12/02 Font	2m2f110yE Hdl			GD	£2954

Total win prize-money £2954

Going: Sf: 0-0 GS: 0-0 Gd: 1-2 GF: - Fm: 0-0
Distance: 2m/2m3: 1-2 2m4-2m7: 0-0 3m+: 0-0
Track: LH: 1-2 RH: 0-0 Tight: 1-1 Gall: 0-1
Aids: Bl: 0-0 Vi: 0-0 Tstrap: 0-0
Best Rating: 125 12/02 Font 2m2f110y good Hdl

Twice a winner over middle distances on Flat for John Dunlop; changed hands for 85,000gns at the sales; won at Fontwell on hurdles bow; killed in Triumph Hurdle. (DEAD)

Old Feathers (IRE)
109   105+
6-y-o b g Hernando (FR)-Undiscovered (Tap On Wood)
Jonjo O Neill (P Haley 28/9) John Connor

Placings:5531/5F310 (2563)
2002/03: 16⁵G, 20²G, 21³G, 22¹S, 24⁹GS,

	Starts	1st	2nd	3rd	Win & Pl
Hurdles	5	1	0	1	7521
Career Total	9	2	0	2	11002
105 11/02 Uttx	2m6f110yD(0-125)HHdl			SFT	£5434
96 4/01 Muss	2m4f F(0-95)HHdl			G-F	£2838

Total win prize-money £8273

Going: Sf: 1-1 GS: 0-1 Gd: 0-3 GF: - Fm: 0-0
Distance: 2m/2m3: 0-1 2m4-2m7: 1-3 3m+: 0-1
Track: LH: 1-5 RH: 0-0 Tight: 0-1 Gall: 0-1
Aids: Bl: 0-0 Vi: 0-0 Tstrap: 0-0
Best Rating: 105 11/02 Uttx 2m6f110y soft Hdl

Modest chaser; successful on fast and soft ground, he is at his best over two and a half miles plus. Winner at Uttoxeter in November.

Old Hush Wing (IRE)
97(102h)   (100h)105+
10-y-o b g Tirol-Saneena (Kris)
Mrs S J Smith Mrs B Ramsden

Placings:4/1O521/5223136/13334/11005/6U454B6-4
(4691)
2002/03: 19⁴GF,

	Starts	1st	2nd	3rd	Win & Pl
Hurdles	1	0	0	0	371
Career Total	31	6	3	5	29214
112 12/00 Hntg	2m5f110yF Hdl			SFT	£1789
122 11/00 Hayd	2m4f F Hdl			HVY	£2019
128 11/99 Sedg	2m5f110yB HHdl			GD	£6273
125 11/98 Sedg	2m5f110yB HHdl			G-S	£6677
106 5/98 Sedg	2m5f110yE Hdl			GD	£2425
115 11/97 Sedg	2m5f110yE Hdl			GD	£2705

Total win prize-money £21890

Going: Sf: 0-0 GS: 0-0 Gd: 0-0 GF: - Fm: 0-1
Distance: 2m/2m3: 0-0 2m4-2m7: 0-1 3m+: 0-0
Track: LH: 0-0 RH: 0-1 Tight: 0-1 Gall: 0-0
Aids: Bl: 0-0 Vi: 0-0 Tstrap: 0-0
Best Rating: 130 1/00 Wrck 2m4f110y soft Hdl

Modest hurdler/chaser; likes sedgefield; best over two and a half miles; opened his account over fences on third start at favourite track in May; acts on soft/heavy ground but is getting a bit long in the tooth now.

Old King Coal
78f   68f
7-y-o b g Miners Lamp-Mill Shine (Milan)
R M Stronge G B Barlow

Placings:6 (1670)
2002/03: 17⁶S,

	Starts	1st	2nd	3rd	Win & Pl
NH Flat	1	0	0	0	0
Career Total	1	0	0	0	0

Going: Sf: 0-1 GS: 0-0 Gd: 0-0 GF: - Fm: 0-0
Distance: 2m/2m3: 0-1 2m4-2m7: 0-0 3m+: 0-0
Track: LH: 0-1 RH: 0-0 Tight: 0-1 Gall: 0-0
Aids: Bl: 0-0 Vi: 0-0 Tstrap: 0-0
Best Rating: 68 10/02 Bang 2m1f soft NHF

Old Marsh (IRE)
113   126
7-y-o b g Grand Lodge (USA)-Lolly Dolly (Alleged (USA))
Miss Venetia Williams Seasons And Paradise

Placings:4/4020-131125CF04 (3727)
2002/03: 16¹G, 17³S, 16¹GF, 16¹GF, 16²GF, 16⁵G, 17⁹GS, 20⁴GS,
19⁹GS, 16⁴G,

	Starts	1st	2nd	3rd	Win & Pl
Hurdles	10	3	1	1	13731
Career Total	15	3	2	1	17019
110 7/02 Worc	2m D Hdl			G-F	£3601
120 7/02 Uttx	2m E Hdl			G-F	£3464
119 5/02 Aint	2m110y D Hdl			GD	£3523

Total win prize-money £10589

Going: Sf: 0-1 GS: 0-3 Gd: 1-3 GF: - Fm: 2-3
Distance: 2m/2m3: 3-8 2m4-2m7: 0-2 3m+: 0-0
Track: LH: 3-7 RH: 0-3 Tight: 1-4 Gall: 0-0
Aids: Bl: 0-3 Vi: 0-0 Tstrap: 0-5
Best Rating: 126 2/03 Kemp 2m good Hdl

Fair handicap hurdler; effective at around two miles; suited by fast ground; has worn a tongue tie and blinkers; front-runner.

Old Nosey (IRE)
99   89
7-y-o b g Muharib (USA)-Regent Star (Prince Regent (FR))
B Mactaggart (D T Hughes 13/9) The Potassium Partnership

Placings:4000-0566365F6002 (4621)
2002/03: 16⁹GY, 16⁵F, 16⁶GY, 16⁶GF, 17³F, 20⁶G, 20⁵G, 20⁷GS,
16⁶GS, 20⁴GS, 16⁰G, 20²GF,

	Starts	1st	2nd	3rd	Win & Pl
NH Flat	1	0	0	1	344
Hurdles	11	0	1	0	1124
Career Total	16	0	1	1	1726

Going: Sf: 0-0 GS: 0-3 Gd: 0-3 GF: - Fm: 0-4
Distance: 2m/2m3: 0-7 2m4-2m7: 0-5 3m+: 0-0
Track: LH: 0-5 RH: 0-3 Tight: 0-3 Gall: 0-0
Aids: Bl: 0-1 Vi: 0-0 Tstrap: 0-0
Best Rating: 89 8/02 Dpat 2m1f172y firm NHF

Plating-class hurdler; ex-Irish; best effort in Britain when second in a weak novices handicap at Carlisle in April 2003; stays two and a half miles.

Old Rolla (IRE)
101   97
5-y-o b g Old Vic-Criswood (IRE) (Chromite (USA))

C Grant A Dawson

Placings:0033006 (4752)
2002/03: 16⁰HY, 16⁰S, 24³HY, 24³S, 24⁰S, 24⁰S, 24⁶G,

	Starts	1st	2nd	3rd	Win & Pl
NH Flat	1	0	0	0	0
Hurdles	6	0	0	2	1279
Career Total	7	0	0	2	1279

Going: Sf: 0-6 GS: 0-0 Gd: 0-1 GF: - Fm: 0-0
Distance: 2m/2m3: 0-2 2m4-2m7: 0-0 3m+: 0-5
Track: LH: 0-6 RH: 0-1 Tight: 0-0 Gall: 0-2
Aids: Bl: 0-0 Vi: 0-0 Tstrap: 0-0
Best Rating: 91 2/03 Ayr 3m110y soft Hdl

Modest staying novice hurdler; easily best effort when a distant third in a three-mile Ayr novice on testing ground.

Old Rouvel (USA)
101   126
12-y-o b g Riverman (USA)-Marie De Russy (FR) (Sassafras (FR))
A King Mrs R D Cowell

Placings:2421P/2P20/5134/61514-060 (4456)
2002/03: 23⁹G, 24⁶S, 24⁹G,

	Starts	1st	2nd	3rd	Win & Pl
Hurdles	3	0	0	0	165
Career Total	21	4	4	1	30529
133 12/01 Kemp	3m110y C(0-135)HHdl			GD	£7182
126 11/01 Chep	3m B(0-150)HHdl			G-S	£6827
128 1/01 Kemp	3m110y D(0-120)HHdl			SFT	£5164
113 3/98 Hntg	2m5f110yE Hdl			GD	£2565

Total win prize-money £21740

Going: Sf: 0-1 GS: 0-0 Gd: 0-2 GF: - Fm: 0-0
Distance: 2m/2m3: 0-0 2m4-2m7: 0-0 3m+: 0-3
Track: LH: 0-2 RH: 0-1 Tight: 0-1 Gall: 0-0
Aids: Bl: 0-0 Vi: 0-0 Tstrap: 0-0
Best Rating: 133 4/02 Aint 3m110y good Hdl

Useful staying hurdler; not the most consistent sort; seems well suited by a flat, right-handed track; handles good ground or easier; best when fresh; stays three miles.

Old Tim (IRE)
98   95
10-y-o b/br g Poet s Dream (IRE)-Settled (Blue Cashmere)
S Kirk M G White

Placings:4000/0/22240/0F4-1 (2067)
2002/03: 21¹GS,

	Starts	1st	2nd	3rd	Win & Pl
Hurdles	1	1	0	0	2300
Career Total	15	1	3	0	5519
95 11/02 MRas	2m5f110yG(0-90)HHdl			G-S	£2299

Total win prize-money £2300

Going: Sf: 0-0 GS: 1-1 Gd: 0-0 GF: - Fm: 0-0
Distance: 2m/2m3: 0-0 2m4-2m7: 1-1 3m+: 0-0
Track: LH: 0-0 RH: 1-1 Tight: 1-1 Gall: 0-0
Aids: Bl: 0-0 Vi: 0-0 Tstrap: 0-0
Best Rating: 95 11/02 MRas 2m5f110y gd-sft Hdl

Inconsistent typoe in Ireland, won on his debut here for new trainer in poor selling hurdle in bad ground at Market Rasen in November.

Olde Oak
93(95h)   (76h)52
9-y-o ch g Precocious-Quisissanno (Be My Guest (USA))
B Ellison Mrs Jean Stapleton

Placings:/04U5506P-04P   (0624)
2002/03: 16⁰G, 17⁴HY, 17⁵GF,

	Starts	1st	2nd	3rd	Win & Pl
Chases	3	0	0	0	263
Career Total	11	0	0	0	263

Going: Sf: 0-1 GS: 0-0 Gd: 0-1 GF: - Fm: 0-1
Distance: 2m/2m3: 0-3 2m4-2m7: 0-0 3m+: 0-0
Track: LH: 0-2 RH: 0-1 Tight: 0-3 Gall: 0-0
Aids: Bl: 0-0 Vi: 0-0 Tstrap: 0-3
Best Rating: 76   8/01   Sthl   2m   gd-fm   Hdl

Ole Gunnar (IRE)
93   73
11-y-o b g Le Bavard (FR)-Rareitess (Rarity)
M S Wilesmith   M S Wilesmith

Placings:P-3   (0510)
2002/03: 20³G,

	Starts	1st	2nd	3rd	Win & Pl
Hurdles	1	0	0	1	386
Career Total	2	0	0	1	386

Going: Sf: 0-0 GS: 0-0 Gd: 0-1 GF: - Fm: 0-0
Distance: 2m/2m3: 0-0 2m4-2m7: 0-1 3m+: 0-0
Track: LH: 0-1 RH: 0-0 Tight: 0-0 Gall: 0-0
Aids: Bl: 0-0 Vi: 0-0 Tstrap: 0-0
Best Rating: 66   6/02   Worc   2m4f   good   Hdl

Olitheaga
82   85
8-y-o ch g Safawan-Lyaaric (Privy Seal)
C J Mann   Property Racing Partnership

Placings:12-P0   (4568)
2002/03: 19²G, 22⁰GF,

	Starts	1st	2nd	3rd	Win & Pl
Hurdles	2	0	0	0	
Career Total	4	1	1	0	2625
96 5/01 Hntg 2m110y H NHF				G-F	£1729
				Total win prize-money	£1729

Going: Sf: 0-0 GS: 0-0 Gd: 0-1 GF: - Fm: 0-1
Distance: 2m/2m3: 0-0 2m4-2m7: 0-2 3m+: 0-0
Track: LH: 0-1 RH: 0-1 Tight: 0-0 Gall: 0-0
Aids: Bl: 0-0 Vi: 0-0 Tstrap: 0-0
Best Rating: 96   10/01   Bang   2m1f   good   Hdl

Won a bumper at Huntingdon in 2001; has lost his way since; struggled to land the odds in a very weak novices hurdle at Cartmel in May in first time blinkers.

Oliver Cromwell (IRE)
104(110h)   (131h)122
8-y-o br g Mandalus-Gemini Gale (Strong Gale)
P R Hedger   Howard Spooner

Placings:556U513/221P1/P223301-06305302   (3599)
2002/03: 23⁹G, 21⁶GS, 20³G, 22⁰S, 24⁵S, 24³G, 19⁰GS, 24²S,

	Starts	1st	2nd	3rd	Win & Pl
Hurdles	3	0	0	0	275
Chases	5	0	1	2	3685
Career Total	27	4	5	5	45719
131 4/02 Chel 3m B(0-145)HHdl			GD	£10871	
122 2/01 Kemp 2m5f C(0-130)HHdl			G-S	£14072	
129 1/01 Extr 2m3f E(0-115)HHdl			HVY	£3136	
98 3/00 Towc 2m E(0-105)HHdl			GD	£2562	
			Total win prize-money		£30642

Going: Sf: 0-3 GS: 0-2 Gd: 0-3 GF: - Fm: 0-0
Distance: 2m/2m3: 0-0 2m4-2m7: 0-3 3m+: 0-5
Track: LH: 0-3 RH: 0-5 Tight: 0-2 Gall: 0-0
Aids: Bl: 0-1 Vi: 0-0 Tstrap: 0-0
Best Rating: 131 4/02 Chel 3m   good   Hdl

Fair novice chaser; stays three miles and should be suited by further; acts on ground good or softer.

Olivety
93   92
8-y-o b g Lighter-Star Of Tycoon (Tycoon Ii)
K A Ryan   Mr & Mrs K Hughes

Placings:5/02/3P-4   (1562)
2002/03: 22⁴G,

	Starts	1st	2nd	3rd	Win & Pl
Hurdles	1	0	0	0	293
Career Total	6	0	1	1	1171

Going: Sf: 0-0 GS: 0-0 Gd: 0-1 GF: - Fm: 0-0
Distance: 2m/2m3: 0-0 2m4-2m7: 0-1 3m+: 0-0
Track: LH: 0-1 RH: 0-0 Tight: 0-1 Gall: 0-0
Aids: Bl: 0-0 Vi: 0-0 Tstrap: 0-0
Best Rating: 101 11/99 Weth 2m   good   NHF

Modest form in bumpers and novice hurdles. Handles heavy, but may prefer a sound surface.

Olivier (USA)
101   103+
5-y-o ch g Theatrical-Izara (USA) (Blushing John (USA))
Miss Venetia Williams   You Can Be Sure

Placings:2-63   (1924)
2002/03: 17⁶G, 21³GS,

	Starts	1st	2nd	3rd	Win & Pl
NH Flat	1	0	0	0	0
Hurdles	1	0	0	1	545
Career Total	3	0	1	1	1561

Going: Sf: 0-0 GS: 0-1 Gd: 0-1 GF: - Fm: 0-0
Distance: 2m/2m3: 0-1 2m4-2m7: 0-1 3m+: 0-0
Track: LH: 0-0 RH: 0-2 Tight: 0-0 Gall: 0-0
Aids: Bl: 0-0 Vi: 0-0 Tstrap: 0-0
Best Rating: 110 4/02 Prth 2m110y   good   NHF

Modest bumper and hurdles form on a sound surface.

Ollar House (IRE)
75   41
12-y-o b g Zaffaran (USA)-Lavengaddy (Balgaddy)
J Barclay   Jim Barclay

Placings:0/PP/P-3P   (0378)
2002/03: 24³GF, 27⁶G,

	Starts	1st	2nd	3rd	Win & Pl
Hurdles	2	0	0	1	433
Career Total	6	0	0	1	433

Going: Sf: 0-0 GS: 0-0 Gd: 0-1 GF: - Fm: 0-1
Distance: 2m/2m3: 0-0 2m4-2m7: 0-0 3m+: 0-2
Track: LH: 0-1 RH: 0-1 Tight: 0-1 Gall: 0-0
Aids: Bl: 0-0 Vi: 0-0 Tstrap: 0-0
Best Rating: 82 12/98 Punc 2m   soft   NHF

Moderate form over hurdles.

Ollie Magern
101   109
5-y-o b g Alderbrook-Outfield (Monksfield)
N A Twiston-Davies (F Jordan 15/1)   Roger Nicholls

Placings:0002   (4568)
2002/03: 17⁰G, 16⁰GS, 16⁰S, 22²GF,

	Starts	1st	2nd	3rd	Win & Pl
NH Flat	2	0	0	0	0
Hurdles	2	0	1	0	1311
Career Total	4	0	1	0	1311

Going: Sf: 0-1 GS: 0-1 Gd: 0-1 GF: - Fm: 0-1
Distance: 2m/2m3: 0-3 2m4-2m7: 0-1 3m+: 0-0
Track: LH: 0-1 RH: 0-2 Tight: 0-1 Gall: 0-2
Aids: Bl: 0-0 Vi: 0-0 Tstrap: 0-0
Best Rating: 91 4/03 Strf 2m6f110y gd-fm Hdl

Modest novice hurdler; consistent form over staying distances; likes to force the pace; considered best with cut in the ground but handles good to firm; stays well.

Ollies Boy (IRE)
12-y-o br g Electric-Kilcor Rose (Pitpan)
Miss Caroline Barclay   Jamie Alexander

Placings:5/PPU3P55/PU0302F544P/0P002/2000P3-
                                                            (0005)
2002/03: 20³G,

	Starts	1st	2nd	3rd	Win & Pl
Chases	1	0	0	1	254
Career Total	30	0	3	3	5135

Going: Sf: 0-0 GS: 0-0 Gd: 0-1 GF: - Fm: 0-0
Distance: 2m/2m3: 0-0 2m4-2m7: 0-1 3m+: 0-0
Track: LH: 0-1 RH: 0-0 Tight: 0-0 Gall: 0-1
Aids: Bl: 0-0 Vi: 0-0 Tstrap: 0-0
Best Rating: 86 3/00 Kels 2m1f   gd-sft   Ch

Olney Lad
96   83
4-y-o b g Democratic (USA)-Alipampa (IRE) (Glenstal (USA))
Mrs P Robeson (R Guest 1/10)   T H Rossiter

Placings:55   (4399)
2002/03: 16⁵G, 16⁵GF,

	Starts	1st	2nd	3rd	Win & Pl
Hurdles	2	0	0	0	0
Career Total	2	0	0	0	0

Going: Sf: 0-0 GS: 0-0 Gd: 0-1 GF: - Fm: 0-1
Distance: 2m/2m3: 0-2 2m4-2m7: 0-0 3m+: 0-0
Track: LH: 0-1 RH: 0-1 Tight: 0-0 Gall: 0-1
Aids: Bl: 0-0 Vi: 0-0 Tstrap: 0-0
Best Rating: 83 3/03 Hayd 2m   gd-fm Hdl

Modest form over hurdles so far; seems suited by a sound surface.

Omni Cosmo Touch (USA)
77(97c)
7-y-o b g Trempolino (USA)-Wooden Pudden (USA) (Top Ville)
Mrs S J Smith (O Sherwood 23/5)   Mrs S Smith

Placings:221122/51412RR-6R6R   (1637)
2002/03: 24⁶GF, 20ᴿG, 17⁶GF, 17⁶S,

	Starts	1st	2nd	3rd	Win & Pl
Hurdles	4	0	0	0	0
Career Total	**17**	**4**	**5**	**0**	**22369**
120 6/01 Worc 2m4f C(0-135)HHdl	GD	£5525			
120 5/01 Ling 2m3f110yD(0-125)HHdl	G-F	£7250			
111 10/00 Tntn 2m1f E Hdl	GD	£2891			
98 9/00 Worc 2m E Hdl	G-F	£1904			

Total win prize-money £17571

Going:	Sf: 0-1 GS: 0-0 Gd: 0-1 GF: - Fm: 0-2
Distance:	2m/2m3: 0-2 2m4-2m7: 0-1 3m+: 0-1
Track:	LH: 0-3 RH: 0-1 Tight: 0-0 Gall: 0-0
Aids:	Bl: 0-0 Vi: 0-0 Tstrap: 0-0
Best Rating:	120 6/01 Worc 2m4f good Hdl

Showed progressive form over hurdles but has become most reluctant to race and cannot be trusted. Effective on a sound surface. Stays an extended two miles three furlongs.

Omniscient (IRE)

4-y-o b f Distinctly North (USA)-Mystic Shadow (IRE) (Mtoto)
Mrs P N Dutfield The Carpetbaggers

Placings:F   (1327)
2002/03: 16ᶠG,

	Starts	1st	2nd	3rd	Win & Pl
Hurdles	1	0	0	0	
Career Total	**1**	**0**	**0**	**0**	

Going:	Sf: 0-0 GS: 0-0 Gd: 0-1 GF: - Fm: 0-0
Distance:	2m/2m3: 0-1 2m4-2m7: 0-0 3m+: 0-0
Track:	LH: 0-1 RH: 0-0 Tight: 0-0 Gall: 0-0
Aids:	Bl: 0-0 Vi: 0-0 Tstrap: 0-0
Best Rating:	0 9/02 Plum 2m good Hdl

Winner at two, well held on the Flat at three.

On A Deal

89   90

5-y-o b g Teenoso (USA)-Gale Spring (IRE) (Strong Gale)
R J Hodges Unity Farm Holiday Centre Ltd

Placings:04O5   (3782)
2002/03: 16⁶S, 17⁴S, 16⁰GS, 17⁵GS,

	Starts	1st	2nd	3rd	Win & Pl
NH Flat	4	0	0	0	0
Career Total	**4**	**0**	**0**	**0**	**0**

Going:	Sf: 0-2 GS: 0-2 Gd: 0-0 GF: - Fm: 0-0
Distance:	2m/2m3: 0-4 2m4-2m7: 0-0 3m+: 0-0
Track:	LH: 0-0 RH: 0-3 Tight: 0-0 Gall: 0-0
Aids:	Bl: 0-0 Vi: 0-0 Tstrap: 0-0
Best Rating:	99 1/03 Tntn 2m1f soft NHF

Novice hurdler; inclined to run freely in his bumpers; some promise over hurdles; stays two miles six and should stay further; appears to act on most ground.

On A Full Wager

74   65

6-y-o b g Homo Sapien-Ntombi (Trasi s Son)
P Bowen R Owen

Placings:40000P   (3120)
2002/03: 17⁴GF, 16⁰GF, 16⁰S, 16⁰S, 20⁰PS,

	Starts	1st	2nd	3rd	Win & Pl
NH Flat	2	0	0	0	0
Hurdles	4	0	0	0	0

Career Total	6	0	0	0	0

Going:	Sf: 0-4 GS: 0-0 Gd: 0-0 GF: - Fm: 0-2
Distance:	2m/2m3: 0-4 2m4-2m7: 0-2 3m+: 0-0
Track:	LH: 0-4 RH: 0-2 Tight: 0-0 Gall: 0-2
Aids:	Bl: 0-0 Vi: 0-0 Tstrap: 0-0
Best Rating:	85 6/02 Hrfd 2m1f gd-fm NHF

On Appeal (IRE)

79   34

7-y-o b g Buckskin (FR)-Little Quince (Laurence O)
D M Grissell Pps Racing

Placings:6-0   (1786)
2002/03: 22⁹GS,

	Starts	1st	2nd	3rd	Win & Pl
Hurdles	1	0	0	0	0
Career Total	**2**	**0**	**0**	**0**	**0**

Going:	Sf: 0-0 GS: 0-1 Gd: 0-0 GF: - Fm: 0-0
Distance:	2m/2m3: 0-0 2m4-2m7: 0-1 3m+: 0-0
Track:	LH: 0-0 RH: 0-1 Tight: 0-0 Gall: 0-0
Aids:	Bl: 0-0 Vi: 0-0 Tstrap: 0-0
Best Rating:	100 5/01 Folk 2m1f110y gd-sft NHF

On Approval

92f   58f

4-y-o b g First Trump-Gymcrak Lovebird (Taufan (USA))
T D Easterby K C Partnership

Placings:600   (4593)
2002/03: 16⁶G, 16⁰GF, 16⁰G,

	Starts	1st	2nd	3rd	Win & Pl
NH Flat	3	0	0	0	0
Career Total	**3**	**0**	**0**	**0**	**0**

Going:	Sf: 0-0 GS: 0-0 Gd: 0-2 GF: - Fm: 0-1
Distance:	2m/2m3: 0-3 2m4-2m7: 0-0 3m+: 0-0
Track:	LH: 0-3 RH: 0-0 Tight: 0-0 Gall: 0-0
Aids:	Bl: 0-1 Vi: 0-0 Tstrap: 0-0
Best Rating:	58 3/03 Weth 2m good NHF

Started favourite for bumper at Wetherby in March but finished well beaten.

On Ice (IRE)

7-y-o ch g Pursuit Of Love-Ice Chocolate (USA) (Icecapade (USA))
F P Murtagh Mrs Anna Kenny

Placings:PP/0P-P   (1527)
2002/03: 17⁵G,

	Starts	1st	2nd	3rd	Win & Pl
Hurdles	1	0	0	0	0
Career Total	**5**	**0**	**0**	**0**	**0**

Going:	Sf: 0-0 GS: 0-0 Gd: 0-1 GF: - Fm: 0-0
Distance:	2m/2m3: 0-1 2m4-2m7: 0-0 3m+: 0-0
Track:	LH: 0-1 RH: 0-0 Tight: 0-1 Gall: 0-0
Aids:	Bl: 0-0 Vi: 0-0 Tstrap: 0-0
Best Rating:	0 10/02 Sedg 2m1f good Hdl

On The Bone

11-y-o b m Lyphento (USA)-Lydia Languish (Hotfoot)

R Harvey K And A K Smith

Placings:6S-P   (0055)
2002/03: 24ᴾG,

	Starts	1st	2nd	3rd	Win & Pl
Chases	1	0	0	0	
Career Total	**3**	**0**	**0**	**0**	**0**

Going:	Sf: 0-0 GS: 0-0 Gd: 0-1 GF: - Fm: 0-0
Distance:	2m/2m3: 0-0 2m4-2m7: 0-0 3m+: 0-1
Track:	LH: 0-1 RH: 0-0 Tight: 0-1 Gall: 0-0
Aids:	Bl: 0-0 Vi: 0-0 Tstrap: 0-0
Best Rating:	

On The Day (IRE)

102   98

6-y-o ch g Roselier (FR)-Solar Jet (Mandalus)
L Lungo R A Bartlett

Placings:3-32P3   (4392)
2002/03: 20³GS, 27²S, 24ᴾHY, 24³G,

	Starts	1st	2nd	3rd	Win & Pl
Hurdles	4	0	1	2	2050
Career Total	**5**	**0**	**1**	**3**	**2439**

Going:	Sf: 0-2 GS: 0-1 Gd: 0-1 GF: - Fm: 0-0
Distance:	2m/2m3: 0-0 2m4-2m7: 0-1 3m+: 0-3
Track:	LH: 0-3 RH: 0-1 Tight: 0-1 Gall: 0-1
Aids:	Bl: 0-0 Vi: 0-0 Tstrap: 0-0
Best Rating:	98 12/02 Sedg 3m3f110y soft Hdl

Modest staying novice hurdler.

On The Game

8-y-o b m Unfuwain (USA)-All Glorious (Crowned Prince (USA))
D C O Brien Mrs V O Brien

Placings:0/0P-F   (2254)
2002/03: 22ᶠHY,

	Starts	1st	2nd	3rd	Win & Pl
Hurdles	1	0	0	0	
Career Total	**4**	**0**	**0**	**0**	

Going:	Sf: 0-1 GS: 0-0 Gd: 0-0 GF: - Fm: 0-0
Distance:	2m/2m3: 0-0 2m4-2m7: 0-1 3m+: 0-0
Track:	LH: 0-0 RH: 0-1 Tight: 0-1 Gall: 0-0
Aids:	Bl: 0-0 Vi: 0-0 Tstrap: 0-0
Best Rating:	0 12/02 Folk 2m1f110y heavy Hdl

On The Luce

6-y-o b g Karinga Bay-Lirchur (Lir)
L Lungo S H C Racing

Placings:60-P   (0041)
2002/03: 16ᴾGS,

	Starts	1st	2nd	3rd	Win & Pl
Hurdles	1	0	0	0	
Career Total	**3**	**0**	**0**	**0**	**0**

Going:	Sf: 0-0 GS: 0-1 Gd: 0-0 GF: - Fm: 0-0
Distance:	2m/2m3: 0-0 2m4-2m7: 0-0 3m+: 0-0
Track:	LH: 0-1 RH: 0-0 Tight: 0-1 Gall: 0-0
Aids:	Bl: 0-0 Vi: 0-0 Tstrap: 0-0
Best Rating:	85 1/02 Newc 2m soft NHF

On The Run (IRE)

108(102h)   (90h)**90**

9-y-o ch m Don t Forget Me-Chepstow House (USA)
(Northern Baby (CAN))
D J Wintle D A Thorpe

Placings:00/206/632000/023F20/34061000-223424UP
(1551)
2002/03: 16²GF, 16²S, 17³GF, 16⁴GF, 19²GF, 20⁴G, 20ᵁF, 19⁸G,

	Starts	1st	2nd	3rd	Win & Pl
Hurdles	3	0	2	1	1621
Chases	5	0	1	0	1761
Career Total	33	1	7	4	8933
85 8/01 Sthl 2m   G Hdl   G-F £1570

Total win prize-money £1571

Going:	Sf: 0-1 GS: 0-0 Gd: 0-2 GF: - Fm: 0-5
Distance:	2m/2m3: 0-6 2m4-2m7: 0-2 3m+: 0-0
Track:	LH: 0-4 RH: 0-4 Tight: 0-4 Gall: 0-1
Aids:	Bl: 0-0 Vi: 0-0 Tstrap: 0-8
Best Rating:	97 7/00 Worc 2m gd-fm Hdl

Plating class, she is effective on a flat left-handed track and is best over two miles on fast ground. Has shown improvement since racing with her tongue tied. Does not find much off the bridle.

Onassis

100   **88**

6-y-o b g Roselier (FR)-Jack s The Girl (IRE) (Supreme Leader)
O Sherwood P Joe Davis & Peter McNeil

Placings:352PP3   (4704)
2002/03: 16³GS, 17⁵S, 21²S, 24⁴S, 21²S, 20³G,

	Starts	1st	2nd	3rd	Win & Pl
NH Flat	1	0	0	1	336
Hurdles	5	0	1	1	1957
Career Total	6	0	1	2	2293

Going:	Sf: 0-4 GS: 0-1 Gd: 0-1 GF: - Fm: 0-0
Distance:	2m/2m3: 0-2 2m4-2m7: 0-3 3m+: 0-1
Track:	LH: 0-4 RH: 0-2 Tight: 0-3 Gall: 0-1
Aids:	Bl: 0-1 Vi: 0-0 Tstrap: 0-1
Best Rating:	82 1/03 Plum 2m5f soft Hdl

Some ability over hurdles, but looks short of pace.

Oncourse (IRE)

78   **43**

7-y-o b g Toulon-Slaney Jazz (Orchestra)
R D Tudor (Miss F M Crowley 6/9) R D Tudor

Placings:1-P0   (3596)
2002/03: 24ᴾGF, 17⁰S,

	Starts	1st	2nd	3rd	Win & Pl
Hurdles	2	0	0	0	
Career Total	3	1	0	0	3339
102 7/01 Dund 2m135y NHF   FRM £3338

Total win prize-money £3339

Going:	Sf: 0-1 GS: 0-0 Gd: 0-0 GF: - Fm: 0-1
Distance:	2m/2m3: 0-1 2m4-2m7: 0-0 3m+: 0-1
Track:	LH: 0-0 RH: 0-1 Tight: 0-1 Gall: 0-0
Aids:	Bl: 0-0 Vi: 0-0 Tstrap: 0-0
Best Rating:	102 7/01 Dund 2m135y firm NHF

One A Dackie

91f   **68f**

4-y-o b f Lord Americo-Oriel Dream (Oats)

Ferdy Murphy Jack Iddon

Placings:6   (4404)
2002/03: 16⁶GF,

	Starts	1st	2nd	3rd	Win & Pl
NH Flat	1	0	0	0	0
Career Total	1	0	0	0	0

Going:	Sf: 0-0 GS: 0-0 Gd: 0-0 GF: - Fm: 0-1
Distance:	2m/2m3: 0-1 2m4-2m7: 0-0 3m+: 0-0
Track:	LH: 0-1 RH: 0-0 Tight: 0-0 Gall: 0-0
Aids:	Bl: 0-0 Vi: 0-0 Tstrap: 0-0
Best Rating:	68 3/03 Hayd 2m gd-fm NHF

One Five Eight

52f

4-y-o b g Alflora (IRE)-Dark Nightingale (Strong Gale)
M W Easterby J W P Curtis

Placings:0   (4594)
2002/03: 16⁰G,

	Starts	1st	2nd	3rd	Win & Pl
NH Flat	1	0	0	0	
Career Total	1	0	0	0	

Going:	Sf: 0-0 GS: 0-0 Gd: 0-1 GF: - Fm: 0-0
Distance:	2m/2m3: 0-1 2m4-2m7: 0-0 3m+: 0-0
Track:	LH: 0-1 RH: 0-0 Tight: 0-0 Gall: 0-0
Aids:	Bl: 0-0 Vi: 0-0 Tstrap: 0-0
Best Rating:	52 4/03 Hexm 2m110y good NHF

One For Me

104   **92d**

5-y-o br m Tragic Role (USA)-Chantallee s Pride (Mansooj)
Jean-Rene Auvray M J Lewin

Placings:1P   (1792)
2002/03: 16¹G, 16ᴾS,

	Starts	1st	2nd	3rd	Win & Pl
Hurdles	2	1	0	0	4433
Career Total	2	1	0	0	4433
92 10/02 Strf 2m110y D Hdl   GD £4433

Total win prize-money £4433

Going:	Sf: 0-1 GS: 0-0 Gd: 1-1 GF: - Fm: 0-0
Distance:	2m/2m3: 1-2 2m4-2m7: 0-0 3m+: 0-0
Track:	LH: 1-1 RH: 0-1 Tight: 1-1 Gall: 0-0
Aids:	Bl: 0-0 Vi: 0-0 Tstrap: 0-0
Best Rating:	92 10/02 Strf 2m110y good Hdl

Surprise winner on her hurdles debut in October 2002.

One For Philip

95f   **90f**

5-y-o b m Blushing Flame (USA)-Ile De Danse (Ile De Bourbon (USA))
L Lungo S W Transport (swindon) Ltd

Placings:423   (2560)
2002/03: 17⁴S, 17²GF, 16³GF,

	Starts	1st	2nd	3rd	Win & Pl
NH Flat	3	0	1	1	906
Career Total	3	0	1	1	906

Going:	Sf: 0-1 GS: 0-0 Gd: 0-0 GF: - Fm: 0-2
Distance:	2m/2m3: 0-3 2m4-2m7: 0-0 3m+: 0-0
Track:	LH: 0-1 RH: 0-2 Tight: 0-3 Gall: 0-0
Aids:	Bl: 0-0 Vi: 0-0 Tstrap: 0-0

Best Rating: 90 12/02 Muss 2m   gd-fm NHF

Fair form to make the frame in bumpers.

One For You (IRE)

6-y-o b m Blues Traveller (IRE)-Steel Duchess (IRE) (Yashgan)
Jean-Rene Auvray The One For You Partnership

Placings:P/0   (1382)
2002/03: 17⁰GF,

	Starts	1st	2nd	3rd	Win & Pl
NH Flat	1	0	0	0	
Career Total	2	0	0	0	

Going:	Sf: 0-0 GS: 0-0 Gd: 0-0 GF: - Fm: 0-1
Distance:	2m/2m3: 0-1 2m4-2m7: 0-0 3m+: 0-0
Track:	LH: 0-0 RH: 0-1 Tight: 0-0 Gall: 0-0
Aids:	Bl: 0-0 Vi: 0-0 Tstrap: 0-0
Best Rating:	0 10/02 Hrfd 2m1f gd-fm NHF

One In The Eye

10-y-o br g Arrasas (USA)-Mingalles (Prince De Galles)
Jamie Poulton Ormonde Racing

Placings:2/56/0P/46321600/PP   (1747)
2002/03: 16ᴾG, 21ᴾS,

	Starts	1st	2nd	3rd	Win & Pl
Hurdles	2	0	0	0	
Career Total	15	1	2	1	3223
88 1/00 Folk 2m1f110yG(0-90)HHdl SFT £1557

Total win prize-money £1558

Going:	Sf: 0-1 GS: 0-0 Gd: 0-1 GF: - Fm: 0-0
Distance:	2m/2m3: 0-1 2m4-2m7: 0-1 3m+: 0-0
Track:	LH: 0-2 RH: 0-0 Tight: 0-2 Gall: 0-0
Aids:	Bl: 0-0 Vi: 0-0 Tstrap: 0-2
Best Rating:	88 1/00 Folk 2m1f110y soft Hdl

One Knight (IRE)

121(111h)   (134h)**159+**

7-y-o ch g Roselier (FR)-Midnights Daughter (IRE) (Long Pond)
P J Hobbs R Gibbs

Placings:131/1136-13111   (4110)
2002/03: 19¹S, 24³S, 23¹GS, 23¹GS, 24¹G,

	Starts	1st	2nd	3rd	Win & Pl
Chases	5	4	0	1	112848
Career Total	8	8	0	3	133782
159 3/03 Chel 3m110y A Ch   GD £81200
138 1/03 Extr 2m7f110yE Ch   G-S £4849
119 12/02 Extr 2m7f110yD Ch   G-S £5518
151 11/02 Chep 2m5f110yA Ch   SFT £17980
134 11/01 Chep 2m4f   A Hdl   G-F £10500
119 10/01 Chep 2m4f   E Hdl   SFT £2569
119 3/01 Newb 2m110y H NHF   HVY £2660
116 11/00 Winc 2m   H NHF   G-S £1645

Total win prize-money £126922

Going:	Sf: 1-2 GS: 2-2 Gd: 1-1 GF: - Fm: 0-0
Distance:	2m/2m3: 0-0 2m4-2m7: 1-1 3m+: 3-4
Track:	LH: 2-3 RH: 2-2 Tight: 0-0 Gall: 1-2
Aids:	Bl: 0-0 Vi: 0-0 Tstrap: 0-0
Best Rating:	159 3/03 Chel 3m110y good Ch

Very smart novice chaser; won three times over fences before wonderful effort to make all in the 2003 Royal &

SunAlliance Chase at the 2003 Festival; suited by forcing tactics and acts on any ground.

One More Native (IRE)

93f **94f**

6-y-o ch g Be My Native (USA)-Romany Fortune (Sunyboy)
J L Needham Miss Joanna Needham

Placings:*34* (3370)
2002/03: 16³GS, 16⁴G,

	Starts	1st	2nd	3rd	Win & Pl
NH Flat	2	0	0	1	341
Career Total	2	0	0	1	341

Going: Sf: 0-0 GS: 0-1 Gd: 0-1 GF: - Fm: 0-0
Distance: 2m/2m3: 0-2 2m4-2m7: 0-0 3m+: 0-0
Track: LH: 0-2 RH: 0-0 Tight: 0-2 Gall: 0-0
Aids: Bl: 0-0 Vi: 0-0 Tstrap: 0-0
Best Rating: 94 11/02 Sthl 2m gd-sft NHF

Some ability in moderate bumpers.

One More Stride

71 **32**

7-y-o gr g Beveled (USA)-Gem Of Gold (Jellaby)
H E Haynes (C R Cox 1/5) N A Phillips

Placings:*00/P600* (3545)
2002/03: 16⁶GF, 17⁶S, 19⁰GS, 19⁰G,

	Starts	1st	2nd	3rd	Win & Pl
Hurdles	3	0	0	0	0
Chases	1	0	0	0	0
Career Total	6	0	0	0	0

Going: Sf: 0-1 GS: 0-1 Gd: 0-1 GF: - Fm: 0-1
Distance: 2m/2m3: 0-3 2m4-2m7: 0-1 3m+: 0-0
Track: LH: 0-1 RH: 0-3 Tight: 0-1 Gall: 0-1
Aids: Bl: 0-0 Vi: 0-0 Tstrap: 0-0
Best Rating: 76 2/01 Towc 2m heavy NHF

One Nation (IRE)

94(104c) (110c)**114**

8-y-o br g Be My Native (USA)-Diklers Run (Deep Run)
Miss H C Knight The Earl Cadogan

Placings:*3/24F211/144134/23-P300* (3288)
2002/03: 19⁹GS, 21³S, 21⁹G, 17⁹GS,

	Starts	1st	2nd	3rd	Win & Pl
Hurdles	3	0	0	1	1221
Chases	1	0	0	0	0
Career Total	19	4	3	4	25514
129	1/01	Winc	2m		D(0-125)HHdl	SFT £5187
121	10/00	Hrfd	2m1f		D(0-120)HHdl	GD £2977
115	4/00	Winc	2m		E Hdl	G-S £2604
112	3/00	Hntg	2m110y		E Hdl	SFT £2440

Total win prize-money £13208

Going: Sf: 0-1 GS: 0-2 Gd: 0-1 GF: - Fm: 0-0
Distance: 2m/2m3: 0-2 2m4-2m7: 0-2 3m+: 0-0
Track: LH: 0-1 RH: 0-3 Tight: 0-1 Gall: 0-1
Aids: Bl: 0-0 Vi: 0-0 Tstrap: 0-0
Best Rating: 131 2/01 Asct 2m4f heavy Hdl

Formerly a useful hurdler, he had shown promise over fences. Pulled up on his first start for over a year at Taunton in November 2002 and was then returned to hurdles and has questions to answer. All his wins so far have been at around two miles on right-handed tracks.

One Night Out (IRE)

106(116h) (135h)**129**

7-y-o b/br g Jamesmead-Deladeuce (Le Bavard (FR))
W P Mullins Roderick Ryan

Placings:*215/131452121-146U6F2* (4740a)
2002/03: 17¹S, 24⁴S, 17⁶S, 18⁰S, 20⁶GY, 29⁵G, 20²G,

	Starts	1st	2nd	3rd	Win & Pl
Chases	7	1	1	0	20346
Career Total	19	6	4	1	56988
129	11/02	Fair	2m1f	Ch		SFT £7975
129	4/02	Punc	3m	Hdl		YLD £7407
135	3/02	Punc	2m6f	Hdl		SFT £7407
119	12/01	Punc	2m4f	Hdl		SFT £6399
127	5/01	Gowr	2m	NHF		GD £4451
129	2/01	Fair	2m	NHF		HVY £3895

Total win prize-money £37537

Going: Sf: 1-4 GS: 0-0 Gd: 0-2 GF: - Fm: 0-0
Distance: 2m/2m3: 1-3 2m4-2m7: 0-2 3m+: 0-2
Track: LH: 0-1 RH: 1-4 Tight: 0-0 Gall: 0-0
Aids: Bl: 0-0 Vi: 0-0 Tstrap: 0-0
Best Rating: 135 3/02 Punc 2m6f soft Hdl

Fairly useful Irish-trained novice chaser; formerly decent hurdler; effective from 2m to 3m, but probably suited by farther than 2m; jumped poorly when stepped up in class and 4th to Jair Du Cochet in Grade A Feltham Novices Chase at Kempton; suited by soft ground; best when held up.

One Of The Natives (IRE)

93 **90d**

9-y-o b g Be My Native (USA)-Take Me Home (Amoristic (USA))
Miss H C Knight Miss Judy Pimblett

Placings:*50/P/P34F-0P* (0213)
2002/03: 24⁰GF, 19⁹G,

	Starts	1st	2nd	3rd	Win & Pl
Chases	2	0	0	0	
Career Total	9	0	0	1	976

Going: Sf: 0-0 GS: 0-0 Gd: 0-1 GF: - Fm: 0-0
Distance: 2m/2m3: 0-1 2m4-2m7: 0-0 3m+: 0-1
Track: LH: 0-0 RH: 0-2 Tight: 0-1 Gall: 0-0
Aids: Bl: 0-0 Vi: 0-0 Tstrap: 0-0
Best Rating: 95 2/02 Tntn 3m soft Ch

One Up (IRE)

90 **57**

5-y-o b m Bob Back (USA)-Strong Desire (IRE) (Strong Gale)
M Todhunter (Cathal McCarthy 17/11) Steve Baron

Placings:*005* (4661)
2002/03: 16⁰S, 16⁰S, 17⁵GF,

	Starts	1st	2nd	3rd	Win & Pl
Hurdles	3	0	0	0	0
Career Total	3	0	0	0	0

Going: Sf: 0-2 GS: 0-0 Gd: 0-0 GF: - Fm: 0-1
Distance: 2m/2m3: 0-3 2m4-2m7: 0-0 3m+: 0-0
Track: LH: 0-1 RH: 0-2 Tight: 0-0 Gall: 0-0
Aids: Bl: 0-0 Vi: 0-0 Tstrap: 0-0
Best Rating: 57 4/03 Carl 2m1f gd-fm Hdl

Onefourseven

100 **91**

10-y-o b g Jumbo Hirt (USA)-Dominance (Dominion)
P C Haslam J Roundtree

Placings:*2224500-0* (1722)
2002/03: 23⁹G,

	Starts	1st	2nd	3rd	Win & Pl
Hurdles	1	0	0	0	
Career Total	8	0	3	0	2588

Going: Sf: 0-0 GS: 0-0 Gd: 0-1 GF: - Fm: 0-0
Distance: 2m/2m3: 0-0 2m4-2m7: 0-1 3m+: 0-0
Track: LH: 0-1 RH: 0-0 Tight: 0-0 Gall: 0-0
Aids: Bl: 0-0 Vi: 0-0 Tstrap: 0-0
Best Rating: 85 11/01 Newc 2m4f good Hdl

Poor novice hurdler; stays 3m; effective on fast ground.

Oneofourown (IRE)

97 (55h)**95**

12-y-o ch g Varshan-Twinkling (Star Appeal)
S Donohoe T Hyland

Placings:*040412006/6052365340413 5U2/2050526F34305 1/00P6U035/25P40PU215-5636563U41U* (4657a)
2002/03: 24⁵GF, 24⁴S, 24³GF, 24⁶GF, 24⁵G, 25⁶F, 24³GF, 26⁴S, 28⁴S, 24¹G, 25⁰GF,

	Starts	1st	2nd	3rd	Win & Pl
Chases	11	1	4	2	6889
Career Total	68	5	7	8	43844
95	3/03	Dpat	3m	(0-102)HCh	GD £5600
95	4/02	Fair	3m1f	(0-109)HCh	G-Y £8000
94	4/00	Fair	3m1f	(0-109)HCh	G-Y £5500
108	3/99	Naas	3m	Ch	Y-S £3989
97	2/98	Thur	3m	(0-116)HHdl	SFT £2978

Total win prize-money £26089

Going: Sf: 0-3 GS: 0-0 Gd: 1-2 GF: - Fm: 0-6
Distance: 2m/2m3: 0-0 2m4-2m7: 0-0 3m+: 1-11
Track: LH: 0-2 RH: 0-5 Tight: 0-1 Gall: 0-0
Aids: Bl: 1-11 Vi: 0-0 Tstrap: 0-9
Best Rating: 110 4/99 Punc 3m1f yield Ch

Oneoftwo

6-y-o ch m Bold Arrangement-Celtic Waters (Celtic Cone)
Mrs J C McGregor Mrs Dorothy Thomson

Placings:*0P* (1417)
2002/03: 16⁰GF, 22⁸GF,

	Starts	1st	2nd	3rd	Win & Pl
NH Flat	1	0	0	0	
Hurdles	1	0	0	0	
Career Total	2	0	0	0	

Going: Sf: 0-0 GS: 0-0 Gd: 0-0 GF: - Fm: 0-2
Distance: 2m/2m3: 0-1 2m4-2m7: 0-1 3m+: 0-0
Track: LH: 0-1 RH: 0-1 Tight: 0-1 Gall: 0-0
Aids: Bl: 0-0 Vi: 0-0 Tstrap: 0-0
Best Rating: 22 9/02 Prth 2m110y gd-fm NHF

Onethreesixsqadron

5-y-o b g Bandmaster (USA)-Paprika (IRE) (The Parson)
A G Newcombe Lavis Medical Systems

Placings:*0* (0737)

2002/03: 17⁰GF,

	Starts	1st	2nd	3rd	Win & Pl
NH Flat	1	0	0	0	
Career Total	1	0	0	0	

Going: Sf: 0-0 GS: 0-0 Gd: 0-0 GF: - Fm: 0-1
Distance: 2m/2m3: 0-1 2m4-2m7: 0-0 3m+: 0-0
Track: LH: 0-1 RH: 0-0 Tight: 0-1 Gall: 0-0
Aids: Bl: 0-0 Vi: 0-0 Tstrap: 0-0
Best Rating: 0 7/02 NAbb 2m1f gd-fm NHF

Oneway (IRE)
101   103
6-y-o b g Bob s Return (IRE)-Rendezvous (Lorenzaccio)
M G Rimell Mark Rimell

Placings:05245 (4228)
2002/03: 17⁰G, 19⁵GS, 17²GS, 19⁴GS, 25⁵GF,

	Starts	1st	2nd	3rd	Win & Pl
NH Flat	1	0	0	0	0
Hurdles	4	0	1	0	1696
Career Total	5	0	1	0	1696

Going: Sf: 0-0 GS: 0-3 Gd: 0-1 GF: - Fm: 0-1
Distance: 2m/2m3: 0-2 2m4-2m7: 0-2 3m+: 0-1
Track: LH: 0-4 RH: 0-1 Tight: 0-1 Gall: 0-0
Aids: Bl: 0-0 Vi: 0-0 Tstrap: 0-0
Best Rating: 103 3/03 Donc 2m3f110y gd-sft Hdl

Placed in a point-to-point; has shown modest form in novice hurdles.

Only Little
106
5-y-o ch m Sula Bula-Chicory (Vaigly Great)
D P Keane Conkwell Grange Stud Ltd

Placings:PP (2193)
2002/03: 16⁵PS, 17⁷GS,

	Starts	1st	2nd	3rd	Win & Pl
Hurdles	2	0	0	0	
Career Total	2	0	0	0	

Going: Sf: 0-1 GS: 0-1 Gd: 0-0 GF: - Fm: 0-0
Distance: 2m/2m3: 0-2 2m4-2m7: 0-0 3m+: 0-0
Track: LH: 0-1 RH: 0-1 Tight: 0-1 Gall: 0-0
Aids: Bl: 0-0 Vi: 0-0 Tstrap: 0-0
Best Rating: 0 11/02 Tntn 2m1f gd-sft Hdl

Only Once
106   118
8-y-o b g King s Ride-Rambling Gold (Little Buskins)
L Lungo Ashleybank Investments Limited

Placings:11 (4305)
2002/03: 27¹HY, 25¹G,

	Starts	1st	2nd	3rd	Win & Pl
Chases	2	2	0	0	9784
Career Total	2	2	0	0	9784
118 3/03 Kels 3m1f		D Ch		GD	£5838
97 1/03 Sedg 3m3f		E Ch		HVY	£3945
				Total win prize-money	£9784

Going: Sf: 1-1 GS: 0-0 Gd: 1-1 GF: - Fm: 0-0
Distance: 2m/2m3: 0-0 2m4-2m7: 0-0 3m+: 2-2
Track: LH: 2-2 RH: 0-0 Tight: 2-2 Gall: 0-0
Aids: Bl: 0-0 Vi: 0-0 Tstrap: 0-0
Best Rating: 118 3/03 Kels 3m1f good Ch

Winning Irish pointer; winner of his first two starts over fences in this country, but finished lame on the second occasion; stays 3m 3f; acts on good and soft ground.

Only One Matty (IRE)
84   96
6-y-o b g Satco (FR)-Poundworld (IRE) (Orchestra)
Mrs K Walton (C Roche 12/8) The White Liners

Placings:040000-33400 (2140)
2002/03: 16³YS, 24³YS, 18⁴GF, 22⁰G, 16⁰GS,

	Starts	1st	2nd	3rd	Win & Pl
Hurdles	5	0	0	2	1380
Career Total	11	0	0	2	1655

Going: Sf: 0-0 GS: 0-1 Gd: 0-1 GF: - Fm: 0-1
Distance: 2m/2m3: 0-4 2m4-2m7: 0-1 3m+: 0-1
Track: LH: 0-1 RH: 0-0 Tight: 0-0 Gall: 0-1
Aids: Bl: 0-1 Vi: 0-0 Tstrap: 0-3
Best Rating: 100 5/01 Fair 2m good NHF

Only When Provoked (IRE)
102   75
5-y-o b g General Monash (USA)-Lyzia (IRE) (Lycius (USA))
A Streeter The Saturday Lunchtime Syndicate

Placings:6340033-35P (0562)
2002/03: 16³GS, 20⁵G, 19⁹GF,

	Starts	1st	2nd	3rd	Win & Pl
Hurdles	3	0	0	1	288
Career Total	10	0	0	4	1240

Going: Sf: 0-0 GS: 0-1 Gd: 0-1 GF: - Fm: 0-0
Distance: 2m/2m3: 0-1 2m4-2m7: 0-2 3m+: 0-0
Track: LH: 0-1 RH: 0-2 Tight: 0-1 Gall: 0-0
Aids: Bl: 0-0 Vi: 0-1 Tstrap: 0-3
Best Rating: 75 5/02 Towc 2m gd-sft Hdl

Only Words (USA)
105   82
6-y-o ch g Shuailaan (USA)-Conversation Piece (USA) (Seeking The Gold (USA))
A J Lockwood Mrs Lynne Lumley

Placings:500356-202001252402P0 (4260)
2002/03: 16²GS, 16⁰G, 20²GF, 17⁰GF, 21⁰G, 17¹G, 16²HY, 16⁵GS, 17²S, 17⁴S, 16⁹G, 17⁹HY, 19⁹S, 21⁰G,

	Starts	1st	2nd	3rd	Win & Pl
Hurdles	14	1	5	0	6014
Career Total	20	1	5	0	6260
82 10/02 Sedg 2m1f		G(0-90)HHdl		GD	£2289
				Total win prize-money	£2289

Going: Sf: 0-5 GS: 0-2 Gd: 1-5 GF: - Fm: 0-2
Distance: 2m/2m3: 1-11 2m4-2m7: 0-3 3m+: 0-0
Track: LH: 1-13 RH: 0-1 Tight: 1-9 Gall: 0-1
Aids: Bl: 0-1 Vi: 0-0 Tstrap: 0-0
Best Rating: 82 2/03 Sedg 2m1f heavy Hdl

Plating-class hurdler; acts on soft.

Only You
100   76
7-y-o b g Gildoran-Outfield (Monksfield)
N A Twiston-Davies Roger Nicholls

Placings:0FP/5U00554PU4326-33 (0324)
2002/03: 20³GF, 20³G,

	Starts	1st	2nd	3rd	Win & Pl
Hurdles	2	0	0	2	675
Career Total	18	0	1	3	1485

Going: Sf: 0-0 GS: 0-0 Gd: 0-1 GF: - Fm: 0-1
Distance: 2m/2m3: 0-0 2m4-2m7: 0-2 3m+: 0-0
Track: LH: 0-2 RH: 0-0 Tight: 0-0 Gall: 0-0
Aids: Bl: 0-0 Vi: 0-0 Tstrap: 0-0
Best Rating: 76 5/02 Worc 2m4f good Hdl

Modest maiden including selling company. Suited by two and a half miles and fast ground.

Ontos (GER)
111   120+
7-y-o b/br g Super Abound (USA)-Onestep (GER) (Konigsstuhl (GER))
A Scott (Ronald O Leary 6/9) Miss Victoria Scott Jnr

Placings:P/0002344-F4F5511145140433434 (4470)
2002/03: 17⁵YS, 16⁴S, 16⁵GY, 16⁵GF, 16¹GF, 17¹GF, 16¹GF, 16⁴GF, 16⁵G, 16¹S, 17⁴HY, 17⁰G, 16⁴G, 20³HY, 16³G, 18⁴GS, 18³G, 16⁴G,

	Starts	1st	2nd	3rd	Win & Pl
Hurdles	19	4	0	3	23416
Career Total	27	4	1	4	25625
120 11/02 Kels 2m110y		D(0-125)HHdl		SFT	£4043
110 9/02 Prth 2m110y		D Hdl		G-F	£4303
108 9/02 Sedg 2m1f		E Hdl		G-F	£2968
102 8/02 Hntg 2m110y		F Hdl		G-F	£2223
				Total win prize-money	£13537

Going: Sf: 1-4 GS: 0-1 Gd: 0-6 GF: - Fm: 3-5
Distance: 2m/2m3: 4-18 2m4-2m7: 0-1 3m+: 0-0
Track: LH: 2-11 RH: 2-5 Tight: 2-7 Gall: 1-2
Aids: Bl: 0-0 Vi: 0-0 Tstrap: 0-0
Best Rating: 120 4/03 Aint 2m110y good Hdl

Fair novice hurdler; ex-Irish; in good form in the autumn of 2002; consistent efforts since; effective on most types of ground.

Onwardsandupwards (IRE)
90f
4-y-o b/br g Un Desperado (FR)-Kalifornia Katie (IRE) (Sharp Charter)
P F Nicholls Paul K Barber

Placings:1 (3337)
2002/03: 17¹S,

	Starts	1st	2nd	3rd	Win & Pl
NH Flat	1	1	0	0	2562
Career Total	1	1	0	0	2562
90 1/03 Tntn 2m1f		H NHF		SFT	£2562
				Total win prize-money	£2562

Going: Sf: 1-1 GS: 0-0 Gd: 0-0 GF: - Fm: 0-0
Distance: 2m/2m3: 1-1 2m4-2m7: 0-0 3m+: 0-0
Track: LH: 0-0 RH: 0-0 Tight: 0-0 Gall: 0-0
Aids: Bl: 0-0 Vi: 0-0 Tstrap: 0-0
Best Rating: 90 1/03 Tntn 2m1f soft NHF

Justified favouritism when narrow winner of soft ground bumper at Taunton on his racecourse debut January 2003.

Oo Ee Be
7-y-o b g Whittingham (IRE)-Miss Derby (USA) (Master Derby (USA))

Mrs N J Hughes L J Bridge

Placings:050304/5/00204-50   (4288)
2002/03: 16⁵GS, 20⁹GF,

	Starts	1st	2nd	3rd	Win & Pl
Chases	2	0	0	0	0
Career Total	14	0	1	1	1105

Going:	Sf: 0-0 GS: 0-1 Gd: 0-0 GF: - Fm: 0-1
Distance:	2m/2m3: 0-1 2m4-2m7: 0-1 3m+: 0-0
Track:	LH: 0-0 RH: 0-2 Tight: 0-0 Gall: 0-0
Aids:	Bl: 0-0 Vi: 0-0 Tstrap: 0-0
Best Rating:	81 3/00 Extr 2m1f110y gd-fm Hdl

Oodachee
107

4-y-o b g Marju (IRE)-Lady Marguerrite (Blakeney)
C F Swan Modreeny Syndicate

Placings:23   (4651a)
2002/03: 16²G, 16³F,

	Starts	1st	2nd	3rd	Win & Pl
NH Flat	2	0	1	1	1045
Career Total	2	0	1	1	1045

Going:	Sf: 0-0 GS: 0-0 Gd: 0-1 GF: - Fm: 0-0
Distance:	2m/2m3: 0-2 2m4-2m7: 0-0 3m+: 0-0
Track:	LH: 0-1 RH: 0-0 Tight: 0-0 Gall: 0-0
Aids:	Bl: 0-0 Vi: 0-0 Tstrap: 0-0
Best Rating:	98 4/03 Cork 2m firm NHF

Irish trained gelding;placed in bumpers on a sound surface.

Oops (IRE)
65   57

4-y-o b g In The Wings-Atsuko (IRE) (Mtoto)
A J Lidderdale (J G Given 5/8) M J Dawson

Placings:0   (3312)
2002/03: 17⁹GS,

	Starts	1st	2nd	3rd	Win & Pl
Hurdles	1	0	0	0	0
Career Total	1	0	0	0	0

Going:	Sf: 0-0 GS: 0-1 Gd: 0-0 GF: - Fm: 0-0
Distance:	2m/2m3: 0-1 2m4-2m7: 0-0 3m+: 0-0
Track:	LH: 0-0 RH: 0-1 Tight: 0-0 Gall: 0-0
Aids:	Bl: 0-0 Vi: 0-0 Tstrap: 0-0
Best Rating:	57 1/03 Extr 2m1f gd-sft Hdl

Opal Ridge
89f   95f

6-y-o ch g Jupiter Island-The Beginning (Goldhill)
P R Webber D I Bare

Placings:4   (2627)
2002/03: 16⁴S,

	Starts	1st	2nd	3rd	Win & Pl
NH Flat	1	0	0	0	0
Career Total	1	0	0	0	0

Going:	Sf: 0-1 GS: 0-0 Gd: 0-0 GF: - Fm: 0-0
Distance:	2m/2m3: 0-1 2m4-2m7: 0-0 3m+: 0-0
Track:	LH: 0-1 RH: 0-0 Tight: 0-0 Gall: 0-0
Aids:	Bl: 0-0 Vi: 0-0 Tstrap: 0-0
Best Rating:	95 12/02 Uttx 2m soft NHF

Winning pointer, showed some ability on debut under Rules in bumper at Uttoxeter in December.

Opal'Lou (FR)
107   103d

7-y-o b m Garde Royale-Calligraphie (FR) (Rb Chesne)
P F Nicholls Formpave Ltd

Placings:5060/250040F/32363636-25332   (4717)
2002/03: 19²GS, 19⁵S, 20³G, 22³G, 25²F,

	Starts	1st	2nd	3rd	Win & Pl
Chases	5	0	2	2	4117
Career Total	24	0	4	6	11992

Going:	Sf: 0-1 GS: 0-0 Gd: 0-2 GF: - Fm: 0-1
Distance:	2m/2m3: 0-1 2m4-2m7: 0-3 3m+: 0-1
Track:	LH: 0-0 RH: 0-4 Tight: 0-3 Gall: 0-0
Aids:	Bl: 0-0 Vi: 0-0 Tstrap: 0-0
Best Rating:	105 12/02 Extr 2m3f110y gd-sft Ch

Modest chaser; effective at around two and a half miles; has become disappointing.

Open Ground (IRE)
92   106

6-y-o ch g Common Grounds-Poplina (USA) (Roberto (USA))
Ian Williams The Net Partnership

Placings:61161405/055110-4P00F   (4088)
2002/03: 20⁴S, 16⁶GS, 16⁶HY, 16⁶S, 16⁶GS,

	Starts	1st	2nd	3rd	Win & Pl
Hurdles	5	0	0	0	1058
Career Total	19	5	0	0	17077
116	3/02	Newb	2m110y C(0-130)HHdl		SFT £5512
118	1/01	Wwck	2m	D Hdl	SFT £4777
110	11/00	MRas	2m1f110yE Hdl		SFT £2534
89	11/00	Wwck	2m	E Hdl	HVY £2261
				Total win prize-money £15085	

Going:	Sf: 0-3 GS: 0-2 Gd: 0-0 GF: - Fm: 0-0
Distance:	2m/2m3: 0-4 2m4-2m7: 0-1 3m+: 0-0
Track:	LH: 0-5 RH: 0-0 Tight: 0-1 Gall: 0-1
Aids:	Bl: 0-1 Vi: 0-3 Tstrap: 0-0
Best Rating:	118 1/01 Donc 2m110y good Hdl

Fair dual-purpose performer; confirmed mudlark, but won on fast ground on the Flat in 2002; effective at around two miles; has been successful in a visor; has worn blinkers.

Open Invitation (IRE)
(53h)   (15h) 26

9-y-o b g Hollow Hand-Nohoval Jane (Amoristic (USA))
Mrs J C McGregor (Mrs D Thomson 21/6) Mrs Dorothy Thomson

Placings:PP0-P40P   (1308)
2002/03: 24⁵GF, 20⁴GS, 20⁹GF, 20⁸GF,

	Starts	1st	2nd	3rd	Win & Pl
Hurdles	2	0	0	0	0
Chases	2	0	0	0	0
Career Total	7	0	0	0	0

Going:	Sf: 0-0 GS: 0-1 Gd: 0-0 GF: - Fm: 0-0
Distance:	2m/2m3: 0-0 2m4-2m7: 0-3 3m+: 0-1
Track:	LH: 0-1 RH: 0-3 Tight: 0-0 Gall: 0-0
Aids:	Bl: 0-0 Vi: 0-0 Tstrap: 0-0
Best Rating:	26 5/01 Chel 2m110y good Ch

Opening Bat

7-y-o b g Batshoof-Absalantra (Absalom)
Miss Z C Davison Mrs Gail Davison

Placings:000-P   (0111)
2002/03: 16⁸GS,

	Starts	1st	2nd	3rd	Win & Pl
Hurdles	1	0	0	0	
Career Total	4	0	0	0	

Going:	Sf: 0-0 GS: 0-1 Gd: 0-0 GF: - Fm: 0-0
Distance:	2m/2m3: 0-1 2m4-2m7: 0-0 3m+: 0-0
Track:	LH: 0-0 RH: 0-1 Tight: 0-0 Gall: 0-0
Aids:	Bl: 0-0 Vi: 0-0 Tstrap: 0-0
Best Rating:	54 12/01 Folk 2m1f110y soft NHF

Optimism (FR)
65f   80f

5-y-o b g Roakarad-Miss Daisy (FR) (Shirley Heights)
R H Alner P M De Wilde

Placings:03   (4364)
2002/03: 16⁰G, 17³F,

	Starts	1st	2nd	3rd	Win & Pl
NH Flat	2	0	0	1	267
Career Total	2	0	0	1	267

Going:	Sf: 0-0 GS: 0-0 Gd: 0-1 GF: - Fm: 0-1
Distance:	2m/2m3: 0-2 2m4-2m7: 0-0 3m+: 0-0
Track:	LH: 0-0 RH: 0-1 Tight: 0-0 Gall: 0-0
Aids:	Bl: 0-0 Vi: 0-0 Tstrap: 0-0
Best Rating:	80 3/03 Tntn 2m1f firm NHF

Improved on debut when third in five runner firm ground bumper at Taunton March 2003.

Optimistic Chris
111(104h)   (109h) 120

8-y-o b g Pharly (FR)-Gay Twenties (Lord Gayle (USA))
Mrs J Candlish (A Streeter 28/10) Optimistic Racing

Placings:1416/235P36/004523/15101-4326P   (2475)
2002/03: 21⁴G, 17³GF, 20²S, 20⁶GS, 16⁶GS,

	Starts	1st	2nd	3rd	Win & Pl
Chases	5	0	1	1	3874
Career Total	26	5	3	4	27713
109	4/02	Bang	2m1f110yD Ch	GD	£4485
100	12/01	Ludl	2m4f	D(0-115)HCh	GD £4238
109	9/01	MRas	2m3f110yE(0-115)HHdl	SFT	£3178
112	2/99	Kels	2m110y C Hdl	SFT	£5359
96	12/98	Uttx	2m	G Hdl	SFT £1658
				Total win prize-money £18919	

Going:	Sf: 0-1 GS: 0-2 Gd: 0-1 GF: - Fm: 0-1
Distance:	2m/2m3: 0-2 2m4-2m7: 0-3 3m+: 0-0
Track:	LH: 0-4 RH: 0-1 Tight: 0-2 Gall: 0-2
Aids:	Bl: 0-0 Vi: 0-0 Tstrap: 0-0
Best Rating:	120 10/02 Bang 2m4f110y soft Ch

Won three races over fences on 2001/2002 and turned in a career best effort at Bangor in April 2002. Has continued to run well since. Has won from two miles one and a half furlongs to two and a half miles. Acts on good to firm and soft ground.

Optimistic Thinker
83(104h)

9-y-o ch g Beveled (USA)-Racemosa (Town Crier)

T R George M R C Opperman

Placings: 1*0*2P61P/**2223**/412P1UP6/P234014P-4PPPP
                 (4693)
2002/03: 16⁴GF, 16⁶S, 16⁸S, 17⁸G, 17⁹G,

	Starts	1st	2nd	3rd	Win & Pl
Hurdles	1	0	0	0	0
Chases	4	0	0	0	0
Career Total	32	5	6	2	21409
115 1/02 Hntg	2m110y	D(0-115)HCh		G-S	£3893
118 11/00 Uttx	2m	D Ch		HVY	£3944
113 10/00 Hntg	2m110y	E(0-105)HCh		G-F	£3052
103 3/99 NAbb	2m1f	F(0-100)HHdl		SFT	£1760
109 10/98 MRas	1m5f110yH NHF			HVY	£1234
			Total win prize-money £13886

Going:	Sf: 0-2 GS: 0-0 Gd: 0-2 GF: - Fm: 0-1
Distance:	2m/2m3: 0-5 2m4-2m7: 0-0 3m+: 0-1
Track:	LH: 0-3 RH: 0-2 Tight: 0-3 Gall: 0-0
Aids:	Bl: 0-1 Vi: 0-0 Tstrap: 0-0
Best Rating:	118 11/00 Uttx 2m heavy Ch

A winner of a bumper, over hurdles and over fences; made a winning return to fences in January 2002 after some moderate efforts over hurdles; acts on most types of ground and is effective at around two miles; bang out of form of late.

Optimum Night
78f   64f

4-y-o b g Superlative-Black Bess (Hasty Word)
P D Niven Mrs H M Lipscomb

Placings: *0*   **(3969)**
2002/03: 16⁰S,

	Starts	1st	2nd	3rd	Win & Pl
NH Flat	1	0	0	0	
Career Total	1	0	0	0	

Going:	Sf: 0-1 GS: 0-0 Gd: 0-0 GF: - Fm: 0-0
Distance:	2m/2m3: 0-1 2m4-2m7: 0-0 3m+: 0-0
Track:	LH: 0-1 RH: 0-0 Tight: 0-1 Gall: 0-0
Aids:	Bl: 0-0 Vi: 0-0 Tstrap: 0-0
Best Rating:	64 3/03 Catt 2m soft NHF

Oracle Des Mottes (FR)
98   96+

4-y-o b g Signe Divin (USA)-Daisy Des Mottes (FR) (Abdonski (FR))
P F Nicholls Mark Tincknell

Placings: 2303   **(3312)**
2002/03: 17²S, 16³GS, 17⁰S, 17³GS,

	Starts	1st	2nd	3rd	Win & Pl
Hurdles	4	0	1	2	2185
Career Total	4	0	1	2	2185

Going:	Sf: 0-2 GS: 0-2 Gd: 0-0 GF: - Fm: 0-0
Distance:	2m/2m3: 0-4 2m4-2m7: 0-0 3m+: 0-0
Track:	LH: 0-0 RH: 0-4 Tight: 0-1 Gall: 0-0
Aids:	Bl: 0-0 Vi: 0-0 Tstrap: 0-0
Best Rating:	96 1/03 Extr 2m1f gd-sft Hdl

French import; modest juvenile hurdler; acts on soft ground.

Orake Prince

4-y-o b g Bluegrass Prince (IRE)-Kiri Te (Liboi (USA))
J G Portman D A Drake

Placings: PP   **(4220)**
2002/03: 16⁸GS, 19⁸GF,

	Starts	1st	2nd	3rd	Win & Pl
Hurdles	2	0	0	0	
Career Total	2	0	0	0	

Going:	Sf: 0-0 GS: 0-1 Gd: 0-0 GF: - Fm: 0-1
Distance:	2m/2m3: 0-1 2m4-2m7: 0-1 3m+: 0-0
Track:	LH: 0-1 RH: 0-1 Tight: 0-1 Gall: 0-0
Aids:	Bl: 0-0 Vi: 0-0 Tstrap: 0-0
Best Rating:	0 3/03 Hrfd 2m3f110y gd-fm Hdl

Orange Order (IRE)
101 (110c)   (115c) 86

10-y-o ch g Generous (IRE)-Fleur D Oranger (Northfields (USA))
G M Moore Mrs A Roddis

Placings: 6P/62106504/013502060L00/11615062/11354331 50/4214123F3-P5P336P33P0   **(4795)**
2002/03: 20⁵GS, 20⁵G, 22²G, 21³GF, 21³G, 21⁶G, 26⁸GF, 27³G, 21³GF, 21⁹G, 21⁰GF,

	Starts	1st	2nd	3rd	Win & Pl
Hurdles	3	0	0	0	0
Chases	8	0	0	4	2793
Career Total	60	10	5	10	37602
101 7/01 Wolv	2m4f110yE Ch		G-F	£3376
115 6/01 MRas	2m4f	E Ch	G-F	£3851
119 9/00 Sedg	2m5f110yD(0-120)HHdl		GD	£3575
114 5/00 Weth	2m	E(0-115)HHdl	G-S	£2485
101 5/00 Sedg	2m1f	F(0-100)HHdl	G-F	£2492
102 9/99 Sedg	2m1f	G(0-95)HHdl	G-F	£2066
102 7/99 Sedg	2m1f	G(0-95)HHdl	G-F	£1884
100 7/99 Sedg	2m1f	F(0-100)HHdl	G-F	£2010
109 6/98 Tral	2m	(0-102)Hdl	GD	£2382
102 9/97 Clon	2m	Hdl	Y-S	£2543
			Total win prize-money £26666

Going:	Sf: 0-0 GS: 0-1 Gd: 0-6 GF: - Fm: 0-4
Distance:	2m/2m3: 0-0 2m4-2m7: 0-9 3m+: 0-2
Track:	LH: 0-10 RH: 0-1 Tight: 0-8 Gall: 0-0
Aids:	Bl: 0-0 Vi: 0-0 Tstrap: 0-0
Best Rating:	119 9/00 Sedg 2m5f110y good Hdl

Plating-class hurdler; Sedgefield specialist over hurdles, ordinary handicap chaser, best at distances short of three miles.

Orange Tree Lad
98   77

5-y-o b g Tragic Role (USA)-Adorable Cherub (USA) (Halo (USA))
Mrs Jane Galpin Mrs Jane Galpin

Placings: P033343506U   **(4525)**
2002/03: 16⁸S, 16⁹G, 17³S, 17³S, 17³G, 19⁴GS, 16³S, 17⁵S, 16⁶GS, 17⁶GF, 16⁰G,

	Starts	1st	2nd	3rd	Win & Pl
Hurdles	11	0	0	4	1329
Career Total	11	0	0	4	1329

Going:	Sf: 0-5 GS: 0-2 Gd: 0-3 GF: - Fm: 0-1
Distance:	2m/2m3: 0-10 2m4-2m7: 0-1 3m+: 0-0
Track:	LH: 0-5 RH: 0-6 Tight: 0-3 Gall: 0-0
Aids:	Bl: 0-0 Vi: 0-0 Tstrap: 0-0
Best Rating:	77 1/03 Ludl 2m soft Hdl

Plating-class hurdler.

Orangerie (IRE)
(106h)   (112 h)

5-y-o b g Darshaan-Fleur D Oranger (Northfields (USA))

P J Hobbs Richard Green (fine Paintings)

Placings: 4-1204U2365   **(4776)**
2002/03: 16¹GF, 22²GS, 24⁰GS, 20⁴HY, 18⁰S, 16²HY, 19³GS, 20⁶G, 20⁵G,

	Starts	1st	2nd	3rd	Win & Pl
Hurdles	9	1	2	1	12087
Career Total	10	1	2	1	12422
119 10/02 Chel	2m110y	D Hdl		G-F	£7586
			Total win prize-money £7586

Going:	Sf: 0-3 GS: 0-3 Gd: 0-2 GF: - Fm: 1-1
Distance:	2m/2m3: 1-4 2m4-2m7: 0-4 3m+: 0-1
Track:	LH: 1-3 RH: 0-5 Tight: 0-3 Gall: 0-0
Aids:	Bl: 0-7 Vi: 0-0 Tstrap: 0-0
Best Rating:	119 11/02 Winc 2m6f gd-sft Hdl

Fair hurdler; effective at up to two miles six furlongs; acts on a sound surface, but is also effective with cut; often wears blinkers; is probably not a straight forward ride.

Orapa
69   31

4-y-o b g Spectrum (IRE)-African Dance (USA) (El Gran Senor (USA))
Julian Poulton (Sir Michael Stoute 27/5) Ian Frazer

Placings: 0   **(3830)**
2002/03: 16⁰G,

	Starts	1st	2nd	3rd	Win & Pl
Hurdles	1	0	0	0	
Career Total	1	0	0	0	

Going:	Sf: 0-0 GS: 0-0 Gd: 0-1 GF: - Fm: 0-0
Distance:	2m/2m3: 0-1 2m4-2m7: 0-0 3m+: 0-0
Track:	LH: 0-1 RH: 0-0 Tight: 0-1 Gall: 0-0
Aids:	Bl: 0-0 Vi: 0-0 Tstrap: 0-0
Best Rating:	31 2/03 Weth 2m good Hdl

Orbicularis (IRE)
87   75

7-y-o b g Supreme Leader-Liffey Travel (Le Bavard (FR))
R F Fisher Great Head House Estates Limited

Placings: 0*00*-000   **(1959)**
2002/03: 16⁰G, 22⁰S, 20⁰S,

	Starts	1st	2nd	3rd	Win & Pl
Hurdles	3	0	0	0	
Career Total	6	0	0	0	

Going:	Sf: 0-2 GS: 0-0 Gd: 0-1 GF: - Fm: 0-0
Distance:	2m/2m3: 0-1 2m4-2m7: 0-2 3m+: 0-0
Track:	LH: 0-3 RH: 0-0 Tight: 0-1 Gall: 0-0
Aids:	Bl: 0-0 Vi: 0-0 Tstrap: 0-0
Best Rating:	87 10/01 Carl 2m1f gd-sft NHF

Orchard Fields (IRE)
101   109d

6-y-o b g Lord Americo-Art Lover (IRE) (Over The River (FR))
Mrs P Sly P J Turner

Placings: 0*6*-14500   **(4786)**
2002/03: 20¹S, 20⁴HY, 23⁵GS, 20⁰G, 22⁰G,

	Starts	1st	2nd	3rd	Win & Pl
Hurdles	5	1	0	0	4664
Career Total	7	1	0	0	4664
109 11/02 Leic	2m4f110yD Hdl		SFT	£4260
			Total win prize-money £4261

Going:	Sf: 1-2 GS: 0-1 Gd: 0-2 GF: - Fm: 0-0
Distance:	2m/2m3: 0-0 2m4-2m7: 1-5 3m+: 0-0
Track:	LH: 0-2 RH: 1-2 Tight: 0-0 Gall: 0-0
Aids:	Bl: 0-0 Vi: 0-0 Tstrap: 0-0
Best Rating:	109 11/02 Leic 2m4f110y soft Hdl

Made a winning debut over hurdles in a slowly run novice event at Leicester in November 2002. Held since.

Orchestra's Boy (IRE)

95   89

8-y-o b g Homo Sapien-Ballycurnane Lady (Orchestra)
Mrs A M Thorpe   Mrs A M Thorpe

Placings: 0200-22   (1697)
2002/03: 22²GF, 24²GF,

	Starts	1st	2nd	3rd	Win & Pl
Hurdles	2	0	2	0	2856
Career Total	6	0	3	0	3278

Going:	Sf: 0-0 GS: 0-0 Gd: 0-0 GF: - Fm: 0-2
Distance:	2m/2m3: 0-0 2m4-2m7: 0-1 3m+: 0-1
Track:	LH: 0-1 RH: 0-1 Tight: 0-1 Gall: 0-0
Aids:	Bl: 0-0 Vi: 0-0 Tstrap: 0-0
Best Rating:	93 7/01 Worc 2m good NHF

Probably achieved little when a well-beaten runner-up to the same horse in a couple of three-runner evetns at Uttoxeter and Taunton in October 2002.

Orient Bay (IRE)

106   71

8-y-o b g Commanche Run-East Link (IRE) (Over The River (FR))
M Sheppard   R W Guilding

Placings: 4/U-PR44P33U   (4636)
2002/03: 24PG, 25RG, 254S, 244S, 25PG, 243GF, 253GF, 24UG,

	Starts	1st	2nd	3rd	Win & Pl
Chases	8	0	0	2	2488
Career Total	10	0	0	2	2488

Going:	Sf: 0-2 GS: 0-0 Gd: 0-4 GF: - Fm: 0-2
Distance:	2m/2m3: 0-0 2m4-2m7: 0-0 3m+: 0-8
Track:	LH: 0-2 RH: 0-6 Tight: 0-3 Gall: 0-0
Aids:	Bl: 0-0 Vi: 0-0 Tstrap: 0-0
Best Rating:	92 5/00 Prth 2m110y gd-sft NHF

Point-to-point winner in 2002 but only moderate form in chases; has shown a tendency to jump left handed.

Orient Express (IRE)

95(80h)   (92h)85

6-y-o b g Blues Traveller (IRE)-Oriental Splendour (Runnett)
Mrs L Richards (J T Gifford 24/9)   Mrs Lydia Richards

Placings: 00332PP   (2604)
2002/03: 16⁰GF, 16⁰GF, 18³GF, 16³G, 18²GF, 18PGS, 16PGS,

	Starts	1st	2nd	3rd	Win & Pl
Hurdles	3	0	0	1	424
Chases	4	0	1	1	1439
Career Total	7	0	1	2	1863

Going:	Sf: 0-0 GS: 0-2 Gd: 0-1 GF: - Fm: 0-4
Distance:	2m/2m3: 0-7 2m4-2m7: 0-0 3m+: 0-0
Track:	LH: 0-4 RH: 0-1 Tight: 0-5 Gall: 0-0
Aids:	Bl: 0-0 Vi: 0-0 Tstrap: 0-0

Best Rating:	92 8/02 Font 2m2f110y gd-fm Hdl

Modest novice hurdler, placed on his first two starts over fences.

Oriental Style (IRE)

106   102+

9-y-o r g Indian Ridge-Bazaar Promise (Native Bazaar)
M R Hoad (P R Rodford 27/1)   Leon Best

Placings: 55033/55042U442123/54/651P4B3-21400 (4188)
2002/03: 27²GS, 20¹S, 264HY, 25⁰GS, 28⁰G,

	Starts	1st	2nd	3rd	Win & Pl
Hurdles	1	0	0	0	0
Chases	4	1	1	0	8602
Career Total	31	3	4	4	19901
102	12/02	Uttx	2m4f	D(0-115)HCh	SFT	£6174
100	1/02	Wwck	2m4f110yF(0-90)HCh		SFT	£2705
92	3/99	NAbb	2m5f110yE(0-115)HCh		SFT	£2788
			Total win prize-money £11668			

Going:	Sf: 1-2 GS: 0-2 Gd: 0-1 GF: - Fm: 0-0
Distance:	2m/2m3: 0-0 2m4-2m7: 1-1 3m+: 0-4
Track:	LH: 1-1 RH: 0-3 Tight: 0-3 Gall: 0-0
Aids:	Bl: 1-5 Vi: 0-0 Tstrap: 0-0
Best Rating:	102 12/02 Uttx 2m4f soft Ch

Modest chaser, soft ground and two and a half miles suit and won in those conditions at Uttoxeter in December 2002. Usually blinkered.

Orlando Sunrise (IRE)

(96h)   (93h)77

6-y-o ch m Dolphin Street (FR)-Miss Belgravia (USA) (Smarten (USA))
Ian Williams   Charles Eden

Placings: 3060-00   (0840)
2002/03: 16⁰GF, 19⁰GF,

	Starts	1st	2nd	3rd	Win & Pl
Hurdles	2	0	0	0	0
Career Total	6	0	0	1	471

Going:	Sf: 0-0 GS: 0-0 Gd: 0-0 GF: - Fm: 0-2
Distance:	2m/2m3: 0-2 2m4-2m7: 0-0 3m+: 0-0
Track:	LH: 0-2 RH: 0-0 Tight: 0-2 Gall: 0-0
Aids:	Bl: 0-1 Vi: 0-0 Tstrap: 0-0
Best Rating:	93 10/01 Strf 2m110y gd-sft Hdl

Regressive form over hurdles for Ian Williams; modest fourth on chasing debut at Southwell July 2003 on first start for new yard.

Orleans (IRE)

8-y-o b g Scenic-Guest House (What A Guest)
S J Robinson   S J Robinson

Placings: 03/5/2OO-F   (4107)
2002/03: 27FS,

	Starts	1st	2nd	3rd	Win & Pl
Chases	1	0	0	0	
Career Total	7	0	1	1	910

Going:	Sf: 0-1 GS: 0-0 Gd: 0-0 GF: - Fm: 0-0
Distance:	2m/2m3: 0-0 2m4-2m7: 0-0 3m+: 0-1
Track:	LH: 0-1 RH: 0-0 Tight: 0-1 Gall: 0-0
Aids:	Bl: 0-1 Vi: 0-0 Tstrap: 0-0
Best Rating:	92 6/01 Worc 2m gd-fm Hdl

Orswell Crest

109   115

9-y-o b g Crested Lark-Slave s Bangle (Prince Rheingold)
P J Hobbs   The Mane Chance Partnership

Placings: 0/063/0245U-1133314   (4765)
2002/03: 25¹G, 25¹G, 24³GS, 25³S, 23³G, 25¹G, 31⁴G,

	Starts	1st	2nd	3rd	Win & Pl
Chases	7	3	3	1	51066
Career Total	16	3	1	4	53167
113	4/03	Ayr	3m1f	B HCh	GD	£21255
115	11/02	Aint	3m1f	D(0-115)HCh	GD	£14218
108	11/02	Winc	3m1f110yD(0-110)HCh		GD	£10188
			Total win prize-money £45663			

Going:	Sf: 0-1 GS: 0-1 Gd: 3-5 GF: - Fm: 0-0
Distance:	2m/2m3: 0-0 2m4-2m7: 0-0 3m+: 3-7
Track:	LH: 2-3 RH: 1-3 Tight: 1-1 Gall: 0-1
Aids:	Bl: 0-0 Vi: 0-0 Tstrap: 0-0
Best Rating:	115 11/02 Aint 3m1f good Ch

Fair staying novice chaser; won at Wincanton and Aintree in November 2002 on decent ground and landed a novices handicap at Ayr in April 2003; effective on good and softer; stays three and a quarter miles; likes flat tracks.

Oscail An Doras (IRE)

99   78

14-y-o ch g Avocat-Candora (Cantab)
P Bowen   R G Miles

Placings: 50000/120631F33/131625/06111144/P4553PF04 4/00P/00 (0784)
2002/03: 23⁰GF, 21⁰GF,

	Starts	1st	2nd	3rd	Win & Pl
Chases	2	0	0	0	
Career Total	43	8	2	5	33851
117	3/99	Hntg	2m110y	D(0-125)HCh	SFT	£3873
113	2/99	Hntg	2m110y	D(0-125)HCh	G-S	£3968
108	1/99	Muss	2m	E(0-115)HCh	SFT	£3470
101	12/98	Hntg	2m110y	F(0-115)HCh	SFT	£2670
112	5/96	Hrfd	2m3f	E Ch	GD	£2944
102	5/96	Hrfd	2m3f	E Ch	FRM	£2690
105	3/96	Hrfd	2m	E Ch	SFT	£2677
92	5/95	Hntg	2m110y	E Hdl	FRM	£2355
			Total win prize-money £24952			

Going:	Sf: 0-0 GS: 0-0 Gd: 0-0 GF: - Fm: 0-2
Distance:	2m/2m3: 0-0 2m4-2m7: 0-1 3m+: 0-1
Track:	LH: 0-2 RH: 0-0 Tight: 0-0 Gall: 0-0
Aids:	Bl: 0-0 Vi: 0-0 Tstrap: 0-0
Best Rating:	117 4/99 MRas 2m1f110y good Ch

Oscar Mac

4-y-o b g Double Eclipse (IRE)-Stravano (Handsome Sailor)
Mrs L Williamson   Mrs G E McCrea

Placings: 00PP   (4219)
2002/03: 16⁰GS, 17⁰G, 17PS, 17PGF,

	Starts	1st	2nd	3rd	Win & Pl
NH Flat	2	0	0	0	0
Hurdles	2	0	0	0	0
Career Total	4	0	0	0	

Going:	Sf: 0-1 GS: 0-1 Gd: 0-1 GF: - Fm: 0-1
Distance:	2m/2m3: 0-4 2m4-2m7: 0-0 3m+: 0-0
Track:	LH: 0-2 RH: 0-2 Tight: 0-1 Gall: 0-0
Aids:	Bl: 0-0 Vi: 0-0 Tstrap: 0-0

Best Rating: 50 2/03 Weth 2m   gd-sft NHF

Oscar Performance (IRE)

97(99h)   (98+h)**112+**

8-y-o gr g Roselier (FR)-Miss Iverk (Torus)
R H Buckler Twentyman

Placings:P000-0123P   (3732)
2002/03: 16⁶G, 20¹GS, 23²GS, 24³GS, 24ᴾG,

	Starts	1st	2nd	3rd	Win & Pl
Hurdles	2	1	0	0	3297
Chases	3	0	1	1	2209
Career Total	9	1	1	1	5506
87 6/02 Uttx	2m4f110yD Hdl			G-S	£3297

Total win prize-money £3297

Going: Sf: 0-0 GS: 1-2 Gd: 0-2 GF: - Fm: 0-1
Distance: 2m/2m3: 0-1 2m4-2m7: 1-1 3m+: 0-3
Track: LH: 1-2 RH: 0-1 Tight: 0-0 Gall: 0-0
Aids: Bl: 0-0 Vi: 0-0 Tstrap: 0-0
Best Rating: 112 1/03 Kemp 3m   gd-sft Ch

Ex-Irish, he put up improved form to win a Towcester novice hurdle in May 2002.

Oscar Wilde

                                              86

11-y-o b g Arctic Lord-Topsy Bee (Be Friendly)
R H Alner Paul Green

Placings:50/422/F014F/0P2-0   (0058)
2002/03: 16⁶G,

	Starts	1st	2nd	3rd	Win & Pl
Chases	1	0	0	0	
Career Total	14	1	3	0	10540
108 11/99 Winc	2m5f	E(0-105)HCh		GD	£5381

Total win prize-money £5381

Going: Sf: 0-0 GS: 0-0 Gd: 0-1 GF: - Fm: 0-0
Distance: 2m/2m3: 0-1 2m4-2m7: 0-0 3m+: 0-0
Track: LH: 0-0 RH: 0-1 Tight: 0-0 Gall: 0-0
Aids: Bl: 0-0 Vi: 0-0 Tstrap: 0-0
Best Rating: 108 11/99 Winc 2m5f   good Ch

Fair chaser at trips around two miles five on a sound surface. Disappointing since returning from a lengthy absence.

Oscarsexpress

6-y-o ch m Gunner B-Anchor Express (Carlingford Castle)
D Burchell D A Malam

Placings:600-P   (0072)
2002/03: 26ᴾGF,

	Starts	1st	2nd	3rd	Win & Pl
Hurdles	1	0	0	0	
Career Total	4	0	0	0	0

Going: Sf: 0-0 GS: 0-0 Gd: 0-0 GF: - Fm: 0-1
Distance: 2m/2m3: 0-0 2m4-2m7: 0-0 3m+: 0-1
Track: LH: 0-0 RH: 0-1 Tight: 0-0 Gall: 0-0
Aids: Bl: 0-0 Vi: 0-0 Tstrap: 0-0
Best Rating: 77 2/02 Wwck 2m   heavy NHF

Ososhot

108   **102**

10-y-o b g Teenoso (USA)-Duckdown (Blast)

A J Wilson Favourites Racing

Placings:1/U/52564F5/060113-0F2003   (4318)
2002/03: 16⁶G, 22ᶠGS, 23²GS, 22⁰GS, 22⁰HY, 24³G,

	Starts	1st	2nd	3rd	Win & Pl
Hurdles	6	0	1	1	2588
Career Total	21	3	2	2	12401
114 1/02 Winc	2m6f	D(0-115)HHdl		G-S	£3556
104 12/01 Winc	2m6f	F(0-100)HHdl		GD	£2709
116 3/99 Ludl	2m	H NHF		SFT	£1493

Total win prize-money £7759

Going: Sf: 0-2 GS: 0-3 Gd: 0-1 GF: - Fm: 0-0
Distance: 2m/2m3: 0-1 2m4-2m7: 0-4 3m+: 0-1
Track: LH: 0-3 RH: 0-3 Tight: 0-1 Gall: 0-0
Aids: Bl: 0-0 Vi: 0-0 Tstrap: 0-0
Best Rating: 116 11/00 MRas 2m1f110y gd-sft Hdl

Fair staying hurdler; effective at two miles six; acts on good and soft ground.

Otahuna

100   **73**

7-y-o b g Selkirk (USA)-Stara (Star Appeal)
J A Moore J A Moore

Placings:P/P/P0220   (1325)
2002/03: 16ᴾS, 17⁰G, 17²G, 17²GF, 17⁰GF,

	Starts	1st	2nd	3rd	Win & Pl
Hurdles	5	0	2	0	1494
Career Total	7	0	2	0	1494

Going: Sf: 0-1 GS: 0-0 Gd: 0-2 GF: - Fm: 0-2
Distance: 2m/2m3: 0-5 2m4-2m7: 0-0 3m+: 0-0
Track: LH: 0-4 RH: 0-1 Tight: 0-4 Gall: 0-0
Aids: Bl: 0-0 Vi: 0-0 Tstrap: 0-0
Best Rating: 86 3/00 Catt 2m   gd-fm Hdl

Turned in an improved effort when runner-up in a selling hurdle at Cartmel in August.

Otterington Girl

7-y-o b m Noble Patriarch-Bidweaya (USA) (Lear Fan (USA))
Miss S E Hall Mrs D S Wilkinson

Placings:5/00   (4793)
2002/03: 17⁰GF, 17⁰GF,

	Starts	1st	2nd	3rd	Win & Pl
Hurdles	2	0	0	0	
Career Total	3	0	0	0	0

Going: Sf: 0-0 GS: 0-0 Gd: 0-0 GF: - Fm: 0-2
Distance: 2m/2m3: 0-2 2m4-2m7: 0-0 3m+: 0-0
Track: LH: 0-1 RH: 0-1 Tight: 0-1 Gall: 0-0
Aids: Bl: 0-0 Vi: 0-0 Tstrap: 0-0
Best Rating: 0 4/03 Sedg 2m1f   gd-fm Hdl

Ottoman (IRE)

73f   **88+f**

6-y-o b g Sadler s Wells (USA)-Morning Devotion (USA) (Affirmed (USA))
G A Swinbank D J Lever

Placings:0   (0328)
2002/03: 16⁰G,

	Starts	1st	2nd	3rd	Win & Pl
NH Flat	1	0	0	0	
Career Total	1	0	0	0	

Going: Sf: 0-0 GS: 0-0 Gd: 0-1 GF: - Fm: 0-0
Distance: 2m/2m3: 0-1 2m4-2m7: 0-0 3m+: 0-0
Track: LH: 0-1 RH: 0-0 Tight: 0-0 Gall: 0-0
Aids: Bl: 0-0 Vi: 0-0 Tstrap: 0-0
Best Rating: 88 5/02 Worc 2m   good NHF

Bred to win a Derby, ran green on bumper debut.

Oudalmuteena (IRE)

72(102h)   (94h)**38**

8-y-o b g Lahib (USA)-Roxy Music (IRE) (Song)
C J Gray Riverdance Consortium

Placings:040/060123P400P/4P04400-0   (0036)
2002/03: 17⁰G,

	Starts	1st	2nd	3rd	Win & Pl
Chases	1	0	0	0	
Career Total	22	1	1	1	4143
88 12/00 Extr	2m3f	F(0-100)HHdl		HVY	£2548

Total win prize-money £2548

Going: Sf: 0-0 GS: 0-0 Gd: 0-1 GF: - Fm: 0-0
Distance: 2m/2m3: 0-1 2m4-2m7: 0-0 3m+: 0-0
Track: LH: 0-0 RH: 0-1 Tight: 0-0 Gall: 0-0
Aids: Bl: 0-0 Vi: 0-0 Tstrap: 0-0
Best Rating: 94 2/02 Winc 2m   soft Hdl

Oulton Broad

105   **104**

7-y-o b g Midyan (USA)-Lady Quachita (USA) (Sovereign Dancer (USA))
R Ford (M R Hoad 14/5) The Haydock Club

Placings:55F31111P/000PP/003060P4P-641412U631
                                              (1611)
2002/03: 17⁶G, 19⁴G, 20¹GS, 22⁴G, 20¹GF, 20²G, 16ᵁGS, 20⁶G, 20³GF, 23¹G,

	Starts	1st	2nd	3rd	Win & Pl
Hurdles	9	3	1	1	15329
Chases	1	0	0	0	0
Career Total	33	7	1	3	31019
104 10/02 Hayd	2m7f110yD(0-115)HHdl		GD	£4257
105 6/02 Uttx	2m4f110yD(0-120)HHdl		G-F	£5330
104 6/02 Prth	2m4f110yD(0-115)HHdl		G-S	£3396
122 4/00 Asct	2m4f	C(0-130)HHdl		SFT	£6402
102 3/00 Hrfd	2m3f110yD(0-120)HHdl		GD	£3497
115 2/00 Folk	2m1f110yF(0-95)HHdl		SFT	£2366
106 2/00 Hrfd	2m3f110yF Hdl		GD	£2534

Total win prize-money £27784

Going: Sf: 0-0 GS: 1-2 Gd: 1-6 GF: - Fm: 1-2
Distance: 2m/2m3: 0-2 2m4-2m7: 2-7 3m+: 1-1
Track: LH: 2-5 RH: 1-5 Tight: 0-3 Gall: 0-0
Aids: Bl: 0-0 Vi: 0-0 Tstrap: 0-0
Best Rating: 122 4/00 Asct 2m4f   soft Hdl

A fair handicap hurdler from two and a half to three, running well in the summer of 2002. Acts on soft, but handles good ground.

Our Armageddon (NZ)

114   **131+**

6-y-o b g Sky Chase (NZ)-Monte D Oro (NZ) (Cache Of Gold (USA))
R C Guest (N B Mason 25/1) Leslie John Garrett

Placings:21311   (4412)
2002/03: 17²GS, 16¹S, 16³GS, 17¹GS, 17¹G,

	Starts	1st	2nd	3rd	Win & Pl
Hurdles	5	3	1	1	16321

Career Total	5	3	1	1		16321
131	3/03	MRas	2m1f110yC Hdl		GD	£7036
119	3/03	Carl	2m1f	E Hdl	G-S	£3640
110	12/02	Newc	2m	E Hdl	SFT	£3555

Total win prize-money £14232

Going:	Sf: 1-1 GS: 1-3 Gd: 1-1 GF: - Fm: 0-0
Distance:	2m/2m3: 3-5 2m4-2m7: 0-0 3m+: 0-0
Track:	LH: 1-2 RH: 2-3 Tight: 1-2 Gall: 1-2
Aids:	Bl: 0-0 Vi: 0-0 Tstrap: 0-0
Best Rating:	131 3/03 MRas 2m1f110y good Hdl

Decent novice hurdler; goes well on a soft surface but equally at home on good; successful for the third time in four starts when adding to his record at Market Rasen in March.

Our Barrick (IRE)

7-y-o b g Sharp Charter-Mimmsie Starr (Pitskelly)
J Neville G L Greenhaf

Placings:0P/P   (0685)
2002/03: 21PG,

	Starts	1st	2nd	3rd	Win & Pl
Chases	1	0	0	0	
Career Total	3	0	0	0	

Going:	Sf: 0-0 GS: 0-0 Gd: 0-1 GF: - Fm: 0-0
Distance:	2m/2m3: 0-0 2m4-2m7: 0-1 3m+: 0-0
Track:	LH: 0-1 RH: 0-0 Tight: 0-1 Gall: 0-0
Aids:	Bl: 0-0 Vi: 0-0 Tstrap: 0-0
Best Rating:	45 1/01 Kemp 2m soft NHF

Our Boy (IRE)

8-y-o b g Convinced-Miss Polymer (Doulab (USA))
J G Cromwell Denis J Reddan

Placings:00/63/213P0F-02   (4745a)
2002/03: 26QG, 25ZG,

	Starts	1st	2nd	3rd	Win & Pl
Chases	2	0	1	0	1558
Career Total	12	1	2	2	8163
100	5/01	Navn	3m	Ch	GD £4173

Total win prize-money £4173

Going:	Sf: 0-0 GS: 0-0 Gd: 0-2 GF: - Fm: 0-0
Distance:	2m/2m3: 0-0 2m4-2m7: 0-0 3m+: 0-2
Track:	LH: 0-1 RH: 0-0 Tight: 0-0 Gall: 0-1
Aids:	Bl: 0-0 Vi: 0-0 Tstrap: 0-2
Best Rating:	106 5/01 Fair 3m1f good Ch

Irish hunter chase/point-to-point winner; stays three miles; acts on soft ground; often tongue tied.

Our Destiny
65   42

5-y-o b g Mujadil (USA)-Superspring (Superlative)
D Burchell (M A Buckley 20/7) Three Acres Racing

Placings:0   (0437)
2002/03: 16QG,

	Starts	1st	2nd	3rd	Win & Pl
Hurdles	1	0	0	0	
Career Total	1	0	0	0	

Going:	Sf: 0-0 GS: 0-0 Gd: 0-1 GF: - Fm: 0-0
Distance:	2m/2m3: 0-1 2m4-2m7: 0-0 3m+: 0-0
Track:	LH: 0-1 RH: 0-0 Tight: 0-0 Gall: 0-0

Aids: Bl: 0-0 Vi: 0-0 Tstrap: 0-0
Best Rating: 42 6/02 Uttx 2m good Hdl

Our Dream (IRE)
93f   81f

4-y-o b f Bob Back (USA)-Baybush (Boreen (FR))
Mrs M Reveley Scart Stud

Placings:5   (3747)
2002/03: 16QG,

	Starts	1st	2nd	3rd	Win & Pl
NH Flat	1	0	0	0	0
Career Total	1	0	0	0	0

Going:	Sf: 0-0 GS: 0-0 Gd: 0-1 GF: - Fm: 0-0
Distance:	2m/2m3: 0-1 2m4-2m7: 0-0 3m+: 0-0
Track:	LH: 0-0 RH: 0-1 Tight: 0-0 Gall: 0-1
Aids:	Bl: 0-0 Vi: 0-0 Tstrap: 0-0
Best Rating:	81 2/03 Hntg 2m110y good NHF

Our Ethel
85   71

5-y-o ch m Be My Chief (USA)-Annes Gift (Ballymoss)
Mrs M Reveley Minster Commercials

Placings:10-00   (4357)
2002/03: 16QG, 16QGF,

	Starts	1st	2nd	3rd	Win & Pl
NH Flat	2	0	0	0	
Career Total	4	1	0	0	2321
86	2/02	Muss	2m	H NHF	SFT £2320

Total win prize-money £2321

Going:	Sf: 0-0 GS: 0-0 Gd: 0-1 GF: - Fm: 0-1
Distance:	2m/2m3: 0-2 2m4-2m7: 0-0 3m+: 0-0
Track:	LH: 0-1 RH: 0-1 Tight: 0-0 Gall: 0-0
Aids:	Bl: 0-0 Vi: 0-0 Tstrap: 0-0
Best Rating:	86 2/03 Ludl 2m good NHF

From a good family, she made a winning debut on soft ground in a Musselburgh bumper, Fbruary 2002; showed little on hurdling bow at Wetherby in May 2003.

Our Imperial Bay (USA)
90   97d

4-y-o b g Smart Strike (CAN)-Heat Lightning (USA) (Summer Squall (USA))
Mrs A J Perrett A P Jones & Mrs M D Jones

Placings:65   (3804)
2002/03: 16QG, 16QS,

	Starts	1st	2nd	3rd	Win & Pl
Hurdles	2	0	0	0	0
Career Total	2	0	0	0	0

Going:	Sf: 0-1 GS: 0-0 Gd: 0-1 GF: - Fm: 0-0
Distance:	2m/2m3: 0-2 2m4-2m7: 0-0 3m+: 0-0
Track:	LH: 0-2 RH: 0-0 Tight: 0-1 Gall: 0-0
Aids:	Bl: 0-2 Vi: 0-0 Tstrap: 0-0
Best Rating:	97 12/02 Newb 2m110y good Hdl

Middle-distance winner on the Flat; has been tried in both blinkers and a visor over hurdles.

Our Jolly Swagman
110   122

8-y-o b g Thowra (FR)-Queens Dowry (Dominion)

J W Mullins F G Matthews

Placings:50P6/U0P121/54131PU26-PPP3012P1   (4624)
2002/03: 26PS, 29PS, 26PHY, 20QS, 26QS, 251S, 26ZGS, 24PG, 261GF,

	Starts	1st	2nd	3rd	Win & Pl
Chases	9	2	1	1	11687
Career Total	28	6	3	2	28161
117	4/03	NAbb	3m2f110yD(0-115)HCh	G-F £6403
87	2/03	Folk	3m1f	F(0-90)HCh	SFT £3523
103	1/02	Plum	2m4f	D(0-125)HCh	HVY £3916
93	12/01	Plum	3m2f	F(0-110)HCh	GD £3916
87	4/01	Plum	3m2f	F(0-90)HCh	SFT £3038
77	1/01	Plum	3m2f	F(0-90)HCh	G-S £3094

Total win prize-money £23890

Going:	Sf: 1-6 GS: 0-1 Gd: 0-1 GF: - Fm: 1-1
Distance:	2m/2m3: 0-0 2m4-2m7: 0-1 3m+: 2-8
Track:	LH: 1-8 RH: 1-1 Tight: 2-6 Gall: 0-0
Aids:	Bl: 0-0 Vi: 1-1 Tstrap: 0-0
Best Rating:	117 4/03 NAbb 3m2f110y gd-fm Ch

Fair staying chaser; improved form when swapping usual cheekpieces for a visor when winning at Newton Abbot in April 2003; went on to complete hat-trick; goes well at Plumpton; acts on all types of ground; stays three and a quarter miles.

Our Kev (IRE)
96

7-y-o b g Be My Native (USA)-Sunbath (Krayyan)
B G Powell Mrs Jean R Bishop

Placings:06P0-P   (1793)
2002/03: 21PS,

	Starts	1st	2nd	3rd	Win & Pl
Hurdles	1	0	0	0	
Career Total	5	0	0	0	0

Going:	Sf: 0-1 GS: 0-0 Gd: 0-0 GF: - Fm: 0-0
Distance:	2m/2m3: 0-0 2m4-2m7: 0-0 3m+: 0-0
Track:	LH: 0-0 RH: 0-1 Tight: 0-0 Gall: 0-0
Aids:	Bl: 0-0 Vi: 0-0 Tstrap: 0-0
Best Rating:	96 3/02 Newb 3m110y soft Hdl

Our Kris

11-y-o b g Kris-Our Reverie (USA) (J O Tobin (USA))
C J Bennett C J Bennett

Placings:1143F20/P4665333/565P0P/0314120/5242P3/PP 0P005/0   (3843)
2002/03: 24QG,

	Starts	1st	2nd	3rd	Win & Pl
Hurdles	1	0	0	0	
Career Total	42	4	4	6	33186
103	9/98	MRas	3m	C(0-130)HHdl	GD £4224
103	7/98	Sedg	3m3f110yE(0-110)HHdl	G-S £2726
127	12/95	Chel	2m1f	C Hdl	GD £3707
122	11/95	Newb	2m110y	C Hdl	GD £3879

Total win prize-money £14538

Going:	Sf: 0-0 GS: 0-0 Gd: 0-1 GF: - Fm: 0-0
Distance:	2m/2m3: 0-0 2m4-2m7: 0-0 3m+: 0-1
Track:	LH: 0-0 RH: 0-1 Tight: 0-0 Gall: 0-0
Aids:	Bl: 0-0 Vi: 0-0 Tstrap: 0-0
Best Rating:	132 3/96 Aint 2m110y good Hdl

Our Man Flin (IRE)

10-y-o br g Mandalus-Flinging (Good Times (ITY))

Miss E C M Neyens The Flindicate

Placings:*0/43*P0/606P3/0P/6-0   (0029)
2002/03: 21ºGF,

	Starts	1st	2nd	3rd	Win & Pl
Chases	1	0	0	0	
Career Total	14	0	0	2	373

Going:	Sf: 0-0 GS: 0-0 Gd: 0-0 GF: - Fm: 0-1
Distance:	2m/2m3: 0-0 2m4-2m7: 0-1 3m+: 0-0
Track:	LH: 0-1 RH: 0-0 Tight: 0-0 Gall: 0-1
Aids:	Bl: 0-0 Vi: 0-0 Tstrap: 0-0
Best Rating:	89 12/98 Towc 2m soft Hdl

Our Osca (IRE)

7-y-o b g Supreme Leader-Mayrhofen (Don)
P R Johnson P Johnson

Placings:PP   (2134)
2002/03: 20ºGS, 21ºG,

	Starts	1st	2nd	3rd	Win & Pl
Hurdles	2	0	0	0	
Career Total	2	0	0	0	

Going:	Sf: 0-0 GS: 0-1 Gd: 0-1 GF: - Fm: 0-0
Distance:	2m/2m3: 0-0 2m4-2m7: 0-2 3m+: 0-0
Track:	LH: 0-1 RH: 0-1 Tight: 0-1 Gall: 0-0
Aids:	Bl: 0-0 Vi: 0-0 Tstrap: 0-0
Best Rating:	0 11/02 Ludl 2m5f good Hdl

Our Tommy
97   92

10-y-o ch g Ardross-Ina s Farewell (Random Shot)
A E Price (C J Price 12/2) Mrs H L Price

Placings:F/P501-6223PP   (4528)
2002/03: 24ºGS, 20ºS, 20ºS, 20ºGS, 20ºGF, 24ºG,

	Starts	1st	2nd	3rd	Win & Pl
Chases	6	0	2	1	3154
Career Total	11	1	2	1	7200
92	3/02	Wwck	2m4f110y		E(0-105)HCh
GD	£4046				

Total win prize-money £4046

Going:	Sf: 0-2 GS: 0-2 Gd: 0-1 GF: - Fm: 0-1
Distance:	2m/2m3: 0-0 2m4-2m7: 0-4 3m+: 0-2
Track:	LH: 0-2 RH: 0-4 Tight: 0-2 Gall: 0-0
Aids:	Bl: 0-0 Vi: 0-0 Tstrap: 0-0
Best Rating:	92 3/03 Leic 2m4f110y gd-sft Ch

Moderate chaser; winning pointer; a shock winner of a novices handicap chase at Warwick in March 2002; best at two and a half miles; likes good or soft ground.

Our Vic (IRE)
112   142+

5-y-o b g Old Vic-Shabra Princess (Buckskin (FR))
M C Pipe D A Johnson

Placings:111   (3478)
2002/03: 17¹S, 19¹S, 16¹GS,

	Starts	1st	2nd	3rd	Win & Pl
Hurdles	3	3	0	0	14169
Career Total	3	3	0	0	14169
147	2/03	Winc	2m	D(0-125)HHdl	G-S £5073
128	1/03	Tntn	2m3f110y	D Hdl	SFT £5427
118	12/02	Extr	2m1f	E Hdl	SFT £3668

Total win prize-money £14169

Very useful hurdler; winning pointer, he has made a good impression over hurdles, winning his first three races easily from the front. Acts on soft ground.

Ourman (IRE)

7-y-o b g Good Thyne (USA)-Magic Minstrel (Pitpan)
Mrs A Bell (T P Tate 4/5) Mrs A Bell

Placings:*0633/12C-U3U*   (4572)
2002/03: 26⁴UG, 27³G, 24⁴UG,

	Starts	1st	2nd	3rd	Win & Pl
Chases	3	0	0	1	220
Career Total	10	1	1	3	5296
102	1/02	Sedg	3m3f	E Ch	HVY £3045

Total win prize-money £3045

Going:	Sf: 0-0 GS: 0-0 Gd: 0-3 GF: - Fm: 0-0
Distance:	2m/2m3: 0-0 2m4-2m7: 0-0 3m+: 0-3
Track:	LH: 0-3 RH: 0-0 Tight: 0-2 Gall: 0-0
Aids:	Bl: 0-0 Vi: 0-0 Tstrap: 0-1
Best Rating:	102 3/02 Ayr 3m1f heavy Ch

Lightly raced maiden, has shown ability in bumpers and hurdles; got off the mark on his chasing debut at Sedgefield in January 2002; has since competed in points and hunter chases; stays three and a half miles; acts on soft ground.

Out Of The Shadows
106   113

7-y-o gr m Rock Hopper-Shadows Of Silver (Carwhite)
Mrs M Reveley Ms Linda Redmond

Placings:*0/03/F1416-3053134P424*   (4549)
2002/03: 16³GS, 16⁵G, 16⁵GF, 16³G, 16¹G, 16³GS, 16⁴G, 19²GS, 16⁴GS, 16²GF, 16⁴G,

	Starts	1st	2nd	3rd	Win & Pl
Hurdles	11	1	1	3	10427
Career Total	19	3	1	4	17692
112	11/02	Hayd	2m	D(0-120)HHdl	GD £3737
112	1/02	Donc	2m110y	E Hdl	GD £3290
107	11/01	Hayd	2m	D Hdl	GD £3535

Total win prize-money £10563

Going:	Sf: 0-0 GS: 0-3 Gd: 1-5 GF: - Fm: 0-3
Distance:	2m/2m3: 1-10 2m4-2m7: 0-1 3m+: 0-0
Track:	LH: 1-11 RH: 0-0 Tight: 0-0 Gall: 0-2
Aids:	Bl: 0-0 Vi: 0-0 Tstrap: 0-0
Best Rating:	113 3/03 Weth 2m gd-fm Hdl

Fair handicap hurdler; acts on good ground and is effective at around two miles.

Ouzel (IRE)
93   77

7-y-o b m Mandalus-Dipper s Gift (IRE) (Salluceva)
C W Thornton Geoff Bonson

Placings:5/P0/4   (1810)
2002/03: 16⁴G,

	Starts	1st	2nd	3rd	Win & Pl
Hurdles	1	0	0	0	337
Career Total	4	0	0	0	337

Going:
Going:	Sf: 0-0 GS: 0-0 Gd: 0-1 GF: - Fm: 0-0
Distance:	2m/2m3: 0-0 1 GF: - Fm: 0-0
Track:	LH: 0-1 RH: 0-0 Tight: 1-1 Gall: 0-0
Aids:	Bl: 0-0 Vi: 0-0 Tstrap: 0-0
Best Rating:	84 4/00 Carl 2m1f gd-sft NHF

Over Anxious (IRE)
112   123+

7-y-o ch g Over The River (FR)-Legal Statement (IRE) (Strong Statement (USA))
Jonjo O Neill Paul Green

Placings:06-2   (1922)
2002/03: 19²GS,

	Starts	1st	2nd	3rd	Win & Pl
Hurdles	1	0	1	0	1280
Career Total	3	0	1	0	1280

Going:	Sf: 0-0 GS: 0-1 Gd: 0-0 GF: - Fm: 0-0
Distance:	2m/2m3: 0-1 2m4-2m7: 0-0 3m+: 0-0
Track:	LH: 0-1 RH: 0-0 Tight: 0-0 Gall: 0-1
Aids:	Bl: 0-0 Vi: 0-0 Tstrap: 0-0
Best Rating:	117 3/02 Newb 3m110y gd-sft Hdl

Fair novice hurdler; a point-to-point winner in Ireland; he made a highly promising debut over three miles, subsequently disqualified; ran well on seasonal debut when runner-up back at Newbury; suited by cut in the ground; his future lies over fences.

Over Bridge
95   67

5-y-o b g Overbury (IRE)-Celtic Bridge (Celtic Cone)
Mrs S M Johnson I K Johnson

Placings:*00500PR00*   (4194)
2002/03: 16⁵GF, 16⁰GF, 17⁵GF, 16⁰GS, 17⁰S, 19⁰S, 17⁸G, 17⁰GS, 21⁰G,

	Starts	1st	2nd	3rd	Win & Pl
NH Flat	3	0	0	0	0
Hurdles	6	0	0	0	0
Career Total	9	0	0	0	0

Going:	Sf: 0-2 GS: 0-2 Gd: 0-2 GF: - Fm: 0-3
Distance:	2m/2m3: 0-7 2m4-2m7: 0-2 3m+: 0-0
Track:	LH: 0-3 RH: 0-6 Tight: 0-1 Gall: 0-0
Aids:	Bl: 0-0 Vi: 0-0 Tstrap: 0-0
Best Rating:	83 7/02 NAbb 2m1f gd-fm NHF

Over Charged (IRE)
56

6-y-o b g Over The River (FR)-Rookery Lady (IRE) (Callernish)
J M Jefferson Richard Collins

Placings:3PP0-P   (0066)
2002/03: 21ºGF,

	Starts	1st	2nd	3rd	Win & Pl
Hurdles	1	0	0	0	
Career Total	5	0	0	1	327

Going:	Sf: 0-0 GS: 0-0 Gd: 0-0 GF: - Fm: 0-1
Distance:	2m/2m3: 0-0 2m4-2m7: 0-0 1 3m+: 0-0
Track:	LH: 0-1 RH: 0-0 Tight: 0-1 Gall: 0-0
Aids:	Bl: 0-0 Vi: 0-0 Tstrap: 0-0
Best Rating:	56 2/02 Newc 2m4f soft Hdl

Over Easy (IRE)

9-y-o ch g Tremblant-Tell A Tale (Le Bavard (FR))
G C Evans   N Morgan

Placings:0050/0/P   (3951)
2002/03: 16⁰GS,

	Starts	1st	2nd	3rd	Win & Pl
Chases	1	0	0	0	
Career Total	6	0	0	0	

Going:	Sf: 0-0 GS: 0-1 Gd: 0-0 GF: - Fm: 0-0
Distance:	2m/2m3: 0-1 2m4-2m7: 0-0 3m+: 0-0
Track:	LH: 0-0 RH: 0-1 Tight: 0-0 Gall: 0-0
Aids:	Bl: 0-0 Vi: 0-0 Tstrap: 0-0
Best Rating:	73 3/00 Thur 2m soft Hdl

Over The Burn

102   **93**

11-y-o b g Over The River (FR)-Sharp Vixen (Laurence O)
B Mactaggart   Boysaday Racing

Placings:P555/0/401P/PP-33P   (1415)
2002/03: 25³GS, 25³G, 25⁵GF,

	Starts	1st	2nd	3rd	Win & Pl
Chases	3	0	0	2	1055
Career Total	14	1	0	2	3804
83 2/01 Carl 3m110y E Hdl				SFT	£2521
			Total win prize-money £2521		

Going:	Sf: 0-0 GS: 0-1 Gd: 0-1 GF: - Fm: 0-1
Distance:	2m/2m3: 0-0 2m4-2m7: 0-0 3m+: 0-3
Track:	LH: 0-3 RH: 0-0 Tight: 0-1 Gall: 0-0
Aids:	Bl: 0-0 Vi: 0-0 Tstrap: 0-0
Best Rating:	93 5/02 Hexm 3m1f good Ch

Over The Counter (IRE)

7-y-o b m Persian Bold-Scotia Rose (Tap On Wood)
E A Elliott   Eric A Elliott

Placings:052/121/0   (3868)
2002/03: 16⁰GS,

	Starts	1st	2nd	3rd	Win & Pl
Hurdles	1	0	0	0	
Career Total	7	2	2	0	7294
104 6/00 Uttx 2m D Hdl				G-F	£3006
90 5/00 Newc 2m E Hdl				G-F	£2775
			Total win prize-money £5782		

Going:	Sf: 0-0 GS: 0-1 Gd: 0-0 GF: - Fm: 0-0
Distance:	2m/2m3: 0-1 2m4-2m7: 0-0 3m+: 0-0
Track:	LH: 0-1 RH: 0-0 Tight: 0-0 Gall: 0-1
Aids:	Bl: 0-0 Vi: 0-0 Tstrap: 0-0
Best Rating:	106 5/00 Hexm 2m good Hdl

Over The First (IRE)

106(111h)   (130h)**122**

8-y-o b/br g Orchestra-Ruby Lodge (Peacock (FR))
C F Swan   Trotters Ind Trading Syndicate

Placings:0030/135015016/031610PU5310-0U21141F40
              (4071a)
2002/03: 16⁶S, 16ᵁYS, 20²S, 16¹HY, 16¹S, 16⁴HY, 20¹S, 19⁵S, 16⁴HY, 19⁰HY,

	Starts	1st	2nd	3rd	Win & Pl
Hurdles	9	3	1	0	34286

Chases	1	0	0	0	0
Career Total	35	9	1	4	70457
130	1/03	Navn	2m4f		HHdl	SFT	£12662
119	11/02	Fair	2m		HHdl	SFT	£15153
115	11/02	Clon	2m	(67-109)HHdl	HVY	£3809
119	3/02	Navn	2m1f	(0-127)HCh	SH	£7975
126	11/01	Cork	2m	(0-109)HCh	Y-S	£6677
104	10/01	Tipp	2m	Ch	HVY	£5842
120	1/01	Thur	2m	Hdl	HVY	£6677
116	11/00	Thur	2m	Hdl	SFT	£2760
104	8/00	Tral	2m1f	NHF	SFT	£3588
					Total win prize-money £65145	

Going:	Sf: 3-9 GS: 0-0 Gd: 0-0 GF: - Fm: 0-0
Distance:	**2m/2m3: 2-8** 2m4-2m7: 1-2 3m+: 0-0
Track:	LH: 1-4 RH: 1-2 Tight: 0-0 Gall: 0-0
Aids:	Bl: 0-0 Vi: 0-0 Tstrap: 0-0
Best Rating:	**130** 1/03 Navn 2m4f soft Hdl

Decent Irish handicap hurdler/chaser; effective at around two miles; goes well on a soft surface.

Over The Hill (IRE)

89(106h)   (90h)**88+**

11-y-o b g Over The River (FR)-Joint Equity (Callernish)
S J Magnier   A Hartgrove

Placings:P/12PUP/3F0R/526113023   (4795)
2002/03: 27⁵G, 22²G, 22⁶GF, 21¹G, 27¹G, 27³S, 27⁰S, 21²G, 21³GF,

	Starts	1st	2nd	3rd	Win & Pl
Hurdles	9	2	2	2	8011
Career Total	19	3	3	3	10854
90	10/02 Sedg	3m3f110yF(0-100)HHdl	GD	£2618
78	10/02 Sedg	2m5f110yG(0-90)HHdl	GD	£2170
87	5/99 Ctml	3m2f	H Ch	GD	£1943
		Total win prize-money £6731		

Going:	Sf: 0-2 GS: 0-0 Gd: 2-5 GF: - Fm: 0-2
Distance:	2m/2m3: 0-0 2m4-2m7: 1-5 3m+: 1-4
Track:	**LH: 2-9** RH: 0-0 **Tight: 2-9** Gall: 0-0
Aids:	**Bl: 2-7** Vi: 0-0 Tstrap: 0-0
Best Rating:	93 4/00 Ayr 3m3f110y good Ch

Plating-class hurdler/chaser; won twice at Sedgefield in October 2002; stays 3m 3f but effective at shorter; acts on a sound surface; has worn blinkers.

Over The Storm (IRE)

104   **124**

6-y-o b g Over The River (FR)-Naas (Ballymore)
Miss H C Knight   Hogarth Racing

Placings:1230   (4113)
2002/03: 24¹G, 24²GS, 24³S, 32⁰G,

	Starts	1st	2nd	3rd	Win & Pl
Chases	4	1	1	1	8046
Career Total	4	1	1	1	8046
112	12/02 Donc	3m	D Ch	GD	£4904
		Total win prize-money £4905		

Going:	Sf: 0-1 GS: 0-1 Gd: 1-2 GF: - Fm: 0-0
Distance:	2m/2m3: 0-0 2m4-2m7: 0-0 **3m+: 1-4**
Track:	**LH: 1-2** RH: 0-2 Tight: 0-1 **Gall: 1-2**
Aids:	Bl: 0-0 Vi: 0-0 Tstrap: 0-0
Best Rating:	124 2/03 Tntn 3m soft Ch

Modest novice chaser; winning Irish pointer; stays three miles and looks the sort to get much further; may be best on good ground.

Over The Water (IRE)

95   **111**

11-y-o gr g Over The River (FR)-Shanacloon Lass (General Ironside)
R H Alner   The Droop Partners

Placings:P260/036/311/R3561/513F/02PP50-3   (0178)
2002/03: 25³GF,

	Starts	1st	2nd	3rd	Win & Pl
Chases	1	0	0	0	666
Career Total	26	4	2	5	23231
111	10/00 Winc	2m5f	F(0-110)HCh	G-S	£5135
110	4/00 Ludl	2m4f	F(0-115)HCh	GD	£5850
114	11/98 Winc	2m5f	E Ch	GD	£3192
123	11/98 Kemp	2m4f110yD Ch	G-S	£3735
		Total win prize-money £17913		

Going:	Sf: 0-0 GS: 0-0 Gd: 0-0 GF: - Fm: 0-1
Distance:	2m/2m3: 0-0 2m4-2m7: 0-0 3m+: 0-1
Track:	LH: 0-0 RH: 0-1 Tight: 0-0 Gall: 0-0
Aids:	Bl: 0-0 Vi: 0-0 Tstrap: 0-0
Best Rating:	123 11/98 Kemp 2m4f110y gd-sft Ch

Fair front-running chaser, best on good or softer at short of three miles.

Over To You Bert

88   **59**

4-y-o b g Overbury (IRE)-Silvers Era (Balidar)
Mrs P N Dutfield   Unity Farm Holiday Centre Ltd

Placings:0   (2339)
2002/03: 13⁰S,

	Starts	1st	2nd	3rd	Win & Pl
NH Flat	1	0	0	0	
Career Total	1	0	0	0	

Going:	Sf: 0-1 GS: 0-0 Gd: 0-0 GF: - Fm: 0-0
Distance:	2m/2m3: 0-0 2m4-2m7: 0-0 3m+: 0-0
Track:	LH: 0-0 RH: 0-1 Tight: 0-0 Gall: 0-0
Aids:	Bl: 0-0 Vi: 0-0 Tstrap: 0-0
Best Rating:	44 12/02 Extr 1m5f soft NHF

Over Zealous (IRE)

113   (59h)**107**

11-y-o ch g Over The River (FR)-Chatty Di (Le Bavard (FR))
John R Upson   Middleham Park Racing X

Placings:0000/245/U11112/22P4RP/05361PPP-322411
              (4151)
2002/03: 25⁰GS, 27³S, 30²GS, 26²S, 24⁴HY, 26¹GS, 29¹G,

	Starts	1st	2nd	3rd	Win & Pl
Chases	7	2	1	1	11470
Career Total	33	7	6	2	31820
107	3/03 Wwck	3m5f	E(0-110)HCh	GD	£4030
106	2/03 Chep	3m2f110yF(0-90)HCh	G-S	£3688
97	1/02 Wwck	3m	F(0-95)HCh	SFT	£2705
98	1/00 Newc	3m6f	D(0-125)HCh	SFT	£3753
93	12/99 Sedg	3m3f	F(0-110)HCh	G-S	£3579
95	11/99 Newc	3m	F(0-90)HCh	G-S	£2866
93	11/99 Sedg	3m3f	F(0-100)HCh	G-S	£2670
		Total win prize-money £23294		

Going:	Sf: 0-3 GS: 1-3 Gd: 1-1 GF: - Fm: 0-0
Distance:	2m/2m3: 0-0 2m4-2m7: 0-0 **3m+: 2-7**
Track:	**LH: 2-5** RH: 0-1 Tight: 0-2 Gall: 0-2
Aids:	**Bl: 2-7** Vi: 0-0 Tstrap: 0-0
Best Rating:	107 3/03 Wwck 3m5f good Ch

Moderate handicap chaser; genuine and stays very well; best on ground good and softer.

Overlord (IRE)

87   **70**

6-y-o b g Lord Americo-Straddler s Hill (IRE) (Torus)
B De Haan The Longheade Partnership

Placings:000   (3780)
2002/03: 16⁰G, 16⁶S, 22⁰GS,

	Starts	1st	2nd	3rd	Win & Pl
NH Flat	1	0	0	0	0
Hurdles	2	0	0	0	0
Career Total	3	0	0	0	

Going:	Sf: 0-1 GS: 0-1 Gd: 0-1 GF: - Fm: 0-0
Distance:	2m/2m3: 0-2 2m4-2m7: 0-1 3m+: 0-0
Track:	LH: 0-1 RH: 0-2 Tight: 0-0 Gall: 0-1
Aids:	Bl: 0-0 Vi: 0-0 Tstrap: 0-0
Best Rating:	85 11/02 Winc 2m good NHF

Oversman

88(74c)   **89**

10-y-o b g Keen-Jamaican Punch (IRE) (Shareef Dancer (USA))
M J M Evans Mrs J Z Munday

Placings:025/14033/2040421231/0001222363/6P4P0P/5540
23P00-466P   (0511)
2002/03: 16⁴GF, 16⁶G, 16⁶G, 20⁰S,

	Starts	1st	2nd	3rd	Win & Pl
Hurdles	2	0	0	0	0
Chases	2	0	0	0	0
Career Total	46	4	7	6	14784
102	1/00	Sedg	2m1f	G(0-95)HHdl	SFT	£1589
91	2/99	Donc	2m110y	G Hdl	G-F	£1646
91	1/99	Muss	2m	G Hdl	G-S	£2248
85	5/97	Weth	2m	E Hdl	G-S	£2232
				Total win prize-money £7716		

Going:	Sf: 0-1 GS: 0-0 Gd: 0-2 GF: - Fm: 0-1
Distance:	2m/2m3: 0-3 2m4-2m7: 0-1 3m+: 0-0
Track:	LH: 0-2 RH: 0-2 Tight: 0-0 Gall: 0-0
Aids:	Bl: 0-4 Vi: 0-0 Tstrap: 0-3
Best Rating:	106 1/00 Muss 2m good Hdl

Plating-class hurdler/chaser.

Overstrand (IRE)

102   **109**

4-y-o b g In The Wings-Vaison La Romaine (Arctic Tern (USA))
Mrs M Reveley (Mrs A J Perrett 14/10) F F Racing Services Partnership IV

Placings:360   (4130)
2002/03: 16⁵G, 16⁶G, 17⁰G,

	Starts	1st	2nd	3rd	Win & Pl
Hurdles	3	0	0	1	1111
Career Total	3	0	0	1	1111

Going:	Sf: 0-0 GS: 0-1 Gd: 0-2 GF: - Fm: 0-0
Distance:	2m/2m3: 0-3 2m4-2m7: 0-0 3m+: 0-0
Track:	LH: 0-3 RH: 0-0 Tight: 0-0 Gall: 0-2
Aids:	Bl: 0-0 Vi: 0-0 Tstrap: 0-0
Best Rating:	109 3/03 Chel 2m1f good Hdl

Fair middle-distance performer on the Flat; has shown form over hurdles at around two miles.

Owen Roe (IRE)

98(100h)   (107h)**91**

6-y-o b g Blues Traveller (IRE)-Faye (Monsanto (FR))
Mrs H Dalton Paternosters Racing

Placings:6/62300-1P2U   (2504)
2002/03: 18¹GF, 21P GF, 17²G, 21U GS,

	Starts	1st	2nd	3rd	Win & Pl
Hurdles	1	0	1	0	840
Chases	3	1	0	0	2898
Career Total	10	1	2	1	5178
91	9/02	Font	2m2f	F Ch	G-F	£2898
				Total win prize-money £2898		

Going:	Sf: 0-0 GS: 0-1 Gd: 0-1 GF: 1-2
Distance:	2m/2m3: 1-2 2m4-2m7: 0-2 3m+: 0-0
Track:	LH: 0-2 RH: 0-1 Tight: 1-2 Gall: 0-0
Aids:	Bl: 0-0 Vi: 0-0 Tstrap: 0-0
Best Rating:	107 12/02 Hrfd 2m1f good Hdl

Maiden on the Flat and over hurdles, made a winning debut over fences at Fontwell in September 2002. Acts on a sound surface and is effective at around two miles two.

Owen's Pet (IRE)

83(73h)   (94h)**99**

9-y-o b g Alphabatim (USA)-Ballinlovane (Le Moss)
R T Phillips Archmold Ltd

Placings:63/P023-6   (0114)
2002/03: 25⁶GS,

	Starts	1st	2nd	3rd	Win & Pl
Chases	1	0	0	0	0
Career Total	7	0	1	2	2379

Going:	Sf: 0-0 GS: 0-1 Gd: 0-0 GF: - Fm: 0-0
Distance:	2m/2m3: 0-0 2m4-2m7: 0-0 3m+: 0-1
Track:	LH: 0-0 RH: 0-1 Tight: 0-0 Gall: 0-0
Aids:	Bl: 0-0 Vi: 0-0 Tstrap: 0-0
Best Rating:	99 4/02 Carl 3m2f gd-sft Ch

Former Irish point winner. Modest form over hurdles before running well on chasing debut at Carlisle in April 2002.

Owthorpe Hill

9-y-o br g Scorpio (FR)-Star Route (Owen Dudley)
John A Harris Mrs Margaret Marston

Placings:0/PP-P   (0089)
2002/03: 22P G,

	Starts	1st	2nd	3rd	Win & Pl
Hurdles	1	0	0	0	
Career Total	4	0	0	0	

Going:	Sf: 0-0 GS: 0-0 Gd: 0-1 GF: - Fm: 0-0
Distance:	2m/2m3: 0-0 2m4-2m7: 0-1 3m+: 0-0
Track:	LH: 0-0 RH: 0-0 Tight: 0-0 Gall: 0-0
Aids:	Bl: 0-0 Vi: 0-0 Tstrap: 0-0
Best Rating:	12 3/00 Donc 2m110y good NHF

Oxendale

10-y-o ch g Primitive Rising (USA)-Saucy Moon (Saucy Kit)
R Dench Mrs S Dench

Placings:0   (0311)
2002/03: 26⁰G,

	Starts	1st	2nd	3rd	Win & Pl
Chases	1	0	0	0	

Career Total   1   0   0   0

Owen Roe continued — (top right)

Career Total   1   0   0   0

Oxidor (IRE)

96   **87**

8-y-o br g Be My Native (USA)-Euroblend (IRE) (The Parson)
C P Morlock D And Mrs H Woodhall

Placings:0/000015/6360015-30530   (2104)
2002/03: 22³G, 24⁰G, 27⁵S, 24³GS, 26⁶GS,

	Starts	1st	2nd	3rd	Win & Pl
Hurdles	5	0	0	2	1019
Career Total	19	2	0	3	6890
90	3/02	Hntg	3m2f	E(0-110)HHdl	G-F	£2492
96	2/01	Uttx	2m6f110yF(0-105)HHdl	SFT	£3041
			Total win prize-money £5534		

Going:	Sf: 0-1 GS: 0-2 Gd: 0-2 GF: - Fm: 0-0
Distance:	2m/2m3: 0-0 2m4-2m7: 0-1 3m+: 0-4
Track:	LH: 0-2 RH: 0-3 Tight: 0-1 Gall: 0-1
Aids:	Bl: 0-5 Vi: 0-0 Tstrap: 0-5
Best Rating:	100 11/99 Weth 2m good NHF

Shock winner in low-grade company at Huntingdon in March. Likes fast ground.

Oyster Bay

95   **85**

7-y-o b m Mandalus-Holy Times (IRE) (The Parson)
A Streeter Martin Jump

Placings:0/510P6030-4   (0111)
2002/03: 16⁴GS,

	Starts	1st	2nd	3rd	Win & Pl
Hurdles	1	0	0	0	0
Career Total	10	1	0	1	2277
97	11/01	Uttx	2m	H NHF	SFT	£1953
			Total win prize-money £1953		

Going:	Sf: 0-0 GS: 0-1 Gd: 0-0 GF: - Fm: 0-0
Distance:	2m/2m3: 0-1 2m4-2m7: 0-0 3m+: 0-0
Track:	LH: 0-0 RH: 0-1 Tight: 0-0 Gall: 0-0
Aids:	Bl: 0-0 Vi: 0-0 Tstrap: 0-0
Best Rating:	97 11/01 Uttx 2m soft NHF

Plating class hurdler who handles soft ground.

Oyster Shell (IRE)

76   **64**

6-y-o b g Be My Native (USA)-Judys View (King s Ride)
N J Henderson The Oyster Shell Partnership

Placings:6   (3780)
2002/03: 22⁶GS,

	Starts	1st	2nd	3rd	Win & Pl
Hurdles	1	0	0	0	0
Career Total	1	0	0	0	0

Going:	Sf: 0-0 GS: 0-1 Gd: 0-0 GF: - Fm: 0-0
Distance:	2m/2m3: 0-0 2m4-2m7: 0-1 3m+: 0-0
Track:	LH: 0-0 RH: 0-1 Tight: 0-0 Gall: 0-0
Aids:	Bl: 0-0 Vi: 0-0 Tstrap: 0-0
Best Rating:	64 2/03 Extr 2m6f110y gd-sft Hdl

Ozzie Jones

106   **123**

12-y-o b g Formidable (USA)-Distant Relation (Great Nephew)
K R Pearce Keith R Pearce

Placings:4516552P50F/4500/3453/**22021214**/131432114/1
26P16/46P31331-4132   (0734)
2002/03: 25⁴GF, 24¹GF, 24³GF, 26²GF,

	Starts	1st	2nd	3rd	Win & Pl
Chases	4	1	1	1	7346
Career Total	54	12	8	8	60892
116 6/02	Strf	3m	H Ch		G-F	£3562
120 4/02	Strf	3m	H Ch		GD	£3020
123 8/01	Sthl	3m110y	E(0-115)HCh		G-F	£4368
123 9/00	Plum	3m2f	D(0-125)HCh		GD	£3789
107 5/00	Ludl	3m	H Ch		GD	£2404
123 10/99	Plum	3m2f	C(0-130)HCh		G-F	£7215
110 10/99	Ludl	3m	E(0-115)HHdl		G-F	£3464
123 7/99	Wolv	3m1f	D(0-120)HCh		G-F	£3934
127 5/99	Hrfd	3m1f110yE(0-115)HCh		GD	£3631
125 9/98	Hntg	3m	D(0-110)HCh		G-F	£2906
109 7/98	Bang	3m110y	E(0-115)HCh		GD	£4162
80 10/94	Ludl	2m	Hdl		FRM	£1987

Total win prize-money £44447

Going: Sf: 0-0 GS: 0-0 Gd: 0-0 GF: - Fm: 1-4
Distance: 2m/2m3: 0-0 2m4-2m7: 0-0 **3m+: 1-4**
Track: LH: 1-3 RH: 0-1 Tight: 1-3 Gall: 0-0
Aids: Bl: 0-0 Vi: 0-0 Tstrap: 0-0
Best Rating: 127 5/99 Hrfd 3m1f110y good Ch

Fair fast ground staying handicap chaser, he is usually most effective in the first half of the season. Shows his form blinkered or not, and should continue to find winning opportunities. Clear cut winner of hunter chase at Stratford April 2002 and followed up at the same course in June.

Pachinco

90   **60**

5-y-o ch g Bluebird (USA)-Lady Philippa (IRE) (Taufan (USA))
J G M O Shea K A Ayres

Placings:P0PP   (4608)
2002/03: 17⁷PS, 17⁰GS, 16⁷G, 17⁷PG,

	Starts	1st	2nd	3rd	Win & Pl
Hurdles	4	0	0	0	
Career Total	4	0	0	0	

Going: Sf: 0-1 GS: 0-1 Gd: 0-2 GF: - Fm: 0-0
Distance: 2m/2m3: 0-4 2m4-2m7: 0-0 3m+: 0-0
Track: LH: 0-1 RH: 0-3 Tight: 0-1 Gall: 0-1
Aids: Bl: 0-0 Vi: 0-0 Tstrap: 0-1
Best Rating: 60 3/03 Carl 2m1f gd-sft Hdl

Runner-up in a very weak three-runner novices hurdle at Cartmel in May; well beaten in selling company previously.

Pacific Alliance (IRE)

99   **86**

7-y-o b g Fayruz-La Gravotte (FR) (Habitat)
M Wigham Michael Wigham

Placings:53515   (1699)
2002/03: 16⁸GF, 19²GF, 16⁵F, 17¹G, 17⁵GF,

	Starts	1st	2nd	3rd	Win & Pl
Hurdles	5	1	0	1	2552
Career Total	5	1	0	1	2552
86 10/02	MRas	2m1f110yG(0-95)HHdl		gd-sft	

Total win prize-money £2268

Going: Sf: 0-0 GS: 0-0 Gd: 1-1 GF: - Fm: 0-4
Distance: 2m/2m3: 1-5 2m4-2m7: 0-0 3m+: 0-0
Track: LH: 0-1 RH: 1-4 Tight: 1-2 Gall: 0-1
Aids: Bl: 0-1 Vi: 0-0 Tstrap: 0-0
Best Rating: 86 10/02 MRas 2m1f110y good Hdl

Selling hurdler, acts on good ground and is effective at around two miles.

Pacifyc (IRE)

102   **91**

8-y-o b g Brief Truce (USA)-Ocean Blue (IRE) (Bluebird (USA))
John A Harris Mrs A E Harris

Placings:P1P00-240206   (1563)
2002/03: 19²GF, 20⁴GF, 22⁹GF, 17²GS, 19⁰GF, 17⁶G,

	Starts	1st	2nd	3rd	Win & Pl
Hurdles	6	0	2	0	1470
Career Total	10	1	2	0	3143
98 9/01	MRas	2m1f110yG Hdl		G-F	£1673

Total win prize-money £1673

Going: Sf: 0-0 GS: 0-1 Gd: 0-1 GF: - Fm: 0-4
Distance: 2m/2m3: 0-2 2m4-2m7: 0-4 3m+: 0-0
Track: LH: 0-2 RH: 0-4 Tight: 0-5 Gall: 0-0
Aids: Bl: 0-0 Vi: 0-0 Tstrap: 0-0
Best Rating: 98 9/01 MRas 2m1f110y gd-fm Hdl

Of little account on the Flat, but he has had wind problems and a tongue-strap may have been the key in helping him make a winning hurdling debut in a seller at Market Rasen in September.

Pack Leader (IRE)

97   **91**

7-y-o b g Muharib (USA)-Royal Broderick (IRE) (Lancastrian)
Jonjo O Neill John Connor

Placings:0P050   (4786)
2002/03: 24⁰S, 22⁵S, 20⁵S, 28⁵G, 22⁰G,

	Starts	1st	2nd	3rd	Win & Pl
Hurdles	5	0	0	0	0
Career Total	5	0	0	0	0

Going: Sf: 0-3 GS: 0-0 Gd: 0-2 GF: - Fm: 0-0
Distance: 2m/2m3: 0-0 2m4-2m7: 0-3 3m+: 0-2
Track: LH: 0-2 RH: 0-2 Tight: 0-1 Gall: 0-0
Aids: Bl: 0-0 Vi: 0-0 Tstrap: 0-2
Best Rating: 91 11/02 Hayd 2m4f soft Hdl

Modest hurdler.

Paco Venture (IRE)

(108h)   **(119 h)100+**

8-y-o b g Supreme Leader-Ethelsdaughter (Deep Run)
Miss Venetia Williams (G M Lyons 9/6) Ashleybank Investments Limited

Placings:4/00/26-035511212150   (4171)
2002/03: 19⁰G, 20³G, 20⁵SH, 16⁵S, 24¹G, 22¹GF, 23²G, 24¹GF, 20²GS, 24¹GS, 21⁵S, 22⁰S,

	Starts	1st	2nd	3rd	Win & Pl
Hurdles	12	4	3	1	23969
Career Total	17	4	3	1	25061
119 12/02	Bang	3m	C(0-135)HHdl		G-S	£7527
109 10/02	Tntn	3m110y	D Hdl		G-F	£4396
106 10/02	Uttx	2m6f110yD Hdl		G-F	£5600
104 9/02	Worc	3m	H Hdl		GD	£2233

Total win prize-money £19756

Paddies Boy (IRE)

91(97h)   **99**

8-y-o ch g Astronef-Bushfield Lady (Le Bavard (FR))
J J Lambe H Muldoon

Placings:043P50/0/42-3P64P0151   (4534a)
2002/03: 24³S, 24⁴PY, 20⁶SH, 21⁴GF, 21⁰G, 17⁹G, 24¹S, 25⁶G, 24¹GF,

	Starts	1st	2nd	3rd	Win & Pl
Hurdles	3	0	0	0	0
Chases	6	2	0	1	10735
Career Total	18	2	1	2	12417
101 4/03	Gowr	3m	(0-95)HCh		G-F	£6720
94 3/03	Dpat	3m	Ch		SFT	£3584

Total win prize-money £10305

Going: Sf: 1-2 GS: 0-0 Gd: 0-3 GF: - Fm: 1-2
Distance: 2m/2m3: 0-1 2m4-2m7: 0-3 **3m+: 2-5**
Track: LH: 0-6 **RH: 1-1** Tight: 0-4 Gall: 0-0
Aids: Bl: 0-1 Vi: 0-0 Tstrap: 0-0
Best Rating: 101 4/03 Gowr 3m gd-fm Ch

Irish hunter chaser.

Paddy For Paddy (IRE)

9-y-o b g Mandalus-Lady Rerico (Pamroy)
G L Landau Mrs Jane Thornton

Placings:12P   (4480)
2002/03: 25¹S, 25²G, 25PG,

	Starts	1st	2nd	3rd	Win & Pl
Chases	3	1	1	0	2646
Career Total	3	1	1	0	2646
100 2/03	Folk	3m1f	H Ch		SFT	£1554

Total win prize-money £1554

Going: Sf: 1-1 GS: 0-0 Gd: 0-2 GF: - Fm: 0-0
Distance: 2m/2m3: 0-0 2m4-2m7: 0-0 **3m+: 1-3**
Track: LH: 0-1 **RH: 1-2** Tight: 1-2 Gall: 0-0
Aids: Bl: 0-1 Vi: 0-0 Tstrap: 0-0
Best Rating: 100 3/03 Extr 3m1f110y good Ch

Consistent performer who won three times between the flags; returned from two year absence to win three mile hunter chase at Folkestone February 2003; just touched off at Exeter the following month; acts on ground good and softer; seems sure to win more hunter chases.

Paddy Maguire (IRE)

85   **52**

10-y-o b g Mazaad-Knocknagow (Buckskin (FR))
Mrs A M Naughton W M Wanless

Placings:5050/0305/35P6   (4372)
2002/03: 22³S, 20⁴HY, 20⁵PG, 21⁶G,

	Starts	1st	2nd	3rd	Win & Pl
Hurdles	3	0	0	1	442
Chases	1	0	0	0	0
Career Total	12	0	0	2	868

Going: Sf: 0-3 GS: 1-2 Gd: 1-4 GF: - Fm: 2-2
Distance: 2m/2m3: 0-2 2m4-2m7: 1-6 **3m+: 3-4**
Track: **LH: 3-9** RH: 1-1 Tight: 2-3 Gall: 0-1
Aids: Bl: 0-0 Vi: 0-0 Tstrap: 0-0
Best Rating: 119 12/02 Bang 3m gd-sft Hdl

Fair hurdler; in fine form in 2002/3; stays three miles; does not want the ground too soft; will make a chaser.

Going: Sf: 0-3 GS: 0-0 Gd: 0-1 GF: - Fm: 0-0
Distance: 2m/2m3: 0-0 2m4-2m7: 0-0 4 3m+: 0-0
Track: LH: 0-3 RH: 0-1 Tight: 0-0 Gall: 0-1
Aids: Bl: 0-0 Vi: 0-0 Tstrap: 0-0
Best Rating: 75 10/99 Weth 3m1f good Hdl

Paddy The Driver (IRE)

81　　90

7-y-o b g Grand Plaisir (IRE)-Jude s Hollow (IRE) (Hollow Hand)
J D Frost Torquay Boyz Racing Syndicate

Placings:40/64306P-6　(0735)
2002/03: 17⁶GF,

	Starts	1st	2nd	3rd	Win & Pl
Hurdles	1	0	0	0	0
Career Total	9	0	0	1	866

Going: Sf: 0-0 GS: 0-0 Gd: 0-0 GF: - Fm: 0-1
Distance: 2m/2m3: 0-1 2m4-2m7: 0-0 3m+: 0-0
Track: LH: 0-1 RH: 0-0 Tight: 0-0 Gall: 0-0
Aids: Bl: 0-0 Vi: 0-0 Tstrap: 0-0
Best Rating: 90 7/01 NAbb 2m1f gd-fm Hdl

Paddy The Optimist (IRE)

92　　86

7-y-o b g Leading Counsel (USA)-Erne Duchess (IRE) (Duky)
T R George M R C Opperman

Placings:6-66　(2548)
2002/03: 16⁸S, 17⁶HY,

	Starts	1st	2nd	3rd	Win & Pl
Hurdles	2	0	0	0	0
Career Total	3	0	0	0	0

Going: Sf: 0-2 GS: 0-0 Gd: 0-0 GF: - Fm: 0-0
Distance: 2m/2m3: 0-2 2m4-2m7: 0-0 3m+: 0-0
Track: LH: 0-1 RH: 0-1 Tight: 0-0 Gall: 0-0
Aids: Bl: 0-0 Vi: 0-0 Tstrap: 0-0
Best Rating: 86 12/02 Folk 2m1f110y heavy Hdl

Paddy The Piper (IRE)

107f　　110f

6-y-o b g Witness Box (USA)-Divine Dibs (Raise You Ten)
L Lungo Devey Group Limited

Placings:3-211　(4357)
2002/03: 16²HY, 16¹G, 16¹GF,

	Starts	1st	2nd	3rd	Win & Pl
NH Flat	3	2	1	0	4641
Career Total	4	2	1	1	5149
110 3/03 Weth	2m		H NHF	G-F	£2037
100 2/03 Catt	2m		H NHF	GD	£2058

Total win prize-money £4095

Going: Sf: 0-1 GS: 0-0 Gd: 1-1 GF: - Fm: 1-1
Distance: 2m/2m3: 2-3 2m4-2m7: 0-0 3m+: 0-0
Track: LH: 2-3 RH: 0-0 Tight: 1-1 Gall: 0-0
Aids: Bl: 0-0 Vi: 0-0 Tstrap: 0-0
Best Rating: 110 3/03 Weth 2m gd-fm NHF

Has shown ability in bumpers and broke his duck at Catterick in February; followed up under a penalty at Wetherby the following month; acts on a soft surface.

Paddy's Profiles (IRE)

76　　16

9-y-o b g Euphemism-Dame Niamh (IRE) (Buckskin (FR))
Miss K M George Stableline

Placings:0/004/65-0005　(4515)
2002/03: 19⁰GS, 17⁰GS, 21⁰G, 17⁵GF,

	Starts	1st	2nd	3rd	Win & Pl
Hurdles	4	0	0	0	0
Career Total	10	0	0	0	0

Going: Sf: 0-0 GS: 0-2 Gd: 0-1 GF: - Fm: 0-1
Distance: 2m/2m3: 0-3 2m4-2m7: 0-1 3m+: 0-0
Track: LH: 0-0 RH: 0-4 Tight: 0-0 Gall: 0-0
Aids: Bl: 0-0 Vi: 0-0 Tstrap: 0-0
Best Rating: 79 1/01 Tntn 2m3f110y soft Hdl

Paddy's Thyme (IRE)

97　　71

7-y-o gr g Good Thyne (USA)-Nanny Kehoe (IRE) (Sexton Blake)
Ferdy Murphy Paddy O Donnell

Placings:055/09FU2　(4376)
2002/03: 16⁰GS, 23⁵F, 16⁰G, 27²G,

	Starts	1st	2nd	3rd	Win & Pl
Hurdles	2	0	1	0	766
Chases	2	0	0	0	
Career Total	7	0	1	0	766

Going: Sf: 0-0 GS: 0-1 Gd: 0-3 GF: - Fm: 0-0
Distance: 2m/2m3: 0-2 2m4-2m7: 0-0 3m+: 0-2
Track: LH: 0-1 RH: 0-3 Tight: 0-1 Gall: 0-2
Aids: Bl: 0-0 Vi: 0-0 Tstrap: 0-0
Best Rating: 89 11/00 Chel 2m110y gd-sft NHF

Failed to get round in two starts over fences; runner-up in bad novices hurdle at Sedgefield in March.

Paddy's Wolf

12-y-o b g Little Wolf-Paddy s Delight (Paddy s Birthday)
Grahame A Dedman Grahame A Dedman

Placings:4PP/0P/UPP-P　(0315)
2002/03: 21⁰G,

	Starts	1st	2nd	3rd	Win & Pl
Chases	1	0	0	0	
Career Total	9	0	0	0	251

Going: Sf: 0-0 GS: 0-0 Gd: 0-1 GF: - Fm: 0-0
Distance: 2m/2m3: 0-0 2m4-2m7: 0-1 3m+: 0-0
Track: LH: 0-0 RH: 0-1 Tight: 0-1 Gall: 0-0
Aids: Bl: 0-0 Vi: 0-0 Tstrap: 0-0
Best Rating: 55 3/00 Font 2m2f110y gd-fm Hdl

Paddyspearl

32

9-y-o b g Henbit (USA)-La Furze (Winden)
A W Carroll A Bayman

Placings:00P/PP0PP3-FPP　(0682)
2002/03: 16³GS, 16⁶GS, 16⁶G, 17⁶G,

	Starts	1st	2nd	3rd	Win & Pl
Chases	4	0	0	1	623
Career Total	12	0	0	1	623

Going: Sf: 0-0 GS: 0-2 Gd: 0-2 GF: - Fm: 0-0
Distance: 2m/2m3: 0-4 2m4-2m7: 0-0 3m+: 0-0
Track: LH: 0-3 RH: 0-1 Tight: 0-2 Gall: 0-0
Aids: Bl: 0-0 Vi: 0-0 Tstrap: 0-0
Best Rating: 32 5/02 Fknm 2m110y gd-sft Ch

Pagan Leader (IRE)

10-y-o b g Supreme Leader-Dawning Glory (Hittite Glory)
P T Dalton Mrs Julie Martin

Placings:0/0P/4P6UP00/P/P　(3090)
2002/03: 24⁵PG,

	Starts	1st	2nd	3rd	Win & Pl
Chases	1	0	0	0	
Career Total	12	0	0	0	230

Going: Sf: 0-0 GS: 0-0 Gd: 0-1 GF: - Fm: 0-0
Distance: 2m/2m3: 0-0 2m4-2m7: 0-0 3m+: 0-1
Track: LH: 0-1 RH: 0-0 Tight: 0-0 Gall: 0-1
Aids: Bl: 0-0 Vi: 0-0 Tstrap: 0-0
Best Rating: 62 5/99 Towc 3m gd-fm Hdl

Pailitas (GER)

107　　69

6-y-o b g Lomitas-Pradera (GER) (Abary (GER))
Ian Williams C N Barnes

Placings:0P0P-120060　(4573)
2002/03: 16¹GF, 16²GF, 16⁶GF, 17⁰GF, 17⁵GF, 16⁰GF,

	Starts	1st	2nd	3rd	Win & Pl
Hurdles	6	1	1	0	2779
Career Total	10	1	1	0	2779
77 6/02 Hntg	2m110y		6g(0-95)HHdl	G-F	£1661

Total win prize-money £1662

Going: Sf: 0-0 GS: 0-0 Gd: 0-0 GF: - Fm: 1-6
Distance: 2m/2m3: 1-6 2m4-2m7: 0-0 3m+: 0-0
Track: LH: 0-4 RH: 1-2 Tight: 0-3 Gall: 1-1
Aids: Bl: 0-0 Vi: 0-0 Tstrap: 0-0
Best Rating: 83 6/02 Uttx 2m gd-fm Hdl

Selling-class hurdler; best at two miles; acts on fast ground.

Pakochino (IRE)

59

11-y-o ch g Moscow Society (USA)-Tossy Lass (Le Bavard (FR))
Robert John Osborne P T McNicholas

Placings:004/P00/500-050O　(1621)
2002/03: 24⁵S, 22⁵G, 20⁰G, 16⁰GS,

	Starts	1st	2nd	3rd	Win & Pl
Hurdles	4	0	0	0	
Career Total	13	0	0	0	163

Going: Sf: 0-1 GS: 0-1 Gd: 0-2 GF: - Fm: 0-0
Distance: 2m/2m3: 0-4 2m4-2m7: 0-2 3m+: 0-1
Track: LH: 0-1 RH: 0-0 Tight: 0-1 Gall: 0-0
Aids: Bl: 0-0 Vi: 0-0 Tstrap: 0-0
Best Rating: 85 9/98 Gway 2m heavy NHF

Palace Parade (USA)

75

13-y-o ch g Cure The Blues (USA)-Parasail (USA) (In Reality)
A G Hobbs T D H Hughes

Placings:F6U6045/5P0/365UP2/UP0042/43P10U/05PP0/4/16/00P-P   (0652)
2002/03: 26PGF,

	Starts	1st	2nd	3rd	Win & Pl
Chases	1	0	0		
Career Total	40	2	2	2	5403
86	5/00	Font	3m2f110yH Ch		GD £1484
92	1/98	Wind	2m6f110yG(0-95)HHdl		GD £2132

Total win prize-money £3617

Going: Sf: 0-0 GS: 0-0 Gd: 0-0 GF: - Fm: 0-1
Distance: 2m/2m3: 0-0 2m4-2m7: 0-0 3m+: 0-1
Track: LH: 0-1 RH: 0-0 Tight: 0-0 Gall: 0-0
Aids: Bl: 0-0 Vi: 0-0 Tstrap: 0-0
Best Rating: 92 1/98 Wind 2m6f110y good Hdl

Palacio (IRE)

69   **52**

6-y-o ch g Erin s Isle-Gayle Gal (Lord Gayle (USA))
E McNamara Alexander McCarthy

Placings:000   (1126a)
2002/03: 17DYS, 20OGF, 17OG,

	Starts	1st	2nd	3rd	Win & Pl
Hurdles	3	0	0	0	
Career Total	3	0	0	0	

Going: Sf: 0-0 GS: 0-0 Gd: 0-1 GF: - Fm: 0-1
Distance: 2m/2m3: 0-2 2m4-2m7: 0-1 3m+: 0-0
Track: LH: 0-3 RH: 0-0 Tight: 0-1 Gall: 0-0
Aids: Bl: 0-0 Vi: 0-0 Tstrap: 0-0
Best Rating: 52 8/02 Tral 2m1f good Hdl

Palais (IRE)

85   **81**

8-y-o b g Darshaan-Dance Festival (Nureyev (USA))
John A Harris J South

Placings:46000/300/P6P-1020   (4786)
2002/03: 24¹GS, 26⁰GF, 22²G, 22⁹G,

	Starts	1st	2nd	3rd	Win & Pl
Hurdles	4	1	1	0	4777
Career Total	15	1	1	1	5197
73	8/02	MRas	3m	D Hdl	G-S £3851

Total win prize-money £3851

Going: Sf: 0-0 GS: 1-1 Gd: 0-2 GF: - Fm: 0-1
Distance: 2m/2m3: 0-0 2m4-2m7: 0-0 3m+: 1-2
Track: LH: 0-0 RH: 1-2 Tight: 1-1 Gall: 0-1
Aids: Bl: 0-0 Vi: 0-0 Tstrap: 0-0
Best Rating: 93 10/99 Strf 2m110y gd-fm Hdl

Modest hurdler; won over three miles at Market Rasen in August 2002; runner up there in novices handicap on return to action in March.

Palarshan (FR)

115(101h)   (133h)**144+**

5-y-o b/br g Darshaan-Palavera (FR) (Bikala)
H D Daly Mrs A L Wood

Placings:131-22311   (4134)
2002/03: 16²G, 16²G, 19³S, 16¹GS, 16¹G,

	Starts	1st	2nd	3rd	Win & Pl
Chases	5	2	2	1	55191
Career Total	8	4	2	2	66378
144	3/03	Chel	2m110y	A HCh	GD £43500
131	2/03	Leic	2m	E Ch	G-S £4745
140	4/02	Chel	2m1f	B Hdl	G-F £8541
	8/01	Pard	1m6f	Hdl	GD £542

Total win prize-money £57328

Going: Sf: 0-1 GS: 1-1 Gd: 1-3 GF: - Fm: 0-0
Distance: 2m/2m3: 2-4 2m4-2m7: 0-1 3m+: 0-0
Track: LH: 1-2 RH: 1-3 Tight: 0-0 Gall: 1-1
Aids: Bl: 0-0 Vi: 0-0 Tstrap: 0-0
Best Rating: 144 3/03 Chel 2m110y good Ch

Very useful chaser; winner on the Flat in France and over hurdles in the Czech Republic; useful novice chaser in 2002/3, he won the Grand Annual at the Cheltenham Festival; probably best at two miles, although does shape as though further will suit in time; suited by good ground; should continue to progress.

Pallingham Lad (IRE)

13-y-o b g Torenaga-Star Mill (Milan)
Miss Emma Oliver (Mrs Lynne Jones 12/5) Roger Oliver

Placings:050/P   (0347)
2002/03: 26PGS,

	Starts	1st	2nd	3rd	Win & Pl
Chases	1	0	0	0	
Career Total	4	0	0	0	

Going: Sf: 0-0 GS: 0-1 Gd: 0-0 GF: - Fm: 0-0
Distance: 2m/2m3: 0-0 2m4-2m7: 0-0 3m+: 0-1
Track: LH: 0-1 RH: 0-0 Tight: 0-1 Gall: 0-0
Aids: Bl: 0-0 Vi: 0-0 Tstrap: 0-1
Best Rating: 90 6/95 Uttx 2m gd-fm NHF

Palm Beach (IRE)

4-y-o ch c Pennekamp (USA)-Crystal Bright (Bold Lad (IRE))
D J S Cosgrove Ms S A Ravenhall

Placings:FP   (1756)
2002/03: 16FGF, 16PG,

	Starts	1st	2nd	3rd	Win & Pl
Hurdles	2	0	0	0	
Career Total	2	0	0	0	

Going: Sf: 0-0 GS: 0-0 Gd: 0-1 GF: - Fm: 0-1
Distance: 2m/2m3: 0-2 2m4-2m7: 0-0 3m+: 0-0
Track: LH: 0-1 RH: 0-1 Tight: 0-0 Gall: 0-1
Aids: Bl: 0-0 Vi: 0-0 Tstrap: 0-1
Best Rating: 0 11/02 Wwck 2m good Hdl

Palua

106   **139+**

6-y-o b g Sri Pekan (USA)-Reticent Bride (IRE) (Shy Groom (USA))
Miss E C Lavelle (I A Balding 19/10) Mark Barrett And Partners

Placings:4-2120   (4131)

2002/03: 20²GS, 20¹HY, 24²G, 24⁹G,

	Starts	1st	2nd	3rd	Win & Pl
Hurdles	4	1	2	0	14053
Career Total	5	1	2	0	14861
111	2/03	Folk	2m4f110yE Hdl		HVY £3689

Total win prize-money £3689

Going: Sf: 1-1 GS: 0-1 Gd: 0-2 GF: - Fm: 0-0
Distance: 2m/2m3: 0-0 2m4-2m7: 1-2 3m+: 0-2
Track: LH: 0-2 RH: 1-2 Tight: 1-1 Gall: 0-1
Aids: Bl: 0-0 Vi: 0-0 Tstrap: 0-0
Best Rating: 139 2/03 Kemp 3m110y good Hdl

Promising hurdler; runner-up in the Cesarewitch on his final start of the 2001 turf season; lightly-raced over hurdles, creditable 2nd to Deano s Beeno (giving 8lb) in the Rendlesham at Kempton in Fennuary; enigmatic character who travels well but finds little off the bit; acts on good and heavy ground; stays 3m.

Pamela Anshan

106(94h)   (66 h)**96**

6-y-o b m Anshan-Have Form (Haveroid)
S C Burrough (P R Rodford 27/1) Mrs Christine Priest

Placings:5555-606P42   (4360)
2002/03: 16⁶GS, 17⁰GS, 19⁶GS, 19⁷G, 19⁴S, 19²F,

	Starts	1st	2nd	3rd	Win & Pl
Hurdles	2	0	0	0	0
Chases	4	0	1	0	1587
Career Total	10	0	1	0	1587

Going: Sf: 0-1 GS: 0-3 Gd: 0-1 GF: - Fm: 0-1
Distance: 2m/2m3: 0-4 2m4-2m7: 0-2 3m+: 0-0
Track: LH: 0-0 RH: 0-6 Tight: 0-1 Gall: 0-0
Aids: Bl: 0-0 Vi: 0-0 Tstrap: 0-0
Best Rating: 96 3/03 Extr 2m3f110y soft Ch

Poor maiden hurdler and chaser.

Pampered Gale (IRE)

9-y-o b g Strong Gale-Pampered Russian (Deep Run)
J M Turner J M Turner

Placings:3464/643/245P5/6   (0311)
2002/03: 26⁶G,

	Starts	1st	2nd	3rd	Win & Pl
Chases	1	0	0	0	0
Career Total	13	0	1	2	2979

Going: Sf: 0-0 GS: 0-0 Gd: 0-1 GF: - Fm: 0-0
Distance: 2m/2m3: 0-0 2m4-2m7: 0-0 3m+: 0-1
Track: LH: 0-0 RH: 0-1 Tight: 0-1 Gall: 0-0
Aids: Bl: 0-0 Vi: 0-0 Tstrap: 0-0
Best Rating: 93 5/00 Ludl 3m good Ch

Pangeran (USA)

11-y-o ch g Forty Niner (USA)-Smart Heiress (USA) (Vaguely Noble)
Neil King Mrs Jill McVay

Placings:42622505/423U/3622/143UU/31P3/32460-53   (0403)
2002/03: 24⁵GF, 22³GF,

	Starts	1st	2nd	3rd	Win & Pl
Chases	2	0	0	1	251

Career Total	32	2	7	7	9758
106 5/00 Uttx	2m5f	H Ch		GD	£1742
92 5/99 Folk	2m5f	H Ch		G-F	£1472

Total win prize-money £3214

Going: Sf: 0-0 GS: 0-0 Gd: 0-0 GF: - Fm: 0-2
Distance: 2m/2m3: 0-0 2m4-2m7: 0-1 3m+: 0-1
Track: LH: 0-0 RH: 0-2 Tight: 0-1 Gall: 0-1
Aids: Bl: 0-0 Vi: 0-0 Tstrap: 0-0
Best Rating: 106 5/00 Uttx 2m5f good Ch

Hunter chaser; multiple winner between the flags; best at three miles, but effective at shorter; best on a sound surface.

Panmure (IRE)
98   88
7-y-o b g Alphabatim (USA)-Serjitak (Saher)
P D Niven (N J Henderson 5/3) P D Niven

Placings:304-040P0U   (4776)
2002/03: 19⁰G, 19⁴S, 17⁰G, 20⁵S, 22⁰G, 20⁰U,

	Starts	1st	2nd	3rd	Win & Pl
Hurdles	5	0	0	0	0
Chases	1	0	0	0	0
Career Total	9	0	0	1	608

Going: Sf: 0-2 GS: 0-0 Gd: 0-4 GF: - Fm: 0-0
Distance: 2m/2m3: 0-2 2m4-2m7: 0-4 3m+: 0-0
Track: LH: 0-2 RH: 0-3 Tight: 0-1 Gall: 0-0
Aids: Bl: 0-0 Vi: 0-0 Tstrap: 0-1
Best Rating: 104 10/01 Chel 2m110y good NHF

Panooras Lord (IRE)
94   93
9-y-o b g Topanoora-Ladyship (Windjammer (USA))
J S Wainwright J S Wainwright

Placings:6320/5P0200010/U0/1PP046/0005-F50 (0665)
2002/03: 16⁵S, 16⁶G, 17⁵GF, 22⁰GF,

	Starts	1st	2nd	3rd	Win & Pl
Hurdles	4	0	0	0	0
Career Total	28	2	2	1	5118
98 6/00 Fknm	2m	G(0-90)HHdl		GD	£1876
87 4/99 Hntg	2m110y	G(0-100)HHdl		G-F	£1926

Total win prize-money £3802

Going: Sf: 0-0 GS: 0-0 Gd: 0-2 GF: - Fm: 0-2
Distance: 2m/2m3: 0-3 2m4-2m7: 0-1 3m+: 0-0
Track: LH: 0-3 RH: 0-1 Tight: 0-2 Gall: 0-1
Aids: Bl: 0-0 Vi: 0-0 Tstrap: 0-1
Best Rating: 98 6/00 Fknm 2m good Hdl

Panto
52f   20f
6-y-o b g Lepanto (GER)-Sherzine (Gorytus (USA))
M Hill Singing In The Rain

Placings:0   (2378)
2002/03: 16⁰S,

	Starts	1st	2nd	3rd	Win & Pl
NH Flat	1	0	0	0	0
Career Total	1	0	0	0	0

Going: Sf: 0-1 GS: 0-0 Gd: 0-0 GF: - Fm: 0-0
Distance: 2m/2m3: 0-1 2m4-2m7: 0-0 3m+: 0-0
Track: LH: 0-1 RH: 0-0 Tight: 0-0 Gall: 0-0
Aids: Bl: 0-0 Vi: 0-0 Tstrap: 0-0
Best Rating: 20 12/02 Wwck 2m soft NHF

Paperising
108(108h)   (128h)148
11-y-o b g Primitive Rising (USA)-Eye Bee Aitch (Move Off)
N G Richards The Jockeys Whips

Placings:1040/2411215P/51F111/4F/5112P/01P14-125
                                              (2509)
2002/03: 22¹G, 25²G, 20⁵G,

	Starts	1st	2nd	3rd	Win & Pl
Hurdles	1	0	0	0	0
Chases	2	1	1	0	9485
Career Total	33	13	4	0	100158
149 5/02 Kels	2m6f110yC(0-130)HCh		GD	£6643
128 3/02 Carl	2m4f	D(0-125)HHdl	GS	£3575
142 2/02 Ayr	2m4f	B(0-145)HCh	HVY	£12431
141 2/01 Uttx	3m	C(0-130)HCh	SFT	£6741
135 1/01 Ayr	2m4f	D(0-140)HCh	GS	£9742
138 4/98 Ayr	3m1f	C HCh	GD	£25330
138 3/98 Bang	3m110y	D Ch	G-S	£4377
137 3/98 Ayr	3m1f	D Ch	G-S	£3626
121 2/98 Kels	3m1f	D Ch	G-S	£4021
119 2/97 Carl	2m4f110yE Hdl		SFT	£2738
110 12/96 Hexm	3m	E Hdl	G-S	£2805
106 12/96 Sedg	2m5f110yE Hdl		GD	£1935
94 3/96 Carl	2m1f	H NHF	GD	£1479

Total win prize-money £85446

Going: Sf: 0-0 GS: 0-0 Gd: 1-3 GF: - Fm: 0-0
Distance: 2m/2m3: 0-0 2m4-2m7: 1-2 3m+: 0-1
Track: LH: 1-3 RH: 0-0 Tight: 1-1 Gall: 0-0
Aids: Bl: 0-0 Vi: 0-0 Tstrap: 0-0
Best Rating: 149 5/02 Weth 3m1f good Ch

Smart handicap chaser/hurdler, he has had something of an interrupted career through injury, but has a decent strike rate since 1998; best on soft ground at up to three miles and is suited by sharpish left-handed tracks.

Paperprophet
108   124+
5-y-o b g Glory Of Dancer-Living Legend (ITY) (Archway (IRE))
N G Richards The Jockeys Whips

Placings:3112   (2766)
2002/03: 16³G, 17¹GS, 20¹S, 20²GS,

	Starts	1st	2nd	3rd	Win & Pl
NH Flat	1	0	0	1	324
Hurdles	3	2	1	0	12111
Career Total	4	2	1	1	12435
110 11/02 Ayr	2m4f	D(0-110)HHdl	SFT	£4420
97 10/02 Bang	2m1f	E Hdl	G-S	£3038

Total win prize-money £7458

Going: Sf: 1-1 GS: 1-2 Gd: 0-1 GF: - Fm: 0-0
Distance: 2m/2m3: 1-2 2m4-2m7: 1-2 3m+: 0-0
Track: LH: 2-3 RH: 0-1 Tight: 1-2 Gall: 0-0
Aids: Bl: 0-0 Vi: 0-0 Tstrap: 0-0
Best Rating: 121 12/02 Muss 2m4f gd-sft Hdl

Never reached a racecourse when trained by Mark Johnston. Built on a promising start to his career when third in a Worcester bumper when winning novice hurdles at Bangor October 2002 and at Ayr the following month. Suited by soft ground.

Paperweight
70   43
7-y-o b m In The Wings-Crystal Reay (Sovereign Dancer (USA))
Miss K M George A B Parr

Placings:00FP/60/0   (0574)

2002/03: 22⁰G,

	Starts	1st	2nd	3rd	Win & Pl
Hurdles	1	0	0	0	0
Career Total	7	0	0	0	0

Going: Sf: 0-0 GS: 0-0 Gd: 0-1 GF: - Fm: 0-0
Distance: 2m/2m3: 0-0 2m4-2m7: 0-1 3m+: 0-0
Track: LH: 0-1 RH: 0-0 Tight: 0-1 Gall: 0-0
Aids: Bl: 0-0 Vi: 0-0 Tstrap: 0-0
Best Rating: 70 5/00 Ludl 2m good Hdl

Paphian Bay
80f   61f
5-y-o b g Karinga Bay-Bichette (Lidhame)
Ferdy Murphy S Hubbard Rodwell

Placings:0   (3528)
2002/03: 16⁰G,

	Starts	1st	2nd	3rd	Win & Pl
NH Flat	1	0	0	0	0
Career Total	1	0	0	0	0

Going: Sf: 0-0 GS: 0-0 Gd: 0-1 GF: - Fm: 0-0
Distance: 2m/2m3: 0-1 2m4-2m7: 0-0 3m+: 0-0
Track: LH: 0-1 RH: 0-0 Tight: 0-0 Gall: 0-1
Aids: Bl: 0-0 Vi: 0-0 Tstrap: 0-0
Best Rating: 61 2/03 Newb 2m110y good NHF

Parable
89   75
7-y-o b g Midyan (USA)-Top Table (Shirley Heights)
Mrs P Sly Robin Sturgess

Placings:06   (2493)
2002/03: 16⁰GS, 16⁶S,

	Starts	1st	2nd	3rd	Win & Pl
Hurdles	2	0	0	0	0
Career Total	2	0	0	0	0

Going: Sf: 0-1 GS: 0-1 Gd: 0-0 GF: - Fm: 0-0
Distance: 2m/2m3: 0-2 2m4-2m7: 0-0 3m+: 0-0
Track: LH: 0-2 RH: 0-0 Tight: 0-0 Gall: 0-1
Aids: Bl: 0-0 Vi: 0-0 Tstrap: 0-0
Best Rating: 75 12/02 Donc 2m110y soft Hdl

Little signs of ability so far.

Parade Racer
12-y-o b g Derring Rose-Dusky Damsel (Sahib)
Tim Butt Tim Butt

Placings:56/PP42F153/F/PP43444P/3/3203-11P (4107)
2002/03: 25¹GS, 20¹GF, 27⁴S,

	Starts	1st	2nd	3rd	Win & Pl
Chases	3	2	0	0	4619
Career Total	27	3	2	5	12766
99 5/02 Prth	2m4f110yH Ch		G-F	£2743
104 5/02 Kels	3m1f	H Ch	G-S	£1876
82 1/97 Towc	2m5f	G(0-95)HHdl	G-S	£2232

Total win prize-money £6852

Going: Sf: 0-1 GS: 1-1 Gd: 0-0 GF: - Fm: 1-1
Distance: 2m/2m3: 0-0 2m4-2m7: 1-1 3m+: 1-2
Track: LH: 1-2 RH: 1-1 Tight: 1-2 Gall: 0-0
Aids: Bl: 0-0 Vi: 0-0 Tstrap: 0-0
Best Rating: 104 5/02 Kels 3m1f gd-sft Ch

Fair pointer/hunter chaser, stays three miles. Acts on any ground.

Paradisio (FR)

7-y-o b g Albert Du Berlais (FR)-Pretty Lady (FR) (Le Gregol (FR))
W J Tolhurst   W J Tolhurst

Placings:11/3F344/5   (4671)
2002/03: 24⁵G,

	Starts	1st	2nd	3rd	Win & Pl
Chases	1	0	0	0	
Career Total	8	2	0	2	13784
4/00 Pau	2m1f	Ch		GD	£3842
3/00 Pau	2m110y	Hdl		GD	£3362

Total win prize-money £7204

Going: Sf: 0-0 GS: 0-0 Gd: 0-1 GF: - Fm: 0-0
Distance: 2m/2m3: 0-0 2m4-2m7: 0-0 3m+: 0-1
Track: LH: 0-1 RH: 0-0 Tight: 0-1 Gall: 0-0
Aids: Bl: 0-0 Vi: 0-0 Tstrap: 0-0
Best Rating: 73   4/03   Fknm   3m110y   good   Ch

Parahandy (IRE)

13-y-o b g Lancastrian-Dishcloth (Fury Royal)
Giles Smyly   G E Dowty

Placings:2246/UF11/4P345/1/224224/53-025   (4565)
2002/03: 33⁰GF, 26²GS, 24⁵GF,

	Starts	1st	2nd	3rd	Win & Pl
Chases	3	0	1	0	420
Career Total	25	3	7	2	30110
125 11/99 NAbb	3m2f110yB(0-140)HCh	G-S			£8439
127 4/98 Winc	3m1f110yE Ch		G-S		£3226
133 4/98 Font	3m2f110yE(0-115)HCh	G-S			£3377

Total win prize-money £15043

Going: Sf: 0-0 GS: 0-1 Gd: 0-0 GF: - Fm: 0-2
Distance: 2m/2m3: 0-0 2m4-2m7: 0-0 3m+: 0-3
Track: LH: 0-3 RH: 0-0 Tight: 0-1 Gall: 0-1
Aids: Bl: 0-0 Vi: 0-0 Tstrap: 0-0
Best Rating: 133   4/98   Font   3m2f110y   gd-sft   Ch

He had a luckless season, finishing second four times and being caught close home at Fontwell in February. A thorough stayer; suited by cut in the ground.

Pardini (USA)
94   94

4-y-o b g Quest For Fame-Noblissima (IRE) (Sadler s Wells (USA))
M F Harris   Let s Live Racing

Placings:4   (4084)
2002/03: 16⁴GS,

	Starts	1st	2nd	3rd	Win & Pl
Hurdles	1	0	0	0	429
Career Total	1	0	0	0	429

Going: Sf: 0-0 GS: 0-1 Gd: 0-0 GF: - Fm: 0-0
Distance: 2m/2m3: 0-1 2m4-2m7: 0-0 3m+: 0-0
Track: LH: 0-1 RH: 0-0 Tight: 0-1 Gall: 0-0
Aids: Bl: 0-0 Vi: 0-0 Tstrap: 0-0
Best Rating: 86   3/03   Strf   2m110y   gd-sft   Hdl

Pardishar (IRE)
104   100

5-y-o b g Kahyasi-Parapa (IRE) (Akarad (FR))
G L Moore   Mike Charlton And Rodger Sargent

Placings:0-5   (0263)
2002/03: 16⁵G,

	Starts	1st	2nd	3rd	Win & Pl
Hurdles	1	0	0	0	0
Career Total	2	0	0	0	0

Going: Sf: 0-0 GS: 0-0 Gd: 0-1 GF: - Fm: 0-0
Distance: 2m/2m3: 0-1 2m4-2m7: 0-0 3m+: 0-0
Track: LH: 0-1 RH: 0-0 Tight: 0-1 Gall: 0-0
Aids: Bl: 0-0 Vi: 0-0 Tstrap: 0-1
Best Rating: 102   5/02   Aint   2m110y   good   Hdl

A winner on the Flat for Sir Michael Stoute, he is yet to race over hurdles.

Pardon What
100(98h)   (90dh)96

7-y-o b g Theatrical Charmer-Tree Poppy (Rolfe (USA))
B G Powell   Mrs A Ellis

Placings:3f UP54014P   (4528)
2002/03: 16³G, 16¹S, 25⁰G, 20⁸S, 20⁵S, 21⁴S, 20⁰HY, 20¹S, 19⁴G, 24ᴾG,

	Starts	1st	2nd	3rd	Win & Pl
NH Flat	2	1	0	1	1747
Hurdles	5	0	0	0	0
Chases	3	1	0	0	5291
Career Total	10	2	0	1	7038
96 3/03 Bang	2m4f110yE(0-105)HCh	SFT			£4858
108 6/02 Worc	2m	H NHF	SFT		£1519

Total win prize-money £6378

Going: Sf: 2-6 GS: 0-0 Gd: 0-4 GF: - Fm: 0-0
Distance: 2m/2m3: 1-2 2m4-2m7: 1-6 3m+: 0-2
Track: LH: 2-9 RH: 0-1 Tight: 1-2 Gall: 0-0
Aids: Bl: 0-0 Vi: 0-0 Tstrap: 0-0
Best Rating: 108   6/02   Worc   2m   soft   NHF

Moderate chaser, winner at Bangor on debut; effective at two and a half miles; acts on soft ground.

Pardus (FR)
                87

7-y-o b g Unfuwain (USA)-Provacatrice (USA) (Irish River (FR))
Mario Hofer   Stall Konigsforst

Placings:15F   (3269)
2002/03: 19¹HY, 19⁵HY, 17ᶠHY,

	Starts	1st	2nd	3rd	Win & Pl
Hurdles	3	1	0	0	5117
Career Total	3	1	0	0	5117
11/02 Stra	2m3f	Hdl	HVY		£4123

Total win prize-money £4123

Going: Sf: 1-3 GS: 0-0 Gd: 0-0 GF: - Fm: 0-0
Distance: 2m/2m3: 1-2 2m4-2m7: 0-1 3m+: 0-0
Track: LH: 0-1 RH: 0-0 Tight: 0-1 Gall: 0-0
Aids: Bl: 0-0 Vi: 0-0 Tstrap: 0-0
Best Rating: 87   1/03   Folk   2m1f110y   heavy   Hdl

Paris Latino (FR)
                72f

4-y-o b g Nikos-Tarbelissima (FR) (Tarbes (FR))
C Tizzard   R G Tizzard

Placings:00   (2574)
2002/03: 12⁰GS, 12⁰G,

	Starts	1st	2nd	3rd	Win & Pl
NH Flat	2	0	0	0	
Career Total	2	0	0	0	

Going: Sf: 0-0 GS: 0-1 Gd: 0-1 GF: - Fm: 0-0
Distance: 2m/2m3: 0-0 2m4-2m7: 0-0 3m+: 0-0
Track: LH: 0-2 RH: 0-0 Tight: 0-0 Gall: 0-0
Aids: Bl: 0-0 Vi: 0-0 Tstrap: 0-0
Best Rating: 72   11/02   Newb   1m4f110y   gd-sft   NHF

Paris Pike (IRE)
(103h)   (118h)147

11-y-o b g Satco (FR)-Bouise (Royal Buck)
Ferdy Murphy   Major & Mrs Ivan Straker

Placings:4104/4344.32212/1121111/2P66FP-F50   (4164)
2002/03: 24ᶠG, 20⁵G, 24⁰GS,

	Starts	1st	2nd	3rd	Win & Pl
Hurdles	2	0	0	0	0
Chases	1	0	0	0	0
Career Total	29	8	5	2	103592
158 4/00 Ayr	4m1f	A HCh	GD		£42000
153 3/00 Uttx	3m2f	C HCh	GD		£18395
140 3/00 Kels	3m1f	B(0-150)HCh	G-S		£8513
138 2/00 Kels	3m1f	C Ch	G-S		£7150
110 11/99 Kels	3m1f	D Ch	GD		£4221
101 5/99 Prth	3m110y	E Hdl	HVY		£2990
115 2/99 Clon	3m	Hdl	SFT		£3069
106 10/97 Leop	2m4f	NHF	G-Y		£4069

Total win prize-money £90408

Going: Sf: 0-0 GS: 0-1 Gd: 0-2 GF: - Fm: 0-0
Distance: 2m/2m3: 0-0 2m4-2m7: 0-1 3m+: 0-2
Track: LH: 0-3 RH: 0-0 Tight: 0-0 Gall: 0-2
Aids: Bl: 0-0 Vi: 0-0 Tstrap: 0-0
Best Rating: 158   4/00   Ayr   4m1f   good   Ch

Very useful staying chaser; winner of the 2000 Scottish National, but he has not won since and has had his problems; likes decent ground; good effort over hurdles at Wetherby in February.

Parish Oak
106(108h)   (80h)96

8-y-o b g Rakaposhi King-Poppy s Pride (Uncle Pokey)
Ian Williams   Mrs M Mann

Placings:05P0/U001-PP01U1   (4787)
2002/03: 16¹GS, 20ᴾS, 21ᴾS, 20ᴿGS, 20¹GS, 20ᵁGF, 20¹G,

	Starts	1st	2nd	3rd	Win & Pl
Hurdles	2	1	0	0	2573
Chases	5	2	0	0	8395
Career Total	14	3	0	0	10967
96 4/03 MRas	2m4f	E(0-105)HCh	GD		£4186
87 3/03 Wwck	2m4f110yE(0-105)HCh	G-S			£4208
81 4/02 Towc	2m	E(0-105)HHdl	G-S		£2572

Total win prize-money £10968

Going: Sf: 0-2 GS: 2-3 Gd: 1-1 GF: - Fm: 0-1
Distance: 2m/2m3: 1-1 2m4-2m7: 2-6 3m+: 0-0
Track: LH: 1-2 RH: 2-5 Tight: 1-3 Gall: 0-0
Aids: Bl: 0-0 Vi: 0-0 Tstrap: 1-2
Best Rating: 96   4/03   MRas   2m4f   good   Ch

Moderate hurdler/chaser; stays two and a half miles; handles cut in the ground.

Parisian Eire (IRE)

4-y-o gr g Paris House-La Fille De Feu (Never So Bold)

N A Smith P E T Chandler

Placings:PP00P   (3926)
2002/03: 16PHY, 16PS, 16OHY, 16OHY, 20PG,

	Starts	1st	2nd	3rd	Win & Pl
Hurdles	5	0	0	0	
Career Total	5	0	0	0	

Going: Sf: 0-4 GS: 0-0 Gd: 0-1 GF: - Fm: 0-0
Distance: 2m/2m3: 0-4 2m4-2m7: 0-1 3m+: 0-0
Track: LH: 0-2 RH: 0-3 Tight: 0-0 Gall: 0-1
Aids: Bl: 0-1 Vi: 0-0 Tstrap: 0-0
Best Rating: 0   3/03   Hntg   2m4f110y   good   Hdl

Park City
105   **94**

4-y-o b g Slip Anchor-Cryptal (Persian Bold)
P J Hobbs (P Howling 6/7) Jack Joseph

Placings:B3021P503   (4573)
2002/03: 16RGF, 16JGF, 16OG, 16JG, 16JS, 19PG, 16JS, 17OGF, 16JGF,

	Starts	1st	2nd	3rd	Win & Pl
Hurdles	9	1	1	2	4979
Career Total	9	1	1	2	4979
85	12/02	Wwck	2m		F(0-100)HHdl SFT £2541

Total win prize-money £2541

Going: Sf: 1-2 GS: 0-0 Gd: 0-3 GF: - Fm: 0-4
Distance: 2m/2m3: 1-8 2m4-2m7: 0-1 3m+: 0-0
Track: LH: 1-4 RH: 0-5 Tight: 0-2 Gall: 0-2
Aids: Bl: 0-0 Vi: 0-0 Tstrap: 0-0
Best Rating: 91   4/03   Strf   2m110y   gd-fm   Hdl

Modest handicap hurdler; effective at around two miles and on good and soft ground.

Park End

11-y-o ch g Bairn (USA)-Abdera (Ahonoora)
N J Legg Miss M D Burrough

Placings:0/0   (4390)
2002/03: 19OF,

	Starts	1st	2nd	3rd	Win & Pl
Chases	1	0	0	0	
Career Total	2	0	0	0	

Going: Sf: 0-0 GS: 0-0 Gd: 0-0 GF: 0-0 - Fm: 0-1
Distance: 2m/2m3: 0-0 2m4-2m7: 0-1 3m+: 0-0
Track: LH: 0-0 RH: 0-1 Tight: 0-0 Gall: 0-0
Aids: Bl: 0-0 Vi: 0-0 Tstrap: 0-0
Best Rating: 56   12/96   Uttx   2m   gd-sft   NHF

Park Lane Freddie
91   **88**

5-y-o b g Nalchik (USA)-Kathy s Role (Rolfe (USA))
J Mackie Mrs Nigel Batho

Placings:00600   (4567)
2002/03: 17OG, 16OG, 17RGS, 19JGF, 20PGF,

	Starts	1st	2nd	3rd	Win & Pl
NH Flat	3	0	0	0	0
Hurdles	2	0	0	0	0
Career Total	5	0	0	0	0

Going: Sf: 0-0 GS: 0-1 Gd: 0-2 GF: - Fm: 0-2
Distance: 2m/2m3: 0-3 2m4-2m7: 0-2 3m+: 0-0

Track: LH: 0-3 RH: 0-2 Tight: 0-3 Gall: 0-0
Aids: Bl: 0-0 Vi: 0-0 Tstrap: 0-1
Best Rating: 88   12/02   Bang   2m1f   gd-sft   NHF

Well held in bumpers and novice hurdles.

Park Place (IRE)
94(77c)   (60c)**90**

8-y-o gr g Husyan (USA)-Iron Mermaid (General Ironside)
J I A Charlton W F Trueman

Placings:105/665-0434   (4776)
2002/03: 16OG, 20JS, 25JGF, 20JG,

	Starts	1st	2nd	3rd	Win & Pl
Hurdles	3	0	0	1	984
Chases	1	0	0	0	0
Career Total	10	1	0	1	2902
112	5/00	Prth	2m110y		H NHF G-S £1918

Total win prize-money £1918

Going: Sf: 0-1 GS: 0-0 Gd: 0-2 GF: - Fm: 0-1
Distance: 2m/2m3: 0-1 2m4-2m7: 0-2 3m+: 0-1
Track: LH: 0-2 RH: 0-2 Tight: 0-1 Gall: 0-0
Aids: Bl: 0-0 Vi: 0-0 Tstrap: 0-0
Best Rating: 112   5/00   Prth   2m110y   gd-sft   NHF

Moderate novice hurdler; stayed three miles; acted on a sound surface; (DEAD)

Parlour Game
108(105h)   (112h)**107**

7-y-o br m Petoski-Henry s True Love (Random Shot)
H D Daly T F F Nixon

Placings:31F0/63P55-F4U32P2   (4024)
2002/03: 20FGS, 20JGS, 20UGS, 19JGS, 20JGS, 20PG, 25JS,

	Starts	1st	2nd	3rd	Win & Pl
Chases	7	0	2	1	3978
Career Total	16	1	2	3	7332
117	1/01	Sthl	2m		E Hdl HVY £2590

Total win prize-money £2590

Going: Sf: 0-1 GS: 0-5 Gd: 0-1 GF: - Fm: 0-0
Distance: 2m/2m3: 0-0 2m4-2m7: 0-6 3m+: 0-1
Track: LH: 0-2 RH: 0-5 Tight: 0-3 Gall: 0-2
Aids: Bl: 0-0 Vi: 0-0 Tstrap: 0-0
Best Rating: 117   1/01   Sthl   2m   heavy   Hdl

Won a Southwell novice hurdle in Janaury 2001, but things have not really gone her way since; easy winner of handicap bow over fences at Uttoxeter in April; stays two and a half miles; suited by soft ground.

Parsifal
109   **82**

4-y-o b g Sadler s Wells (USA)-Moss (USA) (Woodman (USA))
J Howard Johnson (J G Given 21/10) Dick Thackeray

Placings:00P6   (4517)
2002/03: 16JG, 17OGS, 16PGS, 17PG,

	Starts	1st	2nd	3rd	Win & Pl
Hurdles	4	0	0	0	0
Career Total	4	0	0	0	0

Going: Sf: 0-0 GS: 0-2 Gd: 0-2 GF: - Fm: 0-0
Distance: 2m/2m3: 0-4 2m4-2m7: 0-0 3m+: 0-0
Track: LH: 0-2 RH: 0-2 Tight: 0-2 Gall: 0-1
Aids: Bl: 0-0 Vi: 0-0 Tstrap: 0-0
Best Rating: 66   4/03   Sedg   2m1f   good   Hdl

Moderate novice hurdler; ran best race on latest start when close third in handicap company at Sedgefield in May.

Parsons Boy

14-y-o ch g The Parson-Kylogue Daisy (Little Buskins)
P H Morris P H Morris

Placings:060660P/26511113/1103/6PP1P13/3354233P/P4
064P/1/12P-0   (3521)
2002/03: 22OGS,

	Starts	1st	2nd	3rd	Win & Pl
Chases	1	0	0	0	
Career Total	45	10	3	7	52922
84	5/01	Hexm	3m1f		H Ch SFT £2688
88	4/01	Hayd	3m		F(0-105)HCh SFT £3601
129	4/98	Bang	3m110y		D(0-125)HCh SFT £5015
126	3/98	Bang	3m110y		D(0-125)HCh G-S £4443
127	11/96	Hayd	3m4f110yB(0-140)HCh GD £6729
124	11/96	Carl	3m		D(0-125)HCh GD £4535
108	3/96	Bang	3m110y		D Ch HVY £4071
116	3/96	Newc	3m		E Ch SFT £3165
102	2/96	Weth	3m110y		D Ch G-S £3821
103	2/96	Kels	3m1f		E Ch SFT £3050

Total win prize-money £41121

Going: Sf: 0-1 GS: 0-1 Gd: 0-0 GF: - Fm: 0-0
Distance: 2m/2m3: 0-0 2m4-2m7: 0-1 3m+: 0-0
Track: LH: 0-1 RH: 0-0 Tight: 0-0 Gall: 0-0
Aids: Bl: 0-0 Vi: 0-0 Tstrap: 0-0
Best Rating: 129   4/98   Worc   2m7f110y   gd-sft   Ch

Parsons Pride (IRE)
70   **35**

7-y-o b g Persian Mews-First Prize (IRE) (The Parson)
C Weedon Colin Weedon

Placings:30PP   (3920)
2002/03: 16JG, 16OG, 24PGS, 18PS,

	Starts	1st	2nd	3rd	Win & Pl
NH Flat	2	0	0	1	284
Hurdles	2	0	0	0	0
Career Total	4	0	0	1	284

Going: Sf: 0-1 GS: 0-1 Gd: 0-2 GF: - Fm: 0-0
Distance: 2m/2m3: 0-3 2m4-2m7: 0-0 3m+: 0-1
Track: LH: 0-2 RH: 0-1 Tight: 0-1 Gall: 0-0
Aids: Bl: 0-0 Vi: 0-0 Tstrap: 0-0
Best Rating: 91   9/02   Worc   2m   good   NHF

Party Animal (IRE)
104   **93+**

11-y-o b g Buckskin (FR)-More Chat (Torenaga)
K C Bailey Racing Club Kcb

Placings:453/23/1U/3-P   (3824)
2002/03: 26PGS,

	Starts	1st	2nd	3rd	Win & Pl
Chases	1	0	0	0	
Career Total	9	1	1	3	5155
110	11/00	Hrfd	3m1f110yF(0-90)HCh G-S £2710

Total win prize-money £2710

Going: Sf: 0-0 GS: 0-1 Gd: 0-0 GF: - Fm: 0-0
Distance: 2m/2m3: 0-0 2m4-2m7: 0-0 3m+: 0-1
Track: LH: 0-1 RH: 0-0 Tight: 0-0 Gall: 0-0
Aids: Bl: 0-0 Vi: 0-0 Tstrap: 0-0
Best Rating: 110   11/01   Wwck   3m2f   good   Ch

Lightly raced, he won an amateur handicap chase at Hereford November 2000, but was off the track for 11 months after falling next time; broke blood vessel when pulled up at Chepstow February 2003; has obviously been difficult to train.

Party Games (IRE)
94   **82**

6-y-o b g King s Ride-Shady Miss (Mandamus)
D M Grissell   Gregory Barker

Placings:4-5   (1582)
2002/03: 18⁴G, 21⁵G,

	Starts	1st	2nd	3rd	Win & Pl
NH Flat	1	0	0	0	0
Hurdles	1	0	0	0	0
Career Total	2	0	0	0	0

Going: Sf: 0-0 GS: 0-0 Gd: 0-2 GF: - Fm: 0-0
Distance: 2m/2m3: 0-1 2m4-2m7: 0-1 3m+: 0-0
Track: LH: 0-2 RH: 0-0 Tight: 0-1 Gall: 0-0
Aids: Bl: 0-0 Vi: 0-0 Tstrap: 0-0
Best Rating: 85   10/02 Plum 2m5f   good   Hdl

Party Lad (IRE)
            94

10-y-o b g King s Ride-Lantern Lass (Monksfield)
N A Twiston-Davies   Mrs R Mackness

Placings:03/P10/0624F2/1U4PP-P   (0114)
2002/03: 25ᴾGS,

	Starts	1st	2nd	3rd	Win & Pl
Chases	1	0	0	0	
Career Total	17	2	2	1	11046
85	5/01 Hexm	3m1f	E Ch		SFT £3399
98	1/00 Cork	2m	Hdl		SH £3864

Total win prize-money £7264

Going: Sf: 0-0 GS: 0-1 Gd: 0-0 GF: - Fm: 0-0
Distance: 2m/2m3: 0-0 2m4-2m7: 0-0 3m+: 0-1
Track: LH: 0-0 RH: 0-1 Tight: 0-0 Gall: 0-0
Aids: Bl: 0-0 Vi: 0-0 Tstrap: 0-0
Best Rating: 111   1/99 Naas 2m   heavy   Hdl

Modest chaser, stays three miles, acts on soft ground. Not the best of jumpers.

Paso Fino (IRE)
75f   **59f**

4-y-o b g Alzao (USA)-Kentucky Fall (FR) (Lead On Time (USA))
J R Norton   Mrs H Rafter

Placings:00   (4788)
2002/03: 16⁰S, 17⁰G,

	Starts	1st	2nd	3rd	Win & Pl
NH Flat	2	0	0	0	
Career Total	2	0	0	0	

Going: Sf: 0-1 GS: 0-0 Gd: 0-1 GF: - Fm: 0-0
Distance: 2m/2m3: 0-2 2m4-2m7: 0-0 3m+: 0-0
Track: LH: 0-1 RH: 0-1 Tight: 0-2 Gall: 0-0
Aids: Bl: 0-0 Vi: 0-0 Tstrap: 0-0
Best Rating: 59   3/03 Catt 2m   soft   NHF

Pass Me By
105f   **95f**

4-y-o b g Balnibarbi-Errol Emerald (Dom Racine (FR))
T D Walford   Mrs M Cooper

Placings:104   (4230)
2002/03: 16¹G, 17⁰GS, 16⁴GF,

	Starts	1st	2nd	3rd	Win & Pl
NH Flat	3	1	0	0	2975

Career Total	3	1	0	0	2975
93	1/03 Muss 2m	H NHF		GD	£2975

Total win prize-money £2975

Going: Sf: 0-0 GS: 0-1 Gd: 1-1 GF: - Fm: 0-1
Distance: 2m/2m3: 1-3 2m4-2m7: 0-0 3m+: 0-0
Track: LH: 0-1 RH: 1-2 Tight: 1-1 Gall: 0-0
Aids: Bl: 0-0 Vi: 0-0 Tstrap: 0-0
Best Rating: 104   3/03 Carl   2m1f   gd-sft   NHF

Made quite an impressive debut in a bumper at Musselburgh in January 2003; badly hampered next time.

Passenger Omar (IRE)
68   **55**

5-y-o b g Safety Catch (USA)-Princess Douglas (Bishop Of Orange)
Noel T Chance   Mrs V Griffiths

Placings:R0   (3528)
2002/03: 16ᴿHY, 16⁰G,

	Starts	1st	2nd	3rd	Win & Pl
NH Flat	2	0	0	0	
Career Total	2	0	0	0	

Going: Sf: 0-1 GS: 0-0 Gd: 0-1 GF: - Fm: 0-0
Distance: 2m/2m3: 0-2 2m4-2m7: 0-0 3m+: 0-0
Track: LH: 0-2 RH: 0-0 Tight: 0-0 Gall: 0-2
Aids: Bl: 0-0 Vi: 0-0 Tstrap: 0-2
Best Rating: 77   2/03 Newb 2m110y   good   NHF

Passereau (FR)
111   **117**

7-y-o b g Fijar Tango (FR)-Becebege (FR) (Iron Duke (FR))
C N Kellett   Sean A Taylor

Placings:0412/06P354005U1644F/0P21322P5PP51-PU6222361310P2   (4348)
2002/03: 20ᴾS, 17ᵁGF, 20⁶G, 17²GF, 17²S, 20²GF, 16³G, 17⁶GF, 17¹GS, 16³S, 16¹S, 16⁶S, 16⁶G, 20²GF,

	Starts	1st	2nd	3rd	Win & Pl
Chases	14	2	4	2	19495
Career Total	46	6	8	4	51548
117	1/03 Fknm	2m110y D(0-120)HCh		SFT	£7335
115	10/02 Bang	2m1f110yE(0-110)HCh		G-S	£4914
103	4/02 MRas	2m4f	E(0-105)HCh		G-F £3744
95	11/01 Plum	2m1f	F(0-110)HCh		G-S £2912
99	2/01 Bang	2m1f110yD(0-110)HCh		HVY	£4212
	1/00 Pau	2m2f	Hdl		HVY £5764

Total win prize-money £28882

Going: Sf: 1-5 GS: 1-1 Gd: 0-3 GF: - Fm: 0-5
Distance: 2m/2m3: 2-10 2m4-2m7: 0-4 3m+: 0-0
Track: LH: 2-4 RH: 0-6 Tight: 2-8 Gall: 0-1
Aids: Bl: 0-0 Vi: 0-0 Tstrap: 0-0
Best Rating: 117   3/03 Wwck 2m4f110y   gd-fm   Ch

Fair chaser; often let down by his jumping; best at distances up to two and a half miles; appears to act on all types of ground; has worn visor and tongue tie.

Pateley (IRE)
78(105c)   (107c)**75**

9-y-o b g Cataldi-Suir Venture (Roselier (FR))
John R Upson   K Hancock & P M Haslam

Placings:64103/00B1023564/2253R60/62233PF04-P0   (0822)
2002/03: 24ᴾG, 16⁹GF,

	Starts	1st	2nd	3rd	Win & Pl

	Starts	1st	2nd	3rd	Win & Pl
Hurdles	1	0	0	0	0
Chases	1	0	0	0	0
Career Total	33	2	5	5	14331
112	11/99 Thur	2m	Hdl		Y-S £2217
102	1/99 Fair	2m	NHF		HVY £2762

Total win prize-money £4980

Going: Sf: 0-0 GS: 0-0 Gd: 0-1 GF: - Fm: 0-0
Distance: 2m/2m3: 0-1 2m4-2m7: 0-0 3m+: 0-1
Track: LH: 0-2 RH: 0-0 Tight: 0-1 Gall: 0-0
Aids: Bl: 0-1 Vi: 0-0 Tstrap: 0-0
Best Rating: 120   11/00 Chel 2m5f   gd-sft   Hdl

Not the most straightforward customer, he has shown ability over hurdles and fences since coming from Ireland.

Patriarch (IRE)

7-y-o b g Alphabatim (USA)-Strong Language (Formidable (USA))
M Pitman   Malcolm C Denmark

Placings:13/502132/P   (3517)
2002/03: 23ᴾGS,

	Starts	1st	2nd	3rd	Win & Pl
Hurdles	1	0	0	0	
Career Total	9	2	2	2	21707
135	2/01 Wwck	2m5f	B Hdl		SFT £9217
117	2/00 Newb	2m110y	B NHF		G-S £7670

Total win prize-money £16887

Going: Sf: 0-0 GS: 0-1 Gd: 0-0 GF: - Fm: 0-0
Distance: 2m/2m3: 0-0 2m4-2m7: 0-0 3m+: 0-1
Track: LH: 0-1 RH: 0-0 Tight: 0-0 Gall: 0-0
Aids: Bl: 0-0 Vi: 0-0 Tstrap: 0-0
Best Rating: 135   2/01 Wwck 2m5f   soft   Hdl

Patriarch Express
114f   **123f**

6-y-o b g Noble Patriarch-Jaydeeglen (Bay Express)
G A Harker   A P Muir

Placings:2-1100   (4115)
2002/03: 16¹GF, 16¹G, 16⁰G, 16⁰G,

	Starts	1st	2nd	3rd	Win & Pl
NH Flat	4	2	0	0	7131
Career Total	5	2	1	0	7617
111	10/02 Chel	2m110y H NHF		GD	£4127
107	9/02 Prth	2m110y H NHF		G-F	£3003

Total win prize-money £7131

Going: Sf: 0-0 GS: 0-0 Gd: 1-3 GF: - Fm: 1-1
Distance: 2m/2m3: 2-4 2m4-2m7: 0-0 3m+: 0-0
Track: LH: 1-3 RH: 1-1 Tight: 0-0 Gall: 0-1
Aids: Bl: 0-0 Vi: 0-0 Tstrap: 0-0
Best Rating: 123   3/03 Chel 2m110y   good   NHF

Decent bumper horse, comfortable winner at Perth in September 2002 before following up at Cheltenham.

Patricksnineteenth (IRE)
97f   **112f**

6-y-o b g Mister Lord (USA)-Many Miracles (Le Moss)
P R Webber   The Large G & T Partnership

Placings:310   (4481)
2002/03: 16³GS, 16¹HY, 17⁰G,

	Starts	1st	2nd	3rd	Win & Pl
NH Flat	3	1	0	1	2960

Career Total	3	1	0	1	2960
111	2/03	Sand	2m110y	H NHF	HVY £2656

Total win prize-money £2657

Going: Sf: 1-1 GS: 0-1 Gd: 0-1 GF: - Fm: 0-0
Distance: 2m/2m3: 1-3 2m4-2m7: 0-0 3m+: 0-0
Track: LH: 0-1 RH: 1-1 Tight: 0-0 Gall: 0-0
Aids: Bl: 0-0 Vi: 0-0 Tstrap: 0-0
Best Rating: 112 1/03 Hayd 2m   gd-sft NHF

Winner of a bumper on only his second outing; looks quite useful; acts on heavy ground.

Patriot Games (IRE)
102   139+
9-y-o b g Polish Patriot (USA)-It s Now Or Never (High Line)
C F Swan J P McManus

Placings:04140/45/30/12P43-403161   (4475)
2002/03: 17⁴GY, 17⁰GS, 20³G, 16¹F, 16⁶GF, 20¹G,

	Starts	1st	2nd	3rd	Win & Pl
Hurdles	6	2	0	1	32087
Career Total	20	4	1	3	54059
139	4/03	Aint	2m4f	A HHdl	GD £23200
125	9/02	Punc	2m	Hdl	FRM £7407
126	5/01	Navn	2m	HHdl	GD £8911
111	2/98	Naas	2m	Hdl	Y-S £2680

Total win prize-money £42199

Going: Sf: 0-0 GS: 0-1 Gd: 1-2 GF: - Fm: 1-2
Distance: 2m/2m3: 0-0 2m4-2m7: 1-2 3m+: 0-0
Track: LH: 1-1 RH: 1-2 Tight: 1-2 Gall: 0-0
Aids: Bl: 0-0 Vi: 0-0 Tstrap: 0-0
Best Rating: 139 4/03 Aint 2m4f   good Hdl

Useful Irish handicap hurdler; recorded a fourth career win in Class A event at Aintree but finished lame; stays two and a half miles.

Pats Future
24f
4-y-o ch f King s Signet (USA)-Bedelia (Mr Fluorocarbon)
S C Burrough (P R Rodford 28/1) P R Rodford

Placings:00   (3782)
2002/03: 17⁰S, 17⁰GS,

	Starts	1st	2nd	3rd	Win & Pl
NH Flat	2	0	0	0	
Career Total	2	0	0	0	

Going: Sf: 0-1 GS: 0-1 Gd: 0-0 GF: - Fm: 0-0
Distance: 2m/2m3: 0-2 2m4-2m7: 0-0 3m+: 0-0
Track: LH: 0-0 RH: 0-0 Tight: 0-0 Gall: 0-0
Aids: Bl: 0-0 Vi: 0-0 Tstrap: 0-0
Best Rating: 24 1/03 Tntn 2m1f   soft NHF

Pauls Dream (IRE)

8-y-o ch g Deep Society-Pampered Sally (Paddy s Stream)
P Monteith A Irvine

Placings:PP-P   (1986)
2002/03: 22ᴾS,

	Starts	1st	2nd	3rd	Win & Pl
Hurdles	1	0	0	0	
Career Total	3	0	0	0	

Going: Sf: 0-1 GS: 0-0 Gd: 0-0 GF: - Fm: 0-0
Distance: 2m/2m3: 0-0 2m4-2m7: 0-1 3m+: 0-0
Track: LH: 0-0 RH: 0-0 Tight: 0-0 Gall: 0-0

Aids: Bl: 0-0 Vi: 0-0 Tstrap: 0-0
Best Rating: 0 11/02 Ayr 2m6f   soft Hdl

Pauls Legacy

7-y-o ch g Nicholas Bill-Extremity (Quayside)
J D Frost N W Lake

Placings:0   (4514)
2002/03: 22⁰GF,

	Starts	1st	2nd	3rd	Win & Pl
Hurdles	1	0	0	0	
Career Total	1	0	0	0	

Going: Sf: 0-0 GS: 0-0 Gd: 0-0 GF: - Fm: 0-1
Distance: 2m/2m3: 0-0 2m4-2m7: 0-1 3m+: 0-0
Track: LH: 0-0 RH: 0-1 Tight: 0-0 Gall: 0-0
Aids: Bl: 0-0 Vi: 0-0 Tstrap: 0-0
Best Rating: 0 4/03 Extr 2m6f110y gd-fm Hdl

Paulton
89
10-y-o b g Lugana Beach-Runcina (Runnett)
K Bishop Slabs And Lucan

Placings:P4630423/1322/2520P/000/6641/3264150-P
(0088)
2002/03: 20ᴾG,

	Starts	1st	2nd	3rd	Win & Pl
Hurdles	1	0	0	0	
Career Total	32	3	6	4	10539
89	11/01	Extr	2m1f	G(0-95)HHdl	G-F £1802
78	4/01	Extr	2m1f	G(0-95)HHdl	G-S £1932
75	5/97	Extr	2m2f	G Hdl	GD £1818

Total win prize-money £5554

Going: Sf: 0-0 GS: 0-0 Gd: 0-1 GF: - Fm: 0-0
Distance: 2m/2m3: 0-0 2m4-2m7: 0-1 3m+: 0-0
Track: LH: 0-1 RH: 0-0 Tight: 0-0 Gall: 0-0
Aids: Bl: 0-0 Vi: 0-0 Tstrap: 0-0
Best Rating: 92 11/98 Tntn 2m3f110y   good Hdl

Handicap hurdler, acts on most types of ground and is effective over two miles.

Pauntley Gofa
102(108h)   (112h)113+
7-y-o b g Afzal-Gotageton (Oats)
J L Spearing Clapham & Partners

Placings:2/260/10P1F3-4313   (0696)
2002/03: 16⁴GF, 16³GF, 17¹GF, 20³G,

	Starts	1st	2nd	3rd	Win & Pl
Hurdles	1	0	0	0	
Chases	3	1	0	2	5403
Career Total	14	3	2	3	13665
112	6/02	MRas	2m1f110yD Ch	G-F	£4309
109	11/01	Ludl	2m	D Hdl	G-F £3558
112	5/01	MRas	2m1f110yE Hdl	GD	£2914

Total win prize-money £10783

Going: Sf: 0-0 GS: 0-0 Gd: 0-1 GF: - Fm: 1-3
Distance: 2m/2m3: 1-3 2m4-2m7: 0-1 3m+: 0-0
Track: LH: 0-0 RH: 1-4 Tight: 1-2 Gall: 0-0
Aids: Bl: 0-0 Vi: 0-0 Tstrap: 0-0
Best Rating: 113 7/02 MRas 2m4f   good Ch

A big backward sort, he took time to come to himself but got off the mark on his third outing over hurdles. Scored again at Ludlow in November 2001. Best suited by two miles and a sound surface. Successful over fences in June 2002.

Pavey Ark (IRE)
96f   96f
5-y-o b g King s Ride-Splendid Run (Deep Run)
James Moffatt Mr & Mrs A G Milligan

Placings:052   (4594)
2002/03: 16⁰HY, 17⁵G, 16²G,

	Starts	1st	2nd	3rd	Win & Pl
NH Flat	3	0	1	0	544
Career Total	3	0	1	0	544

Going: Sf: 0-1 GS: 0-0 Gd: 0-2 GF: - Fm: 0-0
Distance: 2m/2m3: 0-3 2m4-2m7: 0-0 3m+: 0-0
Track: LH: 0-3 RH: 0-0 Tight: 0-1 Gall: 0-0
Aids: Bl: 0-0 Vi: 0-0 Tstrap: 0-0
Best Rating: 96 4/03 Hexm 2m110y   good NHF

Modest form in bumpers.

Pawn Broker
96   98+
6-y-o ch g Selkirk (USA)-Dime Bag (High Line)
D R C Elsworth Raymond Tooth

Placings:6   (2770)
2002/03: 16⁶HY,

	Starts	1st	2nd	3rd	Win & Pl
Hurdles	1	0	0	0	0
Career Total	1	0	0	0	0

Going: Sf: 0-1 GS: 0-0 Gd: 0-0 GF: - Fm: 0-0
Distance: 2m/2m3: 0-1 2m4-2m7: 0-0 3m+: 0-0
Track: LH: 0-1 RH: 0-0 Tight: 0-0 Gall: 0-1
Aids: Bl: 0-0 Vi: 0-0 Tstrap: 0-0
Best Rating: 98 12/02 Newb 2m110y   heavy Hdl

Paxford Jack
109(106h)   (102h)118
7-y-o ch g Alflora (IRE)-Rakajack (Rakaposhi King)
M F Harris Mrs Ruth Nelmes

Placings:3333U/40341P40-55212510P   (4472)
2002/03: 16⁵G, 21⁵G, 24²GS, 21¹G, 25²S, 24⁵S, 24¹GS, 32⁰G, 21ᴾG,

	Starts	1st	2nd	3rd	Win & Pl
Hurdles	1	0	0	0	0
Chases	8	2	2	5	46458
Career Total	22	3	2	5	51586
118	2/03	Hayd	3m	B(0-140)HCh	G-S £11557
105	12/02	Chel	2m5f	B Ch	GD £29000
98	1/02	Folk	2m1f110yD(0-115)HHdl	HVY £3286

Total win prize-money £43844

Going: Sf: 0-2 GS: 1-2 Gd: 1-5 GF: - Fm: 0-0
Distance: 2m/2m3: 0-1 2m4-2m7: 1-3 3m+: 1-5
Track: LH: 2-8 RH: 0-1 Tight: 0-3 Gall: 1-4
Aids: Bl: 0-0 Vi: 0-0 Tstrap: 0-0
Best Rating: 118 2/03 Hayd 3m   gd-sft Ch

Fair chaser; progressive; effective at three miles; suited by soft ground; jumps well.

Paxford Lady
98   70
6-y-o b m Alflora (IRE)-Rakajack (Rakaposhi King)
M F Harris Warwick Racecourse Owners Club

Placings:500PP-P   (0076)
2002/03: 19ᴾGF,

	Starts	1st	2nd	3rd	Win & Pl
Hurdles	1	0	0	0	
Career Total	6	0	0	0	0

Going: Sf: 0-0 GS: 0-0 Gd: 0-0 GF: - Fm: 0-1
Distance: 2m/2m3: 0-0 2m4-2m7: 0-1 3m+: 0-0
Track: LH: 0-0 RH: 0-1 Tight: 0-0 Gall: 0-0
Aids: Bl: 0-1 Vi: 0-0 Tstrap: 0-0
Best Rating: 70 12/01 Folk 2m1f110y heavy NHF

First worthwhile form over fences when well beaten runner-up in weak mares only handicap in soft ground at Uttoxeter in April.

Paxford Trooper

9-y-o b g Gunner B-Say Shanaz (Tickled Pink)
M F Harris M Harris

Placings:5/P0-P		(0273)
2002/03: 22PGF,

	Starts	1st	2nd	3rd	Win & Pl
Hurdles	1	0	0	0	
Career Total	4	0	0	0	0

Going: Sf: 0-0 GS: 0-0 Gd: 0-0 GF: - Fm: 0-1
Distance: 2m/2m3: 0-0 2m4-2m7: 0-1 3m+: 0-0
Track: LH: 0-1 RH: 0-0 Tight: 0-1 Gall: 0-0
Aids: Bl: 0-0 Vi: 0-0 Tstrap: 0-0
Best Rating: 87 5/98 Worc 2m gd-fm NHF

Paylander
### 102										90

7-y-o ch g Karinga Bay-Bichette (Lidhame)
G L Moore Bryan Pennick

Placings:642		(4279)
2002/03: 16⁶G, 16⁴S, 20²GF,

	Starts	1st	2nd	3rd	Win & Pl
Hurdles	3	0	1	0	674
Career Total	3	0	1	0	674

Going: Sf: 0-1 GS: 0-0 Gd: 0-1 GF: - Fm: 0-1
Distance: 2m/2m3: 0-2 2m4-2m7: 0-1 3m+: 0-0
Track: LH: 0-2 RH: 0-0 Tight: 0-3 Gall: 0-0
Aids: Bl: 0-0 Vi: 0-0 Tstrap: 0-0
Best Rating: 90 3/03 Font 2m4f gd-fm Hdl

Lightly-raced hurdler; has shown form in the lowest grade; acts on decent ground; stays two and a half miles.

Paymaster (NZ)
### 102(100h)					(103h)103

8-y-o ch g Norman Pentaquad (USA)-Tivy (NZ) (Noble Bijou (USA))
Miss H C Knight A Auer J Collins And J Eddis

Placings:3155-2PF		(1690)
2002/03: 20²GF, 16²GF, 20²G,

	Starts	1st	2nd	3rd	Win & Pl
Chases	3	0	1	0	916
Career Total	7	1	1	2	5552
103 11/01 Extr	2m3f	D Hdl		G-F	£4075
			Total win prize-money £4076		

Going: Sf: 0-0 GS: 0-0 Gd: 0-1 GF: - Fm: 0-2
Distance: 2m/2m3: 0-1 2m4-2m7: 0-2 3m+: 0-2
Track: LH: 0-1 RH: 0-2 Tight: 0-0 Gall: 0-2
Aids: Bl: 0-0 Vi: 0-0 Tstrap: 0-2

Best Rating: 103 6/02 Hntg 2m4f110y gd-fm Ch

A New Zealand import, he confirmed the promise shown on his hurdling debut in October with a win a month later in a novices hurdle at Exeter. Has struggled over fences; suited to at least two miles three furlongs on a sound surface.

Paynestown Lad (IRE)
### 98										86

7-y-o b g Bravefoot-Athy Lady (Welsh Captain)
Miss C J E Caroe Miss C J E Caroe

Placings:006P6U1		(4634)
2002/03: 16⁰G, 16⁰GS, 16⁶HY, 16⁰HY, 20⁶GF, 22ᵁGF, 21¹GF,

	Starts	1st	2nd	3rd	Win & Pl
Hurdles	7	1	0	0	3484
Career Total	7	1	0	0	3484
86 4/03 Plum	2m5f	E Hdl		G-F	£3484
			Total win prize-money £3484		

Going: Sf: 0-2 GS: 0-1 Gd: 0-1 GF: - Fm: 1-3
Distance: 2m/2m3: 0-4 2m4-2m7: 1-3 3m+: 0-0
Track: LH: 1-3 RH: 0-4 Tight: 1-3 Gall: 0-1
Aids: Bl: 0-0 Vi: 0-0 Tstrap: 0-0
Best Rating: 86 4/03 Plum 2m5f gd-fm Hdl

Plating-class hurdler; first worthwhile form when slightly fortunate winner of a novice hurdle at Plumpton in April 2003; stays two miles five; effective on good to firm.

Pc's Eurocruiser (IRE)
### 98										73

7-y-o b g Fayruz-Kuwait Night (Morston (FR))
A Crook Andy Crook Racing Jumps Partnership

Placings:0OP/055261/P00033-43		(0349)
2002/03: 16⁴GF, 16³G,

	Starts	1st	2nd	3rd	Win & Pl
Hurdles	2	0	0	1	282
Career Total	17	1	1	3	4006
82 9/00 MRas	2m1f110yF(0-100)HHdl		G-F	£2747
			Total win prize-money £2748		

Going: Sf: 0-0 GS: 0-0 Gd: 0-1 GF: - Fm: 0-1
Distance: 2m/2m3: 0-2 2m4-2m7: 0-0 3m+: 0-0
Track: LH: 0-1 RH: 0-1 Tight: 0-1 Gall: 0-0
Aids: Bl: 0-0 Vi: 0-0 Tstrap: 0-0
Best Rating: 86 2/02 Fknm 2m gd-sft Hdl

Moderate hurdler. Acts on a sound surface and is effective over two miles.

Peacemaker (IRE)
### 101										66

11-y-o br g Strong Gale-Gamonda (Gala Performance (USA))
J R Cornwall J R Cornwall

Placings:00P3/404/040P/P22035/121222F5F4-005P3		(4690)

2002/03: 20⁰GS, 24⁰G, 21⁵G, 24⁵PG, 25³G,

	Starts	1st	2nd	3rd	Win & Pl
Chases	5	0	0	1	532
Career Total	32	2	6	3	18753
86 7/01 Strf	2m5f110yE(0-105)HCh	GD	£3328		
86 6/01 Fknm	2m5f110yF(0-100)HCh	G-F	£3562		
			Total win prize-money £6891		

Going: Sf: 0-0 GS: 0-1 Gd: 0-4 GF: - Fm: 0-0
Distance: 2m/2m3: 0-0 2m4-2m7: 0-2 3m+: 0-3

Track: LH: 0-2 RH: 0-3 Tight: 0-3 Gall: 0-1
Aids: Bl: 0-0 Vi: 0-0 Tstrap: 0-0
Best Rating: 98 9/01 Strf 3m gd-fm Ch

Peacock Theatre
### 102										36

5-y-o b g Red Rainbow-Fine Art (IRE) (Tate Gallery (USA))
Edward C Sexton (A Streeter 30/6) Leo Fitzpatrick

Placings:0104050-36P000		(2740a)
2002/03: 20³G, 20⁶G, 24⁷S, 22⁰GF, 16⁰YS, 20⁰S,

	Starts	1st	2nd	3rd	Win & Pl
Hurdles	6	0	0	1	306
Career Total	13	1	0	1	1867
83 9/01 MRas	2m1f110yG Hdl		SFT	£1561
			Total win prize-money £1561		

Going: Sf: 0-2 GS: 0-0 Gd: 0-2 GF: - Fm: 0-1
Distance: 2m/2m3: 0-1 2m4-2m7: 0-4 3m+: 0-1
Track: LH: 0-4 RH: 0-0 Tight: 0-0 Gall: 0-0
Aids: Bl: 0-4 Vi: 0-0 Tstrap: 0-0
Best Rating: 83 5/02 Uttx 2m4f110y good Hdl

Pealings (IRE)
### 95										112

11-y-o gr g Wood Chanter-Ten-Cents (Taste Of Honey)
Ferdy Murphy Geoff Hubbard Racing

Placings:0U644/031135510/4P2122010/2R44025/0065/2P1144024-45		(1622)
2002/03: 21⁴G, 24⁵GS,

	Starts	1st	2nd	3rd	Win & Pl
Chases	2	0	0	0	521
Career Total	45	7	7	2	48530
112 1/02 Plum	3m2f	E Ch	HVY	£3262	
112 1/02 Fknm	3m110y D Ch		SFT	£4161	
125 3/99 Ling	2m3f110yC(0-135)HHdl	G-S	£7262		
126 12/98 Uttx	2m4f110yB(0-145)HHdl	SFT	£5094		
111 2/98 Asct	2m4f E(0-120)HHdl	GD	£3680		
106 10/97 Hntg	2m4f110yE Hdl	G-F	£2530		
104 10/97 Hntg	2m4f110yE Hdl	GD	£2372		
			Total win prize-money £28365		

Going: Sf: 0-0 GS: 0-1 Gd: 0-1 GF: - Fm: 0-0
Distance: 2m/2m3: 0-0 2m4-2m7: 0-1 3m+: 0-1
Track: LH: 0-2 RH: 0-0 Tight: 0-1 Gall: 0-0
Aids: Bl: 0-0 Vi: 0-0 Tstrap: 0-0
Best Rating: 129 2/00 Asct 2m4f soft Hdl

A one-time decent handicap hurdler, he won two ordinary novices chases in January 2002. Stays three miles, acts in soft ground.

Pearliwhirl
### 91f										67f

4-y-o b f Alflora (IRE)-Pearlossa (Teenoso (USA))
W Jenks W Jenks

Placings:0		(4404)
2002/03: 16⁰GF,

	Starts	1st	2nd	3rd	Win & Pl
NH Flat	1	0	0	0	
Career Total	1	0	0	0	

Going: Sf: 0-0 GS: 0-0 Gd: 0-0 GF: - Fm: 0-0
Distance: 2m/2m3: 0-1 2m4-2m7: 0-0 3m+: 0-0
Track: LH: 0-1 RH: 0-0 Tight: 0-0 Gall: 0-0
Aids: Bl: 0-0 Vi: 0-0 Tstrap: 0-0
Best Rating: 67 3/03 Hayd 2m gd-fm NHF

Showed some ability on bumper debut.

Peartree House (IRE)
101   112

9-y-o b g Simply Majestic (USA)-Fashion Front (Habitat)
D W Chapman (Mrs M Reveley 25/11) J M Chapman

Placings:3561-15U0   (2131)
2002/03: 16¹G, 16⁵GF, 16ᵁGS, 16⁹G,

	Starts	1st	2nd	3rd	Win & Pl
Hurdles	4	1	0	0	3696
Career Total	8	2	0	1	7256
112 8/02	Prth	2m110y G Hdl		GD	£3696
112 4/02	Plum	2m	E Hdl	G-F	£3167

Total win prize-money £6864

Going:	Sf: 0-0 GS: 0-1 Gd: 1-2 GF: - Fm: 0-1
Distance:	2m/2m3: 1-4 2m4-2m7: 0-0 3m+: 0-0
Track:	LH: 0-1 RH: 1-3 Tight: 0-0 Gall: 0-0
Aids:	Bl: 0-0 Vi: 0-0 Tstrap: 0-0
Best Rating:	112 8/02 Prth 2m110y good Hdl

A useful handicapper on the Flat in his prime, he is not the force of old but has proved by forcing tactics in weak company over hurdles. Ran out an easy winner of a Perth seller in August.

Peasedown Tofana
99   76

10-y-o b m Teenoso (USA)-Hatherley (Deep Run)
R H Alner Sir Richard Sutton

Placings:55435/P/P-2P0   (1555)
2002/03: 25⁵G, 23²G, 23⁹GF, 25⁰G,

	Starts	1st	2nd	3rd	Win & Pl
Hurdles	1	0	0	0	0
Chases	3	0	1	0	982
Career Total	10	0	1	1	1329

Going:	Sf: 0-0 GS: 0-0 Gd: 0-3 GF: - Fm: 0-1
Distance:	2m/2m3: 0-0 2m4-2m7: 0-0 3m+: 0-4
Track:	LH: 0-2 RH: 0-1 Tight: 0-0 Gall: 0-0
Aids:	Bl: 0-0 Vi: 0-0 Tstrap: 0-0
Best Rating:	83 8/98 NAbb 2m1f gd-fm NHF

Winning pointer, well beaten when runner-up in a novice chase in May 2002.

Pebble Moon
(102h)   (92h)100

7-y-o gr g Efisio-Jazz (Sharrood (USA))
Miss Lucinda V Russell J D I Bell

Placings:0411F3/0054/2F0P40UF01P-P   (0022)
2002/03: 20ᴾG,

	Starts	1st	2nd	3rd	Win & Pl
Chases	1	0	0	0	0
Career Total	22	3	1	1	11725
74 3/02	Ayr	2m4f	E Ch	HVY	£3840
97 1/00	Font	2m6f110yF(0-110)HHdl		GD	£2170
94 1/00	Plum	2m	D Hdl	HVY	£3545

Total win prize-money £9556

Going:	Sf: 0-0 GS: 0-0 Gd: 0-1 GF: - Fm: 0-0
Distance:	2m/2m3: 0-0 2m4-2m7: 0-1 3m+: 0-0
Track:	LH: 0-1 RH: 0-0 Tight: 0-0 Gall: 0-0
Aids:	Bl: 0-0 Vi: 0-1 Tstrap: 0-0
Best Rating:	100 5/01 Extr 2m3f110y gd-sft Ch

Success came early in his hurdle career with a double in very different conditions. He then lost his way and dropped right down the weights until he was able to bring home the goods in a weak event in March 2002.

Peccadillo (IRE)
113   135

9-y-o br g Un Desperado (FR)-First Mistake (Posse (USA))
R H Alner Dwight Makins

Placings:60/63212/315/2133143F-11430P15   (4792)
2002/03: 21¹G, 20¹GF, 21⁴G, 20³G, 20⁰G, 21ᴾS, 19¹G, 20⁵G,

	Starts	1st	2nd	3rd	Win & Pl
Chases	8	3	0	1	28210
Career Total	26	7	3	6	51944
135 4/03	Asct	2m3f110yD(0-125)HCh		GD	£10341
134 9/02	Hntg	2m4f110yC(0-135)HCh		G-F	£7995
133 9/02	Uttx	2m5f	D(0-125)HCh	GD	£5411
135 12/01	Winc	2m5f	F(0-115)HCh	G-F	£4075
120 12/01	Winc	2m5f	F(0-110)HCh	G-F	£4173
115 12/00	Winc	2m	E(0-115)HCh	G-S	£4290
99 3/00	Folk	2m	F(0-100)HCh	G-F	£2422

Total win prize-money £38710

Going:	Sf: 0-1 GS: 0-0 Gd: 2-6 GF: - Fm: 1-1
Distance:	2m/2m3: 0-0 2m4-2m7: 3-8 3m+: 0-0
Track:	LH: 1-1 RH: 2-7 Tight: 0-0 Gall: 1-1
Aids:	Bl: 0-0 Vi: 0-0 Tstrap: 0-0
Best Rating:	135 4/03 Asct 2m3f110y good Ch

Useful handicap chaser, he is at his best when able to establish an uncontested lead; jumps well, acts on fast ground and goes particularly well at Wincanton.

Peejay Hobbs
104   95+

5-y-o ch g Alhijaz-Hicklam Millie (Absalom)
C J Gray (P G Murphy 10/6) S C Botham

Placings:3430F-0251216   (1113)
2002/03: 21ᶠGS, 22⁰G, 22²G, 16⁵GF, 20¹G, 20²GF, 22¹GF, 24⁶GF,

	Starts	1st	2nd	3rd	Win & Pl
Hurdles	8	2	2	0	5487
Career Total	12	2	2	2	6095
95 8/02	NAbb	2m6f	F Hdl	G-F	£2226
95 7/02	Wolv	2m4f110yG Hdl		GD	£1937

Total win prize-money £4164

Going:	Sf: 0-0 GS: 0-1 Gd: 1-3 GF: - Fm: 1-4
Distance:	2m/2m3: 0-1 2m4-2m7: 2-6 3m+: 0-1
Track:	LH: 2-6 RH: 0-2 Tight: 2-3 Gall: 0-0
Aids:	Bl: 0-0 Vi: 0-0 Tstrap: 0-0
Best Rating:	95 8/02 NAbb 2m6f gd-fm Hdl

Modest hurdler, successful in selling and claiming company in the summer of 2002. Stays two and three-quarter miles.

Peewit Bridge

11-y-o ch g Gildoran-Electric Panic (Chukaroo)
S A Brookshaw The Gilbert Partnership

Placings:20F365/66P4342312/134065/PPP   (0442)
2002/03: 20ᴾF, 25ᴾG, 21ᴾS,

	Starts	1st	2nd	3rd	Win & Pl
Chases	3	0	0	0	
Career Total	25	2	3	4	12366
109 11/00	Leic	2m4f110yF(0-100)HCh		G-S	£2899
101 3/00	Leic	2m4f110yE(0-115)HCh		G-S	£3120

Total win prize-money £6019

Going:	Sf: 0-1 GS: 0-0 Gd: 0-1 GF: - Fm: 0-1
Distance:	2m/2m3: 0-0 2m4-2m7: 0-2 3m+: 0-1
Track:	LH: 0-2 RH: 0-1 Tight: 0-0 Gall: 0-0
Aids:	Bl: 0-0 Vi: 0-0 Tstrap: 0-0
Best Rating:	109 11/00 Leic 2m4f110y gd-sft Ch

Peeyoutwo
95   70

8-y-o b g Golden Heights-Nyika (Town And Country)
Mrs D A Hamer Power Units (1953) Ltd

Placings:100P-0   (3780)
2002/03: 22⁰GS,

	Starts	1st	2nd	3rd	Win & Pl
Hurdles	1	0	0	0	
Career Total	5	1	0	0	2170
91 8/01	NAbb	2m1f	H NHF	G-F	£2170

Total win prize-money £2170

Going:	Sf: 0-0 GS: 0-1 Gd: 0-0 GF: - Fm: 0-0
Distance:	2m/2m3: 0-0 2m4-2m7: 0-1 3m+: 0-0
Track:	LH: 0-0 RH: 0-1 Tight: 0-0 Gall: 0-0
Aids:	Bl: 0-0 Vi: 0-0 Tstrap: 0-0
Best Rating:	97 10/01 Chel 2m110y good NHF

Lightly-raced since winning a Newton Abbot bumper on debut August 2001; has given the impression he fails to stay 2m 4f over hurdles.

Peggy Hacket (IRE)
84   56

6-y-o b m Alflora (IRE)-Radical Lady (Radical)
N B Mason N B Mason

Placings:400P   (3265)
2002/03: 16⁴HY, 20⁰S, 20⁰GS, 19ᴾGS,

	Starts	1st	2nd	3rd	Win & Pl
NH Flat	1	0	0	0	0
Hurdles	3	0	0	0	0
Career Total	4	0	0	0	0

Going:	Sf: 0-2 GS: 0-2 Gd: 0-0 GF: - Fm: 0-0
Distance:	2m/2m3: 0-1 2m4-2m7: 0-3 3m+: 0-0
Track:	LH: 0-3 RH: 0-1 Tight: 0-0 Gall: 0-1
Aids:	Bl: 0-0 Vi: 0-0 Tstrap: 0-0
Best Rating:	65 11/02 Hexm 2m110y heavy NHF

Peggy Sioux (IRE)
92   75

6-y-o b m Little Bighorn-Gayable (Gay Fandango (USA))
J I A Charlton John Hogg

Placings:300-25   (2556)
2002/03: 16²HY, 20⁵GF,

	Starts	1st	2nd	3rd	Win & Pl
NH Flat	1	0	1	0	502
Hurdles	1	0	0	0	0
Career Total	5	0	1	1	834

Going:	Sf: 0-1 GS: 0-0 Gd: 0-1 GF: - Fm: 0-1
Distance:	2m/2m3: 0-1 2m4-2m7: 0-1 3m+: 0-0
Track:	LH: 0-1 RH: 0-1 Tight: 0-1 Gall: 0-0
Aids:	Bl: 0-0 Vi: 0-0 Tstrap: 0-0
Best Rating:	93 11/02 Hexm 2m110y heavy NHF

Promising efforts in bumpers.

Peggy's Prince
93f   88f

5-y-o b g Morpeth-Prudent Peggy (Kambalda)
J D Frost Mrs J McCormack

Placings:3   (4601)
2002/03: 17³GF,

	Starts	1st	2nd	3rd	Win & Pl
NH Flat	1	0	0	1	466

Career Total	1	0	0	1	466

Going: Sf: 0-0 GS: 0-0 Gd: 0-0 GF: - Fm: 0-1
Distance: 2m/2m3: 0-1 2m4-2m7: 0-0 3m+: 0-0
Track: LH: 0-0 RH: 0-1 Tight: 0-0 Gall: 0-0
Aids: Bl: 0-0 Vi: 0-0 Tstrap: 0-0
Best Rating: 88 4/03 Extr 2m1f gd-fm NHF

Out of a mare who won over three miles over fences; modest third on bumper debut.

Peggys Delight
94   77

8-y-o ch m Minster Son-Chasers Bar (Oats)
J R Turner J E Swiers

Placings:00/000P5/00-0 (0331)
2002/03: 20^0G,

	Starts	1st	2nd	3rd	Win & Pl
Hurdles	1	0	0	0	0
Career Total	10	0	0	0	0

Going: Sf: 0-0 GS: 0-0 Gd: 0-1 GF: - Fm: 0-0
Distance: 2m/2m3: 0-0 2m4-2m7: 0-1 3m+: 0-0
Track: LH: 0-1 RH: 0-0 Tight: 0-0 Gall: 0-0
Aids: Bl: 0-0 Vi: 0-0 Tstrap: 0-1
Best Rating: 80 5/02 Weth 2m4f110y good Hdl

Pego
58f

5-y-o b m Syrtos-Romantic Melody (Battle Hymn)
G F Bridgwater D Aymes

Placings:00-0 (0686)
2002/03: 16^0GF,

	Starts	1st	2nd	3rd	Win & Pl
NH Flat	1	0	0	0	
Career Total	3	0	0	0	

Going: Sf: 0-0 GS: 0-0 Gd: 0-0 GF: - Fm: 0-1
Distance: 2m/2m3: 0-1 2m4-2m7: 0-0 3m+: 0-0
Track: LH: 0-0 RH: 0-0 Tight: 0-0 Gall: 0-0
Aids: Bl: 0-0 Vi: 0-0 Tstrap: 0-0
Best Rating: 58 7/02 Strf 2m110y gd-fm NHF

Pele Mele (FR)
84   82

8-y-o b g Tel Quel (FR)-Star System (FR) (Northern Treat (USA))
Miss Venetia Williams Cheltenham Racing Ltd

Placings:00-U00 (2586)
2002/03: 17^0US, 16^0S, 17^0GS,

	Starts	1st	2nd	3rd	Win & Pl
Hurdles	3	0	0	0	
Career Total	5	0	0	0	

Going: Sf: 0-2 GS: 0-1 Gd: 0-0 GF: - Fm: 0-0
Distance: 2m/2m3: 0-3 2m4-2m7: 0-0 3m+: 0-0
Track: LH: 0-2 RH: 0-1 Tight: 0-2 Gall: 0-0
Aids: Bl: 0-0 Vi: 0-0 Tstrap: 0-0
Best Rating: 82 3/02 Winc 2m good Hdl

Pele Mele

7-y-o b/br g Milieu-Hiltie Skiltie (Liberated)

A M Crow Mrs H G Peplinski

Placings:60-0PP0P (1735)
2002/03: 20^0G, 16^0GF, 20^0G, 24^0S, 16^PS,

	Starts	1st	2nd	3rd	Win & Pl
Hurdles	4	0	0	0	0
Chases	1	0	0	0	0
Career Total	7	0	0	0	0

Going: Sf: 0-2 GS: 0-0 Gd: 0-2 GF: - Fm: 0-1
Distance: 2m/2m3: 0-2 2m4-2m7: 0-2 3m+: 0-1
Track: LH: 0-3 RH: 0-2 Tight: 0-1 Gall: 0-0
Aids: Bl: 0-0 Vi: 0-0 Tstrap: 0-1
Best Rating: 85 4/02 Carl 2m1f good NHF

Pelota Vasca

7-y-o b m Relief Pitcher-Valls D Andorra (Free State)
M R Bosley J P Carrington

Placings:60/00P (0777)
2002/03: 16^0G, 17^0G, 20^PGF,

	Starts	1st	2nd	3rd	Win & Pl
NH Flat	2	0	0	0	0
Hurdles	1	0	0	0	0
Career Total	5	0	0	0	0

Going: Sf: 0-0 GS: 0-0 Gd: 0-2 GF: - Fm: 0-1
Distance: 2m/2m3: 0-2 2m4-2m7: 0-1 3m+: 0-0
Track: LH: 0-3 RH: 0-0 Tight: 0-1 Gall: 0-0
Aids: Bl: 0-0 Vi: 0-0 Tstrap: 0-0
Best Rating: 62 7/00 Worc 2m good NHF

Pen-Almozon
(80h)   (62h)

7-y-o ch h Almoojid-Cornish Mona Lisa (Damsire Unregistered)
N J Hawke P Mann

Placings:0000F04 (4253)
2002/03: 17^0HY, 19^0GS, 22^0HY, 24^0HY, 25^FGS, 24^0GS, 23^4G,

	Starts	1st	2nd	3rd	Win & Pl
NH Flat	1	0	0	0	0
Hurdles	4	0	0	0	0
Chases	2	0	0	0	458
Career Total	7	0	0	0	458

Going: Sf: 0-3 GS: 0-3 Gd: 0-1 GF: - Fm: 0-0
Distance: 2m/2m3: 0-2 2m4-2m7: 0-1 3m+: 0-4
Track: LH: 0-3 RH: 0-0 Tight: 0-2 Gall: 0-0
Aids: Bl: 0-0 Vi: 0-0 Tstrap: 0-0
Best Rating: 74 11/02 NAbb 2m1f heavy NHF

Pendant
72(103h)   7

8-y-o b g Warning-Emerald (USA) (El Gran Senor (USA))
Mrs J Candlish Friends R Four

Placings:3P104/00/6PP-P3 (4705)
2002/03: 20^0GF, 21^3G,

	Starts	1st	2nd	3rd	Win & Pl
Hurdles	1	0	0	0	0
Chases	1	0	0	1	627
Career Total	12	1	0	1	3355
96	1/00 Catt	2m3f	E Hdl	GD	£2362

Total win prize-money £2362

Going: Sf: 0-0 GS: 0-0 Gd: 0-1 GF: - Fm: 0-1
Distance: 2m/2m3: 0-0 2m4-2m7: 0-2 3m+: 0-0
Track: LH: 0-2 RH: 0-0 Tight: 0-1 Gall: 0-1
Aids: Bl: 0-0 Vi: 0-0 Tstrap: 0-1
Best Rating: 96 4/00 MRas 2m5f110y gd-fm Hdl

Winner on the flat and over hurdles in the past but of little account nowadays.

Pendle Hill
101   112

8-y-o gr g Roscoe Blake-Pendle Princess (Broxted)
P Beaumont N W A Bannister

Placings:4003/665002610/5224640 (4773)
2002/03: 25^5S, 20^2HY, 20^2S, 24^4G, 21^6GS, 20^4GS, 20^0G,

	Starts	1st	2nd	3rd	Win & Pl
Chases	7	0	2	0	4148
Career Total	20	1	3	1	8013
98	2/01 Newc	2m4f	E Hdl	HVY	£2555

Total win prize-money £2555

Going: Sf: 0-3 GS: 0-2 Gd: 0-2 GF: - Fm: 0-0
Distance: 2m/2m3: 0-0 2m4-2m7: 0-5 3m+: 0-2
Track: LH: 0-5 RH: 0-2 Tight: 0-1 Gall: 0-4
Aids: Bl: 0-0 Vi: 0-0 Tstrap: 0-0
Best Rating: 112 11/02 Carl 2m4f heavy Ch

Modest hurdler chaser; successful over hurdles over two and a half miles; has shown ability over fences at around the same distance; goes well in the mud.

Pendragon

11-y-o b g Bold Fox-Celtic Royale (Celtic Cone)
Mrs Sarah Faulks Mrs Sarah Faulks

Placings:26-F (0031)
2002/03: 33^FGF,

	Starts	1st	2nd	3rd	Win & Pl
Chases	1	0	0	0	
Career Total	3	0	1	0	621

Going: Sf: 0-0 GS: 0-0 Gd: 0-0 GF: - Fm: 0-1
Distance: 2m/2m3: 0-0 2m4-2m7: 0-0 3m+: 0-1
Track: LH: 0-1 RH: 0-0 Tight: 0-0 Gall: 0-1
Aids: Bl: 0-0 Vi: 0-0 Tstrap: 0-0
Best Rating: 86 3/02 Towc 3m1f soft Ch

Modest pointer/hunter chaser, suited by good ground or softer.

Penge Point (IRE)
92   73

6-y-o br g Lord Americo-Broken Boots (IRE) (King s Ride)
A King Lady Harris

Placings:2000 (3779)
2002/03: 16^2G, 16^0HY, 19^0G, 19^0GS,

	Starts	1st	2nd	3rd	Win & Pl
NH Flat	2	0	1	0	684
Hurdles	2	0	0	0	
Career Total	4	0	1	0	684

Going: Sf: 0-1 GS: 0-1 Gd: 0-2 GF: - Fm: 0-0
Distance: 2m/2m3: 0-4 2m4-2m7: 0-0 3m+: 0-0
Track: LH: 0-2 RH: 0-2 Tight: 0-0 Gall: 0-1
Aids: Bl: 0-0 Vi: 0-0 Tstrap: 0-0
Best Rating: 101 11/02 Winc 2m good NHF

Stayed on for second on his debut.

Penguin Bay

95(77c)   (55c)**84**
7-y-o b g Rock Hopper-Corn Lily (Aragon)
N Wilson (Mrs M Reveley 9/8) Mrs Susan McDonald

Placings:330/3030-50604200   (4711)
2002/03: 20⁵GS, 16⁹GF, 21⁶GF, 16⁹G, 17⁴GF, 16²F, 16⁹G, 16⁹GF,

	Starts	1st	2nd	3rd	Win & Pl
Hurdles	7	0	1	0	868
Chases	1	0	0	0	0
Career Total	15	0	1	4	2100

Going:	Sf: 0-0 GS: 0-1 Gd: 0-2 GF: - Fm: 0-5
Distance:	2m/2m3: 0-6 2m4-2m7: 0-2 3m+: 0-0
Track:	LH: 0-7 RH: 0-1 Tight: 0-2 Gall: 0-0
Aids:	Bl: 0-4 Vi: 0-0 Tstrap: 0-0
Best Rating:	107 5/00 Hntg 2m110y gd-sft NHF

Placed form in very modest company over hurdles.

Penneless Dancer

69   **36**
4-y-o b g Pennekamp (USA)-Villella (Sadler s Wells (USA))
M E Sowersby (M Blanshard 23/8) Neville Saunders

Placings:00   (2304)
2002/03: 16⁹G, 16⁹GS,

	Starts	1st	2nd	3rd	Win & Pl
Hurdles	2	0	0	0	
Career Total	2	0	0	0	

Going:	Sf: 0-0 GS: 0-1 Gd: 0-1 GF: - Fm: 0-0
Distance:	2m/2m3: 0-2 2m4-2m7: 0-0 3m+: 0-0
Track:	LH: 0-2 RH: 0-0 Tight: 0-2 Gall: 0-0
Aids:	Bl: 0-0 Vi: 0-0 Tstrap: 0-0
Best Rating:	36 11/02 Catt 2m good Hdl

Penninoir

(76h)   (73h)
7-y-o br m Royal Fountain-The Pride Of Pokey (Uncle
Pokey)
Mrs S C Bradburne R H Black

Placings:00P0P50-FP5PP   (3770)
2002/03: 17⁶G, 21⁸PS, 24⁵G, 16⁹P, 25⁸GS,

	Starts	1st	2nd	3rd	Win & Pl
Chases	5	0	0	0	0
Career Total	12	0	0	0	0

Going:	Sf: 0-1 GS: 0-1 Gd: 0-3 GF: - Fm: 0-0
Distance:	2m/2m3: 0-2 2m4-2m7: 0-1 3m+: 0-2
Track:	LH: 0-3 RH: 0-2 Tight: 0-3 Gall: 0-0
Aids:	Bl: 0-0 Vi: 0-2 Tstrap: 0-0
Best Rating:	73 3/02 Kels 2m6f110y soft Hdl

Modest hurdler yet to prove her stamina.

Penny Pass (IRE)

4-y-o b g Pennekamp (USA)-Belle Etoile (FR) (Lead On
Time (USA))
M C Pipe (Sir Mark Prescott 5/9) John Brown & Megan
Dennis

Placings:PP   (3148)
2002/03: 16⁶G, 16⁸HY,

	Starts	1st	2nd	3rd	Win & Pl
Hurdles	2	0	0	0	

Career Total   2   0   0   0

Going:	Sf: 0-1 GS: 0-0 Gd: 0-1 GF: - Fm: 0-0
Distance:	2m/2m3: 0-2 2m4-2m7: 0-0 3m+: 0-0
Track:	LH: 0-2 RH: 0-0 Tight: 0-0 Gall: 0-0
Aids:	Bl: 0-0 Vi: 0-0 Tstrap: 0-0
Best Rating:	0 1/03 Chep 2m110y heavy Hdl

Penny Pictures (IRE)

106   **127+**
4-y-o b c Theatrical-Copper Creek (Habitat)
M C Pipe (J G Given 15/8) Terry Neill

Placings:311   (4539)
2002/03: 16³GS, 17¹S, 16¹G,

	Starts	1st	2nd	3rd	Win & Pl
Hurdles	3	2	0	1	8450
Career Total	3	2	0	1	8450
106 4/03	Ludl	2m	E Hdl	GD	£4186
127 3/03	Bang	2m1f	E Hdl	SFT	£3493
			Total win prize-money £7680		

Going:	Sf: 1-1 GS: 0-1 Gd: 1-1 GF: - Fm: 0-0
Distance:	2m/2m3: 2-3 2m4-2m7: 0-0 3m+: 0-0
Track:	LH: 1-1 RH: 1-2 Tight: 1-1 Gall: 0-0
Aids:	Bl: 0-0 Vi: 0-0 Tstrap: 0-0
Best Rating:	127 3/03 Bang 2m1f soft Hdl

Fair handicapper on the Flat; ran well on hurdles debut and
easy winner of next two starts; keen sort; suited by good
ground; effective over two miles; will need to learn to settle if
he is going to reach his full potential over hurdles.

Pennyago (IRE)

80f   **64f**
6-y-o b g Good Thyne (USA)-Boro Penny (Normandy)
Mrs H Dalton Trevor Hemmings

Placings:0   (3412)
2002/03: 16⁹GS,

	Starts	1st	2nd	3rd	Win & Pl
NH Flat	1	0	0	0	
Career Total	1	0	0	0	

Going:	Sf: 0-0 GS: 0-1 Gd: 0-0 GF: - Fm: 0-0
Distance:	2m/2m3: 0-1 2m4-2m7: 0-0 3m+: 0-0
Track:	LH: 0-1 RH: 0-0 Tight: 0-0 Gall: 0-0
Aids:	Bl: 0-0 Vi: 0-0 Tstrap: 0-0
Best Rating:	65 2/03 Weth 2m gd-sft NHF

Pennyahei

12-y-o b m Malaspina-Pennyazena (Pamroy)
S A Brookshaw Miss H Brookshaw

Placings:P/UO6P065P4/2203220530/5P0F2041U/4466026
0/P-5   (4026)
2002/03: 25⁵S,

	Starts	1st	2nd	3rd	Win & Pl
Chases	1	0	0	0	0
Career Total	39	6	1	2	10307
92 3/00	Uttx	3m2f	F(0-110)HCh	GD	£3835
			Total win prize-money £3835		

Going:	Sf: 0-1 GS: 0-0 Gd: 0-0 GF: - Fm: 0-0
Distance:	2m/2m3: 0-0 2m4-2m7: 0-0 3m+: 0-1
Track:	LH: 0-0 RH: 0-1 Tight: 0-0 Gall: 0-0

Aids:	Bl: 0-0 Vi: 0-0 Tstrap: 0-0
Best Rating:	92 5/00 Hrfd 3m1f110y good Ch

Winning chaser/decent pointer.

Pennys From Heaven

104   **89**
9-y-o gr g Generous (IRE)-Heavenly Cause (USA) (Grey
Dawn Ii)
Miss T M Ide Miss Tracey Ide

Placings:05/040/023-53430326   (0913)
2002/03: 17⁵G, 17⁹GS, 17⁴G, 17³G, 20⁰GF, 19³G, 17²GF, 19⁶GS,

	Starts	1st	2nd	3rd	Win & Pl
Hurdles	8	0	1	3	2140
Career Total	16	0	2	4	3623

Going:	Sf: 0-0 GS: 0-2 Gd: 0-4 GF: - Fm: 0-2
Distance:	2m/2m3: 0-5 2m4-2m7: 0-3 3m+: 0-0
Track:	LH: 0-4 RH: 0-4 Tight: 0-5 Gall: 0-0
Aids:	Bl: 0-0 Vi: 0-0 Tstrap: 0-0
Best Rating:	95 3/98 Kels 2m110y good Hdl

Modest form in a sporadic hurdling career. Showed
improved form when twice placed in novice hurdles in April
2002. Should be suited by two and a half miles.

Penthouse Minstrel

9-y-o b/br g Seven Hearts-Pantemeron (Heres)
Miss N Stephens (C J Gray 1/6) Bob Andrews

Placings:542P-PP   (3479)
2002/03: 22⁸P, 25⁸GS,

	Starts	1st	2nd	3rd	Win & Pl
Hurdles	1	0	0	0	0
Chases	1	0	0	0	0
Career Total	6	0	1	0	691

Going:	Sf: 0-0 GS: 0-1 Gd: 0-0 GF: - Fm: 0-1
Distance:	2m/2m3: 0-0 2m4-2m7: 0-1 3m+: 0-1
Track:	LH: 0-1 RH: 0-1 Tight: 0-1 Gall: 0-0
Aids:	Bl: 0-0 Vi: 0-0 Tstrap: 0-0
Best Rating:	96 5/01 Winc 2m6f gd-fm Hdl

Won maiden open point April 2003; twice tapped for speed
in the space of three days in 2m 4f hunter chases the following month.

Pentland Squire

87   **55**
12-y-o b g Belfort (FR)-Sparkler Superb (Grisaille)
Miss C J E Caroe Miss C J E Caroe

Placings:00/032355/12222122/05321/P304/F4-005P
                                                                  (4143)
2002/03: 16⁰GF, 16⁰G, 16⁵GF, 16⁸G,

	Starts	1st	2nd	3rd	Win & Pl
Hurdles	4	0	0	0	0
Career Total	31	3	8	4	14164
113 4/00	Hexm	2m	E(0-115)HHdl	GD	£2688
106 12/97	Sedg	2m1f	E(0-100)HHdl	GD	£2346
98 9/97	Carl	2m1f	F(0-100)HHdl	G-F	£2276
			Total win prize-money £7310		

Going:	Sf: 0-1 GS: 0-0 Gd: 0-2 GF: - Fm: 0-1
Distance:	2m/2m3: 0-4 2m4-2m7: 0-0 3m+: 0-0
Track:	LH: 0-3 RH: 0-1 Tight: 0-1 Gall: 0-0
Aids:	Bl: 0-0 Vi: 0-0 Tstrap: 0-0

Career Total   2   0   0   0

Best Rating: 115 3/00 Weth 2m   gd-sft Hdl

Pepe Galvez (SWE)
105   119

6-y-o br g Mango Express-Mango Sampaquita (SWE) (Colombian Friend (USA))
Mrs L C Taylor Mrs D Barnett

Placings:213215   (4608)
2002/03: 16²GF, 17¹GS, 17³GS, 16²G, 16¹G, 17⁵G,

	Starts	1st	2nd	3rd	Win & Pl
Hurdles	6	2	2	1	15493
Career Total	6	2	2	1	15493
119 3/03 Newb 2m110y D Hdl				GD	£5291
100 11/02 Tntn 2m1f E Hdl				G-S	£3540
				Total win prize-money £8832	

Going:	Sf: 0-0 GS: 1-2 Gd: 1-3 GF: - Fm: 0-1
Distance:	2m/2m3: 2-6 2m4-2m7: 0-0 3m+: 0-0
Track:	LH: 1-4 RH: 1-2 Tight: 1-2 Gall: 1-3
Aids:	Bl: 0-0 Vi: 0-0 Tstrap: 0-0
Best Rating:	119 3/03 Newb 2m110y good Hdl

Decent novice hurdler; suited by two miles; acts on decent ground.

Peppercorn (GER)
101   121

6-y-o b g Big Shuffle (USA)-Pasca (GER) (Lagunas)
F Doumen Peter Battel

Placings:36P   (3619)
2002/03: 16³S, 16⁶S, 16⁶HY,

	Starts	1st	2nd	3rd	Win & Pl
Hurdles	3	0	0	1	1463
Career Total	3	0	0	1	1463

Going:	Sf: 0-3 GS: 0-0 Gd: 0-0 GF: - Fm: 0-0
Distance:	2m/2m3: 0-3 2m4-2m7: 0-0 3m+: 0-0
Track:	LH: 0-1 RH: 0-2 Tight: 0-0 Gall: 0-1
Aids:	Bl: 0-1 Vi: 0-0 Tstrap: 0-0
Best Rating:	121 11/02 Newb 2m110y soft Hdl

Group class on the Flat in Germany; he has shown promise over hurdles, but has yet to get his head in front.

Peppercorn Prince

6-y-o b g General Wade-Lady Regent (Wolver Hollow)
Miss E C Lavelle Mrs S Metcalfe

Placings:P   (4760)
2002/03: 18ᴾGF,

	Starts	1st	2nd	3rd	Win & Pl
NH Flat	1	0	0	0	
Career Total	1	0	0	0	

Going:	Sf: 0-0 GS: 0-0 Gd: 0-0 GF: - Fm: 0-1
Distance:	2m/2m3: 0-1 2m4-2m7: 0-0 3m+: 0-0
Track:	LH: 0-1 RH: 0-0 Tight: 0-1 Gall: 0-0
Aids:	Bl: 0-0 Vi: 0-0 Tstrap: 0-0
Best Rating:	0 4/03 Font 2m2f110y gd-fm NHF

Per Amore (IRE)
106(110h)   (121h)121

5-y-o ch g General Monash (USA)-Danny s Miracle (Superlative)

P J Hobbs Mrs J F Deithrick

Placings:323311-221003   (4734)
2002/03: 16²S, 16²F, 16¹GS, 17⁰HY, 16⁰G, 16³GF,

	Starts	1st	2nd	3rd	Win & Pl
Hurdles	6	1	2	1	7416
Career Total	12	3	3	4	16356
121 11/02 Winc 2m	E(0-115)HHdl			G-S	£3428
103 4/02 Ludl 2m	E Hdl			G-F	£3020
109 4/02 Ludl 2m	D Hdl			GD	£3900
			Total win prize-money £10350		

Going:	Sf: 0-2 GS: 1-1 Gd: 0-1 GF: - Fm: 0-2
Distance:	2m/2m3: 1-6 2m4-2m7: 0-0 3m+: 0-0
Track:	LH: 0-4 RH: 1-2 Tight: 0-1 Gall: 0-1
Aids:	Bl: 1-5 Vi: 0-0 Tstrap: 0-0
Best Rating:	121 11/02 Winc 2m gd-sft Hdl

Useful handicap hurdler; acts on all ground except extremes; has been blinkered when winning; won back-to-back novice chases at Huntingdon and Newton Abbot May/June 2003; stays 21 furlongs.

Perange (FR)
105   128

7-y-o ch g Perrault-La Mesange (FR) (Olmeto)
P F Nicholls Mrs J Stewart

Placings:0060541/313321-54F1   (4694)
2002/03: 19⁵S, 26⁴GS, 21FS, 21¹G,

	Starts	1st	2nd	3rd	Win & Pl
Chases	4	1	0	0	5896
Career Total	17	4	1	3	36147
112 4/03 NAbb 2m5f110yD(0-125)HCh			GD	£5460	
131 2/02 Font 2m4f C Ch			SFT	£6230	
112 10/01 Uttx 2m D Ch			G-S	£4875	
3/01 Autl 2m3f110y HHdl			HVY	£9699	
			Total win prize-money £26264		

Going:	Sf: 0-2 GS: 0-1 Gd: 1-1 GF: - Fm: 0-0
Distance:	2m/2m3: 0-2 2m4-2m7: 1-2 3m+: 0-1
Track:	LH: 1-1 RH: 0-2 Tight: 1-3 Gall: 0-0
Aids:	Bl: 0-0 Vi: 0-0 Tstrap: 0-0
Best Rating:	131 2/02 Font 2m4f soft Ch

Fair handicap chaser; suited by soft ground; has won on faster but jumped right when doing so; effective at two and a half miles.

Perchancer (IRE)
95   118

7-y-o ch g Perugino (USA)-Irish Hope (Nishapour (FR))
P C Haslam N P Green

Placings:3/1F24-5   (1298)
2002/03: 16⁵GF,

	Starts	1st	2nd	3rd	Win & Pl
Hurdles	1	0	0	0	
Career Total	6	1	1	1	4432
116 11/01 Weth 2m4f110yE Hdl			GD	£2744	
			Total win prize-money £2744		

Going:	Sf: 0-0 GS: 0-0 Gd: 0-0 GF: - Fm: 0-1
Distance:	2m/2m3: 0-1 2m4-2m7: 0-0 3m+: 0-0
Track:	LH: 0-0 RH: 0-1 Tight: 0-0 Gall: 0-0
Aids:	Bl: 0-0 Vi: 0-0 Tstrap: 0-0
Best Rating:	118 4/02 Strf 2m110y good Hdl

Modest hurdler. Best around two and a half miles. Acts on a sound surface. Mixes hurdling with runs on the All-Weather.

Perching (IRE)
105   73

9-y-o b g Strong Gale-Fiona s Blue (Crash Course)
P Butler John Plackett

Placings:50/UF0412/P5-02   (4702)
2002/03: 25⁰GF, 26²GF,

	Starts	1st	2nd	3rd	Win & Pl
Chases	2	0	1	0	960
Career Total	12	1	2	0	7548
108 3/00 Ling 3m D Ch			GD	£4186	
			Total win prize-money £4186		

Going:	Sf: 0-0 GS: 0-0 Gd: 0-0 GF: - Fm: 0-2
Distance:	2m/2m3: 0-0 2m4-2m7: 0-0 3m+: 0-2
Track:	LH: 0-1 RH: 0-1 Tight: 0-2 Gall: 0-0
Aids:	Bl: 0-0 Vi: 0-0 Tstrap: 0-0
Best Rating:	113 4/00 Font 2m6f good Ch

Plating-class chaser; lightly raced in recent seasons; has shown only moderate form; best on a sound surface; stays three miles; has worn cheekpieces.

Percipient
82f   77f

5-y-o b g Pennekamp (USA)-Annie Albright (USA) (Verbatim (USA))
G Thorner Graham Thorner

Placings:5   (1670)
2002/03: 17⁵S,

	Starts	1st	2nd	3rd	Win & Pl
NH Flat	1	0	0	0	0
Career Total	1	0	0	0	0

Going:	Sf: 0-1 GS: 0-0 Gd: 0-0 GF: - Fm: 0-0
Distance:	2m/2m3: 0-1 2m4-2m7: 0-0 3m+: 0-0
Track:	LH: 0-1 RH: 0-0 Tight: 0-1 Gall: 0-0
Aids:	Bl: 0-0 Vi: 0-0 Tstrap: 0-0
Best Rating:	77 10/02 Bang 2m1f soft NHF

Percy Basil

4-y-o b g Petoski-Madam-M (Tina s Pet)
Ian Williams C B Compton

Placings:0   (3789)
2002/03: 17⁰G,

	Starts	1st	2nd	3rd	Win & Pl
NH Flat	1	0	0	0	
Career Total	1	0	0	0	

Going:	Sf: 0-0 GS: 0-0 Gd: 0-1 GF: - Fm: 0-0
Distance:	2m/2m3: 0-1 2m4-2m7: 0-0 3m+: 0-0
Track:	LH: 0-0 RH: 0-1 Tight: 0-0 Gall: 0-0
Aids:	Bl: 0-0 Vi: 0-0 Tstrap: 0-0
Best Rating:	0 2/03 Hrfd 2m1f good NHF

Percy Beck
(99h)   (87+h)

7-y-o ch g Minster Son-Kate O Kirkham (Le Bavard (FR))
P Needham P Needham

Placings:000/05UP-251460U   (3913)
2002/03: 17²GF, 16⁵G, 16¹GS, 16⁴G, 17⁶GF, 16⁰G, 20⁰US,

	Starts	1st	2nd	3rd	Win & Pl
Hurdles	6	1	1	0	2545
Chases	1	0	0	0	0

Career Total	14	1	1	0	2545
83	5/02	Weth	2m		F(0-100)HHdl	G-S	£1911

Total win prize-money £1911

Going:	Sf: 0-1 GS: 1-1 Gd: 0-3 GF: - Fm: 0-2
Distance:	2m/2m3: 1-6 2m4-2m7: 0-1 3m+: 0-0
Track:	LH: 1-5 RH: 0-2 Tight: 0-2 Gall: 0-0
Aids:	Bl: 0-0 Vi: 0-0 Tstrap: 0-0
Best Rating:	83 5/02 Weth 2m gd-sft Hdl

Modest hurdler, turned in a much improved effort when breaking his duck in handicap company at Wetherby in May.

Percy Braithwaite (IRE)

72(100c)

11-y-o b g Kahyasi-Nasseem (FR) (Zeddaan)
Mrs P Ford W E Donohue, K Marritt, K R Ford

Placings:41001U/22362530/3P234/464411/23F46P/04445
200-606   (2771)
2002/03: 26⁶G, 24⁰G, 19⁶HY,

	Starts	1st	2nd	3rd	Win & Pl
Hurdles	3	0	0	0	0
Career Total	42	4	6	5	22153
101	4/00	Hntg	2m110y	D(0-115)HCh	GD	£4048
86	2/00	Ludl	2m	E(0-100)HCh	GD	£2873
107	4/97	Ludl	2m	E Hdl	FRM	£2248
102	1/97	Ludl	2m	E Hdl	G-F	£2682

Total win prize-money £11852

Going:	Sf: 0-1 GS: 0-0 Gd: 0-2 GF: - Fm: 0-0
Distance:	2m/2m3: 0-1 2m4-2m7: 0-0 3m+: 0-2
Track:	LH: 0-1 RH: 0-2 Tight: 0-0 Gall: 0-1
Aids:	Bl: 0-0 Vi: 0-0 Tstrap: 0-0
Best Rating:	112 5/97 Ludl 2m gd-fm Hdl

Did well in his first season over hurdles for new trainer Pam Whittle, and will pay his way again, despite apparently poor form recently. Never put into the race at Hereford in October, he paid the penalty for duelling up front with a rival next time. His saddle slipped on his next start, and he had no chance at the weights latest. Races keenly, and may be best with strong handling.

Percy Parkeeper

106   120

10-y-o b g Teenoso (USA)-True Clown (True Song)
N A Twiston-Davies Mr & Mrs Peter Orton

Placings:1224/F40213F/3454/0113450PP-124333 (4775)
2002/03: 17¹GF, 16²GF, 20⁴GF, 20³G, 24³G, 24³G,

	Starts	1st	2nd	3rd	Win & Pl
Chases	6	1	3	3	14584
Career Total	30	5	4	6	35699
121	9/02	Strf	2m1f110yD(0-120)HCh	G-F	£5473
123	10/01	Hrfd	2m	E(0-115)HCh	GD	£3376
119	9/01	Prth	2m	E(0-115)HCh	GD	£5369
124	2/99	Kemp	2m5f	D Hdl	GD	£3009
107	1/98	Hntg	2m110y	H NHF	G-S	£1402

Total win prize-money £18631

Going:	Sf: 0-0 GS: 0-0 Gd: 0-3 GF: - Fm: 1-3
Distance:	2m/2m3: 1-2 2m4-2m7: 0-2 3m+: 0-2
Track:	LH: 1-2 RH: 0-4 Tight: 1-1 Gall: 0-0
Aids:	Bl: 0-0 Vi: 0-0 Tstrap: 0-0
Best Rating:	124 2/99 Kemp 2m5f good Hdl

Fair handicap chaser; yet to win beyond an extended 2m but does stay much further; best on good ground; likes to dominate; has worn blinkers.

Perfect Fellow

93   133

9-y-o b g Teamster-G W Supermare (Rymer)
Miss H C Knight The Unlucky For Some Partnership

Placings:10/11/0/31/41-1F   (1966)
2002/03: 20¹G, 20⁶GS,

	Starts	1st	2nd	3rd	Win & Pl
Chases	2	1	0	0	12852
Career Total	11	6	0	1	34414
133	10/02	Chel	2m4f110yC(0-135)HCh	GD	£12852
133	12/01	Kemp	2m4f110yD(0-120)HCh	GD	£10676
116	12/00	Folk	2m5f	D Ch	SFT	£3848
126	1/99	Folk	2m6f110yE Hdl	HVY	£2427
108	12/98	Strf	2m6f110yE Hdl	SFT	£2250
90	3/98	NAbb	2m1f	H NHF	SFT	£1236

Total win prize-money £33289

Going:	Sf: 0-0 GS: 0-1 Gd: 1-1 GF: - Fm: 0-0
Distance:	2m/2m3: 0-0 2m4-2m7: 1-2 3m+: 0-0
Track:	LH: 1-2 RH: 0-0 Tight: 0-0 Gall: 1-2
Aids:	Bl: 0-0 Vi: 0-0 Tstrap: 0-0
Best Rating:	133 10/02 Chel 2m4f110y good Ch

Useful chaser; was off the track for a year after December 2000, but bounced back to score in game style at Kempton on Boxing Day. After another absence, he won nicely at Cheltenham in October 2002.

Perfect Liaison

103f   95f

6-y-o b g Alflora (IRE)-Connie s Pet (National Trust)
R H Alner Neil & Susie Dalgren

Placings:06   (4444)
2002/03: 17⁰GS, 16⁶G,

	Starts	1st	2nd	3rd	Win & Pl
NH Flat	2	0	0	0	0
Career Total	2	0	0	0	0

Going:	Sf: 0-0 GS: 0-1 Gd: 0-1 GF: - Fm: 0-0
Distance:	2m/2m3: 0-2 2m4-2m7: 0-0 3m+: 0-0
Track:	LH: 0-0 RH: 0-2 Tight: 0-0 Gall: 0-0
Aids:	Bl: 0-0 Vi: 0-0 Tstrap: 0-0
Best Rating:	95 4/03 Asct 2m110y good NHF

Periwinkle Lad (IRE)

112   (94c)103

6-y-o b g Perugino (USA)-Bold Kate (Bold Lad (IRE))
E McNamara We Didn t Name Him Syndicate

Placings:S/000000-026U003030132166602013   (4729a)
2002/03: 16⁰YS, 17²YS, 16⁶SH, 16⁴GF, 17⁰GF, 16⁰G, 16³GF, 16⁰F, 16³F, 16⁰GS, 22¹S, 20³S, 22²HY, 20¹HY, 20⁶YS, 22⁶YS, 20⁰S, 18²S, 22⁰Y, 24¹GF, 22³G,

	Starts	1st	2nd	3rd	Win & Pl
Hurdles	18	3	2	4	24228
Chases	3	0	1	0	1247
Career Total	28	3	3	4	25475
102	4/03	List	3m	(81-123)HHdl	G-F	£9918
95	12/02	Tram	2m4f	(60-88)HHdl	HVY	£3809
85	11/02	Thur	2m6f110y	(60-88)HHdl	SFT	£3809

Total win prize-money £17539

Going:	Sf: 2-6 GS: 0-1 Gd: 0-2 GF: - Fm: 1-6
Distance:	2m/2m3: 0-11 2m4-2m7: 2-9 3m+: 1-1
Track:	LH: 0-5 RH: 0-3 Tight: 0-1 Gall: 0-0
Aids:	Bl: 0-8 Vi: 0-0 Tstrap: 0-0
Best Rating:	103 4/03 Fair 2m6f good Hdl

Moderate Irish novice hurdler; acts on any ground.

Perk Alert (IRE)

103   82

9-y-o b g Executive Perk-Clondo Blue (IRE) (Miners Lamp)
A King Mrs Dawn Perrett

Placings:210/3033F/4/P061   (4221)
2002/03: 22²PS, 24⁰S, 23⁶S, 25¹SF,

	Starts	1st	2nd	3rd	Win & Pl
Chases	4	1	0	0	3445
Career Total	13	2	1	3	7069
76	3/03	Hrfd	3m1f110yF(0-90)HCh	G-F	£3445
106	12/98	Wwck	2m	H NHF	SFT	£1444

Total win prize-money £4890

Going:	Sf: 0-3 GS: 0-0 Gd: 0-0 GF: - Fm: 1-1
Distance:	2m/2m3: 0-0 2m4-2m7: 0-1 3m+: 1-3
Track:	LH: 0-1 RH: 1-3 Tight: 0-1 Gall: 0-1
Aids:	Bl: 0-0 Vi: 0-0 Tstrap: 0-0
Best Rating:	118 11/98 Wwck 2m soft NHF

Plating-class staying chaser; suited by fast ground.

Perkys Pride (IRE)

103   102

7-y-o b g Executive Perk-Josie Mac (Pitpan)
M C Pipe (Michael Cunningham 16/10) D A Johnson

Placings:3/2/23⁄1311035-500P064   (4553)
2002/03: 16⁵S, 16⁰S, 17⁰G, 22⁶GS, 17⁰S, 17⁶G, 22⁴G,

	Starts	1st	2nd	3rd	Win & Pl
Hurdles	7	0	0	0	784
Career Total	18	3	2	4	24260
124	1/02	Navn	2m6f	Hdl	Y-S	£7196
121	12/01	Navn	2m2f	Hdl	Y-S	£5842
108	11/01	DRoy	2m	NHF	YLD	£5008

Total win prize-money £18047

Going:	Sf: 0-3 GS: 0-1 Gd: 0-3 GF: - Fm: 0-0
Distance:	2m/2m3: 0-5 2m4-2m7: 0-2 3m+: 0-0
Track:	LH: 0-4 RH: 0-3 Tight: 0-1 Gall: 0-2
Aids:	Bl: 0-0 Vi: 0-0 Tstrap: 0-0
Best Rating:	125 4/02 Fair 2m4f gd-yld Hdl

Fair hurdler; ex-Irish; yet to find his form for new yard; well beaten when gambled on in an extended two mile handicap at Exeter March 2003; acts on a soft surface, stays two miles six.

Perouse

101   105

5-y-o ch g Alderbrook-Track Angel (Ardoon)
P F Nicholls (L Lungo 9/12) J Dickson

Placings:221-0211   (4716)
2002/03: 16⁰GS, 16²G, 17¹F, 16¹F,

	Starts	1st	2nd	3rd	Win & Pl
Hurdles	4	2	1	0	8982
Career Total	7	3	3	0	11685
105	4/03	Winc	2m	E Hdl	FRM	£3521
86	4/03	Tntn	2m1f	E Hdl	FRM	£3906
93	4/02	Hexm	2m110y	H NHF	GD	£1701

Total win prize-money £9128

Going:	Sf: 0-0 GS: 0-1 Gd: 0-1 GF: - Fm: 2-2
Distance:	2m/2m3: 2-4 2m4-2m7: 0-0 3m+: 0-0
Track:	LH: 0-2 RH: 2-2 Tight: 1-1 Gall: 0-0
Aids:	Bl: 0-0 Vi: 0-0 Tstrap: 0-0
Best Rating:	112 4/02 Carl 2m1f good NHF

Fair novice hurdler; three times winner on a sound surface; best at two miles at present.

Persian Bandit (IRE)

5-y-o b g Idris (IRE)-Ce Soir (Northern Baby (CAN))
J R Jenkins   Mrs Wendy Jenkins

Placings:0P-   (0007)
2002/03: 16^{P}G,

	Starts	1st	2nd	3rd	Win & Pl
Hurdles	1	0	0	0	
Career Total	2	0	0	0	

Going: Sf: 0-0 GS: 0-0 Gd: 0-1 GF: - Fm: 0-0
Distance: 2m/2m3: 0-1 2m4-2m7: 0-0 3m+: 0-0
Track: LH: 0-1 RH: 0-0 Tight: 0-1 Gall: 0-0
Aids: Bl: 0-0 Vi: 0-1 Tstrap: 0-0
Best Rating:

Persian King (IRE)
108   121

6-y-o ch g Persian Bold-Queen s Share (Main Reef)
J A B Old   W E Sturt

Placings:5/66-23110   (1692)
2002/03: 17^{2}G, 17^{3}GF, 16^{1}G, 16^{1}GF, 16^{9}G,

	Starts	1st	2nd	3rd	Win & Pl
Hurdles	5	2	1	1	8427
Career Total	8	2	1	1	8427
115 10/02 Chep 2m110y D Hdl				G-F	£4143
90 9/02 Worc 2m			E Hdl	GD	£2982
			Total win prize-money £7126		

Going: Sf: 0-0 GS: 0-0 Gd: 1-3 GF: - Fm: 1-2
Distance: 2m/2m3: 2-5 2m4-2m7: 0-0 3m+: 0-0
Track: LH: 2-5 RH: 0-0 Tight: 0-2 Gall: 0-0
Aids: Bl: 0-0 Vi: 0-0 Tstrap: 0-0
Best Rating: 115 10/02 Chep 2m110y   gd-fm   Hdl

Fair hurdler; winner of a low-grade maiden hurdle at Worcester September 2002 and followed up at Chepstow; capable of better; acts on a sound surface.

Persian Point
80   79

7-y-o ch g Persian Bold-Kind Thoughts (Kashmir Ii)
Mrs A Duffield   Clarks New Town

Placings:5/46   (0697)
2002/03: 16^{4}GS, 19^{6}G,

	Starts	1st	2nd	3rd	Win & Pl
Hurdles	2	0	0	0	0
Career Total	3	0	0	0	0

Going: Sf: 0-0 GS: 0-1 Gd: 0-1 GF: - Fm: 0-0
Distance: 2m/2m3: 0-1 2m4-2m7: 0-1 3m+: 0-0
Track: LH: 0-1 RH: 0-1 Tight: 0-1 Gall: 0-0
Aids: Bl: 0-0 Vi: 0-0 Tstrap: 0-0
Best Rating: 79 4/01 Muss 2m1f   gd-fm   Hdl

Persian Pride (IRE)
95   96+

5-y-o ch g Barathea (IRE)-Glenarff (USA) (Irish River (FR))
P W Harris (P J Hobbs 10/6)   Dr Jamal Ahmadzadeh

Placings:2   (0520)

2002/03: 17^{2}G,

	Starts	1st	2nd	3rd	Win & Pl
Hurdles	1	0	1	0	1068
Career Total	1	0	1	0	1068

Going: Sf: 0-0 GS: 0-0 Gd: 0-1 GF: - Fm: 0-0
Distance: 2m/2m3: 0-1 2m4-2m7: 0-0 3m+: 0-0
Track: LH: 0-1 RH: 0-0 Tight: 0-1 Gall: 0-0
Aids: Bl: 0-0 Vi: 0-0 Tstrap: 0-0
Best Rating: 90 6/02 NAbb 2m1f   good   Hdl

Persian Waters (IRE)
112   137+

7-y-o b g Persian Bold-Emerald Waters (King s Lake (USA))
J R Fanshawe   Paul Green

Placings:1224/200/230   (4112)
2002/03: 21^{2}G, 22^{3}GS, 21^{0}G,

	Starts	1st	2nd	3rd	Win & Pl
Hurdles	3	0	1	1	5522
Career Total	10	1	4	1	20136
115 11/99 Hntg 2m110y C Hdl				G-F	£5327
			Total win prize-money £5327		

Going: Sf: 0-0 GS: 0-1 Gd: 0-2 GF: - Fm: 0-0
Distance: 2m/2m3: 0-0 2m4-2m7: 0-3 3m+: 0-0
Track: LH: 0-1 RH: 0-2 Tight: 0-0 Gall: 0-1
Aids: Bl: 0-0 Vi: 0-0 Tstrap: 0-0
Best Rating: 134 2/03 Winc 2m6f   gd-sft   Hdl

Useful handicap hurdler; fair staying handicapper on the level; was absent from the track after running on the Flat in June 2001 until returning with good efforts in a decent handicap hurdles early in 2003; stays two miles five; suited by a sound surface, but does handle softer ground

Persona Pride

9-y-o gr g St Enodoc-Le Jour Fortune (Twilight Alley)
Mrs B Brown   Percy Priday

Placings:P64P-PP   (4026)
2002/03: 24^{P}S, 25^{P}S,

	Starts	1st	2nd	3rd	Win & Pl
Chases	2	0	0	0	
Career Total	6	0	0	0	0

Going: Sf: 0-2 GS: 0-0 Gd: 0-0 GF: - Fm: 0-0
Distance: 2m/2m3: 0-0 2m4-2m7: 0-0 3m+: 0-2
Track: LH: 0-0 RH: 0-2 Tight: 0-0 Gall: 0-0
Aids: Bl: 0-0 Vi: 0-0 Tstrap: 0-0
Best Rating: 80 3/02 Hrfd 3m1f110y   good   Ch

Personal Assurance
103   112

6-y-o b g Un Desperado (FR)-Steel Typhoon (General Ironside)
Jonjo O Neill   Christopher W T Johnston

Placings:3233154   (4602)
2002/03: 17^{3}G, 17^{2}GS, 16^{3}GS, 21^{3}S, 16^{1}HY, 16^{5}S, 21^{4}G,

	Starts	1st	2nd	3rd	Win & Pl
NH Flat	3	0	1	2	1096
Hurdles	4	1	0	1	7490
Career Total	7	1	1	3	8586
112 2/03 Sand 2m110y D Hdl				HVY	£5414
			Total win prize-money £5415		

Going: Sf: 1-3 GS: 0-2 Gd: 0-2 GF: - Fm: 0-0
Distance: 2m/2m3: 1-5 2m4-2m7: 0-2 3m+: 0-0
Track: LH: 0-2 RH: 1-5 Tight: 0-2 Gall: 0-2
Aids: Bl: 0-0 Vi: 0-1 Tstrap: 0-0
Best Rating: 112 3/03 Uttx   2m   soft   Hdl

Fair bumper/hurdler; won well at Sandown in February 2003; seemingly best at a stiff two miles; likes soft ground.

Persuets (IRE)
77

5-y-o b m Gildoran-Furry Queen (Furry Glen)
J I A Charlton   R A Ross

Placings:4   (4665)
2002/03: 17^{4}GF,

	Starts	1st	2nd	3rd	Win & Pl
NH Flat	1	0	0	0	0
Career Total	1	0	0	0	0

Going: Sf: 0-0 GS: 0-0 Gd: 0-0 GF: - Fm: 0-1
Distance: 2m/2m3: 0-1 2m4-2m7: 0-0 3m+: 0-0
Track: LH: 0-1 RH: 0-0 Tight: 0-0 Gall: 0-0
Aids: Bl: 0-0 Vi: 0-0 Tstrap: 0-0
Best Rating: 92 4/03 Carl   2m1f   gd-fm   NHF

Bumper performer; showed promise on her debut on fast ground.

Pertemps (IRE)

10-y-o ch g Good Thyne (USA)-Julia s Pauper (Pauper)
Ian Williams   Pertemps Group Limited

Placings:600F5/3522224P6/1-0   (4118)
2002/03: 24^{0}G,

	Starts	1st	2nd	3rd	Win & Pl
Chases	1	0	0	0	
Career Total	16	1	4	1	6477
91 6/01 Hrfd			3m1f110yG(0-90)HCh	FRM	£3283
			Total win prize-money £3283		

Going: Sf: 0-0 GS: 0-0 Gd: 0-1 GF: - Fm: 0-0
Distance: 2m/2m3: 0-0 2m4-2m7: 0-0 3m+: 0-1
Track: LH: 0-0 RH: 0-1 Tight: 0-0 Gall: 0-1
Aids: Bl: 0-0 Vi: 0-1 Tstrap: 0-0
Best Rating: 91 6/01 Hrfd   3m1f110y   firm   Ch

Pertemps Boycott (IRE)
99   62

5-y-o b g Indian Ridge-Coupe D Hebe (Ile De Bourbon (USA))
H Alexander   Alastair Baillie

Placings:03P30P04-3P014P0P5   (4518)
2002/03: 16^{3}G, 16^{P}GF, 19^{0}GF, 20^{1}GF, 21^{4}S, 22^{P}G, 20^{9}GF, 20^{P}G, 21^{5}G,

	Starts	1st	2nd	3rd	Win & Pl
Hurdles	9	1	0	1	2212
Career Total	17	1	0	3	2704
71 6/02 Hexm			2m4f110yG(0-95)HHdl	G-F	£1981
			Total win prize-money £1981		

Going: Sf: 0-1 GS: 0-0 Gd: 0-4 GF: - Fm: 1-4
Distance: 2m/2m3: 0-2 2m4-2m7: 1-7 3m+: 0-0
Track: LH: 1-6 RH: 0-3 Tight: 0-5 Gall: 0-1
Aids: Bl: 0-0 Vi: 0-0 Tstrap: 0-0
Best Rating: 71 6/02 Hexm   2m4f110y   gd-fm   Hdl

Plating-class hurdler; showed little before winning a selling hurdle at Hexham in June 2002; has shown little since and is not one to place much faith in.

Pertemps Cindrella

98(93c)   (91c)**81**

8-y-o ch m Almoojid-Cinderella Derek (Hittite Glory)
B D Leavy J A Provan

Placings:*33060/P030/0F522250/5F012200P4-204361*
                                                          (3939)
2002/03: 20²G, 16⁰HY, 20⁴HY, 16³HY, 16²S, 22¹S,

	Starts	1st	2nd	3rd	Win & Pl
Hurdles	5	0	1	1	962
Chases	1	1	0	0	4316
Career Total	33	2	6	4	10965
91	3/03	MRas	2m6f110yE(0-105)HCh	SFT	£4315
82	11/01	Uttx	2m	G(0-90)HHdl	HVY	£1897
				Total win prize-money	£6213

Going:	Sf: 1-5 GS: 0-0 Gd: 0-1 GF: - Fm: 0-0
Distance:	2m/2m3: 0-3 2m4-2m7: 1-3 3m+: 0-0
Track:	LH: 0-5 RH: 1-1 Tight: 1-1 Gall: 0-2
Aids:	Bl: 0-1 Vi: 0-0 Tstrap: 0-0
Best Rating:	91 3/03 MRas 2m6f110y soft Ch

Plating-class hurdler; suited by testing conditions, she won a poor selling hurdle at Uttoxeter in November; had luck on her side when making a winning debut over fences at Market Rasen in March.

Pertemps Flash

65f   **52f**

5-y-o gr g Silca Blanka (IRE)-Fast Market (Petong)
A D Smith Pertemps Group Limited

Placings:*0P*   (0823)
2002/03: 16⁰GF, 16⁰GF,

	Starts	1st	2nd	3rd	Win & Pl
NH Flat	2	0	0	0	
Career Total	2	0	0	0	

Going:	Sf: 0-0 GS: 0-0 Gd: 0-0 GF: - Fm: 0-2
Distance:	2m/2m3: 0-2 2m4-2m7: 0-0 3m+: 0-0
Track:	LH: 0-2 RH: 0-0 Tight: 0-0 Gall: 0-0
Aids:	Bl: 0-0 Vi: 0-0 Tstrap: 0-0
Best Rating:	52 5/02 Worc 2m gd-fm NHF

Pertemps Jardine (IRE)

67   **40**

5-y-o b/br g General Monash (USA)-Indescent Blue (Bluebird (USA))
Mrs A M Thorpe S A Douch

Placings:*U0P*   (2175)
2002/03: 16⁰G, 21⁰GS, 16⁰S,

	Starts	1st	2nd	3rd	Win & Pl
Hurdles	3	0	0	0	
Career Total	3	0	0	0	

Going:	Sf: 0-1 GS: 0-1 Gd: 0-1 GF: - Fm: 0-0
Distance:	2m/2m3: 0-2 2m4-2m7: 0-1 3m+: 0-0
Track:	LH: 0-3 RH: 0-0 Tight: 0-0 Gall: 0-1
Aids:	Bl: 0-0 Vi: 0-0 Tstrap: 0-0
Best Rating:	40 11/02 Chel 2m5f gd-sft Hdl

Pertemps Machine

4-y-o b g Danzig Connection (USA)-Shamrock Dancer (IRE) (Dance Of Life (USA))
A D Smith Pertemps Group Limited

Placings:*P*   (0971)
2002/03: 16⁶GS,

	Starts	1st	2nd	3rd	Win & Pl
Hurdles	1	0	0	0	
Career Total	1	0	0	0	

Going:	Sf: 0-0 GS: 0-1 Gd: 0-0 GF: - Fm: 0-0
Distance:	2m/2m3: 0-1 2m4-2m7: 0-0 3m+: 0-0
Track:	LH: 0-1 RH: 0-0 Tight: 0-1 Gall: 0-0
Aids:	Bl: 0-0 Vi: 0-0 Tstrap: 0-0
Best Rating:	0 8/02 Strf 2m110y gd-sft Hdl

Pertemps Silenus

5-y-o b g Silca Blanka (IRE)-Silvie (Kind Of Hush)
A D Smith Pertemps Group Limited

Placings:*00-0PP*   (3598)
2002/03: 18⁰S, 17⁵S, 17⁶S,

	Starts	1st	2nd	3rd	Win & Pl
NH Flat	1	0	0	0	0
Hurdles	2	0	0	0	0
Career Total	5	0	0	0	

Going:	Sf: 0-3 GS: 0-0 Gd: 0-0 GF: - Fm: 0-0
Distance:	2m/2m3: 0-3 2m4-2m7: 0-0 3m+: 0-0
Track:	LH: 0-1 RH: 0-2 Tight: 0-1 Gall: 0-0
Aids:	Bl: 0-0 Vi: 0-0 Tstrap: 0-0
Best Rating:	69 2/02 Sand 2m110y soft NHF

Pertemps Susie

100   **92**

7-y-o b m Gildoran-Brilliant Future (Welsh Saint)
Ian Williams Martin Green

Placings:*006/164-05325*   (4683)
2002/03: 17⁰GS, 19⁵S, 17³F, 19²GF, 21⁵GF,

	Starts	1st	2nd	3rd	Win & Pl
Hurdles	5	0	1	1	1798
Career Total	11	1	1	1	3985
95	5/01	Extr	2m1f	H NHF	FRM £2187
				Total win prize-money	£2188

Going:	Sf: 0-1 GS: 0-1 Gd: 0-0 GF: - Fm: 0-3
Distance:	2m/2m3: 0-3 2m4-2m7: 0-2 3m+: 0-0
Track:	LH: 0-1 RH: 0-4 Tight: 0-1 Gall: 0-1
Aids:	Bl: 0-0 Vi: 0-0 Tstrap: 0-0
Best Rating:	95 5/01 Extr 2m1f firm NHF

Won firm ground bumper at Exeter May 2001; two good efforts over hurdles at same course in the spring of 2003; best at distances short of two and a half miles; acts on fast ground.

Pertemps Timmy

83f   **88f**

5-y-o b g Petoski-Brilliant Future (Welsh Saint)
A Streeter Pertemps Group Limited

Placings:*3-3*   (0517)
2002/03: 16³S,

	Starts	1st	2nd	3rd	Win & Pl
NH Flat	1	0	0	1	217

Pertino

107(108h)   (113h)**117**

7-y-o b g Terimon-Persian Fountain (IRE) (Persian Heights)
J M Jefferson W Fouracres, T Pryke & D Willis

Placings:*5412153/P0056P/P0F12205212-5412120*   (4523)
2002/03: 18⁵GS, 16⁴GF, 16¹GF, 16²GF, 17¹G, 17²G, 16⁹G,

	Starts	1st	2nd	3rd	Win & Pl
Hurdles	2	0	0	0	317
Chases	5	2	2	0	10613
Career Total	31	6	7	1	29494
117	10/02	Sthl	2m1f	E Ch	GD £4315
106	9/02	Hexm	2m110y	E Ch	G-F £3357
112	4/02	Carl	2m1f	D(0-120)HHdl	GD £3486
106	10/01	Kels	2m110y	C(0-115)HHdl	GD £2821
120	2/00	Muss	2m	D Hdl	G-S £3087
104	1/00	Newc	2m	E Hdl	SFT £2558
				Total win prize-money	£19627

Going:	Sf: 0-0 GS: 0-1 Gd: 1-3 GF: - Fm: 1-3
Distance:	2m/2m3: 2-7 2m4-2m7: 0-0 3m+: 0-0
Track:	LH: 2-7 RH: 0-0 Tight: 0-2 Gall: 0-0
Aids:	Bl: 0-0 Vi: 0-0 Tstrap: 0-0
Best Rating:	120 2/00 Muss 2m gd-sft Hdl

Fair hurdler. Took well to chasing in the autumn of 2002, winning twice and running well otherwise. Suited by a sound surface, has worn sheepskin cheekpieces.

Pescetto Lady (IRE)

99   **107**

5-y-o b m Toulon-Glenpatrick Peach (IRE) (Lafontaine (USA))
Mrs John Harrington Mrs Eileen Queally

Placings:*0-S21F*   (1967)
2002/03: 16⁵GY, 16²GF, 16¹F, 16⁶GS,

	Starts	1st	2nd	3rd	Win & Pl
NH Flat	1	0	0	0	
Hurdles	3	1	1	0	6663
Career Total	5	1	1	0	6663
90	9/02	List	2m	Hdl	FRM £5533
				Total win prize-money	£5534

Going:	Sf: 0-0 GS: 0-1 Gd: 0-0 GF: - Fm: 1-2
Distance:	2m/2m3: 1-4 2m4-2m7: 0-0 3m+: 0-0
Track:	LH: 1-2 RH: 0-0 Tight: 0-0 Gall: 0-0
Aids:	Bl: 0-0 Vi: 0-0 Tstrap: 0-0
Best Rating:	94 9/02 Klny 2m gd-fm Hdl

Irish novice hurdler, winner in September 2002 and successful on the Flat next time.

Pessimistic Dick

113   **121**

10-y-o b g Derrylin-Tycoon Moon (Tycoon Ii)
H Morrison Frank Flynn And Richard Madden

Placings:*5505/262P4533/P1036F30F52/PP0P/P534-14511115P5*
                                                          (4603)
2002/03: 23¹GF, 23⁴GF, 26⁵GF, 26¹G, 27¹G, 26¹GF, 24¹GF, 24⁵G, 32⁸G, 26⁵G,

Pertemps Machine

Career Total   2   0   2   444

Going:	Sf: 0-1 GS: 0-0 Gd: 0-0 GF: - Fm: 0-0
Distance:	2m/2m3: 0-1 2m4-2m7: 0-0 3m+: 0-0
Track:	LH: 0-1 RH: 0-0 Tight: 0-0 Gall: 0-0
Aids:	Bl: 0-0 Vi: 0-0 Tstrap: 0-0
Best Rating:	88 6/02 Worc 2m soft NHF

Placed in ordinary bumpers.

	Starts	1st	2nd	3rd	Win & Pl
Chases	10	5	0	0	29410
Career Total	41	6	3	5	38583

121	10/02	Chel	3m110y	E(0-125)HCh	G-F	£7829
113	10/02	Carl	3m2f	D(0-115)HCh	G-F	£6678
103	9/02	Sedg	3m3f	D(0-115)HCh	GD	£4680
98	8/02	Ctml	3m2f	D(0-120)HCh	GD	£5200
90	6/02	Worc	2m7f110yE(0-110)HCh	G-F	£3757
75	9/99	Carl	2m4f110yE Ch	G-F	£3096

Total win prize-money £31240

Going: Sf: 0-0 GS: 0-0 Gd: 2-5 GF: - Fm: 3-5
Distance: 2m/2m3: 0-0 2m4-2m7: 0-0 3m+: 5-10
Track: LH: 4-9 RH: 1-1 Tight: 2-4 Gall: 1-3
Aids: Bl: 0-0 Vi: 0-0 Tstrap: 0-0
Best Rating: 121 10/02 Chel 3m110y   gd-fm   Ch

Modest staying handicap chaser; not always the most consistent, but in fine form in the summer and autumn of 2002 with five victories in staying handicap chases; has been in the grip of the Handicapper since; suited by three miles plus and the ground good or faster.

Petanque (IRE)
94   117
7-y-o b g King s Ride-Phargara (IRE) (Phardante (FR))
N J Henderson   P J D Pottinger

Placings: 1-5146   (4328)
2002/03: 16⁵GS, 19¹GS, 16⁴HY, 16⁶G,

	Starts	1st	2nd	3rd	Win & Pl
NH Flat	1	0	0	0	0
Hurdles	3	1	0	0	6280
Career Total	5	2	0	0	8030

| 117 | 1/03 | Donc | 2m3f110yD Hdl | G-S | £5863 |
| 105 | 12/01 | Hntg | 2m110y H NHF | G-S | £1750 |

Total win prize-money £7613

Going: Sf: 0-1 GS: 1-2 Gd: 0-1 GF: - Fm: 0-0
Distance: 2m/2m3: 0-3 2m4-2m7: 1-1 3m+: 0-0
Track: LH: 1-3 RH: 0-1 Tight: 0-0 Gall: 0-2
Aids: Bl: 0-0 Vi: 0-0 Tstrap: 0-0
Best Rating: 117 1/03 Donc 2m3f110y gd-sft Hdl

Useful novice hurdler; bumper winner; effective over trips of around two and half miles and handles cut in the ground, but disappointed when tried on heavy.

Petara (IRE)
68   32
8-y-o ch g Petardia-Romangoddess (IRE) (Rhoman Rule (USA))
J S Wainwright   Wisma Partnership

Placings: 0/0P   (4412)
2002/03: 17⁰GS, 17⁷PG,

	Starts	1st	2nd	3rd	Win & Pl
Hurdles	2	0	0	0	
Career Total	3	0	0	0	

Going: Sf: 0-0 GS: 0-1 Gd: 0-1 GF: - Fm: 0-0
Distance: 2m/2m3: 0-2 2m4-2m7: 0-0 3m+: 0-0
Track: LH: 0-0 RH: 0-2 Tight: 0-1 Gall: 0-0
Aids: Bl: 0-0 Vi: 0-0 Tstrap: 0-0
Best Rating: 58 7/99 Sedg 2m1f gd-fm Hdl

Poor Flat performer who has shown nothing over hurdles.

Pete The Parson (IRE)
79   98d
14-y-o b g The Parson-Gemelek (Menelek)

J A B Old   Www.Theracingforum.Co.Uk

Placings: 23/33/03U1211/621123/5360/5P63/5F6/36FP43-P05P   (3572)
2002/03: 20⁶G, 18⁹G, 21⁵HY, 20⁸S,

	Starts	1st	2nd	3rd	Win & Pl
Chases	4	0	0	0	480
Career Total	38	5	4	9	38792

138	1/98	Chel	2m5f	B HCh	G-S	£8184
140	12/97	Towc	2m110y	D(0-125)HCh	SFT	£3665
123	4/96	Extr	2m2f	D(0-125)HCh	GD	£3915
118	3/96	Chep	2m3f110yE Ch	G-S	£2914
111	2/96	Chep	2m110y E Ch	SFT	£3078

Total win prize-money £21759

Going: Sf: 0-2 GS: 0-0 Gd: 0-2 GF: - Fm: 0-0
Distance: 2m/2m3: 0-1 2m4-2m7: 0-3 3m+: 0-0
Track: LH: 0-2 RH: 0-1 Tight: 0-0 Gall: 0-2
Aids: Bl: 0-0 Vi: 0-0 Tstrap: 0-0
Best Rating: 144 1/98 Chel 2m5f gd-sft Ch

Veteran handicap chaser, he is effective on good and soft ground, and stays two miles five furlongs. Not always the most reliable jumper.

Peter's Two Fun (FR)
104   97
6-y-o b g Funambule (USA)-Spinner s Mate (FR) (Miller s Mate)
M C Pipe   P A Deal

Placings: F30P/25S543-231202034520P   (3254)
2002/03: 22²G, 22³G, 20¹G, 22²GF, 22⁹GF, 26²GF, 19⁰GF, 22³F, 25⁴G, 20⁵GS, 21²G, 22⁰GS, 21⁸HY,

	Starts	1st	2nd	3rd	Win & Pl
Hurdles	13	1	4	2	7281
Career Total	23	1	5	4	12728
99	6/02 Worc 2m4f	E Hdl	GD	£2702

Total win prize-money £2702

Going: Sf: 0-1 GS: 0-2 Gd: 1-5 GF: - Fm: 0-5
Distance: 2m/2m3: 0-0 2m4-2m7: 1-11 3m+: 0-2
Track: LH: 1-5 RH: 0-7 Tight: 0-2 Gall: 0-0
Aids: Bl: 0-0 Vi: 1-11 Tstrap: 0-0
Best Rating: 99 6/02 NAbb 2m6f gd-fm Hdl

Front-running hurdler. Ran the opposition ragged when winning a poor maiden hurdle over two and a half miles at Worcester June 2002. In the frame since.

Peterson's Cay (IRE)
92   89
5-y-o b g Grand Lodge (USA)-Columbian Sand (IRE) (Salmon Leap (USA))
Mrs M Reveley   Lucayan Stud

Placings: 42-435P4   (4355)
2002/03: 16⁴G, 16³GS, 16⁵G, 19⁹GS, 20⁴GF,

	Starts	1st	2nd	3rd	Win & Pl
NH Flat	2	0	0	1	636
Hurdles	3	0	0	0	272
Career Total	7	0	1	1	1420

Going: Sf: 0-0 GS: 0-2 Gd: 0-2 GF: - Fm: 0-1
Distance: 2m/2m3: 0-3 2m4-2m7: 0-2 3m+: 0-0
Track: LH: 0-3 RH: 0-2 Tight: 0-0 Gall: 0-0
Aids: Bl: 0-1 Vi: 0-0 Tstrap: 0-0
Best Rating: 95 12/02 Muss 2m gd-sft NHF

Flat-bred but looked short of speed in bumpers; satisfactory debut over hurdles in January but disappointed afterwards.

Peteuresque (USA)
93   92
6-y-o ch g Peteski (CAN)-Miss Ultimo (USA) (Screen King (USA))
R H Buckler   Woodland Flowers

Placings: 4/6-P6   (3443)
2002/03: 16⁶S, 16⁶HY,

	Starts	1st	2nd	3rd	Win & Pl
Hurdles	2	0	0	0	0
Career Total	4	0	0	0	0

Going: Sf: 0-2 GS: 0-0 Gd: 0-0 GF: - Fm: 0-0
Distance: 2m/2m3: 0-2 2m4-2m7: 0-0 3m+: 0-0
Track: LH: 0-2 RH: 0-0 Tight: 0-0 Gall: 0-0
Aids: Bl: 0-0 Vi: 0-0 Tstrap: 0-0
Best Rating: 99 4/01 Winc 2m soft Hdl

Petite Aimee (IRE)

5-y-o b m Toulon-Midnight Seeker (Status Seeker)
J S Haldane   J Kyle

Placings: P   (4778)
2002/03: 16⁰G,

	Starts	1st	2nd	3rd	Win & Pl
NH Flat	1	0	0	0	
Career Total	1	0	0	0	

Going: Sf: 0-0 GS: 0-0 Gd: 0-1 GF: - Fm: 0-0
Distance: 2m/2m3: 0-1 2m4-2m7: 0-0 3m+: 0-0
Track: LH: 0-0 RH: 0-1 Tight: 0-0 Gall: 0-0
Aids: Bl: 0-0 Vi: 0-0 Tstrap: 0-0
Best Rating: 0 4/03 Prth 2m110y good NHF

Petite Risk
99
9-y-o ch m Risk Me (FR)-Technology (FR) (Top Ville)
D M Lloyd   D M Lloyd

Placings: 1213/03/F220042U2/32500/U2112113-U (2362)
2002/03: 20⁰S,

	Starts	1st	2nd	3rd	Win & Pl
Hurdles	1	0	0	0	
Career Total	29	6	8	4	22245

90	3/02	Ludl	2m	F Hdl	G-S	£2649
99	3/02	Hntg	2m110y G Hdl	SFT	£1657
95	12/01	Leic	2m	G Hdl	GD	£1981
89	12/01	Hrfd	2m1f	G Hdl	GD	£1897
112	3/98	Ludl	2m	E Hdl	G-S	£2684
116	3/98	Plum	2m1f	F Hdl	GD	£1935

Total win prize-money £12805

Going: Sf: 0-1 GS: 0-0 Gd: 0-0 GF: - Fm: 0-0
Distance: 2m/2m3: 0-0 2m4-2m7: 0-1 3m+: 0-0
Track: LH: 0-1 RH: 0-0 Tight: 0-0 Gall: 0-0
Aids: Bl: 0-0 Vi: 0-0 Tstrap: 0-0
Best Rating: 125 3/99 Winc 2m good Hdl

In fine heart in lowly hurdles in 2001/02, effective on soft ground.

Petolinski
109   100
5-y-o b g Petoski-Olnistar (FR) (Balsamo (FR))
J S King   R B Denny

Placings: 60-00130P   (4252)

2002/03: 20⁰GS, 20⁰S, 20¹S, 20⁹HY, 25⁰HY, 22ᴾG,

	Starts	1st	2nd	3rd	Win & Pl
Hurdles	6	1	0	1	3718
Career Total	8	1	0	1	3718
100 12/02 Chep	2m4f	E Hdl		SFT	£2912

Total win prize-money £2912

Going: Sf: 1-4 GS: 0-1 Gd: 0-1 GF: 0-0 Fm: 0-0
Distance: 2m2/m3: 0-0 2m4-2m7: 1-5 3m+: 0-1
Track: LH: 1-3 RH: 0-2 Tight: 0-0 Gall: 0-0
Aids: Bl: 0-0 Vi: 0-0 Tstrap: 0-0
Best Rating: 100 12/02 Leic 2m4f110y heavy Hdl

Tremendous improvement when shock 33/1 winner of two and a half mile novice hurdle at Chepstow November 2002. The form could be suspect.

Petongski

54   18

5-y-o b g Petong-Madam Petoski (Petoski)
D W Barker P Asquith

Placings:0   (2473)
2002/03: 16⁰G,

	Starts	1st	2nd	3rd	Win & Pl
Hurdles	1	0	0	0	
Career Total	1	0	0	0	

Going: Sf: 0-0 GS: 0-0 Gd: 0-1 GF: 0-0 Fm: 0-0
Distance: 2m2/m3: 0-1 2m4-2m7: 0-0 3m+: 0-0
Track: LH: 0-1 RH: 0-0 Tight: 0-0 Gall: 0-1
Aids: Bl: 0-0 Vi: 0-0 Tstrap: 0-0
Best Rating: 11 12/02 Donc 2m110y good Hdl

Petrea

8-y-o b m St Ninian-Polypodium (Politico (USA))
W M Burnell W M Burnell

Placings:50/00PP-3   (0392)
2002/03: 24³G,

	Starts	1st	2nd	3rd	Win & Pl
Chases	1	0	0	1	435
Career Total	7	0	0	1	435

Going: Sf: 0-0 GS: 0-0 Gd: 0-0 GF: 0-1 Fm: 0-0
Distance: 2m2/m3: 0-0 2m4-2m7: 0-0 3m+: 0-1
Track: LH: 0-1 RH: 0-0 Tight: 0-1 Gall: 0-0
Aids: Bl: 0-0 Vi: 0-0 Tstrap: 0-0
Best Rating: 88 5/02 Strf 3m good Ch

Petros Chief

6-y-o b g Factual (USA)-Dancing Ballerina (Record Run)
Miss M E Rowland Mrs R A Murrell

Placings:0PP   (2476)
2002/03: 16⁰GF, 20ᴾS, 19⁷GS,

	Starts	1st	2nd	3rd	Win & Pl
NH Flat	1	0	0	0	0
Hurdles	2	0	0	0	0
Career Total	3	0	0	0	

Going: Sf: 0-1 GS: 0-1 Gd: 0-0 GF: - Fm: 0-1
Distance: 2m2/m3: 0-1 2m4-2m7: 0-2 3m+: 0-0
Track: LH: 0-3 RH: 0-0 Tight: 0-0 Gall: 0-0
Aids: Bl: 0-0 Vi: 0-0 Tstrap: 0-0
Best Rating: 62 8/02 Worc 2m gd-fm NHF

Petticoat Lil (IRE)

83   64

7-y-o b m Petoski-Heresy (IRE) (Black Minstrel)
R Mathew Robin Mathew

Placings:0/P056   (4320)
2002/03: 16ᴾGS, 16⁹GS, 17⁵S, 17⁶G,

	Starts	1st	2nd	3rd	Win & Pl
Hurdles	4	0	0	0	
Career Total	5	0	0	0	0

Going: Sf: 0-1 GS: 0-2 Gd: 0-1 GF: - Fm: 0-0
Distance: 2m2/m3: 0-4 2m4-2m7: 0-0 3m+: 0-0
Track: LH: 0-3 RH: 0-1 Tight: 0-2 Gall: 0-1
Aids: Bl: 0-0 Vi: 0-1 Tstrap: 0-0
Best Rating: 64 3/03 Bang 2m1f good Hdl

Pettree (IRE)

109   108+

9-y-o ch g King Persian-Whackers World (Whistling Deer)
N A Twiston-Davies Pettifer Group Limited

Placings:U02/6623FP/1UU-64052   (4636)
2002/03: 20⁶GS, 20⁴G, 26ᴾS, 24⁵GS, 24²G,

	Starts	1st	2nd	3rd	Win & Pl
Chases	5	0	1	0	1355
Career Total	17	1	3	1	7991
108 11/01 Wwck	2m4f110yD(0-125)HCh	GD	£4153		

Total win prize-money £4154

Going: Sf: 0-1 GS: 0-2 Gd: 0-2 GF: - Fm: 0-0
Distance: 2m2/m3: 0-0 2m4-2m7: 0-2 3m+: 0-3
Track: LH: 0-4 RH: 0-1 Tight: 0-2 Gall: 0-0
Aids: Bl: 0-1 Vi: 0-0 Tstrap: 0-0
Best Rating: 114 2/00 Newb 3m110y gd-sft Hdl

Modest chaser; inclined to be let down by his jumping; often loses his place during his races; acts on good ground; stays 3m.

Peveril Pendragon

9-y-o b g Emarati (USA)-Princess Siham (Chabrias (FR))
G B Balding Mrs E A Haycock

Placings:40414/552456P43/PP   (3547)
2002/03: 17ᴾHY, 16ᴾG,

	Starts	1st	2nd	3rd	Win & Pl
Chases	2	0	0	0	
Career Total	16	1	1	1	6536
104 3/98 Newb	2m110y C Hdl	SFT	£4081		

Total win prize-money £4081

Going: Sf: 0-1 GS: 0-0 Gd: 0-0 GF: - Fm: 0-0
Distance: 2m2/m3: 0-2 2m4-2m7: 0-0 3m+: 0-0
Track: LH: 0-1 RH: 0-1 Tight: 0-1 Gall: 0-0
Aids: Bl: 0-0 Vi: 0-0 Tstrap: 0-2
Best Rating: 104 3/98 Newb 2m110y soft Hdl

Pewter Light (IRE)

82   58

6-y-o gr g Roselier (FR)-Luminous Light (Cardinal Flower)
B J M Ryall I & Mrs K G Fawcett

Placings:PP0   (4311)
2002/03: 24ᴾHY, 22ᴾGS, 21⁰G,

	Starts	1st	2nd	3rd	Win & Pl
Hurdles	3	0	0	0	
Career Total	3	0	0	0	

Going: Sf: 0-1 GS: 0-1 Gd: 0-1 GF: - Fm: 0-0
Distance: 2m/m3: 0-0 2m4-2m7: 0-2 3m+: 0-1
Track: LH: 0-2 RH: 0-1 Tight: 0-0 Gall: 0-1
Aids: Bl: 0-0 Vi: 0-0 Tstrap: 0-0
Best Rating: 58 3/03 Newb 2m5f good Hdl

Phantom Mist

7-y-o b m Opera Ghost-Titian Mist (Town And Country)
M Salaman M J Lewin

Placings:0-U   (0737)
2002/03: 17ᵁGF,

	Starts	1st	2nd	3rd	Win & Pl
NH Flat	1	0	0	0	
Career Total	2	0	0	0	

Going: Sf: 0-0 GS: 0-0 Gd: 0-0 GF: - Fm: 0-1
Distance: 2m2/m3: 0-1 2m4-2m7: 0-0 3m+: 0-0
Track: LH: 0-1 RH: 0-0 Tight: 0-1 Gall: 0-0
Aids: Bl: 0-0 Vi: 0-0 Tstrap: 0-0
Best Rating: 0 7/02 NAbb 2m1f gd-fm NHF

Phar Breeze (IRE)

89   70

8-y-o b m Phardante (FR)-Glamorous Gale (Strong Gale)
Mrs J M Mann Mrs J M Mann

Placings:000/060R6F06-51P0BP   (3834)
2002/03: 20⁵G, 16¹GS, 17ᴾS, 16⁹GS, 22ᴮGS, 20ᴾG,

	Starts	1st	2nd	3rd	Win & Pl
Hurdles	6	1	0	0	4017
Career Total	17	1	0	0	4017
94 11/02 Sthl	2m	D Hdl	G-S	£4017	

Total win prize-money £4017

Going: Sf: 0-1 GS: 1-3 Gd: 0-2 GF: - Fm: 0-0
Distance: 2m/m3: 1-3 2m4-2m7: 0-3 3m+: 0-0
Track: LH: 1-4 RH: 0-2 Tight: 1-3 Gall: 0-1
Aids: Bl: 0-0 Vi: 0-0 Tstrap: 0-0
Best Rating: 94 11/02 Sthl 2m gd-sft Hdl

Unplaced in 12 starts before winning a weak novice hurdle at Southwell in November 2002.

Phar City (IRE)

100(103h)   (90h)102

6-y-o b g Phardante (FR)-Aunty Dawn (IRE) (Strong Gale)
R H Buckler Mrs Timothy Lewis

Placings:6/503P5021   (4701)
2002/03: 16⁵G, 21⁰GS, 20³GS, 24ᴾS, 24⁵HY, 22⁴GS, 21²HY, 20¹GF,

	Starts	1st	2nd	3rd	Win & Pl
NH Flat	1	0	0	0	0
Hurdles	6	0	1	0	1486
Chases	1	1	0	0	3318
Career Total	9	1	1	0	4804
102 4/03 Plum	2m4f	F Ch	G-F	£3318	

Total win prize-money £3318

Going: Sf: 0-4 GS: 0-2 Gd: 0-1 GF: - Fm: 1-1
Distance: 2m2/m3: 0-1 2m4-2m7: 1-5 3m+: 0-2
Track: LH: 1-7 RH: 0-1 Tight: 1-3 Gall: 0-1
Aids: Bl: 0-0 Vi: 0-0 Tstrap: 0-0
Best Rating: 102 4/03 Plum 2m4f gd-fm Ch

Moderate hurdler/chaser; got off the mark on his chase debut; suited by fast ground; stays two miles five.

Phar Echo (IRE)

101   **46**

12-y-o b g Phardante (FR)-Borecca (Boreen (FR))
Mrs H O Graham   Mrs H O Graham

Placings:04/3041310P/5232/12F0F015/420523505/004400
/03156-1U6P065   (2164)
2002/03: 25¹G, 25UGF, 30⁶G, 20⁰G, 27⁰G, 27⁶S, 27⁵S,

	Starts	1st	2nd	3rd	Win & Pl
Chases	7	1	0	0	3276
Career Total	**49**	**6**	**5**	**5**	**27842**
83	4/02	Hexm	3m1f	F(0-100)HCh	GD	£3276
80	3/02	Hexm	4m	F(0-100)HCh	HVY	£3916
106	3/99	Ayr	2m6f	F(0-110)HHdl	SFT	£2815
101	10/98	Carl	3m110y	E(0-115)HHdl	HVY	£2388
99	3/97	Ayr	2m	D(0-110)HHdl	SFT	£2933
95	1/97	Ayr	2m4f	D(0-110)HHdl	GD	£3218

Total win prize-money £18546

Going: Sf: 0-2 GS: 0-0 Gd: 1-4 GF: - Fm: 0-1
Distance: 2m/2m3: 0-0 2m4-2m7: 0-1 3m+: 1-6
Track: LH: 1-6 RH: 0-0 Tight: 0-3 Gall: 0-0
Aids: Bl: 1-6 Vi: 0-0 Tstrap: 0-0
Best Rating: 106 3/99 Ayr 2m6f soft Hdl

Moderate staying chaser, suited by extreme distances. Acts on good and heavy ground. Usually blinkered.

Phar From A Fiddle (IRE)

107(103h)   (107h)**130**

7-y-o b/br g Phardante (FR)-Lucycello (Monksfield)
P F Nicholls   Mrs J Stewart

Placings:0U2/22114444-45   (0917)
2002/03: 20⁴GS, 24⁵GS,

	Starts	1st	2nd	3rd	Win & Pl
Chases	2	0	0	0	3250
Career Total	**13**	**2**	**3**	**0**	**29817**
130	11/01	Winc	3m1f110yD(0-110)HCh	GD	£6955
130	10/01	Chel	2m4f110yD(0-110)HCh	GD	£8697

Total win prize-money £15652

Going: Sf: 0-0 GS: 0-2 Gd: 0-0 GF: - Fm: 0-0
Distance: 2m/2m3: 0-0 2m4-2m7: 0-1 3m+: 0-1
Track: LH: 0-0 RH: 0-2 Tight: 0-1 Gall: 0-0
Aids: Bl: 0-0 Vi: 0-0 Tstrap: 0-0
Best Rating: 130 11/01 Chel 2m4f110y good Ch

Useful chaser; thought not to want the ground too soft. Stays three miles plus.

Phar From Chance

101   **96**

8-y-o ch g Phardante (FR)-Chancer s Last (Foggy Bell)
P F Nicholls   B C Marshall

Placings:5-P331FU5F0   (1701)
2002/03: 20PGF, 21³GF, 26³GF, 26¹GF, 26⁶G, 25UF, 24⁵F, 24FF,
24⁰GF,

	Starts	1st	2nd	3rd	Win & Pl
Chases	9	1	0	2	4103
Career Total	**10**	**1**	**0**	**2**	**4103**
96	8/02	NAbb	3m2f110yF(0-100)HCh	G-F	£2912

Total win prize-money £2912

Going: Sf: 0-0 GS: 0-0 Gd: 0-1 GF: - Fm: 1-8
Distance: 2m/2m3: 0-0 2m4-2m7: 0-2 3m+: 1-7
Track: LH: 1-3 RH: 0-4 Tight: 1-7 Gall: 0-0
Aids: Bl: 0-0 Vi: 0-0 Tstrap: 0-0
Best Rating: 96 8/02 NAbb 3m2f110y gd-fm Ch

Moderate handicap chaser, stays beyond three miles and acts on a sound surface.

Phar From Fair (IRE)

100   **106+**

6-y-o b g Phardante (FR)-Wintry Shower (Strong Gale)
L Wells   Mrs Carrie Zetter-Wells

Placings:4-11024   (2984)
2002/03: 17¹GF, 17¹GF, 16⁰GS, 17²HY, 18⁴HY,

	Starts	1st	2nd	3rd	Win & Pl
NH Flat	3	2	0	0	3738
Hurdles	2	0	1	0	1041
Career Total	**6**	**2**	**1**	**0**	**4779**
95	10/02	Hrfd	2m1f	H NHF	G-F	£1869
86	9/02	Hrfd	2m1f	H NHF	G-F	£1869

Total win prize-money £3738

Going: Sf: 0-2 GS: 0-1 Gd: 0-0 GF: - Fm: 2-2
Distance: 2m/2m3: 2-5 2m4-2m7: 0-0 3m+: 0-0
Track: LH: 0-2 RH: 2-3 Tight: 0-2 Gall: 0-0
Aids: Bl: 0-0 Vi: 0-0 Tstrap: 0-0
Best Rating: 106 12/02 Folk 2m1f110y heavy Hdl

Promising debut in Ascot bumper April 2002. Successful twice at Hereford in September and October under A P McCoy. Ability over hurdles, acts on good and heavy ground.

Phar From Frosty (IRE)

98   **92+**

6-y-o br g Phardante (FR)-Cold Evening (IRE) (Strong Gale)
C R Egerton   Mrs Sandra A Roe

Placings:014F   (2693)
2002/03: 17⁰G, 16¹GS, 19⁴GS, 19FGS,

	Starts	1st	2nd	3rd	Win & Pl
NH Flat	2	1	0	0	2352
Hurdles	2	0	0	0	0
Career Total	**4**	**1**	**0**	**0**	**2352**
90	11/02	Ludl	2m	H NHF	G-S	£2352

Total win prize-money £2352

Going: Sf: 0-0 GS: 1-3 Gd: 0-1 GF: - Fm: 0-0
Distance: 2m/2m3: 1-2 2m4-2m7: 0-2 3m+: 0-0
Track: LH: 0-1 RH: 1-3 Tight: 0-1 Gall: 0-0
Aids: Bl: 0-0 Vi: 0-0 Tstrap: 0-0
Best Rating: 90 12/02 Donc 2m3f110y gd-sft Hdl

Won bumper at Ludlow November 2002; appears to stay 3m 3f over hurdles; acts on good to soft.

Phar Glory (IRE)

    93

8-y-o b g Phardante (FR)-Prudent Rose (IRE) (Strong Gale)
A J Lidderdale   George Ward

Placings:001-2   (0246)
2002/03: 22²G,

	Starts	1st	2nd	3rd	Win & Pl
Hurdles	1	0	1	0	930
Career Total	**4**	**1**	**1**	**0**	**3604**
90	4/02	Chep	2m4f	E Hdl	G-F	£2674

Total win prize-money £2674

Going: Sf: 0-0 GS: 0-0 Gd: 0-1 GF: - Fm: 0-0
Distance: 2m/2m3: 0-0 2m4-2m7: 0-1 3m+: 0-0
Track: LH: 0-0 RH: 0-1 Tight: 0-0 Gall: 0-0
Aids: Bl: 0-0 Vi: 0-0 Tstrap: 0-0
Best Rating: 93 5/02 Extr 2m6f110y good Hdl

Moderate hurdler; won a weak novice hurdle at Chepstow in April 2002. Stays two and a half miles plus, should make a chaser.

Phar To Co (IRE)

8-y-o b m Phardante (FR)-Roseowen (Derring Rose)
K Goldsworthy   Greenacre Racing Partnership Ltd

Placings:F   (4541)
2002/03: 24FG,

	Starts	1st	2nd	3rd	Win & Pl
Chases	1	0	0	0	
Career Total	**1**	**0**	**0**	**0**	

Going: Sf: 0-0 GS: 0-0 Gd: 0-1 GF: - Fm: 0-0
Distance: 2m/2m3: 0-0 2m4-2m7: 0-0 3m+: 0-1
Track: LH: 0-0 RH: 0-1 Tight: 0-1 Gall: 0-0
Aids: Bl: 0-0 Vi: 0-0 Tstrap: 0-0
Best Rating: 0 4/03 Ludl 3m good Ch

Pharagon (IRE)

41

5-y-o b g Phardante (FR)-Hogan (IRE) (Black Minstrel)
Mrs C J Kerr   Mrs C J Kerr

Placings:000   (4772)
2002/03: 14⁰GS, 16⁰GS, 16⁰G,

	Starts	1st	2nd	3rd	Win & Pl
NH Flat	2	0	0	0	0
Hurdles	1	0	0	0	
Career Total	**3**	**0**	**0**	**0**	

Going: Sf: 0-0 GS: 0-2 Gd: 0-1 GF: - Fm: 0-0
Distance: 2m/2m3: 0-0 2m4-2m7: 0-0 3m+: 0-0
Track: LH: 0-1 RH: 0-2 Tight: 0-1 Gall: 0-0
Aids: Bl: 0-0 Vi: 0-0 Tstrap: 0-0
Best Rating: 26 12/02 Ayr 1m6f gd-sft NHF

Pharailde

82   **44**

5-y-o ch m Phardante (FR)-Canal Street (Oats)
M J Roberts   Mike Roberts

Placings:0003   (4757)
2002/03: 18⁰GF, 18⁰S, 20⁰G, 22³GF,

	Starts	1st	2nd	3rd	Win & Pl
NH Flat	2	0	0	0	
Hurdles	2	0	0	1	510
Career Total	**4**	**0**	**0**	**1**	**510**

Going: Sf: 0-1 GS: 0-0 Gd: 0-1 GF: - Fm: 0-2
Distance: 2m/2m3: 0-2 2m4-2m7: 0-2 3m+: 0-0
Track: LH: 0-3 RH: 0-1 Tight: 0-3 Gall: 0-1
Aids: Bl: 0-0 Vi: 0-0 Tstrap: 0-0
Best Rating: 56 5/02 Font 2m2f110y gd-fm NHF

Plating-class novice hurdler; best on a sound surface.

Pharaoh Hatshepsut (IRE)

5-y-o b m Definite Article-Maid Of Mourne (Fairy King (USA))
R A Fahey   Mike Flynn

Placings:P   (2265)
2002/03: 16^PHY,

	Starts	1st	2nd	3rd	Win & Pl
Hurdles	1	0	0	0	
Career Total	1	0	0	0	

Going: Sf: 0-1 GS: 0-0 Gd: 0-0 GF: - Fm: 0-0
Distance: 2m/2m3: 0-1 2m4-2m7: 0-0 3m+: 0-0
Track: LH: 0-1 RH: 0-0 Tight: 0-1 Gall: 0-0
Aids: Bl: 0-0 Vi: 0-0 Tstrap: 0-0
Best Rating: 0   12/02 Kels   2m110y   heavy   Hdl

Pharaway Citizen (IRE)

105(101h)   (100h)**113**
8-y-o ch g Phardante (FR)-Boreen Citizen (Boreen (FR))
T R George Pharaway Partnership

Placings:P32-3PP1P53   (4624)
2002/03: 23³S, 24^PGS, 25^PG, 22¹S, 23^PG, 22⁵G, 26³GF,

	Starts	1st	2nd	3rd	Win & Pl
Hurdles	2	0	0	1	375
Chases	5	1	0	1	9721
Career Total	10	1	1	3	11457
113	2/03	Newb	2m6f110yD(0-120)HCh	SFT	£8736

Total win prize-money £8736

Going: Sf: 1-2 GS: 0-1 Gd: 0-3 GF: - Fm: 0-1
Distance: 2m/2m3: 0-0 **2m4-2m7:** 1-2 3m+: 0-5
Track: LH: **1-3** RH: 0-4 Tight: 0-3 **Gall:** 1-1
Aids: Bl: 0-0 Vi: 0-0 Tstrap: 0-0
Best Rating: 113   2/03   Newb   2m6f110y   soft   Ch

Fair chaser; successful between the flags in Ireland; won a moderate handicap chase on his second start over fences; stays two miles six; acts on soft and good to firm ground.

Pharbeit (IRE)

95   **78**
6-y-o b g King s Ride-Phargara (IRE) (Phardante (FR))
E L James Lady Thompson

Placings:060   (4442)
2002/03: 16⁰S, 16⁶S, 20⁰G,

	Starts	1st	2nd	3rd	Win & Pl
NH Flat	2	0	0	0	0
Hurdles	1	0	0	0	0
Career Total	3	0	0	0	0

Going: Sf: 0-2 GS: 0-0 Gd: 0-1 GF: - Fm: 0-0
Distance: 2m/2m3: 0-2 2m4-2m7: 0-1 3m+: 0-0
Track: LH: 0-2 RH: 0-1 Tight: 0-0 Gall: 0-1
Aids: Bl: 0-1 Vi: 0-0 Tstrap: 0-0
Best Rating: 84   12/02   Uttx   2m   soft   NHF

Novice hurdler; yet to prove he stays further than two miles; wears blinkers.

Pharbeitfrome (IRE)

109   **92**
9-y-o b g Phardante (FR)-Asigh Glen (Furry Glen)
N Wilson (D E Cantillon 6/10) W Stone

Placings:0/00F310F/P04P/0UPF43-31PP3F1U05 (4687)
2002/03: 16³GS, 17¹GF, 19^PGF, 19^PG, 16³GF, 20^FG, 16¹HY, 16^UGS, 16⁰HY, 17⁵G,

	Starts	1st	2nd	3rd	Win & Pl
Hurdles	1	0	0	0	0
Chases	9	2	0	2	7798

Career Total | 28 | 3 | 0 | 4 | 11742
83 | 1/03 | Sedg | 2m110y | F(0-90)HCh | HVY | £3297
83 | 6/02 | MRas | 2m1f110yF(0-100)HCh | G-F | £3388
99 | 3/00 | Dpat | 2m2f | Ch | SFT | £2345

Total win prize-money £9031

Going: Sf: 1-2 GS: 0-2 Gd: 0-3 GF: - Fm: 1-3
Distance: **2m/2m3:** 2-8 2m4-2m7: 0-2 3m+: 0-0
Track: LH: 1-5 RH: 1-5 **Tight: 2-9** Gall: 0-0
Aids: Bl: 0-0 Vi: 0-0 **Tstrap: 2-10**
Best Rating: 99   3/00   Dpat   2m2f   soft   Ch

Moderate handicap chaser; not the best of jumpers; acts on all types of ground; best at distances short of 2m4f.

Phardante Flyer (IRE)

80(89h)   **64**
9-y-o ch g Phardante (FR)-Shannon Lek (Menelek)
P J Hobbs Mrs Karola Vann

Placings:2/1141141/24/2P-04   (4767)
2002/03: 17⁰G, 20⁴G,

	Starts	1st	2nd	3rd	Win & Pl
Hurdles	2	0	0	0	646
Career Total	14	5	3	0	38900
144	4/00	Aint	2m110y	A Hdl	GD	£21000
123	2/00	Ludl	2m	E Hdl	GD	£2352
120	1/00	Winc	2m	E Hdl	G-S	£2205
114	11/99	Wwck	2m	H NHF	GD	£1856
113	11/99	Sand	2m110y	H NHF	GD	£1658

Total win prize-money £29071

Going: Sf: 0-0 GS: 0-0 Gd: 0-2 GF: - Fm: 0-0
Distance: 2m/2m3: 0-1 2m4-2m7: 0-1 3m+: 0-0
Track: LH: 0-1 RH: 0-1 Tight: 0-0 Gall: 0-1
Aids: Bl: 0-0 Vi: 0-0 Tstrap: 0-0
Best Rating: 144   4/00   Aint   2m110y   good   Hdl

Fair hurdler; goes well on good ground, but effective with cut; best over two miles; formerly useful but lightly raced in recent seasons; finished lame in novice chase in May 2003.

Pharlen's Dream (IRE)

66   **31**
7-y-o b m Phardante (FR)-Local Dream (Deep Run)
R H Buckler R H Buckler

Placings:0-0PPU6   (4272)
2002/03: 16⁰GS, 18^PS, 21^PS, 20^UHY, 16⁶G,

	Starts	1st	2nd	3rd	Win & Pl
NH Flat	1	0	0	0	0
Hurdles	4	0	0	0	0
Career Total	6	0	0	0	0

Going: Sf: 0-3 GS: 0-1 Gd: 0-1 GF: - Fm: 0-0
Distance: 2m/2m3: 0-3 2m4-2m7: 0-2 3m+: 0-0
Track: LH: 0-4 RH: 0-1 Tight: 0-2 Gall: 0-0
Aids: Bl: 0-2 Vi: 0-0 Tstrap: 0-0
Best Rating: 37   11/02   Sthl   2m   gd-sft   NHF

Pharly Reef

105   **102**
11-y-o b g Pharly (FR)-Hay Reef (Mill Reef (USA))
D Burchell Mrs Ruth Burchell

Placings:6020/00612/4U26621/1154/S35065-6102 (0729)
2002/03: 17⁶G, 16¹S, 16⁶GF, 16²GF,

	Starts	1st	2nd	3rd	Win & Pl
Hurdles	4	1	1	0	5378

Career Total | 30 | 5 | 5 | 1 | 24217
102 | 6/02 | Uttx | 2m | D(0-115)HHdl | SFT | £3276
113 | 11/99 | Chep | 2m110y | D(0-125)HHdl | SFT | £2845
109 | 7/99 | Strf | 2m110y | C(0-130)HHdl | GD | £4926
98 | 4/99 | Bang | 2m1f | F(0-100)HHdl | GD | £3858
82 | 12/96 | Fknm | 2m | G(0-95)HHdl | GD | £2733

Total win prize-money £17640

Going: Sf: 1-1 GS: 0-1 Gd: 0-1 GF: - Fm: 0-2
Distance: **2m/2m3:** 1-4 2m4-2m7: 0-0 3m+: 0-0
Track: LH: **1-4** RH: 0-0 Tight: 0-3 Gall: 0-0
Aids: Bl: 0-0 Vi: 0-0 Tstrap: 0-0
Best Rating: 113   11/99   Chep   2m110y   soft   Hdl

Modest hurdler around two miles who is entering the veteran stage; goes well on good and soft ground.

Pharmistice (IRE)

12-y-o b g Phardante (FR)-Lucylet (Kinglet)
Miss N Stirling (Mrs P C Stirling 29/5) Mrs P C Stirling

Placings:006/10/2140/0/4-13   (4508)
2002/03: 25¹GF, 25³G,

	Starts	1st	2nd	3rd	Win & Pl
Chases	2	1	0	1	3434
Career Total	13	3	1	1	9370
102	5/02	Kels	3m1f	H Ch	G-F	£2999
83	11/97	Kels	2m6f110yD(0-125)HHdl	G-F	£2738
82	12/96	Kels	2m6f110yE Hdl	GD	£2346

Total win prize-money £8084

Going: Sf: 0-0 GS: 0-0 Gd: 0-1 GF: - Fm: 1-1
Distance: 2m/2m3: 0-0 2m4-2m7: 0-0 **3m+:** 1-2
Track: LH: 1-2 RH: 0-0 Tight: 1-2 Gall: 0-0
Aids: Bl: 0-0 Vi: 0-0 Tstrap: 0-0
Best Rating: 102   4/03   Kels   3m1f   good   Ch

Pharpost (IRE)

107(97h)   (100h)**119+**
8-y-o b g Phardante (FR)-Branstown Lady (Deep Run)
Miss Venetia Williams D E Harrison

Placings:136/41-2F3F424   (4254)
2002/03: 25²G, 25^FG, 24³S, 21^FGS, 21⁴GS, 22³S, 19⁴G,

	Starts	1st	2nd	3rd	Win & Pl
Chases	7	0	2	1	8770
Career Total	12	2	2	2	13288
100	11/01	Strf	2m6f110yE Hdl	SFT	£2618
114	11/00	Ludl	2m	H NHF	GD	£1652

Total win prize-money £4270

Going: Sf: 0-2 GS: 0-2 Gd: 0-3 GF: - Fm: 0-0
Distance: 2m/2m3: 0-2 2m4-2m7: 0-4 3m+: 0-3
Track: LH: 0-4 RH: 0-3 Tight: 0-1 Gall: 0-3
Aids: Bl: 0-0 Vi: 0-0 Tstrap: 0-0
Best Rating: 126   11/02   Winc   3m1f110y   good   Ch

Modest chaser; stays 3m, suited by the ground good or softer; likes to be held up but often finds little under pressure.

Phartodante (IRE)

64   **7**
6-y-o b m Phardante (FR)-Hennywood (IRE) (Henbit (USA))
Mrs L C Jewell Mrs Linda Jewell

Placings:0P   (4634)
2002/03: 16⁰GF, 21^PGF,

	Starts	1st	2nd	3rd	Win & Pl
NH Flat	1	0	0	0	0
Hurdles	1	0	0	0	0
Career Total	2	0	0	0	0

Going: Sf: 0-0 GS: 0-0 Gd: 0-0 GF: - Fm: 0-2
Distance: 2m/2m3: 0-1 2m4-2m7: 0-1 3m+: 0-0
Track: LH: 0-1 RH: 0-1 Tight: 0-1 Gall: 0-1
Aids: Bl: 0-0 Vi: 0-0 Tstrap: 0-0
Best Rating: 58 3/03 Hntg 2m110y gd-fm NHF

Phase Eight Girl
98   78

7-y-o b m Warrshan (USA)-Bugsy s Sister (Aragon)
J Hetherton Peter Urquhart

Placings:363P0046/4124544-313   (1167)
2002/03: 20³G, 26¹GF, 21³G,

	Starts	1st	2nd	3rd	Win & Pl
Hurdles	3	1	0	2	2943
Career Total	18	2	1	4	6417

78	8/02	Hntg	3m2f	F(0-95)HHdl	G-F	£2262
77	5/01	Hntg	2m110y	G(0-95)HHdl	G-F	£1736
			Total win prize-money £3998

Going: Sf: 0-0 GS: 0-0 Gd: 0-2 GF: - Fm: 1-1
Distance: 2m/2m3: 0-0 2m4-2m7: 0-2 3m+: 1-1
Track: LH: 0-2 RH: 1-1 Tight: 0-2 Gall: 1-1
Aids: Bl: 0-0 Vi: 0-0 Tstrap: 0-0
Best Rating: 78 8/02 Hntg 3m2f gd-fm Hdl

Small mare, winning hurdler who needs fast ground. Stays well.

Phildari (IRE)
109(107h)   (108h)103

7-y-o b g Shardari-Philosophical (Welsh Chanter)
P R Webber Michael Coghlan

Placings:00/022423-34P5242   (4701)
2002/03: 20³GF, 20⁴G, 21⁴PS, 16⁵GS, 24²GF, 24⁴G, 20²GF,

	Starts	1st	2nd	3rd	Win & Pl
Hurdles	3	0	0	1	841
Chases	4	0	2	0	2649
Career Total	15	0	5	2	7898

Going: Sf: 0-1 GS: 0-1 Gd: 0-2 GF: - Fm: 0-3
Distance: 2m/2m3: 0-1 2m4-2m7: 0-4 3m+: 0-2
Track: LH: 0-2 RH: 0-5 Tight: 0-2 Gall: 0-2
Aids: Bl: 0-0 Vi: 0-0 Tstrap: 0-6
Best Rating: 108 10/02 Chep 2m4f good Hdl

Modest chaser; improved over hurdles for the fitting of a tongue tie; often placed but yet to win; acts on good and soft ground; stays three miles; has worn cheekpieces.

Philtre (IRE)
98   67

9-y-o b g Phardante (FR)-Forest Gale (Strong Gale)
Mrs H L Needham J D Callow

Placings:2P3U/1311046-P   (0414)
2002/03: 28⁶GF,

	Starts	1st	2nd	3rd	Win & Pl
Chases	1	0	0	0	
Career Total	12	3	1	2	16372

110	6/01	Worc	2m7f110yE Ch		G-F	£3190
110	6/01	Strf	H Ch		G-F	£8287
110	5/01	Hntg	3m	E Ch	GD	£3731
				Total win prize-money £15209

Going: Sf: 0-0 GS: 0-0 Gd: 0-0 GF: - Fm: 0-1
Distance: 2m/2m3: 0-0 2m4-2m7: 0-0 3m+: 0-1
Track: LH: 0-1 RH: 0-0 Tight: 0-1 Gall: 0-0
Aids: Bl: 0-0 Vi: 0-0 Tstrap: 0-0

Best Rating: 110 6/01 Worc 2m7f110y gd-fm Ch

Useful hunter chaser and point winner, he won a modest novice chase in the summer of 2001. Needs a sound surface and stays three and a half miles.

Phinda Forest (IRE)
80   40

4-y-o br f Charnwood Forest (IRE)-Shatalia (USA) (Shahrastani (USA))
W Storey (I A Balding 12/9) Gremlin Racing

Placings:00P   (4517)
2002/03: 16⁰G, 16⁰GS, 17⁰G,

	Starts	1st	2nd	3rd	Win & Pl
Hurdles	3	0	0	0	
Career Total	3	0	0	0	

Going: Sf: 0-0 GS: 0-1 Gd: 0-2 GF: - Fm: 0-0
Distance: 2m/2m3: 0-3 2m4-2m7: 0-0 3m+: 0-0
Track: LH: 0-2 RH: 0-1 Tight: 0-3 Gall: 0-0
Aids: Bl: 0-0 Vi: 0-0 Tstrap: 0-0
Best Rating: 47 2/03 Muss 2m good Hdl

Phoenix Phlyer

9-y-o b g Ardross-Brown Coast (Oats)
D Pipe John Duggan

Placings:500/005023/020P34312/00-0   (0032)
2002/03: 21⁰GF,

	Starts	1st	2nd	3rd	Win & Pl
Chases	1	0	0	0	
Career Total	21	1	3	3	8586

| 108 | 4/01 | Extr | 2m3f110yF(0-95)HCh | G-S | £3447 |
| | | | | Total win prize-money £3448 |

Going: Sf: 0-0 GS: 0-0 Gd: 0-0 GF: - Fm: 0-1
Distance: 2m/2m3: 0-0 2m4-2m7: 0-0 3m+: 0-0
Track: LH: 0-1 RH: 0-0 Tight: 0-0 Gall: 0-1
Aids: Bl: 0-0 Vi: 0-1 Tstrap: 0-0
Best Rating: 108 4/01 Extr 2m3f110y gd-sft Ch

Photographer (USA)
90   101

5-y-o b/br g Mountain Cat (USA)-Clickety Click (USA) (Sovereign Dancer (USA))
Mrs N Smith Tony Hayward, Barry Fulton, Jamie Bruce

Placings:404-5   (0097)
2002/03: 18⁵GF,

	Starts	1st	2nd	3rd	Win & Pl
Hurdles	1	0	0	0	0
Career Total	4	0	0	0	0

Going: Sf: 0-0 GS: 0-0 Gd: 0-0 GF: - Fm: 0-1
Distance: 2m/2m3: 0-1 2m4-2m7: 0-0 3m+: 0-0
Track: LH: 0-1 RH: 0-0 Tight: 0-1 Gall: 0-0
Aids: Bl: 0-0 Vi: 0-0 Tstrap: 0-0
Best Rating: 101 2/02 Kemp 2m good Hdl

Moderate novice hurdler.

Phylozzo

7-y-o ch m Michelozzo (USA)-Phyllida Fox (Healaugh Fox)
C J Price Mrs C W Middleton

Placings:0-P   (0901)
2002/03: 20⁰G,

	Starts	1st	2nd	3rd	Win & Pl
Hurdles	1	0	0	0	
Career Total	2	0	0	0	

Going: Sf: 0-0 GS: 0-0 Gd: 0-1 GF: - Fm: 0-0
Distance: 2m/2m3: 0-0 2m4-2m7: 0-1 3m+: 0-0
Track: LH: 0-1 RH: 0-0 Tight: 0-0 Gall: 0-0
Aids: Bl: 0-0 Vi: 0-0 Tstrap: 0-0
Best Rating: 0 8/02 Worc 2m4f good Hdl

Physical Force

5-y-o b g Casteddu-Kaiserlinde (GER) (Frontal)
D W Chapman (J R Best 11/10) David W Chapman

Placings:P   (1480)
2002/03: 20⁰GF,

	Starts	1st	2nd	3rd	Win & Pl
Hurdles	1	0	0	0	
Career Total	1	0	0	0	

Going: Sf: 0-0 GS: 0-0 Gd: 0-0 GF: - Fm: 0-1
Distance: 2m/2m3: 0-0 2m4-2m7: 0-1 3m+: 0-0
Track: LH: 0-0 RH: 0-1 Tight: 0-0 Gall: 0-1
Aids: Bl: 0-0 Vi: 0-0 Tstrap: 0-0
Best Rating: 0 10/02 Hntg 2m4f110y gd-fm Hdl

Physical Graffiti (USA)
103   95

6-y-o b g Mister Baileys-Gleaming Water (USA) (Pago Pago)
J A B Old Nigel Dempster

Placings:04/40-F14   (3949)
2002/03: 19⁵S, 16¹HY, 19⁴S,

	Starts	1st	2nd	3rd	Win & Pl
Hurdles	3	1	0	0	5288
Career Total	7	1	0	0	5616

| 95 | 2/03 | Leic | 2m | E(0-105)HHdl | HVY | £4914 |
| | | | | Total win prize-money £4914 |

Going: Sf: 1-3 GS: 0-0 Gd: 0-0 GF: - Fm: 0-0
Distance: 2m/2m3: 1-2 2m4-2m7: 0-1 3m+: 0-0
Track: LH: 0-0 RH: 1-3 Tight: 0-1 Gall: 0-0
Aids: Bl: 0-0 Vi: 0-0 Tstrap: 0-0
Best Rating: 95 2/03 Leic 2m heavy Hdl

Generally moderate; some signs of ability; won at Leicester in February 2003; acts on very soft ground; should stay further than two miles.

Piccadilly
109(108h)   (98 h)84

8-y-o ch m Belmez (USA)-Polly s Pear (USA) (Sassafras (FR))
Miss Kate Milligan S Ward

Placings:505234/5325/631U233-1523F   (1217)
2002/03: 24¹G, 22⁵GF, 25²GS, 25³GF, 26⁶G,

	Starts	1st	2nd	3rd	Win & Pl
Hurdles	1	0	0	0	2758
Chases	4	0	1	1	2188
Career Total	22	2	4	6	10618

98	5/02	Sthl	3m110y	E(0-105)HHdl	GD	£2758
87	8/01	Sthl	3m110y	G Hdl	G-F	£1575
				Total win prize-money £4333

Going: Sf: 0-0 GS: 0-1 Gd: 1-2 GF: - Fm: 0-2
Distance: 2m/2m3: 0-0 2m4-2m7: 0-1 **3m+: 1-4**
Track: **LH: 1-2** RH: 0-3 Tight: 1-4 Gall: 0-0
Aids: Bl: 0-0 Vi: 0-0 Tstrap: 0-0
Best Rating: 98 5/02 Sthl 3m110y good Hdl

Moderate hurdler/chaser; stays three miles; best on a sound surface.

Piccolina

11-y-o ch m Phardante (FR)-Highland Chain (Furry Glen)
G J Smith (R T Phillips 26/5) The Very Picky Partnership

Placings:04/5F   (1220)
2002/03: 20⁵GF, 21⁵G,

	Starts	1st	2nd	3rd	Win & Pl
Hurdles	2	0	0	0	0
Career Total	4	0	0	0	0

Going: Sf: 0-0 GS: 0-0 Gd: 0-1 GF: - Fm: 0-0
Distance: 2m/2m3: 0-0 2m4-2m7: 0-0 3m+: 0-0
Track: LH: 0-2 RH: 0-0 Tight: 0-1 Gall: 0-0
Aids: Bl: 0-0 Vi: 0-0 Tstrap: 0-0
Best Rating: 0 9/02 Sthl 2m5f110y good Hdl

Piccolo Lady

4-y-o b f Piccolo-Tonic Chord (La Grange Music)
M Wigham Charles Alan McKechnie

Placings:P   (1641)
2002/03: 16⁵G,

	Starts	1st	2nd	3rd	Win & Pl
Hurdles	1	0	0	0	
Career Total	1	0	0	0	

Going: Sf: 0-0 GS: 0-0 Gd: 0-1 GF: - Fm: 0-0
Distance: 2m/2m3: 0-1 2m4-2m7: 0-0 3m+: 0-0
Track: LH: 0-0 RH: 0-0 Tight: 0-1 Gall: 0-0
Aids: Bl: 0-0 Vi: 0-0 Tstrap: 0-0
Best Rating: 0 10/02 Kemp 2m good Hdl

Picket Piece
118

12-y-o br g Shareef Dancer (USA)-Jouvencelle (Rusticaro (FR))
N A Twiston-Davies H R Mould

Placings:4/665111325/22130400/3F3220115/0P6B20-
                                                    (0014)
2002/03: 25⁹GS,

	Starts	1st	2nd	3rd	Win & Pl
Chases	1	0	0	0	
Career Total	33	6	6	4	62319
124 3/01	Sand	3m110y	C(0-135)HCh	SFT	£7377
124 2/01	Leic	2m7f110yE(0-115)HCh	SFT	£3836
138 11/99	Newb	2m3f	B(0-140)HHdl	G-S	£20832
116 2/99	Newb	2m110y	D(0-115)HHdl	G-S	£3028
120 1/99	Chel	2m1f	D(0-120)HHdl	SFT	£4758
94 1/99	Ludl	2m	E(0-105)HHdl	SFT	£2372

Total win prize-money £42205

Going: Sf: 0-0 GS: 0-1 Gd: 0-0 GF: - Fm: 0-0
Distance: 2m/2m3: 0-0 2m4-2m7: 0-0 3m+: 0-1
Track: LH: 0-0 RH: 0-0 Tight: 0-0 Gall: 0-0
Aids: Bl: 0-0 Vi: 0-0 Tstrap: 0-0
Best Rating: 138 11/00 MRas 2m5f110y gd-sft Hdl

Fair chaser; suited by easy ground, he tries hard and stays three miles.

Picture Mee
14

5-y-o b m Aragon-Heemee (On Your Mark)
M A Barnes J M Carlyle

Placings:0F-PP   (0618)
2002/03: 16⁶GS, 16⁶GF,

	Starts	1st	2nd	3rd	Win & Pl
Hurdles	2	0	0	0	
Career Total	4	0	0	0	

Going: Sf: 0-0 GS: 0-1 Gd: 0-0 GF: - Fm: 0-1
Distance: 2m/2m3: 0-2 2m4-2m7: 0-0 3m+: 0-0
Track: LH: 0-2 RH: 0-0 Tight: 0-0 Gall: 0-0
Aids: Bl: 0-0 Vi: 0-0 Tstrap: 0-1
Best Rating: 0 6/02 Hexm 2m110y gd-fm Hdl

Picture Palace
100   109+

5-y-o ch g Salse (USA)-Moviegoer (Pharly (FR))
T R George Mrs V Beeching,Alan Waller,James Layton

Placings:22220343-P5431   (4218)
2002/03: 16⁸S, 21⁵S, 19⁴G, 16³S, 26¹GF,

	Starts	1st	2nd	3rd	Win & Pl
Hurdles	5	1	0	1	5008
Career Total	13	1	4	3	13315
102 3/03	Hrfd	3m2f	E(0-110)HHdl	G-F	£3528

Total win prize-money £3528

Going: Sf: 0-3 GS: 0-0 Gd: 0-1 GF: - Fm: 1-1
Distance: 2m/2m3: 0-2 2m4-2m7: 0-0 **3m+: 1-1**
Track: LH: 0-1 **RH: 1-4** Tight: 0-0 Gall: 0-1
Aids: **Bl: 1-5** Vi: 0-0 Tstrap: 0-0
Best Rating: 108 11/01 Chel 2m110y good Hdl

Modest hurdler; stays really well; winner at Hereford in March and Southwell two months later.

Pierre Precieuse
97f   78f

4-y-o ch f Bijou D Inde-Time Or Never (FR) (Dowsing (USA))
J S Goldie J S Morrison

Placings:066   (4778)
2002/03: 16⁹GS, 16⁸S, 16⁶G,

	Starts	1st	2nd	3rd	Win & Pl
NH Flat	3	0	0	0	0
Career Total	3	0	0	0	0

Going: Sf: 0-1 GS: 0-1 Gd: 0-1 GF: - Fm: 0-0
Distance: 2m/2m3: 0-3 2m4-2m7: 0-0 3m+: 0-0
Track: LH: 0-2 RH: 0-1 Tight: 0-0 Gall: 0-0
Aids: Bl: 0-0 Vi: 0-0 Tstrap: 0-0
Best Rating: 78 4/03 Prth 2m110y good NHF

Pietro Bembo (IRE)
106   102+

9-y-o b g Midyan (USA)-Cut No Ice (Great Nephew)
P C Ritchens (Miss E C Lavelle 9/11) Fraser Miller Racing

Placings:0/42613125/F4100/0P5401/43-60   (2370)
2002/03: 16⁶G, 16⁹S,

	Starts	1st	2nd	3rd	Win & Pl
Hurdles	2	0	0	0	525

Career Total 24 4 2 2 28474

133 3/01	Asct	2m110y	B(0-140)HHdl	HVY	£7254
133 2/00	Kemp	2m	C(0-135)HHdl	SFT	£10481
130 3/99	Folk	2m1f110yE	HHdl	G-S	£2488
133 12/98	Winc	2m	E(0-100)HHdl	SFT	£2528

Total win prize-money £22751

Going: Sf: 0-1 GS: 0-0 Gd: 0-1 GF: - Fm: 0-0
Distance: 2m/2m3: 0-2 2m4-2m7: 0-0 3m+: 0-0
Track: LH: 0-0 RH: 0-2 Tight: 0-0 Gall: 0-0
Aids: Bl: 0-0 Vi: 0-0 Tstrap: 0-0
Best Rating: 133 3/01 Asct 2m110y heavy Hdl

Useful hurdler/moderate chaser; likes to force the pace; best on soft ground, but acts on faster; yet to prove he stays three miles.

Pikestaff (USA)
98   93d

5-y-o ch g Diesis-Navarene (USA) (Known Fact (USA))
M A Barnes (T D Barron 1/5) J M Carlyle

Placings:0002   (4616)
2002/03: 22⁰G, 16⁶S, 16⁶S, 17²GF,

	Starts	1st	2nd	3rd	Win & Pl
Hurdles	4	0	1	0	1084
Career Total	4	0	1	0	1084

Going: Sf: 0-2 GS: 0-0 Gd: 0-1 GF: - Fm: 0-0
Distance: 2m/2m3: 0-3 2m4-2m7: 0-1 3m+: 0-0
Track: LH: 0-3 RH: 0-1 Tight: 0-0 Gall: 0-1
Aids: Bl: 0-0 Vi: 0-0 Tstrap: 0-0
Best Rating: 93 4/03 Carl 2m1f gd-fm Hdl

Plating-class hurdler; poor form before runner-up in weak event at Carlisle; suited by fast ground.

Pilgrim Goose (IRE)
73   59

5-y-o ch g Rainbows For Life (CAN)-Across The Ring (IRE) (Auction Ring (USA))
Jedd O Keeffe (J R Best 19/10) G McMahon

Placings:0   (2473)
2002/03: 16⁰G,

	Starts	1st	2nd	3rd	Win & Pl
Hurdles	1	0	0	0	
Career Total	1	0	0	0	

Going: Sf: 0-0 GS: 0-0 Gd: 0-1 GF: - Fm: 0-0
Distance: 2m/2m3: 0-1 2m4-2m7: 0-0 3m+: 0-0
Track: LH: 0-1 RH: 0-0 Tight: 0-0 Gall: 0-1
Aids: Bl: 0-0 Vi: 0-0 Tstrap: 0-0
Best Rating: 52 12/02 Donc 2m110y good Hdl

Pillaging Pict
114   126

8-y-o ch g Primitive Rising (USA)-Carat Stick (Gold Rod)
J B Walton Messrs F T Walton

Placings:F63415F311-31351P   (4751)
2002/03: 22³G, 17¹S, 16³S, 20⁵GS, 22¹GS, 20⁶G,

	Starts	1st	2nd	3rd	Win & Pl
Chases	6	2	0	2	18554
Career Total	16	5	0	4	36078
126 3/03	Kels	2m6f110yC(0-130)HCh	G-S	£11482
126 11/02	Kels	2m1f	D(0-115)HCh	SFT	£4823
114 4/02	Prth	2m4f110yD(0-115)HCh	GD	£5863
105 4/02	Carl	2m4f	E(0-100)HCh	SFT	£3867
101 1/02	Catt	2m	E(0-105)HCh	G-S	£6071

Total win prize-money £32107

Going: Sf: 1-2 GS: 1-2 Gd: 0-2 GF: - Fm: 0-0
Distance: 2m/2m3: 1-2 2m4-2m7: 1-4 3m+: 0-0
Track: LH: 2-5 RH: 0-1 Tight: 2-3 Gall: 0-1
Aids: Bl: 0-0 Vi: 0-0 Tstrap: 0-0
Best Rating: 126 3/03 Kels 2m6f110y gd-sft Ch

Fair chaser; stays two and three-quarter miles; appreciates cut, but does not want it too soft.

Pillar Of Fire (IRE)

103(101c)   (103c) 101

9-y-o gr g Roselier (FR)-Cousin Flo (True Song)
Ian Williams Paul Robson

Placings:633/40101/02**P4PF04P**-O0100   (4159)
2002/03: 20⁰GS, 20⁶S, 21¹G, 22⁶S, 22⁹G,

	Starts	1st	2nd	3rd	Win & Pl
Hurdles	5	1	0		6344
Career Total	22	3	1	2	15497
101	10/02	MRas	2m5f110yD(0-125)HHdl	GD	£6344
103	4/01	MRas	2m3f110yD(0-120)HHdl	G-S	£3932
100	12/00	MRas	2m3f110yF Hdl	G-S	£2562

Total win prize-money £12839

Going: Sf: 0-2 GS: 0-1 Gd: 1-2 GF: - Fm: 0-0
Distance: 2m/2m3: 0-0 **2m4-2m7: 1-5** 3m+: 0-0
Track: LH: 0-3 **RH: 1-1** Tight: 1-1 Gall: 0-0
Aids: Bl: 0-0 Vi: 0-0 Tstrap: 0-0
Best Rating: 103 4/01 MRas 2m3f110y gd-sft Hdl

At his best over hurdles at Market Rasen, he is effective at around two miles five. Has not shown much over fences.

Piltdown Chimes

8-y-o b m Arctic Lord-Houston Belle (Milford)
J R Best Mrs F A Veasey

Placings:0P/P-P   (0434)
2002/03: 20⁰PGF,

	Starts	1st	2nd	3rd	Win & Pl
Hurdles	1	0	0	0	
Career Total	4	0	0	0	

Going: Sf: 0-0 GS: 0-0 Gd: 0-0 GF: - Fm: 0-1
Distance: 2m/2m3: 0-0 2m4-2m7: 0-0 3m+: 0-1
Track: LH: 0-0 RH: 0-0 Tight: 0-0 Gall: 0-1
Aids: Bl: 0-0 Vi: 0-0 Tstrap: 0-0
Best Rating: 52 11/00 Tntn 2m1f good NHF

Pimlico (IRE)

91f   96f

5-y-o ch g Imp Society (USA)-Willow Gale (Strong Gale)
J T Gifford John Plackett

Placings:50   (1995)
2002/03: 17⁵GS, 16⁰GS,

	Starts	1st	2nd	3rd	Win & Pl
NH Flat	2	0	0	0	0
Career Total	2	0	0	0	0

Going: Sf: 0-0 GS: 0-2 Gd: 0-0 GF: - Fm: 0-0
Distance: 2m/2m3: 0-2 2m4-2m7: 0-0 3m+: 0-0
Track: LH: 0-1 RH: 0-1 Tight: 0-1 Gall: 0-0
Aids: Bl: 0-0 Vi: 0-0 Tstrap: 0-0
Best Rating: 96 11/02 Chel 2m110y gd-sft NHF

Well held in bumpers.

Pingo Hill (IRE)

96   78

11-y-o ch g Salt Dome (USA)-Andarta (Ballymore)
J Mackie R J Wright

Placings:000113FP0**PF5**/45435/112P5/6065/PP-14 (1083)
2002/03: 19¹GF, 20⁴GF,

	Starts	1st	2nd	3rd	Win & Pl
Hurdles	2	1	0		1687
Career Total	30	5	1	2	15132
78	6/02	MRas	2m3f110yG(0-90)HHdl	G-F	£1687
101	7/98	Bang	2m4f	E(0-115)HHdl	GD	£3582
96	5/98	Hntg	2m5f110yG(0-95)HHdl	G-F	£1898
111	7/96	Wxfd	2m4f	Hdl	YLD	£2648
98	6/96	Limk	2m2f	Hdl	GD	£3530

Total win prize-money £13347

Going: Sf: 0-0 GS: 0-0 Gd: 0-0 GF: - Fm: 1-2
Distance: 2m/2m3: 0-0 **2m4-2m7: 1-2** 3m+: 0-0
Track: LH: 0-0 **RH: 1-2** Tight: **1-1** Gall: 0-1
Aids: Bl: 0-0 Vi: 0-0 Tstrap: 0-0
Best Rating: 111 7/96 Wxfd 2m4f yield Hdl

Plating-class chaser; best around two and a half miles; acts on a sound surface.

Pip Moss

103   85

8-y-o ch g Le Moss-My Aisling (John De Coombe)
J A B Old Mrs Jim Old

Placings:0/5F-0063   (4096)
2002/03: 16⁹GS, 16⁶S, 22⁶GS, 19³HY,

	Starts	1st	2nd	3rd	Win & Pl
Hurdles	4	0	0	1	837
Career Total	7	0	0	1	837

Going: Sf: 0-2 GS: 0-2 Gd: 0-0 GF: - Fm: 0-0
Distance: 2m/2m3: 0-2 2m4-2m7: 0-2 3m+: 0-0
Track: LH: 0-2 RH: 0-0 Tight: 0-1 Gall: 0-1
Aids: Bl: 0-0 Vi: 0-0 Tstrap: 0-0
Best Rating: 95 12/01 NAbb 2m1f heavy NHF

Moderate efforts in bumpers and hurdles.

Pip's Brave

68   9

7-y-o b g Be My Chief (USA)-Pipistrelle (Shareef Dancer (USA))
L A Dace Luke Dace

Placings:P/0   (1869)
2002/03: 18⁰GS,

	Starts	1st	2nd	3rd	Win & Pl
Hurdles	1	0	0	0	
Career Total	2	0	0	0	

Going: Sf: 0-0 GS: 0-1 Gd: 0-0 GF: - Fm: 0-0
Distance: 2m/2m3: 0-1 2m4-2m7: 0-0 3m+: 0-0
Track: LH: 0-1 RH: 0-0 Tight: 0-1 Gall: 0-0
Aids: Bl: 0-0 Vi: 0-0 Tstrap: 0-1
Best Rating: 9 11/02 Font 2m2f110y gd-sft Hdl

Pipers Lament

92f   71f

4-y-o ch g Hamas (IRE)-Highland Rhapsody (IRE) (Kris)
R Ford Holding Partnership

Placings:4   (4269)

2002/03: 16⁴GF,

	Starts	1st	2nd	3rd	Win & Pl
NH Flat	1	0	0	0	0
Career Total	1	0	0	0	0

Going: Sf: 0-0 GS: 0-0 Gd: 0-0 GF: - Fm: 0-1
Distance: 2m/2m3: 0-1 2m4-2m7: 0-0 3m+: 0-0
Track: LH: 0-1 RH: 0-0 Tight: 0-1 Gall: 0-0
Aids: Bl: 0-0 Vi: 0-0 Tstrap: 0-0
Best Rating: 71 3/03 Sthl 2m gd-fm NHF

Pirandello (IRE)

110   107

5-y-o ch g Shalford (IRE)-Scenic Villa (Top Ville)
K C Bailey (Miss K B Boutflower 21/12) Quicksilver Racing Partnership

Placings:611   (4573)
2002/03: 16⁶G, 16¹GF, 16¹GF,

	Starts	1st	2nd	3rd	Win & Pl
Hurdles	3	2	0		9549
Career Total	3	2	0	0	9549
107	4/03	Strf	2m110y D(0-110)HHdl	G-F	£5850
90	3/03	Hntg	2m110y E Hdl	G-F	£3698

Total win prize-money £9549

Going: Sf: 0-0 GS: 0-0 Gd: 0-1 GF: - Fm: 2-2
Distance: **2m/2m3: 2-3** 2m4-2m7: 0-0 3m+: 0-0
Track: LH: 1-1 RH: 1-2 Tight: 1-1 Gall: 1-1
Aids: Bl: 0-0 Vi: 0-0 Tstrap: 0-0
Best Rating: 107 4/03 Strf 2m110y gd-fm Hdl

Modest novice hurdler; progressive; winner at Huntingdon in March and at Stratford the following month; suited by fast ground and two miles.

Pirate King (IRE)

33   54

6-y-o g g Eurobus-Shakie Lady (Tug Of War)
C P Morlock Pell-Mell Partners

Placings:0PP   (3265)
2002/03: 16⁶G, 21³S, 19⁶GS,

	Starts	1st	2nd	3rd	Win & Pl
Hurdles	3	0	0	0	
Career Total	3	0	0	0	

Going: Sf: 0-1 GS: 0-1 Gd: 0-1 GF: - Fm: 0-0
Distance: 2m/2m3: 0-1 2m4-2m7: 0-2 3m+: 0-0
Track: LH: 0-2 RH: 0-1 Tight: 0-0 Gall: 0-0
Aids: Bl: 0-0 Vi: 0-0 Tstrap: 0-0
Best Rating: 54 11/02 Winc 2m good Hdl

Pizarro (IRE)

113   147

6-y-o ch g Broken Hearted-Our Swan Lady (Swan s Rock)
E J O Grady Edward Wallace

Placings:1/1f-1312F   (4473)
2002/03: 20¹S, 20³YS, 20¹S, 21²G, 24⁶G,

	Starts	1st	2nd	3rd	Win & Pl
Hurdles	5	2	1	1	44493
Career Total	8	5	1	1	73615
132	2/03	DRoy	2m4f	Hdl	SFT	£5376
147	11/02	Navn	2m4f	Hdl	SFT	£14355
152	3/02	Chel	2m110y	A NHF	G-S	£18000
127	2/02	Naas	2m	NHF	HVY	£4444
126	4/01	Fair	2m	NHF	SFT	£6677

Total win prize-money £48855

Going: Sf: 2-2 GS: 0-0 Gd: 0-2 GF: - Fm: 0-0
Distance: 2m/2m3: 0-0 2m4-2m7: 2-4 3m+: 0-1
Track: LH: 1-4 RH: 0-0 Tight: 0-1 Gall: 0-1
Aids: Bl: 0-0 Vi: 0-0 Tstrap: 0-0
Best Rating: 152 3/02 Chel 2m110y gd-sft NHF

Winner of the 2002 Champion Bumper at Cheltenham; has progressed into high-class novice hurdler and finished second after being promoted a place in the Royal & SunAlliance Novices Hurdle at the 2003 Festival; early casualty at Aintree; stays two and a half miles; suited by soft ground; top-class prospect.

Place Above (IRE)
90   45
7-y-o b g Alphabatim (USA)-Lucky Pit (Pitpan)
E A Elliott Eric A Elliott

Placings:05 (3989)
2002/03: 20⁰GS, 24⁵S,

	Starts	1st	2nd	3rd	Win & Pl
Hurdles	2	0	0	0	0
Career Total	2	0	0	0	

Going: Sf: 0-1 GS: 0-1 Gd: 0-0 GF: - Fm: 0-0
Distance: 2m/2m3: 0-0 2m4-2m7: 0-1 3m+: 0-1
Track: LH: 0-1 RH: 0-1 Tight: 0-1 Gall: 0-0
Aids: Bl: 0-0 Vi: 0-0 Tstrap: 0-0
Best Rating: 45 2/03 Ayr 2m4f gd-sft Hdl

Placid Man (IRE)
106   130+
9-y-o br g Un Desperado (FR)-Sparkling Gale (IRE) (Strong Gale)
N J Henderson Highclere Thoroughbred Racing Ltd

Placings:2/3/P1 (2986)
2002/03: 19⁶S, 20¹HY,

	Starts	1st	2nd	3rd	Win & Pl
Chases	2	1	0	0	4085
Career Total	4	1	1	1	5426
130 1/03 Font 2m4f	E Ch		HVY	£4085	
		Total win prize-money	£4085		

Going: Sf: 1-2 GS: 0-0 Gd: 0-0 GF: - Fm: 0-0
Distance: 2m/2m3: 0-0 2m4-2m7: 1-2 3m+: 0-0
Track: LH: 0-0 RH: 0-0 Tight: 1-1 Gall: 0-0
Aids: Bl: 0-0 Vi: 0-0 Tstrap: 0-0
Best Rating: 130 1/03 Font 2m4f heavy Ch

An Irish point winner, runner-up in a bumper over there and ran well enough on his hurdling debut at Doncaster back in January 2001; returned from nearly two years off in late 2002 and won on heavy ground at Fontwell in January 2003.

Plain Chant
64
6-y-o b g Doyoun-Sing Softly (Luthier)
B J Llewellyn S Harrison

Placings:000P-P (0207)
2002/03: 16⁶G,

	Starts	1st	2nd	3rd	Win & Pl
Hurdles	1	0	0	0	
Career Total	5	0	0	0	

Going: Sf: 0-0 GS: 0-0 Gd: 0-1 GF: - Fm: 0-0
Distance: 2m/2m3: 0-1 2m4-2m7: 0-0 3m+: 0-0
Track: LH: 0-0 RH: 0-1 Tight: 0-0 Gall: 0-0
Aids: Bl: 0-0 Vi: 0-0 Tstrap: 0-0

Best Rating: 64 11/01 Plum 2m good Hdl

Plaisance (GER)
89   80
4-y-o b f Monsun (GER)-Pariana (USA) (Bering)
J R Jenkins Jack McGrath

Placings:F23P (4637)
2002/03: 16⁶GS, 18²S, 17³G, 16⁶GF,

	Starts	1st	2nd	3rd	Win & Pl
Hurdles	4	0	1	1	1477
Career Total	4	0	1	1	1477

Going: Sf: 0-1 GS: 0-1 Gd: 0-1 GF: - Fm: 0-1
Distance: 2m/2m3: 0-4 2m4-2m7: 0-0 3m+: 0-0
Track: LH: 0-3 RH: 0-1 Tight: 0-4 Gall: 0-0
Aids: Bl: 0-0 Vi: 0-0 Tstrap: 0-0
Best Rating: 80 3/03 Folk 2m1f110y good Hdl

Fair maiden hurdler.

Planet Ireland (IRE)
11-y-o b g Mandalus-Seapatrick (The Parson)
Mrs J M Hollands Mrs C J Kerr

Placings:PP/5040U/4PFP/PS06-5 (0260)
2002/03: 20⁶G, 20⁵GF,

	Starts	1st	2nd	3rd	Win & Pl
Chases	2	0	0	0	0
Career Total	16	0	0	0	460

Going: Sf: 0-0 GS: 0-0 Gd: 0-1 GF: - Fm: 0-1
Distance: 2m/2m3: 0-0 2m4-2m7: 0-2 3m+: 0-0
Track: LH: 0-1 RH: 0-1 Tight: 0-0 Gall: 0-1
Aids: Bl: 0-0 Vi: 0-0 Tstrap: 0-0
Best Rating: 70 5/02 Prth 2m4f110y gd-fm Ch

Plantaganet (FR)
88f   93f
5-y-o br g Cadoudal (FR)-Ever Young (FR) (Royal Charter (FR))
Ian Williams Sir Robert Ogden

Placings:00 (4444)
2002/03: 16⁶G, 16⁶G,

	Starts	1st	2nd	3rd	Win & Pl
NH Flat	2	0	0	0	
Career Total	2	0	0	0	

Going: Sf: 0-0 GS: 0-0 Gd: 0-2 GF: - Fm: 0-0
Distance: 2m/2m3: 0-2 2m4-2m7: 0-0 3m+: 0-0
Track: LH: 0-0 RH: 0-2 Tight: 0-0 Gall: 0-0
Aids: Bl: 0-0 Vi: 0-0 Tstrap: 0-0
Best Rating: 93 2/03 Kemp 2m good NHF

Plantageant
63
6-y-o ch g Superlative-International Star (IRE) (Astronef)
N B Mason N B Mason

Placings:PP0/0- (0004)
2002/03: 16⁶G,

	Starts	1st	2nd	3rd	Win & Pl
Hurdles	1	0	0	0	

Career Total   4   0   0   0

Going: Sf: 0-0 GS: 0-0 Gd: 0-1 GF: - Fm: 0-0
Distance: 2m/2m3: 0-1 2m4-2m7: 0-0 3m+: 0-0
Track: LH: 0-1 RH: 0-0 Tight: 0-0 Gall: 0-1
Aids: Bl: 0-0 Vi: 0-0 Tstrap: 0-1
Best Rating:

Plastic Paddy (IRE)
97f   115f
6-y-o b g Beau Sher-Vultang Lady (Le Bavard (FR))
D P Keane W Clifford

Placings:12 (3623)
2002/03: 16¹S, 16²HY,

	Starts	1st	2nd	3rd	Win & Pl
NH Flat	2	1	1	0	2712
Career Total	2	1	1	0	2712
110 12/02 Uttx 2m	H NHF		SFT	£1953	
		Total win prize-money	£1953		

Going: Sf: 1-2 GS: 0-0 Gd: 0-0 GF: - Fm: 0-0
Distance: 2m/2m3: 1-2 2m4-2m7: 0-0 3m+: 0-0
Track: LH: 1-1 RH: 0-1 Tight: 0-0 Gall: 0-0
Aids: Bl: 0-0 Vi: 0-0 Tstrap: 0-0
Best Rating: 115 2/03 Sand 2m110y heavy NHF

Chasing-bred, but doing very well in bumpers; acts very well on testing ground; should stay well.

Platonic-My-Eye (IRE)
95(102c)   (126c)115
10-y-o ch g Over The River (FR)-Love-In-A-Mist (Paddy's Stream)
Jonjo O Neill J P McManus

Placings:0/1U30/F2500P/FP1F6/111P-4 (0396)
2002/03: 27⁴GF,

	Starts	1st	2nd	3rd	Win & Pl
Hurdles	1	0	0	0	318
Career Total	21	5	1	1	22839
116 9/01 Strf 3m	D(0-125)HCh	G-F	£6968		
111 5/01 Weth 3m1f	D Hdl	FRM	£3444		
115 5/01 Prth 3m110y	E Hdl	SFT	£3041		
116 2/01 Ludl 2m4f	F(0-100)HCh	GD	£4202		
94 9/98 Gway 2m1f	Ch	HVY	£2989		
	Total win prize-money	£20645			

Going: Sf: 0-0 GS: 0-0 Gd: 0-0 GF: - Fm: 0-1
Distance: 2m/2m3: 0-0 2m4-2m7: 0-0 3m+: 0-1
Track: LH: 0-1 RH: 0-0 Tight: 0-1 Gall: 0-0
Aids: Bl: 0-0 Vi: 0-0 Tstrap: 0-0
Best Rating: 116 9/01 Strf 3m gd-fm Ch

Playaway (IRE)
94   77
9-y-o b g Black Minstrel-Actually Stell (Deep Run)
O Brennan Mrs Pat Brennan

Placings:06/0-0P (0566)
2002/03: 17⁰GF, 17⁶GF,

	Starts	1st	2nd	3rd	Win & Pl
Hurdles	2	0	0	0	
Career Total	5	0	0	0	0

Going: Sf: 0-0 GS: 0-0 Gd: 0-0 GF: - Fm: 0-2
Distance: 2m/2m3: 0-2 2m4-2m7: 0-0 3m+: 0-0

Career Total   4   0   0   0

Track: LH: 0-0 RH: 0-2 Tight: 0-2 Gall: 0-0
Aids: Bl: 0-0 Vi: 0-0 Tstrap: 0-0
Best Rating: 97   6/00   MRas   2m1f110y   gd-fm   NHF

Playing Away

8-y-o ch m Northern Game-Ottery News (Pony Express)
O J Carter   O J Carter

Placings:P/PP-R   (0693)
2002/03: 25PS,

	Starts	1st	2nd	3rd	Win & Pl
Hurdles	1	0	0	0	
Career Total	4	0	0	0	

Going: Sf: 0-1 GS: 0-0 Gd: 0-0 GF: - Fm: 0-0
Distance: 2m/2m3: 0-0 2m4-2m7: 0-0 3m+: 0-1
Track: LH: 0-1 RH: 0-0 Tight: 0-1 Gall: 0-0
Aids: Bl: 0-0 Vi: 0-0 Tstrap: 0-0
Best Rating: 0   7/02   Wolv   3m1f   soft   Hdl

Plenty Courage

105(108c)   (77c)92

9-y-o ch g Gildoran-Fastlass (Celtic Cone)
F S Storey   F S Storey

Placings:035111F/406P31/605F0/0255212510P34-246000525   (4618)
2002/03: 21²GF, 20⁴GF, 21⁶G, 17⁰HY, 20⁹GS, 19⁰S, 21⁵G, 22²G, 20⁵GF,

	Starts	1st	2nd	3rd	Win & Pl
Hurdles	8	0	1	0	1300
Chases	1	0	1	0	930
Career Total	40	6	5	3	24798
107	11/01	Ayr	2m4f	C(0-130)HHdl	G-S	£5148
107	10/01	Sedg	2m5f110yD(0-125)HHdl	GD	£3265
114	4/00	Carl	2m4f110yD(0-125)HHdl	SFT	£3388
100	3/99	Hexm	2m	E Hdl	G-S	£2427
106	3/99	Ayr	2m	F Hdl	SFT	£2145
102	2/99	Muss	2m	H NHF	G-F	£1702
				Total win prize-money £18076		

Going: Sf: 0-2 GS: 0-1 Gd: 0-3 GF: - Fm: 0-3
Distance: 2m/2m3: 0-2 2m4-2m7: 0-7 3m+: 0-3
Track: LH: 0-7 RH: 0-2 Tight: 0-5 Gall: 0-0
Aids: Bl: 0-0 Vi: 0-0 Tstrap: 0-0
Best Rating: 114   4/00   Carl   2m4f110y   soft   Hdl

Moderate handicap hurdler; best when ridden with forcing tactics; stays two miles six; suited by good or softer; looked only modest over fences in the spring of 2002; has worn cheekpieces.

Plenty Inn Hand

(96h)   (87dh)

7-y-o b g Alflora (IRE)-Shean Deas (Le Moss)
H D Daly   Patrick Burling Developments Ltd

Placings:303P0   (4194)
2002/03: 20³S, 20⁰S, 20³HY, 16⁰S, 21⁰G,

	Starts	1st	2nd	3rd	Win & Pl
Hurdles	5	0	0	2	1343
Career Total	5	0	0	2	1343

Going: Sf: 0-4 GS: 0-0 Gd: 0-1 GF: - Fm: 0-0
Distance: 2m/2m3: 0-1 2m4-2m7: 0-4 3m+: 0-0
Track: LH: 0-3 RH: 0-2 Tight: 0-0 Gall: 0-1
Aids: Bl: 0-0 Vi: 0-0 Tstrap: 0-0
Best Rating: 87   11/02   Uttx   2m4f110y   soft   Hdl

Plumbob (IRE)

14-y-o br g Bob Back (USA)-Naujella (Malinowski (USA))
Mrs F Browne   Mrs John Duncan

Placings:14200/6045503F53/00F043414204034/2/426/21U4/F1625/30500313122/46023/1-U   (0031)
2002/03: 33UGF,

	Starts	1st	2nd	3rd	Win & Pl
Chases	1	0	0	0	
Career Total	61	7	9	8	33586
85	6/01	Hexm	2m4f110yE(0-115)HCh	G-S	£3493
105	2/00	Newc	3m	F(0-105)HHdl	HVY	£2033
104	1/00	Newc	2m4f	G(0-95)HHdl	SFT	£1557
123	11/98	Hexm	2m4f110yG(0-90)HHdl	HVY	£2127
104	5/97	Uttx	2m5f	D Ch	G-S	£3468
106	12/94	Newc	2m4f	(0-125)HHdl	GD	£2738
77	8/92	Tral	2m	Hdl	G-Y	£3548
				Total win prize-money £18969		

Going: Sf: 0-0 GS: 0-1 Gd: 0-0 GF: - Fm: 0-1
Distance: 2m/2m3: 0-0 2m4-2m7: 0-0 3m+: 0-1
Track: LH: 0-1 RH: 0-0 Tight: 0-0 Gall: 0-1
Aids: Bl: 0-0 Vi: 0-0 Tstrap: 0-0
Best Rating: 123   11/98   Hexm   2m4f110y   heavy   Hdl

Plumier (FR)

5-y-o b g Beyssac (FR)-Plume Rose (FR) (Rose Laurel)
Jonjo O Neill   Sir Robert Ogden

Placings:5P   (3928)
2002/03: 16⁵S, 26PG,

	Starts	1st	2nd	3rd	Win & Pl
NH Flat	1	0	0	0	0
Hurdles	1	0	0	0	0
Career Total	2	0	0	0	0

Going: Sf: 0-1 GS: 0-0 Gd: 0-1 GF: - Fm: 0-0
Distance: 2m/2m3: 0-1 2m4-2m7: 0-0 3m+: 0-1
Track: LH: 0-0 RH: 0-2 Tight: 0-0 Gall: 0-1
Aids: Bl: 0-0 Vi: 0-0 Tstrap: 0-0
Best Rating: 64   2/03   Asct   2m110y   soft   NHF

Well-made type, well beaten in bumpers.

Pluto

103   (63c)72

8-y-o b g Sharpo-No More Rosies (Warpath)
A Robson   A Robson

Placings:0/03P/266P/F0P60-64453   (1499)
2002/03: 22⁶G, 21⁴G, 20⁴GF, 22⁵GF, 24³G,

	Starts	1st	2nd	3rd	Win & Pl
Hurdles	5	0	0	1	310
Career Total	18	0	1	2	1338

Going: Sf: 0-0 GS: 0-0 Gd: 0-3 GF: - Fm: 0-2
Distance: 2m/2m3: 0-0 2m4-2m7: 0-4 3m+: 0-1
Track: LH: 0-5 RH: 0-0 Tight: 0-3 Gall: 0-0
Aids: Bl: 0-5 Vi: 0-0 Tstrap: 0-2
Best Rating: 74   11/00   Ayr   2m6f   soft   Hdl

Plutocrat

111   128

7-y-o b g Polar Falcon (USA)-Choire Mhor (Dominion)
L Lungo   A W Jack

Placings:00P111/0P0P/6612P3-2002152   (4618)
2002/03: 16²G, 16⁹G, 22⁹HY, 24²GF, 20¹GS, 18⁵G, 20²GF,

	Starts	1st	2nd	3rd	Win & Pl
Hurdles	7	1	3	0	17355
Career Total	23	5	4	1	31849
128	12/02	Muss	2m4f	C(0-135)HHdl	G-S	£12267
122	11/01	Newc	2m	E(0-115)HHdl	G-S	£2541
106	2/00	Sand	2m110y	E(0-115)HHdl	SFT	£3575
94	1/00	Muss	2m	G(0-95)HHdl	GD	£2338
72	1/00	Muss	2m	G Hdl	SFT	£2324
				Total win prize-money £23045		

Going: Sf: 0-1 GS: 1-1 Gd: 0-3 GF: - Fm: 0-2
Distance: 2m/2m3: 0-3 2m4-2m7: 1-3 3m+: 0-1
Track: LH: 0-4 RH: 1-3 Tight: 1-5 Gall: 0-0
Aids: Bl: 0-0 Vi: 0-0 Tstrap: 0-0
Best Rating: 128   4/03   Carl   2m4f   gd-fm   Hdl

Decent hurdler; effective from two to three miles; suited by hold-up tactics off a strong pace; acts on most types of ground.

Poachers Run (IRE)

101(95c)   (79c)91

8-y-o b m Executive Perk-Rugged Run (Deep Run)
G M Moore   D J Bushell

Placings:115110/2250P40/5F045-P3P1U50   (2494)
2002/03: 25PG, 24³G, 20PGS, 21¹GF, 21UG, 21⁵S, 19⁰S,

	Starts	1st	2nd	3rd	Win & Pl
Hurdles	6	1	0	1	4076
Chases	1	0	0	0	
Career Total	25	5	2	1	14945
91	10/02	Sedg	2m5f110yD(0-125)HHdl	G-F	£3682
106	1/00	Sedg	2m5f110yE Hdl	SFT	£2537
97	1/00	Sedg	2m5f110yE Hdl	SFT	£2502
106	11/99	Hexm	2m	H NHF	GD	£1618
105	10/99	Carl	2m1f	H NHF	SFT	£1710
				Total win prize-money £12052		

Going: Sf: 0-2 GS: 0-1 Gd: 0-3 GF: - Fm: 1-1
Distance: 2m/2m3: 0-2 2m4-2m7: 1-5 3m+: 0-2
Track: LH: 1-7 RH: 0-0 Tight: 1-5 Gall: 0-0
Aids: Bl: 0-3 Vi: 0-0 Tstrap: 0-0
Best Rating: 112   11/00   Hayd   2m7f110y   soft   Hdl

Handicap hurdler; has won at up to two miles five; acts on good and soft ground.

Poaching (IRE)

76f   55f

5-y-o b g Gone Fishin-Riveress (Dunphy)
Mrs A Duffield   Mrs Ann Duffield

Placings:00   (4437)
2002/03: 17⁰G, 16⁰G,

	Starts	1st	2nd	3rd	Win & Pl
NH Flat	2	0	0	0	
Career Total	2	0	0	0	

Going: Sf: 0-0 GS: 0-0 Gd: 0-2 GF: - Fm: 0-0
Distance: 2m/2m3: 0-2 2m4-2m7: 0-0 3m+: 0-0
Track: LH: 0-2 RH: 0-0 Tight: 0-1 Gall: 0-0
Aids: Bl: 0-0 Vi: 0-0 Tstrap: 0-0
Best Rating: 55   10/02   Sedg   2m1f   good   NHF

Point

92   110

6-y-o b g Polish Precedent (USA)-Sixslip (USA) (Diesis)
W Jenks   Mrs W P Jenks

Column 1

Placings:*140*-02   (2002)
2002/03: 16⁰G, 20²S,

	Starts	1st	2nd	3rd	Win & Pl
Hurdles	2	0	1	0	1180
Career Total	5	1	1	0	3387

104 1/02 Newc 2m   H NHF   SFT £1568
Total win prize-money £1568

Going: Sf: 0-1 GS: 0-0 Gd: 0-1 GF: - Fm: 0-0
Distance: 2m/2m3: 0-1 2m4-2m7: 0-1 3m+: 0-0
Track: LH: 0-2 RH: 0-0 Tight: 0-0 Gall: 0-0
Aids: Bl: 0-0 Vi: 0-0 Tstrap: 0-0
Best Rating: 113 4/02 Aint 2m1f   good   NHF

Easy winner of his bumper debut, held in better company.

Point Of Origin (IRE)
72   35
6-y-o b h Caerleon (USA)-Aptostar (USA) (Fappiano (USA))
K A Morgan   Get Em Off

Placings:4/45PP   (1669)
2002/03: 20⁴G, 24⁵GS, 20ᴾGF, 20ᴾS,

	Starts	1st	2nd	3rd	Win & Pl
Hurdles	4	0	0	0	0
Career Total	5	0	0	0	0

Going: Sf: 0-1 GS: 0-1 Gd: 0-1 GF: - Fm: 0-1
Distance: 2m/2m3: 0-0 2m4-2m7: 0-3 3m+: 0-1
Track: LH: 0-3 RH: 0-1 Tight: 0-2 Gall: 0-0
Aids: Bl: 0-0 Vi: 0-0 Tstrap: 0-0
Best Rating: 94 11/00 Hrfd 2m1f   gd-sft   Hdl

Polar Champ
116(111c)   (134c)133
10-y-o b g Polar Falcon (USA)-Ceramic (USA) (Raja Baba (USA))
M C Pipe   The Reims Partnership

Placings:441200/54000/1111111430P/4101-31112142PU3   (4623)
2002/03: 24³GF, 26¹G, 24¹GF, 26¹GF, 26²GF, 23¹G, 24⁴S, 33²S, 34ᴾS, 36ᵁG, 27³GF,

	Starts	1st	2nd	3rd	Win & Pl
Hurdles	3	0	0	2	2029
Chases	8	4	3	0	22495
Career Total	37	14	3	3	62948

134	10/02	Extr	2m7f110yD Ch		GD	£4959
107	7/02	NAbb	3m2f110yE Ch		G-F	£4026
117	6/02	Strf	3m	E Ch	G-F	£3575
127	6/02	NAbb	3m2f110yD Ch		GD	£4017
116	3/02	NAbb	3m3f	F Hdl		GD	£2254
130	1/02	Leic	2m4f110yF Hdl		SFT	£3125
155	10/00	Towc	3m	C(0-135)HHdl	G-S	£4745
141	8/00	Worc	3m	C(0-135)HHdl	G-F	£6710
154	7/00	NAbb	3m3f	C(0-130)HHdl	G-F	£4654
135	6/00	NAbb	2m6f	D(0-120)HHdl	G-F	£2887
134	6/00	Strf	3m3f	C(0-125)HHdl	GD	£3185
129	5/00	Uttx	3m110y	F(0-105)HHdl	G-F	£2051
113	5/00	Uttx	2m4f110yG(0-100)HHdl		G-F	£1715
115	12/98	Bang	2m1f	E Hdl	G-S	£2358

Total win prize-money £50264

Going: Sf: 0-3 GS: 0-0 Gd: 2-3 GF: - Fm: 2-5
Distance: 2m/2m3: 0-0 2m4-2m7: 0-0 **3m+: 4-11**
Track: **LH: 3-10** RH: 1-1 **Tight: 3-5** Gall: 0-1
Aids: Bl: 0-0 Vi: **4-9** Tstrap: 0-0
Best Rating: 155 10/00 Towc 3m   gd-sft   Hdl

Useful hurdler/chaser; in prolific form in 2002 winning six times; goes well at Newton Abbot; suited by marathon trips; acts well on decent ground, but goes on a soft surface; often fitted with a visor.

Column 2

Polar Gunner
77   35
6-y-o b g Gunner B-Polar Belle (Arctic Lord)
J M Jefferson   Mrs M E Dixon

Placings:4000   (3816)
2002/03: 16⁴G, 22⁰G, 16⁰S, 19⁰G,

	Starts	1st	2nd	3rd	Win & Pl
NH Flat	1	0	0	0	0
Hurdles	3	0	0	0	0
Career Total	4	0	0	0	0

Going: Sf: 0-1 GS: 0-0 Gd: 0-3 GF: - Fm: 0-0
Distance: 2m/2m3: 0-3 2m4-2m7: 0-1 3m+: 0-0
Track: LH: 0-4 RH: 0-0 Tight: 0-2 Gall: 0-1
Aids: Bl: 0-0 Vi: 0-0 Tstrap: 0-2
Best Rating: 83 4/02 Hexm 2m110y   good   NHF

Polar Red
115   150
6-y-o ch g Polar Falcon (USA)-Sharp Top (Sharpo)
M C Pipe   Lady Clarke

Placings:222110-P000   (4476)
2002/03: 16ᴾHY, 16⁰G, 17⁰G, 16⁰G,

	Starts	1st	2nd	3rd	Win & Pl
Hurdles	4	0	0	0	0
Career Total	10	2	3	0	41424

154	3/02	Sand	2m110y	B(0-150)HHdl	G-S	£26100
153	1/02	Chel	2m1f	D(0-120)HHdl	HVY	£9360

Total win prize-money £35460

Going: Sf: 0-1 GS: 0-0 Gd: 0-3 GF: - Fm: 0-0
Distance: 2m/2m3: 0-4 2m4-2m7: 0-0 3m+: 0-0
Track: LH: 0-3 RH: 0-1 Tight: 0-1 Gall: 0-2
Aids: Bl: 0-0 Vi: 0-4 Tstrap: 0-0
Best Rating: 154 3/02 Sand 2m110y   gd-sft   Hdl

Smart hurdler; impressive winner of a handicap at Cheltenham in January 2002 and landed a massive gamble in the Imperial Cup at Sandown; has not recaptured that form in 2002/03; suited by cut in the ground; usually wears a visor.

Polaris Flame (IRE)

10-y-o b m Mandalus-Polar Crash (Crash Course)
Mrs D Foster   Mrs M E Foster

Placings:P2/02/1435/1F3323-1302031   (4745a)
2002/03: 25¹YS, 25³YS, 24⁰S, 25²YS, 26⁰G, 24³GF, 25¹G,

	Starts	1st	2nd	3rd	Win & Pl
Chases	7	2	1	2	13908
Career Total	21	4	4	6	29612

105	4/03	Fair	3m1f	Ch	GD	£6720
109	5/02	Kbgn	3m1f	(0-102)HCh	Y-S	£4233
107	5/01	Fair	3m1f	Ch	GD	£6677
89	5/00	Punc	2m4f	Ch	G-F	£3312

Total win prize-money £20943

Going: Sf: 0-1 GS: 0-0 Gd: 1-2 GF: - Fm: 0-1
Distance: 2m/2m3: 0-0 2m4-2m7: 0-0 **3m+: 2-7**
Track: LH: 0-1 **RH: 1-5** Tight: 0-0 Gall: 0-1
Aids: Bl: 0-0 Vi: 0-0 Tstrap: 0-0
Best Rating: 121 2/01 Fair 3m1f   yield   Ch

Modest Irish-trained pointer/hunter chaser; stays three miles one; probably best on a sound surface.

Column 3

Poliantas (FR)
121   156
6-y-o b g Rasi Brasak-Popie D Ecorcei (FR) (Balsamo (FR))
P F Nicholls   Mark Tincknell

Placings:212P331/112121-212651   (4604)
2002/03: 20²GS, 21¹GS, 21²GS, 21⁶GS, 21⁵G, 21¹G,

	Starts	1st	2nd	3rd	Win & Pl
Chases	6	2	2	0	77215
Career Total	19	8	6	2	133325

156	4/03	Chel	2m5f	A HCh	GD	£29000
149	12/02	Winc	2m5f	B HCh	G-S	£17922
135	4/02	Sand	3m110y	B Ch	GD	£16337
101	3/02	Tntn	2m3f	D Ch	SFT	£4777
126	2/02	Sand	2m4f110yD Ch		SFT	£4845
	6/01	Pari	2m1f	Hdl	G-S	£10669
	4/01	Nanc	2m1f	Hdl	HLD	£3880
	10/00	Pari	2m1f	Hdl	HVY	£4365

Total win prize-money £91797

Going: Sf: 0-0 GS: 1-4 Gd: 1-2 GF: - Fm: 0-0
Distance: 2m/2m3: 0-0 **2m4-2m7: 2-6** 3m+: 0-0
Track: LH: 1-4 RH: 1-2 Tight: 0-0 **Gall: 1-4**
Aids: Bl: 0-0 Vi: 0-0 Tstrap: 0-0
Best Rating: 156 4/03 Chel 2m5f   good   Ch

Smart chaser; runner-up in the Thomas Pink in November 2002, and won a good race at Wincanton next time; returned to form winning a valuable prize at Cheltenham in April; stays three miles, but best at around two and a half; effective on good and soft ground.

Policastro

5-y-o b g Anabaa (USA)-Belle Arrivee (Bustino)
Miss K M George (P Mitchell 1/2)   Miss K George

Placings:P   (3931)
2002/03: 20ᴾS,

	Starts	1st	2nd	3rd	Win & Pl
Hurdles	1	0	0	0	
Career Total	1	0	0	0	

Going: Sf: 0-1 GS: 0-0 Gd: 0-0 GF: - Fm: 0-0
Distance: 2m/2m3: 0-0 2m4-2m7: 0-1 3m+: 0-0
Track: LH: 0-0 RH: 0-0 Tight: 0-1 Gall: 0-0
Aids: Bl: 0-0 Vi: 0-0 Tstrap: 0-0
Best Rating: 0 3/03 Font 2m4f   soft   Hdl

Polish Baron (IRE)
83   113
6-y-o b g Barathea (IRE)-Polish Mission (Polish Precedent (USA))
J White   Nick Quesnel

Placings:1156/121F41P0-3   (0099)
2002/03: 20³GF,

	Starts	1st	2nd	3rd	Win & Pl
Hurdles	1	0	0	1	341
Career Total	13	5	1	1	19098

103	2/02	Hntg	2m110y	F Hdl	SFT	£1895
113	12/01	Font	2m2f110yG Hdl		GD	£3094
110	5/01	NAbb	2m1f	D(0-125)HHdl	G-F	£4134
107	1/01	Plum	2m	E Hdl	SFT	£1918
107	11/00	Hntg	2m110y	B Hdl	G-S	£6857

Total win prize-money £17900

Going: Sf: 0-0 GS: 0-0 Gd: 0-0 GF: - Fm: 0-1
Distance: 2m/2m3: 0-0 2m4-2m7: 0-1 3m+: 0-0
Track: LH: 0-0 RH: 0-0 Tight: 0-1 Gall: 0-0
Aids: Bl: 0-0 Vi: 0-0 Tstrap: 0-0

Best Rating: 113 12/01 Font 2m2f110y good Hdl

He has a good winning record over hurdles at a modest level at two-two and a quarter miles. Acts on fast ground, but is suited by softer.

Polish Cloud (FR)
103   105

6-y-o gr g Bering-Batchelor s Button (FR) (Kenmare (FR))
T R George Mrs Grace Frankel & Partners

Placings:10243   (4776)
2002/03: 16¹S, 19⁰GS, 16²S, 19⁴G, 20³G,

	Starts	1st	2nd	3rd	Win & Pl
Hurdles	5	1	1	1	5638
Career Total	5	1	1	1	5638
95 12/02 Donc	2m110y E Hdl			SFT	£3102

Total win prize-money £3102

Going: Sf: 1-2 GS: 0-1 Gd: 0-2 GF: - Fm: 0-0
Distance: 2m/2m3: 1-3 2m4-2m7: 0-2 3m+: 0-0
Track: LH: 1-4 RH: 0-1 Tight: 0-0 Gall: 1-3
Aids: Bl: 0-0 Vi: 0-0 Tstrap: 0-0
Best Rating: 104 3/03 Newb 2m110y soft Hdl

Modest hurdler; Polish import; best over two miles, although stays further; acts on good and soft ground.

Polish Flame
112   126d

5-y-o b g Blushing Flame (USA)-Lady Emm (Emarati (USA))
Mrs M Reveley O Brien Kent Racing & Falcon Assets

Placings:6114-60200   (4164)
2002/03: 20⁶G, 20⁰GS, 20²HY, 23⁰GS, 24⁰GS,

	Starts	1st	2nd	3rd	Win & Pl
Hurdles	5	0	1	0	3126
Career Total	9	2	1	0	11012
115 12/01 Newc	2m	D Hdl		G-S	£3386
110 11/01 Ayr	2m	E Hdl		G-S	£2999

Total win prize-money £6387

Going: Sf: 0-1 GS: 0-3 Gd: 0-1 GF: - Fm: 0-0
Distance: 2m/2m3: 0-4 2m4-2m7: 0-3 3m+: 0-2
Track: LH: 0-5 RH: 0-0 Tight: 0-0 Gall: 0-1
Aids: Bl: 0-0 Vi: 0-0 Tstrap: 0-0
Best Rating: 128 12/01 Chep 2m110y gd-sft Hdl

Decent hurdler; suited by cut in the ground; stays 2m 4f; dual Flat winner.

Polish Legend
85   64

4-y-o b g Polish Precedent (USA)-Chita Rivera (Chief Singer)
R J Baker M A Swift, A J Chapman And T Warden

Placings:044   (4510)
2002/03: 17⁰S, 17⁴F, 17⁴GF,

	Starts	1st	2nd	3rd	Win & Pl
Hurdles	3	0	0	0	632
Career Total	3	0	0	0	632

Going: Sf: 0-1 GS: 0-0 Gd: 0-0 GF: - Fm: 0-2
Distance: 2m/2m3: 0-3 2m4-2m7: 0-0 3m+: 0-0
Track: LH: 0-0 RH: 0-3 Tight: 0-2 Gall: 0-0
Aids: Bl: 0-0 Vi: 0-0 Tstrap: 0-0
Best Rating: 64 4/03 Extr 2m1f gd-fm Hdl

Failed to justify support in the market when fourth on firm ground at Taunton second start.

Polish Paddy (IRE)
99   88+

5-y-o b g Priolo (USA)-Polish Widow (Polish Precedent (USA))
J W Mullins Denis J Barry

Placings:050006014-1   (0379)
2002/03: 25⁴G, 21¹G,

	Starts	1st	2nd	3rd	Win & Pl
Hurdles	2	1	0	0	1721
Career Total	10	2	0	0	3471
88 5/02 Hntg	2m5f110yG(0-95)HHdl		GD	£1720
80 4/02 Tntn	3m110y G(0-95)HHdl		GD	£1750

Total win prize-money £3471

Going: Sf: 0-0 GS: 0-0 Gd: 0-1 GF: - Fm: 0-0
Distance: 2m/2m3: 0-0 2m4-2m7: 1-1 3m+: 0-1
Track: LH: 0-0 RH: 1-1 Tight: 0-0 Gall: 1-1
Aids: Bl: 0-1 Vi: 1-1 Tstrap: 0-0
Best Rating: 88 5/02 Hntg 2m5f110y good Hdl

Modest selling-class hurdler. Scored at Taunton and Huntingdon in the spring of 2002, both times in a visor. Looks to need trips of around three miles and fast ground.

Polish Pilot (IRE)
106(103h)   (76h)80

8-y-o b g Polish Patriot (USA)-Va Toujours (Alzao (USA))
J R Cornwall J R Cornwall

Placings:3321602/43P0040/4P0P531543P4-2P4P03045534454   (4689)
2002/03: 16⁶G, 17⁴S, 16⁴GS, 16⁶PGF, 17⁰G, 17³GF, 17⁰G, 16⁴G, 20⁵GS, 16⁵GS, 16³GS, 16⁴G, 17⁴GS, 17⁴GF, 17⁵G, 17⁴G,

	Starts	1st	2nd	3rd	Win & Pl
Hurdles	1	0	0	0	0
Chases	14	0	1	2	3573
Career Total	41	2	3	7	12008
76 1/02 Sthl	2m	F(0-95)HHdl		G-S	£2352
105 11/99 Worc	2m	E(0-105)HHdl		GD	£2267

Total win prize-money £4620

Going: Sf: 0-1 GS: 0-5 Gd: 0-7 GF: - Fm: 0-2
Distance: 2m/2m3: 0-14 2m4-2m7: 0-1 3m+: 0-0
Track: LH: 0-9 RH: 0-6 Tight: 0-9 Gall: 0-3
Aids: Bl: 0-0 Vi: 0-0 Tstrap: 0-0
Best Rating: 105 11/99 Worc 2m good Hdl

Very moderate hurdler/chaser; best at around two miles.

Polish Spirit
103(97h)   (101h)99

8-y-o b g Emarati (USA)-Gentle Star (Comedy Star (USA))
B R Millman (P J Hobbs 14/7) Mrs Izabel Palmer

Placings:44F00-213   (0730)
2002/03: 17²GS, 21¹G, 21³GF,

	Starts	1st	2nd	3rd	Win & Pl
Hurdles	1	0	1	0	732
Chases	2	1	0	1	3484
Career Total	8	1	1	1	4503
101 7/02 Strf	2m5f110yF Ch		GD	£2824

Total win prize-money £2824

Going: Sf: 0-0 GS: 0-1 Gd: 1-1 GF: - Fm: 0-1
Distance: 2m/2m3: 0-1 2m4-2m7: 1-2 3m+: 0-0
Track: LH: 1-3 RH: 0-0 Tight: 1-3 Gall: 0-0
Aids: Bl: 1-3 Vi: 0-0 Tstrap: 0-0
Best Rating: 101 7/02 Strf 2m5f110y good Ch

He has won over fences, but looks a quirky sort.

Polished
92   81

4-y-o ch g Danzig Connection (USA)-Glitter (FR) (Reliance Ii)
R C Guest (K O Cunningham-Brown 13/9) N B Mason

Placings:5   (4405)
2002/03: 16⁵G,

	Starts	1st	2nd	3rd	Win & Pl
Hurdles	1	0	0	0	0
Career Total	1	0	0	0	0

Going: Sf: 0-0 GS: 0-0 Gd: 0-1 GF: - Fm: 0-0
Distance: 2m/2m3: 0-1 2m4-2m7: 0-0 3m+: 0-0
Track: LH: 0-1 RH: 0-0 Tight: 0-0 Gall: 0-0
Aids: Bl: 0-0 Vi: 0-0 Tstrap: 0-0
Best Rating: 81 3/03 Hexm 2m110y good Hdl

Hinted at ability on hurdles debut at Hexham in March.

Politburo
99(94h)

8-y-o b g Presidium-Kitty Come Home (Monsanto (FR))
J T Gifford Mrs J F Hall

Placings:0/0/005FP501-4PP   (4430)
2002/03: 16⁶G, 20⁶G, 20⁶GF,

	Starts	1st	2nd	3rd	Win & Pl
Chases	3	0	0	0	0
Career Total	13	1	0	0	3416
97 4/02 Plum	2m1f	E Ch		G-F	£3415

Total win prize-money £3416

Going: Sf: 0-0 GS: 0-0 Gd: 0-2 GF: - Fm: 0-1
Distance: 2m/2m3: 0-1 2m4-2m7: 0-2 3m+: 0-0
Track: LH: 0-1 RH: 0-2 Tight: 0-2 Gall: 0-1
Aids: Bl: 0-0 Vi: 0-0 Tstrap: 0-0
Best Rating: 97 4/02 Plum 2m1f gd-fm Ch

Did not take to hurdling, but landed a weak novices chase second time out on a sound surface.

Politely
66f   33f

5-y-o b m Tragic Role (USA)-Polly Worth (Wolver Hollow)
H Morrison Dr Nigel Knott

Placings:0   (4197)
2002/03: 16⁰G,

	Starts	1st	2nd	3rd	Win & Pl
NH Flat	1	0	0	0	
Career Total	1	0	0	0	

Going: Sf: 0-0 GS: 0-0 Gd: 0-1 GF: - Fm: 0-0
Distance: 2m/2m3: 0-1 2m4-2m7: 0-0 3m+: 0-0
Track: LH: 0-0 RH: 0-1 Tight: 0-0 Gall: 0-0
Aids: Bl: 0-0 Vi: 0-0 Tstrap: 0-0
Best Rating: 33 3/03 Ludl 2m good NHF

Political Cruise
81f   70f

5-y-o b g Royal Fountain-Political Mill (Politico (USA))
R Nixon G R S Nixon

Placings:040   (3507)
2002/03: 16⁶S, 16⁴HY, 16⁰HY,

	Starts	1st	2nd	3rd	Win & Pl
NH Flat	3	0	0	0	0
Career Total	3	0	0	0	0

Going: Sf: 0-3 GS: 0-0 Gd: 0-0 GF: - Fm: 0-0
Distance: 2m/2m3: 0-3 2m4-2m7: 0-0 3m+: 0-0
Track: LH: 0-3 RH: 0-0 Tight: 0-0 Gall: 0-0
Aids: Bl: 0-1 Vi: 0-0 Tstrap: 0-0
Best Rating: 70   1/03   Ayr   2m   heavy   NHF

Political Sox

110(100c)   (77c)97

9-y-o br g Mirror Boy-Political Mill (Politico (USA))
R Nixon   G R S Nixon

Placings:640/466000425P340/605100/05005230322340-
4643P01120044364   (4752)
2002/03: 16⁴G, 17⁶G, 22⁴GF, 24³GS, 17⁵S, 20⁴S, 18¹HY, 20¹S,
16²HY, 17⁰HY, 16⁶GS, 22⁴GS, 20⁴S, 20³G, 22⁶G, 24⁴G,

	Starts	1st	2nd	3rd	Win & Pl
Hurdles	12	2	1		9774
Chases	4	0	0	1	1053
Career Total	52	3	5	6	19489
97	12/02	Newc	2m4f	F Hdl	SFT	£2926
95	12/02	Kels	2m2f	F(0-90)HHdl	HVY	£3458
84	2/01	Kels	2m110y	F(0-100)HHdl	SFT	£2772

Total win prize-money £9156

Going: Sf: 2-7 GS: 0-3 Gd: 0-5 GF: - Fm: 0-1
Distance: 2m/2m3: 1-7 2m4-2m7: 1-7 3m+: 0-2
Track: LH: 2-14 RH: 0-2 Tight: 1-7 Gall: 1-2
Aids: Bl: 0-0 Vi: 0-0 Tstrap: 0-0
Best Rating: 97   1/03   Ayr   2m   heavy   Hdl

Plating-class hurdler; best around two and a half miles; suited by soft ground, but acts on faster.

Polka

78   82

8-y-o b g Slip Anchor-Peace Dance (Bikala)
V G Greenway   V G Greenway

Placings:00060P-0P   (0628)
2002/03: 17⁰S, 22ᴾGF,

	Starts	1st	2nd	3rd	Win & Pl
Hurdles	2	0	0	0	
Career Total	8	0	0	0	0

Going: Sf: 0-1 GS: 0-0 Gd: 0-0 GF: - Fm: 0-1
Distance: 2m/2m3: 0-1 2m4-2m7: 0-1 3m+: 0-0
Track: LH: 0-2 RH: 0-0 Tight: 0-2 Gall: 0-0
Aids: Bl: 0-0 Vi: 0-0 Tstrap: 0-0
Best Rating: 82   11/01   Tntn   2m1f   good   Hdl

Polligana

99   90

7-y-o b g Lugana Beach-Pollibrig (Politico (USA))
V R A Dartnall   W Westacott

Placings:00023-P0F5   (4622)
2002/03: 24ᴾHY, 17⁰GS, 22ᶠG, 22⁵GF,

	Starts	1st	2nd	3rd	Win & Pl
Hurdles	4	0	0	0	
Career Total	9	0	1	1	1334

Going: Sf: 0-1 GS: 0-1 Gd: 0-1 GF: - Fm: 0-1
Distance: 2m/2m3: 0-1 2m4-2m7: 0-2 3m+: 0-1
Track: LH: 0-2 RH: 0-2 Tight: 0-1 Gall: 0-0
Aids: Bl: 0-0 Vi: 0-0 Tstrap: 0-0
Best Rating: 103   4/02   Winc   2m6f   good   Hdl

Modest novice hurdler; acts on good ground; effective at two miles six.

Polly Live Wire

9-y-o b m El Conquistador-Flash Wire (Flatbush)
Mrs K D Day   A A Day

Placings:F0F0PPP/PPF4P-P   (0317)
2002/03: 34ᴾG,

	Starts	1st	2nd	3rd	Win & Pl
Chases	1	0	0	0	
Career Total	13	0	0	0	145

Going: Sf: 0-0 GS: 0-0 Gd: 0-1 GF: - Fm: 0-0
Distance: 2m/2m3: 0-0 2m4-2m7: 0-0 3m+: 0-1
Track: LH: 0-1 RH: 0-0 Tight: 0-0 Gall: 0-0
Aids: Bl: 0-0 Vi: 0-0 Tstrap: 0-0
Best Rating: 51   7/00   Strf   3m   gd-fm   Ch

Poly Amanshaa (IRE)

105(99h)   (100h)116

11-y-o b/br g Nashamaa-Mombones (Lord Gayle (USA))
M C Banks   M C Banks

Placings:005143/22/3532/312/0515414P/02U/24-142P   (4570)
2002/03: 16¹GS, 21⁴G, 19²G, 20ᴾG,

	Starts	1st	2nd	3rd	Win & Pl
Chases	4	1	0		8451
Career Total	32	5	7	4	30849
110	12/02	Donc	2m110y	D(0-115)HCh	G-S	£4754
113	1/00	Donc	2m3f110yD Ch		GD	£4134
111	12/99	Fknm	2m5f110yD Ch		GD	£3635
97	5/98	Towc	2m	D(0-125)HHdl	G-F	£2805
91	4/96	Fknm	2m	E(0-100)HHdl	GD	£2885

Total win prize-money £18214

Going: Sf: 0-0 GS: 1-1 Gd: 0-3 GF: - Fm: 0-0
Distance: 2m/2m3: 1-1 2m4-2m7: 0-3 3m+: 0-0
Track: LH: 1-3 RH: 0-1 Tight: 0-2 Gall: 1-1
Aids: Bl: 0-0 Vi: 0-0 Tstrap: 0-0
Best Rating: 118   1/01   Donc   2m3f110y   good   Ch

Fair chaser; overcame a lengthy abscence when recording a third career win over fences at Doncaster in December; acts well on all goings bar extremes.

Polydamas

(96c)   (119c)76

11-y-o b g Last Tycoon-Graecia Magna (USA) (Private Account (USA))
Dr P Pritchard   David & Lesley Byrne

Placings:340/33131026/11P1/55030P0P-P   (0147)
2002/03: 24ᴾGF,

	Starts	1st	2nd	3rd	Win & Pl
Hurdles	1	0	0	0	
Career Total	24	5	1	5	23749
130	1/00	Ludl	2m	E Ch	GD	£2873
132	12/99	Ludl	2m	E Ch	GD	£3192
132	11/99	Wwck	2m4f	D Ch	GD	£4085
108	3/98	Ludl	2m	E Hdl	GD	£2584
122	11/97	Newb	2m110y	C Hdl	SFT	£4240

Total win prize-money £16976

Going: Sf: 0-0 GS: 0-0 Gd: 0-0 GF: - Fm: 0-1
Distance: 2m/2m3: 0-0 2m4-2m7: 0-0 3m+: 0-1
Track: LH: 0-1 RH: 0-0 Tight: 0-0 Gall: 0-0
Aids: Bl: 0-0 Vi: 0-0 Tstrap: 0-0
Best Rating: 133   4/98   Asct   2m4f   gd-sft   Hdl

Polyphony (USA)

104   75

9-y-o b g Cox s Ridge (USA)-Populi (USA) (Star Envoy (USA))
D C O Brien   Mrs V O Brien

Placings:5/32400/66/36F6P/PP65-26   (4188)
2002/03: 22²S, 28⁶G,

	Starts	1st	2nd	3rd	Win & Pl
Hurdles	2	0	1	0	700
Career Total	19	0	2	2	2149

Going: Sf: 0-1 GS: 0-0 Gd: 0-1 GF: - Fm: 0-0
Distance: 2m/2m3: 0-0 2m4-2m7: 0-1 3m+: 0-1
Track: LH: 0-1 RH: 0-1 Tight: 0-2 Gall: 0-0
Aids: Bl: 0-0 Vi: 0-0 Tstrap: 0-0
Best Rating: 90   1/99   Folk   2m6f110y   heavy   Hdl

Plating-class hurdler/chaser; runner-up in a seller at Fontwell in March 2003; has worn headgear.

Pontius

106(98h)   (107h)111

6-y-o b g Terimon-Coole Pilate (Celtic Cone)
N A Twiston-Davies   H R Mould

Placings:033-53FF3BP31   (4774)
2002/03: 20⁵G, 23³G, 24ᶠG, 25ᶠG, 23³G, 21ᴮG, 20ᴾGS, 22³G, 27¹G,

	Starts	1st	2nd	3rd	Win & Pl
Hurdles	3	1	0	1	7280
Chases	6	0	0	2	1465
Career Total	12	1	0	5	9732
107	4/03	Prth	3m3f	D(0-125)HHdl	GD	£6942

Total win prize-money £6942

Going: Sf: 0-0 GS: 0-1 Gd: 1-8 GF: - Fm: 0-0
Distance: 2m/2m3: 0-0 2m4-2m7: 0-5 3m+: 1-4
Track: LH: 0-6 RH: 0-2 Tight: 0-1 Gall: 0-2
Aids: Bl: 0-0 Vi: 0-0 Tstrap: 0-0
Best Rating: 107   4/03   Prth   3m3f   good   Hdl

Modest chaser/hurdler; has shown ability over fences but has had problems getting round; stays three miles plus; seems to appreciate good ground.

Pontypool

9-y-o gr g Absalom-Girl s Brigade (Brigadier Gerard)
R E Peacock   Derek And Jean Clee

Placings:0/000/0P0   (2565)
2002/03: 20⁶GF, 20ᴾG, 17⁰GS,

	Starts	1st	2nd	3rd	Win & Pl
Hurdles	3	0	0	0	
Career Total	6	0	0	0	

Going: Sf: 0-0 GS: 0-1 Gd: 0-1 GF: - Fm: 0-1
Distance: 2m/2m3: 0-1 2m4-2m7: 0-2 3m+: 0-0
Track: LH: 0-3 RH: 0-0 Tight: 0-1 Gall: 0-0
Aids: Bl: 0-0 Vi: 0-0 Tstrap: 0-0
Best Rating: 69   3/00   Chep   2m110y   good   NHF

Poppet

104   85

7-y-o gr m Terimon-Combe Hill (Crozier)
N J Henderson   Gibson, Goddard, Hamer & Hawkes

Placings:01   (4222)

2002/03: 19⁰GS, 17¹GF,

	Starts	1st	2nd	3rd	Win & Pl
Hurdles	2	1	0	0	3458
Career Total	2	1	0	0	3458
85 3/03 Hrfd	2m1f	E Hdl		G-F	£3458

Total win prize-money £3458

Going:	Sf: 0-0 GS: 0-1 Gd: 0-0 GF: - Fm: 1-1	
Distance:	2m/2m3: 1-1 2m4-2m7: 0-1 3m+: 0-0	
Track:	LH: 0-0 RH: 1-2 Tight: 0-1 Gall: 0-0	
Aids:	Bl: 0-0 Vi: 0-0 Tstrap: 0-0	
Best Rating:	85 3/03 Hrfd 2m1f	gd-fm Hdl

Moderate hurdler; acts on a sound surface.

Poppy's Progress
78f   **67f**

6-y-o ch m Carlton (GER)-Countess Blakeney (Baron Blakeney)
T D McCarthy Philip Sheehan

Placings:06   (3432)
2002/03: 16⁰GS, 18⁶S,

	Starts	1st	2nd	3rd	Win & Pl
NH Flat	2	0	0	0	0
Career Total	2	0	0	0	0

Going:	Sf: 0-1 GS: 0-1 Gd: 0-0 GF: - Fm: 0-0	
Distance:	2m/2m3: 0-2 2m4-2m7: 0-0 3m+: 0-0	
Track:	LH: 0-1 RH: 0-1 Tight: 0-1 Gall: 0-1	
Aids:	Bl: 0-0 Vi: 0-0 Tstrap: 0-0	
Best Rating:	55 12/02 Hntg 2m110y	gd-sft NHF

Popsi's Cloggs
98

11-y-o ch g Joli Wasfi (USA)-Popsi s Poppet (Hill Clown (USA))
R Curtis The Popsi Partners

Placings:3O/10/PP2P32/2U1P-P   (1785)
2002/03: 25PGF,

	Starts	1st	2nd	3rd	Win & Pl
Chases	1	0	0	0	
Career Total	15	2	3	2	11774
95 3/02 Sand	3m110y	D(0-115)HCh	GD	£5772
95 5/98 Extr	2m2f	H NHF	GD	£1486

Total win prize-money £7259

Going:	Sf: 0-0 GS: 0-0 Gd: 0-0 GF: - Fm: 0-1	
Distance:	2m/2m3: 0-0 2m4-2m7: 0-0 3m+: 0-1	
Track:	LH: 0-0 RH: 0-1 Tight: 0-1 Gall: 0-0	
Aids:	Bl: 0-0 Vi: 0-0 Tstrap: 0-0	
Best Rating:	98 12/01 Folk 3m1f	good Ch

Moderate chaser; scored at Sandown in March 2002. Suited by three miles and a sound surface.

Porak (IRE)
106   **123**

6-y-o ch g Perugino (USA)-Gayla Orchestra (Lord Gayle (USA))
G L Moore Allen, Manley, Prichard, Russell

Placings:242-120   (3180)
2002/03: 16¹GS, 16²S, 16⁰G,

	Starts	1st	2nd	3rd	Win & Pl
Hurdles	3	1	1	0	7710
Career Total	6	1	3	0	9669
123 11/02 Asct	2m110y	D Hdl	G-S	£5213

Total win prize-money £5213

Going: Sf: 0-1 GS: 1-1 Gd: 0-1 GF: - Fm: 0-0
Distance: 2m/2m3: 1-3 2m4-2m7: 0-0 3m+: 0-0
Track: LH: 0-0 RH: 1-3 Tight: 0-0 Gall: 0-0
Aids: Bl: 0-0 Vi: 0-0 Tstrap: 0-0
Best Rating: 123 11/02 Asct 2m110y   gd-sft Hdl

Fair novice hurdler; won very nicely at Ascot in November 2002; effective over two miles with cut in the ground.

Porlock Castle

10-y-o b g Thowra (FR)-Miss Melmore (Nishapour (FR))
P C Ritchens P Ritchens

Placings:03506430/1PP/PP   (1602)
2002/03: 18PGF, 19PG,

	Starts	1st	2nd	3rd	Win & Pl
Chases	2	0	0	0	
Career Total	13	1	0	2	3264
94 6/98 Hrfd	2m	E Ch	GD	£2710

Total win prize-money £2710

Going:	Sf: 0-0 GS: 0-0 Gd: 0-1 GF: - Fm: 0-1	
Distance:	2m/2m3: 0-1 2m4-2m7: 0-1 3m+: 0-0	
Track:	LH: 0-1 RH: 0-0 Tight: 0-1 Gall: 0-0	
Aids:	Bl: 0-0 Vi: 0-0 Tstrap: 0-0	
Best Rating:	94 6/98 Hrfd 2m	good Ch

Porlock Hill

9-y-o b g Petoski-Gay Ticket (New Member)
J Scott (Mrs Sue Popham 8/5) G T Lever

Placings:P/FFP/4RP-UP   (4480)
2002/03: 24UGF, 25PG,

	Starts	1st	2nd	3rd	Win & Pl
Chases	2	0	0	0	
Career Total	9	0	0	0	212

Going:	Sf: 0-0 GS: 0-0 Gd: 0-1 GF: - Fm: 0-1	
Distance:	2m/2m3: 0-0 2m4-2m7: 0-0 3m+: 0-0	
Track:	LH: 0-2 RH: 0-0 Tight: 0-1 Gall: 0-0	
Aids:	Bl: 0-0 Vi: 0-0 Tstrap: 0-0	
Best Rating:	62 7/01 Worc 2m	soft Ch

Pornic (FR)
104(100c)   **(108c)98**

9-y-o b g Shining Steel-Marie De Geneve (FR) (Nishapour (FR))
A Crook John Sinclair (haulage) Ltd

Placings:11436233/P5F053324223/110326431/50064033P
PP-14332   (3122)
2002/03: 17¹GS, 16⁴GS, 17³HY, 16³G, 16²HY,

	Starts	1st	2nd	3rd	Win & Pl
Hurdles	5	1	1	2	5162
Career Total	45	6	6	12	41492
98 11/02 Carl	2m1f	E(0-110)HHdl	G-S	£2870
98 4/01 MRas	2m1f110yE(0-115)HCh	G-S	£4078
108 6/00 Prth	2m	E(0-115)HCh	SFT	£4095
110 5/00 MRas	2m1f110yD(0-120)HCh	G-F	£4192
5/98 Autl	2m2f	Ch	SFT	£10101

Total win prize-money £25338

Going:	Sf: 0-2 GS: 1-2 Gd: 0-1 GF: - Fm: 0-0	
Distance:	2m/2m3: 1-5 2m4-2m7: 0-0 3m+: 0-0	
Track:	LH: 0-3 RH: 1-2 Tight: 0-0 Gall: 0-2	
Aids:	Bl: 0-0 Vi: 0-0 Tstrap: 0-0	
Best Rating:	114 3/99 Newc 2m110y	soft Ch

Moderate handicap hurdler/chaser. Effective over two miles, handles heavy.

Port Moresby (IRE)
89   **83+**

5-y-o b g Tagula (IRE)-Santana Lady (IRE) (Blakeney)
N A Callaghan Martin Moore

Placings:04-P5   (2712)
2002/03: 16PS, 16⁵GS,

	Starts	1st	2nd	3rd	Win & Pl
Hurdles	2	0	0	0	0
Career Total	4	0	0	0	0

Going:	Sf: 0-1 GS: 0-1 Gd: 0-0 GF: - Fm: 0-0	
Distance:	2m/2m3: 0-2 2m4-2m7: 0-0 3m+: 0-0	
Track:	LH: 0-1 RH: 0-1 Tight: 0-0 Gall: 0-0	
Aids:	Bl: 0-0 Vi: 0-0 Tstrap: 0-0	
Best Rating:	86 12/02 Winc 2m	gd-sft Hdl

A useful Flat performer, has shown little over hurdles.

Port Valenska (IRE)

10-y-o b g Roi Danzig (USA)-Silvera (Ribero)
Matthew Vick (Dr P Pritchard 26/5) Matthew Vick

Placings:0P00/50030000/0PP-0   (4390)
2002/03: 19⁰F,

	Starts	1st	2nd	3rd	Win & Pl
Chases	1	0	0	0	
Career Total	16	0	0	1	246

Going:	Sf: 0-0 GS: 0-0 Gd: 0-0 GF: - Fm: 0-1	
Distance:	2m/2m3: 0-0 2m4-2m7: 0-1 3m+: 0-0	
Track:	LH: 0-0 RH: 0-1 Tight: 0-0 Gall: 0-0	
Aids:	Bl: 0-1 Vi: 0-0 Tstrap: 0-1	
Best Rating:	54 9/97 MRas 2m1f110y	good Hdl

Portobello King (IRE)

8-y-o br g King s Ride-Raw Courage (IRE) (The Parson)
D J Wintle L & P Partnership

Placings:605/P   (3310)
2002/03: 19PGS,

	Starts	1st	2nd	3rd	Win & Pl
Hurdles	1	0	0	0	
Career Total	4	0	0	0	0

Going:	Sf: 0-0 GS: 0-1 Gd: 0-0 GF: - Fm: 0-0	
Distance:	2m/2m3: 0-2 2m4-2m7: 0-0 3m+: 0-0	
Track:	LH: 0-0 RH: 0-1 Tight: 0-0 Gall: 0-0	
Aids:	Bl: 0-0 Vi: 0-0 Tstrap: 0-0	
Best Rating:	81 4/00 NAbb 2m1f	heavy NHF

Posh Pearl
107   **96**

8-y-o b/br m Rakaposhi King-Rim Of Pearl (Rymer)
Miss Venetia Williams David Jenks

Placings:11125/F3   (4366)
2002/03: 19¹HY, 20⁰G,

	Starts	1st	2nd	3rd	Win & Pl
Hurdles	2	0	0	1	742

Career Total	7	3	1	1	12955
120 3/01 Wwck	2m	H NHF		HVY	£1967
111 12/00 Tntn	2m1f	H NHF		SFT	£1694
116 11/00 Extr	2m1f	H NHF		G-S	£1652

Total win prize-money £5313

Going:	Sf: 0-1 GS: 0-0 Gd: 0-1 GF: - Fm: 0-0
Distance:	2m/2m3: 0-0 2m4-2m7: 0-2 3m+: 0-0
Track:	LH: 0-0 RH: 0-2 Tight: 0-1 Gall: 0-0
Aids:	Bl: 0-0 Vi: 0-0 Tstrap: 0-0
Best Rating:	120 4/01 Kemp 2m good NHF

Useful bumper performer 2000/1; refused to settle when falling on hurdling debut at Taunton March 2003; better efforts since; stays two and a half miles.

Posh Stick

96   71

6-y-o b m Rakaposhi King-Carat Stick (Gold Rod)
J B Walton Messrs F T Walton

Placings:000-0PP0250   (4750)
2002/03: 16⁰G, 17⁵S, 27⁵S, 21⁰HY, 16²G, 17⁵S, 24⁰G,

	Starts	1st	2nd	3rd	Win & Pl
NH Flat	1	0	0	0	0
Hurdles	6	0	1	0	756
Career Total	10	0	1	0	756

Going:	Sf: 0-3 GS: 0-0 Gd: 0-4 GF: - Fm: 0-0
Distance:	2m/2m3: 0-4 2m4-2m7: 0-1 3m+: 0-2
Track:	LH: 0-6 RH: 0-1 Tight: 0-5 Gall: 0-0
Aids:	Bl: 0-0 Vi: 0-0 Tstrap: 0-0
Best Rating:	86 3/02 Ayr 2m heavy NHF

Positive Profile (IRE)

82   90

5-y-o b g Definite Article-Leyete Gulf (IRE) (Slip Anchor)
P C Haslam Chelgate Public Relations Ltd

Placings:30   (2476)
2002/03: 16³GS, 19⁰GS,

	Starts	1st	2nd	3rd	Win & Pl
Hurdles	2	0	0	1	613
Career Total	2	0	0	1	613

Going:	Sf: 0-0 GS: 0-2 Gd: 0-0 GF: - Fm: 0-0
Distance:	2m/2m3: 0-2 2m4-2m7: 0-1 3m+: 0-0
Track:	LH: 0-2 RH: 0-0 Tight: 0-0 Gall: 0-0
Aids:	Bl: 0-0 Vi: 0-0 Tstrap: 0-0
Best Rating:	90 11/02 Weth 2m gd-sft Hdl

Useful staying handicapper on the Flat; lightly-raced over hurdles, but looks to need about two and a half miles.

Possible Pardon (NZ)

109   128

9-y-o b g lades (FR)-Wonderful Excuse (NZ) (Alibhai (NZ))
P J Hobbs B Pike

Placings:245/1144-216F10   (3946)
2002/03: 26²GS, 27¹GS, 29⁶GS, 25⁶GS, 24¹HY, 30⁰S,

	Starts	1st	2nd	3rd	Win & Pl
Chases	6	2	1	0	14428
Career Total	13	4	2	0	23225
128 1/03 Chep	3m	D(0-125)HCh	HVY	£5902
122 11/02 Tntn	3m3f	D(0-115)HCh	G-S	£6890
113 1/02 Font	3m2f110y	E(0-110)HCh		

GD £3304
105 11/01 Plum 3m2f D(0-110)HCh G-S £3818
Total win prize-money £19915

Going:	Sf: 1-2 GS: 1-4 Gd: 0-0 GF: - Fm: 0-0
Distance:	2m/2m3: 0-0 2m4-2m7: 0-0 3m+: 2-6
Track:	LH: 1-2 RH: 1-3 Tight: 1-2 Gall: 0-0
Aids:	Bl: 0-0 Vi: 0-0 Tstrap: 0-0
Best Rating:	128 1/03 Chep 3m heavy Ch

A fair staying handicap chaser, he stays further than three miles and acts on ground good or softer.

Pot Red

95   61

13-y-o ch g Noalto-Frieda s Joy (Proverb)
R Johnson M E Broad

Placings:PF/4FPP/005P   (1216)
2002/03: 25⁰GF, 21⁰GF, 21⁵G, 21ᴾG,

	Starts	1st	2nd	3rd	Win & Pl
Chases	4	0	0	0	0
Career Total	10	0	0	0	255

Going:	Sf: 0-0 GS: 0-0 Gd: 0-2 GF: - Fm: 0-2
Distance:	2m/2m3: 0-0 2m4-2m7: 0-3 3m+: 0-1
Track:	LH: 0-4 RH: 0-0 Tight: 0-2 Gall: 0-0
Aids:	Bl: 0-0 Vi: 0-0 Tstrap: 0-0
Best Rating:	69 12/99 Catt 2m good Ch

Potentate (USA)

97   (84c) 120

12-y-o b/br g Capote (USA)-Gay Fantastic (Ela-Mana-Mou)
M C Pipe Jim Weeden

Placings:1011/13011/30311/001121412/0310443/PU60P01
P0P/P505251-4   (0196)
2002/03: 16¹G, 16⁴F,

	Starts	1st	2nd	3rd	Win & Pl
Hurdles	2	1	0	0	1918
Career Total	48	15	3	5	97311
120 4/02 Plum	2m	F Hdl	GD	£1918
119 3/01 Ling	2m	D(0-120)HCh	HVY	£6792
137 12/99 Winc	2m5f	B Ch	SFT	£9725
161 4/99 Chep	2m110y	B Hdl	SFT	£6905
138 2/99 Hayd	2m	C Ch	SFT	£5868
142 12/98 Chep	2m3f110y	D Ch	HVY	£3805
118 12/98 Plum	2m	E Ch	SFT	£3387
158 4/98 Chep	2m110y	B Hdl	HVY	£7195
154 3/98 Newb	2m110y	B HHdl	G-S	£5195
143 3/97 Chep	2m110y	B Hdl	G-S	£6947
141 3/97 Chep	2m4f110yC(0-130)HHdl	G-S	£5637
125 11/96 Chep	2m110y D(0-120)HHdl	G-S	£2784
114 4/96 Chep	2m110y	E Hdl	SFT	£2766
111 3/96 Chep	2m110y	E Hdl	SFT	£2472
120 12/95 Chep	2m110y	D Hdl	SFT	£3247

Total win prize-money £74649

Going:	Sf: 0-0 GS: 0-0 Gd: 0-0 GF: 1-1 GF: - Fm: 0-0
Distance:	2m/2m3: 1-2 2m4-2m7: 0-0 3m+: 0-0
Track:	LH: 1-2 RH: 0-0 Tight: 1-1 Gall: 0-0
Aids:	Bl: 0-0 Vi: 0-0 Tstrap: 0-0
Best Rating:	161 4/99 Ayr 2m soft Hdl

Fair hurdler; nothing like the force of old; effective on any ground, he has an excellent record at Chepstow.

Potoffairies (IRE)

95(109h)   (108h) 94+

8-y-o ch g Montelimar (USA)-Ladycastle (Pitpan)
Mrs S A Bramall Mrs S A Bramall

Placings:25246/11622/P420-330   (3297a)
2002/03: 24³S, 24³HY, 24⁶S,

	Starts	1st	2nd	3rd	Win & Pl
Hurdles	1	0	0	1	1877
Chases	2	0	0	1	750
Career Total	17	2	5	2	15540
110 11/00 Ayr	2m4f	D(0-120)HHdl	G-S	£3042
109 11/00 Carl	2m4f110yF(0-100)HHdl	HVY	£2324

Total win prize-money £5366

Going:	Sf: 0-3 GS: 0-0 Gd: 0-0 GF: - Fm: 0-0
Distance:	2m/2m3: 0-0 2m4-2m7: 0-0 3m+: 0-3
Track:	LH: 0-3 RH: 0-0 Tight: 0-1 Gall: 0-0
Aids:	Bl: 0-0 Vi: 0-0 Tstrap: 0-0
Best Rating:	116 1/01 Ayr 3m110y gd-sft Hdl

Fair Irish handicap hurdler. Stays three miles. Acts on soft ground.

Poussin Bleu

6-y-o b m Henbit (USA)-Blue Point (IRE) (On Your Mark)
J Mackie Mrs S M Shone

Placings:S   (1494)
2002/03: 17⁵GS,

	Starts	1st	2nd	3rd	Win & Pl
NH Flat	1	0	0	0	
Career Total	1	0	0	0	

Going:	Sf: 0-0 GS: 0-1 Gd: 0-0 GF: - Fm: 0-0
Distance:	2m/2m3: 0-1 2m4-2m7: 0-0 3m+: 0-0
Track:	LH: 0-1 RH: 0-0 Tight: 0-1 Gall: 0-0
Aids:	Bl: 0-0 Vi: 0-0 Tstrap: 0-0
Best Rating:	0 10/02 Bang 2m1f gd-sft NHF

Powder Creek (IRE)

83f   108f

6-y-o b g Little Bighorn-Our Dorcet (Condorcet (FR))
Mrs M Reveley T M McKain

Placings:230-1   (0328)
2002/03: 16¹G,

	Starts	1st	2nd	3rd	Win & Pl
NH Flat	1	1	0	0	1595
Career Total	4	1	1	1	2299
108 5/02 Worc	2m	H NHF	GD	£1594

Total win prize-money £1595

Going:	Sf: 0-0 GS: 0-0 Gd: 1-1 GF: - Fm: 0-0
Distance:	2m/2m3: 1-1 2m4-2m7: 0-0 3m+: 0-0
Track:	LH: 1-1 RH: 0-0 Tight: 0-0 Gall: 0-0
Aids:	Bl: 0-0 Vi: 0-0 Tstrap: 0-0
Best Rating:	108 5/02 Worc 2m good NHF

Appreciated the top of the ground when winning Worcester bumper May 2002, stepping up on previous form.

Power And Demand

87   65

6-y-o b g Formidable (USA)-Mazurkanova (Song)
Miss M Bragg Friends Of Rock Park

Placings:P0030-0PP66   (1546)
2002/03: 17⁰GF, 17ᴾGF, 17ᴾG, 17⁶F, 19⁶F,

	Starts	1st	2nd	3rd	Win & Pl
Hurdles	5	0	0	0	0
Career Total	10	0	0	1	545

Going:	Sf: 0-0 GS: 0-0 Gd: 0-1 GF: - Fm: 0-4
Distance:	2m/2m3: 0-4 2m4-2m7: 0-1 3m+: 0-0
Track:	LH: 0-3 RH: 0-2 Tight: 0-4 Gall: 0-0
Aids:	Bl: 0-0 Vi: 0-0 Tstrap: 0-0
Best Rating:	86 2/02 Tntn 2m1f soft Hdl

Modest hurdler, he likes cut in the ground.

Power Hit (USA)
95   51

7-y-o b g Leo Castelli (USA)-Rajana (USA) (Rajab (USA))
K Bishop G A Doble

Placings:220/23P/PP0   (4465)
2002/03: 24PS, 17PGS, 24PF,

	Starts	1st	2nd	3rd	Win & Pl
Hurdles	3	0	0		
Career Total	9	0	3	1	3234

Going:	Sf: 0-1 GS: 0-1 Gd: 0-0 GF: - Fm: 0-1
Distance:	2m/2m3: 0-1 2m4-2m7: 0-0 3m+: 0-2
Track:	LH: 0-0 RH: 0-3 Tight: 0-2 Gall: 0-0
Aids:	Bl: 0-2 Vi: 0-0 Tstrap: 0-0
Best Rating:	102 9/99 Extr 2m1f gd-sft Hdl

Power Unit
108(97h)   (91h)113+

8-y-o ch g Risk Me (FR)-Hazel Bee (Starch Reduced)
Mrs D A Hamer Power Units (1953) Ltd

Placings:2204-351440   (4614)
2002/03: 17PG, 16PG, 19PS, 16PHY, 20PGS, 21PG,

	Starts	1st	2nd	3rd	Win & Pl
Hurdles	2	0	0		408
Chases	4	1	0	0	6552
Career Total	10	1	2	1	8461
105 1/03 Tntn 2m3f D(0-110)HCh SFT £5703

Total win prize-money £5704

Going:	Sf: 1-2 GS: 0-1 Gd: 0-3 GF: - Fm: 0-0
Distance:	2m/2m3: 1-4 2m4-2m7: 0-2 3m+: 0-0
Track:	LH: 0-4 RH: 1-2 Tight: 1-2 Gall: 0-1
Aids:	Bl: 0-0 Vi: 0-0 Tstrap: 0-0
Best Rating:	105 2/03 Chep 2m110y heavy Ch

Fair hurdler/chaser; won 2m 3f novice hurdle at Taunton January 2003; not inconvenienced by a drop back to 2m when winning handicap chase at Worcester May 2003; seems to handle any ground.

Powernglory (IRE)
(88c)   (88c)

12-y-o ch g Accordion-Fairfield Springs (Miami Springs)
J Neville J C Campbell

Placings:UPP0/P/P05-P   (0693)
2002/03: 25PS,

	Starts	1st	2nd	3rd	Win & Pl
Hurdles	1	0	0	0	
Career Total	9	0	0	0	0

Going:	Sf: 0-1 GS: 0-0 Gd: 0-0 GF: 0-0 Fm: 0-0
Distance:	2m/2m3: 0-0 2m4-2m7: 0-0 3m+: 0-1
Track:	LH: 0-1 RH: 0-0 Tight: 0-0 Gall: 0-0
Aids:	Bl: 0-0 Vi: 0-0 Tstrap: 0-1
Best Rating:	78 5/01 Chel 2m110y good Ch

Poynder Park (IRE)

12-y-o b g Mandalus-So Deep (Deep Run)
Mrs J Williamson Len Stevenson

Placings:PP/2   (4664)
2002/03: 24²GF,

	Starts	1st	2nd	3rd	Win & Pl
Chases	1	0	1	0	444
Career Total	3	0	1	0	444

Going:	Sf: 0-0 GS: 0-0 Gd: 0-0 GF: - Fm: 0-1
Distance:	2m/2m3: 0-0 2m4-2m7: 0-0 3m+: 0-1
Track:	LH: 0-0 RH: 0-1 Tight: 0-0 Gall: 0-0
Aids:	Bl: 0-0 Vi: 0-0 Tstrap: 0-0
Best Rating:	84 4/03 Carl 3m gd-fm Ch

Moderate hunter/pointer; stays three miles; suited by fast ground; wears cheekpieces.

Prah Sands
90   106

10-y-o b g Henbit (USA)-Minor Furlong (Native Bazaar)
C Tizzard R P & S H Richards

Placings:0/4325P/2PPP42-025P   (0652)
2002/03: 19PG, 21²GF, 20⁵GF, 26PGF,

	Starts	1st	2nd	3rd	Win & Pl
Chases	4	0	1	0	1308
Career Total	16	0	4	1	6926

Going:	Sf: 0-0 GS: 0-0 Gd: 0-1 GF: - Fm: 0-3
Distance:	2m/2m3: 0-0 2m4-2m7: 0-3 3m+: 0-1
Track:	LH: 0-1 RH: 0-3 Tight: 0-1 Gall: 0-1
Aids:	Bl: 0-2 Vi: 0-2 Tstrap: 0-0
Best Rating:	107 11/00 Tntn 2m3f gd-sft Ch

Former winning pointer. Has become generally disappointing under Rules. Often wears headgear.

Prairie Minstrel (USA)
100   100d

9-y-o b g Regal Intention (CAN)-Prairie Sky (USA) (Gone West (USA))
R Dickin E R C Beech & B Wilkinson

Placings:2223125P152/0025025622/21F111P/3-0021P60   (4787)

2002/03: 20PG, 19PG, 20²GF, 20¹G, 20PGS, 19⁶G, 20PG,

	Starts	1st	2nd	3rd	Win & Pl
Chases	7	1	1	0	5824
Career Total	36	7	11	2	33447
100	12/02 Leic	2m4f110yD(0-115)HCh		GD	£4758
106	8/99 Sthl	2m4f110yE(0-105)HCh		G-F	£3125
97	8/99 MRas	2m4f	D Ch	G-F	£4413
104	7/99 MRas	2m4f	D Ch	G-F	£3795
109	5/99 Hntg	2m4f110yE Ch		G-F	£2860
88	3/98 Wwck	2m	F(0-100)HHdl	SFT	£2244
92	11/97 Wind	2m	E Hdl	GD	£2407

Total win prize-money £23604

Going:	Sf: 0-0 GS: 0-1 Gd: 1-5 GF: - Fm: 0-1
Distance:	2m/2m3: 0-2 2m4-2m7: 1-5 3m+: 0-0
Track:	LH: 0-2 RH: 1-5 Tight: 0-1 Gall: 0-0
Aids:	Bl: 0-0 Vi: 0-0 Tstrap: 0-0
Best Rating:	109 5/99 Hntg 2m4f110y gd-fm Ch

In fine form in the summer of 1999 until breaking down; steadily finding his form since returning and scored at Leicester in December 2002; suited by two and a half miles and the ground good or faster; has run badly of late.

Prairie Run (IRE)
101   85+

7-y-o ch m Montelimar (USA)-Lady Leona (Leander)
L Lungo Riverstown Racing Syndicate

Placings:343-212   (0581)
2002/03: 21²GF, 16¹G, 16²G,

	Starts	1st	2nd	3rd	Win & Pl
Hurdles	3	1	2	0	3970
Career Total	6	1	2	2	4651
83 6/02 Hexm 2m110y E Hdl		GD	£2509

Total win prize-money £2510

Going:	Sf: 0-0 GS: 0-0 Gd: 1-2 GF: - Fm: 0-1
Distance:	2m/2m3: 1-2 2m4-2m7: 0-1 3m+: 0-0
Track:	LH: 1-3 RH: 0-0 Tight: 0-1 Gall: 0-0
Aids:	Bl: 0-0 Vi: 0-0 Tstrap: 0-0
Best Rating:	93 1/02 Newc 2m soft NHF

A half-sister to a winning hurdler, she has shown modest ability on soft ground in bumpers and on fast ground over hurdles.

Prairie Star
98   106

8-y-o br g Landyap (USA)-Stars And Stripes (Royalty)
R H Buckler The Crop Circle

Placings:0300   (4252)
2002/03: 17PGS, 19³GS, 22PGS, 22PG,

	Starts	1st	2nd	3rd	Win & Pl
Hurdles	4	0	0	1	544
Career Total	4	0	0	1	544

Going:	Sf: 0-0 GS: 0-3 Gd: 0-1 GF: - Fm: 0-0
Distance:	2m/2m3: 0-2 2m4-2m7: 0-2 3m+: 0-0
Track:	LH: 0-1 RH: 0-3 Tight: 0-2 Gall: 0-0
Aids:	Bl: 0-0 Vi: 0-0 Tstrap: 0-0
Best Rating:	101 1/03 Extr 2m3f gd-sft Hdl

Prancing Blade
118   79

10-y-o b g Broadsword (USA)-Sparkling Cinders (Netherkelly)
N A Twiston-Davies Gavin Macecheri

Placings:60/C4P0F6/222112F06/31115U4F/-PP-2434214FPP00P   (3846)
2002/03: 20²G, 24⁴GS, 23³S, 24⁴G, 23²G, 24¹GF, 24⁴GF, 24PGS, 24PG, 25PGS, 24PHY, 24PS, 24PG,

	Starts	1st	2nd	3rd	Win & Pl
Chases	13	1	2	1	15229
Career Total	40	6	6	2	43365
125	9/02 Prth	3m	(0-115)HCh	GF	£8862
131	10/00 MRas	2m1f110yC Ch		GD	£7215
128	9/00 Chep	2m3f110yC Ch		GD	£6743
116	5/00 Bang	2m1f110yC Ch		GD	£3510
116	10/99 Worc	2m2f	E Hdl	G-F	£2402
104	10/99 Hexm	2m	E Hdl	GD	£2364

Total win prize-money £31097

Going:	Sf: 0-3 GS: 0-3 Gd: 0-5 GF: - Fm: 1-2
Distance:	2m/2m3: 0-0 2m4-2m7: 0-1 3m+: 1-12
Track:	LH: 0-7 RH: 1-6 Tight: 0-3 Gall: 0-1
Aids:	Bl: 0-0 Vi: 0-0 Tstrap: 0-0
Best Rating:	131 10/00 MRas 2m1f110y good Ch

Fair handicap chaser; stays three miles; acts on a sound surface.

Prate Box (IRE)

13-y-o b g Ela-Mana-Mou-Prattle On (Ballymore)
Mrs P Chamings Mrs Peter Corbett

Placings:*U/06*033110/2602/0006441311F0/21F2/PPP/F-P   **(0032)**
2002/03: 21PGF,

	Starts	1st	2nd	3rd	Win & Pl
Chases	1	0	0	0	
Career Total	34	6	4	3	30410

129	11/97	Chep	2m3f110yC(0-135)HCh	G-S	£6905
123	3/97	Fair	2m4f	(0-109)HCh	GD	£4747
123	3/97	Naas	2m40y	(0-109)HCh	Y-S	£3051
113	1/97	Punc	2m	(0-109)HCh	Y-S	£3730
127	2/95	Clon	2m	Hdl	HVY	£3051
110	11/94	Clon	2m	Hdl	Y-S	£2446

Total win prize-money £23933

Going:	Sf: 0-0 GS: 0-0 Gd: 0-0 GF: - Fm: 0-1
Distance:	2m/2m3: 0-0 2m4-2m7: 0-1 3m+: 0-0
Track:	LH: 0-1 RH: 0-0 Tight: 0-0 Gall: 0-1
Aids:	Bl: 0-0 Vi: 0-0 Tstrap: 0-0
Best Rating:	131 1/98 Kemp 2m4f110y gd-sft Ch

Prayerful
61   40

4-y-o b f Syrtos-Pure Formality (Forzando)
B N Doran P N Exton

Placings:0U0   **(4086)**
2002/03: 16QS, 21US, 19QGS,

	Starts	1st	2nd	3rd	Win & Pl
Hurdles	3	0	0	0	
Career Total	3	0	0	0	

Going:	Sf: 0-2 GS: 0-0 Gd: 0-0 GF: - Fm: 0-0
Distance:	2m/2m3: 0-2 2m4-2m7: 0-1 3m+: 0-0
Track:	LH: 0-2 RH: 0-1 Tight: 0-1 Gall: 0-0
Aids:	Bl: 0-0 Vi: 0-0 Tstrap: 0-0
Best Rating:	40 3/03 Strf 2m3f gd-sft Hdl

Precious Bane (IRE)
87   86

5-y-o b g Bigstone (IRE)-Heavenward (USA) (Conquistador
Cielo (USA))
B P J Baugh M W & A N Harris

Placings:6060-0655   **(1442)**
2002/03: 17QGF, 20PGF, 16SGY, 22SF,

	Starts	1st	2nd	3rd	Win & Pl
NH Flat	1	0	0	0	0
Hurdles	3	0	0	0	0
Career Total	8	0	0	0	0

Going:	Sf: 0-0 GS: 0-0 Gd: 0-0 GF: 0-0 Fm: 0-3
Distance:	2m/2m3: 0-2 2m4-2m7: 0-2 3m+: 0-0
Track:	LH: 0-1 RH: 0-2 Tight: 0-0 Gall: 0-0
Aids:	Bl: 0-0 Vi: 0-0 Tstrap: 0-0
Best Rating:	87 8/02 Gway 2m gd-yld NHF

Has shown little so far.

Precious Moments
91f   88f

7-y-o b m Polar Falcon (USA)-Brassy Nell (Dunbeath (USA))
J A Moore J A Moore

Placings:*30-0*   **(0409)**
2002/03: 17QGF,

	Starts	1st	2nd	3rd	Win & Pl
NH Flat	1	0	0	0	
Career Total	3	0	0	1	208

Going:	Sf: 0-0 GS: 0-0 Gd: 0-0 GF: - Fm: 0-1
Distance:	2m/2m3: 0-1 2m4-2m7: 0-0 3m+: 0-0
Track:	LH: 0-0 RH: 0-1 Tight: 0-1 Gall: 0-0
Aids:	Bl: 0-0 Vi: 0-0 Tstrap: 0-0
Best Rating:	88 10/01 Fknm 2m soft NHF

Precious Music (IRE)
107   127

10-y-o br g Orchestra-Precious Petra (Bing Ii)
Gerard Farrell Thomas Farrell

Placings:*500/03/*1105/461-11F00P   **(3424a)**
2002/03: 241S, 241YS, 24FHY, 24QS, 24QG, 28PSH,

	Starts	1st	2nd	3rd	Win & Pl
Chases	6	2	0	0	15951
Career Total	18	5	0	1	28385

119	12/02	Navn	3m	(0-135)HCh	Y-S	£7975
108	11/02	Naas	3m	(0-116)HCh	SFT	£7975
127	9/01	Rosc	3m100y	Ch	GD	£5008
119	12/00	Navn	2m2f	Hdl	HVY	£4416
91	11/00	Dpat	2m1f172y	NHF	SFT	£2345

Total win prize-money £27720

Going:	Sf: 1-3 GS: 0-0 Gd: 0-0 GF: - Fm: 0-0
Distance:	2m/2m3: 0-0 2m4-2m7: 0-0 3m+: 2-6
Track:	LH: 2-5 RH: 0-0 Tight: 0-0 Gall: 0-1
Aids:	Bl: 0-0 Vi: 0-0 Tstrap: 0-0
Best Rating:	127 9/01 Rosc 3m100y good Ch

Irish handicap chaser, effective over three miles on soft
ground.

Preferred (IRE)
98   86

5-y-o b g Distant Relative-Fruhlingserwachen (USA) (Irish
River (FR))
O Sherwood (R Hannon 17/5) R J Brennan & N J
Hemmington

Placings:335036   **(1089)**
2002/03: 17QG, 16QGF, 16SGF, 19QGF, 18QGF, 16QGF,

	Starts	1st	2nd	3rd	Win & Pl
Hurdles	6	0	0	3	1221
Career Total	6	0	0	3	1221

Going:	Sf: 0-0 GS: 0-0 Gd: 0-0 GF: - Fm: 0-5
Distance:	2m/2m3: 0-6 2m4-2m7: 0-0 3m+: 0-0
Track:	LH: 0-4 RH: 0-2 Tight: 0-2 Gall: 0-1
Aids:	Bl: 0-2 Vi: 0-0 Tstrap: 0-0
Best Rating:	86 7/02 Worc 2m gd-fm Hdl

A fair Flat performer, he lacks stamina over hurdles.

Prelotte (IRE)

4-y-o b g Nicolotte-Prepare (IRE) (Millfontaine)
J Neville Ron Bartlett

Placings:*0*   **(2172)**
2002/03: 14QGS,

	Starts	1st	2nd	3rd	Win & Pl
NH Flat	1	0	0	0	

Career Total   1   0   0   0

Going:	Sf: 0-0 GS: 0-1 Gd: 0-0 GF: - Fm: 0-0
Distance:	2m/2m3: 0-0 2m4-2m7: 0-0 3m+: 0-0
Track:	LH: 0-1 RH: 0-0 Tight: 0-0 Gall: 0-0
Aids:	Bl: 0-0 Vi: 0-0 Tstrap: 0-0
Best Rating:	0 11/02 Wwck 1m6f gd-sft NHF

Prelude To Fame (USA)
81   107

10-y-o b g Affirmed (USA)-Dance Call (USA) (Nijinsky
(CAN))
Mrs A C Tate M Tate

Placings:13602/2/1056F/23U4/060PP0/42-0   **(1754)**
2002/03: 16QG,

	Starts	1st	2nd	3rd	Win & Pl
Hurdles	1	0	0	0	
Career Total	24	2	4	2	9256

118	11/98	MRas	2m5f110yE(0-115)HHdl	G-S	£2740
91	8/96	Ctml	2m1f110yE Hdl	GD	£2215

Total win prize-money £4955

Going:	Sf: 0-0 GS: 0-0 Gd: 0-1 GF: - Fm: 0-0
Distance:	2m/2m3: 0-1 2m4-2m7: 0-0 3m+: 0-0
Track:	LH: 0-1 RH: 0-0 Tight: 0-0 Gall: 0-0
Aids:	Bl: 0-0 Vi: 0-0 Tstrap: 0-0
Best Rating:	118 12/99 Weth 2m7f gd-sft Hdl

Modest hurdler; stays two miles five furlongs.

Premier Ambitions
95   73

5-y-o b g Bin Ajwaad (IRE)-Good Thinking (USA) (Raja
Baba (USA))
M E Sowersby (W J Haggas 8/6) M E Sowersby

Placings:U0006405   **(4373)**
2002/03: 17UGS, 16QGS, 20QHY, 17QS, 16SGS, 16QGF, 17QG, 17SG,

	Starts	1st	2nd	3rd	Win & Pl
Hurdles	8	0	0	0	0
Career Total	8	0	0	0	0

Going:	Sf: 0-2 GS: 0-3 Gd: 0-3 GF: - Fm: 0-0
Distance:	2m/2m3: 0-7 2m4-2m7: 0-1 3m+: 0-0
Track:	LH: 0-6 RH: 0-2 Tight: 0-6 Gall: 0-0
Aids:	Bl: 0-0 Vi: 0-0 Tstrap: 0-0
Best Rating:	74 1/03 Catt 2m good Hdl

All-Weather Flat winner but only plating-class over hurdles.

Premier Boy (IRE)
80   71

5-y-o b g Blues Traveller (IRE)-Little Min (Nebbiolo)
B S Rothwell Premier Protection Services Ltd

Placings:30P00-06   **(0504)**
2002/03: 16QG, 17RG,

	Starts	1st	2nd	3rd	Win & Pl
Hurdles	2	0	0	0	0
Career Total	7	0	0	1	374

Going:	Sf: 0-0 GS: 0-0 Gd: 0-2 GF: - Fm: 0-0
Distance:	2m/2m3: 0-2 2m4-2m7: 0-0 3m+: 0-0
Track:	LH: 0-2 RH: 0-0 Tight: 0-0 Gall: 0-0
Aids:	Bl: 0-2 Vi: 0-0 Tstrap: 0-2
Best Rating:	71 10/01 Kels 2m110y good Hdl

Premier Drive (IRE)

112(110h)   (121h)117

10-y-o ch g Black Minstrel-Ballyanihan (Le Moss)
G M Moore A W Sergeant

Placings:*U6665/600315/21153P1/322F32111P-F533F0*

(3833)

2002/03: 20FG, 16GS, 20GHY, 20GHY, 20FS, 20OG,

	Starts	1st	2nd	3rd	Win & Pl
Chases	6	0	0	2	4019
Career Total	**34**	**7**	**4**	**6**	**33323**
117	3/02	Hexm	2m110y E Ch		HVY	£3107
108	2/02	Leic	2m4f110yE Ch		SFT	£3094
122	1/02	Leic	2m4f110yD Ch		GD	£4403
121	4/01	Weth	2m4f110yD Hdl		G-S	£3395
121	12/00	Weth	2m4f110yE(0-105)HHdl		SFT	£2702
115	11/00	Weth	2m4f110yD Hdl		HVY	£3250
99	1/00	Tram	2m		NHF	Y-S	£2760

Total win prize-money £22712

Going:	Sf: 0-4 GS: 0-0 Gd: 0-2 GF: - Fm: 0-0
Distance:	2m/2m3: 0-1 2m4-2m7: 0-5 3m+: 0-0
Track:	LH: 0-6 RH: 0-0 Tight: 0-1 Gall: 0-1
Aids:	Bl: 0-0 Vi: 0-0 Tstrap: 0-0
Best Rating:	**122** 1/02 Leic 2m4f110y good Ch

Fair chaser; effective from two to two and a half miles; acts on ground good or softer; suited by forcing tactics

Premier Estate (IRE)

101   91d

6-y-o b g Satco (FR)-Kettleby (IRE) (Tale Quale)
R Rowe Mrs Jacky Field

Placings:*6-05334U*

(4186)

2002/03: 21OG, 21GS, 21GS, 20GHY, 20GS, 17OG,

	Starts	1st	2nd	3rd	Win & Pl
Hurdles	6	0	0	2	999
Career Total	**7**	**0**	**0**	**2**	**999**

Going:	Sf: 0-4 GS: 0-0 Gd: 0-2 GF: - Fm: 0-0
Distance:	2m/2m3: 0-1 2m4-2m7: 0-5 3m+: 0-0
Track:	LH: 0-2 RH: 0-3 Tight: 0-4 Gall: 0-0
Aids:	Bl: 0-0 Vi: 0-0 Tstrap: 0-0
Best Rating:	**98** 2/02 Font 2m2f110y soft NHF

Premier Generation (IRE)

96(95h)   (113h)105

10-y-o b g Cadeaux Genereux-Bristle (Thatch (USA))
Dr P Pritchard Ray Edwards

Placings:00/23/1211020/402/05001303/00550045-4P4

(0852)

2002/03: 16GF, 20PGF, 21GF,

	Starts	1st	2nd	3rd	Win & Pl
Chases	3	0	0	0	349
Career Total	**33**	**4**	**4**	**3**	**31681**
120	12/00	Ludl	2m	E Ch	SFT	£3493
141	2/99	Kemp	2m	A Hdl	SFT	£9465
124	12/98	Wwck	2m	E Hdl	SFT	£3036
112	11/98	Chel	2m110y	D(0-110)HHdl	G-S	£7457

Total win prize-money £23453

Going:	Sf: 0-0 GS: 0-0 Gd: 0-0 GF: - Fm: 0-3
Distance:	2m/2m3: 0-1 2m4-2m7: 0-2 3m+: 0-0
Track:	LH: 0-3 RH: 0-0 Tight: 0-3 Gall: 0-0
Aids:	Bl: 0-0 Vi: 0-0 Tstrap: 0-0
Best Rating:	**141** 2/99 Kemp 2m soft Hdl

Modest chaser; formerly useful hurdler; best around two miles on soft ground.

Premiere Foulee (FR)

98   78

8-y-o ch m Sillery (USA)-Dee (Caerleon (USA))
F Jordan Warwick Davis

Placings:PP00P/P/004/223-02P2P40

(2779)

2002/03: 20OGF, 18²GF, 25⁵GF, 24²F, 19⁵S, 18⁴G, 24⁰S,

	Starts	1st	2nd	3rd	Win & Pl
Hurdles	7	0	2	0	1641
Career Total	**19**	**0**	**4**	**1**	**3494**

Going:	Sf: 0-2 GS: 0-0 Gd: 0-1 GF: - Fm: 0-4
Distance:	2m/2m3: 0-2 2m4-2m7: 0-2 3m+: 0-3
Track:	LH: 0-3 RH: 0-3 Tight: 0-4 Gall: 0-0
Aids:	Bl: 0-1 Vi: 0-0 Tstrap: 0-0
Best Rating:	**78** 10/01 Ludl 3m gd-fm Hdl

Moderate maiden hurdler. Runner-up in two and a quarter mile seller at Fontwell September 2002. Bounced back after a dismal display next time to again be runner-up over three miles at Ludlow the following month. Tends not to find an awful lot off the bridle.

Presenting Henry (IRE)

5-y-o b g Presenting-Sleeven Lady (Crash Course)
P J Hobbs Mrs Karola Vann

Placings:40

(3319)

2002/03: 17⁴G, 21OGS,

	Starts	1st	2nd	3rd	Win & Pl
NH Flat	1	0	0	0	0
Hurdles	1	0	0	0	0
Career Total	**2**	**0**	**0**	**0**	**0**

Going:	Sf: 0-0 GS: 0-1 Gd: 0-1 GF: - Fm: 0-0
Distance:	2m/2m3: 0-1 2m4-2m7: 0-1 3m+: 0-0
Track:	LH: 0-0 RH: 0-2 Tight: 0-0 Gall: 0-0
Aids:	Bl: 0-0 Vi: 0-0 Tstrap: 0-0
Best Rating:	**97** 10/02 Extr 2m1f good NHF

Presenting Mist (IRE)

78

5-y-o ch m Presenting-Blackwater Mist (IRE) (King s Ride)
C F Swan Capt D G Swan

Placings:060

(4424a)

2002/03: 16⁰S, 16⁶S, 16⁰F,

	Starts	1st	2nd	3rd	Win & Pl
NH Flat	3	0	0	0	0
Career Total	**3**	**0**	**0**	**0**	**0**

Going:	Sf: 0-2 GS: 0-0 Gd: 0-0 GF: - Fm: 0-1
Distance:	2m/2m3: 0-3 2m4-2m7: 0-0 3m+: 0-0
Track:	LH: 0-0 RH: 0-1 Tight: 0-0 Gall: 0-0

Press To Sting

94   94d

14-y-o b g Scorpio (FR)-Olive Press (Ragapan)
A H Mactaggart Mrs A H Mactaggart

Placings:0/P/46FPP6/3UP/142P0-P646

(1560)

2002/03: 24PGF, 20RGF, 25⁴GF, 25RG,

	Starts	1st	2nd	3rd	Win & Pl
Chases	4	0	0	0	0
Career Total	**20**	**1**	**1**	**2**	**7113**
100	10/01	Carl	2m4f	D Ch	G-S	£4465

Total win prize-money £4466

Going:	Sf: 0-0 GS: 0-0 Gd: 0-1 GF: - Fm: 0-3
Distance:	2m/2m3: 0-0 2m4-2m7: 0-1 3m+: 0-3
Track:	LH: 0-3 RH: 0-1 Tight: 0-1 Gall: 0-0
Aids:	Bl: 0-0 Vi: 0-0 Tstrap: 0-0
Best Rating:	**100** 10/01 Carl 2m4f gd-sft Ch

Pressionage

4-y-o b f Puissance-My Girl (Mon Tresor)
H S Howe Jonathan Leigh

Placings:P

(1366)

2002/03: 17PF,

	Starts	1st	2nd	3rd	Win & Pl
Hurdles	1	0	0	0	
Career Total	**1**	**0**	**0**	**0**	

Going:	Sf: 0-0 GS: 0-0 Gd: 0-0 GF: - Fm: 0-1
Distance:	2m/2m3: 0-1 2m4-2m7: 0-0 3m+: 0-0
Track:	LH: 0-0 RH: 0-1 Tight: 0-0 Gall: 0-0
Aids:	Bl: 0-0 Vi: 0-0 Tstrap: 0-1
Best Rating:	**0** 10/02 Extr 2m1f firm Hdl

Prestige Lord (IRE)

11-y-o b g Lord Americo-Fiona s Wish (Wishing Star)
Miss L J C Sweeting C R R Sweeting

Placings:0

(0033)

2002/03: 25⁰GF,

	Starts	1st	2nd	3rd	Win & Pl
Chases	1	0	0	0	
Career Total	**1**	**0**	**0**	**0**	

Going:	Sf: 0-0 GS: 0-0 Gd: 0-0 GF: - Fm: 0-1
Distance:	2m/2m3: 0-0 2m4-2m7: 0-0 3m+: 0-1
Track:	LH: 0-1 RH: 0-0 Tight: 0-0 Gall: 0-1
Aids:	Bl: 0-0 Vi: 0-0 Tstrap: 0-0
Best Rating:	**47** 5/02 Chel 3m1f110y gd-fm Ch

Presto

90   92

6-y-o b g Namaqualand (USA)-Polish Dancer (USA) (Malinowski (USA))
Mrs Merrita Jones Speed 2911 Ltd

Placings:2/50020-P40

(4371)

2002/03: 22⁰G, 16⁴S, 16⁰G,

	Starts	1st	2nd	3rd	Win & Pl
Hurdles	3	0	0	0	406

Career Total   9   0   2   0   1986

Going: Sf: 0-1 GS: 0-0 Gd: 0-2 GF: - Fm: 0-0
Distance: 2m/2m3: 0-2 2m4-2m7: 0-1 3m+: 0-0
Track: LH: 0-1 RH: 0-2 Tight: 0-0 Gall: 0-1
Aids: Bl: 0-3 Vi: 0-0 Tstrap: 0-2
Best Rating: 92 3/02 Tntn 2m1f   soft   Hdl

Modest hurdler, probably stays beyond two miles.

Presuming Ed (IRE)

10-y-o b g Nordico (USA)-Top Knot (High Top)
James R Tuck R W Lewis

Placings:3-6   (0033)
2002/03: 25⁶GF,

	Starts	1st	2nd	3rd	Win & Pl
Chases	1	0	0	0	0
Career Total	2	0	0	1	308

Going: Sf: 0-0 GS: 0-0 Gd: 0-0 GF: - Fm: 0-1
Distance: 2m/2m3: 0-0 2m4-2m7: 0-0 3m+: 0-1
Track: LH: 0-1 RH: 0-0 Tight: 0-0 Gall: 0-1
Aids: Bl: 0-0 Vi: 0-0 Tstrap: 0-0
Best Rating: 95 3/02 Extr 2m3f110y good   Ch

Fragile, lightly-raced hunter chaser/pointer. Stays three miles, acts on any ground.

Priceless Sam

12-y-o b m Silly Prices-Samonia (Rolfe (USA))
Mrs S M Barker J W Barker

Placings:5/2   (3968)
2002/03: 25²S,

	Starts	1st	2nd	3rd	Win & Pl
Chases	1	0	1	0	438
Career Total	2	0	1	0	438

Going: Sf: 0-1 GS: 0-0 Gd: 0-0 GF: - Fm: 0-0
Distance: 2m/2m3: 0-0 2m4-2m7: 0-0 3m+: 0-1
Track: LH: 0-1 RH: 0-0 Tight: 0-1 Gall: 0-0
Aids: Bl: 0-0 Vi: 0-0 Tstrap: 0-0
Best Rating: 95 3/03 Catt 3m1f110y soft   Ch

Winner of two points but runs infrequently; runner-up in a moderate hunters chase at Catterick in March.

Pride Of Pennker (IRE)

88   49

10-y-o b m Glacial Storm (USA)-Quitrentina (Green Shoon)
G A Ham C F Caple

Placings:0P0P/4P12400/640/FP3UP/P3454P   (2782)
2002/03: 24⁸S, 18³G, 21⁴GF, 19⁵GF, 22⁴G, 24⁵S,

	Starts	1st	2nd	3rd	Win & Pl
Chases	6	0	0	1	1302
Career Total	25	1	1	2	5528
75 10/98 Tntn 2m3f110yE Hdl				FRM	£2669

Total win prize-money £2669

Going: Sf: 0-2 GS: 0-0 Gd: 0-2 GF: - Fm: 0-2
Distance: 2m/2m3: 0-2 2m4-2m7: 0-0 3m+: 0-2
Track: LH: 0-2 RH: 0-2 Tight: 0-5 Gall: 0-0
Aids: Bl: 0-0 Vi: 0-0 Tstrap: 0-0
Best Rating: 86 10/98 Ludl 2m5f110y gd-fm   Hdl

Poor handicap chaser; best at distances short of 3m.

Pride Of The Park (FR)

91   67

4-y-o b g Marju (IRE)-Taj Victory (Final Straw)
Mrs N Macauley R J Hayward

Placings:6   (1336)
2002/03: 16⁶GF,

	Starts	1st	2nd	3rd	Win & Pl
Hurdles	1	0	0	0	0
Career Total	1	0	0	0	0

Going: Sf: 0-0 GS: 0-0 Gd: 0-0 GF: - Fm: 0-1
Distance: 2m/2m3: 0-1 2m4-2m7: 0-0 3m+: 0-0
Track: LH: 0-0 RH: 0-1 Tight: 0-0 Gall: 0-1
Aids: Bl: 0-1 Vi: 0-0 Tstrap: 0-0
Best Rating: 68 9/02 Hntg 2m110y gd-fm Hdl

Pridewood Fuggle

(106h)   (89h)
13-y-o b g Little Wolf-Quick Reply (Tarqogan)
R J Price Mrs B Morris

Placings:302/PP/0313045/361163540/FP20PP0/40003616-
165420F0UP   (3822)
2002/03: 20¹G, 19⁶G, 22⁵GS, 19⁴GF, 20²S, 17⁰GF, 22⁵GF, 19⁰S, 19ᵁG, 20⁵GS,

	Starts	1st	2nd	3rd	Win & Pl
Hurdles	8	1	1	0	3322
Chases	2	0	0	0	0
Career Total	46	5	3	6	18053
89 5/02 Bang 2m4f G(0-95)HHdl		GD	£2604
84 4/02 Uttx 2m4f110yG(0-90)HHdl		GD	£1981
99 2/00 Hrfd 2m1f C(0-115)HHdl		GD	£2769
94 1/00 Tntn 2m3f110yF(0-100)HHdl		G-S	£2678
88 3/99 Chep 2m110y G(0-95)HHdl		HVY	£2248

Total win prize-money £12281

Going: Sf: 0-2 GS: 0-2 Gd: 1-3 GF: - Fm: 0-3
Distance: 2m/2m3: 0-3 2m4-2m7: 1-7 3m+: 0-0
Track: LH: 1-6 RH: 0-0 Tight: 1-5 Gall: 0-0
Aids: Bl: 0-0 Vi: 0-0 Tstrap: 0-0
Best Rating: 99 2/00 Hrfd 2m1f   good Hdl

Modest two-mile handicap hurdler; best with cut in the ground when given a patient ride; in good heart in 2002; stays two miles three.

Priestfield Boy (IRE)

83   64

6-y-o b g Un Desperado (FR)-Sandbank (IRE) (Kambalda)
C P Morlock The Shouting Men

Placings:00-F50P   (2118)
2002/03: 20⁶GF, 16⁵G, 16⁶G, 20⁶GS,

	Starts	1st	2nd	3rd	Win & Pl
Hurdles	4	0	0	0	0
Career Total	6	0	0	0	0

Going: Sf: 0-0 GS: 0-1 Gd: 0-2 GF: - Fm: 0-1
Distance: 2m/2m3: 0-2 2m4-2m7: 0-2 3m+: 0-0
Track: LH: 0-3 RH: 0-1 Tight: 0-3 Gall: 0-0
Aids: Bl: 0-1 Vi: 0-0 Tstrap: 0-1
Best Rating: 64 9/02 Plum 2m   good   Hdl

Priests Bridge (IRE)

112   129

7-y-o ch m Mr Ditton-Paddys Gale (Strong Gale)

N A Twiston-Davies Geoffrey & Donna Keeys

Placings:12213012B   (4456)
2002/03: 17¹GS, 17²G, 20²S, 20¹S, 24³G, 20⁹GS, 24¹GS, 23²G, 24⁸G,

	Starts	1st	2nd	3rd	Win & Pl
NH Flat	2	1	1	0	2496
Hurdles	7	2	2	1	23155
Career Total	9	3	3	1	25651
122 2/03 Kemp 3m110y D Hdl		G-S	£5255
122 11/02 Uttx 2m4f110yE Hdl		SFT	£3489
125 10/02 Bang 2m1f H NHF		G-S	£1873

Total win prize-money £10618

Going: Sf: 1-2 GS: 2-3 Gd: 0-4 GF: - Fm: 0-0
Distance: 2m/2m3: 1-2 2m4-2m7: 1-3 3m+: 1-4
Track: LH: 2-7 RH: 1-2 Tight: 1-2 Gall: 0-1
Aids: Bl: 0-0 Vi: 0-0 Tstrap: 0-0
Best Rating: 129 3/03 Hayd 2m7f110y good   Hdl

Irish point winner; useful novice hurdler; stays 3m; effective in soft ground; front runner; tough.

Primarosa

74   41+

4-y-o ch f Atraf-Prim Lass (Reprimand)
John A Harris Mrs Susan M Lee

Placings:0   (1323)
2002/03: 17⁰GF,

	Starts	1st	2nd	3rd	Win & Pl
Hurdles	1	0	0	0	0
Career Total	1	0	0	0	0

Going: Sf: 0-0 GS: 0-0 Gd: 0-0 GF: - Fm: 0-1
Distance: 2m/2m3: 0-1 2m4-2m7: 0-0 3m+: 0-0
Track: LH: 0-0 RH: 0-1 Tight: 0-1 Gall: 0-0
Aids: Bl: 0-0 Vi: 0-0 Tstrap: 0-0
Best Rating: 41 9/02 MRas 2m1f110y gd-fm Hdl

Primaticcio (IRE)

8-y-o b g Priolo (USA)-Martinova (Martinmas)
D L Williams (V J Hughes 10/5) D L Williams

Placings:04/2-1111   (0414)
2002/03: 21¹GF, 21¹GF, 21¹G, 28¹GF,

	Starts	1st	2nd	3rd	Win & Pl
Chases	4	4	0	0	26053
Career Total	7	4	1	0	27096
126 6/02 Strf 3m4f B Ch		G-F	£17680
125 5/02 Folk 2m5f H Ch		GD	£1976
110 5/02 Winc 2m5f H Ch		G-F	£3575
104 5/02 Chel 2m5f H Ch		G-F	£2821

Total win prize-money £26053

Going: Sf: 0-0 GS: 0-0 Gd: 1-1 GF: - Fm: 3-3
Distance: 2m/2m3: 0-0 2m4-2m7: 3-3 3m+: 1-1
Track: LH: 2-2 RH: 2-2 Tight: 2-2 Gall: 1-1
Aids: Bl: 0-0 Vi: 2-2 Tstrap: 0-0
Best Rating: 126 6/02 Strf 3m4f   gd-fm   Ch

Progressive hunter chaser. Completed a four-timer when winning the Justitia Champion Hunters Chase at Stratford June 2002. Likes fast ground, wears headgear.

Prime Attraction

103   85+

6-y-o gr m Primitive Rising (USA)-My Friend Melody (Sizzling Melody)
W M Brisbourne Positive Partners

Placings: *100-*12U   **(1609)**
2002/03: 16¹G, 16²G, 20ᵁG,

	Starts	1st	2nd	3rd	Win & Pl
NH Flat	1	1	0	0	1547
Hurdles	2	0	1	0	839
Career Total	**6**	**2**	**1**	**0**	**3856**
103	6/02	Hexm	2m110y	H NHF		GD	£1547
83	7/01	Uttx	2m	H NHF		G-F	£1470

Total win prize-money £3017

Going:	Sf: 0-0 GS: 0-0 Gd: 1-3 GF: - Fm: 0-0
Distance:	2m/2m3: 1-2 2m4-2m7: 0-1 3m+: 0-0
Track:	LH: 1-3 RH: 0-0 Tight: 0-0 Gall: 0-0
Aids:	Bl: 0-0 Vi: 0-0 Tstrap: 0-0
Best Rating:	103 6/02 Hexm 2m110y good NHF

Winner twice in bumpers, acts on good ground. Runner-up on her hurdling debut in October 2002.

Prime Minister
104   85

9-y-o ch g Be My Chief (USA)-Classic Design (Busted)
G E Jones G Elwyn Jones

Placings: P/6045-33P04   **(4486)**
2002/03: 17³GF, 16³GF, 16PS, 16⁹GF, 17⁴GF,

	Starts	1st	2nd	3rd	Win & Pl
Hurdles	5	0	0	2	724
Career Total	**10**	**0**	**0**	**2**	**724**

Going:	Sf: 0-1 GS: 0-0 Gd: 0-0 GF: - Fm: 0-4
Distance:	2m/2m3: 0-5 2m4-2m7: 0-0 3m+: 0-0
Track:	LH: 0-3 RH: 0-2 Tight: 0-0 Gall: 0-0
Aids:	Bl: 0-0 Vi: 0-0 Tstrap: 0-0
Best Rating:	78 4/03 Hrfd 2m1f gd-fm Hdl

Plating-class hurdler, acts on fast ground; does not truly stay 2m.

Primero (IRE)
91   98

9-y-o b g Lycius (USA)-Pipitina (Bustino)
P F Nicholls Mrs Maureen Emery

Placings: PPP/U3P/133514F-U50F   **(0922)**
2002/03: 26ᵁGF, 21⁵GF, 23⁹GF, 26⁶GF,

	Starts	1st	2nd	3rd	Win & Pl
Chases	4	0	0	0	0
Career Total	**17**	**2**	**0**	**3**	**10463**
98	8/01	Font	3m2f110yF(0-90)HCh	G-F	£3542
98	6/01	Strf	2m5f110yD(0-110)HCh	G-F	£4436

Total win prize-money £7979

Going:	Sf: 0-0 GS: 0-0 Gd: 0-0 GF: - Fm: 0-4
Distance:	2m/2m3: 0-0 2m4-2m7: 0-1 3m+: 0-3
Track:	LH: 0-3 RH: 0-0 Tight: 0-3 Gall: 0-0
Aids:	Bl: 0-2 Vi: 0-0 Tstrap: 0-4
Best Rating:	98 8/01 Font 3m2f110y gd-fm Ch

Moderate staying chaser, suited by fast ground, has had jumping problems.

Primitive Satin

8-y-o ch g Primitive Rising (USA)-Satinanda (Leander)
R Tate R Tate

Placings: PU41-25   **(0319)**
2002/03: 25²GS, 26⁵G,

	Starts	1st	2nd	3rd	Win & Pl
Chases	2	0	1	0	660
Career Total	**6**	**1**	**1**	**0**	**2227**

80	4/02	Hexm	3m1f	H Ch	GD	£1566

Total win prize-money £1567

Going:	Sf: 0-0 GS: 0-1 Gd: 0-1 GF: - Fm: 0-0
Distance:	2m/2m3: 0-0 2m4-2m7: 0-0 3m+: 0-2
Track:	LH: 0-2 RH: 0-0 Tight: 0-0 Gall: 0-0
Aids:	Bl: 0-2 Vi: 0-0 Tstrap: 0-0
Best Rating:	80 5/02 Hexm 3m1f gd-sft Ch

Fair pointer who got off the mark under Rules at Hexham in April. stays three miles plus, acts on any ground, has worn blinkers.

Primitive Son
84   84

6-y-o b g Primitive Rising (USA)-Bramcote Centenary (Alleging (USA))
N Wilson Dennis Simpson

Placings: 56064   **(4715)**
2002/03: 17⁵G, 23⁹GS, 21⁰GS, 20⁶GF, 20⁴GF,

	Starts	1st	2nd	3rd	Win & Pl
NH Flat	1	0	0	0	0
Hurdles	4	0	0	0	0
Career Total	**5**	**0**	**0**	**0**	**0**

Going:	Sf: 0-0 GS: 0-2 Gd: 0-1 GF: - Fm: 0-2
Distance:	2m/2m3: 0-1 2m4-2m7: 0-4 3m+: 0-0
Track:	LH: 0-4 RH: 0-1 Tight: 0-2 Gall: 0-0
Aids:	Bl: 0-0 Vi: 0-0 Tstrap: 0-0
Best Rating:	84 3/03 Weth 2m4f110y gd-fm Hdl

Primitive Way

11-y-o b g Primitive Rising (USA)-Potterway (Velvet Prince)
C Storey (Miss S E Forster 29/5) The Hon Gerald Maitland-Carew

Placings: 6213353P04P-2440   **(4552)**
2002/03: 25²G, 24⁴GF, 25⁴GF, 27⁹G,

	Starts	1st	2nd	3rd	Win & Pl
Chases	4	0	1	0	1825
Career Total	**15**	**1**	**2**	**3**	**10497**
90	10/01	Kels	3m1f	E Ch	GD	£3201

Total win prize-money £3201

Going:	Sf: 0-0 GS: 0-0 Gd: 0-2 GF: - Fm: 0-2
Distance:	2m/2m3: 0-0 2m4-2m7: 0-0 3m+: 0-4
Track:	LH: 0-3 RH: 0-1 Tight: 0-1 Gall: 0-0
Aids:	Bl: 0-3 Vi: 0-0 Tstrap: 0-0
Best Rating:	104 4/02 Hexm 3m1f good Ch

Winning pointer, he got off the mark under Rules at Kelso in October 2001, but struggled in better company after that. Acts on good ground and is effective at three miles plus. Usually wears blinkers.

Prince Albert
105   94

5-y-o ch g Rock City-Russell Creek (Sandy Creek)
J R Jenkins H Thomas

Placings: 2-2   **(1448)**
2002/03: 16²G,

	Starts	1st	2nd	3rd	Win & Pl
Hurdles	1	0	1	0	1254
Career Total	**2**	**0**	**2**	**0**	**2179**

Going:	Sf: 0-0 GS: 0-0 Gd: 0-1 GF: - Fm: 0-0
Distance:	2m/2m3: 0-1 2m4-2m7: 0-0 3m+: 0-0

Track:	LH: 0-1 RH: 0-0 Tight: 0-1 Gall: 0-0
Aids:	Bl: 0-0 Vi: 0-0 Tstrap: 0-0
Best Rating:	94 10/02 Fknm 2m good Hdl

Modest Flat performer, respectable efforts so far over hurdles.

Prince Among Men
108   116+

6-y-o b g Robellino (USA)-Forelino (USA) (Trempolino (USA))
N G Richards Jim Ennis

Placings: 1212/330-12341   **(4686)**
2002/03: 17¹G, 16²GS, 16³GS, 16⁴GS, 17¹GF,

	Starts	1st	2nd	3rd	Win & Pl
Hurdles	5	2	1	1	7393
Career Total	**12**	**4**	**3**	**3**	**16284**
111	4/03	MRas	2m1f110yG	Hdl	G-F	£2517
104	11/02	Hrfd	2m1f	G Hdl	GD	£2261
106	10/00	Ludl	2m	E Hdl	G-F	£2807
106	8/00	Worc	2m	E Hdl	G-F	£2775

Total win prize-money £10361

Going:	Sf: 0-0 GS: 0-3 Gd: 1-1 GF: - Fm: 1-1
Distance:	2m/2m3: 2-5 2m4-2m7: 0-0 3m+: 0-0
Track:	LH: 0-3 RH: 2-2 Tight: 1-1 Gall: 0-1
Aids:	Bl: 0-0 Vi: 0-0 Tstrap: 0-0
Best Rating:	112 12/02 Ayr 2m gd-sft Hdl

Fair hurdler; suited by trips of around two miles and handles cut in the ground, but looks better on a sound surface; consistent.

Prince Atraf
88   69

4-y-o b g Atraf-Forest Fantasy (Rambo Dancer (CAN))
B R Millman H Gooding

Placings: 0   **(2329)**
2002/03: 16⁰GS,

	Starts	1st	2nd	3rd	Win & Pl
Hurdles	1	0	0	0	
Career Total	**1**	**0**	**0**	**0**	

Going:	Sf: 0-0 GS: 0-1 Gd: 0-0 GF: - Fm: 0-0
Distance:	2m/2m3: 0-1 2m4-2m7: 0-0 3m+: 0-0
Track:	LH: 0-0 RH: 0-1 Tight: 0-0 Gall: 0-0
Aids:	Bl: 0-0 Vi: 0-0 Tstrap: 0-0
Best Rating:	69 12/02 Winc 2m gd-sft Hdl

Prince De Berry
(94c)   (57c)

12-y-o ch g Ballacashtal (CAN)-Hoonah (FR) (Luthier)
G A Ham N G Ahier

Placings: 0464/U4/652P0F402/130/323/2311046P/U062P3 201-0   **(0037)**
2002/03: 22⁰G,

	Starts	1st	2nd	3rd	Win & Pl
Hurdles	1	0	0	0	
Career Total	**39**	**4**	**6**	**5**	**8037**
	4/02	LES	2m	HHdl	G-S	£1200
	8/00	LES	2m	HHdl	G-F	£1050
	8/00	LES	2m4f	HHdl	G-F	£1050
	7/98	LES	2m	Hdl	G-F	£900

Total win prize-money £4200

Going:	Sf: 0-0 GS: 0-0 Gd: 0-1 GF: - Fm: 0-0
Distance:	2m/2m3: 0-0 2m4-2m7: 0-1 3m+: 0-0
Track:	LH: 0-0 RH: 0-1 Tight: 0-0 Gall: 0-0

Aids: Bl: 0-0 Vi: 0-0 Tstrap: 0-0
Best Rating: 83 1/95   Sand 2m110y   soft   Hdl

Prince De Galles
104   84

10-y-o b g Prince Des Coeurs (USA)-Royal Brush (King Of Spain)
P Bowen Homebred Racing

Placings:0/2600221U30P/FFF04506-501P44P   (4465)
2002/03: 24⁵G, 24⁰G, 24¹S, 24⁶G, 24⁴G, 25⁵HY, 24²PF,

	Starts	1st	2nd	3rd	Win & Pl
Hurdles	7	1	0	0	3095
Career Total	27	2	3	1	9809
93	6/02 Uttx 3m110y E(0-105)HHdl SFT £2660
97	11/00 Ludl 3m F(0-105)HHdl GD £3493
					Total win prize-money £6154

Going: Sf: 1-2 GS: 0-0 Gd: 0-4 GF: - Fm: 0-1
Distance: 2m/2m3: 0-0 2m4-2m7: 0-0 3m+: 1-7
Track: LH: 1-3 RH: 0-3 Tight: 0-3 Gall: 0-0
Aids: Bl: 1-4 Vi: 0-0 Tstrap: 0-0
Best Rating: 99 6/00 Uttx 2m4f110y good Hdl

Moderate handicap hurdler; best in soft ground; stays well; needs blinkers.

Prince Dimitri
102   117

4-y-o ch g Desert King (IRE)-Pinta (IRE) (Ahonoora)
M C Pipe (D Nicholls 12/8) Lucayan Stud

Placings:1F024   (4637)
2002/03: 16¹S, 16⁷HY, 16⁰G, 16²G, 16⁴GF,

	Starts	1st	2nd	3rd	Win & Pl
Hurdles	5	1	1	0	5308
Career Total	5	1	1	0	5308
110	12/02 Wwck 2m E Hdl SFT £3213
					Total win prize-money £3213

Going: Sf: 1-2 GS: 0-0 Gd: 0-2 GF: - Fm: 0-1
Distance: 2m/2m3: 1-5 2m4-2m7: 0-0 3m+: 0-0
Track: LH: 1-5 RH: 0-0 Tight: 0-1 Gall: 0-0
Aids: Bl: 0-0 Vi: 0-2 Tstrap: 0-0
Best Rating: 117 1/03 Wwck 2m   heavy Hdl

Fair juvenile hurdler; effective on soft ground; has worn a visor.

Prince Dorcet (IRE)
85   64

7-y-o b g Asir-Lady Dorcet (Condorcet (FR))
J I A Charlton J I A Charlton

Placings:3000   (4661)
2002/03: 17³GF, 16⁶G, 16⁰G, 17⁰GF,

	Starts	1st	2nd	3rd	Win & Pl
NH Flat	2	0	0	1	284
Hurdles	2	0	0	0	0
Career Total	4	0	0	1	284

Going: Sf: 0-0 GS: 0-0 Gd: 0-2 GF: - Fm: 0-2
Distance: 2m/2m3: 0-4 2m4-2m7: 0-0 3m+: 0-0
Track: LH: 0-2 RH: 0-2 Tight: 0-1 Gall: 0-0
Aids: Bl: 0-0 Vi: 0-0 Tstrap: 0-0
Best Rating: 87 10/02 Carl 2m1f   gd-fm NHF

Prince Dundee (FR)
98(98c)   (108c)107

8-y-o ch g Ecossais (FR)-Princesse Normande (FR) (Belgio (FR))
J Neville Beacon Estates Ltd

Placings:26/2036/0315322/0P4U0UF0-P0P004   (0770)
2002/03: 17PGF, 20⁴GF, 20PGS, 16⁴GF, 22⁸GF, 20⁴GF,

	Starts	1st	2nd	3rd	Win & Pl
Hurdles	6	0	0	0	0
Career Total	27	1	4	3	7617
106	12/00 Folk 2m1f110yD(0-110)HHdl HVY £2957
					Total win prize-money £2958

Going: Sf: 0-0 GS: 0-1 Gd: 0-0 GF: - Fm: 0-5
Distance: 2m/2m3: 0-2 2m4-2m7: 0-4 3m+: 0-0
Track: LH: 0-5 RH: 0-1 Tight: 0-1 Gall: 0-0
Aids: Bl: 0-5 Vi: 0-0 Tstrap: 0-2
Best Rating: 107 4/01 Tntn   2m3f110y gd-fm Hdl

Fair handicap hurdler at around two and a half miles. Handles fast ground and soft. Yet to click over fences.

Prince Highlight (IRE)
98(102h)   (111h)99

8-y-o b g Lord Americo-Madamme Highlights (Andretti)
Ferdy Murphy Mrs M B Scholey

Placings:30215/02553-02P4F33F   (4614)
2002/03: 18⁰GS, 20²GS, 20PG, 21⁴S, 16³G, 21³G, 21FG,

	Starts	1st	2nd	3rd	Win & Pl
Hurdles	1	0	0	0	0
Chases	7	0	1	2	2991
Career Total	18	1	3	4	12519
107	4/01 Hayd 2m D Hdl SFT £3945
					Total win prize-money £3946

Going: Sf: 0-1 GS: 0-2 Gd: 0-5 GF: - Fm: 0-0
Distance: 2m/2m3: 0-3 2m4-2m7: 0-5 3m+: 0-0
Track: LH: 0-7 RH: 0-1 Tight: 0-4 Gall: 0-3
Aids: Bl: 0-1 Vi: 0-0 Tstrap: 0-0
Best Rating: 111 11/01 Hayd   2m4f   good Hdl

Modest novice chaser; sole win came over hurdles in April 2001; has struggled to make an impact over fences and looks one to tread carefully with.

Prince Minata (IRE)
86   85

8-y-o b g Machiavellian (USA)-Aminata (Glenstal (USA))
P W Hiatt P W Hiatt

Placings:P0/P/30-0   (1231)
2002/03: 16⁹G,

	Starts	1st	2nd	3rd	Win & Pl
Hurdles	1	0	0	0	0
Career Total	6	0	0	1	340

Going: Sf: 0-0 GS: 0-0 Gd: 0-1 GF: - Fm: 0-0
Distance: 2m/2m3: 0-1 2m4-2m7: 0-0 3m+: 0-0
Track: LH: 0-1 RH: 0-0 Tight: 0-0 Gall: 0-0
Aids: Bl: 0-0 Vi: 0-0 Tstrap: 0-0
Best Rating: 85 9/01 Sedg 2m1f   good Hdl

Prince Nicholas
101   106

8-y-o ch g Midyan (USA)-Its My Turn (Palm Track)
K W Hogg Auldyn Stud Ltd

Placings:244/2345-13P   (1294)
2002/03: 26¹GS, 22³G, 24PGF,

	Starts	1st	2nd	3rd	Win & Pl
Hurdles	3	1	0	1	3916
Career Total	10	1	2	2	6022
106	6/02 Ctml 3m2f D Hdl G-S £3380
					Total win prize-money £3380

Going: Sf: 0-0 GS: 1-1 Gd: 0-1 GF: - Fm: 0-1
Distance: 2m/2m3: 0-0 2m4-2m7: 0-1 3m+: 1-2
Track: LH: 1-2 RH: 0-1 Tight: 1-2 Gall: 0-0
Aids: Bl: 0-0 Vi: 0-0 Tstrap: 0-0
Best Rating: 106 6/02 Ctml 3m2f   gd-sft Hdl

A 12-furlong winner on the Flat, has run well in novice hurdles and scored over three mile two at Cartmel in June 2002.

Prince Of Aragon
91   82

7-y-o b g Aragon-Queens Welcome (Northfields (USA))
D M Grissell Robin Smith

Placings:00/205-0   (0200)
2002/03: 16⁰GF,

	Starts	1st	2nd	3rd	Win & Pl
Hurdles	1	0	0	0	
Career Total	6	0	1	0	740

Going: Sf: 0-0 GS: 0-0 Gd: 0-0 GF: - Fm: 0-0
Distance: 2m/2m3: 0-1 2m4-2m7: 0-0 3m+: 0-0
Track: LH: 0-1 RH: 0-0 Tight: 0-0 Gall: 0-0
Aids: Bl: 0-0 Vi: 0-0 Tstrap: 0-0
Best Rating: 82 4/02 Uttx 2m   gd-fm Hdl

Poor hurdle form.

Prince Of Slane
92f   100f

4-y-o b g Prince Daniel (USA)-Singing Slane (Cree Song)
C Grant J H Richardson

Placings:2   (4788)
2002/03: 17²G,

	Starts	1st	2nd	3rd	Win & Pl
NH Flat	1	0	1	0	580
Career Total	1	0	1	0	580

Going: Sf: 0-0 GS: 0-0 Gd: 0-1 GF: - Fm: 0-0
Distance: 2m/2m3: 0-1 2m4-2m7: 0-0 3m+: 0-0
Track: LH: 0-0 RH: 0-1 Tight: 0-1 Gall: 0-0
Aids: Bl: 0-0 Vi: 0-0 Tstrap: 0-0
Best Rating: 100 4/03 MRas 2m1f110y good NHF

Half-brother to Hunting Slane, six times a winner over hurdles for same stable; finished clear second best on debut in modest bumper at Market Rasen in April.

Prince Omid (USA)
88   62

6-y-o b g Shuailaan (USA)-Matilda The Hun (USA) (Young Bob (USA))
Mrs Merrita Jones Speed 2911 Ltd

Placings:0   (0171)
2002/03: 16⁰G,

	Starts	1st	2nd	3rd	Win & Pl
Hurdles	1	0	0	0	
Career Total	1	0	0	0	

Going: Sf: 0-0 GS: 0-0 Gd: 0-1 GF: - Fm: 0-0
Distance: 2m/2m3: 0-1 2m4-2m7: 0-0 3m+: 0-0
Track: LH: 0-1 RH: 0-0 Tight: 0-1 Gall: 0-0
Aids: Bl: 0-0 Vi: 0-0 Tstrap: 0-0
Best Rating: 66   5/02   Sthl   2m   good   Hdl

Prince On The Ter

84(88c)   (59c)93

8-y-o b g Terimon-Princess Constanza (Relkino)
C L Popham   C L Popham

Placings:5/0000/030PUP00P-056P   (0986)
2002/03: 16⁰GF, 21⁵G, 21⁶GF, 26ᴾGF,

	Starts	1st	2nd	3rd	Win & Pl
Hurdles	2	0	0	0	0
Chases	2	0	0	0	0
Career Total	18	0	0	1	356

Going: Sf: 0-0 GS: 0-0 Gd: 0-1 GF: - Fm: 0-3
Distance: 2m/2m3: 0-1 2m4-2m7: 0-2 3m+: 0-1
Track: LH: 0-4 RH: 0-0 Tight: 0-2 Gall: 0-0
Aids: Bl: 0-0 Vi: 0-0 Tstrap: 0-0
Best Rating: 100   5/01   Fair   2m2f   good   NHF

Prince Sandrovitch (IRE)

9-y-o b g Camden Town-Devon Royale (Le Prince)
Mrs Jane Galpin   Mrs C D Farmer

Placings:5/264135/P   (0032)
2002/03: 21ᴾGF,

	Starts	1st	2nd	3rd	Win & Pl
Chases	1	0	0	0	
Career Total	8	1	1	1	3836
96 2/00 Chep 2m110y E Hdl				SFT	£2824

Total win prize-money £2825

Going: Sf: 0-0 GS: 0-0 Gd: 0-0 GF: - Fm: 0-1
Distance: 2m/2m3: 0-0 2m4-2m7: 0-1 3m+: 0-0
Track: LH: 0-1 RH: 0-0 Tight: 0-0 Gall: 0-1
Aids: Bl: 0-0 Vi: 0-0 Tstrap: 0-0
Best Rating: 102   3/00   Chep   2m110y   gd-sft   Hdl

Prince Shaamaal

97   90

5-y-o b g Shaamit (IRE)-Princess Alaska (Northern State (USA))
K Bell   The Upshire Racing Partnership

Placings:U05   (3596)
2002/03: 19ᵁGF, 19⁰GS, 17⁵S,

	Starts	1st	2nd	3rd	Win & Pl
Hurdles	3	0	0	0	0
Career Total	3	0	0	0	0

Going: Sf: 0-1 GS: 0-1 Gd: 0-0 GF: - Fm: 0-1
Distance: 2m/2m3: 0-2 2m4-2m7: 0-1 3m+: 0-0
Track: LH: 0-1 RH: 0-2 Tight: 0-1 Gall: 0-1
Aids: Bl: 0-0 Vi: 0-0 Tstrap: 0-0
Best Rating: 72   2/03   Tntn   2m1f   soft   Hdl

Prince Skyburd

            73

12-y-o b g Domynsky-Burntwood Lady (Royal Buck)

Mrs P M A Avison   Mrs P M A Avison

Placings:45P00/1113U3/5P465/66151524/51F50/PP523PP
-P   (0699)
2002/03: 17ᴾGF,

	Starts	1st	2nd	3rd	Win & Pl
Chases	1	0	0	0	
Career Total	37	6	2	3	21921
85 5/00 Hexm 2m110y F(0-105)HCh				G-F	£3146
84 12/99 Muss 2m F(0-95)HCh				G-S	£2762
77 11/99 Sedg 2m110y HCh				GD	£2726
97 10/96 Bang 2m1f110yE(0-115)HCh				G-F	£3818
100 9/96 Worc 2m E(0-100)HCh				G-F	£3081
93 8/96 Sedg 2m110y E Ch				G-F	£2905

Total win prize-money £18439

Going: Sf: 0-0 GS: 0-0 Gd: 0-0 GF: - Fm: 0-1
Distance: 2m/2m3: 0-1 2m4-2m7: 0-0 3m+: 0-1
Track: LH: 0-0 RH: 0-1 Tight: 0-1 Gall: 0-0
Aids: Bl: 0-0 Vi: 0-0 Tstrap: 0-0
Best Rating: 100   9/96   Worc   2m   gd-fm   Ch

Plating-class handicap chaser, best at two miles on decent ground.

Prince Slayer

107   84

7-y-o b g Batshoof-Top Sovereign (High Top)
T P McGovern   Ahmed Abdel-Khaleq

Placings:2P3/6-63   (3809)
2002/03: 16⁶GS, 16³S,

	Starts	1st	2nd	3rd	Win & Pl
Hurdles	2	0	0	1	742
Career Total	6	0	1	2	1644

Going: Sf: 0-1 GS: 0-1 Gd: 0-0 GF: - Fm: 0-0
Distance: 2m/2m3: 0-2 2m4-2m7: 0-0 3m+: 0-0
Track: LH: 0-2 RH: 0-0 Tight: 0-2 Gall: 0-0
Aids: Bl: 0-0 Vi: 0-0 Tstrap: 0-0
Best Rating: 103   2/01   Plum   2m   soft   Hdl

Fair novice hurdler, but still a maiden.

Prince Sorinieres (FR)

105   125

8-y-o br g Valanjou (FR)-Somewhat Better (Rheingold)
M C Pipe   The Arthur White Partnership

Placings:11/111F422F30/P/P-5P1   (4466)
2002/03: 25⁵GS, 24ᴾHY, 24¹F,

	Starts	1st	2nd	3rd	Win & Pl
Chases	3	1	0	0	7020
Career Total	17	8	2	1	46510
125 4/03 Tntn 3m D(0-120)HCh			FRM	£7020
8/99 Mesl 2m1f110y Ch				SFT	£4306
6/99 Toul 2m1f110y Ch				GD	£4844
5/99 Mesl 2m1f110y Ch				SFT	£3767
3/99 Toul 2m1f110y Hdl				VS	£11841
3/99 Chol 2m1f Hdl				VS	£3229

Total win prize-money £35007

Going: Sf: 0-1 GS: 0-1 Gd: 0-0 GF: - Fm: 1-1
Distance: 2m/2m3: 0-0 2m4-2m7: 0-0 3m+: 1-3
Track: LH: 0-1 RH: 1-2 Tight: 1-1 Gall: 0-0
Aids: Bl: 0-0 Vi: 0-0 Tstrap: 0-0
Best Rating: 138   11/99   Towc   2m110y   good   Ch

Fair chaser; formerly trained in France; won first race since coming to this country four years ago at Taunton in early April 2003; just beaten by the progressive Banjo Hill at Exeter next time; effective at three miles; acts on most types of ground.

Prince Wot A Mess (IRE)

100   100

12-y-o ch g Buckskin (FR)-Valary (Roman Warrior)
D Broad   Patrick Anthony Burke

Placings:0/0P00/5F/000/34632415/30645/6-20UP2 (1358a)
2002/03: 24²GF, 20⁰GF, 25ᵁGF, 27ᴾG, 25²F,

	Starts	1st	2nd	3rd	Win & Pl
Chases	5	0	2	0	2798
Career Total	29	1	3	3	9071
87 10/99 Thur 2m6f (0-102)HCh			G-Y	£3080

Total win prize-money £3080

Going: Sf: 0-0 GS: 0-0 Gd: 0-1 GF: - Fm: 0-4
Distance: 2m/2m3: 0-0 2m4-2m7: 0-1 3m+: 0-4
Track: LH: 0-1 RH: 0-3 Tight: 0-1 Gall: 0-0
Aids: Bl: 0-0 Vi: 0-0 Tstrap: 0-0
Best Rating: 90   10/00   Thur   2m6f   yld-sft   Ch

Moderate irish chaser; stays two miles six furlongs; acts on easy ground.

Princess Claudia (IRE)

97   89d

5-y-o b m Kahyasi-Shamarra (FR) (Zayyani)
M F Harris   Peter E Clinton

Placings:244   (4635)
2002/03: 16²GF, 19⁴GF, 19⁴GF,

	Starts	1st	2nd	3rd	Win & Pl
Hurdles	3	0	1	0	1475
Career Total	3	0	1	0	1475

Going: Sf: 0-0 GS: 0-0 Gd: 0-0 GF: - Fm: 0-3
Distance: 2m/2m3: 0-3 2m4-2m7: 0-0 3m+: 0-0
Track: LH: 0-2 RH: 0-1 Tight: 0-2 Gall: 0-0
Aids: Bl: 0-0 Vi: 0-0 Tstrap: 0-0
Best Rating: 89   4/03   Extr   2m3f   gd-fm   Hdl

Moderate novice hurdler; likely to stay 2m 4f.

Princess Hatie

68f

4-y-o b f Petoski-Culm Country (Town And Country)
P R Hedger   Bill Broomfield

Placings:0   (3673)
2002/03: 18⁰GS,

	Starts	1st	2nd	3rd	Win & Pl
NH Flat	1	0	0	0	
Career Total	1	0	0	0	

Going: Sf: 0-0 GS: 0-1 Gd: 0-0 GF: - Fm: 0-0
Distance: 2m/2m3: 0-1 2m4-2m7: 0-0 3m+: 0-0
Track: LH: 0-1 RH: 0-0 Tight: 0-1 Gall: 0-0
Aids: Bl: 0-0 Vi: 0-0 Tstrap: 0-0
Best Rating: 0   2/03   Font   2m2f110y   gd-sft   NHF

Princess Pushy

72f   58f

6-y-o b m Broadsword (USA)-Phrase n Cold (IRE) (Strong Statement (USA))
D L Williams   Gumbrills Racing Partnership

Placings:00   (0436)

2002/03: 17^OG, 16^OGF,

	Starts	1st	2nd	3rd	Win & Pl
NH Flat	2	0	0	0	
Career Total	2	0	0	0	

Going: Sf: 0-0 GS: 0-0 Gd: 0-1 GF: - Fm: 0-1
Distance: 2m/2m3: 0-2 2m4-2m7: 0-0 3m+: 0-1
Track: LH: 0-0 RH: 0-2 Tight: 0-1 Gall: 0-1
Aids: Bl: 0-0 Vi: 0-0 Tstrap: 0-0
Best Rating: 58   6/02   Hntg   2m110y   gd-fm   NHF

Princess Ria (IRE)

6-y-o b m Petong-Walking Saint (Godswalk (USA))
M E Sowersby   M E Sowersby

Placings:3-PP   (2099)
2002/03: 17^PS, 19^PG,

	Starts	1st	2nd	3rd	Win & Pl
Hurdles	2	0	0	0	
Career Total	3	0	0	1	338

Going: Sf: 0-1 GS: 0-0 Gd: 0-1 GF: - Fm: 0-0
Distance: 2m/2m3: 0-2 2m4-2m7: 0-0 3m+: 0-0
Track: LH: 0-2 RH: 0-0 Tight: 0-2 Gall: 0-0
Aids: Bl: 0-0 Vi: 0-0 Tstrap: 0-0
Best Rating: 0   11/02   Catt   2m3f   good   Hdl

Princess Sophie
100   73

5-y-o b m Tragic Role (USA)-Octavia (Sallust)
K W Hogg   K W Hogg

Placings:0P-405F   (4793)
2002/03: 17⁴GS, 16^OG, 17⁵GF, 17^FGF,

	Starts	1st	2nd	3rd	Win & Pl
Hurdles	4	0	0	0	0
Career Total	6	0	0	0	0

Going: Sf: 0-0 GS: 0-1 Gd: 0-1 GF: - Fm: 0-2
Distance: 2m/2m3: 0-4 2m4-2m7: 0-0 3m+: 0-0
Track: LH: 0-3 RH: 0-1 Tight: 0-3 Gall: 0-0
Aids: Bl: 0-0 Vi: 0-0 Tstrap: 0-0
Best Rating: 73   7/02   MRas   2m1f110y   gd-fm   Hdl

Plating-class novice hurdler; took a fatal fall at Sedgefield in April 2003. (DEAD)

Princess Stephanie
86f   57f

5-y-o b m Shaab-Waterloo Princess (IRE) (Le Moss)
M J Gingell   Dave (Ben) Heath

Placings:0   (4672)
2002/03: 16^OG,

	Starts	1st	2nd	3rd	Win & Pl
NH Flat	1	0	0	0	
Career Total	1	0	0	0	

Going: Sf: 0-0 GS: 0-0 Gd: 0-1 GF: - Fm: 0-0
Distance: 2m/2m3: 0-1 2m4-2m7: 0-0 3m+: 0-0
Track: LH: 0-1 RH: 0-0 Tight: 0-1 Gall: 0-0
Aids: Bl: 0-0 Vi: 0-0 Tstrap: 0-0
Best Rating: 57   4/03   Fknm   2m   good   NHF

Princess Symphony (IRE)
107(94h)   (109 h)129

7-y-o ch m Lashkari-Hemmingford Grey (Sexton Blake)
E Sheehy   Donal Whelan

Placings:01/405502-012F3122P10   (4727a)
2002/03: 20^OG, 24¹YS, 24²S, 22^FHY, 25³S, 20¹HY, 20²S, 20²S, 24^PYS, 22¹S, 29^OG,

	Starts	1st	2nd	3rd	Win & Pl
Hurdles	3	1	1	0	5215
Chases	8	2	2	1	32494
Career Total	19	4	4	1	42991
129 3/03 Limk 2m6f		Ch		SFT	£16883
123 12/02 Limk 2m4f		Ch		HVY	£7196
109 5/02 Kbgn 3m		Hdl		Y-S	£4233
105 10/00 Gowr 2m		NHF		SFT	£3864

Total win prize-money £32176

Going: Sf: 2-7 GS: 0-0 Gd: 0-2 GF: - Fm: 0-0
Distance: 2m/2m3: 0-0 **2m4-2m7: 2-6** 3m+: 1-5
Track: LH: 0-4 **RH: 1-4** Tight: 0-1 Gall: 0-0
Aids: Bl: 0-1 Vi: 0-0 Tstrap: 0-0
Best Rating: 129   3/03   Limk   2m6f   soft   Ch

Fair Irish-trained chaser; stays three miles; acts on soft.

Princesse Grec (FR)
96(102h)   (78h)72

5-y-o ch m Grand Tresor (FR)-Perimele (FR) (Mon Fils)
Dr P Pritchard   The Honfleur Syndicate

Placings:00P0P00-4256200PPU56   (4695)
2002/03: 20⁴G, 16²S, 20⁵GF, 24⁶G, 16²GS, 16^OG, 16^OG, 21^PGS, 18^PS, 32^UG, 19⁵GF, 16⁶G,

	Starts	1st	2nd	3rd	Win & Pl
Hurdles	6	0	2	0	1648
Chases	6	0	0	0	0
Career Total	19	0	2	0	1648

Going: Sf: 0-2 GS: 0-2 Gd: 0-6 GF: - Fm: 0-2
Distance: 2m/2m3: 0-7 2m4-2m7: 0-3 3m+: 0-2
Track: LH: 0-10 RH: 0-1 Tight: 0-4 Gall: 0-2
Aids: Bl: 0-0 Vi: 0-0 Tstrap: 0-0
Best Rating: 78   8/02   Strf   2m110y   gd-sft   Hdl

Ordinary form in novice hurdles and chases; suited by soft ground.

Priory Gardens (IRE)

9-y-o b g Broken Hearted-Rosy O Leary (Majetta)
Mrs N S Sharpe   M D Jones

Placings:0/P   (4021)
2002/03: 17^PS,

	Starts	1st	2nd	3rd	Win & Pl
Hurdles	1	0	0	0	
Career Total	2	0	0	0	

Going: Sf: 0-1 GS: 0-0 Gd: 0-0 GF: - Fm: 0-0
Distance: 2m/2m3: 0-1 2m4-2m7: 0-0 3m+: 0-0
Track: LH: 0-0 RH: 0-1 Tight: 0-0 Gall: 0-0
Aids: Bl: 0-0 Vi: 0-0 Tstrap: 0-0
Best Rating: 31   8/00   Worc   2m   gd-fm   Hdl

Priory Wood
41

7-y-o ch m Gunner B-Penlea Lady (Leading Man)
Mrs H Dalton   Mrs S G Addinsell

Placings:100-P   (2099)
2002/03: 19^PG,

	Starts	1st	2nd	3rd	Win & Pl
Hurdles	1	0	0	0	
Career Total	4	1	0	0	1596
87 12/01 Hrfd		H NHF		SFT	£1596

Total win prize-money £1596

Going: Sf: 0-0 GS: 0-0 Gd: 0-1 GF: - Fm: 0-0
Distance: 2m/2m3: 0-1 2m4-2m7: 0-0 3m+: 0-0
Track: LH: 0-1 RH: 0-0 Tight: 0-1 Gall: 0-0
Aids: Bl: 0-0 Vi: 0-0 Tstrap: 0-1
Best Rating: 87   12/01   Hrfd   2m1f   soft   NHF

Made a winning debut in a Hereford bumper; held over hurdles.

Private Percival
94   91

10-y-o b g Arrasas (USA)-Romacina (Roman Warrior)
Jamie Poulton   J Logan

Placings:0/464P4/0-63   (2128)
2002/03: 20⁶GS, 17³S,

	Starts	1st	2nd	3rd	Win & Pl
Chases	2	0	0	1	564
Career Total	9	0	0	1	1507

Going: Sf: 0-1 GS: 0-1 Gd: 0-0 GF: - Fm: 0-0
Distance: 2m/2m3: 0-1 2m4-2m7: 0-1 3m+: 0-0
Track: LH: 0-2 RH: 0-0 Tight: 0-2 Gall: 0-0
Aids: Bl: 0-0 Vi: 0-0 Tstrap: 0-0
Best Rating: 91   11/02   Plum   2m1f   soft   Ch

Plating-class chaser; acts on soft.

Private Pete

10-y-o ch g Gunner B-Vedra (IRE) (Carlingford Castle)
Lady Connell   Sir Michael Connell

Placings:P/1-30   (4459)
2002/03: 25³S, 21^OG,

	Starts	1st	2nd	3rd	Win & Pl
Chases	2	0	0	1	222
Career Total	4	1	0	1	2361
91 3/02 Leic 2m7f110yH Ch				SFT	£2138

Total win prize-money £2139

Going: Sf: 0-1 GS: 0-0 Gd: 0-1 GF: - Fm: 0-0
Distance: 2m/2m3: 0-0 2m4-2m7: 0-1 3m+: 0-1
Track: LH: 0-1 RH: 0-1 Tight: 0-2 Gall: 0-0
Aids: Bl: 0-0 Vi: 0-0 Tstrap: 0-0
Best Rating: 91   2/03   Folk   3m1f   soft   Ch

Hunter chaser/ pointer; acts on soft ground.

Private Seal
23

8-y-o b g King s Signet (USA)-Slender (Aragon)
Julian Poulton   Russell Reed

Placings:B0/6/0   (1504)
2002/03: 17^OG,

	Starts	1st	2nd	3rd	Win & Pl
Hurdles	1	0	0	0	

Career Total   **4**   **0**   **0**   **0**   **0**

Going:	Sf: 0-0 GS: 0-0 Gd: 0-1 GF: - Fm: 0-0
Distance:	2m/2m3: 0-1 2m4-2m7: 0-0 3m+: 0-0
Track:	LH: 0-1 RH: 0-0 Tight: 0-0 Gall: 0-0
Aids:	Bl: 0-0 Vi: 0-0 Tstrap: 0-1
Best Rating:	45 4/99 Plum 2m1f gd-sft Hdl

Private Treaty

5-y-o b m Contract Law (USA)-Inbisat (Beldale Flutter (USA))
S A Brookshaw Swift Racing

Placings:00P   **(2445)**
2002/03: 17⁹GS, 16⁰G, 16ᴾG,

	Starts	1st	2nd	3rd	Win & Pl
NH Flat	2	0	0	0	
Hurdles	1	0	0	0	0
Career Total	**3**	**0**	**0**	**0**	

Going:	Sf: 0-0 GS: 0-1 Gd: 0-2 GF: - Fm: 0-0
Distance:	2m/2m3: 0-3 2m4-2m7: 0-0 3m+: 0-0
Track:	LH: 0-1 RH: 0-2 Tight: 0-1 Gall: 0-0
Aids:	Bl: 0-0 Vi: 0-0 Tstrap: 0-2
Best Rating:	0 12/02 Ludl 2m good Hdl

Prize Dancer (FR)
64   85

5-y-o ch g Suave Dancer (USA)-Spot Prize (USA) (Seattle Dancer (USA))
M E Sowersby (D R C Elsworth 26/7) The Prize Guys Partnership

Placings:60-P0   **(1743)**
2002/03: 24ᴾGF, 16⁰GS,

	Starts	1st	2nd	3rd	Win & Pl
Hurdles	2	0	0	0	
Career Total	**4**	**0**	**0**	**0**	**0**

Going:	Sf: 0-0 GS: 0-1 Gd: 0-0 GF: - Fm: 0-1
Distance:	2m/2m3: 0-1 2m4-2m7: 0-0 3m+: 0-1
Track:	LH: 0-1 RH: 0-1 Tight: 0-1 Gall: 0-0
Aids:	Bl: 0-0 Vi: 0-0 Tstrap: 0-0
Best Rating:	85 2/02 Kemp 2m good Hdl

A winner over 14 furlongs on the level, he was suited by fast ground on the Flat. Disappointing so far over hurdles.

Pro Bono (IRE)

13-y-o ch g Tale Quale-Quality Suite (Prince Hansel)
M G Hazell W F Caudwell

Placings:00030100/4F3P2521/F3PU321/31U4P/34315U/654/02F2P36/14-PPP   **(4059)**
2002/03: 25ᴾGS, 24ᴾS, 26ᴾGS,

	Starts	1st	2nd	3rd	Win & Pl
Chases	3	0	0	0	
Career Total	**50**	**6**	**5**	**8**	**20775**
96	5/01	Strf	3m	H Ch	G-F	£3374
104	2/99	Fknm	2m5f110yH Ch		G-S	£2168
100	2/98	Fknm	2m5f110yH Ch		GD	£2158
100	4/97	Chel	2m110y H Ch		GD	£2190
98	3/96	Fknm	2m5f110yH Ch		G-F	£2440
107	4/95	Thur	2m	Hdl		GD	£2204
				Total win prize-money £14536

Going:	Sf: 0-1 GS: 0-2 Gd: 0-0 GF: - Fm: 0-0

Distance:	2m/2m3: 0-0 2m4-2m7: 0-0 3m+: 0-3
Track:	LH: 0-2 RH: 0-1 Tight: 0-0 Gall: 0-1
Aids:	Bl: 0-0 Vi: 0-0 Tstrap: 0-0
Best Rating:	110 5/98 Sthl 2m4f110y good Ch

Pro Dancer (USA)
97   113

5-y-o b/br h Pleasant Tap (USA)-Shihama (USA) (Shadeed (USA))
P M J Doyle James A Duggan

Placings:23333-F34601   **(4581a)**
2002/03: 16ᶠGF, 16³Gd, 16⁴G, 16⁶GY, 16⁰G, 16¹GF,

	Starts	1st	2nd	3rd	Win & Pl
Hurdles	6	1	0	1	8277
Career Total	**11**	**1**	**1**	**5**	**12152**
113	4/03	List	2m		G-F	£4928
				Total win prize-money £4929

Going:	Sf: 0-0 GS: 0-0 Gd: 0-2 GF: - Fm: 1-3
Distance:	**2m/2m3: 1-6** 2m4-2m7: 0-0 3m+: 0-0
Track:	**LH: 1-4** RH: 0-0 Tight: 0-1 Gall: 0-0
Aids:	Bl: 0-0 Vi: 0-0 Tstrap: 0-0
Best Rating:	113 4/03 List 2m gd-fm Hdl

Modest Irish hurdler; acts on fast ground.

Probus Lady
85   61

6-y-o ch m Good Times (ITY)-Decoyanne (Decoy Boy)
K Bishop E G M Beard

Placings:P   **(0345)**
2002/03: 22ᴾGS,

	Starts	1st	2nd	3rd	Win & Pl
Hurdles	1	0	0	0	
Career Total	**1**	**0**	**0**	**0**	

Going:	Sf: 0-0 GS: 0-1 Gd: 0-0 GF: - Fm: 0-0
Distance:	2m/2m3: 0-0 2m4-2m7: 0-1 3m+: 0-0
Track:	LH: 0-1 RH: 0-0 Tight: 0-1 Gall: 0-0
Aids:	Bl: 0-0 Vi: 0-0 Tstrap: 0-0
Best Rating:	

Probus Lord
102   104

8-y-o b g Rough Stones-Decoyanne (Decoy Boy)
K Bishop E G M Beard

Placings:05/P-0P   **(0510)**
2002/03: 24⁰G, 20ᴾG,

	Starts	1st	2nd	3rd	Win & Pl
Hurdles	2	0	0	0	
Career Total	**5**	**0**	**0**	**0**	**0**

Going:	Sf: 0-0 GS: 0-0 Gd: 0-2 GF: - Fm: 0-0
Distance:	2m/2m3: 0-0 2m4-2m7: 0-0 3m+: 0-1
Track:	LH: 0-1 RH: 0-1 Tight: 0-0 Gall: 0-0
Aids:	Bl: 0-0 Vi: 0-0 Tstrap: 0-0
Best Rating:	77 12/99 Ludl 2m gd-sft NHF

Runner-up in stamina test run in soft ground at Newton Abbot in April 2003 and again over 3m 2f on fast ground at Hereford in June.

Procedure (USA)
(88c)

7-y-o b/br g Strolling Along (USA)-Bold Courtesan (USA) (Bold Bidder)

J A B Old W E Sturt

Placings:60206-3   **(3818)**
2002/03: 16³GS,

	Starts	1st	2nd	3rd	Win & Pl
Chases	1	0	0	1	730
Career Total	**6**	**0**	**1**	**1**	**1485**

Going:	Sf: 0-0 GS: 0-1 Gd: 0-0 GF: - Fm: 0-0
Distance:	2m/2m3: 0-1 2m4-2m7: 0-0 3m+: 0-0
Track:	LH: 0-0 RH: 0-1 Tight: 0-0 Gall: 0-0
Aids:	Bl: 0-0 Vi: 0-0 Tstrap: 0-0
Best Rating:	109 1/02 Tntn 2m1f soft Hdl

Modest hurdler; successful twice on the Flat; well beaten on chase debut.

Professor Cool (IRE)

10-y-o b g Cataldi-Frostbite (Prince Tenderfoot (USA))
R J Price R J Price

Placings:10/32231/P   **(0147)**
2002/03: 24ᴾGF,

	Starts	1st	2nd	3rd	Win & Pl
Hurdles	1	0	0	0	
Career Total	**8**	**2**	**2**	**2**	**6163**
118	3/99	Donc	2m4f	E Hdl	G-S	£2582
102	2/98	Font	2m2f	H NHF	GD	£1329
				Total win prize-money £3912

Going:	Sf: 0-0 GS: 0-0 Gd: 0-0 GF: - Fm: 0-1
Distance:	2m/2m3: 0-0 2m4-2m7: 0-0 3m+: 0-1
Track:	LH: 0-1 RH: 0-0 Tight: 0-0 Gall: 0-0
Aids:	Bl: 0-0 Vi: 0-0 Tstrap: 0-0
Best Rating:	118 3/99 Donc 2m4f gd-sft Hdl

Profiler (USA)
91   75

8-y-o b g Capote (USA)-Magnificent Star (USA) (Silver Hawk (USA))
Ferdy Murphy Mrs J Morgan

Placings:55/2046444/0U1F1/PPPP3U-6PU3BP0   **(4588)**
2002/03: 16⁶S, 19ᴾG, 21ᵁS, 16³HY, 22ᴾG, 22ᴾS, 20⁰G,

	Starts	1st	2nd	3rd	Win & Pl
Chases	7	0	0	1	471
Career Total	**27**	**2**	**1**	**2**	**7248**
96	1/01	Donc	2m4f	E Hdl	GD	£2254
111	10/00	Folk	2m	E Ch	G-F	£2808
				Total win prize-money £5062

Going:	Sf: 0-4 GS: 0-0 Gd: 0-3 GF: - Fm: 0-0
Distance:	2m/2m3: 0-3 2m4-2m7: 0-3 3m+: 0-1
Track:	LH: 0-5 RH: 0-2 Tight: 0-6 Gall: 0-0
Aids:	Bl: 0-2 Vi: 0-0 Tstrap: 0-0
Best Rating:	111 10/00 Folk 2m gd-fm Ch

Plating-class chaser; winner on the flat, over hurdles and fences; needs a sound surface and goes well from two miles to two miles four.

Prokofiev (USA)
112(102c)   (122c)125+

7-y-o br g Nureyev (USA)-Aviara (USA) (Cox's Ridge (USA))
Jonjo O Neill Mrs Sylvia Darlington

Placings:14/5520010/52350344-616305P1   **(4563)**
2002/03: 24⁶S, 22¹S, 21⁶S, 22³HY, 20⁹S, 21⁵G, 22ᴾS, 24¹GF,

	Starts	1st	2nd	3rd	Win & Pl
Hurdles	8	2	0	1	15471

Career Total	25	4	2	3	35813
125	4/03	Bang	3m	D(0-120)HHdl	G-F	£5619
125	12/02	Sand	2m6f	C(0-130)HHdl	SFT	£7442
134	2/01	Newc	2m4f	B(0-140)HHdl	HVY	£6366
109	12/99	Wwck	2m	C Hdl	SFT	£5912

Total win prize-money £25341

Going:	Sf: 1-6 GS: 0-0 Gd: 0-1 GF: - Fm: 1-1
Distance:	2m/2m3: 0-0 2m4-2m7: 1-6 3m+: 1-2
Track:	LH: 1-5 RH: 1-3 Tight: 1-1 Gall: 0-1
Aids:	Bl: 2-6 Vi: 0-0 Tstrap: 0-2
Best Rating:	134 2/01 Newc 2m4f heavy Hdl

Fair hurdler; not a straightforward ride; stays two miles six and is suited by soft ground; has worn a tongue tie and blinkers.

Prologue (IRE)

96   77

12-y-o b g Mandalus-Advance Notice (Le Bavard (FR))
Mrs L Williamson (Trainer Unknown 19/5) R Greenway

Placings:0000/P/355P   (0785)
2002/03: 23³G, 20⁵GF, 22⁵GF, 26⁶GF,

	Starts	1st	2nd	3rd	Win & Pl
Chases	4	0	0	1	479
Career Total	9	0	0	1	479

Going:	Sf: 0-0 GS: 0-0 Gd: 0-1 GF: - Fm: 0-3
Distance:	2m/2m3: 0-0 2m4-2m7: 0-3 3m+: 0-1
Track:	LH: 0-2 RH: 0-2 Tight: 0-2 Gall: 0-0
Aids:	Bl: 0-0 Vi: 0-0 Tstrap: 0-0
Best Rating:	77 6/02 MRas 2m4f gd-fm Ch

Prominent Profile (IRE)

105   99

10-y-o ch g Mazaad-Nakuru (IRE) (Mandalus)
N A Twiston-Davies The Son Partnership

Placings:10113034/13FU4/050U50-U1P4   (3900)
2002/03: 22¹¹G, 18¹G, 20⁴S, 20⁴PS,

	Starts	1st	2nd	3rd	Win & Pl
Chases	4	1	0	0	6972
Career Total	23	5	0	3	31364
99	12/02	Newb	2m2f110yD(0-120)HCh	£6162
135	10/99	Chep	2m3f110yD Ch	SFT	£4182
146	1/99	Weth	2m4f110yD Hdl	SFT	£3038
132	12/98	Chep	2m110y A NHF	HVY	£6280
115	10/98	Chel	2m110y H NHF	G-S	£1940

Total win prize-money £21602

Going:	Sf: 0-2 GS: 0-0 Gd: 1-2 GF: - Fm: 0-0
Distance:	2m/2m3: 1-1 2m4-2m7: 0-3 3m+: 0-0
Track:	LH: 1-3 RH: 0-0 Tight: 0-1 Gall: 1-2
Aids:	Bl: 0-0 Vi: 0-0 Tstrap: 0-0
Best Rating:	146 1/99 Weth 2m4f110y soft Hdl

Modest chaser, former very useful novice hurdler; dropped considerably in the handicap prior to scoring at Newbury in December 2002; effective at up to two and a half miles; acts on soft ground; has worn blinkers.

Promising (FR)

101   75

5-y-o ch m Ashkalani (IRE)-Sea Thunder (Salse (USA))
M C Chapman Mrs S M Richards

Placings:4620F0   (4525)
2002/03: 16⁴G, 16⁶G, 16²G, 17⁰GS, 17⁷G, 16⁰G,

	Starts	1st	2nd	3rd	Win & Pl
Hurdles	6	0	1	0	680
Career Total	6	0	1	0	680

Going:	Sf: 0-0 GS: 0-1 Gd: 0-0 GF: - Fm: 0-0
Distance:	2m/2m3: 0-6 2m4-2m7: 0-0 3m+: 0-0
Track:	LH: 0-4 RH: 0-2 Tight: 0-4 Gall: 0-0
Aids:	Bl: 0-0 Vi: 0-0 Tstrap: 0-0
Best Rating:	75 10/02 Strf 2m110y good Hdl

Plating-class hurdler; effective over two miles on good ground.

Proper Squire (USA)

105(109h)   (122 h)120

6-y-o b g Bien Bien (USA)-La Cumbre (Sadler s Wells (USA))
C J Mann The Icy Fire Partnership

Placings:214P-1313400   (4456)
2002/03: 22¹¹GF, 21³G, 24¹¹G, 24³G, 24⁴G, 25⁰G, 24⁰G,

	Starts	1st	2nd	3rd	Win & Pl
Hurdles	7	2	0	2	11214
Career Total	11	3	1	2	16301
121	11/02	Kemp	3m110y D(0-120)HHdl	GD	£5330
112	5/02	Font	2m6f110yE(0-110)HHdl	G-F	£2562
110	12/01	Strf	2m6f110yE Hdl	SFT	£3125

Total win prize-money £11018

Going:	Sf: 0-0 GS: 0-0 Gd: 1-6 GF: - Fm: 1-1
Distance:	2m/2m3: 0-0 2m4-2m7: 1-2 3m+: 1-5
Track:	LH: 1-5 RH: 1-2 Tight: 1-3 Gall: 0-3
Aids:	Bl: 0-2 Vi: 0-0 Tstrap: 0-0
Best Rating:	122 12/02 Chel 3m good Hdl

Useful handicap hurdler, fair chaser; has performed creditably since being switched to fences; stays three miles; best on fast ground, but acts on heavy.

Property Zone

104   102

5-y-o b g Cool Jazz-Prime Property (IRE) (Tirol)
C Grant (M W Easterby 19/10) Mrs A Meller

Placings:60554-06F332141   (4754)
2002/03: 16⁰GF, 17⁵GF, 17⁷GS, 16³G, 16⁹GS, 16²GS, 16¹G,
16⁴GF, 16¹G,

	Starts	1st	2nd	3rd	Win & Pl
Hurdles	8	2	1	2	13300
Chases	1	0	0	0	0
Career Total	14	2	1	2	13300
102	4/03	Prth	2m110y D(0-120)HHdl	GD	£7104
99	3/03	Donc	2m110y E(0-105)HHdl	G-S	£3552

Total win prize-money £10657

Going:	Sf: 0-0 GS: 1-4 Gd: 1-2 GF: - Fm: 0-3
Distance:	2m/2m3: 2-9 2m4-2m7: 0-0 3m+: 0-0
Track:	LH: 1-6 RH: 1-3 Tight: 0-2 Gall: 1-3
Aids:	Bl: 0-0 Vi: 0-0 Tstrap: 0-0
Best Rating:	102 4/03 Prth 2m110y good Hdl

Plating-class hurdler; acts on good to soft ground; effective over two miles.

Prospector's Cove

76   29

10-y-o b g Dowsing (USA)-Pearl Cove (Town And Country)
J M Bradley Saracen Racing

Placings:406/0   (1231)
2002/03: 16⁰G,

	Starts	1st	2nd	3rd	Win & Pl
Hurdles	1	0	0	0	

Career Total	4	0	0	0	0

Going:	Sf: 0-0 GS: 0-0 Gd: 0-0 GF: - Fm: 0-0
Distance:	2m/2m3: 0-0 2m4-2m7: 0-0 3m+: 0-0
Track:	LH: 0-1 RH: 0-0 Tight: 0-0 Gall: 0-0
Aids:	Bl: 0-0 Vi: 0-0 Tstrap: 0-0
Best Rating:	102 3/98 Plum 2m1f good Hdl

Protagonist

105   110

5-y-o b/br g In The Wings-Fatah Flare (USA) (Alydar (USA))
P R Webber Milbourne Lodge Partnership

Placings:0401-6010P   (3295)
2002/03: 16⁸GF, 17⁰G, 21¹S, 21⁰G, 19⁷GS,

	Starts	1st	2nd	3rd	Win & Pl
Hurdles	5	1	0	0	6438
Career Total	9	2	0	0	10911
110	12/02	Kemp	2m5f	C(0-135)HHdl	SFT	£6438
104	3/02	Newb	2m110y	D(0-110)HHdl	G-S	£4134

Total win prize-money £10572

Going:	Sf: 1-1 GS: 0-1 Gd: 0-2 GF: - Fm: 0-1
Distance:	2m/2m3: 0-2 2m4-2m7: 1-3 3m+: 0-0
Track:	LH: 0-3 RH: 1-2 Tight: 0-0 Gall: 0-1
Aids:	Bl: 0-0 Vi: 0-0 Tstrap: 0-0
Best Rating:	110 12/02 Kemp 2m5f soft Hdl

Stepped up on earlier efforts when successful on his handicap debut in March 2002 and later scored at Kempton. Stays two miles five and acts with cut in the ground.

Protocol (IRE)

108   95

9-y-o b g Taufan (USA)-Ukraine s Affair (USA) (The Minstrel (CAN))
Mrs S Lamyman P Lamyman

Placings:43/2450422/006/246015500   (4157)
2002/03: 17²G, 16⁴G, 16⁶GS, 16⁰GS, 17¹GS, 16⁵HY, 16⁵GS,
16⁶HY, 17⁰G,

	Starts	1st	2nd	3rd	Win & Pl
Hurdles	9	1	1	0	3361
Career Total	21	1	4	1	8089
99	12/02	MRas	2m1f110yG(0-95)HHdl	G-S	£2425

Total win prize-money £2426

Going:	Sf: 0-2 GS: 1-4 Gd: 0-3 GF: - Fm: 0-0
Distance:	2m/2m3: 1-9 2m4-2m7: 0-0 3m+: 0-0
Track:	LH: 0-5 RH: 1-4 Tight: 1-4 Gall: 0-3
Aids:	Bl: 0-0 Vi: 0-0 Tstrap: 1-9
Best Rating:	109 3/00 Donc 2m110y good Hdl

Moderate hurdler, won a selling handicap hurdle at Market Rasen in December.

Proud Cavalier

7-y-o b g Pharly (FR)-Midnight Flit (Bold Lad (IRE))
Jean-Rene Auvray S J Edwards

Placings:0/PF   (0613)
2002/03: 16⁰GF, 16⁶GF,

	Starts	1st	2nd	3rd	Win & Pl
Hurdles	2	0	0	0	
Career Total	3	0	0	0	

Going:	Sf: 0-0 GS: 0-0 Gd: 0-0 GF: - Fm: 0-2
Distance:	2m/2m3: 0-2 2m4-2m7: 0-0 3m+: 0-0
Track:	LH: 0-1 RH: 0-1 Tight: 0-0 Gall: 0-0

Aids: Bl: 0-0 Vi: 0-0 Tstrap: 0-0
Best Rating: 0 6/02 Worc 2m   gd-fm Hdl

Proud Fountain (IRE)

10-y-o br g Royal Fountain-Proud Polly (IRE) (Pollerton)
J W Hughes Mrs Murray Scott

Placings:0/0/061P-0   (4508)
2002/03: 25[0]G,

	Starts	1st	2nd	3rd	Win & Pl
Chases	1	0	0	0	
Career Total	7	1	0	0	1694

80 11/01 Hntg 3m2f G(0-95)HHdl GD £1694
Total win prize-money £1694

Going: Sf: 0-0 GS: 0-0 Gd: 0-1 GF: - Fm: 0-0
Distance: 2m/2m3: 0-0 2m4-2m7: 0-0 3m+: 0-1
Track: LH: 0-1 RH: 0-0 Tight: 0-1 Gall: 0-0
Aids: Bl: 0-0 Vi: 0-0 Tstrap: 0-0
Best Rating: 80 11/01 Hntg 3m2f good Hdl

Proud Monk
89   69

10-y-o gr g Aragon-Silent Sister (Kind Of Hush)
Jean-Rene Auvray S J Edwards

Placings:05/00   (0326)
2002/03: 16[9]GS, 16[9]G,

	Starts	1st	2nd	3rd	Win & Pl
Hurdles	2	0	0	0	
Career Total	4	0	0	0	0

Going: Sf: 0-0 GS: 0-1 Gd: 0-1 GF: - Fm: 0-0
Distance: 2m/2m3: 0-2 2m4-2m7: 0-0 3m+: 0-0
Track: LH: 0-1 RH: 0-1 Tight: 0-0 Gall: 0-0
Aids: Bl: 0-0 Vi: 0-0 Tstrap: 0-1
Best Rating: 70 5/02 Worc 2m good Hdl

Proud Peer (IRE)
96f   88f

5-y-o ch g Mister Lord (USA)-Raffeen Pride (Shackleton)
M Pitman G C Stevens

Placings:55   (3556)
2002/03: 16[5]GS, 18[5]HY,

	Starts	1st	2nd	3rd	Win & Pl
NH Flat	2	0	0	0	0
Career Total	2	0	0	0	0

Going: Sf: 0-1 GS: 0-1 Gd: 0-0 GF: - Fm: 0-0
Distance: 2m/2m3: 0-2 2m4-2m7: 0-0 3m+: 0-0
Track: LH: 0-1 RH: 0-1 Tight: 0-1 Gall: 0-0
Aids: Bl: 0-0 Vi: 0-0 Tstrap: 0-0
Best Rating: 88 1/03 Kemp 2m gd-sft NHF

Decent fifth on debut, but found the ground too soft next time when well beaten.

Proud Western (USA)
54   53

5-y-o b/br g Gone West (USA)-Proud Lou (USA) (Proud Clarion)

B Ellison Spring Cottage Syndicate

Placings:00-0   (3156)
2002/03: 16[6]G,

	Starts	1st	2nd	3rd	Win & Pl
Hurdles	1	0	0	0	
Career Total	3	0	0	0	

Going: Sf: 0-0 GS: 0-0 Gd: 0-1 GF: - Fm: 0-0
Distance: 2m/2m3: 0-1 2m4-2m7: 0-0 3m+: 0-0
Track: LH: 0-0 RH: 0-1 Tight: 0-1 Gall: 0-0
Aids: Bl: 0-0 Vi: 0-0 Tstrap: 0-0
Best Rating: 53 3/02 Catt 2m gd-sft Hdl

Provence Dreamer
94   76

6-y-o b g Alflora (IRE)-Kilbragh Dreamer (IRE) (Decent Fellow)
Jonjo O Neill Mrs Jonjo O Neill

Placings:22P53   (4355)
2002/03: 17[2]G, 17[2]S, 24[5]HY, 21[5]GS, 20[3]GF,

	Starts	1st	2nd	3rd	Win & Pl
NH Flat	2	0	2	0	1112
Hurdles	3	0	0	1	544
Career Total	5	0	2	1	1655

Going: Sf: 0-2 GS: 0-1 Gd: 0-1 GF: - Fm: 0-1
Distance: 2m/2m3: 0-2 2m4-2m7: 0-2 3m+: 0-1
Track: LH: 0-3 RH: 0-2 Tight: 0-3 Gall: 0-0
Aids: Bl: 0-0 Vi: 0-0 Tstrap: 0-0
Best Rating: 104 10/02 MRas 2m1f110y good NHF

Runner-up in bumpers on good to soft ground; modest form over hurdles; looks a stayer.

Proverbial Gray
101   73

6-y-o ro m Norton Challenger-Clove Bud (Beau Charmeur (FR))
D R Gandolfo D R Gandolfo Ltd

Placings:500-506403S   (4679)
2002/03: 16[5]GS, 17[9]GS, 17[6]S, 17[4]HY, 17[0]F, 16[3]G, 16[5]GF,

	Starts	1st	2nd	3rd	Win & Pl
Hurdles	7	0	0	1	353
Career Total	10	0	0	1	353

Going: Sf: 0-2 GS: 0-2 Gd: 0-1 GF: - Fm: 0-2
Distance: 2m/2m3: 0-7 2m4-2m7: 0-0 3m+: 0-0
Track: LH: 0-3 RH: 0-4 Tight: 0-3 Gall: 0-1
Aids: Bl: 0-0 Vi: 0-0 Tstrap: 0-0
Best Rating: 75 10/02 Bang 2m1f gd-sft Hdl

Plating-class hurdler; tends to pull hard.

Provocative (FR)
98f   121f

5-y-o b/br g Useful (FR)-All Blue (FR) (Noir Et Or)
M Todhunter Sir Robert Ogden

Placings:23   (4411)
2002/03: 16[2]G, 16[3]G,

	Starts	1st	2nd	3rd	Win & Pl
NH Flat	2	0	1	1	881
Career Total	2	0	1	1	881

Going: Sf: 0-0 GS: 0-0 Gd: 0-2 GF: - Fm: 0-0

Distance: 2m/2m3: 0-2 2m4-2m7: 0-0 3m+: 0-0
Track: LH: 0-2 RH: 0-0 Tight: 0-0 Gall: 0-0
Aids: Bl: 0-0 Vi: 0-0 Tstrap: 0-0
Best Rating: 121 3/03 Hayd 2m good NHF

Prudish Lass

6-y-o b m Warcraft (USA)-Bella Delite (Uncle Pokey)
A J Lidderdale Goforbroke

Placings:0   (3174)
2002/03: 16[9]GS,

	Starts	1st	2nd	3rd	Win & Pl
NH Flat	1	0	0	0	
Career Total	1	0	0	0	

Going: Sf: 0-0 GS: 0-1 Gd: 0-0 GF: - Fm: 0-0
Distance: 2m/2m3: 0-1 2m4-2m7: 0-0 3m+: 0-0
Track: LH: 0-1 RH: 0-0 Tight: 0-0 Gall: 0-0
Aids: Bl: 0-0 Vi: 0-0 Tstrap: 0-0
Best Rating: 0 1/03 Hayd 2m gd-sft NHF

Ptarmigan

6-y-o ch g Rock Hopper-Tee Gee Jay (Northern Tempest (USA))
T T Clement Future Electrical Services Ltd

Placings:0-0   (4122)
2002/03: 16[9]G,

	Starts	1st	2nd	3rd	Win & Pl
NH Flat	1	0	0	0	
Career Total	2	0	0	0	

Going: Sf: 0-0 GS: 0-0 Gd: 0-1 GF: - Fm: 0-0
Distance: 2m/2m3: 0-1 2m4-2m7: 0-0 3m+: 0-0
Track: LH: 0-0 RH: 0-1 Tight: 0-0 Gall: 0-1
Aids: Bl: 0-0 Vi: 0-0 Tstrap: 0-0
Best Rating: 45 10/01 Hntg 2m110y good NHF

Ptolomy
71f   68f

6-y-o ch g Presidium-Moonwalker (Night Shift (USA))
J G Fitzgerald N H T Wrigley

Placings:6   (0205)
2002/03: 16[6]GF,

	Starts	1st	2nd	3rd	Win & Pl
NH Flat	1	0	0	0	0
Career Total	1	0	0	0	0

Going: Sf: 0-0 GS: 0-0 Gd: 0-0 GF: - Fm: 0-1
Distance: 2m/2m3: 0-1 2m4-2m7: 0-0 3m+: 0-0
Track: LH: 0-1 RH: 0-0 Tight: 0-0 Gall: 0-0
Aids: Bl: 0-0 Vi: 0-0 Tstrap: 0-0
Best Rating: 68 5/02 Worc 2m gd-fm NHF

Pucks Court
53f   4f

6-y-o b g Nomadic Way (USA)-Miss Puck (Tepukei)
I A Brown W Brown

Placings:P00   (1709)
2002/03: 17[P]GF, 17[9]G, 17[0]G,

	Starts	1st	2nd	3rd	Win & Pl
NH Flat	3	0	0	0	
Career Total	3	0	0	0	

Going:	Sf: 0-0 GS: 0-0 Gd: 0-2 GF: - Fm: 0-1
Distance:	2m/2m3: 0-3 2m4-2m7: 0-0 3m+: 0-0
Track:	LH: 0-2 RH: 0-1 Tight: 0-3 Gall: 0-0
Aids:	Bl: 0-0 Vi: 0-0 Tstrap: 0-0
Best Rating:	4 10/02 Sedg 2m1f good NHF

Pucks Way

4-y-o b g Nomadic Way (USA)-Adventurous Lady (Roman Warrior)
D G Bridgwater Miss E E Hill

Placings:5 (1453)
2002/03: 16⁵F,

	Starts	1st	2nd	3rd	Win & Pl
Hurdles	1	0	0	0	0
Career Total	1	0	0	0	0

Going:	Sf: 0-0 GS: 0-0 Gd: 0-0 GF: - Fm: 0-1
Distance:	2m/2m3: 0-1 2m4-2m7: 0-0 3m+: 0-0
Track:	LH: 0-1 RH: 0-0 Tight: 0-0 Gall: 0-0
Aids:	Bl: 0-0 Vi: 0-0 Tstrap: 0-0
Best Rating:	0 10/02 Ludl 2m firm Hdl

Pudlicott Mill (IRE)
53

4-y-o b g Definite Article-Mimining (Tower Walk)
M F Harris M Harris

Placings:P (0838)
2002/03: 16PGF,

	Starts	1st	2nd	3rd	Win & Pl
Hurdles	1	0	0	0	
Career Total	1	0	0	0	

Going:	Sf: 0-0 GS: 0-0 Gd: 0-0 GF: - Fm: 0-0
Distance:	2m/2m3: 0-1 2m4-2m7: 0-0 3m+: 0-0
Track:	LH: 0-1 RH: 0-0 Tight: 0-1 Gall: 0-0
Aids:	Bl: 0-0 Vi: 0-0 Tstrap: 0-0
Best Rating:	0 7/02 Strf 2m110y gd-fm Hdl

Puntal (FR)
114   146

7-y-o b g Bering-Saveur (Ardross)
M C Pipe Terry Neill

Placings:32P2224/05600-1111F122010P (4462)
2002/03: 16¹G, 17¹G, 16¹G, 16¹GF, 18FVS, 17¹GS, 16²S, 16²GS, 16⁰G, 16¹G, 21⁰G, 20²G,

	Starts	1st	2nd	3rd	Win & Pl
Hurdles	12	6	2	0	68589
Career Total	24	6	6	1	103928

146	2/03	Kemp	2m	A Hdl	GD	£17400
149	7/02	MRas	2m1f110yB(0-140)HHdl		G-S	£23200
140	5/02	Strf	2m110y	D Hdl	G-F	£4322
134	5/02	Worc	2m	E Hdl	GD	£2709
124	5/02	Hrfd	2m1f	E Hdl	GD	£3188
122	5/02	Sthl	2m	D Hdl	GD	£3469

Total win prize-money £54290

Going:	Sf: 0-1 GS: 1-2 Gd: 4-7 GF: - Fm: 1-1
Distance:	2m/2m3: 6-10 2m4-2m7: 0-2 3m+: 0-0
Track:	LH: 3-6 RH: 3-5 Tight: 3-4 Gall: 0-2
Aids:	Bl: 0-0 Vi: 0-0 Tstrap: 0-0
Best Rating:	149 12/02 Asct 2m110y soft Hdl

Smart novice hurdler; has shown good form at around two miles, but promises to stay further; seems to act on good and soft ground; best with forcing tactics.

Purbeck Wonder

7-y-o ro g Riverwise (USA)-Blue Wonder (Idiots Delight)
N R Mitchell Mrs Margaret Speed

Placings:P-P (0205)
2002/03: 16PGF,

	Starts	1st	2nd	3rd	Win & Pl
NH Flat	1	0	0	0	
Career Total	2	0	0	0	

Going:	Sf: 0-0 GS: 0-0 Gd: 0-0 GF: - Fm: 0-1
Distance:	2m/2m3: 0-1 2m4-2m7: 0-0 3m+: 0-0
Track:	LH: 0-1 RH: 0-0 Tight: 0-0 Gall: 0-0
Aids:	Bl: 0-0 Vi: 0-0 Tstrap: 0-0
Best Rating:	0 5/02 Worc 2m gd-fm NHF

Pure Brief (IRE)
86(99h)   (82h)74

6-y-o b g Brief Truce (USA)-Epure (Bellypha)
A Streeter Mrs V D Gandola-Gray

Placings:U000-1P5535 (1504)
2002/03: 16¹GF, 16PGS, 17⁵GF, 17⁵G, 17³GF, 17⁵G,

	Starts	1st	2nd	3rd	Win & Pl
Hurdles	6	1	0	1	4267
Career Total	10	1	0	1	4267
82	7/02 Uttx 2m E(0-110)HHdl			G-F	£3770

Total win prize-money £3770

Going:	Sf: 0-0 GS: 0-1 Gd: 0-2 GF: - Fm: 1-3
Distance:	2m/2m3: 1-6 2m4-2m7: 0-0 3m+: 0-0
Track:	LH: 1-5 RH: 0-1 Tight: 0-3 Gall: 0-0
Aids:	Bl: 1-3 Vi: 0-3 Tstrap: 0-0
Best Rating:	82 9/02 MRas 2m1f110y gd-fm Hdl

Poor hurdler; wore blinkers for the first time when lucky winner of a handicap hurdle at Uttoxeter in July 2002.

Pure Fun (IRE)
104   109+

6-y-o b g Lord Americo-Rath Caola (Neltino)
P J Hobbs Miss I D Du Pre

Placings:10055244-04140421 (4720)
2002/03: 22⁰G, 19⁴GF, 24¹F, 24⁴F, 20⁰GS, 19⁴GS, 21²G, 22¹F,

	Starts	1st	2nd	3rd	Win & Pl
Hurdles	8	2	1	0	10582
Career Total	16	3	2	0	13910
105	4/03 Winc 2m6f E(0-105)HHdl			FRM	£3542
109	10/02 Ludl 3m D(0-115)HHdl			FRM	£5348
95	8/01 Worc 2m H NHF			G-F	£1449

Total win prize-money £10339

Going:	Sf: 0-0 GS: 0-2 Gd: 0-2 GF: - Fm: 2-4
Distance:	2m/2m3: 0-0 2m4-2m7: 1-6 3m+: 1-2
Track:	LH: 0-0 RH: 2-2 Tight: 0-2 Gall: 0-0
Aids:	Bl: 0-0 Vi: 0-0 Tstrap: 0-0
Best Rating:	109 10/02 Ludl 3m firm Hdl

modest hurdler; fast ground bumper winner; appreciated step up to three miles when winning a three-runner race at Ludlow October 2002; good efforts in the summer of 2003; considered a chaser in the making.

Pure Grit (IRE)

13-y-o b g Sheer Grit-Shuil Eile (Deep Run)
G D Hanmer Mrs B L Shaw

Placings:366/P/6 (0503)
2002/03: 26⁶G,

	Starts	1st	2nd	3rd	Win & Pl
Chases	1	0	0	0	0
Career Total	5	0	0	1	257

Going:	Sf: 0-0 GS: 0-0 Gd: 0-1 GF: - Fm: 0-0
Distance:	2m/2m3: 0-0 2m4-2m7: 0-0 3m+: 0-1
Track:	LH: 0-1 RH: 0-0 Tight: 0-1 Gall: 0-0
Aids:	Bl: 0-0 Vi: 0-0 Tstrap: 0-0
Best Rating:	96 2/96 Thur 2m yld-sft NHF

Pure Mischief (IRE)
105   93

4-y-o b g Alhaarth (IRE)-Bellissi (IRE) (Bluebird (USA))
Miss J Feilden J F Thomas

Placings:3U610 (4637)
2002/03: 16³GS, 16US, 16⁶HY, 16¹HY, 16⁹GF,

	Starts	1st	2nd	3rd	Win & Pl
Hurdles	5	1	0	1	3043
Career Total	5	1	0	1	3043
93	3/03 Plum 2m F Hdl			HVY	£2548

Total win prize-money £2548

Going:	Sf: 1-3 GS: 0-1 Gd: 0-0 GF: - Fm: 0-1
Distance:	2m/2m3: 1-5 2m4-2m7: 0-0 3m+: 0-0
Track:	LH: 1-5 RH: 0-0 Tight: 1-3 Gall: 0-0
Aids:	Bl: 0-0 Vi: 0-0 Tstrap: 0-0
Best Rating:	93 3/03 Plum 2m heavy Hdl

Winning claiming hurdler; acts on heavy.

Purser Pete (IRE)
72f   50f

7-y-o b g Jurado (USA)-Roselita (Deep Run)
Miss Lucinda V Russell Girls On Tour

Placings:00 (1989)
2002/03: 16⁹GF, 16⁶S,

	Starts	1st	2nd	3rd	Win & Pl
NH Flat	2	0	0	0	
Career Total	2	0	0	0	

Going:	Sf: 0-1 GS: 0-0 Gd: 0-0 GF: - Fm: 0-0
Distance:	2m/2m3: 0-2 2m4-2m7: 0-0 3m+: 0-0
Track:	LH: 0-1 RH: 0-1 Tight: 0-0 Gall: 0-0
Aids:	Bl: 0-0 Vi: 0-0 Tstrap: 0-1
Best Rating:	53 9/02 Prth 2m110y gd-fm NHF

Pusey Sance

5-y-o br g Puissance-Pusey Street (Native Bazaar)
B L Lay B L Lay

Placings:PU (1814)
2002/03: 16PG, 17UG,

	Starts	1st	2nd	3rd	Win & Pl
Hurdles	2	0	0	0	
Career Total	2	0	0	0	

Going:	Sf: 0-0 GS: 0-0 Gd: 0-2 GF: - Fm: 0-0

Distance: 2m/2m3: 0-2 2m4-2m7: 0-0 3m+: 0-0
Track: LH: 0-1 RH: 0-1 Tight: 0-1 Gall: 0-0
Aids: Bl: 0-0 Vi: 0-0 Tstrap: 0-0
Best Rating: 0   11/02 Hrfd   2m1f   good   Hdl

Putsometnby (IRE)

106(106h)   (113h)131

7-y-o ch g Phardante (FR)-Bobs My Uncle (Deep Run)
Jonjo O Neill (K F O Brien 13/10) Getjar Limited

Placings:0S0021233025-022F2132132U5   (4307)
2002/03: 20⁴GY, 24²G, 20²YS, 22FY, 22²GY, 25¹GF, 20³GF, 24²F, 20¹G, 27³G, 24²G, 24UG, 32⁵G,

	Starts	1st	2nd	3rd	Win & Pl
Hurdles	2	0	1	0	883
Chases	11	2	4	2	38786
Career Total	25	3	8	4	48080
116	10/02	Limk	2m4f	Ch		GD	£8972
95	8/02	Kbgn	3m1f	Ch		G-F	£5503
104	8/01	Tral	2m1f	Hdl		GD	£4451

Total win prize-money £18927

Going: Sf: 0-0 GS: 0-0 Gd: 1-6 GF: - Fm: 1-3
Distance: 2m/2m3: 0-0 2m4-2m7: 1-6 3m+: 1-7
Track: LH: 0-4 **RH: 1-4** Tight: 0-2 Gall: 0-2
Aids: Bl: 0-1 Vi: 0-0 Tstrap: 0-0
Best Rating: 131 3/03 Donc 3m   good   Ch

Fair handicap chaser; acts on good or faster ground; stays three miles.

Putup Or Shutup (IRE)

109   106

7-y-o br g Religiously (USA)-Nights Crack (Callernish)
K C Bailey Les McLaughlin

Placings:0¹122245-42153   (3133)
2002/03: 22⁴S, 20²GS, 21¹GS, 25⁵S, 24³S,

	Starts	1st	2nd	3rd	Win & Pl
Hurdles	5	1	1	1	5627
Career Total	12	2	4	1	9089
106	11/02	Ludl	2m5f	E Hdl		G-S	£3542
103	10/01	Fknm	2m	H NHF		SFT	£1452

Total win prize-money £4996

Going: Sf: 0-2 GS: 1-2 Gd: 0-1 GF: - Fm: 0-0
Distance: 2m/2m3: 0-0 **2m4-2m7:** 1-3 3m+: 0-2
Track: LH: 0-2 **RH: 1-3** Tight: 0-0 Gall: 0-0
Aids: Bl: 0-0 Vi: 0-0 Tstrap: 0-0
Best Rating: 106 11/02 Ludl 2m5f   gd-sft   Hdl

Modest hurdler; stays two miles five furlongs; acts on soft ground.

Puzzleman

(89h)   (67h)69

10-y-o ch g Henbit (USA)-Floreamus (Quayside)
D J Caro E McMichael & P Evans

Placings:40P/26/4/4P5P00P-P   (0109)
2002/03: 21PGF,

	Starts	1st	2nd	3rd	Win & Pl
Hurdles	1	0	0	0	
Career Total	14	0	1	0	1082

Going: Sf: 0-0 GS: 0-0 Gd: 0-0 GF: - Fm: 0-1
Distance: 2m/2m3: 0-0 2m4-2m7: 0-0 3m+: 0-0
Track: LH: 0-0 RH: 0-1 Tight: 0-0 Gall: 0-0
Aids: Bl: 0-0 Vi: 0-0 Tstrap: 0-0

Best Rating: 94   2/00   Ludl   2m5f   gd-fm   Hdl

Pythagoras

86(101h)   (81h)73

6-y-o ch g Kris-Tricorne (Green Desert (USA))
M Sheppard Mike Drake, Tim Doxsey, Ray Hitchin

Placings:2306-64   (4525)
2002/03: 16⁶S, 16⁴G,

	Starts	1st	2nd	3rd	Win & Pl
Hurdles	2	0	0	0	
Career Total	6	0	1	1	909

Going: Sf: 0-1 GS: 0-0 Gd: 0-1 GF: - Fm: 0-0
Distance: 2m/2m3: 0-2 2m4-2m7: 0-0 3m+: 0-0
Track: LH: 0-1 RH: 0-1 Tight: 0-1 Gall: 0-0
Aids: Bl: 0-0 Vi: 0-0 Tstrap: 0-0
Best Rating: 81 4/03 Uttx 2m   good   Hdl

Plating-class hurdler; acts on a sound surface.

Qandil (USA)

7-y-o ch g Riverman (USA)-Confirmed Affair (USA) (Affirmed (USA))
Miss J Feilden Mrs S McGuiness

Placings:P   (2239)
2002/03: 16PS,

	Starts	1st	2nd	3rd	Win & Pl
Hurdles	1	0	0	0	
Career Total	1	0	0	0	

Going: Sf: 0-1 GS: 0-0 Gd: 0-0 GF: - Fm: 0-0
Distance: 2m/2m3: 0-1 2m4-2m7: 0-0 3m+: 0-0
Track: LH: 0-1 RH: 0-0 Tight: 0-0 Gall: 0-1
Aids: Bl: 0-0 Vi: 0-0 Tstrap: 0-0
Best Rating: 0   11/02 Newb 2m110y   soft   Hdl

Qobtaan (USA)

34

4-y-o b g Capote (USA)-Queen s Gallery (USA) (Forty Niner (USA))
M R Bosley (A J Chamberlain 13/11) Inca Financial Services

Placings:00   (2374)
2002/03: 16⁰GS, 16⁰S,

	Starts	1st	2nd	3rd	Win & Pl
Hurdles	2	0	0	0	
Career Total	2	0	0	0	

Going: Sf: 0-1 GS: 0-1 Gd: 0-0 GF: - Fm: 0-0
Distance: 2m/2m3: 0-2 2m4-2m7: 0-0 3m+: 0-0
Track: LH: 0-2 RH: 0-0 Tight: 0-0 Gall: 0-1
Aids: Bl: 0-1 Vi: 0-0 Tstrap: 0-0
Best Rating: 0   12/02 Wwck 2m   soft   Hdl

Quabmatic

106   104

10-y-o b g Pragmatic-Good Skills (Bustino)
K Bishop Eric s Friends Racing Partnership

Placings:4/543533/540/426101/0/16P-PP03311   (4256)
2002/03: 19³G, 19PGS, 20⁴S, 19³S, 19⁴GS, 19¹S, 17¹G,

	Starts	1st	2nd	3rd	Win & Pl
Hurdles	7	2	0	2	9819

Career Total 27   5   1   5   20284

102	3/03	Extr	2m1f	D(0-115)HHdl	GD	£4823
104	2/03	Tntn	2m3f110yE(0-110)HHdl	SFT	£4046
98	11/01	Uttx	2m4f110yG(0-115)HHdl	SFT	£2618
104	4/00	Extr	2m1f110yG(0-105)HHdl	HVY	£2928
104	3/00	Tntn	2m3f110yE(0-115)HHdl	GD	£3209

Total win prize-money £17625

Going: Sf: 1-3 GS: 0-2 Gd: 1-2 GF: - Fm: 0-0
Distance: 2m/2m3: 1-2 2m4-2m7: 1-5 3m+: 0-0
Track: LH: 0-1 **RH: 2-6 Tight:** 1-3 Gall: 0-0
Aids: Bl: 0-0 Vi: 0-0 Tstrap: 0-0
Best Rating: 104 2/03 Tntn 2m3f110y soft   Hdl

Moderate hurdler; came back from these leg problems to win first time out over two and a half miles at Uttoxeter in November 2001; returned to form with back-to-back victories in February and March 2003; stays two and a half miles; acts on ground good and softer.

Quainton Hills

(99c)   (121c)79

9-y-o b g Gildoran-Spin Again (Royalty)
D R Stoddart D R Stoddart

Placings:203/42F12U/4234-PP0   (3865)
2002/03: 21PS, 24²S, 19⁰GS,

	Starts	1st	2nd	3rd	Win & Pl
Hurdles	3	0	0	0	
Career Total	16	1	4	2	9670
112	1/01	Leic	2m7f110yF Ch		SFT	£2824

Total win prize-money £2824

Going: Sf: 0-2 GS: 0-1 Gd: 0-0 GF: - Fm: 0-0
Distance: 2m/2m3: 0-0 2m4-2m7: 0-2 3m+: 0-1
Track: LH: 0-1 RH: 0-2 Tight: 0-0 Gall: 0-0
Aids: Bl: 0-0 Vi: 0-0 Tstrap: 0-0
Best Rating: 112 1/01 Leic 2m7f110y soft   Ch

A half-brother to Party Politics, he stays three miles but can be a sketchy jumper.

Quality First (IRE)

112(113h)   (111h)133

10-y-o b g Un Desperado (FR)-Vipsania (General Ironside)
Mrs H Dalton (Paul Nolan 6/10) Felix Sheridan

Placings:5/R0L00/0001001513130F2F4/P4313204-4B2F01042163   (4714)
2002/03: 20⁰HY, 20⁴G, 24⁸S, 21²S, 17FSH, 16⁹GF, 21¹HY, 24⁰G, 20⁴G, 21²S, 20¹G, 21⁶G, 25³GF,

	Starts	1st	2nd	3rd	Win & Pl
Hurdles	3	0	0	0	650
Chases	10	2	2	1	31642
Career Total	43	7	4	5	71539
133	3/03	Bang	2m4f110yC(0-135)HCh	GD	£10595
127	1/03	Chel	2m5f	C(0-130)HCh	HVY	£11424
104	2/02	Navn	2m	(0-120)HHdl	SFT	£6349
125	11/00	Naas	2m3f	(0-130)HCh	Y-S	£4416
110	9/00	List	2m3f	Ch	HVY	£4968
116	8/00	Tral	2m4f	Ch	Y-S	£3864
75	6/00	Navn	2m	(0-102)HHdl	GD	£3312

Total win prize-money £44929

Going: Sf: 1-5 GS: 0-0 Gd: 1-5 GF: - Fm: 0-2
Distance: 2m/2m3: 0-2 **2m4-2m7:** 2-8 3m+: 0-3
Track: **LH: 2-9** RH: 0-0 Tight: 1-2 Gall: 1-2
Aids: Bl: 0-0 Vi: 0-0 Tstrap: 0-0
Best Rating: 133 4/03 Aint 2m5f110y good   Ch

Useful chaser; fair hurdler; ex-Irish; best over trips of around two and a half miles; suited by soft ground, effective on good.

Quantum Lady

86   **49**

5-y-o b m Mujadil (USA)-Folly Finnesse (Joligeneration)
J D Frost   N W Lake

Placings:02   **(1800)**
2002/03: 16⁰G, 17²S,

	Starts	1st	2nd	3rd	Win & Pl
Hurdles	2	0	1	0	630
Career Total	2	0	1	0	630

Going:	Sf: 0-1 GS: 0-0 Gd: 0-1 GF: - Fm: 0-0
Distance:	2m/2m3: 0-2 2m4-2m7: 0-0 3m+: 0-0
Track:	LH: 0-2 RH: 0-0 Tight: 0-1 Gall: 0-0
Aids:	Bl: 0-0 Vi: 0-0 Tstrap: 0-0
Best Rating:	49 11/02 NAbb 2m1f soft Hdl

Plating-class hurdler.

Quarter Masters (IRE)

105   **93**

4-y-o b g Mujadil (USA)-Kentucky Wildcat (Be My Guest (USA))
G M Moore   The Dowdstown Boy S

Placings:P601300P   **(3490)**
2002/03: 17²S, 17⁶G, 16⁰GF, 16¹S, 20³GS, 16⁰S, 17⁰GS, 20⁶GS,

	Starts	1st	2nd	3rd	Win & Pl
Hurdles	8	1	0	1	3443
Career Total	8	1	0	1	3443
93 11/02 Ayr	2m	E Hdl		SFT	£2989

Total win prize-money £2989

Going:	Sf: 1-3 GS: 0-3 Gd: 0-1 GF: - Fm: 0-1
Distance:	2m/2m3: 1-6 2m4-2m7: 0-2 3m+: 0-0
Track:	LH: 1-8 RH: 0-0 Tight: 0-3 Gall: 0-1
Aids:	Bl: 0-0 Vi: 0-0 Tstrap: 0-0
Best Rating:	93 11/02 Ayr 2m soft Hdl

Fair juvenile hurdler, winner at Ayr in November 2002; acts on soft ground.

Quarterstaff

108   **110**

9-y-o b g Charmer-Quaranta (Hotfoot)
C R Wilson   Mrs J Wilson (durham)

Placings:36P/2C33P2-23U21   **(4396)**
2002/03: 20²GF, 21³G, 25⁴G, 25²GF, 24¹G,

	Starts	1st	2nd	3rd	Win & Pl
Chases	5	1	2	1	12597
Career Total	14	1	4	4	15765
106 3/03 Carl	3m	D(0-115)HCh	GD	£8612

Total win prize-money £8613

Going:	Sf: 0-0 GS: 0-0 Gd: 1-3 GF: - Fm: 0-2
Distance:	2m/2m3: 0-0 2m4-2m7: 0-2 3m+: 1-3
Track:	LH: 0-3 RH: 1-2 Tight: 0-2 Gall: 0-0
Aids:	Bl: 0-0 Vi: 0-0 Tstrap: 0-0
Best Rating:	106 3/03 Carl 3m good Ch

Modest chaser; former point-to-pointer who has been placed a number of times in novice chases; looked booked for first success under Rules when giving his rider little chance two out in a handicap at Catterick in January; narrowly beaten after a blunder two out at Wetherby in March; finally broke his duck under Rules at Carlisle a week later.

Quatermass

7-y-o b g Karinga Bay-Panchellita (USA) (Pancho Villa (USA))
A Hollingsworth   Kombined Motor Services Ltd

Placings:0/00P-P   **(0273)**
2002/03: 22⁰GF,

	Starts	1st	2nd	3rd	Win & Pl
Hurdles	1	0	0	0	
Career Total	5	0	0	0	

Going:	Sf: 0-0 GS: 0-0 Gd: 0-0 GF: - Fm: 0-1
Distance:	2m/2m3: 0-0 2m4-2m7: 0-0 3m+: 0-0
Track:	LH: 0-1 RH: 0-0 Tight: 0-1 Gall: 0-0
Aids:	Bl: 0-0 Vi: 0-0 Tstrap: 0-0
Best Rating:	50 6/01 Worc 2m good NHF

Quazar (IRE)

116   **157**

5-y-o b g Inzar (USA)-Evictress (IRE) (Sharp Victor (USA))
Jonjo O Neill   C D Carr

Placings:1111P12011-32010104   **(4478)**
2002/03: 16³G, 16²GS, 16⁶S, 20¹GS, 16⁰G, 20¹G, 21⁹G, 20⁴G,

	Starts	1st	2nd	3rd	Win & Pl
Hurdles	8	2	1	1	48348
Career Total	18	9	2	1	186675
152 3/03 Hayd	2m4f	B HHdl	GD	£15065
146 1/03 Hayd	2m4f	B HHdl	G-S	£10933
137 4/02 Punc	2m	Hdl	GD	£41901
137 4/02 Aint	2m110y	A Hdl	GD	£58000
132 1/02 Wwck	2m	B Hdl	SFT	£8736
117 11/01 Weth	2m	A Hdl	GD	£10627
116 10/01 Chel	2m110y	B Hdl	GD	£6857
108 9/01 Bang	2m1f	D Hdl	GD	£3402
89 8/01 Bang	2m1f	B Hdl	GD	£3052

Total win prize-money £158576

Going:	Sf: 0-1 GS: 1-2 Gd: 1-5 GF: - Fm: 0-0
Distance:	2m/2m3: 0-4 2m4-2m7: 2-4 3m+: 0-0
Track:	LH: 2-6 RH: 0-2 Tight: 0-1 Gall: 0-2
Aids:	Bl: 0-0 Vi: 0-0 Tstrap: 2-8
Best Rating:	156 4/03 Aint 2m4f good Hdl

Smart hurdler, he was a useful juvenile, landing big-race successes at Aintree and Punchestown; relished the step up to two miles four when winning at Haydock in January 2003, and again won at the course over the trip in early March; unable to defy top-weight in the Coral Cup; fair effort in Grade One event at Aintree; wears a tongue tie; acts on good/good to soft ground.

Quedex

104   **100**

7-y-o b g Deploy-Alwal (Pharly (FR))
R J Price (E L James 5/7) Fox And Cub Partnership

Placings:225431   **(4635)**
2002/03: 17²S, 17²S, 24⁵S, 21⁴S, 19³GF, 19¹GF,

	Starts	1st	2nd	3rd	Win & Pl
Hurdles	6	1	2	1	6041
Career Total	6	1	2	1	6041
100 4/03 Strf	2m3f	F Hdl	G-F	£3010

Total win prize-money £3010

Going:	Sf: 0-4 GS: 0-0 Gd: 0-0 GF: - Fm: 1-2
Distance:	2m/2m3: 1-3 2m4-2m7: 0-2 3m+: 0-1
Track:	LH: 1-2 RH: 0-4 Tight: 1-2 Gall: 0-1
Aids:	Bl: 0-0 Vi: 0-0 Tstrap: 0-0
Best Rating:	101 1/03 Tntn 2m1f soft Hdl

Moderate hurdler; fair stayer on the Flat; finally got off the mark over hurdles when winning modest maiden at Stratford April 2003; acts on a sound surface; should be suited by two and a half miles plus.

Queen Of Araghty

6-y-o ch m Phardante (FR)-Queen s Darling (Le Moss)
M Todhunter   Tim Kilroe

Placings:03-650   **(0418)**
2002/03: 16⁶G, 20⁵GF, 22⁰HY,

	Starts	1st	2nd	3rd	Win & Pl
NH Flat	1	0	0	0	0
Hurdles	2	0	0	0	0
Career Total	5	0	0	1	357

Going:	Sf: 0-1 GS: 0-0 Gd: 0-1 GF: - Fm: 0-1
Distance:	2m/2m3: 0-1 2m4-2m7: 0-2 3m+: 0-0
Track:	LH: 0-2 RH: 0-1 Tight: 0-1 Gall: 0-0
Aids:	Bl: 0-0 Vi: 0-0 Tstrap: 0-0
Best Rating:	85 4/02 Carl 2m1f good NHF

Queen Of Jazz

85f   **66f**

6-y-o b m Sovereign Water (FR)-When The Saints (Bay Express)
Mrs H Dalton   Kinnersley Optimists

Placings:00   **(0560)**
2002/03: 17⁰S, 17⁰GF,

	Starts	1st	2nd	3rd	Win & Pl
NH Flat	2	0	0	0	
Career Total	2	0	0	0	

Going:	Sf: 0-1 GS: 0-0 Gd: 0-0 GF: - Fm: 0-1
Distance:	2m/2m3: 0-2 2m4-2m7: 0-0 3m+: 0-0
Track:	LH: 0-1 RH: 0-1 Tight: 0-1 Gall: 0-0
Aids:	Bl: 0-0 Vi: 0-0 Tstrap: 0-0
Best Rating:	66 6/02 Hrfd 2m1f gd-fm NHF

Queen's Banquet

94f   **96f**

6-y-o b m Glacial Storm (USA)-Culinary (Tower Walk)
P R Webber   M S C Thurgood

Placings:300O   **(4611)**
2002/03: 17³S, 16⁰G, 16⁰G, 17⁰G,

	Starts	1st	2nd	3rd	Win & Pl
NH Flat	4	0	0	1	401
Career Total	4	0	0	1	401

Going:	Sf: 0-1 GS: 0-0 Gd: 0-3 GF: - Fm: 0-0
Distance:	2m/2m3: 0-2 2m4-2m7: 0-0 3m+: 0-0
Track:	LH: 0-2 RH: 0-1 Tight: 0-0 Gall: 0-1
Aids:	Bl: 0-0 Vi: 0-0 Tstrap: 0-0
Best Rating:	96 4/03 Chel 2m1f good NHF

Decent third on debut, but has not gone the right way since.

Queen's Pageant

109   **106**

9-y-o ch m Risk Me (FR)-Mistral s Dancer (Shareef Dancer (USA))
J L Spearing   Mrs Robert Heathcote

Placings:0431-5510020   (4171)
2002/03: 19⁰G, 21⁵G, 19¹GS, 20⁰GS, 19⁰GS, 20²HY, 22⁰S,

	Starts	1st	2nd	3rd	Win & Pl
Hurdles	7	1	1	0	6097
Career Total	11	2	1	1	9595
104 11/02 Tntn	2m3f110yD(0-120)HHdl		G-S	£4550
95 4/02 Hrfd	2m3f110yE Hdl		G-F	£3080

Total win prize-money £7630

Going: Sf: 0-2 GS: 1-3 Gd: 0-2 GF: - Fm: 0-0
Distance: 2m/2m3: 0-0 **2m4-2m7: 1-7** 3m+: 0-0
Track: LH: 0-0 **RH: 1-5** Tight: 1-4 Gall: 0-0
Aids: Bl: 0-0 Vi: 0-0 Tstrap: 0-0
Best Rating: 106 2/03 Sand 2m4f110y heavy Hdl

Fair hurdler; best at around two and a half miles; acts on both fast and heavy ground; has gone well in cheekpieces.

Queens Harbour (IRE)

92   91

9-y-o b g Brush Aside (USA)-Queenie Kelly (The Parson)
N J Henderson   Philip Matton

Placings:1314/0/06   (4173)
2002/03: 16⁰GS, 20⁶S,

	Starts	1st	2nd	3rd	Win & Pl
Hurdles	2	0	0	0	0
Career Total	7	2	0	1	5674
117 3/99 Newb	2m110y H NHF		SFT	£1752
101 12/98 Towc	2m	H NHF	SFT	£1308

Total win prize-money £3061

Going: Sf: 0-1 GS: 0-1 Gd: 0-0 GF: - Fm: 0-0
Distance: 2m/2m3: 0-1 2m4-2m7: 0-1 3m+: 0-0
Track: LH: 0-2 RH: 0-0 Tight: 0-0 Gall: 0-1
Aids: Bl: 0-0 Vi: 0-0 Tstrap: 0-0
Best Rating: 132 3/99 Chel 2m110y gd-sft NHF

One time smart bumper horse; has had leg trouble and was reappearing after a long absence when running with credit at Doncaster in January 2003; best on soft ground; capable of a good deal better if remaining sound.

Queensland Bay

75f   54f

4-y-o ch f Primitive Rising (USA)-Hysteria (Prince Bee)
T D Easterby   C H Stevens

Placings:06   (3570)
2002/03: 16⁰HY, 17⁶HY,

	Starts	1st	2nd	3rd	Win & Pl
NH Flat	2	0	0	0	0
Career Total	2	0	0	0	0

Going: Sf: 0-2 GS: 0-0 Gd: 0-0 GF: - Fm: 0-0
Distance: 2m/2m3: 0-2 2m4-2m7: 0-0 3m+: 0-0
Track: LH: 0-2 RH: 0-0 Tight: 0-0 Gall: 0-0
Aids: Bl: 0-0 Vi: 0-0 Tstrap: 0-0
Best Rating: 54 2/03 Sedg 2m1f heavy NHF

Queensway (IRE)

97   74

11-y-o b g Pennine Walk-Polaregina (FR) (Rex Magna (FR))
R M Carson   Mrs P Carson

Placings:12013/3445P21/1422/4FU100/561F35600-P52P   (1752)
2002/03: 17⁰GF, 17⁵S, 16²GF, 17⁰GS,

	Starts	1st	2nd	3rd	Win & Pl
Chases	4	0	1	0	840

Career Total   **35**   **6**   **5**   **3**   **24607**

103 8/01 Strf	2m1f110yF(0-105)HCh	G-F	£4160
101 10/00 Ludl	2m	G(0-95)HCh	G-F	£2730
107 8/99 Prth	2m	F(0-100)HCh	G-F	£4182
87 4/99 Kels	2m1f	E Ch	G-F	£3582
100 4/98 Sedg	2m1f	E Hdl	SFT	£2582
111 5/97 Prth	2m110y H NHF	G-S	£1020

Total win prize-money £18258

Going: Sf: 0-1 GS: 0-1 Gd: 0-0 GF: - Fm: 0-2
Distance: 2m/2m3: 0-4 2m4-2m7: 0-0 3m+: 0-0
Track: LH: 0-2 RH: 0-2 Tight: 0-3 Gall: 0-1
Aids: Bl: 0-0 Vi: 0-0 Tstrap: 0-4
Best Rating: 111 5/97 Prth 2m110y gd-sft NHF

Poor chaser, best on fast ground at around two miles.

Quetal (IRE)

10-y-o ch g Buckskin (FR)-Cantafleur (Cantab)
Mrs Laura J Young   Miss K J Kitching

Placings:2F44/F6P/11-10   (4133)
2002/03: 24¹S, 26⁰G,

	Starts	1st	2nd	3rd	Win & Pl
Chases	2	1	0	0	1974
Career Total	11	3	1	0	15255
129 2/03 Newb	3m	H Ch	SFT	£1974
115 4/02 Aint	3m1f	B Ch	GD	£10822
104 3/02 Wwck	3m2f	H Ch	GD	£1176

Total win prize-money £13973

Going: Sf: 1-1 GS: 0-0 Gd: 0-1 GF: - Fm: 0-0
Distance: 2m/2m3: 0-0 2m4-2m7: 0-0 3m+: 1-2
Track: LH: 1-2 RH: 0-0 Tight: 0-0 Gall: 1-2
Aids: Bl: 0-0 Vi: 0-0 Tstrap: 0-0
Best Rating: 129 2/03 Newb 3m soft Ch

Winning pointer and hunter chaser; loves soft ground; a little disappointing in 2003.

Quibble

58   58

6-y-o ch g Lammtarra (USA)-Blou Dan (USA) (Damascus (USA))
A Bailey   Www.Mark-Kilner-Racing.Com (16)

Placings:06   (2185)
2002/03: 16⁰S, 16⁶GS,

	Starts	1st	2nd	3rd	Win & Pl
Hurdles	2	0	0	0	0
Career Total	2	0	0	0	0

Going: Sf: 0-1 GS: 0-1 Gd: 0-0 GF: - Fm: 0-0
Distance: 2m/2m3: 0-2 2m4-2m7: 0-0 3m+: 0-0
Track: LH: 0-2 RH: 0-0 Tight: 0-0 Gall: 0-0
Aids: Bl: 0-0 Vi: 0-0 Tstrap: 0-0
Best Rating: 58 11/02 Ayr 2m soft Hdl

Quickswood (IRE)

          105

10-y-o b g Yashgan-Up To Trix (Over The River (FR))
C R Barwell   Harvey Spack

Placings:440/4P056431/01P220202/UFP3100/0PP000500
310-P   (0268)
2002/03: 27⁰GF,

	Starts	1st	2nd	3rd	Win & Pl
Hurdles	1	0	0	0	
Career Total	40	4	4	3	21017
105 2/02 Wwck	2m5f	D(0-120)HHdl	HVY	£3598

---

113 2/01 Newb	3m110y	C(0-130)HHdl	SFT	£5733
110 6/99 Worc	3m	F(0-100)HHdl	G-S	£2111
101 5/99 Hrfd	3m2f	E Hdl	GD	£2070

Total win prize-money £13513

Going: Sf: 0-0 GS: 0-0 Gd: 0-0 GF: - Fm: 0-1
Distance: 2m/2m3: 0-0 2m4-2m7: 0-0 3m+: 0-1
Track: LH: 0-1 RH: 0-0 Tight: 0-1 Gall: 0-0
Aids: Bl: 0-0 Vi: 0-1 Tstrap: 0-0
Best Rating: 113 2/01 Newb 3m110y soft Hdl

Modest handicap hurdler. Suited by three miles and acts on most types of ground.

Quiet Celebration

6-y-o b m Superpower-Quiet Amusement (USA) (Regal And Royal (USA))
Miss K M George   Nigel Gooding

Placings:0P   (0775)
2002/03: 16⁰GF, 16⁸GF,

	Starts	1st	2nd	3rd	Win & Pl
NH Flat	1	0	0	0	0
Hurdles	1	0	0	0	0
Career Total	2	0	0	0	0

Going: Sf: 0-0 GS: 0-0 Gd: 0-0 GF: - Fm: 0-2
Distance: 2m/2m3: 0-2 2m4-2m7: 0-0 3m+: 0-0
Track: LH: 0-1 RH: 0-0 Tight: 0-0 Gall: 0-0
Aids: Bl: 0-0 Vi: 0-0 Tstrap: 0-0
Best Rating: 19 7/02 Strf 2m110y gd-fm NHF

Quiet Moments (IRE)

10-y-o b g Ron s Victory (USA)-Saint Cynthia (Welsh Saint)
Miss P Fitton   Pigs Might Fly Syndicate

Placings:5P5503/02432153/606011PP00/4P   (0210)
2002/03: 25⁴GS, 25⁸PS,

	Starts	1st	2nd	3rd	Win & Pl
Chases	2	0	0	0	0
Career Total	26	3	2	3	11940
88 12/98 Font	3m2f110yE(0-110)HCh	SFT	£4014
88 12/98 Uttx	3m	E(0-105)HCh	G-S	£3243
84 3/98 Hrfd	3m2f	F(0-95)HHdl	G-F	£2626

Total win prize-money £9884

Going: Sf: 0-1 GS: 0-1 Gd: 0-0 GF: - Fm: 0-0
Distance: 2m/2m3: 0-0 2m4-2m7: 0-0 3m+: 0-2
Track: LH: 0-1 RH: 0-1 Tight: 0-0 Gall: 0-0
Aids: Bl: 0-0 Vi: 0-0 Tstrap: 0-0
Best Rating: 88 12/98 Font 3m2f110y soft Ch

Quiet Water (IRE)

91(109h)   (112 h)112+

7-y-o br g Lord Americo-Sirana (Al Sirat (USA))
P J Hobbs   (M J Wilkinson 11/5)   Network Training 4

Placings:040/450-103110   (4441)
2002/03: 21¹GS, 19⁰S, 19³S, 21¹G, 19¹G, 20⁰G,

	Starts	1st	2nd	3rd	Win & Pl
Hurdles	6	3	0	1	12362
Career Total	12	3	0	1	12692
105 3/03 Newb	2m3f	E(0-110)HHdl	GD	£3682
100 2/03 Ludl	2m5f	D(0-120)HHdl	GD	£5642
89 5/02 Hntg	2m5f110yE(0-110)HHdl	G-F	£2415

Total win prize-money £11739

Column 1

Going:	Sf: 0-2 GS: 0-0 Gd: 2-3 GF: - Fm: 1-1
Distance:	2m/2m3: 1-1 **2m4-2m7: 2-5** 3m+: 0-0
Track:	LH: 1-1 **RH: 2-5** Tight: 0-2 Gall: 2-2
Aids:	Bl: 0-0 Vi: 0-0 Tstrap: 0-0
Best Rating:	**105** 3/03 Newb 2m3f good Hdl

Modest, improving handicap hurdler; made winning chasing debut when beating Miss Cool in 2m 5f novice chase at Newton Abbot July 2003; can defy a penalty; stays 2m 5f; suited by a sound surface.

Quinta Lad

5-y-o b g Alhijaz-Jersey Belle (Distant Relative)
J R Norton (J Balding 14/8) J M Lacey

Placings:00O   (2473)
2002/03: 17⁰S, 16⁰GS, 16⁰G,

	Starts	1st	2nd	3rd	Win & Pl
Hurdles	3	0	0	0	
Career Total	3	0	0	0	

Going:	Sf: 0-1 GS: 0-1 Gd: 0-1 GF: - Fm: 0-0
Distance:	2m/2m3: 0-3 2m4-2m7: 0-0 3m+: 0-0
Track:	LH: 0-3 RH: 0-0 Tight: 0-1 Gall: 0-1
Aids:	Bl: 0-0 Vi: 0-0 Tstrap: 0-0
Best Rating:	**0** 12/02 Donc 2m110y good Hdl

Quintrell Downs

92   95

8-y-o b g Efisio-Nineteenth Of May (Homing)
T R George Mr & Mrs D A Gamble

Placings:000/13/3   (1556)
2002/03: 17³G,

	Starts	1st	2nd	3rd	Win & Pl
Hurdles	1	0	0	1	609
Career Total	6	1	0	2	3707
94	7/99	Wolv	2m	E(0-105)HHdl	G-F £2692

Total win prize-money £2693

Going:	Sf: 0-0 GS: 0-0 Gd: 0 GF: - Fm: 0-0
Distance:	2m/2m3: 0-1 2m4-2m7: 0-0 3m+: 0-0
Track:	LH: 0-0 RH: 0-1 Tight: 0-0 Gall: 0-0
Aids:	Bl: 0-0 Vi: 0-0 Tstrap: 0-0
Best Rating:	**95** 10/02 Hrfd 2m1f good Hdl

Quit The Pack (IRE)

66

5-y-o b/br g Grand Lodge (USA)-Treasure (IRE) (Treasure Kay)
R N Bevis Ewson Contractors And Steve Corbett

Placings:00P-P   (2131)
2002/03: 16²G,

	Starts	1st	2nd	3rd	Win & Pl
Hurdles	1	0	0	0	
Career Total	4	0	0	0	

Going:	Sf: 0-0 GS: 0-0 Gd: 0-1 GF: - Fm: 0-0
Distance:	2m/2m3: 0-1 2m4-2m7: 0-0 3m+: 0-0
Track:	LH: 0-0 RH: 0-1 Tight: 0-0 Gall: 0-0
Aids:	Bl: 0-0 Vi: 0-0 Tstrap: 0-0
Best Rating:	**71** 2/02 Ludl 2m soft Hdl

Quizzical

(99h)   (87h)
5-y-o ch g Indian Ridge-Mount Row (Alzao (USA))

Column 2

John G Carr James Hepburn

Placings:FP-06320000   (4246a)
2002/03: 17⁰G, 20⁶GF, 20³GS, 16²G, 16⁹F, 21⁹G, 21⁹GS, 20⁹S,

	Starts	1st	2nd	3rd	Win & Pl
Hurdles	8	0	1	1	1582
Career Total	10	0	1	1	1582

Going:	Sf: 0-1 GS: 0-2 Gd: 0-3 GF: - Fm: 0-2
Distance:	2m/2m3: 0-3 2m4-2m7: 0-5 3m+: 0-0
Track:	LH: 0-3 RH: 0-2 Tight: 0-0 Gall: 0-2
Aids:	Bl: 0-0 Vi: 0-0 Tstrap: 0-0
Best Rating:	**98** 3/02 Wxfd 2m soft Hdl

Poor maiden hurdler, flattered by a literal reading of his placed form in a seller at Perth in August.

Racingformclub Boy

68   21

4-y-o ch g Blushing Flame (USA)-Sonoco (Song)
P S McEntee Dave Anderson

Placings:P0P   (2325)
2002/03: 16⁰GS, 16⁰GS, 17⁸S,

	Starts	1st	2nd	3rd	Win & Pl
Hurdles	3	0	0	0	
Career Total	3	0	0	0	

Going:	Sf: 0-1 GS: 0-2 Gd: 0-0 GF: - Fm: 0-0
Distance:	2m/2m3: 0-3 2m4-2m7: 0-0 3m+: 0-0
Track:	LH: 0-1 RH: 0-2 Tight: 0-2 Gall: 0-1
Aids:	Bl: 0-0 Vi: 0-2 Tstrap: 0-0
Best Rating:	**27** 11/02 Fknm 2m gd-sft Hdl

Radar (IRE)

113(99h)   (93 h)118+

8-y-o b g Petardia-Soignee (Night Shift (USA))
Miss S E Forster C Storey

Placings:345/321/0112F4-53541   (3569)
2002/03: 16⁵GF, 16³G, 21⁵G, 16⁴S, 16¹HY,

	Starts	1st	2nd	3rd	Win & Pl
Hurdles	2	0	0	1	626
Chases	3	1	0	0	4358
Career Total	17	4	2	3	21027
118	2/03	Sedg	2m110y	E(0-110)HChc	HVY £4046
103	3/02	Sedg	2m110y	D Ch	SFT £3844
105	3/02	Sedg	2m110y	C Ch	SFT £6077
107	8/00	Worc	2m	E Hdl	G-F £2756

Total win prize-money £16725

Going:	Sf: 1-2 GS: 0-0 Gd: 0-2 GF: - Fm: 0-1
Distance:	2m/2m3: 1-4 2m4-2m7: 0-1 3m+: 0-0
Track:	LH: 1-4 RH: 0-1 Tight: 1-4 Gall: 0-0
Aids:	Bl: 0-0 Vi: 0-0 Tstrap: 0-0
Best Rating:	**118** 2/03 Sedg 2m110y heavy Ch

Modest hurdler/chaser; a winner on the Flat; been successful over hurdles and fences; effective over two miles; acts on most types of ground.

Radbrook Hall

82f   56f

4-y-o b g Teenoso (USA)-Sarah s Venture (Averof)
M W Easterby S Hughes & J Southway

Placings:0   (3883)
2002/03: 16⁰GS,

	Starts	1st	2nd	3rd	Win & Pl
NH Flat	1	0	0	0	

Column 3

Career Total	1 0 0 0

Going:	Sf: 0-1 GS: 0-1 Gd: 0-0 GF: - Fm: 0-0
Distance:	2m/2m3: 0-1 2m4-2m7: 0-0 3m+: 0-0
Track:	LH: 0-1 RH: 0-0 Tight: 0-0 Gall: 0-1
Aids:	Bl: 0-0 Vi: 0-0 Tstrap: 0-0
Best Rating:	**56** 3/03 Donc 2m110y gd-sft NHF

Radcliffe (IRE)

95   96

6-y-o b g Supreme Leader-Marys Course (Crash Course)
Miss Venetia Williams M L Shone

Placings:610⁶   (3784)
2002/03: 16⁶GS, 16¹GS, 16⁹S, 19⁶G,

	Starts	1st	2nd	3rd	Win & Pl
NH Flat	3	1	0	0	2009
Hurdles	1	0	0	0	0
Career Total	4	1	0	0	2009
108	12/02	Fknm	2m	H NHF	G-S £2009

Total win prize-money £2009

Going:	Sf: 0-1 GS: 1-1 Gd: 0-2 GF: - Fm: 0-0
Distance:	2m/2m3: 1-3 2m4-2m7: 0-1 3m+: 0-0
Track:	**LH: 1-1** RH: 0-3 **Tight: 1-1** Gall: 0-0
Aids:	Bl: 0-0 Vi: 0-0 Tstrap: 0-0
Best Rating:	**108** 12/02 Fknm 2m gd-sft NHF

Easy winner of poor Fakenham bumper; runner-up in novice hurdle May 2003; probably stays 3m 2f.

Radical Jack

(73h)   (47h)
6-y-o b g Presidium-Luckifosome (Smackover)
C W Fairhurst Mrs B J Boocock

Placings:00-PPU   (4351)
2002/03: 16⁶PG, 20⁹S, 16ᵁGF,

	Starts	1st	2nd	3rd	Win & Pl
Hurdles	1	0	0	0	0
Chases	2	0	0	0	0
Career Total	5	0	0	0	

Going:	Sf: 0-1 GS: 0-0 Gd: 0-1 GF: - Fm: 0-1
Distance:	2m/2m3: 0-2 2m4-2m7: 0-1 3m+: 0-0
Track:	LH: 0-1 RH: 0-2 Tight: 0-1 Gall: 0-0
Aids:	Bl: 0-0 Vi: 0-0 Tstrap: 0-0
Best Rating:	**47** 9/01 Sedg 2m1f gd-fm Hdl

Radlett (IRE)

8-y-o b g Supreme Leader-Classical Friend (IRE) (Lidhame)
A M Hales Andrew L Cohen

Placings:0/0/F   (2629)
2002/03: 16⁵S,

	Starts	1st	2nd	3rd	Win & Pl
Hurdles	1	0	0	0	
Career Total	3	0	0	0	

Going:	Sf: 0-1 GS: 0-0 Gd: 0-0 GF: - Fm: 0-0
Distance:	2m/2m3: 0-1 2m4-2m7: 0-0 3m+: 0-0
Track:	LH: 0-1 RH: 0-0 Tight: 0-0 Gall: 0-0
Aids:	Bl: 0-0 Vi: 0-0 Tstrap: 0-0
Best Rating:	**79** 3/00 Newb 2m110y gd-fm NHF

Career Total   1   0   0   0

Radley Park (IRE)

60   **8**

4-y-o b g Vettori (IRE)-Livry (USA) (Lyphard (USA))
E W Tuer (P J Makin 10/9) Far Distant Partnership

Placings:00   (4156)
2002/03: 16⁰GS, 17⁹G,

	Starts	1st	2nd	3rd	Win & Pl
Hurdles	2	0	0	0	
Career Total	2	0	0	0	

Going: Sf: 0-0 GS: 0-1 Gd: 0-1 GF: - Fm: 0-0
Distance: 2m/2m3: 0-2 2m4-2m7: 0-0 3m+: 0-0
Track: LH: 0-1 RH: 0-1 Tight: 0-1 Gall: 0-1
Aids: Bl: 0-0 Vi: 0-0 Tstrap: 0-0
Best Rating: 8 3/03 MRas 2m1f110y good Hdl

Raffles Rooster

109   **129**

11-y-o ch g Galetto (FR)-Singapore Girl (FR) (Lyphard (USA))
Miss Venetia Williams Mark A Leatham

Placings:35/232/142U1/251/51F01326/31524-5222 (3093)
2002/03: 25⁵GS, 24²S, 24²S, 24²G,

	Starts	1st	2nd	3rd	Win & Pl
Chases	4	0	3		6184
Career Total	30	6	9	4	52638
126	12/01 Sand	3m110y D(0-120)HCh	G-S	£7150
125	2/01 Towc	3m1f	C(0-130)HCh	HVY £5941
125	11/00 NAbb	3m2f110yC(0-130)HCh	HVY £7315
119	3/00 Tntn	3m	F(0-105)HCh	GD £4777
108	2/99 Tntn	3m	E(0-115)HCh	G-S £3875
115	11/98 Font	2m3f	E Ch	SFT £2786

Total win prize-money £31845

Going: Sf: 0-2 GS: 0-1 Gd: 0-1 GF: - Fm: 0-0
Distance: 2m/2m3: 0-0 2m4-2m7: 0-0 3m+: 0-4
Track: LH: 0-4 RH: 0-0 Tight: 0-0 Gall: 0-1
Aids: Bl: 0-0 Vi: 0-0 Tstrap: 0-0
Best Rating: 129 12/02 Hayd 3m soft Ch

Useful chaser; once a useful Flat handicapper, he is a capable chaser. Suited by hold-up tactics and a test of stamina, although he does not find a great deal off the bit. Acts on any ground softer than good.

Ragasah

5-y-o b m Glory Of Dancer-Slight Risk (Risk Me (FR))
Miss Gay Kelleway E Oertel

Placings:F   (1448)
2002/03: 16⁵G,

	Starts	1st	2nd	3rd	Win & Pl
Hurdles	1	0	0	0	
Career Total	1	0	0	0	

Going: Sf: 0-0 GS: 0-0 Gd: 0-1 GF: - Fm: 0-0
Distance: 2m/2m3: 0-1 2m4-2m7: 0-0 3m+: 0-0
Track: LH: 0-1 RH: 0-0 Tight: 0-1 Gall: 0-0
Aids: Bl: 0-0 Vi: 0-0 Tstrap: 0-0
Best Rating: 0 10/02 Fknm 2m good Hdl

Ragdale Hall (USA)

108   **124+**

6-y-o b g Bien Bien (USA)-Gift Of Dance (USA) (Trempolino (USA))

J Joseph (P J Hobbs 11/9) Jack Joseph

Placings:2-2132422141   (4639)
2002/03: 16²GF, 16¹G, 16³GF, 17²GF, 16⁴G, 18²GF, 17²GF, 19¹GF, 20⁴G, 16¹GF,

	Starts	1st	2nd	3rd	Win & Pl
Hurdles	10	3	4	1	17506
Career Total	11	3	5	1	18294
121	4/03 Strf	2m110y D(0-125)HHdl	G-F	£4849
105	9/02 Hrfd	2m3f110yE Hdl	G-F	£3195
96	6/02 Uttx	2m	E Hdl	GD £2639

Total win prize-money £10684

Going: Sf: 0-0 GS: 0-0 Gd: 1-3 GF: - Fm: 2-7
Distance: 2m/2m3: 2-8 2m4-2m7: 1-2 3m+: 0-0
Track: LH: 2-7 RH: 1-3 Tight: 1-5 Gall: 0-0
Aids: Bl: 0-0 Vi: 0-0 Tstrap: 0-2
Best Rating: 121 4/03 Strf 2m110y gd-fm Hdl

Fair hurdler; effective from two to two and a half miles and suited by a sound surface.

Raglan Nightfire

90f   **83f**

5-y-o ch g New Reputation-Ophiuchus (Nader)
K O Cunningham-Brown Danebury Racing Stables Limited

Placings:5000   (2045)
2002/03: 16⁵S, 16⁰G, 18⁰S, 17⁰HY,

	Starts	1st	2nd	3rd	Win & Pl
NH Flat	4	0	0	0	0
Career Total	4	0	0	0	0

Going: Sf: 0-3 GS: 0-0 Gd: 0-1 GF: - Fm: 0-0
Distance: 2m/2m3: 0-4 2m4-2m7: 0-0 3m+: 0-0
Track: LH: 0-4 RH: 0-0 Tight: 0-1 Gall: 0-0
Aids: Bl: 0-0 Vi: 0-0 Tstrap: 0-0
Best Rating: 83 6/02 Worc 2m soft NHF

Ragu

94   **85**

5-y-o b m Contract Law (USA)-Mamworth (Funny Man)
Ferdy Murphy Raj Patel

Placings:0323-5432004   (4616)
2002/03: 16⁵GS, 20⁴GS, 20³G, 21²HY, 21⁰G, 21⁰G, 17⁴GF,

	Starts	1st	2nd	3rd	Win & Pl
Hurdles	7	0	1	1	2257
Career Total	11	0	2	3	3332

Going: Sf: 0-1 GS: 0-2 Gd: 0-3 GF: - Fm: 0-1
Distance: 2m/2m3: 0-3 2m4-2m7: 0-4 3m+: 0-0
Track: LH: 0-4 RH: 0-3 Tight: 0-4 Gall: 0-2
Aids: Bl: 0-0 Vi: 0-0 Tstrap: 0-0
Best Rating: 86 4/02 Fknm 2m good NHF

Modest novice hurdler; stays two miles five; acts in good and heavy ground.

Rain Doctor

9-y-o ch g Lycius (USA)-Rain Date (USA) (Blushing Groom (FR))
K Robson Mrs M Armstrong

Placings:20/PP/U-   (0005)
2002/03: 20⁰G,

	Starts	1st	2nd	3rd	Win & Pl
Chases	1	0	0	0	

Career Total   5   0   1   0   476

Going: Sf: 0-0 GS: 0-0 Gd: 0-1 GF: - Fm: 0-0
Distance: 2m/2m3: 0-0 2m4-2m7: 0-1 3m+: 0-0
Track: LH: 0-1 RH: 0-0 Tight: 0-0 Gall: 0-1
Aids: Bl: 0-0 Vi: 0-0 Tstrap: 0-1
Best Rating: 95 10/99 Hexm 2m good NHF

Rainbow Chase (IRE)

102   **96**

5-y-o b g Rainbow Quest (USA)-Fayrooz (USA) (Gulch (USA))
S J Magnier Fergus Jones

Placings:0404-54630P   (4591)
2002/03: 16⁵HY, 16⁴GS, 16⁶G, 16³G, 17⁰G, 16⁰G,

	Starts	1st	2nd	3rd	Win & Pl
Hurdles	6	0	0	1	356
Career Total	10	0	0	1	617

Going: Sf: 0-1 GS: 0-1 Gd: 0-4 GF: - Fm: 0-0
Distance: 2m/2m3: 0-6 2m4-2m7: 0-0 3m+: 0-0
Track: LH: 0-6 RH: 0-0 Tight: 0-2 Gall: 0-2
Aids: Bl: 0-0 Vi: 0-0 Tstrap: 0-1
Best Rating: 96 2/03 Catt 2m good Hdl

Very limited ability over hurdles so far and has started life in handicap company from a harsh mark.

Rainbow Dance (IRE)

107(109h)   (124+h)**116**

7-y-o ch g Rainbows For Life (CAN)-Nishila (USA) (Green Dancer (USA))
Jonjo O Neill Mrs G Smith

Placings:05325 4/00 f26562-1212335   (1929)
2002/03: 25²G, 21¹GF, 24²G, 20²GS, 21³GS, 20³GS, 20⁵G,

	Starts	1st	2nd	3rd	Win & Pl
Hurdles	4	2	2	0	9776
Chases	4	0	1	2	3746
Career Total	21	3	5	3	19953
120	6/02 Worc	2m4f	C(0-135)HHdl	GD	£5109
124	5/02 Ludl	2m5f	E(0-105)HHdl	G-F	£3150
104	7/01 Tipp	2m	NHF	GD	£3895

Total win prize-money £12154

Going: Sf: 0-0 GS: 0-3 Gd: 1-4 GF: - Fm: 1-1
Distance: 2m/2m3: 0-0 2m4-2m7: 2-6 3m+: 0-2
Track: LH: 1-5 RH: 1-2 Tight: 0-5 Gall: 0-0
Aids: Bl: 2-6 Vi: 0-0 Tstrap: 0-1
Best Rating: 124 5/02 Ludl 2m5f gd-fm Hdl

Modest hurdler, who has reportedly suffered from breathing problems. Looked an improved performer in first-time blinkers when winning at Ludlow in May 2002, but beaten under a penalty next time. Bounced back to form when winning handicap at Worcester June 2002. Jumped adequately when runner-up on chasing debut at Bangor in October but disappointing since. Effective on fast ground.

Rainbow River (IRE)

109   **110**

5-y-o ch g Rainbows For Life (CAN)-Shrewd Girl (USA) (Sagace (FR))
M C Chapman Patrick Darcy

Placings:2114   (4412)

2002/03: 17²GS, 16¹G, 21¹¹GF, 17⁴G,

	Starts	1st	2nd	3rd	Win & Pl
Hurdles	4	2	1	0	8865
Career Total	4	2	1	0	8865
98	3/03 Ludl	2m5f	E Hdl	G-F	£3799
110	3/03 Fknm	2m	E Hdl	GD	£3528

Total win prize-money £7327

Going:	Sf: 0-0 GS: 0-1 Gd: 1-2 GF: - Fm: 1-1
Distance:	2m/2m3: 1-3 2m4-2m7: 1-1 3m+: 0-0
Track:	LH: 1-1 RH: 1-3 **Tight: 1-3** Gall: 0-0
Aids:	Bl: 0-0 Vi: 0-0 Tstrap: 0-0
Best Rating:	110 3/03 Fknm 2m good Hdl

Fair novice hurdler; acts on decent ground; effective at up to two miles five.

Rainbow Spirit (IRE)
99   100

6-y-o b g Rainbows For Life (CAN)-Merrie Moment (IRE) (Taufan (USA))
H Alexander Mrs L J Bowers

Placings:515-P4P   (0564)
2002/03: 22ᴾGS, 24⁴GF, 19ᴾG,

	Starts	1st	2nd	3rd	Win & Pl
Hurdles	3	0	0	0	317
Career Total	6	1	0	0	3131
100	2/02 Muss	3m	E Hdl	G-S	£2814

Total win prize-money £2814

Going:	Sf: 0-0 GS: 0-1 Gd: 0-0 GF: - Fm: 0-0
Distance:	2m/2m3: 0-0 2m4-2m7: 0-2 3m+: 0-1
Track:	LH: 0-1 RH: 0-2 Tight: 0-2 Gall: 0-0
Aids:	Bl: 0-0 Vi: 0-0 Tstrap: 0-2
Best Rating:	100 4/02 Hrfd 3m2f gd-fm Hdl

A stayer on the Flat, showed the benefit of the step up to three miles when scoring at Musselburgh in February. Seems to handle any ground.

Rainbow Star (FR)
(94h)   (74h)48

9-y-o b/br g Saumarez-In The Star (FR) (In Fijar (USA))
Mrs P Ford W E Donohue

Placings:221P/214P5/4P11F/1P/P000P-R03P   (1206)
2002/03: 16ᴾGS, 20ᴾGF, 26³GF, 26ᴾG,

	Starts	1st	2nd	3rd	Win & Pl
Hurdles	3	0	0	1	363
Chases	1	0	0	0	
Career Total	25	5	3	1	13486
106	5/00 Hrfd	3m3f110yG Hdl		GD	£1974
105	1/00 Plum	2m5f	G Hdl	SFT	£2292
99	1/00 Tntn	2m3f110yG Hdl		SFT	£1519
116	5/98 NAbb	2m1f	D Hdl	G-F	£2832
99	3/98 NAbb	2m1f	F Hdl	SFT	£1962

Total win prize-money £10580

Going:	Sf: 0-0 GS: 0-1 Gd: 0-1 GF: - Fm: 0-2
Distance:	2m/2m3: 0-1 2m4-2m7: 0-1 3m+: 0-2
Track:	LH: 0-4 RH: 0-0 Tight: 0-1 Gall: 0-0
Aids:	Bl: 0-0 Vi: 0-0 Tstrap: 0-0
Best Rating:	116 5/98 NAbb 2m1f gd-fm Hdl

Rainbow Sun
(88h)   (72+h)

7-y-o ch g Minster Son-Rillin (Ribston)
N M Babbage John Cantrill

Placings:40-00P0   (4536)
2002/03: 19⁰GF, 16⁰G, 21ᴾS, 24⁰G,

	Starts	1st	2nd	3rd	Win & Pl
Hurdles	4	0	0	0	
Career Total	6	0	0	0	0

Going:	Sf: 0-1 GS: 0-0 Gd: 0-2 GF: - Fm: 0-1
Distance:	2m/2m3: 0-1 2m4-2m7: 0-2 3m+: 0-1
Track:	LH: 0-0 RH: 0-4 Tight: 0-0 Gall: 0-0
Aids:	Bl: 0-0 Vi: 0-0 Tstrap: 0-0
Best Rating:	91 4/02 Wwck 2m gd-fm NHF

Rainbows Aglitter
108   119

6-y-o ch g Rainbows For Life (CAN)-Chalet Waldegg (Monsanto (FR))
D R Gandolfo Nigel Stafford

Placings:1/12324P-233020   (4323)
2002/03: 17²GS, 21³G, 16³S, 17⁹G, 16²S, 16⁹G,

	Starts	1st	2nd	3rd	Win & Pl
Hurdles	6	0	2	2	10544
Career Total	13	2	4	3	18710
114	10/01 Sthl	2m	E Hdl	GD	£2247
105	1/01 Kemp	2m	H NHF	SFT	£1683

Total win prize-money £3931

Going:	Sf: 0-2 GS: 0-1 Gd: 0-3 GF: - Fm: 0-0
Distance:	2m/2m3: 0-5 2m4-2m7: 0-1 3m+: 0-0
Track:	LH: 0-4 RH: 0-2 Tight: 0-1 Gall: 0-3
Aids:	Bl: 0-0 Vi: 0-0 Tstrap: 0-0
Best Rating:	119 3/03 Winc 2m soft Hdl

Fair handicap hurdler; effective at up to two miles five; acts on good and soft ground.

Raincheck

12-y-o b g Mtoto-Lashing (USA) (Storm Bird (CAN))
Mrs Georgina Worsley Mrs Georgina Worsley

Placings:FP0PLPP2/FUU52P/14/PP/P/P   (0316)
2002/03: 21ᴾG,

	Starts	1st	2nd	3rd	Win & Pl
Chases	1	0	0	0	
Career Total	20	1	2	0	3159
108	2/98 Folk	2m5f	H Ch	G-F	£1067

Total win prize-money £1067

Going:	Sf: 0-0 GS: 0-0 Gd: 0-1 GF: - Fm: 0-0
Distance:	2m/2m3: 0-0 2m4-2m7: 0-1 3m+: 0-0
Track:	LH: 0-0 RH: 0-1 Tight: 0-1 Gall: 0-0
Aids:	Bl: 0-0 Vi: 0-0 Tstrap: 0-1
Best Rating:	108 2/98 Folk 2m5f gd-fm Ch

Rainforest (IRE)
84   86

8-y-o b/br g Be My Native (USA)-Nanny Kehoe (IRE) (Sexton Blake)
P R Webber The Royal Ascot Racing Club

Placings:43/0   (2234)
2002/03: 16⁰G,

	Starts	1st	2nd	3rd	Win & Pl
Chases	1	0	0	0	
Career Total	3	0	0	1	406

Going:	Sf: 0-0 GS: 0-0 Gd: 0-1 GF: - Fm: 0-0
Distance:	2m/2m3: 0-1 2m4-2m7: 0-0 3m+: 0-0
Track:	LH: 0-0 RH: 0-1 Tight: 0-0 Gall: 0-0
Aids:	Bl: 0-0 Vi: 0-0 Tstrap: 0-0
Best Rating:	109 2/00 Asct 2m110y soft NHF

	Starts	1st	2nd	3rd	Win & Pl
Hurdles	4	0	0	0	
Career Total	6	0	0	0	0

Going:	Sf: 0-1 GS: 0-0 Gd: 0-2 GF: - Fm: 0-1
Distance:	2m/2m3: 0-1 2m4-2m7: 0-2 3m+: 0-1
Track:	LH: 0-0 RH: 0-4 Tight: 0-0 Gall: 0-0
Aids:	Bl: 0-0 Vi: 0-0 Tstrap: 0-0
Best Rating:	91 4/02 Wwck 2m gd-fm NHF

Rainton

7-y-o gr g Kasakov-Strathleven (My Swanee)
Miss N Stirling (J R Turner 19/5) Mrs P C Stirling

Placings:0/003P05U/00P-0   (4506)
2002/03: 25⁰G,

	Starts	1st	2nd	3rd	Win & Pl
Chases	1	0	0	0	
Career Total	12	0	0	1	500

Going:	Sf: 0-0 GS: 0-0 Gd: 0-1 GF: - Fm: 0-0
Distance:	2m/2m3: 0-0 2m4-2m7: 0-0 3m+: 0-1
Track:	LH: 0-1 RH: 0-0 Tight: 0-1 Gall: 0-0
Aids:	Bl: 0-0 Vi: 0-0 Tstrap: 0-0
Best Rating:	74 4/03 Kels 3m1f good Ch

Raisa's Gold (IRE)

5-y-o b m Goldmark (USA)-Princess Raisa (Indian King (USA))
B S Rothwell Brian Rothwell

Placings:F-P   (0581)
2002/03: 16ᴾG,

	Starts	1st	2nd	3rd	Win & Pl
Hurdles	1	0	0	0	
Career Total	2	0	0	0	

Going:	Sf: 0-0 GS: 0-0 Gd: 0-1 GF: - Fm: 0-0
Distance:	2m/2m3: 0-1 2m4-2m7: 0-0 3m+: 0-0
Track:	LH: 0-1 RH: 0-0 Tight: 0-0 Gall: 0-0
Aids:	Bl: 0-0 Vi: 0-0 Tstrap: 0-0
Best Rating:	0 6/02 Hexm 2m110y good Hdl

Raise A Gale (IRE)

9-y-o b/br m Strong Gale-Raise A Rose (IRE) (Cardinal Flower)
Miss E Hill (S E H Sherwood 14/7) R G Langley

Placings:030050/F123   (4361)
2002/03: 24ᶠG, 23¹GF, 24²GF, 24³F,

	Starts	1st	2nd	3rd	Win & Pl
Chases	4	1	1	1	5251
Career Total	10	1	1	2	5699
100	6/02 Worc	2m7f110yE Ch		G-F	£3088

Total win prize-money £3089

Going:	Sf: 0-0 GS: 0-0 Gd: 0-1 GF: - Fm: 1-3
Distance:	2m/2m3: 0-0 2m4-2m7: 0-0 **3m+: 1-4**
Track:	**LH: 1-3** RH: 0-1 Tight: 0-3 Gall: 0-0
Aids:	Bl: 0-0 Vi: 0-0 Tstrap: 0-0
Best Rating:	100 7/02 Strf 3m gd-fm Ch

Ex-pointer and winning novice chaser; acts on fast ground; stays at least three miles.

Raise A McGregor
97(82h)   (74h)84

7-y-o br g Perpendicular-Gregory s Lady (Meldrum)
Mrs S J Smith Keith Nicholson

Placings:3O0/04-P00   (2103)
2002/03: 16ᴾG, 20⁰HY, 16⁰G,

	Starts	1st	2nd	3rd	Win & Pl
Hurdles	3	0	0	0	
Career Total	8	0	0	1	213

Going: Sf: 0-1 GS: 0-0 Gd: 0-2 GF: - Fm: 0-0
Distance: 2m/2m3: 0-2 2m4-2m7: 0-1 3m+: 0-0
Track: LH: 0-3 RH: 0-0 Tight: 0-1 Gall: 0-0
Aids: Bl: 0-0 Vi: 0-0 Tstrap: 0-0
Best Rating: 95   7/00   Worc   2m   gd-fm   NHF

Pulled up on chasing debut May 2003; not disgraced in 2m novices handicap next time.

Raise Your Glass (IRE)

4-y-o b/br g Namaqualand (USA)-Toast And Honey (IRE) (Glow (USA))
C W Thornton   Mrs M Blacker

Placings:060   (4778)
2002/03: 14⁰G5, 16⁶G, 16⁰G,

	Starts	1st	2nd	3rd	Win & Pl
NH Flat	3	0	0	0	0
Career Total	3	0	0	0	0

Going: Sf: 0-0 GS: 0-1 Gd: 0-2 GF: - Fm: 0-0
Distance: 2m/2m3: 0-2 2m4-2m7: 0-0 3m+: 0-0
Track: LH: 0-2 RH: 0-1 Tight: 0-0 Gall: 0-0
Aids: Bl: 0-0 Vi: 0-0 Tstrap: 0-0
Best Rating: 66   4/03   Newc   2m   good   NHF

Raiseapearl
78   **44**
8-y-o b/br g Pocketed (USA)-Little Anthem (True Song)
R D Wylie   Mrs S Blane

Placings:06   (2763)
2002/03: 20⁰G, 20⁶S,

	Starts	1st	2nd	3rd	Win & Pl
Hurdles	2	0	0	0	0
Career Total	2	0	0	0	0

Going: Sf: 0-1 GS: 0-0 Gd: 0-1 GF: - Fm: 0-0
Distance: 2m/2m3: 0-0 2m4-2m7: 0-2 3m+: 0-0
Track: LH: 0-2 RH: 0-0 Tight: 0-0 Gall: 0-0
Aids: Bl: 0-0 Vi: 0-0 Tstrap: 0-0
Best Rating: 44   12/02   Hayd   2m4f   good   Hdl

Rajah Eman (IRE)

5-y-o b g Sri Pekan (USA)-Jungle Book (IRE) (Ballad Rock)
R Allan (C A Dwyer 21/6)   The J R and R Ownership

Placings:FP   (1162)
2002/03: 16²GS, 17²GF,

	Starts	1st	2nd	3rd	Win & Pl
Hurdles	2	0	0	0	0
Career Total	2	0	0	0	0

Going: Sf: 0-0 GS: 0-1 Gd: 0-0 GF: - Fm: 0-1
Distance: 2m/2m3: 0-2 2m4-2m7: 0-0 3m+: 0-0
Track: LH: 0-1 RH: 0-1 Tight: 0-1 Gall: 0-0
Aids: Bl: 0-0 Vi: 0-0 Tstrap: 0-0
Best Rating: 0   9/02   Sedg   2m1f   gd-fm   Hdl

Rajati (USA)

8-y-o b g Chief s Crown (USA)-Charming Life (NZ) (Sir Tristram)

R J Rowsell   R J Rowsell

Placings:5404116342513/00025PF5/365600253F/6 (4736)
2002/03: 24⁶GF,

	Starts	1st	2nd	3rd	Win & Pl
Chases	1	0	0	0	0
Career Total	32	3	3	4	13539
114 3/99 Chep 2m110y C HHdl			SFT	£4531
104 12/98 Newc 2m E Hdl			SFT	£2274
87 11/98 Ludl 2m G Hdl			GD	£1674
Total win prize-money £8479				

Going: Sf: 0-0 GS: 0-0 Gd: 0-0 GF: - Fm: 0-1
Distance: 2m/2m3: 0-0 2m4-2m7: 0-0 3m+: 0-1
Track: LH: 0-1 RH: 0-0 Tight: 0-0 Gall: 0-0
Aids: Bl: 0-0 Vi: 0-0 Tstrap: 0-0
Best Rating: 114   3/99   Chep   2m110y   soft   Hdl

Rakalackey
101f   **106+f**
5-y-o br g Rakaposhi King-Celtic Slave (Celtic Cone)
H D Daly   B G Hellyer

Placings:55   (4155)
2002/03: 17³GS, 16⁵G,

	Starts	1st	2nd	3rd	Win & Pl
NH Flat	2	0	0	0	0
Career Total	2	0	0	0	0

Going: Sf: 0-0 GS: 0-1 Gd: 0-1 GF: - Fm: 0-0
Distance: 2m/2m3: 0-2 2m4-2m7: 0-0 3m+: 0-0
Track: LH: 0-2 RH: 0-0 Tight: 0-1 Gall: 0-0
Aids: Bl: 0-0 Vi: 0-0 Tstrap: 0-0
Best Rating: 106   3/03   Wwck   2m   good   NHF

A half-brother to Young Spartacus; has shown promise when finishing fifth in both his bumpers.

Rakaposhi Lass
91   **97+**
7-y-o b m Rakaposhi King-Ballysax Lass (Main Reef)
M C Pipe   D A Johnson

Placings:1111   (1090)
2002/03: 17¹G, 16¹GF, 16¹GF, 22¹GF,

	Starts	1st	2nd	3rd	Win & Pl
NH Flat	3	3	0	0	5664
Hurdles	1	1	0	0	2940
Career Total	4	4	0	0	8604
97 8/02 NAbb 2m6f E Hdl			G-F	£2940
127 7/02 Worc 2m H NHF			G-F	£1818
124 6/02 Worc 2m H NHF			G-F	£1577
106 6/02 NAbb 2m1f H NHF			GD	£2268
Total win prize-money £8605				

Going: Sf: 0-0 GS: 0-0 Gd: 1-1 GF: - Fm: 3-3
Distance: 2m/2m3: 3-3 2m4-2m7: 1-1 3m+: 0-0
Track: LH: 4-4 RH: 0-0 Tight: 2-2 Gall: 0-0
Aids: Bl: 0-0 Vi: 0-0 Tstrap: 0-0
Best Rating: 127   7/02   Worc   2m   gd-fm   NHF

A useful pointer, successful in three bumpers in midsummer 2002. Completed a four-timer on hurdling debut.Acts on fast ground.

Rakaposhi Raid
107(82c)   (45c)**76**
7-y-o b m Rakaposhi King-Minty Muncher (Idiots Delight)
N B Mason   N B Mason

Placings:0005235045-54   (1015)

2002/03: 21⁵G, 24⁴G,

	Starts	1st	2nd	3rd	Win & Pl
Hurdles	1	0	0	0	311
Chases	1	0	0	0	0
Career Total	12	0	1	1	1135

Going: Sf: 0-0 GS: 0-0 Gd: 0-2 GF: - Fm: 0-0
Distance: 2m/2m3: 0-0 2m4-2m7: 0-1 3m+: 0-1
Track: LH: 0-1 RH: 0-1 Tight: 0-1 Gall: 0-0
Aids: Bl: 0-0 Vi: 0-1 Tstrap: 0-1
Best Rating: 76   2/02   Newc   3m   soft   Hdl

Plating-class hurdler, stays two miles-four, has been held over three miles to date. Suited by soft ground.

Rakassa
90f   **88f**
5-y-o ch m Ballet Royal (USA)-Shafayif (Ela-Mana-Mou)
H J Manners   H J Manners

Placings:00530   (4481)
2002/03: 16⁵G, 16⁰G, 16⁵S, 14³GF, 17⁰G,

	Starts	1st	2nd	3rd	Win & Pl
NH Flat	5	0	0	1	283
Career Total	5	0	0	1	283

Going: Sf: 0-1 GS: 0-0 Gd: 0-3 GF: - Fm: 0-1
Distance: 2m/2m3: 0-4 2m4-2m7: 0-0 3m+: 0-0
Track: LH: 0-2 RH: 0-1 Tight: 0-0 Gall: 0-1
Aids: Bl: 0-0 Vi: 0-0 Tstrap: 0-0
Best Rating: 88   4/03   Aint   2m1f   good   NHF

Raleagh Native (IRE)
101(87h)   (57h)**108d**
10-y-o ch g Be My Native (USA)-Lagan Valley Rose (Avocat)
Miss A M Newton-Smith   John Grist

Placings:1P/1F6/04/06F3P2-2U6F0   (4441)
2002/03: 20²G, 20²S, 20ᵁHY, 20⁴S, 20⁴S, 20⁴G,

	Starts	1st	2nd	3rd	Win & Pl
Hurdles	1	0	0	0	0
Chases	5	0	2	0	2231
Career Total	18	2	2	1	10119
126 10/98 Worc 2m2f E Hdl			SFT	£2477
121 11/97 MRas 2m4f D Ch			GD	£3834
Total win prize-money £6312				

Going: Sf: 0-4 GS: 0-0 Gd: 0-2 GF: - Fm: 0-0
Distance: 2m/2m3: 0-0 2m4-2m7: 0-6 3m+: 0-0
Track: LH: 0-4 RH: 0-2 Tight: 0-0 Gall: 0-0
Aids: Bl: 0-0 Vi: 0-0 Tstrap: 0-0
Best Rating: 126   10/98   Worc   2m2f   soft   Hdl

Lightly-raced moderate chaser, let down more than once by his jumping.

Ramblees Holly
101   **92**
5-y-o ch g Alfie Dickins-Lucky Holly (General David)
R S Wood   R S Wood

Placings:30-0630P650   (4711)
2002/03: 16⁰G, 16⁶GF, 19³GF, 16⁰G, 20ᴾHY, 16⁶G, 17⁵S, 16⁰GF,

	Starts	1st	2nd	3rd	Win & Pl
NH Flat	2	0	0	0	0
Hurdles	6	0	0	1	678

Column 1

Career Total	10	0	0	2	934

Going:	Sf: 0-2 GS: 0-2 Gd: 0-1 GF: - Fm: 0-3
Distance:	2m/2m3: 0-6 2m4-2m7: 0-2 3m+: 0-0
Track:	LH: 0-6 RH: 0-2 Tight: 0-4 Gall: 0-0
Aids:	Bl: 0-0 Vi: 0-0 Tstrap: 0-0
Best Rating:	92 11/02 Weth 2m gd-sft Hdl

Took a novices' hurdle in soft ground at Sedgefield in May; not disgraced under a penalty since; stays three miles.

Rambling Home (IRE)

11-y-o br g Orchestra-Rambling Ivy (Mandalus)
T R George Mrs Charlie Hughes

Placings:P   (3954)
2002/03: 20PGS,

	Starts	1st	2nd	3rd	Win & Pl
Chases	1	0	0	0	
Career Total	1	0	0	0	

Going:	Sf: 0-0 GS: 0-1 Gd: 0-0 GF: - Fm: 0-0
Distance:	2m/2m3: 0-0 2m4-2m7: 0-1 3m+: 0-0
Track:	LH: 0-0 RH: 0-1 Tight: 0-0 Gall: 0-0
Aids:	Bl: 0-0 Vi: 0-0 Tstrap: 0-0
Best Rating:	0 3/03 Leic 2m4f110y gd-sft Ch

Ramirez (IRE)

100f   100f

5-y-o ch g Royal Abjar (USA)-Flooding (USA) (Irish River (FR))
M Pitman Autofour Engineering

Placings:200   (4444)
2002/03: 17²S, 17⁰HY, 16⁰G,

	Starts	1st	2nd	3rd	Win & Pl
NH Flat	3	0	1	0	732
Career Total	3	0	1	0	732

Going:	Sf: 0-2 GS: 0-0 Gd: 0-1 GF: - Fm: 0-0
Distance:	2m/2m3: 0-3 2m4-2m7: 0-0 3m+: 0-0
Track:	LH: 0-0 RH: 0-2 Tight: 0-1 Gall: 0-0
Aids:	Bl: 0-0 Vi: 0-0 Tstrap: 0-0
Best Rating:	100 1/03 Tntn 2m1f soft NHF

Defied burly appearance when narrowly beaten at Taunton in soft ground on bumper debut January 2003. Held afterwards.

Random Harvest (IRE)

108   121

14-y-o br g Strong Gale-Bavello (Le Bavard (FR))
Mrs M Reveley C C Buckley

Placings:5/426/24120PU/B5324/U14121130/1/PP1245PP/
F321600F-0P23P461351   (4796)
2002/03: 20⁴G, 20⁶GS, 26²GS, 24³G, 24⁵GS, 24⁶GS,
23¹GF, 24³G, 25⁴GF, 28¹GF,

	Starts	1st	2nd	3rd	Win & Pl
Chases	11	2	1	2	25333
Career Total	53	10	8	5	99546
121	4/03	Sedg	3m4f	D(0-125)HCh	G-F	12110
116	3/03	Weth	2m7f110yD(0-125)HCh		G-F	£6792
138	12/01	Weth	3m1f	C(0-130)HCh	SFT	£7560
136	11/00	Weth	3m1f	D(0-125)HCh	SFT	£3828

Column 2

129	12/99	Weth	2m7f	D Hdl	G-S	£3207
150	12/98	Weth	3m1f	B HCh	SFT	£14732
150	12/98	Weth	3m1f	B(0-145)HCh	GD	£7100
137	10/98	MRas	3m1f	C(0-130)HCh	G-S	£6905
122	5/98	Weth	3m1f	C(0-135)HCh	G-F	£4719
118	1/97	Carl	2m4f110yD(0-120)HCh		GD	£3566

Total win prize-money £70523

Going:	Sf: 0-0 GS: 0-4 Gd: 0-3 GF: - Fm: 2-4
Distance:	2m/2m3: 0-0 2m4-2m7: 0-0 3m+: 2-9
Track:	LH: 1-10 RH: 0-0 Tight: 1-1 Gall: 0-5
Aids:	Bl: 0-0 Vi: 0-0 Tstrap: 0-0
Best Rating:	153 1/99 Hayd 3m soft Ch

Fair handicap chaser; well into the veteran stage; goes well at Wetherby and recorded his seventh win there in March 2003; best at around three miles on soft ground, although does handle a faster surface.

Random Native (IRE)

105f   102f

5-y-o br g Be My Native (USA)-Random Wind (Random Shot)
T J Fitzgerald (J G Fitzgerald 18/1) Jim Ennis

Placings:0-131   (4665)
2002/03: 16¹G, 16³GF, 17¹GF,

	Starts	1st	2nd	3rd	Win & Pl
NH Flat	3	2	0	1	4469
Career Total	4	2	0	1	4469
102	4/03	Carl	2m1f	H NHF	G-F	£2119
100	1/03	Catt	2m	H NHF	GD	£2058

Total win prize-money £4178

Going:	Sf: 0-0 GS: 0-0 Gd: 1-1 GF: - Fm: 1-2
Distance:	2m/2m3: 2-3 2m4-2m7: 0-0 3m+: 0-0
Track:	LH: 1-2 RH: 1-1 Tight: 1-1 Gall: 0-0
Aids:	Bl: 0-0 Vi: 0-0 Tstrap: 0-0
Best Rating:	102 4/03 Carl 2m1f gd-fm NHF

Modest bumper performer; took ordinary bumpers at Catterick in January and Carlisle in April 2003; given a lot to do when third at Wetherby in between; acts on a sound surface; looks a fair prospect.

Randrich

6-y-o b m Alflora (IRE)-Randama (Akarad (FR))
P M Rich P M Rich

Placings:P-P   (2174)
2002/03: 20PS,

	Starts	1st	2nd	3rd	Win & Pl
Hurdles	1	0	0	0	
Career Total	2	0	0	0	

Going:	Sf: 0-1 GS: 0-0 Gd: 0-0 GF: - Fm: 0-0
Distance:	2m/2m3: 0-0 2m4-2m7: 0-1 3m+: 0-0
Track:	LH: 0-1 RH: 0-0 Tight: 0-0 Gall: 0-0
Aids:	Bl: 0-0 Vi: 0-0 Tstrap: 0-0
Best Rating:	0 11/02 Chep 2m4f soft Hdl

Randy (GER)

105   77

5-y-o gr g Neshad (USA)-Regal Beauty (GER) (Windwurf (GER))
M C Pipe M C Pipe

Placings:P0PP   (3445)

Column 3

2002/03: 19⁵GS, 19⁰GS, 16⁶PS, 16⁶PHY,

	Starts	1st	2nd	3rd	Win & Pl
Hurdles	4	0	0	0	
Career Total	4	0	0	0	

Going:	Sf: 0-2 GS: 0-2 Gd: 0-0 GF: - Fm: 0-0
Distance:	2m/2m3: 0-3 2m4-2m7: 0-1 3m+: 0-0
Track:	LH: 0-1 RH: 0-3 Tight: 0-1 Gall: 0-0
Aids:	Bl: 0-0 Vi: 0-0 Tstrap: 0-0
Best Rating:	77 12/02 Tntn 2m3f110y gd-sft Hdl

Selling hurdler; seemed to appreciate first run on a sound surface when fourth at Newton Abbot June 2003.

Raneen Nashwan

96   94

7-y-o b g Nashwan (USA)-Raneen Alwatar (Sadler s Wells (USA))
R J Baker M Channon

Placings:F0020-4063   (0649)
2002/03: 16⁴GF, 20⁰G, 17⁶GF, 17³GF,

	Starts	1st	2nd	3rd	Win & Pl
Hurdles	4	0	0	1	526
Career Total	9	0	1	1	1326

Going:	Sf: 0-0 GS: 0-0 Gd: 0-1 GF: - Fm: 0-3
Distance:	2m/2m3: 0-3 2m4-2m7: 0-1 3m+: 0-0
Track:	LH: 0-2 RH: 0-2 Tight: 0-1 Gall: 0-0
Aids:	Bl: 0-1 Vi: 0-0 Tstrap: 0-0
Best Rating:	94 5/02 Winc 2m gd-fm Hdl

Moderate hurdler, suited by cut in the ground. Has a tendency to hinder himself by racing too keenly.

Ranelagh Gray (IRE)

102   86

6-y-o gr g Roselier (FR)-Bea Marie (IRE) (King s Ride)
Miss Venetia Williams Christopher Drury

Placings:05P50   (4311)
2002/03: 18⁰S, 16⁵GS, 21⁵PS, 16⁵G, 21⁹G,

	Starts	1st	2nd	3rd	Win & Pl
NH Flat	2	0	0	0	0
Hurdles	3	0	0	0	0
Career Total	5	0	0	0	0

Going:	Sf: 0-2 GS: 0-1 Gd: 0-2 GF: - Fm: 0-0
Distance:	2m/2m3: 0-3 2m4-2m7: 0-2 3m+: 0-0
Track:	LH: 0-3 RH: 0-2 Tight: 0-1 Gall: 0-3
Aids:	Bl: 0-0 Vi: 0-0 Tstrap: 0-0
Best Rating:	86 2/03 Hntg 2m110y good Hdl

Ranger Sloane

11-y-o ch g Gunner B-Lucky Amy (Lucky Wednesday)
G Fierro G Fierro

Placings:0P/36661F040/4113004/3043604336/34562/43/P
                                               (1830)
2002/03: 16⁶PHY,

	Starts	1st	2nd	3rd	Win & Pl
Hurdles	1	0	0	0	
Career Total	36	3	1	8	15251
103	12/97	Hayd	2m	C(0-135)HHdl	SFT	£3225
97	12/97	Sthl	2m	E(0-115)HHdl	GD	£2238
86	2/97	Hrfd	2m1f	F(0-90)HHdl	G-S	£2570

Total win prize-money £8033

Going:	Sf: 0-1 GS: 0-0 Gd: 0-0 GF: - Fm: 0-0
Distance:	2m/2m3: 0-1 2m4-2m7: 0-0 3m+: 0-0
Track:	LH: 0-1 RH: 0-0 Tight: 0-0 Gall: 0-0
Aids:	Bl: 0-0 Vi: 0-0 Tstrap: 0-0
Best Rating:	105 12/98 Hntg 2m110y soft Hdl

Rapid Liner

96(99c)   (81c)**66**

10-y-o b g Skyliner-Stellaris (Star Appeal)
B G Powell (J Gallagher 19/3) Mrs G Elliott And G Jarvie

Placings:00P6035/5P5/00006/P00P0/00PP-602 (4629)
2002/03: 16⁶GF, 19⁰GF, 21²GF,

	Starts	1st	2nd	3rd	Win & Pl
Hurdles	3	0	1	0	700
Career Total	27	0	1	1	997

Going:	Sf: 0-0 GS: 0-0 Gd: 0-0 GF: - Fm: 0-3
Distance:	2m/2m3: 0-2 2m4-2m7: 0-1 3m+: 0-0
Track:	LH: 0-1 RH: 0-2 Tight: 0-1 Gall: 0-0
Aids:	Bl: 0-0 Vi: 0-0 Tstrap: 0-0
Best Rating:	71 4/01 Font 2m2f good Ch

Poor hurdler/chaser; only worthwhile form when runner-up in Plumpton seller in April 2003.

Rapier

90   **98**

9-y-o b g Sharpo-Sahara Breeze (Ela-Mana-Mou)
A Streeter Greencard Golfers

Placings:10/356/2-5 (0051)
2002/03: 20⁵G,

	Starts	1st	2nd	3rd	Win & Pl
Hurdles	1	0	0	0	0
Career Total	7	1	1	1	3163
106 12/98 Ayr	2m		E Hdl	G-S	£2407
			Total win prize-money £2408		

Going:	Sf: 0-0 GS: 0-0 Gd: 0-1 GF: - Fm: 0-0
Distance:	2m/2m3: 0-2 2m4-2m7: 0-1 3m+: 0-0
Track:	LH: 0-1 RH: 0-0 Tight: 0-1 Gall: 0-0
Aids:	Bl: 0-0 Vi: 0-0 Tstrap: 0-0
Best Rating:	106 12/98 Ayr 2m gd-sft Hdl

Selling hurdler these days.

Rapt (IRE)

89   **73**

5-y-o b g Septieme Ciel (USA)-Dream Play (USA) (Blushing Groom (FR))
M A Barnes (P W D Arcy 15/5) Thirdtimelucky

Placings:0P00 (4507)
2002/03: 17⁰GF, 16²S, 16⁰GS, 16⁰G,

	Starts	1st	2nd	3rd	Win & Pl
Hurdles	4	0	0	0	
Career Total	4	0	0	0	

Going:	Sf: 0-1 GS: 0-1 Gd: 0-1 GF: - Fm: 0-1
Distance:	2m/2m3: 0-4 2m4-2m7: 0-0 3m+: 0-0
Track:	LH: 0-4 RH: 0-0 Tight: 0-3 Gall: 0-1
Aids:	Bl: 0-0 Vi: 0-0 Tstrap: 0-0
Best Rating:	38 7/02 Sedg 2m1f gd-fm Hdl

Rarchnamara (IRE)

95(108h)   (109h)**84**

8-y-o b g Commanche Run-Knollwood Court (Le Jean)

Ferdy Murphy John Duddy

Placings:400/42122322-4U (3565)
2002/03: 20⁴GF, 27⁰HY,

	Starts	1st	2nd	3rd	Win & Pl
Chases	2	0	0	0	418
Career Total	13	1	5	1	7087
103 6/01 Hexm 2m4f110yE(0-105)HHdl			G-S	£2626	
			Total win prize-money £2626		

Going:	Sf: 0-1 GS: 0-0 Gd: 0-0 GF: - Fm: 0-1
Distance:	2m/2m3: 0-0 2m4-2m7: 0-1 3m+: 0-1
Track:	LH: 0-1 RH: 0-1 Tight: 0-2 Gall: 0-0
Aids:	Bl: 0-0 Vi: 0-0 Tstrap: 0-0
Best Rating:	109 12/01 Hexm 3m soft Hdl

Rare Genius (USA)

92

7-y-o ch g Beau Genius (CAN)-Aunt Nola (USA) (Olden Times)
Ian Williams The Second Heyfleet Partnership

Placings:2-0 (1922)
2002/03: 19⁰GS,

	Starts	1st	2nd	3rd	Win & Pl
Hurdles	1	0	0	0	
Career Total	2	0	1	0	690

Going:	Sf: 0-0 GS: 0-1 Gd: 0-0 GF: - Fm: 0-0
Distance:	2m/2m3: 0-1 2m4-2m7: 0-0 3m+: 0-0
Track:	LH: 0-1 RH: 0-0 Tight: 0-0 Gall: 0-1
Aids:	Bl: 0-0 Vi: 0-0 Tstrap: 0-0
Best Rating:	92 7/01 Strf 2m3f gd-fm Hdl

Rare Occurance

13-y-o b g Damister (USA)-Superior Quality (Star Appeal)
A W Carroll R H Harris

Placings:62/50/3044/51P/6/PP (0442)
2002/03: 20⁰GF, 21⁸S,

	Starts	1st	2nd	3rd	Win & Pl
Chases	2	0	0	0	
Career Total	14	1	1	1	5986
99 3/99 Ling	2m4f110yE Ch		G-S	£3485	
			Total win prize-money £3485		

Going:	Sf: 0-1 GS: 0-0 Gd: 0-0 GF: - Fm: 0-1
Distance:	2m/2m3: 0-0 2m4-2m7: 0-2 3m+: 0-0
Track:	LH: 0-2 RH: 0-0 Tight: 0-0 Gall: 0-0
Aids:	Bl: 0-0 Vi: 0-0 Tstrap: 0-0
Best Rating:	111 12/94 Kemp 2m soft Hdl

Rare Ouzel (IRE)

110   **101**

7-y-o b g Be My Native (USA)-Ring Ouzel (IRE) (Deep Run)
A J Martin Daniel Harnett

Placings:040/0-1021F (3085a)
2002/03: 16¹GY, 20⁰S, 21²G, 18¹HY, 16FS,

	Starts	1st	2nd	3rd	Win & Pl
NH Flat	1	1	0	0	3598
Hurdles	4	1	1	0	13346
Career Total	9	2	1	0	17219
101 12/02 Leop	2m2f	(74-116)HHdl	HVY	£9171	
95 5/02 Baln	2m	NHF	G-Y	£3598	
			Total win prize-money £12770		

| Going: | Sf: 1-3 GS: 0-0 Gd: 0-1 GF: - Fm: 0-0 |

Distance:	2m/2m3: 2-3 2m4-2m7: 0-2 3m+: 0-0
Track:	LH: 1-3 RH: 0-1 Tight: 0-0 Gall: 0-1
Aids:	Bl: 0-0 Vi: 0-0 Tstrap: 0-0
Best Rating:	101 12/02 Leop 2m2f heavy Hdl

Fair hurdler; winner of a Leopardstown handicap hurdle at Christmas; acts well on soft ground; stays two and a half miles.

Rare Presence (IRE)

92   **77**

4-y-o b g Sadler s Wells (USA)-Celebrity Style (USA) (Seeking The Gold (USA))
C P Morlock (D K Weld 16/10) The Shouting Men

Placings:004 (4184)
2002/03: 16⁰HY, 17⁰GS, 17⁴G,

	Starts	1st	2nd	3rd	Win & Pl
Hurdles	3	0	0	0	0
Career Total	3	0	0	0	0

Going:	Sf: 0-1 GS: 0-1 Gd: 0-1 GF: - Fm: 0-0
Distance:	2m/2m3: 0-3 2m4-2m7: 0-0 3m+: 0-0
Track:	LH: 0-0 RH: 0-3 Tight: 0-1 Gall: 0-0
Aids:	Bl: 0-1 Vi: 0-0 Tstrap: 0-0
Best Rating:	77 3/03 Folk 2m1f110y good Hdl

Moderate hurdler; limited potential; has worn blinkers.

Rasko (FR)

98   **106+**

7-y-o gr g Kadalko (FR)-Fagaras (FR) (Kenmare (FR))
T Doumen (F Doumen 29/11) Ecurie Passing

Placings:103243/51344 (2569)
2002/03: 20⁵VS, 19¹HY, 18³HY, 19⁴HY, 24⁴G,

	Starts	1st	2nd	3rd	Win & Pl
Hurdles	4	1	0	1	18933
Chases	1	0	0	0	650
Career Total	11	2	1	3	85729
10/02 Pari	2m3f	Hdl	HVY	£6773	
9/99 Autl	2m2f	Hdl	VS	£15070	
			Total win prize-money £21843		

Going:	Sf: 1-3 GS: 0-0 Gd: 0-1 GF: - Fm: 0-0
Distance:	2m/2m3: 1-3 2m4-2m7: 0-1 3m+: 0-1
Track:	LH: 0-2 RH: 0-0 Tight: 0-0 Gall: 0-1
Aids:	Bl: 0-0 Vi: 0-0 Tstrap: 0-0
Best Rating:	106 12/02 Newb 3m good Ch

French-trained hurdler/chaser; twice a winner over hurdles in France at around two and a quarter miles; goes well in the mud.

Rathbawn Prince (IRE)

109   (110h)**144**

11-y-o ch g All Haste (USA)-Ellis Town (Camden Town)
D T Hughes T J Culhane

Placings:141/55100/133200/0P2P3214U/21115U55P/2056 F0-0F43P0 (4727a)
2002/03: 21⁰GY, 16FS, 16⁴Y, 24³G, 25PG, 29⁰G,

	Starts	1st	2nd	3rd	Win & Pl
Hurdles	1	0	0	0	0
Chases	5	0	0	1	6669
Career Total	44	8	5	4	83664
145 11/00 DRoy	2m2f	Ch	G-Y	£10400	
122 10/00 Thur	2m6f	Ch	Y-S	£4416	
121 10/00 Fair	2m2f	Hdl	G-Y	£3864	
130 2/00 Fair	2m2f	Ch	HVY	£4692	

105	10/98 Fair	2m	Hdl	YLD	£2989
120	3/98 Navn	2m	NHF	Y-S	£2680
119	4/97 Punc	2m	NHF	GD	£6782
107	10/96 Punc	2m	NHF	GD	£3177

Total win prize-money £39001

Going: Sf: 0-1 GS: 0-0 Gd: 0-3 GF: - Fm: 0-0
Distance: 2m/2m3: 0-2 2m4-2m7: 0-1 3m+: 0-0
Track: LH: 0-3 RH: 0-1 Tight: 0-1 Gall: 0-1
Aids: Bl: 0-0 Vi: 0-0 Tstrap: 0-0
Best Rating: 157 5/01 Fair 3m5f good Ch

Smart Irish staying chaser; runner-up in the 2001 Irish National, been lightly raced since; has won on a sound surface but effective on heavy; has worn blinkers on one single occasion.

Rathgar Beau (IRE)
118(113h) (133h)**149**
7-y-o b/br g Beau Sher-Salerina (Orchestra)
E Sheehy One-O-Eight Racing Club

Placings:165F212312523-2B43213211F (4477)
2002/03: 16²YS, 17⁶YS, 17⁴S, 16³S, 16²S, 17¹HY, 17³S, 16²YS, 16¹Y, 16¹HY, 16⁶G,

	Starts	1st	2nd	3rd	Win & Pl
Chases	11	3	3	2	36760
Career Total	24	6	7	4	61673

144	3/03 Naas	2m	Ch	HVY	£8441
139	2/03 Thur	2m	Ch	YLD	£6272
105	12/02 Limk	2m1f	Ch	HVY	£7196
126	1/02 Thur	2m	Hdl	Y-S	£5079
122	11/01 Thur	2m	Hdl	Y-S	£5008
122	12/00 Fair	2m	NHF	SFT	£3312

Total win prize-money £35311

Going: Sf: 2-6 GS: 0-0 Gd: 0-1 GF: - Fm: 0-0
Distance: 2m/2m3: 3-11 2m4-2m7: 0-0 3m+: 0-0
Track: LH: 1-5 RH: 0-0 Tight: 0-1 Gall: 0-0
Aids: Bl: 0-0 Vi: 0-0 Tstrap: 0-0
Best Rating: 144 3/03 Naas 2m heavy Ch

Very useful Irish novice chaser; suited by two miles and loves the mud.

Rathgibbon (IRE)
93 **95**
12-y-o b g Phardante (FR)-Harp Song (Auction Ring (USA))
Mrs L C Jewell (Neil King 30/5) Mrs M B Stephens

Placings:005222245/114413214350/0600015334/05066P5 44431PU460/PU6532651222/55344163/PPP5 (1626)
2002/03: 16⁸G, 21⁸G, 24⁶G, 21⁵GS,

	Starts	1st	2nd	3rd	Win & Pl
Chases	4	0	0	0	0
Career Total	72	8	9	8	40083

95	1/01 Plum	2m4f	F(0-105)HCh	G-S	£2996
95	3/00 Plum	2m4f	F(0-110)HCh	GD	£2762
104	12/98 Punc	2m	(0-123)HCh	SH	£4782
121	11/97 Naas	2m3f	Ch	SH	£4408
121	11/96 Tipp	2m4f	(0-123)HHdl	SFT	£2824
115	10/96 Tipp	2m4f	(0-130)HHdl	SFT	£2824
91	7/96 Wxfd	2m4f	Hdl	GD	£2881
105	7/96 Tipp	2m	NHF	G-F	£3001

Total win prize-money £26442

Going: Sf: 0-0 GS: 0-1 Gd: 0-3 GF: - Fm: 0-0
Distance: 2m/2m3: 0-1 2m4-2m7: 0-2 3m+: 0-1
Track: LH: 0-1 RH: 0-3 Tight: 0-2 Gall: 0-1
Aids: Bl: 0-0 Vi: 0-3 Tstrap: 0-3
Best Rating: 121 11/97 Naas 2m3f sft-hvy Ch

Ratified
102(101c) (89c)**60**
6-y-o b g Not In Doubt (USA)-Festival Of Magic (USA) (Clever Trick (USA))
M C Chapman Twinacre Nurseries Ltd

Placings:0004024U54305-052000245000 (2688)
2002/03: 16⁶G, 17⁵HY, 17²GS, 17⁰GF, 17⁰G, 17⁰GF, 24²GF, 20⁴GF, 22⁶G, 21⁰GS, 16⁰G, 17⁰GS,

	Starts	1st	2nd	3rd	Win & Pl
Hurdles	10	0	2	0	2760
Chases	2	0	0	0	
Career Total	25	0	3	1	6007

Going: Sf: 0-1 GS: 0-3 Gd: 0-4 GF: - Fm: 0-4
Distance: 2m/2m3: 0-8 2m4-2m7: 0-3 3m+: 0-1
Track: LH: 0-7 RH: 0-5 Tight: 0-9 Gall: 0-2
Aids: Bl: 0-0 Vi: 0-0 Tstrap: 0-0
Best Rating: 89 2/02 Wrck 2m110y soft Ch

Very modest placed form over hurdles and fences.

Raunchy (IRE)
101(99c) (111c)**110**
9-y-o br g Be My Native (USA)-Dirty Diana (Boreen (FR))
Jonjo O Neill (J E Mulhern 26/7) J P McManus

Placings:1/22/63F/504325-202 (1071)
2002/03: 24²YS, 24⁹GF, 22²G,

	Starts	1st	2nd	3rd	Win & Pl
Hurdles	3	0	2	0	2054
Career Total	15	1	5	2	10704

118	3/99 Leop	2m	NHF	SFT	£3069

Total win prize-money £3069

Going: Sf: 0-0 GS: 0-0 Gd: 0-1 GF: - Fm: 0-1
Distance: 2m/2m3: 0-2 2m4-2m7: 0-1 3m+: 0-2
Track: LH: 0-1 RH: 0-0 Tight: 0-1 Gall: 0-0
Aids: Bl: 0-0 Vi: 0-0 Tstrap: 0-0
Best Rating: 128 12/99 Leop 2m4f soft Hdl

One time bumper winner, modest form over hurdles, suited by three miles.

Ravenswood (IRE)
106 **137**
6-y-o b g Warning-Green Lucia (Green Dancer (USA))
M C Pipe D A Johnson

Placings:236111-P0624 (4102)
2002/03: 24⁵YS, 22⁰S, 21⁶S, 24²G, 25⁴G,

	Starts	1st	2nd	3rd	Win & Pl
Hurdles	5	0	1	0	5604
Career Total	11	3	2	1	49999

137	4/02 Ayr	2m6f	B(0-150)HHdl	GD	£6988
131	4/02 Aint	2m4f	A HHdl	GD	£23200
124	3/02 Newb	2m110y	C(0-130)HHdl	G-S	£12815

Total win prize-money £43005

Going: Sf: 0-3 GS: 0-0 Gd: 0-2 GF: - Fm: 0-0
Distance: 2m/2m3: 0-0 2m4-2m7: 0-2 3m+: 0-3
Track: LH: 0-1 RH: 0-2 Tight: 0-0 Gall: 0-2
Aids: Bl: 0-0 Vi: 0-0 Tstrap: 0-5
Best Rating: 137 3/03 Chel 3m1f110y good Hdl

Very useful staying hurdler; completed a hat-trick in the spring of 2002; effective at two miles but stays three; acts on good to soft ground; wears a tongue tie.

Raving Lord (IRE)
79 **50**
6-y-o b g Lord Americo-Miss Kertina (IRE) (Orchestra)
J P Dodds Tom Batey

Placings:65540P (3325)
2002/03: 16⁸GF, 17⁵GF, 16⁵G, 16⁴S, 19⁰GS, 16⁸G,

	Starts	1st	2nd	3rd	Win & Pl
NH Flat	4	0	0	0	0
Hurdles	2	0	0	0	0
Career Total	6	0	0	0	0

Going: Sf: 0-1 GS: 0-1 Gd: 0-2 GF: - Fm: 0-2
Distance: 2m/2m3: 0-6 2m4-2m7: 0-0 3m+: 0-0
Track: LH: 0-3 RH: 0-3 Tight: 0-0 Gall: 0-0
Aids: Bl: 0-0 Vi: 0-0 Tstrap: 0-0
Best Rating: 93 11/02 Ayr 2m soft NHF

Raw Silk
111 **119+**
5-y-o b g Rudimentary (USA)-Misty Silks (Scottish Reel)
M Todhunter (Jonjo O Neill 24/8) The Cartmel Syndicate

Placings:0420020111-3440232 (1808)
2002/03: 16³G, 17⁴G, 20⁴S, 17⁹G, 16²G, 18³S, 16²G,

	Starts	1st	2nd	3rd	Win & Pl
Hurdles	7	0	2	2	3194
Career Total	17	3	4	2	12055

97	4/02 Newc	2m	F Hdl	FRM	£2079
94	4/02 Fknm	2m	D(0-110)HHdl	GD	£3410
93	3/02 Fknm	2m	G(0-90)HHdl	GD	£1857

Total win prize-money £7347

Going: Sf: 0-2 GS: 0-0 Gd: 0-5 GF: - Fm: 0-0
Distance: 2m/2m3: 0-6 2m4-2m7: 0-1 3m+: 0-0
Track: LH: 0-7 RH: 0-0 Tight: 0-3 Gall: 0-0
Aids: Bl: 0-4 Vi: 0-0 Tstrap: 0-1
Best Rating: 105 11/02 Hayd 2m good Hdl

Fair hurdler; recorded fourth career win at Cartmel in May 2003; best on decent ground; best at around two miles.

Ray River
(97h) (66h)
11-y-o b g Waki River (FR)-Mrs Feathers (Pyjama Hunt)
K G Wingrove M M Foulger

Placings:5104401/55643406/31650/04/000-0620FP3 (1377)
2002/03: 20⁰G, 19⁶G, 22²GF, 25⁰G, 23²GF, 20⁰G, 25³GF,

	Starts	1st	2nd	3rd	Win & Pl
Hurdles	4	0	1	0	564
Chases	3	0	0	1	554
Career Total	32	3	1	3	8002

84	2/98 Font	2m6f110y	G(0-95)HHdl	GD	£2170
86	4/96 Uttx	2m4f110y	G(0-95)HHdl	G-F	£2141
81	10/95 Worc	2m	G HHdl	GD	£2038

Total win prize-money £6350

Going: Sf: 0-0 GS: 0-0 Gd: 0-4 GF: - Fm: 0-3
Distance: 2m/2m3: 0-0 2m4-2m7: 0-4 3m+: 0-3
Track: LH: 0-5 RH: 0-2 Tight: 0-2 Gall: 0-0
Aids: Bl: 0-2 Vi: 0-0 Tstrap: 0-0
Best Rating: 88 12/95 Donc 2m110y gd-fm Hdl

Raybaan (IRE)
78 **52**
4-y-o b g Flying Spur (AUS)-Genetta (Green Desert (USA))
M H Tompkins Kenneth Macpherson

Placings:0   (4605)
2002/03: 17⁰G,

	Starts	1st	2nd	Win & Pl
Hurdles	1	0	0	0
Career Total	1	0	0	0

Going:	Sf: 0-0 GS: 0-0 Gd: 0-1 GF: - Fm: 0-0
Distance:	2m/2m3: 0-1 2m4-2m7: 0-0 3m+: 0-0
Track:	LH: 0-1 RH: 0-0 Tight: 0-0 Gall: 0-1
Aids:	Bl: 0-0 Vi: 0-0 Tstrap: 0-0
Best Rating:	52 4/03 Chel 2m1f good Hdl

Raybrook (IRE)

8-y-o ch g Moscow Society (USA)-Vesper Time (The Parson)
Mrs L B Normile   John Findlay

Placings:2/05-PP   (0373)
2002/03: 20PGF, 18PG,

	Starts	1st	2nd	3rd	Win & Pl
Hurdles	2	0	0	0	
Career Total	5	0	1	0	416

Going:	Sf: 0-0 GS: 0-0 Gd: 0-1 GF: - Fm: 0-0
Distance:	2m/2m3: 0-1 2m4-2m7: 0-1 3m+: 0-0
Track:	LH: 0-1 RH: 0-1 Tight: 0-1 Gall: 0-0
Aids:	Bl: 0-0 Vi: 0-0 Tstrap: 0-1
Best Rating:	96 7/00 Worc 2m good NHF

Rayware Boy (IRE)
99   80

7-y-o b g Scenic-Amata (USA) (Nodouble (USA))
D Shaw   Rayton Racing

Placings:0256F0/05/1051U3-06230R0   (4157)
2002/03: 16⁰G, 16⁶G, 17²GF, 16³GS, 16⁰G, 16⁶G, 17⁰G,

	Starts	1st	2nd	3rd	Win & Pl
Hurdles	7	0	1	1	1382
Career Total	21	2	2	2	7668
92	1/02	Donc	2m110y	F(0-100)HHdl	SFT £2754
82	12/01	Bang	2m1f	F(0-100)HHdl	G-S £2086

Total win prize-money £4841

Going:	Sf: 0-0 GS: 0-1 Gd: 0-5 GF: - Fm: 0-1
Distance:	2m/2m3: 0-7 2m4-2m7: 0-0 3m+: 0-0
Track:	LH: 0-6 RH: 0-1 Tight: 0-5 Gall: 0-0
Aids:	Bl: 0-1 Vi: 0-6 Tstrap: 0-0
Best Rating:	92 3/02 Donc 2m110y gd-sft Hdl

Modest handicap hurdler, acts on soft ground and wears a visor; has refused to race.

Razer Blade
93   (121h)120

8-y-o b g Teenoso (USA)-Sparkling Cinders (Netherkelly)
N J Henderson   The Liars Poker Partnership

Placings:1/12525/3-13F   (4569)
2002/03: 21¹S, 22³G, 24FG,

	Starts	1st	2nd	3rd	Win & Pl
Chases	3	1	0	1	6732
Career Total	10	3	2	2	18428
120	3/03	Winc	2m5f	D Ch	SFT £5642
129	11/00	Kemp	2m	D Hdl	SFT £3737
135	4/00	Ayr	2m	H NHF	GD £3071

Total win prize-money £12451

Going:	Sf: 1-1 GS: 0-0 Gd: 0-2 GF: - Fm: 0-0

Distance:	2m/2m3: 0-0 2m4-2m7: 1-2 3m+: 0-1
Track:	LH: 0-2 RH: 1-1 Tight: 0-1 Gall: 0-1
Aids:	Bl: 0-0 Vi: 0-0 Tstrap: 0-0
Best Rating:	140 2/01 Kemp 2m5f gd-sft Hdl

Winner of a bumper and over hurdles and now a fair novice chaser; probably a fortunate winner on his second start over fences and has not jumped with any fluency; stays three miles; handles good ground, but may be better with cut.

Razzmatazz (IRE)
77   57

9-y-o br g Camden Town-Sallys Wish (Proverb)
J Howard Johnson   George Thursby

Placings:00/00000550000/0   (4373)
2002/03: 17⁰G,

	Starts	1st	2nd	3rd	Win & Pl
Hurdles	1	0	0	0	
Career Total	11	0	0	0	

Going:	Sf: 0-0 GS: 0-0 Gd: 0-1 GF: - Fm: 0-0
Distance:	2m/2m3: 0-1 2m4-2m7: 0-0 3m+: 0-0
Track:	LH: 0-1 RH: 0-0 Tight: 0-1 Gall: 0-0
Aids:	Bl: 0-0 Vi: 0-0 Tstrap: 0-0
Best Rating:	92 12/00 Navn 2m heavy NHF

Reach The Clouds (IRE)
104(97h)   (95h)101

11-y-o b g Lord Americo-Dusky Stream (Paddy s Stream)
John R Upson   Middleham Park Racing Ix

Placings:0P0F63/1302325230/1325152/1323241/4F64432
20/522432F035-F42232   (4276)
2002/03: 20⁵G, 17⁶G, 17⁴GS, 20²S, 16²GS, 19³G, 16²G,

	Starts	1st	2nd	3rd	Win & Pl
Chases	7	0	3	1	4923
Career Total	55	5	15	11	52321
118	4/00	Chel	2m110y	C(0-135)HCh	SFT £10244
115	10/99	Bang	2m11f110yF(0-110)HCh		G-S £4045
109	4/99	Plum	2m2f	F(0-110)HCh	G-S £2932
107	11/98	Folk	2m	E(0-100)HCh	G-S £3436
82	10/97	Plum	2m1f	E(0-100)HHdl	GD £2511

Total win prize-money £23170

Going:	Sf: 0-1 GS: 0-2 Gd: 0-4 GF: - Fm: 0-0
Distance:	2m/2m3: 0-5 2m4-2m7: 0-2 3m+: 0-0
Track:	LH: 0-6 RH: 0-1 Tight: 0-3 Gall: 0-0
Aids:	Bl: 0-0 Vi: 0-0 Tstrap: 0-0
Best Rating:	118 5/01 Sthl 2m gd-fm Ch

Moderate chaser; suited by two miles or a bit further with some give in the ground.

Reachforthestars

7-y-o b m Royal Fountain-China s Way (USA) (Native Uproar (USA))
J Mackie   Fools Who Dream

Placings:00/P   (3830)
2002/03: 16PG,

	Starts	1st	2nd	3rd	Win & Pl
Hurdles	1	0	0	0	
Career Total	3	0	0	0	

Going:	Sf: 0-0 GS: 0-0 Gd: 0-1 GF: - Fm: 0-0

Distance:	2m/2m3: 0-1 2m4-2m7: 0-0 3m+: 0-0
Track:	LH: 0-1 RH: 0-0 Tight: 0-0 Gall: 0-0
Aids:	Bl: 0-0 Vi: 0-0 Tstrap: 0-0
Best Rating:	40 4/01 MRas 2m1f110y heavy NHF

Real Chief (IRE)
84f   83f

5-y-o b g Caerleon (USA)-Greek Air (IRE) (Ela-Mana-Mou)
Miss M E Rowland   Miss M E Rowland

Placings:00S   (0724)
2002/03: 17⁰G, 16⁰GS, 16⁵G,

	Starts	1st	2nd	3rd	Win & Pl
NH Flat	3	0	0	0	
Career Total	3	0	0	0	

Going:	Sf: 0-0 GS: 0-1 Gd: 0-2 GF: - Fm: 0-0
Distance:	2m/2m3: 0-3 2m4-2m7: 0-0 3m+: 0-0
Track:	LH: 0-2 RH: 0-1 Tight: 0-1 Gall: 0-0
Aids:	Bl: 0-0 Vi: 0-0 Tstrap: 0-0
Best Rating:	83 5/02 Hrfd 2m1f good NHF

Real Estate
92(101h)   (94h)88

9-y-o b g High Estate-Haitienne (FR) (Green Dancer (USA))
J S King   Robert Skillen

Placings:4122130/451560040/04FP0/06F221300-
60U42035   (4700)
2002/03: 16⁶G, 19⁰GS, 20UGS, 20⁴G, 20²G, 20⁰G, 21³G, 21⁵GF,

	Starts	1st	2nd	3rd	Win & Pl
Hurdles	4	0	0	1	846
Chases	4	0	1	0	1341
Career Total	38	4	5	3	30476
92	2/02	Ludl	2m4f	E(0-110)HCh	GD £4433
139	11/98	Asct	2m110y	B(0-145)HHdl	G-S £6716
125	2/98	Uttx	2m	D Hdl	SFT £3777
131	11/97	Asct	2m110y	B Hdl	G-S £4901

Total win prize-money £19850

Going:	Sf: 0-0 GS: 0-2 Gd: 0-5 GF: - Fm: 0-0
Distance:	2m/2m3: 0-1 2m4-2m7: 0-7 3m+: 0-0
Track:	LH: 0-2 RH: 0-6 Tight: 0-3 Gall: 0-2
Aids:	Bl: 0-0 Vi: 0-0 Tstrap: 0-0
Best Rating:	139 11/98 Asct 2m110y gd-sft Hdl

Plating-class hurdler/chaser; best over two and a half miles on good ground or softer.

Real Fire (IRE)
99(98h)   (73h)75

9-y-o b g Astronef-Golden Arum (Home Guard (USA))
R Johnson   Robert Johnson

Placings:331202P/4PPP040245P602400/0/0P/040510-
0P3040404304204   (4432)
2002/03: 16⁶G, 16⁸G, 27PG, 20³GF, 19⁰GF, 21⁴G, 21⁹G, 27⁴S,
21⁰GS, 16⁴GS, 21³S, 24⁰G, 21⁴HY, 16²S, 27⁰S, 16⁴G,

	Starts	1st	2nd	3rd	Win & Pl
Hurdles	12	0	1	1	1280
Chases	4	0	0	1	1251
Career Total	48	2	5	4	10137
73	10/01	Sedg	2m5f110yG(0-95)HHdl		GD £1862
77	9/97	Prth	2m110y	E Hhl	G-F £2558

Total win prize-money £4420

Going:	Sf: 0-5 GS: 0-2 Gd: 0-7 GF: - Fm: 0-2
Distance:	2m/2m3: 0-5 2m4-2m7: 0-7 3m+: 0-4
Track:	LH: 0-13 RH: 0-3 Tight: 0-11 Gall: 0-3
Aids:	Bl: 0-7 Vi: 0-2 Tstrap: 0-5

Best Rating: 82 10/97 Carl 2m1f   gd-fm   Hdl

Moderate hurdler/chaser.

Real Shady

93   **89**

6-y-o b g Bob s Return (IRE)-Madam Margeaux (IRE) (Ardross)
M W Easterby Lord Daresbury

Placings: 1/400-PP2   (4408)
2002/03: 19PG, 16PG, 16²G,

	Starts	1st	2nd	3rd	Win & Pl
Hurdles	3	0	1	0	1045
Career Total	7	1	1	0	2634

90 1/01 Newc 2m   H NHF   SFT   £1589
                        Total win prize-money £1589

Going: Sf: 0-0 GS: 0-0 Gd: 0-3 GF: - Fm: 0-0
Distance: 2m/2m3: 0-2 2m4-2m7: 0-1 3m+: 0-0
Track: LH: 0-2 RH: 0-1 Tight: 0-2 Gall: 0-0
Aids: Bl: 0-0 Vi: 0-0 Tstrap: 0-0
Best Rating: 107 11/01 Weth 2m   good   NHF

Plating-class hurdler; bumper winner; acts on soft ground; effective over two miles.

Real Sharp (IRE)

84   **39**

5-y-o br g Son Of Sharp Shot (IRE)-Lady By Chance (IRE) (Never Got A Chance)
S E H Sherwood The Perseverance Mob

Placings: 6040   (4527)
2002/03: 16PGS, 19PG, 194S, 20PG,

	Starts	1st	2nd	3rd	Win & Pl
NH Flat	1	0	0	0	0
Hurdles	3	0	0	0	269
Career Total	4	0	0	0	269

Going: Sf: 0-1 GS: 0-1 Gd: 0-2 GF: - Fm: 0-0
Distance: 2m/2m3: 0-1 2m4-2m7: 0-3 3m+: 0-0
Track: LH: 0-1 RH: 0-3 Tight: 0-0 Gall: 0-0
Aids: Bl: 0-0 Vi: 0-0 Tstrap: 0-0
Best Rating: 66 11/02 Ludl 2m   gd-sft   NHF

Moderate hurdler; has shown little in four starts under Rules.

Real Value (IRE)

12-y-o b g Matching Pair-Silent Verb (Proverb)
Mrs D M Grissell Cockerell Cowing Racing

Placings: 12F2/P05513/F20P-021F   (4615)
2002/03: 25PS, 26²GS, 23¹GS, 26PG,

	Starts	1st	2nd	3rd	Win & Pl
Chases	4	1	1	0	6510
Career Total	18	3	4	1	28993

108 3/03 Leic 2m7f110yH Ch   G-S £5486
131 2/01 Sand 3m110y B(0-140)HCh SFT £9948
121 3/00 Newb 3m   H Ch   SFT £1557
                        Total win prize-money £16992

Going: Sf: 0-1 GS: 1-2 Gs: 0-1 GF: - Fm: 0-0
Distance: 2m/2m3: 0-0 2m4-2m7: 0-0 3m+: 1-4
Track: LH: 0-1 RH: 1-2 Tight: 0-1 Gall: 0-1
Aids: Bl: 0-0 Vi: 0-0 Tstrap: 0-0
Best Rating: 136 3/00 Chel 3m2f110y gd-fm   Ch

Fair hunter chaser; thorough stayer; seems to handle any ground; can make mistakes.

Realslim Shady

71   **28**

5-y-o gr g Gran Alba (USA)-Shy Hiker (Netherkelly)
A C Whillans M J Norman

Placings: 0   (4749)
2002/03: 20PG,

	Starts	1st	2nd	3rd	Win & Pl
Hurdles	1	0	0	0	
Career Total	1	0	0	0	

Going: Sf: 0-0 GS: 0-0 Gd: 0-1 GF: - Fm: 0-0
Distance: 2m/2m3: 0-1 2m4-2m7: 0-1 3m+: 0-0
Track: LH: 0-0 RH: 0-1 Tight: 0-0 Gall: 0-0
Aids: Bl: 0-0 Vi: 0-0 Tstrap: 0-0
Best Rating: 28 4/03 Prth 2m4f110y good   Hdl

Reasonable Reserve (IRE)

107   **101+**

6-y-o ch g Fourstars Allstar (USA)-Alice O Malley (The Parson)
C F Swan Seamus Mannion

Placings: 0006-403   (1015)
2002/03: 204YS, 20PY, 243G,

	Starts	1st	2nd	3rd	Win & Pl
NH Flat	2	0	0	0	196
Hurdles	1	0	0	1	623
Career Total	7	0	0	1	819

Going: Sf: 0-0 GS: 0-0 Gd: 0-1 GF: - Fm: 0-0
Distance: 2m/2m3: 0-0 2m4-2m7: 0-2 3m+: 0-1
Track: LH: 0-0 RH: 0-1 Tight: 0-0 Gall: 0-0
Aids: Bl: 0-1 Vi: 0-0 Tstrap: 0-0
Best Rating: 91 4/02 Clon 2m4f   gd-yld   NHF

Modest novice hurdler when trained by Charlie Swan in Ireland; caused 40/1 shock when rallying to beat two penalised rivals in Worcester 3m novice hurdle June 2003; showed that that was no fluke when completing a hat-trick over the same course and distance the following month; likes fast ground; stays well.

Reasoning

5-y-o ch m Selkirk (USA)-Attribute (Warning)
B S Rothwell Cleaning And Paper Disposables Ltd

Placings: P   (1568)
2002/03: 19PG,

	Starts	1st	2nd	3rd	Win & Pl
Hurdles	1	0	0	0	
Career Total	1	0	0	0	

Going: Sf: 0-0 GS: 0-0 Gd: 0-1 GF: - Fm: 0-0
Distance: 2m/2m3: 0-0 2m4-2m7: 0-1 3m+: 0-0
Track: LH: 0-0 RH: 0-0 Tight: 0-1 Gall: 0-0
Aids: Bl: 0-0 Vi: 0-0 Tstrap: 0-0
Best Rating: 0 10/02 MRas 2m3f110y good   Hdl

Rebel Clown

5-y-o gr g King s Signet (USA)-Castle Cary (Castle Keep)
N J Hawke Mrs D A Wetherall

Placings: 00   (0737)
2002/03: 17PG, 17PGF,

	Starts	1st	2nd	3rd	Win & Pl
NH Flat	2	0	0	0	
Career Total	2	0	0	0	

Going: Sf: 0-0 GS: 0-0 Gd: 0-1 GF: - Fm: 0-1
Distance: 2m/2m3: 0-2 2m4-2m7: 0-0 3m+: 0-0
Track: LH: 0-2 RH: 0-0 Tight: 0-2 Gall: 0-0
Aids: Bl: 0-0 Vi: 0-0 Tstrap: 0-0
Best Rating: 0 7/02 NAbb 2m1f   gd-fm   NHF

Rebel Raider (IRE)

100   **93**

4-y-o b g Mujadil (USA)-Emily s Pride (Shirley Heights)
B N Pollock (Patrick J Flynn 31/10) S G B Morrison

Placings: C   (4539)
2002/03: 16CG,

	Starts	1st	2nd	3rd	Win & Pl
Hurdles	1	0	0	0	
Career Total	1	0	0	0	

Going: Sf: 0-0 GS: 0-0 Gd: 0-1 GF: - Fm: 0-0
Distance: 2m/2m3: 0-1 2m4-2m7: 0-0 3m+: 0-0
Track: LH: 0-0 RH: 0-1 Tight: 0-0 Gall: 0-0
Aids: Bl: 0-0 Vi: 0-0 Tstrap: 0-0
Best Rating: 0 4/03 Ludl 2m   good   Hdl

Moderate hurdler; clearly second best on all three outings since being carried out on his British debut.

Rebel Reprieve (IRE)

7-y-o b g Rich Rebel (USA)-Reprieved Run (Deep Run)
S A Brookshaw Mrs John Fearnall

Placings: P   (0491)
2002/03: 24PHY,

	Starts	1st	2nd	3rd	Win & Pl
Chases	1	0	0	0	
Career Total	1	0	0	0	

Going: Sf: 0-1 GS: 0-0 Gd: 0-0 GF: - Fm: 0-0
Distance: 2m/2m3: 0-0 2m4-2m7: 0-0 3m+: 0-1
Track: LH: 0-1 RH: 0-0 Tight: 0-0 Gall: 0-0
Aids: Bl: 0-0 Vi: 0-0 Tstrap: 0-0
Best Rating:

Rebel's Gift

88   **56**

10-y-o b g Genuine Gift (CAN)-Princess Veronica (Rebel Prince)
F P Murtagh S R Bainbridge & Mrs G Bainbridge

Placings: 0P5/4FPP00104/6010F60/3303PP-0PP5 (4434)
2002/03: 22PGF, 20PHY, 20PS, 20PG,

	Starts	1st	2nd	3rd	Win & Pl
Hurdles	4	0	0	0	0
Career Total	29	2	0	3	5294

78 10/00 Kels 2m6f110yF(0-105)HHdl GD £2786
78 2/00 Catt 2m3f   G(0-90)HHdl   GD £1617
                        Total win prize-money £4403

Going: Sf: 0-2 GS: 0-0 Gd: 0-1 GF: - Fm: 0-1
Distance: 2m/2m3: 0-0 2m4-2m7: 0-0 3m+: 0-0

Track: LH: 0-4 RH: 0-0 Tight: 0-1 Gall: 0-2
Aids: Bl: 0-0 Vi: 0-0 Tstrap: 0-0
Best Rating: 78 9/01 Sedg 2m5f110y good Hdl

Plating-class hurdler. Best form around two miles six furlongs but is out of form at present..

Recess (IRE)
105   106

7-y-o b/br g Approach The Bench (IRE)-Storms-Of-Life (Strong Gale)
J T Gorman   Mrs S Andrews

Placings:000P46-54400450FF   (4500a)
2002/03: 16⁶G, 16⁴S, 16⁴SH, 16⁰S, 16⁰YS, 16⁴GS, 18⁵HY, 16⁰S, 16⁴S, 16⁷GY,

	Starts	1st	2nd	3rd	Win & Pl
NH Flat	3	0	0	0	466
Hurdles	7	0	0	0	900
Career Total	16	0	0	0	1636

Going: Sf: 0-5 GS: 0-1 Gd: 0-1 GF: - Fm: 0-0
Distance: 2m/2m3: 0-10 2m4-2m7: 0-0 3m+: 0-0
Track: LH: 0-4 RH: 0-2 Tight: 0-0 Gall: 0-0
Aids: Bl: 0-7 Vi: 0-0 Tstrap: 0-0
Best Rating: 106 11/02 Chel 2m110y gd-sft Hdl

Very modest hurdles form in Ireland. Did not do too badly in a novice handicap at Cheltenham in November 2002.

Red Adhere
89(57c)   (52c)42

8-y-o b g Insan (USA)-By The Lake (Tyrant (USA))
N B Mason   Mrs D B Mason

Placings:P/000P5-   (0006)
2002/03: 20⁵G,

	Starts	1st	2nd	3rd	Win & Pl
Hurdles	1	0	0	0	0
Career Total	6	0	0	0	0

Going: Sf: 0-0 GS: 0-0 Gd: 0-1 GF: - Fm: 0-0
Distance: 2m/2m3: 0-0 2m4-2m7: 0-1 3m+: 0-0
Track: LH: 0-1 RH: 0-0 Tight: 0-0 Gall: 0-1
Aids: Bl: 0-1 Vi: 0-0 Tstrap: 0-0
Best Rating: 42 4/02 Newc 2m4f good Hdl

Modest dual-purpose performer.

Red Afgem
84f   63f

6-y-o ch m Afzal-Preacher s Gem (The Parson)
Mrs S M Johnson   Mrs P A Wallis

Placings:030   (0560)
2002/03: 16⁰GF, 16³GS, 17⁰GF,

	Starts	1st	2nd	3rd	Win & Pl
NH Flat	3	0	0	1	240
Career Total	3	0	0	1	240

Going: Sf: 0-0 GS: 0-1 Gd: 0-0 GF: - Fm: 0-0
Distance: 2m/2m3: 0-3 2m4-2m7: 0-0 3m+: 0-0
Track: LH: 0-2 RH: 0-1 Tight: 0-1 Gall: 0-0
Aids: Bl: 0-0 Vi: 0-0 Tstrap: 0-0
Best Rating: 63 6/02 Hrfd 2m1f gd-fm NHF

Well beaten on fast ground on bumper debut but improved performance on good to soft when third at Southwell in spring 2002.

Red Alert Man (IRE)
97(79h)   (77h)76

7-y-o ch g Sharp Charter-Tukurua (Noalto)
Mrs L Williamson   Halewood International Ltd

Placings:006/F0F0P-44PP563U1   (4705)
2002/03: 16⁴S, 16⁴S, 16⁰G, 16⁰HY, 16⁵S, 16⁶GS, 20³S, 17⁰G, 21³G,

	Starts	1st	2nd	3rd	Win & Pl
Chases	9	1	0	1	5504
Career Total	17	1	0	1	5504
76 4/03 Uttx	2m5f	E Ch		GD	£4389
		Total win prize-money			£4389

Going: Sf: 0-5 GS: 0-1 Gd: 1-3 GF: - Fm: 0-0
Distance: 2m/2m3: 0-7 2m4-2m7: 1-2 3m+: 0-0
Track: LH: 1-5 RH: 0-4 Tight: 0-4 Gall: 0-0
Aids: Bl: 1-5 Vi: 0-0 Tstrap: 0-0
Best Rating: 79 3/01 Hayd 2m heavy NHF

Selling-class chaser; stays two and a half miles; acts well on good ground.

Red And Dangerous

8-y-o b g Afzal-Flori Wonder (Floriana)
Mrs D A Hamer   Mrs J E Harries

Placings:0P-PP   (1195)
2002/03: 20⁰GF, 19⁰GF,

	Starts	1st	2nd	3rd	Win & Pl
Hurdles	2	0	0	0	0
Career Total	4	0	0	0	0

Going: Sf: 0-0 GS: 0-0 Gd: 0-0 GF: - Fm: 0-2
Distance: 2m/2m3: 0-0 2m4-2m7: 0-2 3m+: 0-0
Track: LH: 0-1 RH: 0-1 Tight: 0-0 Gall: 0-0
Aids: Bl: 0-0 Vi: 0-0 Tstrap: 0-0
Best Rating: 0 9/02 Hrfd 2m3f110y gd-fm Hdl

Red Ark
108   137

10-y-o ch g Gunner B-Minim (Rymer)
R C Guest (N B Mason 14/2)   Mrs D B Mason

Placings:00P/560641132112121B/12P14202F2/4P501100U-0606P   (4479)
2002/03: 20⁰GS, 16⁶S, 24⁰G, 16⁶G, 36⁰G,

	Starts	1st	2nd	3rd	Win & Pl
Chases	5	0	0	0	1441
Career Total	43	10	7	1	90624
143 2/02 Sand	2m	C(0-135)HCh		SFT	£10140
134 1/02 Donc	2m110y	B(0-150)HCh		SFT	£10344
143 11/00 Newb	2m4f	B(0-145)HCh		SFT	£15648
115 9/00 MRas	2m3f110y	E(0-115)HHdl		G-F	£2808
140 4/00 Aint	2m4f	C HCh		GD	£11407
129 3/00 Sand	2m	C Ch		GD	£7403
119 1/00 Donc	2m110y	E(0-105)HCh		GD	£3282
115 1/00 Leic	2m7f110yD(0-110)HCh			GD	£5980
109 11/99 Catt	2m	F(0-100)HHdl		G-F	£2705
104 11/99 Newc	2m4f	F(0-90)HHdl		GD	£2305
		Total win prize-money			£72026

Going: Sf: 0-1 GS: 0-1 Gd: 0-3 GF: - Fm: 0-0
Distance: 2m/2m3: 0-2 2m4-2m7: 0-1 3m+: 0-2
Track: LH: 0-3 RH: 0-2 Tight: 0-1 Gall: 0-2
Aids: Bl: 0-0 Vi: 0-0 Tstrap: 0-3
Best Rating: 143 2/02 Sand 2m soft Ch

Useful chaser; best over two miles, but does stay further; suited by soft ground; usually wears a tongue tie, and has also been tried in cheekpieces.

Red Blazer
110   141d

12-y-o ch g Bustino-Klewraye (Lord Gayle (USA))
Miss H C Knight   Miss H Knight

Placings:120/3/112/131P5/2F52/F2/21R11-1235   (3728)
2002/03: 20¹GS, 16²G, 21³GS, 16⁶G,

	Starts	1st	2nd	3rd	Win & Pl
Chases	4	1	1	1	15776
Career Total	27	9	7	3	72607
141 11/02 Hntg	2m4f110yC(0-130)HCh		G-S	£8073
134 2/02 Hntg	2m4f110yD Ch		G-S	£4143
141 1/02 Kemp	2m	C Ch	GD	£6890
139 11/01 Kemp	2m	D Ch	GD	£4095
144 2/98 Hayd	2m	B Hdl	GD	£10211
145 12/97 Uttx	2m4f110yB(0-145)HHdl		G-S	£4769
133 1/97 Leic	2m4f110y Hdl		G-S	£3548
114 12/96 Towc	2m	E Hdl	HVY	£2897
115 2/95 Asct	2m110y H NHF		HVY	£2620
		Total win prize-money			£47250

Going: Sf: 0-0 GS: 1-2 Gd: 0-2 GF: - Fm: 0-0
Distance: 2m/2m3: 0-2 2m4-2m7: 1-2 3m+: 0-0
Track: LH: 0-1 RH: 1-3 Tight: 0-0 Gall: 1-2
Aids: Bl: 0-0 Vi: 0-0 Tstrap: 0-0
Best Rating: 148 4/98 Asct 3m gd-sft Hdl

Very useful handicap chaser; acts on good, soft and heavy ground; stays two and a half miles; jumps well.

Red Blooded (IRE)
94(48h)   (10h)78

6-y-o b g River Falls-Volkova (Green Desert (USA))
Mrs L C Jewell   J S S Hollins

Placings:0P5   (3925)
2002/03: 16⁶S, 20⁰GS, 16⁵G,

	Starts	1st	2nd	3rd	Win & Pl
Hurdles	1	0	0	0	0
Chases	1	0	0	0	0
Career Total	3	0	0	0	0

Going: Sf: 0-1 GS: 0-1 Gd: 0-1 GF: - Fm: 0-0
Distance: 2m/2m3: 0-2 2m4-2m7: 0-1 3m+: 0-0
Track: LH: 0-1 RH: 0-1 Tight: 0-1 Gall: 0-1
Aids: Bl: 0-0 Vi: 0-0 Tstrap: 0-2
Best Rating: 78 3/03 Hntg 2m110y good Ch

Red Brae

6-y-o b g Rakaposhi King-Sayshar (Saylar)
Jonjo O Neill   C D Carr

Placings:5/04-P   (2512)
2002/03: 20⁰G,

	Starts	1st	2nd	3rd	Win & Pl
Hurdles	1	0	0	0	0
Career Total	4	0	0	0	0

Going: Sf: 0-0 GS: 0-0 Gd: 0-1 GF: - Fm: 0-0
Distance: 2m/2m3: 0-0 2m4-2m7: 0-1 3m+: 0-0
Track: LH: 0-1 RH: 0-0 Tight: 0-0 Gall: 0-0
Aids: Bl: 0-1 Vi: 0-0 Tstrap: 0-0
Best Rating: 100 3/02 Chep 2m110y soft NHF

Red Brook Lad

8-y-o ch g Nomadic Way (USA)-Silently Yours (USA) (Silent Screen (USA))

C St V Fox C St V Fox

Placings: P053060/UF2   (4390)
2002/03: 22^UG, 25^FGS, 19²F,

	Starts	1st	2nd	3rd	Win & Pl
Chases	3	0	1	0	1136
Career Total	10	0	1	1	1446

Going:	Sf: 0-0 GS: 0-1 Gd: 0-1 GF: - Fm: 0-1
Distance:	2m/2m3: 0-0 2m4-2m7: 0-0 3m+: 0-0
Track:	LH: 0-0 RH: 0-3 Tight: 0-0 Gall: 0-0
Aids:	Bl: 0-0 Vi: 0-0 Tstrap: 0-0
Best Rating:	100 3/03 Extr 2m3f110y firm Ch

Fair hunter chaser; prolific winning pointer; stays three miles one; unlikely to stay further; suited by a sound surface.

Red Canyon (IRE)
112   98

6-y-o b g Zieten (USA)-Bayazida (Bustino)
A G Hobbs (B I Case 30/5) Miss Jayne Brace & Gwyn Brace

Placings: 0/04000435P-001114425   (1640)
2002/03: 26^PG, 20^UG, 21^UG, 20¹GF, 22¹GF, 22¹GF, 22⁴GF, 24⁴G, 24²F, 21⁵G,

	Starts	1st	2nd	3rd	Win & Pl
Hurdles	10	3	1	1	10275
Career Total	19	3	1	1	10704
98 8/02 NAbb 2m6f	E(0-110)HHdl		G-F	£2884	
95 7/02 Strf 2m6f110y	E(0-110)HHdl		G-F	£3209	
79 6/02 Worc 2m4f	E(0-105)HHdl		G-F	£2653	

Total win prize-money £8747

Going:	Sf: 0-0 GS: 0-0 Gd: 0-5 GF: - Fm: 3-5
Distance:	2m/2m3: 0-0 **2m4-2m7: 3-7** 3m+: 0-3
Track:	LH: 3-6 RH: 0-3 Tight: 2-3 Gall: 0-1
Aids:	Bl: 0-1 Vi: 0-0 Tstrap: 0-0
Best Rating:	98 10/02 Ludl 3m firm Hdl

Middle-distance Flat winner and moderate hurdler; stays well; acts on fast ground.

Red Dancer (FR)
107   105

7-y-o b g Red Paradise-Majestic Dancer (FR) (What A Guest)
C Olehla (T Civel 2/6) Staj Wrbna

Placings: F00P42F3P40F0/26P224520/01434P12-21U2026   (1940)
2002/03: 21²G, 25¹G, 25^UF, 19²G, 25⁹G, 26⁹HY, 31⁶GS,

	Starts	1st	2nd	3rd	Win & Pl
Chases	7	1	3	0	11767
Career Total	37	3	9	2	37147
6/02 Sluz 3m1f	Ch	GD	£2899	
10/01 Brat 3m1f	Ch	G-S	£813	
7/01 Brat 3m3f110y	Ch	GD	£1264	

Total win prize-money £4976

Going:	Sf: 0-1 GS: 0-1 Gd: 1-4 GF: - Fm: 0-1
Distance:	2m/2m3: 0-0 2m4-2m7: 0-2 **3m+: 1-5**
Track:	LH: 0-2 RH: 0-1 Tight: 0-0 Gall: 0-0
Aids:	Bl: 0-0 Vi: 0-0 Tstrap: 0-0
Best Rating:	108 11/02 Chel 3m7f gd-sft Ch

Czech-trained chaser. Successful over three miles one in Poland in June.

Red Diamond

4-y-o br g Mind Games-Sandicroft Jewel (Grey Desire)

Miss K M George Stableline

Placings: P   (1756)
2002/03: 16^PG,

	Starts	1st	2nd	3rd	Win & Pl
Hurdles	1	0	0	0	
Career Total	1	0	0	0	

Going:	Sf: 0-0 GS: 0-0 Gd: 0-1 GF: - Fm: 0-0
Distance:	2m/2m3: 0-1 2m4-2m7: 0-0 3m+: 0-0
Track:	LH: 0-1 RH: 0-0 Tight: 0-0 Gall: 0-0
Aids:	Bl: 0-0 Vi: 0-0 Tstrap: 0-0
Best Rating:	0 11/02 Wwck 2m good Hdl

Red Emperor
96   99

9-y-o b g Emperor Fountain-Golden Curd (FR) (Nice Havrais (USA))
R C Guest (N B Mason 5/12) N B Mason

Placings: 3043535652611523/0060U1436U05/512632P156-3531P50   (4165)
2002/03: 24⁶G, 26³G, 26⁵S, 28³S, 24¹GS, 28^PS, 24⁵S, 24⁰GS,

	Starts	1st	2nd	3rd	Win & Pl
Chases	8	1	0	2	4499
Career Total	45	6	4	8	25577
99 11/02 Newc 3m	F(0-90)HCh	G-S	£3292	
98 3/02 Newc 3m	F(0-100)HCh	HVY	£2989	
99 11/01 Newc 3m	F(0-90)HCh	G-S	£2597	
94 11/00 Newc 3m	F(0-90)HCh	G-S	£2457	
93 2/00 Carl 2m4f110y	F(0-110)HCh	HVY	£3526	
81 1/00 Sthl 3m110y	F(0-90)HCh	G-S	£2643	

Total win prize-money £17505

Going:	Sf: 0-4 GS: 1-2 Gd: 0-2 GF: - Fm: 0-0
Distance:	2m/2m3: 0-0 2m4-2m7: 0-0 **3m+: 1-8**
Track:	LH: 1-5 RH: 0-3 Tight: 0-2 Gall: 1-3
Aids:	Bl: 1-8 Vi: 0-0 Tstrap: 1-6
Best Rating:	99 11/02 Newc 3m gd-sft Ch

Fair handicapper chaser; stays three miles plus; effective on soft ground; likes Newcastle; usually wears blinkers and tongue tie.

Red Ensign
69f   73f

6-y-o ch g Lancastrian-Medway Queen (Pitpan)
Mrs L C Jewell Mrs S Stanier

Placings: 00   (4431)
2002/03: 18⁰S, 18⁰GF,

	Starts	1st	2nd	3rd	Win & Pl
NH Flat	2	0	0	0	
Career Total	2	0	0	0	

Going:	Sf: 0-1 GS: 0-0 Gd: 0-0 GF: - Fm: 0-0
Distance:	2m/2m3: 0-2 2m4-2m7: 0-0 3m+: 0-0
Track:	LH: 0-2 RH: 0-0 Tight: 0-0 Gall: 0-0
Aids:	Bl: 0-0 Vi: 0-0 Tstrap: 0-0
Best Rating:	73 3/03 Plum 2m2f gd-fm NHF

Red Flyer (IRE)
98   98

4-y-o br g Catrail (USA)-Marostica (ITY) (Stone)
P C Haslam Mrs C Barclay

Placings: 122FP   (4573)
2002/03: 16¹GS, 16²GS, 16²G, 18^FG, 16^PGF,

	Starts	1st	2nd	3rd	Win & Pl
Hurdles	5	1	2	0	6863

Career Total	5	1	2	0	6863
98 11/02 Newc 2m	D Hdl	G-S	£4173	

Total win prize-money £4173

Going:	Sf: 0-0 GS: 1-2 Gd: 0-2 GF: - Fm: 0-1
Distance:	**2m/2m3: 1-5** 2m4-2m7: 0-0 3m+: 0-0
Track:	LH: 1-4 RH: 0-1 Tight: 0-4 Gall: 1-1
Aids:	Bl: 0-0 Vi: 0-0 Tstrap: 0-0
Best Rating:	98 3/03 Kels 2m2f good Hdl

Modest novice hurdler; best over two miles and acts on any ground.

Red Forest (IRE)

4-y-o b g Charnwood Forest (IRE)-High Atlas (Shirley Heights)
W Clay (B W Hills 24/7) P Riley

Placings: PP   (1205)
2002/03: 16^PGF, 16^PG,

	Starts	1st	2nd	3rd	Win & Pl
Hurdles	2	0	0	0	
Career Total	2	0	0	0	

Going:	Sf: 0-0 GS: 0-0 Gd: 0-1 GF: - Fm: 0-1
Distance:	2m/2m3: 0-2 2m4-2m7: 0-0 3m+: 0-0
Track:	LH: 0-2 RH: 0-0 Tight: 0-1 Gall: 0-0
Aids:	Bl: 0-0 Vi: 0-0 Tstrap: 0-0
Best Rating:	0 9/02 Uttx 2m good Hdl

Red Gauntlet

10-y-o b g Wonderful Surprise-Border Minstrel (Menelek)
Mrs A C Hamilton (B Mactaggart 26/5) Mrs M A Bowie

Placings: F   (4309)
2002/03: 25^FG,

	Starts	1st	2nd	3rd	Win & Pl
Chases	1	0	0	0	
Career Total	1	0	0	0	

Going:	Sf: 0-0 GS: 0-0 Gd: 0-1 GF: - Fm: 0-0
Distance:	2m/2m3: 0-0 2m4-2m7: 0-0 3m+: 0-1
Track:	LH: 0-1 RH: 0-0 Tight: 0-1 Gall: 0-0
Aids:	Bl: 0-0 Vi: 0-0 Tstrap: 0-0
Best Rating:	90 3/03 Kels 3m1f good Ch

Red Genie
95   75

5-y-o ch g Primitive Rising (USA)-Marsden Rock (Tina s Pet)
R C Guest (N B Mason 25/10) N B Mason

Placings: 3404   (4411)
2002/03: 16³G, 17⁴GF, 16⁰GS, 16⁴G,

	Starts	1st	2nd	3rd	Win & Pl
NH Flat	4	0	0	1	261
Career Total	4	0	0	1	261

Going:	Sf: 0-0 GS: 0-0 Gd: 0-1 GF: - Fm: 0-2
Distance:	2m/2m3: 0-4 2m4-2m7: 0-0 3m+: 0-0
Track:	LH: 0-3 RH: 0-1 Tight: 0-1 Gall: 0-0
Aids:	Bl: 0-0 Vi: 0-0 Tstrap: 0-0
Best Rating:	85 3/03 Hexm 2m110y good NHF

Moderate form in bumpers; only plating-class over hurdles.

Red Gold

90

9-y-o ch g Sula Bula-Ruby Celebration (New Member)
Andrew Turnell Mrs C C Williams

Placings:0563PF/0F4-P (3916)
2002/03: 24PS,

	Starts	1st	2nd	3rd	Win & Pl
Chases	1	0	0	0	
Career Total	10	0	0	1	673

Going:	Sf: 0-1 GS: 0-0 Gd: 0-0 GF: - Fm: 0-0
Distance:	2m/2m3: 0-0 2m4-2m7: 0-0 3m+: 0-1
Track:	LH: 0-0 RH: 0-1 Tight: 0-0 Gall: 0-0
Aids:	Bl: 0-0 Vi: 0-0 Tstrap: 0-0
Best Rating:	104 1/01 Leic 2m4f110y soft Ch

Red Guard

105(96h) (107+h)**124**

9-y-o ch g Soviet Star (USA)-Zinzara (USA) (Stagedoor Johnny)
J T Gifford L A Hooper

Placings:4552/062140/11/0410P/622234F1-2F5P331F2 (4682)
2002/03: 202GF, 18FG, 19SG, 20PGS, 253GS, 223G, 241S, 24FG, 242GF,

	Starts	1st	2nd	3rd	Win & Pl
Hurdles	2	0	0	0	0
Chases	7	1	2	2	10978
Career Total	34	6	7	3	52031
124	1/03	Hntg	3m	D(0-120)HCh	SFT	£5950
109	4/02	Font	2m6f	C Ch	G-F	£7345
138	1/01	Asct	2m110y	B HHdl	SFT	£10185
133	10/99	Weth	2m	C(0-135)HHdl	G-F	£5018
120	10/99	Font	2m2f110yC(0-135)HHdl	GD	£4719
124	12/98	Sand	2m110y	D(0-115)HHdl	GD	£4924

Total win prize-money £38145

Going:	Sf: 1-1 GS: 0-2 Gd: 0-4 GF: - Fm: 0-2
Distance:	2m/2m3: 0-2 2m4-2m7: 0-0 3m+: 1-4
Track:	LH: 0-5 RH: 1-3 Tight: 0-3 Gall: 1-5
Aids:	Bl: 0-0 Vi: 0-0 Tstrap: 0-0
Best Rating:	138 1/01 Asct 2m110y soft Hdl

Fair chaser; acts on most types of ground; effective at up to three miles; has not always convinced in a finish and needs to come late; has worn sheepskin cheekpieces and blinkers

Red Halo

104 **110**

4-y-o b c Be My Guest (USA)-Pray (IRE) (Priolo (USA))
M C Pipe (R Hannon 13/7) Terry Neill

Placings:111P0 (4605)
2002/03: 171S, 161GS, 171GF, 16PG, 170GS,

	Starts	1st	2nd	3rd	Win & Pl
Hurdles	5	3	0	0	11876
Career Total	5	3	0	0	11876
110	8/02	Bang	2m1f	E Hdl	G-F	£3672
95	8/02	Strf	2m110y	D Hdl	G-S	£5053
110	8/02	Bang	2m1f	E Hdl	SFT	£3150

Total win prize-money £11877

Going:	Sf: 1-1 GS: 1-1 Gd: 0-2 GF: - Fm: 1-1
Distance:	2m/2m3: 3-5 2m4-2m7: 0-0 3m+: 0-0
Track:	LH: 3-5 RH: 0-0 Tight: 3-4 Gall: 0-1
Aids:	Bl: 0-0 Vi: 0-0 Tstrap: 0-0
Best Rating:	110 8/02 Bang 2m1f gd-fm Hdl

Completed an early-season hat-trick, odds-on each time;

---

pulled-up twice since due to poor jumping; best at around two miles; acts on soft and fast ground.

Red Hare (NZ)

103(98h)

9-y-o ch g Famous Star-Mutual Belle (NZ) (Western Bay (NZ))
Miss K Marks (N J Henderson 30/10) Nick Shutts

Placings:420/01PF6146-F3261PP2 (4705)
2002/03: 22FGF, 263GF, 23FG, 25RG, 241GF, 25PG, 28PG, 212G,

	Starts	1st	2nd	3rd	Win & Pl
Hurdles	1	0	0	0	0
Chases	7	1	2	1	7839
Career Total	19	3	3	1	16908
103	10/02	Tntn	3m	E(0-105)HCh	G-F	£4712
96	11/01	Kemp	3m110y	D(0-120)HHdl	GD	£5352
95	6/01	Fknm	2m4f	E Hdl	G-F	£2891

Total win prize-money £12957

Going:	Sf: 0-0 GS: 0-0 Gd: 0-5 GF: - Fm: 1-3
Distance:	2m/2m3: 0-0 2m4-2m7: 0-2 3m+: 1-6
Track:	LH: 0-4 RH: 1-3 Tight: 1-2 Gall: 0-0
Aids:	Bl: 0-0 Vi: 0-0 Tstrap: 0-0
Best Rating:	105 11/00 Wrwck 2m soft Hdl

Plating-class chaser; stays three miles; acts on decent ground.

Red Hot Indian (IRE)

104(99h) (100h)**88**

10-y-o b g Little Bighorn-Pepper Cannister (Lord Gayle (USA))
N B Mason Mrs D B Mason

Placings:1/43235/43213/P24/431-6001F644 (1737)
2002/03: 186GS, 196GS, 209GS, 211G, 17FG, 176G, 204G, 204GS,

	Starts	1st	2nd	3rd	Win & Pl
Hurdles	2	0	0	0	0
Chases	6	1	0	0	5057
Career Total	25	4	3	5	19218
88	8/02	Ctml	2m5f110yE(0-105)HCh	GD	£4306
100	4/02	MRas	2m1f110yG	HD	G-F	£1736
111	2/00	Hntg	2m4f110yD(0-120)HHdl	SFT	£5421
106	4/98	Prth	2m110y H NHF	HVY	£2066

Total win prize-money £13529

Going:	Sf: 0-0 GS: 0-4 Gd: 1-4 GF: - Fm: 0-0
Distance:	2m/2m3: 0-4 2m4-2m7: 1-4 3m+: 0-0
Track:	LH: 1-7 RH: 0-1 Tight: 1-2 Gall: 0-0
Aids:	Bl: 1-7 Vi: 0-0 Tstrap: 1-5
Best Rating:	111 3/00 Newb 2m5f soft Hdl

Modest hunter chase form, and successful in a selling hurdle at Easter 2002. Looked reluctant when opening his account over fences in a handicap at Cartmel in August.

Red Hot Robbie

102 **81**

10-y-o ch g Gildoran-Quarry Machine (Laurence O)
Mrs N S Sharpe J V C Davenport

Placings:0/P63P (2349)
2002/03: 24PGS, 206G, 223G, 24PGS,

	Starts	1st	2nd	3rd	Win & Pl
Hurdles	4	0	0	1	636
Career Total	5	0	0	1	636

Going:	Sf: 0-0 GS: 0-1 Gd: 0-3 GF: - Fm: 0-0
Distance:	2m/2m3: 0-0 2m4-2m7: 0-2 3m+: 0-2
Track:	LH: 0-3 RH: 0-0 Tight: 0-3 Gall: 0-0

Aids:	Bl: 0-0 Vi: 0-0 Tstrap: 0-0
Best Rating:	81 10/02 Strf 2m6f110y good Hdl

Best effort so far when third in a modest 22 furlong maiden hurdle at Stratford October 2002.

Red Hustler (IRE)

103(84h) (47h)**88+**

7-y-o ch g Husyan (USA)-Isoldes Tower (Balliol)
C Grant W Raw

Placings:056-5F231 (4712)
2002/03: 205HY, 16FG, 162S, 163G, 161GF,

	Starts	1st	2nd	3rd	Win & Pl
Chases	5	1	1	1	6641
Career Total	8	1	1	1	6641
88	4/03	Weth	2m	E Ch	G-F	£4354

Total win prize-money £4354

Going:	Sf: 0-2 GS: 0-0 Gd: 0-0 GF: - Fm: 1-1
Distance:	2m/2m3: 1-4 2m4-2m7: 0-1 3m+: 0-0
Track:	LH: 1-4 RH: 0-1 Tight: 0-2 Gall: 0-1
Aids:	Bl: 0-0 Vi: 0-0 Tstrap: 0-0
Best Rating:	88 4/03 Weth 2m gd-fm Ch

Moderate chaser; off the mark in weak four-runner event at Wetherby in April 2003.

Red Jupiter

(70h) (9h)

6-y-o b g Jupiter Island-Glen Dancer (Furry Glen)
R C Guest (N B Mason 13/11) N B Mason

Placings:0-6P066P (4356)
2002/03: 206G, 20PG, 210G, 20PGS, 226S, 20PGF,

	Starts	1st	2nd	3rd	Win & Pl
Hurdles	5	0	0	0	0
Chases	1	0	0	0	0
Career Total	7	0	0	0	0

Going:	Sf: 0-1 GS: 0-1 Gd: 0-3 GF: - Fm: 0-1
Distance:	2m/2m3: 0-0 2m4-2m7: 0-6 3m+: 0-0
Track:	LH: 0-5 RH: 0-1 Tight: 0-3 Gall: 0-0
Aids:	Bl: 0-1 Vi: 0-0 Tstrap: 0-0
Best Rating:	78 4/02 Weth 2m gd-fm NHF

Red Knight (IRE)

100f

5-y-o b/br g Goldmark (USA)-Dafwan (Nashwan (USA))
C Roche Michael A O Riordan

Placings:10 (4481)
2002/03: 181Y, 170G,

	Starts	1st	2nd	3rd	Win & Pl
NH Flat	2	1	0	0	3584
Career Total	2	1	0	0	3584
100	3/03	Clon	2m2f	NHF	YLD	£3584

Total win prize-money £3584

Going:	Sf: 0-0 GS: 0-0 Gd: 0-0 GF: - Fm: 0-0
Distance:	2m/2m3: 1-2 2m4-2m7: 0-0 3m+: 0-0
Track:	LH: 0-0 RH: 0-0 Tight: 0-0 Gall: 0-0
Aids:	Bl: 0-0 Vi: 0-0 Tstrap: 0-0
Best Rating:	100 3/03 Clon 2m2f yield NHF

Red Lion (FR)

101 **95d**

6-y-o ch g Lion Cavern (USA)-Mahogany River (Irish River (FR))

N J Henderson (B J Meehan 27/9) W H Ponsonby

Placings:30340   **(4752)**
2002/03: 16³GS, 20⁰S, 16³G, 21⁴GF, 24⁰G,

	Starts	1st	2nd	3rd	Win & Pl
Hurdles	5	0	0	2	1684
Career Total	5	0	0	2	1684

Going: Sf: 0-1 GS: 0-1 Gd: 0-2 GF: - Fm: 0-1
Distance: 2m/2m3: 0-2 2m4-2m7: 0-2 3m+: 0-1
Track: LH: 0-1 RH: 0-3 Tight: 0-2 Gall: 0-1
Aids: Bl: 0-0 Vi: 0-0 Tstrap: 0-2
Best Rating: 99 2/03 Winc 2m   gd-sft   Hdl

Modest middle-distance/stayer on the Flat; made a decent hurdling debut at Wincanton in February 2003, but has not gone on from that; acts on a sound surface.

Red Magic (FR)

5-y-o b/br h Grand Lodge (USA)-Ma Priere (FR) (Highest Honor (FR))
M C Pipe   Terry Neill

Placings:P   **(2445)**
2002/03: 16ᴾG,

	Starts	1st	2nd	3rd	Win & Pl
Hurdles	1	0	0	0	
Career Total	1	0	0	0	

Going: Sf: 0-0 GS: 0-0 Gd: 0-1 GF: - Fm: 0-0
Distance: 2m/2m3: 0-1 2m4-2m7: 0-0 3m+: 0-0
Track: LH: 0-0 RH: 0-1 Tight: 0-0 Gall: 0-0
Aids: Bl: 0-0 Vi: 0-1 Tstrap: 0-0
Best Rating: 0   12/02 Ludl   2m   good   Hdl

Red Mail (USA)
104(84h)   (59h)**90**

5-y-o b g Red Ransom (USA)-Seattle Byline (USA) (Slew City Slew (USA))
M A Barnes   T A Barnes

Placings:0-5P0053   **(4660)**
2002/03: 16⁵S, 16⁶GS, 16⁶S, 17⁰G, 21⁵S, 20³GF,

	Starts	1st	2nd	3rd	Win & Pl
Hurdles	4	0	0	0	0
Chases	2	0	0	1	690
Career Total	7	0	0	1	690

Going: Sf: 0-2 GS: 0-1 Gd: 0-2 GF: - Fm: 0-1
Distance: 2m/2m3: 0-4 2m4-2m7: 0-2 3m+: 0-0
Track: LH: 0-5 RH: 0-1 Tight: 0-3 Gall: 0-1
Aids: Bl: 0-0 Vi: 0-0 Tstrap: 0-0
Best Rating: 83 4/03 Sedg 2m5f   good   Ch

Poor hurdler/chaser; limited promise over fences; stays two miles five, but shapes as if further will suit.

Red Man (IRE)
87   **97**

6-y-o ch g Toulon-Jamie s Lady (Ashmore (FR))
M Todhunter   A Slack

Placings:500   **(3769)**
2002/03: 16⁵GS, 21⁰HY, 20⁰GS,

	Starts	1st	2nd	3rd	Win & Pl
Hurdles	3	0	0	0	0
Career Total	3	0	0	0	0

Red Marauder
(105h)   (120+h)**155**

13-y-o ch g Gunner B-Cover Your Money (Precipice Wood)
R C Guest (N B Mason 30/11) N B Mason

Placings:1212/3/1/111/16F0/14552F1/4   **(3797)**
2002/03: 24⁴S,

	Starts	1st	2nd	3rd	Win & Pl
Hurdles	1	0	0	0	388
Career Total	21	9	3	1	392206

145	4/01	Aint	4m4f	A HCh		HVY£310000
138	9/00	MRas	3m	C(0-135)HHdl	G-F	£6909
145	2/00	Weth	2m4f110yB HCh		SFT	£10348
152	11/98	Asct	2m3f110yA HCh		GD	£29177
141	11/98	Carl	2m4f110yC(0-135)HCh		SFT	£4697
133	10/98	Worc	2m4f110yC(0-130)HCh		SFT	£5224
129	12/97	Hexm	2m110y E Ch		SFT	£3234
103	11/93	Ayr	2m	Hdl		GD	£2200
89	10/93	Hexm	2m	Hdl		SFT	£1733
					Total win prize-money £373526

Going: Sf: 0-1 GS: 0-0 Gd: 0-0 GF: - Fm: 0-0
Distance: 2m/2m3: 0-0 2m4-2m7: 0-0 3m+: 0-1
Track: LH: 0-1 RH: 0-0 Tight: 0-0 Gall: 0-1
Aids: Bl: 0-0 Vi: 0-0 Tstrap: 0-0
Best Rating: 152 11/98 Asct 2m3f110y good   Ch

Very useful chaser; earned his place in history when avoiding all the melee to come home virtually alone in the 2001 Grand National; stays very well; best on soft ground; caught the eye on his return from injury over hurdles at Newcastle in February 2003. He was subsequently retired.

Red Marsala
91f   **64f**

5-y-o b/br g Tragic Role (USA)-Southend Scallywag (Tina s Pet)
R C Guest   N B Mason

Placings:0   **(3998)**
2002/03: 16⁰G,

	Starts	1st	2nd	3rd	Win & Pl
NH Flat	1	0	0	0	
Career Total	1	0	0	0	

Going: Sf: 0-0 GS: 0-0 Gd: 0-1 GF: - Fm: 0-0
Distance: 2m/2m3: 0-1 2m4-2m7: 0-0 3m+: 0-0
Track: LH: 0-1 RH: 0-0 Tight: 0-0 Gall: 0-0
Aids: Bl: 0-0 Vi: 0-0 Tstrap: 0-0
Best Rating: 64 3/03 Weth 2m   good   NHF

Half-brother to two winners for the stable; showed ability though well beaten in the end in bumper at Wetherby in March on debut.

Red Minster
99(66h)   (17h)**94**

6-y-o b g Minster Son-Minty Muncher (Idiots Delight)
R C Guest (N B Mason 14/2) N B Mason

Placings:000-0031P33   **(3993)**
2002/03: 22⁰G, 16⁶S, 16³HY, 16¹HY, 24²S, 20³S, 25³G,

	Starts	1st	2nd	3rd	Win & Pl
Hurdles	1	0	0	0	0
Chases	6	1	0	3	5849

Career Total	10	1	0	3	5849
94	1/03 Newc 2m110y E(0-105)HCh	HVY	£3958
		Total win prize-money £3959

Going: Sf: 1-5 GS: 0-0 Gd: 0-2 GF: - Fm: 0-0
Distance: 2m/2m3: 1-3 2m4-2m7: 0-2 3m+: 0-2
Track: LH: 1-5 RH: 0-2 Tight: 0-1 Gall: 1-2
Aids: Bl: 0-0 Vi: 0-0 Tstrap: 0-0
Best Rating: 94 1/03 Newc 2m110y heavy   Ch

Moderate chaser; acts well on a soft surface; has won over two miles, but gets further; goes well in cheekpieces.

Red Neck

12-y-o ch m Nishapour (FR)-Roda Haxan (Huntercombe)
John Moore   Mrs C E Goldsworthy

Placings:3162P4/P/43/5-25P   **(4736)**
2002/03: 24²GF, 19⁵G, 24⁰GF,

	Starts	1st	2nd	3rd	Win & Pl
Chases	3	0	1	0	430
Career Total	13	1	2	2	5009
106	7/97 Worc 2m4f D Hdl		G-F	£2966
		Total win prize-money £2966

Going: Sf: 0-0 GS: 0-0 Gd: 0-1 GF: - Fm: 0-2
Distance: 2m/2m3: 0-0 2m4-2m7: 0-1 3m+: 0-2
Track: LH: 0-2 RH: 0-1 Tight: 0-0 Gall: 0-0
Aids: Bl: 0-0 Vi: 0-0 Tstrap: 0-3
Best Rating: 106 7/97 Worc 2m4f   gd-fm   Hdl

Red Nose Lady
99   **97**

6-y-o b m Teenoso (USA)-Red Rambler (Rymer)
J M Jefferson   Mrs M E Dixon

Placings:225P-546P   **(2705)**
2002/03: 16⁵HY, 20⁵G, 20⁴HY, 20⁶HY, 20ᴾHY,

	Starts	1st	2nd	3rd	Win & Pl
NH Flat	1	0	0	0	0
Hurdles	4	0	0	0	0
Career Total	8	0	2	0	1018

Going: Sf: 0-3 GS: 0-1 Gd: 0-1 GF: - Fm: 0-0
Distance: 2m/2m3: 0-1 2m4-2m7: 0-4 3m+: 0-0
Track: LH: 0-3 RH: 0-2 Tight: 0-0 Gall: 0-0
Aids: Bl: 0-0 Vi: 0-0 Tstrap: 0-0
Best Rating: 97 11/02 Hexm 2m4f110y heavy   Hdl

Moderate hurdler; handles testing ground.

Red Oassis
100(49h)   (13h)**82**

12-y-o ch g Rymer-Heron s Mirage (Grey Mirage)
M J M Evans   Mrs J Z Munday

Placings:00F/4U10/P022-54U1   **(4276)**
2002/03: 20⁵S, 16⁴G, 20ᵁG, 16¹G,

	Starts	1st	2nd	3rd	Win & Pl
Chases	4	1	0	0	3675
Career Total	15	2	2	0	8127
82	3/03 Chep 2m110y F(0-100)HCh	GD	£3416
76	3/01 Wwck 2m110y F(0-90)HCh	HVY	£2538
		Total win prize-money £5954

Going: Sf: 0-1 GS: 0-0 Gd: 1-3 GF: - Fm: 0-0
Distance: 2m/2m3: 1-2 2m4-2m7: 0-2 3m+: 0-0
Track: LH: 1-1 RH: 0-3 Tight: 0-0 Gall: 0-1
Aids: Bl: 0-0 Vi: 0-0 Tstrap: 0-0
Best Rating: 86 3/02 Uttx 2m   heavy   Ch

Winning point to pointer. Fair efforts under Rules over fences. Suited by two miles and good to soft ground but handles heavy. A careless jumper.

Red Perk (IRE)

73

6-y-o b g Executive Perk-Supreme View (Supreme Leader)
N B Mason N B Mason

Placings:*0-52*   (1184)
2002/03: 20⁵G, 26²G,

	Starts	1st	2nd	3rd	Win & Pl
Hurdles	2	0	1	0	826
Career Total	3	0	1	0	826

Going:	Sf: 0-0 GS: 0-0 Gd: 0-2 GF: - Fm: 0-0
Distance:	2m/2m3: 0-0 2m4-2m7: 0-1 3m+: 0-1
Track:	LH: 0-2 RH: 0-0 Tight: 0-1 Gall: 0-0
Aids:	Bl: 0-0 Vi: 0-0 Tstrap: 0-0
Best Rating:	73 9/02 Sthl 3m2f good Hdl

Plating-class hurdler; stays well.

Red Raja

10-y-o b/br g Persian Heights-Jenny Splendid (John Splendid)
H J Manners (C R Cox 4/3) C R Cox

Placings:01251510/223/64465/0653/6/P30   (4523)
2002/03: 16⁶G, 16³GF, 16⁶G,

	Starts	1st	2nd	3rd	Win & Pl
Chases	3	0	0	1	621
Career Total	24	3	3	3	46245
133	3/97	Newb	2m110y	D(0-125)HHdl	GD	£3317
127	2/97	Wind	2m	B Hdl	GD	£7546
112	12/96	Folk	2m1f110yE Hdl	G-S	£2427

Total win prize-money £13291

Going:	Sf: 0-0 GS: 0-1 Gd: 0-1 GF: - Fm: 0-1
Distance:	2m/2m3: 0-3 2m4-2m7: 0-0 3m+: 0-0
Track:	LH: 0-2 RH: 0-1 Tight: 0-0 Gall: 0-0
Aids:	Bl: 0-0 Vi: 0-0 Tstrap: 0-0
Best Rating:	133 12/97 Chel 2m4f110y good Hdl

Red Rampage

100(91h)   (87h)**105**

8-y-o b g King s Ride-Mighty Fly (Comedy Star (USA))
R C Guest (N B Mason 8/2) N B Mason

Placings:U40042464/5042031420P-5O3F1PC31P (4765)
2002/03: 21⁵G, 20°HY, 20³HY, 25°HY, 24¹S, 33⁸S, 24°HY, 30³G, 26¹S, 31°G,

	Starts	1st	2nd	3rd	Win & Pl
Chases	10	2	0	2	11176
Career Total	30	3	3	3	18159
105	3/03	Carl	3m2f	E(0-110)HCh	SFT	£4582
104	12/02	Newc	3m	E(0-115)HCh	SFT	£4305
105	3/02	Catt	3m1f110yE(0-100)HCh	G-S	£3113

Total win prize-money £12002

Going:	Sf: 2-7 GS: 0-0 Gd: 0-3 GF: - Fm: 0-0
Distance:	2m/2m3: 0-0 2m4-2m7: 0-3 3m+: 2-7
Track:	LH: 1-6 RH: 1-3 Tight: 0-3 Gall: 1-2
Aids:	Bl: 2-10 Vi: 0-0 Tstrap: 2-8
Best Rating:	105 3/03 Carl 3m2f soft Ch

Modest handicap chaser; stays at least three miles two; acts on a soft surface; usually wears a tongue tie and blinkers.

Red Rebel

11-y-o gr g Scallywag-Little Red Flower (Blakeney)
Mrs Caroline Bailey Mrs M E Moody

Placings:1FP/4UR/U-1F10   (4443)
2002/03: 24¹GF, 24⁶G, 16¹GS, 19⁶G,

	Starts	1st	2nd	3rd	Win & Pl
Chases	4	2	0	0	5600
Career Total	11	3	0	0	7132
91	3/03	Leic	2m	H Ch	G-S	£2611
91	5/02	Hntg	3m	H Ch	G-F	£2989
108	5/98	Uttx	3m2f	H Ch	GD	£1433

Total win prize-money £7033

Going:	Sf: 0-0 GS: 1-1 Gd: 0-2 GF: - Fm: 1-1
Distance:	2m/2m3: 1-1 2m4-2m7: 0-1 3m+: 1-2
Track:	LH: 0-0 RH: 2-4 Tight: 0-0 Gall: 1-2
Aids:	Bl: 0-0 Vi: 0-0 Tstrap: 0-0
Best Rating:	108 5/98 Uttx 3m2f good Ch

Fair pointer/hunter chaser; acts on any ground.

Red Return (IRE)

92   **82**

6-y-o ch g Bob s Return (IRE)-Kerrie s Pearl (Proverb)
L A Dace Exors of the Late Mr Eddie Davess

Placings:*50*   (1250)
2002/03: 16⁵GF, 16⁶G,

	Starts	1st	2nd	3rd	Win & Pl
NH Flat	2	0	0	0	0
Career Total	2	0	0	0	0

Going:	Sf: 0-0 GS: 0-0 Gd: 0-1 GF: - Fm: 0-1
Distance:	2m/2m3: 0-2 2m4-2m7: 0-0 3m+: 0-0
Track:	LH: 0-2 RH: 0-0 Tight: 0-0 Gall: 0-0
Aids:	Bl: 0-0 Vi: 0-0 Tstrap: 0-0
Best Rating:	82 6/02 Worc 2m gd-fm NHF

Signs of ability in both bumper starts; not disgraced when fourth in 3m novice hurdle at Worcester on hurdling bow June 2003.

Red Rooney

4-y-o b g Astronef-Mica Male (ITY) (Law Society (USA))
P Butler Homewoodgate Racing Club

Placings:P   (3177)
2002/03: 16°G,

	Starts	1st	2nd	3rd	Win & Pl
Hurdles	1	0	0	0	
Career Total	1	0	0	0	

Going:	Sf: 0-0 GS: 0-0 Gd: 0-1 GF: - Fm: 0-0
Distance:	2m/2m3: 0-1 2m4-2m7: 0-0 3m+: 0-0
Track:	LH: 0-0 RH: 0-1 Tight: 0-0 Gall: 0-0
Aids:	Bl: 0-0 Vi: 0-0 Tstrap: 0-0
Best Rating:	0 1/03 Kemp 2m good Hdl

Red Socialite (IRE)

102   **108+**

6-y-o ch g Moscow Society (USA)-Dees Darling (IRE) (King Persian)
D R Gandolfo Starlight Racing

Placings:*05-401*   (4311)
2002/03: 17⁴HY, 21⁰S, 21¹G,

	Starts	1st	2nd	3rd	Win & Pl
Hurdles	3	1	0	0	7123
Career Total	5	1	0	0	7123
108	3/03	Newb	2m5f	D Hdl	GD	£6815

Total win prize-money £6815

Going:	Sf: 0-2 GS: 0-0 Gd: 1-1 GF: - Fm: 0-0
Distance:	2m/2m3: 0-1 2m4-2m7: 1-2 3m+: 0-0
Track:	LH: 1-3 RH: 0-0 Tight: 0-1 Gall: 1-1
Aids:	Bl: 0-0 Vi: 0-0 Tstrap: 0-0
Best Rating:	108 3/03 Newb 2m5f good Hdl

Fair novice hurdler; caused a 40/1 surprise at Newbury in March 2003; stays 2m 5f and handles any ground.

Red Square Dawn

97   **77**

7-y-o b m Derrylin-Raise The Dawn (Rymer)
Mrs L Williamson Halewood International Ltd

Placings:020/P0P6420-0202053   (4708)
2002/03: 25⁰G, 20⁰G, 20⁴GS, 20⁹GF, 20²GF, 21⁰G, 22⁵GF, 20³G,

	Starts	1st	2nd	3rd	Win & Pl
Hurdles	8	0	2	1	2323
Career Total	17	0	4	1	3558

Going:	Sf: 0-0 GS: 0-1 Gd: 0-4 GF: - Fm: 0-3
Distance:	2m/2m3: 0-0 2m4-2m7: 0-7 3m+: 0-0
Track:	LH: 0-6 RH: 0-1 Tight: 0-2 Gall: 0-0
Aids:	Bl: 0-5 Vi: 0-1 Tstrap: 0-0
Best Rating:	77 4/03 Uttx 2m4f110y good Hdl

Plating-class; modest form in novice hurdles; possibly best at around two miles; acts on decent ground.

Red Square Ice

97   **71**

8-y-o b g Scallywag-Arctic Rymes (Rymer)
G Barnett J T Stimpson

Placings:06   (2134)
2002/03: 22⁰S, 21⁶G,

	Starts	1st	2nd	3rd	Win & Pl
Hurdles	2	0	0	0	0
Career Total	2	0	0	0	0

Going:	Sf: 0-1 GS: 0-0 Gd: 0-1 GF: - Fm: 0-0
Distance:	2m/2m3: 0-0 2m4-2m7: 0-2 3m+: 0-0
Track:	LH: 0-1 RH: 0-1 Tight: 0-0 Gall: 0-0
Aids:	Bl: 0-0 Vi: 0-0 Tstrap: 0-0
Best Rating:	71 11/02 Ludl 2m5f good Hdl

Red Square Island

70

8-y-o ch g Jupiter Island-Queen Of The Nile (Hittite Glory)
Mrs L Williamson Miss Judy Eaton

Placings:P000-P   (0185)
2002/03: 16°G,

	Starts	1st	2nd	3rd	Win & Pl
Hurdles	1	0	0	0	
Career Total	5	0	0	0	

Going:	Sf: 0-0 GS: 0-0 Gd: 0-1 GF: - Fm: 0-0
Distance:	2m/2m3: 0-1 2m4-2m7: 0-0 3m+: 0-0
Track:	LH: 0-1 RH: 0-0 Tight: 0-0 Gall: 0-0
Aids:	Bl: 0-1 Vi: 0-0 Tstrap: 0-0
Best Rating:	70 2/02 Ludl 2m gd-sft Hdl

Red Square King

75(87h)   (69dh)**7**
5-y-o ch g Sure Blade (USA)-Patscilla (Squill (USA))
Mrs L Williamson Halewood International Ltd

Placings:050-505P   (1620)
2002/03: 16⁵G, 16⁹GF, 21⁵GF, 21⁷F,

	Starts	1st	2nd	3rd	Win & Pl
Hurdles	4	0	0	0	0
Career Total	7	0	0	0	0

Going:	Sf: 0-0 GS: 0-0 Gd: 0-1 GF: - Fm: 0-3
Distance:	2m/2m3: 0-3 2m4-2m7: 0-1 3m+: 0-0
Track:	LH: 0-2 RH: 0-2 Tight: 0-0 Gall: 0-1
Aids:	Bl: 0-0 Vi: 0-0 Tstrap: 0-0
Best Rating:	71 6/02 Uttx 2m good Hdl

Poor novice hurdler/chaser.

Red Square Man (IRE)

69(92h)   (91 h)**30**
8-y-o b g Rashar (USA)-November Tide (Laurence O)
Mrs L Williamson Halewood International Ltd

Placings:05/4P663P   (2943)
2002/03: 17⁴G, 17⁷GS, 16⁶G, 20⁶S, 17³G, 16⁸S,

	Starts	1st	2nd	3rd	Win & Pl
Hurdles	6	0	0	1	714
Career Total	8	0	0	1	714

Going:	Sf: 0-2 GS: 0-1 Gd: 0-3 GF: - Fm: 0-0
Distance:	2m/2m3: 0-5 2m4-2m7: 0-1 3m+: 0-0
Track:	LH: 0-4 RH: 0-2 Tight: 0-2 Gall: 0-0
Aids:	Bl: 0-0 Vi: 0-0 Tstrap: 0-0
Best Rating:	91 10/02 Hayd 2m good Hdl

Red Stranger (FR)

                                                               74
6-y-o b g Le Balafre (FR)-Abeille Royale (USA) (Turn To Mars (USA))
M C Pipe Terry Neill

Placings:0/0300524PPP-   (0010)
2002/03: 25⁶G,

	Starts	1st	2nd	3rd	Win & Pl
Hurdles	1	0	0	0	
Career Total	11	0	1	1	1054

Going:	Sf: 0-0 GS: 0-0 Gd: 0-1 GF: - Fm: 0-0
Distance:	2m/2m3: 0-0 2m4-2m7: 0-0 3m+: 0-1
Track:	LH: 0-0 RH: 0-0 Tight: 0-0 Gall: 0-0
Aids:	Bl: 0-0 Vi: 0-0 Tstrap: 0-1
Best Rating:	84 6/01 NAbb 2m1f good NHF

Red Striker

115   **145**
9-y-o ch g Gunner B-Cover Your Money (Precipice Wood)
R C Guest (N B Mason 25/1) N B Mason

Placings:45/2222211110/2F1215141152/0P1PP-5022U
                                                               (4479)
2002/03: 20⁵GS, 26⁶GS, 20⁹HY, 20²G, 36⁸UG,

	Starts	1st	2nd	3rd	Win & Pl
Chases	5	0	2	0	8965
Career Total	34	10	10	0	102127

147	1/02	Hayd	3m	A HCh	SFT	£26100
141	4/01	Aint	2m4f	C HCh	SFT	£15925
133	3/01	Hntg	2m5f110yD(0-125)HHdl	SFT	£3666
142	1/01	Newc	2m4f	A Ch	SFT	£14500
133	11/00	Carl	2m	D Ch	SFT	£4153
124	10/00	Kels	2m1f	E Ch	G-S	£2990
118	2/00	Bang	2m1f	E Hdl	G-S	£2828
118	2/00	Muss	2m4f	F(0-100)HHdl	G-S	£2743
115	1/00	Sthl	2m4f110yE(0-105)HHdl	G-S	£2506
105	11/99	Kels	2m6f110yE(0-105)HHdl	GD	£2815
			Total win prize-money £78227

Going:	Sf: 0-1 GS: 0-2 Gd: 0-2 GF: - Fm: 0-0
Distance:	2m/2m3: 0-0 2m4-2m7: 0-3 3m+: 0-2
Track:	LH: 0-5 RH: 0-0 Tight: 0-1 Gall: 0-0
Aids:	Bl: 0-0 Vi: 0-0 Tstrap: 0-5
Best Rating:	147 1/02 Hayd 3m soft Ch

Very useful chaser; best over two and a half miles, but does stay three; suited by soft ground; does tend to make the odd mistake; Richard Guest gets on very well with him; wears a tongue tie.

Red Sun

108   **112**
6-y-o b g Foxhound (USA)-Superetta (Superlative)
J Mackie (A Streeter 30/10) Bulls Head Racing Club

Placings:F6P/32FP662-216231043   (4691)
2002/03: 16²G, 17¹GF, 17⁵GF, 16²GF, 16³G, 19¹S, 17⁹GS, 17⁴G, 19³GF,

	Starts	1st	2nd	3rd	Win & Pl
Hurdles	9	2	2	2	12110
Career Total	19	2	4	3	14477

112	12/02	Donc	2m3f110yD(0-115)HHdl	SFT	£3857
100	6/02	MRas	2m1f110yE Hdl	G-F	£2702
			Total win prize-money £6560

Going:	Sf: 1-1 GS: 0-1 Gd: 0-3 GF: - Fm: 1-4
Distance:	2m/2m3: 1-7 2m4-2m7: 1-2 3m+: 0-0
Track:	LH: 1-5 RH: 1-4 Tight: 1-5 Gall: 0-1
Aids:	Bl: 0-0 Vi: 0-0 Tstrap: 0-0
Best Rating:	112 12/02 Donc 2m3f110y soft Hdl

Fair hurdler; acts on both soft and fast ground; stays two miles three.

Red Tyrant

100   **88**
5-y-o b g Minster Son-By The Lake (Tyrant (USA))
R C Guest (N B Mason 29/1) Mason Jobe

Placings:5006034   (4590)
2002/03: 16⁵G, 16⁰S, 16⁹HY, 16⁸S, 20⁹GF, 16³G, 20⁴G,

	Starts	1st	2nd	3rd	Win & Pl
NH Flat	4	0	0	0	0
Hurdles	3	0	0	1	523
Career Total	7	0	0	1	523

Going:	Sf: 0-3 GS: 0-0 Gd: 0-3 GF: - Fm: 0-1
Distance:	2m/2m3: 0-5 2m4-2m7: 0-2 3m+: 0-0
Track:	LH: 0-7 RH: 0-0 Tight: 0-1 Gall: 0-0
Aids:	Bl: 0-0 Vi: 0-0 Tstrap: 0-0
Best Rating:	92 3/03 Catt 2m soft NHF

Red Uno (IRE)

82f   **71f**
6-y-o ch g Executive Perk-Hogan s Cherry (General Ironside)
N B Mason N B Mason

Placings:00   (2117)
2002/03: 16⁸GF, 17⁰G,

	Starts	1st	2nd	3rd	Win & Pl
NH Flat	2	0	0	0	
Career Total	2	0	0	0	

Going:	Sf: 0-0 GS: 0-0 Gd: 0-1 GF: - Fm: 0-1
Distance:	2m/2m3: 0-2 2m4-2m7: 0-0 3m+: 0-0
Track:	LH: 0-0 RH: 0-1 Tight: 0-0 Gall: 0-0
Aids:	Bl: 0-0 Vi: 0-0 Tstrap: 0-0
Best Rating:	74 9/02 Prth 2m110y gd-fm NHF

Red Will Danagher (IRE)

98   **89**
6-y-o b g Glacial Storm (USA)-Clodas Pet (IRE) (Andretti)
John Allen John Allen

Placings:P020   (3595)
2002/03: 22⁸G, 20⁰GS, 20²HY, 20⁰HY,

	Starts	1st	2nd	3rd	Win & Pl
Hurdles	4	0	1	0	1688
Career Total	4	0	1	0	1688

Going:	Sf: 0-2 GS: 0-1 Gd: 0-1 GF: - Fm: 0-0
Distance:	2m/2m3: 0-2 2m4-2m7: 0-4 3m+: 0-0
Track:	LH: 0-2 RH: 0-2 Tight: 0-1 Gall: 0-0
Aids:	Bl: 0-0 Vi: 0-0 Tstrap: 0-0
Best Rating:	79 1/03 Leic 2m4f110y heavy Hdl

Moderate novice hurdler; stays 2m 6f.

Red Wine

109   **122**
4-y-o b g Hamas (IRE)-Red Bouquet (Reference Point)
J A Osborne Paul J Dixon

Placings:310   (4130)
2002/03: 16⁹HY, 16¹S, 17⁰G,

	Starts	1st	2nd	3rd	Win & Pl
Hurdles	3	1	0	1	5906
Career Total	3	1	0	1	5906

| 118 | 2/03 | Newb | 2m110y | D Hdl | SFT | £5115 |
| | | | Total win prize-money £5116 |

Going:	Sf: 1-2 GS: 0-0 Gd: 0-1 GF: - Fm: 0-0
Distance:	2m/2m3: 1-3 2m4-2m7: 0-0 3m+: 0-0
Track:	LH: 1-2 RH: 0-1 Tight: 0-0 Gall: 1-2
Aids:	Bl: 0-0 Vi: 0-0 Tstrap: 0-0
Best Rating:	122 3/03 Chel 2m1f good Hdl

Fair hurdler; won November Handicap on Flat; third on hurdles debut before winning in good style at Newbury; held in the Triumph Hurdle; acts on good and heavy ground.

Redde (IRE)

103(116h)   (119h)**110+**
8-y-o ch g Classic Memory-Stoney Broke (Pauper)
R J Smith M Stock,D Jackson,R W Hibberd,C Harrison

Placings:2110/F51P21-P   (0113)
2002/03: 24⁰GS,

	Starts	1st	2nd	3rd	Win & Pl
Hurdles	1	0	0	0	
Career Total	8	4	2	0	21273

119	3/02	Chep	2m4f	C(0-135)HHdl	G-S	£5018
116	1/02	Carl	2m1f	D Hdl	HVY	£3526
123	2/01	Newb	2m110y	B NHF	SFT	£8190
110	11/00	Chep	2m110y	H NHF	HVY	£1505
			Total win prize-money £18239

Going: Sf: 0-0 GS: 0-1 Gd: 0-0 GF: - Fm: 0-0
Distance: 2m/2m3: 0-0 2m4-2m7: 0-0 3m+: 0-1
Track: LH: 0-0 RH: 0-1 Tight: 0-0 Gall: 0-0
Aids: Bl: 0-0 Vi: 0-0 Tstrap: 0-0
Best Rating: 123 2/01   Newb 2m110y   soft   NHF

Modest handicap hurdler; won very poor 2m 7f novice chase in bad ground at Uttoxeter May 2003; goes well in soft/heavy ground.

Redemption

114   146

8-y-o b g Sanglamore (USA)-Ypha (USA) (Lyphard (USA))
N A Twiston-Davies (P R Webber 1/2) John Duggan &
Michael Purtill

Placings:60460/31150F/2FF116/12136P-3F5F4   (4604)
2002/03: 16³HY, 16²HY, 16⁵G, 16²HY, 21⁴G,

	Starts	1st	2nd	3rd	Win & Pl
Chases	5	0	0	1	6191
Career Total	28	6	2	3	49293
145 11/01 Asct	2m		B HCh		G-F £13380
149 10/01 Weth	2m4f110yB(0-145)HCh			GD	£9064
135 1/01 Weth	2m4f		E Ch		HVY £3003
133 1/01 Plum	2m4f		E Ch		G-S £2964
121 2/00 Ludl	2m		E Hdl		GD £2352
118 12/99 Weth	2m		D Hdl		G-S £3460
			Total win prize-money £34224		

Going: Sf: 0-3 GS: 0-0 Gd: 0-2 GF: - Fm: 0-0
Distance: 2m/2m3: 0-4 2m4-2m7: 0-1 3m+: 0-0
Track: LH: 0-2 RH: 0-3 Tight: 0-0 Gall: 0-1
Aids: Bl: 0-1 Vi: 0-0 Tstrap: 0-0
Best Rating: 149 1/02   Asct 2m   good   Ch

Useful chaser; stays two and a half miles but probably better over two miles in a strongly-run race; acts on any ground, although arguably best on good or slightly softer; not the safest of jumpers; has worn blinkers.

Redgrave Wolf

99   75

10-y-o ch m Little Wolf-Redgrave Rose (Tug Of War)
K Bishop Barford Park Racing

Placings:3/000600/20255/12/P0/0-244P   (2167)
2002/03: 25²GS, 25⁴G, 24⁴GS, 26⁸G,

	Starts	1st	2nd	3rd	Win & Pl
Chases	4	0	1	0	1397
Career Total	21	1	4	1	5716
85 5/99 Towc	3m	F(0-100)HHdl		G-F	£1807
			Total win prize-money £1807		

Going: Sf: 0-0 GS: 0-2 Gd: 0-2 GF: - Fm: 0-0
Distance: 2m/2m3: 0-0 2m4-2m7: 0-0 3m+: 0-4
Track: LH: 0-1 RH: 0-3 Tight: 0-1 Gall: 0-0
Aids: Bl: 0-0 Vi: 0-0 Tstrap: 0-0
Best Rating: 85 5/99   Extr 2m6f   gd-fm   Hdl

Redhouse Chevalier

4-y-o b g Pursuit Of Love-Trampolo (USA) (Trempolino (USA))
J R Adam James R Adam

Placings:00P   (4306)
2002/03: 16⁸G, 16⁹GS, 18⁵G,

	Starts	1st	2nd	3rd	Win & Pl
NH Flat	2	0	0	0	0
Hurdles	1	0	0	0	0
Career Total	3	0	0	0	

Going: Sf: 0-0 GS: 0-1 Gd: 0-2 GF: - Fm: 0-0
Distance: 2m/2m3: 0-3 2m4-2m7: 0-0 3m+: 0-0
Track: LH: 0-2 RH: 0-1 Tight: 0-2 Gall: 0-0
Aids: Bl: 0-0 Vi: 0-0 Tstrap: 0-0
Best Rating: 47 2/03   Ayr   2m   gd-sft   NHF

Redmire

9-y-o b m Nomadic Way (USA)-Decent Sort (Decent Fellow)
Miss V J Parvin J H Hewitt

Placings:4-0   (0083)
2002/03: 25⁰GS,

	Starts	1st	2nd	3rd	Win & Pl
Chases	1	0	0	0	
Career Total	2	0	0	0	84

Going: Sf: 0-0 GS: 0-1 Gd: 0-0 GF: - Fm: 0-0
Distance: 2m/2m3: 0-0 2m4-2m7: 0-0 3m+: 0-1
Track: LH: 0-1 RH: 0-0 Tight: 0-0 Gall: 0-0
Aids: Bl: 0-0 Vi: 0-0 Tstrap: 0-0
Best Rating: 65 4/02   MRas 3m1f   good   Ch

Redouble

100   81

7-y-o b g First Trump-Sunflower Seed (Mummy s Pet)
E L James (B R Millman 22/6) E James

Placings:0/0060202-254004444550   (4429)
2002/03: 21²F, 20⁵S, 20⁴GF, 22⁹GF, 22⁸GF, 19⁴F, 20⁴G, 19⁴GF, 20⁴HY, 19⁵GS, 21⁵G, 21⁰GF,

	Starts	1st	2nd	3rd	Win & Pl
Hurdles	12	0	1	0	747
Career Total	20	0	3	0	2249

Going: Sf: 0-2 GS: 0-1 Gd: 0-2 GF: - Fm: 0-7
Distance: 2m/2m3: 0-1 2m4-2m7: 0-11 3m+: 0-0
Track: LH: 0-8 RH: 0-3 Tight: 0-7 Gall: 0-0
Aids: Bl: 0-3 Vi: 0-1 Tstrap: 0-1
Best Rating: 90 10/02   Extr   2m3f   firm   Hdl

Modest maiden hurdler, stays two and a half miles and acts on soft ground.

Redskin Raider (IRE)

(98h)   (105h)

7-y-o b g Commanche Run-Sheltered (IRE) (Strong Gale)
T R George Mrs Christine Davies

Placings:00/0033P20-P   (3346)
2002/03: 23³S,

	Starts	1st	2nd	3rd	Win & Pl
Chases	1	0	0	0	
Career Total	10	0	1	2	1956

Going: Sf: 0-1 GS: 0-0 Gd: 0-0 GF: - Fm: 0-0
Distance: 2m/2m3: 0-0 2m4-2m7: 0-0 3m+: 0-1
Track: LH: 0-0 RH: 0-0 Tight: 0-0 Gall: 0-0
Aids: Bl: 0-0 Vi: 0-0 Tstrap: 0-0
Best Rating: 105 4/02   Winc   2m6f   good   Hdl

Reduski

65   65

8-y-o b g Thethingaboutitis (USA)-Call Me Daisy (Callernish)

A J Deakin A J Deakin

Placings:P50P0   (0908)
2002/03: 22⁸GF, 16⁵GS, 16⁹S, 25⁸S, 17⁹GS,

	Starts	1st	2nd	3rd	Win & Pl
Hurdles	5	0	0	0	0
Career Total	5	0	0	0	0

Going: Sf: 0-2 GS: 0-2 Gd: 0-0 GF: - Fm: 0-1
Distance: 2m/2m3: 0-3 2m4-2m7: 0-1 3m+: 0-1
Track: LH: 0-4 RH: 0-1 Tight: 0-4 Gall: 0-0
Aids: Bl: 0-0 Vi: 0-0 Tstrap: 0-0
Best Rating: 65 5/02   Sthl   2m   gd-sft   Hdl

Redwood Grove (USA)

96   90d

7-y-o b g Woodman (USA)-Ikebana (IRE) (Sadler s Wells (USA))
Miss G Browne (N A Gaselee 5/12) Bryan Mathieson

Placings:1435/06P50046-P4000P   (3778)
2002/03: 24⁸G, 16⁴HY, 16⁶S, 20⁰HY, 16⁰HY, 24⁸GS,

	Starts	1st	2nd	3rd	Win & Pl
Hurdles	6	0	0	0	0
Career Total	18	1	0	1	3849
117 11/00 Wwck	2m	E Hdl		SFT	£2119
		Total win prize-money £2120			

Going: Sf: 0-4 GS: 0-1 Gd: 0-1 GF: - Fm: 0-0
Distance: 2m/2m3: 0-3 2m4-2m7: 0-1 3m+: 0-2
Track: LH: 0-2 RH: 0-4 Tight: 0-0 Gall: 0-0
Aids: Bl: 0-0 Vi: 0-0 Tstrap: 0-0
Best Rating: 119 3/01   Newb   2m110y   heavy   Hdl

Fair hurdler, but has failed to progress from a winning debut. Seems to handle most ground, but did not appear to take to chasing in autumn 2001.

Reel Dancer

86   73

6-y-o b g Minshaanshu Amad (USA)-Sister Rosarii (USA) (Properantes (USA))
B De Haan The Play 4 Partnership

Placings:632-26   (3593)
2002/03: 20²HY, 16⁶HY,

	Starts	1st	2nd	3rd	Win & Pl
Hurdles	2	0	1	0	646
Career Total	5	0	2	1	1440

Going: Sf: 0-2 GS: 0-0 Gd: 0-0 GF: - Fm: 0-0
Distance: 2m/2m3: 0-1 2m4-2m7: 0-0 3m+: 0-0
Track: LH: 0-0 RH: 0-2 Tight: 0-1 Gall: 0-0
Aids: Bl: 0-0 Vi: 0-0 Tstrap: 0-0
Best Rating: 107 2/02   Sand   2m110y   soft   NHF

Placed form in bumpers and hurdles. Acts on soft/heavy ground.

Reel Handsome

97   61

11-y-o ch g Handsome Sailor-Reel Chance (Proverb)
C T Pogson C T Pogson

Placings:PPB360/3SP452/P4PU35F266400-3004324PU   (4264)
2002/03: 16⁵G, 17⁹GF, 16⁹GF, 21⁴G, 22³GF, 17²G, 17⁴GS, 21⁸S, 20⁰GF,

	Starts	1st	2nd	3rd	Win & Pl
Chases	9	0	1	2	3776
Career Total	34	0	3	5	9260

Going:	Sf: 0-1 GS: 0-1 Gd: 0-3 GF: - Fm: 0-4
Distance:	2m2m3: 0-3 2m4-2m7: 0-0
Track:	LH: 0-6 RH: 0-3 Tight: 0-5 Gall: 0-1
Aids:	Bl: 0-0 Vi: 0-0 Tstrap: 0-9
Best Rating:	86 10/02 Sthl 2m1f good Ch

Long standing maiden over fences, slow.

Reflective Way

103   **92**

10-y-o ch m Mirror Boy-Craigie Way (Palm Track)
A C Whillans Duncan D Stewart

Placings: P0234-11P   **(0619)**
2002/03: 25¹G, 24¹GS, 25⁵GF,

	Starts	1st	2nd	3rd	Win & Pl
Chases	3	2	0	0	8797
Career Total	8	2	1	1	11204
92	6/02	Prth	3m	D Ch	G-S	£5124
92	5/02	Hexm	3m1f	E(0-105)HCh	GD	£3672

Total win prize-money £8797

Going:	Sf: 0-0 GS: 1-1 Gd: 1-1 GF: - Fm: 0-1
Distance:	2m2m3: 0-0 2m4-2m7: 0-0 3m+: 2-3
Track:	LH: 1-2 RH: 1-1 Tight: 0-0 Gall: 0-0
Aids:	Bl: 0-0 Vi: 0-0 Tstrap: 0-0
Best Rating:	92 6/02 Prth 3m gd-sft Ch

Improved over fences during the spring of 2002 and scored twice in the spring. Suited to trips of around three miles and fast ground.

Reflex Blue

108   **86**

6-y-o b g Ezzoud (IRE)-Briggsmaid (Elegant Air)
R J Price Fox And Cub Partnership

Placings: 460006-23344   **(2063)**
2002/03: 16²G, 17³GF, 21³F, 214F, 19⁴S,

	Starts	1st	2nd	3rd	Win & Pl
Hurdles	5	0	1	2	1881
Career Total	11	0	1	2	1881

Going:	Sf: 0-1 GS: 0-0 Gd: 0-1 GF: - Fm: 0-3
Distance:	2m2m3: 0-2 2m4-2m7: 0-3 3m+: 0-0
Track:	LH: 0-1 RH: 0-4 Tight: 0-0 Gall: 0-0
Aids:	Bl: 0-0 Vi: 0-5 Tstrap: 0-0
Best Rating:	86 10/02 Hrld 2m1f gd-fm Hdl

Runner-up in a big field in a two mile seller at Worcester September 2002. Stays further.

Reflex Courier (IRE)

113   **99**

11-y-o b g Over The River (FR)-Thornpark Lady (Mandalus)
John R Upson Martin Tucker & Jim Bath

Placings: 425PBPF0/11PP23/314254/14PU36-P41350   **(4165)**

2002/03: 22⁵S, 224S, 24¹S, 24⁹S, 235GS, 240GS,

	Starts	1st	2nd	3rd	Win & Pl
Chases	6	1	0	1	6311
Career Total	32	5	3	4	25717
99	11/02	Hayd	3m	D(0-115)HCh	SFT	£5075
96	11/01	Hayd	2m6f	F(0-110)HCh	GD	£3601
104	11/00	Leic	2m7f110yF(0-110)HCh	G-S	£2678
104	11/99	MRas	3m1f	F(0-105)HCh	G-S	£3018

93	10/99	Bang	3m110y	F(0-105)HCh	SFT	£3875

Total win prize-money £18248

Going:	Sf: 1-4 GS: 0-2 Gd: 0-0 GF: - Fm: 0-0
Distance:	2m2m3: 0-0 2m4-2m7: 0-2 3m+: 1-4
Track:	LH: 1-5 RH: 0-1 Tight: 0-1 Gall: 0-1
Aids:	Bl: 0-0 Vi: 0-0 Tstrap: 0-0
Best Rating:	104 11/00 Leic 2m7f110y gd-sft Ch

Moderate chaser; stays 3m; acts on good ground or softer; seems best held up for a late run.

Reflex Reaction (IRE)

(86c)   (29c)**62**

8-y-o b g Arapahos (FR)-Beswick Paper Lady (Giolla Mear)
John R Upson Mrs Sheree Tucker

Placings: 0/05P/2P/P440-PP   **(0789)**
2002/03: 26P, 26PGF,

	Starts	1st	2nd	3rd	Win & Pl
Hurdles	1	0	0	0	0
Chases	1	0	0	0	0
Career Total	12	0	1	0	999

Going:	Sf: 0-0 GS: 0-0 Gd: 0-0 GF: - Fm: 0-1
Distance:	2m2m3: 0-0 2m4-2m7: 0-0 3m+: 0-2
Track:	LH: 0-1 RH: 0-1 Tight: 0-1 Gall: 0-0
Aids:	Bl: 0-0 Vi: 0-0 Tstrap: 0-0
Best Rating:	74 10/00 Towc 2m5f gd-fm Hdl

Regal Ali (IRE)

49   **13**

4-y-o ch g Ali-Royal (IRE)-Depeche (FR) (King s Lake (USA))
G A Ham (John Berry 23/1) N G Ahier

Placings: 0P0   **(4463)**
2002/03: 16⁰S, 17²G, 17⁰F,

	Starts	1st	2nd	3rd	Win & Pl
Hurdles	3	0	0	0	
Career Total	3	0	0	0	

Going:	Sf: 0-1 GS: 0-0 Gd: 0-1 GF: - Fm: 0-1
Distance:	2m2m3: 0-3 2m4-2m7: 0-0 3m+: 0-0
Track:	LH: 0-1 RH: 0-2 Tight: 0-1 Gall: 0-0
Aids:	Bl: 0-0 Vi: 0-0 Tstrap: 0-0
Best Rating:	24 4/03 Tntn 2m1f firm Hdl

Regal Applause

80   **41**

4-y-o b f Royal Applause-Panchellita (USA) (Pancho Villa (USA))
M R Hoad (G L Moore 22/7) Mrs J A Ewer

Placings: 00   **(2417)**
2002/03: 17⁰S, 18⁰G,

	Starts	1st	2nd	3rd	Win & Pl
Hurdles	2	0	0	0	
Career Total	2	0	0	0	

Going:	Sf: 0-1 GS: 0-0 Gd: 0-1 GF: - Fm: 0-0
Distance:	2m2m3: 0-2 2m4-2m7: 0-0 3m+: 0-0
Track:	LH: 0-1 RH: 0-1 Tight: 0-2 Gall: 0-0
Aids:	Bl: 0-0 Vi: 0-0 Tstrap: 0-0
Best Rating:	41 11/02 Folk 2m1f110y soft Hdl

Regal Chance

96   **92+**

10-y-o b g Cisto (FR)-Regal Flutter (Henry The Seventh)
A King Mrs A A Shutes

Placings: 0/0/FP2001   **(3929)**
2002/03: 19⁵G, 19⁵GS, 16²S, 19⁰G, 16⁵S, 20¹G,

	Starts	1st	2nd	3rd	Win & Pl
Chases	6	1	1	0	4881
Career Total	8	1	1	0	4881
94	3/03	Hntg	2m4f110yF(0-90)HCh	GD	£3412

Total win prize-money £3413

Going:	Sf: 0-2 GS: 0-1 Gd: 1-3 GF: - Fm: 0-0
Distance:	2m2m3: 0-5 2m4-2m7: 1-1 3m+: 0-0
Track:	LH: 0-1 RH: 1-5 Tight: 0-1 Gall: 1-1
Aids:	Bl: 0-0 Vi: 0-0 Tstrap: 0-0
Best Rating:	94 3/03 Hntg 2m4f110y good Ch

Moderate. lightly-raced chaser; stays two and a half miles; acts on good ground or softer.

Regal Exit (FR)

110(104h)   (126h)**127**

7-y-o ch g Exit To Nowhere (USA)-Regalante (Gairloch)
N J Henderson Brian Buckley

Placings: 1312/6000-12010P   **(4458)**
2002/03: 16¹G, 16²GS, 16⁶G, 19¹G, 21⁰G, 16⁰G,

	Starts	1st	2nd	3rd	Win & Pl
Hurdles	1	0	0	0	0
Chases	5	2	1	0	9706
Career Total	14	4	2	1	38925
126	3/03	Donc	2m3f	E Ch	GD	£4043
118	12/02	Ludl	2m	E Ch	GD	£4095
134	3/00	Newb	2m110y	D Hdl	SFT	£3835
130	1/00	Chel	2m1f	B Hdl	SFT	£7020

Total win prize-money £18993

Going:	Sf: 0-0 GS: 0-1 Gd: 2-5 GF: - Fm: 0-0
Distance:	2m2m3: 2-5 2m4-2m7: 0-1 3m+: 0-0
Track:	LH: 1-4 RH: 1-2 Tight: 1-3 Gall: 0-2
Aids:	Bl: 0-0 Vi: 0-0 Tstrap: 0-0
Best Rating:	140 3/00 Chel 2m1f gd-fm Hdl

Decent hurdler/novice chaser; runner-up in the 2000 Triumph Hurdle, but has had training setbacks; fair form over fences in 2002/03; stays 2m 4f; effective on a sound surface.

Regal Gale (IRE)

9-y-o b g Strong Gale-Diklers Queen (IRE) (The Parson)
J Wade John Wade

Placings: 6P/2P/P   **(1707)**
2002/03: 21PG,

	Starts	1st	2nd	3rd	Win & Pl
Chases	1	0	0	0	
Career Total	5	0	1	0	964

Going:	Sf: 0-0 GS: 0-0 Gd: 0-0 GF: - Fm: 0-0
Distance:	2m2m3: 0-0 2m4-2m7: 0-1 3m+: 0-0
Track:	LH: 0-1 RH: 0-0 Tight: 0-1 Gall: 0-0
Aids:	Bl: 0-0 Vi: 0-0 Tstrap: 0-0
Best Rating:	105 5/00 Uttx 2m6f110y good Hdl

Regal Holly

111(96h)   (118h)**121+**

8-y-o b m Gildoran-Pusey Street (Native Bazaar)

C J Mann Dr David Harris & Peter Simpson

Placings:1123/111135/034F00F5-212221   (4170)
2002/03: 21²GS, 25¹S, 22²S, 24²S, 20²G, 21¹S,

	Starts	1st	2nd	3rd	Win & Pl
Chases	6	2	4	0	29422
Career Total	24	8	5	3	72826

121	3/03	Uttx	2m5f	A HCh		SFT	£18600
121	12/02	Folk	3m1f	E Ch		SFT	£3487
130	2/01	Asct	2m4f	B(0-150)HHdl		HVY	£20923
123	1/01	Font	2m2f110yD(0-125)HHdl			SFT	£4231
120	12/00	MRas	2m3f110yD(0-125)HHdl			G-S	£7410
98	11/00	Catt	2m3f	F Hdl		GD	£1438
106	7/99	Worc	2m	H NHF		G-F	£1563
106	6/99	Worc	2m	H NHF		G-S	£1378

Total win prize-money £59034

Going: Sf: 2-4 GS: 0-1 Gd: 0-1 GF: - Fm: 0-0
Distance: 2m2m3: 0-0 2m4-2m7: 1-4 3m+: 1-2
Track: LH: 1-2 RH: 1-3 Tight: 1-4 Gall: 0-0
Aids: Bl: 2-5 Vi: 0-0 Tstrap: 0-0
Best Rating: 130 2/01 Asct 2m4f heavy Hdl

Fair chaser; successful in bumpers, she was a useful handicapper over hurdles; fair novice chaser; suited by ease in the ground; stays three miles.

Regal Hymn

8-y-o b g Regal Embers (IRE)-It s Only Her (French Marny)
Mrs Barbara Waring A D Peachey

Placings:P   (0194)
2002/03: 21ᴾF,

	Starts	1st	2nd	3rd	Win & Pl
Hurdles	1	0	0	0	
Career Total	1	0	0	0	

Going: Sf: 0-0 GS: 0-0 Gd: 0-0 GF: - Fm: 0-1
Distance: 2m/2m3: 0-0 2m4-2m7: 0-1 3m+: 0-0
Track: LH: 0-1 RH: 0-0 Tight: 0-0 Gall: 0-0
Aids: Bl: 0-0 Vi: 0-0 Tstrap: 0-0
Best Rating: 0 5/02 Wwck 2m5f firm Hdl

Regal Light

(69h)   (69h)
8-y-o gr g Gran Alba (USA)-Light Of Zion (Pieces Of Eight)
J C Tuck J W Storkey

Placings:0PP6   (4567)
2002/03: 19ᴾGS, 20ᴾS, 19ᴾGS, 20⁶GF,

	Starts	1st	2nd	3rd	Win & Pl
Hurdles	4	0	0	0	
Career Total	4	0	0	0	

Going: Sf: 0-1 GS: 0-2 Gd: 0-0 GF: - Fm: 0-1
Distance: 2m/2m3: 0-2 2m4-2m7: 0-2 3m+: 0-0
Track: LH: 0-2 RH: 0-2 Tight: 0-1 Gall: 0-0
Aids: Bl: 0-0 Vi: 0-0 Tstrap: 0-0
Best Rating: 69 4/03 Bang 2m4f gd-fm Hdl

Regal River (IRE)

112(89h)   (83h)103
6-y-o b g Over The River (FR)-My Friend Fashion (Laurence O)
John R Upson Middleham Park Racing Xix

Placings:005P10-F231P   (3251)
2002/03: 20ᶠS, 26²HY, 24³S, 23¹S, 26ᴾS,

	Starts	1st	2nd	3rd	Win & Pl
Chases	5	1	1	1	5031
Career Total	11	2	1	1	7702

103	1/03	Leic	2m7f110yF(0-90)HCh	SFT	£3435
82	3/02	Towc	3m	F(0-100)HHdl	SFT	£2670

Total win prize-money £6106

Going: Sf: 1-5 GS: 0-0 Gd: 0-0 GF: - Fm: 0-0
Distance: 2m/2m3: 0-0 2m4-2m7: 0-1 3m+: 1-4
Track: LH: 0-4 RH: 1-1 Tight: 0-0 Gall: 0-0
Aids: Bl: 0-0 Vi: 0-0 Tstrap: 0-0
Best Rating: 103 1/03 Leic 2m7f110y soft Ch

Modest handicap hurdler/chaser. Acts on a soft surface and is well suited by three miles.

Regal Statesman (NZ)

85(97h)   (49h)56
10-y-o br g Vice Regal (NZ)-Hykit (NZ) (Swinging Junior)
O Brennan Lady Anne Bentinck

Placings:0/2PP/412PPP64-4405   (4341)
2002/03: 20⁴G, 17⁴GF, 24⁰G, 20⁵GF,

	Starts	1st	2nd	3rd	Win & Pl
Hurdles	1	0	0	0	
Chases	3	0	0	0	374
Career Total	16	1	2	0	5709

89	5/01	Weth	2m7f	D Hdl	FRM	£3549

Total win prize-money £3549

Going: Sf: 0-0 GS: 0-0 Gd: 0-2 GF: - Fm: 0-2
Distance: 2m/2m3: 0-1 2m4-2m7: 0-2 3m+: 0-1
Track: LH: 0-3 RH: 0-1 Tight: 0-2 Gall: 0-2
Aids: Bl: 0-0 Vi: 0-0 Tstrap: 0-0
Best Rating: 98 5/00 MRas 2m1f110y gd-fm Hdl

Regal Term (IRE)

59f   16f
5-y-o b g Welsh Term-Regal Hostess (King s Ride)
R Dickin R G & R A Whitehead

Placings:0   (2947)
2002/03: 16⁰S,

	Starts	1st	2nd	3rd	Win & Pl
NH Flat	1	0	0	0	
Career Total	1	0	0	0	

Going: Sf: 0-1 GS: 0-0 Gd: 0-0 GF: - Fm: 0-0
Distance: 2m/2m3: 0-1 2m4-2m7: 0-0 3m+: 0-0
Track: LH: 0-0 RH: 0-1 Tight: 0-0 Gall: 0-0
Aids: Bl: 0-0 Vi: 0-0 Tstrap: 0-0
Best Rating: 16 1/03 Ludl 2m soft NHF

Regal Tribute

5-y-o b g Tragic Role (USA)-Hushlet (Governor General)
R C Guest (N B Mason 12/11) N B Mason

Placings:00   (4357)
2002/03: 16⁰GS, 16⁰GF,

	Starts	1st	2nd	3rd	Win & Pl
NH Flat	2	0	0	0	
Career Total	2	0	0	0	

Going: Sf: 0-0 GS: 0-1 Gd: 0-0 GF: - Fm: 0-1
Distance: 2m/2m3: 0-2 2m4-2m7: 0-0 3m+: 0-0
Track: LH: 0-2 RH: 0-0 Tight: 0-1 Gall: 0-0

Aids: Bl: 0-0 Vi: 0-0 Tstrap: 0-0
Best Rating: 0 4/03 Newc 2m good NHF

Regal Vision (IRE)

97(101h)   (101h)105+
6-y-o b g Emperor Jones (USA)-Shining Eyes (USA) (Mr Prospector (USA))
C G Cox The Lucky For Some Partnership

Placings:0/U124P34030-54640   (4441)
2002/03: 19⁵GS, 19⁴S, 24⁶G, 21⁴G, 20⁰G,

	Starts	1st	2nd	3rd	Win & Pl
Hurdles	5	0	0	0	570
Career Total	16	1	1	2	4487

105	8/01	Bang	2m4f	F Hdl	GD	£2268

Total win prize-money £2268

Going: Sf: 0-1 GS: 0-0 Gd: 0-3 GF: - Fm: 0-1
Distance: 2m/2m3: 0-0 2m4-2m7: 0-4 3m+: 0-1
Track: LH: 0-1 RH: 0-4 Tight: 0-1 Gall: 0-0
Aids: Bl: 0-4 Vi: 0-0 Tstrap: 0-0
Best Rating: 105 4/02 Hntg 2m5f110y gd-fm Hdl

Won a weak maiden hurdle at Bangor August 2001; unseated rider on chasing debut May 2003 but his jumping stood him in good stead when springing 40/1 shock next time; needs a test of stamina on a sound surface.

Regar (IRE)

98   84
11-y-o b g Buckskin (FR)-Pass Thurn (Trimmingham)
Brian McNichol Brian McNichol

Placings:000/0P60/F-U2   (0402)
2002/03: 20ᶠG, 20ᵁGF, 20²GF,

	Starts	1st	2nd	3rd	Win & Pl
Chases	3	0	1	0	450
Career Total	10	0	1	0	450

Going: Sf: 0-0 GS: 0-0 Gd: 0-1 GF: - Fm: 0-2
Distance: 2m/2m3: 0-0 2m4-2m7: 0-3 3m+: 0-0
Track: LH: 0-2 RH: 0-1 Tight: 0-0 Gall: 0-1
Aids: Bl: 0-0 Vi: 0-0 Tstrap: 0-0
Best Rating: 76 6/02 Hexm 2m4f110y gd-fm Ch

Poor chaser; stays 2m 4f.

Regardez-Moi

89   64
6-y-o b m Distinctly North (USA)-Tomard (Thatching)
Miss M Bragg Friends Of Rock Park

Placings:6B56665   (4626)
2002/03: 17⁶S, 17⁸S, 19⁵GS, 17⁶GS, 22⁶GF, 19⁶GF, 17⁵GF,

	Starts	1st	2nd	3rd	Win & Pl
Hurdles	7	0	0	0	
Career Total	7	0	0	0	

Going: Sf: 0-2 GS: 0-2 Gd: 0-0 GF: - Fm: 0-3
Distance: 2m/2m3: 0-6 2m4-2m7: 0-1 3m+: 0-0
Track: LH: 0-1 RH: 0-6 Tight: 0-3 Gall: 0-0
Aids: Bl: 0-0 Vi: 0-0 Tstrap: 0-0
Best Rating: 64 3/03 Winc 2m6f gd-fm Hdl

Poor hurdler; does not appear to stay 2m 6f.

Regency Red (IRE)

102   84
5-y-o ch g Dolphin Street (FR)-Future Romance (Distant Relative)

R Ford (M D I Usher 27/7) Mrs J M Russell

Placings:30   (1735)
2002/03: 20³G, 16⁰S,

	Starts	1st	2nd	3rd	Win & Pl
Hurdles	2	0	0	1	622
Career Total	2	0	0	1	622

Going:	Sf: 0-1 GS: 0-0 Gd: 0-1 GF: - Fm: 0-0
Distance:	2m/2m3: 0-1 2m4-2m7: 0-1 3m+: 0-0
Track:	LH: 0-1 RH: 0-1 Tight: 0-1 Gall: 0-0
Aids:	Bl: 0-0 Vi: 0-0 Tstrap: 0-0
Best Rating:	84 8/02 Prth 2m4f110y good Hdl

Quirky plater on the Flat. Shaped well on his hurdles debut but far from sure to progress.

Regents Walk (IRE)
105f   103+f
5-y-o b g Phardante (FR)-Raw Courage (IRE) (The Parson)
B De Haan Mrs D Vaughan

Placings:3   (4269)
2002/03: 16³GF,

	Starts	1st	2nd	3rd	Win & Pl
NH Flat	1	0	0	1	281
Career Total	1	0	0	1	281

Going:	Sf: 0-0 GS: 0-0 Gd: 0-0 GF: - Fm: 0-1
Distance:	2m/2m3: 0-1 2m4-2m7: 0-0 3m+: 0-0
Track:	LH: 0-1 RH: 0-0 Tight: 0-1 Gall: 0-0
Aids:	Bl: 0-0 Vi: 0-0 Tstrap: 0-0
Best Rating:	103 3/03 Sthl 2m gd-fm NHF

Showed modest ability in bumpers on fast ground.

Reggae Rhythm (IRE)
100(75c)   (88c)81
9-y-o b g Be My Native (USA)-Invery Lady (Sharpen Up)
R N Bevis (Noel T Chance 7/5) Peter J Doyle

Placings:00053 13363/0020PF00/66231B465/025-050P2P
                                               (4566)
2002/03: 18⁰G, 17⁵S, 19⁰S, 21PHY, 16²G, 20PGF,

	Starts	1st	2nd	3rd	Win & Pl
Hurdles	6	0	1	0	766
Career Total	36	2	4	5	12373
105	1/01	Tram	2m	Hdl	HVY	£4451
102	11/98	Clon	2m	NHF	SFT	£1942

Total win prize-money £6395

Going:	Sf: 0-3 GS: 0-0 Gd: 0-1 GF: - Fm: 0-2
Distance:	2m/2m3: 0-3 2m4-2m7: 0-3 3m+: 0-0
Track:	LH: 0-4 RH: 0-2 Tight: 0-3 Gall: 0-1
Aids:	Bl: 0-0 Vi: 0-0 Tstrap: 0-0
Best Rating:	113 11/01 Tram 2m yield Hdl

An ex-Irish gelding who won over hurdles in his native country but failed to get off the mark over fences. Now with Noel Chance. Acts on soft/heavy ground.

Reggie Buck (USA)
104   96
9-y-o b/br g Alleged (USA)-Hello Memphis (USA) (Super Concorde (USA))
J Mackie Fools Who Dream

Placings:P0/25146/05121225/203UP2300/16U1215355-06656003   (4484)

2002/03: 17⁰G, 17⁶S, 17⁶GS, 16⁵G, 16⁶S, 16⁰GS, 16⁰G, 17³GF,

	Starts	1st	2nd	3rd	Win & Pl
Hurdles	8	0	0	1	1447
Career Total	42	6	7	4	33190
114	11/01	Weth	2m	D(0-125)HHdl	GD	£3445
114	10/01	Sthl	2m	E(0-115)HHdl	GD	£2912
113	5/01	Hntg	2m110y	F(0-105)HHdl	GD	£2922
113	1/00	Catt	2m	D(0-120)HHdl	GD	£5547
100	12/99	Leic	2m	D(0-110)HHdl	GD	£2332
99	1/99	Donc	2m110y	F(0-110)HHdl	GD	£2066

Total win prize-money £19226

Going:	Sf: 0-2 GS: 0-2 Gd: 0-3 GF: - Fm: 0-1
Distance:	2m/2m3: 0-8 2m4-2m7: 0-0 3m+: 0-0
Track:	LH: 0-7 RH: 0-1 Tight: 0-4 Gall: 0-0
Aids:	Bl: 0-1 Vi: 0-0 Tstrap: 0-0
Best Rating:	114 12/01 Hntg 2m110y gd-sft Hdl

Modest; one time fair handicap hurdler; took advantage of a lenient mark when clear cut winner at Hexham in April; acts well on good ground; effective at around two miles; has been tried in blinkers.

Reign Dance
12-y-o ch g Kinglet-Gay Criselle (Decoy Boy)
Mrs D H McCarthy Mrs D H McCarthy

Placings:13/44P/PP/P-P   (0313)
2002/03: 25PG,

	Starts	1st	2nd	3rd	Win & Pl
Chases	1	0	0	0	
Career Total	9	1	0	1	2127
100	3/98	Leic	2m4f110yH	Ch	SFT	£1968

Total win prize-money £1968

Going:	Sf: 0-0 GS: 0-0 Gd: 0-1 GF: - Fm: 0-0
Distance:	2m/2m3: 0-0 2m4-2m7: 0-0 3m+: 0-1
Track:	LH: 0-0 RH: 0-1 Tight: 0-1 Gall: 0-0
Aids:	Bl: 0-0 Vi: 0-0 Tstrap: 0-0
Best Rating:	100 3/98 Towc 2m6f gd-fm Ch

Reivers Moon
95   75
4-y-o b/br f Midnight Legend-Here Comes Tibby (Royal Fountain)
W Amos W Amos

Placings:016   (4665)
2002/03: 14⁰GS, 17¹G, 17⁶GF,

	Starts	1st	2nd	3rd	Win & Pl
NH Flat	3	1	0	0	2220
Career Total	3	1	0	0	2220
89	3/03	Carl	2m1f	H NHF	GD	£2220

Total win prize-money £2220

Going:	Sf: 0-0 GS: 0-1 Gd: 1-1 GF: - Fm: 0-1
Distance:	2m/2m3: 1-2 2m4-2m7: 0-0 3m+: 0-0
Track:	LH: 0-1 RH: 1-2 Tight: 0-0 Gall: 0-0
Aids:	Bl: 0-0 Vi: 0-0 Tstrap: 0-0
Best Rating:	89 3/03 Carl 2m1f good NHF

Moderate bumper performer; took a slowly-run bumper in clear cut fashion at Carlisle in March; well beaten on the same track next time; runner-up in modest company on hurdling bow at Sedgefield in May.

Relative Delight
77   31
5-y-o b m Distant Relative-Pasja (IRE) (Posen (USA))
John A Harris Mick Rowley

Placings:006F-000   (2688)
2002/03: 16⁰HY, 19⁰S, 17⁰GS,

	Starts	1st	2nd	3rd	Win & Pl
Hurdles	3	0	0	0	0
Career Total	7	0	0	0	0

Plating-class hurdler, stays two and a half miles, acts on soft ground.

Reliance Leader
72   30
7-y-o ch g Weld-Swift Messenger (Giolla Mear)
D L Williams Reliance Car Hire Services Ltd

Placings:00-P00   (4568)
2002/03: 20PHY, 21⁰G, 22⁰GF,

	Starts	1st	2nd	3rd	Win & Pl
Hurdles	3	0	0	0	0
Career Total	5	0	0	0	0

Going:	Sf: 0-1 GS: 0-0 Gd: 0-1 GF: - Fm: 0-0
Distance:	2m/2m3: 0-0 2m4-2m7: 0-3 3m+: 0-0
Track:	LH: 0-2 RH: 0-1 Tight: 0-1 Gall: 0-1
Aids:	Bl: 0-0 Vi: 0-0 Tstrap: 0-0
Best Rating:	30 4/03 Strf 2m6f110y gd-fm Hdl

Religious Lass (IRE)
68   34
5-y-o b m Religiously (USA)-Carolin Lass (IRE) (Carlingford Castle)
Colin S McKeever David Adair

Placings:50-6   (1386)
2002/03: 20⁶GF,

	Starts	1st	2nd	3rd	Win & Pl
Hurdles	1	0	0	0	0
Career Total	3	0	0	0	0

Going:	Sf: 0-0 GS: 0-0 Gd: 0-0 GF: - Fm: 0-1
Distance:	2m/2m3: 0-0 2m4-2m7: 0-1 3m+: 0-0
Track:	LH: 0-1 RH: 0-0 Tight: 0-0 Gall: 0-0
Aids:	Bl: 0-0 Vi: 0-0 Tstrap: 0-0
Best Rating:	34 10/02 Hexm 2m4f110y gd-fm Hdl

Remember Star
77(95h)   (80h)81
10-y-o ch m Don t Forget Me-Star Girl Gay (Lord Gayle (USA))
A D Smith Duckhaven Stud

Placings:60604P/000P304/404023344/260PP5110/10440/031601-0P00   (0822)
2002/03: 17⁰GS, 21PGF, 16⁰GF, 16⁰GF,

	Starts	1st	2nd	3rd	Win & Pl
Hurdles	2	0	0	0	0
Chases	2	0	0	0	0
Career Total	46	5	2	4	13604
81	11/01	Extr	2m3f110yF(0-95)HCh	G-F	£3692
80	10/01	Extr	2m1f	G(0-95)HHdl	G-F	£1813
85	5/00	Extr	2m1f	G(0-95)HHdl	FRM	£1834
85	3/00	Extr	2m1f110yG Hdl	G-F	£1939
72	3/00	Extr	2m1f110y	G(0-95)HHdl	

G-S £1599

Total win prize-money £10879

Going:	Sf: 0-0 GS: 0-1 Gd: 0-0 GF: - Fm: 0-3
Distance:	2m/2m3: 0-3 2m4-2m7: 0-1 3m+: 0-0
Track:	LH: 0-4 RH: 0-0 Tight: 0-3 Gall: 0-0
Aids:	Bl: 0-0 Vi: 0-0 Tstrap: 0-0
Best Rating:	85 5/00 Extr 2m1f firm Hdl

Selling hurdler, suited by fast ground and likes Exeter.

Remington (IRE)
104   100
5-y-o ch g Indian Ridge-Sea Harrier (Grundy)
Mrs A M Thorpe (Mrs S D Williams 11/5) S A Douch

Placings:0-5032   (4191)
2002/03: 16⁵GF, 16⁹GS, 16³G, 16²G,

	Starts	1st	2nd	3rd	Win & Pl
NH Flat	2	0	0	0	0
Hurdles	2	0	1	1	1800
Career Total	**5**	**0**	**1**	**1**	**1800**

Going:	Sf: 0-0 GS: 0-1 Gd: 0-2 GF: - Fm: 0-1
Distance:	2m/2m3: 0-4 2m4-2m7: 0-3 3m+: 0-1
Track:	LH: 0-1 RH: 0-3 Tight: 0-0 Gall: 0-0
Aids:	Bl: 0-0 Vi: 0-0 Tstrap: 0-0
Best Rating:	101 2/03 Ludl 2m good Hdl

Modest novice hurdler; acts on a sound surface.

Renaloo (IRE)
109   91
8-y-o gr g Tremblant-Rare Flower (Decent Fellow)
R Rowe Tim Clowes

Placings:50046/006/056-F521F331P   (4360)
2002/03: 20⁶G, 20⁵G, 16²S, 16¹S, 16⁶HY, 18³S, 18²S, 16¹G, 19⁶F,

	Starts	1st	2nd	3rd	Win & Pl
Chases	9	2	1	2	10480
Career Total	**20**	**2**	**1**	**2**	**10480**
91 3/03 Folk 2m		E(0-110)HCh		GD	£4095
91 1/03 Folk 2m		E(0-105)HCh		SFT	£4075

Total win prize-money £8171

Going:	Sf: 1-5 GS: 0-0 Gd: 1-3 GF: - Fm: 0-1
Distance:	2m/2m3: 2-7 2m4-2m7: 0-2 3m+: 0-0
Track:	LH: 0-0 RH: 2-6 Tight: 2-9 Gall: 0-0
Aids:	Bl: 0-0 Vi: 0-0 Tstrap: 0-0
Best Rating:	99 11/99 Wwck 2m good NHF

Modest chaser, effective at 2m and acts on any ground; suited by positive tactics.

Renzo (IRE)
95   114
10-y-o g Alzao (USA)-Watership (USA) (Foolish Pleasure (USA))
John A Harris Cleartherm Ltd

Placings:1F2240/23220/U/60F24-41040   (2690)
2002/03: 16⁴G, 19¹GF, 19⁰GS, 16⁴S, 19⁰GS,

	Starts	1st	2nd	3rd	Win & Pl
Hurdles	5	1	0	0	6695
Career Total	**22**	**3**	**2**	**6**	**24890**
114 6/02 MRas	2m3f110yC(0-130)HHdl		G-F	£5512
139 11/98 Asct	2m110y C Hdl		G-S	£3940

Total win prize-money £9452

Going:	Sf: 0-1 GS: 0-2 Gd: 0-1 GF: - Fm: 1-1
Distance:	2m/2m3: 0-2 2m4-2m7: 1-3 3m+: 0-0
Track:	LH: 0-2 RH: 1-3 Tight: 1-3 Gall: 0-1

| Aids: | Bl: 0-0 Vi: 0-0 Tstrap: 0-0 |
| Best Rating: | 139 2/99 Asct 2m110y   gd-sft   Hdl |

Modest hurdler, stayer on the Flat, he won on his hurdling debut but failed to add to that over hurdles until winning at Market Rasen in June 2002. He has plenty of ability, but also a mind of his own. Acts on any ground and stays two and a half miles.

Replacement Pet (IRE)
6-y-o b m Petardia-Richardstown Lass (IRE) (Muscatite)
H S Howe Mrs Ruth Egan

Placings:0   (0520)
2002/03: 17⁰G,

	Starts	1st	2nd	3rd	Win & Pl
Hurdles	1	0	0	0	
Career Total	**1**	**0**	**0**	**0**	

Going:	Sf: 0-0 GS: 0-0 Gd: 0-1 GF: - Fm: 0-0
Distance:	2m/2m3: 0-1 2m4-2m7: 0-0 3m+: 0-0
Track:	LH: 0-1 RH: 0-0 Tight: 0-1 Gall: 0-0
Aids:	Bl: 0-0 Vi: 0-0 Tstrap: 0-0
Best Rating:	

Repulse Bay (IRE)
88   58
5-y-o b g Barathea (IRE)-Bourbon Topsy (Ile De Bourbon (USA))
J S Goldie J S Goldie

Placings:30P-00   (4019)
2002/03: 16⁰G, 16⁰S,

	Starts	1st	2nd	3rd	Win & Pl
Hurdles	2	0	0	0	
Career Total	**5**	**0**	**0**	**1**	**429**

Going:	Sf: 0-1 GS: 0-0 Gd: 0-1 GF: - Fm: 0-0
Distance:	2m/2m3: 0-2 2m4-2m7: 0-0 3m+: 0-0
Track:	LH: 0-2 RH: 0-0 Tight: 0-0 Gall: 0-1
Aids:	Bl: 0-0 Vi: 0-0 Tstrap: 0-0
Best Rating:	60 3/03 Ayr 2m soft Hdl

Repunzel
86(105h)   (95h)95
8-y-o b m Carlingford Castle-Hi-Rise Lady (Sunyboy)
N A Gaselee Michael Watt

Placings:20/0641/F05/64UP0P13-F0152   (4154)
2002/03: 17⁵S, 16⁰G, 17¹HY, 18⁵S, 16²G,

	Starts	1st	2nd	3rd	Win & Pl
Chases	5	1	1	0	4085
Career Total	**22**	**3**	**2**	**1**	**11673**
95 1/03 Plum 2m1f		F(0-90)HCh		HVY	£3081
95 1/02 Plum 2m		D(0-115)HHdl		HVY	£3304
98 4/00 Plum	2m	D Hdl		G-S	£2811

Total win prize-money £9196

Going:	Sf: 1-3 GS: 0-0 Gd: 0-2 GF: - Fm: 0-0
Distance:	2m/2m3: 1-5 2m4-2m7: 0-0 3m+: 0-0
Track:	LH: 1-3 RH: 0-1 Tight: 1-3 Gall: 0-1
Aids:	Bl: 0-0 Vi: 0-0 Tstrap: 0-0
Best Rating:	98 4/00 Plum 2m gd-sft Hdl

Modest handicap hurdler/chaser, suited by soft ground over two miles.

Repute
73f   69f
5-y-o b g Unfuwain (USA)-Someone Special (Habitat)
G A Swinbank Scotnorth Racing Ltd

Placings:000   (3883)
2002/03: 16⁰HY, 16⁰G, 16⁰GS,

	Starts	1st	2nd	3rd	Win & Pl
NH Flat	3	0	0	0	
Career Total	**3**	**0**	**0**	**0**	

Going:	Sf: 0-1 GS: 0-1 Gd: 0-1 GF: - Fm: 0-0
Distance:	2m/2m3: 0-3 2m4-2m7: 0-0 3m+: 0-0
Track:	LH: 0-3 RH: 0-0 Tight: 0-1 Gall: 0-1
Aids:	Bl: 0-0 Vi: 0-0 Tstrap: 0-0
Best Rating:	69 1/03 Newc 2m heavy NHF

Top-class Flat pedigree but picked up cheaply at three and well beaten on debut in bumpers.

Requestor
98   95+
8-y-o br g Distinctly North (USA)-Bebe Altesse (GER) (Alpenkonig (GER))
T J Fitzgerald (J G Fitzgerald 22/2) Marquesa De Moratalla

Placings:00461   (4434)
2002/03: 16⁰S, 16⁰G, 20⁴G, 20⁶GS, 20¹G,

	Starts	1st	2nd	3rd	Win & Pl
Hurdles	5	1	0	0	2527
Career Total	**5**	**1**	**0**	**0**	**2527**
95 4/03 Newc 2m4f		G(0-95)HHdl		GD	£2527

Total win prize-money £2527

Going:	Sf: 0-1 GS: 0-1 Gd: 1-3 GF: - Fm: 0-0
Distance:	2m/2m3: 0-2 2m4-2m7: 1-3 3m+: 0-0
Track:	LH: 1-4 RH: 0-1 Tight: 0-1 Gall: 1-3
Aids:	Bl: 0-0 Vi: 0-0 Tstrap: 1-1
Best Rating:	95 4/03 Newc 2m4f good Hdl

Moderate hurdler; stays two and a half miles; best on a sound surface.

Rescator (FR)
99   88
7-y-o gr g Saint Estephe (FR)-La Narquoise (FR) (Al Nasr (FR))
Mrs S J Smith Mrs S Smith

Placings:1/420P/6643   (4641)
2002/03: 23⁶GS, 21⁶GS, 20⁴GS, 19³GF,

	Starts	1st	2nd	3rd	Win & Pl
Hurdles	4	0	0	1	754
Career Total	**9**	**1**	**1**	**1**	**3522**
109 1/00 Font	2m2f110yH NHF		G-S	£1792

Total win prize-money £1792

Going:	Sf: 0-0 GS: 0-3 Gd: 0-0 GF: - Fm: 0-1
Distance:	2m/2m3: 0-1 2m4-2m7: 0-3 3m+: 0-0
Track:	LH: 0-3 RH: 0-1 Tight: 0-2 Gall: 0-1
Aids:	Bl: 0-0 Vi: 0-0 Tstrap: 0-0
Best Rating:	119 1/01 Plum 2m5f soft Hdl

Point and bumper winner; finished lame on the first time he had run on fast ground when third in 2m 3f maiden hurdle at Stratford April 2003.

Rescindo (IRE)
105   108
4-y-o b g Revoque (IRE)-Mystic Dispute (IRE) (Magical Strike (USA))

M C Pipe Joy And Valentine Feerick

Placings:224 (4463)
2002/03: 16²GS, 16²G, 17⁴F,

	Starts	1st	2nd	3rd	Win & Pl
Hurdles	3	0	2	0	3091
Career Total	3	0	2	0	3091

Going:	Sf: 0-0 GS: 0-1 Gd: 0-1 GF: Fm: 0-1
Distance:	2m/2m3: 0-3 2m4-2m7: 0-0 3m+: 0-0
Track:	LH: 0-0 RH: 0-3 Tight: 0-1 Gall: 0-0
Aids:	Bl: 0-0 Vi: 0-0 Tstrap: 0-0
Best Rating:	96 2/03 Winc 2m gd-sft Hdl

Moderate hurdler; still a maiden; shown form at around 2m; acts on decent ground; wears a visor.

Researcher
99   88

4-y-o ch f Cosmonaut-Rest (Dance In Time (CAN))
Miss Venetia Williams (R M Beckett 27/5) Mrs Kathy Stuart

Placings:6226 (4152)
2002/03: 16⁶GS, 17²HY, 16²G, 16⁶G,

	Starts	1st	2nd	3rd	Win & Pl
Hurdles	4	0	2	0	2479
Career Total	4	0	2	0	2479

Going:	Sf: 0-1 GS: 0-2 Gd: 0-1 GF: Fm: 0-0
Distance:	2m/2m3: 0-4 2m4-2m7: 0-0 3m+: 0-0
Track:	LH: 0-3 RH: 0-1 Tight: 0-3 Gall: 0-0
Aids:	Bl: 0-0 Vi: 0-0 Tstrap: 0-0
Best Rating:	86 1/03 Sthl 2m gd-sft Hdl

Modest juvenile hurdler; runner-up in minor events at Southwell and Folkstone January 2003; got off the mark in a weakly contested mares only event at Exeter at the end of April.

Reseda (IRE)
95f   100+f

6-y-o b g Rock Hopper-Sweet Mignonette (Tina s Pet)
R T Phillips R S Williams

Placings:11 (0436)
2002/03: 17¹G, 16¹GF,

	Starts	1st	2nd	3rd	Win & Pl
NH Flat	2	2	0	0	3415
Career Total	2	2	0	0	3415
100 6/02	Hntg	2m110y H NHF		G-F	£1556
100 5/02	Extr	2m1f H NHF		GD	£1858
		Total win prize-money £3416			

Going:	Sf: 0-0 GS: 0-0 Gd: 1-1 GF: Fm: 1-1
Distance:	2m/2m3: 2-2 2m4-2m7: 0-0 3m+: 0-0
Track:	LH: 0-0 RH: 2-2 Tight: 0-0 Gall: 1-1
Aids:	Bl: 0-0 Vi: 0-0 Tstrap: 0-0
Best Rating:	100 6/02 Hntg 2m110y gd-fm NHF

Moderate dual bumper winner; acts on a sound surface.

Resistance (IRE)
98   89

6-y-o br g Phardante (FR)-Shean Hill (IRE) (Bar Dexter (USA))
G A Ham Sally and Tom Dalley and Dave Durbin

Placings:3/160-4F6 (2586)
2002/03: 19⁴GS, 20⁵S, 17⁶GS,

	Starts	1st	2nd	3rd	Win & Pl
Hurdles	3	0	0	0	420

Career Total   7   1   0   1   2478
99 5/01 Extr   2m1f   H NHF   GD   £1785
                        Total win prize-money £1785

Going:	Sf: 0-1 GS: 0-2 Gd: 0-0 GF: Fm: 0-0
Distance:	2m/2m3: 0-2 2m4-2m7: 0-1 3m+: 0-0
Track:	LH: 0-1 RH: 0-1 Tight: 0-0 Gall: 0-0
Aids:	Bl: 0-0 Vi: 0-0 Tstrap: 0-0
Best Rating:	106 5/01 Hntg 2m110y gd-fm NHF

Modest bumper performer; moderate efforts over hurdles.

Ressource (FR)
96   83

4-y-o b c Broadway Flyer (USA)-Rayonne (Sadler s Wells (USA))
G L Moore The Straight Forward Partnership Ii

Placings:05424306 (4079)
2002/03: 16⁰G, 16⁵S, 17⁴S, 17²GS, 16⁴HY, 16³S, 16⁰G, 16⁸HY,

	Starts	1st	2nd	3rd	Win & Pl
Hurdles	8	0	1	1	1270
Career Total	8	0	1	1	1270

Going:	Sf: 0-5 GS: 0-1 Gd: 0-2 GF: Fm: 0-0
Distance:	2m/2m3: 0-8 2m4-2m7: 0-0 3m+: 0-0
Track:	LH: 0-3 RH: 0-5 Tight: 0-5 Gall: 0-1
Aids:	Bl: 0-0 Vi: 0-0 Tstrap: 0-0
Best Rating:	83 2/03 Plum 2m soft Hdl

Ex-French, runner-up in a selling novice hurdle before unseating and being remounted when set for third in a juvenile hurdle at Plumpton. Acts on soft ground and looks capable of improvement.

Restless Wind (IRE)
109   113

11-y-o b g Celio Rufo-Trulos (Three Dons)
G B Balding The Kingfisher Partnership

Placings:3UP/F5/340123-413521 (4682)
2002/03: 23⁴G, 24¹G, 24³G, 27⁵GS, 25²GF, 24¹GF,

	Starts	1st	2nd	3rd	Win & Pl
Chases	6	2	1	1	15692
Career Total	17	3	2	4	23037
113 4/03	Hntg	3m	D(0-120)HCh	G-F	£5460
113 11/02	Kemp	3m	D(0-120)HCh	GD	£6922
96 3/02	Tntn	3m	F(0-90)Ch	SFT	£3150
		Total win prize-money £15533			

Going:	Sf: 0-0 GS: 0-0 Gd: 1-3 GF: Fm: 1-2
Distance:	2m/2m3: 0-0 2m4-2m7: 0-0 3m+: 2-6
Track:	LH: 0-0 RH: 2-6 Tight: 0-2 Gall: 1-1
Aids:	Bl: 0-0 Vi: 0-0 Tstrap: 0-0
Best Rating:	113 4/03 Hntg 3m gd-fm Ch

Modest handicap chaser, stays three miles and acts on most types of ground.

Ret Frem (IRE)
(81h)   (36h) 79

10-y-o b g Posen (USA)-New Light (Reform)
A G Blackmore A G Blackmore

Placings:262/414/3/000/640645/0P056F6-2 (0153)
2002/03: 24²G,

	Starts	1st	2nd	3rd	Win & Pl
Chases	1	0	1	0	904
Career Total	24	1	3	1	5198
82 9/97	Prth	2m4f110yE Hdl		G-F	£2772
		Total win prize-money £2772			

Going:	Sf: 0-0 GS: 0-0 Gd: 0-1 GF: Fm: 0-0
Distance:	2m/2m3: 0-0 2m4-2m7: 0-0 3m+: 0-1
Track:	LH: 0-1 RH: 0-0 Tight: 0-1 Gall: 0-0
Aids:	Bl: 0-0 Vi: 0-0 Tstrap: 0-0
Best Rating:	85 5/00 Font 2m2f110y good Hdl

Plating-class chaser; stays two and a half miles; best on a sound surface.

Return The Call (IRE)

6-y-o b g Bob Back (USA)-Ring Four (IRE) (Supreme Leader)
Miss H C Knight H Stephen Smith & Harold Winton

Placings:0-0 (1660)
2002/03: 22⁰G,

	Starts	1st	2nd	3rd	Win & Pl
Hurdles	1	0	0	0	
Career Total	2	0	0	0	

Going:	Sf: 0-0 GS: 0-0 Gd: 0-1 GF: Fm: 0-0
Distance:	2m/2m3: 0-0 2m4-2m7: 0-1 3m+: 0-0
Track:	LH: 0-0 RH: 0-1 Tight: 0-0 Gall: 0-0
Aids:	Bl: 0-0 Vi: 0-0 Tstrap: 0-0
Best Rating:	65 11/01 Sand 2m110y gd-sft NHF

Returning
96   133

7-y-o b m Bob s Return (IRE)-Buck Comtess (USA) (Spend A Buck (USA))
Miss H C Knight Harold Winton

Placings:0001/4F3P511P23P/11112243F-43P (3178)
2002/03: 16⁴GS, 20³S, 21²FG,

	Starts	1st	2nd	3rd	Win & Pl
Hurdles	1	0	0	0	0
Chases	2	0	1	0	2798
Career Total	27	7	3	4	54153
137 11/01	Asct	2m3f110yB Ch		GD	£9464
133 11/01	Sand	2m D Ch		G-S	£4936
114 10/01	Tntn	2m3f D Ch		FRM	£5538
111 10/01	Extr	2m1f110yE Ch		G-F	£3526
110 12/00	Hrfd	2m3f110yF(0-105)HHdl		HVY	£3344
104 12/00	Tntn	2m3f110yD(0-120)HHdl		SFT	£2970
97 4/00	Carl	2m4f110yE(0-105)HHdl		SFT	£2912
		Total win prize-money £32692			

Going:	Sf: 0-1 GS: 0-1 Gd: 0-1 GF: Fm: 0-0
Distance:	2m/2m3: 0-1 2m4-2m7: 0-2 3m+: 0-0
Track:	LH: 0-0 RH: 0-3 Tight: 0-0 Gall: 0-0
Aids:	Bl: 0-0 Vi: 0-0 Tstrap: 0-0
Best Rating:	137 12/01 Sand 2m gd-sft Ch

Useful chaser; ex-Irish mare, winner three times over hurdles in 2000/1. Took well to fences in the autumn of 2001, winning four times before having her limitations exposed. She has won on fast ground, but looks ideally suited by cut. Stays two and a half miles.

Revelino (IRE)
88   51

4-y-o b g Revoque (IRE)-Forelino (USA) (Trempolino (USA))
Miss S J Wilton (E A L Dunlop 14/10) John Pointon And Sons

Placings:004 (4219)
2002/03: 16⁰GS, 16⁰GS, 17⁴GF,

	Starts	1st	2nd	3rd	Win & Pl
Hurdles	3	0	0	0	260

| Career Total | 3 | 0 | 0 | 0 | 260 |

Going: Sf: 0-0 GS: 0-2 Gd: 0-0 GF: - Fm: 0-1
Distance: 2m/2m3: 0-3 2m4-2m7: 0-0 3m+: 0-0
Track: LH: 0-2 RH: 0-1 Tight: 0-1 Gall: 0-1
Aids: Bl: 0-0 Vi: 0-0 Tstrap: 0-0
Best Rating: 68   3/03   Hrfd   2m1f   gd-fm   Hdl

Reverse Charge

99(109h)   (121dh)96

11-y-o b g Teenoso (USA)-Ebb And Flo (Forlorn River)
C Grant   Ian W Glenton

Placings:0/31P20000/1211120/PP05OP/210062-03P3F0
                             (3517)
2002/03: 22⁰S, 25³GS, 33PS, 25³S, 24FHY, 23⁰GS,

	Starts	1st	2nd	3rd	Win & Pl
Hurdles	2	0	0	0	0
Chases	4	0	0	2	1457
Career Total	34	6	5	3	38938

121	12/01	Hayd	2m6f	B(0-140)HHdl	SFT	£8238
128	1/00	Wwck	2m4f110yB	HHdl	SFT	£7264
130	12/99	Weth	2m7f	C(0-130)HHdl	G-S	£4857
116	12/99	Newc	2m4f	C(0-135)HHdl	SFT	£5272
105	11/99	MRas	2m1f110yF(0-110)HHdl	G-S	£2290
92	7/98	MRas	2m1f110yF Hdl		G-F	£1469
				Total win prize-money £29392

Going: Sf: 0-4 GS: 0-2 Gd: 0-0 GF: - Fm: 0-0
Distance: 2m/2m3: 0-0 2m4-2m7: 0-1 3m+: 0-5
Track: LH: 0-5 RH: 0-1 Tight: 0-2 Gall: 0-1
Aids: Bl: 0-0 Vi: 0-2 Tstrap: 0-1
Best Rating: 130   12/99   Weth   2m7f   gd-sft   Hdl

Moderate but tough staying hurdler, he is suited by soft ground. Has not looked quite as good over fences despite some fair efforts. Has been tried in a visor, tongue tie and cheekpieces.

Reverse Swing

108   80d

6-y-o b m Charmer-Milly Kelly (Murrayfield)
Mrs H Dalton (Mrs P Sly 9/10) The Herons Partnership

Placings:060-5051F006   (4679)
2002/03: 17⁵GF, 17⁰GF, 20⁵G, 16¹GS, 16FG, 17⁰G, 16⁸GF, 16⁶GF,

	Starts	1st	2nd	3rd	Win & Pl
Hurdles	8	1	0	0	3494
Career Total	11	1	0	0	3494

| 80 | 11/02 | Winc | 2m | E(0-100)HHdl | G-S | £3493 |
| | | | | Total win prize-money £3494 |

Going: Sf: 0-0 GS: 1-1 Gd: 0-3 GF: - Fm: 0-4
Distance: 2m/2m3: 1-7 2m4-2m7: 0-1 3m+: 0-0
Track: LH: 0-1 RH: 1-7 Tight: 0-3 Gall: 0-1
Aids: Bl: 0-0 Vi: 0-0 Tstrap: 0-0
Best Rating: 80   12/02   Ludl   2m   good   Hdl

Poor novice hurdler; acts on good.

Reviewer (IRE)

110   128

5-y-o b g Sadler s Wells (USA)-Clandestina (USA) (Secretariat (USA))
H Morrison   Martyn Meade

Placings:21P-0320   (4323)
2002/03: 17⁰GS, 16³GS, 16²GS, 16⁰G,

	Starts	1st	2nd	3rd	Win & Pl
Hurdles	4	0	1	1	5436
Career Total	7	1	2	1	9831

| 128 | 2/02 | MRas | 2m1f110yD Hdl | G-S | £3612 |
| | | | | Total win prize-money £3612 |

Going: Sf: 0-1 GS: 0-2 Gd: 0-1 GF: - Fm: 0-0
Distance: 2m/2m3: 0-4 2m4-2m7: 0-0 3m+: 0-0
Track: LH: 0-3 RH: 0-1 Tight: 0-0 Gall: 0-3
Aids: Bl: 0-0 Vi: 0-0 Tstrap: 0-0
Best Rating: 128   3/03   Newb   2m110y   soft   Hdl

Useful dual-purpose performer; suited by two miles and good or easy ground; a keen sort.

Revitalize

92   82

5-y-o b g Lion Cavern (USA)-Belle Et Deluree (USA) (The Minstrel (CAN))
D G McArdle   Grafton Street Syndicate

Placings:002-0046P0   (1833a)
2002/03: 16⁰HY, 19⁰YS, 17⁴G, 16⁶GF, 20⁵S, 18⁰GY,

	Starts	1st	2nd	3rd	Win & Pl
Hurdles	6	0	0	0	0
Career Total	9	0	1	0	1161

Going: Sf: 0-2 GS: 0-0 Gd: 0-1 GF: - Fm: 0-1
Distance: 2m/2m3: 0-5 2m4-2m7: 0-1 3m+: 0-0
Track: LH: 0-3 RH: 0-1 Tight: 0-1 Gall: 0-0
Aids: Bl: 0-1 Vi: 0-1 Tstrap: 0-0
Best Rating: 95   12/01   Thur   2m   heavy   Hdl

Reynolds House (IRE)

(79h)   (45h)

9-y-o ch g Glacial Storm (USA)-Lucky House (Pollerton)
A E Jessop   Mrs Gloria Jessop

Placings:0P00/00/00-PP   (3110)
2002/03: 17P0GF, 16PS,

	Starts	1st	2nd	3rd	Win & Pl
Hurdles	1	0	0	0	0
Chases	1	0	0	0	0
Career Total	10	0	0	0	0

Going: Sf: 0-1 GS: 0-0 Gd: 0-0 GF: - Fm: 0-1
Distance: 2m/2m3: 0-2 2m4-2m7: 0-0 3m+: 0-0
Track: LH: 0-0 RH: 0-2 Tight: 0-1 Gall: 0-0
Aids: Bl: 0-1 Vi: 0-0 Tstrap: 0-0
Best Rating: 73   10/00   Chep   2m4f   gd-sft   Hdl

Rhapsody In Blue (IRE)

107(99h)   (90 h)73

8-y-o b g Magical Strike (USA)-Palace Blue (IRE) (Dara Monarch)
R Ford   Bricks, Bills & Beer

Placings:6300/00036/P/P30F121420-F120   (3916)
2002/03: 21FS, 20¹HY, 24²G, 24⁰S,

	Starts	1st	2nd	3rd	Win & Pl
Hurdles	1	1	0	0	2310
Chases	3	0	1	0	1281
Career Total	24	3	3	3	7555

90	1/03	Newc	2m4f	G(0-95)HHdl	HVY	£2310
83	12/01	Tntn	3m110y	G(0-90)HHdl	G-S	£1722
				Total win prize-money £4032

Going: Sf: 1-3 GS: 0-0 Gd: 0-1 GF: - Fm: 0-0
Distance: 2m/2m3: 0-0 2m4-2m7: 1-2 3m+: 0-2

Track: LH: 1-2 RH: 0-2 Tight: 0-1 Gall: 1-1
Aids: Bl: 0-0 Vi: 0-0 Tstrap: 1-4
Best Rating: 99   3/99   Newb   2m110y   gd-fm   Hdl

Poor chaser; plating-class hurdler; effective from two and a half to three miles; handles good ground, but better on softer.

Rhetoric (IRE)

99   66

4-y-o b g Desert King (IRE)-Squaw Talk (USA) (Gulch (USA))
D G Bridgwater (J H M Gosden 10/5) Alan A Wright

Placings:60P6P40   (4629)
2002/03: 16⁶GF, 16⁰GS, 17PS, 16⁶HY, 26PS, 24⁴F, 21⁰GF,

	Starts	1st	2nd	3rd	Win & Pl
Hurdles	7	0	0	0	177
Career Total	7	0	0	0	177

Going: Sf: 0-3 GS: 0-1 Gd: 0-0 GF: - Fm: 0-3
Distance: 2m/2m3: 0-4 2m4-2m7: 0-1 3m+: 0-2
Track: LH: 0-2 RH: 0-5 Tight: 0-2 Gall: 0-1
Aids: Bl: 0-0 Vi: 0-0 Tstrap: 0-0
Best Rating: 66   4/03   Tntn   3m110y   firm   Hdl

Rhinestone Cowboy (IRE)

114   161+

7-y-o b g Be My Native (USA)-Monumental Gesture (Head For Heights)
Jonjo O Neill   Mrs John Magnier

Placings:12-111113   (4099)
2002/03: 16¹GS, 16¹S, 17¹G, 16¹GS, 16¹GS, 16³G,

	Starts	1st	2nd	3rd	Win & Pl
NH Flat	1	1	0	0	10570
Hurdles	5	4	0	1	94657
Career Total	8	6	1	1	114577

161	2/03	Winc	2m	A Hdl	G-S	£29750
151	2/03	Weth	2m	A Hdl	G-S	£17400
117	12/02	Chel	2m1f	B Hdl	GD	£10230
131	11/02	Newb	2m110y	D Hdl	SFT	£4277
131	11/02	Chel	2m110y	A NHF	G-S	£10570
131	2/02	Asct	2m110y	N HHF	SFT	£2450
				Total win prize-money £74677

Going: Sf: 1-1 GS: 3-3 Gd: 1-2 GF: - Fm: 0-0
Distance: 2m/2m3: 5-6 2m4-2m7: 0-0 3m+: 0-0
Track: LH: 4-5 RH: 1-1 Tight: 0-0 Gall: 2-2
Aids: Bl: 0-0 Vi: 0-0 Tstrap: 0-0
Best Rating: 161   3/03   Chel   2m110y   good   Hdl

Top-class, exceptionally promising hurdler; narrowly beaten in the Festival bumper in 2002; winner of bumper on return to action at Cheltenham in November, he has since won novice hurdles at Newbury, Cheltenham and a Grade Two at Wetherby before running out a most impressive winner of the Kingwell Hurdle at Wincanton on first appearance in senior company; did not jump fluently when third in the Champion Hurdle; effective at around 2m; acts on good and soft ground; usually held up; likely to prove better than bare form.

Rhythm Hill (IRE)

93   89

8-y-o b m Orchestra-Cantafleur (Cantab)
Mrs S J Smith (George Stewart 3/7) Aaron Metcalfe

Placings:00⁵-005   (3834)

2002/03: 20^Y, 20^G, 20^SG,

	Starts	1st	2nd	3rd	Win & Pl
NH Flat	1	0	0	0	0
Hurdles	2	0	0	0	0
Career Total	**6**	**0**	**0**	**0**	0

Going: Sf: 0-0 GS: 0-0 Gd: 0-2 GF: - Fm: 0-0
Distance: 2m/2m3: 0-0 2m4-2m7: 0-3 3m+: 0-0
Track: LH: 0-1 RH: 0-0 Tight: 0-0 Gall: 0-0
Aids: Bl: 0-0 Vi: 0-0 Tstrap: 0-2
Best Rating: 89 2/03 Weth 2m4f110y good Hdl

Rhythm King

77(96h)   (86h)**93**
8-y-o b g Rakaposhi King-Minim (Rymer)
J A B Old Mrs J A Fowler/the Kentish Men

Placings:00/600-U0FU0   (4154)
2002/03: 19^UG, 16^OG, 16^FGS, 20^UGS, 16^OG,

	Starts	1st	2nd	3rd	Win & Pl
Hurdles	1	0	0	0	0
Chases	4	0	0	0	0
Career Total	**10**	**0**	**0**	**0**	0

Going: Sf: 0-0 GS: 0-3 Gd: 0-2 GF: - Fm: 0-0
Distance: 2m/2m3: 0-4 2m4-2m7: 0-1 3m+: 0-0
Track: LH: 0-3 RH: 0-2 Tight: 0-0 Gall: 0-1
Aids: Bl: 0-0 Vi: 0-0 Tstrap: 0-0
Best Rating: 93 3/03 Wwck 2m4f110y gd-sft Ch

Rianatta (IRE)

4-y-o b f Nicolotte-Asturiana (Julio Mariner)
P Butler Homewoodgate Racing Club

Placings:000   (3918)
2002/03: 16^OG, 16^OHY, 18OS,

	Starts	1st	2nd	3rd	Win & Pl
Hurdles	3	0	0	0	0
Career Total	**3**	**0**	**0**	**0**	0

Going: Sf: 0-2 GS: 0-0 Gd: 0-1 GF: - Fm: 0-0
Distance: 2m/2m3: 0-3 2m4-2m7: 0-0 3m+: 0-0
Track: LH: 0-2 RH: 0-1 Tight: 0-2 Gall: 0-0
Aids: Bl: 0-0 Vi: 0-0 Tstrap: 0-0
Best Rating: 0 3/03 Font 2m2f110y soft Hdl

Ribbon Of Light

29
5-y-o b g Spectrum (IRE)-Brush Away (Ahonoora)
Ian Williams A L R Morton

Placings:0-P   (0800)
2002/03: 17^PS,

	Starts	1st	2nd	3rd	Win & Pl
Hurdles	1	0	0	0	0
Career Total	**2**	**0**	**0**	**0**	0

Going: Sf: 0-1 GS: 0-0 Gd: 0-0 GF: - Fm: 0-0
Distance: 2m/2m3: 0-1 2m4-2m7: 0-0 3m+: 0-0
Track: LH: 0-0 RH: 0-0 Tight: 0-1 Gall: 0-0
Aids: Bl: 0-0 Vi: 0-1 Tstrap: 0-0
Best Rating: 29 11/01 Newb 2m110y good Hdl

Ricardo

112(109h)   (129h)**140**
9-y-o b g Sanglamore (USA)-Nurica (USA) (Nureyev (USA))
Brian Nolan Patrick Whelan

Placings:P10116P/503321/0-23U4400   (4498a)
2002/03: 16²S, 17³HY, 16US, 17⁴S, 16⁴YS, 16⁹G, 16⁰GY,

	Starts	1st	2nd	3rd	Win & Pl
Hurdles	1	0	0	0	0
Chases	6	0	1	1	9527
Career Total	**21**	**4**	**2**	**3**	52069
145	2/01	Leop	2m		HHdl	HVY £13104
128	3/99	Newb	2m110y		C(0-130)HHdl	SFT £4549
111	2/99	Uttx	2m		D Hdl	HVY £3777
110	12/98	Towc	2m		E Hdl	SFT £2512

Total win prize-money £23945

Going: Sf: 0-4 GS: 0-0 Gd: 0-1 GF: - Fm: 0-0
Distance: 2m/2m3: 0-7 2m4-2m7: 0-0 3m+: 0-0
Track: LH: 0-5 RH: 0-0 Tight: 0-0 Gall: 0-0
Aids: Bl: 0-1 Vi: 0-0 Tstrap: 0-0
Best Rating: 145 2/01 Leop 2m heavy Hdl

Very useful Irish novice chaser; formerly decent hurdler; best over 2m; suited by cut in the ground.

Riccarton

94(100h)   (83 h)**88**
10-y-o b g Nomination-Legendary Dancer (Shareef Dancer (USA))
D C Turner Mrs M E Turner

Placings:560/12603/06455P-4322535   (4627)
2002/03: 17⁴GF, 16³GF, 16²GF, 16⁹G, 19⁵F, 17³G, 21⁵GF,

	Starts	1st	2nd	3rd	Win & Pl
Hurdles	1	0	0	0	0
Chases	6	0	2	2	3926
Career Total	**21**	**1**	**3**	**3**	7967
89	9/99	Tntn	2m3f110yD Hdl		G-F	£2626

Total win prize-money £2626

Going: Sf: 0-0 GS: 0-0 Gd: 0-2 GF: - Fm: 0-5
Distance: 2m/2m3: 0-6 2m4-2m7: 0-1 3m+: 0-0
Track: LH: 0-5 RH: 0-2 Tight: 0-6 Gall: 0-0
Aids: Bl: 0-0 Vi: 0-0 Tstrap: 0-0
Best Rating: 99 11/99 Chel 2m110y good Hdl

Low-grade chaser, in the frame in the summer of 2002.

Rice Point

10-y-o b g Gold Dust-My Kizzy (The Ditton)
John Squire John Squire

Placings:P-P   (0034)
2002/03: 16^PGF,

	Starts	1st	2nd	3rd	Win & Pl
Chases	1	0	0	0	0
Career Total	**2**	**0**	**0**	**0**	0

Going: Sf: 0-0 GS: 0-0 Gd: 0-0 GF: - Fm: 0-1
Distance: 2m/2m3: 0-1 2m4-2m7: 0-0 3m+: 0-0
Track: LH: 0-1 RH: 0-0 Tight: 0-0 Gall: 0-1
Aids: Bl: 0-0 Vi: 0-0 Tstrap: 0-0

Richie's Delight (IRE)

99(102h)   (100h)**106**
10-y-o br g Phardante (FR)-Johnstown Love (IRE) (Golden Love)

Ferdy Murphy Geoff Hubbard Racing

Placings:S/405452P/351S42312F1/44P43364/4P022-U434232242P0   (2168)
2002/03: 16^UG, 20⁴G, 20³S, 20⁴GF, 20²G, 20³S, 20²GF, 20²GF, 21⁴GF, 21²GS, 24^PGS, 19⁰GS,

	Starts	1st	2nd	3rd	Win & Pl
Hurdles	10	0	3	2	3872
Chases	2	0	1	0	1163
Career Total	**44**	**3**	**9**	**6**	24994
99	4/00	Hntg	2m4f110yE Ch		GD	£3180
119	11/99	Hntg	2m4f110yD Ch		G-F	£4177
96	8/99	Hntg	2m4f110yE Hdl		G-F	£2835

Total win prize-money £10192

Going: Sf: 0-2 GS: 0-3 Gd: 0-3 GF: - Fm: 0-4
Distance: 2m/2m3: 0-2 2m4-2m7: 0-9 3m+: 0-1
Track: LH: 0-9 RH: 0-3 Tight: 0-3 Gall: 0-3
Aids: Bl: 0-0 Vi: 0-0 Tstrap: 0-0
Best Rating: 119 12/99 Leic 2m4f110y gd-fm Ch

Moderate hurdler/chaser, acts on any ground, particularly suited by two and a half miles at Huntingdon.

Rickham Glory

5-y-o b g Past Glories-Rickham Bay (Snow Warning)
H E Haynes Miss Alison Joy

Placings:000   (4542)
2002/03: 16^OGS, 16^OGS, 16^OG,

	Starts	1st	2nd	3rd	Win & Pl
NH Flat	3	0	0	0	
Career Total	**3**	**0**	**0**	**0**	

Going: Sf: 0-0 GS: 0-2 Gd: 0-1 GF: - Fm: 0-0
Distance: 2m/2m3: 0-3 2m4-2m7: 0-0 3m+: 0-0
Track: LH: 0-1 RH: 0-2 Tight: 0-0 Gall: 0-0
Aids: Bl: 0-0 Vi: 0-0 Tstrap: 0-0
Best Rating: 0 4/03 Ludl 2m good NHF

Ricko (NZ)

106   **104**
9-y-o b g Defensive Play (USA)-Native Hawk (NZ) (War Hawk)
B G Powell D & J Newell

Placings:42212F/0-364F211F5   (1690)
2002/03: 16³S, 17⁶G, 21⁴GF, 21^FGF, 20²GS, 21¹GF, 21¹GF, 21^FGF, 20⁵G,

	Starts	1st	2nd	3rd	Win & Pl
Chases	9	2	1	1	20510
Career Total	**16**	**3**	**4**	**1**	25007
100	9/02	Strf	2m5f110yD Ch		G-F	£5375
107	8/02	NAbb	2m5f110yB HCh		G-F	£12722
	6/00	Trap	1m4f110y Hdl		HVY	£1393

Total win prize-money £19492

Going: Sf: 0-1 GS: 0-1 Gd: 0-2 GF: - Fm: 2-5
Distance: 2m/2m3: 0-0 **2m4-2m7: 2-7** 3m+: 0-0
Track: **LH: 2-9** RH: 0-0 Tight: 2-6 Gall: 0-1
Aids: Bl: 0-0 Vi: 0-0 Tstrap: 0-0
Best Rating: 110 1/01 Plum 2m soft Hdl

Front-running novice chaser. Possibly unlucky when falling two out whilst still in the lead at Newton Abbot July 2002 but had luck on his side when scoring at Newton Abbot. Followed up at Stratford; acts on any ground.

Ricky B

81   **71**
7-y-o b g Rakaposhi King-Fililode (Mossberry)

M Wellings The 1471 Racing Partnership

Placings:*00*/00PP5-400   (1702)
2002/03: 20⁴G, 16⁹G, 19⁹GF,

	Starts	1st	2nd	3rd	Win & Pl
Hurdles	3	0	0	0	0
Career Total	10	0	0	0	0

Going:	Sf: 0-0 GS: 0-0 Gd: 0-2 GF: - Fm: 0-1
Distance:	2m/2m3: 0-2 2m4-2m7: 0-2 3m+: 0-0
Track:	LH: 0-2 RH: 0-1 Tight: 0-2 Gall: 0-0
Aids:	Bl: 0-0 Vi: 0-0 Tstrap: 0-0
Best Rating:	71 5/02 Uttx 2m4f110y good Hdl

Ridapour (IRE)

88   81

4-y-o b g Kahyasi-Ridiyara (IRE) (Persian Bold)
D J Wintle (A De Royer-Dupre 11/10) Frinton Bloodstock

Placings:*3*   (4567)
2002/03: 20³GF,

	Starts	1st	2nd	3rd	Win & Pl
Hurdles	1	0	0	1	573
Career Total	1	0	0	1	573

Going:	Sf: 0-0 GS: 0-0 Gd: 0-0 GF: - Fm: 0-1
Distance:	2m/2m3: 0-0 2m4-2m7: 0-1 3m+: 0-0
Track:	LH: 0-1 RH: 0-0 Tight: 0-1 Gall: 0-0
Aids:	Bl: 0-0 Vi: 0-0 Tstrap: 0-0
Best Rating:	79 4/03 Bang 2m4f gd-fm Hdl

Moderate hurdler; shapes as though he needs further than two miles; now qualified for handicaps.

Riders Revenge (IRE)

92f   104f

5-y-o b g Norwich-Paico Ana (Paico)
P M J Doyle J Halley

Placings:*300*   (2285a)
2002/03: 16⁹YS, 16⁹GS, 16⁹SH,

	Starts	1st	2nd	3rd	Win & Pl
NH Flat	3	0	0	1	344
Career Total	3	0	0	1	344

Going:	Sf: 0-0 GS: 0-1 Gd: 0-0 GF: - Fm: 0-0
Distance:	2m/2m3: 0-3 2m4-2m7: 0-0 3m+: 0-0
Track:	LH: 0-1 RH: 0-1 Tight: 0-0 Gall: 0-0
Aids:	Bl: 0-0 Vi: 0-0 Tstrap: 0-0
Best Rating:	104 10/02 Thur 2m yld-sft NHF

Ran well to be third first time out in an 18 runner bumper on a soft surface. Held subsequently.

Ridgeway (IRE)

8-y-o b g Indian Ridge-Regal Promise (Pitskelly)
Miss J E Foster (M W Easterby 15/10) Stuart Hardy

Placings:*32/55-4412*   (4417)
2002/03: 17⁴GF, 17⁴G, 25¹S, 25²G,

	Starts	1st	2nd	3rd	Win & Pl
Hurdles	2	0	0	0	370
Chases	2	1	1	0	1806
Career Total	8	1	2	1	3812
102 3/03 Catt 3m1f110yH Ch				SFT	£1423
				Total win prize-money £1424	

Going:	Sf: 1-1 GS: 0-0 Gd: 0-2 GF: - Fm: 0-1
Distance:	2m/2m3: 0-2 2m4-2m7: 0-0 3m+: 1-2
Track:	LH: 1-2 RH: 0-2 Tight: 1-4 Gall: 0-0
Aids:	Bl: 0-0 Vi: 0-0 Tstrap: 0-0
Best Rating:	104 12/00 Donc 2m110y gd-sft Hdl

Modest hunter chaser; best over trips of three miles plus and acts on any ground; tends to make mistakes.

Ridgeway Lad

98   83

5-y-o ch g Primo Dominie-Phyliel (USA) (Lyphard (USA))
T D Easterby David & Steven Dudley

Placings:*4*   (0407)
2002/03: 17⁴GF,

	Starts	1st	2nd	3rd	Win & Pl
Hurdles	1	0	0	0	0
Career Total	1	0	0	0	0

Going:	Sf: 0-0 GS: 0-0 Gd: 0-0 GF: - Fm: 0-0
Distance:	2m/2m3: 0-1 2m4-2m7: 0-0 3m+: 0-0
Track:	LH: 0-0 RH: 0-1 Tight: 0-1 Gall: 0-0
Aids:	Bl: 0-0 Vi: 0-0 Tstrap: 0-0
Best Rating:	79 6/02 MRas 2m1f110y gd-fm Hdl

Riding High

65f

4-y-o ch f Afzal-Upper Mount Street (IRE) (Strong Gale)
C P Morlock Mrs Hugh Maitland-Jones

Placings:*60*   (3432)
2002/03: 17⁹HY, 18⁹S,

	Starts	1st	2nd	3rd	Win & Pl
NH Flat	2	0	0	0	0
Career Total	2	0	0	0	0

Going:	Sf: 0-2 GS: 0-0 Gd: 0-0 GF: - Fm: 0-0
Distance:	2m/2m3: 0-2 2m4-2m7: 0-0 3m+: 0-0
Track:	LH: 0-1 RH: 0-1 Tight: 0-2 Gall: 0-0
Aids:	Bl: 0-0 Vi: 0-0 Tstrap: 0-0
Best Rating:	0 2/03 Font 2m2f110y soft NHF

Rift Valley (IRE)

109(106h)   (117 h)127+

8-y-o b g Good Thyne (USA)-Necochea (Julio Mariner)
P J Hobbs Mrs Kathy Stuart

Placings:*4210/6446020/11111-00U016*   (4441)
2002/03: 22⁰S, 21⁰G, 24ᵁG, 22⁰GS, 22¹F, 20⁶G,

	Starts	1st	2nd	3rd	Win & Pl
Hurdles	6	1	0	0	5395
Career Total	22	7	2	0	30438
117 3/03 Extr 2m6f110yD(0-125)HHdl FRM £5395					
117 8/01 Worc 2m4f D(0-125)HHdl G-F £4238					
115 8/01 Worc 3m C(0-135)HHdl G-F £5363					
110 7/01 Wolv 2m4f110yD(0-125)HHdl G-F £6727					
117 7/01 MRas 2m1f110yK(0-105)HHdl GD £3206					
108 6/01 Worc 2m4f E(0-105)HHdl GD £2534					
98 12/99 Ludl 2m H NHF G-S £1763					
				Total win prize-money £29228	

Going:	Sf: 0-1 GS: 0-1 Gd: 0-3 GF: - Fm: 1-1
Distance:	2m/2m3: 0-0 2m4-2m7: 1-5 3m+: 0-1
Track:	LH: 0-2 RH: 1-4 Tight: 0-1 Gall: 0-1
Aids:	Bl: 0-0 Vi: 1-3 Tstrap: 0-1
Best Rating:	117 3/03 Extr 2m6f110y firm Hdl

Useful hurdler; progressive performer in modest company

over hurdles in the summer of 2001, winning five on the bounce; won twice over fences in the summer of 2003; stays 3m; acts on fast ground; jumps badly to his right; best in a visor.

Rigadoon (IRE)

111(100h)   (84h)97d

7-y-o b g Be My Chief (USA)-Loucoum (FR) (Iron Duke (FR))
M W Easterby C Buckton, K Mercer & A Ford

Placings:*1F0/6/55354-4P23231PP5P*   (4690)
2002/03: 20⁴GF, 25⁵GF, 25²GF, 23³GF, 20²GS, 27³S, 24¹GS, 25⁸S, 25⁸S, 28⁶G, 25⁸G,

	Starts	1st	2nd	3rd	Win & Pl
Chases	11	1	2	2	7841
Career Total	20	2	2	3	11736
97 12/02 Hntg 3m E(0-105)HCh G-S £3721					
102 11/99 Weth 2m D Hdl GD £2914					
				Total win prize-money £6636	

Going:	Sf: 0-3 GS: 1-2 Gd: 0-2 GF: - Fm: 0-4
Distance:	2m/2m3: 0-0 2m4-2m7: 0-2 3m+: 1-9
Track:	LH: 0-6 RH: 1-4 Tight: 0-7 Gall: 1-1
Aids:	Bl: 1-11 Vi: 0-0 Tstrap: 0-0
Best Rating:	102 11/99 Weth 2m good Hdl

Moderate chaser; often in the frame over fences, and won first race since November 1999 at Huntingdon in December 2002. Stays three miles, does not want the ground too soft.

Right

103(81c)   (61c)101

8-y-o b m Teenoso (USA)-Left (Remainder Man)
D McCain Mrs D McCain

Placings:*5F1-F2P3P2*   (4320)
2002/03: 17⁵S, 17²GS, 16⁶HY, 21³HY, 20²S, 17²G,

	Starts	1st	2nd	3rd	Win & Pl
Hurdles	4	0	2	0	1435
Chases	2	0	0	1	855
Career Total	9	1	2	1	4558
101 3/02 Bang 2m1f F Hdl SFT £2268					
				Total win prize-money £2268	

Going:	Sf: 0-4 GS: 0-1 Gd: 0-1 GF: - Fm: 0-0
Distance:	2m/2m3: 0-4 2m4-2m7: 0-2 3m+: 0-0
Track:	LH: 0-5 RH: 0-1 Tight: 0-4 Gall: 0-1
Aids:	Bl: 0-1 Vi: 0-0 Tstrap: 0-0
Best Rating:	101 12/02 Bang 2m1f gd-sft Hdl

Moderate hurdler; off the mark in weak claiming hurdle at Bangor in March 2002. Soon tailed off on chasing bow and lacks the size to make much of an impact over fences.

Rightsaidfred

15-y-o b g Lighter-Ladybank (Dear Gazelle)
Miss A M Newton-Smith P A Bull

Placings:*1/FF2/1112BF/132P0/P3126/12-1*   (0313)
2002/03: 25¹G,

	Starts	1st	2nd	3rd	Win & Pl
Chases	1	1	0	0	1926
Career Total	23	8	5	2	43674
107 5/02 Folk 3m1f H Ch GD £1926					
112 3/02 Plum 3m2f H Ch G-S £1148					
136 1/01 Winc 3m1f110yD(0-125)HCh G-S £5343					
132 12/99 Folk 3m2f D(0-125)HCh GD £3710					
136 1/99 Newb 3m2f110yC(0-135)HCh HVY £10866					
121 11/98 Folk 3m2f E(0-110)HCh G-S £4260					
113 11/98 Plum 3m1f110yD(0-120)HCh SFT £4143					
95 5/95 Folk 3m2f H Ch GD £1774					

Total win prize-money £33171

Going: Sf: 0-0 GS: 0-0 Gd: 1-1 GF: - Fm: 0-0
Distance: 2m/2m3: 0-0 2m4-2m7: 0-0 **3m+:** 1-1
Track: LH: 0-0 **RH:** 1-1 **Tight:** 1-1 Gall: 0-0
Aids: Bl: 0-0 Vi: 0-0 Tstrap: 0-0
Best Rating: 136 1/01 Winc 3m1f110y soft   Ch

A sprightly veteran, he jumps well and stays. In good heart in point-to-points in the spring of 2002 before winning a hunter chase at Folkestone.

Rigmarole

115(100c)   (101+c)**128**
5-y-o b g Fairy King (USA)-Cattermole (USA) (Roberto (USA))
P F Nicholls D J & F A Jackson

Placings:1463011-302002   (3727)
2002/03: 18³GF, 17⁰GS, 16²G, 16⁰G, 16⁰GS, 16²G,

	Starts	1st	2nd	3rd	Win & Pl
Hurdles	6	0	2	1	6122
Career Total	13	3	2	2	16558
126 4/02 Sedg	2m1f	E Hdl		G-F	£2576
104 4/02 Weth	2m	E Hdl		G-F	£3220
109 12/01 Weth	2m	D Hdl		G-S	£3759

Total win prize-money £9555

Going: Sf: 0-0 GS: 0-2 Gd: 0-3 GF: - Fm: 0-1
Distance: 2m/2m3: 0-6 2m4-2m7: 0-0 3m+: 0-0
Track: LH: 0-2 RH: 0-4 Tight: 0-2 Gall: 0-0
Aids: Bl: 0-0 Vi: 0-0 Tstrap: 0-5
Best Rating: 128 2/03 Kemp 2m   good   Hdl

Fair hurdler, ex-French; suited by trips of around two miles and fast ground; wears a tongue tie.

Rigolade (USA)

106(103c)   (107c)**36**
7-y-o b g Dayjur (USA)-Arewehavingfunyet (USA) (Sham (USA))
N F Glynn Noel Glynn

Placings:04000/0P4-210011P   (1938)
2002/03: 24²G, 20¹GF, 20⁵GY, 20⁰G, 26¹G, 24¹F, 24⁸G,

	Starts	1st	2nd	3rd	Win & Pl
Hurdles	4	1	1	0	4582
Chases	3	2	0	0	10803
Career Total	15	3	1	0	15913
107 9/02 List	3m	(0-102)HCh		FRM	£6773
100 9/02 Uttx	3m2f	E Ch		GD	£4030
94 8/02 Bang	2m4f	E(0-105)HHdl		G-F	£3786

Total win prize-money £14589

Going: Sf: 0-0 GS: 0-0 Gd: 1-4 GF: - Fm: 2-2
Distance: 2m/2m3: 0-0 2m4-2m7: 1-3 **3m+:** 2-4
Track: **LH:** 3-5 RH: 0-0 **Tight:** 1-1 Gall: 0-1
Aids: **Bl:** 3-6 Vi: 0-0 Tstrap: 0-0
Best Rating: 109 5/00 Punc 2m   yield   NHF

Irish handicap chaser/hurdler, stays well. Winner at Bangor over hurdles and Uttoxeter and Listowel in the late summer of 2002.

Rimosa

100   **91**
8-y-o b m Miners Lamp-Crosa (Crozier)
A P Jones A P Jones

Placings:00/PF035U-55P4   (0698)
2002/03: 17⁵G, 16⁵G, 19⁰G, 17⁴GF,

	Starts	1st	2nd	3rd	Win & Pl
Hurdles	4	0	0	0	0

Career Total   12   0   0   1   393

Going: Sf: 0-0 GS: 0-0 Gd: 0-3 GF: - Fm: 0-1
Distance: 2m/2m3: 0-3 2m4-2m7: 0-1 3m+: 0-0
Track: LH: 0-0 RH: 0-4 Tight: 0-1 Gall: 0-0
Aids: Bl: 0-0 Vi: 0-0 Tstrap: 0-0
Best Rating: 91 5/02 Extr 2m1f   good   Hdl

Ring De Sou (FR)

(79h)   (69h)
6-y-o b g Ajdayt (USA)-Ring Ann (IRE) (Auction Ring (USA))
M C Pipe Trevor Painting

Placings:000/4RR15P-0   (0576)
2002/03: 17⁰G,

	Starts	1st	2nd	3rd	Win & Pl
Hurdles	1	0	0	0	
Career Total	10	1	0	0	9215
6/01 Autl	2m1f110y Ch		VS		£6305

Total win prize-money £6305

Going: Sf: 0-0 GS: 0-0 Gd: 0-1 GF: - Fm: 0-0
Distance: 2m/2m3: 0-1 2m4-2m7: 0-0 3m+: 0-0
Track: LH: 0-1 RH: 0-0 Tight: 0-1 Gall: 0-0
Aids: Bl: 0-0 Vi: 0-1 Tstrap: 0-0
Best Rating: 78 6/02 NAbb 2m1f   good   Hdl

Rio Grande (IRE)

                                             74
9-y-o b g Un Desperado (FR)-Liffey s Choice (Little Buskins)
C R Barwell Tony Fiorillo

Placings:10/PP/0-3   (0035)
2002/03: 22³G,

	Starts	1st	2nd	3rd	Win & Pl
Hurdles	1	0	0	1	350
Career Total	6	1	0	1	3584
90 9/99 Gway	2m	NHF		SFT	£3234

Total win prize-money £3234

Going: Sf: 0-0 GS: 0-0 Gd: 0-1 GF: - Fm: 0-0
Distance: 2m/2m3: 0-2 2m4-2m7: 0-1 3m+: 0-0
Track: LH: 0-0 RH: 0-1 Tight: 0-0 Gall: 0-0
Aids: Bl: 0-0 Vi: 0-0 Tstrap: 0-1
Best Rating: 90 9/99 Gway 2m   soft   NHF

Moderate hurdler; has apparently had his fair share of training problems since winning a bumper in soft ground at Galway in September 1999.

Rio Real (IRE)

98   **96**
7-y-o b g Case Law-Fine Flame (Le Prince)
J Mackie Mrs Sue Adams

Placings:33321/2/1634   (1830)
2002/03: 16¹G, 16⁵GS, 16³G, 16⁴HY,

	Starts	1st	2nd	3rd	Win & Pl
Hurdles	4	1	0	1	2302
Career Total	10	2	2	4	6381
93 5/02 Towc	2m	G Hdl		GD	£1862
94 12/99 Uttx	2m	G Hdl		SFT	£1679

Total win prize-money £3541

Going: Sf: 0-1 GS: 0-1 Gd: 1-2 GF: - Fm: 0-0
Distance: **2m/2m3:** 1-4 2m4-2m7: 0-0 3m+: 0-0
Track: LH: 0-3 **RH:** 1-1 Tight: 0-1 Gall: 0-0
Aids: Bl: 0-0 **Vi:** 1-4 Tstrap: 0-0
Best Rating: 104 11/00 Leic 2m   heavy   Hdl

Lightly-raced, plating class hurdler, suited by good ground or softer. Usually wears headgear.

Rio Tinto

                                             94
8-y-o gr g Gran Alba (USA)-Hollow Creek (Tarqogan)
W Jenks Mrs Diane Snowden

Placings:24/50F30/055115-P   (0037)
2002/03: 22ᴾG,

	Starts	1st	2nd	3rd	Win & Pl
Hurdles	1	0	0	0	
Career Total	14	1	1	1	6660
94 3/02 Sthl	3m110y	F(0-100)HHdl		HVY	£3161
94 3/02 Hrfd	3m2f	F(0-95)HHdl		GD	£2509

Total win prize-money £5671

Going: Sf: 0-0 GS: 0-0 Gd: 0-1 GF: - Fm: 0-0
Distance: 2m/2m3: 0-0 2m4-2m7: 0-1 3m+: 1-0
Track: LH: 0-0 RH: 0-1 Tight: 0-0 Gall: 0-0
Aids: Bl: 0-0 Vi: 0-1 Tstrap: 0-0
Best Rating: 97 1/00 Ludl 2m   gd-sft   NHF

Modest hurdler, successful in low-grade compan y at Southwell and Hereford early in 2002. Stays three miles plus and effective on good ground.

Riothamus (IRE)

68f   **102f**
5-y-o b g Supreme Leader-Kemchee (Kemal (FR))
Ferdy Murphy RP Racing

Placings:1   (3917)
2002/03: 17¹GS,

	Starts	1st	2nd	3rd	Win & Pl
NH Flat	1	1	0	0	2009
Career Total	1	1	0	0	2009
108 3/03 Carl	2m1f	H NHF		G-S	£2009

Total win prize-money £2009

Going: Sf: 0-0 GS: 1-1 Gd: 0-0 GF: - Fm: 0-0
Distance: **2m/2m3:** 1-1 2m4-2m7: 0-0 3m+: 0-0
Track: LH: 0-0 **RH:** 1-1 Tight: 0-0 Gall: 0-0
Aids: Bl: 0-0 Vi: 0-0 Tstrap: 0-0
Best Rating: 108 3/03 Carl 2m1f   gd-sft   NHF

Made a successful racecourse bow in a run-of-the-mill bumper at Carlisle in March 2003. acts on easy ground.

Rise Above (IRE)

9-y-o b m Simply Great (FR)-La Tanque (USA) (Last Raise (USA))
J Cullinan R J Matthews

Placings:4F0F/000330/4-P   (0379)
2002/03: 21ᴾG,

	Starts	1st	2nd	3rd	Win & Pl
Hurdles	1	0	0	0	
Career Total	12	0	0	2	466

Going: Sf: 0-0 GS: 0-0 Gd: 0-1 GF: - Fm: 0-0
Distance: 2m/2m3: 0-0 2m4-2m7: 0-1 3m+: 0-0
Track: LH: 0-0 RH: 0-1 Tight: 0-0 Gall: 0-1
Aids: Bl: 0-0 Vi: 0-0 Tstrap: 0-0
Best Rating: 69 11/99 Sedg 2m5f110y good Hdl

Rising Generation (FR)

105(102c)   (131dc)**114**
6-y-o ch g Risen Star (USA)-Queen s Victory (FR)

(Carmarthen (FR))
N G Richards Alistair Duff

Placings:43/2112F5/1131143P-54P52   (4691)
2002/03: 17⁵S, 19⁴G, 20⁴S, 16⁵G, 19²GF,

	Starts	1st	2nd	3rd	Win & Pl
Hurdles	4	0	1	0	2023
Chases	1	0	0	0	0
Career Total	21	6	3	3	35441

131	1/02	Hrfd	2m3f	E Ch		SFT	£3302
	10/01	Nanc	2m3f	Hdl	VS	£4364
	9/01	Crao	2m2f110y	Ch	SFT	£5819

Total win prize-money £23151

Going:	Sf: 0-2 GS: 0-0 Gd: 0-2 GF: - Fm: 0-1
Distance:	2m2m3: 0-2 2m4-2m7: 0-3 3m+: 0-0
Track:	LH: 0-1 RH: 0-4 Tight: 0-2 Gall: 0-0
Aids:	Bl: 0-0 Vi: 0-0 Tstrap: 0-0
Best Rating:	131 1/02 Hrfd 2m3f soft Ch

Moderate hurdler; winning chaser, stays 2m 5f; acts on fast ground; not the most consistent.

Risk Accessor (IRE)
114   (148h)142

8-y-o b g Commanche Run-Bellatollah (Bellman (FR))
C Roche J P McManus

Placings:22/21251323/11F2331F2-40223   (4458)
2002/03: 22⁴Y, 20⁴GS, 20²SH, 16²G, 16³G,

	Starts	1st	2nd	3rd	Win & Pl
Chases	5	0	2	1	29658
Career Total	24	5	9	5	120868

128	2/02	Thur	2m	Ch	HVY	£6349
130	1/01	Thur	2m6f	Ch	YLD	£7790
146	5/01	Fair	2m4f	Hdl	G-Y	£14677
130	1/01	Naas	2m4f	Hdl	SFT	£18346
135	10/00	Fair	2m4f	Hdl	G-Y	£4416

Total win prize-money £51580

Going:	Sf: 0-0 GS: 0-1 Gd: 0-2 GF: - Fm: 0-0
Distance:	2m/2m3: 0-2 2m4-2m7: 0-3 3m+: 0-0
Track:	LH: 0-3 RH: 0-2 Tight: 0-1 Gall: 0-2
Aids:	Bl: 0-0 Vi: 0-0 Tstrap: 0-1
Best Rating:	148 4/01 Fair 2m4f soft Hdl

Useful handicap chaser; stays two miles six, but effective at shorter; looks best on a soft surface; has worn a tongue tie.

Risk Of Lightning

7-y-o ch m Risk Me (FR)-Lightning Legend (Lord Gayle (USA))
Miss Z C Davison Highly Charged Partnership

Placings:0   (3747)
2002/03: 16⁶G,

	Starts	1st	2nd	3rd	Win & Pl
NH Flat	1	0	0	0	
Career Total	1	0	0	0	

Going:	Sf: 0-0 GS: 0-0 Gd: 0-1 GF: - Fm: 0-0
Distance:	2m/2m3: 0-1 2m4-2m7: 0-0 3m+: 0-0
Track:	LH: 0-0 RH: 0-1 Tight: 0-0 Gall: 0-1
Aids:	Bl: 0-0 Vi: 0-0 Tstrap: 0-0
Best Rating:	0 2/03 Hntg 2m110y good NHF

Risker (USA)
93   66

4-y-o b g Gone West (USA)-Trampoli (USA) (Trempolino (USA))

J Joseph (P J Hobbs 28/9) Jack Joseph

Placings:F056   (4637)
2002/03: 17⁵G, 16⁰G, 16⁵G, 16⁶GF,

	Starts	1st	2nd	3rd	Win & Pl
Hurdles	4	0	0	0	314
Career Total	4	0	0	0	314

Going:	Sf: 0-0 GS: 0-0 Gd: 0-3 GF: - Fm: 0-1
Distance:	2m/2m3: 0-4 2m4-2m7: 0-0 3m+: 0-0
Track:	LH: 0-4 RH: 0-0 Tight: 0-3 Gall: 0-0
Aids:	Bl: 0-0 Vi: 0-0 Tstrap: 0-0
Best Rating:	80 9/02 NAbb 2m1f good Hdl

Shown a little over hurdles, but not the best of jumpers.

Risky Girl
66   32

8-y-o gr m Risk Me (FR)-Jove s Voodoo (USA) (Northern Jove (CAN))
H J Manners H J Manners

Placings:13/6-0   (0367)
2002/03: 17⁰S,

	Starts	1st	2nd	3rd	Win & Pl
Hurdles	1	0	0	0	
Career Total	4	1	0	1	2811

88	11/98	Hrfd	2m1f	E Hdl	GD	£2556

Total win prize-money £2556

Going:	Sf: 0-1 GS: 0-0 Gd: 0-0 GF: - Fm: 0-0
Distance:	2m/2m3: 0-1 2m4-2m7: 0-0 3m+: 0-0
Track:	LH: 0-1 RH: 0-0 Tight: 0-1 Gall: 0-0
Aids:	Bl: 0-0 Vi: 0-0 Tstrap: 0-0
Best Rating:	89 12/98 Font 2m2f110y gd-sft Hdl

Risky Reef
121   137

6-y-o ch g Risk Me (FR)-Pas De Reef (Pas De Seul)
Andrew Lee Ergon Syndicate

Placings:14-3211   (4476)
2002/03: 16³HY, 16²HY, 16¹S, 16¹G,

	Starts	1st	2nd	3rd	Win & Pl
Hurdles	4	2	1	1	33460
Career Total	6	3	1	1	42428

137	4/03	Aint	2m110y	A HHdl	GD	£23200
133	1/03	Thur	2m	Hdl	SFT	£6272
121	12/01	Limk	2m	Hdl	SFT	£7862

Total win prize-money £37336

Going:	Sf: 1-3 GS: 0-0 Gd: 1-1 GF: - Fm: 0-0
Distance:	2m/2m3: 2-4 2m4-2m7: 0-0 3m+: 0-0
Track:	LH: 1-1 RH: 1-1 Tight: 1-1 Gall: 0-0
Aids:	Bl: 0-0 Vi: 0-0 Tstrap: 0-0
Best Rating:	137 4/03 Aint 2m110y good Hdl

Useful Irish-trained hurdler; followed up a Thurles success in January with victory in a valuable handicap at Aintree; suited by two miles and decent ground; very consistent.

Risky Way
105   99

7-y-o b g Risk Me (FR)-Hot Sunday Sport (Star Appeal)
B S Rothwell Mike Gosse

Placings:104300/2/32U42P-U212   (4783)
2002/03: 16⁰U, 16²G, 16¹G, 17²G,

	Starts	1st	2nd	3rd	Win & Pl
Chases	4	1	2	0	7802
Career Total	19	2	5	2	14050

99	2/03	Catt	2m	D(0-115)HCh	GD	£5343
85	9/99	MRas	2m1f110yG Hdl		G-F	£1688

Total win prize-money £7031

Going:	Sf: 0-0 GS: 0-0 Gd: 1-4 GF: - Fm: 0-0
Distance:	2m/2m3: 1-4 2m4-2m7: 0-0 3m+: 0-0
Track:	LH: 1-3 RH: 0-1 Tight: 1-3 Gall: 0-1
Aids:	Bl: 0-0 Vi: 0-0 Tstrap: 0-0
Best Rating:	99 2/03 Catt 2m good Ch

Moderate chaser; selling hurdle winner on fast ground, he has run to a similar level of ability over fences, suited by a sound surface.

Rith Dubh (IRE)
135d

11-y-o b g Black Minstrel-Deep Bonnie (Deep Run)
Jonjo O Neill J P McManus

Placings:1/52560/52420/11/2366/23223221214-0P (4101)
2002/03: 25⁰G, 24⁰PG,

	Starts	1st	2nd	3rd	Win & Pl
Chases	2	0	0	0	
Career Total	30	5	10	3	57952

135	3/02	Chel	4m	B Ch	G-S	£26000
121	2/02	Hntg	3m	C(0-125)HCh	SFT	£6857
127	6/99	Tipp	2m1f	Hdl	GD	£3376
105	6/99	Wxfd	2m	Hdl	G-F	£2639
112	3/97	Thur	2m2f	NHF	GD	£2712

Total win prize-money £41587

Going:	Sf: 0-0 GS: 0-0 Gd: 0-2 GF: - Fm: 0-0
Distance:	2m/2m3: 0-0 2m4-2m7: 0-0 3m+: 0-2
Track:	LH: 0-2 RH: 0-0 Tight: 0-0 Gall: 0-2
Aids:	Bl: 0-2 Vi: 0-0 Tstrap: 0-0
Best Rating:	135 4/02 Punc 3m1f gd-yld Ch

Useful ex-Irish staying chaser; ended a series of frustrating runs with a useful win at Huntingdon at the start of 2002; was given a superb ride to win the National Hunt Chase at the 2002 Festival; has a tendency to down tools when the pressure is applied; acts on everything but extremes of ground and stays really well; usually wears blinkers.

Ritual
110(94h)   (83h)110

8-y-o ch g Selkirk (USA)-Pure Formality (Forzando)
Miss Jacqueline S Doyle The Four X

Placings:14F020/5/21F2-13P   (2486)
2002/03: 16¹G, 16³GS, 16⁶P,G,

	Starts	1st	2nd	3rd	Win & Pl
Chases	3	1	0	1	6486
Career Total	14	3	3	1	15003

110	11/02	Folk	2m	D(0-125)HCh	GD	£5356
102	12/01	Hntg	2m110y	F(0-105)HCh	G-S	£2569
104	10/99	Font	2m2f110yE Hdl		GD	£1987

Total win prize-money £9913

Going:	Sf: 0-0 GS: 0-1 Gd: 1-2 GF: - Fm: 0-0
Distance:	2m/2m3: 1-3 2m4-2m7: 0-0 3m+: 0-0
Track:	LH: 0-2 RH: 1-1 Tight: 1-1 Gall: 0-1
Aids:	Bl: 0-0 Vi: 0-0 Tstrap: 0-0
Best Rating:	113 4/00 Asct 2m110y good Hdl

Modest chaser; winner on the Flat and over hurdles for Simon Dow, he was sent straight into handicaps when sent chasing by his new yard and has rewarded connections with a couple of victories. Suited by two miles and soft ground.

River Amora (IRE)
100(89h)   (86h)76

8-y-o b g Willie Joe (IRE)-That s Amora (Paddy s Stream)

P Butler Mrs P A Wood

Placings:055200034U660134-30563535P536   (2983)
2002/03: 20⁴G, 20³GF, 20⁹G, 20⁵GF, 22⁶GF, 20³GF, 20⁵G, 26³GF, 19⁵G, 21²GF, 18⁵G, 20³S, 22⁵HY,

	Starts	1st	2nd	3rd	Win & Pl
Hurdles	1	0	0	0	0
Chases	12	0	0	4	2472
Career Total	28	1	1	6	7295
88	4/02	Plum	2m4f	F Ch		£2557

Total win prize-money £2558

Going:	Sf: 0-2 GS: 0-0 Gd: 0-5 GF: - Fm: 0-6
Distance:	2m/2m3: 0-1 2m4-2m7: 0-11 3m+: 0-1
Track:	LH: 0-5 RH: 0-3 Tight: 0-11 Gall: 0-1
Aids:	Bl: 0-0 Vi: 0-2 Tstrap: 0-0
Best Rating:	88 9/02 Plum 2m4f good Ch

Moderate, lightly-raced hurdler/chaser. Suited by good/fast ground. Usually amateur ridden.

River Bailiff (IRE)
97   **72**
7-y-o ch g Over The River (FR)-Rath Caola (Neltino)
J Howard Johnson (S Garrott 22/5) S Garrott

Placings:464655   (4660)
2002/03: 26⁴G, 16⁶G, 21⁴S, 16⁶G, 16⁵G, 20⁵GF,

	Starts	1st	2nd	3rd	Win & Pl
Chases	6	0	0	0	410
Career Total	6	0	0	0	410

Going:	Sf: 0-1 GS: 0-0 Gd: 0-4 GF: - Fm: 0-1
Distance:	2m/2m3: 0-3 2m4-2m7: 0-3 3m+: 0-0
Track:	LH: 0-4 RH: 0-2 Tight: 0-2 Gall: 0-1
Aids:	Bl: 0-1 Vi: 0-0 Tstrap: 0-0
Best Rating:	79 2/03 Weth 2m good Ch

River Bann (USA)
98   **110+**
6-y-o ch g Irish River (FR)-Spiritual Star (USA) (Soviet Star (USA))
Mrs Jane Galpin Mrs C D Farmer

Placings:46423   (3856)
2002/03: 17⁴GS, 19⁶GS, 17⁴S, 19²GS, 17³GS,

	Starts	1st	2nd	3rd	Win & Pl
Hurdles	5	0	1	1	2611
Career Total	5	0	1	1	2611

Going:	Sf: 0-1 GS: 0-4 Gd: 0-0 GF: - Fm: 0-0
Distance:	2m/2m3: 0-5 2m4-2m7: 0-0 3m+: 0-0
Track:	LH: 0-0 RH: 0-5 Tight: 0-3 Gall: 0-0
Aids:	Bl: 0-0 Vi: 0-0 Tstrap: 0-0
Best Rating:	105 1/03 Extr 2m3f gd-sft Hdl

Modest hurdler; best over trips beyond two miles.

River Bug (IRE)
103   **127**
9-y-o ch g Over The River (FR)-Fiona s Wish (Wishing Star)
Jamie Poulton Ormonde Racing

Placings:050/1P1-320P114   (4172)
2002/03: 24³GS, 29²S, 32⁵GS, 26⁷HY, 26¹HY, 26¹GS, 34⁴S,

	Starts	1st	2nd	3rd	Win & Pl
Chases	7	2	1	1	20879
Career Total	13	4	1	1	42999
127	2/03	Plum	3m2f	E(0-115)Ch	G-S	£5382
105	1/03	Folk	3m2f	F(0-100)HCh	HVY	£3367

---

106 3/02 Font 3m4f D(0-125)HCh SFT £17615
86 3/02 Towc 3m1f F(0-100)HCh SFT £4504

Total win prize-money £30869

Going:	Sf: 1-4 GS: 1-3 Gd: 0-0 GF: - Fm: 0-0
Distance:	2m/2m3: 0-0 2m4-2m7: 0-0 3m+: 2-7
Track:	LH: 1-3 RH: 1-3 Tight: 2-4 Gall: 0-0
Aids:	Bl: 1-2 Vi: 0-0 Tstrap: 0-0
Best Rating:	127 2/03 Plum 3m2f gd-sft Ch

Ex-Irish; landed the Southern National at Fontwell in March 2002; stays 3m 4f; suited by soft ground; has worn blinkers.

River Captain (USA)
(109h)   **(102h)**
10-y-o ch g Riverman (USA)-Katsura (USA) (Northern Dancer)
A Scott P Swift,I Bennett,H Harrison,Mrs L Lamb

Placings:40/210-55F   (1558)
2002/03: 21⁵GF, 20⁵G, 17⁵G,

	Starts	1st	2nd	3rd	Win & Pl
Hurdles	2	0	0	0	0
Chases	1	0	0	0	0
Career Total	8	1	1	0	4366
100	12/01	Kels	2m110y	E Hdl	G-S	£3346

Total win prize-money £3346

Going:	Sf: 0-0 GS: 0-0 Gd: 0-2 GF: - Fm: 0-1
Distance:	2m/2m3: 0-1 2m4-2m7: 0-2 3m+: 0-0
Track:	LH: 0-2 RH: 0-1 Tight: 0-2 Gall: 0-0
Aids:	Bl: 0-0 Vi: 0-0 Tstrap: 0-0
Best Rating:	102 8/02 Prth 2m4f110y good Hdl

Decent novice hurdler, comfortable winner at Kelso in December. Handles cut in the ground. Leading when falling on his chasing debut in October 2002.

River City (IRE)
108   **117**
6-y-o b g Norwich-Shuil Na Lee (IRE) (Phardante (FR))
Noel T Chance Mrs S Rowley-Williams & Partners

Placings:01-2511P4   (4323)
2002/03: 19²GF, 20⁵G, 17¹S, 16¹GS, 16⁵S, 16⁴G,

	Starts	1st	2nd	3rd	Win & Pl
Hurdles	6	2	1	0	9691
Career Total	8	3	1	0	12400
103	1/03	Donc	2m110y	E Hdl	G-S	£3581
110	11/02	NAbb	2m1f	E Hdl	SFT	£3613
100	4/02	Asct	2m110y	H NHF	G-F	£2709

Total win prize-money £9904

Going:	Sf: 1-2 GS: 1-1 Gd: 0-2 GF: - Fm: 0-0
Distance:	2m/2m3: 2-4 2m4-2m7: 0-2 3m+: 0-0
Track:	LH: 2-5 RH: 0-1 Tight: 1-2 Gall: 1-3
Aids:	Bl: 0-0 Vi: 0-0 Tstrap: 0-0
Best Rating:	117 3/03 Newb 2m110y good Hdl

Fair hurdler; suited by 2m, but may stay further; acts on any ground; possesses plenty of scope.

River Gold
92   **80**
9-y-o ch g River God (USA)-Lady St Clair (Young Generation)
M Pitman C B Hoffman

Placings:660/53540/3PP/P-54   (4265)
2002/03: 20⁵G, 24⁴GF,

	Starts	1st	2nd	3rd	Win & Pl
Chases	2	0	0	0	296
Career Total	14	0	0	2	1759

Going:	Sf: 0-0 GS: 0-0 Gd: 0-1 GF: - Fm: 0-1
Distance:	2m/2m3: 0-0 2m4-2m7: 0-1 3m+: 0-1
Track:	LH: 0-1 RH: 0-1 Tight: 0-1 Gall: 0-1
Aids:	Bl: 0-0 Vi: 0-0 Tstrap: 0-0
Best Rating:	105 2/99 Asct 2m110y gd-sft NHF

River Joy (IRE)
77f   **76f**
5-y-o b g Norwich-Vanessa s Palace (Quayside)
Noel T Chance C Green & J Dennis

Placings:000   (3789)
2002/03: 16⁵GS, 17⁰HY, 17⁰G,

	Starts	1st	2nd	3rd	Win & Pl
NH Flat	3	0	0	0	
Career Total	3	0	0	0	

Going:	Sf: 0-1 GS: 0-1 Gd: 0-1 GF: - Fm: 0-0
Distance:	2m/2m3: 0-3 2m4-2m7: 0-0 3m+: 0-0
Track:	LH: 0-3 RH: 0-3 Tight: 0-1 Gall: 0-0
Aids:	Bl: 0-0 Vi: 0-0 Tstrap: 0-3
Best Rating:	76 2/03 Folk 2m1f110y heavy NHF

River Marshal (IRE)
94f   **93f**
5-y-o b g Synefos (USA)-Marshallstown (Callernish)
M W Easterby Lord Manton

Placings:623   (3412)
2002/03: 14⁶GS, 16²G, 16³GS,

	Starts	1st	2nd	3rd	Win & Pl
NH Flat	3	0	1	1	936
Career Total	3	0	1	1	936

Going:	Sf: 0-0 GS: 0-2 Gd: 0-1 GF: - Fm: 0-0
Distance:	2m/2m3: 0-2 2m4-2m7: 0-0 3m+: 0-0
Track:	LH: 0-3 RH: 0-0 Tight: 0-1 Gall: 0-0
Aids:	Bl: 0-1 Vi: 0-0 Tstrap: 0-0
Best Rating:	97 1/03 Catt 2m good NHF

Moderate bumper performer; blinkered when runner-up in a very ordinary bumper at Catterick in January (hung badly). Well beaten third at Wetherby two weeks later.

River Mere
95   **90**
9-y-o b g River God (USA)-Rupert s Daughter (Rupert Bear)
Mrs L Williamson Mrs J E Webster

Placings:502/PP4P-054   (4669)
2002/03: 16⁰GF, 16⁵G, 16⁴G,

	Starts	1st	2nd	3rd	Win & Pl
Hurdles	3	0	0	0	419
Career Total	10	0	1	0	849

Going:	Sf: 0-0 GS: 0-0 Gd: 0-2 GF: - Fm: 0-1
Distance:	2m/2m3: 0-3 2m4-2m7: 0-0 3m+: 0-0
Track:	LH: 0-3 RH: 0-2 Tight: 0-1 Gall: 0-0
Aids:	Bl: 0-0 Vi: 0-0 Tstrap: 0-0
Best Rating:	91 10/00 Ludl 2m gd-fm NHF

Plating-class novice hurdler; acts on fast ground; free running sort who is not getting home in his races.

River Mist (IRE)
45f   **78f**
4-y-o ch f Over The River (FR)-Minature Miss (Move Off)

D Eddy Mrs H Scotto

Placings:*2*   (4397)
2002/03: 17²G,

	Starts	1st	2nd	3rd	Win & Pl
NH Flat	1	0	1	0	634
Career Total	1	0	1	0	634

Going: Sf: 0-0 GS: 0-0 Gd: 0-1 GF: - Fm: 0-0
Distance: 2m/2m3: 0-1 2m4-2m7: 0-0 3m+: 0-0
Track: LH: 0-0 RH: 0-1 Tight: 0-0 Gall: 0-0
Aids: Bl: 0-0 Vi: 0-0 Tstrap: 0-0
Best Rating: 78   3/03   Carl   2m1f   good   NHF

Jumping bred; runner-up in slowly-run bumper on debut at Carlisle in March 2003.

River Ness

108(79c)   (56c)110
7-y-o br g Buckskin (FR)-Stubbin Moor (Kinglet)
N G Richards Dr Kenneth S Fraser

Placings:*P/022011-22524P5*   (4774)
2002/03: 22²GS, 21²G, 20⁵S, 16²HY, 21⁴HY, 21⁵G, 27⁵G,

	Starts	1st	2nd	3rd	Win & Pl
Hurdles	6	0	3	0	4032
Chases	1	0	0	0	428
Career Total	14	2	5	0	12058
100 4/02 Prth			3m110y D Hdl		GD £3731
100 3/02 Sedg			2m5f110y		E Hdl SFT

£2618

Total win prize-money £6349

Going: Sf: 0-3 GS: 0-1 Gd: 0-3 GF: - Fm: 0-0
Distance: 2m/2m3: 0-1 2m4-2m7: 0-5 3m+: 0-1
Track: LH: 0-6 RH: 0-0 Tight: 0-5 Gall: 0-0
Aids: Bl: 0-0 Vi: 0-0 Tstrap: 0-0
Best Rating: 110   1/03   Ayr   2m   heavy   Hdl

Modest hurdler; disappointed on chase debut; stays three miles; handles good ground or softer.

River Of Wishes

5-y-o b m Riverwise (USA)-Wishful Dream (Crawter)
C W Mitchell C W Mitchell

Placings:*0*   (3630)
2002/03: 16⁰S,

	Starts	1st	2nd	3rd	Win & Pl
NH Flat	1	0	0	0	
Career Total	1	0	0	0	

Going: Sf: 0-1 GS: 0-0 Gd: 0-0 GF: - Fm: 0-0
Distance: 2m/2m3: 0-1 2m4-2m7: 0-0 3m+: 0-0
Track: LH: 0-0 RH: 0-1 Tight: 0-0 Gall: 0-0
Aids: Bl: 0-0 Vi: 0-0 Tstrap: 0-0
Best Rating: 0   2/03   Asct   2m110y   soft   NHF

River Pilot

103   124
9-y-o b g Unfuwain (USA)-Cut Ahead (Kalaglow)
C J Mann (Noel Meade 21/7) Terry Grove

Placings:*1231/02222/5/P1233-F0544*   (3743)
2002/03: 16⁵FY, 20⁰G, 20⁵GF, 16⁴HY, 16⁴G,

	Starts	1st	2nd	3rd	Win & Pl
Chases	5	0	0	0	1150
Career Total	20	3	6	3	26562
123 8/01 Gway			2m1f		Ch Y-S £6955

129	4/99	Punc	2m		Hdl		YLD	£6752
114	5/98	Navn	2m		Hdl		Y-S	£3573

Total win prize-money £17282

Going: Sf: 0-1 GS: 0-0 Gd: 0-2 GF: - Fm: 0-1
Distance: 2m/2m3: 0-3 2m4-2m7: 0-2 3m+: 0-0
Track: LH: 0-1 RH: 0-2 Tight: 0-0 Gall: 0-1
Aids: Bl: 0-0 Vi: 0-0 Tstrap: 0-0
Best Rating: 129   4/99   Punc   2m   yield   Hdl

Fair ex-Irish chaser, best at around two miles; suited by soft ground.

River Pirate (IRE)

107   110
6-y-o b g Un Desperado (FR)-Kigali (IRE) (Torus)
N J Henderson Riverwood Racing II

Placings:*3335*   (4051)
2002/03: 16³G, 16³S, 16³HY, 16⁵HY,

	Starts	1st	2nd	3rd	Win & Pl
NH Flat	2	0	0	2	714
Hurdles	2	0	0	1	833
Career Total	4	0	0	3	1547

Going: Sf: 0-3 GS: 0-0 Gd: 0-1 GF: - Fm: 0-0
Distance: 2m/2m3: 0-4 2m4-2m7: 0-0 3m+: 0-0
Track: LH: 0-0 RH: 0-4 Tight: 0-0 Gall: 0-0
Aids: Bl: 0-0 Vi: 0-0 Tstrap: 0-0
Best Rating: 106   2/03   Sand   2m110y   heavy   Hdl

Fair bumper/hurdle form; won two novice hurdles in May; acts on most types of ground; should stay beyond 2m 1f.

River Rambler

94f   61f
4-y-o ch f River Falls-Horsepower (Superpower)
J R Norton J Norton

Placings:*0*   (4357)
2002/03: 16⁰GF,

	Starts	1st	2nd	3rd	Win & Pl
NH Flat	1	0	0	0	
Career Total	1	0	0	0	

Going: Sf: 0-0 GS: 0-0 Gd: 0-0 GF: - Fm: 0-1
Distance: 2m/2m3: 0-1 2m4-2m7: 0-0 3m+: 0-0
Track: LH: 0-1 RH: 0-0 Tight: 0-0 Gall: 0-0
Aids: Bl: 0-0 Vi: 0-0 Tstrap: 0-0
Best Rating: 63   3/03   Weth   2m   gd-fm   NHF

River Reine (IRE)

70   48
4-y-o br f Lahib (USA)-Talahari (IRE) (Roi Danzig (USA))
E W Tuer (B W Hills 25/10) E Tuer

Placings:*0*   (2182)
2002/03: 16⁰GS,

	Starts	1st	2nd	3rd	Win & Pl
Hurdles	1	0	0	0	
Career Total	1	0	0	0	

Going: Sf: 0-0 GS: 0-1 Gd: 0-0 GF: - Fm: 0-0
Distance: 2m/2m3: 0-1 2m4-2m7: 0-0 3m+: 0-0
Track: LH: 0-1 RH: 0-0 Tight: 0-0 Gall: 0-0
Aids: Bl: 0-0 Vi: 0-0 Tstrap: 0-0
Best Rating: 51   11/02   Weth   2m   gd-sft   Hdl

River Rising

100(91h)   (85dh)82
9-y-o br g Primitive Rising (USA)-Dragons Daughter (Mandrake Major)
C R Wilson W R Wilson

Placings:*P/430-0*   (4225)
2002/03: 20⁰GF,

	Starts	1st	2nd	3rd	Win & Pl
Hurdles	1	0	0	0	
Career Total	5	0	0	1	424

Going: Sf: 0-0 GS: 0-0 Gd: 0-0 GF: - Fm: 0-1
Distance: 2m/2m3: 0-0 2m4-2m7: 0-1 3m+: 0-0
Track: LH: 0-1 RH: 0-0 Tight: 0-0 Gall: 0-0
Aids: Bl: 0-0 Vi: 0-0 Tstrap: 0-0
Best Rating: 85   5/01   Sedg   2m5f110y   good   Hdl

River Shamrock (IRE)

93(107h)   (87h)96
9-y-o ch g Alphabatim (USA)-High Feather (Nishapour (FR))
Seamus O Farrell Seamus O Farrell

Placings:*530S00/00/0000544263-0435006*   (4584a)
2002/03: 24⁰S, 24⁴YS, 24³G, 24⁴S, 25⁰S, 24⁰YS, 20⁶GF,

	Starts	1st	2nd	3rd	Win & Pl
Hurdles	2	0	0	0	245
Chases	5	0	0	1	2442
Career Total	25	0	1	3	6020

Going: Sf: 0-3 GS: 0-0 Gd: 0-1 GF: - Fm: 0-1
Distance: 2m/2m3: 0-0 2m4-2m7: 0-1 3m+: 0-1
Track: LH: 0-3 RH: 0-3 Tight: 0-0 Gall: 0-1
Aids: Bl: 0-2 Vi: 0-0 Tstrap: 0-0
Best Rating: 96   11/02   Chel   3m110y   good   Ch

River Slave (IRE)

111   93
9-y-o b/br g Over The River (FR)-Sally Slave (Paddy s Stream)
T R George Richard J B Blake

Placings:*10/P24P/3323P*   (3622)
2002/03: 21³S, 26³HY, 23²S, 20³S, 24⁴PS,

	Starts	1st	2nd	3rd	Win & Pl
Chases	5	0	1	3	2977
Career Total	11	1	2	3	5859
113 2/00 Carl			2m1f		H NHF HVY £1694

Total win prize-money £1694

Going: Sf: 0-5 GS: 0-0 Gd: 0-0 GF: - Fm: 0-0
Distance: 2m/2m3: 0-0 2m4-2m7: 0-2 3m+: 0-3
Track: LH: 0-2 RH: 0-3 Tight: 0-1 Gall: 0-0
Aids: Bl: 0-0 Vi: 0-0 Tstrap: 0-0
Best Rating: 113   2/00   Carl   2m1f   heavy   NHF

Fair chaser. Stays well, acts in soft ground.

River Styx (IRE)

102(88h)   (85h)85
8-y-o ch g Over The River (FR)-Money For Honey (New Brig)
D McCain The Bankhouse Confederacy

Placings:*000/2600/00442330-P332124*   (4351)
2002/03: 17⁵HY, 17³GS, 16³G, 16²G, 16¹G, 16²G, 16⁴GF,

	Starts	1st	2nd	3rd	Win & Pl
Hurdles	1	0	0	1	434
Chases	6	1	2	1	11024
Career Total	**22**	**1**	**4**	**4**	**15301**
85	2/03	Muss	2m		D(0-110)HCh	GD	£6643

Total win prize-money £6643

Going: Sf: 0-1 GS: 0-1 Gd: 1-4 GF: - Fm: 0-1
Distance: 2m/2m3: 1-7 2m4-2m7: 0-0 3m+: 0-0
Track: LH: 0-5 RH: 1-2 Tight: 1-4 Gall: 0-1
Aids: Bl: 1-4 Vi: 0-0 Tstrap: 1-6
Best Rating: 106 5/00 Aint 2m110y gd-fm Hdl

Moderate novice chaser; suited by two miles and good ground; off the mark at the 20th attempt at Musselburgh in February.

River Surprise (IRE)

10-y-o b g Over The River (FR)-Reelin Surprise (Royal Match)
Mike Lurcock Mike Lurcock

Placings:P (4487)
2002/03: 16PGF,

	Starts	1st	2nd	3rd	Win & Pl
Chases	1	0	0	0	
Career Total	**1**	**0**	**0**	**0**	

Going: Sf: 0-0 GS: 0-0 Gd: 0-0 GF: - Fm: 0-1
Distance: 2m/2m3: 0-1 2m4-2m7: 0-0 3m+: 0-0
Track: LH: 0-0 RH: 0-1 Tight: 0-0 Gall: 0-0
Aids: Bl: 0-0 Vi: 0-0 Tstrap: 0-0
Best Rating: 0 4/03 Hrfd 2m gd-fm Ch

River Trix (IRE)

109(83h)   (100h)99
9-y-o b g Riverhead (USA)-Game Trix (Buckskin (FR))
D J Caro The Viva Vialli Partnership

Placings:0/0P2/UPP20-0503 (4735)
2002/03: 24QGS, 20FS, 20PS, 19JGF,

	Starts	1st	2nd	3rd	Win & Pl
Hurdles	2	0	0	0	0
Chases	2	0	0	1	378
Career Total	**13**	**0**	**2**	**1**	**2006**

Going: Sf: 0-2 GS: 0-1 Gd: 0-0 GF: - Fm: 0-1
Distance: 2m/2m3: 0-0 2m4-2m7: 0-3 3m+: 0-1
Track: LH: 0-1 RH: 0-2 Tight: 0-1 Gall: 0-2
Aids: Bl: 0-0 Vi: 0-0 Tstrap: 0-0
Best Rating: 100 4/01 Winc 2m6f soft Hdl

Moderate front-running chaser; won 2m 4f maiden chase at Hexham May 2003; stays 3m 2f; acts on good and soft ground.

River Wye (IRE)

116
11-y-o b g Jareer (USA)-Sun Gift (Guillaume Tell (USA))
G H Yardley Woodsfield Wanderers

Placings:64325/01P/241/224612U1F/32112/303/6064-P
(1667)
2002/03: 20PS,

	Starts	1st	2nd	3rd	Win & Pl
Chases	1	0	0	0	
Career Total	**33**	**6**	**7**	**4**	**42331**
133	3/00	Bang	2m4f110yC(0-135)HCh	GD	£7247
133	2/00	Kemp	2m4f110yC(0-130)HCh	SFT	£10481

135	2/99	Bang	2m1f110yD(0-110)HCh	G-S	£3696
119	12/98	Ludl	2m	E Ch	G-S	£2775
117	5/98	Bang	2m1f	E(0-110)HHdl	GD	£2879
105	2/97	Strf	2m3f	(0-105)Hdl	GD	£2368

Total win prize-money £29448

Going: Sf: 0-1 GS: 0-0 Gd: 0-0 GF: - Fm: 0-0
Distance: 2m/2m3: 0-0 2m4-2m7: 0-1 3m+: 0-0
Track: LH: 0-1 RH: 0-0 Tight: 0-1 Gall: 0-0
Aids: Bl: 0-0 Vi: 0-0 Tstrap: 0-0
Best Rating: 135 2/99 Bang 2m1f110y gd-sft Ch

A useful chaser a couple of seasons ago, he has failed to show much this season. Suited by trips from two to two and a half miles and the ground good or softer.

Riverblue (IRE)

105
7-y-o b g Bluebird (USA)-La Riveraine (USA) (Riverman (USA))
D J Wintle Mrs Joan L Egan

Placings:2P-P (3269)
2002/03: 17PHY,

	Starts	1st	2nd	3rd	Win & Pl
Hurdles	1	0	0	0	
Career Total	**3**	**0**	**1**	**0**	**935**

Going: Sf: 0-1 GS: 0-0 Gd: 0-0 GF: - Fm: 0-0
Distance: 2m/2m3: 0-1 2m4-2m7: 0-0 3m+: 0-0
Track: LH: 0-0 RH: 0-1 Tight: 0-1 Gall: 0-0
Aids: Bl: 0-0 Vi: 0-0 Tstrap: 0-1
Best Rating: 105 6/01 Strf 2m110y gd-fm Hdl

Useful handicapper on the Flat on a fast surface, ran well on fast on his debut but twice pulled up on heavy ground.

Riverlord

98(83h)   (42h)78
9-y-o b g River God (USA)-Sultry (Sula Bula)
P R Rodford Miss S J Burgin

Placings:00/P6-044P (0732)
2002/03: 20QGF, 23JG, 23JGF, 21PGF,

	Starts	1st	2nd	3rd	Win & Pl
Hurdles	1	0	0	0	0
Chases	3	0	0	0	483
Career Total	**8**	**0**	**0**	**0**	**483**

Going: Sf: 0-0 GS: 0-0 Gd: 0-1 GF: - Fm: 0-3
Distance: 2m/2m3: 0-0 2m4-2m7: 0-2 3m+: 0-2
Track: LH: 0-4 RH: 0-0 Tight: 0-1 Gall: 0-0
Aids: Bl: 0-0 Vi: 0-0 Tstrap: 0-0
Best Rating: 78 5/02 Worc 2m7f110y good Ch

Riverside Lodge (IRE)

73
9-y-o b g Riverhead (USA)-Huricane Dodo (Sexton Blake)
R D E Woodhouse R Priestley Developments Co Ltd

Placings:0PP/FP1PFPP/PP50/P3P-P (0065)
2002/03: 27PGF,

	Starts	1st	2nd	3rd	Win & Pl
Chases	1	0	0	0	
Career Total	**18**	**1**	**0**	**1**	**5496**
80	12/99	Catt	2m3f	F(0-100)HCh	GD	£4900

Total win prize-money £4900

Going: Sf: 0-0 GS: 0-0 Gd: 0-0 GF: - Fm: 0-1
Distance: 2m/2m3: 0-0 2m4-2m7: 0-0 3m+: 0-1
Track: LH: 0-1 RH: 0-0 Tight: 0-1 Gall: 0-0
Aids: Bl: 0-0 Vi: 0-0 Tstrap: 0-0
Best Rating: 80 12/99 Catt 2m3f good Ch

Moderate chaser, he has had a real problem getting round. A sound surface seems to help.

Riviere

58   93+
8-y-o ch m Meadowbrook-Cimarron (Carnival Dancer)
E W Tuer R G Fairs

Placings:04/16/0-0-1 (4139)
2002/03: 24JS,

	Starts	1st	2nd	3rd	Win & Pl
Hurdles	1	1	0	0	3416
Career Total	**7**	**2**	**0**	**0**	**5005**
93	3/03	Hexm	3m	E Hdl	SFT	£3416
111	1/00	Muss	2m	H NHF	SFT	£1589

Total win prize-money £5005

Going: Sf: 1-1 GS: 0-0 Gd: 0-0 GF: - Fm: 0-0
Distance: 2m/2m3: 0-0 2m4-2m7: 0-0 3m+: 1-1
Track: LH: 1-1 RH: 0-0 Tight: 0-0 Gall: 0-0
Aids: Bl: 0-0 Vi: 0-0 Tstrap: 0-0
Best Rating: 111 1/00 Muss 2m soft NHF

Moderate hurdler; bumper winner in the past; shock winner on first start for new stable in false-run novices' hurdle over three miles in bad ground at Hexham in March 2003.

Roaming Ronan (IRE)

70
5-y-o b g Sri Pekan (USA)-Maradata (IRE) (Shardari)
R W Thomson R W Thomson

Placings:4503P-P (0251)
2002/03: 20PG, 16PGF,

	Starts	1st	2nd	3rd	Win & Pl
Hurdles	2	0	0	0	
Career Total	**6**	**0**	**0**	**1**	**398**

Going: Sf: 0-0 GS: 0-0 Gd: 0-1 GF: - Fm: 0-1
Distance: 2m/2m3: 0-1 2m4-2m7: 0-1 3m+: 0-0
Track: LH: 0-1 RH: 0-0 Tight: 0-0 Gall: 0-1
Aids: Bl: 0-0 Vi: 0-0 Tstrap: 0-0
Best Rating: 70 3/02 Kels 2m2f heavy Hdl

Rob Leach

90   128
6-y-o b g Robellino (USA)-Arc Empress Jane (IRE) (Rainbow Quest (USA))
G L Moore Richard Green (fine Paintings)

Placings:262/1431126-510 (2245)
2002/03: 16SGS, 16JHY, 16QS,

	Starts	1st	2nd	3rd	Win & Pl
Hurdles	3	1	0	0	7085
Career Total	**13**	**4**	**3**	**1**	**51441**
127	11/02	Asct	2m110y	C(0-130)HHdl	HVY	£7085
122	12/01	Sand	2m110y	A(0-150)HHdl	SFT	£31900
116	11/01	Plum	2m	D Hdl	GD	£3721
108	9/01	Plum	2m	E Hdl	G-S	£2520

Total win prize-money £45226

Going: Sf: 1-2 GS: 0-1 Gd: 0-0 GF: - Fm: 0-0
Distance: 2m/2m3: 1-3 2m4-2m7: 0-0 3m+: 0-0

Track: LH: 0-1 RH: 1-2 Tight: 0-0 Gall: 0-1
Aids: Bl: 0-1 Vi: 0-0 Tstrap: 0-0
Best Rating: 128 12/01 Newb 2m110y gd-sft Hdl

Useful hurdler; improved with experience over hurdles; took a valuable handicap at Sandown when fitted with blinkers for the first time. Possibly a better effort when second in a conditions event at Newbury, he was then held at Kempton in a decent handicap. Disappointing on his return in November 2002, but scored next time out. Handles good ground and heavy and obviously likes a sharp track.

Rob Mine (IRE)

11-y-o b g Roselier (FR)-Noddi Fliw (Jasmine Star)
C Sporborg Christopher Sporborg

Placings:000/2/F6/1 (4031)
2002/03: 24¹S,

	Starts	1st	2nd	3rd	Win & Pl
Chases	1	1	0	0	4076
Career Total	7	1	1	0	4448
93 3/03 Sand	3m110y H Ch			SFT	£4075

Total win prize-money £4076

Going: Sf: 1-1 GS: 0-0 Gd: 0-0 GF: - Fm: 0-0
Distance: 2m/2m3: 0-0 2m4-2m7: 0-0 3m+: 1-1
Track: LH: 0-0 RH: 1-1 Tight: 0-0 Gall: 0-0
Aids: Bl: 0-0 Vi: 0-0 Tstrap: 0-0
Best Rating: 101 2/00 Chep 3m soft Ch

Hunter chaser/point-to-pointer; acts on soft ground.

Robber (IRE)
98   87

6-y-o ch g Un Desperado (FR)-Christy s Girl (IRE) (Buckskin (FR))
P J Hobbs The Hedonists

Placings:04-5030F0 (4606)
2002/03: 21⁵S, 20⁰HY, 19³GS, 24⁰G, 22⁵G, 24⁰G,

	Starts	1st	2nd	3rd	Win & Pl
Hurdles	6	0	0	1	542
Career Total	8	0	0	1	542

Going: Sf: 0-2 GS: 0-1 Gd: 0-3 GF: - Fm: 0-0
Distance: 2m/2m3: 0-1 2m4-2m7: 0-3 3m+: 0-2
Track: LH: 0-3 RH: 0-3 Tight: 0-0 Gall: 0-1
Aids: Bl: 0-0 Vi: 0-0 Tstrap: 0-0
Best Rating: 92 3/02 Wwck 2m gd-sft NHF

Moderate hurdler; does not find too much off the bridle.

Robber Baron (IRE)
104   122+

6-y-o ch g Un Desperado (FR)-N T Nad (Welsh Pageant)
Miss H C Knight The Radicals Partnership

Placings:1/3226-1P (1939)
2002/03: 19¹GS, 16²G,

	Starts	1st	2nd	3rd	Win & Pl
Hurdles	2	1	0	0	5457
Career Total	7	2	2	1	12813
121 11/02 Extr	2m3f	D Hdl		G-S	£5456
110 3/01 Hntg	2m110y H NHF			SFT	£1806

Total win prize-money £7263

Going: Sf: 0-0 GS: 1-1 Gd: 0-1 GF: - Fm: 0-0
Distance: 2m/2m3: 1-2 2m4-2m7: 0-0 3m+: 0-0
Track: LH: 0-1 RH: 1-1 Tight: 0-0 Gall: 0-0
Aids: Bl: 0-0 Vi: 0-0 Tstrap: 0-0
Best Rating: 121 11/02 Extr 2m3f gd-sft Hdl

Fair hurdler; got off the mark on his debut in a Huntingdon bumper in March 2001, before a fair third in a Listed event at Cheltenham. Runner-up to useful sorts twice over hurdles. Won on his reappearance in 2002/2003 season. Acts on good and soft ground. His future looks to lie over fences.

Robbie Can Can
98   91

4-y-o b g Robellino (USA)-Can Can Lady (Anshan)
A W Carroll (J G Given 30/10) K F Coleman

Placings:5410 (3571)
2002/03: 17⁵S, 16⁴GS, 16¹HY, 16⁰HY,

	Starts	1st	2nd	3rd	Win & Pl
Hurdles	4	1	0	0	2983
Career Total	4	1	0	0	2983
91 1/03 Chep	2m110y F Hdl			HVY	£2688

Total win prize-money £2688

Going: Sf: 1-3 GS: 0-1 Gd: 0-0 GF: - Fm: 0-0
Distance: 2m/2m3: 1-4 2m4-2m7: 0-0 3m+: 0-0
Track: LH: 1-2 RH: 0-2 Tight: 0-1 Gall: 0-0
Aids: Bl: 0-0 Vi: 0-0 Tstrap: 0-0
Best Rating: 91 1/03 Chep 2m110y heavy Hdl

He was given a fine tactical ride when winning a novices claiming hurdle at Chepstow in January 2003; suited by soft ground.

Robbie's Adventure
96   67

9-y-o ch g Le Coq D Or-Mendick Adventure (Mandrake Major)
D L Williams Symbol Of Success Racing

Placings:04/0P045103/P3F134P/325-P4F3PP003P4 (4702)
2002/03: 24²GF, 26⁴G, 27⁵S, 26³HY, 26⁶HY, 22⁶S, 25⁰S, 26⁰GS, 25³GF, 25⁶G, 26⁴GF,

	Starts	1st	2nd	3rd	Win & Pl
Chases	11	0	0	2	1420
Career Total	31	2	1	6	8948
86 1/01 Tntn	3m	F(0-95)HCh	HVY		£3139
86 2/00 Folk	2m1f110yG(0-90)HHdl	SFT			£1547

Total win prize-money £4687

Going: Sf: 0-5 GS: 0-1 Gd: 0-2 GF: - Fm: 0-3
Distance: 2m/2m3: 0-0 2m4-2m7: 0-1 3m+: 0-10
Track: LH: 0-5 RH: 0-4 Tight: 0-6 Gall: 0-1
Aids: Bl: 0-0 Vi: 0-4 Tstrap: 0-0
Best Rating: 86 1/01 Tntn 3m heavy Ch

Poor staying chaser. Acts on an easy surface. Not the best of jumpers. Has run well in a visor.

Robbo
114(104h)   (132h)140

9-y-o b g Robellino (USA)-Basha (USA) (Chief s Crown (USA))
Mrs M Reveley The Scarth Racing Partnership

Placings:1120/332221106/U21123115/0124363/042P006-01331054PU (4479)
2002/03: 25⁰S, 20¹GS, 22³HY, 23³HY, 24¹G, 24⁰G, 24⁵S, 24⁴GS, 34⁴S, 36⁴G,

	Starts	1st	2nd	3rd	Win & Pl
Hurdles	5	1	0	2	7125
Chases	5	1	0	0	8141
Career Total	46	11	8	7	118247
140 1/03 Donc	3m	C(0-130)HCh	GD	£8141
127 11/02 Newc	2m4f	D(0-125)HHdl	G-S	£5031
149 11/00 Kels	3m1f	B(0-140)HCh	SFT	£8990
147 3/00 Carl	2m4f110yC Ch		HVY	£7560

---

142 2/00 Newc	2m4f	B(0-140)HCh	HVY	£10432
108 11/99 Kels	2m6f110yE Ch		GD	£3355
113 11/99 Ayr	2m4f	D Ch		GD	£3951
133 2/99 Newc	2m4f	B(0-140)HHdl	G-S	£6937
134 2/99 Newc	2m4f	C(0-130)HHdl	SFT	£5790
118 1/98 Newc	2m	E Hdl	G-S	£2368
116 1/98 Ayr	2m	E Hdl	SFT	£2248

Total win prize-money £64807

Going: Sf: 0-5 GS: 1-2 Gd: 1-3 GF: - Fm: 0-0
Distance: 2m/2m3: 0-0 2m4-2m7: 1-3 3m+: 1-7
Track: LH: 2-9 RH: 0-1 Tight: 0-3 Gall: 2-4
Aids: Bl: 0-1 Vi: 0-2 Tstrap: 0-0
Best Rating: 149 12/00 Chel 2m5f soft Ch

Useful chaser/decent hurdler; suited by good ground or softer; stays three miles; often wears a visor or cheekpieces; can appear a little quirky; tends to be best when coming from off the pace.

Robella
(99h)   (72h)

7-y-o ch m Keen-Afrabela (African Sky)
K A Morgan Mrs Gilly Willett

Placings:03/60034300-F (1449)
2002/03: 16²G,

	Starts	1st	2nd	3rd	Win & Pl
Chases	1	0	0	0	
Career Total	11	0	0	3	1276

Going: Sf: 0-0 GS: 0-0 Gd: 0-1 GF: - Fm: 0-0
Distance: 2m/2m3: 0-1 2m4-2m7: 0-0 3m+: 0-0
Track: LH: 0-1 RH: 0-0 Tight: 0-1 Gall: 0-0
Aids: Bl: 0-0 Vi: 0-0 Tstrap: 0-0
Best Rating: 72 1/02 Sthl 2m gd-sft Hdl

Weak form at around two miles over hurdles.

Robert The Bruce
106   111

8-y-o ch g Distinct Native-Kawarau Queen (Taufan (USA))
L Lungo G G Fraser

Placings:333/31/2-2 (4037)
2002/03: 20²S,

	Starts	1st	2nd	3rd	Win & Pl
Hurdles	1	0	1	0	1490
Career Total	7	1	2	4	6399
96 5/00 Hexm	2m	E Hdl		GD	£2443

Total win prize-money £2444

Going: Sf: 0-1 GS: 0-0 Gd: 0-0 GF: - Fm: 0-0
Distance: 2m/2m3: 0-0 2m4-2m7: 0-1 3m+: 0-0
Track: LH: 0-1 RH: 0-0 Tight: 0-0 Gall: 0-0
Aids: Bl: 0-0 Vi: 0-0 Tstrap: 0-0
Best Rating: 111 3/03 Ayr 2m4f soft Hdl

Modest hurdler; acts on good or softer.

Roberty Bob (IRE)
112(68h)   (96 h)121

8-y-o ch g Bob Back (USA)-Inesdela (Wolver Hollow)
H D Daly P J H Wills

Placings:43222/311-1423533 (4057)
2002/03: 26¹G, 24⁴GS, 24²HY, 24³S, 26⁵S, 26³HY, 29³GS,

	Starts	1st	2nd	3rd	Win & Pl
Hurdles	1	0	0	1	1045
Chases	6	1	1	2	10298
Career Total	15	3	4	5	39971
133 5/02 Uttx	3m2f	D Ch		GD	£4368

133	3/02	Uttx	3m2f	B HCh	HVY	£19110
125	3/02	Towc	2m6f	D Ch	SFT	£5538
				Total win prize-money £29016		

Going:	Sf: 0-4 GS: 0-2 Gd: 1-1 GF: - Fm: 0-0
Distance:	2m/2m3: 0-0 2m4-2m7: 0-0 3m+: 1-7
Track:	LH: 1-5 RH: 0-2 Tight: 0-1 Gall: 0-1
Aids:	Bl: 0-0 Vi: 0-0 Tstrap: 0-0
Best Rating:	133 11/02 Bang 3m110y heavy Ch

Fair consistent chaser; goes well at Uttoxeter; stays 3m 5f; suited by soft ground.

Robins Meg

7-y-o b m Skyliner-Home Dove (Homeboy)
M E Sowersby Mrs Jean W Robinson

Placings:30-00U (4688)
2002/03: 17OGF, 16OG, 19UGF,

	Starts	1st	2nd	3rd	Win & Pl
NH Flat	2	0	0	0	0
Hurdles	1	0	0	0	0
Career Total	5	0	0	1	228

Going:	Sf: 0-0 GS: 0-0 Gd: 0-1 GF: - Fm: 0-2
Distance:	2m/2m3: 0-2 2m4-2m7: 0-1 3m+: 0-0
Track:	LH: 0-1 RH: 0-2 Tight: 0-2 Gall: 0-0
Aids:	Bl: 0-0 Vi: 0-0 Tstrap: 0-0
Best Rating:	82 9/01 MRas 2m1f110y soft NHF

Robins Pride (IRE)
105   71

13-y-o b g Treasure Hunter-Barney s Sister (Abednego)
C L Popham Richard Weeks, P Littlejohns, A Staple

Placings:30/P0054/22F1521201/P22P3U2/P3312353F/PU 44142204F/053640624P1/655641U6U/00043-550P4342
(4735)
2002/03: 24⁴S, 21⁵GS, 22⁰HY, 26⁶GS, 16⁴G, 19³F, 21⁴GF, 19²GF,

	Starts	1st	2nd	3rd	Win & Pl
Chases	8	0	1	1	1361
Career Total	77	7	12	9	41016
89	1/01	Tntn	2m	F(0-110)HCh	HVY	£3493
99	4/00	Winc	2m	E(0-115)HCh	G-S	£4270
105	12/98	Winc	2m	D(0-125)HCh	SFT	£3512
102	12/97	Winc	2m	D(0-125)HCh	G-S	£3626
110	3/96	NAbb	2m1f	F(0-100)HHdl	SFT	£2589
100	1/96	Winc	2m	F Hdl	G-S	£2617
84	5/95	Ctml	2m1f110yE Hdl	GD	£2416
				Total win prize-money £22528		

Going:	Sf: 0-2 GS: 0-2 Gd: 0-1 GF: - Fm: 0-3
Distance:	2m/2m3: 0-2 2m4-2m7: 0-4 3m+: 0-2
Track:	LH: 0-5 RH: 0-2 Tight: 0-3 Gall: 0-0
Aids:	Bl: 0-8 Vi: 0-0 Tstrap: 0-0
Best Rating:	114 1/98 Asct 2m gd-sft Ch

Plating-class chaser; fair sort in his prime, but into the veteran stage now and on the decline; runner-up in selling chase Chepstow April 2003; stays three miles; loves the mud.

Roboastar (USA)
97   90

6-y-o b/br g Green Dancer (USA)-Sweet Alabastar (USA) (Gulch (USA))
P G Murphy Mrs John Spielman

Placings:404R0-4R (0505)
2002/03: 20⁴GF, 24⁸RG,

	Starts	1st	2nd	3rd	Win & Pl
Hurdles	2	0	0	0	0

Career Total	7	0	0	0	0

Going:	Sf: 0-0 GS: 0-0 Gd: 0-1 GF: - Fm: 0-1
Distance:	2m/2m3: 0-0 2m4-2m7: 0-1 3m+: 0-1
Track:	LH: 0-2 RH: 0-0 Tight: 0-0 Gall: 0-0
Aids:	Bl: 0-0 Vi: 0-0 Tstrap: 0-0
Best Rating:	90 10/01 Strf 2m110y gd-sft Hdl

Robsand (IRE)

14-y-o b g Sandalay-Remindful (Bargello)
A L Shaw A L Shaw

Placings:00/3/40423/24365P/4300P/F (0218)
2002/03: 25FG,

	Starts	1st	2nd	3rd	Win & Pl
Chases	1	0	0	0	0
Career Total	20	0	2	4	7761

Going:	Sf: 0-0 GS: 0-0 Gd: 0-1 GF: - Fm: 0-0
Distance:	2m/2m3: 0-0 2m4-2m7: 0-0 3m+: 0-1
Track:	LH: 0-0 RH: 0-1 Tight: 0-0 Gall: 0-0
Aids:	Bl: 0-0 Vi: 0-0 Tstrap: 0-0
Best Rating:	120 2/97 Towc 3m1f gd-sft Ch

Robyn Alexander (IRE)
106   124

5-y-o ch m Sharifabad (IRE)-Flagship Ahoy (IRE) (Accordion)
P F Nicholls (V Bowens 10/6) A P Brady

Placings:0-5252310F31 (4362)
2002/03: 16⁵G, 16²S, 16⁵S, 16²SH, 16³S, 18¹S, 17⁰GS, 16⁶GS, 17³G, 19¹F,

	Starts	1st	2nd	3rd	Win & Pl
NH Flat	4	0	2	0	1865
Hurdles	6	2	0	2	11578
Career Total	11	2	2	2	13443
112	3/03	Tntn	2m3f110yD(0-115)HHdl	FRM	£5118
105	12/02	Font	2m2f110yD Hdl	SFT	£5122
				Total win prize-money £10241		

Going:	Sf: 1-4 GS: 0-2 Gd: 0-2 GF: - Fm: 1-1
Distance:	2m/2m3: 1-9 2m4-2m7: 1-1 3m+: 0-0
Track:	LH: 1-3 RH: 1-4 Tight: 2-2 Gall: 0-2
Aids:	Bl: 0-0 Vi: 0-0 Tstrap: 0-0
Best Rating:	112 3/03 Tntn 2m3f110y firm Hdl

Modest hurdler; ex-Irish; handles soft ground; appreciated a sounder surface when easy winner of uncompetitive handicap at Taunton March 2003.

Rocastle Lad (IRE)
106

7-y-o gr g Roselier (FR)-Ivory Queen (Teenoso (USA))
N J Hawke N J McMullan And N R Packer

Placings:0-0PP (2453)
2002/03: 16⁰G, 17⁵GS, 19²GS,

	Starts	1st	2nd	3rd	Win & Pl
NH Flat	1	0	0	0	0
Hurdles	2	0	0	0	0
Career Total	4	0	0	0	

Going:	Sf: 0-0 GS: 0-2 Gd: 0-1 GF: - Fm: 0-0
Distance:	2m/2m3: 0-2 2m4-2m7: 0-1 3m+: 0-0

Track:	LH: 0-1 RH: 0-2 Tight: 0-2 Gall: 0-0
Aids:	Bl: 0-0 Vi: 0-0 Tstrap: 0-0
Best Rating:	40 11/01 NAbb 2m1f good NHF

Roccioso
76   72

6-y-o br g Pelder (IRE)-Priory Bay (Petong)
J C Fox Mrs J A Cleary

Placings:PP0/PP030-00 (0367)
2002/03: 16⁶GS, 17⁰S,

	Starts	1st	2nd	3rd	Win & Pl
Hurdles	2	0	0	0	0
Career Total	10	0	0	1	254

Going:	Sf: 0-1 GS: 0-1 Gd: 0-0 GF: - Fm: 0-0
Distance:	2m/2m3: 0-2 2m4-2m7: 0-0 3m+: 0-0
Track:	LH: 0-1 RH: 0-1 Tight: 0-1 Gall: 0-0
Aids:	Bl: 0-0 Vi: 0-0 Tstrap: 0-0
Best Rating:	73 12/00 Newb 2m110y soft Hdl

Very modest maiden hurdler.

Rock Bleu (FR)
35f   93f

5-y-o ch g Epervier Bleu-Egeria (FR) (Baly Rockette)
A Parker Mr & Mrs Raymond Anderson Green

Placings:006 (4397)
2002/03: 14⁰GS, 17⁰S, 17⁶G,

	Starts	1st	2nd	3rd	Win & Pl
NH Flat	3	0	0	0	0
Career Total	3	0	0	0	0

Going:	Sf: 0-1 GS: 0-1 Gd: 0-1 GF: - Fm: 0-0
Distance:	2m/2m3: 0-2 2m4-2m7: 0-0 3m+: 0-0
Track:	LH: 0-1 RH: 0-2 Tight: 0-0 Gall: 0-0
Aids:	Bl: 0-0 Vi: 0-0 Tstrap: 0-0
Best Rating:	93 3/03 Carl 2m1f soft NHF

Chasing-type; well beaten in bumpers.

Rock Crystal
72f   38f

4-y-o b g Joligeneration-Rusty Rock (Ayres Rock)
J L Spearing Masonaires

Placings:000 (4542)
2002/03: 16⁶S, 17⁰G, 16⁶G,

	Starts	1st	2nd	3rd	Win & Pl
NH Flat	3	0	0	0	0
Career Total	3	0	0	0	0

Going:	Sf: 0-1 GS: 0-0 Gd: 0-2 GF: - Fm: 0-0
Distance:	2m/2m3: 0-3 2m4-2m7: 0-0 3m+: 0-0
Track:	LH: 0-0 RH: 0-3 Tight: 0-0 Gall: 0-0
Aids:	Bl: 0-0 Vi: 0-0 Tstrap: 0-0
Best Rating:	38 1/03 Ludl 2m soft NHF

Rock Garden (IRE)
100f   94f

4-y-o br f Bigstone (IRE)-Woodland Garden (Godswalk (USA))
R F Johnson Houghton R F Johnson Houghton

Placings:1340 (4611)
2002/03: 14¹GS, 13³S, 16⁴GF, 17⁰G,

	Starts	1st	2nd	3rd	Win & Pl
NH Flat	4	1	0	1	3156
Career Total	4	1	0	1	**3156**

88 11/02 Wwck 1m6f   H NHF   G-S   £2765

Total win prize-money £2765

Going: Sf: 0-1 GS: 1-1 Gd: 0-1 GF: - Fm: 0-1
Distance: 2m/2m3: 0-2 2m4-2m7: 0-0 3m+: 0-1
Track: LH: 1-3 RH: 0-1 Tight: 0-0 Gall: 0-1
Aids: Bl: 0-0 Vi: 0-0 Tstrap: 0-0
Best Rating: 94 3/03 Hayd 2m gd-fm NHF

Modest bumper performer; dam is an unraced half-sister to a French Group Two winner stayed on well to win a moderate-looking junior bumper at Warwick in November 2002; twice ran well in defeat subsequently under a penalty; acts on easy and fast ground.

Rock Rose
106(97h)   (87h)83
10-y-o b m Arctic Lord-Ovington Court (Prefairy)
B J M Ryall (C Tizzard 12/12) Mrs Angela Davis

Placings:5U5/P602O3/3BU214P-46545   (4293)
2002/03: 22[4]G, 27[6]GS, 19[5]GS, 24[4]GS, 25[5]GF,

	Starts	1st	2nd	3rd	Win & Pl
Hurdles	1	0	0	0	332
Chases	4	0	0	0	432
Career Total	21	1	2	2	**9076**

100 2/02 Tntn 3m   D Ch   SFT   £5284

Total win prize-money £5285

Going: Sf: 0-0 GS: 0-3 Gd: 0-1 GF: - Fm: 0-1
Distance: 2m/2m3: 0-1 2m4-2m7: 0-1 3m+: 0-3
Track: LH: 0-0 RH: 0-5 Tight: 0-2 Gall: 0-0
Aids: Bl: 0-0 Vi: 0-0 Tstrap: 0-0
Best Rating: 100 2/02 Tntn 3m soft Ch

Has shown ability over both hurdles and fences in modest company. Won a decent chase over three miles in February 2002.

Rock Springs
5-y-o b g Rock City-Riva La Belle (Ron s Victory (USA))
C W Fairhurst Mrs B J Boocock

Placings:0-0P   (3166)
2002/03: 16[0]GS, 25[0]G,

	Starts	1st	2nd	3rd	Win & Pl
NH Flat	1	0	0	0	0
Hurdles	1	0	0	0	0
Career Total	3	0	0	0	**0**

Going: Sf: 0-0 GS: 0-1 Gd: 0-1 GF: - Fm: 0-0
Distance: 2m/2m3: 0-1 2m4-2m7: 0-0 3m+: 0-1
Track: LH: 0-1 RH: 0-1 Tight: 0-2 Gall: 0-0
Aids: Bl: 0-0 Vi: 0-0 Tstrap: 0-0
Best Rating: 0 1/03 Catt 3m1f110y good Hdl

Rock'n Cold (IRE)
97(107h)   (107h)100+
5-y-o b g Bigstone (IRE)-Unalaska (IRE) (High Estate)
R M H Cowell (T R George 21/12) C Akers

Placings:5213-PP131   (4675)
2002/03: 16[6]HY, 20[8]PS, 16[1]S, 17[3]G, 17[1]GF,

	Starts	1st	2nd	3rd	Win & Pl
Hurdles	5	2	0	1	6072
Career Total	9	3	1	2	**10062**

100 4/03 Hrfd 2m1f   G Hdl   G-F   £2338
100 3/03 Catt 2m   G Hdl   SFT   £2436
109 3/02 MRas 2m1ff110yE Hdl   G-S   £2765

Total win prize-money £7539

Going: Sf: 1-3 GS: 0-0 Gd: 0-1 GF: - Fm: 1-1
Distance: 2m/2m3: 2-4 2m4-2m7: 0-1 3m+: 0-0
Track: LH: 1-2 RH: 1-3 Tight: 1-2 Gall: 0-0
Aids: Bl: 0-0 Vi: 0-1 Tstrap: 0-0
Best Rating: 109 3/02 Chep 2m110y soft Hdl

Fair hurdler; won selling races either side of good third in handicap company at Market Rasen in March; acts on soft and fast ground; effective over two miles; wears cheekpieces.

Rockcliffe Gossip
111   112
11-y-o ch g Phardante (FR)-Clonmello (Le Bavard (FR))
N A Twiston-Davies Mrs Caroline Beresford-Wylie

Placings:322/222501/22152U335/U33P4/0322335P2-4165601   (4765)
2002/03: 25[4]GF, 24[1]GS, 24[6]GF, 24[5]HY, 32[6]GS, 24[0]GS, 31[1]G,

	Starts	1st	2nd	3rd	Win & Pl
Chases	7	2	0	0	26589
Career Total	39	4	11	8	**49199**

112 4/03 Prth 3m7f   E(0-110)HCh   GD   £15515
114 10/02 Bang 3m3f   D(0-120)HCh   G-S   £10773
94 10/99 Towc 2m6f   E Ch   GD   £2739
118 4/99 Uttx 2m4f110yE(0-115)HHdl   G-S   £3225

Total win prize-money £32253

Going: Sf: 0-1 GS: 1-3 Gd: 1-1 GF: - Fm: 0-2
Distance: 2m/2m3: 0-0 2m4-2m7: 0-0 3m+: 2-7
Track: LH: 1-2 RH: 0-4 Tight: 1-1 Gall: 0-0
Aids: Bl: 0-0 Vi: 0-0 Tstrap: 0-0
Best Rating: 118 4/99 Uttx 2m4f110y gd-sft Hdl

Modest chaser; out-and-out stayer who is often tapped for speed; stays extreme distances; suited by a little ease in the ground.

Rocket Radar
12-y-o b g Vouchsafe-Courtney Pennant (Angus)
Mrs J Hughes Mrs J Hughes

Placings:4/1/34/4P6/421-153   (3848)
2002/03: 25[1]G, 28[5]GF, 27[3]G,

	Starts	1st	2nd	3rd	Win & Pl
Chases	3	1	0	1	2751
Career Total	13	3	1	2	**7584**

105 5/02 Hrfd 3m1f110yH Ch   GD   £2320
96 4/02 Ludl 3m   H Ch   GD   £2800
100 4/99 Worc 2m7f110yH Ch   G-S   £1193

Total win prize-money £6314

Going: Sf: 0-0 GS: 0-0 Gd: 1-2 GF: - Fm: 0-1
Distance: 2m/2m3: 0-0 2m4-2m7: 0-1 3m+: 1-3
Track: LH: 0-0 RH: 1-2 Tight: 0-2 Gall: 0-0
Aids: Bl: 0-0 Vi: 0-0 Tstrap: 0-0
Best Rating: 105 5/02 Hrfd 3m1f110y good Ch

Fair hunter chaser; stays three miles; likes yielding ground, but has also won on good to firm.

Rockette
72   14
8-y-o ch m Rock Hopper-Primulette (Mummy s Pet)
A J Chamberlain Lord Goldicote

Placings:0/050U/0   (0882)
2002/03: 16[0]S,

	Starts	1st	2nd	3rd	Win & Pl
Hurdles	1	0	0	0	0
Career Total	6	0	0	0	**0**

Going: Sf: 0-1 GS: 0-0 Gd: 0-0 GF: - Fm: 0-0
Distance: 2m/2m3: 0-1 2m4-2m7: 0-0 3m+: 0-0
Track: LH: 0-1 RH: 0-0 Tight: 0-1 Gall: 0-0
Aids: Bl: 0-0 Vi: 0-0 Tstrap: 0-0
Best Rating: 79 9/00 Worc 2m gd-fm Hdl

Rockfield Lane (IRE)
(96h)   (91h)
7-y-o b/br g Sharifabad (IRE)-Suir Surprise (Rusticaro (FR))
G F Bridgwater (P M J Doyle 5/10) Michael Appleby

Placings:0/045504P000   (2712)
2002/03: 16[0]S, 16[4]YS, 16[5]GF, 16[5]F, 16[0]GF, 16[4]GF, 21[8]GS, 16[0]S, 17[0]G, 16[0]GS,

	Starts	1st	2nd	3rd	Win & Pl
NH Flat	3	0	0	0	
Hurdles	7	0	0	0	221
Career Total	11	0	0	0	**221**

Going: Sf: 0-2 GS: 0-2 Gd: 0-1 GF: - Fm: 0-4
Distance: 2m/2m3: 0-9 2m4-2m7: 0-1 3m+: 0-0
Track: LH: 0-2 RH: 0-3 Tight: 0-1 Gall: 0-0
Aids: Bl: 0-0 Vi: 0-0 Tstrap: 0-0
Best Rating: 93 7/02 Gway 2m soft NHF

Plating-class hurdler; tailed-off on chase debut; no worthwhile form since arriving from Ireland in 2002; has worn visor.

Rockford (IRE)
96   82
7-y-o b g King s Ride-Pampered Russian (Deep Run)
A King M R Deeley

Placings:03/P6450   (4488)
2002/03: 21[P]S, 25[8]S, 24[4]GS, 26[5]G, 26[0]GF,

	Starts	1st	2nd	3rd	Win & Pl
Hurdles	5	0	0	0	404
Career Total	7	0	0	1	**654**

Going: Sf: 0-2 GS: 0-1 Gd: 0-1 GF: - Fm: 0-1
Distance: 2m/2m3: 0-2 2m4-2m7: 0-1 3m+: 0-4
Track: LH: 0-2 RH: 0-3 Tight: 0-0 Gall: 0-1
Aids: Bl: 0-0 Vi: 0-1 Tstrap: 0-0
Best Rating: 92 4/01 Newb 2m110y soft NHF

Rockview (IRE)
92(73h)   (60h)71
8-y-o b g Mandalus-Saltee Star (Arapaho)
M E Sowersby (R H York 24/8) M E Sowersby

Placings:00/00/R/00P432R-4P5R6RF   (1166)
2002/03: 16[4]GS, 18[P]GF, 16[5]GF, 16[6]G, 16[6]GF, 23[8]G, 21[2]G,

	Starts	1st	2nd	3rd	Win & Pl
Hurdles	1	0	0	0	0
Chases	6	0	0	0	242
Career Total	19	0	1	1	**1680**

Going: Sf: 0-0 GS: 0-0 Gd: 0-4 GF: - Fm: 0-3
Distance: 2m/2m3: 0-5 2m4-2m7: 0-1 3m+: 0-1
Track: LH: 0-6 RH: 0-0 Tight: 0-4 Gall: 0-0

Aids: Bl: 0-0 Vi: 0-0 Tstrap: 0-0
Best Rating: 71 7/02 Wolv 2m good Ch

Moderate ex-Irish chaser. Handles any ground.

Rocky Balboa

11-y-o b g Buckley-Midnight Pansy (Deadly Nightshade)
W Davies Bill Davies

Placings:0/P0/PPP (1898)
2002/03: 23⁶G, 24⁴S, 27⁶PS,

	Starts	1st	2nd	3rd	Win & Pl
Hurdles	1	0	0	0	0
Chases	2	0	0	0	
Career Total	**6**	**0**	**0**		

Going: Sf: 0-2 GS: 0-0 Gd: 0-1 GF: - Fm: 0-0
Distance: 2m/2m3: 0-0 2m4-2m7: 0-0 3m+: 0-3
Track: LH: 0-3 RH: 0-0 Tight: 0-2 Gall: 0-0
Aids: Bl: 0-0 Vi: 0-0 Tstrap: 0-0
Best Rating: 65 3/97 Bang 2m1f good NHF

Rocky Island

101   110

6-y-o b g Rock Hopper-Queen s Eyot (Grundy)
J Mackie Mrs Sue Adams

Placings:033030/60012311-P40 (1943)
2002/03: 20⁵G, 20⁴G, 21⁹G,

	Starts	1st	2nd	3rd	Win & Pl
Hurdles	3	0	0	0	275
Career Total	**17**	**3**	**1**	**4**	**11806**
110 4/02	Uttx	2m4f110yE(0-110)HHdl		GD	£3570
102 3/02	Newb	2m3f	E(0-110)HHdl	SFT	£3342
93 2/02	Uttx	2m	G Hdl	HVY	£2002
				Total win prize-money £8915	

Going: Sf: 0-0 GS: 0-0 Gd: 0-3 GF: - Fm: 0-0
Distance: 2m/2m3: 0-0 2m4-2m7: 0-3 3m+: 0-0
Track: LH: 0-3 RH: 0-0 Tight: 0-0 Gall: 0-1
Aids: Bl: 0-0 Vi: 0-0 Tstrap: 0-0
Best Rating: 110 4/02 Uttx 2m4f110y good Hdl

Modest hurdler. Suited by two and a half miles and soft ground. Bought for 5,000gns after winning a seller at Uttoxeter and has proved a shrewd buy.

Rodalko (FR)

108   106

5-y-o b g Kadalko (FR)-Darling Rose (FR) (Rose Laurel)
O Sherwood J Palmer-Brown

Placings:02-F14P0P (4692)
2002/03: 21⁵FS, 21¹G, 19⁴G, 22⁵PG, 21⁰GS, 22⁹G,

	Starts	1st	2nd	3rd	Win & Pl
Hurdles	6	1	1	0	3941
Career Total	**8**	**1**	**1**	**0**	**4435**
100 11/02	Ludl	2m5f	E Hdl	GD	£3562
				Total win prize-money £3562	

Going: Sf: 0-1 GS: 0-0 Gd: 0-2 GF: - Fm: 0-0
Distance: 2m/2m3: 0-0 2m4-2m7: 1-5 3m+: 0-0
Track: LH: 0-4 RH: 1-2 Tight: 0-4 Gall: 0-1
Aids: Bl: 0-0 Vi: 0-0 Tstrap: 0-0
Best Rating: 106 12/02 Newb 2m3f good Hdl

Modest hurdler; shaped well in a couple of bumpers, before falling on his hurdling debut. Made all next time, stays two miles five. Acts on good.

Rodber (USA)

96   94+

7-y-o ch g Rodrigo De Triano (USA)-Berceau (USA) (Alleged (USA))
Mrs L B Normile K J Fehilly And A K Collins

Placings:43-3P4P (3769)
2002/03: 16³S, 20⁴GS, 20⁴HY, 20²GS,

	Starts	1st	2nd	3rd	Win & Pl
NH Flat	1	0	0	1	288
Hurdles	3	0	0	0	280
Career Total	**6**	**0**	**0**	**2**	**1313**

Going: Sf: 0-2 GS: 0-2 Gd: 0-0 GF: - Fm: 0-0
Distance: 2m/2m3: 0-1 2m4-2m7: 0-3 3m+: 0-0
Track: LH: 0-4 RH: 0-0 Tight: 0-0 Gall: 0-0
Aids: Bl: 0-0 Vi: 0-0 Tstrap: 0-0
Best Rating: 110 11/02 Ayr 2m soft NHF

Roddy The Vet (IRE)

91   92

5-y-o ch g Be My Native (USA)-Caronia (IRE) (Cardinal Flower)
A Ennis (Sean O O Brien 10/10) Lady Wates

Placings:0-16040 (4058)
2002/03: 16¹G, 16⁶GS, 21⁰GS, 22⁴GS, 21⁰S,

	Starts	1st	2nd	3rd	Win & Pl
NH Flat	1	1	0	0	4868
Hurdles	4	0	0	0	321
Career Total	**6**	**1**	**0**	**0**	**5189**
102 10/02	Gowr	2m	NHF	GD	£4868
				Total win prize-money £4868	

Going: Sf: 0-1 GS: 0-3 Gd: 1-1 GF: - Fm: 0-0
Distance: 2m/2m3: 1-2 2m4-2m7: 0-3 3m+: 0-0
Track: LH: 0-3 RH: 0-1 Tight: 0-1 Gall: 0-1
Aids: Bl: 0-0 Vi: 0-0 Tstrap: 0-0
Best Rating: 102 10/02 Gowr 2m good NHF

Ex-Irish-trained novice hurdler; won a bumper at Gowran Park in October 2002 but no immediate promise over hurdles in Britain.

Rodiak

94   74

4-y-o b g Distant Relative-Misty Silks (Scottish Reel)
Bob Jones The Rodiak Partnership

Placings:3224 (1380)
2002/03: 16³GS, 18²G, 16²GF, 17⁴GF,

	Starts	1st	2nd	3rd	Win & Pl
Hurdles	4	0	2	1	2942
Career Total	**4**	**0**	**2**	**1**	**2942**

Going: Sf: 0-0 GS: 0-1 Gd: 0-1 GF: - Fm: 0-2
Distance: 2m/2m3: 0-4 2m4-2m7: 0-0 3m+: 0-0
Track: LH: 0-3 RH: 0-1 Tight: 0-3 Gall: 0-0
Aids: Bl: 0-0 Vi: 0-2 Tstrap: 0-0
Best Rating: 74 9/02 Strf 2m110y gd-fm Hdl

Moderate form in hurdles on varying ground.

Rodolfo

95f   104f

5-y-o b g Tragic Role (USA)-Be Discreet (Junius (USA))
O Sherwood P Joe Davis

Placings:1-063 (4788)

2002/03: 16⁰GS, 16⁶G, 17³G,

	Starts	1st	2nd	3rd	Win & Pl
NH Flat	3	0	0	1	290
Career Total	**4**	**1**	**0**	**1**	**2089**
104 4/02	MRas	2m1f110yH NHF		GD	£1799
				Total win prize-money £1799	

Going: Sf: 0-0 GS: 0-1 Gd: 0-2 GF: - Fm: 0-0
Distance: 2m/2m3: 0-3 2m4-2m7: 0-0 3m+: 0-0
Track: LH: 0-0 RH: 0-3 Tight: 0-1 Gall: 0-0
Aids: Bl: 0-0 Vi: 0-0 Tstrap: 0-0
Best Rating: 104 4/03 MRas 2m1f110y good NHF

A half-brother to Gothenburg; won a Market Rasen bumper in April 2002; well beaten third in same race a year later.

Rodrigo (IRE)

(101h)

10-y-o b g Good Thyne (USA)-Magic Minstrel (Pitpan)
Ian Williams Mark F Sheasby

Placings:64134212/4220650/1/36U65P6/0PP3-P (0336)
2002/03: 20²G,

	Starts	1st	2nd	3rd	Win & Pl
Chases	1	0	0	0	
Career Total	**28**	**3**	**4**	**3**	**13892**
102 5/99	Clon	2m4f	Hdl	SFT	£3222
114 2/98	Clon	2m4f	Hdl	Y-S	£1935
102 10/97	Fair	2m	NHF	GD	£3051
				Total win prize-money £8211	

Going: Sf: 0-0 GS: 0-0 Gd: 0-1 GF: - Fm: 0-0
Distance: 2m/2m3: 0-0 2m4-2m7: 0-1 3m+: 0-0
Track: LH: 0-0 RH: 0-0 Tight: 0-0 Gall: 0-0
Aids: Bl: 0-0 Vi: 0-0 Tstrap: 0-0
Best Rating: 122 3/98 Fair 2m4f yield Hdl

Ex-Irish hurdler, does not look one to trust.

Rody (IRE)

84   57

6-y-o b/br g Foxhound (USA)-Capable Kate (IRE) (Alzao (USA))
I R Brown (F Jordan 24/9) I R Brown

Placings:FPP-605PP0P (4675)
2002/03: 17⁶G, 19⁰GF, 20⁵G, 24⁰PS, 24⁴PGF, 18⁰GF, 17⁰GF,

	Starts	1st	2nd	3rd	Win & Pl
Hurdles	7	0	0	0	0
Career Total	**10**	**0**	**0**	**0**	**0**

Going: Sf: 0-1 GS: 0-0 Gd: 0-2 GF: - Fm: 0-4
Distance: 2m/2m3: 0-3 2m4-2m7: 0-2 3m+: 0-2
Track: LH: 0-4 RH: 0-3 Tight: 0-2 Gall: 0-0
Aids: Bl: 0-0 Vi: 0-0 Tstrap: 0-0
Best Rating: 55 6/02 Hrfd 2m1f good Hdl

Roebucks Way

20f

5-y-o b g Shaamit (IRE)-Alwal (Pharly (FR))
D Shaw Swann Racing Ltd

Placings:0 (2142)
2002/03: 14⁰GS,

	Starts	1st	2nd	3rd	Win & Pl
NH Flat	1	0	0	0	
Career Total	**1**	**0**	**0**	**0**	

Going: Sf: 0-0 GS: 0-1 Gd: 0-0 GF: - Fm: 0-0
Distance: 2m/2m3: 0-0 2m4-2m7: 0-0 3m+: 0-0

Track: LH: 0-1 RH: 0-0 Tight: 0-0 Gall: 0-0
Aids: Bl: 0-0 Vi: 0-0 Tstrap: 0-0
Best Rating: 20   11/02   Newc   1m6f   gd-sft   NHF

Rogue Spirit

100   **102**

7-y-o b g Petong-Quick Profit (Formidable (USA))
S L Keightley (R M Stronge 6/5) Mrs C C Regalado-Gonzalez

Placings: 35434B25F0-45   (0111)
2002/03: 17⁴G, 16⁵GS,

	Starts	1st	2nd	3rd	Win & Pl
Hurdles	2	0	0	0	0
Career Total	12	0	1	2	1819

Going: Sf: 0-0 GS: 0-1 Gd: 0-1 GF: - Fm: 0-0
Distance: 2m/2m3: 0-2 2m4-2m7: 0-0 3m+: 0-0
Track: LH: 0-0 RH: 0-1 Tight: 0-1 Gall: 0-0
Aids: Bl: 0-2 Vi: 0-0 Tstrap: 0-0
Best Rating: 102   6/01   Strf   2m110y   gd-fm   Hdl

Rohan

98   **89**

7-y-o gr g Norton Challenger-Acushla Macree (Mansingh (USA))
R F Johnson Houghton Mrs R F Johnson Houghton

Placings: 06/5-02   (4277)
2002/03: 16⁰G, 20²GF,

	Starts	1st	2nd	3rd	Win & Pl
Hurdles	2	0	1	0	1088
Career Total	5	0	1	0	1088

Going: Sf: 0-0 GS: 0-0 Gd: 0-1 GF: - Fm: 0-1
Distance: 2m/2m3: 0-1 2m4-2m7: 0-1 3m+: 0-0
Track: LH: 0-0 RH: 0-1 Tight: 0-1 Gall: 0-1
Aids: Bl: 0-0 Vi: 0-0 Tstrap: 0-1
Best Rating: 104   10/00   Extr   2m1f   good   NHF

Lightly-raced maiden hurdler; has shown only moderate form so far; stays two and a half miles; acts on decent ground.

Roi De Danse

54

8-y-o ch g Komaite (USA)-Princess Lucy (Local Suitor (USA))
Miss Z C Davison Mrs J Irvine

Placings: 0/0-0   (0057)
2002/03: 17⁰G,

	Starts	1st	2nd	3rd	Win & Pl
Hurdles	1	0	0	0	
Career Total	3	0	0	0	

Going: Sf: 0-0 GS: 0-0 Gd: 0-1 GF: - Fm: 0-0
Distance: 2m/2m3: 0-1 2m4-2m7: 0-0 3m+: 0-0
Track: LH: 0-0 RH: 0-1 Tight: 0-1 Gall: 0-0
Aids: Bl: 0-0 Vi: 0-0 Tstrap: 0-0
Best Rating: 46   5/00   Worc   2m   good   Hdl

Roky Star (FR)

98   **86**

6-y-o b g Start Fast (FR)-Rosydolie (FR) (Dhausli (FR))

M R Bosley N Turner, D Kelly, D Merricks, R Jones

Placings: 33/0130-6344   (3274)
2002/03: 16⁶G, 19³S, 22⁴HY, 22⁴HY,

	Starts	1st	2nd	3rd	Win & Pl
Hurdles	4	0	0	1	550
Career Total	10	1	0	4	3511
106 11/01 Folk	2m1f110yH NHF			SFT	£1641

Total win prize-money £1642

Going: Sf: 0-3 GS: 0-0 Gd: 0-1 GF: - Fm: 0-0
Distance: 2m/2m3: 0-1 2m4-2m7: 0-3 3m+: 0-0
Track: LH: 0-1 RH: 0-3 Tight: 0-2 Gall: 0-0
Aids: Bl: 0-0 Vi: 0-0 Tstrap: 0-1
Best Rating: 106   11/01   Folk   2m1f110y   soft   NHF

Bumper winner, modest hurdler at around two and a half miles.

Role Model

101   **82**

7-y-o b m Tragic Role (USA)-Emerald Gulf (IRE) (Wassl)
J Neville D T Phillips

Placings: 30/2/3   (0902)
2002/03: 20³G,

	Starts	1st	2nd	3rd	Win & Pl
Hurdles	1	0	0	1	419
Career Total	4	0	1	2	1194

Going: Sf: 0-0 GS: 0-0 Gd: 0-1 GF: - Fm: 0-0
Distance: 2m/2m3: 0-0 2m4-2m7: 0-1 3m+: 0-0
Track: LH: 0-1 RH: 0-0 Tight: 0-0 Gall: 0-0
Aids: Bl: 0-0 Vi: 0-0 Tstrap: 0-0
Best Rating: 82   8/02   Worc   2m4f   good   Hdl

Plating-class hurdler; may have blown up on first start for new stable in two and a half mile Worcester seller August 2002.

Rolex Free (ARG)

76   **63**

5-y-o ch g Friul (ARG)-Karolera (ARG) (Kaljerry (ARG))
Mrs L C Taylor Mrs L C Taylor

Placings: 6   (3729)
2002/03: 16⁶G,

	Starts	1st	2nd	3rd	Win & Pl
Hurdles	1	0	0	0	450
Career Total	1	0	0	0	450

Going: Sf: 0-0 GS: 0-0 Gd: 0-1 GF: - Fm: 0-0
Distance: 2m/2m3: 0-1 2m4-2m7: 0-0 3m+: 0-0
Track: LH: 0-0 RH: 0-1 Tight: 0-0 Gall: 0-0
Aids: Bl: 0-0 Vi: 0-0 Tstrap: 0-0
Best Rating: 63   2/03   Kemp   2m   good   Hdl

Rolfe (NZ)

83

13-y-o b g Tom s Shu (USA)-Tredia (NZ) (Mussorgsky)
Dr P Pritchard Mrs T Pritchard

Placings: 34502/31115P3/P/P0P011626/64324305P0/0001 3100/P62615U-P   (0359)
2002/03: 24⁷GS,

	Starts	1st	2nd	3rd	Win & Pl
Hurdles	1	0	0	0	
Career Total	48	8	4	6	25910
83 7/01 Worc	2m4f	G(0-90)HHdl		SFT	£1638
83 10/00 Sthl	2m	G(0-95)HHdl		HVY	£1515

83	8/00	NAbb	2m1f	F(0-100)HHdl	G-S	£2555
103	3/99	Ludl	2m	F Hdl	GD	£2339
108	3/99	Donc	2m4f	G Hdl	G-S	£1716
110	6/96	Uttx	2m4f110yC Hdl		G-F	£4494
	5/96	Uttx	2m	E Hdl	GD	£2389
	5/96	Strf	2m110y	E(0-100)HHdl	G-F	£2598

Total win prize-money £19246

Going: Sf: 0-0 GS: 0-1 Gd: 0-0 GF: - Fm: 0-0
Distance: 2m/2m3: 0-0 2m4-2m7: 0-0 3m+: 0-1
Track: LH: 0-1 RH: 0-0 Tight: 0-1 Gall: 0-0
Aids: Bl: 0-0 Vi: 0-0 Tstrap: 0-0
Best Rating: 116   4/99   Ludl   2m   good   Hdl

Rolfes Delight

104(95h)   (56h)**90**

11-y-o b g Rolfe (USA)-Idiot s Run (Idiots Delight)
A E Jones Miss Sophie Parmentier

Placings: 5/16/PP-1F0515PP   (3855)
2002/03: 21¹GF, 24⁵GS, 20⁵S, 22⁵GF, 25¹F, 24⁵GF, 25⁵G, 24⁴GS,

	Starts	1st	2nd	3rd	Win & Pl
Hurdles	2	0	0	0	
Chases	6	2	0	0	7944
Career Total	13	3	0	0	9406
90 10/02 Winc	3m1f110yF(0-95)HCh			FRM	£3692
89 5/02 Winc	2m5f	E(0-100)HCh		G-F	£4251
100 5/00 Bang	3m110y	H Ch		G-S	£1462

Total win prize-money £9407

Going: Sf: 0-1 GS: 0-2 Gd: 0-1 GF: - Fm: 2-4
Distance: 2m/2m3: 0-0 2m4-2m7: 1-3 3m+: 1-5
Track: LH: 0-3 RH: 2-5 Tight: 0-4 Gall: 0-0
Aids: Bl: 0-0 Vi: 0-0 Tstrap: 0-0
Best Rating: 100   5/00   Bang   3m110y   gd-sft   Ch

Moderate chaser; landed a low-grade novices handicap chase at Wincanton in May 2002 and added to that over the same track in October; returned from three month absence to land 3m 1f selling handicap chase at Hereford June 2003; stays three miles plus; acts on fast ground.

Roll With It (IRE)

10-y-o b g Royal Fountain-Deirdre Elizabeth (Salluceva)
I Anderson Ian Anderson

Placings: 05/6263/000300660/20/33   (0145)
2002/03: 24³G, 24³GF,

	Starts	1st	2nd	3rd	Win & Pl
Chases	2	0	0	2	446
Career Total	19	0	2	4	2140

Going: Sf: 0-0 GS: 0-0 Gd: 0-1 GF: - Fm: 0-1
Distance: 2m/2m3: 0-0 2m4-2m7: 0-0 3m+: 0-2
Track: LH: 0-2 RH: 0-0 Tight: 0-1 Gall: 0-0
Aids: Bl: 0-0 Vi: 0-0 Tstrap: 0-0
Best Rating: 94   7/98   Klny   2m1f   gd-yld   NHF

A thorough stayer between the flags who ran respectably in hunter chases in May 2002.

Roller Blade

110   **121**

9-y-o b g Broadsword (USA)-Sparkling Cinders (Netherkelly)
N A Twiston-Davies Advanced Marketing Services Ltd

Placings: 40610/1F6P551/52620/F-15PU314PFR   (3879)
2002/03: 16²G, 16¹G, 25⁵G, 20⁶G, 22⁴UG, 17³S, 25¹GF, 24⁴GF, 25⁵G, 21⁶F, 24⁶RG,

	Starts	1st	2nd	3rd	Win & Pl
Chases	11	2	0	1	9353

Career Total	28	5	2	1		17107
120	9/02	Hrfd	3m1f110yE(0-105)HCh	G-F	£3974
105	5/02	Sthl	2m	E(0-100)HCh	GD	£3142
105	3/00	Tntn	2m3f110yG(0-100)HHdl	GD	£1770
99	5/99	Uttx	2m	E Hdl	G-F	£2620
115	3/99	Ludl	2m	H NHF	GD	£1451
				Total win prize-money £12961		

Going:	Sf: 0-1 GS: 0-1 Gd: 1-7 GF: - Fm: 1-2
Distance:	2m/2m3: 1-3 2m4-2m7: 0-3 3m+: 1-5
Track:	LH: 1-5 RH: 1-6 Tight: 1-3 Gall: 0-2
Aids:	Bl: 0-0 Vi: 0-0 Tstrap: 0-0
Best Rating:	120 10/02 Kemp 3m gd-fm Ch

Fair handicap chaser; acts on a sound surface; stays three miles.

Rolling Maul (IRE)
98   58
8-y-o b g Simply Great (FR)-Soyez Sage (FR) (Grundy)
Miss C J E Caroe Miss C J E Caroe

Placings:30/040255/05410F00030/200050364P-50P343

                                 (4632)

2002/03: 20⁵GF, 20⁰G, 24⁰GF, 24³G, 25⁴G, 26³GF,

	Starts	1st	2nd	3rd	Win & Pl
Chases	6	0	0	2	1926
Career Total	35	1	2	9	9983
82	7/00	Baln	2m4f	(0-95)HHdl	G-F	£3312
				Total win prize-money £3312		

Going:	Sf: 0-0 GS: 0-0 Gd: 0-3 GF: - Fm: 0-3
Distance:	2m/2m3: 0-0 2m4-2m7: 0-2 3m+: 0-4
Track:	LH: 0-2 RH: 0-3 Tight: 0-4 Gall: 0-2
Aids:	Bl: 0-3 Vi: 0-0 Tstrap: 0-0
Best Rating:	97 11/00 Navn 2m4f soft Ch

Poor maiden chaser; tends to run in snatches.

Rolling River (IRE)
97(84h)   (49h)91
6-y-o b g Over The River (FR)-Paddy s Dancer (Paddy s Stream)
J Wade John Wade

Placings:053   (2474)

2002/03: 20⁰GF, 27⁵S, 24³G,

	Starts	1st	2nd	3rd	Win & Pl
Hurdles	2	0	0	0	0
Chases	1	0	0	1	755
Career Total	3	0	0	1	755

Going:	Sf: 0-1 GS: 0-0 Gd: 0-0 GF: - Fm: 0-1
Distance:	2m/2m3: 0-0 2m4-2m7: 0-1 3m+: 0-2
Track:	LH: 0-3 RH: 0-0 Tight: 0-1 Gall: 0-1
Aids:	Bl: 0-0 Vi: 0-0 Tstrap: 0-0
Best Rating:	91 12/02 Donc 3m good Ch

Point winner, shaped well when third on chasing debut at Doncaster in December. Looks a stayer in the making.

Rolling Tide (IRE)
87   107
7-y-o b g Alphabatim (USA)-St.Cristoph (The Parson)
N J Henderson B T Stewart-Brown

Placings:2/1-0P   (2687)

2002/03: 16⁰S, 21³S,

	Starts	1st	2nd	3rd	Win & Pl
Hurdles	2	0	0	0	
Career Total	4	1	1	0	3225
107	2/02	Ludl	2m	E Hdl	G-S	£2677
				Total win prize-money £2678		

Going:	Sf: 0-2 GS: 0-0 Gd: 0-0 GF: - Fm: 0-0
Distance:	2m/2m3: 0-1 2m4-2m7: 0-1 3m+: 0-0
Track:	LH: 0-1 RH: 0-1 Tight: 0-0 Gall: 0-1
Aids:	Bl: 0-0 Vi: 0-0 Tstrap: 0-0
Best Rating:	107 2/02 Ludl 2m gd-sft Hdl

Modest hurdler; won an ordinary novice hurdle in February 2002 in good style. Held since.

Roma Road
85   68
7-y-o b g Syrtos-Fair Cruise (Cruise Missile)
R J Smith Oliver Ryan & Mrs Gill Ryan

Placings:250   (3167)

2002/03: 16²GF, 16⁵HY, 16⁶G,

	Starts	1st	2nd	3rd	Win & Pl
NH Flat	3	0	1	0	562
Career Total	3	0	1	0	562

Going:	Sf: 0-1 GS: 0-0 Gd: 0-0 GF: 0-1
Distance:	2m/2m3: 0-3 2m4-2m7: 0-0 3m+: 0-0
Track:	LH: 0-3 RH: 0-0 Tight: 0-1 Gall: 0-0
Aids:	Bl: 0-0 Vi: 0-0 Tstrap: 0-0
Best Rating:	102 5/02 Chep 2m110y gd-fm NHF

Hung badly when short-headed in a bumper on his debut.

Roman Candle (IRE)
101   82
7-y-o b g Sabrehill (USA)-Penny Banger (IRE) (Pennine Walk)
Mrs Lucinda Featherstone Largesse Racing

Placings:00F-6U05220F5   (4669)

2002/03: 16⁶S, 17⁰GF, 16⁰GF, 19⁵GF, 17²GF, 16²GF, 17⁰GF, 16FF, 16⁵G,

	Starts	1st	2nd	3rd	Win & Pl
Hurdles	9	0	2	0	1748
Career Total	12	0	2	0	1748

Going:	Sf: 0-1 GS: 0-0 Gd: 0-0 GF: 0-7
Distance:	2m/2m3: 0-9 2m4-2m7: 0-0 3m+: 0-0
Track:	LH: 0-6 RH: 0-3 Tight: 0-4 Gall: 0-0
Aids:	Bl: 0-0 Vi: 0-0 Tstrap: 0-0
Best Rating:	84 8/02 Worc 2m gd-fm Hdl

Moderate maiden hurdler.

Roman Court (IRE)
95   88
5-y-o b g Witness Box (USA)-Small Iron (General Ironside)
R H Alner Lady Talbot Of Malahide

Placings:62   (4514)

2002/03: 16⁶G, 22²GF,

	Starts	1st	2nd	3rd	Win & Pl
NH Flat	1	0	0	0	0
Hurdles	1	0	1	0	872
Career Total	2	0	1	0	872

Going:	Sf: 0-0 GS: 0-0 Gd: 0-1 GF: - Fm: 0-1
Distance:	2m/2m3: 0-1 2m4-2m7: 0-1 3m+: 0-0
Track:	LH: 0-1 RH: 0-1 Tight: 0-0 Gall: 0-0
Aids:	Bl: 0-0 Vi: 0-0 Tstrap: 0-0
Best Rating:	89 3/03 Chep 2m110y good NHF

Half-brother to winning pointer; shaped as if he needed further when well beaten second in two and three quarter mile maiden hurdle at Exeter April 2003.

Roman King (IRE)
102   95
8-y-o b g Sadler s Wells (USA)-Romantic Feeling (Shirley Heights)
Mrs J Candlish (P F Nicholls 1/2) Centaur Racing Ltd

Placings:F345226166F   (4173)

2002/03: 17FS, 17³G, 20⁴G, 16⁵S, 16²GS, 16²HY, 16⁶GS, 16¹HY, 16⁶HY, 16⁶GS, 20⁶S,

	Starts	1st	2nd	3rd	Win & Pl
Hurdles	11	1	2	1	5485
Career Total	11	1	2	1	5485
95	2/03	Uttx	2m	G Hdl	HVY	£2457
				Total win prize-money £2457		

Going:	Sf: 1-6 GS: 0-3 Gd: 0-2 GF: - Fm: 0-0
Distance:	2m/2m3: 1-9 2m4-2m7: 0-2 3m+: 0-0
Track:	LH: 1-5 RH: 0-6 Tight: 0-2 Gall: 0-1
Aids:	Bl: 0-0 Vi: 0-0 Tstrap: 0-0
Best Rating:	95 2/03 Uttx 2m heavy Hdl

Moderate hurdler; took a seller at Uttoxeter in February; acts on heavy ground.

Roman Outlaw
102   103
11-y-o gr g Alias Smith (USA)-Roman Moor (Owen Anthony)
Mrs K Walton Mrs K Walton

Placings:344/200441/4/0/623P/4211PU55P-P1650UP1P   (4765)

2002/03: 27⁵PS, 24¹HY, 24⁶HY, 25⁵HY, 24⁰S, 32US, 20⁰G, 24¹G, 31PG,

	Starts	1st	2nd	3rd	Win & Pl
Chases	9	2	0	0	9072
Career Total	33	5	3	2	22679
103	4/03	Newc	3m	D(0-120)HCh	GD	£5733
106	1/03	Newc	3m	F(0-100)HCh	HVY	£3339
105	1/02	Newc	3m6f	D(0-125)HCh	SFT	£4104
106	12/01	Newc	3m6f	F(0-110)HCh	G-S	£3386
102	4/98	Hexm	2m4f110yE Hdl	HVY	£2789
				Total win prize-money £19354		

Going:	Sf: 1-6 GS: 0-0 Gd: 1-3 GF: - Fm: 0-0
Distance:	2m/2m3: 0-0 2m4-2m7: 0-1 3m+: 2-8
Track:	LH: 2-7 RH: 0-1 Tight: 0-1 Gall: 2-4
Aids:	Bl: 1-6 Vi: 0-0 Tstrap: 0-0
Best Rating:	109 11/97 Weth 2m good NHF

Modest staying chaser, best at Newcastle and recorded fourth win there in April; unreliable though.

Roman Way
?   ?
7-y-o ch g Gildoran-Olympian Princess (Master Owen)
R W Powell R W Powell

Placings:P   (4506)

2002/03: 25PG,

	Starts	1st	2nd	3rd	Win & Pl
Chases	1	0	0	0	
Career Total	1	0	0	0	

Going:	Sf: 0-0 GS: 0-0 Gd: 0-1 GF: 0-0
Distance:	2m/2m3: 0-0 2m4-2m7: 0-0 3m+: 0-1
Track:	LH: 0-1 RH: 0-0 Tight: 0-1 Gall: 0-0
Aids:	Bl: 0-0 Vi: 0-0 Tstrap: 0-0
Best Rating:	0 4/03 Kels 3m1f good Ch

Romannie (BEL)

74   **62**

4-y-o b f Piccolo-Green Land (BEL) (Hero s Honor (USA))
G M Moore (Mrs S A Watt 26/11) Major E J Watt

Placings: P000   (2161)
2002/03: 17PG, 16OGF, 16OG, 17OS,

	Starts	1st	2nd	3rd	Win & Pl
Hurdles	4	0	0	0	
Career Total	4	0	0	0	

Going:	Sf: 0-1 GS: 0-0 Gd: 0-2 GF: - Fm: 0-1
Distance:	2m2/m3: 0-4 2m4-2m7: 0-0 3m+: 0-0
Track:	LH: 0-4 RH: 0-0 Tight: 0-3 Gall: 0-0
Aids:	Bl: 0-0 Vi: 0-0 Tstrap: 0-0
Best Rating:	57 10/02 Kels 2m10y gd-fm Hdl

Romantic Hero (IRE)

103   (78h) **116+**

7-y-o b g Supreme Leader-Right Love (Golden Love)
N A Gaselee Simon Harrap

Placings: 43/F41-FPP21   (4271)
2002/03: 22FS, 18PG, 21PS, 20²S, 24¹G,

	Starts	1st	2nd	3rd	Win & Pl
Chases	5	2	1	0	5280
Career Total	10	2	1	1	11476
116	3/03	Chep	3m	F(0-100)HCh	GD 3584
107	3/02	Newb	2m2f110yD(0-110)HCh	G-S	5616
				Total win prize-money £9200	

Going:	Sf: 0-3 GS: 0-0 Gd: 1-2 GF: - Fm: 0-0
Distance:	2m2/m3: 0-1 2m4-2m7: 0-0 3m+: 1-1
Track:	LH: 1-3 RH: 0-0 Tight: 0-1 Gall: 0-2
Aids:	Bl: 1-2 Vi: 0-0 Tstrap: 0-0
Best Rating:	116 3/03 Chep 3m good Ch

Fair, lightly-raced chaser; stays three miles; suited by soft ground.

Romany Chat

11-y-o b g Backchat (USA)-Ranee s Song (True Song)
Mrs Rosemary Gasson Mrs Rosemary Gasson

Placings: PP/0143P-64P   (0414)
2002/03: 21PGF, 25⁴S, 28PGF,

	Starts	1st	2nd	3rd	Win & Pl
Chases	3	0	0	0	528
Career Total	10	1	0	1	3870
101	5/01	Chel	2m5f	H Ch	GD 2535
				Total win prize-money £2535	

Going:	Sf: 0-1 GS: 0-0 Gd: 0-0 GF: - Fm: 0-2
Distance:	2m2/m3: 0-0 2m4-2m7: 0-1 3m+: 0-2
Track:	LH: 0-2 RH: 0-1 Tight: 0-1 Gall: 0-1
Aids:	Bl: 0-0 Vi: 0-0 Tstrap: 0-0
Best Rating:	101 2/02 Hntg 3m gd-sft Ch

Winning pointer, he goes on most ground.

Romany Dream

90   **56**

5-y-o b m Nomadic Way (USA)-Half Asleep (Quiet Fling (USA))
R Dickin The Snoozy Partnership

Placings: f0   (4733)

2002/03: 16¹GF, 16OGF,

	Starts	1st	2nd	3rd	Win & Pl
NH Flat	1	1	0	0	2037
Hurdles	1	0	0	0	0
Career Total	2	1	0	0	2037
82	3/03	Wwck	2m	H NHF	G-F £2037
				Total win prize-money £2037	

Going:	Sf: 0-0 GS: 0-0 Gd: 0-0 GF: - Fm: 1-2
Distance:	2m2/m3: 1-2 2m4-2m7: 0-0 3m+: 0-0
Track:	LH: 1-2 RH: 0-0 Tight: 0-0 Gall: 0-0
Aids:	Bl: 0-0 Vi: 0-0 Tstrap: 0-0
Best Rating:	82 3/03 Wwck 2m gd-fm NHF

Won a Warwick bumper on her debut.

Romany Fair (IRE)

4-y-o b g Blues Traveller (IRE)-Fantasticus (IRE) (Lycius (USA))
C E N Smith (W S Cunningham 18/5) J D T Smith

Placings: P   (0797)
2002/03: 17PGS,

	Starts	1st	2nd	3rd	Win & Pl
Hurdles	1	0	0	0	
Career Total	1	0	0	0	

Going:	Sf: 0-0 GS: 0-1 Gd: 0-0 GF: - Fm: 0-0
Distance:	2m2/m3: 0-1 2m4-2m7: 0-0 3m+: 0-0
Track:	LH: 0-0 RH: 0-1 Tight: 0-1 Gall: 0-0
Aids:	Bl: 0-0 Vi: 0-0 Tstrap: 0-0
Best Rating:	0 8/02 Ctml 2m1f110y good Hdl

Romany Hill

101 (67c)   (14c) **89**

8-y-o b g Nomadic Way (USA)-Snarry Hill (Vitiges (FR))
J M Jefferson Capt M S Bagley

Placings: 00/P665405/0P0-43341P0   (3814)
2002/03: 19⁴S, 22³GS, 26³GF, 21⁴G, 20¹GF, 20PG, 16OG,

	Starts	1st	2nd	3rd	Win & Pl
Hurdles	6	1	0	2	5569
Chases	1	0	0	0	0
Career Total	19	1	0	2	5569
89	9/02	Prth	2m4f110yF(0-100)HHdl	G-F	£4186
				Total win prize-money £4186	

Going:	Sf: 0-1 GS: 0-1 Gd: 0-3 GF: - Fm: 1-2
Distance:	2m2/m3: 0-2 2m4-2m7: 1-4 3m+: 0-1
Track:	LH: 0-4 RH: 1-2 Tight: 0-4 Gall: 0-1
Aids:	Bl: 0-0 Vi: 0-1 Tstrap: 0-0
Best Rating:	89 9/02 Prth 2m4f110y gd-fm Hdl

Moderate staying novice hurdler, suited by cut in the ground. In good form in the autumn of 2002.

Romany Lass

78   **58**

7-y-o b m Romany Rye-Furnace Lass Vii (Damsire Unregistered)
W Storey Richardson Kelly O Gara Partnership

Placings: 0-04   (0475)
2002/03: 16OG, 17⁴GS,

	Starts	1st	2nd	3rd	Win & Pl
Hurdles	2	0	0	0	301
Career Total	3	0	0	0	301

Going:	Sf: 0-0 GS: 0-1 Gd: 0-1 GF: - Fm: 0-0

Distance:	2m/2m3: 0-2 2m4-2m7: 0-0 3m+: 0-0
Track:	LH: 0-2 RH: 0-0 Tight: 0-1 Gall: 0-0
Aids:	Bl: 0-0 Vi: 0-0 Tstrap: 0-0
Best Rating:	58 6/02 Ctml 2m1f110y gd-sft Hdl

Rome (IRE)

85f   **87f**

4-y-o br g Singspiel (IRE)-Ela Romara (Ela-Mana-Mou)
G P Enright G R Macdonald, K Fitchie, M Enright

Placings: 615   (4788)
2002/03: 16OG, 141GF, 17⁵G,

	Starts	1st	2nd	3rd	Win & Pl
NH Flat	3	1	0	0	1981
Career Total	3	1	0	0	1981
87	3/03	Hrfd	1m6f	H NHF	G-F £1981
				Total win prize-money £1981	

Going:	Sf: 0-0 GS: 0-0 Gd: 0-2 GF: - Fm: 1-1
Distance:	2m/2m3: 0-2 2m4-2m7: 0-0 3m+: 0-0
Track:	LH: 0-0 RH: 0-2 Tight: 0-1 Gall: 0-0
Aids:	Bl: 0-0 Vi: 0-0 Tstrap: 0-0
Best Rating:	87 3/03 Hrfd 1m6f gd-fm NHF

Flat-bred half-brother to the useful Foyer out of the Nassau Stakes winner Ela Romara; took a bumper at Hereford in March 2003.

Romero

105 (115h)   (131h) **118**

7-y-o b g Robellino (USA)-Casamurrae (Be My Guest (USA))
Miss E C Lavelle Fraser Miller Racing

Placings: 1126201/234004/2124000042-446351U440   (4324)
2002/03: 24⁴GS, 16⁴G, 17⁶GS, 19³GS, 22⁵GS, 22¹S, 22UG, 27⁴S, 22⁴S, 24OG,

	Starts	1st	2nd	3rd	Win & Pl
Hurdles	2	0	0	0	1076
Chases	8	1	1	0	8740
Career Total	33	5	6	2	52223
117	11/02	Newb	2m6f110yD(0-120)HCh	SFT	£6500
131	11/01	Asct	2m110y B(0-150)HHdl	GD	£7121
123	4/00	Asct	2m110y C HHdl	GD	£4414
119	11/99	Asct	2m110y B Hdl	GD	£6742
109	10/99	Asct	2m110y C Hdl	GD	£4788
				Total win prize-money £30066	

Going:	Sf: 1-3 GS: 0-4 Gd: 0-3 GF: - Fm: 0-0
Distance:	2m/2m3: 0-2 2m4-2m7: 1-5 3m+: 0-3
Track:	LH: 1-5 RH: 0-5 Tight: 0-2 Gall: 1-6
Aids:	Bl: 0-0 Vi: 1-7 Tstrap: 1-4
Best Rating:	131 11/01 Sand 2m110y gd-sft Hdl

Fair chaser/hurdler; won his first race over fences in a handicap at Newbury in November 2002; goes really well on good ground but handles soft; had a good record at Ascot over hurdles; effective at up to two miles six; has worn a tongue tie and a visor.

Romil Star (GER)

103   **70**

6-y-o b g Chief s Crown (USA)-Romelia (USA) (Woodman (USA))
R D Wylie M R Johnson

Placings: 004-10   (0375)
2002/03: 16¹GF, 16OG,

	Starts	1st	2nd	3rd	Win & Pl
Hurdles	2	1	0	0	3445
Career Total	5	1	0	0	3445

94 5/02 Prth 2m110y E(0-105)HHdl G-F £3445
Total win prize-money £3445

Going:	Sf: 0-0 GS: 0-0 Gd: 0-1 GF: - Fm: 1-1				
Distance:	**2m/2m3: 1-2** 2m4-2m7: 0-0 3m+: 0-0				
Track:	LH: 0-1 RH: **1-1** Tight: 0-1 Gall: 0-0				
Aids:	Bl: 0-0 Vi: 0-0 Tstrap: 0-0				
Best Rating:	**94** 5/02 Prth 2m110y gd-fm Hdl				

A Flat winner in Germany who progressed over hurdles to win on his handicap debut at Perth in May 2002. Races freely and handles any ground.

Ron Miel (IRE)

9-y-o b g Brush Aside (USA)-Try Le Reste (IRE) (Le Moss)
M Rodda P Senter

Placings:P   (0218)
2002/03: 25PG,

	Starts	1st	2nd	3rd	Win & Pl
Chases	1	0	0	0	
Career Total	1	0	0	0	

Going:	Sf: 0-0 GS: 0-0 Gd: 0-1 GF: - Fm: 0-0				
Distance:	2m/2m3: 0-0 2m4-2m7: 0-0 3m+: 0-1				
Track:	LH: 0-0 RH: 0-1 Tight: 0-0 Gall: 0-0				
Aids:	Bl: 0-0 Vi: 0-0 Tstrap: 0-0				
Best Rating:	**0** 5/02 Hrfd 3m1f110y good Ch				

Ronans Choice (IRE)
87

10-y-o b g Yashgan-Petite Port (IRE) (Decent Fellow)
G M McCourt Mrs Kathy Stuart

Placings:602PG/61-PPP   (0730)
2002/03: 25PG, 23PGF, 21PGF,

	Starts	1st	2nd	3rd	Win & Pl
Chases	3	0	0	0	
Career Total	10	1	0	0	3698
87	4/02	Font	3m2f110yF(0-100)HCh	g-f	£2786
			Total win prize-money £2786		

Going:	Sf: 0-0 GS: 0-0 Gd: 0-0 GF: 1- Fm: 0-0				
Distance:	2m/2m3: 0-0 2m4-2m7: 0-1 3m+: 0-2				
Track:	LH: 0-2 RH: 0-1 Tight: 0-0 Gall: 0-0				
Aids:	Bl: 0-3 Vi: 0-0 Tstrap: 0-1				
Best Rating:	**87** 4/02 Font 3m2f110y gd-fm Ch				

Lightly-raced ex-Irish pointer. Got off the mark when fitted with blinkers for the first time at Fontwell in April 2002 but has struggled since. Stays well, seems to handles any ground.

Roobihoo (IRE)
98f   83f

4-y-o b g Norwich-Griffinstown Lady (Over The River (FR))
C Grant Mrs H E Aitkin

Placings:55   (4778)
2002/03: 16⁵G, 16⁵G,

	Starts	1st	2nd	3rd	Win & Pl
NH Flat	2	0	0	0	0
Career Total	2	0	0	0	0

Going:	Sf: 0-0 GS: 0-0 Gd: 0-2 GF: - Fm: 0-0				
Distance:	2m/2m3: 0-2 2m4-2m7: 0-0 3m+: 0-0				
Track:	LH: 0-1 RH: 0-1 Tight: 0-0 Gall: 0-0				

Roofer (IRE)
83   66

5-y-o b m Barathea (IRE)-Castlerahan (IRE) (Thatching)
Miss K M George (B R Millman 6/7) M J Watson

Placings:0P   (2945)
2002/03: 16⁰GS, 21PS,

	Starts	1st	2nd	3rd	Win & Pl
Hurdles	2	0	0	0	
Career Total	2	0	0	0	

Going:	Sf: 0-1 GS: 0-1 Gd: 0-0 GF: - Fm: 0-0				
Distance:	2m/2m3: 0-1 2m4-2m7: 0-1 3m+: 0-0				
Track:	LH: 0-1 RH: 0-1 Tight: 0-0 Gall: 0-0				
Aids:	Bl: 0-0 Vi: 0-0 Tstrap: 0-0				
Best Rating:	**66** 11/02 Wwck 2m gd-sft Hdl				

Rooftop

7-y-o b g Thatching-Top Berry (High Top)
W Storey Gremlin Racing

Placings:B3300/00P/P-   (0004)
2002/03: 16PG,

	Starts	1st	2nd	3rd	Win & Pl
Hurdles	1	0	0	0	
Career Total	9	0	0	2	569

Going:	Sf: 0-0 GS: 0-0 Gd: 0-0 GF: - Fm: 0-0				
Distance:	2m/2m3: 0-1 2m4-2m7: 0-0 3m+: 0-0				
Track:	LH: 0-1 RH: 0-0 Tight: 0-0 Gall: 0-1				
Aids:	Bl: 0-0 Vi: 0-0 Tstrap: 0-0				
Best Rating:	**89** 9/99 Cork 2m gd-fm Hdl				

Rookery Lad
104   92

5-y-o b g Makbul-Wayzgoose (USA) (Diesis)
C N Kellett (B D Leavy 5/10) John O Donovan

Placings:00600402   (4679)
2002/03: 16⁰G, 17⁰GF, 16⁶GF, 16⁰G, 16⁹GF, 16⁴G, 22⁰G, 16²GF,

	Starts	1st	2nd	3rd	Win & Pl
NH Flat	1	0	0	0	0
Hurdles	7	0	1	0	690
Career Total	8	0	1	0	690

Going:	Sf: 0-0 GS: 0-0 Gd: 0-4 GF: - Fm: 0-4				
Distance:	2m/2m3: 0-7 2m4-2m7: 0-1 3m+: 0-0				
Track:	LH: 0-5 RH: 0-2 Tight: 0-0 Gall: 0-2				
Aids:	Bl: 0-0 Vi: 0-0 Tstrap: 0-0				
Best Rating:	**71** 4/03 Hntg 2m110y gd-fm Hdl				

Moderate handicap hurdler; improved form since joining present connections; has run consistently well in better company since winning 2m novices Huntingdon seller May 2003; appeared to stay 2m 6f when runner-up at Stratford in July.

Rooster

8-y-o b g Roi Danzig (USA)-Jussoli (Don)
Mrs Julie Read Mrs P King

Placings:35/4125/F-P43   (4667)
2002/03: 16PGS, 21⁴G, 21³G,

	Starts	1st	2nd	3rd	Win & Pl
Chases	3	0	0	1	476
Career Total	10	1	1	2	7488
113	3/00	Donc	2m110y E(0-105)HHdl	GD	£5551
			Total win prize-money £5551		

Going:	Sf: 0-0 GS: 0-1 Gd: 0-2 GF: - Fm: 0-0				
Distance:	2m/2m3: 0-1 2m4-2m7: 0-2 3m+: 0-0				
Track:	LH: 0-2 RH: 0-1 Tight: 0-2 Gall: 0-0				
Aids:	Bl: 0-0 Vi: 0-0 Tstrap: 0-0				
Best Rating:	**113** 3/00 Newc 2m good Hdl				

Poor hunter chaser; best on a sound surface; stays two miles five.

Rooster Booster
123   178+

9-y-o gr g Riverwise (USA)-Came Cottage (Nearly A Hand)
P J Hobbs Terry Warner

Placings:0/23F1332/3PF2323P/5542214-111112   (4478)
2002/03: 16¹G, 16¹GS, 17¹G, 16¹HY, 16¹G, 20²G,

	Starts	1st	2nd	3rd	Win & Pl
Hurdles	6	5	1	0	299831
Career Total	29	7	7	6	416056
178	3/03	Chel	2m110y A Hdl	GD	£174000
161	2/03	Sand	2m110y B Hdl	HVY	£12180
163	12/02	Chel	2m1f A Hdl	GD	£43500
170	11/02	Chel	2m110y A HHdl	G-S	£29000
166	10/02	Kemp	2m B Hdl	GD	£8151
155	3/02	Chel	2m1f A HHdl	GD	£33000
120	1/00	Tntn	2m1f D Hdl	SFT	£4284
			Total win prize-money £304116		

Going:	Sf: 1-1 GS: 1-1 Gd: 3-4 GF: - Fm: 0-0				
Distance:	**2m/2m3: 5-5** 2m4-2m7: 0-0 3m+: 0-1				
Track:	LH: 3-4 RH: 2-2 Tight: 0-1 **Gall: 1-1**				
Aids:	Bl: 0-0 Vi: 0-0 Tstrap: 0-0				
Best Rating:	**178** 3/03 Chel 2m110y good Hdl				

The 2003 Champion hurdler; after several near misses, he landed the 2002 County Hurdle at Cheltenham; improved significantly in 2002/2003, winning his first four starts including the Bula Hurdle at Cheltenham; slightly disappointing when only narrowly winning Agfa Hurdle at Sandown in heavy ground but an easy winner of the 2003 Champion Hurdle back on good; somewhat unlucky narrow loser of Grade 1 at Aintree; stays 2 1/2 miles but suited by strongly-run 2m; effective on good or soft ground, possibly not at his best on heavy; consistent and goes well at Cheltenham.

Rooster's Reunion
96f   96f

4-y-o gr g Presenting-Court Town (Camden Town)
D R Gandolfo Terry Warner

Placings:02   (4275)
2002/03: 14⁰GS, 16²G,

	Starts	1st	2nd	3rd	Win & Pl
NH Flat	2	0	1	0	568
Career Total	2	0	1	0	568

Going:	Sf: 0-0 GS: 0-1 Gd: 0-1 GF: - Fm: 0-0				
Distance:	2m/2m3: 0-2 2m4-2m7: 0-0 3m+: 0-0				
Track:	LH: 0-2 RH: 0-0 Tight: 0-0 Gall: 0-0				
Aids:	Bl: 0-0 Vi: 0-0 Tstrap: 0-0				
Best Rating:	**96** 3/03 Chep 2m110y good NHF				

Moderate bumper performer; acts on good.

Roppongi Dancer

95   **72**

4-y-o b f Mtoto-Ice Chocolate (USA) (Icecapade (USA))
Mrs M Reveley Andy Peake

Placings:5600   (2473)
2002/03: 17⁵GS, 17⁶G, 16⁰G, 16⁰G,

	Starts	1st	2nd	3rd	Win & Pl
Hurdles	4	0	0	0	0
Career Total	4	0	0	0	0

Going:	Sf: 0-0 GS: 0-1 Gd: 0-3 GF: - Fm: 0-0
Distance:	2m/2m3: 0-4 2m4-2m7: 0-0 3m+: 0-0
Track:	LH: 0-3 RH: 0-1 Tight: 0-3 Gall: 0-1
Aids:	Bl: 0-0 Vi: 0-0 Tstrap: 0-0
Best Rating:	72 8/02 Sedg 2m1f good Hdl

Plating-class hurdler; should stay further than two miles one.

Rosa Gallica

72f   **45f**

7-y-o ch m Sula Bula-Armonit (Town Crier)
Miss H C Knight Mrs J Hodgkiss

Placings:0   (0149)
2002/03: 16⁰GF,

	Starts	1st	2nd	3rd	Win & Pl
NH Flat	1	0	0	0	
Career Total	1	0	0	0	

Going:	Sf: 0-0 GS: 0-0 Gd: 0-0 GF: - Fm: 0-1
Distance:	2m/2m3: 0-1 2m4-2m7: 0-0 3m+: 0-0
Track:	LH: 0-1 RH: 0-0 Tight: 0-0 Gall: 0-0
Aids:	Bl: 0-0 Vi: 0-0 Tstrap: 0-0
Best Rating:	45 5/02 Chep 2m110y gd-fm NHF

Rosaker (USA)

107   **148**

6-y-o b g Pleasant Tap (USA)-Rose Crescent (USA) (Nijinsky (CAN))
Noel Meade High Street Ceathar Syndicate

Placings:5110   (4097)
2002/03: 16⁵SH, 16¹S, 20¹Y, 16⁰G,

	Starts	1st	2nd	3rd	Win & Pl
Hurdles	4	2	0	0	24919
Career Total	4	2	0	0	24919
148	2/03	Naas	2m4f		Hdl	YLD £19415
114	12/02	Fair	2m		Hdl	SFT £5503
					Total win prize-money £24919

Going:	Sf: 1-1 GS: 0-0 Gd: 0-1 GF: - Fm: 0-0
Distance:	2m/2m3: 1-3 2m4-2m7: 1-1 3m+: 0-0
Track:	LH: 0-1 RH: 1-2 Tight: 0-0 Gall: 0-0
Aids:	Bl: 0-0 Vi: 0-0 Tstrap: 0-0
Best Rating:	148 2/03 Naas 2m4f yield Hdl

Very useful Irish-trained novice hurdler; winner on the Flat in Dubai; suited by 2m 4f and likely to get farther; effective with cut in the ground.

Rosalee Royale

11-y-o ch m Out Of Hand-Miss Ark Royal (Broadsword (USA))
Mrs S Kittow Mrs S Kittow

Placings:00/0/6/6   (4487)
2002/03: 16⁶GF,

	Starts	1st	2nd	3rd	Win & Pl
Chases	1	0	0	0	0
Career Total	5	0	0	0	0

Going:	Sf: 0-0 GS: 0-0 Gd: 0-0 GF: - Fm: 0-1
Distance:	2m/2m3: 0-1 2m4-2m7: 0-0 3m+: 0-0
Track:	LH: 0-0 RH: 0-1 Tight: 0-0 Gall: 0-0
Aids:	Bl: 0-0 Vi: 0-0 Tstrap: 0-0
Best Rating:	55 3/96 Wwck 2m good NHF

Rosalyons (IRE)

93(103h)   (96h)**82**

9-y-o gr g Roselier (FR)-Coffee Shop (Bargello)
Mrs H O Graham Mrs H O Graham

Placings:5/06000/011U330PP4F-050353614P   (4305)
2002/03: 21⁰G, 22⁵G, 21⁰G, 22³HY, 25⁵S, 25³S, 24⁶S, 22¹GS, 22⁴S, 25⁶G,

	Starts	1st	2nd	3rd	Win & Pl
Hurdles	5	1	0	0	5065
Chases	5	0	0	2	1373
Career Total	27	3	0	4	13341
96	3/03	Kels	2m6f110yD(0-115)HHdl	G-S	£4797
102	10/01	Carl	2m4f	E(0-105)HHdl	SFT	£2609
85	10/01	Kels	2m6f110yF(0-110)HHdl	G-S	£2716
					Total win prize-money £10123

Going:	Sf: 0-5 GS: 1-1 Gd: 0-4 GF: - Fm: 0-0
Distance:	2m/2m3: 0-0 2m4-2m7: 1-6 3m+: 0-4
Track:	LH: 1-10 RH: 0-0 Tight: 1-5 Gall: 0-1
Aids:	Bl: 0-0 Vi: 0-0 Tstrap: 0-0
Best Rating:	102 12/01 Kels 2m6f110y gd-sft Hdl

Moderate hurdler/chaser; stays three miles; has won on soft and good to soft.

Rosarian (IRE)

109   **122**

6-y-o b g Fourstars Allstar (USA)-Only A Rose (Glint Of Gold)
V R A Dartnall A & D Enterprises (poole) Ltd

Placings:4213-4431311F   (4609)
2002/03: 22⁴S, 24⁴HY, 19³G, 22¹GS, 24³G, 27¹S, 24¹G, 24⁶G,

	Starts	1st	2nd	3rd	Win & Pl
Hurdles	8	3	0	2	16255
Career Total	12	4	1	3	18931
122	3/03	Newb	3m110y	D Hdl	GD	£5193
114	3/03	Font	3m3f	E Hdl	SFT	£3451
119	1/03	Winc	2m6f	D(0-115)HHdl	G-S	£5460
115	1/02	Font	2m2f110yH HHdl	GD	£1680
					Total win prize-money £15785

Going:	Sf: 1-3 GS: 1-1 Gd: 1-4 GF: - Fm: 0-0
Distance:	2m/2m3: 0-0 2m4-2m7: 1-3 3m+: 2-5
Track:	LH: 1-4 RH: 1-3 Tight: 1-1 Gall: 1-3
Aids:	Bl: 0-0 Vi: 0-1 Tstrap: 0-0
Best Rating:	123 2/02 Asct 2m110y soft NHF

Fair novice hurdler; stays 3m plus; acts in soft ground, but reportedly better on a good surface.

Rosco

109   **117**

9-y-o b g Roscoe Blake-Silva Linda (Precipice Wood)
J T Gifford Miss J Semple

Placings:2/33223341/43226/21-4512   (4609)
2002/03: 20⁴HY, 22⁵HY, 20¹G, 24²G,

	Starts	1st	2nd	3rd	Win & Pl
Hurdles	4	1	1	0	12870

Career Total	20	3	7	5	30007
120	4/03	Asct	2m4f	D(0-125)HHdl	GD	£7215
115	10/01	Plum	3m1f110yD(0-120)HHdl	SFT	£3526
109	4/00	Strf	2m6f110yE Hdl	GD	£2660
					Total win prize-money £13401

Going:	Sf: 0-2 GS: 0-0 Gd: 1-2 GF: - Fm: 0-0
Distance:	2m/2m3: 0-0 2m4-2m7: 1-3 3m+: 0-1
Track:	LH: 0-1 RH: 1-3 Tight: 0-0 Gall: 0-1
Aids:	Bl: 0-0 Vi: 0-0 Tstrap: 0-0
Best Rating:	121 3/00 Sand 2m4f110y good Hdl

Fair handicap hurdler; looks a real chasing type; returned from a long break to run well at Sandown in February 2003, showing he retains all of his ability; again ran well next time before scoring at Ascot when fitted with cheekpieces; stays three miles, but effective at shorter; acts on ground ranging from good to heavy.

Rose Bowl Boy (IRE)

79f   **52f**

5-y-o ch g Lahib (USA)-Danita (IRE) (Roi Danzig (USA))
C J Mann The Rose Bowl Partnership

Placings:000   (3903)
2002/03: 16⁰HY, 16⁰GS, 16⁰S,

	Starts	1st	2nd	3rd	Win & Pl
NH Flat	3	0	0	0	
Career Total	3	0	0	0	

Going:	Sf: 0-2 GS: 0-1 Gd: 0-0 GF: - Fm: 0-0
Distance:	2m/2m3: 0-3 2m4-2m7: 0-0 3m+: 0-0
Track:	LH: 0-2 RH: 0-1 Tight: 0-0 Gall: 0-2
Aids:	Bl: 0-0 Vi: 0-0 Tstrap: 0-0
Best Rating:	49 1/03 Kemp 2m gd-sft NHF

Rose D'April (FR)

107   **115d**

6-y-o gr g April Night (FR)-Rose De Hoc (FR) (Rose Laurel)
L Lungo Ashleybank Investments Limited

Placings:0/120-151P0   (4304)
2002/03: 17¹HY, 16⁵S, 20¹G, 20⁰GS, 22⁰G,

	Starts	1st	2nd	3rd	Win & Pl
Hurdles	5	2	0	0	6372
Career Total	9	3	1	0	8457
115	1/03	Muss	2m4f	E(0-100)HHdl	GD	£3347
104	11/02	Carl	2m1f	E Hdl	HVY	£3024
102	12/01	Catt	2m	N HHdl	GD	£1631
					Total win prize-money £8003

Going:	Sf: 1-2 GS: 0-1 Gd: 1-2 GF: - Fm: 0-0
Distance:	2m/2m3: 1-2 2m4-2m7: 1-3 3m+: 0-0
Track:	LH: 0-3 RH: 2-2 Tight: 1-2 Gall: 0-1
Aids:	Bl: 0-0 Vi: 0-0 Tstrap: 0-0
Best Rating:	115 1/03 Muss 2m4f good Hdl

Modest hurdler; big sort, bumper winner; scored twice over hurdles; stays two miles four.

Rose Tina

99(101h)   (84h)**95**

6-y-o b m Tina s Pet-Rosevear (IRE) (Contract Law (USA))
B G Powell (E A Wheeler 24/11) Church Racing Partnership

Placings:U66/40450-0036224   (4598)
2002/03: 16⁵S, 21⁰HY, 21³GS, 20⁶G, 22²G, 19²F, 19⁴GF,

	Starts	1st	2nd	3rd	Win & Pl
Hurdles	4	0	0	1	1503

Chases	3	0	2	0	2942
Career Total	15	0	2	1	4721

Going: Sf: 0-2 GS: 0-1 Gd: 0-2 GF: - Fm: 0-2
Distance: 2m/2m3: 0-3 2m4-2m7: 0-4 3m+: 0-0
Track: LH: 0-2 RH: 0-4 Tight: 0-4 Gall: 0-0
Aids: Bl: 0-0 Vi: 0-0 Tstrap: 0-0
Best Rating: 91　3/03　Font　2m6f　good　Ch

Has shown only modest form over fences so far.

Rosecharmer
95　　　　　　73

6-y-o ch m Charmer-Rosie Cone (Celtic Cone)
Mrs P Sly　Thorney Racing Club

Placings:000-6606P　　　　　　　(3834)
2002/03: 21⁶GS, 20⁶GS, 19⁰GS, 22⁶HY, 20⁰G,

	Starts	1st	2nd	3rd	Win & Pl
Hurdles	5	0	0	0	0
Career Total	8	0	0	0	0

Going: Sf: 0-1 GS: 0-3 Gd: 0-1 GF: - Fm: 0-0
Distance: 2m/2m3: 0-0 2m4-2m7: 0-5 3m+: 0-0
Track: LH: 0-3 RH: 0-2 Tight: 0-1 Gall: 0-1
Aids: Bl: 0-0 Vi: 0-0 Tstrap: 0-0
Best Rating: 75　4/02　Fknm　2m　good　NHF

Rosegrove Rooster

6-y-o b g Henbit (USA)-Cornbelt (Oats)
D J Caro　Joe Roper

Placings:00-P　　　　　　　　(4567)
2002/03: 20⁰GF,

	Starts	1st	2nd	3rd	Win & Pl
Hurdles	1	0	0	0	
Career Total	3	0	0	0	

Going: Sf: 0-0 GS: 0-0 Gd: 0-0 GF: - Fm: 0-1
Distance: 2m/2m3: 0-0 2m4-2m7: 0-1 3m+: 0-0
Track: LH: 0-1 RH: 0-0 Tight: 0-1 Gall: 0-0
Aids: Bl: 0-0 Vi: 0-0 Tstrap: 0-0
Best Rating: 72　3/02　Ludl　2m　soft　NHF

Roselier Bell (IRE)
(84h)　　　　　(44h)

10-y-o b g Roselier (FR)-Bell Walks Fancy (Entre Chat)
B J Llewellyn　B J Llewellyn

Placings:0/033F30/34042F/0600.5/0P-0PP　(3225)
2002/03: 24⁰S, 22⁶HY, 27⁰HY,

	Starts	1st	2nd	3rd	Win & Pl
Hurdles	2	0	0	0	
Chases	1	0	0	0	
Career Total	23	0	1	4	2663

Going: Sf: 0-3 GS: 0-0 Gd: 0-0 GF: - Fm: 0-0
Distance: 2m/2m3: 0-0 2m4-2m7: 0-1 3m+: 0-2
Track: LH: 0-1 RH: 0-2 Tight: 0-3 Gall: 0-0
Aids: Bl: 0-0 Vi: 0-0 Tstrap: 0-0
Best Rating: 105　1/99　Punc　3m　heavy　Hdl

Rosemead Tye
81(87c)　　　　　(50+c)52

7-y-o b m Kasakov-Nouvelle Cuisine (Yawa)

J A Moore　Mrs J M Moore

Placings:0P0P0　　　　　　　(4666)
2002/03: 16⁶GS, 20⁰GF, 16⁰G, 16⁵S, 16⁰G,

	Starts	1st	2nd	3rd	Win & Pl
NH Flat	1	0	0	0	0
Hurdles	4	0	0	0	0
Career Total	5	0	0	0	

Going: Sf: 0-1 GS: 0-1 Gd: 0-1 GF: - Fm: 0-1
Distance: 2m/2m3: 0-4 2m4-2m7: 0-1 3m+: 0-0
Track: LH: 0-4 RH: 0-1 Tight: 0-4 Gall: 0-0
Aids: Bl: 0-0 Vi: 0-0 Tstrap: 0-3
Best Rating: 52　2/03　Catt　2m　good　Hdl

Plating-class hurdler; yet to show any worthwhile form; tailed off on chasing debut.

Rosencrantz (IRE)
112　　　　　　115

11-y-o b g Sadler s Wells (USA)-Rosananti (Blushing Groom (FR))
Miss Venetia Williams　M J Fenn

Placings:0/1112F3P10/P43/5FU11/4P-1312P5　(0970)
2002/03: 16¹GS, 20³GF, 16¹HY, 20²G, 20⁰GF, 17⁵S,

	Starts	1st	2nd	3rd	Win & Pl
Chases	6	2	1		10741
Career Total	26	8	2	3	36046
115	6/02	Uttx	2m	D(0-120)HCh	HVY	£4368
111	5/02	Towc	2m110y	F(0-100)HCh	G-S	£3445
121	7/99	Wolv	2m	C(0-130)HCh	G-S	£6995
100	6/99	Strf	2m4f	E(0-115)HCh	G-F	£2960
124	3/97	Asct	2m110y	C(0-135)HHdl	GD	£4856
111	11/96	Tntn	2m1f	E Hdl	G-F	£2358
110	10/96	Winc	2m	E Hdl	G-F	£2635
94	5/96	Chep	2m110y	E Hdl	G-F	£2486
				Total win prize-money £30104		

Going: Sf: 1-2 GS: 1-1 Gd: 0-1 GF: - Fm: 0-2
Distance: 2m/2m3: 2-3 2m4-2m7: 0-1 3m+: 0-0
Track: LH: 1-4 RH: 1-2 Tight: 0-2 Gall: 0-0
Aids: Bl: 0-0 Vi: 0-0 Tstrap: 0-0
Best Rating: 124　3/97　Asct　2m110y　good　Hdl

Modest chaser, lightly raced recently. Possibly best at two miles.

Roseta Pearl (IRE)
83　　　　　　59

7-y-o gr m Roselier (FR)-Brown Pearl (Tap On Wood)
Mrs S Wall　Mrs S Wall

Placings:3F5　　　　　　　(4213)
2002/03: 26³S, 25⁵F5, 22⁵G,

	Starts	1st	2nd	3rd	Win & Pl
Chases	3	0	0	1	624
Career Total	3	0	0	1	624

Going: Sf: 0-2 GS: 0-0 Gd: 0-1 GF: - Fm: 0-0
Distance: 2m/2m3: 0-2 2m4-2m7: 0-1 3m+: 0-2
Track: LH: 0-0 RH: 0-1 Tight: 0-2 Gall: 0-0
Aids: Bl: 0-0 Vi: 0-0 Tstrap: 0-2
Best Rating: 59　3/03　Font　2m6f　good　Ch

Rosewood (GER)
　　　　　　82

4-y-o b f Eagle Eyed (USA)-Rhode Island (GER) (Waajib)
C Von Der Recke　Dr Stephen & Elizabeth Eversfield

Placings:F　　　　　　　(2637)
2002/03: 16⁵S,

	Starts	1st	2nd	3rd	Win & Pl
Hurdles	1	0	0	0	
Career Total	1	0	0	0	

Going: Sf: 0-1 GS: 0-0 Gd: 0-0 GF: - Fm: 0-0
Distance: 2m/2m3: 0-1 2m4-2m7: 0-0 3m+: 0-0
Track: LH: 0-1 RH: 0-0 Tight: 0-0 Gall: 0-0
Aids: Bl: 0-0 Vi: 0-0 Tstrap: 0-0
Best Rating: 82　12/02　Wwck　2m　soft　Hdl

Rosey Boy (IRE)
96　　　　　　103

10-y-o gr g Roselier (FR)-Rossian (Silent Spring)
H Morrison　Mrs Panda Christie & M S Wilson

Placings:434P4210/P/510UF　　　(4120)
2002/03: 24⁵G, 26¹S, 24⁰G, 25¹G, 26⁶G,

	Starts	1st	2nd	3rd	Win & Pl
Hurdles	4	1	0	0	3332
Chases	1	0	0	0	
Career Total	14	2	1	1	6997
103	12/02	Hrfd	3m2f	F(0-100)HHdl	SFT	£3332
103	3/99	Font	3m3f	E Hdl	SFT	£2267
				Total win prize-money £5600		

Going: Sf: 1-1 GS: 0-0 Gd: 0-4 GF: - Fm: 0-0
Distance: 2m/2m3: 0-0 2m4-2m7: 0-0 3m+: 1-5
Track: LH: 0-1 RH: 1-4 Tight: 0-0 Gall: 0-2
Aids: Bl: 0-1 Vi: 0-0 Tstrap: 0-0
Best Rating: 103　12/02　Hrfd　3m2f　soft　Hdl

Modest staying hurdler, winner at Hereford in December 2002 on his second run after a long absence. Acts on soft ground.

Rosidavis (IRE)
93f　　　　　　86f

5-y-o ch g Roselier (FR)-Zalara (Zalazl (USA))
R F Fisher　Great Head House Estates Limited

Placings:22P　　　　　　　(1389)
2002/03: 17²GF, 16²GF, 16⁰GF,

	Starts	1st	2nd	3rd	Win & Pl
NH Flat	3	0	2	0	1050
Career Total	3	0	2	0	1050

Going: Sf: 0-0 GS: 0-0 Gd: 0-0 GF: - Fm: 0-3
Distance: 2m/2m3: 0-3 2m4-2m7: 0-0 3m+: 0-0
Track: LH: 0-3 RH: 0-0 Tight: 0-1 Gall: 0-0
Aids: Bl: 0-0 Vi: 0-0 Tstrap: 0-0
Best Rating: 86　9/02　Hexm　2m110y　gd-fm　NHF

Modest form in bumpers on fast ground.

Rosie Redman (IRE)
101　　　　　　81

6-y-o gr m Roselier (FR)-Carbia s Last (Palm Track)
J R Turner　Miss S J Turner

Placings:3-54454　　　　　　(4406)
2002/03: 16⁵S, 22⁴HY, 20⁴G, 24⁵S, 20⁴G,

	Starts	1st	2nd	3rd	Win & Pl
Hurdles	5	0	0	0	468
Career Total	6	0	0	1	686

Going: Sf: 0-3 GS: 0-0 Gd: 0-2 GF: - Fm: 0-0
Distance: 2m/2m3: 0-1 2m4-2m7: 0-3 3m+: 0-1

Track: LH: 0-4 RH: 0-1 Tight: 0-1 Gall: 0-1
Aids: Bl: 0-0 Vi: 0-0 Tstrap: 0-0
Best Rating: 97 11/01 Weth 2m good NHF

Moderate maiden hurdler; jumping-bred; very limited ability in bumpers and novices hurdles.

Rospo

7-y-o b/br g Tromeros-East Gale (Oats)
Mrs L B Normile Mrs K B Mactaggart

Placings:0-FP (1911)
2002/03: 16⁶G, 16⁹S,

	Starts	1st	2nd	3rd	Win & Pl
Hurdles	2	0	0	0	
Career Total	3	0	0	0	

Going: Sf: 0-1 GS: 0-0 Gd: 0-1 GF: - Fm: 0-0
Distance: 2m/2m3: 0-2 2m4-2m7: 0-0 3m+: 0-0
Track: LH: 0-2 RH: 0-0 Tight: 0-1 Gall: 0-0
Aids: Bl: 0-0 Vi: 0-0 Tstrap: 0-0
Best Rating: 21 3/02 Catt 2m gd-sft NHF

Ross Cottage

11-y-o b g Hyrossi-Flavias Cottage (Marcus Superbus)
T Long P R Bateman

Placings:36 (0395)
2002/03: 26³G, 28⁶G,

	Starts	1st	2nd	3rd	Win & Pl
Chases	2	0	0	1	286
Career Total	2	0	0	1	286

Going: Sf: 0-0 GS: 0-0 Gd: 0-2 GF: - Fm: 0-0
Distance: 2m/2m3: 0-0 2m4-2m7: 0-0 3m+: 0-2
Track: LH: 0-2 RH: 0-0 Tight: 0-1 Gall: 0-0
Aids: Bl: 0-0 Vi: 0-0 Tstrap: 0-0
Best Rating: 80 5/02 Uttx 3m2f good Ch

Ross Minster (IRE)
128

9-y-o ro g Roselier (FR)-Face To Face (The Parson)
P J Hobbs The Country Side

Placings:62/150121/53P1352/1235501-P (1852)
2002/03: 25⁹G,

	Starts	1st	2nd	3rd	Win & Pl
Chases	1	0	0	0	
Career Total	23	6	4	3	33487

128	4/02	Chep	3m2f110yD(0-120)HCh	G-S	£4124
124	11/01	NAbb	3m2f110yD(0-120)HCh	SFT	£3767
121	1/01	Chep	3m2f110yE(0-115)HCh	G-S	£3104
121	4/00	Uttx	3m2f	E Ch	HVY	£5540
120	2/00	Winc	3m1f110yD Ch	G-S	£4348
115	11/99	Towc	3m	D Hdl	GD	£3051

Total win prize-money £23936

Going: Sf: 0-0 GS: 0-0 Gd: 0-1 GF: - Fm: 0-0
Distance: 2m/2m3: 0-0 2m4-2m7: 0-0 3m+: 0-1
Track: LH: 0-0 RH: 0-1 Tight: 0-0 Gall: 0-0
Aids: Bl: 0-0 Vi: 0-0 Tstrap: 0-0
Best Rating: 128 4/02 Chep 3m2f110y gd-sft Ch

Useful staying handicap chaser. Has won with and without blinkers. Needs strong handling. Acts on soft ground and good to soft. Stays three and a quarter miles.

Ross Moff (IRE)
114   141

10-y-o b g Good Thyne (USA)-Miss Kamsy (Kambalda)
A J Martin Seamus Ross

Placings:00/5 f23220/111311/121/F5F53F (4727a)
2002/03: 17⁵SH, 25⁵G, 20⁵SH, 16⁵G, 25³G, 29⁵G,

	Starts	1st	2nd	3rd	Win & Pl
Chases	6	0	0	1	6978
Career Total	24	8	4	3	90055

129	2/01	Thur	2m	Ch	Y-S	€5564
111	1/01	Leop	2m5f	Ch	SFT	£10483
140	4/00	Fair	2m	Hdl	G-Y	£15600
148	4/00	Aint	3m110y	B HHdl	GD	£14716
139	2/00	Punc	2m	Hdl	Y-S	£10400
127	1/00	Navn	2m6f	Hdl	SFT	£4692
119	12/99	DRoy	2m	Hdl	HVY	£2464
104	1/99	DRoy	2m	NHF	HVY	£2455

Total win prize-money €66376

Going: Sf: 0-0 GS: 0-0 Gd: 0-4 GF: - Fm: 0-0
Distance: 2m/2m3: 0-2 2m4-2m7: 0-1 3m+: 0-3
Track: LH: 0-3 RH: 0-3 Tight: 0-1 Gall: 0-2
Aids: Bl: 0-0 Vi: 0-0 Tstrap: 0-6
Best Rating: 148 4/00 Aint 3m110y good Hdl

Useful chaser; stays three miles, but effective at shorter; likes soft ground; worn a tongue tie recently.

Ross Park (IRE)
83   80

7-y-o b g Roselier (FR)-La Christyana (IRE) (The Parson)
J Howard Johnson Gordon Brown/bert Watson

Placings:4-06F (2101)
2002/03: 24⁰S, 20⁶HY, 25⁷G,

	Starts	1st	2nd	3rd	Win & Pl
Hurdles	3	0	0	0	0
Career Total	4	0	0	0	0

Going: Sf: 0-2 GS: 0-0 Gd: 0-1 GF: - Fm: 0-0
Distance: 2m/2m3: 0-0 2m4-2m7: 0-1 3m+: 0-0
Track: LH: 0-2 RH: 0-1 Tight: 0-1 Gall: 0-0
Aids: Bl: 0-0 Vi: 0-0 Tstrap: 0-1
Best Rating: 80 3/02 Hexm 3m heavy Hdl

Plating-class hurdler; held when crashing out on handicap debut at Catterick in November.

Ross Will (IRE)
84   75

9-y-o b g Satco (FR)-Jayells Dream (Space King)
Ian Williams Mark F Sheasby

Placings:2/P00P (4786)
2002/03: 24⁵HY, 16⁰GS, 20⁰HY, 22⁵G,

	Starts	1st	2nd	3rd	Win & Pl
Hurdles	4	0	0	0	
Career Total	5	0	1	0	640

Going: Sf: 0-2 GS: 0-1 Gd: 0-1 GF: - Fm: 0-0
Distance: 2m/2m3: 0-1 2m4-2m7: 0-2 3m+: 0-0
Track: LH: 0-2 RH: 0-1 Tight: 0-1 Gall: 0-1
Aids: Bl: 0-0 Vi: 0-0 Tstrap: 0-0
Best Rating: 89 3/00 DRoy 2m gd-yld NHF

Plating-class hurdler; runner-up in an Irish bumper; shown little in three hurdles starts in Britain; started favourite at Market Rasen in April but was fatally injured. (DEAD)

Rosscarbery Grey (IRE)

5-y-o gr g Gothland (FR)-Millroad (Buckskin (FR))
S T Lewis Simon T Lewis

Placings:00 (4224)
2002/03: 16⁰G, 14⁰GF,

	Starts	1st	2nd	3rd	Win & Pl
NH Flat	2	0	0	0	
Career Total	2	0	0	0	

Going: Sf: 0-0 GS: 0-0 Gd: 0-1 GF: - Fm: 0-1
Distance: 2m/2m3: 0-1 2m4-2m7: 0-0 3m+: 0-0
Track: LH: 0-1 RH: 0-0 Tight: 0-0 Gall: 0-0
Aids: Bl: 0-0 Vi: 0-0 Tstrap: 0-0
Best Rating: 0 3/03 Hrfd 1m6f gd-fm NHF

Rosslea (IRE)
112   125+

5-y-o b g Roselier (FR)-Burren Gale (IRE) (Strong Gale)
Miss H C Knight Jim Lewis

Placings:P230 (4109)
2002/03: 20⁰HY, 20²S, 22³GS, 21⁰G,

	Starts	1st	2nd	3rd	Win & Pl
Hurdles	4	0	1	1	2885
Career Total	4	0	1	1	2885

Going: Sf: 0-2 GS: 0-1 Gd: 0-1 GF: - Fm: 0-0
Distance: 2m/2m3: 0-2 2m4-2m7: 0-2 3m+: 0-0
Track: LH: 0-2 RH: 0-2 Tight: 0-0 Gall: 0-1
Aids: Bl: 0-0 Vi: 0-0 Tstrap: 0-0
Best Rating: 125 12/02 Uttx 2m4f110y soft Hdl

Irish point winner; in the frame in novice hurdles; stays two miles six; acts with give in the ground.

Rostropovich (IRE)
117   155

6-y-o gr g Sadler s Wells (USA)-Infamy (Shirley Heights)
M F Morris M A Kilduff

Placings:13316/14005-452424021 (4789)
2002/03: 16⁴GF, 24⁵S, 24²YS, 24⁴S, 24²SH, 24⁴YS, 25⁰G, 24²G, 24¹GF,

	Starts	1st	2nd	3rd	Win & Pl
Hurdles	9	1	3	0	50208
Career Total	19	4	3	2	78923

155	4/03	Sand	3m	B Hdl	G-F	£29000
137	5/01	Fair	2m	Hdl	GD	£10483
124	4/01	Cork	2m	Hdl	Y-S	£6120
109	1/01	Naas	2m	Hdl	SFT	£5564

Total win prize-money £51170

Going: Sf: 0-2 GS: 0-0 Gd: 0-2 GF: - Fm: 1-2
Distance: 2m/2m3: 0-1 2m4-2m7: 0-0 3m+: 1-8
Track: LH: 0-6 RH: 0-0 Tight: 0-1 Gall: 0-2
Aids: Bl: 0-0 Vi: 0-0 Tstrap: 0-8
Best Rating: 155 4/03 Sand 3m gd-fm Hdl

High-class hurdler; won valuable event at Sandown April 2003; suited by 3m; acts on good and soft ground; usually wears a tongue strap; has worn cheekpieces.

Rotuma (IRE)
101   82

4-y-o b g Tagula (IRE)-Cross Question (USA) (Alleged (USA))

M Dods Denton Hall Racing Ltd

Placings:563433 (4352)
2002/03: 16⁵GF, 16⁶S, 16⁹GS, 16⁴GS, 17³G, 16⁵GF,

	Starts	1st	2nd	3rd	Win & Pl
Hurdles	6	0	0	3	1889
Career Total	6	0	0	3	1889

Going: Sf: 0-1 GS: 0-2 Gd: 0-1 GF: - Fm: 0-2
Distance: 2m/2m3: 0-2 2m4-2m7: 0-0 3m+: 0-0
Track: LH: 0-6 RH: 0-0 Tight: 0-2 Gall: 0-2
Aids: Bl: 0-0 Vi: 0-2 Tstrap: 0-0
Best Rating: 89 10/02 Weth 2m   gd-fm Hdl

Very limited ability in juvenile hurdles.

Rough Tiger (IRE)

10-y-o ch g Glacial Storm (USA)-Mourne Trix (Golden Love)
F A Hutsby Mrs Ian McKie

Placings:F (3952)
2002/03: 23⁶GS,

	Starts	1st	2nd	3rd	Win & Pl
Chases	1	0	0	0	
Career Total	1	0	0	0	

Going: Sf: 0-0 GS: 0-1 Gd: 0-0 GF: - Fm: 0-0
Distance: 2m/2m3: 0-0 2m4-2m7: 0-0 3m+: 0-1
Track: LH: 0-0 RH: 0-1 Tight: 0-0 Gall: 0-0
Aids: Bl: 0-0 Vi: 0-0 Tstrap: 0-0
Best Rating: 98 3/03 Leic 2m7f110y gd-sft Ch

Round The Bend

11-y-o b g Revolutionary (USA)-No Love (Bustiki)
Miss Louise Allan F Allan

Placings:25 (0403)
2002/03: 20²GF, 22⁵GF,

	Starts	1st	2nd	3rd	Win & Pl
Chases	2	0	1	0	416
Career Total	2	0	1	0	416

Going: Sf: 0-0 GS: 0-0 Gd: 0-0 GF: - Fm: 0-2
Distance: 2m/2m3: 0-0 2m4-2m7: 0-2 3m+: 0-0
Track: LH: 0-0 RH: 0-2 Tight: 0-1 Gall: 0-1
Aids: Bl: 0-0 Vi: 0-0 Tstrap: 0-0
Best Rating: 81 6/02 MRas 2m6f110y gd-fm Ch

Modest pointer/hunter chaser, handles fast ground.

Route Barree (FR)
78   52

5-y-o ch g Exit To Nowhere (USA)-Star Des Evees (FR) (Moulin)
S Dow Byerley Bloodstock

Placings:36-6 (3963)
2002/03: 16⁶S,

	Starts	1st	2nd	3rd	Win & Pl
Hurdles	1	0	0	0	0
Career Total	3	0	0	1	435

Going: Sf: 0-1 GS: 0-0 Gd: 0-0 GF: - Fm: 0-0
Distance: 2m/2m3: 0-1 2m4-2m7: 0-0 3m+: 0-0
Track: LH: 0-1 RH: 0-0 Tight: 0-1 Gall: 0-0
Aids: Bl: 0-0 Vi: 0-0 Tstrap: 0-0
Best Rating: 77 9/01 Plum 2m   gd-fm Hdl

Route One (IRE)

10-y-o b g Welsh Term-Skylin (Skyliner)
D Frankland D Frankland

Placings:1/2241/1F466/0/023221 (4443)
2002/03: 16⁹GF, 16²G, 20³S, 16²GS, 20²GF, 19¹G,

	Starts	1st	2nd	3rd	Win & Pl
Chases	6	1	3	1	5804
Career Total	17	4	5	1	14326
97	4/03	Asct	2m3f110yH Ch	GD	£2954
105	5/99	Towc	E Hdl	G-F	£2985
106	4/99	Hrfd	2m1f E Hdl	G-F	£2578
106	4/97	MRas	1m5f110yH NHF	GD	£1402

Total win prize-money £9921

Going: Sf: 0-1 GS: 0-1 Gd: 1-2 GF: - Fm: 0-2
Distance: 2m/2m3: 0-3 2m4-2m7: 1-3 3m+: 0-0
Track: LH: 0-2 RH: 1-4 Tight: 0-2 Gall: 0-1
Aids: Bl: 0-0 Vi: 0-0 Tstrap: 0-0
Best Rating: 106 4/99 Hrfd 2m1f   gd-fm Hdl

Modest hunter chaser; consistent sort; best form at around two and a half miles; likes fast ground.

Route Sixty Six (IRE)
98(106h)   (110h)85

7-y-o b m Brief Truce (USA)-Lyphards Goddess (IRE) (Lyphard s Special (USA))
Jedd O Keeffe Wetherby Racing Bureau 47

Placings:0F12/322PP-U10PP (3868)
2002/03: 17ᵁG, 16¹S, 16⁹G, 16⁶G, 16⁶GS,

	Starts	1st	2nd	3rd	Win & Pl
Hurdles	1	0	0	0	0
Chases	4	1	0	0	5872
Career Total	14	2	3	1	15726
85	11/02	Ayr	2m	D Ch	SFT	£5872
90	1/01	Muss	2m	E Hdl	GD	£2362

Total win prize-money £8235

Going: Sf: 1-1 GS: 0-1 Gd: 0-3 GF: - Fm: 0-0
Distance: 2m/2m3: 1-5 2m4-2m7: 0-0 3m+: 0-0
Track: LH: 1-4 RH: 0-1 Tight: 0-3 Gall: 0-1
Aids: Bl: 0-0 Vi: 0-0 Tstrap: 0-0
Best Rating: 110 12/01 Kemp 2m   good Hdl

Plating-class hurdler/chaser; suited by good ground, two miles, a sharp track and being held up.

Roveretto
102(109h)   (135h)127

8-y-o b g Robellino (USA)-Spring Flyer (IRE) (Waajib)
Mrs M Reveley Codan Trust Company Limited

Placings:222/5112/F013/40-56261134 (3748)
2002/03: 23⁵GS, 25⁶GS, 22⁵S, 24⁸G, 16¹G, 16¹G, 20³GS, 20⁴G,

	Starts	1st	2nd	3rd	Win & Pl
Hurdles	4	0	1	0	4684
Chases	4	2	0	1	12867
Career Total	21	5	5	2	35087
102	1/03	Muss	2m	E Ch	GD	£4647
123	1/03	Muss	2m	D Ch	GD	£5369
142	12/00	Muss	3m	D(0-125)HHdl	GD	£5050
124	1/00	Catt	2m3f	E Hdl	GD	£2362
122	12/99	Muss	2m4f	E Hdl	G-S	£2905

Total win prize-money £20336

Going: Sf: 0-1 GS: 0-2 Gd: 2-5 GF: - Fm: 0-0
Distance: 2m/2m3: 2-2 2m4-2m7: 0-3 3m+: 0-3
Track: LH: 0-4 RH: 2-4 Tight: 2-2 Gall: 0-2

Aids: Bl: 0-0 Vi: 0-0 Tstrap: 0-0
Best Rating: 142 12/00 Muss 3m   good Hdl

Useful novice chaser in 2002/3; winner at Musselburgh on his first two runs before finishing third in better company; best on good ground around a sharp track; effective at two miles; probably stays three.

Rovestar
84   55

12-y-o b g Le Solaret (FR)-Gilberts Choice (My Swanee)
C L Popham The Rovestar Partnership

Placings:04/453000/61003/360R451412/4231310052/2332
05315336/11422P0FPU/0310413415-0P0600 (4528)
2002/03: 16⁰S, 27⁰GS, 24⁰S, 19⁶S, 24⁰S, 24⁰G,

	Starts	1st	2nd	3rd	Win & Pl
Chases	6	0	0	0	
Career Total	71	11	7	12	57532
109	4/02	Tntn	3m	D(0-120)HCh	GD	£7020
105	1/02	Tntn	3m	E(0-110)HCh	SFT	£3640
100	11/01	Chep	2m110y	E(0-115)HCh	G-S	£3307
109	5/00	Towc	2m110y	D(0-125)HCh	SFT	£3848
109	5/00	Towc	2m110y	E(0-115)HCh	SFT	£3198
109	2/00	Towc	2m110y	D(0-120)HCh	SFT	£3861
113	2/99	Towc	2m110y	D(0-120)HCh	SFT	£3658
108	11/98	Wwck	2m	D(0-125)HCh	SFT	£3415
112	4/98	Winc	2m	E(0-115)HCh	G-S	£3550
112	3/98	NAbb	2m110y	F(0-100)HCh	SFT	£2448
94	11/96	Wwck	2m	E(0-100)HHdl	GD	£2692

Total win prize-money £40640

Going: Sf: 0-4 GS: 0-1 Gd: 0-1 GF: - Fm: 0-0
Distance: 2m/2m3: 0-2 2m4-2m7: 0-0 3m+: 0-4
Track: LH: 0-2 RH: 0-4 Tight: 0-4 Gall: 0-0
Aids: Bl: 0-4 Vi: 0-0 Tstrap: 0-0
Best Rating: 113 2/99 Towc 2m110y soft Ch

Fair handicap chaser, goes really well at Towcester and excels in soft ground. Stays three miles, is effective over shorter.

Roxby Explorer
96(95c)   (85c)90

7-y-o b g Aragon-Super Blues (Welsh Captain)
O Sherwood F B O T Racing

Placings:/33F-4FFP0P25P (4683)
2002/03: 16⁴GF, 20⁰FG, 21⁴S, 20⁵PS, 16⁰HY, 16⁸S, 17²G, 21⁵G, 21⁸GF,

	Starts	1st	2nd	3rd	Win & Pl
Hurdles	6	0	1	0	1069
Chases	3	0	0	0	287
Career Total	13	1	1	2	3784
100	10/01	Sedg	2m1f	H NHF	G-S	£1620

Total win prize-money £1621

Going: Sf: 0-4 GS: 0-0 Gd: 0-3 GF: - Fm: 0-2
Distance: 2m/2m3: 0-4 2m4-2m7: 0-5 3m+: 0-0
Track: LH: 0-1 RH: 0-7 Tight: 0-5 Gall: 0-2
Aids: Bl: 0-5 Vi: 0-0 Tstrap: 0-0
Best Rating: 100 10/01 Sedg 2m1f gd-sft NHF

Moderate hurdler; acts on good and soft ground; effective at around two miles; wears blinkers.

Royal Allegiance
82(83h)   (35h)51

8-y-o ch g Kris-Wilayif (USA) (Danzig (USA))
P Wegmann R Koniger

Placings:P00003006/4013005000/00P0-P53 (4638)
2002/03: 16⁵S, 17⁵GF, 17³G,

	Starts	1st	2nd	3rd	Win & Pl
Hurdles	1	0	0	0	0
Chases	2	0	0	1	1239
Career Total	26	1	0	3	5041

85 10/00 Strf 2m110y F(0-100)HHdl G-S £2828
Total win prize-money £2828

Going:	Sf: 0-1 GS: 0-0 Gd: 0-1 GF: - Fm: 0-1
Distance:	2m/2m3: 0-3 2m4-2m7: 0-0 3m+: 0-1
Track:	LH: 0-3 RH: 0-0 Tight: 0-2 Gall: 0-0
Aids:	Bl: 0-1 Vi: 0-0 Tstrap: 0-0
Best Rating:	85 10/00 Strf 2m110y gd-sft Hdl

Royal Alphabet (IRE)

115f   126f

5-y-o b g King s Theatre (IRE)-A-To-Z (IRE) (Ahonoora)
W P Mullins Dr Tim Mahony

Placings: 101   (4658a)
2002/03: 16¹GY, 16⁶G, 16¹GF,

	Starts	1st	2nd	3rd	Win & Pl
NH Flat	3	2	0	0	13991
Career Total	3	2	0	0	13991

114 4/03 Fair 2m NHF G-F £8064
107 8/02 Gway 2m NHF G-Y £5926
Total win prize-money £13991

Going:	Sf: 0-0 GS: 0-0 Gd: 0-1 GF: - Fm: 1-1
Distance:	2m/2m3: 2-3 2m4-2m7: 0-0 3m+: 0-0
Track:	LH: 0-1 RH: 1-1 Tight: 0-1 Gall: 0-0
Aids:	Bl: 0-0 Vi: 0-0 Tstrap: 0-0
Best Rating:	126 3/03 Chel 2m110y good NHF

Royal Arrow (USA)

98   79

7-y-o b g Dayjur (USA)-Buy The Firm (USA) (Affirmed (USA))
Ferdy Murphy Oak Wood Racing

Placings: 4FF6/5553500-240   (1384)
2002/03: 16²G, 17⁴HY, 16⁹GF,

	Starts	1st	2nd	3rd	Win & Pl
Hurdles	3	0	1	0	563
Career Total	14	0	1	1	792

Going:	Sf: 0-0 GS: 0-0 Gd: 0-1 GF: - Fm: 0-1
Distance:	2m/2m3: 0-3 2m4-2m7: 0-0 3m+: 0-0
Track:	LH: 0-3 RH: 0-0 Tight: 0-2 Gall: 0-0
Aids:	Bl: 0-0 Vi: 0-0 Tstrap: 0-0
Best Rating:	79 5/02 Fknm 2m good Hdl

Moderate hurdler. Has yet to win in this country.

Royal Artist

86   67

7-y-o b g Royal Academy (USA)-Council Rock (General Assembly (USA))
M Brittain Holgate Racing Club

Placings: 6   (1375)
2002/03: 17⁶GF,

	Starts	1st	2nd	3rd	Win & Pl
Hurdles	1	0	0	0	0
Career Total	1	0	0	0	0

Going:	Sf: 0-0 GS: 0-0 Gd: 0-0 GF: - Fm: 0-1
Distance:	2m/2m3: 0-1 2m4-2m7: 0-0 3m+: 0-0
Track:	LH: 0-1 RH: 0-0 Tight: 0-1 Gall: 0-0

Aids:	Bl: 0-0 Vi: 0-0 Tstrap: 0-0
Best Rating:	67 10/02 Sedg 2m1f gd-fm Hdl

Fair handicapper best at seven furlongs on the Flat but on the downgrade now and well beaten on hurdling bow.

Royal Auclair (FR)

110   (96h) 155

6-y-o ch g Garde Royale-Carmonera (FR) (Carmont (FR))
M C Pipe Clive D Smith

Placings: 531115/F111-440   (4100)
2002/03: 21⁴GS, 24⁴G, 24⁹G,

	Starts	1st	2nd	3rd	Win & Pl
Chases	3	0	0	0	5045
Career Total	13	6	0	1	98200

152 3/02 Chel 2m5f A Ch GD £42000
139 1/02 Chel 2m5f B HCh HVY £12720
119 12/01 Extr 2m1f110yC Ch G-S £8515
143 2/01 Sand 2m110y D Hdl HVY £4270
12/00 Engh 2m1f110y Hdl HVY £10567
11/00 Engh 2m1f110y Hdl HVY £9606
Total win prize-money £87680

Going:	Sf: 0-0 GS: 0-1 Gd: 0-2 GF: - Fm: 0-0
Distance:	2m/2m3: 0-0 2m4-2m7: 0-1 3m+: 0-2
Track:	LH: 0-2 RH: 0-1 Tight: 0-0 Gall: 0-2
Aids:	Bl: 0-0 Vi: 0-0 Tstrap: 0-0
Best Rating:	155 2/03 Newb 3m good Ch

Smart chaser; a leading novice in 2001/2, making all in the Cathcart at the Festival; a little disappointing in 2003; stays three miles; acts on good and soft ground.

Royal Barge

112 (102h)   (101h) 109

13-y-o b g Nearly A Hand-April Airs (Grey Mirage)
P Bowen Mrs Miriam Sullivan

Placings: 3263/2311113321P/U20/P-4143   (1936)
2002/03: 20⁴GF, 25¹GF, 24⁴G, 24³GS,

	Starts	1st	2nd	3rd	Win & Pl
Hurdles	2	0	0	0	291
Chases	2	1	0	1	5000
Career Total	23	6	4	6	29824

109 8/02 MRas 3m1f E(0-110)HCh G-F £4439
120 12/98 Extr 3m2f D(0-125)HCh SFT £5034
109 7/98 Sedg 3m3f D Ch GD £3533
114 7/98 Worc 2m7f110yF(0-105)HCh GD £2798
117 6/98 Sthl 3m110y E(0-110)HHdl GD £2305
93 5/98 Ctml 2m6f D Hdl G-F £2992
Total win prize-money £21106

Going:	Sf: 0-0 GS: 0-2 Gd: 0-0 GF: - Fm: 1-2
Distance:	2m/2m3: 0-0 2m4-2m7: 0-1 3m+: 1-3
Track:	LH: 0-1 RH: 1-3 Tight: 1-3 Gall: 0-0
Aids:	Bl: 0-0 Vi: 0-0 Tstrap: 0-0
Best Rating:	120 12/98 Extr 3m2f soft Ch

Fair handicap chaser. Stays well and likes to force the pace. Best on right-handed courses. Acts on a sound surface but has scored once in the soft.

Royal Beluga (USA)

111 (107h)   120

6-y-o b g Rahy (USA)-Navratilovna (USA) (Nureyev (USA))
T R George M R C Opperman

Placings: 24/5236-320011532152   (4614)
2002/03: 16³GF, 17²GF, 17⁰GF, 16⁰GS, 17¹HY, 20¹GS, 20⁵S, 20³GS, 20²S, 18¹G, 20⁵G, 21²G,

	Starts	1st	2nd	3rd	Win & Pl
Hurdles	4	0	1	1	1125

Going:	Sf: 0-0 GS: 0-0 Gd: 0-1 GF: - Fm: 0-1

Chases	8	3	2	1	24516
Career Total	18	3	5	3	27884

117 3/03 Newb 2m2f110yD(0-110)HCh GD £5720
106 1/03 Ludl 2m4f E(0-105)HCh G-S £5291
99 11/02 Bang 2m1f110yE(0-105)HCh HVY £4231
Total win prize-money £15243

Going:	Sf: 1-3 GS: 1-3 Gd: 1-3 GF: - Fm: 0-3
Distance:	2m/2m3: 2-6 2m4-2m7: 1-6 3m+: 0-0
Track:	LH: 2-6 RH: 1-6 Tight: 2-5 Gall: 1-4
Aids:	Bl: 0-0 Vi: 0-1 Tstrap: 0-0
Best Rating:	120 4/03 Chel 2m5f good Ch

Fair handicap chaser; consistent with three wins 2002/3; possibly best on soft ground; stays two and a half miles; has worn a visor.

Royal Buckingham (IRE)

66

8-y-o b g Erdelistan (FR)-French Class (The Parson)
J A Moore J A Moore

Placings: 10/00/P0P-PUP   (0778)
2002/03: 16⁵G, 16⁴G, 18⁰GF,

	Starts	1st	2nd	3rd	Win & Pl
Hurdles	3	0	0	0	
Career Total	10	1	0	0	1806

107 1/00 Ludl 2m H NHF GD £1806
Total win prize-money £1806

Going:	Sf: 0-0 GS: 0-0 Gd: 0-2 GF: - Fm: 0-1
Distance:	2m/2m3: 0-3 2m4-2m7: 0-0 3m+: 0-0
Track:	LH: 0-3 RH: 0-0 Tight: 0-1 Gall: 0-0
Aids:	Bl: 0-0 Vi: 0-0 Tstrap: 0-0
Best Rating:	107 1/00 Ludl 2m good NHF

Royal Cascade (IRE)

9-y-o b g River Falls-Relative Stranger (Cragador)
B A McMahon Mrs J McMahon

Placings: P   (3268)
2002/03: 16⁰GS,

	Starts	1st	2nd	3rd	Win & Pl
Hurdles	1	0	0	0	
Career Total	1	0	0	0	

Going:	Sf: 0-0 GS: 0-1 Gd: 0-0 GF: - Fm: 0-0
Distance:	2m/2m3: 0-1 2m4-2m7: 0-0 3m+: 0-0
Track:	LH: 0-1 RH: 0-0 Tight: 0-0 Gall: 0-1
Aids:	Bl: 0-0 Vi: 0-0 Tstrap: 0-0
Best Rating:	0 1/03 Donc 2m110y gd-sft Hdl

Royal Casino (IRE)

95f   77f

6-y-o b g Kasmayo-Gambling Princess Vii (Damsire Unregistered)
O Brennan O Brennan

Placings: 60   (4594)
2002/03: 16⁶GF, 16⁰G,

	Starts	1st	2nd	3rd	Win & Pl
NH Flat	2	0	0	0	0
Career Total	2	0	0	0	0

Going:	Sf: 0-0 GS: 0-0 Gd: 0-0 GF: 0-1 Fm: 0-1

Distance: 2m/2m3: 0-2 2m4-2m7: 0-0 3m+: 0-0
Track: LH: 0-2 RH: 0-0 Tight: 0-0 Gall: 0-0
Aids: Bl: 0-0 Vi: 0-0 Tstrap: 0-0
Best Rating: 77 3/03 Weth 2m gd-fm NHF

Royal Castle (IRE)

105(110h)   (126 h)**110+**

9-y-o b g Caerleon (USA)-Sun Princess (English Prince)
Mrs K Walton (M H Tompkins 8/7) Stan Clough and
Dudley Bendall

Placings:223/11500/1/P-010P   (4563)
2002/03: 24⁹GF, 21¹G, 20⁹G, 24⁸GF,

	Starts	1st	2nd	3rd	Win & Pl
Hurdles	4	1	0	0	4030
Career Total	14	4	2	1	15803
117	10/02	Sedg	2m5f110yD(0-125)HHdl	GD	£4030
126	7/00	Strf	2m6f110yE(0-115)HHdl	G-F	£3542
114	12/99	Donc	2m4f	E Hdl	G-F	£3113
109	11/99	Towc	2m5f	E Hdl	GD	£2775

Total win prize-money £13461

Going: Sf: 0-0 GS: 0-0 Gd: 1-2 GF: - Fm: 0-2
Distance: 2m/2m3: 0-0 2m4-2m7: 1-2 3m+: 0-0
Track: LH: 1-3 RH: 0-1 Tight: 1-4 Gall: 0-0
Aids: Bl: 0-0 Vi: 0-0 Tstrap: 0-0
Best Rating: 137 3/00 Chel 2m5f good Hdl

Fair hurdler at around two and a half miles; won three runner 2m 5f novice chase in soft ground at Sedgefield May
2003 and followed up at Cartmel; acts on a sound surface.

Royal Ceti (FR)

6-y-o b/br g Garde Royale-Mira Ceti (FR) (Carvin)
M C Pipe (E Lellouche 28/9) B Boutboul

Placings:1FF   (3141)
2002/03: 18¹VS, 18⁵FVS, 17⁵S,

	Starts	1st	2nd	3rd	Win & Pl
Hurdles	3	1	0	0	15313
Career Total	3	1	0	0	15313
9/02	Autl	2m2f	Hdl	VS £15313	

Total win prize-money £15313

Going: Sf: 0-1 GS: 0-0 Gd: 0-0 GF: - Fm: 0-0
Distance: 2m/2m3: 1-3 2m4-2m7: 0-0 3m+: 0-0
Track: LH: 0-0 RH: 0-1 Tight: 0-1 Gall: 0-0
Aids: Bl: 0-0 Vi: 0-0 Tstrap: 0-0
Best Rating: 0 1/03 Tntn 2m1f soft Hdl

Royal Charlie

75f   **69f**

6-y-o br g Royal Fountain-Cool View (Kinglet)
L Lungo D G Pryde

Placings:0   (3174)
2002/03: 16⁹GS,

	Starts	1st	2nd	3rd	Win & Pl
NH Flat	1	0	0	0	
Career Total	1	0	0	0	

Going: Sf: 0-0 GS: 0-1 Gd: 0-0 GF: - Fm: 0-0
Distance: 2m/2m3: 0-1 2m4-2m7: 0-0 3m+: 0-0
Track: LH: 0-1 RH: 0-0 Tight: 0-0 Gall: 0-0
Aids: Bl: 0-0 Vi: 0-0 Tstrap: 0-0
Best Rating: 69 1/03 Hayd 2m gd-sft NHF

Royal China (IRE)

95   **84**

5-y-o b g Aristocracy-Luan Causca (Pampapaul)
Miss H C Knight David Zeffman

Placings:0405   (4595)
2002/03: 17⁹G, 17⁴G, 21⁹GS, 22⁵GF,

	Starts	1st	2nd	3rd	Win & Pl
NH Flat	1	0	0	0	0
Hurdles	3	0	0	0	333
Career Total	4	0	0	0	333

Going: Sf: 0-0 GS: 0-1 Gd: 0-2 GF: - Fm: 0-1
Distance: 2m/2m3: 0-2 2m4-2m7: 0-2 3m+: 0-0
Track: LH: 0-0 RH: 0-4 Tight: 0-0 Gall: 0-0
Aids: Bl: 0-0 Vi: 0-0 Tstrap: 0-0
Best Rating: 84 4/03 Extr 2m6f110y gd-fm Hdl

Royal County Buck (IRE)

99   (101h)**111**

8-y-o b g Good Thyne (USA)-Little Quince (Laurence O)
A J Martin Dunsany Racing Syndicate

Placings:0000/41233-6005046   (3137)
2002/03: 17⁶YS, 20⁹HY, 17⁹S, 18⁵S, 16⁰YS, 20⁴HY, 24⁶S,

	Starts	1st	2nd	3rd	Win & Pl
Chases	7	0	0	0	393
Career Total	16	1	1	2	6280
103	6/01	Dpat	2m4f110y		NHF FRM
£3338					

Total win prize-money £3339

Going: Sf: 0-5 GS: 0-0 Gd: 0-0 GF: - Fm: 0-0
Distance: 2m/2m3: 0-4 2m4-2m7: 0-2 3m+: 0-1
Track: LH: 0-1 RH: 0-3 Tight: 0-1 Gall: 0-0
Aids: Bl: 0-0 Vi: 0-0 Tstrap: 0-2
Best Rating: 103 6/01 Dpat 2m4f110y firm NHF

Royal Crimson

12-y-o b g Danehill (USA)-Fine Honey (USA) (Drone (USA))
Mrs F E Needham Major R R Alers-Hankey

Placings:0/3501/52P/5FP114/040/130P14/P320/3P (4777)
2002/03: 24³S, 31⁸PG,

	Starts	1st	2nd	3rd	Win & Pl
Chases	2	0	0	1	627
Career Total	29	5	2	4	20164
107	2/00	Muss	2m4f	E(0-115)HCh	GD	£4550
101	10/99	Hexm	2m10y	F(0-100)HCh	GD	£2862
100	3/98	Hexm	2m110y	E Ch	GD	£3284
107	3/98	Catt	2m3f	E Ch	G-S	£2979
106	2/96	Muss	2m	E Hdl	G-F	£2154

Total win prize-money £15831

Going: Sf: 0-1 GS: 0-0 Gd: 0-1 GF: - Fm: 0-0
Distance: 2m/2m3: 0-0 2m4-2m7: 0-0 3m+: 0-0
Track: LH: 0-0 RH: 0-1 Tight: 0-0 Gall: 0-0
Aids: Bl: 0-0 Vi: 0-0 Tstrap: 0-0
Best Rating: 107 2/00 Muss 2m4f good Ch

On the downgrade and well beaten on return in hunter
chase company.

Royal Emperor (IRE)

116   **156**

7-y-o gr g Roselier (FR)-Boreen Bro (Boreen (FR))

Mrs S J Smith Widdop Wanderers

Placings:30/03P/6F243-1121122   (4473)
2002/03: 24¹S, 24¹GS, 24²GS, 23¹HY, 23¹GS, 25²G, 24²G,

	Starts	1st	2nd	3rd	Win & Pl
Hurdles	7	4	3	0	58365
Career Total	17	4	4	3	61241
147	2/03	Hayd	2m7f110yB HHdl	G-S	£12651
143	12/02	Weth	2m7f	C(0-130)HHdl	HVY	£6812
125	11/02	Carl	3m110y	E Hdl	G-S	£3591
115	10/02	Carl	3m110y	E Hdl	SFT	£3262

Total win prize-money £26317

Going: Sf: 2-2 GS: 2-3 Gd: 0-2 GF: - Fm: 0-0
Distance: 2m/2m3: 0-0 2m4-2m7: 1-1 3m+: 3-6
Track: LH: 2-5 RH: 2-2 Tight: 0-1 Gall: 0-2
Aids: Bl: 0-0 Vi: 0-0 Tstrap: 0-0
Best Rating: 156 4/03 Aint 3m110y good Hdl

Smart staying novice hurdler, progressing really well; narrow runner-up in Pertemps Handicap Final at Cheltenham in
2003; beaten by top-class novice when runner-up in Grade
One at Aintree; suited by soft ground; stays three miles;
tough and genuine.

Royal Enclosure (IRE)

74   **51**

5-y-o b g Royal Academy (USA)-Hi Bettina (Henbit (USA))
Mrs S M Johnson Geoff Jay

Placings:500-0   (4283)
2002/03: 16⁹GF,

	Starts	1st	2nd	3rd	Win & Pl
Hurdles	1	0	0	0	0
Career Total	4	0	0	0	0

Going: Sf: 0-0 GS: 0-0 Gd: 0-0 GF: - Fm: 0-1
Distance: 2m/2m3: 0-1 2m4-2m7: 0-0 3m+: 0-0
Track: LH: 0-0 RH: 0-1 Tight: 0-0 Gall: 0-0
Aids: Bl: 0-0 Vi: 0-0 Tstrap: 0-1
Best Rating: 65 10/01 Ludl 2m gd-fm Hdl

Royal Entrance (IRE)

10-y-o b g Don t Forget Me-Royal Miami (Miami Springs)
M Rodda P Senter

Placings:P/00/P   (4526)
2002/03: 24⁸PG,

	Starts	1st	2nd	3rd	Win & Pl
Chases	1	0	0	0	
Career Total	4	0	0	0	

Going: Sf: 0-0 GS: 0-0 Gd: 0-1 GF: - Fm: 0-0
Distance: 2m/2m3: 0-0 2m4-2m7: 0-0 3m+: 0-1
Track: LH: 0-1 RH: 0-0 Tight: 0-0 Gall: 0-0
Aids: Bl: 0-0 Vi: 0-0 Tstrap: 0-0
Best Rating: 56 5/99 Tipp 2m4f gd-fm Ch

Royal Event

102   **105**

12-y-o ch g Rakaposhi King-Upham Reunion (Paridel)
D R Gandolfo A E Frost

Placings:013/223120/4212/21PP/P2/3140550/P33P216-P4
                                        (0346)

2002/03: 20PG, 214GS,

	Starts	1st	2nd	3rd	Win & Pl
Chases	2	0	0	0	314
Career Total	35	6	8	5	37995
105 3/02 Winc 2m5f	E(0-110)HCh		SFT		£4251
109 11/00 Winc 2m5f	E(0-115)HCh		G-S		£5304
121 10/98 Strf 2m5f110yC(0-135)HCh		GD		£5215
121 12/97 Sthl 2m	E Ch		GD		£3288
104 1/97 Wind 2m	D(0-120)HHdl		G-F		£2945
112 2/96 Nott 2m	H NHF		G-S		£1229
		Total win prize-money £22233

Going:	Sf: 0-0 GS: 0-1 Gd: 0-1 GF: - Fm: 0-0
Distance:	2m2m3: 0-0 2m4-2m7: 0-2 3m+: 0-0
Track:	LH: 0-2 RH: 0-0 Tight: 0-1 Gall: 0-0
Aids:	Bl: 0-0 Vi: 0-0 Tstrap: 0-0
Best Rating:	121 10/98 Strf 2m5f110y good Ch

Modest handicapper; successful at Wincanton in March 2002; best at around two and a half miles; sound surface is essential.

Royal Feelings

101(97h)   (70h)84

9-y-o b g Feelings (FR)-Wedderburn (Royalty)
Mrs D Thomson The Good To Soft Firm

Placings:0600/5404/00-4224F   (0915)
2002/03: 244GF, 242GS, 252GF, 204G, 20PGS,

	Starts	1st	2nd	3rd	Win & Pl
Chases	5	0	2	0	3159
Career Total	15	0	2	0	3398

Going:	Sf: 0-0 GS: 0-2 Gd: 0-1 GF: - Fm: 0-2
Distance:	2m2m3: 0-0 2m4-2m7: 0-2 3m+: 0-3
Track:	LH: 0-1 RH: 0-4 Tight: 0-1 Gall: 0-0
Aids:	Bl: 0-0 Vi: 0-0 Tstrap: 0-0
Best Rating:	85 10/99 Kels 2m110y good Hdl

Maiden hurdler/ chaser.

Royal Gillie

71f

6-y-o br m Royal Fountain-Gilmansleuch (IRE) (Mandalus)
Mrs J K M Oliver Miss J S Peat

Placings:0   (4593)
2002/03: 16DG,

	Starts	1st	2nd	3rd	Win & Pl
NH Flat	1	0	0	0	
Career Total	1	0	0	0	

Going:	Sf: 0-0 GS: 0-0 Gd: 0-1 GF: - Fm: 0-0
Distance:	2m2m3: 0-1 2m4-2m7: 0-0 3m+: 0-0
Track:	LH: 0-1 RH: 0-0 Tight: 0-0 Gall: 0-0
Aids:	Bl: 0-0 Vi: 0-0 Tstrap: 0-0
Best Rating:	71 4/03 Hexm 2m110y good NHF

Royal Hand

13-y-o b g Nearly A Hand-Royal Rushes (Royal Palace)
C N Kellett Mrs Helen Herrick

Placings:00PP05/0U2FF0PF544/3FF435352/PP36F1P3P0
0/PPP/P   (0563)
2002/03: 20PGF,

	Starts	1st	2nd	3rd	Win & Pl
Chases	1	0	0	0	
Career Total	41	1	2	5	5102
73 12/99 Leic 2m4f110yG(0-90)HHdl		GD		£1814
		Total win prize-money £1814

Going:	Sf: 0-0 GS: 0-0 Gd: 0-0 GF: - Fm: 0-1
Distance:	2m2m3: 0-0 2m4-2m7: 0-1 3m+: 0-0
Track:	LH: 0-0 RH: 0-0 Tight: 0-1 Gall: 0-0
Aids:	Bl: 0-0 Vi: 0-0 Tstrap: 0-0
Best Rating:	82 12/95 Towc 2m soft NHF

Royal Hector (GER)

100   100

4-y-o b g Hector Protector (USA)-Rudolfina (CAN) (Pleasant Colony (USA))
A G Hobbs (C Von Der Recke 24/11) Three Counties Racing 2

Placings:25500   (4152)
2002/03: 162GS, 165G, 165GS, 169G, 169G,

	Starts	1st	2nd	3rd	Win & Pl
Hurdles	5	0	1	0	1392
Career Total	5	0	1	0	1392

Going:	Sf: 0-0 GS: 0-2 Gd: 0-3 GF: - Fm: 0-0
Distance:	2m2m3: 0-5 2m4-2m7: 0-0 3m+: 0-0
Track:	LH: 0-3 RH: 0-2 Tight: 0-1 Gall: 0-2
Aids:	Bl: 0-0 Vi: 0-0 Tstrap: 0-0
Best Rating:	98 3/03 Hntg 2m110y good Hdl

Jumps debut in Britain saw him finish second at Fakenham. Effective at two miles.

Royal Jake (IRE)

111   135

9-y-o b g Jolly Jake (NZ)-Wee Mite (Menelek)
Noel Meade Gerard Callaghan

Placings:3601/203F200/212105-106132000   (4472)
2002/03: 201YS, 220Y, 228HY, 171GF, 173SH, 162SH, 240S, 169G, 210G,

	Starts	1st	2nd	3rd	Win & Pl
Chases	9	2	1	1	19387
Career Total	26	5	5	3	48419
111 9/02 Cork 2m1f	Ch		G-F		£7975
125 5/02 Klny 2m4f	Ch		Y-S		£7975
122 3/02 Punc 2m	HCh		SFT		£11165
98 12/01 Fair 2m2f	Ch		YLD		£6677
85 4/00 DRoy 2m	Hdl		G-F		£2760
		Total win prize-money £36553

Going:	Sf: 0-2 GS: 0-0 Gd: 0-2 GF: - Fm: 1-1
Distance:	2m2m3: 1-4 2m4-2m7: 1-4 3m+: 0-1
Track:	LH: 1-4 RH: 0-4 Tight: 0-1 Gall: 0-1
Aids:	Bl: 1-4 Vi: 0-0 Tstrap: 0-0
Best Rating:	135 12/02 Punc 2m sft-hvy Ch

Decent Irish handicap chaser; effective at up to two and a half miles; acts on soft and fast ground; has worn blinkers.

Royal Meg

1f

5-y-o b/br m Emperor Jones (USA)-Queen s Eyot (Grundy)
Mrs M Reveley W G McHarg

Placings:00   (2391)
2002/03: 169GS, 14DGS,

	Starts	1st	2nd	3rd	Win & Pl
NH Flat	2	0	0	0	
Career Total	2	0	0	0	

Going:	Sf: 0-0 GS: 0-2 Gd: 0-0 GF: - Fm: 0-0
Distance:	2m2m3: 0-1 2m4-2m7: 0-0 3m+: 0-0
Track:	LH: 0-2 RH: 0-0 Tight: 0-0 Gall: 0-0
Aids:	Bl: 0-0 Vi: 0-0 Tstrap: 0-0

Best Rating:	0 12/02 Ayr 1m6f gd-sft NHF

Royal Mystery

83

4-y-o ch f King s Signet (USA)-Miss Caradon (IRE) (Prince Rupert (FR))
H S Howe Kevin Daniel Crabb

Placings:0P   (2195)
2002/03: 16DS, 17PGS,

	Starts	1st	2nd	3rd	Win & Pl
Hurdles	2	0	0	0	
Career Total	2	0	0	0	

Going:	Sf: 0-1 GS: 0-1 Gd: 0-0 GF: - Fm: 0-0
Distance:	2m2m3: 0-2 2m4-2m7: 0-0 3m+: 0-0
Track:	LH: 0-0 RH: 0-2 Tight: 0-1 Gall: 0-0
Aids:	Bl: 0-0 Vi: 0-0 Tstrap: 0-0
Best Rating:	0 11/02 Tntn 2m1f gd-sft Hdl

Royal Partnership (IRE)

(98h)   (83h)

7-y-o b g Royal Academy (USA)-Go Honey Go (General Assembly (USA))
D L Williams Reliance Car Hire Services Ltd

Placings:000P0/5P30-PPP0   (1128)
2002/03: 24PGF, 20PG, 16PGF, 17DGF,

	Starts	1st	2nd	3rd	Win & Pl
Hurdles	1	0	0	0	0
Chases	3	0	0	0	0
Career Total	13	0	0	1	458

Going:	Sf: 0-0 GS: 0-0 Gd: 0-1 GF: - Fm: 0-3
Distance:	2m2m3: 0-2 2m4-2m7: 0-1 3m+: 0-1
Track:	LH: 0-1 RH: 0-3 Tight: 0-3 Gall: 0-1
Aids:	Bl: 0-1 Vi: 0-0 Tstrap: 0-1
Best Rating:	89 1/01 Tntn 2m1f heavy Hdl

Royal Plum

98

7-y-o ch g Inchinor-Miss Plum (Ardross)
Mrs M Reveley Lucayan Stud

Placings:6/210/0501245-0   (1611)
2002/03: 23DG,

	Starts	1st	2nd	3rd	Win & Pl
Hurdles	1	0	0	0	
Career Total	12	2	2	0	6357
98 1/02 Muss 3m	E(0-105)HHdl		GD		£3514
111 7/00 Worc 2m	H NHF		GD		£1456
		Total win prize-money £4970

Going:	Sf: 0-0 GS: 0-0 Gd: 0-1 GF: - Fm: 0-0
Distance:	2m2m3: 0-0 2m4-2m7: 0-0 3m+: 0-1
Track:	LH: 0-1 RH: 0-0 Tight: 0-0 Gall: 0-0
Aids:	Bl: 0-0 Vi: 0-0 Tstrap: 0-0
Best Rating:	111 7/00 Worc 2m good NHF

Moderate hurdler; stays three miles; acts on good ground.

Royal Predica (FR)

110   149

9-y-o ch g Tip Moss (FR)-Girl Vamp (FR) (Kaldoun (FR))
M C Pipe P A Deal, J S Dale & A Stennett

Placings:1/344F2131P/4211FF/2PPP/2122P500-10P

(4791)

2002/03: 24¹G, 36⁶G, 29⁵G,

	Starts	1st	2nd	3rd	Win & PI
Chases	3	1	0	0	29000
Career Total	31	7	6	2	113516
149	3/03	Chel	3m110y	B(0-140)HCh	GD	£29000
142	6/01	NAbb	2m5f110yD(0-125)HCh	GD	£4085
147	2/00	Wwck	2m4f	B(0-140)HCh	SFT	£8784
129	1/00	Wwck	2m4f	C(0-135)HCh	SFT	£7117
136	4/99	Aint	2m4f	C HCh	G-S	£11235
98	1/99	Plum	2m	E Ch	HVY	£2915
	7/97	Diep	1m7f	Hdl	FRM	£3591
					Total win prize-money £66728

Going: Sf: 0-0 GS: 0-0 Gd: 1-3 GF: - Fm: 0-0
Distance: 2m/2m3: 0-0 2m4-2m7: 0-0 3m+: 1-3
Track: LH: 1-2 RH: 0-1 Tight: 0-1 Gall: 1-1
Aids: Bl: 0-0 Vi: 0-0 Tstrap: 1-3
Best Rating: 149 3/03 Chel 3m110y good Ch

Smart chaser when on song; stays three miles; ran out a surprise winner of the Fulke Walwyn/Kim Muir at the 2003 Cheltenham Festival; failed to stay in the National; suited by good or softer ground; wears a tongue strap.

Royal Pretence

6-y-o b m Royal Fountain-Just Pretend (Sayyaf)
G F Edwards (Miss Lucinda V Russell 15/5) G F Edwards

Placings:00-PP5

(0868)

2002/03: 20⁵GF, 22³GF, 22⁵GF,

	Starts	1st	2nd	3rd	Win & PI
Hurdles	3	0	0	0	0
Career Total	5	0	0	0	0

Going: Sf: 0-0 GS: 0-0 Gd: 0-0 GF: - Fm: 0-3
Distance: 2m/2m3: 0-0 2m4-2m7: 0-3 3m+: 0-0
Track: LH: 0-2 RH: 0-1 Tight: 0-2 Gall: 0-0
Aids: Bl: 0-1 Vi: 0-0 Tstrap: 0-0
Best Rating: 54 4/02 Carl 2m1f good NHF

Royal Racer (FR)

93   88d

5-y-o b g Danehill (USA)-Green Rosy (USA) (Green Dancer (USA))
J R Best Mr & Mrs R Dawbarn

Placings:0P600

(4669)

2002/03: 16⁰HY, 16⁷HY, 16⁶S, 16⁰G, 16⁹G,

	Starts	1st	2nd	3rd	Win & PI
Hurdles	5	0	0	0	0
Career Total	5	0	0	0	0

Going: Sf: 0-3 GS: 0-0 Gd: 0-2 GF: - Fm: 0-0
Distance: 2m/2m3: 0-3 2m4-2m7: 0-0 3m+: 0-0
Track: LH: 0-2 RH: 0-3 Tight: 0-1 Gall: 0-1
Aids: Bl: 0-0 Vi: 0-0 Tstrap: 0-0
Best Rating: 88 12/02 Newb 2m10y heavy Hdl

Royal Rapport

90   84

10-y-o ch g Rich Charlie-Miss Camellia (Sonnen Gold)
T Wall (Mrs J A Wall 6/5) T Wall

Placings:21/5005/P-PPP4

(0513)

2002/03: 24⁶GF, 20⁴S, 21⁴S, 16⁴S,

	Starts	1st	2nd	3rd	Win & PI
Chases	4	0	0	0	265

Career Total   11   1   1   0   3271
86   9/96 Hexm 2m   E Hdl   FRM £2322
                        Total win prize-money £2322

Going: Sf: 0-3 GS: 0-0 Gd: 0-0 GF: - Fm: 0-1
Distance: 2m/2m3: 0-1 2m4-2m7: 0-2 3m+: 0-1
Track: LH: 0-3 RH: 0-1 Tight: 0-2 Gall: 0-0
Aids: Bl: 0-1 Vi: 0-2 Tstrap: 0-0
Best Rating: 86 9/96 Hexm 2m firm Hdl

Royal Reward (IRE)

79   75

9-y-o b g King s Ride-Fatima Rose (The Parson)
M Todhunter Mrs Kate Hall

Placings:20P04/UU0/56040-

(0006)

2002/03: 20⁰G,

	Starts	1st	2nd	3rd	Win & PI
Hurdles	1	0	0	0	
Career Total	13	0	1	0	444

Going: Sf: 0-0 GS: 0-0 Gd: 0-1 GF: - Fm: 0-0
Distance: 2m/2m3: 0-0 2m4-2m7: 0-1 3m+: 0-0
Track: LH: 0-1 RH: 0-0 Tight: 0-0 Gall: 0-1
Aids: Bl: 0-0 Vi: 0-0 Tstrap: 0-0
Best Rating: 106 11/99 Weth 2m good NHF

Royal Rocket (IRE)

91f   75f

6-y-o b m King s Ride-Carol s Cracker (IRE) (Persian Mews)
Miss Venetia Williams Miss L M Rochford

Placings:5

(4404)

2002/03: 16⁵GF,

	Starts	1st	2nd	3rd	Win & PI
NH Flat	1	0	0	0	0
Career Total	1	0	0	0	0

Going: Sf: 0-0 GS: 0-0 Gd: 0-0 GF: - Fm: 0-1
Distance: 2m/2m3: 0-1 2m4-2m7: 0-0 3m+: 0-0
Track: LH: 0-1 RH: 0-0 Tight: 0-0 Gall: 0-0
Aids: Bl: 0-0 Vi: 0-0 Tstrap: 0-0
Best Rating: 75 3/03 Hayd 2m gd-fm NHF

Chasing-bred mare; showed some ability on bumper debut.

Royal Rosa (FR)

113f   123+f

4-y-o ch g Garde Royale-Crystalza (FR) (Crystal Palace (FR))
N J Henderson Million In Mind Partnership (12)

Placings:161

(4053)

2002/03: 12¹G, 16⁶HY, 16¹HY,

	Starts	1st	2nd	3rd	Win & PI
NH Flat	3	2	0	0	5191
Career Total	3	2	0	0	5191
123	3/03	Sand	2m110y	H NHF	HVY	£2383
98	12/02	Newb	1m4f110yH NHF	GD	£2807
					Total win prize-money £5191

Going: Sf: 1-2 GS: 0-0 Gd: 1-1 GF: - Fm: 0-0
Distance: 2m/2m3: 1-2 2m4-2m7: 0-0 3m+: 0-0
Track: LH: 1-1 RH: 1-2 Tight: 0-0 Gall: 0-0
Aids: Bl: 0-0 Vi: 0-0 Tstrap: 0-0
Best Rating: 123 3/03 Sand 2m110y heavy NHF

Useful bumper performer; gained third win from four runs in Punchestown bumper in April 2003; acts on good ground or softer.

Royal Snoopy (IRE)

10-y-o b/br g Royal Fountain-Lovely Snoopy (IRE) (Phardante (FR))
Mrs F E Needham (C J Mann 23/8) Michael D Abrahams

Placings:1303/50F43/034115511/62FU20/21323-36F22

(4520)

2002/03: 24³GF, 20⁶G, 24⁵FGF, 22²GF, 27²G,

	Starts	1st	2nd	3rd	Win & PI
Chases	5	0	2	1	2546
Career Total	34	6	6	7	46531
106	5/01	Hntg	3m	E Ch	G-F	£3523
124	3/00	Sand	2m6f	D(0-120)HHdl	GF	£7345
124	2/00	Winc	2m6f	C(0-135)HHdl	GD	£8502
121	11/99	MRas	3m5f110yF Hdl	G-S	£1975
116	11/99	Sand	2m6f	E(0-105)HHdl	GD	£3403
107	1/98	Fair	2m	NHF	SFT	£2680
					Total win prize-money £27429

Going: Sf: 0-0 GS: 0-0 Gd: 0-2 GF: - Fm: 0-3
Distance: 2m/2m3: 0-0 2m4-2m7: 0-2 3m+: 0-3
Track: LH: 0-3 RH: 0-1 Tight: 0-3 Gall: 0-0
Aids: Bl: 0-5 Vi: 0-0 Tstrap: 0-0
Best Rating: 129 2/01 Ludl 2m4f gd-sft Ch

Modest pointer/hunter chaser; formerly a decent handicap chaser, but not entirely straightforward; possibly best when allowed to dominate; seems to handle any ground, but best on a sound surface; usually wears blinkers.

Royal Tommy (IRE)

91   100

11-y-o b g Royal Fountain-Cherry Token (Prince Hansel)
R H Buckler L G Kimber

Placings:PP2211/P211/P1B034/15P01-P5066P

(3946)

2002/03: 31⁵GS, 24⁵S, 29⁹HY, 33⁶S, 26⁹HY, 30⁰S,

	Starts	1st	2nd	3rd	Win & PI
Chases	6	0	0	0	326
Career Total	27	7	3	1	53839
125	3/02	Chep	3m5f110yD(0-120)HCh	SFT	£4407
125	12/01	Hayd	3m4f110yC(0-135)HCh	SFT	£12792
125	12/00	Chep	3m2f110yC(0-130)HCh	HVY	£10348
125	2/00	Bang	3m6f	D(0-120)HCh	G-S	£5050
125	2/00	Towc	3m1f	C(0-130)HCh	SFT	£6910
106	4/99	Towc	2m6f	E Ch	SFT	£2819
88	4/99	Hrfd	3m1f110yE Ch	GF	£3485
					Total win prize-money £45812

Going: Sf: 0-5 GS: 0-1 Gd: 0-0 GF: - Fm: 0-0
Distance: 2m/2m3: 0-0 2m4-2m7: 0-0 3m+: 0-6
Track: LH: 0-5 RH: 0-1 Tight: 0-0 Gall: 0-1
Aids: Bl: 0-2 Vi: 0-0 Tstrap: 0-0
Best Rating: 125 3/02 Chep 3m5f110y soft Ch

Moderate staying chaser; scored in a decent chase over three and a half miles at Haydock in December 2001, and added to that when dropped in class at Chepstow in March 2002; suited by soft ground; has worn blinkers; inconsistent.

Royal Wanderer (IRE)

100   97

5-y-o ch g Royal Abjar (USA)-Rose n Reason (IRE) (Reasonable (FR))
C R Wilson Bill Martin

Placings:653314406343P

(4669)

2002/03: 16⁶G, 19⁵G, 17³G⁰, 17³G, 17¹G, 17⁴GF, 16⁴GF, 16⁰GS, 19⁶GS, 16³G, 16⁴G, 16³G, 16⁶PG,

	Starts	1st	2nd	3rd	Win & Pl
Hurdles	13	1	0	4	7203
Career Total	13	1	0	4	7203
87 8/02 Ctml	2m1f110yE Hdl			GD	£3920

Total win prize-money £3920

Going: Sf: 0-0 GS: 0-2 Gd: 1-8 GF: - Fm: 0-3
Distance: 2m/2m3: 1-12 2m4-2m7: 0-1 3m+: 0-0
Track: LH: 1-9 RH: 0-4 Tight: 1-11 Gall: 0-0
Aids: Bl: 0-0 Vi: 0-0 Tstrap: 0-0
Best Rating: 100 4/03 Fknm 2m good Hdl

Moderate hurdler; effective on good ground; looks best at around two miles.

Royale Angela (FR)

11-y-o ch g Garde Royale-Santa Angela (FR) (Son Of Silver)
J Neville Gallagher Enterprises Ltd

Placings: 126F3/2111120/020/10015P4/22P03/PP (0359)
2002/03: 24PGS, 24PGS,

	Starts	1st	2nd	3rd	Win & Pl
Hurdles	2	0	0	0	
Career Total	29	7	6	2	35865
128 2/00 Newc 3m	D(0-125)HHdl			SFT	£2879
125 11/99 NAbb 2m6f	D(0-125)HHdl			SFT	£2983
127 2/98 Uttx	2m6f110yC(0-135)HHdl			SFT	£10942
118 1/98 Plum 2m4f				HVY	£2910
105 12/97 Plum 2m4f	F(0-105)HHdl			SFT	£1970
106 12/97 Worc 2m4f	D(0-125)HHdl			SFT	£2756
106 10/95 Bang 2m1f	D Hdl			G-S	£2920

Total win prize-money £27363

Going: Sf: 0-0 GS: 0-2 Gd: 0-0 GF: - Fm: 0-0
Distance: 2m/2m3: 0-0 2m4-2m7: 0-0 3m+: 0-2
Track: LH: 0-1 RH: 0-1 Tight: 0-1 Gall: 0-0
Aids: Bl: 0-0 Vi: 0-0 Tstrap: 0-0
Best Rating: 133 3/00 Chel 3m1f110y good Hdl

Fair staying hurdler, effective in soft ground.

Royale De Vassy (FR)

103　　　　130

9-y-o b m Royal Charter (FR)-Bayalika (FR) (Kashtan (FR))
Miss Venetia Williams Len Jakeman,J Davies,R Downes & J Lewis

Placings: 61/3P33F02/12331230/613U-P660 (4101)
2002/03: 24PG, 24BGS, 24PGS, 24PG,

	Starts	1st	2nd	3rd	Win & Pl
Chases	4	0	0	0	900
Career Total	25	4	3	7	80092
141 12/01 Chel	3m1f110yB HCh			GD	£28496
136 11/00 Chel	3m110y E(0-135)HCh			G-S	£7605
119 5/00 Uttx 3m	B HCh			GD	£10348
5/99 LE L 2m1f	Ch			GD	£3767

Total win prize-money £50216

Going: Sf: 0-0 GS: 0-2 Gd: 0-2 GF: - Fm: 0-0
Distance: 2m/2m3: 0-0 2m4-2m7: 0-0 3m+: 0-4
Track: LH: 0-4 RH: 0-0 Tight: 0-0 Gall: 0-1
Aids: Bl: 0-0 Vi: 0-0 Tstrap: 0-0
Best Rating: 141 12/01 Chel 3m1f110y good Ch

Useful handicap chaser; sound jumper; stays beyond three miles but has enough pace to be effective over shorter distances; acts on good and good to soft ground.

Royaloutlook

6-y-o br g Royal Fountain-Broad Outlook (Broadsword (USA))
G A Harker Malcolm Smith

Placings: 404P (4659)
2002/03: 16⁴HY, 16⁰G, 17⁴G, 20PGF,

	Starts	1st	2nd	3rd	Win & Pl
NH Flat	3	0	0	0	0
Hurdles	1	0	0	0	0
Career Total	4	0	0	0	0

Going: Sf: 0-1 GS: 0-0 Gd: 0-2 GF: - Fm: 0-1
Distance: 2m/2m3: 0-3 2m4-2m7: 0-1 3m+: 0-0
Track: LH: 0-2 RH: 0-2 Tight: 0-1 Gall: 0-0
Aids: Bl: 0-0 Vi: 0-0 Tstrap: 0-0
Best Rating: 91 1/03 Ayr 2m heavy NHF

Backed when well beaten on bumper debut; well beaten since, including over hurdles.

Royaltino (IRE)

11-y-o b g Neltino-Royal Well (Royal Vulcan)
Miss T McCurrich Miss T McCurrich

Placings: 1/2F310/11/2136/022P/P2 (3962)
2002/03: 24PGS, 24²S,

	Starts	1st	2nd	3rd	Win & Pl
Chases	2	0	1	0	666
Career Total	18	5	5	2	64007
10/98 Engh 2m3f	Ch			VS	£15152
4/98 Engh 2m3f	Hdl			HVY	£10101
3/98 Vire 2m3f	Hdl			HLD	£3030
117 2/97 Kemp 2m5f	D Hdl			GD	£2969
103 2/96 Wwck 2m	H NHF			GD	£1867

Total win prize-money £33119

Going: Sf: 0-1 GS: 0-1 Gd: 0-0 GF: - Fm: 0-0
Distance: 2m/2m3: 0-0 2m4-2m7: 0-0 3m+: 0-2
Track: LH: 0-1 RH: 0-1 Tight: 0-2 Gall: 0-0
Aids: Bl: 0-0 Vi: 0-0 Tstrap: 0-0
Best Rating: 119 3/97 Chel 2m5f gd-fm Hdl

Modest hunter chaser; acts in soft ground; former useful hurdler when trained in France.

Roymillon (GER)

108　　　　87

9-y-o b g Milesius (USA)-Royal Slope (USA) (His Majesty (USA))
D J Wintle John W Egan/graham Brown

Placings: 005/06551403-514 (1817)
2002/03: 22⁵GF, 26¹GF, 26⁴G,

	Starts	1st	2nd	3rd	Win & Pl
Hurdles	3	1	0	0	2498
Career Total	14	2	0	1	4834
87 9/02 Hntg 3m2f	F(0-90)HHdl			G-F	£2234
85 7/01 Worc 3m	F(0-100)HHdl			GD	£1946

Total win prize-money £4180

Going: Sf: 0-0 GS: 0-0 Gd: 0-1 GF: - Fm: 1-2
Distance: 2m/2m3: 0-0 2m4-2m7: 0-1 3m+: 1-2
Track: LH: 0-1 RH: 1-2 Tight: 0-1 Gall: 1-1
Aids: Bl: 0-0 Vi: 0-0 Tstrap: 0-0
Best Rating: 87 9/02 Hntg 3m2f gd-fm Hdl

A one-time decent performer in Germany, he has won over hurdles in this country but looks a moody character. Stays very well and is suited by coming from off the pace.

Royrace

56

11-y-o b g Wace (USA)-Royal Tycoon (Tycoon Ii)
W M Brisbourne Andrew Evans

Placings: 0P5P5/54P/350P03P4U/FP02P0P04/3PP/0P-P (0891)
2002/03: 20PS,

	Starts	1st	2nd	3rd	Win & Pl
Chases	1	0	0	0	
Career Total	32	0	1	3	2501

Going: Sf: 0-1 GS: 0-0 Gd: 0-0 GF: - Fm: 0-0
Distance: 2m/2m3: 0-0 2m4-2m7: 0-1 3m+: 0-0
Track: LH: 0-1 RH: 0-0 Tight: 0-1 Gall: 0-0
Aids: Bl: 0-0 Vi: 0-0 Tstrap: 0-0
Best Rating: 89 10/98 Bang 2m4f good Hdl

Rubon Prince (IRE)

37

12-y-o ch g Kambalda-Oh Clare (Laurence O)
N B Mason N B Mason

Placings: 4U0/63534302PU3/423503U24454240/P/U0-P (1062)
2002/03: 23PG,

	Starts	1st	2nd	3rd	Win & Pl
Chases	1	0	0	0	
Career Total	34	0	4	6	8009

Going: Sf: 0-0 GS: 0-0 Gd: 0-1 GF: - Fm: 0-0
Distance: 2m/2m3: 0-0 2m4-2m7: 0-0 3m+: 0-1
Track: LH: 0-1 RH: 0-0 Tight: 0-0 Gall: 0-0
Aids: Bl: 0-0 Vi: 0-0 Tstrap: 0-0
Best Rating: 83 9/97 Carl 2m1f gd-fm NHF

Ruby Gale (IRE)

(110h)　　(128h)133

7-y-o b g Lord Americo-Well Over (Over The River (FR))
P F Nicholls Mrs Angela Tincknell

Placings: 0/1210212-F6 (1782)
2002/03: 17FG, 19⁶G,

	Starts	1st	2nd	3rd	Win & Pl
Chases	2	0	0	0	0
Career Total	10	3	3	0	13822
120 3/02 Extr 2m3f	E Hdl			GD	£2828
116 12/01 Extr 2m3f	E Hdl			GD	£2922
102 11/01 NAbb 2m1f	H NHF			GD	£2289

Total win prize-money £8008

Going: Sf: 0-0 GS: 0-0 Gd: 0-2 GF: - Fm: 0-0
Distance: 2m/2m3: 0-1 2m4-2m7: 0-1 3m+: 0-0
Track: LH: 0-0 RH: 0-2 Tight: 0-0 Gall: 0-0
Aids: Bl: 0-0 Vi: 0-0 Tstrap: 0-0
Best Rating: 133 10/02 Extr 2m1f110y good Ch

Fair chaser/hurdler; reproduced his winning bumper form in 2001/02, scoring twice over two miles over at Exeter. Sure to be in the shake-up when falling on his chase debut in October 2002. Travels well and is suited by good ground.

Rudetski

98　　　　92

6-y-o b g Rudimentary (USA)-Butosky (Busted)
M Dods A F & P Monk

Placings: 005 (2558)

2002/03: 16⁰GS, 16⁰GS, 16⁵GF,

	Starts	1st	2nd	3rd	Win & Pl
Hurdles	3	0	0	0	0
Career Total	3	0	0	0	0

Going: Sf: 0-0 GS: 0-2 Gd: 0-0 GF: - Fm: 0-1
Distance: 2m/2m3: 0-3 2m4-2m7: 0-0 3m+: 0-0
Track: LH: 0-2 RH: 0-1 Tight: 0-1 Gall: 0-1
Aids: Bl: 0-0 Vi: 0-0 Tstrap: 0-0
Best Rating: 92 12/02 Muss 2m   gd-fm Hdl

Rudge Hill

77   39

7-y-o b g Almushmmir-Time After Time (High Award)
G A Ham Martin Smith (frome)

Placings:00-P   (2196)
2002/03: 19⁰GS,

	Starts	1st	2nd	3rd	Win & Pl
Chases	1	0	0	0	
Career Total	3	0	0	0	

Going: Sf: 0-0 GS: 0-1 Gd: 0-0 GF: - Fm: 0-0
Distance: 2m/2m3: 0-1 2m4-2m7: 0-0 3m+: 0-0
Track: LH: 0-2 RH: 0-1 Tight: 0-1 Gall: 0-1
Aids: Bl: 0-0 Vi: 0-0 Tstrap: 0-0
Best Rating: 0 11/02 Tntn 2m3f   gd-sft Ch

No worthwhile form in bumpers and a chase.

Rudi Knight

111(105h)   (132h)119

8-y-o ch g Rudimentary (USA)-Fleeting Affair (Hotfoot)
Miss Venetia Williams Derek And Jean Clee

Placings:413512362/3302122/0054-533   (3315)
2002/03: 20⁵G, 19³S, 19³GS,

	Starts	1st	2nd	3rd	Win & Pl
Hurdles	1	0	0	0	0
Chases	2	0	0	2	1502
Career Total	23	3	5	6	33581
130	2/01	Kemp	2m	C(0-135)HHdl	G-S	£10676
119	1/00	Font	2m2f110yC(0-135)HHdl	G-S	£6142
107	7/99	NAbb	2m1f	E Hdl	G-F	£2671

Total win prize-money £19490

Going: Sf: 0-1 GS: 0-1 Gd: 0-1 GF: - Fm: 0-0
Distance: 2m/2m3: 0-0 2m4-2m7: 0-3 3m+: 0-0
Track: LH: 0-2 RH: 0-1 Tight: 0-0 Gall: 0-0
Aids: Bl: 0-0 Vi: 0-0 Tstrap: 0-0
Best Rating: 138 3/01 Newb 2m110y   heavy Hdl

Decent hurdler, winning novice chaser, but does not look a natural; recorded second win over fences at Market Rasen in July 2003; stays two and a half miles; seems to act on most types of ground; often held up in his races.

Rudi's Charm

91f   90f

6-y-o b g Rudimentary (USA)-Irene s Charter (Persian Bold)
J A Moore J A Moore

Placings:50   (3160)
2002/03: 16⁵GF, 16⁰G,

	Starts	1st	2nd	3rd	Win & Pl
NH Flat	2	0	0	0	0
Career Total	2	0	0	0	0

Going: Sf: 0-0 GS: 0-0 Gd: 0-1 GF: - Fm: 0-1

Distance: 2m/2m3: 0-2 2m4-2m7: 0-0 3m+: 0-0
Track: LH: 0-0 RH: 0-0 Tight: 0-2 Gall: 0-0
Aids: Bl: 0-0 Vi: 0-0 Tstrap: 0-0
Best Rating: 90 12/02 Muss 2m   gd-fm NHF

Rudi's Pleasure (IRE)

105(113h)   (106h)101

8-y-o ch g Buckskin (FR)-Kind Sir She Said (Decent Fellow)
E McNamara Robert Butler

Placings:0060/3160260335/46002321430-24242642444F
(4730a)
2002/03: 24²Y, 22⁴G, 20²YS, 22⁴G, 24²F, 21⁶G, 24⁴HY, 20²HY, 20⁴S, 24⁴SH, 24⁴Y, 22⁶G,

	Starts	1st	2nd	3rd	Win & Pl
Hurdles	7	0	3	0	6843
Chases	5	0	1	0	2737
Career Total	37	2	7	5	31943
106	12/01	Limk	2m4f	(0-116)HHdl	SFT	£8395
100	6/00	Tral	2m4f	(0-109)HHdl	SH	£3588

Total win prize-money £11983

Going: Sf: 0-3 GS: 0-0 Gd: 0-4 GF: - Fm: 0-1
Distance: 2m/2m3: 0-0 2m4-2m7: 0-7 3m+: 0-5
Track: LH: 0-1 RH: 0-3 Tight: 0-0 Gall: 0-1
Aids: Bl: 0-0 Vi: 0-0 Tstrap: 0-0
Best Rating: 113 11/00 Chel 2m5f   gd-sft Hdl

Modest irish hurdler/chaser; stays two a ahlf miles; best on soft ground.

Rudolf Rassendyll (IRE)

106(100h)   (103h)119

8-y-o b g Supreme Leader-Chantel Rouge (Boreen (FR))
Miss Venetia Williams Mrs C S Wilson

Placings:060-51412   (4028)
2002/03: 19⁵G, 20¹S, 20⁴S, 19¹GS, 24²S,

	Starts	1st	2nd	3rd	Win & Pl
Hurdles	2	1	0	0	2702
Chases	3	1	1	0	8165
Career Total	8	2	1	0	10867
119	2/03	Chep	2m3f110yD(0-120)HCh	G-S	£5635
103	1/03	Hntg	2m4f110yF(0-95)HHdl	SFT	£2702

Total win prize-money £8338

Going: Sf: 1-3 GS: 1-1 Gd: 0-1 GF: - Fm: 0-0
Distance: 2m/2m3: 0-0 2m4-2m7: 2-4 3m+: 0-1
Track: LH: 1-1 RH: 1-4 Tight: 0-0 Gall: 1-1
Aids: Bl: 0-0 Vi: 0-0 Tstrap: 0-0
Best Rating: 119 2/03 Chep 2m3f110y gd-sft Ch

Fair chaser/hurdler; won a novice handicap hurdle at Huntingdon in January 2003, and a handicap chase at Chepstow the following month; stays two and a half miles; acts on soft ground.

Rufius (IRE)

111   78

10-y-o b g Celio Rufo-In View Lass (Tepukei)
P Kelsall Peter Kelsall

Placings:4000/000P3/OP055F/55240-2124216P0 (4614)
2002/03: 23²G, 24¹GF, 20²G, 20⁴GS, 20²G, 25¹S, 23⁶GS, 22⁵S, 21⁰G,

	Starts	1st	2nd	3rd	Win & Pl
Chases	9	2	3	0	22444
Career Total	29	2	4	1	24790
104	12/02	Chel	3m1f110yD(0-120)HCh	SFT	£11221

| 100 | 9/02 | Hntg | 3m | E Ch | G-F | £3526 |

Total win prize-money £14748

Going: Sf: 1-2 GS: 0-2 Gd: 0-4 GF: - Fm: 1-1
Distance: 2m/2m3: 0-0 2m4-2m7: 0-5 3m+: 2-4
Track: LH: 1-6 RH: 1-3 Tight: 0-0 Gall: 2-6
Aids: Bl: 0-0 Vi: 0-0 Tstrap: 0-0
Best Rating: 104 12/02 Chel 3m1f110y soft Ch

Moderate chaser; best at trips around two and a half to three miles; acts on a sound surface, although is effective on soft.

Rugged Man (IRE)

100   89

5-y-o b h Topanoora-The Grey (GER) (Pentathlon)
Graham John McKeever F Thompson

Placings:0-3500430   (1298)
2002/03: 17⁵HY, 17⁵G, 16⁰G, 20⁰Y, 21⁴G, 19³GF, 16⁰GF,

	Starts	1st	2nd	3rd	Win & Pl
Hurdles	7	0	0	2	961
Career Total	8	0	0	2	961

Going: Sf: 0-1 GS: 0-0 Gd: 0-3 GF: - Fm: 0-2
Distance: 2m/2m3: 0-5 2m4-2m7: 0-2 3m+: 0-0
Track: LH: 0-3 RH: 0-1 Tight: 0-3 Gall: 0-0
Aids: Bl: 0-3 Vi: 0-0 Tstrap: 0-0
Best Rating: 89 6/02 Ctml 2m1f110y heavy Hdl

Poor novice hurdler.

Rugged River (IRE)

115   137

8-y-o b g Over The River (FR)-Early Dalus (IRE) (Mandalus)
R H Alner Miss H J Flower

Placings:351P/13PP3   (3898)
2002/03: 26¹HY, 26³S, 29²HY, 24²HY, 24³S,

	Starts	1st	2nd	3rd	Win & Pl
Chases	5	1	0	2	13611
Career Total	9	2	0	3	21985
133	11/02	NAbb	3m2f110yC(0-130)HCh	HVY	£7368
130	12/00	Extr	2m1f110yC H	HVY	£7805

Total win prize-money £15173

Going: Sf: 1-5 GS: 0-0 Gd: 0-0 GF: - Fm: 0-0
Distance: 2m/2m3: 0-0 2m4-2m7: 0-0 3m+: 1-5
Track: LH: 1-4 RH: 0-1 Tight: 1-1 Gall: 0-3
Aids: Bl: 0-0 Vi: 0-0 Tstrap: 0-0
Best Rating: 137 12/02 Chep 3m2f110y soft Ch

Useful staying chaser; broke down at Ascot in December 2000; successful on his first start since being pin-fired when narrow winner of extended three and a quarter mile handicap at Newton Abbot November 2002; mixed efforts in better company subsequently; stays three miles two; likes the mud.

Rugged Ruben

6-y-o b g Minshaanshu Amad (USA)-Kiri Te (Liboi (USA))
J W Mullins Mrs M M Rayner

Placings:5PP   (1582)
2002/03: 17⁵G, 20⁵G, 21⁰G,

	Starts	1st	2nd	3rd	Win & Pl
NH Flat	1	0	0	0	0
Hurdles	2	0	0	0	0
Career Total	3	0	0	0	0

Going: Sf: 0-0 GS: 0-0 Gd: 0-2 GF: - Fm: 0-1

Distance:	2m/2m3: 0-1 2m4-2m7: 0-2 3m+: 0-0
Track:	LH: 0-1 RH: 0-1 Tight: 0-2 Gall: 0-0
Aids:	Bl: 0-0 Vi: 0-0 Tstrap: 0-0
Best Rating:	70 9/02 Hrfd 2m1f gd-fm NHF

Rum Pointer (IRE)
110   134

7-y-o b g Turtle Island (IRE)-Osmunda (Mill Reef (USA))
R H Buckler K C B Mackenzie

Placings:432112/P-42260F   (4102)
2002/03: 20⁴S, 22²GS, 24²S, 23⁶GS, 22⁰HY, 25²FG,

	Starts	1st	2nd	3rd	Win & Pl
Hurdles	6	0	2	0	9254
Career Total	13	2	4	1	26555
130 1/01 Donc 2m4f	A Hdl			GD	£9600
119 1/01 Wwck 2m5f	D Hdl			SFT	£3874
				Total win prize-money £13474

Going:	Sf: 0-3 GS: 0-2 Gd: 0-1 GF: - Fm: 0-0
Distance:	2m/2m3: 0-0 2m4-2m7: 0-3 3m+: 0-3
Track:	LH: 0-4 RH: 0-2 Tight: 0-0 Gall: 0-2
Aids:	Bl: 0-0 Vi: 0-0 Tstrap: 0-0
Best Rating:	134 12/02 Chel 3m soft Hdl

Useful hurdler at around two miles four to three miles; has stamina in abundance; best on an easy surface.

Run For Eileen (IRE)

8-y-o b m Cataldi-Deep Dawn Run (Deep Run)
A Sadik A Sadik

Placings:FP   (1812)
2002/03: 20²S, 17²G,

	Starts	1st	2nd	3rd	Win & Pl
Hurdles	2	0	0	0	
Career Total	2	0	0	0	

Going:	Sf: 0-1 GS: 0-0 Gd: 0-1 GF: - Fm: 0-0
Distance:	2m/2m3: 0-1 2m4-2m7: 0-1 3m+: 0-0
Track:	LH: 0-1 RH: 0-1 Tight: 0-1 Gall: 0-0
Aids:	Bl: 0-0 Vi: 0-0 Tstrap: 0-0
Best Rating:	0 11/02 Hrfd 2m1f good Hdl

Run For Paddy
107(111h)   (146h) 147d

7-y-o b g Michelozzo (USA)-Deep Selection (IRE) (Deep Run)
Mrs H Dalton B Perkins

Placings:230/3111263/23411P1P-1PP   (4469)
2002/03: 24¹GF, 21⁵GS, 25⁵G,

	Starts	1st	2nd	3rd	Win & Pl
Chases	3	1	0	0	13579
Career Total	21	7	3	4	59500
147 10/02 Chep 3m	B(0-145)HChc		G-F	£13578
140 4/02 MRas 3m1f	D Ch		GD	£4907
140 3/02 Donc 2m3f110yD Ch			G-S	£4368
111 2/02 Fknm 3m110y D Ch			G-S	£3874
132 10/00 Chel 2m5f	B(0-145)HHdl		GD	£8414
118 9/00 Uttx 2m6f110yC Hdl			G-S	£4771
107 9/00 Font 2m2f110yE Hdl			G-S	£2782
				Total win prize-money £42695

Going:	Sf: 0-0 GS: 0-1 Gd: 0-1 GF: - Fm: 1-1
Distance:	2m/2m3: 0-0 2m4-2m7: 0-1 3m+: 1-2
Track:	LH: 1-3 RH: 0-0 Tight: 0-1 Gall: 0-1
Aids:	Bl: 0-0 Vi: 0-0 Tstrap: 0-0
Best Rating:	156 12/00 Chel 2m5f110y soft Hdl

Very useful chaser when on song; stays three miles; acts on both good to firm and good to soft ground.

Run For The Boys

7-y-o ch g Michelozzo (USA)-Horns Lodge (High Line)
C J Mann Charlie Mann

Placings:0-0P   (2547)
2002/03: 16⁰G, 22⁰HY,

	Starts	1st	2nd	3rd	Win & Pl
NH Flat	1	0	0	0	0
Hurdles	1	0	0	0	0
Career Total	3	0	0	0	

Going:	Sf: 0-1 GS: 0-0 Gd: 0-1 GF: - Fm: 0-0
Distance:	2m/2m3: 0-1 2m4-2m7: 0-1 3m+: 0-0
Track:	LH: 0-0 RH: 0-2 Tight: 0-1 Gall: 0-0
Aids:	Bl: 0-0 Vi: 0-0 Tstrap: 0-0
Best Rating:	86 2/02 Kemp 2m good NHF

Runaway Bishop (USA)
100(107h)   (94h)94

8-y-o b/br g Lear Fan (USA)-Valid Linda (USA) (Valid Appeal (USA))
J R Cornwall (Mrs A Duffield 6/9) J R Cornwall

Placings:230/322342313/F/242-3423334   (2500)
2002/03: 24³GS, 17⁴GF, 24²G, 21³S, 17³GF, 25³GS, 24⁴GS,

	Starts	1st	2nd	3rd	Win & Pl
Hurdles	5	0	1	3	1645
Chases	2	0	0	1	1220
Career Total	23	1	7	9	14080
96 3/00 Folk 2m5f	D Ch		G-F	£4036
				Total win prize-money £4037

Going:	Sf: 0-1 GS: 0-3 Gd: 0-1 GF: - Fm: 0-2
Distance:	2m/2m3: 0-2 2m4-2m7: 0-1 3m+: 0-4
Track:	LH: 0-4 RH: 0-3 Tight: 0-5 Gall: 0-0
Aids:	Bl: 0-3 Vi: 0-2 Tstrap: 0-0
Best Rating:	109 4/00 Font 2m6f good Ch

Fair chaser, plating class hurdler. Stays three miles over hurdles. Has won at up to two miles five over fences. Acts on a sound surface.

Runaway Ralph
    (84c)   (62c)

9-y-o ch g Rolfe (USA)-Swift Messenger (Giolla Mear)
D L Williams D L Williams

Placings:0/06/4PU   (0478)
2002/03: 20⁴GF, 19⁰G, 26ᵁGS,

	Starts	1st	2nd	3rd	Win & Pl
Hurdles	1	0	0	0	0
Chases	2	0	0	0	237
Career Total	6	0	0	0	237

Going:	Sf: 0-0 GS: 0-1 Gd: 0-1 GF: - Fm: 0-1
Distance:	2m/2m3: 0-0 2m4-2m7: 0-1 3m+: 0-1
Track:	LH: 0-1 RH: 0-1 Tight: 0-2 Gall: 0-0
Aids:	Bl: 0-0 Vi: 0-0 Tstrap: 0-0
Best Rating:	62 5/02 Font 2m4f gd-fm Ch

Runner Bean
105(97h)   (84h)105

9-y-o b/br g Henbit (USA)-Bean Alainn (Candy Cane)

R Lee H F P Foods Limited

Placings:51f634P/403P-424P21   (4684)
2002/03: 16⁴S, 19²S, 16⁴S, 16⁰S, 17²G, 16¹GF,

	Starts	1st	2nd	3rd	Win & Pl
Chases	6	1	2	0	9647
Career Total	17	3	2	2	14048
98 4/03 Hntg 2m110y	D(0-115)HCh	G-F	£5852
114 11/99 Ludl 2m	H NHF		GD	£1542
105 5/99 Uttx 2m	H NHF		G-F	£1763
				Total win prize-money £9158

Going:	Sf: 0-4 GS: 0-0 Gd: 0-1 GF: - Fm: 1-1
Distance:	2m/2m3: 1-6 2m4-2m7: 0-0 3m+: 0-0
Track:	LH: 0-1 RH: 1-5 Tight: 0-2 Gall: 1-1
Aids:	Bl: 0-0 Vi: 0-0 Tstrap: 0-0
Best Rating:	114 11/99 Ludl 2m good NHF

Moderate novice chaser; took a novices handicap at Huntingdon in April; stays two and a half miles but best over shorter; acts on any ground.

Running Battle

7-y-o br m Lepanto (GER)-Running Cool (Record Run)
N J Hawke C G Newman

Placings:0P-P   (0035)
2002/03: 22⁰G,

	Starts	1st	2nd	3rd	Win & Pl
Hurdles	1	0	0	0	
Career Total	3	0	0	0	

Going:	Sf: 0-0 GS: 0-0 Gd: 0-1 GF: - Fm: 0-0
Distance:	2m/2m3: 0-0 2m4-2m7: 0-1 3m+: 0-0
Track:	LH: 0-0 RH: 0-2 Tight: 0-0 Gall: 0-0
Aids:	Bl: 0-0 Vi: 0-0 Tstrap: 0-0
Best Rating:	66 11/01 Extr 2m1f gd-fm NHF

Running De Cerisy (FR)
    (107h)

9-y-o ch g Lightning (FR)-Niloq (FR) (Nikos)
Miss S J Wilton John Pointon And Sons

Placings:1F1133P04/041/FPP/65112132432403-PP   (4413)
2002/03: 20²GS, 17²G,

	Starts	1st	2nd	3rd	Win & Pl
Chases	2	0	0	0	
Career Total	31	7	3	5	27009
110 8/01 NAbb 2m1f	F Hdl		G-F	£2296
102 7/01 MRas 2m1f110yF(0-105)HCh		G-S	£4251
114 7/01 Wolv 2m	G Hdl		G-S	£1621
110 11/98 Hrfd 2m	E(0-100)HCh		GD	£3126
114 9/97 NAbb 2m1f	E Hdl		SFT	£2148
108 8/97 Worc 2m	E Hdl		G-F	£2250
6/97 Autl 1m7f	Hdl		SFT	£7295
				Total win prize-money £22987

Going:	Sf: 0-0 GS: 0-1 Gd: 0-1 GF: - Fm: 0-0
Distance:	2m/2m3: 0-1 2m4-2m7: 0-1 3m+: 0-0
Track:	LH: 0-0 RH: 0-2 Tight: 0-2 Gall: 0-0
Aids:	Bl: 0-0 Vi: 0-0 Tstrap: 0-0
Best Rating:	114 8/01 NAbb 2m1f good Hdl

Modest chaser/fair hurdler; best over two miles; acts on most types of ground.

Running Machine (IRE)

105(100h)   (96 h)**101**

6-y-o b g Classic Memory-Foxborough Lady (Crash Course)
A M Hales Andrew L Cohen

Placings:03F3F336   (3927)
2002/03: 19⁰G, 21³S, 27FS, 24³GS, 24FHY, 23³GS, 21³S, 24⁶G,

	Starts	1st	2nd	3rd	Win & Pl
Hurdles	5	0	0	2	878
Chases	3	0	0	2	1369
Career Total	8	0	0	4	2246

Going:	Sf: 0-4 GS: 0-2 Gd: 0-2 GF: - Fm: 0-0
Distance:	2m/2m3: 0-0 2m4-2m7: 0-3 3m+: 0-5
Track:	LH: 0-4 RH: 0-4 Tight: 0-5 Gall: 0-1
Aids:	Bl: 0-0 Vi: 0-0 Tstrap: 0-7
Best Rating:	101 2/03 Folk 2m5f soft Ch

Moderate novice hurdler; modest third on his first two starts over fences; stays three miles; wears a tongue tie.

Running Man (FR)

106(109h)   (124 h)**136**

9-y-o ch g General Holme (USA)-Rudolfina (Pharly (FR))
P R Webber Mrs C A Waters

Placings:F14P/355/211/1F154   (4781)
2002/03: 16¹GF, 16FGF, 16¹GF, 16⁵G, 16⁴GF,

	Starts	1st	2nd	3rd	Win & Pl
Hurdles	2	1	0	0	3801
Chases	3	1	0	0	12381
Career Total	15	5	1	1	28118
133	10/02 Kemp	2m	B(0-140)HCh	G-F	£10881
129	8/02 Hntg	2m110y	E(0-110)HHdl	G-F	£2926
123	8/00 Prth	2m	D Ch	GD	£4026
109	6/00 Folk	2m	E Ch	GD	£3164
123	1/99 Muss	2m	E Hdl	G-S	£2022
			Total win prize-money £23021

Going:	Sf: 0-0 GS: 0-0 Gd: 0-1 GF: - Fm: 2-4
Distance:	2m/2m3: 2-5 2m4-2m7: 0-0 3m+: 0-0
Track:	LH: 0-0 RH: 2-5 Tight: 0-0 Gall: 1-1
Aids:	Bl: 0-0 Vi: 0-0 Tstrap: 0-0
Best Rating:	133 10/02 Kemp 2m gd-fm Ch

Useful chaser/hurdler; keen front-runner; races at around the minimum trip, effective on a sound surface; suited by right-handed tracks.

Running Moss

108   **110**

11-y-o ch g Le Moss-Run n Fly (Deep Run)
A H Mactaggart Mrs A H Mactaggart

Placings:P62/344412/P314/1321-3P4   (2263)
2002/03: 22³S, 28PS, 25⁴HY,

	Starts	1st	2nd	3rd	Win & Pl
Chases	3	0	0	1	2067
Career Total	20	4	3	4	44889
110	3/02 Kels	4m	C(0-135)HCh	HVY	£24534
103	11/01 Kels	2m6f110yD(0-120)HCh	GD	£5148
109	11/00 Catt	3m1f110yF(0-110)HCh	G-S	£4192
97	12/99 Sedg	3m3f	E Ch	SFT	£3299
			Total win prize-money £37175

Going:	Sf: 0-3 GS: 0-0 Gd: 0-0 GF: - Fm: 0-0
Distance:	2m/2m3: 0-0 2m4-2m7: 0-1 3m+: 0-2
Track:	LH: 0-3 RH: 0-0 Tight: 0-3 Gall: 0-0
Aids:	Bl: 0-0 Vi: 0-0 Tstrap: 0-0
Best Rating:	113 12/02 Kels 3m1f heavy Ch

Suited by a strongly-run race, he is a three-mile staying chaser who has been effective on a soft surface and good ground.

Running Mute

108   **98**

9-y-o b g Roscoe Blake-Rose Albertine (Record Token)
Mrs S H Shirley-Beavan J E M Vestey

Placings:1   (0503)
2002/03: 26¹G,

	Starts	1st	2nd	3rd	Win & Pl
Chases	1	1	0	0	2301
Career Total	1	1	0	0	2301
79	6/02 Ctml	3m2f	H Ch	GD	£2301
			Total win prize-money £2301

Going:	Sf: 0-0 GS: 0-0 Gd: 1-1 GF: - Fm: 0-0
Distance:	2m/2m3: 0-0 2m4-2m7: 0-0 3m+: 1-1
Track:	LH: 1-1 RH: 0-0 Tight: 1-1 Gall: 0-0
Aids:	Bl: 0-0 Vi: 0-0 Tstrap: 0-0
Best Rating:	79 6/02 Ctml 3m2f good Ch

Moderate performer; has won plenty of points; runner-up in a handicap chase last time; stays three miles; acts on a sound surface.

Running Times (USA)

(104h)   (121h)

6-y-o b g Brocco (USA)-Concert Peace (USA) (Hold Your Peace (USA))
H J Manners (M C Pipe 14/5) H J Manners

Placings:04/122401-1P   (4346)
2002/03: 19¹G, 16PGF,

	Starts	1st	2nd	3rd	Win & Pl
Hurdles	1	1	0	0	2002
Chases	1	0	0	0	0
Career Total	10	3	2	0	10243
121	5/02 Hrfd	2m3f110yG Hdl	GD	£2002
116	3/02 Chep	2m4f	F Hdl	SFT	£2016
102	5/01 Sedg	2m5f110yE Hdl	GD	£2786
			Total win prize-money £6804

Going:	Sf: 0-0 GS: 0-0 Gd: 1-1 GF: - Fm: 0-1
Distance:	2m/2m3: 0-1 2m4-2m7: 1-1 3m+: 0-0
Track:	LH: 0-1 RH: 1-1 Tight: 0-0 Gall: 0-0
Aids:	Bl: 0-0 Vi: 1-2 Tstrap: 0-0
Best Rating:	121 5/02 Hrfd 2m3f110y good Hdl

Suited by good ground, he is a useful plater over hurdles and was sold out of the Pipe yard after winning in May 2002.

Runningwiththemoon

79   **58**

7-y-o b g Homo Sapien-Ardeal (Ardross)
C C Bealby Mrs S M V Bealby

Placings:6P   (1907)
2002/03: 16⁶GF, 20PGS,

	Starts	1st	2nd	3rd	Win & Pl
NH Flat	1	0	0	0	0
Hurdles	1	0	0	0	0
Career Total	2	0	0	0	0

Going:	Sf: 0-0 GS: 0-1 Gd: 0-0 GF: - Fm: 0-1
Distance:	2m/2m3: 0-1 2m4-2m7: 0-1 3m+: 0-0
Track:	LH: 0-2 RH: 0-0 Tight: 0-1 Gall: 0-0
Aids:	Bl: 0-0 Vi: 0-0 Tstrap: 0-0
Best Rating:	0 11/02 Stfd 2m4f110y gd-sft Hdl

Rupert

89f   **64f**

6-y-o ch g Arzanni-High Affair (High Line)
S G Griffiths S G Griffiths

Placings:60   (1606)
2002/03: 16⁶GF, 16⁰G,

	Starts	1st	2nd	3rd	Win & Pl
NH Flat	2	0	0	0	0
Career Total	2	0	0	0	0

Going:	Sf: 0-0 GS: 0-0 Gd: 0-1 GF: - Fm: 0-1
Distance:	2m/2m3: 0-2 2m4-2m7: 0-0 3m+: 0-0
Track:	LH: 0-2 RH: 0-0 Tight: 0-0 Gall: 0-0
Aids:	Bl: 0-0 Vi: 0-0 Tstrap: 0-0
Best Rating:	64 10/02 Chep 2m110y gd-fm NHF

Rush 'n Tear

12-y-o b g Rushmere-May Singer (Record Run)
Mrs A A Hawkins Mrs A A Hawkins

Placings:4/3UP/0   (0311)
2002/03: 26⁰G,

	Starts	1st	2nd	3rd	Win & Pl
Chases	1	0	0	0	0
Career Total	5	0	0	1	320

Going:	Sf: 0-0 GS: 0-0 Gd: 0-1 GF: - Fm: 0-0
Distance:	2m/2m3: 0-0 2m4-2m7: 0-0 3m+: 0-1
Track:	LH: 0-0 RH: 0-1 Tight: 0-1 Gall: 0-0
Aids:	Bl: 0-0 Vi: 0-0 Tstrap: 0-0
Best Rating:	66 5/99 Folk 2m5f gd-fm Ch

Rush'N'Run

84f   **64f**

4-y-o b g Kasakov-Runfawit Pet (Welsh Saint)
D Carroll John R Ashcroft

Placings:000   (4357)
2002/03: 16⁰G, 17⁰HY, 16⁰GF,

	Starts	1st	2nd	3rd	Win & Pl
NH Flat	3	0	0	0	
Career Total	3	0	0	0	

Going:	Sf: 0-1 GS: 0-0 Gd: 0-1 GF: - Fm: 0-1
Distance:	2m/2m3: 0-3 2m4-2m7: 0-0 3m+: 0-0
Track:	LH: 0-3 RH: 0-0 Tight: 0-2 Gall: 0-0
Aids:	Bl: 0-0 Vi: 0-0 Tstrap: 0-0
Best Rating:	66 1/03 Catt 2m good NHF

Rushen Raider

101   **73**

11-y-o br g Reprimand-Travel Storm (Lord Gayle (USA))
P Needham P Needham

Placings:SP00/12/615/U22260/3P021050/40246306F00-30   (1706)
2002/03: 24³G, 21⁰G,

	Starts	1st	2nd	3rd	Win & Pl
Hurdles	2	0	0	1	421
Career Total	36	3	6	3	14769
103	9/00 Sedg	2m5f110yD(0-120)HHdl	SFT	£2892
112	9/98 Sedg	2m5f110yD(0-120)HHdl	GD	£2726
104	5/97 MRas	2m1f110yE Hdl	G-F	£2547
			Total win prize-money £8167

Going: Sf: 0-0 GS: 0-0 Gd: 0-2 GF: - Fm: 0-0
Distance: 2m/2m3: 0-0 2m4-2m7: 0-1 3m+: 0-1
Track: LH: 0-2 RH: 0-0 Tight: 0-1 Gall: 0-0
Aids: Bl: 0-0 Vi: 0-0 Tstrap: 0-0
Best Rating: 115 9/99 Sedg 2m5f110y gd-fm Hdl

Modest staying hurdler; goes well at Sedgefield.

Rushing Again

93(76h)   73
8-y-o br g Rushmere-Saunders Grove (IRE) (Sunyboy)
Dr P Pritchard   The Shooting Stars

Placings:20-P4234U4PP4P   (4627)
2002/03: 20⁴GS, 26⁴GF, 24²GF, 24³G, 24⁴G, 25⁰G, 21⁴S, 26²GS, 26⁵S, 24⁴F, 21⁴GF,

	Starts	1st	2nd	3rd	Win & Pl
Chases	11	0	1	1	5896
Career Total	13	0	2	1	6613

Going: Sf: 0-2 GS: 0-2 Gd: 0-3 GF: - Fm: 0-4
Distance: 2m/2m3: 0-0 2m4-2m7: 0-3 3m+: 0-8
Track: LH: 0-8 RH: 0-2 Tight: 0-3 Gall: 0-5
Aids: Bl: 0-0 Vi: 0-0 Tstrap: 0-0
Best Rating: 100 3/02 Font 3m3f   soft   Hdl

Winning pointer; runner-up in a weak novice hurdle in March 2002; modest placed efforts over fences in 2002/3; stays well.

Russell House (IRE)

106(105h)   (103h)108
7-y-o b/br g Roselier (FR)-Salufair (Salluceva)
A King   Mrs L Field

Placings:52/36200-3FP1P6   (4558)
2002/03: 25³G, 30⁵GS, 29⁸GS, 24¹G, 24⁹GS, 25⁶G,

	Starts	1st	2nd	3rd	Win & Pl
Chases	6	1	0	1	4758
Career Total	13	1	2	2	7542
108	1/03	Donc	3m	E(0-115)HCh	GD £4122
				Total win prize-money £4122

Going: Sf: 0-0 GS: 0-3 Gd: 1-3 GF: - Fm: 0-0
Distance: 2m/2m3: 0-0 2m4-2m7: 0-0 3m+: 1-6
Track: LH: 1-3 RH: 0-3 Tight: 0-0 Gall: 1-2
Aids: Bl: 0-1 Vi: 0-0 Tstrap: 0-0
Best Rating: 108 1/03 Donc 3m   good   Ch

Fair hurdler/chaser; looks an out and out stayer who appreciates a severe test of stamina. Finished distressed when finally opening his account at Doncaster in January and pulled up next time.

Russell Road (IRE)

94   112
11-y-o b g Phardante (FR)-Burren Gale (IRE) (Strong Gale)
A King   Mrs L Field

Placings:115/31321/12/00/0P3P   (3833)
2002/03: 25⁰GS, 22²G, 24³GS, 20⁰G,

	Starts	1st	2nd	3rd	Win & Pl
Chases	4	0	0	1	666
Career Total	16	5	2	3	22429
130	11/99	Extr	2m6f110yD Ch		G-S £5353
137	3/99	Sand	2m6f	D Hdl	G-S £4416
109	12/98	Towc	2m5f	D Hdl	SFT £3099
111	12/98	Towc	2m	H NHF	GD £1318
110	12/97	Towc	2m	H NHF	SFT £1360
				Total win prize-money £15548

Going: Sf: 0-0 GS: 0-2 Gd: 0-2 GF: - Fm: 0-0
Distance: 2m/2m3: 0-0 2m4-2m7: 0-3 3m+: 0-2
Track: LH: 0-2 RH: 0-2 Tight: 0-0 Gall: 0-1
Aids: Bl: 0-0 Vi: 0-0 Tstrap: 0-1
Best Rating: 137 3/99 Sand 2m6f   gd-sft Hdl

Fair handicap chaser; returned from two years off in December 2002; gradually finding some form; stays two miles six; suited by good to soft ground.

Russian Court

102   95
7-y-o b g Soviet Lad (USA)-Court Town (Camden Town)
S E H Sherwood (D R Gandolfo 16/1) Rosemary Viscountess Boyne

Placings:4/06/3616540-540131F   (4088)
2002/03: 17⁵GS, 16⁴HY, 22⁰GF, 16¹S, 17³GS, 17¹GS, 16⁵GS,

	Starts	1st	2nd	3rd	Win & Pl
Hurdles	7	2	0	1	8259
Career Total	17	3	0	2	11747
95	2/03	Tntn	2m1f	E(0-105)HHdl	G-S £4046
89	1/03	Ludl	2m	G(0-95)HHdl	SFT £3146
87	10/01	Plum	2m	F(0-100)HHdl	SFT £2639
				Total win prize-money £9832

Going: Sf: 1-2 GS: 1-4 Gd: 0-0 GF: - Fm: 0-1
Distance: 2m/2m3: 2-6 2m4-2m7: 0-1 3m+: 0-0
Track: LH: 0-5 RH: 2-2 Tight: 1-5 Gall: 0-0
Aids: Bl: 0-0 Vi: 0-0 Tstrap: 0-0
Best Rating: 95 2/03 Tntn 2m1f   gd-sft Hdl

Plating-class hurdler; suited by two miles and soft ground; needs to come late off a strong pace and do it all on the bridle.

Russian Dancer

99   (85h)79
7-y-o b g Petoski-Merry Minuet (Trumpeter)
Jedd O Keeffe   Paul & Anne Sellars

Placings:65/P-5   (3772)
2002/03: 21⁵GS,

	Starts	1st	2nd	3rd	Win & Pl
Chases	1	0	0	0	0
Career Total	4	0	0	0	0

Going: Sf: 0-0 GS: 0-1 Gd: 0-0 GF: - Fm: 0-0
Distance: 2m/2m3: 0-2 2m4-2m7: 0-1 3m+: 0-0
Track: LH: 0-1 RH: 0-0 Tight: 0-0 Gall: 0-0
Aids: Bl: 0-0 Vi: 0-0 Tstrap: 0-0
Best Rating: 85 4/01 Weth 2m4f110y gd-sft Hdl

Russian Gigolo (IRE)

104   103d
6-y-o b g Toulon-Nanogan (Tarqogan)
N A Twiston-Davies Mrs Caroline Beresford-Wylie

Placings:4006-25230P4   (4764)
2002/03: 20²GS, 20⁵S, 19²G, 22³HY, 20⁰GS, 20⁵HY, 24⁴G,

	Starts	1st	2nd	3rd	Win & Pl
Hurdles	7	0	2	1	4266
Career Total	11	0	2	1	4266

Going: Sf: 0-3 GS: 0-2 Gd: 0-2 GF: - Fm: 0-0
Distance: 2m/2m3: 0-1 2m4-2m7: 0-5 3m+: 0-1
Track: LH: 0-4 RH: 0-3 Tight: 0-1 Gall: 0-1
Aids: Bl: 0-0 Vi: 0-0 Tstrap: 0-0
Best Rating: 111 10/02 Bang 2m4f   gd-sft Hdl

Modest novice hurdler; acts on a soft surface; stays two miles six.

Russian Prince (IRE)

8-y-o b g Soviet Lad (USA)-Sweet Goodbye (Petorius)
S R Bolton (B S Rothwell 8/5) J Flint

Placings:600/0/F-P6   (0403)
2002/03: 21⁶GS, 20⁷GF, 22⁶GF,

	Starts	1st	2nd	3rd	Win & Pl
Hurdles	2	0	0	0	0
Chases	1	0	0	0	0
Career Total	7	0	0	0	0

Going: Sf: 0-0 GS: 0-1 Gd: 0-0 GF: - Fm: 0-2
Distance: 2m/2m3: 0-0 2m4-2m7: 0-3 3m+: 0-0
Track: LH: 0-1 RH: 0-2 Tight: 0-1 Gall: 0-0
Aids: Bl: 0-0 Vi: 0-0 Tstrap: 0-0
Best Rating: 81 6/02 MRas 2m6f110y gd-fm Ch

Russian River

66   63
11-y-o b g Sulaafah (USA)-Ninotchka (Niniski (USA))
J J Bridger   J J Bridger

Placings:P0P/0PP500/04FP/156205P032/6P0/000-F0
                                                   (2129)
2002/03: 18⁶GS, 16⁰S,

	Starts	1st	2nd	3rd	Win & Pl
Hurdles	2	0	0	0	0
Career Total	31	1	2	1	3464
86	9/99	Font	2m2f110yG(0-95)HHdl	GD £1865
				Total win prize-money £1865

Going: Sf: 0-1 GS: 0-1 Gd: 0-0 GF: - Fm: 0-0
Distance: 2m/2m3: 0-2 2m4-2m7: 0-0 3m+: 0-0
Track: LH: 0-2 RH: 0-0 Tight: 0-2 Gall: 0-0
Aids: Bl: 0-0 Vi: 0-0 Tstrap: 0-0
Best Rating: 86 4/00 Winc 2m   gd-sft Hdl

Rust En Vrede

104   80
4-y-o b g Royal Applause-Souveniers (Relko)
D Carroll (J L Eyre 15/6) Alan Mann

Placings:3050   (4573)
2002/03: 16³G, 17⁰GS, 16⁵GF, 16⁰GF,

	Starts	1st	2nd	3rd	Win & Pl
Hurdles	4	0	0	1	850
Career Total	4	0	0	1	850

Going: Sf: 0-0 GS: 0-1 Gd: 0-1 GF: - Fm: 0-2
Distance: 2m/2m3: 0-4 2m4-2m7: 0-0 3m+: 0-0
Track: LH: 0-2 RH: 0-2 Tight: 0-2 Gall: 0-0
Aids: Bl: 0-0 Vi: 0-0 Tstrap: 0-0
Best Rating: 84 2/03 Muss 2m   good   Hdl

Moderate maiden on the Flat; has shown just fair form over hurdles.

Rustic Revelry

10-y-o b g Afzal-Country Festival (Town And Country)
R H York   R H York

Placings:00000/45/5F4/216/36O6005-B62536   (0695)

2002/03: 16⁸GF, 16⁶G, 21²G, 16⁵S, 21³GF, 22⁶G,

	Starts	1st	2nd	3rd	Win & Pl
Chases	6	0	1	1	1637
Career Total	26	1	2	2	4176
89 5/00 Folk	2m5f	H Ch		GD	£1456

Total win prize-money £1456

Going:	Sf: 0-1 GS: 0-1 Gd: 0-3 GF: - Fm: 0-2
Distance:	2m/2m3: 0-3 2m4-2m7: 0-3 3m+: 0-2
Track:	LH: 0-3 RH: 0-3 Tight: 0-2 Gall: 0-1
Aids:	Bl: 0-4 Vi: 0-0 Tstrap: 0-0
Best Rating:	100 5/00 Hntg 2m4f110y good Ch

Hunter chaser; prolific winner between the flags; likes a sound surface, but acts with cut; stays three miles, but effective at shorter; wears blinkers.

Rusty Alntyne (IRE)

5-y-o ch g Rashar (USA)-Sky Rainbow (IRE) (Henbit (USA))
G M Moore Dr C I Emmerson

Placings:0-005PP (3965)
2002/03: 16⁹GF, 17⁰G, 24⁵GS, 25⁸G, 16⁸S,

	Starts	1st	2nd	3rd	Win & Pl
NH Flat	2	0	0	0	0
Hurdles	3	0	0	0	0
Career Total	6	0	0	0	0

Going:	Sf: 0-1 GS: 0-1 Gd: 0-2 GF: - Fm: 0-1
Distance:	2m/2m3: 0-3 2m4-2m7: 0-0 3m+: 0-2
Track:	LH: 0-5 RH: 0-0 Tight: 0-3 Gall: 0-0
Aids:	Bl: 0-0 Vi: 0-0 Tstrap: 0-0
Best Rating:	75 4/02 Carl 2m1f good NHF

Rusty Fellow

13-y-o b g Rustingo-Sallisses (Pamroy)
Mrs G M Shail Mrs G M Shail

Placings:32P3/23263/443P/54P5/610OPP-610 (0314)
2002/03: 33⁶GF, 30¹GF, 31⁰G,

	Starts	1st	2nd	3rd	Win & Pl
Chases	3	1	0	0	2205
Career Total	26	2	3	5	6795
95 5/02 Hntg	3m6f110yH Ch				£2205
95 5/01 Hntg	3m6f110yH Ch			G-F	£1631

Total win prize-money £3836

Going:	Sf: 0-0 GS: 0-0 Gd: 0-1 GF: - Fm: 1-2
Distance:	2m/2m3: 0-0 2m4-2m7: 0-0 3m+: 1-3
Track:	LH: 0-1 RH: 1-2 Tight: 0-0 Gall: 1-2
Aids:	Bl: 0-0 Vi: 0-0 Tstrap: 0-0
Best Rating:	100 4/98 Chel 3m1f110y good Ch

Modest hunter chaser, stays very well, acts on any ground. Runs in snatches.

Rutledge Red (IRE)
105   109
7-y-o gr g Roselier (FR)-Katebeaujolais (Politico (USA))
J M Jefferson Ashleybank Investments Limited

Placings:0P2-01112 (1907)
2002/03: 20⁰G, 19¹GF, 19¹GF, 20¹GS, 20²GS,

	Starts	1st	2nd	3rd	Win & Pl
Hurdles	5	3	1	0	12607
Career Total	8	3	2	0	13572
111 10/02 Fknm	2m4f	D Hdl		G-S	£3708
112 10/02 MRas	2m3f110yD Hdl			G-F	£4407
100 8/02 MRas	2m3f110yE Hdl			G-F	£3195

Total win prize-money £11311

Going:	Sf: 0-0 GS: 1-2 Gd: 0-1 GF: - Fm: 2-2
Distance:	2m/2m3: 0-0 2m4-2m7: 3-5 3m+: 0-0
Track:	LH: 1-3 RH: 2-2 Tight: 3-4 Gall: 0-0
Aids:	Bl: 0-0 Vi: 0-0 Tstrap: 0-0
Best Rating:	112 11/02 Sthl 2m4f110y gd-sft Hdl

Fair novice hurdler; completed a hat-trick in the autumn of 2002 with two wins at Market Rasen and one at Fakenham; suited by at least two and a half miles; has won on good to firm and soft ground.

Ryalux (IRE)
113(104h)   (119h)154
10-y-o b g Riverhead (USA)-Kings De Lema (IRE) (King s Ride)
A Crook William Lomas

Placings:221/12F111/3331P/22223F21-312231 (4557)
2002/03: 24³GF, 25¹S, 25²HY, 24²G, 24³G, 33¹G,

	Starts	1st	2nd	3rd	Win & Pl
Chases	6	2	2	2	104633
Career Total	28	9	10	6	158626
154 4/03 Ayr	4m1f	A HCh		GD	£63800
139 11/02 Ayr	3m1f	C(0-135)HCh		SFT	£10080
134 4/02 Prth	3m	B HCh		GD	£12203
129 1/01 Weth	2m4f110yD(0-125)HCh			G-S	£4160
125 3/00 Carl	2m	D Ch		G-S	£4368
109 3/00 Newc	2m4f	E Ch		GD	£3152
129 2/00 Newc	2m4f	E Ch		SFT	£3087
104 5/99 Hexm	2m1f	E Hdl		SFT	£2526
109 3/99 Newc	2m4f	E Hdl		GD	£2253

Total win prize-money £105630

Going:	Sf: 1-2 GS: 0-0 Gd: 1-3 GF: - Fm: 0-1
Distance:	2m/2m3: 0-0 2m4-2m7: 0-0 3m+: 2-6
Track:	LH: 2-4 RH: 0-2 Tight: 0-1 Gall: 0-1
Aids:	Bl: 0-0 Vi: 0-0 Tstrap: 0-0
Best Rating:	154 4/03 Ayr 4m1f good Ch

Very useful chaser; consistent; just touched off in the Great Yorkshire Chase at Doncaster in January 2003 and ran well in the Racing Post Chase; posted a career-best effort when stepped up to four miles one to land the Scottish National; stays well; acts on most types of ground.

Ryan's Gold (IRE)
78   50
5-y-o b g Distant View (USA)-Kathleen s Dream (USA) (Last Tycoon)
B Mactaggart Appletreehall Racing Group

Placings:P00 (2764)
2002/03: 16⁸S, 16⁹GF, 20⁰GS,

	Starts	1st	2nd	3rd	Win & Pl
Hurdles	3	0	0	0	
Career Total	3	0	0	0	

Going:	Sf: 0-1 GS: 0-1 Gd: 0-0 GF: - Fm: 0-1
Distance:	2m/2m3: 0-2 2m4-2m7: 0-1 3m+: 0-0
Track:	LH: 0-1 RH: 0-2 Tight: 0-3 Gall: 0-0
Aids:	Bl: 0-0 Vi: 0-0 Tstrap: 0-0
Best Rating:	50 12/02 Muss 2m4f gd-sft Hdl

Ryders Storm (USA)
98   115d
4-y-o b/br g Dynaformer (USA)-Justicara (Rusticaro (FR))
T R George (M C Pipe 29/10) Ryder Racing Ltd

Placings:1114P (4460)
2002/03: 18¹G, 17¹G, 18¹GF, 16⁴GF, 16⁶G,

	Starts	1st	2nd	3rd	Win & Pl
Hurdles	5	3	0	0	10522
Career Total	5	3	0	0	10522
93 9/02 Font	2m2f110yE Hdl			G-F	£2926
115 9/02 Bang	2m1f	D Hdl		GD	£3997
95 8/02 Font	2m2f110yE Hdl			GD	£3010

Total win prize-money £9934

Going:	Sf: 0-0 GS: 0-0 Gd: 2-3 GF: - Fm: 1-2
Distance:	2m/2m3: 3-5 2m4-2m7: 0-0 3m+: 0-0
Track:	LH: 3-5 RH: 0-0 Tight: 3-4 Gall: 0-0
Aids:	Bl: 0-0 Vi: 0-1 Tstrap: 0-0
Best Rating:	115 9/02 Bang 2m1f good Hdl

Fair front-running juvenile hurdler, winner of his first three starts early in the season; not a fluent hurdler; acts on a sound surface.

Rydon Lane (IRE)
98   95
7-y-o br g Toca Madera-Polocracy (IRE) (Aristocracy)
Mrs S D Williams D C Coard

Placings:0/004446-4F51P (3778)
2002/03: 19⁴G, 21⁵HY, 22⁵GS, 19¹GS, 24⁵GS,

	Starts	1st	2nd	3rd	Win & Pl
Hurdles	4	1	0	0	3145
Chases	1	0	0	0	0
Career Total	12	1	0	0	3595
95 1/03 Extr	2m3f	F(0-100)HHdl		G-S	£2838

Total win prize-money £2839

Going:	Sf: 0-1 GS: 1-3 Gd: 0-1 GF: - Fm: 0-0
Distance:	2m/2m3: 1-2 2m4-2m7: 0-2 3m+: 0-1
Track:	LH: 0-1 RH: 1-4 Tight: 0-1 Gall: 0-0
Aids:	Bl: 0-0 Vi: 0-0 Tstrap: 0-0
Best Rating:	98 12/02 Winc 2m6f gd-sft Hdl

Moderate hurdler; won a handicap at Exeter in January. Stays two miles six.

Rye Rum (IRE)
83   50
12-y-o br g Strong Gale-Eimers Pet (Paddy s Stream)
J W F Aynsley J W F Aynsley

Placings:0PP/PPP/P/PPP/P2/6035/P0LPP-5PP (0619)
2002/03: 20⁵GF, 20⁰G, 25⁶GF,

	Starts	1st	2nd	3rd	Win & Pl
Chases	3	0	0	0	0
Career Total	24	0	1	1	1253

Going:	Sf: 0-0 GS: 0-0 Gd: 0-1 GF: - Fm: 0-2
Distance:	2m/2m3: 0-0 2m4-2m7: 0-2 3m+: 0-1
Track:	LH: 0-3 RH: 0-0 Tight: 0-0 Gall: 0-0
Aids:	Bl: 0-0 Vi: 0-0 Tstrap: 0-0
Best Rating:	57 6/99 Hexm 2m4f110y gd-fm Ch

Saafend Rocket (IRE)
96   83
5-y-o b/br g Distinctly North (USA)-Simple Annie (Simply Great (FR))
R Lee (Andrew Reid 5/8) Richard Lee

Placings:6F (2131)
2002/03: 16⁶GS, 16⁶G,

	Starts	1st	2nd	3rd	Win & Pl
Hurdles	2	0	0	0	0
Career Total	2	0	0	0	0

Going: Sf: 0-0 GS: 0-1 Gd: 0-1 GF: - Fm: 0-0
Distance: 2m/2m3: 0-2 2m4-2m7: 0-0 3m+: 0-0
Track: LH: 0-0 RH: 0-2 Tight: 0-0 Gall: 0-0
Aids: Bl: 0-0 Vi: 0-0 Tstrap: 0-0
Best Rating: 80 11/02 Ludl 2m good Hdl

Sabadilla (USA)
109 117
9-y-o b g Sadler s Wells (USA)-Jasmina (USA) (Forli (ARG))
Patrick Michael Verling (M R Bosley 24/1) W Coleman

Placings:05561 (4648a)
2002/03: 16⁵S, 19⁵GS, 17⁵HY, 16⁶G, 16¹F,

	Starts	1st	2nd	3rd	Win & Pl
Hurdles	5	1	0	0	7169
Career Total	5	1	0	0	7169
99	4/03 Cork 2m	(81-116)HHdl		FRM	£7168

Total win prize-money £7169

Going: Sf: 0-2 GS: 0-1 Gd: 0-1 GF: - Fm: 1-1
Distance: 2m/2m3: 1-5 2m4-2m7: 0-0 3m+: 0-0
Track: LH: 0-1 RH: 0-2 Tight: 0-0 Gall: 0-1
Aids: Bl: 0-0 Vi: 0-0 Tstrap: 0-0
Best Rating: 99 4/03 Cork 2m firm Hdl

Sabi Sand
103(94h) (81h)97
7-y-o b m Minster Son-Radical Lady (Radical)
R C Guest (N B Mason 26/12) N B Mason

Placings:00006-2014411P (4170)
2002/03: 22²GS, 23⁰G, 26¹HY, 24⁴GS, 25⁴S, 24¹S, 25¹S, 21⁹S,

	Starts	1st	2nd	3rd	Win & Pl
Hurdles	1	0	0	0	0
Chases	7	3	1	0	13920
Career Total	13	3	1	0	13920
97	3/03 Catt 3m1f110yE(0-100)HCh			SFT	£4069
94	2/03 Newc 3m E(0-110)HCh			SFT	£4400
97	11/02 Uttx 3m2f F(0-100)HCh			HVY	£3445

Total win prize-money £11915

Going: Sf: 3-5 GS: 0-2 Gd: 0-1 GF: - Fm: 0-0
Distance: 2m/2m3: 0-0 2m4-2m7: 1-3 3m+: 3-5
Track: LH: 3-5 RH: 0-3 Tight: 0-0 Gall: 1-2
Aids: Bl: 0-0 Vi: 0-0 Tstrap: 0-0
Best Rating: 97 3/03 Catt 3m1f110y soft Ch

Moderate chaser; stays well; suited by soft ground; successful at Newcastle in February and Catterick a week later.

Saby (FR)
102(89h) (86 h)114
5-y-o b/br g Sassanian (USA)-Valy Flett (FR) (Pietru (FR))
P J Hobbs Setsquare Recruitment

Placings:424022-36002 (4695)
2002/03: 17⁵S, 17⁶S, 16⁹HY, 19⁰GF, 16²G,

	Starts	1st	2nd	3rd	Win & Pl
Hurdles	4	0	0	1	765
Chases	1	0	1	0	1251
Career Total	11	0	4	1	8249

Going: Sf: 0-3 GS: 0-0 Gd: 0-1 GF: - Fm: 0-0
Distance: 2m/2m3: 0-5 2m4-2m7: 0-0 3m+: 0-0
Track: LH: 0-2 RH: 0-3 Tight: 0-3 Gall: 0-0
Aids: Bl: 0-0 Vi: 0-0 Tstrap: 0-0
Best Rating: 114 4/03 NAbb 2m110y good Ch

Selling-class hurdler, modest chaser; goes well at around two miles; acts on decent ground.

Sackville (IRE)
108 (130h)165
10-y-o b g Satco (FR)-Sackville Street (Ete Indien (USA))
Miss F M Crowley Seamus O Farrell

Placings:01 1/13123111/5221111111/131335FF-2151 (2918a)
2002/03: 20³HY, 24¹G, 24⁵HY, 22¹HY,

	Starts	1st	2nd	3rd	Win & Pl
Chases	4	2	1	0	47963
Career Total	33	18	4	5	352262
137	1/03 Tram 2m6f Ch			HVY	£10551
156	12/02 Hayd 3m A Ch			GD	£31000
162	11/01 Weth 3m1f A Ch			GD	£29000
145	5/01 Fair 2m4f Ch			GD	£34354
162	4/01 Leop 3m HCh			SH	£37500
157	4/01 Fair 2m4f Ch			SFT	£19334
143	2/01 Naas 2m4f Ch			Y-S	£15725
165	2/01 Leop 2m5f Ch			HVY	£38951
149	1/01 Naas 3m Ch			SFT	£18346
145	12/00 Fair 2m4f Ch			Y-S	£23400
137	11/00 Chel 3m110y B Ch			GD	£10530
161	4/00 Aint 3m110y A Hdl			GD	£27000
136	3/00 Navn 2m6f Hdl			YLD	£4692
126	3/00 Gowr 2m Hdl			YLD	£4416
140	1/00 Fair 2m4f Hdl			SFT	£4416
111	9/99 List 2m6f Hdl			Y-S	£6776
119	10/98 Gowr 2m4f NHF			Y-S	£4782
101	8/98 Tral 2m1f NHF			GD	£2989

Total win prize-money £323770

Going: Sf: 1-3 GS: 0-0 Gd: 1-1 GF: - Fm: 0-0
Distance: 2m/2m3: 0-0 2m4-2m7: 1-2 3m+: 1-2
Track: LH: 1-2 RH: 1-2 Tight: 0-0 Gall: 0-0
Aids: Bl: 0-0 Vi: 0-0 Tstrap: 0-0
Best Rating: 165 2/01 Leop 2m5f heavy Ch

High-class staying chaser; unbeaten as a novice in 2000/1; won the Charlie Hall Chase at Wetherby in November 2001; best ever effort to beat Bobby Grant (rec 10lb) in Tommy Whittle at Haydock in December; effective at 3m; seems to handle any ground; jumps left; possibly not suited by being rushed along in top-class company.

Sacrifice

8-y-o b g Arctic Lord-Kellyann (Jellaby)
T Long Mike Cornish

Placings:501-324313 (4678)
2002/03: 16³GF, 20²F, 16⁴GS, 20³GF, 16¹GF, 19³GF,

	Starts	1st	2nd	3rd	Win & Pl
Chases	6	1	1	3	3116
Career Total	9	2	1	3	5415
100	4/03 Hrfd 2m H Ch			G-F	£1540
85	4/02 Hrfd 2m3f H Ch			GD	£2299

Total win prize-money £3840

Going: Sf: 0-0 GS: 0-0 Gd: 0-0 GF: - Fm: 1-5
Distance: 2m/2m3: 1-4 2m4-2m7: 0-2 3m+: 0-0
Track: LH: 0-2 RH: 1-4 Tight: 0-1 Gall: 0-1
Aids: Bl: 0-0 Vi: 0-0 Tstrap: 0-0
Best Rating: 100 4/03 Hrfd 2m gd-fm Ch

Moderate hunter chaser at two to two and a half miles.

Sacundai (IRE)
121 164
6-y-o b g Hernando (FR)-Shahdiza (USA) (Blushing Groom (FR))
E J O Grady Malm Syndicate

Placings:15121255-41111 (4478)

2002/03: 20⁴YS, 20¹S, 16¹Y, 16¹Y, 20¹G,

	Starts	1st	2nd	3rd	Win & Pl
Hurdles	5	4	0	0	127264
Career Total	13	7	2	0	178218
164	4/03 Aint 2m4f A Hdl			GD	£87000
148	3/03 Limk 2m Hdl			YLD	£7688
155	2/03 Gowr 2m Hdl			YLD	£23214
138	1/03 Naas 2m4f Hdl			SFT	£8441
136	12/01 Leop 2m Hdl			YLD	£20967
105	10/01 Tipp 2m Hdl			HVY	£7862
99	5/01 Tipp 2m Hdl			G-F	£4451

Total win prize-money £159627

Going: Sf: 1-1 GS: 0-0 Gd: 1-1 GF: - Fm: 0-0
Distance: 2m/2m3: 2-2 2m4-2m7: 2-3 3m+: 0-0
Track: LH: 1-2 RH: 0-0 Tight: 1-1 Gall: 0-0
Aids: Bl: 0-0 Vi: 0-0 Tstrap: 0-0
Best Rating: 164 4/03 Aint 2m4f good Hdl

High-class Irish-trained hurdler; had luck on his side when narrowly defeating Rooster Booster in Grade One hurdle at Aintree; loves soft ground, although he did break his duck on a sound surface; stays two and a half miles.

Sad Mad Bad (USA)
102(98h) (101h)105
9-y-o b g Sunny s Halo (CAN)-Quite Attractive (USA) (Well Decorated (USA))
Mrs M Reveley P D Savill

Placings:11410/13111060/312P25/40062U32/311FP-414000PP (4557)
2002/03: 24⁴S, 25¹GS, 25⁴GS, 26⁹S, 24⁰GS, 34⁴S, 33⁶G,

	Starts	1st	2nd	3rd	Win & Pl
Hurdles	2	0	0	0	0
Chases	6	1	0	0	5630
Career Total	40	11	4	4	91820
121	11/02 Weth 3m1f D(0-125)HCh			G-S	£4615
121	11/01 Plum 3m5f C(0-130)HCh			GD	£13340
121	1/01 Uttx 3m2f E(0-115)HCh			G-S	£6500
128	1/00 Uttx 2m4f B(0-140)HCh			SFT	£23200
112	3/99 Carl 2m4f110yC Ch			SFT	£5472
124	2/99 MRas 2m4f D Ch			SFT	£4027
131	12/98 Bang 2m4f110yD Ch			G-S	£3582
104	11/98 MRas 2m4f D Ch			G-S	£4608
125	2/98 Hayd 2m C HHdl			GD	£5083
120	11/97 Newc 2m D Hdl			GD	£2841
117	11/97 MRas 2m1f110yD Hdl			GD	£2999

Total win prize-money £76269

Going: Sf: 0-4 GS: 1-3 Gd: 0-1 GF: - Fm: 0-0
Distance: 2m/2m3: 0-2 2m4-2m7: 0-0 3m+: 1-8
Track: LH: 1-7 RH: 0-1 Tight: 0-0 Gall: 0-3
Aids: Bl: 0-0 Vi: 0-3 Tstrap: 0-0
Best Rating: 131 12/98 Bang 2m4f110y gd-sft Ch

Fair chaser at his best; not the easiest of rides; stays extreme distances; victorious in the Sussex National at Plumpton in 2001; has worn a visor; acts on soft ground.

Saddler's Quest
89 77
6-y-o b g Saddlers Hall (IRE)-Seren Quest (Rainbow Quest (USA))
C P Morlock The Fairy Story Partnership

Placings:0 (3847)
2002/03: 16⁰G,

	Starts	1st	2nd	3rd	Win & Pl
Hurdles	1	0	0	0	
Career Total	1	0	0	0	

Going: Sf: 0-0 GS: 0-0 Gd: 0-1 GF: - Fm: 0-0

Saddlers Boy
75f

5-y-o b g Saddlers Hall (IRE)-Miss Poll Flinders (Swing Easy (USA))
K C Bailey Norcroft Park Stud

Placings:0 (1923)
2002/03: 12⁰GS,

	Starts	1st	2nd	3rd	Win & Pl
NH Flat	1	0	0	0	
Career Total	1	0	0	0	

Going: Sf: 0-0 GS: 0-0 Gd: 0-0 GF: - Fm: 0-0
Distance: 2m/2m3: 0-0 2m4-2m7: 0-0 3m+: 0-0
Track: LH: 0-1 RH: 0-0 Tight: 0-0 Gall: 0-0
Aids: Bl: 0-0 Vi: 0-0 Tstrap: 0-0
Best Rating: 85 11/02 Newb 1m4f110y gd-sft NHF

Sadler's Cove (FR)
84   74

5-y-o b g King s Theatre (IRE)-Mine D Or (FR) (Posse (USA))
B G Powell Gallagher Equine Ltd

Placings:000 (4561)
2002/03: 21⁰G, 19⁰GF, 20⁰GF,

	Starts	1st	2nd	3rd	Win & Pl
Hurdles	3	0	0	0	
Career Total	3	0	0	0	

Going: Sf: 0-0 GS: 0-0 Gd: 0-1 GF: - Fm: 0-2
Distance: 2m/2m3: 0-0 2m4-2m7: 0-3 3m+: 0-0
Track: LH: 0-2 RH: 0-1 Tight: 0-1 Gall: 0-1
Aids: Bl: 0-0 Vi: 0-0 Tstrap: 0-0
Best Rating: 74 4/03 Hrfd 2m3f110y gd-fm Hdl

Sadler's Realm
(82h)   (67h)98

10-y-o b g Sadler s Wells (USA)-Rensaler (USA) (Stop The Music (USA))
P J Hobbs B D Racing

Placings:02/2012111220/1403043/3321/P551-4PF (3642)
2002/03: 19⁴HY, 19⁵S, 21ᶠGS,

	Starts	1st	2nd	3rd	Win & Pl
Chases	3	0	0	0	565
Career Total	30	7	6	4	56028
131	4/02	Chep	2m3f110yD(0-125)HCh	G-S	£4085
122	2/01	Sand	2m4f110yD Ch	SFT	£4982
141	12/98	Chep	2m4f110yB(0-140)HHdl	GD	£5319
111	1/98	Extr	2m3f110yD(0-125)HHdl	HVY	£3340
115	12/97	Chep	2m110y E(0-120)HHdl	HVY	£2320
108	12/97	Extr	2m2f	F(0-105)HHdl	£2176
114	11/97	Kemp	2m	F(0-100)HHdl	G-S	£1898
			Total win prize-money £24120		

Going: Sf: 0-2 GS: 0-1 Gd: 0-0 GF: - Fm: 0-0
Distance: 2m/2m3: 0-1 2m4-2m7: 0-2 3m+: 0-0
Track: LH: 0-1 RH: 0-2 Tight: 0-1 Gall: 0-0
Aids: Bl: 0-0 Vi: 0-0 Tstrap: 0-0
Best Rating: 141 2/99 Newb 2m110y good Hdl

Moderate two and a half mile chase; acts on soft ground and a sound surface; out of form of late.

Sadler's Secret (IRE)
107   113

8-y-o b g Sadler s Wells (USA)-Athyka (USA) (Secretariat (USA))
A J Deakin (M C Pipe 4/7) A J Deakin

Placings:F42143350/013/4203330PP/0043P-30P21233204 (3744)
2002/03: 27³S, 20⁰G, 22ᴾGF, 24²F, 20¹G, 24²G, 27³S, 23³S, 24²S, 24⁰S, 26⁴G,

	Starts	1st	2nd	3rd	Win & Pl
Hurdles	11	1	3	3	9521
Career Total	37	3	5	10	22287
110	11/02	Hayd	2m4f	E(0-110)HHdl	GD	£3575
118	4/00	Tntn	2m1f	F(0-110)HHdl	G-S	£2926
107	12/98	Plum	2m1f	E Hdl	SFT	£2512
				Total win prize-money £9014	

Going: Sf: 0-5 GS: 0-1 Gd: 1-4 GF: - Fm: 0-2
Distance: 2m/2m3: 1-6 2m4-2m7: 1-3 3m+: 0-8
Track: LH: 1-6 RH: 0-0 Tight: 0-5 Gall: 0-1
Aids: Bl: 0-1 Vi: 0-1 Tstrap: 0-1
Best Rating: 124 12/00 Tntn 3m110y soft Hdl

Safari Paradise (FR)
115   116

6-y-o ch g Red Paradise-Safari Liz (USA) (Hawaii)
M C Pipe (T Civel 19/10) P Deal, J Dale, T Neill

Placings:600555640/F442505FP-U00640300 (4606)
2002/03: 21ᵁⱽS, 23⁰VS, 19⁶GS, 16⁴HY, 17⁰S, 21³G, 22⁰HY, 24⁰G,

	Starts	1st	2nd	3rd	Win & Pl
Hurdles	6	0	0	1	2866
Chases	3	0	0	0	0
Career Total	27	0	1	1	49722

Going: Sf: 0-3 GS: 0-1 Gd: 0-2 GF: - Fm: 0-0
Distance: 2m/2m3: 0-3 2m4-2m7: 0-4 3m+: 0-2
Track: LH: 0-3 RH: 0-4 Tight: 0-1 Gall: 0-2
Aids: Bl: 0-0 Vi: 0-1 Tstrap: 0-0
Best Rating: 116 2/03 Kemp 2m5f good Hdl

Fair ex-French hurdler/chaser; has shown only modest form over hurdles since coming to Britain; subject of an unsuccessful gamble when stepped up in trip in February 2003; disappointing since; seems best on soft ground.

Safe Enough (IRE)
103   97

7-y-o ch g Safety Catch (USA)-Godfreys Cross (IRE) (Fine Blade (USA))
J T Gifford D S Norden & R S Norden

Placings:00/3/4-01 (1431)
2002/03: 16⁶GF, 21¹GF,

	Starts	1st	2nd	3rd	Win & Pl
Hurdles	2	1	0	0	3445
Career Total	6	1	0	1	3906
97	10/02	Plum	2m5f	E(0-110)HHdl	G-F	£3445
				Total win prize-money £3445	

Going: Sf: 0-0 GS: 0-0 Gd: 0-0 GF: - Fm: 1-2
Distance: 2m/2m3: 0-1 2m4-2m7: 1-1 3m+: 0-0
Track: LH: 1-1 RH: 0-1 Tight: 1-1 Gall: 0-1
Aids: Bl: 0-0 Vi: 0-0 Tstrap: 0-0
Best Rating: 101 10/00 Chep 2m110y gd-sft Hdl

Modest hurdler, stays two miles-five, acts on fast ground.

Safe Shot
76   43

4-y-o b g Salse (USA)-Optaria (Song)
Mrs J C McGregor (Mrs D Thomson 16/9) The Boozers Brigade

Placings:000 (4749)
2002/03: 16⁹G, 17⁰GS, 20⁰G,

	Starts	1st	2nd	3rd	Win & Pl
Hurdles	3	0	0	0	
Career Total	3	0	0	0	

Going: Sf: 0-0 GS: 0-1 Gd: 0-2 GF: - Fm: 0-0
Distance: 2m/2m3: 0-2 2m4-2m7: 0-1 3m+: 0-0
Track: LH: 0-0 RH: 0-3 Tight: 0-1 Gall: 0-0
Aids: Bl: 0-0 Vi: 0-0 Tstrap: 0-0
Best Rating: 43 2/03 Muss 2m good Hdl

Saffron Sun
107(104h)   (106h)113

8-y-o b g Landyap (USA)-Saffron Bun (Sit In The Corner (USA))
J D Frost Mrs J F Bury

Placings:000/3F005/01432613-60P124F (4779)
2002/03: 23⁶GS, 19⁰GS, 24²S, 23¹G, 23²F, 21⁴G, 20ᶠGF,

	Starts	1st	2nd	3rd	Win & Pl
Chases	7	1	1	0	9275
Career Total	23	3	2	3	17057
113	3/03	Extr	2m7f110yD(0-110)HCh	GD	£5954
104	4/02	Extr	2m1f	E Hdl	FRM	£3066
92	6/01	NAbb	2m1f	F(0-100)HHdl	GD	£2667
				Total win prize-money £11687	

Going: Sf: 0-1 GS: 0-1 Gd: 1-3 GF: - Fm: 0-2
Distance: 2m/2m3: 0-0 2m4-2m7: 0-0 3m+: 1-4
Track: LH: 0-1 RH: 1-6 Tight: 0-1 Gall: 0-1
Aids: Bl: 0-0 Vi: 0-0 Tstrap: 0-0
Best Rating: 113 3/03 Extr 2m7f110y good Ch

Modest novice chaser; stays three miles and suited by fast ground.

Safi

8-y-o b g Generous (IRE)-Jasarah (IRE) (Green Desert (USA))
D McCain D McCain

Placings:PP/335003104/0204524U6/0-60 (1546)
2002/03: 16⁶GS, 19⁰F,

	Starts	1st	2nd	3rd	Win & Pl
Hurdles	2	0	0	0	
Career Total	23	1	2	3	4720
92	12/99	Donc	2m110y G Hdl	G-F	£1864
				Total win prize-money £1864	

Going: Sf: 0-0 GS: 0-0 Gd: 0-0 GF: - Fm: 0-2
Distance: 2m/2m3: 0-1 2m4-2m7: 0-1 3m+: 0-0
Track: LH: 0-1 RH: 0-1 Tight: 0-1 Gall: 0-0
Aids: Bl: 0-1 Vi: 0-0 Tstrap: 0-2
Best Rating: 92 5/00 Hrfd 2m3f110y good Hdl

Hunter chaser; has been let down by his jumping.

Saga Royale (FR)
88   77

7-y-o b m Garde Royale-Passionnante (FR) (Dike (USA))
D C O Brien Mrs V O Brien

Placings:644/06/40004-5R (4186)
2002/03: 21⁵S, 17ᴿG,

	Starts	1st	2nd	3rd	Win & Pl
Hurdles	2	0	0	0	0
Career Total	12	0	0	0	273

Going: Sf: 0-1 GS: 0-0 Gd: 0-1 GF: - Fm: 0-0
Distance: 2m/2m3: 0-1 2m4-2m7: 0-1 3m+: 0-0
Track: LH: 0-1 RH: 0-1 Tight: 0-2 Gall: 0-0
Aids: Bl: 0-0 Vi: 0-0 Tstrap: 0-0
Best Rating: 77 2/03 Plum 2m5f soft Hdl

Sage Dancer (USA)
94(105h) (105h)99
6-y-o b g Green Dancer (USA)-Sophonisbe (Wollow)
C Grant (D K Weld 22/8) C E Whiteley

Placings:0/2154P (4257)
2002/03: 16²GY, 16¹G, 16⁵GF, 17⁴GS, 16⁶G,

	Starts	1st	2nd	3rd	Win & Pl
Hurdles	3	1	1	0	7595
Chases	2	0	0	0	615
Career Total	6	1	1	0	8210
94 8/02 Cork 2m		Hdl		GD	£5926

Total win prize-money £5926

Going: Sf: 0-0 GS: 0-1 Gd: 1-2 GF: - Fm: 0-1
Distance: 2m/2m3: 1-5 2m4-2m7: 0-0 3m+: 0-0
Track: LH: 0-3 RH: 0-0 Tight: 0-2 Gall: 0-0
Aids: Bl: 0-0 Vi: 0-0 Tstrap: 0-0
Best Rating: 105 8/02 Tipp 2m gd-fm Hdl

Sahem (IRE)
99 97
6-y-o b g Sadler s Wells (USA)-Sumava (IRE) (Sure Blade (USA))
D Eddy Robert Gray

Placings:22142460 (2420)
2002/03: 16²G, 16²GF, 17¹GF, 16⁴GF, 22²S, 20⁴S, 16⁶GS, 21⁰S,

	Starts	1st	2nd	3rd	Win & Pl
NH Flat	4	1	2	0	2734
Hurdles	4	0	1	0	1104
Career Total	8	1	3	0	3838
97 7/02 Sedg 2m1f		H NHF		G-F	£1841

Total win prize-money £1841

Going: Sf: 0-3 GS: 0-1 Gd: 0-1 GF: - Fm: 1-3
Distance: 2m/2m3: 1-2 2m4-2m7: 0-3 3m+: 0-0
Track: LH: 1-7 RH: 0-1 Tight: 1-3 Gall: 0-2
Aids: Bl: 0-0 Vi: 0-0 Tstrap: 0-0
Best Rating: 97 11/02 Newc 2m4f soft Hdl

Bumper winner, has been placed over hurdles.

Sahhar
101 87
10-y-o ch g Sayf El Arab (USA)-Native Magic (Be My Native (USA))
B D Leavy Mrs Margaret Underwood

Placings:4/6F/0126340/6/510/03-260465 (4706)
2002/03: 16²G, 16⁶G, 16⁹S, 19⁴G, 16⁶G, 20⁵G,

	Starts	1st	2nd	3rd	Win & Pl
Hurdles	6	0	1	0	790
Career Total	22	2	2	2	5846
91 11/00 Ludl 2m		G Hdl		GD	£1981
88 8/98 Worc 2m		G(0-95)HHdl		G-F	£1744

Total win prize-money £3725

Going: Sf: 0-1 GS: 0-0 Gd: 0-5 GF: - Fm: 0-0
Distance: 2m/2m3: 0-5 2m4-2m7: 0-1 3m+: 0-0
Track: LH: 0-4 RH: 0-2 Tight: 0-2 Gall: 0-0
Aids: Bl: 0-0 Vi: 0-0 Tstrap: 0-0
Best Rating: 91 6/01 Worc 2m gd-fm Hdl

Selling plater over hurdles.

Saidai (IRE)
86f 74f
5-y-o b g Roselier (FR)-V Soske Gale (IRE) (Strong Gale)
Jonjo O Neill Mrs M C Sweeney

Placings:6 (3789)
2002/03: 17⁶G,

	Starts	1st	2nd	3rd	Win & Pl
NH Flat	1	0	0	0	0
Career Total	1	0	0	0	0

Going: Sf: 0-0 GS: 0-0 Gd: 0-1 GF: - Fm: 0-0
Distance: 2m/2m3: 0-1 2m4-2m7: 0-0 3m+: 0-0
Track: LH: 0-0 RH: 0-1 Tight: 0-0 Gall: 0-0
Aids: Bl: 0-0 Vi: 0-0 Tstrap: 0-0
Best Rating: 77 2/03 Hrfd 2m1f good NHF

Chasing-type, well beaten on debut in bumper at Hereford in February.

Sailor Jack (USA)
94 96
7-y-o b g Green Dancer (USA)-Chateaubrook (USA) (Alleged (USA))
D McCain D McCain

Placings:66136/4056/122-54 (0894)
2002/03: 21⁵GF, 20⁴S,

	Starts	1st	2nd	3rd	Win & Pl
Hurdles	2	0	0	0	375
Career Total	14	2	2	1	5496
92 5/01 Tntn 2m3f110y H		G(0-100)HHdl		FRM	£1785
82 1/00 Catt 2m		G Hdl		GD	£1708

Total win prize-money £3494

Going: Sf: 0-1 GS: 0-0 Gd: 0-0 GF: - Fm: 0-1
Distance: 2m/2m3: 0-0 2m4-2m7: 0-2 3m+: 0-0
Track: LH: 0-2 RH: 0-1 Tight: 0-2 Gall: 0-0
Aids: Bl: 0-1 Vi: 0-0 Tstrap: 0-0
Best Rating: 96 6/01 Prth 3m110y firm Hdl

Saint Joseph
101
13-y-o ch g Lir-Kimberley Ann (St Columbus)
Miss S Young B R J Young

Placings:2/6432/05114/1B4/0634-P (0039)
2002/03: 19⁰G,

	Starts	1st	2nd	3rd	Win & Pl
Chases	1	0	0	0	
Career Total	18	3	2	2	10866
110 3/01 Extr 2m3f110yH Ch				HVY	£2271
100 4/00 Tntn 3m		H Ch		G-S	£2891
94 3/00 Tntn 3m		H Ch		SFT	£3003

Total win prize-money £8166

Going: Sf: 0-0 GS: 0-0 Gd: 0-1 GF: - Fm: 0-0
Distance: 2m/2m3: 0-0 2m4-2m7: 0-1 3m+: 0-0
Track: LH: 0-0 RH: 0-1 Tight: 0-0 Gall: 0-0
Aids: Bl: 0-0 Vi: 0-0 Tstrap: 0-0
Best Rating: 110 3/01 Extr 2m3f110y heavy Ch

Saint Par (FR)
112(103h) (118h)112
5-y-o gr g Saint Preuil (FR)-Paris Or (FR) (Noir Et Or)
P F Nicholls Prd Holdings Limited

Placings:454/233433111-P044243 (4696)
2002/03: 20⁰G, 20⁰S, 20⁴S, 19⁴GS, 21²S, 24⁴G, 26³G,

	Starts	1st	2nd	3rd	Win & Pl
Hurdles	2	0	0	0	0
Chases	5	0	1	1	3466
Career Total	19	3	2	5	33243
118 4/02 Ayr 2m		C Hdl		GD	£5180
111 3/02 Uttx 2m		D Hdl		HVY	£3445
100 3/02 Chep 2m4f		D Hdl		G-S	£3552

Total win prize-money £12178

Going: Sf: 0-3 GS: 0-1 Gd: 0-3 GF: - Fm: 0-0
Distance: 2m/2m3: 0-0 2m4-2m7: 0-5 3m+: 0-2
Track: LH: 0-4 RH: 0-3 Tight: 0-3 Gall: 0-0
Aids: Bl: 0-4 Vi: 0-0 Tstrap: 0-0
Best Rating: 118 4/02 Ayr 2m good Hdl

Ex-French; modest novice chaser; stays two and a half miles; acts well in the mud; has worn blinkers.

Saint Romble (FR)
110 100
6-y-o b g Sassanian (USA)-Limatge (FR) (Trac)
P J Hobbs M G St Quinton

Placings:1/0064-P2123P4 (4327)
2002/03: 21⁰GF, 16²GS, 19²S, 16³G, 18⁴S, 18⁴G,

	Starts	1st	2nd	3rd	Win & Pl
Chases	7	1	2	1	10657
Career Total	12	2	2	1	20764
100 12/02 Asct 2m		D(0-110)HCh		G-S	£6776
4/01 Engh 2m110y		Hdl		HVY	£9699

Total win prize-money £16475

Going: Sf: 0-2 GS: 1-1 Gd: 0-3 GF: - Fm: 0-1
Distance: 2m/2m3: 1-6 2m4-2m7: 0-1 3m+: 0-0
Track: LH: 0-2 RH: 1-4 Tight: 0-3 Gall: 0-1
Aids: Bl: 0-0 Vi: 0-0 Tstrap: 0-0
Best Rating: 100 12/02 Asct 2m gd-sft Ch

Modest chaser; flattered by winning distance when scoring at Ascot in December 2002; probably a lucky winner of Class F classified chase at Worcester May 2003; effective at two to two and a half miles; acts on good and soft ground.

Saintsaire (FR)
103 125
4-y-o b g Apeldoorn (FR)-Pro Wonder (FR) (The Wonder (FR))
N J Henderson (P Lefevre 24/5) Anthony Speelman

Placings:1350 (4130)
2002/03: 16¹G, 17³GS, 16⁵G, 17⁰G,

	Starts	1st	2nd	3rd	Win & Pl
Hurdles	4	1	0	1	8145
Career Total	4	1	0	1	8145
122 12/02 Newb 2m110y		D Hdl		GD	£4095

Total win prize-money £4095

Going: Sf: 0-0 GS: 0-1 Gd: 1-3 GF: - Fm: 0-0
Distance: 2m/2m3: 1-4 2m4-2m7: 0-0 3m+: 0-0
Track: LH: 1-3 RH: 0-1 Tight: 0-0 Gall: 1-3
Aids: Bl: 0-0 Vi: 0-0 Tstrap: 0-0
Best Rating: 125 1/03 Chel 2m1f gd-sft Hdl

Useful juvenile hurdler; winner on the Flat in France; created a very good impression on debut at Newbury; held in better races subsequently; acts in good and soft ground.

Saitensohn (GER)

115   **131**

5-y-o b/br h Monsun (GER)-Saite (GER) (Marduk (GER))
Jonjo O Neill (C Von Der Recke 1/2) Harold A Via Jr

Placings:521110   (4109)
2002/03: 17⁵S, 17²S, 19¹GS, 21¹S, 22¹HY, 21⁰G,

	Starts	1st	2nd	3rd	Win & Pl
Hurdles	4	3	0		17443
Chases	2	0	1	0	3497
Career Total	6	3	1	0	20940
115 2/03 Sand 2m6f	C Hdl			HVY	£6438
128 11/02 Newb 2m3f	C Hdl			SFT	£6844
123 11/02 Newb 2m3f	D Hdl			G-S	£4160

Total win prize-money £17443

Going:	Sf: 2-4 GS: 1-1 Gd: 0-1 GF: - Fm: 0-0
Distance:	2m/2m3: 1-3 2m4-2m7: 2-3 3m+: 0-0
Track:	LH: 2-3 RH: 1-1 Tight: 0-0 Gall: 2-3
Aids:	Bl: 0-0 Vi: 0-0 Tstrap: 0-0
Best Rating:	128 11/02 Newb 2m5f soft Hdl

Useful former German-trained novice hurdler, beaten in a couple of chases in Germany; won on all three visits to Britain before joining his current handler; stays two miles six; acts well on soft ground.

Salaman (FR)

100   **66**

11-y-o b g Saumarez-Merry Sharp (Sharpen Up)
D C O Brien D C O Brien

Placings:03/60412P/P045/252004/404/05P500-564PP32   (4465)
2002/03: 27⁵GF, 22⁶GF, 22⁴GS, 22⁸HY, 22⁸S, 28³G, 24²F,

	Starts	1st	2nd	3rd	Win & Pl
Hurdles	7	0	1	1	1237
Career Total	34	1	1	2	6031
97 2/98 Folk	2m6f110yE(0-115)HHdl	G-F	£2427

Total win prize-money £2427

Going:	Sf: 0-2 GS: 0-1 Gd: 0-1 GF: - Fm: 0-3
Distance:	2m/2m3: 0-0 2m4-2m7: 0-4 3m+: 0-3
Track:	LH: 0-2 RH: 0-4 Tight: 0-7 Gall: 0-0
Aids:	Bl: 0-0 Vi: 0-5 Tstrap: 0-5
Best Rating:	97 3/99 Folk 2m6f110y gd-sft Hdl

Plating-class hurdler; without a win since February 1998; stays 2m 6f and best on fast ground.

Saler Sal

6-y-o ch m Primitive Rising (USA)-Portonia (Ascertain (USA))
P D Niven (Jonjo O Neill 12/6) C D Carr

Placings:PPP   (1372)
2002/03: 24⁸GF, 21⁸G, 21⁸GF,

	Starts	1st	2nd	3rd	Win & Pl
Hurdles	2	0	0	0	0
Chases	1	0	0	0	0
Career Total	3	0	0		0

Going:	Sf: 0-0 GS: 0-0 Gd: 0-1 GF: - Fm: 0-2
Distance:	2m/2m3: 0-0 2m4-2m7: 0-2 3m+: 0-1
Track:	LH: 0-2 RH: 0-1 Tight: 0-2 Gall: 0-0
Aids:	Bl: 0-0 Vi: 0-0 Tstrap: 0-0
Best Rating:	0 10/02 Sedg 2m5f gd-fm Ch

No signs of ability to date.

Salford

106   **94**

8-y-o ch g Salse (USA)-Bustellina (Busted)
N J Hawke Mrs D A Wetherall

Placings:PP/02/51F1P030/**P1PP**-U4P122   (4627)
2002/03: 22ᵁGS, 24⁴G, 24⁸HY, 21¹GF, 25²GF, 21²GF,

	Starts	1st	2nd	3rd	Win & Pl
Hurdles	1	0	0	0	0
Chases	5	1	2	0	6640
Career Total	22	4	3	1	17942
94 3/03 Winc 2m5f	E(0-110)HCh	G-F	£3900
94 5/01 Winc 2m5f	F(0-100)HCh	G-F	£4160
99 12/00 Ludl 2m5f	E(0-105)HHdl	SFT	£2891
83 10/00 Extr 2m3f	E(0-115)HHdl	GD	£3198

Total win prize-money £14149

Going:	Sf: 0-1 GS: 0-1 Gd: 0-1 GF: - Fm: 1-3
Distance:	2m/2m3: 0-0 2m4-2m7: 1-3 3m+: 0-3
Track:	LH: 0-1 RH: 1-5 Tight: 0-2 Gall: 0-1
Aids:	Bl: 0-0 Vi: 0-0 Tstrap: 0-0
Best Rating:	99 12/00 Ludl 2m5f soft Hdl

Moderate handicap chaser; best around two and a half miles; suited by fast ground.

Salgrado (NZ)

85   **72**

7-y-o ch g Prince Salieri (AUS)-Musing (Music Maestro)
Jonjo O Neill Ray & Sue Dodd Partnership

Placings:00   (4328)
2002/03: 16⁹S, 16⁹G,

	Starts	1st	2nd	3rd	Win & Pl
Hurdles	2	0	0	0	
Career Total	2	0	0	0	

Going:	Sf: 0-1 GS: 0-0 Gd: 0-1 GF: - Fm: 0-0
Distance:	2m/2m3: 0-2 2m4-2m7: 0-0 3m+: 0-0
Track:	LH: 0-2 RH: 0-0 Tight: 0-0 Gall: 0-2
Aids:	Bl: 0-0 Vi: 0-0 Tstrap: 0-0
Best Rating:	72 3/03 Newb 2m110y good Hdl

Salhood

106f   **99+f**

4-y-o b g Capote (USA)-Princess Haifa (USA) (Mr Prospector (USA))
S Gollings J B Webb

Placings:20   (4481)
2002/03: 16²GF, 17⁰G,

	Starts	1st	2nd	3rd	Win & Pl
NH Flat	2	0	1	0	562
Career Total	2	0	1	0	562

Going:	Sf: 0-0 GS: 0-0 Gd: 0-1 GF: - Fm: 0-1
Distance:	2m/2m3: 0-2 2m4-2m7: 0-0 3m+: 0-0
Track:	LH: 0-1 RH: 0-0 Tight: 0-1 Gall: 0-0
Aids:	Bl: 0-0 Vi: 0-0 Tstrap: 0-0
Best Rating:	98 3/03 Sthl 2m gd-fm NHF

Bought out of Marcus Tregoning s stable for 11,000 gns; won seven runner Chepstow bumper third start; acts on fast ground.

Salient Point (IRE)

6-y-o gr m Sri Pekan (USA)-Tajarib (IRE) (Last Tycoon)
Mrs K M Lamb Mrs K M Lamb

Placings:P   (0158)
2002/03: 16⁸G,

	Starts	1st	2nd	3rd	Win & Pl
Hurdles	1	0	0	0	
Career Total	1	0	0	0	

Salierious (NZ)

94   **70**

8-y-o ch g Prince Salieri (AUS)-Analaw (NZ) (Diplomatic Agent (USA))
J C Tuck The Lammas Partnership

Placings:360/00P/062666-0PP00   (0840)
2002/03: 20⁰G, 21²G, 22⁸GF, 16⁹GF, 19⁰GF,

	Starts	1st	2nd	3rd	Win & Pl
Hurdles	5	0	0	0	
Career Total	17	0	1	1	786

Going:	Sf: 0-0 GS: 0-0 Gd: 0-2 GF: - Fm: 0-3
Distance:	2m/2m3: 0-2 2m4-2m7: 0-3 3m+: 0-0
Track:	LH: 0-4 RH: 0-1 Tight: 0-2 Gall: 0-1
Aids:	Bl: 0-0 Vi: 0-3 Tstrap: 0-0
Best Rating:	103 10/99 Tntn 2m1f gd-fm NHF

Salim

70   **56**

6-y-o b g Salse (USA)-Moviegoer (Pharly (FR))
J E Long J F Reeves

Placings:0P   (2728)
2002/03: 17⁰HY, 16⁸PHY,

	Starts	1st	2nd	3rd	Win & Pl
Hurdles	2	0	0	0	
Career Total	2	0	0	0	

Going:	Sf: 0-2 GS: 0-0 Gd: 0-0 GF: - Fm: 0-0
Distance:	2m/2m3: 0-2 2m4-2m7: 0-0 3m+: 0-0
Track:	LH: 0-0 RH: 0-2 Tight: 0-1 Gall: 0-0
Aids:	Bl: 0-0 Vi: 0-0 Tstrap: 0-0
Best Rating:	0 12/02 Leic 2m heavy Hdl

Salix Bay

89   **56**

7-y-o b g Karinga Bay-Willow Gale (Strong Gale)
P Butler John Plackett

Placings:660   (3821)
2002/03: 20⁶S, 21⁶S, 23⁰GS,

	Starts	1st	2nd	3rd	Win & Pl
Hurdles	1	0	0	0	0
Chases	2	0	0	0	0
Career Total	3	0	0	0	0

Going:	Sf: 0-2 GS: 0-1 Gd: 0-0 GF: - Fm: 0-0
Distance:	2m/2m3: 0-0 2m4-2m7: 0-2 3m+: 0-1
Track:	LH: 0-1 RH: 0-2 Tight: 0-1 Gall: 0-0
Aids:	Bl: 0-0 Vi: 0-0 Tstrap: 0-0
Best Rating:	56 2/03 Folk 2m5f soft Ch

Salix Dancer

80   **101**

6-y-o b g Shareef Dancer (USA)-Willowbank (Gay Fandango (USA))
H J Collingridge The Hamilton Partnership

Placings:03-3   (2016)
2002/03: 16³HY,

	Starts	1st	2nd	3rd	Win & Pl
Hurdles	1	0	0	1	547
Career Total	3	0	0	2	941

Going: Sf: 0-1 GS: 0-0 Gd: 0-0 GF: - Fm: 0-0
Distance: 2m/2m3: 0-1 2m4-2m7: 0-0 3m+: 0-0
Track: LH: 0-0 RH: 0-1 Tight: 0-0 Gall: 0-0
Aids: Bl: 0-0 Vi: 0-0 Tstrap: 0-0
Best Rating: 101 3/02 Hntg 2m110y   gd-fm Hdl

Modest level of form over hurdles and an unlikely improver.

Salliemak

75f   **47f**

5-y-o b m Makbul-Glenbrook Fort (Fort Nayef)
A J Wilson Tim Leadbeater

Placings:0   (2117)
2002/03: 17⁰G,

	Starts	1st	2nd	3rd	Win & Pl
NH Flat	1	0	0	0	
Career Total	1	0	0	0	

Going: Sf: 0-0 GS: 0-0 Gd: 0-1 GF: - Fm: 0-0
Distance: 2m/2m3: 0-1 2m4-2m7: 0-0 3m+: 0-0
Track: LH: 0-0 RH: 0-0 Tight: 0-0 Gall: 0-0
Aids: Bl: 0-0 Vi: 0-0 Tstrap: 0-0
Best Rating: 48 11/02 Aint 2m1f   good NHF

Sally Scally

11-y-o ch m Scallywag-Petite Cone (Celtic Cone)
Miss T Jackson H L Thompson

Placings:3⁴40666620P/6460/PPP/6/2-3P4   (4592)
2002/03: 21³GF, 27⁸S, 25⁴G,

	Starts	1st	2nd	3rd	Win & Pl
Chases	3	0	0	1	330
Career Total	22	0	2	2	1873

Going: Sf: 0-1 GS: 0-0 Gd: 0-1 GF: - Fm: 0-1
Distance: 2m/2m3: 0-0 2m4-2m7: 0-1 3m+: 0-2
Track: LH: 0-3 RH: 0-0 Tight: 0-2 Gall: 0-0
Aids: Bl: 0-0 Vi: 0-0 Tstrap: 0-0
Best Rating: 120 2/98 Winc 2m   gd-fm Hdl

Modest hunter chaser, looks best at around two miles-five. Acts on a sound surface.

Sally's Pride

81f   **78f**

6-y-o gr m Norton Challenger-Another Scally (Scallywag)
Mrs H Dalton F A Dickinson

Placings:6   (2505)
2002/03: 16⁶GS,

	Starts	1st	2nd	3rd	Win & Pl
NH Flat	1	0	0	0	
Career Total	1	0	0	0	

Going: Sf: 0-0 GS: 0-1 Gd: 0-0 GF: - Fm: 0-0
Distance: 2m/2m3: 0-1 2m4-2m7: 0-0 3m+: 0-0
Track: LH: 0-1 RH: 0-0 Tight: 0-0 Gall: 0-0
Aids: Bl: 0-0 Vi: 0-0 Tstrap: 0-0
Best Rating: 78 12/02 Fknm 2m   gd-sft NHF

Sally's Twins

105(99c)   (70c)**70**

10-y-o b m Dowsing (USA)-Bird Of Love (Ela-Mana-Mou)
A R Dicken D W Shaw

Placings:364/3660/P/644PP3-005P3222F06204   (3811)
2002/03: 21⁰GF, 21⁰G, 21⁵G, 21³PG, 24³GF, 24²GF, 25²G, 20²HY, 21⁶S, 24⁰HY, 20⁶G, 21³HY, 24⁰G, 25⁴G,

	Starts	1st	2nd	3rd	Win & Pl
Hurdles	9	0	2	1	2398
Chases	5	0	2	0	2164
Career Total	28	0	4	4	7621

Going: Sf: 0-4 GS: 0-0 Gd: 0-7 GF: - Fm: 0-3
Distance: 2m/2m3: 0-0 2m4-2m7: 0-8 3m+: 0-6
Track: LH: 0-11 RH: 0-3 Tight: 0-8 Gall: 0-0
Aids: Bl: 0-0 Vi: 0-0 Tstrap: 0-0
Best Rating: 101 12/96 Ling 2m110y   gd-sft Hdl

Plating class hurdler/chaser.

Salmon Ladder (USA)

112   **100**

11-y-o b h Bering-Ballerina Princess (USA) (Mr Prospector (USA))
A J Martin Nicholas Butterly

Placings:0400/320-3502   (4749)
2002/03: 18³S, 20⁵S, 16⁰Y, 20²G,

	Starts	1st	2nd	3rd	Win & Pl
Hurdles	4	0	1	1	2350
Career Total	11	0	2	2	4141

Going: Sf: 0-2 GS: 0-0 Gd: 0-1 GF: - Fm: 0-0
Distance: 2m/2m3: 0-2 2m4-2m7: 0-2 3m+: 0-0
Track: LH: 0-1 RH: 0-2 Tight: 0-0 Gall: 0-0
Aids: Bl: 0-0 Vi: 0-0 Tstrap: 0-0
Best Rating: 110 6/01 Tral 2m1f   gd-fm Hdl

Moderate hurdler; smart Flat horse in England in his prime; now trained in Ireland; runner-up at Perth in April and June; acts on good ground; stays two and a half miles.

Saloup

78   **87**

5-y-o b m Wolfhound (USA)-Sarcita (Primo Dominie)
O Sherwood Raymond Tooth

Placings:642-0   (0333)
2002/03: 16⁰G,

	Starts	1st	2nd	3rd	Win & Pl
Hurdles	1	0	0	0	
Career Total	4	0	1	0	1163

Going: Sf: 0-0 GS: 0-0 Gd: 0-1 GF: - Fm: 0-0
Distance: 2m/2m3: 0-0 2m4-2m7: 0-0 3m+: 0-0
Track: LH: 0-1 RH: 0-0 Tight: 0-0 Gall: 0-0
Aids: Bl: 0-0 Vi: 0-0 Tstrap: 0-0
Best Rating: 87 4/02 Ludl 2m   gd-fm Hdl

Stayed on quite nicely on her third run over hurdles.

Salt Hill King

83   **66**

6-y-o b g Rakaposhi King-Domtony (Martinmas)
Ferdy Murphy Peter Botham

Placings:0P-00   (3120)
2002/03: 19⁰GS, 20⁵S,

	Starts	1st	2nd	3rd	Win & Pl
Hurdles	2	0	0	0	
Career Total	4	0	0	0	

Going: Sf: 0-1 GS: 0-1 Gd: 0-0 GF: - Fm: 0-0
Distance: 2m/2m3: 0-0 2m4-2m7: 0-2 3m+: 0-0
Track: LH: 0-0 RH: 0-2 Tight: 0-1 Gall: 0-1
Aids: Bl: 0-0 Vi: 0-0 Tstrap: 0-0
Best Rating: 66 12/02 MRas 2m3f110y   gd-sft Hdl

Saltis (IRE)

82(94c)   (75c)**37**

11-y-o ch g Salt Dome (USA)-Mrs Tittlemouse (Nonoalco (USA))
Mrs Jane Galpin Mrs Jane Galpin

Placings:03320303/4354/0550F4/1-06U00P   (0902)
2002/03: 16⁵GF, 21⁶GF, 16⁴UGF, 20⁸GS, 20⁸GF, 20⁸PG,

	Starts	1st	2nd	3rd	Win & Pl
Hurdles	2	0	0	0	0
Chases	4	0	0	0	0
Career Total	25	1	1	5	4584
75	4/02	Hrfd	2m	H Ch	G-F £1907

Total win prize-money £1908

Going: Sf: 0-0 GS: 0-1 Gd: 0-1 GF: - Fm: 0-4
Distance: 2m/2m3: 0-2 2m4-2m7: 0-4 3m+: 0-0
Track: LH: 0-5 RH: 0-1 Tight: 0-1 Gall: 0-1
Aids: Bl: 0-1 Vi: 0-0 Tstrap: 0-0
Best Rating: 79 4/97 Ludl 2m5f110y   gd-fm Hdl

Acts on the top of the ground and won a two-mile hunter chase in April 2002. Probably best at around two and a half miles.

Salton Mare (IRE)

72f   **36f**

5-y-o b m Houmayoun (FR)-Cygnet Wood (IRE) (Toca Madera)
A J Lockwood John L Holdroyd

Placings:6   (0833)
2002/03: 17⁶GF,

	Starts	1st	2nd	3rd	Win & Pl
NH Flat	1	0	0	0	0
Career Total	1	0	0	0	0

Going: Sf: 0-0 GS: 0-0 Gd: 0-0 GF: - Fm: 0-1
Distance: 2m/2m3: 0-1 2m4-2m7: 0-0 3m+: 0-0
Track: LH: 0-1 RH: 0-0 Tight: 0-1 Gall: 0-0
Aids: Bl: 0-0 Vi: 0-0 Tstrap: 0-0
Best Rating: 36 7/02 Sedg 2m1f   gd-fm NHF

Salvage

98(101h)   (100h)**97**

8-y-o b g Kahyasi-Storm Weaver (USA) (Storm Bird (CAN))
Mrs J C McGregor (Mrs D Thomson 16/5) Mrs E R Sneddon

Placings:031/33/254P23B4/344P535-P3056425   (4773)
2002/03: 18⁸GS, 16³GF, 16⁰HY, 17⁵GS, 20⁶GS, 20⁴G, 16²G, 20⁵G,

	Starts	1st	2nd	3rd	Win & Pl
Hurdles	2	0	0	0	0
Chases	6	0	1	1	3909
Career Total	28	1	3	7	13131

93 4/99 Carl 2m1f E Hdl GD £2612
Total win prize-money £2612

Going: Sf: 0-1 GS: 0-3 Gd: 0-3 GF: - Fm: 0-1
Distance: 2m/2m3: 0-5 2m4-2m7: 0-3 3m+: 0-0
Track: LH: 0-4 RH: 0-4 Tight: 0-2 Gall: 0-2
Aids: Bl: 0-0 Vi: 0-0 Tstrap: 0-0
Best Rating: 105 9/00 Prth 2m110y heavy Hdl

Plating-class hurdler/chaser; suited by fast ground.

Sam Adamson
108(95h)   (63h)93+
8-y-o br g Domitor (USA)-Sardine (Saritamer (USA))
J W Mullins M Jenkins

Placings:600/000P0/45   (4641)
2002/03: 19[4]GF, 19[5]GF,

	Starts	1st	2nd	3rd	Win & Pl
Hurdles	2	0	0	0	295
Career Total	10	0	0	0	295

Going: Sf: 0-0 GS: 0-0 Gd: 0-0 GF: - Fm: 0-2
Distance: 2m/2m3: 0-2 2m4-2m7: 0-0 3m+: 0-0
Track: LH: 0-1 RH: 0-1 Tight: 0-1 Gall: 0-0
Aids: Bl: 0-0 Vi: 0-0 Tstrap: 0-0
Best Rating: 81 11/00 Wwck 2m soft Hdl

Plating-class chaser; stays two miles five; acts on good to firm.

Sam Quale (IRE)
96   123
11-y-o ch g Tale Quale-Samanthabrownthorn (Mandalus)
B Ellison E J Berry

Placings:0/1241UP/U1FF504-6P3   (0357)
2002/03: 25[6]GS, 24[4]G, 20[3]GS,

	Starts	1st	2nd	3rd	Win & Pl
Chases	3	0	0	1	647
Career Total	17	3	1	1	13797

123 12/01 MRas 2m6f110yF(0-110)HCh SFT £4208
123 2/01 Newc 2m4f E Ch HVY £3620
105 10/00 Sthl 3m110y E Ch SFT £3612
Total win prize-money £11441

Going: Sf: 0-0 GS: 0-2 Gd: 0-1 GF: - Fm: 0-0
Distance: 2m/2m3: 0-0 2m4-2m7: 0-1 3m+: 0-2
Track: LH: 0-3 RH: 0-0 Tight: 0-3 Gall: 0-0
Aids: Bl: 0-0 Vi: 0-2 Tstrap: 0-0
Best Rating: 123 12/01 MRas 2m6f110y soft Ch

Soft-ground handicap chaser. Stays two and three-quarter miles.

Sam Rockett
101   92
10-y-o b g Petong-Art Deco (Artaius (USA))
P J Hobbs L G Kennard

Placings:600100/2114126/3P/F00040/6054552114/004012 4-4053   (0870)
2002/03: 22[4]G, 22[9]G, 27[5]GF, 27[3]GF,

	Starts	1st	2nd	3rd	Win & Pl
Hurdles	4	0	0	1	419
Career Total	42	7	4	2	20755

92 8/01 NAbb 3m3f F(0-105)HHdl GD £2961
91 9/00 Hrfd 3m2f E(0-115)HHdl G-F £3090

90 8/00 Font 2m4f F(0-100)HHdl G-F £2289
104 11/97 NAbb 2m1f E(0-110)HHdl G-F £2253
91 9/97 NAbb 2m1f G Hdl GD £1784
100 8/97 NAbb 2m1f G(0-95)HHdl G-F £1860
82 1/97 Tntn 2m1f G Hdl G-F £1857
Total win prize-money £16098

Going: Sf: 0-0 GS: 0-0 Gd: 0-2 GF: - Fm: 0-2
Distance: 2m/2m3: 0-0 2m4-2m7: 0-2 3m+: 0-2
Track: LH: 0-4 RH: 0-0 Tight: 0-4 Gall: 0-0
Aids: Bl: 0-4 Vi: 0-0 Tstrap: 0-0
Best Rating: 104 11/97 NAbb 2m1f gd-fm Hdl

Moderate handicap hurdler; needs marathon distances these days; acts on ground good or faster.

Sam's Profiles
104   73
9-y-o b g Infantry-Lady De-Lacy (Pitpan)
Miss K M George Miss K George

Placings:6/55PP-P2   (4706)
2002/03: 21[8]GS, 21[8]G, 20[2]G,

	Starts	1st	2nd	3rd	Win & Pl
Hurdles	2	0	1	0	718
Chases	1	0	0	0	0
Career Total	7	0	1	0	718

Going: Sf: 0-0 GS: 0-1 Gd: 0-2 GF: - Fm: 0-0
Distance: 2m/2m3: 0-0 2m4-2m7: 0-3 3m+: 0-0
Track: LH: 0-2 RH: 0-1 Tight: 0-1 Gall: 0-0
Aids: Bl: 0-0 Vi: 0-1 Tstrap: 0-0
Best Rating: 87 1/01 Extr 2m1f heavy Hdl

Plating-class hurdler; has won a point-to-point; acts well on decent ground; stays three miles.

Samara Song
90   61
10-y-o ch g Savahra Sound-Hosting (Thatching)
Ian Williams R J Turton

Placings:360/U0/0   (1231)
2002/03: 16[9]G,

	Starts	1st	2nd	3rd	Win & Pl
Hurdles	1	0	0	0	
Career Total	6	0	0	1	363

Going: Sf: 0-0 GS: 0-0 Gd: 0-1 GF: - Fm: 0-0
Distance: 2m/2m3: 0-1 2m4-2m7: 0-0 3m+: 0-0
Track: LH: 0-1 RH: 0-0 Tight: 0-0 Gall: 0-0
Aids: Bl: 0-0 Vi: 0-0 Tstrap: 0-0
Best Rating: 75 11/96 Wind 2m good Hdl

Samarardo
79   84
6-y-o b g Son Pardo-Kinlet Vision (IRE) (Vision (USA))
N A Dunger N A Dunger

Placings:0400-0P   (0681)
2002/03: 18[0]GF, 22[8]GF,

	Starts	1st	2nd	3rd	Win & Pl
Hurdles	2	0	0	0	
Career Total	6	0	0	0	

Going: Sf: 0-0 GS: 0-0 Gd: 0-0 GF: - Fm: 0-2
Distance: 2m/2m3: 0-1 2m4-2m7: 0-0 3m+: 0-0
Track: LH: 0-2 RH: 0-0 Tight: 0-2 Gall: 0-0
Aids: Bl: 0-0 Vi: 0-0 Tstrap: 0-0

Best Rating: 84 12/01 Donc 2m110y good Hdl

Samasakhan (IRE)
105   118
7-y-o b h Slip Anchor-Samarzana (USA) (Blushing Groom (FR))
P Hughes Gerald Love

Placings:00000530/002643-531202045   (4582a)
2002/03: 20[5]YS, 20[3]Y, 22[1]YS, 19[2]GF, 24[6]S, 21[2]GS, 24[0]S, 24[4]S, 24[5]GF,

	Starts	1st	2nd	3rd	Win & Pl
Hurdles	9	1	2	1	14211
Career Total	23	1	3	3	17091

103 7/02 Kbgn 2m6f Hdl Y-S £3809
Total win prize-money £3810

Going: Sf: 0-3 GS: 0-1 Gd: 0-0 GF: - Fm: 0-2
Distance: 2m/2m3: 0-1 2m4-2m7: 1-4 3m+: 0-4
Track: LH: 0-3 RH: 0-2 Tight: 0-1 Gall: 0-1
Aids: Bl: 0-0 Vi: 0-0 Tstrap: 0-0
Best Rating: 118 11/02 Chel 2m5f gd-sft Hdl

Fair Irish handicap hurdler; probably stays three miles; does not want the ground too soft.

Samby
101f   108f
5-y-o ch g Anshan-Mossy Fern (Le Moss)
O Sherwood R Waters

Placings:221   (4190)
2002/03: 14[2]GS, 18[2]S, 17[1]G,

	Starts	1st	2nd	3rd	Win & Pl
NH Flat	3	1	2	0	3386
Career Total	3	1	2	0	3386

100 3/03 Folk 2m1f110yH NHF GD £1960
Total win prize-money £1960

Going: Sf: 0-1 GS: 0-1 Gd: 1-1 GF: - Fm: 0-0
Distance: 2m/2m3: 1-2 2m4-2m7: 0-0 3m+: 0-0
Track: LH: 0-2 RH: 1-1 Tight: 1-2 Gall: 0-0
Aids: Bl: 0-0 Vi: 0-0 Tstrap: 0-0
Best Rating: 108 11/02 Wwck 1m6f gd-sft NHF

Bumper winner; game; should stay 2m 4f over hurdles.

Sammagefromtenesse (IRE)
106   82
6-y-o b g Petardia-Canoora (Ahonoora)
N F Glynn N F Glynn

Placings:6000/000000-P360P0   (4452a)
2002/03: 16[8]SH, 16[3]G, 20[6]G, 17[0]GS, 16[8]S, 16[9]G,

	Starts	1st	2nd	3rd	Win & Pl
Hurdles	6	0	0	1	436
Career Total	16	0	0	1	436

Going: Sf: 0-1 GS: 0-1 Gd: 0-3 GF: - Fm: 0-0
Distance: 2m/2m3: 0-5 2m4-2m7: 0-1 3m+: 0-0
Track: LH: 0-3 RH: 0-0 Tight: 0-2 Gall: 0-0
Aids: Bl: 0-1 Vi: 0-0 Tstrap: 0-0
Best Rating: 92 7/01 Slig 2m good Hdl

Sammy Samba
102   100+
5-y-o b g Be My Chief (USA)-Peggy Spencer (Formidable (USA))

P J Hobbs Aubrey & Christine Loze/D Charlesworth

Placings:3-1P56112F (1780)
2002/03: 17¹GF, 20⁰GS, 20⁵GF, 16⁶GF, 19¹F, 22¹F, 21²F, 22²GS,

	Starts	1st	2nd	3rd	Win & Pl
NH Flat	1	1	0	0	2247
Hurdles	7	2	1	0	7237
Career Total	9	3	1	1	9711
100	10/02	Extr	2m6f110yE(0-100)HHdl	FRM	£3202
89	10/02	Extr	2m3f	E(0-105)HHdl	FRM £3062
92	7/02	NAbb	2m1f	H NHF	G-F £2247

Total win prize-money £8513

Going:	Sf: 0-0 GS: 0-2 Gd: 0-0 GF: - Fm: 3-6
Distance:	2m/2m3: 2-3 2m4-2m7: 1-5 3m+: 0-0
Track:	LH: 1-3 RH: 2-5 Tight: 1-2 Gall: 0-0
Aids:	Bl: 0-0 Vi: 0-0 Tstrap: 1-2
Best Rating:	100 10/02 Ludl 2m5f firm Hdl

Moderate hurdler; reported to have had a breathing problem when pulled up on his hurdling debut and then choked next start. Fitted with tongue-tie when winning 17 and 19 furlong handicaps on firm ground at Exeter in October 2002.

Samon (GER)
100(119h)   (145h)**119+**
6-y-o ch g Monsun (GER)-Savanna (GER) (Sassafras (FR))
M C Pipe The Macca & Growler Partnership

Placings:10-0325 (4475)
2002/03: 16⁵S, 20³GS, 21²G, 20⁵G,

	Starts	1st	2nd	3rd	Win & Pl
Hurdles	4	0	1	1	19574
Career Total	6	1	1	1	22607
145	1/02	Tntn	2m1f	E Hdl	SFT £3033

Total win prize-money £3033

Going:	Sf: 0-1 GS: 0-1 Gd: 0-2 GF: - Fm: 0-0
Distance:	2m/2m3: 0-1 2m4-2m7: 0-3 3m+: 0-0
Track:	LH: 0-3 RH: 0-1 Tight: 0-1 Gall: 0-1
Aids:	Bl: 0-0 Vi: 0-0 Tstrap: 0-0
Best Rating:	145 3/03 Chel 2m5f good Hdl

Very useful ex-German hurdler; stays two miles five; acts on soft and good ground; runner-up in the Coral Cup at the Cheltenham Festival; faced simple task on chasing bow at Southwell in May 2003; should take high rank.

Samsaam (IRE)
108   **133**
6-y-o b g Sadler s Wells (USA)-Azyaa (Kris)
M C Pipe Matt Archer & Miss Jean Broadhurst

Placings:41P-052 (4441)
2002/03: 17⁰G, 20⁵HY, 20²G,

	Starts	1st	2nd	3rd	Win & Pl
Hurdles	3	0	1	0	2220
Career Total	6	1	1	0	4978
108	3/02	Winc	2m	E Hdl	GD £2758

Total win prize-money £2758

Going:	Sf: 0-1 GS: 0-0 Gd: 0-2 GF: - Fm: 0-0
Distance:	2m/2m3: 0-1 2m4-2m7: 0-2 3m+: 0-0
Track:	LH: 0-1 RH: 0-2 Tight: 0-0 Gall: 0-1
Aids:	Bl: 0-3 Vi: 0-0 Tstrap: 0-2
Best Rating:	119 4/03 Asct 2m4f good Hdl

Fair hurdler; Group Three winner on the Flat for John Dunlop; stays two and a half miles; has worn blinkers or a visor and been tongue tied.

Samson Des Galas (FR)
93f   **90f**
5-y-o b/br g Agent Bleu (FR)-Sarema (FR) (Primo Dominie)
R Ford J & G Sporting Partners

Placings:6 (3412)
2002/03: 16⁶GS,

	Starts	1st	2nd	3rd	Win & Pl
NH Flat	1	0	0	0	0
Career Total	1	0	0	0	0

Going:	Sf: 0-0 GS: 0-1 Gd: 0-0 GF: - Fm: 0-0
Distance:	2m/2m3: 0-1 2m4-2m7: 0-0 3m+: 0-0
Track:	LH: 0-1 RH: 0-0 Tight: 0-0 Gall: 0-0
Aids:	Bl: 0-0 Vi: 0-0 Tstrap: 0-0
Best Rating:	91 2/03 Weth 2m gd-sft NHF

Glimmer of ability on first ever outing in a bumper at Wetherby in February.

Samuel Charles
81   **48**
5-y-o b g Green Desert (USA)-Hejraan (USA) (Alydar (USA))
Miss Venetia Williams Mrs C T Dakin

Placings:5006 (4212)
2002/03: 17⁵S, 16⁰GS, 17⁰GS, 18⁶G,

	Starts	1st	2nd	3rd	Win & Pl
NH Flat	2	0	0	0	0
Hurdles	2	0	0	0	0
Career Total	4	0	0	0	0

Going:	Sf: 0-1 GS: 0-2 Gd: 0-1 GF: - Fm: 0-0
Distance:	2m/2m3: 0-4 2m4-2m7: 0-0 3m+: 0-0
Track:	LH: 0-2 RH: 0-2 Tight: 0-3 Gall: 0-0
Aids:	Bl: 0-0 Vi: 0-0 Tstrap: 0-0
Best Rating:	97 11/02 Hrfd 2m1f soft NHF

Samuel Wilderspin
109   **137**
11-y-o b g Henbit (USA)-Littoral (Crash Course)
R Lee Steve Smith

Placings:106/321143/6122P1/130/24P130/1512FP-23540P (4603)
2002/03: 24²G, 26³GS, 33⁵S, 24⁴GS, 24⁰G, 26⁶G,

	Starts	1st	2nd	3rd	Win & Pl
Chases	6	0	1	1	7048
Career Total	36	9	6	5	81011
142	2/02	Hayd	3m	B(0-140)HCh	HVY £9653
140	11/01	Chel	3m110y	E(0-135)HCh	GD £8736
136	2/01	Weth	3m1f	C(0-135)HCh	SFT £6780
130	5/99	Towc	3m1f	E Ch	SFT £3156
119	4/99	Wwck	3m2f	D Ch	SFT £4465
116	1/99	Wwck	2m4f110yD Ch	SFT	£4695
134	2/98	Wwck	2m4f110yB Hdl	GD	£6807
111	1/98	Donc	2m4f	D Hdl	GD £4136
118	2/97	Wwck	2m	H NHF	GD £1028

Total win prize-money £49461

Going:	Sf: 0-1 GS: 0-2 Gd: 0-3 GF: - Fm: 0-0
Distance:	2m/2m3: 0-2 2m4-2m7: 0-0 3m+: 0-6
Track:	LH: 0-6 RH: 0-0 Tight: 0-0 Gall: 0-5
Aids:	Bl: 0-0 Vi: 0-0 Tstrap: 0-6
Best Rating:	142 2/02 Hayd 3m heavy Ch

Very useful chaser; best at around three miles; stays well; acts on soft ground; runs well fresh; wears a tongue tie.

Samule
13-y-o gr g Another Realm-Dancing Kathleen (Green God)
Mrs A E Harding Mrs A E Harding

Placings:25/1P (0403)
2002/03: 20¹GF, 22²GF,

	Starts	1st	2nd	3rd	Win & Pl
Chases	2	1	0	0	2048
Career Total	4	1	1	0	2381
86	5/02	Strf	2m4f	H Ch	G-F £2047

Total win prize-money £2048

Going:	Sf: 0-0 GS: 0-0 Gd: 0-0 GF: - Fm: 1-2
Distance:	2m/2m3: 0-0 2m4-2m7: 1-2 3m+: 0-0
Track:	LH: 1-1 RH: 0-1 Tight: 1-2 Gall: 0-0
Aids:	Bl: 0-0 Vi: 0-0 Tstrap: 1-2
Best Rating:	92 3/98 Winc 2m5f gd-sft Ch

Lightly raced in recent years, won a novices' hunter chase at Stratford over two and a half miles May 2002.

San Dimas (USA)
94   **95**
6-y-o gr g Distant View (USA)-Chrystophard (USA) (Lypheor)
R Allan Mrs R P Aggio

Placings:4/4P4026033-0135P4 (4621)
2002/03: 17⁰GF, 22¹GF, 22³G, 16⁵S, 22⁰S, 20⁴GF,

	Starts	1st	2nd	3rd	Win & Pl
Hurdles	6	1	0	1	4031
Career Total	16	1	1	3	5259
95	10/02	Kels	2m6f110y	E Hdl	G-F £3445

Total win prize-money £3445

Going:	Sf: 0-0 GS: 0-0 Gd: 0-1 GF: - Fm: 1-3
Distance:	2m/2m3: 0-2 2m4-2m7: 1-4 3m+: 0-0
Track:	LH: 1-4 RH: 0-2 Tight: 1-5 Gall: 0-0
Aids:	Bl: 0-0 Vi: 1-5 Tstrap: 0-0
Best Rating:	95 10/02 Kels 2m6f110y gd-fm Hdl

Moderate hurdler; goes well at Kelso; stays two miles six; acts on a sound surface; usually wears a visor, but has worn cheekpieces.

San Francisco
103   **95**
9-y-o b g Aragon-Sirene Bleu Marine (USA) (Secreto (USA))
A C Whillans C Bird

Placings:32030/00213/25534/P04133U3052/3466110F3-5P5P446325 (4763)
2002/03: 16⁵S, 20⁰G, 25⁵GS, 20⁵S, 20⁴S, 20⁴S, 20⁶S, 20³S, 16²S, 16⁵G,

	Starts	1st	2nd	3rd	Win & Pl
Chases	10	0	1	1	3072
Career Total	45	4	5	10	26827
99	3/02	Ayr	2m	F(0-95)HCh	SFT £2936
89	3/02	Ayr	2m	F(0-95)HCh	HVY £4273
94	12/00	Newc	2m110y	F(0-90)Ch	SFT £2380
99	3/99	Ayr	2m	D(0-110)HHdl	SFT £2882

Total win prize-money £12473

Going:	Sf: 0-7 GS: 0-1 Gd: 0-2 GF: - Fm: 0-0
Distance:	2m/2m3: 0-3 2m4-2m7: 0-6 3m+: 0-1
Track:	LH: 0-9 RH: 0-1 Tight: 0-1 Gall: 0-1
Aids:	Bl: 0-0 Vi: 0-0 Tstrap: 0-4
Best Rating:	103 2/01 Kels 2m1f soft Ch

Moderate handicap chaser; handles testing ground; best at around two miles.

San Giorgio

100   **68**

14-y-o b g Lighter-Gold Willow (Goldfella)
P Kelsall Peter Kelsall

Placings:*0*/P32P/121604U/4P23/20/260/053045300/00035
03-056P   (1784)
2002/03: 26⁹GF, 24⁵G, 26⁶GF, 24ᴾGS,

	Starts	1st	2nd	3rd	Win & Pl
Hurdles	4	0	0	0	0
Career Total	41	2	5	6	14159
94 11/95 Chel	3m1f110yB HHdl		G-S		£4856
79 9/95 Worc	3m	F Hdl	G-F		£1996
			Total win prize-money £6852		

Going:	Sf: 0-0 GS: 0-1 Gd: 0-1 GF: - Fm: 0-2
Distance:	2m/2m3: 0-0 2m4-2m7: 0-0 3m+: 0-4
Track:	LH: 0-1 RH: 0-3 Tight: 0-1 Gall: 0-2
Aids:	Bl: 0-1 Vi: 0-0 Tstrap: 0-0
Best Rating:	102 10/98 Hntg 3m2f good Hdl

San Marco (IRE)

105

5-y-o b g Brief Truce (USA)-Nuit Des Temps (Sadler s Wells
(USA))
Mrs P Sly (C Collins 5/8) R Brazier

Placings:P03-P   (1625)
2002/03: 20ᴾGS,

	Starts	1st	2nd	3rd	Win & Pl
Hurdles	1	0	0	0	
Career Total	4	0	0	1	429

Going:	Sf: 0-0 GS: 0-1 Gd: 0-0 GF: - Fm: 0-0
Distance:	2m/2m3: 0-0 2m4-2m7: 0-1 3m+: 0-0
Track:	LH: 0-1 RH: 0-0 Tight: 0-1 Gall: 0-0
Aids:	Bl: 0-0 Vi: 0-0 Tstrap: 0-0
Best Rating:	105 1/02 Tram 2m sft-hvy Hdl

San Marino (IRE)

91   **86**

7-y-o b g Torus-Lousion (Lucifer (USA))
Miss Venetia Williams P Ryan

Placings:*4*-3FF   (3788)
2002/03: 21³HY, 16ᶠS, 19ᶠG,

	Starts	1st	2nd	3rd	Win & Pl
Chases	3	0	0	1	652
Career Total	4	0	0	1	652

Going:	Sf: 0-2 GS: 0-0 Gd: 0-1 GF: - Fm: 0-0
Distance:	2m/2m3: 0-2 2m4-2m7: 0-1 3m+: 0-0
Track:	LH: 0-0 RH: 0-3 Tight: 0-1 Gall: 0-0
Aids:	Bl: 0-0 Vi: 0-0 Tstrap: 0-0
Best Rating:	88 10/01 Fknm 2m soft NHF

San Peire (FR)

98   **107+**

6-y-o b g Cyborg (FR)-Shakapoura (FR) (Shakapour)
J Howard Johnson Comtake-Welding Engineering
Specialists

Placings:*0*605-3P021   (4376)
2002/03: 20³G, 19ᴾGS, 19⁹G, 16²GS, 27¹G,

	Starts	1st	2nd	3rd	Win & Pl
Hurdles	5	1	1	1	3797
Career Total	9	1	1	1	3797

---

101 3/03	Sedg	3m3f110yF Hdl	GD	£2681
		Total win prize-money £2681		

Going:	Sf: 0-1 GS: 0-1 Gd: 1-3 GF: - Fm: 0-0
Distance:	2m/2m3: 0-3 2m4-2m7: 0-1 3m+: 1-1
Track:	LH: 1-5 RH: 0-0 Tight: 1-4 Gall: 0-0
Aids:	Bl: 0-0 Vi: 0-0 Tstrap: 0-0
Best Rating:	101 3/03 Sedg 3m3f110y good Hdl

Modest novice hurdler; much improved since stepping up to
extreme distances; turned a poor novices hurdle into a
procession at Sedgefield in March; effortless winner of a
handicap back there in May.

San Suru (GER)

80   **77**

9-y-o b h Surumu (GER)-Sweet Virtue (USA) (Halo (USA))
Mario Hofer Stall Jenny

Placings:PP0/1101/11/124-6335   (3640)
2002/03: 20⁶G, 20³S, 17³S, 16⁵GS,

	Starts	1st	2nd	3rd	Win & Pl
Hurdles	4	0	0	2	3588
Career Total	16	6	1	2	46186
8/01 Badn	2m4f165y		Hdl	GD	
£9772					
8/00 Manh	2m		Hdl	GD	£2581
6/00 Hamb	2m1f		Hdl	SFT	£4194
4/00 Manh	2m2f		Hdl	GD	£3226
10/99 Gels	2m1f		Hdl	SFT	£2166
8/99 Dort	2m		Hdl	GD	£1986
		Total win prize-money £23925			

Going:	Sf: 0-2 GS: 0-1 Gd: 0-1 GF: - Fm: 0-0
Distance:	2m/2m3: 0-2 2m4-2m7: 0-2 3m+: 0-0
Track:	LH: 0-0 RH: 0-2 Tight: 0-0 Gall: 0-0
Aids:	Bl: 0-1 Vi: 0-0 Tstrap: 0-0
Best Rating:	76 2/03 Winc 2m gd-sft Hdl

Multiple winner on the sand and over hurdles in Germany;
acts on good and soft ground; he finished down the field in
the Supreme Novices on his second appearance in Britain;
stays two and a half miles; acts on good or softer.

Sanderstead

79   **56**

4-y-o b g So Factual (USA)-Charnwood Queen (Cadeaux
Genereux)
K G Wingrove (K A Morgan 7/9) First In Racing
Partnership

Placings:*0*P   (3545)
2002/03: 16⁶GF, 19ᴾG,

	Starts	1st	2nd	3rd	Win & Pl
Hurdles	2	0	0	0	
Career Total	2	0	0	0	

Going:	Sf: 0-0 GS: 0-0 Gd: 0-1 GF: - Fm: 0-1
Distance:	2m/2m3: 0-1 2m4-2m7: 0-1 3m+: 0-0
Track:	LH: 0-1 RH: 0-1 Tight: 0-1 Gall: 0-0
Aids:	Bl: 0-1 Vi: 0-0 Tstrap: 0-0
Best Rating:	56 9/02 Strf 2m110y gd-fm Hdl

Sandholes (IRE)

111   **104+**

7-y-o gr m Tirol-Caroline Lady (JPN) (Caro)
Miss Lucinda V Russell Mrs Edith S Russell

Placings:662/2212/P40-221   (0495)
2002/03: 20²GF, 20²GS, 16¹GS,

	Starts	1st	2nd	3rd	Win & Pl
Hurdles	3	1	2	0	6627

Career Total	13	2	6	0	12741
104 6/02 Prth	2m110y D(0-115)HHdl	G-S		£4294
90 8/00 Slig	2m	Hdl	YLD	£2760
		Total win prize-money £7055		

Going:	Sf: 0-0 GS: 1-2 Gd: 0-0 GF: - Fm: 0-1
Distance:	2m/2m3: 1-1 2m4-2m7: 0-2 3m+: 0-0
Track:	LH: 0-0 RH: 1-3 Tight: 0-0 Gall: 0-0
Aids:	Bl: 0-0 Vi: 0-0 Tstrap: 0-0
Best Rating:	104 6/02 Prth 2m110y gd-sft Hdl

Modest ex-Irish hurdler, won over the minimum trip on easy
ground in August 2000 and went missing from then until
spring 2002. Seems to handle any ground.

Sandoran

103(101h)   **103**

10-y-o b g Gildoran-Party Miss (West Partisan)
M Hill Singing In The Rain

Placings:*05*400/F5PF4446F241/0P4151016/6526203/2402
3225-P1   (4695)
2002/03: 16²GS, 16¹G,

	Starts	1st	2nd	3rd	Win & Pl
Hurdles	1	0	0	0	0
Chases	1	1	0	0	4066
Career Total	43	5	7	2	25535
103 4/03 NAbb	2m110y E(0-105)HCh	GD	£4065
106 3/00 NAbb	2m6f	D(0-125)HHdl	GD	£2919
101 2/00 Tntn	2m3f110yE(0-115)HHdl	SFT	£3073
96 1/00 Tntn	2m3f110yF(0-105)HHdl	SFT	£2506
98 4/99 Extr	2m1f110yE(0-105)HHdl	SFT	£2276
		Total win prize-money £14841		

Going:	Sf: 0-0 GS: 0-1 Gd: 1-1 GF: - Fm: 0-0
Distance:	2m/2m3: 1-2 2m4-2m7: 0-0 3m+: 0-0
Track:	LH: 1-2 RH: 0-0 Tight: 1-1 Gall: 0-0
Aids:	Bl: 0-0 Vi: 0-0 Tstrap: 0-0
Best Rating:	106 3/00 NAbb 2m6f good Hdl

Plating-class chaser; stays two miles-six although effective
at shorter; handles any ground.

Sands Rising

98   **88**

6-y-o b g Primitive Rising (USA)-Celtic Sands (Celtic Cone)
R Johnson T L A Robson

Placings:*00*-030434   (4304)
2002/03: 16⁶GS, 21³S, 16⁹GS, 20⁴HY, 24³S, 22⁴G,

	Starts	1st	2nd	3rd	Win & Pl
Hurdles	6	0	0	2	1615
Career Total	8	0	0	2	1615

Going:	Sf: 0-3 GS: 0-2 Gd: 0-1 GF: - Fm: 0-0
Distance:	2m/2m3: 0-2 2m4-2m7: 0-3 3m+: 0-1
Track:	LH: 0-6 RH: 0-0 Tight: 0-2 Gall: 0-4
Aids:	Bl: 0-0 Vi: 0-0 Tstrap: 0-0
Best Rating:	88 3/03 Kels 2m6f110y good Hdl

Limited ability over hurdles to date.

Sandy Duff

94   **107+**

9-y-o ch g Scottish Reel-Not Enough (Balinger)
J D Frost The Tuesday Syndicate

Placings:*10*/211P/2336P/113502-F5   (4694)
2002/03: 19ᶠG, 21⁵G,

	Starts	1st	2nd	3rd	Win & Pl
Chases	2	0	0	0	0
Career Total	19	5	3	3	24320

127	10/01	Sthl	2m	E Ch	GD	£3357
111	5/01	Ling	2m	E Ch	G-F	£3549
121	1/00	Donc	2m110y	E Hdl	GD	£2814
121	12/99	Folk	2m1f110yE Hdl		SFT	£2512
116	1/99	Ludl	2m	H NHF	SFT	£1546
				Total win prize-money £13779

Going: Sf: 0-0 GS: 0-0 Gd: 0-2 GF: - Fm: 0-0
Distance: 2m/2m3: 0-0 2m4-2m7: 0-2 3m+: 0-0
Track: LH: 0-1 RH: 0-1 Tight: 0-1 Gall: 0-0
Aids: Bl: 0-0 Vi: 0-0 Tstrap: 0-0
Best Rating: 133 12/00 Kemp 2m   gd-sft Ch

Modest chaser; disappointing when well backed in first-time blinkers at Newton Abbot May 2003; suited by 2m and a sound surface.

Sandywell George
97   76+

8-y-o ch g Zambrano-Farmcote Air (True Song)
L P Grassick David Lloyd & Mrs Carole Lloyd

Placings: *0/004*P/P603P-6U0PP5   (4709)
2002/03: 27⁶GF, 22ᵁGF, 19⁰G, 24⁴PS, 24⁴G,

	Starts	1st	2nd	3rd	Win & Pl
Hurdles	6	0	0	0	0
Career Total	16	0	0	1	454

Going: Sf: 0-1 GS: 0-0 Gd: 0-2 GF: - Fm: 0-3
Distance: 2m/2m3: 0-0 2m4-2m7: 0-3 3m+: 0-3
Track: LH: 0-5 RH: 0-1 Tight: 0-3 Gall: 0-0
Aids: Bl: 0-0 Vi: 0-0 Tstrap: 0-0
Best Rating: 87 1/01 Chep 2m110y   gd-sft NHF

Modest novice hurdler who has had plenty of chances; twice no match for the winner when runner-up over 2m 4f at Worcester June 2003; acts on a sound surface; does not appear to stay 3m.

Santa Lucia
95(106h)   (100h)

7-y-o b m Namaqualand (USA)-Villasanta (Corvaro (USA))
M Dods J A Wynn-Williams

Placings: F/60241-042335   (4509)
2002/03: 16⁰G, 20⁴S, 20²G, 19³GS, 21³G, 22⁵G,

	Starts	1st	2nd	3rd	Win & Pl
Hurdles	6	0	1	2	1729
Career Total	12	1	2	2	6443
100	4/02	Prth	2m4f110yD Hdl		GD	£3718
				Total win prize-money £3718

Going: Sf: 0-1 GS: 0-1 Gd: 0-4 GF: - Fm: 0-0
Distance: 2m/2m3: 0-1 2m4-2m7: 0-5 3m+: 0-0
Track: LH: 0-5 RH: 0-1 Tight: 0-3 Gall: 0-1
Aids: Bl: 0-0 Vi: 0-0 Tstrap: 0-1
Best Rating: 100 4/02 Prth 2m4f110y   good Hdl

Modest selling hurdler; well beaten third on chasing bow at Sedgefield in July; suited by fast ground but handles softer; stays two and a half miles.

Santella Boy (USA)
100(86h)   (50h)80+

11-y-o b g Turkoman (USA)-Dream Creek (USA) (The Minstrel (CAN))
Miss C Dyson Miss C Dyson

Placings: 36/351321142F4/**112132**/0PP4P254/P0/00423/04 633-014   (1041)
2002/03: 23⁹GF, 26¹GF, 26⁴GF,

	Starts	1st	2nd	3rd	Win & Pl
Chases	3	1	0	0	2933

80	8/02	NAbb	3m2f110yF(0-90)HCh		G-F	£2933
117	7/97	Sthl	3m110y E Ch		G-F	£3593
117	6/97	Uttx	2m7f	D Ch	G-F	£3420
113	5/97	Extr	2m7f110yD Ch		GD	£3550
97	9/96	Extr	2m6f	E(0-110)HHdl	FRM	£2611
103	8/96	Hntg	2m4f110yE Hdl		G-F	£2192
94	6/96	MRas	3m	D Hdl	G-F	£2974
				Total win prize-money £21276

Going: Sf: 0-0 GS: 0-0 Gd: 0-0 GF: - Fm: 1-3
Distance: 2m/2m3: 0-0 2m4-2m7: 0-0 3m+: 1-3
Track: LH: 1-2 RH: 0-0 Tight: 1-2 Gall: 0-0
Aids: Bl: 0-0 Vi: 0-0 Tstrap: 0-0
Best Rating: 117 7/97 Sthl 3m110y   gd-fm Ch

Very modest chaser, stays well.

Santenay (FR)
101(126h)   (160h)114+

5-y-o b g Mister Mat (FR)-Guigone (FR) (Esprit Du Nord (USA))
P F Nicholls The Hon Mrs Townshend

Placings: 522P14-11201   (4780)
2002/03: 16¹GF, 16¹G, 16²S, 16⁹G, 16¹GF,

	Starts	1st	2nd	3rd	Win & Pl
Hurdles	5	3	1	0	81558
Career Total	11	4	3	0	89102
142	4/03	Sand	2m110y B Hdl		G-F	£34800
146	1/03	Winc	2m	A HHdl	GD	£20300
142	10/02	Chep	2m110y B HHdl		G-F	£9958
116	3/02	Winc	2m	E Hdl	GD	£2758
				Total win prize-money £67816

Going: Sf: 0-1 GS: 0-0 Gd: 1-2 GF: - Fm: 2-2
Distance: 2m/2m3: 3-5 2m4-2m7: 0-0 3m+: 0-0
Track: LH: 1-2 RH: 2-3 Tight: 0-0 Gall: 0-0
Aids: Bl: 0-0 Vi: 0-0 Tstrap: 0-0
Best Rating: 160 12/02 Kemp 2m   soft Hdl

High-class ex-French hurdler; made rapid progress over timber in 2002/3; best efforts when highly creditable 3l runner-up to Intersky Falcon in Christmas Hurdle at Kempton in December and 7l winner of valuable Concept Hurdle at Sandown in April; handles any ground; goes particularly well at Wincanton.

Saone Et Loire (FR)
70   84

6-y-o b m Always Fair (USA)-Saone (USA) (Bering)
M C Pipe Yvonne Reynolds & Roger Stanley

Placings: 23/4362401-P0   (1932)
2002/03: 16⁶G, 17⁰GS,

	Starts	1st	2nd	3rd	Win & Pl
Hurdles	2	0	0	0	
Career Total	11	1	2	2	3385
84	3/02	Tntn	2m1f	G Hdl	SFT	£1694
				Total win prize-money £1694

Going: Sf: 0-0 GS: 0-1 Gd: 0-1 GF: - Fm: 0-0
Distance: 2m/2m3: 0-2 2m4-2m7: 0-0 3m+: 0-0
Track: LH: 0-1 RH: 0-1 Tight: 0-1 Gall: 0-0
Aids: Bl: 0-0 Vi: 0-2 Tstrap: 0-2
Best Rating: 85 2/01 Tntn 2m1f   heavy Hdl

Plating-class hurdler, finished last in the French 1000 guineas, before going to Martin Pipe. Acts on soft ground.

Saorsie
106   102

5-y-o b g Emperor Jones (USA)-Exclusive Lottery

(Presidium)
J C Fox Lord Mutton Racing Partnership

Placings: 0500-B10644   (4186)
2002/03: 16⁸GF, 17¹GF, 16⁹G, 17⁵HY, 16⁴GS, 17⁴G,

	Starts	1st	2nd	3rd	Win & Pl
Hurdles	6	1	0	0	3457
Career Total	10	1	0	0	3457
88	7/02	NAbb	2m1f	F(0-100)HHdl	G-F	£2926
				Total win prize-money £2926

Going: Sf: 0-1 GS: 0-1 Gd: 0-2 GF: - Fm: 1-2
Distance: 2m/2m3: 1-6 2m4-2m7: 0-0 3m+: 0-0
Track: LH: 1-4 RH: 0-2 Tight: 1-4 Gall: 0-0
Aids: Bl: 0-1 Vi: 0-0 Tstrap: 0-0
Best Rating: 88 7/02 NAbb 2m1f   gd-fm Hdl

Moderate handicap hurdler; came back to form when landing a touch at Worcester May 2003 and won again the following month at Newton Abbot; best at around two miles; acts on good to firm and good to soft; does not find a lot off the bridle.

Saragann (IRE)
114(113h)   (134h)123

8-y-o b g Danehill (USA)-Sarfiya (IRE) (Doyoun)
P J Hobbs Jay Dee Bloodstock Limited

Placings: 235PPP6/4U44113/2131-02P12UF3450 (3181)
2002/03: 16⁶S, 20²GF, 20⁶GS, 17¹S, 17²GF, 16ᵁG, 20⁵G, 16³GS, 19⁴GS, 21⁵HY, 20⁰G,

	Starts	1st	2nd	3rd	Win & Pl
Hurdles	2	0	1	0	2062
Chases	9	1	1	1	13527
Career Total	29	5	4	4	72720
120	8/02	Strf	2m1f110yD(0-125)HCh		SFT	£6838
134	8/01	Sthl	2m	C(0-130)HHdl	G-F	£4810
130	6/01	Worc	2m	B(0-140)HHdl	G-F	£14384
124	1/01	Kemp	2m4f110yE(0-115)HCh		SFT	£3737
115	11/00	Carl	2m	E Ch	SFT	£3146
				Total win prize-money £32917

Going: Sf: 1-3 GS: 0-3 Gd: 0-3 GF: - Fm: 0-2
Distance: 2m/2m3: 1-6 2m4-2m7: 0-5 3m+: 0-0
Track: LH: 1-8 RH: 0-3 Tight: 1-3 Gall: 0-2
Aids: Bl: 0-0 Vi: 0-0 Tstrap: 0-0
Best Rating: 134 6/02 Worc 2m4f   gd-fm Hdl

Fair chaser, stays two and a half miles, but effective over shorter; acts on any ground.

Sarah's Son (IRE)

8-y-o b g Be My Native (USA)-Call Me Ruby (IRE) (Callernish)
Miss Kate Milligan (John R Upson 19/5) P G Forster

Placings: P/P   (0829)
2002/03: 21⁸GF,

	Starts	1st	2nd	3rd	Win & Pl
Hurdles	1	0	0	0	
Career Total	2	0	0	0	

Going: Sf: 0-0 GS: 0-0 Gd: 0-0 GF: - Fm: 0-1
Distance: 2m/2m3: 0-0 2m4-2m7: 0-1 3m+: 0-0
Track: LH: 0-1 RH: 0-0 Tight: 0-1 Gall: 0-0
Aids: Bl: 0-0 Vi: 0-0 Tstrap: 0-1
Best Rating: 0 7/02 Sedg 2m5f110y   gd-fm Hdl

Saras Delight

11-y-o b g Idiots Delight-Lady Bess (Straight Lad)

Major General C A Ramsay Major General C A Ramsay

Placings:06/03F3/3U1233/15/5/F-PP3   (4777)
2002/03: 25PG, 27PG, 31³G,

	Starts	1st	2nd	3rd	Win & Pl
Chases	3	0	0	1	626
Career Total	19	2	1	6	9212
100 4/00 Newc 3m		F(0-105)HCh		G-S	£2902
101 12/98 Hrfd	3m1f110yF Ch			G-S	£2125
		Total win prize-money £5027			

Going: Sf: 0-0 GS: 0-0 Gd: 0-3 GF: - Fm: 0-0
Distance: 2m/2m3: 0-0 2m4-2m7: 0-0 3m+: 0-3
Track: LH: 0-2 RH: 0-0 Tight: 0-1 Gall: 0-0
Aids: Bl: 0-0 Vi: 0-0 Tstrap: 0-0
Best Rating: 101 1/99 Winc 3m1f110y soft   Ch

Plating-class hunter chaser; stays three miles; suited by cut in the ground.

Sarasota (IRE)
97   78
8-y-o b g Lord Americo-Ceoltoir Dubh (Black Minstrel)
P Bowen F W & E P Ridge

Placings:060P/02P05-P   (4418)
2002/03: 22PG,

	Starts	1st	2nd	3rd	Win & Pl
Hurdles	1	0	0	0	
Career Total	10	0	1	0	793

Going: Sf: 0-0 GS: 0-0 Gd: 0-1 GF: - Fm: 0-0
Distance: 2m/2m3: 0-0 2m4-2m7: 0-1 3m+: 0-0
Track: LH: 0-0 RH: 0-0 Tight: 0-0 Gall: 0-0
Aids: Bl: 0-0 Vi: 0-0 Tstrap: 0-0
Best Rating: 84 5/01 NAbb 2m1f   gd-fm Hdl

Sarasota Storm
86   92+
11-y-o b g Petoski-Challanging (Mill Reef (USA))
J D Frost Miss H S Robarts

Placings:P2P0/P/UP/5341/221-2   (0998)
2002/03: 22²GF,

	Starts	1st	2nd	3rd	Win & Pl
Hurdles	1	0	1	0	1099
Career Total	15	2	4	1	9134
89 8/01 NAbb 2m6f		F(0-110)HHdl		GD	£2919
80 10/00 Extr	2m6f110yF(0-100)HHdl			GD	£2450
		Total win prize-money £5369			

Going: Sf: 0-0 GS: 0-0 Gd: 0-0 GF: - Fm: 0-1
Distance: 2m/2m3: 0-0 2m4-2m7: 0-1 3m+: 0-0
Track: LH: 0-1 RH: 0-0 Tight: 0-0 Gall: 0-0
Aids: Bl: 0-0 Vi: 0-0 Tstrap: 0-0
Best Rating: 92 8/02 NAbb 2m6f   gd-fm Hdl

Saratov (GER)
110
4-y-o b g Acatenango (GER)-Sovereign Touch (IRE) (Pennine Walk)
Jonjo O Neill P Piller

Placings:F   (3252)
2002/03: 16FHY,

	Starts	1st	2nd	3rd	Win & Pl
Hurdles	1	0	0	0	
Career Total	1	0	0	0	

Going: Sf: 0-1 GS: 0-0 Gd: 0-0 GF: - Fm: 0-0
Distance: 2m/2m3: 0-1 2m4-2m7: 0-0 3m+: 0-0
Track: LH: 0-1 RH: 0-0 Tight: 0-0 Gall: 0-0
Aids: Bl: 0-0 Vi: 0-0 Tstrap: 0-0
Best Rating: 110 1/03 Wwck 2m   heavy Hdl

Every chance when fell at the last on hurdles debut; effective in heavy ground.

Saratov
101   93+
5-y-o b g Rudimentary (USA)-Sarabah (IRE) (Ela-Mana-Mou)
G A Swinbank J David Abell

Placings:3   (0566)
2002/03: 17³GF,

	Starts	1st	2nd	3rd	Win & Pl
Hurdles	1	0	0	1	386
Career Total	1	0	0	1	386

Going: Sf: 0-0 GS: 0-0 Gd: 0-0 GF: - Fm: 0-1
Distance: 2m/2m3: 0-0 2m4-2m7: 0-1 3m+: 0-0
Track: LH: 0-0 RH: 0-1 Tight: 0-1 Gall: 0-0
Aids: Bl: 0-0 Vi: 0-0 Tstrap: 0-0
Best Rating: 93 6/02 MRas 2m1f110y gd-fm Hdl

Formerly useful Flat racer; modest hurdles debut in June 2002.

Sarena Special
6-y-o b g Lucky Guest-Lariston Gale (Pas De Seul)
J D Frost Sarena Mfg Ltd

Placings:5/P-P   (0367)
2002/03: 17PS,

	Starts	1st	2nd	3rd	Win & Pl
Hurdles	1	0	0	0	
Career Total	3	0	0	0	0

Going: Sf: 0-1 GS: 0-0 Gd: 0-0 GF: - Fm: 0-0
Distance: 2m/2m3: 0-1 2m4-2m7: 0-0 3m+: 0-0
Track: LH: 0-1 RH: 0-0 Tight: 0-1 Gall: 0-0
Aids: Bl: 0-0 Vi: 0-0 Tstrap: 0-0
Best Rating: 75 10/00 Kemp 2m   gd-sft Hdl

Sargasso Sea
104f   109f
6-y-o gr g Greensmith-Sea Spice (Precipice Wood)
J A B Old Miss S Blumberg

Placings:341   (4005)
2002/03: 16³S, 16⁴GS, 16¹S,

	Starts	1st	2nd	3rd	Win & Pl
NH Flat	3	1	0	1	2281
Career Total	3	1	0	1	2281
109 3/03 Winc	2m	H NHF		SFT	£1995
		Total win prize-money £1995			

Going: Sf: 1-2 GS: 0-1 Gd: 0-0 GF: - Fm: 0-0
Distance: 2m/2m3: 1-3 2m4-2m7: 0-0 3m+: 0-0
Track: LH: 0-1 RH: 1-2 Tight: 0-0 Gall: 0-0
Aids: Bl: 0-0 Vi: 0-0 Tstrap: 0-0
Best Rating: 109 3/03 Winc 2m   soft   NHF

Bumper winner; suited by soft ground and will need a test of stamina over hurdles.

Sarn
91   73
4-y-o b g Atraf-Covent Garden Girl (Sizzling Melody)
A Bailey S A Pritchard

Placings:5P   (2182)
2002/03: 16⁵S, 16PGS,

	Starts	1st	2nd	3rd	Win & Pl
Hurdles	2	0	0	0	0
Career Total	2	0	0	0	0

Going: Sf: 0-1 GS: 0-1 Gd: 0-0 GF: - Fm: 0-0
Distance: 2m/2m3: 0-2 2m4-2m7: 0-0 3m+: 0-0
Track: LH: 0-2 RH: 0-0 Tight: 0-0 Gall: 0-0
Aids: Bl: 0-0 Vi: 0-0 Tstrap: 0-0
Best Rating: 73 11/02 Ayr 2m   soft   Hdl

Sarteano
88
9-y-o ch m Anshan-Daisy Girl (Main Reef)
G J Smith (D Shaw 12/5) F K Baxter

Placings:0P   (0667)
2002/03: 20⁰GF, 20PGF,

	Starts	1st	2nd	3rd	Win & Pl
Hurdles	2	0	0	0	
Career Total	2	0	0	0	

Going: Sf: 0-0 GS: 0-0 Gd: 0-0 GF: - Fm: 0-2
Distance: 2m/2m3: 0-0 2m4-2m7: 0-2 3m+: 0-0
Track: LH: 0-2 RH: 0-0 Tight: 0-0 Gall: 0-0
Aids: Bl: 0-0 Vi: 0-0 Tstrap: 0-0
Best Rating: 62 6/02 Worc 2m4f   gd-fm Hdl

Sasha Star (IRE)
102   60
5-y-o b g Namaqualand (USA)-Trojan Relation (Trojan Fen)
G Brown T And J A Curry

Placings:04605-304P   (1747)
2002/03: 16³GF, 16PGF, 22⁴GF, 21PS,

	Starts	1st	2nd	3rd	Win & Pl
Hurdles	4	0	0	1	237
Career Total	9	0	0	1	237

Going: Sf: 0-1 GS: 0-0 Gd: 0-0 GF: - Fm: 0-3
Distance: 2m/2m3: 0-2 2m4-2m7: 0-2 3m+: 0-0
Track: LH: 0-3 RH: 0-1 Tight: 0-2 Gall: 0-1
Aids: Bl: 0-3 Vi: 0-0 Tstrap: 0-0
Best Rating: 60 6/02 NAbb 2m6f   gd-fm Hdl

Beaten in selling hurdles at up to 22 furlongs.

Saspys Lad
111   113+
6-y-o b g Faustus (USA)-Legendary Lady (Reprimand)
W M Brisbourne K J Oulton

Placings:0003/05133-12F011   (1218)
2002/03: 17¹G, 17²GF, 16FGF, 18⁹GF, 16¹GF, 17¹G,

	Starts	1st	2nd	3rd	Win & Pl
Hurdles	6	3	1		11699
Career Total	15	4	1	3	14647
113 9/02 Sthl	2m1f	D(0-115)HHdl		GD	£4065
102 8/02 Uttx	2m	D(0-125)HHdl		G-F	£4121
88 6/02 NAbb	2m1f	F(0-100)HHdl		GD	£2646
79 2/02 Fknm	2m	G(0-90)HHdl		G-S	£1892
		Total win prize-money £12725			

Going: Sf: 0-0 GS: 0-0 Gd: 2-2 GF: - Fm: 1-3
Distance: 2m/2m3: 3-6 2m4-2m7: 0-0 3m+: 0-0
Track: LH: 3-5 RH: 0-1 Tight: 1-2 Gall: 0-0
Aids: Bl: 0-0 Vi: 0-0 Tstrap: 0-0
Best Rating: 113 9/02 Sthl 2m1f   good   Hdl

Modest hurdler; regular in selling company, winning at Fakenham in February and Class F handicap at Newton Abbot in June 2002. In the process of showing vastly improved form when falling at the last with a clear lead at Uttoxeter in July and made amends with a couple of comfortable wins. Acts on a sound surface.

Satanas (FR)

67(79h)   (85h)7
5-y-o b g Dress Parade-Oiseau Noir (FR) (Rex Magna (FR))
O Sherwood M G St Quinton

Placings:00-P65P   (4428)
2002/03: 17PGS, 19GGS, 18SS, 25PGF,

	Starts	1st	2nd	3rd	Win & Pl
Hurdles	4	0	0	0	0
Career Total	6	0	0	0	0

Going: Sf: 0-1 GS: 0-2 Gd: 0-0 GF: - Fm: 0-1
Distance: 2m/2m3: 0-2 2m4-2m7: 0-1 3m+: 0-1
Track: LH: 0-2 RH: 0-1 Tight: 0-2 Gall: 0-0
Aids: Bl: 0-0 Vi: 0-0 Tstrap: 0-0
Best Rating: 88 2/02 Kemp 2m   good   NHF

Has shown very little in bumpers and novice hurdles.

Satanta

88   55
6-y-o b g Cosmonaut-Expensive Gift (Record Token)
J W Mullins Mrs M M Rayner

Placings:06P-0   (0444)
2002/03: 21PGS, 19GG,

	Starts	1st	2nd	3rd	Win & Pl
Hurdles	2	0	0	0	0
Career Total	4	0	0	0	0

Going: Sf: 0-0 GS: 0-1 Gd: 0-0 GF: - Fm: 0-0
Distance: 2m/2m3: 0-0 2m4-2m7: 0-2 3m+: 0-0
Track: LH: 0-0 RH: 0-2 Tight: 0-0 Gall: 0-0
Aids: Bl: 0-0 Vi: 0-0 Tstrap: 0-0
Best Rating: 63 8/01 NAbb 2m1f   gd-fm NHF

Satchmo (IRE)

101   102
11-y-o b g Satco (FR)-Taradale (Torus)
E J O Grady R A H Perkins

Placings:21U/24F211FP/066-30   (4100)
2002/03: 20³YS, 24⁰G,

	Starts	1st	2nd	3rd	Win & Pl
Chases	2	0	0	1	2045
Career Total	16	3	3	1	34004
147 3/01	Hntg	2m4f110yB HCh		SFT	£10328
147 2/01	Kemp	2m4f110yC(0-130)HCh		GD	£10871
136 3/00	Sand	2m4f110yH Ch		G-F	£2436
		Total win prize-money £23636			

Going: Sf: 0-0 GS: 0-0 Gd: 0-1 GF: - Fm: 0-0
Distance: 2m/2m3: 0-0 2m4-2m7: 0-1 3m+: 0-1
Track: LH: 0-1 RH: 0-0 Tight: 0-0 Gall: 0-1
Aids: Bl: 0-0 Vi: 0-0 Tstrap: 0-0
Best Rating: 147 3/01 Hntg 2m4f110y soft   Ch

Useful chaser; formerly trained by Gardie Grissell; absent for 14 months before finishing third at Gowran in February 2003; effective at two and a half miles; acts on good and soft ground.

Satshoon (IRE)

103(107c)   (133c)110
10-y-o b g Satco (FR)-Tudor Lady (Green Shoon)
P F Nicholls Mick Coburn

Placings:221U11/P1-116040   (4029)
2002/03: 23¹G, 25¹GS, 25⁶GS, 25⁰GS, 24⁴S, 24⁰S,

	Starts	1st	2nd	3rd	Win & Pl
Hurdles	1	0	0	0	345
Chases	5	2	0	0	6968
Career Total	14	6	2	0	27233
133 11/02	Extr	2m7f110yD(0-125)HCh	GD	£6968
125 12/01	Winc	3m1f110yD(0-120)HCh	GD	£5187
129 4/01	Winc	3m1f110yD	SFT	£4988
123 4/01	Winc	3m1f110yE Ch	SFT	£3757
119 1/01	Font	2m4f	E Ch	SFT	£3318
		Total win prize-money £24219			

Going: Sf: 0-2 GS: 1-3 Gd: 1-1 GF: - Fm: 0-0
Distance: 2m/2m3: 0-0 2m4-2m7: 0-0 3m+: 2-6
Track: LH: 0-0 RH: 2-6 Tight: 0-1 Gall: 0-0
Aids: Bl: 2-6 Vi: 0-0 Tstrap: 0-0
Best Rating: 133 11/02 Winc 3m1f110y gd-sft Ch

Decent handicap chaser; effective at around 3m and acts on good and soft ground; rattled up a hat-trick in novice hurdles in the summer of 2003; unsuited by left-handed course and fast ground at Stratford next time; usually wears blinkers.

Saucy Kirina

93   58
6-y-o b m Regal Embers (IRE)-Eleri (Rolfe (USA))
Mrs P Ford W E Donohue

Placings:0P/PP6P-00   (0444)
2002/03: 16⁰G, 19⁰G,

	Starts	1st	2nd	3rd	Win & Pl
Hurdles	2	0	0	0	0
Career Total	8	0	0	0	0

Going: Sf: 0-0 GS: 0-0 Gd: 0-2 GF: - Fm: 0-0
Distance: 2m/2m3: 0-2 2m4-2m7: 0-1 3m+: 0-0
Track: LH: 0-1 RH: 0-1 Tight: 0-1 Gall: 0-0
Aids: Bl: 0-0 Vi: 0-1 Tstrap: 0-0
Best Rating: 58 6/02 Hrfd 2m3f110y good   Hdl

Pulled up in four of first five starts over timber.

Saucy Night

(78c)   (44c)61
7-y-o ch g Anshan-Kiss In The Dark (Starry Night (USA))
C C Bealby Exors Of The Late R E N Gardiner

Placings:00P-0P   (0380)
2002/03: 16⁰G, 26⁰G,

	Starts	1st	2nd	3rd	Win & Pl
Hurdles	1	0	0	0	0
Chases	1	0	0	0	0
Career Total	5	0	0	0	0

Going: Sf: 0-0 GS: 0-0 Gd: 0-2 GF: - Fm: 0-0
Distance: 2m/2m3: 0-2 2m4-2m7: 0-0 3m+: 0-1
Track: LH: 0-1 RH: 0-1 Tight: 0-1 Gall: 0-1
Aids: Bl: 0-0 Vi: 0-0 Tstrap: 0-0
Best Rating: 61 12/01 Donc 2m4f   good   Hdl

Saumarez Park

54f
5-y-o b g Magic Ring (IRE)-Rocquaine Bay (Morston (FR))
G L Moore The Warrenwood Racing Partnership

Placings:0   (1923)
2002/03: 12⁰GS,

	Starts	1st	2nd	3rd	Win & Pl
NH Flat	1	0	0	0	0
Career Total	1	0	0	0	0

Going: Sf: 0-0 GS: 0-1 Gd: 0-0 GF: - Fm: 0-0
Distance: 2m/2m3: 0-0 2m4-2m7: 0-0 3m+: 0-0
Track: LH: 0-1 RH: 0-0 Tight: 0-0 Gall: 0-0
Aids: Bl: 0-0 Vi: 0-0 Tstrap: 0-0
Best Rating: 70 11/02 Newb 1m4f110y gd-sft NHF

Savannah Mo (IRE)

103   92+
8-y-o ch m Husyan (USA)-Sweet Start (Candy Cane)
J N R Billinge J N R Billinge & Mrs M M Wilson

Placings:00/012PP/0P02621   (4016)
2002/03: 24⁰S, 27PS, 27⁰S, 24²HY, 27⁶HY, 20²S, 22¹S,

	Starts	1st	2nd	3rd	Win & Pl
Hurdles	7	1	2	0	5130
Career Total	14	2	3	0	8358
92 3/03	Ayr	2m6f	E(0-110)HHdl	SFT	£3484
83 11/00	Ayr	2m6f	E Hdl	SFT	£2548
		Total win prize-money £6032			

Going: Sf: 1-7 GS: 0-0 Gd: 0-0 GF: - Fm: 0-0
Distance: 2m/2m3: 0-0 2m4-2m7: 1-2 3m+: 0-5
Track: LH: 1-7 RH: 0-0 Tight: 0-3 Gall: 0-1
Aids: Bl: 0-0 Vi: 0-0 Tstrap: 0-0
Best Rating: 92 3/03 Ayr 2m6f   soft   Hdl

Plating-class hurdler; best at around two and a half miles; acts on soft ground.

Save The Planet

72
6-y-o b m Environment Friend-Geoffreys Bird (Master Willie)
P Monteith P Monteith

Placings:0/60P05-0   (0185)
2002/03: 16⁰G,

	Starts	1st	2nd	3rd	Win & Pl
Hurdles	1	0	0	0	0
Career Total	7	0	0	0	0

Going: Sf: 0-0 GS: 0-0 Gd: 0-1 GF: - Fm: 0-0
Distance: 2m/2m3: 0-1 2m4-2m7: 0-0 3m+: 0-0
Track: LH: 0-1 RH: 0-0 Tight: 0-0 Gall: 0-0
Aids: Bl: 0-0 Vi: 0-1 Tstrap: 0-0
Best Rating: 72 4/02 Newc 2m   firm   Hdl

Sawa-Id

10-y-o b g Anshan-Bermuda Lily (Dunbeath (USA))
Mrs Caroline Bailey John Nicholls (banbury) Ltd

Placings:214233/13220R/2322/010223UR1RR/L   (4565)
2002/03: 24¹GF,

	Starts	1st	2nd	3rd	Win & Pl
Chases	1	0	0	0	0
Career Total	28	4	9	5	28384
98 2/01	Fknm	3m110y D Ch	SFT	£4636

83	6/00	Baln	2m1f		Ch	G-Y	£4029
112	5/98	Rosc	2m		Hdl	GD	£2829
116	1/98	Fair	2m		Hdl	HVY	£2680
					Total win prize-money		£14176

Going:	Sf: 0-0 GS: 0-0 Gd: 0-0 GF: - Fm: 0-1
Distance:	2m/2m3: 0-2 2m4-2m7: 0-0 3m+: 0-1
Track:	LH: 0-1 RH: 0-0 Tight: 0-1 Gall: 0-0
Aids:	Bl: 0-1 Vi: 0-0 Tstrap: 0-0
Best Rating:	130 11/98 Fair 2m soft Hdl

Sawlajan (USA)
87

12-y-o ch g Woodman (USA)-Crafty Satin (USA) (Crimson Satan)
Mrs T J McInnes Skinner Mrs T J McInnes Skinner

Placings:0/2/230312B/0123011440P/60-P (0731)
2002/03: 22PGF,

	Starts	1st	2nd	3rd	Win & Pl
Hurdles	1	0	0	0	
Career Total	23	4	4	3	24906

120	9/00	Worc	2m4f	C(0-135)HHdl	G-F	£6862
120	8/00	Worc	2m4f	C(0-120)HHdl	G-F	£4121
115	6/00	Strf	2m110y	D(0-120)HHdl	G-S	£3562
102	8/99	Strf	2m6f110yD	Hdl	GD	£3148
				Total win prize-money		£17695

Going:	Sf: 0-0 GS: 0-0 Gd: 0-0 GF: - Fm: 0-1
Distance:	2m/2m3: 0-2 2m4-2m7: 0-0 3m+: 0-1
Track:	LH: 0-1 RH: 0-0 Tight: 0-1 Gall: 0-0
Aids:	Bl: 0-1 Vi: 0-0 Tstrap: 0-0
Best Rating:	120 9/00 Worc 2m4f gd-fm Hdl

Saxon Duke

12-y-o b g Saxon Farm-Bucks Princess (Buckskin (FR))
Mrs M J McGuinness L J McGuinness

Placings:610/F3212314/22F21/13234B/F1/F0302343-0 (3855)
2002/03: 24PGS,

	Starts	1st	2nd	3rd	Win & Pl
Chases	1	0	0	0	
Career Total	33	6	7	7	43306

123	3/01	Wwck	3m5f	C(0-135)HCh	SFT	£6987
113	10/99	Chel	3m110y	E(0-125)HCh	GD	£4833
115	1/99	Extr	2m7f110yE(0-115)HCh		HVY	£3038
106	4/98	Extr	2m7f110yE(0-100)HCh		SFT	£3441
98	12/97	Tntn	3m	F(0-105)HCh	GD	£2822
111	2/96	Nott	2m	N HNF	G-S	£1236
				Total win prize-money		£22359

Going:	Sf: 0-0 GS: 0-1 Gd: 0-0 GF: - Fm: 0-0
Distance:	2m/2m3: 0-0 2m4-2m7: 0-0 3m+: 0-1
Track:	LH: 0-0 RH: 0-1 Tight: 0-1 Gall: 0-0
Aids:	Bl: 0-0 Vi: 0-0 Tstrap: 0-0
Best Rating:	125 3/98 Hntg 3m soft Ch

A dour stayer, he goes well under testing conditions.

Saxon Mill
109 **101+**

8-y-o ch g Saxon Farm-Djellaba (Decoy Boy)
Mrs Pippa Bickerton David Bickerton

Placings:2602/403/0P24P-130 (3262)
2002/03: 17IS, 19³GS, 16⁹GS,

	Starts	1st	2nd	3rd	Win & Pl
Hurdles	3	1	0	1	4675
Career Total	15	1	3	2	7529

| 101 | 12/02 | MRas | 2m1f110yD | Hdl | SFT | £3900 |
| | | | | Total win prize-money | | £3900 |

Going:	Sf: 1-1 GS: 0-2 Gd: 0-0 GF: - Fm: 0-0
Distance:	2m/2m3: 1-2 2m4-2m7: 0-1 3m+: 0-0
Track:	LH: 1-1 RH: 1-2 Tight: 1-2 Gall: 0-1
Aids:	Bl: 0-1 Vi: 0-0 Tstrap: 0-0
Best Rating:	101 12/02 MRas 2m3f110y gd-sft Hdl

Modest hurdler, finally broke his duck at Market Rasen in December, effective over two and a half miles in soft ground.

Saxon Queen
95(86c) (63c)**90**

9-y-o b m Lord Bud-Saxon Slave (Be Friendly)
G Prodromou George Prodromou

Placings:44450/2S646F4241-1P64 (1450)
2002/03: 20¹G, 19PGF, 20⁶G, 16⁴G,

	Starts	1st	2nd	3rd	Win & Pl
Hurdles	4	1	0	0	2077
Career Total	19	2	2	0	4886

90	5/02	Fknm	2m4f	F(0-95)HHdl	GD	£1818
84	4/02	Hntg	2m110y	G(0-90)HHdl	G-F	£1733
				Total win prize-money		£3552

Going:	Sf: 0-0 GS: 0-0 Gd: 1-3 GF: - Fm: 0-1
Distance:	2m/2m3: 0-1 2m4-2m7: 1-3 3m+: 0-0
Track:	LH: 1-3 RH: 0-1 Tight: 1-4 Gall: 0-0
Aids:	Bl: 0-0 Vi: 0-0 Tstrap: 0-0
Best Rating:	90 5/02 Fknm 2m4f good Hdl

Winner of a point-to-point in May 2000, she has made the frame in selling hurdles.

Saxon Spirit

7-y-o ch g Saxon Farm-Miss Date (Mandamus)
I R Brown I R Brown

Placings:0-000P (4482)
2002/03: 16⁰G, 17⁰S, 16⁰S, 19PGF,

	Starts	1st	2nd	3rd	Win & Pl
NH Flat	2	0	0	0	0
Hurdles	2	0	0	0	0
Career Total	5	0	0	0	

Going:	Sf: 0-2 GS: 0-0 Gd: 0-1 GF: - Fm: 0-1
Distance:	2m/2m3: 0-3 2m4-2m7: 0-1 3m+: 0-0
Track:	LH: 0-2 RH: 0-2 Tight: 0-0 Gall: 0-0
Aids:	Bl: 0-0 Vi: 0-0 Tstrap: 0-0
Best Rating:	75 4/02 Ludl 2m gd-fm NHF

Say Again (IRE)
105(117h) (135 h)**129**

7-y-o gr g Celio Rufo-Tricias Pet (Mandalus)
Paul Nolan Sean Duggan

Placings:306/13F212244-1212420 (4136)
2002/03: 16¹S, 16²S, 16¹YS, 16²S, 17⁴HY, 20²S, 17⁰G,

	Starts	1st	2nd	3rd	Win & Pl
Hurdles	4	2	1	0	72193
Chases	3	0	2	0	4320
Career Total	19	4	6	2	90674

135	8/02	Gway	2m	HHdl	Y-S	£55935
116	1/02	Navn	2m	HHdl	SFT	£12760
114	11/01	Tram	2m	(0-95)Hdl	YLD	£4729
103	5/01	Tram	2m	Hdl	G-F	£4451
				Total win prize-money		£77879

Going:	Sf: 1-5 GS: 0-0 Gd: 0-1 GF: - Fm: 0-0
Distance:	2m/2m3: 2-6 2m4-2m7: 0-1 3m+: 0-0
Track:	LH: 1-4 RH: 1-1 Tight: 0-0 Gall: 0-1
Aids:	Bl: 0-0 Vi: 0-0 Tstrap: 0-0
Best Rating:	135 8/02 Gway 2m yld-sft Hdl

Very useful hurdler, but just modest over fences so far; likes soft ground; seemingly best at two to two and a half miles.

Saywhen
96 **48**

11-y-o br g Say Primula-Practicality (Weavers Hall)
Mrs A Price Mrs A Price

Placings:05406P4U4-4F044 (1615)
2002/03: 24⁴GF, 23FG, 23⁹G, 24⁴F, 20⁴F,

	Starts	1st	2nd	3rd	Win & Pl
Chases	5	0	0	0	1122
Career Total	14	0	0	0	2023

Going:	Sf: 0-0 GS: 0-0 Gd: 0-2 GF: - Fm: 0-3
Distance:	2m/2m3: 0-0 2m4-2m7: 0-1 3m+: 0-4
Track:	LH: 0-2 RH: 0-3 Tight: 0-3 Gall: 0-0
Aids:	Bl: 0-0 Vi: 0-0 Tstrap: 0-5
Best Rating:	80 3/02 Ludl 3m gd-sft Ch

Winning pointer/maiden chaser.

Scally Tag

10-y-o gr m Scallywag-Miss Mo Jo (Vaigly Great)
M Smith Malcolm Smith

Placings:0P/SP-P (0449)
2002/03: 16PG,

	Starts	1st	2nd	3rd	Win & Pl
Hurdles	1	0	0	0	
Career Total	5	0	0	0	

Going:	Sf: 0-0 GS: 0-0 Gd: 0-1 GF: - Fm: 0-0
Distance:	2m/2m3: 0-1 2m4-2m7: 0-0 3m+: 0-0
Track:	LH: 0-1 RH: 0-0 Tight: 0-0 Gall: 0-0
Aids:	Bl: 0-0 Vi: 0-0 Tstrap: 0-0
Best Rating:	7 11/98 Carl 2m1f soft NHF

Scallybuck (IRE)
101 (105h)**94d**

11-y-o br g Scallywag-Miss McNight (Master Buck)
R H Buckler (Michael Hourigan 6/9) D R Fear

Placings:0060F4554/0000/321440162P2/12243132665356/55242U6632F6P-24450F065364P (2667)
2002/03: 25²YS, 22⁴S, 20⁴S, 24⁵YS, 22⁰GY, 25FYS, 22⁰GF, 22⁶GF, 25⁶GF, 24⁶G, 21⁴GS, 26⁶S,

	Starts	1st	2nd	3rd	Win & Pl
Hurdles	1	0	0	0	
Chases	12	0	1	1	4289
Career Total	64	4	10	6	50409

115	7/00	Kbgn	2m7f	HCh	G-F	£10400
99	5/00	DRoy	3m	(0-123)HCh	YLD	£13000
92	9/99	List	2m3f	(0-102)HCh	Y-S	£4312
85	6/99	Kbgn	3m1f	(0-102)HCh	GD	£2915
				Total win prize-money		£30629

Going:	Sf: 0-3 GS: 0-1 Gd: 0-2 GF: - Fm: 0-3
Distance:	2m/2m3: 0-0 2m4-2m7: 0-6 3m+: 0-7
Track:	LH: 0-0 RH: 0-6 Tight: 0-0 Gall: 0-0
Aids:	Bl: 0-2 Vi: 0-0 Tstrap: 0-0
Best Rating:	116 8/00 Gway 2m6f good Ch

Scamp

93f   **91f**

4-y-o b f Selkirk (USA)-Cut And Run (Slip Anchor)
H D Daly (D E Cantillon 18/12) Million In Mind Partnership (12)

Placings:*201*   (4600)
2002/03: 12²G, 16⁹G, 17¹GF,

	Starts	1st	2nd	3rd	Win & Pl
NH Flat	3	1	1	0	3826
Career Total	3	1	1	0	3826

86 4/03 Extr 2m1f H NHF G-F £3024
Total win prize-money £3024

Going:	Sf: 0-0 GS: 0-0 Gd: 0-2 GF: - Fm: 1-1
Distance:	2m/2m3: 1-2 2m4-2m7: 0-0 3m+: 0-0
Track:	LH: 0-0 RH: 1-2 Tight: 0-0 Gall: 0-1
Aids:	Bl: 0-0 Vi: 0-0 Tstrap: 0-0
Best Rating:	91 12/02 Newb 1m4f110y good NHF

Half-brother to the stayer Ski Run; awarded fast ground bumper after being short-headed at Exeter April 2003; runner-up next time.

Scarborough Fair (IRE)

97   **105**

6-y-o b g Synefos (USA)-Hue N Cry (IRE) (Denel (FR))
Jonjo O Neill Sir Robert Ogden

Placings:*0-30P*   (3147)
2002/03: 24³S, 21⁰GS, 24PHY,

	Starts	1st	2nd	3rd	Win & Pl
Hurdles	3	0	0	1	378
Career Total	4	0	0	1	378

Going:	Sf: 0-2 GS: 0-1 Gd: 0-0 GF: - Fm: 0-0
Distance:	2m/2m3: 0-0 2m4-2m7: 0-1 3m+: 0-2
Track:	LH: 0-3 RH: 0-0 Tight: 0-0 Gall: 0-1
Aids:	Bl: 0-0 Vi: 0-0 Tstrap: 0-0
Best Rating:	105 11/02 Chep 3m soft Hdl

Showed a marked improvement on his hurdling debut over three miles at Newbury in March 2002 when third at Chepstow in November. Well beaten since.

Scarface

103   **84**

6-y-o ch h Hernando (FR)-Scarlatine (IRE) (Alzao (USA))
A G Hobbs Three Counties Racing

Placings:*0P600*   (4252)
2002/03: 16⁰S, 20PHY, 16⁶S, 19⁰S, 22⁰G,

	Starts	1st	2nd	3rd	Win & Pl
Hurdles	5	0	0	0	0
Career Total	5	0	0	0	0

Going:	Sf: 0-4 GS: 0-0 Gd: 0-1 GF: - Fm: 0-0
Distance:	2m/2m3: 0-2 2m4-2m7: 0-3 3m+: 0-0
Track:	LH: 0-1 RH: 0-4 Tight: 0-1 Gall: 0-1
Aids:	Bl: 0-0 Vi: 0-0 Tstrap: 0-0
Best Rating:	84 1/03 Hntg 2m110y soft Hdl

Moderate hurdler; a winner on the Flat in Germany; shown limited promise over hurdles.

Scarletti (GER)

108   **117+**

6-y-o ch g Master Willie-Solidago (USA) (Decies)
Jonjo O Neill Strathayr Publishing Ltd

Placings:2-2214122   (4767)
2002/03: 16²GS, 16²GF, 16²GF, 16¹GS, 17⁴GF, 16¹G, 16²G, 20²G,

	Starts	1st	2nd	3rd	Win & Pl
Hurdles	8	2	5	0	19764
Career Total	8	2	5	0	19764

114 9/02 Worc 2m D(0-115)HHdl GD £4342
86 8/02 Prth 2m110y D Hdl G-S £4888
Total win prize-money £9230

Going:	Sf: 0-0 GS: 1-2 Gd: 1-3 GF: - Fm: 0-3
Distance:	2m/2m3: 2-7 2m4-2m7: 0-1 3m+: 0-0
Track:	LH: 1-4 RH: 1-4 Tight: 0-2 Gall: 0-0
Aids:	Bl: 0-0 Vi: 0-0 **Tstrap: 1-2**
Best Rating:	114 10/02 Chel 2m110y good Hdl

Modest hurdler; stays two and a half miles; acts on ground either side of good; consistent.

Scattiehattie

8-y-o gr m Arzanni-Kiki Star (Some Hand)
M Hill Mrs Caroline Greenslade

Placings:*P*   (0574)
2002/03: 22PG,

	Starts	1st	2nd	3rd	Win & Pl
Hurdles	1	0	0	0	0
Career Total	1	0	0	0	0

Going:	Sf: 0-0 GS: 0-0 Gd: 0-0 GF: - Fm: 0-0
Distance:	2m/2m3: 0-0 2m4-2m7: 0-1 3m+: 0-0
Track:	LH: 0-1 RH: 0-0 Tight: 0-1 Gall: 0-0
Aids:	Bl: 0-0 Vi: 0-0 Tstrap: 0-0
Best Rating:	0 6/02 NAbb 2m6f good Hdl

Scenic Storm (IRE)

     84

8-y-o b g Scenic-Sit Elnaas (USA) (Sir Ivor)
Ferdy Murphy Leeds Plywood And Doors Ltd

Placings:*0/004/0P45P-P*   (2132)
2002/03: 24PG,

	Starts	1st	2nd	3rd	Win & Pl
Chases	1	0	0	0	0
Career Total	10	0	0	0	339

Going:	Sf: 0-0 GS: 0-0 Gd: 0-1 GF: - Fm: 0-0
Distance:	2m/2m3: 0-0 2m4-2m7: 0-0 3m+: 0-1
Track:	LH: 0-0 RH: 0-1 Tight: 0-1 Gall: 0-0
Aids:	Bl: 0-0 Vi: 0-0 Tstrap: 0-0
Best Rating:	84 2/02 Fknm 3m110y gd-sft Ch

Very ordinary hurdling form in plating-class company to date.

Scented Air

106   **113**

6-y-o b m Lion Cavern (USA)-Jungle Rose (Shirley Heights)
J D Czerpak (P W Hiatt 24/3) Stampede Racing

Placings:*120104*   (4780)
2002/03: 16¹G, 16²G, 16³GS, 16¹G, 16⁹GS, 16⁴GF,

	Starts	1st	2nd	3rd	Win & Pl
Hurdles	6	2	1	0	10443
Career Total	6	2	1	0	10443

100 12/02 Ludl 2m E(0-110)HHdl GD £4056
87 10/02 Strf 2m110y G Hdl GD £2303
Total win prize-money £6359

Going:	Sf: 0-0 GS: 0-2 Gd: 2-3 GF: - Fm: 0-1

Schedule B

78   **57**

5-y-o ch g Dancing Spree (USA)-Jolizal (Good Times (ITY))
R Hollinshead Andrew Lawrence

Placings:*5*   (1008)
2002/03: 20⁵GF,

	Starts	1st	2nd	3rd	Win & Pl
Hurdles	1	0	0	0	0
Career Total	1	0	0	0	0

Going:	Sf: 0-0 GS: 0-0 Gd: 0-0 GF: - Fm: 0-1
Distance:	2m/2m3: 0-0 2m4-2m7: 0-1 3m+: 0-0
Track:	LH: 0-1 RH: 0-0 Tight: 0-1 Gall: 0-0
Aids:	Bl: 0-0 Vi: 0-0 Tstrap: 0-0
Best Rating:	61 8/02 Bang 2m4f gd-fm Hdl

Schemer (IRE)

75   **80**

8-y-o ch g Samhoi (USA)-Gambling Princess Vii (Damsire Unregistered)
Mrs S J Smith Mrs S Smith

Placings:*3/000-P2P0*   (1006)
2002/03: 20PGS, 21²GF, 16PG, 20⁹GF,

	Starts	1st	2nd	3rd	Win & Pl
Hurdles	3	0	1	0	549
Chases	1	0	0	0	0
Career Total	8	0	1	1	763

Going:	Sf: 0-0 GS: 0-1 Gd: 0-1 GF: - Fm: 0-2
Distance:	2m/2m3: 0-1 2m4-2m7: 0-3 3m+: 0-0
Track:	LH: 0-4 RH: 0-0 Tight: 0-2 Gall: 0-0
Aids:	Bl: 0-0 Vi: 0-0 Tstrap: 0-0
Best Rating:	95 9/00 Worc 2m gd-fm NHF

Runner-up in poor selling hurdle over an extended 21 furlongs at Southwell July 2002.

Schoolhouse Walk

5-y-o b g Mistertopogigo (IRE)-Restandbejoyful (Takachiho)
Mrs S Lamyman P Lamyman

Placings:*4000*   (1627)
2002/03: 17⁴GF, 16⁹G, 17⁹GF, 16⁹GS,

	Starts	1st	2nd	3rd	Win & Pl
NH Flat	4	0	0	0	0
Career Total	4	0	0	0	0

Going:	Sf: 0-0 GS: 0-1 Gd: 0-1 GF: - Fm: 0-2
Distance:	2m/2m3: 0-4 2m4-2m7: 0-0 3m+: 0-0
Track:	LH: 0-2 RH: 0-2 Tight: 0-3 Gall: 0-0
Aids:	Bl: 0-0 Vi: 0-0 Tstrap: 0-0
Best Rating:	87 6/02 MRas 2m1f110y gd-fm NHF

Schuh Venture (IRE)

91   **84**

8-y-o b g Little Bighorn-Elegant Miss (Prince Tenderfoot (USA))

Now, modest hurdler; best at around two miles; acts on good ground; likes to race prominently.

	Sf: 0-0 GS: 1-2 Gd: 1-2 Tight: 1-2 Gall: 0-1
Track:	LH: 1-4 RH: 1-2 **Tight: 1-2** Gall: 0-1
Aids:	Bl: 0-0 Vi: 0-0 Tstrap: 0-0
Best Rating:	113 4/03 Sand 2m110y gd-fm Hdl

Dr P Pritchard Not Going To Cheltenham Partnership

Placings:*40/5P02/P566P*   (4004)
2002/03: 22^FG, 20⁵S, 16⁶S, 19⁶S, 22^PS,

	Starts	1st	2nd	3rd	Win & Pl
Hurdles	5	0	0	0	575
Career Total	11	0	1	0	1211

Going:	Sf: 0-4 GS: 0-0 Gd: 0-1 GF: - Fm: 0-0
Distance:	2m2m3: 0-0 2m4-2m7: 0-3 3m+: 0-0
Track:	LH: 0-3 RH: 0-2 Tight: 0-0 Gall: 0-0
Aids:	Bl: 0-0 Vi: 0-0 Tstrap: 0-0
Best Rating:	94 10/00 Aint 2m110y good Hdl

Scola Gravaca (IRE)
82   49
5-y-o ch g Petardia-Mystery Bid (Auction Ring (USA))
Mrs L Wadham (K A Morgan 16/5) The Badlingham Syndicate

Placings:*00-000*   (4117)
2002/03: 16⁶GF, 17⁰HY, 16⁰G,

	Starts	1st	2nd	3rd	Win & Pl
NH Flat	1	0	0	0	0
Hurdles	2	0	0	0	0
Career Total	5	0	0		0

Going:	Sf: 0-1 GS: 0-0 Gd: 0-0 GF: - Fm: 0-1
Distance:	2m2m3: 0-3 2m4-2m7: 0-0 3m+: 0-0
Track:	LH: 0-0 RH: 0-3 Tight: 0-1 Gall: 0-1
Aids:	Bl: 0-0 Vi: 0-1 Tstrap: 0-1
Best Rating:	80 3/02 Hntg 2m110y gd-fm NHF

Scolardy (IRE)
92   144d
5-y-o b g Turtle Island (IRE)-Emerald Pendant (Nebos (GER))
W P Mullins David Flynn

Placings:*012121-00*   (4099)
2002/03: 16⁰G, 16⁰G,

	Starts	1st	2nd	3rd	Win & Pl
Hurdles	2	0	0	0	
Career Total	8	3	2	0	69000
144	3/02	Chel	2m1f	A Hdl	GD £52200
122	1/02	Thur	2m	Hdl	Y-S £6138
110	11/01	Thur	2m	Hdl	Y-S £3895
			Total win prize-money £62233

Going:	Sf: 0-0 GS: 0-0 Gd: 0-2 GF: - Fm: 0-0
Distance:	2m2m3: 0-2 2m4-2m7: 0-0 3m+: 0-0
Track:	LH: 0-2 RH: 0-0 Tight: 0-0 Gall: 0-1
Aids:	Bl: 0-0 Vi: 0-0 Tstrap: 0-0
Best Rating:	144 3/02 Chel 2m1f good Hdl

Very useful juvenile hurdler in 2001/02; consistent in Ireland before running away with the 2002 Triumph Hurdle; suffered a setback early in the 2002/3 season and showed little sign of former ability on return; suited by 2m; goes well on good ground, but handles much softer.

Scolboa (IRE)
92   91
6-y-o gr m Bob s Return (IRE)-Dont Rough It (Pragmatic)
I R Ferguson Meter Syndicate

Placings:*55600520*   (4774)
2002/03: 16⁵S, 20⁵S, 20⁶S, 18⁰YS, 24⁰HY, 20⁵Y, 22²G, 27⁰G,

	Starts	1st	2nd	3rd	Win & Pl
NH Flat	1	0	0	0	0

Hurdles	7	0	1	0	935
Career Total	8	0	1	0	935

Going:	Sf: 0-4 GS: 0-0 Gd: 0-2 GF: - Fm: 0-0
Distance:	2m2m3: 0-2 2m4-2m7: 0-4 3m+: 0-2
Track:	LH: 0-1 RH: 0-0 Tight: 0-0 Gall: 0-0
Aids:	Bl: 0-0 Vi: 0-0 Tstrap: 0-0
Best Rating:	91 3/03 Dpat 2m6f good Hdl

Scoop (IRE)
77(101h)   (97h)75
7-y-o b m Scenic-Big Story (Cadeaux Genereux)
G M Moore Major E J Watt

Placings:*5633/P/21P32-0*   (0184)
2002/03: 16⁰G,

	Starts	1st	2nd	3rd	Win & Pl
Chases	1	0	0	0	
Career Total	11	1	2	3	4743
97	5/01	Hexm	2m	F(0-110)HHdl	G-F £1848
			Total win prize-money £1848

Going:	Sf: 0-0 GS: 0-0 Gd: 0-1 GF: - Fm: 0-0
Distance:	2m2m3: 0-1 2m4-2m7: 0-0 3m+: 0-0
Track:	LH: 0-1 RH: 0-0 Tight: 0-0 Gall: 0-0
Aids:	Bl: 0-0 Vi: 0-0 Tstrap: 0-0
Best Rating:	97 6/01 Prth 2m110y firm Hdl

Scoop Thirty Nine
94   67
5-y-o b m Petoski-Welsh Clover (Cruise Missile)
Mrs E Slack Mrs Evelyn Slack

Placings:*P0-6P16*   (4711)
2002/03: 21⁶GF, 20⁵S, 17¹G, 16⁶GF,

	Starts	1st	2nd	3rd	Win & Pl
Hurdles	4	1	0	0	2436
Career Total	6	1	0	0	2436
64	3/03	Sedg	2m1f	G(0-90)HHdl	GD £2436
			Total win prize-money £2436

Going:	Sf: 0-1 GS: 0-0 Gd: 1-1 GF: - Fm: 0-2
Distance:	2m2m3: 1-2 2m4-2m7: 0-2 3m+: 0-0
Track:	LH: 1-4 RH: 0-0 Tight: 1-2 Gall: 0-1
Aids:	Bl: 0-0 Vi: 0-0 Tstrap: 0-0
Best Rating:	67 4/03 Weth 2m gd-fm Hdl

Scoring Pedigree (IRE)
100   109
11-y-o b g King Luthier-Quick Romance (Lucky Brief)
J W Mullins Wilsford Racing Partnership

Placings:*01340/1P/225/3/3345/2345F12P23P2-462F*   (2011)
2002/03: 20⁴GF, 24⁶GS, 21²G, 23^FGF,

	Starts	1st	2nd	3rd	Win & Pl
Chases	4	0	1	0	2454
Career Total	31	3	7	6	25337
102	11/01	Folk	2m5f	F(0-90)Ch	GD £3493
117	11/97	Kemp	2m5f	D Hdl	G-F £2857
106	12/96	Bang	2m1f	H NHF	GD £1658
			Total win prize-money £8009

Going:	Sf: 0-0 GS: 0-1 Gd: 0-1 GF: - Fm: 0-2
Distance:	2m2m3: 0-0 2m4-2m7: 0-2 3m+: 0-0
Track:	LH: 0-1 RH: 0-2 Tight: 0-2 Gall: 0-0
Aids:	Bl: 0-0 Vi: 0-2 Tstrap: 0-0

Best Rating: 128 3/97 Chel 2m110y gd-fm NHF

Modest hurdler, fair chaser who has had his share of problems. Finally got off the mark over fences in November 2001 when dropping in grade, and continued to run well subsequently without winning. Effective at up to two miles-six over fences. Does not want the ground too soft, has worn a visor.

Scotia Nostra (IRE)
95   96
11-y-o b g High Estate-Crown Witness (Crowned Prince (USA))
Miss Venetia Williams Favourites Racing

Placings:*1400/P112F52/100P/3F*   (4324)
2002/03: 24³GS, 24^FG,

	Starts	1st	2nd	3rd	Win & Pl
Chases	2	0	0		1580
Career Total	17	4	2	1	31528
129	2/00	Hayd	3m	B(0-140)HCh	HVY £10491
122	11/98	Carl	2m4f110yD Ch		HVY £3598
122	11/98	Ayr	2m5f110yD(0-110)HCh		G-S £3756
117	12/97	Thur	2m	Hdl	SH £3730
			Total win prize-money £21576

Going:	Sf: 0-0 GS: 0-1 Gd: 0-1 GF: - Fm: 0-0
Distance:	2m2m3: 0-0 2m4-2m7: 0-0 3m+: 0-2
Track:	LH: 0-2 RH: 0-0 Tight: 0-1 Gall: 0-1
Aids:	Bl: 0-0 Vi: 0-0 Tstrap: 0-0
Best Rating:	131 12/98 Chel 2m5f good Ch

Fair chaser; stays three miles; acts on good and heavy ground; ran well in March 2003 after a near three-year absence.

Scotish Law (IRE)
102   101
5-y-o ch g Case Law-Scotia Rose (Tap On Wood)
P R Chamings Inhurst Farm Stables Partnership

Placings:*023*   (4285)
2002/03: 16⁰GS, 19²S, 21³GF,

	Starts	1st	2nd	3rd	Win & Pl
Hurdles	3	0	1	1	1659
Career Total	3	0	1	1	1659

Going:	Sf: 0-1 GS: 0-1 Gd: 0-0 GF: - Fm: 0-1
Distance:	2m2m3: 0-2 2m4-2m7: 0-2 3m+: 0-0
Track:	LH: 0-0 RH: 0-3 Tight: 0-0 Gall: 0-0
Aids:	Bl: 0-0 Vi: 0-0 Tstrap: 0-0
Best Rating:	91 3/03 Ludl 2m5f gd-fm Hdl

Big improvement on hurdling debut when runner-up to easy winner Throwaline over extended 19 furlongs at Hereford on soft ground; seemed to have his fair share of weight when third on handicap debut at Exeter May 2003; keen going sort and unseated rider and bolted before start next time; not disgraced when runner-up to the improving Too Technical at Stratford in July.

Scotmail Boy (IRE)
104   94
10-y-o b g Over The River (FR)-Princess Paula (Smoggy)
J Howard Johnson George Tobitt

Placings:*05P/5000P/2P13212/61P3/02P06P-045342*   (4662)
2002/03: 24⁰GS, 30⁴GF, 20⁵G, 32³S, 21⁴G, 26²GF,

	Starts	1st	2nd	3rd	Win & Pl
Chases	6	0	1	1	3595
Career Total	31	3	5	3	27143
106	11/00	Carl	3m2f	C(0-130)HCh	SFT £6760

96	3/00	Sedg	2m5f	E Ch		G-F	£3342
93	1/00	Sedg	3m3f	E Ch		SFT	£2658
					Total win prize-money		£12762

Going: Sf: 0-1 GS: 0-1 Gd: 0-3 GF: - Fm: 0-1
Distance: 2m/2m3: 0-0 2m4-2m7: 0-2 3m+: 0-4
Track: LH: 0-5 RH: 0-1 Tight: 0-2 Gall: 0-0
Aids: Bl: 0-0 Vi: 0-0 Tstrap: 0-0
Best Rating: 120 11/01 Carl 3m2f heavy Ch

Moderate chaser; third in the John Hughes Trophy Chase at Aintree on his final start of the 2000/2001, but suffered in the handicap as a result and modest form since; a sound jumper, he acts on any ground, stays well and is probably best without blinkers nowadays.

Scotmail Lad (IRE)
111 117
9-y-o b g Ilium-Nicholas Ferry (Floriferous)
G M Moore Gordon Brown/bert Watson

Placings:041/3134115135/52406/222236322/P362245211
PP-36324 (4436)
2002/03: 20³S, 20⁶HY, 20⁵S, 22²GS, 24⁴G,

	Starts	1st	2nd	3rd	Win & Pl
Chases	5	0	1	2	6245
Career Total	44	7	11	8	42321

120	3/02	MRas	2m4f	E Ch		SFT	£3419
114	2/02	Leic	2m4f110yE(0-105)HCh			SFT	£3627
122	3/99	Kels	2m6fl110yE(0-120)HHdl			SFT	£2892
125	1/99	Weth	2m4f110yE(0-105)HHdl			HVY	£2066
123	12/98	Ayr	2m4f	E Hdl		HVY	£2794
100	10/98	Carl	2m1f	E Hdl		HVY	£2458
100	3/98	Hexm	2m	H NHF		GD	£1455
				Total win prize-money			£18711

Going: Sf: 0-3 GS: 0-1 Gd: 0-1 GF: - Fm: 0-0
Distance: 2m/2m3: 0-0 2m4-2m7: 0-4 3m+: 0-1
Track: LH: 0-4 RH: 0-1 Tight: 0-2 Gall: 0-1
Aids: Bl: 0-3 Vi: 0-0 Tstrap: 0-1
Best Rating: 127 3/99 Newc 3m soft Hdl

Fair chaser; best over two and a half miles; suited by soft ground; has worn a visor or blinkers; suited by forcing tactics.

Scotmail Park
4-y-o b g Presidium-Miss Tri Colour (Shavian)
G M Moore Gordon Brown/bert Watson

Placings:PP (3912)
2002/03: 16⁶S, 17⁷GS,

	Starts	1st	2nd	3rd	Win & Pl
Hurdles	2	0	0	0	
Career Total	2	0	0	0	

Going: Sf: 0-1 GS: 0-1 Gd: 0-0 GF: - Fm: 0-0
Distance: 2m/2m3: 0-2 2m4-2m7: 0-0 3m+: 0-0
Track: LH: 0-1 RH: 0-1 Tight: 0-0 Gall: 0-1
Aids: Bl: 0-0 Vi: 0-0 Tstrap: 0-0
Best Rating: 0 3/03 Carl 2m1f gd-sft Hdl

Scots Grey
111 (115h) (131h) 142
8-y-o gr g Terimon-Misowni (Niniski (USA))
N J Henderson W H Ponsonby

Placings:2165/445110320-122133F (4557)
2002/03: 20¹GS, 20²GS, 19²S, 20¹GS, 20³G, 20³G, 33³G

	Starts	1st	2nd	3rd	Win & Pl
Chases	7	2	2	2	34996

	Career Total	20	5	4	3	55930
133	2/03	Kemp	2m4f110yD Ch		G-S	£7150
132	11/02	Hntg	2m4f110yD Ch		G-S	£4732
125	12/01	Asct	2m4f	E(0-115)HHdl	GD	£6987
120	12/01	Ludl	2m	F(0-110)HHdl	GD	£3474
120	11/00	MRas	2m4f110yE Hdl		G-S	£2634
			Total win prize-money			£24979

Going: Sf: 0-1 GS: 2-3 Gd: 0-3 GF: - Fm: 0-0
Distance: 2m/2m3: 0-0 2m4-2m7: 2-6 3m+: 0-1
Track: LH: 0-3 RH: 2-4 Tight: 0-0 Gall: 1-3
Aids: Bl: 0-0 Vi: 0-0 Tstrap: 0-0
Best Rating: 142 3/03 Chel 2m4f110y good Ch

Progressive handicap hurdler in 2001/2; jumped soundly when winning on chase debut at Huntingdon in November; ran well against potentially top-class opponents subsequently, and scored again at Kempton; all his wins have been on right-handed tracks; stays two and a half miles, handles good ground or softer; likes to make the running.

Scottie York
80 49
7-y-o b g Noble Patriarch-Devon Dancer (Shareef Dancer (USA))
P Monteith James Shaw

Placings:0/000/05 (0454)
2002/03: 16⁵GF, 20⁶G,

	Starts	1st	2nd	3rd	Win & Pl
Hurdles	2	0	0	0	0
Career Total	5	0	0	0	0

Going: Sf: 0-0 GS: 0-0 Gd: 0-1 GF: - Fm: 0-1
Distance: 2m/2m3: 0-1 2m4-2m7: 0-1 3m+: 0-0
Track: LH: 0-1 RH: 0-1 Tight: 0-1 Gall: 0-0
Aids: Bl: 0-0 Vi: 0-0 Tstrap: 0-0
Best Rating: 68 10/99 Weth 2m gd-fm Hdl

Scottish Clover
10-y-o ch m Scottish Reel-National Clover (National Trust)
Mrs H Dalton Michael H Ings

Placings:4PP (3346)
2002/03: 23⁴G, 25²PS, 23⁵PS,

	Starts	1st	2nd	3rd	Win & Pl
Chases	3	0	0	0	317
Career Total	3	0	0	0	317

Going: Sf: 0-2 GS: 0-0 Gd: 0-1 GF: - Fm: 0-0
Distance: 2m/2m3: 0-0 2m4-2m7: 0-0 3m+: 0-3
Track: LH: 0-0 RH: 0-3 Tight: 0-0 Gall: 0-0
Aids: Bl: 0-0 Vi: 0-0 Tstrap: 0-0
Best Rating: 0 1/03 Leic 2m7f110y soft Ch

Scottish Dance
99 98
6-y-o ch m Bustino-Highland Lyric (Rymer)
N J Henderson Stephen Owen

Placings:2122-0610 (4326)
2002/03: 19⁹GS, 16⁶GS, 19¹G, 21⁰G,

	Starts	1st	2nd	3rd	Win & Pl
Hurdles	4	1	0	0	5119
Career Total	8	2	3	0	8313

98	2/03	Hrfd	2m3f110yD Hdl		GD	£5118
98	1/02	Hntg	2m110y H NHF		G-S	£1603
			Total win prize-money			£6722

Going: Sf: 0-0 GS: 0-2 Gd: 1-2 GF: - Fm: 0-0
Distance: 2m/2m3: 0-1 2m4-2m7: 1-3 3m+: 0-0
Track: LH: 0-1 RH: 1-3 Tight: 0-1 Gall: 0-1
Aids: Bl: 0-0 Vi: 0-0 Tstrap: 0-1
Best Rating: 100 2/02 Ludl 2m good NHF

Bumper winner; fair novice hurdler; stays two and a half miles; effective on good ground.

Scottish Memories (IRE)
113 160
7-y-o ch g Houmayoun (FR)-Interj (Salmon Leap (USA))
Noel Meade Mrs Mary Halligan

Placings:20011-51240 (4099)
2002/03: 16⁵GF, 16¹HY, 20²SH, 16⁴YS, 16⁹G,

	Starts	1st	2nd	3rd	Win & Pl
Hurdles	5	1	1	0	23238
Career Total	10	3	2	0	79890

154	11/02	DRoy	2m	Hdl		HVY	£11963
154	4/02	Punc	2m	Hdl		YLD	£32233
153	4/02	Fair	2m	Hdl		G-Y	£23128
				Total win prize-money			£67325

Going: Sf: 1-1 GS: 0-0 Gd: 0-1 GF: - Fm: 0-1
Distance: 2m/2m3: 1-4 2m4-2m7: 0-1 3m+: 0-0
Track: LH: 0-2 RH: 0-1 Tight: 0-0 Gall: 0-0
Aids: Bl: 0-0 Vi: 0-0 Tstrap: 0-0
Best Rating: 160 12/02 Fair 2m4f sft-hvy Hdl

High-class Irish hurdler; looked set for the top when winning a couple of Graded races in the spring of 2002 and valid excuses for defeats by Intersky Falcon (needed race), Limestone Lad (trip and ground) and Like-A-Butterfly (interrupted preparation); effective from 2m to 2m 4f; acts on heavy ground, but reportedly prefers a sound surface.

Scottish Roots
8-y-o b g Roscoe Blake-Lothian Queen (Scorpio (FR))
C R Egerton Mrs C N Weatherby & Lady Daresbury

Placings:350-PP (0335)
2002/03: 23⁸G, 23⁷G,

	Starts	1st	2nd	3rd	Win & Pl
Hurdles	2	0	0	0	
Career Total	5	0	0	1	208

Going: Sf: 0-0 GS: 0-0 Gd: 0-2 GF: - Fm: 0-0
Distance: 2m/2m3: 0-0 2m4-2m7: 0-1 3m+: 0-1
Track: LH: 0-2 RH: 0-0 Tight: 0-0 Gall: 0-0
Aids: Bl: 0-1 Vi: 0-0 Tstrap: 0-0
Best Rating: 102 10/01 Chel 2m110y good NHF

Scottish Song
96 80
10-y-o b g Niniski (USA)-Miss Saint-Cloud (Nonoalco (USA))
Mrs M Reveley Mrs M Reveley

Placings:1/1/4/000/03 (4168)
2002/03: 16⁹G, 20³GS,

	Starts	1st	2nd	3rd	Win & Pl
Hurdles	2	0	0	1	648
Career Total	8	2	0	1	6521

117	5/98	Leop	2m	NHF		G-F	£2978
108	3/98	Leop	2m	NHF		G-Y	£2680
				Total win prize-money			£5658

Going: Sf: 0-0 GS: 0-1 Gd: 0-1 GF: - Fm: 0-0

Distance:	2m/2m3: 0-1 2m4-2m7: 0-1 3m+: 0-0
Track:	LH: 0-2 RH: 0-2 Tight: 0-0 Gall: 0-1
Aids:	Bl: 0-0 Vi: 0-0 Tstrap: 0-0
Best Rating:	117 5/98 Leop 2m gd-fm NHF

Plating-class hurdler; stayed two and a half miles. (DEAD)

Scotton Green

106   **125d**

12-y-o ch g Ardross-Grange Hill Girl (Workboy)
T D Easterby The I.B. & B.D.F. Partnership

Placings:0P0/52/F31011/220211226P/23P21130/2FP5225 3/PP225U30-P50FR4   **(3093)**
2002/03: 26PS, 25SS, 27GGS, 31FGS, 33RS, 24⁴G,

	Starts	1st	2nd	3rd	Win & Pl
Chases	6	0	0	0	626
Career Total	51	7	13	5	122571
122	2/00	Newc	4m1f	B(0-150)HCh	HVY	£29000
116	2/00	Catt	3m6f	C(0-130)HCh	GD	£7052
126	1/99	Catt	3m11f110yE Ch		SFT	£4266
112	12/98	Hayd	3m	D(0-110)HCh	SFT	£3793
111	1/98	Ayr	3m110y	D(0-110)HHdl	G-S	£2897
97	1/98	Weth	2m4f110yF(0-105)HHdl	SFT	£2150
94	11/97	Aint	2m4f	E(0-110)HHdl	GD	£2710
			Total win prize-money £51871

Going:	Sf: 0-3 GS: 0-2 Gd: 0-1 GF: - Fm: 0-0
Distance:	2m/2m3: 0-0 2m4-2m7: 0-0 3m+: 0-6
Track:	LH: 0-4 RH: 0-2 Tight: 0-3 Gall: 0-1
Aids:	Bl: 0-5 Vi: 0-0 Tstrap: 0-0
Best Rating:	126 2/99 Uttx 3m2f heavy Ch

Useful chaser; tough stayer, he was trained for the Tote Northern National at Newcastle in February 2001 and beat everything bar the progressive novice Narrow Water. An excellent third from 17lb outside the handicap in the Whitbread Gold Cup on his final start, he ran his best race last term when third in the Midlands Grand National. Ran well for a long way in the Becher Chase but refused when exhausted at Market Rasen on Boxing Day. Acts well on soft ground.

Scowlin Brig

99(95h)   **73**

7-y-o ch g Minster Son-Gideonscleuch (Beverley Boy)
F P Murtagh D McLeod

Placings:05/P505-63P353   **(2421)**
2002/03: 21⁶GF, 21³G, 24⁴G, 27³G, 25⁵HY, 27³S,

	Starts	1st	2nd	3rd	Win & Pl
Hurdles	1	0	0	0	0
Chases	5	0	0	3	1757
Career Total	12	0	0	3	1757

Going:	Sf: 0-2 GS: 0-0 Gd: 0-3 GF: - Fm: 0-1
Distance:	2m/2m3: 0-0 2m4-2m7: 0-2 3m+: 0-4
Track:	LH: 0-6 RH: 0-0 Tight: 0-5 Gall: 0-0
Aids:	Bl: 0-0 Vi: 0-0 Tstrap: 0-0
Best Rating:	76 2/01 Sedg 2m1f soft NHF

Has not shown much over fences.

Scrapman

97   **82**

10-y-o ch g Backchat (USA)-Saila Thims (Alias Smith (USA))
G A Swinbank S Bell

Placings:0/040   **(0616)**
2002/03: 16⁰G, 17⁴G, 20⁰GF,

	Starts	1st	2nd	3rd	Win & Pl
Hurdles	3	0	0	0	281

Career Total	4	0	0	0	281

Going:	Sf: 0-0 GS: 0-0 Gd: 0-2 GF: - Fm: 0-1
Distance:	2m/2m3: 0-2 2m4-2m7: 0-1 3m+: 0-0
Track:	LH: 0-3 RH: 0-0 Tight: 0-1 Gall: 0-0
Aids:	Bl: 0-0 Vi: 0-0 Tstrap: 0-0
Best Rating:	82 6/02 Ctml 2m1f110y good Hdl

Lightly-raced maiden hurdler.

Scratch The Dove

101   **96**

6-y-o b m Henbit (USA)-Coney Dove (Celtic Cone)
C J Price Cecil J Price

Placings:400-2P1543   **(4194)**
2002/03: 20²S, 19⁴PG, 20¹HY, 16⁵G, 21⁴GS, 21³G,

	Starts	1st	2nd	3rd	Win & Pl
Hurdles	6	1	1	1	6273
Career Total	9	1	1	1	6273
96	11/02	Leic	2m4f110yE(0-105)HHdl	HVY	£4104
			Total win prize-money £4105

Going:	Sf: 1-2 GS: 0-1 Gd: 0-3 GF: - Fm: 0-0
Distance:	2m/2m3: 0-1 2m4-2m7: 1-5 3m+: 0-0
Track:	LH: 0-1 RH: 1-5 Tight: 0-1 Gall: 0-0
Aids:	Bl: 0-0 Vi: 0-0 Tstrap: 0-0
Best Rating:	96 3/03 Ludl 2m5f good Hdl

Narrow winner of a weak mares novices hurdle in heavy ground in November 2002. Stays two and a half miles.

Scravels

76   **53**

4-y-o ch g Elmaamul (USA)-Defined Feature (IRE) (Nabeel Dancer (USA))
J K Price (Dr J D Scargill 7/8) J K Price

Placings:06F   **(4021)**
2002/03: 16⁰HY, 19⁶G, 17⁷S,

	Starts	1st	2nd	3rd	Win & Pl
Hurdles	3	0	0	0	0
Career Total	3	0	0	0	0

Going:	Sf: 0-2 GS: 0-0 Gd: 0-1 GF: - Fm: 0-0
Distance:	2m/2m3: 0-2 2m4-2m7: 0-1 3m+: 0-0
Track:	LH: 0-1 RH: 0-2 Tight: 0-0 Gall: 0-0
Aids:	Bl: 0-0 Vi: 0-0 Tstrap: 0-0
Best Rating:	53 3/03 Hrfd 2m1f soft Hdl

Scrumpy

81f   **45f**

4-y-o b g Sir Harry Lewis (USA)-Superfina (USA) (Fluorescent Light (USA))
S E H Sherwood Mrs Strachan,Graham,Boyne,Lywood,Parkes

Placings:0   **(4122)**
2002/03: 16⁰G,

	Starts	1st	2nd	3rd	Win & Pl
NH Flat	1	0	0	0	
Career Total	1	0	0	0	

Going:	Sf: 0-0 GS: 0-0 Gd: 0-1 GF: - Fm: 0-0
Distance:	2m/2m3: 0-1 2m4-2m7: 0-0 3m+: 0-0
Track:	LH: 0-0 RH: 0-1 Tight: 0-0 Gall: 0-1
Aids:	Bl: 0-0 Vi: 0-0 Tstrap: 0-0
Best Rating:	45 3/03 Hntg 2m110y good NHF

Scruton

9-y-o b g Cruise Missile-My Martina (My Swallow)
R Ford (Trainer Unknown 12/5) Mrs J M Russell

Placings:P   **(0503)**
2002/03: 26RG,

	Starts	1st	2nd	3rd	Win & Pl
Chases	1	0	0	0	
Career Total	1	0	0	0	

Going:	Sf: 0-0 GS: 0-0 Gd: 0-1 GF: - Fm: 0-0
Distance:	2m/2m3: 0-0 2m4-2m7: 0-0 3m+: 0-1
Track:	LH: 0-1 RH: 0-0 Tight: 0-0 Gall: 0-0
Aids:	Bl: 0-0 Vi: 0-0 Tstrap: 0-0
Best Rating:	0 6/02 Ctml 3m2f good Ch

Sculptor

97   **96**

4-y-o b g Salse (USA)-Classic Colleen (IRE) (Sadler s Wells (USA))
C J Mann (G A Butler 16/8) Magic Moments

Placings:0   **(3287)**
2002/03: 17⁰GS,

	Starts	1st	2nd	3rd	Win & Pl
Hurdles	1	0	0	0	
Career Total	1	0	0	0	

Going:	Sf: 0-0 GS: 0-1 Gd: 0-0 GF: - Fm: 0-0
Distance:	2m/2m3: 0-1 2m4-2m7: 0-0 3m+: 0-0
Track:	LH: 0-1 RH: 0-0 Tight: 0-0 Gall: 0-1
Aids:	Bl: 0-0 Vi: 0-0 Tstrap: 0-0
Best Rating:	76 1/03 Chel 2m1f gd-sft Hdl

Modest hurdler; stiff task on hurdles debut, but good second at Wincanton on second start.

Scurra

4-y-o b g Spectrum (IRE)-Tamnia (Green Desert (USA))
A C Whillans (R Wilman 28/10) Mrs L M Whillans

Placings:PP   **(3771)**
2002/03: 16⁶GS, 16⁶GS,

	Starts	1st	2nd	3rd	Win & Pl
Hurdles	2	0	0	0	
Career Total	2	0	0	0	

Going:	Sf: 0-0 GS: 0-2 Gd: 0-0 GF: - Fm: 0-0
Distance:	2m/2m3: 0-2 2m4-2m7: 0-0 3m+: 0-0
Track:	LH: 0-2 RH: 0-0 Tight: 0-0 Gall: 0-0
Aids:	Bl: 0-0 Vi: 0-0 Tstrap: 0-0
Best Rating:	0 2/03 Ayr 2m gd-sft Hdl

Sea Drifting

109(110h)   **(123h)128**

6-y-o b g Slip Anchor-Theme (IRE) (Sadler s Wells (USA))
K A Morgan (Ferdy Murphy 25/1) Mr & Mrs S Giles & Mr & Mrs J Taqvi

Placings:110/114P32-F33134252   **(4613)**
2002/03: 20⁵S, 21³S, 20⁵S, 24¹GS, 21³GS, 24⁴G, 22²GF, 25⁵G, 25²G,

	Starts	1st	2nd	3rd	Win & Pl
Chases	9	1	2	3	27207
Career Total	18	5	3	4	48379

117	12/02	Muss	3m	D Ch	G-S £6662
114	12/01	Ayr	2m	E Hdl	SFT £2544
126	11/01	Newc	2m4f	D Hdl	G-S £3328
112	2/01	Weth	2m	H NHF	SFT £1701
108	1/01	Ludl	2m	H NHF	SFT £2065

Total win prize-money £16303

Going:	Sf: 0-3 GS: 1-2 Gd: 0-3 GF: - Fm: 0-1
Distance:	2m/2m3: 0-0 2m4-2m7: 0-5 3m+: 1-4
Track:	LH: 0-8 RH: **1-1** Tight: **1-3** Gall: 0-5
Aids:	Bl: 0-0 Vi: 0-0 Tstrap: 0-0
Best Rating:	**128** 3/03 Chel 3m110y good Ch

Useful novice chaser, previously decent bumper horse and novice hurdler; has shown ability over fences, being successful at Musselburgh in December 2002 and running well at the Festival; acts on soft ground although handles faster; stays three miles; has worn cheekpieces.

Sea Ferry (IRE)
90(112h)   (116h)91
7-y-o b g Ilium-Nicholas Ferry (Floriferous)
Noel T Chance   A D Weller

Placings:121/21P-45   (2663)
2002/03: 24⁴GS, 22⁵S,

	Starts	1st	2nd	3rd	Win & Pl
Hurdles	1	0	0	0	329
Chases	1	0	0	0	0
Career Total	8	3	2	0	13453
116	11/01	Chep	3m	C(0-130)HHdl	SFT £5434
111	2/01	Plum	2m5f	D Hdl	SFT £3656
111	11/00	Folk	2m4f110y F Hdl		HVY £1827

Total win prize-money £10917

Going:	Sf: 0-1 GS: 0-1 Gd: 0-0 GF: - Fm: 0-0
Distance:	2m/2m3: 0-0 2m4-2m7: 0-1 3m+: 0-1
Track:	LH: 0-0 RH: 0-1 Tight: 0-2 Gall: 0-0
Aids:	Bl: 0-0 Vi: 0-0 Tstrap: 0-0
Best Rating:	**116** 11/01 Chep 3m soft Hdl

Lightly-raced, progressive staying hurdler. Stays three miles and acts on soft ground.

Sea Haitch Em

8-y-o ch g Norton Challenger-One Way Circuit (Windjammer (USA))
Miss Lisa Llewellyn   V J Hughes

Placings:5000/045-2   (3954)
2002/03: 20²GS,

	Starts	1st	2nd	3rd	Win & Pl
Chases	1	0	1	0	668
Career Total	8	0	1	0	668

Going:	Sf: 0-0 GS: 0-1 Gd: 0-0 GF: - Fm: 0-0
Distance:	2m/2m3: 0-0 2m4-2m7: 0-1 3m+: 0-0
Track:	LH: 0-0 RH: 0-1 Tight: 0-0 Gall: 0-0
Aids:	Bl: 0-0 Vi: 0-0 Tstrap: 0-0
Best Rating:	**96** 3/03 Leic 2m4f110y gd-sft Ch

Sea Maize
79f   40f
5-y-o b m Sea Raven (IRE)-Dragons Daughter (Mandrake Major)
C R Wilson   W R Wilson

Placings:00   (4672)
2002/03: 16⁵GF, 16⁶G,

	Starts	1st	2nd	3rd	Win & Pl
NH Flat	2	0	0	0	

Career Total	2	0	0	0

Going:	Sf: 0-0 GS: 0-0 Gd: 0-1 GF: - Fm: 0-1
Distance:	2m/2m3: 0-2 2m4-2m7: 0-0 3m+: 0-0
Track:	LH: 0-2 RH: 0-0 Tight: 0-1 Gall: 0-0
Aids:	Bl: 0-0 Vi: 0-0 Tstrap: 0-0
Best Rating:	**40** 3/03 Weth 2m gd-fm NHF

Sea Mark
108   109+
7-y-o ro g Warning-Mettlesome (Lomond (USA))
C Grant   Akv Cladding Fabrications Ltd

Placings:40-41P4   (0768)
2002/03: 16⁴G, 17¹GF, 17⁸GF, 17⁴GF,

	Starts	1st	2nd	3rd	Win & Pl
Hurdles	4	1	0	0	2994
Career Total	6	1	0	0	3428
105	6/02	MRas	2m1f110y E Hdl		G-F £2723

Total win prize-money £2723

Going:	Sf: 0-0 GS: 0-0 Gd: 0-1 GF: - Fm: 1-3
Distance:	2m/2m3: 1-4 2m4-2m7: 0-0 3m+: 0-0
Track:	LH: 0-2 RH: **1-2** Tight: **1-4** Gall: 0-0
Aids:	Bl: **1-3** Vi: 0-0 Tstrap: 0-0
Best Rating:	**107** 5/02 Aint 2m110y good Hdl

Modest hurdler; suited by a sound surface.

Sea Pearl
42
9-y-o b m Derring Rose-Tillside Brig (New Brig)
Mrs S P Stretton   Mr & Mrs Stretton

Placings:56P/P00-6P   (0559)
2002/03: 22⁶GS, 26⁸GF,

	Starts	1st	2nd	3rd	Win & Pl
Hurdles	2	0	0	0	0
Career Total	8	0	0	0	0

Going:	Sf: 0-0 GS: 0-1 Gd: 0-0 GF: - Fm: 0-1
Distance:	2m/2m3: 0-0 2m4-2m7: 0-1 3m+: 0-1
Track:	LH: 0-1 RH: 0-0 Tight: 0-1 Gall: 0-0
Aids:	Bl: 0-0 Vi: 0-0 Tstrap: 0-0
Best Rating:	**92** 12/00 Tntn 2m1f soft NHF

Sea Princess
41f
6-y-o b m Sea Raven (IRE)-Mighty Miss (Doc Marten)
M E Sowersby   M E Sowersby

Placings:0-P   (0361)
2002/03: 16⁶GS,

	Starts	1st	2nd	3rd	Win & Pl
NH Flat	1	0	0	0	
Career Total	2	0	0	0	

Going:	Sf: 0-0 GS: 0-1 Gd: 0-0 GF: - Fm: 0-0
Distance:	2m/2m3: 0-1 2m4-2m7: 0-0 3m+: 0-0
Track:	LH: 0-1 RH: 0-0 Tight: 0-1 Gall: 0-0
Aids:	Bl: 0-0 Vi: 0-0 Tstrap: 0-0
Best Rating:	**41** 4/02 Weth 2m gd-fm NHF

Sea Spirit

11-y-o gr m Nearly A Hand-Uncornered (USA) (Silver Series (USA))

Career Total	2	0	0	0

Miss Emma Kelley   Miss Emma Kelley

Placings:4   (0347)
2002/03: 26⁴GS,

	Starts	1st	2nd	3rd	Win & Pl
Chases	1	0	0	0	0
Career Total	1	0	0	0	0

Going:	Sf: 0-0 GS: 0-1 Gd: 0-0 GF: - Fm: 0-0
Distance:	2m/2m3: 0-0 2m4-2m7: 0-0 3m+: 0-1
Track:	LH: 0-1 RH: 0-0 Tight: 0-1 Gall: 0-0
Aids:	Bl: 0-0 Vi: 0-0 Tstrap: 0-0
Best Rating:	**47** 5/02 NAbb 3m2f110y gd-sft Ch

Sea Tarth
89
12-y-o gr m Nicholas Bill-Seajan (Mandamus)
T R Kinsey   Mrs T R Kinsey

Placings:122623400/440F340511/0U210/00P2/6-0 (0322)
2002/03: 24⁰G,

	Starts	1st	2nd	3rd	Win & Pl
Hurdles	1	0	0	0	0
Career Total	30	4	5	2	13023
77	8/99	Worc	2m7f110y E Ch		SFT £3036
91	4/99	Worc	3m	F(0-100)HHdl	G-S £2409
86	4/99	Hrfd	3m2f	E(0-105)HHdl	G-F £2431
108	5/97	Bang	2m1f	H NHF	GD £1287

Total win prize-money £9164

Going:	Sf: 0-0 GS: 0-0 Gd: 0-1 GF: - Fm: 0-0
Distance:	2m/2m3: 0-0 2m4-2m7: 0-0 3m+: 0-1
Track:	LH: 0-1 RH: 0-0 Tight: 0-0 Gall: 0-0
Aids:	Bl: 0-0 Vi: 0-0 Tstrap: 0-0
Best Rating:	**108** 5/97 Bang 2m1f good NHF

Sea Urchin

10-y-o b g Scallywag-Sailor s Shanty (Dubassoff (USA))
Mrs H J Wiegersma   J H Philips

Placings:P   (0247)
2002/03: 19⁰G,

	Starts	1st	2nd	3rd	Win & Pl
Chases	1	0	0	0	
Career Total	1	0	0	0	

Going:	Sf: 0-0 GS: 0-0 Gd: 0-1 GF: - Fm: 0-0
Distance:	2m/2m3: 0-0 2m4-2m7: 0-0 3m+: 0-0
Track:	LH: 0-0 RH: 0-1 Tight: 0-0 Gall: 0-0
Aids:	Bl: 0-0 Vi: 0-0 Tstrap: 0-0
Best Rating:	**0** 5/02 Extr 2m3f110y good Ch

Seabrook Lad

12-y-o b g Derrylin-Moll (Rugantino)
Mrs F Kehoe   Seabrook Partners

Placings:005/4F0214/634/5U20115/23U2/PP/6P0-233 (4451)
2002/03: 24²GF, 24³G, 24³G,

	Starts	1st	2nd	3rd	Win & Pl
Chases	3	0	1	2	1525
Career Total	31	3	5	4	18721
115	3/99	Ludl	3m	F(0-115)HCh	GD £4758
114	2/99	Ludl	2m4f	F(0-100)HCh	GD £2671
102	3/97	Hntg	2m5f110y E Hdl		G-F £2867

Total win prize-money £10298

Going:	Sf: 0-0 GS: 0-0 Gd: 0-2 GF: - Fm: 0-1				
Distance:	2m/2m3: 0-0 2m4-2m7: 0-0 3m+: 0-3				
Track:	LH: 0-0 RH: 0-3 Tight: 0-1 Gall: 0-2				
Aids:	Bl: 0-0 Vi: 0-0 Tstrap: 0-0				
Best Rating:	119 5/99 Ludl 3m gd-fm Ch				

Fair pointer/hunter chaser, consistent sort; suited by a sound surface, although acts on softer; stays three miles.

Seahorse Boy (IRE)

6-y-o b g Petardia-Million At Dawn (IRE) (Fayruz)
Mrs A C Tate R C Smith

Placings:PP-P   (1713)
2002/03: 16PG,

	Starts	1st	2nd	3rd	Win & Pl
Hurdles	1	0	0	0	
Career Total	3	0	0	0	

Going:	Sf: 0-0 GS: 0-0 Gd: 0-1 GF: - Fm: 0-0				
Distance:	2m/2m3: 0-1 2m4-2m7: 0-0 3m+: 0-0				
Track:	LH: 0-1 RH: 0-0 Tight: 0-1 Gall: 0-0				
Aids:	Bl: 0-0 Vi: 0-0 Tstrap: 0-0				
Best Rating:	0 10/02 Strf 2m110y good Hdl				

Sealed Orders

6-y-o ch m Bustino-Royal Seal (Privy Seal)
Mrs S Lamyman J J Greenwood

Placings:P   (4355)
2002/03: 20PGF,

	Starts	1st	2nd	3rd	Win & Pl
Hurdles	1	0	0	0	
Career Total	1	0	0	0	

Going:	Sf: 0-0 GS: 0-0 Gd: 0-0 GF: - Fm: 0-1				
Distance:	2m/2m3: 0-0 2m4-2m7: 0-1 3m+: 0-0				
Track:	LH: 0-1 RH: 0-0 Tight: 0-0 Gall: 0-0				
Aids:	Bl: 0-0 Vi: 0-0 Tstrap: 0-0				
Best Rating:	0 3/03 Weth 2m4f110y gd-fm Hdl				

Sean At The Ivy (FR)

4-y-o b g Nikos-Matelica (FR) (Rb Chesne)
P F Nicholls Mrs J Stewart

Placings:P   (3673)
2002/03: 18PGS,

	Starts	1st	2nd	3rd	Win & Pl
NH Flat	1	0	0	0	
Career Total	1	0	0	0	

Going:	Sf: 0-0 GS: 0-1 Gd: 0-0 GF: - Fm: 0-0				
Distance:	2m/2m3: 0-1 2m4-2m7: 0-0 3m+: 0-0				
Track:	LH: 0-1 RH: 0-0 Tight: 0-1 Gall: 0-0				
Aids:	Bl: 0-0 Vi: 0-0 Tstrap: 0-0				
Best Rating:	0 2/03 Font 2m2f110y gd-sft NHF				

Sean's Minstrel (IRE)

10-y-o gr g Black Minstrel-Gala Star (Gail Star)

Mrs D M Grissell G J D Wragg

Placings:FP/6   (0383)
2002/03: 24PG,

	Starts	1st	2nd	3rd	Win & Pl
Chases	1	0	0	0	0
Career Total	3	0	0	0	0

Going:	Sf: 0-0 GS: 0-0 Gd: 0-1 GF: - Fm: 0-0				
Distance:	2m/2m3: 0-0 2m4-2m7: 0-0 3m+: 0-0				
Track:	LH: 0-0 RH: 0-1 Tight: 0-0 Gall: 0-1				
Aids:	Bl: 0-0 Vi: 0-0 Tstrap: 0-0				
Best Rating:					

Search And Destroy (USA)

111(105h)   (107h)**118**
5-y-o b/br g Sky Classic (CAN)-Hunt The Thimble (USA) (Turn And Count (USA))
T R George Mrs R E R Rumboll

Placings:246-1030   (3643)
2002/03: 16TG, 16PG, 16PG, 16PGS,

	Starts	1st	2nd	3rd	Win & Pl
Hurdles	4	1	0	1	4241
Career Total	7	1	1	1	5307
107	12/02	Donc	2m110y	F(0-100)HHdl	GD	£3136
				Total win prize-money £3136		

Going:	Sf: 0-1 GS: 0-1 Gd: 1-2 GF: - Fm: 0-0				
Distance:	2m/2m3: 1-4 2m4-2m7: 0-0 3m+: 0-0				
Track:	LH: 1-1 RH: 0-3 Tight: 0-1 Gall: 1-1				
Aids:	Bl: 0-0 Vi: 0-0 Tstrap: 0-0				
Best Rating:	107 1/03 Muss 2m good Hdl				

Fair novice chaser; progressive form on fast ground; effective at up to two and a half miles; best on a sound surface.

Search N' Destroy (NZ)

8-y-o b g Heroicity (AUS)-Nassa Charm (NZ) (Nassipour (USA))
Lady Connell Sir Michael Connell

Placings:0-P   (0985)
2002/03: 17PGF,

	Starts	1st	2nd	3rd	Win & Pl
Hurdles	1	0	0	0	
Career Total	2	0	0	0	

Going:	Sf: 0-0 GS: 0-0 Gd: 0-0 GF: - Fm: 0-1				
Distance:	2m/2m3: 0-1 2m4-2m7: 0-0 3m+: 0-0				
Track:	LH: 0-1 RH: 0-0 Tight: 0-0 Gall: 0-0				
Aids:	Bl: 0-0 Vi: 0-0 Tstrap: 0-0				
Best Rating:	66 12/01 Towc 2m heavy NHF				

Seasmith

89   **72**
8-y-o br/gr g Greensmith-Sea Spice (Precipice Wood)
L Lungo J M Crichton

Placings:0/440-46F00   (4591)
2002/03: 26FGS, 20FHY, 16FHY, 16PG, 16PG,

	Starts	1st	2nd	3rd	Win & Pl
Hurdles	4	0	0	0	260
Chases	1	0	0	0	0
Career Total	9	0	0	0	531

Going:	Sf: 0-3 GS: 0-1 Gd: 0-1 GF: - Fm: 0-0				
Distance:	2m/2m3: 0-3 2m4-2m7: 0-1 3m+: 0-1				
Track:	LH: 0-4 RH: 0-1 Tight: 0-1 Gall: 0-0				
Aids:	Bl: 0-0 Vi: 0-0 Tstrap: 0-0				
Best Rating:	97 1/02 Carl 2m1f heavy Hdl				

Has run with credit over hurdles in the mud.

Season Express

(89h)   (70 h)
8-y-o ch g Vital Season-Coach Rd Express (Pony Express)
C Tizzard G F Gingell

Placings:464   (4718)
2002/03: 20FGF, 22FGF, 22FF,

	Starts	1st	2nd	3rd	Win & Pl
Hurdles	3	0	0	0	272
Career Total	3	0	0	0	272

Going:	Sf: 0-0 GS: 0-0 Gd: 0-0 GF: - Fm: 0-3				
Distance:	2m/2m3: 0-0 2m4-2m7: 0-3 3m+: 0-0				
Track:	LH: 0-0 RH: 0-2 Tight: 0-1 Gall: 0-0				
Aids:	Bl: 0-0 Vi: 0-0 Tstrap: 0-0				
Best Rating:	70 4/03 Extr 2m6f110y gd-fm Hdl				

Modest form over hurdles so far.

Seasquill (AUS)

97   **86**
8-y-o br g Squill (USA)-Sea Surge (AUS) (Rolle)
Ferdy Murphy G Wilson,T Murphy & B Harrison Burcombe

Placings:40660P   (4338)
2002/03: 16FS, 17FHY, 16FGF, 16FG, 17FHY, 20FGF,

	Starts	1st	2nd	3rd	Win & Pl
Hurdles	6	0	0	0	708
Career Total	6	0	0	0	708

Going:	Sf: 0-3 GS: 0-0 Gd: 0-1 GF: - Fm: 0-2				
Distance:	2m/2m3: 0-5 2m4-2m7: 0-1 3m+: 0-0				
Track:	LH: 0-2 RH: 0-4 Tight: 0-3 Gall: 0-1				
Aids:	Bl: 0-0 Vi: 0-0 Tstrap: 0-0				
Best Rating:	86 1/03 Muss 2m good Hdl				

Seattle Art (USA)

106(90h)   (63h)**90**
9-y-o b g Seattle Slew (USA)-Artiste (Artaius (USA))
P Monteith I Bell

Placings:0/0P/65553010F/63/52P00430FPP35U1-04140   (0917)
2002/03: 16PGS, 20FG, 22TG, 21FGF, 24PGS,

	Starts	1st	2nd	3rd	Win & Pl
Chases	5	1	0	0	5077
Career Total	34	2	3	4	15309
89	7/02	MRas	2m6f110yE(0-105)HCh	GD	£4452
83	4/02	Hexm	2m4f110yF(0-95)HCh	GD	£3192
81	2/00	Muss	2m	E Ch	G-S	£3071
				Total win prize-money £10716		

Going:	Sf: 0-0 GS: 0-2 Gd: 1-2 GF: - Fm: 0-1				
Distance:	2m/2m3: 0-1 2m4-2m7: 1-3 3m+: 0-1				
Track:	LH: 0-3 RH: 1-2 Tight: 1-2 Gall: 0-0				
Aids:	Bl: 0-0 Vi: 0-0 Tstrap: 0-0				
Best Rating:	89 8/02 Prth 3m gd-sft Ch				

Moderate chaser, handles a left handed track but is suited by a right-handed track and good ground.

Seattle Lad (IRE)

11-y-o ch g Krayyan-Zedosa s Pet (Prince Bee)
M A Allen Mrs V J Davey

Placings:0PP-P   (0123)
2002/03: 27PGF,

	Starts	1st	2nd	3rd	Win & Pl
Hurdles	1	0	0	0	
Career Total	4	0	0	0	

Going:	Sf: 0-0 GS: 0-0 Gd: 0-0 GF: - Fm: 0-1
Distance:	2m/2m3: 0-0 2m4-2m7: 0-0 3m+: 0-1
Track:	LH: 0-0 RH: 0-0 Tight: 0-1 Gall: 0-0
Aids:	Bl: 0-0 Vi: 0-0 Tstrap: 0-0
Best Rating:	0 5/02 Font 3m3f gd-fm Hdl

Second Pick (IRE)
66   42

7-y-o b g Doubletour (USA)-Wurli (Wolver Hollow)
R J Armson R J Armson

Placings:000P-PPPP   (0438)
2002/03: 21PGS, 16PGF, 20PG, 20PGS, 23PG,

	Starts	1st	2nd	3rd	Win & Pl
Hurdles	3	0	0	0	0
Chases	2	0	0	0	0
Career Total	8	0	0	0	

Going:	Sf: 0-0 GS: 0-2 Gd: 0-2 GF: - Fm: 0-1
Distance:	2m/2m3: 0-1 2m4-2m7: 0-4 3m+: 0-0
Track:	LH: 0-3 RH: 0-2 Tight: 0-1 Gall: 0-1
Aids:	Bl: 0-0 Vi: 0-0 Tstrap: 0-0
Best Rating:	34 1/02 Kemp 2m soft NHF

Second Tenor (IRE)
99   71

6-y-o b m Glacial Storm (USA)-Rustic Path (Proverb)
D Brace David Brace

Placings:3   (1010)
2002/03: 203GF,

	Starts	1st	2nd	3rd	Win & Pl
Hurdles	1	0	0	1	436
Career Total	1	0	0	1	436

Going:	Sf: 0-0 GS: 0-0 Gd: 0-0 GF: - Fm: 0-1
Distance:	2m/2m3: 0-0 2m4-2m7: 0-1 3m+: 0-0
Track:	LH: 0-1 RH: 0-0 Tight: 0-0 Gall: 0-0
Aids:	Bl: 0-0 Vi: 0-0 Tstrap: 0-0
Best Rating:	71 8/02 Bang 2m4f gd-fm Hdl

Secret Alliance (IRE)

11-y-o b g Royal Fountain-Hardy Polly (Pollerton)
P C Handley P C & S E Handley

Placings:5-1   (4640)
2002/03: 211G,

	Starts	1st	2nd	3rd	Win & Pl
Chases	1	1	0	0	3484
Career Total	2	1	0	0	3484
91 4/03 Strf	2m5f110yH Ch			GD	£3484

Total win prize-money £3484

Going:	Sf: 0-0 GS: 0-0 Gd: 1-1 GF: - Fm: 0-0
Distance:	2m/2m3: 0-0 2m4-2m7: 1-1 3m+: 0-0
Track:	LH: 1-1 RH: 0-0 Tight: 1-1 Gall: 0-0
Aids:	Bl: 0-0 Vi: 0-0 Tstrap: 0-0
Best Rating:	91 4/03 Strf 2m5f110y good Ch

Returned after nearly a year off to win a point in April 2003; followed up by causing 25/1 shock in 2m 5f hunter chase at Stratford; acts on good ground; best at 3m.

Secret Conquest
100   82

6-y-o b m Secret Appeal-Mohibbah (USA) (Conquistador Cielo (USA))
G M Moore Keith Nicholson

Placings:40P   (3963)
2002/03: 174GF, 170GF, 16PS,

	Starts	1st	2nd	3rd	Win & Pl
Hurdles	3	0	0	0	0
Career Total	3	0	0	0	0

Going:	Sf: 0-1 GS: 0-0 Gd: 0-0 GF: - Fm: 0-2
Distance:	2m/2m3: 0-3 2m4-2m7: 0-0 3m+: 0-0
Track:	LH: 0-3 RH: 0-0 Tight: 0-3 Gall: 0-0
Aids:	Bl: 0-0 Vi: 0-0 Tstrap: 0-0
Best Rating:	82 9/02 Sedg 2m1f gd-fm Hdl

Modest seven furlong handicapper on the Flat. Looks to have stamina limitations over hurdles.

Secret Drinker (IRE)
110(100h)   (78h)85

7-y-o b g Husyan (USA)-Try Le Reste (IRE) (Le Moss)
O Sherwood S Channing-Williams

Placings:0/005221-55323P   (4438)
2002/03: 245GS, 235S, 263S, 242S, 293G, 24PG,

	Starts	1st	2nd	3rd	Win & Pl
Chases	6	0	1	2	2888
Career Total	13	1	3	2	6561
78 3/02 Plum	3m1f110yF(0-95)HHdl		G-S	£2278	

Total win prize-money £2279

Going:	Sf: 0-3 GS: 0-1 Gd: 0-2 GF: - Fm: 0-0
Distance:	2m/2m3: 0-0 2m4-2m7: 0-0 3m+: 0-6
Track:	LH: 0-2 RH: 0-4 Tight: 0-1 Gall: 0-1
Aids:	Bl: 0-0 Vi: 0-0 Tstrap: 0-0
Best Rating:	85 3/03 Wwck 3m5f good Ch

Moderate chaser; stays three miles plus; acts on a soft surface; lacks a turn of foot.

Secret Flutter (IRE)
97   83

4-y-o b f Entrepreneur-Spend A Rubble (USA) (Spend A Buck (USA))
J G Portman Captain Francis Burne

Placings:3010   (3148)
2002/03: 173GS, 180G, 161S, 160HY,

	Starts	1st	2nd	3rd	Win & Pl
Hurdles	4	1	0	1	2265
Career Total	4	1	0	1	2265
83 12/02 Uttx	2m		G Hdl	SFT	£1988

Total win prize-money £1988

Going:	Sf: 1-2 GS: 0-1 Gd: 0-1 GF: - Fm: 0-0
Distance:	2m/2m3: 1-4 2m4-2m7: 0-0 3m+: 0-0
Track:	LH: 1-3 RH: 0-1 Tight: 0-2 Gall: 0-0
Aids:	Bl: 0-0 Vi: 0-0 Tstrap: 0-0
Best Rating:	83 12/02 Uttx 2m soft Hdl

Wide margin winner of a poor selling hurdle in the mud at Uttoxeter in December.

Secret Mission
81f   65f

7-y-o b m Infantry-Scudding (Cruise Missile)
Ms A E Embiricos Miss Judith Ann Knapman

Placings:05   (1063)
2002/03: 160GF, 165GF,

	Starts	1st	2nd	3rd	Win & Pl
NH Flat	2	0	0	0	0
Career Total	2	0	0	0	0

Going:	Sf: 0-0 GS: 0-0 Gd: 0-0 GF: - Fm: 0-2
Distance:	2m/2m3: 0-2 2m4-2m7: 0-0 3m+: 0-0
Track:	LH: 0-1 RH: 0-1 Tight: 0-0 Gall: 0-1
Aids:	Bl: 0-0 Vi: 0-0 Tstrap: 0-0
Best Rating:	74 8/02 Worc 2m gd-fm NHF

Secret Progress (IRE)
96   (80h)107

7-y-o ch g Safety Catch (USA)-Lady Progress (Proverb)
I A Duncan Anthony McAlister

Placings:0000-40F23   (3328)
2002/03: 174YS, 200S, 22FYS, 202S, 243G,

	Starts	1st	2nd	3rd	Win & Pl
Hurdles	2	0	0	0	196
Chases	3	0	1	1	2097
Career Total	9	0	1	1	2293

Going:	Sf: 0-2 GS: 0-0 Gd: 0-1 GF: - Fm: 0-0
Distance:	2m/2m3: 0-1 2m4-2m7: 0-3 3m+: 0-1
Track:	LH: 0-1 RH: 0-2 Tight: 0-1 Gall: 0-0
Aids:	Bl: 0-0 Vi: 0-0 Tstrap: 0-0
Best Rating:	107 12/02 DRoy 2m4f soft Ch

Irish chaser, best at around two and a half miles.

Secret Sentiment
85   77

5-y-o b m Mark Of Esteem (IRE)-Sahara Baladee (USA) (Shadeed (USA))
A B Coogan A B Coogan

Placings:65P-P0   (0407)
2002/03: 17PG, 170GF,

	Starts	1st	2nd	3rd	Win & Pl
Hurdles	2	0	0	0	0
Career Total	5	0	0	0	0

Going:	Sf: 0-0 GS: 0-0 Gd: 0-1 GF: - Fm: 0-1
Distance:	2m/2m3: 0-2 2m4-2m7: 0-0 3m+: 0-0
Track:	LH: 0-0 RH: 0-2 Tight: 0-2 Gall: 0-0
Aids:	Bl: 0-0 Vi: 0-0 Tstrap: 0-0
Best Rating:	82 2/02 Sand 2m110y heavy Hdl

Secret Truth

14-y-o ch m Nestor-Another Nitty (Country Retreat)
Andrew J Martin Andrew J Martin

Placings:PPPPP/5/3P3P/4PPP/P152PP-P4   (0392)
2002/03: 16PGF, 244G,

	Starts	1st	2nd	3rd	Win & Pl
Chases	2	0	0	0	0
Career Total	22	1	1	2	3664

86 5/01 Strf 2m5f110yH Ch G-F £2530
Total win prize-money £2531

Going: Sf: 0-0 GS: 0-0 Gd: 0-1 GF: - Fm: 0-1
Distance: 2m/2m3: 0-1 2m4-2m7: 0-0 3m+: 0-1
Track: LH: 0-2 RH: 0-0 Tight: 0-1 Gall: 0-1
Aids: Bl: 0-0 Vi: 0-0 Tstrap: 0-0
Best Rating: 90 5/02 Strf 3m good Ch

Hunter chaser who has shown her best form on fast ground. Reportedly retired.

Secret's Out
95   88
7-y-o b g Polish Precedent (USA)-Secret Obsession (USA) (Secretariat (USA))
F Lloyd F Lloyd

Placings:0033/235/060542223030-03425 (1716)
2002/03: 19QS, 163GF, 164G, 162G, 165G,

	Starts	1st	2nd	3rd	Win & Pl
Hurdles	5	0	1	1	1311
Career Total	24	0	5	6	6218

Going: Sf: 0-1 GS: 0-0 Gd: 0-3 GF: - Fm: 0-1
Distance: 2m/2m3: 0-5 2m4-2m7: 0-0 3m+: 0-0
Track: LH: 0-5 RH: 0-0 Tight: 0-3 Gall: 0-0
Aids: Bl: 0-0 Vi: 0-0 Tstrap: 0-0
Best Rating: 96 9/00 Uttx 2m gd-sft Hdl

Moderate form in novice and handicap hurdles.

Secrete Contract
81   74
5-y-o b g Contract Law (USA)-Secret Account (Blakeney)
Miss A M Newton-Smith The Secrete Society Partnership

Placings:PP0-00 (0097)
2002/03: 17QG, 18QGF,

	Starts	1st	2nd	3rd	Win & Pl
Hurdles	2	0	0	0	
Career Total	5	0	0	0	

Going: Sf: 0-0 GS: 0-0 Gd: 0-1 GF: - Fm: 0-1
Distance: 2m/2m3: 0-2 2m4-2m7: 0-0 3m+: 0-0
Track: LH: 0-1 RH: 0-1 Tight: 0-2 Gall: 0-0
Aids: Bl: 0-1 Vi: 0-0 Tstrap: 0-1
Best Rating: 74 5/02 Font 2m2f110y gd-fm Hdl

Securon Dancer
68   40
5-y-o b m Emperor Jones (USA)-Gena Ivor (USA) (Sir Ivor)
R Rowe Mrs R A Proctor

Placings:0 (0425)
2002/03: 18QGF,

	Starts	1st	2nd	3rd	Win & Pl
Hurdles	1	0	0	0	
Career Total	1	0	0	0	

Going: Sf: 0-0 GS: 0-0 Gd: 0-0 GF: - Fm: 0-1
Distance: 2m/2m3: 0-1 2m4-2m7: 0-0 3m+: 0-0
Track: LH: 0-1 RH: 0-0 Tight: 0-1 Gall: 0-0
Aids: Bl: 0-0 Vi: 0-0 Tstrap: 0-0
Best Rating: 40 6/02 Font 2m2f110y gd-fm Hdl

Securon Rose (IRE)
72
7-y-o gr m Roselier (FR)-Hand Me Down (Cheval)
R Rowe Mrs R A Proctor

Placings:00/56050- (0010)
2002/03: 25QG,

	Starts	1st	2nd	3rd	Win & Pl
Hurdles	1	0	0	0	
Career Total	7	0	0	0	

Going: Sf: 0-0 GS: 0-0 Gd: 0-0 GF: 0-1 Fm: 0-0
Distance: 2m/2m3: 0-0 2m4-2m7: 0-0 3m+: 0-1
Track: LH: 0-0 RH: 0-0 Tight: 0-0 Gall: 0-0
Aids: Bl: 0-0 Vi: 0-0 Tstrap: 0-0
Best Rating: 82 1/01 Kemp 2m soft NHF

Lightly raced hurdler. Raced mainly at trips around two and a half miles. Modest form to date.

See More Business (IRE)
118   171
13-y-o b g Seymour Hicks (FR)-Miss Redlands (Dubassoff (USA))
P F Nicholls Paul K Barber & Sir Robert Ogden

Placings:111/122F/3111C/41P31/11141/1515/FP135-2110 (4132)
2002/03: 242S, 261S, 251GS, 269G,

	Starts	1st	2nd	3rd	Win & Pl
Chases	4	2	1	0	63919
Career Total	35	18	3	3	699722

171	2/03	Winc	3m1f110yA Ch	G-S	£23800
166	12/02	Chep	3m2f110yA HCh	SFT	£23800
171	2/02	Winc	3m1f110yA Ch	G-S	£16770
178	1/01	Chel	3m1f110yA Ch	SFT	£49125
178	10/00	Weth	3m1f A Ch	SFT	£27000
	4/00	Aint	3m A Ch	GD	£46900
178	2/00	Newb	3m B Ch	G-S	£31000
178	12/99	Kemp	3m A Ch	SFT	£65500
175	10/99	Weth	3m1f A Ch	G-S	£23800
172	3/99	Chel	3m2f110yA Ch	G-S	£149600
172	12/98	Weth	3m A HCh	GD	£20305
172	1/98	Chel	3m1f110yB Ch	G-S	£16937
168	12/97	Kemp	3m A Ch	SFT	£64374
158	12/97	Chel	3m A HCh	SFT	£18606
133	11/96	Chep	3m2f110yA Ch	G-S	£13786
148	12/95	Sand	2m6f A Hdl	GD	£9555
130	11/95	Winc	2m6f C Hdl	GD	£3727
134	11/95	Chep	2m4f110yD Hdl	G-S	£2845

Total win prize-money £607433

Going: Sf: 1-2 GS: 1-1 Gd: 0-1 GF: - Fm: 0-0
Distance: 2m/2m3: 0-0 2m4-2m7: 0-0 3m+: 2-4
Track: LH: 1-2 RH: 1-1 Tight: 0-0 Gall: 0-1
Aids: Bl: 2-4 Vi: 0-0 Tstrap: 0-0
Best Rating: 178 1/01 Chel 3m1f110y soft Ch

Evergreen top-class chaser; winner of the Gold Cup in 1999 and 3rd in 2002; good return to action at Down Royal in November 2002; won the Rehearsal Chase at Chepstow for a third time in December and scored again at Wincanton in February; stays 3m 2f; acts on soft and good but does not want the ground too fast; usually wears blinkers.

See More Snow
95   86
6-y-o b g Seymour Hicks (FR)-Snow Child (Mandrake Major)
W G M Turner E Goody

Placings:64/6-435033 (4292)
2002/03: 174F, 163G, 205GS, 199GS, 173G, 163GF,

	Starts	1st	2nd	3rd	Win & Pl
Hurdles	6	0	0	3	1522
Career Total	9	0	0	3	1522

Going: Sf: 0-0 GS: 0-2 Gd: 0-2 GF: - Fm: 0-2
Distance: 2m/2m3: 0-4 2m4-2m7: 0-2 3m+: 0-0
Track: LH: 0-2 RH: 0-4 Tight: 0-2 Gall: 0-0
Aids: Bl: 0-0 Vi: 0-1 Tstrap: 0-0
Best Rating: 89 3/03 Winc 2m gd-fm Hdl

Moderate hurdler; best at around two miles.

See More Stars
84   76
6-y-o b g Seymour Hicks (FR)-China s Way (USA) (Native Uproar (USA))
J Mackie Fools Who Dream

Placings:P-P50 (0390)
2002/03: 20PGF, 175S, 16QGS,

	Starts	1st	2nd	3rd	Win & Pl
Hurdles	3	0	0	0	0
Career Total	4	0	0	0	0

Going: Sf: 0-1 GS: 0-1 Gd: 0-0 GF: - Fm: 0-1
Distance: 2m/2m3: 0-2 2m4-2m7: 0-1 3m+: 0-0
Track: LH: 0-3 RH: 0-0 Tight: 0-1 Gall: 0-0
Aids: Bl: 0-0 Vi: 0-0 Tstrap: 0-0
Best Rating: 76 5/02 Bang 2m1f soft Hdl

See My Girl
77f   48f
5-y-o gr m Terimon-Nessfield (Tumble Wind (USA))
M A Barnes J Duckworth

Placings:00 (3775)
2002/03: 16QG, 16QGS,

	Starts	1st	2nd	3rd	Win & Pl
NH Flat	2	0	0	0	
Career Total	2	0	0	0	

Going: Sf: 0-0 GS: 0-1 Gd: 0-1 GF: - Fm: 0-0
Distance: 2m/2m3: 0-2 2m4-2m7: 0-0 3m+: 0-0
Track: LH: 0-1 RH: 0-1 Tight: 0-0 Gall: 0-0
Aids: Bl: 0-0 Vi: 0-0 Tstrap: 0-0
Best Rating: 48 2/03 Ayr 2m gd-sft NHF

See You Around
101(86h)   (94h)92
8-y-o b g Sharp Deal-Seeborg (Lepanto (GER))
C Tizzard The Infamous Five

Placings:0320P25P/4SP64U22P-2560532 (4271)
2002/03: 212GS, 165GS, 20PHY, 20QGS, 255GS, 263GS, 242G,

	Starts	1st	2nd	3rd	Win & Pl
Chases	7	0	2	1	2902
Career Total	24	0	6	2	7027

Going: Sf: 0-1 GS: 0-5 Gd: 0-1 GF: - Fm: 0-0
Distance: 2m/2m3: 0-1 2m4-2m7: 0-3 3m+: 0-3
Track: LH: 0-2 RH: 0-4 Tight: 0-1 Gall: 0-0
Aids: Bl: 0-1 Vi: 0-1 Tstrap: 0-0
Best Rating: 109 12/00 Folk 2m1f110y heavy NHF

Modest hurdler/novice chaser; suited to soft/heavy ground; stays three miles plus.

See You Man

58f   **68f**

5-y-o b g Young Freeman (USA)-Shepani (New Member)
C Tizzard   J A G Meaden

Placings:0   (4296)
2002/03: 16⁰GF,

	Starts	1st	2nd	3rd	Win & Pl
NH Flat	1	0	0	0	
Career Total	1	0	0	0	

Going:	Sf: 0-0 GS: 0-0 Gd: 0-0 GF: - Fm: 0-1
Distance:	2m/2m3: 0-1 2m4-2m7: 0-0 3m+: 0-0
Track:	LH: 0-0 RH: 0-1 Tight: 0-0 Gall: 0-0
Aids:	Bl: 0-0 Vi: 0-0 Tstrap: 0-0
Best Rating:	68 3/03 Winc 2m gd-fm NHF

See You Sometime

114   **142**

8-y-o b g Sharp Deal-Shepani (New Member)
J W Mullins   J A G Meaden

Placings:43435/3111132-4101   (4607)
2002/03: 21⁴S, 22¹GS, 21⁹G, 21¹G,

	Starts	1st	2nd	3rd	Win & Pl
Hurdles	4	2	0	0	28523
Career Total	16	6	1	4	70380
142	4/03	Chel	2m5f110yB HHdl	GD	
142	2/03	Winc	2m6f	C(0-135)HHdl	G-S £16008
140	12/01	Newb	2m5f	B Hdl	G-S £9993
132	11/01	Chel	2m5f	C(0-135)HHdl	GD £18118
121	6/01	Strf	2m6f110yD Hdl	G-F	£3796
118	5/01	Folk	2m4f110yF(0-100)HHdl	G-F	£2037
				Total win prize-money £61148

Going:	Sf: 0-1 GS: 1-1 Gd: 1-2 GF: - Fm: 0-0
Distance:	2m/2m3: 0-0 2m4-2m7: 2-4 3m+: 0-0
Track:	LH: 1-3 RH: 1-1 Tight: 0-0 Gall: 1-3
Aids:	Bl: 0-0 Vi: 0-0 Tstrap: 0-0
Best Rating:	142 4/03 Chel 2m5f110y good Hdl

Very useful front-running hurdler; effective at up to two miles six furlongs and may stay further; acts on a sound surface but handles cut.

Seebald (GER)

120   **165**

8-y-o b g Mulberry (FR)-Spartina (USA) (Northern Baby (CAN))
M C Pipe   The Macca & Growler Partnership

Placings:110/2630/111111122-222F21   (4790)
2002/03: 17²G, 16²S, 16²G, 16FG, 20²G, 16¹G,

	Starts	1st	2nd	3rd	Win & Pl
Chases	6	1	4	0	130340
Career Total	22	10	7	1	258863
165	4/03	Sand	2m	B Ch	GD £59500
155	1/02	Wwck	2m4f110yC Ch	SFT	£8385
153	12/01	Asct	2m3f110yA Ch	GD £16375
156	11/01	Chel	2m	A Ch	GD £18000
131	10/01	Chel	2m	C Ch	GD £10272
123	6/01	MRas	2m1f110yD Ch	G-F	£6045
117	6/01	Hrfd	2m	E Ch	FRM £3159
117	5/01	Hrfd	2m	E Ch	GD £3297
133	2/00	Newb	2m110y C Hdl	G-S	£5226
123	1/00	Tntn	2m1f	E Hdl	G-S £2513
				Total win prize-money £132773

Going:	Sf: 0-1 GS: 0-0 Gd: 1-5 GF: - Fm: 0-0
Distance:	2m/2m3: 1-5 2m4-2m7: 0-1 3m+: 0-0
Track:	LH: 0-2 RH: 1-4 Tight: 0-1 Gall: 0-1

Aids:	Bl: 0-0 Vi: 0-0 Tstrap: 0-0
Best Rating:	165 4/03 Sand 2m good Ch

High-class chaser; won his first seven races in the 2001/02 season before a good 2nd in the Arkle; good efforts in defeat this term, including when still bang there in the Champion Chase when falling two out; runner-up to easy winner in Martell Cup at Aintree; beat Cenkos (rec 4lb) in valuable event at Sandown in April; effective from 2m to 2m 4f; acts on good and soft ground; room for improvement in his jumping; genuine and consistent.

Seef

88(86h)   (67h)**80**

9-y-o b g Slip Anchor-Compton Lady (USA) (Sovereign Dancer (USA))
J S King   Mrs S Horton

Placings:20/60006/1435/35324/002352-1PP556U   (4702)
2002/03: 26¹G, 24⁹GF, 23⁹G, 25⁵GF, 23⁵GF, 25⁸GF, 26ᵁGF,

	Starts	1st	2nd	3rd	Win & Pl
Chases	7	1	0		3380
Career Total	29	2	4	4	13027
80	5/02	Folk	3m2f	E Ch	GD £3380
99	5/99	Extr	2m6f	E Hdl	G-F £2915
				Total win prize-money £6295

Going:	Sf: 0-0 GS: 0-0 Gd: 1-2 GF: - Fm: 0-5
Distance:	2m/2m3: 0-0 2m4-2m7: 0-0 3m+: 1-7
Track:	LH: 0-2 RH: 1-5 Tight: 1-3 Gall: 0-1
Aids:	Bl: 0-0 Vi: 0-0 Tstrap: 0-0
Best Rating:	99 10/99 Winc 2m6f gd-fm Hdl

Modest hurdler/fair chaser; best over staying distances; acts on a sound surface.

Seem Of Gold

97   **78**

7-y-o b m Gold Dust-Shepani (New Member)
J W Mullins   J A G Meaden

Placings:00/B160506-660   (1620)
2002/03: 22⁵GF, 24⁵G, 21⁰F,

	Starts	1st	2nd	3rd	Win & Pl
Hurdles	3	0	0	0	0
Career Total	12	1	0	0	2282
84	6/01	NAbb	2m1f	H NHF	GD £2282
				Total win prize-money £2282

Going:	Sf: 0-0 GS: 0-0 Gd: 0-1 GF: - Fm: 0-2
Distance:	2m/2m3: 0-0 2m4-2m7: 0-2 3m+: 0-1
Track:	LH: 0-1 RH: 0-2 Tight: 0-0 Gall: 0-0
Aids:	Bl: 0-0 Vi: 0-0 Tstrap: 0-0
Best Rating:	85 12/01 Tntn 2m1f gd-sft Hdl

Sefton Blake

104   **79**

9-y-o b g Roscoe Blake-Rainbow Lady (Jaazeiro (USA))
R D Wylie   M R Johnson

Placings:404P6/55243616/112P0/415P56/0P46-6   (4710)
2002/03: 23⁶GF,

	Starts	1st	2nd	3rd	Win & Pl
Hurdles	1	0	0	0	
Career Total	29	4	2	1	12549
93	8/00	Sthl	3m110y E Ch	G-F	£3133
93	11/99	Catt	3m1f110yE(0-115)HHdl	G-F	£2304
93	5/99	Ctml	2m6f	F(0-95)HHdl	GD £3100
84	4/99	Sedg	2m5f110yG(0-100)HHdl	FRM £2164
				Total win prize-money £10702

Going:	Sf: 0-0 GS: 0-0 Gd: 0-0 GF: - Fm: 0-1

Distance:	2m/2m3: 0-0 2m4-2m7: 0-1 3m+: 0-0
Track:	LH: 0-1 RH: 0-0 Tight: 0-0 Gall: 0-0
Aids:	Bl: 0-0 Vi: 0-0 Tstrap: 0-0
Best Rating:	96 11/99 Kels 2m6f110y good Hdl

Sefton Lodge

4-y-o b g Barathea (IRE)-Pine Needle (Kris)
Andrew Reid (C N Allen 26/2) J L Guillambert

Placings:P0   (2503)
2002/03: 17⁵S, 16⁹GS,

	Starts	1st	2nd	3rd	Win & Pl
Hurdles	2	0	0	0	
Career Total	2	0	0	0	

Going:	Sf: 0-1 GS: 0-1 Gd: 0-0 GF: - Fm: 0-0
Distance:	2m/2m3: 0-2 2m4-2m7: 0-0 3m+: 0-0
Track:	LH: 0-1 RH: 0-1 Tight: 0-2 Gall: 0-0
Aids:	Bl: 0-0 Vi: 0-0 Tstrap: 0-0
Best Rating:	0 12/02 Fknm 2m gd-sft Hdl

Seixo Branco

105(92h)   (129h)**129**

7-y-o b g Saddlers' Hall (IRE)-Gift Of Glory (FR) (Niniski (USA))
C R Egerton   Elite Racing Club

Placings:16/1250/012   (3157)
2002/03: 16⁸S, 17¹S, 16²G,

	Starts	1st	2nd	3rd	Win & Pl
Hurdles	1	0	0	0	
Chases	2	1	1	0	7612
Career Total	9	3	2	0	20577
129	12/02	MRas	2m1f110yD Ch	SFT	£5960
140	12/00	Sthl	2m4f110yD(0-125)HHdl	SFT	£2908
116	3/00	Font	2m4f	E Hdl	G-S	£2618
				Total win prize-money £11487

Going:	Sf: 1-2 GS: 0-0 Gd: 0-1 GF: - Fm: 0-0
Distance:	2m/2m3: 1-3 2m4-2m7: 0-0 3m+: 0-0
Track:	LH: 0-1 RH: 1-2 Tight: 1-2 Gall: 0-1
Aids:	Bl: 0-0 Vi: 0-0 Tstrap: 0-0
Best Rating:	140 2/01 Asct 2m4f heavy Hdl

Useful novice chaser; formerly decent hurdler; effective from two to two and a half miles; best on soft ground; off the track for 19 months after April 2001.

Seize The Day (IRE)

97   **79**

15-y-o b g Lomond (USA)-Cheerful Heart (Petingo)
M J Coombe   Mrs N M Coombe

Placings:000/51211/550123/0-00   (2455)
2002/03: 24⁰G, 24⁰GS,

	Starts	1st	2nd	3rd	Win & Pl
Hurdles	2	0	0	0	
Career Total	17	4	2	1	11266
114	1/99	Winc	2m6f	C(0-115)HHdl	SFT £2878
112	4/98	Hntg	2m5f110yE(0-115)HHdl	G-S £2390
104	4/98	Winc	F(0-105)HHdl	G-S £2374
95	3/98	Hntg	2m5f110yG(0-90)HHdl	GD £1968
				Total win prize-money £9610

Going:	Sf: 0-0 GS: 0-1 Gd: 0-1 GF: - Fm: 0-0
Distance:	2m/2m3: 0-0 2m4-2m7: 0-0 3m+: 0-2
Track:	LH: 0-0 RH: 0-2 Tight: 0-0 Gall: 0-0
Aids:	Bl: 0-0 Vi: 0-0 Tstrap: 0-0
Best Rating:	119 3/99 Hntg 3m2f gd-sft Hdl

Fair handicap hurdler. Has won at up to two miles six furlongs. Acts on soft ground.

Sekwana (POL)

66   **19**

4-y-o b f Duke Valentino-Surmia (POL) (Demon Club (POL))
Miss A M Newton-Smith Sharon Nelson,Christine Davies,H Le Fanu

Placings:P   (4148)
2002/03: 16PG,

	Starts	1st	2nd	3rd	Win & Pl
Hurdles	1	0	0	0	
Career Total	1	0	0	0	

Going:	Sf: 0-0 GS: 0-0 Gd: 0-1 GF: - Fm: 0-0
Distance:	2m/2m3: 0-1 2m4-2m7: 0-0 3m+: 0-0
Track:	LH: 0-1 RH: 0-0 Tight: 0-1 Gall: 0-0
Aids:	Bl: 0-0 Vi: 0-0 Tstrap: 0-0
Best Rating:	0 3/03 Fknm 2m good Hdl

Sel

106   **95**

5-y-o b m Salse (USA)-Frog (Akarad (FR))
G L Moore John Hetherington

Placings:4032252-6236   (2351)
2002/03: 16²G, 16⁶S, 17²GS, 20³S, 16⁶GS,

	Starts	1st	2nd	3rd	Win & Pl
Hurdles	5	0	2	1	2395
Career Total	11	0	4	2	4323

Going:	Sf: 0-2 GS: 0-2 Gd: 0-1 GF: - Fm: 0-0
Distance:	2m/2m3: 0-4 2m4-2m7: 0-1 3m+: 0-0
Track:	LH: 0-2 RH: 0-3 Tight: 0-4 Gall: 0-0
Aids:	Bl: 0-5 Vi: 0-0 Tstrap: 0-0
Best Rating:	95 11/02 Folk 2m1f110y gd-sft Hdl

Modest hurdler, handles soft ground but suited by faster. Usually wears blinkers.

Self Defense

122   **160**

6-y-o b h Warning-Dansara (Dancing Brave (USA))
Miss E C Lavelle (M Zilber 18/8) Fraser Miller Racing

Placings:43324P   (4478)
2002/03: 16⁴S, 20³S, 16³GS, 16²HY, 16⁴G, 20PG,

	Starts	1st	2nd	3rd	Win & Pl
Hurdles	6	0	1	2	27358
Career Total	6	0	1	2	27358

Going:	Sf: 0-3 GS: 0-1 Gd: 0-2 GF: - Fm: 0-0
Distance:	2m/2m3: 0-4 2m4-2m7: 0-2 3m+: 0-0
Track:	LH: 0-3 RH: 0-3 Tight: 0-1 Gall: 0-1
Aids:	Bl: 0-0 Vi: 0-0 Tstrap: 0-0
Best Rating:	160 3/03 Chel 2m1f110y good Hdl

Very useful and progressive ex-French novice hurdler; best effort so far a surprising and game narrow defeat by Rooster Booster in the 2003 Agfa Hurdle at Sandown, and showed that was no fluke when fourth in the Champion Hurdle; stays 2m 4f and seems well suited by a stiff 2m in testing conditions.

Semah's Parc

     50f

5-y-o b g Pure Melody (USA)-Semah s Dream (Gunner B)

Mrs A M Naughton J P Hames

Placings:0   (1243)
2002/03: 16⁵GF,

	Starts	1st	2nd	3rd	Win & Pl
NH Flat	1	0	0	0	
Career Total	1	0	0	0	

Going:	Sf: 0-0 GS: 0-0 Gd: 0-0 GF: - Fm: 0-1
Distance:	2m/2m3: 0-1 2m4-2m7: 0-0 3m+: 0-0
Track:	LH: 0-1 RH: 0-0 Tight: 0-1 Gall: 0-0
Aids:	Bl: 0-0 Vi: 0-0 Tstrap: 0-0
Best Rating:	50 9/02 Hexm 2m110y gd-fm NHF

Semliki

10-y-o b g Nearly A Hand-River Culm (Royal Salmon)
A D Peachey P Spittle

Placings:P-P   (4059)
2002/03: 26PGS,

	Starts	1st	2nd	3rd	Win & Pl
Chases	1	0	0	0	
Career Total	2	0	0	0	

Going:	Sf: 0-0 GS: 0-1 Gd: 0-0 GF: - Fm: 0-0
Distance:	2m/2m3: 0-0 2m4-2m7: 0-0 3m+: 0-1
Track:	LH: 0-1 RH: 0-0 Tight: 0-0 Gall: 0-0
Aids:	Bl: 0-0 Vi: 0-0 Tstrap: 0-0
Best Rating:	0 3/03 Wwck 3m2f gd-sft Ch

Senor Eduardo

82f   **98f**

6-y-o gr g Terimon-Jasmin Path (Warpath)
S Gollings R L Houlton

Placings:005-5   (2505)
2002/03: 16⁵GS,

	Starts	1st	2nd	3rd	Win & Pl
NH Flat	1	0	0	0	0
Career Total	4	0	0	0	0

Going:	Sf: 0-0 GS: 0-1 Gd: 0-0 GF: - Fm: 0-0
Distance:	2m/2m3: 0-1 2m4-2m7: 0-0 3m+: 0-0
Track:	LH: 0-1 RH: 0-0 Tight: 0-1 Gall: 0-0
Aids:	Bl: 0-0 Vi: 0-0 Tstrap: 0-0
Best Rating:	98 2/02 Wwck 2m soft NHF

Senor Gigo

78f   **53f**

5-y-o b g Mistertopogigo (IRE)-Lady Carol (Lord Gayle (USA))
A Scott Andy Scott

Placings:00   (1982)
2002/03: 17⁰GF, 16⁰HY,

	Starts	1st	2nd	3rd	Win & Pl
NH Flat	2	0	0	0	
Career Total	2	0	0	0	

Going:	Sf: 0-1 GS: 0-0 Gd: 0-0 GF: - Fm: 0-1
Distance:	2m/2m3: 0-2 2m4-2m7: 0-0 3m+: 0-0
Track:	LH: 0-1 RH: 0-1 Tight: 0-0 Gall: 0-0
Aids:	Bl: 0-0 Vi: 0-0 Tstrap: 0-0
Best Rating:	53 10/02 Carl 2m1f gd-fm NHF

Senor Hurst

78   **54**

8-y-o b g Young Senor (USA)-Broadhurst (Workboy)
Mrs P Sly Mrs P M Sly

Placings:02P0/0/623F432/00   (0698)
2002/03: 17⁰GF, 17⁰GF,

	Starts	1st	2nd	3rd	Win & Pl
Hurdles	2	0	0	0	
Career Total	14	0	3	2	3358

Going:	Sf: 0-0 GS: 0-0 Gd: 0-0 GF: - Fm: 0-2
Distance:	2m/2m3: 0-2 2m4-2m7: 0-0 3m+: 0-0
Track:	LH: 0-0 RH: 0-2 Tight: 0-2 Gall: 0-0
Aids:	Bl: 0-0 Vi: 0-0 Tstrap: 0-0
Best Rating:	87 7/00 MRas 2m1f110y good Hdl

Senora Honoria

66f   **47f**

5-y-o b m Perpendicular-Star Thyme (Point North)
J Mackie R M Mitchell

Placings:0   (1910)
2002/03: 16⁰GS,

	Starts	1st	2nd	3rd	Win & Pl
NH Flat	1	0	0	0	
Career Total	1	0	0	0	

Going:	Sf: 0-0 GS: 0-1 Gd: 0-0 GF: - Fm: 0-0
Distance:	2m/2m3: 0-1 2m4-2m7: 0-0 3m+: 0-0
Track:	LH: 0-1 RH: 0-0 Tight: 0-1 Gall: 0-0
Aids:	Bl: 0-0 Vi: 0-0 Tstrap: 0-0
Best Rating:	47 11/02 Sthl 2m gd-sft NHF

Sense Of Adventure

10-y-o ch g Lord Bud-Mistral Magic (Crofter (USA))
H B Hodge H B Hodge

Placings:P   (4671)
2002/03: 24PG,

	Starts	1st	2nd	3rd	Win & Pl
Chases	1	0	0	0	
Career Total	1	0	0	0	

Going:	Sf: 0-0 GS: 0-0 Gd: 0-1 GF: - Fm: 0-0
Distance:	2m/2m3: 0-0 2m4-2m7: 0-0 3m+: 0-1
Track:	LH: 0-1 RH: 0-0 Tight: 0-1 Gall: 0-0
Aids:	Bl: 0-0 Vi: 0-0 Tstrap: 0-0
Best Rating:	0 4/03 Fknm 3m110y good Ch

Lightly-raced pointer; did not jump well when pulled up on debut under Rules.

Sento (IRE)

107   **108+**

5-y-o ch g Persian Bold-Esclava (USA) (Nureyev (USA))
A King Mrs M C Sweeney

Placings:1006041   (4622)
2002/03: 17¹GF, 16⁰GS, 16⁰HY, 16⁶GS, 16⁰G, 20⁴GF, 22¹GF,

	Starts	1st	2nd	3rd	Win & Pl
NH Flat	2	1	0	0	2191
Hurdles	5	1	0	0	6213
Career Total	7	2	0	0	8404
104	4/03	NAbb	2m6f	E(0-105)HHdl	G-F	£5928
108	8/02	NAbb	2m1f	H NHF	G-F	£2191

Total win prize-money £8119

Going:	Sf: 0-1 GS: 0-2 Gd: 0-1 GF: - Fm: 2-3
Distance:	2m/2m3: 1-5 2m4-2m7: 1-2 3m+: 0-0
Track:	LH: 2-6 RH: 0-1 Tight: 2-2 Gall: 0-3
Aids:	Bl: 0-0 Vi: 0-0 Tstrap: 0-0
Best Rating:	108 8/02 NAbb 2m1f gd-fm NHF

Modest hurdler; has been held since raised 11lb after showing improved form when stepped up to 2m 6f to win at Newton Abbot April 2003; suited by fast ground, but acts with cut.

September Harvest (USA)

85   50

7-y-o ch g Mujtahid (USA)-Shawgatny (USA) (Danzig Connection (USA))
Mrs S Lamyman P Lamyman

Placings:4/600664F/0060646-P6   (1621)
2002/03: 17³G, 16⁶GS,

	Starts	1st	2nd	3rd	Win & Pl
Hurdles	2	0	0	0	0
Career Total	17	0	0	0	209

Going:	Sf: 0-0 GS: 0-1 Gd: 0-1 GF: - Fm: 0-0
Distance:	2m/2m3: 0-2 2m4-2m7: 0-0 3m+: 0-0
Track:	LH: 0-2 RH: 0-0 Tight: 0-1 Gall: 0-0
Aids:	Bl: 0-0 Vi: 0-0 Tstrap: 0-0
Best Rating:	84 12/00 Donc 2m110y heavy Hdl

September Moon

101   95

5-y-o b m Bustino-Lunabelle (Idiots Delight)
Mrs A M Thorpe (J Neville 27/11) Miss Derien Edwards

Placings:40001F   (4757)
2002/03: 17⁴GS, 16⁹G, 21⁰GS, 20⁰S, 22¹GF, 22⁵GF,

	Starts	1st	2nd	3rd	Win & Pl
NH Flat	2	0	0	0	0
Hurdles	4	1	0	0	4534
Career Total	6	1	0	0	4534
95 4/03 Extr 2m6f110yE Hdl			G-F	£4533	
			Total win prize-money £4534		

Going:	Sf: 0-1 GS: 0-2 Gd: 0-1 GF: - Fm: 1-2
Distance:	2m/2m3: 0-2 2m4-2m7: 1-4 3m+: 0-0
Track:	LH: 0-4 RH: 1-2 Tight: 0-2 Gall: 0-0
Aids:	Bl: 0-0 Vi: 0-0 Tstrap: 0-0
Best Rating:	95 4/03 Extr 2m6f110y gd-fm Hdl

Supported at long odds when showing improved form to win 22 furlong fast ground novice hurdle at Exeter April 2003.

Serendipity (FR)

10-y-o b g Mtoto-Bint Damascus (USA) (Damascus (USA))
Miss L V Davis Miss Louise Davis

Placings:U10/4/P   (1616)
2002/03: 24⁵PF,

	Starts	1st	2nd	3rd	Win & Pl
Hurdles	1	0	0	0	0
Career Total	5	1	0	0	2654
105 2/98 Ludl 2m		E Hdl	GD	£2654	
			Total win prize-money £2654		

Going:	Sf: 0-0 GS: 0-0 Gd: 0-0 GF: - Fm: 0-1
Distance:	2m/2m3: 0-0 2m4-2m7: 0-0 3m+: 0-1

Track:	LH: 0-0 RH: 0-1 Tight: 0-0 Gall: 0-0
Aids:	Bl: 0-0 Vi: 0-0 Tstrap: 0-0
Best Rating:	105 2/98 Ludl 2m good Hdl

Serenus (USA)

113(102c)   (132dc)109

10-y-o b g Sunshine Forever (USA)-Curl And Set (USA) (Nijinsky (CAN))
D R C Elsworth W V & Mrs E S Robins

Placings:3511F60/114304/21304/1322U14/420465/534060
443-002200034   (4596)
2002/03: 19⁰GS, 16⁶S, 19²GS, 16²S, 21⁰G, 21⁰G, 16⁰HY, 19³F,
19⁴GF,

	Starts	1st	2nd	3rd	Win & Pl
Hurdles	9	0	2	1	5046
Career Total	49	7	6	7	93863
137	2/00	Kemp	2m4f110yA Ch		G-S	£13200
121	11/99	Newb	2m1f	D Ch	G-F	£4500
147	12/98	Kemp	2m	B(0-145)HHdl	SFT	£6957
133	12/97	Kemp	2m	B HHdl	SFT	£6768
122	12/97	Hntg	2m110y	D(0-125)HHdl	GD	£2735
117	12/96	Ling	2m110y	A Hdl	G-S	£9735
112	12/96	Font	2m2f110yE Hdl		GD	£2364
			Total win prize-money £46260		

Going:	Sf: 0-3 GS: 0-2 Gd: 0-2 GF: - Fm: 0-2
Distance:	2m/2m3: 0-5 2m4-2m7: 0-4 3m+: 0-0
Track:	LH: 0-2 RH: 0-7 Tight: 0-2 Gall: 0-2
Aids:	Bl: 0-0 Vi: 0-0 Tstrap: 0-0
Best Rating:	149 12/00 Kemp 2m gd-sft Hdl

Modest hurdler these days; stays two and a half miles; acts on most types of ground; has a good record at Kempton.

Serious Position (IRE)

96   91

8-y-o ch g Orchestra-Lady Temba (Callernish)
D R Stoddart D R Stoddart

Placings:5P6P4P/0PP336P-544   (1896)
2002/03: 16⁵GF, 16⁴G, 16⁴GS,

	Starts	1st	2nd	3rd	Win & Pl
Hurdles	3	0	0	0	618
Career Total	16	0	0	2	1962

Going:	Sf: 0-0 GS: 0-1 Gd: 0-1 GF: - Fm: 0-1
Distance:	2m/2m3: 0-3 2m4-2m7: 0-0 3m+: 0-0
Track:	LH: 0-1 RH: 0-2 Tight: 0-0 Gall: 0-2
Aids:	Bl: 0-0 Vi: 0-0 Tstrap: 0-0
Best Rating:	91 10/02 Hayd 2m good Hdl

Moderate hurdler; pulled up five times from first nine starts over hurdles, but showed a measure of ability in the spring of 2002.

Serious Trust

85   68

10-y-o b g Alzao (USA)-Mill Line (Mill Reef (USA))
Mrs L C Jewell Peter J Allen

Placings:0/020-56   (0909)
2002/03: 21⁵S, 24⁸GS,

	Starts	1st	2nd	3rd	Win & Pl
Hurdles	2	0	0	0	0
Career Total	6	0	1	0	449

Going:	Sf: 0-1 GS: 0-1 Gd: 0-0 GF: - Fm: 0-0

Distance:	2m/2m3: 0-0 2m4-2m7: 0-1 3m+: 0-1
Track:	LH: 0-0 RH: 0-2 Tight: 0-2 Gall: 0-0
Aids:	Bl: 0-0 Vi: 0-0 Tstrap: 0-0
Best Rating:	68 7/01 Wolv 2m4f110y gd-fm Hdl

Serotonin

86   100

4-y-o b g Barathea (IRE)-Serotina (IRE) (Mtoto)
Jonjo O Neill (R Charlton 25/8) Mike Browne

Placings:2F   (3590)
2002/03: 17²HY, 16²HY,

	Starts	1st	2nd	3rd	Win & Pl
Hurdles	2	0	1	0	3614
Career Total	2	0	1	0	3614

Going:	Sf: 0-2 GS: 0-0 Gd: 0-0 GF: - Fm: 0-0
Distance:	2m/2m3: 0-2 2m4-2m7: 0-0 3m+: 0-0
Track:	LH: 0-1 RH: 0-1 Tight: 0-0 Gall: 0-1
Aids:	Bl: 0-0 Vi: 0-0 Tstrap: 0-0
Best Rating:	100 1/03 Chel 2m1f heavy Hdl

Decent sort at around ten furlongs on the Flat; destroyed at Sandown on second start over hurdles. (DEAD)

Serraval (FR)

99   87+

5-y-o ch m Sanglamore (USA)-Saone (USA) (Bering)
B S Rothwell J T Brown

Placings:F-2364   (1089)
2002/03: 16²GF, 17³G, 17⁶GF, 16⁴GF,

	Starts	1st	2nd	3rd	Win & Pl
Hurdles	4	0	1	1	1252
Career Total	5	0	1	1	1252

Going:	Sf: 0-0 GS: 0-0 Gd: 0-1 GF: - Fm: 0-3
Distance:	2m/2m3: 0-4 2m4-2m7: 0-0 3m+: 0-0
Track:	LH: 0-3 RH: 0-1 Tight: 0-1 Gall: 0-1
Aids:	Bl: 0-0 Vi: 0-0 Tstrap: 0-0
Best Rating:	87 8/02 Sedg 2m1f good Hdl

Plating-class hurdler. Looked a shade unlucky when runner-up in maiden hurdle at Worcester July 2002. Held subsequently.

Sertorius (IRE)

89   69

6-y-o b g Sharifabad (IRE)-Nomun Nofun (Creative Plan (USA))
P T Dalton Mrs Julie Martin

Placings:0/P0-PP00PF0P   (4705)
2002/03: 20⁵PGF, 21⁹PG, 20⁰S, 16⁰G, 24⁵PG, 20⁴PGF, 16⁰G, 21⁰PG,

	Starts	1st	2nd	3rd	Win & Pl
Hurdles	3	0	0	0	0
Chases	5	0	0	0	0
Career Total	11	0	0	0	0

Going:	Sf: 0-1 GS: 0-0 Gd: 0-0 GF: - Fm: 0-2
Distance:	2m/2m3: 0-2 2m4-2m7: 0-5 3m+: 0-1
Track:	LH: 0-7 RH: 0-1 Tight: 0-0 Gall: 0-3
Aids:	Bl: 0-0 Vi: 0-0 Tstrap: 0-1
Best Rating:	69 12/02 Donc 2m110y good Ch

Seskin-View (IRE)

8-y-o b/br m Buckskin (FR)-Honeyview (IRE) (Forties Field (FR))

Ferdy Murphy S L & M A Hubbard Rodwell

Placings:*00/60* (2134)
2002/03: 16⁶S, 21⁰G,

	Starts	1st	2nd	3rd	Win & Pl
Hurdles	2	0	0	0	0
Career Total	4	0	0	0	0

Going:	Sf: 0-1 GS: 0-0 Gd: 0-1 GF: - Fm: 0-0
Distance:	2m/2m3: 0-1 2m4-2m7: 0-1 3m+: 0-0
Track:	LH: 0-1 RH: 0-1 Tight: 0-0 Gall: 0-0
Aids:	Bl: 0-0 Vi: 0-0 Tstrap: 0-0
Best Rating:	59 5/99 Clon 2m soft NHF

Set Dance (IRE)
101   76

7-y-o b g Suave Dancer (USA)-La Courant (USA) (Little Current (USA))
E L James Miss Helen Pease

Placings:*000PP-2P00* (0625)
2002/03: 17²G, 22⁶GF, 16⁶GF, 17⁹GF,

	Starts	1st	2nd	3rd	Win & Pl
Hurdles	4	0	1	0	646
Career Total	9	0	1	0	646

Going:	Sf: 0-0 GS: 0-0 Gd: 0-1 GF: - Fm: 0-3
Distance:	2m/2m3: 0-3 2m4-2m7: 0-1 3m+: 0-0
Track:	LH: 0-0 RH: 0-4 Tight: 0-2 Gall: 0-1
Aids:	Bl: 0-0 Vi: 0-0 Tstrap: 0-0
Best Rating:	76 5/02 Folk 2m1f110y good Hdl

Setting Sun
103   93

10-y-o ch g Generous (IRE)-Suntrap (USA) (Roberto (USA))
N Waggott Mrs J Waggott

Placings:*60322/0P/001/0P/44450* (3154)
2002/03: 16⁴GS, 20⁴G, 22⁴G, 20⁵S, 20⁰G,

	Starts	1st	2nd	3rd	Win & Pl
Hurdles	5	0	0	0	1154
Career Total	17	1	2	1	6114
100 2/00 Muss 3m	D(0-110)HHdl G-S £3250
	Total win prize-money £3250

Going:	Sf: 0-1 GS: 0-1 Gd: 0-3 GF: - Fm: 0-0
Distance:	2m/2m3: 0-1 2m4-2m7: 0-4 3m+: 0-0
Track:	LH: 0-2 RH: 0-3 Tight: 0-2 Gall: 0-0
Aids:	Bl: 0-0 Vi: 0-0 Tstrap: 0-0
Best Rating:	105 3/98 Newc 2m gd-fm Hdl

Modest staying hurdler, handles a sound surface but suited by a little cut. Stays three miles.

Seven Mile Gale (IRE)

11-y-o b g Strong Gale-Moonlight Romance (Teenoso (USA))
N G Richards Southport s Adelphi Hotel

Placings:*500/5/F111/F* (0583)
2002/03: 20⁶G,

	Starts	1st	2nd	3rd	Win & Pl
Chases	1	0	0	0	
Career Total	9	3	0	0	10160
119 8/99 Prth 2m4f110y(0-110)HCh	G-F £4162
104 7/99 Sedg 2m110y E Ch	G-F £2791

---

115 6/99 Hexm 2m4f110yE Ch G-F £3206
Total win prize-money £10161

Going:	Sf: 0-0 GS: 0-0 Gd: 0-1 GF: - Fm: 0-0
Distance:	2m/2m3: 0-0 2m4-2m7: 0-1 3m+: 0-0
Track:	LH: 0-1 RH: 0-1 Tight: 0-0 Gall: 0-0
Aids:	Bl: 0-1 Vi: 0-0 Tstrap: 0-0
Best Rating:	119 8/99 Prth 2m4f110y gd-fm Ch

Sevensider (IRE)
95   51

5-y-o b/br g Satco (FR)-Pretty Beau (IRE) (Beau Charmeur (FR))
M W Easterby Abbots Salford Caravan Park

Placings:*060000P* (4108)
2002/03: 16⁰G, 16⁶HY, 16⁹GS, 19⁰GS, 16⁹S, 25⁰G, 17⁹S,

	Starts	1st	2nd	3rd	Win & Pl
NH Flat	2	0	0	0	0
Hurdles	5	0	0	0	0
Career Total	7	0	0	0	0

Going:	Sf: 0-3 GS: 0-2 Gd: 0-2 GF: - Fm: 0-0
Distance:	2m/2m3: 0-6 2m4-2m7: 0-0 3m+: 0-1
Track:	LH: 0-7 RH: 0-0 Tight: 0-3 Gall: 0-2
Aids:	Bl: 0-1 Vi: 0-0 Tstrap: 0-0
Best Rating:	71 11/02 Weth 2m heavy NHF

Severn Air
88f   80f

5-y-o b m Alderbrook-Mariner s Air (Julio Mariner)
J L Spearing Mrs Peter Badger

Placings:*60* (4060)
2002/03: 16⁶G, 16⁹S,

	Starts	1st	2nd	3rd	Win & Pl
NH Flat	2	0	0	0	0
Career Total	2	0	0	0	0

Going:	Sf: 0-1 GS: 0-0 Gd: 0-1 GF: - Fm: 0-0
Distance:	2m/2m3: 0-2 2m4-2m7: 0-0 3m+: 0-0
Track:	LH: 0-1 RH: 0-1 Tight: 0-0 Gall: 0-1
Aids:	Bl: 0-0 Vi: 0-0 Tstrap: 0-0
Best Rating:	80 2/03 Hntg 2m110y good NHF

Best effort on third start in bumpers.

Severn Magic

10-y-o b m Buckley-La Margarite (Bonne Noel)
D Thomas R Packer

Placings:*P-5* (0055)
2002/03: 24⁵G,

	Starts	1st	2nd	3rd	Win & Pl
Chases	1	0	0	0	0
Career Total	2	0	0	0	0

Going:	Sf: 0-0 GS: 0-0 Gd: 0-0 GF: - Fm: 0-0
Distance:	2m/2m3: 0-0 2m4-2m7: 0-0 3m+: 0-1
Track:	LH: 0-1 RH: 0-0 Tight: 0-1 Gall: 0-0
Aids:	Bl: 0-1 Vi: 0-0 Tstrap: 0-0
Best Rating:	60 5/02 Bang 3m110y good Ch

Seymour Chance
84   66

7-y-o ch m Seymour Hicks (FR)-City s Sister (Maystreak)

Mrs G S Rees Mrs C J Black

Placings:*0-4630400P* (3490)
2002/03: 16⁴GS, 17⁶GF, 16³GF, 16⁶G, 16⁴S, 16⁹G, 20⁹GS,

	Starts	1st	2nd	3rd	Win & Pl
NH Flat	3	0	0	1	316
Hurdles	5	0	0	0	279
Career Total	9	0	0	1	595

Going:	Sf: 0-1 GS: 0-2 Gd: 0-3 GF: - Fm: 0-2
Distance:	2m/2m3: 0-6 2m4-2m7: 0-2 3m+: 0-0
Track:	LH: 0-5 RH: 0-2 Tight: 0-5 Gall: 0-0
Aids:	Bl: 0-0 Vi: 0-1 Tstrap: 0-0
Best Rating:	75 7/02 Strf 2m110y gd-fm NHF

Sh Boom
114   143

5-y-o b g Alderbrook-Muznah (Royal And Regal (USA))
Jonjo O Neill T G K Construction Ltd

Placings:*61-11215P* (4462)
2002/03: 16¹HY, 20¹S, 21²G, 20¹G, 21⁵G, 20⁹G,

	Starts	1st	2nd	3rd	Win & Pl
NH Flat	1	1	0	0	2478
Hurdles	5	2	1	0	14662
Career Total	8	4	1	0	18862
126 3/03 Hntg 2m4f110yE Hdl	GD £3766
133 12/02 Uttx 2m4f110yE Hdl	SFT £3669
100 11/02 Weth 2m H NHF	HVY £2478
98 4/02 Towc 2m H NHF	GD £1722
	Total win prize-money £11636

Going:	Sf: 2-2 GS: 0-0 Gd: 1-4 GF: - Fm: 0-0
Distance:	2m/2m3: 1-1 2m4-2m7: 2-5 3m+: 0-0
Track:	LH: 2-4 RH: 1-2 Tight: 0-1 Gall: 1-2
Aids:	Bl: 0-0 Vi: 0-0 Tstrap: 0-0
Best Rating:	143 3/03 Chel 2m5f good Hdl

Useful half-brother to smart Stayers' Hurdle winner Anzum; did well in bumpers, winning twice; most convincing winner over hurdling bow at Uttoxeter in December and ran very well in top company afterwards; stays 2m 5f; acts on good and soft ground.

Shaadiva
100   81

5-y-o b m Shaamit (IRE)-Kristal Diva (Kris)
A King Cheltenham Racing Ltd

Placings:*0043* (4755)
2002/03: 16⁹S, 16⁰G, 16⁴GF, 18³GF,

	Starts	1st	2nd	3rd	Win & Pl
NH Flat	2	0	0	0	0
Hurdles	2	0	0	1	782
Career Total	4	0	0	1	782

Going:	Sf: 0-1 GS: 0-0 Gd: 0-1 GF: - Fm: 0-2
Distance:	2m/2m3: 0-4 2m4-2m7: 0-0 3m+: 0-0
Track:	LH: 0-2 RH: 0-2 Tight: 0-2 Gall: 0-1
Aids:	Bl: 0-0 Vi: 0-0 Tstrap: 0-0
Best Rating:	82 4/03 Font 2m2f110y gd-fm Hdl

Plating-class novice hurdler; acts on a sound surface.

Shade Lucky

7-y-o ch g Gildoran-Snowy Autumn (Deep Run)
B J M Ryall J F Tucker

Placings:*00-PP* (2073)

2002/03: 19^{P}GS, 22^{P}GS,

	Starts	1st	2nd	3rd	Win & Pl
Hurdles	2	0	0	0	
Career Total	4	0	0	0	

Going: Sf: 0-0 GS: 0-2 Gd: 0-0 GF: - Fm: 0-0
Distance: 2m/2m3: 0-1 2m4-2m7: 0-1 3m+: 0-0
Track: LH: 0-1 RH: 0-1 Tight: 0-0 Gall: 0-1
Aids: Bl: 0-0 Vi: 0-0 Tstrap: 0-0
Best Rating: 67 12/01 NAbb 2m1f   heavy NHF

Shaded (IRE)

94   64

9-y-o b g Night Shift (USA)-Sarsaparilla (FR) (Shirley Heights)
D J Minty D J Minty

Placings:06FP0/00P200P/00P0434534P/0/000301-FPP0   (4693)
2002/03: 19^{1}FS, 16^{2}HY, 19^{P}HY, 17^{0}G,

	Starts	1st	2nd	3rd	Win & Pl
Hurdles	3	0	0	0	0
Chases	1	0	0	0	0
Career Total	34	1	1	3	3192

75   10/01 Tntn   2m3f110yG(0-90)HHdl   FRM £1690
                  Total win prize-money £1691

Going: Sf: 0-3 GS: 0-0 Gd: 0-1 GF: - Fm: 0-0
Distance: 2m/2m3: 0-3 2m4-2m7: 0-1 3m+: 0-0
Track: LH: 0-2 RH: 0-2 Tight: 0-3 Gall: 0-0
Aids: Bl: 0-0 Vi: 0-0 Tstrap: 0-0
Best Rating: 75 10/01 Tntn   2m3f110y   firm   Hdl

Plating-class hurdler; finished lame when winning a modest Taunton seller in October 2001; supported at long odds when running best race since returning in 2m 6f selling handicap at Newton Abbot May 2003; should do better over shorter trips.

Shadow Catcher

83   69+

6-y-o b g Missed Flight-Welgenco (Welsh Saint)
E W Tuer D R Obank

Placings:00-500   (2103)
2002/03: 17^{5}GF, 16^{0}G, 16^{0}G,

	Starts	1st	2nd	3rd	Win & Pl
Hurdles	3	0	0	0	0
Career Total	5	0	0	0	0

Going: Sf: 0-0 GS: 0-0 Gd: 0-2 GF: - Fm: 0-1
Distance: 2m/2m3: 0-3 2m4-2m7: 0-0 3m+: 0-0
Track: LH: 0-2 RH: 0-1 Tight: 0-2 Gall: 0-0
Aids: Bl: 0-0 Vi: 0-0 Tstrap: 0-0
Best Rating: 69 10/02 Kels   2m110y   good   Hdl

Shady Affair (IRE)

86(97c)   28

12-y-o b g Black Minstrel-Golden Ice (Golden Love)
R N Bevis Mrs S J Clutton

Placings:PP/25516UP-50P0   (3811)
2002/03: 20^{5}GS, 20^{0}G, 24^{P}G, 25^{0}G,

	Starts	1st	2nd	3rd	Win & Pl
Hurdles	3	0	0	0	0
Chases	1	0	0	0	0
Career Total	13	1	1	0	4528

82   11/01 Bang   2m1f110yE(0-105)HCh   SFT   £3607
                Total win prize-money £3608

Going: Sf: 0-0 GS: 0-1 Gd: 0-3 GF: - Fm: 0-0
Distance: 2m/2m3: 0-0 2m4-2m7: 0-2 3m+: 0-2
Track: LH: 0-2 RH: 0-2 Tight: 0-3 Gall: 0-0
Aids: Bl: 0-0 Vi: 0-0 Tstrap: 0-0
Best Rating: 82 11/01 Bang 2m1f110y soft   Ch

Shady Anne

101   85

5-y-o ch m Derrylin-Juno Away (Strong Gale)
F Jordan D Pugh

Placings:1-61050P   (4091)
2002/03: 16^{1}GS, 17^{5}GF, 17^{1}S, 16^{9}HY, 20^{5}S, 21^{0}S, 19^{P}HY,

	Starts	1st	2nd	3rd	Win & Pl
NH Flat	4	2	0	0	3618
Hurdles	3	0	0	0	0
Career Total	7	2	0	0	3618

106 10/02 Bang   2m1f   H NHF   SFT £1881
93   4/02 Towc   2m   H NHF   G-S £1736
               Total win prize-money £3618

Going: Sf: 1-5 GS: 1-1 Gd: 0-0 GF: - Fm: 0-1
Distance: 2m/2m3: 2-4 2m4-2m7: 0-3 3m+: 0-0
Track: LH: 1-3 RH: 1-4 Tight: 1-2 Gall: 0-0
Aids: Bl: 0-0 Vi: 0-0 Tstrap: 0-0
Best Rating: 106 10/02 Bang 2m1f   soft   NHF

Won a weak bumper on her debut, but won a much better one in good style on her third start. Acts well in the soft. held over hurdles.

Shady Grey

90f   80f

5-y-o gr m Minster Son-Yemaail (IRE) (Shaadi (USA))
Miss S E Forster A Dawson

Placings:600   (3991)
2002/03: 16^{6}HY, 16^{0}G, 17^{0}S,

	Starts	1st	2nd	3rd	Win & Pl
NH Flat	3	0	0	0	0
Career Total	3	0	0	0	0

Going: Sf: 0-2 GS: 0-0 Gd: 0-1 GF: - Fm: 0-0
Distance: 2m/2m3: 0-3 2m4-2m7: 0-0 3m+: 0-0
Track: LH: 0-1 RH: 0-2 Tight: 0-1 Gall: 0-0
Aids: Bl: 0-0 Vi: 0-0 Tstrap: 0-0
Best Rating: 80 1/03 Ayr   2m   heavy NHF

Shady Man

90   78

5-y-o b g Shaamit (IRE)-Miss Hardy (Formidable (USA))
N G Richards Trevor Hemmings

Placings:0-P602   (3355)
2002/03: 17^{0}G, 16^{6}S, 16^{0}GS, 16^{2}HY,

	Starts	1st	2nd	3rd	Win & Pl
Hurdles	4	0	1	0	1040
Career Total	5	0	1	0	1040

Going: Sf: 0-2 GS: 0-1 Gd: 0-1 GF: - Fm: 0-0
Distance: 2m/2m3: 0-4 2m4-2m7: 0-0 3m+: 0-0
Track: LH: 0-4 RH: 0-0 Tight: 0-1 Gall: 0-2
Aids: Bl: 0-0 Vi: 0-0 Tstrap: 0-0
Best Rating: 78 1/03 Newc 2m   heavy Hdl

First worthwhile form when runner-up in a novices handicap hurdle at Newcastle in January.

Shaffishayes

103   86

11-y-o ch g Clantime-Mischievous Miss (Niniski (USA))
Mrs M Reveley P Davidson-Brown

Placings:F4-04333U2F   (4433)
2002/03: 16^{0}GS, 16^{4}G, 16^{3}S, 16^{3}HY, 16^{3}S, 16^{U}S, 17^{2}G, 16^{F}G,

	Starts	1st	2nd	3rd	Win & Pl
Hurdles	8	0	1	3	1863
Career Total	10	0	1	3	1863

Going: Sf: 0-4 GS: 0-3 Gd: 0-3 GF: - Fm: 0-0
Distance: 2m/2m3: 0-8 2m4-2m7: 0-0 3m+: 0-0
Track: LH: 0-7 RH: 0-1 Tight: 0-2 Gall: 0-4
Aids: Bl: 0-0 Vi: 0-0 Tstrap: 0-0
Best Rating: 95 10/01 Aint   2m110y   good   Hdl

Plating-class veteran; effective at two miles; acts on decent ground.

Shah (IRE)

98   82

10-y-o b g King Persian-Gay And Sharp (Fine Blade (USA))
P Kelsall Peter Kelsall

Placings:00P0P/1/45-P1   (0329)
2002/03: 16^{P}GS, 16^{1}G,

	Starts	1st	2nd	3rd	Win & Pl
Chases	2	1	0	0	2979
Career Total	10	2	0	0	6951

89   5/02 Worc   2m   F(0-95)HCh   GD   £2978
78   10/00 Ludl   2m4f   D(0-110)HCh   G-F   £3711
             Total win prize-money £6691

Going: Sf: 0-0 GS: 0-1 Gd: 1-1 GF: - Fm: 0-0
Distance: 2m/2m3: 1-2 2m4-2m7: 0-0 3m+: 0-0
Track: LH: 1-1 RH: 0-1 Tight: 0-0 Gall: 0-0
Aids: Bl: 0-0 Vi: 0-0 Tstrap: 0-0
Best Rating: 89 5/02 Worc 2m   good   Ch

Plating-class chaser. Scored on second start for new trainer at Worcester May 2002. Effective at up to two and a half miles. Likes fast ground.

Shahboor (USA)

104(106h)   (123h)111

9-y-o b g Zilzal (USA)-Iva Reputation (USA) (Sir Ivor)
Mrs P Robeson Sir Evelyn De Rothschild

Placings:0/24160/12104233/325F3435-21   (4523)
2002/03: 17^{2}GS, 16^{1}G,

	Starts	1st	2nd	3rd	Win & Pl
Chases	2	1	1	0	5865
Career Total	24	4	5	5	27536

111 4/03 Uttx   2m   E Ch   GD   £4114
125 5/99 Uttx   2m   C(0-135)HHdl   GD   £4440
125 5/99 Strf   2m110y D(0-120)HHdl   G-S   £3860
106 5/98 Uttx   2m   E(0-100)HHdl   G-F   £2547
            Total win prize-money £14962

Going: Sf: 0-0 GS: 0-1 Gd: 1-1 GF: - Fm: 0-0
Distance: 2m/2m3: 1-2 2m4-2m7: 0-0 3m+: 0-0
Track: LH: 1-1 RH: 0-1 Tight: 0-1 Gall: 0-0
Aids: Bl: 0-0 Vi: 0-0 Tstrap: 0-0
Best Rating: 125 5/99 Uttx   2m   good   Hdl

Modest novice chaser; decent handicap hurdler in his time; finished runner-up at Market Rasen on his first outing for over two years and followed up with an impressive victory at Uttoxeter; acts on most types of ground; best at two miles; looks well handicapped over fences.

Shake Eddie Shake (IRE)

87   **69**

6-y-o b g Blues Traveller (IRE)-Fortune Teller (Troy)
H S Howe C I A Slocock

Placings:05/PPP-P040   (4693)
2002/03: 19PGS, 17OGS, 194F, 17OG,

	Starts	1st	2nd	3rd	Win & Pl
Hurdles	4	0	0	0	335
Career Total	9	0	0	0	335

Going:	Sf: 0-0 GS: 0-2 Gd: 0-1 GF: - Fm: 0-1
Distance:	2m2/m3: 0-3 2m4-2m7: 0-1 3m+: 0-0
Track:	LH: 0-1 RH: 0-3 Tight: 0-3 Gall: 0-0
Aids:	Bl: 0-0 Vi: 0-0 Tstrap: 0-0
Best Rating:	69 3/03 Tntn 2m3f110y firm Hdl

Poor novice hurdler.

Shakwaa

72   **50**

4-y-o ch f Lion Cavern (USA)-Shadha (USA) (Devil s Bag (USA))
E A Elliott (M R Channon 17/5) Eric A Elliott

Placings:00   (4156)
2002/03: 17OGS, 17OG,

	Starts	1st	2nd	3rd	Win & Pl
Hurdles	2	0	0	0	
Career Total	2	0	0	0	

Going:	Sf: 0-0 GS: 0-1 Gd: 0-1 GF: - Fm: 0-0
Distance:	2m/m3: 0-2 2m4-2m7: 0-0 3m+: 0-0
Track:	LH: 0-0 RH: 0-2 Tight: 0-1 Gall: 0-0
Aids:	Bl: 0-0 Vi: 0-0 Tstrap: 0-0
Best Rating:	47 3/03 Carl 2m1f gd-sft Hdl

Shalaal (USA)

81   **80**

9-y-o b g Sheikh Albadou-One Fine Day (USA) (Quadratic (USA))
M C Chapman Eric Knowles

Placings:620/1P/000050500/51114203300/54-4P (3366)
2002/03: 164GS, 16PGS,

	Starts	1st	2nd	3rd	Win & Pl
Chases	2	0	0	0	275
Career Total	29	4	2	2	20340
116	6/00	Hrfd	2m1f	F(0-105)HHdl	G-F £3627
106	6/00	Uttx	2m	F(0-110)HHdl	G-F £1932
97	5/00	Ctml	2m	F(0-120)HHdl	G-S £3185
97	5/98	Ctml	2m1f110yD	(0-120)HHdl	G-F £2736
				Total win prize-money	£11480

Going:	Sf: 0-0 GS: 0-2 Gd: 0-0 GF: - Fm: 0-0
Distance:	2m/m3: 0-2 2m4-2m7: 0-0 3m+: 0-0
Track:	LH: 0-2 RH: 0-0 Tight: 0-2 Gall: 0-0
Aids:	Bl: 0-0 Vi: 0-0 Tstrap: 0-0
Best Rating:	116 6/00 Hrfd 2m1f gd-fm Hdl

Plating-class chaser; completed a hat-trick over hurdles in the summer of 2000 but, after a promising start over fences has not really progressed. Does not want extremes of going.

Shalaines Pride (IRE)

94   **74**

10-y-o b g Yashgan-Swifts Butterfly (Furry Glen)

T P McGovern M Ferron

Placings:3P06/4PPFP   (4428)
2002/03: 194GF, 20OGF, 21PG, 21FS, 25PGF,

	Starts	1st	2nd	3rd	Win & Pl
Hurdles	4	0	0	0	0
Chases	1	0	0	0	0
Career Total	9	0	0	1	185

Going:	Sf: 0-1 GS: 0-0 Gd: 0-1 GF: - Fm: 0-3
Distance:	2m/m3: 0-0 2m4-2m7: 0-4 3m+: 0-1
Track:	LH: 0-3 RH: 0-1 Tight: 0-2 Gall: 0-0
Aids:	Bl: 0-0 Vi: 0-0 Tstrap: 0-3
Best Rating:	93 6/98 Worc 2m gd-fm NHF

Shalako (USA)

106   **118+**

5-y-o ch g Kingmambo (USA)-Sporades (USA) (Vaguely Noble)
P J Hobbs D J Jones

Placings:141   (3141)
2002/03: 171GS, 164S, 171S,

	Starts	1st	2nd	3rd	Win & Pl
Hurdles	3	2	0	0	10181
Career Total	3	2	0	0	10181
113	1/03	Tntn	2m1f	E Hdl	SFT £4615
118	11/02	Tntn	2m1f	D Hdl	G-S £4316
				Total win prize-money	£8931

Going:	Sf: 1-2 GS: 1-1 Gd: 0-0 GF: - Fm: 0-0
Distance:	2m/m3: 2-3 2m4-2m7: 0-0 3m+: 0-0
Track:	LH: 0-0 RH: 2-3 Tight: 2-2 Gall: 0-0
Aids:	Bl: 0-0 Vi: 0-0 Tstrap: 0-0
Best Rating:	118 11/02 Tntn 2m1f gd-sft Hdl

Fair novice hurdler; suited by two miles and cut in the ground; goes well at Taunton.

Shalbeblue (IRE)

98(105h)   (110h)**95**

6-y-o b g Shalford (IRE)-Alberjas (IRE) (Sure Blade (USA))
B Ellison Four Clubs

Placings:3534P/16632116-63023233   (4794)
2002/03: 16SG, 173S, 20OGS, 16ZG, 163G, 16ZG, 163G, 213GF,

	Starts	1st	2nd	3rd	Win & Pl
Hurdles	4	0	1	1	2685
Chases	4	0	1	3	3903
Career Total	21	3	3	7	18475
108	3/02	Sedg	2m1f	E(0-110)HHdl	SFT £2548
110	2/02	Sedg	2m1f	E Hdl	SFT £2583
111	10/01	Sedg	2m1f	E Hdl	G-S £2576
				Total win prize-money	£7707

Going:	Sf: 0-1 GS: 0-1 Gd: 0-5 GF: - Fm: 0-1
Distance:	2m/m3: 0-6 2m4-2m7: 0-2 3m+: 0-0
Track:	LH: 0-5 RH: 0-3 Tight: 0-7 Gall: 0-0
Aids:	Bl: 0-8 Vi: 0-0 Tstrap: 0-0
Best Rating:	112 1/01 Donc 2m110y good Hdl

Moderate chaser; mixes Flat racing with hurdling; little impact over fences so far; looks best at around two miles; suited by cut in the ground but handles faster; usually wears blinkers or cheekpieces.

Shaluji (IRE)

104f   **91f**

6-y-o b m Montelimar (USA)-Shuil Alanna (Furry Glen)
Mrs M Reveley T M McKain

Placings:50P   (3167)
2002/03: 165GS, 16PS, 16PG,

	Starts	1st	2nd	3rd	Win & Pl
NH Flat	3	0	0	0	0
Career Total	3	0	0	0	0

Going:	Sf: 0-1 GS: 0-0 Gd: 0-1 GF: - Fm: 0-0
Distance:	2m/m3: 0-3 2m4-2m7: 0-0 3m+: 0-0
Track:	LH: 0-3 RH: 0-0 Tight: 0-1 Gall: 0-0
Aids:	Bl: 0-0 Vi: 0-0 Tstrap: 0-0
Best Rating:	91 11/02 Weth 2m gd-sft NHF

Shaman

97   **90**

6-y-o b g Fraam-Magic Maggie (Beveled (USA))
G L Moore (B A Pearce 13/5) Paul Chapman

Placings:P60   (4733)
2002/03: 17PHY, 165S, 16OGF,

	Starts	1st	2nd	3rd	Win & Pl
Hurdles	3	0	0	0	0
Career Total	3	0	0	0	0

Going:	Sf: 0-2 GS: 0-0 Gd: 0-0 GF: - Fm: 0-1
Distance:	2m/m3: 0-3 2m4-2m7: 0-0 3m+: 0-0
Track:	LH: 0-2 RH: 0-1 Tight: 0-2 Gall: 0-0
Aids:	Bl: 0-0 Vi: 0-0 Tstrap: 0-0
Best Rating:	90 12/02 Folk 2m1f110y heavy Hdl

Moderate novice hurdler.

Shamawan (IRE)

121   **144**

8-y-o b g Kris-Shamawna (IRE) (Darshaan)
Jonjo O Neill J P McManus

Placings:050/020/3P632/2112-F132   (3286)
2002/03: 16FGS, 161HY, 16JS, 212GS,

	Starts	1st	2nd	3rd	Win & Pl
Chases	4	1	1	1	25293
Career Total	19	3	5	3	41321
136	11/02	Asct	2m	B(0-145)HCh	HVY £10992
119	3/02	MRas	2m1f110yD Ch	G-S £5936
126	3/02	Hntg	2m110y	D(0-115)HCh	SFT £3893
				Total win prize-money	£20823

Going:	Sf: 1-2 GS: 0-2 Gd: 0-0 GF: - Fm: 0-0
Distance:	2m/m3: 1-3 2m4-2m7: 0-1 3m+: 0-0
Track:	LH: 0-2 RH: 1-2 Tight: 0-1 Gall: 0-1
Aids:	Bl: 0-0 Vi: 0-0 Tstrap: 0-0
Best Rating:	141 1/03 Chel 2m5f gd-sft Ch

Very useful handicap chaser; acts on soft ground; effective at around two miles to two miles five; not the most fluent of jumpers; progressed well in 2002/03.

Shamel

82   **32**

7-y-o b g Unfuwain (USA)-Narjis (USA) (Blushing Groom (FR))
C J Price Glyn Byard

Placings:P   (3173)
2002/03: 20PGS,

	Starts	1st	2nd	3rd	Win & Pl
Hurdles	1	0	0	0	
Career Total	1	0	0	0	

Going:	Sf: 0-0 GS: 0-1 Gd: 0-0 GF: - Fm: 0-0

Distance:	2m/2m3: 0-0 2m4-2m7: 0-1 3m+: 0-0
Track:	LH: 0-1 RH: 0-0 Tight: 0-0 Gall: 0-0
Aids:	Bl: 0-0 Vi: 0-0 Tstrap: 0-0
Best Rating:	0 1/03 Hayd 2m4f gd-sft Hdl

Shameless

72   **33**

6-y-o ch g Prince Daniel (USA)-Level Edge (Beveled (USA))
H Alexander   Mrs L Lever

Placings: 4025-PPPP0P   (4710)
2002/03: 21PS, 27PS, 17PHY, 24PS, 16OS, 23PGF,

	Starts	1st	2nd	3rd	Win & Pl
Hurdles	6	0	0	0	
Career Total	10	0	1	0	506

Going:	Sf: 0-5 GS: 0-0 Gd: 0-0 GF: - Fm: 0-1
Distance:	2m/2m3: 0-2 2m4-2m7: 0-2 3m+: 0-2
Track:	LH: 0-6 RH: 0-0 Tight: 0-4 Gall: 0-1
Aids:	Bl: 0-0 Vi: 0 Tstrap: 0-0
Best Rating:	89 3/02 Sthl 2m heavy NHF

Shampooed (IRE)

113(97h)   (100h)**114**

9-y-o b m Law Society (USA)-White Cap S (Shirley Heights)
R Dickin   Warwick Members Racing Club

Placings: 001/200/010511/114561300/4102553641-P162250   (3620)
2002/03: 20PG, 16¹GF, 17PGS, 16²GS, 18²G, 19⁵G, 16⁶S,

	Starts	1st	2nd	3rd	Win & Pl
Chases	7	1	2	0	7524
Career Total	38	10	4	2	42943
109	5/02	Worc	2m	E(0-110)HCh	G-F	£3368
99	4/02	Wwck	2m110y	E Ch	G-F	£3458
111	5/01	Strf	2m1f110yD Ch		G-S	£4403
113	2/01	Wwck	2m	C(0-130)HHdl	SFT	£5135
116	5/00	Hrfd	2m3f110yD(0-120)HHdl		G-S	£3071
116	5/00	Towc	2m	D(0-125)HHdl	SFT	£3211
109	4/00	Wwck	2m110y	D(0-120)HHdl	GD	£3568
92	3/00	Wwck	2m	F(0-100)HHdl	SFT	£1960
98	12/99	Wwck	2m	F(0-110)HHdl	SFT	£1996
94	3/98	Clon		Hdl	YLD	£2382
					Total win prize-money £32555	

Going:	Sf: 0-1 GS: 0-2 Gd: 0-3 GF: - Fm: 1-1
Distance:	2m/2m3: 1-6 2m4-2m7: 0-1 3m+: 0-0
Track:	LH: 1-6 RH: 0-1 Tight: 0-1 Gall: 0-1
Aids:	Bl: 0-1 Vi: 1-5 Tstrap: 0-0
Best Rating:	116 3/01 Strf 2m110y soft Hdl

Modest hurdler/chaser; multiple winner in her time; very game; effective on a sound surface but best when the mud is flying; stays 2m 4f; has worn a visor.

Shamsan (IRE)

106(106c)   (100+c)**116**

6-y-o ch g Night Shift (USA)-Awayil (USA) (Woodman (USA))
J Joseph (P J Hobbs 6/11) Jack Joseph

Placings: 03/1212116600-221222312246   (4734)
2002/03: 16²G, 16²S, 17¹GF, 20²GF, 20²GF, 21²GF, 20³G, 20¹G, 20²GF, 24²G, 16⁴GF, 16⁶GF,

	Starts	1st	2nd	3rd	Win & Pl
Hurdles	7	1	4	0	9406
Chases	5	1	3	1	10534
Career Total	24	6	9	2	35633
96	9/02	Plum	2m4f	D Ch	GD	£5538
113	6/02	Hrfd	2m1f	E(0-110)HHdl	G-F	£3402

118	7/01	NAbb	2m1f	D Hdl	GD	£3376
106	7/01	Strf	2m110y	D Hdl	GD	£3472
110	6/01	Hrfd	2m1f	E Hdl	FRM	£2712
113	5/01	Sthl	2m	E Hdl	FRM	£3662
					Total win prize-money £22164	

Going:	Sf: 0-1 GS: 0-0 Gd: 1-4 GF: - Fm: 1-7
Distance:	2m/2m3: 1-6 2m4-2m7: 1-5 3m+: 0-1
Track:	LH: 1-10 RH: 1-2 Tight: 1-6 Gall: 0-0
Aids:	Bl: 1-3 Vi: 0-0 Tstrap: 0-2
Best Rating:	121 6/01 Strf 2m110y gd-fm Hdl

Fair hurdler/modest chaser; multiple novice hurdle winner in his time; has shown ability over fences, winning a modest event at Plumpton; needs ground good or faster; stays two and a half miles; sometimes wears blinkers; best held up.

Shane

60   **22**

5-y-o ch g Aragon-Angel Fire (Nashwan (USA))
F P Murtagh   F P Murtagh

Placings: PPP-0   (1076)
2002/03: 17⁰G,

	Starts	1st	2nd	3rd	Win & Pl
Hurdles	1	0	0	0	
Career Total	4	0	0	0	

Going:	Sf: 0-0 GS: 0-0 Gd: 0-1 GF: - Fm: 0-0
Distance:	2m/2m3: 0-1 2m4-2m7: 0-0 3m+: 0-0
Track:	LH: 0-1 RH: 0-0 Tight: 0-1 Gall: 0-0
Aids:	Bl: 0-0 Vi: 0-0 Tstrap: 0-0
Best Rating:	25 8/02 Ctml 2m1f110y good Hdl

Shannon Gale (IRE)

(103h)   (104h)**120d**

11-y-o b g Strong Gale-Shannon Spray (Le Bavard (FR))
C Roche   J P McManus

Placings: 00/00021/14P/252F/231P202/02P046-PPP000   (4472)
2002/03: 27PGS, 28PSH, 21PHY, 20⁰Y, 24⁰GY, 21⁰G,

	Starts	1st	2nd	3rd	Win & Pl
Hurdles	2	0	0	0	
Chases	4	0	0	0	
Career Total	33	3	7	1	63785
117	11/00	Navn	2m4f	Ch	SFT	£4968
116	12/98	Leop	3m	HHdl	HVY	£8445
110	12/96	Leop	2m	NHF	YLD	£3177
					Total win prize-money £16592	

Going:	Sf: 0-1 GS: 0-1 Gd: 0-1 GF: - Fm: 0-0
Distance:	2m/2m3: 0-2 2m4-2m7: 0-3 3m+: 0-3
Track:	LH: 0-4 RH: 0-1 Tight: 0-2 Gall: 0-0
Aids:	Bl: 0-0 Vi: 0-0 Tstrap: 0-0
Best Rating:	137 3/99 Chel 3m1f110y gd-sft Hdl

Useful Irish staying chaser; gets three miles plus; effective on soft ground; disappointing in 2002/2003.

Shannon Light (IRE)

100   **100**

11-y-o b/br g Electric-Shannon Lass (Callernish)
N R Mitchell   N R Mitchell

Placings: 00202/3/0/0P/2506410F-2P   (0578)
2002/03: 27²S, 22PG,

	Starts	1st	2nd	3rd	Win & Pl
Hurdles	2	0	1	0	838
Career Total	19	1	4	1	6876
101	3/02	Chep	3m	D(0-120)HHdl	SFT	£3575

Total win prize-money £3575

Going:	Sf: 0-1 GS: 0-0 Gd: 0-1 GF: - Fm: 0-0
Distance:	2m/2m3: 0-0 2m4-2m7: 0-1 3m+: 0-1
Track:	LH: 0-2 RH: 0-0 Tight: 0-2 Gall: 0-0
Aids:	Bl: 0-0 Vi: 0-0 Tstrap: 0-0
Best Rating:	104 5/97 Tipp 2m4f yld-sft NHF

Modest form over hurdles. Has won on heavy ground, handles faster.

Shannon Quest (IRE)

104(107c)   (90c)**90**

7-y-o b/br g Zaffaran (USA)-Carrick Shannon (Green Shoon)
O Sherwood   Ledwidge Best Fforde

Placings: 0/030436F-2P5423F5P   (4597)
2002/03: 16²G, 16PG, 16⁵G, 16⁴G, 16²G, 16³G, 20FGF, 20⁵G, 17PGF,

	Starts	1st	2nd	3rd	Win & Pl
Hurdles	1	0	0	0	
Chases	8	0	2	1	3325
Career Total	17	0	2	3	4502

Going:	Sf: 0-0 GS: 0-0 Gd: 0-7 GF: - Fm: 0-2
Distance:	2m/2m3: 0-7 2m4-2m7: 0-2 3m+: 0-0
Track:	LH: 0-2 RH: 0-7 Tight: 0-4 Gall: 0-3
Aids:	Bl: 0-8 Vi: 0-0 Tstrap: 0-0
Best Rating:	96 5/02 Folk 2m good Ch

Plating-class hurdler/chaser; sometimes wears blinkers; effective at around two miles, probably gets two miles six; not a straightforward ride.

Shannon's Dream

61

7-y-o gr m Anshan-Jenny s Call (Petong)
Mrs Barbara Waring   Hugh J Shapter

Placings: 00PP-0P   (2315)
2002/03: 17⁰GS, 20PHY,

	Starts	1st	2nd	3rd	Win & Pl
Hurdles	2	0	0	0	
Career Total	6	0	0	0	

Going:	Sf: 0-1 GS: 0-1 Gd: 0-0 GF: - Fm: 0-0
Distance:	2m/2m3: 0-1 2m4-2m7: 0-1 3m+: 0-0
Track:	LH: 0-0 RH: 0-2 Tight: 0-1 Gall: 0-0
Aids:	Bl: 0-0 Vi: 0-0 Tstrap: 0-0
Best Rating:	26 6/01 Worc 2m gd-fm Hdl

Shannon's Pride (IRE)

103   **120+**

7-y-o gr g Roselier (FR)-Spanish Flame (IRE) (Spanish Place (USA))
N G Richards   J Hales

Placings: 3-113   (4304)
2002/03: 22¹S, 20¹GS, 22³G,

	Starts	1st	2nd	3rd	Win & Pl
Hurdles	3	2	0	1	6818
Career Total	4	2	0	2	7675
120	12/02	Ayr	2m4f	E Hdl	G-S	£3052
112	11/02	Ayr	2m6f	E Hdl	SFT	£3094
					Total win prize-money £6146	

Going:	Sf: 1-1 GS: 1-1 Gd: 0-1 GF: - Fm: 0-0

Distance:	2m/2m3: 0-0 2m4-2m7: 2-3 3m+: 0-0		
Track:	LH: 2-3 RH: 0-0 Tight: 0-1 Gall: 0-0		
Aids:	Bl: 0-0 Vi: 0-0 Tstrap: 0-0		
Best Rating:	120 12/02 Ayr	2m4f	gd-sft Hdl

Promising novice hurdler, stays 2m 6f and should stay further; suited by cut in the ground and will make a nice chaser in time.

Shardam (IRE)

116(110h)   (115h)135

6-y-o b g Shardari-Knockea Hill (Buckskin (FR))
N A Twiston-Davies Howard Parker

Placings:2526262-31U21512   (4469)
2002/03: 19³G, 24¹S, 24¹G, 19²G, 22¹S, 24⁵G, 24¹GS, 25²G,

	Starts	1st	2nd	3rd	Win & Pl
Hurdles	2	1	0	1	3176
Chases	6	2	2	0	23529
Career Total	15	3	6	1	29845
125	2/03 Chep	3m	D Ch		G-S	£5713
129	12/02 Font	2m6f	D Ch		SFT	£6864
108	11/02 Chep	3m	F Hdl		SFT	£2646

Total win prize-money £15224

Going:	Sf: 2-2 GS: 1-1 Gd: 0-5 GF: - Fm: 0-0
Distance:	2m/2m3: 0-1 2m4-2m7: 1-2 3m+: 2-5
Track:	LH: 2-4 RH: 0-3 Tight: 1-4 Gall: 0-1
Aids:	Bl: 0-0 Vi: 0-0 Tstrap: 0-0
Best Rating:	135 4/03 Aint 3m1f good Ch

Useful chaser; runner-up in valuable handicap at Aintree in April; acts on good and soft ground; stays three miles; tough and progressive.

Share Options (IRE)

12-y-o b/br g Executive Perk-Shannon Belle (Pollerton)
P Jones Steve Hammond

Placings:53/1F5124P/PP121P6/1142322/2PR4/P (3848)
2002/03: 27⁰G,

	Starts	1st	2nd	3rd	Win & Pl
Chases	1	0	0	0	
Career Total	28	6	6	2	35029
127	11/98 Uttx	3m2f	D(0-125)HCh	GD	£4835
127	10/98 MRas	3m1f	D(0-125)HCh	HVY	£4323
119	4/98 Weth	3m1f	D(0-110)HCh	G-S	£3964
108	12/97 Weth	3m1f	D Ch	SFT	£3678
104	1/97 Catt	3m1f110yE Hdl		GD	£2931
100	10/96 Weth	2m4f110yD Hdl		GD	£3107

Total win prize-money £22840

Going:	Sf: 0-0 GS: 0-0 Gd: 0-1 GF: - Fm: 0-0
Distance:	2m/2m3: 0-0 2m4-2m7: 0-3 3m+: 0-1
Track:	LH: 0-0 RH: 0-1 Tight: 0-1 Gall: 0-0
Aids:	Bl: 0-0 Vi: 0-0 Tstrap: 0-0
Best Rating:	127 2/99 Hayd 3m soft Ch

Shared-Interest

(75h)
9-y-o ch m Interrex (CAN)-La Campagnola (Hubble Bubble)
K Bishop David J Adams

Placings:0/P0-P   (3945)
2002/03: 19⁰S,

	Starts	1st	2nd	3rd	Win & Pl
Hurdles	1	0	0	0	
Career Total	4	0	0	0	

Going:	Sf: 0-0 GS: 0-0 Gd: 0-0 GF: - Fm: 0-0

Distance:	2m/2m3: 0-1 2m4-2m7: 0-0 3m+: 0-0		
Track:	LH: 0-0 RH: 0-1 Tight: 0-0 Gall: 0-0		
Aids:	Bl: 0-0 Vi: 0-0 Tstrap: 0-0		
Best Rating:	32 2/99 Winc 2m		gd-sft NHF

Shareef (FR)

101(103h)   (123h)132

6-y-o b g Port Lyautey (FR)-Saralik (Salse (USA))
A King (J W Mullins 3/6) Mrs Jeni Fisher

Placings:1/5U12P44-P3U22   (2054)
2002/03: 20⁰G, 19³G, 22⁰GF, 19²G, 16²G,

	Starts	1st	2nd	3rd	Win & Pl
Hurdles	3	0	0	1	524
Chases	2	0	2	0	3443
Career Total	13	2	3	1	9636
114	10/01 Winc	2m6f	E Hdl	GD	£2275
91	4/01 Newb	2m110y H NHF	SFT	£1750

Total win prize-money £4025

Going:	Sf: 0-0 GS: 0-0 Gd: 0-4 GF: - Fm: 0-0
Distance:	2m/2m3: 0-1 2m4-2m7: 0-4 3m+: 0-0
Track:	LH: 0-2 RH: 0-3 Tight: 0-1 Gall: 0-0
Aids:	Bl: 0-0 Vi: 0-0 Tstrap: 0-0
Best Rating:	132 11/02 Extr 2m3f110y good Ch

Useful chaser/fair hurdler; best on a soundish surface; sound debut over fences behind Montreal at Exeter.

Sharimage (IRE)

12-y-o ch g Luxury Image-Even Fort (Even Money)
Miss A Nolan Mrs R Mackness

Placings:4003P0FF242220/64150/1P3/P   (3548)
2002/03: 25⁰G,

	Starts	1st	2nd	3rd	Win & Pl
Chases	1	0	0	0	
Career Total	23	2	4	2	7455
96	5/99 DRoy	3m	Ch	G-F	£2455
100	3/99 Dpat	3m	Ch	HVY	£1994

Total win prize-money £4450

Going:	Sf: 0-0 GS: 0-0 Gd: 0-1 GF: - Fm: 0-0
Distance:	2m/2m3: 0-0 2m4-2m7: 0-0 3m+: 0-1
Track:	LH: 0-0 RH: 0-1 Tight: 0-0 Gall: 0-0
Aids:	Bl: 0-0 Vi: 0-0 Tstrap: 0-0
Best Rating:	107 3/98 DRoy 2m good Ch

Sharlom (IRE)

90(103h)   (85h)65+

6-y-o br g Shardari-Sarahs Music (IRE) (Orchestra)
R D E Woodhouse (Mrs M Stirk 23/5) R D E Woodhouse

Placings:05PF0P-PP6U443   (1402)
2002/03: 20⁰G, 21⁰G, 21⁶GF, 21ᵁGF, 22⁴GF, 24⁴GF, 16³GF,

	Starts	1st	2nd	3rd	Win & Pl
Hurdles	2	0	0	1	260
Chases	5	0	0	0	588
Career Total	13	0	0	1	848

Going:	Sf: 0-0 GS: 0-0 Gd: 0-2 GF: - Fm: 0-5
Distance:	2m/2m3: 0-1 2m4-2m7: 0-5 3m+: 0-1
Track:	LH: 0-5 RH: 0-2 Tight: 0-2 Gall: 0-1
Aids:	Bl: 0-1 Vi: 0-0 Tstrap: 0-0
Best Rating:	85 10/02 Uttx 2m gd-fm Hdl

Achieved first placing when third in a selling hurdle at Uttoxeter in October.

Sharmadan (FR)

54f   65f

7-y-o ch g Zayyani-Sharmada (FR) (Zeddaan)
K A Morgan H A Blenkhorn

Placings:0-0   (3167)
2002/03: 16⁶G,

	Starts	1st	2nd	3rd	Win & Pl
NH Flat	1	0	0	0	
Career Total	2	0	0	0	

Going:	Sf: 0-0 GS: 0-0 Gd: 0-1 GF: - Fm: 0-0
Distance:	2m/2m3: 0-2 2m4-2m7: 0-0 3m+: 0-0
Track:	LH: 0-1 RH: 0-0 Tight: 0-1 Gall: 0-0
Aids:	Bl: 0-0 Vi: 0-0 Tstrap: 0-0
Best Rating:	65 6/01 Worc 2m good NHF

Sharmy (IRE)

104   110

7-y-o ro g Caerleon (USA)-Petticoat Lane (Ela-Mana-Mou)
Ian Williams T J & Mrs H Parrott

Placings:525224-31F5   (4449)
2002/03: 16³GS, 16¹GS, 16⁶GS, 16⁵G,

	Starts	1st	2nd	3rd	Win & Pl
Hurdles	4	1	0	1	3798
Career Total	10	1	3	1	8532
100	11/02 Hntg	2m110y E Hdl	G-S	£2996

Total win prize-money £2996

Going:	Sf: 0-0 GS: 1-3 Gd: 0-1 GF: - Fm: 0-0
Distance:	2m/2m3: 1-4 2m4-2m7: 0-0 3m+: 0-0
Track:	LH: 0-1 RH: 1-3 Tight: 0-0 Gall: 1-1
Aids:	Bl: 0-0 Vi: 0-0 Tstrap: 0-0
Best Rating:	116 4/02 Aint 2m110y good Hdl

Modest, lightly-raced novice hurdler; effective over two miles; acts well with cut in the ground.

Sharp Belline (IRE)

109   114

6-y-o b g Robellino (USA)-Moon Watch (Night Shift (USA))
John A Harris Townville C C Racing Club

Placings:01402/063304624-1240   (1321)
2002/03: 24¹GS, 26²HY, 24⁴G, 24⁰GF,

	Starts	1st	2nd	3rd	Win & Pl
Hurdles	4	1	1	0	5306
Career Total	18	2	3	2	12902
114	5/02 Sthl	3m110y D(0-120)HHdl	G-S	£3523
117	2/01 Donc	2m4f	E Hdl	GD	£2508

Total win prize-money £6032

Going:	Sf: 0-1 GS: 1-1 Gd: 0-1 GF: - Fm: 0-1
Distance:	2m/2m3: 0-0 2m4-2m7: 0-0 3m+: 1-4
Track:	LH: 1-3 RH: 0-1 Tight: 1-3 Gall: 0-0
Aids:	Bl: 0-0 Vi: 0-0 Tstrap: 0-0
Best Rating:	117 2/01 Donc 2m4f good Hdl

Modest hurdler; only small but she is all heart. Stays three miles and acts on a sound surface, has won on good to soft ground, but does not have much in the way of a turn of foot.

Sharp City

4-y-o b g Rock City-Mary Miller (Sharpo)
A C Whillans I Campbell

Placings:P   (1806)
2002/03: 16⁰G,

	Starts	1st	2nd	3rd	Win & Pl
Hurdles	1	0	0	0	
Career Total	1	0	0	0	

Going: Sf: 0-0 GS: 0-0 Gd: 0-1 GF: - Fm: 0-0
Distance: 2m2m3: 0-1 2m4-2m7: 0-0 3m+: 0-0
Track: LH: 0-1 RH: 0-0 Tight: 0-0 Gall: 0-0
Aids: Bl: 0-0 Vi: 0-0 Tstrap: 0-0
Best Rating: 0   11/02   Hayd   2m   good   Hdl

Sharp Embrace

10-y-o ch g Broadsword (USA)-Running Kiss (Deep Run)
Miss Susan Rodman   Miss Susan Rodman

Placings:40P/005P032FP/3-P5   (0191)
2002/03: 24PG, 245GF,

	Starts	1st	2nd	3rd	Win & Pl
Chases	2	0	0	0	0
Career Total	15	0	1	2	1532

Going: Sf: 0-0 GS: 0-0 Gd: 0-1 GF: - Fm: 0-0
Distance: 2m2m3: 0-1 2m4-2m7: 0-0 3m+: 0-0
Track: LH: 0-1 RH: 0-0 Tight: 0-0 Gall: 0-0
Aids: Bl: 0-0 Vi: 0-0 Tstrap: 0-0
Best Rating: 84   9/98   Bang   3m110y   good   Ch

Sharp Gossip (IRE)

7-y-o b g College Chapel-Idle Gossip (Runnett)
J R Weymes (J A R Toller 25/9)   Neil Palamountain

Placings:P   (2185)
2002/03: 16PGS,

	Starts	1st	2nd	3rd	Win & Pl
Hurdles	1	0	0	0	
Career Total	1	0	0	0	

Going: Sf: 0-0 GS: 0-1 Gd: 0-0 GF: - Fm: 0-0
Distance: 2m2m3: 0-1 2m4-2m7: 0-0 3m+: 0-0
Track: LH: 0-1 RH: 0-0 Tight: 0-0 Gall: 0-0
Aids: Bl: 0-0 Vi: 0-0 Tstrap: 0-0
Best Rating: 0   11/02   Weth   2m   gd-sft   Hdl

Sharp Hand
98   **75**

7-y-o ch g Handsome Sailor-Sharp Glance (IRE) (Deep Run)
J G M O Shea   N M Lowe

Placings:00P6535   (4486)
2002/03: 17OGS, 17OS, 19FG, 17FS, 17SG, 16SG, 17SGF,

	Starts	1st	2nd	3rd	Win & Pl
NH Flat	2	0	0	0	0
Hurdles	5	0	0	1	500
Career Total	7	0	0	1	500

Going: Sf: 0-2 GS: 0-1 Gd: 0-3 GF: - Fm: 0-1
Distance: 2m2m3: 0-6 2m4-2m7: 0-1 3m+: 0-0
Track: LH: 0-1 RH: 0-6 Tight: 0-1 Gall: 0-0
Aids: Bl: 0-0 Vi: 0-0 Tstrap: 0-0
Best Rating: 83   12/02   Bang   2m1f   gd-sft   NHF

Selling hurdler; seems best on ground good or faster.

Sharp Seal
99   **79**

9-y-o b g Broadsword (USA)-Little Beaver (Privy Seal)
M Madgwick   J D Brownrigg

Placings:P-3U42FP5   (4359)
2002/03: 193F, 22UGS, 214S, 202S, 22FHY, 22PS, 245F,

	Starts	1st	2nd	3rd	Win & Pl
Chases	7	0	1	1	2593
Career Total	8	0	1	1	2593

Going: Sf: 0-4 GS: 0-1 Gd: 0-0 GF: - Fm: 0-2
Distance: 2m2m3: 0-1 2m4-2m7: 0-5 3m+: 0-1
Track: LH: 0-0 RH: 0-3 Tight: 0-7 Gall: 0-1
Aids: Bl: 0-0 Vi: 0-0 Tstrap: 0-0
Best Rating: 91   12/02   Font   2m4f   soft   Ch

Moderate novice chaser; stays three miles; acts on soft ground.

Sharp Single (IRE)
97   **74**

7-y-o b m Supreme Leader-Pollyville (Pollerton)
P Beaumont   W L Smith

Placings:PPPP   (3958)
2002/03: 20PG, 16PG, 16PG, 17PS,

	Starts	1st	2nd	3rd	Win & Pl
Hurdles	4	0	0	0	
Career Total	4	0	0	0	

Going: Sf: 0-1 GS: 0-0 Gd: 0-3 GF: - Fm: 0-0
Distance: 2m2m3: 0-3 2m4-2m7: 0-1 3m+: 0-0
Track: LH: 0-3 RH: 0-1 Tight: 0-3 Gall: 0-0
Aids: Bl: 0-0 Vi: 0-0 Tstrap: 0-0
Best Rating: 0   3/03   Bang   2m1f   soft   Hdl

Sharp Soprano

4-y-o b f Mon Tresor-Gentle Star (Comedy Star (USA))
B R Millman   Mrs Izabel Palmer

Placings:U   (1461)
2002/03: 16UF,

	Starts	1st	2nd	3rd	Win & Pl
Hurdles	1	0	0	0	
Career Total	1	0	0	0	

Going: Sf: 0-0 GS: 0-0 Gd: 0-0 GF: - Fm: 0-1
Distance: 2m2m3: 0-1 2m4-2m7: 0-0 3m+: 0-0
Track: LH: 0-0 RH: 0-1 Tight: 0-0 Gall: 0-0
Aids: Bl: 0-0 Vi: 0-0 Tstrap: 0-0
Best Rating: 0   10/02   Winc   2m   firm   Hdl

Sharp Steel
97(94h)   (84h)**95+**

8-y-o ch g Beveled (USA)-Shift Over (USA) (Night Shift (USA))
Miss S J Wilton   John Pointon And Sons

Placings:400-5P653   (4317)
2002/03: 16SGF, 16PG, 16RS, 16SG, 173G,

	Starts	1st	2nd	3rd	Win & Pl
Hurdles	3	0	0	0	0
Chases	2	0	0	1	828
Career Total	8	0	0	1	828

Sharp Word (IRE)
     78f

4-y-o br g Needle Gun (IRE)-Pas De Mot (Tender King)
T P Tate   T P Tate

Placings:6   (2391)
2002/03: 14RGS,

	Starts	1st	2nd	3rd	Win & Pl
NH Flat	1	0	0	0	0
Career Total	1	0	0	0	0

Going: Sf: 0-0 GS: 0-1 Gd: 0-0 GF: - Fm: 0-0
Distance: 2m2m3: 0-0 2m4-2m7: 0-0 3m+: 0-0
Track: LH: 0-1 RH: 0-0 Tight: 0-0 Gall: 0-0
Aids: Bl: 0-0 Vi: 0-0 Tstrap: 0-0
Best Rating: 75   12/02   Ayr   1m6f   gd-sft   NHF

Sharpaman

8-y-o b g Mandalus-Sharp Glance (IRE) (Deep Run)
S H Shirley-Beavan   S H Shirley-Beavan

Placings:F   (0502)
2002/03: 26FG,

	Starts	1st	2nd	3rd	Win & Pl
Chases	1	0	0	0	
Career Total	1	0	0	0	

Going: Sf: 0-0 GS: 0-0 Gd: 0-1 GF: - Fm: 0-0
Distance: 2m2m3: 0-0 2m4-2m7: 0-0 3m+: 0-1
Track: LH: 0-1 RH: 0-0 Tight: 0-1 Gall: 0-0
Aids: Bl: 0-0 Vi: 0-0 Tstrap: 0-0
Best Rating: 0   6/02   Ctml   3m2f   good   Ch

Sharpastrizam (NZ)
105   (57h)**109**

8-y-o b g Try To Stop Me-Atristazam (NZ) (Zamazaan (FR))
P Beaumont   Trevor Hemmings

Placings:2F060P/11P1211551-44044   (4763)
2002/03: 164GS, 164GS, 19PG, 164G, 164G,

	Starts	1st	2nd	3rd	Win & Pl
Chases	5	0	0	0	2182
Career Total	21	6	2	0	27599
112 4/02 Prth	2m		C(0-130)HCh	GD	£7111
111 1/02 Donc	2m110y		E(0-105)HCh	GD	£3201
96 12/01 Catt	2m		F(0-105)HCh	GD	£3024
96 11/01 Weth	2m		D(0-110)HCh	GD	£4153
92 5/01 Bang	2m1f110y		F(0-95)HCh	GD	£3486
91 5/01 Sthl	2m		F(0-100)HCh	FRM	£2775
				Total win prize-money	£23752

Going: Sf: 0-0 GS: 0-2 Gd: 0-3 GF: - Fm: 0-0
Distance: 2m2m3: 0-5 2m4-2m7: 0-0 3m+: 0-0
Track: LH: 0-4 RH: 0-1 Tight: 0-2 Gall: 0-1
Aids: Bl: 0-0 Vi: 0-0 Tstrap: 0-0
Best Rating: 112   12/02   Donc   2m110y   gd-sft   Ch

Moderate chaser; has rather been let down by his jumping since switching to fences but was a good third in 2m novices handicap at Worcester June 2003; landed similar event over course and distance next time; seems best when held up; acts on good ground; probably best at 2m.

Fair chaser, enjoyed a fine season in novice chases in 2001/02, suited by around two miles on a sound surface.

Sharpaten (IRE)

110 (115c)128

8-y-o b g Scenic-Sloane Ranger (Sharpen Up)
C J Mann (P Hughes 19/10) The Baron Rouge Partnership

Placings:233164/62632110/560400/162542F-030053240
(3727)
2002/03: 21⁰S, 16³GF, 16⁰YS, 16⁰F, 16⁵S, 19³G, 16²GS, 16⁴GS, 16⁰G,

	Starts	1st	2nd	3rd	Win & Pl
Hurdles	8	0	1	2	6839
Chases	1	0	0	0	0
Career Total	36	4	6	5	51954
115 5/01	Wxfd	2m	Ch		Y-S £6677
140 4/00	Aint	2m110y	B HHdl		GD £19500
128 3/00	Leop	2m	(0-144)HHdl		Y-S £4968
111 3/99	Limk	2m1f	Hdl		SH £2700

Total win prize-money £33846

Going: Sf: 0-2 GS: 0-2 Gd: 0-2 GF: - Fm: 0-2
Distance: 2m/2m3: 0-8 2m4-2m7: 0-1 3m+: 0-0
Track: LH: 0-4 RH: 0-2 Tight: 0-1 Gall: 0-0
Aids: Bl: 0-0 Vi: 0-0 Tstrap: 0-0
Best Rating: 142 10/00 Gowr 2m   soft   Hdl

Decent ex-Irish handicap hurdler; suited by two miles; acts on good and soft ground.

Sharvie

92 65

6-y-o b g Rock Hopper-Heresheis (Free State)
C J Hemsley Wychwood Racing Partnership

Placings:6000P4 (4675)
2002/03: 16⁶GF, 22⁰S, 21⁰G, 16⁰S, 16⁶G, 17⁴GF,

	Starts	1st	2nd	3rd	Win & Pl
Hurdles	6	0	0	0	0
Career Total	6	0	0	0	0

Going: Sf: 0-2 GS: 0-0 Gd: 0-2 GF: - Fm: 0-2
Distance: 2m/2m3: 0-4 2m4-2m7: 0-2 3m+: 0-0
Track: LH: 0-4 RH: 0-2 Tight: 0-0 Gall: 0-0
Aids: Bl: 0-1 Vi: 0-0 Tstrap: 0-0
Best Rating: 65 4/03 Hrfd 2m1f   gd-fm   Hdl

Poor novice hurdler; stays really well.

Shaydeylaydeh (IRE)

64 41

4-y-o b f Shaddad (USA)-Spirito Libro (USA) (Lear Fan (USA))
C N Allen J R Bamforth

Placings:0 (1893)
2002/03: 16⁰GS,

	Starts	1st	2nd	3rd	Win & Pl
Hurdles	1	0	0	0	
Career Total	1	0	0	0	

Going: Sf: 0-0 GS: 0-1 Gd: 0-0 GF: - Fm: 0-0
Distance: 2m/2m3: 0-1 2m4-2m7: 0-0 3m+: 0-0
Track: LH: 0-0 RH: 0-1 Tight: 0-0 Gall: 0-1
Aids: Bl: 0-0 Vi: 0-0 Tstrap: 0-0
Best Rating: 35 11/02 Hntg 2m110y   gd-sft   Hdl

Shays Lane (IRE)

101(93h) (78h)92+

9-y-o b g The Bart (USA)-Continuity Lass (Continuation)
Ferdy Murphy Mrs C McKeane

Placings:0000-54 (4503)
2002/03: 25⁵G, 25⁴G,

	Starts	1st	2nd	3rd	Win & Pl
Chases	2	0	0	0	415
Career Total	6	0	0	0	415

Going: Sf: 0-0 GS: 0-0 Gd: 0-2 GF: - Fm: 0-0
Distance: 2m/2m3: 0-4 2m4-2m7: 0-0 3m+: 0-2
Track: LH: 0-2 RH: 0-0 Tight: 0-2 Gall: 0-0
Aids: Bl: 0-0 Vi: 0-0 Tstrap: 0-0
Best Rating: 78 11/01 Weth 2m   good   Hdl

Moderate but improving chaser; successful at Hexham in May and followed up the following month; stays very well; acts on fast ground.

Shazal

101 74

6-y-o b m Afzal-Isolationist (Welsh Pageant)
J N R Billinge Mr & Mrs D Nimmo

Placings:0-00F6 (4504)
2002/03: 16⁰S, 16⁰G, 16⁰FS, 16⁶G,

	Starts	1st	2nd	3rd	Win & Pl
Hurdles	4	0	0	0	0
Career Total	5	0	0	0	0

Going: Sf: 0-2 GS: 0-0 Gd: 0-2 GF: - Fm: 0-0
Distance: 2m/2m3: 0-4 2m4-2m7: 0-0 3m+: 0-0
Track: LH: 0-3 RH: 0-1 Tight: 0-3 Gall: 0-0
Aids: Bl: 0-0 Vi: 0-0 Tstrap: 0-0
Best Rating: 65 4/03 Kels 2m110y   good   Hdl

Plating-class hurdler; shock winner of a low-grade handicap at Perth in June 2003; acts on good ground.

She Wont Scream

5-y-o b m Desert Dirham (USA)-Silent Scream (IRE) (Lahib (USA))
C J Hemsley (Mrs J A Saunders 3/8) R J Barrett

Placings:PUR (1246)
2002/03: 16⁵G, 16⁰GF, 24⁰RG,

	Starts	1st	2nd	3rd	Win & Pl
NH Flat	1	0	0	0	
Hurdles	2	0	0	0	
Career Total	3	0	0	0	

Going: Sf: 0-0 GS: 0-0 Gd: 0-2 GF: - Fm: 0-1
Distance: 2m/2m3: 0-2 2m4-2m7: 0-0 3m+: 0-1
Track: LH: 0-3 RH: 0-0 Tight: 0-1 Gall: 0-0
Aids: Bl: 0-0 Vi: 0-0 Tstrap: 0-0
Best Rating: 0 9/02 Worc 3m   good   Hdl

She's A Corker (IRE)

104 78

8-y-o b/br m Jurado (USA)-Lean Over (Over The River (FR))
D L Williams (Miss C F Elliott 8/6) Richard Cook Limited

Placings:4650PP/UP1P (1817)

2002/03: 24ᵁG, 26ᴾG, 22¹G, 26ᴾG,

	Starts	1st	2nd	3rd	Win & Pl
Hurdles	2	1	0	0	4134
Chases	2	0	0	0	0
Career Total	10	1	0	0	4390
78 10/02	Strf	2m6f110yD Hdl		GD £4134

Total win prize-money £4134

Going: Sf: 0-0 GS: 0-0 Gd: 1-4 GF: - Fm: 0-0
Distance: 2m/2m3: 0-0 2m4-2m7: 1-1 3m+: 0-3
Track: LH: 1-3 RH: 0-1 Tight: 1-3 Gall: 0-0
Aids: Bl: 0-0 Vi: 0-0 Tstrap: 0-0
Best Rating: 81 11/00 Thur 2m6f110y heavy   Hdl

Won a couple of points in 2002 prior to failing to complete in two hunter chases. Apparently only having a pipe-opener prior to going chasing when landing a weakly contested 22 furlong maiden hurdle at Stratford October 2002.

She's Our Native (IRE)

101f 103f

5-y-o b m Be My Native (USA)-More Dash (IRE) (Strong Gale)
P J Hobbs Ian Brice

Placings:21 (4197)
2002/03: 17²S, 16¹G,

	Starts	1st	2nd	3rd	Win & Pl
NH Flat	2	1	1	0	2762
Career Total	2	1	1	0	2762
101 3/03	Ludl	2m	H NHF		GD £1960

Total win prize-money £1960

Going: Sf: 0-1 GS: 0-0 Gd: 1-1 GF: - Fm: 0-0
Distance: 2m/2m3: 1-2 2m4-2m7: 0-0 3m+: 0-0
Track: LH: 0-0 RH: 1-1 Tight: 0-0 Gall: 0-0
Aids: Bl: 0-0 Vi: 0-0 Tstrap: 0-0
Best Rating: 101 3/03 Ludl 2m   good   NHF

She's Yours

4-y-o ch f Whittingham (IRE)-Flood s Hot Stuff (Chilibang)
A J Chamberlain (B G Powell 13/11) A J Chamberlain

Placings:06 (4737)
2002/03: 12⁰G, 16⁶GF,

	Starts	1st	2nd	3rd	Win & Pl
NH Flat	2	0	0	0	0
Career Total	2	0	0	0	0

Going: Sf: 0-0 GS: 0-1 Gd: 0-0 GF: - Fm: 0-1
Distance: 2m/2m3: 0-1 2m4-2m7: 0-0 3m+: 0-0
Track: LH: 0-2 RH: 0-0 Tight: 0-0 Gall: 0-0
Aids: Bl: 0-0 Vi: 0-0 Tstrap: 0-0
Best Rating: 0 4/03 Chep 2m110y   gd-fm   NHF

Sheep Stealer

66 36

15-y-o gr g Absalom-Kilroe s Calin (Be Friendly)
R E Peacock R E Peacock

Placings:001603/F/3/0F06313/6002/P/5433P/0604600P/00
(0682)
2002/03: 20⁰G, 17⁰G,

	Starts	1st	2nd	3rd	Win & Pl
Hurdles	1	0	0	0	0
Chases	1	0	0	0	0

Career Total	35	2	1	6	7625
95	4/96	Extr	2m2f	F(0-105)HHdl	G-F £2193
85	3/93	Catt	2m	Hdl	GD £1764

Total win prize-money £3957

Going:	Sf: 0-0 GS: 0-0 Gd: 0-2 GF: - Fm: 0-0
Distance:	2m/2m3: 0-1 2m4-2m7: 0-0 3m+: 0-0
Track:	LH: 0-2 RH: 0-0 Tight: 0-2 Gall: 0-0
Aids:	Bl: 0-0 Vi: 0-0 Tstrap: 0-0
Best Rating:	98 5/94 Bang 2m1f110y gd-fm Ch

Sheila McKenzie

6-y-o b m Aragon-Lady Quachita (USA) (Sovereign Dancer (USA))
C O King C O King

Placings:P-P (4089)
2002/03: 24PGS,

	Starts	1st	2nd	3rd	Win & Pl
Chases	1	0	0	0	
Career Total	2	0	0	0	

Going:	Sf: 0-0 GS: 0-1 Gd: 0-0 GF: - Fm: 0-0
Distance:	2m/2m3: 0-0 2m4-2m7: 0-0 3m+: 0-1
Track:	LH: 0-1 RH: 0-0 Tight: 0-1 Gall: 0-0
Aids:	Bl: 0-0 Vi: 0-0 Tstrap: 0-0
Best Rating:	0 3/03 Strf 3m gd-sft Ch

Shellin Hill (IRE)

96(86h)   (87h)67
9-y-o ch g Sharp Victor (USA)-Queenspay (Sandhurst Prince)
R J Price My Left Foot Racing Syndicate

Placings:000/0532.00402P6/0423424F0P622-621FP3P043F4P (4614)
2002/03: 17RG, 17²G, 17¹G, 16FGF, 19PG, 16³G, 16PG, 20QG, 16⁴GS, 19³S, 16FS, 19⁴F, 21PG,

	Starts	1st	2nd	3rd	Win & Pl
Chases	13	1	1	2	6453
Career Total	40	1	7	4	13540
96	9/02	Sthl	2m1f	HCh	4 £3049

Total win prize-money £3050

Going:	Sf: 0-2 GS: 0-1 Gd: 1-8 GF: - Fm: 0-0
Distance:	2m/2m3: 1-11 2m4-2m7: 0-2 3m+: 0-0
Track:	LH: 1-5 RH: 0-8 Tight: 0-4 Gall: 0-1
Aids:	Bl: 0-0 Vi: 0-0 Tstrap: 0-0
Best Rating:	97 6/01 Worc 2m good Ch

Modest chaser, suited by two miles and fast ground. Off the mark at the 30th attempt when taking a weak handicap at Southwell in September 2002.

Sheltering (IRE)

11-y-o b g Strong Gale-Lady Brenda (IRE) (Crash Course)
E J O Grady Mrs Stewart Catherwood

Placings:5/1112/1131F/1111/312U41-110F (4459)
2002/03: 25¹YS, 24¹YS, 26QG, 21FG,

	Starts	1st	2nd	3rd	Win & Pl
Chases	4	2	0	0	12097
Career Total	24	14	2	2	99841
139	2/03	Leop	3m	Ch	Y-S £7616
135	1/03	Punc	3m1f	Ch	Y-S £4480
113	4/02	Punc	3m1f	Ch	GD £9969
140	1/02	Punc	3m1f	Ch	SH £5503
135	4/01	Fair	3m1f	Ch	SH £10483

146	2/01	Fair	3m1f	Ch	YLD £4173
150	2/01	Leop	3m	Ch	HVY £6677
139	5/00	Punc	3m1f	Ch	GD £10400
127	2/00	Fair	3m1f	Ch	HVY £3312
127	1/00	Fair	3m1f	Ch	SFT £3312
107	5/99	Gowr	3m	Ch	YLD £3683
128	4/99	Fair	3m1f	Ch	G-Y £6138
121	3/99	Wxfd	3m	Ch	Y-S £3069
103	3/99	Limk	2m6f	Ch	SFT £3222

Total win prize-money £82041

Going:	Sf: 0-0 GS: 0-0 Gd: 0-2 GF: - Fm: 0-0
Distance:	2m/2m3: 0-0 2m4-2m7: 0-0 3m+: 2-3
Track:	LH: 1-3 RH: 1-1 Tight: 0-1 Gall: 0-1
Aids:	Bl: 0-0 Vi: 0-0 Tstrap: 0-0
Best Rating:	150 2/01 Leop 3m heavy Ch

Useful Irish hunter chaser; stays well; suited by soft ground; disappointed in the 2003 Cheltenham Foxhunters .

Shelu

56   94
5-y-o b g Good Thyne (USA)-Nearly Married (Nearly A Hand)
Ferdy Murphy Raj Patel

Placings:0-003P (4590)
2002/03: 16QGS, 26QG, 24³S, 20PG,

	Starts	1st	2nd	3rd	Win & Pl
NH Flat	1	0	0	0	0
Hurdles	3	0	0	1	488
Career Total	5	0	0	1	488

Going:	Sf: 0-1 GS: 0-1 Gd: 0-2 GF: - Fm: 0-0
Distance:	2m/2m3: 0-1 2m4-2m7: 0-1 3m+: 0-2
Track:	LH: 0-2 RH: 0-2 Tight: 0-0 Gall: 0-2
Aids:	Bl: 0-0 Vi: 0-0 Tstrap: 0-0
Best Rating:	94 3/03 Hexm 3m soft Hdl

First signs of ability when third in three mile novices hurdle in bad ground at Hexham in March.

Shemardi

(93h)   (72h)
6-y-o b g Jumbo Hirt (USA)-Masirah (Dunphy)
M Madgwick J D Brownrigg

Placings:000/05005640-00F4U02 (4217)
2002/03: 20QGS, 22QGS, 19FS, 20⁴HY, 17UHY, 20⁵S, 22QG,

	Starts	1st	2nd	3rd	Win & Pl
Hurdles	4	0	1	0	790
Chases	3	0	0	0	314
Career Total	18	0	1	0	1104

Going:	Sf: 0-4 GS: 0-2 Gd: 0-1 GF: - Fm: 0-0
Distance:	2m/2m3: 0-2 2m4-2m7: 0-5 3m+: 0-0
Track:	LH: 0-2 RH: 0-2 Tight: 0-6 Gall: 0-0
Aids:	Bl: 0-0 Vi: 0-0 Tstrap: 0-0
Best Rating:	82 3/02 Font 2m4f soft Hdl

Shemdani (IRE)

104   133
6-y-o b g Unfuwain (USA)-Shemaka (IRE) (Nishapour (FR))
M C Pipe Mr & Mrs M Bovingdon & C Langley

Placings:112-61 (3624)
2002/03: 16RGS, 16¹S,

	Starts	1st	2nd	3rd	Win & Pl
Hurdles	2	1	0	0	4979
Career Total	5	3	1	0	13115

124	2/03	Asct	2m110y	D(0-120)HHdl	SFT £4979
128	3/02	MRas	2m1f110yE Hdl		G-S £3304
102	1/02	Donc	2m110y	D Hdl	SFT £3472

Total win prize-money £11755

Going:	Sf: 1-1 GS: 0-1 Gd: 0-0 GF: - Fm: 0-0
Distance:	2m/2m3: 1-2 2m4-2m7: 0-0 3m+: 0-0
Track:	LH: 0-1 RH: 1-1 Tight: 0-0 Gall: 0-1
Aids:	Bl: 0-0 Vi: 0-0 Tstrap: 0-0
Best Rating:	128 3/02 MRas 2m1f110y gd-sft Hdl

Useful ex-French hurdler; made a successful debut over hurdles in Britain on soft ground and proved different class under a positive ride in a similar event next time; neck runner-up on his handicap debut at Ascot in April and took advantage of favourable mark when successful there in February.

Shemill

63f   70f
5-y-o b g Spectrum (IRE)-Shemaleyah (Lomond (USA))
D Eddy I R Clements

Placings:0-00 (3167)
2002/03: 16QGF, 16QG,

	Starts	1st	2nd	3rd	Win & Pl
NH Flat	2	0	0	0	
Career Total	3	0	0	0	

Going:	Sf: 0-0 GS: 0-0 Gd: 0-1 GF: - Fm: 0-1
Distance:	2m/2m3: 0-2 2m4-2m7: 0-0 3m+: 0-0
Track:	LH: 0-2 RH: 0-0 Tight: 0-1 Gall: 0-0
Aids:	Bl: 0-0 Vi: 0-0 Tstrap: 0-0
Best Rating:	70 4/02 Carl 2m1f good NHF

Shenandoah (IRE)

92   83
7-y-o b m Supreme Leader-Gold Label (Deep Run)
P J Hobbs Bob Jevon

Placings:50/233UP (1784)
2002/03: 20²G, 22³GF, 24³G, 22UG, 24PGS,

	Starts	1st	2nd	3rd	Win & Pl
Hurdles	5	0	1	2	1801
Career Total	7	0	1	2	1801

Going:	Sf: 0-0 GS: 0-1 Gd: 0-3 GF: - Fm: 0-1
Distance:	2m/2m3: 0-0 2m4-2m7: 0-3 3m+: 0-2
Track:	LH: 0-3 RH: 0-2 Tight: 0-1 Gall: 0-0
Aids:	Bl: 0-0 Vi: 0-0 Tstrap: 0-0
Best Rating:	95 12/00 Tntn 2m1f soft NHF

Modest staying hurdler; acts on a sound surface; it is thought that her future will eventually lie in three mile chases.

Shenoso

8-y-o b m Teenoso (USA)-Mossy Morning (Le Moss)
M A Barnes M Barnes

Placings:P (0451)
2002/03: 16PG,

	Starts	1st	2nd	3rd	Win & Pl
Hurdles	1	0	0	0	
Career Total	1	0	0	0	

Going:	Sf: 0-0 GS: 0-0 Gd: 0-1 GF: - Fm: 0-0
Distance:	2m/2m3: 0-1 2m4-2m7: 0-0 3m+: 0-0
Track:	LH: 0-1 RH: 0-0 Tight: 0-0 Gall: 0-0

Aids: Bl: 0-0 Vi: 0-0 Tstrap: 0-0
Best Rating: 0   6/02   Hexm   2m110y   good   Hdl

Shepherds Rest (IRE)

106(88h)   (57h)**110**

11-y-o b g Accordion-Mandy s Last (Krayyan)
C P Morlock   The Odd Dozen

Placings:062640223/231U220/0322/P45P02/53322112215
P01/346P003PP0/PP023241331434 11-F1252P5   (2500)
2002/03: 27FGS, 261G, 262G, 245S, 252G, 24FG, 245GS,

	Starts	1st	2nd	3rd	Win & Pl
Hurdles	1	0	0	0	0
Chases	6	1	2	0	7089
Career Total	73	10	17	11	65239
110 6/02	Uttx	3m2f		D(0-120)HCh	GD	£4340
110 4/02	Uttx	3m2f		E(0-110)HCh	G-F	£3601
100 4/02	Wwck	3m110y		E(0-105)HCh	G-F	£4078
102 10/01	Folk	2m5f		F(0-95)HCh	GD	£3406
89 8/01	Ctml	2m5f110yF(0-110)HCh			GD	£4192
107 4/00	Uttx	2m4f110yE(0-115)HCh			SFT	£2824
117 3/00	Newb	2m4f		D(0-125)HCh	SFT	£7091
119 1/00	Kemp	2m4f110yE(0-115)HCh			GD	£3477
116 1/00	Wwck	2m4f		E(0-115)HCh	SFT	£3198
106 12/96	Ling	2m110y		E(0-110)HHdl	G-S	£2364

Total win prize-money £38575

Going: Sf: 0-1 GS: 0-1 Gd: 1-4 GF: - Fm: 0-1
Distance: 2m/2m3: 0-0 2m4-2m7: 0-0 **3m+: 1-7**
Track: LH: **1-5** RH: 0-2 Tight: 0-5 Gall: 0-0
Aids: Bl: 0-0 Vi: **1-7** Tstrap: 0-0
Best Rating: 119   2/00   Wwck   2m4f   soft   Ch

Modest handicap chaser, he has developed stamina with age and now gets three and a quarter miles. He likes to be held up, finds little off the bridle, and seems best on a sound surface these days although he handles cut.

Sherbet Lad (IRE)

112   **104**

7-y-o b g Cataldi-She s Foolish (IRE) (Callernish)
V R A Dartnall   Lisa Mackenzie, M Foxon & J Darbishire

Placings:02U3-01   (4032)
2002/03: 16PGS, 20THY,

	Starts	1st	2nd	3rd	Win & Pl
Hurdles	2	1	0	0	5054
Career Total	6	1	1	1	5915
104 3/03	Sand	2m4f110yD Hdl		HVY	£5053

Total win prize-money £5054

Going: Sf: 1-1 GS: 0-1 Gd: 0-0 GF: - Fm: 0-0
Distance: 2m/2m3: 0-1 **2m4-2m7: 1-1** 3m+: 0-0
Track: LH: 0-0 **RH: 1-2** Tight: 0-0 Gall: 0-0
Aids: Bl: 0-0 Vi: 0-0 Tstrap: 0-0
Best Rating: 104   3/03   Sand   2m4f110y   heavy   Hdl

Moderate novice hurdler, stays two and a half miles; effective in testing ground.

Sherfield Lass

71   **23**

5-y-o b m Tina s Pet-Mindyerownbusiness (IRE) (Roselier (FR))
Mrs H Dalton   W D Edwards

Placings:0   (4404)
2002/03: 16QGF,

	Starts	1st	2nd	3rd	Win & Pl
NH Flat	1	0	0	0	

Career Total   1   0   0   0

Going: Sf: 0-0 GS: 0-0 Gd: 0-0 GF: - Fm: 0-1
Distance: 2m/2m3: 0-1 2m4-2m7: 0-0 3m+: 0-0
Track: LH: 0-1 RH: 0-0 Tight: 0-0 Gall: 0-0
Aids: Bl: 0-0 Vi: 0-0 Tstrap: 0-0
Best Rating: 53   3/03   Hayd   2m   gd-fm   NHF

Sherngold (IRE)

92   **65**

5-y-o b m Shernazar-Portanob (IRE) (Be My Native (USA))
R H Alner   Mrs M A T Potter

Placings:0F036   (4426)
2002/03: 16QHY, 16FGS, 22QGS, 17FGF, 16RGF,

	Starts	1st	2nd	3rd	Win & Pl
NH Flat	1	0	0	0	0
Hurdles	4	0	0	1	532
Career Total	5	0	0	1	532

Going: Sf: 0-1 GS: 0-2 Gd: 0-0 GF: - Fm: 0-2
Distance: 2m/2m3: 0-2 2m4-2m7: 0-1 3m+: 0-0
Track: LH: 0-2 RH: 0-3 Tight: 0-1 Gall: 0-0
Aids: Bl: 0-0 Vi: 0-0 Tstrap: 0-0
Best Rating: 65   3/03   Hrfd   2m1f   gd-fm   Hdl

Sherwood Rose (IRE)

81   **66**

7-y-o gr m Mandalus-Cronlier (Roselier (FR))
K C Bailey   Peter Granger

Placings:0/0-0   (1849)
2002/03: 22QG,

	Starts	1st	2nd	3rd	Win & Pl
Hurdles	1	0	0	0	
Career Total	3	0	0	0	

Going: Sf: 0-0 GS: 0-0 Gd: 0-1 GF: - Fm: 0-0
Distance: 2m/2m3: 0-0 2m4-2m7: 0-1 3m+: 0-0
Track: LH: 0-0 RH: 0-0 Tight: 0-0 Gall: 0-0
Aids: Bl: 0-0 Vi: 0-0 Tstrap: 0-0
Best Rating: 70   2/02   Wwck   2m   heavy   NHF

Shesgottohaveit (IRE)

4-y-o b f Flying Spur (AUS)-Carousel Mall (IRE) (Soughaan (USA))
P Mitchell   Mrs Joy Johnson

Placings:0P   (2012)
2002/03: 16QG, 16PHY,

	Starts	1st	2nd	3rd	Win & Pl
Hurdles	2	0	0	0	
Career Total	2	0	0	0	

Going: Sf: 0-1 GS: 0-0 Gd: 0-1 GF: - Fm: 0-0
Distance: 2m/2m3: 0-2 2m4-2m7: 0-0 3m+: 0-0
Track: LH: 0-1 RH: 0-1 Tight: 0-1 Gall: 0-0
Aids: Bl: 0-0 Vi: 0-0 Tstrap: 0-0
Best Rating: 0   11/02   Leic   2m   heavy   Hdl

Generally well beaten on the Flat.

Career Total   1   0   0   0

Sheskinqueen (IRE)

62   **49**

8-y-o b m Black Monday-Our Lady Sofie (Ile De Bourbon (USA))
R Wilman   R Wilman

Placings:50142060-00   (3573)
2002/03: 16QGS, 16QHY,

	Starts	1st	2nd	3rd	Win & Pl
Hurdles	2	0	0	0	
Career Total	10	1	1	0	3303
95 7/01	Worc	2m		E Hdl	SFT	£2513

Total win prize-money £2513

Going: Sf: 0-1 GS: 0-1 Gd: 0-0 GF: - Fm: 0-0
Distance: 2m/2m3: 0-2 2m4-2m7: 0-0 3m+: 0-0
Track: LH: 0-1 RH: 0-1 Tight: 0-1 Gall: 0-0
Aids: Bl: 0-0 Vi: 0-0 Tstrap: 0-1
Best Rating: 103   1/02   Hntg   2m110y   gd-sft   Hdl

Shifting Moon

109(80c)   (83c)**82**

11-y-o b g Night Shift (USA)-Moonscape (Ribero)
F Jordan   Mrs K Roberts-Hindle

Placings:2104500/0PP204031F/61211233P/0631/P001406
33634/00610534446/0P22050U3P-404125350U0   (1805)
2002/03: 16RS, 20QGF, 224GF, 221GF, 202S, 20RGF, 243GF, 20RG, 22QGF, 23UG, 20RG,

	Starts	1st	2nd	3rd	Win & Pl
Hurdles	11	1	1	1	6179
Career Total	74	9	7	10	38500
91 7/02	Strf	2m6f110yD(0-115)HHdl		G-F	£4186
100 9/00	Bang	2m4f	F(0-110)HHdl		G-F	£4251
95 11/99	NAbb	2m1f	E(0-115)HHdl		G-S	£2906
108 7/98	Strf	2m110y	D(0-125)HHdl		G-F	£3496
91 8/97	Ctml	2m1f110yD(0-120)HHdl		G-F	£2784
89 8/97	NAbb	2m1f	E(0-110)HHdl		G-F	£2179
89 8/97	NAbb	2m1f	E(0-110)HHdl		G-F	£2116
77 4/97	Tntn	2m1f	E(0-115)HHdl		FRM	£2200
102 8/95	NAbb	2m1f	D Hdl		G-F	£2532

Total win prize-money £26654

Going: Sf: 0-2 GS: 0-0 Gd: 0-3 GF: - Fm: 1-6
Distance: 2m/2m3: 0-1 **2m4-2m7: 1-8** 3m+: 0-2
Track: **LH: 1-11** RH: 0-0 Tight: **1-6** Gall: 0-0
Aids: Bl: 0-0 Vi: 0-0 Tstrap: **1-11**
Best Rating: 108   7/98   Strf   2m110y   gd-fm   Hdl

Plating-class hurdler; stays 2m 6f; suited by hold up tactics; has proved a flop over fences.

Shii-Take's Girl

58

5-y-o ch m Deploy-Super Sally (Superlative)
M E Sowersby   The Wolds Partnership

Placings:50-P   (0765)
2002/03: 21PGF,

	Starts	1st	2nd	3rd	Win & Pl
Hurdles	1	0	0	0	
Career Total	3	0	0	0	0

Going: Sf: 0-0 GS: 0-0 Gd: 0-0 GF: - Fm: 0-1
Distance: 2m/2m3: 0-0 2m4-2m7: 0-0 3m+: 0-0
Track: LH: 0-1 RH: 0-0 Tight: 0-1 Gall: 0-0
Aids: Bl: 0-0 Vi: 0-0 Tstrap: 0-0
Best Rating: 59   3/02   Hayd   2m   good   Hdl

Shilo (IRE)

9-y-o ch g Roselier (FR)-Cathedral Street (Boreen Beag)
P D Williams Mrs D J Hughes

Placings:00/P   (0819)
2002/03: 23PGF,

	Starts	1st	2nd	3rd	Win & Pl
Chases	1	0	0	0	
Career Total	3	0	0	0	

Going:	Sf: 0-0 GS: 0-0 Gd: 0-0 GF: - Fm: 0-1
Distance:	2m2/m3: 0-0 2m4-2m7: 0-0 3m+: 0-1
Track:	LH: 0-1 RH: 0-0 Tight: 0-0 Gall: 0-0
Aids:	Bl: 0-0 Vi: 0-0 Tstrap: 0-0
Best Rating:	88 2/00 Asct 2m110y soft NHF

Shinda Mondial

87f   80f

5-y-o b h French Gondolier (USA)-Off And On (Touching
Wood (USA))
A R Dicken Stephen Ramsay

Placings:556   (1477)
2002/03: 16⁵GF, 16⁵GF, 17⁶GF,

	Starts	1st	2nd	3rd	Win & Pl
NH Flat	3	0	0	0	0
Career Total	3	0	0	0	0

Going:	Sf: 0-0 GS: 0-0 Gd: 0-0 GF: - Fm: 0-3
Distance:	2m2/m3: 0-3 2m4-2m7: 0-0 3m+: 0-0
Track:	LH: 0-2 RH: 0-1 Tight: 0-0 Gall: 0-0
Aids:	Bl: 0-0 Vi: 0-0 Tstrap: 0-0
Best Rating:	80 9/02 Hexm 2m110y gd-fm NHF

Shining Leader (IRE)

90(87h)   (62h)70+

12-y-o b g Supreme Leader-Shining Run (Deep Run)
M J Gingell Ian Clements

Placings:6F453P   (1330)
2002/03: 20⁶G, 16⁶G, 24⁴GS, 16⁵GF, 18³GF, 17⁶G,

	Starts	1st	2nd	3rd	Win & Pl
Hurdles	2	0	0	0	296
Chases	4	0	0	1	414
Career Total	6	0	0	1	710

Going:	Sf: 0-0 GS: 0-1 Gd: 0-3 GF: - Fm: 0-2
Distance:	2m2/m3: 0-4 2m4-2m7: 0-1 3m+: 0-1
Track:	LH: 0-2 RH: 0-3 Tight: 0-5 Gall: 0-1
Aids:	Bl: 0-0 Vi: 0-0 Tstrap: 0-0
Best Rating:	70 9/02 Font 2m2f gd-fm Ch

A winning pointer, he has shown modest form under Rules.

Shining Tyne

99   91

9-y-o b g Primitive Rising (USA)-Shining Bann (Bargello)
R Johnson David Blythe

Placings:0/00F/6RPP03/6423F-445652322   (4753)
2002/03: 20⁴S, 20⁴GS, 24⁵G, 24⁶G, 24⁴S, 22²S, 20³GS, 24²G, 24²G,

	Starts	1st	2nd	3rd	Win & Pl
Chases	9	0	3	1	7628

Career Total   24   0   4   3   12648

Going:	Sf: 0-3 GS: 0-2 Gd: 0-4 GF: - Fm: 0-0
Distance:	2m2/m3: 0-0 2m4-2m7: 0-4 3m+: 0-5
Track:	LH: 0-7 RH: 0-2 Tight: 0-1 Gall: 0-7
Aids:	Bl: 0-0 Vi: 0-0 Tstrap: 0-0
Best Rating:	91 4/03 Prth 3m good Ch

Moderate maiden chaser; stays 2m 4f, acts on soft ground;
has worn tongue tie and cheekpieces.

Shipley Mill

91   71

7-y-o b g St Ninian-Shipley Bridge (Town And Country)
J T Gifford Mrs J T Gifford

Placings:5P0-F0   (0379)
2002/03: 17⁶G, 21⁰G,

	Starts	1st	2nd	3rd	Win & Pl
Hurdles	2	0	0	0	
Career Total	5	0	0	0	0

Going:	Sf: 0-0 GS: 0-0 Gd: 0-0 GF: - Fm: 0-0
Distance:	2m2/m3: 0-1 2m4-2m7: 0-1 3m+: 0-0
Track:	LH: 0-0 RH: 0-2 Tight: 0-1 Gall: 0-1
Aids:	Bl: 0-0 Vi: 0-0 Tstrap: 0-0
Best Rating:	92 11/01 Sand 2m110y gd-sft NHF

Shobrooke Mill

10-y-o ch g Shaab-Jubilee Leigh (Hubble Bubble)
Mrs S Prouse Mrs S Prouse

Placings:U/U342-6U   (0395)
2002/03: 21⁶GF, 28⁰G,

	Starts	1st	2nd	3rd	Win & Pl
Chases	2	0	0	0	0
Career Total	7	0	1	1	853

Going:	Sf: 0-0 GS: 0-0 Gd: 0-1 GF: - Fm: 0-1
Distance:	2m2/m3: 0-0 2m4-2m7: 0-1 3m+: 0-1
Track:	LH: 0-2 RH: 0-0 Tight: 0-1 Gall: 0-1
Aids:	Bl: 0-0 Vi: 0-0 Tstrap: 0-0
Best Rating:	95 4/02 Extr 2m7f110y firm Ch

Fair hunter/point-to-pointer. Stays three miles, handles most
ground.

Shooting Light (IRE)

110   (130h)169

10-y-o b g Shernazar-Church Light (Caerleon (USA))
M C Pipe J M Brown & M J Blackburn

Placings:1213/24004/526/36B2365/3132350/111P-5P
                                                        (2685)
2002/03: 27⁵GS, 24⁸S,

	Starts	1st	2nd	3rd	Win & Pl
Chases	2	0	0	0	1500
Career Total	32	6	5	6	175101

169	12/01	Asct	3m110y A HCh	GD	£32500
161	11/01	Chel	2m4f110yA HCh	GD	£58000
155	10/01	Chel	2m4f110yC(0-135)HCh	GD	£13013
132	11/00	Asct	2m3f110yB Ch	SFT	£9350
126	1/97	Chel	2m1f A Hdl	G-F	£9779
114	11/96	Sand	2m110y D Hdl	GD	£2801

Total win prize-money £125444

Going:	Sf: 0-1 GS: 0-1 Gd: 0-0 GF: - Fm: 0-0
Distance:	2m2/m3: 0-0 2m4-2m7: 0-0 3m+: 0-2

Track: LH: 0-1 RH: 0-1 Tight: 0-0 Gall: 0-1
Aids: Bl: 0-0 Vi: 0-2 Tstrap: 0-0
Best Rating: 169 12/01 Asct 3m110y   good Ch

High-class chaser; joined Martin Pipe at the start of 2001/02,
when easy winner of the Thomas Pink Gold Cup and Tote
Silver Cup; pulled up lame in the Gold Cup; well held this
term; stays three miles, effective over shorter; has won on
good ground and soft; usually wears a visor.

Short Change (IRE)

99   105

4-y-o b g Revoque (IRE)-Maafi Esm (Polish Precedent
(USA))
A W Carroll (B J Meehan 13/6) Dennis & Andrew Deacon

Placings:12B0   (2329)
2002/03: 17¹G, 16²F, 16BGS, 16⁰GS,

	Starts	1st	2nd	3rd	Win & Pl
Hurdles	4	1	1	0	4591
Career Total	4	1	1	0	4591

102 10/02 Hrfd 2m1f   E Hdl   GD   £3507
Total win prize-money £3507

Going:	Sf: 0-0 GS: 0-2 Gd: 1-1 GF: - Fm: 0-1
Distance:	2m2/m3: 1-4 2m4-2m7: 0-0 3m+: 0-0
Track:	LH: 0-1 RH: 1-3 Tight: 0-0 Gall: 0-0
Aids:	Bl: 0-0 Vi: 0-0 Tstrap: 0-0
Best Rating:	102 11/02 Chel 2m110y gd-sft Hdl

Modest hurdler; made a successful start to his hurdling
career when turning over the well-regarded Le Duc at
Hereford October 2002. May have had a tough task under a
penalty when second to Adecco at Ludlow the following
week.

Shoshoni Warrior (IRE)

104   92+

7-y-o b g Commanche Run-Delko (Decent Fellow)
Jonjo O Neill (Ms Caroline Hutchinson 15/5) J P
McManus

Placings:3-1P34P   (3914)
2002/03: 16¹G, 19PG, 24³S, 24⁴S, 20PGS,

	Starts	1st	2nd	3rd	Win & Pl
NH Flat	1	1	0	0	0
Hurdles	4	0	0	1	1088
Career Total	6	1	0	2	1732

Going:	Sf: 0-2 GS: 0-1 Gd: 1-2 GF: - Fm: 0-0
Distance:	2m2/m3: 1-1 2m4-2m7: 0-2 3m+: 0-2
Track:	LH: 0-0 RH: 0-4 Tight: 0-1 Gall: 0-0
Aids:	Bl: 0-0 Vi: 0-0 Tstrap: 0-0
Best Rating:	104 4/02 Fair 2m yield NHF

Moderate hurdler; dead-heated in a Gowran Park bumper
on good ground May 2002. Could have found the ground too
soft when third in three mile novice hurdle at Taunton
January 2003.

Shotgun Willy (IRE)

110   168

9-y-o ch g Be My Native (USA)-Minorettes Girl (Strong Gale)
P F Nicholls C G Roach

Placings:52/1111/11312/32P2-1P5   (4557)
2002/03: 28¹G, 36PG, 33⁵G,

	Starts	1st	2nd	3rd	Win & Pl
Chases	3	1	0	0	66550
Career Total	18	8	4	2	218474

168	3/03	Hayd	3m4f110yA HCh	GD	£63800
160	2/01	Newb	3m B Ch	SFT	£29750
152	11/00	Newb	3m A Ch	G-S	£29750
146	10/00	Winc	3m1f110yD Ch	G-S	£4192
144	3/00	Chep	3m A Hdl	HVY	£9600
147	2/00	Uttx	3m110y C Hdl	SFT	£5466
135	1/00	Uttx	3m110y D Hdl	SFT	£3997
126	11/99	Winc	2m6f C Hdl	GD	£5303
			Total win prize-money £151861		

Going: Sf: 0-0 GS: 0-0 Gd: 1-3 GF: - Fm: 0-0
Distance: 2m/2m3: 0-0 2m4-2m7: 0-0 3m+: 1-3
Track: LH: 1-3 RH: 0-0 Tight: 0-1 Gall: 0-0
Aids: Bl: 0-1 Vi: 0-0 Tstrap: 0-0
Best Rating: 168 3/03 Hayd 3m4f110y good Ch

High-class staying chaser; a leading novice in 2000/1; ran a blinder when second in the Scottish National in April 2002, before landing the Red Square Vodka Gold Cup at Haydock in March 2003 after nearly a year off the track; ran no race at all when pulled up in the Grand National; well-beaten fifth in first-time blinkers in the Scottish National a week later; stays four miles; effective on good and soft ground.

Should Be Fun

6-y-o ch m Milieu-Our Dessa (Derek H)
Miss S E Forster C Storey

Placings:000   (1633)
2002/03: 16⁶G, 16⁶GF, 24⁸S,

	Starts	1st	2nd	3rd	Win & Pl
NH Flat	2	0	0	0	0
Hurdles	1	0	0	0	0
Career Total	3	0	0	0	

Going: Sf: 0-1 GS: 0-0 Gd: 0-1 GF: - Fm: 0-1
Distance: 2m/2m3: 0-2 2m4-2m7: 0-0 3m+: 0-1
Track: LH: 0-2 RH: 0-1 Tight: 0-0 Gall: 0-0
Aids: Bl: 0-0 Vi: 0-0 Tstrap: 0-0
Best Rating: 40 6/02 Hexm 2m110y good NHF

Shoulton (IRE)

(81h)   (35h)
6-y-o br g Aristocracy-Jay Joy (Double U Jay)
G H Yardley Mrs S Tainton

Placings:05-000U   (4321)
2002/03: 16⁰HY, 24⁰HY, 24⁰GS, 24⁰G,

	Starts	1st	2nd	3rd	Win & Pl
NH Flat	1	0	0	0	0
Hurdles	2	0	0	0	0
Chases	1	0	0	0	0
Career Total	6	0	0	0	

Going: Sf: 0-2 GS: 0-1 Gd: 0-1 GF: - Fm: 0-0
Distance: 2m/2m3: 0-1 2m4-2m7: 0-0 3m+: 0-3
Track: LH: 0-3 RH: 0-1 Tight: 0-1 Gall: 0-1
Aids: Bl: 0-0 Vi: 0-0 Tstrap: 0-0
Best Rating: 64 12/02 Newb 2m110y heavy NHF

Show The Way
100   85
5-y-o ch g Hernando (FR)-Severine (USA) (Trempolino (USA))
J R Jenkins Uk Packaging Supplies Ltd

Placings:40-033P20   (4143)
2002/03: 17⁰G, 16³GF, 18³GF, 20⁰G, 16²GS, 16⁰G,

	Starts	1st	2nd	3rd	Win & Pl
Hurdles	6	0	1	2	1267
Career Total	8	0	1	2	1267

Going: Sf: 0-0 GS: 0-1 Gd: 0-3 GF: - Fm: 0-2
Distance: 2m/2m3: 0-5 2m4-2m7: 0-1 3m+: 0-0
Track: LH: 0-3 RH: 0-2 Tight: 0-5 Gall: 0-1
Aids: Bl: 0-0 Vi: 0-5 Tstrap: 0-0
Best Rating: 85 10/02 Fknm 2m gd-sft Hdl

Makes the frame in very moderate races over hurdles, but looks a hard ride and is a weak finisher.

Showpiece
112   132
5-y-o b g Selkirk (USA)-Hawayah (IRE) (Shareef Dancer (USA))
C J Mann (W J Haggas 7/10) C S G Limited

Placings:4   (3527)
2002/03: 16⁴G,

	Starts	1st	2nd	3rd	Win & Pl
Hurdles	1	0	0	0	568
Career Total	1	0	0	0	568

Going: Sf: 0-0 GS: 0-0 Gd: 0-1 GF: - Fm: 0-0
Distance: 2m/2m3: 0-1 2m4-2m7: 0-0 3m+: 0-1
Track: LH: 0-1 RH: 0-0 Tight: 0-0 Gall: 0-1
Aids: Bl: 0-0 Vi: 0-0 Tstrap: 0-0
Best Rating: 102 2/03 Newb 2m110y good Hdl

Useful hurdler, in good form in the summer of 2003; suited by trips of around two miles and acts on most types of ground.

Showtime Shirley
55
5-y-o ch m First Trump-Wollow Maid (Wollow)
A Bailey Sandybrow Stables Ltd

Placings:0006-0   (0269)
2002/03: 16⁰GF,

	Starts	1st	2nd	3rd	Win & Pl
Hurdles	1	0	0	0	0
Career Total	5	0	0	0	0

Going: Sf: 0-0 GS: 0-0 Gd: 0-0 GF: - Fm: 0-0
Distance: 2m/2m3: 0-1 2m4-2m7: 0-0 3m+: 0-0
Track: LH: 0-1 RH: 0-0 Tight: 0-1 Gall: 0-0
Aids: Bl: 0-0 Vi: 0-1 Tstrap: 0-0
Best Rating: 55 12/01 Catt 2m soft Hdl

Shrilanka (IRE)
90(88h)   (66h)55
7-y-o b m Lashkari-Lady Nerak (Pitpan)
P J Hobbs Mr & Mrs A J Heywood

Placings:4-0555   (4636)
2002/03: 21⁰S, 20⁵HY, 19⁵GS, 24⁵G,

	Starts	1st	2nd	3rd	Win & Pl
Hurdles	3	0	0	0	0
Chases	1	0	0	0	0
Career Total	5	0	0	0	323

Going: Sf: 0-2 GS: 0-1 Gd: 0-1 GF: - Fm: 0-0
Distance: 2m/2m3: 0-1 2m4-2m7: 0-2 3m+: 0-1
Track: LH: 0-2 RH: 0-2 Tight: 0-1 Gall: 0-0
Aids: Bl: 0-0 Vi: 0-0 Tstrap: 0-0

Best Rating: 84 5/01 Tipp 2m2f heavy NHF

Shu Gaa (IRE)

10-y-o ch g Salse (USA)-River Reem (USA) (Irish River (FR))
C Goulding Mrs M A J Johnson

Placings:10411/3/4F3F4F0/545630/14P43/0P-P   (0316)
2002/03: 21⁰G,

Chases	1	0	0	0	0
Career Total	27	4	0	4	24646

112	5/00	Bang	2m4f110yD(0-120)HCh	GD	£7475
116	4/97	Ayr	2m C HHdl	GD	£4402
106	3/97	Chep	2m110y C HHdl	G-S	£3488
101	12/96	Hayd	2m C HHdl	G-S	£2955
			Total win prize-money £18321		

Going: Sf: 0-0 GS: 0-0 Gd: 0-1 GF: - Fm: 0-0
Distance: 2m/2m3: 0-0 2m4-2m7: 0-1 3m+: 0-0
Track: LH: 0-0 RH: 0-1 Tight: 0-1 Gall: 0-0
Aids: Bl: 0-0 Vi: 0-0 Tstrap: 0-0
Best Rating: 116 5/97 Hayd 2m good Hdl

Shuil Back (IRE)
90   51
6-y-o b m Bob Back (USA)-Shuil Ar Aghaidh (The Parson)
A J Lidderdale George Ward

Placings:3-P   (4527)
2002/03: 20⁰G,

	Starts	1st	2nd	3rd	Win & Pl
Hurdles	1	0	0	0	0
Career Total	2	0	0	1	246

Going: Sf: 0-0 GS: 0-0 Gd: 0-1 GF: - Fm: 0-0
Distance: 2m/2m3: 0-0 2m4-2m7: 0-1 3m+: 0-0
Track: LH: 0-1 RH: 0-0 Tight: 0-0 Gall: 0-0
Aids: Bl: 0-0 Vi: 0-0 Tstrap: 0-0
Best Rating: 82 4/02 Towc 2m good NHF

Daughter of a smart staying mare, likely to need a test of stamina in time.

Shuil Tsarina (IRE)
88f
5-y-o b m King s Ride-Shuil Realt (IRE) (Jolly Jake (NZ))
J M Jefferson Mrs K S Gaffney & Mrs Alix Stevenson

Placings:03   (1824)
2002/03: 16⁰G, 16³HY,

	Starts	1st	2nd	3rd	Win & Pl
NH Flat	2	0	0	1	251
Career Total	2	0	0	1	251

Going: Sf: 0-1 GS: 0-0 Gd: 0-1 GF: - Fm: 0-0
Distance: 2m/2m3: 0-2 2m4-2m7: 0-0 3m+: 0-0
Track: LH: 0-2 RH: 0-0 Tight: 0-0 Gall: 0-0
Aids: Bl: 0-0 Vi: 0-0 Tstrap: 0-0
Best Rating: 88 11/02 Hexm 2m110y heavy NHF

Shuttleworth (IRE)
103   106
9-y-o br g Be My Native (USA)-Cool Princess (Proverb)
C C Bealby Michael Hill

Placings:453214600/01U32-265P   (3939)
2002/03: 22^2S, 24^6G, 24^5GS, 22^8S,

	Starts	1st	2nd	3rd	Win & Pl
Chases	4	0	1	0	1684
Career Total	18	2	3	2	12122

87	10/01	Sthl	3m110y	E Ch	GD £3149
116	11/00	Thur	2m6f110y	Hdl	HVY £3864

Total win prize-money £7013

Going: Sf: 0-2 GS: 0-1 Gd: 0-1 GF: - Fm: 0-0
Distance: 2m/2m3: 0-0 2m4-2m7: 0-2 3m+: 0-2
Track: LH: 0-1 RH: 0-3 Tight: 0-2 Gall: 0-1
Aids: Bl: 0-0 Vi: 0-0 Tstrap: 0-0
Best Rating: 116 11/00 Thur 2m6f110y heavy Hdl

Modest chaser; lightly-raced, best effort over fences when runner-up at Market Rasen in December. handles testing ground.

Shylock (IRE)

9-y-o b g Buckskin (FR)-Sly Maid (Rapid River)
T H Caldwell (M F Morris 19/5) T H Caldwell

Placings:000P/4   (4664)
2002/03: 24^4GF,

	Starts	1st	2nd	3rd	Win & Pl
Chases	1	0	0	0	111
Career Total	5	0	0	0	111

Going: Sf: 0-0 GS: 0-0 Gd: 0-0 GF: - Fm: 0-1
Distance: 2m/2m3: 0-0 2m4-2m7: 0-0 3m+: 0-1
Track: LH: 0-0 RH: 0-1 Tight: 0-0 Gall: 0-0
Aids: Bl: 0-0 Vi: 0-0 Tstrap: 0-0
Best Rating: 55 5/99 Naas 2m good Hdl

Siamo Disperati

5-y-o ch g Aragon-Jambo (Rambo Dancer (CAN))
Miss M Bragg W H Whitley

Placings:0P   (3779)
2002/03: 16^0G, 19^PGS,

	Starts	1st	2nd	3rd	Win & Pl
Hurdles	2	0	0	0	
Career Total	2	0	0	0	

Going: Sf: 0-0 GS: 0-2 Gd: 0-0 GF: - Fm: 0-0
Distance: 2m/2m3: 0-2 2m4-2m7: 0-0 3m+: 0-0
Track: LH: 0-0 RH: 0-2 Tight: 0-0 Gall: 0-0
Aids: Bl: 0-0 Vi: 0-0 Tstrap: 0-0
Best Rating: 0 2/03 Extr 2m3f gd-sft Hdl

Sigma Run (IRE)

(79h)   (65h)90
14-y-o b g The Parson-Splendid Run (Deep Run)
Dr P Pritchard The Shooting Stars

Placings:54/1F63FUB/350F56U/01531FP4/1213F553123/0
F364261P6/412P2P0430/P321232404450/02603343P1P04
U44203-P   (0058)
2002/03: 16^PG,

	Starts	1st	2nd	3rd	Win & Pl
Chases	1	0	0	0	
Career Total	88	10	10	14	51947

90	10/01	Ludl	2m	G(0-95)HCh	G-F £2926
97	7/00	MRas	2m1f110y	F(0-110)HCh	GD £3510
88	6/99	MRas	2m1f110y	D(0-125)HCh	GD £3764
105	10/98	Extr	2m1f	E(0-115)HCh	GD £3485
108	10/97	Hrfd	2m	F(0-105)HCh	GD £2710
95	6/97	Sthl	2m	E(0-115)HCh	G-F £3842
95	5/97	Ludl	2m	E Ch	G-F £2892
93	11/96	Leic	2m1f	E Ch	G-F £3246
67	10/96	Ludl	2m	E Hdl	FRM £2192
92	11/94	MRas	1m5f110y	NHF	GD £1940

Total win prize-money £30508

Going: Sf: 0-0 GS: 0-0 Gd: 0-1 GF: - Fm: 0-0
Distance: 2m/2m3: 0-1 2m4-2m7: 0-3 3m+: 0-0
Track: LH: 0-0 RH: 0-1 Tight: 0-1 Gall: 0-0
Aids: Bl: 0-0 Vi: 0-0 Tstrap: 0-0
Best Rating: 108 10/97 Hrfd 2m good Ch

A fair sort in modest handicap chases at up to two and a half miles, but needs a sound surface and is not altogether consistent. Best going right-handed.

Signed And Dated (USA)

81   66
4-y-o b g Red Ransom (USA)-Libeccio (NZ) (Danzatore (CAN))
Mrs E Slack A Slack

Placings:P0F   (4793)
2002/03: 16^PG, 17^0G, 17^FGF,

	Starts	1st	2nd	3rd	Win & Pl
Hurdles	3	0	0	0	
Career Total	3	0	0	0	

Going: Sf: 0-0 GS: 0-0 Gd: 0-2 GF: - Fm: 0-0
Distance: 2m/2m3: 0-3 2m4-2m7: 0-0 3m+: 0-0
Track: LH: 0-3 RH: 0-0 Tight: 0-2 Gall: 0-0
Aids: Bl: 0-0 Vi: 0-0 Tstrap: 0-0
Best Rating: 55 4/03 Sedg 2m1f good Hdl

Sijujama (IRE)

97   80d
8-y-o b g Torus-Knights Bounty (IRE) (Henbit (USA))
Miss Lucinda V Russell Major R B H Young

Placings:00000/P0F/P3-2344PP   (2387)
2002/03: 16^2GS, 16^3G, 20^4G, 20^4GF, 23^9GF, 21^PGS,

	Starts	1st	2nd	3rd	Win & Pl
Chases	6	0	1	1	3826
Career Total	16	0	1	2	4152

Going: Sf: 0-0 GS: 0-2 Gd: 0-2 GF: - Fm: 0-2
Distance: 2m/2m3: 0-2 2m4-2m7: 0-3 3m+: 0-1
Track: LH: 0-2 RH: 0-3 Tight: 0-1 Gall: 0-0
Aids: Bl: 0-0 Vi: 0-0 Tstrap: 0-0
Best Rating: 102 11/99 Naas 2m yld-sft Hdl

Modest form when placed over fences so far.

Sikasso (USA)

105   102
7-y-o b/br g Silver Hawk (USA)-Silken Doll (USA) (Chieftain II)
G A Swinbank Blyth,Buttery,Rider and Wilson

Placings:3323/30333   (4591)
2002/03: 16^3S, 16^9G, 17^3GS, 16^3GS, 16^3G,

	Starts	1st	2nd	3rd	Win & Pl
Hurdles	5	0	0	4	2161
Career Total	9	0	1	7	3273

Going: Sf: 0-1 GS: 0-2 Gd: 0-2 GF: - Fm: 0-0
Distance: 2m/2m3: 0-5 2m4-2m7: 0-0 3m+: 0-0
Track: LH: 0-3 RH: 0-2 Tight: 0-1 Gall: 0-2
Aids: Bl: 0-0 Vi: 0-0 Tstrap: 0-0
Best Rating: 104 12/00 Muss 2m good NHF

Moderate novice hurdler, no great battler.

Silchester Dream

83   42
5-y-o ch m Karinga Bay-Raghill Hannah (Buckskin (FR))
C G Cox The Silchester Racing Club

Placings:004   (4222)
2002/03: 12^8G, 16^0G, 17^4GF,

	Starts	1st	2nd	3rd	Win & Pl
NH Flat	2	0	0	0	0
Hurdles	1	0	0	0	266
Career Total	3	0	0	0	266

Going: Sf: 0-0 GS: 0-0 Gd: 0-2 GF: - Fm: 0-1
Distance: 2m/2m3: 0-2 2m4-2m7: 0-3 3m+: 0-0
Track: LH: 0-1 RH: 0-2 Tight: 0-0 Gall: 0-0
Aids: Bl: 0-0 Vi: 0-0 Tstrap: 0-0
Best Rating: 78 12/02 Newb 1m4f110y good NHF

Silence Reigns

(90h)   (92h)114
9-y-o b g Saddlers Hall (IRE)-Rensaler (USA) (Stop The Music (USA))
P F Nicholls C G Roach

Placings:0/16310/0/1412P-FU6   (4553)
2002/03: 20^6G, 20^UG, 22^6G,

	Starts	1st	2nd	3rd	Win & Pl
Hurdles	1	0	0	0	0
Chases	2	0	0	0	0
Career Total	15	4	1	1	32675

126	12/01	Chep	2m3f110yD Ch	G-S	£4163
139	11/01	Chep	2m110y E Ch	SFT	£3415
127	3/00	Ludl	2m E Hdl	G-S	£2880
127	11/99	Chel	2m110y A Hdl	GD	£9525

Total win prize-money £19985

Going: Sf: 0-0 GS: 0-0 Gd: 0-3 GF: - Fm: 0-0
Distance: 2m/2m3: 0-0 2m4-2m7: 0-3 3m+: 0-0
Track: LH: 0-3 RH: 0-0 Tight: 0-0 Gall: 0-1
Aids: Bl: 0-0 Vi: 0-0 Tstrap: 0-0
Best Rating: 143 2/02 Sand 2m4f110y gd-sft Ch

Former smart hurdler; very useful novice chaser in 2001/2, absent after February; failed to complete on two runs over fences March 2003; well beaten over hurdles in April; suited by good or soft ground; stays two and a half miles.

Silent Action (USA)

98(89h)   76
11-y-o b/br g Greinton-Heather Bee (USA) (Drone (USA))
N A Smith Mrs G C List

Placings:25/00036/334/63P/03F53/0P5000060-5P5044   (1099)
2002/03: 20^5G, 20^PG, 22^5GF, 20^UGF, 26^4GF, 26^4GF,

	Starts	1st	2nd	3rd	Win & Pl
Hurdles	6	0	0	0	0
Career Total	33	0	1	6	2856

Going: Sf: 0-0 GS: 0-0 Gd: 0-2 GF: - Fm: 0-4
Distance: 2m/2m3: 0-0 2m4-2m7: 0-4 3m+: 0-2
Track: LH: 0-6 RH: 0-0 Tight: 0-1 Gall: 0-0

Aids: Bl: 0-0 Vi: 0-0 Tstrap: 0-6
Best Rating: 96 2/96 Punc 2m   soft   NHF

Won two modest points spring 2003; well beaten under Rules.

Silent Appeal

96f   97f

6-y-o b m Alflora (IRE)-Silent Surrender (Nearly A Hand)
Simon Earle Festival Racing (uk) Limited

Placings:24   (3113)
2002/03: 17²HY, 17⁴HY,

	Starts	1st	2nd	3rd	Win & Pl
NH Flat	2	0	1	0	548
Career Total	2	0	1	0	548

Going: Sf: 0-2 GS: 0-0 Gd: 0-0 GF: - Fm: 0-0
Distance: 2m/2m3: 0-2 2m4-2m7: 0-0 3m+: 0-0
Track: LH: 0-0 RH: 0-2 Tight: 0-2 Gall: 0-0
Aids: Bl: 0-0 Vi: 0-0 Tstrap: 0-0
Best Rating: 97 12/02 Folk 2m1f110y heavy NHF

Silent Guest (IRE)

75   39

10-y-o b g Don t Forget Me-Guest House (What A Guest)
J D Frost R C Burridge

Placings:2164/53P/565/0200224/60-0   (3825)
2002/03: 16⁰GS,

	Starts	1st	2nd	3rd	Win & Pl
Hurdles	1	0	0	0	
Career Total	20	1	4	1	5770
87 11/96 Newc 2m E Hdl G-F £2274

Total win prize-money £2274

Going: Sf: 0-0 GS: 0-1 Gd: 0-0 GF: - Fm: 0-0
Distance: 2m/2m3: 0-1 2m4-2m7: 0-0 3m+: 0-0
Track: LH: 0-1 RH: 0-0 Tight: 0-0 Gall: 0-0
Aids: Bl: 0-0 Vi: 0-0 Tstrap: 0-0
Best Rating: 87 11/96 Newc 2m   gd-fm Hdl

Silent Gunner

5-y-o ch g Gunner B-Quiet Dawn (Lighter)
J S King T L Morshead

Placings:0   (4275)
2002/03: 16⁰G,

	Starts	1st	2nd	3rd	Win & Pl
NH Flat	1	0	0	0	
Career Total	1	0	0	0	

Going: Sf: 0-0 GS: 0-0 Gd: 0-1 GF: - Fm: 0-0
Distance: 2m/2m3: 0-1 2m4-2m7: 0-0 3m+: 0-0
Track: LH: 0-1 RH: 0-0 Tight: 0-0 Gall: 0-0
Aids: Bl: 0-0 Vi: 0-0 Tstrap: 0-0
Best Rating: 0 3/03 Chep 2m110y good NHF

Silent Hunter

(70h)   (40h)

7-y-o ch g Lion Cavern (USA)-Zealous Kitten (USA) (The Minstrel (CAN))
M J Ryan The Beach Boys

Placings:0/00PPPPF-   (0009)

2002/03: 26⁶G,

	Starts	1st	2nd	3rd	Win & Pl
Chases	1	0	0	0	
Career Total	8	0	0	0	

Going: Sf: 0-0 GS: 0-0 Gd: 0-1 GF: - Fm: 0-0
Distance: 2m/2m3: 0-0 2m4-2m7: 0-0 3m+: 0-1
Track: LH: 0-1 RH: 0-2 Tight: 0-1 Gall: 0-0
Aids: Bl: 0-1 Vi: 0-0 Tstrap: 0-1
Best Rating: 54 3/01 Hntg 2m110y soft NHF

Poor chase/hurdles form.

Silent Snipe

107(93h)   (51h)63

10-y-o ch g Jendali (USA)-Sasol (Bustino)
Miss L C Siddall Mrs D Ibbotson

Placings:P665P60P3010-U014P0130P   (4662)
2002/03: 25⁰G, 25⁰G, 251GF, 254GF, 23⁰G, 26⁰GF, 251GF, 26³GF, 27⁰G, 26⁶GF,

	Starts	1st	2nd	3rd	Win & Pl
Hurdles	1	0	0	0	0
Chases	9	2	0	1	7047
Career Total	22	3	0	2	10528
82 10/02 Hexm 3m1f F(0-100)HCh G-F £3150
85 6/02 Hexm 3m1f F(0-95)HCh G-F £2702
80 4/02 Hexm 3m1f E Ch G-F £3217

Total win prize-money £9070

Going: Sf: 0-0 GS: 0-0 Gd: 0-4 GF: - Fm: 2-6
Distance: 2m/2m3: 0-0 2m4-2m7: 0-0 3m+: 2-10
Track: LH: 2-8 RH: 0-2 Tight: 0-1 Gall: 0-0
Aids: Bl: 0-0 Vi: 0-0 Tstrap: 0-0
Best Rating: 85 6/02 Hexm 3m1f   gd-fm Ch

Plating-class chaser; winning pointer; suited by three miles plus and fast ground; goes well at Hexham.

Silent Sound (IRE)

100   87

7-y-o b g Be My Guest (USA)-Whist Awhile (Caerleon (USA))
C Tizzard (Mrs S A Liddiard 4/12) Mrs P Tizzard

Placings:026   (4733)
2002/03: 19⁰GS, 16²GF, 16⁶GF,

	Starts	1st	2nd	3rd	Win & Pl
Hurdles	3	0	1	0	790
Career Total	3	0	1	0	790

Going: Sf: 0-0 GS: 0-1 Gd: 0-0 GF: - Fm: 0-2
Distance: 2m/2m3: 0-3 2m4-2m7: 0-0 3m+: 0-0
Track: LH: 2-2 RH: 0-1 Tight: 0-1 Gall: 0-0
Aids: Bl: 0-0 Vi: 0-0 Tstrap: 0-0
Best Rating: 87 3/03 Plum 2m   gd-fm Hdl

Plating-class hurdler; acts on fast ground.

Silent Voice (IRE)

10

6-y-o ch g Unfuwain (USA)-Symeterie (USA) (Seattle Song (USA))
Sir John Barlow Bt Sir John & Lady Barlow

Placings:0-P   (0267)
2002/03: 20⁰G,

	Starts	1st	2nd	3rd	Win & Pl
Hurdles	1	0	0	0	
Career Total	2	0	0	0	

Going: Sf: 0-0 GS: 0-1 Gd: 0-1 GF: - Fm: 0-0
Distance: 2m/2m3: 0-0 2m4-2m7: 0-0 3m+: 0-0
Track: LH: 0-1 RH: 0-0 Tight: 0-1 Gall: 0-0
Aids: Bl: 0-0 Vi: 0-0 Tstrap: 0-0
Best Rating: 0 5/02 Aint 2m4f   good Hdl

Silk St Bridget

6-y-o b m Rock Hopper-Silk St James (Pas De Seul)
W M Brisbourne The Bridget Partnership

Placings:P   (2233)
2002/03: 16⁰PS,

	Starts	1st	2nd	3rd	Win & Pl
Hurdles	1	0	0	0	
Career Total	1	0	0	0	

Going: Sf: 0-1 GS: 0-0 Gd: 0-0 GF: - Fm: 0-0
Distance: 2m/2m3: 0-1 2m4-2m7: 0-0 3m+: 0-0
Track: LH: 0-0 RH: 0-1 Tight: 0-0 Gall: 0-0
Aids: Bl: 0-0 Vi: 0-0 Tstrap: 0-0
Best Rating: 0 11/02 Leic 2m   soft Hdl

Silk St John

82

9-y-o b g Damister (USA)-Silk St James (Pas De Seul)
W M Brisbourne C R S Partners

Placings:0/2-0   (2200)
2002/03: 16⁰S,

	Starts	1st	2nd	3rd	Win & Pl
Hurdles	1	0	0	0	
Career Total	3	0	1	0	694

Going: Sf: 0-1 GS: 0-0 Gd: 0-0 GF: - Fm: 0-0
Distance: 2m/2m3: 0-1 2m4-2m7: 0-0 3m+: 0-0
Track: LH: 0-1 RH: 0-0 Tight: 0-0 Gall: 0-0
Aids: Bl: 0-0 Vi: 0-0 Tstrap: 0-0
Best Rating: 91 01/01 Hntg 2m110y good Hdl

Has shown ability over hurdles and should be capable of scoring over two miles on good ground.

Silk Trader

105   113

8-y-o b g Nomadic Way (USA)-Money Run (Deep Run)
J Mackie The Festival Dream Partnership

Placings:40/61U3/31400403163110-504414   (4734)
2002/03: 16⁵HY, 16⁶S, 16⁴HY, 16⁵HY, 16¹HY, 16⁴GF,

	Starts	1st	2nd	3rd	Win & Pl
Hurdles	6	1	0	4	5922
Career Total	26	6	0	4	25751
113 3/03 Sand 2m110y E(0-115)HHdl HVY £4732
113 3/03 Towc 2m D(0-125)HHdl G-S £5174
104 3/02 Sand 2m110y D(0-115)HHdl G-S £4231
108 12/01 Leic 2m F(0-100)HHdl SFT £3146
113 5/01 Wwck 2m3f E(0-115)HHdl GD £2660
100 2/01 Uttx 2m D Hdl SFT £2849

Total win prize-money £22794

Going: Sf: 1-5 GS: 0-0 Gd: 0-0 GF: - Fm: 0-0
Distance: 2m/2m3: 1-6 2m4-2m7: 0-0 3m+: 0-0
Track: LH: 0-3 RH: 1-3 Tight: 0-0 Gall: 0-1
Aids: Bl: 0-0 Vi: 0-0 Tstrap: 0-0
Best Rating: 113 3/03 Sand 2m110y heavy Hdl

Modest handicap hurdler; has won over two miles three, but is probably better over two miles; acts on good to soft ground.

Silken Memories

8-y-o b g Past Glories-Ribonny (FR) (Fast Hilarious (USA))
R Shiels   R Shiels

Placings:4030/P   (0765)
2002/03: 21ᴾGF,

	Starts	1st	2nd	3rd	Win & Pl
Hurdles	1	0	0	0	
Career Total	5	0	0	1	235

Going:	Sf: 0-0 GS: 0-0 Gd: 0-0 GF: - Fm: 0-1	
Distance:	2m2m3: 0-0 2m4-2m7: 0-0 3m+: 0-0	
Track:	LH: 0-1 RH: 0-0 Tight: 0-1 Gall: 0-0	
Aids:	Bl: 0-0 Vi: 0-0 Tstrap: 0-0	
Best Rating:	84 3/00 Hntg 2m110y gd-fm NHF	

Silken Pearls

89   97+

7-y-o b m Leading Counsel (USA)-River Pearl (Oats)
L Lungo   P E Truscott

Placings:4-110   (3228)
2002/03: 16¹HY, 22¹S, 21⁰HY,

	Starts	1st	2nd	3rd	Win & Pl
NH Flat	1	1	0	0	1757
Hurdles	2	1	0	0	4027
Career Total	4	2	0	0	5784
97	11/02 Kels	2m6f110yD Hdl		SFT	£4026
104	11/02 Hexm	2m110y H NHF		HVY	£1757
			Total win prize-money £5784		

Going:	Sf: 2-3 GS: 0-0 Gd: 0-0 GF: - Fm: 0-0	
Distance:	2m2m3: 1-1 2m4-2m7: 1-2 3m+: 0-0	
Track:	LH: 2-3 RH: 0-0 Tight: 1-2 Gall: 0-0	
Aids:	Bl: 0-0 Vi: 0-0 Tstrap: 0-0	
Best Rating:	104 11/02 Hexm 2m110y heavy NHF	

Winner of a bumper and a novices hurdle at Kelso in November but has run poorly since.

Silken Thyne

105   125

7-y-o b g Good Thyne (USA)-Padykin (Bustino)
C C Bealby   T P Radford

Placings:4/211P   (2614)
2002/03: 19²GF, 22¹S, 23¹GS, 24²S,

	Starts	1st	2nd	3rd	Win & Pl
Hurdles	4	2	1	0	9107
Career Total	5	2	1	0	9365
115	12/02 Weth	2m7f	D Hdl	G-S	£3981
131	11/02 Uttx	2m6f110yE Hdl		SFT	£3769
			Total win prize-money £7751		

Going:	Sf: 1-2 GS: 1-1 Gd: 0-0 GF: - Fm: 0-1	
Distance:	2m2m3: 0-0 2m4-2m7: 2-3 3m+: 0-1	
Track:	LH: 2-2 RH: 0-2 Tight: 0-1 Gall: 0-0	
Aids:	Bl: 0-0 Vi: 0-0 Tstrap: 0-0	
Best Rating:	131 11/02 Uttx 2m6f110y soft Hdl	

Fair hurdler; improving sort and getting better the further he goes. Gamely landed a maiden hurdle over an extended two-mile-six at Uttoxeter in November 2002, followed up at Wetherby but was pulled up and dismounted subsequently. Acts on soft.

Silly Boy

8-y-o ch g Crested Lark-Sutton Lass (Politico (USA))

R C Harper   R C Harper

Placings:PF   (2689)
2002/03: 20ᴾGS, 17ᶠS,

	Starts	1st	2nd	3rd	Win & Pl
Chases	2	0	0	0	
Career Total	2	0	0	0	

Going:	Sf: 0-1 GS: 0-1 Gd: 0-0 GF: - Fm: 0-0	
Distance:	2m2m3: 0-1 2m4-2m7: 0-1 3m+: 0-0	
Track:	LH: 0-0 RH: 0-2 Tight: 0-1 Gall: 0-1	
Aids:	Bl: 0-0 Vi: 0-0 Tstrap: 0-0	
Best Rating:	0 4/03 Plum 2m4f gd-fm Ch	

Winning ex-pointer with a poor completion record, but no form under Rules.

Silogue (IRE)

94   73+

6-y-o b/br g Distinctly North (USA)-African Bloom (African Sky)
O Brennan   O Brennan

Placings:5   (1133)
2002/03: 19⁵GF,

	Starts	1st	2nd	3rd	Win & Pl
Hurdles	1	0	0	0	0
Career Total	1	0	0	0	0

Going:	Sf: 0-0 GS: 0-0 Gd: 0-0 GF: - Fm: 0-1	
Distance:	2m2m3: 0-0 2m4-2m7: 0-1 3m+: 0-0	
Track:	LH: 0-0 RH: 0-1 Tight: 0-1 Gall: 0-0	
Aids:	Bl: 0-0 Vi: 0-0 Tstrap: 0-0	
Best Rating:	40 8/02 MRas 2m3f110y gd-fm Hdl	

Silva Venture (IRE)

84   73

6-y-o b m Mandalus-Miss The Post (Bustino)
L Lungo   Elite Racing Club

Placings:0-000   (4408)
2002/03: 16⁰GS, 17⁰GS, 16⁰G,

	Starts	1st	2nd	3rd	Win & Pl
NH Flat	1	0	0	0	0
Hurdles	2	0	0	0	0
Career Total	4	0	0	0	

Going:	Sf: 0-0 GS: 0-2 Gd: 0-1 GF: - Fm: 0-0	
Distance:	2m2m3: 0-0 2m4-2m7: 0-0 3m+: 0-0	
Track:	LH: 0-2 RH: 0-1 Tight: 0-0 Gall: 0-0	
Aids:	Bl: 0-0 Vi: 0-0 Tstrap: 0-0	
Best Rating:	63 4/02 Hexm 2m110y good NHF	

First worthwhile form when well beaten fourth in modest novices hurdle at Hexham in April.

Silver Birch (IRE)

106   109

6-y-o b g Clearly Bust-All Gone (Giolla Mear)
P F Nicholls   Paul K Barber

Placings:4113   (3948)
2002/03: 24⁴S, 20¹S, 25¹HY, 24³S,

	Starts	1st	2nd	3rd	Win & Pl
Hurdles	4	2	0	1	10367
Career Total	4	2	0	1	10367
100	1/03 Plum	3m1f110yD Hdl		HVY	£5473
109	11/02 Chep	2m4f	D Hdl	SFT	£4231
			Total win prize-money £9705		

Going:	Sf: 2-4 GS: 0-0 Gd: 0-0 GF: - Fm: 0-0	
Distance:	2m2m3: 0-0 2m4-2m7: 1-1 3m+: 1-3	
Track:	LH: 1-2 RH: 0-1 Tight: 0-0 Gall: 0-0	
Aids:	Bl: 0-0 Vi: 0-0 Tstrap: 0-0	
Best Rating:	109 11/02 Chep 2m4f soft Hdl	

Modest staying hurdler; Irish Point winner; suited by two and a half to three miles plus and a soft surface; best held up; disappointing in slowly-run race at Exeter when attempting a hat-trick.

Silver Buzzard (USA)

112   108

4-y-o b/br g Silver Hawk (USA)-Stellarina (USA) (Pleasant Colony (USA))
Jonjo O Neill (M R Channon 7/11) International Plywood Plc

Placings:521446   (4325)
2002/03: 16⁵GF, 18²GF, 16¹G, 16⁴HY, 22⁴HY, 19⁶G,

	Starts	1st	2nd	3rd	Win & Pl
Hurdles	6	1	1	0	6317
Career Total	6	1	1	0	6317
91	11/02 Hayd	2m	D Hdl	GD	£4111
			Total win prize-money £4111		

Going:	Sf: 0-2 GS: 0-0 Gd: 1-2 GF: - Fm: 0-2	
Distance:	**2m/2m3: 1-5** 2m4-2m7: 0-1 3m+: 0-0	
Track:	**LH: 1-4** RH: 0-2 Tight: 0-2 Gall: 0-1	
Aids:	Bl: 0-0 Vi: 0-0 Tstrap: 0-0	
Best Rating:	105 3/03 Sand 2m6f heavy Hdl	

Fair hurdler, suited by a soft surface and stays 2m 6f, although is effective over shorter.

Silver Charmer

105   111

4-y-o b f Charmer-Sea Dart (Air Trooper)
H S Howe   John Bull

Placings:F34041F0   (4610)
2002/03: 16ᶠGF, 16³GS, 16⁴S, 17⁰G, 17⁴HY, 19¹G, 20ᶠG, 21⁰G,

	Starts	1st	2nd	3rd	Win & Pl
Hurdles	8	1	0	1	7967
Career Total	8	1	0	1	7967
105	3/03 Newb	2m3f	D(0-115)HHdl	GD	£4823
			Total win prize-money £4823		

Going:	Sf: 0-2 GS: 0-1 Gd: 1-4 GF: - Fm: 0-1	
Distance:	**2m/2m3: 1-6** 2m4-2m7: 0-2 3m+: 0-0	
Track:	**LH: 1-8** RH: 0-0 Tight: 0-2 **Gall: 1-5**	
Aids:	Bl: 0-0 Vi: 0-0 Tstrap: 0-0	
Best Rating:	111 4/03 Aint 2m4f good Hdl	

Fair juvenile hurdler; still in contention when falling two out in Grade 2 event at Aintree; acts on most types of ground; stays two miles three.

Silver Charter (USA)

99   87

4-y-o b g Silver Hawk (USA)-Pride Of Darby (USA) (Danzig (USA))
G B Balding   Argent Racing

Placings:26040   (4450)
2002/03: 16²GS, 16⁶GS, 16⁰G, 19⁴G, 21⁰G,

	Starts	1st	2nd	3rd	Win & Pl
Hurdles	5	0	1	0	1661
Career Total	5	0	1	0	1661

Going:	Sf: 0-0 GS: 0-2 Gd: 0-3 GF: - Fm: 0-0	

Distance:	2m/2m3: 0-4 2m4-2m7: 0-1 3m+: 0-0
Track:	LH: 0-2 RH: 0-3 Tight: 0-0 Gall: 0-4
Aids:	Bl: 0-0 Vi: 0-0 Tstrap: 0-0
Best Rating:	87 11/02 Hntg 2m110y gd-sft Hdl

Moderate hurdler; effective on good to soft.

Silver Chevalier (IRE)

99   **80**

5-y-o gr g Petong-Princess Eurolink (Be My Guest (USA))
Mrs D A Hamer (B Llewellyn 9/8) Mrs D A Hamer

Placings:06P5-0PP0P   (1058)
2002/03: 16⁰GF, 19⁰G, 20⁵S, 16⁶GS, 24⁶GF,

	Starts	1st	2nd	3rd	Win & Pl
Hurdles	5	0	0	0	0
Career Total	9	0	0	0	0

Going:	Sf: 0-1 GS: 0-1 Gd: 0-1 GF: - Fm: 0-2
Distance:	2m/2m3: 0-2 2m4-2m7: 0-2 3m+: 0-1
Track:	LH: 0-3 RH: 0-2 Tight: 0-0 Gall: 0-0
Aids:	Bl: 0-0 Vi: 0-0 Tstrap: 0-0
Best Rating:	80 4/02 Ludl 2m gd-fm Hdl

Silver Chieftan (IRE)

100f   **86f**

5-y-o gr g Be My Native (USA)-Mystery Rose (Roselier (FR))
P J Hobbs P A Newey

Placings:0   (4329)
2002/03: 16⁰G,

	Starts	1st	2nd	3rd	Win & Pl
NH Flat	1	0	0	0	
Career Total	1	0	0	0	

Going:	Sf: 0-0 GS: 0-0 Gd: 0-1 GF: - Fm: 0-0
Distance:	2m/2m3: 0-1 2m4-2m7: 0-0 3m+: 0-0
Track:	LH: 0-1 RH: 0-0 Tight: 0-0 Gall: 0-1
Aids:	Bl: 0-0 Vi: 0-0 Tstrap: 0-0
Best Rating:	86 3/03 Newb 2m110y good NHF

Silver Dancer (IRE)

79   **45**

7-y-o gr g Roselier (FR)-Fancy Step (Step Together (USA))
M G Rimell Mark Rimell

Placings:050U   (4225)
2002/03: 16⁰S, 20⁵HY, 26⁰G, 20ᵁGF,

	Starts	1st	2nd	3rd	Win & Pl
NH Flat	1	0	0	0	0
Hurdles	3	0	0	0	0
Career Total	4	0	0	0	0

Going:	Sf: 0-2 GS: 0-0 Gd: 0-1 GF: - Fm: 0-1
Distance:	2m/2m3: 0-1 2m4-2m7: 0-2 3m+: 0-1
Track:	LH: 0-2 RH: 0-2 Tight: 0-0 Gall: 0-0
Aids:	Bl: 0-0 Vi: 0-0 Tstrap: 0-0
Best Rating:	46 12/02 Wwck 2m soft NHF

Very moderate form so far.

Silver Gift

(106h)   (97h)

6-y-o b m Rakaposhi King-Kellsboro Kate (Paddy s Stream)
G Fierro G Fierro

Placings:0040/PP360P3-0FP52211U141PP04100   (4759)
2002/03: 20⁰G, 21⁵FS, 19⁶PGF, 22⁵GF, 24²G, 26²GF, 27¹G, 24¹GF, 26ᵁGF, 24¹G, 22⁴GF, 26¹GF, 24⁴S, 27⁵S, 26⁹GF, 27⁴GF, 26¹GF, 24⁰G, 27⁹GF,

	Starts	1st	2nd	3rd	Win & Pl
Hurdles	18	5	2	0	16683
Chases	1	0	0	0	0
Career Total	30	5	2	2	17647
97	4/03	Hrfd	3m2f	E(0-105)HHdl	G-F	£3568
97	10/02	Hntg	3m2f	E(0-110)HHdl	G-F	£2884
94	9/02	Worc	3m	F(0-100)HHdl	GD	£2828
84	8/02	Worc	3m	F(0-95)HHdl	G-F	£2653
81	8/02	Sedg	3m3f110yE(0-110)HHdl	GD	£2891
				Total win prize-money £14825

Going:	Sf: 0-3 GS: 0-0 Gd: 2-5 GF: - Fm: 3-11
Distance:	2m/2m3: 0-0 2m4-2m7: 0-5 3m+: 5-14
Track:	LH: 3-12 RH: 2-5 Tight: 1-6 Gall: 1-2
Aids:	Bl: 0-0 Vi: 0-0 Tstrap: 0-0
Best Rating:	97 4/03 Hrfd 3m2f gd-fm Hdl

Modest staying handicap hurdler; suited by extreme distances; acts on ground good and faster.

Silver Groom (IRE)

13-y-o gr g Shy Groom (USA)-Rustic Lawn (Rusticaro (FR))
David M Easterby Ms K P Barron

Placings:132P/14020/14350/06/254/5P-3   (0416)
2002/03: 24³GF,

	Starts	1st	2nd	3rd	Win & Pl
Chases	1	0	0	1	548
Career Total	22	3	3	3	29841
140	11/96	Asct	2m110y	B HHdl	G-F	£4992
140	11/95	Sand	2m110y	B(0-145)HHdl	G-F	£4947
111	11/94	Strf	2m110y	Hdl	G-S	£2164
				Total win prize-money £12104

Going:	Sf: 0-0 GS: 0-0 Gd: 0-0 GF: - Fm: 0-1
Distance:	2m/2m3: 0-0 2m4-2m7: 0-0 3m+: 0-1
Track:	LH: 0-1 RH: 0-0 Tight: 0-1 Gall: 0-0
Aids:	Bl: 0-0 Vi: 0-0 Tstrap: 0-0
Best Rating:	145 2/97 Newb 2m110y good Hdl

Silver Howe

99   **99**

10-y-o gr g Move Off-Vinovia (Ribston)
D Moffatt The C J G Partnership

Placings:0000600/6065O2466/402P42/46222P/102340640 -240P5   (1072)
2002/03: 22²G, 22⁴GS, 16⁶G, 20⁵GS, 17⁵G,

	Starts	1st	2nd	3rd	Win & Pl
Hurdles	5	0	1	0	1064
Career Total	42	1	8	1	11103
97	5/01	Bang	2m4f	E Hdl	GD	£3104
				Total win prize-money £3105

Going:	Sf: 0-0 GS: 0-2 Gd: 0-3 GF: - Fm: 0-0
Distance:	2m/2m3: 0-2 2m4-2m7: 0-3 3m+: 0-0
Track:	LH: 0-5 RH: 0-0 Tight: 0-4 Gall: 0-0
Aids:	Bl: 0-0 Vi: 0-3 Tstrap: 0-0
Best Rating:	99 5/02 Kels 2m6f110y good Hdl

Moderate hurdler; has shown some ability and has made the frame often, but has only ever won once and now looks well past his best.

Silver Jack (IRE)

70f   **96f**

5-y-o gr g Roselier (FR)-Consharon (IRE) (Strong Gale)

M Todhunter B Batey

Placings:6   (3775)
2002/03: 16⁶GS,

	Starts	1st	2nd	3rd	Win & Pl
NH Flat	1	0	0	0	0
Career Total	1	0	0	0	0

Going:	Sf: 0-0 GS: 0-1 Gd: 0-0 GF: - Fm: 0-0
Distance:	2m/2m3: 0-1 2m4-2m7: 0-0 3m+: 0-0
Track:	LH: 0-1 RH: 0-0 Tight: 0-0 Gall: 0-0
Aids:	Bl: 0-0 Vi: 0-0 Tstrap: 0-0
Best Rating:	96 2/03 Ayr 2m gd-sft NHF

Silver Knight

113   **119**

5-y-o gr g Simply Great (FR)-Hysteria (Prince Bee)
T D Easterby C H Stevens

Placings:16-0122163303   (4764)
2002/03: 16⁰G, 20¹HY, 20²GS, 21²S, 25¹G, 24⁶GS, 20³GS, 24³GS, 24⁰G, 24³G,

	Starts	1st	2nd	3rd	Win & Pl
Hurdles	10	2	2	3	14489
Career Total	12	3	2	3	16676
112	1/03	Catt	3m1f110yE Hdl	GD	£3590
107	11/02	Hexm	2m4f110yE Hdl	HVY	£3003
109	3/02	Donc	2m110y H NHF	G-S	£2186
				Total win prize-money £8780

Going:	Sf: 1-2 GS: 0-4 Gd: 1-4 GF: - Fm: 0-0
Distance:	2m/2m3: 0-1 2m4-2m7: 1-4 3m+: 1-5
Track:	LH: 2-9 RH: 0-1 Tight: 1-3 Gall: 0-3
Aids:	Bl: 0-1 Vi: 0-0 Tstrap: 0-0
Best Rating:	119 3/03 Newc 3m gd-sft Hdl

Fair novice hurdler; not a fluent jumper; game; stays 3m; acts on good ground or softer; has worn blinkers.

Silver Man

82   **46**

9-y-o gr g Silver Owl-What An Experience (Chance Meeting)
D C Turner Mrs M E Turner

Placings:P4   (1157)
2002/03: 21⁰PGF, 16⁴G,

	Starts	1st	2nd	3rd	Win & Pl
Chases	2	0	0	0	305
Career Total	2	0	0	0	305

Going:	Sf: 0-0 GS: 0-0 Gd: 0-1 GF: - Fm: 0-1
Distance:	2m/2m3: 0-1 2m4-2m7: 0-1 3m+: 0-0
Track:	LH: 0-2 RH: 0-0 Tight: 0-2 Gall: 0-0
Aids:	Bl: 0-0 Vi: 0-0 Tstrap: 0-0
Best Rating:	0 9/02 NAbb 2m110y good Ch

Silver Pot Black

8-y-o gr g Ron s Victory (USA)-Haunting (Lord Gayle (USA))
Miss L Day William John Day

Placings:543/F2000/0-P   (0145)
2002/03: 24⁰PGF,

	Starts	1st	2nd	3rd	Win & Pl
Chases	1	0	0	0	
Career Total	10	0	1	1	891

| Going: | Sf: 0-0 GS: 0-0 Gd: 0-0 GF: - Fm: 0-1 |

Distance: 2m/2m3: 0-0 2m4-2m7: 0-0 3m+: 0-1
Track: LH: 0-1 RH: 0-0 Tight: 0-0 Gall: 0-0
Aids: Bl: 0-0 Vi: 0-0 Tstrap: 0-0
Best Rating: 102 3/00 Tntn 3m110y good Hdl

Silver Risks (FR)
80   **57**
5-y-o gr m Take Risks (FR)-Turkansa (FR) (Baby Turk)
D R Gandolfo Starlight Racing

Placings:0-0000 (2372)
2002/03: 17⁹G, 20⁹GF, 20⁹G, 16⁸S,

	Starts	1st	2nd	3rd	Win & Pl
Hurdles	4	0	0	0	
Career Total	5	0	0	0	

Going: Sf: 0-1 GS: 0-0 Gd: 0-2 GF: - Fm: 0-1
Distance: 2m/2m3: 0-2 2m4-2m7: 0-2 3m+: 0-0
Track: LH: 0-4 RH: 0-0 Tight: 0-2 Gall: 0-0
Aids: Bl: 0-1 Vi: 0-0 Tstrap: 0-0
Best Rating: 51 6/02 NAbb 2m1f good Hdl

Silver Sleeve (IRE)
97(95c)   (90c)**65**
11-y-o b g Taufan (USA)-Sable Coated (Caerleon (USA))
Mrs H M Bridges Mrs H M Bridges

Placings:F0002035/4124430/P/0060-6UP40423040 (4119)
2002/03: 19⁶G, 20⁴GF, 19⁶GF, 174⁻F, 16⁹G, 174⁻S, 20²HY, 173⁻HY, 18⁹S, 174⁻S, 16⁹G,

	Starts	1st	2nd	3rd	Win & Pl
Hurdles	9	0	1	1	1281
Chases	2	0	0	0	0
Career Total	31	1	3	3	5284
84 7/96 Strf	2m3f	E(0-100)HHdl	G-F		£2178

Total win prize-money £2178

Going: Sf: 0-5 GS: 0-0 Gd: 0-3 GF: - Fm: 0-3
Distance: 2m/2m3: 0-7 2m4-2m7: 0-4 3m+: 0-0
Track: LH: 0-2 RH: 0-9 Tight: 0-3 Gall: 0-2
Aids: Bl: 0-4 Vi: 0-0 Tstrap: 0-0
Best Rating: 90 3/02 Extr 2m3f110y good Ch

Plating-class hurdler, a hard ride.

Silver Socks
84(112h)   (111h)**95**
6-y-o gr g Petong-Tasmim (Be My Guest (USA))
M W Easterby Mrs Angela K Geraghty

Placings:054/313143-3P (1978)
2002/03: 16³G, 16⁵HY,

	Starts	1st	2nd	3rd	Win & Pl
Chases	2	0	0	1	588
Career Total	11	2	0	4	8675
110 1/02 Muss	2m	E Hdl	GD		£2730
111 12/01 Hayd	2m	E(0-105)HHdl	SFT		£3052

Total win prize-money £5782

Going: Sf: 0-1 GS: 0-0 Gd: 0-1 GF: - Fm: 0-0
Distance: 2m/2m3: 0-2 2m4-2m7: 0-0 3m+: 0-0
Track: LH: 0-2 RH: 0-0 Tight: 0-0 Gall: 0-0
Aids: Bl: 0-2 Vi: 0-0 Tstrap: 0-0
Best Rating: 112 2/02 Newc 2m soft Hdl

Moderate hurdler; suited by soft ground; has worn blinkers.

Silver Steel
92(111h)   (123h)**126**
8-y-o b g Shernazar-Yldizlar (Star Appeal)
C Roche J P McManus

Placings:524/32314/5F11F1U53-1205 (4172)
2002/03: 24¹S, 22²S, 24⁹G, 34⁵S,

	Starts	1st	2nd	3rd	Win & Pl
Hurdles	2	1	1	0	14736
Chases	2	0	0	0	2500
Career Total	21	5	3	3	56434
123 11/02 Navn	3m	HHdl	SFT	£13558
127 1/02 Leop	2m5f	Ch	Y-S	£11963
127 1/01 Navn	2m4f	Ch	YLD	£7790
121 12/01 Thur	3m	Ch	HVY	£6677
120 12/00 Leop	2m2f	Hdl	SH	£5520

Total win prize-money £45508

Going: Sf: 1-3 GS: 0-0 Gd: 0-1 GF: - Fm: 0-0
Distance: 2m/2m3: 0-0 2m4-2m7: 0-1 3m+: 1-3
Track: LH: 1-3 RH: 0-0 Tight: 0-0 Gall: 0-1
Aids: Bl: 0-0 Vi: 0-0 Tstrap: 0-0
Best Rating: 127 1/02 Leop 2m5f yld-sft Ch

Useful Irish chaser/hurdler; stays 4m, but effective over shorter; suited by soft ground.

Silver Streak (IRE)
142
9-y-o gr g Roselier (FR)-Vulcash (IRE) (Callernish)
J T Gifford Mrs Timothy Pilkington

Placings:2/422013/33P5/52411P2-P (1679)
2002/03: 21²GF,

	Starts	1st	2nd	3rd	Win & Pl
Hurdles	1	0	0	0	
Career Total	19	3	5	3	32808
132 12/01 Chel	3m1f110yB Ch	GD	£12018
120 11/01 Weth	3m1f D Ch	GD	£4069
128 3/00 Sand	2m4f110yD Hdl	GD	£4426

Total win prize-money £20515

Going: Sf: 0-0 GS: 0-0 Gd: 0-0 GF: - Fm: 0-0
Distance: 2m/2m3: 0-0 2m4-2m7: 0-1 3m+: 0-0
Track: LH: 0-1 RH: 0-0 Tight: 0-0 Gall: 0-1
Aids: Bl: 0-0 Vi: 0-0 Tstrap: 0-0
Best Rating: 132 12/01 Chel 3m1f110y good Ch

A winner over hurdles, but struggled in better company over fences until hitting form late in 2001. Stays three miles plus and best on good ground.

Silver Stud (FR)
99   **107**
4-y-o b c Double Bed (FR)-Pointe Argentee (Pas De Seul)
F Doumen Mme M-J Levesque

Placings:0322026F (3590)
2002/03: 18⁰S, 15³VS, 16²VS, 18²HY, 18⁰HY, 16²HY, 18⁶VS, 19⁶VS,

	Starts	1st	2nd	3rd	Win & Pl
Hurdles	8	0	3	1	21596
Career Total	8	0	3	1	21596

Going: Sf: 0-4 GS: 0-0 Gd: 0-0 GF: - Fm: 0-0
Distance: 2m/2m3: 0-6 2m4-2m7: 0-1 3m+: 0-0
Track: LH: 0-2 RH: 0-2 Tight: 0-1 Gall: 0-0
Aids: Bl: 0-0 Vi: 0-0 Tstrap: 0-0
Best Rating: 100 2/03 Sand 2m110y heavy Hdl

Fair French juvenile; runner-up at Sandown in February; acts well on soft ground.

Silver Tarn (IRE)
88   **68**
5-y-o gr/ro m Parthian Springs-Mary Kate (Callernish)
R H Alner Mr & Mrs D Bennett

Placings:PP4 (4270)
2002/03: 20⁰HY, 19⁰G, 164⁻G,

	Starts	1st	2nd	3rd	Win & Pl
Hurdles	3	0	0	0	389
Career Total	3	0	0	0	389

Going: Sf: 0-1 GS: 0-0 Gd: 0-2 GF: - Fm: 0-0
Distance: 2m/2m3: 0-1 2m4-2m7: 0-2 3m+: 0-0
Track: LH: 0-2 RH: 0-1 Tight: 0-0 Gall: 0-0
Aids: Bl: 0-0 Vi: 0-0 Tstrap: 0-0
Best Rating: 68 3/03 Chep 2m110y good Hdl

A half-brother to the moderate winning staying chaser Mr Timbrology. should do better over fences.

Silver Thyne (IRE)
94   **81**
11-y-o br g Good Thyne (USA)-Fitz s Buck (Master Buck)
R J Hodges R A Ford

Placings:145012P2/1P/2 (0105)
2002/03: 16²GF,

	Starts	1st	2nd	3rd	Win & Pl
Hurdles	1	0	1	0	613
Career Total	11	3	3	6	16946
120 5/99 Strf	2m110y C(0-135)HHdl	GD	£5790
123 3/97 Wwck	2m4f110yE Hdl	GD	£2197
114 5/96 NAbb	2m1f H NHF	SFT	£1369

Total win prize-money £9357

Going: Sf: 0-0 GS: 0-0 Gd: 0-0 GF: - Fm: 0-1
Distance: 2m/2m3: 0-1 2m4-2m7: 0-0 3m+: 0-0
Track: LH: 0-0 RH: 0-1 Tight: 0-0 Gall: 0-0
Aids: Bl: 0-0 Vi: 0-0 Tstrap: 0-0
Best Rating: 123 3/97 Uttx 2m4f110y gd-fm Hdl

One-time decent hurdler, off for three years and runner-up in a seller on his return.

Silver Tonic
65   **55**
7-y-o gr g Petong-Princess Eurolink (Be My Guest (USA))
J M Bradley (A G Hobbs 1/8) Brian Henderson

Placings:P0P (2445)
2002/03: 22²S, 16⁰G, 16⁰PG,

	Starts	1st	2nd	3rd	Win & Pl
Hurdles	3	0	0	0	
Career Total	3	0	0	0	

Going: Sf: 0-1 GS: 0-0 Gd: 0-2 GF: - Fm: 0-0
Distance: 2m/2m3: 0-2 2m4-2m7: 0-1 3m+: 0-0
Track: LH: 0-1 RH: 0-2 Tight: 0-1 Gall: 0-0
Aids: Bl: 0-0 Vi: 0-0 Tstrap: 0-0
Best Rating: 55 11/02 Ludl 2m good Hdl

Silvertown
109   **130**
8-y-o b g Danehill (USA)-Docklands (USA) (Theatrical)
L Lungo R J Gilbert & Sw Transport (swindon) Ltd

Placings:5106P-030111 (4663)
2002/03: 19³S, 21³S, 19⁰GS, 20¹G, 171⁻GF, 17¹GF,

	Starts	1st	2nd	3rd	Win & Pl
Hurdles	6	3	0	1	16389

Career Total	11	4	0	1	19357
130 4/03 Carl 2m1f	D(0-120)HHdl			G-F	£4599
120 4/03 Hrfd 2m1f	D(0-115)HHdl			G-F	£7454
120 3/03 Carl 2m4f	E(0-110)HHdl			GD	£3864
105 5/01 Newc 2m	E Hdl			G-F	£2968
				Total win prize-money	£18885

Going: Sf: 0-2 GS: 0-1 Gd: 1-1 GF: - Fm: 2-2
Distance: 2m/2m3: 2-2 2m4-2m7: 1-4 3m+: 0-0
Track: LH: 0-3 RH: 3-3 Tight: 0-0 Gall: 0-0
Aids: Bl: 0-0 Vi: 0-0 Tstrap: 0-0
Best Rating: 130 4/03 Carl 2m1f gd-fm Hdl

Useful hurdler; in fine form in the spring of 2003, completing a hat-trick in handicap hurdles and winning another two on the Flat; stays two and a half miles and suited by fast ground; likes to dominate.

Simber Hill (IRE)

111   **122**

9-y-o ch g Phardante (FR)-Princess Wager (Pollerton)
P J Hobbs (A King 14/5) C de P Berry, C Moore, P Rowe

Placings:105/25213/3F333545-31132215F3   (4753)
2002/03: 25⁵GS, 25³G, 24¹G, 21⁴GF, 23³GF, 26²G, 25²G, 24¹GF, 24⁵S, 24⁴F, 24³G,

	Starts	1st	2nd	3rd	Win & Pl
Chases	11	3	2	3	22034
Career Total	26	5	4	8	32165
122 10/02 Tntn 3m	D Ch			G-F	£5362
121 7/02 Uttx 3m	D(0-120)HCh			G-F	£6909
109 7/02 Strf 3m	E(0-110)HCh			GD	£4186
108 3/00 Newb 3m110y	D Hdl			G-F	£3770
108 12/98 Bang 2m1f	H NHF			G-S	£1266
				Total win prize-money	£21495

Going: Sf: 0-1 GS: 0-1 Gd: 1-5 GF: - Fm: 2-4
Distance: 2m/2m3: 0-0 2m4-2m7: 0-0 3m+: 3-11
Track: LH: 2-4 RH: 1-7 Tight: 2-4 Gall: 0-0
Aids: Bl: 2-9 Vi: 0-0 Tstrap: 0-0
Best Rating: 122 10/02 Tntn 3m gd-fm Ch

Fair chaser; stays three miles; inclined to be let down by his jumping; best on a sound surface; wears blinkers.

Simons Castle (IRE)

95(84h)   (54h)**87**

10-y-o b g Scenic-Miss Toot (Ardross)
J D Frost Ides Of March Racing

Placings:13/202123/13630/3U0P/542623-05   (0681)
2002/03: 19⁹G, 22⁵GF,

	Starts	1st	2nd	3rd	Win & Pl
Hurdles	1	0	0	0	0
Chases	1	0	0	0	0
Career Total	25	3	5	6	21664
133 10/98 Towc 2m	C(0-135)HHdl			G-S	£4096
124 2/98 Ling 2m110y	F Hdl			G-S	£2262
115 1/97 Punc 2m	NHF			YLD	£3051
				Total win prize-money	£9410

Going: Sf: 0-0 GS: 0-0 Gd: 0-1 GF: - Fm: 0-1
Distance: 2m/2m3: 0-0 2m4-2m7: 0-2 3m+: 0-0
Track: LH: 0-1 RH: 0-1 Tight: 0-1 Gall: 0-0
Aids: Bl: 0-0 Vi: 0-0 Tstrap: 0-0
Best Rating: 133 10/98 Towc 2m gd-sft Hdl

Plating-class chaser; appreciates cut in the ground.

Simoski

88   **69+**

6-y-o b g Petoski-Miss Simone (Ile De Bourbon (USA))
N A Twiston-Davies N A Twiston-Davies

Placings:0/0-03FU0   (2943)
2002/03: 16⁹GF, 19³GF, 19⁵G, 16¹⁰G, 16⁰S,

	Starts	1st	2nd	3rd	Win & Pl
Hurdles	4	0	0	1	432
Chases	1	0	0	0	0
Career Total	7	0	0	1	432

Going: Sf: 0-1 GS: 0-0 Gd: 0-2 GF: - Fm: 0-2
Distance: 2m/2m3: 0-3 2m4-2m7: 0-2 3m+: 0-0
Track: LH: 0-1 RH: 0-4 Tight: 0-1 Gall: 0-0
Aids: Bl: 0-0 Vi: 0-0 Tstrap: 0-0
Best Rating: 72 10/02 Hrfd 2m3f110y gd-fm Hdl

Simply Better

10-y-o b g Roscoe Blake-Pure-Lite (Imperial Fling (USA))
Mrs G M Shail Carl Spate

Placings:4/46/000/0   (0029)
2002/03: 21⁰GF,

	Starts	1st	2nd	3rd	Win & Pl
Chases	1	0	0	0	
Career Total	7	0	0	0	309

Going: Sf: 0-0 GS: 0-0 Gd: 0-0 GF: - Fm: 0-1
Distance: 2m/2m3: 0-0 2m4-2m7: 0-1 3m+: 0-0
Track: LH: 0-1 RH: 0-0 Tight: 0-0 Gall: 0-1
Aids: Bl: 0-0 Vi: 0-0 Tstrap: 0-0
Best Rating: 79 6/99 Tipp 2m1f good NHF

Simply Da Best (IRE)

107

5-y-o b g Lake Coniston (IRE)-Sakala (NZ) (Gold And Ivory (USA))
Mrs John Harrington (S J Magnier 26/9) Joseph G Rafferty

Placings:1-65   (4658a)
2002/03: 16⁶GF, 16⁵GF,

	Starts	1st	2nd	3rd	Win & Pl
NH Flat	2	0	0	0	
Career Total	3	1	0	0	1590
100 3/02 Hntg 2m110y	H NHF			G-F	£1590
				Total win prize-money	£1590

Going: Sf: 0-0 GS: 0-0 Gd: 0-0 GF: - Fm: 0-2
Distance: 2m/2m3: 0-2 2m4-2m7: 0-0 3m+: 0-0
Track: LH: 0-0 RH: 0-2 Tight: 0-0 Gall: 0-0
Aids: Bl: 0-0 Vi: 0-0 Tstrap: 0-1
Best Rating: 107 4/03 Fair 2m gd-fm NHF

Sprint-bred. Landed an old fashioned gamble in easy fashion on his debut at Huntingdon in March 2002. Held since.

Simply Remy

86   **56**

5-y-o ch g Chaddleworth (IRE)-Exemplaire (FR) (Polish Precedent (USA))
John Berry Simply 2000

Placings:0   (4635)
2002/03: 19⁰GF,

	Starts	1st	2nd	3rd	Win & Pl
Hurdles	1	0	0	0	
Career Total	1	0	0	0	

Going: Sf: 0-0 GS: 0-0 Gd: 0-0 GF: - Fm: 0-1
Distance: 2m/2m3: 0-1 2m4-2m7: 0-0 3m+: 0-0
Track: LH: 0-1 RH: 0-0 Tight: 0-1 Gall: 0-0
Aids: Bl: 0-0 Vi: 0-0 Tstrap: 0-0
Best Rating: 56 4/03 Strf 2m3f gd-fm Hdl

Simply Supreme (IRE)

110   **133+**

6-y-o b g Supreme Leader-Some Gift (Avocat)
Mrs S J Smith Trevor Hemmings

Placings:130-111244   (4473)
2002/03: 22¹S, 20¹S, 20¹S, 20²GS, 23⁴G, 24⁴G,

	Starts	1st	2nd	3rd	Win & Pl
Hurdles	6	3	1	0	21791
Career Total	9	4	1	1	23872
133 12/02 Hayd 2m4f	D Hdl			SFT	£4160
133 11/02 Hayd 2m4f	D Hdl			SFT	£3835
122 11/02 Kels 2m6f110y	E Hdl			SFT	£3588
111 12/01 Bang 2m1f	H Hdl			G-S	£1746
				Total win prize-money	£13330

Going: Sf: 3-3 GS: 0-1 Gd: 0-2 GF: - Fm: 0-0
Distance: 2m/2m3: 0-0 2m4-2m7: 3-4 3m+: 0-2
Track: LH: 3-6 RH: 0-0 Tight: 1-2 Gall: 0-0
Aids: Bl: 0-0 Vi: 0-0 Tstrap: 0-0
Best Rating: 133 12/02 Hayd 2m4f soft Hdl

Bumper winner; won his first three starts over hurdles, two over the brush hurdles at Haydock; stays two and a half miles; effective in soft ground; front-runner; will make a chaser.

Simply The One (IRE)

77(93h)   **71d**

6-y-o ch g Simply Great (FR)-Lady Mearlane (Giolla Mear)
Mrs H Dalton A J Brazier

Placings:454-25FPP   (4707)
2002/03: 16⁴GS, 24²GS, 19⁵S, 24⁴G, 21²G, 26⁹G,

	Starts	1st	2nd	3rd	Win & Pl
Hurdles	1	0	0	0	0
Chases	5	0	1	0	1264
Career Total	8	0	1	0	1617

Going: Sf: 0-1 GS: 0-2 Gd: 0-3 GF: - Fm: 0-0
Distance: 2m/2m3: 0-2 2m4-2m7: 0-1 3m+: 0-3
Track: LH: 0-3 RH: 0-3 Tight: 0-1 Gall: 0-2
Aids: Bl: 0-2 Vi: 0-0 Tstrap: 0-0
Best Rating: 80 12/01 Newb 2m3f gd-sft Hdl

Moderate novice chaser; stays three miles; acts on good to soft ground.

Sinalco (USA)

76f   **70f**

5-y-o b g Quest For Fame-Sin Lucha (USA) (Northfields (USA))
Mrs L B Normile A K Collins

Placings:605   (4039)
2002/03: 16⁸HY, 16⁰G, 16⁵S,

	Starts	1st	2nd	3rd	Win & Pl
NH Flat	3	0	0	0	0
Career Total	3	0	0	0	0

Going: Sf: 0-2 GS: 0-0 Gd: 0-1 GF: - Fm: 0-0

Distance: 2m/2m3: 0-3 2m4-2m7: 0-0 3m+: 0-0
Track: LH: 0-3 RH: 0-0 Tight: 0-1 Gall: 0-0
Aids: Bl: 0-0 Vi: 0-0 Tstrap: 0-0
Best Rating: 70 3/03 Ayr 2m soft NHF

Sing Solo (IRE)
(76h) **106**

8-y-o ch g Be My Native (USA)-Caesonia (Buckskin (FR))
P J Hobbs T A Curran

Placings:5240/3P0/B1FP0-02 (1462)
2002/03: 19⁰GF, 21²F,

	Starts	1st	2nd	3rd	Win & Pl
Chases	2	0	1	0	1491
Career Total	14	1	2	1	8107
106 11/01 Tntn	2m3f		E(0-105)HCh		£5398
Total win prize-money £5398					

Going: Sf: 0-0 GS: 0-0 Gd: 0-0 GF: - Fm: 0-2
Distance: 2m/2m3: 0-1 2m4-2m7: 0-1 3m+: 0-0
Track: LH: 0-0 RH: 0-2 Tight: 0-0 Gall: 0-0
Aids: Bl: 0-0 Vi: 0-0 Tstrap: 0-0
Best Rating: 106 11/01 Tntn 2m3f good Ch

Modest chaser, stays two miles-three, acts on good ground. Has raced mostly on right-handed tracks.

Singing Sand
99 **105**

13-y-o b g Orchestra-Noss Head (New Brig)
P Monteith Hamilton House Limited

Placings:06/036203/033F1122/23P3P4/0/52F33222/03531 U6P4/030121F32-5665 (1306)
2002/03: 20⁵GF, 17⁶GS, 17⁶GF, 16⁵GF,

	Starts	1st	2nd	3rd	Win & Pl
Chases	4	0	0	0	0
Career Total	53	5	10	12	32994
105 9/01 Uttx	2m	F(0-100)HCh	G-F	£2933
102 7/01 MRas	2m1f110yF(0-110)HCh	GD	£3607
101 10/00 Kels	2m1f	E(0-115)HCh	SFT	£3250
128 3/97 Ayr	2m	E Ch	SFT	£3119
100 2/97 Muss	2m	E(0-100)HCh	G-F	£2976
Total win prize-money £15886				

Going: Sf: 0-0 GS: 0-1 Gd: 0-0 GF: - Fm: 0-3
Distance: 2m/2m3: 0-3 2m4-2m7: 0-1 3m+: 0-0
Track: LH: 0-1 RH: 0-3 Tight: 0-2 Gall: 0-0
Aids: Bl: 0-0 Vi: 0-0 Tstrap: 0-0
Best Rating: 128 4/97 Ayr 2m good Ch

He is an effective sort in modest handicap chases over two miles in the north, but is no world-beater and is not too easy to predict.

Single Sourcing (IRE)
107 **98**

12-y-o b g Good Thyne (USA)-Lady Albron (Royal Match)
A C Whillans G L Harrow

Placings:142P/P/P1PP3P/F304241/FPPP3/41146-3 (4036)
2002/03: 25³S,

	Starts	1st	2nd	3rd	Win & Pl
Chases	1	0	0	1	933
Career Total	28	5	2	4	29543
101 11/01 Kels	3m4f	F(0-110)HCh	G-S	£4212
98 10/01 Aint	3m1f	F(0-105)HCh	GD	£5232
102 1/99 Ayr	2m5f110yC HCh	HVY	£10480
94 5/97 Uttx	2m	E Hdl	G-S	£2389
103 5/95 Uttx	2m	H NHF	G-F	£1805

Total win prize-money £24120

Going: Sf: 0-1 GS: 0-0 Gd: 0-0 GF: - Fm: 0-0
Distance: 2m/2m3: 0-0 2m4-2m7: 0-0 3m+: 0-1
Track: LH: 0-1 RH: 0-0 Tight: 0-0 Gall: 0-0
Aids: Bl: 0-0 Vi: 0-0 Tstrap: 0-0
Best Rating: 108 10/95 Newb 2m110y good NHF

Modest staying handicap chaser; took a veterans' race at Cartmel in May; stays extremely well; acts on most types of ground; has broken blood vessels.

Single Trigger (IRE)
80f **75f**

5-y-o ch m Ela-Mana-Mou-Tycoon Aly (IRE) (Last Tycoon)
H E Haynes Miss Sally R Haynes

Placings:0006 (4224)
2002/03: 16⁸GF, 16⁶G, 16⁰S, 14⁸GF,

	Starts	1st	2nd	3rd	Win & Pl
NH Flat	4	0	0	0	0
Career Total	4	0	0	0	0

Going: Sf: 0-1 GS: 0-0 Gd: 0-0 GF: 0-1 Fm: 0-2
Distance: 2m/2m3: 0-3 2m4-2m7: 0-0 3m+: 0-1
Track: LH: 0-2 RH: 0-0 Tight: 0-0 Gall: 0-0
Aids: Bl: 0-1 Vi: 0-1 Tstrap: 0-1
Best Rating: 82 3/03 Hrfd 1m6f gd-fm NHF

Singoverthesea
7-y-o b g Sea Raven (IRE)-Pentland Beauty (Remainder Man)
J R Jenkins R B Hill

Placings:U (3742)
2002/03: 16⁰G,

	Starts	1st	2nd	3rd	Win & Pl
Hurdles	1	0	0	0	
Career Total	1	0	0	0	

Going: Sf: 0-0 GS: 0-0 Gd: 0-0 GF: 0-1 Fm: 0-0
Distance: 2m/2m3: 0-1 2m4-2m7: 0-0 3m+: 0-0
Track: LH: 0-0 RH: 0-1 Tight: 0-0 Gall: 0-1
Aids: Bl: 0-0 Vi: 0-0 Tstrap: 0-0
Best Rating: 0 2/03 Hntg 2m110y good Hdl

Sinnerman (IRE)
73 **33**

7-y-o gr g Roselier (FR)-Madam Beau (Le Tricolore)
C J Hemsley Keith McKay

Placings:0 (4311)
2002/03: 21⁰G,

	Starts	1st	2nd	3rd	Win & Pl
Hurdles	1	0	0	0	
Career Total	1	0	0	0	

Going: Sf: 0-0 GS: 0-0 Gd: 0-0 GF: 0-1 Fm: 0-0
Distance: 2m/2m3: 0-0 2m4-2m7: 0-1 3m+: 0-0
Track: LH: 0-1 RH: 0-0 Tight: 0-0 Gall: 0-1
Aids: Bl: 0-0 Vi: 0-0 Tstrap: 0-0
Best Rating: 33 3/03 Newb 2m5f good Hdl

Sip Of Brandy (IRE)
10-y-o ch g Sharp Charter-Manhattan Brandy (Frankincense)

W J G Hughes Greenacre Racing Partnership Ltd

Placings:P44PP/PP/1 (4541)
2002/03: 24¹G,

	Starts	1st	2nd	3rd	Win & Pl
Chases	1	1	0	0	2968
Career Total	8	1	0	0	3161
95 4/03 Ludl	3m	H Ch	GD	£2968
Total win prize-money £2968				

Going: Sf: 0-0 GS: 0-0 Gd: 1-1 GF: - Fm: 0-0
Distance: 2m/2m3: 0-0 2m4-2m7: 0-0 3m+: 1-1
Track: LH: 1-1 RH: 1-1 Tight: 1-1 Gall: 0-0
Aids: Bl: 0-0 Vi: 0-0 Tstrap: 0-0
Best Rating: 95 4/03 Ludl 3m good Ch

Sprang 33/1 shock when landing modest three mile hunter chase at Ludlow April 2003.

Sir Albert (GER)
87 **103+**

4-y-o b c Dashing Blade-Santa Augusta (Esclavo (FR))
C Von Der Recke Quadriga Gmbh

Placings:12 (0797)
2002/03: 17⁷GS, 16²S,

	Starts	1st	2nd	3rd	Win & Pl
Hurdles	2	1	1	0	4916
Career Total	2	1	1	0	4916
110 7/02 MRas	2m1f110yD Hdl	G-S	£4241
Total win prize-money £4241				

Going: Sf: 0-1 GS: 1-1 Gd: 0-0 GF: - Fm: 0-0
Distance: 2m/2m3: 1-2 2m4-2m7: 0-0 3m+: 0-0
Track: LH: 0-0 RH: 1-1 Tight: 1-1 Gall: 0-0
Aids: Bl: 0-0 Vi: 0-0 Tstrap: 0-0
Best Rating: 110 7/02 MRas 2m1f110y gd-sft Hdl

German-trained colt, easy winner of an early-season juvenile hurdle at Market Rasen.

Sir Alfred
100 **95**

4-y-o b g Royal Academy (USA)-Magnificent Star (USA) (Silver Hawk (USA))
A King (B R Millman 15/8) W A Harrison-Allan & D Bellamy

Placings:P514 (4559)
2002/03: 16⁸S, 16⁵G, 16¹GF, 16⁴G,

	Starts	1st	2nd	3rd	Win & Pl
Hurdles	4	1	0	0	5497
Career Total	4	1	0	0	5497
95 3/03 Hayd	2m	D Hdl	G-F	£4927
Total win prize-money £4927				

Going: Sf: 0-0 GS: 0-0 Gd: 0-2 GF: - Fm: 1-1
Distance: 2m/2m3: 1-4 2m4-2m7: 0-0 3m+: 0-0
Track: LH: 1-3 RH: 0-1 Tight: 0-0 Gall: 0-1
Aids: Bl: 0-0 Vi: 0-0 Tstrap: 0-0
Best Rating: 95 3/03 Hayd 2m gd-fm Hdl

Modest juvenile hurdler; fair middle-distance handicapper on the Flat; won a novice event on fast ground at Haydock in March 2003.

Sir Bob (IRE)
108 **119**

11-y-o br g Aristocracy-Wilden (Will Somers)
Mrs H Dalton (K C Bailey 4/5) Mrs Lucia Farmer

Placings:02/4200/313112/F342/2U5/124P4-P23 (3820)
2002/03: 26⁸G, 24²GS, 23⁸GS,

Column 1

	Starts	1st	2nd	3rd	Win & Pl
Chases	3	0	1	1	2770
Career Total	27	4	7	4	25351

128	11/01	Towc	2m6f	D Ch	SFT	£5304
128	3/99	Carl	3m110y	E Hdl	SFT	£2318
128	2/99	Carl	3m110y	E Hdl	HVY	£2472
108	11/98	Newc	3m	E Hdl	G-S	£2379

Total win prize-money £12473

Going:	Sf: 0-0 GS: 0-2 Gd: 0-1 GF: - Fm: 0-0
Distance:	2m/2m3: 0-0 2m4-2m7: 0-0 3m+: 0-3
Track:	LH: 0-2 RH: 0-1 Tight: 0-1 Gall: 0-0
Aids:	Bl: 0-1 Vi: 0-0 Tstrap: 0-0
Best Rating:	128 11/01 Towc 2m6f soft Ch

Fair chaser; stays well; goes well in soft ground; has worn blinkers.

Sir Cumference

107   100

7-y-o b g Sir Harry Lewis (USA)-Puki Puki (Roselier (FR))
Miss H C Knight   Richard Lissack

Placings:6P511   (4636)
2002/03: 23⁶GS, 24⁰PG, 24⁵GS, 24¹G, 24¹G,

	Starts	1st	2nd	3rd	Win & Pl
Chases	5	2	0	0	8974
Career Total	5	2	0	0	8974

100	4/03	Strf	3m	F(0-100)HCh	GD	£3514
92	4/03	Ludl	3m	D(0-110)HCh	GD	£5460

Total win prize-money £8974

Going:	Sf: 0-0 GS: 0-2 Gd: 2-3 GF: - Fm: 0-0
Distance:	2m/2m3: 0-0 2m4-2m7: 0-0 3m+: 2-5
Track:	LH: 1-2 RH: 1-3 Tight: 2-3 Gall: 0-1
Aids:	Bl: 0-0 Vi: 0-0 Tstrap: 0-0
Best Rating:	100 4/03 Strf 3m good Ch

Moderate chaser; dual point-to-point winner; won 3m novices handicap chase at Ludlow April 2003; followed up in Class F handicap at Stratford next time; considered best suited to left-handed tracks; likes good ground.

Sir Edward Burrow (IRE)

101   93

5-y-o b g Distinctly North (USA)-Alalja (IRE) (Entitled)
W Storey   W Storey

Placings:450-P6F   (4168)
2002/03: 19⁰GS, 16⁶GS, 20⁰FGS,

	Starts	1st	2nd	3rd	Win & Pl
Hurdles	3	0	0	0	0
Career Total	6	0	0	0	308

Going:	Sf: 0-0 GS: 0-3 Gd: 0-0 GF: - Fm: 0-0
Distance:	2m/2m3: 0-2 2m4-2m7: 0-1 3m+: 0-0
Track:	LH: 0-3 RH: 0-0 Tight: 0-1 Gall: 0-1
Aids:	Bl: 0-0 Vi: 0-0 Tstrap: 0-0
Best Rating:	93 12/01 Weth 2m gd-sft Hdl

Sir Frosty

97   131

10-y-o b g Arctic Lord-Snowy Autumn (Deep Run)
B J M Ryall   J F Tucker

Placings:1341-11U   (4557)
2002/03: 32¹GS, 33¹S, 33⁰G,

	Starts	1st	2nd	3rd	Win & Pl
Chases	3	2	0	0	22923

Column 2

Career Total	7	4	0	1	33922

125	1/03	Chel	4m1f	B(0-145)HCh	SFT	£12620
131	12/02	Extr	4m	D(0-125)HCh	G-S	£10302
122	1/02	Tntn	3m3f	C(0-130)HCh	SFT	£7020
127	10/01	Hrfd	3m1f110yE Ch		SFT	£2941

Total win prize-money £32885

Going:	Sf: 1-1 GS: 1-1 Gd: 0-1 GF: - Fm: 0-0
Distance:	2m/2m3: 0-0 2m4-2m7: 0-0 3m+: 2-3
Track:	LH: 1-2 RH: 1-1 Tight: 0-0 Gall: 1-1
Aids:	Bl: 0-0 Vi: 0-0 Tstrap: 2-3
Best Rating:	131 12/02 Extr 4m gd-sft Ch

Fair chaser, stays 4m 1f; usually wears a tongue tie; goes well fresh; effective on soft ground.

Sir Hamelin (IRE)

80

6-y-o b g Hernando (FR)-Georgia Stephens (USA) (The Minstrel (CAN))
M C Pipe   A S Helaissi

Placings:P/4000-P   (0770)
2002/03: 20⁰GF,

	Starts	1st	2nd	3rd	Win & Pl
Hurdles	1	0	0	0	0
Career Total	6	0	0	0	0

Going:	Sf: 0-0 GS: 0-0 Gd: 0-0 GF: - Fm: 0-1
Distance:	2m/2m3: 0-0 2m4-2m7: 0-1 3m+: 0-0
Track:	LH: 0-1 RH: 0-0 Tight: 0-0 Gall: 0-0
Aids:	Bl: 0-0 Vi: 0-1 Tstrap: 0-1
Best Rating:	80 5/01 Sthl 2m firm Hdl

Sir Henbue

7-y-o ch g Henbit (USA)-Owena Deep (Deep Run)
Mark Campion   The Sir Henbue Partnership

Placings:PO-0P   (3938)
2002/03: 16⁰G, 21⁰GS,

	Starts	1st	2nd	3rd	Win & Pl
NH Flat	1	0	0	0	0
Hurdles	1	0	0	0	0
Career Total	4	0	0	0	

Going:	Sf: 0-0 GS: 0-1 Gd: 0-1 GF: - Fm: 0-0
Distance:	2m/2m3: 0-1 2m4-2m7: 0-1 3m+: 0-0
Track:	LH: 0-1 RH: 0-1 Tight: 0-2 Gall: 0-0
Aids:	Bl: 0-0 Vi: 0-0 Tstrap: 0-0
Best Rating:	63 7/01 Worc 2m good NHF

Sir Homo (IRE)

79   52

9-y-o b g Homo Sapien-Deise Lady (Le Bavard (FR))
E W Tuer   E Tuer

Placings:00660P/F0P-P0   (2697)
2002/03: 21⁰PS, 17⁰S,

	Starts	1st	2nd	3rd	Win & Pl
Hurdles	2	0	0	0	
Career Total	11	0	0	0	

Going:	Sf: 0-2 GS: 0-0 Gd: 0-0 GF: - Fm: 0-0
Distance:	2m/2m3: 0-1 2m4-2m7: 0-0 3m+: 0-0
Track:	LH: 0-2 RH: 0-0 Tight: 0-2 Gall: 0-0
Aids:	Bl: 0-0 Vi: 0-0 Tstrap: 0-0
Best Rating:	98 6/00 Naas 2m3f yield NHF

Column 3

Sir Lamb

104   98+

7-y-o gr g Rambo Dancer (CAN)-Caroline Lamb (Hotfoot)
Miss S E Hall   C Platts

Placings:130/02056-1   (0400)
2002/03: 20¹GF,

	Starts	1st	2nd	3rd	Win & Pl
Hurdles	1	1	0	0	2321
Career Total	9	2	1	1	5532

98	6/02	Hexm	2m4f110yE Hdl	G-F	£2320
109	10/00	Carl	2m1f	H NHF	G-S	£2023

Total win prize-money £4344

Going:	Sf: 0-0 GS: 0-0 Gd: 0-0 GF: - Fm: 1-1
Distance:	2m/2m3: 0-0 2m4-2m7: 1-1 3m+: 0-0
Track:	LH: 1-1 RH: 0-0 Tight: 0-0 Gall: 0-0
Aids:	Bl: 0-0 Vi: 1-1 Tstrap: 0-0
Best Rating:	109 10/00 Carl 2m1f gd-sft NHF

Moderate hurdler; stays two and a half miles; acts on good to soft ground; has looked less than keen on occasions..

Sir Mouse

91   94

7-y-o gr g Phardante (FR)-Place Stephanie (IRE) (Hatim (USA))
R Rowe   Capt A Pratt

Placings:2-3P   (4310)
2002/03: 20³S, 24⁰PG,

	Starts	1st	2nd	3rd	Win & Pl
Hurdles	2	0	0	1	514
Career Total	3	0	1	1	1196

Going:	Sf: 0-1 GS: 0-0 Gd: 0-1 GF: - Fm: 0-0
Distance:	2m/2m3: 0-0 2m4-2m7: 0-1 3m+: 0-1
Track:	LH: 0-1 RH: 0-0 Tight: 0-1 Gall: 0-1
Aids:	Bl: 0-0 Vi: 0-0 Tstrap: 0-0
Best Rating:	102 11/01 Font 2m4f gd-sft Hdl

Moderate novice hurdler; stays two and a half miles; should get further.

Sir Ninja (IRE)

76(86h)   (94h)74

6-y-o b g Turtle Island (IRE)-The Poachers Lady (IRE) (Salmon Leap (USA))
S Kirk (G Brown 28/5)   Hargood Limited

Placings:5003-55   (0370)
2002/03: 16⁶F, 16⁵S,

	Starts	1st	2nd	3rd	Win & Pl
Chases	2	0	0	0	0
Career Total	6	0	0	1	396

Going:	Sf: 0-1 GS: 0-0 Gd: 0-0 GF: - Fm: 0-1
Distance:	2m/2m3: 0-2 2m4-2m7: 0-0 3m+: 0-0
Track:	LH: 0-2 RH: 0-0 Tight: 0-1 Gall: 0-0
Aids:	Bl: 0-0 Vi: 0-0 Tstrap: 0-0
Best Rating:	94 4/02 Hexm 2m110y gd-fm Hdl

Useful ten-furlong handicapper on the Flat on his day. Has yet to show the same level of form over hurdles.

Sir Norman

109(90h)   (78h)112

8-y-o b g Arctic Lord-Moy Ran Lady (Black Minstrel)
R D E Woodhouse   M A Sawyer

Placings: 0/000P6PP-5512232   (4712)
2002/03: 25⁵GF, 23⁵GF, 21¹S, 20²GS, 20²S, 16³G, 16²GF,

	Starts	1st	2nd	3rd	Win & Pl
Chases	7	1	3	1	9953
Career Total	15	1	3	1	9953
96	11/02 Ayr		2m5f1110yD(0-110)HCh	SFT	£5057
				Total win prize-money £5057	

Going: Sf: 1-2 GS: 0-1 Gd: 0-1 GF: - Fm: 0-3
Distance: 2m/2m3: 0-2 2m4-2m7: 1-3 3m+: 0-2
Track: LH: 1-5 RH: 0-1 Tight: 0-1 Gall: 0-1
Aids: Bl: 0-0 Vi: 0-0 Tstrap: 1-6
Best Rating: 96 11/02 Ayr 2m5f1110y soft Ch

Moderate chaser; little show in bumpers or over hurdles, but has done better over fences so far, winning at Ayr in November 2002 and Kelso in 2003; effective on decent ground.

Sir Pelinore

67   25

8-y-o b g Caerleon (USA)-Soemba (General Assembly (USA))
Mrs A M Woodrow Mrs Ann Woodrow

Placings: 0-PB0   (3926)
2002/03: 24⁵PGS, 16⁸G, 20⁹G,

	Starts	1st	2nd	3rd	Win & Pl
Hurdles	3	0	0	0	
Career Total	4	0	0	0	

Going: Sf: 0-0 GS: 0-1 Gd: 0-2 GF: - Fm: 0-0
Distance: 2m/2m3: 0-1 2m4-2m7: 0-1 3m+: 0-1
Track: LH: 0-0 RH: 0-3 Tight: 0-0 Gall: 0-2
Aids: Bl: 0-0 Vi: 0-0 Tstrap: 0-0
Best Rating: 55 5/01 Folk 2m1f110y gd-sft NHF

Sir Rembrandt (IRE)

118(106h)   (113h)148+

7-y-o b g Mandalus-Sue s A Lady (Le Moss)
R H Alner A & D Enterprises (poole) Ltd

Placings: 32021-11   (2465)
2002/03: 22¹GS, 25¹G,

	Starts	1st	2nd	3rd	Win & Pl
Chases	2	2	0	0	20220
Career Total	7	3	2	1	27197
148	12/02 Chel		3m1f110yA Ch	GD	£14500
130	11/02 Newb		2m6f110yD Ch	G-S	£5720
113	3/02 Newb		3m110y D Hdl	SFT	£4563
				Total win prize-money £24783	

Going: Sf: 0-0 GS: 1-1 Gd: 1-1 GF: - Fm: 0-0
Distance: 2m/2m3: 0-0 2m4-2m7: 1-1 3m+: 1-1
Track: LH: 2-2 RH: 0-0 Tight: 0-0 Gall: 2-2
Aids: Bl: 0-0 Vi: 0-0 Tstrap: 0-0
Best Rating: 148 12/02 Chel 3m1f110y good Ch

Very useful chaser; showed promise in bumpers; good stayer over hurdles, winning at Newbury. Made a successful chasing debut back at that venue in November in a decent race, then finished second in a Grade Two race at Cheltenham. Stays three miles one; acts on good or softer; he is making up into a fine chaser.

Sir Risky (IRE)

90(93h)   (78h)76

10-y-o b g Treasure Kay-Social Butterfly (USA) (Sir Ivor)
B J Llewelyn Robert Emmanuel

Placings: 00000000/410000P0006/504332665P03/5033400
/004600-460F344   (1617)

2002/03: 16⁴GF, 17⁶GF, 16⁹GF, 17⁶G, 17³F, 19⁴F, 16⁴F,

	Starts	1st	2nd	3rd	Win & Pl
Hurdles	2	0	0	1	332
Chases	5	0	0	0	545
Career Total	51	1	1	6	6933
84	5/98 Wxfd		2m	(0-116)Hdl	GD	£2978
				Total win prize-money £2978	

Going: Sf: 0-0 GS: 0-0 Gd: 0-1 GF: - Fm: 0-6
Distance: 2m/2m3: 0-7 2m4-2m7: 0-0 3m+: 0-0
Track: LH: 0-3 RH: 0-4 Tight: 0-2 Gall: 0-1
Aids: Bl: 0-0 Vi: 0-0 Tstrap: 0-0
Best Rating: 88 8/00 Wxfd 2m2f yield Hdl

Poor maiden hurdler and chaser.

Sir Robbo (IRE)

103   72

9-y-o b g Glacial Storm (USA)-Polly s Slipper (Pollerton)
N A Twiston-Davies Melton Pets Direct Ltd

Placings: U03/01P1005546/1/525FP-1P   (0215)
2002/03: 25¹GF, 25⁵G,

	Starts	1st	2nd	3rd	Win & Pl
Chases	2	1	0	0	3900
Career Total	21	4	1	4	14497
99	5/02 Hrfd		3m1f110yE(0-105)HCh	G-F	£3900
99	5/00 Hrfd		2m3f	D Ch	GD	£3900
96	10/99 Hrfd		2m1f	D Hdl	GF	£2892
96	6/99 Hrfd		2m1f	D Hdl	GD	£2801
				Total win prize-money £13493	

Going: Sf: 0-0 GS: 0-0 Gd: 0-1 GF: - Fm: 1-1
Distance: 2m/2m3: 0-0 2m4-2m7: 0-0 3m+: 1-2
Track: LH: 0-0 RH: 1-2 Tight: 0-0 Gall: 0-0
Aids: Bl: 0-0 Vi: 0-0 Tstrap: 0-0
Best Rating: 101 4/99 Towc 2m good NHF

All his wins over hurdles and fences have come at Hereford; stays three miles plus; likes fast ground.

Sir Rowland Hill (IRE)

101f   97f

4-y-o b g Kahyasi-Zaila (IRE) (Darshaan)
Ferdy Murphy A G Chappell

Placings: 21   (4593)
2002/03: 16²GF, 16¹G,

	Starts	1st	2nd	3rd	Win & Pl
NH Flat	2	1	1	0	2456
Career Total	2	1	1	0	2456
92	4/03 Hexm		2m110y H NHF	GD	£1904
				Total win prize-money £1904	

Going: Sf: 0-0 GS: 0-0 Gd: 0-1 GF: - Fm: 0-1
Distance: 2m/2m3: 1-2 2m4-2m7: 0-0 3m+: 0-0
Track: LH: 1-2 RH: 0-0 Tight: 0-0 Gall: 0-0
Aids: Bl: 0-0 Vi: 0-0 Tstrap: 0-0
Best Rating: 92 4/03 Hexm 2m110y good NHF

Useful bumper performer; has won one of his three starts so far, being placed on the other two occasions; effective at two miles, will stay further; acts on good ground.

Sir Ruscott (IRE)

107   100d

9-y-o b g Mister Lord (USA)-Clash Moss (Le Moss)
J R Norton Mrs Y Ruscoe

Placings: 0412505-010556   (4141)
2002/03: 25⁰G, 24¹S, 27⁰S, 24⁵HY, 24⁵GS, 24⁶S,

	Starts	1st	2nd	3rd	Win & Pl
Hurdles	6	1	0	0	3712
Career Total	13	2	1	0	6747
97	11/02 Leic	3m	D(0-115)HHdl	SFT	£3711
101	11/01 Sedg	3m3f110yE Hdl		SFT	£2338
				Total win prize-money £6050	

Going: Sf: 1-4 GS: 0-1 Gd: 0-1 GF: - Fm: 0-0
Distance: 2m/2m3: 0-0 2m4-2m7: 0-0 3m+: 1-6
Track: LH: 0-4 RH: 1-2 Tight: 0-2 Gall: 0-1
Aids: Bl: 0-0 Vi: 1-6 Tstrap: 0-0
Best Rating: 101 12/01 Hexm 3m soft Hdl

Modest hurdler, stays very well and appreciates soft ground. Winner at Leicester in December but is unreliable.

Sir Storm (IRE)

109(110h)   (114h)122d

7-y-o b g Ore-Yonder Bay (IRE) (Trimmingham)
G M Moore J R F (management Consultants) Ltd

Placings: 301P2P-2123235   (3835)
2002/03: 17²S, 16¹HY, 20⁴G, 16³G, 16²GH, 16³HY, 16⁵G,

	Starts	1st	2nd	3rd	Win & Pl
Chases	7	1	3	2	15215
Career Total	13	2	4	3	19229
109	11/02 Weth	2m	D(0-110)HCh	HVY	£5092
114	11/01 Bang	2m1f	E Hdl	G-S	£2828
				Total win prize-money £7921	

Going: Sf: 1-4 GS: 0-0 Gd: 0-3 GF: - Fm: 0-0
Distance: 2m/2m3: 1-6 2m4-2m7: 0-1 3m+: 0-0
Track: LH: 1-7 RH: 0-0 Tight: 0-1 Gall: 0-1
Aids: Bl: 0-0 Vi: 1-6 Tstrap: 0-0
Best Rating: 122 12/02 Hayd 2m good Ch

Fair novice chaser; he took well to fences in the autumn of 2002, winning on heavy ground and running into a couple of top-class prospects otherwise; has been known to break blood vessels and well below form last two starts.

Sir Toby (IRE)

112   (86h)122

10-y-o bl g Strong Gale-Petite Deb (Cure The Blues (USA))
R Rowe Capt A Pratt

Placings: 0430/530/3F2-1114   (2729)
2002/03: 20¹GF, 20¹G, 20¹G, 20⁴GS,

	Starts	1st	2nd	3rd	Win & Pl
Chases	4	3	0	0	17741
Career Total	14	3	1	3	20952
122	11/02 Leic	2m4f110yC(0-130)HCh	GD	£8073
122	11/02 Kemp	2m4f110yD Ch	GD	£5316
107	10/02 Hntg	2m4f110y(0-105)HCh	G-F	£3536
				Total win prize-money £16926	

Going: Sf: 0-0 GS: 0-1 Gd: 2-2 GF: - Fm: 1-1
Distance: 2m/2m3: 0-0 2m4-2m7: 3-4 3m+: 0-0
Track: LH: 0-0 RH: 3-4 Tight: 0-0 Gall: 1-1
Aids: Bl: 0-0 Vi: 0-0 Tstrap: 0-0
Best Rating: 122 11/02 Leic 2m4f110y good Ch

Fair chaser; completed a hat-trick in autumn 2002; suited by two and a half miles and a right-handed track; acts on a sound surface.

Sir Valentine (IRE)

102   99

9-y-o b g Be My Native (USA)-Turnvella (Tumble Wind (USA))
R Rowe Capt A Pratt

Placings: 0/0530P/121004/0130/U13-U03   (2667)

2002/03: 30ᵁGS, 32ᴾGS, 26³S,

	Starts	1st	2nd	3rd	Win & Pl
Chases	3	0	0	1	736
Career Total	22	4	1	4	17119
99	3/02 Font	3m2f110yE(0-110)HCh		SFT	£3374
99	10/00 Plum	3m2f	D(0-110)HCh	SFT	£4060
96	12/99 Plum	3m1f110yE(0-105)HHdl		GD	£2285
96	11/99 Plum	2m5f	F(0-100)HHdl	G-F	£2355
			Total win prize-money £12074		

Going: Sf: 0-1 GS: 0-2 Gd: 0-0 GF: - Fm: 0-0
Distance: 2m/2m3: 0-0 2m4-2m7: 0-0 3m+: 0-3
Track: LH: 0-0 RH: 0-2 Tight: 0-1 Gall: 0-1
Aids: Bl: 0-0 Vi: 0-0 Tstrap: 0-0
Best Rating: 99   3/02   Font   3m4f   soft   Ch

Fair handicap chaser, stays well and likes soft ground. Goes well fresh.

Sir Walter (IRE)

106(108c)   (79c)100
10-y-o b g The Bart (USA)-Glenbalda (Kambalda)
A G Hobbs J Parfitt

Placings:0000/0/044346F023/0304/PFF0200U6412361344
6134-6240   (0511)

	Starts	1st	2nd	3rd	Win & Pl
Hurdles	1	0	0	0	0
Chases	3	0	1	0	851
Career Total	45	3	4	6	12302
105	3/02 Wwck	2m	F(0-100)HHdl	G-S	£2159
97	12/01 Ludl	2m	F Hdl	GD	£2383
91	10/01 MRas	2m1f110yG(0-95)HHdl		GD	£1680
			Total win prize-money £6224		

Going: Sf: 0-1 GS: 0-0 Gd: 0-2 GF: - Fm: 0-0
Distance: 2m/2m3: 0-3 2m4-2m7: 0-1 3m+: 0-0
Track: LH: 0-3 RH: 0-1 Tight: 0-2 Gall: 0-0
Aids: Bl: 0-0 Vi: 0-0 Tstrap: 0-0
Best Rating: 105   3/02   Wwck   2m   gd-sft   Hdl

Modest hurdler; suited by two miles and a sound surface, travels well in his races; runner-up over fences in May 2002; pulled up in all three of his points in 2003.

Sir Williamwallace (IRE)

10-y-o br g Strong Gale-Kemchee (Kemal (FR))
J G M O Shea Gary Roberts

Placings:00560000/F133F0/14626633/4P0PPP-
P0630452P26P   (1715)
2002/03: 25ᴾGF, 20ᵁGF, 23ᴿGF, 25³G, 23⁹GF, 26⁴GF, 19⁵GF,
24²GF, 25ᴾGF, 26²GF, 19⁶G, 28ᴾGS,

	Starts	1st	2nd	3rd	Win & Pl
Chases	12	0	2	1	3435
Career Total	40	2	3	5	12975
77	5/00 Dpat	2m2f	(0-95)HCh	GD	£3174
75	7/99 Wxfd	2m	(0-95)HCh	FRM	£3683
			Total win prize-money £6857		

Going: Sf: 0-0 GS: 0-1 Gd: 0-2 GF: - Fm: 0-9
Distance: 2m/2m3: 0-1 2m4-2m7: 0-2 3m+: 0-9
Track: LH: 0-9 RH: 0-3 Tight: 0-3 Gall: 0-1
Aids: Bl: 0-0 Vi: 0-5 Tstrap: 0-0
Best Rating: 84   9/00   Dpat   2m2f   good   Ch

Modest ex-Irish chaser who is more effective on a sound surface. Stays three miles plus.

Sireric (IRE)

106(108h)   (106h)103
13-y-o b g Asir-Twice Regal (Royal Prerogative)
R Johnson C H P Bell

Placings:0321/000/03/316213/F4U0P0/4221P2/33243-
205411241220   (4164)
2002/03: 27²GF, 30⁴G, 27⁵S, 30⁴GS, 27¹S, 27¹S, 24²HY, 27⁴HY,
24¹HY, 24²S, 24²GS, 24⁰GS,

	Starts	1st	2nd	3rd	Win & Pl
Hurdles	5	1	2	0	7953
Chases	7	2	2	0	10868
Career Total	44	7	10	7	44945
103	1/03 Newc	3m	E(0-110)HCh	HVY	£5040
100	12/02 Sedg	3m3f	F(0-95)HCh	SFT	£3386
98	12/02 Sedg	3m3f110yD(0-115)HHdl		SFT	£4459
97	1/01 Newc	3m	E(0-115)HCh	HVY	£3391
108	3/98 Hexm	4m	D(0-120)HCh	SFT	£4272
108	12/97 Sedg	3m3f	E(0-110)HCh	SFT	£3738
109	4/95 Hexm	3m	E Hdl	HVY	£2578
			Total win prize-money £26869		

Going: Sf: 3-7 GS: 0-3 Gd: 0-1 GF: - Fm: 0-1
Distance: 2m/2m3: 0-0 2m4-2m7: 0-0 3m+: 3-12
Track: LH: 3-10 RH: 0-1 Tight: 2-5 Gall: 1-5
Aids: Bl: 0-0 Vi: 0-0 Tstrap: 0-0
Best Rating: 109   4/95   Hexm   3m   heavy   Hdl

Modest hurdler/chaser; stays marathon trips; acts on a soft surface; suited by forcing tactics.

Sirinndi (IRE)

82(76c)   68
9-y-o b g Shahrastani (USA)-Sinntara (IRE) (Lashkari)
Miss K Marks Nick Shutts

Placings:0/630/0/54100654/00-P36   (3445)
2002/03: 16ᴾS, 20³HY, 16⁶HY,

	Starts	1st	2nd	3rd	Win & Pl
Hurdles	3	0	0	1	324
Career Total	18	1	0	2	2261
90	12/00 Chep	2m4f	G Hdl	HVY	£1526
			Total win prize-money £1526		

Going: Sf: 0-3 GS: 0-0 Gd: 0-0 GF: - Fm: 0-0
Distance: 2m/2m3: 0-2 2m4-2m7: 0-1 3m+: 0-0
Track: LH: 0-2 RH: 0-1 Tight: 0-0 Gall: 0-0
Aids: Bl: 0-0 Vi: 0-0 Tstrap: 0-0
Best Rating: 90   12/00   Chep   2m4f   heavy   Hdl

Third in a seller at Leicester in December.

Sissinghurst Star (IRE)

72(96h)   (74h)87
8-y-o b g Moscow Society (USA)-Raplist (Arapaho)
R Dickin Brian Clifford

Placings:0/60P0/60305-35PP5   (1113)
2002/03: 16³F, 16⁵G, 16ᴾGF, 21ᴾGF, 24⁵GF,

	Starts	1st	2nd	3rd	Win & Pl
Hurdles	1	0	0	0	0
Chases	4	0	0	1	476
Career Total	15	0	0	2	938

Going: Sf: 0-0 GS: 0-0 Gd: 0-1 GF: - Fm: 0-4
Distance: 2m/2m3: 0-3 2m4-2m7: 0-1 3m+: 0-2
Track: LH: 0-4 RH: 0-1 Tight: 0-1 Gall: 0-0
Aids: Bl: 0-3 Vi: 0-2 Tstrap: 0-0
Best Rating: 87   5/02   Wwck   2m110y   firm   Ch

Sissinghurst Storm (IRE)

90   75
5-y-o b/br m Good Thyne (USA)-Mrs Hill (Strong Gale)
R Dickin Brian Clifford

Placings:03   (4568)
2002/03: 17⁰G, 22³GF,

	Starts	1st	2nd	3rd	Win & Pl
NH Flat	1	0	0	0	0
Hurdles	1	0	0	1	656
Career Total	2	0	0	1	656

Going: Sf: 0-0 GS: 0-0 Gd: 0-1 GF: - Fm: 0-1
Distance: 2m/2m3: 0-1 2m4-2m7: 0-1 3m+: 0-0
Track: LH: 0-1 RH: 0-1 Tight: 0-1 Gall: 0-0
Aids: Bl: 0-0 Vi: 0-0 Tstrap: 0-0
Best Rating: 75   4/03   Strf   2m6f110y   gd-fm   Hdl

Novice hurdler; finished third on hurdles debut at Stratford in April 2003.

Sister Amy

6-y-o gr m Gods Solution-Amys Sister (Silly Prices)
J R Turner J Edward Boynton

Placings:00   (4593)
2002/03: 16⁰GF, 16⁰G,

	Starts	1st	2nd	3rd	Win & Pl
NH Flat	2	0	0	0	0
Career Total	2	0	0	0	0

Going: Sf: 0-0 GS: 0-0 Gd: 0-1 GF: - Fm: 0-1
Distance: 2m/2m3: 0-2 2m4-2m7: 0-0 3m+: 0-0
Track: LH: 0-2 RH: 0-0 Tight: 0-0 Gall: 0-0
Aids: Bl: 0-0 Vi: 0-0 Tstrap: 0-0
Best Rating: 72   3/03   Weth   2m   gd-fm   NHF

Sister Anna

90   69
5-y-o br m Gildoran-Take The Veil (Monksfield)
T D Walford Anthony Preston

Placings:206   (4522)
2002/03: 16²G, 17⁰G, 16⁶G,

	Starts	1st	2nd	3rd	Win & Pl
NH Flat	2	0	1	0	708
Hurdles	1	0	0	0	0
Career Total	3	0	1	0	708

Going: Sf: 0-0 GS: 0-0 Gd: 0-3 GF: - Fm: 0-0
Distance: 2m/2m3: 0-3 2m4-2m7: 0-0 3m+: 0-0
Track: LH: 0-2 RH: 0-1 Tight: 0-1 Gall: 0-0
Aids: Bl: 0-0 Vi: 0-0 Tstrap: 0-0
Best Rating: 88   3/03   Weth   2m   good   NHF

Novice hurdler; jumping bred; runner-up first time in bumper at Wetherby in March, but well beaten since.

Sister Charlotte

8-y-o ch m Gildoran-Sharlinda (Deep Run)
J C Tuck M J Howard

Placings:00P-P   (0273)
2002/03: 22ᴾGF,

	Starts	1st	2nd	3rd	Win & Pl
Hurdles	1	0	0	0	
Career Total	4	0	0	0	

Going:	Sf: 0-0 GS: 0-0 Gd: 0-0 GF: - Fm: 0-1
Distance:	2m/2m3: 0-0 2m4-2m7: 0-0 3m+: 0-0
Track:	LH: 0-1 RH: 0-0 Tight: 0-1 Gall: 0-0
Aids:	Bl: 0-0 Vi: 0-0 Tstrap: 0-0
Best Rating:	68 11/01 Extr 2m1f gd-fm NHF

Sister Superior (IRE)

(103h)   (101h)**77**

8-y-o b m Supreme Leader-Nicat (Wolver Hollow)
S Gollings The High Five Partnership

Placings:*02263500516/35P-22503***P5**   (4416)
2002/03: 19²G, 20²HY, 20⁵S, 20⁹HY, 19³G, 21³PS, 25⁵G,

	Starts	1st	2nd	3rd	Win & Pl
Hurdles	4	0	2	0	2099
Chases	3	0	0	1	622
Career Total	21	1	4	3	23960
109 3/01	Newb	2m5f		HHdl	HVY £17400
				Total win prize-money £17400

Going:	Sf: 0-4 GS: 0-0 Gd: 0-3 GF: - Fm: 0-0
Distance:	2m/2m3: 0-1 2m4-2m7: 0-5 3m+: 0-1
Track:	LH: 0-4 RH: 0-3 Tight: 0-2 Gall: 0-0
Aids:	Bl: 0-0 Vi: 0-0 Tstrap: 0-0
Best Rating:	111 6/00 Uttx 2m good NHF

Modest hurdler; distant third on chasing debut; stays 2m 6f; acts on good ground and softer.

Sister Valenthyne (IRE)

72f

6-y-o ch m Good Thyne (USA)-Coteri Run (Deep Run)
S Gollings Mrs M A Hall

Placings:*0P-3*   (1494)
2002/03: 17³GS,

	Starts	1st	2nd	3rd	Win & Pl
NH Flat	1	0	0	1	268
Career Total	3	0	0	1	268

Going:	Sf: 0-0 GS: 0-1 Gd: 0-0 GF: - Fm: 0-0
Distance:	2m/2m3: 0-1 2m4-2m7: 0-0 3m+: 0-0
Track:	LH: 0-1 RH: 0-0 Tight: 0-1 Gall: 0-0
Aids:	Bl: 0-0 Vi: 0-0 Tstrap: 0-0
Best Rating:	72 2/02 Donc 2m110y soft NHF

Six Clerks (IRE)

10-y-o b g Shadeed (USA)-Skidmore Girl (USA) (Vaguely Noble)
Mrs S M Odell W J Odell

Placings:*0421330/52325263/6P5P46/30F3FP/05530535-20PP*   (4443)
2002/03: 16²GF, 22⁶G, 24⁶S, 19⁹G,

	Starts	1st	2nd	3rd	Win & Pl
Chases	4	0	1	0	1050
Career Total	39	1	5	8	9150
89 2/97	Catt	2m		F Hdl	GD £2029
				Total win prize-money £2029

Going: Sf: 0-1 GS: 0-0 Gd: 0-2 GF: - Fm: 0-1

Distance:	2m/2m3: 0-1 2m4-2m7: 0-2 3m+: 0-1
Track:	LH: 0-2 RH: 0-2 Tight: 0-0 Gall: 0-2
Aids:	Bl: 0-0 Vi: 0-4 Tstrap: 0-0
Best Rating:	99 3/97 MRas 2m1f110y good Hdl

Modest hunter chaser on a long losing run.

Six Of One

95   **85**

5-y-o b g Kahyasi-Ten To Six (Night Shift (USA))
R Rowe (E Danel 15/10) Mrs R A Proctor

Placings:*6660*   (4371)
2002/03: 17⁶HY, 21⁶G, 20⁶HY, 16⁶G,

	Starts	1st	2nd	3rd	Win & Pl
Hurdles	4	0	0	0	177
Career Total	4	0	0	0	177

Going:	Sf: 0-2 GS: 0-0 Gd: 0-2 GF: - Fm: 0-0
Distance:	2m/2m3: 0-2 2m4-2m7: 0-2 3m+: 0-0
Track:	LH: 0-0 RH: 0-4 Tight: 0-1 Gall: 0-0
Aids:	Bl: 0-0 Vi: 0-0 Tstrap: 0-0
Best Rating:	85 3/03 Sand 2m4f110y heavy Hdl

An ex-French middle-distance winner on the Flat; acts on good ground; has worn blinkers.

Six Pack (IRE)

78   **55**

5-y-o ch g Royal Abjar (USA)-Regal Entrance (Be My Guest (USA))
Andrew Turnell J J Canny

Placings:*50*   (2200)
2002/03: 17⁵G, 16⁰S,

	Starts	1st	2nd	3rd	Win & Pl
Hurdles	2	0	0	0	0
Career Total	2	0	0	0	0

Going:	Sf: 0-1 GS: 0-0 Gd: 0-1 GF: - Fm: 0-0
Distance:	2m/2m3: 0-2 2m4-2m7: 0-0 3m+: 0-0
Track:	LH: 0-2 RH: 0-0 Tight: 0-0 Gall: 0-0
Aids:	Bl: 0-0 Vi: 0-0 Tstrap: 0-0
Best Rating:	55 9/02 Sthl 2m1f good Hdl

Sixo (IRE)

113f   **130f**

6-y-o gr g Roselier (FR)-Miss Mangaroo (Oats)
M C Pipe Matt Archer & Miss Jean Broadhurst

Placings:*113*   (3528)
2002/03: 17¹HY, 16¹HY, 16³G,

	Starts	1st	2nd	3rd	Win & Pl
NH Flat	3	2	0	1	7065
Career Total	3	2	0	1	7065
125 12/02	Newb	2m110y	H NHF		HVY £2646
109 11/02	NAbb	2m1f	H NHF		HVY £2219
				Total win prize-money £4865

Going:	Sf: 2-2 GS: 0-0 Gd: 0-1 GF: - Fm: 0-0
Distance:	2m/2m3: 2-3 2m4-2m7: 0-0 3m+: 0-0
Track:	LH: 2-3 RH: 0-0 Tight: 1-1 Gall: 1-2
Aids:	Bl: 0-0 Vi: 0-0 Tstrap: 0-0
Best Rating:	130 2/03 Newb 2m110y good NHF

Useful bumper performer; out of a mare who won at two and a half miles over hurdles; clear-cut winner of heavy ground bumpers in late 2002. besten on faster ground.

Skenfrith

103   **83**

4-y-o b g Atraf-Hobbs Choice (Superpower)
Miss S E Forster (A Berry 2/5) C Storey

Placings:*00302*   (4659)
2002/03: 16⁰GS, 16³GS, 17⁰G, 20²GF,

	Starts	1st	2nd	3rd	Win & Pl
Hurdles	5	0	1	1	1558
Career Total	5	0	1	1	1558

Going:	Sf: 0-0 GS: 0-3 Gd: 0-1 GF: - Fm: 0-0
Distance:	2m/2m3: 0-4 2m4-2m7: 0-1 3m+: 0-0
Track:	LH: 0-3 RH: 0-2 Tight: 0-3 Gall: 0-1
Aids:	Bl: 0-0 Vi: 0-0 Tstrap: 0-0
Best Rating:	83 4/03 Carl 2m4f gd-fm Hdl

Plating-class hurdler; stays two and a half miles; acts on fast and easy ground.

Skibb (IRE)

106   **118**

6-y-o b g Be My Native (USA)-Inch Lady (Bulldozer)
M F Morris Mrs A M Daly

Placings:*54-3014434*   (4462)
2002/03: 17³YS, 16⁰HY, 18¹YS, 16⁴S, 16⁴Y, 20³Y, 20⁴G,

	Starts	1st	2nd	3rd	Win & Pl
Hurdles	7	1	0	2	11651
Career Total	9	1	0	2	11848
118 1/03	Punc	2m2f		Hdl	Y-S £7168
				Total win prize-money £7169

Going:	Sf: 0-2 GS: 0-0 Gd: 0-1 GF: - Fm: 0-0
Distance:	2m/2m3: 1-5 2m4-2m7: 0-2 3m+: 0-0
Track:	LH: 0-2 RH: 0-3 Tight: 0-1 Gall: 0-0
Aids:	Bl: 0-0 Vi: 0-0 Tstrap: 0-0
Best Rating:	118 1/03 Punc 2m2f yld-sft Hdl

Decent Irish-trained novice hurdler; acts on a soft surface; stays two and a half miles.

Skiddaw Gale

80(81h)   (56h)**59+**

9-y-o b g Strong Gale-Whimbrel (Dara Monarch)
M A Barnes M Barnes

Placings:*0/56560/4P04P0P6-P5*   (0450)
2002/03: 20⁰GF, 16³G,

	Starts	1st	2nd	3rd	Win & Pl
Chases	2	0	0	0	0
Career Total	16	0	0	0	0

Going:	Sf: 0-0 GS: 0-0 Gd: 0-0 GF: - Fm: 0-1
Distance:	2m/2m3: 0-1 2m4-2m7: 0-1 3m+: 0-0
Track:	LH: 0-2 RH: 0-0 Tight: 0-0 Gall: 0-0
Aids:	Bl: 0-0 Vi: 0-0 Tstrap: 0-1
Best Rating:	74 6/00 Hexm 2m gd-fm Hdl

Skiddaw Rose (IRE)

100   **76**

7-y-o gr m Terimon-Whimbrel (Dara Monarch)
M A Barnes John Wills

Placings:*06/00*PP-44030300   (2103)
2002/03: 16⁴GF, 16⁴GF, 17⁰GF, 16³GF, 17⁰GF, 16³G, 17⁰G, 16⁰G,

	Starts	1st	2nd	3rd	Win & Pl
Hurdles	8	0	0	2	1066
Career Total	14	0	0	2	1066

Going:	Sf: 0-0 GS: 0-0 Gd: 0-3 GF: - Fm: 0-5
Distance:	2m/2m3: 0-8 2m4-2m7: 0-0 3m+: 0-0
Track:	LH: 0-6 RH: 0-2 Tight: 0-4 Gall: 0-0
Aids:	Bl: 0-0 Vi: 0-0 Tstrap: 0-0
Best Rating:	76 10/02 Hexm 2m110y good Hdl

Poor novice hurdler; habitual front runner.

Skillwise

94   **103**

11-y-o b g Buckley-Calametta (Oats)
T D Easterby Chris D Calvert

Placings:*0/012252U51/3/02142P5/412264U16/432P34100*
U-PP565 (2495)
2002/03: 25^PGS, 25^PGS, 24⁴S, 27⁶GS, 26⁵GS,

	Starts	1st	2nd	3rd	Win & Pl
Chases	5	0	0	0	975
Career Total	42	6	8	3	59488
126	3/02	Donc	3m2f	B(0-145)HCh	G-S	£20640
123	4/01	Hayd	2m6f	B(0-140)HCh	SFT	£10093
114	11/00	Newc	3m	D(0-125)HCh	SFT	£3809
120	11/99	Weth	3m1f	D Ch	GD	£3925
114	4/98	Ayr	2m4f	C HHdl	GD	£4289
107	10/97	Sedg	2m1f	H NHF	GD	£1035
				Total win prize-money £43792

Going:	Sf: 0-1 GS: 0-4 Gd: 0-0 GF: - Fm: 0-0
Distance:	2m/2m3: 0-0 2m4-2m7: 0-0 3m+: 0-5
Track:	LH: 0-4 RH: 0-1 Tight: 0-3 Gall: 0-2
Aids:	Bl: 0-0 Vi: 0-0 Tstrap: 0-0
Best Rating:	126 3/02 Donc 3m2f gd-sft Ch

Moderate handicap chaser. Seemingly effective on any ground, he stays beyond three miles.

Skinsey Finnegan (IRE)

111   **109**

9-y-o b g Fresh Breeze (USA)-Rose Of Solway (Derring Rose)
C A Dwyer Casino Racing Partnership

Placings:*23/3431225423* (4756)
2002/03: 16³GS, 19⁴GS, 21³GS, 16¹S, 16²G, 16²GS, 16⁵S, 16⁴GF, 17²GF, 18³GF,

	Starts	1st	2nd	3rd	Win & Pl
Chases	10	1	3	3	9958
Career Total	12	1	4	4	10613
109	12/02	Folk	2m	F(0-90)HCh	GD	£3425
				Total win prize-money £3426

Going:	Sf: 1-2 GS: 0-3 Gd: 0-2 GF: - Fm: 0-3
Distance:	2m/2m3: 1-8 2m4-2m7: 0-2 3m+: 0-0
Track:	LH: 0-5 RH: 1-4 Tight: 1-6 Gall: 0-2
Aids:	Bl: 0-0 Vi: 0-0 Tstrap: 1-7
Best Rating:	109 4/03 Plum 2m1f gd-fm Ch

Modest chaser; winning pointer; placed in bumpers in 2000; placed over fences before winning at Folkestone in December 2002; just caught at Doncaster the following month; effective at two miles, stays further.

Skiora

63   **70**

6-y-o br m Petoski-Coral Delight (Idiots Delight)
A J Wilson The Up And Running Partnership

Placings:*0-3U04P* (4626)
2002/03: 16³GF, 16^UGS, 16⁶GS, 16⁴GF, 17^PGF,

	Starts	1st	2nd	3rd	Win & Pl
NH Flat	1	0	0	1	240

| Hurdles | 4 | 0 | 0 | 0 | 0 |
| Career Total | 6 | 0 | 0 | 1 | 240 |

Going:	Sf: 0-0 GS: 0-2 Gd: 0-0 GF: - Fm: 0-3
Distance:	2m/2m3: 0-5 2m4-2m7: 0-0 3m+: 0-0
Track:	LH: 0-3 RH: 0-2 Tight: 0-1 Gall: 0-0
Aids:	Bl: 0-1 Vi: 0-0 Tstrap: 0-0
Best Rating:	82 5/02 Worc 2m gd-fm NHF

Has shown ability in bumpers and hurdles on varying ground.

Skipmantoo (IRE)

8-y-o ch g Pips Pride-Sports Post Lady (IRE) (M Double M (USA))
Miss C Dyson Miss C Dyson

Placings:*U0-P* (2565)
2002/03: 17^PGS,

	Starts	1st	2nd	3rd	Win & Pl
Hurdles	1	0	0	0	
Career Total	3	0	0	0	

Going:	Sf: 0-0 GS: 0-1 Gd: 0-0 GF: - Fm: 0-0
Distance:	2m/2m3: 0-1 2m4-2m7: 0-0 3m+: 0-0
Track:	LH: 0-1 RH: 0-0 Tight: 0-1 Gall: 0-0
Aids:	Bl: 0-0 Vi: 0-0 Tstrap: 0-1
Best Rating:	50 5/01 Hntg 2m110y gd-fm NHF

Skippers Cleuch (IRE)

105   **122**

9-y-o b g Be My Native (USA)-Cloughoola Lady (Black Minstrel)
L Lungo Ashleybank Investments Limited

Placings:*111/1111P/11U0* (4101)
2002/03: 22¹HY, 20¹GS, 20^UHY, 24⁰G,

	Starts	1st	2nd	3rd	Win & Pl
Chases	4	2	0	0	10209
Career Total	12	9	0	0	31866
122	12/02	Weth	2m4f110yD Ch	G-S	£5152
112	11/02	Kels	2m6f110yD Ch	HVY	£5057
151	1/01	Newc	2m4f	B Hdl	SFT	£6873
132	12/00	Newc	2m4f	E Hdl	SFT	£2723
138	12/00	Ayr	2m	E Hdl	SFT	£2380
120	11/00	Ayr	2m	E Hdl	SFT	£1974
138	4/00	Carl	2m1f	H NHF	G-S	£1652
126	3/00	Carl	2m1f	H NHF	G-S	£4465
124	3/00	Ayr	2m	H NHF	HVY	£1589
				Total win prize-money £31867

Going:	Sf: 1-2 GS: 1-1 Gd: 0-1 GF: - Fm: 0-0
Distance:	2m/2m3: 0-0 2m4-2m7: 2-3 3m+: 0-1
Track:	LH: 2-4 RH: 0-0 Tight: 1-1 Gall: 0-1
Aids:	Bl: 0-0 Vi: 0-0 Tstrap: 0-1
Best Rating:	151 1/01 Newc 2m4f soft Hdl

Useful novice chaser, but not quite living up to expectations; won his first seven outings over hurdles and first two over fences; stays 2m 6f; effective on soft ground.

Skram

96(97h)   (76h)**116**

10-y-o b g Rambo Dancer (CAN)-Skarberg (FR) (Noir Et Or)
R Dickin W P Evans & Mrs D L Weaver

Placings:*F14552P20/122236224412/16010P/P2003425224*
5/11U21113245/250F51204-5P (0327)

2002/03: 20⁵G, 20^PG,

	Starts	1st	2nd	3rd	Win & Pl
Chases	2	0	0	0	
Career Total	61	11	16	3	63413
113	7/01	Strf	2m4f	D(0-125)HCh	GD	£7280
115	9/00	Strf	2m4f	D(0-120)HCh	GD	£4017
115	8/00	Worc	2m4f110yD Ch	G-F	£4147
117	7/00	Strf	2m1f110yE Ch	G-F	£3103
112	6/00	Worc	2m4f110yD(0-110)HCh	G-F	£4069
105	5/00	Wwck	2m	E Ch	G-F	£2948
101	2/99	Font	2m2f110yE(0-115)HHdl	SFT	£7327
107	5/98	Hntg	2m2f110yD(0-125)HHdl	G-F	£2931
107	4/98	Font	2m2f110yE(0-110)HHdl	G-S	£2427
97	9/97	Font	2m2f110yF(0-105)HHdl	GD	£2048
77	8/96	Font	2m2f110yE Hdl	G-F	£2175
				Total win prize-money £42475

Going:	Sf: 0-0 GS: 0-0 Gd: 0-2 GF: - Fm: 0-0
Distance:	2m/2m3: 0-0 2m4-2m7: 0-2 3m+: 0-0
Track:	LH: 0-2 RH: 0-0 Tight: 0-1 Gall: 0-0
Aids:	Bl: 0-0 Vi: 0-0 Tstrap: 0-0
Best Rating:	117 9/00 MRas 2m6f110y gd-fm Ch

Fair handicap chaser; at his best from two-two and a half miles; likes fast ground and shows his best form in the summer months.

Sky To Sea (FR)

105   **104+**

5-y-o b g Adieu Au Roi (IRE)-Urban Sky (FR) (Groom Dancer (USA))
M J Grassick Miss Christine Tsui

Placings:*2* (2558)
2002/03: 16²GF,

	Starts	1st	2nd	3rd	Win & Pl
Hurdles	1	0	1	0	1299
Career Total	1	0	1	0	1299

Going:	Sf: 0-0 GS: 0-0 Gd: 0-0 GF: - Fm: 0-1
Distance:	2m/2m3: 0-1 2m4-2m7: 0-0 3m+: 0-0
Track:	LH: 0-0 RH: 0-0 Tight: 0-1 Gall: 0-0
Aids:	Bl: 0-0 Vi: 0-0 Tstrap: 0-0
Best Rating:	104 12/02 Muss 2m gd-fm Hdl

A winner on the Flat in Ireland, he showed ability on his hurdling debut at Musselburgh.

Skycab (IRE)

110   **136**

11-y-o b g Montelimar (USA)-Sams Money (Pry)
J T Gifford P H Betts (holdings) Ltd

Placings:*4/522411/4225/2162140115/P0P4P/51-331P311* (4792)
2002/03: 20³GS, 19³HY, 24¹GS, 24^PS, 25³GS, 20¹G, 20¹G,

	Starts	1st	2nd	3rd	Win & Pl
Chases	7	3	0	3	36040
Career Total	35	10	6	3	92293
136	4/03	Sand	2m4f110yB(0-145)HCh	GD	£17400
135	4/03	Strf	2m4f	C(0-130)HCh	GD	£8287
133	12/02	Fknm	3m110y	D(0-125)HCh	G-S	£6630
132	10/01	Sthl	2m4f110yD(0-120)HCh	GD	£6841
135	4/00	Strf	2m4f	C(0-130)HCh	GD	£6500
135	4/00	Asct	2m4f110yB(0-130)HCh	SFT	£13812
129	12/99	Hntg	2m4f110yE Ch	G-S	£3613
127	11/99	Sand	2m	D Ch	GD	£4401
127	4/98	MRas	2m3f110yD Hdl	SFT	£3315
127	4/98	Fknm	2m	E(0-100)HHdl	G-S	£1400
				Total win prize-money £73803

| Going: | Sf: 0-2 GS: 1-3 Gd: 2-2 GF: - Fm: 0-0 |
| Distance: | 2m/2m3: 0-0 2m4-2m7: 2-4 3m+: 1-3 |

Track: LH: 2-3 RH: 1-4 **Tight:** 2-2 Gall: 0-1
Aids: Bl: 0-0 Vi: 0-0 Tstrap: 0-0
Best Rating: 136 4/03 Sand 2m4f110y good Ch

Useful handicap chaser; stays three miles; acts on most types of ground; gave Josh Gifford a winner with his last runner at Sandown in April.

Skylander

85   74

7-y-o b g Thethingaboutitis (USA)-Mesembryanthemum (Warpath)
B J Llewellyn G I Isaac

Placings:06-5   (0443)
2002/03: 18GG, 17GG,

	Starts	1st	2nd	3rd	Win & Pl
NH Flat	1	0	0	0	0
Hurdles	1	0	0	0	0
Career Total	3	0	0	0	0

Going: Sf: 0-0 GS: 0-0 Gd: 0-2 GF: - Fm: 0-0
Distance: 2m/2m3: 0-2 2m4-2m7: 0-0 3m+: 0-0
Track: LH: 0-1 RH: 0-1 Tight: 0-0 Gall: 0-0
Aids: Bl: 0-0 Vi: 0-0 Tstrap: 0-0
Best Rating: 85 4/02 Plum 2m2f good NHF

Skylarker (USA)

87   75

5-y-o b g Sky Classic (CAN)-O My Darling (USA) (Mr Prospector (USA))
W S Kittow (C F Wall 23/9) Midd Shire Racing

Placings:55   (4270)
2002/03: 17SG, 16SG,

	Starts	1st	2nd	3rd	Win & Pl
Hurdles	2	0	0	0	0
Career Total	2	0	0	0	0

Going: Sf: 0-1 GS: 0-0 Gd: 0-1 GF: - Fm: 0-0
Distance: 2m/2m3: 0-2 2m4-2m7: 0-0 3m+: 0-0
Track: LH: 0-1 RH: 0-1 Tight: 0-0 Gall: 0-0
Aids: Bl: 0-0 Vi: 0-0 Tstrap: 0-0
Best Rating: 75 12/02 Tntn 2m1f soft Hdl

Slaney Fox (IRE)

83   103

6-y-o b m Foxhound (USA)-Mean To Me (Homing)
Mrs John Harrington Mrs J Rees

Placings:0142O2-013050   (1967)
2002/03: 16OS, 161G, 163GF, 16GG, 16SHY, 16GGS,

	Starts	1st	2nd	3rd	Win & Pl
NH Flat	2	1	0	0	3810
Hurdles	4	0	0	1	494
Career Total	10	1	1	1	5417
94 8/02 Tral 2m		NHF		GD	3809

Total win prize-money £3810

Going: Sf: 0-2 GS: 0-1 Gd: 1-2 GF: - Fm: 0-1
Distance: 2m/2m3: 1-6 2m4-2m7: 0-0 3m+: 0-0
Track: LH: 0-1 RH: 0-0 Tight: 0-0 Gall: 0-0
Aids: Bl: 0-0 Vi: 0-0 Tstrap: 0-0
Best Rating: 103 9/02 Klny 2m gd-fm Hdl

Irish novice hurdler; effective over two miles on good ground.

Slasher Jack (IRE)

78(97h)   (77h)66

12-y-o b g Alzao (USA)-Sherkraine (Shergar)
Mrs D Thomson The Boozers Brigade

Placings:24/1550/60510PP06P/650634P5-5P   (0182)
2002/03: 17SGS, 25PG,

	Starts	1st	2nd	3rd	Win & Pl
Chases	2	0	0	0	0
Career Total	26	2	1	1	6614
97 11/00 Kels 2m2f	F(0-90)HHdl		SFT	£2873
97 1/00 Muss 2m	E Hdl		GD	£2415

Total win prize-money £5288

Going: Sf: 0-0 GS: 0-1 Gd: 0-1 GF: - Fm: 0-0
Distance: 2m/2m3: 0-1 2m4-2m7: 0-0 3m+: 0-1
Track: LH: 0-2 RH: 0-0 Tight: 0-1 Gall: 0-0
Aids: Bl: 0-0 Vi: 0-0 Tstrap: 0-0
Best Rating: 97 11/00 Kels 2m2f soft Hdl

He has ability, but also has a mind of his own.

Sledmere (IRE)

8-y-o ch g Shalford (IRE)-Jazirah (Main Reef)
George R Moscrop George R Moscrop

Placings:005PP/F-UU   (0260)
2002/03: 25UGS, 20UGF,

	Starts	1st	2nd	3rd	Win & Pl
Chases	2	0	0	0	0
Career Total	8	0	0	0	0

Going: Sf: 0-0 GS: 0-1 Gd: 0-0 GF: - Fm: 0-1
Distance: 2m/2m3: 0-0 2m4-2m7: 0-1 3m+: 0-0
Track: LH: 0-1 RH: 0-1 Tight: 0-0 Gall: 0-0
Aids: Bl: 0-0 Vi: 0-0 Tstrap: 0-0
Best Rating: 72 7/00 Uttx 2m4f110y gd-fm Hdl

Sleeping Music (FR)

91(71h)   (23h)66

6-y-o b g Sleeping Car (FR)-Music Sobre (FR) (Crowned Music (USA))
J R Best Edward Charles Brooke

Placings:P504/23054-4PP6   (1452)
2002/03: 164GF, 21PGF, 22PG, 20PG,

	Starts	1st	2nd	3rd	Win & Pl
Hurdles	1	0	0	0	0
Chases	3	0	0	0	211
Career Total	13	0	1	1	5012

Going: Sf: 0-0 GS: 0-0 Gd: 0-2 GF: - Fm: 0-2
Distance: 2m/2m3: 0-1 2m4-2m7: 0-3 3m+: 0-0
Track: LH: 0-3 RH: 0-0 Tight: 0-2 Gall: 0-0
Aids: Bl: 0-3 Vi: 0-0 Tstrap: 0-0
Best Rating: 66 7/02 Worc 2m gd-fm Ch

Sleepy River (IRE)

94   27

12-y-o ch g Over The River (FR)-Shreelane (Laurence O)
Miss Kate Milligan The Aunts

Placings:0103/005010/0050/1F14/36P3606/11/15P343-FPP   (4375)
2002/03: 243G, 24FGF, 24PGS, 28PG,

	Starts	1st	2nd	3rd	Win & Pl
Chases	4	0	1	0	464

Career Total 36   7   0   5   24812

104	11/01	Newc	3m	D(0-125)HCh	GD	£4075
96	11/00	Wwck	3m110y	E(0-105)HCh	HVY	£2886
96	10/00	Wwck	3m2f	F(0-105)HCh	SFT	£2467
109	11/98	Kels	2m6f110yD(0-125)HHdl		HVY	£2749
114	10/98	Kels	2m6f110yD(0-125)HHdl		SFT	£2871
113	3/97	Tipp	2m4f	(0-123)HHdl	G-Y	£4069
108	1/96	Tram	2m	Hdl	SFT	£2295

Total win prize-money £21414

Going: Sf: 0-0 GS: 0-1 Gd: 0-2 GF: - Fm: 0-1
Distance: 2m/2m3: 0-0 2m4-2m7: 0-0 3m+: 0-4
Track: LH: 0-3 RH: 0-1 Tight: 0-1 Gall: 0-2
Aids: Bl: 0-0 Vi: 0-0 Tstrap: 0-0
Best Rating: 115 4/96 Punc 2m2f soft Hdl

Moderate staying chaser; goes well at Warwick; likes soft ground.

Sleepytime Tim

19f

7-y-o b g Henbit (USA)-Cloncoose (IRE) (Remainder Man)
J A Moore J A Moore

Placings:0-0P   (0687)
2002/03: 16OG, 16PGF,

	Starts	1st	2nd	3rd	Win & Pl
NH Flat	2	0	0	0	0
Career Total	3	0	0	0	0

Going: Sf: 0-0 GS: 0-0 Gd: 0-1 GF: - Fm: 0-1
Distance: 2m/2m3: 0-2 2m4-2m7: 0-0 3m+: 0-0
Track: LH: 0-1 RH: 0-0 Tight: 0-0 Gall: 0-0
Aids: Bl: 0-0 Vi: 0-0 Tstrap: 0-1
Best Rating: 19 6/02 Hexm 2m110y good NHF

Sleeting

96(100c)   (69c)71

10-y-o ch g Lycius (USA)-Pluvial (Habat)
J Gallagher Horses Away Racing Club

Placings:3505060/2F443604/133000/01403/62060306554-0P0224   (1616)
2002/03: 21OGG, 16PGF, 17PGF, 22²G, 21²G, 24⁴F,

	Starts	1st	2nd	3rd	Win & Pl
Hurdles	4	0	2	0	1264
Chases	2	0	0	0	0
Career Total	43	2	4	6	9156
90	11/00	Tntn 2m1f	G(0-90)HHdl	GD	£1599
98	9/99	Sedg 2m1f	E Hdl	GD	£2267

Total win prize-money £3868

Going: Sf: 0-0 GS: 0-0 Gd: 0-1 GF: - Fm: 0-5
Distance: 2m/2m3: 0-2 2m4-2m7: 0-3 3m+: 0-1
Track: LH: 0-5 RH: 0-1 Tight: 0-4 Gall: 0-0
Aids: Bl: 0-0 Vi: 0-0 Tstrap: 0-0
Best Rating: 98 10/99 Sedg 2m1f gd-fm Hdl

Moderate hurdler; acts on well on good ground and is suited by around two miles six furlongs.

Sleight

94f   78f

4-y-o ch f Bob s Return (IRE)-Jolejester (Relkino)
W Jenks W Jenks

Placings:44   (4343)
2002/03: 16⁴S, 16⁴GF,

	Starts	1st	2nd	3rd	Win & Pl
NH Flat	2	0	0	0	0
Career Total	2	0	0	0	0

Going:	Sf: 0-1 GS: 0-0 Gd: 0-0 GF: - Fm: 0-1
Distance:	2m/2m3: 0-2 2m4-2m7: 0-0 3m+: 0-1
Track:	LH: 0-1 RH: 0-0 Tight: 0-0 Gall: 0-1
Aids:	Bl: 0-0 Vi: 0-0 Tstrap: 0-0
Best Rating:	83 3/03 Wwck 2m soft NHF

Sleight Of Hand (IRE)

80(87h)   (69h)**38**

10-y-o b g Hollow Hand-Marand (Damsire Unknown)
J S King Alan Lee

Placings:60/3060/33/P5P/5P45-FP550   (3741)
2002/03: 20FGF, 20PG, 23SG, 19SG, 20QG,

	Starts	1st	2nd	3rd	Win & Pl
Hurdles	1	0	0	0	0
Chases	4	0	0	0	0
Career Total	20	0	0	3	1252

Going:	Sf: 0-0 GS: 0-0 Gd: 0-4 GF: - Fm: 0-1
Distance:	2m/2m3: 0-4 2m4-2m7: 0-3 3m+: 0-1
Track:	LH: 0-0 RH: 0-5 Tight: 0-1 Gall: 0-1
Aids:	Bl: 0-0 Vi: 0-0 Tstrap: 0-2
Best Rating:	92 10/99 Font 2m6f110y good Hdl

Slewmore (IRE)

12-y-o br g Mister Majestic-Lola s Pet (Ahonoora)
Richard Mathias (Mrs D A Hamer 24/10) Richard Mathias

Placings:050000/00005010/1306623F000/05033435/03040
43000000/411/F400-53630   (4678)
2002/03: 20SF, 19JGF, 17SGS, 16JF, 19QGF,

	Starts	1st	2nd	3rd	Win & Pl
Chases	5	0	0	2	873
Career Total	58	4	1	9	16905
63	7/00	Baln	2m1f	(0-102)HCh	G-F	£4416
54	7/00	Wxfd	2m	(0-95)HCh	FRM	£3588
96	5/97	Dpat	2m1f172y	(0-109)HHdl	GD	£2034
94	3/97	Thur	2m	(0-116)HHdl	GD	£2712
				Total win prize-money £12752

Going:	Sf: 0-0 GS: 0-1 Gd: 0-0 GF: - Fm: 0-4
Distance:	2m/2m3: 0-4 2m4-2m7: 0-1 3m+: 0-0
Track:	LH: 0-2 RH: 0-3 Tight: 0-2 Gall: 0-0
Aids:	Bl: 0-0 Vi: 0-0 Tstrap: 0-1
Best Rating:	96 5/97 Dpat 2m1f172y good Hdl

Dual winner over both hurdles and fences in Ireland; moderate hunter chaser now; acts on ground good or faster; best at around two miles.

Sliema (IRE)

85   **60**

5-y-o b g Desert Style (IRE)-Ascoli (Skyliner)
O Sherwood John Marks

Placings:00-0   (0242)
2002/03: 17QG,

	Starts	1st	2nd	3rd	Win & Pl
Hurdles	1	0	0	0	
Career Total	3	0	0	0	

Going:	Sf: 0-0 GS: 0-0 Gd: 0-0 GF: 0-1 Fm: 0-0
Distance:	2m/2m3: 0-1 2m4-2m7: 0-0 3m+: 0-0
Track:	LH: 0-0 RH: 0-1 Tight: 0-0 Gall: 0-0
Aids:	Bl: 0-0 Vi: 0-0 Tstrap: 0-0
Best Rating:	85 4/02 Weth 2m gd-fm NHF

Sliema Creek

9-y-o gr g Beveled (USA)-Sea Farer Lake (Gairloch)
V Thompson V Thompson

Placings:U3221600160/0010300PB50P/P-P   (0085)
2002/03: 25PGS,

	Starts	1st	2nd	3rd	Win & Pl
Chases	1	0	0	0	
Career Total	25	3	2	2	9333
75	10/98	Sedg	2m5f	E Ch	GD	£3176
94	3/98	Hntg	2m110y	G Hdl	SFT	£1870
94	10/97	Worc	2m	E Hdl	SFT	£2279
				Total win prize-money £7326

Going:	Sf: 0-0 GS: 0-1 Gd: 0-0 GF: - Fm: 0-0
Distance:	2m/2m3: 0-0 2m4-2m7: 0-0 3m+: 0-1
Track:	LH: 0-1 RH: 0-0 Tight: 0-0 Gall: 0-0
Aids:	Bl: 0-0 Vi: 0-0 Tstrap: 0-0
Best Rating:	94 3/98 Hntg 2m110y soft Hdl

Slingshot

7-y-o b g Seymour Hicks (FR)-Flower Of Tintern (Free State)
M G Rimell Mark Rimell

Placings:00P   (3784)
2002/03: 16QS, 16QG, 19PG,

	Starts	1st	2nd	3rd	Win & Pl
NH Flat	2	0	0	0	
Hurdles	1	0	0	0	
Career Total	3	0	0	0	

Going:	Sf: 0-1 GS: 0-0 Gd: 0-2 GF: - Fm: 0-0
Distance:	2m/2m3: 0-2 2m4-2m7: 0-1 3m+: 0-0
Track:	LH: 0-2 RH: 0-1 Tight: 0-1 Gall: 0-0
Aids:	Bl: 0-0 Vi: 0-0 Tstrap: 0-0
Best Rating:	65 1/03 Sthl 2m good NHF

Slip Away

94(91h)   (39h)**50**

10-y-o gr g Jumbo Hirt (USA)-Au Pair (Runnymede)
Ms Liz Harrison David Alan Harrison

Placings:40/5/2P-4505   (0830)
2002/03: 26QG, 25SGF, 27QGF, 27SGF,

	Starts	1st	2nd	3rd	Win & Pl
Hurdles	1	0	0	0	
Chases	3	0	0	0	242
Career Total	9	0	1	0	1297

Going:	Sf: 0-0 GS: 0-0 Gd: 0-0 GF: - Fm: 0-3
Distance:	2m/2m3: 0-0 2m4-2m7: 0-0 3m+: 0-4
Track:	LH: 0-4 RH: 0-0 Tight: 0-3 Gall: 0-0
Aids:	Bl: 0-2 Vi: 0-0 Tstrap: 0-0
Best Rating:	72 10/97 Carl 2m1f firm NHF

Slip The Net (IRE)

85   **67**

9-y-o b g Slip Anchor-Circus Ring (High Top)
M J Weeden Malcolm Green

Placings:6/00/6   (2338)
2002/03: 19QS,

	Starts	1st	2nd	3rd	Win & Pl
Hurdles	1	0	0	0	0

| Career Total | 4 | 0 | 0 | 0 | 0 |

Going:	Sf: 0-1 GS: 0-0 Gd: 0-0 GF: - Fm: 0-0
Distance:	2m/2m3: 0-1 2m4-2m7: 0-0 3m+: 0-0
Track:	LH: 0-0 RH: 0-1 Tight: 0-0 Gall: 0-0
Aids:	Bl: 0-0 Vi: 0-0 Tstrap: 0-0
Best Rating:	87 3/99 Newb 2m110y gd-fm Hdl

Slip The Ring

84   **62**

9-y-o ch g Belmez (USA)-Sixslip (USA) (Diesis)
Miss K Marks Nick Shutts

Placings:S52250/565-FP   (4707)
2002/03: 20FGS, 26PG,

	Starts	1st	2nd	3rd	Win & Pl
Chases	2	0	0	0	
Career Total	11	0	2	0	1532

Going:	Sf: 0-0 GS: 0-1 Gd: 0-1 GF: - Fm: 0-0
Distance:	2m/2m3: 0-0 2m4-2m7: 0-1 3m+: 0-1
Track:	LH: 0-1 RH: 0-1 Tight: 0-0 Gall: 0-0
Aids:	Bl: 0-0 Vi: 0-0 Tstrap: 0-0
Best Rating:	108 10/00 MRas 2m3f110y good Hdl

Sloane Street (FR)

102   **82**

4-y-o b g Sadler s Wells (USA)-Shy Danceuse (FR) (Groom Dancer (USA))
D J Caro (A Fabre 3/6) The Yes - No - Wait   Sorries

Placings:FP005320   (4566)
2002/03: 16FGF, 16PGS, 16QGS, 17SHY, 16JG, 16JG, 20QGF,

	Starts	1st	2nd	3rd	Win & Pl
Hurdles	8	0	1	1	2171
Career Total	8	0	1	1	2171

Going:	Sf: 0-1 GS: 0-3 Gd: 0-2 GF: - Fm: 0-2
Distance:	2m/2m3: 0-7 2m4-2m7: 0-1 3m+: 0-0
Track:	LH: 0-5 RH: 0-3 Tight: 0-1 Gall: 0-3
Aids:	Bl: 0-0 Vi: 0-1 Tstrap: 0-0
Best Rating:	89 11/02 Chel 2m110y gd-sft Hdl

Placed on the Flat in France but has shown nothing over hurdles here.

Slooghy (FR)

105   **127**

7-y-o br g Missolonghi (USA)-Lady Charrecey (FR) (Fin Bon)
N J Henderson P A Deal

Placings:4/0-3221B   (3880)
2002/03: 21JS, 22BHY, 22PHY, 24JG, 24BGS,

	Starts	1st	2nd	3rd	Win & Pl
Hurdles	5	1	2	1	9155
Career Total	7	1	2	1	12065
127	2/03	Newb	3m110y	C(0-130)HHdl	GD	£6426
				Total win prize-money £6426

Going:	Sf: 0-3 GS: 0-1 Gd: 1-1 GF: - Fm: 0-0
Distance:	2m/2m3: 0-2 2m4-2m7: 0-3 3m+: 1-2
Track:	LH: 1-4 RH: 0-1 Tight: 0-2 Gall: 1-3
Aids:	Bl: 0-0 Vi: 0-0 Tstrap: 0-0
Best Rating:	127 2/03 Newb 3m110y good Hdl

Useful handicap hurdler; successful at Newbury in February 2003 and unlucky next time; stays three miles; acts on good and heavy ground.

Small Shots
63

6-y-o br g Roselier (FR)-My Adventure (IRE) (Strong Gale)
C R Egerton B G Pomford

Placings:0 (2476)
2002/03: 19GS,

	Starts	1st	2nd	3rd	Win & Pl
Hurdles	1	0	0	0	
Career Total	1	0	0	0	

Going: Sf: 0-0 GS: 0-1 Gd: 0-0 GF: - Fm: 0-0
Distance: 2m/2m3: 0-0 2m4-2m7: 0-1 3m+: 0-0
Track: LH: 0-1 RH: 0-0 Tight: 0-0 Gall: 0-0
Aids: Bl: 0-0 Vi: 0-0 Tstrap: 0-0
Best Rating: 63 12/02 Donc 2m3f110y gd-sft Hdl

Smart Guy
102 **84**

11-y-o ch g Gildoran-Talahache Bridge (New Brig)
Mrs L C Jewell Mrs P S Donkin

Placings:0/0P0F/0P0003U6U02U0/5U65P/3P3432633/U21 0P5P-PP5FO61P2P30P2 (4756)
2002/03: 21FG, 19PGF, 24SG, 21FGS, 18OGS, 22SG, 20IS, 20FS, 22SS, 16PG, 20SG, 24OG, 20PGF, 18SGF,

	Starts	1st	2nd	3rd	Win & Pl
Chases	14	1	2	1	7528
Career Total	53	2	5	7	16702
81	12/02 Font	2m4f	F(0-100)HCh	SFT	£4832
79	12/01 Font	2m4f	F(0-100)HCh	GD	£3055
				Total win prize-money	£7888

Going: Sf: 1-3 GS: 0-2 Gd: 0-6 GF: - Fm: 0-3
Distance: 2m/2m3: 0-4 2m4-2m7: 1-8 3m+: 0-2
Track: LH: 0-5 RH: 0-4 Tight: 1-9 Gall: 0-2
Aids: Bl: 0-0 Vi: 0-0 Tstrap: 0-0
Best Rating: 91 3/99 Font 2m3f soft Ch

Modest chaser; only two wins both came over two and a half miles at Fontwell; acts on any ground.

Smart Lord
95(103c) (71c)**74**

12-y-o br g Arctic Lord-Lady Catcher (Free Boy)
M R Bosley The Blowingstone Partnership

Placings:5050/303545P/20FP/0/43/3/36223-0554 (2443)
2002/03: 20OG, 17SG, 17SS, 16KGS,

	Starts	1st	2nd	3rd	Win & Pl
Hurdles	3	0	0	0	0
Chases	1	0	0	0	273
Career Total	28	0	3	6	5996

Going: Sf: 0-1 GS: 0-1 Gd: 0-2 GF: - Fm: 0-0
Distance: 2m/2m3: 0-3 2m4-2m7: 0-1 3m+: 0-0
Track: LH: 0-2 RH: 0-0 Tight: 0-1 Gall: 0-1
Aids: Bl: 0-0 Vi: 0-2 Tstrap: 0-2
Best Rating: 91 3/96 Folk 2m1f110y gd-fm NHF

Modest performer over hurdles, regularly in the frame over fences, but is proving hard to win with.

Smart Play (USA)

10-y-o gr g Sovereign Dancer (USA)-Casessa (USA) (Caro)
A J Lidderdale Doubleprint

Placings:P (1582)
2002/03: 21PG,

	Starts	1st	2nd	3rd	Win & Pl
Hurdles	1	0	0	0	
Career Total	1	0	0	0	

Going: Sf: 0-0 GS: 0-0 Gd: 0-1 GF: - Fm: 0-0
Distance: 2m/2m3: 0-0 2m4-2m7: 0-1 3m+: 0-0
Track: LH: 0-1 RH: 0-0 Tight: 0-0 Gall: 0-0
Aids: Bl: 0-0 Vi: 0-0 Tstrap: 0-0
Best Rating: 0 10/02 Plum 2m5f good Hdl

Smart Squall (USA)
81 **61**

8-y-o b h Summer Squall (USA)-Greek Wedding (USA) (Blushing Groom (FR))
A J Lidderdale George Ward

Placings:03/0P (3335)
2002/03: 19OGS, 24PS,

	Starts	1st	2nd	3rd	Win & Pl
Hurdles	2	0	0	0	
Career Total	4	0	0	1	404

Going: Sf: 0-1 GS: 0-1 Gd: 0-0 GF: - Fm: 0-0
Distance: 2m/2m3: 0-1 2m4-2m7: 0-0 3m+: 0-1
Track: LH: 0-0 RH: 0-2 Tight: 0-0 Gall: 0-0
Aids: Bl: 0-0 Vi: 0-0 Tstrap: 0-0
Best Rating: 99 3/00 Hrfd 2m3f110y good Hdl

Formerly decent on the Flat, he has not shown much in limited opportunities over hurdles.

Smarty (IRE)
102(101h) (102h)**104**

10-y-o b/br g Royal Fountain-Cahernane Girl (Bargello)
M Pitman Mrs T Brown

Placings:0036P/45F11P11/132P2/12035PP-05 (2115)
2002/03: 31OGS, 27SGS,

	Starts	1st	2nd	3rd	Win & Pl
Chases	2	0	0	0	1625
Career Total	27	6	3	3	169594
91	11/01 Plum	2m5f	E Hdl	G-S	£2387
133	12/00 Leic	2m7f110yD(0-125)HCh		G-S	£4192
140	3/99 Uttx	3m2f	C HCh	G-S	£18643
135	2/99 Hntg	3m	D(0-120)HCh	G-S	£5836
123	1/99 Leic	2m7f110yF(0-110)HCh		SFT	£3262
118	12/98 Wwck	3m2f	E Ch	G-S	£2846
				Total win prize-money	£37168

Going: Sf: 0-0 GS: 0-2 Gd: 0-0 GF: - Fm: 0-0
Distance: 2m/2m3: 0-0 2m4-2m7: 0-0 3m+: 0-2
Track: LH: 0-2 RH: 0-0 Tight: 0-1 Gall: 0-0
Aids: Bl: 0-1 Vi: 0-0 Tstrap: 0-0
Best Rating: 140 3/99 Uttx 3m2f gd-sft Ch

Useful staying chaser on his day; ran a blinder when narrowly beaten under 12st in the Sussex National in 2001 and topped that effort when runner-up in the Grand National to Red Marauder; made a winning return to hurdles in November 2001, before finishing second over the National fences again in the Becher Chase, but he has been well held since; suited by good to soft ground; often wears blinkers or visor.

Smashing Time (USA)

5-y-o b m Smart Strike (CAN)-Broken Peace (USA) (Devil s Bag (USA))

M C Chapman Eric Knowles

Placings:P0 (4412)
2002/03: 17PGS, 17OG,

	Starts	1st	2nd	3rd	Win & Pl
Hurdles	2	0	0	0	
Career Total	2	0	0	0	

Going: Sf: 0-0 GS: 0-1 Gd: 0-1 GF: - Fm: 0-0
Distance: 2m/2m3: 0-2 2m4-2m7: 0-0 3m+: 0-0
Track: LH: 0-0 RH: 0-2 Tight: 0-2 Gall: 0-0
Aids: Bl: 0-0 Vi: 0-0 Tstrap: 0-0
Best Rating: 0 3/03 MRas 2m1f110y good Hdl

Smetherds Tom
95 **64**

9-y-o b g Dortino-Nellie s Joy Vii (Damsire Unregistered)
N R Mitchell Mrs J C Duffy

Placings:6UPP30 (4695)
2002/03: 16KS, 22US, 20PHY, 16PS, 19SF, 16OG,

	Starts	1st	2nd	3rd	Win & Pl
Chases	6	0	0	1	856
Career Total	6	0	0	1	856

Going: Sf: 0-4 GS: 0-0 Gd: 0-1 GF: - Fm: 0-0
Distance: 2m/2m3: 0-4 2m4-2m7: 0-2 3m+: 0-0
Track: LH: 0-2 RH: 0-2 Tight: 0-6 Gall: 0-0
Aids: Bl: 0-0 Vi: 0-0 Tstrap: 0-0
Best Rating: 59 4/03 Tntn 2m3f firm Ch

Smile Pleeze (IRE)

11-y-o b g Naheez (USA)-Harkin Park (Pollerton)
M R Daniell Miss S Troughton

Placings:66F/50/5/40P-4 (0033)
2002/03: 25KGF,

	Starts	1st	2nd	3rd	Win & Pl
Chases	1	0	0	0	302
Career Total	10	0	0	0	302

Going: Sf: 0-0 GS: 0-0 Gd: 0-0 GF: - Fm: 0-1
Distance: 2m/2m3: 0-0 2m4-2m7: 0-0 3m+: 0-1
Track: LH: 0-1 RH: 0-0 Tight: 0-0 Gall: 0-0
Aids: Bl: 0-0 Vi: 0-0 Tstrap: 0-0
Best Rating: 95 3/02 Chel 3m2f110y good Ch

Winning pointer, best on a sound surface although has won on good to soft.

Smiling Thru

11-y-o b g Reference Point-Ever Genial (Brigadier Gerard)
P Grindey (T H Caldwell 19/5) Peter Grindey

Placings:P-PP (1334)
2002/03: 26PG, 24FGF,

	Starts	1st	2nd	3rd	Win & Pl
Chases	2	0	0	0	
Career Total	3	0	0	0	

Going: Sf: 0-0 GS: 0-0 Gd: 0-0 GF: 0-1 Fm: 0-1
Distance: 2m/2m3: 0-0 2m4-2m7: 0-0 3m+: 0-2
Track: LH: 0-1 RH: 0-0 Tight: 0-1 Gall: 0-1
Aids: Bl: 0-0 Vi: 0-0 Tstrap: 0-0
Best Rating: 0 9/02 Hntg 3m gd-fm Ch

Smith's Perk (IRE)

10-y-o b g Executive Perk-Sister Of Slane (The Parson)
Mrs L C Jewell Mrs A Emanuel

Placings:106/2/PP/0/5PP6   (4341)
2002/03: 21⁵HY, 20⁶S, 25⁵G, 20⁶GF,

	Starts	1st	2nd	3rd	Win & Pl
Hurdles	2	0	0	0	0
Chases	2	0	0	0	0
Career Total	11	1	1	0	2329

101 12/97 Hntg 2m110y H NHF   GD £1413
Total win prize-money £1413

Going:	Sf: 0-2 GS: 0-0 Gd: 0-0 GF: - Fm: 0-1
Distance:	2m/2m3: 0-0 2m4-2m7: 0-3 3m+: 0-1
Track:	LH: 0-1 RH: 0-2 Tight: 0-3 Gall: 0-1
Aids:	Bl: 0-1 Vi: 0-0 Tstrap: 0-4
Best Rating:	107 2/98 Newb 2m110y good NHF

Smiths Landing
107   117+

6-y-o b g Primitive Rising (USA)-Landing Power (Hills Forecast)
Mrs S J Smith Billy McCullough

Placings:6464512   (4715)
2002/03: 16⁶G, 19⁴GS, 16⁶S, 19⁴G, 20⁵GS, 20¹G, 20²GF,

	Starts	1st	2nd	3rd	Win & Pl
NH Flat	1	0	0	0	0
Hurdles	6	1	1	0	5143
Career Total	7	1	1	0	5143

111 3/03 Hexm 2m4f110yE(0-105)HHdl GD £3794
Total win prize-money £3794

Going:	Sf: 0-1 GS: 0-2 Gd: 1-3 GF: - Fm: 0-1
Distance:	2m/2m3: 0-4 2m4-2m7: 1-3 3m+: 0-0
Track:	LH: 1-7 RH: 0-0 Tight: 0-2 Gall: 0-1
Aids:	Bl: 0-0 Vi: 0-0 Tstrap: 0-0
Best Rating:	114 4/03 Weth 2m4f110y gd-fm Hdl

Fair novice hurdler; jumped much better than previously when getting off the mark at Hexham in March; progressive since and recorded another victory in handicap company at Wetherby in May; stays two and a half miles and should get further; handles fast ground.

Smiths Wynd

11-y-o gr g Alias Smith (USA)-Carrapateira (Gunner B)
R Shiels R Shiels

Placings:P3FP/6/P/2-0   (0402)
2002/03: 20²G, 20⁹GF,

	Starts	1st	2nd	3rd	Win & Pl
Chases	2	0	1	0	508
Career Total	8	0	1	1	1033

Going:	Sf: 0-0 GS: 0-0 Gd: 0-1 GF: - Fm: 0-1
Distance:	2m/2m3: 0-0 2m4-2m7: 0-2 3m+: 0-1
Track:	LH: 0-2 RH: 0-0 Tight: 0-0 Gall: 0-1
Aids:	Bl: 0-0 Vi: 0-0 Tstrap: 0-0
Best Rating:	78 2/99 Muss 3m good Ch

Smokestack (IRE)
91   91

7-y-o b g Lord Americo-Chiminee Fly (Proverb)
J A B Old M Lovatt/c Jenkins

Placings:054-30   (4252)
2002/03: 16³S, 22¹⁰G,

	Starts	1st	2nd	3rd	Win & Pl
Hurdles	2	0	0	1	892
Career Total	5	0	0	1	1224

Going:	Sf: 0-1 GS: 0-0 Gd: 0-1 GF: - Fm: 0-0
Distance:	2m/2m3: 0-1 2m4-2m7: 0-1 3m+: 0-0
Track:	LH: 0-1 RH: 0-2 Tight: 0-0 Gall: 0-0
Aids:	Bl: 0-0 Vi: 0-0 Tstrap: 0-0
Best Rating:	91 12/02 Sand 2m110y soft Hdl

Smooth Passage
69   34

4-y-o b g Suave Dancer (USA)-Flagship (Rainbow Quest (USA))
J Gallagher Colin Rashbrook

Placings:0   (4084)
2002/03: 16⁸GS,

	Starts	1st	2nd	3rd	Win & Pl
Hurdles	1	0	0	0	0
Career Total	1	0	0	0	0

Going:	Sf: 0-0 GS: 0-1 Gd: 0-0 GF: - Fm: 0-0
Distance:	2m/2m3: 0-1 2m4-2m7: 0-0 3m+: 0-0
Track:	LH: 0-1 RH: 0-0 Tight: 0-1 Gall: 0-0
Aids:	Bl: 0-0 Vi: 0-0 Tstrap: 0-0
Best Rating:	34 3/03 Strf 2m110y gd-sft Hdl

Smooth Sailing
100   104

8-y-o gr g Beveled (USA)-Sea Farer Lake (Gairloch)
K McAuliffe A R Parrish

Placings:10/PP451-22   (0326)
2002/03: 16²GF, 16²G,

	Starts	1st	2nd	3rd	Win & Pl
Hurdles	2	0	2	0	1608
Career Total	9	2	2	0	7278

99 3/02 Plum 2m F(0-90)Hdl GD £2341
90 1/00 Leic 2m E Hdl SFT £3328
Total win prize-money £5670

Going:	Sf: 0-0 GS: 0-0 Gd: 0-1 GF: - Fm: 0-1
Distance:	2m/2m3: 0-2 2m4-2m7: 0-0 3m+: 0-0
Track:	LH: 0-2 RH: 0-0 Tight: 0-0 Gall: 0-0
Aids:	Bl: 0-0 Vi: 0-0 Tstrap: 0-0
Best Rating:	105 5/02 Worc 2m good Hdl

Fair hurdler, suited by fast ground and two miles.

Smudge (IRE)
96   98

6-y-o br g Be My Native (USA)-Crash Call (Crash Course)
R Ford Mrs Brenda Siddall

Placings:0-P06   (2507)
2002/03: 16⁹PG, 19⁹GS, 16⁶G,

	Starts	1st	2nd	3rd	Win & Pl
Hurdles	3	0	0	0	0
Career Total	4	0	0	0	0

Going:	Sf: 0-0 GS: 0-1 Gd: 0-2 GF: - Fm: 0-0
Distance:	2m/2m3: 0-3 2m4-2m7: 0-0 3m+: 0-0
Track:	LH: 0-3 RH: 0-0 Tight: 0-0 Gall: 0-0
Aids:	Bl: 0-0 Vi: 0-1 Tstrap: 0-0
Best Rating:	98 12/02 Hayd 2m good Hdl

Smyslov
93   72

5-y-o b g Rainbow Quest (USA)-Vlaanderen (IRE) (In The Wings)
P R Webber Trevor Sharman

Placings:553-0   (0663)
2002/03: 16⁰GF,

	Starts	1st	2nd	3rd	Win & Pl
Hurdles	1	0	0	0	0
Career Total	4	0	0	1	432

Going:	Sf: 0-0 GS: 0-0 Gd: 0-0 GF: - Fm: 0-1
Distance:	2m/2m3: 0-0 2m4-2m7: 0-0 3m+: 0-0
Track:	LH: 0-1 RH: 0-0 Tight: 0-0 Gall: 0-0
Aids:	Bl: 0-0 Vi: 0-1 Tstrap: 0-0
Best Rating:	90 4/02 Ludl 2m gd-fm Hdl

Fair handicapper on the Flat but disappointing over hurdles until a better effort on his third attempt.

Snails Castle (IRE)
86   91

4-y-o b g Danehill (USA)-Bean Island (USA) (Afleet (CAN))
E W Tuer (N A Callaghan 6/6) Shore Property

Placings:03   (1413)
2002/03: 16⁵GF, 16³GF,

	Starts	1st	2nd	3rd	Win & Pl
Hurdles	2	0	0	1	596
Career Total	2	0	0	1	596

Going:	Sf: 0-0 GS: 0-0 Gd: 0-0 GF: - Fm: 0-2
Distance:	2m/2m3: 0-2 2m4-2m7: 0-0 3m+: 0-0
Track:	LH: 0-1 RH: 0-1 Tight: 0-1 Gall: 0-0
Aids:	Bl: 0-0 Vi: 0-0 Tstrap: 0-0
Best Rating:	86 10/02 Kels 2m110y gd-fm Hdl

Poor form when placed in juvenile hurdle at Kelso in October.

Snake Goddess
51

5-y-o b m Primo Dominie-Shoshone (Be My Chief (USA))
D W P Arbuthnot The Sfs Partnership

Placings:0P00-P   (0331)
2002/03: 20⁷G,

	Starts	1st	2nd	3rd	Win & Pl
Hurdles	1	0	0	0	
Career Total	5	0	0	0	

Going:	Sf: 0-0 GS: 0-0 Gd: 0-1 GF: - Fm: 0-0
Distance:	2m/2m3: 0-0 2m4-2m7: 0-1 3m+: 0-0
Track:	LH: 0-1 RH: 0-0 Tight: 0-0 Gall: 0-0
Aids:	Bl: 0-0 Vi: 0-1 Tstrap: 0-0
Best Rating:	51 4/02 Font 2m2f110y gd-fm Hdl

Snapper
93(92h)   (70h)65

12-y-o b g Gunner B-Fortalice (Saucy Kit)
Mrs L B Normile L B N Racing Club

Placings:6/4036/143/56P61UP0/0505PU-514   (0496)
2002/03: 22⁵G, 24¹GF, 24⁴GS,

	Starts	1st	2nd	3rd	Win & Pl
Hurdles	2	1	0	0	3031
Chases	1	0	0	0	516

Career Total	25	3	0	2	9421
70	5/02 Prth	3m110y	E Hdl	G-F	£3031
94	12/00 Ayr	3m5f	E(0-115)HCh	SFT	£2834
103	5/99 Prth	2m4f110yH Ch		HVY	£2190
			Total win prize-money £8055		

Going: Sf: 0-0 GS: 0-1 Gd: 0-1 GF: - Fm: 1-1
Distance: 2m/2m3: 0-0 2m4-2m7: 0-0 **3m+: 1-2**
Track: LH: 0-1 **RH: 1-2** Tight: 0-1 Gall: 0-0
Aids: **Bl: 1-2** Vi: 0-0 Tstrap: 0-0
Best Rating: 103 5/99 Prth 2m4f110y heavy Ch

Modest staying handicapper, seems better over hurdles. Acts on any ground and has run his better races on galloping tracks. Usually wears blinkers.

Snipe

103f   **95f**

5-y-o ch g Anshan-Flexwing (Electric)
G A Butler   T D Holland-Martin

Placings:04   (4329)
2002/03: 16⁰HY, 16⁴G,

	Starts	1st	2nd	3rd	Win & Pl
NH Flat	2	0	0	0	0
Career Total	2	0	0	0	0

Going: Sf: 0-1 GS: 0-0 Gd: 0-1 GF: - Fm: 0-0
Distance: 2m/2m3: 0-2 2m4-2m7: 0-0 3m+: 0-0
Track: LH: 0-1 RH: 0-1 Tight: 0-0 Gall: 0-1
Aids: Bl: 0-0 Vi: 0-0 Tstrap: 0-0
Best Rating: 95 3/03 Newb 2m110y good NHF

Sniper

103   **76**

11-y-o ch g Gunner B-Highfrith (Deep Run)
F P Murtagh   Hurst Farm Racing

Placings:00P/64S3P362U00/21122445P/P356PPP/1P0P6
6P/20P32PP4-P305P   (4409)
2002/03: 27⁰PG, 21³G, 27⁰G, 25⁵PG, 25⁵G,

	Starts	1st	2nd	3rd	Win & Pl
Chases	5	0	0	1	663
Career Total	50	3	6	5	20954
76	10/00 Sedg	3m3f	F(0-90)HCh	G-S	£2808
110	11/98 Kels	3m1f	D Ch	SFT	£5107
107	10/98 Kels	3m1f	D Ch	SFT	£3468
			Total win prize-money £11384		

Going: Sf: 0-1 GS: 0-0 Gd: 0-3 GF: - Fm: 0-1
Distance: 2m/2m3: 0-0 2m4-2m7: 0-1 3m+: 0-4
Track: LH: 0-5 RH: 0-0 Tight: 0-4 Gall: 0-0
Aids: Bl: 0-0 Vi: 0-0 Tstrap: 0-1
Best Rating: 110 11/98 Kels 3m1f soft Ch

Modest staying chaser. Best on good to soft.

Snizort (USA)

69   **28**

5-y-o b g Bahri (USA)-Ava Singstheblues (USA) (Dixieland Band (USA))
M E Sowersby   Racing Ladies

Placings:P04   (1420)
2002/03: 24⁵GS, 17⁰GF, 24⁴GF,

	Starts	1st	2nd	3rd	Win & Pl
Hurdles	3	0	0	0	319
Career Total	3	0	0	0	319

Going: Sf: 0-0 GS: 0-1 Gd: 0-0 GF: - Fm: 0-2

Snow Cloud

9-y-o b m Today And Tomorrow-Fancy Pages (Touch Paper)
R Brotherton   R D Evans

Placings:P   (2565)
2002/03: 17⁵GS,

	Starts	1st	2nd	3rd	Win & Pl
Hurdles	1	0	0	0	
Career Total	1	0	0	0	

Going: Sf: 0-0 GS: 0-0 Gd: 0-0 GF: - Fm: 0-0
Distance: 2m/2m3: 0-1 2m4-2m7: 0-0 3m+: 0-0
Track: LH: 0-1 RH: 0-0 Tight: 0-1 Gall: 0-0
Aids: Bl: 0-0 Vi: 0-0 Tstrap: 0-0
Best Rating: 0 12/02 Bang 2m1f gd-sft Hdl

Snow Partridge (USA)

101   (67h)**81**

9-y-o ch g Arctic Tern (USA)-Lady Sharp (FR) (Sharpman)
Mrs L C Taylor   T Chamberlain

Placings:52130/FP53035F   (4632)
2002/03: 22⁵G, 19⁰PS, 20⁵GS, 19⁴G, 20⁴GS, 20³GF, 24⁵G, 26⁵GF,

	Starts	1st	2nd	3rd	Win & Pl
Hurdles	2	0	0	0	0
Chases	6	0	0	2	1576
Career Total	13	1	1	3	5080
106	7/00 Worc	2m4f	E Hdl	G-F	£2324
			Total win prize-money £2324		

Going: Sf: 0-1 GS: 0-2 Gd: 0-3 GF: - Fm: 0-2
Distance: 2m/2m3: 0-1 2m4-2m7: 0-5 3m+: 0-2
Track: LH: 0-2 RH: 0-5 Tight: 0-4 Gall: 0-0
Aids: Bl: 0-1 Vi: 0-0 Tstrap: 0-0
Best Rating: 106 7/00 Worc 2m4f gd-fm Hdl

Snowboy (IRE)

11-y-o br g Celio Rufo-Laurestown Rose (Derring Rose)
Mrs J M Bailey   Mrs J M Bailey

Placings:56P0U0/43P3PU/54F-2   (0312)
2002/03: 21²G,

	Starts	1st	2nd	3rd	Win & Pl
Chases	1	0	1	0	654
Career Total	16	0	1	2	2046

Going: Sf: 0-0 GS: 0-0 Gd: 0-0 GF: - Fm: 0-0
Distance: 2m/2m3: 0-0 2m4-2m7: 0-1 3m+: 0-0
Track: LH: 0-0 RH: 0-1 Tight: 0-1 Gall: 0-0
Aids: Bl: 0-0 Vi: 0-0 Tstrap: 0-0
Best Rating: 94 11/97 Ludl 2m good NHF

Snowmore

103   **114**

7-y-o ch m Glacial Storm (USA)-Royal Typhoon (Royal Fountain)

Mrs S J Smith   Paul J Dixon

Placings:4622412P0-2110442P   (4774)
2002/03: 21²GF, 21¹GF, 21¹G, 21⁰G, 20⁴GS, 19⁴GS, 24²GS, 27⁰G,

	Starts	1st	2nd	3rd	Win & Pl
Hurdles	8	2	2	0	13631
Career Total	17	3	5	0	17616
105	10/02 Sthl	2m5f110yC(0-130)HHdl	GD	£6890
99	8/02 Sthl	2m5f110yE(0-110)HHdl	G-F	£3410
83	11/01 Catt	2m3f	F Hdl	G-F	£1907
			Total win prize-money £12208		

Going: Sf: 0-0 GS: 0-3 Gd: 1-3 GF: - Fm: 1-2
Distance: 2m/2m3: 0-0 **2m4-2m7: 2-6** 3m+: 0-2
Track: **LH: 2-5** RH: 0-2 Tight: 0-3 Gall: 0-1
Aids: Bl: 0-0 Vi: 0-0 Tstrap: 0-0
Best Rating: 112 3/03 MRas 3m gd-sft Hdl

Modest hurdler, stays two miles-five, suited by a sound surface and positive tactics; recorded third win over Southwell s mini-fences in May but finished lame.

Snowtre (IRE)

80f   **59f**

6-y-o b g Glacial Storm (USA)-Forest Gale (Strong Gale)
Mrs H L Needham   J D Callow

Placings:0   (0660)
2002/03: 16⁰GF,

	Starts	1st	2nd	3rd	Win & Pl
NH Flat	1	0	0	0	
Career Total	1	0	0	0	

Going: Sf: 0-0 GS: 0-0 Gd: 0-0 GF: - Fm: 0-0
Distance: 2m/2m3: 0-1 2m4-2m7: 0-0 3m+: 0-0
Track: LH: 0-1 RH: 0-0 Tight: 0-0 Gall: 0-0
Aids: Bl: 0-0 Vi: 0-0 Tstrap: 0-0
Best Rating: 63 6/02 Worc 2m gd-fm NHF

So Tempted

4-y-o br f So Factual (USA)-Bystrouska (Gorytus (USA))
N Wilson   J Watson

Placings:SF   (4269)
2002/03: 17⁵HY, 16⁶GF,

	Starts	1st	2nd	3rd	Win & Pl
NH Flat	2	0	0	0	
Career Total	2	0	0	0	

Going: Sf: 0-1 GS: 0-0 Gd: 0-0 GF: - Fm: 0-1
Distance: 2m/2m3: 0-2 2m4-2m7: 0-0 3m+: 0-0
Track: LH: 0-0 RH: 0-0 Tight: 0-2 Gall: 0-0
Aids: Bl: 0-0 Vi: 0-0 Tstrap: 0-0
Best Rating: 0 3/03 Sthl 2m gd-fm NHF

Soap Stone

90   **57**

8-y-o b m Gunner B-Tzarina (USA) (Gallant Romeo (USA))
Miss A M Newton-Smith   G V Gann

Placings:RR/00505/R005   (4703)
2002/03: 20⁵G, 16⁰GF, 21⁰GF, 16⁵GF,

	Starts	1st	2nd	3rd	Win & Pl
Hurdles	4	0	0	0	0
Career Total	11	0	0	0	0

Going: Sf: 0-0 GS: 0-0 Gd: 0-1 GF: - Fm: 0-3

Distance: 2m/2m3: 0-2 2m4-2m7: 0-2 3m+: 0-0
Track: LH: 0-3 RH: 0-1 Tight: 0-4 Gall: 0-0
Aids: Bl: 0-1 Vi: 0-0 Tstrap: 0-4
Best Rating: 68 10/99 Towc 2m   good   Hdl

Soaring Monarch
92   **87**

8-y-o b g Rakaposhi King-Flying Faith (Rymer)
J T Gifford Ivybrook Partners

Placings:0/0/00F30P0-UFF6P00   (4568)
2002/03: 19UGS, 22FGS, 21FS, 20PS, 24FGS, 22QG, 22QG,

	Starts	1st	2nd	3rd	Win & Pl
Hurdles	4	0	0	0	0
Chases	3	0	0	0	0
Career Total	16	0	0	1	610

Going: Sf: 0-2 GS: 0-3 Gd: 0-1 GF: - Fm: 0-1
Distance: 2m/2m3: 0-0 2m4-2m7: 0-0 3m+: 0-1
Track: LH: 0-2 RH: 0-4 Tight: 0-4 Gall: 0-1
Aids: Bl: 0-0 Vi: 0-0 Tstrap: 0-0
Best Rating: 102 12/00 Kemp 2m   gd-sft   Hdl

Modest maiden hurdler, has yet to complete over fences.

Sober Hill
92   **89**

5-y-o b g Komaite (USA)-Mamoda (Good Times (ITY))
N B Mason N B Mason

Placings:50022-4026   (1072)
2002/03: 16AG, 16QG, 17ZG, 17RG,

	Starts	1st	2nd	3rd	Win & Pl
Hurdles	4	0	1	0	1068
Career Total	9	0	3	0	2124

Going: Sf: 0-0 GS: 0-1 Gd: 0-3 GF: - Fm: 0-0
Distance: 2m/2m3: 0-0 2m4-2m7: 0-0 3m+: 0-0
Track: LH: 0-3 RH: 0-1 Tight: 0-2 Gall: 0-0
Aids: Bl: 0-0 Vi: 0-0 Tstrap: 0-2
Best Rating: 89 8/02 Ctml 2m1f1f110y   good   Hdl

In the frame in selling hurdles, but looks an awkward ride.

Socialist (USA)
                                                67

7-y-o b g Hermitage (USA)-Social Missy (USA) (Raised
Socially (USA))
G Brown Mrs Carol Ann Brown

Placings:500/50FP5-   (0007)
2002/03: 16SG,

	Starts	1st	2nd	3rd	Win & Pl
Hurdles	1	0	0	0	0
Career Total	8	0	0	0	0

Going: Sf: 0-0 GS: 0-0 Gd: 0-1 GF: - Fm: 0-0
Distance: 2m/2m3: 0-1 2m4-2m7: 0-0 3m+: 0-0
Track: LH: 0-1 RH: 0-0 Tight: 0-1 Gall: 0-0
Aids: Bl: 0-0 Vi: 0-0 Tstrap: 0-0
Best Rating: 67 5/01 Hntg 2m110y   gd-fm   Hdl

Society Buck (IRE)
81   **81**

6-y-o b g Moscow Society (USA)-Bucks Grove (IRE)
(Buckskin (FR))

M W Easterby Abbots Salford Caravan Park

Placings:0-1040   (3227)
2002/03: 17IGF, 17PS, 16FGS, 17QHY,

	Starts	1st	2nd	3rd	Win & Pl
NH Flat	2	1	0	0	1848
Hurdles	2	0	0	0	306
Career Total	5	1	0	0	2154
89	7/02	Sedg	2m1f	H NHF	G-F £1848

Total win prize-money £1848

Going: Sf: 0-2 GS: 0-1 Gd: 0-0 GF: - Fm: 1-1
Distance: 2m/2m3: 1-4 2m4-2m7: 0-0 3m+: 0-0
Track: LH: 1-3 RH: 0-1 Tight: 1-2 Gall: 0-0
Aids: Bl: 0-0 Vi: 0-0 Tstrap: 0-0
Best Rating: 89 10/02 Carl 2m1f   soft   NHF

Unplaced on his debut, he got off the mark second time out
at Sedgefield. Bred to stay. Acts on good to firm ground.
Held subsequently.

Socute

8-y-o b m Tina s Pet-Cute Pam (Pamroy)
J W Mullins The Not So Blonde Partnership

Placings:5   (0488)
2002/03: 24SHY,

	Starts	1st	2nd	3rd	Win & Pl
Hurdles	1	0	0	0	0
Career Total	1	0	0	0	0

Going: Sf: 0-1 GS: 0-0 Gd: 0-0 GF: - Fm: 0-0
Distance: 2m/2m3: 0-0 2m4-2m7: 0-0 3m+: 0-0
Track: LH: 0-1 RH: 0-0 Tight: 0-0 Gall: 0-0
Aids: Bl: 0-0 Vi: 0-0 Tstrap: 0-0
Best Rating:

Sodelk
89   **80**

9-y-o ch m Interrex (CAN)-Summoned By Bells (Stanford)
J E Long Mick Robinson

Placings:000/L4/50F2P60/PP3RU54PU55P-0U520LP5L
                                                  (2307)
2002/03: 16QGS, 16UG, 20SG, 19ZF, 16QG, 22LGS, 18PGS, 16FS,
21LHY,

	Starts	1st	2nd	3rd	Win & Pl
Hurdles	8	0	1	0	1240
Chases	1	0	0	0	0
Career Total	33	0	2	1	2307

Going: Sf: 0-2 GS: 0-3 Gd: 0-3 GF: - Fm: 0-1
Distance: 2m/2m3: 0-6 2m4-2m7: 0-3 3m+: 0-0
Track: LH: 0-4 RH: 0-4 Tight: 0-6 Gall: 0-1
Aids: Bl: 0-0 Vi: 0-0 Tstrap: 0-0
Best Rating: 81 1/02 Leic 2m   soft   Hdl

Modest maiden hurdler whose best effort was on heavy
ground. Has shown signs of temperament.

Soeur Fontenail (FR)
110(98h)   (10th)**117**

6-y-o b m Turgeon (USA)-Fontanalia (FR) (Rex Magna
(FR))
N J Hawke La Connection Francaise

Placings:P65/2432310-31224316P   (4570)

2002/03: 17RG, 17IG, 17ZGS, 16ZGS, 19SGS, 19RG, 17IS, 16PG,
20PG,

	Starts	1st	2nd	3rd	Win & Pl
Chases	9	2	2	2	17141
Career Total	19	3	4	4	24204
113	2/03	Plum	2m1f	D Ch	SFT £6841
120	10/02	Plum	2m1f	D(0-110)HCh	GD £5378
101	3/02	NAbb	2m1f	E Hdl	GD £3052

Total win prize-money £15272

Going: Sf: 1-1 GS: 0-3 Gd: 1-5 GF: - Fm: 0-0
Distance: 2m/2m3: 2-7 2m4-2m7: 0-2 3m+: 0-0
Track: LH: 2-6 RH: 0-3 Tight: 2-4 Gall: 0-1
Aids: Bl: 0-0 Vi: 0-0 Tstrap: 0-0
Best Rating: 120 11/02 Winc 2m   gd-sft   Ch

Fair chaser; effective at around 2m, stays 2m 3f; acts on
good and soft ground; has worn cheekpieces.

Sofisio
107   **93**

6-y-o ch g Efisio-Legal Embrace (CAN) (Legal Bid (USA))
Miss S J Wilton John Pointon And Sons

Placings:0/5U543-6502   (0778)
2002/03: 17FGF, 16SGF, 16QG, 16ZGF,

	Starts	1st	2nd	3rd	Win & Pl
Hurdles	4	0	1	0	596
Career Total	10	0	1	1	1219

Going: Sf: 0-0 GS: 0-0 Gd: 0-1 GF: - Fm: 0-3
Distance: 2m/2m3: 0-4 2m4-2m7: 0-0 3m+: 0-0
Track: LH: 0-3 RH: 0-1 Tight: 0-0 Gall: 0-0
Aids: Bl: 0-0 Vi: 0-0 Tstrap: 0-4
Best Rating: 93 12/01 Ludl 2m   good   Hdl

Moderate hurdler who races in tongue tie and blinkers.

Soho Fields (IRE)
105   **103**

6-y-o b g Good Thyne (USA)-Rosie Owen (IRE) (Roselier
(FR))
Miss H C Knight The Earl Cadogan

Placings:1054   (3845)
2002/03: 16IGS, 19PG, 17RS, 21LG,

	Starts	1st	2nd	3rd	Win & Pl
Hurdles	4	1	0	0	5539
Career Total	4	1	0	0	5539
103	11/02	Ludl	2m	D Hdl	G-S £4706

Total win prize-money £4706

Going: Sf: 0-1 GS: 1-1 Gd: 0-2 GF: - Fm: 0-0
Distance: 2m/2m3: 1-3 2m4-2m7: 0-1 3m+: 0-0
Track: LH: 0-2 RH: 1-2 Tight: 0-0 Gall: 0-2
Aids: Bl: 0-0 Vi: 0-0 Tstrap: 0-0
Best Rating: 103 12/02 Newb 2m3f   good   Hdl

Modest hurdler; won on his debut at Ludlow; has the scope
to develop into a chaser in time.

Sol Chance
84f   **93f**

4-y-o ch g Jupiter Island-Super Sol (Rolfe (USA))
R S Brookhouse R S Brookhouse

Placings:6   (3644)
2002/03: 16PGS,

	Starts	1st	2nd	3rd	Win & Pl
NH Flat	1	0	0	0	0
Career Total	1	0	0	0	0

Going: Sf: 0-0 GS: 0-1 Gd: 0-0 GF: - Fm: 0-0
Distance: 2m/2m3: 0-1 2m4-2m7: 0-0 3m+: 0-0
Track: LH: 0-0 RH: 0-1 Tight: 0-0 Gall: 0-0
Aids: Bl: 0-0 Vi: 0-0 Tstrap: 0-0
Best Rating: 93   2/03 Winc 2m   gd-sft NHF

Sol Music

11-y-o ch g Southern Music-Tyqueen (Tycoon Ii)
Mrs V M Graham The G & P Partnership

Placings: 0/55/245212/03551120/5P55600/131-0111 (4390)
2002/03: 21⁰GF, 16¹G, 20¹GS, 19¹F,

		Starts	1st	2nd	3rd	Win & Pl
Chases		4	3	0	0	9362
Career Total		31	8	4	2	28078
107	3/03	Extr	2m3f110yH Ch		FRM	£3692
114	3/03	Leic	2m4f110yH Ch		G-S	£2660
107	5/02	Towc	2m110y H Ch		GD	£3010
107	3/02	Extr	2m3f110yH Ch		GD	£2156
110	5/01	NAbb	2m110y E(0-115)HCh		G-F	£3410
126	3/99	Hrfd	2m E Ch		G-S	£3160
118	3/99	Tntn	2m110y F(0-100)HCh		SFT	£3241
113	4/98	Hrfd	2m1f E Hdl		SFT	£2641
			Total win prize-money £23972			

Going: Sf: 0-0 GS: 1-1 Gd: 1-1 GF: - Fm: 1-2
Distance: 2m/2m3: 1-1 **2m4-2m7: 2-3** 3m+: 0-0
Track: LH: 0-1 **RH: 3-3** Tight: 0-0 Gall: 0-1
Aids: Bl: 0-0 Vi: 0-0 Tstrap: 0-0
Best Rating: 126   3/99 Hrfd 2m   gd-sft Ch

A front-running hunter chaser, seems best in the spring on a right-handed track; suited by two miles and handles any ground.

Soldershire
95   91

6-y-o b g Weld-Dishcloth (Fury Royal)
S Dow P McCarthy

Placings: 0-3P (1793)
2002/03: 18⁰G, 18³G, 21PS,

	Starts	1st	2nd	3rd	Win & Pl
NH Flat	1	0	0	0	0
Hurdles	2	0	0	1	444
Career Total	3	0	0	1	444

Going: Sf: 0-1 GS: 0-0 Gd: 0-2 GF: - Fm: 0-0
Distance: 2m/2m3: 0-2 2m4-2m7: 0-1 3m+: 0-0
Track: LH: 0-2 RH: 0-1 Tight: 0-1 Gall: 0-0
Aids: Bl: 0-0 Vi: 0-0 Tstrap: 0-0
Best Rating: 91   10/02 Font 2m2f110y good Hdl

Showed a hint of promise in a weak race on hurdle debut at Fontwell.

Soldier Of Rome (IRE)
98   103

6-y-o b g Satco (FR)-Queens Tricks (Le Bavard (FR))
P R Hedger Howard Spooner

Placings: F33P-P00 (2334)
2002/03: 21PS, 16⁰G, 22⁰S,

	Starts	1st	2nd	3rd	Win & Pl
Hurdles	3	0	0	0	
Career Total	7	0	0	2	1053

Going: Sf: 0-2 GS: 0-0 Gd: 0-1 GF: - Fm: 0-0
Distance: 2m/2m3: 0-1 2m4-2m7: 0-2 3m+: 0-0
Track: LH: 0-0 RH: 0-3 Tight: 0-0 Gall: 0-0
Aids: Bl: 0-0 Vi: 0-0 Tstrap: 0-0
Best Rating: 103 1/02 Donc 2m4f   soft Hdl

A lightly-raced maiden over hurdles, he has run with credit, including when third at Doncaster in January 2002. Should stay further. Acts on an easy surface.

Soldier's Song

10-y-o b m Infantry-Top Soprano (High Top)
R J Hodges Lt Col E L Stocker

Placings: 00/PP-P (0036)
2002/03: 17PG,

	Starts	1st	2nd	3rd	Win & Pl
Chases	1	0	0	0	
Career Total	5	0	0	0	

Going: Sf: 0-0 GS: 0-0 Gd: 0-1 GF: - Fm: 0-0
Distance: 2m/2m3: 0-1 2m4-2m7: 0-0 3m+: 0-0
Track: LH: 0-0 RH: 0-1 Tight: 0-0 Gall: 0-0
Aids: Bl: 0-0 Vi: 0-0 Tstrap: 0-0
Best Rating: 55   3/98 Winc 2m   good Hdl

Solid Land (FR)
92   93+

4-y-o b f Solid Illusion (USA)-Tip Land (FR) (Tip Moss (FR))
P F Nicholls (A Hosselet 24/9) Mrs J Stewart

Placings: 63F4 (3236)
2002/03: 15⁶S, 18³VS, 16⁶S, 16⁴S,

	Starts	1st	2nd	3rd	Win & Pl
Hurdles	4	0	0	1	5959
Career Total	4	0	0	1	5959

Going: Sf: 0-3 GS: 0-0 Gd: 0-0 GF: - Fm: 0-0
Distance: 2m/2m3: 0-3 2m4-2m7: 0-0 3m+: 0-0
Track: LH: 0-2 RH: 0-0 Tight: 0-1 Gall: 0-0
Aids: Bl: 0-0 Vi: 0-0 Tstrap: 0-0
Best Rating: 93   12/02 Wwck 2m   soft Hdl

Solo Dancer
94   65

5-y-o ch m Sayaarr (USA)-Oiseval (National Trust)
Mrs H M Bridges Mrs H M Bridges

Placings: 0F630P-6PFFP3 (4626)
2002/03: 22⁶G, 24PS, 17FG, 17FGS, 16PHY, 17³GF,

	Starts	1st	2nd	3rd	Win & Pl
Hurdles	6	0	0	1	553
Career Total	12	0	0	2	902

Going: Sf: 0-2 GS: 0-1 Gd: 0-2 GF: - Fm: 0-1
Distance: 2m/2m3: 0-4 2m4-2m7: 0-1 3m+: 0-1
Track: LH: 0-3 RH: 0-3 Tight: 0-1 Gall: 0-0
Aids: Bl: 0-0 Vi: 0-0 Tstrap: 0-0
Best Rating: 70   12/01 Winc 2m   good Hdl

Plating-class hurdler; modest form over hurdles so far; has worn cheekpieces.

Solsgirth

12-y-o br g Ardross-Lillie s Brig (New Brig)

N W Alexander Jamie Alexander

Placings: 0P/013P/**13F5P3P53/1112F36263/6001F3U/P523 PP4/0024PP-P** (4018)
2002/03: 21PS,

		Starts	1st	2nd	3rd	Win & Pl
Chases		1	0	0	0	
Career Total		46	6	4	8	33778
95	1/00	Ayr	2m E(0-115)HCh		SFT	£3211
109	11/98	Hexm	2m4f110yF(0-105)HCh		HVY	£3063
99	11/98	Kels	2m1f D(0-120)HCh		SFT	£3387
98	10/98	Kels	2m1f E(0-115)HCh		SFT	£3139
88	11/97	Ayr	2m4f D(0-110)HCh		G-S	£3636
92	2/97	Ayr	2m E(0-100)HHdl		SFT	£2626
			Total win prize-money £19065			

Going: Sf: 0-1 GS: 0-0 Gd: 0-0 GF: - Fm: 0-0
Distance: 2m/2m3: 0-0 2m4-2m7: 0-1 3m+: 0-0
Track: LH: 0-1 RH: 0-0 Tight: 0-0 Gall: 0-0
Aids: Bl: 0-0 Vi: 0-0 Tstrap: 0-1
Best Rating: 115 12/98 Ayr 3m1f   gd-sft Ch

Moderate ability over hurdles and fences, he stays three miles, but his wins in recent seasons have been over shorter. Very much suited by soft ground.

Solvang (IRE)
60   88

11-y-o b g Carlingford Castle-Bramble Bird (Pitpan)
F Jordan Miss E M V England

Placings: 10/1132FP3PP/10201613/232125/45F6/05-PP5P (1199)
2002/03: 20PS, 23PGF, 225GF, 19PGF,

		Starts	1st	2nd	3rd	Win & Pl
Hurdles		1	0	0	0	0
Chases		3	0	0	0	0
Career Total		35	7	5	4	46451
130	11/99	Aint	2m4f C(0-130)HCh		GD	£7067
110	10/98	Winc	2m6f E Hdl		G-F	£2206
126	8/98	Tral	2m4f HCh		GD	£11260
121	6/98	Rosc	3m100y Ch		G-Y	£2382
125	7/97	Klny	2m4f Ch		Y-S	£3391
113	6/97	Clon	2m2f Ch		GD	£2712
109	4/97	Fair	2m2f NHF		G-F	£6287
			Total win prize-money £35309			

Going: Sf: 0-1 GS: 0-0 Gd: 0-0 GF: - Fm: 0-3
Distance: 2m/2m3: 0-1 2m4-2m7: 0-2 3m+: 0-1
Track: LH: 0-2 RH: 0-1 Tight: 0-1 Gall: 0-0
Aids: Bl: 0-0 Vi: 0-0 Tstrap: 0-4
Best Rating: 130 12/99 Leic 2m4f110y good Ch

Ex-Irish, he made the frame in a couple of Cheltenham handicaps in the autumn before winning at Aintree. Disappointed at Leicester over Christmas. Suited by patient handling, he is consistent and should continue to pay his way.

Solway Breeze (IRE)
92   50

10-y-o b m King s Ride-Spicey Cut (Cut Above)
Ms Liz Harrison David Alan Harrison

Placings: 225/331P10/F4UP/3312-UPP (4765)
2002/03: 24US, 25PS, 31PG,

		Starts	1st	2nd	3rd	Win & Pl
Chases		3	0	0	0	
Career Total		20	3	3	4	15689
98	3/02	Ayr	3m1f D Ch		SFT	£4367
116	1/00	Hayd	2m6f D Hdl		SFT	£3666
97	12/99	Hexm	3m E Hdl		HVY	£2658
			Total win prize-money £10691			

Going: Sf: 0-2 GS: 0-0 Gd: 0-1 GF: - Fm: 0-0
Distance: 2m/2m3: 0-0 2m4-2m7: 0-0 3m+: 0-3
Track: LH: 0-2 RH: 0-1 Tight: 0-0 Gall: 0-1
Aids: Bl: 0-0 Vi: 0-0 Tstrap: 0-0
Best Rating: 116 1/00 Hayd 2m6f soft Hdl

Solway Coaster

88(82c)   (51c)39

10-y-o b g Jumbo Hirt (USA)-Lady Mag (Silver Season)
Ms Liz Harrison David Alan Harrison

Placings:460   (0916)
2002/03: 20⁴GF, 20⁶GF, 20⁹GS,

	Starts	1st	2nd	3rd	Win & Pl
Hurdles	1	0	0	0	0
Chases	2	0	0	0	168
Career Total	3	0	0	0	168

Going: Sf: 0-0 GS: 0-1 Gd: 0-0 GF: - Fm: 0-2
Distance: 2m/2m3: 0-0 2m4-2m7: 0-3 3m+: 0-0
Track: LH: 0-2 RH: 0-1 Tight: 0-0 Gall: 0-0
Aids: Bl: 0-0 Vi: 0-0 Tstrap: 0-1
Best Rating: 51 6/02 Hexm 2m4f110y gd-fm Ch

Solway Donal (IRE)

98   75

10-y-o b m Celio Rufo-Knockaville (Crozier)
Ms Liz Harrison David Alan Harrison

Placings:0FP/55/06P40PU316P-UPP635   (4794)
2002/03: 20ᵁGF, 24ᴾGF, 21ᴾG, 25⁶G, 20³GF, 21⁵GF,

	Starts	1st	2nd	3rd	Win & Pl
Chases	6	0	0	1	669
Career Total	22	1	0	2	3670

72 1/02 Sedg 2m110y F(0-90)HCh HVY £2499
Total win prize-money £2499

Going: Sf: 0-0 GS: 0-0 Gd: 0-2 GF: - Fm: 0-4
Distance: 2m/2m3: 0-0 2m4-2m7: 0-4 3m+: 0-2
Track: LH: 0-4 RH: 0-2 Tight: 0-2 Gall: 0-0
Aids: Bl: 0-0 Vi: 0-0 Tstrap: 0-0
Best Rating: 80 1/02 Catt 3m1f110y gd-sft Ch

Plating-class chaser; poor form in 2002/2003; handles heavy ground, but has won on good.

Solway Gale (IRE)

88   71

6-y-o b m Husyan (USA)-Some Gale (Strong Gale)
Ms Liz Harrison David Alan Harrison

Placings:60-063056   (4392)
2002/03: 20⁹GF, 20⁶G, 16³G, 16⁰G, 20⁵S, 24⁶G,

	Starts	1st	2nd	3rd	Win & Pl
Hurdles	6	0	0	1	530
Career Total	8	0	0	1	530

Going: Sf: 0-1 GS: 0-0 Gd: 0-4 GF: - Fm: 0-1
Distance: 2m/2m3: 0-2 2m4-2m7: 0-3 3m+: 0-1
Track: LH: 0-2 RH: 0-4 Tight: 0-4 Gall: 0-0
Aids: Bl: 0-0 Vi: 0-0 Tstrap: 0-0
Best Rating: 77 2/02 Muss 2m soft NHF

Poor form in novice hurdles.

Solway Gorge

7-y-o ch g Jumbo Hirt (USA)-Kilkenny Gorge (Deep Run)

Ms Liz Harrison David Alan Harrison

Placings:00P   (4376)
2002/03: 16⁹GF, 16⁹GF, 27⁵G,

	Starts	1st	2nd	3rd	Win & Pl
NH Flat	2	0	0	0	0
Hurdles	1	0	0	0	0
Career Total	3	0	0	0	

Going: Sf: 0-0 GS: 0-0 Gd: 0-1 GF: - Fm: 0-2
Distance: 2m/2m3: 0-2 2m4-2m7: 0-0 3m+: 0-1
Track: LH: 0-2 RH: 0-1 Tight: 0-1 Gall: 0-0
Aids: Bl: 0-0 Vi: 0-0 Tstrap: 0-0
Best Rating: 31 9/02 Prth 2m110y gd-fm NHF

Solway Minstrel

92   79

6-y-o ch g Jumbo Hirt (USA)-Spicey Cut (Cut Above)
Ms Liz Harrison David Alan Harrison

Placings:0   (1243)
2002/03: 16⁹GF,

	Starts	1st	2nd	3rd	Win & Pl
NH Flat	1	0	0	0	
Career Total	1	0	0	0	

Going: Sf: 0-0 GS: 0-0 Gd: 0-0 GF: - Fm: 0-1
Distance: 2m/2m3: 0-1 2m4-2m7: 0-0 3m+: 0-0
Track: LH: 0-1 RH: 0-0 Tight: 0-0 Gall: 0-0
Aids: Bl: 0-0 Vi: 0-0 Tstrap: 0-0
Best Rating: 38 9/02 Hexm 2m110y gd-fm NHF

Novice hurdler; stays three miles; acts on a sound surface.

Solway Plain

97(97h)   (76h)97

9-y-o br g King s Ride-Oh Dear (Paico)
Ms Liz Harrison David Alan Harrison

Placings:5635400-5PPP   (0915)
2002/03: 25⁵GS, 24⁵GF, 22ᴾGF, 20⁵GS,

	Starts	1st	2nd	3rd	Win & Pl
Chases	4	0	0	0	0
Career Total	11	0	0	1	440

Going: Sf: 0-0 GS: 0-2 Gd: 0-0 GF: - Fm: 0-2
Distance: 2m/2m3: 0-0 2m4-2m7: 0-2 3m+: 0-2
Track: LH: 0-2 RH: 0-2 Tight: 0-1 Gall: 0-0
Aids: Bl: 0-0 Vi: 0-0 Tstrap: 0-0
Best Rating: 76 3/02 Ayr 2m6f heavy Hdl

Plating-class chaser.

Solway Rose

94   104

9-y-o ch m Minster Son-Lady Mag (Silver Season)
Ms Liz Harrison David Alan Harrison

Placings:346/31P/3F301/PUP1U4-P244U   (3126)
2002/03: 26ᴾS, 24²S, 26⁴HY, 25⁴GS, 24ᵁHY,

	Starts	1st	2nd	3rd	Win & Pl
Chases	5	0	1	0	2885
Career Total	22	3	1	4	16196

105 3/02 Ayr 3m1f D(0-125)HCh HVY £4745
105 10/00 Carl 3m2f D(0-120)HCh G-S £3786
100 6/99 Prth 3m110y E Hdl G-S £2724
Total win prize-money £11255

Going: Sf: 0-4 GS: 0-1 Gd: 0-0 GF: - Fm: 0-0
Distance: 2m/2m3: 0-0 2m4-2m7: 0-0 3m+: 0-5
Track: LH: 0-3 RH: 0-2 Tight: 0-0 Gall: 0-2
Aids: Bl: 0-0 Vi: 0-0 Tstrap: 0-0
Best Rating: 105 11/02 Newc 3m soft Ch

Moderate staying chaser, suited by easy ground. Handles the mud.

Somayda (IRE)

54   28

8-y-o b g Last Tycoon-Flame Of Tara (Artaius (USA))
Miss Jacqueline S Doyle The Somayda Partnership

Placings:0P-0P   (2712)
2002/03: 16⁸S, 16⁵G,

	Starts	1st	2nd	3rd	Win & Pl
Hurdles	2	0	0	0	
Career Total	4	0	0	0	

Going: Sf: 0-1 GS: 0-1 Gd: 0-0 GF: - Fm: 0-0
Distance: 2m/2m3: 0-2 2m4-2m7: 0-0 3m+: 0-0
Track: LH: 0-1 RH: 0-1 Tight: 0-1 Gall: 0-1
Aids: Bl: 0-0 Vi: 0-0 Tstrap: 0-1
Best Rating: 28 3/02 Winc 2m good Hdl

Some Go West (IRE)

9-y-o b g Un Desperado (FR)-Costly Lady (Bold Lad (IRE))
Neil King Simon Bullimore

Placings:5/520P614/0255P/332-UP   (0313)
2002/03: 24ᵁG, 25ᴾG,

	Starts	1st	2nd	3rd	Win & Pl
Chases	2	0	0	0	
Career Total	18	1	3	2	6765

102 2/00 Donc 2m3f110yE(0-105)HCh GD £3055
Total win prize-money £3055

Going: Sf: 0-0 GS: 0-0 Gd: 0-2 GF: - Fm: 0-0
Distance: 2m/2m3: 0-0 2m4-2m7: 0-0 3m+: 0-2
Track: LH: 0-1 RH: 0-1 Tight: 0-2 Gall: 0-0
Aids: Bl: 0-0 Vi: 0-0 Tstrap: 0-0
Best Rating: 102 5/01 Folk 3m1f good Ch

Some Operator (IRE)

99   91

9-y-o b g Lord Americo-Rathvilly Flier (Peacock (FR))
T Wall Michael Doocey

Placings:50/UU434U0/00300-02   (4641)
2002/03: 16⁶G, 19²GF,

	Starts	1st	2nd	3rd	Win & Pl
Hurdles	2	0	1	0	860
Career Total	16	0	1	2	2264

Going: Sf: 0-0 GS: 0-0 Gd: 0-1 GF: - Fm: 0-1
Distance: 2m/2m3: 0-2 2m4-2m7: 0-0 3m+: 0-0
Track: LH: 0-1 RH: 0-1 Tight: 0-1 Gall: 0-0
Aids: Bl: 0-0 Vi: 0-0 Tstrap: 0-0
Best Rating: 99 10/99 Chep 2m110y soft Hdl

Moderate hurdler; showed ability in 1999; relatively lightly-raced since; settled much better when springing 25/1 shock in low grade novices handicap hurdle at Stratford May 2003.

Some Story (IRE)

72   40

7-y-o b g Mandalus-April Lilly (Deep Run)

Mrs V J Makin R G Makin

Placings:00U   (1826)
2002/03: 24^DGF, 16^DG, 22US,

	Starts	1st	2nd	3rd	Win & Pl
Hurdles	3	0	0	0	
Career Total	3	0	0	0	

Going:	Sf: 0-1 GS: 0-0 Gd: 0-1 GF: - Fm: 0-1
Distance:	2m/2m3: 0-1 2m4-2m7: 0-0 3m+: 0-1
Track:	LH: 0-3 RH: 0-0 Tight: 0-1 Gall: 0-0
Aids:	Bl: 0-0 Vi: 0-0 Tstrap: 0-0
Best Rating:	40 10/02 Kels 2m110y good Hdl

Some Tool

65   **42**

6-y-o b g Jupiter Island-Melodys Daughter (Sizzling Melody)
John A Harris M F Schofield

Placings:00   (0725)
2002/03: 17^DGF, 16^DGF,

	Starts	1st	2nd	3rd	Win & Pl
Hurdles	2	0	0	0	
Career Total	2	0	0	0	

Going:	Sf: 0-0 GS: 0-0 Gd: 0-0 GF: - Fm: 0-2
Distance:	2m/2m3: 0-2 2m4-2m7: 0-0 3m+: 0-0
Track:	LH: 0-1 RH: 0-1 Tight: 0-2 Gall: 0-0
Aids:	Bl: 0-0 Vi: 0-0 Tstrap: 0-0
Best Rating:	44 7/02 Strf 2m110y gd-fm Hdl

Somemanforoneman (IRE)

97(108c)   (90c)**93**

9-y-o b g Asir-Wintry Shower (Strong Gale)
R S Brookhouse (C J Mann 17/1) R S Brookhouse

   Placings:4500/352430/63301F646263/011232F/055P420-
P4F6P   (4609)
2002/03: 27^PGS, 24⁴HY, 24^FHY, 24⁶GS, 24^PG,

	Starts	1st	2nd	3rd	Win & Pl
Hurdles	2	0	0	0	0
Chases	3	0	0	0	568
Career Total	41	3	5	6	32944
145	11/00	Asct	3m110y	C(0-130)HCh	G-S	£6646
130	10/00	Wwck	2m4f110yD	Ch	SFT	£4030
105	12/99	Clon	2m6f	(0-95)Hdl	SH	£3388
				Total win prize-money £14064		

Going:	Sf: 0-2 GS: 0-2 Gd: 0-1 GF: - Fm: 0-0
Distance:	2m/2m3: 0-0 2m4-2m7: 0-0 3m+: 0-5
Track:	LH: 0-4 RH: 0-1 Tight: 0-1 Gall: 0-2
Aids:	Bl: 0-4 Vi: 0-0 Tstrap: 0-0
Best Rating:	145 11/00 Asct 3m110y gd-sft Ch

Moderate ex-Irish handicap chaser, very useful early on in Britain; suited by cut in the ground; stays three miles, effective at two and a half, usually wears blinkers.

Somerton (POL)

5-y-o b g Saphir (GER)-Sobota (POL) (Pawiment (POL))
T R George Mrs S Nelson,Allan Stennett,Terry Warner

Placings:PP   (3141)
2002/03: 19^PGS, 17^PS,

	Starts	1st	2nd	3rd	Win & Pl
Hurdles	2	0	0	0	

Career Total   **2**   **0**   **0**   **0**

Going:	Sf: 0-1 GS: 0-1 Gd: 0-0 GF: - Fm: 0-0
Distance:	2m/2m3: 0-2 2m4-2m7: 0-0 3m+: 0-0
Track:	LH: 0-1 RH: 0-1 Tight: 0-1 Gall: 0-1
Aids:	Bl: 0-0 Vi: 0-0 Tstrap: 0-0
Best Rating:	0 1/03 Tntn 2m1f soft Hdl

Something Dandy (IRE)

102(110h)   (121h)**104**

10-y-o b g Brush Aside (USA)-Hawthorn Dandy (Deep Run)
J A B Old Blomeley/Iovatt Partnership

Placings:00/F0U/2240/520-5641342112   (4608)
2002/03: 24⁵G, 22⁶G, 20⁴GF, 24¹G, 23³G, 20⁴G, 26²G, 24¹G,
24¹GS, 17²G,

	Starts	1st	2nd	3rd	Win & Pl
Hurdles	5	1	1	0	6618
Chases	5	2	1	1	11409
Career Total	22	3	5	1	21207
101	11/02	Tntn	3m	E(0-105)HCh	G-S	£3640
101	11/02	Kemp	3m	D(0-110)HCh	GD	£5908
98	7/02	Worc	3m	E(0-100)HHdl	GD	£2905
				Total win prize-money £12453		

Going:	Sf: 0-0 GS: 1-1 Gd: 2-8 GF: - Fm: 0-1
Distance:	2m/2m3: 0-1 2m4-2m7: 0-3 3m+: 3-6
Track:	LH: 1-7 RH: 2-3 Tight: 1-2 Gall: 0-1
Aids:	Bl: 0-0 Vi: 0-0 Tstrap: 0-0
Best Rating:	121 4/03 Chel 2m1f good Hdl

Fair novice hurdler/chaser at around two and a half to three miles; acts on good or faster ground.

Something Happened (NZ)

                   88

10-y-o b g Cache Of Gold (USA)-Iseki (NZ) (Brazen Bay (AUS))
O Brennan Michael Lowe

Placings:5/0/3-P   (4225)
2002/03: 20^PGF,

	Starts	1st	2nd	3rd	Win & Pl
Hurdles	1	0	0	0	
Career Total	4	0	0	1	507

Going:	Sf: 0-0 GS: 0-0 Gd: 0-0 GF: - Fm: 0-1
Distance:	2m/2m3: 0-0 2m4-2m7: 0-1 3m+: 0-0
Track:	LH: 0-1 RH: 0-0 Tight: 0-0 Gall: 0-0
Aids:	Bl: 0-0 Vi: 0-0 Tstrap: 0-0
Best Rating:	88 5/01 Weth 2m7f firm Hdl

Something Special

5-y-o b g Petong-My Dear Watson (Chilibang)
H E Haynes Miss Sally R Haynes

Placings:P   (0512)
2002/03: 16^PS,

	Starts	1st	2nd	3rd	Win & Pl
Hurdles	1	0	0	0	
Career Total	1	0	0	0	

Going:	Sf: 0-1 GS: 0-0 Gd: 0-0 GF: - Fm: 0-0
Distance:	2m/2m3: 0-1 2m4-2m7: 0-0 3m+: 0-0

Track:	LH: 0-1 RH: 0-0 Tight: 0-0 Gall: 0-0
Aids:	Bl: 0-0 Vi: 0-0 Tstrap: 0-0
Best Rating:	

Somosierra (IRE)

8-y-o gr g Paris House-Island Heather (IRE) (Salmon Leap (USA))
V Thompson V Thompson

Placings:00/P-P   (0080)
2002/03: 16^PGS,

	Starts	1st	2nd	3rd	Win & Pl
Hurdles	1	0	0	0	
Career Total	4	0	0	0	

Going:	Sf: 0-0 GS: 0-1 Gd: 0-0 GF: - Fm: 0-0
Distance:	2m/2m3: 0-1 2m4-2m7: 0-0 3m+: 0-0
Track:	LH: 0-1 RH: 0-0 Tight: 0-0 Gall: 0-0
Aids:	Bl: 0-1 Vi: 0-0 Tstrap: 0-0
Best Rating:	34 4/99 Kels 2m110y gd-fm Hdl

Son Of A Gun

100   **88**

9-y-o b g Gunner B-Sola Mia (Tolomeo)
M J Polglase (J Neville 25/5) Ron Spore & Michael Crompton

Placings:312223/330-360P4100   (4666)
2002/03: 16³G, 17⁶GS, 25⁵HY, 24^PHY, 19⁴GS, 16¹G, 20⁰G, 16⁰G,

	Starts	1st	2nd	3rd	Win & Pl
Hurdles	8	1	0	1	2827
Career Total	17	2	3	5	9641
88	3/03	Fknm	2m	G(0-90)HHdl	GD	£2382
101	9/99	MRas	1m5f110yH	NHF	G-F	£1595
				Total win prize-money £3977		

Going:	Sf: 0-2 GS: 0-2 Gd: 1-4 GF: - Fm: 0-0
Distance:	2m/2m3: 1-4 2m4-2m7: 0-2 3m+: 0-2
Track:	LH: 1-6 RH: 0-2 Tight: 1-3 Gall: 0-1
Aids:	Bl: 0-0 Vi: 0-0 Tstrap: 0-0
Best Rating:	126 12/99 Chep 2m110y heavy NHF

Plating-class hurdler; best on a sound surface; rather inconsistent.

Son Of Anshan

10-y-o b g Anshan-Anhaar (Ela-Mana-Mou)
G Tuer G Tuer

Placings:0321F11/33P/314P3223/4450/P4/5213-311U   (4459)

2002/03: 23³GS, 27¹S, 27¹G, 21^UG,

	Starts	1st	2nd	3rd	Win & Pl
Chases	4	2	0	1	3917
Career Total	32	7	4	8	29426
104	3/03	Sedg	3m3f	H Ch	GD	£1540
113	3/03	Sedg	3m3f	H Ch	SFT	£1533
85	3/02	Sedg	3m3f	H Ch	SFT	£1498
113	11/98	Uttx	3m	D Ch	GD	£4370
133	3/97	Kels	2m	D Hdl	GD	£2815
121	3/97	Ayr	2m	E Hdl	SFT	£2134
109	12/96	Newc	2m	E Hdl	GD	£2337
				Total win prize-money £16229		

Going:	Sf: 1-1 GS: 0-1 Gd: 1-2 GF: - Fm: 0-0
Distance:	2m/2m3: 0-0 2m4-2m7: 0-1 3m+: 2-3
Track:	LH: 2-3 RH: 0-1 Tight: 2-3 Gall: 0-1
Aids:	Bl: 0-0 Vi: 0-0 Tstrap: 2-4

Best Rating: 133 3/97 Kels 2m2f good Hdl

Fair hunter chaser; one-time decent novice over fences; won two Sedgefield hunter chases in March 2003; stays well; acts on good or softer; usually tongue tied.

Son Of Light (IRE)
106(101h)   (113h)113

8-y-o br g Hollow Hand-Leaney Kamscort (Kambalda)
Miss Venetia Williams (A Streeter 12/8) Mrs Rosemary Bateman

Placings:432420/114/304P660-523112   (4624)
2002/03: 24⁵GF, 22²GF, 22³GF, 26¹GF, 26¹GF, 26²GF,

	Starts	1st	2nd	3rd	Win & Pl
Chases	6	2	2	1	12416
Career Total	22	4	4	3	20333
113	8/02	Sthl	3m2f		E Ch	G-F	£4368
113	7/02	Uttx	3m2f		E Ch	G-F	£4410
106	10/00	Sthl	2m		E Hdl	G-S	£2226
107	9/00	Strf	2m110y		E Hdl	GD	£2743

Total win prize-money £13747

Going:	Sf: 0-0 GS: 0-0 Gd: 0-0 GF: - Fm: 2-6
Distance:	2m/2m3: 0-0 2m4-2m7: 0-0 3m+: 2-4
Track:	LH: 2-3 RH: 0-3 Tight: 0-4 Gall: 0-0
Aids:	Bl: 0-0 Vi: 0-0 Tstrap: 0-0
Best Rating:	113 8/02 Sthl 3m2f gd-fm Ch

Moderate chaser; won twice over hurdles in the autumn of 2000; finally broke his duck over fences at Uttoxeter in July 2002 and followed up at August next month; effective at three miles two; likes a sound surface.

Son Of Ross
93(84c)   (22c)43

9-y-o b g Minster Son-Nancy Ardross (Ardross)
R W Thomson R W Thomson

Placings:0/00/4005/41PP00-U560   (0453)
2002/03: 22⁴UG, 24⁵GF, 27⁶G, 24⁹G,

	Starts	1st	2nd	3rd	Win & Pl
Hurdles	4	0	0	0	0
Career Total	17	1	0	0	2898
70	6/01 Prth		3m110y	E Hdl	G-F	£2898

Total win prize-money £2898

Going:	Sf: 0-0 GS: 0-0 Gd: 0-3 GF: - Fm: 0-1
Distance:	2m/2m3: 0-0 2m4-2m7: 0-1 3m+: 0-3
Track:	LH: 0-3 RH: 0-1 Tight: 0-2 Gall: 0-0
Aids:	Bl: 0-0 Vi: 0-0 Tstrap: 0-0
Best Rating:	70 6/01 Prth 3m110y gd-fm Hdl

Son Of Snurge (FR)
101   81

7-y-o b g Snurge-Swift Spring (FR) (Bluebird (USA))
W G Young W G Young

Placings:PP/F4662400P554000335   (4590)
2002/03: 22⁵GF, 20⁴G, 22⁵G, 16⁵S, 20⁵HY, 20⁴S, 20⁵G, 20⁹GS, 24²HY, 24⁵HY, 24⁵HY, 20⁴HY, 24⁹G, 22⁰GS, 27⁰S, 21³G, 20⁴G, 20⁵G,

	Starts	1st	2nd	3rd	Win & Pl
Hurdles	18	0	1	2	1912
Career Total	20	0	1	2	1912

Going:	Sf: 0-8 GS: 0-2 Gd: 0-7 GF: - Fm: 0-1
Distance:	2m/2m3: 0-1 2m4-2m7: 0-12 3m+: 0-5
Track:	LH: 0-17 RH: 0-1 Tight: 0-8 Gall: 0-1
Aids:	Bl: 0-0 Vi: 0-0 Tstrap: 0-0
Best Rating:	81 4/03 Hexm 2m4f110y good Hdl

Poor hurdler; placed several times but has never looked like winning; stays 3m.

Sonevafushi (FR)
121   126

5-y-o b g Ganges (USA)-For Kicks (FR) (Top Ville)
Miss Venetia Williams B C Dice

Placings:130-1220460   (4475)
2002/03: 20¹G, 18²G, 17²HY, 16⁰G, 20⁴S, 16⁶S, 20⁰G,

	Starts	1st	2nd	3rd	Win & Pl
Hurdles	7	1	2	0	15873
Career Total	10	2	2	1	20568
105	5/02	Sthl	2m4f110yE Hdl		GD	£2667
115	1/02	Newb	2m110y D Hdl		G-S	£4179

Total win prize-money £6847

Going:	Sf: 0-3 GS: 0-1 Gd: 1-4 GF: - Fm: 0-0
Distance:	2m/2m3: 0-4 2m4-2m7: 1-3 3m+: 0-0
Track:	LH: 1-5 RH: 0-1 Tight: 1-3 Gall: 0-2
Aids:	Bl: 0-0 Vi: 0-0 Tstrap: 0-0
Best Rating:	129 1/03 Chel 2m1f heavy Hdl

Decent handicap hurdler; does not find much off the bridle; has won over two miles and two and a half on a sound surface; has worn blinkers.

Sonic Girl (IRE)
(75h)   (60h)

8-y-o ch m Boyne Valley-So Ladylike (Malinowski (USA))
N M Babbage B Babbage

Placings:040600/4002000/0-60PP   (4024)
2002/03: 16⁶S, 16⁹HY, 16⁶S, 25⁶PS,

	Starts	1st	2nd	3rd	Win & Pl
Hurdles	2	0	0	0	0
Chases	2	0	0	0	0
Career Total	18	0	1	0	1368

Going:	Sf: 0-0 GS: 0-1 Gd: 0-0 GF: - Fm: 0-0
Distance:	2m/2m3: 0-3 2m4-2m7: 0-0 3m+: 0-0
Track:	LH: 0-1 RH: 0-3 Tight: 0-1 Gall: 0-0
Aids:	Bl: 0-1 Vi: 0-0 Tstrap: 0-0
Best Rating:	84 8/00 Rosc 2m firm NHF

Sonny Jim
109   84

5-y-o b g Timeless Times (USA)-Allesca (Alleging (USA))
M D I Usher (Jonjo O Neill 4/5) Miss D G Kerr

Placings:0F622010440-532323046   (4425)
2002/03: 16⁵GS, 21³S, 16²S, 16⁵S, 19²GS, 18⁵S, 21⁰HY, 19⁴HY, 16⁶GF,

	Starts	1st	2nd	3rd	Win & Pl
Hurdles	9	0	2	3	4178
Career Total	20	1	4	3	9558
89	2/02	Plum	2m	F Hdl	HVY	£2247

Total win prize-money £2247

Going:	Sf: 0-6 GS: 0-2 Gd: 0-0 GF: - Fm: 0-1
Distance:	2m/2m3: 0-5 2m4-2m7: 0-4 3m+: 0-0
Track:	LH: 0-8 RH: 0-1 Tight: 0-6 Gall: 0-0
Aids:	Bl: 0-1 Vi: 0-1 Tstrap: 0-0
Best Rating:	91 2/03 Font 2m2f110y soft Hdl

Moderate handicap hurdler; sprang 40/1 surprise when winning Class F handicap at Worcester June 2003; unsuited by fast ground; stays 2m 4f.

Soon Or Late
86   72

5-y-o ch g Kris-Silky Heights (IRE) (Head For Heights)
Miss J A Camacho Bernard Bloom

Placings:0   (1568)
2002/03: 19⁰G,

	Starts	1st	2nd	3rd	Win & Pl
Hurdles	1	0	0	0	
Career Total	1	0	0	0	

Going:	Sf: 0-0 GS: 0-0 Gd: 0-1 GF: - Fm: 0-0
Distance:	2m/2m3: 0-0 2m4-2m7: 0-1 3m+: 0-0
Track:	LH: 0-0 RH: 0-1 Tight: 0-1 Gall: 0-0
Aids:	Bl: 0-0 Vi: 0-0 Tstrap: 0-0
Best Rating:	72 10/02 MRas 2m3f110y good Hdl

Sorbiediditmyway (IRE)
58f

4-y-o b g Sorbie Tower (IRE)-Wamdha (IRE) (Thatching)
B G Powell Mrs Liz Nelson

Placings:0   (3673)
2002/03: 18⁰GS,

	Starts	1st	2nd	3rd	Win & Pl
NH Flat	1	0	0	0	
Career Total	1	0	0	0	

Going:	Sf: 0-0 GS: 0-1 Gd: 0-0 GF: - Fm: 0-0
Distance:	2m/2m3: 0-1 2m4-2m7: 0-0 3m+: 0-0
Track:	LH: 0-1 RH: 0-0 Tight: 0-1 Gall: 0-0
Aids:	Bl: 0-1 Vi: 0-0 Tstrap: 0-0
Best Rating:	0 2/03 Font 2m2f110y gd-sft NHF

Sorely Missed (IRE)
86

8-y-o br g Yashgan-Well Honey (Al Sirat (USA))
R Dickin Mrs M Payne

Placings:60P/0P613334-4PPP   (4267)
2002/03: 19⁴GF, 20⁰G, 16⁶HY, 24⁰GF,

	Starts	1st	2nd	3rd	Win & Pl
Hurdles	2	0	0	0	0
Chases	2	0	0	0	375
Career Total	15	1	0	3	5134
78	11/01	Wwck	2m3f	F(0-100)HHdl	GD	£2059

Total win prize-money £2059

Going:	Sf: 0-1 GS: 0-0 Gd: 0-1 GF: - Fm: 0-2
Distance:	2m/2m3: 0-2 2m4-2m7: 0-1 3m+: 0-1
Track:	LH: 0-2 RH: 0-2 Tight: 0-1 Gall: 0-0
Aids:	Bl: 0-0 Vi: 0-1 Tstrap: 0-0
Best Rating:	87 10/00 Chep 2m110y gd-sft NHF

Sorrento King
108(105h)   (99h)108

6-y-o ch g First Trump-Star Face (African Sky)
Mrs M Reveley B Padgett, K Bennett & A Davies

Placings:4203U3102-33411F   (4690)
2002/03: 16³GF, 16⁹G, 16⁴G, 21³GF, 21¹GF, 25⁶G,

	Starts	1st	2nd	3rd	Win & Pl
Chases	6	2	0	2	8838
Career Total	15	3	2	4	14828
108	10/02	Sedg	2m5f	E Ch	G-F	£3711

87	9/02	Sedg	2m5f	E Ch		GD	£3701
99	12/01	Kels	2m110y	E Hdl		G-S	£3346
					Total win prize-money £10760		

Going:	Sf: 0-0 GS: 0-0 Gd: 1-4 GF: - Fm: 1-2
Distance:	2m/2m3: 0-3 **2m4-2m7:** 2-2 3m+: 0-1
Track:	LH: **2-5** RH: 0-1 Tight: **2-6** Gall: 0-0
Aids:	Bl: 0-0 Vi: 0-0 Tstrap: 0-0
Best Rating:	**108** 10/02 Sedg 2m5f gd-fm Ch

Modest chaser; has won over hurdles, now novice chasing, succesful at Perth and Sedgefield. Effective at around two miles five and acts on fast ground.

Sossus Vlei

102   **114d**

7-y-o b g Inchinor-Sassalya (Sassafras (FR))
P Winkworth   P Winkworth

Placings:300-20225   (3999)
2002/03: 16²G, 16⁶S, 16²S, 16²S, 16⁵S,

	Starts	1st	2nd	3rd	Win & Pl
Hurdles	5	0	3	0	4235
Career Total	8	0	3	1	5211

Going:	Sf: 0-4 GS: 0-0 Gd: 0-1 GF: - Fm: 0-0
Distance:	2m/2m3: 0-5 2m4-2m7: 0-0 3m+: 0-0
Track:	LH: 0-4 RH: 0-1 Tight: 0-2 Gall: 0-0
Aids:	Bl: 0-0 Vi: 0-0 Tstrap: 0-0
Best Rating:	**134** 2/02 Newb 2m110y soft Hdl

Fair novice hurdler; one-time decent performer on the Flat; acts in soft ground; rather frustrating.

Sound Of Cheers

107(103h)   (109h)**99**

6-y-o br g Zilzal (USA)-Martha Stevens (USA) (Super Concorde (USA))
F Kirby   Fred Kirby

Placings:061023-44P542620   (4591)
2002/03: 20⁴HY, 21⁴S, 19⁵G, 20⁵HY, 19⁴G, 21²S, 16⁶G, 16²G, 16⁹G,

	Starts	1st	2nd	3rd	Win & Pl
Hurdles	1	0	0	0	0
Chases	8	0	2	0	3402
Career Total	15	1	3	1	7239
105	1/02	Newc	2m4f	E Hdl		SFT	£2667
					Total win prize-money £2667		

Going:	Sf: 0-4 GS: 0-0 Gd: 0-5 GF: - Fm: 0-0
Distance:	2m/2m3: 0-5 2m4-2m7: 0-4 3m+: 0-0
Track:	LH: 0-8 RH: 0-1 Tight: 0-4 Gall: 0-1
Aids:	Bl: 0-0 Vi: 0-0 Tstrap: 0-5
Best Rating:	**109** 3/02 Sedg 2m1f soft Hdl

Modest chaser; stays two and a half miles and should get further; acts on soft/heavy ground.

Sounds Cool

98(102c)   (84c)**84**

7-y-o b g Savahra Sound-Lucky Candy (Lucky Wednesday)
A Streeter   Formula One Racing

Placings:0/00500F/U126P33-44P   (1197)
2002/03: 17⁴G, 17⁴G, 19⁶GF,

	Starts	1st	2nd	3rd	Win & Pl
Hurdles	3	0	0	0	0
Career Total	17	1	1	2	3238
74	6/01	MRas	2m1f110yG(0-90)HHdl	G-F	£1645
				Total win prize-money £1645	

Sounds Promising

8-y-o b g Profilic-Blakeney Sound (Blakeney)
R Wilman   John Burton

Placings:P   (0152)
2002/03: 23⁶G,

	Starts	1st	2nd	3rd	Win & Pl
Hurdles	1	0	0	0	
Career Total	1	0	0	0	

Going:	Sf: 0-0 GS: 0-0 Gd: 0-1 GF: - Fm: 0-0
Distance:	2m/2m3: 0-0 2m4-2m7: 0-0 3m+: 0-1
Track:	LH: 0-1 RH: 0-0 Tight: 0-1 Gall: 0-0
Aids:	Bl: 0-0 Vi: 0-0 Tstrap: 0-0
Best Rating:	**0** 5/02 Fknm 2m7f110y good Hdl

Sounds Strong (IRE)

14-y-o br g Strong Gale-Jazz Bavard (Le Bavard (FR))
Miss A Armitage   N W A Bannister

Placings:2/1F/1F16P/222FPFF/03/21UF/6   (0477)
2002/03: 26⁶GS,

	Starts	1st	2nd	3rd	Win & Pl
Chases	1	0	0	0	0
Career Total	22	4	5	1	22912
104	5/00	Kels	3m1f	H Ch		G-F	£1848
134	12/96	Ling	3m	C(0-135)HCh	G-S	£4878
129	10/96	Weth	3m1f	B(0-140)HCh	GD	£4471
125	11/95	Chel	3m110y	C Ch		GD	£4788
					Total win prize-money £15985		

Going:	Sf: 0-0 GS: 0-1 Gd: 0-0 GF: - Fm: - 0-0
Distance:	2m/2m3: 0-0 2m4-2m7: 0-0 3m+: 0-1
Track:	LH: 0-1 RH: 0-0 Tight: 0-1 Gall: 0-0
Aids:	Bl: 0-0 Vi: 0-0 Tstrap: 0-0
Best Rating:	**134** 5/97 Wwck 3m2f good Ch

Soundtrack (IRE)

100   **114**

10-y-o b g Orchestra-Misty Boosh (Tarboosh (USA))
Miss Venetia Williams   J M Kinnear

Placings:22f11125/34111F/P0P-6   (4738)
2002/03: 24⁶GF,

	Starts	1st	2nd	3rd	Win & Pl
Chases	1	0	0	0	0
Career Total	18	7	3	0	27884
121	3/01	Plum	3m2f	E Ch	HVY	£3055
130	2/01	Tntn	3m	D Ch	HVY	£5715
140	1/01	Plum	3m2f	E Ch	HVY	£3318
123	10/99	Strf	2m6f110yD Hdl	G-F	£3717
120	10/99	Bang	2m4f	E Hdl	G-S	£2295
119	9/99	Hrfd	2m3f110yE Hdl	GD	£2472
98	9/99	Carl	2m1f	H NHF	G-F	£1647
				Total win prize-money £22221	

Going:	Sf: 0-0 GS: 0-0 Gd: 0-0 GF: - Fm: 0-1
Distance:	2m/2m3: 0-0 2m4-2m7: 0-0 3m+: 0-1
Track:	LH: 0-1 RH: 0-0 Tight: 0-0 Gall: 0-0

| **Aids:** | Bl: 0-0 Vi: 0-0 Tstrap: 0-0 |
| **Best Rating:** | **140** 1/01 Plum 3m2f   heavy   Ch |

Fair chaser; an out-and-out stayer; did well in novice chases at the beginning of 2001, winning three times on heavy ground; lightly raced since and has dropped significantly in the handicap.

Soundz Of Muzic (IRE)

94   **91**

8-y-o b m Supreme Leader-Southern Princess (Black Minstrel)
A J Martin   Mrs Anne Chambers-Ryan

Placings:0U00P0-5534B0134   (4754)
2002/03: 20⁵HY, 16⁵S, 16³SH, 16⁴HY, 16⁶SH, 16⁰HY, 16¹S, 16³GY, 16⁴G,

	Starts	1st	2nd	3rd	Win & Pl
NH Flat	1	0	0	0	0
Hurdles	8	1	0	2	6429
Career Total	15	1	0	2	6429
81	3/03	Thur	2m	(67-95)HHdl	SFT	£4480
					Total win prize-money £4481		

Going:	Sf: 1-5 GS: 0-0 Gd: 0-1 GF: - Fm: 0-0
Distance:	2m/2m3: 1-8 2m4-2m7: 0-1 3m+: 0-0
Track:	LH: 0-0 RH: 1-5 Tight: 0-0 Gall: 0-0
Aids:	Bl: 0-0 Vi: 0-0 Tstrap: 0-0
Best Rating:	**91** 3/03 Cork 2m gd-yld Hdl

Moderate Irish-trained hurdler; suited by two miles; acts on soft ground.

South West Express (IRE)

86(88h)   (35h)**42**

11-y-o ch g Executive Perk-Bohemian Girl (Pardao)
Mrs D Thomas   Mrs D Thomas

Placings:0/500/5521030/3022U1/12263FP/PP56/P00PF30 4356-03P0   (4735)
2002/03: 22⁰GF, 19³G, 26⁵HY, 19⁰GF,

	Starts	1st	2nd	3rd	Win & Pl
Hurdles	1	0	0	0	0
Chases	3	0	0	1	371
Career Total	43	3	5	6	15264
89	11/99	Leic	2m4f110yF(0-100)HCh	G-F	£3379
88	3/99	Tntn	2m110y F(0-105)HCh	SFT	£2775
72	12/97	Leic	2m4f110yG(0-90)HHdl	SFT	£2108
				Total win prize-money £8262	

Going:	Sf: 0-1 GS: 0-0 Gd: 0-1 GF: - Fm: 0-2
Distance:	2m/2m3: 0-0 2m4-2m7: 0-3 3m+: 0-1
Track:	LH: 0-4 RH: 0-0 Tight: 0-1 Gall: 0-0
Aids:	Bl: 0-0 Vi: 0-0 Tstrap: 0-0
Best Rating:	**92** 3/00 Tntn 2m110y good Ch

Very modest handicap chaser these days.

South West Won

5-y-o b g Bedford (USA)-Wood Heath (Heres)
Miss Sheena West   B Cockerill

Placings:6   (4760)
2002/03: 18⁶GF,

	Starts	1st	2nd	3rd	Win & Pl
NH Flat	1	0	0	0	0
Career Total	1	0	0	0	0

(continued)

Going:	Sf: 0-0 GS: 0-0 Gd: 0-0 GF: - Fm: 0-1
Distance:	2m/2m3: 0-1 2m4-2m7: 0-0 3m+: 0-1
Track:	LH: 0-1 RH: 0-0 Tight: 0-1 Gall: 0-0
Aids:	
Best Rating:	0 4/03 Font 2m2f110y gd-fm NHF

Southdown House
99   **95d**
7-y-o b m Husyan (USA)-Inger-Lea (Record Run)
R Rowe   Southdown Holdings Limited

Placings:4243   (4187)
2002/03: 17⁴HY, 20²HY, 20⁴S, 20³G,

	Starts	1st	2nd	3rd	Win & Pl
NH Flat	1	0	0	0	0
Hurdles	3	0	1	1	2013
Career Total	4	0	1	1	2013

Going:	Sf: 0-3 GS: 0-0 Gd: 0-1 GF: - Fm: 0-0
Distance:	2m/2m3: 0-1 2m4-2m7: 0-0 3m+: 0-0
Track:	LH: 0-1 RH: 0-2 Tight: 0-3 Gall: 0-0
Aids:	Bl: 0-0 Vi: 0-0 Tstrap: 0-0
Best Rating:	95 2/03 Chep 2m4f heavy Hdl

Moderate hurdler; stays two and a half miles.

Southern Dunes
69   **12**
7-y-o b g Ardkinglass-Leprechaun Lady (Royal Blend)
G Fierro   G Fierro

Placings:PP/0P0P0P-P06   (1924)
2002/03: 16⁵GF, 17⁰G, 21⁶GS,

	Starts	1st	2nd	3rd	Win & Pl
Hurdles	3	0	0	0	0
Career Total	11	0	0	0	0

Going:	Sf: 0-0 GS: 0-1 Gd: 0-1 GF: - Fm: 0-1
Distance:	2m/2m3: 0-2 2m4-2m7: 0-0 3m+: 0-0
Track:	LH: 0-1 RH: 0-2 Tight: 0-0 Gall: 0-0
Aids:	Bl: 0-1 Vi: 0-0 Tstrap: 0-0
Best Rating:	55 12/01 Donc 2m110y good Hdl

Southern Ridge
93(66c)   (40c)**69**
12-y-o b g Indian Ridge-Southern Sky (Comedy Star (USA))
A S T Holdsworth   N J Holdsworth

Placings:60066/22145/66/00P/0F02-03   (0573)
2002/03: 17⁰GS, 17³G,

	Starts	1st	2nd	3rd	Win & Pl
Hurdles	2	0	0	1	324
Career Total	21	1	3	1	4356
97	9/96	NAbb	2m1f	E Hdl	GD £2326

Total win prize-money £2327

Going:	Sf: 0-0 GS: 0-0 Gd: 0-1 GF: - Fm: 0-0
Distance:	2m/2m3: 0-2 2m4-2m7: 0-0 3m+: 0-0
Track:	LH: 0-2 RH: 0-0 Tight: 0-0 Gall: 0-0
Aids:	Bl: 0-0 Vi: 0-0 Tstrap: 0-0
Best Rating:	97 9/96 NAbb 2m1f good Hdl

Plating class hurdler, suited by two miles and good ground.

Southern Star (IRE)
115   (128h)**145**
8-y-o ch g Montelimar (USA)-Flying Pegus (Beau Chapeau)

Miss H C Knight   Trevor Hemmings

Placings:13/23113/11U34P2-202000   (4479)
2002/03: 27²GS, 26⁹GS, 26²S, 28⁹G, 24⁹G, 36⁹G,

	Starts	1st	2nd	3rd	Win & Pl
Chases	6	0	2	0	19223
Career Total	20	5	4	4	70850
144	10/01	Chel	3m110y	C Ch	£8346
114	10/01	Bang	2m4f110yD Ch	GD	£4309
132	2/01	Hntg	2m4f110yB Hdl	G-S	£8970
133	1/01	Winc	2m	E Hdl	G-S	£2047
123	10/99	Hntg	2m110y	H NHF	£1842

Total win prize-money £25516

Going:	Sf: 0-1 GS: 0-2 Gd: 0-3 GF: - Fm: 0-0
Distance:	2m/2m3: 0-0 2m4-2m7: 0-0 3m+: 0-6
Track:	LH: 0-6 RH: 0-0 Tight: 0-1 Gall: 0-4
Aids:	Bl: 0-0 Vi: 0-0 Tstrap: 0-0
Best Rating:	145 12/02 Chel 3m2f110y soft Ch

Useful chaser; acts on most types of ground; stays 3m 4f.

Southern-Be-George
93(106h)   (95h)**76**
8-y-o b g Be My Chief (USA)-Southern Sky (Comedy Star (USA))
W G M Turner   A Wilkinson

Placings:P435/0P44P/215/11-0PP4   (0435)
2002/03: 24⁰G, 27⁵GF, 20⁵GS, 20⁴GF,

	Starts	1st	2nd	3rd	Win & Pl
Hurdles	2	0	0	0	0
Chases	2	0	0	0	229
Career Total	18	3	1	1	10299
95	8/01	Hrfd	2m3f110yF(0-100)HHdl	G-F	£2901
87	8/01	Sthl	2m4f110yF(0-110)HHdl	G-F	£2947
89	5/00	Extr	2m6f E(0-105)HHdl	G-F	£2957

Total win prize-money £8807

Going:	Sf: 0-0 GS: 0-1 Gd: 0-1 GF: - Fm: 0-2
Distance:	2m/2m3: 0-0 2m4-2m7: 0-2 3m+: 0-2
Track:	LH: 0-3 RH: 0-1 Tight: 0-3 Gall: 0-1
Aids:	Bl: 0-0 Vi: 0-0 Tstrap: 0-0
Best Rating:	95 9/01 Hrfd 2m3f110y gd-fm Hdl

Southerncrosspatch
105   **87**
12-y-o ch g Ra Nova-Southern Bird (Shiny Tenth)
Mrs Barbara Waring   E S Chivers

Placings:0/040/0125F3P/111P/3PP204P4/03422P/133424 4022-P60P42   (4683)
2002/03: 24⁸GS, 24⁶GS, 26⁵S, 23⁸GS, 24⁴GF, 21²GF,

	Starts	1st	2nd	3rd	Win & Pl
Hurdles	6	0	1	0	1444
Career Total	45	5	8	5	28703
101	6/01	NAbb	3m3f	E(0-115)HHdl	GD £3038
101	6/98	Strf	2m4f	E(0-115)HCh	G-S £2921
86	6/98	Sthl	3m110y	F(0-105)HCh	GD £3777
107	6/98	Worc	2m4f110yE(0-100)HCh	G-F	£3315
87	8/97	Sthl	3m110y	E Hdl	G-F £2322

Total win prize-money £15375

Going:	Sf: 0-0 GS: 0-3 Gd: 0-0 GF: - Fm: 0-2
Distance:	2m/2m3: 0-0 2m4-2m7: 0-2 3m+: 0-4
Track:	LH: 0-3 RH: 0-3 Tight: 0-3 Gall: 0-1
Aids:	Bl: 0-0 Vi: 0-0 Tstrap: 0-0
Best Rating:	107 6/98 Worc 2m4f110y gd-fm Ch

Moderate handicap hurdler these days; has won three times over fences in the past.

Southerndown (IRE)
110(97h)   (88h)**90+**
10-y-o ch g Montelimar (USA)-Country Melody (IRE) (Orchestra)
R Lee   Mrs Bill Neale And John Jackson

Placings:05/62265504/P5261055/040/4002260553033- 2F524111440   (2944)
2002/03: 25²G, 24⁵GS, 25⁵GF, 23²GF, 26⁴GF, 26¹GF, 24¹G, 26¹G, 24⁴GF, 24⁴GS, 24⁰GS,

	Starts	1st	2nd	3rd	Win & Pl
Hurdles	1	0	0	0	433
Chases	10	3	2	0	14480
Career Total	45	4	7	3	22876
98	10/02	Sthl	3m2f	F(0-100)HCh	GD £3334
90	9/02	Bang	3m110y	E(0-100)HCh	GD £5027
98	8/02	Sthl	3m2f	E Ch	G-F £3672
80	8/99	Hntg	3m2f	F(0-90)HHdl	G-F £1955

Total win prize-money £13992

Going:	Sf: 0-0 GS: 0-3 Gd: 2-3 GF: - Fm: 1-5
Distance:	2m/2m3: 0-0 2m4-2m7: 0-0 3m+: 3-11
Track:	LH: 3-7 RH: 0-4 Tight: 1-6 Gall: 0-0
Aids:	Bl: 0-0 Vi: 0-0 Tstrap: 0-0
Best Rating:	98 10/02 Sthl 3m2f good Ch

Plating-class staying hurdler and chaser; suited by good ground or faster; stays extreme distances.

Sovereign
106   **93**
9-y-o b m Interrex (CAN)-Shiny Penny (Glint Of Gold)
J F Panvert   J F Panvert

Placings:5524342/6220604060P5/60P6P66550500023303/ 610015/0-41003246632   (4668)
2002/03: 20⁴G, 19¹G, 22⁰G, 22⁰GF, 22³GF, 19²GF, 19⁴GF, 24⁶GF, 24⁶F, 22³F, 20²G,

	Starts	1st	2nd	3rd	Win & Pl
Hurdles	11	1	2	2	7313
Career Total	56	3	7	6	16983
93	6/02	Hrfd	2m3f110yE(0-110)HHdl	GD £3465
92	9/00	Hrfd	2m3f110yE Hdl	G-F £2992
90	5/00	Fknm	2m7f110yE Hdl	FRM £2229

Total win prize-money £8687

Going:	Sf: 0-0 GS: 0-0 Gd: 1-4 GF: - Fm: 0-7
Distance:	2m/2m3: 0-0 2m4-2m7: 1-9 3m+: 0-2
Track:	LH: 0-5 RH: 1-6 Tight: 0-9 Gall: 0-0
Aids:	Bl: 0-0 Vi: 0-0 Tstrap: 0-0
Best Rating:	93 4/03 Fknm 2m4f good Hdl

Plating-class hurdler; consistent; likes the ground good or faster; stays two and a half miles.

Sovereign Gold
77   **64**
6-y-o b g Rakaposhi King-Page Of Gold (Goldhill)
D R Gandolfo   K W Bell & Son Ltd

Placings:0-0   (3182)
2002/03: 21⁰G,

	Starts	1st	2nd	3rd	Win & Pl
Hurdles	1	0	0	0	
Career Total	2	0	0	0	

Going:	Sf: 0-0 GS: 0-0 Gd: 0-1 GF: - Fm: 0-0
Distance:	2m/2m3: 0-0 2m4-2m7: 0-0 3m+: 0-0
Track:	LH: 0-0 RH: 0-1 Tight: 0-0 Gall: 0-0
Aids:	Bl: 0-0 Vi: 0-0 Tstrap: 0-0
Best Rating:	88 11/01 Sand 2m110y gd-sft NHF

Sovereign Grit (IRE)
51

13-y-o ch g Sheer Grit-Gorryelm (Arctic Slave)
Mrs L C Jewell Mrs A Greengrow

Placings:20/40/P63-P   (0123)
2002/03: 27PGF,

	Starts	1st	2nd	3rd	Win & Pl
Hurdles	1	0	0	0	
Career Total	8	0	1	1	1219

Going:	Sf: 0-0 GS: 0-0 Gd: 0-0 GF: - Fm: 0-1
Distance:	2m2m3: 0-0 2m4-2m7: 0-0 3m+: 0-1
Track:	LH: 0-0 RH: 0-0 Tight: 0-0 Gall: 0-0
Aids:	Bl: 0-0 Vi: 0-0 Tstrap: 0-0
Best Rating:	96 4/96 Thur 2m gd-yld NHF

Poor form over both types of obstacle.

Sovereign State (IRE)
109   89

6-y-o b g Soviet Lad (USA)-Portree (Slip Anchor)
J A Moore (Miss S E Hall 27/9) J A Moore

Placings:4P063   (4666)
2002/03: 164GS, 16PHY, 16QG, 19QG, 16QGF,

	Starts	1st	2nd	3rd	Win & Pl
Hurdles	5	0	0	1	714
Career Total	5	0	0	1	714

Going:	Sf: 0-1 GS: 0-1 Gd: 0-3 GF: - Fm: 0-0
Distance:	2m2m3: 0-5 2m4-2m7: 0-0 3m+: 0-0
Track:	LH: 0-4 RH: 0-1 Tight: 0-3 Gall: 0-0
Aids:	Bl: 0-0 Vi: 0-0 Tstrap: 0-0
Best Rating:	80 4/03 Fknm 2m good Hdl

Plating-class hurdler; keen sort; seems best on a sound surface; goes well on a sharp track; has worn a visor.

Sovereign's Gift
99   95+

7-y-o ch m Elegant Monarch-Cadeau D Aragon (Aragon)
Mrs S D Williams B W Gillbard

Placings:000/05030-4252P2   (4290)
2002/03: 174GF, 172GF, 225GF, 222G, 24PF, 222GF,

	Starts	1st	2nd	3rd	Win & Pl
Hurdles	6	0	3	0	3356
Career Total	14	0	3	1	3737

Going:	Sf: 0-0 GS: 0-0 Gd: 0-1 GF: - Fm: 0-5
Distance:	2m2m3: 0-2 2m4-2m7: 0-3 3m+: 0-1
Track:	LH: 0-4 RH: 0-2 Tight: 0-5 Gall: 0-0
Aids:	Bl: 0-0 Vi: 0-0 Tstrap: 0-0
Best Rating:	95 9/02 NAbb 2m6f good Hdl

Moderate hurdler; winning plater on the Flat; put stamina to good use when winning 2m 1f mares only novice hurdle at Newton Abbot June 2003; stays 2m 6f; acts on a sound surface.

Spaghetti Junction
101   103

5-y-o ch m Sir Harry Lewis (USA)-Up The Junction (IRE) (Treasure Kay)
R H Alner Paul Murphy

Placings:1P340   (4610)
2002/03: 161S, 17PHY, 193S, 214G, 21QG,

	Starts	1st	2nd	3rd	Win & Pl
Hurdles	5	1	0	1	7077
Career Total	5	1	0	1	7077
106 11/02 Hayd 2m		D Hdl		SFT	£3770

Total win prize-money £3770

Going:	Sf: 1-3 GS: 0-0 Gd: 0-2 GF: - Fm: 0-0
Distance:	2m2m3: 1-3 2m4-2m7: 0-2 3m+: 0-0
Track:	LH: 1-3 RH: 0-2 Tight: 0-1 Gall: 0-2
Aids:	Bl: 0-0 Vi: 0-0 Tstrap: 0-0
Best Rating:	106 11/02 Hayd 2m soft Hdl

Modest hurdler; acts on both decent and soft ground.

Spainkris
109   105

4-y-o b g Kris-Pennycairn (Last Tycoon)
A Crook (X Nakkachdji 9/11) M Wainright

Placings:05U16   (4399)
2002/03: 16QHY, 165GS, 16UG, 171G, 16QGF,

	Starts	1st	2nd	3rd	Win & Pl
Hurdles	5	1	0	0	5586
Career Total	5	1	0	0	5586
104 3/03 MRas		2m1f110yD Hdl		GD	£4836

Total win prize-money £4836

Going:	Sf: 0-1 GS: 0-1 Gd: 1-2 GF: - Fm: 0-1
Distance:	2m2m3: 1-5 2m4-2m7: 0-0 3m+: 0-0
Track:	LH: 0-4 RH: 1-1 Tight: 1-1 Gall: 0-0
Aids:	Bl: 0-0 Vi: 0-0 Tstrap: 0-0
Best Rating:	105 3/03 Hayd 2m good Hdl

Modest hurdler; fair Flat performer in France; effective over two miles; acts on good and heavy ground.

Spandau (NZ)
95   83

9-y-o br g Fiesta Star (AUS)-Koru (NZ) (Diplomatic Agent (USA))
J C Tuck M Tuck

Placings:00P/2600/1/P-P0530   (4566)
2002/03: 17PG, 17QGS, 165HY, 179HY, 20QGF,

	Starts	1st	2nd	3rd	Win & Pl
Hurdles	5	0	0	1	413
Career Total	14	1	1	1	3830
95 5/00 Hrfd		2m1f D(0-110)HHdl		GD	£2762

Total win prize-money £2763

Going:	Sf: 0-2 GS: 0-1 Gd: 0-1 GF: - Fm: 0-1
Distance:	2m2m3: 0-4 2m4-2m7: 0-1 3m+: 0-0
Track:	LH: 0-5 RH: 0-0 Tight: 0-4 Gall: 0-0
Aids:	Bl: 0-0 Vi: 0-0 Tstrap: 0-0
Best Rating:	95 5/00 Hrfd 2m1f good Hdl

Modest hurdler, lightly raced since winning at Hereford in May 2002.

Spanish Archer (IRE)
97 (100c)   44

8-y-o b g Spanish Place (USA)-Bow Gello (Bargello)
L Waring (P J Hobbs 14/9) Mrs J Waring

Placings:6f0000/02213/P-P13P5043403P05   (2779)
2002/03: 25PG, 211S, 213GF, 23PG, 23QGF, 26QGF, 224G, 20QG, 224F, 17QGS, 173GS, 16PS, 19QGS, 245S,

	Starts	1st	2nd	3rd	Win & Pl
Hurdles	7	0	0	2	728

	Chases	7	1	0	1	3504
Career Total		26	3	2	4	10825
70 6/02 Uttx		2m5f	F(0-90)HCh		SFT	£2674
87 10/00 Folk		2m5f	F(0-95)HCh		G-F	£2387
99 11/99 Tntn		2m1f	H NHF		GD	£1680

Total win prize-money £6742

Going:	Sf: 1-3 GS: 0-2 Gd: 0-4 GF: - Fm: 0-5
Distance:	2m2m3: 0-4 2m4-2m7: 1-5 3m+: 0-5
Track:	LH: 1-7 RH: 0-6 Tight: 0-6 Gall: 0-0
Aids:	Bl: 0-0 Vi: 0-0 Tstrap: 0-1
Best Rating:	99 11/99 Tntn 2m1f good NHF

Plating-class chaser; only third best when gifted a modest handicap chase at Uttoxeter in June 2002; acts on any ground.

Spanish Main (IRE)
97   111

9-y-o b g Spanish Place (USA)-Willow Grouse (Giolla Mear)
N A Twiston-Davies C B Sanderson

Placings:454/21U3111/1333F1U0/3U0P5-3415   (4765)
2002/03: 273S, 264HY, 301S, 315G,

	Starts	1st	2nd	3rd	Win & Pl
Chases	4	1	0	1	13442
Career Total	27	7	1	6	53929
111 3/03 Extr		3m6f110yD(0-125)HCh		SFT	£10880
131 2/01 Uttx		3m2f	B HCh		HVY	£12640
107 10/00 Extr		2m7f110yD Ch		GD	£3770
124 4/00 Chel		3m	D(0-120)HHdl		SFT	£7247
113 3/00 Font		3m4f	E Hdl		G-S	£2394
112 10/00 Asct		3m	C HHdl		G-S	£5694
93 10/99 Strf		2m6f110yE Hdl		G-S	£2057

Total win prize-money £44705

Going:	Sf: 1-3 GS: 0-0 Gd: 0-1 GF: - Fm: 0-0
Distance:	2m2m3: 0-0 2m4-2m7: 0-0 3m+: 1-4
Track:	LH: 0-1 RH: 1-2 Tight: 0-1 Gall: 0-0
Aids:	Bl: 0-0 Vi: 0-0 Tstrap: 0-0
Best Rating:	131 2/01 Uttx 3m2f heavy Ch

Fair chaser; stays 3m 6f; won Devon National at Exeter March 2003 (outstaying tiring rivals from off the pace); needs soft ground and extreme distances to perform at his best; has worn a visor and tongue tie.

Spark Of Life
87   95

6-y-o b m Rainbows For Life (CAN)-Sparkly Girl (IRE) (Danehill (USA))
T D McCarthy James Etheridge

Placings:3-5   (0735)
2002/03: 175GF,

	Starts	1st	2nd	3rd	Win & Pl
Hurdles	1	0	0	0	0
Career Total	2	0	0	1	495

Going:	Sf: 0-0 GS: 0-0 Gd: 0-0 GF: - Fm: 0-1
Distance:	2m2m3: 0-1 2m4-2m7: 0-0 3m+: 0-0
Track:	LH: 0-1 RH: 0-0 Tight: 0-1 Gall: 0-0
Aids:	Bl: 0-0 Vi: 0-0 Tstrap: 0-0
Best Rating:	95 11/01 Extr 2m1f gd-fm Hdl

Sparkey Smith (IRE)

11-y-o b g Mister Majestic-Jim Says (Jaazeiro (USA))
Major General C A Ramsay (C F Swan 29/8) Will Ramsay

Placings:0/001P/041P0/00221321F300/21153F006/244-020064   (3582)

2002/03: 20⁰S, 20²GF, 17⁹V, 22⁴GF, 20⁶GF, 24⁴G,

	Starts	1st	2nd	3rd	Win & Pl
Hurdles	1	0	0	0	
Chases	5	0	1	0	3730
Career Total	40	6	6	3	36884
130	6/00	Wxfd	2m4f	(0-109)HCh	YLD	£3864
129	5/00	Clon	2m2f	(0-102)HCh	GD	£3036
100	8/99	Tram	2m	(0-109)HCh	G-F	£4928
90	6/99	Baln	2m1f	Ch	G-F	£3529
123	8/98	Tram	2m	(0-130)HHdl	G-F	£5978
108	3/98	Leop	2m	Hdl	G-Y	£2680

Total win prize-money £24017

Going: Sf: 0-1 GS: 0-0 Gd: 0-1 GF: - Fm: 0-3
Distance: 2m/2m3: 0-1 2m4-2m7: 0-4 3m+: 0-1
Track: LH: 0-1 RH: 0-3 Tight: 0-1 Gall: 0-0
Aids: Bl: 0-0 Vi: 0-0 Tstrap: 0-0
Best Rating: 130 6/00 Wxfd 2m4f   yield   Ch

Sparkling Cascade (IRE)

101   70

11-y-o b m Royal Fountain-Yukon Law (Goldhill)
A G Newcombe A G Newcombe

Placings:320/P62-2P52   (1080)
2002/03: 24²GS, 26⁶GF, 26⁵GF, 26⁹G,

	Starts	1st	2nd	3rd	Win & Pl
Chases	4	0	2	0	2203
Career Total	10	0	4	1	4563

Going: Sf: 0-0 GS: 0-1 Gd: 0-1 GF: - Fm: 0-2
Distance: 2m/2m3: 0-0 2m4-2m7: 0-0 3m+: 0-4
Track: LH: 0-3 RH: 0-0 Tight: 0-3 Gall: 0-0
Aids: Bl: 0-0 Vi: 0-0 Tstrap: 0-0
Best Rating: 92 8/00 NAbb 2m110y good Ch

Moderate chaser; placed in low-grade chases at Newton Abbot, Southwell and Fontwell in 2002; stays three miles; probably best suited by a sound surface.

Sparkling Embers

8-y-o b g Regal Embers (IRE)-Lady Pia (Pia Fort)
C J Price Gerald Davies

Placings:PPU-PP   (0214)
2002/03: 17⁵GF, 19⁹GS,

	Starts	1st	2nd	3rd	Win & Pl
Hurdles	2	0	0	0	
Career Total	5	0	0	0	

Going: Sf: 0-0 GS: 0-0 Gd: 0-1 GF: - Fm: 0-1
Distance: 2m/2m3: 0-1 2m4-2m7: 0-1 3m+: 0-0
Track: LH: 0-0 RH: 0-2 Tight: 0-0 Gall: 0-0
Aids: Bl: 0-0 Vi: 0-0 Tstrap: 0-0
Best Rating: 0 5/02 Hrfd 2m3f110y good   Hdl

Sparkling Jess

81f   38f

4-y-o b f Alderbrook-Tasmin Gayle (IRE) (Strong Gale)
M J Roberts Mike Roberts

Placings:00   (3930)
2002/03: 17⁰HY, 16⁹G,

	Starts	1st	2nd	3rd	Win & Pl
NH Flat	2	0	0	0	
Career Total	2	0	0	0	

Going: Sf: 0-1 GS: 0-0 Gd: 0-1 GF: - Fm: 0-0
Distance: 2m/2m3: 0-2 2m4-2m7: 0-0 3m+: 0-0
Track: LH: 0-0 RH: 0-2 Tight: 0-1 Gall: 0-1
Aids: Bl: 0-0 Vi: 0-0 Tstrap: 0-0
Best Rating: 38 3/03 Hntg 2m110y good NHF

Sparkling Lass

(86h)   (45h)

9-y-o gr m Nicholas Bill-Sparkling Time (USA) (Olden Times)
N G Ayliffe R A Bimson

Placings:050P/06F52/00450544/04P004-000   (4623)
2002/03: 19⁰GS, 22⁰G, 27⁰GF,

	Starts	1st	2nd	3rd	Win & Pl
Hurdles	3	0	0	0	
Career Total	26	0	1	0	924

Going: Sf: 0-0 GS: 0-1 Gd: 0-1 GF: - Fm: 0-1
Distance: 2m/2m3: 0-0 2m4-2m7: 0-2 3m+: 0-1
Track: LH: 0-1 RH: 0-2 Tight: 0-2 Gall: 0-0
Aids: Bl: 0-0 Vi: 0-0 Tstrap: 0-0
Best Rating: 88 4/01 Winc 2m6f   soft Hdl

Moderate hurdler/chaser.

Sparkling Sword

91   56

8-y-o gr m Broadsword (USA)-Sparkling Time (USA) (Olden Times)
Miss Venetia Williams Mrs M Horton

Placings:12/3-0   (0340)
2002/03: 24⁹G,

	Starts	1st	2nd	3rd	Win & Pl
Hurdles	1	0	0	0	
Career Total	4	1	1	1	5354
107	10/00	Wwck	2m	H NHF	SFT	£1575

Total win prize-money £1575

Going: Sf: 0-0 GS: 0-0 Gd: 0-1 GF: - Fm: 0-0
Distance: 2m/2m3: 0-0 2m4-2m7: 0-0 3m+: 0-1
Track: LH: 0-0 RH: 0-1 Tight: 0-0 Gall: 0-0
Aids: Bl: 0-0 Vi: 0-0 Tstrap: 0-0
Best Rating: 120 12/00 Chep 2m110y soft NHF

A half-sister to the stayers Sparkling Buck and Sparkling Cone, she has shown plenty of ability in bumpers. Suited by soft ground.

Sparky Gayle (IRE)

13-y-o b g Strong Gale-Baybush (Boreen (FR))
A Parker Mr & Mrs Raymond Anderson Green

Placings:2/12221001/13254/111111/4342/3P31/0602U/P20/01-3 (4552)
2002/03: 27³G,

	Starts	1st	2nd	3rd	Win & Pl
Chases	1	0	0	1	550
Career Total	39	12	8	5	116087
128	4/02	Kels	3m1f	H Ch	G-F	£2670
150	4/99	Ayr	2m4f	B HCh	HVY	£10328
147	4/97	Ayr	2m4f	B HCh	GD	£14490
155	3/97	Chel	2m5f	B Ch	GD	£32850
140	2/97	Ayr	2m4f	D Ch	SFT	£3808
126	1/97	Carl	2m	D Ch	G-F	£3707
135	11/96	Newc	2m4f	C Ch	GD	£5340
114	11/96	Ayr	2m	D Ch	GD	£3675
127	11/95	Ayr	2m4f	D(0-120)HHdl	GD	£3615
107	4/95	Carl	2m4f110y	E Hdl	FRM	

£2480

| 121 | 1/95 | Ayr | 2m4f | D Hdl | SFT | £2983 |
| | 5/94 | Dpat | 2m1f172y NHF | | GD | £1479 |

Total win prize-money £87429

Going: Sf: 0-0 GS: 0-0 Gd: 0-1 GF: - Fm: 0-0
Distance: 2m/2m3: 0-0 2m4-2m7: 0-0 3m+: 0-1
Track: LH: 0-1 RH: 0-0 Tight: 0-0 Gall: 0-0
Aids: Bl: 0-0 Vi: 0-0 Tstrap: 0-1
Best Rating: 155 3/97 Chel 2m5f   good Ch

Fair hunter chaser nowadays; won the Cathcart Chase at the Cheltenham Festival in 1997. Stays three miles one; better at shorter; acts on any ground.

Special Agenda (IRE)

111(86h)   (90h)117

9-y-o b g Torus-Easter Blade (IRE) (Fine Blade (USA))
C J Mann Mrs L G Turner

Placings:445/P1132O3F2/222PU202P6-14UP56   (3942)
2002/03: 16¹GS, 17⁴GS, 17⁴GS, 16⁸GS, 17⁵GS, 17⁶S,

	Starts	1st	2nd	3rd	Win & Pl
Chases	6	1	0	0	4660
Career Total	28	3	7	2	22788
124	5/02	NAbb	2m110y	D(0-115)HCh	G-S	£3922
122	11/00	Hrfd	2m	E(0-105)HCh	SFT	£2804
119	11/00	Plum	2m1f	E Ch	SFT	£3346

Total win prize-money £10074

Going: Sf: 0-1 GS: 1-5 Gd: 0-0 GF: - Fm: 0-0
Distance: 2m/2m3: 1-6 2m4-2m7: 0-0 3m+: 0-0
Track: LH: 1-5 RH: 0-1 Tight: 1-5 Gall: 0-1
Aids: Bl: 0-0 Vi: 0-0 Tstrap: 0-0
Best Rating: 124 5/02 NAbb 2m110y gd-sft Ch

Modest chaser/hurdler; has shown good form with cut in the ground; effective at around two miles.

Special Conquest

100f   103+f

5-y-o b g El Conquistador-Kellys Special (Netherkelly)
J W Mullins F G Matthews

Placings:1   (4628)
2002/03: 17¹GF,

	Starts	1st	2nd	3rd	Win & Pl
NH Flat	1	1	0	0	3206
Career Total	1	1	0	0	3206
103	4/03	NAbb	2m1f	H NHF	G-F	£3206

Total win prize-money £3206

Going: Sf: 0-0 GS: 0-0 Gd: 0-0 GF: - Fm: 1-1
Distance: 2m/2m3: 1-1 2m4-2m7: 0-0 3m+: 0-0
Track: LH: 1-1 RH: 0-0 Tight: 1-1 Gall: 0-0
Aids: Bl: 0-0 Vi: 0-0 Tstrap: 0-0
Best Rating: 103 4/03 NAbb 2m1f   gd-fm NHF

Half-brother to staying chaser Kellys Conquest; won a bumper at Newton Abbot on his racecourse debut. Acts on fast.

Special Constable

5-y-o b/br g Derrylin-Lavenham s Last (Rymer)
B I Case Case Racing Partnership

Placings:0P   (3319)
2002/03: 14⁰GS, 21⁹GS,

	Starts	1st	2nd	3rd	Win & Pl
NH Flat	1	0	0	0	0

Hurdles	1	0	0	0
Career Total	2	0	0	0

Going:	Sf: 0-0 GS: 0-2 Gd: 0-0 GF: - Fm: 0-0
Distance:	2m/2m3: 0-0 2m4-2m7: 0-1 3m+: 0-0
Track:	LH: 0-1 RH: 0-1 Tight: 0-0 Gall: 0-0
Aids:	Bl: 0-0 Vi: 0-0 Tstrap: 0-0
Best Rating:	62 11/02 Wwck 1m6f gd-sft NHF

Special Present

108   **110+**

5-y-o ch g Presenting-Pitts Special (Pitpan)
L Wells Mrs Carrie Zetter-Wells

Placings:220-211   **(1409)**
2002/03: 16²G, 16¹GF, 18¹G,

	Starts	1st	2nd	3rd	Win & Pl
NH Flat	1	0	1	0	648
Hurdles	2	2	0	1	7255
Career Total	6	2	3	0	9207
110	10/02	Font	2m2f110yE Hdl		GD	£3108
106	9/02	Strf	2m110y D Hdl		G-F	£4147

Total win prize-money £7255

Going:	Sf: 0-0 GS: 0-0 Gd: 1-2 GF: - Fm: 1-1
Distance:	2m/2m3: 2-3 2m4-2m7: 0-0 3m+: 0-0
Track:	LH: 2-3 RH: 0-0 Tight: 2-2 Gall: 0-0
Aids:	Bl: 0-0 Vi: 0-0 Tstrap: 0-0
Best Rating:	110 10/02 Font 2m2f110y good Hdl

Regularly placed in bumpers, he made a successful transition to hurdles in 2002, winning his first two starts. Tragically, he suffered fatal injuries on the second occasion. (DEAD)

Specialism

62   **19**

5-y-o ch g Spectrum (IRE)-Waft (USA) (Topsider (USA))
M J Gingell (T Keddy 14/7) Miss K D Francis

Placings:0   **(2310)**
2002/03: 16⁰HY,

	Starts	1st	2nd	3rd	Win & Pl
Hurdles	1	0	0	0	
Career Total	1	0	0	0	

Going:	Sf: 0-1 GS: 0-0 Gd: 0-0 GF: - Fm: 0-0
Distance:	2m/2m3: 0-1 2m4-2m7: 0-0 3m+: 0-0
Track:	LH: 0-1 RH: 0-0 Tight: 0-1 Gall: 0-0
Aids:	Bl: 0-0 Vi: 0-0 Tstrap: 0-0
Best Rating:	0 12/02 Plum 2m heavy Hdl

Specialize

110   **106**

11-y-o b g Faustus (USA)-Scholastika (GER) (Alpenkonig (GER))
K R Burke P A Brazier

Placings:606/PP3/11124302P5212/112130650220/P14310
0P/P0011163-5P0P4402P6   **(1208)**
2002/03: 24⁵GF, 24⁴GS, 20⁹GF, 24⁸GF, 20⁴GF, 21⁴G, 21⁹G, 26²G, 21⁸GF, 21⁶G,

	Starts	1st	2nd	3rd	Win & Pl
Chases	10	1	0	0	2590
Career Total	57	12	8	5	66789
119	8/01	Sedg	2m5f	D(0-125)HCh	G-F	£4056
118	7/01	Strf	2m4f	E(0-115)HCh	GD	£4707
107	7/01	Sedg	2m5f	F(0-110)HCh	G-F	£4348
119	12/00	Fknm	3m110y	D(0-120)HCh	G-S	£4260

119	10/00	Strf	2m4f	F(0-110)HCh	SFT	£4257
124	6/99	Uttx	2m5f	C(0-135)HCh	G-S	£6905
121	5/99	Fknm	3m110y	D(0-120)HCh	G-F	£6602
121	5/99	Uttx	2m4f	D(0-125)HCh	G-F	£4396
121	4/99	Uttx	2m5f	D(0-110)HCh	G-S	£4513
95	5/98	Worc	2m	F(0-105)HHdl	G-F	£2285
97	5/98	Hrfd	2m1f	C(0-100)HHdl	GD	£2442
91	5/98	Uttx	2m	G(0-95)HHdl	GD	£1710

Total win prize-money £50488

Going:	Sf: 0-0 GS: 0-1 Gd: 0-4 GF: - Fm: 0-5
Distance:	2m/2m3: 0-0 2m4-2m7: 0-6 3m+: 0-4
Track:	LH: 0-10 RH: 0-0 Tight: 0-7 Gall: 0-0
Aids:	Bl: 0-2 Vi: 0-3 Tstrap: 0-0
Best Rating:	124 6/99 Uttx 2m5f gd-sft Ch

Modest handicap chaser who has gone well for Tony McCoy in the past. Stays well but is becoming disappointing and his placed form at Cartmel in August 2002 is probably as good as he is now. Best on fast ground.

Spectrometer

117   **149+**

6-y-o ch g Rainbow Quest (USA)-Selection Board (Welsh Pageant)
P J Hobbs Concertina Racing

Placings:21124-25222135   **(4456)**
2002/03: 16²S, 17⁵GS, 18²G, 19²G, 20²G, 17¹G, 21³G, 24⁵G,

	Starts	1st	2nd	3rd	Win & Pl
Hurdles	8	1	4	1	40277
Career Total	13	3	6	1	48494
140	12/02	Chel	2m1f	C(0-135)HHdl	GD	£16892
117	7/01	Worc	2m	D Hdl	GD	£3307
104	7/01	Strf	2m3f	E Hdl	G-F	£2415

Total win prize-money £22615

Going:	Sf: 0-1 GS: 0-1 Gd: 1-6 GF: - Fm: 0-0
Distance:	2m/2m3: 1-5 2m4-2m7: 0-2 3m+: 0-1
Track:	LH: 1-7 RH: 0-1 Tight: 0-5 Gall: 1-2
Aids:	Bl: 0-0 Vi: 0-0 Tstrap: 0-0
Best Rating:	149 4/03 Aint 3m110y good Hdl

Very useful handicap hurdler; likes good/fast ground but also handles softer; stays three miles.

Spectroscope (IRE)

119   **137**

4-y-o b g Spectrum (IRE)-Paloma Bay (IRE) (Alzao (USA))
Jonjo O Neill Mrs G Smith

Placings:1B4112   **(4460)**
2002/03: 16¹G, 16⁸GS, 16⁴G, 16¹GS, 17¹G, 16²G,

	Starts	1st	2nd	3rd	Win & Pl
Hurdles	6	3	1	0	91958
Career Total	6	3	1	0	91958
137	3/03	Chel	2m1f	A Hdl	GD	£58000
121	3/03	Kemp	2m	D Hdl	G-S	£5005
112	10/02	Kemp	2m	D Hdl	G-F	£4348

Total win prize-money £67354

Going:	Sf: 0-0 GS: 1-2 Gd: 2-4 GF: - Fm: 0-0
Distance:	2m/2m3: 3-6 2m4-2m7: 0-0 3m+: 0-0
Track:	LH: 1-3 RH: 2-3 Tight: 0-1 Gall: 1-1
Aids:	Bl: 0-0 Vi: 0-0 Tstrap: 0-0
Best Rating:	137 4/03 Aint 2m110y good Hdl

Very useful juvenile hurdler; twice a winner at Kempton; game winner of the Triumph Hurdle at Cheltenham; runner-up under a penalty at Aintree; suited by good and yielding ground; tough sort; should stay 2m 4f.

Speed Board (IRE)

11-y-o b g Waajib-Pitty Pal (USA) (Caracolero (USA))
Dennis Pugh (F Flood 3/6) Dennis Pugh

Placings:04002O536/P000/00215025P/10010050/0105P55
04P1P/0F31P10/0PP055P36-0333U   **(3548)**
2002/03: 20⁰GY, 24³S, 25³YS, 24³YS, 25⁰G,

	Starts	1st	2nd	3rd	Win & Pl
Chases	5	0	0	3	2307
Career Total	65	7	3	6	35084
107	2/01	Naas	2m4f	(0-116)HCh	SH	£6677
96	12/00	Navn	2m4f	(0-123)HCh	HVY	£5880
101	3/00	Wxfd	3m	(0-109)HCh	YLD	£3864
106	5/99	Gowr	3m1f	(0-116)HHdl	GD	£4910
108	1/99	Fair	2m6f	(0-116)HHdl	HVY	£3069
101	5/98	Fair	3m	(0-109)HHdl	Y-S	£2680
96	1/98	DRoy	2m4f	(0-109)HHdl	SFT	£1489

Total win prize-money £28570

Going:	Sf: 0-1 GS: 0-0 Gd: 0-1 GF: - Fm: 0-0
Distance:	2m/2m3: 0-0 2m4-2m7: 0-1 3m+: 0-4
Track:	LH: 0-1 RH: 0-1 Tight: 0-0 Gall: 0-0
Aids:	Bl: 0-5 Vi: 0-0 Tstrap: 0-0
Best Rating:	108 1/99 Fair 2m6f heavy Hdl

Speed Venture

105   **101**

6-y-o b g Owington-Jade Venture (Never So Bold)
J Mackie Wall Racing Partners

Placings:13345-0005410   **(4159)**
2002/03: 19⁰GS, 16⁰S, 16⁰GS, 17⁵GS, 16⁴G, 19¹S, 22⁰G,

	Starts	1st	2nd	3rd	Win & Pl
Hurdles	7	1	0	0	5298
Career Total	12	2	0	2	8832
101	3/03	Hrfd	2m3f110yD(0-120)HHdl		SFT	£5297
99	11/01	Uttx	2m	E Hdl		SFT	£2758

Total win prize-money £8056

Going:	Sf: 1-2 GS: 0-3 Gd: 0-2 GF: - Fm: 0-0
Distance:	2m/2m3: 0-5 2m4-2m7: 1-2 3m+: 0-0
Track:	LH: 0-5 RH: 1-1 Tight: 0-2 Gall: 0-1
Aids:	Bl: 0-0 Vi: 1-4 Tstrap: 1-7
Best Rating:	101 3/03 Hrfd 2m3f110y soft Hdl

Moderate hurdler; stays 2m 3f; acts on soft ground.

Spendid (IRE)

109(121h)   (152dh)**145**

11-y-o b g Tidaro (USA)-Spendapromise (Goldhill)
A King Mrs Stewart Catherwood

Placings:201311/11642321/11122P1/F225154/0P/2322461
6-30130   **(4791)**
2002/03: 25³GS, 25⁰GS, 26¹GS, 33³G, 29⁰G,

	Starts	1st	2nd	3rd	Win & Pl
Hurdles	2	0	0	1	3300
Chases	3	1	0	1	24359
Career Total	43	13	10	5	203916
145	12/02	Donc	3m2f	B(0-140)HCh	G-S	£12259
152	4/02	Asct	3m	A Hdl	G-F	£17400
157	2/00	Winc	3m1f110yB Ch		GD	£17306
161	4/99	Aint	3m1f	A Ch		GD	£26775
144	12/98	Chel	3m1f110yC Ch		GD	£7230
134	11/98	Chel	3m110y	B Ch	G-S	£9530
124	10/98	Weth	3m1f	C Ch		GD	£4770
144	4/98	Chel	2m5f110yB HHdl		HVY	£6208
132	11/97	Chel	2m5f	E(0-130)HHdl	GD	£2788
130	11/97	Towc	2m5f	D(0-125)HHdl	G-S	£2912
119	2/97	Towc	2m	E Hdl	SFT	£1976
116	1/97	MRas	2m3f110yE Hdl		GD	£2700

111 9/96 List 2m NHF GD £3884
Total win prize-money £115741

Going: Sf: 0-0 GS: 1-3 Gd: 0-2 GF: - Fm: 0-0
Distance: 2m2/m3: 0-0 2m4-2m7: 0-0 3m+: 1-5
Track: LH: 1-4 RH: 0-1 Tight: 0-0 Gall: 1-2
Aids: Bl: 0-0 Vi: 0-0 Tstrap: 0-0
Best Rating: 161 4/99 Aint 3m1f good Ch

Very useful chaser/smart hurdler; successful at Doncaster in December 2002; not seen again until third in the Scottish National at Ayr in April 2003; had shown high-class form over hurdles in the previous couple of seasons; stays four miles; acts on fast and soft ground.

Speriamo (IRE)
65   **34**
7-y-o b g Mandalus-Mares Eat Oats (Ovac (ITY))
G Brown The Ever Smiling Partnership

Placings:0-60 (1592)
2002/03: 16⁶GF, 22⁰G,

	Starts	1st	2nd	3rd	Win & Pl
Hurdles	2	0	0	0	0
Career Total	3	0	0	0	0

Going: Sf: 0-0 GS: 0-0 Gd: 0-0 GF: - Fm: 0-1
Distance: 2m2/m3: 0-1 2m4-2m7: 0-1 3m+: 0-0
Track: LH: 0-1 RH: 0-1 Tight: 0-1 Gall: 0-0
Aids: Bl: 0-0 Vi: 0-0 Tstrap: 0-0
Best Rating: 34 10/02 Plum 2m gd-fm Hdl

Spider Boy
6-y-o b g Jupiter Island-Great Dilemma (Vaigly Great)
Miss Z C Davison Highly Charged Partnership

Placings:00-03 (4350)
2002/03: 16⁰GF, 16³GF,

	Starts	1st	2nd	3rd	Win & Pl
NH Flat	2	0	0	1	291
Career Total	4	0	0	1	291

Going: Sf: 0-1 GS: 0-0 Gd: 0-0 GF: - Fm: 0-1
Distance: 2m2/m3: 0-2 2m4-2m7: 0-0 3m+: 0-0
Track: LH: 0-2 RH: 0-0 Tight: 0-0 Gall: 0-1
Aids: Bl: 0-2 Vi: 0-0 Tstrap: 0-0
Best Rating: 84 3/03 Wwck 2m gd-fm NHF

Spider Music
91   **88**
7-y-o ch g Orchestra-Muffet s Spider (Rymer)
Ferdy Murphy Mrs F D McInnes Skinner

Placings:03-3O36 (4228)
2002/03: 20³HY, 20⁰GS, 20³G, 25⁶GF,

	Starts	1st	2nd	3rd	Win & Pl
Hurdles	4	0	0	2	1340
Career Total	6	0	0	3	1623

Going: Sf: 0-1 GS: 0-1 Gd: 0-1 GF: - Fm: 0-1
Distance: 2m2/m3: 0-0 2m4-2m7: 0-3 3m+: 0-1
Track: LH: 0-2 RH: 0-2 Tight: 0-0 Gall: 0-1
Aids: Bl: 0-2 Vi: 0-0 Tstrap: 0-0
Best Rating: 102 2/02 Kemp 2m good NHF

Has shown ability in bumpers and hurdles.

Spilaw (FR)
100(92h)   **(73h)74**
7-y-o b g Sky Lawyer (FR)-Spinage (FR) (Village Star (FR))
John Allen Avon Estates Ltd

Placings:1/045/2614200400F0/00040U0130-53326446 (4118)
2002/03: 16⁵S, 17³GS, 21³GS, 20²S, 21⁶S, 26⁴S, 26⁴GS, 24⁶G,

	Starts	1st	2nd	3rd	Win & Pl
Chases	8	0	1	2	2754
Career Total	34	3	3	3	26134

95 11/01 Folk 2m F(0-95)HCh GD £2541
11/00 Engh 2m2f Ch HLD £6244
4/99 Toul 1m7f Hdl VS £3229
Total win prize-money £12014

Going: Sf: 0-4 GS: 0-3 Gd: 0-1 GF: - Fm: 0-0
Distance: 2m2/m3: 0-2 2m4-2m7: 0-3 3m+: 0-3
Track: LH: 0-3 RH: 0-5 Tight: 0-3 Gall: 0-1
Aids: Bl: 0-0 Vi: 0-0 Tstrap: 0-0
Best Rating: 95 11/01 Folk 2m good Ch

Poor handicap chaser; looks to stay about three miles.

Spinaround
5-y-o br g Terimon-Re-Spin (Gildoran)
N A Gaselee D R Stoddart

Placings:00 (4212)
2002/03: 16⁰HY, 18⁰G,

	Starts	1st	2nd	3rd	Win & Pl
NH Flat	1	0	0	0	0
Hurdles	1	0	0	0	0
Career Total	2	0	0	0	0

Going: Sf: 0-1 GS: 0-0 Gd: 0-0 GF: - Fm: 0-0
Distance: 2m2/m3: 0-2 2m4-2m7: 0-0 3m+: 0-0
Track: LH: 0-1 RH: 0-1 Tight: 0-1 Gall: 0-0
Aids: Bl: 0-0 Vi: 0-0 Tstrap: 0-0
Best Rating: 86 2/03 Sand 2m110y heavy NHF

Spinning Silver
77   **53**
8-y-o b g Nearly A Hand-Paid Elation (Pia Fort)
D J Minty D J Minty

Placings:00/FP-0PF6 (1236)
2002/03: 17⁰S, 20⁵GF, 22⁶GF, 20⁶G,

	Starts	1st	2nd	3rd	Win & Pl
Hurdles	4	0	0	0	0
Career Total	8	0	0	0	0

Going: Sf: 0-1 GS: 0-0 Gd: 0-1 GF: - Fm: 0-2
Distance: 2m2/m3: 0-1 2m4-2m7: 0-0 3m+: 0-0
Track: LH: 0-4 RH: 0-0 Tight: 0-2 Gall: 0-0
Aids: Bl: 0-0 Vi: 0-0 Tstrap: 0-0
Best Rating: 60 5/02 NAbb 2m1f soft Hdl

Spinofski
109   **128**
8-y-o b g Petoski-Spin Again (Royalty)
P R Webber D R Stoddart

Placings:45/RF3131/4R434110-22U2205 (4324)
2002/03: 24²G, 22²G, 26⁵S, 25²GS, 24²S, 24⁶G, 24⁵G,

	Starts	1st	2nd	3rd	Win & Pl
Chases	7	0	4	0	12966
Career Total	23	4	4	3	40790

126 2/02 Kemp 3m D(0-125)HCh G-S £7085
117 1/02 Hntg 3m D(0-120)HCh G-S £3991
118 4/01 MRas 2m4f F(0-105)HCh HVY £4158
104 3/01 Newb 2m2f110yD(0-110)HCh HVY £7345
Total win prize-money £22579

Going: Sf: 0-2 GS: 0-1 Gd: 0-4 GF: - Fm: 0-0
Distance: 2m2/m3: 0-0 2m4-2m7: 0-1 3m+: 0-6
Track: LH: 0-4 RH: 0-3 Tight: 0-0 Gall: 0-4
Aids: Bl: 0-0 Vi: 0-0 Tstrap: 0-0
Best Rating: 128 2/03 Sand 3m110y soft Ch

Useful staying chaser; effective on most types of ground, especially soft; stays three miles.

Spinontheriver (IRE)
10-y-o b g Over The River (FR)-Spindle Tree (Laurence O)
Lady Susan Watson Lady Susan Watson

Placings:P4/P (3090)
2002/03: 24⁰PG,

	Starts	1st	2nd	3rd	Win & Pl
Chases	1	0	0	0	0
Career Total	3	0	0	0	222

Going: Sf: 0-0 GS: 0-0 Gd: 0-0 GF: - Fm: 0-0
Distance: 2m2/m3: 0-0 2m4-2m7: 0-0 3m+: 0-1
Track: LH: 0-1 RH: 0-0 Tight: 0-0 Gall: 0-1
Aids: Bl: 0-0 Vi: 0-0 Tstrap: 0-0
Best Rating: 53 12/99 Sedg 3m3f soft Ch

Spinosa
5-y-o br m Afzal-Rosewater (Waterfall)
Mrs P Sly T M Fowler

Placings:5 (4672)
2002/03: 16⁵G,

	Starts	1st	2nd	3rd	Win & Pl
NH Flat	1	0	0	0	0
Career Total	1	0	0	0	0

Going: Sf: 0-0 GS: 0-0 Gd: 0-0 GF: - Fm: 0-0
Distance: 2m2/m3: 0-1 2m4-2m7: 0-0 3m+: 0-0
Track: LH: 0-1 RH: 0-0 Tight: 0-1 Gall: 0-0
Aids: Bl: 0-0 Vi: 0-0 Tstrap: 0-0
Best Rating: 63 4/03 Fknm 2m good NHF

Spirit Leader (IRE)
120   **154**
7-y-o b/br m Supreme Leader-That s The Spirit (Mandalus)
Mrs John Harrington D Thompson

Placings:4413/22222212-231511 (4136)
2002/03: 16²S, 16³HY, 16¹S, 16⁵S, 16¹G, 17¹G,

	Starts	1st	2nd	3rd	Win & Pl
Hurdles	6	3	1	1	157096
Career Total	18	5	8	2	186919

154 3/03 Chel 2m1f A HHdl GD £37700
144 2/03 Newb 2m110y A HHdl GD £69600
136 12/02 Sand 2m110y A(0-150)HHdl SFT £40600
125 3/02 Punc 2m Hdl SFT £6138
125 4/01 Gowr 2m NHF Y-S £4173
Total win prize-money £158211

Going: Sf: 1-4 GS: 0-0 Gd: 2-2 GF: - Fm: 0-0
Distance: 2m2/m3: 3-6 2m4-2m7: 0-0 3m+: 0-0

Track:	LH: 2-3 RH: 1-1 Tight: 0-0 Gall: 2-2
Aids:	Bl: 0-0 Vi: 0-0 Tstrap: 0-0
Best Rating:	154 3/03 Chel 2m1f good Hdl

Smart, tough, progressive Irish-trained handicap hurdler; landed the valuable William Hill Handicap Hurdle at Sandown in December 2002 and the Tote Gold Trophy and County Hurdle in 2003; effective at around two miles; acts on fast but well suited by soft ground.

Spirit Of Destiny

6-y-o ch m Riverwise (USA)-Tearful Sarah (Rugantino)
C W Mitchell   C W Mitchell

Placings:00-P   (1849)
2002/03: 22^PG,

	Starts	1st	2nd	3rd	Win & Pl
Hurdles	1	0	0	0	
Career Total	3	0	0	0	

Going:	Sf: 0-0 GS: 0-0 Gd: 0-1 GF: - Fm: 0-0
Distance:	2m/2m3: 0-0 2m4-2m7: 0-1 3m+: 0-0
Track:	LH: 0-0 RH: 0-1 Tight: 0-1 Gall: 0-0
Aids:	Bl: 0-0 Vi: 0-0 Tstrap: 0-0
Best Rating:	63 3/02 Winc 2m soft NHF

Spirit Of Love (USA)
106   100

8-y-o ch g Trempolino (USA)-Dream Mary (USA) (Marfa (USA))
E W Tuer   E Tuer

Placings:45-41F   (0561)
2002/03: 23⁴G, 22¹G, 24^FGF,

	Starts	1st	2nd	3rd	Win & Pl
Hurdles	3	1	0	0	3178
Career Total	5	1	0	0	3452
100 6/02	Ctml	2m6f	F(0-95)HHdl		GD	£3178

Total win prize-money £3178

Going:	Sf: 0-0 GS: 0-0 Gd: 1-2 GF: - Fm: 0-1
Distance:	2m/2m3: 0-0 2m4-2m7: 1-2 3m+: 0-1
Track:	LH: 1-2 RH: 0-1 Tight: 1-2 Gall: 0-0
Aids:	Bl: 0-0 Vi: 0-0 Tstrap: 0-0
Best Rating:	100 6/02 MRas 3m gd-fm Hdl

Moderate hurdler; formerly high-class stayer on the Flat; effortless winner at Cartmel but fell fatally next time. (DEAD)

Spirit Of Tenby (IRE)
95   80

6-y-o b g Tenby-Asturiana (Julio Mariner)
A G Hobbs (C J Mann 30/6)   Furnish With Abbey

Placings:3210-P6006P00   (2130)
2002/03: 16^PG, 17^PG, 20⁰GF, 16⁰G, 22⁶G, 17^PGF, 21⁰G, 24⁰G,

	Starts	1st	2nd	3rd	Win & Pl
Hurdles	8	0	0	0	
Career Total	12	1	1	0	5001
97 6/01	Prth	2m110y D Hdl		G-F	£3493

Total win prize-money £3494

Going:	Sf: 0-0 GS: 0-0 Gd: 0-6 GF: - Fm: 0-2
Distance:	2m/2m3: 0-4 2m4-2m7: 0-3 3m+: 0-1
Track:	LH: 0-5 RH: 0-3 Tight: 0-3 Gall: 0-1
Aids:	Bl: 0-0 Vi: 0-1 Tstrap: 0-0
Best Rating:	97 6/01 Prth 2m110y gd-fm Hdl

Spirit Ofthe Green (IRE)
93f   82f

5-y-o b g Detroit Sam (FR)-Golden Hearted (Corvaro (USA))
L Wells   Jazz Knight Partnership

Placings:5   (4190)
2002/03: 17⁵G,

	Starts	1st	2nd	3rd	Win & Pl
NH Flat	1	0	0	0	0
Career Total	1	0	0	0	0

Going:	Sf: 0-0 GS: 0-0 Gd: 0-1 GF: - Fm: 0-0
Distance:	2m/2m3: 0-0 2m4-2m7: 0-0 3m+: 0-0
Track:	LH: 0-0 RH: 0-1 Tight: 0-1 Gall: 0-0
Aids:	Bl: 0-0 Vi: 0-0 Tstrap: 0-0
Best Rating:	82 3/03 Folk 2m1f110y good NHF

Splash And Dash (IRE)

8-y-o ch g Arcane (USA)-Quilty Rose (Buckskin (FR))
Mrs S J Hickman   Maurice Smith

Placings:1   (4089)
2002/03: 24¹GS,

	Starts	1st	2nd	3rd	Win & Pl
Chases	1	1	0	0	3543
Career Total	1	1	0	0	3543
97 3/03	Strf	3m	H Ch		G-S	£3542

Total win prize-money £3543

Going:	Sf: 0-0 GS: 1-1 Gd: 0-0 GF: - Fm: 0-0
Distance:	2m/2m3: 0-0 2m4-2m7: 0-0 3m+: 1-1
Track:	LH: 1-1 RH: 0-0 Tight: 1-1 Gall: 0-0
Aids:	Bl: 0-0 Vi: 0-0 Tstrap: 0-0
Best Rating:	97 3/03 Strf 3m gd-sft Ch

Hunter chaser; made winning start under Rules at Stratford in March 2003; won three from five in points; acts on good and good to soft.

Splodge
79

12-y-o b g Oedipus Complex-Gardella (Garnered)
N A Callaghan   Miss Sarah L Judge

Placings:FP/5PP-PP   (0356)
2002/03: 25^PGS, 24^PGS,

	Starts	1st	2nd	3rd	Win & Pl
Chases	2	0	0	0	
Career Total	7	0	0	0	0

Going:	Sf: 0-0 GS: 0-2 Gd: 0-0 GF: - Fm: 0-0
Distance:	2m/2m3: 0-0 2m4-2m7: 0-0 3m+: 0-2
Track:	LH: 0-1 RH: 0-1 Tight: 0-1 Gall: 0-0
Aids:	Bl: 0-2 Vi: 0-0 Tstrap: 0-0
Best Rating:	79 5/01 Font 3m2f110y gd-fm Ch

Spoof (IRE)
100   105

8-y-o b g Good Thyne (USA)-Wraparound Sue (Touch Paper)
L Lungo   The Hookers

Placings:503060/511/4F00214-5256   (2927)

2002/03: 24⁵G, 27²S, 20⁵GS, 24⁶HY,

	Starts	1st	2nd	3rd	Win & Pl
Hurdles	4	0	1	0	1568
Career Total	20	3	2	1	15293
105 3/02	Ayr	2m6f	E(0-110)HHdl		HVY	£2712
105 4/01	Prth	2m4f110yD(0-110)HHdl		HVY	£6474
104 1/01	Ayr	3m110y D(0-110)HHdl		G-S	£3409

Total win prize-money £12596

Going:	Sf: 0-2 GS: 0-1 Gd: 0-1 GF: - Fm: 0-0
Distance:	2m/2m3: 0-0 2m4-2m7: 0-1 3m+: 0-3
Track:	LH: 0-4 RH: 0-0 Tight: 0-1 Gall: 0-0
Aids:	Bl: 0-0 Vi: 0-0 Tstrap: 0-0
Best Rating:	105 3/02 Ayr 2m6f heavy Hdl

Fair hurdler. Likes to get his toe in. Stays three miles.

Sporazene (IRE)
120   139

4-y-o gr g Cozzene (USA)-Sporades (USA) (Vaguely Noble)
P F Nicholls (A Fabre 3/9)   Ged Mason & David Jackson

Placings:331   (4559)
2002/03: 16³GS, 16³GS, 16¹G,

	Starts	1st	2nd	3rd	Win & Pl
Hurdles	3	1	0	2	9592
Career Total	3	1	0	2	9592
112 4/03	Ayr	2m	C Hdl		GD	£7403

Total win prize-money £7404

Going:	Sf: 0-0 GS: 0-2 Gd: 1-1 GF: - Fm: 0-0
Distance:	2m/2m3: 1-3 2m4-2m7: 0-0 3m+: 0-0
Track:	LH: 1-3 RH: 0-0 Tight: 0-0 Gall: 0-0
Aids:	Bl: 0-0 Vi: 0-0 Tstrap: 0-0
Best Rating:	112 4/03 Ayr 2m good Hdl

Useful novice hurdler; middle-distance winner on the Flat in France; beaten favourite twice at Wetherby over hurdles before easily getting off the mark in weak event at Ayr; not a fluent jumper as yet.

Sporting Chance

11-y-o ch g Ikdam-Tumbling Ego (Abednego)
A G Hobbs (Ms J Channon 15/5)   Furnish With Abbey

Placings:5000/P/P-3004   (0730)
2002/03: 19³G, 25⁰GF, 23⁰GF, 21⁴GF,

	Starts	1st	2nd	3rd	Win & Pl
Chases	4	0	0	1	574
Career Total	10	0	0	1	574

Going:	Sf: 0-0 GS: 0-0 Gd: 0-1 GF: - Fm: 0-3
Distance:	2m/2m3: 0-0 2m4-2m7: 0-2 3m+: 0-2
Track:	LH: 0-2 RH: 0-2 Tight: 0-1 Gall: 0-0
Aids:	Bl: 0-0 Vi: 0-0 Tstrap: 0-0
Best Rating:	77 7/02 Strf 2m5f110y gd-fm Ch

Sporting Gesture
86   88

6-y-o ch g Safawan-Polly Packer (Reform)
M W Easterby   Steve Hull

Placings:0   (1743)
2002/03: 16⁰GS,

	Starts	1st	2nd	3rd	Win & Pl
Hurdles	1	0	0	0	
Career Total	1	0	0	0	

Going:	Sf: 0-0 GS: 0-1 Gd: 0-0 GF: - Fm: 0-0

Distance: 2m/2m3: 0-1 2m4-2m7: 0-0 3m+: 0-0
Track: LH: 0-1 RH: 0-0 Tight: 0-0 Gall: 0-0
Aids: Bl: 0-0 Vi: 0-0 Tstrap: 0-0
Best Rating: 88 11/02 Weth 2m gd-sft Hdl

Sportsman (IRE)
97 **99**

4-y-o b g Sri Pekan (USA)-Ardent Range (IRE) (Archway (IRE))
M W Easterby The Shooting Syndicate

Placings:6253 (2247)
2002/03: 17[6]GF, 16[2]GF, 16[5]G, 16[3]GS,

	Starts	1st	2nd	3rd	Win & Pl
Hurdles	4	0	1	1	1852
Career Total	4	0	1	1	1852

Going: Sf: 0-0 GS: 0-1 Gd: 0-1 GF: - Fm: 0-2
Distance: 2m/2m3: 0-2 2m4-2m7: 0-0 3m+: 0-0
Track: LH: 0-3 RH: 0-1 Tight: 0-0 Gall: 0-1
Aids: Bl: 0-3 Vi: 0-0 Tstrap: 0-0
Best Rating: 99 10/02 Weth 2m gd-fm Hdl

Has shown ability in juvenile hurdles.

Spot The Native (IRE)
103(93h) (82h)**82d**

7-y-o ch g Be My Native (USA)-Shannon Foam (Le Bavard (FR))
Mrs S J Smith Trevor Hemmings

Placings:0/500-33002UUP4 (4227)
2002/03: 17[3]G, 20[3]GS, 20[0]G, 16[0]G, 27[2]HY, 24[U]G, 25[U]G, 25[P]S, 25[4]GF,

	Starts	1st	2nd	3rd	Win & Pl
Hurdles	3	0	0	2	1058
Chases	6	0	1	0	1535
Career Total	13	0	1	2	2593

Going: Sf: 0-2 GS: 0-1 Gd: 0-5 GF: - Fm: 0-1
Distance: 2m/2m3: 0-2 2m4-2m7: 0-2 3m+: 0-5
Track: LH: 0-6 RH: 0-3 Tight: 0-6 Gall: 0-1
Aids: Bl: 0-0 Vi: 0-0 Tstrap: 0-0
Best Rating: 93 4/01 Ayr 2m gd-fm NHF

Very moderate form over hurdles and fences, runner-up in a stamina test at Sedgefield in January.

Spot Thedifference (IRE)
110 (87h)**135**

10-y-o b g Lafontaine (USA)-Spotted Choice (IRE) (Callernish)
E Bolger J P McManus

Placings:P13F/220/4142/311126UP-6U0 (4727a)
2002/03: 26[6]G, 21[1]G, 29[0]G,

	Starts	1st	2nd	3rd	Win & Pl
Chases	3	0	0	0	600
Career Total	22	5	4	2	43102
130	6/01	Kbgn	3m1f	(0-123)HCh	GD	£10483
119	6/01	Rosc	3m100y	(0-116)HCh	GD	£5564
110	5/01	Kbgn	3m1f	Ch	GD	£3895
108	2/01	Thur	3m	Ch	SFT	£4729
100	2/99	Clon	3m	Ch	SFT	£2455

Total win prize-money £27129

Going: Sf: 0-0 GS: 0-0 Gd: 0-3 GF: - Fm: 0-0

Distance: 2m/2m3: 0-2 2m4-2m7: 0-1 3m+: 0-2
Track: LH: 0-2 RH: 0-1 Tight: 0-1 Gall: 0-1
Aids: Bl: 0-0 Vi: 0-0 Tstrap: 0-0
Best Rating: 135 7/01 Kbgn 2m7f good Ch

Useful hunter/handicap chaser at best; stays well; acts on most ground.

Spread The Dream
71f **94f**

5-y-o ch g Alflora (IRE)-Cauchemar (Hot Brandy)
N J Henderson Mrs G M Tregaskes

Placings:2 (4296)
2002/03: 16[2]GF,

	Starts	1st	2nd	3rd	Win & Pl
NH Flat	1	0	1	0	666
Career Total	1	0	1	0	666

Going: Sf: 0-0 GS: 0-0 Gd: 0-0 GF: - Fm: 0-1
Distance: 2m/2m3: 0-1 2m4-2m7: 0-0 3m+: 0-0
Track: LH: 0-0 RH: 0-1 Tight: 0-0 Gall: 0-0
Aids: Bl: 0-0 Vi: 0-0 Tstrap: 0-0
Best Rating: 94 3/03 Winc 2m gd-fm NHF

Runner-up in fast-ground bumper on debut.

Spread The Word
11-y-o b m Deploy-Apply (King s Lake (USA))
Mrs O Bush Mrs Pam Pengelly

Placings:55/P (3479)
2002/03: 25[P]GS,

	Starts	1st	2nd	3rd	Win & Pl
Chases	1	0	0	0	
Career Total	3	0	0	0	0

Going: Sf: 0-0 GS: 0-1 Gd: 0-0 GF: - Fm: 0-0
Distance: 2m/2m3: 0-1 2m4-2m7: 0-0 3m+: 0-0
Track: LH: 0-1 RH: 0-0 Tight: 0-0 Gall: 0-0
Aids: Bl: 0-0 Vi: 0-0 Tstrap: 0-0
Best Rating: 89 2/97 Winc 2m yield Hdl

Spree Vision
104 **86**

7-y-o b g Suave Dancer (USA)-Regent s Folly (IRE) (Touching Wood (USA))
P Monteith I Bell

Placings:6/30620/653-22163P050 (4019)
2002/03: 16[2]GS, 20[2]G, 16[1]GS, 16[6]GS, 16[3]HY, 20[P]HY, 16[0]GS, 17[5]GS, 16[0]S,

	Starts	1st	2nd	3rd	Win & Pl
Hurdles	9	1	2	1	7592
Career Total	18	1	3	3	8920
105	11/02	Newc	2m	D Hdl	G-S	£3945

Total win prize-money £3946

Going: Sf: 0-3 GS: 1-5 Gd: 0-1 GF: - Fm: 0-0
Distance: 2m/2m3: 1-7 2m4-2m7: 0-2 3m+: 0-0
Track: LH: 1-6 RH: 0-3 Tight: 0-0 Gall: 1-1
Aids: Bl: 0-0 Vi: 0-0 Tstrap: 0-1
Best Rating: 105 11/02 Newc 2m gd-sft Hdl

Modest novice hurdler, in good form on the Flat and just denied at Perth in August; got off the mark at Newcastle in November over two miles; seems best on good to soft ground.

Sprightley Pip (IRE)
12-y-o gr g Roselier (FR)-Owen s Rose (Master Owen)
P Williams Mrs D J Hughes

Placings:500/4/20/103-PP (0245)
2002/03: 33[P]GF, 25[P]G,

	Starts	1st	2nd	3rd	Win & Pl
Chases	2	0	0	0	
Career Total	11	1	1	1	3353
91	5/01	Strf	3m	H Ch	G-F	£1904

Total win prize-money £1905

Going: Sf: 0-0 GS: 0-0 Gd: 0-1 GF: - Fm: 0-1
Distance: 2m/2m3: 0-0 2m4-2m7: 0-0 3m+: 0-2
Track: LH: 0-1 RH: 0-1 Tight: 0-0 Gall: 0-1
Aids: Bl: 0-0 Vi: 0-0 Tstrap: 0-0
Best Rating: 106 11/97 Chep 2m4f110y gd-sft Hdl

Spring Dawn
105 **113**

8-y-o gr g Arzanni-Another Spring (Town Crier)
N J Henderson W H Ponsonby

Placings:34/45/3230 (4146)
2002/03: 16[3]GS, 17[2]GS, 17[3]GS, 16[0]G,

	Starts	1st	2nd	3rd	Win & Pl
Hurdles	4	0	1	2	2239
Career Total	8	0	1	3	2499

Going: Sf: 0-0 GS: 0-3 Gd: 0-1 GF: - Fm: 0-0
Distance: 2m/2m3: 0-4 2m4-2m7: 0-0 3m+: 0-0
Track: LH: 0-2 RH: 0-2 Tight: 0-3 Gall: 0-1
Aids: Bl: 0-0 Vi: 0-0 Tstrap: 0-0
Best Rating: 113 11/02 Tntn 2m1f gd-sft Hdl

Modest hurdler; suited by easy ground.

Spring Double (IRE)
96 **87**

12-y-o br g Seclude (USA)-Solar Jet (Mandalus)
N A Twiston-Davies Mrs Lorna Berryman

Placings:06/1340511P2/4333/22P313/63432PP43/1000P-6 (0147)
2002/03: 24[6]GF,

	Starts	1st	2nd	3rd	Win & Pl
Hurdles	1	0	0	0	0
Career Total	36	5	4	9	28898
104	11/01	Kemp	3m110y	D(0-120)HHdl	GD	£4446
110	4/99	Uttx	3m	D(0-125)HCh	G-S	£4416
126	3/97	Newb	2m5f	D Hdl	G-S	£3467
105	2/97	Hrfd	2m3f110yE(0-105)HHdl		SFT	£2337
110	5/96	Uttx	2m	H NHF	GD	£1763

Total win prize-money £16429

Going: Sf: 0-0 GS: 0-0 Gd: 0-0 GF: - Fm: 0-1
Distance: 2m/2m3: 0-0 2m4-2m7: 0-0 3m+: 0-1
Track: LH: 0-1 RH: 0-0 Tight: 0-0 Gall: 0-0
Aids: Bl: 0-1 Vi: 0-0 Tstrap: 0-0
Best Rating: 126 3/97 Newb 2m5f gd-sft Hdl

Spring Gale (IRE)
12-y-o b g Strong Gale-Orospring (Tesoro Mio)
J M Turner J M Turner

Placings:3/012151P/2121243/22523P32/62/124/21-R3 (0313)

2002/03: 24ᴿG, 25³G,

	Starts	1st	2nd	3rd	Win & Pl
Chases	2	0	0	1	275
Career Total	32	7	11	5	38865
115 5/01 Folk	3m1f	H Ch		GD	£1934
105 5/00 Fknm	3m110y	H Ch		FRM	£1473
127 12/97 Strf	2m5f110yD Ch			SFT	£4770
132 11/97 Uttx	2m4f	D(0-125)HCh		G-S	£3468
115 3/97 Donc	2m4f	E Hdl		G-F	£2679
111 1/97 Tntn	2m3f110yD Hdl			G-F	£3137
110 10/96 Font	2m6f110yE Hdl			GD	£2595
			Total win prize-money £20059		

Going:	Sf: 0-0 GS: 0-0 Gd: 0-2 GF: - Fm: 0-0
Distance:	2m/2m3: 0-0 2m4-2m7: 0-0 3m+: 0-2
Track:	LH: 0-1 RH: 0-1 Tight: 0-2 Gall: 0-0
Aids:	Bl: 0-0 Vi: 0-0 Tstrap: 0-0
Best Rating:	132 1/98 Chel 2m5f gd-sft Ch

Decent pointer/hunter chaser, but is sometimes reluctant to start.

Spring Grove (IRE)
105(108c)   (132c)112
8-y-o b g Mandalus-Lucy Lorraine (IRE) (Buckskin (FR))
R H Alner H V Perry

Placings: 1/52153/123313/FUPP34-P46   (4596)
2002/03: 21ᴾG, 20⁴G, 19⁶GF,

	Starts	1st	2nd	3rd	Win & Pl
Hurdles	2	0	0	0	381
Chases	1	0	0	0	0
Career Total	21	4	2	5	21255
132 2/01 Leic	2m	E Ch		SFT	£3413
124 1/00 Kemp	2m	D Ch		G-S	£4959
125 2/00 Font	2m2f110yE Hdl			SFT	£2537
108 3/99 Chep	2m110y	H NHF		G-S	£1856
			Total win prize-money £12768		

Going:	Sf: 0-0 GS: 0-0 Gd: 0-2 GF: - Fm: 0-1
Distance:	2m/2m3: 0-1 2m4-2m7: 0-2 3m+: 0-0
Track:	LH: 0-2 RH: 0-1 Tight: 0-1 Gall: 0-0
Aids:	Bl: 0-0 Vi: 0-0 Tstrap: 0-0
Best Rating:	132 12/01 Winc 2m5f good Ch

Modest hurdler/chaser; winner of a bumper, over hurdles and over fences; acts well on a soft surface and is effective at around two to two and a half miles.

Spring Pursuit
86   85
7-y-o b g Rudimentary (USA)-Pursuit Of Truth (USA) (Irish River (FR))
R J Price E G Bevan

Placings: 560   (2507)
2002/03: 17⁵GS, 16⁶S, 16⁰G,

	Starts	1st	2nd	3rd	Win & Pl
Hurdles	3	0	0	0	0
Career Total	3	0	0	0	0

Going:	Sf: 0-1 GS: 0-1 Gd: 0-1 GF: - Fm: 0-0
Distance:	2m/2m3: 0-3 2m4-2m7: 0-0 3m+: 0-0
Track:	LH: 0-2 RH: 0-1 Tight: 0-1 Gall: 0-0
Aids:	Bl: 0-0 Vi: 0-0 Tstrap: 0-0
Best Rating:	85 12/02 Wwck 2m soft Hdl

Spring Rock
57f   55f
6-y-o b g Rock Hopper-Shaft Of Sunlight (Sparkler)
R M Whitaker R M Whitaker

Placings: 00   (1639)
2002/03: 16⁰GF, 17⁰S,

	Starts	1st	2nd	3rd	Win & Pl
NH Flat	2	0	0	0	
Career Total	2	0	0	0	

Going:	Sf: 0-1 GS: 0-0 Gd: 0-0 GF: 0-0 Fm: 0-1
Distance:	2m/2m3: 0-2 2m4-2m7: 0-0 3m+: 0-0
Track:	LH: 0-1 RH: 0-1 Tight: 0-0 Gall: 0-0
Aids:	Bl: 0-0 Vi: 0-0 Tstrap: 0-0
Best Rating:	59 9/02 Hexm 2m110y gd-fm NHF

Springbok Attitude
101   70
6-y-o b g Pharly (FR)-Tugra (FR) (Baby Turk)
B Llewellyn Mrs M Llewellyn

Placings: 000/00042P0P-PPP00023   (1455)
2002/03: 16⁸GF, 17⁷G, 16⁸S, 16⁸GF, 16⁰GF, 20⁰GF, 17²F, 16³F,

	Starts	1st	2nd	3rd	Win & Pl
Hurdles	8	0	1	1	1102
Career Total	19	0	2	1	1950

Going:	Sf: 0-1 GS: 0-0 Gd: 0-1 GF: - Fm: 0-6
Distance:	2m/2m3: 0-7 2m4-2m7: 0-1 3m+: 0-0
Track:	LH: 0-5 RH: 0-3 Tight: 0-0 Gall: 0-0
Aids:	Bl: 0-1 Vi: 0-0 Tstrap: 0-0
Best Rating:	84 9/01 Strf 2m110y gd-fm Hdl

Placed in selling hurdles.

Springer The Lad
81(94h)   (90h)43
6-y-o ch g Carlton (GER)-Also Kirsty (Twilight Alley)
D M Grissell Mrs Christine Notley

Placings: 04P6-34P   (4028)
2002/03: 17³S, 21⁴HY, 24⁴S,

	Starts	1st	2nd	3rd	Win & Pl
Hurdles	1	0	0	1	415
Chases	2	0	0	0	326
Career Total	7	0	0	1	741

Going:	Sf: 0-3 GS: 0-0 Gd: 0-0 GF: - Fm: 0-0
Distance:	2m/2m3: 0-1 2m4-2m7: 0-1 3m+: 0-1
Track:	LH: 0-0 RH: 0-3 Tight: 0-2 Gall: 0-0
Aids:	Bl: 0-0 Vi: 0-0 Tstrap: 0-0
Best Rating:	90 11/02 Folk 2m1f110y soft Hdl

Springfield Gilda (IRE)
5-y-o b m Gildoran-Ledee (Le Bavard (FR))
S Gollings Mrs M A Hall

Placings: 052-2P   (1908)
2002/03: 17³G, 16⁸GS,

	Starts	1st	2nd	3rd	Win & Pl
NH Flat	1	0	1	0	624
Hurdles	1	0	0	0	0
Career Total	5	0	2	0	1086

Going:	Sf: 0-0 GS: 0-1 Gd: 0-1 GF: - Fm: 0-0
Distance:	2m/2m3: 0-2 2m4-2m7: 0-0 3m+: 0-0
Track:	LH: 0-2 RH: 0-1 Tight: 0-2 Gall: 0-0

Aids:	Bl: 0-0 Vi: 0-0 Tstrap: 0-0
Best Rating:	87 9/02 NAbb 2m1f good NHF

Has shown progressive if modest form in bumpers.

Springfield Rex
90
12-y-o ch g Oedipus Complex-Scarlet Coon (Tycoon Ii)
D E Ingle The Extreme Team

Placings: 15/300-P   (0163)
2002/03: 20ᴾGF,

	Starts	1st	2nd	3rd	Win & Pl
Chases	1	0	0	0	
Career Total	6	1	0	1	2234
90 5/00 Aint	3m1f	H Ch		G-F	£1751
			Total win prize-money £1752		

Going:	Sf: 0-0 GS: 0-0 Gd: 0-0 GF: - Fm: 0-1
Distance:	2m/2m3: 0-0 2m4-2m7: 0-1 3m+: 0-0
Track:	LH: 0-1 RH: 0-0 Tight: 0-0 Gall: 0-0
Aids:	Bl: 0-0 Vi: 0-0 Tstrap: 0-0
Best Rating:	90 5/01 Strf 3m gd-fm Ch

Springfield Scally
122   138
10-y-o ch g Scallywag-Ledee (Le Bavard (FR))
S Gollings Anne Campbell-Aintree Racecourse

Placings: 21114113246/222U33616/5324541220/F00-14035100   (4456)
2002/03: 24¹S, 25⁴GS, 22⁰S, 21³S, 23⁵GS, 24¹GS, 25⁰G, 24⁹G,

	Starts	1st	2nd	3rd	Win & Pl
Hurdles	8	2	0	1	28799
Career Total	41	9	8	5	90493
138 3/03 Donc	3m110y	B(0-140)HHdl		G-S	£13639
138 11/02 Chep	3m	B(0-150)HHdl		SFT	£10145
145 2/01 Uttx	2m6f110yC(0-135)HHdl			HVY	£10426
132 3/00 Uttx	2m6f110yB(0-140)HHdl			GD	£10692
112 1/99 MRas	3m	E Hdl		SFT	£2337
96 12/98 MRas	2m3f110yF Hdl			SFT	£2304
108 10/98 Fknm	2m	H NHF		SFT	£1143
103 9/98 MRas	1m5f110yH NHF			GD	£1255
103 9/98 Worc	2m	H NHF		G-F	£1716
			Total win prize-money £53661		

Going:	Sf: 1-3 GS: 1-3 Gd: 0-2 GF: - Fm: 0-0
Distance:	2m/2m3: 0-2 2m4-2m7: 0-2 3m+: 2-6
Track:	LH: 2-8 RH: 0-0 Tight: 0-1 **Gall: 1-3**
Aids:	Bl: 0-0 Vi: 0-0 Tstrap: 0-0
Best Rating:	145 2/01 Uttx 2m6f110y heavy Hdl

Useful handicap hurdler; stays three miles; acts on soft/heavy ground; tremendously genuine; likes to front-run; recorded sixth career win over hurdles at Doncaster in March 2003.

Springford (IRE)
11-y-o b g King s Ride-Tickenor Wood (Le Bavard (FR))
Mrs Caroline Keevil M J O Connor

Placings: 00P/224521P/3006-5   (0245)
2002/03: 25⁵G,

	Starts	1st	2nd	3rd	Win & Pl
Chases	1	0	0	0	0
Career Total	15	1	3	1	8004
92 3/00 Towc	2m6f	D Ch		GD	£4143
			Total win prize-money £4144		

Going:	Sf: 0-0 GS: 0-0 Gd: 0-1 GF: - Fm: 0-0
Distance:	2m/2m3: 0-0 2m4-2m7: 0-0 3m+: 0-1

Track:	LH: 0-0 RH: 0-1 Tight: 0-0 Gall: 0-0
Aids:	Bl: 0-0 Vi: 0-0 Tstrap: 0-0
Best Rating:	106 11/99 Hrfd 3m1f110y good Ch

Springwell Albert (IRE)

7-y-o ch g Alphabatim (USA)-Red Bit (IRE) (Henbit (USA))
C Grant Birotex

Placings:00UP-PP					(4661)
2002/03: 20PGF, 17PGF,					

	Starts	1st	2nd	3rd	Win & Pl
Hurdles	2	0	0	0	
Career Total	6	0	0	0	

Going:	Sf: 0-0 GS: 0-0 Gd: 0-0 GF: - Fm: 0-2
Distance:	2m/2m3: 0-1 2m4-2m7: 0-1 3m+: 0-0
Track:	LH: 0-1 RH: 0-1 Tight: 0-0 Gall: 0-0
Aids:	Bl: 0-0 Vi: 0-0 Tstrap: 0-0
Best Rating:	83 1/02 Muss 2m good NHF

Springwell Bob

70   **49**

7-y-o b g Alflora (IRE)-Gokatiego (Huntercombe)
C Grant Birotex

Placings:0P					(4659)
2002/03: 16PS, 20PGF,					

	Starts	1st	2nd	3rd	Win & Pl
Hurdles	2	0	0	0	
Career Total	2	0	0	0	

Going:	Sf: 0-1 GS: 0-0 Gd: 0-0 GF: - Fm: 0-1
Distance:	2m/2m3: 0-1 2m4-2m7: 0-1 3m+: 0-0
Track:	LH: 0-1 RH: 0-1 Tight: 0-0 Gall: 0-0
Aids:	Bl: 0-0 Vi: 0-0 Tstrap: 0-0
Best Rating:	49 12/02 Weth 2m soft Hdl

Springwood White

100   **72**

9-y-o gr g Sharkskin Suit (USA)-Kale Brig (New Brig)
J L Gledson J L Gledson

Placings:P-U003					(4592)
2002/03: 20UGF, 20PGF, 16PG, 253G,					

	Starts	1st	2nd	3rd	Win & Pl
Chases	4	0	0	1	224
Career Total	5	0	0	1	224

Going:	Sf: 0-0 GS: 0-0 Gd: 0-2 GF: - Fm: 0-2
Distance:	2m/2m3: 0-1 2m4-2m7: 0-2 3m+: 0-1
Track:	LH: 0-4 RH: 0-0 Tight: 0-0 Gall: 0-0
Aids:	Bl: 0-0 Vi: 0-0 Tstrap: 0-0
Best Rating:	72 4/03 Hexm 3m1f good Ch

Winning pointer; tried to make all when third in modest novices handicap chase at Hexham in June; stays three miles; acts on fast ground.

Spud One

108   **102**

6-y-o b g Lord Americo-Red Dusk (Deep Run)
O Sherwood R K Carvill

Placings:12515P2					(4716)
2002/03: 171GS, 172G, 165GS, 161G, 185G, 16PG, 162F,					

	Starts	1st	2nd	3rd	Win & Pl
NH Flat	2	1	1	0	2401
Hurdles	5	1	1	0	4682
Career Total	7	2	2	0	7083
97	2/03	Hntg	2m110y	E Hdl	GD	£3676
101	11/02	Folk	2m1f110yH	NHF	G-S	£1841

Total win prize-money £5517

Going:	Sf: 0-0 GS: 1-2 Gd: 1-4 GF: - Fm: 0-1
Distance:	2m/2m3: 2-7 2m4-2m7: 0-0 3m+: 0-0
Track:	LH: 0-3 RH: 2-4 Tight: 1-3 Gall: 1-2
Aids:	Bl: 0-0 Vi: 0-0 Tstrap: 0-0
Best Rating:	104 12/02 Hrfd 2m1f good NHF

Fair novice hurdler; bumper winner; suited by ground good or faster; has looked a difficult ride on occasions.

Spuddler's Dream

82f   **82f**

6-y-o ch g Michelozzo (USA)-Keep On Dreaming (Sunyboy)
P F Nicholls Richard Barber

Placings:0					(0219)
2002/03: 17OG,					

	Starts	1st	2nd	3rd	Win & Pl
NH Flat	1	0	0	0	
Career Total	1	0	0	0	

Going:	Sf: 0-0 GS: 0-0 Gd: 0-1 GF: - Fm: 0-0
Distance:	2m/2m3: 0-1 2m4-2m7: 0-0 3m+: 0-0
Track:	LH: 0-0 RH: 0-1 Tight: 0-0 Gall: 0-0
Aids:	Bl: 0-0 Vi: 0-0 Tstrap: 0-0
Best Rating:	82 5/02 Hrfd 2m1f good NHF

Spumante Prince

6-y-o b g Tromeros-Asti Spumante (FR) (Fireside Chat (USA))
G Barnett J S Bickerton

Placings:00P					(3847)
2002/03: 16OGF, 16OGF, 16PG,					

	Starts	1st	2nd	3rd	Win & Pl
NH Flat	2	0	0	0	0
Hurdles	1	0	0	0	0
Career Total	3	0	0	0	0

Going:	Sf: 0-0 GS: 0-0 Gd: 0-1 GF: - Fm: 0-2
Distance:	2m/2m3: 0-3 2m4-2m7: 0-0 3m+: 0-0
Track:	LH: 0-2 RH: 0-1 Tight: 0-0 Gall: 0-0
Aids:	Bl: 0-0 Vi: 0-1 Tstrap: 0-0
Best Rating:	0 2/03 Ludl 2m good Hdl

Spy Boy (IRE)

91(96h)   (48h)**42**

7-y-o b g Balla Cove-Spy Girl (Tanfirion)
S T Lewis Simon T Lewis

Placings:3/F04440/53301U005U-P000O634P04000PP					(3957)
2002/03: 21UG, 20PGF, 16OGF, 19OGF, 16OGF, 20OGF, 23FGF, 243S, 234G, 17PG, 19OG, 20OGS, 16OS, 19OGS, 24OS, 26PGS, 17PS,					

	Starts	1st	2nd	3rd	Win & Pl
Hurdles	9	0	0	0	0
Chases	8	0	0	1	1214
Career Total	33	1	0	4	5105
80	10/01	Font	2m4f	F Hdl	G-S	£2373

Total win prize-money £2373

Going:	Sf: 0-4 GS: 0-3 Gd: 0-4 GF: - Fm: 0-6
Distance:	2m/2m3: 0-5 2m4-2m7: 0-7 3m+: 0-5
Track:	LH: 0-13 RH: 0-4 Tight: 0-7 Gall: 0-1
Aids:	Bl: 0-4 Vi: 0-0 Tstrap: 0-0
Best Rating:	88 7/00 Worc 2m gd-fm NHF

Plating-class hurdler, best on soft.

Squandamania

93   **60**

10-y-o b g Ela-Mana-Mou-Garden Pink (FR) (Bellypha)
J R Norton Jaffa Racing Syndicate

Placings:3005/3522/5644213/F261311/P00P060-R55055					(4104)
2002/03: 16RHY, 205GS, 2115S, 24OHY, 20SS, 27SS,					

	Starts	1st	2nd	3rd	Win & Pl
Hurdles	6	0	0	0	0
Career Total	35	4	4	4	17463
108	2/01	Sedg	2m1f	F(0-110)HHdl	G-S	£3038
101	2/01	Sedg	2m1f	D(0-120)HHdl	SFT	£5193
104	12/00	Sedg	2m1f	F(0-110)HHdl	SFT	£2383
101	2/00	Sedg	2m1f	F(0-110)HHdl	G-S	£2775

Total win prize-money £13392

Going:	Sf: 0-5 GS: 0-1 Gd: 0-0 GF: - Fm: 0-0
Distance:	2m/2m3: 0-1 2m4-2m7: 0-3 3m+: 0-2
Track:	LH: 0-6 RH: 0-0 Tight: 0-2 Gall: 0-2
Aids:	Bl: 0-0 Vi: 0-1 Tstrap: 0-0
Best Rating:	108 2/01 Sedg 2m1f gd-sft Hdl

Plating-class hurdler; suited by a strongly-run two miles, he goes bery well at Sedgefield.

Square One (IRE)

9-y-o b m Mandalus-Deep Dollar (Deep Run)
C C Bealby Mrs Russell Price

Placings:1/033PP-P					(0114)
2002/03: 25PGS,					

	Starts	1st	2nd	3rd	Win & Pl
Chases	1	0	0	0	
Career Total	7	1	0	2	2810
89	3/01	MRas	3m1f	H Ch	HVY	£1380

Total win prize-money £1381

Going:	Sf: 0-0 GS: 0-1 Gd: 0-0 GF: - Fm: 0-0
Distance:	2m/2m3: 0-0 2m4-2m7: 0-0 3m+: 0-1
Track:	LH: 0-0 RH: 0-1 Tight: 0-0 Gall: 0-0
Aids:	Bl: 0-1 Vi: 0-0 Tstrap: 0-0
Best Rating:	89 3/01 MRas 3m1f heavy Ch

Squeeze (IRE)

49f   **83f**

5-y-o b g Old Vic-Petaluma Pet (Callernish)
B N Pollock Mrs Jenny Dale & J B Dale

Placings:6					(4685)
2002/03: 16OGF,					

	Starts	1st	2nd	3rd	Win & Pl
NH Flat	1	0	0	0	0
Career Total	1	0	0	0	0

Going:	Sf: 0-0 GS: 0-0 Gd: 0-0 GF: - Fm: 0-1
Distance:	2m/2m3: 0-1 2m4-2m7: 0-0 3m+: 0-0
Track:	LH: 0-0 RH: 0-1 Tight: 0-0 Gall: 0-1
Aids:	Bl: 0-0 Vi: 0-0 Tstrap: 0-0
Best Rating:	83 4/03 Hntg 2m110y gd-fm NHF

Squeeze Box (IRE)

103f   **86f**

4-y-o b f Accordion-Spread Your Wings (IRE) (Decent Fellow)

J Howard Johnson Hoggy, Hammy, Hendy and Howy

Placings:*206*   (4593)
2002/03: 16²G, 17⁰G, 16⁶G,

	Starts	1st	2nd	3rd	Win & Pl
NH Flat	3	0	1	0	850
Career Total	3	0	1	0	850

Going:	Sf: 0-0 GS: 0-0 Gd: 0-3 GF: - Fm: 0-0
Distance:	2m/2m3: 0-1 2m4-2m7: 0-0 3m+: 0-0
Track:	LH: 0-1 RH: 0-2 Tight: 0-2 Gall: 0-0
Aids:	Bl: 0-0 Vi: 0-0 Tstrap: 0-0
Best Rating:	86 2/03 Muss 2m good NHF

Runner-up on her debut in a bumper at Musselburgh in February; well beaten subsequently.

Squibnocket (IRE)

                      85+

4-y-o b g Charnwood Forest (IRE)-Serenad Dancer (FR) (Antheus (USA))

T D Easterby D J Power

Placings:*F*   (1739)
2002/03: 16ᶠGS,

	Starts	1st	2nd	3rd	Win & Pl
Hurdles	1	0	0	0	
Career Total	1	0	0	0	

Going:	Sf: 0-0 GS: 0-1 Gd: 0-0 GF: - Fm: 0-0
Distance:	2m/2m3: 0-1 2m4-2m7: 0-0 3m+: 0-0
Track:	LH: 0-0 RH: 0-0 Tight: 0-0 Gall: 0-0
Aids:	Bl: 0-0 Vi: 0-0 Tstrap: 0-0
Best Rating:	80 11/02 Weth 2m gd-sft Hdl

St Bee

97   **35**

8-y-o br g St Ninian-Regal Bee (Royal Fountain)

W G Reed W G Reed

Placings:*0P/U06FPPF45*   (4589)
2002/03: 22ᵁHY, 20⁰GF, 24⁴GS, 24ᶠG, 20ᴾS, 32ᴾS, 25ᶠG, 25⁴G, 25⁵G,

	Starts	1st	2nd	3rd	Win & Pl
Chases	9	0	0	0	0
Career Total	11	0	0	0	0

Going:	Sf: 0-3 GS: 0-1 Gd: 0-4 GF: - Fm: 0-1
Distance:	2m/2m3: 0-0 2m4-2m7: 0-0 3m+: 0-6
Track:	LH: 0-5 RH: 0-4 Tight: 0-0 Gall: 0-0
Aids:	Bl: 0-0 Vi: 0-0 Tstrap: 0-0
Best Rating:	66 4/03 Hexm 3m1f good Ch

St Kilda

71   **65**

6-y-o b m Past Glories-Oiseval (National Trust)

Mrs H M Bridges Mrs H M Bridges

Placings:*03663*   (4077)
2002/03: 16⁶GF, 17³HY, 18⁶HY, 16⁶G, 21³HY,

	Starts	1st	2nd	3rd	Win & Pl
NH Flat	4	0	0	1	269
Hurdles	1	0	0	1	535

Going:	Sf: 0-4 GS: 0-1 Gd: 0-3 GF: - Fm: 0-2

Career Total	5	0	0	2	804

Going:	Sf: 0-3 GS: 0-0 Gd: 0-1 GF: - Fm: 0-1
Distance:	2m/2m3: 0-4 2m4-2m7: 0-1 3m+: 0-0
Track:	LH: 0-3 RH: 0-2 Tight: 0-2 Gall: 0-0
Aids:	Bl: 0-0 Vi: 0-0 Tstrap: 0-0
Best Rating:	82 2/03 Ludl 2m good NHF

St Matthew (USA)

86   **116**

5-y-o b g Lear Fan (USA)-Social Crown (USA) (Chief s Crown (USA))

G M Moore (J W Hills 25/10) Keith Nicholson

Placings:*1214*   (4035)
2002/03: 19¹GS, 20²HY, 21¹HY, 24⁴S,

	Starts	1st	2nd	3rd	Win & Pl
Hurdles	4	2	1	0	8634
Career Total	4	2	1	0	8634
97 2/03 Sedg	2m5f110yE Hdl		HVY		£3619
116 1/03 Donc	2m3f110yE Hdl		G-S		£3532
		Total win prize-money £7152			

Going:	Sf: 1-3 GS: 1-1 Gd: 0-0 GF: - Fm: 0-0
Distance:	2m/2m3: 0-0 **2m4-2m7: 2-3** 3m+: 0-1
Track:	**LH: 2-4** RH: 0-0 **Tight: 1-1** Gall: 0-1
Aids:	Bl: 0-0 Vi: 0-0 Tstrap: 0-0
Best Rating:	116 1/03 Donc 2m3f110y gd-sft Hdl

Fair hurdler on what we ve seen so far; winning two out of three starts; acts well on soft; stays two miles five; has worn blinkers and tongue tie.

St Mellion Par (IRE)

93   **84**

9-y-o ch g Glacial Storm (USA)-Tenerife Sunset (Boreen (FR))

P J Hobbs St Mellion Estates Ltd

Placings:*21350/1340/P5P-6*   (0075)
2002/03: 25⁶GF,

	Starts	1st	2nd	3rd	Win & Pl
Chases	1	0	0	0	0
Career Total	13	2	1	2	10261
121 1/01 Hayd	2m6f	D(0-110)HCh	SFT		£4134
107 1/00 Plum	2m5f	E Hdl	HVY		£2695
		Total win prize-money £6829			

Going:	Sf: 0-0 GS: 0-0 Gd: 0-0 GF: - Fm: 0-1
Distance:	2m/2m3: 0-0 2m4-2m7: 0-0 3m+: 0-1
Track:	LH: 0-0 RH: 0-1 Tight: 0-0 Gall: 0-0
Aids:	Bl: 0-0 Vi: 0-0 Tstrap: 0-0
Best Rating:	121 1/01 Hayd 2m6f soft Ch

St Palais

94   **55**

4-y-o b f Timeless Times (USA)-Crambella (IRE) (Red Sunset)

D L Williams (J Balding 25/8) Gumbrills Racing Partnership

Placings:*026PO04006*   (4574)
2002/03: 16⁰G, 16²GS, 16⁶S, 16ᴾHY, 22⁰HY, 17⁰G, 26⁴G, 21⁰S, 19⁰GF, 22⁶GF,

	Starts	1st	2nd	3rd	Win & Pl
Hurdles	10	0	1	0	1262
Career Total	10	0	1	0	1262

Going:	Sf: 0-4 GS: 0-1 Gd: 0-3 GF: - Fm: 0-2

Distance:	2m/2m3: 0-5 2m4-2m7: 0-4 3m+: 0-1
Track:	LH: 0-5 RH: 0-5 Tight: 0-3 Gall: 0-2
Aids:	Bl: 0-0 Vi: 0-0 Tstrap: 0-0
Best Rating:	63 11/02 Newb 2m110y gd-sft Hdl

Runner-up in a poor juvenile hurdle at Newbury in November.

Stack The Pack (IRE)

83   **86**

6-y-o ch g Good Thyne (USA)-Game Trix (Buckskin (FR))

T R George Mrs Christine Davies

Placings:*01-02*   (3901)
2002/03: 19⁰S, 24²S,

	Starts	1st	2nd	3rd	Win & Pl
Hurdles	2	0	1	0	1622
Career Total	4	1	1	0	4037
105 3/02 NAbb	2m1f	H NHF	GD		£2415
		Total win prize-money £2415			

Going:	Sf: 0-2 GS: 0-0 Gd: 0-0 GF: - Fm: 0-0
Distance:	2m/2m3: 0-0 2m4-2m7: 0-1 3m+: 0-1
Track:	LH: 0-1 RH: 0-1 Tight: 0-1 Gall: 0-1
Aids:	Bl: 0-0 Vi: 0-0 Tstrap: 0-0
Best Rating:	105 3/02 NAbb 2m1f good NHF

Bumper winner; has shown ability over hurdles; probably stays three miles.

Stacky Light (FR)

10-y-o b g Conquistacky (USA)-Lumineuse (BEL) (Lisaro)

D Pipe C M Batterham

Placings:*1P/F-P*   (0078)
2002/03: 25ᴾGF,

	Starts	1st	2nd	3rd	Win & Pl
Chases	1	0	0	0	
Career Total	4	1	0	0	1235
101 5/99 Hrfd	3m1f110yH Ch		G-S		£1234
		Total win prize-money £1235			

Going:	Sf: 0-0 GS: 0-0 Gd: 0-0 GF: - Fm: 0-1
Distance:	2m/2m3: 0-0 2m4-2m7: 0-0 3m+: 0-1
Track:	LH: 0-0 RH: 0-1 Tight: 0-0 Gall: 0-1
Aids:	Bl: 0-0 Vi: 0-0 Tstrap: 0-0
Best Rating:	101 5/99 Hrfd 3m1f110y gd-sft Ch

Stafford King (IRE)

106   **96**

6-y-o b h Nicolotte-Opening Day (Day Is Done)

J G M O Shea The Stafford Syndicate

Placings:*P/23222320*   (1677)
2002/03: 17²S, 16³S, 20²GF, 20²GF, 20²G, 20³GF, 22²GF, 25⁰GF,

	Starts	1st	2nd	3rd	Win & Pl
Hurdles	8	0	5	2	4900
Career Total	9	0	5	2	4900

Going:	Sf: 0-2 GS: 0-0 Gd: 0-1 GF: - Fm: 0-5
Distance:	2m/2m3: 0-2 2m4-2m7: 0-5 3m+: 0-1
Track:	LH: 0-8 RH: 0-0 Tight: 0-2 Gall: 0-1
Aids:	Bl: 0-0 Vi: 0-0 Tstrap: 0-0
Best Rating:	96 7/02 Worc 2m4f good Hdl

Knocking on the door in low grade novice and selling company.

Stage Affair (USA)

117(112h)   (153h)141+

9-y-o b/br g Theatrical-Wooing (USA) (Stagedoor Johnny)
D K Weld Michael W J Smurfit

Placings:1111225/324/2336   (4098)
2002/03: 16²HY, 16³YS, 16³YS, 16⁶G,

	Starts	1st	2nd	3rd	Win & Pl
Hurdles	2	0	1	1	16340
Chases	2	0	0	1	5022
Career Total	14	4	4	3	90209
139 10/99 Tipp	2m	Hdl		SH	£14508
137 8/99 Tral	2m	Hdl		YLD	£6160
125 8/99 Cork	2m	Hdl		Y-S	£4004
110 7/99 Gway	2m	Hdl		G-F	£3989
		Total win prize-money £28664			

Going:	Sf: 0-1 GS: 0-0 Gd: 0-1 GF: - Fm: 0-0
Distance:	2m/2m3: 0-4 2m4-2m7: 0-0 3m+: 0-0
Track:	LH: 0-4 RH: 0-0 Tight: 0-0 Gall: 0-1
Aids:	Bl: 0-1 Vi: 0-0 Tstrap: 0-0
Best Rating:	162 5/00 Punc 2m good Hdl

High-class Irish-trained hurdler and promising novice chaser; highly encouraging third to Schwartzhalle in Grade Two novice event on chasing debut, not disgraced in the Arkle; best over 2m; acts on any ground; sure to improve.

Stage Direction (USA)

94   83

6-y-o b g Theatrical-Carya (USA) (Northern Dancer)
B J Llewellyn The Welsh Valleys Syndicate

Placings:405-01   (0613)
2002/03: 17⁰G, 16¹GF,

	Starts	1st	2nd	3rd	Win & Pl
Hurdles	2	1	0	0	2345
Career Total	5	1	0	0	2345
84 6/02 Worc	2m	F Hdl		G-F	£2345
		Total win prize-money £2345			

Going:	Sf: 0-0 GS: 0-0 Gd: 0-1 GF: - Fm: 1-1
Distance:	2m/2m3: 1-2 2m4-2m7: 0-0 3m+: 0-0
Track:	LH: 1-2 RH: 0-0 Tight: 0-1 Gall: 0-0
Aids:	Bl: 0-0 Vi: 0-0 Tstrap: 0-0
Best Rating:	84 6/02 Worc 2m gd-fm Hdl

Plating-class hurdler; won two mile novices claimer at Worcester June 2002. Likes fast ground.

Stakeholder (IRE)

80   58

5-y-o ch g Priolo (USA)-Island Goddess (Godswalk (USA))
M Sheppard M J Drake

Placings:035-000   (2111)
2002/03: 17⁰S, 16⁰GS, 16⁰G,

	Starts	1st	2nd	3rd	Win & Pl
Hurdles	3	0	0	0	
Career Total	6	0	0	1	256

Going:	Sf: 0-1 GS: 0-1 Gd: 0-1 GF: - Fm: 0-0
Distance:	2m/2m3: 0-3 2m4-2m7: 0-0 3m+: 0-0
Track:	LH: 0-2 RH: 0-1 Tight: 0-2 Gall: 0-1
Aids:	Bl: 0-0 Vi: 0-0 Tstrap: 0-0
Best Rating:	95 4/02 Carl 2m1f good NHF

Shaped with promise in bumpers, one of which was a Graded event. Held over hurdles.

Stalky

4-y-o ch f Bahamian Bounty-La Noisette (Rock Hopper)
G F Bridgwater (Mrs N Macauley 2/5) Aubrey Ellis

Placings:P   (1004)
2002/03: 17ᴾGF,

	Starts	1st	2nd	3rd	Win & Pl
Hurdles	1	0	0	0	
Career Total	1	0	0	0	

Going:	Sf: 0-0 GS: 0-0 Gd: 0-0 GF: - Fm: 0-1
Distance:	2m/2m3: 0-1 2m4-2m7: 0-0 3m+: 0-0
Track:	LH: 0-0 RH: 0-1 Tight: 0-1 Gall: 0-0
Aids:	Bl: 0-0 Vi: 0-0 Tstrap: 0-0
Best Rating:	0 8/02 Bang 2m1f gd-fm Hdl

Stalky Dove

6-y-o b m Homo Sapien-Sally s Dove (Celtic Cone)
W M Brisbourne Mrs J M Russell

Placings:460   (4404)
2002/03: 16⁴G, 16⁶GF, 16⁰GF,

	Starts	1st	2nd	3rd	Win & Pl
NH Flat	3	0	0	0	0
Career Total	3	0	0	0	0

Going:	Sf: 0-0 GS: 0-0 Gd: 0-0 GF: - Fm: 0-2
Distance:	2m/2m3: 0-3 2m4-2m7: 0-0 3m+: 0-0
Track:	LH: 0-1 RH: 0-2 Tight: 0-0 Gall: 0-1
Aids:	Bl: 0-0 Vi: 0-0 Tstrap: 0-0
Best Rating:	85 2/03 Ludl 2m good NHF

Runner-up behind a useful sort in bumper at Hexham in April on fourth start (poached long lead).

Stallone

99   86

6-y-o ch g Brief Truce (USA)-Bering Honneur (USA) (Bering)
N Wilson (D Nicholls 16/8) Mrs N C Wilson

Placings:635F5   (4433)
2002/03: 16⁶G, 17³GS, 16⁵G, 16⁶FS, 16⁵G,

	Starts	1st	2nd	3rd	Win & Pl
Hurdles	5	0	0	1	498
Career Total	5	0	0	1	498

Going:	Sf: 0-1 GS: 0-1 Gd: 0-3 GF: - Fm: 0-0
Distance:	2m/2m3: 0-5 2m4-2m7: 0-0 3m+: 0-0
Track:	LH: 0-3 RH: 0-2 Tight: 0-3 Gall: 0-1
Aids:	Bl: 0-0 Vi: 0-0 Tstrap: 0-1
Best Rating:	92 11/02 MRas 2m1f110y gd-sft Hdl

Regressive on the Flat, well beaten over hurdles so far.

Stamparland Hill

91(99c)   (140c)112

8-y-o b g Gildoran-Woodland Flower (Furry Glen)
J M Jefferson Ashleybank Investments Limited

Placings:355/1321FP3P-04P   (4524)
2002/03: 20⁰GS, 19⁴GS, 16⁰G,

	Starts	1st	2nd	3rd	Win & Pl
Hurdles	3	0	0	0	550
Career Total	14	2	1	3	8917
130 1/02 Weth	2m	E Ch		G-S	£3342
93 9/01 Sedg	2m1f	E Hdl		GD	£2380
		Total win prize-money £5723			

Stand Aside

104   114

7-y-o b g In The Wings-Honourable Sheba (USA) (Roberto (USA))
J T Gifford Chris Hardy

Placings:2205/235   (3147)
2002/03: 20²HY, 22³HY, 24⁵HY,

	Starts	1st	2nd	3rd	Win & Pl
Hurdles	3	0	1	1	1913
Career Total	7	0	3	1	3829

Going:	Sf: 0-3 GS: 0-0 Gd: 0-0 GF: - Fm: 0-0
Distance:	2m/2m3: 0-0 2m4-2m7: 0-2 3m+: 0-1
Track:	LH: 0-1 RH: 0-2 Tight: 0-1 Gall: 0-0
Aids:	Bl: 0-0 Vi: 0-0 Tstrap: 0-0
Best Rating:	114 12/02 Folk 2m6f110y heavy Hdl

Has shown ability in novice hurdles, although he carries his head rather high. Acts on soft ground. Stays two miles six and a half furlongs.

Stand Easy (IRE)

103(91h)   (77h)109

10-y-o b g Buckskin (FR)-Geeaway (Gala Performance (USA))
J R Cornwall (J G Portman 7/3) J R Cornwall

Placings:1/3355222/25303-FP0433   (4613)
2002/03: 26⁵HY, 23⁸GS, 24⁰HY, 22⁴S, 26³S, 25³G,

	Starts	1st	2nd	3rd	Win & Pl
Hurdles	3	0	0	1	435
Chases	3	0	0	1	2409
Career Total	19	1	4	6	11896
98 4/99 NAbb	2m1f	H NHF		SFT	£1397
		Total win prize-money £1397			

Going:	Sf: 0-4 GS: 0-1 Gd: 0-1 GF: - Fm: 0-0
Distance:	2m/2m3: 0-0 2m4-2m7: 0-1 3m+: 0-5
Track:	LH: 0-4 RH: 0-2 Tight: 0-2 Gall: 0-1
Aids:	Bl: 0-0 Vi: 0-0 Tstrap: 0-0
Best Rating:	113 11/99 Chep 2m110y gd-sft NHF

Moderate staying chaser; surprise winner over an extended three miles in the mud at Uttoxeter in April; better that effort under a penalty in similar conditions two weeks later.

Standiford Girl (IRE)

87   58

6-y-o b m Standiford (USA)-Pennine Girl (IRE) (Pennine Walk)
L A Dace Luke Dace

Placings:0-P00   (4081)
2002/03: 16ᴾS, 21⁰GS, 16⁰HY,

	Starts	1st	2nd	3rd	Win & Pl
Hurdles	3	0	0	0	
Career Total	4	0	0	0	

Going:	Sf: 0-2 GS: 0-1 Gd: 0-0 GF: - Fm: 0-0
Distance:	2m/2m3: 0-2 2m4-2m7: 0-0 3m+: 0-1

Modest hurdler; mixes hurdling and chasing; is a fair sort over hurdles and quite decent over fences; acts on good and soft ground; has never won beyond two miles one.

Track: LH: 0-2 RH: 0-1 Tight: 0-2 Gall: 0-1
Aids: Bl: 0-0 Vi: 0-0 Tstrap: 0-0
Best Rating: 59   10/01 Tntn   2m1f   firm   Hdl

Standing Applause (USA)

94

5-y-o b/br g Theatrical-Pent (USA) (Mr Prospector (USA))
Mrs A J Hamilton-Fairley   Mrs A Hamilton-Fairley

Placings:P05   (0614)
2002/03: 20PGF, 20OG, 205GF,

	Starts	1st	2nd	3rd	Win & Pl
Hurdles	3	0	0	0	0
Career Total	3	0	0	0	0

Going: Sf: 0-0 GS: 0-0 Gd: 0-1 GF: - Fm: 0-2
Distance: 2m/2m3: 0-0 2m4-2m7: 0-3 3m+: 0-0
Track: LH: 0-3 RH: 0-0 Tight: 0-0 Gall: 0-0
Aids: Bl: 0-0 Vi: 0-0 Tstrap: 0-3
Best Rating: 78   6/02 Worc   2m4f   gd-fm   Hdl

Standing Bloom

105   99

7-y-o ch m Presidium-Rosie Cone (Celtic Cone)
Mrs P Sly   The Stablemates

Placings:4536/065P-032140   (4326)
2002/03: 16OGF, 173S, 20²GS, 21¹HY, 204HY, 21OG,

	Starts	1st	2nd	3rd	Win & Pl
Hurdles	6	1	1	1	4922
Career Total	14	1	1	2	5159
99	1/03 Wwck	2m5f	F(0-90)Hdl	HVY	£2828
			Total win prize-money £2828

Going: Sf: 1-3 GS: 0-1 Gd: 0-1 GF: - Fm: 0-1
Distance: 2m/2m3: 0-2 **2m4-2m7: 1-4** 3m+: 0-0
Track: **LH: 1-4** RH: 0-2 Tight: 0-1 Gall: 0-2
Aids: Bl: 0-0 Vi: 0-0 Tstrap: 0-0
Best Rating: 102   4/01 Kemp   2m   good   NHF

Modest novice hurdler; stays two miles five; effective in heavy ground.

Stanley Island

6-y-o b g Stani (USA)-Teminny (Grey Love)
M Sheppard   Mrs C Regan

Placings:PP   (1553)
2002/03: 16PGF, 19PG,

	Starts	1st	2nd	3rd	Win & Pl
Hurdles	2	0	0	0	0
Career Total	2	0	0	0	0

Going: Sf: 0-0 GS: 0-0 Gd: 0-1 GF: - Fm: 0-1
Distance: 2m/2m3: 0-1 2m4-2m7: 0-1 3m+: 0-0
Track: LH: 0-1 RH: 0-1 Tight: 0-0 Gall: 0-0
Aids: Bl: 0-0 Vi: 0-0 Tstrap: 0-0
Best Rating: 0   10/02 Hrfd   2m3f110y   good   Hdl

Stanley Park

95   73

5-y-o ch g Bold Arrangement-Queen Buzzard (Buzzard s Bay)
J R Weymes   Miss K Buckle

Placings:00P   (4715)
2002/03: 16OG, 16OG, 20PGF,

	Starts	1st	2nd	3rd	Win & Pl
NH Flat	1	0	0	0	0
Hurdles	2	0	0	0	0
Career Total	3	0	0	0	0

Going: Sf: 0-0 GS: 0-0 Gd: 0-2 GF: - Fm: 0-1
Distance: 2m/2m3: 0-2 2m4-2m7: 0-1 3m+: 0-0
Track: LH: 0-3 RH: 0-0 Tight: 0-1 Gall: 0-0
Aids: Bl: 0-0 Vi: 0-0 Tstrap: 0-0
Best Rating: 57   3/03 Hexm   2m110y   good   Hdl

First form when well beaten third in modest novices hurdle at Sedgefield in May 2003.

Stanmore (IRE)

105   107

11-y-o b g Aristocracy-Lady Go Marching (USA) (Go Marching (USA))
Mrs J A Saunders   Mr & Mrs Simon E Bown

Placings:500/3U21P51F0/313PF2P1/423/6153/1P4010-P4321143144   (2121)
2002/03: 22PGF, 204GS, 213GF, 21²GF, 21¹GF, 241GF, 204GF, 213G, 241GS, 244GS, 244GS,

	Starts	1st	2nd	3rd	Win & Pl
Chases	11	3	1	2	20967
Career Total	44	10	4	7	49125
107	10/02 Fknm	3m110y	E(0-110)HCh	G-S	£5148
99	9/02 Strf	3m	D(0-125)HCh	G-F	£8138
99	8/02 Sthl	2m5f110yF(0-105)HCh		G-F	£3770
99	11/01 Leic	2m4f110yF(0-100)HCh		G-S	£3125
88	5/01 Hntg	3m	H Ch	G-F	£1820
99	5/00 MRas	2m6f110yH Ch		G-S	£1976
106	5/99 Hrfd	2m3f110yE Hdl		GD	£2560
130	5/98 Strf	2m6f110yC(0-135)HCh		G-S	£5182
112	12/97 Wwck	2m4f110yD(0-110)HCh		G-S	£3551
103	10/97 Chel	2m4f110yD(0-110)HCh		GD	£3876
			Total win prize-money £39151

Going: Sf: 0-0 GS: 1-4 Gd: 0-1 GF: - Fm: 2-6
Distance: 2m/2m3: 0-0 2m4-2m7: 1-7 **3m+: 2-4**
Track: **LH: 3-8** RH: 0-3 **Tight: 2-5** Gall: 0-2
Aids: Bl: 0-0 Vi: 0-0 Tstrap: 0-0
Best Rating: 130   5/98 Strf   2m5f110y   gd-fm   Ch

Modest handicap chaser, in good heart in the second half of 2002 with wins at Southwell, Stratford and Fakenham. Suited by forcing tactics, stays three miles and handles cut in the ground, but is best suited by fast.

Stantonbury Park

84f   72f

6-y-o gr g Neltino-True Divine (True Song)
S J Gilmore   Brian Gurney

Placings:0   (1696)
2002/03: 16OG,

	Starts	1st	2nd	3rd	Win & Pl
NH Flat	1	0	0	0	0
Career Total	1	0	0	0	0

Going: Sf: 0-0 GS: 0-0 Gd: 0-1 GF: - Fm: 0-0
Distance: 2m/2m3: 0-1 2m4-2m7: 0-0 3m+: 0-0
Track: LH: 0-1 RH: 0-0 Tight: 0-0 Gall: 0-0
Aids: Bl: 0-0 Vi: 0-0 Tstrap: 0-0
Best Rating: 72   10/02 Chel   2m110y   good   NHF

Stantons Church

96   71

6-y-o b g Homo Sapien-Valkyrie Reef (Miramar Reef)
H D Daly   Michael Lowe

Placings:545P   (4338)
2002/03: 165GS, 164G, 175S, 20PGF,

	Starts	1st	2nd	3rd	Win & Pl
Hurdles	4	0	0	0	0
Career Total	4	0	0	0	0

Going: Sf: 0-1 GS: 0-1 Gd: 0-1 GF: - Fm: 0-1
Distance: 2m/2m3: 0-3 2m4-2m7: 0-1 3m+: 0-0
Track: LH: 0-0 RH: 0-4 Tight: 0-1 Gall: 0-1
Aids: Bl: 0-0 Vi: 0-0 Tstrap: 0-0
Best Rating: 84   12/02 Ludl   2m   good   Hdl

Staple Sound

80   50

6-y-o b g Alflora (IRE)-Loch Scavaig (IRE) (The Parson)
James Moffatt (W McKeown 25/11)   Mrs G A Turnbull

Placings:00-000P   (4435)
2002/03: 17OS, 20OHY, 16OGS, 20PG,

	Starts	1st	2nd	3rd	Win & Pl
NH Flat	1	0	0	0	0
Hurdles	3	0	0	0	0
Career Total	6	0	0	0	0

Going: Sf: 0-2 GS: 0-1 Gd: 0-1 GF: - Fm: 0-0
Distance: 2m/2m3: 0-2 2m4-2m7: 0-2 3m+: 0-0
Track: LH: 0-3 RH: 0-1 Tight: 0-0 Gall: 0-0
Aids: Bl: 0-0 Vi: 0-0 Tstrap: 0-0
Best Rating: 83   10/02 Carl   2m1f   soft   NHF

Star Angler (IRE)

97f

5-y-o b g Supreme Leader-So Pink (IRE) (Deep Run)
H D Daly   Lady Knutsford

Placings:2   (4090)
2002/03: 16²GS,

	Starts	1st	2nd	3rd	Win & Pl
NH Flat	1	0	1	0	1084
Career Total	1	0	1	0	1084

Going: Sf: 0-0 GS: 0-1 Gd: 0-0 GF: - Fm: 0-0
Distance: 2m/2m3: 0-1 2m4-2m7: 0-0 3m+: 0-0
Track: LH: 0-0 RH: 0-0 Tight: 0-0 Gall: 0-0
Aids: Bl: 0-0 Vi: 0-0 Tstrap: 0-0
Best Rating: 99   3/03 Strf   2m110y   gd-sft   NHF

Star Blakeney

101   78+

10-y-o b g Blakeney-Trikkala Star (Tachypous)
B D Leavy   Barry Leavy

Placings:00/600/0**P530P**/P-P1063   (1172)
2002/03: 20PGS, 22¹GF, 21OG, 20PGF, 22³GF,

	Starts	1st	2nd	3rd	Win & Pl
Hurdles	4	1	0	1	2308
Chases	1	0	0	0	0
Career Total	17	1	0	2	2872
78	6/02 Uttx	2m6f110yG(0-90)HHdl	G-F	£1974
			Total win prize-money £1974

Going: Sf: 0-0 GS: 0-1 Gd: 0-1 GF: - Fm: 1-3
Distance: 2m/2m3: 0-0 **2m4-2m7: 1-5** 3m+: 0-0
Track: LH: **1-4** RH: 0-1 Tight: 0-3 Gall: 0-1
Aids: Bl: 0-0 Vi: 0-0 **Tstrap: 1-5**
Best Rating: 82 11/96 Hayd 2m   good   Hdl

Star Catcher (IRE)
67
7-y-o b g Toulon-Paper Merchant (Hays)
B G Powell L J Brotherton

Placings:00/PP-P0   (3120)
2002/03: 24PS, 20⁵S,

	Starts	1st	2nd	3rd	Win & Pl
Hurdles	2	0	0	0	
Career Total	6	0	0	0	

Going: Sf: 0-2 GS: 0-0 Gd: 0-0 GF: - Fm: 0-0
Distance: 2m/2m3: 0-0 2m4-2m7: 0-1 3m+: 0-1
Track: LH: 0-0 RH: 0-2 Tight: 0-1 Gall: 0-1
Aids: Bl: 0-0 Vi: 0-0 Tstrap: 0-1
Best Rating: 54 10/00 Fknm 2m   good   NHF

Star Control (IRE)
94(93c)   (71c)77
9-y-o gr m Phardante (FR)-Grey Star (General Ironside)
H J Evans Mrs Jane Evans

Placings:0U0/66/0F0P3-005   (0789)
2002/03: 20⁹GF, 22⁰GF, 26⁵GF,

	Starts	1st	2nd	3rd	Win & Pl
Hurdles	3	0	0	0	0
Career Total	13	0	0	1	382

Going: Sf: 0-0 GS: 0-0 Gd: 0-0 GF: - Fm: 0-3
Distance: 2m/2m3: 0-0 2m4-2m7: 0-2 3m+: 0-1
Track: LH: 0-3 RH: 0-0 Tight: 0-1 Gall: 0-0
Aids: Bl: 0-0 Vi: 0-0 Tstrap: 0-0
Best Rating: 87 5/00 Uttx 2m4f110y   gd-fm Hdl

Star Councel (IRE)
110(101c)   (60c)96
7-y-o b m Leading Counsel (USA)-Black Avenue (IRE)
(Strong Gale)
B S Rothwell Mrs Liz Hunt

Placings:00/455 1314436P00440P-5C0P524201   (4267)
2002/03: 21⁵GS, 20⁵HY, 22⁵S, 16⁵PGF, 27⁵S, 21²S, 19⁴GS, 24²G, 22⁰GS, 24¹GF,

	Starts	1st	2nd	3rd	Win & Pl
Hurdles	6	1	2	0	6112
Chases	4	0	0	0	
Career Total	29	3	2	2	17851
95 3/03 Sthl	3m110y F(0-100)HHdl			G-F	£3584
100 9/01 List	2m4f Hdl			G-F	£6004
98 8/01 Slig	2m4f NHF			SH	£3338

Total win prize-money £12927

Going: Sf: 0-5 GS: 0-2 Gd: 0-2 GF: - Fm: 1-1
Distance: 2m/2m3: 0-1 2m4-2m7: 0-6 **3m+: 1-3**
Track: LH: **1-9** RH: 0-1 Tight: **1-6** Gall: 0-0
Aids: Bl: 0-0 Vi: 0-0 Tstrap: 0-0
Best Rating: 100 9/01 List 2m4f   gd-fm Hdl

Moderate hurdler; stays three miles, acts on any ground.

Star Dynasty (IRE)
94
6-y-o b g Bering-Siwaayib (Green Desert (USA))
D McCain Clayton Bigley Partnership Ltd

Placings:042-2P   (0056)
2002/03: 16²G, 17⁵G,

	Starts	1st	2nd	3rd	Win & Pl
Hurdles	2	0	1	0	744
Career Total	5	0	2	0	1676

Going: Sf: 0-0 GS: 0-0 Gd: 0-2 GF: - Fm: 0-0
Distance: 2m/2m3: 0-2 2m4-2m7: 0-0 3m+: 0-0
Track: LH: 0-2 RH: 0-0 Tight: 0-1 Gall: 0-0
Aids: Bl: 0-0 Vi: 0-0 Tstrap: 0-0
Best Rating: 94 4/02 Hexm 2m110y   good   Hdl

Above average ten-furlong maiden on the Flat who is finding his feet over hurdles. Handles soft ground.

Star Jack (FR)
115   130
8-y-o b g Epervier Bleu-Little Point (FR) (Le Nain Jaune (FR))
T J Fitzgerald (J G Fitzgerald 26/12) Mr & Mrs Raymond Anderson Green

Placings:1115/3213/PF/PP1P-P022311PP   (4557)
2002/03: 22⁸PG, 16⁰G, 16²GS, 20²GS, 24³GS, 16¹S, 16¹GS, 16⁶GS, 33⁸PG,

	Starts	1st	2nd	3rd	Win & Pl
Hurdles	1	0	0	0	0
Chases	8	7	3	1	37875
Career Total	23	7	3	3	84265
130 11/02 Weth	2m B(0-150)HCh		G-S	£10916
129 11/02 Ayr	2m C(0-130)HCh		SFT	£7975
124 4/02 Ayr	2m4f B HCh		GD	£10397
1/00 Pau	2m110y Hdl		GD	£6244
2/99 Pau	2m2f110y Ch		HVY	£15070
1/99 Pau	2m1f Ch		GD	£6459
10/98 Toul	2m1f110y Hdl		HVY	£4041

Total win prize-money £61104

Going: Sf: 1-1 GS: 1-5 Gd: 0-3 GF: - Fm: 0-0
Distance: **2m/2m3: 2-5** 2m4-2m7: 0-2 3m+: 0-2
Track: LH: **2-7** RH: 0-2 Tight: 0-3 Gall: 0-0
Aids: Bl: 0-0 Vi: 0-0 Tstrap: 0-5
Best Rating: 130 11/02 Weth 2m   gd-sft Ch

Useful handicap chaser; tends to have two ways of running; often wears tongue-strap and sheepskin cheekpieces; best over two/two and a half miles; effective on most types of ground.

Star Of Raven
6-y-o b m Sea Raven (IRE)-Lucy At The Minute (Silly Prices)
Joss Saville Joss Saville

Placings:000-F   (4592)
2002/03: 25²G,

	Starts	1st	2nd	3rd	Win & Pl
Chases	1	0	0	0	
Career Total	4	0	0	0	

Going: Sf: 0-0 GS: 0-0 Gd: 0-1 GF: - Fm: 0-0
Distance: 2m/2m3: 0-0 2m4-2m7: 0-0 3m+: 0-1
Track: LH: 0-1 RH: 0-0 Tight: 0-0 Gall: 0-0
Aids: Bl: 0-0 Vi: 0-0 Tstrap: 0-0
Best Rating: 72 4/03 Hexm 3m1f   good   Ch

Star Of Wonder (FR)
94   73
8-y-o ch m The Wonder (FR)-Teardrops Fall (FR) (Law Society (USA))
John Allen John Allen, Michael Gray, Vicki Jameson

Placings:F600501P/P63U5-0PP00336P00   (4116)
2002/03: 17⁰G, 17²GF, 16⁵PS, 16⁰G, 16⁰HY, 16³GS, 16³G, 16⁶GS, 16⁵PHY, 19⁰GS, 21⁰G,

	Starts	1st	2nd	3rd	Win & Pl
Hurdles	9	0	0	2	783
Chases	2	0	0	0	0
Career Total	24	1	0	3	3888
89 4/00 Plum	2m D Hdl		G-S	£2811

Total win prize-money £2811

Going: Sf: 0-3 GS: 0-2 Gd: 0-5 GF: - Fm: 0-1
Distance: 2m/2m3: 0-9 2m4-2m7: 0-2 3m+: 0-0
Track: LH: 0-6 RH: 0-5 Tight: 0-4 Gall: 0-1
Aids: Bl: 0-1 Vi: 0-3 Tstrap: 0-0
Best Rating: 89 4/00 Plum 2m   gd-sft Hdl

Modest hurdler; placed in sellers.

Star Of Wonder
97   104
5-y-o b m Celtic Swing-Meant To Be (Morston (FR))
Lady Herries Lady Mary Mumford

Placings:1125-435   (0611)
2002/03: 18⁴GF, 22³GF, 20⁵GF,

	Starts	1st	2nd	3rd	Win & Pl
Hurdles	3	0	1	1	492
Career Total	7	2	1	1	7288
99 10/01 Winc	2m D Hdl		G-F	£3283
95 9/01 Font	2m2f110yE Hdl		G-F	£2408

Total win prize-money £5691

Going: Sf: 0-0 GS: 0-0 Gd: 0-0 GF: - Fm: 0-3
Distance: 2m/2m3: 0-1 2m4-2m7: 0-2 3m+: 0-0
Track: LH: 0-3 RH: 0-0 Tight: 0-2 Gall: 0-0
Aids: Bl: 0-0 Vi: 0-0 Tstrap: 0-0
Best Rating: 104 4/02 Asct 2m110y   gd-fm Hdl

Moderate hurdler. Two miles on fast ground are her ideal conditions.

Star Protector (FR)
97   106
4-y-o b c Hector Protector (USA)-Frustration (Salse (USA))
R M Stronge (J W Hills 30/8) Sir Clement Freud

Placings:314   (1968)
2002/03: 16³G, 16¹GS, 16⁴GS,

	Starts	1st	2nd	3rd	Win & Pl
Hurdles	3	1	0	1	5923
Career Total	3	1	0	1	5923
102 11/02 Asct	2m110y D Hdl		G-S	£4433

Total win prize-money £4433

Going: Sf: 0-0 GS: 1-2 Gd: 0-1 GF: - Fm: 0-0
Distance: **2m/2m3: 1-3** 2m4-2m7: 0-0 3m+: 0-0
Track: LH: 0-1 **RH: 1-2** Tight: 0-0 Gall: 0-0
Aids: Bl: 0-0 Vi: 0-0 Tstrap: 0-0
Best Rating: 103 11/02 Chel 2m110y   gd-sft Hdl

Useful Juvenile hurdler, effective at around two miles and goes well with cut in the ground.

Star Seventeen
90   59
5-y-och mRock City-WestminsterWaltz(DanceInTime (CAN))

T H Caldwell (P W D Arcy 8/10) M J Caldwell

Placings:6000P   **(4022)**
2002/03: 16⁰GF, 16⁰GS, 16⁰G, 17⁰GS, 19⁰S,

	Starts	1st	2nd	3rd	Win & $
Hurdles	5	0	0	0	0
Career Total	5	0	0	0	0

Going: Sf: 0-1 GS: 0-2 Gd: 0-1 GF: - Fm: 0-1
Distance: 2m/2m3: 0-4 2m4-2m7: 0-1 3m+: 0-0
Track: LH: 0-2 RH: 0-3 Tight: 0-1 Gall: 0-1
Aids: Bl: 0-0 Vi: 0-0 Tstrap: 0-0
Best Rating: 59 8/02 Hntg 2m110y gd-fm Hdl

Star Time (IRE)

4-y-o b g Fourstars Allstar (USA)-Punctual (Lead On Time (USA))
A G Hobbs Furnish With Abbey

Placings:0P   **(2317)**
2002/03: 12⁰GS, 16⁰PHY,

	Starts	1st	2nd	3rd	Win & $
NH Flat	1	0	0	0	0
Hurdles	1	0	0	0	0
Career Total	2	0	0	0	

Going: Sf: 0-1 GS: 0-1 Gd: 0-0 GF: - Fm: 0-0
Distance: 2m/2m3: 0-1 2m4-2m7: 0-0 3m+: 0-0
Track: LH: 0-1 RH: 0-1 Tight: 0-0 Gall: 0-0
Aids: Bl: 0-0 Vi: 0-0 Tstrap: 0-0
Best Rating: 52 11/02 Newb 1m4f110y gd-sft NHF

Star Trooper (IRE)
103   98

7-y-o b/br g Brief Truce (USA)-Star Cream (Star Appeal)
Miss S E Forster (E McNamara 23/9) C Storey

Placings:0040/000023500/0000220630-041210002 **(4663)**
2002/03: 16⁹GF, 16⁴F, 17¹S, 18²HY, 17¹S, 16⁹G, 18⁰GS, 21⁰G, 17²GF,

	Starts	1st	2nd	3rd	Win & $
Hurdles	9	2	2	0	8293
Career Total	32	2	5	2	12289
101	12/02	Sedg	2m1f	E(0-110)HHdl	SFT	£3346
84	11/02	Sedg	2m1f	G(0-95)HHdl	SFT	£2100

Total win prize-money £5446

Going: Sf: 2-3 GS: 0-1 Gd: 0-2 GF: - Fm: 0-3
Distance: 2m/2m3: 2-8 2m4-2m7: 0-1 3m+: 0-0
Track: LH: 2-7 RH: 0-1 Tight: 2-6 Gall: 0-0
Aids: Bl: 0-1 Vi: 0-0 Tstrap: 0-0
Best Rating: 107 8/00 Tral 2m1f soft Hdl

Moderate hurdler, ex-Irish; won twice at Sedgefield in late 2002; best around two miles; suited by soft ground; also handles faster going; has worn cheekpieces.

Starcross Sadie
64f   38f

5-y-o b m Saddlers Hall (IRE)-Starr Danias (USA) (Sensitive Prince (USA))
R A Fahey D M Beresford

Placings:0   **(2450)**
2002/03: 16⁰G,

	Starts	1st	2nd	3rd	Win & $
NH Flat	1	0	0	0	
Career Total	1	0	0	0	

Aids: Bl: 0-0 Vi: 0-0 Tstrap: 0-0
Best Rating: 38 12/02 Ludl 2m   good   NHF

Starry Mary
92   73

5-y-o b m Deploy-Darling Splodge (Elegant Air)
E L James The Westenholz Family

Placings:00   **(3138)**
2002/03: 16⁰S, 21⁰S,

	Starts	1st	2nd	3rd	Win & $
Hurdles	2	0	0	0	
Career Total	2	0	0	0	

Going: Sf: 0-2 GS: 0-0 Gd: 0-0 GF: - Fm: 0-0
Distance: 2m/2m3: 0-1 2m4-2m7: 0-1 3m+: 0-0
Track: LH: 0-1 RH: 0-1 Tight: 0-0 Gall: 0-0
Aids: Bl: 0-0 Vi: 0-0 Tstrap: 0-0
Best Rating: 73 12/02 Wwck 2m   soft   Hdl

Stars Delight (IRE)
101   113

6-y-o ch g Fourstars Allstar (USA)-Celtic Cygnet (Celtic Cone)
G L Moore (Mrs L C Jewell 9/6) Leon Best

Placings:050-40311   **(4358)**
2002/03: 17⁴G, 16⁰HY, 16³HY, 20¹S, 19¹F,

	Starts	1st	2nd	3rd	Win & $
NH Flat	1	0	0	0	
Hurdles	4	2	0	1	8748
Career Total	8	2	0	1	8748
100	3/03	Tntn	2m3f110yE Hdl	FRM	£4348
109	3/03	Font	2m4f	E Hdl	SFT	£3598

Total win prize-money £7947

Going: Sf: 1-3 GS: 0-0 Gd: 0-1 GF: - Fm: 1-1
Distance: 2m/2m3: 0-3 2m4-2m7: 2-2 3m+: 0-0
Track: LH: 0-1 RH: 1-3 Tight: 2-3 Gall: 0-1
Aids: Bl: 0-0 Vi: 0-0 Tstrap: 0-0
Best Rating: 109 3/03 Font 2m4f   soft   Hdl

Modest hurdler; won two modest 2m 4f novice hurdles on contrasting ground in March 2003; acts on soft and firm going.

Stars Out Tonight (IRE)
110(107h)   (137h)137

6-y-o b g Insan (USA)-Go And Tell (Kemal (FR))
Miss H C Knight Jim Lewis

Placings:0/11004-131P   **(4110)**
2002/03: 17¹G, 16³GS, 25¹GS, 24²G,

	Starts	1st	2nd	3rd	Win & $
Chases	4	2	0	1	14185
Career Total	10	4	0	1	22239
125	2/03	Winc	3m1f110yD Ch	G-S	£5642
137	10/02	Extr	2m1f110yD Ch	GD	£5243
115	11/01	Kemp	2m	D Hdl	GD	£3412
108	10/01	Chel	2m110y	H NHF	GD	£3948

Total win prize-money £18247

Going: Sf: 0-0 GS: 1-2 Gd: 1-2 GF: - Fm: 0-0
Distance: 2m/2m3: 1-2 2m4-2m7: 0-0 3m+: 1-2
Track: LH: 0-2 RH: 2-2 Tight: 0-0 Gall: 0-2

Aids: Bl: 0-0 Vi: 0-0 Tstrap: 0-0
Best Rating: 137 10/02 Extr 2m1f110y good   Ch

Useful novice chaser; stays three miles plus; suited by good ground or a bit softer; jumps well; likes to race prominently; progressive.

Starting Again
94   120

9-y-o b g Petoski-Lynemore (Nearly A Hand)
H D Daly Mr & Mrs M P Wiggin

Placings:1/32/21PF2313-5   **(1607)**
2002/03: 19⁰G,

	Starts	1st	2nd	3rd	Win & $
Chases	1	0	0	0	
Career Total	12	3	3	3	16809
120	4/02	Ludl	2m4f	D(0-115)HCh	GD	£6500
106	10/01	Ludl	2m4f	E Ch	G-F	£3386
105	12/98	Ludl	2m	H NHF	G-S	£1318

Total win prize-money £11206

Going: Sf: 0-0 GS: 0-0 Gd: 0-1 GF: - Fm: 0-0
Distance: 2m/2m3: 0-0 2m4-2m7: 0-1 3m+: 0-0
Track: LH: 0-1 RH: 0-0 Tight: 0-0 Gall: 0-0
Aids: Bl: 0-0 Vi: 0-0 Tstrap: 0-0
Best Rating: 120 4/02 Ludl 2m4f   good   Ch

Modest chaser; bumper winner and ex-pointer. Placed over hurdles, he made a good start to his chasing career, winning at Ludlow twice. acts on fast and easy ground.

Starzaan (IRE)
116   132

4-y-o b g Darshaan-Stellina (IRE) (Caerleon (USA))
H Morrison (P F I Cole 25/10) Ben Arbib

Placings:4104   **(4460)**
2002/03: 16⁴G, 17¹HY, 17⁰G, 16⁴G,

	Starts	1st	2nd	3rd	Win & $
Hurdles	4	1	0	0	9322
Career Total	4	1	0	0	9322
116	1/03	Folk	2m1f110yE Hdl	HVY	£3507

Total win prize-money £3507

Going: Sf: 1-1 GS: 0-0 Gd: 0-3 GF: - Fm: 0-0
Distance: 2m/2m3: 1-4 2m4-2m7: 0-0 3m+: 0-0
Track: LH: 0-3 RH: 1-1 Tight: 1-2 Gall: 0-2
Aids: Bl: 0-0 Vi: 0-0 Tstrap: 0-0
Best Rating: 128 4/03 Aint 2m110y good   Hdl

Useful juvenile hurdler; easy winner at Folkestone on second run; fourth in Grade Two at Aintree; acts in heavy ground; successful on fast ground on the Flat.

Stash The Cash (IRE)

12-y-o b g Persian Bold-Noble Girl (Be Friendly)
Miss A Armitage (P Beaumont 26/5) Mrs P A H Hartley

Placings:002/525452212122050/20211141/30P3034/31P3 62/P2P404220/6P4/P   **(0477)**
2002/03: 26⁰PGS,

	Starts	1st	2nd	3rd	Win & $
Chases	1	0	0	0	
Career Total	52	7	13	5	37371
101	11/98	Hexm	2m110y	E Ch	HVY	£3234
125	4/97	Kels	2m110y	D(0-125)HHdl	G-F	£4788
122	1/97	Ayr	2m	E(0-125)HHdl	GD	£2901
123	12/96	Muss	2m	E(0-110)HHdl	G-F	£2584
106	12/96	Kels	2m2f	D(0-125)HHdl	GD	£3271

99 2/96 Kels 2m2f D(0-125)HHdl SFT £2857
100 1/96 Ayr   2m   F Hdl   GD   £2193
Total win prize-money £21830

Going: Sf: 0-0 GS: 0-1 Gd: 0-0 GF: - Fm: 0-0
Distance: 2m/2m3: 0-0 2m4-2m7: 0-0 3m+: 0-1
Track: LH: 0-1 RH: 0-0 Tight: 0-1 Gall: 0-0
Aids: Bl: 0-0 Vi: 0-0 Tstrap: 0-1
Best Rating: 125 2/98 Weth 2m good Hdl

State Affairs (IRE)

7-y-o ch g Political Merger (USA)-Bridewell Belle (Saulingo)
R Hollinshead Mrs Dianne E Edwards

Placings:00/PPP (4482)
2002/03: 20PGS, 19PS, 19PGF,

	Starts	1st	2nd	3rd	Win & Pl
Hurdles	3	0	0	0	
Career Total	5	0	0	0	

Going: Sf: 0-1 GS: 0-1 Gd: 0-0 GF: - Fm: 0-1
Distance: 2m/2m3: 0-0 2m4-2m7: 0-3 3m+: 0-0
Track: LH: 0-1 RH: 0-2 Tight: 0-0 Gall: 0-0
Aids: Bl: 0-0 Vi: 0-0 Tstrap: 0-0
Best Rating: 72 3/00 Ludl 2m good NHF

State Casino

6-y-o b m State Diplomacy (USA)-Nod And A Wink (Casino Boy)
Miss L C Siddall Podso Racing

Placings:0-P0PPP (3801)
2002/03: 16PG, 17UGF, 16PG, 21PHY, 24PS,

	Starts	1st	2nd	3rd	Win & Pl
NH Flat	2	0	0	0	0
Hurdles	3	0	0	0	0
Career Total	6	0	0	0	

Going: Sf: 0-2 GS: 0-0 Gd: 0-2 GF: - Fm: 0-1
Distance: 2m/2m3: 0-3 2m4-2m7: 0-1 3m+: 0-1
Track: LH: 0-4 RH: 1 Tight: 0-0 Gall: 0-1
Aids: Bl: 0-0 Vi: 0-0 Tstrap: 0-0
Best Rating: 0 2/03 Newc 3m soft Hdl

State Of Balance
77f

5-y-o ch m Mizoram (USA)-Equilibrium (Statoblest)
K Bell North Farm Stud

Placings:60 (4431)
2002/03: 17PS, 18PGF,

	Starts	1st	2nd	3rd	Win & Pl
NH Flat	2	0	0	0	0
Career Total	2	0	0	0	

Going: Sf: 0-1 GS: 0-0 Gd: 0-0 GF: - Fm: 0-1
Distance: 2m/2m3: 0-2 2m4-2m7: 0-0 3m+: 0-0
Track: LH: 0-1 RH: 0-0 Tight: 0-0 Gall: 0-0
Aids: Bl: 0-0 Vi: 0-0 Tstrap: 0-0
Best Rating: 77 1/03 Tntn 2m1f soft NHF

Stateley Lord (IRE)
(87h)   (65h)
7-y-o b/br g Good Thyne (USA)-Sixfoursix (Balinger)

G L Moore John B Hobbs

Placings:UP0P-P (3110)
2002/03: 16PS,

	Starts	1st	2nd	3rd	Win & Pl
Chases	1	0	0	0	
Career Total	5	0	0	0	

Going: Sf: 0-1 GS: 0-0 Gd: 0-0 GF: - Fm: 0-0
Distance: 2m/2m3: 0-1 2m4-2m7: 0-0 3m+: 0-0
Track: LH: 0-0 RH: 0-1 Tight: 0-1 Gall: 0-0
Aids: Bl: 0-0 Vi: 0-0 Tstrap: 0-1
Best Rating: 65 3/02 Newb 2m3f soft Hdl

Little sign of ability in three novice hurdles at up to two miles six furlongs.

Statim
109   120

4-y-o b f Marju (IRE)-Rapid Repeat (IRE) (Exactly Sharp (USA))
M J P O Brien (L M Cumani 14/8) Sanguine Syndicate

Placings:22220 (4460)
2002/03: 16²SH, 16²S, 16²YS, 16²HY, 16⁰G,

	Starts	1st	2nd	3rd	Win & Pl
Hurdles	5	0	4	0	8104
Career Total	5	0	4	0	8104

Going: Sf: 0-2 GS: 0-0 Gd: 0-1 GF: - Fm: 0-0
Distance: 2m/2m3: 0-5 2m4-2m7: 0-0 3m+: 0-0
Track: LH: 0-3 RH: 0-1 Tight: 0-1 Gall: 0-0
Aids: Bl: 0-4 Vi: 0-0 Tstrap: 0-0
Best Rating: 120 2/03 Fair 2m yld-sft Hdl

Useful juvenile hurdler in Ireland, runner-up on first four starts; middle-distance winner on the Flat for Luca Cumani; effective on fast ground and in soft; has worn blinkers.

Station Island (IRE)
101   77
6-y-o ch g Roselier (FR)-Sweet Tulip (Beau Chapeau)
J Mackie J S Harlow

Placings:5 (4122)
2002/03: 16⁵G,

	Starts	1st	2nd	3rd	Win & Pl
NH Flat	1	0	0	0	0
Career Total	1	0	0	0	

Going: Sf: 0-0 GS: 0-0 Gd: 0-1 GF: - Fm: 0-0
Distance: 2m/2m3: 0-1 2m4-2m7: 0-0 3m+: 0-0
Track: LH: 0-0 RH: 0-1 Tight: 0-0 Gall: 0-1
Aids: Bl: 0-0 Vi: 0-0 Tstrap: 0-0
Best Rating: 77 3/03 Hntg 2m110y good NHF

Irish point winner; half-brother to Truckers Tavern; runner-up in a modest novices hurdle at Wetherby in May 2003; stays well.

Stay Lucky (NZ)

14-y-o b g Sir Sydney (NZ)-Against The Odds (NZ) (Harbor Prince (USA))
Simon Bloss J G Phillips

Placings:423/3/5PP2/00335/3P/P (0190)
2002/03: 24PGF,

	Starts	1st	2nd	3rd	Win & Pl
Chases	1	0	0	0	
Career Total	16	0	2	5	9433

Going: Sf: 0-0 GS: 0-0 Gd: 0-0 GF: - Fm: 0-1
Distance: 2m/2m3: 0-0 2m4-2m7: 0-0 3m+: 0-1
Track: LH: 0-0 RH: 0-1 Tight: 0-0 Gall: 0-1
Aids: Bl: 0-0 Vi: 0-0 Tstrap: 0-0
Best Rating: 126 12/96 Ling 3m gd-sft Ch

Steady Eddy
77   87

11-y-o ch g Scorpio (FR)-Moaning Jenny (Privy Seal)
N A Twiston-Davies N A Twiston-Davies

Placings:13/4O21/UPU031P-P6 (0555)
2002/03: 24PG, 25RGF,

	Starts	1st	2nd	3rd	Win & Pl
Chases	2	0	0	0	0
Career Total	15	1	0	0	6984
87 4/02 Uttx	3m	G(0-90)HCh	GD	£2317	
99 9/00 Worc	3m	F Hdl	G-F	£1869	
108 8/98 Worc	2m	H NHF	GD	£1203	
				Total win prize-money £5389	

Going: Sf: 0-0 GS: 0-0 Gd: 0-1 GF: - Fm: 0-1
Distance: 2m/2m3: 0-0 2m4-2m7: 0-0 3m+: 0-2
Track: LH: 0-1 RH: 0-0 Tight: 0-0 Gall: 0-0
Aids: Bl: 0-0 Vi: 0-0 Tstrap: 0-0
Best Rating: 108 8/98 Worc 2m good NHF

Plating-class chaser; won a selling handicap at Uttoxeter. Likes good ground, stays three miles.

Steel Bells (IRE)

14-y-o br g Mandalus-Lucy s Pal (Random Shot)
A W Froggatt (Trainer Unknown 12/5) Julian Robbins

Placings:0/004/P (0317)
2002/03: 34PG,

	Starts	1st	2nd	3rd	Win & Pl
Chases	1	0	0	0	
Career Total	5	0	0	0	

Going: Sf: 0-0 GS: 0-0 Gd: 0-1 GF: - Fm: 0-0
Distance: 2m/2m3: 0-0 2m4-2m7: 0-0 3m+: 0-0
Track: LH: 0-1 RH: 0-0 Tight: 0-0 Gall: 0-0
Aids: Bl: 0-0 Vi: 0-0 Tstrap: 0-0
Best Rating: 79 2/95 Font 2m2f soft Hdl

Steel Edge (IRE)
(97h)

9-y-o ch g Torus-Lasting Impression (Proverb)
Miss Venetia Williams Worcester Racing Club

Placings:215/P54335/UF (3927)
2002/03: 25UG, 24FG,

	Starts	1st	2nd	3rd	Win & Pl
Chases	2	0	0	0	
Career Total	11	1	1	2	3571
109 2/00 Folk	2m1f110yH NHF		SFT	£1599	
				Total win prize-money £1600	

Going: Sf: 0-0 GS: 0-0 Gd: 0-2 GF: - Fm: 0-0
Distance: 2m/2m3: 0-0 2m4-2m7: 0-0 3m+: 0-2
Track: LH: 0-0 RH: 0-2 Tight: 0-0 Gall: 0-1
Aids: Bl: 0-0 Vi: 0-0 Tstrap: 0-0
Best Rating: 109 4/00 Font 2m2f110y good NHF

Steel Mill (IRE)

83(103h)   (82+h)**67**

8-y-o gr g Roselier (FR)-Chatmando (IRE) (Mandalus)
D J Caro   Mrs J F Billington

Placings:000/PP63P-325   (2003)
2002/03: 25PG, 253GF, 222GS, 255G,

	Starts	1st	2nd	3rd	Win & Pl
Hurdles	3	0	1	1	1285
Chases	1	0	0	0	0
Career Total	11	0	1	2	1659

Going: Sf: 0-0 GS: 0-1 GF: 0-2 GF: - Fm: 0-1
Distance: 2m/2m3: 0-0 2m4-2m7: 0-1 3m+: 0-3
Track: LH: 0-1 RH: 0-2 Tight: 0-1 Gall: 0-0
Aids: Bl: 0-0 Vi: 0-0 Tstrap: 0-0
Best Rating: 86   3/01   Wwck 2m   heavy   NHF

Moderate form in bumpers, over hurdles and over fences. Stays well.

Steel Rigg (IRE)

97   **73**

11-y-o ch g Lancastrian-Cute Play (Salluceva)
Mrs A Hamilton   Ian Hamilton

Placings:2403/6P10/3/02F2F6/4   (0453)
2002/03: 244G,

	Starts	1st	2nd	3rd	Win & Pl
Hurdles	1	0	0	0	0
Career Total	14	1	2	2	4434
85 4/99 Hexm 2m4f110yE Hdl		GD		£2176	

Total win prize-money £2176

Going: Sf: 0-0 GS: 0-0 GF: 0-1 GF: - Fm: 0-0
Distance: 2m/2m3: 0-0 2m4-2m7: 0-0 3m+: 0-1
Track: LH: 0-1 RH: 0-0 Tight: 0-0 Gall: 0-0
Aids: Bl: 0-0 Vi: 0-0 Tstrap: 0-1
Best Rating: 89   6/00   Prth   3m   soft   Ch

Stennikov (IRE)

102   **114**

7-y-o b g Good Thyne (USA)-Belle Bavard (Le Bavard (FR))
P F Nicholls   B C Marshall

Placings:41603-240   (3153)
2002/03: 192G, 204S, 240HY,

	Starts	1st	2nd	3rd	Win & Pl
Hurdles	3	0	1	0	1386
Career Total	8	1	1	1	3531
108 10/01 Chep 2m110y H NHF			SFT	£1722	

Total win prize-money £1722

Going: Sf: 0-2 GS: 0-0 GF: 0-1 GF: - Fm: 0-0
Distance: 2m/2m3: 0-0 2m4-2m7: 0-2 3m+: 0-1
Track: LH: 0-2 RH: 0-1 Tight: 0-1 Gall: 0-0
Aids: Bl: 0-0 Vi: 0-0 Tstrap: 0-0
Best Rating: 114   10/02   MRas   2m3f110y   good   Hdl

Fair maiden hurdler.

Step In Line (IRE)

11-y-o gr g Step Together (USA)-Ballycahan Girl (Bargello)
Mrs Ruth Hayter   J K Braithwaite

Placings:00/3P0P3/4462243464P1/33132330FP/00303214
P/650365-0   (0032)
2002/03: 21PGF,

	Starts	1st	2nd	3rd	Win & Pl
Chases	1	0	0	0	

Career Total   45   3   4   11   19132
95   8/00   NAbb   2m5f110yF(0-105)HCh   GD   £3454
95   6/99   NAbb   2m110y F(0-105)HCh   GD   £4396
99   3/99   NAbb   2m110y F Ch   SFT   £2362

Total win prize-money £10214

Going: Sf: 0-0 GS: 0-0 GF: 0-0 GF: - Fm: 0-1
Distance: 2m/2m3: 0-0 2m4-2m7: 0-1 3m+: 0-0
Track: LH: 0-1 RH: 0-0 Tight: 0-0 Gall: 0-1
Aids: Bl: 0-0 Vi: 0-0 Tstrap: 0-0
Best Rating: 99   3/99   NAbb   2m110y   soft   Ch

Step In Silver (IRE)

(95h)   (88h)

7-y-o gr g Step Together (USA)-Seagate (IRE) (Decent Fellow)
Jonjo O Neill   Ray & Sue Dodd Partnership

Placings:0604-PPP   (4537)
2002/03: 20PGS, 22PGS, 24PG,

	Starts	1st	2nd	3rd	Win & Pl
Hurdles	2	0	0	0	0
Chases	1	0	0	0	0
Career Total	7	0	0	0	0

Going: Sf: 0-0 GS: 0-2 GF: 0-1 GF: - Fm: 0-0
Distance: 2m/2m3: 0-0 2m4-2m7: 0-2 3m+: 0-1
Track: LH: 0-0 RH: 0-3 Tight: 0-1 Gall: 0-0
Aids: Bl: 0-0 Vi: 0-0 Tstrap: 0-0
Best Rating: 88   4/02   Bang   2m4f   good   Hdl

Step On Eyre (IRE)

13-y-o b g Step Together (USA)-Jane Eyre (Master Buck)
S Wynne   J E Stockton

Placings:00/115/151/222P331/22111P/042435/6P16/641P
2-4P4   (4565)
2002/03: 224GS, 25PG, 244GF,

	Starts	1st	2nd	3rd	Win & Pl
Chases	3	0	0	0	680
Career Total	39	10	7	3	71561
130	12/01	Bang	4m1f	D(0-120)HCh	SFT	£4494
134	2/01	Bang	3m6f	D(0-120)HCh	HVY	£5209
154	2/99	Hayd	3m	B(0-145)HCh	HVY	£12518
148	1/99	Weth	3m1f	B HCh	HVY	£8130
127	12/98	Bang	2m4f110yD(0-120)HCh	G-S	£4299
117	4/98	Towc	2m6f	E Ch	G-S	£2921
123	4/97	Punc	2m	Hdl	GD	£4747
111	11/96	Tipp	2m	Hdl	SFT	£2824
121	6/95	Tipp	2m	NHF	Y-S	£2712
112	5/95	Tipp	2m4f	NHF	GD	£2712

Total win prize-money £50571

Going: Sf: 0-0 GS: 0-1 GF: 0-1 GF: - Fm: 0-1
Distance: 2m/2m3: 0-0 2m4-2m7: 0-1 3m+: 0-2
Track: LH: 0-3 RH: 0-0 Tight: 0-1 Gall: 0-0
Aids: Bl: 0-0 Vi: 0-0 Tstrap: 0-0
Best Rating: 154   2/99   Hayd   3m   soft   Ch

One time useful handicap chaser; winning pointer; goes well under testing conditions but is inconsistent; stays four miles plus.

Step Quick (IRE)

9-y-o ch g All Haste (USA)-Little Steps (Step Together (USA))
W Bryan (P Bowen 12/5) David A Smith

Placings:60/222   (4678)
2002/03: 242S, 242GF, 192GF,

	Starts	1st	2nd	3rd	Win & Pl
Chases	3	0	3	0	2244
Career Total	5	0	3	0	2244

Going: Sf: 0-1 GS: 0-0 GF: 0-0 GF: - Fm: 0-2
Distance: 2m/2m3: 0-1 2m4-2m7: 0-0 3m+: 0-2
Track: LH: 0-2 RH: 0-1 Tight: 0-2 Gall: 0-0
Aids: Bl: 0-0 Vi: 0-0 Tstrap: 0-0
Best Rating: 93   10/99   Tntn   2m1f   gd-fm   NHF

Modest hunter Chaser; stays three miles; acts on fast ground.

Stepastray

6-y-o gr g Alhijaz-Wandering Stranger (Petong)
R E Barr   D Thomson

Placings:P   (2517)
2002/03: 16PS,

	Starts	1st	2nd	3rd	Win & Pl
Hurdles	1	0	0	0	
Career Total	1	0	0	0	

Going: Sf: 0-1 GS: 0-0 GF: 0-0 GF: - Fm: 0-0
Distance: 2m/2m3: 0-1 2m4-2m7: 0-0 3m+: 0-0
Track: LH: 0-1 RH: 0-0 Tight: 0-0 Gall: 0-1
Aids: Bl: 0-0 Vi: 0-0 Tstrap: 0-0
Best Rating: 0   12/02   Newc   2m   soft   Hdl

Steppes

66(92h)   (78h)**89**

8-y-o b g Jendali (USA)-Asoness (Laxton)
M J Gingell   T Alexander And G S Plastow

Placings:001PPP   (4709)
2002/03: 21DG, 21DGF, 241G, 26PG, 20PGS, 24PG,

	Starts	1st	2nd	3rd	Win & Pl
Hurdles	5	1	0	0	2226
Chases	1	0	0	0	0
Career Total	6	1	0	0	2226
78 9/02 Worc 3m		F Hdl		GD	£2226

Total win prize-money £2226

Going: Sf: 0-0 GS: 0-1 GF: 1-4 GF: - Fm: 0-1
Distance: 2m/2m3: 0-0 2m4-2m7: 0-3 3m+: 1-3
Track: LH: 1-6 RH: 0-0 Tight: 0-2 Gall: 0-0
Aids: Bl: 0-0 Vi: 0-0 Tstrap: 0-0
Best Rating: 78   9/02   Worc   3m   Hdl

Plating-class chaser; caused 50/1 shock when winning a three mile maiden hurdle at Worcester September 2002 in three subsequent runs.

Steppes Of Gold (IRE)

97f   **108+f**

6-y-o b g Moscow Society (USA)-Trysting Place (He Loves Me)
N G Richards   Independent Twine Manufacturing Co Ltd

Placings:1   (4437)
2002/03: 161G,

	Starts	1st	2nd	3rd	Win & Pl
NH Flat	1	1	0	0	2065
Career Total	1	1	0	0	2065
108 4/03 Newc 2m		H NHF		GD	£2065

Total win prize-money £2065

Going:	Sf: 0-0 GS: 0-0 Gd: 1-1 GF: - Fm: 0-0
Distance:	2m/2m3: 1-1 2m4-2m7: 0-0 3m+: 0-0
Track:	LH: 1-1 RH: 0-0 Tight: 0-0 Gall: 0-0
Aids:	Bl: 0-0 Vi: 0-0 Tstrap: 0-0
Best Rating:	108 4/03 Newc 2m good NHF

Got off the mark on debut when winning a fair Newcastle bumper; effective on a sound surface; should make a decent hurdler/ chaser in time.

Sterling Dot Com (IRE)

93(96h)   (116h)**85**

7-y-o b g Roselier (FR)-Daddy s Folly (Le Moss)
P J Hobbs Sterling Racing Syndicate

Placings: 3/134-F540P   (3314)
2002/03: 24FS, 24⁵G, 24⁴HY, 24⁰GS, 25PGS,

	Starts	1st	2nd	3rd	Win & Pl
Chases	5	0	0	0	375
Career Total	9	1	0	2	4446
116 12/01 Wwck 2m5f		E Hdl		SFT	£2844
			Total win prize-money £2845

Going:	Sf: 0-2 GS: 0-2 Gd: 0-1 GF: - Fm: 0-0
Distance:	2m/2m3: 0-0 2m4-2m7: 0-0 3m+: 0-5
Track:	LH: 0-3 RH: 0-2 Tight: 0-1 Gall: 0-0
Aids:	Bl: 0-1 Vi: 0-0 Tstrap: 0-0
Best Rating:	116 12/01 Wwck 2m5f soft Hdl

Plating-class performer; has not jumped well on his chasing starts to date. Stays two miles five; acts on soft ground.

Sterling Stewart (IRE)

108(109h)   (112h)**125+**

8-y-o b g Insan (USA)-Kyle Eile (IRE) (Callernish)
M Pitman Ron George

Placings: 03U3F2P/61PF30U15-232   (1540)
2002/03: 17²G, 21³GF, 20²GF,

	Starts	1st	2nd	3rd	Win & Pl
Chases	3	0	2	1	5532
Career Total	19	2	3	4	21596
114 4/02 Asct	2m3f110yC Ch		G-F	£6012
112 12/01 Newb 2m3f	D(0-125)HHdl		G-S	£5375
			Total win prize-money £11389

Going:	Sf: 0-0 GS: 0-0 Gd: 0-1 GF: - Fm: 0-2
Distance:	2m/2m3: 0-1 2m4-2m7: 0-2 3m+: 0-0
Track:	LH: 0-3 RH: 0-0 Tight: 0-2 Gall: 0-0
Aids:	Bl: 0-0 Vi: 0-0 Tstrap: 0-0
Best Rating:	127 10/02 Weth 2m4f110y gd-fm Ch

Fair hurdler around two miles four. Of similar ability over fences. Acts on any ground.

Stero Heights (IRE)

101   **99**

8-y-o b g Shirley Heights-Trystero (Shareef Dancer (USA))
D Broad W A Barrett

Placings: 3/000P0-50142112   (1517a)
2002/03: 17⁵YS, 24⁰S, 20¹G, 18⁴GY, 20²GF, 21¹G, 20¹G, 20²G,

	Starts	1st	2nd	3rd	Win & Pl
Hurdles	8	3	2	0	14395
Career Total	14	3	2	1	14636
92 10/02 Rosc	2m4f	(60-95)HHdl	GD	£4024
92 9/02 Sedg	2m5f110yE(0-105)HHdl	GD	£2947
76 7/02 Baln	2m4f	(60-88)HHdl	GD	£4233
				Total win prize-money £11205

Going:	Sf: 0-1 GS: 0-0 Gd: 3-4 GF: - Fm: 0-1
Distance:	2m/2m3: 0-2 2m4-2m7: 3-5 3m+: 0-1
Track:	LH: 1-1 RH: 0-0 Tight: 1-1 Gall: 0-0
Aids:	Bl: 0-2 Vi: 0-0 Tstrap: 3-8
Best Rating:	99 10/02 Limk 2m4f good Hdl

Irish-trained gelding; acts on good ground; stays an extended 21 furlongs.

Steve Ford

14-y-o gr g Another Realm-Sky Miss (Skymaster)
Mrs S S Harbour P J Morgan

Placings: 60/P/30F0V3/5140450/U632/15223/1123/U5P/P0
P-F   (0032)
2002/03: 21FGF,

	Starts	1st	2nd	3rd	Win & Pl
Chases	1	0	0	0	
Career Total	36	4	4	5	19259
110 5/98 Worc	2m4f110yD(0-125)HCh	G-F	£4235
105 5/98 Winc	2m5f	E(0-100)HCh	GD	£3480
99 5/97 Uttx	2m4f110yD(0-125)HHdl	GD	£2913
97 5/95 Worc	2m	E(0-110)HHdl	GD	£2547
			Total win prize-money £13176

Going:	Sf: 0-0 GS: 0-0 Gd: 0-0 GF: - Fm: 0-1
Distance:	2m/2m3: 0-0 2m4-2m7: 0-1 3m+: 0-0
Track:	LH: 0-1 RH: 0-0 Tight: 0-0 Gall: 0-1
Aids:	Bl: 0-0 Vi: 0-0 Tstrap: 0-0
Best Rating:	110 5/98 Worc 2m4f110y gd-fm Ch

Steve The Fish (IRE)

85(86c)   (89c)**49**

7-y-o ch g Dry Dock-Country Clothing (Salluceva)
J A B Old W E Sturt

Placings: 06/05FF2-P5U   (2774)
2002/03: 24PGS, 20⁵GS, 22US,

	Starts	1st	2nd	3rd	Win & Pl
Hurdles	1	0	0	0	0
Chases	2	0	0	0	0
Career Total	10	0	1	0	558

Going:	Sf: 0-1 GS: 0-2 Gd: 0-0 GF: - Fm: 0-0
Distance:	2m/2m3: 0-0 2m4-2m7: 0-2 3m+: 0-1
Track:	LH: 0-1 RH: 0-1 Tight: 0-0 Gall: 0-1
Aids:	Bl: 0-0 Vi: 0-0 Tstrap: 0-0
Best Rating:	98 3/02 Towc 2m5f gd-sft Ch

Moderate novice hurdler/chaser; stays two miles five; acts on easy ground.

Stewart's Lad

80   **97**

6-y-o b g Well Beloved-Moneyacre (Veloski)
B D Leavy S H Riley

Placings: 0453F-0   (1754)
2002/03: 16⁰G,

	Starts	1st	2nd	3rd	Win & Pl
Hurdles	1	0	0	0	
Career Total	6	0	0	1	386

Going:	Sf: 0-0 GS: 0-0 Gd: 0-1 GF: - Fm: 0-0
Distance:	2m/2m3: 0-1 2m4-2m7: 0-0 3m+: 0-0
Track:	LH: 0-1 RH: 0-0 Tight: 0-0 Gall: 0-0
Aids:	Bl: 0-0 Vi: 0-0 Tstrap: 0-0

| Best Rating: | 97 4/02 Uttx 2m good Hdl |

Has shown ability in novice hurdles.

Stila (IRE)

4-y-o b f Desert Style (IRE)-Noorajo (IRE) (Ahonoora)
B W Duke (J S Bolger 17/10) Brendan W Duke Racing

Placings: P   (3918)
2002/03: 18PS,

	Starts	1st	2nd	3rd	Win & Pl
Hurdles	1	0	0	0	
Career Total	1	0	0	0	

Going:	Sf: 0-1 GS: 0-0 Gd: 0-0 GF: - Fm: 0-0
Distance:	2m/2m3: 0-1 2m4-2m7: 0-0 3m+: 0-0
Track:	LH: 0-1 RH: 0-0 Tight: 0-1 Gall: 0-0
Aids:	Bl: 0-0 Vi: 0-0 Tstrap: 0-0
Best Rating:	0 3/03 Font 2m2f110y soft Hdl

Ex-Irish; plating-class maiden on the Flat; pulled up on hurdling debut.

Still Speedy (IRE)

94f   **95f**

6-y-o b g Toulon-Gorge (Mount Hagen (FR))
Noel T Chance Still, Simpson & Castledine

Placings: 004   (4737)
2002/03: 16⁵G, 16⁶G, 16⁴GF,

	Starts	1st	2nd	3rd	Win & Pl
NH Flat	3	0	0	0	0
Career Total	3	0	0	0	0

Going:	Sf: 0-0 GS: 0-0 Gd: 0-2 GF: - Fm: 0-1
Distance:	2m/2m3: 0-3 2m4-2m7: 0-0 3m+: 0-0
Track:	LH: 0-1 RH: 0-2 Tight: 0-0 Gall: 0-0
Aids:	Bl: 0-0 Vi: 0-0 Tstrap: 0-0
Best Rating:	95 11/02 Winc 2m good NHF

Has shown ability in bumpers; does not look a straightforward ride.

Sting Like A Bee (IRE)

96   **76**

4-y-o b c Ali-Royal (IRE)-Hidden Agenda (FR) (Machiavellian (USA))
J S Goldie (H R A Cecil 22/8) The Newton Arms

Placings: 005356   (4507)
2002/03: 16⁰G, 16⁰GS, 16⁵G, 16³G, 16⁵S, 16⁶G,

	Starts	1st	2nd	3rd	Win & Pl
Hurdles	6	0	0	1	353
Career Total	6	0	0	1	353

Going:	Sf: 0-3 GS: 0-1 Gd: 0-2 GF: - Fm: 0-0
Distance:	2m/2m3: 0-6 2m4-2m7: 0-0 3m+: 0-0
Track:	LH: 0-6 RH: 0-0 Tight: 0-2 Gall: 0-1
Aids:	Bl: 0-0 Vi: 0-0 Tstrap: 0-3
Best Rating:	76 1/03 Catt 2m good Hdl

Plating-class hurdler; disappointing maiden on the Flat; only small and best effort when third in selling hurdle at Catterick in January; usually wears a tongue strap.

Stitch-B (IRE)

(94h)   (74h)

10-y-o ch g Naheez (USA)-Sea View (Quayside)

P Beaumont The Foulrice Twenty

Placings: 0000/013/3002/00-P   (0563)
2002/03: 20PGF,

	Starts	1st	2nd	3rd	Win & Pl
Chases	1	0	0	0	
Career Total	14	1	1	2	3963
79	6/99	Wxfd	2m4f	Hdl	G-F	£2639

Total win prize-money £2640

Going: Sf: 0-0 GS: 0-0 Gd: 0-0 GF: 0-1
Distance: 2m/2m3: 0-0 2m4-2m7: 0-1 3m+: 0-0
Track: LH: 0-0 RH: 0-0 Tight: 0-1 Gall: 0-0
Aids: Bl: 0-0 Vi: 0-0 Tstrap: 0-0
Best Rating: 89 12/00 Muss 3m   good   Hdl

Stockers Pride

(97h)   (106h)
8-y-o b g Sula Bula-Fille De Soleil (Sunyboy)
S Woodman J D Sells

Placings: 062313-PFP   (3552)
2002/03: 22PGS, 26FHY, 26PS,

	Starts	1st	2nd	3rd	Win & Pl
Hurdles	1	0	0	0	0
Chases	2	0	0	0	0
Career Total	9	1	1	2	3968
106	1/02	Plum	3m1f110yE Hdl	HVY	£2572

Total win prize-money £2573

Going: Sf: 0-2 GS: 0-1 Gd: 0-0 GF: 0-0
Distance: 2m/2m3: 0-0 2m4-2m7: 0-1 3m+: 0-2
Track: LH: 0-3 RH: 0-0 Tight: 0-3 Gall: 0-0
Aids: Bl: 0-0 Vi: 0-0 Tstrap: 0-0
Best Rating: 106 1/02 Plum 3m1f110y heavy Hdl

Modest novice hurdler, stays well and acts in the mud.

Stocks 'n Shares

95   78
7-y-o b m Jupiter Island-Norstock (Norwick (USA))
J White The Norstock Partnership

Placings: 0/0500   (2288)
2002/03: 17OG, 17SG, 21OGS, 17OG,

	Starts	1st	2nd	3rd	Win & Pl
NH Flat	1	0	0	0	0
Hurdles	3	0	0	0	0
Career Total	5	0	0	0	0

Going: Sf: 0-0 GS: 0-1 Gd: 0-3 GF: 0-0
Distance: 2m/2m3: 0-3 2m4-2m7: 0-1 3m+: 0-0
Track: LH: 0-1 RH: 0-3 Tight: 0-0 Gall: 0-0
Aids: Bl: 0-0 Vi: 0-0 Tstrap: 0-1
Best Rating: 82 12/02 Hrfd 2m1f   good   Hdl

Winner of a poor selling hurdle at Hereford in December 2002.

Stone Cold

111(103h)   (97h)107
6-y-o ch g Inchinor-Vaula (Henbit (USA))
T D Easterby Six Diamonds Partnership

Placings: 45551040/0525P021F51-643462222   (4353)
2002/03: 16⁶GF, 20⁴G, 16³S, 16⁴S, 16⁶GS, 20²G, 20²G, 20²G, 23⁹GF,

	Starts	1st	2nd	3rd	Win & Pl
Chases	9	0	4	1	8260
Career Total	28	3	6	1	20925
97	4/02	MRas	2m1f110y	E(0-105)HCh	

G-F £3786
97 3/02 Donc 2m110y D(0-110)HCh   SFT   £4160
97 2/01 Sedg 2m1f   D(0-95)HHdl   SFT   £2009

Total win prize-money £9955

Going: Sf: 0-2 GS: 0-1 Gd: 0-4 GF: - Fm: 0-2
Distance: 2m/2m3: 0-4 2m4-2m7: 0-4 3m+: 0-1
Track: LH: 0-6 RH: 0-2 Tight: 0-3 Gall: 0-2
Aids: Bl: 0-8 Vi: 0-0 Tstrap: 0-0
Best Rating: 107 3/03 Weth 2m7f110y gd-fm   Ch

Modest handicap chaser; stays three miles; usually blinkered and suffers from secondcitis; acts on any ground; consistent.

Stone Mountain (IRE)

67   37
11-y-o gr g Mandalus-Dora Frost (Stradavinsky)
C J Down Miss K Penning

Placings: 00/PP0   (2671)
2002/03: 23PG, 19PG, 17OS,

	Starts	1st	2nd	3rd	Win & Pl
Hurdles	1	0	0	0	0
Chases	2	0	0	0	0
Career Total	5	0	0	0	0

Going: Sf: 0-1 GS: 0-0 Gd: 0-2 GF: - Fm: 0-0
Distance: 2m/2m3: 0-1 2m4-2m7: 0-1 3m+: 0-0
Track: LH: 0-0 RH: 0-3 Tight: 0-0 Gall: 0-0
Aids: Bl: 0-0 Vi: 0-0 Tstrap: 0-0
Best Rating: 70 12/98 Ludl 2m   gd-sft NHF

Stonehenge (IRE)

89(100h)   (91dh)77
6-y-o b g Caerleon (USA)-Sharata (IRE) (Darshaan)
D Burchell (A King 22/10) Three Acres Racing

Placings: 5P0/512535PP05-06PP0   (2061)
2002/03: 17OG, 20⁶G, 20PGS, 19PG, 17OS,

	Starts	1st	2nd	3rd	Win & Pl
Hurdles	2	0	0	0	0
Chases	3	0	0	0	0
Career Total	18	1	1	1	4155
95	6/01	NAbb	2m6f	F(0-105)HHdl	GD	£2793

Total win prize-money £2793

Going: Sf: 0-1 GS: 0-1 Gd: 0-3 GF: - Fm: 0-0
Distance: 2m/2m3: 0-3 2m4-2m7: 0-2 3m+: 0-0
Track: LH: 0-1 RH: 0-4 Tight: 0-1 Gall: 0-1
Aids: Bl: 0-0 Vi: 0-2 Tstrap: 0-0
Best Rating: 95 6/01 NAbb 2m6f   gd-fm   Hdl

Stonehill Prospect

39
9-y-o b m Lightning Dealer-Ditchling Beacon (High Line)
C J Gray G V Alderman

Placings: 0/04-5   (0369)
2002/03: 17⁵S,

	Starts	1st	2nd	3rd	Win & Pl
Hurdles	1	0	0	0	0
Career Total	4	0	0	0	0

Going: Sf: 0-1 GS: 0-0 Gd: 0-0 GF: - Fm: 0-0
Distance: 2m/2m3: 0-1 2m4-2m7: 0-3 3m+: 0-0
Track: LH: 0-1 RH: 0-0 Tight: 0-1 Gall: 0-0

Aids: Bl: 0-0 Vi: 0-0 Tstrap: 0-0
Best Rating: 60 4/01 Font 2m2f110y good   Hdl

Stoneravinmad

78
5-y-o ch g Never So Bold-Premier Princess (Hard Fought)
Mrs E Slack Mrs Evelyn Slack

Placings: 0U00   (4406)
2002/03: 20⁶S, 27US, 21OS, 20⁴G,

	Starts	1st	2nd	3rd	Win & Pl
Hurdles	4	0	0	0	0
Career Total	4	0	0	0	0

Going: Sf: 0-3 GS: 0-0 Gd: 0-1 GF: - Fm: 0-0
Distance: 2m/2m3: 0-0 2m4-2m7: 0-3 3m+: 0-1
Track: LH: 0-4 RH: 0-0 Tight: 0-2 Gall: 0-1
Aids: Bl: 0-0 Vi: 0-0 Tstrap: 0-0
Best Rating: 44 11/02 Newc 2m4f   soft   Hdl

Stonesby (IRE)

11-y-o b g The Bart (USA)-Maid In The Mist (Pry)
Geoffrey Deacon Mrs J M Duckett

Placings: 03/F3136/30245146/P/P   (3955)
2002/03: 20PGS,

	Starts	1st	2nd	3rd	Win & Pl
Chases	1	0	0	0	
Career Total	17	2	1	4	9058
96	2/99	Muss	2m	D(0-110)HCh	G-F	£3616
88	12/97	Catt	2m3f	E Hdl	GD	£2444

Total win prize-money £6061

Going: Sf: 0-0 GS: 0-1 Gd: 0-0 GF: - Fm: 0-0
Distance: 2m/2m3: 0-0 2m4-2m7: 0-1 3m+: 0-0
Track: LH: 0-0 RH: 0-1 Tight: 0-0 Gall: 0-0
Aids: Bl: 0-0 Vi: 0-0 Tstrap: 0-0
Best Rating: 96 2/99 Muss 2m   gd-fm   Ch

Stoney Path

104   94
8-y-o b m Petoski-Lampstone (Ragstone)
A King The Golden Anorak Partnership

Placings: 450/2/P001-1   (0324)
2002/03: 20¹G,

	Starts	1st	2nd	3rd	Win & Pl
Hurdles	1	1	0	0	2646
Career Total	9	2	1	0	6863
94	5/02	Worc	2m4f	E(0-100)HHdl	GD	£2646
89	4/02	Hrfd	2m3f110yE(0-105)HHdl	GD	£3430

Total win prize-money £6076

Going: Sf: 0-0 GS: 0-0 Gd: 1-1 GF: - Fm: 0-0
Distance: 2m/2m3: 0-0 2m4-2m7: 1-1 3m+: 0-0
Track: LH: 1-1 RH: 0-0 Tight: 0-0 Gall: 0-0
Aids: Bl: 0-0 Vi: 0-0 Tstrap: 0-0
Best Rating: 94 5/02 Worc 2m4f   good   Hdl

Modest hurdler, effective on fast ground. Won novices handicap at Hereford April 2002. Finished lame when following up at Worcester next month.

Stoney River (IRE)

9-y-o b g Riverhead (USA)-Another Space (Brave Invader (USA))

Ms Alison Christmas P England

Placings:U/33P-P   (0166)
2002/03: 25PGF,

	Starts	1st	2nd	3rd	Win & Pl
Chases	1	0	0	0	
Career Total	5	0	0	2	1134

Going:	Sf: 0-0 GS: 0-0 Gd: 0-0 GF: - Fm: 0-1
Distance:	2m2m3: 0-0 2m4-2m7: 0-0 3m+: 0-1
Track:	LH: 0-1 RH: 0-0 Tight: 0-0 Gall: 0-0
Aids:	Bl: 0-0 Vi: 0-0 Tstrap: 0-1
Best Rating:	90 5/01 Font 3m2f110y gd-fm Ch

Stop The Music (IRE)

67   35

7-y-o b g Lord Americo-Brace Yourself (Castle Keep)
S E H Sherwood The Hon Mrs S Sherwood

Placings:45-0   (1601)
2002/03: 20QG,

	Starts	1st	2nd	3rd	Win & Pl
Hurdles	1	0	0	0	
Career Total	3	0	0	0	0

Going:	Sf: 0-0 GS: 0-0 Gd: 0-1 GF: - Fm: 0-0
Distance:	2m2m3: 0-0 2m4-2m7: 0-1 3m+: 0-0
Track:	LH: 0-1 RH: 0-0 Tight: 0-0 Gall: 0-0
Aids:	Bl: 0-0 Vi: 0-0 Tstrap: 0-0
Best Rating:	86 1/02 Ludl 2m good NHF

Stopwatch (IRE)

98(104h)   (63h)90

8-y-o b g Lead On Time (USA)-Rose Bonbon (FR) (High Top)
Mrs L C Jewell The Stopwatch Partnership

Placings:03015/5P40/3542500/64360016-3F022UFF0   (4119)
2002/03: 21³GF, 17FGF, 19QGF, 20²G, 20²GS, 19US, 19FG, 16FG, 16QG,

	Starts	1st	2nd	3rd	Win & Pl
Hurdles	4	0	0	1	345
Chases	5	0	2	0	2894
Career Total	33	2	3	4	10861
82	3/02	Hntg	2m110y F(0-100)HHdl		G-F £1848
104	4/99	Plum	2m1f E(0-105)HHdl		GD £2302

Total win prize-money £4151

Going:	Sf: 0-1 GS: 0-1 Gd: 0-4 GF: - Fm: 0-3
Distance:	2m2m3: 0-5 2m4-2m7: 0-4 3m+: 0-0
Track:	LH: 0-0 RH: 0-8 Tight: 0-5 Gall: 0-3
Aids:	Bl: 0-0 Vi: 0-0 Tstrap: 0-0
Best Rating:	104 4/99 Chel 2m1f good Hdl

Moderate chaser; effective at two and a half miles; not the best of jumpers.

Storm A Brewing

99   72

7-y-o ch g Glacial Storm (USA)-Southern Squaw (Buckskin (FR))
R M Stronge Mrs Bernice Stronge

Placings:20-004   (4347)
2002/03: 22QG, 26QG, 25⁴GF,

	Starts	1st	2nd	3rd	Win & Pl
Hurdles	3	0	0	0	275

Career Total	5	0	1	0	907

Going:	Sf: 0-1 GS: 0-0 Gd: 0-1 GF: - Fm: 0-1
Distance:	2m/2m3: 0-0 2m4-2m7: 0-1 3m+: 0-2
Track:	LH: 0-2 RH: 0-1 Tight: 0-0 Gall: 0-0
Aids:	Bl: 0-0 Vi: 0-0 Tstrap: 0-0
Best Rating:	98 1/02 Ludl 2m good NHF

Out of half-sister to Docklands Express; runner-up in bumper on debut; gradually improving in staying novice hurdles; may do better in handicaps.

Storm Ahead (IRE)

86(104h)   (64h)63

9-y-o b g Glacial Storm (USA)-Little Slip (Super Slip)
A Parker (N G Richards 25/9) It s A Bargain Syndicate

Placings:04320/0000/F425P-06P0P   (4776)
2002/03: 22QG, 16⁶GF, 16PGF, 20QG, 20PG,

	Starts	1st	2nd	3rd	Win & Pl
Hurdles	4	0	0	0	0
Chases	1	0	0	0	0
Career Total	19	0	2	1	1930

Going:	Sf: 0-0 GS: 0-0 Gd: 0-3 GF: - Fm: 0-2
Distance:	2m/2m3: 0-2 2m4-2m7: 0-3 3m+: 0-0
Track:	LH: 0-3 RH: 0-2 Tight: 0-1 Gall: 0-0
Aids:	Bl: 0-0 Vi: 0-0 Tstrap: 0-2
Best Rating:	101 11/99 Dpat 2m1f87y yield NHF

Plating-class chaser.

Storm Boxer (IRE)

105

5-y-o b/br g Glacial Storm (USA)-Sarakin (IRE) (Buckskin (FR))
P Mullins Mrs Helen Mullins

Placings:10   (4115)
2002/03: 16¹YS, 16QG,

	Starts	1st	2nd	3rd	Win & Pl
NH Flat	2	1	0	0	5825
Career Total	2	1	0	0	5825
114	1/03	Leop	2m	NHF	Y-S £5824

Total win prize-money £5825

Going:	Sf: 0-0 GS: 0-0 Gd: 0-1 GF: - Fm: 0-0
Distance:	2m/2m3: 1-2 2m4-2m7: 0-0 3m+: 0-0
Track:	LH: 0-1 RH: 0-0 Tight: 0-0 Gall: 0-0
Aids:	Bl: 0-0 Vi: 0-0 Tstrap: 0-0
Best Rating:	122 3/03 Chel 2m110y good NHF

Storm Castle (IRE)

11-y-o b g Carlingford Castle-Strong Rum (Strong Gale)
Miss J Wickens Noel Cronin

Placings:21P2/034P630/0/2-126U   (4133)
2002/03: 25¹G, 26²G, 28⁶GF, 26UG,

	Starts	1st	2nd	3rd	Win & Pl
Chases	4	1	1	0	3978
Career Total	17	2	4	2	14127
92	5/02	Extr	3m1f110yH Ch		GD £3536
116	2/99	Tntn	3m110y D Hdl		G-S £2644

Total win prize-money £6180

Going:	Sf: 0-0 GS: 0-0 Gd: 1-3 GF: - Fm: 0-1
Distance:	2m/2m3: 0-0 2m4-2m7: 0-0 3m+: 1-4
Track:	LH: 0-2 RH: 1-2 Tight: 0-2 Gall: 0-1
Aids:	Bl: 0-0 Vi: 0-0 Tstrap: 0-0

Best Rating:	120 4/99 Chel 2m5f110y good Hdl

Useful pointer/hunter chaser; suited by a sound surface; stays three miles one.

Storm Damage (IRE)

103   126

11-y-o b g Waajib-Connaught Lace (Connaught)
P F Nicholls Major A M J Shaw

Placings:65113/00/F21245/33112334/3132305/3422150/20
64B10-22351   (3592)
2002/03: 24²GS, 24²S, 31³GS, 27⁵S, 24¹S,

	Starts	1st	2nd	3rd	Win & Pl
Chases	5	1	2	1	14501
Career Total	47	9	9	10	117804
126	2/03	Sand	3m110y E Ch	SFT	£6942
135	3/02	Sand	3m110y C(0-135)HCh	GD	£6987
135	2/01	Sand	3m110y B(0-145)HCh	HVY	£20825
135	11/99	Chep	2m3f110yC(0-130)HCh	SFT	£6006
139	1/99	Chep	2m4f110yB(0-145)HCh	SFT	£10386
139	12/98	Chep	2m4f110yC(0-130)HCh	HVY	£4955
116	1/98	Wind	2m E Ch	GD	£2921
119	2/96	Clon	2m Hdl	SFT	£2295
117	2/96	Gowr	2m Hdl	Y-S	£3177

Total win prize-money £64498

Going:	Sf: 1-3 GS: 0-2 Gd: 0-0 GF: - Fm: 0-0
Distance:	2m/2m3: 0-0 2m4-2m7: 0-0 3m+: 1-5
Track:	LH: 0-2 RH: 1-3 Tight: 0-1 Gall: 0-0
Aids:	Bl: 1-3 Vi: 0-0 Tstrap: 0-0
Best Rating:	139 1/99 Kemp 2m4f110y soft Ch

Decent staying chaser; had conditions in his favour when winning a sub-standard renewal of the Agfa Chase at Sandown in February 2001; shade disappointing after that success, but won back at Sandown in March 2002 and when winning the Royal Artillery Gold Cup in February 2003; stays three miles plus; acts on soft ground; sometimes blinkered.

Storm Kitten (IRE)

64   33

5-y-o br m Catrail (USA)-Mbunda (Mtoto)
Miss K M George Miss K George

Placings:600-0   (1928)
2002/03: 16QGS,

	Starts	1st	2nd	3rd	Win & Pl
Hurdles	1	0	0	0	
Career Total	4	0	0	0	0

Going:	Sf: 0-0 GS: 0-1 Gd: 0-0 GF: - Fm: 0-0
Distance:	2m/2m3: 0-0 2m4-2m7: 0-0 3m+: 0-0
Track:	LH: 0-0 RH: 0-1 Tight: 0-0 Gall: 0-0
Aids:	Bl: 0-0 Vi: 0-0 Tstrap: 0-0
Best Rating:	67 1/02 Tntn 2m1f soft NHF

Storm Man (IRE)

11-y-o br g Glacial Storm (USA)-Devon Royale (Le Prince)
Miss Charlotte Williams C W M Cornelius

Placings:5/060/0/0-0   (0193)
2002/03: 20QF,

	Starts	1st	2nd	3rd	Win & Pl
Chases	1	0	0	0	
Career Total	7	0	0	0	0

Going:	Sf: 0-0 GS: 0-0 Gd: 0-0 GF: - Fm: 0-1				
Distance:	2m/2m3: 0-0 2m4-2m7: 0-1 3m+: 0-0				
Track:	LH: 0-1 RH: 0-0 Tight: 0-0 Gall: 0-0				
Aids:	Bl: 0-0 Vi: 0-0 Tstrap: 0-0				
Best Rating:	83 9/97 DRoy 2m gd-fm NHF				

Storm Of Gold (IRE)

10-y-o b g Glacial Storm (USA)-Tipperary Tartan (Rarity)
D L Williams (Miss C F Elliott 22/5) Reliance Car Hire Services Ltd

Placings:235/11320/21F/0020/61PP-26P4P66   (4215)
2002/03: 25²S, 31⁶G, 25⁵G, 25⁴S, 26⁹GS, 24⁶S, 28⁶G,

	Starts	1st	2nd	3rd	Win & Pl
Chases	7	0	1	0	856
Career Total	26	4	5	2	24444
101 2/02 Ludl 3m7f H Ch	G-S	£2618			
124 12/99 MRas 3m1f E Ch	G-S	£3070			
124 12/98 Uttx 2m4f110yE Hdl	G-S	£1966			
121 11/98 Hayd 2m4f D Hdl	G-S	£2885			
	Total win prize-money £10540				

Going:	Sf: 0-3 GS: 0-1 Gd: 0-3 GF: - Fm: 0-0				
Distance:	2m/2m3: 0-0 2m4-2m7: 0-0 3m+: 0-7				
Track:	LH: 0-1 RH: 0-5 Tight: 0-3 Gall: 0-0				
Aids:	Bl: 0-0 Vi: 0-1 Tstrap: 0-0				
Best Rating:	134 3/99 Sand 2m4f110y soft Hdl				

Moderate hunter chaser; stays very well but may not be the most hearty.

Storm Prince (IRE)
97   95

6-y-o ch g Prince Of Birds (USA)-Petersford Girl (IRE) (Taufan (USA))
J L Spearing D J Oseman

Placings:2113P0/0506   (4058)
2002/03: 16⁰S, 16⁵S, 16⁹GS, 21⁶S,

	Starts	1st	2nd	3rd	Win & Pl
Hurdles	4	0	0	0	0
Career Total	10	2	1	1	7092
118 11/00 Hrfd 2m1f E Hdl	G-S	£2723			
116 10/00 Wwck 2m D Hdl	SFT	£3048			
	Total win prize-money £5772				

Going:	Sf: 0-3 GS: 0-1 Gd: 0-0 GF: - Fm: 0-0				
Distance:	2m/2m3: 0-3 2m4-2m7: 0-1 3m+: 0-0				
Track:	LH: 0-4 RH: 0-0 Tight: 0-0 Gall: 0-1				
Aids:	Bl: 0-0 Vi: 0-0 Tstrap: 0-0				
Best Rating:	118 12/00 Newb 2m110y soft Hdl				

Successful in a couple of novice hurdles in 2000. Lightly raced and modest form since. Effective at around two miles, and acts well with cut in the ground.

Storm Tiger (IRE)
(106h)   (101h)103

12-y-o b g Strong Gale-Happy Party (Invited (USA))
C G Cox Mrs S Warren

Placings:4000/0042P1/05641122/350645F2/412643F1351
4F3321/1431431522/50422F44233PU-P30F   (1379)
2002/03: 16⁶PGF, 17³GF, 17⁰GF, 16⁶GF,

	Starts	1st	2nd	3rd	Win & Pl
Hurdles	2	0	0	1	290
Chases	2	0	0	0	
Career Total	70	10	11	10	54720
108 8/00 Ctml 2m1f110yD(0-120)HCh	G-S	£3809			
113 7/00 Sthl 2m F(0-105)HCh	G-F	£4056			
113 5/00 Hntg 2m110y F(0-105)HCh	G-S	£2846			
104 4/00 Hayd 2m D(0-120)HCh	GD	£7215			
96 12/99 Hntg 2m110y F(0-105)HCh	G-S	£2565			
96 11/99 Ludl 2m E(0-105)HCh	GD	£3485			
102 5/99 Worc 2m E(0-105)HHdl	G-F	£2031			
92 2/98 Towc 2m E(0-110)HHdl	GD	£2460			
89 1/98 Wind 2m F(0-105)HHdl	GD	£2076			
87 3/97 Wind 2m F(0-105)HHdl	GD	£2104			
	Total win prize-money £32649				

Going:	Sf: 0-0 GS: 0-0 Gd: 0-0 GF: - Fm: 0-4				
Distance:	2m/2m3: 0-4 2m4-2m7: 0-0 3m+: 0-0				
Track:	LH: 0-1 RH: 0-3 Tight: 0-1 Gall: 0-0				
Aids:	Bl: 0-0 Vi: 0-4 Tstrap: 0-0				
Best Rating:	113 10/01 Hrfd 2m good Ch				

Moderate, consistent handicapper chaser around two miles on the smaller tracks, he won four times in the middle of 2000, but has tended to find one or two to beat him since. Prefers decent ground and jumps soundly. Usually wears a visor.

Storm Valley (IRE)

11-y-o b g Strong Gale-Windy Run (Deep Run)
J R Cornwall J R Cornwall

Placings:0P0/56/650UP5P4/133/P1PP-F5U   (4263)
2002/03: 21⁶G, 22⁵S, 24ᵁGF,

	Starts	1st	2nd	3rd	Win & Pl
Chases	3	0	0	0	
Career Total	23	2	0	2	7877
95 10/01 Sthl 3m110y F(0-100)HCh	GD	£2940			
86 9/00 Plum 2m4f D(0-110)HCh	G-F	£3770			
	Total win prize-money £6710				

Going:	Sf: 0-1 GS: 0-0 Gd: 0-1 GF: - Fm: 0-1				
Distance:	2m/2m3: 0-0 2m4-2m7: 0-2 3m+: 0-1				
Track:	LH: 0-2 RH: 0-1 Tight: 0-2 Gall: 0-0				
Aids:	Bl: 0-0 Vi: 0-0 Tstrap: 0-1				
Best Rating:	95 10/01 Sthl 3m110y good Ch				

Storm Wizard (IRE)
83

6-y-o b g Catrail (USA)-Society Ball (Law Society (USA))
D G Bridgwater Colin Rashbrook

Placings:0-0   (4021)
2002/03: 17⁰S,

	Starts	1st	2nd	3rd	Win & Pl
Hurdles	1	0	0	0	
Career Total	2	0	0	0	

Going:	Sf: 0-1 GS: 0-0 Gd: 0-0 GF: - Fm: 0-0				
Distance:	2m/2m3: 0-1 2m4-2m7: 0-0 3m+: 0-0				
Track:	LH: 0-0 RH: 0-1 Tight: 0-0 Gall: 0-0				
Aids:	Bl: 0-0 Vi: 0-0 Tstrap: 0-0				
Best Rating:	83 5/01 Font 2m2f110y gd-fm Hdl				

Stormdancer (IRE)

6-y-o ch g Bluebird (USA)-Unspoiled (Tina s Pet)
Mrs Lucinda Featherstone Largesse Racing

Placings:PPP   (4372)
2002/03: 16⁶GS, 20⁵S, 21⁷G,

	Starts	1st	2nd	3rd	Win & Pl
Hurdles	3	0	0	0	
Career Total	3	0	0	0	

Going:	Sf: 0-1 GS: 0-1 Gd: 0-1 GF: - Fm: 0-0				
Distance:	2m/2m3: 0-1 2m4-2m7: 0-2 3m+: 0-0				
Track:	LH: 0-2 RH: 0-1 Tight: 0-1 Gall: 0-1				
Aids:	Bl: 0-0 Vi: 0-0 Tstrap: 0-0				
Best Rating:	0 3/03 Sedg 2m5f110y good Hdl				

Stormez (FR)
116(108h)   (140h)158

6-y-o b g Ezzoud (IRE)-Stormy Scene (USA) (Storm Bird (CAN))
M C Pipe D A Johnson

Placings:02163011541033-112110111222   (4791)
2002/03: 23¹GF, 23¹G, 21²GS, 32¹GF, 27¹GS, 26⁹GS, 24¹G, 24¹G, 24¹G, 32²G, 33²G, 29²G,

	Starts	1st	2nd	3rd	Win & Pl
Chases	12	7	4	0	173620
Career Total	26	11	5	3	269371
143 2/03 Kemp 3m C Ch	GD	£12753			
145 2/03 Newb 3m C Ch	GD	£8287			
139 1/03 Kemp 3m C Ch	GD	£8346			
150 11/02 Chel 3m3f110yA HCh	G-S	£34800			
141 6/02 Uttx 4m110y B(0-140)HCh	G-F	£32500			
111 5/02 Worc 2m7f110yE Ch	GD	£3190			
122 5/02 Worc 2m7f110yD Ch	G-F	£5362			
134 2/02 Asct 3m C Hdl	SFT	£5005			
140 11/01 Engh 2m3f Hdl	HVY	£31038			
11/01 Engh 2m2f Hdl	HVY	£17459			
7/01 Autl 2m3f110y Hdl	G-S	£19399			
	Total win prize-money £178141				

Going:	Sf: 0-0 GS: 1-3 Gd: 4-7 GF: - Fm: 2-2				
Distance:	2m/2m3: 0-0 2m4-2m7: 0-1 3m+: 7-11				
Track:	LH: 4-8 RH: 2-3 Tight: 0-1 Gall: 2-4				
Aids:	Bl: 0-0 Vi: 0-0 Tstrap: 7-12				
Best Rating:	158 4/03 Ayr 4m1f good Ch				

Smart novice chaser, successful seven times and runner-up in National Hunt Challenge Cup at Cheltenham, Scottish National and attheraces Gold Cup; stays four miles; only small, but usually jumps soundly; at his best on decent ground; has won on a soft surface; usually wears a tongue tie.

Stormhill Stag
104(96h)   (92h)119

11-y-o b g Buckley-Sweet Sirenia (Al Sirat (USA))
R Lee R Taylor

Placings:2112/426431F/534P0/2230F/1220113-5P422   (4254)
2002/03: 22⁵S, 19⁸GS, 20⁴HY, 19²GS, 19²G,

	Starts	1st	2nd	3rd	Win & Pl
Hurdles	1	0	0	0	0
Chases	4	0	2	0	3915
Career Total	33	6	9	4	37421
118 3/02 Newb 2m4f D(0-125)HCh	G-S	£9512			
120 1/02 Towc 2m110y D(0-120)HCh	HVY	£5083			
106 5/01 Extr 2m3f110yF(0-95)HCh	G-S	£3248			
110 1/99 Font 2m8f110yF(0-110)HHdl	SFT	£2845			
113 6/97 Sthl 2m H NHF	G-S	£1203			
115 5/97 Uttx 2m H NHF	G-F	£1287			
	Total win prize-money £23178				

Going:	Sf: 0-2 GS: 0-2 Gd: 0-1 GF: - Fm: 0-0				
Distance:	2m/2m3: 0-0 2m4-2m7: 0-5 3m+: 0-0				
Track:	LH: 0-2 RH: 0-3 Tight: 0-1 Gall: 0-0				
Aids:	Bl: 0-0 Vi: 0-0 Tstrap: 0-0				
Best Rating:	120 3/02 Chep 2m3f110y gd-sft Ch				

Fair chaser; effective at up to 3m; best with give in the ground.

Stormy Beech

107   **93**

7-y-o b g Glacial Storm (USA)-Cheeny s Brig (New Brig)
R Johnson (B Mactaggart 1/5) Peter & Paul Kelly

Placings:0/P00-P0052613102   **(4108)**
2002/03: 22^PGS, 17^PG, 24^PS, 20⁵HY, 17²S, 16⁶S, 16¹G, 16⁹HY, 17¹HY, 16⁹G, 17²S,

	Starts	1st	2nd	3rd	Win & Pl
Hurdles	11	2	2	1	7317
Career Total	15	2	2	1	7317

93	2/03	Sedg	2m1f	F(0-95)HHdl	HVY	£2730
84	1/03	Catt	2m	G(0-90)HHdl	GD	£2471

Total win prize-money £5201

Going:	Sf: 1-7 GS: 0-1 Gd: 1-3 GF: - Fm: 0-0
Distance:	2m/2m3: 2-8 2m4-2m7: 0-2 3m+: 0-1
Track:	LH: 2-10 RH: 0-1 Tight: 2-6 Gall: 0-2
Aids:	Bl: 2-8 Vi: 0-0 Tstrap: 0-0
Best Rating:	93 2/03 Sedg 2m1f heavy Hdl

Moderate hurdler; much improved effort when easy winner at Catterick in January 2003 and followed up at Sedgefield the following month; acts on soft and good; usually wears blinkers.

Stormy Lord (IRE)

112   **129**

7-y-o br g Lord Americo-Decent Shower (Decent Fellow)
J Wade John Wade

Placings:00/323-215131   **(4354)**
2002/03: 16²GF, 17¹GF, 16⁵G, 16¹GS, 16³GS, 20¹GF,

	Starts	1st	2nd	3rd	Win & Pl
Hurdles	6	3	1	1	21546
Career Total	11	3	2	3	23501

112	3/03	Weth	2m4f110yD(0-125)HHdl	G-F	£5512
114	12/02	Ayr	2m C(0-135)HHdl	G-F	£8190
116	10/02	Carl	2m1f E Hdl	G-F	£3220

Total win prize-money £16922

Going:	Sf: 0-0 GS: 1-2 Gd: 0-1 GF: - Fm: 2-3
Distance:	2m/2m3: 2-5 2m4-2m7: 1-1 3m+: 0-0
Track:	LH: 2-4 RH: 1-2 Tight: 0-0 Gall: 0-0
Aids:	Bl: 0-0 Vi: 0-0 Tstrap: 0-0
Best Rating:	129 2/03 Weth 2m gd-sft Hdl

Fair hurdler, on the upgrade; made it three wins from last six starts with all the way win at Wetherby in March; stays two and a half miles.

Stormy Pass

56   **36**

6-y-o b g Dolphin Street (FR)-Noble Choice (Dahar (USA))
P R Webber Mrs P Sherwood

Placings:000P-0   **(1601)**
2002/03: 20⁰G,

	Starts	1st	2nd	3rd	Win & Pl
Hurdles	1	0	0	0	
Career Total	5	0	0	0	

Going:	Sf: 0-0 GS: 0-0 Gd: 0-1 GF: - Fm: 0-0
Distance:	2m/2m3: 0-0 2m4-2m7: 0-0 3m+: 0-0
Track:	LH: 0-1 RH: 0-0 Tight: 0-0 Gall: 0-0
Aids:	Bl: 0-0 Vi: 0-1 Tstrap: 0-1
Best Rating:	86 5/01 Folk 2m1f110y gd-sft NHF

Stormy Skye (IRE)

107(106h)   (122h)**115**

7-y-o b g Bluebird (USA)-Canna (Caerleon (USA))
G L Moore Mrs J Moore,Mrs J Agnew,T Pollock

Placings:435122/102P/36300536-234F33F3   **(4427)**
2002/03: 21²G, 20³HY, 22⁴S, 20^FGS, 20³GS, 20³GS, 25^FG, 26³GF,

	Starts	1st	2nd	3rd	Win & Pl
Chases	8	0	1	4	5584
Career Total	26	2	4	8	25952

122	11/00	Asct	2m110y C(0-135)HHdl	SFT	£8365
108	2/00	Plum	2m E Hdl	SFT	£2534

Total win prize-money £10900

Going:	Sf: 0-2 GS: 0-3 Gd: 0-2 GF: - Fm: 0-1
Distance:	2m/2m3: 0-0 2m4-2m7: 0-6 3m+: 0-2
Track:	LH: 0-3 RH: 0-3 Tight: 0-7 Gall: 0-0
Aids:	Bl: 0-5 Vi: 0-0 Tstrap: 0-0
Best Rating:	125 2/01 Kemp 2m5f gd-sft Hdl

Fair novice chaser; stays two and three-quarter miles; acts on soft ground; a hard ride.

Stormyfairweather (IRE)

11-y-o b g Strong Gale-Game Sunset (Menelek)
N J Henderson Mrs Christopher Hanbury

Placings:62011/110P/2133112/P1/5/P   **(4324)**
2002/03: 24^PG,

	Starts	1st	2nd	3rd	Win & Pl
Chases	1	0	0	0	
Career Total	20	8	3	2	111058

163	3/00	Chel	2m5f	A Ch	G-F	£36000
150	3/99	Chel	2m5f	A Ch	G-S	£32700
120	2/99	Donc	3m	E Ch	G-F	£2999
133	11/98	Chel	2m4f110yB Ch	GD	£9394
129	11/97	Newb	2m110y B(0-140)HHdl	SFT	£5492
120	5/97	Towc	2m	D Hdl	SFT	£2966
114	4/97	Chel	2m5f110yE(0-105)HHdl	G-F	£2996
101	3/97	Towc	2m5f	E Hdl	G-F	£2722

Total win prize-money £95271

Going:	Sf: 0-0 GS: 0-0 Gd: 0-1 GF: - Fm: 0-0
Distance:	2m/2m3: 0-0 2m4-2m7: 0-0 3m+: 0-1
Track:	LH: 0-1 RH: 0-0 Tight: 0-0 Gall: 0-1
Aids:	Bl: 0-0 Vi: 0-0 Tstrap: 0-0
Best Rating:	163 3/00 Chel 2m5f gd-fm Ch

Smart chaser; dual winner of the Cathcart at Cheltenham; not seen after returning home lame after the Heinenken Gold Cup at Punchestown in May 2000 until March 2003; best on decent ground; proven up to three miles and a furlong.

Straight On (IRE)

12-y-o b/br g Tremblant-Maybird (Royalty)
H B Hodge (Mrs S A Hodge 22/5) A H B Hodge

Placings:0/00003/104O0612/2U31/4P-24   **(0313)**
2002/03: 24²G, 25⁴G,

	Starts	1st	2nd	3rd	Win & Pl
Chases	2	0	1	0	429
Career Total	22	3	3	2	9199

105	2/98	Fknm	3m110y D Ch	GD	£3313
98	9/96	Dpat	2m1f172y (0-102)HHdl	FRM	£1765
98	5/96	Dpat	2m6f	Hdl	G-F	£1588

Total win prize-money £6667

Going:	Sf: 0-0 GS: 0-0 Gd: 0-2 GF: - Fm: 0-0

Distance:	2m/2m3: 0-0 2m4-2m7: 0-0 3m+: 0-2
Track:	LH: 0-1 RH: 0-1 Tight: 0-0 Gall: 0-0
Aids:	Bl: 0-0 Vi: 0-0 Tstrap: 0-0
Best Rating:	109 1/98 Hntg 3m gd-sft Ch

Strait Talking (FR)

100   **86**

5-y-o b g Bering-Servia (Le Marmot (FR))
Jedd O Keeffe E Rider

Placings:040-06302F021   **(4666)**
2002/03: 16⁶G, 16⁶HY, 16³GS, 16⁶S, 16²G, 16^FS, 16⁰G, 16²G, 16¹G,

	Starts	1st	2nd	3rd	Win & Pl
Hurdles	8	1	2	1	4337
Chases	1	0	0	0	
Career Total	12	1	2	1	4337

88	4/03	Fknm	2m	G(0-90)HHdl	GD	£2367

Total win prize-money £2367

Going:	Sf: 0-3 GS: 0-1 Gd: 1-5 GF: - Fm: 0-0
Distance:	2m/2m3: 1-9 2m4-2m7: 0-0 3m+: 0-0
Track:	LH: 1-9 RH: 0-0 Tight: 1-4 Gall: 0-2
Aids:	Bl: 0-0 Vi: 0-0 Tstrap: 0-0
Best Rating:	88 4/03 Fknm 2m good Hdl

Selling-class hurdler; runner-up at Catterick and Uttoxeter in 2003 before scoring at Fakenham; fell on only chase start; acts on good ground; stays two mileslikes a sharp track; front-runner.

Stratco (IRE)

103(99h)   (111h)**128**

9-y-o b/br g Satco (FR)-No Slow (King s Ride)
W W Dennis W W Dennis

Placings:000/25/P0/03102140-16   **(0666)**
2002/03: 23¹G, 21⁶GF,

	Starts	1st	2nd	3rd	Win & Pl
Chases	2	1	0	0	3757
Career Total	17	3	2	1	12039

128	5/02	Extr	2m7f110yE Ch	GD	£3757
111	10/01	Extr	2m3f	E(0-105)HHdl	G-F	£2730
110	6/01	NAbb	2m6f	D Hdl	G-F	£3241

Total win prize-money £9729

Going:	Sf: 0-0 GS: 0-0 Gd: 1-1 GF: - Fm: 0-1
Distance:	2m/2m3: 0-0 2m4-2m7: 0-0 3m+: 1-1
Track:	LH: 0-1 RH: 1-1 Tight: 0-0 Gall: 0-0
Aids:	Bl: 0-0 Vi: 0-0 Tstrap: 0-0
Best Rating:	128 5/02 Extr 2m7f110y good Ch

Fair staying hurdler. Made quite an impressive start over fences when winning at Exeter May 2002 over two miles seven and a half furlong.. Acts on fast ground.

Strategic Course (USA)

7-y-o b g Alleged (USA)-Danlu (USA) (Danzig (USA))
C J Teague B Batey

Placings:00   **(1243)**
2002/03: 17⁰GF, 16⁰GF,

	Starts	1st	2nd	3rd	Win & Pl
NH Flat	2	0	0	0	
Career Total	2	0	0	0	

Going:	Sf: 0-0 GS: 0-0 Gd: 0-0 GF: - Fm: 0-2
Distance:	2m/2m3: 0-2 2m4-2m7: 0-0 3m+: 0-0

Track: LH: 0-2 RH: 0-0 Tight: 0-1 Gall: 0-0
Aids: Bl: 0-1 Vi: 0-1 Tstrap: 0-0
Best Rating: 0   9/02   Hexm 2m110y   gd-fm NHF

Strath Fillan

92   61

5-y-o b m Dolphin Street (FR)-Adarama (IRE) (Persian Bold)
H J Collingridge (W J Musson 22/10) L M Power

Placings:0-6600   (4338)
2002/03: 16⁶GF, 16⁸GF, 16⁹G, 20⁹GF,

	Starts	1st	2nd	3rd	Win & Pl
Hurdles	4	0	0	0	0
Career Total	5	0	0	0	0

Going: Sf: 0-1 GS: 0-0 Gd: 0-1 GF: - Fm: 0-3
Distance: 2m/2m3: 0-3 2m4-2m7: 0-1 3m+: 0-0
Track: LH: 0-3 RH: 0-1 Tight: 0-2 Gall: 0-1
Aids: Bl: 0-0 Vi: 0-0 Tstrap: 0-0
Best Rating: 73   3/02   Hntg 2m110y   gd-fm Hdl

Strawberry Hill (IRE)

103   88

9-y-o b g Lancastrian-Tudor Lady (Green Shoon)
Miss V Scott (A Scott 8/4) Exors of the late Andy Scott

Placings:546P-5P526   (4776)
2002/03: 21⁵GF, 21⁹S, 16⁵G, 17⁷G, 20⁶G,

	Starts	1st	2nd	3rd	Win & Pl
Hurdles	5	0	1	0	1509
Career Total	9	0	1	0	1509

Going: Sf: 0-1 GS: 0-0 Gd: 0-3 GF: - Fm: 0-1
Distance: 2m/2m3: 0-2 2m4-2m7: 0-3 3m+: 0-0
Track: LH: 0-4 RH: 0-1 Tight: 0-3 Gall: 0-0
Aids: Bl: 0-0 Vi: 0-0 Tstrap: 0-0
Best Rating: 88   4/03   Sedg 2m1f   good Hdl

Moderate hurdler; showed little worthwhile form before finishing second at Sedgefield in April 2003; connections appear to be struggling to find his trip.

Strawman

102(93h)   (79h)92

6-y-o b g Ela-Mana-Mou-Oatfield (Great Nephew)
C N Kellett (J G Given 22/6) J E Titley

Placings:44P4P/60660-4FP6U312P   (1289)
2002/03: 21⁴G, 21⁶G, 22⁸GF, 26⁶GF, 20⁴G, 17³GF, 18¹G, 21²G, 26⁸GF,

	Starts	1st	2nd	3rd	Win & Pl
Chases	9	1	1	1	5689
Career Total	19	1	1	1	6151
92	8/02	Font	2m2f	E Ch	GD £4007

Total win prize-money £4008

Going: Sf: 0-0 GS: 0-0 Gd: 1-5 GF: - Fm: 0-4
Distance: 2m/2m3: 1-2 2m4-2m7: 0-5 3m+: 0-2
Track: LH: 0-6 RH: 0-1 Tight: 1-6 Gall: 0-0
Aids: Bl: 0-0 Vi: 0-1 Tstrap: 0-0
Best Rating: 92   9/02   Sedg 2m5f   good Ch

Well held in modest company over hurdles and over fences until finding a very weak three-runner chase on a Bank Holiday Monday in 2002. Genuine sort.

Streamsforth Lad (IRE)

(100h)   (88h)

6-y-o b g Be My Native (USA)-Protrial (Proverb)
S A Brookshaw T G K Construction Ltd

Placings:00-263P50P44   (4488)
2002/03: 16²F, 16⁶G, 16³GS, 16⁸G, 16⁵S, 21⁹G, 21⁸G, 21⁴GF, 26⁴GF,

	Starts	1st	2nd	3rd	Win & Pl
NH Flat	2	0	1	0	739
Hurdles	7	0	0	1	1291
Career Total	11	0	1	1	2030

Going: Sf: 0-1 GS: 0-1 Gd: 0-4 GF: - Fm: 0-3
Distance: 2m/2m3: -5 2m4-2m7: 0-3 3m+: 0-1
Track: LH: 0-3 RH: 0-6 Tight: 0-0 Gall: 0-0
Aids: Bl: 0-0 Vi: 0-0 Tstrap: 0-0
Best Rating: 92   10/02   Chel 2m110y   good NHF

Signs of ability in bumpers but has not really lived up to that promise over timber.

Streamstown (IRE)

87   149

9-y-o b/br g Rashar (USA)-Lady Torsil (Torus)
Ferdy Murphy Haydock Park National Hunt Partnership

Placings:3104100/540551212/4F21115/56P1P0-0 (2244)
2002/03: 20⁹GS,

	Starts	1st	2nd	3rd	Win & Pl
Chases	1	0	0	0	
Career Total	30	8	3	1	87969
149	2/02	Uttx	3m4f	A HCh	HVY £40600
144	1/01	Weth	3m1f	B HCh	G-S £10056
143	11/00	Hayd	3m	E(0-115)HCh	HVY £3510
128	11/00	Aint	2m4f	D(0-125)HCh	G-S £7280
102	3/00	Clon	2m4f	Ch	G-Y £4416
98	2/00	Punc	2m4f	(0-116)HCh	SFT £4968
110	3/99	Gowr	2m4f	Hdl	YLD £2700
104	1/99	Naas	2m	NHF	HVY £2762

Total win prize-money £76294

Going: Sf: 0-0 GS: 0-1 Gd: 0-0 GF: - Fm: 0-0
Distance: 2m/2m3: 0-0 2m4-2m7: 0-1 3m+: 0-0
Track: LH: 0-1 RH: 0-0 Tight: 0-0 Gall: 0-1
Aids: Bl: 0-0 Vi: 0-0 Tstrap: 0-0
Best Rating: 149   2/02   Uttx 3m4f   heavy Ch

Very useful ex-Irish chaser, after falling at Aintree on his British debut he improved to win three in a row, including a valuable Wetherby handicap. His limitations were exposed in the De Vere Gold Cup, and againin 2001 in the Charlie Hall Chase and Hennessy, but testing conditions saw him win the National Trial at Uttoxeter in February 2002; lightly raced since. Stays three miles plus. Acts on soft ground.

Street Fighter (FR)

8-y-o b g Subotica (FR)-American Order (USA) (Slew O Gold (USA))
Jonjo O Neill Tony Eaves

Placings:2P/0-P   (1563)
2002/03: 17⁸G,

	Starts	1st	2nd	3rd	Win & Pl
Hurdles	1	0	0	0	
Career Total	4	0	1	0	681

Going: Sf: 0-0 GS: 0-0 Gd: 0-1 GF: - Fm: 0-0

Distance: 2m/2m3: 0-1 2m4-2m7: 0-0 3m+: 0-0
Track: LH: 0-0 RH: 0-1 Tight: 0-1 Gall: 0-0
Aids: Bl: 0-1 Vi: 0-1 Tstrap: 0-1
Best Rating: 95   1/99   Tntn 2m1f   soft Hdl

Street Magic (IRE)

96   88

6-y-o b m Jolly Jake (NZ)-Corrie s Duchess (IRE) (Burslem)
N A Twiston-Davies The Alchemists

Placings:60F5-23   (1849)
2002/03: 20²G, 22³G,

	Starts	1st	2nd	3rd	Win & Pl
Hurdles	2	0	1	1	1539
Career Total	6	0	1	1	1539

Going: Sf: 0-0 GS: 0-0 Gd: 0-2 GF: - Fm: 0-0
Distance: 2m/2m3: 0-0 2m4-2m7: 0-2 3m+: 0-0
Track: LH: 0-1 RH: 0-1 Tight: 0-0 Gall: 0-0
Aids: Bl: 0-0 Vi: 0-0 Tstrap: 0-0
Best Rating: 88   11/02   Winc 2m6f   good Hdl

Keen sort, modest form over hurdles.

Street Smart (IRE)

94   85

7-y-o gr g Roselier (FR)-College Street (IRE) (Strong Gale)
C J Mann Mrs L G Turner

Placings:00P-00PP   (3778)
2002/03: 24⁵GS, 22⁰HY, 24⁸S, 24⁸GS,

	Starts	1st	2nd	3rd	Win & Pl
Hurdles	4	0	0	0	
Career Total	7	0	0	0	

Going: Sf: 0-2 GS: 0-2 Gd: 0-0 GF: - Fm: 0-0
Distance: 2m/2m3: 0-0 2m4-2m7: 0-1 3m+: 0-3
Track: LH: 0-0 RH: 0-4 Tight: 0-3 Gall: 0-0
Aids: Bl: 0-0 Vi: 0-0 Tstrap: 0-0
Best Rating: 85   12/02   Folk 2m6f110y   heavy Hdl

Street Walker (IRE)

74   63

7-y-o b m Dolphin Street (FR)-Foolish Dame (USA) (Foolish Pleasure (USA))
W Storey D O Cremin

Placings:P500/05/646-00   (2161)
2002/03: 17⁰GS, 17⁰S,

	Starts	1st	2nd	3rd	Win & Pl
Hurdles	2	0	0	0	
Career Total	11	0	0	0	0

Going: Sf: 0-1 GS: 0-1 Gd: 0-0 GF: - Fm: 0-0
Distance: 2m/2m3: 0-2 2m4-2m7: 0-0 3m+: 0-0
Track: LH: 0-2 RH: 0-0 Tight: 0-2 Gall: 0-0
Aids: Bl: 0-0 Vi: 0-0 Tstrap: 0-0
Best Rating: 63   11/01   Sedg 2m1f   soft Hdl

Streetwise Kid (IRE)

4-y-o b g Dolphin Street (FR)-Perfect Answer (Keen)
C Roberts (J Neville 3/1) F J Ayres

	Placings:*00*PU				(4445)

2002/03: 12⁰GS, 16⁶S, 16⁶G, 16⁴G,

	Starts	1st	2nd	3rd	Win & Pl
NH Flat	2	0	0	0	0
Hurdles	2	0	0	0	0
Career Total	4	0	0	0	

Going:	Sf: 0-1 GS: 0-1 Gd: 0-2 GF: - Fm: 0-0
Distance:	2m/2m3: 0-3 2m4-2m7: 0-0 3m+: 0-0
Track:	LH: 0-1 RH: 0-0 Tight: 0-0 Gall: 0-0
Aids:	Bl: 0-0 Vi: 0-0 Tstrap: 0-0
Best Rating:	49 11/02 Newb 1m4f110y gd-sft NHF

Stretching (IRE)

10-y-o br g Contract Law (USA)-Mrs Mutton (Dancer s Image (USA))
Miss Joanne Priest M A Lloyd

Placings:4/P/0050062006342154/0356053360/5 (0416)
2002/03: 24⁵GF,

	Starts	1st	2nd	3rd	Win & Pl
Chases	1	0	0	0	0
Career Total	29	1	2	4	4531
80 2/99 Tntn 2m1f G(0-95)HHdl G-S £1565					
				Total win prize-money £1565	

Going:	Sf: 0-0 GS: 0-0 Gd: 0-0 GF: - Fm: 0-1
Distance:	2m/2m3: 0-0 2m4-2m7: 0-0 3m+: 0-1
Track:	LH: 0-1 RH: 0-0 Tight: 0-0 Gall: 0-0
Aids:	Bl: 0-0 Vi: 0-0 Tstrap: 0-0
Best Rating:	84 11/99 Uttx 2m gd-sft Hdl

Strewth

9-y-o b g Cruise Missile-Storm Foot (Import)
Mrs L Pomfret A Witcomb

Placings:00P/0/P6 (4565)
2002/03: 20⁵GS, 24⁶GF,

	Starts	1st	2nd	3rd	Win & Pl
Chases	2	0	0	0	0
Career Total	6	0	0	0	0

Going:	Sf: 0-0 GS: 0-1 Gd: 0-0 GF: - Fm: 0-1
Distance:	2m/2m3: 0-0 2m4-2m7: 0-1 3m+: 0-1
Track:	LH: 0-1 RH: 0-1 Tight: 0-1 Gall: 0-0
Aids:	Bl: 0-0 Vi: 0-0 Tstrap: 0-0
Best Rating:	76 5/00 Chel 2m5f good Ch

Strictly Speaking (IRE)

100   **102**

6-y-o b g Sri Pekan (USA)-Gaijin (Caerleon (USA))
P F I Cole P F I Cole Ltd

Placings:0340-6P (2307)
2002/03: 19⁶GS, 21⁵PHY,

	Starts	1st	2nd	3rd	Win & Pl
Hurdles	2	0	0	0	0
Career Total	6	0	0	1	682

Going:	Sf: 0-1 GS: 0-1 Gd: 0-0 GF: - Fm: 0-0
Distance:	2m/2m3: 0-1 2m4-2m7: 0-1 3m+: 0-0
Track:	LH: 0-2 RH: 0-0 Tight: 0-0 Gall: 0-1
Aids:	Bl: 0-0 Vi: 0-0 Tstrap: 0-0

Best Rating: 112 1/02 Newb 2m3f gd-sft Hdl

A winner on the Flat, he stays two miles three furlongs over hurdles and acts on good to soft ground.

Stromian House (IRE)

72

7-y-o br g Rock Hopper-Strike Home (Be My Guest (USA))
A D Smith David M Williams

Placings:00/0P-4PP (2334)
2002/03: 22⁴G, 21⁵PS, 22⁵PS,

	Starts	1st	2nd	3rd	Win & Pl
Hurdles	3	0	0	0	0
Career Total	7	0	0	0	0

Going:	Sf: 0-2 GS: 0-0 Gd: 0-1 GF: - Fm: 0-0
Distance:	2m/2m3: 0-0 2m4-2m7: 0-3 3m+: 0-0
Track:	LH: 0-1 RH: 0-2 Tight: 0-1 Gall: 0-0
Aids:	Bl: 0-0 Vi: 0-0 Tstrap: 0-0
Best Rating:	81 5/00 Hntg 2m110y gd-sft NHF

Stromness (USA)

108(113h)   (149 h)**130**

6-y-o ch g Trempolino (USA)-Caithness (USA) (Roberto (USA))
A King Lady Harris

Placings:5225/25112241-613633 (4439)
2002/03: 25⁶GS, 24¹S, 23³GS, 20⁶GS, 24³G, 24³G,

	Starts	1st	2nd	3rd	Win & Pl
Hurdles	6	1	0	3	26686
Career Total	18	4	5	3	88348
149 12/02 Chel 3m B Hdl				SFT £12435	
153 4/02 Aint 3m110y A Hdl				GD £34800	
130 1/02 Kemp 2m5f D Hdl				G-S £5073	
121 1/02 Font 2m6f110yE Hdl				GD £2730	
			Total win prize-money £55039		

Going:	Sf: 1-1 GS: 0-3 Gd: 0-2 GF: - Fm: 0-0
Distance:	2m/2m3: 0-0 2m4-2m7: 0-1 3m+: 1-5
Track:	LH: 1-3 RH: 0-2 Tight: 0-1 Gall: 1-1
Aids:	Bl: 0-0 Vi: 0-0 Tstrap: 0-1
Best Rating:	153 4/02 Aint 3m110y good Hdl

Smart staying hurdler; only small; best recent effort 7l defeat of Rum Pointer (rec 8lb) in Spa Hurdle at Cheltenham in December 2002; has persistently suffered from wind problems and returned after third soft palate operation to win weakly contested four-runner novice chase at Worcester July 2003; suited to 3m; acts on good and soft ground, although better on the former.

Strong Arrow (IRE)

101(95c)   (91c)**87**

10-y-o b g Strong Gale-Caesonia (Buckskin (FR))
J A Supple (Ferdy Murphy 23/11) Geoff Hubbard Racing

Placings:2/6P2/4F21P3F5/P100F/3-202536164 (4279)
2002/03: 23²G, 23⁹G, 24²GF, 24⁵G, 20³S, 20⁶GF, 20¹G, 20⁶GS, 20⁴GF,

	Starts	1st	2nd	3rd	Win & Pl
Hurdles	8	1	2	1	5569
Chases	1	0	0	0	0
Career Total	27	3	5	3	16930
87 10/02 Fknm 2m4f E(0-105)HHdl GD £3711					
121 10/00 Sthl 2m4f110yF(0-110)HCh SFT £2723					
121 1/00 Wwck 2m4f D Ch SFT £4631					
				Total win prize-money £11067	

Going:	Sf: 0-1 GS: 0-1 Gd: 1-4 GF: - Fm: 0-3
Distance:	2m/2m3: 0-0 **2m4-2m7:** 1-6 3m+: 0-3
Track:	**LH: 1-5** RH: 0-2 **Tight: 1-5** Gall: 0-1
Aids:	Bl: 0-0 Vi: 0-0 Tstrap: 0-0
Best Rating:	121 10/00 Sthl 2m4f110y soft Ch

Strong Decision (IRE)

97   **91+**

6-y-o br g Mandalus-Francois s Crumpet (IRE) (Strong Gale)
M C Banks M C Banks

Placings:504-2 (4681)
2002/03: 21²GF,

	Starts	1st	2nd	3rd	Win & Pl
Hurdles	1	0	1	0	1036
Career Total	4	0	1	0	1036

Going:	Sf: 0-0 GS: 0-0 Gd: 0-0 GF: - Fm: 0-1
Distance:	2m/2m3: 0-0 2m4-2m7: 0-1 3m+: 0-0
Track:	LH: 0-0 RH: 0-1 Tight: 0-0 Gall: 0-1
Aids:	Bl: 0-0 Vi: 0-0 Tstrap: 0-0
Best Rating:	108 12/01 Newb 2m110y good NHF

Some ability in bumpers; runner- up in modest event on hurdling bow at Huntingdon in April; should stay well.

Strong Finish

86(96h)   (68h)**74**

8-y-o ch g Montelimar (USA)-Atlantic View (Crash Course)
P W Hiatt Paul Porter

Placings:00P/0400-P45455423 (1482)
2002/03: 22⁵GF, 22⁴GF, 22⁵GS, 24⁴GF, 22⁵GF, 21⁵GF, 21⁴G, 24²GF, 24³GF,

	Starts	1st	2nd	3rd	Win & Pl
Hurdles	5	0	0	0	322
Chases	4	0	1	1	1787
Career Total	16	0	1	1	2109

Going:	Sf: 0-0 GS: 0-1 Gd: 0-1 GF: - Fm: 0-7
Distance:	2m/2m3: 0-0 2m4-2m7: 0-6 3m+: 0-3
Track:	LH: 0-6 RH: 0-3 Tight: 0-6 Gall: 0-2
Aids:	Bl: 0-0 Vi: 0-0 Tstrap: 0-2
Best Rating:	77 7/02 Strf 2m6f110y gd-fm Hdl

Moderate hurdler/chaser.

Strong Flow (IRE)

110(110h)   (130+h)**147+**

6-y-o br g Over The River (FR)-Stormy Skies (Strong Gale)
P F Nicholls B C Marshall

Placings:21 (3852)
2002/03: 24²GS, 24¹GS,

	Starts	1st	2nd	3rd	Win & Pl
Hurdles	2	1	1	0	5309
Career Total	2	1	1	0	5309
130 2/03 Tntn 3m110y E Hdl				G-S £4452	
				Total win prize-money £4453	

Going:	Sf: 0-0 GS: 1-2 Gd: 0-0 GF: - Fm: 0-0
Distance:	2m/2m3: 0-0 2m4-2m7: 0-0 **3m+:** 1-2
Track:	LH: 0-0 **RH: 1-1** Tight: 1-2 Gall: 0-0
Aids:	Bl: 0-0 Vi: 0-0 Tstrap: 0-0
Best Rating:	130 2/03 Tntn 3m110y gd-sft Hdl

Very useful hurdler turned chaser; Irish point winner; did not hang around making the transition from hurdles to fences; easily got off the mark at the second attempt over hurdles in February 2003; has won both starts over fences, the second

one in handicap company; stays three miles plus; acts on good ground; jumps well and is progressive.

Strong King (IRE)

109

(2h)

9-y-o b/br g Strong Gale-Mrs Simpson (Kinglet)
R Ford (Mrs Carrie Ford 12/5) D W Watson

Placings:00/0/0/P-P   (0438)
2002/03: 23PG,

	Starts	1st	2nd	3rd	Win & Pl
Chases	1	0	0	0	
Career Total	5	0	0	0	

Going:	Sf: 0-0 GS: 0-0 Gd: 0-1 GF: - Fm: 0-0
Distance:	2m/2m3: 0-0 2m4-2m7: 0-1 3m+: 0-0
Track:	LH: 0-1 RH: 0-0 Tight: 0-0 Gall: 0-0
Aids:	Bl: 0-0 Vi: 0-1 Tstrap: 0-0
Best Rating:	69 1/01 Ayr 2m4f gd-sft Hdl

Strong Magic (IRE)

111   92

11-y-o br g Strong Gale-Baybush (Boreen (FR))
J R Cornwall   J R Cornwall

Placings:00/5/503040/4536F542/30/B3FB1123220-
5042224405   (4528)
2002/03: 20PS, 24OGS, 244S, 212GF, 202GS, 242GS, 244GS,
234GS, 22OG, 245G,

	Starts	1st	2nd	3rd	Win & Pl
Chases	10	0	3	6	10220
Career Total	40	2	7	5	35033
100 11/01 Aint	3m1f		D(0-115)HCh	G-S	£10627
107 11/01 Hntg	3m		F(0-105)HCh	GD	£2625
				Total win prize-money £13253

Going:	Sf: 0-2 GS: 0-5 Gd: 0-2 GF: - Fm: 0-1
Distance:	2m/2m3: 0-0 2m4-2m7: 0-4 3m+: 0-6
Track:	LH: 0-7 RH: 0-3 Tight: 0-4 Gall: 0-1
Aids:	Bl: 0-0 Vi: 0-0 Tstrap: 0-0
Best Rating:	107 11/01 Hntg 3m good Ch

Modest chaser; stays three miles; best on a sound surface; jumps well generally.

Strong Paladin (IRE)

105   114

12-y-o b g Strong Gale-Kalanshoe (Random Shot)
N A Gaselee   Mrs Angela Brodie

Placings:50/6011/F53332/3F233/32334/312/1224-33614
    (4603)
2002/03: 223G, 243G, 25PGS, 261GF, 264G,

	Starts	1st	2nd	3rd	Win & Pl
Chases	5	1	0	2	8938
Career Total	34	5	6	12	60101
114 3/03 Font	3m2f110yD(0-125)HCh			G-F	£5993
127 10/01 Font	2m6f		D(0-120)HCh	G-S	£6922
109 10/00 Folk	3m1f		F(0-100)HCh	G-F	£2656
110 3/97 Font	2m2f110yE Hdl			G-F	£2385
97 2/97 Tntn	2m3f110yD Hdl			G-S	£2567
				Total win prize-money £20524

Going:	Sf: 0-0 GS: 0-1 Gd: 0-3 GF: - Fm: 1-1
Distance:	2m/2m3: 0-0 2m4-2m7: 0-1 3m+: 1-4
Track:	LH: 0-1 RH: 0-2 Tight: 1-2 Gall: 0-1
Aids:	Bl: 0-0 Vi: 0-0 Tstrap: 0-0
Best Rating:	127 12/01 Kemp 3m good Ch

Fair chaser; a little one-paced; stays 3m 2f; acts on both fast and easy surfaces.

Strong Resolve (IRE)

105   93

7-y-o gr g Roselier (FR)-Farmerette (Teofane)
J Barclay   Nigel Shepherd

Placings:62F3UP50-P333545P541P   (4168)
2002/03: 24PGF, 163G, 223S, 203S, 205HY, 204GS, 165GS, 24PS,
165GS, 204GS, 16¹S, 20PGS,

	Starts	1st	2nd	3rd	Win & Pl
Hurdles	12	1	0	3	4868
Career Total	20	1	1	4	6135
93 3/03 Ayr	2m		F Hdl	SFT	£2670
				Total win prize-money £2671

Going:	Sf: 1-5 GS: 0-5 Gd: 0-1 GF: - Fm: 0-1
Distance:	2m/2m3: 1-4 2m4-2m7: 0-6 3m+: 0-2
Track:	LH: 1-9 RH: 0-3 Tight: 0-2 Gall: 0-1
Aids:	Bl: 0-0 Vi: 0-0 Tstrap: 0-0
Best Rating:	100 12/01 Ayr 2m soft Hdl

Has shown ability in hurdles on soft and fast ground. Stays two and a half miles.

Strong Tartan (IRE)

109(78h)   (90h)108+

9-y-o br g Strong Gale-Kemchee (Kemal (FR))
A Parker   Mr & Mrs Raymond Anderson Green

Placings:0153F/132F-33FP   (4752)
2002/03: 223GF, 253G, 22FS, 24PG,

	Starts	1st	2nd	3rd	Win & Pl
Hurdles	2	0	0	1	530
Chases	2	0	0	1	1042
Career Total	13	2	1	4	9457
103 11/01 Ayr	2m5f110yD(0-110)HCh			GD	£4251
100 1/00 Muss	2m		H NHF	SFT	£1599
				Total win prize-money £5851

Going:	Sf: 0-1 GS: 0-0 Gd: 0-2 GF: - Fm: 0-1
Distance:	2m/2m3: 0-0 2m4-2m7: 0-2 3m+: 0-2
Track:	LH: 0-3 RH: 0-1 Tight: 0-3 Gall: 0-0
Aids:	Bl: 0-0 Vi: 0-0 Tstrap: 0-0
Best Rating:	103 1/02 Muss 3m soft Ch

Modest hurdler/chaser; raised a total of 20lb after back-to-back wins at Hexham and Perth in the summer of 2003; probably only just stays 3m; acts on good to firm and soft ground.

Strong Vision (IRE)

85   109

12-y-o b g Strong Gale-Deep Vision (Deep Run)
K C Bailey   I F W Buchan

Placings:2/F22/32/4PP-32PPP   (0785)
2002/03: 223GS, 23PGF, 26PG, 26PGF, 26PGF,

	Starts	1st	2nd	3rd	Win & Pl
Chases	5	0	1	1	2380
Career Total	14	0	5	2	9939

Going:	Sf: 0-0 GS: 0-1 Gd: 0-1 GF: - Fm: 0-3
Distance:	2m/2m3: 0-2 2m4-2m7: 0-1 3m+: 0-4
Track:	LH: 0-4 RH: 0-1 Tight: 0-1 Gall: 0-0
Aids:	Bl: 0-4 Vi: 0-0 Tstrap: 0-0
Best Rating:	124 3/99 Asct 3m110y gd-fm Ch

Modest chaser; stays three miles; acts on soft, but handles faster ground.

Strongtrooper (IRE)

109   107

8-y-o b g Doubletour (USA)-Moss Gale (Strong Gale)
O Sherwood   Beckwith, Milne, Munro Partnership

Placings:4/10/FPF341F-6   (4694)
2002/03: 216G,

	Starts	1st	2nd	3rd	Win & Pl
Chases	1	0	0	0	0
Career Total	11	2	0	1	8350
89 4/02 Uttx	2m5f		E-Ch	G-S	£4264
106 11/00 Ludl	2m5f		E Hdl	GD	£2723
				Total win prize-money £6987

Going:	Sf: 0-0 GS: 0-0 Gd: 0-1 GF: - Fm: 0-0
Distance:	2m/2m3: 0-0 2m4-2m7: 0-1 3m+: 0-0
Track:	LH: 0-1 RH: 0-0 Tight: 0-1 Gall: 0-0
Aids:	Bl: 0-0 Vi: 0-0 Tstrap: 0-0
Best Rating:	107 4/00 Font 2m2f110y good NHF

Modest but progressive chaser; has had his problems but ran much better when runner-up at Wetherby in May; went one better at Market Rasen the following month; stays well.

Studio Thirty

91   75

11-y-o gr g Rock City-Chepstow Vale (USA) (Key To The Mint (USA))
R J Price   Derek & Cheryl Holder

Placings:5F0P/1165546/146224243/534460PP/05P0/4220-
00P   (4484)
2002/03: 19OG, 16OG, 17PGF,

	Starts	1st	2nd	3rd	Win & Pl
Hurdles	3	0	0	0	
Career Total	39	3	5	2	15153
89 12/98 Hrfd	2m1f		D(0-120)HHdl	G-S	£2731
85 12/97 Hrfd	2m1f		E(0-100)HHdl	SFT	£2934
79 12/97 Hrfd	2m3f110yF(0-100)HHdl			GD	£2122
				Total win prize-money £7787

Going:	Sf: 0-0 GS: 0-0 Gd: 0-2 GF: - Fm: 0-1
Distance:	2m/2m3: 0-2 2m4-2m7: 0-1 3m+: 0-0
Track:	LH: 0-0 RH: 0-3 Tight: 0-0 Gall: 0-1
Aids:	Bl: 0-0 Vi: 0-0 Tstrap: 0-0
Best Rating:	93 5/01 Hrfd 2m3f110y good Hdl

Moderate hurdler; effective between two miles and two miles four; acts on a sound surface.

Sturm Und Drang

99(99h)   (91 h)87+

9-y-o ch g Selkirk (USA)-Historiette (Chief s Crown (USA))
C J Down (J D Frost 22/6) B Reeder

Placings:0006/02-652   (4733)
2002/03: 17PG, 165GF, 162GF,

	Starts	1st	2nd	3rd	Win & Pl
Hurdles	1	0	1	0	1092
Chases	2	0	0	0	
Career Total	9	0	2	0	1968

Going:	Sf: 0-0 GS: 0-0 Gd: 0-1 GF: - Fm: 0-2
Distance:	2m/2m3: 0-3 2m4-2m7: 0-0 3m+: 0-0
Track:	LH: 0-2 RH: 0-1 Tight: 0-1 Gall: 0-0
Aids:	Bl: 0-0 Vi: 0-0 Tstrap: 0-0
Best Rating:	91 4/03 Chep 2m110y gd-fm Hdl

Modest, lightly-raced hurdler; let down by his jumping in a couple of outings over fences for Jimmy Frost summer 2002; jumped better on return to fences when well beaten third at Worcester in July 2003; suited by a sound surface.

Stylino (USA)

89   77

6-y-o ch g Trempolino (USA)-Smartly Styled (USA) (Cox s Ridge (USA))
C C Bealby R S Hunnisett

Placings:0444224P0/425-4PP   (0624)
2002/03: 20⁴GF, 21⁸GS, 17⁶GF,

	Starts	1st	2nd	3rd	Win & Pl
Chases	3	0	0	0	321
Career Total	15	0	3	0	45286

Going:	Sf: 0-0 GS: 0-1 Gd: 0-0 GF: - Fm: 0-2	
Distance:	2m/2m3: 0-1 2m4-2m7: 0-2 3m+: 0-0	
Track:	LH: 0-1 RH: 0-2 Tight: 0-0 Gall: 0-0	
Aids:	Bl: 0-1 Vi: 0-0 Tstrap: 0-1	
Best Rating:	77 6/02 MRas 2m4f gd-fm Ch	

Stylish Fella (USA)

83   65

5-y-o b g Irish River (FR)-Dariela (USA) (Manila (USA))
D G Bridgwater R B Sayers

Placings:4P0-5PP0   (0882)
2002/03: 19⁵GF, 24⁴G, 20⁴G, 16⁹S,

	Starts	1st	2nd	3rd	Win & Pl
Hurdles	4	0	0	0	0
Career Total	7	0	0	0	

Going:	Sf: 0-1 GS: 0-0 Gd: 0-2 GF: - Fm: 0-1	
Distance:	2m/2m3: 0-1 2m4-2m7: 0-0 3m+: 0-0	
Track:	LH: 0-3 RH: 0-1 Tight: 0-2 Gall: 0-0	
Aids:	Bl: 0-2 Vi: 0-0 Tstrap: 0-0	
Best Rating:	65 6/02 Hrfd 2m3f110y gd-fm Hdl	

Suave Frankie

76   77

7-y-o ch g Suave Dancer (USA)-Francia (Legend Of France (USA))
I W McInnes I W McInnes

Placings:P64606205-P   (0186)
2002/03: 20⁵G, 24⁸G,

	Starts	1st	2nd	3rd	Win & Pl
Hurdles	2	0	0	0	
Career Total	10	0	1	0	548

Going:	Sf: 0-0 GS: 0-0 Gd: 0-2 GF: - Fm: 0-0	
Distance:	2m/2m3: 0-0 2m4-2m7: 0-1 3m+: 0-1	
Track:	LH: 0-2 RH: 0-0 Tight: 0-0 Gall: 0-1	
Aids:	Bl: 0-0 Vi: 0-0 Tstrap: 0-0	
Best Rating:	77 4/02 Newc 2m4f good Hdl	

Suba Lin

14-y-o b m Sula Bula-Tula Lin (Tula Rocket)
Mrs C Atyeo Mrs C Atyeo

Placings:P   (0176)
2002/03: 21⁸GF,

	Starts	1st	2nd	3rd	Win & Pl
Chases	1	0	0	0	
Career Total	1	0	0	0	

| Going: | Sf: 0-0 GS: 0-0 Gd: 0-0 GF: - Fm: 0-1 | |

Subiaco (GER)

105   102

6-y-o b h Monsun (GER)-So Sedulous (USA) (The Minstrel (CAN))
B J Curley (A Schutz 26/10) Mrs B J Curley

Placings:5F   (3619)
2002/03: 16⁵GS, 16⁵HY,

	Starts	1st	2nd	3rd	Win & Pl
Hurdles	2	0	0	0	0
Career Total	2	0	0	0	0

Going:	Sf: 0-0 GS: 0-1 Gd: 0-0 GF: - Fm: 0-0	
Distance:	2m/2m3: 0-2 2m4-2m7: 0-0 3m+: 0-0	
Track:	LH: 0-1 RH: 0-1 Tight: 0-0 Gall: 0-1	
Aids:	Bl: 0-0 Vi: 0-0 Tstrap: 0-0	
Best Rating:	102 1/03 Donc 2m110y gd-sft Hdl	

Such Phun

87   61

5-y-o b m Karinga Bay-Bugsy s Sister (Aragon)
J Hetherton Peter Urquhart

Placings:6-503066   (2447)
2002/03: 16⁵G, 17⁰GF, 17³S, 17⁰G, 19⁶G, 21⁶G,

	Starts	1st	2nd	3rd	Win & Pl
NH Flat	2	0	0	0	0
Hurdles	4	0	0	1	650
Career Total	7	0	0	1	650

Going:	Sf: 0-1 GS: 0-0 Gd: 0-4 GF: - Fm: 0-1	
Distance:	2m/2m3: 0-2 2m4-2m7: 0-1 3m+: 0-0	
Track:	LH: 0-3 RH: 0-3 Tight: 0-4 Gall: 0-0	
Aids:	Bl: 0-0 Vi: 0-0 Tstrap: 0-0	
Best Rating:	72 4/02 Hexm 2m110y good NHF	

Suck Your Thumb

9-y-o b m Teenoso (USA)-Onaway (Commanche Run)
N A Twiston-Davies N A Twiston-Davies

Placings:5/PPP-P   (1926)
2002/03: 16⁸GS,

	Starts	1st	2nd	3rd	Win & Pl
Hurdles	1	0	0	0	
Career Total	5	0	0	0	0

Going:	Sf: 0-0 GS: 0-1 Gd: 0-0 GF: - Fm: 0-0	
Distance:	2m/2m3: 0-1 2m4-2m7: 0-0 3m+: 0-0	
Track:	LH: 0-0 RH: 0-1 Tight: 0-0 Gall: 0-0	
Aids:	Bl: 0-0 Vi: 0-0 Tstrap: 0-0	
Best Rating:	100 5/00 Bang 2m1f good NHF	

Sud Bleu (FR)

118   127

5-y-o b g Pistolet Bleu (IRE)-Sudaka (FR) (Garde Royale)
P F Nicholls Barry Marshall & Terry Warner

Placings:043200-13204355   (3894)

Stylino (USA) — continued

Distance:	2m/2m3: 0-0 2m4-2m7: 0-1 3m+: 0-0	
Track:	LH: 0-0 RH: 0-1 Tight: 0-0 Gall: 0-0	
Aids:	Bl: 0-0 Vi: 0-0 Tstrap: 0-0	
Best Rating:	0 5/02 Winc 2m5f gd-fm Ch	

2002/03: 17¹G, 16³G, 16²S, 16⁶S, 17⁴HY, 17³S, 22⁵GS, 18⁵GS,

	Starts	1st	2nd	3rd	Win & Pl
Hurdles	8	1	1	2	13120
Career Total	14	1	2	3	21198
121 10/02 Extr 2m1f   D Hdl   GD £4329
Total win prize-money £4329

Going:	Sf: 0-4 GS: 0-2 Gd: 1-2 GF: - Fm: 0-0	
Distance:	2m/2m3: 1-7 2m4-2m7: 0-1 3m+: 0-0	
Track:	LH: 0-4 RH: 1-4 Tight: 0-2 Gall: 0-2	
Aids:	Bl: 0-0 Vi: 0-0 Tstrap: 0-0	
Best Rating:	127 1/03 Tntn 2m1f soft Hdl	

Decent novice hurdler; ex-French; suited by two miles and acts on soft ground, but looks best on good; consistent but does not find much off the bridle.

Sudden Shock (GER)

104(106h)   (150h)139

8-y-o br g Motley (USA)-Santalina (Relko)
Jonjo O Neill Darren C Mercer

Placings:11/312212/122216126/06PP12-FF34210   (4557)
2002/03: 25⁶G, 20⁵S, 21³GS, 25⁴GS, 24²G, 32¹G, 33⁰G,

	Starts	1st	2nd	3rd	Win & Pl
Hurdles	1	0	0	1	8250
Chases	6	1	1	0	30131
Career Total	30	9	9	2	184885
139 3/03 Chel 4m   B Ch   GD £26100
134 4/02 Aint 3m110y A HHdl GD £23200
11/00 Siro 2m4f   Hdl   HVY £16266
9/00 Maia 2m4f110y   Hdl   GD £35785
5/00 Badn 2m4f165y   Hdl   HVY £9677
11/99 Turi 2m2f   Hdl   SFT £10935
8/99 Gels 2m1f   Hdl   SFT £2708
4/99 Gels 2m   Hdl   HVY £2166
3/99 Gels 2m   Hdl   HVY £2166
Total win prize-money £129003

Going:	Sf: 0-1 GS: 0-2 Gd: 1-4 GF: - Fm: 0-0	
Distance:	2m/2m3: 0-0 2m4-2m7: 0-0 3m+: 1-5	
Track:	LH: 1-3 RH: 0-4 Tight: 0-1 Gall: 1-2	
Aids:	Bl: 0-0 Vi: 0-0 Tstrap: 0-0	
Best Rating:	148 4/02 Sand 3m good Hdl	

Very useful novice chaser, former smart hurdler; confidence seemed to take a knock after falls in first two chases; successful for the first time over fences in National Hunt Challenge Cup at Cheltenham in 2003; stays 4m; acts on good ground and softer.

Suez Tornado (IRE)

10-y-o ch g Mujtahid (USA)-So Stylish (Great Nephew)
K Tork (B R Johnson 12/6) K Tork

Placings:06/B200/022-55PP   (4082)
2002/03: 26²G, 26⁵G, 26⁵G, 20⁰GF, 26⁰S,

	Starts	1st	2nd	3rd	Win & Pl
Chases	5	0	1	0	1040
Career Total	13	0	3	0	3300

Going:	Sf: 0-1 GS: 0-0 Gd: 0-3 GF: - Fm: 0-1	
Distance:	2m/2m3: 0-0 2m4-2m7: 0-1 3m+: 0-4	
Track:	LH: 0-2 RH: 0-2 Tight: 0-5 Gall: 0-0	
Aids:	Bl: 0-5 Vi: 0-0 Tstrap: 0-0	
Best Rating:	84 12/00 Ludl 2m soft Hdl	

Suhail (IRE)

56

7-y-o b g Wolfhound (USA)-Sharayif (IRE) (Green Desert (USA))
Jane Southcombe Mark Savill

Placings:0 (1814)
2002/03: 17⁰G,

	Starts	1st	2nd	3rd	Win & Pl
Hurdles	1	0	0	0	
Career Total	1	0	0	0	

Going:	Sf: 0-0 GS: 0-0 Gd: 0-1 GF: - Fm: 0-0
Distance:	2m/2m3: 0-1 2m4-2m7: 0-0 3m+: 0-0
Track:	LH: 0-0 RH: 0-1 Tight: 0-0 Gall: 0-0
Aids:	Bl: 0-0 Vi: 0-0 Tstrap: 0-1
Best Rating:	0 11/02 Hrfd 2m1f good Hdl

Sulaban

7-y-o b m Sula Bula-Mariban (Mummy s Pet)
B J M Ryall B J M Ryall

Placings:0-PP (4514)
2002/03: 19⁶GS, 22⁸GF,

	Starts	1st	2nd	3rd	Win & Pl
Hurdles	1	0	0	0	
Chases	1	0	0	0	0
Career Total	3	0	0	0	

Going:	Sf: 0-0 GS: 0-1 Gd: 0-0 GF: - Fm: 0-1
Distance:	2m/2m3: 0-0 2m4-2m7: 0-2 3m+: 0-0
Track:	LH: 0-0 RH: 0-2 Tight: 0-0 Gall: 0-0
Aids:	Bl: 0-0 Vi: 0-0 Tstrap: 0-0
Best Rating:	66 11/01 Extr 2m1f gd-fm NHF

Sullane Storm (IRE)

103 **96**

8-y-o b g Glacial Storm (USA)-Heather Point (Pollerton)
M C Pipe Sean Lucey

Placings:0U5433P-PPU011 (4738)
2002/03: 25ᴾGS, 24ᴾGS, 26ᵁGS, 30⁸S, 24¹HY, 24¹GF,

	Starts	1st	2nd	3rd	Win & Pl
Chases	6	2	0	2	7652
Career Total	13	2	0	2	9922
93	4/03	Chep	3m	E(0-110)HCh	G-F	£4221
96	3/03	Tntn	3m	F(0-90)Ch	HVY	£3430
				Total win prize-money £7652		

Going:	Sf: 1-2 GS: 0-3 Gd: 0-0 GF: - Fm: 1-1
Distance:	2m/2m3: 0-0 2m4-2m7: 0-0 3m+: 2-6
Track:	LH: 1-2 RH: 1-4 Tight: 1-1 Gall: 0-0
Aids:	Bl: 0-0 Vi: 0-0 Tstrap: 0-0
Best Rating:	106 12/01 Limk 2m6f heavy Ch

Moderate chaser; ex-Irish; won a weakly contested contest at Taunton March 2003; all out to follow up at Chepstow on fast ground the following month; inclined to make mistakes; acts on soft ground.

Sullys Hope

115 **118**

6-y-o b g Rock Hopper-Super Sally (Superlative)
Nick Williams Mrs Jane Kelly

Placings:PP0F/0202321341010-0P434 (2468)
2002/03: 16⁰G, 19ᴾG, 16⁴G, 16³S, 17⁶G,

	Starts	1st	2nd	3rd	Win & Pl
Hurdles	5	0	0	1	3706
Career Total	22	3	3	3	20712
115	3/02	Strf	2m110y	D(0-125)HHdl	G-S	£7514
115	12/01	Strf	2m110y	D Hdl	SFT	£3822
106	11/01	Strf	2m110y	F(0-100)HHdl	SFT	£2765
				Total win prize-money £14101		

Going:	Sf: 0-1 GS: 0-0 Gd: 0-4 GF: - Fm: 0-0
Distance:	2m/2m3: 0-2 2m4-2m7: 0-3 3m+: 0-0
Track:	LH: 0-5 RH: 0-0 Tight: 0-1 Gall: 0-2
Aids:	Bl: 0-0 Vi: 0-0 Tstrap: 0-0
Best Rating:	118 12/02 Chel 2m1f good Hdl

Fair chaser; a different horse at Stratford and has gained all three of his wins there. Suited by two miles and soft ground.

Sulphur Springs (IRE)

107 **145**

11-y-o ch g Don t Forget Me-Short Wave (FR) (Trepan (FR))
M C Pipe P A D Scouller

Placings:0/056P25/22F3P22/45533/066/1/PS1111161-30P (1335)
2002/03: 24³GF, 28⁹GF, 20ᴾGF,

	Starts	1st	2nd	3rd	Win & Pl
Chases	3	0	0	1	1308
Career Total	35	7	5	4	113669
145	4/02	Strf	2m4f	C(0-130)HCh	GD	£7124
140	9/01	MRas	2m6f110yCh	SFT	£7665
130	9/01	NAbb	3m2f110yD(0-120)HCh	G-F	£3997
130	7/01	Strf	3m	E(0-115)HCh	GD	£4920
135	4/01	MRas	2m6f110yE(0-105)HCh	G-F	£4160
121	6/01	Strf	3m	H Ch	G-F	£1337
100	4/01	MRas	2m6f110yH Ch	G-S	£1266
				Total win prize-money £30471		

Going:	Sf: 0-0 GS: 0-0 Gd: 0-0 GF: - Fm: 0-3
Distance:	2m/2m3: 0-0 2m4-2m7: 0-1 3m+: 0-2
Track:	LH: 0-2 RH: 0-1 Tight: 0-2 Gall: 0-1
Aids:	Bl: 0-0 Vi: 0-0 Tstrap: 0-3
Best Rating:	145 4/02 Strf 2m4f good Ch

Very useful handicap chaser. Won six times in 2001, lightly-raced since. Acts on most types of ground and stays three miles.

Sumboy (IRE)

9-y-o gr g Aristocracy-Sign O The Season (Strong Gale)
J F Panvert J F Panvert

Placings:5PPBPP-P (0114)
2002/03: 25ᴾGS,

	Starts	1st	2nd	3rd	Win & Pl
Chases	1	0	0	0	
Career Total	7	0	0	0	0

Going:	Sf: 0-0 GS: 0-1 Gd: 0-0 GF: - Fm: 0-0
Distance:	2m/2m3: 0-0 2m4-2m7: 0-0 3m+: 0-1
Track:	LH: 0-0 RH: 0-1 Tight: 0-0 Gall: 0-0
Aids:	Bl: 0-0 Vi: 0-0 Tstrap: 0-0
Best Rating:	0 5/02 Towc 3m1f gd-sft Ch

Summer Bounty

102 **93**

7-y-o b g Lugana Beach-Tender Moment (IRE) (Caerleon (USA))
F Jordan Tim Powell

Placings:55P/24/000-40F (2112)
2002/03: 16⁴G, 16⁹GS, 20⁶G,

	Starts	1st	2nd	3rd	Win & Pl
Hurdles	3	0	0	0	271
Career Total	11	0	1	0	1046

Going:	Sf: 0-0 GS: 0-1 Gd: 0-2 GF: - Fm: 0-0
Distance:	2m/2m3: 0-2 2m4-2m7: 0-1 3m+: 0-0
Track:	LH: 0-3 RH: 0-0 Tight: 0-0 Gall: 0-0
Aids:	Bl: 0-0 Vi: 0-0 Tstrap: 0-0
Best Rating:	93 11/02 Chel 2m110y gd-sft Hdl

Ineffective over hurdles.

Summer Break (IRE)

74 **70**

6-y-o ch m Foxhound (USA)-Out In The Sun (USA) (It s Freezing (USA))
Anthony Mullins (W J Musson 5/12) Mrs A F Mee

Placings:131/5000000-P4 (2315)
2002/03: 16⁰G, 20⁴HY,

	Starts	1st	2nd	3rd	Win & Pl
Hurdles	2	0	0	0	0
Career Total	12	2	0	1	7658
111	1/01	Fknm	2m	D Hdl	SFT	£3265
110	11/00	Clon	2m	Hdl	HVY	£3312
				Total win prize-money £6578		

Going:	Sf: 0-1 GS: 0-0 Gd: 0-1 GF: - Fm: 0-0
Distance:	2m/2m3: 0-1 2m4-2m7: 0-1 3m+: 0-0
Track:	LH: 0-1 RH: 0-1 Tight: 0-0 Gall: 0-0
Aids:	Bl: 0-0 Vi: 0-0 Tstrap: 0-0
Best Rating:	111 1/01 Fknm 2m soft Hdl

Plating-class hurdler. Acts well on a soft surface and is effective at around two miles, but well beaten in 2001/2.

Summer Cherry (USA)

79 **77**

6-y-o b g Summer Squall (USA)-Cherryrob (USA) (Roberto (USA))
Jamie Poulton Jamie Poulton

Placings:0/0-0 (1723)
2002/03: 16⁹GS,

	Starts	1st	2nd	3rd	Win & Pl
Hurdles	1	0	0	0	
Career Total	3	0	0	0	

Going:	Sf: 0-0 GS: 0-1 Gd: 0-0 GF: - Fm: 0-0
Distance:	2m/2m3: 0-0 2m4-2m7: 0-0 3m+: 0-0
Track:	LH: 0-0 RH: 0-1 Tight: 0-0 Gall: 0-0
Aids:	Bl: 0-0 Vi: 0-0 Tstrap: 0-0
Best Rating:	82 1/01 Kemp 2m soft Hdl

Summer Villa

85 **34**

11-y-o b m Nomination-Maravilla (Mandrake Major)
K G Wingrove A F Maiden

Placings:00/33202532/235501442306/5U2060/00-00 (0778)
2002/03: 16⁰S, 16⁰GF,

	Starts	1st	2nd	3rd	Win & Pl
Hurdles	2	0	0	0	

Career Total	32	1	6	5	6509
79 8/97 MRas 2m1f110y				F(0-100)HHdl	
G-F £1982					

Total win prize-money £1982

Going: Sf: 0-1 GS: 0-0 Gd: 0-0 GF: - Fm: 0-1
Distance: 2m/2m3: 0-0 2m4-2m7: 0-0 3m+: 0-0
Track: LH: 0-2 RH: 0-0 Tight: 0-0 Gall: 0-0
Aids: Bl: 0-1 Vi: 0-0 Tstrap: 0-1
Best Rating: 81 5/97 Wwck 2m   gd-fm Hdl

Sumut

67f   82f

4-y-o b g Hamas (IRE)-Simaat (USA) (Mr Prospector (USA))
G A Swinbank Elsa Crankshaw & G Allan Ii

Placings:0   (3775)
2002/03: 16⁰GS,

	Starts	1st	2nd	3rd	Win & Pl
NH Flat	1	0	0	0	
Career Total	1	0	0	0	

Going: Sf: 0-0 GS: 0-1 Gd: 0-0 GF: - Fm: 0-0
Distance: 2m/2m3: 0-1 2m4-2m7: 0-0 3m+: 0-0
Track: LH: 0-1 RH: 0-0 Tight: 0-0 Gall: 0-0
Aids: Bl: 0-0 Vi: 0-0 Tstrap: 0-0
Best Rating: 82 2/03 Ayr 2m   gd-sft NHF

Sun Bird (IRE)

108   113

5-y-o ch g Prince Of Birds (USA)-Summer Fashion
(Moorestyle)
R Allan Mrs R P Aggio

Placings:2   (1911)
2002/03: 16²S,

	Starts	1st	2nd	3rd	Win & Pl
Hurdles	1	0	1	0	1132
Career Total	1	0	1	0	1132

Going: Sf: 0-1 GS: 0-0 Gd: 0-0 GF: - Fm: 0-0
Distance: 2m/2m3: 0-1 2m4-2m7: 0-0 3m+: 0-0
Track: LH: 0-1 RH: 0-0 Tight: 0-0 Gall: 0-0
Aids: Bl: 0-0 Vi: 0-0 Tstrap: 0-0
Best Rating: 113 11/02 Kels 2m110y   soft Hdl

Useful novice hurdler; good debut performance when runner-up at Kelso in November and has twice run well there since; effective at two miles; acts on fast ground.

Sun King

106   107

6-y-o ch g Zilzal (USA)-Opus One (Slip Anchor)
Mrs M Reveley The Mary Reveley Racing Club

Placings:4/21S015-11232P0   (4524)
2002/03: 16¹GF, 16¹G, 17²GF, 20³GF, 17²GS, 19³GS, 16⁰G,

	Starts	1st	2nd	3rd	Win & Pl
Hurdles	7	2	2	1	10127
Career Total	14	4	3	1	15938
86 5/02 Towc 2m			D Hdl	GD	£3150
107 5/02 Weth 2m			E Hdl	G-F	£2562
96 4/02 MRas 2m3f110y			D Hdl	G-F	£3780
94 6/01 Worc 2m			H NHF	G-F	£1536

Total win prize-money £11029

Going: Sf: 0-0 GS: 0-2 Gd: 1-2 GF: - Fm: 1-3
Distance: 2m/2m3: 2-6 2m4-2m7: 0-1 3m+: 0-0
Track: LH: 1-4 RH: 1-3 Tight: 0-3 Gall: 0-0

Aids: Bl: 0-0 Vi: 0-0 Tstrap: 0-0
Best Rating: 107 8/02 MRas 2m1f110y gd-sft Hdl

Fair novice hurdler, effective on fast ground and stays two and a half miles.

Sunczech (IRE)

13-y-o b m Sunyboy-Miss Prague (Mon Capitaine)
Mrs S S Harbour S C Clark

Placings:3/P/654   (4216)
2002/03: 24⁶G, 20⁵GS, 20⁴G,

	Starts	1st	2nd	3rd	Win & Pl
Chases	3	0	0	0	0
Career Total	5	0	0	1	148

Going: Sf: 0-0 GS: 0-1 Gd: 0-2 GF: - Fm: 0-0
Distance: 2m/2m3: 0-0 2m4-2m7: 0-2 3m+: 0-1
Track: LH: 0-1 RH: 0-1 Tight: 0-2 Gall: 0-0
Aids: Bl: 0-1 Vi: 0-0 Tstrap: 0-0
Best Rating: 85 2/99 Folk 2m5f   gd-sft Ch

Sundance Sid (IRE)

84   65

7-y-o b g Phardante (FR)-The Kid s Sister (Black Minstrel)
Miss E C Lavelle Remenham Racing

Placings:0PF0060-0   (0200)
2002/03: 16⁰GF,

	Starts	1st	2nd	3rd	Win & Pl
Hurdles	1	0	0	0	
Career Total	8	0	0	0	0

Going: Sf: 0-0 GS: 0-0 Gd: 0-0 GF: - Fm: 0-1
Distance: 2m/2m3: 0-1 2m4-2m7: 0-0 3m+: 0-0
Track: LH: 0-1 RH: 0-0 Tight: 0-0 Gall: 0-0
Aids: Bl: 0-0 Vi: 0-1 Tstrap: 0-0
Best Rating: 65 4/02 Extr 2m1f   firm Hdl

Sundawn Lady

95   86

5-y-o b m Faustus (USA)-Game Domino (Derring Rose)
C P Morlock Michael Padfield & Philip Dean

Placings:00225   (4681)
2002/03: 16⁰S, 17⁵S, 20²G, 22²GF, 21⁵GF,

	Starts	1st	2nd	3rd	Win & Pl
NH Flat	2	0	0	0	0
Hurdles	3	0	2	0	2401
Career Total	5	0	2	0	2401

Going: Sf: 0-2 GS: 0-0 Gd: 0-1 GF: - Fm: 0-2
Distance: 2m/2m3: 0-2 2m4-2m7: 0-3 3m+: 0-0
Track: LH: 0-1 RH: 0-3 Tight: 0-2 Gall: 0-1
Aids: Bl: 0-0 Vi: 0-0 Tstrap: 0-0
Best Rating: 86 4/03 Strf 2m6f110y gd-fm Hdl

Plating-class hurdler; appears suited by a sound surface; effective at around two miles six.

Sunday Habits (IRE)

105   88+

9-y-o ch g Montelimar (USA)-Robertina (USA) (Roberto (USA))
D P Keane D P Keane

Aids: Bl: 0-0 Vi: 0-0 Tstrap: 0-0
Best Rating: 107 8/02 MRas 2m1f110y gd-sft Hdl

Placings:400/0P05-1U					(4702)
2002/03: 26¹GF, 26ᵁGF,					

	Starts	1st	2nd	3rd	Win & Pl
Chases	2	1	0	0	3159
Career Total	9	1	0	0	3351
81 4/03 Plum 3m2f			F(0-95)HCh	G-F	£3159

Total win prize-money £3159

Going: Sf: 0-0 GS: 0-0 Gd: 0-0 GF: - Fm: 1-2
Distance: 2m/2m3: 0-0 2m4-2m7: 0-0 3m+: 1-2
Track: LH: 1-2 RH: 0-0 Tight: 1-2 Gall: 0-0
Aids: Bl: 0-0 Vi: 0-0 Tstrap: 0-0
Best Rating: 81 4/03 Plum 3m2f   gd-fm Ch

Plating-class chaser; won weak Plumpton event on British debut in April 2003 after showing limited ability in Ireland; stays three miles two.

Sunday Rain (USA)

103(110h)   (102h)97+

6-y-o b g Summer Squall (USA)-Oxava (FR) (Antheus (USA))
Miss Lucinda V Russell Peter K Dale Ltd

Placings:233P0/352400-1331230305   (4591)
2002/03: 16¹G, 20³S, 16⁴G, 16¹GF, 16²GF, 16³GF, 16⁰G, 20³GS, 19⁰GS, 16⁵G,

	Starts	1st	2nd	3rd	Win & Pl
Hurdles	10	2	1	4	10171
Career Total	21	2	3	7	17817
97 6/02 Hexm 2m110y D Hdl				G-F	£3472
98 4/02 Hexm 2m110y E Hdl				GD	£2604

Total win prize-money £6076

Going: Sf: 0-1 GS: 0-2 Gd: 1-4 GF: - Fm: 1-3
Distance: 2m/2m3: 2-7 2m4-2m7: 0-3 3m+: 0-0
Track: LH: 2-10 RH: 0-0 Tight: 0-2 Gall: 0-1
Aids: Bl: 0-0 Vi: 0-0 Tstrap: 0-0
Best Rating: 111 12/00 Chel 2m1f   soft Hdl

Moderate chaser/fair handicap hurdler; tried in chases recently; best at around two miles, seems to act on ground good or faster.

Sungates (IRE)

88   77

7-y-o ch g Glacial Storm (USA)-Live It Up (Le Coq D Or)
A J Lidderdale Team George Ii

Placings:2-65   (2079)
2002/03: 24⁶S, 24⁵HY,

	Starts	1st	2nd	3rd	Win & Pl
Hurdles	2	0	0	0	0
Career Total	3	0	1	0	559

Going: Sf: 0-2 GS: 0-0 Gd: 0-0 GF: - Fm: 0-0
Distance: 2m/2m3: 0-0 2m4-2m7: 0-0 3m+: 0-0
Track: LH: 0-1 RH: 0-1 Tight: 0-0 Gall: 0-0
Aids: Bl: 0-0 Vi: 0-0 Tstrap: 0-0
Best Rating: 95 5/01 Hrfd 2m1f   good NHF

Sungio

103   104

5-y-o b g Halling (USA)-Time Or Never (FR) (Dowsing (USA))
B G Powell Mrs Rachel A Powell

Placings:660-P41PP4P   (2307)
2002/03: 17⁵GF, 16⁴G, 20¹G, 19³G, 21³PG, 18⁴GS, 21⁵HY,

	Starts	1st	2nd	3rd	Win & Pl
Hurdles	7	1	0	0	3136

Career Total	10	1	0	0	3136
104 10/02 Font	2m4f	F Hdl		GD	£3136

Total win prize-money £3136

Going: Sf: 0-1 GS: 0-1 Gd: 1-4 GF: - Fm: 0-1
Distance: 2m/2m3: 0-4 **2m4-2m7: 1-3** 3m+: 0-0
Track: LH: 0-4 RH: 0-2 **Tight: 1-4** Gall: 0-0
Aids: Bl: 0-0 Vi: 0-0 Tstrap: 0-0
Best Rating: 104 11/02 Font 2m2f110y gd-sft Hdl

Moderate novice hurdler. Off the mark in weak race at Fontwell in October. Stays two and a half miles.

Sunlit Boy

11-y-o ch g Ardross-Sunlit River (Roi Soleil)
J J Bridger J J Bridger

Placings:5PP/P3P0/0P (4080)
2002/03: 20⁰GS, 26ᴾS,

	Starts	1st	2nd	3rd	Win & Pl
Chases	2	0	0	0	
Career Total	9	0	0	1	650

Going: Sf: 0-1 GS: 0-1 Gd: 0-0 GF: - Fm: 0-0
Distance: 2m/2m3: 0-0 2m4-2m7: 0-1 3m+: 0-1
Track: LH: 0-1 RH: 0-1 Tight: 0-1 Gall: 0-0
Aids: Bl: 0-0 Vi: 0-0 Tstrap: 0-0
Best Rating: 92 12/98 Wwck 2m soft NHF

Sunne Lord (IRE)
78   68

6-y-o b g Mister Lord (USA)-Happy Party (Invited (USA))
A King Mrs S Warren

Placings:000 (4482)
2002/03: 16⁰S, 17⁰S, 19⁰GF,

	Starts	1st	2nd	3rd	Win & Pl
NH Flat	2	0	0	0	0
Hurdles	1	0	0	0	0
Career Total	3	0	0	0	

Going: Sf: 0-2 GS: 0-0 Gd: 0-0 GF: - Fm: 0-1
Distance: 2m/2m3: 0-2 2m4-2m7: 0-1 3m+: 0-0
Track: LH: 0-1 RH: 0-0 Tight: 0-0 Gall: 0-0
Aids: Bl: 0-0 Vi: 0-0 Tstrap: 0-0
Best Rating: 87 12/02 Wwck 2m soft NHF

Sunny Sombrero
70f   58f

6-y-o b m Contract Law (USA)-Vitry (Vitiges (FR))
Dr P Pritchard B S Hicks

Placings:00 (0724)
2002/03: 16⁰GF, 16⁰G,

	Starts	1st	2nd	3rd	Win & Pl
NH Flat	2	0	0	0	
Career Total	2	0	0	0	

Going: Sf: 0-0 GS: 0-0 Gd: 0-0 GF: - Fm: 0-1
Distance: 2m/2m3: 0-2 2m4-2m7: 0-0 3m+: 0-0
Track: LH: 0-2 RH: 0-0 Tight: 0-0 Gall: 0-0
Aids: Bl: 0-0 Vi: 0-0 Tstrap: 0-0
Best Rating: 58 7/02 Worc 2m good NHF

Sunnyarjun
88   65

5-y-o ch g Afzal-Hush Tina (Tina s Pet)
J C Tuck J C Tuck

Placings:000 (4635)
2002/03: 16⁰GS, 16⁰G, 19⁰GF,

	Starts	1st	2nd	3rd	Win & Pl
NH Flat	1	0	0	0	0
Hurdles	2	0	0	0	0
Career Total	3	0	0	0	

Going: Sf: 0-0 GS: 0-1 Gd: 0-1 GF: - Fm: 0-1
Distance: 2m/2m3: 0-3 2m4-2m7: 0-0 3m+: 0-0
Track: LH: 0-1 RH: 0-2 Tight: 0-1 Gall: 0-0
Aids: Bl: 0-0 Vi: 0-0 Tstrap: 0-0
Best Rating: 73 1/03 Kemp 2m gd-sft NHF

Sunnyside Royale (IRE)
85   61

4-y-o b g Ali-Royal (IRE)-Kuwah (IRE) (Be My Guest (USA))
M W Easterby S Durkin, P Earnshaw & J Greenan

Placings:00 (2182)
2002/03: 16⁰G, 16⁰GS,

	Starts	1st	2nd	3rd	Win & Pl
Hurdles	2	0	0	0	
Career Total	2	0	0	0	

Going: Sf: 0-0 GS: 0-1 Gd: 0-1 GF: - Fm: 0-0
Distance: 2m/2m3: 0-2 2m4-2m7: 0-0 3m+: 0-0
Track: LH: 0-2 RH: 0-0 Tight: 0-0 Gall: 0-0
Aids: Bl: 0-0 Vi: 0-0 Tstrap: 0-0
Best Rating: 61 11/02 Hayd 2m good Hdl

Sunridge Fairy (IRE)
107   93

4-y-o b f Definite Article-Foxy Fairy (IRE) (Fairy King (USA))
Ronald Thompson (Miss K Marks 23/11) J B Slatcher

Placings:111411405 (4262)
2002/03: 17¹G, 17¹G, 17¹GF, 16⁴G, 16¹HY, 16¹G, 17⁴HY, 16⁰GS, 17⁵G,

	Starts	1st	2nd	3rd	Win & Pl
Hurdles	9	5	0	0	13597
Career Total	9	5	0	0	13597

93	11/02	Catt	2m	G Hdl	GD	£2009
91	11/02	Leic	2m	G Hdl	HVY	£2268
93	9/02	Hrfd	2m1f	G Hdl	G-F	£2124
98	8/02	Ctml	2m1f110yE Hdl		GD	£3472
88	8/02	Sedg	2m1f	E Hdl	GD	£2968

Total win prize-money £12842

Going: Sf: 1-2 GS: 0-1 Gd: 3-5 GF: - Fm: 1-1
Distance: **2m/2m3: 5-9** 2m4-2m7: 0-0 3m+: 0-0
Track: **LH: 3-7** RH: 2-2 **Tight: 3-6** Gall: 0-1
Aids: Bl: 0-0 Vi: 0-0 Tstrap: 0-0
Best Rating: 98 8/02 Ctml 2m1f110y good Hdl

Moderate hurdler; dual selling winner on the All-Weather, made a successful bow over hurdles at Sedgefield in August and followed up in game fashion at Cartmel in August. Again gave her all when completing the hat-trick in a seller at Hereford in September, after which she was sold. Held in a better race on her first start for her new yard before winning sellers at Leicester and Catterick in November after which she changed stables for a third time.

Sunridge Rose
80   42

5-y-o b m Piccolo-Floral Spark (Forzando)
Andrew Reid A S Reid

Placings:P-0PP (0269)
2002/03: 17⁰G, 16ᴾGF, 16ᴾGF,

	Starts	1st	2nd	3rd	Win & Pl
Hurdles	3	0	0	0	
Career Total	4	0	0	0	

Going: Sf: 0-0 GS: 0-0 Gd: 0-1 GF: - Fm: 0-2
Distance: 2m/2m3: 0-3 2m4-2m7: 0-0 3m+: 0-0
Track: LH: 0-2 RH: 0-1 Tight: 0-2 Gall: 0-0
Aids: Bl: 0-0 Vi: 0-0 Tstrap: 0-0
Best Rating: 42 5/02 Folk 2m1f110y good Hdl

Sunrise Special (IRE)

10-y-o b g Petorius-Break Of Day (On Your Mark)
P R Rodford Mrs G Landrigan And R Scott

Placings:043FF6211/2620321332/FP4P1311F2/PP053/P (1839)
2002/03: 24ᴾS,

	Starts	1st	2nd	3rd	Win & Pl
Chases	1	0	0	0	
Career Total	35	6	6	6	42650

125	3/00	Chep	2m3f110yC(0-135)HCh	G-S	£10478
125	3/00	Chep	2m3f110yD(0-120)HCh	HVY	£3757
108	1/00	Tntn	2m3f	D(0-110)HCh	G-S	£4309
109	3/99	Extr	2m1f110yD(0-120)HHdl	SFT	£2786
96	4/98	Extr	2m3f110yE(0-110)HHdl	SFT	£2802
101	4/98	Extr	2m2f	E(0-100)HHdl	SFT	£2448

Total win prize-money £26582

Going: Sf: 0-1 GS: 0-0 Gd: 0-0 GF: - Fm: 0-0
Distance: 2m/2m3: 0-0 2m4-2m7: 0-0 3m+: 0-1
Track: LH: 0-1 RH: 0-0 Tight: 0-0 Gall: 0-0
Aids: Bl: 0-1 Vi: 0-0 Tstrap: 0-0
Best Rating: 125 3/00 Chep 2m3f110y gd-sft Ch

Sunshan

7-y-o b g Anshan-Kyrenia Sunset (CYP) (Lucky Look (CYP))
T Long Unity Farm Holiday Centre Ltd

Placings:60/6565 (4678)
2002/03: 20⁶G, 19⁵F, 19⁶G, 19⁵GF,

	Starts	1st	2nd	3rd	Win & Pl
Chases	4	0	0	0	0
Career Total	6	0	0	0	0

Going: Sf: 0-0 GS: 0-0 Gd: 0-2 GF: - Fm: 0-2
Distance: 2m/2m3: 0-1 2m4-2m7: 0-3 3m+: 0-0
Track: LH: 0-0 RH: 0-3 Tight: 0-1 Gall: 0-0
Aids: Bl: 0-0 Vi: 0-0 Tstrap: 0-2
Best Rating: 79 4/03 Asct 2m3f110y good Ch

Sunshine Boy
81 (107h)   (94h) 60

7-y-o b g Cadeaux Genereux-Sahara Baladee (USA) (Shadeed (USA))
Miss E C Lavelle David Cliff And Philippa Clunes

Placings:P0/51122/26-P3P   (4692)
2002/03: 22PGS, 18JG, 22PG,

	Starts	1st	2nd	3rd	Win & Pl
Hurdles	3	0	0	1	782
Career Total	12	2	3	1	9065
100 6/00 Fknm	2m7f110yF(0-100)HHdl		GD		£2671
93 5/00 Worc	2m4f	F(0-100)HHdl	GD		£2065

Total win prize-money £4737

Going:	Sf: 0-0 GS: 0-1 Gd: 0-2 GF: - Fm: 0-0
Distance:	2m/2m3: 0-1 2m4-2m7: 0-2 3m+: 0-0
Track:	LH: 0-2 RH: 0-1 Tight: 0-0 Gall: 0-0
Aids:	Bl: 0-0 Vi: 0-0 Tstrap: 0-0
Best Rating:	100 7/01 Worc 3m good Hdl

Moderate hurdler; stays 3m; suited by a decent surface.

Sunshine Heights
79f   62f
6-y-o b m Golden Heights-Turners Keep (Just A Monarch)
P R Hedger Chris Silverthorne

Placings:66   (1201)
2002/03: 16GF, 17GF,

	Starts	1st	2nd	3rd	Win & Pl
NH Flat	2	0	0	0	0
Career Total	2	0	0	0	0

Going:	Sf: 0-0 GS: 0-0 Gd: 0-0 GF: - Fm: 0-2
Distance:	2m/2m3: 0-2 2m4-2m7: 0-0 3m+: 0-0
Track:	LH: 0-1 RH: 0-1 Tight: 0-0 Gall: 0-0
Aids:	Bl: 0-0 Vi: 0-0 Tstrap: 0-0
Best Rating:	70 8/02 Worc 2m gd-fm NHF

Sunshine Leader (IRE)
108(106h)   (100h)100
8-y-o b m Supreme Leader-Cherry Run (Deep Run)
E L James Mrs D C Samworth

Placings:1232/231330-236   (2762)
2002/03: 16²HY, 25³S, 24⁶S,

	Starts	1st	2nd	3rd	Win & Pl
Chases	3	0	1	1	1992
Career Total	13	2	4	5	14658
100 12/01 Leic	2m4f110yD Hdl		SFT		£3562
87 6/00 Cork	2m4f	NHF	GD		£3864

Total win prize-money £7426

Going:	Sf: 0-3 GS: 0-0 Gd: 0-0 GF: - Fm: 0-0
Distance:	2m/2m3: 0-1 2m4-2m7: 0-0 3m+: 0-2
Track:	LH: 0-2 RH: 0-1 Tight: 0-1 Gall: 0-0
Aids:	Bl: 0-0 Vi: 0-0 Tstrap: 0-0
Best Rating:	100 11/02 Weth 2m heavy Ch

Moderate hurdler; strongly-made mare, very consistent, but has only a solitary victory at Leicester in December 2001 to her name since arriving from Ireland. Stays two and a half miles. Failed the stamina test of three miles one on her second run over fences. Has won on good and acts on soft ground.

Suntas (IRE)
89(92h)   (98h)112
8-y-o b m Riberetto-Shuil (IRE) (Meneval (USA))
T R George Mr & Mrs D A Gamble

Placings:0/32244/42214P2-140PP   (4151)
2002/03: 30¹GS, 32⁴GS, 26⁶S, 29⁴GS, 29⁷G,

	Starts	1st	2nd	3rd	Win & Pl
Chases	5	1	0	0	9424

Career Total	18	2	5	1	24456
120 11/02 Hntg	3m6f110yD(0-120)HCh		G-S		£8631
115 1/02 Hntg	3m	E Ch		G-S	£3164

Total win prize-money £11795

Going:	Sf: 0-1 GS: 1-3 Gd: 0-1 GF: - Fm: 0-0
Distance:	2m/2m3: 0-0 2m4-2m7: 0-0 3m+: 1-5
Track:	LH: 0-3 RH: 1-2 Tight: 0-0 Gall: 1-2
Aids:	Bl: 0-0 Vi: 0-0 Tstrap: 0-0
Best Rating:	120 11/02 Hntg 3m6f110y gd-sft Ch

Fair chaser; she stays very well over fences; suited by good to soft ground.

Sunuvugun
100   64
11-y-o b g Gunner B-Final Melody (Final Straw)
Mrs D Thomson Discounted Cashflow

Placings:3PP/2043/15P/PFP24P/PPP-P54P   (0695)
2002/03: 25PGS, 25⁵GF, 20⁴GS, 22PG,

	Starts	1st	2nd	3rd	Win & Pl
Chases	4	0	0	0	521
Career Total	23	1	2	2	6574
88 9/99 Kels	3m1f	E Ch		G-F	£2786

Total win prize-money £2786

Going:	Sf: 0-0 GS: 0-2 Gd: 0-1 GF: - Fm: 0-0
Distance:	2m/2m3: 0-0 2m4-2m7: 0-2 3m+: 0-0
Track:	LH: 0-2 RH: 0-2 Tight: 0-2 Gall: 0-0
Aids:	Bl: 0-0 Vi: 0-0 Tstrap: 0-0
Best Rating:	94 12/97 Hntg 2m110y gd-sft NHF

Super Blue (IRE)
6-y-o b m Supreme Leader-Tip Marie (IRE) (Celio Rufo)
P F Nicholls Mrs Angela Tincknell

Placings:06P   (3147)
2002/03: 17⁰G, 17⁶HY, 24PHY,

	Starts	1st	2nd	3rd	Win & Pl
NH Flat	2	0	0	0	0
Hurdles	1	0	0	0	0
Career Total	3	0	0	0	0

Going:	Sf: 0-2 GS: 0-0 Gd: 0-1 GF: - Fm: 0-0
Distance:	2m/2m3: 0-0 2m4-2m7: 0-0 3m+: 0-1
Track:	LH: 0-2 RH: 0-1 Tight: 0-1 Gall: 0-0
Aids:	Bl: 0-0 Vi: 0-0 Tstrap: 0-0
Best Rating:	75 10/02 Extr 2m1f good NHF

Super Dollar (IRE)
100(104h)   (104h)105
7-y-o ch g Great Commotion (USA)-L Americaine (USA) (Verbatim (USA))
K C Bailey The Not Over Big Partnership

Placings:66441/B230043/51505-3F   (0513)
2002/03: 17³GF, 16⁵S,

	Starts	1st	2nd	3rd	Win & Pl
Chases	2	0	0	1	748
Career Total	19	2	1	3	9732
104 6/01 Strf	2m3f	F(0-110)HHdl	G-F		£3262
105 4/00 Fknm	2m	D(0-110)HHdl	GD		£2837

Total win prize-money £6099

Going:	Sf: 0-1 GS: 0-0 Gd: 0-0 GF: - Fm: 0-1
Distance:	2m/2m3: 0-2 2m4-2m7: 0-0 3m+: 0-0
Track:	LH: 0-2 RH: 0-0 Tight: 0-1 Gall: 0-0
Aids:	Bl: 0-0 Vi: 0-0 Tstrap: 0-0

| Best Rating: | 105 5/02 Strf 2m1f110y gd-fm Ch |

A winner over hurdles and acts on a sound surface. Effective at around two and a half miles.

Super Dolphin
97   73
4-y-o ch g Dolphin Street (FR)-Supergreen (Superlative)
T P Tate T P Tate

Placings:00066   (4669)
2002/03: 16⁰S, 16⁹GS, 16⁰GS, 16⁶S, 16⁶G,

	Starts	1st	2nd	3rd	Win & Pl
Hurdles	5	0	0	0	0
Career Total	5	0	0	0	0

Going:	Sf: 0-2 GS: 0-2 Gd: 0-1 GF: - Fm: 0-0
Distance:	2m/2m3: 0-5 2m4-2m7: 0-0 3m+: 0-0
Track:	LH: 0-5 RH: 0-0 Tight: 0-3 Gall: 0-0
Aids:	Bl: 0-0 Vi: 0-0 Tstrap: 0-0
Best Rating:	73 3/03 Catt 2m soft Hdl

Super Fellow (IRE)
111   (114h)130
9-y-o b g Shy Groom (USA)-Killough (Lord Gayle (USA))
Denis P Murphy P M Dwyer

Placings:0504323/12643354/211F/02006/53012154 (4474)
2002/03: 17⁵S, 20³SH, 20⁰YS, 26¹GF, 23²F, 24¹G, 24⁵HY, 25⁴G,

	Starts	1st	2nd	3rd	Win & Pl
Chases	8	2	1	1	24769
Career Total	32	5	5	5	40257
112 11/02 Chel	3m110y B Ch		GD		£13764
107 8/02 NAbb	3m2f110yD Ch		G-F		£4678
120 6/99 Navn	2m4f	HHdl	G-F		£4603
122 5/99 Cfml	2m1f110yD Hdl		GD		£3160
103 5/98 Dund	2m135y	Hdl		G-Y	£1935

Total win prize-money £28143

Going:	Sf: 0-2 GS: 0-0 Gd: 1-2 GF: - Fm: 1-2
Distance:	2m/2m3: 0-1 2m4-2m7: 0-3 3m+: 2-4
Track:	LH: 2-6 RH: 0-0 Tight: 1-2 Gall: 1-1
Aids:	Bl: 1-3 Vi: 0-0 Tstrap: 2-7
Best Rating:	131 11/00 Naas 2m sft-hvy Hdl

Fair Irish-trained novice chaser; successful at Newton Abbot and Cheltenham in 2002; stays an extended three and a quarter miles; prefers a sound surface; wears a tongue tie.

Super Gran (IRE)
5-y-o b m Grand Plaisir (IRE)-Caldeon Mist (IRE) (Le Moss)
R Johnson Robert Johnson

Placings:P   (1242)
2002/03: 16PGF,

	Starts	1st	2nd	3rd	Win & Pl
NH Flat	1	0	0	0	
Career Total	1	0	0	0	

Going:	Sf: 0-0 GS: 0-0 Gd: 0-0 GF: - Fm: 0-1
Distance:	2m/2m3: 0-1 2m4-2m7: 0-0 3m+: 0-0
Track:	LH: 0-1 RH: 0-0 Tight: 0-0 Gall: 0-0
Aids:	Bl: 0-0 Vi: 0-0 Tstrap: 0-0
Best Rating:	0 9/02 Hexm 2m110y gd-fm NHF

Super Nomad
106(103h)   (112h)122
8-y-o b g Nomadic Way (USA)-Super Sue (Lochnager)

M W Easterby Brian Hutchinson & David & Steven Dudley

Placings:245/05315136123/214P/**1F452123-5FP2422**

(4687)

2002/03: 16⁵G, 16⁶S, 19⁹G, 19²G, 16⁴G, 16²G, 17²G,

	Starts	1st	2nd	3rd	Win & Pl
Hurdles	1	0	0	0	535
Chases	6	3	0		8888
Career Total	**33**	**6**	**8**	**4**	**43892**
122	2/02	Newc	2m110y	E Ch		SFT	£3055
106	11/01	Kels	2m1f	E Ch		GD	£3445
128	11/00	Aint	2m4f	C(0-135)HHdl	G-S	£10871
121	3/00	Newc	2m4f	D(0-110)HHdl	GD	£3256
112	1/00	Donc	2m110y	F(0-100)HHdl	G-F	£2138
107	12/99	Newc	2m4f	E Hdl		SFT	£2690

Total win prize-money £25458

Going:	Sf: 0-1 GS: 0-0 Gd: 0-6 GF: - Fm: 0-0
Distance:	2m/2m3: 0-7 2m4-2m7: 0-0 3m+: 0-0
Track:	LH: 0-5 RH: 0-2 Tight: 0-3 Gall: 0-1
Aids:	Bl: 0-0 Vi: 0-0 Tstrap: 0-1
Best Rating:	128 11/00 Aint 2m4f gd-sft Hdl

Fair handicap chaser; effective at two to two and a half miles and seems to act on any ground; returned after a break to finish game runner-up in a two and a half mile handicap chase at Doncaster in January 2003; has worn a tongue tie.

Super Rapier (IRE)

96(71c)   (22c)82+

11-y-o b g Strong Gale-Misty Venture (Foggy Bell)
Ferdy Murphy Exors Of The Late G A Hubbard

Placings:46343/3052F33/5113/3634/0P6/60006-1345

(0986)

2002/03: 27¹GF, 23³GS, 24⁴G, 26⁵GF,

	Starts	1st	2nd	3rd	Win & Pl
Hurdles	4	1	0	1	2367
Career Total	**32**	**3**	**1**	**9**	**15073**
82	5/02	Font	3m3f	G(0-95)HHdl	G-F	£1939
107	5/98	Uttx	2m5f	E(0-115)HCh	G-F	£2866
107	5/98	Fknm	2m5f110yE(0-110)HCh	GD	£4298

Total win prize-money £9103

Going:	Sf: 0-0 GS: 0-1 Gd: 0-1 GF: - Fm: 1-2
Distance:	2m/2m3: 0-0 2m4-2m7: 0-0 **3m+: 1-4**
Track:	LH: 0-3 RH: 0-0 **Tight: 1-2** Gall: 0-0
Aids:	Bl: 0-0 **Vi: 1-2** Tstrap: 0-0
Best Rating:	107 5/98 Uttx 2m5f gd-fm Ch

Plating-class handicap hurdler. Stays beyond three miles and acts on a sound surface.

Super Road Train

103f

4-y-o b g Petoski-Foehn Gale (IRE) (Strong Gale)
L Wells David Knox

Placings:1

(4431)

2002/03: 18¹GF,

	Starts	1st	2nd	3rd	Win & Pl
NH Flat	1	1	0	0	3562
Career Total	**1**	**1**	**0**	**0**	**3562**
102	3/03	Plum	2m2f	H NHF	G-F	£3562

Total win prize-money £3562

Going:	Sf: 0-0 GS: 0-0 Gd: 0-0 GF: - Fm: 1-1
Distance:	2m/2m3: 1-1 2m4-2m7: 0-0 3m+: 0-0
Track:	**LH: 1-1** RH: 0-0 Tight: 0-0 Gall: 0-0
Aids:	Bl: 0-0 Vi: 0-0 Tstrap: 0-0
Best Rating:	102 3/03 Plum 2m2f gd-fm NHF

Made a winning bumper debut; acts on fast ground.

Super Sammy

100   93

7-y-o br m Mesleh-Super Sue (Lochnager)
M W Easterby Whitestonecliffe Racing Partnership

Placings:0/311642-022316026

(4406)

2002/03: 16⁵G, 16²S, 19²G, 19³GS, 16¹HY, 21⁶HY, 16⁹GS, 20²G,
20⁶G,

	Starts	1st	2nd	3rd	Win & Pl
Hurdles	9	1	3	1	6775
Career Total	**16**	**3**	**4**	**2**	**12406**
92	1/03	Newc	2m	E Hdl	HVY	£3438
105	1/02	Newc	2m	H NHF	SFT	£1988
96	12/01	Donc	2m110y	H NHF	GD	£2562

Total win prize-money £7989

Going:	Sf: 1-3 GS: 0-2 Gd: 0-4 GF: - Fm: 0-0
Distance:	**2m/2m3: 1-5** 2m4-2m7: 0-4 3m+: 0-0
Track:	**LH: 1-8** RH: 0-1 Tight: 0-3 Gall: 1-2
Aids:	Bl: 0-0 Vi: 0-0 Tstrap: 0-0
Best Rating:	105 1/02 Newc 2m soft NHF

Modest hurdler; stays two and a half miles; effective on ground from good to heavy; successful in bumpers and over hurdles, but becoming increasingly unreliable.

Super Satco (IRE)

5-y-o b g Satco (FR)-Brae (IRE) (Runnett)
Edward Butler W Hitchen

Placings:50

(1995)

2002/03: 16⁵GF, 16⁰GS,

	Starts	1st	2nd	3rd	Win & Pl
NH Flat	2	0	0	0	0
Career Total	**2**	**0**	**0**	**0**	**0**

Going:	Sf: 0-0 GS: 0-1 Gd: 0-0 GF: - Fm: 0-1
Distance:	2m/2m3: 0-2 2m4-2m7: 0-0 3m+: 0-0
Track:	LH: 0-2 RH: 0-0 Tight: 0-0 Gall: 0-0
Aids:	Bl: 0-0 Vi: 0-0 Tstrap: 0-0
Best Rating:	87 9/02 Hexm 2m110y gd-fm NHF

Showed a little ability in bumpers.

Superb Leader (IRE)

103(100h)   (103h)104

9-y-o b g Supreme Leader-Emmagreen (Green Shoon)
Miss Venetia Williams The Geisha Girls

Placings:2P4P/43241

(4317)

2002/03: 17⁴GS, 20⁵GS, 17²S, 20⁴GS, 17¹G,

	Starts	1st	2nd	3rd	Win & Pl
Hurdles	1	0	0	0	0
Chases	4	1	1	1	8097
Career Total	**9**	**1**	**2**	**1**	**8549**
104	3/03	Bang	2m1f110y	D Ch	GD	£5378

Total win prize-money £5379

Going:	Sf: 0-1 GS: 0-3 Gd: 1-1 GF: - Fm: 0-0
Distance:	**2m/2m3: 1-3** 2m4-2m7: 0-2 3m+: 0-0
Track:	**LH: 1-4** RH: 0-1 **Tight: 1-4** Gall: 0-0
Aids:	Bl: 0-0 Vi: 0-0 Tstrap: 0-0
Best Rating:	107 11/99 Chep 2m110y gd-sft NHF

Lightly-raced; shaped well after a lengthy absence when fourth at Bangor in December 2002; jumped adequately until tiring in the closing stages on chasing debut over two and a half miles at Ludlow the following month and finished runner-up at Bangor in February.

Superior Weapon (IRE)

94   98d

9-y-o b g Riverhead (USA)-Ballytrustan Maid (IRE) (Orchestra)
F P Murtagh Hendy And Hammy Partnership

Placings:P/6353100-2PP

(2001)

2002/03: 24²GF, 25²PGF, 22⁸S,

	Starts	1st	2nd	3rd	Win & Pl
Chases	3	0	1	0	1692
Career Total	**11**	**1**	**1**	**2**	**6386**
98	3/02	Kels	2m1f	E Ch	SFT	£3796

Total win prize-money £3796

Going:	Sf: 0-1 GS: 0-0 Gd: 0-0 GF: - Fm: 0-2
Distance:	2m/2m3: 0-0 2m4-2m7: 0-1 3m+: 0-0
Track:	LH: 0-2 RH: 0-1 Tight: 0-0 Gall: 0-0
Aids:	Bl: 0-0 Vi: 0-0 Tstrap: 0-3
Best Rating:	98 5/02 Prth 3m gd-fm Ch

Moderate chaser; winner twice in point-to-points up to three miles in the mud; handles any ground, usually tongue tied.

Supershot (IRE)

73f   56f

5-y-o b g Son Of Sharp Shot (IRE)-One To Two (IRE) (Astronef)
O Brennan O Brennan

Placings:0

(2477)

2002/03: 16⁰GS,

	Starts	1st	2nd	3rd	Win & Pl
NH Flat	1	0	0	0	
Career Total	**1**	**0**	**0**	**0**	

Going:	Sf: 0-0 GS: 0-1 Gd: 0-0 GF: - Fm: 0-0
Distance:	2m/2m3: 0-1 2m4-2m7: 0-0 3m+: 0-0
Track:	LH: 0-1 RH: 0-0 Tight: 0-0 Gall: 0-1
Aids:	Bl: 0-0 Vi: 0-0 Tstrap: 0-0
Best Rating:	59 12/02 Donc 2m110y gd-sft NHF

Superstar Express (IRE)

86   73

6-y-o br g Jurado (USA)-Easter Bee (IRE) (Phardante (FR))
J I A Charlton J I A Charlton

Placings:000-0600

(4616)

2002/03: 16⁰GS, 16⁶G, 16⁰G, 17⁰GF,

	Starts	1st	2nd	3rd	Win & Pl
NH Flat	1	0	0	0	0
Hurdles	3	0	0	0	0
Career Total	**7**	**0**	**0**	**0**	**0**

Going:	Sf: 0-1 GS: 0-0 Gd: 0-2 GF: - Fm: 0-1
Distance:	2m/2m3: 0-4 2m4-2m7: 0-0 3m+: 0-0
Track:	LH: 0-3 RH: 0-1 Tight: 0-1 Gall: 0-0
Aids:	Bl: 0-0 Vi: 0-0 Tstrap: 0-0
Best Rating:	80 3/02 Hntg 2m110y gd-fm NHF

Supraluna

88   84

4-y-o ch f Classic Cliche (IRE)-Spring Flyer (IRE) (Waajib)
Mrs M Reveley Codan Trust Company Limited

Placings:00   (4404)
2002/03: 14⁰GS, 16⁰GF,

	Starts	1st	2nd	3rd	Win & Pl
NH Flat	2	0	0	0	
Career Total	2	0	0	0	

Going:	Sf: 0-0 GS: 0-1 Gd: 0-0 GF: - Fm: 0-1
Distance:	2m/2m3: 0-1 2m4-2m7: 0-0 3m+: 0-0
Track:	LH: 0-2 RH: 0-0 Tight: 0-0 Gall: 0-0
Aids:	Bl: 0-0 Vi: 0-0 Tstrap: 0-0
Best Rating:	62 3/03 Hayd 2m gd-fm NHF

Half-sister to winning hurdlers Miss Tango and Roveretto; showed nothing in two bumpers for Mary Reveley; fitted with an eyeshield when runner-up in modest Newton Abbot novice hurdle June 2003 on first run for Martin Pipe.

Supreme Attraction (IRE)

89   **85+**

6-y-o b m Supreme Leader-Tourist Attraction (IRE) (Polleton)
Noel T Chance Mrs Norma Kelly

Placings:01-3   (2442)
2002/03: 20³GS,

	Starts	1st	2nd	3rd	Win & Pl
Hurdles	1	0	0	1	577
Career Total	3	1	0	1	2474
101 2/02 Wwck 2m		H NHF		HVY	£1897

Total win prize-money £1897

Going:	Sf: 0-0 GS: 0-1 Gd: 0-0 GF: - Fm: 0-0
Distance:	2m/2m3: 0-0 2m4-2m7: 0-1 3m+: 0-0
Track:	LH: 0-0 RH: 0-1 Tight: 0-0 Gall: 0-1
Aids:	Bl: 0-0 Vi: 0-0 Tstrap: 0-0
Best Rating:	101 2/02 Wwck 2m heavy NHF

Winner of a bumper, she ran well to be third on her hurdling debut. Acts on good to soft ground.

Supreme Being (IRE)

103   **112**

6-y-o b g Supreme Leader-Parsonetta (The Parson)
Michael Cunningham Mrs B Lynch

Placings:0⁄503441064-053660   (3767a)
2002/03: 21⁰HY, 25⁰SH, 20³HY, 20⁶S, 20⁶HY, 20⁰YS,

	Starts	1st	2nd	3rd	Win & Pl
Hurdles	6	0	0	1	1380
Career Total	16	1	0	2	9762
111 1/02 Fair 2m2f		Hdl		Y-S	£5932

Total win prize-money £5933

Going:	Sf: 0-4 GS: 0-0 Gd: 0-0 GF: - Fm: 0-0
Distance:	2m/2m3: 0-0 2m4-2m7: 0-0 6-8 3m+: 0-0
Track:	LH: 0-2 RH: 0-3 Tight: 0-0 Gall: 0-0
Aids:	Bl: 0-3 Vi: 0-0 Tstrap: 0-0
Best Rating:	112 4/02 Punc 2m4f yield Hdl

Supreme Breeze (IRE)

106   **91**

8-y-o b g Supreme Leader-Merry Breeze (Strong Gale)
Ferdy Murphy The Supreme Three

Placings:0⁄21530/PF252F2-U456233   (4765)
2002/03: 25ᵁGS, 25⁴G, 24⁵HY, 24⁶G, 25²S, 25³GF, 31³G,

	Starts	1st	2nd	3rd	Win & Pl
Chases	7	0	1	2	5104
Career Total	20	1	5	3	12975
95 11/00 Newc 2m4f		E Hdl		SFT	£2478

Total win prize-money £2478

Going:	Sf: 0-2 GS: 0-1 Gd: 0-3 GF: - Fm: 0-1
Distance:	2m/2m3: 0-0 2m4-2m7: 0-0 3m+: 0-7
Track:	LH: 0-5 RH: 0-1 Tight: 0-3 Gall: 0-2
Aids:	Bl: 0-3 Vi: 0-0 Tstrap: 0-0
Best Rating:	97 12/00 Weth 2m4f110y soft Hdl

Plating-class staying chaser; stays three miles seven; acts on any ground.

Supreme Buccaneer (IRE)

9-y-o b g Supreme Leader-Night Blade (Fine Blade (USA))
Mrs S M Johnson I K Johnson

Placings:0⁄0P-5PP   (2234)
2002/03: 20⁵GS, 19⁵PGS, 16⁶G,

	Starts	1st	2nd	3rd	Win & Pl
Chases	3	0	0	0	0
Career Total	6	0	0	0	0

Going:	Sf: 0-0 GS: 0-2 Gd: 0-1 GF: - Fm: 0-0
Distance:	2m/2m3: 0-2 2m4-2m7: 0-1 3m+: 0-0
Track:	LH: 0-1 RH: 0-2 Tight: 0-0 Gall: 0-0
Aids:	Bl: 0-0 Vi: 0-0 Tstrap: 0-0
Best Rating:	75 5/99 Chep 2m110y good NHF

Supreme Catch (IRE)

105(103h)   (121h)**126**

6-y-o b g Supreme Leader-Lucky Trout (Beau Charmeur (FR))
Miss H C Knight Bucknall Street Partnership

Placings:12-512   (2488)
2002/03: 19⁵G, 20¹GS, 21²G,

	Starts	1st	2nd	3rd	Win & Pl
Chases	3	1	1	0	16642
Career Total	5	2	2	0	20314
128 11/02 Hntg	2m4f110yD Ch			G-S	£5642
126 3/02 Font	2m4f	E Hdl		SFT	£2530

Total win prize-money £8173

Going:	Sf: 0-0 GS: 1-1 Gd: 0-2 GF: - Fm: 0-0
Distance:	2m/2m3: 0-0 2m4-2m7: 1-3 3m+: 0-0
Track:	LH: 0-1 RH: 1-2 Tight: 0-0 Gall: 1-2
Aids:	Bl: 0-0 Vi: 0-0 Tstrap: 0-0
Best Rating:	128 11/02 Hntg 2m4f110y gd-sft Ch

Useful chaser; ex-Irish pointer, made a winning debut over hurdles at Fontwell. Second next time. He made a fair chasing debut before winning at Huntingdon next time. A good second over 21 furlongs at Cheltenham in December. Acts on soft ground.

Supreme Charm (IRE)

99   **136d**

11-y-o b g Sovereign Water (FR)-Welsh Charmer (Welsh Captain)
K C Bailey P J Vogt

Placings:1⁄14506/212111121/211316/420413FP/3163U6/24 U2214650-5   (1725)

2002/03: 24⁵GS,

	Starts	1st	2nd	3rd	Win & Pl
Chases	1	0	0	0	0
Career Total	46	14	8	4	124687
136 12/01 Donc	3m2f	B(0-140)HCh		GD	£11242
138 11/00 Chel	3m7f	B Ch		SFT	£21255
135 2/00 Leic	2m7f110yD(0-125)HCh			G-S	£7085
131 3/99 Asct	2m3f110yC HCh			G-F	£13810
124 1/99 Ludl	2m	E Ch		G-S	£2866
108 12/98 Ludl	2m	D Ch		GD	£3581
130 4/98 Asct	2m4f	D Hdl		SFT	£3777
128 4/98 Asct	3m	C(0-135)HHdl		GD	£5152
123 12/97 Extr	2m2f	D Hdl		SFT	£3841
118 11/97 Asct	2m4f	C Hdl		SFT	£3582
114 11/97 Asct	2m4f	E(0-105)HHdl		SFT	£3598
96 9/97 Strf	2m6f110yD Hdl			G-F	£3038
102 7/96 Bell	2m1f	NHF		GD	£3685
98 6/96 Slig	2m	NHF		YLD	£2824

Total win prize-money £89341

Going:	Sf: 0-0 GS: 0-1 Gd: 0-0 GF: - Fm: 0-0
Distance:	2m/2m3: 0-0 2m4-2m7: 0-0 3m+: 0-1
Track:	LH: 0-0 RH: 0-1 Tight: 0-0 Gall: 0-0
Aids:	Bl: 0-0 Vi: 0-0 Tstrap: 0-0
Best Rating:	138 11/00 Chel 3m7f soft Ch

Useful chaser; sound jumper, he won the Sporting Index Chase over Cheltenham s cross-country course in November 2000. A thorough stayer, he won over three miles two at Doncaster in December 2001 and finished a fine fifth in the 2002 National. Acts on any ground and is probably best with patient tactics employed.

Supreme Class

6-y-o ch g Arrasas (USA)-Gabitats Dominion (Gabitat)
G N Alford G N Alford

Placings:00P   (0725)
2002/03: 17⁰GF, 16⁰GF, 16⁶GF,

	Starts	1st	2nd	3rd	Win & Pl
NH Flat	2	0	0	0	0
Hurdles	1	0	0	0	0
Career Total	3	0	0	0	

Going:	Sf: 0-0 GS: 0-0 Gd: 0-0 GF: - Fm: 0-3
Distance:	2m/2m3: 0-3 2m4-2m7: 0-0 3m+: 0-0
Track:	LH: 0-1 RH: 0-1 Tight: 0-0 Gall: 0-0
Aids:	Bl: 0-0 Vi: 0-0 Tstrap: 0-0
Best Rating:	36 6/02 Hrfd 2m1f gd-fm NHF

Supreme Craft (IRE)

7-y-o b m Warcraft (USA)-Phantom Thistle (Deep Run)
Mrs S M Johnson (Ms A E Embiricos 3/6) I K Johnson

Placings:600   (0771)
2002/03: 16⁶GF, 16⁰GF, 24⁰GF,

	Starts	1st	2nd	3rd	Win & Pl
NH Flat	2	0	0	0	0
Hurdles	1	0	0	0	0
Career Total	3	0	0	0	0

Going:	Sf: 0-0 GS: 0-0 Gd: 0-0 GF: - Fm: 0-3
Distance:	2m/2m3: 0-2 2m4-2m7: 0-0 3m+: 0-1
Track:	LH: 0-2 RH: 0-1 Tight: 0-0 Gall: 0-1
Aids:	Bl: 0-0 Vi: 0-0 Tstrap: 0-0
Best Rating:	75 6/02 Hntg 2m110y gd-fm NHF

Supreme Dawn (IRE)

96f   **96f**

6-y-o b g Supreme Leader-Tudor Dawn (Deep Run)
A J Lidderdale George Ward

Placings:4-43   (2627)
2002/03: 17⁴G, 16³S,

	Starts	1st	2nd	3rd	Win & Pl
NH Flat	2	0	0	1	279
Career Total	3	0	0	1	279

Going: Sf: 0-1 GS: 0-0 Gd: 0-1 GF: - Fm: 0-0
Distance: 2m/2m3: 0-2 2m4-2m7: 0-0 3m+: 0-0
Track: LH: 0-1 RH: 0-1 Tight: 0-0 Gall: 0-0
Aids: Bl: 0-0 Vi: 0-0 Tstrap: 0-0
Best Rating: 96 12/02 Uttx 2m   soft   NHF

Half-brother to smart hurdler Dawn Leader amongst others, has run with credit in bumpers.

Supreme Developer (IRE)

97   **125**

6-y-o b g Supreme Leader-Bettys The Boss (IRE) (Deep Run)
Anthony Mullins Mrs A N Durkan

Placings:161-23210   (4097)
2002/03: 20²SH, 16³HY, 16²S, 18¹YS, 16⁹G,

	Starts	1st	2nd	3rd	Win & Pl
Hurdles	5	1	2	1	9379
Career Total	8	3	2	1	25787
120	2/03	Navn	2m2f	Hdl		Y-S	£6272
125	4/02	Punc	2m	NHF		GD	£11963
118	1/02	Fair	2m	NHF		Y-S	£4444

Total win prize-money £22681

Going: Sf: 0-2 GS: 0-0 Gd: 0-1 GF: - Fm: 0-0
Distance: 2m/2m3: 1-4 2m4-2m7: 0-1 3m+: 0-0
Track: LH: 0-3 RH: 0-1 Tight: 0-0 Gall: 0-0
Aids: Bl: 0-0 Vi: 0-0 Tstrap: 0-0
Best Rating: 126 3/02 Chel 2m110y   gd-sft   NHF

Useful Irish-trained novice hurdler; bumper winner; suited by two miles two and ground good or softer; likes to race prominently.

Supreme Fortune (IRE)

107(113h)   **99**

9-y-o b g Supreme Leader-Lucylet (Kinglet)
Mrs M Reveley The Supreme Partnership

Placings:2034/133515113555/02U14P/003352066-036222241   (4432)
2002/03: 18⁹GS, 20³G, 16⁶G, 20²G, 21²GS, 21²S, 19²G, 16⁴G, 16¹G,

	Starts	1st	2nd	3rd	Win & Pl
Hurdles	5	0	2	1	1590
Chases	4	1	2	0	7774
Career Total	40	6	7	7	41392
99	4/03	Newc	2m110y	E Ch		GD	£4075
124	1/01	Hayd	2m	B(0-140)HHdl		SFT	£8392
117	2/00	Catt	2m3f	D Hdl		GD	£3198
121	1/00	Newc	2m	B Hdl		SFT	£6857
124	12/99	Newc	2m	F(0-105)HHdl		SFT	£2305
110	5/99	Aint	2m110y	D Hdl		G-S	£2905

Total win prize-money £27736

Supreme Glory (IRE)

110   **140**

10-y-o b g Supreme Leader-Pentlows (Sheer Grit)
P G Murphy C J L Moorsom

Placings:221FP4/521343/1415-4P502   (4479)
2002/03: 26⁴S, 29⁹HY, 24⁵G, 28⁹G, 36²G,

	Starts	1st	2nd	3rd	Win & Pl
Chases	5	0	1	0	135750
Career Total	21	4	4	2	226605
147	12/01	Chep	3m5f110yA HCh		G-S	£43500
140	11/01	Strf	3m4f	D(0-125)HCh		SFT	£4160
138	12/00	Extr	4m	D(0-120)HCh		HVY	£8352
123	12/99	Wwck	3m1f110yD Ch		SFT	£6222

Total win prize-money £62236

Going: Sf: 0-2 GS: 0-0 Gd: 0-3 GF: - Fm: 0-0
Distance: 2m/2m3: 0-0 2m4-2m7: 0-0 3m+: 0-5
Track: LH: 0-5 RH: 0-0 Tight: 0-1 Gall: 0-1
Aids: Bl: 0-0 Vi: 0-0 Tstrap: 0-0
Best Rating: 147 2/02 Newb 3m   soft   Ch

Useful stayer; he has a good record when racing over marathon distances and took the Welsh National in 2001; stayed on from a long way back when runner-up in the 2003 Grand National; suited by testing conditions; jumps soundly.

Supreme Hill (IRE)

105   **121+**

6-y-o br g Supreme Leader-Regents Prancer (Prince Regent (FR))
C J Mann J E Brown

Placings:1522-324   (3265)
2002/03: 20³S, 20²S, 19⁴GS,

	Starts	1st	2nd	3rd	Win & Pl
Hurdles	3	0	1	1	3297
Career Total	7	1	3	1	8136
121	12/01	Wwck	2m	H NHF		SFT	£1708

Total win prize-money £1708

Going: Sf: 0-2 GS: 0-1 Gd: 0-0 GF: - Fm: 0-0
Distance: 2m/2m3: 0-0 2m4-2m7: 0-3 3m+: 0-0
Track: LH: 0-2 RH: 0-1 Tight: 0-0 Gall: 0-0
Aids: Bl: 0-0 Vi: 0-0 Tstrap: 0-0
Best Rating: 121 12/01 Wwck 2m   soft   NHF

Decent bumper performer and had shown promise over hurdles; stays two and a half miles; acts on soft ground.

Supreme Irony (IRE)

106(93h)   (101h)**95**

10-y-o b g Supreme Leader-Florenanti (Floriferous)
M J Roberts Mike Roberts

Placings:0051/004/B4/5PP36-33U0   (0685)
2002/03: 24³GS, 20³GS, 24ᵁGF, 21⁹G,

	Starts	1st	2nd	3rd	Win & Pl
Chases	4	0	0	2	1444
Career Total	18	1	0	3	4363
105	4/99	Folk	2m1f110yH NHF		G-F	£1483

Total win prize-money £1483

Going: Sf: 0-1 GS: 0-2 Gd: 1-6 GF: - Fm: 0-0
Distance: 2m/2m3: 1-5 2m4-2m7: 0-0 3m+: 0-0
Track: LH: 1-8 RH: 0-1 Tight: 0-4 Gall: 1-2
Aids: Bl: 0-0 Vi: 0-0 Tstrap: 0-0
Best Rating: 127 12/01 Hayd 2m4f   soft   Hdl

Moderate hurdler/chaser; if not as good as he was, he showed ability on his chasing debut and got off the mark over fences at Newcastle in early April.

Supreme Lad (IRE)

114

9-y-o b g Supreme Leader-April Shade (Harwell)
M W Easterby Lord Daresbury & The Hon Mrs E Greenall

Placings:24311/5-FP   (2113)
2002/03: 22ᶠGS, 25ᴾG,

	Starts	1st	2nd	3rd	Win & Pl
Chases	2	0	0	0	
Career Total	8	2	1	1	7344
124	3/00	Donc	2m4f	E Hdl		G-S	£2688
124	1/00	Weth	2m4f110yD Hdl		SFT	£3367

Total win prize-money £6055

Going: Sf: 0-0 GS: 0-1 Gd: 0-1 GF: - Fm: 0-0
Distance: 2m/2m3: 0-0 2m4-2m7: 0-1 3m+: 0-1
Track: LH: 0-1 RH: 0-1 Tight: 0-2 Gall: 0-0
Aids: Bl: 0-0 Vi: 0-0 Tstrap: 0-0
Best Rating: 124 3/00 Donc 2m4f   gd-sft   Hdl

Off the track for a long time after winning over hurdles in the spring of 2000, he was close enough when falling two out in a novice chase in October 2002.

Supreme Lass (IRE)

87   **70**

7-y-o b m Supreme Leader-Falas Lass (Belfalas)
G M Moore Ean Muller

Placings:2401-0P0   (3830)
2002/03: 19⁰G, 16ᴾGS, 16⁰G,

	Starts	1st	2nd	3rd	Win & Pl
Hurdles	3	0	0	0	
Career Total	7	1	1	0	2129
99	3/02	Donc	2m110y	H NHF		SFT	£1666

Total win prize-money £1666

Going: Sf: 0-0 GS: 0-1 Gd: 0-2 GF: - Fm: 0-0
Distance: 2m/2m3: 0-3 2m4-2m7: 0-0 3m+: 0-0
Track: LH: 0-3 RH: 0-0 Tight: 0-1 Gall: 0-1
Aids: Bl: 0-0 Vi: 0-0 Tstrap: 0-0
Best Rating: 99 3/02 Donc 2m110y   soft   NHF

Supreme Native (IRE)

105   **109**

7-y-o b g Be My Native (USA)-Ballough Bui (IRE) (Supreme Leader)
P F Nicholls Mrs Angela Tincknell

Placings:2/233-32P   (1660)
2002/03: 16³GS, 17²F, 22ᴾG,

	Starts	1st	2nd	3rd	Win & Pl
Hurdles	3	0	1	1	1590
Career Total	7	0	3	3	2873

Going: Sf: 0-0 GS: 0-0 Gd: 0-1 GF: - Fm: 0-2
Distance: 2m/2m3: 0-2 2m4-2m7: 0-1 3m+: 0-0

Track: LH: 0-1 RH: 0-2 Tight: 0-1 Gall: 0-0
Aids: Bl: 0-0 Vi: 0-0 Tstrap: 0-0
Best Rating: 109 10/02 Chep 2m110y   gd-fm   Hdl

Placed in bumpers and hurdles. Suited by good ground, but seems a little short of pace.

Supreme Optimist (IRE)

103   **103**

6-y-o b g Supreme Leader-Armagale (IRE) (Strong Gale)
N G Richards H R C Catherwood

Placings: 50-033   (2657)
2002/03: 17⁰G, 16³S, 16³GS,

	Starts	1st	2nd	3rd	Win & Pl
Hurdles	3	0	0	2	1006
Career Total	5	0	0	2	1006

Going: Sf: 0-1 GS: 0-1 Gd: 0-1 GF: - Fm: 0-0
Distance: 2m/2m3: 0-3 2m4-2m7: 0-0 3m+: 0-0
Track: LH: 0-3 RH: 0-0 Tight: 0-2 Gall: 0-0
Aids: Bl: 0-0 Vi: 0-0 Tstrap: 0-0
Best Rating: 108 11/02 Kels 2m110y   soft   Hdl

Moderate hurdler; has only shown moderate form to date; acts on soft ground.

Supreme Piper (IRE)

105   **107**

5-y-o b g Supreme Leader-Whistling Doe (Whistling Deer)
P J Hobbs Mrs Karola Vann

Placings: 34226   (4048)
2002/03: 16³G, 17⁴G, 19²S, 22²GS, 20⁶HY,

	Starts	1st	2nd	3rd	Win & Pl
NH Flat	1	0	0	1	306
Hurdles	4	0	2	0	4395
Career Total	5	0	2	1	4701

Going: Sf: 0-2 GS: 0-1 Gd: 0-2 GF: - Fm: 0-0
Distance: 2m/2m3: 0-2 2m4-2m7: 0-0 3m+: 0-0
Track: LH: 0-2 RH: 0-3 Tight: 0-1 Gall: 0-1
Aids: Bl: 0-0 Vi: 0-0 Tstrap: 0-0
Best Rating: 107 1/03 Tntn 2m3f110y   soft   Hdl

Fair maiden hurdler; effective at up to two miles six; acts well on soft ground.

Supreme Prince (IRE)

109   **146+**

6-y-o b g Supreme Leader-Strong Serenade (IRE) (Strong Gale)
P J Hobbs Mrs Karola Vann

Placings: 1-11103   (4473)
2002/03: 20¹G, 20¹S, 22¹GS, 21⁰G, 24³G,

	Starts	1st	2nd	3rd	Win & Pl
Hurdles	5	3	0	1	35372
Career Total	6	4	0	1	37182
132	2/03	Winc	2m6f	B Hdl	G-S	£9256
146	11/02	Chep	2m4f	A Hdl	SFT	£13685
132	10/02	Chep	2m4f	E Hdl	GD	£3630
117	10/01	Extr	2m1f	H NHF	G-S	£1809

Total win prize-money £28382

Going: Sf: 1-1 GS: 1-1 Gd: 1-3 GF: - Fm: 0-0
Distance: 2m/2m3: 0-0 2m4-2m7: 3-4 3m+: 0-1
Track: LH: 2-4 RH: 1-1 Tight: 0-1 Gall: 0-1

Useful novice hurdler; successful in his only bumper at Exeter October 2001; not seen until making an impressive hurdling debut over two and a half miles at Chepstow October 2002; followed up in equally good style in the Persian War at the same course the following month, but not impressive at Wincanton; good seventh in the Royal & SunAlliance; acts on good or softer; stays 2m 6f; has the makings of a high-class staying hurdler.

Supreme Priority (IRE)

86   **78**

5-y-o b g Supreme Leader-Kakemona (Kambalda)
Jonjo O Neill Mrs Stewart Catherwood

Placings: 03300   (3871)
2002/03: 16⁰S, 16³HY, 22³HY, 24⁰GS, 19⁰S,

	Starts	1st	2nd	3rd	Win & Pl
NH Flat	2	0	0	1	378
Hurdles	3	0	0	1	496
Career Total	5	0	0	2	874

Going: Sf: 0-4 GS: 0-1 Gd: 0-0 GF: - Fm: 0-0
Distance: 2m/2m3: 0-3 2m4-2m7: 0-1 3m+: 0-1
Track: LH: 0-3 RH: 0-2 Tight: 0-1 Gall: 0-2
Aids: Bl: 0-0 Vi: 0-0 Tstrap: 0-0
Best Rating: 101 12/02 Newb 2m110y   heavy   NHF

Supreme Quest (IRE)

112   **116**

7-y-o b g Supreme Leader-Hazy River (Over The River (FR))
Jonjo O Neill R & E H Investments Ltd

Placings: 1/002PB1U-21P   (1210)
2002/03: 24²G, 27¹GF, 24⁰G,

	Starts	1st	2nd	3rd	Win & Pl
Hurdles	3	1	1	0	4378
Career Total	11	3	2	0	14010
116	5/02	Strf	3m3f	D(0-115)HHdl	G-F	£3486
114	4/02	Uttx	3m110y	E(0-100)HHdl	GD	£3178
94	4/00	Fair	2m2f	NHF	G-Y	£5888

Total win prize-money £12552

Going: Sf: 0-0 GS: 0-0 Gd: 0-2 GF: - Fm: 1-1
Distance: 2m/2m3: 0-0 2m4-2m7: 0-0 3m+: 1-3
Track: LH: 1-3 RH: 0-0 Tight: 1-2 Gall: 0-0
Aids: Bl: 0-0 Vi: 1-1 Tstrap: 0-0
Best Rating: 116 9/02 Uttx 3m110y   good   Hdl

Fair novice hurdler around three miles who lacks scope. Wears a visor and acts on most types of ground.

Supreme Silence (IRE)

(98c)   **(57c)**

6-y-o b g Bluebird (USA)-Why So Silent (Mill Reef (USA))
Jedd O Keeffe Wetherby Racing Bureau 50

Placings: P/5651PPP0-03P   (1385)
2002/03: 21³G, 24³G, 25⁰GF,

	Starts	1st	2nd	3rd	Win & Pl
Hurdles	1	0	0	0	0
Chases	2	0	0	1	774
Career Total	12	1	0	1	3171

88 | 6/01 | Hexm | 2m4f110yE Hdl | | GD | £2397

Total win prize-money £2398

Going: Sf: 0-0 GS: 0-0 Gd: 0-2 GF: - Fm: 0-1
Distance: 2m/2m3: 0-0 2m4-2m7: 0-1 3m+: 0-2
Track: LH: 0-3 RH: 0-0 Tight: 0-2 Gall: 0-0
Aids: Bl: 0-1 Vi: 0-0 Tstrap: 0-0
Best Rating: 88 6/01 Hexm 2m4f110y   good   Hdl

Won a novice hurdle at Hexham in the summer of 2001 over two and a half miles. Showed he stays three miles when third on his chasing debut. Best on a sound surface.

Supreme Soviet

108   **90d**

13-y-o ch g Presidium-Sylvan Song (Song)
A C Whillans Mrs L M Whillans

Placings: 050/46/F32220/24204/16203/114014/5350P141/564P03000P/32022010P-13P24P3P   (4409)
2002/03: 24¹GF, 24³GS, 23⁸G, 25²GF, 25⁴G, 25⁵PGS, 27³G, 25⁵PG,

	Starts	1st	2nd	3rd	Win & Pl
Chases	8	1	2	1	10946
Career Total	62	8	10	7	48433
93	5/02	Prth	3m	D(0-115)HCh	G-F	£7052
98	2/02	Muss	3m	E(0-105)HCh	SFT	£3396
109	3/00	Carl	2m4f110yF(0-110)HCh	G-S	£4738
104	2/00	Muss	3m	F(0-95)HCh	G-S	£2938
113	12/98	Ayr	2m4f	E(0-105)HCh	HVY	£3187
116	6/98	Prth	2m4f110yE(0-115)HCh	GF	£4143
111	5/98	Kels	2m6f110yE Ch	GF	£2424
90	5/97	Prth	2m4f110yE Hdl	SFT	£2747

Total win prize-money £30628

Going: Sf: 0-0 GS: 0-2 Gd: 0-4 GF: - Fm: 1-2
Distance: 2m/2m3: 0-0 2m4-2m7: 0-0 3m+: 1-8
Track: LH: 0-6 RH: 1-2 Tight: 0-4 Gall: 0-0
Aids: Bl: 0-0 Vi: 0-0 Tstrap: 0-0
Best Rating: 116 6/98 Prth 2m4f110y   gd-fm   Ch

Moderate three-mile chaser, acts on any ground.

Supreme Storm (IRE)

99(98h)   (92h)**108+**

8-y-o b g Supreme Leader-Angolass (Al Sirat (USA))
B G Powell P Keane

Placings: 40/0030-41P   (0506)
2002/03: 19⁴G, 20¹G, 20⁰PG,

	Starts	1st	2nd	3rd	Win & Pl
Chases	3	1	0	0	3383
Career Total	9	1	0	0	4046
108	5/02	Hntg	2m4f110yE(0-100)HCh	GD	£3162

Total win prize-money £3162

Going: Sf: 0-0 GS: 0-0 Gd: 1-3 GF: - Fm: 0-0
Distance: 2m/2m3: 0-1 2m4-2m7: 1-2 3m+: 0-0
Track: LH: 0-1 RH: 1-2 Tight: 0-0 Gall: 1-1
Aids: Bl: 0-0 Vi: 0-0 Tstrap: 0-0
Best Rating: 108 5/02 Hntg 2m4f110y   good   Ch

Supreme Toss (IRE)

111   **137+**

7-y-o b g Supreme Leader-Sleemana (Prince Hansel)
R T Phillips The Coin Tossers

Placings: 3f-111   (3404)
2002/03: 21¹S, 20¹HY, 24¹HY,

	Starts	1st	2nd	3rd	Win & Pl
Hurdles	3	3	0	0	13727

		Starts	1st	2nd	3rd	Win & Pl
Career Total		5	4	0	1	15956

137	2/03	Uttx	3m110y	D Hdl	HVY	£5138
127	12/02	Leic	2m4f110yD Hdl		HVY	£5239
120	12/02	Wwck	2m5f	E Hdl	SFT	£3349
98	3/02	Wwck	2m	H NHF	G-S	£1981
			Total win prize-money			£15708

Going: Sf: 3-3 GS: 0-0 Gd: 0-0 GF: - Fm: 0-0
Distance: 2m/2m3: 0-0 **2m4-2m7: 2-2** 3m+: 1-1
Track: LH: 2-2 RH: 1-1 Tight: 0-0 Gall: 0-0
Aids: Bl: 0-0 Vi: 0-0 Tstrap: 0-0
Best Rating: 137 2/03 Uttx 3m110y heavy Hdl

Progressive staying novice hurdler; off the mark on only his second-ever outing in a bumper at Warwick in March; won three times over hurdles in December 2002 and January 2003; stays three miles; acts on soft or heavy ground.

Supremely Bright

6-y-o b m Supreme Leader-Oh So Bright (Celtic Cone)
M J Ryan P Picton-Warlow

Placings:00 (4060)
2002/03: 16⁰G, 16⁰S,

	Starts	1st	2nd	3rd	Win & Pl
NH Flat	2	0	0	0	
Career Total	2	0	0	0	

Going: Sf: 0-1 GS: 0-0 Gd: 0-1 GF: - Fm: 0-0
Distance: 2m/2m3: 0-2 2m4-2m7: 0-0 3m+: 0-0
Track: LH: 0-1 RH: 0-0 Tight: 0-0 Gall: 0-1
Aids: Bl: 0-0 Vi: 0-0 Tstrap: 0-0
Best Rating: 0 3/03 Wwck 2m soft NHF

Supremely Red (IRE)
84 89
6-y-o b g Supreme Leader-Her Name Was Lola (Pitskelly)
D A Rees (M C Pipe 14/6) D A Rees & P Harris

Placings:4-3P100P (4338)
2002/03: 22³GF, 22PGS, 22¹G, 22⁹GS, 22⁰S, 20PGF,

			Starts	1st	2nd	3rd	Win & Pl
Hurdles			6	1	0	1	2961
Career Total			7	1	0	1	2961
89	6/02	NAbb	2m6f	E Hdl		GD	£2961
			Total win prize-money				£2961

Going: Sf: 0-1 GS: 0-2 Gd: 1-1 GF: - Fm: 0-2
Distance: 2m/2m3: 0-0 **2m4-2m7: 1-6** 3m+: 0-0
Track: LH: 1-2 RH: 0-4 Tight: 1-2 Gall: 0-1
Aids: Bl: 0-0 **Vi: 1-4** Tstrap: 0-0
Best Rating: 89 6/02 NAbb 2m6f good Hdl

Plating-class hurdler; stays two miles six; acts on a sound surface.

Surabaya (FR)
104(97c) (65c)62
8-y-o ch m Galetto (FR)-Silver Sea (FR) (Gay Mecene (USA))
F Jordan Supercraft Structures Limited

Placings:23P0P/P0200/40P54P/5PF46FPP-0P603P6 (1616)
2002/03: 20⁰G, 21PGF, 22⁶GF, 22⁹G, 26³GF, 24PG, 24⁶F,

	Starts	1st	2nd	3rd	Win & Pl
Hurdles	5	0	0	1	319
Chases	2	0	0	0	0

	Starts	1st	2nd	3rd	Win & Pl
Career Total	31	0	2	2	1331

Going: Sf: 0-0 GS: 0-0 Gd: 0-2 GF: - Fm: 0-5
Distance: 2m/2m3: 0-0 2m4-2m7: 0-4 3m+: 0-3
Track: LH: 0-5 RH: 0-2 Tight: 0-3 Gall: 0-1
Aids: Bl: 0-2 Vi: 0-0 Tstrap: 0-0
Best Rating: 100 9/99 Hrfd 2m1f good Hdl

Sure Future
109 120+
7-y-o b g Kylian (USA)-Lady Ever-So-Sure (Malicious)
R M Stronge The Test Valley Partnership

Placings:34046/336/5450122-43121 (2725)
2002/03: 25⁴HY, 19³GS, 22¹HY, 20²S, 24¹S,

			Starts	1st	2nd	3rd	Win & Pl
Hurdles			5	2	1	1	13730
Career Total			20	3	3	4	20301
120	12/02	Kemp	3m110y	C(0-135)HHdl	SFT		£6380
117	12/02	Folk	2m6f110yE(0-105)HHdl		HVY		£4153
103	3/02	Newb	2m5f	E(0-105)HHdl	SFT		£3640
			Total win prize-money				£14174

Going: Sf: 2-4 GS: 0-1 Gd: 0-0 GF: - Fm: 0-0
Distance: 2m/2m3: 0-2 2m4-2m7: 1-3 3m+: 1-2
Track: LH: 0-0 **RH: 2-5** Tight: 1-2 Gall: 0-0
Aids: Bl: 0-0 Vi: 0-0 Tstrap: 0-1
Best Rating: 120 12/02 Kemp 3m110y soft Hdl

Fair hurdler; stays three miles and loves soft ground; very consistent; has worn a tongue tie.

Sure Touch
76
6-y-o ch g Sure Blade (USA)-Welsh Lustre (IRE) (Mandalus)
Jonjo O Neill Mrs L R Lovell

Placings:03-FP5 (2073)
2002/03: 20⁰G, 21PS, 22⁵GS,

	Starts	1st	2nd	3rd	Win & Pl
Hurdles	3	0	0	0	0
Career Total	5	0	0	1	308

Going: Sf: 0-1 GS: 0-1 Gd: 0-0 GF: - Fm: 0-0
Distance: 2m/2m3: 0-0 2m4-2m7: 0-3 3m+: 0-0
Track: LH: 0-1 RH: 0-2 Tight: 0-0 Gall: 0-0
Aids: Bl: 0-0 Vi: 0-0 Tstrap: 0-0
Best Rating: 92 4/02 Wwck 2m gd-fm NHF

Showed ability in bumpers in the spring of 2002. Held over hurdles.

Surefast
105(99h) (80h)90
8-y-o ch g Nearly A Hand-Meldon Lady (Ballymoss)
S C Burrough (P R Rodford 23/1) Brian Derrick

Placings:0/00/60F0U55-300636 (4359)
2002/03: 20³GF, 20⁰G, 21⁰HY, 17⁶G, 24³GS, 24⁶F,

	Starts	1st	2nd	3rd	Win & Pl
Hurdles	4	0	0	1	563
Chases	2	0	0	0	678
Career Total	16	0	0	2	1241

Going: Sf: 0-1 GS: 0-1 Gd: 0-2 GF: - Fm: 0-2
Distance: 2m/2m3: 0-1 2m4-2m7: 0-3 3m+: 0-0
Track: LH: 0-3 RH: 0-3 Tight: 0-2 Gall: 0-0
Aids: Bl: 0-0 Vi: 0-0 Tstrap: 0-0
Best Rating: 90 2/03 Tntn 3m gd-sft Ch

Very modest novice hurdler/chaser; stays two and a half miles; unsuited by fast ground.

Surprising
105(103c) (116c)113
8-y-o b g Primitive Rising (USA)-Ascot Lass (Touching Wood (USA))
P J Hobbs M G St Quinton

Placings:4/212P/1133221-103420005 (4609)
2002/03: 23¹G, 25⁰GS, 25³G, 24⁴GS, 24²S, 22⁰HY, 22⁰GS, 25⁰G, 24⁵G,

			Starts	1st	2nd	3rd	Win & Pl
Hurdles			6	1	0	0	12800
Chases			3	0	1	1	2533
Career Total			21	5	5	3	64168
137	5/02	Hayd	2m7f110yB HHdl		GD		£12247
135	4/02	Prth	3m110y	B Hdl	GD		£8978
121	11/01	Kemp	2m5f	D Hdl	GD		£3558
112	10/01	Plum	2m5f	E Hdl	SFT		£2481
118	10/00	Extr	2m1f	H NHF	GD		£1652
			Total win prize-money				£28918

Going: Sf: 0-2 GS: 0-3 Gd: 1-4 GF: - Fm: 0-0
Distance: 2m/2m3: 0-0 2m4-2m7: 0-2 **3m+: 1-7**
Track: LH: 1-5 RH: 0-4 Tight: 0-0 Gall: 0-4
Aids: **Bl: 1-7** Vi: 0-0 Tstrap: 0-0
Best Rating: 137 5/02 Hayd 2m7f110y good Hdl

Formerly very useful staying hurdler; but has become disappointing; has not taken to chasing; acts on decent ground, but goes on soft; described as a stuffy sort, he idles in front; wears blinkers.

Sursum Corda
12-y-o b g Idiots Delight-Childhay (Roi Soleil)
John Wall M Ward-Thomas

Placings:4/2/342F3211/4252R14/2112330/030/P1P231-35343 (4572)
2002/03: 16³G, 21⁵G, 20³GS, 20⁴GF, 24³G,

			Starts	1st	2nd	3rd	Win & Pl
Chases			5	0	0	3	1224
Career Total			38	7	8	9	42245
107	4/02	Asct	2m3f110yH Ch		G-F		£2947
90	5/01	Folk	2m5f	H Ch	GD		£1909
123	12/99	Hayd	2m	B(0-140)HCh	HVY		£10113
120	11/99	Wwck	2m	D(0-125)HCh	GD		£4042
112	3/99	Hntg	2m4f110yE Ch		SFT		£2997
94	4/98	Hntg	2m110y	E Hdl	G-S		£2434
116	4/98	Extr	2m3f110yE Hdl		SFT		£2889
			Total win prize-money				£27324

Going: Sf: 0-0 GS: 0-1 Gd: 0-3 GF: - Fm: 0-1
Distance: 2m/2m3: 0-1 2m4-2m7: 0-3 3m+: 0-1
Track: LH: 0-1 RH: 0-4 Tight: 0-3 Gall: 0-0
Aids: Bl: 0-0 Vi: 0-0 Tstrap: 0-5
Best Rating: 126 2/00 Sand 2m4f110y gd-sft Ch

Hunter chaser; formerly a decent hurdler/chaser; effective over two and two and a half miles; suited by a sound surafce; wears tongue tie.

Susan Wintour (IRE)
6-y-o gr m Roselier (FR)-Fine Artist (Fine Blade (USA))
H D Daly M Ward-Thomas

Placings:04-P (1666)
2002/03: 20PS,

	Starts	1st	2nd	3rd	Win & Pl
Hurdles	1	0	0	0	

Career Total   3   0   0   0   0

Going:	Sf: 0-1 GS: 0-0 Gd: 0-0 GF: - Fm: 0-0
Distance:	2m/2m3: 0-0 2m4-2m7: 0-1 3m+: 0-0
Track:	LH: 0-1 RH: 0-0 Tight: 0-1 Gall: 0-0
Aids:	Bl: 0-0 Vi: 0-0 Tstrap: 0-0
Best Rating:	71 3/02 Uttx 2m heavy NHF

Susan's Boy
74

7-y-o b g Minster Son-Nancy Ardross (Ardross)
R Dickin T Joyce

Placings:54-0   (2476)
2002/03: 19⁰GS,

	Starts	1st	2nd	3rd	Win & Pl
Hurdles	1	0	0	0	
Career Total	3	0	0	0	0

Going:	Sf: 0-0 GS: 0-1 Gd: 0-0 GF: - Fm: 0-0
Distance:	2m/2m3: 0-0 2m4-2m7: 0-1 3m+: 0-0
Track:	LH: 0-1 RH: 0-0 Tight: 0-0 Gall: 0-0
Aids:	Bl: 0-0 Vi: 0-0 Tstrap: 0-0
Best Rating:	82 5/01 NAbb 2m1f gd-fm NHF

Susejebha (IRE)
96(91c)   (83c)**76**

7-y-o ch m Magical Wonder (USA)-Tribute To Viqueen (Furry Glen)
Mrs T White (M C Pipe 13/8) Dr Ian R Shenkin

Placings:245260/606/34633
2002/03: 22³GS, 16⁴GF, 20⁶G, 22³GF, 16³F,

	Starts	1st	2nd	3rd	Win & Pl
Hurdles	3	0	0	3	973
Chases	2	0	0	0	0
Career Total	14	0	2	3	2238

Going:	Sf: 0-0 GS: 0-1 Gd: 0-1 GF: - Fm: 0-3
Distance:	2m/2m3: 0-2 2m4-2m7: 0-3 3m+: 0-0
Track:	LH: 0-5 RH: 0-0 Tight: 0-3 Gall: 0-0
Aids:	Bl: 0-0 Vi: 0-0 Tstrap: 0-0
Best Rating:	83 7/02 NAbb 2m110y gd-fm Ch

Still a maiden over both hurdles and fences.

Susie Sinatra
89   **78**

7-y-o ch m Jupiter Island-Noire Small (USA) (Elocutionist (USA))
Ian Williams M Murphy

Placings:3/45/6P-6   (0089)
2002/03: 22⁶G,

	Starts	1st	2nd	3rd	Win & Pl
Hurdles	1	0	0	0	0
Career Total	6	0	0	1	251

Going:	Sf: 0-0 GS: 0-0 Gd: 0-0 GF: - Fm: 0-0
Distance:	2m/2m3: 0-0 2m4-2m7: 0-1 3m+: 0-0
Track:	LH: 0-1 RH: 0-0 Tight: 0-0 Gall: 0-0
Aids:	Bl: 0-0 Vi: 0-0 Tstrap: 0-0
Best Rating:	89 11/00 Hrfd 2m1f gd-sft NHF

Suspendid (IRE)
108   **121+**

10-y-o b g Yashgan-Spendapromise (Goldhill)
R Lee (C R Egerton 30/6) Stockton Heath Racing

Placings:/0/11P0/143-PP0211   (4538)
2002/03: 32⁵GF, 20⁶G, 24⁶G, 20²GF, 20¹G, 20¹G,

	Starts	1st	2nd	3rd	Win & Pl
Chases	6	2	1	0	16592
Career Total	15	6	1	1	31082
116 4/03	Ludl	2m4f	D(0-120)HCh	GD	£6727
109 4/03	Ludl	2m4f	D(0-115)HCh	GD	£7800
114 9/01	Prth	2m4f110yE Ch	GD	£4901
113 9/00	Hrfd	2m3f110yE Hdl	G-S	£2170
106 6/00	Strf	2m110y E Hdl	G-S	£2702
94 6/99	Rosc	2m	NHF	G-F	£2455
			Total win prize-money £26756

Going:	Sf: 0-0 GS: 0-0 Gd: 2-4 GF: - Fm: 0-2
Distance:	2m/2m3: 0-0 2m4-2m7: 2-4 3m+: 0-2
Track:	LH: 0-1 RH: 2-4 Tight: 2-5 Gall: 0-0
Aids:	Bl: 0-0 Vi: 0-0 Tstrap: 0-0
Best Rating:	121 4/02 Chel 2m5f gd-fm Ch

Modest handicap chaser; has had blood-vessel problems; suited by 2m 4f; jumps well; acts on a sound surface.

Swan Knight (USA)
103   **123**

7-y-o b/br g Sadler s Wells (USA)-Shannkara (IRE) (Akarad (FR))
R A Fahey (R J White 27/5) J J Staunton

Placings:1P2/0-0526   (4323)
2002/03: 17⁰GS, 16⁵G, 16²GS, 16⁶G,

	Starts	1st	2nd	3rd	Win & Pl
Hurdles	4	0	1	0	3077
Career Total	8	1	2	0	8721
127 2/01	Winc	2m	D Hdl	GD	£3969
			Total win prize-money £3969

Going:	Sf: 0-0 GS: 0-2 Gd: 0-2 GF: - Fm: 0-0
Distance:	2m/2m3: 0-4 2m4-2m7: 0-0 3m+: 0-0
Track:	LH: 0-4 RH: 0-0 Tight: 0-2 Gall: 0-2
Aids:	Bl: 0-0 Vi: 0-0 Tstrap: 0-0
Best Rating:	127 2/01 Winc 2m good Hdl

Fair hurdler; effective at two miles; best on good ground.

Swaneys Hill (IRE)

7-y-o b g Shernazar-Why Me Linda (IRE) (Nashamaa)
F Lloyd (W Clay 4/5) F Lloyd

Placings:0-00P   (3493)
2002/03: 16⁶G, 17⁰GS, 17⁷GS,

	Starts	1st	2nd	3rd	Win & Pl
NH Flat	2	0	0	0	0
Hurdles	2	0	0	0	0
Career Total	4	0	0	0	0

Going:	Sf: 0-0 GS: 0-2 Gd: 0-1 GF: - Fm: 0-0
Distance:	2m/2m3: 0-3 2m4-2m7: 0-0 3m+: 0-0
Track:	LH: 0-3 RH: 0-0 Tight: 0-2 Gall: 0-0
Aids:	Bl: 0-0 Vi: 0-0 Tstrap: 0-0
Best Rating:	75 2/02 Wwck 2m soft NHF

Swansea Bay
119(93h)   (89h)**135**

7-y-o b g Jurado (USA)-Slave s Bangle (Prince Rheingold)

P Bowen Peter Bowling

Placings:26244/130-04211116116P   (3188)
2002/03: 25⁵GF, 24⁴GS, 26²GF, 23¹GF, 24¹S, 23¹G, 23¹G, 24⁶GF, 25¹G, 25¹G, 24⁶S, 25⁵PGS,

	Starts	1st	2nd	3rd	Win & Pl
Chases	12	6	1	0	55625
Career Total	20	7	3	1	58888
135 11/02	Winc	3m1f110yA(0-150)HCh	GD	£29000
128 10/02	Winc	3m1f110yE(0-110)HCh	GD	£4936
122 9/02	Worc	2m7f110yG(0-135)HCh	GD	£7413
106 8/02	Worc	2m7f110yE(0-105)HCh	GD	£3555
105 8/02	Bang	3m110y D(0-115)HCh	SFT	£5964
111 7/02	Worc	2m7f110yF(0-100)HCh	G-F	£3059
89 9/01	Worc	3m F Hdl	G-F	£1883
			Total win prize-money £55813

Going:	Sf: 1-2 GS: 0-2 Gd: 4-4 GF: - Fm: 1-4
Distance:	2m/2m3: 0-0 2m4-2m7: 0-0 3m+: 6-12
Track:	LH: 4-7 RH: 2-5 Tight: 1-3 Gall: 0-0
Aids:	Bl: 0-0 Vi: 0-0 Tstrap: 0-0
Best Rating:	135 11/02 Winc 3m1f110y good Ch

Useful chaser; moderate hurdler, but progressive over fences and completed a four-timer in handicaps during the summer of 2002; won at Wincanton in October and followed up there in the Badger Brewery; held since; stays three miles; acts on fast ground but has won on soft; wears sheepskin cheekpieces.

Swansea Gold (IRE)

12-y-o ch m Torus-Show M How (Ashmore (FR))
Miss Hilary Handel Miss Hilary Handel

Placings:2/5415/150O2/4U/P   (4361)
2002/03: 24²F,

	Starts	1st	2nd	3rd	Win & Pl
Chases	1	0	0	0	
Career Total	13	2	2	0	9349
90 5/99	Extr	2m6f110yF(0-100)HCh	G-F	£3805
88 2/99	Font	3m2f110yF(0-95)HCh	SFT	£2981
			Total win prize-money £6786

Going:	Sf: 0-0 GS: 0-0 Gd: 0-0 GF: - Fm: 0-1
Distance:	2m/2m3: 0-0 2m4-2m7: 0-0 3m+: 0-1
Track:	LH: 0-0 RH: 0-1 Tight: 0-1 Gall: 0-0
Aids:	Bl: 0-0 Vi: 0-0 Tstrap: 0-0
Best Rating:	103 5/97 Strf 3m good Ch

Swazi Prince
86f   **65f**

4-y-o b g Rakaposhi King-Swazi Princess (IRE) (Brush Aside (USA))
N A Gaselee Mrs P T Orchart

Placings:0   (4155)
2002/03: 16⁰G,

	Starts	1st	2nd	3rd	Win & Pl
NH Flat	1	0	0	0	
Career Total	1	0	0	0	

Going:	Sf: 0-0 GS: 0-0 Gd: 0-1 GF: - Fm: 0-0
Distance:	2m/2m3: 0-1 2m4-2m7: 0-0 3m+: 0-0
Track:	LH: 0-1 RH: 0-0 Tight: 0-0 Gall: 0-0
Aids:	Bl: 0-0 Vi: 0-0 Tstrap: 0-0
Best Rating:	65 3/03 Wwck 2m good NHF

Sweeping Storm (IRE)

90   **70**

6-y-o ch g Glacial Storm (USA)-Sweeping Gold (Quayside)
J Wade   John Wade

Placings: 3   (1471)
2002/03: 17³GF,

	Starts	1st	2nd	3rd	Win & Pl
Hurdles	1	0	0	1	460
Career Total	1	0	0	1	460

Going: Sf: 0-0 GS: 0-0 Gd: 0-0 GF: - Fm: 0-1
Distance: 2m/2m3: 0-1 2m4-2m7: 0-0 3m+: 0-0
Track: LH: 0-0 RH: 0-1 Tight: 0-0 Gall: 0-0
Aids: Bl: 0-0 Vi: 0-0 Tstrap: 0-0
Best Rating: 76 10/02 Carl 2m1f   gd-fm   Hdl

Has hinted at a small amount of ability over hurdles.

Sweet Auburn (IRE)

46

7-y-o b/br g Tidaro (USA)-Sweet View (King s Ride)
Mrs B K Thomson   Mrs B K Thomson

Placings: 5P0   (2420)
2002/03: 16⁵HY, 20ᴾHY, 21⁰S,

	Starts	1st	2nd	3rd	Win & Pl
NH Flat	1	0	0	0	0
Hurdles	2	0	0	0	0
Career Total	3	0	0	0	0

Going: Sf: 0-3 GS: 0-0 Gd: 0-0 GF: - Fm: 0-0
Distance: 2m/2m3: 0-1 2m4-2m7: 0-2 3m+: 0-0
Track: LH: 0-2 RH: 0-1 Tight: 0-1 Gall: 0-0
Aids: Bl: 0-0 Vi: 0-0 Tstrap: 0-0
Best Rating: 73 11/02 Weth 2m   heavy   NHF

Sweet Bird (FR)

92   **96**

6-y-o ch g Epervier Bleu-Sweet Virginia (FR) (Tapioca Ii)
A M Hales   Andrew L Cohen

Placings: 3/40-56   (3595)
2002/03: 21⁵GS, 20⁶HY,

	Starts	1st	2nd	3rd	Win & Pl
Hurdles	2	0	0	0	0
Career Total	5	0	0	1	210

Going: Sf: 0-1 GS: 0-1 Gd: 0-0 GF: - Fm: 0-0
Distance: 2m/2m3: 0-0 2m4-2m7: 0-2 3m+: 0-0
Track: LH: 0-0 RH: 0-2 Tight: 0-0 Gall: 0-0
Aids: Bl: 0-0 Vi: 0-0 Tstrap: 0-0
Best Rating: 99 1/02 Towc 2m   heavy   Hdl

A half-brother to useful chaser and hurdler Sweet Duke, he has only run to a modest level over hurdles to date; Stays two miles; acts on a soft surface.

Sweet Diversion (IRE)

82f   **89f**

4-y-o b g Carroll House-Serocco Wind (Roi Guillaume (FR))
P F Nicholls   Mr & Mrs Ian Marshall

Placings: 22   (4364)

2002/03: 17²HY, 17²F,

	Starts	1st	2nd	3rd	Win & Pl
NH Flat	2	0	2	0	1132
Career Total	2	0	2	0	1132

Going: Sf: 0-1 GS: 0-0 Gd: 0-0 GF: - Fm: 0-1
Distance: 2m/2m3: 0-2 2m4-2m7: 0-0 3m+: 0-0
Track: LH: 0-0 RH: 0-1 Tight: 0-1 Gall: 0-0
Aids: Bl: 0-0 Vi: 0-0 Tstrap: 0-0
Best Rating: 89 2/03 Folk 2m1f110y   heavy   NHF

Showed ability in debut in a soft ground bumper when runner-up; also second when 4/11 on firm ground at Taunton next time.

Sweet Lord (IRE)

(84h)   **(80h)**

12-y-o ch g Aristocracy-Sweet And Fleet (Whistling Deer)
J A B Old   Alan & Linda Bird

Placings: 4/30260P/F441/1/3/4   (0771)
2002/03: 24¹GF,

	Starts	1st	2nd	3rd	Win & Pl
Hurdles	1	0	0	0	0
Career Total	14	2	1	2	21068
124	11/99 Wwck	3m1f110yC(0-130)HCh		GD	£6710
128	3/99 Asct	3m110y	B Ch	G-F	£11568

Total win prize-money £18278

Going: Sf: 0-0 GS: 0-0 Gd: 0-0 GF: - Fm: 0-1
Distance: 2m/2m3: 0-0 2m4-2m7: 0-0 3m+: 0-1
Track: LH: 0-1 RH: 0-0 Tight: 0-0 Gall: 0-0
Aids: Bl: 0-0 Vi: 0-0 Tstrap: 0-0
Best Rating: 128 3/99 Asct 3m110y   gd-fm   Ch

Sweet Milly

98   **81**

8-y-o b m Milieu-Another Joyful (Rubor)
J E Dixon   Mrs S F Dixon

Placings: 0/FPP/4630P4434   (4661)
2002/03: 16⁴G, 16⁶G, 16³GS, 16⁶G, 16ᴾHY, 16⁴G, 16⁴GS, 16³HY, 17⁴GF,

	Starts	1st	2nd	3rd	Win & Pl
Hurdles	9	0	0	2	1235
Career Total	13	0	0	2	1235

Going: Sf: 0-2 GS: 0-2 Gd: 0-4 GF: - Fm: 0-1
Distance: 2m/2m3: 0-9 2m4-2m7: 0-0 3m+: 0-0
Track: LH: 0-7 RH: 0-2 Tight: 0-1 Gall: 0-0
Aids: Bl: 0-0 Vi: 0-0 Tstrap: 0-0
Best Rating: 81 1/03 Ayr 2m   heavy   Hdl

Plating-class novice hurdler; very limited ability to date; seems best with cut in the ground.

Sweet Minuet

101   **85**

6-y-o b m Minshaanshu Amad (USA)-Sweet N Twenty (High Top)
M Madgwick   W E Baird

Placings: 3006P/4306-441   (4755)
2002/03: 19⁴HY, 20⁴G, 18¹GF,

	Starts	1st	2nd	3rd	Win & Pl
Hurdles	3	1	0	0	4288
Career Total	12	1	0	2	5056
84	4/03 Font	2m2f110yE Hdl		G-F	£3584

Total win prize-money £3584

Going: Sf: 0-1 GS: 0-0 Gd: 0-1 GF: - Fm: 1-1
Distance: 2m/2m3: 1-1 2m4-2m7: 0-2 3m+: 0-0
Track: LH: 1-1 RH: 0-2 Tight: 1-2 Gall: 0-0
Aids: Bl: 0-0 Vi: 0-0 Tstrap: 0-0
Best Rating: 85 11/01 Wwck 2m5f   good   Hdl

Modest novice hurdler; stays two miles-five; acts on any ground.

Sweet Senorita

97(106c)   (146?c)**107?**

8-y-o b m Young Senor (USA)-Sweet N Twenty (High Top)
M C Pipe   D A Johnson

Placings: 1P21141151211/212/611-P40U3   (1578)
2002/03: 22ᴾGF, 17⁴GF, 16⁹GF, 16ᵁGF, 16³G,

	Starts	1st	2nd	3rd	Win & Pl
Hurdles	5	0	0	1	444
Career Total	24	11	4	1	36110
117	7/01 Worc	2m	E Ch	GD	£2999
136	6/01 NAbb	2m110y	E Ch	GD	£3351
133	5/00 Uttx	2m	D(0-125)HHdl	GD	£3432
135	4/00 Strf	2m110y	D(0-110)HHdl	GD	£3024
117	3/00 Bang	2m1f	F Hdl	GD	£2331
131	2/00 Leic	2m	F Hdl	G-S	£2793
93	1/00 Plum	2m	F Hdl	HVY	£2485
112	12/99 MRas	2m1f110yG Hdl		GD	£1616
115	10/99 Ludl	2m	G Hdl	G-F	£2113
108	9/99 Extr	2m1f	G(0-95)HHdl	G-S	£1798
99	8/99 NAbb	2m1f	G Hdl	G-F	£1987

Total win prize-money £27930

Going: Sf: 0-0 GS: 0-0 Gd: 0-1 GF: - Fm: 0-4
Distance: 2m/2m3: 0-4 2m4-2m7: 0-1 3m+: 0-0
Track: LH: 0-4 RH: 0-1 Tight: 0-4 Gall: 0-0
Aids: Bl: 0-0 Vi: 0-0 Tstrap: 0-0
Best Rating: 141 6/00 Worc 2m   gd-fm   Hdl

Modest, prolific front-running hurdler, she made a successful switch to fences but was off the track for over a year before returning over hurdles in the summer of 2002. Best around two miles, she handles most types of ground and is notably tough, but does not seem to be as good as she was.

Sweet Sensation

76   **37**

8-y-o ch m Carlingford Castle-Pink Sensation (Sagaro)
C Grant   Mrs A Meller

Placings: 0434-0P0U   (4798)
2002/03: 20⁰G, 22ᴾS, 19⁰G, 17ᵁGF,

	Starts	1st	2nd	3rd	Win & Pl
Hurdles	4	0	0	0	
Career Total	8	0	0	1	227

Going: Sf: 0-1 GS: 0-0 Gd: 0-2 GF: - Fm: 0-1
Distance: 2m/2m3: 0-2 2m4-2m7: 0-2 3m+: 0-0
Track: LH: 0-4 RH: 0-0 Tight: 0-3 Gall: 0-0
Aids: Bl: 0-0 Vi: 0-0 Tstrap: 0-0
Best Rating: 99 5/01 Newc 2m   gd-fm   NHF

Sweet Serenata

65

8-y-o gr m Keen-Serenata (Larrinaga)
M E Sowersby   R D Seldon

Placings: 4P35/0PF022/504050-P   (0331)
2002/03: 20ᴾG,

	Starts	1st	2nd	3rd	Win & Pl
Hurdles	1	0	0	0	
Career Total	17	0	2	1	1268

Going: Sf: 0-0 GS: 0-0 Gd: 0-1 GF: - Fm: 0-0
Distance: 2m/2m3: 0-0 2m4-2m7: 0-1 3m+: 0-0
Track: LH: 0-1 RH: 0-0 Tight: 0-0 Gall: 0-0
Aids: Bl: 0-0 Vi: 0-0 Tstrap: 0-0
Best Rating: 78 11/00 Catt 2m3f   good   Hdl

Swift Pearl (IRE)

109   **93**

10-y-o b g Persian Mews-Laurestown Rose (Derring Rose)
T M Walsh Edward Cawley

Placings:5/0F00-20⁵51   (0916)
2002/03: 16²S, 16⁰S, 20⁵HY, 19⁵YS, 20¹GS,

	Starts	1st	2nd	3rd	Win & Pl
NH Flat	3	0	1	0	982
Hurdles	2	1	0	0	3416
Career Total	10	1	1	0	4397
101	8/02	Prth	2m4f110y		G-S £3415

Total win prize-money £3416

Going: Sf: 0-3 GS: 1-1 Gd: 0-0 GF: - Fm: 0-0
Distance: 2m/2m3: 0-0 **2m4-2m7: 1-2** 3m+: 0-0
Track: LH: 0-1 RH: **1-1** Tight: 0-0 Gall: 0-0
Aids: Bl: 0-0 Vi: 0-0 Tstrap: 0-0
Best Rating: 101 8/02 Prth 2m4f110y gd-sft Hdl

Modest form in bumpers, opened his account in a modest event at Perth in August.

Swift Rose (IRE)

                                             37

6-y-o b m Roselier (FR)-Clonarctic Slave (Sir Mordred)
Paul Nolan (Ferdy Murphy 30/4) Thomas A Byrne

Placings:00000   (3979a)
2002/03: 16⁰G, 20⁰S, 16⁵S, 17⁰S,

	Starts	1st	2nd	3rd	Win & Pl
NH Flat	1	0	0	0	0
Hurdles	4	0	0	0	0
Career Total	5	0	0	0	

Going: Sf: 0-4 GS: 0-0 Gd: 0-1 GF: - Fm: 0-0
Distance: 2m/2m3: 0-3 2m4-2m7: 0-2 3m+: 0-0
Track: LH: 0-1 RH: 0-1 Tight: 0-0 Gall: 0-0
Aids: Bl: 0-0 Vi: 0-0 Tstrap: 0-0
Best Rating: 36 3/03 Dpat 2m1f172y soft Hdl

Swift Swallow

84f   **94f**

5-y-o ch g Missed Flight-Alhargah (Be My Guest (USA))
O Brennan Richard J Marshall

Placings:3   (4685)
2002/03: 16³GF,

	Starts	1st	2nd	3rd	Win & Pl
NH Flat	1	0	0	1	276
Career Total	1	0	0	1	276

Going: Sf: 0-0 GS: 0-0 Gd: 0-0 GF: - Fm: 0-1
Distance: 2m/2m3: 0-1 2m4-2m7: 0-0 3m+: 0-0
Track: LH: 0-0 RH: 0-1 Tight: 0-0 Gall: 0-1
Aids: Bl: 0-0 Vi: 0-0 Tstrap: 0-0
Best Rating: 94 4/03 Hntg 2m110y gd-fm NHF

Looked very short of experience when well beaten third first time in a bumper at Huntingdon in April.

Swincombe (IRE)

100   **115**

8-y-o b g Good Thyne (USA)-Gladtogetit (Green Shoon)
R H Alner (Miss Emma Kelley 22/5) T J Whitley

Placings:0121P   (3142)
2002/03: 21⁰GF, 24¹GF, 26²G, 25¹GS, 27⁰S,

	Starts	1st	2nd	3rd	Win & Pl
Chases	5	2	1	0	9727
Career Total	5	2	1	0	9727
115	12/02	Winc	3m1f110yD(0-125)HCh	G-S	£7757
102	5/02	Chep	3m H Ch	G-F	£1397

Total win prize-money £9156

Going: Sf: 0-1 GS: 1-1 Gd: 0-1 GF: - Fm: 1-2
Distance: 2m/2m3: 0-0 2m4-2m7: 0-1 **3m+: 2-4**
Track: LH: 1-3 RH: 1-2 Tight: 0-1 Gall: 0-1
Aids: Bl: 0-0 Vi: 0-0 Tstrap: 0-0
Best Rating: 115 12/02 Winc 3m1f110y gd-sft Ch

Fair chaser; former pointer; effective on fast ground; stays three miles two.

Swing West (USA)

97(95h)   **4**

9-y-o b h Gone West (USA)-Danlu (USA) (Danzig (USA))
N F Glynn N F Glynn

Placings:212002/35U0006/5PF20U25/03U0F/0022450515
PP0PPP-300P0P   (4453a)
2002/03: 20³G, 24⁰G, 16⁰SH, 20⁰S, 24⁰S, 20⁰G,

	Starts	1st	2nd	3rd	Win & Pl
Hurdles	1	0	0	0	0
Chases	5	0	0	1	1060
Career Total	48	2	7	3	16736
91	11/01	Tram	2m4f	(0-102)HCh	YLD £5286
112	12/97	Ling	2m110y E Hdl	G-S £2546

Total win prize-money £7832

Going: Sf: 0-2 GS: 0-0 Gd: 0-2 GF: - Fm: 0-1
Distance: 2m/2m3: 0-1 2m4-2m7: 0-3 3m+: 0-2
Track: LH: 0-3 RH: 0-3 Tight: 0-2 Gall: 0-0
Aids: Bl: 0-3 Vi: 0-0 Tstrap: 0-0
Best Rating: 113 1/98 Newc 2m   gd-sft Hdl

Swinging The Blues (IRE)

85   **69**

9-y-o b g Bluebird (USA)-Winsong Melody (Music Maestro)
C A Dwyer Mrs Shelley Dwyer

Placings:55/030-0   (0349)
2002/03: 16⁰G,

	Starts	1st	2nd	3rd	Win & Pl
Hurdles	1	0	0	0	
Career Total	6	0	0	1	270

Going: Sf: 0-0 GS: 0-0 Gd: 0-0 GF: - Fm: 0-0
Distance: 2m/2m3: 0-1 2m4-2m7: 0-0 3m+: 0-0
Track: LH: 0-1 RH: 0-0 Tight: 0-1 Gall: 0-1
Aids: Bl: 0-0 Vi: 0-1 Tstrap: 0-0
Best Rating: 89 11/98 Hntg 2m110y gd-sft Hdl

Middle-distance Flat winner, very lightly raced over hurdles.

Sword Lady

88f   **73f**

5-y-o b m Broadsword (USA)-Speckyfoureyes (Blue Cashmere)

Mrs S D Williams Berry Racing

Placings:6   (4628)
2002/03: 17⁶GF,

	Starts	1st	2nd	3rd	Win & Pl
NH Flat	1	0	0	0	0
Career Total	1	0	0	0	0

Going: Sf: 0-0 GS: 0-0 Gd: 0-0 GF: - Fm: 0-1
Distance: 2m/2m3: 0-1 2m4-2m7: 0-0 3m+: 0-0
Track: LH: 0-1 RH: 0-0 Tight: 0-1 Gall: 0-0
Aids: Bl: 0-0 Vi: 0-0 Tstrap: 0-0
Best Rating: 73 4/03 NAbb 2m1f   gd-fm NHF

Sylcan Express

98   **76**

10-y-o br g Sylvan Express-Dercanny (Derek H)
C N Kellett Vince, Ady, Bob And Rich

Placings:300/0P40P/105/00U0P/0000440P3-04   (0379)
2002/03: 20⁰G, 21⁴G,

	Starts	1st	2nd	3rd	Win & Pl
Hurdles	2	0	0	0	0
Career Total	27	1	0	2	2887
89	10/99	Towc	2m5f	E(0-105)HHdl	GD £2390

Total win prize-money £2390

Going: Sf: 0-0 GS: 0-0 Gd: 0-2 GF: - Fm: 0-0
Distance: 2m/2m3: 0-2 2m4-2m7: 0-2 3m+: 0-0
Track: LH: 0-1 RH: 0-1 Tight: 0-0 Gall: 0-1
Aids: Bl: 0-0 Vi: 0-0 Tstrap: 0-0
Best Rating: 92 2/98 Muss 2m   good NHF

Sylv

68   **27**

5-y-o b m Ridgewood Ben-High Commotion (IRE) (Taufan (USA))
J G Portman Miss R Wakeford

Placings:06   (1036)
2002/03: 16⁰GF, 18⁶GF,

	Starts	1st	2nd	3rd	Win & Pl
Hurdles	2	0	0	0	0
Career Total	2	0	0	0	0

Going: Sf: 0-0 GS: 0-0 Gd: 0-0 GF: - Fm: 0-2
Distance: 2m/2m3: 0-2 2m4-2m7: 0-0 3m+: 0-0
Track: LH: 0-2 RH: 0-0 Tight: 0-1 Gall: 0-0
Aids: Bl: 0-0 Vi: 0-0 Tstrap: 0-0
Best Rating: 27 7/02 Worc 2m   gd-fm Hdl

Sylva Bounty

4-y-o br g Bahamian Bounty-Spriolo (Priolo (USA))
B P J Baugh (C E Brittain 17/9) Stan Baugh

Placings:PP   (4219)
2002/03: 16⁶G, 17⁶GF,

	Starts	1st	2nd	3rd	Win & Pl
Hurdles	2	0	0	0	
Career Total	2	0	0	0	

Going: Sf: 0-0 GS: 0-0 Gd: 0-1 GF: - Fm: 0-1
Distance: 2m/2m3: 0-2 2m4-2m7: 0-0 3m+: 0-0
Track: LH: 0-1 RH: 0-0 Tight: 0-1 Gall: 0-0
Aids: Bl: 0-0 Vi: 0-0 Tstrap: 0-0
Best Rating: 0 3/03 Hrfd 2m1f   gd-fm Hdl

Sylva Legend (USA)

(104h)   (102h)
7-y-o b g Lear Fan (USA)-Likeashot (CAN) (Gun Shot)
R J Baker M A Swift, A J Chapman And T Warden

Placings:2322566-143134   (2006)
2002/03: 16¹GF, 17⁴G, 17³G, 22¹GF, 22³GF, 21⁴G,

	Starts	1st	2nd	3rd	Win & Pl
Hurdles	5	2	0	2	6977
Chases	1	0	0	0	361
Career Total	13	2	3	3	10709
102 6/02 NAbb 2m6f D Hdl				G-F	£3276
102 5/02 Chep 2m110y E(0-105)HHdl				G-F	£2618
Total win prize-money £5894					

Going: Sf: 0-0 GS: 0-0 Gd: 0-3 GF: - Fm: 2-3
Distance: 2m/2m3: 1-3 2m4-2m7: 1-3 3m+: 0-0
Track: LH: 2-4 RH: 0-2 Tight: 1-4 Gall: 0-0
Aids: Bl: 0-0 Vi: 0-0 Tstrap: 0-0
Best Rating: 102 8/02 NAbb 2m6f gd-fm Hdl

Fair efforts in novice hurdles, winning a minor handicap at Chepstow in May 2002. Won 22 furlong novice hurdle at Newton Abbot June 2002, held next time. Handles most types of ground.

Sylvan Twister

71   44
4-y-o br c First Trump-Storm Party (IRE) (Bluebird (USA))
P Mitchell Georgia Partnership

Placings:F0   (4184)
2002/03: 16⁵S, 17⁹G,

	Starts	1st	2nd	3rd	Win & Pl
Hurdles	2	0	0	0	
Career Total	2	0	0	0	

Going: Sf: 0-1 GS: 0-0 Gd: 0-1 GF: - Fm: 0-0
Distance: 2m/2m3: 0-2 2m4-2m7: 0-0 3m+: 0-0
Track: LH: 0-1 RH: 0-1 Tight: 0-2 Gall: 0-0
Aids: Bl: 0-0 Vi: 0-0 Tstrap: 0-0
Best Rating: 44 3/03 Folk 2m1f110y good Hdl

Sylviajazz

4-y-o b f Alhijaz-Dispol Princess (IRE) (Cyrano De Bergerac)
Miss J Feilden J W Jenkins

Placings:0   (3236)
2002/03: 16⁹S,

	Starts	1st	2nd	3rd	Win & Pl
Hurdles	1	0	0	0	
Career Total	1	0	0	0	

Going: Sf: 0-1 GS: 0-0 Gd: 0-0 GF: - Fm: 0-0
Distance: 2m/2m3: 0-1 2m4-2m7: 0-0 3m+: 0-0
Track: LH: 0-1 RH: 0-0 Tight: 0-1 Gall: 0-0
Aids: Bl: 0-0 Vi: 0-0 Tstrap: 0-0
Best Rating: 0 1/03 Fknm 2m soft Hdl

Sylviesbuck (IRE)

89   91
6-y-o b g Kasmayo-Sylvies Missiles (IRE) (Buckskin (FR))
G M Moore Mrs I I Plumb

Placings:2500   (3816)
2002/03: 16²HY, 22⁵HY, 16⁹G, 19⁹G,

	Starts	1st	2nd	3rd	Win & Pl
NH Flat	1	0	1	0	708
Hurdles	3	0	0	0	
Career Total	4	0	1	0	708

Going: Sf: 0-2 GS: 0-1 Gd: 0-1 GF: - Fm: 0-0
Distance: 2m/2m3: 0-3 2m4-2m7: 0-1 3m+: 0-0
Track: LH: 0-4 RH: 0-0 Tight: 0-1 Gall: 0-0
Aids: Bl: 0-0 Vi: 0-0 Tstrap: 0-0
Best Rating: 91 2/03 Hayd 2m gd-sft Hdl

Irish point winner, showed promise in his only bumper, but well beaten over hurdles.

Ta Ta For Now

100(104h)   (101h)90
6-y-o b g Ezzoud (IRE)-Exit Laughing (Shaab)
P Beaumont Mrs V M Stewart

Placings:05F0P-1443003   (3964)
2002/03: 20¹G, 24⁴GF, 22⁴S, 20³S, 24⁹G, 21⁰GS, 25³S,

	Starts	1st	2nd	3rd	Win & Pl
Hurdles	5	1	0	1	3232
Chases	2	0	0	1	626
Career Total	12	1	0	2	3858
101 4/02 Hexm 2m4f110yE Hdl			GD	£2520
Total win prize-money £2520				

Going: Sf: 0-3 GS: 0-1 Gd: 1-2 GF: - Fm: 0-1
Distance: 2m/2m3: 0-0 2m4-2m7: 1-4 3m+: 0-3
Track: LH: 1-5 RH: 0-2 Tight: 0-3 Gall: 0-0
Aids: Bl: 0-0 Vi: 0-0 Tstrap: 0-0
Best Rating: 101 12/02 Ayr 2m4f soft Hdl

Moderate form in bumpers and over hurdles so far, winner of a novice hurdle at Hexham but erratic over fences so far.

Taakid (USA)

107   108
8-y-o b g Diesis-Tanwi (Vision (USA))
Mrs S J Smith Daggers Drawn

Placings:660/360305/301P/55F-1255325313   (1495)
2002/03: 16¹GS, 16²GF, 17⁵GS, 16⁵G, 20³GS, 16²GF, 17⁵G, 21³G, 21¹GF, 20³G,

	Starts	1st	2nd	3rd	Win & Pl
Chases	10	2	2	3	12627
Career Total	26	3	2	6	17060
95 10/02 Sedg 2m5f D(0-115)HCh			G-F	£4667
93 5/02 Hexm 2m110y E(0-105)HCh			G-S	£3465
95 7/00 Wolv 2m4f110yE Ch			GD	£3386
Total win prize-money £11519				

Going: Sf: 0-0 GS: 1-3 Gd: 0-4 GF: - Fm: 1-3
Distance: 2m/2m3: 1-6 2m4-2m7: 1-4 3m+: 0-0
Track: LH: 2-10 RH: 0-0 Tight: 1-5 Gall: 0-0
Aids: Bl: 0-0 Vi: 0-0 Tstrap: 0-0
Best Rating: 96 10/02 Hexm 2m4f110y good Ch

Modest handicap chaser; quite impressive on return at Southwell in May; stays two miles five and acts on any ground but is ideally suited by firm.

Table Mountain

96   109+
7-y-o ch g Rock Hopper-Comtec Princess (Gulf Pearl)
C Weedon Bill Hinge

Placings:3222/P-1   (1603)
2002/03: 16¹G,

	Starts	1st	2nd	3rd	Win & Pl
Hurdles	1	1	0	0	3543
Career Total	6	1	3	1	5919
98 10/02 Chep 2m110y E Hdl			GD	£3542
Total win prize-money £3543				

Hurdles	3	0	0	0
Career Total	4	0	1	0

Going: Sf: 0-0 GS: 0-0 Gd: 1-1 GF: - Fm: 0-0
Distance: 2m/2m3: 1-1 2m4-2m7: 0-0 3m+: 0-0
Track: LH: 1-1 RH: 0-0 Tight: 0-0 Gall: 0-0
Aids: Bl: 0-0 Vi: 0-0 Tstrap: 0-0
Best Rating: 120 4/01 Asct 2m110y heavy NHF

Showed promise in bumpers, and came from well back to win a Chepstow novice hurdle in October 2002.

Taboo Tee

98(102h)   (94h)74
7-y-o br m Teenoso (USA)-Temporary Affair (Mandalus)
O Sherwood The Taboo Team

Placings:4/044256-PP60   (1593)
2002/03: 20²G, 21⁵GS, 20⁶G, 23⁹G,

	Starts	1st	2nd	3rd	Win & Pl
Hurdles	1	0	0	0	0
Chases	3	0	0	0	0
Career Total	11	0	1	0	1386

Going: Sf: 0-0 GS: 0-1 Gd: 0-3 GF: - Fm: 0-0
Distance: 2m/2m3: 0-2 2m4-2m7: 0-3 3m+: 0-1
Track: LH: 0-3 RH: 0-1 Tight: 0-3 Gall: 0-0
Aids: Bl: 0-0 Vi: 0-0 Tstrap: 0-0
Best Rating: 94 12/01 Winc 2m good Hdl

Plating-class maiden hurdler who stays two and a half miles and is effective on good/soft ground. Pulled up on chasing debut in spring of 2002.

Tacin (IRE)

111   119+
6-y-o b g Supreme Leader-Nicat (Wolver Hollow)
B G Powell Mrs Jean R Bishop

Placings:3F   (3901)
2002/03: 21³GS, 24⁵S,

	Starts	1st	2nd	3rd	Win & Pl
Hurdles	2	0	0	1	872
Career Total	2	0	0	1	872

Going: Sf: 0-1 GS: 0-1 Gd: 0-0 GF: - Fm: 0-0
Distance: 2m/2m3: 0-0 2m4-2m7: 0-1 3m+: 0-1
Track: LH: 0-1 RH: 0-1 Tight: 0-0 Gall: 0-1
Aids: Bl: 0-0 Vi: 0-0 Tstrap: 0-0
Best Rating: 107 1/03 Kemp 2m5f gd-sft Hdl

Irish point winner; has shown ability in staying novice hurdles.

Tacita

82   49
8-y-o ch m Gunner B-Taco (High Season)
M D McMillan M D McMillan

Placings:40/3P-040   (4217)
2002/03: 24⁹G, 20⁴G, 22⁹G,

	Starts	1st	2nd	3rd	Win & Pl
Hurdles	3	0	0	0	316
Career Total	7	0	0	1	691

Going: Sf: 0-1 GS: 0-0 Gd: 0-2 GF: - Fm: 0-0
Distance: 2m/2m3: 0-0 2m4-2m7: 0-3 3m+: 0-1
Track: LH: 0-1 RH: 0-2 Tight: 0-1 Gall: 0-0
Aids: Bl: 0-0 Vi: 0-0 Tstrap: 0-0
Best Rating: 89 12/00 Ludl 2m soft NHF

She showed promise in bumpers in soft ground at Ludlow and did not disgrace herself on her debut over hurdles in November at Stratford.

Tacolino (FR)

114   **119+**

9-y-o ch g Royal Charter (FR)-Tamilda (FR) (Rose Laurel)
O Brennan (A L T Moore 8/11) John Sheridan

Placings:40/0035/30406/F1460F215/P3-00F51   (4687)
2002/03: 16⁰G, 16⁰G, 16⁰F, 20⁵G, 17¹G,

	Starts	1st	2nd	3rd	Win & Pl
Chases	5	1	0	0	5857
Career Total	27	3	1	3	19198
99 4/03	MRas	2m1f110y	D(0-115)HCh		
GD £5856					
109 12/00	Fair	2m100y	(0-116)HCh	Y-S	£5520
89 5/00	Rosc	2m	(0-123)HCh	FRM	£4416

Total win prize-money £15793

Going: Sf: 0-0 GS: 0-0 Gd: 1-4 GF: - Fm: 0-1
Distance: 2m/2m3: 1-4 2m4-2m7: 0-1 3m+: 0-0
Track: LH: 0-1 RH: 1-2 Tight: 1-2 Gall: 0-0
Aids: Bl: 0-0 Vi: 0-0 Tstrap: 0-3
Best Rating: 109 12/00 Fair 2m100y yld-sft Ch

Modest ex-Irish chaser; stays 2m 4f; seems to act on most types of going.

Tactful Remark (USA)

113   **124+**

7-y-o ch g Lord At War (ARG)-Right Word (USA) (Verbatim (USA))
M C Pipe Professor D B A Silk & Mrs Heather Silk

Placings:113P3   (4524)
2002/03: 16¹S, 17¹GF, 17³HY, 17²G, 16³G,

	Starts	1st	2nd	3rd	Win & Pl
Hurdles	5	2	0	2	7655
Career Total	5	2	0	2	7655
131 6/02	NAbb	2m1f	D Hdl	G-F	£3469
131 6/02	Worc	2m	E Hdl	SFT	£2765

Total win prize-money £6235

Going: Sf: 1-2 GS: 0-0 Gd: 0-2 GF: - Fm: 1-1
Distance: 2m/2m3: 2-5 2m4-2m7: 0-0 3m+: 0-0
Track: LH: 2-4 RH: 0-1 Tight: 1-2 Gall: 0-1
Aids: Bl: 0-0 Vi: 0-0 Tstrap: 0-0
Best Rating: 131 6/02 NAbb 2m1f gd-fm Hdl

Decent novice hurdler; had found it more difficult to front-run in handicap company; suited by 2m; acts on any ground.

Tadzio

90f   **77f**

4-y-o bl g Mtoto-Fresher (Fabulous Dancer (USA))
P R Webber Mrs R Philipps

Placings:0   (4122)
2002/03: 16⁰G,

	Starts	1st	2nd	3rd	Win & Pl
NH Flat	1	0	0	0	
Career Total	1	0	0	0	

Going: Sf: 0-0 GS: 0-0 Gd: 0-0 GF: - Fm: 0-0
Distance: 2m/2m3: 0-1 2m4-2m7: 0-0 3m+: 0-0
Track: LH: 0-0 RH: 0-1 Tight: 0-0 Gall: 0-1
Aids: Bl: 0-0 Vi: 0-0 Tstrap: 0-1
Best Rating: 43 3/03 Hntg 2m110y good NHF

Taffs Well

94   **103**

10-y-o b g Dowsing (USA)-Zahiah (So Blessed)

B Ellison Ronald McCulloch

Placings:F2-021   (0956)
2002/03: 16⁰GS, 17²GF, 17¹G,

	Starts	1st	2nd	3rd	Win & Pl
Hurdles	3	1	1	0	3728
Career Total	5	1	2	0	4476
103 8/02	Sedg	2m1f	E Hdl	GD	£2884

Total win prize-money £2884

Going: Sf: 0-0 GS: 0-1 Gd: 1-1 GF: - Fm: 0-1
Distance: 2m/2m3: 1-3 2m4-2m7: 0-0 3m+: 0-0
Track: LH: 1-3 RH: 0-0 Tight: 1-3 Gall: 0-0
Aids: Bl: 0-0 Vi: 0-0 Tstrap: 0-0
Best Rating: 103 8/02 Sedg 2m1f good Hdl

Moderate hurdler; acts on a sound surface; twice finished runner-up in novices hurdles before enjoying an easy success at Sedgefield in August 2002.

Tagar (FR)

98(105h)   (95h)**89**

6-y-o b g Fijar Tango (FR)-Fight For Arfact (Salmon Leap (USA))
N J Henderson P J Orme

Placings:3640/522-340   (3624)
2002/03: 19³GS, 16⁴S, 16⁰S,

	Starts	1st	2nd	3rd	Win & Pl
Hurdles	3	0	0	1	640
Career Total	10	0	2	2	8897

Going: Sf: 0-2 GS: 0-1 Gd: 0-0 GF: - Fm: 0-0
Distance: 2m/2m3: 0-3 2m4-2m7: 0-0 3m+: 0-0
Track: LH: 0-1 RH: 0-2 Tight: 0-0 Gall: 0-2
Aids: Bl: 0-0 Vi: 0-0 Tstrap: 0-0
Best Rating: 124 3/02 Newb 2m110y gd-sft Hdl

Disappointing novice hurdler; ex-French; stays two and a half miles; suited by soft ground.

Tagula Sun (IRE)

81f   **80f**

5-y-o b g Tagula (IRE)-Dee-Lady (Deploy)
Jean-Rene Auvray Mrs Christine Fennell

Placings:00-4   (0436)
2002/03: 16⁴GF,

	Starts	1st	2nd	3rd	Win & Pl
NH Flat	1	0	0	0	0
Career Total	3	0	0	0	0

Going: Sf: 0-0 GS: 0-0 Gd: 0-0 GF: - Fm: 0-1
Distance: 2m/2m3: 0-1 2m4-2m7: 0-0 3m+: 0-0
Track: LH: 0-0 RH: 0-1 Tight: 0-0 Gall: 0-1
Aids: Bl: 0-0 Vi: 0-0 Tstrap: 0-1
Best Rating: 80 6/02 Hntg 2m110y gd-fm NHF

Tahrima

87f   **67f**

4-y-o b f Slip Anchor-Khandjar (Kris)
C A Dwyer Mrs Shelley Dwyer

Placings:0   (3747)
2002/03: 16⁰G,

	Starts	1st	2nd	3rd	Win & Pl
NH Flat	1	0	0	0	
Career Total	1	0	0	0	

Tail Gunner

4-y-o gr g Vague Shot-Plum Blossom (USA) (Gallant Romeo (USA))
K A Morgan (S C Williams 23/7) Mrs Celia Miller

Placings:U   (1323)
2002/03: 17ᵁGF,

	Starts	1st	2nd	3rd	Win & Pl
Hurdles	1	0	0	0	
Career Total	1	0	0	0	

Going: Sf: 0-0 GS: 0-0 Gd: 0-0 GF: - Fm: 0-1
Distance: 2m/2m3: 0-1 2m4-2m7: 0-0 3m+: 0-0
Track: LH: 0-0 RH: 0-1 Tight: 0-1 Gall: 0-0
Aids: Bl: 0-0 Vi: 0-0 Tstrap: 0-0
Best Rating: 0 9/02 MRas 2m1f110y gd-fm Hdl

Taillefer (FR)

81(105h)   (104h)**57**

7-y-o b g Cyborg (FR)-Tourka (FR) (Rose Laurel)
M E D Francis Mrs Merrick Francis Iii

Placings:0F503123126/0-PBPP6213   (4173)
2002/03: 21ᴾGS, 20ᴾGS, 22ᴾS, 24ᴾS, 22⁶GS, 22²HY, 20¹HY, 20³S,

	Starts	1st	2nd	3rd	Win & Pl
Hurdles	5	1	1		8168
Chases	3	0	0	0	0
Career Total	20	3	3	3	21795
102 2/03	Sand	2m4f110yD(0-120)HHdl	HVY	£5027
122 3/01	Hntg	2m4f110yE Ch	SFT	£3276
9/00	Fntb	2m3f	Ch	GD	£3362

Total win prize-money £11666

Going: Sf: 1-5 GS: 0-3 Gd: 0-0 GF: - Fm: 0-0
Distance: 2m/2m3: 0-0 2m4-2m7: 1-7 3m+: 0-1
Track: LH: 0-4 RH: 1-4 Tight: 0-1 Gall: 0-2
Aids: Bl: 0-0 Vi: 0-0 Tstrap: 0-0
Best Rating: 122 3/01 Hayd 2m6f heavy Ch

Modest handicap hurdler; has won over fences, but failed to progress over the larger obstacles; effective at around two and a half miles; acts on good and soft ground.

Tailored (IRE)

9-y-o b g King s Ride-Hook s Close (Kemal (FR))
R H Alner Pell-Mell Partners

Placings:4332/1/F   (1853)
2002/03: 21ᶠG,

	Starts	1st	2nd	3rd	Win & Pl
Chases	1	0	0	0	
Career Total	6	1	1	2	10723
118 12/00	Kemp	2m4f110yC(0-130)HCh	G-S	£9139

Total win prize-money £9139

Going: Sf: 0-0 GS: 0-0 Gd: 0-1 GF: - Fm: 0-0
Distance: 2m/2m3: 0-0 2m4-2m7: 0-1 3m+: 0-0
Track: LH: 0-0 RH: 0-1 Tight: 0-0 Gall: 0-0
Aids: Bl: 0-0 Vi: 0-0 Tstrap: 0-0
Best Rating: 118 12/00 Kemp 2m4f110y gd-sft Ch

Won over fences at Kempton over Christmas 2000, but was

not seen again until falling at Wincanton in November 2002. Acts on good to soft ground.

Tails I Win

4-y-o b g Petoski-Spinayab (King Of Spain)
J W Mullins J H Mead

Placings:0   (4053)
2002/03: 16⁰HY,

	Starts	1st	2nd	3rd	Win & Pl
NH Flat	1	0	0	0	
Career Total	1	0	0	0	

Going:	Sf: 0-1 GS: 0-0 Gd: 0-0 GF: - Fm: 0-0
Distance:	2m2/m3: 0-1 2m4-2m7: 0-0 3m+: 0-0
Track:	LH: 0-0 RH: 0-1 Tight: 0-0 Gall: 0-0
Aids:	Bl: 0-0 Vi: 0-0 Tstrap: 0-0
Best Rating:	**0** 3/03 Sand 2m110y heavy NHF

Takagi (IRE)

118(105h)   (132h)**151**
8-y-o b g Husyan (USA)-Ballyclough Gale (Strong Gale)
E J O Grady D Cox

Placings:0/2/3f145/3U311F2152-1P2P230   (4727a)
2002/03: 24¹S, 26PGS, 24²SH, 28PSH, 25²YS, 24³GY, 29⁰G,

	Starts	1st	2nd	3rd	Win & Pl
Hurdles	1	0	0	1	795
Chases	6	1	2	0	39492
Career Total	24	6	5	4	109393
150	11/02	Navn	3m	HCh		SFT	£25920
143	3/02	Navn	3m	HCh		SH	£15950
143	1/02	Naas	3m	Ch		SH	£17944
126	1/02	Naas	2m3f	Ch		YLD	£7831
123	1/01	Naas	2m3f	Hdl		SFT	£5564
135	12/00	Gowr	2m2f	NHF		HVY	£3588
				Total win prize-money £76800

Going:	Sf: 1-1 GS: 0-1 Gd: 0-1 GF: - Fm: 0-0
Distance:	2m/2m3: 0-0 2m4-2m7: 0-0 3m+: 1-7
Track:	LH: 1-3 RH: 0-3 Tight: 0-0 Gall: 0-1
Aids:	Bl: 0-0 Vi: 0-0 Tstrap: 0-0
Best Rating:	**151** 2/03 Fair 3m1f yld-sft Ch

Smart Irish chaser; stays beyond three miles; effective in soft ground.

Take A Drop (IRE)

103   **111d**
8-y-o b g Farhaan-Misquested (Lord Ha Ha)
Seamus O Farrell Seamus O Farrell

Placings:0000600/454340P2-00f16P5400   (4582a)
2002/03: 16⁰GF, 20⁰G, 16¹G, 20¹GF, 16PYS, 21PG, 21⁵GS, 24⁴HY, 24⁰S, 24⁰GF,

	Starts	1st	2nd	3rd	Win & Pl
NH Flat	1	1	0	0	4445
Hurdles	9	1	0	0	5308
Career Total	25	2	1	1	12053
99	8/02	Tram	2m	Hdl		G-F	£4233
109	8/02	Cork	2m	NHF		GD	£4444
				Total win prize-money £8678

Going:	Sf: 0-2 GS: 0-1 Gd: 1-3 GF: - Fm: 1-3
Distance:	2m/2m3: 1-3 2m4-2m7: 1-4 3m+: 0-3
Track:	LH: 0-2 RH: 0-1 Tight: 0-0 Gall: 0-2
Aids:	Bl: 0-0 Vi: 0-0 Tstrap: 0-0
Best Rating:	**111** 11/02 Chel 2m5f gd-sft Hdl

Modest Irish hurdler, winner twice in August 2002.

Take A Rain Check (IRE)

66   **33**
6-y-o b m Rainbows For Life (CAN)-Just A Second (Jimsun)
C J Drewe The Coskett Partnership

Placings:PP-PP0   (4574)
2002/03: 18PHY, 20PHY, 22⁰GF,

	Starts	1st	2nd	3rd	Win & Pl
Hurdles	3	0	0	0	
Career Total	5	0	0	0	

Going:	Sf: 0-2 GS: 0-0 Gd: 0-0 GF: - Fm: 0-1
Distance:	2m/2m3: 0-2 2m4-2m7: 0-2 3m+: 0-0
Track:	LH: 0-2 RH: 0-1 Tight: 0-0 Gall: 0-0
Aids:	Bl: 0-0 Vi: 0-0 Tstrap: 0-0
Best Rating:	**33** 4/03 Strf 2m6f110y gd-fm Hdl

Take Control (IRE)

105   **146**
9-y-o b g Roselier (FR)-Frosty Fairy (Paddy s Stream)
M C Pipe D A Johnson

Placings:0501/113101/11225130/36P4P51-04F0P6 (4557)
2002/03: 26⁰GS, 24⁴G, 29PHY, 28⁰G, 34PS, 33⁶G,

	Starts	1st	2nd	3rd	Win & Pl
Chases	6	0	0	0	4150
Career Total	31	9	2	3	154902
153	4/02	Ayr	4m1f	A HCh		GD	£60000
131	2/01	Wwck	3m2f	C Ch		SFT	£7046
138	11/00	NAbb	3m2f110y	C Ch		HVY	£5768
143	10/00	Extr	2m3f110y	D Ch		SFT	£5655
145	4/00	Chel	3m	B(0-145)HHdl		SFT	£10582
126	2/00	Plum	2m5f	D Hdl		SFT	£3797
117	12/99	Hayd	2m7f110yD(0-110)HHdl		SFT	£3257
112	12/99	Winc	2m6f	F(0-100)HHdl		GD	£2472
118	2/99	Naas	2m3f	NHF		SFT	£3069
				Total win prize-money £101649

Going:	Sf: 0-2 GS: 0-1 Gd: 0-3 GF: - Fm: 0-0
Distance:	2m/2m3: 0-0 2m4-2m7: 0-0 3m+: 0-6
Track:	LH: 0-6 RH: 0-0 Tight: 0-0 Gall: 0-1
Aids:	Bl: 0-0 Vi: 0-1 Tstrap: 0-0
Best Rating:	**153** 4/02 Ayr 4m1f good Ch

Very useful chaser; won the Scottish Grand National in 2002; relishes testing conditions, but also effective on a sound surface; stays four miles; inconsistent; has worn visor.

Take Flite

109   **123**
6-y-o b g Cadeaux Genereux-Green Seed (IRE) (Lead On Time (USA))
Anthony Mullins Sean J Murphy

Placings:2613-03324102F0   (4742a)
2002/03: 16⁰YS, 16³GF, 17³G, 16²G, 16⁴GF, 16¹G, 16⁰S, 16²HY, 16⁶G, 16⁰G,

	Starts	1st	2nd	3rd	Win & Pl
Hurdles	10	1	2	2	15369
Career Total	14	2	3	3	23707
112	10/02	Cork	2m	Hdl		GD	£8773
115	3/02	Fair	2m	Hdl		G-Y	£6349
				Total win prize-money £15123

Going:	Sf: 0-2 GS: 0-0 Gd: 1-5 GF: - Fm: 0-2
Distance:	2m/2m3: 1-10 2m4-2m7: 0-0 3m+: 0-0
Track:	LH: 0-3 RH: 0-3 Tight: 0-1 Gall: 0-0
Aids:	Bl: 0-0 Vi: 0-0 Tstrap: 0-0

Best Rating: 123 4/03 Aint 2m110y good Hdl

Fair Irish-trained hurdler; suited by two miles and the ground good or softer.

Take Heed

105   **86**
7-y-o b g Warning-Tunaria (USA) (Lyphard (USA))
K A Morgan Roemex Ltd

Placings:U/0FP-05122606   (4186)
2002/03: 16⁰GF, 17⁵S, 16¹G, 16²GS, 16²G, 16⁶G, 16⁰GS, 17⁶G,

	Starts	1st	2nd	3rd	Win & Pl
Hurdles	8	1	2	0	5514
Career Total	12	1	2	0	5514
88	11/02	Kemp	2m	E(0-100)HHdl		GD	£3591
				Total win prize-money £3591

Going:	Sf: 0-1 GS: 0-2 Gd: 1-4 GF: - Fm: 0-1
Distance:	2m/2m3: 1-8 2m4-2m7: 0-0 3m+: 0-0
Track:	LH: 0-5 RH: 1-3 Tight: 0-0 Gall: 0-1
Aids:	Bl: 0-0 Vi: 0-0 Tstrap: 1-7
Best Rating:	**88** 11/02 Kemp 2m good Hdl

Moderate novice hurdler, winner at Kempton in November 2002, suited by a sound surface.

Take My Side (IRE)

11-y-o b g Be My Native (USA)-Fight For It (Strong Gale)
Mrs P Townsley Paul Townsley

Placings:6501U43/35353U0/P/PP-U4F   (4080)
2002/03: 21US, 20⁴GS, 26PS,

	Starts	1st	2nd	3rd	Win & Pl
Chases	3	0	0	0	515
Career Total	20	1	0	4	5087
111	1/98	Plum	2m4f	E Hdl		HVY	£2637
				Total win prize-money £2637

Going:	Sf: 0-2 GS: 0-1 Gd: 0-0 GF: - Fm: 0-0
Distance:	2m/2m3: 0-2 2m4-2m7: 0-2 3m+: 0-0
Track:	LH: 0-2 RH: 0-0 Tight: 0-3 Gall: 0-0
Aids:	Bl: 0-0 Vi: 0-0 Tstrap: 0-0
Best Rating:	**114** 3/98 Sand 2m4f110y good Ch

Take The Brush (IRE)

9-y-o b m Brush Aside (USA)-Ballywilliam Girl (Royal Match)
J White Nick Quesnel

Placings:0/P-FP   (0272)
2002/03: 18FGF, 20PGF,

	Starts	1st	2nd	3rd	Win & Pl
Chases	2	0	0	0	
Career Total	4	0	0	0	

Going:	Sf: 0-0 GS: 0-0 Gd: 0-0 GF: - Fm: 0-2
Distance:	2m/2m3: 0-0 2m4-2m7: 0-0 3m+: 0-0
Track:	LH: 0-1 RH: 0-0 Tight: 0-2 Gall: 0-0
Aids:	Bl: 0-0 Vi: 0-0 Tstrap: 0-0
Best Rating:	**0** 5/02 Strf 2m4f gd-fm Ch

Take The Stand (IRE)

105(100h)   (97h)**129+**
7-y-o b g Witness Box (USA)-Denys Daughter (IRE) (Crash

Course)
Ian Williams C M Kinane

Placings:00/64224135-P211 (4427)
2002/03: 24PGS, 23²GS, 24¹G, 26¹GF,

	Starts	1st	2nd	3rd	Win & PI
Chases	4	2	1	0	15050
Career Total	14	3	3	1	19600
124 3/03 Plum 3m2f D Ch				G-F	£6890
119 3/03 Fknm 3m110y D Ch				GD	£6440
92 9/01 Worc 3m F Hdl				G-F	£1876
				Total win prize-money	£15206

Going: Sf: 0-0 GS: 0-2 Gd: 1-1 GF: - Fm: 1-1
Distance: 2m/2m3: 0-0 2m4-2m7: 0-0 3m+: 2-4
Track: LH: 2-3 RH: 0-1 Tight: 2-3 Gall: 0-0
Aids: Bl: 0-0 Vi: 0-0 Tstrap: 0-0
Best Rating: 124 3/03 Plum 3m2f gd-fm Ch

Progressive chaser; won back-to-back novice chases and Fakenham and Plumpton March 2003; with winner and going well when falling five out in Summer National at Uttoxeter; made amends next time when winning a handicap at Newton Abbot; stays well; likes fast ground.

Takeyourtime
103   95
8-y-o b m Hatim (USA)-Wand Of Youth (Mandamus)
A Scott Andy Scott

Placings:0664062/024-433220P5 (3352)
2002/03: 20⁴G, 20³GS, 24³GS, 20²GS, 20²G, 16⁰HY, 24PHY, 20⁵HY,

	Starts	1st	2nd	3rd	Win & PI
Hurdles	8	0	2	2	3244
Career Total	18	0	4	2	15228

Going: Sf: 0-3 GS: 0-3 Gd: 0-2 GF: - Fm: 0-0
Distance: 2m/2m3: 0-1 2m4-2m7: 0-5 3m+: 0-2
Track: LH: 0-6 RH: 0-2 Tight: 0-0 Gall: 0-2
Aids: Bl: 0-0 Vi: 0-0 Tstrap: 0-0
Best Rating: 112 4/01 Aint 2m4f soft Hdl

Very moderate novice hurdler; stays three miles; acts on most types of ground.

Taking (FR)
94   92
7-y-o gr g Take Risks (FR)-Sonning (FR) (Moulin)
C N Kellett Sean A Taylor

Placings:P265033/565640364621/P0F22-503621P3P (2015)
2002/03: 16⁵GS, 16⁰GF, 16³G, 19⁶GF, 20²GS, 21¹GF, 21⁰GF, 21³GF, 20⁰GF,

	Starts	1st	2nd	3rd	Win & PI
Chases	9	1	1	2	5202
Career Total	33	2	5	5	36583
92 7/02 Sthl 2m5f110yF(0-95)HCh				G-F	£3087
87 2/01 Folk 2m F(0-90)HCh				SFT	£2926
				Total win prize-money	£6013

Going: Sf: 0-0 GS: 0-2 Gd: 0-1 GF: - Fm: 1-6
Distance: 2m/2m3: 0-4 2m4-2m7: 1-5 3m+: 0-0
Track: LH: 1-6 RH: 0-3 Tight: 0-1 Gall: 0-0
Aids: Bl: 1-5 Vi: 0-0 Tstrap: 0-0
Best Rating: 92 7/02 Sthl 2m5f110y gd-fm Ch

Moderate chaser; French import, improved form since tried in blinkers and won a handicap over an extended 21 furlongs at Southwell July 2002. Seems to act on any ground, best held up.

Taksina
83   43
4-y-o b f Wace (USA)-Quago (New Member)
R H Buckler Mrs Timothy Lewis

Placings:0056 (4626)
2002/03: 18⁰HY, 17⁰HY, 18⁵S, 17⁵GF,

	Starts	1st	2nd	3rd	Win & PI
NH Flat	2	0	0	0	0
Hurdles	2	0	0	0	0
Career Total	4	0	0	0	0

Going: Sf: 0-3 GS: 0-0 Gd: 0-0 GF: - Fm: 0-1
Distance: 2m/2m3: 0-4 2m4-2m7: 0-0 3m+: 0-0
Track: LH: 0-3 RH: 0-1 Tight: 0-4 Gall: 0-0
Aids: Bl: 0-0 Vi: 0-0 Tstrap: 0-0
Best Rating: 45 2/03 Folk 2m1f110y heavy NHF

Talaria (IRE)
7-y-o ch m Petardia-Million At Dawn (IRE) (Fayruz)
C J Teague Richardson Kelly O Gara Partnership

Placings:P0PP (1237)
2002/03: 17⁵GS, 17⁰G, 17PGF, 16PGF,

	Starts	1st	2nd	3rd	Win & PI
Hurdles	4	0	0	0	
Career Total	4	0	0	0	

Going: Sf: 0-0 GS: 0-1 Gd: 0-1 GF: - Fm: 0-2
Distance: 2m/2m3: 0-4 2m4-2m7: 0-0 3m+: 0-0
Track: LH: 0-4 RH: 0-0 Tight: 0-3 Gall: 0-0
Aids: Bl: 0-0 Vi: 0-0 Tstrap: 0-1
Best Rating: 0 9/02 Hexm 2m110y gd-fm Hdl

Talarive (USA)
117   128
7-y-o ch g Riverman (USA)-Estala (Be My Guest (USA))
P D Niven (Jonjo O Neill 7/12) Ian G M Dalgleish

Placings:00000/4P00/425023-2112322P (4049)
2002/03: 16²S, 16¹HY, 16¹HY, 16²GS, 20³GS, 16²GS, 18²GS, 16PHY,

	Starts	1st	2nd	3rd	Win & PI
Hurdles	8	2	4	1	20476
Career Total	23	2	6	2	23530
114 1/03 Ayr 2m D(0-125)HHdl				HVY	£4745
105 12/02 Leic 2m F(0-100)HHdl				HVY	£3513
				Total win prize-money	£8258

Going: Sf: 2-4 GS: 0-4 Gd: 0-0 GF: - Fm: 0-0
Distance: 2m/2m3: 2-4 2m4-2m7: 0-1 3m+: 0-0
Track: LH: 1-6 RH: 1-2 Tight: 0-1 Gall: 0-0
Aids: Bl: 0-0 Vi: 0-0 Tstrap: 0-0
Best Rating: 128 3/03 Kels 2m2f gd-sft Hdl

Fair ex-Irish hurdler; stays two and a half miles, but effective over shorter; suited by testing ground; very consistent.

Talathath (FR)
97(74h)   75
11-y-o b g Soviet Star (USA)-Mashmoon (USA) (Habitat)
M J Wilkinson R G & R A Whitehead

Placings:321411/2124265U055/0P0404P20/30F5311/42P3 0/0022-6U (0993)
2002/03: 22⁶GF, 26UGF,

	Starts	1st	2nd	3rd	Win & PI
Chases	2	0	0	0	0

Career Total	44	6	8	4	31907
97 11/99 Tntn 2m3f110yD(0-120)HHdl				GD	£2913
89 11/99 Kemp 2m5f E(0-115)HHdl				G-F	£5277
127 9/97 Worc 2m5f D(0-140)HHdl				G-F	£4948
114 4/97 MRas 2m3f110yD Hdl				GD	£3156
118 4/97 Chel 2m1f D Hdl				G-F	£2957
116 3/97 Winc 2m F Hdl				G-F	£1917
				Total win prize-money	£21171

Going: Sf: 0-0 GS: 0-0 Gd: 0-0 GF: - Fm: 0-2
Distance: 2m/2m3: 0-0 2m4-2m7: 0-1 3m+: 0-1
Track: LH: 0-1 RH: 0-1 Tight: 0-2 Gall: 0-0
Aids: Bl: 0-0 Vi: 0-0 Tstrap: 0-0
Best Rating: 127 9/97 Worc 2m4f gd-fm Hdl

Talbot Lad
94(99h)   (89h)97
7-y-o b g Weld-Greenacres Girl (Tycoon Ii)
S A Brookshaw M J Talbot

Placings:202255020-35P0423526 (4704)
2002/03: 17³G, 20⁵G, 20PG, 16⁰S, 19⁴G, 17²S, 16³G, 17⁵G, 20²GF, 20⁶G,

	Starts	1st	2nd	3rd	Win & PI
Hurdles	5	0	1	1	1601
Chases	5	0	1	1	2600
Career Total	19	0	6	2	6770

Going: Sf: 0-2 GS: 0-0 Gd: 0-7 GF: - Fm: 0-1
Distance: 2m/2m3: 0-6 2m4-2m7: 0-4 3m+: 0-0
Track: LH: 0-6 RH: 0-4 Tight: 0-5 Gall: 0-0
Aids: Bl: 0-0 Vi: 0-0 Tstrap: 0-10
Best Rating: 102 4/02 Ludl 2m good Hdl

Placed in bumpers and over hurdles; modest placed efforts so far over fences; stays 2m 4f.

Tale Bridge (IRE)
10-y-o b g Tale Quale-Loobagh Bridge (River Beauty)
Mrs O Bush (Miss M Lakin 22/5) J Grant Cann

Placings:0600/P3P (4480)
2002/03: 26PG, 25³S, 25PG,

	Starts	1st	2nd	3rd	Win & PI
Chases	3	0	0	1	208
Career Total	7	0	0	1	208

Going: Sf: 0-1 GS: 0-0 Gd: 0-2 GF: - Fm: 0-0
Distance: 2m/2m3: 0-0 2m4-2m7: 0-0 3m+: 0-3
Track: LH: 0-2 RH: 0-1 Tight: 0-1 Gall: 0-0
Aids: Bl: 0-0 Vi: 0-0 Tstrap: 0-0
Best Rating: 78 3/03 Winc 3m1f110y soft Ch

Talent Star
6-y-o b g Mizoram (USA)-Bells Of Longwick (Myjinski (USA))
A W Carroll Gordon W Day

Placings:P (1575)
2002/03: 16PG,

	Starts	1st	2nd	3rd	Win & PI
Hurdles	1	0	0	0	
Career Total	1	0	0	0	

Going: Sf: 0-0 GS: 0-0 Gd: 0-1 GF: - Fm: 0-0
Distance: 2m/2m3: 0-1 2m4-2m7: 0-0 3m+: 0-0

Track: LH: 0-1 RH: 0-0 Tight: 0-1 Gall: 0-0
Aids: Bl: 0-0 Vi: 0-0 Tstrap: 0-0
Best Rating: 0 10/02 Strf 2m110y good Hdl

Tales Of Bounty (IRE)

106(105c) (121c)123

8-y-o b g Ela-Mana-Mou-Tales Of Wisdom (Rousillon (USA))
P F Nicholls H B Geddes

Placings:36532/100/31/2-1014 (3851)
2002/03: 24¹GS, 25⁰GS, 24¹GS, 24⁴GS,

	Starts	1st	2nd	3rd	Win & Pl
Hurdles	2	1	0	0	3444
Chases	2	1	0	0	5214
Career Total	15	4	2	3	20842
121 12/02 Tntn	3m	D Ch		G-S	£4875
121 11/02 Extr	3m110y	E(0-110)HHdl		G-S	£3444
123 4/01 Winc	2m6f	D(0-120)HHdl		SFT	£4225
116 11/99 Extr	2m1f	E Hdl		G-S	£3297
				Total win prize-money	£15841

Going: Sf: 0-0 GS: 2-4 Gd: 0-0 GF: - Fm: 0-0
Distance: 2m/2m3: 0-0 2m4-2m7: 0-0 3m+: 2-4
Track: LH: 0-1 RH: 2-3 Tight: 1-2 Gall: 0-1
Aids: Bl: 0-0 Vi: 0-0 Tstrap: 0-0
Best Rating: 123 4/01 Winc 2m6f soft Hdl

Useful staying handicap hurdler and chaser; won 3m novice chase at Taunton December 2002; stays three miles; acts on soft ground.

Talk On Corners (IRE)

84 44

8-y-o b m Alphabatim (USA)-Shannon Lass (Callernish)
N R Mitchell (John Brassil 26/2) Michael Green

Placings:0F0000/00P-00PP (4720)
2002/03: 16⁰HY, 16⁰S, 18⁰YS, 22⁰F,

	Starts	1st	2nd	3rd	Win & Pl
NH Flat	1	0	0	0	
Hurdles	3	0	0	0	
Career Total	13	0	0	0	

Going: Sf: 0-2 GS: 0-0 Gd: 0-0 GF: - Fm: 0-1
Distance: 2m/2m3: 0-3 2m4-2m7: 0-1 3m+: 0-0
Track: LH: 0-0 RH: 0-1 Tight: 0-0 Gall: 0-0
Aids: Bl: 0-0 Vi: 0-0 Tstrap: 0-0
Best Rating: 64 1/02 Punc 2m yld-sft Hdl

Tall Tale (IRE)

98 69+

11-y-o b g Tale Quale-Prudent Rose (IRE) (Strong Gale)
R Johnson The Jolly Boys Partnership

Placings:52/34P/PP0425520/03UP4/345340F34-35354U40P64P1 (4409)
2002/03: 25³G, 25⁵G, 26³G, 27⁵G, 25⁴HY, 24ᵁGS, 27⁴S, 25⁰G, 27⁰HY, 27⁶HY, 32⁴S, 25¹G,

	Starts	1st	2nd	3rd	Win & Pl
Chases	13	1	0	2	4492
Career Total	41	1	3	7	11607
74 3/03 Hexm	3m1f	G(0-90)HCh		GD	£2681
				Total win prize-money	£2681

Going: Sf: 0-6 GS: 0-1 Gd: 1-6 GF: - Fm: 0-0
Distance: 2m/2m3: 0-0 2m4-2m7: 0-0 3m+: 1-13

Track: LH: 1-13 RH: 0-0 Tight: 0-7 Gall: 0-1
Aids: Bl: 0-0 Vi: 0-5 Tstrap: 0-0
Best Rating: 98 10/01 Kels 3m1f good Ch

Poor staying chaser; finally broke his duck at Hexham in March; acts on good.

Tallenoe

(3113)

4-y-o b f Rudimentary (USA)-Tino-Ella (Bustino)
P R Webber Miss Tina Miller

Placings:0 (3113)
2002/03: 17⁰HY,

	Starts	1st	2nd	3rd	Win & Pl
NH Flat	1	0	0	0	
Career Total	1	0	0	0	

Going: Sf: 0-1 GS: 0-0 Gd: 0-0 GF: - Fm: 0-0
Distance: 2m/2m3: 0-1 2m4-2m7: 0-0 3m+: 0-0
Track: LH: 0-0 RH: 0-1 Tight: 0-1 Gall: 0-0
Aids: Bl: 0-0 Vi: 0-0 Tstrap: 0-0
Best Rating: 0 1/03 Folk 2m1f110y heavy NHF

Tallison

73f

5-y-o ch g First Trump-Clare Celeste (Coquelin (USA))
P F Nicholls Neil Smith

Placings:5-0 (0523)
2002/03: 17⁰G,

	Starts	1st	2nd	3rd	Win & Pl
NH Flat	1	0	0	0	
Career Total	2	0	0	0	0

Going: Sf: 0-0 GS: 0-0 Gd: 0-1 GF: - Fm: 0-0
Distance: 2m/2m3: 0-1 2m4-2m7: 0-0 3m+: 0-0
Track: LH: 0-1 RH: 0-0 Tight: 0-0 Gall: 0-0
Aids: Bl: 0-0 Vi: 0-0 Tstrap: 0-0
Best Rating: 73 4/02 MRas 2m1f110y good NHF

Tallow Bay (IRE)

102 (51h)106d

8-y-o b g Glacial Storm (USA)-Minimum Choice (IRE) (Miners Lamp)
Mrs S Wall Mrs S Wall

Placings:000/5054600/243F25U2P-6116P5 (4085)
2002/03: 25⁶G, 21¹S, 21¹HY, 24⁶S, 26⁶GS, 20⁵GS,

	Starts	1st	2nd	3rd	Win & Pl
Chases	6	2	0	0	7660
Career Total	25	2	3	1	13142
106 1/03 Folk	2m5f	E Ch		HVY	£4238
104 1/03 Folk	2m5f	F(0-95)HCh		SFT	£3421
				Total win prize-money	£7660

Going: Sf: 2-3 GS: 0-2 Gd: 0-1 GF: - Fm: 0-0
Distance: 2m/2m3: 0-0 2m4-2m7: 2-3 3m+: 0-3
Track: LH: 0-2 RH: 2-4 Tight: 2-5 Gall: 0-0
Aids: Bl: 0-0 Vi: 0-0 Tstrap: 0-0
Best Rating: 109 4/00 Asct 2m110y soft NHF

Fair handicap chaser, but did not get off the mark over fences until winning twice at Folkestone in January 2003. Goes well there and prefers stiff tracks and soft ground. Stays three miles.

Tamango (FR)

104(102h) (117h)117

6-y-o gr g Klimt (FR)-Tipmosa (FR) (Tip Moss (FR))
P J Hobbs The Brushmakers

Placings:32401-2223F3 (4596)
2002/03: 19²G, 16²G, 17²GS, 20³HY, 16²HY, 19³GF,

	Starts	1st	2nd	3rd	Win & Pl
Hurdles	3	0	2	1	4602
Chases	3	0	1	1	3839
Career Total	11	1	4	3	12222
103 4/02 Tntn	2m1f	E Hdl		G-S	£2800
				Total win prize-money	£2800

Going: Sf: 0-2 GS: 0-1 Gd: 0-2 GF: - Fm: 0-1
Distance: 2m/2m3: 0-5 2m4-2m7: 0-1 3m+: 0-0
Track: LH: 0-1 RH: 0-4 Tight: 0-2 Gall: 0-0
Aids: Bl: 0-0 Vi: 0-0 Tstrap: 0-0
Best Rating: 118 2/02 Font 2m2f110y soft NHF

Modest hurdler; fair novice chaser, successful twice in May 2003; just touched off in hat-trick bid at Stratford in July; acts well on fast ground; stays two and a half miles; has room for improvement in his jumping.

Tambo (IRE)

97 95

8-y-o b g Shardari-Carmen Lady (Torus)
M Bradstock Mark Tamburro

Placings:040221/40/3P-P2 (4430)
2002/03: 21ᴾS, 20²GF,

	Starts	1st	2nd	3rd	Win & Pl
Chases	2	0	1	0	1728
Career Total	12	1	3	1	6563
113 3/00 Plum	2m5f	E Hdl		GD	£2450
				Total win prize-money	£2450

Going: Sf: 0-1 GS: 0-0 Gd: 0-0 GF: - Fm: 0-1
Distance: 2m/2m3: 0-0 2m4-2m7: 0-2 3m+: 0-0
Track: LH: 0-2 RH: 0-0 Tight: 0-0 Gall: 0-0
Aids: Bl: 0-0 Vi: 0-0 Tstrap: 0-0
Best Rating: 116 3/00 Donc 2m4f gd-sft Hdl

Modest handicap chaser; has run well in 2002/3 after a year off; all out to win a 2m 6f handicap chase at Fontwell May 2003; acts on fast ground.

Taming (IRE)

109 135d

7-y-o ch g Lycius (USA)-Black Fighter (USA) (Secretariat (USA))
Miss Venetia Williams Oakview Racing

Placings:6F2/P003/5-25111031113F0 (4112)
2002/03: 17²GG, 16⁵S, 16¹GS, 16¹GS, 20¹G, 17⁰GS, 16³G, 20¹GS, 21¹G, 21¹GS, 20³HY, 20ᶠHY, 21⁰G,

	Starts	1st	2nd	3rd	Win & Pl
Hurdles	13	6	1	2	31259
Career Total	21	6	2	3	32538
135 11/02 Chel	2m5f	B Hdl		G-S	£9744
135 10/02 Chel	2m5f	C Hdl		GD	£7297
125 10/02 Hntg	2m4f110yD Hdl			G-F	£3649
135 7/02 Worc	2m4f	E Hdl		GD	£2842
122 7/02 Wolv	2m	E Hdl		G-S	£2905
108 6/02 Uttx	2m	E Hdl		G-S	£2667
				Total win prize-money	£29105

Going: Sf: 0-3 GS: 3-4 Gd: 2-4 GF: - Fm: 1-2
Distance: 2m/2m3: 2-6 2m4-2m7: 4-7 3m+: 0-0
Track: LH: 5-8 RH: 1-5 Tight: 1-3 Gall: 3-4
Aids: Bl: 0-0 Vi: 0-0 Tstrap: 0-0
Best Rating: 135 11/02 Chel 2m5f gd-sft Hdl

Useful hurdler; successful six times on decent ground in 2002 but below par on a softer surface subsequently; suited by two and a half miles.

Tana River (IRE)
113   131+
7-y-o b g Over The River (FR)-Home In The Glen (Furry Glen)
Miss E C Lavelle The Frisky Fillies

Placings:22111   (4048)
2002/03: 20²G, 20²S, 19¹GS, 20¹HY, 20¹HY,

	Starts	1st	2nd	3rd	Win & Pl
Hurdles	5	3	2	0	40503
Career Total	5	3	2	0	40503
131 3/03	Sand	2m4f110yA HHdl		HVY	£29000
110 1/03	Leic	2m4f110yD Hdl		HVY	£5486
109 12/02	Extr	2m3f	E Hdl	G-S	£3598
			Total win prize-money		£38084

Going: Sf: 2-3 GS: 1-1 Gd: 0-1 GF: - Fm: 0-0
Distance: 2m/2m3: 1-1 **2m4-2m7: 2-4** 3m+: 0-0
Track: LH: 0-2 **RH: 3-3** Tight: 0-0 Gall: 0-0
Aids: Bl: 0-0 Vi: 0-0 Tstrap: 0-0
Best Rating: **131** 3/03 Sand 2m4f110y heavy Hdl

Fair novice hurdler; effective at two and a half miles and acts on a soft surface.

Tango Royal (FR)
110(109c)   (129c)120
7-y-o gr g Royal Charter (FR)-Nazia (FR) (Zino)
M C Pipe B A Kilpatrick

Placings:01310112/03154F4/600-FF06635   (4256)
2002/03: 16⁶G, 17⁵FS, 16⁶S, 17⁶S, 19⁶GS, 19³S, 17⁷G,

	Starts	1st	2nd	3rd	Win & Pl
Hurdles	5	0	0	1	748
Chases	2	0	0	0	0
Career Total	25	5	1	3	116139
9/00	Comp	2m1f110y Hdl		G-S	£3362
3/00	Autl	2m4f110y Ch		VS	£28818
3/00	Autl	2m1f110y Ch		HVY	£28818
11/99	Engh	2m1f	Ch	HLD	£10764
10/99	Toul	2m1f110y Ch		SFT	£4844
			Total win prize-money		£76606

Going: Sf: 0-3 GS: 0-2 Gd: 0-2 GF: - Fm: 0-0
Distance: 2m/2m3: 0-6 2m4-2m7: 0-1 3m+: 0-0
Track: LH: 0-3 RH: 0-4 Tight: 0-1 Gall: 0-2
Aids: Bl: 0-0 Vi: 0-0 Tstrap: 0-5
Best Rating: **139** 11/00 Autl 2m6f heavy Ch

Fair hurdler/chaser; ex-French; lost his way over fences with jumping problems; got off the mark in this country when winning strongly-run 2m handicap hurdle at Stratford May 2003; looks best suited by trips of around 2m; effective on soft ground; has worn a tongue tie.

Tanikos (FR)
100   101
4-y-o b g Nikos-Tamana (USA) (Northern Baby (CAN))
N J Henderson Studwell Two Partnership

Placings:130   (4130)
2002/03: 17¹HY, 16³G, 17⁰G,

	Starts	1st	2nd	3rd	Win & Pl
Hurdles	3	1	0	1	5002
Career Total	3	1	0	1	5002
11/02	Pari	2m1f	Hdl	HVY	£4418
			Total win prize-money		£4418

Going: Sf: 1-1 GS: 0-0 Gd: 0-2 GF: - Fm: 0-0
Distance: **2m/2m3: 1-3** 2m4-2m7: 0-0 3m+: 0-0
Track: LH: 0-2 RH: 0-0 Tight: 0-0 Gall: 0-1
Aids: Bl: 0-0 Vi: 0-0 Tstrap: 0-0
Best Rating: **101** 2/03 Weth 2m good Hdl

Moderate juvenile hurdler; winner in heavy ground in French provinces in November; no excuse when only third on much better ground at Wetherby in February (forced to make the running).

Tanners Court
6-y-o b g Framlington Court-True Nell (Neltino)
Miss C Dyson Miss C Dyson

Placings:0030   (4190)
2002/03: 17⁰G, 16⁰S, 16³GS, 17⁰G,

	Starts	1st	2nd	3rd	Win & Pl
NH Flat	4	0	0	1	342
Career Total	4	0	0	1	342

Going: Sf: 0-1 GS: 0-0 Gd: 0-2 GF: - Fm: 0-0
Distance: 2m/2m3: 0-4 2m4-2m7: 0-0 3m+: 0-0
Track: LH: 0-2 RH: 0-2 Tight: 0-1 Gall: 0-0
Aids: Bl: 0-0 Vi: 0-0 Tstrap: 0-0
Best Rating: **92** 1/03 Kemp 2m gd-sft NHF

Tanners Friend
6-y-o b m Environment Friend-Glenn s Slipper (Furry Glen)
Miss C Dyson Miss C Dyson

Placings:0000P   (4187)
2002/03: 17⁰GS, 17⁰S, 16⁰GS, 16⁰G, 20⁰G,

	Starts	1st	2nd	3rd	Win & Pl
NH Flat	4	0	0	0	0
Hurdles	1	0	0	0	0
Career Total	5	0	0	0	0

Going: Sf: 0-1 GS: 0-2 Gd: 0-2 GF: - Fm: 0-0
Distance: 2m/2m3: 0-4 2m4-2m7: 0-1 3m+: 0-0
Track: LH: 0-1 RH: 0-3 Tight: 0-2 Gall: 0-0
Aids: Bl: 0-0 Vi: 0-0 Tstrap: 0-0
Best Rating: **79** 2/03 Ludl 2m good NHF

Tantabank
66f
5-y-o b g Primitive Rising (USA)-Rua Ros (IRE) (Roselier (FR))
Mrs S J Smith R Preston

Placings:0   (1982)
2002/03: 16⁰HY,

	Starts	1st	2nd	3rd	Win & Pl
NH Flat	1	0	0	0	0
Career Total	1	0	0	0	0

Going: Sf: 0-1 GS: 0-0 Gd: 0-0 GF: - Fm: 0-0
Distance: 2m/2m3: 0-1 2m4-2m7: 0-0 3m+: 0-0
Track: LH: 0-1 RH: 0-0 Tight: 0-0 Gall: 0-0
Aids: Bl: 0-0 Vi: 0-0 Tstrap: 0-0
Best Rating: **66** 11/02 Weth 2m heavy NHF

Tap Dance
103   65
5-y-o ch g Dancing Spree (USA)-Trachelium (Formidable (USA))

M E Sowersby (Miss S E Hall 1/11) Paul Clifton

Placings:20P2P-022006PP0   (4686)
2002/03: 16⁰S, 21²GF, 21²G, 20⁰GF, 23⁰G, 21⁶HY, 25⁵G, 27⁵G, 17⁰GF,

	Starts	1st	2nd	3rd	Win & Pl
Hurdles	9	0	2	0	1670
Career Total	14	0	4	0	3148

Going: Sf: 0-2 GS: 0-0 Gd: 0-4 GF: - Fm: 0-3
Distance: 2m/2m3: 0-2 2m4-2m7: 0-5 3m+: 0-2
Track: LH: 0-8 RH: 0-1 Tight: 0-7 Gall: 0-0
Aids: Bl: 0-1 Vi: 0-1 Tstrap: 0-0
Best Rating: **85** 8/02 Sedg 2m5f110y good Hdl

Exposed novice hurdler. Effective at two miles two furlongs and acts on heavy ground.

Tap Dancer (IRE)
74   56
5-y-o b g Sadler s Wells (USA)-Watch Out (USA) (Mr Prospector (USA))
B G Powell The A T P Racing Partnership

Placings:006-5P   (0972)
2002/03: 16⁵GF, 16⁶GS,

	Starts	1st	2nd	3rd	Win & Pl
Hurdles	2	0	0	0	0
Career Total	5	0	0	0	0

Going: Sf: 0-0 GS: 0-1 Gd: 0-0 GF: - Fm: 0-1
Distance: 2m/2m3: 0-2 2m4-2m7: 0-0 3m+: 0-0
Track: LH: 0-2 RH: 0-0 Tight: 0-1 Gall: 0-0
Aids: Bl: 0-0 Vi: 0-0 Tstrap: 0-0
Best Rating: **56** 7/02 Worc 2m gd-fm Hdl

Tap The Stone (IRE)
66   24
4-y-o b g Bigstone (IRE)-Wadeyaa (Green Desert (USA))
J S Wainwright Barry J Ross

Placings:0P0   (2120)
2002/03: 16⁰GF, 16⁶S, 16⁰GS,

	Starts	1st	2nd	3rd	Win & Pl
Hurdles	3	0	0	0	0
Career Total	3	0	0	0	0

Going: Sf: 0-1 GS: 0-1 Gd: 0-0 GF: - Fm: 0-1
Distance: 2m/2m3: 0-3 2m4-2m7: 0-0 3m+: 0-0
Track: LH: 0-3 RH: 0-0 Tight: 0-1 Gall: 0-1
Aids: Bl: 0-0 Vi: 0-1 Tstrap: 0-0
Best Rating: **25** 11/02 Fknm 2m gd-sft Hdl

Tarasco (FR)
106(105h)   (133h)122+
7-y-o b g Deploy-Moucha (FR) (Fabulous Dancer (USA))
P R Webber Mrs D Ridley

Placings:13205-F5111   (4562)
2002/03: 20⁵S, 19⁵G, 16¹G, 17¹GS, 17¹GF,

	Starts	1st	2nd	3rd	Win & Pl
Chases	5	3	0	0	15373
Career Total	10	4	1	1	26391
122 4/03	Bang	2m1f110yD Ch		G-F	£5629
123 3/03	MRas	2m1f110yD Ch		G-S	£5687
105 3/03	Hntg	2m110y E Ch		GD	£4056
130 12/01	Bang	2m1f	E Hdl	G-S	£2807
			Total win prize-money		£18180

Going: Sf: 0-1 GS: 1-1 Gd: 1-2 GF: - Fm: 1-1
Distance: 2m/2m3: 3-4 2m4m-2m7: 0-1 3m+: 0-0
Track: LH: 1-3 RH: 2-2 Tight: 2-3 Gall: 1-1
Aids: Bl: 0-0 Vi: 2-2 Tstrap: 0-0
Best Rating: 133 1/02   Wwck 2m   soft   Hdl

Fair chaser; ex-French, he won three times on varying ground in the spring of 2003; has worn a visor.

Tarashani (IRE)

90   84

5-y-o ch g Primo Dominie-Tarakana (USA) (Shahrastani (USA))
B Ellison Eddie Kirtland/Bob Bowden

Placings:006-444   (2425)
2002/03: 18⁴S, 16⁴HY, 17⁴S,

	Starts	1st	2nd	3rd	Win & Pl
Hurdles	3	0	0	0	263
Career Total	6	0	0	0	263

Going: Sf: 0-3 GS: 0-0 Gd: 0-0 GF: - Fm: 0-0
Distance: 2m/2m3: 0-3 2m4m-2m7: 0-0 3m+: 0-0
Track: LH: 0-3 RH: 0-0 Tight: 0-2 Gall: 0-0
Aids: Bl: 0-0 Vi: 0-0 Tstrap: 0-0
Best Rating: 84 11/02   Weth 2m   heavy   Hdl

Plating-class maiden on the Flat and over hurdles.

Tarbolton Moss

92(104h)   (101h)112

8-y-o b m Le Moss-Priceless Peril (Silly Prices)
M Todhunter Mrs David Marshall

Placings:0505/40331212-42P13   (4307)
2002/03: 20⁴S, 25²S, 26⁶HY, 25¹GS, 32³G,

	Starts	1st	2nd	3rd	Win & Pl
Chases	5	1	1	1	12417
Career Total	17	3	3	3	20518
112 2/03	Ayr	3m1f		E Ch	G-S £4036
101 3/02	Kels	3m3f		F(0-95)HHdl	SFT £2999
93 2/02	Newc	3m		F(0-100)HHdl	SFT £1904

Total win prize-money £8941

Going: Sf: 0-3 GS: 1-1 Gd: 0-1 GF: - Fm: 0-0
Distance: 2m/2m3: 0-0 2m4m-2m7: 0-1 3m+: 1-4
Track: LH: 1-3 RH: 0-2 Tight: 0-2 Gall: 0-0
Aids: Bl: 0-0 Vi: 0-0 Tstrap: 0-0
Best Rating: 112 2/03   Ayr 3m1f   gd-sft   Ch

Modest hurdler; stays three miles plus; appreciates soft ground.

Tarboush

102   89

6-y-o b g Polish Precedent (USA)-Barboukh (Night Shift (USA))
B G Powell (N A Callaghan 21/12) Gallagher Equine Ltd

Placings:6032   (4463)
2002/03: 16⁶GS, 16⁰G, 16³G, 17²F,

	Starts	1st	2nd	3rd	Win & Pl
Hurdles	4	0	1	1	1681
Career Total	4	0	1	1	1681

Going: Sf: 0-0 GS: 0-1 Gd: 0-2 GF: - Fm: 0-1
Distance: 2m/2m3: 0-4 2m4m-2m7: 0-0 3m+: 0-0
Track: LH: 0-0 RH: 0-4 Tight: 0-1 Gall: 0-0
Aids: Bl: 0-0 Vi: 0-0 Tstrap: 0-0
Best Rating: 89 3/03   Ludl 2m   good   Hdl

Fair hurdler; acts on any ground; suited by forcing tactics

Tardar (NZ)

108   125+

7-y-o br g Prince Ferdinand-La Magnifique (NZ) (Kampala)
Jonjo O Neill Ray & Sue Dodd Partnership

Placings:3110   (4112)
2002/03: 16³GS, 16¹S, 16¹HY, 21⁰G,

	Starts	1st	2nd	3rd	Win & Pl
Hurdles	4	2	0	1	9537
Career Total	4	2	0	1	9537
125 2/03	Chep	2m110y	D Hdl	HVY	£5034
120 12/02	Chep	2m110y	D Hdl	SFT	£3926

Total win prize-money £8960

Going: Sf: 2-2 GS: 0-1 Gd: 0-0 GF: - Fm: 0-0
Distance: 2m/2m3: 2-3 2m4m-2m7: 0-1 3m+: 0-0
Track: LH: 2-4 RH: 0-0 Tight: 0-0 Gall: 0-1
Aids: Bl: 0-0 Vi: 0-0 Tstrap: 0-0
Best Rating: 125 2/03   Chep 2m110y   heavy   Hdl

Useful novice hurdler; formerly a winner on the Flat in Australia and New Zealand; best over two miles and suited by soft ground; progressive.

Tardissima

64f   17f

5-y-o ch m River Falls-Chilibang Bang (Chilibang)
Mrs H O Graham R D Graham

Placings:00   (0584)
2002/03: 16⁰GF, 16⁰G,

	Starts	1st	2nd	3rd	Win & Pl
NH Flat	2	0	0	0	
Career Total	2	0	0	0	

Going: Sf: 0-0 GS: 0-0 Gd: 0-0 GF: - Fm: 0-1
Distance: 2m/2m3: 0-2 2m4m-2m7: 0-0 3m+: 0-0
Track: LH: 0-1 RH: 0-1 Tight: 0-0 Gall: 0-0
Aids: Bl: 0-0 Vi: 0-0 Tstrap: 0-0
Best Rating: 17 5/02   Prth 2m110y   gd-fm   NHF

Tarongo (FR)

104   81

5-y-o b g Tel Quel (FR)-Rainbow Rainbow (Vision (USA))
Mrs L C Taylor Mrs L C Taylor

Placings:PP-PF2   (4638)
2002/03: 19⁰GF, 19⁰F, 17²G,

	Starts	1st	2nd	3rd	Win & Pl
Hurdles	1	0	0	0	0
Chases	2	0	1	0	2478
Career Total	5	0	1	0	2478

Going: Sf: 0-0 GS: 0-0 Gd: 0-0 GF: - Fm: 0-2
Distance: 2m/2m3: 0-2 2m4m-2m7: 0-1 3m+: 0-0
Track: LH: 0-1 RH: 0-2 Tight: 0-2 Gall: 0-0
Aids: Bl: 0-0 Vi: 0-0 Tstrap: 0-0
Best Rating: 0 4/03   Strf 2m1f110y   good   Ch

Tarongoshy (IRE)

88   77

6-y-o ch m Over The River (FR)-October Lady (Lucifer (USA))
M Pitman Mrs David Laing

Placings:24P0-05P   (4681)
2002/03: 17⁰HY, 24⁵GF, 21⁸GF,

	Starts	1st	2nd	3rd	Win & Pl
Hurdles	3	0	0	0	0

Career Total   7   0   1   0   460

Going: Sf: 0-1 GS: 0-0 Gd: 0-0 GF: - Fm: 0-2
Distance: 2m/2m3: 0-1 2m4m-2m7: 0-1 3m+: 0-1
Track: LH: 0-1 RH: 0-2 Tight: 0-2 Gall: 0-1
Aids: Bl: 0-2 Vi: 0-0 Tstrap: 0-0
Best Rating: 94 1/02   Folk 2m1f110y   soft   NHF

Tarski

98   100+

9-y-o ch g Polish Precedent (USA)-Illusory (King s Lake (USA))
W S Kittow Midd Shire Racing

Placings:66-10102P   (1620)
2002/03: 16¹GF, 16⁰GS, 17¹GF, 16⁰G, 19⁰F, 21⁰F,

	Starts	1st	2nd	3rd	Win & Pl
Hurdles	6	2	1	0	6020
Career Total	8	2	1	0	6020
89 8/02	NAbb	2m1f	F Hdl	G-F	£2205
93 7/02	Worc	2m	E Hdl	G-F	£2940

Total win prize-money £5145

Going: Sf: 0-0 GS: 0-1 Gd: 0-1 GF: - Fm: 2-4
Distance: 2m/2m3: 2-5 2m4m-2m7: 0-1 3m+: 0-0
Track: LH: 2-4 RH: 0-2 Tight: 1-2 Gall: 0-0
Aids: Bl: 0-0 Vi: 0-1 Tstrap: 0-0
Best Rating: 100 10/02   Extr 2m3f   firm   Hdl

Modest hurdler; sprang 25/1 shock when landing 2m maiden hurdle at Worcester July 2002; scored again in a claimer at Newton Abbot the following month; appreciated step up to 2m 4f when winning Worcester selling handicap July 2003; acts on ground good and faster.

Tarxien

110(109h)   (142h)153

9-y-o b g Kendor (FR)-Tanz (IRE) (Sadler s Wells (USA))
M C Pipe B A Kilpatrick

Placings:4/443/54302/4111111B2-1121F2   (4554)
2002/03: 20¹GS, 19¹S, 21²S, 20¹HY, 21²G, 20²G,

	Starts	1st	2nd	3rd	Win & Pl
Chases	6	3	2	0	76840
Career Total	24	9	4	2	134344
153 2/03	Sand	2m4f110yA	Ch	HVY	£34100
153 12/02	Asct	2m3f110yA	Ch	SFT	£18000
145 11/02	Chel	2m4f110yB	Ch	G-S	£12354
134 12/01	Asct	3m	B Hdl	GD	£11340
140 11/01	Chel	2m5f	B Hdl	GD	£8736
136 9/01	Worc	2m4f	C(0-135)HHdl	G-F	£5554
126 8/01	NAbb	2m6f	E Hdl	G-F	£2954
130 8/01	MRas	2m3f110yC(0-130)HHdl		G-F	£6179
125 7/01	NAbb	2m6f	C(0-130)HHdl	GD	£4867

Total win prize-money £104086

Going: Sf: 2-3 GS: 1-1 Gd: 0-2 GF: - Fm: 0-0
Distance: 2m/2m3: 0-0 2m4m-2m7: 3-6 3m+: 0-0
Track: LH: 1-4 RH: 2-2 Tight: 0-0 Gall: 1-3
Aids: Bl: 0-0 Vi: 0-0 Tstrap: 3-6
Best Rating: 153 2/03   Sand 2m4f110y   heavy   Ch

Very useful novice hurdler; has shown high-class form in novice chases, including when landing the Scilly Isles Novices Chase at Sandown in February 2003; jumped poorly prior to falling in Cathcart at Cheltenham; did not jump that well when runner-up at Ayr subsequently; stays three miles, but effective at shorter; acts well on a soft surface, but is probably better on faster ground; wears a tongue tie.

Tasbok (IRE)

(104h) (95h)**75**

8-y-o b g Posen (USA)-Go Honey Go (General Assembly (USA))

R Rowe Sports Turf Management Ltd

Placings:6050233-5PF (2255)

2002/03: 21³G, 22⁵GF, 20ᴾGS, 21ᶠS,

	Starts	1st	2nd	3rd	Win & Pl
Hurdles	3	0	0	1	357
Chases	1	0	0	0	0
Career Total	**10**	**0**	**1**	**2**	**1890**

Going: Sf: 0-1 GS: 0-1 Gd: 0-1 GF: - Fm: 0-1
Distance: 2m/2m3: 0-0 2m4-2m7: 0-4 3m+: 0-0
Track: LH: 0-1 RH: 0-3 Tight: 0-2 Gall: 0-0
Aids: Bl: 0-0 Vi: 0-0 Tstrap: 0-0
Best Rating: **95** 4/02 Asct 2m110y gd-fm Hdl

Taskmaster

115+

6-y-o b g Alflora (IRE)-Travail Girl (Forties Field (FR))

P J Hobbs Andrew P Wyer

Placings:0-F (1603)

2002/03: 16ᶠG,

	Starts	1st	2nd	3rd	Win & Pl
Hurdles	1	0	0	0	
Career Total	**2**	**0**	**0**	**0**	

Going: Sf: 0-0 GS: 0-0 Gd: 0-1 GF: - Fm: 0-0
Distance: 2m/2m3: 0-1 2m4-2m7: 0-0 3m+: 0-0
Track: LH: 0-1 RH: 0-0 Tight: 0-0 Gall: 0-0
Aids: Bl: 0-0 Vi: 0-0 Tstrap: 0-0
Best Rating: **104** 10/02 Chep 2m110y good Hdl

Tathmin

102(103c) (96c)**82**

10-y-o b g Weldnaas (USA)-Alcassa (FR) (Satingo)

A King Miss J M Bodycote

Placings:0053/10/000/1105212-**122335355** (4340)

2002/03: 23¹G, 23²G, 23²GF, 26³G, 26³GF, 24⁵GS, 24³G, 22⁵G, 26⁵GF,

	Starts	1st	2nd	3rd	Win & Pl
Hurdles	5	0	0	2	1232
Chases	4	1	2	1	6771
Career Total	**25**	**5**	**4**	**4**	**23745**

102	5/02	Weth	2m7f110y	D Ch	GD	£4147
102	11/01	Extr	3m110y	E(0-115)HHdl	G-F	£3234
95	5/01	Hrfd	2m3f110y	F(0-110)HHdl	GD	£3643
98	5/01	Winc	2m6f	F(0-100)HHdl	G-F	£3584
78	5/97	Hrfd	2m1f	E(0-100)HHdl	GD	£2332

Total win prize-money £16941

Going: Sf: 0-0 GS: 0-1 Gd: 1-5 GF: - Fm: 0-3
Distance: 2m/2m3: 0-0 2m4-2m7: 0-2 **3m+: 1-7**
Track: LH: 0-4 RH: 0-4 Tight: 0-2 Gall: 0-2
Aids: Bl: 0-5 Vi: 0-1 Tstrap: 0-0
Best Rating: **102** 6/02 Worc 2m7f110y gd-fm Ch

Plating-class hurdler; moderate chaser; best on a sound surface; usually blinkered.

Taxbuster

(95h) (75h)

11-y-o b g Welsh Captain-Indian Cash (Indian Ruler)

N B Thomson Taxbusters

Placings:43/2/0P0036/46/0000-F (0036)

2002/03: 17ᶠG,

	Starts	1st	2nd	3rd	Win & Pl
Chases	1	0	0	0	
Career Total	**16**	**0**	**1**	**2**	**854**

Going: Sf: 0-0 GS: 0-0 Gd: 0-1 GF: - Fm: 0-0
Distance: 2m/2m3: 0-1 2m4-2m7: 0-0 3m+: 0-0
Track: LH: 0-0 RH: 0-1 Tight: 0-0 Gall: 0-0
Aids: Bl: 0-0 Vi: 0-0 Tstrap: 0-0
Best Rating: **110** 3/00 Winc 2m gd-sft Hdl

Te Akau Dan (NZ)

9-y-o b g Dance Floor (USA)-Bellandaan (NZ) (Standaan (FR))

S G Griffiths S G Griffiths

Placings:P040/0**PF**0P/PP/PP-P (0840)

2002/03: 19ᴾGF,

	Starts	1st	2nd	3rd	Win & Pl
Hurdles	1	0	0	0	
Career Total	**14**	**0**	**0**	**0**	**0**

Going: Sf: 0-0 GS: 0-0 Gd: 0-0 GF: - Fm: 0-1
Distance: 2m/2m3: 0-1 2m4-2m7: 0-0 3m+: 0-0
Track: LH: 0-1 RH: 0-0 Tight: 0-1 Gall: 0-0
Aids: Bl: 0-0 Vi: 0-0 Tstrap: 0-0
Best Rating: **66** 2/99 Hrfd 2m3f110y good Hdl

Tea Box (IRE)

12-y-o b g Meneval (USA)-Elteetee (Paddy s Stream)

M A Kemp M A Kemp

Placings:00/U04**0**5/1/31/1FP-3 (0154)

2002/03: 24³G,

	Starts	1st	2nd	3rd	Win & Pl
Chases	1	0	0	1	214
Career Total	**14**	**3**	**0**	**2**	**5883**

110	4/02	Fknm	3m110y	H Ch	GD	£2161
90	5/00	Hexm	2m4f110y	H Ch	GD	£1237
93	4/00	Newc	2m4f	H Ch	G-S	£1813

Total win prize-money £5214

Going: Sf: 0-0 GS: 0-0 Gd: 0-1 GF: - Fm: 0-0
Distance: 2m/2m3: 0-0 2m4-2m7: 0-0 3m+: 0-1
Track: LH: 0-1 RH: 0-0 Tight: 0-1 Gall: 0-0
Aids: Bl: 0-0 Vi: 0-0 Tstrap: 0-0
Best Rating: **110** 4/02 Fknm 3m110y good Ch

Useful pointer/hunter chaser with high strike rate. Stays three miles, does not want the ground too soft.

Tea Time (IRE)

8-y-o b g Glacial Storm (USA)-Blaze Of Hope (IRE) (Le Moss)

R T Phillips Colin Pocock

Placings:P-P (0035)

2002/03: 22ᴾG,

	Starts	1st	2nd	3rd	Win & Pl
Hurdles	1	0	0	0	
Career Total	**2**	**0**	**0**	**0**	

Going: Sf: 0-0 GS: 0-0 Gd: 0-1 GF: - Fm: 0-0
Distance: 2m/2m3: 0-0 2m4-2m7: 0-1 3m+: 0-0
Track: LH: 0-0 RH: 0-1 Tight: 0-0 Gall: 0-0
Aids: Bl: 0-0 Vi: 0-0 Tstrap: 0-0
Best Rating:

Teaatral

105(114h) (157dh)**124**

9-y-o b g Saddlers Hall (IRE)-La Cabrilla (Carwhite)

C R Egerton Bernard Gover Bloodstock Trading Ltd

Placings:210112/013110/**U**3111/P412P56/5430PP-5 (2846)

2002/03: 24⁵S,

	Starts	1st	2nd	3rd	Win & Pl
Hurdles	1	0	0	0	523
Career Total	**31**	**10**	**3**	**3**	**132645**

164	2/01	Sand	2m110y	B Hdl	HVY	£13468
164	4/00	Asct	3m	A Hdl	GD	£18600
158	2/00	Kemp	3m110y	A HHdl	SFT	£13200
162	2/00	Asct	2m4f	B(0-150)HHdl	SFT	£20579
150	2/99	Sand	2m6f	A HHdl	G-S	£26800
148	1/99	Kemp	2m5f	C(0-135)HHdl	HVY	£5628
131	12/98	Leic	2m4f110y	D(0-120)HHdl	SFT	£3002
105	4/98	Hrfd	2m1f	E Hdl	G-S	£2624
110	4/98	Tntn	2m1f	E(0-115)HHdl	GD	£2710
111	1/98	Folk	2m1f110y	E Hdl	G-S	£1976

Total win prize-money £108588

Going: Sf: 0-1 GS: 0-0 Gd: 0-0 GF: - Fm: 0-0
Distance: 2m/2m3: 0-0 2m4-2m7: 0-0 3m+: 0-1
Track: LH: 0-1 RH: 0-0 Tight: 0-0 Gall: 0-1
Aids: Bl: 0-1 Vi: 0-0 Tstrap: 0-0
Best Rating: **164** 2/01 Kemp 3m110y gd-sft Hdl

A useful staying hurdler, high-class at his best, he showed his versatility when winning over the minimum trip at Sandown in February 2001; disappointing in 2001/02; has won weak novice chases at Huntingdon in May and Market Rasen the following month; has only ever won on right-handed tracks; suited by soft ground, he usually wears blinkers.

Teal Bay

11-y-o b m Scallywag-Centaura (Centaurus)

P A Jones P A Jones

Placings:0/43/BF63/5 (0278)

2002/03: 24⁵S,

	Starts	1st	2nd	3rd	Win & Pl
Chases	1	0	0	0	0
Career Total	**8**	**0**	**0**	**2**	**660**

Going: Sf: 0-1 GS: 0-0 Gd: 0-0 GF: - Fm: 0-0
Distance: 2m/2m3: 0-0 2m4-2m7: 0-0 3m+: 0-1
Track: LH: 0-1 RH: 0-0 Tight: 0-1 Gall: 0-0
Aids: Bl: 0-0 Vi: 0-0 Tstrap: 0-0
Best Rating: **88** 4/98 Chep 2m4f110y heavy Hdl

Tealby

98 **109+**

6-y-o b m Efisio-Al Raja (King s Lake (USA))

Mrs L Wadham The Dyball Partnership

Placings:21214-122 (2706)

2002/03: 16¹GS, 17²G, 16²GS,

	Starts	1st	2nd	3rd	Win & Pl
Hurdles	3	1	2	0	7451
Career Total	**8**	**3**	**4**	**0**	**11482**

92	12/02	Sthl	2m	E Hdl	G-S	£2961
95	7/01	Worc	2m	H NHF	GD	£1494

109 6/01 MRas 2m1f110yH NHF   G-F £1589
Total win prize-money £6045

Going:	Sf: 0-0 GS: 1-2 Gd: 0-1 GF: - Fm: 0-0
Distance:	**2m/2m3: 1-3** 2m4-2m7: 0-0 3m+: 0-0
Track:	**LH: 1-2** RH: 0-1 Tight: **1-1** Gall: 0-1
Aids:	Bl: 0-0 Vi: 0-0 Tstrap: 0-0
Best Rating:	**109** 12/02 Chel 2m1f good Hdl

Modest hurdler; dual bumper winner, easy winner over hurdles at Southwell in December 2002 and second to Rhinestone Cowboy next time; acts on most ground; consistent.

Team Captain

94   **94d**
9-y-o ch g Teamster-Silly Sausage (Silly Answer)
C J Down P J Hickman

Placings:0IP/2PF2122-2U46   (4293)
2002/03: 21²GF, 28⁴G, 27⁴G, 25⁶GF,

	Starts	1st	2nd	3rd	Win & Pl
Chases	4	0	1	0	1100
Career Total	13	1	5	0	5805
100 3/02 Winc 3m1f110y				H Ch	GD
£1684					

Total win prize-money £1684

Going:	Sf: 0-0 GS: 0-0 Gd: 0-2 GF: - Fm: 0-2
Distance:	2m/2m3: 0-0 2m4-2m7: 0-1 3m+: 0-3
Track:	LH: 0-1 RH: 0-3 Tight: 0-2 Gall: 0-0
Aids:	Bl: 0-0 Vi: 0-0 Tstrap: 0-0
Best Rating:	**105** 5/02 Strf 3m4f good Ch

Moderate hunter/pointer, he stays three miles and acts on fast ground.

Teddy Mac (IRE)

6-y-o b g Commanche Run-Fraudulento (Orchestra)
C Weedon Alf Chadwick

Placings:PF   (3920)
2002/03: 24²G, 18⁹S,

	Starts	1st	2nd	3rd	Win & Pl
Hurdles	2	0	0	0	
Career Total	2	0	0	0	

Going:	Sf: 0-1 GS: 0-0 Gd: 0-1 GF: - Fm: 0-0
Distance:	2m/2m3: 0-1 2m4-2m7: 0-0 3m+: 0-1
Track:	LH: 0-2 RH: 0-0 Tight: 0-1 Gall: 0-0
Aids:	Bl: 0-0 Vi: 0-0 Tstrap: 0-0
Best Rating:	**0** 3/03 Font 2m2f110y soft Hdl

Tedo (IRE)

5-y-o ch g Beveled (USA)-Gunner Girl (Gunner B)
J Neville J Neville

Placings:P-P   (0105)
2002/03: 16⁰GF,

	Starts	1st	2nd	3rd	Win & Pl
Hurdles	1	0	0	0	
Career Total	2	0	0	0	

Going:	Sf: 0-0 GS: 0-0 Gd: 0-0 GF: - Fm: 0-1
Distance:	2m/2m3: 0-1 2m4-2m7: 0-0 3m+: 0-0
Track:	LH: 0-0 RH: 0-1 Tight: 0-0 Gall: 0-0
Aids:	Bl: 0-0 Vi: 0-0 Tstrap: 0-0
Best Rating:	**0** 5/02 Ludl 2m gd-fm Hdl

Tedstone Fox

11-y-o b g Bold Fox-Royal Wren (Blast)
Miss R S Reynolds Mrs E Weaver

Placings:P/FFP0-0P   (0247)
2002/03: 16⁰GF, 19⁸G,

	Starts	1st	2nd	3rd	Win & Pl
Chases	2	0	0	0	
Career Total	7	0	0	0	

Going:	Sf: 0-0 GS: 0-0 Gd: 0-1 GF: - Fm: 0-1
Distance:	2m/2m3: 0-2 2m4-2m7: 0-1 3m+: 0-0
Track:	LH: 0-1 RH: 0-1 Tight: 0-0 Gall: 0-1
Aids:	Bl: 0-0 Vi: 0-0 Tstrap: 0-0
Best Rating:	**75** 6/01 Strf 2m5f110y gd-fm Ch

Tee-Jay (IRE)

110(89c)   (94c)**104**
7-y-o ch g Un Desperado (FR)-N T Nad (Welsh Pageant)
M D Hammond T J Equestrian Ltd

Placings:03/5131PP-5P03032   (4410)
2002/03: 20⁵S, 20⁶S, 16⁸G, 19³GS, 24⁰G, 24³GS, 20²G,

	Starts	1st	2nd	3rd	Win & Pl
Hurdles	4	0	1	2	2609
Chases	3	0	0	0	
Career Total	15	2	1	4	9455
111 2/02 Muss 2m4f		D Hdl		G-S	£3510
108 12/01 Catt 2m3f		E Hdl		SFT	£2492

Total win prize-money £6002

Going:	Sf: 0-2 GS: 0-2 Gd: 0-3 GF: - Fm: 0-0
Distance:	2m/2m3: 0-2 2m4-2m7: 0-3 3m+: 0-2
Track:	LH: 0-4 RH: 0-3 Tight: 0-4 Gall: 0-1
Aids:	Bl: 0-0 Vi: 0-0 Tstrap: 0-0
Best Rating:	**111** 2/02 Muss 2m4f gd-sft Hdl

Moderate hurdler, stays two and a half miles, suited by soft ground; made little impact when tried over fences.

Teelin

96f   **101f**
6-y-o b g Neltino-Slieve League (IRE) (Roselier (FR))
P R Webber Andrew Jenkins

Placings:3   (4275)
2002/03: 16³G,

	Starts	1st	2nd	3rd	Win & Pl
NH Flat	1	0	0	1	284
Career Total	1	0	0	1	284

Going:	Sf: 0-0 GS: 0-0 Gd: 0-1 GF: - Fm: 0-0
Distance:	2m/2m3: 0-1 2m4-2m7: 0-0 3m+: 0-0
Track:	LH: 0-1 RH: 0-0 Tight: 0-0 Gall: 0-0
Aids:	Bl: 0-0 Vi: 0-0 Tstrap: 0-0
Best Rating:	**101** 3/03 Chep 2m110y good NHF

Teelin Bay (IRE)

11-y-o b g Be My Native (USA)-Fahy Quay (Quayside)
Miss Pauline Robson Mr & Mrs Raymond Anderson Green

Placings:00/0/21P/42PP/1/U1-4   (0161)
2002/03: 25⁴G,

	Starts	1st	2nd	3rd	Win & Pl
Chases	1	0	0	0	0

Career Total   14   3   2   0   11313
115 4/02 Ayr 3m3f110yH Ch   GD £3038
113 4/01 Ayr 3m3f110yH Ch   GD £3900
90 11/98 Kels 2m6f110yE Hdl   HVY £2374
Total win prize-money £9312

Going:	Sf: 0-0 GS: 0-0 Gd: 0-1 GF: - Fm: 0-0
Distance:	2m/2m3: 0-0 2m4-2m7: 0-0 3m+: 0-1
Track:	LH: 0-1 RH: 0-0 Tight: 0-1 Gall: 0-0
Aids:	Bl: 0-0 Vi: 0-0 Tstrap: 0-1
Best Rating:	**115** 4/02 Ayr 3m3f110y good Ch

Hunter chaser; lightly raced; stays three miles three furlongs and is effective on a soft surface.

Tees Components

117   **152+**
8-y-o b g Risk Me (FR)-Lady Warninglid (Ela-Mana-Mou)
Mrs M Reveley Tees Components Ltd

Placings:211/11-1213   (3884)
2002/03: 24¹GS, 16²S, 24¹GS, 23³G,

	Starts	1st	2nd	3rd	Win & Pl
Hurdles	4	2	1	1	25850
Career Total	9	6	2	1	41201
152 1/03 Donc 3m110y		A Hdl		G-S	£17400
152 11/02 Newc 3m		D Hdl		G-S	£4056
134 12/01 Chep 2m110y		A NHF		G-S	£9000
123 11/01 Weth 2m		H NHF		GD	£2359
120 2/00 Weth 2m		H NHF		SFT	£1862
129 11/99 Weth 2m		H NHF		GD	£1618

Total win prize-money £36295

Going:	Sf: 0-1 GS: 2-2 Gd: 0-1 GF: - Fm: 0-0
Distance:	2m/2m3: 0-1 2m4-2m7: 0-0 **3m+: 2-3**
Track:	**LH: 2-4** RH: 0-0 Tight: 0-0 **Gall: 2-3**
Aids:	Bl: 0-0 Vi: 0-0 Tstrap: 0-0
Best Rating:	**152** 1/03 Donc 3m110y gd-sft Hdl

Very useful hurdler/bumper horse and stayer on the Flat who made an impressive hurdling bow over three miles at Newcastle in November 2002, jumping soundly; maintained a decent level of form subsequently; stays three miles; needs the mud.

Teeton Priceless

8-y-o b m Broadsword (USA)-Teeton Frolic (Sunley Builds)
Mrs Joan Tice Mrs Joan Tice

Placings:UF   (4089)
2002/03: 23ᵁLS, 24ᶠGS,

	Starts	1st	2nd	3rd	Win & Pl
Chases	2	0	0	0	
Career Total	2	0	0	0	

Going:	Sf: 0-0 GS: 0-2 Gd: 0-0 GF: - Fm: 0-0
Distance:	2m/2m3: 0-0 2m4-2m7: 0-0 3m+: 0-2
Track:	LH: 0-1 RH: 0-1 Tight: 0-1 Gall: 0-0
Aids:	Bl: 0-0 Vi: 0-0 Tstrap: 0-0
Best Rating:	**0** 3/03 Strf 3m gd-sft Ch

Tefi

86   **72**
5-y-o ch g Efisio-Masuri Kabisa (USA) (Ascot Knight (CAN))
S R Bowring Simon Mapletoft Partnership

Placings:P   (0407)
2002/03: 17⁰GF,

	Starts	1st	2nd	3rd	Win & Pl
Hurdles	1	0	0	0	

Career Total   1   0   0   0

Going: Sf: 0-0 GS: 0-0 Gd: 0-0 GF: - Fm: 0-1
Distance: 2m/2m3: 0-1 2m4-2m7: 0-0 3m+: 0-0
Track: LH: 0-0 RH: 0-1 Tight: 0-1 Gall: 0-0
Aids: Bl: 0-0 Vi: 0-0 Tstrap: 0-0
Best Rating: 0   6/02   MRas   2m1f110y   gd-fm   Hdl

Teguise

85(84h)   (48h)50
7-y-o ch m Tigani-The Ranee (Royal Palace)
B Ellison   Mrs Cheryl L Owen

Placings: 0P00/00003   (1075)
2002/03: 16⁰G, 17⁰GS, 19⁰GF, 20⁰G, 26³G,

	Starts	1st	2nd	3rd	Win & Pl
Hurdles	3	0	0	0	0
Chases	2	0	0	1	645
Career Total	9	0	0	1	645

Going: Sf: 0-0 GS: 0-1 Gd: 0-3 GF: - Fm: 0-1
Distance: 2m/2m3: 0-2 2m4-2m7: 0-2 3m+: 0-1
Track: LH: 0-3 RH: 0-2 Tight: 0-4 Gall: 0-0
Aids: Bl: 0-0 Vi: 0-0 Tstrap: 0-2
Best Rating: 57   7/00   Sedg   2m1f   gd-fm   NHF

Tejano Gold (USA)

13-y-o ch g Tejano (USA)-Nelli Forli (USA) (Broadway Forli
(USA))
F L Matthews   J E Wood

Placings: 00F4FP3/13254F1301/31542205204/41F203/462
22212/2/14P/3/PP   (3955)
2002/03: 20⁵GS, 20⁰GS,

	Starts	1st	2nd	3rd	Win & Pl
Chases	2	0	0	0	0
Career Total	49	7	11	6	39715
107 12/99 Ludl	2m4f	E(0-115)HCh		G-S	£3566
110 12/97 MRas	2m1f110yD Ch			HVY	£3834
122 12/96 Uttx	2m	C(0-130)HHdl		SFT	£3550
113 9/95 Bang	2m1f	C(0-130)HHdl		GD	£3371
110 3/95 Ludl	2m	E(0-115)HHdl		GD	£2598
104 1/95 Nott	2m	D(0-120)HHdl		SFT	£3010
104 9/94 Worc	2m	Hdl		G-S	£1944
		Total win prize-money £21873			

Going: Sf: 0-1 GS: 0-1 Gd: 0-0 GF: - Fm: 0-0
Distance: 2m/2m3: 0-0 2m4-2m7: 0-2 3m+: 0-0
Track: LH: 0-1 RH: 0-1 Tight: 0-1 Gall: 0-0
Aids: Bl: 0-0 Vi: 0-0 Tstrap: 0-0
Best Rating: 122   4/97   Worc   2m   soft   Hdl

Tejaque

8-y-o b m Lord Of Arabia-Devil s Gold (Goldfella)
Mrs N S Sharpe   B W Farthing

Placings: P   (0727)
2002/03: 22ᴾGF,

	Starts	1st	2nd	3rd	Win & Pl
Hurdles	1	0	0	0	0
Career Total	1	0	0	0	0

Going: Sf: 0-0 GS: 0-0 Gd: 0-0 GF: - Fm: 0-1
Distance: 2m/2m3: 0-0 2m4-2m7: 0-1 3m+: 0-0
Track: LH: 0-1 RH: 0-0 Tight: 0-1 Gall: 0-0

Aids: Bl: 0-0 Vi: 0-0 Tstrap: 0-0
Best Rating: 0   7/02   Strf   2m6f110y   gd-fm   Hdl

Telemoss (IRE)

105(117h)   (154h)140+
9-y-o b g Montelimar (USA)-Shan s Moss (Le Moss)
N G Richards   Ashleybank Investments Limited

Placings: 15/021/1121244-1114   (3395)
2002/03: 20¹S, 22¹HY, 16¹HY, 20⁴HY,

	Starts	1st	2nd	3rd	Win & Pl
Chases	4	3	0	0	16302
Career Total	16	8	3	0	61131
138 1/03 Newc	2m110y E Ch			HVY	£3997
125 12/02 Kels	2m6f110yE Ch			HVY	£4147
117 11/02 Ayr	2m D Ch			SFT	£5407
140 12/01 Hayd	2m4f	B HHdl		SFT	£11921
130 10/01 Weth	2m	C(0-135)HHdl		GD	£5430
127 5/01 Hexm	2m4f110yD(0-125)HHdl			SFT	£3570
124 2/01 Kels	2m2f	E Hdl		SFT	£2912
105 11/99 Hayd	2m	H NHF		GD	£1934
		Total win prize-money £39322			

Going: Sf: 3-4 GS: 0-0 Gd: 0-0 GF: - Fm: 0-0
Distance: 2m/2m3: 1-1 2m4-2m7: 2-3 3m+: 0-0
Track: LH: 3-3 RH: 0-1 Tight: 1-1 Gall: 1-1
Aids: Bl: 0-0 Vi: 0-0 Tstrap: 0-0
Best Rating: 154   3/02   Chel   3m   good   Hdl

Smart novice chaser; formerly high-class hurdler, best over trips of around two and a half miles;effective on good ground, but very much suited by soft; unbeaten over fences until breaking a blood-vessel and reportedly injuring a knee at Sandown in February 2003.

Telimar Prince (IRE)

116   137
7-y-o b g Montelimar (USA)-Blakica (Sexton Blake)
J T Gifford   Mrs Angela Brodie

Placings: 0/61-1232   (3670)
2002/03: 19¹GS, 17²G, 16³HY, 20²GS,

	Starts	1st	2nd	3rd	Win & Pl
Hurdles	4	1	2	1	24440
Career Total	7	2	2	1	26971
130 11/02 Newb	2m3f	C(0-130)HHdl		G-S	£6922
124 3/02 Font	2m4f	E Hdl		SFT	£2530
		Total win prize-money £9454			

Going: Sf: 0-1 GS: 1-2 Gd: 0-1 GF: - Fm: 0-0
Distance: 2m/2m3: 1-3 2m4-2m7: 0-1 3m+: 0-0
Track: LH: 1-2 RH: 0-1 Tight: 0-0 Gall: 1-2
Aids: Bl: 0-0 Vi: 0-0 Tstrap: 0-0
Best Rating: 140   2/03   Sand   2m110y   heavy   Hdl

Progressive and very useful handicap hurdler; acts on a soft surface and stays two and a half miles.

Tell Me Why (IRE)

(99h)   (97h)115
7-y-o gr g Roselier (FR)-Clonarctic Slave (Sir Mordred)
P R Webber   Mrs C A Waters

Placings: 5-2   (2638)
2002/03: 24²GS,

	Starts	1st	2nd	3rd	Win & Pl
Chases	1	0	1	0	2380
Career Total	2	0	1	0	2380

Going: Sf: 0-0 GS: 0-1 Gd: 0-0 GF: - Fm: 0-0
Distance: 2m/2m3: 0-0 2m4-2m7: 0-0 3m+: 0-1

Track: LH: 0-1 RH: 0-0 Tight: 0-0 Gall: 0-0
Aids: Bl: 0-0 Vi: 0-0 Tstrap: 0-0
Best Rating: 116   12/02   Wwck   3m110y   gd-sft   Ch

Modest chaser; full-brother to a winning staying hurdler, he showed plenty of promise when second in a novice chase before Christmas.

Telmar Flyer

6-y-o gr m Neltino-Flying Mistress (Lear Jet)
J Cullinan   Dodson & Partners

Placings: 00-F0PP   (3554)
2002/03: 16⁰GS, 16ᶠGF, 16⁰G, 20ᴾGS, 16ᴾHY,

	Starts	1st	2nd	3rd	Win & Pl
NH Flat	3	0	0	0	0
Hurdles	2	0	0	0	0
Career Total	6	0	0	0	0

Going: Sf: 0-1 GS: 0-2 Gd: 0-1 GF: - Fm: 0-1
Distance: 2m/2m3: 0-4 2m4-2m7: 0-1 3m+: 0-0
Track: LH: 0-2 RH: 0-3 Tight: 0-1 Gall: 0-2
Aids: Bl: 0-0 Vi: 0-0 Tstrap: 0-0
Best Rating: 73   10/02   Chel   2m110y   good   NHF

Teme Valley

92(105h)   (110 h)63
9-y-o br g Polish Precedent (USA)-Sudeley (Dancing Brave
(USA))
J Howard Johnson   Chris Heron

Placings: 065U01/0F60132211/550150/00020016-4001001
(4521)
2002/03: 16⁴GF, 16⁰GF, 22⁰S, 17¹S, 16⁰G, 16⁰G, 17¹G,

	Starts	1st	2nd	3rd	Win & Pl
Hurdles	7	2	0	0	8941
Career Total	37	8	3	1	28078
110 4/03 Sedg	2m1f	D(0-120)HHdl		GD	£4904
103 11/02 Sedg	2m1f	D(0-115)HHdl		SFT	£4036
110 4/02 Sedg	2m1f	D(0-115)HHdl		G-F	£3276
115 1/01 Catt	2m3f	F(0-110)HHdl		G-S	£2373
121 4/00 Sedg	2m1f	E(0-115)HHdl		GD	£2394
116 3/00 Sedg	2m1f	F(0-110)HHdl		G-F	£2677
110 12/99 Sedg	2m1f	F(0-110)HHdl		G-S	£2460
96 4/99 Sedg	2m1f	E Hdl		G-S	£2495
		Total win prize-money £24617			

Going: Sf: 1-2 GS: 0-0 Gd: 1-3 GF: - Fm: 0-2
Distance: 2m/2m3: 2-6 2m4-2m7: 0-1 3m+: 0-0
Track: LH: 2-7 RH: 0-0 Tight: 2-5 Gall: 0-0
Aids: Bl: 0-0 Vi: 0-0 Tstrap: 0-1
Best Rating: 121   4/00   Sedg   2m1f   good   Hdl

Modest hurdler; a winner seven times at his favoured Sedgefield; does not want the ground too soft; effective at around two miles.

Temper Lad (USA)

105   100
8-y-o b g Riverman (USA)-Dokki (USA) (Northern Dancer)
J Joseph   Jack Joseph

Placings: P11331/6210P3404/00/5404-2   (0102)
2002/03: 22²GF,

	Starts	1st	2nd	3rd	Win & Pl
Hurdles	1	0	1	0	732
Career Total	22	4	2	3	18872
129 10/99 Chep	2m110y C Hdl			GD	£4658
116 4/99 Strf	2m110y D(0-110)HHdl			GD	£2612
110 9/98 Hntg	2m110y E Hdl			G-F	£2326

| 105 | 9/98 | Strf | 2m110y | E Hdl | | GD | £2318 |

Total win prize-money £11915

Going: Sf: 0-0 GS: 0-0 Gd: 0-0 GF: - Fm: 0-1
Distance: 2m2/2m3: 0-0 2m4-2m7: 0-1 3m+: 0-0
Track: LH: 0-1 RH: 0-0 Tight: 0-1 Gall: 0-0
Aids: Bl: 0-0 Vi: 0-0 Tstrap: 0-1
Best Rating: 130 1/00 Kemp 2m5f good Hdl

Moderate hurdler; acts on a sound surface.

Temple Dog (IRE)
105   **121**

7-y-o ch g Un Desperado (FR)-Shower (King s Lake (USA))
T P Tate The Ivy Syndicate

Placings:4/103-111   **(4167)**
2002/03: 16¹GS, 16¹S, 16¹GS,

	Starts	1st	2nd	3rd	Win & Pl
Hurdles	3	3	0	0	11257
Career Total	7	4	0	1	13258
125	3/03	Newc	2m	E Hdl		G-S	£3464
118	12/02	Hayd	2m	D Hdl		SFT	£4719
116	12/02	Ayr	2m	E Hdl		G-S	£3073
131	2/02	Ayr	2m	H NHF		HVY	£1739

Total win prize-money £12997

Going: Sf: 1-1 GS: 2-2 Gd: 0-0 GF: - Fm: 0-0
Distance: 2m2/2m3: 3-3 2m4-2m7: 0-0 3m+: 0-0
Track: LH: 3-3 RH: 0-0 Tight: 0-0 Gall: 1-1
Aids: Bl: 0-0 Vi: 0-0 Tstrap: 0-0
Best Rating: 131 2/02 Ayr 2m heavy NHF

Fair hurdler; previously decent bumper horse; an easy winner in heavy ground at Ayr in February and ran well at Cheltenham, but beaten on faster ground under a penalty next time; made a winning debut over hurdles at Ayr in December 2002 and followed up at Haydock later the same month.

Temples Time (IRE)
91   **74**

5-y-o b m Distinctly North (USA)-Midnight Patrol (Ashmore (FR))
R Brotherton W M Rollett

Placings:5-44P   **(0510)**
2002/03: 16⁴GF, 16⁴G, 20⁴G,

	Starts	1st	2nd	3rd	Win & Pl
Hurdles	3	0	0	0	0
Career Total	4	0	0	0	0

Going: Sf: 0-0 GS: 0-0 Gd: 0-0 GF: - Fm: 0-1
Distance: 2m2/2m3: 0-0 2m4-2m7: 0-1 3m+: 0-0
Track: LH: 0-3 RH: 0-0 Tight: 0-0 Gall: 0-0
Aids: Bl: 0-0 Vi: 0-0 Tstrap: 0-0
Best Rating: 84 5/02 Worc 2m gd-fm Hdl

Tempo (IRE)
(67h)   (39h)**83**

11-y-o b g Satco (FR)-Arabian Sands (Pollerton)
Ian Williams C N Barnes

Placings:5/ 1224/2313142F/230U/5/FP/0P0FP6651UP-U
    (0350)
2002/03: 21ᵁG,

	Starts	1st	2nd	3rd	Win & Pl
Chases	1	0	0	0	
Career Total	32	4	5	3	23752
83	4/02	Plum	2m1f	G(0-90)HCh		G-F	£2268
132	2/98	Thur	2m	Ch		YLD	£2382

| 130 | 2/98 | Clon | 2m4f | Ch | Y-S | £2978 |
| 119 | 5/96 | Gowr | 2m | NHF | GD | £2824 |

Total win prize-money £10454

Going: Sf: 0-0 GS: 0-0 Gd: 0-1 GF: - Fm: 0-0
Distance: 2m2/2m3: 0-0 2m4-2m7: 0-1 3m+: 0-0
Track: LH: 0-1 RH: 0-0 Tight: 0-1 Gall: 0-0
Aids: Bl: 0-0 Vi: 0-0 Tstrap: 0-0
Best Rating: 136 4/98 Fair 2m4f gd-yld Ch

Ex-Irish chaser, now selling class. Seems best when making the running.

Ten Fourteen (IRE)

8-y-o ch g Ore-Yonder Bay (IRE) (Trimmingham)
Miss Z C Davison Mrs J Irvine

Placings:000/0/P-P   **(0246)**
2002/03: 21ᴾGS, 22ᴾG,

	Starts	1st	2nd	3rd	Win & Pl
Hurdles	2	0	0	0	
Career Total	6	0	0	0	

Going: Sf: 0-0 GS: 0-1 Gd: 0-1 GF: - Fm: 0-0
Distance: 2m2/2m3: 0-0 2m4-2m7: 0-2 3m+: 0-0
Track: LH: 0-0 RH: 0-2 Tight: 0-0 Gall: 0-0
Aids: Bl: 0-0 Vi: 0-0 Tstrap: 0-0
Best Rating: 47 2/00 Clon 2m2f sft-hvy NHF

Tenacious Star (IRE)

5-y-o b g Fourstars Allstar (USA)-Saltee Sound (IRE) (Buckskin (FR))
Ferdy Murphy The Sgs Partnership

Placings:0PP   **(3911)**
2002/03: 16⁵S, 22ᴾHY, 17ᴾGS,

	Starts	1st	2nd	3rd	Win & Pl
NH Flat	1	0	0	0	0
Hurdles	2	0	0	0	0
Career Total	3	0	0	0	0

Going: Sf: 0-2 GS: 0-1 Gd: 0-0 GF: - Fm: 0-0
Distance: 2m2/2m3: 0-2 2m4-2m7: 0-1 3m+: 0-0
Track: LH: 0-2 RH: 0-1 Tight: 0-0 Gall: 0-0
Aids: Bl: 0-0 Vi: 0-0 Tstrap: 0-0
Best Rating: 77 11/02 Ayr 2m soft NHF

Tender Tangle
81   **63**

8-y-o ch g Crested Lark-Red Tango (Legal Tender)
F Jordan Mrs P M Pugh

Placings:PP-0FU   **(0663)**
2002/03: 16ᴾGS, 16⁹G, 16ᶠS, 16ᵁGF,

	Starts	1st	2nd	3rd	Win & Pl
Hurdles	4	0	0	0	
Career Total	5	0	0	0	

Going: Sf: 0-1 GS: 0-1 Gd: 0-1 GF: - Fm: 0-0
Distance: 2m2/2m3: 0-4 2m4-2m7: 0-0 3m+: 0-0
Track: LH: 0-2 RH: 0-2 Tight: 0-0 Gall: 0-0
Aids: Bl: 0-0 Vi: 0-0 Tstrap: 0-0
Best Rating: 63 5/02 Towc 2m good Hdl

Tender Touch (IRE)
98(98h)   (74h)**79**

8-y-o gr m Weldnaas (USA)-Moments Peace (Adonijah)
Miss Kate Milligan J D Gordon

Placings:23545/B00/6632322054/105464-555303   **(4377)**
2002/03: 16⁵GF, 19⁵GF, 20⁵GF, 20³HY, 16⁶S, 16³G,

	Starts	1st	2nd	3rd	Win & Pl
Hurdles	5	0	0	1	270
Chases	1	0	0	1	667
Career Total	30	1	4	5	7443
82	11/01	Kels	2m110y	G Hdl		GD	£2702

Total win prize-money £2702

Going: Sf: 0-2 GS: 0-0 Gd: 0-1 GF: - Fm: 0-3
Distance: 2m2/2m3: 0-3 2m4-2m7: 0-3 3m+: 0-0
Track: LH: 0-4 RH: 0-0 Tight: 0-2 Gall: 0-1
Aids: Bl: 0-0 Vi: 0-0 Tstrap: 0-0
Best Rating: 84 4/02 Prth 2m110y good Hdl

Moderate chaser; did not achieve much when winning 2m1f handicap at Southwell June 2003; best at two miles and yet to convince she stays further; effective on decent ground.

Tenerife Flyer
71   **56**

5-y-o ch m Rock City-Nobleata (Dunbeath (USA))
J R Norton K Swift

Placings:000P-00   **(2473)**
2002/03: 19⁰G, 16⁰G,

	Starts	1st	2nd	3rd	Win & Pl
Hurdles	2	0	0	0	
Career Total	6	0	0	0	

Going: Sf: 0-0 GS: 0-0 Gd: 0-2 GF: - Fm: 0-0
Distance: 2m2/2m3: 0-2 2m4-2m7: 0-0 3m+: 0-0
Track: LH: 0-2 RH: 0-0 Tight: 0-1 Gall: 0-1
Aids: Bl: 0-0 Vi: 0-0 Tstrap: 0-0
Best Rating: 60 2/02 MRas 2m1f110y gd-sft Hdl

Tennessee Twist (IRE)

13-y-o b g Buckskin (FR)-Darjoy (Darantus)
M Williamson (Mrs L Williamson 5/6) Halewood International Ltd

Placings:420/2141/P1/FP/31F/U/0PPPP/3-034P   **(3962)**
2002/03: 33⁰GF, 34³G, 26⁴GS, 24ᴾS,

	Starts	1st	2nd	3rd	Win & Pl
Chases	4	0	0	1	444
Career Total	25	4	2	3	24996
128	11/98	Chel	3m3f110y	B HCh		GD	£10191
140	2/97	Chep	3m	C Ch		GD	£5411
124	2/96	Towc	3m	E Hdl		HVY	£2452
117	11/95	Newb	3m110y	C Hdl		GD	£3603

Total win prize-money £21661

Going: Sf: 0-1 GS: 0-1 Gd: 0-1 GF: - Fm: 0-1
Distance: 2m2/2m3: 0-0 2m4-2m7: 0-0 3m+: 0-4
Track: LH: 0-4 RH: 0-0 Tight: 0-2 Gall: 0-4
Aids: Bl: 0-0 Vi: 0-0 Tstrap: 0-0
Best Rating: 140 2/97 Chep 3m good Ch

One-time decent handicapper, now hunter chaser. Stays well. Acts on a sound surface.

Tenshookmen (IRE)

112   **112**

9-y-o ch g Cardinal Flower-April Rise (Prominer)
W F Codd (W J Codd 12/5) W J Codd

Placings:*6201/P505/441140630-0P110465P*   (4657a)
2002/03: 20⁵GY, 19⁵F, 18¹YS, 18¹S, 20⁵GS, 20⁴HY, 21⁶YS, 20⁵GF, 25⁵GF,

	Starts	1st	2nd	3rd	Win & Pl
Chases	9	2	0	0	12009
Career Total	26	5	1	1	33521

109	11/02	Punc	2m2f	(0-116)HCh	SFT	£6773
98	10/02	Thur	2m2f	(0-95)HCh	Y-S	£4868
112	10/01	Punc	2m4f	(0-109)HCh	YLD	£6677
106	9/01	List	2m3f	Ch	G-F	£7790
105	4/00	List	3m	Ch	Y-S	£4416
				Total win prize-money £30524

Going: Sf: 1-2 GS: 0-1 Gd: 0-0 GF: - Fm: 0-3
Distance: 2m/2m3: 2-3 2m4-2m7: 0-5 3m+: 0-1
Track: LH: 0-2 RH: 2-5 Tight: 0-0 Gall: 0-1
Aids: Bl: 0-0 Vi: 0-0 Tstrap: 0-0
Best Rating: 112 4/03 Tram 2m4f   gd-fm Ch

Winning chaser in Ireland, effective at up to three miles, but effective at shorter, acts on a soft surface.

Tensile (IRE)

108(105c)   (121c)**136**

8-y-o b g Tenby-Bonnie Isle (Pitcairn)
P J Hobbs D Charlesworth

Placings:*1/1211P/343P201-41F1331355*   (4400)
2002/03: 23⁴G, 21¹GS, 21⁶G, 24¹GF, 26³GF, 20³G, 20¹GF, 20³S, 22⁵GF, 22⁵GF,

	Starts	1st	2nd	3rd	Win & Pl
Hurdles	6	1	0	2	13572
Chases	4	2	0	1	10473
Career Total	23	8	2	5	66051

132	10/02	Uttx	2m4f110yC(0-130)HHdl	G-F	£7150
120	7/02	Strf	3m	D Ch	G-F	£5590
120	5/02	NAbb	2m5f110yD Ch	G-S	£4163
139	3/02	Hayd	2m6f	C(0-135)HHdl	GD	£6929
144	12/00	Hayd	B HHdl	HVY	£12174
144	12/00	Chep	2m4f	C(0-130)HHdl	HVY	£8716
132	11/00	Tntn	2m3f110yF(0-110)HHdl	GD	£2564
110	11/99	Leic	2m	E Hdl	G-S	£2945
				Total win prize-money £50234

Going: Sf: 0-2 GS: 1-1 Gd: 0-3 GF: - Fm: 2-4
Distance: 2m/2m3: 0-4 2m4-2m7: 2-7 3m+: 1-3
Track: LH: 3-10 RH: 0-0 Tight: 2-4 Gall: 0-0
Aids: Bl: 0-0 Vi: 0-0 Tstrap: 0-0
Best Rating: 144 12/00 Hayd 2m4f   heavy Hdl

Useful handicap hurdler; winner of novice chases in the summer of 2002 but not a natural jumper; stays three miles; acts on most types of ground.

Tentsmuir

92   **75**

7-y-o b m Arctic Lord-Deep Pier (Deep Run)
D W Whillans D McComb

Placings:*10-P04*   (4750)
2002/03: 20⁵G, 20⁵HY, 24⁴G,

	Starts	1st	2nd	3rd	Win & Pl
Hurdles	3	0	0	0	474
Career Total	5	1	0	0	2406

| 95 | 1/02 | Newc | 2m | H NHF | SFT | £1932 |
| | | | | Total win prize-money £1932 |

Going: Sf: 0-1 GS: 0-0 Gd: 0-0 GF: - Fm: 0-0

Distance: 2m/2m3: 0-0 2m4-2m7: 0-2 3m+: 0-1
Track: LH: 0-1 RH: 0-2 Tight: 0-1 Gall: 0-0
Aids: Bl: 0-0 Vi: 0-0 Tstrap: 0-0
Best Rating: 95 1/02 Newc 2m   soft NHF

Plating-class hurdler; bumper winner on racecourse debut; first sign of ability since when second in modest event at Perth; stays three miles; seems to act on most ground.

Teorban (POL)

94   **84**

4-y-o b c Don Corleone-Tabaka (POL) (Pyjama Hunt)
M Pitman Something In The City Partnership

Placings:*6*   (4337)
2002/03: 16⁶GF,

	Starts	1st	2nd	3rd	Win & Pl
Hurdles	1	0	0	0	0
Career Total	1	0	0	0	0

Going: Sf: 0-0 GS: 0-0 Gd: 0-0 GF: - Fm: 0-1
Distance: 2m/2m3: 0-1 2m4-2m7: 0-0 3m+: 0-0
Track: LH: 0-0 RH: 0-1 Tight: 0-0 Gall: 0-1
Aids: Bl: 0-0 Vi: 0-0 Tstrap: 0-0
Best Rating: 70 3/03 Hntg 2m110y   gd-fm Hdl

Terdad (USA)

110(87c)   (54c)**92**

10-y-o ch g Lomond (USA)-Istiska (FR) (Irish River (FR))
M C Chapman Tremousser Partnership

Placings:*1142/1040/332116336/052062203/0001551615-50F004P06340*   (4686)
2002/03: 19⁵GS, 17⁰GF, 19⁶F, 17⁰G, 16⁶G, 22⁴GF, 20⁶GF, 21⁰G, 19⁶GS, 16³S, 16⁴GF, 17⁰GF,

	Starts	1st	2nd	3rd	Win & Pl
Hurdles	10	0	0	1	348
Chases	2	0	0	0	580
Career Total	48	8	5	6	28877

115	12/01	Catt	2m3f	F(0-110)HHdl	SFT	£1890
111	10/01	Sedg	2m1f	F Hdl	GD	£1974
106	8/01	MRas	2m1f110yG(0-95)HHdl	G-F	£1785
118	12/99	Hntg	2m110y	D(0-125)HHdl	G-F	£5204
111	11/99	Wwck	2m	G Hdl	GD	£1637
109	5/98	Prth	2m110y	E(0-105)HHdl	G-F	£2892
93	9/97	Prth	2m110y	E Hdl	G-F	£2633
91	8/97	Sedg	2m1f	E Hdl	G-F	£2304
				Total win prize-money £20320

Going: Sf: 0-1 GS: 0-2 Gd: 0-3 GF: - Fm: 0-6
Distance: 2m/2m3: 0-6 2m4-2m7: 0-6 3m+: 0-0
Track: LH: 0-4 RH: 0-8 Tight: 0-7 Gall: 0-1
Aids: Bl: 0-6 Vi: 0-1 Tstrap: 0-0
Best Rating: 118 12/99 Hntg 2m110y   good Hdl

Plating-class hurdler; stays three miles; acts on any going.

Terek (GER)

109   **104**

7-y-o ch g Irish River (FR)-Turbaine (USA) (Trempolino (USA))
R T Phillips Mrs Claire Smith

Placings:*2P-424*   (3185)
2002/03: 16⁴GS, 16²G, 16⁴GS,

	Starts	1st	2nd	3rd	Win & Pl
Hurdles	3	0	1	0	1456
Career Total	5	0	2	0	2270

Going: Sf: 0-0 GS: 0-2 Gd: 0-1 GF: - Fm: 0-0

Distance: 2m/2m3: 0-3 2m4-2m7: 0-0 3m+: 0-0
Track: LH: 0-1 RH: 0-2 Tight: 0-0 Gall: 0-2
Aids: Bl: 0-0 Vi: 0-0 Tstrap: 0-0
Best Rating: 106 12/02 Donc 2m110y   good Hdl

Group Three winner on the Flat in Germany, suited by cut in the ground; good efforts over hurdles so far; finally broke duck with a hard fought success at Cartmel in July; has a tendency to race keenly.

Teridove

6-y-o b g Terimon-Flakey Dove (Oats)
C J Price Mrs M Price

Placings:*00*   (2675)
2002/03: 16⁶G, 17⁰S,

	Starts	1st	2nd	3rd	Win & Pl
NH Flat	2	0	0	0	
Career Total	2	0	0	0	

Going: Sf: 0-1 GS: 0-0 Gd: 0-1 GF: - Fm: 0-0
Distance: 2m/2m3: 0-2 2m4-2m7: 0-0 3m+: 0-0
Track: LH: 0-0 RH: 0-2 Tight: 0-0 Gall: 0-0
Aids: Bl: 0-0 Vi: 0-0 Tstrap: 0-0
Best Rating: 58 11/02 Ludl 2m   good NHF

Out of Champion Hurdle winner Flakey Dove.

Terimon's Dream

65   **35**

6-y-o gr g Terimon-I Have A Dream (SWE) (Mango Express)
A W Carroll John McKenna

Placings:*0*   (2166)
2002/03: 16⁰GS,

	Starts	1st	2nd	3rd	Win & Pl
Hurdles	1	0	0	0	
Career Total	1	0	0	0	

Going: Sf: 0-0 GS: 0-1 Gd: 0-0 GF: - Fm: 0-0
Distance: 2m/2m3: 0-1 2m4-2m7: 0-0 3m+: 0-0
Track: LH: 0-1 RH: 0-0 Tight: 0-0 Gall: 0-0
Aids: Bl: 0-0 Vi: 0-0 Tstrap: 0-0
Best Rating: 35 11/02 Wwck 2m   gd-sft Hdl

Terino

101   **59**

7-y-o b g Terimon-Ashmo (Ashmore (FR))
A E Jessop A Jessop

Placings:*500-500004*   (4679)
2002/03: 16⁵G, 16⁹GF, 22⁸GS, 19⁰S, 16⁹GF, 16⁴GF,

	Starts	1st	2nd	3rd	Win & Pl
Hurdles	6	0	0	0	0
Career Total	9	0	0	0	0

Going: Sf: 0-1 GS: 0-1 Gd: 0-1 GF: - Fm: 0-3
Distance: 2m/2m3: 0-4 2m4-2m7: 0-2 3m+: 0-0
Track: LH: 0-2 RH: 0-4 Tight: 0-4 Gall: 0-2
Aids: Bl: 0-0 Vi: 0-0 Tstrap: 0-0
Best Rating: 91 12/01 Hntg 2m110y   gd-sft NHF

Modest bumper form; only plating-class over hurdles.

Termonfeckin

5-y-o b g Runnett-Crimson Sol (Crimson Beau)

P W Hiatt Phil Kelly

Placings:336   (1010)
2002/03: 17³GF, 16³GF, 20⁶GF,

	Starts	1st	2nd	3rd	Win & Pl
NH Flat	2	0	0	2	539
Hurdles	1	0	0	0	0
Career Total	3	0	0	2	539

Going: Sf: 0-0 GS: 0-0 Gd: 0-0 GF: - Fm: 0-3
Distance: 2m/2m3: 0-2 2m4-2m7: 0-1 3m+: 0-0
Track: LH: 0-0 RH: 0-1 Tight: 0-2 Gall: 0-0
Aids: Bl: 0-0 Vi: 0-0 Tstrap: 0-0
Best Rating: 88   7/02   Strf   2m110y   gd-fm   NHF

Tertullian (IRE)
79   77
4-y-o b g Petorius-Fiddes (IRE) (Alzao (USA))
S Dow (R Hannon 14/10) J R May

Placings:0   (2568)
2002/03: 16⁰G,

	Starts	1st	2nd	3rd	Win & Pl
Hurdles	1	0	0	0	
Career Total	1	0	0	0	

Going: Sf: 0-0 GS: 0-0 Gd: 0-1 GF: - Fm: 0-0
Distance: 2m/2m3: 0-1 2m4-2m7: 0-0 3m+: 0-0
Track: LH: 0-1 RH: 0-0 Tight: 0-0 Gall: 0-1
Aids: Bl: 0-0 Vi: 0-0 Tstrap: 0-0
Best Rating: 75   12/02   Newb   2m110y   good   Hdl

Tesora Mia

7-y-o ch m Mon Tresor-Rocky Affair (Clear Run)
M Wellings Mrs G Lancina

Placings:0P   (3546)
2002/03: 16⁰GS, 19⁰G,

	Starts	1st	2nd	3rd	Win & Pl
NH Flat	1	0	0	0	0
Hurdles	1	0	0	0	0
Career Total	2	0	0	0	0

Going: Sf: 0-0 GS: 0-1 Gd: 0-1 GF: - Fm: 0-0
Distance: 2m/2m3: 0-1 2m4-2m7: 0-1 3m+: 0-0
Track: LH: 0-0 RH: 0-2 Tight: 0-0 Gall: 0-0
Aids: Bl: 0-0 Vi: 0-0 Tstrap: 0-0
Best Rating: 1   11/02   Ludl   2m   gd-sft   NHF

Test Of Loyalty
102(94h)   (71h)83
9-y-o b g Niniski (USA)-River Chimes (Forlorn River)
J N R Billinge Hilton Racing Partnership

Placings:0/P/0364P206-4116544   (4773)
2002/03: 16⁴GS, 16¹G, 17¹G, 16⁶GF, 16⁵G, 17⁴G, 20⁴G,

	Starts	1st	2nd	3rd	Win & Pl
Chases	7	2	0	0	10591
Career Total	17	2	1	1	12387
93	9/02	Sthl	2m1f	E(0-105)HCh	GD	£4036
85	6/02	Prth	2m	F(0-100)HCh	G-S	£5382

Total win prize-money £9419

Going: Sf: 0-0 GS: 1-2 Gd: 1-4 GF: - Fm: 0-1
Distance: 2m/2m3: 2-6 2m4-2m7: 0-1 3m+: 0-0
Track: LH: 1-4 RH: 1-3 Tight: 0-2 Gall: 0-0

Aids: Bl: 0-0 Vi: 0-0 Tstrap: 0-0
Best Rating: 93   9/02   Sthl   2m1f   good   Ch

Moderate handicap chaser; best at around two miles; acts on most types of ground; suited by a flat track.

Texas Ranger
104   128
5-y-o b g Mtoto-Favorable Exchange (USA) (Exceller (USA))
C J Mann The Whitcoombe Partnership

Placings:2-1111054300   (4109)
2002/03: 18¹GF, 16¹GF, 20¹GS, 20¹GF, 21⁰GY, 21⁵HY, 21⁴GS, 20³HY, 21⁰G, 21⁰G,

	Starts	1st	2nd	3rd	Win & Pl
Hurdles	10	4	0	1	22849
Career Total	11	4	1	1	25477
128	6/02	Worc	2m4f	C(0-135)HHdl	G-F	£6702
125	5/02	Fknm	2m4f	E Hdl	G-S	£2989
121	5/02	Worc	2m	E Hdl	G-F	£2660
115	5/02	Font	2m2f110yE Hdl		G-F	£2572

Total win prize-money £14925

Going: Sf: 0-2 GS: 1-2 Gd: 0-2 GF: - Fm: 3-3
Distance: 2m/2m3: 2-2 2m4-2m7: 2-8 3m+: 0-0
Track: LH: 4-8 RH: 0-1 Tight: 2-2 Gall: 0-3
Aids: Bl: 0-0 Vi: 0-0 Tstrap: 0-0
Best Rating: 128   6/02   Worc   2m4f   gd-fm   Hdl

Useful novice hurdler; in fine form in the summer of 2002; stays two miles four furlongs; best on a sound surface, although has shown form with cut in the ground.

Thalys (GER)

(95h)   (107+h)
5-y-o bl g Gold And Ivory (USA)-Tachira (Faraway Times (USA))
Mrs H Dalton J Hales

Placings:0-23212   (0777)
2002/03: 16²GF, 17³S, 17²GF, 19¹GF, 20²GF,

	Starts	1st	2nd	3rd	Win & Pl
Hurdles	5	1	3	1	7284
Career Total	6	1	3	1	7284
107	7/02	MRas	2m3f110yD Hdl		G-F	£4144

Total win prize-money £4144

Going: Sf: 0-1 GS: 0-0 Gd: 0-0 GF: - Fm: 1-4
Distance: 2m/2m3: 0-3 2m4-2m7: 1-2 3m+: 0-0
Track: LH: 0-3 RH: 1-2 Tight: 1-3 Gall: 0-0
Aids: Bl: 0-0 Vi: 0-0 Tstrap: 1-3
Best Rating: 107   7/02   MRas   2m3f110y   gd-fm   Hdl

Winner on the Flat in native Germany; opened his account over hurdles at Market Rasen in July 2002; ran too freely when pulled up after going clear on chasing debut at Worcester July 2003.

Thames (IRE)
90f   111f
5-y-o b g Over The River (FR)-Aon Dochas (IRE) (Strong Gale)
N J Henderson Trevor Hemmings

Placings:34   (4481)
2002/03: 16³G, 17⁴G,

	Starts	1st	2nd	3rd	Win & Pl
NH Flat	2	0	0	1	1795
Career Total	2	0	0	1	1795

Going: Sf: 0-0 GS: 0-0 Gd: 0-2 GF: - Fm: 0-0
Distance: 2m/2m3: 0-2 2m4-2m7: 0-0 3m+: 0-0

Track: LH: 0-1 RH: 0-0 Tight: 0-0 Gall: 0-0
Aids: Bl: 0-0 Vi: 0-0 Tstrap: 0-0
Best Rating: 111   4/03   Aint   2m1f   good   NHF

Has shown a fair level of ability in bumpers.

Thanx Directory (IRE)
99f   84f
4-y-o ch f Mukaddamah (USA)-Scanno s Choice (IRE) (Pennine Walk)
T J Etherington S Calladene

Placings:031   (4343)
2002/03: 14⁰GS, 16³S, 16¹GF,

	Starts	1st	2nd	3rd	Win & Pl
NH Flat	3	1	0	1	2246
Career Total	3	1	0	1	2246
84	3/03	Hntg	2m110y	H NHF	G-F	£1960

Total win prize-money £1960

Going: Sf: 0-1 GS: 0-1 Gd: 0-0 GF: - Fm: 1-1
Distance: 2m/2m3: 1-2 2m4-2m7: 0-0 3m+: 0-0
Track: LH: 0-2 RH: 1-1 Tight: 0-0 Gall: 1-1
Aids: Bl: 0-0 Vi: 0-0 Tstrap: 0-0
Best Rating: 84   3/03   Hntg   2m110y   gd-fm   NHF

Bumper winner; acts on fast ground.

Thari (USA)
109(117h)   (119h)125
6-y-o b g Silver Hawk (USA)-Magic Slipper (Habitat)
Noel Meade D P Sharkey

Placings:124012-142F4001   (4740a)
2002/03: 22¹S, 21⁴GF, 20²YS, 20⁵S, 20⁴SH, 21⁰G, 24⁰G, 20¹G,

	Starts	1st	2nd	3rd	Win & Pl
Hurdles	2	0	0	0	0
Chases	6	2	1	0	53063
Career Total	14	4	3	0	91373
125	4/03	Fair	2m4f	Ch	GD	£41327
118	9/02	Gway	2m6f	Ch	SFT	£7196
129	4/02	Fair	2m4f	Hdl	G-Y	£13957
122	12/01	Leop	2m	Hdl	YLD	£7512

Total win prize-money £69992

Going: Sf: 1-2 GS: 0-0 Gd: 1-3 GF: - Fm: 0-1
Distance: 2m/2m3: 0-0 2m4-2m7: 2-7 3m+: 0-1
Track: LH: 0-2 RH: 2-5 Tight: 0-1 Gall: 0-1
Aids: Bl: 0-0 Vi: 0-0 Tstrap: 0-0
Best Rating: 145   4/02   Punc   2m4f   good   Hdl

Very useful hurdler/fair chaser; stays two and a three-quarter miles; suited by cut in the ground; has worn a tongue tie.

That's Fine
103   107
8-y-o ch g Good Thyne (USA)-Wing On (Quayside)
R T Phillips The After Eights

Placings:53/123-025   (3778)
2002/03: 22⁰HY, 24²S, 24⁵GS,

	Starts	1st	2nd	3rd	Win & Pl
Hurdles	3	0	1	0	1160
Career Total	8	1	2	2	4206
96	12/01	Folk	2m1f110yH NHF	SFT	£1568

Total win prize-money £1568

Going: Sf: 0-2 GS: 0-1 Gd: 0-0 GF: - Fm: 0-0
Distance: 2m/2m3: 0-0 2m4-2m7: 0-1 3m+: 0-2
Track: LH: 0-0 RH: 0-3 Tight: 0-2 Gall: 0-0
Aids: Bl: 0-0 Vi: 0-0 Tstrap: 0-0

Best Rating: 107 1/03 Trtn 3m110y soft   Hdl

Modest hurdler; improved to win his third start in a Folkestone bumper. Appreciated a step up to three miles when second in a Class E handicap at Taunton January 2003 despite being hampered on the home turn.

Thatcham Island

74   **20**

10-y-o ch m Jupiter Island-Floreal (Formidable (USA))
Mrs L P Baker Michael W Baker

Placings:0044/0033221P/35500/PP0P   (4425)
2002/03: 24²GF, 22PGS, 17⁰HY, 16FGF,

	Starts	1st	2nd	3rd	Win & Pl
Hurdles	4	0	0	0	
Career Total	21	1	2	3	3405
83 3/00 Towc 2m		G Hdl		GD	£1631
					Total win prize-money £1631

Going:	Sf: 0-1 GS: 0-1 Gd: 1-3 GF: - Fm: 0-2
Distance:	2m/2m3: 0-2 2m4-2m7: 0-1 3m+: 0-1
Track:	LH: 0-1 RH: 0-3 Tight: 0-4 Gall: 0-0
Aids:	Bl: 0-1 Vi: 0-0 Tstrap: 0-0
Best Rating:	83 5/00 Fknm 2m4f firm Hdl

Thatcher Rock

89

7-y-o b g High Estate-Bellifontaine (FR) (Bellypha)
Jonjo O Neill D J Deer

Placings:0/406-P   (2211)
2002/03: 17PS,

	Starts	1st	2nd	3rd	Win & Pl
Hurdles	1	0	0	0	
Career Total	5	0	0	0	0

Going:	Sf: 0-1 GS: 0-0 Gd: 0-0 GF: - Fm: 0-0
Distance:	2m/2m3: 0-1 2m4-2m7: 0-0 3m+: 0-0
Track:	LH: 0-1 RH: 0-0 Tight: 0-1 Gall: 0-0
Aids:	Bl: 0-0 Vi: 0-0 Tstrap: 0-0
Best Rating:	89 3/02 Extr 2m3f good Hdl

Thatchers Longshot

72f   **69f**

6-y-o ch g Gunner B-Formidable Lady (Formidable (USA))
S A Brookshaw S A Brookshaw

Placings:6   (0517)
2002/03: 16⁶S,

	Starts	1st	2nd	3rd	Win & Pl
NH Flat	1	0	0	0	0
Career Total	1	0	0	0	0

Going:	Sf: 0-1 GS: 0-0 Gd: 0-0 GF: - Fm: 0-0
Distance:	2m/2m3: 0-1 2m4-2m7: 0-0 3m+: 0-0
Track:	LH: 0-0 RH: 0-0 Tight: 0-1 Gall: 0-0
Aids:	Bl: 0-0 Vi: 0-0 Tstrap: 0-0
Best Rating:	69 6/02 Worc 2m soft NHF

Thats All Folks

110(99h)   (107h)**114**

6-y-o b g Alhijaz-So It Goes (Free State)
M Todhunter (P F Nicholls 14/5) The Cartmel Syndicate

Placings:3100/04F2315-6231F22   (0951)

2002/03: 19⁶G, 21²HY, 17³GS, 16¹G, 17FGF, 21²GF, 21²G,

	Starts	1st	2nd	3rd	Win & Pl
Hurdles	1	0	0	0	
Chases	6	1	3	1	9884
Career Total	18	3	4	3	19088
108 6/02 Hexm 2m110y D(0-125)HCh			GD	£5508
114 4/02 Hrfd 2m3f D Ch			G-F	£4153
114 1/01 Trtn 2m1f E Hdl			HVY	£2046
					Total win prize-money £11709

Going:	Sf: 0-1 GS: 0-1 Gd: 1-3 GF: - Fm: 0-2
Distance:	2m/2m3: 1-3 2m4-2m7: 0-4 3m+: 0-0
Track:	LH: 1-5 RH: 0-2 Tight: 0-5 Gall: 0-0
Aids:	Bl: 0-0 Vi: 0-0 Tstrap: 0-0
Best Rating:	114 8/02 Sedg 2m5f good Ch

Fair chaser, effective at around two miles but stays further.

Thats The Crack (IRE)

9-y-o b g King s Ride-Mighty Crack (Deep Run)
Alan J Brown Alan J Brown

Placings:4PP6/2/1-P   (4508)
2002/03: 25PG,

	Starts	1st	2nd	3rd	Win & Pl
Chases	1	0	0	0	
Career Total	7	1	1	0	4996
96 5/01 Ling 2m4f110yF(0-90)HCh			G-F	£3486
					Total win prize-money £3486

Going:	Sf: 0-0 GS: 0-0 Gd: 0-0 GF: - Fm: 0-0
Distance:	2m/2m3: 0-0 2m4-2m7: 0-0 3m+: 0-1
Track:	LH: 0-1 RH: 0-0 Tight: 0-1 Gall: 0-0
Aids:	Bl: 0-0 Vi: 0-0 Tstrap: 0-0
Best Rating:	96 5/01 Ling 2m4f110y gd-fm Ch

Thatsforeel

10-y-o b g Scottish Reel-That Space (Space King)
Miss Joanne Tremain C J Hitchings

Placings:2/32PPP0-1   (4526)
2002/03: 24¹G,

	Starts	1st	2nd	3rd	Win & Pl
Chases	1	1	0	0	1547
Career Total	8	1	2	1	4460
87 4/03 Uttx 3m		H Ch		GD	£1547
					Total win prize-money £1547

Going:	Sf: 0-0 GS: 0-0 Gd: 1-1 GF: - Fm: 0-0
Distance:	2m/2m3: 0-0 2m4-2m7: 0-0 3m+: 1-1
Track:	LH: 1-1 RH: 0-0 Tight: 0-0 Gall: 0-0
Aids:	Bl: 0-0 Vi: 0-0 Tstrap: 0-0
Best Rating:	112 4/01 Winc 3m1f110y soft Ch

A winning pointer/hunter chaser; effective in soft ground.

The Alleycat (IRE)

98(86h)   (79h)**91**

12-y-o b g Tidaro (USA)-Allitess (Mugatpura)
R Ford (J S Haldane 25/7) David Bostock

Placings:0F/61152150-0051   (4699)
2002/03: 17⁰GF, 16⁰GF, 17⁵G, 17¹GF,

	Starts	1st	2nd	3rd	Win & Pl
Hurdles	1	0	0	0	0
Chases	3	1	0	0	2587
Career Total	14	4	1	0	15035
91 4/03 Plum 2m1f G(0-90)HCh			G-F	£2586

Going:	Sf: 0-1 GS: 0-1 Gd: 1-3 GF: - Fm: 0-2

(continues)

2002/03: 19⁶G, 21²HY, 17³GS, 16¹G, 17FGF, 21²GF, 21²G,

92 7/01 Sedg 2m110y E(0-115)HCh			G-F	£3363
86 6/01 Prth 2m F(0-100)HCh			G-F	£4823
80 5/01 Hntg 2m4f110yF(0-100)HCh			G-F	£2990
				Total win prize-money £13764

Going:	Sf: 0-0 GS: 0-0 Gd: 0-1 GF: - Fm: 1-3
Distance:	2m/2m3: 1-4 2m4-2m7: 0-0 3m+: 0-0
Track:	LH: 1-3 RH: 0-1 Tight: 1-4 Gall: 0-0
Aids:	Bl: 0-0 Vi: 0-0 Tstrap: 0-0
Best Rating:	92 7/01 Sedg 2m110y gd-fm Ch

Plating-class chaser; multiple winning pointer in his time; likes fast ground; effective at around two miles.

The Bajan Bandit (IRE)

108(104h)   (134h)**144**

8-y-o b g Commanche Run-Sunrise Highway Vii (Damsire Unregistered)
L Lungo Ashleybank Investments Limited

Placings:1/111/11101-112PP   (4110)
2002/03: 20¹HY, 21¹GS, 22²GS, 25PGS, 24²G,

	Starts	1st	2nd	3rd	Win & Pl
Chases	5	2	1	0	14197
Career Total	14	10	1	0	58434
144 12/02 Ayr 2m5f110yE Ch			G-S	£3770
120 11/02 Carl 2m4f D Ch			HVY	£5307
131 4/02 Ayr 2m4f C Hdl			GD	£5570
134 2/02 Ayr 2m4f E Hdl			HVY	£3108
126 11/01 Carl 2m1f E Hdl			HVY	£2531
115 11/01 Ayr 2m E Hdl			G-S	£2597
147 4/01 Aint 2m1f A NHF			HVY	£18000
142 12/00 Chep 2m110y A NHF			SFT	£9000
129 11/00 Ayr 2m H NHF			SFT	£1767
108 4/00 Ayr 2m1f H NHF			G-S	£1662
				Total win prize-money £53315

Going:	Sf: 1-1 GS: 1-3 Gd: 0-1 GF: - Fm: 0-0
Distance:	2m/2m3: 0-0 2m4-2m7: 2-3 3m+: 0-2
Track:	LH: 1-4 RH: 1-1 Tight: 0-0 Gall: 0-1
Aids:	Bl: 0-0 Vi: 0-0 Tstrap: 0-0
Best Rating:	147 4/01 Aint 2m1f heavy NHF

Very useful novice chaser; a top-class bumper horse and also very decent over hurdles; has looked to need a trip since switched to fences; stays at least 2m 4f; goes very well on heavy ground; not at his best when pulled up twice early in 2003.

The Bandit (IRE)

101   **89**

6-y-o b g Un Desperado (FR)-Sweet Friendship (Alleging (USA))
Miss E C Lavelle R J Lavelle

Placings:0-0F62   (4338)
2002/03: 17⁰G, 19FGS, 19⁶GS, 20²GF,

	Starts	1st	2nd	3rd	Win & Pl
Hurdles	4	0	1	0	1141
Career Total	5	0	1	0	1141

Going:	Sf: 0-0 GS: 0-2 Gd: 0-1 GF: - Fm: 0-1
Distance:	2m/2m3: 0-3 2m4-2m7: 0-1 3m+: 0-0
Track:	LH: 0-0 RH: 0-4 Tight: 0-0 Gall: 0-1
Aids:	Bl: 0-0 Vi: 0-0 Tstrap: 0-0
Best Rating:	102 2/02 Kemp 2m good NHF

Plating-class novice hurdler; probably stays 2m 4f.

The Barge (IRE)

87   **66**

10-y-o b g Un Desperado (FR)-Marble Owen (Master Owen)
J White   Mrs P A White

Placings:3/B3100/0000/P5P/P6623-26   (4699)
2002/03: 20²S, 17⁶GF,

	Starts	1st	2nd	3rd	Win & Pl
Chases	2	0	1	0	1245
Career Total	20	1	2	3	5931
115	2/99 Thur	2m6f		Hdl	HVY £2455

Total win prize-money £2455

Going:	Sf: 0-1 GS: 0-0 Gd: 0-0 GF: - Fm: 0-1
Distance:	2m/2m3: 0-1 2m4-2m7: 0-1 3m+: 0-0
Track:	LH: 0-1 RH: 0-0 Tight: 0-2 Gall: 0-0
Aids:	Bl: 0-2 Vi: 0-0 Tstrap: 0-0
Best Rating:	115 2/99 Thur 2m6f heavy Hdl

Plating-class chaser; acts on soft ground; stays two and a half miles; jumps well.

The Beyton Bear (IRE)

7-y-o b g Dromod Hill-Reffian (IRE) (Henbit (USA))
J N R Billinge   J N R Billinge

Placings:0-P   (4014)
2002/03: 16⁵PS,

	Starts	1st	2nd	3rd	Win & Pl
Hurdles	1	0	0	0	
Career Total	2	0	0	0	

Going:	Sf: 0-1 GS: 0-0 Gd: 0-0 GF: - Fm: 0-0
Distance:	2m/2m3: 0-1 2m4-2m7: 0-0 3m+: 0-0
Track:	LH: 0-1 RH: 0-0 Tight: 0-0 Gall: 0-0
Aids:	Bl: 0-0 Vi: 0-0 Tstrap: 0-0
Best Rating:	79 10/01 Sthl 2m good NHF

The Big'Un

109   **90**

9-y-o b g Green-Fingered-Lismore (Relkino)
G L Moore   The P G Partnership

Placings:P243/46-P63   (4118)
2002/03: 21⁵PS, 20⁶G, 24³G,

	Starts	1st	2nd	3rd	Win & Pl
Chases	3	0	0	1	497
Career Total	9	0	1	2	2737

Going:	Sf: 0-1 GS: 0-0 Gd: 0-2 GF: - Fm: 0-0
Distance:	2m/2m3: 0-0 2m4-2m7: 0-2 3m+: 0-1
Track:	LH: 0-0 RH: 0-3 Tight: 0-1 Gall: 0-2
Aids:	Bl: 0-2 Vi: 0-0 Tstrap: 0-0
Best Rating:	103 3/00 Font 2m4f gd-sft Ch

The Biker (IRE)

99   **127+**

6-y-o br g Arctic Lord-Glenravel (Lucifer (USA))
M C Pipe   D A Johnson

Placings:13-11   (2041)
2002/03: 16¹S, 17¹HY,

	Starts	1st	2nd	3rd	Win & Pl
Hurdles	2	2	0	0	7618
Career Total	4	3	0	1	16894

127	11/02 NAbb	2m1f	D Hdl	HVY	£3997
126	11/02 Uttx	2m	E Hdl	SFT	£3620
115	4/02 Fair	2m	NHF	G-Y	£7619

Total win prize-money £15239

Going:	Sf: 2-2 GS: 0-0 Gd: 0-0 GF: - Fm: 0-0
Distance:	2m/2m3: 2-2 2m4-2m7: 0-0 3m+: 0-0
Track:	LH: 2-2 RH: 0-0 Tight: 1-1 Gall: 0-0
Aids:	Bl: 0-0 Vi: 0-0 Tstrap: 0-0
Best Rating:	127 11/02 NAbb 2m1f heavy Hdl

Fair novice hurdler; bumper winner in Ireland, suited by two miles and acts on soft ground; effective under forcing tactics.

The Biscuit

94   **71**

9-y-o ch m Nomadic Way (USA)-Not To Worry (USA) (Stevward)
B Mactaggart   K Bruce

Placings:0/00-2   (1294)
2002/03: 24²GF,

	Starts	1st	2nd	3rd	Win & Pl
Hurdles	1	0	1	0	1272
Career Total	4	0	1	0	1272

Going:	Sf: 0-0 GS: 0-0 Gd: 0-0 GF: - Fm: 0-1
Distance:	2m/2m3: 0-0 2m4-2m7: 0-0 3m+: 0-1
Track:	LH: 0-0 RH: 0-1 Tight: 0-0 Gall: 0-0
Aids:	Bl: 0-0 Vi: 0-0 Tstrap: 0-1
Best Rating:	71 12/01 Muss 2m4f gd-fm Hdl

Moderate novice hurdler; stays two miles four; acts on fast ground.

The Bo'Sun

81f   **82f**

6-y-o b g Charmer-Sailors Joy (Handsome Sailor)
A E Jessop   Mrs Gloria Jessop

Placings:00   (4685)
2002/03: 16⁹GS, 16⁹GF,

	Starts	1st	2nd	3rd	Win & Pl
NH Flat	2	0	0	0	
Career Total	2	0	0	0	

Going:	Sf: 0-0 GS: 0-1 Gd: 0-0 GF: - Fm: 0-1
Distance:	2m/2m3: 0-2 2m4-2m7: 0-0 3m+: 0-0
Track:	LH: 0-1 RH: 0-1 Tight: 0-1 Gall: 0-0
Aids:	Bl: 0-0 Vi: 0-0 Tstrap: 0-0
Best Rating:	82 4/03 Hntg 2m110y gd-fm NHF

The Boiler White (IRE)

15-y-o ch g Deep Run-Cill Dara (Lord Gayle (USA))
E W Froggatt   E W Froggatt

Placings:00/101240301316F0/P2F006P2/P/P/CP-P (0317)
2002/03: 34⁶PG,

	Starts	1st	2nd	3rd	Win & Pl
Chases	1	0	0	0	
Career Total	29	4	3	2	15456
106	3/95 Nott	3m3f110yF(0-105)HCh	SFT	£2684
106	2/95 Hayd	2m4f	D Ch	HVY	£4105
115	11/94 Wind	2m6f110y Hdl	G-S	£2024
107	10/94 Uttx	2m4f110y Hdl	G-F	£2421

Total win prize-money £11237

The Bold Abbot

13-y-o b g Derring Rose-Canford Abbas (Hasty Word)
Miss Sarah West   Miss S West

Placings:0P0/54/U3/4-3   (0033)
2002/03: 25³GF,

	Starts	1st	2nd	3rd	Win & Pl
Chases	1	0	0	1	604
Career Total	9	0	0	2	816

Going:	Sf: 0-0 GS: 0-0 Gd: 0-0 GF: - Fm: 0-1
Distance:	2m/2m3: 0-0 2m4-2m7: 0-0 3m+: 0-1
Track:	LH: 0-1 RH: 0-0 Tight: 0-0 Gall: 0-1
Aids:	Bl: 0-0 Vi: 0-0 Tstrap: 0-0
Best Rating:	89 4/00 Towc 2m6f good Ch

The Bongo Man (IRE)

108   **110d**

10-y-o b g Be My Native (USA)-Fight For It (Strong Gale)
D J Wintle   Hugh M Duffy

Placings:1/3360/6123350/064412124F/016/2P0PF-P6310P0   (4415)
2002/03: 17⁵PS, 16⁶GF, 21³GS, 24¹F, 24⁹GS, 22²HY, 17⁰G,

	Starts	1st	2nd	3rd	Win & Pl
Hurdles	7	1	0	1	3953
Career Total	39	6	4	5	40989
110	10/02 Tntn	3m110y	E(0-110)HHdl	FRM	£3402
118	9/00 Clon	2m4f	(0-109)HHdl	GD	£2760
117	11/99 Tram	2m	(0-109)HCh	YLD	£6160
109	9/99 Tram		Ch	G-Y	£2926
118	9/98 Clon	2m	(0-102)HHdl	GD	£2540
115	4/97 Punc	2m	NHF	GD	£6782

Total win prize-money £24572

Going:	Sf: 0-2 GS: 0-1 Gd: 0-1 GF: - Fm: 1-3
Distance:	2m/2m3: 0-3 2m4-2m7: 0-2 3m+: 1-2
Track:	LH: 0-3 RH: 1-4 Tight: 1-4 Gall: 0-0
Aids:	Bl: 0-0 Vi: 0-0 Tstrap: 1-3
Best Rating:	120 10/98 Gowr 2m yld-sft Hdl

Modest hurdler, has shown form over fences in Ireland; acts on most types of ground; effective at up to three miles.

The Boozing Brief (USA)

80   **58**

10-y-o b g Turkoman (USA)-Evening Silk (USA) (Damascus (USA))
Miss C Dyson   Miss C Dyson

Placings:22U/020/05002P/554/P6P   (4635)
2002/03: 20⁶G, 20⁶G, 19⁷GF,

	Starts	1st	2nd	3rd	Win & Pl
Hurdles	3	0	0	0	0
Career Total	18	0	4	0	2364

Going:	Sf: 0-0 GS: 0-0 Gd: 0-0 GF: - Fm: 0-1
Distance:	2m/2m3: 0-1 2m4-2m7: 0-2 3m+: 0-0
Track:	LH: 0-2 RH: 0-1 Tight: 0-2 Gall: 0-1

Aids: Bl: 0-0 Vi: 0-0 Tstrap: 0-3
Best Rating: 84 3/98 Sedg 2m1f   gd-sft Hdl

Plating-class hurdler; lightly raced in recent seasons; wears tongue tie.

The Brewer

88   77

11-y-o ch g Dunbeath (USA)-Bell Cord (Beldale Flutter (USA))
J C Tuck J C T Racing Club

Placings:024/00003022/33111313/5440332U0/3FF402/004
002-61   (1789)
2002/03: 16⁶G, 22¹GS,

	Starts	1st	2nd	3rd	Win & Pl
Hurdles	2	1	0	0	2184
Career Total	42	5	6	8	21393
77	11/02	Folk	2m6f110yG(0-95)HHdl	G-S	£2184
107	3/98	Extr	2m2f	D(0-120)HHdl	SFT	£2804
107	11/97	Extr	2m3f	E(0-100)HHdl	GD	£2700
93	10/97	Extr	2m3f	F(0-105)HHdl	GD	£2766
87	10/97	Hrlnd	2m3f110yF(0-95)HHdl	G-F	£2094
			Total win prize-money £12548		

Going: Sf: 0-0 GS: 1-1 Gd: 0-1 GF: - Fm: 0-0
Distance: 2m/2m3: 0-0 **2m4-2m7: 1-1** 3m+: 0-0
Track: LH: 0-1 **RH: 1-1 Tight: 1-2** Gall: 0-0
Aids: Bl: 0-0 Vi: 0-0 Tstrap: 0-0
Best Rating: 107 3/98 Extr 2m2f   soft Hdl

Plating-class chaser; gained first win for four and a half years in November 2002; best suited by soft these days.

The Broken Man

10-y-o b g Rakaposhi King-School Run (Deep Run)
Mrs R L Elliot (Miss Louise Wood 19/5) D Davidson

Placings:0/60   (4506)
2002/03: 25⁶S, 25⁰G,

	Starts	1st	2nd	3rd	Win & Pl
Chases	2	0	0	0	0
Career Total	3	0	0	0	0

Going: Sf: 0-1 GS: 0-0 Gd: 0-1 GF: - Fm: 0-0
Distance: 2m/2m3: 0-0 2m4-2m7: 0-0 3m+: 0-2
Track: LH: 0-2 RH: 0-0 Tight: 0-2 Gall: 0-0
Aids: Bl: 0-0 Vi: 0-0 Tstrap: 0-0
Best Rating: 76 3/03 Catt 3m1f110y soft Ch

The Bunny Boiler (IRE)

107(110h)   (137 h)145d

9-y-o b g Tremblant-Danny s Charm (IRE) (Arapahos (FR))
Noel Meade The Usual Suspects Syndicate

Placings:2¹¹⁵210/FU00U21/5312F11-21P00U0   (4791)
2002/03: 24²S, 24¹YS, 29²HY, 24⁰SH, 24⁰G, 36¹U, 29⁰G,

	Starts	1st	2nd	3rd	Win & Pl
Hurdles	2	1	1	0	15926
Chases	5	0	0	0	0
Career Total	27	7	5	1	175144
137	12/02	Navn	3m	HHdl	Y-S	£11963
145	4/02	Fair	3m5f	HCh	G-Y	£65693
145	3/02	Uttx	4m2f	A HCh	HVY	£49600
122	12/01	Thur	2m6f	Hdl	HVY	£5008
118	1/01	DRoy	3m	Ch	G-Y	£6677
113	3/00	Naas	3m	Hdl	Y-S	£3588
84	5/99	Dpat	2m4f110y	NHF	GD	£1994

Total win prize-money £144524

Going: Sf: 0-2 GS: 0-0 Gd: 0-3 GF: - Fm: 0-0
Distance: 2m2/2m3: 0-0 2m4-2m7: 0-0 **3m+: 1-7**
Track: **LH: 1-5** RH: 0-2 Tight: 0-1 Gall: 0-1
Aids: Bl: 0-0 Vi: 0-0 Tstrap: 0-0
Best Rating: 145 4/02 Fair 3m5f   gd-yld Ch

Very useful chaser; won the Midlands and Irish Grand Nationals in 2002, but largely disappointing in 2003; stays extreme distances; acts on soft and heavy ground.

The Byedein (IRE)

89   72

6-y-o b m Alflora (IRE)-Southern Squaw (Buckskin (FR))
A H Mactaggart A H Mactaggart

Placings:00-505255   (4750)
2002/03: 16⁵GF, 22⁰S, 16⁵HY, 16²G, 20⁵GF, 24⁵G,

	Starts	1st	2nd	3rd	Win & Pl
NH Flat	1	0	0	0	0
Hurdles	5	0	1	0	1060
Career Total	8	0	1	0	1060

Going: Sf: 0-2 GS: 0-0 Gd: 0-2 GF: - Fm: 0-2
Distance: 2m/2m3: 0-3 2m4-2m7: 0-2 3m+: 0-1
Track: LH: 0-3 RH: 0-3 Tight: 0-3 Gall: 0-0
Aids: Bl: 0-0 Vi: 0-0 Tstrap: 0-0
Best Rating: 74 4/03 Prth 3m110y good Hdl

Plating-class hurdler; has shown some ability in bumpers and novice hurdles; looks essentially a stayer.

The Car Chaser (IRE)

75   27

5-y-o ch g Great Marquess-Bright Diamond (Never So Bold)
A M Hales Andrew L Cohen

Placings:000   (1869)
2002/03: 16⁰G, 16⁰G, 18⁰GS,

	Starts	1st	2nd	3rd	Win & Pl
NH Flat	2	0	0	0	0
Hurdles	1	0	0	0	0
Career Total	3	0	0	0	0

Going: Sf: 0-0 GS: 0-1 Gd: 0-1 GF: - Fm: 0-1
Distance: 2m2/2m3: 0-3 2m4-2m7: 0-0 3m+: 0-0
Track: LH: 0-3 RH: 0-0 Tight: 0-1 Gall: 0-0
Aids: Bl: 0-0 Vi: 0-0 Tstrap: 0-0
Best Rating: 91 10/02 Chep 2m110y good NHF

The Cardiff Bay

69   23

9-y-o b g St Ninian-Comarch (Ancient Monro)
Mrs Merrita Jones G J Hicks

Placings:03P0/P/5-6   (0175)
2002/03: 21⁶GF,

	Starts	1st	2nd	3rd	Win & Pl
Chases	1	0	0	0	0
Career Total	7	0	0	1	235

Going: Sf: 0-0 GS: 0-0 Gd: 0-0 GF: - Fm: 0-1
Distance: 2m2/2m3: 0-0 2m4-2m7: 0-1 3m+: 0-0
Track: LH: 0-0 RH: 0-1 Tight: 0-0 Gall: 0-0
Aids: Bl: 0-0 Vi: 0-0 Tstrap: 0-0
Best Rating: 78 1/00 Towc 2m   heavy NHF

The Cottonwool Kid

89   81

11-y-o b g Blakeney-Relatively Smart (Great Nephew)
Mrs Merrita Jones Stephen Appelbee

Placings:50/0/5005000/F000/610/6-00P   (0994)
2002/03: 22⁰GF, 22⁰GF, 22⁶GF,

	Starts	1st	2nd	3rd	Win & Pl
Hurdles	3	0	0	0	
Career Total	21	1	0	0	2984
90	10/00	Tntn	3m110y	F(0-110)HHdl	GD	£2983
			Total win prize-money £2984		

Going: Sf: 0-0 GS: 0-0 Gd: 0-0 GF: - Fm: 0-3
Distance: 2m2/2m3: 0-0 2m4-2m7: 0-3 3m+: 0-0
Track: LH: 0-2 RH: 0-1 Tight: 0-2 Gall: 0-0
Aids: Bl: 0-0 Vi: 0-0 Tstrap: 0-0
Best Rating: 90 10/00 Tntn 3m110y   good Hdl

The Count (FR)

96   69

4-y-o b g Sillery (USA)-Dear Countess (FR) (Fabulous Dancer (USA))
F P Murtagh (Andrew Reid 3/7) Jack The Lads

Placings:300P   (4405)
2002/03: 16³S, 16⁹GS, 17⁰GS, 16⁶G,

	Starts	1st	2nd	3rd	Win & Pl
Hurdles	4	0	0	1	323
Career Total	4	0	0	1	323

Going: Sf: 0-1 GS: 0-2 Gd: 0-1 GF: - Fm: 0-0
Distance: 2m2/2m3: 0-4 2m4-2m7: 0-0 3m+: 0-0
Track: LH: 0-2 RH: 0-2 Tight: 0-2 Gall: 0-0
Aids: Bl: 0-0 Vi: 0-0 Tstrap: 0-0
Best Rating: 55 11/02 Kels 2m110y   soft Hdl

The Crooked Oak

(107c)
11-y-o ch g Fearless Action (USA)-Life Goes On (Pharly (FR))
Keith Thomas Keith Thomas

Placings:2/400P/0343/0U4/PU5/56/41410U040-F   (0085)
2002/03: 25⁵GS,

	Starts	1st	2nd	3rd	Win & Pl
Chases	1	0	0	0	
Career Total	27	2	1	2	7544
96	6/01	Hexm	3m1f	E(0-105)HCh	GD	£3204
75	5/01	Hexm	2m4f110yF Ch		G-F	£2115
			Total win prize-money £5321		

Going: Sf: 0-0 GS: 0-1 Gd: 0-0 GF: - Fm: 0-0
Distance: 2m2/2m3: 0-0 2m4-2m7: 0-0 3m+: 0-1
Track: LH: 0-1 RH: 0-0 Tight: 0-0 Gall: 0-0
Aids: Bl: 0-0 Vi: 0-0 Tstrap: 0-0
Best Rating: 97 11/96 Carl 2m1f   good NHF

Modest stayer winning over fences; held over hurdles; best on a sound surface.

The Croppy Boy

85   44

11-y-o b g Arctic Lord-Deep Cut (Deep Run)
Mrs N S Sharpe J V C Davenport

Placings:5400/0/454P/F4P-P430   (1677)
2002/03: 23⁵G, 24⁴G, 26³G, 25⁰GF,

	Starts	1st	2nd	3rd	Win & Pl
Hurdles	3	0	0	1	423

Chases	1	0	0	0	0
Career Total	16	0	0	1	741

Going:	Sf: 0-0 GS: 0-0 Gd: 0-3 GF: - Fm: 0-1
Distance:	2m/2m3: 0-0 2m4-2m7: 0-0 3m+: 0-4
Track:	LH: 0-4 RH: 0-0 Tight: 0-0 Gall: 0-1
Aids:	Bl: 0-0 Vi: 0-0 Tstrap: 0-0
Best Rating:	85 11/96 Wwck 2m good NHF

The Culdee (IRE)
105   125d

7-y-o ch g Phardante (FR)-Deep Inagh (Deep Run)
F Flood   C E Falls

Placings:0/00025f31/1001000023-230000   (4729a)
2002/03: 21²HY, 24³HY, 24⁰G, 16⁰Y, 25⁰G, 22⁰G,

	Starts	1st	2nd	3rd	Win & Pl
Hurdles	6	0	1	1	5736
Career Total	25	4	3	3	52973
118	12/01 Leop	2m2f	(0-120)HHdl	YLD	£9173
117	10/01 Gway	2m	HHdl	SH	£18346
97	4/01 Fair	2m	(67-140)HHdl	SFT	£6677
103	11/00 DRoy	2m	NHF	Y-S	£4140
			Total win prize-money £38337

Going:	Sf: 0-3 GS: 0-0 Gd: 0-2 GF: - Fm: 0-0
Distance:	2m/2m3: 0-1 2m4-2m7: 0-2 3m+: 0-3
Track:	LH: 0-4 RH: 0-1 Tight: 0-0 Gall: 0-1
Aids:	Bl: 0-0 Vi: 0-0 Tstrap: 0-0
Best Rating:	125 10/02 Gway 2m5f190y heavy Hdl

Useful hurdler; stays three miles; acts well on soft ground.

The Dangler (IRE)

10-y-o b g Feelings (FR)-Royal Typhoon (Royal Fountain)
Mrs Laura J Young (J D Frost 15/7)   Capt Alex Michael

Placings:550P02P/222U/2132066-531P00   (4459)
2002/03: 22⁵G, 16²G, 21¹GF, 24⁵G, 21⁰G,

	Starts	1st	2nd	3rd	Win & Pl
Hurdles	1	0	0	0	0
Chases	5	1	6	1	3938
Career Total	24	2	6	2	14765
93	6/02 NAbb	2m5f110yE(0-105)HCh	G-F	£3461
86	6/01 NAbb	2m110y F(0-105)HCh	G-S	£3360
		Total win prize-money £6821

Going:	Sf: 0-1 GS: 0-0 Gd: 0-3 GF: - Fm: 1-2
Distance:	2m/2m3: 0-2 2m4-2m7: 1-3 3m+: 0-1
Track:	LH: 1-4 RH: 0-2 Tight: 1-4 Gall: 0-0
Aids:	Bl: 0-0 Vi: 0-0 Tstrap: 0-0
Best Rating:	93 6/02 NAbb 2m5f110y gd-fm Ch

Fair handicap/hunter chaser; stays 21 furlongs; effective at shorter; acts on a sound surface.

The Dark Flasher (IRE)
112   124

6-y-o b h Lucky Guest-Perpignan (Rousillon (USA))
C F Swan   N O Flaherty

Placings:1343204F-0632000F43   (4742a)
2002/03: 16⁰S, 16⁶S, 16³YS, 18²S, 16⁰S, 16⁰YS, 16⁶S, 16⁴GY, 16³G,

	Starts	1st	2nd	3rd	Win & Pl
Hurdles	10	0	1	2	9325
Career Total	18	1	2	4	17581
111	11/01 Naas	2m	Hdl	Y-S	£4729

Total win prize-money £4730

Going:	Sf: 0-6 GS: 0-0 Gd: 0-1 GF: - Fm: 0-0
Distance:	2m/2m3: 0-10 2m4-2m7: 0-0 3m+: 0-0
Track:	LH: 0-4 RH: 0-3 Tight: 0-0 Gall: 0-0
Aids:	Bl: 0-0 Vi: 0-0 Tstrap: 0-0
Best Rating:	124 4/03 Fair 2m good Hdl

Useful Irish-trained handicap hurdler; effective at two miles and acts on good ground, but handles heavy.

The Dark Lord (IRE)
104   91+

6-y-o b g Lord Americo-Khalkeys Shoon (Green Shoon)
Mrs L Wadham   A E Pakenham

Placings:42   (4051)
2002/03: 16⁴G, 16²HY,

	Starts	1st	2nd	3rd	Win & Pl
Hurdles	2	0	1	0	1510
Career Total	2	0	1	0	1510

Going:	Sf: 0-1 GS: 0-0 Gd: 0-1 GF: - Fm: 0-0
Distance:	2m/2m3: 0-2 2m4-2m7: 0-0 3m+: 0-0
Track:	LH: 0-0 RH: 0-2 Tight: 0-0 Gall: 0-1
Aids:	Bl: 0-0 Vi: 0-0 Tstrap: 0-0
Best Rating:	90 2/03 Hntg 2m110y good Hdl

Moderate hurdler; easy winner of maiden hurdle in June 2003; effective at 2m4f.

The Duckpond (IRE)
101

6-y-o ch g Bob s Return (IRE)-Miss Gosling (Prince Bee)
J A B Old   W E Sturt

Placings:4-4F   (2572)
2002/03: 16⁴HY, 19⁰FG,

	Starts	1st	2nd	3rd	Win & Pl
NH Flat	1	0	0	0	0
Hurdles	1	0	0	0	0
Career Total	3	0	0	0	0

Going:	Sf: 0-1 GS: 0-0 Gd: 0-1 GF: - Fm: 0-0
Distance:	2m/2m3: 0-2 2m4-2m7: 0-0 3m+: 0-0
Track:	LH: 0-2 RH: 0-0 Tight: 0-0 Gall: 0-1
Aids:	Bl: 0-1 Vi: 0-0 Tstrap: 0-0
Best Rating:	107 2/02 Sand 2m110y soft NHF

The Eens
98(72h)   (18h)85

11-y-o b g Rakaposhi King-Snippet (Ragstone)
D McCain   Shaw Hill Golf Club (sage Cott Props Ltd

Placings:5064/26P4P1/124231U0/4P440522143/4623P5P/03623541313-P44465   (4401)
2002/03: 24⁰G, 22⁴G, 25⁴HY, 28⁴S, 24⁶S, 24⁵GF,

	Starts	1st	2nd	3rd	Win & Pl
Chases	6	0	0	1	1023
Career Total	53	6	7	7	35180
90	4/02 Uttx	3m2f	E(0-110)HCh	G-S	£4221
85	3/02 MRas	3m1f	F(0-95)HCh	SFT	£3031
101	3/00 Carl	2m4f	E(0-115)HHdl	HVY	£2436
95	3/99 Uttx	3m2f	F(0-110)HCh	HVY	£3631
105	11/98 Hayd	2m	C(0-130)HCh	SFT	£4697
94	3/98 Bang	2m4f110yD Ch	G-S	£3598
			Total win prize-money £21616

Going:	Sf: 0-3 GS: 0-0 Gd: 0-2 GF: - Fm: 0-1
Distance:	2m/2m3: 0-0 2m4-2m7: 0-1 3m+: 0-5

Track:	LH: 0-4 RH: 0-2 Tight: 0-3 Gall: 0-0
Aids:	Bl: 0-0 Vi: 0-0 Tstrap: 0-0
Best Rating:	105 11/98 Hayd 2m soft Ch

Moderate chaser; he is normally a sound jumper; needs cut in the ground to be seen at his best; stays three miles.

The Equaliser

6-y-o b g Alflora (IRE)-My Charade (Cawston s Clown)
M J Roberts   Mike Roberts

Placings:6B   (2253)
2002/03: 18⁶GF, 20⁸HY,

	Starts	1st	2nd	3rd	Win & Pl
NH Flat	1	0	0	0	0
Hurdles	1	0	0	0	0
Career Total	2	0	0	0	0

Going:	Sf: 0-1 GS: 0-0 Gd: 0-0 GF: - Fm: 0-1
Distance:	2m/2m3: 0-1 2m4-2m7: 0-1 3m+: 0-0
Track:	LH: 0-1 RH: 0-1 Tight: 0-2 Gall: 0-0
Aids:	Bl: 0-0 Vi: 0-0 Tstrap: 0-0
Best Rating:	90 5/02 Font 2m2f110y gd-fm NHF

The Fairy Flag (IRE)
74   50

5-y-o ch m Inchinor-Good Reference (IRE) (Reference Point)
A Bailey   Mrs V Farrington

Placings:115-PP5   (4798)
2002/03: 20⁰S, 16⁰GF, 17⁵GF,

	Starts	1st	2nd	3rd	Win & Pl
Hurdles	3	0	0	0	0
Career Total	6	2	0	0	7817
97	11/01 Sand	2m110y D Hdl	G-S	£4212
97	11/01 Hayd	2m	D Hdl	SFT	£3605
			Total win prize-money £7817

Going:	Sf: 0-1 GS: 0-0 Gd: 0-0 GF: - Fm: 0-2
Distance:	2m/2m3: 0-2 2m4-2m7: 0-1 3m+: 0-0
Track:	LH: 0-3 RH: 0-0 Tight: 0-1 Gall: 0-0
Aids:	Bl: 0-1 Vi: 0-0 Tstrap: 0-0
Best Rating:	97 11/01 Sand 2m110y gd-sft Hdl

Plating-class hurdler; dual winner as a juvenile in 2001; lightly-raced since; suited by two miles on soft ground.

The Fenman
90   82d

5-y-o b g Mazaad-Dalgorian (IRE) (Lancastrian)
C N Kellett   D H & Mrs R E Muir

Placings:000-P200230000   (4525)
2002/03: 16⁰GF, 17²S, 16⁰S, 16⁰GS, 19²S, 19³G, 25⁰G, 21⁰G, 22⁰G, 16⁰G,

	Starts	1st	2nd	3rd	Win & Pl
Hurdles	10	0	2	1	1848
Career Total	13	0	2	1	1848

Going:	Sf: 0-3 GS: 0-1 Gd: 0-5 GF: - Fm: 0-1
Distance:	2m/2m3: 0-5 2m4-2m7: 0-4 3m+: 0-1
Track:	LH: 0-6 RH: 0-3 Tight: 0-4 Gall: 0-1
Aids:	Bl: 0-3 Vi: 0-0 Tstrap: 0-0
Best Rating:	82 2/03 Hrfd 2m3f110y good Hdl

Plating-class hurdler; stays two and a half miles.

The Flyer (IRE)

109   **118**

6-y-o b g Blues Traveller (IRE)-National Ballet (Shareef Dancer (USA))
Miss S J Wilton   John Pointon And Sons

Placings:1314/0301201320-2142   (2640)
2002/03: 20²G, 19¹G, 22⁴S, 21²S,

	Starts	1st	2nd	3rd	Win & Pl
Hurdles	4	1	2	0	11323
Career Total	18	5	4	3	24964

118	11/02	Hrfd	2m3f110y		D(0-125)HHdl	GD	£6987
101	2/02	Hrfd	2m1f		D(0-115)HHdl	HVY	£3381
101	12/01	Hrfd	2m1f		E(0-115)HHdl	GD	£2968
97	11/00	Uttx	2m		E Hdl	HVY	£2303
97	9/00	MRas	2m1f110yG Hdl			G-F	£1561
					Total win prize-money £17201		

Going:	Sf: 0-2 GS: 0-0 Gd: 0-0 GF: - Fm: 0-0
Distance:	2m/2m3: 0-0 2m4-2m7: 1-4 3m+: 0-0
Track:	LH: 0-3 RH: 1-1 Tight: 0-0 Gall: 0-0
Aids:	Bl: 0-0 Vi: 0-0 Tstrap: 0-0
Best Rating:	118 12/02 Wwck 2m5f soft Hdl

Fair handicap hurdler, stays two and a half miles. Three times a winner at Hereford. Acts on all types of ground.

The French Furze (IRE)

100(119h)   (150h)**124+**

9-y-o ch g Be My Guest (USA)-Exciting (Mill Reef (USA))
N G Richards   Jim Ennis

Placings:1261131PP/P2060/2110P/222065/2223304-02651F   (4377)
2002/03: 16⁹G, 16²GS, 17⁶G, 16⁵GS, 21¹S, 16⁶G,

	Starts	1st	2nd	3rd	Win & Pl
Hurdles	4	0	1	0	13125
Chases	2	1	0	0	3887
Career Total	38	7	11	2	120138

124	3/03	Sedg	2m5f	E Ch	SFT	£3887
146	1/02	Chel	2m1f	B(0-145)HHdl	G-S	£10140
141	1/00	Hayd	2m	B(0-145)HHdl	SFT	£6652
134	2/98	Hntg	2m11y0	C Hdl	GD	£4202
137	11/97	Chel	2m11y0	B Hdl	GD	£5121
135	11/97	Plum	2m1f	G-F		£2385
96	8/97	Tram	2m	Hdl	GD	£2712
					Total win prize-money £35101	

Going:	Sf: 1-1 GS: 0-2 Gd: 0-3 GF: - Fm: 0-0
Distance:	2m/2m3: 0-5 2m4-2m7: 1-1 3m+: 0-0
Track:	LH: 1-6 RH: 0-0 Tight: 1-2 Gall: 0-2
Aids:	Bl: 0-0 Vi: 0-0 Tstrap: 0-0
Best Rating:	153 1/02 Leop 2m heavy Hdl

Smart hurdler/novice chaser; front runner suited by two miles and soft ground; finished runner-up for the third year in a row in the Fighting Fifth at Newcastle in November 2002; straightforward task when making successful chase debut at Sedgefield in March 2003 despite jumping left-handed; in front but under pressure when falling at the last fence at the same track two weeks later.

The Full Nelson (IRE)

101   **68**

8-y-o b/br g Supreme Leader-Quivering Melody (Lord Ha Ha)
Mrs Jane Galpin   The Artemis Partnership

Placings:0/216002/P6000460   (4083)

2002/03: 22⁶S, 20⁶S, 22⁰GS, 22⁰S, 22⁰GS, 24⁴GS, 22⁶S, 25⁰HY,

	Starts	1st	2nd	3rd	Win & Pl
Hurdles	8	0	0	0	273
Career Total	15	1	2	0	3151

111	11/00	Towc	2m	H NHF	SFT	£1512
				Total win prize-money £1512		

Going:	Sf: 0-5 GS: 0-3 Gd: 0-0 GF: - Fm: 0-0
Distance:	2m/2m3: 0-0 2m4-2m7: 0-6 3m+: 0-2
Track:	LH: 0-6 RH: 0-1 Tight: 0-4 Gall: 0-0
Aids:	Bl: 0-1 Vi: 0-3 Tstrap: 0-0
Best Rating:	111 11/00 Towc 2m soft NHF

Fair handicap hurdler, stays two and a half miles. Three times a winner at Hereford. Acts on all types of ground.

The Funky Monkey (IRE)

7-y-o gr g Roselier (FR)-Rumups Debut (IRE) (Good Thyne (USA))
A Parker   Mr & Mrs Raymond Anderson Green

Placings:00-20P   (3987)
2002/03: 17²GF, 17⁰S, 20²S,

	Starts	1st	2nd	3rd	Win & Pl
NH Flat	2	0	1	0	569
Hurdles	1	0	0	0	0
Career Total	5	0	1	0	569

Going:	Sf: 0-2 GS: 0-0 Gd: 0-0 GF: - Fm: 0-1
Distance:	2m/2m3: 0-2 2m4-2m7: 0-1 3m+: 0-0
Track:	LH: 0-0 RH: 0-3 Tight: 0-0 Gall: 0-0
Aids:	Bl: 0-0 Vi: 0-0 Tstrap: 0-0
Best Rating:	101 10/02 Carl 2m1f gd-fm NHF

Some ability in bumpers and will make a chaser one day.

The Gambling Lady

7-y-o b/br m General Gambul-Coach Rd Express (Pony Express)
C Tizzard   G F Gingell

Placings:P-PF   (3245)
2002/03: 24²HY, 21⁵HY,

	Starts	1st	2nd	3rd	Win & Pl
Hurdles	2	0	0	0	
Career Total	3	0	0	0	

Going:	Sf: 0-2 GS: 0-0 Gd: 0-0 GF: - Fm: 0-0
Distance:	2m/2m3: 0-0 2m4-2m7: 0-1 3m+: 0-1
Track:	LH: 0-2 RH: 0-0 Tight: 0-1 Gall: 0-0
Aids:	Bl: 0-0 Vi: 0-0 Tstrap: 0-1
Best Rating:	0 1/03 Plum 2m5f heavy Hdl

The Gatherer (IRE)

(116h)   (125h)**129+**

9-y-o b g Be My Native (USA)-Reaper s Run (Deep Run)
A L T Moore   J P McManus

Placings:332/5120/145/42F1620-FF3F0   (4136)
2002/03: 16⁶GF, 17⁵S, 16⁹S, 16⁵YS, 17⁰G,

	Starts	1st	2nd	3rd	Win & Pl
Hurdles	2	0	0	0	0
Chases	3	0	0	1	795
Career Total	22	3	4	3	69154

142	1/02	Leop	2m	Hdl	Y-S	£7975
139	10/00	Gowr	2m	(0-135)HHdl	SFT	£10400
103	2/00	Punc	2m	Hdl	Y-S	£4140
				Total win prize-money £22515		

The Gene Genie

101(95c)   (97+c)**104**

8-y-o b g Syrtos-Sally Maxwell (Roscoe Blake)
R J Hodges   Mrs Carol Taylor

Placings:32506/13230/21232243P-5532   (2783)
2002/03: 17⁵GS, 19⁵GS, 16⁴GS, 17²S,

	Starts	1st	2nd	3rd	Win & Pl
Hurdles	2	0	1	1	2043
Chases	2	0	0	0	0
Career Total	23	2	7	6	17272

103	12/01	Winc	2m	(0-120)HHdl	GD	£5213
91	12/00	Hrfd	2m1f	G Hdl	HVY	£2023
				Total win prize-money £7236		

Going:	Sf: 0-1 GS: 0-3 Gd: 0-0 GF: - Fm: 0-0
Distance:	2m/2m3: 0-4 2m4-2m7: 0-0 3m+: 0-0
Track:	LH: 0-1 RH: 0-3 Tight: 0-3 Gall: 0-0
Aids:	Bl: 0-0 Vi: 0-0 Tstrap: 0-0
Best Rating:	113 1/01 Tntn 2m1f soft Hdl

Moderate, consistent handicap hurdler, but acts on good ground or softer and is best at around two miles.

The Gopher (IRE)

105   **108**

14-y-o ch g General View-Egg Shells (Miami Springs)
D J Wintle   John W Egan

Placings:50/00006O0215/B103P341P/031U22414/11B31S3 3/44122160F/3332F240PP/40641F-5411P   (1583)
2002/03: 23⁵GF, 23⁴GF, 26¹GF, 26¹G, 26⁶G,

	Starts	1st	2nd	3rd	Win & Pl
Chases	5	2	0	0	11843
Career Total	67	13	7	9	87552

108	9/02	Plum	3m2f	D(0-120)HCh	GD	£6825
108	8/02	Sthl	3m2f	D(0-115)HCh	G-F	£5018
108	9/01	Hrfd	2m3f	F(0-110)HCh	G-F	£4056
135	8/99	Sthl	3m110y	D(0-125)HCh	G-F	£4513
128	6/99	MRas	2m4f	C(0-135)HCh	G-F	£7035
129	8/98	Worc	2m7f110yD(0-125)HCh		G-F	£3685
124	6/98	MRas	3m1f	D(0-120)HCh	GD	£4648
122	5/98	Uttx	2m	C(0-130)HCh	G-F	£4947
114	11/97	Wwck	2m2f	C(0-135)HCh	GD	£5014
106	9/97	NAbb	2m2f110yD(0-120)HCh		SFT	£3338
110	4/97	List	2m6f110y (0-109)HCh		G-F	£4069
110	9/96	List	2m2f	Ch	GD	£4237
108	4/95	Baln	3m	Hdl	YLD	£2204
				Total win prize-money £59592		

Going:	Sf: 0-0 GS: 0-0 Gd: 1-2 GF: - Fm: 1-3
Distance:	2m/2m3: 0-0 2m4-2m7: 0-0 3m+: 2-5
Track:	LH: 2-5 RH: 0-0 Tight: 1-2 Gall: 0-0
Aids:	Bl: 2-4 Vi: 0-0 Tstrap: 0-0
Best Rating:	135 8/99 Sthl 3m110y gd-fm Ch

Veteran chaser who is consistent but slow. Has won over trips of around two and a half miles, but looks better suited by further. Best on a sound surface, ususally blinkered.

The Granby (IRE)

106(105c)   (145c)**130**

9-y-o b g Insan (USA)-Elteetee (Paddy s Stream)

Mrs M Reveley Revival Racing Ltd

Placings:*4063*/2F11111/**3311**U-6403   **(3880)**
2002/03: 24⁶GF, 23⁴GS, 24⁰G, 24³GS,

	Starts	1st	2nd	3rd	Win & Pl
Hurdles	4	0	0	1	4098
Career Total	20	7	1	4	31405
135 2/02	Donc	3m	E Ch		SFT	£3354
117 12/01	Muss	3m	D Ch		GD	£4231
135 4/00	Ayr	2m4f	C Hdl		GD	£5572
135 1/00	Donc	3m	D Hdl		G-F	£3493
124 1/00	Catt	2m	E Hdl		GD	£2835
127 12/99	Catt	2m3f	E Hdl		G-F	£1940
112 10/99	Sedg	2m1f	D Hdl		GD	£3168

Total win prize-money £24595

Going: Sf: 0-0 GS: 0-2 Gd: 0-1 GF: - Fm: 0-1
Distance: 2m/2m3: 0-0 2m4-2m7: 0-0 3m+: 0-4
Track: LH: 0-3 RH: 0-1 Tight: 0-1 Gall: 0-2
Aids: Bl: 0-0 Vi: 0-0 Tstrap: 0-0
Best Rating: 135 2/02 Donc 3m soft Ch

Useful chaser/hurdler; stays three miles; did most of his winning over hurdles on a sound surface but has won over fences on good to soft/soft ground.

The Grandson (IRE)
14

8-y-o b g Husyan (USA)-Tarary (Boreen (FR))
S T Lewis Simon T Lewis

Placings:P0P-PP   **(1058)**
2002/03: 19⁰S, 24⁰GF,

	Starts	1st	2nd	3rd	Win & Pl
Hurdles	2	0	0	0	
Career Total	5	0	0	0	

Going: Sf: 0-1 GS: 0-0 Gd: 0-0 GF: - Fm: 0-1
Distance: 2m/2m3: 0-1 2m4-2m7: 0-0 3m+: 0-1
Track: LH: 0-2 RH: 0-0 Tight: 0-1 Gall: 0-0
Aids: Bl: 0-0 Vi: 0-0 Tstrap: 0-0
Best Rating: 17 4/02 Tntn 2m1f gd-sft Hdl

The Greenkeeper (IRE)

10-y-o b g Beau Sher-Hurricane Hattie (Strong Gale)
C Tizzard Mrs N G Smyth

Placings:P/P6F-   **(0009)**
2002/03: 26⁶G,

	Starts	1st	2nd	3rd	Win & Pl
Chases	1	0	0	0	
Career Total	4	0	0	0	0

Going: Sf: 0-0 GS: 0-0 Gd: 0-1 GF: - Fm: 0-0
Distance: 2m/2m3: 0-0 2m4-2m7: 0-0 3m+: 0-1
Track: LH: 0-1 RH: 0-0 Tight: 0-1 Gall: 0-0
Aids: Bl: 0-0 Vi: 0-0 Tstrap: 0-0
Best Rating:

The Grey Baron

6-y-o gr g Baron Blakeney-Topsy Bee (Be Friendly)
A Ennis The A T P Racing Partnership

Placings:PP   **(3346)**
2002/03: 24⁰G, 23⁰S,

	Starts	1st	2nd	3rd	Win & Pl
Chases	2	0	0	0	
Career Total	2	0	0	0	

Going: Sf: 0-1 GS: 0-0 Gd: 0-1 GF: - Fm: 0-0
Distance: 2m/2m3: 0-0 2m4-2m7: 0-0 3m+: 0-2
Track: LH: 0-1 RH: 0-1 Tight: 0-0 Gall: 0-1
Aids: Bl: 0-0 Vi: 0-0 Tstrap: 0-2
Best Rating: 0 1/03 Leic 2m7f110y soft Ch

The Grey Butler (IRE)
104f   97f

6-y-o gr g Roselier (FR)-Georgic (Tumble Gold)
B De Haan Mrs D Vaughan

Placings:34   **(4444)**
2002/03: 16³S, 16⁴G,

	Starts	1st	2nd	3rd	Win & Pl
NH Flat	2	0	0	1	349
Career Total	2	0	0	1	349

Going: Sf: 0-1 GS: 0-0 Gd: 0-1 GF: - Fm: 0-0
Distance: 2m/2m3: 0-2 2m4-2m7: 0-0 3m+: 0-0
Track: LH: 0-0 RH: 0-2 Tight: 0-0 Gall: 0-0
Aids: Bl: 0-0 Vi: 0-0 Tstrap: 0-0
Best Rating: 97 4/03 Asct 2m110y good NHF

Moderate performer; showed ability on debut when third in a weak bumper at Ascot in February; fourth in another Ascot bumper next time.

The Grey Dyer (IRE)
107(105h)   (120h)120

9-y-o gr g Roselier (FR)-Tawny Kate (IRE) (Crash Course)
L Lungo Ashleybank Investments Limited

Placings:05/52/421/**UF132**-2F1PP2   **(4589)**
2002/03: 20²S, 24⁶GS, 25¹GS, 33⁶S, 20⁰HY, 25²G,

	Starts	1st	2nd	3rd	Win & Pl
Chases	6	1	2	0	9583
Career Total	18	3	5	1	18387
120 12/02	Ayr	3m1f	D(0-125)HCh	G-S	£6792
109 11/01	Weth	2m4f110yF(0-110)HHdl	GD	£2478
105 4/01	Prth	2m4f110yD Hdl	HVY	£2828

Total win prize-money £12099

Going: Sf: 0-3 GS: 1-2 Gd: 0-1 GF: - Fm: 0-0
Distance: 2m/2m3: 0-0 2m4-2m7: 0-2 3m+: 0-2 3m+: 1-4
Track: LH: 1-5 RH: 0-1 Tight: 0-1 Gall: 0-2
Aids: Bl: 0-0 Vi: 0-0 Tstrap: 0-0
Best Rating: 120 12/02 Ayr 3m1f gd-sft Ch

Decent novice chaser, winner at Ayr in December but pulled up next time and ran badly at Newcastle in January 2003.

The Guinea Stamp

4-y-o b g Overbury (IRE)-Gagajulu (Al Hareb (USA))
A Berry (S A Brookshaw 17/3) Dingley Dell Racing Ltd

Placings:00PP   **(4219)**
2002/03: 16⁰G, 16⁰G, 17⁰S, 17⁰GF,

	Starts	1st	2nd	3rd	Win & Pl
NH Flat	2	0	0	0	0
Hurdles	2	0	0	0	0
Career Total	4	0	0	0	

Going: Sf: 0-2 GS: 0-0 Gd: 0-1 GF: - Fm: 0-1
Distance: 2m/2m3: 0-4 2m4-2m7: 0-0 3m+: 0-0
Track: LH: 0-2 RH: 0-2 Tight: 0-2 Gall: 0-0
Aids: Bl: 0-0 Vi: 0-0 Tstrap: 0-0
Best Rating: 21 1/03 Ludl 2m soft NHF

The Hearty Joker (IRE)
107   101+

8-y-o b g Broken Hearted-Furryway (Furry Glen)
B G Powell Mrs Marygold O Kelly

Placings:P0/P6P422-4323236   **(3145)**
2002/03: 20²GS, 21⁴GF, 20³GF, 21²GF, 20³G, 21²S, 20³G, 19⁶S,

	Starts	1st	2nd	3rd	Win & Pl
Chases	8	0	3	3	6026
Career Total	15	0	4	3	7448

Going: Sf: 0-2 GS: 0-1 Gd: 0-2 GF: - Fm: 0-3
Distance: 2m/2m3: 0-1 2m4-2m7: 0-7 3m+: 0-0
Track: LH: 0-0 RH: 0-5 Tight: 0-6 Gall: 0-0
Aids: Bl: 0-0 Vi: 0-0 Tstrap: 0-0
Best Rating: 88 4/02 Hntg 2m4f110y gd-fm Ch

Moderate, consistent chaser; finally broke his duck when 10lb wrong in modest 2m6f handicap at Market Rasen in July 2003; limitations exposed under penalty next time; suited by a sound surface.

The Honey Guide

7-y-o gr g Homo Sapien-The Whirlie Weevil (Scallywag)
Mrs L B Normile Mrs J Olivier

Placings:0P   **(4749)**
2002/03: 17⁰S, 20⁰G,

	Starts	1st	2nd	3rd	Win & Pl
NH Flat	1	0	0	0	0
Hurdles	1	0	0	0	0
Career Total	2	0	0	0	

Going: Sf: 0-1 GS: 0-0 Gd: 0-1 GF: - Fm: 0-0
Distance: 2m/2m3: 0-1 2m4-2m7: 0-1 3m+: 0-0
Track: LH: 0-0 RH: 0-2 Tight: 0-0 Gall: 0-0
Aids: Bl: 0-0 Vi: 0-0 Tstrap: 0-0
Best Rating: 31 10/02 Carl 2m1f soft NHF

The Joker (IRE)
98f   112+f

5-y-o ch g Montelimar (USA)-How Doudo (Oats)
J K Magee J Killen

Placings:5114   **(3507)**
2002/03: 17⁵GF, 17¹YS, 16¹HY, 16⁴HY,

	Starts	1st	2nd	3rd	Win & Pl
NH Flat	4	2	0	0	5277
Career Total	4	2	0	0	5277
112 1/03	Ayr	2m	H NHF	HVY	£1890
109 12/02	Dpat	2m1f172y NHF	Y-S	£3386

Total win prize-money £5277

Going: Sf: 1-2 GS: 0-0 Gd: 0-0 GF: - Fm: 0-1
Distance: 2m/2m3: 2-4 2m4-2m7: 0-0 3m+: 0-0
Track: LH: 1-2 RH: 0-0 Tight: 0-0 Gall: 0-0
Aids: Bl: 0-0 Vi: 0-0 Tstrap: 0-0
Best Rating: 112 1/03 Ayr 2m heavy NHF

Modest, dual bumper winner; acts on soft ground.

The Kerry Rebel (IRE)

102(91h)   (66h)**69**

10-y-o b g Gallant Knight-Symphony Orchestra (Orchestra)
Miss G Browne (R Curtis 8/6) Mrs Rhona Alexander

Placings:P/P0000/0/0/00P/0-P00**432**   (1228)
2002/03: 24^PG, 24^DG, 24⁰G, 21⁴GF, 26³GF, 24²G,

	Starts	1st	2nd	3rd	Win & Pl
Hurdles	3	0	0	0	
Chases	3	0	1	1	1963
Career Total	18	0	1	1	1963

Going:	Sf: 0-0 GS: 0-0 Gd: 0-4 GF: - Fm: 0-2
Distance:	2m/2m3: 0-0 2m4-2m7: 0-1 3m+: 0-5
Track:	LH: 0-6 RH: 0-0 Tight: 0-3 Gall: 0-0
Aids:	Bl: 0-1 Vi: 0-0 Tstrap: 0-0
Best Rating:	74 5/97 Gowr 2m good NHF

Very moderate staying chaser, suited by a sound surface and improving with experience.

The Kew Tour (IRE)

105   **114**

7-y-o ch g Un Desperado (FR)-Drivers Bureau (Proverb)
Mrs S J Smith Keith Nicholson

Placings:640-1**12**   (4764)
2002/03: 25¹G, 20¹GF, 24²G,

	Starts	1st	2nd	3rd	Win & Pl
Hurdles	3	2	1	0	9412
Career Total	6	2	1	0	9756
108	3/03	Weth	2m4f110yE Hdl		G-F	£3532
92	3/03	Weth	3m1f	F(0-100)HHdl	GD	£3041
				Total win prize-money £6575		

Going:	Sf: 0-0 GS: 0-0 Gd: 1-2 GF: - Fm: 1-1
Distance:	2m/2m3: 0-0 2m4-2m7: 1-1 3m+: 1-2
Track:	LH: 2-2 RH: 0-1 Tight: 0-0 Gall: 0-0
Aids:	Bl: 0-0 Vi: 0-0 Tstrap: 0-0
Best Rating:	114 4/03 Prth 3m110y good Hdl

Moderate hurdler; winning pointer in Ireland; made a successful hurdling bow here at Wetherby in March and had no difficulty following up there in a weak event two weeks later; acts on a sound surface; looks a potential chaser.

The Laird's Entry (IRE)

86   **111**

8-y-o b g King s Ride-Balancing Act (Balinger)
L Lungo Ashleybank Investments Limited

Placings:3315-**6**   (0156)
2002/03: 22⁶G,

	Starts	1st	2nd	3rd	Win & Pl
Hurdles	1	0	0	0	0
Career Total	5	1	0	2	4066
111	1/02	Catt	2m3f	D Hdl	SFT	£3360
				Total win prize-money £3360		

Going:	Sf: 0-0 GS: 0-0 Gd: 0-0 GF: 0-1 GF: - Fm: 0-0
Distance:	2m/2m3: 0-0 2m4-2m7: 0-1 3m+: 0-0
Track:	LH: 0-1 RH: 0-0 Tight: 0-0 Gall: 0-0
Aids:	Bl: 0-0 Vi: 0-0 Tstrap: 0-0
Best Rating:	111 1/02 Catt 2m3f soft Hdl

Modest hurdler; lovely big chasing type from the family of Granville Again and Morley Street, he got off the mark on his second start over hurdles at Catterick in February 2002. Highly regarded, he is suited by two and a half miles and give in the ground and will make a very nice chaser.

The Lambton Worm

(97h)   (88h)

9-y-o b g Superpower-Springwell (Miami Springs)
G F Edwards G F Edwards

Placings:054035/00/4050/500-6**P**   (0648)
2002/03: 17⁶G, 21^PGF,

	Starts	1st	2nd	3rd	Win & Pl
Hurdles	1	0	0	0	0
Chases	1	0	0	0	0
Career Total	17	0	0	1	395

Going:	Sf: 0-0 GS: 0-0 Gd: 0-1 GF: - Fm: 0-1
Distance:	2m/2m3: 0-1 2m4-2m7: 0-1 3m+: 0-0
Track:	LH: 0-2 RH: 0-0 Tight: 0-2 Gall: 0-0
Aids:	Bl: 0-0 Vi: 0-0 Tstrap: 0-0
Best Rating:	93 1/99 Catt 2m soft Hdl

The Land Agent

105   **108**

12-y-o b g Town And Country-Notinhand (Nearly A Hand)
J W Mullins D I Bare

Placings:31/20/53424311/PP431224U5/U2441453/2U4P/5
6F004-43103P6**431**   (4676)
2002/03: 25⁴GF, 21³GS, 20¹GF, 21⁰G, 20³GS, 27^PGS, 18⁶G,
21⁴G, 20³S, 19¹GF,

	Starts	1st	2nd	3rd	Win & Pl
Chases	10	2	0	3	12942
Career Total	50	7	6	8	102535
104	4/03	Hrfd	2m3f	E(0-110)HCh	G-F	£4468
109	6/02	Strf	2m4f	D(0-115)HCh	G-F	£4371
145	2/00	Winc	2m5f	B Ch	G-S	£10432
144	1/99	Winc	2m5f	B Ch	G-S	£10162
139	4/98	Sand	2m4f110yC HCh	G-S	£14975
139	4/98	Asct	2m3f110yC Ch	G-S	£5924
128	4/96	NAbb	2m1f	H NHF	SFT	£1509
				Total win prize-money £51844		

Going:	Sf: 0-1 GS: 0-4 Gd: 0-2 GF: - Fm: 2-3
Distance:	2m/2m3: 1-2 2m4-2m7: 1-6 3m+: 0-2
Track:	LH: 1-5 RH: 1-5 Tight: 1-4 Gall: 0-2
Aids:	Bl: 0-0 Vi: 0-0 Tstrap: 0-0
Best Rating:	145 2/00 Winc 2m5f gd-sft Ch

Modest chaser nowadays, formerly useful,; effective at around two and a half miles; acts on most types of ground.

The Last Cast

102   **120+**

4-y-o ch g Prince Of Birds (USA)-Atan s Gem (USA)
(Sharpen Up)
C R Egerton D P Barrie

Placings:53**111**   (2885)
2002/03: 16⁵G, 16³S, 17¹S, 17¹S, 17¹HY,

	Starts	1st	2nd	3rd	Win & Pl
Hurdles	5	3	0	1	16410
Career Total	5	3	0	1	16410
120	1/03	Chel	2m1f	B Hdl	HVY	£9526
106	12/02	MRas	2m1f110yE Hdl	SFT	£3094
96	11/02	Bang	2m1f	E Hdl	SFT	£3136
				Total win prize-money £15756		

Going:	Sf: 3-4 GS: 0-0 Gd: 0-1 GF: - Fm: 0-0
Distance:	2m/2m3: 3-5 2m4-2m7: 0-0 3m+: 0-0
Track:	LH: 2-2 RH: 1-3 Tight: 2-2 Gall: 1-1
Aids:	Bl: 0-0 Vi: 0-0 Tstrap: 0-0
Best Rating:	120 1/03 Chel 2m1f heavy Hdl

Fair juvenile hurdler; completed a hat-trick at Bangor, Market Rasen and Cheltenham; suited by forcing tactics; effective in soft ground.

The Last Mohican

97   **99d**

4-y-o b g Common Grounds-Arndilly (Robellino (USA))
P Howling P Woodward

Placings:435**2204**   (4681)
2002/03: 16⁴GS, 16⁵S, 16⁵GS, 19²GS, 17²G, 16⁰G, 21⁴GF,

	Starts	1st	2nd	3rd	Win & Pl
Hurdles	7	0	2	1	1937
Career Total	7	0	2	1	1937

Going:	Sf: 0-1 GS: 0-3 Gd: 0-2 GF: - Fm: 0-1
Distance:	2m/2m3: 0-5 2m4-2m7: 0-2 3m+: 0-0
Track:	LH: 0-5 RH: 0-2 Tight: 0-2 Gall: 0-2
Aids:	Bl: 0-0 Vi: 0-0 Tstrap: 0-0
Best Rating:	95 2/03 Donc 2m3f110y gd-sft Hdl

Moderate hurdler; effective from two to two and a half miles; acts on good and soft ground.

The Last Shout (IRE)

10-y-o b g Yashgan-Apia Sunshine (Simbir)
Mrs Mair Hughes B R Hughes

Placings:0/**P**   (0029)
2002/03: 21^PGF,

	Starts	1st	2nd	3rd	Win & Pl
Chases	1	0	0	0	
Career Total	2	0	0	0	

Going:	Sf: 0-0 GS: 0-0 Gd: 0-0 GF: - Fm: 0-1
Distance:	2m/2m3: 0-0 2m4-2m7: 0-1 3m+: 0-0
Track:	LH: 0-1 RH: 0-0 Tight: 0-0 Gall: 0-1
Aids:	Bl: 0-0 Vi: 0-0 Tstrap: 0-0
Best Rating:	44 10/98 Fair 2m yield Hdl

The Leader

102   **105+**

10-y-o b g Ardross-Leading Line (Leading Man)
P R Chamings Inhurst Farm Stables Partnership

Placings:546P/31U644/2541355/P2P441200-02010**P**   (4023)
2002/03: 16⁰G, 26²HY, 24⁰S, 16¹HY, 18⁶S, 16^PS,

	Starts	1st	2nd	3rd	Win & Pl
Chases	6	1	1	0	4627
Career Total	32	4	4	2	17913
105	1/03	Folk	2m	F(0-100)HCh	HVY	£3374
105	1/02	Folk	2m	F(0-100)HCh	SFT	£3250
105	1/01	Folk	2m	F(0-100)HCh	HVY	£2478
102	1/00	Folk	2m	E Ch	SFT	£2866
				Total win prize-money £11971		

Going:	Sf: 1-5 GS: 0-0 Gd: 0-1 GF: - Fm: 0-0
Distance:	2m/2m3: 1-4 2m4-2m7: 0-0 3m+: 0-2
Track:	LH: 0-1 RH: 1-4 Tight: 1-5 Gall: 0-0
Aids:	Bl: 0-0 Vi: 0-0 Tstrap: 0-0
Best Rating:	105 1/03 Folk 2m heavy Ch

Modest chaser; runs by far his best races at Folkestone and has gained all four of his wins there. Suited by two miles and soft ground.

The Leazes

86f   **61f**

4-y-o b g Shaamit (IRE)-Air Of Elegance (Elegant Air)
A Dickman The Maroon Stud

Placings:PP   (4665)
2002/03: 16PG, 17PGF,

	Starts	1st	2nd	3rd	Win & Pl
NH Flat	2	0	0	0	
Career Total	2	0	0	0	

Going:	Sf: 0-0 GS: 0-0 Gd: 0-1 GF: - Fm: 0-1
Distance:	2m/2m3: 0-2 2m4-2m7: 0-0 3m+: 0-0
Track:	LH: 0-1 RH: 0-1 Tight: 0-0 Gall: 0-0
Aids:	Bl: 0-0 Vi: 0-0 Tstrap: 0-0
Best Rating:	0 4/03 Carl 2m1f gd-fm NHF

The Lyme Volunteer (IRE)

104   **115**

6-y-o b m Zaffaran (USA)-Dooley O Brien (The Parson)
O Sherwood The Chamberlain Addiscott Partnership

Placings:6-053321251   (4673)
2002/03: 18GG, 18FGF, 19JF, 25JGF, 24SGS, 24IG, 24SS, 24SS, 26IGF,

	Starts	1st	2nd	3rd	Win & Pl
NH Flat	1	0	0	0	
Hurdles	8	2	2	2	13873
Career Total	9	2	2	2	13873
106	4/03	Hrfd	3m2f	E Hdl		G-F	£3438
113	11/02	Ludl	3m	E(0-105)HHdl		GD	£4550
				Total win prize-money £7989

Going:	Sf: 0-2 GS: 0-1 Gd: 1-1 GF: - Fm: 1-5
Distance:	2m/2m3: 0-3 2m4-2m7: 0-0 3m+: 2-6
Track:	LH: 0-3 RH: 2-6 Tight: 0-3 Gall: 0-1
Aids:	Bl: 0-0 Vi: 0-0 Tstrap: 0-0
Best Rating:	115 12/02 Asct 3m soft Hdl

Fair novice hurdler; stays 3m 2f; acts on fast and soft ground.

The Major (NZ)

88   **121**

10-y-o ch g Try To Stop Me-Equation (NZ) (Palatable (USA))
J R Cornwall J R Cornwall

Placings:232U1/444P11113-P35F   (2115)
2002/03: 21PG, 20JG, 20GGS, 27FGS,

	Starts	1st	2nd	3rd	Win & Pl
Chases	4	0	0	1	2376
Career Total	18	5	2	3	33321
133	12/01	Newc	2m4f	D(0-125)HCh		G-S	£4085
125	11/01	Ayr	2m4f	D(0-120)HCh		G-S	£4111
118	10/01	Bang	3m110y	D(0-120)HCh		GD	£6825
118	10/01	Uttx	2m5f	D(0-120)HCh		G-S	£4875
120	2/01	Uttx	2m	D(0-120)HCh		HVY	£5070
				Total win prize-money £24966

Going:	Sf: 0-0 GS: 0-2 Gd: 0-2 GF: - Fm: 0-0
Distance:	2m/2m3: 0-0 2m4-2m7: 0-3 3m+: 0-1
Track:	LH: 0-3 RH: 0-1 Tight: 0-2 Gall: 0-2
Aids:	Bl: 0-0 Vi: 0-0 Tstrap: 0-0
Best Rating:	133 12/01 Newc 2m4f gd-sft Ch

Fair chaser, won four in a row in 2001 before the run came to an end on heavy ground. Has changed stables and out of form since.

The Manse Brae (IRE)

104(103h)   (113h)**120+**

7-y-o b g Roselier (FR)-Decent Preacher (Decent Fellow)
J M Jefferson Ashleybank Investments Limited

Placings:04411-15611   (3813)
2002/03: 20IG, 24SGS, 21SG, 24IG, 25IG,

	Starts	1st	2nd	3rd	Win & Pl
Hurdles	1	0	0	0	0
Chases	4	3	0	0	15027
Career Total	10	5	0	0	22070
120	2/03	Catt	3m1f110y	E Ch		GD	£4069
120	1/03	Muss	3m	E Ch		GD	£4696
97	9/02	Bang	2m4f110y	D Ch		GD	£5512
107	4/02	Hexm	2m4f110y	E Hdl		GD	£3276
110	3/02	Carl	2m4f	E(0-105)HHdl		G-S	£3486
				Total win prize-money £21039

Going:	Sf: 0-0 GS: 0-1 Gd: 3-4 GF: - Fm: 0-0
Distance:	2m/2m3: 0-0 2m4-2m7: 1-2 3m+: 2-3
Track:	LH: 2-4 RH: 1-1 Tight: 3-4 Gall: 0-1
Aids:	Bl: 0-0 Vi: 0-0 Tstrap: 0-0
Best Rating:	120 2/03 Catt 3m1f110y good Ch

Fair novice chaser; stays three miles; seems to appreciate good ground; defied a double penalty at Catterick in February.

The Masareti Kid (IRE)

98   **79**

6-y-o b g Commanche Run-Little Crack (IRE) (Lancastrian)
G A Swinbank Ward And Gartzen

Placings:501-15   (1417)
2002/03: 16IGF, 22SGF,

	Starts	1st	2nd	3rd	Win & Pl
NH Flat	1	1	0	0	1827
Hurdles	1	0	0	0	0
Career Total	5	2	0	0	4270
93	9/02	Hexm	2m110y	N HNF		G-F	£1827
104	4/02	Hexm	2m110y	N HNF		G-F	£2443
				Total win prize-money £4270

Going:	Sf: 0-0 GS: 0-0 Gd: 0-0 GF: - Fm: 1-2
Distance:	2m/2m3: 1-1 2m4-2m7: 0-1 3m+: 0-0
Track:	LH: 1-2 RH: 0-0 Tight: 0-1 Gall: 0-0
Aids:	Bl: 0-0 Vi: 0-0 Tstrap: 0-0
Best Rating:	104 4/02 Hexm 2m110y gd-fm NHF

Moderate performer; won two Hexham bumpers for Alan Swinbank in 2002; well held in third place in 2m 6f maiden hurdle at Newton Abbot June 2003 on first run for new stable; acts on good to firm.

The Merriemeade

7-y-o b m Mahrajan-Salmon Spirit (Big Deal)
C J Down Exe Valley Racing

Placings:F   (3138)
2002/03: 21FS,

	Starts	1st	2nd	3rd	Win & Pl
Hurdles	1	0	0	0	
Career Total	1	0	0	0	

Going:	Sf: 0-1 GS: 0-0 Gd: 0-0 GF: - Fm: 0-0
Distance:	2m/2m3: 0-0 2m4-2m7: 0-1 3m+: 0-0
Track:	LH: 0-0 RH: 0-1 Tight: 0-0 Gall: 0-0
Aids:	Bl: 0-0 Vi: 0-0 Tstrap: 0-0

Best Rating: 0   1/03   Ludl   2m5f   soft   Hdl

The Merry Mason (IRE)

100(93h)   (80h)**88**

7-y-o b g Roselier (FR)-Busters Lodge (Antwerp City)
J M Jefferson Ashleybank Investments Limited

Placings:06P-11   (1542)
2002/03: 24IGF, 25IGF,

	Starts	1st	2nd	3rd	Win & Pl
Hurdles	2	2	0	0	5800
Career Total	5	2	0	0	5800
80	10/02	Weth	3m1f	F(0-90)HHdl		G-F	£2341
75	10/02	MRas	3m	F(0-100)HHdl		G-F	£3458
				Total win prize-money £5800

Going:	Sf: 0-0 GS: 0-0 Gd: 0-0 GF: - Fm: 2-2
Distance:	2m/2m3: 0-0 2m4-2m7: 0-0 3m+: 2-2
Track:	LH: 1-1 RH: 1-1 Tight: 1-1 Gall: 0-0
Aids:	Bl: 0-0 Vi: 0-0 Tstrap: 0-0
Best Rating:	80 10/02 Weth 3m1f gd-fm Hdl

Moderate staying hurdler; pulled up on chasing bow; runner-up at Hexham in June next time; stays well; acts on fast ground; not totally reliable.

The Mighty Flynn

56f

4-y-o ch g Botanic (USA)-Owdbetts (IRE) (High Estate)
P Monteith J W D Campbell

Placings:0   (4778)
2002/03: 16QG,

	Starts	1st	2nd	3rd	Win & Pl
NH Flat	1	0	0	0	
Career Total	1	0	0	0	

Going:	Sf: 0-0 GS: 0-0 Gd: 0-1 GF: - Fm: 0-0
Distance:	2m/2m3: 0-1 2m4-2m7: 0-0 3m+: 0-0
Track:	LH: 0-0 RH: 0-1 Tight: 0-0 Gall: 0-0
Aids:	Bl: 0-0 Vi: 0-0 Tstrap: 0-0
Best Rating:	0 4/03 Prth 2m110y good NHF

The Miner

95f   **91f**

5-y-o ch g Hatim (USA)-Glen Morvern (Carlingford Castle)
Miss S E Forster The Wellconnected Partnership

Placings:35   (4665)
2002/03: 16JGF, 17SGF,

	Starts	1st	2nd	3rd	Win & Pl
NH Flat	2	0	0	1	429
Career Total	2	0	0	1	429

Going:	Sf: 0-0 GS: 0-0 Gd: 0-0 GF: - Fm: 0-2
Distance:	2m/2m3: 0-2 2m4-2m7: 0-0 3m+: 0-0
Track:	LH: 0-0 RH: 0-2 Tight: 0-0 Gall: 0-0
Aids:	Bl: 0-0 Vi: 0-0 Tstrap: 0-0
Best Rating:	91 9/02 Prth 2m110y gd-fm NHF

Moderate form in bumpers on a sound surface.

The Minister (IRE)

99   **63**

14-y-o br g Black Minstrel-Miss Hi-Land (Tyrant (USA))
Miss T Jackson H L Thompson

Placings:00/PPP/1U1/P6/P4/PPU/6 (0401)
2002/03: 25⁵GF,

	Starts	1st	2nd	3rd	Win & Pl
Chases	1	0	0		0
Career Total	16	2	0		5695
84 11/95 Catt	2m		F(0-100)HCh	G-F	£2444
87 10/95 Hntg	2m4f110yG(0-95)HCh			FRM	£2940

Total win prize-money £5386

Going:	Sf: 0-0 GS: 0-0 Gd: 0-0 GF: - Fm: 0-1
Distance:	2m/2m3: 0-0 2m4-2m7: 0-0 3m+: 0-1
Track:	LH: 0-1 RH: 0-0 Tight: 0-0 Gall: 0-0
Aids:	Bl: 0-0 Vi: 0-0 Tstrap: 0-0
Best Rating:	94 4/99 Sedg 3m3f firm Ch

The Mog

96   76

4-y-o b g Atraf-Safe Secret (Seclude (USA))
S R Bowring   S R Bowring

Placings:02P (4412)
2002/03: 17⁵S, 20²GF, 17⁶G,

	Starts	1st	2nd	3rd	Win & Pl
Hurdles	3	0	1	0	1038
Career Total	3	0	1	0	1038

Going:	Sf: 0-1 GS: 0-0 Gd: 0-1 GF: - Fm: 0-1
Distance:	2m/2m3: 0-2 2m4-2m7: 0-1 3m+: 0-0
Track:	LH: 0-2 RH: 0-1 Tight: 0-3 Gall: 0-0
Aids:	Bl: 0-0 Vi: 0-0 Tstrap: 0-3
Best Rating:	67 3/03 Sthl 2m4f110y gd-fm Hdl

Plating-class hurdler; poor performer on the Flat; acts on decent ground.

The Moyne Machine (IRE)

105   111

7-y-o b m Elbio-Victoria Hall (Hallgate)
T Doyle (Timothy Doyle 6/3) Patrick J Cantwell

Placings:0P1410/00P0344/5F-06335214 (4170)
2002/03: 16⁰S, 16⁶YS, 20³HY, 16³S, 20⁵S, 16²SH, 18¹SH, 21⁴S,

	Starts	1st	2nd	3rd	Win & Pl
Chases	8	1	1	2	10055
Career Total	23	4	3	3	19319
103 3/03 Thur	2m2f		Ch	SH	£5824
91 2/00 Thur	2m		Hdl	HVY	£3312
92 1/00 Thur	2m		Hdl	SH	£4140

Total win prize-money £13277

Going:	Sf: 0-5 GS: 0-0 Gd: 0-0 GF: - Fm: 0-0
Distance:	2m/2m3: 1-5 2m4-2m7: 0-3 3m+: 0-0
Track:	LH: 0-1 RH: 1-2 Tight: 0-0 Gall: 0-0
Aids:	Bl: 0-0 Vi: 0-0 Tstrap: 0-0
Best Rating:	103 3/03 Thur 2m2f sft-hvy Ch

Modest chaser; stays 2m 2f; effective in soft/heavy ground.

The Names Bond

102   99

5-y-o b g Tragic Role (USA)-Artistic Licence (High Top)
Andrew Turnell   Mrs Claire Hollowood

Placings:25322-6342F (3595)
2002/03: 16⁶G, 17³S, 16⁴G, 16²GF, 0⁷HY,

	Starts	1st	2nd	3rd	Win & Pl
Hurdles	5	0	1	1	1642
Career Total	10	0	4	2	4369

Going:	Sf: 0-2 GS: 0-1 Gd: 0-2 GF: - Fm: 0-0
Distance:	2m/2m3: 0-4 2m4-2m7: 0-1 3m+: 0-0
Track:	LH: 0-4 RH: 0-0 Tight: 0-1 Gall: 0-2
Aids:	Bl: 0-0 Vi: 0-0 Tstrap: 0-0
Best Rating:	99 1/03 Donc 2m110y gd-sft Hdl

Moderate performer, regularly in the frame in hurdle races but has yet to get his head in front.

The Negotiator

112(86h)   (98h)109

9-y-o ch g Nebos (GER)-Baie Des Anges (Pas De Seul)
M A Barnes   T A Barnes

Placings:444P/04422/123/4401331330/5213442213236-52124PPF34 (4751)
2002/03: 16⁵GF, 16²GF, 20¹G, 17²GF, 20⁴GF, 20⁵PS, 16⁵S, 20⁵S, 17³G, 20⁴G,

	Starts	1st	2nd	3rd	Win & Pl
Chases	10	1	2	1	10604
Career Total	45	6	9	9	45360
119 5/02 Weth	2m4f110yD Ch			GD	£3932
110 11/01 Ayr	2m	C(0-130)HCh		GD	£6045
100 6/01 Prth	2m	D Ch		FRM	£4186
102 10/00 Kels	2m110y E(0-115)HHdl			G-S	£2737
103 8/00 Prth	2m110y G Hdl			GD	£2717
100 5/99 Bang	2m4f	D(0-110)HHdl		GD	£3243

Total win prize-money £22861

Going:	Sf: 0-2 GS: 0-1 Gd: 1-3 GF: - Fm: 0-4
Distance:	2m/2m3: 0-5 2m4-2m7: 1-5 3m+: 0-0
Track:	LH: 1-6 RH: 0-4 Tight: 0-4 Gall: 0-1
Aids:	Bl: 0-0 Vi: 0-0 Tstrap: 0-0
Best Rating:	119 6/02 Strf 2m1f110y gd-fm Ch

Fair chaser; effective up to two and a half miles; handles most types of ground.

The Nelson Touch

(93h)   (73h)

6-y-o b g Past Glories-Kellys Special (Netherkelly)
J W Mullins   F G Matthews

Placings:04P6-P0P (2726)
2002/03: 21⁵PS, 20⁵S, 20⁵PHY,

	Starts	1st	2nd	3rd	Win & Pl
Hurdles	3	0	0	0	0
Career Total	7	0	0	0	0

Going:	Sf: 0-3 GS: 0-0 Gd: 0-0 GF: - Fm: 0-0
Distance:	2m/2m3: 0-0 2m4-2m7: 0-3 3m+: 0-0
Track:	LH: 0-2 RH: 0-1 Tight: 0-1 Gall: 0-0
Aids:	Bl: 0-0 Vi: 0-0 Tstrap: 0-0
Best Rating:	86 4/02 Chep 2m4f gd-fm Hdl

The Newsman (IRE)

106(96h)   (101h)115

11-y-o b g Homo Sapien-Miller Fall S (Stubbs Gazette)
G Wareham (Miss S Edwards 3/6) G Wareham

Placings:041/405006/201/4343-23161131 (4756)
2002/03: 21²G, 20³GF, 17¹GF, 17⁵GS, 20¹G, 18¹S, 19³G, 18¹GF,

	Starts	1st	2nd	3rd	Win & Pl
Chases	8	4	1	2	19824
Career Total	24	6	2	4	32915
115 4/03 Font	2m2f	E(0-110)HCh	G-F	£4036
108 3/03 Font	2m2f	E(0-105)HCh	S:FT	£4114
106 12/02 Font	2m2f	E(0-100)HCh	GD	£4114
87 10/02 Plum	2m1f	E(0-100)HCh	G-F	£4004
4/00 Fntb	2m4f	Hdl	SFT	£3074
107 3/98 Font	2m2f110yE Hdl		G-F	£2659

Going:	Sf: 1-1 GS: 0-1 Gd: 1-3 GF: - Fm: 2-3
Distance:	2m/2m3: 3-4 2m4-2m7: 1-4 3m+: 0-0
Track:	LH: 1-3 RH: 0-2 Tight: 4-6 Gall: 0-1
Aids:	Bl: 0-2 Vi: 0-0 Tstrap: 0-0
Best Rating:	115 4/03 Font 2m2f gd-fm Ch

Fair chaser; consistent, but is not the most fluent jumper; likes Fontwell; stays two miles-five, acts on fast ground, has worn blinkers.

The Noble Moor (IRE)

76   57

7-y-o br g Euphemism-Who Says (IRE) (Amazing Bust)
T R George   Mrs Sharon C Nelson

Placings:00-0P (2945)
2002/03: 16⁹G, 21⁵PS,

	Starts	1st	2nd	3rd	Win & Pl
Hurdles	2	0	0	0	
Career Total	4	0	0	0	

Going:	Sf: 0-1 GS: 0-0 Gd: 0-1 GF: - Fm: 0-0
Distance:	2m/2m3: 0-1 2m4-2m7: 0-1 3m+: 0-0
Track:	LH: 0-1 RH: 0-1 Tight: 0-0 Gall: 0-0
Aids:	Bl: 0-0 Vi: 0-0 Tstrap: 0-0
Best Rating:	86 11/01 Sand 2m110y gd-sft NHF

The Nomad

103   110

7-y-o b g Nomadic Way (USA)-Bubbling (Tremblant)
M W Easterby   S H J Brewer

Placings:35/2O55622-2111P1 (4435)
2002/03: 20²G, 17¹G, 17¹GS, 20¹HY, 23⁸GS, 20¹G,

	Starts	1st	2nd	3rd	Win & Pl
Hurdles	6	4	1	0	16091
Career Total	15	4	4	1	18308
108 4/03 Newc	2m4f	E Hdl	GD	£3425
110 12/02 Weth	2m4f110yD(0-110)HHdl		HVY	£4306
108 11/02 MRas	2m1f110yE Hdl		G-S	£3486
98 10/02 Sedg	2m1f	D Hdl	GD	£4186

Total win prize-money £15404

Going:	Sf: 1-1 GS: 1-2 Gd: 2-3 GF: - Fm: 0-0
Distance:	2m/2m3: 2-2 2m4-2m7: 1-4 3m+: 0-0
Track:	LH: 3-5 RH: 1-1 Tight: 2-2 Gall: 1-1
Aids:	Bl: 0-0 Vi: 0-0 Tstrap: 0-0
Best Rating:	110 12/02 Weth 2m4f110y heavy Hdl

Modest novice hurdler; effective from two to two and a half miles and acts on ground good or softer; front runner; goes well for Gino Carenza.

The Norwich Fly (IRE)

106f   107f

6-y-o b m Norwich-The Race Fly (Pollerton)
Miss E C Lavelle (P M J Doyle 8/11) J R Lavelle

Placings:142 (4329)
2002/03: 16¹YS, 16⁴HY, 16²G,

	Starts	1st	2nd	3rd	Win & Pl
NH Flat	3	1	1	0	4645
Career Total	3	1	1	0	4645
107 10/02 Thur	2m		NHF	Y-S	£3386

Total win prize-money £3387

Going: Sf: 0-1 GS: 0-0 Gd: 0-1 GF: - Fm: 0-0
Distance: 2m/2m3: 1-3 2m4-2m7: 0-0 3m+: 0-0
Track: LH: 0-1 RH: 0-0 Tight: 0-0 Gall: 0-1
Aids: Bl: 0-0 Vi: 0-0 Tstrap: 0-0
Best Rating: 107 10/02 Thur 2m   yld-sft NHF

Modest performer; winner of a bumper in Ireland; ran well when runner-up in Newbury bumper on English debut; acts on decent ground.

The October Man

88   77

6-y-o ch g Afzal-Florence May (Grange Melody)
Jonjo O Neill P Byrne

Placings:000   (2055)
2002/03: 16⁰G, 16⁹G, 16⁶G,

	Starts	1st	2nd	3rd	Win & Pl
Hurdles	3	0	0	0	
Career Total	3	0	0	0	

Going: Sf: 0-1 GS: 0-0 Gd: 0-2 GF: - Fm: 0-0
Distance: 2m/2m3: 0-3 2m4-2m7: 0-0 3m+: 0-0
Track: LH: 0-2 RH: 0-1 Tight: 0-0 Gall: 0-0
Aids: Bl: 0-0 Vi: 0-0 Tstrap: 0-0
Best Rating: 71 11/02 Kemp 2m   good Hdl

The Only Option (IRE)

66

8-y-o b m Phardante (FR)-Sirrah Madam (Tug Of War)
R Tate R Tate

Placings:5P-5P   (0335)
2002/03: 24⁴GS, 23⁸G,

	Starts	1st	2nd	3rd	Win & Pl
Hurdles	2	0	0	0	0
Career Total	4	0	0	0	0

Going: Sf: 0-0 GS: 0-1 Gd: 0-1 GF: - Fm: 0-0
Distance: 2m/2m3: 0-0 2m4-2m7: 0-1 3m+: 0-1
Track: LH: 0-2 RH: 0-0 Tight: 0-0 Gall: 0-0
Aids: Bl: 0-0 Vi: 0-0 Tstrap: 0-0
Best Rating: 66 5/01 Sedg 2m5f110y good Hdl

The Other Man (IRE)

78   31

13-y-o b g Remainder Man-Amelioras Gran (Northern Guest (USA))
Miss L C Siddall Miss L C Siddall

Placings:0/00/000053/F5/4U304/33U53P03PU606/00/P06
                                                       (0339)
2002/03: 25ᴾGS, 25⁰S, 25⁶G,

	Starts	1st	2nd	3rd	Win & Pl
Chases	3	0	0	0	0
Career Total	34	0	0	6	3111

Going: Sf: 0-1 GS: 0-1 Gd: 0-1 GF: - Fm: 0-0
Distance: 2m/2m3: 0-0 2m4-2m7: 0-0 3m+: 0-3
Track: LH: 0-1 RH: 0-2 Tight: 0-0 Gall: 0-0
Aids: Bl: 0-0 Vi: 0-0 Tstrap: 0-0
Best Rating: 74 12/98 MRas 3m1f   heavy Ch

The Parsons Dingle

103(94h)   (90h)106

8-y-o ch g Le Moss-Not Enough (Balinger)
P R Webber Tavern Racing

Placings:41/66/2-0414P   (4327)
2002/03: 16⁰G, 16⁴G, 17¹S, 17⁴S, 18⁰G,

	Starts	1st	2nd	3rd	Win & Pl
Chases	5	1	0	0	5867
Career Total	10	2	1	0	8587
106 2/03 Bang	2m1f110yE(0-105)HCh			SFT	£5135
110 3/00 Bang	2m1f	H NHF		GD	£1904
Total win prize-money £7039					

Going: Sf: 1-2 GS: 0-0 Gd: 0-3 GF: - Fm: 0-0
Distance: 2m/2m3: 1-5 2m4-2m7: 0-0 3m+: 0-0
Track: LH: 1-4 RH: 0-1 Tight: 1-3 Gall: 0-2
Aids: Bl: 0-0 Vi: 0-0 Tstrap: 0-0
Best Rating: 110 3/00 Bang 2m1f   good NHF

Modest bumper winner, returned to form when taking a novices handicap chase at Bangor in February in very soft ground.

The Pennys Dropped (IRE)

109   107

6-y-o ch g Bob s Return (IRE)-Shuil Alainn (Levanter)
Jonjo O Neill J P McManus

Placings:0-020F2   (3911)
2002/03: 16⁰G, 18²S, 19⁰GS, 17⁵GS, 17²GS,

	Starts	1st	2nd	3rd	Win & Pl
NH Flat	2	0	1	0	687
Hurdles	3	0	1	0	1120
Career Total	6	0	2	0	1807

Going: Sf: 0-1 GS: 0-3 Gd: 0-1 GF: - Fm: 0-0
Distance: 2m/2m3: 0-4 2m4-2m7: 0-1 3m+: 0-0
Track: LH: 0-4 RH: 0-1 Tight: 0-1 Gall: 0-0
Aids: Bl: 0-0 Vi: 0-0 Tstrap: 0-0
Best Rating: 107 3/03 Carl 2m1f   gd-sft Hdl

Modest hurdler; looked in total charge when crashing out three from home in weak novices hurdle at Bangor in February; runner-up to a useful sort at Carlisle the following month.

The Phair Crier (IRE)

96   114

8-y-o ch g Phardante (FR)-Maul-More (Deep Run)
L Lungo Ashleybank Investments Limited

Placings:13/F14P-0P   (4164)
2002/03: 20⁰GS, 24ᴾGS,

	Starts	1st	2nd	3rd	Win & Pl
Hurdles	2	0	0	0	
Career Total	8	2	0	1	8920
133 1/02 Newc	3m	B Hdl		SFT	£6938
104 1/01 Ayr	2m	H NHF		G-S	£1673
Total win prize-money £8612					

Going: Sf: 0-0 GS: 0-2 Gd: 0-0 GF: - Fm: 0-0
Distance: 2m/2m3: 0-0 2m4-2m7: 0-1 3m+: 0-1
Track: LH: 0-2 RH: 0-0 Tight: 0-0 Gall: 0-1
Aids: Bl: 0-0 Vi: 0-0 Tstrap: 0-0
Best Rating: 133 1/02 Newc 3m   soft Hdl

Useful hurdler and bumper winner; well beaten on handicap debut after lengthy absence; stays three miles and acts on soft ground; has suffered breathing problems.

The Preacher Man (IRE)

8-y-o b g Be My Native (USA)-Frankford Run (Deep Run)
V Thompson V Thompson

Placings:0200/40-U   (3895)
2002/03: 25ᵁGS,

	Starts	1st	2nd	3rd	Win & Pl
Chases	1	0	0	0	
Career Total	7	0	1	0	962

Going: Sf: 0-0 GS: 0-1 Gd: 0-0 GF: - Fm: 0-0
Distance: 2m/2m3: 0-0 2m4-2m7: 0-0 3m+: 0-1
Track: LH: 0-1 RH: 0-0 Tight: 0-1 Gall: 0-0
Aids: Bl: 0-1 Vi: 0-0 Tstrap: 0-0
Best Rating: 100 8/00 Naas 2m3f   firm NHF

The Project

7-y-o b g Prince Of Darkness (IRE)-Kerry Calluna (Celtic Cone)
J C Fox Shirley M & Peter G Palmer

Placings:0-00PP   (3476)
2002/03: 16⁰G, 17⁰GS, 16ᴾG, 22ᴾGS,

	Starts	1st	2nd	3rd	Win & Pl
NH Flat	1	0	0	0	0
Hurdles	3	0	0	0	0
Career Total	5	0	0	0	0

Going: Sf: 0-0 GS: 0-2 Gd: 0-2 GF: - Fm: 0-0
Distance: 2m/2m3: 0-3 2m4-2m7: 0-1 3m+: 0-0
Track: LH: 0-2 RH: 0-2 Tight: 0-1 Gall: 0-1
Aids: Bl: 0-0 Vi: 0-0 Tstrap: 0-0
Best Rating: 81 10/02 Chep 2m110y   good NHF

The Proof

90   73

6-y-o b g Rudimentary (USA)-Indubitable (Sharpo)
G B Balding Miss B Swire

Placings:0-50   (0242)
2002/03: 19⁵GF, 17⁰G,

	Starts	1st	2nd	3rd	Win & Pl
Hurdles	2	0	0	0	0
Career Total	3	0	0	0	0

Going: Sf: 0-0 GS: 0-0 Gd: 0-1 GF: - Fm: 0-1
Distance: 2m/2m3: 0-1 2m4-2m7: 0-1 3m+: 0-0
Track: LH: 0-0 RH: 0-2 Tight: 0-0 Gall: 0-0
Aids: Bl: 0-0 Vi: 0-0 Tstrap: 0-0
Best Rating: 73 5/02 Hrfd 2m3f110y gd-fm Hdl

The Quads

108   (113h)125

11-y-o b g Tinoco-Queen s Royale (Tobrouk (FR))
Ferdy Murphy John Duddy

Placings:430064/531131/605302231300/050124264/P00/4
03240106/03104P40P-P21P5U   (4307)
2002/03: 26ᴾS, 31²GS, 31¹GS, 29ᴾHY, 26⁵HY, 32ᵁG,

	Starts	1st	2nd	3rd	Win & Pl
Chases	6	1	1	0	24838
Career Total	60	8	6	8	104111

125	12/02 Chel	3m7f	C(0-135)HCh	G-S	£13940
125	10/01 Carl	3m2f	D(0-120)HCh	SFT	£4290
125	1/01 Navn	2m4f	HHdl	SFT	£13104
120	10/98 Gowr	3m	HHdl	SH	£14076
121	1/98 Leop	2m3f	HCh	Y-S	£7147
108	4/97 Punc	2m2f	HHdl	GD	£8138
105	3/97 Navn	3m	HHdl	SFT	£5425
99	1/97 Leop	2m6f	(0-130)HHdl	G-Y	£3051
				Total win prize-money	£69177

Going:	Sf: 0-3 GS: 1-2 Gd: 0-1 GF: - Fm: 0-0
Distance:	2m/2m3: 0-0 2m4-2m7: 0-0 3m+: 1-6
Track:	LH: 1-4 RH: 0-1 Tight: 0-0 Gall: 0-0
Aids:	Bl: 1-4 Vi: 0-0 Tstrap: 1-6
Best Rating:	128 1/99 Gowr 3m soft Ch

Fair chaser; stays 3m 7f; has proved well suited to the cross-country races run at Cheltenham this season, winning one and finishing second in the other; regularly tongue tied; wears blinkers.

The Rebel Lady (IRE)
97   86
6-y-o br m Mister Lord (USA)-Arborfield Brook (Over The River (FR))
Miss H C Knight   The Rebel Partnership

Placings:60303   (4536)
2002/03: 18⁶S, 21⁰S, 22³GS, 21⁰G, 24³G,

	Starts	1st	2nd	3rd	Win & Pl
Hurdles	5	0	0	2	1406
Career Total	5	0	0	2	1406

Going:	Sf: 0-2 GS: 0-1 Gd: 0-2 GF: - Fm: 0-0
Distance:	2m/2m3: 0-1 2m4-2m7: 0-3 3m+: 0-1
Track:	LH: 0-2 RH: 0-3 Tight: 0-0 Gall: 0-1
Aids:	Bl: 0-0 Vi: 0-0 Tstrap: 0-0
Best Rating:	91 2/03 Winc 2m6f gd-sft Hdl

Irish point-to-point winner; has shown ability over hurdles.

The Relic (NZ)

8-y-o b g Rua Rukuna (NZ)-Fine Sky (NZ) (Mussorgsky)
Miss H C Knight   Ian David Limited

Placings:P   (1798)
2002/03: 17⁵S,

	Starts	1st	2nd	3rd	Win & Pl
Hurdles	1	0	0	0	
Career Total	1	0	0	0	

Going:	Sf: 0-1 GS: 0-0 Gd: 0-0 GF: 0-0 Fm: 0-0
Distance:	2m/2m3: 0-1 2m4-2m7: 0-0 3m+: 0-0
Track:	LH: 0-1 RH: 0-0 Tight: 0-1 Gall: 0-0
Aids:	Bl: 0-0 Vi: 0-0 Tstrap: 0-0
Best Rating:	0 11/02 NAbb 2m1f soft Hdl

The Renderer

7-y-o b g Homo Sapien-Kingsley (King s Lake (USA))
Miss S J Wilton   John Pointon And Sons

Placings:0   (0823)
2002/03: 16⁰GF,

	Starts	1st	2nd	3rd	Win & Pl
NH Flat	1	0	0	0	
Career Total	1	0	0	0	

The Right Cue (IRE)
80   66
9-y-o b g Torus-Bo Reynella (IRE) (Le Bavard (FR))
P R Rodford   Mrs Christine Priest

Placings:P/0/5/P05-0P   (0444)
2002/03: 20⁰GF, 19⁰G,

	Starts	1st	2nd	3rd	Win & Pl
Hurdles	2	0	0	0	
Career Total	8	0	0	0	0

Going:	Sf: 0-0 GS: 0-0 Gd: 0-0 GF: - Fm: 0-1
Distance:	2m/2m3: 0-0 2m4-2m7: 0-2 3m+: 0-0
Track:	LH: 0-1 RH: 0-1 Tight: 0-0 Gall: 0-0
Aids:	Bl: 0-2 Vi: 0-0 Tstrap: 0-0
Best Rating:	66 4/02 Extr 2m1f firm Hdl

The Rile (IRE)
105(108h)   (122+h)121+
9-y-o ch g Alphabatim (USA)-Donna Chimene (Royal Gunner (USA))
L Lungo   Mr & Mrs Raymond Anderson Green

Placings:0212/64010/0000100-551121   (4015)
2002/03: 20⁵GS, 18⁵S, 20¹GS, 21¹S, 20²S, 20¹S,

	Starts	1st	2nd	3rd	Win & Pl
Hurdles	3	1	0	0	2919
Chases	3	2	1	0	11771
Career Total	22	6	3	0	24068
121 3/03 Ayr	2m4f	E Ch	SFT	£4235
122 1/03 Ayr	2m5f110yD Ch		SFT	£5460
122 11/02 Weth	2m4f110yE(0-110)HHdl	G-S	£2919
117 1/02 Carl	2m4f	D(0-125)HHdl	SFT	£3526
112 2/01 Carl	2m4f110yE Hdl		SFT	£1964
111 3/00 Carl	2m1f	H NHF	HVY	£1704
			Total win prize-money	£19809

Going:	Sf: 2-4 GS: 1-2 Gd: 0-0 GF: - Fm: 0-0
Distance:	2m/2m3: 0-1 2m4-2m7: 3-5 3m+: 0-0
Track:	LH: 3-6 RH: 0-0 Tight: 0-1 Gall: 0-0
Aids:	Bl: 0-0 Vi: 0-0 Tstrap: 0-0
Best Rating:	122 1/03 Ayr 2m5f110y soft Ch

Moderate handicap hurdler/fair chaser; effective in soft ground; stays two and a half miles.

The River Joker (IRE)
106   90d
7-y-o ch g Over The River (FR)-Augustaeliza (IRE) (Callernish)
John R Upson   Graeme P McPherson

Placings:000/FB50P-126P0   (3811)
2002/03: 26¹GS, 20²GS, 24⁶S, 24⁴HY, 25⁰G,

	Starts	1st	2nd	3rd	Win & Pl
Hurdles	5	1	1	0	3197
Career Total	13	1	1	0	3197
89 11/02 Hntg	3m2f	F(0-100)HHdl	G-S	£2289
			Total win prize-money	£2289

Going:	Sf: 0-2 GS: 1-2 Gd: 0-1 GF: - Fm: 0-0
Distance:	2m/2m3: 0-0 2m4-2m7: 0-1 3m+: 1-4

Track:	LH: 0-4 RH: 1-1 Tight: 0-1 Gall: 1-1
Aids:	Bl: 0-0 Vi: 0-0 Tstrap: 0-0
Best Rating:	90 12/02 Weth 2m4f110y gd-sft Hdl

Moderate hurdler; finally got off the mark over hurdles when winning at Huntingdon in November.

The Roan Runner
67   25
5-y-o gr g Nalchik (USA)-Grey Runner (Crofthall)
B P J Baugh   J H Chrimes And Mr & Mrs G W Hannam

Placings:0PP   (1488)
2002/03: 16⁰G, 20⁰G, 20⁰GS,

	Starts	1st	2nd	3rd	Win & Pl
Hurdles	3	0	0	0	
Career Total	3	0	0	0	

Going:	Sf: 0-0 GS: 0-1 Gd: 0-1 GF: - Fm: 0-1
Distance:	2m/2m3: 0-2 2m4-2m7: 0-2 3m+: 0-0
Track:	LH: 0-3 RH: 0-0 Tight: 0-1 Gall: 0-0
Aids:	Bl: 0-0 Vi: 0-1 Tstrap: 0-0
Best Rating:	25 8/02 Uttx 2m gd-fm Hdl

The Roundsills
84d
9-y-o ch g Handsome Sailor-Eye Sight (Roscoe Blake)
M Mullineaux   R Williamson

Placings:25/0004/4256142/0/00-PP   (2708)
2002/03: 16⁶S, 16⁶GS,

	Starts	1st	2nd	3rd	Win & Pl
Hurdles	1	0	0	0	0
Chases	1	0	0	0	0
Career Total	18	1	3	0	6022
95 12/99 Hrfd	2m	E(0-105)HCh	GD	£3243
			Total win prize-money	£3243

Going:	Sf: 0-1 GS: 0-1 Gd: 0-0 GF: - Fm: 0-0
Distance:	2m/2m3: 0-2 2m4-2m7: 0-0 3m+: 0-0
Track:	LH: 0-1 RH: 0-1 Tight: 0-0 Gall: 0-0
Aids:	Bl: 0-0 Vi: 0-0 Tstrap: 0-0
Best Rating:	95 2/00 Ludl 2m good Ch

The Sawdust Kid
109(96h)   (64h)99
9-y-o ch g River God (USA)-Susie s Money (Seymour Hicks (FR))
R H Buckler   Golden Cap

Placings:3/1323P/1654P0-5P2511125P4P6   (4761)
2002/03: 25⁵GF, 26⁶G, 21²G, 23⁵G, 26¹G, 26¹G, 26¹GF, 22²G, 24⁵GF, 24⁵HY, 20⁴G, 26⁶S, 26⁶GF,

	Starts	1st	2nd	3rd	Win & Pl
Chases	13	3	2	0	15947
Career Total	25	5	3	3	22203
102 9/02 Font	3m2f110yE(0-105)HCh	G-F	£4389
100 9/02 Sthl	3m2f	E(0-110)HCh	G-F	£4326
98 8/02 Font	3m2f110yE(0-105)HCh	GD	£4600
104 10/01 Wmc	2m6f	E Hdl	G-F	£2474
98 8/00 Worc	2m	H NHF	G-F	£1473
			Total win prize-money	£17264

Going:	Sf: 0-2 GS: 0-0 Gd: 2-7 GF: - Fm: 1-4
Distance:	2m/2m3: 0-0 2m4-2m7: 0-3 3m+: 3-10
Track:	LH: 1-5 RH: 0-1 Tight: 2-7 Gall: 0-1
Aids:	Bl: 0-1 Vi: 0-0 Tstrap: 0-0
Best Rating:	111 10/00 Chel 3m1f110y good Hdl

Modest, strong-galloping chaser; completed a hat-trick in

dire races in the autumn of 2002; good effort when runner up at Exeter May 2003; stays 3m 2f; acts on fast ground.

The Secretary (IRE)

98   **65**

6-y-o b m Shernazar-Exemplary Fashion (Master Owen)
Mrs H Dalton James Kerr

Placings:0-33P60P   (4709)
2002/03: 16³G, 20³S, 21PS, 16⁶GS, 24⁰S, 24PG,

	Starts	1st	2nd	3rd	Win & Pl
NH Flat	1	0	0	1	257
Hurdles	5	0	0	1	656
Career Total	7	0	0	2	913

Going:	Sf: 0-3 GS: 0-1 Gd: 0-2 GF: - Fm: 0-0
Distance:	2m/2m3: 0-2 2m4-2m7: 0-2 3m+: 0-2
Track:	LH: 0-5 RH: 0-1 Tight: 0-4 Gall: 0-0
Aids:	Bl: 0-0 Vi: 0-0 Tstrap: 0-0
Best Rating:	86 7/02 Worc 2m good NHF

Plating-class hurdler; best form to date when third to a class horse in a novice hurdle at Bangor.

The Sister

88   **84**

6-y-o b m Alflora (IRE)-Donna Farina (Little Buskins)
Jonjo O Neill Mrs R H Thompson

Placings:54   (3996)
2002/03: 20⁵GS, 20⁴G,

	Starts	1st	2nd	3rd	Win & Pl
Hurdles	2	0	0	0	267
Career Total	2	0	0	0	267

Going:	Sf: 0-0 GS: 0-1 Gd: 0-1 GF: - Fm: 0-0
Distance:	2m/2m3: 0-0 2m4-2m7: 0-2 3m+: 0-0
Track:	LH: 0-1 RH: 0-1 Tight: 0-0 Gall: 0-1
Aids:	Bl: 0-0 Vi: 0-0 Tstrap: 0-0
Best Rating:	84 12/02 Hntg 2m4f110y gd-sft Hdl

Plating-class hurdler; showed promise at Huntingdon in December but bitterly disappointing in mares only event at Wetherby in March.

The Sky Is Blue

94   **43**

7-y-o ch g Alflora (IRE)-Mistress Boreen (Boreen (FR))
Mrs P Townsley Paul Townsley

Placings:30P/FPP-4PP   (4569)
2002/03: 16⁴S, 21PHY, 24PS,

	Starts	1st	2nd	3rd	Win & Pl
Chases	3	0	0	0	264
Career Total	9	0	0	1	483

Going:	Sf: 0-2 GS: 0-0 Gd: 0-1 GF: - Fm: 0-0
Distance:	2m/2m3: 0-1 2m4-2m7: 0-1 3m+: 0-1
Track:	LH: 0-1 RH: 0-2 Tight: 0-3 Gall: 0-0
Aids:	Bl: 0-0 Vi: 0-0 Tstrap: 0-1
Best Rating:	92 10/00 Tntn 2m1f good NHF

The Sleeper

86(95h)   (78h)**63**

7-y-o b g Perpendicular-Distant Cherry (General Ironside)
H P Hogarth Hogarth Racing

Placings:00-0000   (3965)
2002/03: 17⁰G, 16⁰GS, 21⁰HY, 16⁰S,

	Starts	1st	2nd	3rd	Win & Pl
NH Flat	1	0	0	0	0
Hurdles	3	0	0	0	0
Career Total	6	0	0	0	

Going:	Sf: 0-2 GS: 0-1 Gd: 0-1 GF: - Fm: 0-0
Distance:	2m/2m3: 0-3 2m4-2m7: 0-0 3m+: 0-0
Track:	LH: 0-4 RH: 0-1 Tight: 0-3 Gall: 0-1
Aids:	Bl: 0-0 Vi: 0-0 Tstrap: 0-0
Best Rating:	78 3/03 Catt 2m soft Hdl

The Stafford Mare (IRE)

70f   **34f**

6-y-o b m Leading Counsel (USA)-Royal Desire (Royal Match)
J G M O Shea N G H Ayliffe

Placings:000   (4275)
2002/03: 16⁰S, 17⁰S, 16⁰G,

	Starts	1st	2nd	3rd	Win & Pl
NH Flat	3	0	0	0	
Career Total	3	0	0	0	

Going:	Sf: 0-2 GS: 0-0 Gd: 0-1 GF: - Fm: 0-0
Distance:	2m/2m3: 0-3 2m4-2m7: 0-0 3m+: 0-0
Track:	LH: 0-1 RH: 0-1 Tight: 0-0 Gall: 0-0
Aids:	Bl: 0-0 Vi: 0-0 Tstrap: 0-0
Best Rating:	34 1/03 Ludl 2m soft NHF

The Staggery Boy (IRE)

105(105h)   **100**

7-y-o b g Shalford (IRE)-Murroe Star (Glenstal (USA))
M R Hoad Foray Racing

Placings:00/000/61056P443-425P44   (4430)
2002/03: 17⁴G, 16²GF, 16⁵G, 19PS, 16⁴G, 20⁴GF,

	Starts	1st	2nd	3rd	Win & Pl
Chases	6	0	1	0	2309
Career Total	20	1	1	1	8246
91	6/01	Navn	2m	(0-102)HHdl	GD £5564
				Total win prize-money	£5565

Going:	Sf: 0-1 GS: 0-0 Gd: 0-3 GF: - Fm: 0-2
Distance:	2m/2m3: 0-4 2m4-2m7: 0-2 3m+: 0-0
Track:	LH: 0-2 RH: 0-4 Tight: 0-5 Gall: 0-0
Aids:	Bl: 0-0 Vi: 0-0 Tstrap: 0-1
Best Rating:	104 11/01 Sedg 2m1f good Hdl

Moderate hurdler/modest novice chaser; won a couple of 2m handicap chases at Newton Abbot in the space of four days in June 2003; acts on good ground unsuited by soft; has worn tongue tie.

The Tall Guy (IRE)

(100h)   (89h)

7-y-o b/br g Zaffaran (USA)-Mullangale (Strong Gale)
N A Twiston-Davies Mrs Jill Scott & Mrs Sarah Macechern

Placings:1//40P-5PF   (3785)
2002/03: 25⁵GF, 19PS, 25PFG,

	Starts	1st	2nd	3rd	Win & Pl
Hurdles	1	0	0	0	307
Chases	2	0	0	0	
Career Total	7	1	0	0	3614

100 4/01 Ayr   2m   H NHF   G-F £3307
      Total win prize-money £3308

Going:	Sf: 0-1 GS: 0-0 Gd: 0-1 GF: - Fm: 0-1
Distance:	2m/2m3: 0-2 2m4-2m7: 0-0 3m+: 0-2
Track:	LH: 0-1 RH: 0-2 Tight: 0-0 Gall: 0-1
Aids:	Bl: 0-0 Vi: 0-0 Tstrap: 0-3
Best Rating:	106 10/01 Carl 2m1f gd-sft NHF

The Tallet

5-y-o ch g Alflora (IRE)-Bustle Em (IRE) (Burslem)
D McCain Mrs N L Spence

Placings:5   (3493)
2002/03: 17⁵GS,

	Starts	1st	2nd	3rd	Win & Pl
Hurdles	1	0	0	0	0
Career Total	1	0	0	0	0

Going:	Sf: 0-0 GS: 0-1 Gd: 0-0 GF: - Fm: 0-0
Distance:	2m/2m3: 0-1 2m4-2m7: 0-0 3m+: 0-0
Track:	LH: 0-1 RH: 0-0 Tight: 0-1 Gall: 0-0
Aids:	Bl: 0-0 Vi: 0-0 Tstrap: 0-0
Best Rating:	0 2/03 Bang 2m1f gd-sft Hdl

The Teuchter

86   **67**

4-y-o b g First Trump-Barefoot Landing (USA) (Cozzene (USA))
N A Dunger (M Johnston 21/9) N A Dunger

Placings:006   (4184)
2002/03: 16⁰HY, 16⁰S, 17⁶G,

	Starts	1st	2nd	3rd	Win & Pl
Hurdles	3	0	0	0	0
Career Total	3	0	0	0	0

Going:	Sf: 0-2 GS: 0-0 Gd: 0-1 GF: - Fm: 0-0
Distance:	2m/2m3: 0-3 2m4-2m7: 0-0 3m+: 0-0
Track:	LH: 0-1 RH: 0-2 Tight: 0-1 Gall: 0-1
Aids:	Bl: 0-0 Vi: 0-0 Tstrap: 0-0
Best Rating:	67 2/03 Newb 2m110y soft Hdl

The Tile Baron (IRE)

97   **80**

6-y-o b g Little Bighorn-Elegant Miss (Prince Tenderfoot (USA))
L Lungo The Tile Barons

Placings:5-000   (3227)
2002/03: 16⁰HY, 16⁰S, 17⁰HY,

	Starts	1st	2nd	3rd	Win & Pl
Hurdles	3	0	0	0	
Career Total	4	0	0	0	0

Going:	Sf: 0-3 GS: 0-0 Gd: 0-0 GF: - Fm: 0-0
Distance:	2m/2m3: 0-3 2m4-2m7: 0-0 3m+: 0-0
Track:	LH: 0-3 RH: 0-0 Tight: 0-2 Gall: 0-1
Aids:	Bl: 0-0 Vi: 0-0 Tstrap: 0-0
Best Rating:	82 3/02 Newc 2m heavy NHF

Plating-class hurdler; first worthwhile form when landing a modest novices handicap hurdle at Cartmel in May 2003; stays well and will be suited by three miles.

The Timberman

11-y-o gr g Grey Desire-Heldigvis (Hot Grove)
Tim Butt Tim Butt

Placings:P5360/F-F (0068)
2002/03: 21FGF,

	Starts	1st	2nd	3rd	Win & Pl
Chases	1	0	0	0	
Career Total	7	0	0	1	449

Going:	Sf: 0-0 GS: 0-0 Gd: 0-0 GF: - Fm: 0-1
Distance:	2m2/m3: 0-0 2m4-2m7: 0-1 3m+: 0-0
Track:	LH: 0-1 RH: 0-0 Tight: 0-1 Gall: 0-0
Aids:	Bl: 0-0 Vi: 0-0 Tstrap: 0-1
Best Rating:	75 5/02 Sedg 2m5f gd-fm Ch

The Tinker

97(72h) (45h)99
8-y-o b g Nomadic Way (USA)-Miss Tino (Relkino)
Mrs S C Bradburne Mrs S Irwin

Placings:00P/600P2P6-FUF32F4 (4407)
2002/03: 16FS, 22UHY, 24FGS, 16³G, 16²G, 17FGS, 16⁴G,

	Starts	1st	2nd	3rd	Win & Pl
Chases	7	0	1	1	3058
Career Total	17	0	2	1	4372

Going:	Sf: 0-2 GS: 0-2 Gd: 0-3 GF: - Fm: 0-0
Distance:	2m2/m3: 0-5 2m4-2m7: 0-1 3m+: 0-1
Track:	LH: 0-4 RH: 0-3 Tight: 0-5 Gall: 0-0
Aids:	Bl: 0-0 Vi: 0-0 Tstrap: 0-0
Best Rating:	99 2/03 Muss 2m good Ch

Modest novice chaser; suited by two miles and ground good or faster; likes to race prominently; still looking for first career win but clear when falling at the last at Ayr in November.

The Toff

68 6
4-y-o b f Overbury (IRE)-Fenian Court (IRE) (John French)
P D Evans Horsehay Racing Club

Placings:060 (3545)
2002/03: 14⁰GS, 16⁶S, 19⁰G,

	Starts	1st	2nd	3rd	Win & Pl
NH Flat	2	0	0	0	0
Hurdles	1	0	0	0	0
Career Total	3	0	0	0	0

Going:	Sf: 0-1 GS: 0-1 Gd: 0-1 GF: - Fm: 0-0
Distance:	2m2/m3: 0-1 2m4-2m7: 0-1 3m+: 0-0
Track:	LH: 0-1 RH: 0-2 Tight: 0-0 Gall: 0-0
Aids:	Bl: 0-0 Vi: 0-1 Tstrap: 0-0
Best Rating:	60 1/03 Ludl 2m soft NHF

The Tube (IRE)

90 60
5-y-o b m Royal Abjar (USA)-Grandeur And Grace (USA) (Septieme Ciel (USA))
P Bowen D R James

Placings:5P-004 (0872)
2002/03: 19⁰GF, 16⁰GF, 17⁴GF,

	Starts	1st	2nd	3rd	Win & Pl
Hurdles	3	0	0	0	0
Career Total	5	0	0	0	0

Going:	Sf: 0-0 GS: 0-0 Gd: 0-0 GF: - Fm: 0-3
Distance:	2m2/m3: 0-2 2m4-2m7: 0-1 3m+: 0-0
Track:	LH: 0-2 RH: 0-1 Tight: 0-1 Gall: 0-0
Aids:	Bl: 0-0 Vi: 0-0 Tstrap: 0-0
Best Rating:	60 4/02 Hrfd 2m1f good Hdl

The Vanliners (HOL)

70 57
4-y-o b g Kadeed (IRE)-For Eve (Forzando)
Mrs H O Graham Mrs H O Graham

Placings:0 (1413)
2002/03: 16⁰GF,

	Starts	1st	2nd	3rd	Win & Pl
Hurdles	1	0	0	0	
Career Total	1	0	0	0	

Going:	Sf: 0-0 GS: 0-0 Gd: 0-0 GF: - Fm: 0-1
Distance:	2m2/m3: 0-1 2m4-2m7: 0-0 3m+: 0-0
Track:	LH: 0-1 RH: 0-0 Tight: 0-0 Gall: 0-0
Aids:	Bl: 0-0 Vi: 0-0 Tstrap: 0-0
Best Rating:	52 10/02 Kels 2m110y gd-fm Hdl

The Villager (IRE)

112(104h) (126+h)131
7-y-o b g Zaffaran (USA)-Kitty Wren (Warpath)
D J Caro Mrs S Tainton

Placings:210/131140-11321P (4469)
2002/03: 20¹G, 24¹HY, 25³G, 20²S, 19¹GS, 25⁶G,

	Starts	1st	2nd	3rd	Win & Pl			
Hurdles	1	1	0	0	4105			
Chases	5	2	1	1	14980			
Career Total	15	7	2	2	32624			
131	1/03	Extr	2m3f110yE	Ch		G-S	£4979	
128	11/02	Bang	3m110y	D Ch		HVY	£4875	
132	10/02	Chep	2m4f	D(0-120)HHdl		GD	£4104	
121	12/01	Hayd	2m4f	D Hdl		SFT	£3770	
115	11/01	Hayd	2m4f	D Hdl		GD	£3861	
109	10/01	Hntg	2m110y	H NHF		GD	£1452	
109	1/01	Donc	2m110y	H NHF		GD	£1771	
				Total win prize-money £24814				

Going:	Sf: 1-2 GS: 1-1 Gd: 1-3 GF: - Fm: 0-0
Distance:	2m2/m3: 0-0 2m4-2m7: 2-3 3m+: 1-3
Track:	LH: 2-5 RH: 1-1 Tight: 1-2 Gall: 0-1
Aids:	Bl: 0-0 Vi: 0-0 Tstrap: 0-0
Best Rating:	132 10/02 Chep 2m4f good Hdl

Useful bumper/hurdle/chase winner; he progressed into a useful novice hurdler in 2001/2; changed stables prior to a winning return at Chepstow; made a winning debut over fences at Bangor; held in better company subsequently but won another novice at Exeter in January; stays three miles, effective at shorter, acts well on good to heavy ground.

The Warrior (IRE)

79 59
7-y-o gr g Willie Joe (IRE)-Fast And Straight (IRE) (Shirley Heights)
T P McGovern A J Loader

Placings:0/0-S0 (0337)
2002/03: 20⁵GF, 16⁰G,

	Starts	1st	2nd	3rd	Win & Pl
Hurdles	2	0	0	0	
Career Total	4	0	0	0	

Going:	Sf: 0-0 GS: 0-0 Gd: 0-1 GF: - Fm: 0-1
Distance:	2m2/m3: 0-1 2m4-2m7: 0-0 3m+: 0-0
Track:	LH: 0-0 RH: 0-1 Tight: 0-1 Gall: 0-0
Aids:	Bl: 0-0 Vi: 0-0 Tstrap: 0-0
Best Rating:	59 5/02 Towc 2m good Hdl

The Welder

(92h) (70h)
9-y-o b g Buckley-Crystal Run Vii (Damsire Unregistered)
V Y Gethin V Y Gethin

Placings:503P60F-P (4640)
2002/03: 21PG,

	Starts	1st	2nd	3rd	Win & Pl
Chases	1	0	0	0	
Career Total	8	0	0	1	241

Going:	Sf: 0-0 GS: 0-0 Gd: 0-1 GF: - Fm: 0-0
Distance:	2m2/m3: 0-0 2m4-2m7: 0-1 3m+: 0-0
Track:	LH: 0-1 RH: 0-0 Tight: 0-1 Gall: 0-0
Aids:	Bl: 0-0 Vi: 0-0 Tstrap: 0-0
Best Rating:	91 3/00 Ludl 2m good NHF

The Whole Hog (IRE)

14-y-o b g Cataldi-Beeston (Our Babu)
K Robson J M B Cookson

Placings:00/5PPP/U2121/1413414/F3PP/56/F/0-6 (0161)
2002/03: 25⁶G,

	Starts	1st	2nd	3rd	Win & Pl			
Chases	1	0	0	0	0			
Career Total	27	5	2	2	19148			
98	11/97	Leic	2m7f110yE(0-110)HCh			G-F	£3464	
99	10/97	Towc	3m1f	E(0-115)HCh		G-F	£2852	
94	5/97	Sedg	3m3f	E Ch		G-F	£3059	
	4/97	NAbb	3m2f110yE Ch			FRM	£2846	
81	3/97	Font	3m2f110yE Ch			G-F	£3132	
				Total win prize-money £15355				

Going:	Sf: 0-0 GS: 0-0 Gd: 0-1 GF: - Fm: 0-0
Distance:	2m2/m3: 0-0 2m4-2m7: 0-0 3m+: 0-1
Track:	LH: 0-1 RH: 0-0 Tight: 0-1 Gall: 0-0
Aids:	Bl: 0-0 Vi: 0-0 Tstrap: 0-0
Best Rating:	99 10/97 Towc 3m1f gd-fm Ch

The Wiley Kalmuck (IRE)

9-y-o b g Be My Native (USA)-Beecom Silk (English Prince)
J M Turner J M Turner

Placings:050002053000/001026400/0P0U0F0010/250P44050-4 (4667)
2002/03: 21⁴G,

	Starts	1st	2nd	3rd	Win & Pl			
Chases	1	0	0	0	158			
Career Total	39	2	3	1	8817			
104	12/00	Muss	3m	F(0-90)HHdl		GD	£1813	
96	9/99	Gowr	3m	(0-102)HHdl		Y-S	£4312	
				Total win prize-money £6126				

Going:	Sf: 0-0 GS: 0-0 Gd: 0-0 GF: - Fm: 0-0
Distance:	2m2/m3: 0-0 2m4-2m7: 0-1 3m+: 0-0
Track:	LH: 0-1 RH: 0-0 Tight: 0-1 Gall: 0-0
Aids:	Bl: 0-0 Vi: 0-0 Tstrap: 0-0

Best Rating: 104 12/00 Muss 3m   good   Hdl

Selling-class hurdler/pointer; in good form in points in the spring of 2003; acts on fast ground.

The Winkster (IRE)

9-y-o b/br g Black Minstrel-Oremus (Marisco)
Mrs D M Grissell Cockerell Cowing Racing

Placings:0/0-P   (0312)
2002/03: 21PG,

	Starts	1st	2nd	3rd	Win & Pl
Chases	1	0	0	0	
Career Total	3	0	0	0	

Going: Sf: 0-0 GS: 0-0 Gd: 0-1 GF: - Fm: 0-0
Distance: 2m/2m3: 0-0 2m4-2m7: 0-1 3m+: 0-0
Track: LH: 0-0 RH: 0-1 Tight: 0-1 Gall: 0-0
Aids: Bl: 0-0 Vi: 0-0 Tstrap: 0-1
Best Rating: 0   5/02 Folk 2m5f   good   Ch

Theatre Call (IRE)
96f   89f
5-y-o b g Old Vic-Jennycomequick (Furry Glen)
J A B Old W E Sturt

Placings:4   (3322)
2002/03: 164GS,

	Starts	1st	2nd	3rd	Win & Pl
NH Flat	1	0	0	0	0
Career Total	1	0	0	0	0

Going: Sf: 0-0 GS: 0-1 Gd: 0-0 GF: - Fm: 0-0
Distance: 2m/2m3: 0-1 2m4-2m7: 0-0 3m+: 0-0
Track: LH: 0-0 RH: 0-1 Tight: 0-0 Gall: 0-0
Aids: Bl: 0-0 Vi: 0-0 Tstrap: 0-0
Best Rating: 89   1/03 Kemp 2m   gd-sft NHF

Theatre Lady (IRE)
83   60
5-y-o b m King s Theatre (IRE)-Littlepace (Indian King (USA))
P D Evans Waterline Racing Club

Placings:60   (2629)
2002/03: 17PG, 160S,

	Starts	1st	2nd	3rd	Win & Pl
Hurdles	2	0	0	0	0
Career Total	2	0	0	0	0

Going: Sf: 0-1 GS: 0-0 Gd: 0-1 GF: - Fm: 0-0
Distance: 2m/2m3: 0-2 2m4-2m7: 0-0 3m+: 0-0
Track: LH: 0-1 RH: 0-1 Tight: 0-0 Gall: 0-0
Aids: Bl: 0-0 Vi: 0-0 Tstrap: 0-0
Best Rating: 64   12/02 Hrfd 2m1f   good   Hdl

Theatre Of Life (IRE)
78   40
4-y-o b g King s Theatre (IRE)-Miss Ironwood (Junius (USA))
G L Moore Danny Bloor

Placings:00   (2195)

2002/03: 17OS, 17OGS,

	Starts	1st	2nd	3rd	Win & Pl
Hurdles	2	0	0	0	
Career Total	2	0	0	0	

Going: Sf: 0-1 GS: 0-1 Gd: 0-0 GF: - Fm: 0-0
Distance: 2m/2m3: 0-2 2m4-2m7: 0-0 3m+: 0-0
Track: LH: 0-0 RH: 0-2 Tight: 0-2 Gall: 0-0
Aids: Bl: 0-0 Vi: 0-0 Tstrap: 0-0
Best Rating: 40   11/02 Folk 2m1f110y soft   Hdl

Theatreland (USA)
(101h)   (112h)
6-y-o b g Dynaformer (USA)-Mime (Cure The Blues (USA))
S E H Sherwood Knightsbridge Bc Glos Ltd & A Clift

Placings:13/0223P-00U   (0508)
2002/03: 24OGF, 27OGF, 23UG,

	Starts	1st	2nd	3rd	Win & Pl
Hurdles	2	0	0	0	0
Chases	1	0	0	0	0
Career Total	10	1	2	2	5835

105 8/00 Worc 2m   E Hdl   G-F £2785
Total win prize-money £2785

Going: Sf: 0-0 GS: 0-0 Gd: 0-1 GF: - Fm: 0-2
Distance: 2m/2m3: 0-0 2m4-2m7: 0-0 3m+: 0-3
Track: LH: 0-3 RH: 0-0 Tight: 0-1 Gall: 0-0
Aids: Bl: 0-0 Vi: 0-0 Tstrap: 0-0
Best Rating: 112 11/01 Kemp 3m110y   good   Hdl

Modest hurdler; lightly-raced on the Flat before making a successful debut over hurdles, but has since found life a little harder. Acts on good to firm and stays three miles, although he has finished with the pace over an extended three miles.

Thebwlboy
85(92h)   (63h)72
10-y-o ch g Interrex (CAN)-Super Melody (Song)
J W Tudor (D C Gibbs 1/5) J W Tudor

Placings:0013220300/00-54P   (0630)
2002/03: 165GF, 164G, 16PGF,

	Starts	1st	2nd	3rd	Win & Pl
Chases	3	0	0	0	0
Career Total	15	1	2	2	5348

85 6/00 NAbb 2m1f   E Hdl   G-F £2359
Total win prize-money £2359

Going: Sf: 0-0 GS: 0-0 Gd: 0-1 GF: - Fm: 0-2
Distance: 2m/2m3: 0-3 2m4-2m7: 0-0 3m+: 0-0
Track: LH: 0-2 RH: 0-1 Tight: 0-1 Gall: 0-1
Aids: Bl: 0-0 Vi: 0-0 Tstrap: 0-0
Best Rating: 89 9/00 Bang 2m1f   gd-fm Hdl

Theicecreamman (IRE)
98   99d
6-y-o ch g Glacial Storm (USA)-Miss Cornetto (IRE) (Parliament)
G Prodromou (L Young 6/2) Mrs L Middleton

Placings:63563013   (4688)
2002/03: 19OYS, 163GS, 165S, 18OGS, 20OS, 19OS, 201SH, 19OGF,

	Starts	1st	2nd	3rd	Win & Pl
NH Flat	3	0	0	1	344
Hurdles	5	1	0	2	5842
Career Total	8	1	0	3	6185

---

99 2/03 Clon 2m4f   Hdl   SH £4480
Total win prize-money £4481

Going: Sf: 0-5 GS: 0-0 Gd: 0-0 GF: - Fm: 0-1
Distance: 2m/2m3: 0-5 2m4-2m7: 1-3 3m+: 0-1
Track: LH: 0-1 RH: 0-2 Tight: 0-1 Gall: 0-0
Aids: Bl: 0-0 Vi: 0-0 Tstrap: 0-0
Best Rating: 104 12/02 Limk 2m4f   soft   Hdl

Ex-Irish novice hurdler; winner of maiden hurdle at Clonmel in February 2003; acted in soft ground; stayed two miles four (DEAD).

Themanfromcarlisle
100   95
7-y-o br g Jupiter Island-Country Mistress (Town And Country)
M Pitman Mrs Elizabeth Pearce

Placings:4-P0014   (4540)
2002/03: 16PS, 16OG, 19OS, 201GF, 214G,

	Starts	1st	2nd	3rd	Win & Pl
Hurdles	4	1	0	0	3959
Chases	1	0	0	0	0
Career Total	6	1	0	0	3959

95 3/03 Font 2m4f   E Hdl   G-F £3536
Total win prize-money £3536

Going: Sf: 0-2 GS: 0-0 Gd: 0-2 GF: - Fm: 1-1
Distance: 2m/2m3: 0-3 2m4-2m7: 1-2 3m+: 0-0
Track: LH: 0-3 RH: 0-1 Tight: 1-2 Gall: 0-2
Aids: Bl: 0-0 Vi: 0-0 Tstrap: 0-0
Best Rating: 95 3/03 Font 2m4f   gd-fm Hdl

Moderate hurdler; acts well on decent ground; stays two and a half miles.

Thepointaboutitis (IRE)
93   112+
6-y-o ch g Case Law-Boston View (IRE) (Simply Great (FR))
John F Gleeson Newtown Mahon Syndicate

Placings:5536-41516   (1939)
2002/03: 17AG, 16IF, 16SG, 17IYS, 16RG,

	Starts	1st	2nd	3rd	Win & Pl
Hurdles	5	2	0	0	10145
Career Total	9	2	0	1	10703

116 10/02 Gowr 2m1f   Hdl   Y-S £5714
96 9/02 Clon 2m   Hdl   FRM £3809
Total win prize-money £9525

Going: Sf: 0-0 GS: 0-0 Gd: 0-3 GF: - Fm: 1-1
Distance: 2m/2m3: 2-5 2m4-2m7: 0-0 3m+: 0-0
Track: LH: 0-2 RH: 0-0 Tight: 0-0 Gall: 0-0
Aids: Bl: 0-0 Vi: 0-0 Tstrap: 0-0
Best Rating: 116 10/02 Gowr 2m1f   yld-sft Hdl

Fair hurdler; ran well in a number of maiden hurdles before getting off the mark at Clonmel in September 2002. Won again at Gowran Park in October and looks on the upgrade; acts on any ground.

Therealbandit (IRE)
105   124+
6-y-o b g Torus-Sunrise Highway Vii (Damsire Unregistered)
M C Pipe D A Johnson

Placings:0631   (4692)
2002/03: 19OS, 17RGS, 20RG, 22IG,

	Starts	1st	2nd	3rd	Win & Pl
Hurdles	4	1	0	1	4182

Career Total   4   1   0   1   4182
114 4/03 NAbb 2m6f   E(0-105)HHdl   GD   £3630
                   Total win prize-money £3630

Going: Sf: 0-1 GS: 0-1 Gd: 1-2 GF: - Fm: 0-0
Distance: 2m/2m3: 0-1 **2m4-2m7: 1-3** 3m+: 0-0
Track: LH: **1-3** RH: 0-1 Tight: **1-3** Gall: 0-0
Aids: Bl: 0-0 Vi: 0-0 Tstrap: 0-0
Best Rating: 114 4/03 NAbb 2m6f   good   Hdl

Fair hurdler; soft ground point winner in Ireland; won three novice hurdles over 2m 6f at Newton Abbot and a 3m 3f handicap at Stratford in April, May and June 2003; acts on soft ground; looks a staying chaser in the making.

Theseus (IRE)

94(109h)   (128h)124

7-y-o b h Danehill (USA)-Graecia Magna (USA) (Private Account (USA))
P Hughes   Sean McCormack

Placings:000/12231040/30220-03420311303   (1564)
2002/03: 17⁵GY, 17³S, 16⁴GF, 20²GF, 17⁰GY, 17³GF, 16¹G, 17¹GF, 16³F, 16⁰S, 17³GS,

	Starts	1st	2nd	3rd	Win & Pl
Chases	11	2	1	4	16048
Career Total	**27**	**4**	**5**	**6**	**36495**
115 9/02	Klny	2m1f	(0-102)HCh	G-F	£5291
101 8/02	Tral	2m	Ch	GD	£5503
120 10/00	Cork	2m	Hdl	SFT	£4416
105 5/00	Cork	2m	Hdl	G-Y	£3864

                Total win prize-money £19074

Going: Sf: 0-2 GS: 0-1 Gd: 1-1 GF: - Fm: 1-5
Distance: **2m/2m3: 2-10** 2m4-2m7: 0-1 3m+: 0-0
Track: LH: 0-1 RH: 0-3 Tight: 0-1 Gall: 0-0
Aids: Bl: 0-0 Vi: 0-0 Tstrap: 0-0
Best Rating: 129 12/00 Leop 2m   sft-hvy Hdl

Fair irish chaser; best at two miles; acts on any ground.

Thesis (IRE)

108   121+

5-y-o ch g Definite Article-Chouette (Try My Best (USA))
Miss Venetia Williams (J A Osborne 22/10) The 1961 Partnership

Placings:2236   (4470)
2002/03: 17²S, 17²S, 16³HY, 16⁶G,

	Starts	1st	2nd	3rd	Win & Pl
Hurdles	4	0	2	1	4586
Career Total	**4**	**0**	**2**	**1**	**4586**

Going: Sf: 0-3 GS: 0-0 Gd: 0-1 GF: - Fm: 0-0
Distance: 2m/2m3: 0-4 2m4-2m7: 0-0 3m+: 0-0
Track: LH: 0-2 RH: 0-2 Tight: 0-4 Gall: 0-0
Aids: Bl: 0-0 Vi: 0-0 Tstrap: 0-0
Best Rating: 125 1/03 Tntn 2m1f   soft   Hdl

Fair novice hurdler; winner on the Flat; got off the mark when convincing winner of maiden hurdle at Worcester May 2003; followed up in a weak event at the same course next time; suited by 2m; acts on any ground.

Theydon Star (NZ)

74   49

6-y-o b g Classic Fame (USA)-Hilarity (NZ) (St Hilarion (USA))
Mrs N Smith   Tony Hayward

Placings:60U-6   (0125)
2002/03: 20⁶GF,

	Starts	1st	2nd	3rd	Win & Pl
Hurdles	1	0	0	0	0
Career Total	**4**	**0**	**0**	**0**	**0**

Going: Sf: 0-0 GS: 0-0 Gd: 0-0 GF: - Fm: 0-1
Distance: 2m/2m3: 0-0 2m4-2m7: 0-1 3m+: 0-0
Track: LH: 0-0 RH: 0-0 Tight: 0-1 Gall: 0-0
Aids: Bl: 0-0 Vi: 0-0 Tstrap: 0-0
Best Rating: 79   8/01   Worc   2m   gd-fm NHF

Thieves'Glen

100f   104f

5-y-o b g Teenoso (USA)-Hollow Creek (Tarqogan)
H Morrison   Panda Christie & Stephanie Gore

Placings:4-534   (4090)
2002/03: 13⁵S, 17³S, 16⁴GS,

	Starts	1st	2nd	3rd	Win & Pl
NH Flat	3	0	0	1	565
Career Total	**4**	**0**	**0**	**1**	**565**

Going: Sf: 0-2 GS: 0-1 Gd: 0-0 GF: - Fm: 0-0
Distance: 2m/2m3: 0-2 2m4-2m7: 0-0 3m+: 0-0
Track: LH: 0-0 RH: 0-2 Tight: 0-0 Gall: 0-0
Aids: Bl: 0-0 Vi: 0-0 Tstrap: 0-0
Best Rating: 104 12/02 Hrfd 2m1f   soft   NHF

A half-brother to Frenchman s Creek, he has shown promise in bumpers.

Think Again (IRE)

88   69

9-y-o b g Long Pond-Either Or (Boreen (FR))
R Craggs   Ray Craggs

Placings:P/0/6P/PSF/P-5055   (2161)
2002/03: 17⁵G, 17⁰G, 20⁵S, 17⁵S,

	Starts	1st	2nd	3rd	Win & Pl
Hurdles	4	0	0	0	0
Career Total	**12**	**0**	**0**	**0**	**0**

Going: Sf: 0-2 GS: 0-0 Gd: 0-2 GF: - Fm: 0-0
Distance: 2m/2m3: 0-3 2m4-2m7: 0-1 3m+: 0-0
Track: LH: 0-4 RH: 0-0 Tight: 0-3 Gall: 0-1
Aids: Bl: 0-0 Vi: 0-0 Tstrap: 0-0
Best Rating: 73   9/00   Sedg   2m1f   good   Hdl

This Thyne

109   103

7-y-o b m Good Thyne (USA)-Dalkey Sound (Crash Course)
Mrs M Reveley   G S Brown

Placings:50P0-60061222F   (2379)
2002/03: 16²GS, 23⁰G, 22⁰G, 26⁶GF, 24¹G, 25²GF, 23²G, 20²S, 20¹FGS,

	Starts	1st	2nd	3rd	Win & Pl
Hurdles	9	1	3	0	6148
Career Total	**13**	**1**	**3**	**0**	**6148**
77 8/02	Prth	3m110y	E(0-100)HHdl	GD	£4046

                Total win prize-money £4046

Going: Sf: 0-1 GS: 0-2 Gd: 1-4 GF: - Fm: 0-2
Distance: 2m/2m3: 0-1 2m4-2m7: 0-0 **3m+: 1-3**
Track: LH: 0-8 **RH: 1-1** Tight: 0-2 Gall: 0-1
Aids: Bl: 0-0 Vi: 0-0 Tstrap: 0-1
Best Rating: 103 11/02 Newc 2m4f   soft   Hdl

Moderate hurdler; showed first form over hurdles when making all in a weak staying hurdle at Perth in August 2002; runner-up three times since.

Thisthatandtother (IRE)

115   148

7-y-o b g Bob Back (USA)-Baden (IRE) (Furry Glen)
P F Nicholls   C G Roach

Placings:2145-1121252   (4555)
2002/03: 16¹G, 16¹G, 20²S, 16¹GS, 16²GS, 16⁵G, 16²G,

	Starts	1st	2nd	3rd	Win & Pl
Hurdles	7	3	3	0	60408
Career Total	**11**	**4**	**4**	**0**	**63794**
148 1/03	Winc	2m	A Hdl	G-S	£23800
117 11/02	Winc	2m	D Hdl	GD	£4881
100 10/02	Winc	2m	D Hdl	GD	£3916
118 2/02	Winc	2m	H NHF	SFT	£1736

                Total win prize-money £34343

Going: Sf: 0-1 GS: 1-2 Gd: 2-4 GF: - Fm: 0-0
Distance: **2m/2m3: 3-6** 2m4-2m7: 0-1 3m+: 0-0
Track: LH: 0-0 **RH: 3-5** Tight: 0-0 Gall: 0-0
Aids: Bl: 0-0 Vi: 0-0 Tstrap: 0-0
Best Rating: 148 4/03 Ayr   2m   good   Hdl

Smart novice hurdler; former useful bumper horse; effective over two miles and did not stay when tried over further; suited by ground good or softer; looks best going right-handed; goes very well at Wincanton.

Thistle Do

95   90d

5-y-o b g College Chapel-Fishki (Niniski (USA))
M D Hammond (L Lungo 14/1) S T Brankin

Placings:0-6P50PP0   (4776)
2002/03: 17⁶S, 27⁵S, 20⁵GS, 16⁰HY, 24⁰P G, 19⁵S, 20⁰G,

	Starts	1st	2nd	3rd	Win & Pl
NH Flat	1	0	0	0	0
Hurdles	6	0	0	0	0
Career Total	**8**	**0**	**0**	**0**	**0**

Going: Sf: 0-4 GS: 0-1 Gd: 0-2 GF: - Fm: 0-0
Distance: 2m/2m3: 0-3 2m4-2m7: 0-2 3m+: 0-2
Track: LH: 0-4 RH: 0-3 Tight: 0-3 Gall: 0-0
Aids: Bl: 0-0 Vi: 0-0 Tstrap: 0-0
Best Rating: 90 12/02 Ayr   2m4f   gd-sft Hdl

Thistlekicker (IRE)

103   79

11-y-o b g Mandalus-Miss Ranova (Giacometti)
Mrs J C McGregor (Mrs D Thomson 17/8) Mrs Jean McGregor

Placings:00/04OP/P2P0/34F0034P2650-010343F050   (4762)
2002/03: 16⁰G, 16¹GF, 16⁰G, 16³GS, 16⁴GF, 17³GF, 17F GF, 16⁰GS, 24⁵G, 16⁰G,

	Starts	1st	2nd	3rd	Win & Pl
Hurdles	10	1	0	2	4076
Career Total	**32**	**1**	**2**	**4**	**6515**
81 5/02	Prth	2m110y	G(0-95)HHdl	G-F	£2954

                Total win prize-money £2954

Going: Sf: 0-0 GS: 0-2 Gd: 0-4 GF: - Fm: 1-4
Distance: **2m/2m3: 1-9** 2m4-2m7: 0-0 3m+: 0-1
Track: LH: 0-4 **RH: 1-6** Tight: 0-3 Gall: 0-0
Aids: Bl: 0-0 Vi: 0-0 Tstrap: 0-0
Best Rating: 81 7/02 MRas 2m1f110y gd-fm Hdl

Plating-class hurdler; suited by fast ground.

Thomas The Doubter

8-y-o gr g Roviris-Doubting Donna (Tom Noddy)
S A Hughes S A Hughes

Placings:*0/FP*   (4736)
2002/03: 21^{F}G, 24^{F}GF,

	Starts	1st	2nd	3rd	Win & Pl
Chases	2	0	0	0	
Career Total	3	0	0	0	

Going: Sf: 0-0 GS: 0-0 Gd: 0-1 GF: - Fm: 0-0
Distance: 2m/2m3: 0-0 2m4-2m7: 0-1 3m+: 0-1
Track: LH: 0-1 RH: 0-1 Tight: 0-1 Gall: 0-0
Aids: Bl: 0-0 Vi: 0-0 Tstrap: 0-0
Best Rating: 0   4/03   Chep   3m   gd-fm   Ch

Thorn In Our Side (IRE)

6-y-o b/br m Detroit Sam (FR)-Aintree Rose (Avocat)
Colin S McKeever Mrs P Sloan

Placings:*P600P*   (1384)
2002/03: 20^{P}Y, 17^{6}G, 16^{9}HY, 16^{0}G, 16^{P}GF,

	Starts	1st	2nd	3rd	Win & Pl
NH Flat	1	0	0	0	0
Hurdles	4	0	0	0	0
Career Total	5	0	0	0	0

Going: Sf: 0-1 GS: 0-0 Gd: 0-2 GF: - Fm: 0-1
Distance: 2m/2m3: 0-4 2m4-2m7: 0-1 3m+: 0-0
Track: LH: 0-2 RH: 0-0 Tight: 0-1 Gall: 0-0
Aids: Bl: 0-0 Vi: 0-0 Tstrap: 0-0
Best Rating: 0   10/02   Hexm   2m110y   gd-fm   Hdl

Thorpeness (IRE)
94   88

4-y-o b c Barathea (IRE)-Brisighella (IRE) (Al Hareb (USA))
J White (C F Wall 17/9) Mrs Elga Moran

Placings:*03*   (2059)
2002/03: 16^{0}G, 17^{3}S,

	Starts	1st	2nd	3rd	Win & Pl
Hurdles	2	0	0	1	497
Career Total	2	0	0	1	497

Going: Sf: 0-1 GS: 0-0 Gd: 0-1 GF: - Fm: 0-0
Distance: 2m/2m3: 0-2 2m4-2m7: 0-0 3m+: 0-0
Track: LH: 0-1 RH: 0-1 Tight: 0-0 Gall: 0-0
Aids: Bl: 0-0 Vi: 0-0 Tstrap: 0-0
Best Rating: 90   11/02   Hrfd   2m1f   soft   Hdl

Stayed on into third on his second run over hurdles.

Thosewerethedays

10-y-o b g Past Glories-Charlotte s Festival (Gala Performance (USA))
Miss Pauline Robson Mrs J D Goodfellow

Placings:*3131FP-13*   (4169)
2002/03: 21^{1}S, 24^{3}GS,

	Starts	1st	2nd	3rd	Win & Pl
Chases	2	1	0	1	2093

Career Total	8	3	0	3	10749
135	3/03	Ayr	2m5f110yH Ch		SFT	£1876
135	2/02	Kemp	2m4f110yD Ch		SFT	£5300
115	12/01	Hrfd	2m	F Ch		GD	£2431

Total win prize-money £9608

Going: Sf: 1-1 GS: 0-1 Gd: 0-0 GF: - Fm: 0-0
Distance: 2m/2m3: 0-0 **2m4-2m7: 1-1** 3m+: 0-1
Track: **LH: 1-2** RH: 0-0 Tight: 0-0 Gall: 0-1
Aids: Bl: 0-0 Vi: 0-0 Tstrap: 0-0
Best Rating: 135 3/03 Ayr   2m5f110y   soft   Ch

Former fair chaser; now competing in hunter chases; best at two and a half miles.

Thoutmosis (USA)
97   100

4-y-o ch g Woodman (USA)-Toujours Elle (USA) (Lyphard (USA))
L Lungo (F Head 10/6) The Border Reivers

Placings:*13*   (4405)
2002/03: 18^{1}G, 16^{3}G,

	Starts	1st	2nd	3rd	Win & Pl
Hurdles	2	1	0	1	4784
Career Total	2	1	0	1	4784
100	3/03	Kels	2m2f	E Hdl		GD	£4186

Total win prize-money £4186

Going: Sf: 0-0 GS: 0-0 Gd: 0-1 GF: - Fm: 0-0
Distance: **2m/2m3: 1-2** 2m4-2m7: 0-0 3m+: 0-0
Track: **LH: 1-2** RH: 0-0 **Tight: 1-1** Gall: 0-0
Aids: Bl: 0-0 Vi: 0-0 Tstrap: 0-0
Best Rating: 100 3/03 Hexm   2m110y   good   Hdl

Modest ex-French novice hurdler; made a winning debut over hurdles at Kelso; stays 2m 2f and suited by good ground; should stay further.

Thread Of Honour (IRE)
97f   95f

6-y-o gr g Roselier (FR)-Sharkezan (IRE) (Double Schwartz)
N J Henderson Sir Stephen Hastings And Partners

Placings:*030*   (3930)
2002/03: 16^{9}G, 16^{3}G, 16^{9}G,

	Starts	1st	2nd	3rd	Win & Pl
NH Flat	3	0	0	1	289
Career Total	3	0	0	1	289

Going: Sf: 0-0 GS: 0-0 Gd: 0-3 GF: - Fm: 0-0
Distance: 2m/2m3: 0-3 2m4-2m7: 0-0 3m+: 0-0
Track: LH: 0-2 RH: 0-1 Tight: 0-1 Gall: 0-1
Aids: Bl: 0-0 Vi: 0-0 Tstrap: 0-0
Best Rating: 95 1/03 Sthl   2m   good   NHF

Three Clouds
53

6-y-o b g Rainbow Quest (USA)-Three Tails (Blakeney)
C N Kellett (G L Moore 16/10) Roland M Wheatley

Placings:*P6-P*   (3231)
2002/03: 23^{P}S,

	Starts	1st	2nd	3rd	Win & Pl
Hurdles	1	0	0	0	
Career Total	3	0	0	0	0

Going: Sf: 0-1 GS: 0-0 Gd: 0-0 GF: - Fm: 0-0

Distance: 2m/2m3: 0-0 2m4-2m7: 0-0 3m+: 0-1
Track: LH: 0-1 RH: 0-0 Tight: 0-1 Gall: 0-0
Aids: Bl: 0-0 Vi: 0-0 Tstrap: 0-0
Best Rating: 53   4/02   Plum   2m   gd-fm   Hdl

Three Days Reign (IRE)
113(88h)   (91h)99

9-y-o br g Camden Town-Little Treat (Miners Lamp)
P D Cundell Entre-Nous

Placings:*2/500/30-3*   (4327)
2002/03: 18^{3}G,

	Starts	1st	2nd	3rd	Win & Pl
Chases	1	0	0	1	880
Career Total	7	0	1	2	1753

Going: Sf: 0-0 GS: 0-0 Gd: 0-1 GF: - Fm: 0-0
Distance: 2m/2m3: 0-1 2m4-2m7: 0-0 3m+: 0-0
Track: LH: 0-1 RH: 0-0 Tight: 0-0 Gall: 0-1
Aids: Bl: 0-0 Vi: 0-0 Tstrap: 0-0
Best Rating: 107 5/99 Chep   2m110y   good   NHF

Moderate chaser/hurdler; lightly-raced in novice hurdles; has taken to fences; raised 11lb after winning 2m 4f handicap at Worcester May 2003; runner-up over 3m at the same course next time.

Three Eagles (USA)
106(108h)   (101h)101

6-y-o ch g Eagle Eyed (USA)-Tertiary (USA) (Vaguely Noble)
A Bailey Granite By Design Ltd

Placings:*50/414026F504P435-13FF*   (1226)
2002/03: 21^{1}F, 19^{3}GF, 20^{F}GF, 20^{F}G,

	Starts	1st	2nd	3rd	Win & Pl
Hurdles	4	1	0	1	3057
Career Total	20	2	1	2	7672
96	5/02	Wwck	2m5f	E(0-110)HHdl		FRM	£2614
101	8/01	Bang	2m4f	F Hdl		G-S	£2268

Total win prize-money £4883

Going: Sf: 0-0 GS: 0-0 Gd: 0-1 GF: - Fm: 1-3
Distance: 2m/2m3: 0-1 **2m4-2m7: 1-3** 3m+: 0-0
Track: **LH: 1-4** RH: 0-0 Tight: 0-2 Gall: 0-0
Aids: Bl: 0-0 Vi: 0-0 Tstrap: 0-0
Best Rating: 107 11/01 Hayd   2m7f110y   good   Hdl

Moderate front-running hurdler; handles most ground and goes well at Bangor; creditable second under top weight on chasing debut in 2m novices handicap at Worcester June on first outing for Martin Pipe.

Three Lions
112   107

6-y-o ch g Jupiter Island-Super Sol (Rolfe (USA))
R S Brookhouse R S Brookhouse

Placings:*32F5-PP01*   (3543)
2002/03: 22^{P}S, 21^{P}GS, 16^{P}S, 17^{1}G,

	Starts	1st	2nd	3rd	Win & Pl
Hurdles	4	1	0	0	3406
Career Total	8	1	1	1	5657
107	2/03	Hrfd	2m1f	E(0-110)HHdl		GD	£3406

Total win prize-money £3406

Going: Sf: 0-2 GS: 0-1 Gd: 1-1 GF: - Fm: 0-0
Distance: **2m/2m3: 1-2** 2m4-2m7: 0-2 3m+: 0-0
Track: LH: 0-2 **RH: 1-2** Tight: 0-0 Gall: 0-0

Aids: Bl: 0-0 Vi: 0-0 Tstrap: 0-0
Best Rating: 118 2/02 Tntn 2m1f   soft   Hdl

Modest hurdler; back to form when winning at Hereford in February 2003; best at two miles; effective on good ground.

Three Saints (IRE)

14-y-o b g Rising-Oh Dora (Even Money)
W G Dutton V Dutton

Placings: 42/3F14/52U4/5P0P/5-3   (0278)
2002/03: 24³S,

	Starts	1st	2nd	3rd	Win & Pl
Chases	1	0	0	1	545
Career Total	16	1	2	2	6659
105 3/96 Bang 2m4f110yE Ch				HVY	£3649

Total win prize-money £3649

Going: Sf: 0-1 GS: 0-0 Gd: 0-0 GF: - Fm: 0-0
Distance: 2m/2m3: 0-0 2m4-2m7: 0-0 3m+: 0-1
Track: LH: 0-1 RH: 0-0 Tight: 0-1 Gall: 0-0
Aids: Bl: 0-0 Vi: 0-0 Tstrap: 0-0
Best Rating: 106 3/95 Navn 2m   heavy   NHF

Once useful under Rules but luckless pointer and poor hunter chaser nowadays.

Three Weeks
100

10-y-o ch g Formidable (USA)-Zilda (FR) (Zino)
M J Wilkinson Edgcote Yacht Club

Placings: 02/560/6413550/03150/2514-P   (0412)
2002/03: 19ᴾGF,

	Starts	1st	2nd	3rd	Win & Pl
Hurdles	1	0	0	0	
Career Total	22	3	2	2	11447
100 11/01 Tntn 2m3f110yF(0-110)HHdl			GD		£2520
93 12/00 Ludl 2m		E(0-115)HHdl	SFT		£3532
113 11/99 Wwck 2m		F(0-100)HHdl	GD		£2080

Total win prize-money £8133

Going: Sf: 0-0 GS: 0-0 Gd: 0-0 GF: - Fm: 0-1
Distance: 2m/2m3: 0-1 2m4-2m7: 0-0 3m+: 0-0
Track: LH: 0-1 RH: 0-0 Tight: 0-1 Gall: 0-0
Aids: Bl: 0-0 Vi: 0-0 Tstrap: 0-0
Best Rating: 113 11/99 Wwck 2m   good   Hdl

Moderate hurdler, his wins have come in ordinary handicap company. Has won on good and soft ground and stays up to two and a half miles.

Threezedzz
101   96

5-y-o ch g Emarati (USA)-Exotic Forest (Dominion)
Mrs P N Dutfield (J M Bradley 15/5) Steve Evans

Placings: 525   (1545)
2002/03: 16⁵GF, 16²G, 17⁵F,

	Starts	1st	2nd	3rd	Win & Pl
Hurdles	3	0	1	0	920
Career Total	3	0	1	0	920

Going: Sf: 0-0 GS: 0-0 Gd: 0-0 GF: 0-1 Fm: 0-2
Distance: 2m/2m3: 0-3 2m4-2m7: 0-0 3m+: 0-0
Track: LH: 0-2 RH: 0-1 Tight: 0-2 Gall: 0-0
Aids: Bl: 0-0 Vi: 0-0 Tstrap: 0-0
Best Rating: 99 9/02 Plum 2m   good   Hdl

Moderate hurdler; best over sprint trips on the Flat but seemed to stay Plumpton s sharp two miles when runner-up over hurdles there in September.

Thrill A Minute (IRE)
100(96h)   (85h)110d

9-y-o b g Be My Native (USA)-Fairy Run (Deep Run)
Jonjo O Neill C D Carr

Placings: 0/25P/02/46114PPP-2PPP   (3489)
2002/03: 28²S, 33ᴾS, 25ᴾGS, 30ᴾS,

	Starts	1st	2nd	3rd	Win & Pl
Chases	4	0	1	0	1252
Career Total	18	2	3	0	9689
110 11/01 Uttx 3m2f	F(0-100)HCh	HVY			£2982
90 10/01 Bang 3m110y	F(0-105)HCh	SFT			£3542

Total win prize-money £6525

Going: Sf: 0-3 GS: 0-1 Gd: 0-0 GF: - Fm: 0-0
Distance: 2m/2m3: 0-0 2m4-2m7: 0-0 3m+: 0-4
Track: LH: 0-1 RH: 0-3 Tight: 0-3 Gall: 0-0
Aids: Bl: 0-0 Vi: 0-0 Tstrap: 0-3
Best Rating: 110 11/01 Uttx 3m2f   heavy   Ch

Modest chaser, effective over three miles plus in soft ground.

Through The Rye
119   142

7-y-o ch g Sabrehill (USA)-Baharlilys (Green Dancer (USA))
E W Tuer Nice To See You Euro-Racing

Placings: 116F/011141-62033P   (4308)
2002/03: 16⁸GS, 16²S, 16⁹G, 16³GS, 17³G, 18ᴾG,

	Starts	1st	2nd	3rd	Win & Pl
Hurdles	6	0	1	2	10703
Career Total	16	6	1	2	38673
133 3/02 Kels 2m2f	C(0-135)HHdl	HVY			£8515
124 3/02 Donc 2m110y	D(0-120)HHdl	SFT			£3486
136 2/02 Sedg 2m1f	E(0-110)HHdl	SFT			£2947
115 2/02 Muss 2m	E(0-110)HHdl	SFT			£5746
122 2/00 Folk 2m1f110yE Hdl		G-S			£2604
122 1/00 Folk 2m1f110yE Hdl		SFT			£2422

Total win prize-money £25720

Going: Sf: 0-1 GS: 0-2 Gd: 0-3 GF: - Fm: 0-0
Distance: 2m/2m3: 0-6 2m4-2m7: 0-0 3m+: 0-0
Track: LH: 0-5 RH: 0-1 Tight: 0-1 Gall: 0-1
Aids: Bl: 0-0 Vi: 0-0 Tstrap: 0-0
Best Rating: 142 3/03 Chel 2m1f   good   Hdl

Useful hurdler; suited by soft ground; effective at up to two and a quarter miles. Excelled himself when third in the County Hurdle in 2003.

Throw The Deuce (IRE)
54

6-y-o b g Desert Style (IRE)-Baileys Bride (IRE) (Shy Groom (USA))
G F Edwards G F Edwards

Placings: 0000/6100F000-P   (2453)
2002/03: 19ᴾGS,

	Starts	1st	2nd	3rd	Win & Pl
Hurdles	1	0	0	0	
Career Total	13	1	0	0	6121
101 7/01 Cork 2m	Hdl		G-F		£6120

Total win prize-money £6121

Going: Sf: 0-0 GS: 0-1 Gd: 0-0 GF: - Fm: 0-0
Distance: 2m/2m3: 0-0 2m4-2m7: 0-1 3m+: 0-0
Track: LH: 0-0 RH: 0-1 Tight: 0-1 Gall: 0-0
Aids: Bl: 0-0 Vi: 0-0 Tstrap: 0-0
Best Rating: 101 7/01 Cork 2m   gd-fm   Hdl

Throwaline
103   114

7-y-o b g Thowra (FR)-Stockline (Capricorn Line)
P J Hobbs Yusof Sepiuddin

Placings: 1-2121   (4757)
2002/03: 18²S, 19¹S, 20²G, 22¹GF,

	Starts	1st	2nd	3rd	Win & Pl
Hurdles	4	2	2	0	10489
Career Total	5	3	2	0	12197
101 4/03 Font 2m6f110yE Hdl			G-F		£3570
107 3/03 Hrfd 2m3f110yE Hdl			SFT		£3490
104 2/02 Winc 2m	H NHF		G-S		£1708

Total win prize-money £8769

Going: Sf: 1-2 GS: 0-0 Gd: 0-1 GF: - Fm: 1-1
Distance: 2m/2m3: 0-1 2m4-2m7: 2-3 3m+: 0-0
Track: LH: 1-3 RH: 1-1 Tight: 1-2 Gall: 0-0
Aids: Bl: 0-0 Vi: 0-0 Tstrap: 0-0
Best Rating: 114 4/03 Ayr 2m4f   good   Hdl

Fair novice hurdler; stays two miles-six; acts on any ground.

Thrower
105   108

12-y-o b g Thowra (FR)-Atlantic Line (Capricorn Line)
W M Brisbourne C M & S J Owen

Placings: 4006/5U2444/113131/0/3U053-2U   (3295)
2002/03: 20²S, 19ᵁGS,

	Starts	1st	2nd	3rd	Win & Pl
Hurdles	2	0	1	0	2080
Career Total	24	4	2	4	22340
135 12/97 Hayd 2m4f	B HHdl	SFT			£6820
132 11/97 Hayd 2m4f	C(0-135)HHdl	GD			£3403
123 11/97 Hayd 2m	D(0-120)HHdl	GD			£2773
130 10/97 Bang 2m1f	E(0-110)HHdl	GD			£3533

Total win prize-money £16532

Going: Sf: 0-1 GS: 0-1 Gd: 0-0 GF: - Fm: 0-0
Distance: 2m/2m3: 0-0 2m4-2m7: 0-2 3m+: 0-0
Track: LH: 0-2 RH: 0-0 Tight: 0-0 Gall: 0-0
Aids: Bl: 0-0 Vi: 0-0 Tstrap: 0-0
Best Rating: 135 12/97 Hayd 2m4f   soft   Hdl

One-time useful hurdler at up to two and a half miles. He has been lightly-raced over hurdles in recent seasons and was killed at Doncaster in January. (DEAD)

Thumper (IRE)
104   96

5-y-o b g Grand Lodge (USA)-Parkeen Princess (He Loves Me)
J Mackie (R Hannon 13/9) Mrs Susan Granger

Placings: 2   (4117)
2002/03: 16²G,

	Starts	1st	2nd	3rd	Win & Pl
Hurdles	1	0	1	0	1070
Career Total	1	0	1	0	1070

Going: Sf: 0-0 GS: 0-0 Gd: 0-1 GF: - Fm: 0-0
Distance: 2m/2m3: 0-1 2m4-2m7: 0-0 3m+: 0-0
Track: LH: 0-0 RH: 0-1 Tight: 0-0 Gall: 0-1
Aids: Bl: 0-0 Vi: 0-0 Tstrap: 0-0
Best Rating: 103 3/03 Hntg 2m10y   good   Hdl

Dual winner on the Flat; good effort when second over an extended two miles on his hurdling debut at Huntingdon in March.

Thunder Canyon (USA)

99   **94**

4-y-o b/br g Gulch (USA)-Naazeq (Nashwan (USA))
N G Richards (M Johnston 21/10) A Newby & D Blott

Placings:5223   **(4668)**
2002/03: 16⁶G, 16²S, 18²G, 20³G,

	Starts	1st	2nd	3rd	Win & Pl
Hurdles	4	0	2	1	2857
Career Total	4	0	2	1	2857

Going:	Sf: 0-1 GS: 0-0 Gd: 0-3 GF: - Fm: 0-0
Distance:	2m/2m3: 0-3 2m4-2m7: 0-1 3m+: 0-0
Track:	LH: 0-1 RH: 0-1 Tight: 0-3 Gall: 0-0
Aids:	Bl: 0-0 Vi: 0-0 Tstrap: 0-0
Best Rating:	94 3/03 Kels 2m2f good Hdl

Moderate hurdler; winning stayer on the Flat; fair efforts over hurdles; acts on any ground.

Thundered (USA)

5-y-o gr g Thunder Gulch (USA)-Lady Lianga (USA) (Secretariat (USA))
G A Swinbank Scotnorth Racing Ltd

Placings:P-P   **(0953)**
2002/03: 17PG,

	Starts	1st	2nd	3rd	Win & Pl
Hurdles	1	0	0	0	
Career Total	2	0	0	0	

Going:	Sf: 0-0 GS: 0-0 Gd: 0-1 GF: - Fm: 0-0
Distance:	2m/2m3: 0-1 2m4-2m7: 0-0 3m+: 0-0
Track:	LH: 0-1 RH: 0-0 Tight: 0-1 Gall: 0-0
Aids:	Bl: 0-0 Vi: 0-0 Tstrap: 0-0
Best Rating:	0 8/02 Sedg 2m1f good Hdl

Thundering Jay-Sea

5-y-o ch m First Trump-Thunder Bug (USA) (Secreto (USA))
J R Jenkins C N & Mrs J C Wright

Placings:0   **(1788)**
2002/03: 17PGS,

	Starts	1st	2nd	3rd	Win & Pl
Hurdles	1	0	0	0	
Career Total	1	0	0	0	

Going:	Sf: 0-0 GS: 0-1 Gd: 0-0 GF: - Fm: 0-0
Distance:	2m/2m3: 0-1 2m4-2m7: 0-0 3m+: 0-0
Track:	LH: 0-0 RH: 0-1 Tight: 0-1 Gall: 0-0
Aids:	Bl: 0-0 Vi: 0-0 Tstrap: 0-0
Best Rating:	0 11/02 Folk 2m1f110y gd-sft Hdl

Thunderpoint (IRE)

102(95h)   (71h)**89**

11-y-o b g Glacial Storm (USA)-Urdite (FR) (Concertino (FR))
R J Price P E Shock

Placings:035/2155P25/1FF1300PP/RP00FP/04R022032F4 24P/0F6041344-2452656   **(4735)**
2002/03: 19²GF, 17⁴GS, 16⁵G, 24²S, 21⁶GF, 20⁵G, 19⁶GF,

	Starts	1st	2nd	3rd	Win & Pl
Chases	7	0	2	0	2363

Career Total		55	4	8	4	20817
86	8/01	Bang	2m4f110yF(0-100)HCh	GD	£4348
107	8/98	MRas	2m1f110yF(0-105)HHdl	G-F	£1912
101	5/98	Hexm	2m	E Hdl	GD	£2033
110	10/97	Sedg	2m1f	D Hdl	GD	£2847
			Total win prize-money £11142		

Going:	Sf: 0-1 GS: 0-1 Gd: 0-2 GF: - Fm: 0-3
Distance:	2m/2m3: 0-3 2m4-2m7: 0-3 3m+: 0-1
Track:	LH: 0-3 RH: 0-4 Tight: 0-4 Gall: 0-0
Aids:	Bl: 0-7 Vi: 0-0 Tstrap: 0-0
Best Rating:	110 2/98 Sedg 2m1f good Hdl

Plating-class chaser; one-time fair handicap hurdler; won 2m 4f novice chase at Bangor August 2001; returned from chasing to land 2m 4f selling handicap hurdle at Chepstow May 2003; showed his versatility by landing 2m 3f handicap chase at Hereford in June despite being 8lb wrong ; acts on ground good and faster.

Thursday-Fourball (IRE)

(96h)   (94h)**40**

9-y-o b g Phardante (FR)-Ashville Lady (IRE) (Le Bavard (FR))
R Curtis Eddie Gloyne

Placings:34FPP/U/26PUP0-U0   **(0246)**
2002/03: 25UGS, 22°G,

	Starts	1st	2nd	3rd	Win & Pl
Hurdles	1	0	0	0	0
Chases	1	0	0	0	0
Career Total	14	0	1	1	1269

Going:	Sf: 0-0 GS: 0-1 Gd: 0-1 GF: - Fm: 0-0
Distance:	2m/2m3: 0-0 2m4-2m7: 0-1 3m+: 0-1
Track:	LH: 0-0 RH: 0-2 Tight: 0-0 Gall: 0-0
Aids:	Bl: 0-0 Vi: 0-0 Tstrap: 0-0
Best Rating:	94 10/01 Plum 3m1f110y soft Hdl

Thwaites Star (IRE)

4-y-o b f Petardia-Monterana (Sallust)
R Johnson (A Berry 16/6) Robert Johnson

Placings:P0FP   **(1323)**
2002/03: 17PG, 17°G, 16FG, 17PGF,

	Starts	1st	2nd	3rd	Win & Pl
Hurdles	4	0	0	0	
Career Total	4	0	0	0	

Going:	Sf: 0-0 GS: 0-0 Gd: 0-3 GF: - Fm: 0-1
Distance:	2m/2m3: 0-4 2m4-2m7: 0-0 3m+: 0-0
Track:	LH: 0-3 RH: 0-1 Tight: 0-3 Gall: 0-0
Aids:	Bl: 0-0 Vi: 0-0 Tstrap: 0-0
Best Rating:	0 9/02 MRas 2m1f110y gd-fm Hdl

Thyme Of Hope

52f   **15f**

5-y-o b m Timeless Times (USA)-Wych Willow (Hard Fought)
Mrs M Reveley The Mary Reveley Racing Club

Placings:0   **(3969)**
2002/03: 16°S,

	Starts	1st	2nd	3rd	Win & Pl
NH Flat	1	0	0	0	
Career Total	1	0	0	0	

Going:	Sf: 0-1 GS: 0-0 Gd: 0-0 GF: - Fm: 0-0
Distance:	2m/2m3: 0-1 2m4-2m7: 0-0 3m+: 0-0
Track:	LH: 0-1 RH: 0-0 Tight: 0-1 Gall: 0-0
Aids:	Bl: 0-0 Vi: 0-0 Tstrap: 0-0
Best Rating:	15 3/03 Catt 2m soft NHF

Thyne Will Tell (IRE)

105(105h)   (126h)**141+**

8-y-o ch g Good Thyne (USA)-Deep Khaletta (Deep Run)
P J Hobbs Mrs J F Deithrick

Placings:1/220/111221-11F4   **(4550)**
2002/03: 21¹GF, 21¹G, 21FGS, 20⁴G,

	Starts	1st	2nd	3rd	Win & Pl
Chases	4	2	0	0	16154
Career Total	14	7	4	0	36898
141	10/02	Strf	2m5f110yC(0-135)HCh	GD	£10530
141	8/02	NAbb	2m5f110yD(0-120)HCh	G-F	£4585
118	9/01	Strf	2m5f110yD Ch	G-F	£4208
116	5/01	NAbb	2m6f	E Hdl	G-F	£3045
120	5/01	Winc	2m6f	E Hdl	G-F	£3283
118	5/01	Hrfd	2m3f110yE Hdl	GD	£2800
110	10/99	Gway	2m	NHF	SFT	£3234
			Total win prize-money £31687		

Going:	Sf: 0-0 GS: 0-1 Gd: 1-2 GF: - Fm: 1-1
Distance:	2m/2m3: 0-0 **2m4-2m7: 2-4** 3m+: 0-0
Track:	**LH: 2-3** RH: 0-1 **Tight: 2-2** Gall: 0-0
Aids:	Bl: 0-0 Vi: 0-0 Tstrap: 0-0
Best Rating:	141 10/02 Strf 2m5f110y good Ch

Useful chaser; lightly raced in recent seasons; best at around 2m 5f; effective on a sound surface; his jumping has room for improvement.

Ti Punch

5-y-o b g Jupiter Island-Caipirinha (IRE) (Strong Gale)
A King Miss K N Roydon

Placings:00P   **(3265)**
2002/03: 17°S, 18°HY, 19PGS,

	Starts	1st	2nd	3rd	Win & Pl
NH Flat	2	0	0	0	0
Hurdles	1	0	0	0	0
Career Total	3	0	0	0	

Going:	Sf: 0-2 GS: 0-1 Gd: 0-0 GF: - Fm: 0-0
Distance:	2m/2m3: 0-2 2m4-2m7: 0-1 3m+: 0-0
Track:	LH: 0-2 RH: 0-1 Tight: 0-0 Gall: 0-0
Aids:	Bl: 0-0 Vi: 0-0 Tstrap: 0-0
Best Rating:	56 11/02 Hrfd 2m1f soft NHF

Tianyi (IRE)

99   **83**

7-y-o b g Mujadil (USA)-Skinity (Rarity)
D J Caro (F Jordan 19/6) Eddie Moss

Placings:P0PP-0050012104   **(2712)**
2002/03: 17°G, 16°GS, 16⁵G, 20°G, 16°GF, 16¹F, 16²G, 17¹GF, 16°GS, 16⁴GS,

	Starts	1st	2nd	3rd	Win & Pl
Hurdles	10	2	1	0	6749
Career Total	14	2	1	0	6749
83	10/02	Tntn	2m1f	F(0-100)HHdl	G-F	£2859
71	10/02	Winc	2m	F(0-95)HHdl	FRM	£3038
			Total win prize-money £5898		

Going: Sf: 0-0 GS: 0-3 Gd: 0-4 GF: - Fm: 2-3
Distance: 2m/2m3: 2-9 2m4-2m7: 0-1 3m+: 0-0
Track: LH: 0-5 RH: 2-5 Tight: 1-4 Gall: 0-0
Aids: Bl: 0-2 Vi: 1-2 Tstrap: 0-0
Best Rating: 83 11/02 Chel 2m110y gd-sft Hdl

Plating-class hurdler; landed a gamble on his first start for Dennis Caro at Wincanton in October 2002. Ran well in defeat next time behind a Pipe improver and was allowed his own way out in front again at Taunton. Suited by two miles and fast ground.

Tibbie Lugs

7-y-o ch g Turbo Speed-Tina s Song (Tina s Pet)
F P Murtagh Miss Shelley Johnstone

Placings:0/0-P   (2000)
2002/03: 20ᴾS,

	Starts	1st	2nd	3rd	Win & Pl
Hurdles	1	0	0	0	
Career Total	3	0	0	0	

Going: Sf: 0-1 GS: 0-0 Gd: 0-0 GF: - Fm: 0-0
Distance: 2m/2m3: 0-0 2m4-2m7: 0-1 3m+: 0-0
Track: LH: 0-1 RH: 0-0 Tight: 0-0 Gall: 0-0
Aids: Bl: 0-0 Vi: 0-0 Tstrap: 0-0
Best Rating: 0 11/02 Hayd 2m4f   soft Hdl

Tickton Flyer
107   **101+**

5-y-o b g Sovereign Water (FR)-Contradictory (Reprimand)
M W Easterby T D Rose & A P Foreman

Placings:2-211253   (2302)
2002/03: 16²GS, 17¹GF, 17¹GF, 16²G, 20⁵HY, 19³GS,

	Starts	1st	2nd	3rd	Win & Pl
NH Flat	3	2	1	0	4154
Hurdles	3	0	1	1	1608
Career Total	7	2	3	1	6316
101	9/02	MRas	2m1f110yH NHF	G-F	£1988
101	6/02	MRas	2m1f110yvH NHF	G-F	£1687
			Total win prize-money £3675		

Going: Sf: 0-1 GS: 0-2 Gd: 0-1 GF: - Fm: 2-2
Distance: 2m/2m3: 2-5 2m4-2m7: 0-1 3m+: 0-0
Track: LH: 0-4 RH: 2-2 Tight: 2-5 Gall: 0-0
Aids: Bl: 0-0 Vi: 0-0 Tstrap: 0-0
Best Rating: 101 9/02 MRas 2m1f110y gd-fm NHF

Fair hurdler; bumper winner; stays two and a half miles and will get further; very much suited by fast ground.

Tidal Reef (IRE)

11-y-o br g Tidaro (USA)-Windsor Reef (Take A Reef)
R Fielder R Fielder

Placings:14/PP5P0056-PP0PP   (4467)
2002/03: 22ᴾG, 23ᴾGS, 26⁹GF, 24ᴾGF, 24ᴾF,

	Starts	1st	2nd	3rd	Win & Pl
Hurdles	4	0	0	0	0
Chases	1	0	0	0	0
Career Total	15	1	0	0	2116
87	5/00	Folk	2m5f	H Ch	GD	£2115
			Total win prize-money £2116		

Going: Sf: 0-0 GS: 0-0 Gd: 0-1 GF: 0-1 Fm: 0-3
Distance: 2m/2m3: 0-0 2m4-2m7: 0-1 3m+: 0-4
Track: LH: 0-3 RH: 0-2 Tight: 0-2 Gall: 0-0
Aids: Bl: 0-1 Vi: 0-0 Tstrap: 0-0

Best Rating: 87 5/00 Folk 2m5f   good Ch

Tied For Time (IRE)

11-y-o b g Montelimar (USA)-Cornamucla (Lucky Guy)
A J Walker S Birkinshaw

Placings:0/05P/015-4   (0403)
2002/03: 22⁴GF,

	Starts	1st	2nd	3rd	Win & Pl
Chases	1	0	0	0	0
Career Total	8	1	0	0	1888
86	5/01	Aint	3m1f	H Ch	GD	£1888
			Total win prize-money £1888		

Going: Sf: 0-0 GS: 0-0 Gd: 0-0 GF: - Fm: 0-1
Distance: 2m/2m3: 0-2 2m4-2m7: 0-1 3m+: 0-0
Track: LH: 0-0 RH: 0-1 Tight: 0-1 Gall: 0-0
Aids: Bl: 0-0 Vi: 0-0 Tstrap: 0-0
Best Rating: 86 6/02 MRas 2m6f110y gd-fm Ch

Tier Worker
70   **52**

7-y-o b g Tenby-On The Tide (Slip Anchor)
T D Easterby D F Sills

Placings:P0   (3515)
2002/03: 16⁶GS, 16⁰GS,

	Starts	1st	2nd	3rd	Win & Pl
Hurdles	2	0	0	0	
Career Total	2	0	0	0	

Going: Sf: 0-0 GS: 0-2 Gd: 0-0 GF: - Fm: 0-0
Distance: 2m/2m3: 0-2 2m4-2m7: 0-0 3m+: 0-0
Track: LH: 0-2 RH: 0-0 Tight: 0-0 Gall: 0-0
Aids: Bl: 0-0 Vi: 0-0 Tstrap: 0-0
Best Rating: 52 2/03 Hayd 2m   gd-sft Hdl

Tierna's Respect

11-y-o b g Respect-Tierna s Pet (Laurence O)
G Chambers R A B Brassey

Placings:54P/U0PF-6   (4390)
2002/03: 19⁶F,

	Starts	1st	2nd	3rd	Win & Pl
Chases	1	0	0	0	0
Career Total	8	0	0	0	254

Going: Sf: 0-0 GS: 0-0 Gd: 0-0 GF: - Fm: 0-1
Distance: 2m/2m3: 0-0 2m4-2m7: 0-1 3m+: 0-0
Track: LH: 0-0 RH: 0-1 Tight: 0-0 Gall: 0-0
Aids: Bl: 0-0 Vi: 0-0 Tstrap: 0-0
Best Rating: 67 6/01 MRas 2m6f110y gd-fm Ch

Tifasi (IRE)
95   **71**

13-y-o b g Shardari-Tikrara (USA) (Assert)
K G Wingrove First In Racing Partnership

Placings:0/4214/6P0432/2/P2613/1322340/040/34P-P0 (0778)
2002/03: 16ᴾS, 16⁰GS,

	Starts	1st	2nd	3rd	Win & Pl
Hurdles	2	0	0	0	

Career Total 32 3 6 5 12429
103 11/99 Wwck 2m2f110yG(0-100)HHdl GD £1660
88 3/99 Catt 2m3f G(0-90)HHdl SFT £2262
7/94 Rosc 2m NHF YLD £2611
Total win prize-money £6533

Going: Sf: 0-1 GS: 0-0 Gd: 0-0 GF: - Fm: 0-1
Distance: 2m/2m3: 0-2 2m4-2m7: 0-0 3m+: 0-0
Track: LH: 0-2 RH: 0-0 Tight: 0-1 Gall: 0-0
Aids: Bl: 0-1 Vi: 0-0 Tstrap: 0-0
Best Rating: 103 1/00 Plum 2m   soft Hdl

Tig Hill
67f

7-y-o b g Tigani-Grange Hill Girl (Workboy)
P Beaumont Geoff Pickering

Placings:0   (1982)
2002/03: 16⁰HY,

	Starts	1st	2nd	3rd	Win & Pl
NH Flat	1	0	0	0	
Career Total	1	0	0	0	

Going: Sf: 0-0 GS: 0-0 Gd: 0-0 GF: - Fm: 0-0
Distance: 2m/2m3: 0-1 2m4-2m7: 0-0 3m+: 0-0
Track: LH: 0-1 RH: 0-0 Tight: 0-0 Gall: 0-0
Aids: Bl: 0-0 Vi: 0-0 Tstrap: 0-0
Best Rating: 67 11/02 Weth 2m   heavy NHF

Tiger Frog (USA)
95   **82**

4-y-o b g French Deputy (USA)-Woodyoubelieveit (USA) (Woodman (USA))
R C Guest (N B Mason 25/1) N B Mason

Placings:6000   (3783)
2002/03: 16⁶G, 16⁰G, 16⁰GS, 17⁰G,

	Starts	1st	2nd	3rd	Win & Pl
Hurdles	4	0	0	0	0
Career Total	4	0	0	0	0

Going: Sf: 0-1 GS: 0-1 Gd: 0-2 GF: - Fm: 0-0
Distance: 2m/2m3: 0-4 2m4-2m7: 0-0 3m+: 0-0
Track: LH: 0-3 RH: 0-1 Tight: 0-0 Gall: 0-2
Aids: Bl: 0-0 Vi: 0-0 Tstrap: 0-0
Best Rating: 82 11/02 Hayd 2m   good Hdl

Well beaten in juvenile hurdles but may be capable of better in time.

Tiger Grass (IRE)
108   **123+**

7-y-o gr g Ezzoud (IRE)-Rustic Lawn (Rusticaro (FR))
M C Pipe (W R Muir 22/5) M J Caddy

Placings:31P/553231106/P0633PP066-P1111223 (1802)
2002/03: 23⁶PG, 21¹S, 22¹G, 26¹GF, 24¹GF, 24²F, 25²G, 22³S,

	Starts	1st	2nd	3rd	Win & Pl
Hurdles	7	4	2	1	17144
Chases	1	0	0	0	
Career Total	30	7	3	6	29166
116	9/02	Prth	3m110y D(0-115)HHdl	G-F	£5525
111	9/02	Hrfd	3m2f E(0-110)HHdl	G-F	£3500
104	9/02	NAbb	2m6f G Hdl	GD	£2170
117	10/02	MRas	2m5f110yG(0-90)HHdl	SFT	£2226
119	10/00	Plum	3m1f110yD(0-120)HHdl	SFT	£3136
116	10/00	Sthl	2m4f110yE(0-115)HHdl	G-S	£2289
115	12/99	Plum	2m E Hdl	HVY	£2582
			Total win prize-money £21429		

Going: Sf: 1-2 GS: 0-0 Gd: 1-3 GF: - Fm: 2-3
Distance: 2m/2m3: 0-0 2m4-2m7: 2-3 3m+: 2-5
Track: LH: 1-3 RH: 3-4 Tight: 2-3 Gall: 0-0
Aids: Bl: 0-0 Vi: 4-7 Tstrap: 0-0
Best Rating: 123 10/02 Extr 3m110y   firm   Hdl

Fair hurdler; slipping down the ratings before taking a Market Rasen seller on his first run for Pipe. Went on to complete a four-timer with wins in ordinary handicaps. Stays well, but requires a lot of driving.

Tiger Rouge
5

8-y-o ch g Kinglet-Lake View Lady (Little Buskins)
M Pitman Mrs Kay Birchenhough

Placings:0P0-P   (0172)
2002/03: 20PG,

	Starts	1st	2nd	3rd	Win & Pl
Hurdles	1	0	0	0	
Career Total	4	0	0	0	

Going: Sf: 0-0 GS: 0-0 Gd: 0-1 GF: - Fm: 0-0
Distance: 2m/2m3: 0-0 2m4-2m7: 0-1 3m+: 0-0
Track: LH: 0-1 RH: 0-0 Tight: 0-1 Gall: 0-0
Aids: Bl: 0-0 Vi: 0-0 Tstrap: 0-0
Best Rating: 63 1/02 Towc 2m   heavy   NHF

Tiger Talk
103(91c)   (79c)**82**

7-y-o ch g Sabrehill (USA)-Tebre (USA) (Sir Ivor)
M E Sowersby The Southwold Set

Placings:U453604P0/2630300063-1351PP052P0645   (4711)
2002/03: 171GF, 163G, 165GS, 171GF, 17PGF, 21PGF, 160G, 175S, 172S, 162G, 199GS, 206GF, 174G, 165GF,

	Starts	1st	2nd	3rd	Win & Pl
Hurdles	10	2	0	1	6455
Chases	4	0	1	0	1490
Career Total	33	2	2	5	11120
89	6/02 MRas	2m1f110yE(0-100)HHdl		G-F	£2635
93	5/02 Sedg	2m1f F(0-100)HHdl		G-F	£2219
				Total win prize-money	£4855

Going: Sf: 0-2 GS: 0-2 Gd: 0-4 GF: - Fm: 2-6
Distance: 2m/2m3: 2-11 2m4-2m7: 0-3 3m+: 0-0
Track: LH: 1-10 RH: 1-4 Tight: 2-9 Gall: 0-0
Aids: Bl: 1-4 Vi: 0-0 Tstrap: 0-0
Best Rating: 98 11/00 Newc 2m   gd-sft   Hdl

Plating-class hurdler/chaser, stays two and a half miles; suited by a sound surface; has worn blinkers.

Tiger Typhoon (IRE)
90(86h)   (76+h)**76**

7-y-o b g Cataldi-Churchtown Breeze (Tarqogan)
R J Hodges Mrs Anna L Sanders

Placings:0/3-03PU3   (4701)
2002/03: 160G, 173GS, 16PGS, 16UGS, 203GF,

	Starts	1st	2nd	3rd	Win & Pl
Hurdles	2	0	0	1	506
Chases	3	0	0	1	474
Career Total	7	0	0	3	1290

Going: Sf: 0-0 GS: 0-3 Gd: 0-1 GF: - Fm: 0-1
Distance: 2m/2m3: 0-4 2m4-2m7: 0-1 3m+: 0-0
Track: LH: 0-1 RH: 0-4 Tight: 0-3 Gall: 0-0

Aids: Bl: 0-0 Vi: 0-0 Tstrap: 0-0
Best Rating: 80 8/01 NAbb 2m1f   gd-fm   NHF

Tigerburningbright (IRE)

9-y-o b g Strong Gale-Ring Road (Giolla Mear)
J R Adam Mrs Ray Calder

Placings:006/PPP   (2180)
2002/03: 20PGS, 22PS, 20PGS,

	Starts	1st	2nd	3rd	Win & Pl
Hurdles	2	0	0	0	0
Chases	1	0	0	0	0
Career Total	6	0	0	0	0

Going: Sf: 0-1 GS: 0-2 Gd: 0-0 GF: - Fm: 0-0
Distance: 2m/2m3: 0-0 2m4-2m7: 0-3 3m+: 0-0
Track: LH: 0-3 RH: 0-0 Tight: 0-2 Gall: 0-0
Aids: Bl: 0-0 Vi: 0-0 Tstrap: 0-0
Best Rating: 103 11/99 Ayr 2m   good   Hdl

Tighten Your Belt (IRE)
111f

6-y-o b g Phardante (FR)-Hi Upham (Deep Run)
Miss Venetia Williams The MerseyClyde Partnership

Placings:13   (4481)
2002/03: 161GS, 173G,

	Starts	1st	2nd	3rd	Win & Pl
NH Flat	2	1	0	1	6823
Career Total	2	1	0	1	6823
111	3/03 Strf	2m110y H NHF		G-S	£3523
				Total win prize-money	£3523

Going: Sf: 0-0 GS: 1-1 Gd: 0-1 GF: - Fm: 0-0
Distance: 2m/2m3: 1-2 2m4-2m7: 0-0 3m+: 0-0
Track: LH: 0-0 RH: 0-0 Tight: 0-0 Gall: 0-0
Aids: Bl: 0-0 Vi: 0-0 Tstrap: 0-0
Best Rating: 111 4/03 Aint 2m1f   good   NHF

Modest bumper performer; winner of a Stratford bumper on his debut under Rules; winner of an Irish point; half-brother to high-class chaser Native Upmanship and looks a fine long term prospect.

Tik-A-Tai (IRE)
108(110c)   (125c)**128**

8-y-o b g Alphabatim (USA)-Carrig Ross (Lord Ha Ha)
O Sherwood The Chamberlain Addiscott Partnership

Placings:1PP/14221P-5313P   (3178)
2002/03: 22G, 213G, 221GS, 223S, 21PG,

	Starts	1st	2nd	3rd	Win & Pl
Hurdles	3	1	0	1	4710
Chases	2	0	0	1	1620
Career Total	14	4	2	2	24166
128	11/02 Font	2m6f110yE(0-110)HHdl		G-S	£3157
128	2/02 Ludl	2m4f D(0-125)HCh		G-S	£5369
118	10/01 Fknm	2m5f110yC Ch		SFT	£6776
123	10/00 Font	2m6f110yE Hdl		G-S	£2338
				Total win prize-money	£17640

Going: Sf: 0-1 GS: 1-1 Gd: 0-3 GF: - Fm: 0-0
Distance: 2m/2m3: 0-0 2m4-2m7: 1-5 3m+: 0-0
Track: LH: 1-4 RH: 0-1 Tight: 1-3 Gall: 0-0
Aids: Bl: 0-0 Vi: 0-0 Tstrap: 0-0
Best Rating: 128 11/02 Font 2m6f110y   gd-sft   Hdl

Fair chaser/hurdler, suited by up to three miles, but not the best of jumpers. Successfully returned to hurdles at Fontwell in November 2002. Stays well and likes cut in the ground.

Tiki Tapu
88f

5-y-o b m Karinga Bay-Hy Wilma (Jalmood (USA))
R J Hodges Mrs C J Coles

Placings:3   (1549)
2002/03: 173F,

	Starts	1st	2nd	3rd	Win & Pl
NH Flat	1	0	0	1	318
Career Total	1	0	0	1	318

Going: Sf: 0-0 GS: 0-0 Gd: 0-0 GF: - Fm: 0-1
Distance: 2m/2m3: 0-1 2m4-2m7: 0-0 3m+: 0-0
Track: LH: 0-0 RH: 0-0 Tight: 0-0 Gall: 0-0
Aids: Bl: 0-0 Vi: 0-0 Tstrap: 0-0
Best Rating: 88 10/02 Tntn 2m1f   firm   NHF

Tikram
113   **139**

6-y-o ch g Lycius (USA)-Black Fighter (USA) (Secretariat (USA))
G L Moore Mike Charlton And Rodger Sargent

Placings:2316/22360-42P4014360   (4475)
2002/03: 164G, 162G, 16PS, 164G, 16PHY, 181G, 164HY, 163G, 16PHY, 20PG,

	Starts	1st	2nd	3rd	Win & Pl
Hurdles	10	1	1	1	37869
Career Total	19	2	4	3	70023
137	12/02 Font	2m2f110yC(0-130)HHdl		GD	£12087
120	1/01 Donc	2m110y C Hdl		GD	£6305
				Total win prize-money	£18392

Going: Sf: 0-4 GS: 0-0 Gd: 1-6 GF: - Fm: 0-0
Distance: 2m/2m3: 1-9 2m4-2m7: 0-0 3m+: 0-0
Track: LH: 1-6 RH: 0-4 Tight: 1-3 Gall: 0-1
Aids: Bl: 0-1 Vi: 0-0 Tstrap: 0-0
Best Rating: 139 2/03 Newb 2m110y   good   Hdl

Useful handicap hurdler; suited by around two miles and acts on soft ground, although is better on good ground; has run well on more than one occasion in some good handicaps but has found winning difficult; got his head in front at Fontwell in December 2002 and ran well in the Tote Gold Trophy; pulled too hard when tried in blinkers.

Tilanjani (IRE)
60

6-y-o ch g Indian Ridge-Tijara (IRE) (Darshaan)
K A Morgan S Giles

Placings:0/46250005-P   (0251)
2002/03: 16PGF,

	Starts	1st	2nd	3rd	Win & Pl
Hurdles	1	0	0	0	
Career Total	10	0	1	0	420

Going: Sf: 0-0 GS: 0-0 Gd: 0-0 GF: - Fm: 0-1
Distance: 2m/2m3: 0-1 2m4-2m7: 0-0 3m+: 0-0
Track: LH: 0-0 RH: 0-1 Tight: 0-0 Gall: 0-0
Aids: Bl: 0-0 Vi: 0-1 Tstrap: 0-0
Best Rating: 80 7/01 Uttx 2m   gd-fm   NHF

Tim's The Man (IRE)
99   93

7-y-o gr g Roselier (FR)-Pindas (Bargello)
C J Mann The Life Of Riley Partnership

Placings:3540-1042   (3938)
2002/03: 16¹HY, 19⁰G, 19⁴S, 21¹²GS,

	Starts	1st	2nd	3rd	Win & Pl
Hurdles	4	1	1	0	5010
Career Total	8	1	1	1	5542
109 11/02 Leic	2m	E Hdl		HVY	£3552
				Total win prize-money	£3552

Going:	Sf: 1-2 GS: 0-1 Gd: 0-1 GF: - Fm: 0-0
Distance:	**2m/2m3: 1-2** 2m4-2m7: 0-2 3m+: 0-0
Track:	LH: 0-0 **RH: 1-3** Tight: 0-2 Gall: 0-1
Aids:	Bl: 0-0 Vi: 0-0 Tstrap: 0-0
Best Rating:	109 11/02 Leic 2m heavy Hdl

Plating-class ex-Irish gelding, winner of a heavy-ground
novice hurdle at Leicester in November 2002; sure to relish
a test of stamina.

Timber Street (IRE)

6-y-o b/br g Montelimar (USA)-Ware Star (IRE) (Torus)
M Pitman Five Arrows Racing

Placings:2P   (1710)
2002/03: 17²GF, 22⁰G,

	Starts	1st	2nd	3rd	Win & Pl
NH Flat	1	0	1	0	534
Hurdles	1	0	0	0	0
Career Total	2	0	1	0	534

Going:	Sf: 0-0 GS: 0-0 Gd: 0-1 GF: - Fm: 0-1
Distance:	2m/2m3: 0-0 2m4-2m7: 0-1 3m+: 0-0
Track:	LH: 0-1 RH: 0-0 Tight: 0-1 Gall: 0-0
Aids:	Bl: 0-0 Vi: 0-0 Tstrap: 0-0
Best Rating:	82 10/02 Hrfd 2m1f gd-fm NHF

Out of an unraced sister to Bradbury Star. Proved no match
for the useful Phar From Fair on his bumper debut at
Hereford October 2002.

Timbourine

5-y-o ch m Hatim (USA)-Persian Symphony (IRE) (Persian
Heights)
C R Wilson A E Lea

Placings:00P   (0916)
2002/03: 16⁰G, 17⁰GF, 20⁰GS,

	Starts	1st	2nd	3rd	Win & Pl
NH Flat	2	0	0	0	0
Hurdles	1	0	0	0	0
Career Total	3	0	0	0	

Going:	Sf: 0-0 GS: 0-1 Gd: 0-0 GF: - Fm: 0-1
Distance:	2m/2m3: 0-2 2m4-2m7: 0-1 3m+: 0-0
Track:	LH: 0-2 RH: 0-1 Tight: 0-0 Gall: 0-0
Aids:	Bl: 0-0 Vi: 0-0 Tstrap: 0-0
Best Rating:	27 6/02 Hexm 2m110y good NHF

Time After Thyne

10-y-o b g Good Thyne (USA)-Lady Solstice (Vital Season)
Ferdy Murphy E Birkbeck & Sir D Landale

Placings:4/06/0/F5P/0-P   (2260)
2002/03: 22²HY,

	Starts	1st	2nd	3rd	Win & Pl
Hurdles	1	0	0	0	
Career Total	9	0	0	0	0

Going:	Sf: 0-1 GS: 0-0 Gd: 0-0 GF: - Fm: 0-0
Distance:	2m/2m3: 0-0 2m4-2m7: 0-1 3m+: 0-0
Track:	LH: 0-1 RH: 0-0 Tight: 0-1 Gall: 0-0
Aids:	Bl: 0-0 Vi: 0-0 Tstrap: 0-0
Best Rating:	99 3/98 Ayr 2m gd-sft NHF

Time Can Tell
81   83

9-y-o ch g Sylvan Express-Stellaris (Star Appeal)
A G Juckes Mrs K C Price

Placings:5/6/3P-60   (0444)
2002/03: 27⁵G, 19⁰G,

	Starts	1st	2nd	3rd	Win & Pl
Hurdles	2	0	0	0	0
Career Total	6	0	0	1	359

Going:	Sf: 0-0 GS: 0-0 Gd: 0-1 GF: - Fm: 0-1
Distance:	2m/2m3: 0-0 2m4-2m7: 0-1 3m+: 0-1
Track:	LH: 0-0 RH: 0-1 Tight: 0-1 Gall: 0-0
Aids:	Bl: 0-0 Vi: 0-0 Tstrap: 0-0
Best Rating:	83 12/01 Hrfd 2m3f110y good Hdl

Time Marches On
98   89

5-y-o b g Timeless Times (USA)-Tees Gazette Girl
(Kalaglow)
Mrs M Reveley Mrs M B Thwaites

Placings:610   (2473)
2002/03: 17⁶G, 16¹S, 16⁰G,

	Starts	1st	2nd	3rd	Win & Pl
Hurdles	3	1	0	0	3471
Career Total	3	1	0	0	3471
89 11/02 Kels	2m110y	G Hdl		SFT	£3471
				Total win prize-money	£3471

Going:	Sf: 1-1 GS: 0-0 Gd: 0-2 GF: - Fm: 0-0
Distance:	**2m/2m3: 1-3** 2m4-2m7: 0-0 3m+: 0-0
Track:	**LH: 1-3** RH: 0-0 **Tight: 1-2** Gall: 0-1
Aids:	Bl: 0-0 Vi: 0-0 Tstrap: 0-0
Best Rating:	89 11/02 Kels 2m110y soft Hdl

Plating-class hurdler; acts on soft.

Time N Tide (IRE)
105   122d

7-y-o b g Namaqualand (USA)-Now Then (Sandford Lad)
Jonjo O Neill Mcourt Fine Meats Ltd & D J Rushen

Placings:6512312/500/53-101P0   (4441)
2002/03: 17¹S, 20⁴HY, 19¹GS, 23⁶GS, 20⁶G,

	Starts	1st	2nd	3rd	Win & Pl
Hurdles	5	2	0	0	10556
Career Total	17	4	2	2	25182
122 1/03 Donc	2m3f110yC(0-135)HHdl	G-S	£7143
121 11/02 Bang	2m1f	E(0-110)HHdl	SFT	£3412
104 4/00 Ludl	2m	D Hdl	GD	£2925
117 1/00 Donc	2m110y	C Hdl	GD	£5876
				Total win prize-money	£19358

Going:	Sf: 1-2 GS: 1-2 Gd: 0-1 GF: - Fm: 0-0
Distance:	2m/2m3: 1-1 2m4-2m7: 1-3 3m+: 0-1

Track:	LH: 2-3 RH: 0-1 Tight: 1-2 Gall: 0-0
Aids:	Bl: 0-0 Vi: 0-0 Tstrap: 0-0
Best Rating:	122 1/03 Donc 2m3f110y gd-sft Hdl

Fair handicap hurdler; stays two and a half miles and acts
on soft ground.

Time Of Flight (IRE)
104   129d

10-y-o ch g Over The River (FR)-Icy Lou (Blue Rullah)
Mrs M Reveley Andy Peake & David Jackson

Placings:150/33UP41/215P4P/25112233F-044   (4229)
2002/03: 16⁰GS, 20⁴G, 16⁴GF,

	Starts	1st	2nd	3rd	Win & Pl
Hurdles	1	0	0	0	0
Chases	2	0	0	0	847
Career Total	27	5	4	4	32755
120 11/01 Weth	2m	C(0-135)HCh	GD	£7085
109 11/01 Carl	2m	D(0-125)HCh	G-S	£3900
127 10/00 Weth	2m4f110yC(0-130)HCh	HVY	£5882
110 3/00 Newc	2m	E Hdl	GD	£2684
111 12/98 Newc	2m	H NHF	SFT	£1318
				Total win prize-money	£20872

Going:	Sf: 0-0 GS: 0-1 Gd: 0-1 GF: - Fm: 0-1
Distance:	2m/2m3: 0-2 2m4-2m7: 0-1 3m+: 0-0
Track:	LH: 0-3 RH: 0-0 Tight: 0-0 Gall: 0-0
Aids:	Bl: 0-0 Vi: 0-0 Tstrap: 0-0
Best Rating:	129 11/01 Weth 2m good Ch

Fair chaser; best over two miles, but does stay further; acts
on ground good or softer; best when held up.

Time Temptress
66

7-y-o b m Timeless Times (USA)-Tangalooma (Hotfoot)
I W McInnes I W McInnes

Placings:4543P/02565-P   (0379)
2002/03: 21²G,

	Starts	1st	2nd	3rd	Win & Pl
Hurdles	1	0	0	0	0
Career Total	11	0	1	1	874

Going:	Sf: 0-0 GS: 0-0 Gd: 0-1 GF: - Fm: 0-0
Distance:	2m/2m3: 0-0 2m4-2m7: 0-1 3m+: 0-0
Track:	LH: 0-0 RH: 0-1 Tight: 0-0 Gall: 0-1
Aids:	Bl: 0-1 Vi: 0-0 Tstrap: 0-0
Best Rating:	74 11/01 Weth 2m7f good Hdl

Time To Parlez
110   78

12-y-o b g Amboise-Image Of War (Warpath)
C J Drewe Mrs J Strange

Placings:00/6/PPP44/P02250/B532P1PP/021UPP4P-
6P0P136024   (4761)
2002/03: 26⁶G, 26⁶G, 32⁰GS, 26⁶HY, 26¹S, 26³S, 24⁶GS, 26⁶GS,
28²G, 26⁴GF,

	Starts	1st	2nd	3rd	Win & Pl
Chases	10	1	1	1	5126
Career Total	40	3	5	2	18173
78 1/03 Plum	3m2f	F(0-90)HCh	SFT	£3276
86 12/01 Towc	3m1f	F(0-110)HCh	HVY	£4438
86 1/01 Font	3m2f110yF(0-100)HCh	SFT	£2847
				Total win prize-money	£10561

Going:	Sf: 1-3 GS: 0-3 Gd: 0-3 GF: - Fm: 0-1
Distance:	2m/2m3: 0-0 2m4-2m7: 0-0 **3m+: 1-10**
Track:	**LH: 1-5** RH: 0-2 Tight: 1-3 Gall: 0-0

Aids: Bl: 0-0 Vi: 0-0 Tstrap: 0-0
Best Rating: 93 12/97 Chep 2m4f110y heavy Hdl

Plating-class chaser; stays well; likes to front run.

Time To Tell

(83h) (55h)
7-y-o b m Keen-Meet Again (Lomond (USA))
B G Powell (Mrs Lydia Pearce 3/2) D Coles, P Moore, J King, J Whittle

Placings: 040P5 (4366)
2002/03: 16⁰G, 16⁴GS, 18⁰S, 22⁸GF, 20⁵G,

	Starts	1st	2nd	3rd	Win & Pl
NH Flat	2	0	0	0	0
Hurdles	3	0	0	0	0
Career Total	5	0	0	0	0

Going: Sf: 0-1 GS: 0-1 Gd: 0-2 GF: - Fm: 0-1
Distance: 2m/2m3: 0-3 2m4-2m7: 0-2 3m+: 0-0
Track: LH: 0-2 RH: 0-3 Tight: 0-2 Gall: 0-0
Aids: Bl: 0-0 Vi: 0-0 Tstrap: 0-0
Best Rating: 83 12/02 Fknm 2m gd-sft NHF

Timeless Chick

100 81
6-y-o ch m Timeless Times (USA)-Be My Bird (Be My Chief (USA))
J L Spearing Be Luckies

Placings: 55343P0-5326 (2067)
2002/03: 17⁵GF, 17³G, 17²G, 21⁶GS,

	Starts	1st	2nd	3rd	Win & Pl
Hurdles	4	0	1	1	970
Career Total	11	0	1	3	1524

Going: Sf: 0-0 GS: 0-1 Gd: 0-2 GF: 0-1 Fm: 0-1
Distance: 2m/2m3: 0-3 2m4-2m7: 0-3 3m+: 0-0
Track: LH: 0-0 RH: 0-4 Tight: 0-2 Gall: 0-0
Aids: Bl: 0-0 Vi: 0-0 Tstrap: 0-0
Best Rating: 84 12/01 Hrfd 2m1f good Hdl

Poor selling hurdler.

Times Past (IRE)

8-y-o b g Commanche Run-Orient Moonbeam (Deep Run)
Mrs Edward Crow M J Parr

Placings: 14-4 (0055)
2002/03: 24⁴G,

	Starts	1st	2nd	3rd	Win & Pl
Chases	1	0	0	0	116
Career Total	3	1	0	0	4398
103 6/01 Navn 2m			NHF		YLD £3895
				Total win prize-money £3895	

Going: Sf: 0-0 GS: 0-0 Gd: 0-1 GF: - Fm: 0-0
Distance: 2m/2m3: 0-3 2m4-2m7: 0-0 3m+: 0-1
Track: LH: 0-1 RH: 0-0 Tight: 0-1 Gall: 0-0
Aids: Bl: 0-0 Vi: 0-0 Tstrap: 0-0
Best Rating: 106 9/01 List 2m gd-fm Hdl

Novice hunter chaser; Irish bumper winner and twice successful between the flags; acts on a sound surafce; stays three miles.

Timidjar (IRE)

108 76
10-y-o b g Doyoun-Timissara (USA) (Shahrastani (USA))
Mrs D Thomas Mrs D Thomas

Placings: 603/236P/2006/26011/1440/0040000-00033 (4679)
2002/03: 16⁰G, 16⁰HY, 19⁰GS, 17³GF, 16³GF,

	Starts	1st	2nd	3rd	Win & Pl
Hurdles	5	0	0	2	853
Career Total	32	3	3	4	9682
100 5/00	Hrfd	2m1f	G(0-95)HHdl	GD	£2100
99 4/00	Hrfd	2m1f	G Hdl	GD	£2159
95 3/00	NAbb	2m1f	F(0-100)HHdl	GD	£1862
				Total win prize-money £6122	

Going: Sf: 0-1 GS: 0-1 Gd: 0-1 GF: - Fm: 0-2
Distance: 2m/2m3: 0-4 2m4-2m7: 0-1 3m+: 0-2
Track: LH: 0-2 RH: 0-3 Tight: 0-1 Gall: 0-1
Aids: Bl: 0-0 Vi: 0-0 Tstrap: 0-0
Best Rating: 102 5/97 Chep 2m110y good Hdl

Selling hurdler; has struggled since completing a hat-trick in the spring of 2000; signs of a return to form in the spring of 2003; acts on good ground.

Timpani (IRE)

98 87+
7-y-o b g Broken Hearted-Queen Kam (IRE) (Kambalda)
M C Pipe John Duggan

Placings: 06/P5-43P0 (1441)
2002/03: 18⁴GF, 24³G, 22²GF, 19⁰F,

	Starts	1st	2nd	3rd	Win & Pl
Hurdles	4	0	0	1	404
Career Total	8	0	0	1	404

Going: Sf: 0-0 GS: 0-0 Gd: 0-1 GF: - Fm: 0-3
Distance: 2m/2m3: 0-2 2m4-2m7: 0-1 3m+: 0-1
Track: LH: 0-3 RH: 0-1 Tight: 0-2 Gall: 0-0
Aids: Bl: 0-0 Vi: 0-0 Tstrap: 0-0
Best Rating: 95 1/01 Kemp 2m soft NHF

Tin Symphony

103f 88f
5-y-o ch m Opera Ghost-Bronze Age (Celtic Cone)
B J M Ryall The Wessex Cornflower Partnership

Placings: U05 (4329)
2002/03: 18ᵁS, 19⁰GS, 16⁵G,

	Starts	1st	2nd	3rd	Win & Pl
NH Flat	3	0	0	0	0
Career Total	3	0	0	0	0

Going: Sf: 0-1 GS: 0-1 Gd: 0-1 GF: - Fm: 0-0
Distance: 2m/2m3: 0-3 2m4-2m7: 0-0 3m+: 0-0
Track: LH: 0-3 RH: 0-0 Tight: 0-2 Gall: 0-1
Aids: Bl: 0-0 Vi: 0-0 Tstrap: 0-0
Best Rating: 88 3/03 Newb 2m110y good NHF

Tina Cooke

91 (89h) (62h) 73
7-y-o gr m Tina s Pet-Up Cooke (Deep Run)
Miss Kate Milligan Mrs J M L Milligan

Placings: 50-P0404P (4418)
2002/03: 16⁰G, 17⁰G, 22⁴S, 16⁰S, 20⁴GF, 22⁸G,

	Starts	1st	2nd	3rd	Win & Pl
Hurdles	6	0	0	0	310

Career Total 8 0 0 0 310

Going: Sf: 0-2 GS: 0-0 Gd: 0-3 GF: - Fm: 0-1
Distance: 2m/2m3: 0-3 2m4-2m7: 0-3 3m+: 0-0
Track: LH: 0-5 RH: 0-0 Tight: 0-4 Gall: 0-1
Aids: Bl: 0-0 Vi: 0-0 Tstrap: 0-0
Best Rating: 85 1/02 Muss 2m good NHF

Held in bumpers and hurdles.

Tina Thyne (IRE)

(99h) (89h)
9-y-o b m Good Thyne (USA)-Tiny Tina (Deep Run)
J G M O Shea (T P Tate 3/5) Gary Roberts

Placings: 12/0042326-5524146 (4465)
2002/03: 21⁵GF, 16⁵HY, 16²HY, 19⁴G, 19¹HY, 16⁴S, 24⁶F,

	Starts	1st	2nd	3rd	Win & Pl
Hurdles	7	1	1	0	5025
Career Total	16	2	4	1	12790
89 3/03	Tntn	2m3f110yE Hdl		HVY	£4322
107 3/00	Uttx	2m	H NHF	GD	£1610
				Total win prize-money £5933	

Going: Sf: 1-4 GS: 0-0 Gd: 0-1 GF: - Fm: 0-2
Distance: 2m/2m3: 0-3 2m4-2m7: 1-3 3m+: 0-1
Track: LH: 0-4 RH: 1-3 Tight: 1-3 Gall: 0-0
Aids: Bl: 0-1 Vi: 0-1 Tstrap: 0-0
Best Rating: 119 4/00 Chel 2m1f soft NHF

Plating-class hurdler; winner of a bumper in 2000; had headgear left off when winning 19 furlong mares only maiden at Taunton March 2003; acts on ground good and softer.

Tina's Indian (IRE)

58
5-y-o b m Indian Ridge-Tina s Charm (IRE) (Hatim (USA))
B G Powell Mrs Chris Harrington

Placings: FU0 (1869)
2002/03: 16⁶GF, 16ᵁG, 18⁰GS,

	Starts	1st	2nd	3rd	Win & Pl
Hurdles	3	0	0	0	0
Career Total	3	0	0	0	0

Going: Sf: 0-0 GS: 0-1 Gd: 0-1 GF: - Fm: 0-1
Distance: 2m/2m3: 0-3 2m4-2m7: 0-0 3m+: 0-0
Track: LH: 0-3 RH: 0-0 Tight: 0-3 Gall: 0-0
Aids: Bl: 0-0 Vi: 0-0 Tstrap: 0-0
Best Rating: 0 11/02 Font 2m2f110y gd-sft Hdl

Tina's Scallywag

97 57
6-y-o br m Baron Blakeney-Southend Scallywag (Tina s Pet)
R C Guest (N B Mason 24/1) N B Mason

Placings: 00006P (3992)
2002/03: 17⁰GF, 20⁶S, 19⁰GS, 16⁰GS, 25⁶G, 25⁶G,

	Starts	1st	2nd	3rd	Win & Pl
NH Flat	1	0	0	0	0
Hurdles	5	0	0	0	0
Career Total	6	0	0	0	0

Going: Sf: 0-1 GS: 0-2 Gd: 0-2 GF: - Fm: 0-1
Distance: 2m/2m3: 0-4 2m4-2m7: 0-2 3m+: 0-2
Track: LH: 0-5 RH: 0-1 Tight: 0-2 Gall: 0-1
Aids: Bl: 0-0 Vi: 0-0 Tstrap: 0-0
Best Rating: 67 9/02 MRas 2m1f110y gd-fm NHF

Tindles Bible

(88h)   (68h)**82**
11-y-o b g Le Coq D Or-Wedderburn (Royalty)
J S Wainwright Keith Jackson

Placings:2262/3F-P446   (2421)
2002/03: 23PGF, 23⁴HY, 27⁴S, 27⁶S,

	Starts	1st	2nd	3rd	Win & Pl
Hurdles	3	0	0	0	0
Chases	1	0	0	0	
Career Total	10	0	3	1	2768

Going:	Sf: 0-3 GS: 0-0 Gd: 0-1 GF: - Fm: 0-0
Distance:	2m/2m3: 0-0 2m4-2m7: 0-2 3m+: 0-2
Track:	LH: 0-4 RH: 0-0 Tight: 0-2 Gall: 0-0
Aids:	Bl: 0-0 Vi: 0-1 Tstrap: 0-0
Best Rating:	103 3/98 Bang 3m gd-sft Hdl

Well-related and lightly raced, he looks only moderate..

Tino (IRE)

108(73h)   (72h)**85**
7-y-o ch g Torus-Delphic Thunder (Viking (USA))
J S King Robert Skillen

Placings:0/00P3536-P10032   (4537)
2002/03: 21PGG, 21¹GF, 25⁰G, 19⁰G, 24³F, 24²G,

	Starts	1st	2nd	3rd	Win & Pl
Chases	6	1	1	1	4675
Career Total	14	1	1	3	5794
85 11/02 Folk	2m5f	F(0-95)HCh	G-F	£4104	

Total win prize-money £4105

Going:	Sf: 0-0 GS: 0-0 Gd: 0-3 GF: - Fm: 1-3
Distance:	2m/2m3: 0-1 2m4-2m7: 1-2 3m+: 0-3
Track:	LH: 0-0 RH: 1-6 Tight: 1-4 Gall: 0-0
Aids:	Bl: 0-0 Vi: 0 Tstrap: 0-0
Best Rating:	90 3/02 Hntg 2m4f110y gd-fm Ch

Very moderate chaser; stays three miles; acts on fast ground.

Tinoveritas (FR)

90f   107f
5-y-o b g Saint Estephe (FR)-Tinorosa (FR) (Concertino (FR))
P F Nicholls C G Roach

Placings:20   (2718)
2002/03: 13²S, 16⁰HY,

	Starts	1st	2nd	3rd	Win & Pl
NH Flat	2	0	1	0	781
Career Total	2	0	1	0	781

Going:	Sf: 0-2 GS: 0-0 Gd: 0-0 GF: - Fm: 0-0
Distance:	2m/2m3: 0-1 2m4-2m7: 0-0 3m+: 0-0
Track:	LH: 0-1 RH: 0-1 Tight: 0-0 Gall: 0-0
Aids:	Bl: 0-0 Vi: 0-0 Tstrap: 0-0
Best Rating:	107 12/02 Extr 1m5f soft NHF

Modest bumper performer; from a winning family; held on well when winning Worcester bumper May 2003; acts on soft ground; will go hurdling in the autumn.

Tiobraid Arann

6-y-o b g Au Bon-Babs Reflection4 Vii (Damsire Unregistered)
A W Carroll Mrs P Izamis

Placings:00   (0660)
2002/03: 16⁰G, 16⁰GF,

	Starts	1st	2nd	3rd	Win & Pl
NH Flat	2	0	0	0	
Career Total	2	0	0	0	

Going:	Sf: 0-0 GS: 0-0 Gd: 0-1 GF: - Fm: 0-1
Distance:	2m/2m3: 0-2 2m4-2m7: 0-0 3m+: 0-0
Track:	LH: 0-2 RH: 0-0 Tight: 0-0 Gall: 0-0
Aids:	Bl: 0-0 Vi: 0-0 Tstrap: 0-0
Best Rating:	0 6/02 Worc 2m gd-fm NHF

Tip Kash (FR)

103   112
6-y-o ch g Kashtan (FR)-Tipas (FR) (Tip Moss (FR))
A M Hales Andrew L Cohen

Placings:0-1443P   (4441)
2002/03: 19¹S, 20⁴HY, 17⁴S, 22³G, 20⁰G,

	Starts	1st	2nd	3rd	Win & Pl
Hurdles	5	1	0	1	5571
Career Total	6	1	0	1	5571
112 11/02 MRas	2m3f110yE Hdl	SFT	£3654		

Total win prize-money £3654

Going:	Sf: 1-3 GS: 0-0 Gd: 0-2 GF: - Fm: 0-0
Distance:	2m/2m3: 0-1 2m4-2m7: 1-4 3m+: 0-0
Track:	LH: 0-1 RH: 1-3 Tight: 1-1 Gall: 0-1
Aids:	Bl: 0-0 Vi: 0-0 Tstrap: 0-0
Best Rating:	112 3/03 MRas 2m6f good Hdl

Modest hurdler; showed ability in one bumper start; effortless winner of a modest novice hurdle at Market Rasen in November 2002, and close third there in handicap company in March; acts on soft ground; stays two miles four.

Tip The Scales

5-y-o b g Dancing Spree (USA)-Keen Melody (USA) (Sharpen Up)
Mrs T J McInnes Skinner Mrs T J McInnes Skinner

Placings:344-00   (4338)
2002/03: 16⁶GS, 20⁰GF,

	Starts	1st	2nd	3rd	Win & Pl
Hurdles	2	0	0	0	
Career Total	5	0	0	1	541

Going:	Sf: 0-0 GS: 0-1 Gd: 0-0 GF: - Fm: 0-1
Distance:	2m/2m3: 0-1 2m4-2m7: 0-1 3m+: 0-0
Track:	LH: 0-1 RH: 0-1 Tight: 0-0 Gall: 0-2
Aids:	Bl: 0-0 Vi: 0-0 Tstrap: 0-0
Best Rating:	92 11/01 Hntg 2m110y good Hdl

Tipp Top Lord (IRE)

6-y-o gr g Mister Lord (USA)-Dark Fluff (Mandalus)
N A Twiston-Davies Mrs R Vaughan

Placings:6   (1633)
2002/03: 24⁶S,

	Starts	1st	2nd	3rd	Win & Pl
Hurdles	1	0	0	0	0
Career Total	1	0	0	0	0

Going:	Sf: 0-1 GS: 0-0 Gd: 0-0 GF: - Fm: 0-0
Distance:	2m/2m3: 0-0 2m4-2m7: 0-0 3m+: 0-1
Track:	LH: 0-0 RH: 0-1 Tight: 0-0 Gall: 0-0

Aids:	Bl: 0-0 Vi: 0-0 Tstrap: 0-0
Best Rating:	0 10/02 Carl 3m110y soft Hdl

Tipsy Mouse (IRE)

103(99h)   (102 h)103
7-y-o ch g Roselier (FR)-Darjoy (Darantus)
Mrs S J Smith (David M O Brien 19/5) Trevor Hemmings

Placings:P00424   (4228)
2002/03: 24PS, 16⁰G, 20⁰GS, 24⁴S, 24²S, 25⁴GF,

	Starts	1st	2nd	3rd	Win & Pl
Hurdles	5	0	1	0	1541
Chases	1	0	0	0	
Career Total	6	0	1	0	1541

Going:	Sf: 0-3 GS: 0-1 Gd: 0-1 GF: - Fm: 0-1
Distance:	2m/2m3: 0-1 2m4-2m7: 0-1 3m+: 0-4
Track:	LH: 0-5 RH: 0-1 Tight: 0-0 Gall: 0-1
Aids:	Bl: 0-0 Vi: 0-0 Tstrap: 0-0
Best Rating:	102 3/03 Carl 3m110y soft Hdl

Moderate novice chaser; winning Irish pointer; successful on second start over fences; open to further improvement; stays three miles one; effective on good ground.

Tiraldo (FR)

10-y-o b g Royal Charter (FR)-Tamilda (FR) (Rose Laurel)
A G Juckes Whistlejacket Partnership

Placings:4/5/22F1F1/23142P2F/40/PP444-5013P   (4409)
2002/03: 26⁵GF, 25⁰GF, 24¹S, 26³GF, 25⁶G,

	Starts	1st	2nd	3rd	Win & Pl
Chases	5	1	0	1	4867
Career Total	28	4	5	2	41666
74 8/02 Strf	3m	E(0-105)HCh	SFT	£4095	
122 11/99 Towc	3m1f	D(0-120)HCh	GD	£6905	
121 2/99 Hntg	2m4f110yD Ch		G-S	£5160	
112 12/98 Strf	2m5f110yD Ch		SFT	£4224	

Total win prize-money £20384

Going:	Sf: 1-1 GS: 0-0 Gd: 0-1 GF: - Fm: 0-3
Distance:	2m/2m3: 0-0 2m4-2m7: 0-0 3m+: 1-5
Track:	LH: 1-3 RH: 0-1 Tight: 1-2 Gall: 0-0
Aids:	Bl: 1-4 Vi: 0-0 Tstrap: 0-0
Best Rating:	126 5/99 Strf 2m5f110y gd-sft Ch

Formerly decent chaser, but very moderate nowadays. Stays three miles, appreciates cut in the ground. goes well at Stratford.

Tirari (IRE)

91   73
4-y-o b f Charnwood Forest (IRE)-Desert Victory (Green Desert (USA))
C R Dore (R C Spicer 17/5) G D J Linder

Placings:U6P00   (4157)
2002/03: 17UGF, 16⁶GF, 16⁶HY, 16⁰G, 17⁰G,

	Starts	1st	2nd	3rd	Win & Pl
Hurdles	5	0	0	0	0
Career Total	5	0	0	0	0

Going:	Sf: 0-1 GS: 0-0 Gd: 0-2 GF: - Fm: 0-2
Distance:	2m/2m3: 0-5 2m4-2m7: 0-0 3m+: 0-0
Track:	LH: 0-1 RH: 0-4 Tight: 0-0 Gall: 0-1
Aids:	Bl: 0-0 Vi: 0-1 Tstrap: 0-0
Best Rating:	73 10/02 Weth 2m gd-fm Hdl

Tirikumba

95   **94**

7-y-o ch m Le Moss-Ntombi (Trasi s Son)
S G Griffiths S G Griffiths

Placings:166   (4611)
2002/03: 16¹G, 16⁶HY, 17⁶G,

	Starts	1st	2nd	3rd	Win & Pl
NH Flat	3	1	0	0	3406
Career Total	3	1	0	0	3406
95	12/02 Ludl	2m	H NHF	GD	£3031

Total win prize-money £3031

Going: Sf: 0-1 GS: 0-0 Gd: 1-2 GF: - Fm: 0-0
Distance: **2m/2m3: 1-3** 2m4-2m7: 0-0 3m+: 0-0
Track: LH: 0-2 **RH: 1-1** Tight: 0-0 Gall: 0-1
Aids: Bl: 0-0 Vi: 0-0 Tstrap: 0-0
Best Rating: **97** 4/03 Chel 2m1f   good   NHF

Successful in a mares bumper at Ludlow on her debut; subsequently highly tried; made satisfactory debut over hurdles when narrowly beaten over 2m 6f at Stratford May 2003; stays well.

Tirley Gale

90   **83**

11-y-o b g Strong Gale-Mascara Vii (Damsire Unregistered)
Miss N Brookes Donald Smith

Placings:000P/0FP35/153P5R6F/04P/04PR-3   (0108)
2002/03: 24³G,

	Starts	1st	2nd	3rd	Win & Pl
Chases	1	0	0	1	373
Career Total	25	1	0	3	5086
98	5/99 Worc	2m7f110yF(0-105)HCh	G-S	£3002

Total win prize-money £3003

Going: Sf: 0-0 GS: 0-0 Gd: 0-0 GF: - Fm: 0-1
Distance: 2m/2m3: 0-0 2m4-2m7: 0-0 3m+: 0-1
Track: LH: 0-0 RH: 0-1 Tight: 0-1 Gall: 0-0
Aids: Bl: 0-0 Vi: 0-0 Tstrap: 0-0
Best Rating: **104** 3/99 Wwck 2m4f110y   good   Ch

Tirley Storm

102(89h)   (66h)**76**

8-y-o b g Tirley Gale-Random Select (Random Shot)
J S Smith Mrs J A Benson

Placings:6/P0044P2P-PP460P00   (3253)
2002/03: 24PGF, 19PG, 20⁴GS, 19⁶GS, 20⁹G, 23PGS, 23⁹S, 20⁹S,

	Starts	1st	2nd	3rd	Win & Pl
Chases	8	0	0	0	424
Career Total	17	0	1	0	2040

Going: Sf: 0-2 GS: 0-3 Gd: 0-2 GF: - Fm: 0-1
Distance: 2m/2m3: 0-2 2m4-2m7: 0-3 3m+: 0-3
Track: LH: 0-2 RH: 0-6 Tight: 0-4 Gall: 0-0
Aids: Bl: 0-0 Vi: 0-0 Tstrap: 0-0
Best Rating: 81 1/01 Donc 2m110y   good   NHF

Moderate form over hurdles and fences so far. Has shown his best form over two and a half miles on good to soft ground.

Tis Gromit

100(101h)   (75h)**75**

9-y-o b m Bedford (USA)-Lac Royale (Lochnager)
Miss Sheena West Mucky Duck Partnership

Placings:0/6P/56323-P6402   (3561)
2002/03: 24PGS, 23⁶GS, 22⁴G, 22⁰HY, 25²S,

	Starts	1st	2nd	3rd	Win & Pl
Hurdles	3	0	0	0	0
Chases	2	0	1	0	1084
Career Total	13	0	2	2	2566

Going: Sf: 0-2 GS: 0-2 Gd: 0-1 GF: - Fm: 0-0
Distance: 2m/2m3: 0-0 2m4-2m7: 0-2 3m+: 0-3
Track: LH: 0-2 RH: 0-2 Tight: 0-4 Gall: 0-0
Aids: Bl: 0-0 Vi: 0-0 Tstrap: 0-0
Best Rating: **90** 4/00 Plum 2m5f   gd-sft   Hdl

Plating-class hurdler/chaser; effective in soft ground; stays three miles.

Tisho

                          85+

7-y-o ch m Sir Harry Lewis (USA)-Sister-In-Law (Legal Tender)
P R Webber Mrs P Scott-Dunn

Placings:134F   (4222)
2002/03: 17¹S, 18³S, 16⁴G, 17FGF,

	Starts	1st	2nd	3rd	Win & Pl
NH Flat	3	1	0	1	2047
Hurdles	1	0	0	0	0
Career Total	4	1	0	1	2047
108	5/02 Bang	2m1f	H NHF	SFT	£1771

Total win prize-money £1771

Going: Sf: 1-2 GS: 0-0 Gd: 0-1 GF: - Fm: 0-1
Distance: **2m/2m3: 1-4** 2m4-2m7: 0-0 3m+: 0-0
Track: **LH: 1-2** RH: 0-2 **Tight: 1-2** Gall: 0-1
Aids: Bl: 0-0 Vi: 0-0 Tstrap: 0-0
Best Rating: **108** 5/02 Bang 2m1f   soft   NHF

Tissifer

104   **115**

7-y-o b g Polish Precedent (USA)-Ingozi (Warning)
Mrs M Reveley (Mrs Lydia Pearce 17/10) T S Child

Placings:1132000-50255F   (4639)
2002/03: 16⁵GS, 16⁰G, 16²GS, 16⁵GS, 17⁵G, 16FGF,

	Starts	1st	2nd	3rd	Win & Pl
Hurdles	6	0	1	0	2186
Career Total	13	2	2	1	9704
111	11/01 NAbb	2m1f	E Hdl	SFT	£2961
110	10/01 Strf	2m110y	E Hdl	G-S	£3293

Total win prize-money £6255

Going: Sf: 0-0 GS: 0-3 Gd: 0-2 GF: - Fm: 0-1
Distance: 2m/2m3: 0-6 2m4-2m7: 0-0 3m+: 0-0
Track: LH: 0-3 RH: 0-3 Tight: 0-2 Gall: 0-2
Aids: Bl: 0-0 Vi: 0-1 Tstrap: 0-0
Best Rating: **124** 12/01 Bang 2m1f   gd-sft   Hdl

Fair hurdler; runner-up at Doncaster in January; inconsistent; suited by soft ground.

Titus Bramble

  (83h)   (66h)**85**

6-y-o b g Puissance-Norska (Northfields (USA))
P C Ritchens Mrs B D Adams

Placings:54431330/UP00PF2254P5-4   (0098)
2002/03: 26⁴GS,

	Starts	1st	2nd	3rd	Win & Pl
Chases	1	0	0	0	236
Career Total	21	1	2	3	8103
80	1/01 Tntn	2m1f	E(0-105)HHdl	HVY	£3062

Total win prize-money £3083

Going: Sf: 0-0 GS: 0-0 Gd: 0-0 GF: - Fm: 0-1
Distance: 2m/2m3: 0-0 2m4-2m7: 0-0 3m+: 0-1
Track: LH: 0-0 RH: 0-0 Tight: 0-1 Gall: 0-0
Aids: Bl: 0-0 Vi: 0-0 Tstrap: 0-0
Best Rating: 85 4/02 Asct 2m3f110y gd-fm   Ch

Plating-class handicap hurdler. Has worn blinkers to winning effect. Has been tried in a tongue-tie, to little effect. Looks best around two and a half miles. Likes to get his toe in.

Tiutchev

117   **170**

10-y-o b g Soviet Star (USA)-Cut Ahead (Kalaglow)
M C Pipe The Liars Poker Partnership

Placings:4FU/U2311/21F1662/111/1061U5/3154-21F0
                         (4647a)
2002/03: 16²HY, 19¹GS, 16FG, 21⁰G,

	Starts	1st	2nd	3rd	Win & Pl
Chases	4	1	1	0	64116
Career Total	32	11	4	2	282448
170	2/03 Asct	2m3f110yA Ch		G-S	£59500
170	2/02 Sand	2m	B HCh	G-S	£10179
170	2/01 Asct	2m3f110yA Ch		SFT	£42575
162	5/00 Punc	2m	A Ch		GD	£24800
164	3/00 Chel	2m	A Ch		GD	£66700
145	1/00 Sand	2m4f110yC Ch		SFT	£7785
144	12/99 Extr	2m1f110yC Ch		G-S	£7220
152	1/99 Kemp	2m	B(0-145)HHdl	HVY	£21280
142	12/98 Chel	2m1f	C(0-135)HHdl	GD	£4622
113	11/97 Chel	2m110y	D(0-110)HHdl	G-F	£7490
117	10/97 Extr	2m1f110yE Hdl		GD	£2326

Total win prize-money £254479

Going: Sf: 0-1 GS: 1-1 Gd: 0-2 GF: - Fm: 0-0
Distance: 2m/2m3: 0-2 **2m4-2m7: 1-2** 3m+: 0-0
Track: LH: 0-1 **RH: 1-2** Tight: 0-0 Gall: 0-1
Aids: Bl: 0-0 Vi: 0-0 Tstrap: 0-0
Best Rating: **170** 2/03 Asct 2m3f110y gd-sft   Ch

Top-class chaser; won the Arkle at Cheltenham Festival in 2000; inconsistent since, largely due to problems with colic, but showed he retains all his ability when jumping well and scoring by 12l from Geos in the Ritz Club Chase at Ascot in February despite carrying condition; effective from 2m to 2m 4f and on good and heavy ground; hard to beat when healthy.

To Be The Best

79(79h)   (61h)**54**

13-y-o ch g Superlative-Early Call (Kind Of Hush)
D A Lamb D A Lamb

Placings:P/P5506/56040PP/4012/P02333/300044P560405
0/5-00   (0832)
2002/03: 17⁰GF, 16⁰GF,

	Starts	1st	2nd	3rd	Win & Pl
Hurdles	1	0	0	0	0
Chases	1	0	0	0	0
Career Total	40	1	2	4	6423
96	9/96 Carl	2m	E Ch	FRM	£2099

Total win prize-money £2099

Going: Sf: 0-0 GS: 0-0 Gd: 0-0 GF: - Fm: 0-2
Distance: 2m/2m3: 0-2 2m4-2m7: 0-0 3m+: 0-0
Track: LH: 0-2 RH: 0-0 Tight: 0-2 Gall: 0-0
Aids: Bl: 0-0 Vi: 0-0 Tstrap: 0-0
Best Rating: 96 9/96 Prth 2m   gd-fm   Ch

To The Future (IRE)
103   97
7-y-o ch g Bob Back (USA)-Lady Graduate (IRE) (Le Bavard (FR))
A Parker Mr & Mrs Raymond Anderson Green

Placings:4454/1-P21P   (3774)
2002/03: 25PG, 25PS, 251S, 25PGS,

	Starts	1st	2nd	3rd	Win & Pl
Chases	4	1	1	0	4976
Career Total	9	2	1	0	6406
97	1/03	Ayr	3m1f	E(0-105)HCh	SFT £3867
97	4/02	Carl	3m2f	H Ch	G-S £1430

Total win prize-money £5298

Going:	Sf: 1-2 GS: 0-1 Gd: 0-1 GF: - Fm: 0-0
Distance:	2m/2m3: 0-0 2m4-2m7: 0-0 3m+: 1-4
Track:	LH: 1-4 RH: 0-0 Tight: 0-1 Gall: 0-0
Aids:	Bl: 0-0 Vi: 0-0 Tstrap: 0-0
Best Rating:	97 1/03 Ayr 3m1f soft Ch

Moderate chaser, ex-hunter chaser, won twice in points before completing the hat-trick in a Carlisle hunter chase in April 2002. Won a novices handicap at Ayr in January; stays well, acts on soft ground.

Toad Hall
92   94
9-y-o b g Henbit (USA)-Candlebright (Lighter)
Mrs L B Normile John Findlay

Placings:60/21/P4   (4766)
2002/03: 20PG, 16PG,

	Starts	1st	2nd	3rd	Win & Pl
Hurdles	1	0	0	0	0
Chases	1	0	0	0	636
Career Total	6	1	1	0	4248
87	8/00	Prth		2m4f110yE Hdl	GD £2555

Total win prize-money £2555

Going:	Sf: 0-0 GS: 0-0 Gd: 0-2 GF: - Fm: 0-0
Distance:	2m/2m3: 0-1 2m4-2m7: 0-1 3m+: 0-0
Track:	LH: 0-1 RH: 0-1 Tight: 0-1 Gall: 0-0
Aids:	Bl: 0-0 Vi: 0-0 Tstrap: 0-0
Best Rating:	94 6/00 Prth 2m4f110y good Hdl

Toberlone
10-y-o b g K-Battery-Elisetta (Monsanto (FR))
J S Haldane J A Riddell

Placings:0/PP/P   (0064)
2002/03: 21PGF,

	Starts	1st	2nd	3rd	Win & Pl
Hurdles	1	0	0	0	0
Career Total	4	0	0	0	

Going:	Sf: 0-0 GS: 0-0 Gd: 0-0 GF: - Fm: 0-1
Distance:	2m/2m3: 0-0 2m4-2m7: 0-1 3m+: 0-0
Track:	LH: 0-1 RH: 0-0 Tight: 0-1 Gall: 0-0
Aids:	Bl: 0-0 Vi: 0-0 Tstrap: 0-0
Best Rating:	

Tobesure (IRE)
106(96c)   (109c)101
9-y-o b g Asir-Princess Citrus (IRE) (Auction Ring (USA))
J I A Charlton Richard Nixon

Placings:250352/64124460/4024P32F-50123603200   (4752)

2002/03: 225GS, 24UG, 221GF, 22UG, 223S, 256G, 24UG, 233GS, 222GS, 22UG, 24UG,

	Starts	1st	2nd	3rd	Win & Pl
Hurdles	11	1	2	2	7733
Career Total	33	2	7	4	15906
93	10/02	Kels	2m6f110yE(0-105)HHdl	G-F	£3549
96	10/00	Kels	2m6f110yE Hdl	GD	£2800

Total win prize-money £6349

Going:	Sf: 0-1 GS: 0-3 Gd: 0-6 GF: - Fm: 1-1
Distance:	2m/2m3: 0-0 2m4-2m7: 1-7 3m+: 0-4
Track:	LH: 1-9 RH: 0-2 Tight: 1-8 Gall: 0-0
Aids:	Bl: 0-0 Vi: 0-0 Tstrap: 0-0
Best Rating:	101 3/03 Kels 2m6f110y gd-sft Hdl

Modest hurdler; stays three miles; goes well at Kelso.

Toby
98   89
10-y-o b g Jendali (USA)-Au Revoir Sailor (Julio Mariner)
N G Richards Taranto De Pol

Placings:4/11P330P/PP/510411120/001P412/4PP   (1561)
2002/03: 20UGS, 20PGF, 22PG,

	Starts	1st	2nd	3rd	Win & Pl
Hurdles	3	0	0	0	0
Career Total	29	8	2	2	27823
110	8/00	Uttx	3m	E Ch	G-F £3615
114	6/00	Worc	2m7f110yD Ch	GD	£3887
118	10/99	Hexm	3m	F(0-100)HHdl	GD £2343
112	9/99	Prth	2m4f110yF(0-100)HHdl	SFT	£4338
100	9/99	Bang	2m4f	F(0-110)HHdl	G-F £4260
109	6/99	Uttx	2m4f110yE(0-115)HHdl	GD	£2368
101	10/97	Kels	2m6f110yG Hdl	G-F	£1896
93	10/97	Bang	2m4f	E Hdl	GD	£2368

Total win prize-money £25081

Going:	Sf: 0-0 GS: 0-1 Gd: 0-1 GF: - Fm: 0-1
Distance:	2m/2m3: 0-0 2m4-2m7: 0-3 3m+: 0-0
Track:	LH: 0-3 RH: 0-0 Tight: 0-1 Gall: 0-0
Aids:	Bl: 0-0 Vi: 0-0 Tstrap: 0-0
Best Rating:	118 10/99 Carl 3m110y good Hdl

Toby Brown
88(98h)   (123h)95
10-y-o b g Arzanni-Forest Nymph (NZ) (Oak Ridge (FR))
A King Allan Stennett And Mrs J M Stennett

Placings:F2053/112U22/42/PP3/360P-2P   (0321)
2002/03: 222GS, 26PG,

	Starts	1st	2nd	3rd	Win & Pl
Chases	2	0	1	0	1460
Career Total	22	2	6	3	15441
116	11/97	MRas	2m4f110yE(0-115)HHdl	GD	£2337
107	9/97	Worc	2m4f	E Hdl	GD	£2495

Total win prize-money £4833

Going:	Sf: 0-0 GS: 0-1 Gd: 0-1 GF: - Fm: 0-0
Distance:	2m/2m3: 0-0 2m4-2m7: 0-1 3m+: 0-1
Track:	LH: 0-1 RH: 0-1 Tight: 0-0 Gall: 0-0
Aids:	Bl: 0-0 Vi: 0-0 Tstrap: 0-0
Best Rating:	137 12/98 Sand 2m6f good Hdl

Moderate handicap hurdler, but lightly raced in recent seasons and has not won since November 1997. Effective at two and a half to three miles and acts on good ground. Pulled up lame on his second chase run in May 2002.

Todays Man
6-y-o b g Bigstone (IRE)-Snowgirl (IRE) (Mazaad)
Mrs Dianne Sayer A Slack

Placings:0P-PP   (1072)
2002/03: 17PG, 17PG,

	Starts	1st	2nd	3rd	Win & Pl
Hurdles	2	0	0	0	
Career Total	4	0	0	0	

Going:	Sf: 0-0 GS: 0-0 Gd: 0-2 GF: - Fm: 0-0
Distance:	2m/2m3: 0-2 2m4-2m7: 0-0 3m+: 0-0
Track:	LH: 0-2 RH: 0-0 Tight: 0-2 Gall: 0-0
Aids:	Bl: 0-0 Vi: 0-0 Tstrap: 0-0
Best Rating:	0 8/02 Ctml 2m1f110y good Hdl

Toddeano
7-y-o b g Perpendicular-Phisus (Henbit (USA))
G Fierro G Fierro

Placings:00-0P   (1928)
2002/03: 16UGF, 16PGS,

	Starts	1st	2nd	3rd	Win & Pl
NH Flat	1	0	0	0	0
Hurdles	1	0	0	0	0
Career Total	4	0	0	0	

Going:	Sf: 0-0 GS: 0-1 Gd: 0-0 GF: - Fm: 0-1
Distance:	2m/2m3: 0-2 2m4-2m7: 0-0 3m+: 0-0
Track:	LH: 0-1 RH: 0-0 Tight: 0-2 Gall: 0-0
Aids:	Bl: 0-0 Vi: 0-0 Tstrap: 0-0
Best Rating:	0 11/02 Ludl 2m gd-sft Hdl

Toejam
100   76
10-y-o ch g Move Off-Cheeky Pigeon (Brave Invader (USA))
R E Barr Mrs R E Barr

Placings:0/45   (4793)
2002/03: 214G, 175GF,

	Starts	1st	2nd	3rd	Win & Pl
Hurdles	2	0	0	0	0
Career Total	3	0	0	0	0

Going:	Sf: 0-0 GS: 0-0 Gd: 0-1 GF: - Fm: 0-1
Distance:	2m/2m3: 0-1 2m4-2m7: 0-1 3m+: 0-0
Track:	LH: 0-2 RH: 0-0 Tight: 0-2 Gall: 0-0
Aids:	Bl: 0-0 Vi: 0-0 Tstrap: 0-0
Best Rating:	72 4/03 Sedg 2m1f gd-fm Hdl

Plating-class hurdler; acts with cut in the ground.

Toft Hall (IRE)
93   53
8-y-o br g Erdelistan (FR)-Countess Christy (Mon Capitaine)
Mrs A Hamilton Ian Hamilton

Placings:F5PPU0   (4589)
2002/03: 20FGS, 27PS, 24PG, 25PG, 25UG, 25UG,

	Starts	1st	2nd	3rd	Win & Pl
Chases	6	0	0	0	0
Career Total	6	0	0	0	0

Going:	Sf: 0-1 GS: 0-1 Gd: 0-4 GF: - Fm: 0-0
Distance:	2m/2m3: 0-0 2m4-2m7: 0-1 3m+: 0-5
Track:	LH: 0-5 RH: 0-1 Tight: 0-3 Gall: 0-1
Aids:	Bl: 0-3 Vi: 0-0 Tstrap: 0-0
Best Rating:	53 4/03 Hexm 3m1f good Ch

Toi Express (IRE)

99(101h)   (100h)109

7-y-o ch g Phardante (FR)-Toi Figures (Deep Run)
P J Hobbs J & B Gibbs & Sons Ltd

Placings:5S/2563-F2311   (1235)
2002/03: 19FG, 16²GF, 17³G, 16¹G, 16¹G,

	Starts	1st	2nd	3rd	Win & Pl
Chases	5	2	1	1	10405
Career Total	11	2	2	2	11815
103 9/02 Worc 2m			E Ch		GD	£4920
95 9/02 NAbb 2m110y E Ch				GD	£3968

|||
Total win prize-money £8888

Going:	Sf: 0-0 GS: 0-0 Gd: 2-4 GF: - Fm: 0-1
Distance:	2m/2m3: 2-5 2m4-2m7: 0-0 3m+: 0-0
Track:	LH: 2-3 RH: 0-2 Tight: 1-2 Gall: 0-0
Aids:	Bl: 0-0 Vi: 0-0 Tstrap: 0-0
Best Rating:	113 6/02 Hrfd 2m gd-fm Ch

Modest chaser; landed a four runner novice chase at
Newton Abbot in September 2002. Appeared lucky to follow-
up at Worcester next time. Best at around two miles. Acts on
a sound surface.

Tolcea (IRE)

76   38

4-y-o ch g Barathea (IRE)-Mosaique Bleue (Shirley Heights)
W Storey (E A L Dunlop 10/5) S Hogg

Placings:P   (3891)
2002/03: 16PGS,

	Starts	1st	2nd	3rd	Win & Pl
Hurdles	1	0	0	0	
Career Total	1	0	0	0	

Going:	Sf: 0-0 GS: 0-1 Gd: 0-0 GF: - Fm: 0-0
Distance:	2m/2m3: 0-1 2m4-2m7: 0-0 3m+: 0-0
Track:	LH: 0-1 RH: 0-0 Tight: 0-1 Gall: 0-0
Aids:	Bl: 0-0 Vi: 0-0 Tstrap: 0-0
Best Rating:	0 3/03 Kels 2m110y gd-sft Hdl

Tollbrae (IRE)

107   97

6-y-o gr g Supreme Leader-Miss Henrietta (IRE) (Step
Together (USA))
N J Henderson R A Bartlett

Placings:14-324   (4032)
2002/03: 20³S, 16²G, 20⁴HY,

	Starts	1st	2nd	3rd	Win & Pl
Hurdles	3	0	1	1	1855
Career Total	5	1	1	1	3556
123 3/02 Hrfd 2m1f			H NHF		SFT	£1701

|||
Total win prize-money £1701

Going:	Sf: 0-2 GS: 0-0 Gd: 0-1 GF: - Fm: 0-0
Distance:	2m/2m3: 0-1 2m4-2m7: 0-2 3m+: 0-0
Track:	LH: 0-1 RH: 0-2 Tight: 0-0 Gall: 0-1
Aids:	Bl: 0-0 Vi: 0-0 Tstrap: 0-0
Best Rating:	123 3/02 Hrfd 2m1f soft NHF

Modest hurdler; soft-ground bumper winner; has shown fair
form over hurdles; acts on good ground, but looks better on
soft.

Tom Costalot (IRE)

106(96h)   (84h)129

8-y-o gr g Black Minstrel-Hop Picker (USA) (Plugged Nickle
(USA))

Mrs Susan Nock Gerard Nock

Placings:6055/B420/351112-311600   (4472)
2002/03: 20³G, 20¹G, 21¹G, 24⁶G, 24⁰G, 21⁰G,

	Starts	1st	2nd	3rd	Win & Pl
Chases	6	2	0	1	15497
Career Total	20	5	2	2	33336
129 12/02 Chel 2m5f		E(0-125)HCh		GD	£9352
129 11/02 Wwck 2m4f110yD(0-125)HCh			GD	£4563
127 2/02 Donc 2m3f110yE(0-105)HCh		SFT	£3302
109 12/01 Leic 2m4f110yD(0-125)HCh		GD	£7672
112 12/01 Winc 2m5f F(0-105)HCh		GD	£3588

|||
Total win prize-money £28477

Going:	Sf: 0-0 GS: 0-0 Gd: 2-6 GF: - Fm: 0-0
Distance:	2m/2m3: 0-0 2m4-2m7: 2-4 3m+: 0-2
Track:	LH: 2-6 RH: 0-0 Tight: 0-1 Gall: 1-3
Aids:	Bl: 0-0 Vi: 0-0 Tstrap: 0-0
Best Rating:	129 12/02 Chel 2m5f good Ch

Useful handicap chaser with a good winning record; jumps
well; suited by trips of around two and a half miles; probably
best on a sound surface, but handles soft.

Tom De Savoie (IRE)

10-y-o br g War Hero-Black Pilot (Linacre)
Mrs Caroline Bailey W G N Barber

Placings:1/2/2F-53   (4671)
2002/03: 23⁵GS, 24³G,

	Starts	1st	2nd	3rd	Win & Pl
Chases	2	0	0	1	411
Career Total	6	1	2	1	3547
98 4/00 Fknm 3m110y H Ch		GD	£2131

|||
Total win prize-money £2132

Going:	Sf: 0-0 GS: 0-1 Gd: 0-1 GF: - Fm: 0-0
Distance:	2m/2m3: 0-0 2m4-2m7: 0-0 3m+: 0-2
Track:	LH: 0-1 RH: 0-1 Tight: 0-1 Gall: 0-0
Aids:	Bl: 0-0 Vi: 0-0 Tstrap: 0-0
Best Rating:	104 3/02 Newb 3m soft Ch

Moderate pointer and hunter chaser; is suited by a sound
surface and three miles.

Tom Fruit

104f   120+f

6-y-o b g Supreme Leader-Forever Mine (IRE) (Phardante
(FR))
T D Easterby David & Steven Dudley

Placings:3221   (3883)
2002/03: 16³GS, 16²GS, 16²HY, 16¹G,

	Starts	1st	2nd	3rd	Win & Pl
NH Flat	4	1	2	1	3528
Career Total	4	1	2	1	3528
120 3/03 Donc 2m110y H NHF		G-S	£2002

|||
Total win prize-money £2002

Going:	Sf: 0-1 GS: 1-3 Gd: 0-0 GF: - Fm: 0-0
Distance:	2m/2m3: 1-4 2m4-2m7: 0-0 3m+: 0-0
Track:	LH: 1-4 RH: 0-0 Tight: 0-0 Gall: 1-2
Aids:	Bl: 0-0 Vi: 0-0 Tstrap: 0-0
Best Rating:	120 3/03 Donc 2m110y gd-sft NHF

Fair bumper performer; big sort, has shown plenty of ability
in bumpers and won very easilt at Doncaster in March on
fourth start.

Tom Pinch (IRE)

14-y-o b g Mandalus-Spanish Royale (Royal Buck)
J R Cornwall J R Cornwall

Placings:2/00/53FF3331U/P4/P23/P6P3-344UP (0723)
2002/03: 21³G, 21⁴G, 22⁴GF, 24⁴G, 23PG,

	Starts	1st	2nd	3rd	Win & Pl
Chases	5	0	0	1	894
Career Total	26	1	2	7	8104
95 4/99 Uttx 3m		G(0-90)HCh		G-S	£2207

|||
Total win prize-money £2208

Going:	Sf: 0-0 GS: 0-0 Gd: 0-4 GF: - Fm: 0-1
Distance:	2m/2m3: 0-0 2m4-2m7: 0-3 3m+: 0-2
Track:	LH: 0-4 RH: 0-1 Tight: 0-4 Gall: 0-0
Aids:	Bl: 0-0 Vi: 0-0 Tstrap: 0-0
Best Rating:	104 4/99 MRas 2m4f soft Ch

Tom The Bomb

7-y-o b g Faustus (USA)-Llanon (Owen Dudley)
D R Wellicome D R Wellicome

Placings:PPPPP   (3429)
2002/03: 20PGF, 26PGF, 21PGS, 19PGS, 22PS,

	Starts	1st	2nd	3rd	Win & Pl
Hurdles	3	0	0	0	0
Chases	2	0	0	0	0
Career Total	5	0	0	0	0

Going:	Sf: 0-1 GS: 0-2 Gd: 0-0 GF: - Fm: 0-2
Distance:	2m/2m3: 0-1 2m4-2m7: 0-3 3m+: 0-1
Track:	LH: 0-3 RH: 0-2 Tight: 0-1 Gall: 0-0
Aids:	Bl: 0-1 Vi: 0-0 Tstrap: 0-0
Best Rating:	0 2/03 Font 2m6f110y soft Hdl

Tom Tygrys

87   63

4-y-o b g Danzig Connection (USA)-Strath Kitten (Scottish
Reel)
P S McEntee Ms Clare Sharp

Placings:654   (1004)
2002/03: 17PGS, 16⁵GF, 17⁴GF,

	Starts	1st	2nd	3rd	Win & Pl
Hurdles	3	0	0	0	283
Career Total	3	0	0	0	283

Going:	Sf: 0-0 GS: 0-1 Gd: 0-0 GF: - Fm: 0-2
Distance:	2m/2m3: 0-3 2m4-2m7: 0-0 3m+: 0-0
Track:	LH: 0-2 RH: 0-1 Tight: 0-3 Gall: 0-0
Aids:	Bl: 0-0 Vi: 0-1 Tstrap: 0-0
Best Rating:	63 8/02 Bang 2m1f gd-fm Hdl

Tom's Lad

10-y-o gr g Scallywag-Menquilla (Menelek)
Lady Connell Lady Connell

Placings:P/P   (1601)
2002/03: 20PG,

	Starts	1st	2nd	3rd	Win & Pl
Hurdles	1	0	0	0	
Career Total	2	0	0	0	

Going:	Sf: 0-0 GS: 0-0 Gd: 0-1 GF: - Fm: 0-0
Distance:	2m/2m3: 0-0 2m4-2m7: 0-1 3m+: 0-0
Track:	LH: 0-1 RH: 0-0 Tight: 0-0 Gall: 0-0
Aids:	Bl: 0-0 Vi: 0-0 Tstrap: 0-0
Best Rating:	0 10/02 Chep 2m4f good Hdl

Tom's Prize

110(84h)   (80h)130

8-y-o ch g Gunner B-Pandora s Prize (Royal Vulcan)
J L Spearing Mrs P Joynes

Placings:0054/U/2514241-F22F110   (4469)
2002/03: 24⁵GS, 23⁴S, 24²HY, 24⁴G, 23¹G, 24¹G, 25⁶G,

	Starts	1st	2nd	3rd	Win & Pl
Chases	7	2	2	0	35208
Career Total	19	4	4	0	47135
125	3/03	Donc	3m	B(0-145)HCh	GD	£22750
130	2/03	Leic	2m7f110y	D(0-125)HCh	SFT	£8528
116	4/02	Strf	3m	D Ch	GD	£4322
109	12/01	Towc	2m6f	D Ch	HVY	£5089

Total win prize-money £40691

Going:	Sf: 1-3 GS: 0-2 Gd: 1-2 GF: - Fm: 0-0
Distance:	2m/2m3: 0-0 2m4-2m7: 0-0 3m+: 2-7
Track:	LH: 1-3 RH: 1-4 Tight: 0-1 Gall: 1-1
Aids:	Bl: 0-0 Vi: 0-0 Tstrap: 0-0
Best Rating:	130 2/03 Leic 2m7f110y soft Ch

Useful handicap chaser; best when able to dominate; stays three miles; acts on any ground.

Tom's River (IRE)

104(97h)   84

11-y-o ch g Over The River (FR)-Nesford (Walshford)
R J Hodges (Mrs M Reveley 4/7) Major A W C Pearn

Placings:120/200/U11P4/4213F/023UU/45415P-
5364PPP43   (4627)
2002/03: 24⁵GS, 30³G, 24⁶G, 24⁴G, 24⁴PS, 24⁴PS, 24⁴PS, 21⁴GF, 21³GF,

	Starts	1st	2nd	3rd	Win & Pl
Hurdles	1	0	0	0	0
Chases	8	0	0	2	2203
Career Total	36	5	4	4	24807
104	1/02	Catt	3m1f110yF(0-100)HCh	G-S	£3514
122	12/99	Catt	3m1f110yF(0-110)HCh	GD	£5004
120	1/99	Catt	3m1f110yF(0-110)HCh	SFT	£3096
101	1/99	Catt	3m1f110yE Ch	GD	£2814
99	2/97	Carl	2m1f	H NHF	SFT	£1035

Total win prize-money £15464

Going:	Sf: 0-3 GS: 0-1 Gd: 0-3 GF: - Fm: 0-2
Distance:	2m/2m3: 0-0 2m4-2m7: 0-2 3m+: 0-7
Track:	LH: 0-3 RH: 0-5 Tight: 0-6 Gall: 0-0
Aids:	Bl: 0-1 Vi: 0-0 Tstrap: 0-0
Best Rating:	122 10/00 Kels 2m6f110y soft Ch

Moderate chaser; fair sort in his prime, but on the downgrade; goes well at Catterick; suited by easy ground.

Tombazaan (IRE)

98   89

7-y-o b m Good Thyne (USA)-Master Nidee (Master Owen)
Graham John McKeever F T Wilson

Placings:31/P4-650   (2657)
2002/03: 19⁶S, 22²YS, 16⁵GS,

	Starts	1st	2nd	3rd	Win & Pl
Hurdles	3	0	0	0	
Career Total	7	1	0	1	2105
107	1/01	Weth	2m	H NHF	HVY	£1610

Total win prize-money £1610

Tomcappagh (IRE)

98   88

12-y-o br g Riberetto-Shuil Suas (Menelek)
Mrs S Wall Mrs S Wall

Placings:F3P3P/4312/F55P/P0UP323P3/0045133U2CP3P
-PP64PP   (4761)
2002/03: 25⁵GS, 25⁵PGF, 26⁵HY, 24⁶GS, 24⁴G, 24⁴PG, 26⁴PGF,

	Starts	1st	2nd	3rd	Win & Pl
Chases	7	0	0	0	535
Career Total	41	2	3	9	12787
86	12/01	Plum	3m2f	F(0-100)HCh	SFT	£4127
103	2/99	Folk	2m5f	H Ch	G-S	£1096

Total win prize-money £5224

Going:	Sf: 0-1 GS: 0-2 Gd: 0-2 GF: - Fm: 0-0
Distance:	2m/2m3: 0-0 2m4-2m7: 0-0 3m+: 0-7
Track:	LH: 0-2 RH: 0-4 Tight: 0-4 Gall: 0-0
Aids:	Bl: 0-0 Vi: 0-0 Tstrap: 0-0
Best Rating:	110 3/99 Strf 3m heavy Ch

Moderate staying chaser, effective in soft ground, stays three miles-two.

Tomenoso

110   108+

5-y-o b g Teenoso (USA)-Guarded Expression (Siberian Express (USA))
Mrs S J Smith Keith Nicholson

Placings:44223-30111   (4618)
2002/03: 17³S, 16⁴G, 16¹G, 21¹G, 20¹GF,

	Starts	1st	2nd	3rd	Win & Pl
Hurdles	5	3	0	1	14626
Career Total	10	3	2	2	16935
108	4/03	Carl	2m4f	D(0-125)HHdl	G-F	£7182
95	3/03	Sedg	2m5f110yE(0-110)HHdl	GD	£3507
101	3/03	Weth	2m	E(0-110)HHdl	GD	£3464

Total win prize-money £14155

Going:	Sf: 0-1 GS: 0-0 Gd: 2-3 GF: - Fm: 1-1
Distance:	2m/2m3: 1-3 2m4-2m7: 2-2 3m+: 0-0
Track:	LH: 2-4 RH: 1-1 Tight: 1-3 Gall: 0-0
Aids:	Bl: 0-0 Vi: 0-0 Tstrap: 0-0
Best Rating:	108 4/03 Carl 2m4f gd-fm Hdl

Modest hurdler; progressive form in 2003 completing a hat-trick at Wetherby, Sedgefield and Carlisle; best on a sound surface but handled the mud; effective at two miles five and should stay further.

Tomfoolary (IRE)

85   74

6-y-o ch g Erin s Isle-Liberty Bird (USA) (Danzatore (CAN))
J A B Old Mrs C H Antrobus

Placings:3/0350-0   (2212)
2002/03: 16⁵S,

	Starts	1st	2nd	3rd	Win & Pl
Hurdles	1	0	0	0	
Career Total	6	0	0	2	677

Going:	Sf: 0-1 GS: 0-0 Gd: 0-0 GF: - Fm: 0-0
Distance:	2m/2m3: 0-1 2m4-2m7: 0-0 3m+: 0-0
Track:	LH: 0-1 RH: 0-0 Tight: 0-0 Gall: 0-1

| Aids: | Bl: 0-0 Vi: 0-0 Tstrap: 0-0 |
| Best Rating: | 94 4/01 Slig 2m heavy NHF |

Tomich (IRE)

(101h)   (87h)124

8-y-o b/br g Lord Americo-Gilt Course (Crash Course)
Miss A M Newton-Smith Julian Smith

Placings:0P/363P1FF-2   (1506)
2002/03: 26²G,

	Starts	1st	2nd	3rd	Win & Pl
Hurdles	1	0	1	0	846
Career Total	10	1	1	2	5910
114	3/02	Winc	2m5f	D Ch	GD	£4309

Total win prize-money £4310

Going:	Sf: 0-0 GS: 0-0 Gd: 0-1 GF: - Fm: 0-0
Distance:	2m/2m3: 0-0 2m4-2m7: 0-0 3m+: 0-1
Track:	LH: 0-1 RH: 0-0 Tight: 0-0 Gall: 0-0
Aids:	Bl: 0-0 Vi: 0-0 Tstrap: 0-0
Best Rating:	114 3/02 Winc 2m5f good Ch

Fair chaser/hurdler; shock winner at Wincanton in March 2002 but a keen sort and not a reliable jumper.

Tommie Swift

25

7-y-o b g Karinga Bay-Marie Swift (Main Reef)
B J Llewellyn B J Llewellyn

Placings:0000-P   (0072)
2002/03: 26⁷PGF,

	Starts	1st	2nd	3rd	Win & Pl
Hurdles	1	0	0	0	
Career Total	5	0	0	0	

Going:	Sf: 0-0 GS: 0-0 Gd: 0-0 GF: - Fm: 0-1
Distance:	2m/2m3: 0-0 2m4-2m7: 0-0 3m+: 0-1
Track:	LH: 0-0 RH: 0-1 Tight: 0-0 Gall: 0-0
Aids:	Bl: 0-0 Vi: 0-0 Tstrap: 0-0
Best Rating:	60 6/01 Worc 2m gd-fm NHF

Tommy Carson

98

8-y-o b g Last Tycoon-Ivory Palm (USA) (Sir Ivor)
Jamie Poulton J Logan

Placings:035P/5424P3045/24/3013352P13440-   (0012)
2002/03: 20⁰G,

	Starts	1st	2nd	3rd	Win & Pl
Chases	1	0	0	0	
Career Total	28	2	3	6	15253
98	1/02	Plum	2m4f	E(0-105)HCh	SFT	£3360
95	9/01	Plum	2m4f	D(0-115)HCh	G-F	£4075

Total win prize-money £7436

Going:	Sf: 0-0 GS: 0-0 Gd: 0-1 GF: - Fm: 0-0
Distance:	2m/2m3: 0-0 2m4-2m7: 0-1 3m+: 0-0
Track:	LH: 0-1 RH: 0-0 Tight: 0-1 Gall: 0-0
Aids:	Bl: 0-0 Vi: 0-0 Tstrap: 0-0
Best Rating:	98 1/02 Plum 2m4f soft Ch

A maiden on the Flat and over hurdles, he has won a couple of minor chases. Seems to handle any ground stays two and a half miles.

Tommy Trooper

100(92c)   (88c)102

8-y-o ch g Infantry-Steady Saunter Vii (Damsire

Column 1

Unregistered)
P F Nicholls Paul K Barber,Mick Coburn,Colin Lewis 1

Placings:*6316/14-0F062*   (3573)
2002/03: 16⁰GS, 16⁵F, 24⁰S, 18⁶S, 16⁰HY,

	Starts	1st	2nd	3rd	Win & Pl
Hurdles	3	0	1	0	1078
Chases	2	1	0	0	
Career Total	11	2	1	1	5514
116 2/02 Font	2m2f110yE Hdl			HVY	£2614
120 2/00 Winc	2m	H NHF		GD	£1575
	Total win prize-money £4190				

Going:	Sf: 0-4 GS: 0-1 Gd: 0-0 GF: - Fm: 0-0
Distance:	2m/2m3: 0-4 2m4-2m7: 0-0 3m+: 0-1
Track:	LH: 0-1 RH: 0-4 Tight: 0-3 Gall: 0-0
Aids:	Bl: 0-0 Vi: 0-0 Tstrap: 0-1
Best Rating:	120 4/00 Aint 2m110y good NHF

Moderate hurdler, useful bumper horse; he missed all of 2001 due to leg trouble; won his hurdles bow at Fontwell in February 2002, modest form since; stays two and a quarter miles; has won on good ground and heavy.

Tommy Wolf

7-y-o ch g Little Wolf-Oneninefive (Sayyaf)
Mrs E B Scott Mrs E B Scott

Placings:*000P*   (0996)
2002/03: 17⁰G, 17⁰GF, 16⁰GF, 22⁶GF,

	Starts	1st	2nd	3rd	Win & Pl
NH Flat	3	0	0	0	0
Hurdles	1	0	0	0	
Career Total	4	0	0	0	

Going:	Sf: 0-0 GS: 0-0 Gd: 0-1 GF: - Fm: 0-3
Distance:	2m/2m3: 0-3 2m4-2m7: 0-1 3m+: 0-0
Track:	LH: 0-1 RH: 0-2 Tight: 0-1 Gall: 0-0
Aids:	Bl: 0-0 Vi: 0-0 Tstrap: 0-0
Best Rating:	69 6/02 Hrfd 2m1f gd-fm NHF

Tomwontpayalot
101   **85+**

4-y-o gr g Overbury (IRE)-Alice Smith (Alias Smith (USA))
B J Eckley Brian Eckley

Placings:*22*   (4444)
2002/03: 14²G, 16²G,

	Starts	1st	2nd	3rd	Win & Pl
NH Flat	2	0	2	0	1301
Career Total	2	0	2	0	1301

Going:	Sf: 0-0 GS: 0-0 Gd: 0-1 GF: - Fm: 0-1
Distance:	2m/2m3: 0-1 2m4-2m7: 0-0 3m+: 0-0
Track:	LH: 0-0 RH: 0-1 Tight: 0-0 Gall: 0-0
Aids:	Bl: 0-0 Vi: 0-0 Tstrap: 0-0
Best Rating:	99 4/03 Asct 2m110y good NHF

Has shown fair form in finishing runner-up on both bumper starts so far.

Tongita

5-y-o b m Petong-Bonita Bee (King Of Spain)
B R Millman (J C McConnochie 3/5) Mrs R E Stocks

Placings:*60-60P*   (3310)
2002/03: 17⁶G, 16⁰HY, 19⁵GS,

	Starts	1st	2nd	3rd	Win & Pl
NH Flat	2	0	0	0	0

Column 2

		Starts	1st	2nd	3rd	Win & Pl
Hurdles	1		0	0	0	0
Career Total	5		0	0	0	0

Going:	Sf: 0-1 GS: 0-1 Gd: 0-1 GF: - Fm: 0-0
Distance:	2m/2m3: 0-3 2m4-2m7: 0-0 3m+: 0-0
Track:	LH: 0-1 RH: 0-2 Tight: 0-1 Gall: 0-1
Aids:	Bl: 0-0 Vi: 0-0 Tstrap: 0-0
Best Rating:	75 3/02 Hntg 2m110y gd-fm NHF

Tonioso
78   **86**

8-y-o b g Teenoso (USA)-Sweet Ryme (Rymer)
Mrs S J Smith Mrs S Smith

Placings:*566*   (1219)
2002/03: 17⁵GF, 17⁶G, 17⁶G,

	Starts	1st	2nd	3rd	Win & Pl
Hurdles	3	0	0	0	0
Career Total	3	0	0	0	0

Going:	Sf: 0-0 GS: 0-0 Gd: 0-2 GF: - Fm: 0-1
Distance:	2m/2m3: 0-3 2m4-2m7: 0-0 3m+: 0-0
Track:	LH: 0-3 RH: 0-0 Tight: 0-1 Gall: 0-0
Aids:	Bl: 0-0 Vi: 0-0 Tstrap: 0-0
Best Rating:	76 8/02 Sthl 2m1f gd-fm Hdl

Tonka
99   **78**

11-y-o b g Mazilier (USA)-Royal Meeting (Dara Monarch)
D R Gandolfo M F Cartwright

Placings:*32/203140/F1F4223503/14/245400/F13600-006*   (3133)
2002/03: 19⁰G, 21⁰GS, 24⁶S,

	Starts	1st	2nd	3rd	Win & Pl
Hurdles	3	0	0	0	0
Career Total	35	4	5	5	26177
110 10/01 MRas	2m5f110yD(0-125)HHdl		GD		£5993
110 2/00 Wwck	2m4f110yC(0-130)HHdl		GD		£5135
106 11/98 Chep	2m110y D(0-135)HHdl		G-S		£2737
107 12/97 Font	2m2f110yD(0-120)HHdl		SFT		£2889
	Total win prize-money £16756				

Going:	Sf: 0-1 GS: 0-1 Gd: 0-1 GF: - Fm: 0-0
Distance:	2m/2m3: 0-0 2m4-2m7: 0-2 3m+: 0-1
Track:	LH: 0-0 RH: 0-3 Tight: 0-0 Gall: 0-1
Aids:	Bl: 0-0 Vi: 0-0 Tstrap: 0-0
Best Rating:	110 10/01 MRas 2m5f110y good Hdl

Plating-class hurdler; game front-runner. He had reportedly lost his confidence before scoring at Market Rasen in October 2001 on his seasonal reappearance, although he has been well held since then. Best at around two miles five furlongs. Has won on various goings but probably appreciates a bit of cut in the ground.

Tonoco
115   **123**

10-y-o b g Teenoso (USA)-Lady Shoco (Montekin)
Mrs S J Smith Trevor Hemmings

Placings:*1/41116P/50211F2/PPP-F2132P01*   (4714)
2002/03: 20⁶G, 16²G, 24¹S, 24³G, 24²GS, 21P S, 21⁰G, 25¹GF,

	Starts	1st	2nd	3rd	Win & Pl
Chases	8	2	2	1	29418
Career Total	25	8	4	1	60728
123 4/03 Weth	3m1f	B(0-150)HCh	G-F	£11362
118 12/02 Hayd	3m	D(0-125)HCh	SFT	£6223
132 3/01 MRas	2m1f110yD Ch		G-S	£5027

Column 3

132	2/01	Carl	2m	D Ch		SFT	£4536
138	2/99	Weth	2m	A Hdl		GD	£9509
133	1/99	Hntg	2m110y	D Hdl		SFT	£2762
132	12/98	Hayd	2m	D Hdl		SFT	£2866
106	4/98	Ayr	2m	H NHF		GD	£3598
				Total win prize-money £45887			

Going:	Sf: 1-2 GS: 0-1 Gd: 0-4 GF: - Fm: 1-1
Distance:	2m/2m3: 0-1 2m4-2m7: 0-3 3m+: 2-4
Track:	LH: 2-8 RH: 0-0 Tight: 0-2 Gall: 0-1
Aids:	Bl: 0-0 Vi: 0-0 Tstrap: 0-0
Best Rating:	138 2/99 Weth 2m good Hdl

Fair chaser; pulled up on all three outings in 2001/2; dropped in the handicap as a result; running well in 2002/3 winning at Haydock and Wetherby, stays three miles; seems to go on most ground; has worn a tongue ite.

Tony The Piler (IRE)
104   **86**

7-y-o br g Tidaro (USA)-Adabiya (IRE) (Akarad (FR))
N G Richards Taranto De Pol

Placings:*0660100B-3254*   (4394)
2002/03: 24³GF, 20⁹HY, 24⁵HY, 20⁴G,

	Starts	1st	2nd	3rd	Win & Pl
Hurdles	4	0	1	1	1328
Career Total	12	1	1	1	1328

Going:	Sf: 0-2 GS: 0-0 Gd: 0-1 GF: - Fm: 0-1
Distance:	2m/2m3: 0-0 2m4-2m7: 0-2 3m+: 0-2
Track:	LH: 0-1 RH: 0-3 Tight: 0-1 Gall: 0-0
Aids:	Bl: 0-0 Vi: 0-0 Tstrap: 0-0
Best Rating:	86 11/02 Carl 2m4f heavy Hdl

Plating-class hurdler, showed his first sign of ability over hurdles when dead-heating in a seller at Musselburgh in February 2002; fair efforts in higher grades since; stays well and acts on soft ground.

Tony Tie
61   **64**

7-y-o b g Ardkinglass-Queen Of The Quorn (Governor General)
J S Goldie Frank Brady

Placings:*0*   (1958)
2002/03: 16⁰S,

	Starts	1st	2nd	3rd	Win & Pl
Hurdles	1	0	0	0	
Career Total	1	0	0	0	

Going:	Sf: 0-1 GS: 0-0 Gd: 0-0 GF: - Fm: 0-0
Distance:	2m/2m3: 0-1 2m4-2m7: 0-0 3m+: 0-0
Track:	LH: 0-1 RH: 0-0 Tight: 0-0 Gall: 0-0
Aids:	Bl: 0-0 Vi: 0-0 Tstrap: 0-0
Best Rating:	64 11/02 Ayr 2m soft Hdl

Too Far To Bridge

6-y-o b g Jupiter Island-Catherine Bridge (Pitpan)
H D Daly J B Sumner

Placings:*P*   (2174)
2002/03: 20P S,

	Starts	1st	2nd	3rd	Win & Pl
Hurdles	1	0	0	0	
Career Total	1	0	0	0	

Going: Sf: 0-1 GS: 0-0 Gd: 0-0 GF: - Fm: 0-0
Distance: 2m/2m3: 0-0 2m4-2m7: 0-1 3m+: 0-0
Track: LH: 0-1 RH: 0-0 Tight: 0-0 Gall: 0-0
Aids: Bl: 0-0 Vi: 0-0 Tstrap: 0-0
Best Rating: 0   11/02 Chep   2m4f   soft   Hdl

Too Forward (IRE)

92   **97**

7-y-o ch g Toulon-One Back (IRE) (Meneval (USA))
M Pitman T L Gibson & D Mathias

Placings:233/F4122100-B0   (4609)
2002/03: 24⁸G, 24⁹G,

	Starts	1st	2nd	3rd	Win & Pl
Hurdles	2	0	0	0	
Career Total	13	2	3	2	21911
137 1/02 Donc	3m110y A Hdl			SFT	£10800
117 12/01 Folk	2m1f110yE Hdl			HVY	£2355
			Total win prize-money £13156		

Going: Sf: 0-0 GS: 0-0 Gd: 0-2 GF: - Fm: 0-0
Distance: 2m/2m3: 0-0 2m4-2m7: 0-0 3m+: 0-2
Track: LH: 0-2 RH: 0-0 Tight: 0-1 Gall: 0-1
Aids: Bl: 0-0 Vi: 0-0 Tstrap: 0-0
Best Rating: 137 1/02 Donc   3m110y   soft   Hdl

Very useful staying hurdler; creditable 7th to Galileo in Royal and SunAlliance Hurdle at Cheltenham Festival in 2002 having been hampered; handles heavy but does not want it too tacky, acts on a sounder surface; stays 3m; does not find a lot of the bit; brought down on return to the action at Aintree in April 2003.

Too Much

5-y-o b m Lugana Beach-Dancing May (Tina s Pet)
J L Spearing Thomas D Goodman

Placings:60PP   (1195)
2002/03: 16⁵GF, 16⁹GF, 16⁶GF, 19⁹GF,

	Starts	1st	2nd	3rd	Win & Pl
NH Flat	2	0	0	0	0
Hurdles	2	0	0	0	0
Career Total	4	0	0	0	0

Going: Sf: 0-0 GS: 0-0 Gd: 0-0 GF: - Fm: 0-4
Distance: 2m/2m3: 0-3 2m4-2m7: 0-1 3m+: 0-0
Track: LH: 0-1 RH: 0-2 Tight: 0-0 Gall: 0-1
Aids: Bl: 0-1 Vi: 0-0 Tstrap: 0-0
Best Rating: 67 7/02 Strf   2m110y   gd-fm   NHF

Too Technical (IRE)

104   **95**

8-y-o b g Archway (IRE)-Another Side (Bold Lad (IRE))
J M Jefferson Richard Collins

Placings:1/30/005   (3508)
2002/03: 16⁶GF, 16⁹G, 16⁵G,

	Starts	1st	2nd	3rd	Win & Pl
Hurdles	3	0	0	0	0
Career Total	6	1	0	1	1807
101 4/00 MRas	1m5f110yH NHF			SFT	£1533
			Total win prize-money £1533		

Going: Sf: 0-0 GS: 0-0 Gd: 0-2 GF: - Fm: 0-1
Distance: 2m/2m3: 0-3 2m4-2m7: 0-0 3m+: 0-0
Track: LH: 0-1 RH: 0-2 Tight: 0-3 Gall: 0-0
Aids: Bl: 0-0 Vi: 0-0 Tstrap: 0-0
Best Rating: 112 5/00 Prth   2m110y   gd-sft   NHF

Moderate hurdler; has improved over hurdles since being stepped up in distance with back-to-back wins over 2m 4f at Hexham and 2m 3f at Stratford; stays well; acts on all types of ground; can continue on the upgrade.

Toorak (USA)

81   **49**

6-y-o b g Irish River (FR)-Just Juliet (USA) (What A Pleasure (USA))
Mrs T J McInnes Skinner Mrs T J McInnes Skinner

Placings:4300-0   (4573)
2002/03: 16⁹GF,

	Starts	1st	2nd	3rd	Win & Pl
Hurdles	1	0	0	0	
Career Total	5	0	0	1	523

Going: Sf: 0-0 GS: 0-0 Gd: 0-0 GF: - Fm: 0-1
Distance: 2m/2m3: 0-1 2m4-2m7: 0-0 3m+: 0-0
Track: LH: 0-1 RH: 0-0 Tight: 0-1 Gall: 0-0
Aids: Bl: 0-0 Vi: 0-0 Tstrap: 0-0
Best Rating: 98 12/01 Hayd   2m   soft   Hdl

Top Ar Aghaidh (IRE)

102f   **92f**

5-y-o b m Topanoora-Shuil Ar Aghaidh (The Parson)
A J Lidderdale George Ward

Placings:1   (0063)
2002/03: 17¹G,

	Starts	1st	2nd	3rd	Win & Pl
NH Flat	1	1	0	0	1761
Career Total	1	1	0	0	1761
92 5/02 Folk	2m1f110yH NHF			GD	£1760
			Total win prize-money £1761		

Going: Sf: 0-0 GS: 0-0 Gd: 1-1 GF: - Fm: 0-0
Distance: 2m/2m3: 1-1 2m4-2m7: 0-0 3m+: 0-0
Track: LH: 0-0 RH: 1-1 Tight: 1-1 Gall: 0-0
Aids: Bl: 0-0 Vi: 0-0 Tstrap: 0-0
Best Rating: 92 5/02 Folk   2m1f110y   good   NHF

Out of a high-class mare; made a winning debut at Folkestone in May 2002.

Top Buck (IRE)

105(105h)   (118h)**132+**

9-y-o b/br g Top Of The World-Orlita (Master Buck)
K C Bailey A N Solomons

Placings:2F/235/1331430-11   (3669)
2002/03: 19¹GS, 20¹GS,

	Starts	1st	2nd	3rd	Win & Pl
Chases	2	2	0	0	10283
Career Total	14	4	2	4	21487
132 2/03 Font	2m4f D Ch			G-S	£5694
128 11/02 Asct	2m3f110yD Ch			G-S	£4589
114 1/02 Winc	2m6f E Hdl			GD	£2859
118 10/01 Extr	2m1f D Hdl			GD	£4238
			Total win prize-money £17381		

Going: Sf: 0-0 GS: 2-2 Gd: 0-0 GF: - Fm: 0-0
Distance: 2m/2m3: 0-0 2m4-2m7: 2-2 3m+: 0-0
Track: LH: 0-0 RH: 1-1 Tight: 1-1 Gall: 0-0
Aids: Bl: 0-0 Vi: 0-0 Tstrap: 0-0
Best Rating: 132 2/03 Font   2m4f   gd-sft   Ch

Useful chaser; stays two miles six; does not want the ground too soft.

Top Light

(68h)   **(19h)76**

7-y-o b g Miners Lamp-Myrtilla (Beldale Flutter (USA))
R H Buckler Robert Long

Placings:0/300PP-P4FF0F   (4633)
2002/03: 21⁵G, 24⁴GF, 24⁶S, 24⁵S, 22⁰S, 20⁶GF,

	Starts	1st	2nd	3rd	Win & Pl
Hurdles	2	0	0	0	0
Chases	4	0	0	0	413
Career Total	12	0	0	1	637

Going: Sf: 0-2 GS: 0-1 Gd: 0-1 GF: - Fm: 0-2
Distance: 2m/2m3: 0-0 2m4-2m7: 0-3 3m+: 0-3
Track: LH: 0-2 RH: 0-4 Tight: 0-5 Gall: 0-0
Aids: Bl: 0-0 Vi: 0-0 Tstrap: 0-0
Best Rating: 76 10/02 Tntn   3m   gd-fm   Ch

Top Nolans (IRE)

90   **70**

5-y-o ch g Topanoora-Lauretta Blue (IRE) (Bluebird (USA))
Miss K Marks (M H Tompkins 26/7) Nick Shutts

Placings:30   (1571)
2002/03: 16³GF, 16⁹G,

	Starts	1st	2nd	3rd	Win & Pl
Hurdles	2	0	0	1	494
Career Total	2	0	0	1	494

Going: Sf: 0-0 GS: 0-0 Gd: 0-1 GF: - Fm: 0-1
Distance: 2m/2m3: 0-2 2m4-2m7: 0-0 3m+: 0-0
Track: LH: 0-2 RH: 0-0 Tight: 0-1 Gall: 0-0
Aids: Bl: 0-0 Vi: 0-0 Tstrap: 0-0
Best Rating: 70 8/02 Uttx   2m   gd-fm   Hdl

A mile winner on heavy ground at Hamilton. A satisfactory start to his hurdling career at Uttoxeter but may have trouble getting the trip.

Top Notch

84f   **87f**

5-y-o br m Alderbrook-Gaygo Lady (Gay Fandango (USA))
K C Bailey Mrs Sharon C Nelson

Placings:60   (2064)
2002/03: 17⁶S, 17⁰S,

	Starts	1st	2nd	3rd	Win & Pl
NH Flat	2	0	0	0	0
Career Total	2	0	0	0	0

Going: Sf: 0-2 GS: 0-0 Gd: 0-0 GF: - Fm: 0-0
Distance: 2m/2m3: 0-2 2m4-2m7: 0-0 3m+: 0-0
Track: LH: 0-1 RH: 0-1 Tight: 0-1 Gall: 0-0
Aids: Bl: 0-0 Vi: 0-0 Tstrap: 0-0
Best Rating: 69 5/02 Bang   2m1f   soft   NHF

Top Of The Class (IRE)

87   **73**

6-y-o b m Rudimentary (USA)-School Mum (Reprimand)
P D Evans P D Evans

Placings:40/5U456-0   (1285)
2002/03: 18⁰GF,

	Starts	1st	2nd	3rd	Win & Pl
Hurdles	1	0	0	0	

Career Total	8	0	0	0	207

Going:	Sf: 0-0 GS: 0-0 Gd: 0-0 GF: - Fm: 0-1
Distance:	2m/2m3: 0-1 2m4-2m7: 0-0 3m+: 0-0
Track:	LH: 0-1 RH: 0-0 Tight: 0-1 Gall: 0-0
Aids:	Bl: 0-0 Vi: 0-1 Tstrap: 0-0
Best Rating:	73 10/01 Aint 2m110y good Hdl

Top Of The Dee
91   **75**

6-y-o ch m Rakaposhi King-Lavenham s Last (Rymer)
Mrs L Williamson Bangor-On-Dee Racing Club

Placings:600-650334236   (1493)
2002/03: 17⁶S, 16⁵GS, 16⁹GF, 20³GF, 17³S, 20⁴GF, 17²GF, 22³GF, 17⁶GS,

	Starts	1st	2nd	3rd	Win & Pl
Hurdles	9	0	1	3	3253
Career Total	12	0	1	3	3253

Going:	Sf: 0-2 GS: 0-2 Gd: 0-1 GF: - Fm: 0-4
Distance:	2m/2m3: 0-6 2m4-2m7: 0-3 3m+: 0-0
Track:	LH: 0-9 RH: 0-0 Tight: 0-5 Gall: 0-0
Aids:	Bl: 0-0 Vi: 0-0 Tstrap: 0-3
Best Rating:	82 7/02 Uttx 2m4f110y gd-fm Hdl

Poor maiden hurdler.

Top Of The Left
79   **70+**

8-y-o b/br g Nomination-Diva Madonna (Chief Singer)
Jonjo O Neill J P McManus

Placings:35/0   (3311)
2002/03: 19⁹GS,

	Starts	1st	2nd	3rd	Win & Pl
Hurdles	1	0	0	0	
Career Total	3	0	0	1	340

Going:	Sf: 0-0 GS: 0-1 Gd: 0-0 GF: - Fm: 0-0
Distance:	2m/2m3: 0-1 2m4-2m7: 0-0 3m+: 0-0
Track:	LH: 0-0 RH: 0-1 Tight: 0-0 Gall: 0-0
Aids:	Bl: 0-0 Vi: 0-0 Tstrap: 0-0
Best Rating:	101 3/01 Hntg 2m4f110y soft Hdl

Top Of The Stack

5-y-o b g Syrtos-Just Hannah (Macmillion)
B N Doran West Mercia Fork Trucks Ltd

Placings:0P   (3350)
2002/03: 16⁰S, 20⁰HY,

	Starts	1st	2nd	3rd	Win & Pl
NH Flat	1	0	0	0	0
Hurdles	1	0	0	0	0
Career Total	2	0	0	0	

Going:	Sf: 0-2 GS: 0-0 Gd: 0-0 GF: - Fm: 0-0
Distance:	2m/2m3: 0-1 2m4-2m7: 0-1 3m+: 0-0
Track:	LH: 0-0 RH: 0-2 Tight: 0-0 Gall: 0-0
Aids:	Bl: 0-0 Vi: 0-0 Tstrap: 0-0
Best Rating:	15 1/03 Ludl 2m soft NHF

Top Saint (IRE)
92   **86**

9-y-o gr g Topanoora-God s Kiss (Godswalk (USA))

Mrs M Reveley Brennan And Rodden

Placings:0/04/005/030/542-0   (0322)
2002/03: 21²GS, 24⁹G,

	Starts	1st	2nd	3rd	Win & Pl
Hurdles	2	0	1	0	566
Career Total	13	0	1	1	1139

Going:	Sf: 0-0 GS: 0-1 Gd: 0-1 GF: - Fm: 0-0
Distance:	2m/2m3: 0-0 2m4-2m7: 0-1 3m+: 0-1
Track:	LH: 0-1 RH: 0-1 Tight: 0-0 Gall: 0-0
Aids:	Bl: 0-0 Vi: 0-0 Tstrap: 0-0
Best Rating:	91 1/00 Sedg 2m1f soft Hdl

Selling-class hurdler, stays well.

Top Stoppa
     46f

5-y-o gr g Environment Friend-Orchid Valley (IRE) (Cyrano De Bergerac)
A Scott Mrs A Scott

Placings:0   (1242)
2002/03: 16⁰GF,

	Starts	1st	2nd	3rd	Win & Pl
NH Flat	1	0	0	0	
Career Total	1	0	0	0	

Going:	Sf: 0-0 GS: 0-0 Gd: 0-0 GF: - Fm: 0-1
Distance:	2m/2m3: 0-1 2m4-2m7: 0-0 3m+: 0-0
Track:	LH: 0-1 RH: 0-0 Tight: 0-0 Gall: 0-0
Aids:	Bl: 0-0 Vi: 0-0 Tstrap: 0-0
Best Rating:	50 9/02 Hexm 2m110y gd-fm NHF

Top Team

7-y-o b m Teamster-Highly Inflammable (USA) (Wind And Wuthering (USA))
Dr P Pritchard Lady Maria Coventry

Placings:0/0/0PPP00-3PP   (0506)
2002/03: 20³GF, 20⁵GS, 20⁶G,

	Starts	1st	2nd	3rd	Win & Pl
Chases	3	0	0	1	620
Career Total	11	0	0	1	620

Going:	Sf: 0-0 GS: 0-1 Gd: 0-1 GF: - Fm: 0-1
Distance:	2m/2m3: 0-0 2m4-2m7: 0-3 3m+: 0-0
Track:	LH: 0-2 RH: 0-1 Tight: 0-2 Gall: 0-0
Aids:	Bl: 0-0 Vi: 0-0 Tstrap: 0-0
Best Rating:	54 7/01 Worc 2m good NHF

Top Trees
83   **69**

5-y-o b g Charnwood Forest (IRE)-Low Line (High Line)
W S Kittow Mrs P E Hawkings

Placings:40   (2194)
2002/03: 17⁴GS, 17⁰GS,

	Starts	1st	2nd	3rd	Win & Pl
Hurdles	2	0	0	0	0
Career Total	2	0	0	0	0

Going:	Sf: 0-0 GS: 0-2 Gd: 0-0 GF: - Fm: 0-0
Distance:	2m/2m3: 0-2 2m4-2m7: 0-0 3m+: 0-0
Track:	LH: 0-0 RH: 0-2 Tight: 0-2 Gall: 0-0
Aids:	Bl: 0-0 Vi: 0-0 Tstrap: 0-0

Best Rating: 69 11/02 Tntn 2m1f gd-sft Hdl

Topol (IRE)
86   **79**

5-y-o br g Topanoora-Kislev (IRE) (Be My Guest (USA))
Miss H C Knight Top Brass Partnership

Placings:0-000   (3779)
2002/03: 17⁰GS, 16⁰GS, 19⁰GS,

	Starts	1st	2nd	3rd	Win & Pl
Hurdles	3	0	0	0	
Career Total	4	0	0	0	

Going:	Sf: 0-0 GS: 0-3 Gd: 0-0 GF: - Fm: 0-0
Distance:	2m/2m3: 0-3 2m4-2m7: 0-0 3m+: 0-0
Track:	LH: 0-2 RH: 0-1 Tight: 0-1 Gall: 0-1
Aids:	Bl: 0-0 Vi: 0-0 Tstrap: 0-0
Best Rating:	80 3/02 Newb 2m110y gd-sft NHF

Topping Lass (IRE)
86   **50**

8-y-o b m Topanoora-Grassed (Busted)
A W Carroll (C Roche 31/8) Miss E J Marley

Placings:3/1U/00-5PL000P   (3814)
2002/03: 16⁵G, 20⁸G, 22ᴸGS, 17⁹GS, 19⁵S, 16⁹HY, 16⁸G,

	Starts	1st	2nd	3rd	Win & Pl
Hurdles	7	0	0	1	
Career Total	11	0	0	1	336

Going:	Sf: 0-2 GS: 0-2 Gd: 0-3 GF: - Fm: 0-0
Distance:	2m/2m3: 0-5 2m4-2m7: 0-2 3m+: 0-0
Track:	LH: 0-4 RH: 0-2 Tight: 0-4 Gall: 0-0
Aids:	Bl: 0-0 Vi: 0-0 Tstrap: 0-6
Best Rating:	99 8/00 Tram 2m gd-fm NHF

Torche (IRE)
99f   **94f**

5-y-o b g Taos (IRE)-Orchette (IRE) (Orchestra)
D J Caro Mrs S Tainton

Placings:4   (4322)
2002/03: 17⁴G,

	Starts	1st	2nd	3rd	Win & Pl
NH Flat	1	0	0	0	0
Career Total	1	0	0	0	0

Going:	Sf: 0-0 GS: 0-0 Gd: 0-1 GF: - Fm: 0-0
Distance:	2m/2m3: 0-1 2m4-2m7: 0-0 3m+: 0-0
Track:	LH: 0-1 RH: 0-0 Tight: 0-0 Gall: 0-0
Aids:	Bl: 0-0 Vi: 0-0 Tstrap: 0-0
Best Rating:	94 3/03 Bang 2m1f good NHF

Torduff Express (IRE)

12-y-o b g Kambalda-Marhabtain (Touching Wood (USA))
P F Nicholls Two Plus Two

Placings:121321/12104/33F/1562P/2131-21U4   (4777)
2002/03: 22²GS, 26¹GS, 36ᵁG, 31⁴G,

	Starts	1st	2nd	3rd	Win & Pl
Chases	4	1	1	0	6361
Career Total	27	9	6	4	107463

130	2/03	Font	3m2f110yH Ch	G-S	£3328
131	4/02	Aint	2m5f110yB Ch	GD	£21645
126	2/02	Font	3m2f110yH Ch	SFT	£6922
112	10/00	Extr	2m6f110yE Hdl	GD	£2540
144	12/98	Asct	3m110y B HCh	G-S	£27230
128	10/98	Plum	3m1f110yC(0-130)HCh	GD	£5257
122	4/98	Sand	3m110y C Ch	G-S	£4598
103	2/98	Font	3m110yE Ch	GD	£3116
103	12/97	Hrfd	3m1f110yE Ch	GD	£2697
				Total win prize-money	£77335

Going: Sf: 0-0 GS: 1-2 Gd: 0-2 GF: - Fm: 0-0
Distance: 2m/2m3: 0-0 2m4-2m7: 0-0 **3m+: 1-3**
Track: LH: 0-2 RH: 0-0 **Tight: 1-2** Gall: 0-0
Aids: **Bl: 1-4** Vi: 0-0 Tstrap: 0-0
Best Rating: 144 12/98 Asct 3m110y gd-sft Ch

Useful hunter chaser; won the Aintree Fox Hunters in 2002 and landed a hunter chase at Fontwell in February 2003; goes well in soft ground; effective in blinkers.

Toreo (FR)

85   63

9-y-o ch g Bakharoff (USA)-Becerrada (FR) (Tip Moss (FR))
J R Adam James R Adam

Placings:3642/00/6/PF   (4019)
2002/03: 20PS, 16FS,

	Starts	1st	2nd	3rd	Win & Pl
Hurdles	2	0	0	0	
Career Total	9	0	1	1	721

Going: Sf: 0-2 GS: 0-0 Gd: 0-0 GF: - Fm: 0-0
Distance: 2m/2m3: 0-1 2m4-2m7: 0-1 3m+: 0-0
Track: LH: 0-2 RH: 0-0 Tight: 0-0 Gall: 0-1
Aids: Bl: 0-0 Vi: 0-0 Tstrap: 0-0
Best Rating: 103 4/99 Hntg 2m110y gd-fm NHF

Tormentoso

96   77

6-y-o b g Catrail (USA)-Chita Rivera (Chief Singer)
A G Hobbs Furnish With Abbey

Placings:00P4PP5/5F06000502350225-0060   (0609)
2002/03: 16DG, 20PG, 16FGF, 16UGF,

	Starts	1st	2nd	3rd	Win & Pl
Hurdles	4	0	0	0	
Career Total	27	0	3	1	1843

Going: Sf: 0-0 GS: 0-0 Gd: 0-2 GF: - Fm: 0-2
Distance: 2m/2m3: 0-3 2m4-2m7: 0-1 3m+: 0-0
Track: LH: 0-3 RH: 0-1 Tight: 0-1 Gall: 0-1
Aids: Bl: 0-0 Vi: 0-0 Tstrap: 0-0
Best Rating: 77 4/02 Hrfd 2m1f good Hdl

Plating-class hurdler, suited by good ground.

Torn Silk

9-y-o b g Top Ville-Cut Velvet (USA) (Northern Dancer)
P England (P F Nicholls 9/6) P England

Placings:01533/05331UF/P421PF2/144564/014F52F1-146P   (4526)
2002/03: 23IS, 20UGS, 25UGS, 24PG,

	Starts	1st	2nd	3rd	Win & Pl
Chases	4	1	0	0	6825
Career Total	37	7	3	4	57829
126	6/02	Worc	2m7f110yC(0-135)HCh	SFT	£6825
125	10/01	Tntn	3m D(0-120)HCh	FRM	£5538

129	6/01	Worc	2m4f110yD(0-120)HCh	G-F	£4114
123	5/00	Worc	2m4f110yB(0-145)HCh	G-F	£10380
123	12/99	Uttx	2m C(0-135)HCh	SFT	£7048
111	1/99	Muss	2m D Ch	SFT	£3762
114	2/98	MRas	2m1f110yC Hdl	GD	£4458
				Total win prize-money	£42128

Going: Sf: 1-1 GS: 0-2 Gd: 0-1 GF: - Fm: 0-0
Distance: 2m/2m3: 0-0 2m4-2m7: 0-1 **3m+: 1-3**
Track: **LH: 1-2** RH: 0-2 Tight: 0-1 Gall: 0-0
Aids: **Bl: 1-2** Vi: 0-0 Tstrap: 0-0
Best Rating: 129 6/01 Worc 2m4f110y gd-fm Ch

One-time decent handicap chaser; on the downgrade and well beaten in hunter chases in 2003.

Torosay (IRE)

66f   99f

5-y-o b g Presenting-Mazuma (IRE) (Mazaad)
N G Richards J Hales

Placings:5   (3917)
2002/03: 17UGS,

	Starts	1st	2nd	3rd	Win & Pl
NH Flat	1	0	0	0	
Career Total	1	0	0	0	

Going: Sf: 0-0 GS: 0-1 Gd: 0-0 GF: - Fm: 0-0
Distance: 2m/2m3: 0-1 2m4-2m7: 0-0 3m+: 0-0
Track: LH: 0-0 RH: 0-1 Tight: 0-0 Gall: 0-0
Aids: Bl: 0-0 Vi: 0-0 Tstrap: 0-0
Best Rating: 105 3/03 Carl 2m1f gd-sft NHF

Fourth in a point; showed ability in bumper at Carlisle in March.

Tortuga Dream (IRE)

75   46

4-y-o b g Turtle Island (IRE)-Tycoon s Catch (IRE) (Thatching)
A Charlton P J Haycock

Placings:0600   (4605)
2002/03: 16UG, 16FHY, 20US, 17UG,

	Starts	1st	2nd	3rd	Win & Pl
Hurdles	4	0	0	0	
Career Total	4	0	0	0	

Going: Sf: 0-2 GS: 0-0 Gd: 0-2 GF: - Fm: 0-0
Distance: 2m/2m3: 0-3 2m4-2m7: 0-1 3m+: 0-0
Track: LH: 0-3 RH: 0-0 Tight: 0-2 Gall: 0-2
Aids: Bl: 0-0 Vi: 0-0 Tstrap: 0-0
Best Rating: 46 4/03 Chel 2m1f good Hdl

Tortugas (FR)

86(91h)   (48h)61d

6-y-o b g Subotica (FR)-Northern Whisper (FR) (Vacarme (USA))
Mrs H Dalton Miss Julia Oakey

Placings:01206/P3P50-044FFF   (4699)
2002/03: 17UG, 17UG, 19UGF, 24FG, 19FG, 17FGF,

	Starts	1st	2nd	3rd	Win & Pl
Hurdles	1	0	0	0	
Chases	5	0	0	0	235
Career Total	16	1	1	1	2970
97	11/00	Tntn	2m1f G Hdl	G-S	£1578
				Total win prize-money	£1579

Torus Star (IRE)

14-y-o b g Torus-Vulstar (Vulgan)
Mrs J Mathias Mrs J Mathias

Placings:0/00P0/PF/06/P   (0218)
2002/03: 25PG,

	Starts	1st	2nd	3rd	Win & Pl
Chases	1	0	0	0	
Career Total	9	0	0	0	

Going: Sf: 0-0 GS: 0-0 Gd: 0-4 GF: - Fm: 0-2
Distance: 2m/2m3: 0-4 2m4-2m7: 0-1 3m+: 0-1
Track: LH: 0-5 RH: 0-1 Tight: 0-3 Gall: 0-0
Aids: Bl: 0-0 Vi: 0-0 Tstrap: 0-0
Best Rating: 97 11/00 Tntn 2m1f gd-sft Hdl

Tory Boy

106   100

8-y-o b g Deploy-Mukhayyalah (Dancing Brave (USA))
M G Quinlan Mrs A W Turner

Placings:P0/121150/65243/06315-1124   (1182)
2002/03: 17IGF, 16IS, 21UGF, 21UG,

	Starts	1st	2nd	3rd	Win & Pl
Hurdles	4	2	1	0	11794
Career Total	22	6	3	2	24031
100	8/02	Strf	2m110y D(0-125)HHdl	SFT	£5057
96	7/02	Sthl	2m D(0-125)HHdl	G-F	£5369
82	8/01	Hntg	2m4f110yG Hdl	G-F	£1549
101	9/99	Sedg	2m5f110yE Hdl	G-F	£2617
72	8/99	Sthl	3m110y E Hdl	G-F	£2221
93	8/99	Strf	2m110y E Hdl	G-F	£2557
				Total win prize-money	£19374

Going: Sf: 1-1 GS: 0-0 Gd: 0-1 GF: - Fm: 1-2
Distance: **2m/2m3: 2-2** 2m4-2m7: 0-2 3m+: 0-0
Track: **LH: 2-4** RH: 0-0 **Tight: 1-1** Gall: 0-0
Aids: Bl: 0-0 Vi: 0-0 Tstrap: 0-0
Best Rating: 111 7/00 Strf 2m6f110y gd-fm Hdl

Modest hurdler, transferred the form that saw him win on the Flat to jumps when winning at Southwell and Stratford in July 2002. Acts on any ground.

Tosawi (IRE)

107   106

7-y-o b g Commanche Run-Deep Satisfaction (Deep Run)
R J Hodges S J Norman

Placings:5/030/04P1421PP-6040032   (3949)
2002/03: 16UG, 21UG, 19UGS, 24UGS, 22UGS, 16UHY, 19US,

	Starts	1st	2nd	3rd	Win & Pl
Hurdles	7	0	1	1	2529
Career Total	20	2	2	2	9180
109	1/02	Tntn	2m3f110yF(0-100)HHdl	SFT	£2714
97	12/01	Extr	2m1f F(0-100)HHdl	GD	£2520
				Total win prize-money	£5235

Going: Sf: 0-2 GS: 0-3 Gd: 0-2 GF: - Fm: 0-0
Distance: 2m/2m3: 0-3 2m4-2m7: 0-3 3m+: 0-1
Track: LH: 0-1 RH: 0-6 Tight: 0-2 Gall: 0-1
Aids: Bl: 0-0 Vi: 0-0 Tstrap: 0-0
Best Rating: 109 1/02 Tntn 2m3f110y soft Hdl

Modest hurdler; acts well on a soft surface; stays two and a half miles.

Toscanini (GER)
107   100
7-y-o b g Goofalik (USA)-Tosca Stella (GER) (Surumu (GER))
D R Gandolfo Mrs John Lee

Placings:3404-5P1   (3949)
2002/03: 16⁵HY, 21ᴾS, 19¹S,

	Starts	1st	2nd	3rd	Win & Pl
Hurdles	3	1	0	0	4859
Career Total	7	1	0	0	5673
100 3/03 Extr 2m3f D(0-115)HHdl SFT £4858					
Total win prize-money £4859					

Going:	Sf: 1-3 GS: 0-0 Gd: 0-0 GF: - Fm: 0-0
Distance:	2m/2m3: 1-2 2m4-2m7: 0-1 3m+: 0-0
Track:	LH: 0-1 RH: 1-2 Tight: 0-0 Gall: 0-1
Aids:	Bl: 0-0 Vi: 0-0 Tstrap: 0-0
Best Rating:	100 3/03 Extr 2m3f soft Hdl

Modeat hurdler; fair Flat form in Germany; described as a bit of a thinker by his trainer was suited to the small field when winning a falsely-run four-runner handicap at Exeter March 2003; acts on soft ground.

Tosheroon (IRE)
108   110
7-y-o b g Good Thyne (USA)-Rare Currency (Rarity)
A M Hales Andrew L Cohen

Placings:13   (1727)
2002/03: 21¹G, 20³GS,

	Starts	1st	2nd	3rd	Win & Pl
Hurdles	2	1	0	1	3880
Career Total	2	1	0	1	3880
110 10/02 Plum 2m5f E Hdl GD £3220					
Total win prize-money £3220					

Going:	Sf: 0-0 GS: 0-1 Gd: 1-1 GF: - Fm: 0-0
Distance:	2m/2m3: 0-0 2m4-2m7: 1-2 3m+: 0-0
Track:	LH: 1-1 RH: 0-1 Tight: 1-1 Gall: 0-0
Aids:	Bl: 0-0 Vi: 0-0 Tstrap: 0-0
Best Rating:	110 11/02 Asct 2m4f gd-sft Hdl

Made a very impressive debut under Rules when winning by ten lengths in a moderate novice hurdle at Plumpton in October 2002, and ran well in defeat on softer ground next time.

Toshiba Times
93(101h)   (98h)97+
7-y-o b g Persian Bold-Kirkby Belle (Bay Express)
M Todhunter (B Ellison 9/8) B Batey

Placings:60P/202132-54   (1529)
2002/03: 16⁵G, 16⁴G,

	Starts	1st	2nd	3rd	Win & Pl
Chases	2	0	0	0	383
Career Total	11	1	3	1	5438
98 9/01 Sedg 2m1f E Hdl G-F £2436					
Total win prize-money £2436					

Going:	Sf: 0-0 GS: 0-0 Gd: 0-2 GF: - Fm: 0-0
Distance:	2m/2m3: 0-2 2m4-2m7: 0-0 3m+: 0-0
Track:	LH: 0-2 RH: 0-0 Tight: 0-2 Gall: 0-0
Aids:	Bl: 0-0 Vi: 0-0 Tstrap: 0-0
Best Rating:	98 10/01 Sedg 2m1f good Hdl

Moderate hurdler/chaser; won a novice hurdle at Sedgefield, but looked less than keen when beaten there in October.

Tosti (FR)
94   86
7-y-o b g Beyssac (FR)-Madame Flibuste (FR) (Rahotep (FR))
C R Egerton K Blackham, T Gould & E De Giles

Placings:1/P-5P   (2549)
2002/03: 26⁵GS, 25ᴾS,

	Starts	1st	2nd	3rd	Win & Pl
Chases	2	0	0	0	0
Career Total	4	1	0	0	3362
4/00 Fntb 2m Hdl SFT £3362					
Total win prize-money £3362					

Going:	Sf: 0-1 GS: 0-1 Gd: 0-0 GF: - Fm: 0-0
Distance:	2m/2m3: 0-0 2m4-2m7: 0-0 3m+: 0-2
Track:	LH: 0-1 RH: 0-1 Tight: 0-1 Gall: 0-0
Aids:	Bl: 0-0 Vi: 0-0 Tstrap: 0-0
Best Rating:	86 12/02 Wwck 3m2f gd-sft Ch

Winning hurdler in France; yet to show much over fences in this country.

Total Eclipse (IRE)
69   8
8-y-o b g Be My Native (USA)-Everdancing (Dance In Time (CAN))
A J Lockwood A J Lockwood

Placings:5P53600/0   (1163)
2002/03: 17⁰GF,

	Starts	1st	2nd	3rd	Win & Pl
Hurdles	1	0	0	0	
Career Total	8	0	0	1	214

Going:	Sf: 0-0 GS: 0-0 Gd: 0-0 GF: - Fm: 0-1
Distance:	2m/2m3: 0-1 2m4-2m7: 0-0 3m+: 0-0
Track:	LH: 0-1 RH: 0-0 Tight: 0-1 Gall: 0-0
Aids:	Bl: 0-0 Vi: 0-0 Tstrap: 0-0
Best Rating:	87 5/00 Extr 2m1f gd-fm NHF

Totally Scottish
106   117
7-y-o b g Mtoto-Glenfinlass (Lomond (USA))
Mrs M Reveley The Phoenix Racing C O

Placings:0002/32451164464402-U21252   (4308)
2002/03: 16ᵁGF, 17²S, 17¹HY, 19²GS, 20⁵GS, 18²G,

	Starts	1st	2nd	3rd	Win & Pl
Hurdles	6	1	3	0	10178
Career Total	24	3	6	1	18557
114 11/02 Carl 2m1f D(0-120)HHdl HVY £3623					
103 10/01 Kels 2m1f10y D(0-125)HHdl G-S £3325					
99 10/01 Carl 2m4f F(0-100)HHdl G-S £2108					
Total win prize-money £9057					

Going:	Sf: 1-2 GS: 0-2 Gd: 0-1 GF: - Fm: 0-1
Distance:	2m/2m3: 1-4 2m4-2m7: 0-2 3m+: 0-0
Track:	LH: 0-4 RH: 1-2 Tight: 0-2 Gall: 0-0
Aids:	Bl: 0-0 Vi: 0-0 Tstrap: 0-0
Best Rating:	117 3/03 Kels 2m2f good Hdl

Fair hurdler; goes well on a stiff track and has a good record at Carlisle; best over two miles.

Totem Dancer
53
10-y-o b m Mtoto-Ballad Opera (Sadler s Wells (USA))
B G Powell G Lloyd

Placings:0/6P/4-P   (1220)
2002/03: 21ᴾG,

	Starts	1st	2nd	3rd	Win & Pl
Hurdles	1	0	0	0	0
Career Total	5	0	0	0	0

Going:	Sf: 0-0 GS: 0-0 Gd: 0-1 GF: - Fm: 0-0
Distance:	2m/2m3: 0-0 2m4-2m7: 0-1 3m+: 0-0
Track:	LH: 0-1 RH: 0-0 Tight: 0-0 Gall: 0-0
Aids:	Bl: 0-0 Vi: 0-0 Tstrap: 0-1
Best Rating:	82 2/00 Muss 2m gd-sft Hdl

Totland Bay (IRE)
(105h)   (107h)
7-y-o br g Phardante (FR)-Seanaphobal Lady (Kambalda)
J W Mullins Ian M McGready

Placings:43040P2-401232232   (4634)
2002/03: 20⁴GF, 23⁰GS, 22¹GF, 22²GF, 22³G, 22²GF, 22²G, 22³G, 21²GF,

	Starts	1st	2nd	3rd	Win & Pl
Hurdles	9	1	4	2	8628
Career Total	16	1	5	3	9620
91 7/02 NAbb 2m6f D Hdl G-F £3581					
Total win prize-money £3582					

Going:	Sf: 0-0 GS: 0-1 Gd: 0-3 GF: - Fm: 1-5
Distance:	2m/2m3: 0-0 2m4-2m7: 1-8 3m+: 0-1
Track:	LH: 1-7 RH: 0-1 Tight: 1-8 Gall: 0-0
Aids:	Bl: 0-0 Vi: 0-0 Tstrap: 0-0
Best Rating:	107 10/02 Font 2m6f110y good Hdl

Modest hurdler, consistent sort, but often finds one or two too good; best on a sound surface; effective at around two miles six furlongs.

Toto Taleca
91   49
6-y-o b m Mtoto-Miss Taleca (Pharly (FR))
M E Sowersby M E Sowersby

Placings:00/4-000P00UP   (4782)
2002/03: 16⁰G, 19⁰G, 19⁴GS, 21ᴾHY, 16⁰G, 17⁰S, 17ᵁGF, 17ᴾG,

	Starts	1st	2nd	3rd	Win & Pl
NH Flat	1	0	0	0	0
Hurdles	7	0	0	0	0
Career Total	11	0	0	0	0

Going:	Sf: 0-2 GS: 0-1 Gd: 0-4 GF: - Fm: 0-1
Distance:	2m/2m3: 0-7 2m4-2m7: 0-1 3m+: 0-0
Track:	LH: 0-6 RH: 0-2 Tight: 0-7 Gall: 0-0
Aids:	Bl: 0-0 Vi: 0-0 Tstrap: 0-0
Best Rating:	75 11/01 Aint 2m1f gd-sft NHF

Touch Closer
89   74
6-y-o b g Inchinor-Ryewater Dream (Touching Wood (USA))
G A Swinbank C N Barnes

Placings:13-060P   (4406)
2002/03: 16⁶GS, 21⁵HY, 16⁰GS, 20ᴾG,

	Starts	1st	2nd	3rd	Win & Pl
Hurdles	4	0	0	0	0
Career Total	6	1	0	1	5123
115 3/02 Ayr 2m H NHF SFT £1673					
Total win prize-money £1673					

Going:	Sf: 0-1 GS: 0-2 Gd: 0-1 GF: - Fm: 0-0
Distance:	2m/2m3: 0-2 2m4-2m7: 0-2 3m+: 0-0

Track: LH: 0-4 RH: 0-0 Tight: 0-1 Gall: 0-1
Aids: Bl: 0-0 Vi: 0-0 Tstrap: 0-0
Best Rating: 135 4/02 Aint 2m1f   good   NHF

Modest novice hurdler; bumper winner; yet to win over timber.

Touch Of Ebony (IRE)

84   62

4-y-o b c Darshaan-Cormorant Wood (Home Guard (USA))
C Roberts (J Neville 28/2) Mrs Theresa O Toole

Placings:000   (3870)
2002/03: 17⁰HY, 17⁰GS, 16⁰S,

	Starts	1st	2nd	3rd	Win & Pl
Hurdles	3	0	0	0	
Career Total	3	0	0	0	

Going: Sf: 0-2 GS: 0-1 Gd: 0-0 GF: - Fm: 0-0
Distance: 2m2m3: 0-3 2m4-2m7: 0-0 3m+: 0-0
Track: LH: 0-1 RH: 0-2 Tight: 0-1 Gall: 0-1
Aids: Bl: 0-0 Vi: 0-0 Tstrap: 0-0
Best Rating: 62 2/03 Newb 2m110y   soft   Hdl

Modest maiden on the Flat and over hurdles.

Tough Terms (IRE)

11-y-o b g Welsh Term-Glenardina (Furry Glen)
Miss V Park D F Donegan

Placings:05/23/UP5/P/1   (0312)
2002/03: 21¹G,

	Starts	1st	2nd	3rd	Win & Pl
Chases	1	1	0	0	2126
Career Total	9	1	1	1	3086
83 5/02 Folk	2m5f	H Ch		GD	£2125

Total win prize-money £2126

Going: Sf: 0-0 GS: 0-0 Gd: 1-1 GF: - Fm: 0-0
Distance: 2m2m3: 0-0 **2m4-2m7: 1-1** 3m+: 0-0
Track: LH: 0-0 **RH: 1-1** Tight: 1-1 Gall: 0-0
Aids: Bl: 0-0 Vi: 0-0 Tstrap: 0-0
Best Rating: 108 11/97 Fair 2m   yield   NHF

Decisive winner of a hunter chase at Folkestone in May 2002.

Toulon Crest (IRE)

94   94

6-y-o b g Toulon-Another Contact (Martin John)
G Prodromou (Donal Hassett 13/7) Alan Macalister

Placings:000P3   (4689)
2002/03: 17⁰HY, 16⁰G, 16⁰G, 24⁶G, 17³G,

	Starts	1st	2nd	3rd	Win & Pl
NH Flat	3	0	0	0	0
Chases	2	0	0	1	833
Career Total	5	0	0	1	833

Going: Sf: 0-1 GS: 0-0 Gd: 0-4 GF: - Fm: 0-0
Distance: 2m2m3: 0-4 2m4-2m7: 0-0 3m+: 0-1
Track: LH: 0-2 RH: 0-3 Tight: 0-4 Gall: 0-1
Aids: Bl: 0-0 Vi: 0-0 Tstrap: 0-1
Best Rating: 94 4/03 MRas 2m1f110y   good   Ch

Modest form in novice chases at up to 3m.

Toulon D'Or (IRE)

86(70h)   (75h)67

6-y-o b g Toulon-Rare Currency (Rarity)
M Pitman Mrs D Salmon

Placings:00-50064P   (2414)
2002/03: 17⁵G, 18⁰GF, 16⁹G, 16⁶G, 20⁴G, 20⁰G,

	Starts	1st	2nd	3rd	Win & Pl
NH Flat	1	0	0	0	0
Hurdles	3	0	0	0	0
Chases	2	0	0	0	321
Career Total	8	0	0	0	321

Going: Sf: 0-0 GS: 0-0 Gd: 0-5 GF: - Fm: 0-1
Distance: 2m/2m3: 0-4 2m4-2m7: 0-2 3m+: 0-0
Track: LH: 0-2 RH: 0-3 Tight: 0-4 Gall: 0-0
Aids: Bl: 0-0 Vi: 0-0 Tstrap: 0-0
Best Rating: 72 11/02 Winc 2m   good   Hdl

Toulon Rouge (IRE)

101   96

6-y-o b m Toulon-Master Nidee (Master Owen)
Ferdy Murphy Racegoers Club Owners Group

Placings:140-6P63161   (4750)
2002/03: 20⁶G, 21⁹GS, 21⁸S, 21³HY, 21¹S, 21⁶G, 24¹G,

	Starts	1st	2nd	3rd	Win & Pl
Hurdles	7	2	0	1	10185
Career Total	10	3	0	1	11746
98 4/03 Prth	3m110y	D Hdl		GD	£6162
89 3/03 Sedg	2m5f110yE Hdl			SFT	£3528
89 1/02 Sedg	2m1f	H Hdl		SFT	£1561

Total win prize-money £11251

Going: Sf: 1-3 GS: 0-1 Gd: 1-3 GF: - Fm: 0-0
Distance: 2m/2m3: 0-0 2m4-2m7: 1-6 3m+: 1-1
Track: LH: 1-6 RH: 1-1 **Tight: 1-4** Gall: 0-0
Aids: Bl: 0-0 Vi: 0-0 Tstrap: 0-0
Best Rating: 103 3/02 Towc 2m   soft   NHF

Moderate hurdler; worked hard to win bumper on racecourse debut at Sedgefield and put disappointing spell behind him when successful at the same track over hurdles in March 2003; stays 2m 5f; acts on soft and heavy.

Toulouse (IRE)

107   114

6-y-o b g Toulon-Neasham (Nishapour (FR))
R H Alner Pell-Mell Partners

Placings:31500   (3779)
2002/03: 16³G, 17¹GS, 16⁵GS, 22⁰GS, 19⁰GS,

	Starts	1st	2nd	3rd	Win & Pl
NH Flat	1	0	0	1	342
Hurdles	4	1	0	0	7085
Career Total	5	1	0	1	7427
114 12/02 Tntn	2m1f	C Hdl		G-S	£7085

Total win prize-money £7085

Going: Sf: 0-0 GS: 1-4 Gd: 0-1 GF: - Fm: 0-0
Distance: **2m/2m3: 1-4** 2m4-2m7: 0-1 3m+: 0-0
Track: LH: 0-0 RH: 1-5 Tight: 1-1 Gall: 0-0
Aids: Bl: 0-0 Vi: 0-0 Tstrap: 0-0
Best Rating: 114 1/03 Winc 2m   gd-sft   Hdl

Promising debut in a bumper, and won well at Taunton on his hurdling debut.

Toulouse-Lautrec (IRE)

103(90h)   (87h)121+

7-y-o ch g Toulon-Bucks Slave (Buckskin (FR))
T R George John French

Placings:6500-131   (2608)
2002/03: 20¹S, 21³G, 24¹S,

	Starts	1st	2nd	3rd	Win & Pl
Chases	3	2	0	1	13482
Career Total	7	2	0	1	13482
123 12/02 Uttx	3m	F(0-90)HCh		SFT	£3484
96 11/02 Uttx	2m4f	E(0-105)HCh		SFT	£4498

Total win prize-money £7982

Going: Sf: 2-2 GS: 0-0 Gd: 0-1 GF: - Fm: 0-0
Distance: 2m/2m3: 0-0 2m4-2m7: 1-2 3m+: 1-1
Track: **LH: 2-3** RH: 0-0 Tight: 0-0 Gall: 0-1
Aids: Bl: 0-0 Vi: 0-0 Tstrap: 0-0
Best Rating: 123 12/02 Uttx   3m   soft   Ch

Fair chaser; made a winning chasing debut in a novices handicap at Uttoxeter in November 2002. Ran well when third at Cheltenham mext time and won again at Uttoxeter a week later. Stays well and handles very testing conditions.

Touring-Turtle (IRE)

95   87

11-y-o gr g Roselier (FR)-Rossian (Silent Spring)
C Tizzard Summer Fun Racing

Placings:0000/002300310020⁰3/PPP/P/33P/432P13P-50
                                                     (0774)
2002/03: 18⁵GF, 23⁹GF,

	Starts	1st	2nd	3rd	Win & Pl
Chases	2	0	0	0	0
Career Total	33	2	3	7	11041
87 12/01 Tntn	2m3f	F(0-95)HCh		G-S	£3181
89 8/97 Dpat	2m6f	(0-102)HHdl		G-F	£1695

Total win prize-money £4877

Going: Sf: 0-0 GS: 0-0 Gd: 0-0 GF: - Fm: 0-2
Distance: 2m/2m3: 0-1 2m4-2m7: 0-0 3m+: 1-1
Track: LH: 0-1 RH: 0-0 Tight: 0-1 Gall: 0-0
Aids: Bl: 0-1 Vi: 0-0 Tstrap: 0-0
Best Rating: 92 6/00 NAbb 3m2f110y   gd-fm   Ch

Moderate novice chaser, winner at Taunton in December. Stays three miles plus.

Tourniquet (IRE)

106   108d

8-y-o b g Torus-Treidlia (Mandalus)
D J Caro D J Williams

Placings:230   (3476)
2002/03: 25²G, 24³HY, 22⁰GS,

	Starts	1st	2nd	3rd	Win & Pl
Hurdles	3	0	1	1	1575
Career Total	3	0	1	1	1575

Going: Sf: 0-1 GS: 0-1 Gd: 0-1 GF: - Fm: 0-0
Distance: 2m/2m3: 0-0 2m4-2m7: 0-1 3m+: 0-2
Track: LH: 0-2 RH: 0-1 Tight: 0-0 Gall: 0-0
Aids: Bl: 0-0 Vi: 0-0 Tstrap: 0-0
Best Rating: 108 11/02 Wwck 3m1f   good   Hdl

Moderate hurdler; winning pointer in Ireland, he has shown promise in staying novice hurdles but may need a sound surface.

Town Crier (IRE)
97   **86+**

8-y-o br g Beau Sher-Ballymacarett (Menelek)
Mrs S J Smith   Trevor Hemmings

Placings:*00/5/F*   (3367)
2002/03: 20^FGS,

	Starts	1st	2nd	3rd	Win & Pl
Hurdles	1	0	0	0	
Career Total	4	0	0	0	0

Going: Sf: 0-0 GS: 0-1 Gd: 0-0 GF: - Fm: 0-0
Distance: 2m/2m3: 0-0 2m4-2m7: 0-0 3m+: 0-0
Track: LH: 0-1 RH: 0-0 Tight: 0-1 Gall: 0-0
Aids: Bl: 0-0 Vi: 0-0 Tstrap: 0-0
Best Rating: 79 3/00 Carl 2m1f   gd-sft NHF

Grand, big type; very easy winner of a novices' hurdle at Uttoxeter in July; should make a useful chaser.

Townie (IRE)
96   **78**

9-y-o ch g Camden Town-Pafelto (Ragapan)
C P Morlock   Reliant Colour

Placings:*03654P/242112/600*   (3744)
2002/03: 24^6G, 24^0S, 26^6G,

	Starts	1st	2nd	3rd	Win & Pl
Hurdles	3	0	0	0	0
Career Total	15	2	3	1	12827
112 11/00 Newb 2m5f	D(0-110)HHdl			G-S	£3250
108 11/00 Kemp 3m110y	E(0-115)HHdl			SFT	£5577

Total win prize-money £8827

Going: Sf: 0-1 GS: 0-0 Gd: 0-2 GF: - Fm: 0-0
Distance: 2m/2m3: 0-2 2m4-2m7: 0-0 3m+: 0-3
Track: LH: 0-0 RH: 0-3 Tight: 0-1 Gall: 0-1
Aids: Bl: 0-0 Vi: 0-0 Tstrap: 0-3
Best Rating: 112 12/00 Kemp 3m110y   gd-sft Hdl

Towns Ender (IRE)
93   **72**

5-y-o b g Zaffaran (USA)-Delway (Fidel)
D J Caro   Mrs S Tainton

Placings:*005*   (4316)
2002/03: 16^0S, 16^0G, 17^5G,

	Starts	1st	2nd	3rd	Win & Pl
NH Flat	2	0	0	0	0
Hurdles	1	0	0	0	0
Career Total	3	0	0	0	0

Going: Sf: 0-0 GS: 0-1 Gd: 0-0 GF: - Fm: 0-0
Distance: 2m/2m3: 0-3 2m4-2m7: 0-0 3m+: 0-0
Track: LH: 0-2 RH: 0-1 Tight: 0-1 Gall: 0-0
Aids: Bl: 0-0 Vi: 0-0 Tstrap: 0-0
Best Rating: 72 3/03 Bang 2m1f   good Hdl

Toy Boy (IRE)
86f   **78f**

5-y-o b g Un Desperado (FR)-Too Sharp (True Song)
Miss H C Knight   Sir Anthony Scott

Placings:*0*   (2444)
2002/03: 16^0GS,

	Starts	1st	2nd	3rd	Win & Pl
NH Flat	1	0	0	0	0
Career Total	1	0	0	0	0

Going: Sf: 0-0 GS: 0-1 Gd: 0-0 GF: - Fm: 0-0
Distance: 2m/2m3: 0-1 2m4-2m7: 0-0 3m+: 0-0
Track: LH: 0-0 RH: 0-1 Tight: 0-0 Gall: 0-1
Aids: Bl: 0-0 Vi: 0-0 Tstrap: 0-0
Best Rating: 78 12/02 Hntg 2m110y   gd-sft NHF

Trabolgan (IRE)
122f   **141f**

5-y-o b g King's Ride-Derrella (Derrylin)
N J Henderson   Trevor Hemmings

Placings:*222*   (4115)
2002/03: 16^2S, 16^2G, 16^2G,

	Starts	1st	2nd	3rd	Win & Pl
NH Flat	3	0	3	0	10563
Career Total	3	0	3	0	10563

Going: Sf: 0-1 GS: 0-0 Gd: 0-2 GF: - Fm: 0-0
Distance: 2m/2m3: 0-3 2m4-2m7: 0-0 3m+: 0-0
Track: LH: 0-2 RH: 0-1 Tight: 0-0 Gall: 0-0
Aids: Bl: 0-0 Vi: 0-0 Tstrap: 0-0
Best Rating: 141 3/03 Chel 2m110y   good NHF

High-class bumper performer; favourite when creditable runner-up in bumpers at Uttoxeter in December and Kempton in February; filled the same position behind Liberman at Cheltenham Festival; acts on good and soft ground.

Track O' Profit (IRE)

11-y-o ch g Kambalda-Teazle (Quayside)
Miss S Young   B R J Young

Placings:*30/P44253632/42P/1U-13*   (4615)
2002/03: 24^1GS, 26^3G,

	Starts	1st	2nd	3rd	Win & Pl
Chases	2	1	0	1	3425
Career Total	18	2	3	4	17032
105 2/03 Tntn 3m	H Ch			G-S	£2394
98 5/01 NAbb 2m5f110yB HCh				G-F	£10290

Total win prize-money £12685

Going: Sf: 0-0 GS: 1-1 Gd: 0-1 GF: - Fm: 0-0
Distance: 2m/2m3: 0-0 2m4-2m7: 0-0 3m+: 1-2
Track: LH: 0-1 RH: 1-1 Tight: 1-1 Gall: 0-1
Aids: Bl: 0-0 Vi: 0-0 Tstrap: 0-0
Best Rating: 105 2/03 Tntn 3m   gd-sft Ch

Fair hunter chaser; stays three miles and best on soft ground.

Trade Dispute (IRE)

11-y-o ro g Ela-Mana-Mou-Safety Feature (Be My Guest (USA))
G Tuer   G Tuer

Placings:*1110/4/1311U/1F31/2/11-P11*   (4520)
2002/03: 25^PGS, 25^1G, 27^1G,

	Starts	1st	2nd	3rd	Win & Pl
Chases	3	2	0	0	4613
Career Total	20	12	1	2	35773
122 4/03 Sedg 3m3f	H Ch			GD	£1519
108 3/03 Kels 3m1f	H Ch			GD	£3094
117 2/02 Muss 3m	H Ch			G-S	£2247
117 2/02 Muss 3m	H Ch			SFT	£2331
121 4/00 Newc 3m	H Ch			G-S	£2681
128 2/00 Catt 3m4f110yH Ch				GD	£3477
125 4/99 Weth 3m1f	H Ch			G-F	£1203
124 3/99 Sedg 3m3f	H Ch			SFT	£1276
113 2/99 Catt 3m4f110yH Ch				GD	£3485
130 9/95 List 2m	Hdl			GD	£3730
108 8/95 Tral 2m	Hdl			G-F	£3730
103 8/95 Rosc 2m	Hdl			G-F	£2373

Total win prize-money £31150

Going: Sf: 0-0 GS: 0-1 Gd: 2-2 GF: - Fm: 0-0
Distance: 2m/2m3: 0-0 2m4-2m7: 0-0 3m+: 2-3
Track: LH: 2-3 RH: 0-0 Tight: 2-2 Gall: 0-0
Aids: Bl: 0-0 Vi: 0-0 Tstrap: 0-0
Best Rating: 135 3/00 Chel 3m2f110y   gd-fm Ch

Decent pointer/hunter chaser; superb strike rate of nine wins from 12 completed starts in hunter chases; usually a sound jumper; stays three miles plus; acts on most types of ground.

Trading Trouble
101(108h)   (125h)**110**

6-y-o b g Petoski-Marielou (FR) (Carwhite)
J M Jefferson   Richard Collins

Placings:*261/22116-3F3*   (3913)
2002/03: 16^3HY, 19FG, 20^3S,

	Starts	1st	2nd	3rd	Win & Pl
Chases	3	0	0	2	1456
Career Total	11	3	3	2	13305
116 3/02 Uttx 2m4f110yD Hdl				HVY	£3484
125 3/02 Uttx 2m4f110yD Hdl				HVY	£3993
98 3/01 Hntg 2m110y H NHF				SFT	£1960

Total win prize-money £9438

Going: Sf: 0-2 GS: 0-0 Gd: 0-1 GF: - Fm: 0-0
Distance: 2m/2m3: 0-2 2m4-2m7: 0-1 3m+: 0-0
Track: LH: 0-2 RH: 0-1 Tight: 0-1 Gall: 0-0
Aids: Bl: 0-0 Vi: 0-0 Tstrap: 0-0
Best Rating: 125 3/02 Uttx 2m4f110y heavy Hdl

Modest novice chaser; bumper and hurdle winner; suited by two and a half miles; best on soft ground.

Traditional (IRE)
90(107h)   (89h)**70**

7-y-o ch g Erin's Isle-Noorajo (IRE) (Ahonoora)
N J Hawke (P J Rothwell 9/10)   Trevor Heayns

Placings:*6/4-00500211065406*   (4692)
2002/03: 16^0YS, 16^0HY, 16^5G, 18^0GY, 16^9GF, 24^2GF, 20^1G, 22^1GF, 22^9GS, 24^6S, 24^5G, 22^4S, 22^0G, 22^6G,

	Starts	1st	2nd	3rd	Win & Pl
Hurdles	14	2	1	0	8503
Career Total	16	2	1	0	8822
92 10/02 Dpat 2m6f	Hdl			G-F	£3809
92 9/02 Dpat 2m4f110y Hdl				GD	£3809

Total win prize-money £7620

Going: Sf: 0-3 GS: 0-1 Gd: 1-5 GF: - Fm: 1-3
Distance: 2m/2m3: 0-5 2m4-2m7: 2-6 3m+: 0-3
Track: LH: 0-3 RH: 0-5 Tight: 0-3 Gall: 0-0
Aids: Bl: 0-1 Vi: 0-0 Tstrap: 0-0
Best Rating: 94 4/02 Fair 2m   yield Hdl

Fair ex-Irish handicap hurdler; yet to win in this country; best on fast ground.

Tragic Ohio
97f   **110+f**

4-y-o b g Tragic Role (USA)-Kiniohio (FR) (Script Ohio (USA))
M C Pipe   Sandicroft Stud I

Placings:*14*   (4275)
2002/03: 17^1GS, 16^4G,

	Starts	1st	2nd	3rd	Win & Pl
NH Flat	2	1	0	0	2058
Career Total	2	1	0	0	2058
110 2/03 Extr 2m1f H NHF				G-S	£2058
				Total win prize-money £2058

Going:	Sf: 0-0 GS: 1-1 Gd: 0-1 GF: - Fm: 0-0
Distance:	2m2m3: 1-2 2m4-2m7: 0-0 3m+: 0-0
Track:	LH: 0-1 RH: 1-1 Tight: 0-0 Gall: 0-0
Aids:	Bl: 0-0 Vi: 0-0 Tstrap: 0-0
Best Rating:	110 2/03 Extr 2m1f gd-sft NHF

Made a winning debut in an Exeter bumper on good to soft ground; beaten on faster next time.

Trained Bythe Best
104   112

5-y-o b m Alderbrook-Princess Moodyshoe (Jalmood (USA))
M C Pipe Mrs Alison C Farrant

Placings:13P3-03P   (2630)
2002/03: 18⁰GF, 20³G, 20ᴾS,

	Starts	1st	2nd	3rd	Win & Pl
Hurdles	3	0	1	0	550
Career Total	7	1	0	3	3788
113 12/01 Font 2m2f110yE Hdl			GD	£2502
				Total win prize-money £2503

Going:	Sf: 0-1 GS: 0-0 Gd: 0-1 GF: - Fm: 0-1
Distance:	2m/2m3: 1-2 2m4-2m7: 0-2 3m+: 0-0
Track:	LH: 0-3 RH: 0-0 Tight: 0-0 Gall: 0-0
Aids:	Bl: 0-0 Vi: 0-0 Tstrap: 0-3
Best Rating:	113 11/02 Hayd 2m4f good Hdl

Modest hurdler; bolted up on her hurdling debut at Fontwell in December 2001, but held subsequently. Won twice on the Flat in the summer of 2002.

Trajectus
67f   29f

6-y-o b m Homo Sapien-Dublin Ferry (Celtic Cone)
Mrs H Dalton Sean Bryan

Placings:P0   (2064)
2002/03: 16ᴾGF, 17⁰S,

	Starts	1st	2nd	3rd	Win & Pl
NH Flat	2	0	0	0	
Career Total	2	0	0	0	

Going:	Sf: 0-1 GS: 0-0 Gd: 0-0 GF: - Fm: 0-1
Distance:	2m/2m3: 0-2 2m4-2m7: 0-0 3m+: 0-0
Track:	LH: 0-1 RH: 0-0 Tight: 0-0 Gall: 0-0
Aids:	Bl: 0-0 Vi: 0-0 Tstrap: 0-0
Best Rating:	29 11/02 Hrfd 2m1f soft NHF

Tramantano
110   126

4-y-o b g Muhtarram (USA)-Hatta Breeze (Night Shift (USA))
N A Twiston-Davies (H Candy 30/10) H R Mould

Placings:14440   (4097)
2002/03: 16¹S, 17⁴G, 16⁴GS, 16⁴G, 16⁰G,

	Starts	1st	2nd	3rd	Win & Pl
Hurdles	5	1	0	0	8877
Career Total	5	1	0	0	8877
110 11/02 Newb 2m110y C Hdl			SFT	£6708
				Total win prize-money £6708

Going:	Sf: 1-1 GS: 0-1 Gd: 0-3 GF: - Fm: 0-0
Distance:	2m/2m3: 1-5 2m4-2m7: 0-0 3m+: 0-0
Track:	LH: 1-4 RH: 0-1 Tight: 0-0 Gall: 1-2

Aids:	Bl: 0-0 Vi: 0-0 Tstrap: 0-2
Best Rating:	123 3/03 Chel 2m110y good Hdl

Useful juvenile hurdler; suited by two miles and good and soft ground; has worn a tongue tie.

Transatlantic (USA)
92   73

5-y-o gr g Dumaani (USA)-Viendra (USA) (Raise A Native)
H D Daly (R F Johnson Houghton 26/10) Mrs A Timpson

Placings:000P   (4677)
2002/03: 16⁰G, 16⁰G, 16⁰GF, 19ᴾGF,

	Starts	1st	2nd	3rd	Win & Pl
Hurdles	4	0	0	0	
Career Total	4	0	0	0	

Going:	Sf: 0-0 GS: 0-0 Gd: 0-2 GF: - Fm: 0-2
Distance:	2m/2m3: 0-3 2m4-2m7: 0-1 3m+: 0-0
Track:	LH: 0-0 RH: 0-4 Tight: 0-0 Gall: 0-1
Aids:	Bl: 0-0 Vi: 0-0 Tstrap: 0-0
Best Rating:	73 3/03 Hntg 2m110y gd-fm Hdl

Plating-class form in novice hurdles so far; headstrong sort and capable of better if settling; needed cut in the ground on the Flat.

Transit
98   97

4-y-o b c Lion Cavern (USA)-Black Fighter (USA) (Secretariat (USA))
B Ellison (H R A Cecil 21/9) Graeme Redpath

Placings:552   (4405)
2002/03: 16⁵S, 16⁵GS, 16²G,

	Starts	1st	2nd	3rd	Win & Pl
Hurdles	3	0	1	0	1196
Career Total	3	0	1	0	1196

Going:	Sf: 0-1 GS: 0-1 Gd: 0-1 GF: - Fm: 0-0
Distance:	2m/2m3: 0-3 2m4-2m7: 0-0 3m+: 0-0
Track:	LH: 0-3 RH: 0-0 Tight: 0-1 Gall: 0-1
Aids:	Bl: 0-0 Vi: 0-0 Tstrap: 0-0
Best Rating:	92 3/03 Hexm 2m110y good Hdl

Modest maiden hurdler; moderate maiden on the Flat; best effort over hurdles when second in ordinary novices event at Hexham in March.

Translucid (USA)
106   118

5-y-o b/br h Woodman (USA)-Gossamer (USA) (Seattle Slew (USA))
C Von Der Recke Bmk Racing

Placings:2216   (3282)
2002/03: 17²VS, 16²GS, 16¹GS, 17⁶GS,

	Starts	1st	2nd	3rd	Win & Pl
Hurdles	4	1	2	0	10923
Career Total	4	1	2	0	10923
117 11/02 Wwck 2m E Hdl			G-S	£3747
				Total win prize-money £3747

Going:	Sf: 0-0 GS: 1-3 Gd: 0-0 GF: - Fm: 0-0
Distance:	2m/2m3: 1-4 2m4-2m7: 0-0 3m+: 0-0
Track:	LH: 1-2 RH: 0-1 Tight: 0-0 Gall: 0-1
Aids:	Bl: 0-0 Vi: 0-0 Tstrap: 0-0
Best Rating:	118 1/03 Chel 2m1f gd-sft Hdl

A keen sort, he won a novice hurdle at Warwick in November 2002.

Travellers Heir (IRE)
102   94

5-y-o ch g Montelimar (USA)-Allaracket (IRE) (The Parson)
H D Daly Mrs Strachan, Griffith, Lewis & Graham

Placings:3-402   (4285)
2002/03: 16⁴G, 16⁰G, 21²GF,

	Starts	1st	2nd	3rd	Win & Pl
NH Flat	1	0	0	0	0
Hurdles	2	0	1	0	1169
Career Total	4	0	1	1	1445

Going:	Sf: 0-0 GS: 0-0 Gd: 0-2 GF: - Fm: 0-1
Distance:	2m/2m3: 0-2 2m4-2m7: 0-1 3m+: 0-0
Track:	LH: 0-1 RH: 0-2 Tight: 0-0 Gall: 0-1
Aids:	Bl: 0-0 Vi: 0-0 Tstrap: 0-0
Best Rating:	94 3/03 Ludl 2m5f gd-fm Hdl

Moderate form in bumpers and hurdles.

Travelling Jack

8-y-o ch g Lyphento (USA)-Lady Magenta (Rolfe (USA))
Mrs Laura J Young M Rowe

Placings:P-5   (4003)
2002/03: 25⁵S,

	Starts	1st	2nd	3rd	Win & Pl
Chases	1	0	0	0	0
Career Total	2	0	0	0	0

Going:	Sf: 0-1 GS: 0-0 Gd: 0-0 GF: - Fm: 0-0
Distance:	2m/2m3: 0-0 2m4-2m7: 0-0 3m+: 0-1
Track:	LH: 0-0 RH: 0-1 Tight: 0-0 Gall: 0-0
Aids:	Bl: 0-0 Vi: 0-0 Tstrap: 0-0
Best Rating:	0 3/03 Winc 3m1f110y soft Ch

Treasure Chest (IRE)
73   81

8-y-o b g Last Tycoon-Sought Out (IRE) (Rainbow Quest (USA))
M C Pipe S A Helaissi

Placings:PP00/3P200F3/4P436R142P3106/26-606 (3245)
2002/03: 22⁶G, 19⁰GS, 21⁶HY,

	Starts	1st	2nd	3rd	Win & Pl
Hurdles	3	0	0	0	0
Career Total	30	2	3	4	8114
98 2/01 Ludl 2m5f G Hdl			G-S	£1960
98 11/00 Wwck 2m3f G(0-95)HHdl			SFT	£1617
				Total win prize-money £3577

Going:	Sf: 0-1 GS: 0-1 Gd: 0-1 GF: - Fm: 0-0
Distance:	2m/2m3: 0-0 2m4-2m7: 0-3 3m+: 0-0
Track:	LH: 0-1 RH: 0-2 Tight: 0-2 Gall: 0-0
Aids:	Bl: 0-0 Vi: 0-0 Tstrap: 0-0
Best Rating:	98 2/01 Ludl 2m5f gd-sft Hdl

Bred to stay and placed on the Flat, he has shown bits and pieces of form over hurdles in modest company. He has ability but is not very reliable and has run some of his better races when amateur or conditional ridden. Stays three miles. Acts on an easy surface. Runs well fresh.

Treasure Dome (IRE)

9-y-o b g Treasure Kay-Royal Saint (USA) (Crimson Satan)
John Whyte The Good Craic Club

Placings:025/441006240/U-P   (4667)
2002/03: 21PG,

	Starts	1st	2nd	3rd	Win & Pl
Chases	1	0	0	0	
Career Total	14	1	2	0	4006
90 7/98 Bell	2m1f			Hdl	G-F £2391
					Total win prize-money £2391

Going:	Sf: 0-0 GS: 0-0 Gd: 0-1 GF: - Fm: 0-0
Distance:	2m/2m3: 0-0 2m4-2m7: 0-1 3m+: 0-0
Track:	LH: 0-1 RH: 0-0 Tight: 0-1 Gall: 0-0
Aids:	Bl: 0-0 Vi: 0-0 Tstrap: 0-0
Best Rating:	101 11/97 Navn 2m gd-yld Hdl

Treasured Coin

96   **76**

5-y-o b g Overbury (IRE)-Slip A Coin (Slip Anchor)
P Bowen Dr D & Mrs C & D & Ms A & J O Brien

Placings:004P0-2P   (1244)
2002/03: 20²GF, 24PG,

	Starts	1st	2nd	3rd	Win & Pl
Hurdles	2	0	1	0	884
Career Total	7	0	1	0	884

Going:	Sf: 0-0 GS: 0-0 Gd: 0-1 GF: - Fm: 0-1
Distance:	2m/2m3: 0-0 2m4-2m7: 0-1 3m+: 0-1
Track:	LH: 0-1 RH: 0-0 Tight: 0-1 Gall: 0-0
Aids:	Bl: 0-0 Vi: 0-0 Tstrap: 0-0
Best Rating:	76 8/02 Font 2m4f gd-fm Hdl

Plating-class hurdler, stays two and a half miles.

Treasured Guest

101   **112**

5-y-o b g Rainbow Quest (USA)-Free Guest (Be My Guest
(USA))
M Halford M Woods

Placings:000-2163010   (1967)
2002/03: 17²GF, 16¹YS, 16⁶Y, 16³G, 16⁹F, 20¹YS, 16⁰GS,

	Starts	1st	2nd	3rd	Win & Pl
Hurdles	7	2	1	1	10877
Career Total	10	2	1	1	10877
105 10/02 Wxfd	2m4f			Hdl	Y-S £3809
102 7/02 Kbgn	2m			Hdl	Y-S £4233
					Total win prize-money £8043

Going:	Sf: 0-0 GS: 0-1 Gd: 0-1 GF: - Fm: 0-2
Distance:	2m/2m3: 1-6 2m4-2m7: 1-1 3m+: 0-0
Track:	LH: 0-2 RH: 0-0 Tight: 0-0 Gall: 0-0
Aids:	Bl: 0-0 Vi: 0-0 Tstrap: 0-0
Best Rating:	112 11/02 Chel 2m110y gd-sft Hdl

Irish novice hurdler, stays two and a half miles, effective in soft ground.

Treble Trouble

94   **63**

7-y-o b g Minster Son-Ferneyhill Lady (Menelek)
C C Bealby Mrs Joan Martin

Placings:0/F-PPFP3P5   (4158)

2002/03: 20PGF, 24PGF, 25FG, 24PGS, 21³S, 16PS, 17⁵GS,

	Starts	1st	2nd	3rd	Win & Pl
Hurdles	3	0	0	0	0
Chases	4	0	0	1	586
Career Total	9	0	0	1	586

Going:	Sf: 0-2 GS: 0-2 Gd: 0-1 GF: - Fm: 0-2
Distance:	2m/2m3: 0-2 2m4-2m7: 0-2 3m+: 0-3
Track:	LH: 0-3 RH: 0-4 Tight: 0-4 Gall: 0-1
Aids:	Bl: 0-0 Vi: 0-0 Tstrap: 0-1
Best Rating:	75 4/02 Fknm 2m5f110y good Ch

Tremallt (IRE)

99(102h)   (102h)**124**

12-y-o b g Henbit (USA)-Secret Romance (Gala
Performance (USA))
T R George Silkword Racing Partnership

Placings:2/226/U12FF1F11/16UP/5146FF/10616-0030
    (4479)
2002/03: 24⁰GS, 24⁰S, 21³S, 36⁰G,

	Starts	1st	2nd	3rd	Win & Pl
Hurdles	1	0	0	0	0
Chases	3	0	0	1	1446
Career Total	32	8	4	1	80946
144 12/01 Kemp	3m	C(0-135)HCh		GD	£29000
102 10/01 MRas	3m	E Hdl		G-S	£3374
144 10/00 Worc	3m	B(0-145)HCh		G-S	£14794
144 10/99 Worc	2m7f110y	C(0-135)HCh		GD	£6807
142 4/99 Uttx	2m4f	D(0-125)HCh		G-S	£4455
134 3/99 Uttx	2m4f	F(0-100)HCh		HVY	£3009
114 2/99 Uttx	2m5f	C HCh		HVY	£7002
107 11/98 Bang	2m4f110y	E(0-105)HCh		SFT	£3598
					Total win prize-money £72042

Going:	Sf: 0-2 GS: 0-1 Gd: 0-1 GF: - Fm: 0-0
Distance:	2m/2m3: 0-0 2m4-2m7: 0-1 3m+: 0-3
Track:	LH: 0-2 RH: 0-2 Tight: 0-1 Gall: 0-0
Aids:	Bl: 0-0 Vi: 0-0 Tstrap: 0-0
Best Rating:	144 12/01 Kemp 3m good Ch

Useful front-running chaser; goes well at Kempton; prone to the odd jumping error; stays three miles; best with a little cut in the ground; has worn visor.

Trenance

87f   **61f**

5-y-o b g Afflora (IRE)-Carmel s Joy (IRE) (Carlingford
Castle)
T R George Mr & Mrs D A Gamble

Placings:0   (4444)
2002/03: 16⁰G,

	Starts	1st	2nd	3rd	Win & Pl
NH Flat	1	0	0	0	
Career Total	1	0	0	0	

Going:	Sf: 0-0 GS: 0-0 Gd: 0-1 GF: - Fm: 0-0
Distance:	2m/2m3: 0-1 2m4-2m7: 0-0 3m+: 0-0
Track:	LH: 0-0 RH: 0-1 Tight: 0-0 Gall: 0-0
Aids:	Bl: 0-0 Vi: 0-0 Tstrap: 0-0
Best Rating:	61 4/03 Asct 2m110y good NHF

Disappointing on debut when down the field in an Ascot bumper.

Trencrom Hill

38f

6-y-o b g Homo Sapien-Sweet On Willie (USA) (Master
Willie)

R J Hodges D F P Racing

Placings:0-0   (1598)
2002/03: 17⁰G,

	Starts	1st	2nd	3rd	Win & Pl
NH Flat	1	0	0	0	
Career Total	2	0	0	0	

Going:	Sf: 0-0 GS: 0-0 Gd: 0-1 GF: - Fm: 0-0
Distance:	2m/2m3: 0-1 2m4-2m7: 0-0 3m+: 0-0
Track:	LH: 0-0 RH: 0-1 Tight: 0-0 Gall: 0-0
Aids:	Bl: 0-0 Vi: 0-0 Tstrap: 0-0
Best Rating:	36 3/02 Newb 2m110y gd-sft NHF

Tresor De Mai (FR)

111   **156**

9-y-o ch g Grand Tresor (FR)-Lady Night (FR) (Pompon
Rouge)
M C Pipe Joe Moran

Placings:1112/151225/4F1334/P224UFP/1P1-430   (4114)
2002/03: 20⁴GS, 19³GS, 20⁰G,

	Starts	1st	2nd	3rd	Win & Pl
Chases	3	0	0	1	13750
Career Total	29	8	5	3	159880
160 2/02 Asct	2m3f110yA Ch			G-S	£37700
153 1/02 Asct	2m3f110yB HCh			GD	£10250
151 12/99 Asct	3m110y B HCh			G-S	£29050
142 1/99 Ling	2m	E Ch		HVY	£2684
10/98 Segr	2m3f	Ch		SFT	£2727
3/98 Vire	2m1f	Hdl		HLD	£2525
11/97 Vire	2m1f	Hdl		GD	£3143
					Total win prize-money £88080

Going:	Sf: 0-0 GS: 0-2 Gd: 0-1 GF: - Fm: 0-0
Distance:	2m/2m3: 0-0 2m4-2m7: 0-3 3m+: 0-0
Track:	LH: 0-1 RH: 0-2 Tight: 0-0 Gall: 0-2
Aids:	Bl: 0-0 Vi: 0-0 Tstrap: 0-0
Best Rating:	160 2/02 Asct 2m3f110y gd-sft Ch

Smart chaser at up to three miles, he is not the best of jumpers, but has run well in decent contests and appears to like Ascot, winning high-class events there in 2002. Best suited by an easy surface.

Tresor Preziniere (FR)

101   **115**

5-y-o b/br g Grand Tresor (FR)-Rose De Martine (FR) (The
Quiet Man (FR))
P J Hobbs Bob Jevon

Placings:050-P05FO1331034F   (4766)
2002/03: 17PG, 18⁰G, 18⁶G, 17FG, 20⁰G, 18¹S, 20³G, 19¹S, 19⁰HY, 18³S, 16⁴GF, 16FG,

	Starts	1st	2nd	3rd	Win & Pl
Hurdles	1	0	0	0	0
Chases	12	2	0	3	9604
Career Total	16	2	0	3	9872
10/02 Ange	Ch			SFT	£3979
8/02 Joss	2m2f	Ch		SFT	£2061
					Total win prize-money £6040

Going:	Sf: 2-4 GS: 0-0 Gd: 0-8 GF: - Fm: 0-1
Distance:	2m/2m3: 2-11 2m4-2m7: 0-2 3m+: 0-0
Track:	LH: 0-1 RH: 0-2 Tight: 0-0 Gall: 0-1
Aids:	Bl: 2-4 Vi: 0-0 Tstrap: 0-0
Best Rating:	115 3/03 Winc 2m gd-fm Ch

Ex-French gelding; well beaten third on British debut; winner of chases at up to 2m 3f; suited by soft ground; wears blinkers.

Tribal County (IRE)
104   106
8-y-o b g Erdelistan (FR)-Kismet Dancer (IRE) (Lancastrian)
Ferdy Murphy (M F Morris 15/5) Anthony O Gorman

Placings:200 f64-000P31   (3987)
2002/03: 20⁵G, 20⁴G, 19⁰G, 24⁴S, 20³G, 20¹S,

	Starts	1st	2nd	3rd	Win & Pl
Hurdles	6	1	0	1	4113
Career Total	12	2	1	1	8705
106 3/03 Carl	2m4f	E Hdl		SFT	£3598
106 11/01 Clon	2m	NHF		YLD	£3338
			Total win prize-money £6937

Going:	Sf: 1-2 GS: 0-0 Gd: 0-4 GF: - Fm: 0-0
Distance:	2m/2m3: 0-0 2m4-2m7: 1-5 3m+: 0-1
Track:	LH: 0-4 RH: 1-4 Tight: 0-1 Gall: 0-0
Aids:	Bl: 0-0 Vi: 0-0 Tstrap: 0-2
Best Rating:	112 5/01 Gowr 2m good NHF

Modest hurdler; ex-Irish, he is effective at around two and a half miles.

Tribal Dancer (IRE)
110(109h)   (118h)118
9-y-o ch g Commanche Run-Cute Play (Salluceva)
Miss Venetia Williams You Can Be Sure

Placings:1/P5/0423115210-24152   (4564)
2002/03: 24²GS, 24⁴S, 24¹GS, 26⁵S, 24²GF,

	Starts	1st	2nd	3rd	Win & Pl
Hurdles	1	0	1	0	1905
Chases	4	1	1	0	8656
Career Total	18	5	4	1	25305
109 2/03 Tntn	3m	E Ch		G-S	£4403
118 2/02 Sand	2m4f110yD(0-120)HHdl		SFT	£4465
104 12/01 Ludl	2m5f	E(0-105)HHdl	GD	£2733
105 11/01 Ludl	3m	F(0-105)HHdl	G-F	£3513
118 4/00 Hntg	2m110y H NHF		GD	£1715
			Total win prize-money £16832

Going:	Sf: 0-2 GS: 1-2 Gd: 0-0 GF: - Fm: 0-1
Distance:	2m/2m3: 0-0 2m4-2m7: 0-0 3m+: 1-5
Track:	LH: 0-2 RH: 1-3 Tight: 1-3 Gall: 0-0
Aids:	Bl: 0-0 Vi: 0-0 Tstrap: 0-0
Best Rating:	118 4/03 Bang 3m110y gd-fm Ch

Fair novice chaser, stays three miles and acts on a sound surface, but has been successful on soft ground.

Tribal Dispute
105   114
6-y-o b g Primitive Rising (USA)-Coral Princess (Imperial Fling (USA))
T D Easterby Mrs Jennifer E Pallister

Placings:4-040212210   (4776)
2002/03: 17⁰G, 17⁴G, 20⁶S, 20²GS, 16¹HY, 16²G, 16²GS, 16¹G, 20⁰G,

	Starts	1st	2nd	3rd	Win & Pl
NH Flat	1	0	0	0	0
Hurdles	8	2	3	0	10804
Career Total	10	2	3	0	10804
113 4/03 Kels	2m110y E Hdl		GD	£3575
106 1/03 Newc	2m	E(0-100)HHdl	HVY	£3380
			Total win prize-money £6955

Going:	Sf: 1-2 GS: 0-2 Gd: 1-5 GF: - Fm: 0-0
Distance:	2m/2m3: 2-6 2m4-2m7: 0-3 3m+: 0-0
Track:	LH: 2-6 RH: 0-3 Tight: 1-4 Gall: 1-3
Aids:	Bl: 0-0 Vi: 0-0 Tstrap: 0-0
Best Rating:	114 3/03 Newc 2m gd-sft Hdl

Fair novice hurdler; suited by cut in the ground effective on faster, effective over two miles, but does stay further; scored at Wetherby in January 2003 and Kelso in April; progressive.

Tribal King (IRE)
109   120
8-y-o b/br g Be My Native (USA)-Island Bridge (Mandalus)
Miss H C Knight Mrs Peter Andrews

Placings:461/15455/23-116P6   (3320)
2002/03: 20¹G, 20¹GS, 22⁶GS, 25⁷G, 24⁶GS,

	Starts	1st	2nd	3rd	Win & Pl
Chases	5	2	0	0	9263
Career Total	15	4	1	1	18863
120 11/02 Weth	2m4f110yD(0-115)HCh	G-S	£5206
93 5/02 Aint	2m4f	D Ch	GD	£4056
103 10/00 Winc	2m	D Hdl	G-S	£3250
122 2/00 Asct	2m110y H NHF	SFT	£2373
			Total win prize-money £14886

Going:	Sf: 0-0 GS: 1-3 Gd: 1-2 GF: - Fm: 0-0
Distance:	2m/2m3: 0-0 2m4-2m7: 2-3 3m+: 0-2
Track:	LH: 2-4 RH: 0-1 Tight: 1-1 Gall: 0-2
Aids:	Bl: 0-0 Vi: 0-0 Tstrap: 0-0
Best Rating:	131 1/01 Asct 2m110y soft Hdl

Fair chaser; missed the second half of the 2001/2 season after breaking a blood vessel , but was successful on his return at Aintree in May and followed up at Wetherby in November. Should stay three miles; acts on good ground or softer.

Tribal Run (IRE)
101   108+
8-y-o ch g Be My Native (USA)-Queen s Run (IRE) (Deep Run)
N G Richards Trevor Hemmings

Placings:6/0P0/PFP-1222   (3511)
2002/03: 25¹HY, 25²HY, 24²S, 30²G,

	Starts	1st	2nd	3rd	Win & Pl
Chases	4	1	3	0	8691
Career Total	11	1	3	0	8691
102 11/02 Hexm	3m1f	F Ch	HVY	£2746
			Total win prize-money £2746

Going:	Sf: 1-3 GS: 0-0 Gd: 0-1 GF: - Fm: 0-0
Distance:	2m/2m3: 0-0 2m4-2m7: 0-0 3m+: 1-4
Track:	LH: 1-4 RH: 0-0 Tight: 0-2 Gall: 0-4
Aids:	Bl: 0-0 Vi: 0-0 Tstrap: 1-4
Best Rating:	108 2/03 Catt 3m6f good Ch

Modest staying novice chaser, won a maiden chase at Hexham in November and has run well since. Acts in testing ground, wears a tongue tie.

Tribal Tract (IRE)
9-y-o b g Alphabatim (USA)-Wiji Damar (Laurence O)
Jonjo O Neill Anne Duchess Of Westminster

Placings:432/3P52P-P   (0114)
2002/03: 25²GS,

	Starts	1st	2nd	3rd	Win & Pl
Chases	1	0	0	0	
Career Total	9	0	2	2	3224

Going:	Sf: 0-0 GS: 0-1 Gd: 0-0 GF: - Fm: 0-0
Distance:	2m/2m3: 0-0 2m4-2m7: 0-0 3m+: 0-1
Track:	LH: 0-0 RH: 0-1 Tight: 0-0 Gall: 0-0
Aids:	Bl: 0-0 Vi: 0-0

| Best Rating: | 100 10/01 Bang 3m110y   soft   Ch |

Tribal Venture (FR)
109   135
5-y-o gr g Dom Alco (FR)-Babacha (FR) (Latnahc (USA))
Ferdy Murphy Network Training Iii

Placings:1-6152631   (4609)
2002/03: 22⁶S, 24¹S, 20⁵GS, 24²GS, 23⁶GS, 25³G, 24¹G,

	Starts	1st	2nd	3rd	Win & Pl
Hurdles	7	2	1	1	32811
Career Total	8	3	1	1	34540
135 4/03 Chel	3m	B(0-145)HHdl	GD	£12818
117 12/02 Asct	3m	C Hdl	SFT	£6792
99 4/02 Towc	2m	H NHF	GD	£1729
			Total win prize-money £21340

Going:	Sf: 1-2 GS: 0-3 Gd: 1-2 GF: - Fm: 0-0
Distance:	2m/2m3: 0-0 2m4-2m7: 0-0 3m+: 2-5
Track:	LH: 1-6 RH: 1-1 Tight: 0-0 Gall: 1-3
Aids:	Bl: 0-0 Vi: 0-0 Tstrap: 0-0
Best Rating:	135 4/03 Chel 3m good Hdl

Useful novice hurdler; third in Pertemps Handicap Final at Cheltenham in 2003; won 3m Class B handicap at the same course the following month; stays 3m 1f; acts on good and soft ground.

Tribal Warrior (IRE)
(104h)   (87h)81
8-y-o b m Muharib (USA)-War Saint (Tug Of War)
N B Mason N B Mason

Placings:000/44260/0065060305012P-4   (1228)
2002/03: 24⁴G,

	Starts	1st	2nd	3rd	Win & Pl
Chases	1	0	0	0	387
Career Total	23	1	2	1	5007
82 4/02 Weth	2m7f	G(0-90)HHdl	GD	£2317
			Total win prize-money £2317

Going:	Sf: 0-0 GS: 0-0 Gd: 0-1 GF: - Fm: 0-0
Distance:	2m/2m3: 0-0 2m4-2m7: 0-0 3m+: 0-1
Track:	LH: 0-1 RH: 0-0 Tight: 0-1 Gall: 0-0
Aids:	Bl: 0-0 Vi: 0-0 Tstrap: 0-1
Best Rating:	97 7/00 Gway 2m good NHF

Plating-class hurdler; short head winner of 23 furlong Wetherby seller on Easter Monday 2002. Probably found two and a half miles inadequate when well beaten second on chasing debut next time.

Tricky Trevor (IRE)
10-y-o b/br g Arctic Lord-Chancer s Last (Foggy Bell)
Mrs H J Cobb Mrs H J Cobb

Placings:3/022P0/5F5F/P   (3950)
2002/03: 23⁸GS,

	Starts	1st	2nd	3rd	Win & Pl
Chases	1	0	0	0	
Career Total	11	0	2	1	1364

Going:	Sf: 0-0 GS: 0-1 Gd: 0-0 GF: - Fm: 0-0
Distance:	2m/2m3: 0-0 2m4-2m7: 0-0 3m+: 0-1
Track:	LH: 0-0 RH: 0-1 Tight: 0-0 Gall: 0-0
Aids:	Bl: 0-0 Vi: 0-0 Tstrap: 0-0
Best Rating:	98 4/98 MRas 1m5f110y soft NHF

Trillionaire

107   **81**

5-y-o ch g Dilum (USA)-Madam Trilby (Grundy)
Miss C J E Caroe Miss N F Thesiger

Placings:05-F4635000P3051   (4786)
2002/03: 18⁶GF, 16⁴GF, 17⁶GF, 19³GF, 22⁵GF, 19⁰GS, 19⁰GS, 21⁰GS, 24⁴HY, 24³GF, 22⁰G, 26⁵GF, 22¹G,

	Starts	1st	2nd	3rd	Win & Pl
Hurdles	13	1	0	2	4425
Career Total	15	1	0	2	4425
79	4/03	MRas	2m6f	F(0-100)HHdl	GD £3144

Total win prize-money £3144

Going:	Sf: 0-1 GS: 0-3 Gd: 1-2 GF: - Fm: 0-7
Distance:	2m/2m3: 0-6 2m4-2m7: 1-4 3m+: 0-3
Track:	LH: 0-8 RH: 0-3 Tight: 0-6 Gall: 0-2
Aids:	Bl: 0-0 Vi: 0-0 Tstrap: 0-0
Best Rating:	79 4/03 MRas 2m6f good Hdl

Plating-class hurdler; finally broke his duck at the 15th attempt at Market Rasen in April 2003; acts on good ground.

Trimstone

66   **17**

6-y-o br g Bandmaster (USA)-Klairover (Smackover)
R J Hodges R J Hodges

Placings:P4   (1800)
2002/03: 16⁰G, 17⁴S,

	Starts	1st	2nd	3rd	Win & Pl
Hurdles	2	0	0	0	0
Career Total	2	0	0	0	0

Going:	Sf: 0-1 GS: 0-0 Gd: 0-1 GF: - Fm: 0-0
Distance:	2m/2m3: 0-2 2m4-2m7: 0-0 3m+: 0-0
Track:	LH: 0-2 RH: 0-0 Tight: 0-2 Gall: 0-0
Aids:	Bl: 0-0 Vi: 0-0 Tstrap: 0-0
Best Rating:	17 11/02 NAbb 2m1f soft Hdl

Trinitro

108   **119**

12-y-o ch g Northern State (USA)-Mrs Waddilove (Bustino)
Rune Haugen Ms Liv Saether Myskja

Placings:3/35202/114/3/14/1F/2/21211-12230   (2467)
2002/03: 21¹GF, 21²S, 22²G, 31³GS, 31⁰GS,

	Starts	1st	2nd	3rd	Win & Pl
Chases	5	1	2	1	17035
Career Total	25	8	7	4	65049
	6/02	Stro	2m5f	Ch	G-F £8154
	9/01	Ovrl	2m5f	Ch	VS £8154
	8/01	Ovrl	2m5f	Ch	SFT £3070
	7/01	Ovrl	2m5f	Ch	HVY £3070
	9/99	Ovrl	2m5f	Ch	HVY £8509
	5/98	Ovrl	1m5f	Ch	GD £2295
	8/96	Ovrl	2m5f	Ch	GD £2548
	7/96	Taby	2m1f110y	Ch	GD £1944

Total win prize-money £37744

Going:	Sf: 0-1 GS: 0-2 Gd: 0-1 GF: - Fm: 1-1
Distance:	2m/2m3: 0-0 2m4-2m7: 1-3 3m+: 0-2
Track:	LH: 0-2 RH: 1-1 Tight: 0-0 Gall: 0-0
Aids:	Bl: 1-5 Vi: 0-0 Tstrap: 0-0
Best Rating:	119 11/02 Chel 3m7f gd-sft Ch

Useful Norwegian-trained chaser; fell at the first in the 2000 Grand National but usually jumps well; stays four miles; wears blinkers; acts on most types of ground.

Trinity Belle (FR)

101   **109**

5-y-o b m Tel Quel (FR)-Razzamatazz (FR) (Always Fair (USA))
G Macaire (E Libaud 19/8) Mme Henri Devin

Placings:1614P   (2124)
2002/03: 17¹S, 18⁶VS, 18¹G, 16⁴S, 17⁶VS,

	Starts	1st	2nd	3rd	Win & Pl
Hurdles	5	2	0	0	9161
Career Total	5	2	0	0	9161
	11/02	Bord	2m2f	Hdl	GD £4417
	8/02	Diep	2m1f	Hdl	SFT £4417

Total win prize-money £8834

Going:	Sf: 1-2 GS: 0-0 Gd: 1-1 GF: - Fm: 0-0
Distance:	2m/2m3: 2-5 2m4-2m7: 0-0 3m+: 0-0
Track:	LH: 0-1 RH: 0-0 Tight: 0-0 Gall: 0-0
Aids:	Bl: 0-0 Vi: 0-0 Tstrap: 0-1
Best Rating:	107 11/02 Plum 2m soft Hdl

Trink Hill

55

5-y-o ch m Good Times (ITY)-Sweet On Willie (USA) (Master Willie)
R J Hodges D F P Racing

Placings:0-5P40P   (3600)
2002/03: 17⁵F, 17⁰S, 16⁴GS, 17⁰S, 24⁰PS,

	Starts	1st	2nd	3rd	Win & Pl
NH Flat	1	0	0	0	0
Hurdles	4	0	0	0	0
Career Total	6	0	0	0	0

Going:	Sf: 0-3 GS: 0-1 Gd: 0-0 GF: - Fm: 0-1
Distance:	2m/2m3: 0-4 2m4-2m7: 0-0 3m+: 0-1
Track:	LH: 0-1 RH: 0-3 Tight: 0-3 Gall: 0-0
Aids:	Bl: 0-0 Vi: 0-0 Tstrap: 0-0
Best Rating:	75 10/02 Tntn 2m1f firm NHF

Trinket (IRE)

99   **101**

5-y-o b g Definite Article-Alamiya (IRE) (Doyoun)
H D Daly Mrs Strachan, Mrs Gabb & Jim Morris

Placings:5-123   (2211)
2002/03: 16¹GF, 16²S, 17³S,

	Starts	1st	2nd	3rd	Win & Pl
NH Flat	1	1	0	0	1679
Hurdles	2	0	1	1	1568
Career Total	4	1	1	1	3247
101	5/02	Worc	2m	H NHF	G-F £1678

Total win prize-money £1679

Going:	Sf: 0-2 GS: 0-0 Gd: 0-0 GF: - Fm: 1-1
Distance:	2m/2m3: 1-3 2m4-2m7: 0-0 3m+: 0-0
Track:	LH: 1-3 RH: 0-0 Tight: 0-1 Gall: 0-0
Aids:	Bl: 0-0 Vi: 0-0 Tstrap: 0-0
Best Rating:	101 11/02 Bang 2m1f soft Hdl

Moderate bumper performer/hurdler; showed promise on his bumper debut in good company at Kempton. Impressive winner at Worcester in May 2002. Placed in nocvice hurdles.

Trinley Moss (IRE)

5-y-o b m Executive Perk-Rosmere (IRE) (Roselier (FR))
J S Haldane J S Haldane

Placings:P   (3771)
2002/03: 16⁶GS,

	Starts	1st	2nd	3rd	Win & Pl
Hurdles	1	0	0	0	
Career Total	1	0	0	0	

Going:	Sf: 0-0 GS: 0-1 Gd: 0-0 GF: - Fm: 0-0
Distance:	2m/2m3: 0-1 2m4-2m7: 0-0 3m+: 0-0
Track:	LH: 0-1 RH: 0-0 Tight: 0-0 Gall: 0-0
Aids:	Bl: 0-0 Vi: 0-0 Tstrap: 0-0
Best Rating:	0 2/03 Ayr 2m gd-sft Hdl

Trio

7-y-o b g Cyrano De Bergerac-May Light (Midyan (USA))
J R Boyle City Industrial Supplies Ltd

Placings:R   (1089)
2002/03: 16⁸GF,

	Starts	1st	2nd	3rd	Win & Pl
Hurdles	1	0	0	0	
Career Total	1	0	0	0	

Going:	Sf: 0-0 GS: 0-0 Gd: 0-0 GF: - Fm: 0-1
Distance:	2m/2m3: 0-1 2m4-2m7: 0-0 3m+: 0-0
Track:	LH: 0-0 RH: 0-1 Tight: 0-0 Gall: 0-1
Aids:	Bl: 0-0 Vi: 0-0 Tstrap: 0-0
Best Rating:	0 8/02 Hntg 2m110y gd-fm Hdl

Trios Venture

(97c)   (93c)

8-y-o ch g Bedford (USA)-Hunting Cottage (Pyjama Hunt)
Miss E C Lavelle Mrs R J Lavelle

Placings:450P2/203PU/2F0P-P   (0379)
2002/03: 21⁰G,

	Starts	1st	2nd	3rd	Win & Pl
Hurdles	1	0	0	0	
Career Total	15	0	3	1	2722

Going:	Sf: 0-0 GS: 0-0 Gd: 0-1 GF: - Fm: 0-0
Distance:	2m/2m3: 0-0 2m4-2m7: 0-1 3m+: 0-0
Track:	LH: 0-0 RH: 0-1 Tight: 0-0 Gall: 0-1
Aids:	Bl: 0-0 Vi: 0-0 Tstrap: 0-0
Best Rating:	89 10/00 Towc 2m gd-sft Hdl

Triple Crown (IRE)

10-y-o b/br g Tidaro (USA)-Noreen Beag (Thatching)
R M Bluck R M Bluck

Placings:0000/00P/P-5   (0108)
2002/03: 24⁵GF,

	Starts	1st	2nd	3rd	Win & Pl
Chases	1	0	0	0	0
Career Total	9	0	0	0	0

Going:	Sf: 0-0 GS: 0-0 Gd: 0-0 GF: - Fm: 0-1
Distance:	2m/2m3: 0-0 2m4-2m7: 0-0 3m+: 0-1
Track:	LH: 0-0 RH: 0-1 Tight: 0-1 Gall: 0-0
Aids:	Bl: 0-0 Vi: 0-0 Tstrap: 0-0
Best Rating:	59 7/99 Bell 2m1f good Hdl

Triple Glory (IRE)
94   **68**

4-y-o b f Goldmark (USA)-Trebles (IRE) (Kenmare (FR))
Mrs P N Dutfield Mrs Pat Scott

Placings:24UP (2005)
2002/03: 16²G, 18⁴GF, 17ᵁG, 17ᴾS,

	Starts	1st	2nd	3rd	Win & Pl
Hurdles	4	0	1	0	1268
Career Total	4	0	1	0	1268

Going:	Sf: 0-1 GS: 0-0 Gd: 0-2 GF: - Fm: 0-1
Distance:	2m/2m3: 0-4 2m4-2m7: 0-0 3m+: 0-1
Track:	LH: 0-2 RH: 0-2 Tight: 0-0 Gall: 0-0
Aids:	Bl: 0-0 Vi: 0-0 Tstrap: 0-0
Best Rating:	68 9/02 Font 2m2f110y gd-fm Hdl

Triple Rum (IRE)
109f   **120f**

6-y-o b g Be My Native (USA)-Pegus Gold (Strong Gale)
James Leavy Mrs Ann M Donnelly

Placings:10 (4115)
2002/03: 16¹S, 16⁹G,

	Starts	1st	2nd	3rd	Win & Pl
NH Flat	2	1	0	0	5825
Career Total	2	1	0	0	5825
120 2/03 Naas 2m	NHF			SFT	£5824
Total win prize-money					£5825

Going:	Sf: 1-1 GS: 0-0 Gd: 0-1 GF: - Fm: 0-0
Distance:	2m/2m3: 1-2 2m4-2m7: 0-0 3m+: 0-0
Track:	LH: 0-1 RH: 0-0 Tight: 0-0 Gall: 0-0
Aids:	Bl: 0-0 Vi: 0-0 Tstrap: 0-0
Best Rating:	120 2/03 Naas 2m soft NHF

Fair irish bumper winner; acts on soft.

Tristan Ludlow (IRE)
104   **115**

7-y-o gr g Roselier (FR)-Surely Madam (Torenaga)
Jonjo O Neill The Blue And White Partnership

Placings:0606-22 (3117)
2002/03: 22²HY, 21²S,

	Starts	1st	2nd	3rd	Win & Pl
Hurdles	2	0	2	0	2174
Career Total	6	0	2	0	2174

Going:	Sf: 0-2 GS: 0-0 Gd: 0-0 GF: - Fm: 0-0
Distance:	2m/2m3: 0-0 2m4-2m7: 0-2 3m+: 0-0
Track:	LH: 0-0 RH: 0-2 Tight: 0-0 Gall: 0-1
Aids:	Bl: 0-0 Vi: 0-0 Tstrap: 0-0
Best Rating:	115 1/03 Hntg 2m5f110y soft Hdl

Fair novice hurdler, stays well, acts in heavy ground. Should make a chaser.

Triumph Of Hope
87   **65**

7-y-o b g Nomadic Way (USA)-Welton Stratagem Vii (Damsire Unregistered)
C Grant D M Robinson

Placings:60 (4435)
2002/03: 20⁶S, 20⁰G,

	Starts	1st	2nd	3rd	Win & Pl
Hurdles	2	0	0	0	0
Career Total	2	0	0	0	0

Going:	Sf: 0-1 GS: 0-0 Gd: 0-1 GF: - Fm: 0-0
Distance:	2m/2m3: 0-0 2m4-2m7: 0-2 3m+: 0-0
Track:	LH: 0-1 RH: 0-0 Tight: 0-0 Gall: 0-1
Aids:	Bl: 0-0 Vi: 0-0 Tstrap: 0-0
Best Rating:	65 3/03 Carl 2m4f soft Hdl

Trivial (IRE)
103(84c)   **(64c)88**

11-y-o b m Rakaposhi King-Miss Rubbish (Rubor)
J E Brockbank T Brockbank

Placings:54UP623-130R53 (4590)
2002/03: 20¹GF, 20³GF, 17⁹HY, 21⁷GS, 20⁵G, 20³G,

	Starts	1st	2nd	3rd	Win & Pl
Hurdles	5	1	0	2	4077
Chases	1	0	0	0	0
Career Total	13	1	1	3	5419
88 5/02 Prth 2m4f110yE Hdl				G-F	£3220
Total win prize-money					£3220

Going:	Sf: 0-1 GS: 0-1 Gd: 0-2 GF: - Fm: 1-2
Distance:	2m/2m3: 0-1 2m4-2m7: 1-5 3m+: 0-0
Track:	LH: 0-3 RH: 1-3 Tight: 0-0 Gall: 0-0
Aids:	Bl: 0-0 Vi: 0-0 Tstrap: 0-0
Best Rating:	88 4/03 Hexm 2m4f110y good Hdl

Plating-class hurdler; former winning pointer, had shown ability over hurdles before scoring at Perth in May 2002; seems to need decent ground.

Trochilidae (IRE)

7-y-o b m Alphabatim (USA)-Quincy Bay (Buckskin (FR))
A J Wilson Mrs M J Wilson

Placings:000-P (2197)
2002/03: 19⁰GS,

	Starts	1st	2nd	3rd	Win & Pl
Hurdles	1	0	0	0	0
Career Total	4	0	0	0	0

Going:	Sf: 0-0 GS: 0-1 Gd: 0-0 GF: - Fm: 0-0
Distance:	2m/2m3: 0-0 2m4-2m7: 0-1 3m+: 0-0
Track:	LH: 0-0 RH: 0-1 Tight: 0-1 Gall: 0-0
Aids:	Bl: 0-0 Vi: 0-0 Tstrap: 0-0
Best Rating:	55 12/01 Hrfd 2m1f soft NHF

Troedrhiwdalar
84   **54**

6-y-o b m Gunner B-Delladear (Sonnen Gold)
Mrs D A Hamer Mrs L G Foster

Placings:0-003P (3852)
2002/03: 16⁹GS, 17⁹G, 17⁰G, 24³GS, 24ᴾGS,

	Starts	1st	2nd	3rd	Win & Pl
NH Flat	2	0	0	0	0
Hurdles	3	0	0	1	376
Career Total	5	0	0	1	376

Going:	Sf: 0-0 GS: 0-2 Gd: 0-2 GF: - Fm: 0-1
Distance:	2m/2m3: 0-3 2m4-2m7: 0-0 3m+: 0-2
Track:	LH: 0-1 RH: 0-4 Tight: 0-1 Gall: 0-0
Aids:	Bl: 0-0 Vi: 0-0 Tstrap: 0-0
Best Rating:	66 5/02 Extr 2m1f good NHF

Trooper
106(98h)   **93**

9-y-o b g Rock Hopper-Silica (USA) (Mr Prospector (USA))
A Crook Colley and Bakes

Placings:14/2P015/2662212/5435303-562P2125P3P3P31 (4797)
2002/03: 16³G, 20⁵GF, 20⁶G, 25²GF, 25⁵GF, 27²G, 27¹G, 27²S, 24⁵GS, 28ᴾS, 27³S, 27ᴾHY, 24³S, 25ᴾGF, 28³G, 27¹GF,

	Starts	1st	2nd	3rd	Win & Pl
Hurdles	3	0	0	1	257
Chases	13	2	3	3	12545
Career Total	36	5	8	6	25627
92 4/03 Sedg 3m3f	E Ch			G-F	£4342
93 10/02 Sedg 3m3f	F(0-90)HCh			GD	£3513
103 12/00 Leic 2m	G Hdl			HVY	£1876
98 3/00 Catt 2m	G Hdl			G-F	£1578
107 1/98 Muss 2m	E Hdl			GD	£2402
Total win prize-money					£13712

Going:	Sf: 0-5 GS: 0-1 Gd: 1-5 GF: - Fm: 1-5
Distance:	2m/2m3: 0-1 2m4-2m7: 0-2 3m+: 2-13
Track:	LH: 2-13 RH: 0-3 Tight: 2-8 Gall: 0-2
Aids:	Bl: 1-14 Vi: 1-2 Tstrap: 0-0
Best Rating:	107 2/98 Weth 2m good Hdl

Plating-class novice chaser; stays three miles-three; goes well on fast ground; likes Sedgefield.

Trooper Collins (IRE)
99   **99**

5-y-o b g Dolphin Street (FR)-Born To Fly (IRE) (Last Tycoon)
Jonjo O Neill Mrs J Carrington

Placings:653P0-043 (1058)
2002/03: 20⁵S, 26⁴GF, 24³GF,

	Starts	1st	2nd	3rd	Win & Pl
Hurdles	3	0	0	1	379
Career Total	8	0	0	2	1022

Going:	Sf: 0-1 GS: 0-0 Gd: 0-0 GF: - Fm: 0-2
Distance:	2m/2m3: 0-0 2m4-2m7: 0-1 3m+: 0-2
Track:	LH: 0-3 RH: 0-0 Tight: 0-0 Gall: 0-0
Aids:	Bl: 0-2 Vi: 0-0 Tstrap: 0-1
Best Rating:	99 1/02 Newb 2m110y gd-sft Hdl

Moderate hurdler; looked set to win three-mile conditional handicap at Worcester August 2002 but did not seem to relish the battle after leading at the last.

Trouble Ahead (IRE)
112   **131**

12-y-o b g Cataldi-Why O Why (Giolla Mear)
Miss Venetia Williams Mrs Sharon C Nelson

Placings:5/3/22111/UP2F11R/330/P1RP-5353 (4751)
2002/03: 25⁵GS, 20⁴GS, 24⁵G, 20³G,

	Starts	1st	2nd	3rd	Win & Pl
Chases	4	0	0	2	4002
Career Total	25	6	3	5	53733
134 3/02 Winc 2m5f	C(0-130)HCh			GD	£6857
151 3/00 Sand 3m110y	C(0-135)HCh			GD	£7085
137 2/00 Sand 3m110y	B(0-145)HCh			GD	£19140
131 5/99 Hrfd 2m3f	D Ch			GD	£3850
136 3/99 Hntg 2m4f110yE Ch				G-S	£2815
133 3/99 Tntn 3m	E Ch			SFT	£3192
Total win prize-money					£42941

Going:	Sf: 0-0 GS: 0-2 Gd: 0-2 GF: - Fm: 0-0

Distance:	2m/2m3: 0-0 2m4-2m7: 0-2 3m+: 0-2
Track:	LH: 0-0 RH: 0-4 Tight: 0-0 Gall: 0-0
Aids:	Bl: 0-0 Vi: 0-0 Tstrap: 0-0
Best Rating:	151 3/00 Sand 3m110y good Ch

Useful chaser; stays three miles; best going right-handed; prone to mistakes; suited by good ground or softer.

Trouble Next Door (IRE)

103(97h)   (85h)107

5-y-o b g Persian Bold-Adjacent (IRE) (Doulab (USA))
N P Littmoden   Mrs Linda Francis

Placings:11-2   (4291)
2002/03: 16²GF,

	Starts	1st	2nd	3rd	Win & Pl
Chases	1	0	1	0	1656
Career Total	3	2	1	0	8026
85	10/01 Ludl	2m		E Hdl	G-F £2957
83	9/01 Plum	2m		D Hdl	G-S £3412
				Total win prize-money £6371

Going:	Sf: 0-0 GS: 0-0 Gd: 0-0 GF: 0-1
Distance:	2m/2m3: 0-1 2m4-2m7: 0-0 3m+: 0-0
Track:	LH: 0-0 RH: 0-1 Tight: 0-0 Gall: 0-0
Aids:	Bl: 0-0 Vi: 0-0 Tstrap: 0-0
Best Rating:	107 3/03 Winc 2m gd-fm Ch

Modest hurdler; took well to hurdling with back-to-back wins at Plumpton and Ludlow on different going; reportedly still a bit on the weak side.

Trouble'N'Strife

66   42

6-y-o b m Endoli (USA)-Midsummer Breeze (Tumble Wind (USA))
Mrs S D Williams   The Pyrford Partnership

Placings:0-65   (0631)
2002/03: 16⁶G, 17⁵GF,

	Starts	1st	2nd	3rd	Win & Pl
Hurdles	2	0	0	0	0
Career Total	3	0	0	0	0

Going:	Sf: 0-0 GS: 0-0 Gd: 0-1 GF: - Fm: 0-1
Distance:	2m/2m3: 0-2 2m4-2m7: 0-0 3m+: 0-0
Track:	LH: 0-2 RH: 0-0 Tight: 0-1 Gall: 0-0
Aids:	Bl: 0-2 Vi: 0-0 Tstrap: 0-0
Best Rating:	42 6/02 Uttx 2m good Hdl

Troubleshooter

92   70

5-y-o b g Ezzoud (IRE)-Oublier L Ennui (FR) (Bellman (FR))
G A Swinbank   Alan Swinbank

Placings:03   (1240)
2002/03: 17⁰GF, 20³GF,

	Starts	1st	2nd	3rd	Win & Pl
Hurdles	2	0	0	1	422
Career Total	2	0	0	1	422

Going:	Sf: 0-0 GS: 0-0 Gd: 0-0 GF: - Fm: 0-2
Distance:	2m/2m3: 0-1 2m4-2m7: 0-1 3m+: 0-0
Track:	LH: 0-2 RH: 0-0 Tight: 0-0 Gall: 0-0
Aids:	Bl: 0-0 Vi: 0-0 Tstrap: 0-0
Best Rating:	70 9/02 Sedg 2m1f gd-fm Hdl

Plating-class hurdler; best on soft ground.

Troysgreen (IRE)

78   23

5-y-o b g Warcraft (USA)-Moylena (Bustomi)
Jonjo O Neill   Ian G M Dalgleish

Placings:0FPPP   (3499)
2002/03: 16⁶G, 23⁷GS, 20⁰GS, 16²GS, 24⁰GS,

	Starts	1st	2nd	3rd	Win & Pl
NH Flat	1	0	0	0	0
Hurdles	4	0	0	0	0
Career Total	5	0	0	0	0

Going:	Sf: 0-0 GS: 0-4 Gd: 0-1 GF: - Fm: 0-0
Distance:	2m/2m3: 0-2 2m4-2m7: 0-2 3m+: 0-1
Track:	LH: 0-3 RH: 0-0 Tight: 0-1 Gall: 0-1
Aids:	Bl: 0-1 Vi: 0-0 Tstrap: 0-0
Best Rating:	80 11/02 Winc 2m good NHF

Truckers Tavern (IRE)

118   167+

8-y-o ch g Phardante (FR)-Sweet Tulip (Beau Chapeau)
Ferdy Murphy   Mrs M B Scholey

Placings:1/111246-3F132   (4132)
2002/03: 25³HY, 24⁵GS, 24¹GS, 24³G, 26²G,

	Starts	1st	2nd	3rd	Win & Pl
Chases	5	1	1	2	121550
Career Total	12	5	2	2	166278
156	1/03 Hayd	3m	A HCh	G-S £34800
148	1/02 Towc	2m110y	B Ch	HVY £13552
119	1/02 Newc	2m110y	E Ch	SFT £3110
115	12/01 Ayr	2m	D Ch	SFT £3887
120	10/00 Weth	2m	C Hdl	HVY £5105
				Total win prize-money £60456

Going:	Sf: 0-2 GS: 1-1 Gd: 0-2 GF: - Fm: 0-0
Distance:	2m/2m3: 0-0 2m4-2m7: 0-0 3m+: 1-5
Track:	LH: 1-4 RH: 0-1 Tight: 0-1 Gall: 0-2
Aids:	Bl: 0-0 Vi: 0-0 Tstrap: 1-4
Best Rating:	167 3/03 Chel 3m2f110y good Ch

High-class chaser; old fashioned chasing type; winner of point-to-points in Ireland; good novice chaser in 2001/2, 4th in the Arkle at Cheltenham; won the Peter Marsh at Haydock in January 2003 from Hussard Collonges (giving 15lb) by 2 1/2l; ran to about same level of form when 9 1/2l 3rd to Valley Henry in Aon Chase at Newbury; 10l second to Best Mate in Cheltenham Gold Cup; stays 3m 2f; suited by soft ground.

True Blue Victory (IRE)

(119h)   (131h)115

7-y-o b g Catrail (USA)-Russian Ribbon (USA) (Nijinsky (CAN))
T M Walsh   William Entenmann

Placings:2/1511-05010   (4049)
2002/03: 20⁰SH, 16⁵HY, 16⁰S, 16¹Y, 16⁰HY,

	Starts	1st	2nd	3rd	Win & Pl
Hurdles	5	1	0	0	8442
Career Total	10	4	1	0	42200
131	2/03 Naas	2m	(88-130)HHdl	YLD £8441
130	12/01 Leop	2m	HHdl	YLD £13104
126	12/01 Fair	2m	HHdl	YLD £15725
114	11/01 Clon	2m	Hdl	YLD £3895
				Total win prize-money £41168

Going:	Sf: 0-3 GS: 0-0 Gd: 0-0 GF: - Fm: 0-0

Distance:	2m/2m3: 1-4 2m4-2m7: 0-1 3m+: 0-0
Track:	LH: 1-3 RH: 0-2 Tight: 0-0 Gall: 0-0
Aids:	Bl: 0-0 Vi: 0-0 Tstrap: 0-0
Best Rating:	131 2/03 Naas 2m yield Hdl

Useful hurdler; effective on yielding ground at around two miles.

True Destiny

101f   92f

6-y-o b m Afzal-Wenrisc (Boreen (FR))
Miss Venetia Williams   Mr & Mrs Peter D Cooper

Placings:10   (4611)
2002/03: 17¹G, 17⁰G,

	Starts	1st	2nd	3rd	Win & Pl
NH Flat	2	1	0	0	1838
Career Total	2	1	0	0	1838
92	3/03 MRas	2m1f110yH NHF	GD	£1837
			Total win prize-money £1838

Going:	Sf: 0-0 GS: 0-0 Gd: 1-2 GF: - Fm: 0-0
Distance:	2m/2m3: 1-2 2m4-2m7: 0-0 3m+: 0-0
Track:	LH: 0-1 RH: 1-1 Tight: 1-1 Gall: 0-1
Aids:	Bl: 0-0 Vi: 0-0 Tstrap: 0-0
Best Rating:	92 3/03 MRas 2m1f110y good NHF

Took a very ordinary mares only bumper on her debut at Market Rasen in March.

True Lies

79   61

6-y-o ch m King s Signet (USA)-Lysithea (Imperial Fling (USA))
C Tizzard   Richard Hedditch

Placings:00/256-000   (3598)
2002/03: 17⁰S, 21⁰HY, 17⁰S,

	Starts	1st	2nd	3rd	Win & Pl
Hurdles	3	0	0	0	
Career Total	8	0	1	0	620

Going:	Sf: 0-0 GS: 0-0 Gd: 0-0 GF: - Fm: 0-0
Distance:	2m/2m3: 0-2 2m4-2m7: 0-1 3m+: 0-0
Track:	LH: 0-1 RH: 0-2 Tight: 0-3 Gall: 0-0
Aids:	Bl: 0-0 Vi: 0-0 Tstrap: 0-0
Best Rating:	76 8/01 Worc 2m gd-fm NHF

True North (IRE)

112   118

8-y-o b g Black Monday-Slip A Loop (The Parson)
L Lungo   Maurice W Chapman

Placings:4/33-P031112   (4139)
2002/03: 24⁶GS, 22⁰S, 20³S, 22¹HY, 24¹HY, 24¹HY, 24²S,

	Starts	1st	2nd	3rd	Win & Pl
Hurdles	7	3	1		12419
Career Total	10	3	1	3	13459
113	1/03 Newc	3m	F(0-100)HHdl	HVY £2646
118	1/03 Ayr	3m110y	D(0-110)HHdl	HVY £4881
112	12/02 Kels	2m6f110yE(0-105)HHdl	HVY £3536
			Total win prize-money £11064

Going:	Sf: 3-6 GS: 0-1 Gd: 0-0 GF: - Fm: 0-0
Distance:	2m/2m3: 0-0 2m4-2m7: 1-3 3m+: 2-4
Track:	LH: 3-7 RH: 0-0 Tight: 1-2 Gall: 1-2
Aids:	Bl: 0-0 Vi: 0-0 Tstrap: 0-0
Best Rating:	118 1/03 Ayr 3m110y heavy Hdl

fair hurdler; looked a stayer in the making on his only outing in a bumper. Showed ability over hurdles after missing a

season and was completing a hat-trick when just hanging on at Newcastle in January.

True Rose (IRE)

103(100h)   (84h)92

7-y-o ch m Roselier (FR)-Naar Chamali (Salmon Leap (USA))
J R Turner Robin Ellerbeck

Placings:501533   (4407)
2002/03: 16⁵S, 21⁹GS, 16¹G, 16⁵G, 16³S, 16⁹G,

	Starts	1st	2nd	3rd	Win & Pl
Hurdles	5	1	0	1	4195
Chases	1	0	0	1	597
Career Total	6	1	0	2	4792
79	2/03	Catt	2m		E Hdl	GD £3710
				Total win prize-money		£3710

Going: Sf: 0-2 GS: 0-1 Gd: 1-3 GF: - Fm: 0-0
Distance: 2m/2m3: 1-5 2m4-2m7: 0-1 3m+: 0-0
Track: LH: 1-6 RH: 0-0 Tight: 1-2 Gall: 0-0
Aids: Bl: 0-0 Vi: 0-0 Tstrap: 0-0
Best Rating: 92 3/03 Hexm 2m110y good Ch

Moderate hurdler; Irish point winner, had luck on her side when taking a mares only novices hurdle at Catterick in February.

Trump Card

103   92+

6-y-o b g Distant Relative-Tell No Lies (High Line)
C F Swan Capt D G Swan

Placings:00/02-004F30¹   (4646a)
2002/03: 16⁶S, 16⁹S, 16⁴S, 20⁵S, 20³G, 16⁹G, 19¹GF,

	Starts	1st	2nd	3rd	Win & Pl
NH Flat	4	1	0	0	4763
Hurdles	3	0	1	0	421
Career Total	11	1	1	1	5958
101	4/03	Cork	2m3f	NHF	G-F	£4480
			Total win prize-money			£4481

Going: Sf: 0-4 GS: 0-0 Gd: 0-2 GF: - Fm: 1-1
Distance: 2m/2m3: 1-5 2m4-2m7: 0-2 3m+: 0-0
Track: LH: 0-1 RH: 0-4 Tight: 0-1 Gall: 0-1
Aids: Bl: 0-2 Vi: 0-0 Tstrap: 0-0
Best Rating: 101 4/03 Cork 2m3f gd-fm NHF

Plating-class Irish-trained hurdler; usually wears blinkers.

Trumper

96(96h)   (91h)82

7-y-o b g First Trump-Sayida-Shahira (Record Run)
J T Gifford Mrs D Day

Placings:0/003400/04502P0-053PP450   (4118)
2002/03: 21⁹G, 21⁵GF, 25³G, 22³G, 26⁶S, 21⁴S, 25⁵S, 24⁹G,

	Starts	1st	2nd	3rd	Win & Pl
Hurdles	1	0	0	0	0
Chases	7	0	0	1	909
Career Total	22	0	1	2	2058

Going: Sf: 0-3 GS: 0-0 Gd: 0-4 GF: - Fm: 0-1
Distance: 2m/2m3: 0-0 2m4-2m7: 0-4 3m+: 0-4
Track: LH: 0-1 RH: 0-5 Tight: 0-7 Gall: 0-0
Aids: Bl: 0-2 Vi: 0-0 Tstrap: 0-0
Best Rating: 91 12/01 Plum 3m1f110y soft Hdl

Plating-class novice chaser; modest hurdler; possibly best over just short of three miles.

Trumpington

100   92

5-y-o ch m First Trump-Brockton Flame (Emarati (USA))
D G Bridgwater R Paul Russell

Placings:6532-63224   (0969)
2002/03: 21⁸GF, 22³GF, 25²S, 24²GF, 22⁴GS,

	Starts	1st	2nd	3rd	Win & Pl
Hurdles	5	0	2	1	2678
Career Total	9	0	3	2	3838

Going: Sf: 0-1 GS: 0-1 Gd: 0-0 GF: - Fm: 0-3
Distance: 2m/2m3: 0-0 2m4-2m7: 0-3 3m+: 0-2
Track: LH: 0-4 RH: 0-1 Tight: 0-3 Gall: 0-0
Aids: Bl: 0-0 Vi: 0-0 Tstrap: 0-0
Best Rating: 92 7/02 Worc 3m gd-fm Hdl

Has shown ability in novice hurdles. Stays well, acts on any ground.

Trusting Paddy (IRE)

100   84

6-y-o b g Synefos (USA)-Homefield Girl (IRE) (Rahotep (FR))
L A Dace D Newman

Placings:5-06443   (4051)
2002/03: 16⁹GS, 16⁶GS, 17⁴HY, 19⁴S, 16³HY,

	Starts	1st	2nd	3rd	Win & Pl
NH Flat	2	0	0	0	0
Hurdles	3	0	0	1	1185
Career Total	6	0	0	1	1185

Going: Sf: 0-3 GS: 0-2 Gd: 0-0 GF: - Fm: 0-0
Distance: 2m/2m3: 0-5 2m4-2m7: 0-0 3m+: 0-0
Track: LH: 0-2 RH: 0-3 Tight: 0-1 Gall: 0-1
Aids: Bl: 0-0 Vi: 0-0 Tstrap: 0-0
Best Rating: 87 1/03 Kemp 2m gd-sft NHF

Plating-class hurdler; acts on soft ground.

Trusting Tom

111   113

8-y-o b g Teamster-Florista (Oats)
C C Bealby T P Radford

Placings:3F2P-124U252   (3953)
2002/03: 22¹GS, 20²GS, 25⁴G, 24ᵁGS, 21²GS, 24⁵G, 20²GS,

	Starts	1st	2nd	3rd	Win & Pl
Chases	7	1	3	0	9738
Career Total	11	1	4	1	11972
108	10/02	MRas	2m6f110yE(0-105)HCh	G-S	£4533
			Total win prize-money		£4534

Going: Sf: 0-0 GS: 1-5 Gd: 0-2 GF: - Fm: 0-0
Distance: 2m/2m3: 0-0 2m4-2m7: 1-4 3m+: 0-3
Track: LH: 0-0 RH: 1-2 Tight: 1-4 Gall: 0-1
Aids: Bl: 0-2 Vi: 0-0 Tstrap: 0-0
Best Rating: 113 12/02 Fknm 2m5f110y gd-sft Ch

Modest novice handicap chaser, stays two miles six; acts on good to soft.

Trustyourinstincts (IRE)

                                                   45

5-y-o ch g Brief Truce (USA)-Mitsubishi Diamond (Tender King)

Seamus O Farrell Seamus O Farrell

Placings:P   (1939)
2002/03: 16⁶G,

	Starts	1st	2nd	3rd	Win & Pl
Hurdles	1	0	0	0	
Career Total	1	0	0	0	

Going: Sf: 0-0 GS: 0-0 Gd: 0-1 GF: - Fm: 0-0
Distance: 2m/2m3: 0-1 2m4-2m7: 0-0 3m+: 0-0
Track: LH: 0-1 RH: 0-0 Tight: 0-0 Gall: 0-0
Aids: Bl: 0-0 Vi: 0-0 Tstrap: 0-0
Best Rating: 0 11/02 Chel 2m110y good Hdl

Try Me And See

84   53

9-y-o ch g Rock City-Al Raja (King s Lake (USA))
A M Crow Einar G Poole

Placings:250/0-050   (2516)
2002/03: 17⁰HY, 23⁵GS, 16⁰S,

	Starts	1st	2nd	3rd	Win & Pl
Hurdles	3	0	0	0	0
Career Total	7	0	1	0	354

Going: Sf: 0-2 GS: 0-1 Gd: 0-0 GF: - Fm: 0-0
Distance: 2m/2m3: 0-2 2m4-2m7: 0-1 3m+: 0-0
Track: LH: 0-2 RH: 0-1 Tight: 0-0 Gall: 0-1
Aids: Bl: 0-0 Vi: 0-0 Tstrap: 0-0
Best Rating: 113 3/98 Chel 2m110y good NHF

Trysull Dream (IRE)

91   63

4-y-o b f Mujadil (USA)-Emma s Whisper (Kind Of Hush)
C A Dwyer Glynn Darrall & Ian Dodd

Placings:5   (1336)
2002/03: 16⁵GF,

	Starts	1st	2nd	3rd	Win & Pl
Hurdles	1	0	0	0	0
Career Total	1	0	0	0	0

Going: Sf: 0-0 GS: 0-0 Gd: 0-0 GF: - Fm: 0-1
Distance: 2m/2m3: 0-2 2m4-2m7: 0-0 3m+: 0-0
Track: LH: 0-0 RH: 0-1 Tight: 0-0 Gall: 0-1
Aids: Bl: 0-0 Vi: 0-0 Tstrap: 0-0
Best Rating: 64 9/02 Hntg 2m110y gd-fm Hdl

Tsanga

92(88h)   (59h)74

11-y-o b g Rakaposhi King-Audrina (Young Generation)
C Grant Garry E West

Placings:00/00043/130/153011130/0016023/PP3/PPP-6453P (0983)
2002/03: 24⁶G, 22⁴GF, 20⁵G, 27³GF, 26⁶GF,

	Starts	1st	2nd	3rd	Win & Pl
Hurdles	1	0	0	0	0
Chases	4	0	0	1	1013
Career Total	38	7	6	7	21716
107	7/99	Sedg	3m3f110yE(0-115)	G-F	£2687
107	9/98	Prth	3m110y E(0-115)HHdl		£3468
107	9/98	Prth	2m4f110yF(0-100)HHdl	GD	£3485
89	8/98	Prth	2m4f110yF(0-100)HHdl	G-F	£2788
92	5/98	Ctml	2m1f110yE(0-90)HHdl	G-F	£3475
77	5/97	Hexm	2m	G(0-95)HHdl	FRM	£2008
			Total win prize-money		£17913

Going: Sf: 0-0 GS: 0-0 Gd: 0-2 GF: - Fm: 0-3
Distance: 2m/2m3: 0-0 2m4-2m7: 0-2 3m+: 0-3
Track: LH: 0-3 RH: 0-2 Tight: 0-4 Gall: 0-0
Aids: Bl: 0-1 Vi: 0-0 Tstrap: 0-5
Best Rating: 107 7/99   Sedg   3m3f110y   gd-fm   Hdl

Tsunami

69(103h)   (87h)77
7-y-o b m Beveled (USA)-Alvecote Lady (Touching Wood (USA))
B D Leavy   S H Riley

Placings:042322320/33154345614-00666U   (4588)
2002/03: 19⁰G, 16⁰G, 17⁶G, 21⁶G, 20⁶G, 20⁴G,

	Starts	1st	2nd	3rd	Win & Pl
Hurdles	4	0	0	0	0
Chases	2	0	0	0	0
Career Total	26	2	4	5	11910
87	11/01	Aint	2m4f		F(0-100)HHdl	G-S	£4602
85	6/01	Worc	2m		F Hdl	G-F	£2030

Total win prize-money £6632

Going: Sf: 0-0 GS: 0-0 Gd: 0-6 GF: - Fm: 0-0
Distance: 2m/2m3: 0-3 2m4-2m7: 0-3 3m+: 0-0
Track: LH: 0-2 RH: 0-4 Tight: 0-1 Gall: 0-0
Aids: Bl: 0-0 Vi: 0-0 Tstrap: 0-0
Best Rating: 87   3/03   Carl   2m4f   good   Hdl

A fair handicap hurdler; stays two and a half miles; has won on good to firm and soft.

Tubber Roads (IRE)

10-y-o b g Un Desperado (FR)-Node (Deep Run)
M G Hazell   W F Caudwell

Placings:30/431/30U0/5631110-P   (0033)
2002/03: 25⁶GF,

	Starts	1st	2nd	3rd	Win & Pl
Chases	1	0	0	0	
Career Total	17	4	0	4	9637
117	3/02	Newb	2m6f110yH Ch		G-S	£2077
111	3/02	Newb	3m	H Ch		SFT	£1918
111	2/02	Fknm	2m5f110yH Ch		G-S	£2167
111	4/00	Fknm	2m5f110yH Ch		GD	£2008

Total win prize-money £8172

Going: Sf: 0-0 GS: 0-0 Gd: 0-0 GF: - Fm: 0-1
Distance: 2m/2m3: 0-0 2m4-2m7: 0-0 3m+: 0-1
Track: LH: 0-1 RH: 0-1 Tight: 0-0 Gall: 0-1
Aids: Bl: 0-0 Vi: 0-0 Tstrap: 0-0
Best Rating: 117   3/02   Newb   2m6f110y   gd-sft   Ch

Hunter chaser, suited by two and a half/three miles, should stay further. Suited by good or good to soft ground.

Tucacas (FR)

109   146
6-y-o gr m Highest Honor (FR)-Three Well (FR) (Sicyos (USA))
M C Pipe   Mrs Belinda Harvey

Placings:611311012-61P0P   (4475)
2002/03: 16⁶G, 21¹¹GS, 22⁶GS, 25⁵G, 20⁶G,

	Starts	1st	2nd	3rd	Win & Pl
Hurdles	5	1	0	0	17790
Career Total	14	6	1	1	68030
146	11/02	Chel	2m5f	C(0-135)HHdl	G-S	£16965
142	4/02	Asct	2m4f	C(0-130)HHdl	G-F	£6418
125	2/02	Sand	2m110y	D Hdl	SFT	£4543
130	1/02	Leic	2m	E Hdl	SFT	£3178
	11/01	Engh	2m2f	Hdl	HVY	£13579

10/01   Engh   2m1f110y Hdl   HLD £12124
Total win prize-money £56809

Going: Sf: 0-0 GS: 1-2 Gd: 0-3 GF: - Fm: 0-0
Distance: 2m/2m3: 0-1 2m4-2m7: 1-3 3m+: 0-1
Track: LH: 1-4 RH: 0-1 Tight: 0-1 Gall: 1-2
Aids: Bl: 0-0 Vi: 0-1 Tstrap: 0-0
Best Rating: 146 11/02   Chel   2m5f   gd-sft   Hdl

Very useful ex-French hurdler; acts on any ground; stays two miles five.

Tucker Fence

58   19
4-y-o br g So Factual (USA)-Daisy Topper (Top Ville)
Ian Emmerson (J Balding 18/11) Ian Emmerson

Placings:0   (3579)
2002/03: 16⁰G,

	Starts	1st	2nd	3rd	Win & Pl
Hurdles	1	0	0	0	
Career Total	1	0	0	0	

Going: Sf: 0-0 GS: 0-0 Gd: 0-1 GF: - Fm: 0-0
Distance: 2m/2m3: 0-1 2m4-2m7: 0-0 3m+: 0-0
Track: LH: 0-0 RH: 0-1 Tight: 0-1 Gall: 0-0
Aids: Bl: 0-0 Vi: 0-0 Tstrap: 0-0
Best Rating: 19   2/03   Muss   2m   good   Hdl

Tudor Gale (IRE)

10-y-o br m Strong Gale-Orra Beg (Dear Gazelle)
A G Juckes   Graham Brown

Placings:0/004P6040/0P/060656R/P-F   (0073)
2002/03: 19⁶GF,

	Starts	1st	2nd	3rd	Win & Pl
Chases	1	0	0	0	
Career Total	20	0	0	0	1425

Going: Sf: 0-0 GS: 0-0 Gd: 0-0 GF: - Fm: 0-0
Distance: 2m/2m3: 0-0 2m4-2m7: 0-0 3m+: 0-0
Track: LH: 0-0 RH: 0-1 Tight: 0-0 Gall: 0-0
Aids: Bl: 0-0 Vi: 0-0 Tstrap: 0-1
Best Rating: 90 12/98   Chep   2m110y   heavy   Hdl

Tudor King (IRE)

101(101h)   (71h)90
9-y-o br g Orchestra-Jane Bond (Good Bond)
J S King   J R Kinloch

Placings:0/00000/4430/06U421FU/4401P260-
601UU03P01   (4633)
2002/03: 20⁶GF, 23⁸GF, 21¹GF, 24⁴GF, 21⁴G, 22⁶GF, 21³F, 24²G,
20⁴GF, 20¹GF,

	Starts	1st	2nd	3rd	Win & Pl
Hurdles	4	0	0	1	486
Chases	6	2	0	0	6412
Career Total	36	4	2	2	15855
90	4/03	Plum	2m4f	F(0-100)HCh	G-F	£3360
90	8/02	Sthl	2m5f110yF(0-90)HCh		G-F	£3052
89	8/01	Uttx	3m	F(0-100)HCh	G-F	£3045
90	10/00	Font	2m2f	C(0-105)HCh	G-S	£3395

Total win prize-money £12852

Going: Sf: 0-0 GS: 0-0 Gd: 0-2 GF: - Fm: 2-8
Distance: 2m/2m3: 0-0 2m4-2m7: 2-7 3m+: 0-3
Track: LH: 2-7 RH: 0-3 Tight: 1-3 Gall: 0-1
Aids: Bl: 0-0 Vi: 0-0 Tstrap: 0-0

Best Rating: 90   4/03   Plum   2m4f   gd-fm   Ch

Moderate chaser/plating-class hurdler; has only won going left-handed; likes fast ground; stays three miles.

Tudor Native

7-y-o b m Distinct Native-Tudorfield Girl (Tudorville)
A Parker   Mrs Cathrine Matthews

Placings:P   (4750)
2002/03: 24⁴G,

	Starts	1st	2nd	3rd	Win & Pl
Hurdles	1	0	0	0	
Career Total	1	0	0	0	

Going: Sf: 0-0 GS: 0-0 Gd: 0-1 GF: - Fm: 0-0
Distance: 2m/2m3: 0-0 2m4-2m7: 0-0 3m+: 0-1
Track: LH: 0-0 RH: 0-1 Tight: 0-0 Gall: 0-0
Aids: Bl: 0-0 Vi: 0-0 Tstrap: 0-0
Best Rating: 0   4/03   Prth   3m110y   good   Hdl

Tudor Nickola

11-y-o ch m Nicholas Bill-Cottage Melody (Super Song)
P D Purdy   P D Purdy

Placings:00/00U/PPP/060/P-UP   (4290)
2002/03: 18⁴GF, 22⁶GF,

	Starts	1st	2nd	3rd	Win & Pl
Hurdles	2	0	0	0	
Career Total	14	0	0	0	0

Going: Sf: 0-0 GS: 0-0 Gd: 0-0 GF: - Fm: 0-2
Distance: 2m/2m3: 0-1 2m4-2m7: 0-1 3m+: 0-0
Track: LH: 0-1 RH: 0-1 Tight: 0-1 Gall: 0-0
Aids: Bl: 0-0 Vi: 0-0 Tstrap: 0-0
Best Rating: 43   1/98   Ling   2m110y   gd-sft   NHF

Tuff Joint (IRE)

61f   82f
5-y-o b/br g Good Thyne (USA)-The Furnituremaker (Mandalus)
C Grant   Trevor Hemmings

Placings:00   (4778)
2002/03: 17⁰GS, 16⁵G,

	Starts	1st	2nd	3rd	Win & Pl
NH Flat	2	0	0	0	
Career Total	2	0	0	0	

Going: Sf: 0-0 GS: 0-1 Gd: 0-1 GF: - Fm: 0-0
Distance: 2m/2m3: 0-2 2m4-2m7: 0-0 3m+: 0-0
Track: LH: 0-0 RH: 0-2 Tight: 0-0 Gall: 0-0
Aids: Bl: 0-0 Vi: 0-0 Tstrap: 0-0
Best Rating: 82 3/03   Carl   2m1f   gd-sft   NHF

Tuftex King

94   75
6-y-o b g Syrtos-More Laughter (Oats)
Ian Williams   Arnie Robinson

Placings:000000O0   (4679)
2002/03: 17⁰G, 16⁶GS, 16⁶S, 17⁰G, 16⁶G, 16⁶G, 17⁰F,
16⁶GF,

	Starts	1st	2nd	3rd	Win & Pl
NH Flat	1	0	0	0	0
Hurdles	8	0	0	0	0
Career Total	9	0	0	0	0

Going: Sf: 0-1 GS: 0-2 Gd: 0-4 GF: - Fm: 0-2
Distance: 2m/2m3: 0-9 2m4-2m7: 0-0 3m+: 0-0
Track: LH: 0-3 RH: 0-6 Tight: 0-2 Gall: 0-4
Aids: Bl: 0-1 Vi: 0-0 Tstrap: 0-0
Best Rating: 87 11/02 Wwck 2m   gd-sft Hdl

Modest hurdles form to date.

Tufty Hopper
103   110
6-y-o b g Rock Hopper-Melancolia (Legend Of France (USA))
Ferdy Murphy (P Howling 10/6) Michael Tufts

Placings:5113F1   (4340)
2002/03: 16⁵GS, 27¹S, 27¹S, 25³G, 24FGS, 26¹GF,

	Starts	1st	2nd	3rd	Win & Pl
Hurdles	6	3	0	1	10685
Career Total	6	3	0	1	10685

112	3/03	Hntg	3m2f	E(0-110)HHdl	G-F	£3464
104	12/02	Sedg	3m3f110yE Hdl		SFT	£3332
104	11/02	Sedg	3m3f110yE Hdl		SFT	£3356
				Total win prize-money £10154		

Going: Sf: 2-2 GS: 0-2 Gd: 0-1 GF: - Fm: 1-1
Distance: 2m/2m3: 0-1 2m4-2m7: 0-0 **3m+: 3-5**
Track: LH: **2-3** RH: 1-3 **Tight: 2-3** Gall: 1-2
Aids: Bl: 0-0 Vi: 0-0 Tstrap: 0-0
Best Rating: 112 3/03 Hntg 3m2f   gd-fm Hdl

M odest handicap hurdler; modest staying handicapper on the Flat; stays 3m 3f; acts on soft and fast ground; not a straightforward ride.

Tulach Ard (IRE)
104   107
8-y-o b g Erdelistan (FR)-Noon Hunting (Green Shoon)
A Parker Mr and Mrs M C Mackenzie

Placings:3/6/432P2-64FU1   (3914)
2002/03: 20⁶GS, 24⁴HY, 20FHY, 21UGS, 201GS,

	Starts	1st	2nd	3rd	Win & Pl
Hurdles	3	1	0	0	4901
Chases	2	0	0	0	0
Career Total	12	1	2	2	7060

| 106 | 3/03 | Carl | 2m4f | D(0-110)HHdl | G-S | £4901 |
| | | | | Total win prize-money £4901 | | |

Going: Sf: 0-2 GS: 1-3 Gd: 0-0 GF: - Fm: 0-0
Distance: 2m/2m3: 0-0 **2m4-2m7: 1-4** 3m+: 0-1
Track: LH: 0-4 **RH: 1-1** Tight: 0-0 Gall: 0-0
Aids: Bl: 0-0 Vi: 0-0 Tstrap: 0-0
Best Rating: 106 3/03 Carl 2m4f   gd-sft Hdl

Modest hurdler; lightly-raced sort with form on good and soft ground in modest hurdles; eventually off the mark at Carlisle in March.

Tullimoss (IRE)
100   77
8-y-o b m Husyan (USA)-Ballynattin Moss (Le Moss)
J N R Billinge Mrs S E Billinge & Mrs C G Braithwaite

Placings:4060-3462F60P0   (4509)
2002/03: 20³GF, 20⁴GF, 22⁶G, 22²S, 20FGS, 24⁶G, 22⁰GS, 22PS, 22⁰G,

	Starts	1st	2nd	3rd	Win & Pl
Hurdles	9	0	1	1	2029

	Starts	1st	2nd	3rd	Win & Pl
Career Total	13	0	1	1	2029

Going: Sf: 0-2 GS: 0-2 Gd: 0-3 GF: - Fm: 0-2
Distance: 2m/2m3: 0-0 2m4-2m7: 0-8 3m+: 0-1
Track: LH: 0-6 RH: 0-3 Tight: 0-5 Gall: 0-0
Aids: Bl: 0-0 Vi: 0-0 Tstrap: 0-1
Best Rating: 77 11/02 Kels 2m6f110y soft Hdl

Modest form in bumpers and novice hurdles.

Tullons Lane
99(78h)   (73h)68
8-y-o b g Riverwise (USA)-Pallanda (Pablond)
N R Mitchell Mrs E Mitchell

Placings:0/05P550/0F45P-P166422P0PP   (4756)
2002/03: 21PG, 18¹GS, 20⁶G, 20⁶S, 16⁴S, 17²HY, 18²S, 20⁰GS, 18⁰S, 21PGF, 18PGF,

	Starts	1st	2nd	3rd	Win & Pl
Chases	11	1	2	0	6273
Career Total	23	1	2	0	6581

| 97 | 11/02 | Font | 2m2f | E(0-110)HCh | G-S | £3766 |
| | | | | Total win prize-money £3766 | | |

Going: Sf: 0-5 GS: 1-2 Gd: 0-2 GF: - Fm: 0-2
Distance: 2m/2m3: 1-6 2m4-2m7: 0-5 3m+: 0-0
Track: LH: 0-2 RH: 0-2 **Tight: 1-10** Gall: 0-0
Aids: Bl: 0-0 Vi: 0-0 Tstrap: 0-0
Best Rating: 97 2/03 Font 2m4f   gd-sft Ch

Plating-class chaser, stays two miles-two, acts on good to soft or heavier ground.

Tulsa (IRE)
79   56
9-y-o b g Priolo (USA)-Lagrion (USA) (Diesis)
L Montague Hall A D Green

Placings:6/3456/0-0   (0349)
2002/03: 16⁰G,

	Starts	1st	2nd	3rd	Win & Pl
Hurdles	1	0	0	0	0
Career Total	7	0	0	1	362

Going: Sf: 0-0 GS: 0-0 Gd: 0-1 GF: - Fm: 0-0
Distance: 2m/2m3: 0-1 2m4-2m7: 0-0 3m+: 0-0
Track: LH: 0-1 RH: 0-0 Tight: 0-1 Gall: 0-0
Aids: Bl: 0-0 Vi: 0-0 Tstrap: 0-0
Best Rating: 96 5/00 Towc 2m   gd-fm Hdl

Tumbleweed Glen (IRE)
100(83h)   (85h)85
7-y-o ch g Mukaddamah (USA)-Mistic Glen (IRE) (Mister Majestic)
P Kelsall Peter Kelsall

Placings:524335U23/34U0000/P50230-642   (4676)
2002/03: 16⁶G, 19⁴GF, 19²GF,

	Starts	1st	2nd	3rd	Win & Pl
Chases	3	0	1	0	1774
Career Total	25	0	4	5	8889

Going: Sf: 0-0 GS: 0-0 Gd: 0-1 GF: - Fm: 0-2
Distance: 2m/2m3: 0-3 2m4-2m7: 0-0 3m+: 0-0
Track: LH: 0-1 RH: 0-2 Tight: 0-0 Gall: 0-0
Aids: Bl: 0-0 Vi: 0-0 Tstrap: 0-0
Best Rating: 106 4/00 Chel 2m1f   soft Hdl

Plating-class hurdler/chaser; missed 2002; fair efforts since returning; stays 2m 4f, effective over shorter, acts on fast ground.

Tunstall (USA)
99   113
4-y-o b g Bahri (USA)-Princess West (GER) (Gone West (USA))
T D Easterby M J Dawson

Placings:125F   (3290)
2002/03: 16¹GF, 16²GS, 16⁵GS, 16²GS,

	Starts	1st	2nd	3rd	Win & Pl
Hurdles	4	1	1	0	7129
Career Total	4	1	1	0	7129

| 101 | 10/02 | Weth | 2m | D Hdl | G-F | £3932 |
| | | | | Total win prize-money £3933 | | |

Going: Sf: 0-0 GS: 0-3 Gd: 0-0 GF: - Fm: 1-1
Distance: **2m/2m3: 1-4** 2m4-2m7: 0-0 3m+: 0-0
Track: LH: 1-3 RH: 0-1 Tight: 0-0 Gall: 0-2
Aids: Bl: 0-0 Vi: 0-0 Tstrap: 0-0
Best Rating: 113 11/02 Weth 2m   gd-sft Hdl

Fair novice hurdler; beat a big field on his hurdles debut at Wetherby in October 2002 and ran very well on return there under a penalty two weeks later; disappointing next time and killed in final-flight fall at Doncaster in January 2003. (DEAD)

Turaath (IRE)
103   103
7-y-o b g Sadler s Wells (USA)-Diamond Field (USA) (Mr Prospector (USA))
P J Hobbs (G M McCourt 17/7) Mrs Kathy Stuart

Placings:05P11-2PP10F   (4004)
2002/03: 21²GF, 20PGS, 20PGF, 19¹S, 20⁰HY, 22²S,

	Starts	1st	2nd	3rd	Win & Pl
Hurdles	6	1	1	0	4708
Career Total	11	3	1	0	9689

103	1/03	Tntn	2m3f110yE(0-105)HHdl	SFT	£3808
94	4/02	MRas	2m5f110yF(0-100)HHdl	GD	£2579
85	4/02	MRas	2m5f110yF(0-95)HHdl	GD	£2401
			Total win prize-money £8789		

Going: Sf: 1-3 GS: 0-1 Gd: 0-0 GF: - Fm: 0-2
Distance: 2m/2m3: 0-0 **2m4-2m7: 1-6** 3m+: 0-0
Track: LH: 0-2 **RH: 1-4** Tight: 1-2 Gall: 0-0
Aids: Bl: 0-0 Vi: 0-0 Tstrap: 0-1
Best Rating: 103 3/03 Winc 2m6f   soft Hdl

Moderate hurdler, he stays two miles five and is effective on good and fast ground. In good heart in the spring of 2002.

Turbo (IRE)
104   106
4-y-o b g Piccolo-By Arrangement (IRE) (Bold Arrangement)
Miss Venetia Williams (G B Balding 25/7) Peter Richardson

Placings:630P   (4460)
2002/03: 17⁶G, 16³S, 17⁰G, 16PG,

	Starts	1st	2nd	3rd	Win & Pl
Hurdles	4	0	0	1	1087
Career Total	4	0	0	1	1087

Going: Sf: 0-1 GS: 0-0 Gd: 0-3 GF: - Fm: 0-0
Distance: 2m/2m3: 0-4 2m4-2m7: 0-0 3m+: 0-0
Track: LH: 0-4 RH: 0-0 Tight: 0-1 Gall: 0-3
Aids: Bl: 0-1 Vi: 0-0 Tstrap: 0-0
Best Rating: 106 2/03 Newb 2m110y soft Hdl

Modest hurdler; not disgraced in the Triumph Hurdle; may be suited by a sharp track.

Turbo Mower

5-y-o b g Turbo Speed-Fruids Park (Royal Fountain)
W G Young W G Young

Placings:*0*-P   (1633)
2002/03: 24PS,

	Starts	1st	2nd	3rd	Win & Pl
Hurdles	1	0	0	0	
Career Total	2	0	0	0	

Going: Sf: 0-1 GS: 0-0 Gd: 0-0 GF: - Fm: 0-0
Distance: 2m/2m3: 0-0 2m4-2m7: 0-0 3m+: 0-1
Track: LH: 0-0 RH: 0-1 Tight: 0-0 Gall: 0-0
Aids: Bl: 0-0 Vi: 0-0 Tstrap: 0-0
Best Rating: 0   10/02 Carl   3m110y   soft   Hdl

Turgeonev (FR)
113   152
8-y-o gr g Turgeon (USA)-County Kerry (FR) (Comrade In Arms)
T D Easterby D F Sills

Placings:05/56121/31P25/41111P0U2-302U6200 (4458)
2002/03: 20³GS, 20⁰GS, 16²GS, 16ᵁG, 16⁶G, 16²G, 16⁹G, 16⁶G,

	Starts	1st	2nd	3rd	Win & Pl
Chases	8	0	2	1	9679
Career Total	29	7	5	2	88162
150	1/02	Asct	2m	A HCh	GD	£34800
138	12/01	Weth	2m	A HCh	G-S	£13500
133	11/01	Weth	2m	B(0-150)HCh	GD	£8895
129	11/01	Newc	2m110y	E(0-115)HCh	GD	£3360
131	11/00	MRas	2m1f110yE Ch	SFT	£3096
122	4/00	MRas	2m1f110yD Hdl	G-F	£3212
126	2/00	Kels	2m110y D Hdl	G-S	£3721

Total win prize-money £70587

Going: Sf: 0-0 GS: 0-3 Gd: 0-5 GF: - Fm: 0-0
Distance: 2m/2m3: 0-6 2m4-2m7: 0-2 3m+: 0-0
Track: LH: 0-6 RH: 0-2 Tight: 0-1 Gall: 0-3
Aids: Bl: 0-0 Vi: 0-0 Tstrap: 0-0
Best Rating: 155 3/02 Chel   2m   gd-sft   Ch

Smart chaser; completed a fine hat-trick towards the end of 2001 including the Castleford Chase at Wetherby; easy winner of the 2002 Victor Chandler, but was outclassed in the Queen Mother Champion Chase and has been held in handicaps since; suited by two miles, does not want the ground too soft.

Turn Back
85   66
4-y-o b f Pivotal-Trachelium (Formidable (USA))
Miss S E Hall C Platts

Placings:60   (4352)
2002/03: 17⁶S, 16⁹GF,

	Starts	1st	2nd	3rd	Win & Pl
Hurdles	2	0	0	0	0
Career Total	2	0	0	0	0

Going: Sf: 0-1 GS: 0-0 Gd: 0-0 GF: - Fm: 0-1
Distance: 2m/2m3: 0-2 2m4-2m7: 0-0 3m+: 0-0
Track: LH: 0-1 RH: 0-1 Tight: 0-1 Gall: 0-0
Aids: Bl: 0-0 Vi: 0-0 Tstrap: 0-0
Best Rating: 66 3/03 Weth   2m   gd-fm   Hdl

Turn Of Phrase (IRE)
97   114+
4-y-o b g Cadeaux Genereux-Token Gesture (IRE) (Alzao (USA))
R A Fahey (D K Weld 25/9) Jacksons Transport (West Riding) Ltd

Placings:50125   (4637)
2002/03: 16⁵GS, 16⁹GS, 16¹GF, 16²GF, 16⁵GF,

	Starts	1st	2nd	3rd	Win & Pl
Hurdles	5	1	1	0	5503
Career Total	5	1	1	0	5503
97	3/03	Weth	2m	E Hdl	G-F	£3464

Total win prize-money £3465

Going: Sf: 0-0 GS: 0-2 Gd: 0-0 GF: - Fm: 1-3
Distance: 2m/2m3: 1-5 2m4-2m7: 0-0 3m+: 0-0
Track: LH: 1-5 RH: 0-0 Tight: 0-2 Gall: 0-0
Aids: Bl: 0-0 Vi: 0-0 Tstrap: 0-0
Best Rating: 101 3/03 Hayd   2m   gd-fm   Hdl

Modest juvenile hurdler; much improved effort when runaway winner in modest company at Wetherby in March and followed up at the same track two months later when blinkered for the first time; game winner on a return there in May; suited by fast ground.

Turn The Tide
83   85
6-y-o b m Derrylin-Mermaid Bay (Jupiter Island)
A King The Octomists

Placings:5F0-52P   (3254)
2002/03: 20⁵GF, 22²F, 21PHY,

	Starts	1st	2nd	3rd	Win & Pl
Hurdles	3	0	1	0	852
Career Total	6	0	1	0	852

Going: Sf: 0-1 GS: 0-0 Gd: 0-0 GF: - Fm: 0-2
Distance: 2m/2m3: 0-0 2m4-2m7: 0-3 3m+: 0-0
Track: LH: 0-1 RH: 0-1 Tight: 0-1 Gall: 0-0
Aids: Bl: 0-0 Vi: 0-0 Tstrap: 0-0
Best Rating: 85 10/02 Winc   2m6f   firm   Hdl

Modest novice hurdler, stays two and a half miles plus, acts on fast ground.

Turn To Blue
67   53
4-y-o b g Bluegrass Prince (IRE)-Alvecote Lady (Touching Wood (USA))
J C Fox Lord Mutton Racing Partnership

Placings:P00   (1918)
2002/03: 16PGF, 16⁰G, 16⁰GS,

	Starts	1st	2nd	3rd	Win & Pl
Hurdles	3	0	0	0	
Career Total	3	0	0	0	

Going: Sf: 0-0 GS: 0-1 Gd: 0-1 GF: - Fm: 0-1
Distance: 2m/2m3: 0-3 2m4-2m7: 0-0 3m+: 0-0
Track: LH: 0-3 RH: 0-0 Tight: 0-1 Gall: 0-1
Aids: Bl: 0-0 Vi: 0-0 Tstrap: 0-0
Best Rating: 53 11/02 Wwck   2m   good   Hdl

Turned Out Nice
99   94
5-y-o b m Ezzoud (IRE)-Green Seed (IRE) (Lead On Time (USA))

P Beaumont (J D Bethell 5/11) Robert Gibbons

Placings:403   (4762)
2002/03: 16⁴GS, 16⁰S, 16³G,

	Starts	1st	2nd	3rd	Win & Pl
Hurdles	3	0	0	1	1168
Career Total	3	0	0	1	1168

Going: Sf: 0-1 GS: 0-1 Gd: 0-1 GF: - Fm: 0-0
Distance: 2m/2m3: 0-3 2m4-2m7: 0-0 3m+: 0-0
Track: LH: 0-2 RH: 0-1 Tight: 0-1 Gall: 0-0
Aids: Bl: 0-0 Vi: 0-0 Tstrap: 0-0
Best Rating: 94 4/03 Prth   2m110y   good   Hdl

Plating-class hurdler; acts on good ground or softer.

Tursal (IRE)

14-y-o b g Fine Blade (USA)-Turlough Pet (Retieme)
A R Campbell (Trainer Unknown 26/5) A R Campbell

Placings:0/0POFF/036/0   (0503)
2002/03: 26⁰G,

	Starts	1st	2nd	3rd	Win & Pl
Chases	1	0	0	0	
Career Total	10	0	0	1	355

Going: Sf: 0-0 GS: 0-0 Gd: 0-1 GF: - Fm: 0-0
Distance: 2m/2m3: 0-0 2m4-2m7: 0-0 3m+: 0-0
Track: LH: 0-1 RH: 0-0 Tight: 0-1 Gall: 0-0
Aids: Bl: 0-0 Vi: 0-0 Tstrap: 0-0
Best Rating: 83 3/97 Hntg   2m5f110y   gd-fm   Hdl

Turtle Dancer (IRE)
100   114
5-y-o b g Turtle Island (IRE)-Love Me Please (IRE) (Darshaan)
B Ellison Ashley Young

Placings:46-16   (1162)
2002/03: 17¹G, 17⁶GF,

	Starts	1st	2nd	3rd	Win & Pl
Hurdles	2	1	0	0	2884
Career Total	4	1	0	0	3489
102	8/02	Sedg	2m1f	E Hdl	GD	£2884

Total win prize-money £2884

Going: Sf: 0-0 GS: 0-0 Gd: 1-1 GF: - Fm: 0-1
Distance: 2m/2m3: 1-2 2m4-2m7: 0-0 3m+: 0-0
Track: LH: 1-2 RH: 0-0 Tight: 1-2 Gall: 0-0
Aids: Bl: 0-0 Vi: 0-0 Tstrap: 0-0
Best Rating: 114 12/01 Fair   2m   yield   Hdl

Modest hurdler; showed useful form in Ireland and scored on his debut for new yard at Sedgefield in August.

Turtle Love (IRE)
104   70
4-y-o b f Turtle Island (IRE)-A Little Loving (He Loves Me)
K A Morgan (Miss V Haigh 30/11) Miss V Haigh

Placings:P60602   (4782)
2002/03: 17⁰G, 16⁶G, 16⁰G, 17⁶G, 16⁰G, 17²G,

	Starts	1st	2nd	3rd	Win & Pl
Hurdles	6	0	1	0	686
Career Total	6	0	1	0	686

Going: Sf: 0-0 GS: 0-0 Gd: 0-6 GF: - Fm: 0-0
Distance: 2m/2m3: 0-6 2m4-2m7: 0-0 3m+: 0-0

Track: LH: 0-5 RH: 0-1 Tight: 0-4 Gall: 0-1
Aids: Bl: 0-1 Vi: 0-0 Tstrap: 0-0
Best Rating: 70 4/03 MRas 2m1f110y good Hdl

Plating-class over hurdles; runner-up in seller at Market Rasen in April.

Turtleback (IRE)

117   137

5-y-o b g Turtle Island (IRE)-Mimicry (Thatch (USA))
E J O Grady D F Desmond

Placings: 13621-21350   (4136)
2002/03: 16²HY, 18¹S, 16³HY, 16⁵YS, 17⁰G,

	Starts	1st	2nd	3rd	Win & Pl
Hurdles	5	1	1	1	15613
Career Total	10	3	2	2	38066

131	11/02	Fair	2m2f	Hdl		SFT	£7975
128	4/02	Punc	2m	Hdl		G-Y	£7975
128	12/01	Leop	2m	Hdl		YLD	£8068
						Total win prize-money £24019

Going: Sf: 1-3 GS: 0-0 Gd: 0-1 GF: - Fm: 0-0
Distance: 2m/2m3: 1-5 2m4-2m7: 0-0 3m+: 0-1
Track: LH: 0-3 RH: 1-1 Tight: 0-0 Gall: 0-1
Aids: Bl: 0-0 Vi: 0-0 Tstrap: 0-0
Best Rating: 137 3/03 Chel 2m1f good Hdl

Useful Irish-trained hurdler; stays two and a quarter miles; suited by cut in the ground.

Tuscan Tempo

72   86

4-y-o ch g Perugino (USA)-Fact Of Time (Known Fact (USA))
G F Edwards (R Hannon 8/8) G F Edwards

Placings: 606FPP   (4251)
2002/03: 17⁶F, 16⁰GS, 17⁶GS, 17⁷GS, 16⁸GS, 17⁰PS,

	Starts	1st	2nd	3rd	Win & Pl
Hurdles	6	0	0	0	0
Career Total	6	0	0	0	0

Going: Sf: 0-0 GS: 0-4 Gd: 0-1 GF: - Fm: 0-1
Distance: 2m/2m3: 0-6 2m4-2m7: 0-0 3m+: 0-0
Track: LH: 0-2 RH: 0-4 Tight: 0-2 Gall: 0-0
Aids: Bl: 0-0 Vi: 0-0 Tstrap: 0-0
Best Rating: 86 1/03 Extr 2m1f gd-sft Hdl

Tuscarora (IRE)

91   79

4-y-o b f Revoque (IRE)-Fresh Look (IRE) (Alzao (USA))
A W Carroll (P C Haslam 15/1) Pursuit Media

Placings: 5   (2098)
2002/03: 16⁵G,

	Starts	1st	2nd	3rd	Win & Pl
Hurdles	1	0	0	0	0
Career Total	1	0	0	0	0

Going: Sf: 0-0 GS: 0-0 Gd: 0-1 GF: - Fm: 0-0
Distance: 2m/2m3: 0-1 2m4-2m7: 0-0 3m+: 0-0
Track: LH: 0-1 RH: 0-0 Tight: 0-1 Gall: 0-0
Aids: Bl: 0-0 Vi: 0-0 Tstrap: 0-0
Best Rating: 79 11/02 Catt 2m good Hdl

Won a sprint seller on the All-Weather; doubtful stayer over hurdles.

Tuska Ridge (IRE)

102(107c)   (97c)95

10-y-o b g Zaffaran (USA)-Mcbrides Reject (Avocat)
J J Lambe Stephen McConville

Placings: 4/2213.1356105P3P/0/2321P53FFU/0FU001400-U1RP02424UR00R0   (4333a)
2002/03: 16⁵UGF, 24¹S, 25⁵YS, 17⁵PSH, 22⁰G, 21²GF, 27⁴G, 21²G, 20⁴GF, 24⁰UF, 24⁴YS, 22⁰S, 20⁰S, 16⁴RY, 24⁰GY,

	Starts	1st	2nd	3rd	Win & Pl
Hurdles	7	0	1	0	1130
Chases	8	1	1	0	8156
Career Total	50	6	6	5	31040

92	5/02	Navn	3m	(0-116)HCh	SFT	£6561
95	12/01	Navn	2m6f	(0-109)HHdl	Y-S	£5564
113	6/00	Strf	3m	E Ch	G-S	£3354
111	10/98	DRoy	2m4f	Hdl	GD	£1494
104	7/98	Klny	2m1f	NHF	G-F	£2989
100	6/98	Tipp	2m1f	NHF	Y-S	£2382
					Total win prize-money £22347

Going: Sf: 1-3 GS: 0-0 Gd: 0-3 GF: - Fm: 0-4
Distance: 2m/2m3: 0-3 2m4-2m7: 0-6 3m+: 1-6
Track: LH: 1-10 RH: 0-0 Tight: 0-3 Gall: 0-0
Aids: Bl: 0-0 Vi: 0-0 Tstrap: 0-0
Best Rating: 113 6/00 Strf 3m gd-sft Ch

Moderate chaser who stays well; acts on soft ground.

Tuxedo Junction (NZ)

105(106h)   (91h)102+

8-y-o b g Little Brown Jug (NZ)-Just Kay (NZ) (St Puckle)
P J Hobbs The Gascoigne Brookes Partnership Iv

Placings: 2404/43P0/341   (0506)
2002/03: 17³GF, 20⁴G, 20¹G,

	Starts	1st	2nd	3rd	Win & Pl
Hurdles	2	0	0	1	450
Chases	1	1	0	0	4076
Career Total	11	1	1	2	5532

| 111 | 6/02 | Worc | 2m4f110yD(0-110)HCh | GD | £4075 |
| | | | | Total win prize-money £4076 |

Going: Sf: 0-0 GS: 0-0 Gd: 1-2 GF: - Fm: 0-1
Distance: 2m/2m3: 0-1 2m4-2m7: 1-2 3m+: 0-0
Track: LH: 1-2 RH: 0-1 Tight: 0-0 Gall: 0-0
Aids: Bl: 0-0 Vi: 0-0 Tstrap: 0-0
Best Rating: 111 6/02 Worc 2m4f110y good Ch

Moderate chaser; has taken to fences well and made a successful chasing debut at Worcester June 2002.

Tweed

57   88

6-y-o ch g Barathea (IRE)-In Perpetuity (Great Nephew)
B Ellison (J R Best 1/1) Paul J Dixon

Placings: 204P/2PP-5   (1747)
2002/03: 21⁵S,

	Starts	1st	2nd	3rd	Win & Pl
Hurdles	1	0	0	0	0
Career Total	8	0	2	0	1666

Going: Sf: 0-1 GS: 0-0 Gd: 0-0 GF: - Fm: 0-0
Distance: 2m/2m3: 0-2 2m4-2m7: 0-1 3m+: 0-0
Track: LH: 0-1 RH: 0-0 Tight: 0-1 Gall: 0-0
Aids: Bl: 0-1 Vi: 0-0 Tstrap: 0-0
Best Rating: 94 1/01 Muss 2m good Hdl

Tweli

97   79

6-y-o b g Deploy-Flying Fantasy (Habitat)
I A Wood Mrs A M Riney

Placings: 32004   (4337)
2002/03: 17³GF, 16²GF, 17⁰G, 17⁰G, 16⁴GF,

	Starts	1st	2nd	3rd	Win & Pl
NH Flat	4	0	1	1	805
Hurdles	1	0	0	0	285
Career Total	5	0	1	1	1090

Going: Sf: 0-0 GS: 0-0 Gd: 0-2 GF: - Fm: 0-3
Distance: 2m/2m3: 0-5 2m4-2m7: 0-0 3m+: 0-0
Track: LH: 0-1 RH: 0-4 Tight: 0-1 Gall: 0-1
Aids: Bl: 0-0 Vi: 0-0 Tstrap: 0-0
Best Rating: 84 3/03 Hntg 2m110y gd-fm Hdl

Moderate placed form in bumpers.

Twice As Good (IRE)

90(83h)   97

9-y-o b g Good Thyne (USA)-Twice As Fluffy (Pollerton)
K C Bailey Graham And Alison Jelley

Placings: 1/0/3324-64PP   (4636)
2002/03: 19⁶G, 23⁴G, 24⁶PG, 24⁶G,

	Starts	1st	2nd	3rd	Win & Pl
Chases	4	0	0	0	264
Career Total	10	1	1	2	3599

| 115 | 4/00 | Hntg | 2m110y | H NHF | GD | £1715 |
| | | | | | Total win prize-money £1715 |

Going: Sf: 0-0 GS: 0-1 Gd: 0-3 GF: - Fm: 0-0
Distance: 2m/2m3: 0-1 2m4-2m7: 0-0 3m+: 0-3
Track: LH: 0-3 RH: 0-3 Tight: 0-2 Gall: 0-0
Aids: Bl: 0-0 Vi: 0-0 Tstrap: 0-0
Best Rating: 115 4/00 Hntg 2m110y good NHF

Twin-Cylinder (IRE)

10-y-o br g Mandalus-Gemini Stone (Le Bavard (FR))
R Lee Richard Lee

Placings: P3   (0446)
2002/03: 19⁰PG, 19³G,

	Starts	1st	2nd	3rd	Win & Pl
Chases	2	0	0	1	469
Career Total	2	0	0	1	469

Going: Sf: 0-0 GS: 0-0 Gd: 0-2 GF: - Fm: 0-0
Distance: 2m/2m3: 0-2 2m4-2m7: 0-0 3m+: 0-0
Track: LH: 0-0 RH: 0-2 Tight: 0-0 Gall: 0-0
Aids: Bl: 0-0 Vi: 0-0 Tstrap: 0-0
Best Rating: 0 6/02 Hrfd 2m3f good Ch

Twiscombe

8-y-o br m Arctic Lord-Flying Cherub (Osiris)
Mrs J G Retter Mrs J G Retter

Placings: 60-P   (0040)
2002/03: 17⁰G,

	Starts	1st	2nd	3rd	Win & Pl
Hurdles	1	0	0	0	0
Career Total	3	0	0	0	0

Going: Sf: 0-0 GS: 0-0 Gd: 0-1 GF: - Fm: 0-0
Distance: 2m/2m3: 0-1 2m4-2m7: 0-0 3m+: 0-0
Track: LH: 0-0 RH: 0-1 Tight: 0-0 Gall: 0-0
Aids: Bl: 0-0 Vi: 0-0 Tstrap: 0-0
Best Rating: 29 4/02 Chel 2m1f good NHF

Twisted Logic (IRE)
109   125
10-y-o b g Tremblant-Logical View (Mandalus)
R H Alner P M De Wilde

Placings:533P3/1P2110151/F63U5/451410U-2533013P215   (4564)
2002/03: 23²G, 25⁵G, 24³GF, 24³GF, 24⁰G, 25¹GS, 23³S, 25⁵GS, 26²GF, 23¹F, 24⁵GF,

	Starts	1st	2nd	3rd	Win & Pl
Chases	11	2	2	3	24329
Career Total	37	9	3	7	65287

125	3/03	Extr	2m7f110yD(0-125)HCh	FRM	£7686
121	12/02	Extr	3m1f110yC(0-135)HCh	G-S	£8320
131	12/01	Extr	3m1f110yC(0-135)HCh	GD	£6994
126	10/01	Chel	3m110y E(0-125)HCh	GD	£7247
136	4/00	Bang	3m110y C(0-135)HCh	G-S	£7410
127	3/00	Font	3m2f110yD(0-125)HCh	G-S	£4616
118	1/00	Wwck	3m1f110yE(0-115)HCh	SFT	£3000
119	12/99	Tntn	3m	F(0-105)HCh	SFT	£3395
106	5/99	Towc	2m6f	E Ch	G-F	£2322

Total win prize-money £51712

Going: Sf: 0-1 GS: 1-2 Gd: 0-3 GF: - Fm: 1-5
Distance: 2m/2m3: 0-0 2m4-2m7: 0-0 3m+: 2-11
Track: LH: 0-5 RH: 2-5 Tight: 0-2 Gall: 0-2
Aids: Bl: 0-0 Vi: 0-0 Tstrap: 0-0
Best Rating: 136 4/00 Bang 3m110y gd-sft Ch

Fair staying chaser; suited to stiff tracks and small fields; acts on most types of ground.

Two For Joy (IRE)
(106h)   (115h)85
8-y-o br m Mandalus-Misty Joy (General Ironside)
C R Egerton Ian Jacombs Sarah Macechern & Partners

Placings:73/121510-F3   (0330)
2002/03: 24²G, 23³G,

	Starts	1st	2nd	3rd	Win & Pl
Chases	2	0	0	1	638
Career Total	10	4	1	2	15377

115	3/02	Towc	3m	D Hdl	G-S	£3507
110	3/02	Extr	2m3f	D Hdl	GD	£3815
100	1/02	Donc	2m4f	E Hdl	GD	£3220
110	11/00	Hrfd	2m1f	H NHF	G-S	£1617

Total win prize-money £12160

Going: Sf: 0-0 GS: 0-0 Gd: 0-2 GF: - Fm: 0-0
Distance: 2m/2m3: 0-0 2m4-2m7: 0-0 3m+: 0-2
Track: LH: 0-1 RH: 0-0 Tight: 0-1 Gall: 0-0
Aids: Bl: 0-0 Vi: 0-0 Tstrap: 0-0
Best Rating: 115 3/02 Towc 3m gd-sft Hdl

Moderate chaser; fair hurdler; stays three miles and is best on a sound surface but out of luck over fences so far.

Two Huge
62   41
5-y-o gr g Norton Challenger-Rainy Miss (IRE) (Cheval)
N A Twiston-Davies The Really Huge Partnership

Placings:0   (4444)
2002/03: 16⁰G,

	Starts	1st	2nd	3rd	Win & Pl
NH Flat	1	0	0	0	

Career Total   1   0   0   0

Going: Sf: 0-0 GS: 0-0 Gd: 0-1 GF: - Fm: 0-0
Distance: 2m/2m3: 0-1 2m4-2m7: 0-0 3m+: 0-0
Track: LH: 0-0 RH: 0-1 Tight: 0-0 Gall: 0-0
Aids: Bl: 0-0 Vi: 0-0 Tstrap: 0-0
Best Rating: 82 4/03 Asct 2m110y good NHF

Two Lords
90   86
11-y-o b g Arctic Lord-Doddycross (Deep Run)
Mrs A C Tate O I F Davies

Placings:00/PP00P/P54140/005224306P0/624U11P4P/PP P000-0035P   (0820)
2002/03: 22⁰G, 24⁰GF, 24³S, 20⁵G, 24⁰GF,

	Starts	1st	2nd	3rd	Win & Pl
Hurdles	5	0	0	1	380
Career Total	44	3	3	2	16301

108	11/00	Hayd	2m7f110yE(0-115)HHdl	SFT	£3623
108	10/00	Ludl	3m	F(0-95)HHdl	G-F	£2765
106	3/99	Ludl	2m5f110yE(0-115)HHdl	SFT	£5454

Total win prize-money £11844

Going: Sf: 0-1 GS: 0-0 Gd: 0-2 GF: - Fm: 0-2
Distance: 2m/2m3: 0-0 2m4-2m7: 0-2 3m+: 0-3
Track: LH: 0-4 RH: 0-1 Tight: 0-1 Gall: 0-0
Aids: Bl: 0-1 Vi: 0-0 Tstrap: 0-5
Best Rating: 108 11/00 Hayd 2m7f110y soft Hdl

Two Tears
103(85h)   (38h)115d
9-y-o gr g Silver Owl-Vomero (NZ) (Church Parade)
N J Hawke M J Disney

Placings:40/2P/4U-5111P4P   (3828)
2002/03: 22⁵GS, 19¹GS, 20¹S, 24¹S, 19⁵S, 19⁴S, 19⁰GS,

	Starts	1st	2nd	3rd	Win & Pl
Hurdles	1	0	0	0	
Chases	6	3	0	0	13789
Career Total	13	3	1	0	15191

115	12/02	Tntn	3m	E(0-105)HCh	SFT	£5118
105	12/02	Bang	2m4f110yE(0-110)HCh	SFT	£4578
102	12/02	Tntn	2m3f	E(0-110)HCh	G-S	£3562

Total win prize-money £13259

Going: Sf: 2-4 GS: 1-3 Gd: 0-0 GF: - Fm: 0-0
Distance: 2m/2m3: 1-3 2m4-2m7: 1-3 3m+: 1-1
Track: LH: 1-2 RH: 2-5 Tight: 3-5 Gall: 0-0
Aids: Bl: 0-0 Vi: 0-0 Tstrap: 0-0
Best Rating: 115 12/02 Tntn 3m soft Ch

Fair chaser; winner at Taunton in December 2002 and defied a penalty in easy fashion at Bangor a week later. Completed the hat-trick back at Taunton; found things tougher having gone up a total of 26lb; stays three miles; effective in soft ground.

Twoforten
85   76
8-y-o b g Robellino (USA)-Grown At Rowan (Gabitat)
P Butler P Butler

Placings:P/40/6-00   (1285)
2002/03: 17⁰GF, 18⁰GF,

	Starts	1st	2nd	3rd	Win & Pl
Hurdles	2	0	0	0	
Career Total	6	0	0	0	0

Going: Sf: 0-0 GS: 0-0 Gd: 0-0 GF: - Fm: 0-2

Distance: 2m/2m3: 0-2 2m4-2m7: 0-0 3m+: 0-0
Track: LH: 0-1 RH: 0-1 Tight: 0-2 Gall: 0-0
Aids: Bl: 0-0 Vi: 0-0 Tstrap: 0-0
Best Rating: 76 9/01 Plum 2m gd-fm Hdl

Twotensforafive
100   84
10-y-o b g Arctic Lord-Sister Of Gold (The Parson)
P R Rodford Mrs Christine Priest

Placings:0000/000300/602P0/F443-P4F31655   (2780)
2002/03: 23⁰GF, 23⁴GF, 22⁵G, 21³G, 19¹G, 19⁶S, 23⁵GS, 19⁵S,

	Starts	1st	2nd	3rd	Win & Pl
Chases	8	1	0	1	3871
Career Total	27	1	1	3	5981

| 84 | 10/02 | Chep | 2m3f110yG(0-90)HCh | GD | £2597 |

Total win prize-money £2597

Going: Sf: 0-2 GS: 0-1 Gd: 1-3 GF: - Fm: 0-2
Distance: 2m/2m3: 0-1 2m4-2m7: 1-4 3m+: 0-3
Track: LH: 1-5 RH: 0-2 Tight: 0-2 Gall: 0-0
Aids: Bl: 0-0 Vi: 0-0 Tstrap: 0-0
Best Rating: 89 7/99 Gway 2m good NHF

Poor chaser, winner of a selling handicap in October 2002.

Twotiming Gent (IRE)
77   69
10-y-o b g Broken Hearted-Dual Express (Giolla Mear)
Niall J Donohoe Niall J Donohoe

Placings:1/PP-0003P   (4374)
2002/03: 16⁰S, 16⁰S, 24⁰Y, 22³G, 27⁰G,

	Starts	1st	2nd	3rd	Win & Pl
Hurdles	5	0	0	1	429
Career Total	8	1	0	1	3465

| 89 | 2/00 | Thur | 2m | NHF | SH | £3036 |

Total win prize-money £3036

Going: Sf: 0-2 GS: 0-0 Gd: 0-2 GF: - Fm: 0-0
Distance: 2m/2m3: 0-2 2m4-2m7: 0-1 3m+: 0-2
Track: LH: 0-2 RH: 0-0 Tight: 0-1 Gall: 0-0
Aids: Bl: 0-2 Vi: 0-0 Tstrap: 0-0
Best Rating: 89 2/00 Thur 2m sft-hvy NHF

Tyndarius (IRE)
107   95
12-y-o b g Mandalus-Lady Rerico (Pamroy)
I W McInnes Alex Shaw

Placings:0/0101P/03U0/2211F/01450P/150-3PPP (4105)
2002/03: 22³S, 25²HY, 24²G, 21⁵S,

	Starts	1st	2nd	3rd	Win & Pl
Chases	4	0	0	1	848
Career Total	28	6	2	2	35367

122	2/02	MRas	2m1f110yD(0-115)HCh	SFT	£4143
122	12/00	Fair	3m1f	HCh	Y-S	£10400
104	3/00	Leop	2m2f	HCh	GD	£5520
104	3/00	Navn	2m1f	Ch	Y-S	£3864
116	4/98	List	2m4f	(0-109)HHdl	Y-S	£2978
103	2/98	Clon	2m4f	Hdl	Y-S	£1935

Total win prize-money £28842

Going: Sf: 0-3 GS: 0-0 Gd: 0-1 GF: - Fm: 0-0
Distance: 2m/2m3: 0-0 2m4-2m7: 0-2 3m+: 1-2
Track: LH: 0-3 RH: 0-1 Tight: 0-3 Gall: 0-1
Aids: Bl: 0-1 Vi: 0-0 Tstrap: 0-0
Best Rating: 122 2/02 MRas 2m1f110y soft Ch

Fair chaser; ex-Irish; effective from two to three miles; acts on ground good or softer; likes to be held up; does tend to make mistakes

Tyrrellspass (IRE)

89   76

6-y-o b g Alzao (USA)-Alpine Chime (IRE) (Tirol)
J D Frost (S Donohoe 7/8) R G Frost

Placings:000P-00   (1231)
2002/03: 16⁶HY, 16⁰YS, 16⁹G,

	Starts	1st	2nd	3rd	Win & Pl
Hurdles	3	0	0		
Career Total	6	0	0		

Going:	Sf: 0-1 GS: 0-0 Gd: 0-1 GF: - Fm: 0-0
Distance:	2m/2m3: 0-3 2m4-2m7: 0-0 3m+: 0-0
Track:	LH: 0-1 RH: 0-0 Tight: 0-0 Gall: 0-0
Aids:	Bl: 0-0 Vi: 0-0 Tstrap: 0-0
Best Rating:	76 7/02 Kbgn 2m yld-sft Hdl

Tysou (FR)

108(108h)   (146h)137

6-y-o b/br g Ajdayt (USA)-Pretty Point (Crystal Glitters (USA))
N J Henderson W J Brown

Placings:2155612110/421300-1331F1   (4548)
2002/03: 16¹GS, 16⁹S, 16⁹G, 16¹GF, 16⁶G, 16¹G,

	Starts	1st	2nd	3rd	Win & Pl
Chases	6	3	0	2	29700
Career Total	22	8	3	3	67652
137	4/03	Ayr	2m	C Ch	GF	£13385
137	3/03	Winc	2m	D Ch	G-F	£5382
135	11/02	Sand	2m	D Ch	G-S	£4777
141	12/01	Donc	2m110y	B(0-140)HHdl	GF	£8112
133	2/01	Muss	2m	D Hdl		£3444
128	2/01	Catt	2m	E Hdl	SFT	£2775
107	11/00	Catt	2m	D Hdl	G-S	£3900
	7/00	Claf	2m	Hdl	SFT	£5764
					Total win prize-money	£47541

Going:	Sf: 0-1 GS: 1-1 Gd: 1-3 GF: - Fm: 1-1
Distance:	2m/2m3: 3-6 2m4-2m7: 0-0 3m+: 0-0
Track:	LH: 1-2 RH: 2-4 Tight: 0-1 Gall: 0-0
Aids:	Bl: 0-0 Vi: 0-0 Tstrap: 0-0
Best Rating:	146 1/02 Kemp 2m gd-sft Hdl

Useful novice chaser; best over two miles; suited by the ground good or softer; just held when tried against the better novices.

Ugie Girl

4-y-o gr f Passing Point (IRE)-Nawtinookey (Uncle Pokey)
A C Whillans G C G Racing Partnership

Placings:0   (4357)
2002/03: 16⁰GF,

	Starts	1st	2nd	3rd	Win & Pl
NH Flat	1	0	0	0	
Career Total	1	0	0	0	

Going:	Sf: 0-0 GS: 0-0 Gd: 0-0 GF: - Fm: 0-1
Distance:	2m/2m3: 0-1 2m4-2m7: 0-0 3m+: 0-0
Track:	LH: 0-1 RH: 0-0 Tight: 0-0 Gall: 0-0
Aids:	Bl: 0-0 Vi: 0-0 Tstrap: 0-0
Best Rating:	0 3/03 Weth 2m gd-fm NHF

Ultimate Gold (IRE)

93(104h)   (103h)78

9-y-o b g Good Thyne (USA)-Golden Mela (Golden Love)
K C Bailey John White

Placings:2623-P3   (2015)
2002/03: 16⁶GS, 20³GF,

	Starts	1st	2nd	3rd	Win & Pl
Chases	2	0	0	1	533
Career Total	6	0	2	2	2489

Going:	Sf: 0-0 GS: 0-1 Gd: 0-0 GF: - Fm: 0-1
Distance:	2m/2m3: 0-1 2m4-2m7: 0-1 3m+: 0-0
Track:	LH: 0-0 RH: 0-2 Tight: 0-0 Gall: 0-0
Aids:	Bl: 0-0 Vi: 0-0 Tstrap: 0-0
Best Rating:	103 3/02 Towc 2m5f gd-sft Hdl

Plating-class hurdler/chaser; stays two and a half miles.

Ulusaba

109(106h)   (106h)97

7-y-o b g Alflora (IRE)-Mighty Fly (Comedy Star (USA))
R C Guest (N B Mason 11/2) N B Mason

Placings:06P/22124/0023133-4456124001461   (3869)
2002/03: 16⁵G, 17⁴G, 17⁴S, 17⁵GF, 16⁶GS, 17³GF, 17²G, 20⁴GF, 16⁹G, 16⁰GF, 17¹GF, 16⁴HY, 16⁹HY, 19¹G,

	Starts	1st	2nd	3rd	Win & Pl
Hurdles	2	1	0	0	4810
Chases	12	2	1	1	10960
Career Total	28	5	5	3	23223
96	2/03	Donc	2m3f	E(0-110)HCh	GD	£3861
104	10/02	MRas	2m1f110yD(0-120)HHdl	G-F	£4810
97	4/02	Sthl	2m1f	E(0-100)HCh	G-F	£3526
106	3/02	Catt	2m	G Hdl	G-S	£1708
88	3/01	MRas	2m1f110yG(0-95)HHdl	GD	£1561
					Total win prize-money	£15466

Going:	Sf: 0-3 GS: 0-1 Gd: 1-5 GF: - Fm: 2-5
Distance:	2m/2m3: 3-13 2m4-2m7: 0-1 3m+: 0-0
Track:	LH: 2-9 RH: 1-5 Tight: 1-7 Gall: 0-1
Aids:	Bl: 3-9 Vi: 0-0 Tstrap: 3-14
Best Rating:	106 3/02 Catt 2m gd-sft Hdl

Moderate handicap chaser; stays 2m 4f; acts on fast ground; wears blinkers and a tongue tie.

Ulvick Star (IRE)

104   71

11-y-o b g Lord Americo-She s Approaching (Ragapan)
M J Gingell Mrs P King

Placings:0/3/P-46P3PU4P   (1542)
2002/03: 20⁴GS, 20⁶GF, 29⁵S, 24³GS, 26⁶GF, 23^UG, 26⁴GF, 25⁶GF,

	Starts	1st	2nd	3rd	Win & Pl
Hurdles	7	0	0	1	593
Chases	1	0	0	0	
Career Total	11	0	0	2	840

Going:	Sf: 0-1 GS: 0-2 Gd: 0-1 GF: - Fm: 0-4
Distance:	2m/2m3: 0-0 2m4-2m7: 0-2 3m+: 0-6
Track:	LH: 0-5 RH: 0-3 Tight: 0-3 Gall: 0-2
Aids:	Bl: 0-0 Vi: 0-1 Tstrap: 0-1
Best Rating:	94 5/00 Hntg 3m good Ch

Very modest hurdler; stays three miles.

Umbopa (USA)

66   17

5-y-o b g Gilded Time (USA)-How Fortunate (CAN) (What Luck (USA))

P Bowen (K R Burke 10/5) The Galloping Punters

Placings:P5   (1800)
2002/03: 16⁶G, 17⁵S,

	Starts	1st	2nd	3rd	Win & Pl
Hurdles	2	0	0	0	0
Career Total	2	0	0	0	0

Going:	Sf: 0-1 GS: 0-0 Gd: 0-1 GF: - Fm: 0-0
Distance:	2m/2m3: 0-2 2m4-2m7: 0-0 3m+: 0-0
Track:	LH: 0-2 RH: 0-0 Tight: 0-1 Gall: 0-0
Aids:	Bl: 0-1 Vi: 0-0 Tstrap: 0-0
Best Rating:	17 11/02 NAbb 2m1f soft Hdl

Umbrella Man (IRE)

105(112h)   (109h)118

7-y-o ch g Insan (USA)-Askasilla (IRE) (Lucky Mickmooch)
Miss H C Knight Mrs J Dollar & Mrs M Hall

Placings:00/2424-5314F2   (4448)
2002/03: 20⁵GS, 16³G, 20¹S, 20⁴GS, 21⁵S, 20²G,

	Starts	1st	2nd	3rd	Win & Pl
Chases	6	1	1	1	10449
Career Total	12	1	3	1	12376
112	1/03	Ludl	2m4f	D(0-115)HCh	SFT	£6873
					Total win prize-money	£6874

Going:	Sf: 1-2 GS: 0-2 Gd: 0-2 GF: - Fm: 0-0
Distance:	2m/2m3: 1-2 2m4-2m7: 0-2 3m+: 0-0
Track:	LH: 0-1 RH: 1-5 Tight: 1-2 Gall: 0-2
Aids:	Bl: 0-0 Vi: 0-0 Tstrap: 0-0
Best Rating:	118 4/03 Ludl 2m4f good Ch

Fair chaser/modest hurdler; successful in a Ludlow handicap chase in January 2003 on only his third run over fences; well suited by soft ground.

Un Jour A Vassy (FR)

110(105h)   (115h)127

8-y-o b g Video Rock (FR)-Bayalika (FR) (Kashtan (FR))
P F Nicholls Mrs Bunty Millard

Placings:64/532F/33U11/1P15330P-2F622   (4466)
2002/03: 24²GF, 20⁵GS, 20⁶GS, 24²G, 24²F,

	Starts	1st	2nd	3rd	Win & Pl
Chases	5	0	3	0	6959
Career Total	24	4	4	5	34489
115	11/01	Tntn	3m110y	D Hdl	GD	£5889
126	5/01	Sthl	2m4f110yB(0-145)HCh	G-F	£10790
115	4/01	Tntn	3m	D (0-110)HCh	G-F	£4046
114	4/01	Fknm	2m5f110yH Ch	G-S	£2298
					Total win prize-money	£23023

Going:	Sf: 0-0 GS: 0-2 Gd: 0-1 GF: - Fm: 0-2
Distance:	2m/2m3: 0-0 2m4-2m7: 0-2 3m+: 0-3
Track:	LH: 0-2 RH: 0-3 Tight: 0-1 Gall: 0-2
Aids:	Bl: 0-0 Vi: 0-0 Tstrap: 0-0
Best Rating:	127 12/01 Winc 3m1f110y good Ch

Fair chaser; effective at two and a half miles; stays three miles on easy tracks; effective on good ground.

Uncle Bert (IRE)

101   91

13-y-o b g Ovac (ITY)-Sweet Gum (USA) (Gummo)
Miss Lucinda V Russell Mrs C G Greig

Placings:5/400361115/345126/F4/31225133314P24/241/P
3325522   (4794)

2002/03: 20ᴾG, 20³GF, 16³GF, 16²G, 20⁵G, 20⁵S, 21²G, 21²GF,

	Starts	1st	2nd	3rd	Win & Pl
Chases	8	0	3	2	6471
Career Total	43	8	8	8	49073
101 10/00 Aint	2m4f	D(0-125)HCh	GD	£12499
103 10/98 Sedg	2m11y	E(0-115)HCh	GD	£3185
101 9/98 Sedg	2m5f	E(0-115)HCh	GD	£3470
103 6/98 Prth	2m	E(0-115)HCh	G-F	£3436
106 11/96 Plum	2m	E(0-115)HCh	SFT	£2906
96 3/96 Font	2m2f	E(0-100)HCh	G-F	£3234
94 3/96 Tntn	2m110y	F(0-105)HCh	GD	£2697
93 2/96 Tntn	2m110y	E(0-100)HCh	G-S	£2927

Total win prize-money £34355

Going:	Sf: 0-1 GS: 0-0 Gd: 0-4 GF: - Fm: 0-3
Distance:	2m/2m3: 0-2 2m4-2m7: 0-6 3m+: 0-0
Track:	LH: 0-5 RH: 0-3 Tight: 0-5 Gall: 0-0
Aids:	Bl: 0-0 Vi: 0-0 Tstrap: 0-0
Best Rating:	106 11/96 Plum 2m soft Ch

Plating-class handicap chaser; one-time useful performer, but in the veteran stage now and without a win for more than two years; stays two and a half miles; acts on a sound surface; suited by a sharp track.

Uncle Clockwise

6-y-o gr g Absalom-Summer Flower (Nomination)
Miss Z C Davison A A Goldson

Placings: PP   (0242)
2002/03: 16ᴾGS, 17ᴾG,

	Starts	1st	2nd	3rd	Win & Pl
Hurdles	2	0	0	0	
Career Total	2	0	0	0	

Going:	Sf: 0-0 GS: 0-1 Gd: 0-1 GF: - Fm: 0-0
Distance:	2m/2m3: 0-2 2m4-2m7: 0-0 3m+: 0-0
Track:	LH: 0-0 RH: 0-2 Tight: 0-0 Gall: 0-0
Aids:	Bl: 0-0 Vi: 0-0 Tstrap: 0-0
Best Rating:	0 5/02 Extr 2m1f good Hdl

Uncle Mick (IRE)

105(106h)   (117h)110
8-y-o b g Ikdam-Kandy Kate (Pry)
C Tizzard D J Hinks

Placings: 5/015/FUF033-F42046021   (4696)
2002/03: 19ᶠG, 22⁴HY, 24²HY, 24⁰G, 24⁴S, 25⁰HY, 25²G, 26³G,

	Starts	1st	2nd	3rd	Win & Pl
Hurdles	6	0	1	0	2729
Chases	3	1	1	0	5388
Career Total	20	2	3	2	13106
101 4/03 NAbb	3m2f110yE Ch	GD	£4124
100 1/01 Plum	3m1f110yE Hdl	HVY	£2387

Total win prize-money £6511

Going:	Sf: 0-5 GS: 0-0 Gd: 1-4 GF: - Fm: 0-0
Distance:	2m/2m3: 0-0 2m4-2m7: 0-3 3m+: 1-6
Track:	LH: 1-6 RH: 0-3 Tight: 1-4 Gall: 0-1
Aids:	Bl: 0-0 Vi: 0-6 Tstrap: 0-0
Best Rating:	117 11/02 Chep 3m heavy Hdl

Modest chaser/hurdler; stays well; appreciates soft ground, but acts on good.

Uncle Teddy (IRE)

101(97h)   (82h)97
10-y-o b g Arctic Cider (USA)-Ishtar (Dike (USA))
Miss E C Lavelle Miss N Henton

Placings: 551/P/50CP41-35125   (1196)
2002/03: 19³G, 20⁵G, 25¹GF, 23²G, 25⁵GF,

	Starts	1st	2nd	3rd	Win & Pl
Chases	5	1	1	1	4621
Career Total	15	3	1	1	10441
91 6/02 Hrfd	3m1f110yG(0-90)HCh	G-F	£3178
97 4/02 Extr	2m3f110yE Ch	FRM	£3962
85 10/99 Towc	2m5f G Hdl	GD	£1562

Total win prize-money £8702

Going:	Sf: 0-0 GS: 0-0 Gd: 0-3 GF: - Fm: 1-2
Distance:	2m/2m3: 0-0 2m4-2m7: 0-2 3m+: 1-3
Track:	LH: 0-1 RH: 1-4 Tight: 0-0 Gall: 0-1
Aids:	Bl: 0-0 Vi: 0-0 Tstrap: 0-0
Best Rating:	97 7/02 Worc 2m7f110y good Ch

Moderate lightly-raced hurdler/chaser. Suited by a sound surface. Took advantage of the odds-on favourite's mistake when winning three runner novice chase at Exeter April 2002.

Uncle Tom

12-y-o b g Scallywag-Reebok (Scottish Rifle)
Mrs M Marfell Mrs M Marfell

Placings: 5   (0218)
2002/03: 25⁵G,

	Starts	1st	2nd	3rd	Win & Pl
Chases	1	0	0	0	0
Career Total	1	0	0	0	0

Going:	Sf: 0-0 GS: 0-0 Gd: 0-1 GF: - Fm: 0-0
Distance:	2m/2m3: 0-0 2m4-2m7: 0-0 3m+: 0-1
Track:	LH: 0-0 RH: 0-1 Tight: 0-0 Gall: 0-1
Aids:	Bl: 0-0 Vi: 0-0 Tstrap: 0-0
Best Rating:	0 5/02 Hrfd 3m1f110y good Ch

Uncle Wallace

101(109h)   (114h)114+
7-y-o b g Neltino-Auntie Dot (Hallodri (ATA))
P R Webber Mrs John Webber

Placings: 40/60420-4334   (3496)
2002/03: 16⁴GF, 18³S, 21³GS, 20⁴GS,

	Starts	1st	2nd	3rd	Win & Pl
Chases	4	0	0	2	2760
Career Total	11	0	1	2	4203

Going:	Sf: 0-1 GS: 0-2 Gd: 0-0 GF: - Fm: 0-1
Distance:	2m/2m3: 0-0 2m4-2m7: 0-2 3m+: 0-0
Track:	LH: 0-1 RH: 0-3 Tight: 0-0 Gall: 0-1
Aids:	Bl: 0-0 Vi: 0-0 Tstrap: 0-0
Best Rating:	114 2/03 Kemp 2m4f110y gd-sft Ch

Fair chaser; son of the useful Auntie Dot; still a maiden but has run with credit in decent company, both over hurdles and fences. Stays two and a half miles, acts on any ground.

Under Construction (IRE)

104   98
5-y-o b g Pennekamp (USA)-Madame Nureyev (USA) (Nureyev (USA))
G A Ham Sally & Tom Dalley

Placings: 30   (2193)
2002/03: 17³S, 17⁰GS,

	Starts	1st	2nd	3rd	Win & Pl
Hurdles	2	0	0	1	556
Career Total	2	0	0	1	556

Going:	Sf: 0-1 GS: 0-1 Gd: 0-0 GF: - Fm: 0-0
Distance:	2m/2m3: 0-2 2m4-2m7: 0-0 3m+: 0-0
Track:	LH: 0-1 RH: 0-1 Tight: 0-2 Gall: 0-0
Aids:	Bl: 0-0 Vi: 0-0 Tstrap: 0-0
Best Rating:	98 11/02 NAbb 2m1f soft Hdl

Modest hurdler; acts on soft ground.

Under The Sand (IRE)

108   127d
6-y-o b g Turtle Island (IRE)-Occupation (Horning)
P J Hobbs R Triple H

Placings: 140/2-6203F00   (4049)
2002/03: 16⁶GS, 16²HY, 16⁶HY, 17³GS, 20ᶠS, 21⁰G, 16⁰HY,

	Starts	1st	2nd	3rd	Win & Pl
Hurdles	7	0	1	1	4666
Career Total	11	1	2	1	14790
122 3/01 Hntg	2m110y E Hdl	SFT	£2933

Total win prize-money £2933

Going:	Sf: 0-4 GS: 0-2 Gd: 0-1 GF: - Fm: 0-0
Distance:	2m/2m3: 0-2 2m4-2m7: 0-2 3m+: 0-0
Track:	LH: 0-1 RH: 0-6 Tight: 0-0 Gall: 0-1
Aids:	Bl: 0-0 Vi: 0-0 Tstrap: 0-0
Best Rating:	129 11/02 Asct 2m110y heavy Hdl

Decent handicap hurdler; acts on soft ground; effective over two miles.

Under The Thumb

91(105h)   (85h)79
9-y-o b g Sunley Builds-Solhoon (Tycoon Ii)
C P Morlock The Two Gingas

Placings: 000/04365/01F10/53P32500-005P0   (2712)
2002/03: 20⁰G, 20⁰GS, 24⁵GS, 19²GS, 16⁹GS,

	Starts	1st	2nd	3rd	Win & Pl
Hurdles	2	0	0	0	0
Chases	3	0	0	0	0
Career Total	26	2	1	3	7728
100 11/00 Ludl	2m	E(0-105)HCh	GD	£3406
101 5/00 Worc	2m	F(0-110)HCh	G-F	£2499

Total win prize-money £5905

Going:	Sf: 0-0 GS: 0-4 Gd: 0-1 GF: - Fm: 0-0
Distance:	2m/2m3: 0-2 2m4-2m7: 0-2 3m+: 0-0
Track:	LH: 0-2 RH: 0-3 Tight: 0-3 Gall: 0-0
Aids:	Bl: 0-0 Vi: 0-0 Tstrap: 0-0
Best Rating:	101 5/00 Worc 2m gd-fm Ch

A winning handicap chaser on two occasions in 2000, but not in the best of form since. Suited by fast ground.

Under Wraps (IRE)

(90h)   (81h)
9-y-o b g In The Wings-Wrapping (Kris)
J Howard Johnson (Jonjo O'Neill 18/12) G Brown

Placings: 400/542122146/11122/0P0-PPPP0   (3915)
2002/03: 24⁵GS, 29ᶠS, 30⁵S, 30ᴾG, 24⁰GS,

	Starts	1st	2nd	3rd	Win & Pl
Hurdles	1	0	0	0	0
Chases	4	0	0	0	0
Career Total	25	5	5	0	25062
120 10/00 Carl	2m4f110yD Ch	GD	£4557

121	5/00	Prth	3m110y	D(0-120)HHdl	GD	£3464
121	5/00	Towc	2m5f	D(0-125)HHdl	SFT	£3334
101	2/00	Ayr	2m6f	E Hdl	HVY	£2905
121	12/99	Uttx	3m110y	F(0-100)HHdl	SFT	£2379

Total win prize-money £16641

Going:	Sf: 0-2 GS: 0-2 Gd: 0-1 GF: - Fm: 0-0
Distance:	2m1/2m3: 0-0 2m4-2m7: 0-0 3m+: 0-5
Track:	LH: 0-3 RH: 0-2 Tight: 0-3 Gall: 0-0
Aids:	Bl: 0-3 Vi: 0-0 Tstrap: 0-0
Best Rating:	129 11/00 Hayd 2m4f heavy Ch

Underley Park (IRE)

(106c)   (101c)**81**

9-y-o ch g Aristocracy-Even Bunny Vii (Damsire Unregistered)

R Ford Richard Ford

Placings:650/56/U/PPP-F   (0478)

2002/03: 26FGS,

	Starts	1st	2nd	3rd	Win & Pl
Hurdles	1	0	0	0	
Career Total	10	0	0	0	0

Going:	Sf: 0-0 GS: 0-1 Gd: 0-0 GF: - Fm: 0-0
Distance:	2m1/2m3: 0-0 2m4-2m7: 0-0 3m+: 0-1
Track:	LH: 0-1 RH: 0-0 Tight: 0-1 Gall: 0-0
Aids:	Bl: 0-0 Vi: 0-0 Tstrap: 0-0
Best Rating:	95 3/99 Hexm 2m gd-sft NHF

Dual point winner; jumped much better than in the past when easily winning maiden hunter chase at Cartmel in May 2003.

Underthescoreboard (IRE)

7-y-o b g Executive Perk-Down The Garden (IRE) (Good Thyne (USA))

Jonjo O Neill Mrs Jonjo O Neill

Placings:P   (0385)

2002/03: 25PGS,

	Starts	1st	2nd	3rd	Win & Pl
Hurdles	1	0	0	0	
Career Total	1	0	0	0	

Going:	Sf: 0-0 GS: 0-1 Gd: 0-0 GF: - Fm: 0-0
Distance:	2m1/2m3: 0-0 2m4-2m7: 0-0 3m+: 0-1
Track:	LH: 0-1 RH: 0-0 Tight: 0-0 Gall: 0-0
Aids:	Bl: 0-0 Vi: 0-0 Tstrap: 0-0
Best Rating:	0 5/02 Weth 3m1f gd-sft Hdl

Ungaretti (GER)

103   105

6-y-o b g Law Society (USA)-Urena (GER) (Dschingis Khan)

Ian Williams Pel Project Management

Placings:30/3032120-404F100   (4563)

2002/03: 234G, 259HY, 254HY, 26FG, 241G, 26QG, 24QGF,

	Starts	1st	2nd	3rd	Win & Pl
Hurdles	7	1	0	2	6380
Career Total	16	2	2	3	11055
105	2/03	Ludl	3m	E(0-110)HHdl	GD	£5655
105	2/02	Hntg	2m4f110y	F(0-100)HHdl	SFT	£2018

Total win prize-money £7674

Going:	Sf: 0-2 GS: 0-0 Gd: 1-4 GF: 0-1

Distance:	2m/2m3: 0-0 2m4-2m7: 0-0 3m+: 1-7
Track:	LH: 0-3 RH: 1-4 Tight: 0-1 Gall: 0-2
Aids:	Bl: 0-0 Vi: 0-0 Tstrap: 0-3
Best Rating:	105 2/03 Ludl 3m good Hdl

Modest hurdler; winner on the Flat in Germany; stays three miles; suited by good ground.

Unleash (USA)

111   129+

4-y-o ch g Benny The Dip (USA)-Lemhi Go (USA) (Lemhi Gold (USA))

P J Hobbs (Sir Mark Prescott 19/9) Mrs David Thompson

Placings:3311   (4637)

2002/03: 163HY, 173GS, 161G, 161GF,

	Starts	1st	2nd	3rd	Win & Pl
Hurdles	4	2	0	2	17560
Career Total	4	2	0	2	17560
126	4/03	Strf	2m110y	B Hdl	G-F	£12122
96	3/03	Ludl	2m	E Hdl	GD	£3669

Total win prize-money £15791

Going:	Sf: 0-1 GS: 0-1 Gd: 1-1 GF: - Fm: 1-1
Distance:	2m/2m3: 2-4 2m4-2m7: 0-0 3m+: 0-0
Track:	LH: 1-1 RH: 1-3 Tight: 1-1 Gall: 0-0
Aids:	Bl: 0-0 Vi: 0-0 Tstrap: 0-0
Best Rating:	126 4/03 Strf 2m110y gd-fm Hdl

Useful winning staying handicapper on the Flat; progressive over hurdles completing a hat-trick in spring 2003; best suited to a sound surface.

Unlimited Free (IRE)

9-y-o ch g Ile De Chypre-Merry Madness (Raise You Ten)

Mrs S Alner (O Sherwood 15/5) The Hon Miss D Harding

Placings:0365/502125P23-465   (4314)

2002/03: 254G, 246GS, 225G,

	Starts	1st	2nd	3rd	Win & Pl
Chases	3	0	0	0	386
Career Total	16	1	3	2	11113
109	1/02	Leic	2m7f110yD(0-110)HCh	GD	£5882

Total win prize-money £5883

Going:	Sf: 0-0 GS: 0-1 Gd: 0-2 GF: - Fm: 0-0
Distance:	2m/2m3: 0-0 2m4-2m7: 0-0 3m+: 1-1
Track:	LH: 0-1 RH: 0-2 Tight: 0-1 Gall: 0-1
Aids:	Bl: 0-0 Vi: 0-0 Tstrap: 0-0
Best Rating:	109 1/02 Donc 3m soft Ch

Modest chaser; lightly raced gelding, acts on good and soft ground.

Unsigned (USA)

104   88

5-y-o b/br g Cozzene (USA)-Striata (USA) (Gone West (USA))

R H Buckler F F Racing Services Partnership II

Placings:0   (0177)

2002/03: 16QGF,

	Starts	1st	2nd	3rd	Win & Pl
Hurdles	1	0	0	0	
Career Total	1	0	0	0	

Going:	Sf: 0-0 GS: 0-0 Gd: 0-0 GF: - Fm: 0-1
Distance:	2m/2m3: 0-1 2m4-2m7: 0-0 3m+: 0-0
Track:	LH: 0-0 RH: 0-1 Tight: 0-0 Gall: 0-0

Aids:	Bl: 0-0 Vi: 0-0 Tstrap: 0-0
Best Rating:	64 5/02 Winc 2m gd-fm Hdl

Plating-class hurdler; well beaten on hurdling debut May 2002; no match for Gebora on next outing at Exeter a year later; appreciated the longer trip when winning 2m 4f novice hurdle at Worcester in June; likes fast ground; looks set for a successful summer campaign.

Untidy Daughter

110   86

4-y-o b f Sabrehill (USA)-Branitska (Mummy s Pet)

B Ellison (R Hannon 29/6) Alderclad Roofing,S Rutter,G Hamilton

Placings:0025051   (4798)

2002/03: 16QGS, 16QGS, 162GS, 175HY, 16QG, 175G, 171GF,

	Starts	1st	2nd	3rd	Win & Pl
Hurdles	7	1	1	0	4554
Career Total	7	1	1	0	4554
82	4/03	Sedg	2m1f	E(0-105)HHdl	G-F	£3373

Total win prize-money £3374

Going:	Sf: 0-1 GS: 0-3 Gd: 0-2 GF: - Fm: 1-1
Distance:	2m/2m3: 1-7 2m4-2m7: 0-0 3m+: 0-0
Track:	LH: 1-7 RH: 0-0 Tight: 1-5 Gall: 0-0
Aids:	Bl: 0-0 Vi: 0-0 Tstrap: 0-0
Best Rating:	82 4/03 Sedg 2m1f gd-fm Hdl

Plating-class hurdler; scored at Sedgefield in April 2003 and again the following month; has worn cheekpieces.

Untold Story (USA)

8-y-o b g Theatrical-Committed Miss (USA) (Key To Content (USA))

G A Ham Colin B Taylor

Placings:00/P   (0214)

2002/03: 19PG,

	Starts	1st	2nd	3rd	Win & Pl
Hurdles	1	0	0	0	
Career Total	3	0	0	0	

Going:	Sf: 0-0 GS: 0-0 Gd: 0-1 GF: - Fm: 0-0
Distance:	2m/2m3: 0-0 2m4-2m7: 0-0 3m+: 0-0
Track:	LH: 0-0 RH: 0-1 Tight: 0-0 Gall: 0-0
Aids:	Bl: 0-0 Vi: 0-0 Tstrap: 0-0
Best Rating:	56 3/00 Tntn 2m3f110y good Hdl

Up In Flames (IRE)

88   65

12-y-o b g Nashamaa-Bella Lucia (Camden Town)

Mrs G S Rees www.mark-kilner-racing.com & T W Wilson

Placings:5230/50/00/036   (4434)

2002/03: 16QG, 173G, 20FG,

	Starts	1st	2nd	3rd	Win & Pl
Hurdles	3	0	0	1	348
Career Total	11	0	1	2	1310

Going:	Sf: 0-0 GS: 0-0 Gd: 0-3 GF: - Fm: 0-0
Distance:	2m/2m3: 0-2 2m4-2m7: 0-1 3m+: 0-0
Track:	LH: 0-3 RH: 0-0 Tight: 0-1 Gall: 0-2
Aids:	Bl: 0-0 Vi: 0-0 Tstrap: 0-3
Best Rating:	101 3/96 Chep 2m110y gd-sft Hdl

Up The Clarets (IRE)

90   **82**

8-y-o b g Petardia-Madeira Lady (On Your Mark)
D McCain Valley Paddocks Racing Limited

Placings:U41515/554404500/6520-3   (0828)
2002/03: 17³GF,

	Starts	1st	2nd	3rd	Win & Pl
Hurdles	1	0	0	1	414
Career Total	20	2	1	1	7060
114	10/98	Hexm	2m	E Hdl	G-S	£2385
106	9/98	Bang	2m1f	D Hdl	GD	£2840

Total win prize-money £5225

Going:	Sf: 0-0 GS: 0-0 Gd: 0-0 GF: - Fm: 0-1
Distance:	2m/2m3: 0-1 2m4-2m7: 0-0 3m+: 0-0
Track:	LH: 0-1 RH: 0-0 Tight: 0-1 Gall: 0-0
Aids:	Bl: 0-0 Vi: 0-0 Tstrap: 0-0
Best Rating:	114 10/98 Hexm 2m gd-sft Hdl

Plating-class, lightly-raced handicap hurdler, best at around the minimum trip on a sound surface.

Up The Glen (IRE)

99   **105**

9-y-o b g Tale Quale-Etrenne (Happy New Year)
R T Phillips Richard Phillips

Placings:16664P/5P-1235   (3853)
2002/03: 20¹HY, 27²S, 20³S, 19⁵GS,

	Starts	1st	2nd	3rd	Win & Pl
Hurdles	4	1	1	1	3267
Career Total	12	2	1	1	4926
105	11/02	Hexm	2m4f110yG(0-90)HHdl	HVY	£1890
104	11/00	Wwck	2m	H NHF	HVY	£1659

Total win prize-money £3549

Going:	Sf: 1-3 GS: 0-1 Gd: 0-0 GF: - Fm: 0-0
Distance:	2m/2m3: 0-0 2m4-2m7: 1-3 3m+: 0-1
Track:	LH: 1-3 RH: 0-1 Tight: 0-2 Gall: 0-1
Aids:	Bl: 0-0 Vi: 0-0 Tstrap: 0-0
Best Rating:	105 11/02 Hexm 2m4f110y heavy Hdl

Moderate hurdler, won a Hexham seller in November 2002 and followed up in similar event at Uttoxeter in April; stays three miles plus; best going left-handed; appreciates heavy ground.

Up The Kyber

70   **72**

6-y-o b g Missed Flight-Najariya (Northfields (USA))
M D Hammond (A Crook 31/5) The Adbrokes Partnership

Placings:30-0P   (2301)
2002/03: 17⁰GS, 16⁵GS,

	Starts	1st	2nd	3rd	Win & Pl
Hurdles	2	0	0	0	
Career Total	4	0	0	1	429

Going:	Sf: 0-0 GS: 0-2 Gd: 0-0 GF: - Fm: 0-0
Distance:	2m/2m3: 0-2 2m4-2m7: 0-0 3m+: 0-0
Track:	LH: 0-1 RH: 0-1 Tight: 0-2 Gall: 0-0
Aids:	Bl: 0-0 Vi: 0-0 Tstrap: 0-0
Best Rating:	72 6/01 Prth 2m110y gd-fm Hdl

Up Your Street

92   **93**

8-y-o b m Petoski-Air Streak (Air Trooper)

J Neville F J Ayres

Placings:5S0/2006PUP22-3   (0115)
2002/03: 24³GS,

	Starts	1st	2nd	3rd	Win & Pl
Hurdles	1	0	0	1	326
Career Total	13	0	3	1	2778

Going:	Sf: 0-0 GS: 0-1 Gd: 0-0 GF: - Fm: 0-0
Distance:	2m/2m3: 0-0 2m4-2m7: 0-0 3m+: 0-1
Track:	LH: 0-0 RH: 0-1 Tight: 0-0 Gall: 0-0
Aids:	Bl: 0-0 Vi: 0-0 Tstrap: 0-0
Best Rating:	93 6/01 Worc 2m4f good Hdl

Moderate hurdler; returned to form when narrowly denied under a low weight at Uttoxeter and Hereford in April 2002.

Upesi

51f

7-y-o b m Regal Embers (IRE)-Dawn Melody (Lighter)
J L Spearing D J Oseman

Placings:00   (1494)
2002/03: 17⁰GF, 17⁰GS,

	Starts	1st	2nd	3rd	Win & Pl
NH Flat	2	0	0	0	
Career Total	2	0	0	0	

Going:	Sf: 0-0 GS: 0-1 Gd: 0-0 GF: - Fm: 0-0
Distance:	2m/2m3: 0-2 2m4-2m7: 0-0 3m+: 0-0
Track:	LH: 0-1 RH: 0-1 Tight: 0-1 Gall: 0-0
Aids:	Bl: 0-0 Vi: 0-0 Tstrap: 0-0
Best Rating:	0 10/02 Bang 2m1f gd-sft NHF

Upgrade

120   **158**

9-y-o b g Be My Guest (USA)-Cantanta (Top Ville)
M C Pipe Matt Archer & Miss Jean Broadhurst

Placings:P15111P/3F0F30/26F126F1/210/6531251-2F5P3   (4604)
2002/03: 21²G, 21⁵GS, 20⁵G, 21⁸G, 21³G,

	Starts	1st	2nd	3rd	Win & Pl
Hurdles	1	0	0	0	0
Chases	4	0	1	1	14300
Career Total	36	9	5	4	213575
158	4/02	Asct	2m3f110yB HCh	G-F	£24900
158	2/02	Winc	2m5f	B Ch	SFT	£10188
158	11/00	Asct	2m3f110yA HCh	SFT	£30000
154	4/00	Chel	2m5f	A Ch	SFT	£21000
150	2/00	Sand	2m4f110yA Ch	GD	£24000
147	3/98	Chel	2m1f	A Hdl	GD	£43460
127	2/98	Sand	2m110y	D Hdl	GD	£2853
140	2/98	Wwck	2m	E Hdl	GD	£2827
133	12/97	Kemp	2m	B Hdl	SFT	£5288

Total win prize-money £164519

Going:	Sf: 0-0 GS: 0-1 Gd: 0-4 GF: - Fm: 0-0
Distance:	2m/2m3: 0-0 2m4-2m7: 0-5 3m+: 0-0
Track:	LH: 0-3 RH: 0-2 Tight: 0-0 Gall: 0-2
Aids:	Bl: 0-2 Vi: 0-0 Tstrap: 0-0
Best Rating:	158 10/02 Winc 2m5f good Ch

High-class chaser but a lazy type; has a tendency to refuse to start or to pull himself up; good reappearance at Wincanton in October 2002 but has blotted his copybook since; suited by forcing tactics; he is best at around two and a half miles and acts on soft ground.

Upon A Thyne (IRE)

6-y-o br m Good Thyne (USA)-Brown Willows (IRE) (Kemal

(FR))
P G Murphy The Golden Anorak Partnership

Placings:40P   (2706)
2002/03: 16⁴G, 17⁰HY, 16⁸GS,

	Starts	1st	2nd	3rd	Win & Pl
NH Flat	2	0	0	0	0
Hurdles	1	0	0	0	0
Career Total	3	0	0	0	0

Going:	Sf: 0-1 GS: 0-1 Gd: 0-1 GF: - Fm: 0-0
Distance:	2m/2m3: 0-2 2m4-2m7: 0-0 3m+: 0-0
Track:	LH: 0-1 RH: 0-2 Tight: 0-1 Gall: 0-0
Aids:	Bl: 0-0 Vi: 0-0 Tstrap: 0-0
Best Rating:	84 11/02 Wwck 2m good NHF

Upright Ima

95f   **77f**

4-y-o b f Perpendicular-Ima Delight (Idiots Delight)
Mrs P Sly Mrs P M Sly

Placings:3   (4343)
2002/03: 16³GF,

	Starts	1st	2nd	3rd	Win & Pl
NH Flat	1	0	0	1	280
Career Total	1	0	0	1	280

Going:	Sf: 0-0 GS: 0-0 Gd: 0-0 GF: - Fm: 0-0
Distance:	2m/2m3: 0-1 2m4-2m7: 0-0 3m+: 0-0
Track:	LH: 0-0 RH: 0-1 Tight: 0-0 Gall: 0-1
Aids:	Bl: 0-0 Vi: 0-0 Tstrap: 0-0
Best Rating:	77 3/03 Hntg 2m110y gd-fm NHF

Third in debut in a bumper; should improve.

Upriver Run

65f   **69f**

4-y-o ch g Alderbrook-Uplift (Bustino)
R Rowe D R L Evans

Placings:000   (4296)
2002/03: 12⁰G, 17⁰GF, 16⁰GF,

	Starts	1st	2nd	3rd	Win & Pl
NH Flat	3	0	0	0	
Career Total	3	0	0	0	

Going:	Sf: 0-1 GS: 0-0 Gd: 0-1 GF: - Fm: 0-0
Distance:	2m/2m3: 0-2 2m4-2m7: 0-0 3m+: 0-0
Track:	LH: 0-1 RH: 0-2 Tight: 0-1 Gall: 0-0
Aids:	Bl: 0-0 Vi: 0-0 Tstrap: 0-0
Best Rating:	69 12/02 Newb 1m4f110y good NHF

Upswing

82   **51**

6-y-o b g Perpendicular-Moorfield Lady (Vicomte)
R Johnson C H P Bell

Placings:00P   (4435)
2002/03: 17⁰GS, 16⁰GS, 20⁰G,

	Starts	1st	2nd	3rd	Win & Pl
Hurdles	3	0	0	0	
Career Total	3	0	0	0	

Going:	Sf: 0-0 GS: 0-2 Gd: 0-1 GF: - Fm: 0-0
Distance:	2m/2m3: 0-2 2m4-2m7: 0-1 3m+: 0-0
Track:	LH: 0-2 RH: 0-1 Tight: 0-0 Gall: 0-2
Aids:	Bl: 0-0 Vi: 0-0 Tstrap: 0-0

Best Rating: 51 3/03 Carl 2m1f gd-sft Hdl

Uptown Lad (IRE)
92   84

4-y-o b g Definite Article-Shoka (FR) (Kaldoun (FR))
R Johnson (Mrs A Duffield 27/9) C Grindell

Placings:0602   (3567)
2002/03: 16⁵S, 16⁶GS, 17⁹HY, 17²HY,

	Starts	1st	2nd	3rd	Win & Pl
Hurdles	4	0	1	0	1460
Career Total	4	0	1	0	1460

Going: Sf: 0-3 GS: 0-1 Gd: 0-0 GF: - Fm: 0-0
Distance: 2m/2m3: 0-4 2m4-2m7: 0-0 3m+: 0-0
Track: LH: 0-4 RH: 0-0 Tight: 0-2 Gall: 0-2
Aids: Bl: 0-0 Vi: 0-0 Tstrap: 0-0
Best Rating: 84 11/02 Newc 2m gd-sft Hdl

Moderate hurdler, very limited ability so far over hurdles.

Urban Hymn (IRE)
91(101h)   (111h)92

7-y-o ch g College Chapel-Soltura (IRE) (Sadler s Wells (USA))
Ferdy Murphy D A Johnson

Placings:140/5P/3053-63464   (4257)
2002/03: 16⁸HY, 17⁷S, 16⁴G, 16⁶G, 16⁴G,

	Starts	1st	2nd	3rd	Win & Pl
Hurdles	2	0	0	1	478
Chases	3	0	0	0	669
Career Total	14	1	0	3	6875
103 2/00 Sand 2m110y D Hdl				G-S	£4329
Total win prize-money £4329					

Going: Sf: 0-2 GS: 0-0 Gd: 0-3 GF: - Fm: 0-0
Distance: 2m/2m3: 0-5 2m4-2m7: 0-0 3m+: 0-0
Track: LH: 0-2 RH: 0-3 Tight: 0-4 Gall: 0-0
Aids: Bl: 0-0 Vi: 0-0 Tstrap: 0-0
Best Rating: 114 5/01 Newc 2m gd-fm Hdl

Moderate chaser/modest hurdler; acts on any ground.

Us Four (IRE)

13-y-o b g Mandalus-Rock Plant (Ovac (ITY))
Miss S A Loggin (S J Magnier 13/5) B O Connell

Placings:0000P0/2600/0300/00P/53/012/0P   (4678)
2002/03: 16⁰G, 19⁰GF,

	Starts	1st	2nd	3rd	Win & Pl
Chases	2	0	0	0	
Career Total	24	1	2	2	2963
87 5/00 Towc 2m110y H Ch				G-F	£1547
Total win prize-money £1547					

Going: Sf: 0-0 GS: 0-0 Gd: 0-1 GF: - Fm: 0-1
Distance: 2m/2m3: 0-2 2m4-2m7: 0-0 3m+: 0-0
Track: LH: 0-0 RH: 0-2 Tight: 0-0 Gall: 0-0
Aids: Bl: 0-1 Vi: 0-0 Tstrap: 0-0
Best Rating: 96 1/97 DRoy 2m gd-yld Hdl

Usk Valley (IRE)
97(88c)   (67c)83

8-y-o b g Tenby-Penultimate (USA) (Roberto (USA))
P R Chamings Inhurst Farm Stables Partnership

Placings:2/20/3/3P05-4F   (4185)
2002/03: 19⁴G, 25⁵G,

	Starts	1st	2nd	3rd	Win & Pl
Chases	2	0	0	0	352
Career Total	10	0	2	2	2097

Going: Sf: 0-0 GS: 0-0 Gd: 0-2 GF: - Fm: 0-0
Distance: 2m/2m3: 0-1 2m4-2m7: 0-0 3m+: 0-1
Track: LH: 0-0 RH: 0-2 Tight: 0-1 Gall: 0-0
Aids: Bl: 0-0 Vi: 0-0 Tstrap: 0-0
Best Rating: 109 2/00 Sand 2m110y soft NHF

Plating-class performer; has shown ability in bumpers and over hurdles, but his runs have been well spread out and he is still very lightly raced; fell in second start over fences.

Va Pensiero (GER)
77   47

4-y-o b c Java Gold (USA)-Velvet Blue (Exactly Sharp (USA))
C Von Der Recke Stall Mohlemberg

Placings:6   (2610)
2002/03: 16⁶S,

	Starts	1st	2nd	3rd	Win & Pl
Hurdles	1	0	0	0	0
Career Total	1	0	0	0	0

Going: Sf: 0-1 GS: 0-0 Gd: 0-0 GF: - Fm: 0-0
Distance: 2m/2m3: 0-1 2m4-2m7: 0-0 3m+: 0-0
Track: LH: 0-1 RH: 0-0 Tight: 0-0 Gall: 0-0
Aids: Bl: 0-0 Vi: 0-0 Tstrap: 0-0
Best Rating: 47 12/02 Uttx 2m soft Hdl

German-trained colt; well beaten in a selling hurdle at Uttoxeter in December 2002.

Vague Idea
110   101

10-y-o gr g Tout Ensemble-Roodle Doodle (Rugantino)
O J Carter (C J Down 1/6) O J Carter

Placings:P6RP/P30-135U665   (4552)
2002/03: 25¹GF, 25⁹G, 21⁵S, 24⁰GF, 20⁶GS, 26⁶GF, 27⁵S,

	Starts	1st	2nd	3rd	Win & Pl
Chases	7	1	0	1	2782
Career Total	14	1	0	2	3111
92 5/02 Hrfd 3m1f110yH Ch				G-F	£2450
Total win prize-money £2450					

Going: Sf: 0-1 GS: 0-1 Gd: 0-2 GF: - Fm: 1-3
Distance: 2m/2m3: 0-0 2m4-2m7: 0-2 3m+: 1-5
Track: LH: 0-5 RH: 1-2 Tight: 0-4 Gall: 0-0
Aids: Bl: 0-0 Vi: 0-0 Tstrap: 0-0
Best Rating: 92 5/02 Hrfd 3m1f110y gd-fm Ch

Modest performer; a bit of a character, he was a fortunate winner at Hereford in May 2002; landed a big gamble when winning at Newton Abbot in June 2003; runner-up at same course next time; stays 3m 2f well; acts on a sound surface; inclined to go left-handed under pressure.

Vaigly North
72   36

5-y-o b m Minshaanshu Amad (USA)-Straight Gold (Vaigly Great)
J A Moore (A G Newcombe 15/7) Mrs J M Moore

Placings:5-036P   (4590)
2002/03: 16⁵GS, 16⁰GS, 16⁹GF, 17⁶GF, 20⁰G,

	Starts	1st	2nd	3rd	Win & Pl
NH Flat	4	0	0	1	225
Hurdles	1	0	0	0	0
Career Total	5	0	0	1	225

Going: Sf: 0-0 GS: 0-2 Gd: 0-1 GF: - Fm: 0-2
Distance: 2m/2m3: 0-4 2m4-2m7: 0-1 3m+: 0-0
Track: LH: 0-4 RH: 0-1 Tight: 0-2 Gall: 0-0
Aids: Bl: 0-0 Vi: 0-0 Tstrap: 0-0
Best Rating: 78 7/02 NAbb 2m1f gd-fm NHF

Valerio
116   139

7-y-o b g Be My Native (USA)-Laurello (Bargello)
N J Henderson Nicholas Cooper

Placings:1/2210-1P50   (4456)
2002/03: 16¹S, 16⁸HY, 22⁵HY, 24⁰G,

	Starts	1st	2nd	3rd	Win & Pl
Hurdles	4	1	0	0	10200
Career Total	9	3	2	0	17861
139 11/02 Newb 2m110y C(0-130)HHdl				SFT	£8700
115 2/02 MRas 2m3f110yD Hdl				G-S	£3640
106 2/01 Winc 2m H NHF				GD	£1729
Total win prize-money £14069					

Going: Sf: 1-3 GS: 0-0 Gd: 0-1 GF: - Fm: 0-0
Distance: 2m/2m3: 1-2 2m4-2m7: 0-1 3m+: 0-1
Track: LH: 1-2 RH: 0-2 Tight: 0-1 Gall: 1-1
Aids: Bl: 0-0 Vi: 0-0 Tstrap: 0-0
Best Rating: 139 11/02 Newb 2m110y soft Hdl

Very useful hurdler; acts on soft and good ground; effective at up to two and a half miles; a potential chaser.

Valeureux
109   109

5-y-o ch g Cadeaux Genereux-La Strada (Niniski (USA))
J Hetherton Eureka Racing

Placings:620-F333   (3771)
2002/03: 17⁵GS, 16⁹GS, 16³GS, 16⁹GS,

	Starts	1st	2nd	3rd	Win & Pl
Hurdles	4	0	0	3	1711
Career Total	7	0	1	3	2501

Going: Sf: 0-0 GS: 0-4 Gd: 0-0 GF: - Fm: 0-0
Distance: 2m/2m3: 0-4 2m4-2m7: 0-0 3m+: 0-0
Track: LH: 0-3 RH: 0-1 Tight: 0-1 Gall: 0-2
Aids: Bl: 0-0 Vi: 0-0 Tstrap: 0-0
Best Rating: 109 1/03 Donc 2m110y gd-sft Hdl

Fair novice hurdler; suited by two miles; acts with cut in the ground; yet to win over timber.

Valfonic
101

5-y-o b g Zafonic (USA)-Valbra (Dancing Brave (USA))
M C Pipe Done It Again

Placings:60U1-11543650P   (3602)
2002/03: 16¹G, 16¹G, 17⁵GF, 17⁴GF, 16³GF, 16⁶GS, 17⁵S, 17⁰S, 19⁸S,

	Starts	1st	2nd	3rd	Win & Pl
Hurdles	9	2	0	1	6459
Career Total	13	3	0	1	9444
111 5/02 Worc 2m E(0-110)HHdl				GD	£3003
96 4/02 Sthl 2m F(0-95)HHdl				GD	£2443
89 4/02 Wwck 2m F(0-95)HHdl				G-F	£2985
Total win prize-money £8432					

Going: Sf: 0-3 GS: 0-1 Gd: 2-2 GF: - Fm: 0-3

Distance:	2m/2m3: 2-8 2m4-2m7: 0-1 3m+: 0-0
Track:	LH: 2-4 RH: 0-5 Tight: 1-6 Gall: 0-0
Aids:	Bl: 0-0 Vi: 0-5 Tstrap: 2-8
Best Rating:	111 6/02 Hrfd 2m1f gd-fm Hdl

Modest hurdler, won on his handicap debut at Warwick in April when encountering fast ground and being fitted with a tongue tie, and followed up next time at Southwell. Showed signs of temperament when overcoming an attempt to head for the paddock at the final flight when completing a hat-trick at Worcester. Disappointing when tried in a visor, may now be in the grip of the Handicapper.

Valhalla (IRE)

97   83

10-y-o b g Brush Aside (USA)-Eimers Pet (Paddy s Stream)
R F Fisher Mrs D Miller

Placings: 3/16/5FP0/44F4/3/6F03-625PU   (0579)
2002/03: 20⁶S, 20²GS, 22⁵HY, 17⁶G, 20ᵁG,

	Starts	1st	2nd	3rd	Win & Pl
Hurdles	5	0	1	0	754
Career Total	21	1	1	3	4308
103	5/97	Uttx	2m	H NHF	GD £1609
				Total win prize-money £1609	

Going:	Sf: 0-2 GS: 0-1 Gd: 0-2 GF: - Fm: 0-0
Distance:	2m/2m3: 0-1 2m4-2m7: 0-4 3m+: 0-0
Track:	LH: 0-5 RH: 0-0 Tight: 0-4 Gall: 0-0
Aids:	Bl: 0-0 Vi: 0-0 Tstrap: 0-2
Best Rating:	103 5/97 Uttx 2m good NHF

Modest handicap hurdler at two/two and a half miles. Not a natural jumper of fences. Acts on a sound surface.

Valhalla Gold

9-y-o ch g Golden Lahab (USA)-Key Harvest (Deep Diver)
B Ellison Mrs Claire Ellison

Placings: P   (1162)
2002/03: 17⁷GF,

	Starts	1st	2nd	3rd	Win & Pl
Hurdles	1	0	0	0	
Career Total	1	0	0	0	

Going:	Sf: 0-0 GS: 0-0 Gd: 0-0 GF: - Fm: 0-1
Distance:	2m/2m3: 0-0 2m4-2m7: 0-0 3m+: 0-0
Track:	LH: 0-1 RH: 0-0 Tight: 0-1 Gall: 0-0
Aids:	Bl: 0-0 Vi: 0-0 Tstrap: 0-0
Best Rating:	0 9/02 Sedg 2m1f gd-fm Hdl

Valigan (IRE)

10-y-o gr g Roselier (FR)-Wonderful Lilly (Prince Hansel)
T P Tate T P Tate

Placings: 6/310231/641150/42F1/241004-4   (3513)
2002/03: 28⁴G,

	Starts	1st	2nd	3rd	Win & Pl
Chases	1	0	0	0	0
Career Total	24	6	3	2	28164
130	12/01	Muss	3m	D(0-120)HCh	G-F £4134
108	2/01	Sedg	3m3f	D Ch	SFT £4010
127	12/99	Muss	3m	D(0-125)HHdl	G-S £5498
135	12/99	Hexm	3m	F(0-105)HHdl	HVY £2343
120	3/99	Ayr	3m110y	D(0-115)HHdl	SFT £3574
106	11/98	Sedg	3m3f110yE Hdl		G-S £2302
				Total win prize-money £21864	

Going:	Sf: 0-0 GS: 0-0 Gd: 0-0 GF: - Fm: 0-0

Distance:	2m/2m3: 0-0 2m4-2m7: 0-0 3m+: 0-1
Track:	LH: 0-1 RH: 0-0 Tight: 0-1 Gall: 0-0
Aids:	Bl: 0-0 Vi: 0-0 Tstrap: 0-0
Best Rating:	135 12/99 Hexm 3m heavy Hdl

One time good-class handicap chaser but on the downgrade and now competing in hunter chases.

Valignani (IRE)

94   114

11-y-o b g Law Society (USA)-When Lit (Northfields (USA))
M C Pipe Codan Trust Company Limited

Placings: 1/111/4212P2P/112FB23302/2F011325054F135/0UPRP500-5PP   (0740)
2002/03: 18⁵GF, 20⁶HY, 25⁶G,

	Starts	1st	2nd	3rd	Win & Pl
Hurdles	3	0	0	0	
Career Total	47	10	8	4	166807
	4/01	Comp	2m4f	Hdl	HVY £6790
	8/00	Claf	2m1f	Hdl	SFT £6244
	7/00	Vich	2m3f110y	Hdl	GD £5283
	6/99	Maia	2m1f110y	Hdl	GD £3645
	5/99	Maia	2m110y	Hdl	GD £3281
	8/98	Maia	2m1f110y	Hdl	GD £7736
	11/97	Turi	2m2f	HHdl	VS £13500
	8/97	Maia	2m1f110y	Hdl	GD £7714
	5/97	Siro	2m2f	HHdl	GD £11571
	11/96	Turi	2m2f	HHdl	G-S £12180
				Total win prize-money £77944	

Going:	Sf: 0-1 GS: 0-0 Gd: 0-1 GF: - Fm: 0-1
Distance:	2m/2m3: 0-1 2m4-2m7: 0-1 3m+: 0-1
Track:	LH: 0-3 RH: 0-0 Tight: 0-2 Gall: 0-0
Aids:	Bl: 0-0 Vi: 0-3 Tstrap: 0-0
Best Rating:	114 11/01 Hayd 2m4f good Hdl

Moderate hurdler/chaser; winner over hurdles in France and Italy, not half as good in England, failing to complete on all starts over fences, and reverting to hurdles late in 2001.

Valjean (IRE)

7-y-o b g Alzao (USA)-Escape Path (Wolver Hollow)
Ms Myfanwy Miles (W M Brisbourne 22/5) P B Miles

Placings: 0/0U-P4   (4487)
2002/03: 16⁶G, 16⁴GF,

	Starts	1st	2nd	3rd	Win & Pl
Hurdles	1	0	0	0	0
Chases	1	0	0	0	0
Career Total	5	0	0	0	0

Going:	Sf: 0-0 GS: 0-0 Gd: 0-0 GF: - Fm: 0-0
Distance:	2m/2m3: 0-2 2m4-2m7: 0-0 3m+: 0-0
Track:	LH: 0-1 RH: 0-1 Tight: 0-0 Gall: 0-0
Aids:	Bl: 0-0 Vi: 0-0 Tstrap: 0-0
Best Rating:	60 4/03 Hrfd 2m gd-fm Ch

Well held in modest company over hurdles.

Valley Henry (IRE)

123   (88h) 166

8-y-o b g Step Together (USA)-Pineway Vii (Damsire Unregistered)
P F Nicholls Paul K Barber

Placings: 15/1134/11FU2F11-114144   (4457)
2002/03: 21¹G, 24¹GS, 25⁴GS, 24¹G, 26⁴G, 25⁴G,

	Starts	1st	2nd	3rd	Win & Pl
Chases	6	3	0	0	105422
Career Total	20	10	1	1	179832

166	2/03	Newb	3m	A Ch	GD £41650
162	12/02	Sand	3m110y	B Ch	G-S £10972
161	10/02	Winc	2m5f	A HCh	GD £23800
158	4/02	Ayr	2m4f	A Ch	GD £15600
99	3/02	Extr	3m1f110yD Ch		GD £5304
153	11/01	Newb	3m	A Ch	GD £17850
124	10/01	Chep	2m3f110yC Ch		GD £6776
140	11/00	Winc	2m6f	C Hdl	SFT £6286
134	11/00	Chep	2m4f	A Hdl	SFT £12000
122	3/00	Leop	2m	NHF	Y-S £3588
				Total win prize-money £143826	

Going:	Sf: 0-0 GS: 1-2 Gd: 2-4 GF: - Fm: 0-0
Distance:	2m/2m3: 0-0 2m4-2m7: 1-1 3m+: 2-5
Track:	LH: 1-4 RH: 2-2 Tight: 0-1 Gall: 1-3
Aids:	Bl: 0-0 Vi: 0-0 Tstrap: 0-0
Best Rating:	166 2/03 Newb 3m good Ch

Top-class chaser; winner of minor events at Wincanton and Sandown this term, but flopped when upped in class at Cheltenham on soft ground; back on a faster surface, won Aon Chase at Newbury (jumping fluently, travelling well and galloping on strongly); good fourth in Cheltenham Gold Cup; stays 3m; needs decent ground.

Valleymore (IRE)

114   129+

7-y-o br g Jolly Jake (NZ)-Glamorous Brush (IRE) (Brush Aside (USA))
S A Brookshaw T G K Construction Ltd

Placings: 042311P   (4400)
2002/03: 16⁶G, 17⁴S, 20²G, 20³S, 20¹GS, 22¹S, 22²GF,

	Starts	1st	2nd	3rd	Win & Pl
NH Flat	1	0	0	0	0
Hurdles	6	2	1	1	23522
Career Total	7	2	1	1	23522
129	3/03	Uttx	2m6f110yB(0-140)HHdl		SFT £9467
121	2/03	Hayd	2m4f	B HHdl	G-S £12412
				Total win prize-money £21634	

Going:	Sf: 1-3 GS: 1-1 Gd: 0-2 GF: - Fm: 0-1
Distance:	2m/2m3: 0-2 2m4-2m7: 2-5 3m+: 0-0
Track:	LH: 2-7 RH: 0-0 Tight: 0-1 Gall: 0-0
Aids:	Bl: 0-0 Vi: 0-0 Tstrap: 0-0
Best Rating:	129 3/03 Uttx 2m6f110y soft Hdl

Fair hurdler; easy winner over brush obstacles at Haydock in February 2003, and followed up at Uttoxeter; pulled up when hating fast ground subsequently; effective at two and a half miles to two miles six; will make a chaser in time.

Valparisa (FR)

5-y-o br m Priolo (USA)-Valuable (FR) (Top Ville)
J Neville J C Parsons

Placings: P   (1494)
2002/03: 17⁷GS,

	Starts	1st	2nd	3rd	Win & Pl
NH Flat	1	0	0	0	
Career Total	1	0	0	0	

Going:	Sf: 0-0 GS: 0-1 Gd: 0-0 GF: - Fm: 0-0
Distance:	2m/2m3: 0-1 2m4-2m7: 0-0 3m+: 0-0
Track:	LH: 0-1 RH: 0-0 Tight: 0-1 Gall: 0-0
Aids:	Bl: 0-0 Vi: 0-0 Tstrap: 0-0
Best Rating:	0 10/02 Bang 2m1f gd-sft NHF

Valuable (IRE)

80f   64f

6-y-o b m Jurado (USA)-Can t Afford It (IRE) (Glow (USA))

Mrs A Duffield Billy Maguire

Placings:*00*   (2560)
2002/03: 16⁰GS, 16⁰GF,

	Starts	1st	2nd	3rd	Win & Pl
NH Flat	2	0	0	0	
Career Total	2	0	0	0	

Going:	Sf: 0-0 GS: 0-1 Gd: 0-0 GF: - Fm: 0-1
Distance:	2m/2m3: 0-2 2m4-2m7: 0-0 3m+: 0-0
Track:	LH: 0-1 RH: 0-1 Tight: 0-1 Gall: 0-0
Aids:	Bl: 0-0 Vi: 0-0 Tstrap: 0-0
Best Rating:	64 12/02 Muss 2m gd-fm NHF

Van De Velde

87   **71**

4-y-o ch g Alhijaz-Lucky Flinders (Free State)
R Wilman Andy Smith

Placings:*000*   (3571)
2002/03: 16⁰GS, 23⁰S, 16⁰HY,

	Starts	1st	2nd	3rd	Win & Pl
Hurdles	3	0	0	0	
Career Total	3	0	0	0	

Going:	Sf: 0-2 GS: 0-1 Gd: 0-0 GF: - Fm: 0-0
Distance:	2m/2m3: 0-2 2m4-2m7: 0-0 3m+: 0-1
Track:	LH: 0-2 RH: 0-1 Tight: 0-2 Gall: 0-0
Aids:	Bl: 0-0 Vi: 0-0 Tstrap: 0-0
Best Rating:	71 12/02 Fknm 2m gd-sft Hdl

Vandas Choice (IRE)

98   **105**

5-y-o b g Sadler s Wells (USA)-Morning Devotion (USA) (Affirmed (USA))
Mrs L B Normile J Petterson

Placings:*43551*   (4772)
2002/03: 14⁴GS, 16³HY, 16⁵GS, 16⁵G, 16¹G,

	Starts	1st	2nd	3rd	Win & Pl
NH Flat	3	0	0	1	271
Hurdles	2	1	0	0	5603
Career Total	5	1	0	1	5874
101	4/03	Prth	2m110y	D Hdl	GD	£5603
Total win prize-money £5603

Going:	Sf: 0-1 GS: 0-2 Gd: 1-2 GF: - Fm: 0-0
Distance:	2m/2m3: 1-4 2m4-2m7: 0-0 3m+: 0-0
Track:	LH: 0-3 RH: 1-2 Tight: 0-0 Gall: 0-0
Aids:	Bl: 0-0 Vi: 0-0 Tstrap: 0-0
Best Rating:	101 4/03 Prth 2m110y good Hdl

Modest bumper performer; got off the mark over hurdles at Perth in April 2003; acts on good ground but handles softer.

Vanormix (FR)

104   **111**

4-y-o gr g Linamix (FR)-Vadsa Honor (FR) (Highest Honor (FR))
M C Pipe (A Fabre 30/6) Jim Weeden

Placings:*2U0114*   (4328)
2002/03: 16²G, 17ᵁHY, 19¹GS, 19¹GS, 16⁴G,

	Starts	1st	2nd	3rd	Win & Pl
Hurdles	6	2	1	0	9199
Career Total	6	2	1	0	9199
111	2/03	Extr	2m3f	E Hdl	G-S	£3737

100 1/03 Extr   2m3f   E Hdl   G-S £3794
Total win prize-money £7532

Going:	Sf: 0-1 GS: 2-2 Gd: 0-3 GF: - Fm: 0-0
Distance:	2m/2m3: 2-6 2m4-2m7: 0-0 3m+: 0-0
Track:	LH: 0-3 RH: 2-3 Tight: 0-0 Gall: 0-3
Aids:	Bl: 0-0 Vi: 0-0 Tstrap: 0-0
Best Rating:	114 1/03 Chel 2m1f heavy Hdl

Modest novice hurdler; stays two miles three; acts on good to soft ground.

Varykinov (IRE)

78(89c)   (91c)**28**

14-y-o b/br g Roselier (FR)-Royal Handful (Some Hand)
M G Rimell Mark Rimell

Placings:*5/34/0P/12/10FB/5/3P-5*   (3827)
2002/03: 24⁵GS,

	Starts	1st	2nd	3rd	Win & Pl
Hurdles	1	0	0	0	
Career Total	15	2	1	2	9099
126	2/99	Hayd	3m	H Ch	SFT	£7035
107	4/98	Worc	2m7f110yH Ch		G-S	£1021
Total win prize-money £8057

Going:	Sf: 0-0 GS: 0-1 Gd: 0-0 GF: - Fm: 0-0
Distance:	2m/2m3: 0-0 2m4-2m7: 0-0 3m+: 0-1
Track:	LH: 0-1 RH: 0-0 Tight: 0-0 Gall: 0-0
Aids:	Bl: 0-1 Vi: 0-0 Tstrap: 0-0
Best Rating:	126 2/99 Hayd 3m soft Ch

Modest hunter chaser these days.

Vegas Vic (IRE)

                                                                        49f

5-y-o b m Old Vic-Princess Breda (IRE) (Long Pond)
G Brown Sean Maguire

Placings:*0*   (2172)
2002/03: 14⁰GS,

	Starts	1st	2nd	3rd	Win & Pl
NH Flat	1	0	0	0	
Career Total	1	0	0	0	

Going:	Sf: 0-0 GS: 0-1 Gd: 0-0 GF: - Fm: 0-0
Distance:	2m/2m3: 0-0 2m4-2m7: 0-0 3m+: 0-0
Track:	LH: 0-1 RH: 0-0 Tight: 0-0 Gall: 0-0
Aids:	Bl: 0-0 Vi: 0-0 Tstrap: 0-0
Best Rating:	50 11/02 Wwck 1m6f gd-sft NHF

Veiled Dancer (IRE)

100(79h)   (71 h)**75**

10-y-o ch g Shareef Dancer (USA)-Fatal Distraction (Formidable (USA))
A S T Holdsworth N J Holdsworth

Placings:*620P/56FPPP/0666P4*   (4215)
2002/03: 22⁰G, 22⁶G, 22⁶G, 25⁶GS, 24⁶G, 28⁴G,

	Starts	1st	2nd	3rd	Win & Pl
Hurdles	3	0	0	0	
Chases	3	0	0	0	336
Career Total	16	0	1	0	942

Going:	Sf: 0-0 GS: 0-1 Gd: 0-5 GF: - Fm: 0-0
Distance:	2m/2m3: 0-0 2m4-2m7: 0-3 3m+: 0-3
Track:	LH: 0-1 RH: 0-4 Tight: 0-1 Gall: 0-1
Aids:	Bl: 0-0 Vi: 0-0 Tstrap: 0-0
Best Rating:	75 3/03 Font 3m4f good Ch

Point winner; maiden over both hurdles and fences; stays well.

Velmez

70(102h)   (78h)**35**

10-y-o ch g Belmez (USA)-Current Raiser (Filiberto (USA))
B J Llewellyn Greg Robinson

Placings:*6006544P/046050/6F02122/P06P-000P*   (1602)
2002/03: 16⁶G, 22⁰G, 22⁰GP, 19⁶G,

	Starts	1st	2nd	3rd	Win & Pl
Hurdles	2	0	0	0	
Chases	2	0	0	0	
Career Total	29	1	3	0	8451
105	6/00	NAbb	2m6f	E Hdl	G-F	£2464
Total win prize-money £2464

Going:	Sf: 0-0 GS: 0-0 Gd: 0-3 GF: - Fm: 0-1
Distance:	2m/2m3: 0-1 2m4-2m7: 0-3 3m+: 0-0
Track:	LH: 0-4 RH: 0-0 Tight: 0-3 Gall: 0-0
Aids:	Bl: 0-4 Vi: 0-0 Tstrap: 0-0
Best Rating:	105 7/00 Worc 3m gd-fm Hdl

Velvet Sword

90   **81**

8-y-o b m Broadsword (USA)-Marney Barle (Julio Mariner)
R Hollinshead Miss S Sharratt

Placings:*005/052*   (0727)
2002/03: 20⁰GF, 20⁵GF, 22⁰GF,

	Starts	1st	2nd	3rd	Win & Pl
Hurdles	3	0	1	0	1495
Career Total	6	0	1	0	1495

Going:	Sf: 0-0 GS: 0-0 Gd: 0-0 GF: - Fm: 0-3
Distance:	2m/2m3: 0-0 2m4-2m7: 0-3 3m+: 0-0
Track:	LH: 0-3 RH: 0-0 Tight: 0-1 Gall: 0-0
Aids:	Bl: 0-0 Vi: 0-0 Tstrap: 0-0
Best Rating:	84 4/01 Newb 2m110y soft NHF

Veneguera (IRE)

108(97c)   **97**

10-y-o b g Satco (FR)-Orlita (Master Buck)
K C Bailey The Sporting Has Beens

Placings:*4006P60/5441440412140/4/0253*62341130464-
P4610P6*   (3117)
2002/03: 24⁶G, 21⁴GF, 22⁶G, 24¹F, 26⁰GS, 26⁶S, 21⁶S,

	Starts	1st	2nd	3rd	Win & Pl
Hurdles	7	1	0	0	3423
Career Total	43	6	3	3	24585
97	10/02	Ludl	3m	F(0-95)HHdl	FRM	£3423
106	10/01	Kemp	2m5f	D(0-125)HHdl	G-S	£5073
106	10/01	Hntg	3m2f	F(0-110)HHdl	GD	£1862
103	3/00	Dpat	2m4f110y	(0-95)HHdl	G-F	£2345
93	11/99	Dpat	2m6f	(0-95)HHdl	YLD	£2002
81	8/99	Naas	2m4f	Hdl	G-F	£3696
Total win prize-money £18402

Going:	Sf: 0-2 GS: 0-1 Gd: 0-2 GF: - Fm: 1-2
Distance:	2m/2m3: 0-0 2m4-2m7: 0-3 3m+: 1-4
Track:	LH: 0-2 RH: 1-5 Tight: 0-1 Gall: 0-3
Aids:	Bl: 0-0 Vi: 0-0 Tstrap: 0-0
Best Rating:	113 6/01 MRas 2m6f110y gd-fm Ch

Moderate hurdler, out-and-out stayer, but a little quirky, he goes particularly well for amateur riders; suited by decent ground; has worn cheekpieces.

Venn Ottery

87(71h)   79+

8-y-o b g Access Ski-Tom s Comedy (Comedy Star (USA))
O J Carter   O J Carter

Placings:P/P/PF-P4P04F0F   (4558)
2002/03: 19⁵GF, 20⁴GF, 16⁶S, 19⁹GF, 16⁴GF, 16⁶GF, 22²G, 25⁵G,

	Starts	1st	2nd	3rd	Win & Pl
Hurdles	2	0	0	0	0
Chases	6	0	0	0	465
Career Total	12	0	0	0	465

Going:	Sf: 0-1 GS: 0-0 Gd: 0-2 GF: - Fm: 0-5
Distance:	2m/2m3: 0-4 2m4-2m7: 0-3 3m+: 0-1
Track:	LH: 0-7 RH: 0-1 Tight: 0-4 Gall: 0-1
Aids:	Bl: 0-0 Vi: 0-0 Tstrap: 0-0
Best Rating:	79 6/02 NAbb 2m110y gd-fm Ch

Headstrong maiden pointer/hunter chaser; acts on a sound surface.

Venture More

95   85

7-y-o br g Green Adventure (USA)-Admire-A-More (Le Coq D Or)
P Monteith   Mrs A F Tullie

Placings:00-0663304   (4504)
2002/03: 18⁰G, 16⁶GF, 16⁶GF, 16³GF, 16³S, 16⁹G, 16⁴G,

	Starts	1st	2nd	3rd	Win & Pl
Hurdles	7	0	0	2	2102
Career Total	9	0	0	2	2102

Going:	Sf: 0-1 GS: 0-0 Gd: 0-3 GF: - Fm: 0-3
Distance:	2m/2m3: 0-7 2m4-2m7: 0-0 3m+: 0-0
Track:	LH: 0-6 RH: 0-1 Tight: 0-3 Gall: 0-0
Aids:	Bl: 0-0 Vi: 0-0 Tstrap: 0-0
Best Rating:	85 4/03 Kels 2m110y good Hdl

Plating-class novice hurdler; placed twice over hurdles; should be suited by a step up in trip.

Venture To Fly (IRE)

97(104h)   (93h)112

9-y-o ch g Roselier (FR)-Fly Run (Deep Run)
N G Richards   Ashleybank Investments Limited

Placings:2325/1134/F-4P   (2387)
2002/03: 20⁴HY, 21²GS,

	Starts	1st	2nd	3rd	Win & Pl
Chases	2	0	0	0	354
Career Total	11	2	2	2	8818
108 1/01	Ayr	2m6f		E Hdl	SFT £2954
117 11/00	Newc	3m		E Hdl	SFT £2583
				Total win prize-money £5537

Going:	Sf: 0-1 GS: 0-0 Gd: 0-0 GF: - Fm: 0-0
Distance:	2m/2m3: 0-0 2m4-2m7: 0-2 3m+: 0-0
Track:	LH: 0-1 RH: 0-1 Tight: 0-0 Gall: 0-0
Aids:	Bl: 0-0 Vi: 0-0 Tstrap: 0-0
Best Rating:	117 1/01 Ayr 3m110y gd-sft Hdl

Modest winner over hurdles, he has been a little disappointing over fences. Acts on soft ground, stays three miles.

Verde Luna

105(101h)   (54h)49

11-y-o ch g Green Desert (USA)-Mamaluna (USA) (Roberto (USA))
A G Hobbs   J Parfitt

Placings:0600106/2133F445/2332435053400/4312012/0/P 060U4/00015066   (2011)
2002/03: 20⁰GF, 21⁰S, 16⁰GS, 26¹GF, 26⁵GF, 19⁰G, 24⁵GF, 23⁸GF,

	Starts	1st	2nd	3rd	Win & Pl
Hurdles	4	0	0	0	0
Chases	4	1	0	0	2940
Career Total	50	5	5	7	20548
79 8/02	Font	3m2f110yF(0-90)HCh	G-F £2940
94 3/99	Font	H Ch	G-F £2390
96 8/98	Sthl	2m4f110yE(0-105)HCh	G-F £2650
87 8/96	NAbb	2m1f	F(0-100)HHdl	G-F £1948
87 4/96	Plum	2m4f	E(0-100)HHdl	FRM £2364
			Total win prize-money £12293

Going:	Sf: 0-1 GS: 0-1 Gd: 0-1 GF: - Fm: 1-5
Distance:	2m/2m3: 0-1 2m4-2m7: 0-3 3m+: 1-4
Track:	LH: 0-3 RH: 0-4 Tight: 1-3 Gall: 0-1
Aids:	Bl: 0-1 Vi: 1-7 Tstrap: 1-3
Best Rating:	100 7/97 Worc 2m good Ch

Modest hurdler/chaser, successful in a Fontwell handicap chase in the summer of 2002. Stays well.

Veridian

104(99c)   (82c)92

10-y-o b g Green Desert (USA)-Alik (FR) (Targowice (USA))
G F Bridgwater (B J Llewellyn 9/8)   John Marks And Dave Allsopp

Placings:F42126/5/14025/15/045006-434PP55   (2131)
2002/03: 17⁴G, 17³S, 16⁴G, 17⁵PG, 20⁵S, 16⁵GS, 16⁵G,

	Starts	1st	2nd	3rd	Win & Pl
Hurdles	5	0	0	1	1011
Chases	2	0	0	0	269
Career Total	27	3	3	1	27635
136 9/00	Bang	2m1f	C(0-135)HHdl	G-F £6825
137 12/99	Kemp	2m	B(0-145)HHdl	SFT £10259
116 3/98	Folk	2m1f110yE Hdl	GD £2630
			Total win prize-money £19714

Going:	Sf: 0-2 GS: 0-1 Gd: 0-4 GF: - Fm: 0-0
Distance:	2m/2m3: 0-6 2m4-2m7: 0-1 3m+: 0-0
Track:	LH: 0-5 RH: 0-2 Tight: 0-3 Gall: 0-0
Aids:	Bl: 0-0 Vi: 0-0 Tstrap: 0-0
Best Rating:	137 12/99 Kemp 2m soft Hdl

Moderate hurdler; stays two and a half miles but is probably better at shorter. Has a fair turn of foot when on song but seems to be on the downgrade. Handles any ground.

Vero Beach

93   88

7-y-o ch g Nicholas Bill-My Moody Girl (IRE) (Alzao (USA))
Mrs S D Williams   Bideford Tool Ltd

Placings:0/5   (4623)
2002/03: 27⁵GF,

	Starts	1st	2nd	3rd	Win & Pl
Hurdles	1	0	0	0	0
Career Total	2	0	0	0	0

Going:	Sf: 0-0 GS: 0-0 Gd: 0-0 GF: - Fm: 0-1
Distance:	2m/2m3: 0-0 2m4-2m7: 0-0 3m+: 0-1
Track:	LH: 0-1 RH: 0-0 Tight: 0-1 Gall: 0-0
Aids:	Bl: 0-0 Vi: 0-0 Tstrap: 0-0
Best Rating:	88 4/03 NAbb 3m3f gd-fm Hdl

Versailles

4-y-o b g Bluegrass Prince (IRE)-Fabulous Pet (Somethingfabulous (USA))

D Burchell (Mrs J R Ramsden 26/7)   Mrs Linda Cognet

Placings:PP   (3177)
2002/03: 17⁵S, 16⁷G,

	Starts	1st	2nd	3rd	Win & Pl
Hurdles	2	0	0	0	
Career Total	2	0	0	0	

Going:	Sf: 0-1 GS: 0-0 Gd: 0-1 GF: - Fm: 0-0
Distance:	2m/2m3: 0-2 2m4-2m7: 0-0 3m+: 0-0
Track:	LH: 0-2 RH: 0-2 Tight: 0-0 Gall: 0-0
Aids:	Bl: 0-0 Vi: 0-0 Tstrap: 0-0
Best Rating:	0 1/03 Kemp 2m good Hdl

Versicium (FR)

100(101h)   (109h)118

9-y-o ch g Mister Sicy (FR)-Verdurine (FR) (General Holme (USA))
M C Pipe   The Arthur White Partnership

Placings:3322U2/10F023U-13P2   (1379)
2002/03: 17¹GF, 17³G, 16²GF, 16²GF,

	Starts	1st	2nd	3rd	Win & Pl
Chases	4	1	1		6204
Career Total	18	2	6	4	15657
118 7/02	Sthl	2m1f	E(0-105)HCh	G-F £4056
109 5/01	NAbb	2m1f	F(0-100)HHdl	G-F £2775
			Total win prize-money £6832

Going:	Sf: 0-0 GS: 0-0 Gd: 0-1 GF: - Fm: 1-3
Distance:	2m/2m3: 1-4 2m4-2m7: 0-3 3m+: 0-0
Track:	LH: 1-3 RH: 0-1 Tight: 0-2 Gall: 0-0
Aids:	Bl: 0-0 Vi: 1-4 Tstrap: 0-0
Best Rating:	118 7/02 Strf 2m1f110y good Ch

Fair front-running low grade handicap hurdler and chaser. Best at two miles and is suited by fast ground.

Vert Espere

111   96

10-y-o ch g Green Adventure (USA)-Celtic Dream (Celtic Cone)
Mrs J Candlish (A Streeter 29/10)   P S Daly

Placings:P/0P000F0/40P5406/2310-25122P   (4713)
2002/03: 20²GF, 24⁵GF, 19¹GF, 21²G, 20²G, 20⁰GF,

	Starts	1st	2nd	3rd	Win & Pl
Hurdles	6	1	3	0	9585
Career Total	25	2	4	1	12830
95 8/02	MRas	2m3f110yD(0-115)HHdl	G-F £4537
90 6/01	Worc	3m	F(0-100)HHdl	GD £2037
			Total win prize-money £6574

Going:	Sf: 0-0 GS: 0-0 Gd: 0-2 GF: - Fm: 1-4
Distance:	2m/2m3: 0-0 2m4-2m7: 1-5 3m+: 0-1
Track:	LH: 0-5 RH: 1-1 Tight: 1-1 Gall: 0-1
Aids:	Bl: 0-0 Vi: 0-0 Tstrap: 0-0
Best Rating:	96 9/02 Worc 2m4f good Hdl

Moderate handicap hurdler; stays three miles; acts on a sound surface.

Very Daring

13-y-o b g Derring Rose-La Verite (Vitiges (FR))
Miss N L Elliott   Miss N L Elliott

Placings:P6/B4364P/03/6005545000000/P-P   (0032)
2002/03: 21⁸GF,

	Starts	1st	2nd	3rd	Win & Pl
Chases	1	0	0	0	

Career Total   25   0   0   2   835

Going: Sf: 0-0 GS: 0-0 Gd: 0-0 GF: - Fm: 0-1
Distance: 2m/2m3: 0-0 2m4-2m7: 0-1 3m+: 0-0
Track: LH: 0-1 RH: 0-0 Tight: 0-0 Gall: 0-1
Aids: Bl: 0-0 Vi: 0-0 Tstrap: 0-0
Best Rating: 83 5/98 Uttx 2m5f   gd-fm Ch

Very Optimistic (IRE)

109f   **110+f**

5-y-o b g Un Desperado (FR)-Bright Future (IRE) (Satco (FR))
Jonjo O Neill Mrs G Smith

Placings:1   (4444)
2002/03: 16¹G,

	Starts	1st	2nd	3rd	Win & Pl
NH Flat	1	1	0	0	2573
Career Total	1	1	0	0	2573
110 4/03 Asct	2m110y H NHF			GD	£2572
Total win prize-money £2573					

Going: Sf: 0-0 GS: 0-0 Gd: 0-0 GF: - Fm: 0-0
Distance: 2m/2m3: 1-1 2m4-2m7: 0-0 3m+: 0-0
Track: LH: 0-0 RH: 1-1 Tight: 0-0 Gall: 0-0
Aids: Bl: 0-0 Vi: 0-0 Tstrap: 0-0
Best Rating: 110 4/03 Asct 2m110y good NHF

Made a good winning debut in a decent Ascot bumper in early April; effective on good ground.

Very Tasty (IRE)

6-y-o ch g Be My Native (USA)-Jasmine Melody (Jasmine Star)
M Todhunter A Slack

Placings:0U-P   (0400)
2002/03: 20PGF,

	Starts	1st	2nd	3rd	Win & Pl
Hurdles	1	0	0	0	
Career Total	3	0	0	0	

Going: Sf: 0-0 GS: 0-0 Gd: 0-0 GF: - Fm: 0-1
Distance: 2m/2m3: 0-0 2m4-2m7: 0-1 3m+: 0-0
Track: LH: 0-0 RH: 0-0 Tight: 0-0 Gall: 0-0
Aids: Bl: 0-0 Vi: 0-0 Tstrap: 0-0
Best Rating: 57 4/02 Carl 2m1f   good NHF

Vetranio (IRE)

85   **67**

6-y-o ch g Hubbly Bubbly (USA)-Cool Charm (Beau Charmeur (FR))
N M Babbage Provex Products Ltd

Placings:660   (3871)
2002/03: 16⁶GS, 18⁶HY, 19⁰S,

	Starts	1st	2nd	3rd	Win & Pl
NH Flat	2	0	0	0	0
Hurdles	1	0	0	0	0
Career Total	3	0	0	0	0

Going: Sf: 0-2 GS: 0-1 Gd: 0-0 GF: - Fm: 0-0
Distance: 2m/2m3: 0-3 2m4-2m7: 0-0 3m+: 0-0
Track: LH: 0-3 RH: 0-0 Tight: 0-1 Gall: 0-1
Aids: Bl: 0-0 Vi: 0-0 Tstrap: 0-0

Best Rating: 88 11/02 Sthl 2m   gd-sft NHF

Viaduct (IRE)

7-y-o b g Archway (IRE)-Decent Essence (Decent Fellow)
Ivor Kingston Ivor Kingston

Placings:050/00043-2334015   (4531a)
2002/03: 28²G, 24³S, 24³SH, 25⁴YS, 26⁹G, 24¹S, 24⁵GF,

	Starts	1st	2nd	3rd	Win & Pl
Chases	7	1	1	2	8774
Career Total	15	1	1	3	10535
85 3/03 Wxfd	3m	Ch		SFT	£4480
Total win prize-money £4481					

Going: Sf: 1-2 GS: 0-0 Gd: 0-2 GF: - Fm: 0-1
Distance: 2m/2m3: 0-0 2m4-2m7: 0-0 3m+: 1-7
Track: LH: 0-2 RH: 1-5 Tight: 0-1 Gall: 0-1
Aids: Bl: 0-1 Vi: 0-0 Tstrap: 1-7
Best Rating: 109 4/02 Punc 3m1f   good   Ch

Modest Irish hunter chaser.

Vic Plum (IRE)

5-y-o b/br m Lord Americo-Naujella (Malinowski (USA))
W G Young W G Young

Placings:000   (3583)
2002/03: 16⁰HY, 14⁰GS, 16⁰G,

	Starts	1st	2nd	3rd	Win & Pl
NH Flat	3	0	0	0	
Career Total	3	0	0	0	

Going: Sf: 0-1 GS: 0-1 Gd: 0-1 GF: - Fm: 0-0
Distance: 2m/2m3: 0-2 2m4-2m7: 0-0 3m+: 0-0
Track: LH: 0-2 RH: 0-1 Tight: 0-1 Gall: 0-0
Aids: Bl: 0-0 Vi: 0-0 Tstrap: 0-0
Best Rating: 26 2/03 Muss 2m   good NHF

Vicar's Lad

85   **65**

7-y-o b g Terimon-Proverbial Rose (Proverb)
N A Twiston-Davies Mrs P Duncan

Placings:405   (3787)
2002/03: 17⁴S, 17⁰G, 26⁵G,

	Starts	1st	2nd	3rd	Win & Pl
NH Flat	2	0	0	0	
Hurdles	1	0	0	0	
Career Total	3	0	0	0	

Going: Sf: 0-1 GS: 0-0 Gd: 0-2 GF: - Fm: 0-0
Distance: 2m/2m3: 0-2 2m4-2m7: 0-0 3m+: 0-1
Track: LH: 0-0 RH: 0-3 Tight: 0-0 Gall: 0-0
Aids: Bl: 0-0 Vi: 0-0 Tstrap: 0-0
Best Rating: 98 11/02 Hrfd 2m1f   soft NHF

Little signs of ability in bumpers and novice hurdles.

Vicars Destiny

97   **99+**

5-y-o b m Sir Harry Lewis (USA)-Church Leap (Pollerton)
Mrs S Lamyman Terence Deal

Placings:4-022314P   (4442)
2002/03: 17³G, 16²G, 16²HY, 20³G, 20¹G, 24⁴S, 20PG,

	Starts	1st	2nd	3rd	Win & Pl
NH Flat	3	0	2	0	1153
Hurdles	4	1	0	1	4331
Career Total	8	1	2	1	5484
97 3/03 Weth	2m4f110yE Hdl			GD	£3474
Total win prize-money £3474					

Going: Sf: 0-2 GS: 0-0 Gd: 1-5 GF: - Fm: 0-0
Distance: 2m/2m3: 0-3 2m4-2m7: 1-3 3m+: 0-1
Track: LH: 1-5 RH: 0-2 Tight: 0-1 Gall: 0-0
Aids: Bl: 0-0 Vi: 0-0 Tstrap: 0-0
Best Rating: 97 3/03 Weth 2m4f110y good Hdl

Moderate hurdler; has shown ability in bumpers; third in mares only novices hurdle on first outing over hurdles at Wetherby in February and took identical event in comfortable fashion there a week later.

Vicentio

4-y-o br g Vettori (IRE)-Smah (Mtoto)
T J Fitzgerald (J G Fitzgerald 25/2) Shaw Thing Partnership

Placings:0060   (4788)
2002/03: 16⁰GS, 16⁰G, 16⁶GF, 17⁰G,

	Starts	1st	2nd	3rd	Win & Pl
NH Flat	4	0	0	0	0
Career Total	4	0	0	0	0

Going: Sf: 0-0 GS: 0-1 Gd: 0-2 GF: - Fm: 0-1
Distance: 2m/2m3: 0-4 2m4-2m7: 0-0 3m+: 0-0
Track: LH: 0-3 RH: 0-1 Tight: 0-2 Gall: 0-0
Aids: Bl: 0-0 Vi: 0-0 Tstrap: 0-0
Best Rating: 77 2/03 Weth 2m   gd-sft NHF

Glimmer of ability in bumpers.

Victor Laszlo

100   **68**

11-y-o b g Ilium-Report Em (USA) (Staff Writer (USA))
R Allan Mrs L A Ogilvie

Placings:6/63064/1205/000/04334P5P0P/2600325454-
40503445   (1308)
2002/03: 17⁴GS, 22⁰GF, 20⁵GF, 22⁰G, 20³GS, 16⁴G, 21⁴G, 20⁵GF,

	Starts	1st	2nd	3rd	Win & Pl
Chases	8	0	0	1	2284
Career Total	41	1	3	5	11242
93 5/98 Prth	2m4f110yE Hdl			G-F	£2835
Total win prize-money £2835					

Going: Sf: 0-0 GS: 0-2 Gd: 0-3 GF: - Fm: 0-3
Distance: 2m/2m3: 0-2 2m4-2m7: 0-0 3m+: 0-0
Track: LH: 0-4 RH: 0-4 Tight: 0-4 Gall: 0-0
Aids: Bl: 0-0 Vi: 0-0 Tstrap: 0-5
Best Rating: 99 5/98 Kels 2m110y gd-fm Hdl

A winner over hurdles but that was over four years ago. Very moderate over fences.

Victoria Ryan (IRE)

86f   **58f**

5-y-o b m Good Thyne (USA)-No Not (Ovac (ITY))
J R Norton G A Hancock & A Parsonage

Placings:00   (4594)
2002/03: 16⁰GF, 16⁰G,

	Starts	1st	2nd	3rd	Win & Pl
NH Flat	2	0	0	0	
Career Total	2	0	0	0	

Going:	Sf: 0-0 GS: 0-0 Gd: 0-1 GF: - Fm: 0-1
Distance:	2m/2m3: 0-2 2m4-2m7: 0-0 3m+: 0-0
Track:	LH: 0-2 RH: 0-0 Tight: 0-0 Gall: 0-0
Aids:	Bl: 0-0 Vi: 0-0 Tstrap: 0-0
Best Rating:	58 4/03 Hexm 2m110y good NHF

Victoria Stone

6-y-o b m Old Vic-Lampstone (Ragstone)
A King Platel & Welch Partnership

Placings:P   (2947)
2002/03: 16PS,

	Starts	1st	2nd	3rd	Win & Pl
NH Flat	1	0	0	0	
Career Total	1	0	0	0	

Going:	Sf: 0-1 GS: 0-0 Gd: 0-0 GF: - Fm: 0-0
Distance:	2m/2m3: 0-1 2m4-2m7: 0-0 3m+: 0-0
Track:	LH: 0-0 RH: 0-1 Tight: 0-0 Gall: 0-0
Aids:	Bl: 0-0 Vi: 0-0 Tstrap: 0-0
Best Rating:	0 1/03 Ludl 2m soft NHF

Victoria's Boy (IRE)

10-y-o b g Denel (FR)-Cloghroe Lady (Hard Boy)
T D Walford David Dickson

Placings:00/00/1526/P506543204-0P   (0784)
2002/03: 24AG, 22PG, 21PGF,

	Starts	1st	2nd	3rd	Win & Pl
Chases	3	0	0	0	0
Career Total	20	1	2	1	5215
102 5/00 Hexm 3m1f		H Ch		G-F	£2366
			Total win prize-money £2366		

Going:	Sf: 0-0 GS: 0-0 Gd: 0-2 GF: - Fm: 0-1
Distance:	2m/2m3: 0-0 2m4-2m7: 0-0 3m+: 0-1
Track:	LH: 0-2 RH: 0-1 Tight: 0-1 Gall: 0-1
Aids:	Bl: 0-0 Vi: 0-0 Tstrap: 0-0
Best Rating:	102 5/00 Hexm 3m1f gd-fm Ch

Winning pointer and hunter chaser; jumps well; best at three miles; effective on fast ground.

Victory Gunner (IRE)

90   67

5-y-o ch g Old Vic-Gunner B Sharp (Gunner B)
C Roberts (J Neville 14/2) Ron Bartlett

Placings:0520   (4481)
2002/03: 16DHY, 16SHY, 172G, 179G,

	Starts	1st	2nd	3rd	Win & Pl
NH Flat	4	0	1	0	560
Career Total	4	0	1	0	560

Going:	Sf: 0-2 GS: 0-0 Gd: 0-2 GF: - Fm: 0-0
Distance:	2m/2m3: 0-4 2m4-2m7: 0-0 3m+: 0-0
Track:	LH: 0-1 RH: 0-2 Tight: 0-1 Gall: 0-1
Aids:	Bl: 0-0 Vi: 0-0 Tstrap: 0-0
Best Rating:	103 2/03 Sand 2m110y heavy NHF

Narrowly beaten in modest Folkestone bumper March 2003; highly tried next time; appeared to find 2m 6f just beyond him on hurdling debut; seems to act on most types of ground.

Victory Roll

97   104

7-y-o b g In The Wings-Persian Victory (IRE) (Persian Bold)
Miss E C Lavelle Sir Gordon Brunton

Placings:004143/01131320-00   (4088)
2002/03: 16PS, 16PGS,

	Starts	1st	2nd	3rd	Win & Pl
Hurdles	2	0	0	0	
Career Total	16	4	1	3	20469
107 12/01 Hntg	2m110y	D(0-125)HHdl		G-S	£8287
110 11/01 Folk	2m1f110yF(0-105)HHdl		SFT	£2681
104 10/01 Folk	2m1f110yF(0-110)HHdl		HVY	£2919
82 1/01 Folk	2m1f110yF(0-115)HHdl		HVY	£2387
			Total win prize-money £16275		

Going:	Sf: 0-1 GS: 0-1 Gd: 0-0 GF: - Fm: 0-0
Distance:	2m/2m3: 0-2 2m4-2m7: 0-0 3m+: 0-0
Track:	LH: 0-1 RH: 0-1 Tight: 0-1 Gall: 0-0
Aids:	Bl: 0-0 Vi: 0-0 Tstrap: 0-0
Best Rating:	110 2/02 Winc 2m soft Hdl

Moderate hurdler; goes particularly well over the extended two miles one furlong on heavy ground at Folkestone, but has shown decent form on other right-handed tracks and acts on a faster surface.

Vidi Caesar (NZ)

(98h)   (84h)

8-y-o b g Racing Is Fun (USA)-Vidi Vici (NZ) (Roman Empire)
R C Guest (N B Mason 20/6) Mark Barrett

Placings:03   (3965)
2002/03: 16DG, 163S,

	Starts	1st	2nd	3rd	Win & Pl
Hurdles	2	0	0	1	559
Career Total	2	0	0	1	559

Going:	Sf: 0-1 GS: 0-0 Gd: 0-0 GF: - Fm: 0-0
Distance:	2m/2m3: 0-2 2m4-2m7: 0-0 3m+: 0-0
Track:	LH: 0-2 RH: 0-0 Tight: 0-1 Gall: 0-0
Aids:	Bl: 0-0 Vi: 0-0 Tstrap: 0-0
Best Rating:	84 3/03 Catt 2m soft Hdl

Placed in testing ground on the Flat in New Zealand; showed some ability when moderate third in novices hurdle at Catterick in March; third again at Cartmel in May; capable of better.

Vigoureux (FR)

97   93

4-y-o b g Villez (USA)-Rouge Folie (FR) (Agent Bleu (FR))
S Gollings Ian Hesketh & John Webb

Placings:2153   (4559)
2002/03: 162HY, 171HY, 16SHY, 163G,

	Starts	1st	2nd	3rd	Win & Pl
Hurdles	4	1	1	1	17041
Career Total	4	1	1	1	17041
11/02 Engh	2m1f110y Hdl		HVY	£10601
		Total win prize-money £10601		

Going:	Sf: 1-3 GS: 0-0 Gd: 0-1 GF: - Fm: 0-0
Distance:	2m/2m3: 1-4 2m4-2m7: 0-0 3m+: 0-0
Track:	LH: 0-2 RH: 0-1 Tight: 0-0 Gall: 0-0
Aids:	Bl: 0-0 Vi: 0-0 Tstrap: 0-0
Best Rating:	93 4/03 Ayr 2m good Hdl

Winning hurdler in France; well held on British debut, but not disgraced when third at Ayr; acts on good and heavy.

Viking Buoy (IRE)

101(91c)   (70c)70

11-y-o ch g Pimpernel s Tune-Clare s Crystal (Tekoah)
Mrs P Townsley Paul Townsley

Placings:S353/2.22UP4132FP/11104023/2263U0/00/03005
3   (4700)
2002/03: 17DHY, 163HY, 18PS, 24DS, 215GF, 213GF,

	Starts	1st	2nd	3rd	Win & Pl
Hurdles	3	0	0	1	539
Chases	3	0	0	0	519
Career Total	37	4	7	7	22822
90 7/98 Wxfd	2m4f	(0-116)HCh	G-F	£3586
111 5/98 Gowr	3m1f	(0-116)HHdl	GD	£4765
98 5/98 Klny	2m4f	(0-109)HCh	Y-S	£2978
107 2/98 Clon	3m	Hdl	Y-S	£1935
			Total win prize-money £13266	

Going:	Sf: 0-4 GS: 0-0 Gd: 0-0 GF: - Fm: 0-2
Distance:	2m/2m3: 0-3 2m4-2m7: 0-3 3m+: 0-1
Track:	LH: 0-2 RH: 0-3 Tight: 0-5 Gall: 0-0
Aids:	Bl: 0-0 Vi: 0-0 Tstrap: 0-0
Best Rating:	111 5/98 Gowr 3m1f good Hdl

Plating-class hurdler/chaser; stays two miles five; seems to act on any ground.

Villa

102f   120+f

7-y-o b g Jupiter Island-Spoonhill Wood (Celtic Cone)
M C Pipe Matt Archer & Miss Jean Broadhurst

Placings:61-1   (2178)
2002/03: 161HY,

	Starts	1st	2nd	3rd	Win & Pl
NH Flat	1	1	0	0	2401
Career Total	3	2	0	0	4718
120 11/02 Chep	2m110y	H NHF		HVY	£2401
108 1/02 Towc	2m	H NHF		HVY	£2317
		Total win prize-money £4718			

Going:	Sf: 1-1 GS: 0-0 Gd: 0-0 GF: - Fm: 0-0
Distance:	2m/2m3: 1-1 2m4-2m7: 0-0 3m+: 0-0
Track:	LH: 1-1 RH: 0-0 Tight: 0-0 Gall: 0-0
Aids:	Bl: 0-0 Vi: 0-0 Tstrap: 0-0
Best Rating:	120 11/02 Chep 2m110y heavy NHF

Fair performer; dual bumper winner on heavy ground; tough sort.

Village Copper

11-y-o b g Town And Country-Culm Valley (Port Corsair)
Mrs Ruth Hayter A Howland Jackson

Placings:06/5-44   (0315)
2002/03: 24AGF, 21AG,

	Starts	1st	2nd	3rd	Win & Pl
Chases	2	0	0	0	110
Career Total	5	0	0	0	110

Going:	Sf: 0-0 GS: 0-0 Gd: 0-1 GF: - Fm: 0-1
Distance:	2m/2m3: 0-0 2m4-2m7: 0-1 3m+: 0-1
Track:	LH: 0-0 RH: 0-2 Tight: 0-1 Gall: 0-1
Aids:	Bl: 0-0 Vi: 0-0 Tstrap: 0-0
Best Rating:	87 4/01 Fknm 3m110y gd-sft Ch

Village King (IRE)

106   143

10-y-o b g Roi Danzig (USA)-Honorine (USA) (Blushing Groom (FR))

P J Hobbs Capt E J Edwards-Heathcote

Placings:45210320/111123122/1336F0/0223F0/001P1-24
(2115)
2002/03: 24²GF, 27⁴GS,

	Starts	1st	2nd	3rd	Win & Pl
Chases	2	0	1	0	7428
Career Total	36	9	8	5	91724

135	4/02	Chel	3m2f110yC(0-135)HCh	G-F	£13071
128	2/02	Font	3m2f110yD(0-125)HCh	SFT	£4153
147	12/99	Chel	2m5f C(0-130)HCh	SFT	£10796
139	3/99	Extr	2m3f E(0-115)HCh	GD	£4040
134	10/98	Chel	2m4f110yD(0-110)HCh	GD	£4856
107	10/98	NAbb	2m5f110yE(0-120)Ch	GD	£3326
107	9/98	Worc	2m7f110yD Ch	G-F	£3556
99	8/98	NAbb	2m110y D Ch	G-F	£3501
112	1/98	Ludl	2m5f110yF Hdl	SFT	£2095

Total win prize-money £49198

Going: Sf: 0-0 GS: 0-1 Gd: 0-0 GF: - Fm: 0-1
Distance: 2m/2m3: 0-0 2m4-2m7: 0-0 3m+: 0-2
Track: LH: 0-2 RH: 0-0 Tight: 0-1 Gall: 0-0
Aids: Bl: 0-0 Vi: 0-0 Tstrap: 0-0
Best Rating: 147 12/99 Chel 2m5f soft Ch

Useful handicap chaser who stays well, he is a somewhat quirky individual and not one to place too much trust in. Successful at Fontwell in February 2002. Pulled up at the Festival, but bounced back at Cheltenham s April meeting. Ran well on his return at Chepstow. Stays three and a quarter miles. Acts on soft and fast ground.

Village Queen (IRE)
83 57
6-y-o ch m Good Thyne (USA)-Lady Henbit (IRE) (Henbit (USA))
P J Hobbs Capt E J Edwards-Heathcote

Placings:00
(2707)
2002/03: 19⁵GS, 16⁹GS,

	Starts	1st	2nd	3rd	Win & Pl
Hurdles	2	0	0	0	
Career Total	2	0	0	0	

Going: Sf: 0-0 GS: 0-2 Gd: 0-0 GF: - Fm: 0-0
Distance: 2m/2m3: 0-1 2m4-2m7: 0-1 3m+: 0-0
Track: LH: 0-0 RH: 0-2 Tight: 0-1 Gall: 0-0
Aids: Bl: 0-0 Vi: 0-0 Tstrap: 0-0
Best Rating: 57 11/02 Tntn 2m3f110y gd-sft Hdl

Villair (IRE)
102(103h) (84h)90
8-y-o b g Valville (FR)-Brackenair (Fairbairn)
C J Mann (D R Stoddart 6/5) Mrs J M Mayo

Placings:3004/00526F-1245F21
(4078)
2002/03: 20⁶GS, 16¹GS, 20²S, 20⁴S, 20⁵S, 17⁶S, 20²GS, 20¹S,

	Starts	1st	2nd	3rd	Win & Pl
Hurdles	1	1	0	0	2016
Chases	7	1	2	0	7145
Career Total	17	2	3	1	9982

98	3/03	Plum	2m4f E(0-110)HCh	SFT	£4065
83	5/02	Towc	2m G Hdl	G-S	£2016

Total win prize-money £6082

Going: Sf: 1-5 GS: 1-3 Gd: 0-0 GF: - Fm: 0-0
Distance: 2m/2m3: 1-2 2m4-2m7: 1-6 3m+: 0-0
Track: LH: 1-4 RH: 1-2 Tight: 1-4 Gall: 0-0
Aids: Bl: 1-3 Vi: 0-0 Tstrap: 0-0
Best Rating: 98 3/03 Plum 2m4f soft Ch

Moderatet hurdler/chaser; stays 2m 4f; does not look keen under pressure.

Vilprano
111 95
12-y-o b g Ra Nova-Village Princess (Rolfe (USA))
James Moffatt (D Moffatt 28/12) The Vilprano Partnership

Placings:0603/313/P012/223625342201/321366/54323216 56/0450141-4535045633300
(4774)
2002/03: 22⁴GS, 24⁵GF, 26³HY, 24⁵G, 22⁰S, 24⁴S, 25⁵G, 23⁶S, 27³HY, 24³S, 24³S, 24⁰GF, 27⁹G,

	Starts	1st	2nd	3rd	Win & Pl
Hurdles	13	0	0	4	2772
Career Total	59	7	9	13	41384

114	1/02	Catt	3m1f110yD(0-115)HHdl	SFT	£5122
107	11/01	Ayr	3m110y D(0-125)HHdl	G-S	£3477
120	12/00	Newc	3m C(0-135)HHdl	SFT	£5086
113	11/99	Bang	3m D(0-125)HHdl	GD	£3574
103	4/99	Bang	3m D(0-125)HHdl	GD	£4474
87	2/98	Newc	3m F(0-105)HHdl	GD	£2102
88	5/96	Ctml	2m6f F(0-95)HHdl	G-F	£2528

Total win prize-money £26366

Going: Sf: 0-7 GS: 0-1 Gd: 0-3 GF: - Fm: 0-2
Distance: 2m/2m3: 0-0 2m4-2m7: 0-2 3m+: 0-11
Track: LH: 0-12 RH: 0-1 Tight: 0-6 Gall: 0-1
Aids: Bl: 0-0 Vi: 0-1 Tstrap: 0-0
Best Rating: 120 12/00 Newc 3m soft Hdl

Moderate hurdler; stays well; acts on a soft surface; has worn cheekpieces.

Vincent Van Gogh (IRE)
100 103
8-y-o b g Executive Perk-Rare Picture (Pollerton)
R J Hodges The Trojan Partnership

Placings:00/P0U2246F1/006521P143P6-126025
(3642)
2002/03: 24¹F, 24²GS, 25⁶GS, 24⁰GS, 21²GS, 21⁵GS,

	Starts	1st	2nd	3rd	Win & Pl
Chases	6	1	2	0	10546
Career Total	29	4	5	1	28193

103	10/02	Tntn	3m D(0-120)HCh	FRM	£5492
100	12/01	Ludl	3m D(0-115)HCh	SFT	£4771
98	12/01	Ludl	3m F(0-100)HCh	GD	£4550
90	4/01	Tntn	2m110y E(0-105)HCh	GD	£3029

Total win prize-money £17843

Going: Sf: 0-0 GS: 0-5 Gd: 0-0 GF: - Fm: 1-1
Distance: 2m/2m3: 0-0 2m4-2m7: 0-2 3m+: 1-4
Track: LH: 0-0 RH: 1-6 Tight: 1-3 Gall: 0-0
Aids: Bl: 0-0 Vi: 0-0 Tstrap: 0-0
Best Rating: 103 2/03 Winc 2m5f gd-sft Ch

Moderate chaser; effective between two and a half and three miles; goes well on fast ground; acts on soft and must go right-handed; has broken blood vessels in the past.

Vino Tinto (IRE)
9-y-o b g Glacial Storm (USA)-Pure Spec (Fine Blade (USA))
Mrs C M Mulhall Mrs C M Mulhall

Placings:00/000000/6640004/0/2-3
(4161)
2002/03: 25³GS,

	Starts	1st	2nd	3rd	Win & Pl
Chases	1	0	0	1	211
Career Total	18	0	1	1	1231

Going: Sf: 0-0 GS: 0-1 Gd: 0-0 GF: - Fm: 0-0
Distance: 2m/2m3: 0-0 2m4-2m7: 0-0 3m+: 0-1

Track: LH: 0-1 RH: 0-1 Tight: 0-1 Gall: 0-0
Aids: Bl: 0-0 Vi: 0-0 Tstrap: 0-0
Best Rating: 89 3/03 MRas 3m1f gd-sft Ch

Former maiden Irish hurdler; winning pointer and narrowly denied in hunter chases.

Violent
78 33
5-y-o b m Deploy-Gentle Irony (Mazilier (USA))
Jamie Poulton Chris Steward

Placings:5-0
(0613)
2002/03: 16⁰GF,

	Starts	1st	2nd	3rd	Win & Pl
Hurdles	1	0	0	0	
Career Total	2	0	0	0	0

Going: Sf: 0-0 GS: 0-0 Gd: 0-0 GF: - Fm: 0-1
Distance: 2m/2m3: 0-1 2m4-2m7: 0-0 3m+: 0-0
Track: LH: 0-1 RH: 0-0 Tight: 0-0 Gall: 0-0
Aids: Bl: 0-0 Vi: 0-0 Tstrap: 0-0
Best Rating: 41 6/02 Worc 2m gd-fm Hdl

Virac Boy (IRE)
102 61
10-y-o b g Tremblant-Supreme Cherry (Buckskin (FR))
Miss G Browne Virac Marketing Ltd

Placings:05P/PP/0P656
(4083)
2002/03: 16⁰GS, 24²P, 25⁶HY, 22⁵S, 25⁶HY,

	Starts	1st	2nd	3rd	Win & Pl
Hurdles	5	0	0	0	
Career Total	10	0	0	0	

Going: Sf: 0-3 GS: 0-1 Gd: 0-1 GF: - Fm: 0-0
Distance: 2m/2m3: 0-0 2m4-2m7: 0-1 3m+: 0-3
Track: LH: 0-1 RH: 0-2 Tight: 0-1 Gall: 0-0
Aids: Bl: 0-0 Vi: 0-0 Tstrap: 0-0
Best Rating: 84 2/99 Wwck 2m gd-sft NHF

# Virgin Soldier (IRE)
104(108h) (128 h)
7-y-o ch g Waajib-Never Been Chaste (Posse (USA))
G A Swinbank J David Abell

Placings:414-1132
(1539)
2002/03: 16¹GF, 17¹G, 16³GF, 16²GF,

	Starts	1st	2nd	3rd	Win & Pl
Hurdles	4	2	1	1	15207
Career Total	7	3	1	1	18933

125	9/02	Bang	2m1f C(0-135)HHdl	GD	£6695
118	9/02	Strf	2m110y D(0-125)HHdl	G-F	£4810
116	12/01	Donc	2m4f E Hdl	GD	£3402

Total win prize-money £14907

Going: Sf: 0-0 GS: 0-0 Gd: 1-1 GF: - Fm: 1-3
Distance: 2m/2m3: 2-4 2m4-2m7: 0-0 3m+: 0-0
Track: LH: 2-3 RH: 0-1 Tight: 2-2 Gall: 0-1
Aids: Bl: 0-0 Vi: 0-0 Tstrap: 0-0
Best Rating: 128 10/02 Weth 2m gd-fm Hdl

Useful hurdler; useful stayer on the Flat; has taken well to hurdles, winning fair handicaps in the autumn of 2002; stays 2m 4f but is effective at shorter; broke his duck over fences on third attempt, his first clear round, at Sedgefield in July; looks most effective on a sound surface.

Virtuoso

93(98h)   (100h)83

9-y-o ch g Suave Dancer (USA)-Creake (Derring Do)
B G Powell The Arkle Bar Partnership

Placings:4115/2F5/254402562/21130406415/3144645-
66646   (3547)
2002/03: 19⁶G, 16⁶S, 19⁶G, 21⁴S, 16⁶G,

	Starts	1st	2nd	3rd	Win & Pl
Hurdles	1	0	0	0	0
Chases	4	0	0	0	314
Career Total	39	6	5	2	32304
115	12/01	Wwck	2m110y	D(0-125)HCh		SFT	£3900
115	4/01	Newb	2m2f110yD Ch		SFT	£3978
115	10/00	Sthl	2m	E(0-115)HCh		SFT	£3454
115	10/00	Sthl	2m	E Ch		HVY	£4192
114	12/97	Wwck	2m	E Hdl		GD	£2773
117	11/97	Uttx	2m	E Hdl		G-S	£2442
				Total win prize-money £20741

Going: Sf: 0-2 GS: 0-0 Gd: 0-3 GF: - Fm: 0-0
Distance: 2m/2m3: 0-4 2m4-2m7: 0-1 3m+: 0-0
Track: LH: 0-3 RH: 0-2 Tight: 0-2 Gall: 0-0
Aids: Bl: 0-0 Vi: 0-0 Tstrap: 0-0
Best Rating: 131 10/98 Weth 2m   good   Hdl

Plating-class handicap chaser, he is effective at trips of around two miles and goes well on ground ranging from good to heavy.

Viscount Bankes

33

5-y-o ch g Clantime-Bee Dee Dancer (Ballacashtal (CAN))
W G M Turner T Lightbowne

Placings:60-P   (4021)
2002/03: 17⁵S,

	Starts	1st	2nd	3rd	Win & Pl
Hurdles	1	0	0	0	0
Career Total	3	0	0	0	0

Going: Sf: 0-1 GS: 0-0 Gd: 0-0 GF: 0-0 Fm: 0-0
Distance: 2m/2m3: 0-1 2m4-2m7: 0-0 3m+: 0-0
Track: LH: 0-0 RH: 0-1 Tight: 0-0 Gall: 0-0
Aids: Bl: 0-0 Vi: 0-0 Tstrap: 0-0
Best Rating: 33 4/02 Hrfd 2m1f   gd-fm Hdl

Visibility (FR)

116   119

4-y-o gr g Linamix (FR)-Visor (USA) (Mr Prospector (USA))
M C Pipe (A Fabre 9/9) Jim Weeden

Placings:32145   (4152)
2002/03: 16⁵S, 17²GS, 16¹HY, 16⁴S, 16⁵G,

	Starts	1st	2nd	3rd	Win & Pl
Hurdles	5	1	1	1	8808
Career Total	5	1	1	1	8808
119	2/03	Leic	2m	D Hdl	HVY	£5135
				Total win prize-money £5135

Going: Sf: 1-3 GS: 0-1 Gd: 0-1 GF: - Fm: 0-0
Distance: 2m/2m3: 1-5 2m4-2m7: 0-0 3m+: 0-0
Track: LH: 0-3 RH: 1-2 Tight: 0-0 Gall: 0-2
Aids: Bl: 0-0 Vi: 0-0 Tstrap: 0-0
Best Rating: 119 2/03 Leic 2m   heavy Hdl

Fair hurdler; ex-French; improving with racing; handles very soft ground well; should stay two and a half miles.

Vital Issue (IRE)

11-y-o b/br g Electric-Dreamello (Bargello)
M J Brown P S Johnson

Placings:1/4412/1UP2/P10   (0414)
2002/03: 25⁶G, 34¹G, 28⁶GF,

	Starts	1st	2nd	3rd	Win & Pl
Chases	3	1	0	0	3105
Career Total	12	4	2	0	13965
108	5/02	Uttx	4m2f	H Ch	GD	£3104
108	6/00	Strf	3m	H Ch	GD	£3770
108	3/98	Carl	3m110y	E Hdl	HVY	£2430
113	3/97	List	2m	NHF	SFT	£2712
			Total win prize-money £12018

Going: Sf: 0-0 GS: 0-0 Gd: 1-2 GF: - Fm: 0-1
Distance: 2m/2m3: 0-0 2m4-2m7: 0-0 3m+: 1-3
Track: LH: 1-3 RH: 0-0 Tight: 0-2 Gall: 0-0
Aids: Bl: 0-0 Vi: 0-0 Tstrap: 0-0
Best Rating: 121 3/98 Uttx 2m4f110y good   Hdl

Hunter chaser, stays marathon trips.

Vitelucy

107   76

4-y-o b f Vettori (IRE)-Classic Line (Last Tycoon)
Miss S J Wilton (A M Balding 12/2) John Pointon And Sons

Placings:42   (4266)
2002/03: 17⁴S, 16²GF,

	Starts	1st	2nd	3rd	Win & Pl
Hurdles	2	0	1	0	1265
Career Total	2	0	1	0	1265

Going: Sf: 0-1 GS: 0-0 Gd: 0-0 GF: - Fm: 0-1
Distance: 2m/2m3: 0-2 2m4-2m7: 0-0 3m+: 0-0
Track: LH: 0-2 RH: 0-0 Tight: 0-2 Gall: 0-0
Aids: Bl: 0-0 Vi: 0-0 Tstrap: 0-0
Best Rating: 76 3/03 Sthl 2m   gd-fm Hdl

Viva Bingo (IRE)

87   46

7-y-o ch g Phardante (FR)-Kitty Frisk (Prince Tenderfoot (USA))
M J Gingell (D P Kelly 20/10) Whistlejacket Partnership

Placings:0-23500PP00   (4679)
2002/03: 16²YS, 16³G, 16⁵G, 16⁶G, 16⁶S, 23⁸S, 17⁶HY, 20⁹GF, 16⁹GF,

	Starts	1st	2nd	3rd	Win & Pl
NH Flat	4	0	1	1	1270
Hurdles	5	0	0	0	0
Career Total	10	0	1	1	1270

Going: Sf: 0-3 GS: 0-0 Gd: 0-3 GF: - Fm: 0-2
Distance: 2m/2m3: 0-7 2m4-2m7: 0-1 3m+: 0-1
Track: LH: 0-4 RH: 0-3 Tight: 0-3 Gall: 0-1
Aids: Bl: 0-0 Vi: 0-0 Tstrap: 0-0
Best Rating: 96 9/02 DRoy 2m   good NHF

Placed in bumpers when trained in Ireland.

Vivaldi Rose (IRE)

93(89c)   (37c)63

8-y-o b m Cataldi-Peaceful Rose (Roselier (FR))
L Lungo Mrs S J Matthews

Placings:0600-P03P4   (4660)
2002/03: 16⁶G, 23⁸G, 21³S, 21⁸G, 20⁴GF,

	Starts	1st	2nd	3rd	Win & Pl
Hurdles	3	0	0	1	473
Chases	2	0	0	0	345
Career Total	9	0	0	1	818

Going: Sf: 0-1 GS: 0-0 Gd: 0-3 GF: - Fm: 0-1
Distance: 2m/2m3: 0-1 2m4-2m7: 0-4 3m+: 0-0
Track: LH: 0-4 RH: 0-1 Tight: 0-2 Gall: 0-0
Aids: Bl: 0-0 Vi: 0-0 Tstrap: 0-0
Best Rating: 87 5/01 Ayr 2m   gd-fm NHF

Plating-class hurdler/chaser, held in weak company; best effort on soft ground.

Vodka Bleu (FR)

99f   117+f

4-y-o b g Pistolet Bleu (IRE)-Viva Vodka (FR) (Crystal Glitters (USA))
M C Pipe (Edward U Hales 12/1) D A Johnson

Placings:11U   (4481)
2002/03: 16¹S, 16¹G, 17ᵁG,

	Starts	1st	2nd	3rd	Win & Pl
NH Flat	3	2	0	0	7666
Career Total	3	2	0	0	7666
117	3/03	Hayd	2m	H NHF	GD	£2065
117	1/03	Leop	2m	NHF	SFT	£5600
			Total win prize-money £7666

Going: Sf: 1-1 GS: 0-0 Gd: 1-2 GF: - Fm: 0-0
Distance: 2m/2m3: 2-3 2m4-2m7: 0-0 3m+: 0-0
Track: LH: 1-1 RH: 0-0 Tight: 0-0 Gall: 0-0
Aids: Bl: 0-0 Vi: 0-0 Tstrap: 0-0
Best Rating: 117 3/03 Hayd 2m   good NHF

Fair performer; winner of a bumper at Leopardstown in January; changed hands for a big sum and followed up at Haydock two months later; unseated rider at halfway when well fancied in Grade Two at Aintree.

Vodka Inferno (IRE)

101   81

6-y-o ch g Moscow Society (USA)-Corrie Lough (IRE) (The Parson)
C R Egerton Magdenta

Placings:03-30P   (3166)
2002/03: 16³GS, 16⁶GS, 25⁸G,

	Starts	1st	2nd	3rd	Win & Pl
NH Flat	2	0	0	1	254
Hurdles	1	0	0	0	0
Career Total	5	0	0	2	599

Going: Sf: 0-0 GS: 0-2 Gd: 0-1 GF: - Fm: 0-0
Distance: 2m/2m3: 0-2 2m4-2m7: 0-0 3m+: 0-1
Track: LH: 0-3 RH: 0-0 Tight: 0-2 Gall: 0-0
Aids: Bl: 0-0 Vi: 0-0 Tstrap: 0-0
Best Rating: 97 11/02 Chel 2m110y gd-sft NHF

Plating-class hurdler; showed ability in bumpers; runner-up in weak novice hurdles at Hexham and Market Rasen in the summer; stays three miles; not a good jumper.

Vol Solitaire (FR)

110(107h)   (141h)152

5-y-o b g Loup Solitaire (USA)-Vol Sauvage (FR) (Always Fair (USA))
P F Nicholls B C Marshall

Placings:4/324315130125-1F1211421   (4554)
2002/03: 17⁵S, 16⁶G, 16¹G, 16²G, 16¹S, 17¹GS, 16⁴G, 16²G, 20¹G.

	Starts	1st	2nd	3rd	Win & Pl
Chases	9	5	2	0	83996
Career Total	22	8	4	3	144966
152 4/03 Ayr	2m4f	A Ch		GD	£21700
135 3/03 Kels	2m1f	C Ch		G-S	£7995
141 12/02 Chel	2m110y	B Ch		SFT	£12495
131 11/02 Wwck	2m110y	C Ch		GD	£7163
126 10/02 Bang	2m1f110yD Ch			SFT	£5408
131 4/02 Chep	2m11f	B HHdl		G-S	£10172
133 1/02 Chel	2m11f	A Hdl		HVY	£15000
113 12/01 Leic	2m	E Hdl		HVY	£3052
				Total win prize-money	£82986

Going: Sf: 2-2 GS: 1-1 Gd: 2-6 GF: - Fm: 0-0
Distance: 2m/2m3: 4-8 2m4-2m7: 1-1 3m+: 0-0
Track: LH: 5-8 RH: 0-1 Tight: 2-3 Gall: 1-2
Aids: Bl: 0-0 Vi: 0-0 Tstrap: 0-0
Best Rating: 152 4/03 Ayr 2m4f good Ch

Smart ex-French novice chaser; thereabouts in good novice company throughout 2002/03 season including beating Golden Alpha at Cheltenham in December; improved for the step up to two miles four when winning valuable novices event at Ayr in April; effective on good ground, ideally suited by testing conditions; very much suited by forcing tactics; jumps well; tough and genuine.

Volano (FR)

111   126

5-y-o b g Pistolet Bleu (IRE)-Vouivre (FR) (Matahawk)
N J Henderson   Thurloe Finsbury

Placings:12P-504F   (4088)
2002/03: 16⁵S, 16⁰HY, 17⁴GS, 16⁶GS,

	Starts	1st	2nd	3rd	Win & Pl
Hurdles	4	0	0	0	1755
Career Total	7	1	1	0	7460
126 2/02 Sand	2m110y D Hdl			SFT	£4348
			Total win prize-money		£4349

Going: Sf: 0-2 GS: 0-2 Gd: 0-0 GF: - Fm: 0-0
Distance: 2m/2m3: 0-4 2m4-2m7: 0-0 3m+: 0-0
Track: LH: 0-3 RH: 0-1 Tight: 0-1 Gall: 0-2
Aids: Bl: 0-0 Vi: 0-0 Tstrap: 0-0
Best Rating: 126 3/03 Strf 2m110y gd-sft Hdl

Useful handicap hurdler; showed an impressive turn of foot to win his hurdle debut in February 2002, but has been held in better company since; acts on a soft surface.

Vrubel (IRE)

82   46

4-y-o ch g Entrenneur-Renzola (Dragonara Palace (USA))
H J Collingridge (N A Callaghan 24/10) V Smith

Placings:P0   (4148)
2002/03: 16⁵HY, 16⁰G,

	Starts	1st	2nd	3rd	Win & Pl
Hurdles	2	0	0	0	
Career Total	2	0	0	0	

Going: Sf: 0-1 GS: 0-0 Gd: 0-1 GF: - Fm: 0-0
Distance: 2m/2m3: 0-2 2m4-2m7: 0-0 3m+: 0-0
Track: LH: 0-1 RH: 0-1 Tight: 0-1 Gall: 0-0
Aids: Bl: 0-0 Vi: 0-0 Tstrap: 0-0
Best Rating: 46 3/03 Fknm 2m good Hdl

Vulcan Lane (NZ)

92   75

6-y-o ch g Star Way-Smudged (NZ) (Nassipour (USA))

N B Mason   N B Mason

Placings:004   (3227)
2002/03: 16⁰S, 16⁰G, 17⁴HY,

	Starts	1st	2nd	3rd	Win & Pl
Hurdles	3	0	0	0	348
Career Total	3	0	0	0	348

Going: Sf: 0-2 GS: 0-0 Gd: 0-1 GF: - Fm: 0-0
Distance: 2m/2m3: 0-3 2m4-2m7: 0-0 3m+: 0-0
Track: LH: 0-2 RH: 0-1 Tight: 0-1 Gall: 0-0
Aids: Bl: 0-0 Vi: 0-0 Tstrap: 0-0
Best Rating: 75 1/03 Sedg 2m1f heavy Hdl

Flat winner in native New Zealand, only modest form over hurdles here so far.

Waders (IRE)

9-y-o b g Good Thyne (USA)-Lochda (Crash Course)
Miss Gayle Evans (Mrs A M Thorpe 14/5) Miss Gayle Evans

Placings:446P/R3P1P/UP0F-5   (4736)
2002/03: 24⁵GF,

	Starts	1st	2nd	3rd	Win & Pl
Chases	1	0	0	0	
Career Total	14	1	0	1	4010
80 8/00 Cttml	3m2f	E Ch		G-S	£3560
			Total win prize-money		£3560

Going: Sf: 0-0 GS: 0-0 Gd: 0-0 GF: - Fm: 0-1
Distance: 2m/2m3: 0-0 2m4-2m7: 0-0 3m+: 0-1
Track: LH: 0-1 RH: 0-0 Tight: 0-0 Gall: 0-0
Aids: Bl: 0-0 Vi: 0-0 Tstrap: 0-0
Best Rating: 100 11/99 Worc 2m gd-sft NHF

Wadsworth (NZ)

102   101

10-y-o b g Kirmann-Guard The Gold (NZ) (Imperial Guard)
B P J Baugh   M W & A N Harris

Placings:30/006P/2311363-36   (0920a)
2002/03: 16³GF, 18⁶Y,

	Starts	1st	2nd	3rd	Win & Pl
Hurdles	2	0	0	1	580
Career Total	15	2	1	5	10073
101 7/01 Wolv	2m	E(0-105)HHdl		G-F	£2940
90 7/01 Wolv	2m	E Hdl		G-S	£2374
			Total win prize-money		£5314

Going: Sf: 0-0 GS: 0-0 Gd: 0-0 GF: - Fm: 0-1
Distance: 2m/2m3: 0-2 2m4-2m7: 0-0 3m+: 0-1
Track: LH: 0-1 RH: 0-1 Tight: 0-0 Gall: 0-0
Aids: Bl: 0-0 Vi: 0-0 Tstrap: 0-0
Best Rating: 101 8/01 Gway 2m2f gd-yld Hdl

Moderate hurdler; stays two miles, acts on any ground.

Waffles Of Amin

74   53

6-y-o b g Owington-Alzianah (Alzao (USA))
S Kirk   S Kirk

Placings:00   (3597)
2002/03: 16⁰G, 17⁰S,

	Starts	1st	2nd	3rd	Win & Pl
Hurdles	2	0	0	0	
Career Total	2	0	0	0	

Going: Sf: 0-1 GS: 0-0 Gd: 0-1 GF: - Fm: 0-0
Distance: 2m/2m3: 0-2 2m4-2m7: 0-0 3m+: 0-0
Track: LH: 0-1 RH: 0-1 Tight: 0-1 Gall: 0-1
Aids: Bl: 0-0 Vi: 0-0 Tstrap: 0-0
Best Rating: 53 12/02 Newb 2m110y good Hdl

Waggy (IRE)

7-y-o b g Cataldi-Energance (IRE) (Salmon Leap (USA))
S E H Sherwood   Mrs A Gordon

Placings:05P   (3787)
2002/03: 16⁰G, 16⁵GF, 26⁰PG,

	Starts	1st	2nd	3rd	Win & Pl
NH Flat	2	0	0	0	0
Hurdles	1	0	0	0	0
Career Total	3	0	0	0	0

Going: Sf: 0-0 GS: 0-0 Gd: 0-0 GF: - Fm: 0-1
Distance: 2m/2m3: 0-2 2m4-2m7: 0-0 3m+: 0-1
Track: LH: 0-1 RH: 0-2 Tight: 0-0 Gall: 0-1
Aids: Bl: 0-0 Vi: 0-0 Tstrap: 0-0
Best Rating: 81 6/02 Hntg 2m110y gd-fm NHF

Wagner (IRE)

96(112h)   (118h)110+

6-y-o b/br g Lure (USA)-Tapaculo (Tap On Wood)
Jonjo O Neill   Ossian Construction Ltd

Placings:21/00120143   (4774)
2002/03: 16⁶G, 17⁰G, 20¹S, 21²S, 20⁰S, 24¹GS, 24⁴GS, 27³G,

	Starts	1st	2nd	3rd	Win & Pl
Hurdles	8	2	1	1	11524
Career Total	10	3	2	1	14678
118 3/03 MRas	3m	D(0-115)HHdl		G-S	£4667
109 10/02 Bang	2m4f	A(0-110)HHdl		SFT	£4134
88 10/00 Hexm	2m	E Hdl		HVY	£2327
			Total win prize-money		£11129

Going: Sf: 1-3 GS: 1-2 Gd: 0-3 GF: - Fm: 0-0
Distance: 2m/2m3: 0-2 2m4-2m7: 1-3 3m+: 1-3
Track: LH: 1-5 RH: 1-2 Tight: 2-4 Gall: 0-1
Aids: Bl: 0-0 Vi: 0-0 Tstrap: 0-0
Best Rating: 118 3/03 MRas 3m gd-sft Hdl

Modest hurdler; injured after some decent form as a juvenile; impressive when winning on seasonal debut at Bangor in October 2002; won again after a break when stepped up to 3m at Market Rasen March 2003; landed 2m 6f handicap at Newton Abbot in June; no match for the improving Captain Zinzan off 11lb higher mark next time; ready winner on chase debut; stays 3m plus; likes soft ground but handles good to firm.

Wahiba Sands

112   154

10-y-o b g Pharly (FR)-Lovely Noor (USA) (Fappiano (USA))
M C Pipe   D A Johnson

Placings:11230/12/112U6/P2125/110022-36643553 (4790)
2002/03: 16⁵S, 24⁵S, 16⁶G, 19⁴GS, 16³G, 20⁵G, 21⁵G, 16³G,

	Starts	1st	2nd	3rd	Win & Pl
Chases	8	0	3	0	37749
Career Total	31	8	7	4	225653
161 12/01 Asct	2m	B HCh		GD	£16825
154 11/01 Asct	2m3f110yA HCh			GD	£30000
141 1/01 Donc	2m110y D Ch			GD	£4088
159 11/99 Asct	2m4f	A Hdl		GD	£15475
161 11/99 Winc	2m	A HHdl		GD	£14875
155 11/98 Newb	2m110y A(0-145)HHdl			SFT	£19290

| 131 | 12/97 | Asct | 2m110y | A Hdl | G-S | £8918 |
| 123 | 12/97 | Leic | 2m | E Hdl | SFT | £2784 |

Total win prize-money £112256

Going: Sf: 0-2 GS: 0-1 Gd: 0-5 GF: - Fm: 0-0
Distance: 2m/2m3: 0-4 2m4-2m7: 0-3 3m+: 0-1
Track: LH: 0-2 RH: 0-6 Tight: 0-1 Gall: 0-1
Aids: Bl: 0-0 Vi: 0-1 Tstrap: 0-0
Best Rating: 161 4/02 Aint 2m4f good Ch

Smart chaser; best form includes defeat of Best Mate in the First National Gold Cup in November 2001 and a length second to Native Upmanship at Aintree in April 2002; well below that form this term including when fitted with cheekpieces or visor; goes particularly well fresh; effective from two miles to two miles five, does not stay three miles; acts on any ground.

Waimea Bay

90f   62f

4-y-o b f Karinga Bay-Smart In Sable (Roscoe Blake)
P R Hedger M McD Hooker

Placings:2   (4697)
2002/03: 17²G,

	Starts	1st	2nd	3rd	Win & Pl
NH Flat	1	0	1	0	856
Career Total	1	0	1	0	856

Going: Sf: 0-0 GS: 0-0 Gd: 0-1 GF: - Fm: 0-0
Distance: 2m/2m3: 0-1 2m4-2m7: 0-0 3m+: 0-0
Track: LH: 0-1 RH: 0-0 Tight: 0-1 Gall: 0-0
Aids: Bl: 0-0 Vi: 0-0 Tstrap: 0-0
Best Rating: 58 4/03 NAbb 2m1f good NHF

Moderate second in a bumper on her debut.

Wain Mountain

102   (114h)138

7-y-o b g Unfuwain (USA)-Mountain Memory (High Top)
J A B Old W J Smith And M D Dudley

Placings:1/5321P/1122-24   (2606)
2002/03: 19³HY, 19⁴GS,

	Starts	1st	2nd	3rd	Win & Pl
Chases	2	0	1	0	3298
Career Total	12	4	4	1	32426
131	1/02	Uttx	3m2f	E Ch	HVY	£3207
128	12/01	Uttx	2m5f	D Ch	SFT	£4104
136	2/01	Hayd	2m7f110yB	HHdl	HVY	£8767
120	2/00	Leic	2m	E Hdl	HVY	£2800

Total win prize-money £18880

Going: Sf: 0-1 GS: 0-0 Gd: 0-0 GF: - Fm: 0-0
Distance: 2m/2m3: 0-0 2m4-2m7: 0-2 3m+: 0-0
Track: LH: 0-1 RH: 0-0 Tight: 0-1 Gall: 0-0
Aids: Bl: 0-0 Vi: 0-0 Tstrap: 0-0
Best Rating: 138 11/02 Chep 2m3f110y heavy Ch

Useful chaser; tough staying hurdler, revels in heavy ground and stays three miles two.

Wainak (USA)

105   87

5-y-o b g Silver Hawk (USA)-Cask (Be My Chief (USA))
Miss Lucinda V Russell (I Semple 21/6) William A Powrie

Placings:50-22342433   (4749)
2002/03: 16²GS, 17²G, 16⁴GF, 16⁴GF, 20²S, 20⁴GS, 20³G,

	Starts	1st	2nd	3rd	Win & Pl
Hurdles	8	0	3	3	6843
Career Total	10	0	3	3	6843

Going: Sf: 0-1 GS: 0-3 Gd: 0-2 GF: - Fm: 0-2
Distance: 2m/2m3: 0-4 2m4-2m7: 0-4 3m+: 0-0
Track: LH: 0-4 RH: 0-4 Tight: 0-2 Gall: 0-0
Aids: Bl: 0-0 Vi: 0-1 Tstrap: 0-0
Best Rating: 91 12/02 Ayr 2m4f gd-sft Hdl

Plating-class hurdler; effective on good ground.

Wait For The Will (USA)

112   115

7-y-o ch g Seeking The Gold (USA)-You d Be Surprised (USA) (Blushing Groom (FR))
G L Moore Rdm Racing

Placings:3/3-2   (0057)
2002/03: 17²G,

	Starts	1st	2nd	3rd	Win & Pl
Hurdles	1	0	1	0	820
Career Total	3	0	1	2	1636

Going: Sf: 0-0 GS: 0-0 Gd: 0-1 GF: - Fm: 0-0
Distance: 2m/2m3: 0-1 2m4-2m7: 0-0 3m+: 0-0
Track: LH: 0-0 RH: 0-1 Tight: 0-1 Gall: 0-0
Aids: Bl: 0-0 Vi: 0-0 Tstrap: 0-0
Best Rating: 104 10/99 Kemp 2m gd-fm Hdl

Fair novice hurdler; ready winner of 2m 1f novice hurdle at Newton Abbot May 2003; ran well in defeat next time; best at around two miles; acts on fast ground; does not always find much for pressure.

Wait For This (IRE)

97(98c)   (105c)105

8-y-o b g Torus-Bar You Try (Bargello)
C J Down J B Radford

Placings:0442/41PP21-4PP00   (1547)
2002/03: 24⁴GF, 28²GF, 25²GF, 22⁰GF, 22⁰F,

	Starts	1st	2nd	3rd	Win & Pl
Hurdles	2	0	0	0	0
Chases	3	0	0	0	108
Career Total	15	2	2	0	7465
105	4/02	Asct	3m110y	H Ch	G-F	£2749
105	5/01	Tntn	3m110y	E Hdl	FRM	£3087

Total win prize-money £5837

Going: Sf: 0-0 GS: 0-0 Gd: 0-0 GF: - Fm: 0-0
Distance: 2m/2m3: 0-0 2m4-2m7: 0-1 3m+: 0-4
Track: LH: 0-3 RH: 0-2 Tight: 0-3 Gall: 0-0
Aids: Bl: 0-1 Vi: 0-0 Tstrap: 0-3
Best Rating: 105 4/02 Asct 3m110y gd-fm Ch

Modest hurdler; winner over hurdles in 2001, hunter chasing in 2002. Stays three miles, appreciates a sound surface.

Wakeup Smiling (IRE)

101f   95f

5-y-o b g Norwich-Blackmiller Lady (Bonne Noel)
Miss E C Lavelle The Wakeup Partnership

Placings:033   (4431)
2002/03: 16⁵HY, 16⁵G, 18³GF,

	Starts	1st	2nd	3rd	Win & Pl
NH Flat	3	0	0	2	845
Career Total	3	0	0	2	845

Going: Sf: 0-1 GS: 0-0 Gd: 0-1 GF: - Fm: 0-1

Distance: 2m/2m3: 0-3 2m4-2m7: 0-0 3m+: 0-0
Track: LH: 0-1 RH: 0-2 Tight: 0-0 Gall: 0-1
Aids: Bl: 0-0 Vi: 0-0 Tstrap: 0-0
Best Rating: 95 3/03 Plum 2m2f gd-fm NHF

Modest form in bumpers.

Walcot Lad (IRE)

99   83

7-y-o b g Jurado (USA)-Butty Miss (Menelek)
B A Pearce Five Men And A Horse

Placings:300/0U0000040-30553   (1178)
2002/03: 22³GF, 19⁴GF, 16⁵GS, 20⁵GF, 16³GF,

	Starts	1st	2nd	3rd	Win & Pl
Hurdles	5	0	0	2	1386
Career Total	17	0	0	3	1598

Going: Sf: 0-0 GS: 0-1 Gd: 0-0 GF: - Fm: 0-4
Distance: 2m/2m3: 0-3 2m4-2m7: 0-2 3m+: 0-0
Track: LH: 0-4 RH: 0-0 Tight: 0-5 Gall: 0-0
Aids: Bl: 0-5 Vi: 0-0 Tstrap: 0-0
Best Rating: 102 1/01 Chep 2m110y gd-sft NHF

Walk On By

101   92

9-y-o gr g Terimon-Try G S (Hotfoot)
J S King Mrs R M Hill

Placings:2362/30P35040/U23243652/1533453/2-326F01P4UP   (1936)
2002/03: 16³GF, 16²S, 16⁶GF, 21²GF, 20⁰S, 22¹G, 20²GF, 19⁴G, 26ᵁG, 24²GS,

	Starts	1st	2nd	3rd	Win & Pl
Hurdles	1	0	0	0	0
Chases	9	1	1	1	5187
Career Total	39	2	7	9	19143
92	8/02	Font	2m6f	F(0-90)HCh	GD	£3867
95	5/00	Font	2m2f	F Ch	GD	£2340

Total win prize-money £6208

Going: Sf: 0-2 GS: 0-1 Gd: 1-3 GF: - Fm: 0-4
Distance: 2m/2m3: 0-3 2m4-2m7: 1-5 3m+: 0-2
Track: LH: 0-7 RH: 0-1 Tight: 1-5 Gall: 0-0
Aids: Bl: 1-6 Vi: 0-0 Tstrap: 0-0
Best Rating: 98 3/98 Winc 2m good Hdl

Modest handicap chaser, effective at up to two miles six, and best suited by a sound surface.

Walk On Seas (IRE)

31   139

8-y-o b g Shardari-Over The Seas (North Summit)
F Doumen Peter Hans Vogt

Placings:220P0/12-0044022
2002/03: 19⁰VS, 19⁰HO, 18⁴HY, 21⁴G, 18⁰HO, 19²VS, 20²VS,

	Starts	1st	2nd	3rd	Win & Pl
Hurdles	7	0	2	0	42004
Career Total	14	1	5	0	79222
	9/01	Autl	2m4f110y	Hdl	SFT	£10669

Total win prize-money £10669

Going: Sf: 0-1 GS: 0-0 Gd: 0-1 GF: - Fm: 0-0
Distance: 2m/2m3: 0-3 2m4-2m7: 0-4 3m+: 0-0
Track: LH: 0-4 RH: 0-0 Tight: 0-0 Gall: 0-1
Aids: Bl: 0-0 Vi: 0-0 Tstrap: 0-1
Best Rating: 139 12/02 Chel 2m5f110y good Hdl

Walter Plinge

105(108c)   (76c)**75**

7-y-o b g Theatrical Charmer-Carousel Zingira (Reesh)
A G Juckes Tony Cocum

Placings:36/5/F0615300-35PPP01   (4706)
2002/03: 21³GF, 21⁵G, 20⁸GF, 24⁸G, 17⁸GS, 21⁰G, 20¹G,

	Starts	1st	2nd	3rd	Win & Pl
Hurdles	5	1	0	0	2513
Chases	2	0	1	0	465
Career Total	18	2	0	3	5223
75	4/03	Uttx	2m4f110yG(0-90)HHdl	GD	£2513
72	7/01	Wolv	2m4f110yG Hdl	G-F	£1570
			Total win prize-money £4084		

Going: Sf: 0-0 GS: 0-1 Gd: 1-4 GF: - Fm: 0-2
Distance: 2m/2m3: 0-1 **2m4-2m7: 1-5** 3m+: 0-1
Track: **LH: 1-7** RH: 0-0 Tight: 0-3 Gall: 0-0
Aids: Bl: 0-0 Vi: 0-0 **Tstrap: 1-2**
Best Rating: 76 5/02 Sedg 2m5f   gd-fm Ch

Plating-class hurdler; has only ever won in selling company; effective at around two and a half miles; acts on good ground.

Walter's Destiny

104   **106**

11-y-o ch g White Prince (USA)-Tearful Sarah (Rugantino)
C W Mitchell C W Mitchell

Placings:60/0505/22P1144/3263401/**F3/3U1UP4P/341-**
P443P3P   (4624)
2002/03: 25⁸G, 25⁴GS, 25⁴GS, 25³GS, 24⁸GS, 25³GF, 26⁸GF,

	Starts	1st	2nd	3rd	Win & Pl
Chases	7	0	0	2	3415
Career Total	39	5	3	7	32031
115	11/01	Extr	2m7f110yD(0-125)HCh	G-F	£5050
114	12/00	Winc	3m1f110yD(0-125)HCh	G-S	£9441
101	4/99	Extr	2m7f	D(0-125)HHdl	G-S	£3078
95	2/98	Ling	2m3f110yF(0-100)HHdl	GD	£2126
86	1/98	Winc	2m6f	F(0-105)HHdl	GD	£2122
			Total win prize-money £21819		

Going: Sf: 0-0 GS: 0-4 Gd: 0-1 GF: - Fm: 0-2
Distance: 2m/2m3: 0-0 2m4-2m7: 0-0 3m+: 0-7
Track: LH: 0-1 RH: 0-6 Tight: 0-1 Gall: 0-0
Aids: Bl: 0-0 Vi: 0-0 Tstrap: 0-0
Best Rating: 115 11/01 Extr 2m7f110y gd-fm Ch

Modest handicap chaser; stays three miles; does not want the ground too soft.

Waltzing Along (IRE)

90f   **96f**

5-y-o b g Presenting-Clyduffe Fairy (Belfalas)
L Lungo Andrew Duncan, Vicky Royds & James Barber

Placings:34   (4593)
2002/03: 16³S, 16⁴G,

	Starts	1st	2nd	3rd	Win & Pl
NH Flat	2	0	0	1	277
Career Total	2	0	0	1	277

Going: Sf: 0-1 GS: 0-0 Gd: 0-1 GF: - Fm: 0-0
Distance: 2m/2m3: 0-2 2m4-2m7: 0-0 3m+: 0-0
Track: LH: 0-2 RH: 0-0 Tight: 0-1 Gall: 0-0
Aids: Bl: 0-0 Vi: 0-0 Tstrap: 0-0
Best Rating: 96 4/03 Hexm 2m110y good NHF

Showed some ability in bumpers.

Wanna Shout

92   **51**

5-y-o b m Missed Flight-Lulu (Polar Falcon (USA))
R Dickin E R C Beech & B Wilkinson

Placings:6-P060   (2168)
2002/03: 16⁸GF, 16⁰G, 16⁶G, 19⁹GS,

	Starts	1st	2nd	3rd	Win & Pl
Hurdles	4	0	0	0	
Career Total	5	0	0	0	

Going: Sf: 0-1 GS: 0-0 Gd: 0-2 GF: - Fm: 0-1
Distance: 2m/2m3: 0-4 2m4-2m7: 0-0 3m+: 0-1
Track: LH: 0-4 RH: 0-0 Tight: 0-1 Gall: 0-0
Aids: Bl: 0-1 Vi: 0-0 Tstrap: 0-0
Best Rating: 51 11/01 Wrwck 2m   good Hdl

War Paint (IRE)

87(72c)   (97c)**44**

11-y-o gr g Zaffaran (USA)-Rosy Posy (IRE) (Roselier (FR))
M Sheppard The Haven Partnership (Cheltenham)

Placings:40/6/4/4-0   (2168)
2002/03: 19⁰GS,

	Starts	1st	2nd	3rd	Win & Pl
Hurdles	1	0	0	0	
Career Total	6	0	0	0	216

Going: Sf: 0-0 GS: 0-1 Gd: 0-0 GF: - Fm: 0-0
Distance: 2m/2m3: 0-1 2m4-2m7: 0-0 3m+: 0-0
Track: LH: 0-1 RH: 0-0 Tight: 0-0 Gall: 0-0
Aids: Bl: 0-0 Vi: 0-0 Tstrap: 0-0
Best Rating: 103 1/99 Donc 2m4f   gd-sft Hdl

War Tune

107   **99**

7-y-o b g Warrshan (USA)-Keen Melody (USA) (Sharpen Up)
B D Leavy (G F Edwards 3/6) The Five Nations Partnership

Placings:04/63/056F32FP20-521   (0614)
2002/03: 21⁵GS, 20²G, 20¹GF,

	Starts	1st	2nd	3rd	Win & Pl
Hurdles	2	1	1	0	5937
Chases	1	0	0	0	0
Career Total	17	1	3	2	8336
95	6/02	Worc	2m4f	E Hdl	G-F	£2681
			Total win prize-money £2681		

Going: Sf: 0-0 GS: 0-1 Gd: 0-1 GF: - Fm: 1-1
Distance: 2m/2m3: 0-2 **2m4-2m7:** 1-4 3m+: 0-0
Track: **LH: 1-3** RH: 0-0 Tight: 0-1 Gall: 0-0
Aids: Bl: 0-0 Vi: 0-0 Tstrap: 0-0
Best Rating: 99 6/02 Uttx 2m4f110y good Hdl

Modest hurdler. Stays two and a half miles, seems effective on most ground.

Ward Seventeen

86f   **75f**

6-y-o b g Supreme Leader-Kerris Melody (Furry Glen)
R S Brookhouse R S Brookhouse

Placings:0   (2064)
2002/03: 17⁰S,

	Starts	1st	2nd	3rd	Win & Pl
NH Flat	1	0	0	0	
Career Total	1	0	0	0	

Wareyth (USA)

67   **28**

4-y-o b/br g Shuailaan (USA)-Bahr Alsalaam (USA) (Riverman (USA))
R H Buckler (Jane Southcombe 2/11) Chris Pugsley

Placings:P0P0U   (4698)
2002/03: 16⁸GS, 17⁰GS, 16⁸GS, 17⁰F, 16ᵁGF,

	Starts	1st	2nd	3rd	Win & Pl
Hurdles	5	0	0	0	
Career Total	5	0	0	0	

Going: Sf: 0-0 GS: 0-3 Gd: 0-0 GF: - Fm: 0-0
Distance: 2m/2m3: 0-5 2m4-2m7: 0-0 3m+: 0-0
Track: LH: 0-2 RH: 0-3 Tight: 0-3 Gall: 0-0
Aids: Bl: 0-0 Vi: 0-0 Tstrap: 0-0
Best Rating: 30 2/03 Extr 2m1f   gd-sft Hdl

Warjan (FR)

110   **131**

6-y-o b g Beaudelaire (USA)-Twilight Mood (USA) (Devil's Bag (USA))
R T Phillips Graeme Love

Placings:325155/0P-1000   (4136)
2002/03: 16¹S, 16⁹S, 16⁹G, 17⁹G,

	Starts	1st	2nd	3rd	Win & Pl
Hurdles	4	1	1	0	7118
Career Total	12	2	1	1	23743
131	11/02	Sand	2m110y	C(0-130)HHdl	SFT	£7117
128	3/01	MRas	2m1f110yD Hdl	GD	£3654
			Total win prize-money £10772		

Going: Sf: 1-2 GS: 0-0 Gd: 0-2 GF: - Fm: 0-0
Distance: 2m/2m3: 1-4 2m4-2m7: 0-0 3m+: 0-0
Track: LH: 0-3 **RH: 1-1** Tight: 0-0 Gall: 0-3
Aids: Bl: 0-0 Vi: 0-0 Tstrap: 0-0
Best Rating: 131 2/03 Newb 2m110y good Hdl

Useful handicap hurdler; suited by two miles; handles cut.

Warm Front

73f   **54f**

6-y-o b m Bustino-Princess Hotpot (IRE) (King's Ride)
Miss H C Knight Mrs Shirley Brasher

Placings:4S!0   (0280)
2002/03: 17⁰S,

	Starts	1st	2nd	3rd	Win & Pl
NH Flat	1	0	0	0	
Career Total	3	0	0	0	0

Going: Sf: 0-1 GS: 0-0 Gd: 0-0 GF: - Fm: 0-0
Distance: 2m/2m3: 0-1 2m4-2m7: 0-0 3m+: 0-0
Track: LH: 0-1 RH: 0-0 Tight: 0-1 Gall: 0-0
Aids: Bl: 0-0 Vi: 0-0 Tstrap: 0-0
Best Rating: 78 2/01 Muss 2m   good NHF

Warminghamsharpish

91   **90+**

6-y-o b m Nalchik (USA)-Tilstock Maid (Rolfe (USA))
W M Brisbourne The Bentley Boys

Placings:*0521*   (1459)
2002/03: 17⁰S, 16⁵G, 16²GF, 16¹F,

	Starts	1st	2nd	3rd	Win & Pl
NH Flat	4	1	1	0	3109
Career Total	**4**	**1**	**1**	**0**	**3109**
86	10/02 Ludl	2m		H NHF	FRM £2586
				Total win prize-money £2587	

Going:	Sf: 0-1 GS: 0-0 Gd: 0-1 GF: - Fm: 1-2	
Distance:	2m/2m3: 1-4 2m4-2m7: 0-0 3m+: 0-0	
Track:	LH: 0-3 RH: 1-1 Tight: 0-1 Gall: 0-0	
Aids:	Bl: 0-0 Vi: 0-0 Tstrap: 0-0	
Best Rating:	92 10/02 Hexm 2m110y	gd-fm NHF

Moderate hurdler/bumper performer; won minor bumper at Ludlow October 2002; first run since; won novice hurdle at same track May 2003; narrow winner under a penalty on her return at Sedgefield in July; handles fast ground.

Warner For Players (IRE)

12-y-o b g Good Thyne (USA)-Bramble Hatch (Pry)
S Wynne David Manning Associates

Placings:*331/5451/36P/200/2/115234-2*   (3491)
2002/03: 20²S,

	Starts	1st	2nd	3rd	Win & Pl
Chases	1	0	1	0	678
Career Total	**21**	**4**	**4**	**4**	**19449**
105	12/01 Hrfd	3m1f110yE Ch		SFT	£3178
110	11/01 MRas	2m4f	E Ch	G-S	£4200
119	2/97 Ling	2m7f	E Hdl	HVY	£2729
111	4/96 NAbb	2m1f	H NHF	G-S	£1313
				Total win prize-money £11421	

Going:	Sf: 0-1 GS: 0-0 Gd: 0-0 GF: - Fm: 0-0	
Distance:	2m/2m3: 0-0 2m4-2m7: 0-1 3m+: 0-0	
Track:	LH: 0-1 RH: 0-0 Tight: 0-1 Gall: 0-0	
Aids:	Bl: 0-0 Vi: 0-0 Tstrap: 0-0	
Best Rating:	137 2/00 Hayd 2m7f110y	heavy Hdl

Hunter chaser nowadays, runner-up at Bangor in February.

Warrbow

12-y-o gr g Fast Frigate-Dam Unregistered (Damsire Unknown)
S Garrott S Garrott

Placings:*P*   (0312)
2002/03: 21ᴾG,

	Starts	1st	2nd	3rd	Win & Pl
Chases	1	0	0	0	
Career Total	**1**	**0**	**0**	**0**	

Going:	Sf: 0-0 GS: 0-0 Gd: 0-1 GF: - Fm: 0-0	
Distance:	2m/2m3: 0-0 2m4-2m7: 0-1 3m+: 0-0	
Track:	LH: 0-0 RH: 0-1 Tight: 0-1 Gall: 0-0	
Aids:	Bl: 0-0 Vi: 0-0 Tstrap: 0-0	
Best Rating:	0 5/02 Folk 2m5f	good Ch

Warren Boy

13-y-o b g Hotfoot-Artaius Rose (FR) (Artaius (USA))

T L Jones F J Ayres

Placings:*1/4F4PP0/0P/0/F*   (0034)
2002/03: 16ᶠGF,

	Starts	1st	2nd	3rd	Win & Pl
Chases	1	0	0	0	
Career Total	**11**	**1**	**0**	**0**	**2383**
99	4/98 Chel	2m110y	H Ch	GD	£2305
				Total win prize-money £2306	

Going:	Sf: 0-0 GS: 0-0 Gd: 0-0 GF: - Fm: 0-1	
Distance:	2m/2m3: 0-1 2m4-2m7: 0-0 3m+: 0-0	
Track:	LH: 0-1 RH: 0-0 Tight: 0-0 Gall: 0-1	
Aids:	Bl: 0-0 Vi: 0-0 Tstrap: 0-0	
Best Rating:	99 4/98 Chel 2m110y	good Ch

Warrlin

106   (70h) **106**

9-y-o b g Warrshan (USA)-Lahin (Rainbow Quest (USA))
C W Fairhurst Glasgow House Racing Syndicate

Placings:*202562360/1523123F/044031134/03200030U0/0 2P3343-2F1*   (1322)
2002/03: 25²GS, 16ᶠGF, 22¹GF,

	Starts	1st	2nd	3rd	Win & Pl
Chases	3	1	1	0	8520
Career Total	**46**	**5**	**8**	**10**	**34001**
87	9/02 MRas	2m6f110yC Ch		G-F	£7540
107	2/00 MRas	2m1f110yF(0-110)HHdl		G-S	£1858
100	2/00 Kels	2m2f	E(0-115)HHdl	G-S	£5850
103	12/98 Sedg	2m1f	E(0-100)HHdl	SFT	£2757
93	8/98 Ctml	2m1f110yE Hdl		G-S	£2477
				Total win prize-money £20485	

Going:	Sf: 0-0 GS: 0-1 Gd: 0-0 GF: - Fm: 1-2	
Distance:	2m/2m3: 0-1 2m4-2m7: 1-1 3m+: 0-1	
Track:	LH: 0-2 RH: 1-1 Tight: 1-1 Gall: 0-0	
Aids:	Bl: 0-0 Vi: 0-0 Tstrap: 0-0	
Best Rating:	109 11/00 Newc 2m	gd-sft Hdl

Modest chaser; winner over hurdles, he has shown fair form over fences. Acts on most types of ground and is effective at around two miles.

Warton Crag

7-y-o b g Tina s Pet-Majestic Form (IRE) (Double Schwartz)
D Moffatt Mrs G A Turnbull

Placings:*0-P*   (0475)
2002/03: 17ᴾGS,

	Starts	1st	2nd	3rd	Win & Pl
Hurdles	1	0	0	0	
Career Total	**2**	**0**	**0**	**0**	

Going:	Sf: 0-0 GS: 0-1 Gd: 0-0 GF: - Fm: 0-0	
Distance:	2m/2m3: 0-1 2m4-2m7: 0-0 3m+: 0-0	
Track:	LH: 0-1 RH: 0-0 Tight: 0-1 Gall: 0-0	
Aids:	Bl: 0-0 Vi: 0-0 Tstrap: 0-0	
Best Rating:	0 6/02 Ctml 2m1f110y	gd-sft Hdl

Wartorn (IRE)

108   **99**

8-y-o b g Warcraft (USA)-Alice Minkthorn (Party Mink)
J S King Miss S Douglas-Pennant

Placings:*450-50022031*   (4004)
2002/03: 19⁵GS, 21⁰S, 17⁰GS, 19²S, 19²S, 21⁰HY, 21³S, 22¹S,

	Starts	1st	2nd	3rd	Win & Pl
Hurdles	8	1	2	1	6198

	Starts	1st	2nd	3rd	Win & Pl
Career Total	**11**	**1**	**2**	**1**	**6198**
98	3/03 Winc	2m6f	F(0-100)HHdl	SFT	£3346
				Total win prize-money £3346	

Going:	Sf: 1-6 GS: 0-2 Gd: 0-0 GF: - Fm: 0-0	
Distance:	2m/2m3: 0-2 2m4-2m7: 1-6 3m+: 0-0	
Track:	LH: 0-4 RH: 1-4 Tight: 0-2 Gall: 0-3	
Aids:	Bl: 0-0 Vi: 0-0 Tstrap: 0-0	
Best Rating:	98 3/03 Winc 2m6f	soft Hdl

Moderate hurdler; stays 3m; seems to act on all types of ground.

Was A Drive (IRE)

96   **81**

9-y-o b g Yashgan-Alan s Rosalinda (Prefairy)
Miss Kate Milligan E C Gordon

Placings:*PP/30P14P-P3F0*   (4588)
2002/03: 20⁰G, 20³HY, 21ᶠS, 20⁰G,

	Starts	1st	2nd	3rd	Win & Pl
Chases	4	0	0	1	542
Career Total	**12**	**1**	**0**	**2**	**4336**
89	3/02 Hexm	2m4f110yF(0-100)HCh		HVY	£3066
				Total win prize-money £3066	

Going:	Sf: 0-2 GS: 0-0 Gd: 0-2 GF: - Fm: 0-0	
Distance:	2m/2m3: 0-0 2m4-2m7: 0-4 3m+: 0-0	
Track:	LH: 0-4 RH: 0-0 Tight: 0-1 Gall: 0-0	
Aids:	Bl: 0-0 Vi: 0-0 Tstrap: 0-0	
Best Rating:	89 3/02 Carl 2m4f	gd-sft Ch

Plating-class chaser, suited by two and a half miles, handles good ground and has won on heavy.

Washington Pink (IRE)

102   **98**

4-y-o b g Tagula (IRE)-Little Red Rose (Precocious)
C Grant (M R Channon 29/5) Ian W Glenton

Placings:*3221340*   (1537)
2002/03: 17³GS, 17²G, 17²G, 16¹G, 16³GF, 16⁴GF, 16⁰GF,

	Starts	1st	2nd	3rd	Win & Pl
Hurdles	7	1	2	2	7556
Career Total	**7**	**1**	**2**	**2**	**7556**
98	9/02 Uttx	2m	D Hdl	GD	£4121
				Total win prize-money £4121	

Going:	Sf: 0-0 GS: 0-1 Gd: 1-3 GF: - Fm: 0-3	
Distance:	2m/2m3: 1-7 2m4-2m7: 0-0 3m+: 0-0	
Track:	LH: 1-5 RH: 0-2 Tight: 0-4 Gall: 0-0	
Aids:	Bl: 0-0 Vi: 0-0 Tstrap: 0-0	
Best Rating:	98 9/02 Uttx 2m	good Hdl

Moderate early-season juvenile hurdler, winner at Uttoxeter; acts on a sound surface.

Wassl Street (IRE)

11-y-o b g Dancing Brave (USA)-One Way Street (Habitat)
R Lee (K A Morgan 15/5) Rex Norton

Placings:*1/41P412/P4/4201/113/P*   (3574)
2002/03: 23ᴾS,

	Starts	1st	2nd	3rd	Win & Pl
Chases	1	0	0	0	
Career Total	**17**	**6**	**2**	**1**	**18252**
108	6/00 MRas	2m4f	E Ch	G-S	£3715
110	5/00 Worc	2m7f110yE Ch		GD	£2983
104	4/00 MRas	2m5f110yF(0-100)HHdl		SFT	£1551
109	3/97 Towc	2m	D(0-120)HHdl	SFT	£2714

107 12/96 Leic 2m4f110yD(0-120)HHdl G-S £3028
111 4/96 Prth 2m4f110yE Hdl SFT £2108
Total win prize-money £16100

Going:	Sf: 0-1 GS: 0-0 Gd: 0-0 GF: - Fm: 0-0
Distance:	2m/2m3: 0-0 2m4-2m7: 0-0 3m+: 0-1
Track:	LH: 0-0 RH: 0-1 Tight: 0-0 Gall: 0-0
Aids:	Bl: 0-0 Vi: 0-0 Tstrap: 0-0
Best Rating:	111 4/96 Prth 2m4f110y soft Hdl

Watch It
84f   80f

5-y-o b g Sea Raven (IRE)-Magic Penny (Sharrood (USA))
M Todhunter Mrs Allison Stamper

Placings:6-04   (4437)
2002/03: 16GS, 164G,

	Starts	1st	2nd	3rd	Win & Pl
NH Flat	2	0	0	0	0
Career Total	3	0	0	0	0

Going:	Sf: 0-0 GS: 0-1 Gd: 0-1 GF: - Fm: 0-0
Distance:	2m/2m3: 0-2 2m4-2m7: 0-0 3m+: 0-0
Track:	LH: 0-2 RH: 0-0 Tight: 0-0 Gall: 0-0
Aids:	Bl: 0-0 Vi: 0-0 Tstrap: 0-0
Best Rating:	80 4/03 Newc 2m good NHF

Modest form in bumpers so far.

Watch The Dove
97   98

6-y-o b g Afzal-Spot The Dove (Riberetto)
C Tizzard Exors of the late L G Tizzard

Placings:024-362246   (4311)
2002/03: 16GS, 206S, 172S, 172S, 174GS, 216G,

	Starts	1st	2nd	3rd	Win & Pl
Hurdles	6	0	2	1	4224
Career Total	9	0	3	1	4914

Going:	Sf: 0-3 GS: 0-1 Gd: 0-2 GF: - Fm: 0-0
Distance:	2m/2m3: 0-4 2m4-2m7: 0-2 3m+: 0-0
Track:	LH: 0-2 RH: 0-4 Tight: 0-2 Gall: 0-1
Aids:	Bl: 0-0 Vi: 0-0 Tstrap: 0-0
Best Rating:	100 3/02 NAbb 2m1f good NHF

Moderate hurdler; from the same family as 1994 Champion Hurdler Flakey Dove; has shown ability in bumpers and novice hurdles; gives the impression he may be best at around two and a half miles.

Watchyourback (NZ)

9-y-o ch g Watchman (NZ)-English Lass (NZ) (English Harbour)
M Trott (Miss K Marks 6/5) M Trott

Placings:23150P/2F   (4667)
2002/03: 242G, 21FG,

	Starts	1st	2nd	3rd	Win & Pl
Chases	2	0	1	0	442
Career Total	8	1	2	1	3102

91 7/00 Wolv 2m4f110yG Hdl GD £1463
Total win prize-money £1463

Going:	Sf: 0-0 GS: 0-0 Gd: 0-2 GF: - Fm: 0-0
Distance:	2m/2m3: 0-0 2m4-2m7: 0-1 3m+: 0-1
Track:	LH: 0-2 RH: 0-0 Tight: 0-0 Gall: 0-0
Aids:	Bl: 0-0 Vi: 0-2 Tstrap: 0-2
Best Rating:	91 7/00 Wolv 2m4f110y good Hdl

Moderate pointer/hunter chaser; stays three miles; acts on a sound surface; not the best of jumpers.

Water Font (IRE)

11-y-o b g Lafontaine (USA)-Belle Savenay (Coquelin (USA))
Mrs J Williamson (Jonjo O Neill 30/6) G & P Barker Ltd/globe Engineering

Placings:4P03P/0043121/1/03FP011P/P24PPU342/P111P-PPP   (3513)
2002/03: 28PG, 32PGF, 28PG,

	Starts	1st	2nd	3rd	Win & Pl
Chases	3	0	0	0	
Career Total	38	8	3	4	42337

115 6/01 Prth 3m C(0-135)HCh G-F £13975
105 6/01 Prth 3m C(0-115)HCh FRM £4979
105 5/01 Newc 3m F(0-90)HCh G-F £3094
105 3/00 Catt 3m1f110yF(0-100)HCh G-F £2626
87 2/00 Muss 3m E(0-105)HCh GD £4290
97 5/98 Uttx 3m110y G(0-105)HHdl G-F £2442
97 4/98 Sedg 2m5f110yE(0-100)HHdl GD £4034
90 3/98 Newc 2m4f G(0-95)HHdl G-F £1668
Total win prize-money £37109

Going:	Sf: 0-0 GS: 0-0 Gd: 0-2 GF: - Fm: 0-1
Distance:	2m/2m3: 0-0 2m4-2m7: 0-0 3m+: 0-3
Track:	LH: 0-2 RH: 0-0 Tight: 0-0 Gall: 0-0
Aids:	Bl: 0-1 Vi: 0-0 Tstrap: 0-0
Best Rating:	115 6/01 Prth 3m gd-fm Ch

Fair staying chaser at his best but poor hunter chaser nowadays.

Water King (USA)
99   89

4-y-o b c Irish River (FR)-Brookshield Baby (IRE) (Sadler s Wells (USA))
G Brown (E A L Dunlop 6/9) Mrs Amanda Killick

Placings:00435   (4631)
2002/03: 16G, 17GHY, 164G, 16G, 16GF,

	Starts	1st	2nd	3rd	Win & Pl
Hurdles	5	0	0	1	1013
Career Total	5	0	0	1	1013

Going:	Sf: 0-2 GS: 0-0 Gd: 0-2 GF: - Fm: 0-1
Distance:	2m/2m3: 0-5 2m4-2m7: 0-0 3m+: 0-0
Track:	LH: 0-2 RH: 0-3 Tight: 0-2 Gall: 0-1
Aids:	Bl: 0-0 Vi: 0-0 Tstrap: 0-0
Best Rating:	89 3/03 Ludl 2m good Hdl

Plating-class hurdler.

Water Sports (IRE)
93   73

5-y-o b m Marju (IRE)-Water Splash (USA) (Little Current (USA))
N A Twiston-Davies (P R Webber 16/1) John Duggan

Placings:00P3   (3923)
2002/03: 16G, 16S, 21PS, 20S,

	Starts	1st	2nd	3rd	Win & Pl
Hurdles	4	0	0	1	385
Career Total	4	0	0	1	385

| Going: | Sf: 0-3 GS: 0-0 Gd: 0-1 GF: - Fm: 0-0 |

Waterberg (IRE)
113(96h)   (92h)120

8-y-o b g Sadler s Wells (USA)-Pretoria (Habitat)
H D Daly R M Kirkland

Placings:1/142/122/161311-2P4044   (4393)
2002/03: 222S, 24PG, 224HY, 22GS, 24GS, 20G,

	Starts	1st	2nd	3rd	Win & Pl
Hurdles	2	0	0	0	654
Chases	4	0	1	0	2842
Career Total	19	7	4	1	36231

118 4/02 Prth 3m C Ch GD £7241
107 4/02 Carl 2m4f C Ch G-F £6987
118 2/02 Ludl 3m D Ch G-S £4134
116 1/01 Hntg 2m4f110yD Hdl GD £3892
119 1/01 Leic 2m4f110yD Hdl HVY £3510
119 12/99 Uttx 2m H NHF SFT £1742
112 4/99 MRas 1m5f110yH NHF SFT £1517
Total win prize-money £29024

Going:	Sf: 0-2 GS: 0-2 Gd: 0-2 GF: - Fm: 0-0
Distance:	2m/2m3: 0-0 2m4-2m7: 0-4 3m+: 0-2
Track:	LH: 0-3 RH: 0-3 Tight: 0-2 Gall: 0-1
Aids:	Bl: 0-2 Vi: 0-0 Tstrap: 0-0
Best Rating:	119 3/01 Hayd 2m4f heavy Hdl

Fair chaser; useful chaser at his best; won three novice chases in the spring of 2002 before his form deteriorated; appreciated a return to 3m with back-to-back wins at Stratford in the summer of 2003; likes fast ground but out of sorts including when tried in blinkers; has broken blood vessels.

Waterhall
92   81

10-y-o b g River God (USA)-Tuneful Queen (Queens Hussar)
J M P Eustace Mrs T S Matthews

Placings:FP/0030255/F/05P26   (4120)
2002/03: 20G, 22GS, 22PHY, 262G, 266G,

	Starts	1st	2nd	3rd	Win & Pl
Hurdles	5	0	2	1	781
Career Total	15	0	2	1	1683

Going:	Sf: 0-1 GS: 0-1 Gd: 0-3 GF: - Fm: 0-0
Distance:	2m/2m3: 0-0 2m4-2m7: 0-3 3m+: 0-2
Track:	LH: 0-1 RH: 0-4 Tight: 0-2 Gall: 0-2
Aids:	Bl: 0-0 Vi: 0-0 Tstrap: 0-0
Best Rating:	84 11/99 MRas 2m1f110y gd-sft Hdl

Waterlily (IRE)
106f   91+f

4-y-o b f Revoque (IRE)-Cochineal (USA) (Vaguely Noble)
M J Wallace Mrs R G Hillen

Placings:1   (4672)
2002/03: 161G,

	Starts	1st	2nd	3rd	Win & Pl
NH Flat	1	1	0	0	1904
Career Total	1	1	0	0	1904

91 4/03 Fknm 2m H NHF GD £1904
Total win prize-money £1904

| Going: | Sf: 0-0 GS: 0-0 Gd: 1-1 GF: - Fm: 0-0 |

Column 1

Distance:	2m/2m3: 1-1 2m4-2m7: 0-0 3m+: 0-0
Track:	LH: 1-1 RH: 0-0 Tight: 1-1 Gall: 0-0
Aids:	Bl: 0-0 Vi: 0-0 Tstrap: 0-0
Best Rating:	91 4/03 Fknm 2m good NHF

Moderate bumper performer; half-sister to two juvenile Flat winners; clear winner on debut in a Fakenham bumper in April 2003; acts on good ground.

Waterloo Park (IRE)

7-y-o b m Alphabatim (USA)-Waterloo Sunset (Deep Run)
P M J Doyle (Noel T Chance 11/5) John I O Byrne

Placings: 100-2P   (0935a)
2002/03: 16²GF, 16PGY,

	Starts	1st	2nd	3rd	Win & Pl
NH Flat	1	0	1	0	480
Hurdles	1	0	0	0	0
Career Total	5	1	1	0	2041
112 11/01 Wwck 2m		H NHF		GD	£1561
			Total win prize-money £1561		

Going:	Sf: 0-0 GS: 0-0 Gd: 0-0 GF: - Fm: 0-1
Distance:	2m/2m3: 0-2 2m4-2m7: 0-0 3m+: 0-0
Track:	LH: 0-1 RH: 0-1 Tight: 0-0 Gall: 0-0
Aids:	Bl: 0-0 Vi: 0-0 Tstrap: 0-0
Best Rating:	112 11/01 Wwck 2m good NHF

Modest performer; made an impressive debut when easily winning a Warwick bumper in November 2001, but was held subsequently.

Watership Down (IRE)

100(97h)   (70h)91
6-y-o b g Dolphin Street (FR)-Persian Myth (Persian Bold)
B G Powell D & J Newell

Placings: 6/064155-5220P   (2080)
2002/03: 23⁵GF, 21²GF, 23²G, 24⁴G, 24³HY,

	Starts	1st	2nd	3rd	Win & Pl
Chases	5	0	2	0	2797
Career Total	12	1	2	0	6148
87 10/01 Sedg 2m5f		E Ch		GD	£3019
			Total win prize-money £3019		

Going:	Sf: 0-1 GS: 0-0 Gd: 0-2 GF: - Fm: 0-2
Distance:	2m/2m3: 0-0 2m4-2m7: 0-1 3m+: 0-4
Track:	LH: 0-2 RH: 0-3 Tight: 0-1 Gall: 0-0
Aids:	Bl: 0-0 Vi: 0-0 Tstrap: 0-0
Best Rating:	91 10/02 Extr 2m7f110y good Ch

Moderate chaser; got off the mark as a four-year-old in a novice chase in October 2001, but has been held in handicaps since. Stays well. Acts on good ground.

Waterspray (AUS)

96   99
5-y-o ch g Lake Coniston (IRE)-Forain (NZ) (Nassipour (USA))
J L Spearing Bache Silk

Placings: 0351   (4468)
2002/03: 16⁰GS, 16³S, 19⁵GS, 17¹F,

	Starts	1st	2nd	3rd	Win & Pl
Hurdles	4	1	0	1	4082
Career Total	4	1	0	1	4082
99 4/03 Tntn 2m1f		E(0-110)HHdl		FRM	£3640
			Total win prize-money £3640		

Going:	Sf: 0-1 GS: 0-2 Gd: 0-0 GF: - Fm: 1-1

Column 2

Distance:	2m/2m3: 1-3 2m4-2m7: 0-1 3m+: 0-0
Track:	LH: 0-3 RH: 1-1 Tight: 1-1 Gall: 0-1
Aids:	Bl: 0-0 Vi: 0-0 Tstrap: 0-0
Best Rating:	99 4/03 Tntn 2m1f firm Hdl

Moderate hurdler; showed ability on the Flat in native Australia; got off the mark on handicap debut at Taunton in early April; acts well on fast; best at around two miles at present.

Watson Lake (IRE)

99f   115f
5-y-o b g Be My Native (USA)-Magneeto (IRE) (Brush Aside (USA))
Noel Meade (Edward U Hales 8/11) John Corr

Placings: 4-210   (4115)
2002/03: 16²S, 16¹HY, 16⁰G,

	Starts	1st	2nd	3rd	Win & Pl
NH Flat	3	1	1	0	5752
Career Total	4	1	1	0	6058
115 11/02 DRoy 2m		NHF		HVY	£4868
			Total win prize-money £4868		

Going:	Sf: 1-2 GS: 0-0 Gd: 0-1 GF: - Fm: 0-0
Distance:	2m/2m3: 1-3 2m4-2m7: 0-0 3m+: 0-0
Track:	LH: 0-1 RH: 0-0 Tight: 0-0 Gall: 0-0
Aids:	Bl: 0-0 Vi: 0-0 Tstrap: 0-0
Best Rating:	115 11/02 DRoy 2m heavy NHF

fair bumper performer; suited by testing ground.

Wave Rock

110(107h)   (124 h)137
8-y-o br g Tragic Role (USA)-Moonscape (Ribero)
P J Hobbs Sterling Racing Syndicate

Placings: 23223413/23U1312F3211F3/141332P1/6523552-12530P4FPU   (4792)
2002/03: 19¹G, 20²G, 21⁵G, 20³GS, 21⁰G, 20PG, 16⁴HY, 16FG, 16PG, 20⁴G,

	Starts	1st	2nd	3rd	Win & Pl
Hurdles	2	1	1	0	5515
Chases	8	0	0	1	13049
Career Total	47	9	10	11	113643
124 5/02 Hrfd	2m3f110yD(0-120)HHdl	GD	£3406		
134 4/01 Ayr	2m	B HCh	G-F	£13474	
134 11/00 Chel	2m	B(0-145)HCh	G-S	£14088	
124 5/00 Punc	2m2f	Ch	GD	£6072	
129 3/00 Hntg	2m110y	E Ch	SFT	£2983	
122 2/00 Chep	2m110y	D Ch	SFT	£4134	
114 11/99 Wwck	2m	D Ch	GD	£4290	
110 8/99 Worc	2m	D(0-125)HHdl	G-S	£3029	
109 2/99 Sand	2m110y	D Hdl	G-S	£2853	
		Total win prize-money £54334			

Going:	Sf: 0-1 GS: 0-1 Gd: 1-8 GF: - Fm: 0-0
Distance:	2m/2m3: 0-3 2m4-2m7: 1-7 3m+: 0-0
Track:	LH: 0-5 RH: 1-5 Tight: 1-1 Gall: 0-3
Aids:	Bl: 1-10 Vi: 0-0 Tstrap: 0-0
Best Rating:	144 4/02 Sand 2m4f110y good Ch

Useful handicap chaser; usually blinkered, he tends to carry his head awkwardly but is genuine; stays two and a half miles and appears to act on any ground; a fine third in the 2002 Thomas Pink Gold Cup.

Waverbeck (IRE)

58f   42f
6-y-o ch m Accordion-Belle Dame (IRE) (Executive Perk)
F S Storey F S Storey

Placings: 50   (2769)

Column 3

2002/03: 16⁵HY, 16⁰GS,

	Starts	1st	2nd	3rd	Win & Pl
NH Flat	2	0	0	0	0
Career Total	2	0	0	0	0

Going:	Sf: 0-1 GS: 0-1 Gd: 0-0 GF: - Fm: 0-0
Distance:	2m/2m3: 0-2 2m4-2m7: 0-0 3m+: 0-0
Track:	LH: 0-1 RH: 0-1 Tight: 0-1 Gall: 0-0
Aids:	Bl: 0-0 Vi: 0-0 Tstrap: 0-0
Best Rating:	42 11/02 Hexm 2m110y heavy NHF

Waynesworld (IRE)

5-y-o b g Petoski-Mariners Mirror (Julio Mariner)
D J Caro F J Mills & W Mills

Placings: 00P   (4527)
2002/03: 16⁰GS, 16⁰GS, 20PG,

	Starts	1st	2nd	3rd	Win & Pl
NH Flat	2	0	0	0	0
Hurdles	1	0	0	0	0
Career Total	3	0	0	0	0

Going:	Sf: 0-0 GS: 0-2 Gd: 0-1 GF: - Fm: 0-0
Distance:	2m/2m3: 0-2 2m4-2m7: 0-1 3m+: 0-0
Track:	LH: 0-2 RH: 0-1 Tight: 0-0 Gall: 0-1
Best Rating:	91 12/02 Donc 2m110y gd-sft NHF

Wayward Buttons

98(90h)   (76h)96
9-y-o b g Nomadic Way (USA)-Lady Buttons (New Brig)
M Todhunter (C P Dennis 15/3) Mrs A W Scott-Harden And Mrs A Nicholson

Placings: 06145PP-45   (4519)
2002/03: 25⁴GS, 21⁵G,

	Starts	1st	2nd	3rd	Win & Pl
Chases	2	0	0	0	0
Career Total	9	1	0	0	3409
95 11/01 Sedg 2m5f		E Ch		SFT	£3090
			Total win prize-money £3091		

Going:	Sf: 0-0 GS: 0-1 Gd: 0-1 GF: - Fm: 0-0
Distance:	2m/2m3: 0-0 2m4-2m7: 0-1 3m+: 0-1
Track:	LH: 0-1 RH: 0-1 Tight: 0-2 Gall: 0-0
Aids:	Bl: 0-0 Vi: 0-0 Tstrap: 0-1
Best Rating:	108 12/01 Muss 3m gd-fm Ch

Moderate winning chaser/pointer; rarely finds as much as he promises and is finding it hard to add to his record; has worn a tongue strap.

Wayward Cove

6-y-o b m Karinga Bay-Wayward Pam (Pamroy)
R J Hodges Mrs E M Charlton

Placings: 0-0F5   (1444)
2002/03: 17⁵GF, 16FGF, 19⁰F,

	Starts	1st	2nd	3rd	Win & Pl
NH Flat	1	0	0	0	0
Hurdles	2	0	0	0	0
Career Total	4	0	0	0	0

Going:	Sf: 0-0 GS: 0-0 Gd: 0-0 GF: - Fm: 0-3
Distance:	2m/2m3: 0-3 2m4-2m7: 0-0 3m+: 0-0
Track:	LH: 0-2 RH: 0-1 Tight: 0-2 Gall: 0-0

Aids: BI: 0-0 Vi: 0-0 Tstrap: 0-0
Best Rating: 72 11/01 Extr 2m1f gd-fm NHF

Wazaro (IRE)

62   62

6-y-o b h Alzao (USA)-Wildbahn (Be My Guest (USA))
C Von Der Recke (H Blume 22/6) Stall Sunderberg

Placings:265   (4086)
2002/03: 17²S, 18⁶G, 19⁵GS,

	Starts	1st	2nd	3rd	Win & Pl
Hurdles	3	0	1	0	1300
Career Total	3	0	1	0	1300

Going: Sf: 0-1 GS: 0-1 Gd: 0-1 GF: - Fm: 0-0
Distance: 2m/2m3: 0-3 2m4-2m7: 0-0 3m+: 0-0
Track: LH: 0-1 RH: 0-1 Tight: 0-2 Gall: 0-0
Aids: BI: 0-0 Vi: 0-0 Tstrap: 0-0
Best Rating: 80 7/02 MRas 2m1f110y soft Hdl

German horse, distant runner-up in a novice hurdle in July 2002.

We'll Make It (IRE)

102   109

5-y-o b g Spectrum (IRE)-Walliser (Niniski (USA))
G L Moore Wayne Barr,John Ripley,D Goff,S Moss

Placings:4342430-0200123   (4634)
2002/03: 16⁵GS, 16²S, 17⁰GS, 20⁹HY, 17¹G, 16²G, 21³GF,

	Starts	1st	2nd	3rd	Win & Pl
Hurdles	7	1	2	1	7904
Career Total	14	1	3	3	10881

109 3/03 Folk 2m1f110yE(0-105)HHdl GD £3474
Total win prize-money £3474

Going: Sf: 0-2 GS: 0-2 Gd: 1-2 GF: - Fm: 0-1
Distance: 2m/2m3: 1-5 2m4-2m7: 0-2 3m+: 0-0
Track: LH: 0-3 RH: 1-4 Tight: 1-2 Gall: 0-1
Aids: BI: 1-6 Vi: 0-0 Tstrap: 0-0
Best Rating: 109 3/03 Folk 2m1f110y good Hdl

Moderate hurdler; effective over two miles; acts on good ground; usually wears blinkers.

Wearerich

78f   55f

6-y-o ch m Alflora (IRE)-Weareagrandmother (Prince Tenderfoot (USA))
P M Rich P M Rich

Placings:0P   (3337)
2002/03: 17⁰S, 17³PS,

	Starts	1st	2nd	3rd	Win & Pl
NH Flat	2	0	0	0	
Career Total	2	0	0	0	

Going: Sf: 0-2 GS: 0-0 Gd: 0-0 GF: - Fm: 0-0
Distance: 2m/2m3: 0-2 2m4-2m7: 0-0 3m+: 0-0
Track: LH: 0-0 RH: 0-1 Tight: 0-0 Gall: 0-0
Aids: BI: 0-0 Vi: 0-0 Tstrap: 0-0
Best Rating: 55 12/02 Hrfd 2m1f soft NHF

Weaver George (IRE)

109(99h)   (94h)112

13-y-o b g Flash Of Steel-Nephrite (Godswalk (USA))
W Storey Regent Decorators Ltd

Placings:F0233241/1100342U/3403F015/15241211123/11223/33F612241/52P26324/64621245/604211111F50-3P426531P05P5P   (4436)
2002/03: 25³GS, 25PG, 26⁴HY, 30²G, 24⁶GS, 21⁵G, 26³G, 25¹G, 26⁶S, 25⁹S, 25⁴HY, 25PGS, 24⁴GS, 24⁴PG,

	Starts	1st	2nd	3rd	Win & Pl
Hurdles	1	0	0	0	365
Chases	13	1	1	2	10712
Career Total	91	20	17	12	115259

118 10/02 Kels 3m1f D(0-125)HCh GD £6773
125 12/01 Kels 3m1f B(0-145)HCh G-S £10707
125 10/01 Kels 3m1f D(0-125)HCh G-S £4173
121 10/01 Carl 3m2f E(0-125)HCh G-S £3477
110 10/01 Kels 3m1f D(0-125)HCh GD £4290
105 10/01 Sedg 2m5f E(0-115)HCh GD £3987
119 11/00 Newc 2m4f D(0-125)HCh SFT £5404
121 4/99 Sedg 2m5f D(0-125)HCh G-S £4432
3/99 Newc 2m4f D(0-125)HCh SFT £3694
118 5/97 Prth 2m4f110yD(0-125)HCh SFT £3436
118 5/97 Sedg 2m5f D(0-125)HCh SFT £3821
118 2/97 Catt 2m E(0-115)HCh G-S £2842
116 2/97 Catt 2m E(0-110)HCh GD £2706
115 1/97 Sedg 2m3f D(0-120)HCh GD £3470
108 12/96 Sedg 2m110y E(0-115)HCh GD £2877
105 5/96 Sedg 2m110y E Ch FRM £2945
105 3/96 Sedg 2m1f E Ch GD £3185
107 12/94 Weth 2m (0-135)HHdl £2565
102 5/94 Weth 2m Hdl G-F £2075
91 4/94 Weth 2m Hdl £2337
Total win prize-money £79203

Going: Sf: 0-4 GS: 0-4 Gd: 1-6 GF: - Fm: 0-0
Distance: 2m/2m3: 0-0 2m4-2m7: 0-0 3m+: 1-13
Track: LH: 1-11 RH: 0-2 Tight: 1-7 Gall: 0-2
Aids: BI: 0-0 Vi: 0-0 Tstrap: 0-0
Best Rating: 129 3/99 Newc 2m4f soft Ch

Fair veteran handicap chaser, stays well; best on good or easy ground; wears cheekpieces.

Weaver Sam

24

8-y-o ch g Ron s Victory (USA)-Grove Star (Upper Case (USA))
K R Burke J Wightman

Placings:203/100/6P0-P   (2350)
2002/03: 20⁵GS,

	Starts	1st	2nd	3rd	Win & Pl
Hurdles	1	0	0	0	
Career Total	10	1	1	1	2023

100 6/99 Hexm 2m H NHF SFT £1367
Total win prize-money £1368

Going: Sf: 0-0 GS: 0-1 Gd: 0-0 GF: - Fm: 0-0
Distance: 2m/2m3: 0-0 2m4-2m7: 0-1 3m+: 0-0
Track: LH: 0-1 RH: 0-0 Tight: 0-1 Gall: 0-0
Aids: BI: 0-0 Vi: 0-0 Tstrap: 0-0
Best Rating: 109 4/99 Aint 2m110y good NHF

Weavers Choice

10-y-o ch g Sunley Builds-Wedding Song (True Song)
Mrs Joan Tice Mrs Joan Tice

Placings:4-P6   (3954)
2002/03: 22PG, 20⁶GS,

	Starts	1st	2nd	3rd	Win & Pl
Chases	2	0	0	0	0
Career Total	3	0	0	0	165

Going: Sf: 0-0 GS: 0-1 Gd: 0-1 GF: - Fm: 0-0
Distance: 2m/2m3: 0-0 2m4-2m7: 0-2 3m+: 0-0
Track: LH: 0-0 RH: 0-2 Tight: 0-0 Gall: 0-0
Aids: BI: 0-0 Vi: 0-0 Tstrap: 0-0
Best Rating: 75 3/02 Leic 2m7f110y soft Ch

Web Master (FR)

87f   103f

5-y-o b g Arctic Tern (USA)-Inesperada (Cariello (FR))
C Grant Miss S J Turner

Placings:30   (4230)
2002/03: 16³GS, 16⁰GF,

	Starts	1st	2nd	3rd	Win & Pl
NH Flat	2	0	0	1	288
Career Total	2	0	0	1	288

Going: Sf: 0-0 GS: 0-1 Gd: 0-0 GF: - Fm: 0-1
Distance: 2m/2m3: 0-2 2m4-2m7: 0-0 3m+: 0-0
Track: LH: 0-2 RH: 0-0 Tight: 0-0 Gall: 0-0
Aids: BI: 0-0 Vi: 0-0 Tstrap: 0-0
Best Rating: 103 2/03 Ayr 2m gd-sft NHF

Moderate French-bred gelding; showed ability on his debut in an Ayr bumper.

Wee Danny (IRE)

105   81+

6-y-o b g Mandalus-Bonne Bouche (Bonne Noel)
L A Dace Luke Dace

Placings:00600-0645   (1042)
2002/03: 17⁰G, 22⁵GF, 27⁴GF, 22⁵GF,

	Starts	1st	2nd	3rd	Win & Pl
Hurdles	4	0	0	0	0
Career Total	9	0	0	0	0

Going: Sf: 0-0 GS: 0-0 Gd: 0-0 GF: - Fm: 0-4
Distance: 2m/2m3: 0-1 2m4-2m7: 0-2 3m+: 0-1
Track: LH: 0-3 RH: 0-1 Tight: 0-4 Gall: 0-0
Aids: BI: 0-0 Vi: 0-0 Tstrap: 0-0
Best Rating: 88 10/01 Fair 2m good NHF

Plating-class novice hurdler; improved form since stepped up to 3m; twice narrowly beaten at Worcester in the summer of 2003; acts on fast ground.

Wee Junior

7-y-o gr g Alflora (IRE)-Sheer Gold (Yankee Gold)
O A Little D W Chilcott

Placings:P   (4736)
2002/03: 24PGF,

	Starts	1st	2nd	3rd	Win & Pl
Chases	1	0	0	0	
Career Total	1	0	0	0	

Going: Sf: 0-0 GS: 0-0 Gd: 0-0 GF: - Fm: 0-1
Distance: 2m/2m3: 0-0 2m4-2m7: 0-0 3m+: 0-1
Track: LH: 0-1 RH: 0-0 Tight: 0-0 Gall: 0-0
Aids: BI: 0-0 Vi: 0-0 Tstrap: 0-0
Best Rating: 0 4/03 Chep 3m gd-fm Ch

Wee Willow

102   71

9-y-o b m Minster Son-Peak Princess (Charlottown)

D W Whillans Chas N Whillans

Placings:050-3443 **(4374)**
2002/03: 26^{3}GS, 22^{4}S, 24^{4}HY, 27^{3}G,

	Starts	1st	2nd	3rd	Win & Pl
Hurdles	4	0	0	2	1284
Career Total	**7**	**0**	**0**	**2**	**1284**

Going: Sf: 0-2 GS: 0-1 Gd: 0-1 GF: - Fm: 0-0
Distance: 2m/2m3: 0-0 2m4-2m7: 0-1 3m+: 0-3
Track: LH: 0-4 RH: 0-0 Tight: 0-3 Gall: 0-1
Aids: Bl: 0-0 Vi: 0-0 Tstrap: 0-0
Best Rating: **71** 3/03 Sedg 3m3f110y good Hdl

Small, lightly-raced mare. Poor form so far.

Weejumpawud

90 **90**
13-y-o b m Jumbo Hirt (USA)-Weewumpawud (King Log)
Miss S E Forster C Storey

Placings:F000/0/4253/132-3 **(0022)**
2002/03: 20^{3}G,

	Starts	1st	2nd	3rd	Win & Pl
Chases	1	0	0	1	517
Career Total	**13**	**1**	**2**	**3**	**5035**

88 5/01 Sedg 2m5f H Ch GD £1620
Total win prize-money £1621

Going: Sf: 0-0 GS: 0-0 Gd: 0-1 GF: - Fm: 0-0
Distance: 2m/2m3: 0-0 2m4-2m7: 0-1 3m+: 0-0
Track: LH: 0-1 RH: 0-0 Tight: 0-0 Gall: 0-0
Aids: Bl: 0-0 Vi: 0-0 Tstrap: 0-0
Best Rating: **90** 4/02 Sedg 2m5f gd-fm Ch

Modest front-running chaser, suited by a sharp track and a sound surface, stays two miles-five.

Weet And See

90(103h) (90dh)**79**
9-y-o b g Lochnager-Simply Style (Baim (USA))
T Wall Ed Weetman (haulage & Storage) Ltd

Placings:5F003/F034056553/026011310661/03600**F**00/06350160P06**P3-5**F41000**6**00 **(1926)**
2002/03: 17^{5}G, 16^{F}GF, 16^{4}GF, 16^{1}S, 16^{0}GF, 17^{0}GF, 16^{0}GS, 16^{6}F, 16^{0}HY, 16^{0}GS,

	Starts	1st	2nd	3rd	Win & Pl
Hurdles	8	1	0	0	1959
Chases	2	0	0	0	0
Career Total	**58**	**6**	**1**	**7**	**17962**

90 7/02 Wolv 2m G Hdl SFT £1958
95 11/01 Uttx 2m F(0-100)HHdl SFT £2737
110 4/00 Uttx 2m E(0-105)HHdl HVY £2663
112 9/99 NAbb 2m1f F(0-110)HHdl G-F £2621
109 7/99 Worc 2m F(0-110)HHdl G-F £1987
102 7/99 NAbb 2m1f F(0-105)HHdl G-S £2779
Total win prize-money £14748

Going: Sf: 1-2 GS: 0-2 Gd: 0-1 GF: - Fm: 0-5
Distance: **2m/2m3: 1-10** 2m4-2m7: 0-0 3m+: 0-0
Track: **LH: 1-7** RH: 0-3 **Tight: 1-4** Gall: 0-0
Aids: Bl: 0-0 Vi: 0-0 Tstrap: 0-0
Best Rating: **112** 9/99 NAbb 2m1f gd-fm Hdl

Plating-class hurdler; still capable in modest company over hurdles as he showed when winning a seller at Wolverhampton in July 2002.

Welburn Boy

92(83h) (61h)**63**
11-y-o b g Kalaglow-Teevano (Blakeney)
M Sheppard K Jones

Placings:*030*/60P/440P**6FF**1450/**23PU510P**/433/003**P-PP**606P **(4706)**
2002/03: 25^{P}S, 26^{P}HY, 20^{6}S, 25^{0}S, 21^{6}G, 20^{P}G,

	Starts	1st	2nd	3rd	Win & Pl
Hurdles	2	0	0	0	0
Chases	4	0	0	0	0
Career Total	**38**	**2**	**1**	**5**	**10049**

90 2/00 Ludl 3m F(0-95)HCh GD £3965
83 3/99 Hrfd 3m2f F(0-95)HHdl G-S £2472
Total win prize-money £6437

Going: Sf: 0-4 GS: 0-0 Gd: 0-2 GF: - Fm: 0-0
Distance: 2m/2m3: 0-0 2m4-2m7: 0-3 3m+: 0-3
Track: LH: 0-4 RH: 0-2 Tight: 0-1 Gall: 0-0
Aids: Bl: 0-6 Vi: 0-0 Tstrap: 0-6
Best Rating: **95** 10/98 Worc 2m2f soft Hdl

A winning pointer, he is only of moderate ability over hurdles and fences.

Welcome Exchange

4-y-o b f Most Welcome-Santarem (USA) (El Gran Senor (USA))
J J Bridger Saddle Up Partnership

Placings:P **(1844)**
2002/03: 16^{P}S,

	Starts	1st	2nd	3rd	Win & Pl
Hurdles	1	0	0	0	
Career Total	**1**	**0**	**0**	**0**	

Going: Sf: 0-1 GS: 0-0 Gd: 0-0 GF: - Fm: 0-0
Distance: 2m/2m3: 0-1 2m4-2m7: 0-0 3m+: 0-0
Track: LH: 0-0 RH: 0-1 Tight: 0-0 Gall: 0-0
Aids: Bl: 0-0 Vi: 0-0 Tstrap: 0-0
Best Rating: **0** 11/02 Sand 2m110y soft Hdl

Welcome News

82f **51f**
5-y-o ch m Bob Back (USA)-Rosie O Keeffe (IRE) (Royal Fountain)
Mrs H Dalton Mrs Caroline Shaw

Placings:*0* **(4060)**
2002/03: 16^{0}S,

	Starts	1st	2nd	3rd	Win & Pl
NH Flat	1	0	0	0	
Career Total	**1**	**0**	**0**	**0**	

Going: Sf: 0-1 GS: 0-0 Gd: 0-0 GF: - Fm: 0-0
Distance: 2m/2m3: 0-1 2m4-2m7: 0-0 3m+: 0-0
Track: LH: 0-1 RH: 0-0 Tight: 0-0 Gall: 0-0
Aids: Bl: 0-0 Vi: 0-0 Tstrap: 0-0
Best Rating: **59** 3/03 Wwck 2m soft NHF

Welcome To Unos

107 **70**
6-y-o ch g Exit To Nowhere (USA)-Royal Loft (Homing)
Mrs M Reveley J & M Leisure / Unos Restaurant

Placings:343/342332 **(4793)**
2002/03: 16^{3}S, 16^{4}G, 16^{2}G, 16^{3}GS, 19^{3}S, 17^{2}GF,

	Starts	1st	2nd	3rd	Win & Pl
Hurdles	6	0	2	3	5598
Career Total	**9**	**0**	**2**	**5**	**7921**

Going: Sf: 0-2 GS: 0-1 Gd: 0-2 GF: - Fm: 0-1
Distance: 2m/2m3: 0-6 2m4-2m7: 0-0 3m+: 0-0
Track: LH: 0-6 RH: 0-0 Tight: 0-5 Gall: 0-0
Aids: Bl: 0-0 Vi: 0-0 Tstrap: 0-0
Best Rating: **105** 2/03 Ayr 2m gd-sft Hdl

Plating-class hurdler; yet to win a race but has been placed a number of times over obstacles; stays two miles-three; acts on any ground.

Weldunfrank

106 **74**
10-y-o br g Weld-Damsong (Petong)
W M Brisbourne Mrs J P McCormack

Placings:*600*/*6*P6/P05U406-2 **(0430)**
2002/03: 16^{2}GF,

	Starts	1st	2nd	3rd	Win & Pl
Hurdles	1	0	1	0	475
Career Total	**14**	**0**	**1**	**0**	**475**

Going: Sf: 0-0 GS: 0-0 Gd: 0-0 GF: - Fm: 0-1
Distance: 2m/2m3: 0-1 2m4-2m7: 0-0 3m+: 0-0
Track: LH: 0-0 RH: 0-1 Tight: 0-0 Gall: 0-1
Aids: Bl: 0-0 Vi: 0-0 Tstrap: 0-0
Best Rating: **89** 5/98 Ludl 2m gd-fm NHF

Plating-class hurdler; acts on fast ground.

Well Chief (GER)

115 **137+**
4-y-o ch g Night Shift (USA)-Wellesiena (GER) (Scenic)
M C Pipe (R Suerland 27/10) D A Johnson

Placings:1123 **(4460)**
2002/03: 17^{1}S, 16^{1}G, 17^{2}G, 16^{3}G,

	Starts	1st	2nd	3rd	Win & Pl
Hurdles	4	2	1	1	56733
Career Total	**4**	**2**	**1**	**1**	**56733**

121 2/03 Kemp 2m A Hdl GD £17400
107 2/03 Tntn 2m1f D Hdl SFT £5232
Total win prize-money £22633

Going: Sf: 1-1 GS: 0-0 Gd: 1-3 GF: - Fm: 0-0
Distance: **2m/2m3: 2-4** 2m4-2m7: 0-0 3m+: 0-0
Track: LH: 0-2 **RH: 2-2 Tight: 1-2** Gall: 0-1
Aids: Bl: 0-0 Vi: 0-0 Tstrap: 0-0
Best Rating: **137** 3/03 Chel 2m1f good Hdl

Useful hurdler; ex-German Group-class performer on the Flat; won well on his hurdles debut and took a muddling Grade 2 at Kempton on his second outing in impressive fashion; beaten a head by Spectroscope in Triumph Hurdle at Cheltenham but only third at Aintree; effective in good and soft ground.

Well Then Now Then (IRE)

105
8-y-o b m Supreme Leader-Northern Dandy (The Parson)
H D Daly Mrs A L Wood

Placings:*2232*/23-115P **(3787)**
2002/03: 24^{1}S, 24^{1}GS, 24^{5}GS, 26^{P}G,

	Starts	1st	2nd	3rd	Win & Pl
Hurdles	4	2	0	0	9167
Career Total	**10**	**2**	**4**	**2**	**12853**

117 12/02 Sthl 3m110y E Hdl G-S £2996
108 11/02 Uttx 3m110y D(0-115)HHdl SFT £5421
Total win prize-money £8417

Going: Sf: 1-1 GS: 1-2 Gd: 0-1 GF: - Fm: 0-0
Distance: 2m/2m3: 0-0 2m4-2m7: 0-0 **3m+: 2-4**
Track: **LH: 2-3** RH: 0-1 **Tight: 1-1** Gall: 0-1
Aids: Bl: 0-0 Vi: 0-0 Tstrap: 0-0
Best Rating: 117 12/02 Sthl 3m110y gd-sft Hdl

Fair staying hurdler; in the frame in each of her first six starts before getting off the mark in a mares handicap hurdle at Uttoxeter in November 2002 and followed up at Southwell the following month. Suited by a real test of stamina.

Wellfranko (IRE)

74   **40**

8-y-o b g Camden Town-Electana (Electrify)
Miss Z C Davison (Ferdy Murphy 25/10) The Secret Circle

Placings:U0001P-00   **(4425)**
2002/03: 16³GS, 16⁵GF,

	Starts	1st	2nd	3rd	Win & Pl
Hurdles	2	0	0	0	
Career Total	8	1	0	0	2667
97 4/02	Uttx 2m	E(0-100)HHdl		G-F	£2667

Total win prize-money £2667

Going: Sf: 0-0 GS: 0-1 Gd: 0-0 GF: - Fm: 0-1
Distance: 2m/2m3: 0-2 2m4-2m7: 0-1 3m+: 0-0
Track: LH: 0-2 RH: 0-0 Tight: 0-2 Gall: 0-0
Aids: Bl: 0-2 Vi: 0-0 Tstrap: 0-0
Best Rating: 97 4/02 Uttx 2m gd-fm Hdl

Showed improved form when winning novices handicap at Uttoxeter in April 2002. Can continue on the upgrade.

Wellie (IRE)

108   **93**

10-y-o b/br g Aristocracy-Sweet View (King s Ride)
S J Gilmore (Mrs K J Gilmore 13/2) S J Gilmore

Placings:06000UP523/54/54U30F4-PP521   **(4735)**
2002/03: 20⁵PS, 16⁶G, 19⁵F, 19²GF, 19¹GF,

	Starts	1st	2nd	3rd	Win & Pl
Chases	5	1	1	0	4242
Career Total	24	1	2	2	7353
93 4/03	Chep 2m3f110yG(0-90)HCh		G-F	£2646

Total win prize-money £2646

Going: Sf: 0-1 GS: 0-0 Gd: 0-0 GF: - Fm: 1-3
Distance: 2m/2m3: 0-3 **2m4-2m7: 1-2** 3m+: 0-0
Track: **LH: 1-1** RH: 0-4 Tight: 0-2 Gall: 0-0
Aids: Bl: 0-0 Vi: 0-0 Tstrap: 0-0
Best Rating: 103 1/01 Donc 2m110y good Ch

Wellington Hall (GER)

78   **99**

5-y-o b g Halling (USA)-Wells Whisper (FR) (Sadler s Wells (USA))
A Charlton (P Schiergen 6/7) Allan Darke & Tom Matthews

Placings:F0P0   **(3624)**
2002/03: 17⁵GS, 16⁶S, 16⁶HY, 16⁶S,

	Starts	1st	2nd	3rd	Win & Pl
Hurdles	4	0	0	0	
Career Total	4	0	0	0	

Going: Sf: 0-3 GS: 0-1 Gd: 0-0 GF: - Fm: 0-0
Distance: 2m/2m3: 0-4 2m4-2m7: 0-0 3m+: 0-0
Track: LH: 0-2 RH: 0-2 Tight: 0-2 Gall: 0-1
Aids: Bl: 0-1 Vi: 0-0 Tstrap: 0-0

Best Rating: 99 11/02 Tntn 2m1f gd-sft Hdl

Wellow (IRE)

(24c)85

7-y-o b g Unblest-Alpine Sunset (Auction Ring (USA))
Miss C J E Caroe D Fish

Placings:P/0PP04000006P055-P6   **(3403)**
2002/03: 19³GF, 16⁸HY,

	Starts	1st	2nd	3rd	Win & Pl
Hurdles	2	0	0	0	0
Career Total	18	0	0	0	0

Going: Sf: 0-1 GS: 0-0 Gd: 0-0 GF: - Fm: 0-1
Distance: 2m/2m3: 0-1 2m4-2m7: 0-1 3m+: 0-0
Track: LH: 0-1 RH: 0-1 Tight: 0-1 Gall: 0-0
Aids: Bl: 0-0 Vi: 0-0 Tstrap: 0-0
Best Rating: 85 3/02 Towc 2m5f gd-sft Hdl

Welsh Border

99   **120d**

5-y-o ch g Zafonic (USA)-Welsh Daylight (Welsh Pageant)
G Prodromou L Cohen

Placings:6-411R6   **(1287)**
2002/03: 17⁴GF, 17¹GS, 17¹GF, 20⁶RG, 18⁶GF,

	Starts	1st	2nd	3rd	Win & Pl
Hurdles	5	2	0	0	6809
Career Total	6	2	0	0	8309
105 8/02	Sthl 2m1f	E Hdl	G-F	£2961
120 8/02	MRas 2m1f110yD Hdl		G-S	£3848

Total win prize-money £6809

Going: Sf: 0-0 GS: 1-1 Gd: 0-1 GF: - Fm: 1-3
Distance: **2m/2m3: 2-4** 2m4-2m7: 0-1 3m+: 0-0
Track: LH: 1-3 RH: 1-2 **Tight: 1-3** Gall: 0-0
Aids: Bl: 0-0 Vi: 0-0 Tstrap: 0-0
Best Rating: 120 8/02 MRas 2m1f110y gd-sft Hdl

Fair novice hurdler; acts on fast and easy ground; stays 2m 1f; can be reluctant to start and is one to treat with caution.

Welsh Dream

103   **101**

6-y-o b g Mtoto-Morgannwg (IRE) (Simply Great (FR))
P C Haslam Mrs B M Hawkins & Mrs C Barclay

Placings:3-2   **(0041)**
2002/03: 16²GS,

	Starts	1st	2nd	3rd	Win & Pl
Hurdles	1	0	1	0	840
Career Total	2	0	1	0	1350

Going: Sf: 0-0 GS: 0-1 Gd: 0-0 GF: - Fm: 0-0
Distance: 2m/2m3: 0-1 2m4-2m7: 0-0 3m+: 0-0
Track: LH: 0-1 RH: 0-0 Tight: 0-1 Gall: 0-0
Aids: Bl: 0-0 Vi: 0-0 Tstrap: 0-0
Best Rating: 101 11/01 Newc 2m gd-sft Hdl

Moderate novice hurdler; lightly raced; broke his duck in a fair race at Cartmel; should stay further than two miles; effective with cut in the ground.

Welsh Main

105   **118+**

6-y-o br g Zafonic (USA)-Welsh Daylight (Welsh Pageant)
S J Magnier Marcus Reeder

Placings:1U-33F21   **(1539)**
2002/03: 16³GF, 16³GS, 16⁶GF, 16²GF, 16¹GF,

	Starts	1st	2nd	3rd	Win & Pl
Hurdles	5	1	1	2	11704
Career Total	7	2	1	2	15036
118 10/02	Weth 2m	B(0-140)HHdl	G-F	£8014
102 3/02	Catt 2m	E Hdl	G-S	£3332

Total win prize-money £11347

Going: Sf: 0-0 GS: 0-1 Gd: 0-0 GF: - Fm: 1-4
Distance: **2m/2m3: 1-5** 2m4-2m7: 0-0 3m+: 0-0
Track: **LH: 1-3** RH: 0-2 Tight: 0-1 Gall: 0-0
Aids: Bl: 0-0 Vi: 0-0 Tstrap: 0-0
Best Rating: 118 10/02 Weth 2m gd-fm Hdl

Fair hurdler; off the mark in a weak, slowly-run event at Catterick in March 2002 and in good form this term before winning at Wetherby. Acts on any ground.

Welsh March (IRE)

91(94h)   (74h)**85**

11-y-o b g Over The River (FR)-Welsh Tan (Welsh Saint)
G M Moore John Robson

Placings:22112/2F15PP/3532/3232121060/253-6F505P   **(3802)**
2002/03: 17⁶S, 16⁶S, 17⁵HY, 16⁶G, 24⁵S, 20⁴S,

	Starts	1st	2nd	3rd	Win & Pl
Hurdles	1	0	0	0	0
Chases	5	0	0	0	0
Career Total	34	5	9	5	40960
118 1/01	Ayr	E(0-115)HCh	G-S	£3416
118 12/00	Hayd 2m	C(0-135)HCh	HVY	£8807
127 11/98	Bang	2m4f110yC(0-130)HCh	SFT	£4879
124 3/98	Ayr	2m E Ch	SFT	£2872
112 12/97	Ayr	2m E Ch	SFT	£2784

Total win prize-money £22760

Going: Sf: 0-5 GS: 0-0 Gd: 0-1 GF: - Fm: 0-0
Distance: 2m/2m3: 0-4 2m4-2m7: 0-1 3m+: 0-1
Track: LH: 0-5 RH: 0-1 Tight: 0-1 Gall: 0-1
Aids: Bl: 0-0 Vi: 0-0 Tstrap: 0-0
Best Rating: 131 4/98 Ayr 2m good Ch

Plating-class chaser, best at two miles with cut in the ground. Suited by a flat track.

Welsh Mistress

4-y-o ch f Master Willie-Llanfihangel Lass (Gildoran)
P D Evans G E Amey

Placings:0U   **(3545)**
2002/03: 16⁹G, 19⁵UG,

	Starts	1st	2nd	3rd	Win & Pl
NH Flat	1	0	0	0	0
Hurdles	1	0	0	0	0
Career Total	2	0	0	0	

Going: Sf: 0-0 GS: 0-0 Gd: 0-0 GF: - Fm: 0-0
Distance: 2m/2m3: 0-1 2m4-2m7: 0-1 3m+: 0-0
Track: LH: 0-1 RH: 0-1 Tight: 0-1 Gall: 0-0
Aids: Bl: 0-0 Vi: 0-0 Tstrap: 0-0
Best Rating: 12 1/03 Sthl 2m good NHF

Welsh Park (IRE)

62

10-y-o ch g Balinger-Welsh Escort (Welsh Captain)
A P James The Festival Racing Partnership

Placings:00000/406.5005313P0/3F036600/UUP0R/FP3004 0-P   **(0740)**

2002/03: 25PG,

	Starts	1st	2nd	3rd	Win & Pl
Hurdles	1	0	0	0	
Career Total	38	1	0	5	4091
98	10/98 Font	2m6f110yF Hdl		GD	£2267

Total win prize-money £2268

Going:	Sf: 0-0 GS: 0-0 Gd: 0-1 GF: - Fm: 0-0
Distance:	2m/2m3: 0-0 2m4-2m7: 0-0 3m+: 0-1
Track:	LH: 0-1 RH: 0-0 Tight: 0-0 Gall: 0-0
Aids:	Bl: 0-0 Vi: 0-0 Tstrap: 0-0
Best Rating:	98 10/98 Font 2m6f110y good Hdl

Wemyss Quest

110(116h)   (129h)116+

8-y-o b g Rainbow Quest (USA)-Wemyss Bight (Dancing Brave (USA))
Ferdy Murphy   Four Blokes

Placings:2515223/21110P0-1   (0563)
2002/03: 201GF,

	Starts	1st	2nd	3rd	Win & Pl
Chases	1	1	0	0	3803
Career Total	15	5	4	1	23650
96	6/02 MRas	2m4f	E Ch	G-F	£3802
129	10/01 Chel	3m1f110yB Hdl		GD	£7117
109	10/01 Weth	3m4f110yD Hdl		GD	£3801
116	6/01 MRas	3m	E Hdl	G-F	£2614
86	8/00 Rosc	2m	NHF	FRM	£3036

Total win prize-money £20373

Going:	Sf: 0-0 GS: 0-0 Gd: 0-0 GF: - Fm: 1-1
Distance:	2m/2m3: 0-0 2m4-2m7: 1-1 3m+: 0-0
Track:	LH: 0-0 RH: 1-1 Tight: 1-1 Gall: 0-0
Aids:	Bl: 0-0 Vi: 0-0 Tstrap: 1-1
Best Rating:	129 10/01 Chel 3m1f110y good Hdl

Fair chaser; returned after a year off with tendon trouble when making all in 3m Worcester handicap chase on first start for new stable despite jumping right; acts on fast ground; goes well when fresh.

Wend's Day (IRE)

106   116

8-y-o br g Brief Truce (USA)-Iswara (USA) (Alleged (USA))
A M Hales   Andrew L Cohen

Placings:144/126   (2603)
2002/03: 161G, 162GS, 206S,

	Starts	1st	2nd	3rd	Win & Pl
Hurdles	3	1	1	0	4259
Career Total	6	2	1	0	6482
116	10/02 Plum	2m	F Hdl	GD	£3108
111	12/99 Donc	2m110y E Hdl		G-S	£1976

Total win prize-money £5085

Going:	Sf: 0-1 GS: 0-1 Gd: 1-1 GF: - Fm: 0-0
Distance:	2m/2m3: 1-2 2m4-2m7: 0-1 3m+: 0-0
Track:	LH: 1-2 RH: 0-1 Tight: 1-2 Gall: 0-0
Aids:	Bl: 0-0 Vi: 0-0 Tstrap: 1-3
Best Rating:	116 10/02 Plum 2m good Hdl

Fair hurdler; winner of a novice hurdle on easy ground in December 1999, he made a good return to hurdles when winning at Plumpton in October 2002, but may have found the race coming too soon when beaten at Fakenham four days later and did not stay in the soft ground next time. Suited by two miles and easy ground, wears a tongue tie.

Wenric Pet

80f   48f

7-y-o br m Petoski-Jervandha (Strong Gale)

J C Tuck   E G R Golledge

Placings:00   (1494)
2002/03: 179G, 179GS,

	Starts	1st	2nd	3rd	Win & Pl
NH Flat	2	0	0	0	
Career Total	2	0	0	0	

Going:	Sf: 0-0 GS: 0-1 Gd: 0-1 GF: - Fm: 0-0
Distance:	2m/2m3: 0-2 2m4-2m7: 0-0 3m+: 0-0
Track:	LH: 0-1 RH: 0-1 Tight: 0-2 Gall: 0-0
Aids:	Bl: 0-0 Vi: 0-0 Tstrap: 0-0
Best Rating:	48 5/02 Folk 2m1f110y good NHF

Wensley Blue (IRE)

89   82

4-y-o b g Blues Traveller (IRE)-Almasa (Faustus (USA))
P C Haslam   Mrs B M Hawkins & R Young

Placings:56   (2182)
2002/03: 175G, 166GS,

	Starts	1st	2nd	3rd	Win & Pl
Hurdles	2	0	0	0	0
Career Total	2	0	0	0	0

Going:	Sf: 0-0 GS: 0-1 Gd: 0-1 GF: - Fm: 0-0
Distance:	2m/2m3: 0-2 2m4-2m7: 0-0 3m+: 0-0
Track:	LH: 0-1 RH: 0-1 Tight: 0-0 Gall: 0-0
Aids:	Bl: 0-0 Vi: 0-0 Tstrap: 0-0
Best Rating:	82 10/02 Hrfd 2m1f good Hdl

Plating-class hurdler; dropped in class won a selling hurdle all out at Hexham in April.

Wensum Dancer

114   92

6-y-o b m Shareef Dancer (USA)-Burning Ambition (Troy)
T Hogan   Patrick Taylor

Placings:0/4221106600F-31666P00   (4498a)
2002/03: 163YS, 161YS, 166GY, 166GF, 166F, 162F, 166GS, 166GY,

	Starts	1st	2nd	3rd	Win & Pl
Hurdles	8	1	0	1	6844
Career Total	20	3	2	1	17737
107	7/02 Limk	2m	(67-102)HHdl	Y-S	£6349
107	7/01 Rosc	2m	(0-102)HHdl	G-F	£4312
107	7/01 Slig	2m	Hdl	GD	£4451

Total win prize-money £15115

Going:	Sf: 0-0 GS: 0-1 Gd: 0-0 GF: - Fm: 0-3
Distance:	2m/2m3: 1-8 2m4-2m7: 0-0 3m+: 0-0
Track:	LH: 0-4 RH: 0-0 Tight: 0-1 Gall: 0-0
Aids:	Bl: 0-0 Vi: 0-0 Tstrap: 1-8
Best Rating:	107 7/02 Limk 2m yld-sft Hdl

Were In Touch (IRE)

    102+f

5-y-o b g Old Vic-Winterland Gale (IRE) (Strong Gale)
P F Nicholls   Paul K Barber

Placings:1   (3556)
2002/03: 181HY,

	Starts	1st	2nd	3rd	Win & Pl
NH Flat	1	1	0	0	3611
Career Total	1	1	0	0	3611
102	2/03 Plum	2m2f	H NHF	HVY	£3610

Total win prize-money £3611

Going:	Sf: 1-1 GS: 0-0 Gd: 0-0 GF: - Fm: 0-0
Distance:	2m/2m3: 1-1 2m4-2m7: 0-0 3m+: 0-0
Track:	LH: 1-1 RH: 0-0 Tight: 0-0 Gall: 0-0
Aids:	Bl: 0-0 Vi: 0-0 Tstrap: 0-0
Best Rating:	102 2/03 Plum 2m2f heavy NHF

Moderate bumper performer; out of an unraced mare; bred for stamina and stayed on stoutly to win a Plumpton bumper on his debut. Will stay three miles in time and is a chaser in the making. Clearly handles testing going.

Were Not Stoppin

105   83

8-y-o b g Mystiko (USA)-Power Take Off (Aragon)
R Bastiman   I B Barker

Placings:5/46-5313526PP   (4354)
2002/03: 165G, 163G, 161GF, 193GF, 225G, 162GF, 176GF, 163S, 20PGF,

	Starts	1st	2nd	3rd	Win & Pl
Hurdles	9	1	1	2	5569
Career Total	12	1	1	2	5569
87	6/02 Uttx	2m	E(0-105)HHdl	G-F	£3630

Total win prize-money £3630

Going:	Sf: 0-1 GS: 0-0 Gd: 0-3 GF: - Fm: 1-5
Distance:	2m/2m3: 1-7 2m4-2m7: 0-2 3m+: 0-0
Track:	LH: 1-8 RH: 0-1 Tight: 0-5 Gall: 0-0
Aids:	Bl: 0-0 Vi: 0-0 Tstrap: 0-0
Best Rating:	87 9/02 Hexm 2m110y gd-fm Hdl

Plating-class novice hurdler, suited by hold up tactics around two miles. Awarded a race at Uttoxeter in June.

Wesley's Lad (IRE)

94   101

9-y-o b/br g Classic Secret (USA)-Galouga (FR) (Lou Piguet (FR))
D Burchell   Brian Williams

Placings:043151/262425321/2P/30-606   (2457)
2002/03: 206S, 190GS, 196GS,

	Starts	1st	2nd	3rd	Win & Pl
Hurdles	3	0	0	0	0
Career Total	22	3	5	3	17933
127	3/99 Strf	2m110y C(0-135)HHdl	HVY	£4930
115	3/98 Plum	2m1f	E Hdl	SFT	£2490
114	1/98 Folk	2m1f110yE Hdl		G-S	£1976

Total win prize-money £9397

Going:	Sf: 0-1 GS: 0-2 Gd: 0-0 GF: - Fm: 0-0
Distance:	2m/2m3: 0-2 2m4-2m7: 0-3 3m+: 0-0
Track:	LH: 0-1 RH: 0-2 Tight: 0-2 Gall: 0-0
Aids:	Bl: 0-0 Vi: 0-0 Tstrap: 0-0
Best Rating:	130 11/99 Leic 2m gd-sft Hdl

Moderate handicap hurdler with cut in the ground, lightly raced in recent seasons.

West Aside (IRE)

(86h)   (66h)

9-y-o b g Brush Aside (USA)-Chancy Belle (Le Bavard (FR))
T P McGovern   B C J Enterprise

Placings:06/00-U   (3824)
2002/03: 26UGS,

	Starts	1st	2nd	3rd	Win & Pl
Chases	1	0	0	0	
Career Total	5	0	0	0	0

Going:	Sf: 0-0 GS: 0-1 Gd: 0-0 GF: - Fm: 0-0
Distance:	2m/2m3: 0-0 2m4-2m7: 0-0 3m+: 0-1

Track: LH: 0-1 RH: 0-0 Tight: 0-0 Gall: 0-0
Aids: Bl: 0-0 Vi: 0-0 Tstrap: 0-0
Best Rating: 66 5/01 Hntg 2m4f110y good Hdl

West Coaster (IRE)
97   88

5-y-o gr g Be My Native (USA)-Donegal Grey (IRE) (Roselier (FR))
Miss H C Knight White Rabbit Partnership

Placings:00-F0360   (4338)
2002/03: 16⁶G, 16⁰S, 16³GS, 19⁶GS, 20⁹GF,

	Starts	1st	2nd	3rd	Win & Pl
Hurdles	5	0	0	1	551
Career Total	7	0	0	1	551

Going: Sf: 0-1 GS: 0-2 Gd: 0-1 GF: - Fm: 0-1
Distance: 2m/2m3: 0-3 2m4-2m7: 0-2 3m+: 0-0
Track: LH: 0-2 RH: 0-3 Tight: 0-1 Gall: 0-3
Aids: Bl: 0-0 Vi: 0-0 Tstrap: 0-0
Best Rating: 89 3/03 Hntg 2m4f110y gd-fm Hdl

First worthwhile form when staying on third at Doncaster in January.

West End Dancer (USA)

6-y-o b m West By West (USA)-Chateau Dancer (USA) (Giacometti)
P S McEntee Mrs R L McEntee

Placings:524541230P/PP   (2320)
2002/03: 20⁵GS, 19⁵S,

	Starts	1st	2nd	3rd	Win & Pl
Hurdles	2	0	0		
Career Total	12	1	2	1	4139
79 1/01 Folk	2m1f110yF(0-100)HHdl		HVY		1866

Total win prize-money £1866

Going: Sf: 0-1 GS: 0-1 Gd: 0-0 GF: - Fm: 0-0
Distance: 2m/2m3: 0-0 2m4-2m7: 0-2 3m+: 0-0
Track: LH: 0-1 RH: 0-1 Tight: 0-2 Gall: 0-0
Aids: Bl: 0-0 Vi: 0-1 Tstrap: 0-0
Best Rating: 79 1/01 Folk 2m1f110y heavy Hdl

West Glory (IRE)

9-y-o b/br g Phardante (FR)-The Kid s Sister (Black Minstrel)
I W McInnes New Century Windows Ltd

Placings:P/P   (4225)
2002/03: 20⁰GF,

	Starts	1st	2nd	3rd	Win & Pl
Hurdles	1	0	0	0	
Career Total	2	0	0	0	

Going: Sf: 0-0 GS: 0-0 Gd: 0-0 GF: - Fm: 0-1
Distance: 2m/2m3: 0-0 2m4-2m7: 0-1 3m+: 0-0
Track: LH: 0-1 RH: 0-0 Tight: 0-0 Gall: 0-0
Aids: Bl: 0-0 Vi: 0-0 Tstrap: 0-0
Best Rating: 0 3/03 Weth 2m4f110y gd-fm Hdl

West Hill Rose (IRE)
104(105h)   (115h)98

8-y-o gr m Roselier (FR)-Clonmeen Official (Official)

V R A Dartnall D G Staddon

Placings:0/035/2114-526P   (3946)
2002/03: 24⁵HY, 23²GS, 26⁶HY, 30⁶S,

	Starts	1st	2nd	3rd	Win & Pl
Hurdles	1	0	0	0	0
Chases	3	0	1	0	1698
Career Total	12	2	2	1	11117
115 2/02 Newb	3m110y C(0-130)HHdl		SFT		£6006
115 1/02 Uttx	3m110y F Hdl		HVY		£1981

Total win prize-money £7987

Going: Sf: 0-3 GS: 0-1 Gd: 0-0 GF: - Fm: 0-0
Distance: 2m/2m3: 0-0 2m4-2m7: 0-0 3m+: 0-4
Track: LH: 0-2 RH: 0-2 Tight: 0-0 Gall: 0-0
Aids: Bl: 0-0 Vi: 0-0 Tstrap: 0-0
Best Rating: 115 2/02 Newb 3m110y soft Hdl

Moderate chaser/fair hurdler; mud-loving staying mare. Relatively lightly raced. Stays three miles. Promising chasing debut at Exeter in December.

West Paces (IRE)
105   102

9-y-o br g Lord Americo-Spanish Royale (Royal Buck)
G B Balding Baldings (training) Ltd

Placings:0PF32   (4537)
2002/03: 19⁰GS, 24⁷S, 21⁶S, 20³G, 24²G,

	Starts	1st	2nd	3rd	Win & Pl
Hurdles	1	0	0	0	
Chases	4	0	1	1	600
Career Total	5	0	1	1	600

Going: Sf: 0-2 GS: 0-1 Gd: 0-2 GF: - Fm: 0-0
Distance: 2m/2m3: 0-1 2m4-2m7: 0-2 3m+: 0-2
Track: LH: 0-0 RH: 0-5 Tight: 0-2 Gall: 0-1
Aids: Bl: 0-0 Vi: 0-0 Tstrap: 0-0
Best Rating: 102 4/03 Ludl 3m good Ch

Moderate, lightly-raced novice chaser; stays 3m 2f; acts on fast ground.

Westcountry Lad

13-y-o b g General Surprise-Charmezzo (Remezzo)
Mrs P Bond L Bond

Placings:5/UP/0/U-5   (0371)
2002/03: 26⁵S,

	Starts	1st	2nd	3rd	Win & Pl
Chases	1	0	0	0	
Career Total	6	0	0	0	

Going: Sf: 0-1 GS: 0-0 Gd: 0-0 GF: - Fm: 0-0
Distance: 2m/2m3: 0-0 2m4-2m7: 0-0 3m+: 0-1
Track: LH: 0-1 RH: 0-0 Tight: 0-1 Gall: 0-0
Aids: Bl: 0-0 Vi: 0-0 Tstrap: 0-0
Best Rating: 65 5/02 NAbb 3m2f110y soft Ch

Westender (FR)
119   164

7-y-o b g In The Wings-Trude (GER) (Windwurf (GER))
M C Pipe Matt Archer & Miss Jean Broadhurst

Placings:P11111022-323   (4555)
2002/03: 17³HY, 16²G, 16³G,

	Starts	1st	2nd	3rd	Win & Pl
Hurdles	3	0	1	2	73302
Career Total	12	5	3	2	158026

151	11/01	Chel	2m110y	A HHdl	GD	£32500
144	10/01	Chel	2m110y	B HHdl	GD	£10432
128	10/01	Chep	2m110y	D Hdl	GD	£3552
119	9/01	Uttx	2m	D Hdl	GD	£3591
125	6/01	Strf	2m110y	D Hdl	G-F	£3848

Total win prize-money £53924

Going: Sf: 0-1 GS: 0-0 Gd: 0-2 GF: - Fm: 0-0
Distance: 2m/2m3: 0-3 2m4-2m7: 0-0 3m+: 0-0
Track: LH: 0-3 RH: 0-0 Tight: 0-0 Gall: 0-1
Aids: Bl: 0-3 Vi: 0-0 Tstrap: 0-0
Best Rating: 164 3/03 Chel 2m110y good Hdl

Smart hurdler; enjoyed very profitable season over hurdles in 2001/2, winning four times and finishing a neck second to Like-A-Butterfly in the 2002 Supreme Novices Hurdle; runner-up in the Champion Hurdle; would have finished closer to Rooster Booster at Cheltenham but for losing ground at the start; found weight concession beyond him when third in the Scottish Champion Hurdle; all form around 2m; suited by a sound surface and reportedly doesn t want it too soft; regularly blinkered.

Western Bluebird (IRE)
98   69

5-y-o b g Bluebird (USA)-Arrastra (Bustino)
Miss Kate Milligan (H Morrison 28/6) The W Bees

Placings:0-00PP   (4434)
2002/03: 16⁰S, 16⁰GS, 25⁶PG, 20⁶G,

	Starts	1st	2nd	3rd	Win & Pl
Hurdles	4	0	0	0	
Career Total	5	0	0	0	

Going: Sf: 0-1 GS: 0-1 Gd: 0-2 GF: - Fm: 0-0
Distance: 2m/2m3: 0-2 2m4-2m7: 0-1 3m+: 0-1
Track: LH: 0-4 RH: 0-0 Tight: 0-1 Gall: 0-3
Aids: Bl: 0-0 Vi: 0-0 Tstrap: 0-0
Best Rating: 70 1/02 Newb 2m110y gd-sft Hdl

Plating-class hurdler; first worthwhile form when narrow winner at Hexham in June 2003; stays two and a half miles; acts on fast ground.

Western Chief (IRE)
103   106

9-y-o b h Caerleon (USA)-Go Honey Go (General Assembly (USA))
D L Williams Miss B W Palmer

Placings:460006/06033524/31111U2/2/2PP-2   (1041)
2002/03: 26²GF,

	Starts	1st	2nd	3rd	Win & Pl
Chases	1	0	1	0	840
Career Total	26	4	5	3	19495
121	5/99	Uttx	2m5f	F(0-100)HCh	G-F	£3022
112	5/99	MRas	2m4f	D Ch	G-F	£4580
97	5/99	Uttx	2m	F(0-100)HHdl	G-F	£2515
98	5/99	Fknm	2m	G(0-95)HHdl	G-F	£1895

Total win prize-money £12014

Going: Sf: 0-0 GS: 0-0 Gd: 0-0 GF: - Fm: 0-0
Distance: 2m/2m3: 0-0 2m4-2m7: 0-0 3m+: 0-0
Track: LH: 0-0 RH: 0-0 Tight: 0-1 Gall: 0-0
Aids: Bl: 0-0 Vi: 0-0 Tstrap: 0-1
Best Rating: 121 5/99 Uttx 2m5f good Ch

Modest, one-time fair handicap chaser, decent run in August 2002 on his first outing over jumps for more than a year.

Western Ridge (FR)
106   97+

6-y-o b g Darshaan-Helvellyn (USA) (Gone West (USA))
B J Llewellyn D H Driscoll

Placings:0-002   (4515)
2002/03: 17⁰S, 16⁰HY, 17²GF,

	Starts	1st	2nd	3rd	Win & Pl
Hurdles	3	0	1	0	1016
Career Total	4	0	1	0	1016

Going: Sf: 0-2 GS: 0-0 Gd: 0-0 GF: - Fm: 0-1
Distance: 2m/2m3: 0-3 2m4-2m7: 0-0 3m+: 0-0
Track: LH: 0-1 RH: 0-2 Tight: 0-1 Gall: 0-0
Aids: Bl: 0-0 Vi: 0-0 Tstrap: 0-0
Best Rating: 78 4/03   Extr   2m1f   gd-fm Hdl

Moderate hold-up hurdler; improved form despite being 5lb wrong when runner-up in 2m novices handicap hurdle at Chepstow May 2003; failed to stay 2m 4f next time but got off the mark over extended 2m at Newton Abbot later that month; followed up over the same course and distance in July; acts on fast ground.

Western Sun

13-y-o b g Sunyboy-Running Valley (Buckskin (FR))
J L Needham J L Needham

Placings:0/00/P/0U0P/R/P0-P   (0075)
2002/03: 25ᴾGF,

	Starts	1st	2nd	3rd	Win & Pl
Chases	1	0	0	0	
Career Total	12	0	0	0	

Going: Sf: 0-0 GS: 0-0 Gd: 0-0 GF: - Fm: 0-0
Distance: 2m/2m3: 0-0 2m4-2m7: 0-0 3m+: 0-0
Track: LH: 0-0 RH: 0-0 Tight: 0-0 Gall: 0-0
Aids: Bl: 0-0 Vi: 0-0 Tstrap: 0-0
Best Rating: 45 9/99   Gway   2m6f   soft   Ch

Westernmost
105   107

5-y-o b g Most Welcome-Dakota Girl (Northern State (USA))
M Todhunter Steve Baron

Placings:S3F52-21222   (1374)
2002/03: 17²HY, 17¹G, 16²GF, 17²G, 21²GF,

	Starts	1st	2nd	3rd	Win & Pl
Hurdles	5	1	4	0	8237
Career Total	10	1	5	1	9716
97 6/02 Ctml 2m1f110yD Hdl				GD	£3653
				Total win prize-money	£3653

Going: Sf: 0-1 GS: 0-0 Gd: 1-2 GF: - Fm: 0-2
Distance: 2m/2m3: 1-4 2m4-2m7: 0-1 3m+: 0-0
Track: LH: 1-5 RH: 0-0 Tight: 1-4 Gall: 0-0
Aids: Bl: 0-0 Vi: 0-0 Tstrap: 0-0
Best Rating: 107 10/02 Sedg 2m5f110y gd-fm Hdl

Modest handicap hurdler, effective at up to two miles five and acts on a sound surface.

Westerton (IRE)

10-y-o b g Glacial Storm (USA)-Killiney Rose (Buckskin (FR))
F A Hutsby Mrs Peter Corbett

Placings:5213410P/25/PF/31   (4161)
2002/03: 24³S, 25¹GS,

	Starts	1st	2nd	3rd	Win & Pl
Chases	2	1	0	1	1759
Career Total	14	3	2	2	7458
90 3/03 MRas 3m1f H Ch				G-S	£1477
112 3/99 Uttx 2m4f110yD Hdl				HVY	£2957
96 10/98 Sedg 2m1f H NHF				G-S	£1255
				Total win prize-money	£5690

Going: Sf: 0-1 GS: 1-1 Gd: 0-0 GF: - Fm: 0-0
Distance: 2m/2m3: 0-0 2m4-2m7: 0-0 3m+: 1-2
Track: LH: 0-1 RH: 1-1 Tight: 1-1 Gall: 0-1
Aids: Bl: 0-0 Vi: 0-0 Tstrap: 0-0
Best Rating: 112 3/99   Uttx   2m4f110y heavy Hdl

Modest hunter chaser; stays three miles; acts well on good ground.

Westfield John

8-y-o b g Little Wolf-Moonbreaker (Twilight Alley)
Ferdy Murphy The Westfielders

Placings:00/000-43   (0397)
2002/03: 20⁴G, 20³GF,

	Starts	1st	2nd	3rd	Win & Pl
Hurdles	1	0	0	0	0
Chases	1	0	0	1	336
Career Total	7	0	0	1	336

Going: Sf: 0-0 GS: 0-0 Gd: 0-1 GF: - Fm: 0-1
Distance: 2m/2m3: 0-0 2m4-2m7: 0-2 3m+: 0-0
Track: LH: 0-2 RH: 0-0 Tight: 0-0 Gall: 0-0
Aids: Bl: 0-0 Vi: 0-0 Tstrap: 0-0
Best Rating: 96 10/00 Chel 2m110y   good NHF

Westgate Run
106   95

6-y-o b m Emperor Jones (USA)-Glowing Reference (Reference Point)
R A Fahey Mark A Leatham

Placings:433102   (2445)
2002/03: 17⁴GF, 17³GF, 21³G, 16¹G, 16⁰GS, 16²G,

	Starts	1st	2nd	3rd	Win & Pl
Hurdles	6	1	1	2	4679
Career Total	6	1	1	2	4679
90 10/02 Hexm 2m110y E Hdl				GD	£2936
				Total win prize-money	£2937

Going: Sf: 0-0 GS: 0-1 Gd: 1-3 GF: - Fm: 0-2
Distance: 2m/2m3: 1-5 2m4-2m7: 0-1 3m+: 0-0
Track: LH: 1-5 RH: 0-1 Tight: 0-1 Gall: 0-0
Aids: Bl: 0-0 Vi: 0-0 Tstrap: 0-0
Best Rating: 91 11/02 Chel 2m110y   gd-sft Hdl

Plating-class hurdler; effective at around two miles and acts on a sound surface; consistent.

Westmeath Lad
76   72

6-y-o ch g Primo Dominie-Re-Release (Baptism)
M Todhunter Jim Ennis

Placings:60-200   (1076)
2002/03: 16²G, 16⁰G, 17⁰G,

	Starts	1st	2nd	3rd	Win & Pl
NH Flat	1	0	1	0	464
Hurdles	2	0	0	0	0
Career Total	5	0	1	0	464

Going: Sf: 0-0 GS: 0-0 Gd: 0-3 GF: - Fm: 0-0
Distance: 2m/2m3: 0-3 2m4-2m7: 0-0 3m+: 0-0
Track: LH: 0-3 RH: 0-0 Tight: 0-1 Gall: 0-0
Aids: Bl: 0-0 Vi: 0-0 Tstrap: 0-0
Best Rating: 100 4/02 Hexm 2m110y   good NHF

Plating-class hurdler; moderate bumper performer.

Westminster City (USA)
75

7-y-o b g Alleged (USA)-Promanade Fan (USA) (Timeless Moment (USA))
Jean-Rene Auvray (G Brown 19/6) D C Roberts

Placings:P30-PP   (0840)
2002/03: 16ᴾGF, 19ᴾGF,

	Starts	1st	2nd	3rd	Win & Pl
Hurdles	2	0	0	0	
Career Total	5	0	0	1	395

Going: Sf: 0-0 GS: 0-0 Gd: 0-0 GF: - Fm: 0-2
Distance: 2m/2m3: 0-2 2m4-2m7: 0-0 3m+: 0-0
Track: LH: 0-2 RH: 0-0 Tight: 0-1 Gall: 0-0
Aids: Bl: 0-0 Vi: 0-0 Tstrap: 0-0
Best Rating: 75 11/01 Plum 2m   gd-sft Hdl

Westmorland (IRE)
105   108+

7-y-o b g Phardante (FR)-Ticking Over (IRE) (Decent Fellow)
L Lungo Maurice W Chapman

Placings:000P/001F1-1   (0186)
2002/03: 24¹G,

	Starts	1st	2nd	3rd	Win & Pl
Hurdles	1	1	0	0	2944
Career Total	10	3	0	0	7816
108 5/02 Hexm 3m F(0-100)HHdl			GD	£2943
97 4/02 Carl 3m110y E(0-105)HHdl			GD	£3108
85 3/02 Sedg 2m5f110yG(0-90)HHdl			SFT	£1764
				Total win prize-money	£7816

Going: Sf: 0-0 GS: 0-0 Gd: 1-1 GF: - Fm: 0-0
Distance: 2m/2m3: 0-0 2m4-2m7: 0-0 3m+: 1-1
Track: LH: 1-1 RH: 0-0 Tight: 0-0 Gall: 0-0
Aids: Bl: 0-0 Vi: 0-0 Tstrap: 0-0
Best Rating: 108 5/02 Hexm 3m   good Hdl

Modest chaser; has improved no end since being faced with a test of stamina with wins at Sedgefield, Carlisle and Hexham in the spring of 2002 despite rising in the handicap. Acts on any ground. Stays three miles.

Weston Court

9-y-o b g Scottish Reel-Lady Westown (Town And Country)
P G Murphy The Weston Court Partnership

Placings:0   (3850)
2002/03: 19⁰GS,

	Starts	1st	2nd	3rd	Win & Pl
Hurdles	1	0	0	0	
Career Total	1	0	0	0	

Going: Sf: 0-0 GS: 0-1 Gd: 0-0 GF: - Fm: 0-0
Distance: 2m/2m3: 0-0 2m4-2m7: 0-1 3m+: 0-0
Track: LH: 0-0 RH: 0-1 Tight: 0-1 Gall: 0-0

Aids: Bl: 0-0 Vi: 0-0 Tstrap: 0-0
Best Rating: 0   2/03   Tntn   2m3f110y   gd-sft   Hdl

Weston Marauder

6-y-o b g Unfuwain (USA)-Rushing River (USA) (Irish River (FR))
M J Gingell M J Gingell

Placings: 0P   (4337)
2002/03: 17⁰G, 16ᴾGF,

	Starts	1st	2nd	3rd	Win & Pl
NH Flat	1	0	0	0	0
Hurdles	1	0	0	0	0
Career Total	2	0	0	0	0

Going: Sf: 0-0 GS: 0-0 Gd: 0-0 GF: - Fm: 0-1
Distance: 2m/2m3: 0-2 2m4-2m7: 0-0 3m+: 0-0
Track: LH: 0-0 RH: 0-2 Tight: 0-0 Gall: 0-1
Aids: Bl: 0-0 Vi: 0-0 Tstrap: 0-0
Best Rating: 0   3/03   Hntg   2m110y   gd-fm   Hdl

Weston Rock

98f   79f

4-y-o b g Double Eclipse (IRE)-Mossberry Fair (Mossberry)
T D Walford Mrs H Spath

Placings: 6   (3160)
2002/03: 16⁶G,

	Starts	1st	2nd	3rd	Win & Pl
NH Flat	1	0	0	0	0
Career Total	1	0	0	0	0

Going: Sf: 0-0 GS: 0-0 Gd: 0-1 GF: - Fm: 0-0
Distance: 2m/2m3: 0-1 2m4-2m7: 0-0 3m+: 0-0
Track: LH: 0-0 RH: 0-1 Tight: 0-1 Gall: 0-0
Aids: Bl: 0-0 Vi: 0-0 Tstrap: 0-0
Best Rating: 79   1/03   Muss   2m   good   NHF

Son of Double Eclipse, stayed on well on debut in bumper at Musselburgh in January.

Westorm (IRE)

80   53

12-y-o b g Strong Gale-Little Peach (Ragapan)
P W Hiatt Miss Maria McKinney

Placings: 000/0000/5P   (0430)
2002/03: 16⁶G, 16ᴾGF,

	Starts	1st	2nd	3rd	Win & Pl
Hurdles	2	0	0	0	0
Career Total	9	0	0	0	0

Going: Sf: 0-0 GS: 0-0 Gd: 0-0 GF: - Fm: 0-2
Distance: 2m/2m3: 0-2 2m4-2m7: 0-0 3m+: 0-0
Track: LH: 0-0 RH: 0-2 Tight: 0-0 Gall: 0-1
Aids: Bl: 0-0 Vi: 0-0 Tstrap: 0-0
Best Rating: 81   1/96   DRoy   2m   yield   Hdl

Westwinds

82

11-y-o b g Vital Season-April s Crook (Crozier)
M J Coombe Mrs N M Coombe

Placings: 4U/15P4-P60   (0555)

2002/03: 21ᴾG, 25⁶G, 25⁹GF,

	Starts	1st	2nd	3rd	Win & Pl
Chases	3	0	0	0	0
Career Total	9	1	0	0	4339
82 5/01 Folk 3m2f E Ch				GD	£3666

Total win prize-money £3666

Going: Sf: 0-0 GS: 0-0 Gd: 0-2 GF: - Fm: 0-1
Distance: 2m/2m3: 0-0 2m4-2m7: 0-1 3m+: 0-2
Track: LH: 0-1 RH: 0-1 Tight: 0-1 Gall: 0-0
Aids: Bl: 0-1 Vi: 0-0 Tstrap: 0-0
Best Rating: 91   1/01   Donc   3m   good   Ch

Whaleef

82   59

5-y-o br g Darshaan-Wilayif (USA) (Danzig (USA))
P R Webber Mrs P Sherwood

Placings: 60   (3115)
2002/03: 17⁶GS, 16⁹S,

	Starts	1st	2nd	3rd	Win & Pl
Hurdles	2	0	0	0	0
Career Total	2	0	0	0	0

Going: Sf: 0-1 GS: 0-0 Gd: 0-1 GF: - Fm: 0-0
Distance: 2m/2m3: 0-1 2m4-2m7: 0-0 3m+: 0-0
Track: LH: 0-0 RH: 0-2 Tight: 0-1 Gall: 0-1
Aids: Bl: 0-0 Vi: 0-0 Tstrap: 0-0
Best Rating: 62   12/02   Tntn   2m1f   gd-sft   Hdl

Decent on the Flat, he showed ability on his hurdling debut at Taunton in December 2002.

Whass Urrp (IRE)

4-y-o b g Desert King (IRE)-Blue Burgee (USA) (Lyphard s Wish (FR))
M E Sowersby (J M Bradley 20/7) I Fox

Placings: P   (3816)
2002/03: 19ᴾG,

	Starts	1st	2nd	3rd	Win & Pl
Hurdles	1	0	0	0	
Career Total	1	0	0	0	

Going: Sf: 0-0 GS: 0-0 Gd: 0-1 GF: - Fm: 0-0
Distance: 2m/2m3: 0-1 2m4-2m7: 0-0 3m+: 0-0
Track: LH: 0-1 RH: 0-0 Tight: 0-1 Gall: 0-0
Aids: Bl: 0-0 Vi: 0-0 Tstrap: 0-1
Best Rating: 0   2/03   Catt   3m2f   good   Hdl

What A Fiddler (IRE)

10-y-o ch g Orchestra-Crowenstown Miss (Over The River (FR))
J S Haldane J S Haldane

Placings: 2/24/5P23/15-16   (4140)
2002/03: 26¹GS, 32⁶S,

	Starts	1st	2nd	3rd	Win & Pl
Chases	2	1	0	0	2730
Career Total	11	2	3	1	7660
89 6/02 Cntrl 3m2f H Ch				G-S	£2730
105 5/01 Hexm 3m1f H Ch				SFT	£2483

Total win prize-money £5213

Going: Sf: 0-1 GS: 1-1 Gd: 0-0 GF: - Fm: 0-0
Distance: 2m/2m3: 0-0 2m4-2m7: 0-0 3m+: 1-2
Track: LH: 1-2 RH: 0-0 Tight: 1-1 Gall: 0-0

Aids: Bl: 0-0 Vi: 0-0 Tstrap: 0-0
Best Rating: 105   5/01   Hexm   3m1f   soft   Ch

Moderate hunter chaser; stays three miles; acts on good ground.

What A Man (IRE)

91   100

6-y-o b g Beau Sher-Cactus Wren (IRE) (Remainder Man)
T R George Paul Green

Placings: 45   (3182)
2002/03: 16⁴S, 21⁵G,

	Starts	1st	2nd	3rd	Win & Pl
NH Flat	1	0	0	0	0
Hurdles	1	0	0	0	537
Career Total	2	0	0	0	537

Going: Sf: 0-1 GS: 0-0 Gd: 0-1 GF: - Fm: 0-0
Distance: 2m/2m3: 0-1 2m4-2m7: 0-1 3m+: 0-0
Track: LH: 0-0 RH: 0-2 Tight: 0-0 Gall: 0-0
Aids: Bl: 0-0 Vi: 0-0 Tstrap: 0-0
Best Rating: 100   1/03   Kemp   2m5f   good   Hdl

Moderate ex-Irish point winner, he showed some promise in a Ludlow bumper but was well beaten in a decent hurdle race at Kempton.

What A Monday

99f   105f

5-y-o b g Beveled (USA)-Raise Memories (Skyliner)
K Bell North Farm Partnership

Placings: 103   (4122)
2002/03: 16¹S, 16⁰G, 16³G,

	Starts	1st	2nd	3rd	Win & Pl
NH Flat	3	1	0	1	1810
Career Total	3	1	0	1	1810
104 6/02 Worc 2m H NHF				SFT	£1523

Total win prize-money £1523

Going: Sf: 1-1 GS: 0-0 Gd: 0-2 GF: - Fm: 0-0
Distance: 2m/2m3: 1-3 2m4-2m7: 0-0 3m+: 0-0
Track: LH: 1-2 RH: 0-1 Tight: 0-0 Gall: 0-2
Aids: Bl: 0-0 Vi: 0-0 Tstrap: 0-0
Best Rating: 105   2/03   Newb   2m110y   good   NHF

Modest performer; has done well in bumpers under his penalty since winning on his debut; effective at two miles; acts on good ground.

What A Wonder (IRE)

98(109h)   (114h)82

8-y-o gr g Roselier (FR)-Lady Abednego Vii (Damsire Unregistered)
Ferdy Murphy The Sheepscar Syndicate

Placings: 0/222121/24U4P01-554540   (4774)
2002/03: 22⁵HY, 24⁵GF, 25⁴G, 26⁵S, 25⁴G, 27⁹G,

	Starts	1st	2nd	3rd	Win & Pl
Hurdles	3	0	0	0	0
Chases	3	0	0	0	623
Career Total	20	3	5	0	17648
116 4/02 Prth 3m110y E(0-105)HHdl				GD	£4654
120 4/01 Prth 3m110y F(0-105)HHdl				HVY	£3514
106 2/01 Muss 3m D(0-110)HHdl				GD	£3458

Total win prize-money £11626

Going: Sf: 0-2 GS: 0-0 Gd: 0-3 GF: - Fm: 0-1
Distance: 2m/2m3: 0-0 2m4-2m7: 0-1 3m+: 0-5

Track: LH: 0-3 RH: 0-2 Tight: 0-3 Gall: 0-0
Aids: Bl: 0-5 Vi: 0-0 Tstrap: 0-0
Best Rating: 120 4/01 Prth 3m110y heavy Hdl

Plating-class hurdler; winner twice over hurdles; made a good start to his chasing career but jumping has let him down; he reverted to hurdles, scoring at Perth in April 2002. Suited by a sharp right-handed track, acts on any ground. Stays three miles.

What You Know (IRE)

105   80

9-y-o b g Be My Guest (USA)-Flamme D Amour (Gift Card (FR))
Mrs D A Hamer Mrs Ashley Davies

Placings: 305/04PP/011000   (3143)
2002/03: 20⁰GF, 16¹G, 19¹F, 16⁶S, 22⁹GS, 19⁰S,

	Starts	1st	2nd	3rd	Win & Pl
Hurdles	6	2	0		4584
Career Total	13	2	0	1	4752
83	10/02	Extr	2m3f	G(0-95)HHdl	FRM	£2282
79	9/02	Worc	2m	G(0-90)HHdl	GD	£2301
				Total win prize-money £4584

Going: Sf: 0-2 GS: 0-1 Gd: 1-1 GF: - Fm: 1-2
Distance: 2m/2m3: 2-3 2m4-2m7: 0-3 3m+: 0-0
Track: LH: 1-3 RH: 1-3 Tight: 0-1 Gall: 0-0
Aids: Bl: 1-3 Vi: 0-0 Tstrap: 0-1
Best Rating: 89 9/98 Hntg 2m110y gd-fm NHF

Plating-class hurdler; did not look a straight forward ride when springing a 66/1 shock in a two mile conditional jockeys selling hurdle at Worcester September 2002. Followed up in a similar event over an extra three furlongs off a 10lb higher mark at Exeter in October.

What You Mean

70

8-y-o ch g Kasakov-Lonely Lass (Headin Up)
J R Norton Michael Ng

Placings: 60/32U256/0/050-50PP   (3812)
2002/03: 20⁵HY, 21⁰S, 16⁹HY, 19⁰G,

	Starts	1st	2nd	3rd	Win & Pl
Hurdles	4	0	0	0	0
Career Total	16	0	2	1	1450

Going: Sf: 0-3 GS: 0-0 Gd: 0-1 GF: - Fm: 0-0
Distance: 2m/2m3: 0-2 2m4-2m7: 0-2 3m+: 0-0
Track: LH: 0-3 RH: 0-1 Tight: 0-2 Gall: 0-1
Aids: Bl: 0-0 Vi: 0-0 Tstrap: 0-0
Best Rating: 94 6/99 Worc 2m gd-fm NHF

What's The Buzz

12-y-o ch g Ardross-Cherry Opal (Saint Denys)
Joss Saville Mrs S Smith

Placings: 5P/0U604/6P0/0   (3968)
2002/03: 25⁰S,

	Starts	1st	2nd	3rd	Win & Pl
Chases	1	0	0	0	
Career Total	11	0	0	0	280

Going: Sf: 0-1 GS: 0-0 Gd: 0-0 GF: - Fm: 0-0
Distance: 2m/2m3: 0-0 2m4-2m7: 0-0 3m+: 0-1
Track: LH: 0-1 RH: 0-0 Tight: 0-1 Gall: 0-0

What's The Count

104   107

7-y-o gr g Theatrical Charmer-Yankee Silver (Yankee Gold)
B R Johnson The Twenty Five Club

Placings: 0/500/P-5342200   (4429)
2002/03: 16⁵G, 20³GS, 22⁴HY, 17²HY, 21²HY, 22⁹HY, 21⁰GF,

	Starts	1st	2nd	3rd	Win & Pl
Hurdles	7	0	2	1	3618
Career Total	12	0	2	1	3618

Going: Sf: 0-4 GS: 0-1 Gd: 0-1 GF: - Fm: 0-1
Distance: 2m/2m3: 0-2 2m4-2m7: 0-5 3m+: 0-0
Track: LH: 0-3 RH: 0-3 Tight: 0-6 Gall: 0-0
Aids: Bl: 0-0 Vi: 0-1 Tstrap: 0-5
Best Rating: 107 2/03 Plum 2m5f heavy Hdl

Modest maiden hurdler; stays two miles five furlongs; acts on a soft surface; often tongue tied.

What's Up Boys (IRE)

160

9-y-o gr g Supreme Leader-Maryville Bick (Malacate (USA))
P J Hobbs R J B Partners

Placings: 62126/11P313/12F1112/14P52-F   (1740)
2002/03: 25⁷GS,

	Starts	1st	2nd	3rd	Win & Pl
Chases	1	0	0	0	
Career Total	24	9	5	2	352390
157	12/01	Newb	3m2f110y		A HCh	SFT
£58000
155	4/01	Aint	3m1f	A Ch	SFT	£50250
141	2/01	Ludl	3m	E Ch	G-S	£3750
123	12/00	Muss	2m4f	D Ch	GD	£4641
149	5/00	Punc	2m4f	Hdl	GD	£24800
149	3/00	Chel	2m5f	A HHdl	GD	£39000
146	12/99	Sand	2m6f	A Hdl	G-S	£9525
119	11/99	Folk	2m4f110yF Hdl		G-S	£1499
104	12/98	Punc	2m	NHF	SH	£2989
				Total win prize-money £194455

Going: Sf: 0-0 GS: 0-1 Gd: 0-0 GF: - Fm: 0-0
Distance: 2m/2m3: 0-0 2m4-2m7: 0-0 3m+: 0-1
Track: LH: 0-1 RH: 0-0 Tight: 0-0 Gall: 0-0
Aids: Bl: 0-1 Vi: 0-0 Tstrap: 0-0
Best Rating: 160 4/02 Aint 4m4f good Ch

High-class chaser; formerly very smart hurdler, including winning the Coral Cup at Cheltenham in 2000 and also winning at Punchestown. He beat Shotgun Willy by a distance at Aintree in 2001 and he ran a fine race for a novice to finish second in the Whitbread. Game winner of the Hennessy on his return, he stays well and is especially effective in soft ground. Fourth in the Welsh National at Christmas, then ran a staying-on race in the Gold Cup and finished a fine second in the Grand National. Took a heavy fall in the Charlie Hall Chase on his reappearance last season and was absent afterwards. Stays well, effective on good ground or softer.

Whatacharlie

100 (79h)   (51h) 52

9-y-o b g Nicholas Bill-Zulu Dancer (Sula Bula)
D P Keane D P Keane

Placings: PF/03   (4702)

2002/03: 19⁰G, 26³GF,

	Starts	1st	2nd	3rd	Win & Pl
Chases	2	0	0	1	480
Career Total	4	0	0	1	480

Going: Sf: 0-0 GS: 0-0 Gd: 0-1 GF: - Fm: 0-0
Distance: 2m/2m3: 0-0 2m4-2m7: 0-1 3m+: 0-1
Track: LH: 0-1 RH: 0-1 Tight: 0-1 Gall: 0-0
Aids: Bl: 0-0 Vi: 0-0 Tstrap: 0-2
Best Rating: 52 4/03 Asct 2m3f110y good Ch

Poor chaser; winning pointer; yet to show any worthwhile form under Rules.

Whatafellow (IRE)

13-y-o ch g Arapahos (FR)-Dara s March (March Parade)
Mrs Edward Crow Gareth Samuel

Placings: 20F/1P/F-43   (4526)
2002/03: 34⁴G, 24³G,

	Starts	1st	2nd	3rd	Win & Pl
Chases	2	0	0	1	221
Career Total	8	1	1	1	3230
105	5/00	Ctml	3m2f	H Ch	G-S	£1964
				Total win prize-money £1964

Going: Sf: 0-0 GS: 0-0 Gd: 0-2 GF: - Fm: 0-0
Distance: 2m/2m3: 0-0 2m4-2m7: 0-0 3m+: 0-2
Track: LH: 0-2 RH: 0-0 Tight: 0-0 Gall: 0-0
Aids: Bl: 0-2 Vi: 0-0 Tstrap: 0-0
Best Rating: 108 3/00 Chel 3m2f110y gd-fm Ch

Multiple winner in points, albeit in easy races; not as effective under Rules; acts on a sound surface.

Whatashock

8-y-o b g Never So Bold-Lady Electric (Electric)
A King J L Frampton

Placings: 00/P   (2585)
2002/03: 23⁰GS,

	Starts	1st	2nd	3rd	Win & Pl
Chases	1	0	0	0	
Career Total	3	0	0	0	

Going: Sf: 0-0 GS: 0-1 Gd: 0-0 GF: - Fm: 0-0
Distance: 2m/2m3: 0-0 2m4-2m7: 0-0 3m+: 0-1
Track: LH: 0-0 RH: 0-1 Tight: 0-0 Gall: 0-0
Aids: Bl: 0-0 Vi: 0-0 Tstrap: 0-0
Best Rating: 98 10/99 Chel 2m110y good NHF

Whatawizard (IRE)

6-y-o br g Hubbly Bubbly (USA)-Justine s Way (USA) (Buffalo Lark (USA))
R Dickin Mrs F Reddick & Mrs C Bloxham

Placings: 00660   (4488)
2002/03: 16⁰S, 20⁰S, 17⁶GS, 24⁶S, 26⁹GF,

	Starts	1st	2nd	3rd	Win & Pl
NH Flat	1	0	0	0	0
Hurdles	4	0	0	0	0
Career Total	5	0	0	0	0

Going: Sf: 0-3 GS: 0-1 Gd: 0-0 GF: - Fm: 0-1
Distance: 2m/2m3: 0-2 2m4-2m7: 0-1 3m+: 0-2
Track: LH: 0-3 RH: 0-2 Tight: 0-1 Gall: 0-1

Aids: Bl: 0-0 Vi: 0-0 Tstrap: 0-0
Best Rating: 57 11/02 Sand 2m110y soft NHF

Whatever For

75f   53f

5-y-o b m Daar Alzamaan (IRE)-Manx Monarch (Dara Monarch)
F P Murtagh F P Murtagh

Placings:0   (2560)
2002/03: 16⁰GF,

	Starts	1st	2nd	3rd	Win & Pl
NH Flat	1	0	0	0	
Career Total	1	0	0	0	

Going: Sf: 0-0 GS: 0-0 Gd: 0-0 GF: 0-1 - Fm: 0-1
Distance: 2m/2m3: 0-1 2m4-2m7: 0-0 3m+: 0-0
Track: LH: 0-0 RH: 0-1 Tight: 0-1 Gall: 0-0
Aids: Bl: 0-0 Vi: 0-0 Tstrap: 0-0
Best Rating: 53 12/02 Muss 2m   gd-fm NHF

Where Eagles Dare (USA)

6-y-o b g Eagle Eyed (USA)-Velveteen (USA) (Pirateer (USA))
M E Sowersby Paul Clifton

Placings:P   (0388)
2002/03: 20⁰GS,

	Starts	1st	2nd	3rd	Win & Pl
Hurdles	1	0	0	0	
Career Total	1	0	0	0	

Going: Sf: 0-0 GS: 0-1 Gd: 0-0 GF: - Fm: 0-0
Distance: 2m/2m3: 0-0 2m4-2m7: 0-1 3m+: 0-0
Track: LH: 0-1 RH: 0-0 Tight: 0-0 Gall: 0-0
Aids: Bl: 0-0 Vi: 0-0 Tstrap: 0-1
Best Rating:

Whereareyounow (IRE)

109(97h)   (115h)133

6-y-o ch g Mister Lord (USA)-Angies Delight (London Gazette)
N A Twiston-Davies H R Mould

Placings:4553420   (4101)
2002/03: 22⁴G, 21⁵GS, 25⁵G, 21³S, 21⁴GS, 24²GS, 24⁰G,

	Starts	1st	2nd	3rd	Win & Pl
Hurdles	2	0	0	0	420
Chases	5	0	1	1	11773
Career Total	7	0	1	1	12193

Going: Sf: 0-1 GS: 0-3 Gd: 0-3 GF: - Fm: 0-0
Distance: 2m/2m3: 0-0 2m4-2m7: 0-4 3m+: 0-3
Track: LH: 0-5 RH: 0-2 Tight: 0-0 Gall: 0-5
Aids: Bl: 0-0 Vi: 0-0 Tstrap: 0-0
Best Rating: 133 1/03 Chel 2m5f   gd-sft Ch

Useful novice chaser; still awaiting his first success; has had a breathing problem in the past; likes to lead; acts well with cut in the ground; gets three miles.

Whether The Storm (IRE)

95   91

7-y-o b g Glacial Storm (USA)-Minimum Choice (IRE) (Miners Lamp)
Miss H C Knight Executive Racing

Placings:3/441/0-44P   (3090)
2002/03: 20⁴GS, 21⁴S, 24⁰G,

	Starts	1st	2nd	3rd	Win & Pl
Chases	3	0	0	0	727
Career Total	8	1	0	1	4596
109 12/00 Newb 2m3f		D Hdl		SFT	£3623

Total win prize-money £3624

Going: Sf: 0-1 GS: 0-1 Gd: 0-1 GF: - Fm: 0-0
Distance: 2m/2m3: 0-0 2m4-2m7: 0-2 3m+: 0-1
Track: LH: 0-2 RH: 0-1 Tight: 0-0 Gall: 0-2
Aids: Bl: 0-0 Vi: 0-0 Tstrap: 0-0
Best Rating: 109 12/00 Newb 2m3f   soft Hdl

Moderate chaser; winner of a novice hurdle in December 2000, after some good efforts in bumpers. Lightly-raced since; acts on soft.

Whispering Holly

79f   45f

4-y-o b g Holly Buoy-Stuart s Gem (Meldrum)
R S Wood R S Wood

Placings:0   (4788)
2002/03: 17⁰G,

	Starts	1st	2nd	3rd	Win & Pl
NH Flat	1	0	0	0	
Career Total	1	0	0	0	

Going: Sf: 0-0 GS: 0-0 Gd: 0-1 GF: - Fm: 0-0
Distance: 2m/2m3: 0-1 2m4-2m7: 0-0 3m+: 0-0
Track: LH: 0-0 RH: 0-1 Tight: 0-1 Gall: 0-0
Aids: Bl: 0-0 Vi: 0-0 Tstrap: 0-0
Best Rating: 14 4/03 MRas 2m1f110y good NHF

Whispering John (IRE)

(104h)   (111h)

7-y-o b g Grand Plaisir (IRE)-London Anne (London Bells (CAN))
P F Nicholls Paul K Barber

Placings:200F   (3669)
2002/03: 19²GS, 21⁰S, 16⁰GS, 20FGS,

	Starts	1st	2nd	3rd	Win & Pl
Hurdles	3	0	1	0	1679
Chases	1	0	0	0	
Career Total	4	0	1	0	1679

Going: Sf: 0-1 GS: 0-3 Gd: 0-0 GF: - Fm: 0-0
Distance: 2m/2m3: 0-2 2m4-2m7: 0-2 3m+: 0-0
Track: LH: 0-1 RH: 0-2 Tight: 0-1 Gall: 0-1
Aids: Bl: 0-0 Vi: 0-0 Tstrap: 0-0
Best Rating: 111 11/02 Extr 2m3f   gd-sft Hdl

Fair hurdler; made the frame in a couple of point to points; second on his chases bow at Exeter in November 2002; held subsequently.

Whistful Suzie (IRE)

92   77

6-y-o ch m Eurobus-Ah Suzie (IRE) (King s Ride)

Mrs S C Bradburne Lord Cochrane And Partners

Placings:006-B65   (1557)
2002/03: 20⁸GF, 20⁶G, 16⁵G,

	Starts	1st	2nd	3rd	Win & Pl
Hurdles	3	0	0	0	0
Career Total	6	0	0	0	0

Going: Sf: 0-0 GS: 0-0 Gd: 0-1 GF: - Fm: 0-2
Distance: 2m/2m3: 0-1 2m4-2m7: 0-2 3m+: 0-0
Track: LH: 0-1 RH: 0-2 Tight: 0-0 Gall: 0-0
Aids: Bl: 0-0 Vi: 0-0 Tstrap: 0-0
Best Rating: 78 3/02 Ayr 2m   heavy NHF

Poor bumper and hurdle form.

Whistling Dixie (IRE)

114   138

7-y-o ch g Forest Wind (USA)-Camdens Gift (Camden Town)
Mrs M Reveley Mrs P D Savill

Placings:12113/216-3406F03   (3396)
2002/03: 16³G, 17⁴GS, 16⁰HY, 16⁶S, 16FHY, 16⁰S, 22³HY,

	Starts	1st	2nd	3rd	Win & Pl
Hurdles	7	0	0	2	15700
Career Total	15	4	2	3	63841
131 11/01 DRoy 2m		(0-135)HHdl		SFT	£26209
127 2/01 Muss 2m		F(0-110)HHdl		GD	£5668
115 1/01 Donc 2m110y		C(0-130)HHdl		GD	£5980
103 12/00 Muss 2m		E Hdl		GD	£1792

Total win prize-money £39650

Going: Sf: 0-5 GS: 0-1 Gd: 0-1 GF: - Fm: 0-0
Distance: 2m/2m3: 0-6 2m4-2m7: 0-1 3m+: 0-0
Track: LH: 0-2 RH: 0-4 Tight: 0-1 Gall: 0-0
Aids: Bl: 0-0 Vi: 0-0 Tstrap: 0-0
Best Rating: 138 12/02 Asct 2m110y heavy Hdl

Useful handicap hurdler; acts on good and soft ground; effective at around two miles; stays two miles six.

Whistling Song

88   42

8-y-o ch m True Song-Sancal (Whistlefield)
R Dickin Haydn Gott And Claire Dickin

Placings:04P-F   (4783)
2002/03: 17FG,

	Starts	1st	2nd	3rd	Win & Pl
Chases	1	0	0	0	
Career Total	4	0	0	0	258

Going: Sf: 0-0 GS: 0-0 Gd: 0-1 GF: - Fm: 0-0
Distance: 2m/2m3: 0-1 2m4-2m7: 0-0 3m+: 0-0
Track: LH: 0-0 RH: 0-1 Tight: 0-1 Gall: 0-0
Aids: Bl: 0-0 Vi: 0-0 Tstrap: 0-0
Best Rating: 75 3/02 Hrfd 3m1f110y good Ch

Poor form over fences; headstrong.

Whitaside (IRE)

100   104

9-y-o b/br g Brush Aside (USA)-Flying Silver (Master Buck)
Mrs S J Smith Ashleybank Investments Limited

Placings:212   (2072)
2002/03: 21²GF, 20¹G, 19²S,

	Starts	1st	2nd	3rd	Win & Pl
Hurdles	3	1	2	0	4805

Career Total	3	1	2	0	4805
104	10/02	Hexm	2m4f110y		E Hdl	GD

£2936

Total win prize-money £2937

Going:	Sf: 0-1 GS: 0-0 Gd: 1-1 GF: - Fm: 0-1
Distance:	2m/2m3: 0-0 **2m4-2m7: 1-3** 3m+: 0-0
Track:	**LH: 1-2** RH: 0-1 Tight: 0-2 Gall: 0-0
Aids:	Bl: 0-0 Vi: 0-0 Tstrap: 0-0
Best Rating:	104 11/02 MRas 2m3f110y soft Hdl

Moderate novice hurdler, shaped with a little promise on his belated debut when runner-up in a modest event at Sedgefield in October. Went one better at Hexham.

White Dove (FR)
97   67+

5-y-o b m Beaudelaire (USA)-Hermine And Pearls (FR) (Shirley Heights)
R Dickin G Clinton

Placings:U634   (1009)
2002/03: 16UGF, 17PG, 19JS, 174GF,

	Starts	1st	2nd	3rd	Win & Pl
Hurdles	4	0	0	1	940
Career Total	4	0	0	1	940

Going:	Sf: 0-0 GS: 0-0 Gd: 0-0 GF: - Fm: 0-2
Distance:	2m/2m3: 0-4 2m4-2m7: 0-0 3m+: 0-0
Track:	LH: 0-3 RH: 0-1 Tight: 0-2 Gall: 0-0
Aids:	Bl: 0-0 Vi: 0-0 Tstrap: 0-0
Best Rating:	67 8/02 Bang 2m1f gd-fm Hdl

White In Front
94(84h)   (69h)90

12-y-o ch g Tina s Pet-Lyaaric (Privy Seal)
Mrs A Price Mrs A Price

Placings:P/20F5P5FF/2240465F43/5062353434/0P503625
65314-334F60   (3136)
2002/03: 163GF, 173GS, 164G, 19FG, 196S, 200S,

	Starts	1st	2nd	3rd	Win & Pl
Chases	6	0	0	2	1776
Career Total	48	1	3	4	14735
95	3/02	Hrfd	2m	E(0-105)HCh	SFT	£4108

Total win prize-money £4108

Going:	Sf: 0-2 GS: 0-1 Gd: 0-2 GF: - Fm: 0-1
Distance:	2m/2m3: 0-5 2m4-2m7: 0-1 3m+: 0-0
Track:	LH: 0-1 RH: 0-5 Tight: 0-2 Gall: 0-0
Aids:	Bl: 0-0 Vi: 0-0 Tstrap: 0-0
Best Rating:	95 3/02 Hrfd 2m soft Ch

Moderate handicap chaser, best at two miles. Only ever runs at Hereford, Ludlow and Bangor-on-Dee.

White Rock Lady
76f

5-y-o b m Rock Hopper-Don t Tell Jean (Petong)
R D E Woodhouse Whitestonecliffe Racing Partnership

Placings:0000   (1609)
2002/03: 16OGF, 16OGF, 20AGF, 20OG,

	Starts	1st	2nd	3rd	Win & Pl
NH Flat	2	0	0	0	
Hurdles	2	0	0	0	
Career Total	4	0	0	0	

Going:	Sf: 0-0 GS: 0-0 Gd: 0-1 GF: - Fm: 0-3
Distance:	2m/2m3: 0-2 2m4-2m7: 0-2 3m+: 0-0

Track:	LH: 0-3 RH: 0-0 Tight: 0-0 Gall: 0-0
Aids:	Bl: 0-0 Vi: 0-0 Tstrap: 0-0
Best Rating:	66 7/02 Strf 2m110y gd-fm NHF

Whitebonnet (IRE)
61

13-y-o b g Rainbow Quest (USA)-Dawn Is Breaking (Import)
C F C Jackson Bogs Hole Racing

Placings:0200P/22501323/20F02500/00P4352/P1515F35/
46P0/6342/P0000-P   (0372)
2002/03: 27PS,

	Starts	1st	2nd	3rd	Win & Pl
Hurdles	1	0	0	0	
Career Total	50	3	8	5	14453
90	1/99	Extr	2m3f110yE(0-115)HHdl	HVY	£2495
81	6/98	NAbb	3m3f	F(0-115)HHdl	GD	£1802
89	1/96	Towc	2m5f	G(0-95)HHdl	SFT	£2052

Total win prize-money £6349

Going:	Sf: 0-1 GS: 0-0 Gd: 0-0 GF: - Fm: 0-0
Distance:	2m/2m3: 0-0 2m4-2m7: 0-0 3m+: 0-1
Track:	LH: 0-1 RH: 0-0 Tight: 0-1 Gall: 0-0
Aids:	Bl: 0-1 Vi: 0-0 Tstrap: 0-0
Best Rating:	95 1/95 Plum 2m1f soft Hdl

Whitenzo (FR)
112(105h)   (140h)140

7-y-o b g Lesotho (USA)-Whitengy (FR) (Olantengy (FR))
P F Nicholls Malcolm Pearce & Gerry Mizel Ii

Placings:00544/5P221112/644251425-540P50   (4791)
2002/03: 25SGS, 26AGS, 24OGS, 24PG, 25SG, 29OG,

	Starts	1st	2nd	3rd	Win & Pl
Chases	6	0	0	0	6500
Career Total	28	4	5	0	78199
114	3/02	Extr	3m110y	E Hdl	GD	£3024
147	2/01	Wwck	2m110y	A Ch	SFT	£15000
149	1/01	Tntn	2m110y	D Ch	HVY	£5292
114	1/01	Font	2m6f	D Ch	SFT	£4494

Total win prize-money £27810

Going:	Sf: 0-0 GS: 0-3 Gd: 0-3 GF: - Fm: 0-0
Distance:	2m/2m3: 0-0 2m4-2m7: 0-0 3m+: 0-6
Track:	LH: 0-5 RH: 0-1 Tight: 0-1 Gall: 0-2
Aids:	Bl: 0-0 Vi: 0-0 Tstrap: 0-0
Best Rating:	150 11/02 Newb 3m2f110y gd-sft Ch

Very useful chaser; acts well on good and soft ground; effective from two miles five to three miles plus; ran two fine races in 2002/3, in the Charlie Hall and the Hennessy, but was undone by a mistake each time; disappointing and pulled up on soft ground at Doncaster in March, and was again below his best at Aintree; frustrating.

Whitfield Warrior
94f   93f

5-y-o ch g Husyan (USA)-Valentines Day (Doctor Pangloss)
J R Turner Yarm Racing Partnership

Placings:4   (3412)
2002/03: 164GS,

	Starts	1st	2nd	3rd	Win & Pl
NH Flat	1	0	0	0	0
Career Total	1	0	0	0	0

Going:	Sf: 0-0 GS: 0-1 Gd: 0-0 GF: - Fm: 0-0
Distance:	2m/2m3: 0-1 2m4-2m7: 0-0 3m+: 0-0
Track:	LH: 0-1 RH: 0-0 Tight: 0-0 Gall: 0-0
Aids:	Bl: 0-0 Vi: 0-0 Tstrap: 0-0

Best Rating:	94	2/03 Weth 2m	gd-sft NHF

Showed some ability when well beaten fourth on his debut in a bumper at Wetherby in February.

Whitley Grange Boy
99(84h)   (55h)74

10-y-o b g Hubbly Bubbly (USA)-Choir (High Top)
A J Lockwood Mrs Carole Sykes

Placings:103/P0-6FU63   (4797)
2002/03: 16SG, 25FS, 21UG, 21SG, 273GF,

	Starts	1st	2nd	3rd	Win & Pl
Chases	5	0	0	1	668
Career Total	10	1	0	2	4193
107	10/99	Weth	2m4f110yD Hdl	G-F	£3187

Total win prize-money £3188

Going:	Sf: 0-1 GS: 0-0 Gd: 0-3 GF: - Fm: 0-1
Distance:	2m/2m3: 0-1 2m4-2m7: 0-2 3m+: 0-0
Track:	LH: 0-5 RH: 0-0 Tight: 0-5 Gall: 0-0
Aids:	Bl: 1-0 Vi: 0-0 Tstrap: 0-0
Best Rating:	107 10/99 Weth 2m4f110y gd-fm Hdl

Plating-class novice chaser; lightly raced of late; best on fast ground; stays well.

Who Cares Wins
108   99

7-y-o ch g Kris-anne Bonny (Ajdal (USA))
J R Jenkins The B C W Partnership

Placings:44/1-P20   (4159)
2002/03: 20PHY, 22PS, 22OG,

	Starts	1st	2nd	3rd	Win & Pl
Hurdles	3	0	1	0	1680
Career Total	6	1	1	0	5054
100	7/01	Strf	2m6f110yD Hdl	GD	£3374

Total win prize-money £3374

Going:	Sf: 0-2 GS: 0-0 Gd: 0-1 GF: - Fm: 0-0
Distance:	2m/2m3: 0-0 2m4-2m7: 0-3 3m+: 0-0
Track:	LH: 0-1 RH: 0-1 Tight: 0-1 Gall: 0-0
Aids:	Bl: 0-0 Vi: 0-0 Tstrap: 0-0
Best Rating:	105 3/01 Hntg 2m110y soft Hdl

Moderate hurdler; lightly raced; stays well and is best on a sound surface.

Who Dares Wins
106(103h)   (112h)79

10-y-o b g Kala Shikari-Sarah s Venture (Averof)
C Grant Mrs A Meller

Placings:322/32202/331363/31/23UP3023-330465   (4140)
2002/03: 269HY, 263HY, 24OHY, 244HY, 26PS, 32PS,

	Starts	1st	2nd	3rd	Win & Pl
Hurdles	1	0	0	0	395
Chases	5	0	0	2	2405
Career Total	30	2	7	12	25610
112	11/00	Uttx	3m2f	F(0-100)HCh	HVY	£2961
106	2/00	Carl	3m2f	D Ch	HVY	£4368

Total win prize-money £7329

Going:	Sf: 0-6 GS: 0-0 Gd: 0-0 GF: - Fm: 0-0
Distance:	2m/2m3: 0-0 2m4-2m7: 0-0 3m+: 0-6
Track:	LH: 0-3 RH: 0-3 Tight: 0-0 Gall: 0-1
Aids:	Bl: 0-0 Vi: 0-0 Tstrap: 0-0
Best Rating:	116 3/99 Carl 3m110y soft Hdl

Modest staying chaser, suited by marathon trips and very soft ground.

Who Is Equiname (IRE)

13-y-o b g Bob Back (USA)-Instanter (Morston (FR))
W J Warner Mrs Judy Wilson

Placings:2203/410203/6/43321/FP1/P-0P   (0209)
2002/03: 21⁰GF, 16⁶G,

	Starts	1st	2nd	3rd	Win & Pl
Chases	2	0	0	0	
Career Total	22	3	4	4	21883
113	12/97	Leic	2m7f110yD(0-125)HCh	GD	£4080
95	4/97	Towc	2m6f	E Ch	G-F	£2560
118	12/94	Kemp	2m	Hdl	SFT	£6555
			Total win prize-money £13195		

Going:	Sf: 0-0 GS: 0-0 Gd: 0-1 GF: - Fm: 0-1
Distance:	2m/2m3: 0-1 2m4-2m7: 0-1 3m+: 0-0
Track:	LH: 0-1 RH: 0-1 Tight: 0-0 Gall: 0-1
Aids:	Bl: 0-2 Vi: 0-0 Tstrap: 0-0
Best Rating:	120 5/97 Worc 2m7f110y soft Ch

Who's The Man

95   51

9-y-o gr g Arzanni-Tommys Dream (Le Bavard (FR))
N M L Ewart N M L Ewart

Placings:0/55-40P   (4505)
2002/03: 24⁴G, 24⁰G, 17⁶G,

	Starts	1st	2nd	3rd	Win & Pl
Chases	3	0	0	0	361
Career Total	6	0	0	0	361

Going:	Sf: 0-0 GS: 0-0 Gd: 0-3 GF: - Fm: 0-0
Distance:	2m/2m3: 0-1 2m4-2m7: 0-0 3m+: 0-2
Track:	LH: 0-1 RH: 0-2 Tight: 0-3 Gall: 0-0
Aids:	Bl: 0-0 Vi: 0-0 Tstrap: 0-0
Best Rating:	65 1/01 Catt 2m gd-sft Hdl

Who's To Say

90(98c)   (88c)57

17-y-o b g Saher-Whisht (Raise You Ten)
Dr P Pritchard Mrs T Pritchard

Placings:00/0331UF/6U5335514/02P413600U3536510/140
241303230/345344363/5PP3222614F063235P/014PU/0/60
05465U0PP-000   (0653)
2002/03: 20⁰S, 22⁹GF, 22⁸GF,

	Starts	1st	2nd	3rd	Win & Pl
Hurdles	3	0	0	0	
Career Total	106	11	8	17	61973
101	9/98	Hntg	2m110y	E(0-115)HCh	G-F	£2860
101	11/97	Wwck	2m	E(0-115)HCh	GD	£2977
127	11/95	Thur	2m	(0-120)HCh	YLD	£2204
123	5/95	Rosc	2m	(0-130)HCh	G-F	£2712
127	4/95	Fair	2m	HCh	F	£6782
120	10/94	Punc	2m	(0-123)HCh	YLD	£2935
124	3/94	Navn	2m	HCh	SH	£6571
106	1/93	Punc	2m	Ch	HVY	£4021
	1/92	Fair	2m2f	HHdl	YLD	£2901
	10/91	Gowr	2m	Hdl	Y-S	£2555
	9/91	Gowr	2m	NHF	soft	£2555
			Total win prize-money £39081		

Going:	Sf: 0-1 GS: 0-0 Gd: 0-0 GF: - Fm: 0-2
Distance:	2m/2m3: 0-0 2m4-2m7: 0-0 3m+: 0-0
Track:	LH: 0-3 RH: 0-0 Tight: 0-2 Gall: 0-0
Aids:	Bl: 0-0 Vi: 0-0 Tstrap: 0-0
Best Rating:	130 5/96 Weth 2m gd-fm Ch

Whose Line Is It

77   39

5-y-o gr g Sharp Deal-Madame Ruby (FR) (Homing)
N J Hawke Mrs D A Wetherall

Placings:623   (4628)
2002/03: 16⁶S, 16²GF, 17³GF,

	Starts	1st	2nd	3rd	Win & Pl
NH Flat	3	0	1	1	1090
Career Total	3	0	1	1	1090

Going:	Sf: 0-1 GS: 0-0 Gd: 0-0 GF: - Fm: 0-2
Distance:	2m/2m3: 0-3 2m4-2m7: 0-0 3m+: 0-0
Track:	LH: 0-2 RH: 0-0 Tight: 0-1 Gall: 0-0
Aids:	Bl: 0-0 Vi: 0-0 Tstrap: 0-0
Best Rating:	94 4/03 NAbb 2m1f gd-fm NHF

Moderate bumper performer; jumping bred; second in Stratford bumper in July 2002; returned from long break to finish third in similar event at Newton Abbot in April 2003.

Widemouth Bay (IRE)

122f   141f

5-y-o br g Be My Native (USA)-Lisaleen River (Over The River (FR))
P J Hobbs Mrs J F Deithrick

Placings:113   (4115)
2002/03: 16¹G, 16¹S, 16³G,

	Starts	1st	2nd	3rd	Win & Pl
NH Flat	3	2	0	1	6794
Career Total	3	2	0	1	6794
113	11/02	Winc	2m	H NHF	GD	£2394
			Total win prize-money £2394		

Going:	Sf: 1-1 GS: 0-0 Gd: 1-2 GF: - Fm: 0-0
Distance:	2m/2m3: 2-3 2m4-2m7: 0-0 3m+: 0-0
Track:	LH: 0-1 RH: 2-2 Tight: 0-0 Gall: 0-0
Aids:	Bl: 0-0 Vi: 0-0 Tstrap: 0-0
Best Rating:	141 3/03 Chel 2m110y good NHF

Useful bumper performer; easy winner on his bumper debut on good ground at Wincanton in November 2002; dead-heated on softer ground at Ludlow next time; third at Cheltenham Festival; genuine sort.

Wild About Harry

94f   103f

6-y-o ch g Romany Rye-Shylyn (Hay Chas)
A R Dicken (L G Cottrell 27/1) Ron Affleck

Placings:400   (4593)
2002/03: 16⁴S, 16⁰GS, 16⁶G,

	Starts	1st	2nd	3rd	Win & Pl
NH Flat	3	0	0	0	0
Career Total	3	0	0	0	0

Going:	Sf: 0-0 GS: 0-1 Gd: 0-1 GF: - Fm: 0-0
Distance:	2m/2m3: 0-3 2m4-2m7: 0-0 3m+: 0-0
Track:	LH: 0-2 RH: 0-1 Tight: 0-0 Gall: 0-0
Aids:	Bl: 0-0 Vi: 0-0 Tstrap: 0-0
Best Rating:	103 12/02 Wwck 2m soft NHF

Wild Bavard (IRE)

11-y-o b g Le Bavard (FR)-Wild Deer (Royal Buck)
A W Congdon A W Congdon

Placings:PUP/4PP/3   (0347)
2002/03: 26³GS,

	Starts	1st	2nd	3rd	Win & Pl
Chases	1	0	0	1	316
Career Total	7	0	0	1	605

Going:	Sf: 0-0 GS: 0-1 Gd: 0-0 GF: - Fm: 0-0
Distance:	2m/2m3: 0-0 2m4-2m7: 0-0 3m+: 0-1
Track:	LH: 0-1 RH: 0-0 Tight: 0-1 Gall: 0-0
Aids:	Bl: 0-0 Vi: 0-0 Tstrap: 0-0
Best Rating:	79 5/02 NAbb 3m2f110y gd-sft Ch

Wild Blade (IRE)

(97h)   (68h)40

10-y-o ch g Meneval (USA)-Tuney Blade (Fine Blade (USA))
Noel T Chance Middleham Park Racing Xvi

Placings:14036/50106/P4006-P   (0114)
2002/03: 25⁶GS,

	Starts	1st	2nd	3rd	Win & Pl
Chases	1	0	0	0	
Career Total	16	2	0	1	3568
94	8/99	Worc	2m4f	F(0-100)HHdl	G-F	£1900
104	5/98	Ludl	2m	H NHF	G-F	£1236
			Total win prize-money £3136		

Going:	Sf: 0-0 GS: 0-1 Gd: 0-0 GF: - Fm: 0-0
Distance:	2m/2m3: 0-0 2m4-2m7: 0-0 3m+: 0-1
Track:	LH: 0-0 RH: 0-1 Tight: 0-0 Gall: 0-0
Aids:	Bl: 0-0 Vi: 0-1 Tstrap: 0-0
Best Rating:	104 5/98 Ludl 2m gd-fm NHF

Modest handicap hurdler.

Wild Dream

112   103+

8-y-o b m Derrylin-Vedra (IRE) (Carlingford Castle)
S Pike Stewart Pike

Placings:3/12-31   (2169)
2002/03: 17³G, 21¹GS,

	Starts	1st	2nd	3rd	Win & Pl
Hurdles	2	1	0	1	4443
Career Total	5	2	1	2	8947
103	11/02	Wwck	2m5f	D Hdl	G-S	£3913
100	6/01	Worc	2m	H NHF	GD	£1515
			Total win prize-money £5429		

Going:	Sf: 0-0 GS: 1-1 Gd: 0-1 GF: - Fm: 0-0
Distance:	2m/2m3: 0-1 2m4-2m7: 1-1 3m+: 0-0
Track:	LH: 1-1 RH: 0-1 Tight: 0-0 Gall: 0-0
Aids:	Bl: 0-0 Vi: 0-0 Tstrap: 0-0
Best Rating:	126 11/01 Chel 2m110y good NHF

Moderate hurdler; tough and useful bumper performer, she won over hurdles at Warwick in November 2002 over two miles five and is very much at home in soft ground.

Wild Hadeer

91   93

9-y-o ch g Hadeer-Wild Moon (USA) (Arctic Tern (USA))
John R Upson The Nap Hand Partnership

Placings:51464/24512/PP00210-0   (0146)
2002/03: 20⁰GF,

	Starts	1st	2nd	3rd	Win & Pl
Hurdles	1	0	0	0	
Career Total	18	3	3	0	10244
93	4/02	Towc	2m	G(0-95)HHdl	G-F	£2009
99	3/00	Towc	2m5f	D(0-120)HHdl	GD	£3133
94	3/99	Catt	2m	E Hdl	SFT	£2915

Total win prize-money £8057

Going:	Sf: 0-0 GS: 0-0 Gd: 0-0 GF: - Fm: 0-1
Distance:	2m/2m3: 0-0 2m4-2m7: 0-1 3m+: 0-0
Track:	LH: 0-1 RH: 0-0 Tight: 0-0 Gall: 0-0
Aids:	Bl: 0-1 Vi: 0-0 Tstrap: 0-0
Best Rating:	104 4/00 Hexm 2m4f110y good Hdl

Moderate hurdler, stays two miles-five, and is effective on good ground or softer. Usually wears blinkers.

Wild Knight (IRE)
103   111
6-y-o b g Jurado (USA)-Knight s Maid (Giolla Mear)
P F Nicholls Hunt & Co (bournemouth) Ltd

Placings:21F4P23   (4772)
2002/03: 17²G, 16¹GF, 22²GS, 20⁴S, 22PGS, 16²GF, 16³G,

	Starts	1st	2nd	3rd	Win & Pl
NH Flat	2	1	1	0	2414
Hurdles	5	0	1	1	1859
Career Total	7	1	2	1	4273
86	10/02	Chep	2m110y	H NHF	G-F	£1883

Total win prize-money £1883

Going:	Sf: 0-1 GS: 0-2 Gd: 0-2 GF: - Fm: 1-2
Distance:	2m/2m3: 1-4 2m4-2m7: 0-3 3m+: 0-0
Track:	LH: 1-2 RH: 0-5 Tight: 0-0 Gall: 0-0
Aids:	Bl: 0-0 Vi: 0-0 Tstrap: 0-0
Best Rating:	111 3/03 Winc 2m gd-fm Hdl

Modest hurdler; former bumper winner; best on a sound surface.

Wild Romance (IRE)
108   125d
8-y-o b g Accordion-Mandy s Last (Krayyan)
D J Wintle B E T Partnership

Placings:60/40110021/3310-F255   (4345)
2002/03: 16PGS, 16²GS, 16⁵S, 16⁵GF,

	Starts	1st	2nd	3rd	Win & Pl
Hurdles	4	0	1	0	1661
Career Total	18	4	2	2	26320
125	12/01	Limk	2m	Hdl	SFT	£7862
124	2/01	Gowr	2m	Hdl	HVY	£5564
90	7/00	Tipp	2m	NHF	G-F	£3032
	6/00	Tipp	2m1f	NHF	G-Y	£3588

Total win prize-money £20048

Going:	Sf: 0-1 GS: 0-2 Gd: 0-0 GF: - Fm: 0-1
Distance:	2m/2m3: 0-4 2m4-2m7: 0-0 3m+: 0-0
Track:	LH: 0-3 RH: 0-1 Tight: 0-0 Gall: 0-0
Aids:	Bl: 0-0 Vi: 0-0 Tstrap: 0-0
Best Rating:	125 12/01 Limk 2m soft Hdl

Fair ex-Irish hurdler; has shown modest ability since coming to Britain; acts on soft ground; effective at around two miles.

Wild Spice (IRE)
111(99h)   (121h)114
8-y-o b g Mandalus-Curry Lunch (Pry)
Miss Venetia Williams M Crabb, B Ead, P May, M Moore

Placings:5330/1/0-1U16052F25   (4438)
2002/03: 22¹G, 20UG, 27¹GF, 20PG, 20⁴GS, 24⁵GS, 26²HY, 24²G, 25²S, 24⁵G,

	Starts	1st	2nd	3rd	Win & Pl
Hurdles	4	2	0	0	7817
Chases	6	0	2	0	2924
Career Total	16	3	2	2	14369
121	5/02	Strf	3m3f	D(0-125)HHdl	G-F	£4127
121	5/02	Extr	2m6f110yD(0-115)HHdl	GD	£3689

---

114 5/00 Hrfd 3m2f E Hdl GD £2600
Total win prize-money £10417

Going:	Sf: 0-2 GS: 0-2 Gd: 1-5 GF: - Fm: 1-1
Distance:	2m/2m3: 0-0 2m4-2m7: 1-4 3m+: 1-6
Track:	LH: 1-6 RH: 1-4 Tight: 1-2 Gall: 0-2
Aids:	Bl: 0-0 Vi: 0-0 Tstrap: 0-0
Best Rating:	121 1/03 Chep 3m2f110y heavy Ch

Modest hurdler/chaser; has not always impressed with his jumping; acts well on a decent surface; stays very well.

Wildfield Rufo (IRE)
108(99c)   (114c)110
8-y-o b g Celio Rufo-Jersey Girl (Hard Boy)
Mrs K Walton Mrs Carol Holroyd

Placings:14-FF2210   (3797)
2002/03: 24²FG, 25²FG, 22²HY, 24²HY, 24¹S, 24⁰S,

	Starts	1st	2nd	3rd	Win & Pl
Hurdles	4	1	2	0	6027
Chases	2	0	0	0	0
Career Total	8	2	2	0	8335
99	2/03	Ayr	3m110y	E Hdl	SFT	£3549
114	3/02	Catt	3m1f110yH Ch	G-S	£1475

Total win prize-money £5025

Going:	Sf: 1-4 GS: 0-0 Gd: 0-2 GF: - Fm: 0-0
Distance:	2m/2m3: 0-0 2m4-2m7: 0-1 3m+: 1-5
Track:	LH: 1-6 RH: 0-0 Tight: 0-1 Gall: 0-1
Aids:	Bl: 0-0 Vi: 0-0 Tstrap: 0-0
Best Rating:	114 3/02 Catt 3m1f110y gd-sft Ch

Modest hurdler/chaser; winner of his only outing in an Irish point; impressive on his hunter chase bow at Catterick in March 2002 but had jumping problems in the autumn and was switched to hurdles in 2003, winning a three mile novices event by a wide margin at Wetherby in May; best on soft ground but handles quicker.

Wilfie Wild
7-y-o b g Nomadic Way (USA)-Wild Child (Grey Ghost)
Mrs Lynne Ward A Jackson

Placings:P   (0083)
2002/03: 25PGS,

	Starts	1st	2nd	3rd	Win & Pl
Chases	1	0	0	0	
Career Total	1	0	0	0	

Going:	Sf: 0-0 GS: 0-1 Gd: 0-0 GF: - Fm: 0-0
Distance:	2m/2m3: 0-0 2m4-2m7: 0-0 3m+: 0-1
Track:	LH: 0-1 RH: 0-0 Tight: 0-0 Gall: 0-0
Aids:	Bl: 0-0 Vi: 0-0 Tstrap: 0-0
Best Rating:	

Wilfram
102   80
6-y-o b g Fraam-Ming Blue (Primo Dominie)
J M Bradley Robert Bailey

Placings:002640   (4622)
2002/03: 16⁰S, 16⁰G, 19²F, 19⁶GF, 22⁴GF, 22⁰GF,

	Starts	1st	2nd	3rd	Win & Pl
Hurdles	6	0	1	0	1666
Career Total	6	0	1	0	1666

Going:	Sf: 0-1 GS: 0-0 Gd: 0-1 GF: - Fm: 0-4
Distance:	2m/2m3: 0-2 2m4-2m7: 0-4 3m+: 0-0

Track:	LH: 0-2 RH: 0-4 Tight: 0-3 Gall: 0-0
Aids:	Bl: 0-0 Vi: 0-0 Tstrap: 0-0
Best Rating:	80 4/03 Strf 2m6f110y gd-fm Hdl

Moderate novice hurdler; suited by two and a half miles; has worn cheekpieces and blinkers.

Wilful Lord (IRE)
80   57
6-y-o b g Lord Americo-Dotties Girl (IRE) (Remainder Man)
J Wade John Wade

Placings:000   (4228)
2002/03: 21⁰GF, 19⁰GS, 25⁰GF,

	Starts	1st	2nd	3rd	Win & Pl
Hurdles	3	0	0	0	
Career Total	3	0	0	0	

Going:	Sf: 0-1 GS: 0-1 Gd: 0-0 GF: - Fm: 0-1
Distance:	2m/2m3: 0-0 2m4-2m7: 0-2 3m+: 0-1
Track:	LH: 0-3 RH: 0-0 Tight: 0-1 Gall: 0-0
Aids:	Bl: 0-0 Vi: 0-0 Tstrap: 0-0
Best Rating:	57 3/03 Weth 3m1f gd-fm Hdl

Will She
66f   24f
5-y-o b m Bollin William-She s A Madam (Kabour)
M E Sowersby Paul Clifton

Placings:000   (0833)
2002/03: 17⁰GF, 16⁰G, 17⁰GF,

	Starts	1st	2nd	3rd	Win & Pl
NH Flat	3	0	0	0	
Career Total	3	0	0	0	

Going:	Sf: 0-0 GS: 0-0 Gd: 0-1 GF: - Fm: 0-2
Distance:	2m/2m3: 0-3 2m4-2m7: 0-0 3m+: 0-0
Track:	LH: 0-2 RH: 0-1 Tight: 0-2 Gall: 0-0
Aids:	Bl: 0-0 Vi: 0-0 Tstrap: 0-3
Best Rating:	24 7/02 Sedg 2m1f gd-fm NHF

Will Tell
100f   93f
5-y-o b g Rainbow Quest (USA)-Guillem (USA) (Nijinsky (CAN))
Mrs S J Smith (T J Etherington 24/11) Apb Racing

Placings:04   (4778)
2002/03: 17⁰G, 16⁴G,

	Starts	1st	2nd	3rd	Win & Pl
NH Flat	2	0	0	0	0
Career Total	2	0	0	0	0

Going:	Sf: 0-0 GS: 0-0 Gd: 0-2 GF: - Fm: 0-0
Distance:	2m/2m3: 0-2 2m4-2m7: 0-0 3m+: 0-0
Track:	LH: 0-0 RH: 0-1 Tight: 0-0 Gall: 0-0
Aids:	Bl: 0-0 Vi: 0-0 Tstrap: 0-0
Best Rating:	93 4/03 Prth 2m110y good NHF

Modest form in bumpers on good ground.

Will'Sillyshankers
77   47
8-y-o b g Silly Prices-Hannah s Song (Saintly Song)
G A Ham D M Drury

Placings:06'00P00P-0P   (0505)
2002/03: 19ᴳG, 24ᴾG,

	Starts	1st	2nd	3rd	Win & Pl
Hurdles	2	0	0	0	
Career Total	10	0	0	0	0

Going: Sf: 0-0 GS: 0-0 Gd: 0-2 GF: - Fm: 0-0
Distance: 2m2m3: 0-0 2m4-2m7: 0-1 3m+: 0-1
Track: LH: 0-1 RH: 0-1 Tight: 0-0 Gall: 0-0
Aids: Bl: 0-0 Vi: 0-0 Tstrap: 0-0
Best Rating: 85 4/01 Winc 2m   soft   NHF

Willa Thyne (IRE)
26
9-y-o br m Good Thyne (USA)-Florella (Royal Fountain)
R Allan Mrs V Scott Watson

Placings:03320P/500/0P6/0P0P-5   (0398)
2002/03: 20ᴾG, 16ᴾGF,

	Starts	1st	2nd	3rd	Win & Pl
Hurdles	2	0	0	0	
Career Total	17	0	1	2	747

Going: Sf: 0-0 GS: 0-0 Gd: 0-1 GF: - Fm: 0-1
Distance: 2m2m3: 0-1 2m4-2m7: 0-1 3m+: 0-0
Track: LH: 0-2 RH: 0-0 Tight: 0-0 Gall: 0-1
Aids: Bl: 0-0 Vi: 0-1 Tstrap: 0-1
Best Rating: 81 11/98 Hexm 2m   heavy   NHF

Lightly-raced longstanding maiden hurdler.

William George (IRE)
90   36
4-y-o b g Turtle Island (IRE)-Lady s Dream (Mazilier (USA))
J Joseph Jack Joseph

Placings:060PU05P   (4425)
2002/03: 16ᴰGS, 18ᴾG, 16ᴾGF, 16ᴾGS, 16ᵁS, 17ᴾGS, 16ᴾG, 16ᴾGF,

	Starts	1st	2nd	3rd	Win & Pl
Hurdles	8	0	0	0	
Career Total	8	0	0	0	0

Going: Sf: 0-1 GS: 0-3 Gd: 0-2 GF: - Fm: 0-2
Distance: 2m2m3: 0-8 2m4-2m7: 0-0 3m+: 0-0
Track: LH: 0-5 RH: 0-3 Tight: 0-3 Gall: 0-2
Aids: Bl: 0-0 Vi: 0-0 Tstrap: 0-0
Best Rating: 66 9/02 Hntg 2m110y   gd-fm   Hdl

Well held over hurdles so far.

William Lionheart
90   74d
9-y-o b g Henbit (USA)-Come To Tea (IRE) (Be My Guest (USA))
Mrs Jane Galpin G P Galpin & Mrs J Dowson

Placings:00004/0/0U54   (3313)
2002/03: 24ᴰGS, 23ᵁHY, 22ᴾHY, 23ᴬGS,

	Starts	1st	2nd	3rd	Win & Pl
Chases	4	0	0	0	373
Career Total	10	0	0	0	373

Going: Sf: 0-1 GS: 0-3 Gd: 0-0 GF: - Fm: 0-0
Distance: 2m2m3: 0-0 2m4-2m7: 0-1 3m+: 0-3
Track: LH: 0-0 RH: 0-3 Tight: 0-2 Gall: 0-0
Aids: Bl: 0-0 Vi: 0-0 Tstrap: 0-0
Best Rating: 74 1/03 Font 2m6f   heavy   Ch

William O'Dee (NZ)
14-y-o br g Exceptionnel-Fiducia O Dee (NZ) (Sir Godfrey (FR))
G Chambers R H Pedrick

Placings:0PP/2F436/4533/03F-4   (0368)
2002/03: 21ᴬS,

	Starts	1st	2nd	3rd	Win & Pl
Chases	1	0	0	0	774
Career Total	16	0	1	4	6204

Going: Sf: 0-1 GS: 0-0 Gd: 0-0 GF: - Fm: 0-0
Distance: 2m2m3: 0-0 2m4-2m7: 0-0 3m+: 0-0
Track: LH: 0-1 RH: 0-0 Tight: 0-1 Gall: 0-0
Aids: Bl: 0-0 Vi: 0-0 Tstrap: 0-0
Best Rating: 112 12/99 Chel 2m5f   good   Ch

Willie Makeit (IRE)
13-y-o b g Coquelin (USA)-Turbina (Tudor Melody)
Mrs A L Tory Mrs A L Tory

Placings:000F0/P26P/P21116332U/45P5/F/1P555/4/40P (4443)
2002/03: 21ᴬGF, 24ᴰG, 19ᴾG,

	Starts	1st	2nd	3rd	Win & Pl
Chases	3	0	0	0	523
Career Total	33	4	3	2	18087

84	5/99	MRas	2m6f110yH Ch	G-F	£2442
90	8/96	Sthl	2m4f110yD(0-105)HCh	GD	£4150
90	8/96	Worc	2m E(0-100)HCh	GD	£2877
88	7/96	Worc	2m E(0-100)HCh	G-F	£3556

Total win prize-money £13025

Going: Sf: 0-0 GS: 0-0 Gd: 0-1 GF: - Fm: 0-2
Distance: 2m2m3: 0-0 2m4-2m7: 0-2 3m+: 0-1
Track: LH: 0-1 RH: 0-2 Tight: 0-1 Gall: 0-0
Aids: Bl: 0-0 Vi: 0-0 Tstrap: 0-0
Best Rating: 90 8/96 Sthl 2m4f110y good   Ch

Veteran hunter chaser, suited by fast ground and stays three miles.

Willoughby Flyer
5-y-o b g Homo Sapien-Jane s Daughter (Pitpan)
John R Upson Willoughby CC Associates Partnership

Placings:50PP   (4347)
2002/03: 25ᴬG, 21ᴰG, 24ᴾG, 25ᴾG,

	Starts	1st	2nd	3rd	Win & Pl
Hurdles	4	0	0	0	
Career Total	4	0	0	0	0

Going: Sf: 0-0 GS: 0-0 Gd: 0-0 GF: 0-2 Fm: -
Distance: 2m2m3: 0-0 2m4-2m7: 0-1 3m+: 0-1
Track: LH: 0-3 RH: 0-1 Tight: 0-1 Gall: 0-0
Aids: Bl: 0-0 Vi: 0-0 Tstrap: 0-0
Best Rating: 0 3/03 Wwck 3m1f   gd-fm   Hdl

Willoughby's Boy (IRE)
78   42
6-y-o b g Night Shift (USA)-Andbell (Trojan Fen)

B Hanbury Mrs G E M Brown

Placings:0   (1890)
2002/03: 16ᴾGS,

	Starts	1st	2nd	3rd	Win & Pl
Hurdles	1	0	0	0	
Career Total	1	0	0	0	0

Going: Sf: 0-0 GS: 0-1 Gd: 0-0 GF: - Fm: 0-0
Distance: 2m2m3: 0-1 2m4-2m7: 0-0 3m+: 0-0
Track: LH: 0-0 RH: 0-0 Tight: 0-0 Gall: 0-1
Aids: Bl: 0-0 Vi: 0-0 Tstrap: 0-0
Best Rating: 44 11/02 Hntg 2m110y   gd-sft Hdl

Willow Run (NZ)
94   80
9-y-o b g Conquistarose (USA)-Crazy Lady (NZ) (One Pound Sterling)
B Ellison Brian Ellison

Placings:6560/1252503-00000   (3508)
2002/03: 16ᴰGF, 17ᴰS, 16ᴰS, 16ᴰG, 16ᴰG,

	Starts	1st	2nd	3rd	Win & Pl
Hurdles	5	0	0	0	
Career Total	16	1	2	1	3671

89	10/01	Sedg	2m1f F(0-95)HHdl	G-S	£2299

Total win prize-money £2300

Going: Sf: 0-2 GS: 0-0 Gd: 0-2 GF: - Fm: 0-1
Distance: 2m2m3: 0-5 2m4-2m7: 0-0 3m+: 0-1
Track: LH: 0-4 RH: 0-1 Tight: 0-3 Gall: 0-1
Aids: Bl: 0-0 Vi: 0-0 Tstrap: 0-0
Best Rating: 89 10/01 Sedg 2m1f   gd-sft Hdl

Willow Wonder
4-y-o ch f Greensmith-Walnut Way (Gambling Debt)
M R Hoad Mr & Mrs D A Gamble

Placings:P   (2005)
2002/03: 17ᴾS,

	Starts	1st	2nd	3rd	Win & Pl
Hurdles	1	0	0	0	
Career Total	1	0	0	0	0

Going: Sf: 0-1 GS: 0-0 Gd: 0-0 GF: - Fm: 0-0
Distance: 2m2m3: 0-1 2m4-2m7: 0-0 3m+: 0-0
Track: LH: 0-0 RH: 0-1 Tight: 0-0 Gall: 0-0
Aids: Bl: 0-0 Vi: 0-0 Tstrap: 0-0
Best Rating: 0 11/02 Folk 2m1f110y soft   Hdl

Wills Perk (IRE)
92   69
8-y-o ch m Executive Perk-Brandy Hill Girl (Green Shoon)
N B Mason N B Mason

Placings:F05PF05-0   (0182)
2002/03: 25ᴾG,

	Starts	1st	2nd	3rd	Win & Pl
Chases	1	0	0	0	
Career Total	8	0	0	0	0

Going: Sf: 0-1 GS: 0-0 Gd: 0-0 GF: - Fm: 0-0
Distance: 2m2m3: 0-2 2m4-2m7: 0-0 3m+: 0-0
Track: LH: 0-1 RH: 0-0 Tight: 0-0 Gall: 0-0
Aids: Bl: 0-0 Vi: 0-0 Tstrap: 0-0
Best Rating: 69 10/01 Carl 2m4f   soft   Ch

Willy Willy

100(90c)   (72c)**93**

10-y-o ch g Master Willie-Monsoon (Royal Palace)
G Brown   Mrs Amanda Killick

Placings:00411663420/113F00/PP551-255P   (2418)
2002/03: 16²GF, 16⁵GS, 19⁵GF, 22⁶G,

	Starts	1st	2nd	3rd	Win & Pl
Hurdles	3	0	1	0	836
Chases	1	0	0	0	0
Career Total	26	5	2	2	20041
93	10/01	Ludl	2m5f	F(0-90)Hdl	G-F	2670
104	8/00	MRas	2m4f	D Ch	G-F	5331
109	7/00	MRas	2m1f110yF(0-105)HCh	G-F	4056
109	10/99	Winc	2m	F(0-100)HHdl	GD	2374
109	9/99	MRas	2m1f110yF(0-100)HHdl	G-F	2318

Total win prize-money £16751

Going: Sf: 0-0 GS: 0-1 Gd: 0-1 GF: - Fm: 0-2
Distance: 2m2m3: 0-2 2m4-2m7: 0-2 3m+: 0-0
Track: LH: 0-2 RH: 0-1 Tight: 0-4 Gall: 0-0
Aids: Bl: 0-0 Vi: 0-0 Tstrap: 0-0
Best Rating: 109   7/00   MRas   2m1f110y   gd-frm   Ch

Modest front-running hurdler, stays two miles-five, suited by fast ground.

Wilton Bridge (IRE)

86   (104h)**104**

9-y-o b g Clearly Bust-Pai-Collect (Paico)
A J Martin   M Heery

Placings:0/000200/00F04112/4F/1313-44UU   (4751)
2002/03: 16⁴SH, 21⁴HY, 21ᵁYS, 20ᵁG,

	Starts	1st	2nd	3rd	Win & Pl
Chases	4	0	0	0	761
Career Total	25	4	2	2	26215
100	12/01	Clon	2m4f	(0-102)HCh	SH	6677
94	11/01	Punc	2m2f	(0-116)HCh	Y-S	7790
107	3/00	Carl	2m4f110yF(0-110)HHdl	G-S	4836
91	3/00	Dpat	3m	(0-95)HCh	G-F	2345

Total win prize-money £21649

Going: Sf: 0-1 GS: 0-0 Gd: 0-1 GF: - Fm: 0-0
Distance: 2m2m3: 0-1 2m4-2m7: 0-3 3m+: 0-0
Track: LH: 0-1 RH: 0-3 Tight: 0-0 Gall: 0-0
Aids: Bl: 0-0 Vi: 0-0 Tstrap: 0-0
Best Rating: 107   3/00   Carl   2m4f110y   gd-sft   Hdl

Moderate Irish chaser; acts on most types of ground, and is effective between two miles two and three miles.

Win Alot

99   **80**

5-y-o b g Aragon-Having Fun (Hard Fought)
S R Bowring   Coverscope Ductwork & Reedkleen Supplies

Placings:P0R531-2P65   (4786)
2002/03: 17²GF, 24²GF, 17⁶G, 22⁵G,

	Starts	1st	2nd	3rd	Win & Pl
Hurdles	4	0	1	0	580
Career Total	10	1	1	1	2608
79	4/02	MRas	2m1f110yG(0-95)HHdl	GD	1750

Total win prize-money £1750

Going: Sf: 0-0 GS: 0-0 Gd: 0-2 GF: - Fm: 0-0
Distance: 2m2m3: 0-2 2m4-2m7: 0-1 3m+: 0-1
Track: LH: 0-1 RH: 0-2 Tight: 0-3 Gall: 0-0
Aids: Bl: 0-0 Vi: 0-0 Tstrap: 0-0
Best Rating: 80   4/03   MRas   2m6f   good   Hdl

Selling hurdler; best around two miles on a sound surface.

Win The Toss

91(89c)   (67c)**47**

11-y-o b g Idiots Delight-Mayfield (USA) (Alleged (USA))
P York   R M Green

Placings:0/0/220554P201/442UP/6004/0-06UP   (4443)
2002/03: 26⁹G, 16⁶GS, 21ᵁG, 19⁸G,

	Starts	1st	2nd	3rd	Win & Pl
Chases	4	0	0	0	0
Career Total	26	1	4	0	4609
94	5/99	Uttx	2m4f110yG(0-100)HHdl	GD	1784

Total win prize-money £1784

Going: Sf: 0-0 GS: 0-1 Gd: 0-3 GF: - Fm: 0-0
Distance: 2m2m3: 0-1 2m4-2m7: 0-2 3m+: 0-1
Track: LH: 0-1 RH: 0-3 Tight: 0-2 Gall: 0-0
Aids: Bl: 0-0 Vi: 0-0 Tstrap: 0-0
Best Rating: 111   5/98   Uttx   2m   gd-sft   NHF

Winchester

108   **126**

8-y-o ch g Gunner B-Tracy Jack (David Jack)
K A Ryan   Mr & Mrs K Hughes

Placings:402/421P/31236   (4461)
2002/03: 22³HY, 19¹G, 25²G, 23³GF, 20⁶G,

	Starts	1st	2nd	3rd	Win & Pl
Chases	5	1	1	2	11060
Career Total	12	2	3	2	15134
111	1/03	Catt	2m3f	D Ch	GD	6851
110	1/01	Catt	3m1f110yE Hdl	G-S	2607

Total win prize-money £9459

Going: Sf: 0-1 GS: 0-0 Gd: 1-3 GF: - Fm: 0-1
Distance: 2m2m3: 1-1 2m4-2m7: 0-2 3m+: 0-2
Track: LH: 1-4 RH: 0-0 Tight: 1-3 Gall: 0-0
Aids: Bl: 0-0 Vi: 0-0 Tstrap: 0-0
Best Rating: 126   3/03   Weth   2m7f110y   gd-frm   Ch

Useful chaser; winner over hurdles; off the track for 21 months before showing promise on his chasing debut; off the mark over fences at Catterick in January; stays three miles plus; acts on soft ground.

Windfola

95f   **71f**

4-y-o b f Sovereign Water (FR)-Sainte Martine (Martinmas)
R D E Woodhouse   Miss J M Slater

Placings:5   (3583)
2002/03: 16⁵G,

	Starts	1st	2nd	3rd	Win & Pl
NH Flat	1	0	0	0	0
Career Total	1	0	0	0	0

Going: Sf: 0-0 GS: 0-0 Gd: 0-1 GF: - Fm: 0-0
Distance: 2m2m3: 0-1 2m4-2m7: 0-0 3m+: 0-0
Track: LH: 0-0 RH: 0-1 Tight: 0-1 Gall: 0-0
Aids: Bl: 0-0 Vi: 0-0 Tstrap: 0-0
Best Rating: 71   2/03   Muss   2m   good   NHF

Windle Brook

102   **98**

11-y-o b g Gildoran-Minigale (Strong Gale)
K C Bailey   Peter Granger

Placings:0/05U63U/422F01/423P1-032PPP   (1593)
2002/03: 19⁰G, 26³G, 23²GF, 24⁸G, 24⁴GS, 23⁸G,

	Starts	1st	2nd	3rd	Win & Pl
Chases	6	0	1	1	1776

	Starts	1st	2nd	3rd	Win & Pl
	Career Total	24	2	4	3	13180
98	4/02	Extr	2m3f110yF(0-95)HCh	FRM	3851
96	9/00	Hntg	3m	F(0-110)HCh	G-F	3250

Total win prize-money £7101

Going: Sf: 0-0 GS: 0-1 Gd: 0-4 GF: - Fm: 0-1
Distance: 2m2m3: 0-0 2m4-2m7: 0-1 3m+: 0-5
Track: LH: 0-4 RH: 0-2 Tight: 0-2 Gall: 0-0
Aids: Bl: 0-0 Vi: 0-0 Tstrap: 0-1
Best Rating: 101   4/97   Worc   2m   gd-fm   NHF

Moderate chaser, he stays three miles on a lively surface.

Windross

107   **134**

11-y-o b g Ardross-Dans Le Vent (Pollerton)
A King   Mrs Peter Prowting

Placings:221140/221F12/3P60/1-PF   (4469)
2002/03: 24ᴾHY, 25ᴾG,

	Starts	1st	2nd	3rd	Win & Pl
Chases	2	0	0	0	
Career Total	19	5	5	1	37914
140	12/01	Newb	3m	D(0-125)HCh	GD	11193
145	2/00	Newb	3m	C Ch	G-S	7595
130	12/99	Uttx	2m5f	D Ch	SFT	4102
124	1/99	Hayd	2m4f	E Hdl	SFT	2340
123	12/98	Wwck	2m3f	E Hdl	G-S	2897

Total win prize-money £28130

Going: Sf: 0-1 GS: 0-0 Gd: 0-1 GF: - Fm: 0-0
Distance: 2m2m3: 0-0 2m4-2m7: 0-0 3m+: 0-2
Track: LH: 0-1 RH: 0-1 Tight: 0-1 Gall: 0-0
Aids: Bl: 0-0 Vi: 0-0 Tstrap: 0-0
Best Rating: 145   2/00   Kemp   3m   gd-sft   Ch

Useful chaser; injured after winning the Mandarin at Newbury in December 2001; absent until returning in February 2003; bounced back to form when winning handicap at Stratford May 2003; stays three miles; acts on good and soft ground.

Windy Valley (IRE)

106(107c)   (97c)**99**

10-y-o gr g Roi Guillaume (FR)-My Bonny Girl (Bonne Noel)
Mrs A J Hamilton-Fairley   Runs In The Family

Placings:0000/000532321322U5/254222/12036U/1032355
242024-PFF24P   (1245)
2002/03: 21ᴾGF, 20ᴾGF, 22ᴾGF, 20²GF, 18⁴G, 24ᴾG,

	Starts	1st	2nd	3rd	Win & Pl
Hurdles	4	0	1	0	1560
Chases	2	0	0	0	0
Career Total	49	3	14	6	23728
99	5/01	Font	2m2f110yF(0-105)HHdl	G-F	2488
93	5/00	Wwck	2m4f110yE(0-115)HHdl	G-F	2710
89	10/98	Font	2m1f172y Hdl	GD	1494

Total win prize-money £6694

Going: Sf: 0-0 GS: 0-0 Gd: 0-2 GF: - Fm: 0-4
Distance: 2m2m3: 0-1 2m4-2m7: 0-4 3m+: 0-1
Track: LH: 0-5 RH: 0-1 Tight: 0-3 Gall: 0-0
Aids: Bl: 0-0 Vi: 0-0 Tstrap: 0-6
Best Rating: 99   5/01   Font   2m2f110y   gd-fm   Hdl

Moderate ex-Irish hurdler/novice chaser, he stays three miles and is effective on fast ground, but is proving very hard to win with.

Winged Angel

103   **104+**

6-y-o ch g Prince Sabo-Silky Heights (IRE) (Head For Heights)

L Lungo Four Up One Down Partnership

Placings:0P-5211   (0579)
2002/03: 20⁵G, 16²G, 20¹G, 20¹G,

	Starts	1st	2nd	3rd	Win & Pl
Hurdles	4	2	1	0	6064
Career Total	6	2	1	0	6064
93	6/02	Hexm 2m4f110yE(0-105)HHdl	GD	£2530
104	6/02	Hexm 2m4f110yE(0-105)HHdl	GD	£2467
			Total win prize-money £4999

Going: Sf: 0-0 GS: 0-0 Gd: 2-4 GF: - Fm: 0-0
Distance: 2m2m3: 0-1 2m4-2m7: 2-3 3m+: 0-0
Track: LH: 2-4 RH: 0-0 Tight: 0-0 Gall: 0-0
Aids: Bl: 0-0 Vi: 0-0 Tstrap: 0-0
Best Rating: 104 6/02 Hexm 2m4f110y good Hdl

Moderate, improving hurdler, successful twice at Hexham in the summer of 2002. Stays two and a half miles.

Winged Hussar
103(110h)   (106h)106
10-y-o b g In The Wings-Akila (FR) (Top Ville)
D R Gandolfo   A E Frost

Placings:2PF2P4-42052   (4317)
2002/03: 17⁴S, 16²S, 17⁰GS, 19⁵G, 17²G,

	Starts	1st	2nd	3rd	Win & Pl
Hurdles	4	0	1	0	1462
Chases	1	0	1	0	1655
Career Total	11	0	4	0	5634

Going: Sf: 0-2 GS: 0-1 Gd: 0-2 GF: - Fm: 0-0
Distance: 2m2m3: 0-4 2m4-2m7: 0-1 3m+: 0-0
Track: LH: 0-3 RH: 0-2 Tight: 0-2 Gall: 0-1
Aids: Bl: 0-0 Vi: 0-0 Tstrap: 0-0
Best Rating: 106 1/03 Ludl 2m soft Hdl

Modest hurdler/chaser; useful on the flat in Ireland; proving hard to win with over hurdles; finds little under pressure.

Winged Lady (GER)
84   54
4-y-o b f Winged Love (IRE)-Wonderful Lady (GER) (Surumu (GER))
A G Juckes   Whistlejacket Partnership

Placings:0   (4084)
2002/03: 16⁰GS,

	Starts	1st	2nd	3rd	Win & Pl
Hurdles	1	0	0	0	0
Career Total	1	0	0	0	0

Going: Sf: 0-0 GS: 0-1 Gd: 0-0 GF: - Fm: 0-0
Distance: 2m2m3: 0-1 2m4-2m7: 0-0 3m+: 0-0
Track: LH: 0-1 RH: 0-0 Tight: 0-1 Gall: 0-0
Aids: Bl: 0-0 Vi: 0-0 Tstrap: 0-0
Best Rating: 0 3/03 Strf 2m110y gd-sft Hdl

Flat winner in Germany; disappointing so far over hurdles.

Wings Of Hope (IRE)
109   93
7-y-o b g Treasure Hunter-She s Got Wings (Bulldozer)
C J Hemsley   Mrs M L Sell

Placings:22535P-FU62535110P   (4677)
2002/03: 22⁴GF, 19ᵁGF, 20⁶G, 20²GF, 20⁵G, 20³GF, 24⁵G, 21¹F, 21¹F, 21⁰G, 19³GF,

	Starts	1st	2nd	3rd	Win & Pl
Hurdles	11	2	1	1	7992

Career Total		17	2	3	2	10011
93	10/02	Ludl 2m5f E(0-105)HHdl	FRM	£3402
86	10/02	Ludl 2m5f F(0-90)Hdl	FRM	£3347
			Total win prize-money £6750

Going: Sf: 0-1 GS: 0-0 Gd: 0-3 GF: - Fm: 2-7
Distance: 2m2m3: 0-0 2m4-2m7: 2-10 3m+: 0-1
Track: LH: 0-6 RH: 2-5 Tight: 0-1 Gall: 0-0
Aids: Bl: 0-0 Vi: 0-0 Tstrap: 0-0
Best Rating: 102 12/01 Strf 2m6f110y soft Hdl

Modest hurdler; stays 2m 5f; acts on fast ground; reportedly difficult to train at home because he is quite a character.

Winn's Pride (IRE)
100   114
12-y-o b g Indian Ridge-Blue Bell Girl (Blakeney)
R Hollinshead   Mrs W L Bailey

Placings:3241460/10/13/3030405/441434252005/U6/U1/10 63-32050   (0779)
2002/03: 20³S, 16²HY, 19⁰GF, 20⁵GF, 24⁰GF,

	Starts	1st	2nd	3rd	Win & Pl
Chases	5	0	1	1	2363
Career Total	43	6	4	7	28741
114	5/01	Bang 2m4f110yD(0-120)HCh	G-S	£6006
114	2/01	Donc 2m3f110yE(0-105)HCh	GD	£3368
111	6/98	Uttx 2m4f110yC(0-110)HHdl	GD	£2389
109	3/97	Uttx 2m6f110yC(0-135)HHdl	GD	£3501
106	5/95	Aint 2m4f F(0-105)HHdl	FRM	£2247
94	2/95	Ludl 2m F Hdl	G-S	£2290
			Total win prize-money £19802

Going: Sf: 0-2 GS: 0-0 Gd: 0-0 GF: - Fm: 0-3
Distance: 2m2m3: 0-2 2m4-2m7: 0-3 3m+: 0-1
Track: LH: 0-4 RH: 0-1 Tight: 0-2 Gall: 0-0
Aids: Bl: 0-0 Vi: 0-0 Tstrap: 0-0
Best Rating: 114 5/01 Bang 2m4f110y gd-sft Ch

Fair chaser, best at around two and a half miles, suited by decent ground.

Winnie
(99h)   (60h)
8-y-o br m Presidium-Sindur (Rolfe (USA))
Miss A M Newton-Smith   John Grist

Placings:00PP0/600334P0005-P40F   (4121)
2002/03: 25⁵G, 22⁸G, 22⁴HY, 17⁰HY, 20⁷G,

	Starts	1st	2nd	3rd	Win & Pl
Hurdles	4	0	0	0	0
Chases	1	0	0	0	0
Career Total	20	0	0	2	597

Going: Sf: 0-2 GS: 0-0 Gd: 0-3 GF: - Fm: 0-0
Distance: 2m2m3: 0-1 2m4-2m7: 0-3 3m+: 0-1
Track: LH: 0-0 RH: 0-4 Tight: 0-2 Gall: 0-1
Aids: Bl: 0-0 Vi: 0-0 Tstrap: 0-0
Best Rating: 82 1/02 Winc 2m6f good Hdl

Winnie The Pooh
(94h)
9-y-o br g Landyap (USA)-Moorland Nell (Neltino)
J D Frost   J E Blake

Placings:024P/F600-062PP   (4695)
2002/03: 17⁰G, 22⁶GF, 22²GF, 17⁸G, 16⁸G,

	Starts	1st	2nd	3rd	Win & Pl
Hurdles	4	0	1	0	840
Chases	1	0	0	0	0
Career Total	13	0	2	0	1490

Going: Sf: 0-0 GS: 0-0 Gd: 0-3 GF: - Fm: 0-2
Distance: 2m2m3: 0-3 2m4-2m7: 0-2 3m+: 0-0
Track: LH: 0-4 RH: 0-1 Tight: 0-4 Gall: 0-0
Aids: Bl: 0-0 Vi: 0-0 Tstrap: 0-0
Best Rating: 92 8/00 NAbb 2m1f good NHF

Winter Brook
5-y-o b m Alderbrook-Oats For Notes (Oats)
G B Balding   H M F McCall

Placings:00   (4222)
2002/03: 12²G, 17⁰GF,

	Starts	1st	2nd	3rd	Win & Pl
NH Flat	1	0	0	0	0
Hurdles	1	0	0	0	0
Career Total	2	0	0	0	0

Going: Sf: 0-0 GS: 0-0 Gd: 0-1 GF: - Fm: 0-1
Distance: 2m2m3: 0-1 2m4-2m7: 0-0 3m+: 0-0
Track: LH: 0-1 RH: 0-1 Tight: 0-0 Gall: 0-0
Aids: Bl: 0-0 Vi: 0-0 Tstrap: 0-0
Best Rating: 50 12/02 Newb 1m4f110y good NHF

Winter Gale (IRE)
11-y-o b/br g Strong Gale-Winter Fox (Martinmas)
M W Easterby   Mrs M E Curtis

Placings:00/4330/P30/11123/02F66-0P6   (0452)
2002/03: 16⁰GF, 24³GS, 20⁶G,

	Starts	1st	2nd	3rd	Win & Pl
Chases	3	0	0	0	0
Career Total	22	3	2	4	15325
106	7/00	Wolv 3m1f E(0-115)HCh	GD	£3978
100	7/00	MRas 2m6f110yF(0-105)HCh	GD	£3770
93	7/00	Worc 2m F(0-95)HCh	GD	£2463
			Total win prize-money £10212

Going: Sf: 0-0 GS: 0-1 Gd: 0-1 GF: - Fm: 0-1
Distance: 2m2m3: 0-1 2m4-2m7: 0-1 3m+: 0-1
Track: LH: 0-3 RH: 0-0 Tight: 0-1 Gall: 0-0
Aids: Bl: 0-0 Vi: 0-0 Tstrap: 0-0
Best Rating: 108 8/00 MRas 3m1f gd-fm Ch

Hunter chaser; without a win since completing a hat-trick in chases in 2000; stays three miles; effective from good to firm to good to soft.

Winter Garden
101(94h)   (100h)101
9-y-o ch g Old Vic-Winter Queen (Welsh Pageant)
Miss Lucinda V Russell   Masons Arms Racing Club/A A Bissett

Placings:013015/6052/2204/R055-650   (3581)
2002/03: 16⁶GS, 16⁵HY, 16⁹G,

	Starts	1st	2nd	3rd	Win & Pl
Hurdles	3	0	0	0	0
Career Total	21	2	3	1	25680
129	4/99	Fair 2m4f Hdl	YLD	£11049
113	1/99	DRoy 2m Hdl	HVY	£2455
			Total win prize-money £13504

Going: Sf: 0-1 GS: 0-1 Gd: 0-1 GF: - Fm: 0-0
Distance: 2m2m3: 0-3 2m4-2m7: 0-0 3m+: 0-0
Track: LH: 0-2 RH: 0-1 Tight: 0-1 Gall: 0-0
Aids: Bl: 0-0 Vi: 0-0 Tstrap: 0-0
Best Rating: 141 5/00 Punc 2m good Hdl

Moderate hurdler/chaser these days; best effort for some time when moderate third at Hexham in April (novices handicap chase).

Winter Whisper (IRE)

8-y-o b g Jurado (USA)-Princess Annabelle (English Prince)
Mrs Susan E Busby   Mrs Susan E Busby

Placings:001P0/**U242P12PP05-P4U0**   (4678)
2002/03: 20ᴾS, 19⁴F, 21ᵁG, 19⁰GF,

	Starts	1st	2nd	3rd	Win & Pl
Chases	4	0	0	0	284
Career Total	**20**	**2**	**3**	**0**	**14392**
98	9/01	Dund	2m3f	Ch		G-F	£5008
102	12/00	Thur	2m	Hdl		SH	£4140

Total win prize-money £9148

Going:	Sf: 0-1 GS: 0-0 Gd: 0-1 GF: - Fm: 0-2
Distance:	2m/2m3: 0-1 2m4-2m7: 0-3 3m+: 0-0
Track:	LH: 0-1 RH: 0-3 Tight: 0-1 Gall: 0-0
Aids:	Bl: 0-0 Vi: 0-0 Tstrap: 0-3
Best Rating:	102 12/00 Thur 2m sft-hvy Hdl

Ex-Irish hunter chaser; acts on any ground.

Wintertide

95   103

7-y-o b g Mtoto-Winter Queen (Welsh Pageant)
C J Mann (R A Fahey 5/7)   J E Brown

Placings:*11/02/42*   (3672)
2002/03: 21⁴G, 22²GS,

	Starts	1st	2nd	3rd	Win & Pl
Hurdles	2	0	1	0	2358
Career Total	**6**	**2**	**2**	**0**	**6233**
109	2/00	Muss	2m	H NHF		G-S	£1683
104	1/00	Catt	2m	H NHF		GD	£1725

Total win prize-money £3410

Going:	Sf: 0-1 GS: 0-1 Gd: 0-1 GF: - Fm: 0-0
Distance:	2m/2m3: 0-2 2m4-2m7: 0-2 3m+: 0-0
Track:	LH: 0-1 RH: 0-1 Tight: 0-1 Gall: 0-0
Aids:	Bl: 0-0 Vi: 0-0 Tstrap: 0-0
Best Rating:	111 2/01 Catt 2m soft NHF

Modest hurdler; winner of bumpers in 2000/01; returned from a spell of Flat racing with a promising efforts in novice hurdles in 2003; acts on easy ground; stays two miles six.

Wise Advice (IRE)

13-y-o b g Duky-Down The Aisle (Godswalk (USA))
M A Kemp   M A Kemp

Placings:2ᴾ12/**3301F2P/206433FF1/5112354235/1313030**
5P/235/0-3P   (4443)
2002/03: 24³GF, 19ᴾG,

	Starts	1st	2nd	3rd	Win & Pl
Chases	2	0	0	1	427
Career Total	**45**	**7**	**7**	**11**	**37134**
113	5/98	Ctml	2m1f110yD(0-125)HCh		G-F	£3516
115	5/98	Prth	2m4f110yE(0-115)HCh		G-F	£4240
104	7/97	MRas	2m4f	D(0-120)HCh		G-F	£3764
108	7/97	Sthl	2m4f110yD(0-120)HCh		G-F	£4198
107	10/96	Hexm	2m4f110y(0-110)HCh		G-F	£3175
102	2/96	Muss	2m4f	F(0-100)HCh		G-F	£3143
96	3/95	Newc	2m110y E Hdl		G-F	£2333

Total win prize-money £24371

Going:	Sf: 0-0 GS: 0-0 Gd: 0-1 GF: - Fm: 0-1

Distance:	2m/2m3: 0-0 2m4-2m7: 0-1 3m+: 0-1
Track:	LH: 0-0 RH: 0-2 Tight: 0-0 Gall: 0-1
Aids:	Bl: 0-0 Vi: 0-0 Tstrap: 0-0
Best Rating:	115 5/98 Prth 2m4f110y gd-fm Ch

Wise King

104   116

13-y-o b g Rakaposhi King-Sunwise (Roi Soleil)
J A B Old   Wise King Partnership

Placings:412/3F2/**2311/311/542/520/5325-F4153**   (4694)
2002/03: 20ᶠGS, 20⁴G, 21¹GS, 19²G, 21³G,

	Starts	1st	2nd	3rd	Win & Pl
Chases	5	1	0	1	12576
Career Total	**28**	**6**	**6**	**5**	**52481**
123	2/03	Winc	2m5f	D(0-120)HCh		G-S	£11115
144	4/99	Asct	2m3f110yB HCh		G-F	£9885
149	2/99	Kemp	2m4f110yD(0-125)HCh		GD	£5038
131	12/97	Sand	2m4f110yD Ch		GD	£4065
124	11/97	Newb	2m110y D(0-110)HHdl		GD	£4810
111	3/96	Uttx	2m	H NHF		GD	£1551

Total win prize-money £36465

Going:	Sf: 0-0 GS: 1-2 Gd: 0-3 GF: - Fm: 0-0
Distance:	2m/2m3: 0-0 **2m4-2m7: 1-5** 3m+: 0-0
Track:	LH: 0-0 **RH: 1-4** Tight: 0-1 Gall: 0-0
Aids:	Bl: 0-0 Vi: 0-0 Tstrap: 0-0
Best Rating:	149 4/00 Asct 2m3f110y good Ch

Fair handicap chaser; now at the veteran stage; does not win very often; at his best at around two and a half miles on good ground.

Wise Man (IRE)

103   (101c)105

8-y-o ch g Mister Lord (USA)-Ballinlonig Star (Black Minstrel)
N W Alexander (A L T Moore 9/9)   Nicholas Alexander

Placings:03/65253-0032   (4304)
2002/03: 22ᴰY, 20⁰GF, 16³S, 22²G,

	Starts	1st	2nd	3rd	Win & Pl
Hurdles	3	0	1	1	2114
Chases	1	0	0	0	0
Career Total	**11**	**0**	**2**	**3**	**4633**

Going:	Sf: 0-1 GS: 0-0 Gd: 0-1 GF: - Fm: 0-1
Distance:	2m/2m3: 0-1 2m4-2m7: 0-3 3m+: 0-0
Track:	LH: 0-2 RH: 0-0 Tight: 0-1 Gall: 0-0
Aids:	Bl: 0-0 Vi: 0-0 Tstrap: 0-0
Best Rating:	105 3/03 Kels 2m6f110y good Hdl

Maiden over hurdles and fences; stays two and a half miles.

Wise Prince (IRE)

11-y-o b g Denel (FR)-Kissowen (Pitpan)
Mrs Edward Crow   David Rogers

Placings:223-33414   (3962)
2002/03: 25³GF, 22³G, 28⁴G, 20¹S, 24⁴S,

	Starts	1st	2nd	3rd	Win & Pl
Chases	5	1	0	2	3965
Career Total	**8**	**1**	**2**	**3**	**5285**
101	2/03	Bang	2m4f110yH Ch		SFT	£2373

Total win prize-money £2373

Going:	Sf: 1-2 GS: 0-0 Gd: 0-2 GF: - Fm: 0-1
Distance:	2m/2m3: 0-0 **2m4-2m7: 1-2** 3m+: 0-3
Track:	**LH: 1-3** RH: 0-0 **Tight: 1-3** Gall: 0-0
Aids:	Bl: 0-0 Vi: 0-0 Tstrap: 0-0

Best Rating:	101 2/03 Bang 2m4f110y soft Ch

Moderate hunter; decisive winner of an ordinary hunter chase at Bangor in February 2003.

Wise Tale

91   78

4-y-o ch g Nashwan (USA)-Wilayif (USA) (Danzig (USA))
P D Niven (M Johnston 5/7)   B Ll Parry

Placings:0F0   (2921)
2002/03: 16⁶S, 16ᶠGS, 16⁰S,

	Starts	1st	2nd	3rd	Win & Pl
Hurdles	3	0	0	0	
Career Total	**3**	**0**	**0**	**0**	

Going:	Sf: 0-2 GS: 0-1 Gd: 0-0 GF: - Fm: 0-0
Distance:	2m/2m3: 0-3 2m4-2m7: 0-0 3m+: 0-0
Track:	LH: 0-3 RH: 0-0 Tight: 0-1 Gall: 0-1
Aids:	Bl: 0-0 Vi: 0-0 Tstrap: 0-0
Best Rating:	73 11/02 Newc 2m soft Hdl

Wishbone Alley (IRE)

66

8-y-o b g Common Grounds-Dul Dul (USA) (Shadeed (USA))
K G Wingrove   M M Foulger

Placings:00P-P   (2061)
2002/03: 17ᴾS,

	Starts	1st	2nd	3rd	Win & Pl
Hurdles	1	0	0	0	
Career Total	**4**	**0**	**0**	**0**	

Going:	Sf: 0-1 GS: 0-0 Gd: 0-0 GF: - Fm: 0-0
Distance:	2m/2m3: 0-1 2m4-2m7: 0-0 3m+: 0-0
Track:	LH: 0-0 RH: 0-1 Tight: 0-0 Gall: 0-0
Aids:	Bl: 0-0 Vi: 0-0 Tstrap: 0-0
Best Rating:	66 9/01 Uttx 2m good Hdl

Wishful Valentine

86   78

7-y-o ch g Riverwise (USA)-Wishful Dream (Crawter)
C W Mitchell   C W Mitchell

Placings:0/000-PP0   (4622)
2002/03: 22ᴾGS, 24ᴾS, 22⁰GF,

	Starts	1st	2nd	3rd	Win & Pl
Hurdles	3	0	0	0	
Career Total	**7**	**0**	**0**	**0**	

Going:	Sf: 0-1 GS: 0-1 Gd: 0-0 GF: - Fm: 0-0
Distance:	2m/2m3: 0-0 2m4-2m7: 0-2 3m+: 0-1
Track:	LH: 0-1 RH: 0-2 Tight: 0-1 Gall: 0-0
Aids:	Bl: 0-0 Vi: 0-0 Tstrap: 0-0
Best Rating:	82 1/01 Kemp 2m soft NHF

Plating-class hurdler; shown little so far.

Wisley Warrior

12-y-o b g Derring Rose-Miss Topem (Mossberry)
C R Willes   T Willes

Placings:66/4530/F1FF/25P23P/B34/P-P   (0031)

2002/03: 33PGF,

	Starts	1st	2nd	3rd	Win & Pl
Chases	1	0	0	0	
Career Total	21	1	2	3	11225

114 3/99 Newb 3m   D(0-115)HCh SFT £3727
Total win prize-money £3727

Going:	Sf: 0-0 GS: 0-0 Gd: 0-0 GF: 0-1
Distance:	2m/2m3: 0-0 2m4-2m7: 0-0 3m+: 0-1
Track:	LH: 0-1 RH: 0-0 Tight: 0-0 Gall: 0-1
Aids:	Bl: 0-0 Vi: 0-0 Tstrap: 0-0
Best Rating:	114 3/99 Newb 3m soft Ch

Witch's Brew
99 ... 104

6-y-o b m Simply Great (FR)-New Broom (IRE) (Brush Aside (USA))
T D Easterby Mrs Bridget Tranmer

Placings:63221423 (4784)
2002/03: 17⁶S, 16³S, 16²HY, 16²G, 16¹G, 21⁴S, 20²G, 19³G,

	Starts	1st	2nd	3rd	Win & Pl
Hurdles	8	1	3	2	7518
Career Total	8	1	3	2	7518

104 2/03 Catt 2m   F(0-95)HHdl GD £2646
Total win prize-money £2646

Going:	Sf: 0-4 GS: 0-0 Gd: 1-4 GF: - Fm: 0-0
Distance:	2m/2m3: 1-5 2m4-2m7: 0-3 3m+: 0-0
Track:	LH: 1-6 RH: 0-2 Tight: 1-5 Gall: 0-1
Aids:	Bl: 0-0 Vi: 0-0 Tstrap: 0-0
Best Rating:	104 2/03 Catt 2m good Hdl

Modest hurdler; defied top weight in mares handicap at Catterick but disliked the tacky ground at Sedgefield in March; acts on good and soft ground.

With A Dash
73f ... 72f

5-y-o ch g Afzal-Oh So Ripe (Deep Run)
N A Twiston-Davies N A Twiston-Davies

Placings:0 (3754)
2002/03: 16⁰G,

	Starts	1st	2nd	3rd	Win & Pl
NH Flat	1	0	0	0	
Career Total	1	0	0	0	

Going:	Sf: 0-0 GS: 0-0 Gd: 0-1 GF: - Fm: 0-0
Distance:	2m/2m3: 0-0 2m4-2m7: 0-0 3m+: 0-0
Track:	LH: 0-0 RH: 0-1 Tight: 0-0 Gall: 0-0
Aids:	Bl: 0-0 Vi: 0-0 Tstrap: 0-0
Best Rating:	72 2/03 Kemp 2m good NHF

With A Twist (GER)
... 120

5-y-o ch g Alwuhush (USA)-Walkona (IRE) (Local Suitor (USA))
C J Mann The Dunnkirk Partnership

Placings:13U2-0F (3294)
2002/03: 17⁰HY, 16²GS,

	Starts	1st	2nd	3rd	Win & Pl
Hurdles	2	0	0	0	
Career Total	6	1	1	1	4960

10/01 Brem 2m   Hdl   HVY £1629
Total win prize-money £1629

Going:	Sf: 0-1 GS: 0-1 Gd: 0-0 GF: - Fm: 0-0
Distance:	2m/2m3: 0-2 2m4-2m7: 0-0 3m+: 0-0
Track:	LH: 0-2 RH: 0-0 Tight: 0-0 Gall: 0-2
Aids:	Bl: 0-0 Vi: 0-0 Tstrap: 0-0
Best Rating:	120 2/02 Hntg 2m10y soft Hdl

Fair hurdler; winner on the Flat and over hurdles in Germany; just missed out in a decent race at Huntingdon on his third outing over hurdles in this country, but was killed at Doncaster in January 2003. (DEAD)

Withcote Jem

8-y-o gr g Norton Challenger-Jem Jen (Great Nephew)
A Scott Mrs S E M Cavenagh

Placings:FO (1731)
2002/03: 16⁶G, 22⁰S,

	Starts	1st	2nd	3rd	Win & Pl
Hurdles	2	0	0	0	
Career Total	2	0	0	0	

Going:	Sf: 0-1 GS: 0-0 Gd: 0-1 GF: - Fm: 0-0
Distance:	2m/2m3: 0-1 2m4-2m7: 0-1 3m+: 0-0
Track:	LH: 0-2 RH: 0-0 Tight: 0-0 Gall: 0-0
Aids:	Bl: 0-0 Vi: 0-0 Tstrap: 0-0
Best Rating:	0 11/02 Kels 2m6f110y soft Hdl

Withcote Welcome

8-y-o gr g Norton Challenger-Welcoming Arms (Free State)
A Scott (B Ellison 5/9) Andy Scott

Placings:P (1977)
2002/03: 23PHY,

	Starts	1st	2nd	3rd	Win & Pl
Hurdles	1	0	0	0	
Career Total	1	0	0	0	

Going:	Sf: 0-1 GS: 0-0 Gd: 0-0 GF: - Fm: 0-0
Distance:	2m/2m3: 0-0 2m4-2m7: 0-1 3m+: 0-0
Track:	LH: 0-1 RH: 0-0 Tight: 0-0 Gall: 0-0
Aids:	Bl: 0-0 Vi: 0-0 Tstrap: 0-0
Best Rating:	0 11/02 Weth 2m7f heavy Hdl

Withcote Wizard

7-y-o gr g Norton Challenger-Roses To Rachel (Artaius (USA))
A Scott Andy Scott

Placings:P4 (1240)
2002/03: 17PG, 20⁴GF,

	Starts	1st	2nd	3rd	Win & Pl
Hurdles	2	0	0	0	0
Career Total	2	0	0	0	0

Going:	Sf: 0-0 GS: 0-0 Gd: 0-1 GF: - Fm: 0-1
Distance:	2m/2m3: 0-1 2m4-2m7: 0-1 3m+: 0-0
Track:	LH: 0-2 RH: 0-0 Tight: 0-1 Gall: 0-0
Aids:	Bl: 0-0 Vi: 0-0 Tstrap: 0-0
Best Rating:	0 10/02 Carl 3m110y soft Hdl

Without A Doubt
95f ... 100f

4-y-o b g Singspiel (IRE)-El Rabab (USA) (Roberto (USA))
M Pitman Malcolm C Denmark

Placings:30 (4329)
2002/03: 16³S, 16⁰G,

	Starts	1st	2nd	3rd	Win & Pl
NH Flat	2	0	0	1	464
Career Total	2	0	0	1	464

Going:	Sf: 0-1 GS: 0-0 Gd: 0-1 GF: - Fm: 0-0
Distance:	2m/2m3: 0-2 2m4-2m7: 0-0 3m+: 0-0
Track:	LH: 0-2 RH: 0-0 Tight: 0-0 Gall: 0-2
Aids:	Bl: 0-0 Vi: 0-0 Tstrap: 0-0
Best Rating:	93 3/03 Newb 2m110y soft NHF

Without Pretense (USA)
88 ... 73

5-y-o b g St Jovite (USA)-Spark Of Success (USA) (Topsider (USA))
N G Ayliffe (D K Weld 23/8) Derek Jones

Placings:0-00P04 (4391)
2002/03: 16⁰GF, 19⁰GS, 17PGS, 16⁰GS, 17⁴F,

	Starts	1st	2nd	3rd	Win & Pl
Hurdles	5	0	0	0	309
Career Total	6	0	0	0	309

Going:	Sf: 0-0 GS: 0-3 Gd: 0-0 GF: - Fm: 0-2
Distance:	2m/2m3: 0-5 2m4-2m7: 0-0 3m+: 0-0
Track:	LH: 0-0 RH: 0-4 Tight: 0-0 Gall: 0-0
Aids:	Bl: 0-0 Vi: 0-0 Tstrap: 0-0
Best Rating:	78 8/02 Kbgn 2m gd-fm Hdl

Plating-class hurdler; improved effort when close fourth in fast ground extended two mile novices handicap at Exeter March 2003.

Witness Time (IRE)
100 ... 97+

7-y-o b g Witness Box (USA)-Lisnacoilla (Beau Chapeau)
B J Eckley Brian Eckley

Placings:304-0551 (3787)
2002/03: 20⁰S, 20⁵S, 20⁵HY, 26¹G,

	Starts	1st	2nd	3rd	Win & Pl
Hurdles	4	1	0	0	3474
Career Total	7	1	0	1	3712

97 2/03 Hrfd 3m2f   E Hdl   GD £3474
Total win prize-money £3474

Going:	Sf: 0-3 GS: 0-0 Gd: 1-1 GF: - Fm: 0-0
Distance:	2m/2m3: 0-0 2m4-2m7: 0-0 3m+: 1-1
Track:	LH: 0-3 RH: 1-1 Tight: 0-0 Gall: 0-0
Aids:	Bl: 0-0 Vi: 0-0 Tstrap: 0-0
Best Rating:	97 2/03 Hrfd 3m2f good Hdl

Modest form in bumpers; much improved effort when landing a three mile two novices hurdle at Hereford in February; potential chaser.

Witney (IRE)
85 ... 73

9-y-o b m Strong Gale-Euroblend (IRE) (The Parson)
P T Dalton Mrs Lucia Farmer

Placings:30/6/0P-040P5 (1220)
2002/03: 22⁰G, 20⁴G, 20⁰GF, 24PGF, 21⁵G,

	Starts	1st	2nd	3rd	Win & Pl
Hurdles	5	0	0	0	276
Career Total	10	0	0	1	506

Going: Sf: 0-0 GS: 0-0 Gd: 0-3 GF: - Fm: 0-2
Distance: 2m/2m3: 0-0 2m4-2m7: 0-4 3m+: 0-1
Track: LH: 0-5 RH: 0-0 Tight: 0-1 Gall: 0-0
Aids: Bl: 0-0 Vi: 0-0 Tstrap: 0-0
Best Rating: 101 3/00 Uttx 2m good NHF

Witney O'Grady (IRE)

(64h)
10-y-o ch g Ring Of Ford-C B M Girl (Diamonds Are Trump (USA))
Miss L V Davis Miss Louise Davis

Placings:0/0/0P5-PP   (4709)
2002/03: 17PGS, 24PG,

	Starts	1st	2nd	3rd	Win & Pl
Hurdles	2	0	0	0	
Career Total	7	0	0	0	0

Going: Sf: 0-0 GS: 0-1 Gd: 0-1 GF: - Fm: 0-0
Distance: 2m/2m3: 0-1 2m4-2m7: 0-0 3m+: 0-1
Track: LH: 0-2 RH: 0-0 Tight: 0-1 Gall: 0-0
Aids: Bl: 0-0 Vi: 0-0 Tstrap: 0-0
Best Rating: 68 4/02 MRas 2m3f110y gd-fm Hdl

Wizadora

8-y-o gr m Safawan-Shrood Biddy (Sharrood (USA))
Mrs S Davies Mrs S Davies

Placings:0PP/P0P00/P4PP/0UPPR-R   (0209)
2002/03: 16RG,

	Starts	1st	2nd	3rd	Win & Pl
Chases	1	0	0	0	
Career Total	18	0	0	0	134

Going: Sf: 0-0 GS: 0-0 Gd: 0-1 GF: - Fm: 0-0
Distance: 2m/2m3: 0-1 2m4-2m7: 0-0 3m+: 0-0
Track: LH: 0-0 RH: 0-1 Tight: 0-0 Gall: 0-0
Aids: Bl: 0-0 Vi: 0-0 Tstrap: 0-1
Best Rating: 79 3/99 Ludl 2m good NHF

Wizard O' Wass

93f   70f
5-y-o ch g Imp Society (USA)-Sabeel (Local Suitor (USA))
J R Turner R C Shedden

Placings:550   (4411)
2002/03: 17SHY, 16SG, 16QG,

	Starts	1st	2nd	3rd	Win & Pl
NH Flat	3	0	0	0	
Career Total	3	0	0	0	0

Going: Sf: 0-1 GS: 0-0 Gd: 0-2 GF: - Fm: 0-0
Distance: 2m/2m3: 0-3 2m4-2m7: 0-0 3m+: 0-0
Track: LH: 0-3 RH: 0-0 Tight: 0-1 Gall: 0-0
Aids: Bl: 0-0 Vi: 0-0 Tstrap: 0-0
Best Rating: 70 3/03 Weth 2m good NHF

Well beaten in bumpers.

Wizardtree

62f   49f
4-y-o ch g Presidium-Snow Tree (Welsh Pageant)
R S Brookhouse R S Brookhouse

Going: Sf: 0-1 GS: 1-2 Gd: 0-2 GF: - Fm: 0-0

Placings:0   (3644)
2002/03: 16QGS,

	Starts	1st	2nd	3rd	Win & Pl
NH Flat	1	0	0	0	
Career Total	1	0	0	0	

Going: Sf: 0-0 GS: 0-1 Gd: 0-0 GF: - Fm: 0-0
Distance: 2m/2m3: 0-1 2m4-2m7: 0-0 3m+: 0-0
Track: LH: 0-0 RH: 0-1 Tight: 0-0 Gall: 0-0
Aids: Bl: 0-0 Vi: 0-0 Tstrap: 0-0
Best Rating: 49 2/03 Winc 2m gd-sft NHF

Wolf Spider

67
6-y-o gr m Norton Challenger-Milly Green (No Loiterer)
A Scott Mrs A Scott

Placings:PP0   (4304)
2002/03: 19PGS, 24PS, 22QG,

	Starts	1st	2nd	3rd	Win & Pl
Hurdles	3	0	0	0	
Career Total	3	0	0	0	

Going: Sf: 0-1 GS: 0-1 Gd: 0-1 GF: - Fm: 0-0
Distance: 2m/2m3: 0-2 2m4-2m7: 0-1 3m+: 0-1
Track: LH: 0-3 RH: 0-0 Tight: 0-2 Gall: 0-1
Aids: Bl: 0-0 Vi: 0-0 Tstrap: 0-0
Best Rating: 0 3/03 Kels 2m6f110y good Hdl

Woman

5-y-o b m Homo Sapien-La Princesse (Le Bavard (FR))
H J Manners H J Manners

Placings:00U   (1995)
2002/03: 16PG, 16UGS,

	Starts	1st	2nd	3rd	Win & Pl
NH Flat	3	0	0	0	
Career Total	3	0	0	0	

Going: Sf: 0-0 GS: 0-1 Gd: 0-1 GF: - Fm: 0-1
Distance: 2m/2m3: 0-3 2m4-2m7: 0-0 3m+: 0-0
Track: LH: 0-2 RH: 0-1 Tight: 0-0 Gall: 0-0
Aids: Bl: 0-0 Vi: 0-0 Tstrap: 0-0
Best Rating: 55 10/02 Chel 2m110y good NHF

Held in all starts to date.

Wonder Weasel (IRE)

112(102h)   (101h)142
10-y-o b g Lancastrian-The She Weasel (Gulf Pearl)
K C Bailey D A Halsall

Placings:513/1/511PP5U-4134F   (4479)
2002/03: 27QGS, 25QGS, 33QS, 28QG, 36QG,

	Starts	1st	2nd	3rd	Win & Pl
Chases	5	1	0	1	18369
Career Total	16	5	0	2	44609
140	12/02 Weth	3m1f	C(0-130)HCh	G-S	£7475
142	12/01 Hayd	3m	D(0-125)HCh	HVY	£6464
142	12/01 Hayd	3m	E(0-115)HCh	SFT	£3558
123	1/01 Donc	2m3f110y	C(0-130)HCh	GD	£7182
120	4/00 Hayd	2m6f	D Ch	GD	£5655
			Total win prize-money		£30336

Going: Sf: 0-1 GS: 1-2 Gd: 0-2 GF: - Fm: 0-0

Distance: 2m/2m3: 0-0 2m4-2m7: 0-0 3m+: 1-5
Track: LH: 1-5 RH: 0-0 Tight: 0-1 Gall: 0-2
Aids: Bl: 0-0 Vi: 0-0 Tstrap: 0-0
Best Rating: 142 3/03 Hayd 3m4f110y good Ch

Useful staying handicap chaser; gets three miles plus; suited by good and soft ground; has worn sheepskin cheekpieces with success.

Wonder Wings

71   34
6-y-o ch g Lir-Ginger Wings (Ginger Boy)
G L Moore D J Forehead

Placings:4   (4760)
2002/03: 18QGF,

	Starts	1st	2nd	3rd	Win & Pl
NH Flat	1	0	0	0	0
Career Total	1	0	0	0	0

Going: Sf: 0-0 GS: 0-0 Gd: 0-0 GF: - Fm: 0-1
Distance: 2m/2m3: 0-1 2m4-2m7: 0-0 3m+: 0-0
Track: LH: 0-1 RH: 0-0 Tight: 0-1 Gall: 0-0
Aids: Bl: 0-0 Vi: 0-0 Tstrap: 0-0
Best Rating: 74 4/03 Font 2m2f110y gd-fm NHF

Wonderful Man

102   89d
7-y-o ch g Magical Wonder (USA)-Gleeful (Sayf El Arab (USA))
R D E Woodhouse M K Oldham

Placings:P640/00-F2235   (4547)
2002/03: 17FGF, 16QGF, 16QGS, 16QG, 16QG,

	Starts	1st	2nd	3rd	Win & Pl
Hurdles	5	0	2	1	2142
Career Total	11	0	2	1	2142

Going: Sf: 0-0 GS: 0-1 Gd: 0-2 GF: - Fm: 0-2
Distance: 2m/2m3: 0-5 2m4-2m7: 0-0 3m+: 0-0
Track: LH: 0-4 RH: 0-1 Tight: 0-1 Gall: 0-0
Aids: Bl: 0-0 Vi: 0-0 Tstrap: 0-0
Best Rating: 89 2/03 Weth 2m good Hdl

Modest, lightly-raced hurdler, suited by fast ground; best when held up.

Wonderful Remark

90   63
7-y-o b m Golden Heights-Queen Of Dreams (Ti King (FR))
G J Smith Mrs Joanne Woods

Placings:00/0P60-0P   (0609)
2002/03: 17QGF, 16PGF,

	Starts	1st	2nd	3rd	Win & Pl
Hurdles	2	0	0	0	
Career Total	8	0	0	0	

Going: Sf: 0-0 GS: 0-0 Gd: 0-0 GF: - Fm: 0-2
Distance: 2m/2m3: 0-2 2m4-2m7: 0-0 3m+: 0-0
Track: LH: 0-1 RH: 0-1 Tight: 0-1 Gall: 0-0
Aids: Bl: 0-1 Vi: 0-0 Tstrap: 0-0
Best Rating: 59 6/02 MRas 2m1f110y gd-fm Hdl

Wontcostalotbut

103(111h)   (114h)105
9-y-o b m Nicholas Bill-Brave Maiden (Three Legs)

B De Haan (M J Wilkinson 6/5) Wontcostalot Partnership

Placings:U36230210/432041532444/22112640/0PP0/3060
33-32100341   (4674)
2002/03: 26³GF, 22²S, 26¹G, 24⁰GS, 24⁰G, 26³GS, 26⁴S, 25¹GF,

	Starts	1st	2nd	3rd	Win & Pl
Hurdles	2	0	1	0	1672
Chases	6	2	0	2	10950
Career Total	47	6	8	9	45923
105	4/03	Hrfd	3m1f110yE Ch		G-F £4932
100	12/02	Font	3m2f110yE Ch		GD £4336
135	12/99	Kemp	3m110y B(0-140)HHdl		SFT £7061
118	11/99	Newb	3m110y C(0-135)HHdl		G-F £4695
108	12/98	NAbb	2m6f (0-125)HHdl		SFT £2684
106	4/98	Uttx	2m4f110yE Hdl		SFT £2211
			Total win prize-money £25920		

Going: Sf: 0-2 GS: 0-2 Gd: 1-2 GF: - Fm: 1-2
Distance: 2m2/2m3: 0-0 2m4-2m7: 0-1 3m+: 2-7
Track: LH: 0-2 RH: 1-2 Tight: 1-4 Gall: 0-1
Aids: Bl: 0-0 Vi: 0-0 Tstrap: 0-0
Best Rating: 135 1/00 Uttx 3m110y soft Hdl

Modest chaser/fair hurdler; loves the mud, but acts on decent ground; stays three miles plus; a little quirky.

Woodfield Gale (IRE)

105   101

10-y-o b g Strong Gale-Excitable Lady (Buckskin (FR))
T D Easterby (Ferdy Murphy 4/6) Frickley Holdings Ltd

Placings:43402/311120/23F1310/453/36PF0-P432622
                                                         (3993)
2002/03: 22²G, 20⁴G, 19³G, 25²GS, 24⁶GS, 25²G, 25²G,

	Starts	1st	2nd	3rd	Win & Pl
Chases	7	0	3	1	4388
Career Total	33	5	6	7	30997
107	2/00	Catt	2m3f	D Ch	GD £4368
115	1/00	Catt	3m110y	D Ch	GD £3159
123	12/98	Newc	2m4f	C HHdl	SFT £5147
110	11/98	Newc	2m4f	D(0-125)HHdl	GD £2836
116	10/98	Weth	2m4f110yD Hdl		SFT £2575
			Total win prize-money £18085		

Going: Sf: 0-0 GS: 0-2 Gd: 0-5 GF: - Fm: 0-0
Distance: 2m2/2m3: 0-1 2m4-2m7: 0-2 3m+: 0-4
Track: LH: 0-6 RH: 0-1 Tight: 0-5 Gall: 0-0
Aids: Bl: 0-1 Vi: 0-0 Tstrap: 0-0
Best Rating: 124 1/99 Donc 2m4f good Hdl

Modest staying chaser, he finished well beaten third on first outing for latest trainer at Catterick in November 2002, but was just caught there the following month; seemed to throw in the towel when just caught at Wetherby in March.

Woodland King (IRE)

91   89

11-y-o b g King s Ride-Bilma (IRE) (Glenstal (USA))
D C Turner Mrs M E Turner

Placings:00FB42/340/0P/P35P   (1593)
2002/03: 26³⁰G, 21³GF, 26⁵G, 23⁰PG,

	Starts	1st	2nd	3rd	Win & Pl
Chases	4	0	0	1	706
Career Total	15	0	1	2	2617

Going: Sf: 0-0 GS: 0-0 Gd: 0-3 GF: - Fm: 0-1
Distance: 2m2/2m3: 0-0 2m4-2m7: 0-1 3m+: 0-3
Track: LH: 0-3 RH: 0-1 Tight: 0-3 Gall: 0-0
Aids: Bl: 0-0 Vi: 0-0 Tstrap: 0-0

Best Rating: 100 4/99 Fair 2m2f yield Ch

Woodland Park (USA)

100   86

5-y-o b g Woodman (USA)-Yemanja (USA) (Alleged (USA))
Mrs D Haine Mrs Solna Thomson Jones

Placings:000-31   (0380)
2002/03: 29³G, 26¹G,

	Starts	1st	2nd	3rd	Win & Pl
Hurdles	2	1	0	1	2768
Career Total	5	1	0	1	2768
86	5/02	Hntg	3m2f	E(0-105)HHdl	GD £2429
			Total win prize-money £2429		

Going: Sf: 0-0 GS: 0-0 Gd: 1-2 GF: - Fm: 0-0
Distance: 2m2/2m3: 0-0 2m4-2m7: 0-0 3m+: 1-1
Track: LH: 0-1 RH: 1-1 Tight: 0-1 Gall: 1-1
Aids: Bl: 0-0 Vi: 0-0 Tstrap: 0-0
Best Rating: 86 5/02 Hntg 3m2f good Hdl

Plating-class hurdler; stays three miles two; acts on good ground.

Woodlands Beau (IRE)

11-y-o b g Beau Sher-Never Intended (Sayyaf)
R H Alner Club Ten

Placings:2U130U22U/234P25PP23U6/2241521U0/03U555
552-42   (0339)
2002/03: 26⁴GF, 25²G,

	Starts	1st	2nd	3rd	Win & Pl
Chases	2	0	1	0	900
Career Total	41	3	11	4	31187
113	1/01	Folk	3m1f	F(0-110)HCh	HVY £6638
113	10/00	Winc	3m1f110yF(0-110)HCh		G-S £5362
117	11/98	Towc	3m1f	D Ch	G-S £3692
			Total win prize-money £15894		

Going: Sf: 0-0 GS: 0-0 Gd: 0-1 GF: - Fm: 0-1
Distance: 2m2/2m3: 0-0 2m4-2m7: 0-1 3m+: 0-2
Track: LH: 0-0 RH: 0-1 Tight: 0-1 Gall: 0-0
Aids: Bl: 0-2 Vi: 0-0 Tstrap: 0-0
Best Rating: 117 3/99 Plum 3m1f110y heavy Ch

Hunter Chaser; suited by three miles plus, soft ground and a right-handed track; usually wears blinkers.

Woodlands Hipower

8-y-o b m Risk Me (FR)-Hallowed (Wolver Hollow)
P A Pritchard Woodlands (worcestershire) Ltd

Placings:0000/U   (0269)
2002/03: 16ᵁGF,

	Starts	1st	2nd	3rd	Win & Pl
Hurdles	1	0	0	0	
Career Total	5	0	0	0	

Going: Sf: 0-0 GS: 0-0 Gd: 0-0 GF: - Fm: 0-1
Distance: 2m2/2m3: 0-0 2m4-2m7: 0-0 3m+: 0-0
Track: LH: 0-1 RH: 0-0 Tight: 0-1 Gall: 0-0
Aids: Bl: 0-0 Vi: 0-0 Tstrap: 0-0
Best Rating: 53 8/99 Hntg 2m110y gd-fm NHF

Woodlands Powergen

10-y-o br g Rich Charlie-Hallowed (Wolver Hollow)
P A Pritchard Woodlands (worcestershire) Ltd

Placings:0/60P/P   (2315)
2002/03: 20ᵖHY,

	Starts	1st	2nd	3rd	Win & Pl
Hurdles	1	0	0	0	
Career Total	5	0	0	0	0

Going: Sf: 0-1 GS: 0-0 Gd: 0-0 GF: - Fm: 0-0
Distance: 2m2/2m3: 0-0 2m4-2m7: 0-1 3m+: 0-0
Track: LH: 0-0 RH: 0-1 Tight: 0-0 Gall: 0-0
Aids: Bl: 0-0 Vi: 0-0 Tstrap: 0-0
Best Rating: 0 12/02 Leic 2m4f110y heavy Hdl

Woodwind Down

105(107h)   (93+h)102

6-y-o b m Piccolo-Bint El Oumara (Al Nasr (FR))
M Todhunter Domino Racing

Placings:066/01P03-3332122P1   (1239)
2002/03: 16³GF, 17³G, 16³G, 16²GF, 16¹GF, 16²G, 16²G, 17⁶G,
20¹GF,

	Starts	1st	2nd	3rd	Win & Pl
Hurdles	5	1	1	3	4660
Chases	4	1	2	0	6006
Career Total	17	3	3	4	14090
93	9/02	Hexm	2m4f110yF(0-95)HHdl		G-F £2380
102	7/02	Sedg	2m110y E Ch		G-F £3731
80	6/01	Prth	2m110y F(0-90)HHdl		FRM £2999
			Total win prize-money £9111		

Going: Sf: 0-0 GS: 0-0 Gd: 0-5 GF: - Fm: 2-4
Distance: 2m2/2m3: 1-8 2m4-2m7: 1-1 3m+: 0-0
Track: LH: 2-8 RH: 0-1 Tight: 1-5 Gall: 0-0
Aids: Bl: 0-0 Vi: 0-3 Tstrap: 0-0
Best Rating: 102 8/02 Sedg 2m110y good Ch

Moderate hurdler, suited by a sound surface. Won on her debut over fences at Sedgefield in July.

Woody's Delight

24f   40f

5-y-o b m Hatim (USA)-Woodram Delight (Idiots Delight)
M A Barnes R B Johnston

Placings:0   (4397)
2002/03: 17⁰G,

	Starts	1st	2nd	3rd	Win & Pl
NH Flat	1	0	0	0	
Career Total	1	0	0	0	

Going: Sf: 0-0 GS: 0-0 Gd: 0-1 GF: - Fm: 0-0
Distance: 2m2/2m3: 0-0 2m4-2m7: 0-0 3m+: 0-0
Track: LH: 0-0 RH: 0-1 Tight: 0-0 Gall: 0-0
Aids: Bl: 0-0 Vi: 0-0 Tstrap: 0-0
Best Rating: 40 3/03 Carl 2m1f good NHF

Woodys Widget

8-y-o b m Rislan (USA)-Woodland Firefly (Min s Baby)
W W Dennis W W Dennis

Placings:P   (0996)

2002/03: 22PGF,

	Starts	1st	2nd	3rd	Win & Pl
Hurdles	1	0	0	0	
Career Total	1	0	0	0	

Going:	Sf: 0-0 GS: 0-0 Gd: 0-0 GF: - Fm: 0-1
Distance:	2m/2m3: 0-0 2m4-2m7: 0-1 3m+: 0-0
Track:	LH: 0-1 RH: 0-0 Tight: 0-1 Gall: 0-0
Aids:	Bl: 0-0 Vi: 0-0 Tstrap: 0-0
Best Rating:	0 8/02 NAbb 2m6f gd-fm Hdl

Woolley
102   79
9-y-o b g Welsh Captain-Singing Hills (Crash Course)
John Allen John Allen

Placings:00F6245/B63243/U0P-4   (0273)
2002/03: 224GF,

	Starts	1st	2nd	3rd	Win & Pl
Hurdles	1	0	0	0	319
Career Total	17	0	2	2	3685

Going:	Sf: 0-0 GS: 0-0 Gd: 0-0 GF: 0-0 Fm: 0-1
Distance:	2m/2m3: 0-0 2m4-2m7: 0-1 3m+: 0-0
Track:	LH: 0-1 RH: 0-0 Tight: 0-1 Gall: 0-0
Aids:	Bl: 0-0 Vi: 0-0 Tstrap: 0-1
Best Rating:	109 3/00 Strf 2m6f110y good Hdl

Woolly Winsome
40
7-y-o br g Lugana Beach-Gay Ming (Gay Meadow)
G Brown Mrs S Clifford

Placings:0P0U0-0   (0059)
2002/03: 17PG,

	Starts	1st	2nd	3rd	Win & Pl
Hurdles	1	0	0	0	
Career Total	6	0	0	0	

Going:	Sf: 0-0 GS: 0-0 Gd: 0-0 GF: 0-1 Fm: 0-0
Distance:	2m/2m3: 0-1 2m4-2m7: 0-0 3m+: 0-0
Track:	LH: 0-0 RH: 0-1 Tight: 0-1 Gall: 0-0
Aids:	Bl: 0-1 Vi: 0-0 Tstrap: 0-0
Best Rating:	40 3/02 Hrfd 2m1f soft Hdl

Modest selling hurdler.

Wor Bobby (IRE)
85f   76f
5-y-o br g Warcraft (USA)-Pil Eagle (FR) (Piling (USA))
B Ellison K M Everitt

Placings:0P   (3357)
2002/03: 16PG, 16PHY,

	Starts	1st	2nd	3rd	Win & Pl
NH Flat	2	0	0	0	
Career Total	2	0	0	0	

Going:	Sf: 0-0 GS: 0-0 Gd: 0-0 GF: 0-1 Fm: 0-0
Distance:	2m/2m3: 0-0 2m4-2m7: 0-1 3m+: 0-0
Track:	LH: 0-2 RH: 0-0 Tight: 0-1 Gall: 0-0
Aids:	Bl: 0-0 Vi: 0-0 Tstrap: 0-0
Best Rating:	80 1/03 Catt 2m good NHF

Workaway
99   94
7-y-o b g Alflora (IRE)-Annicombe Run (Deep Run)
A Parker Mr & Mrs Raymond Anderson Green

Placings:14/540-315265   (4663)
2002/03: 203GF, 161G, 175GS, 162GS, 166S, 175GF,

	Starts	1st	2nd	3rd	Win & Pl
Hurdles	6	1	1	1	5366
Career Total	11	2	1	1	7613
94 10/02 Kels 2m110y D(0-115)HHdl			GD	£4069	
104 11/00 Carl 2m1f H NHF			HVY	£1977	
				Total win prize-money £6047	

Going:	Sf: 0-1 GS: 0-2 Gd: 1-1 GF: - Fm: 0-2
Distance:	2m/2m3: 1-5 2m4-2m7: 0-1 3m+: 0-0
Track:	LH: 1-4 RH: 0-2 Tight: 1-1 Gall: 0-0
Aids:	Bl: 0-0 Vi: 0-0 Tstrap: 0-0
Best Rating:	105 10/01 Carl 2m1f gd-sft NHF

Plating-class hurdler; lightly-raced; acts on good and heavy ground; effective at around two miles; possibly best with a positive ride.

Working Girl
70   70
6-y-o b m Morpeth-Workamiracle (Teamwork)
J D Frost R G Frost

Placings:0003   (4086)
2002/03: 17PG, 16PS, 18PS, 193GS,

	Starts	1st	2nd	3rd	Win & Pl
NH Flat	1	0	0	0	0
Hurdles	3	0	0	1	421
Career Total	4	0	0	1	421

Going:	Sf: 0-2 GS: 0-1 Gd: 0-1 GF: - Fm: 0-0
Distance:	2m/2m3: 0-4 2m4-2m7: 0-0 3m+: 0-0
Track:	LH: 0-2 RH: 0-2 Tight: 0-2 Gall: 0-0
Aids:	Bl: 0-0 Vi: 0-0 Tstrap: 0-0
Best Rating:	70 3/03 Strf 2m3f gd-sft Hdl

Plating-class hurdler.

World Vision (IRE)
89   59
6-y-o ch g Denel (FR)-Dusty Lane (IRE) (Electric)
Ferdy Murphy (C F Swan 25/7) J N Anthony

Placings:430000   (3769)
2002/03: 164GF, 173G, 20PF, 16dGF, 16dGS, 20dGS,

	Starts	1st	2nd	3rd	Win & Pl
NH Flat	4	0	0	1	583
Hurdles	2	0	0	0	0
Career Total	6	0	0	1	583

Going:	Sf: 0-0 GS: 0-2 Gd: 0-1 GF: - Fm: 0-3
Distance:	2m/2m3: 0-4 2m4-2m7: 0-2 3m+: 0-0
Track:	LH: 0-2 RH: 0-1 Tight: 0-1 Gall: 0-0
Aids:	Bl: 0-0 Vi: 0-0 Tstrap: 0-0
Best Rating:	93 7/02 Bell 2m1f good NHF

World Wide Web (IRE)
95(111h)   (125+h)102
7-y-o b g Be My Native (USA)-Meldrum Lass (Buckskin (FR))
Jonjo O Neill J P McManus

Placings:414/56214F5-4005110   (4189)
2002/03: 244G, 22dGS, 19dS, 16dGS, 161HY, 161GS, 16dG,

	Starts	1st	2nd	3rd	Win & Pl
Hurdles	4	2	0	0	9497
Chases	3	0	0	0	368
Career Total	17	4	1	0	22306
127 2/03 Chep 2m110y D(0-125)HHdl G-S				£5050	
120 2/03 Sand 2m110y E(0-115)HHdl HVY				£4446	
117 2/02 DRoy 2m4f Hdl SFT				£3809	
117 12/00 Leop 2m NHF SH				£5520	
				Total win prize-money £18827	

Going:	Sf: 1-2 GS: 1-3 Gd: 0-2 GF: - Fm: 0-0
Distance:	2m/2m3: 2-4 2m4-2m7: 0-2 3m+: 0-1
Track:	LH: 1-4 RH: 1-3 Tight: 0-1 Gall: 0-1
Aids:	Bl: 0-0 Vi: 0-0 Tstrap: 0-0
Best Rating:	127 2/03 Chep 2m110y gd-sft Hdl

Moderate ex-Irish handicap hurdler; suited by around 2m but stays further; won at Sandown and Chepstow in February 2003; acts well on a soft surface.

Worthy Man
64   50
6-y-o b g Homo Sapien-Marnworth (Funny Man)
T R George Mrs W H Walter

Placings:0-P   (3789)
2002/03: 17PG,

	Starts	1st	2nd	3rd	Win & Pl
NH Flat	1	0	0	0	
Career Total	2	0	0	0	

Going:	Sf: 0-0 GS: 0-0 Gd: 0-1 GF: - Fm: 0-0
Distance:	2m/2m3: 0-1 2m4-2m7: 0-0 3m+: 0-0
Track:	LH: 0-0 RH: 0-1 Tight: 0-0 Gall: 0-0
Aids:	Bl: 0-0 Vi: 0-0 Tstrap: 0-0
Best Rating:	55 2/02 Asct 2m110y soft NHF

Wot About Me (IRE)
8-y-o b g Jolly Jake (NZ)-Time Please (Welsh Saint)
Mrs P J Ikin Eamon Spain

Placings:00/F0/FPP-PP   (3951)
2002/03: 21PGF, 16PGS,

	Starts	1st	2nd	3rd	Win & Pl
Chases	2	0	0	0	
Career Total	9	0	0	0	

Going:	Sf: 0-0 GS: 0-1 Gd: 0-0 GF: - Fm: 0-1
Distance:	2m/2m3: 0-1 2m4-2m7: 0-1 3m+: 0-0
Track:	LH: 0-1 RH: 0-1 Tight: 0-0 Gall: 0-0
Aids:	Bl: 0-0 Vi: 0-0 Tstrap: 0-0
Best Rating:	80 11/99 Hayd 2m good NHF

Wot No Cash
93   68
11-y-o gr g Ballacashtal (CAN)-Madame Non (My Swanee)
R C Harper R C Harper

Placings:P5P/F5/P012005PP-35P5   (4699)
2002/03: 183GF, 16dGF, 17PGF, 17dGF,

	Starts	1st	2nd	3rd	Win & Pl
Chases	4	0	0	1	324
Career Total	18	1	1	1	3668
77 5/01 Font 2m2f G(0-90)HCh G-F				£2383	
				Total win prize-money £2384	

Going:	Sf: 0-0 GS: 0-0 Gd: 0-0 GF: - Fm: 0-4
Distance:	2m/2m3: 0-4 2m4-2m7: 0-0 3m+: 0-0
Track:	LH: 0-2 RH: 0-1 Tight: 0-4 Gall: 0-0
Aids:	Bl: 0-0 Vi: 0-0 Tstrap: 0-0
Best Rating:	84 6/01 NAbb 2m110y gd-sft Ch

Plating-class chaser; acts on any ground.

Wotan (IRE)

87   **57**

5-y-o ch g Wolfhound (USA)-Triple Tricks (IRE) (Royal Academy (USA))
R Curtis   A J J Racing

Placings:P0-0				(4032)
2002/03: 20⁰HY,				
	Starts	1st	2nd 3rd Win & Pl
Hurdles	1	0	0 0
Career Total	3	0	0 0

Going:	Sf: 0-1 GS: 0-0 Gd: 0-0 GF: - Fm: 0-0
Distance:	2m/2m3: 0-0 2m4-2m7: 0-0 3m+: 0-0
Track:	LH: 0-0 RH: 0-1 Tight: 0-0 Gall: 0-0
Aids:	Bl: 0-0 Vi: 0-0 Tstrap: 0-0
Best Rating:	57 3/03 Sand 2m4f110y heavy Hdl

Would You Believe

                114+

7-y-o gr g Derrylin-Ramelton (Precipice Wood)
K C Bailey   D Allen

Placings:0/F3				(2638)
2002/03: 23³G, 24³GS,				
	Starts	1st	2nd 3rd Win & Pl
Chases	2	0	0 1 1190
Career Total	3	0	0 1 1190

Going:	Sf: 0-0 GS: 0-0 Gd: 0-1 GF: - Fm: 0-0
Distance:	2m/2m3: 0-0 2m4-2m7: 0-0 3m+: 0-2
Track:	LH: 0-1 RH: 0-1 Tight: 0-0 Gall: 0-0
Aids:	Bl: 0-0 Vi: 0-0 Tstrap: 0-0
Best Rating:	115 12/02 Wwck 3m110y gd-sft Ch

Fell in a novice chase at Leicester on his British debut, fair effort next time.

Wouldn't You Agree (IRE)

95(107h)   (131h)**124+**

7-y-o ch g Toulon-Mention Of Money (Le Bavard (FR))
C Roche   J P McManus

Placings:2-11112					(1990)
2002/03: 16¹S, 16¹GY, 20¹GF, 16¹GF, 21²GS,					
	Starts	1st	2nd	3rd	Win & Pl
NH Flat	1	1	0	0	5503
Hurdles	4	3	1	0	30279
Career Total	6	4	2	0	36685
126 10/02 Tipp		Hdl		G-F	£15153
110 8/02 Tipp	2m4f	Hdl		G-F	£4656
114 8/02 Gway	2m	Hdl		G-Y	£6773
110 7/02 Gway	2m	( )NHF		SFT	£5503
			Total win prize-money £32085

Going:	Sf: 1-1 GS: 0-1 Gd: 0-0 GF: - Fm: 2-2
Distance:	2m/2m3: 3-3 2m4-2m7: 1-2 3m+: 0-0
Track:	LH: 0-1 RH: 1-1 Tight: 0-0 Gall: 0-1
Aids:	Bl: 0-0 Vi: 0-0 Tstrap: 2-2
Best Rating:	131 11/02 Chel 2m5f gd-sft Hdl

Fair irish hurdler; runner-up in a bumper on his only start in 2001, he won a similar contest a year later at Galway and followed up in three hurdle races, winning easily on each occasion. Runner-up at Cheltenham in November. Progressive, stays two and a half miles and acts on soft ground and on a sound surface.

Wrags To Riches (IRE)

101f   **108f**

6-y-o b g Tremblant-Clonea Lady (IRE) (Lord Ha Ha)
K C Bailey   No Illusions Partnership

Placings:052					(2675)
2002/03: 18⁵S, 16⁵G, 17²S,					
	Starts	1st	2nd	3rd	Win & Pl
NH Flat	3	0	1	0	588
Career Total	3	0	1	0	588

Going:	Sf: 0-2 GS: 0-0 Gd: 0-1 GF: - Fm: 0-0
Distance:	2m/2m3: 0-3 2m4-2m7: 0-0 3m+: 0-0
Track:	LH: 0-1 RH: 0-2 Tight: 0-0 Gall: 0-0
Aids:	Bl: 0-0 Vi: 0-0 Tstrap: 0-0
Best Rating:	108 12/02 Hrfd 2m1f soft NHF

Just touched off in a bumper on his second start.

Wrangel (FR)

88(101h)   (85h)**66**

9-y-o ch g Tropular-Swedish Princess (Manado)
B J Llewellyn   Miss Emily Jane Jones

Placings:0/P62/4061320UF0/064210/34-50P06336 (4666)					
2002/03: 17⁵GS, 16⁰GS, 16⁶GS, 17⁰GS, 17⁶GS, 17³GS, 16³G, 16⁶G,					
	Starts	1st	2nd	3rd	Win & Pl
Hurdles	8	0	0	2	820
Career Total	30	2	3	4	9727
100 10/00 Fknm	2m	F(0-105)HHdl		GD	£3331
100 10/99 Strf	2m110y	F(0-100)HHdl		G-S	£2495
			Total win prize-money £5826

Going:	Sf: 0-0 GS: 0-6 Gd: 0-2 GF: - Fm: 0-0
Distance:	2m/2m3: 0-8 2m4-2m7: 0-0 3m+: 0-0
Track:	LH: 0-4 RH: 0-4 Tight: 0-5 Gall: 0-2
Aids:	Bl: 0-0 Vi: 0-0 Tstrap: 0-0
Best Rating:	101 12/99 Donc 2m110y gd-fm Hdl

Plating-class hurdler; best at around two miles; suited by a sound surface.

Wrekengale (IRE)

13-y-o br g Strong Gale-Wrekenogan (Tarqogan)
Neil King   S R Harrison

Placings:00/06/600111/1P/35124P6/32P6330/6PP/32P-3P					
					(0314)
2002/03: 30³GF, 31⁶FG,					
	Starts	1st	2nd	3rd	Win & Pl
Chases	2	0	0	1	315
Career Total	34	5	3	6	27541
106 7/98 Worc	2m7f110yD(0-125)HCh			G-F	£3579
118 5/96 Uttx	3m2f	C(0-130)HCh		G-F	£4429
106 4/96 Asct	3m110y	C HCh		G-F	£7035
93 4/96 Hrfd	3m1f110yF(0-100)HCh			G-F	£3403
101 3/96 Uttx	2m5f	F(0-100)HCh		GD	£2579
			Total win prize-money £21026

| Going: | Sf: 0-0 GS: 0-0 Gd: 0-1 GF: - Fm: 0-1 |
| Distance: | 2m/2m3: 0-0 2m4-2m7: 0-0 3m+: 0-2 |

Track:	LH: 0-0 RH: 0-2 Tight: 0-1 Gall: 0-1
Aids:	Bl: 0-0 Vi: 0-0 Tstrap: 0-2
Best Rating:	118 5/96 Uttx 3m2f gd-fm Ch

Modest pointer/hunter chaser, suited by fast ground, has worn a tongue tie.

Wrens Island (IRE)

107   **105**

9-y-o br g Yashgan-Tipiton (Balboa)
R Dickin   Wholebuild Ltd

Placings:P/P1162P5450-P11P055				(2448)
2002/03: 19⁸GF, 23¹GF, 24¹GF, 23⁹G, 24⁰GF, 20⁵G, 27⁵G,				
	Starts	1st	2nd	3rd	Win & Pl
Chases	7	2	0	0	6978
Career Total	18	4	1	0	13064
105 8/02 Uttx	3m	F(0-100)HCh	G-F	£3412
97 7/02 Worc	2m7f110yE(0-110)HCh	G-F	£3565
102 5/01 Chel	2m110y	H Ch	GD	£3178
100 5/01 Strf	2m4f	H Ch	G-F	£1657
			Total win prize-money £11814

Going:	Sf: 0-0 GS: 0-0 Gd: 0-3 GF: - Fm: 2-4
Distance:	2m/2m3: 0-1 2m4-2m7: 0-1 3m+: 2-5
Track:	LH: 2-4 RH: 0-3 Tight: 0-1 Gall: 0-1
Aids:	Bl: 0-0 Vi: 0-0 Tstrap: 0-0
Best Rating:	105 8/02 Uttx 3m gd-fm Ch

Modest chaser; improved form when winning back-to-back three miles handicaps in July and August 2002; signs of a return to form when runner-up at Worcester June 2003; acts on ground good or faster.

Wun Chai (IRE)

102   **80**

4-y-o b g King s Theatre (IRE)-Flower From Heaven (Baptism)
F Jordan   Graham Brown

Placings:P510				(4573)
2002/03: 17⁸GF, 19⁵S, 17¹GF, 16⁹GF,				
	Starts	1st	2nd	3rd	Win & Pl
Hurdles	4	1	0	0	3374
Career Total	4	1	0	0	3374
80 3/03 Hrfd	2m1f	E Hdl	G-F	£3373
			Total win prize-money £3374

Going:	Sf: 0-1 GS: 0-0 Gd: 0-0 GF: - Fm: 1-3
Distance:	2m/2m3: 1-3 2m4-2m7: 0-1 3m+: 0-0
Track:	LH: 0-2 RH: 1-2 Tight: 0-2 Gall: 0-0
Aids:	Bl: 0-0 Vi: 0-0 Tstrap: 0-0
Best Rating:	80 4/03 Strf 2m110y gd-fm Hdl

Plating-class novice hurdler; suited by fast ground; stays two miles one.

Wunderwood (USA)

                81f

4-y-o b g Faltaat (USA)-Jasoorah (IRE) (Sadler s Wells (USA))
Lady Herries   Tony Perkins

Placings:6				(2574)
2002/03: 12⁶G,				
	Starts	1st	2nd	3rd	Win & Pl
NH Flat	1	0	0	0	0
Career Total	1	0	0	0	0

Going:	Sf: 0-0 GS: 0-0 Gd: 0-1 GF: - Fm: 0-0
Distance:	2m/2m3: 0-0 2m4-2m7: 0-0 3m+: 0-0
Track:	LH: 0-1 RH: 0-0 Tight: 0-0 Gall: 0-0

Aids: Bl: 0-0 Vi: 0-0 Tstrap: 0-0
Best Rating: 81   12/02   Newb   1m4f110y   good   NHF

Wuxi Venture
106   **115**

8-y-o b g Wolfhound (USA)-Push A Button (Bold Lad (IRE))
Miss Venetia Williams R G Leatham

Placings:43242/365162   (4214)
2002/03: 16³HY, 16⁶HY, 16⁵GS, 17¹GS, 16⁶S, 18²G,

	Starts	1st	2nd	3rd	Win & Pl
Hurdles	6	1	1	1	7612
Career Total	11	1	3	2	11415
115 2/03 Bang 2m1f E(0-110)HHdl G-S					£4387
				Total win prize-money	£4388

Going: Sf: 0-3 GS: 1-2 Gd: 0-1 GF: - Fm: 0-0
Distance: 2m/2m3: 1-6 2m4-2m7: 0-0 3m+: 0-0
Track: LH: 1-3 RH: 0-3 Tight: 1-3 Gall: 0-0
Aids: Bl: 0-0 Vi: 0-0 Tstrap: 0-0
Best Rating: 115 3/03 Font 2m2f110y good Hdl

Fair hurdler; suited by ground good or softer; best over two miles.

Wychnor King (IRE)
(77h)   (27h)

9-y-o b/br g Torus-Eva s Fancy (Distinctly (USA))
M Mullineaux Frank Chadwick

Placings:60/0/04-P   (0355)
2002/03: 20ᴾGS,

	Starts	1st	2nd	3rd	Win & Pl
Chases	1	0	0	0	
Career Total	6	0	0	0	400

Going: Sf: 0-0 GS: 0-1 Gd: 0-0 GF: - Fm: 0-0
Distance: 2m/2m3: 0-0 2m4-2m7: 0-1 3m+: 0-0
Track: LH: 0-1 RH: 0-0 Tight: 0-1 Gall: 0-0
Aids: Bl: 0-0 Vi: 0-0 Tstrap: 0-0
Best Rating: 80 2/00 Weth 2m soft NHF

Wychnor Princess (IRE)
51

8-y-o ch m Montelimar (USA)-Forty One (IRE) (Over The River (FR))
L R James C Raine

Placings:0/000P/0U-PP   (0878)
2002/03: 17ᴾGF, 21ᴾG,

	Starts	1st	2nd	3rd	Win & Pl
Hurdles	1	0	0	0	0
Chases	1	0	0	0	0
Career Total	9	0	0	0	

Going: Sf: 0-0 GS: 0-0 Gd: 0-1 GF: - Fm: 0-1
Distance: 2m/2m3: 0-1 2m4-2m7: 0-1 3m+: 0-0
Track: LH: 0-1 RH: 0-1 Tight: 0-2 Gall: 0-0
Aids: Bl: 0-0 Vi: 0-0 Tstrap: 0-0
Best Rating: 73 4/00 MRas 1m5f110y soft NHF

Wynbury Flyer
85   **83**

8-y-o ch g Risk Me (FR)-Woolcana (Some Hand)
R Lee Mrs G P Seymour

Placings:45031443/43614FU1342/0543/F4F-06P   (3366)
2002/03: 19⁰G, 20⁶S, 16²GS,

	Starts	1st	2nd	3rd	Win & Pl
Chases	3	0	0	0	0
Career Total	29	3	1	5	15050
109 2/00 Carl 2m D Ch HVY					£4173
109 12/99 Donc 2m3f110yD Ch G-S					£4261
93 1/99 Catt 2m G Hdl GD					£1646
				Total win prize-money	£10080

Going: Sf: 0-1 GS: 0-1 Gd: 0-1 GF: - Fm: 0-0
Distance: 2m/2m3: 0-2 2m4-2m7: 0-1 3m+: 0-0
Track: LH: 0-1 RH: 0-2 Tight: 0-1 Gall: 0-0
Aids: Bl: 0-0 Vi: 0-0 Tstrap: 0-0
Best Rating: 109 3/00 Kels 2m1f gd-sft Ch

Plating-class chaser; caused a real shock when winning on his second start over fences at Doncaster, deflating some big reputations in the process. Only a respectable effort next time.

Wynyard Dancer

9-y-o b m Minster Son-The White Lion (Flying Tyke)
Mrs G Sunter Mrs G Sunter

Placings:3305/260P/1   (0402)
2002/03: 20¹GF,

	Starts	1st	2nd	3rd	Win & Pl
Chases	1	1	0	0	1575
Career Total	9	1	1	2	2908
74 6/02 Hexm 2m4f110yH Ch G-F					£1575
				Total win prize-money	£1575

Going: Sf: 0-0 GS: 0-0 Gd: 0-0 GF: - Fm: 1-1
Distance: 2m/2m3: 0-0 2m4-2m7: 1-1 3m+: 0-0
Track: LH: 1-1 RH: 0-0 Tight: 0-0 Gall: 0-0
Aids: Bl: 0-0 Vi: 0-0 Tstrap: 0-0
Best Rating: 85 3/99 Hexm 2m gd-sft NHF

Moderate hunter chaser; acts on any ground.

Xaipete (IRE)
111(106h)   (104h)122

11-y-o b g Jolly Jake (NZ)-Rolfete (USA) (Tom Rolfe)
R C Guest (N B Mason 8/2) N B Mason

Placings:000513/5/02341253/43622114211352U/1122320
152244U5301/16411334340453003F/3262F-
306403332326416331F   (4570)
2002/03: 16³G, 19⁰GF, 17⁶G, 16⁴GS, 17⁰GF, 16³G, 16³GF, 16⁵GS,
16²G, 16³GS, 16²S, 17⁶GS, 16¹HY, 16⁶G, 16³G, 16³G, 20¹G,
20ᶠG,

	Starts	1st	2nd	3rd	Win & Pl
Hurdles	8	0	0	4	3003
Chases	11	2	2	3	18811
Career Total	90	15	15	20	100937
122 3/03 Carl 2m4f E(0-110)HCh GD					£4621
113 1/03 Ayr 2m D(0-115)HCh HVY					£5414
120 8/00 Ctml 2m1f110yD(0-125)HHdl GD					£3581
134 8/00 Bang 2m4f110yD(0-125)HCh GD					£5642
123 5/00 Kels 2m110y D(0-125)HHdl GD					£4706
112 4/00 Kels 2m110y D(0-125)HHdl SFT					£2941
127 8/99 Bang 2m4f110yD(0-125)HCh GD					£4810
134 5/99 Aint 2m D(0-125)HCh G-S					£4485
127 5/99 Weth 2m D(0-135)HCh GF					£5572
113 1/99 Muss 2m D(0-125)HCh G-S					£3597
109 12/98 Sedg 2m110y E(0-110)HCh GD					£3488
110 11/98 Sedg 2m110y D(0-110)HCh GD					£3397
105 10/98 Fknm 2m F(0-105)HHdl G-S					£3326
93 11/97 Sedg 2m110y F(0-100)HCh GD					£2784
77 3/96 Sedg 2m1f E Hdl G-F					£2372
				Total win prize-money	£60744

Going: Sf: 1-3 GS: 0-3 Gd: 1-9 GF: - Fm: 0-4
Distance: 2m/2m3: 1-16 2m4-2m7: 1-3 3m+: 0-0
Track: LH: 1-12 RH: 1-7 Tight: 0-8 Gall: 0-3
Aids: Bl: 0-0 Vi: 0-0 Tstrap: 0-0
Best Rating: 134 9/00 Worc 2m gd-fm Ch

Fair hurdler/fair chaser; won 2m 4f handicap hurdle at Worcester July 2003 despite hanging left; effective at up to 2m 4f; acts on most ground.

Xelaroc
83f   **80f**

5-y-o ch m Karinga Bay-Valkyrie Reef (Miramar Reef)
S Gollings Michael Lowe

Placings:0   (3849)
2002/03: 16⁰G,

	Starts	1st	2nd	3rd	Win & Pl
NH Flat	1	0	0	0	
Career Total	1	0	0	0	

Going: Sf: 0-0 GS: 0-0 Gd: 0-1 GF: - Fm: 0-0
Distance: 2m/2m3: 0-1 2m4-2m7: 0-0 3m+: 0-0
Track: LH: 0-0 RH: 0-1 Tight: 0-0 Gall: 0-0
Aids: Bl: 0-0 Vi: 0-0 Tstrap: 0-0
Best Rating: 80 2/03 Ludl 2m good NHF

Xellance (IRE)
109   **98**

6-y-o b g Be My Guest (USA)-Excellent Alibi (USA) (Exceller (USA))
P J Hobbs (B D Leavy 7/2) The Five Nations Partnership

Placings:5000331   (4677)
2002/03: 16⁵G, 16⁰GS, 16⁵S, 20⁰GS, 21³G, 17³GF, 19¹GF,

	Starts	1st	2nd	3rd	Win & Pl
Hurdles	7	1	0	2	4936
Career Total	7	1	0	2	4936
87 4/03 Hrfd 2m3f110yE(0-105)HHdl G-F					£3614
				Total win prize-money	£3614

Going: Sf: 0-1 GS: 0-2 Gd: 0-2 GF: - Fm: 1-2
Distance: 2m/2m3: 0-4 2m4-2m7: 1-3 3m+: 0-0
Track: LH: 0-2 RH: 1-5 Tight: 0-2 Gall: 0-2
Aids: Bl: 0-0 Vi: 0-0 Tstrap: 0-0
Best Rating: 87 4/03 Hrfd 2m3f110y gd-fm Hdl

Plating-class hurdler; multiple winner on the Flat; won at Hereford in April 2003; likes fast ground; suited by distances in excess of 2m; consistent but does not seem to win very often.

Xenophon (IRE)
117   **147+**

7-y-o b g Toulon-Fureen (Furry Glen)
A J Martin Lane Syndicate

Placings:021-211   (4112)
2002/03: 16²S, 16¹S, 21¹G,

	Starts	1st	2nd	3rd	Win & Pl
Hurdles	3	2	1	0	96903
Career Total	6	3	2	0	104139
148 3/03 Chel 2m5f A HHdl GD					£43500
136 1/03 Leop 2m (0-140)HHdl SFT					£51071
106 1/02 Naas 2m3f Hdl SH					£5714
				Total win prize-money	£100286

Going: Sf: 1-2 GS: 0-0 Gd: 1-1 GF: - Fm: 0-0
Distance: 2m/2m3: 1-2 2m4-2m7: 1-1 3m+: 0-0
Track: LH: 2-2 RH: 0-1 Tight: 0-0 Gall: 1-1

Column 1

Aids: Bl: 0-0 Vi: 0-0 Tstrap: 0-0
Best Rating: 148 3/03 Chel 2m5f good Hdl

Smart Irish-trained hurdler; stays two miles five furlongs; acts on soft and good ground; stepped up in class when gaining a surprise win in the valuable Pierse Hurdle in January 2003 and followed up with an impressive win in the Coral Cup at the Cheltenham Festival.

Xerxes (FR)
80f   50f
5-y-o gr g Sir Brink (FR)-Sirta (FR) (Le Pontet (FR))
Jonjo O Neill Sir Robert Ogden

Placings:0   (3930)
2002/03: 16PG,

	Starts	1st	2nd	3rd	Win & Pl
NH Flat	1	0	0	0	
Career Total	1	0	0	0	

Going: Sf: 0-0 GS: 0-0 Gd: 0-1 GF: 0-0 Fm: 0-0
Distance: 2m/2m3: 0-1 2m4-2m7: 0-0 3m+: 0-0
Track: LH: 0-0 RH: 0-1 Tight: 0-0 Gall: 0-1
Aids: Bl: 0-0 Vi: 0-0 Tstrap: 0-0
Best Rating: 50 3/03 Hntg 2m110y good NHF

Xibalba
6-y-o b g Zafonic (USA)-Satanic Dance (FR) (Shareef Dancer (USA))
Mrs M Reveley R Meredith

Placings:P   (4433)
2002/03: 16PG,

	Starts	1st	2nd	3rd	Win & Pl
Hurdles	1	0	0	0	
Career Total	1	0	0	0	

Going: Sf: 0-0 GS: 0-0 Gd: 0-1 GF: 0-0 Fm: 0-0
Distance: 2m/2m3: 0-1 2m4-2m7: 0-0 3m+: 0-0
Track: LH: 0-1 RH: 0-0 Tight: 0-0 Gall: 0-1
Aids: Bl: 0-0 Vi: 0-0 Tstrap: 0-0
Best Rating: 0 4/03 Newc 2m good Hdl

Xtra
84   97+
5-y-o b g Sadler s Wells (USA)-Oriental Mystique (Kris)
J A B Old (L M Cumani 9/7) W E Sturt

Placings:3   (3332)
2002/03: 17³S,

	Starts	1st	2nd	3rd	Win & Pl
Hurdles	1	0	0	1	697
Career Total	1	0	0	1	697

Going: Sf: 0-1 GS: 0-0 Gd: 0-0 GF: 0-0 Fm: 0-0
Distance: 2m/2m3: 0-1 2m4-2m7: 0-0 3m+: 0-0
Track: LH: 0-0 RH: 0-1 Tight: 0-1 Gall: 0-0
Aids: Bl: 0-0 Vi: 0-0 Tstrap: 0-0
Best Rating: 97 1/03 Tntn 2m1f soft Hdl

Moderate novice hurdler; formerly smart performer on the Flat; acts on fast ground, but especially suited by soft

Y-Dug (IRE)
8-y-o b g Wakashan-Jerpoint Sparkle (Roselier (FR))

Column 2

P Bowen Miss Jo Fowler

Placings:0U-P   (0444)
2002/03: 19PG,

	Starts	1st	2nd	3rd	Win & Pl
Hurdles	1	0	0	0	
Career Total	3	0	0	0	

Going: Sf: 0-0 GS: 0-0 Gd: 0-1 GF: 0-0 Fm: 0-0
Distance: 2m/2m3: 0-0 2m4-2m7: 0-1 3m+: 0-0
Track: LH: 0-0 RH: 0-1 Tight: 0-0 Gall: 0-0
Aids: Bl: 0-0 Vi: 0-0 Tstrap: 0-0
Best Rating: 57 5/01 Hntg 2m110y gd-fm NHF

Yaheska (IRE)
87   84
6-y-o b m Prince Of Birds (USA)-How Ya Been (IRE) (Last Tycoon)
J M Bradley J M Bradley

Placings:10F0P-0   (1231)
2002/03: 16³G,

	Starts	1st	2nd	3rd	Win & Pl
Hurdles	1	0	0	0	
Career Total	6	1	0	0	1960
84	9/01	Hrfd	2m1f	G Hdl	G-F £1960
				Total win prize-money	£1960

Going: Sf: 0-0 GS: 0-0 Gd: 0-1 GF: 0-0 Fm: 0-0
Distance: 2m/2m3: 0-1 2m4-2m7: 0-0 3m+: 0-0
Track: LH: 0-1 RH: 0-0 Tight: 0-0 Gall: 0-0
Aids: Bl: 0-0 Vi: 0-0 Tstrap: 0-0
Best Rating: 84 9/01 Hrfd 2m1f gd-fm Hdl

Yakareem (IRE)
103(108h)   (101h)93
7-y-o b g Rainbows For Life (CAN)-Brandywell (Skyliner)
D G Bridgwater Mrs Mary Bridgwater

Placings:0/2120050-3U424221F2P   (2132)
2002/03: 16³G, 17³G, 17⁴GF, 18²G, 17⁴G, 25²GF, 24²F, 24¹F, 24⁴GF, 18²GS, 24²G,

	Starts	1st	2nd	3rd	Win & Pl
Chases	11	1	4	1	9918
Career Total	19	2	6	1	13649
93	10/02	Ludl	3m	F(0-100)HCh	FRM £3731
101	8/01	Hntg	2m110y	F Hdl	G-F £2128
				Total win prize-money	£5859

Going: Sf: 0-1 GS: 0-1 Gd: 0-4 GF: 0-0 Fm: 1-5
Distance: 2m/2m3: 0-6 2m4-2m7: 0-0 3m+: 1-5
Track: LH: 0-4 RH: 1-5 Tight: 1-8 Gall: 0-0
Aids: Bl: 0-0 Vi: 0-0 Tstrap: 0-0
Best Rating: 101 9/01 Sedg 2m1f good Hdl

Moderate chaser; gained due reward for a string of consistent efforts over fences when winning an incident packed four-runner three mile amateur riders handicap chase at Ludlow October 2002. May struggle to stay three miles in a fast run race.

Yankee Crossing (IRE)
76f   76f
5-y-o b g Lord Americo-Ath Leathan (Royal Vulcan)
Jonjo O Neill Trevor Hemmings

Placings:00   (3890)
2002/03: 16PHY, 16⁰G,

Column 3

	Starts	1st	2nd	3rd	Win & Pl
NH Flat	2	0	0	0	
Career Total	2	0	0	0	

Going: Sf: 0-1 GS: 0-0 Gd: 0-1 GF: - Fm: 0-0
Distance: 2m/2m3: 0-2 2m4-2m7: 0-0 3m+: 0-0
Track: LH: 0-1 RH: 0-1 Tight: 0-0 Gall: 0-0
Aids: Bl: 0-0 Vi: 0-0 Tstrap: 0-0
Best Rating: 76 3/03 Hayd 2m good NHF

Yankee Jamie (IRE)
111(105c)   (124c)112
9-y-o b g Strong Gale-Sparkling Opera (Orchestra)
L Lungo R J Gilbert

Placings:6660/P11-PP2111   (3329)
2002/03: 20PGS, 22PS, 25²G, 21¹GS, 25¹S, 24¹G,

	Starts	1st	2nd	3rd	Win & Pl
Hurdles	3	1	1	0	5206
Chases	3	2	0	0	8255
Career Total	13	5	1	0	19551
114	1/03	Muss	3m	E(0-110)HHdl	GD £4075
124	12/02	Ayr	3m1f	E(0-110)HCh	SFT £3601
114	12/02	Ayr	2m5f110yD(0-110)HCh		G-S £4654
103	12/01	Kels	2m6f110yG(0-115)HHdl		G-S £3080
84	11/01	Kels	2m6f110yF(0-100)HHdl		G-S £3010
				Total win prize-money	£18421

Going: Sf: 1-2 GS: 1-2 Gd: 1-2 GF: - Fm: 0-0
Distance: 2m/2m3: 0-0 2m4-2m7: 1-3 3m+: 2-3
Track: LH: 2-4 RH: 1-2 Tight: 1-2 Gall: 0-0
Aids: Bl: 0-0 Vi: 0-0 Tstrap: 0-0
Best Rating: 124 12/02 Ayr 3m1f soft Ch

Fair hurdler/chaser; in fine form in 2002/3; acts on good and soft ground; stays three miles.

Yankie Lord (IRE)
106   88
11-y-o b g Lord Americo-Coolstuff (Over The River (FR))
Mrs J C McGregor The Good To Soft Firm

Placings:12/P1212/P2301/55FFP/0PFPU5431-F2P55P5356   (4751)
2002/03: 24FGF, 16²GF, 17PS, 24⁵GF, 24⁵GS, 20PG, 20⁵G, 20³G, 20⁵G, 20⁶G,

	Starts	1st	2nd	3rd	Win & Pl
Chases	10	0	1	1	2356
Career Total	36	5	5	3	35051
100	2/02	Muss	2m4f	D(0-115)HCh	G-S £5694
131	4/00	Hayd	3m	D(0-125)HCh	GD £7572
118	3/99	Fknm	2m5f110yD(0-120)HCh		GD £4281
130	1/99	Hntg	2m4f110yF(0-105)HCh		SFT £2600
98	2/97	Naas	2m	Ch	SFT £3051
				Total win prize-money	£23201

Going: Sf: 0-1 GS: 0-1 Gd: 0-5 GF: - Fm: 0-3
Distance: 2m/2m3: 0-2 2m4-2m7: 0-5 3m+: 0-3
Track: LH: 0-2 RH: 0-8 Tight: 0-6 Gall: 0-0
Aids: Bl: 0-0 Vi: 0-0 Tstrap: 0-0
Best Rating: 131 4/00 Hayd 3m good Ch

Plating-class chaser; formerly a fair sort but on the downgrade now; probably best when able to dictate over two and a half miles; looks best suited by a sound surface.

Yann's (FR)
105(102h)   (125h)125
7-y-o b g Hellios (USA)-Listen Gyp (USA) (Advocator)
R T Phillips Darren Bloom & Matthew Miller

Placings:0/1103/206S-42212   (3774)
2002/03: 16^4S, 20^2G, 20^2GS, 24^1S, 25^2GS,

	Starts	1st	2nd	3rd	Win & Pl
Hurdles	1				288
Chases	4	1	3	0	10335
Career Total	14	3	4	1	17899

120	2/03	Tntn	3m	D Ch	SFT	£5726
125	1/01	Ludl	2m	E(0-105)HHdl	SFT	£3041
109	11/00	Wwck	2m	E Hdl	SFT	£2119

Total win prize-money £10889

Going: Sf: 1-2 GS: 0-2 Gd: 0-1 GF: - Fm: 0-0
Distance: 2m/2m3: 0-1 2m4-2m7: 0-2 3m+: 1-2
Track: LH: 0-2 RH: 1-3 Tight: 1-2 Gall: 0-1
Aids: Bl: 0-0 Vi: 0-0 Tstrap: 0-0
Best Rating: 125 1/01 Ludl 2m soft Hdl

Fair novice chaser; stays three miles and acts on soft ground; effective under forcing tactics.

Yanus
94 / 101
5-y-o b g Inchinor-Birsay (Bustino)
J S Goldie M Wassall

Placings:25205-256   (1416)
2002/03: 20^2GF, 16^5GF, 16^6GF,

	Starts	1st	2nd	3rd	Win & Pl
Hurdles	3	0	1	0	920
Career Total	8	0	3	0	2631

Going: Sf: 0-0 GS: 0-0 Gd: 0-0 GF: - Fm: 0-3
Distance: 2m/2m3: 0-2 2m4-2m7: 0-1 3m+: 0-0
Track: LH: 0-1 RH: 0-2 Tight: 0-1 Gall: 0-0
Aids: Bl: 0-0 Vi: 0-0 Tstrap: 0-0
Best Rating: 101 4/02 Ayr 2m good Hdl

Moderate novice hurdler, stays two and a half miles and acts on any ground.

Yardbird (IRE)
107f / 93f
4-y-o b g Moonax (IRE)-Princess Lizzie (IRE) (Homo Sapien)
Noel T Chance Gilco

Placings:10   (4743a)
2002/03: 16^1G, 16^9G,

	Starts	1st	2nd	3rd	Win & Pl
NH Flat	2	1	0	0	3416
Career Total	2	1	0	0	3416

93	3/03	Newb	2m110y	H NHF	GD	£3416

Total win prize-money £3416

Going: Sf: 0-0 GS: 0-0 Gd: 1-2 GF: - Fm: 0-0
Distance: 2m/2m3: 1-2 2m4-2m7: 0-0 3m+: 0-0
Track: LH: 1-1 RH: 0-1 Tight: 0-0 Gall: 1-1
Aids: Bl: 0-0 Vi: 0-0 Tstrap: 0-0
Best Rating: 93 3/03 Newb 2m110y good NHF

Moderate bumper performer; dam an unraced half-sister to decent chaser Hoh Warrior; nibbled at in market when making a winning debut at Newbury in March 2003; acts on decent ground.

Yaspleezdo (IRE)
75 / 47
9-y-o ch g Yashgan-By All Means (Pitpan)
G Brown Mel Davies

Placings:0P-0F   (0442)
2002/03: 26^9G, 21^6S,

	Starts	1st	2nd	3rd	Win & Pl
Chases	2	0	0	0	
Career Total	4	0	0	0	

Going: Sf: 0-1 GS: 0-0 Gd: 0-1 GF: - Fm: 0-0
Distance: 2m/2m3: 0-0 2m4-2m7: 0-1 3m+: 0-1
Track: LH: 0-1 RH: 0-1 Tight: 0-1 Gall: 0-0
Aids: Bl: 0-0 Vi: 0-0 Tstrap: 0-0
Best Rating: 47 5/02 Folk 3m2f good Ch

Well held in novice event on chasing debut.

Ydowedoit
57f
5-y-o ch g Bollin William-Scalby Clipper (Sir Mago)
K F Clutterbuck K F Clutterbuck

Placings:0   (4431)
2002/03: 18^0GF,

	Starts	1st	2nd	3rd	Win & Pl
NH Flat	1	0	0	0	
Career Total	1	0	0	0	

Going: Sf: 0-0 GS: 0-0 Gd: 0-0 GF: - Fm: 0-1
Distance: 2m/2m3: 0-1 2m4-2m7: 0-0 3m+: 0-0
Track: LH: 0-1 RH: 0-0 Tight: 0-0 Gall: 0-0
Aids: Bl: 0-0 Vi: 0-0 Tstrap: 0-0
Best Rating: 57 3/03 Plum 2m2f gd-fm NHF

Ydravlis
5-y-o ch m Alflora (IRE)-Levantine Rose (Levanter)
D J S Ffrench Davis Miss Meregan Turner

Placings:PP   (3332)
2002/03: 22^0G, 17^0S,

	Starts	1st	2nd	3rd	Win & Pl
Hurdles	2	0	0	0	
Career Total	2	0	0	0	

Going: Sf: 0-1 GS: 0-0 Gd: 0-1 GF: - Fm: 0-0
Distance: 2m/2m3: 0-1 2m4-2m7: 0-1 3m+: 0-0
Track: LH: 0-1 RH: 0-1 Tight: 0-2 Gall: 0-0
Aids: Bl: 0-0 Vi: 0-0 Tstrap: 0-0
Best Rating: 0 1/03 Tntn 2m1f soft Hdl

Yellow Sky
71 / 26
5-y-o b m Gildoran-Summer Sky (Skyliner)
P F Nicholls Richard Barber

Placings:000   (2706)
2002/03: 16^6G, 17^0GF, 16^9GS,

	Starts	1st	2nd	3rd	Win & Pl
NH Flat	2	0	0	0	
Hurdles	1	0	0	0	
Career Total	3	0	0	0	

Going: Sf: 0-0 GS: 0-1 Gd: 0-1 GF: - Fm: 0-1
Distance: 2m/2m3: 0-3 2m4-2m7: 0-0 3m+: 0-0
Track: LH: 0-2 RH: 0-1 Tight: 0-0 Gall: 0-0
Aids: Bl: 0-0 Vi: 0-0 Tstrap: 0-0
Best Rating: 38 8/02 NAbb 2m1f gd-fm NHF

Yeoman's Point (IRE)
110 / 141
7-y-o b g Sadler s Wells (USA)-Truly Bound (USA) (In Reality)
C Roche J P McManus

Placings:325/1120F-1200   (4456)
2002/03: 20^1S, 25^2GS, 21^0G, 24^0G,

	Starts	1st	2nd	3rd	Win & Pl
Hurdles	4	1	1	0	32125
Career Total	12	3	3	1	57018

136	11/02	Chep	2m4f	B HHdl	SFT	£20300
123	12/01	Fair	2m2f	Hdl	YLD	£7233
118	10/01	Gowr	2m1f	Hdl	YLD	£5842

Total win prize-money £33377

Going: Sf: 1-1 GS: 0-1 Gd: 0-2 GF: - Fm: 0-0
Distance: 2m/2m3: 0-0 **2m4-2m7: 1-2** 3m+: 0-2
Track: **LH: 1-4** RH: 0-0 Tight: 0-1 Gall: 0-2
Aids: Bl: 0-1 Vi: 0-0 Tstrap: 0-0
Best Rating: 141 11/02 Chel 3m1f110y gd-sft Hdl

Very useful handicap hurdler; appears to stay three miles, but is effective at shorter; seems to go well when fresh; acts on most types of ground.

Yer 'Umble (IRE)
75 / 9
12-y-o b g Lafontaine (USA)-Miners Girl (Miners Lamp)
J K Cresswell J K S Cresswell

Placings:60P/5423F00/0046/00164P/000P/6341444/PP03   (4707)
2002/03: 24^2G, 24^4GF, 24^9G, 26^3G,

	Starts	1st	2nd	3rd	Win & Pl
Hurdles	1	0	0	0	0
Chases	3	0	0	1	783
Career Total	35	2	1	3	11549

94	7/00	Strf	3m	D Ch	G-F	£4368
89	3/99	Strf	2m6f110yD Hdl	HVY	£3961	

Total win prize-money £8329

Going: Sf: 0-0 GS: 0-0 Gd: 0-3 GF: - Fm: 0-1
Distance: 2m/2m3: 0-0 2m4-2m7: 0-0 3m+: 0-4
Track: LH: 0-3 RH: 0-1 Tight: 0-1 Gall: 0-0
Aids: Bl: 0-0 Vi: 0-0 Tstrap: 0-0
Best Rating: 94 7/00 Strf 3m gd-fm Ch

Yesyes (IRE)
105 / 110+
8-y-o b g Supreme Leader-Barton Bay (IRE) (Kambalda)
Miss E C Lavelle (Geoffrey Deacon 22/5) The Yomali Partnership

Placings:P01P   (2673)
2002/03: 26^6PG, 19^0GS, 16^1S, 19^6S,

	Starts	1st	2nd	3rd	Win & Pl
Hurdles	3	1	0	0	4251
Chases	1	0	0	0	
Career Total	4	1	0	0	4251

108	11/02	Plum	2m	D HHdl	SFT	£4251

Total win prize-money £4251

Going: Sf: 1-2 GS: 0-1 Gd: 0-1 GF: - Fm: 0-0
Distance: 2m/2m3: 1-2 2m4-2m7: 0-1 3m+: 0-1
Track: LH: 1-2 RH: 0-2 Tight: 1-1 Gall: 0-0
Aids: Bl: 0-0 Vi: 0-0 Tstrap: 0-0
Best Rating: 108 11/02 Plum 2m soft Hdl

Yewcroft Boy

83   **49**

12-y-o ch g Meadowbrook-Another Joyful (Rubor)
A Parker Mrs A J McMath

Placings:46/4/4/4   **(1305)**
2002/03: 20⁴GF,

	Starts	1st	2nd	3rd	Win & Pl
Hurdles	1	0	0	0	322
Career Total	5	0	0	0	529

Going: Sf: 0-0 GS: 0-0 Gd: 0-0 GF: - Fm: 0-1
Distance: 2m/2m3: 0-0 2m4-2m7: 0-1 3m+: 0-0
Track: LH: 0-0 RH: 0-1 Tight: 0-0 Gall: 0-0
Aids: Bl: 0-0 Vi: 0-0 Tstrap: 0-0
Best Rating: 83 1/97 Carl 2m1f gd-fm Hdl

Yob (IRE)

4-y-o b c Common Grounds-First Veil (Primo Dominie)
P D Evans P D Evans

Placings:P   **(0890)**
2002/03: 17ᴾS,

	Starts	1st	2nd	3rd	Win & Pl
Hurdles	1	0	0	0	
Career Total	1	0	0	0	

Going: Sf: 0-1 GS: 0-0 Gd: 0-0 GF: - Fm: 0-0
Distance: 2m/2m3: 0-1 2m4-2m7: 0-0 3m+: 0-0
Track: LH: 0-1 RH: 0-0 Tight: 0-1 Gall: 0-0
Aids: Bl: 0-0 Vi: 0-0 Tstrap: 0-1
Best Rating: 0 8/02 Bang 2m1f soft Hdl

York Rite (AUS)

(99h)   (74+h)

7-y-o ch g Grand Lodge (USA)-Amazaan (NZ) (Zamazaan (FR))
N B Mason N B Mason

Placings:P00-51   **(2118)**
2002/03: 17⁵GF, 20¹GS,

	Starts	1st	2nd	3rd	Win & Pl
Hurdles	2	1	0	0	2212
Career Total	5	1	0	0	2212
74 11/02 Fknm 2m4f		G(0-95)HHdl	G-S		£2212

Total win prize-money £2212

Going: Sf: 0-0 GS: 1-1 Gd: 0-0 GF: - Fm: 0-1
Distance: 2m/2m3: 0-0 2m4-2m7: 1-1 3m+: 0-0
Track: LH: 1-1 RH: 0-1 Tight: 1-2 Gall: 0-0
Aids: Bl: 0-0 Vi: 0-0 Tstrap: 0-0
Best Rating: 74 11/02 Fknm 2m4f gd-sft Hdl

Plating-class hurdler; won well at Fakenham in November.
He stays two mile four and likes soft ground.

Yorkie Morgans

7-y-o b g Manhal-Placid Fury (Sovereign King)
Mrs D A Hamer Ms Diane Morgans

Placings:0PF0   **(4733)**
2002/03: 17⁰GS, 22ᴾGS, 16ꟳG, 16⁰GF,

	Starts	1st	2nd	3rd	Win & Pl
NH Flat	1	0	0	0	0
Hurdles	3	0	0	0	0
Career Total	4	0	0	0	

Yorkshire (IRE)

(105h)   (128 h)

9-y-o ch g Generous (IRE)-Ausherra (USA) (Diesis)
D L Williams P F Moore

Placings:1111132466P6   **(3394)**
2002/03: 20¹GF, 17¹S, 16¹G, 19¹GF, 19¹G, 20³GS, 17²G, 20⁴S, 16⁶S, 21⁶HY, 24ᴾGS, 16⁶HY,

	Starts	1st	2nd	3rd	Win & Pl
Hurdles	11	5	1	0	20121
Chases	1	0	0	1	625
Career Total	12	5	1	1	20746
137 7/02 MRas	2m3f110yD Hdl		GD	£4143
137 7/02 Strf	2m3f	E Hdl	G-F	£3052
125 5/02 Hntg	2m110y E Hdl		GD	£2478
125 5/02 Bang	2m1f	E Hdl	SFT	£2849
107 5/02 Chep	2m4f	D Hdl	G-F	£3659

Total win prize-money £16183

Going: Sf: 1-5 GS: 0-2 Gd: 2-3 GF: - Fm: 2-2
Distance: 2m/2m3: 3-6 2m4-2m7: 2-5 3m+: 0-1
Track: LH: 3-7 RH: 2-5 Tight: 3-5 Gall: 1-3
Aids: Bl: 0-1 Vi: 0-0 Tstrap: 0-0
Best Rating: 137 7/02 MRas 2m3f110y good Hdl

Useful hurdler; good stayer on the Flat, he took advantage
of some uncompetitive novice hurdles in the summer of
2002, winning five in a row. Ran out on his chasing debut,
and has been held back over hurdles, mainly in good company, since. Stays two and a half miles and acts on any
ground.

Yorkshire Edition (IRE)

100   **104**

10-y-o br g Strong Gale-Rent A Card (Raise You Ten)
P F Nicholls Sir Robert Ogden

Placings:541P10/114UP/4FP/3-1P6   **(0662)**
2002/03: 25¹GF, 25ᴾG, 32⁶GF,

	Starts	1st	2nd	3rd	Win & Pl
Chases	3	1	0	0	4329
Career Total	18	5	4	1	22971
104 5/02 Winc	3m1f110yD(0-120)HCh	G-F	£4329
127 11/99 Winc	3m1f110yE(0-105)HCh	GD	£7035
118 10/99 Winc	3m1f110yD Ch	G-F	£3798
91 4/99 Winc	2m6f	E Hdl	GD	£2738
102 12/98 Winc	2m6f	E Hdl	G-S	£2066

Total win prize-money £19967

Going: Sf: 0-0 GS: 0-0 Gd: 0-0 GF: 0-1 Fm: 1-2
Distance: 2m/2m3: 0-0 2m4-2m7: 0-0 3m+: 1-3
Track: LH: 0-0 RH: 1-2 Tight: 0-0 Gall: 0-0
Aids: Bl: 0-0 Vi: 0-0 Tstrap: 0-0
Best Rating: 127 11/99 Winc 3m1f110y Ch

Moderate staying handicap chaser, third after a year off over
three and a half miles at Sedgefield in April 2002.
Appreciated return to a slightly shorter trip when successful
at Wincanton next time. Acts on fast ground.

You Can Call Me Al

80f   **63f**

6-y-o b g Almoojid-Coraletta (Buckley)
O O Neill J A Danahar

Placings:50   **(0660)**
2002/03: 16⁶S, 16⁹GF,

	Starts	1st	2nd	3rd	Win & Pl
NH Flat	2	0	0	0	0
Career Total	2	0	0	0	0

Going: Sf: 0-1 GS: 0-0 Gd: 0-0 GF: - Fm: 0-1
Distance: 2m/2m3: 0-2 2m4-2m7: 0-0 3m+: 0-0
Track: LH: 0-2 RH: 0-0 Tight: 0-0 Gall: 0-0
Aids: Bl: 0-0 Vi: 0-0 Tstrap: 0-0
Best Rating: 63 6/02 Worc 2m gd-fm NHF

You Never Learn

9-y-o b g Aydimour-Briglen (Swing Easy (USA))
Mrs L Wadham Dingley Dell Racing Ltd

Placings:00/5/P6RP-   **(0018)**
2002/03: 16ᴾGS,

	Starts	1st	2nd	3rd	Win & Pl
Chases	1	0	0	0	
Career Total	7	0	0	0	

Going: Sf: 0-0 GS: 0-1 Gd: 0-0 GF: - Fm: 0-0
Distance: 2m/2m3: 0-1 2m4-2m7: 0-0 3m+: 0-0
Track: LH: 0-0 RH: 0-1 Tight: 0-0 Gall: 0-0
Aids: Bl: 0-0 Vi: 0-0 Tstrap: 0-0
Best Rating: 81 3/99 Ludl 2m good NHF

You're A Diamond

5-y-o ch m Superlative-Diamond Tip (Homing)
T P Walshe Mrs Theresa Walshe

Placings:PP   **(1250)**
2002/03: 16ᴾG, 16ᴾG,

	Starts	1st	2nd	3rd	Win & Pl
NH Flat	2	0	0	0	
Career Total	2	0	0	0	

Going: Sf: 0-0 GS: 0-0 Gd: 0-2 GF: - Fm: 0-0
Distance: 2m/2m3: 0-2 2m4-2m7: 0-0 3m+: 0-0
Track: LH: 0-2 RH: 0-0 Tight: 0-0 Gall: 0-0
Aids: Bl: 0-0 Vi: 0-0 Tstrap: 0-0
Best Rating: 0 9/02 Worc 2m good NHF

You're Agoodun

115   **154**

11-y-o ch g Derrylin-Jennie Pat (Rymer)
M C Pipe J S Lammiman

Placings:00000/2R53211/104F2003/114UU2B0/143540P-1P20U   **(4479)**
2002/03: 24¹GS, 24ᴾHY, 28²G, 26⁶G, 36⁶UG,

	Starts	1st	2nd	3rd	Win & Pl
Chases	5	1	1	0	34958
Career Total	40	7	5	3	87208
146 11/02 Asct	3m110y B(0-140)HCh	G-S	£10757
148 11/01 Asct	3m110y B(0-150)HCh	GD	£9854
132 10/00 Hrfd	3m1f110yE Ch	GD	£3493
132 9/00 Hrfd	3m1f110yD Ch	G-S	£3701
142 10/99 Towc	3m C(0-135)HHdl	GD	£4840
138 4/99 Chel	3m D(0-120)HHdl	GD	£5425
130 12/98 Hayd	2m7f110yD(0-110)HHdl	SFT	£2997

Total win prize-money £41069

Going: Sf: 0-1 GS: 1-1 Gd: 0-3 GF: - Fm: 0-0
Distance: 2m/2m3: 0-0 2m4-2m7: 0-0 3m+: 1-5
Track: LH: 0-3 RH: 1-2 Tight: 0-1 Gall: 0-1
Aids: Bl: 0-0 Vi: 1-5 Tstrap: 0-0
Best Rating: 154 3/03   Hayd   3m4f110y   good   Ch

Smart chaser; sometimes let down by his jumping; goes well at Ascot; jumped right when touched off in the Red Square Vodka Gold Cup at Haydock; stays at least three miles three; suited by good ground or softer, usually wears a visor.

You're Special (USA)

109(106h)   (122h)**123+**

6-y-o b g Northern Flagship (USA)-Pillow Mint (USA) (Stagedoor Johnny)
P C Haslam   Les Buckley

Placings:123P14-2   (4166)
2002/03: 20²GS,

	Starts	1st	2nd	3rd	Win & Pl
Chases	1	0	1	0	1236
Career Total	7	2	2	1	9427
121	4/02	Weth	2m4f110yE Hdl		GD	£3143
122	11/01	Newc	2m4f	E Hdl	GD	£2625
				Total win prize-money £5768		

Going: Sf: 0-0 GS: 0-1 Gd: 0-0 GF: - Fm: 0-0
Distance: 2m/2m3: 0-0 2m4-2m7: 0-1 3m+: 0-0
Track: LH: 0-1 RH: 0-0 Tight: 0-0 Gall: 0-1
Aids: Bl: 0-0 Vi: 0-0 Tstrap: 0-0
Best Rating: 122 11/01   MRas   2m5f110y   gd-sft   Hdl

Fair chaser/hurdler; dual winning two and a half mile hurdler, he ran a promising race on his chasing debut at Aintree in May, jumping soundly; won three-horse race at Cartmel easing right down next time; struggled under a double penalty at Hexham in June; acts on most types of ground but not at his best on firm.

Youlneverwalkalone (IRE)

121(117h)   (154h)**156**

9-y-o b g Montelimar (USA)-In My Time (Levmoss)
C Roche   J P McManus

Placings:1/1113/21PF1/3221320-1311P   (4479)
2002/03: 24¹S, 21³G, 24¹S, 24¹G, 36PG,

	Starts	1st	2nd	3rd	Win & Pl
Chases	5	3	0	1	105957
Career Total	22	10	4	4	237682
156	3/03	Chel	3m110y	A HCh	GD	£46400
142	4/03	Leop	3m	HCh	SFT	£42207
147	12/02	Thur	3m	Ch	SFT	£6349
123	1/02	Navn	2m1f	Ch	Y-S	£6773
163	2/01	Gowr	2m	Hdl	HVY	£18346
169	12/00	Fair	2m4f	Hdl	Y-S	£23400
156	2/00	Leop	2m2f	Hdl	YLD	£15600
146	12/99	Leop	2m	Hdl	SH	£14508
123	11/99	Naas	2m4f	Hdl	Y-S	£4004
106	12/98	Leop	2m	NHF	HVY	£4184
				Total win prize-money £181776		

Going: Sf: 2-2 GS: 0-0 Gd: 1-3 GF: - Fm: 0-0
Distance: 2m/2m3: 0-0 2m4-2m7: 0-1 3m+: 3-4
Track: LH: 2-4 RH: 1-1 Tight: 0-1 Gall: 1-2
Aids: Bl: 0-0 Vi: 0-0 Tstrap: 0-0
Best Rating: 169 12/00   Fair   2m4f   yld-sft   Hdl

Very useful chaser; won the National Hunt Handicap Chase at Cheltenham in 2003; suffered a serious leg injury when soon pulled up in the Grand National; travels well in his races; unbeaten over three miles; acts on soft ground.

Young American (IRE)

113   **128d**

7-y-o br g Hamas (IRE)-Banana Peel (Green Dancer (USA))
Jonjo O Neill   J P McManus

Placings:51402/0402/06P03031-261PP6P   (4354)
2002/03: 20²G, 20⁵S, 22¹S, 25PS, 22PGS, 24⁶GS, 20PGF,

	Starts	1st	2nd	3rd	Win & Pl
Hurdles	7	1	1	0	13842
Career Total	24	3	3	2	28876
128	11/02	Hayd	2m6f	B(0-140)HHdl	SFT	£10093
123	4/02	Bang	3m	D(0-120)HHdl	GD	£5687
116	12/99	Leop	2m	Hdl	SH	£4620
				Total win prize-money £20402		

Going: Sf: 1-3 GS: 0-2 Gd: 0-1 GF: - Fm: 0-1
Distance: 2m/2m3: 0-0 **2m4-2m7: 1-5** 3m+: 0-2
Track: **LH: 1-5** RH: 0-2 Tight: 0-0 Gall: 0-1
Aids: Bl: 0-0 Vi: 0-0 Tstrap: 0-0
Best Rating: 129 11/00   Naas   2m   sft-hvy   Hdl

Useful handicap hurdler; stays three miles; acts on good and soft ground; out of form of late.

Young Bounder (FR)

64f   **35f**

4-y-o b/br g Septieme Ciel (USA)-Far But Near (USA) (Far North (CAN))
N A Twiston-Davies   Mrs M E Slade

Placings:0   (3903)
2002/03: 16⁰S,

	Starts	1st	2nd	3rd	Win & Pl
NH Flat	1	0	0	0	
Career Total	1	0	0	0	

Going: Sf: 0-1 GS: 0-0 Gd: 0-0 GF: - Fm: 0-0
Distance: 2m/2m3: 0-1 2m4-2m7: 0-0 3m+: 0-0
Track: LH: 0-1 RH: 0-0 Tight: 0-0 Gall: 0-1
Aids: Bl: 0-0 Vi: 0-0 Tstrap: 0-0
Best Rating: 28 3/03   Newb   2m110y   soft   NHF

Young Buck (IRE)

104(97c)   (48c)**110**

9-y-o ch g Glacial Storm (USA)-Lady Buck (Pollerton)
Ferdy Murphy   Anthony O Gorman

Placings:12/21360/1PP0/06006-4523246   (1815)
2002/03: 21⁴GF, 20⁵G, 19²G, 17³GF, 16²YS, 21⁴GF, 19⁶G,

	Starts	1st	2nd	3rd	Win & Pl
Hurdles	6	0	2	1	3370
Chases	1	0	0	0	233
Career Total	23	3	4	2	20283
119	11/00	DRoy	2m	Hdl	Y-S	£7800
120	11/99	Navn	2m	Hdl	Y-S	£4004
100	10/98	Fair	2m	NHF	YLD	£2690
				Total win prize-money £14494		

Going: Sf: 0-0 GS: 0-0 Gd: 0-3 GF: - Fm: 0-3
Distance: 2m/2m3: 0-2 2m4-2m7: 0-5 3m+: 0-0
Track: LH: 0-3 RH: 0-3 Tight: 0-1 Gall: 0-1
Aids: Bl: 0-3 Vi: 0-0 Tstrap: 0-6
Best Rating: 126 12/99   Punc   2m   soft   Hdl

Modest ex-Irish hurdler/chaser. Suited by cut in the ground.

Young Butt

101   **78**

10-y-o ch g Bold Owl-Cymbal (Ribero)

L A Dace   D Newman

Placings:03/0/P605   (4425)
2002/03: 21PS, 16⁶HY, 17⁰G, 16⁵GF,

	Starts	1st	2nd	3rd	Win & Pl
Hurdles	4	0	0	0	0
Career Total	7	0	0	1	364

Going: Sf: 0-2 GS: 0-0 Gd: 0-1 GF: - Fm: 0-1
Distance: 2m/2m3: 0-3 2m4-2m7: 0-1 3m+: 0-0
Track: LH: 0-3 RH: 0-1 Tight: 0-3 Gall: 0-1
Aids: Bl: 0-2 Vi: 0-0 Tstrap: 0-0
Best Rating: 88 4/00   Plum   2m   gd-sft   Hdl

Young Chevalier

93   **78**

6-y-o b g Alflora (IRE)-Mrs Teasdale (Idiots Delight)
J R Adam   James R Adam

Placings:00/0506-F000   (3159)
2002/03: 20FGS, 20⁰GF, 16⁰GS, 24⁰G,

	Starts	1st	2nd	3rd	Win & Pl
Hurdles	3	0	0	0	0
Chases	1	0	0	0	0
Career Total	10	0	0	0	0

Going: Sf: 0-0 GS: 0-2 Gd: 0-1 GF: - Fm: 0-1
Distance: 2m/2m3: 0-1 2m4-2m7: 0-2 3m+: 0-1
Track: LH: 0-2 RH: 0-2 Tight: 0-2 Gall: 0-1
Aids: Bl: 0-0 Vi: 0-0 Tstrap: 0-0
Best Rating: 78 11/01   Ayr   2m   gd-sft   Hdl

Young Claude

95   **81**

6-y-o b g Le Moss-Deirdres Dream (The Parson)
P Beaumont   Read O Gorman Racing

Placings:033P   (3510)
2002/03: 20⁰S, 23³GS, 25³G, 25PG,

	Starts	1st	2nd	3rd	Win & Pl
Hurdles	4	0	0	2	1125
Career Total	4	0	0	2	1125

Going: Sf: 0-1 GS: 0-1 Gd: 0-2 GF: - Fm: 0-0
Distance: 2m/2m3: 0-0 2m4-2m7: 0-2 3m+: 0-2
Track: LH: 0-4 RH: 0-0 Tight: 0-2 Gall: 0-1
Aids: Bl: 0-0 Vi: 0-0 Tstrap: 0-0
Best Rating: 81 1/03   Catt   3m1f110y   good   Hdl

Plating-class hurdler; half-brother to top staying chaser Young Kenny. Improving with racing but will not be seen to full advantage until he goes over fences.

Young Dalesman

103   **121**

10-y-o br g Teenoso (USA)-Fabulous Molly (Whitstead)
A Streeter   Mrs D F Garrett

Placings:14632/1/02510330/126F14-P4   (1321)
2002/03: 24²GS, 24⁴GF,

	Starts	1st	2nd	3rd	Win & Pl
Hurdles	2	0	0	0	634
Career Total	22	5	3	3	30702
121	3/02	Bang	3m	C(0-135)HHdl	SFT	£5216
121	9/01	MRas	3m	C(0-135)	SFT	£10400
109	8/00	Bang	2m4f	E(0-115)HHdl	GD	£4309
93	5/98	Towc	2m5f	E(0-110)HHdl	G-F	£2547
88	8/97	Bang	2m1f	E Hdl		£2211

Total win prize-money £24685

Going:	Sf: 0-0 GS: 0-1 Gd: 0-0 GF: - Fm: 0-1
Distance:	2m/2m3: 0-0 2m4-2m7: 0-0 3m+: 0-2
Track:	LH: 0-0 RH: 0-2 Tight: 0-1 Gall: 0-0
Aids:	Bl: 0-0 Vi: 0-0 Tstrap: 0-0
Best Rating:	**121** 3/02 Bang 3m soft Hdl

Fair handicap hurdler, he stays three miles and acts on soft ground. Goes well at Bangor and won there for the third time in March 2002.

Young Dancer (IRE)

78f   **100f**

5-y-o b g Eurobus-Misquested (Lord Ha Ha)
V R A Dartnall D G Staddon

Placings:0   (3623)
2002/03: 16[6]HY,

	Starts	1st	2nd	3rd	Win & Pl
NH Flat	1	0	0	0	
Career Total	1	0	0	0	

Going:	Sf: 0-1 GS: 0-0 Gd: 0-0 GF: - Fm: 0-0
Distance:	2m/2m3: 0-1 2m4-2m7: 0-0 3m+: 0-0
Track:	LH: 0-0 RH: 0-1 Tight: 0-0 Gall: 0-0
Aids:	Bl: 0-0 Vi: 0-0 Tstrap: 0-0
Best Rating:	**100** 2/03 Sand 2m110y heavy NHF

Young Devereaux (IRE)

109   **151**

10-y-o b/br g Lord Americo-Miss Iverk (Torus)
P F Nicholls Paul K Barber,Mick Coburn,Colin Lewis 2

Placings:45/31/F11/2-11P   (3628)
2002/03: 16[1]S, 16[1]G, 19[P]GS,

	Starts	1st	2nd	3rd	Win & Pl
Chases	3	2	0	0	77400
Career Total	11	5	1	1	97547
151	1/03	Kemp	2m	A HCh		GD	£46400
141	12/02	Asct	2m	B HCh		SFT	£31000
135	1/00	Folk	2m	E Ch		G-S	£3217
144	1/00	Uttx	2m	D Ch		SFT	£5330
115	12/98	Chep	2m110y	D Hdl		GD	£3116

Total win prize-money £89064

Going:	Sf: 1-1 GS: 0-1 Gd: 1-1 GF: - Fm: 0-0
Distance:	2m/2m3: 2-2 2m4-2m7: 0-1 3m+: 0-0
Track:	LH: 0-0 RH: 2-3 Tight: 0-0 Gall: 0-0
Aids:	Bl: 0-0 Vi: 0-0 Tstrap: 0-0
Best Rating:	**151** 2/03 Asct 2m3f110y gd-sft Ch

Smart but fragile two-mile chaser; winner of handicaps at Ascot and Kempton this term, beating Seebald a length on both occasions; beaten when losing action and pulled up as precaution (returned sound) behind Tiutchev in Ritz Club Chase at Ascot latest; all of his wins have come over two miles, though he does stay further; acts on good and soft ground, but reportedly prefers a sound surface.

Young Joker (IRE)

(105h)   **(95+h)130**

7-y-o b g Jolly Jake (NZ)-Ara View (Rontino)
N A Twiston-Davies Gavin Macechern

Placings:00/33231F-3P   (2240)
2002/03: 19[3]GF, 17[P]GS,

	Starts	1st	2nd	3rd	Win & Pl
Hurdles	1	0	0	1	457

Chases   1   0   0   0   0
Career Total   10   1   1   4   6798
125 4/02 Hrfd 2m3f   E(0-110)HCh   GD   £4231

Total win prize-money £4232

Going:	Sf: 0-0 GS: 0-1 Gd: 0-0 GF: - Fm: 0-1
Distance:	2m/2m3: 0-1 2m4-2m7: 0-0 3m+: 0-0
Track:	LH: 0-1 RH: 0-1 Tight: 0-0 Gall: 0-1
Aids:	Bl: 0-0 Vi: 0-0 Tstrap: 0-0
Best Rating:	**130** 4/02 Hrfd 2m3f gd-fm Ch

Useful chaser; modest placed form over hurdles and fences before winning a Hereford handicap chase by a distance at Easter 2002. Unlucky not to follow up over course and distance next time. Stays two miles three, likes to bowl along in front.

Young Lirrup

85f   **80f**

5-y-o ch g Lir-Blue-Bird Express (Pony Express)
W S Kittow W G Kittow

Placings:0-60   (3337)
2002/03: 17[6]S, 17[0]S,

	Starts	1st	2nd	3rd	Win & Pl
NH Flat	2	0	0	0	0
Career Total	3	0	0	0	0

Going:	Sf: 0-2 GS: 0-0 Gd: 0-0 GF: - Fm: 0-0
Distance:	2m/2m3: 0-2 2m4-2m7: 0-0 3m+: 0-0
Track:	LH: 0-0 RH: 0-1 Tight: 0-0 Gall: 0-0
Aids:	Bl: 0-0 Vi: 0-0 Tstrap: 0-0
Best Rating:	**74** 12/02 Hrfd 2m1f soft NHF

Young Ottoman (IRE)

111(101h)   (125h)**130+**

7-y-o b g Mandalus-Lone Run (Kemal (FR))
V R A Dartnall D G Staddon

Placings:0562/1123-34213   (4113)
2002/03: 22[3]GS, 25[4]G, 24[2]G, 26[1]S, 32[3]G,

	Starts	1st	2nd	3rd	Win & Pl
Chases	5	1	1	2	15573
Career Total	13	3	3	3	23715
122	2/03	Plum	3m2f	D Ch		SFT	£6825
118	1/02	Plum	2m5f	E Hdl		SFT	£2730
101	5/01	Extr	2m6f110yF Hdl		G-S	£2786

Total win prize-money £12341

Going:	Sf: 1-1 GS: 0-1 Gd: 0-3 GF: - Fm: 0-0
Distance:	2m/2m3: 0-0 2m4-2m7: 1-1 3m+: 1-4
Track:	LH: 1-4 RH: 0-0 Tight: 1-1 Gall: 0-3
Aids:	Bl: 0-0 Vi: 0-0 Tstrap: 0-0
Best Rating:	**130** 12/02 Newb 3m good Ch

Very useful novice chaser; third in National Hunt Challenge Cup at Cheltenham; stays 4m; effective in soft ground.

Young Owen

76   **71**

5-y-o b g Balnibarbi-Polly Potter (Pollerton)
R A Fahey Alf Chadwick

Placings:60-5PP   (4014)
2002/03: 16[5]S, 17[5]S, 16[P]S,

	Starts	1st	2nd	3rd	Win & Pl
Hurdles	3	0	0	0	0
Career Total	5	0	0	0	0

Going:	Sf: 0-3 GS: 0-0 Gd: 0-0 GF: - Fm: 0-0
Distance:	2m/2m3: 0-3 2m4-2m7: 0-0 3m+: 0-0
Track:	LH: 0-3 RH: 0-0 Tight: 0-1 Gall: 0-0
Aids:	Bl: 0-0 Vi: 0-0 Tstrap: 0-0
Best Rating:	**71** 11/02 Uttx 2m soft Hdl

Young Spartacus

113   **157**

10-y-o b g Teenoso (USA)-Celtic Slave (Celtic Cone)
H D Daly B G Hellyer

Placings:6161/15102/**11222F**/13211U/306-1   (4114)
2002/03: 20[1]G,

	Starts	1st	2nd	3rd	Win & Pl
Chases	1	1	0	0	43500
Career Total	25	10	5	2	183628
157	3/03	Chel	2m4f110yA HCh		GD	£43500
157	2/01	Kemp	3m	A HCh		GD	£46400
152	1/01	Chel	2m5f	B HCh		SFT	£20800
148	11/00	Chep	2m4f	B HHdl		SFT	£22750
147	12/99	Chep	2m3f110yD Ch		SFT	£3891
136	11/99	Towc	2m110y	E Ch		GD	£3265
133	2/99	Wwck	2m	C(0-135)HHdl		G-S	£4828
128	12/98	Wwck	2m	C(0-130)HHdl		SFT	£5487
119	4/98	Ludl	2m	E Hdl		GD	£2836
120	12/97	Strf	2m110y	E Hdl		SFT	£2710

Total win prize-money £156469

Going:	Sf: 0-0 GS: 0-0 Gd: 1-1 GF: - Fm: 0-0
Distance:	2m/2m3: 0-0 **2m4-2m7**: 1-1 3m+: 0-0
Track:	LH: 1-1 RH: 0-0 Tight: 0-0 **Gall**: 1-1
Aids:	Bl: 0-0 Vi: 0-0 Tstrap: 0-0
Best Rating:	**157** 3/03 Chel 2m4f110y good Ch

High-class chaser; wins include the Ladbroke Trophy Chase at Cheltenham and the 2001 Racing Post Chase; first run for over a year; won the Mildmay of Flete at the 2003 Cheltenham Festival; stays three miles, effective over shorter; effective on soft ground.

Young Steven

12-y-o b g Singing Steven-Adoration (FR) (Dancer s Image (USA))
Mrs J M Hollands Mrs J M Hollands

Placings:003024P/40/3233532/2361/43341/P3P0/5P-35
                                                                    (3582)
2002/03: 25[3]GS, 24[5]G,

	Starts	1st	2nd	3rd	Win & Pl
Chases	2	0	0	1	330
Career Total	33	2	4	10	13330
107	4/00	Kels	3m1f	D Ch		SFT	£3906
99	3/99	Newc	2m4f	H Ch		SFT	£1746

Total win prize-money £5654

Going:	Sf: 0-0 GS: 0-1 Gd: 0-1 GF: - Fm: 0-0
Distance:	2m/2m3: 0-0 2m4-2m7: 0-0 3m+: 0-2
Track:	LH: 0-1 RH: 0-0 Tight: 0-1 Gall: 0-0
Aids:	Bl: 0-0 Vi: 0-0 Tstrap: 0-0
Best Rating:	**108** 5/98 Prth 3m gd-fm Ch

Young Tern

5-y-o b g Young Ern-Turnaway (Runnett)
B J Llewellyn (C G Cox 26/7) B W Parren

Placings:P   (4094)
2002/03: 17[P]HY,

	Starts	1st	2nd	3rd	Win & Pl
Hurdles	1	0	0	0	

Career Total	1	0	0	0

Going: Sf: 0-1 GS: 0-0 Gd: 0-0 GF: - Fm: 0-0
Distance: 2m/2m3: 0-1 2m4-2m7: 0-0 3m+: 0-0
Track: LH: 0-0 RH: 0-1 Tight: 0-1 Gall: 0-0
Aids: Bl: 0-0 Vi: 0-0 Tstrap: 0-0
Best Rating: 0   3/03   Tntn   2m1f   heavy   Hdl

Young Thruster (IRE)

106   **105**

10-y-o b g Over The River (FR)-Bit Of Fashion (Master Owen)
N A Twiston-Davies Gavin Macechern

Placings:326/01231033/11/F/46225P23-6U2   (2167)
2002/03: 25³GS, 26⁶S, 24ᵁGS, 26²G,

	Starts	1st	2nd	3rd	Win & Pl
Chases	4	0	1	1	1531
Career Total	25	4	6	5	26671
97	10/99	Hexm	3m1f		E Ch		GD	£3162
114	5/99	Worc	3m		C(0-130)HHdl		G-S	£5203
107	12/98	Hntg	3m2f		E Hdl		SFT	£2740
105	11/98	NAbb	3m3f		E Hdl		SFT	£2697

Total win prize-money £13804

Going: Sf: 0-1 GS: 0-2 Gd: 0-1 GF: - Fm: 0-0
Distance: 2m/2m3: 0-0 2m4-2m7: 0-0 3m+: 0-4
Track: LH: 0-1 RH: 0-3 Tight: 0-0 Gall: 0-1
Aids: Bl: 0-0 Vi: 0-0 Tstrap: 0-0
Best Rating: 117   10/00   MRas   3m1f   good   Ch

Modest hurdler/chaser, he has had his problems with injury. Returned to good form in the autumn of 2001, he likes marathon trips on good or easy ground.

Young Tomo (IRE)

93   **99**

11-y-o b g Lafontaine (USA)-Siege Queen (Tarqogan)
J Howard Johnson Michael Thompson

Placings:20151/241FP2/4F1/20P/5331FP2-P34   (1532)
2002/03: 27ᴾGF, 25³GF, 27⁴G,

	Starts	1st	2nd	3rd	Win & Pl
Chases	3	0	1		1095
Career Total	27	5	5	3	21732
102	11/01	Sedg	3m3f		F(0-90)HCh		GD	£2947
90	10/99	Sedg	3m3f		F(0-110)HCh		GD	£2882
98	12/98	Muss	3m		E Ch		G-F	£2901
99	2/98	Muss	2m4f		D Hdl		GD	£2895
71	12/97	Sedg	2m5f110yE Hdl				GD	£2022

Total win prize-money £13649

Going: Sf: 0-0 GS: 0-0 Gd: 0-1 GF: - Fm: 0-2
Distance: 2m/2m3: 0-0 2m4-2m7: 0-0 3m+: 0-3
Track: LH: 0-3 RH: 0-0 Tight: 0-0 Gall: 0-0
Aids: Bl: 0-3 Vi: 0-0 Tstrap: 0-0
Best Rating: 105   5/97   Prth   2m110y   gd-sft NHF

Moderate novice chaser at a modest level during the 1998-99 season, he needs fast ground but appears on the downgrade. Scored his first win for two years at Sedgefield in November 2001. Stays well.

Young Will

        47f

4-y-o b g Keen-Barkston Singer (Runnett)
Mrs Lucinda Featherstone Largesse Racing

Placings:0   (1923)

2002/03: 12⁰GS,

	Starts	1st	2nd	3rd	Win & Pl
NH Flat	1	0	0	0	
Career Total	1	0	0	0	

Going: Sf: 0-0 GS: 0-1 Gd: 0-0 GF: - Fm: 0-0
Distance: 2m/2m3: 0-0 2m4-2m7: 0-0 3m+: 0-0
Track: LH: 0-1 RH: 0-0 Tight: 0-0 Gall: 0-0
Aids: Bl: 0-0 Vi: 0-0 Tstrap: 0-0
Best Rating: 60   11/02   Newb   1m4f110y   gd-sft   NHF

Younico

8-y-o b g Nordico (USA)-Young Wilkie (Callernish)
Paul O J Hosgood Paul O J Hosgood

Placings:530364604/6/63-P   (0179)
2002/03: 21ᴾGF,

	Starts	1st	2nd	3rd	Win & Pl
Chases	1	0	0	0	
Career Total	13	0	0	3	1608

Going: Sf: 0-0 GS: 0-0 Gd: 0-0 GF: - Fm: 0-1
Distance: 2m/2m3: 0-0 2m4-2m7: 0-1 3m+: 0-0
Track: LH: 0-0 RH: 0-1 Tight: 0-0 Gall: 0-0
Aids: Bl: 0-0 Vi: 0-0 Tstrap: 0-0
Best Rating: 91   2/00   Catt   2m3f   good   Hdl

Youpeeveecee (IRE)

86   **91**

7-y-o b g Little Bighorn-Godlike (Godswalk (USA))
Mrs J Candlish Greencard Golfers

Placings:042-P436U   (4566)
2002/03: 24ᴾHY, 19⁴G, 19³S, 21⁶G, 20ᵁGF,

	Starts	1st	2nd	3rd	Win & Pl
Hurdles	5	0	0	1	833
Career Total	8	0	1	1	1347

Going: Sf: 0-2 GS: 0-0 Gd: 0-2 GF: - Fm: 0-1
Distance: 2m/2m3: 0-0 2m4-2m7: 0-0 3m+: 0-1
Track: LH: 0-2 RH: 0-3 Tight: 0-1 Gall: 0-0
Aids: Bl: 0-0 Vi: 0-0 Tstrap: 0-0
Best Rating: 97   4/02   MRas   2m1f110y   good   NHF

Modest novice hurdler; has shown signs of temperament; stays two and a half miles.

Your A Gassman (IRE)

103f   **106+f**

5-y-o b g King s Ride-Nish Bar (Callernish)
Ferdy Murphy W J Gott

Placings:3   (4778)
2002/03: 16³G,

	Starts	1st	2nd	3rd	Win & Pl
NH Flat	1	0	0	1	506
Career Total	1	0	0	1	506

Going: Sf: 0-0 GS: 0-0 Gd: 0-1 GF: - Fm: 0-0
Distance: 2m/2m3: 0-1 2m4-2m7: 0-0 3m+: 0-0
Track: LH: 0-0 RH: 0-1 Tight: 0-0 Gall: 0-0
Aids: Bl: 0-0 Vi: 0-0 Tstrap: 0-0
Best Rating: 100   4/03   Prth   2m110y   good   NHF

Modest bumper performer; big type; well backed when third on debut in Perth bumper in Apri; hugely impressive when taking similar event at Southwell three weeks later.

Your My Angel (IRE)

90   **72**

7-y-o b m Commanche Run-Marshtown Fair (IRE) (Camden Town)
Ferdy Murphy S Hubbard Rodwell

Placings:4   (4793)
2002/03: 17⁴GF,

	Starts	1st	2nd	3rd	Win & Pl
Hurdles	1	0	0	0	266
Career Total	1	0	0	0	266

Going: Sf: 0-0 GS: 0-0 Gd: 0-0 GF: - Fm: 0-1
Distance: 2m/2m3: 0-1 2m4-2m7: 0-0 3m+: 0-0
Track: LH: 0-1 RH: 0-0 Tight: 0-1 Gall: 0-0
Aids: Bl: 0-0 Vi: 0-0 Tstrap: 0-0
Best Rating: 71   4/03   Sedg   2m1f   gd-fm   Hdl

Ex-Irish pointer; has shown just moderate performer over hurdles.

Your So Cool

75   **100+**

6-y-o ch g Karinga Bay-Laurel Diver (Celtic Cone)
M C Pipe Matt Archer & Miss Jean Broadhurst

Placings:0-3   (3558)
2002/03: 20³HY,

	Starts	1st	2nd	3rd	Win & Pl
Hurdles	1	0	0	1	527
Career Total	2	0	0	1	527

Going: Sf: 0-1 GS: 0-0 Gd: 0-0 GF: - Fm: 0-0
Distance: 2m/2m3: 0-0 2m4-2m7: 0-1 3m+: 0-0
Track: LH: 0-0 RH: 0-1 Tight: 0-1 Gall: 0-0
Aids: Bl: 0-0 Vi: 0-0 Tstrap: 0-0
Best Rating: 100   2/03   Folk   2m4f110y   heavy   Hdl

Showed ability when blinkered on his hurdling debut on testing ground.

Your Turn Rosie

79   **43**

8-y-o b m Relief Pitcher-Bremhill Rosie (Celtic Cone)
I R Brown I R Brown

Placings:0-0   (0076)
2002/03: 19⁰GF,

	Starts	1st	2nd	3rd	Win & Pl
Hurdles	1	0	0	0	
Career Total	2	0	0	0	

Going: Sf: 0-0 GS: 0-0 Gd: 0-0 GF: - Fm: 0-1
Distance: 2m/2m3: 0-0 2m4-2m7: 0-1 3m+: 0-0
Track: LH: 0-0 RH: 0-1 Tight: 0-0 Gall: 0-0
Aids: Bl: 0-0 Vi: 0-0 Tstrap: 0-0
Best Rating: 43   5/02   Hrfd   2m3f110y   gd-fm   Hdl

Yvanovitch (FR)

94   **98**

5-y-o b g Kaldounevees (FR)-County Kerry (FR) (Comrade In Arms)
Mrs L C Taylor Mrs L C Taylor

Placings:0550   (3902)
2002/03: 16⁹S, 16⁵G, 16⁵G, 16⁹S,

	Starts	1st	2nd	3rd	Win & Pl
Hurdles	4	0	0	0	0
Career Total	4	0	0	0	0

Going: Sf: 0-2 GS: 0-0 Gd: 0-2 GF: - Fm: 0-0
Distance: 2m/2m3: 0-4 2m4-2m7: 0-0 3m+: 0-0
Track: LH: 0-4 RH: 0-0 Tight: 0-0 Gall: 0-4
Aids: Bl: 0-0 Vi: 0-0 Tstrap: 0-0
Best Rating: 98 2/03 Newb 2m10y   good   Hdl

Zaajer (USA)

88   76

7-y-o ch g Silver Hawk (USA)-Crown Quest (USA) (Chief s Crown (USA))
J A B Old W E Sturt

Placings:244P-5   (2288)
2002/03: 17⁵G,

	Starts	1st	2nd	3rd	Win & Pl
Hurdles	1	0	0	0	0
Career Total	5	0	1	0	846

Going: Sf: 0-0 GS: 0-0 Gd: 0-1 GF: - Fm: 0-0
Distance: 2m/2m3: 0-1 2m4-2m7: 0-0 3m+: 0-0
Track: LH: 0-0 RH: 0-1 Tight: 0-0 Gall: 0-0
Aids: Bl: 0-0 Vi: 0-0 Tstrap: 0-0
Best Rating: 90 1/02 Hntg 2m10y gd-sft Hdl

Moderate hurdler; Listed winner on the Flat. Met a useful winner on his hurdles debut at Newton Abbot, before getting beat a long way in heavy ground at Uttoxeter.

Zabadi (IRE)

95   58

11-y-o b g Shahrastani (USA)-Zerzaya (Beldale Flutter (USA))
Miss Venetia Williams Miss V M Williams

Placings:051101/1005052/32F3332F3/52/221222223P206 3/2212111P3-656465   (4023)
2002/03: 20⁶G, 16⁵GS, 20⁶G, 20⁴S, 18⁶S, 16⁵S,

	Starts	1st	2nd	3rd	Win & Pl
Chases	6	0	0	0	313
Career Total	53	9	15	8	100568
119	12/01	Towc	2m110y	D(0-120)HCh	HVY	£5486
113	12/01	Plum	2m4f	D(0-125)HCh	SFT	£3802
119	11/01	Towc	2m110y	F(0-105)HCh	SFT	£3900
117	10/01	Fknm	2m5f110yF(0-100)HCh		SFT	£3435
91	6/00	Uttx	2m4f	D Ch	G-F	£4225
149	11/96	Newb	2m110y	A Hdl	GD	£12100
138	3/96	Aint	2m110y	A Hdl	GD	£28424
139	2/96	Kemp	2m	A Hdl	SFT	£9002
135	1/96	Kemp	2m	D Hdl	GD	£3061

Total win prize-money £73457

Going: Sf: 0-3 GS: 0-1 Gd: 0-2 GF: - Fm: 0-0
Distance: 2m/2m3: 0-3 2m4-2m7: 0-3 3m+: 0-0
Track: LH: 0-3 RH: 0-2 Tight: 0-5 Gall: 0-0
Aids: Bl: 0-0 Vi: 0-0 Tstrap: 0-0
Best Rating: 150 4/97 Ayr 2m   good   Hdl

Plating-class chaser nowadays; one-time smart hurdler, he has proved expensive to follow over fences, though he showed a better attitude in the winter of 2001/2. Suited by two to two and a half miles and soft ground.

Zabriskie Point

85f   52f

4-y-o b f Overbury (IRE)-Brownhill Lass (Sunyboy)
Mrs J C McGregor Drew McClelland

Placings:00   (3583)
2002/03: 16⁰HY, 16⁰G,

	Starts	1st	2nd	3rd	Win & Pl
NH Flat	2	0	0	0	0
Career Total	2	0	0	0	0

Going: Sf: 0-1 GS: 0-0 Gd: 0-1 GF: - Fm: 0-0
Distance: 2m/2m3: 0-2 2m4-2m7: 0-0 3m+: 0-0
Track: LH: 0-1 RH: 0-1 Tight: 0-1 Gall: 0-0
Aids: Bl: 0-0 Vi: 0-0 Tstrap: 0-0
Best Rating: 52 2/03 Muss 2m   good NHF

Zacopani (IRE)

93(105h)   41

11-y-o b g Lafontaine (USA)-Take A Dare (Pragmatic)
R Ford Mr & Mrs T D Williams

Placings:0P0P/041616132/5PF04000P5P/P3300/1F1/P4P 24-0PU   (4409)
2002/03: 24⁰G, 25ᴾGF, 25ᵁG,

	Starts	1st	2nd	3rd	Win & Pl
Chases	3	0	0	0	
Career Total	40	5	2	3	20034
98	7/00	Sedg	3m3f110yF(0-110)HHdl	FRM	£2618
95	5/00	Hexm	3m1f	E Ch	G-F	£3159
101	8/97	Cork	3m	(0-116)HHdl	Y-S	£4069
96	7/97	Klny	2m6f	(0-109)HHdl	G-Y	£3051
101	6/97	Tral	2m	NHF	FRM	£3391

Total win prize-money £16289

Going: Sf: 0-0 GS: 0-0 Gd: 0-2 GF: - Fm: 0-1
Distance: 2m/2m3: 0-0 2m4-2m7: 0-0 3m+: 0-3
Track: LH: 0-1 RH: 0-1 Tight: 0-1 Gall: 0-0
Aids: Bl: 0-3 Vi: 0-0 Tstrap: 0-0
Best Rating: 106 8/97 Tral 2m4f   heavy   Hdl

A real stayer who won on soft ground in Ireland, has looked better suited to fast ground since coming to Britain.

Zafarabad (IRE)

112(89h)   (134h)146

9-y-o gr g Shernazar-Zarafa (Blushing Groom (FR))
P J Hobbs Mrs Elaine Baines

Placings:11141/1323F4/12221U/P03133-1304   (4775)
2002/03: 24¹GF, 24³S, 24⁰G, 24⁴G,

	Starts	1st	2nd	3rd	Win & Pl
Chases	4	1	0	1	24470
Career Total	27	9	4	6	131304
146	10/02	Kemp	3m	B(0-145)HCh	G-F	£17400
140	2/02	Kemp	2m4f110yC(0-130)HCh	G-S	£11212
135	1/00	Hntg	3m	D Ch	GD	£4381
132	11/99	Extr	2m3f	C Ch	G-S	£6385
150	11/98	Newb	2m110y	B Hdl	G-S	£5095
143	4/98	Punc	2m	Hdl	HVY	£26956
142	2/98	Newb	2m110y	C Hdl	GD	£4272
137	1/98	Chel	2m1f	A Hdl	G-S	£9645
134	1/98	Kemp	2m	D Hdl	SFT	£2996

Total win prize-money £88345

Going: Sf: 0-1 GS: 0-0 Gd: 0-2 GF: - Fm: 1-1
Distance: 2m/2m3: 0-0 2m4-2m7: 0-0 3m+: 1-4
Track: LH: 0-0 RH: 1-4 Tight: 0-0 Gall: 0-0
Aids: Bl: 1-4 Vi: 0-0 Tstrap: 0-0
Best Rating: 156 1/99 Leop 2m   heavy   Hdl

Very useful handicap chaser; stays three miles, effective at shorter; acts on a fast surface, but also effective on soft ground; best going right-handed; regularly blinkered.

Zafarelli

79   90

9-y-o gr g Nishapour (FR)-Voltigeuse (USA) (Filiberto (USA))
J R Jenkins The East India Dock Partnership

Placings:403305/400P115P0/PUP665025/142/P056-P0
(0799)
2002/03: 24ᴾG, 21⁰S,

	Starts	1st	2nd	3rd	Win & Pl
Hurdles	2	0	0	0	
Career Total	33	3	2	2	12034
98	5/00	Hntg	2m5f110yD(0-125)HHdl	G-S	£3146
91	1/99	Plum	2m1f	E(0-115)HHdl	HVY	£2740
93	12/98	Folk	2m1f110yE(0-105)HHdl	SFT	£2508

Total win prize-money £8395

Going: Sf: 0-1 GS: 0-0 Gd: 0-1 GF: - Fm: 0-0
Distance: 2m/2m3: 0-0 2m4-2m7: 0-1 3m+: 0-1
Track: LH: 0-1 RH: 0-1 Tight: 0-2 Gall: 0-0
Aids: Bl: 0-0 Vi: 0-0 Tstrap: 0-0
Best Rating: 98 9/00 Plum 2m5f   good   Hdl

In-and-out perfromer who is not genuine.

Zaffamore (IRE)

103(104h)   (97h)126

7-y-o ch g Zaffaran (USA)-Furmore (Furry Glen)
Miss H C Knight Martin Broughton

Placings:0/4/52-1510P2   (4447)
2002/03: 20¹G, 24⁵GS, 20¹S, 20⁰GS, 24ᴾG, 24²G,

	Starts	1st	2nd	3rd	Win & Pl
Chases	6	2	1	0	11225
Career Total	10	2	2	0	12026
126	1/03	Ludl	2m4f	E Ch	SFT	£4953
121	11/02	Ludl	2m4f	E Ch	GD	£4472

Total win prize-money £9425

Going: Sf: 1-1 GS: 0-2 Gd: 1-3 GF: - Fm: 0-0
Distance: 2m/2m3: 0-0 2m4-2m7: 2-3 3m+: 0-3
Track: LH: 0-1 RH: 2-5 Tight: 2-4 Gall: 0-1
Aids: Bl: 0-0 Vi: 0-0 Tstrap: 0-0
Best Rating: 126 4/03 Ludl 3m   good   Ch.

Fair novice chaser; twice successful over two and a half miles at Ludlow; acts on good and soft ground.

Zaffaran In Eden (IRE)

6-y-o ch m Zaffaran (USA)-Edenapa (Peacock (FR))
Colin S McKeever F Thompson

Placings:240   (0949a)
2002/03: 22²Y, 17⁴G, 20⁰HY,

	Starts	1st	2nd	3rd	Win & Pl
NH Flat	1	0	0	0	0
Hurdles	2	0	1	0	883
Career Total	3	0	1	0	883

Going: Sf: 0-1 GS: 0-0 Gd: 0-1 GF: - Fm: 0-0
Distance: 2m/2m3: 0-1 2m4-2m7: 0-2 3m+: 0-0
Track: LH: 0-1 RH: 0-0 Tight: 0-1 Gall: 0-0
Aids: Bl: 0-0 Vi: 0-0 Tstrap: 0-0
Best Rating: 75 6/02 Dpat 2m6f   yield   Hdl

Zaffaran Winds (IRE)

8-y-o b m Zaffaran (USA)-Sharp Winds (Tumble Wind (USA))
Mrs Marilyn Scudamore M Scudamore

Placings:*00605/6F-2*   (0272)
2002/03: 20²GF,

	Starts	1st	2nd	3rd	Win & Pl
Chases	1	0	1	0	630
Career Total	8	0	1	0	630

Going:	Sf: 0-0 GS: 0-0 Gd: 0-0 GF: - Fm: 0-1
Distance:	2m/2m3: 0-0 2m4-2m7: 0-1 3m+: 0-1
Track:	LH: 0-1 RH: 0-0 Tight: 0-1 Gall: 0-0
Aids:	Bl: 0-0 Vi: 0-0 Tstrap: 0-0
Best Rating:	81	4/01	Hayd	2m	soft	Ch

Zaffaranni (IRE)

101(108h)   (103h)120d
7-y-o ch m Zaffaran (USA)-Nimbi (Orchestra)
D J Caro Mrs S Tainton

Placings:*O240/321530-141PUP*   (4674)
2002/03: 24¹GS, 25⁴GS, 20¹GS, 25⁴S, 21ᵁS, 25ᴾGF,

	Starts	1st	2nd	3rd	Win & Pl
Chases	6	2	0	0	11029
Career Total	16	3	2	2	17502
112	12/02	Hntg	2m4f110yD Ch		G-S	£4970
120	11/02	Newb	3m	D(0-110)HCh	G-S	£5694
103	12/01	Ludl	2m5f	D Hdl	GD	£3711

Total win prize-money £14376

Going:	Sf: 0-2 GS: 2-3 Gd: 0-0 GF: - Fm: 0-1
Distance:	2m/2m3: 0-0 2m4-2m7: 1-2 3m+: 1-4
Track:	LH: 1-4 RH: 1-2 Tight: 0-0 Gall: 2-3
Aids:	Bl: 0-0 Vi: 0-0 Tstrap: 0-0
Best Rating:	120	11/02	Newb	3m	gd-sft	Ch

Fair chaser; stays 3m, effective at 2m 4f; acts on good and soft ground; broke down in April.

Zaffre D'Or (IRE)

81f   79f
6-y-o b g Zaffaran (USA)-Massinetta (Bold Lad (IRE))
M Pitman Mrs D Salmon

Placings:*0*   (3903)
2002/03: 16⁰S,

	Starts	1st	2nd	3rd	Win & Pl
NH Flat	1	0	0	0	
Career Total	1	0	0	0	

Going:	Sf: 0-1 GS: 0-0 Gd: 0-0 GF: - Fm: 0-0
Distance:	2m/2m3: 0-1 2m4-2m7: 0-0 3m+: 0-0
Track:	LH: 0-1 RH: 0-0 Tight: 0-0 Gall: 0-1
Aids:	Bl: 0-0 Vi: 0-0 Tstrap: 0-0
Best Rating:	72	3/03	Newb	2m110y	soft	NHF

Zaffre Noir (IRE)

120
7-y-o b g Zaffaran (USA)-Massinetta (Bold Lad (IRE))
M Pitman Mrs D Salmon

Placings:*260/261F31/3054-P*   (0087)
2002/03: 20⁰G,

	Starts	1st	2nd	3rd	Win & Pl
Hurdles	1	0	0	0	
Career Total	14	2	2	2	10643
120	4/01	Winc	2m6f	E Hdl	SFT	£2408
120	12/00	Newb	2m3f	D Hdl	SFT	£3607

Total win prize-money £6016

Going:	Sf: 0-0 GS: 0-0 Gd: 0-1 GF: - Fm: 0-0
Distance:	2m/2m3: 0-0 2m4-2m7: 0-1 3m+: 0-0
Track:	LH: 0-1 RH: 0-0 Tight: 0-0 Gall: 0-0
Aids:	Bl: 0-0 Vi: 0-0 Tstrap: 0-0
Best Rating:	120	12/01	Kemp	2m5f	good	Hdl

Fair hurdler, gets two miles-six but not much further, and appreciates cut in the ground.

Zaggy Lane

108   107
11-y-o b g Prince Of Peace-Meldon Lady (Ballymoss)
S C Burrough (P R Rodford 16/1) E T Wey

Placings:*6/006/5F422/3F111F2/P56/FP306153/3462423P-224425443*   (4738)
2002/03: 24²G, 26²S, 29⁴GS, 30⁴S, 27²S, 28⁴HY, 25⁴GS, 24⁴S, 24³GF,

	Starts	1st	2nd	3rd	Win & Pl
Chases	9	0	3	1	13607
Career Total	44	4	8	6	44756
119	2/01	Wwck	3m5f	F(0-110)HCh	SFT	£3558
123	1/99	Tntn	3m3f	C(0-130)HCh	SFT	£7197
117	12/98	Uttx	3m	D(0-120)HCh	SFT	£3598
112	12/98	NAbb	2m5f110y	(0-100)HCh	SFT	£3080

Total win prize-money £17436

Going:	Sf: 0-5 GS: 0-2 Gd: 0-1 GF: - Fm: 0-1
Distance:	2m/2m3: 0-0 2m4-2m7: 0-0 3m+: 0-9
Track:	LH: 0-7 RH: 0-2 Tight: 0-3 Gall: 0-1
Aids:	Bl: 0-0 Vi: 0-0 Tstrap: 0-0
Best Rating:	123	2/99	Newb	3m2f110y	gd-sft	Ch

Fair staying chaser; suited by marathon trips and soft ground; consistent; does not win very often these days.

Zahaalie (USA)

108   83
11-y-o ch g Zilzal (USA)-Bambee Tt (USA) (Better Bee)
J A Pickering Christian Wroe

Placings:*3612363P/50022225/00P5P/321F040/4*   (4149)
2002/03: 21⁴G,

	Starts	1st	2nd	3rd	Win & Pl
Hurdles	1	0	0	0	0
Career Total	29	2	6	4	9820
94	11/00	Leic	2m4f110yG(0-90)HHdl		HVY	£1932
84	12/97	Bang	2m1f	G Hdl	GD	£2305

Total win prize-money £4238

Going:	Sf: 0-0 GS: 0-0 Gd: 0-1 GF: - Fm: 0-0
Distance:	2m/2m3: 0-0 2m4-2m7: 0-1 3m+: 0-0
Track:	LH: 0-1 RH: 0-0 Tight: 0-0 Gall: 0-0
Aids:	Bl: 0-0 Vi: 0-0 Tstrap: 0-0
Best Rating:	97	3/99	Bang	3m	gd-sft	Hdl

Plating-class hurdler; stays two and a half miles; acts on fast ground.

Zaidaan

102   86
7-y-o b g Ezzoud (IRE)-River Maiden (USA) (Riverman (USA))
D J Wintle (G M McCourt 18/7) It Might Be Ten Partnership

Placings:*1336/2F21056/0P53/21F1U3150/23340024/545/P524F-5*   (0501)
2002/03: 30⁵G,

	Starts	1st	2nd	3rd	Win & Pl
Chases	1	0	0	0	0

Placings:*45/P-1033*   (1447)
2002/03: 16¹GF, 16⁹GF, 16³G, 20³G,

	Starts	1st	2nd	3rd	Win & Pl
Hurdles	4	1	0	2	3032
Career Total	7	1	0	2	3032
80	6/02	Worc	2m	G(0-90)HHdl	G-F	£2387

Total win prize-money £2387

Going:	Sf: 0-0 GS: 0-0 Gd: 0-2 GF: - Fm: 1-2
Distance:	2m/2m3: 1-3 2m4-2m7: 0-1 3m+: 0-0
Track:	LH: 1-4 RH: 0-0 Tight: 0-1 Gall: 0-0
Aids:	Bl: 0-0 Vi: 0-0 Tstrap: 0-0
Best Rating:	90	9/02	Worc	2m	good	Hdl

Plating-class hurdler; landed a gamble in a selling hurdle at Worcester in June 2002 but lame when well beaten next time. Third in a similar event at Worcester for new trainer in September.

Zaleem (IRE)

6-y-o b g Kahyasi-Zallaka (IRE) (Shardari)
Mrs J Candlish N Heath

Placings:*034-P*   (4522)
2002/03: 16⁹G,

	Starts	1st	2nd	3rd	Win & Pl
Hurdles	1	0	0	0	
Career Total	4	0	0	1	283

Going:	Sf: 0-0 GS: 0-0 Gd: 0-1 GF: - Fm: 0-0
Distance:	2m/2m3: 0-1 2m4-2m7: 0-0 3m+: 0-0
Track:	LH: 0-1 RH: 0-0 Tight: 0-0 Gall: 0-0
Aids:	Bl: 0-0 Vi: 0-0 Tstrap: 0-0
Best Rating:	94	12/01	Ludl	2m	good	NHF

Zamat

106   119
7-y-o b g Slip Anchor-Khandjar (Kris)
P Monteith I Bell

Placings:*4360-11105156*   (4308)
2002/03: 16¹G, 18¹S, 16¹S, 17⁰G, 16⁵GS, 16¹GS, 20⁵S, 18⁶G,

	Starts	1st	2nd	3rd	Win & Pl
Hurdles	8	4	0	0	16341
Career Total	12	4	0	1	16805
119	12/03	Ayr	2m	D(0-125)HHdl	G-S	£5512
120	11/02	Kels	2m110y	E Hdl	SFT	£3679
115	11/02	Kels	2m2f	F(0-110)HHdl	SFT	£3419
102	5/02	Kels	2m110y	E(0-105)HHdl	GD	£3731

Total win prize-money £16341

Going:	Sf: 2-3 GS: 1-2 Gd: 1-3 GF: - Fm: 0-0
Distance:	2m/2m3: 4-7 2m4-2m7: 0-1 3m+: 0-0
Track:	LH: 4-8 RH: 0-0 Tight: 3-4 Gall: 0-1
Aids:	Bl: 0-0 Vi: 0-0 Tstrap: 0-0
Best Rating:	120	11/02	Kels	2m110y	soft	Hdl

Fair hurdler, successful four times this season. Suited by two miles; acts on easy ground.

Zamhareer (USA)

80
12-y-o b g Lear Fan (USA)-Awenita (Rarity)
R Ford R Burgess

Placings:*1336/2F21056/0P53/21F1U3150/23340024/545/P524F-5*   (0501)
2002/03: 30⁵G,

	Starts	1st	2nd	3rd	Win & Pl
Chases	1	0	0	0	0

Career Total	42	6	6	6	28300
80	10/01 MRas	3m4f110yF(0-100)HCh		G-S	£3461
109	3/99 Hexm	3m	F(0-110)HHdl	SFT	£2022
106	11/98 Sedg	3m3f	F(0-105)HCh		£2882
113	10/98 Sedg	3m3f110yF(0-100)HHdl		G-S	£2495
120	3/96 Donc	3m110y B HHdl		G-F	£5114
96	11/94 Newc	2m110y Hdl		GD	£2736

Total win prize-money £18711

Going:	Sf: 0-0 GS: 0-0 Gd: 0-1 GF: - Fm: 0-0
Distance:	2m/2m3: 0-0 2m4-2m7: 0-0 3m+: 0-1
Track:	LH: 0-0 RH: 0-0 Tight: 0-0 Gall: 0-0
Aids:	Bl: 0-0 Vi: 0-0 Tstrap: 0-0
Best Rating:	122 3/96 Aint 3m110y good Hdl

Moderate staying chaser, appreciates marathon trips and easy ground.

Zamir

4-y-o ch g Zamindar (USA)-Fairy Flax (IRE) (Dancing Brave (USA))
A Crook (Mrs J R Ramsden 11/5) Ballyleah Bloodstock

Placings:0   (2247)
2002/03: 16ᴼGS,

	Starts	1st	2nd	3rd	Win & Pl
Hurdles	1	0	0	0	
Career Total	1	0	0	0	

Going:	Sf: 0-0 GS: 0-1 Gd: 0-0 GF: - Fm: 0-0
Distance:	2m/2m3: 0-1 2m4-2m7: 0-0 3m+: 0-0
Track:	LH: 0-1 RH: 0-0 Tight: 0-0 Gall: 0-1
Aids:	Bl: 0-0 Vi: 0-0 Tstrap: 0-0
Best Rating:	0 11/02 Newc 2m gd-sft Hdl

Zamorin

80   56

4-y-o b g Zafonic (USA)-Armeria (USA) (Northern Dancer)
P S McEntee (R Charlton 30/4) Keybeam Technology Limited

Placings:00   (2720)
2002/03: 16ᴼGF, 16ᴼS,

	Starts	1st	2nd	3rd	Win & Pl
Hurdles	2	0	0	0	
Career Total	2	0	0	0	

Going:	Sf: 0-1 GS: 0-0 Gd: 0-0 GF: - Fm: 0-1
Distance:	2m/2m3: 0-2 2m4-2m7: 0-0 3m+: 0-0
Track:	LH: 0-1 RH: 0-1 Tight: 0-1 Gall: 0-0
Aids:	Bl: 0-0 Vi: 0-0 Tstrap: 0-0
Best Rating:	54 12/02 Kemp 2m soft Hdl

Zantana Boy (IRE)

89   53

5-y-o ch g Zaffaran (USA)-Ardtana (IRE) (Cidrax (FR))
D J Caro The Carried Away Syndicate

Placings:0   (3623)
2002/03: 16ᴼHY,

	Starts	1st	2nd	3rd	Win & Pl
NH Flat	1	0	0	0	
Career Total	1	0	0	0	

Going:	Sf: 0-1 GS: 0-0 Gd: 0-0 GF: - Fm: 0-0
Distance:	2m/2m3: 0-1 2m4-2m7: 0-0 3m+: 0-0
Track:	LH: 0-0 RH: 0-1 Tight: 0-0 Gall: 0-0

Aids:

Bl: 0-0 Vi: 0-0 Tstrap: 0-0

Best Rating: 0   2/03   Sand   2m110y   heavy NHF

Zapata Highway

71   68

6-y-o ch g Bold Arrangement-Trailing Rose (Undulate (USA))
D R C Elsworth R & H Burridge, M Matheson, A S Wing

Placings:0-0P0   (2218)
2002/03: 16ᴼG, 16ᴾG, 16ᴼS,

	Starts	1st	2nd	3rd	Win & Pl
Hurdles	3	0	0	0	
Career Total	4	0	0	0	

Going:	Sf: 0-1 GS: 0-0 Gd: 0-2 GF: - Fm: 0-0
Distance:	2m/2m3: 0-3 2m4-2m7: 0-0 3m+: 0-0
Track:	LH: 0-1 RH: 0-2 Tight: 0-0 Gall: 0-1
Aids:	Bl: 0-0 Vi: 0-0 Tstrap: 0-0
Best Rating:	68 10/02 Winc 2m good Hdl

Zarbari (IRE)

4-y-o b g Kahyasi-Zarlana (IRE) (Darshaan)
D McCain D McCain

Placings:0   (4665)
2002/03: 17ᴼGF,

	Starts	1st	2nd	3rd	Win & Pl
NH Flat	1	0	0	0	
Career Total	1	0	0	0	

Going:	Sf: 0-0 GS: 0-0 Gd: 0-0 GF: - Fm: 0-1
Distance:	2m/2m3: 0-1 2m4-2m7: 0-0 3m+: 0-0
Track:	LH: 0-0 RH: 0-1 Tight: 0-0 Gall: 0-0
Aids:	Bl: 0-0 Vi: 0-0 Tstrap: 0-1
Best Rating:	44 4/03 Carl 2m1f gd-fm NHF

Zarza Bay (IRE)

90   76

4-y-o b g Hamas (IRE)-Frill (Henbit (USA))
K R Burke Mrs Melba Bryce

Placings:0   (2503)
2002/03: 16ᴼGS,

	Starts	1st	2nd	3rd	Win & Pl
Hurdles	1	0	0	0	
Career Total	1	0	0	0	

Going:	Sf: 0-0 GS: 0-1 Gd: 0-0 GF: - Fm: 0-0
Distance:	2m/2m3: 0-1 2m4-2m7: 0-0 3m+: 0-0
Track:	LH: 0-1 RH: 0-0 Tight: 0-1 Gall: 0-0
Aids:	Bl: 0-0 Vi: 0-0 Tstrap: 0-0
Best Rating:	76 12/02 Fknm 2m gd-sft Hdl

Zelensky (IRE)

4-y-o b g Danehill Dancer (IRE)-Malt Leaf (IRE) (Nearly A Nose (USA))
Jean-Rene Auvray (J A Osborne 27/5) S J Edwards

Placings:P   (3148)
2002/03: 16ᴾHY,

	Starts	1st	2nd	3rd	Win & Pl
Hurdles	1	0	0	0	

Career Total	1	0	0	0

Going:	Bl: 0-0 Vi: 0-0 Tstrap: 0-0
Best Rating:	0 1/03 Chep 2m110y heavy Hdl

Zeloso

104   87

5-y-o b g Alzao (USA)-Silk Petal (Petorius)
M F Harris The Paxford Optimists

Placings:440PP41350P   (4540)
2002/03: 17⁴HY, 17⁴G, 16⁰GS, 16ᴾGF, 16⁴GF, 19¹GF, 19³GF, 20⁵GF, 19ᴼG, 21ᴾG,

	Starts	1st	2nd	3rd	Win & Pl
Hurdles	11	1	0	1	4146
Career Total	11	1	0	1	4146
87	9/02 Hrfd	2m3f110y	F(0-100)HHdl		
G-F	£3115				

Total win prize-money £3115

Going:	Sf: 0-1 GS: 0-1 Gd: 0-3 GF: - Fm: 1-6
Distance:	2m/2m3: 0-7 2m4-2m7: 1-4 3m+: 0-0
Track:	LH: 0-6 RH: 1-5 Tight: 0-6 Gall: 0-3
Aids:	Bl: 0-0 Vi: 1-6 Tstrap: 0-0
Best Rating:	87 9/02 MRas 2m3f110y gd-fm Hdl

Plating-class hurdler; got off the mark when winning at Hereford in September 2002. Acts on decent ground.

Zetagalopon

60   30

5-y-o b m Petong-Azola (IRE) (Alzao (USA))
C L Popham Miss Deborah Bullion

Placings:560-P0   (2712)
2002/03: 17ᴼGS, 16ᴼGS,

	Starts	1st	2nd	3rd	Win & Pl
Hurdles	2	0	0	0	
Career Total	5	0	0	0	0

Going:	Sf: 0-0 GS: 0-2 Gd: 0-0 GF: - Fm: 0-0
Distance:	2m/2m3: 0-2 2m4-2m7: 0-0 3m+: 0-0
Track:	LH: 0-0 RH: 0-2 Tight: 0-0 Gall: 0-0
Aids:	Bl: 0-0 Vi: 0-0 Tstrap: 0-0
Best Rating:	30 9/01 NAbb 2m1f gd-fm Hdl

Ziggy's Way

(102h)   (85h)

8-y-o b g Teenoso (USA)-Onaway (Commanche Run)
Mrs A Barclay Mrs Althea Barclay

Placings:54P/40-P   (3826)
2002/03: 24ᴾGS,

	Starts	1st	2nd	3rd	Win & Pl
Chases	1	0	0	0	
Career Total	6	0	0	0	323

Going:	Sf: 0-0 GS: 0-1 Gd: 0-0 GF: - Fm: 0-0
Distance:	2m/2m3: 0-0 2m4-2m7: 0-0 3m+: 0-1
Track:	LH: 0-1 RH: 0-0 Tight: 0-0 Gall: 0-0
Aids:	Bl: 0-0 Vi: 0-0 Tstrap: 0-0
Best Rating:	99 2/01 Towc 2m heavy NHF

Zilarator (USA)

100

7-y-o b g Zilzal (USA)-Allegedly (USA) (Sir Ivor)
P J Hobbs Jay Dee Bloodstock Limited

Placings:5-2425R   (4622)
2002/03: 20²HY, 16⁴HY, 16²HY, 21⁵S, 22ᴿGF,

	Starts	1st	2nd	3rd	Win & Pl
Hurdles	5	0	2	0	3602
Career Total	6	0	2	0	3602

Going: Sf: 0-4 GS: 0-0 Gd: 0-0 GF: - Fm: 0-1
Distance: 2m/2m3: 0-2 2m4-2m7: 0-3 3m+: 0-0
Track: LH: 0-3 RH: 0-2 Tight: 0-1 Gall: 0-1
Aids: Bl: 0-0 Vi: 0-0 Tstrap: 0-0
Best Rating: 123 2/02 Kemp 2m   gd-sft Hdl

Modest novice hurdler; useful middle-distance handicapper
on the Flat; stays two and a half miles and acts on ground
good or softer; yet to win over timber; sometimes not the
easiest of rides.

Zoffany (IRE)

101   **108+**

6-y-o b g Synefos (USA)-Shining Green (Green Shoon)
M Todhunter Sir Robert Ogden

Placings:10   (3095)
2002/03: 16¹G, 16⁰GS,

	Starts	1st	2nd	3rd	Win & Pl
Hurdles	2	1	0	0	4063
Career Total	2	1	0	0	4063
108 12/02 Hayd 2m		D Hdl		GD	£4062

                         Total win prize-money £4063

Going: Sf: 0-0 GS: 0-1 Gd: 1-1 GF: - Fm: 0-0
Distance: 2m/2m3: 1-2 2m4-2m7: 0-0 3m+: 0-0
Track: LH: 1-2 RH: 0-0 Tight: 0-0 Gall: 0-1
Aids: Bl: 0-0 Vi: 0-0 Tstrap: 0-0
Best Rating: 108 12/02 Hayd 2m   good Hdl

Modest hurdler; fortunate winner on hurdling debut over two
miles at Haydock in December and well beaten next time.

Zoltano (GER)

100   **104**

5-y-o b g In The Wings-Zarella (GER) (Anatas)
M Todhunter Leeds Plywood And Doors Ltd

Placings:42F2   (3103)
2002/03: 16⁴GS, 16²S, 16⁵FS, 16²HY,

	Starts	1st	2nd	3rd	Win & Pl
Hurdles	4	0	2	0	4417
Career Total	4	0	2	0	4417

Going: Sf: 0-3 GS: 0-1 Gd: 0-0 GF: - Fm: 0-0
Distance: 2m/2m3: 0-4 2m4-2m7: 0-0 3m+: 0-0
Track: LH: 0-4 RH: 0-0 Tight: 0-0 Gall: 0-0
Aids: Bl: 0-0 Vi: 0-0 Tstrap: 0-0
Best Rating: 116 12/02 Weth 2m   soft Hdl

Moderate hurdler; winner on the Flat in his native Germany,
has shown promise over hurdles but tends to run too free.
acts on soft ground.

Zsarabak

97(105h)   (111h)**98**

6-y-o br g Soviet Lad (USA)-Moorefield Girl (IRE) (Gorytus
(USA))
Jonjo O Neill C D Carr

Placings:331P0/3223P-1403   (0563)
2002/03: 17¹G, 16⁴G, 16⁸G, 20³GF,

	Starts	1st	2nd	3rd	Win & Pl
Hurdles	3	1	0	0	4859
Chases	1	0	0	1	585
Career Total	14	2	2	5	12836
112 5/02 Bang 2m1f		D(0-115)HHdl		GD	£4329
97 9/00 Bang 2m1f		D Hdl		G-F	£3172

                         Total win prize-money £7501

Going: Sf: 0-0 GS: 0-0 Gd: 1-3 GF: - Fm: 0-1
Distance: 2m/2m3: 1-3 2m4-2m7: 0-1 3m+: 0-0
Track: LH: 1-3 RH: 0-1 Tight: 1-3 Gall: 0-0
Aids: Bl: 0-0 Vi: 0-1 Tstrap: 0-0
Best Rating: 112 5/02 Bang 2m1f   good Hdl

Fair handicap hurdler at his best; well beaten over fences
so far; has broken blood vessels; one to avoid.

Zurs (IRE)

106   **104**

10-y-o b g Tirol-Needy (High Top)
H J Collingridge (Jonjo O Neill 12/12) Mrs M Liston

Placings:0/50/213/4/00031134430-3F26244P   (4639)
2002/03: 17³GF, 16⁶G, 17²G, 20⁶G, 18²GS, 16⁴GS, 16⁴GS, 16ᴾGF,

	Starts	1st	2nd	3rd	Win & Pl
Hurdles	7	0	2	1	5213
Chases	1	0	0	0	0
Career Total	26	3	3	5	28822
118 10/01 Chel	2m110y	E(0-135)HHdl		GD	£7182
112 10/01 Bang	2m1f	F(0-110)HHdl		GD	£5824
112 11/99 Plum	2m	F(0-110)HHdl		G-F	£2818

                         Total win prize-money £15826

Going: Sf: 0-0 GS: 0-3 Gd: 0-3 GF: - Fm: 0-2
Distance: 2m/2m3: 0-7 2m4-2m7: 0-1 3m+: 0-0
Track: LH: 0-5 RH: 0-3 Tight: 0-4 Gall: 0-2
Aids: Bl: 0-0 Vi: 0-0 Tstrap: 0-0
Best Rating: 121 2/02 Kemp 2m   gd-sft Hdl

Moderate hurdler; disappointing of late and is slipping down
the handicap.

Zygo (USA)

23

11-y-o b g Diesis-La Papagena (Habitat)
M Pitman M Pitman

Placings:P/0   (2570)
2002/03: 16⁰G,

	Starts	1st	2nd	3rd	Win & Pl
Hurdles	1	0	0	0	
Career Total	2	0	0	0	

Going: Sf: 0-0 GS: 0-0 Gd: 0-1 GF: - Fm: 0-0
Distance: 2m/2m3: 0-1 2m4-2m7: 0-0 3m+: 0-0
Track: LH: 0-1 RH: 0-0 Tight: 0-0 Gall: 0-1
Aids: Bl: 0-0 Vi: 0-0 Tstrap: 0-0
Best Rating: 0 12/02 Newb 2m110y   good Hdl

Zygomatic

106   **71**

5-y-o ch g Risk Me (FR)-Give Me A Day (Lucky Wednesday)
R F Fisher S P Marsh

Placings:330P0000   (4168)
2002/03: 17³GF, 16³G, 17⁰G, 16ᴾS, 17⁰HY, 16⁹G, 16⁰S, 20⁰GS,

	Starts	1st	2nd	3rd	Win & Pl
NH Flat	3	0	0	2	462
Hurdles	5	0	0	0	0
Career Total	8	0	0	2	462

Going: Sf: 0-3 GS: 0-1 Gd: 0-3 GF: - Fm: 0-1
Distance: 2m/2m3: 0-7 2m4-2m7: 0-1 3m+: 0-0
Track: LH: 0-5 RH: 0-3 Tight: 0-2 Gall: 0-1
Aids: Bl: 0-0 Vi: 0-0 Tstrap: 0-0
Best Rating: 92 6/02 Hexm 2m110y   good NHF

Plating-class novice hurdler; best effort when modest third
at Cartmel in July.

TOP JUMPS OWNERS IN BRITAIN

OWNER	HORSE WITH MOST WIN & PLACE PRIZE-MONEY	WINS-RUNS	WNRS-HORSES	2ND	3RD	4TH	£WIN	£PLACE	£TOTAL
D A Johnson	Stormez	46-168	21-37	22	21	16	577,881	339,220	917,101
J P McManus	Baracouda	33-185	26-64	30	18	12	568,935	184,101	753,036
Jim Lewis	Best Mate	11-27	4-7	4	3	1	413,294	78,233	491,528
Sir Robert Ogden	Ad Hoc	23-117	17-33	18	13	7	271,449	123,204	394,653
Terry Warner	Rooster Booster	14-38	4-8	4	4	4	334,682	49,015	383,698
Dee Racing Syndicate	Monty's Pass	1-1	1-1	0	0	0	348,000	0	348,000
Trevor Hemmings	Goguenard	23-164	12-47	31	15	14	162,874	153,792	316,667
Mrs J Stewart	Cenkos	4-25	4-7	6	1	6	195,760	93,895	289,655
Mrs John Magnier	Native Upmanship	6-10	2-3	1	1	0	159,227	91,750	250,977
Mrs G Smith	Spectroscope	14-33	6-8	6	3	3	168,849	36,475	205,324
Mr & Mrs Raymond Anderson Green	Star Jack	23-104	13-28	16	13	4	143,269	52,239	195,509
Mrs R J Skan	La Landiere	11-24	2-3	5	1	1	170,305	22,654	192,959
N B Mason	Xaipete	27-258	17-57	20	34	21	119,885	71,757	191,643
Ashleybank Investments Limited	Paco Venture	37-98	17-28	10	4	4	165,231	24,650	189,881
The Macca & Growler Partnership	Seebald	2-18	2-3	6	1	1	73,397	92,738	166,135
C G Roach	Shotgun Willy	9-31	6-9	6	1	3	124,566	40,589	165,155
Keith Nicholson	Nickel Sun	23-72	9-14	9	5	8	128,119	29,303	157,422
B A Kilpatrick	Tarxien	9-38	4-7	4	5	3	135,342	22,007	157,350
D Thompson	Spirit Leader	3-3	1-1	0	0	0	147,900	0	147,900
Brian Kearney	Moscow Flyer	1-2	1-1	0	0	0	145,000	0	145,000
Paul K Barber	Valley Henry	9-23	6-7	2	2	3	98,727	44,951	143,678
Robert Lester	Iris's Gift	6-7	1-1	1	0	0	109,057	32,340	141,397
J Hales	Azertyuiop	9-20	5-7	3	4	0	133,127	5,260	138,387
C J L Moorsom	Supreme Glory	0-5	0-1	1	0	1	0	135,750	135,750
Mrs M B Scholey	Truckers Tavern	1-22	1-5	4	5	2	34,800	92,998	127,798
B C Marshall	Vol Solitaire	8-28	4-5	5	3	3	74,105	47,281	121,386
W J Brown	Fondmort	4-12	2-2	2	3	0	81,544	37,054	118,599
Matt Archer & Miss Jean Broadhurst	Westender	6-34	4-12	4	6	3	19,160	98,427	117,588
Axom	Deano's Beeno	3-8	1-1	3	1	0	87,200	29,950	117,150
Halewood International Ltd	Amberleigh House	4-78	3-15	9	12	10	14,830	101,015	115,846
R Gibbs	One Knight	4-5	1-1	0	1	0	109,547	3,300	112,847
Interskyracing.Com & Mrs Jonjo O'Neill	Intersky Falcon	3-4	1-1	0	0	0	104,400	7,500	111,900
William Lomas	Ryalux	2-6	1-1	2	2	0	73,880	30,753	104,633
Mrs Belinda Harvey	Chicuelo	9-28	4-5	2	1	0	96,262	6,055	102,317
Mrs Stewart Catherwood	Keen Leader	6-21	3-5	1	5	0	80,346	21,309	101,655
Mrs Alicia Skene & W S Skene	Ardent Scout	3-11	2-3	3	2	0	66,153	29,305	95,458
The Behrajan Partnership	Behrajan	3-10	2-2	0	3	0	84,171	10,493	94,664
Favourites Racing	Limerick Boy	9-62	7-18	7	13	5	59,547	34,854	94,402
Darren C Mercer	Sudden Shock	8-31	6-6	7	3	1	69,714	21,278	90,992
Terry Neill	Puntal	11-25	3-7	2	1	0	73,845	15,070	88,915
Malm Syndicate	Sacundai	1-2	1-2	0	0	0	87,000	0	87,000
D J & F A Jackson	Epervier d'Or	8-35	5-7	10	3	4	50,150	36,703	86,854
Mark Tincknell	Poliantas	4-13	2-3	3	3	0	53,074	33,542	86,616
The Hon Mrs Townshend	Santenay	3-5	1-1	1	0	0	65,058	16,500	81,558
Thurloe Finsbury	Geos	1-11	1-2	1	2	2	26,800	53,055	79,855
Notalotterry	Kadarann	3-8	1-2	0	2	1	58,592	19,019	77,612
Paul K Barber,Mick Coburn,Colin Lewis 2	Young Devereaux	2-3	1-1	0	0	0	77,400	0	77,400
Mrs E Roberts & Nick Roberts	Chauvinist	2-5	1-1	0	2	0	62,290	13,362	75,652
Major Christopher Hanbury	Irish Hussar	3-13	1-3	1	1	1	55,776	19,654	75,431
Mrs F Montauban	Jair Du Cochet	3-5	1-1	1	0	0	43,577	30,800	74,377

TOP JUMPS TRAINERS IN BRITAIN

WINS-RUNS	%	TRAINER	WIN & PLACE £PRIZE-MONEY	WIN £PRIZE-MONEY	2ND	3RD	£1STAKE	INDIVIDUAL WNRS-HORSES	FIRST-TIME WINS		HURDLES & NH Flat WINS-RUNS	WNRS	CHASES WNS-RUNS	WNRS
190-950	20%	M C Pipe	2,616,700	1,639,346	116	110	+159.99	94-220	48	22%	133-668	20% 70	57-282	20% 28
152-583	26%	P F Nicholls	2,205,056	1,552,746	106	70	+55.19	84-142	44	31%	57-234	24% 38	95-349	27% 52
114-546	21%	Jonjo O'Neill	1,545,414	1,198,144	77	50	+37.22	63-157	26	17%	88-411	21% 49	26-135	19% 15
134-618	22%	P J Hobbs	1,480,859	1,075,242	99	85	+121.40	77-146	35	24%	81-373	22% 50	53-245	22% 31
69-394	18%	N J Henderson	1,072,157	614,239	63	56	+117.30	46-116	22	19%	37-250	15% 26	32-144	22% 21
43-276	16%	Miss H C Knight	891,837	606,257	36	28	+80.47	28-81	17	21%	12-116	10% 10	31-160	19% 18
78-476	16%	Miss Venetia Williams	706,207	449,414	63	68	+147.59	46-113	23	20%	43-251	17% 26	35-225	16% 21
74-352	21%	Mrs S J Smith	641,896	445,481	52	38	+125.55	33-76	15	20%	39-212	18% 20	35-140	25% 16
58-452	13%	Mrs M Reveley	522,329	324,071	55	70	+122.36	40-103	12	12%	34-325	10% 27	24-127	19% 14
43-416	10%	Ferdy Murphy	473,179	244,601	44	56	+166.97	35-115	8	7%	23-236	10% 16	20-180	11% 19
28-203	14%	H D Daly	422,298	306,637	27	30	+49.18	19-57	12	21%	7-88	8% 6	21-115	18% 13
40-275	15%	A King	403,699	210,444	46	34	+15.60	29-71	9	13%	29-187	16% 19	11-88	13% 10
51-343	15%	Ian Williams	396,006	266,063	49	42	+13.05	34-85	14	16%	32-234	14% 24	19-109	17% 13
63-274	23%	L Lungo	364,506	297,545	37	18	+51.14	34-82	19	23%	43-227	19% 26	20-47	43% 12
32-125	26%	R T Phillips	361,726	286,106	19	15	+6.74	14-35	5	14%	21-92	23% 10	11-33	33% 4
5-10	50%	Mrs John Harrington	354,276	350,900	1	0	+31.25	3-6	1	17%	3-6	50% 1	2-4	50% 2
1-1	100%	James Joseph Mangan	348,000	348,000	0	0	+16.00	1-1	1	100%	0-0	0% 0	1-1	100% 1
31-317	10%	N A Twiston-Davies	324,436	161,265	37	42	+77.42	21-82	7	9%	16-167	10% 12	15-150	10% 11
27-245	11%	C J Mann	309,439	149,519	43	36	+4.47	19-61	10	16%	17-156	11% 12	10-89	11% 7
35-272	13%	R H Alner	299,966	190,321	38	35	+38.99	23-74	11	15%	15-152	10% 12	20-120	17% 12
19-192	10%	P R Webber	247,637	115,906	24	24	+83.74	13-61	3	5%	8-107	7% 7	11-85	13% 7
36-140	26%	N G Richards	238,981	148,702	30	13	+25.61	18-43	12	28%	15-85	18% 8	21-55	38% 10
4-27	15%	F Doumen	236,939	205,360	3	3	+7.65	3-13	2	15%	3-18	17% 2	1-9	11% 1
33-155	21%	J Howard Johnson	206,795	172,807	11	12	+3.53	16-41	3	7%	22-103	21% 10	11-52	21% 7
25-184	14%	G L Moore	202,548	121,342	28	19	+26.26	17-49	8	16%	21-148	14% 15	4-36	11% 2
25-189	13%	Mrs H Dalton	184,905	133,091	23	17	+73.74	16-59	7	12%	5-81	6% 5	20-108	19% 12
20-197	10%	J W Mullins	183,784	111,607	21	23	+64.72	14-48	2	4%	11-132	8% 9	9-65	14% 5
22-201	11%	T R George	180,162	116,890	16	27	+22.93	18-63	7	11%	11-116	9% 10	11-85	13% 8
6-67	9%	P G Murphy	175,744	23,123	11	7	+42.57	3-19	1	5%	5-53	9% 3	1-14	7% 1
17-105	16%	Miss E C Lavelle	175,537	111,246	14	9	+31.76	11-34	4	12%	8-67	12% 5	9-38	24% 6
11-151	7%	D McCain	171,047	48,688	15	21	+25.75	8-37	2	5%	5-74	7% 4	6-77	8% 4
2-13	15%	E J O'Grady	169,185	145,000	1	0	+1.00	2-11	2	18%	2-7	29% 2	0-6	0% 0
22-192	11%	K C Bailey	164,914	110,514	13	19	+21.25	16-63	7	11%	13-99	13% 8	9-93	10% 8
13-118	11%	J T Gifford	163,247	106,666	15	17	+31.50	11-32	2	6%	7-63	11% 7	6-55	11% 4
22-218	10%	B G Powell	163,237	111,405	21	25	+31.56	14-56	2	4%	8-133	6% 7	14-85	16% 8
19-157	12%	T D Easterby	155,495	80,127	28	25	+18.90	11-34	1	3%	16-99	16% 9	3-58	5% 2
1-13	8%	A L T Moore	149,917	87,000	1	2	+10.75	1-7	0	0%	0-5	0% 0	1-8	13% 1
22-149	15%	R Rowe	148,740	119,219	10	22	+41.00	12-34	4	12%	7-76	9% 4	15-73	21% 9
8-79	10%	A Crook	148,366	94,516	15	12	+22.82	6-19	1	5%	3-45	7% 3	5-34	15% 3
17-103	17%	M Todhunter	142,290	91,814	22	14	+4.70	12-34	5	15%	10-67	15% 7	7-36	19% 7
2-24	8%	C Roche	141,501	66,700	3	3	+10.50	2-14	1	7%	1-10	10% 1	1-14	7% 1
20-159	13%	G M Moore	141,442	82,503	21	25	+53.25	12-33	3	9%	15-107	14% 10	5-52	10% 2
19-128	15%	R Lee	139,339	88,994	24	8	+13.13	13-28	1	4%	8-59	14% 7	11-69	16% 6
18-96	19%	P Bowen	130,797	101,003	11	5	+10.62	8-24	1	4%	4-60	7% 4	14-36	39% 4
20-91	22%	Noel T Chance	127,409	103,442	9	11	+5.39	9-33	5	15%	20-84	24% 9	0-7	0% 0
20-121	17%	J M Jefferson	125,961	84,878	15	18	+44.15	11-30	4	13%	12-87	14% 7	8-34	24% 4
18-119	15%	P Monteith	120,470	94,477	8	10	+27.01	10-31	2	6%	15-95	16% 7	3-24	13% 3
8-136	6%	P Beaumont	120,253	41,121	12	16	+12.17	5-36	3	8%	4-75	5% 3	4-61	7% 2
18-176	10%	R Dickin	119,090	73,404	24	13	+53.35	12-41	4	10%	8-105	8% 6	10-71	14% 8
23-193	12%	M W Easterby	116,634	69,100	25	17	+66.43	15-51	6	12%	22-137	16% 14	1-56	2% 1

TOP JUMPS JOCKEYS IN BRITAIN

WINS-RIDES	JOCKEY AND DWEST RIDING WEIGHT IN LAST 12 MONTHS	●CONDITIONAL JOCKEY TRAINER GIVING MOST WINNER/WINS-RIDES	ALL RIDES 2ND	3RD	£1 STAKE	WIN & PLACE £PRIZE-MONEY	NH FLAT & HURDLES WINS-RIDES	CHASES WINS-RIDES	FAVOURITES WINS-RIDES	LAST 14 DAYS WINS-RIDES	RIDES SINCE WIN
257-840	31% A P McCoy 10-1	M C Pipe 150-482 31%	132	118	±39.05	2,599,546	169-553	88-287	188-437	7-31	1
147-725	20% R Johnson 10-0	P J Hobbs 73-285 26%	116	111	±115.43	1,735,272	83-439	64-286	82-215	5-35	12
109-478	23% A Dobbin 10-0	L Lungo 34-95 36%	65	43	±74.57	832,830	60-310	49-168	61-145	12-31	4
77-295	26% R Walsh 10-0	P F Nicholls 67-234 29%	49	32	+37.39	1,530,000	36-148	41-147	47-104	8-21	1
77-448	17% M A FitzGerald 10-4	N J Henderson 41-212 19%	71	45	±174.80	962,824	37-274	39-173	49-129	2-18	5
66-548	12% G Lee 10-0	J Howard Johnson 20-68 29%	60	66	±169.55	569,096	42-345	24-203	28-67	0-26	29
62-521	12% A Thornton 10-2	R H Alner 25-150 17%	95	65	±88.28	672,573	23-285	39-236	19-47	2-20	5
61-445	14% W Marston 10-0	Mrs S J Smith 29-112 26%	39	55	±92.16	539,188	41-299	20-146	24-57	3-9	0
60-358	17% B Fenton 10-0	R Rowe 15-99 15%	46	36	+243.88	471,485	30-216	30-142	12-39	3-16	5
59-493	12% L Aspell 10-0	Mrs L Wadham 6-37 16%	59	64	+63.53	616,086	33-320	26-173	13-34	6-21	0
56-388	14% J Culloty 10-0	Miss H C Knight 31-166 19%	46	41	±39.63	900,899	21-228	35-160	21-49	2-8	1
50-487	10% R Thornton 10-0	A King 26-180 14%	69	59	±107.17	535,251	34-318	16-169	10-41	4-27	5
48-249	19% L Cooper 10-0	Jonjo O'Neill 46-231 20%	32	25	±35.18	517,453	37-191	11-58	22-67	0-4	7
48-317	15% B J Crowley 10-0	Miss Venetia Williams 46-262 18%	42	42	±95.85	388,512	26-172	22-145	24-66	1-13	8
46-357	13% S Durack 10-0	Mrs S J Smith 8-29 28%	40	37	+14.97	410,515	36-250	10-107	12-33	1-13	12
42-409	10% T J Murphy 9-10	P F Nicholls 8-34 24%	53	39	±134.91	615,557	19-244	23-165	10-41	3-25	7
41-298	14% ● M Foley 9-9	N J Henderson 15-69 22%	36	26	+26.52	342,239	23-199	18-99	10-36	1-9	4
41-313	13% P Flynn 9-7	P J Hobbs 24-131 18%	38	26	±80.15	326,401	26-205	15-108	15-41	1-12	2
36-317	11% D R Dennis 10-0	Ian Williams 25-177 14%	39	40	±53.89	301,282	22-204	14-113	11-29	2-13	0
36-514	7% R Greene 10-0	K Bishop 12-65 18%	40	50	±231.37	440,952	24-339	12-175	12-31	0-11	36
35-352	10% N Fehily 10-0	C J Mann 22-184 12%	54	50	±36.04	379,636	20-218	15-134	9-38	1-11	4
33-330	10% ● K Renwick 9-11	P Monteith 16-91 18%	36	38	±153.06	257,367	22-230	11-100	13-37	0-20	23
33-384	9% M Bradburne 10-0	H D Daly 12-81 15%	41	39	±94.16	351,773	10-213	23-171	10-29	1-15	7
32-293	11% R Garritty 10-6	G M Moore 15-89 17%	45	51	±108.55	296,169	23-176	9-117	14-41	3-20	1
32-354	9% T Scudamore 10-0	M C Pipe 12-144 8%	34	34	±176.13	294,651	17-235	15-119	15-40	3-15	3
31-211	15% ● W Hutchinson 9-7	Mrs A M Thorpe 8-36 22%	20	29	+50.87	177,932	20-168	11-43	8-22	0-0	7
29-292	10% ● P Robson 9-7	A Parker 3-35 9%	38	36	±136.75	224,297	13-193	16-99	13-31	3-21	0
29-361	8% C Llewellyn 10-0	N A Twiston-Davies 20-208 10%	41	45	±66.97	314,493	16-228	13-133	7-28	1-19	2
28-190	15% ● D Elsworth 9-11	Mrs S J Smith 22-120 18%	28	21	±22.66	273,263	17-143	11-47	11-23	3-15	1
28-259	11% J Crowley 10-0	G A Swinbank 9-63 14%	28	31	±49.10	182,270	18-178	10-81	8-27	1-16	0
28-328	9% T Doyle 10-0	P R Webber 9-74 12%	35	32	±122.16	271,537	18-220	10-108	8-28	2-12	10
28-330	8% R McGrath 10-0	C Grant 5-58 9%	30	41	±120.57	297,049	20-202	8-128	6-18	4-22	6
27-152	18% ● R P McNally 9-4	P F Nicholls 22-73 30%	20	18	±38.07	152,697	17-102	10-50	13-31	3-9	2
27-310	9% P Hide 10-0	G L Moore 10-69 14%	37	16	±86.87	207,694	14-195	13-115	2-16	1-13	4
26-104	25% B J Geraghty 10-3	Jonjo O'Neill 10-33 30%	9	7	+64.85	1,260,920	13-55	13-49	10-21	0-3	4
25-248	10% J M Maguire 10-1	T R George 14-121 12%	28	24	±70.23	214,207	10-152	15-96	9-24	1-10	9
24-184	13% ● P Whelan 9-9	R A Fahey 10-45 22%	25	21	+23.13	159,679	16-143	8-41	8-27	1-10	8
24-268	9% B Hitchcott 9-11	R Dickin 10-53 13%	25	25	±78.28	152,098	14-182	10-86	7-18	0-15	20
23-112	21% Mr Christian Williams 9-11	P F Nicholls 10-42 24%	16	9	±33.99	134,269	2-29	21-83	17-40	0-4	7
23-231	10% J P McNamara 10-4	K C Bailey 7-42 17%	28	23	±50.87	206,344	17-152	6-79	5-15	1-7	1
23-238	10% ● P Aspell 9-9	Mrs M Reveley 13-83 16%	20	36	±87.09	168,820	15-187	8-51	7-30	2-12	1
23-261	9% A Dempsey 10-0	Mrs M Reveley 21-185 11%	29	36	±124.71	246,541	15-202	8-59	9-34	2-14	0
23-292	8% B Harding 10-0	N G Richards 9-54 17%	36	25	±114.94	217,294	8-180	15-112	9-36	1-16	11
22-216	10% D N Russell 10-0	Ferdy Murphy 20-179 11%	17	34	±68.96	340,983	12-118	10-98	5-19	2-8	2
21-137	15% ● A O'Keeffe 9-7	R Lee 9-23 39%	11	21	±13.52	142,884	10-84	11-53	9-23	1-7	1
20-101	20% N Williamson 9-9	Jonjo O'Neill 5-10 50%	9	8	±13.11	527,966	18-63	2-38	9-21	2-4	2
20-124	16% J Tizzard 10-0	P F Nicholls 11-45 24%	17	11	±37.76	224,803	12-73	8-51	10-17	4-11	4
20-208	10% B Storey 10-0	A Parker 7-32 22%	16	27	±110.89	143,771	10-128	10-80	7-16	0-0	24
19-147	13% ● F King 9-12	Mrs M Reveley 15-79 19%	18	21	±52.60	146,820	9-96	10-51	10-22	0-9	38
19-149	13% ● R Flavin 9-11	Jonjo O'Neill 7-25 28%	17	11	±21.24	132,263	13-105	6-44	8-19	1-11	7

RACEFORM JUMP MEDIAN TIMES 2002-2003

Some new distances have been omitted where insufficient data exists to establish a reliable median time.

AINTREE
Chase (Mildmay)

2m	3m 58.7
2m4f	5m 7.3
3m1f	6m 29.2

Chase (National)

2m 6f	5m 40.1
3m3f	7m 15.7
4m4f	9m 8.6

Hurdles

2m110y	4m 7.2
2m4f	4m 55.1
3m110y	6m 11.3

ASCOT
Chase

2m	3m 59.4
2m3f110y	4m 57.3
3m110y	6m 22.8

Hurdles

2m110y	4m 1.6
2m4f	4m 59.6
3m	5m 55.2
3m1f 110y	6m 22.7

AYR
Chase

2m	4m 4.2
2m4f	5m 18.4
2m5f110y	5m 59.8
3m1f	6m 37.9
3m3f110y	7m 7.9
4m1f	8m 20.8

Hurdles

2m	3m 53.8
2m4f	5m 6.3
2m6f	5m 41.6
3m110y	6m 20.8
3m2f110y	6m 37.7

BANGOR
Chase

2m1f110y	4m 25.1
2m4f110y	5m 15.6
3m110y	6m 24.1
3m6f	8m 10.4
4m1f	9m 16.7

Hurdles

2m1f	4m 8.6
2m4f	4m 53.7
3m	5m 54.3

CARLISLE
Chase

2m	4m 13.1
2m4f	5m 15.2
3m	6m 23.9
3m2f	7m 8.5

Hurdles

2m1f	4m 22.5
2m4f110y	5m 16.6

CARTMEL
Chase

2m1f110y	4m 21.6
2m5f110y	5m 22.3
3m2f	6m 39.3

Hurdles

2m1f110y	4m 10.7
2m6f	5m 28.3
3m2f	6m 21.7

CATTERICK
Chase

2m	4m 2.6
2m3f	4m 57.0
3m1f110y	6m 45.7
3m4f110y	7m 27.6

Hurdles

2m	3m 55.4
2m3f	4m 49.0
3m1f110y	6m 34.0

CHELTENHAM (NEW)
Chase

2m110y	4m 10.6
2m5f	5m 28.9
3m1f110y	6m 37.0
3m2f110y	6m 53.3
4m1f	8m 55.7

Hurdles

2m1f	4m 14.6
2m5f110y	5m 28.6
3m110y	6m 2.0

CHELTENHAM (OLD)
Chase

2m	3m 59.3
2m4f110y	5m 12.4
3m1f	6m 28.0
3m3f110y	7m 18.0
4m	8m 23.6

Cross Country Chases

3m	7m 0.7
3m7f	8m 33.3

Hurdles

2m110y	4m 10.6
2m5f	5m 28.9
3m1 f	6m 37.0

CHEPSTOW
Chase

2m110y	4m 19.2
2m3f110y	5m 13.7
3m	6m 17.0
3m2f110y	7m 21.7
3m5f110y	8m 11.0

Hurdles

2m110y	4m 12.8
2m4f	5m 5.1
3m	6m 17.4

DONCASTER
Chase

2m110y	4m 6.8
2m3f110y	4m 59.4
3m	6m 12.7
3m2f	6m 37.8

Hurdles

2m110y	4m 3.3
2m4f	4m 55.5
3m110y	6m 2.4

EXETER
Chase

2m1f110y	4m 20.4
2m3f110y	4m 53.8
2m7f110y	6m 0.6
3m1f110y	6m 24.6

Hurdles

2m1f	4m 7.0
2m3f	4m 33.0
2m6f110y	5m 35.6

FAKENHAM
Chase

2m110y	4m 14.1
2m5f110y	5m 33.6
3m110y	6m 27.9

Hurdles

2m	4m 2.9
2m4f	4m 59.5
2m7f110y	5m 45.3

FOLKESTONE
Chase

2m	4m 9.15
2m5f	5m 31.1
3m1f	6m 32.6
3m2f	6m 44.8
3m7f	8m 0.4

Hurdles

2m1f110y	4m 28.9
2m6f110y	5m57.4

FONTWELL
Chase
2m2f 4m 38.9
3m2f110y 7m 4.2
Hurdles
2m2f110y 4m 33.4
2m6f110y 5m 38.8
3m2f110y 6m 37.5

HAYDOCK
Chase
2m 4m 16.2
2m4f 5m 28.8
3m 6m 34.7
3m4f110y 7m 40.2
4m110y 9m 11.2
Hurdles
2m 3m 59.8
2m4f 5m 8.2
2m6f 5m 49.8
2m7f110y 6m 9.9

HEREFORD
Chase
2m 4m 4.6
2m3f 4m 48.9
3m1f110y 6m 33.8
Hurdles
2m1f 4m 4.2
2m3f110y 4m 48.6
3m2f 6m 29.1

HEXHAM
Chase
2m110y 4m 10.1
2m4f110y 5m 13.7
3m1f 6m 32.8
4m 9m 12.4
Hurdles
2m 4m 14.0
2m4f110y 5m 6.9
3m 6m 11.1

HUNTINGDON
Chase
2m110y 4m 9.2
2m4f110y 5m 4.9
3m 6m 12.0
3m6f110y 8m 7.4
Hurdles
2m110y 3m 56.0
2m4f110y 4m 49.6
2m5f110y 5m 10.0
3m2f 6m 20.6

KELSO
Chase
2m1f 4m 20.5
2m6f110y 5m 55.0

3m1f 6m 27.0
3m4f 7m 24.1
Hurdles
2m110y 4m 1.2
2m2f 4m 31.5
2m6f110y 5m 38.5
3m3f 6m 34.7

KEMPTON
Chase
2m 3m 56.7
2m4f110y 5m 16.0
3m 6m 12.3
Hurdles
2m 3m 57.5
2m5f 5m 16.4
3m110y 6m 13.0

LEICESTER
Chase
2m1f 4m 20.2
2m4f110y 5m 25.5
2m7f110y 6m 12.6
Hurdles
2m 4m 6.3
2m4f110y 5m 21.4
3m 6m 19.7

LINGFIELD
Chase
2m 4m 20.5
2m4f110y 5m 34.8
3m 6m 36.1
Hurdles
2m110y 4m 14.3
2m3f110y 5m10.7
2m7f 6m 13.4

LUDLOW
Chase
2m 4m 4.2
2m4f 5m 6.0
3m 6m 9.4
Hurdles
2m 3m 47.3
2m5f 5m 18.3
3m 5m 55.3

MARKET RASEN
Chase
2m1f110y 4m 28.8
2m4f 5m 6.2
2m6f110y 5m 43.5
3m 6m 28.0
3m1f 6m 34.0
3m4f110y 7m 54.3
4m1f 9m 12.1
Hurdles
2m1f110y 4m16.6
2m3f110y 4m48.8

2m5f110y 5m25.0
3m 6m6.8

MUSSELBURGH
Chase
2m 3m 58.3
2m4f 5m 4.4
3m 6m 10.0
Hurdles
2m 3m 49.8
2m4f 4m 53.5
3m 6m 55.2

NEWBURY
Chase
2m1f 4m 15.9
2m2f110y 5m 42.5
2m4f 5m 12.1
2m6f110y 5m 47.3
3m 6m 10.2
3m2f110y 6m 51.9
Hurdles
2m110y 4m 4.4
2m3f 4m 48.0
2m5f 5m 15.3
3m110y 6m 9.8

NEWCASTLE
Chase
2m110y 4m 14.1
2m4f 5m 15.6
3m 6m 8.2
3m6f 8m 6.2
4m1f 8m 48.1
Hurdles
2m 4m 2.6
2m4f 5m 8.1
3m 6m 6.0

NEWTON ABBOT
Chase
2m110y 4m 7.2
2m5f110y 5m 24.4
3m2f110y 6m 48.7
Hurdles
2m1f 4m 7.1
2m6f 5m 22.2
3m3f 6m 46.0

PERTH
Chase
2m 3m 59.9
2m4f110y 5m 9.8
3m 6m 13.5
Hurdles
2m110y 3m 56.0
2m4f110y 5m 1.6
3m110y 6m 5.4

PLUMPTON
Chase
2m1f 4m 23.8
2m4f 5m 23.6
3m2f 7m 22.4
Hurdles
2m 3m 48.5
2m5f 5m 32.3
3m1f110y 7m 1.3

SANDOWN
Chase
2m 4m 3.2
2m4f110y 5m 21.4
3m110y 6m 31.2
3m5f110y 7m 41.6
Hurdles
2m110y 4m 6.8
2m4f110y 5m 23.6
2m6f 5m 32.8

SEDGEFIELD
Chase
2m110y 4m 9.3
2m5f 5m 19.3
3m3f 7m 2.3
3m4f 7m 11.3
Hurdles
2m1f 4m 2.1
2m5f110y 5m 10.4
3m3f110y 6m 54.9

SOUTHWELL
Chase
Distances have changed so insufficient data available to produce revised median times.

STRATFORD
Chase
2m1f110y 4m 13.5
2m4f 5m 1.2
2m5f110y 5m 23.2
3m 6m 4.1
3m4f 7m 10.10
Hurdles
2m110y 4m 0.3
2m3f 4m 34.9
2m6f110y 5m 33.8
3m3f 6m 33.8

TAUNTON
Chase
2m110y 4m 9.2
2m3f 4m 54.7
3m 6m 16.1
3m3f 7m 18.6
4m2f110y 9m 38.9

Hurdles
2m1f 4m 2.4
2m3f110y 4m 42.7
3m110y 6m 9.5

TOWCESTER
Chase
2m110y 4m 16.3
2m6f 5m 52.2
3m1f 6m 42.3
Hurdles
2m 4m 2.8
2m5f 5m 32.3
3m 6m 16.6

UTTOXETER
Chase
2m 4m 2.2
2m4f 5m 14.5
2m5f 5m 18.4
2m7f 5m 53.3
3m 6m 27.6
3m2f 6m 54.0
4m2f 8m 53.5
Hurdles
2m 3m 51.7
2m4f110y 5m 1.4
2m6f110y 5m 36.5
3m110y 5m 57.9

WARWICK
Chase
2m110y 4m 2.6
2m4f110y 5m 16.8
3m2f 6m 48.9
3m5f 7m 48.9
Hurdles
2m 3m 54.3
2m3f 4m 40.5
2m5f 5m 17.2
3m1f 6m 32.8

WETHERBY
Chase
2m 4m 3.5
2m4f110y 5m 19.5
3m1f 6m 35.1
3m5f 7m 23.1
Hurdles
2m 3m 57.2
2m4f110y 5m 7.5
2m7f 5m 56.2
3m1f 6m 16.3

WINCANTON
Chase
2m 4m 4.4
2m5f 5m 22.5
3m1f110y 6m 45.2
Hurdles
2m 3m 48.0
2m6f 5m 23.6

WORCESTER
Chase
2m 3m 58.7
2m4f110y 5m 16.1
2m7f110y 6m 4.9
Hurdles
2m 3m 50.2
2m2f 4m 22.4
2m4f 4m 53.4
3m 5m 52.5

THOMAS PINK GOLD CUP
(HANDICAP CHASE)
formerly Murphy's & Mackeson Gold Cup
Cheltenham 2m 4f 110y

1993	Bradbury Star	8-11-08	15
1994	Bradbury Star	9-11-11	14
1995	Dublin Flyer	9-11-08	12
1996	Challenger du Luc	6-10-02	12
1997	Senor El Betrutti	8-10-00	9
1998	Cyfor Malta	5-11-03	12
1999	The Outback Way	9-10-00	14
2000	Lady Cricket	6-10-13	15
2001	Shooting Light	8-11-3	14
2002	Stormez	5-10-6	10

FIRST NATIONAL BANK GOLD CUP
(HANDICAP CHASE)
formerly H & T Walker Gold Cup
Ascot 2m 4f

1993	Abandoned due to frost		
1994	Raymylette	7-11-10	11
1995	Sound Man	7-12-00	5
1996	Strong Promise	5-10-05	8
1997	Simply Dashing	9-10-05	15
1998	Red Marauder	8-10-11	11
1999	Nordance Prince	8-10-09	11
2000	Upgrade	6-11-08	4
2001	Wahiba Sands	8-10-4	4
2002	Abandoned due to waterlogging		

HENNESSY COGNAC GOLD CUP
(HANDICAP CHASE)
Newbury 3m 2f 110y

1993	Cogent	9-10-01	9
1994	One Man	6-10-00	16
1995	Couldnt Be Better	8-10-08	11
1996	Coome Hill	7-10-00	11
1997	Suny Bay	8-11-08	14
1998	Teeton Mill	9-10-05	16
1999	Ever Blessed	7-10-00	13
2000	King's Road	7-10-07	17
2001	What's Up Boys	7-10-12	14
2002	Be My Royal	8-10-0	25

TRIPLEPRINT GOLD CUP (HANDICAP CHASE)
Cheltenham 2m 4f

1993	Fragrant Dawn	9-10-02	11
1994	Dublin Flyer	8-10-02	11
1995	Abandoned due to frost		
1996	Addington Boy	8-11-10	10
1997	Senor El Betrutti	8-11-03	9
1998	Northern Starlight	7-10-01	13
1999	Legal Right	6-10-13	9
2000	Go Roger Go	8-11-00	12
2001	Abandoned due to frost		
2002	Fondmort	6-10-5	9

BONUSPRINT CHRISTMAS HURDLE
Kempton 2m

1993	Muse	6-11-07	5
1994	Absaloms's Lady	6-11-02	6
1995	Abandoned due to frost		
1996	Abandoned due to frost		
1997	Kerawi	4-11-07	5
1998	French Holly	7-11-07	5
1999	Dato Star	8-11-07	4
2000	Geos	5-11-07	7

2001	Landing Light	6-11-7	5
2002	Intersky Falcon	5-11-7	6

PERTEMPS KING GEORGE VI CHASE
Kempton 3m

1993	Barton Bank	7-11-10	10
1994	Algan (FR)	6-11-10	9
1995	*One Man	8-11-10	11
1996	One Man	8-11-10	5
1997	See More Business	7-11-10	8
1998	Teeton Mill	9-11-10	9
1999	See More Business	9-11-10	9
2000	First Gold	7-11-10	9
2001	Florida Pearl	9-11-10	8
2002	Best Mate	7-11-10	10

(*Run at Sandown Jan 6th 1996)

CORAL WELSH NATIONAL (HANDICAP CHASE)
Chepstow 3m 6f

1993	Riverside Boy	10-10-00	8
1994	*Master Oats	8-11-06	8
1995	Abandoned due to frost		
1996	Abandoned due to frost		
1997	Earth Summit	9-10-13	14
1998	Kendal Cavalier	8-10-08	14
1999	Edmond	7-10-00	16
2000	Jocks Cross	9-10-04	19
2001	Supreme Glory	8-10-00	13
2002	Mini Sensation	9-10-4	16

(*Run at Newbury)

PIERSE HANDICAP HURDLE
(formerly Ladbroke Handicap Hurdle)
Leopardstown 2m

1994	Atone	7-10-08	25
1995	Anusha	5-10-02	17
1996	Dance Beat	5-09-12	22
1997	Master Tribe	7-10-04	23
1998	Graphic Equaliser	6-10-00	20
1999	Archieve Footage	7-11-08	25
2000	Mantles Prince	6-9-12	14
2001	Grinkov	6-10-07	24
2002	Adamant Approach	8-11-1	26
2003	Xenophon	7-10-11	28

VICTOR CHANDLER HANDICAP CHASE
Ascot 2m

1993	Sybillin	7-10-10	11
1994	*Viking Flagship	7-10-10	4
1995	Martha's Son	8-10-09	8
1996	Big Matt	9-10-04	11
1997	**Ask Tom	8-10-10	8
1998	Jeffell	8-10-11	9
1999	**Call Equiname	9-11-03	7
2000	Nordance Prince	9-10-00	10
2001	Function Dream	9-10-11	10
2002	Turgeonev	7-10-4	8
2003	***Young Devereux	10-10-4	9

(* Run at Warwick)
(**Run at Kempton)
(***Run at Kempton as Tote Exacta Chase)

AGFA DIAMOND (HANDICAP) CHASE
Sandown 3m 110y

1994	Second Schedual	9-10-07	5
1995	Deep Bramble	8-11-10	11
1996	Amtrak Express	9-10-07	3
1997	Dextra Dove	10-11-02	6
1998	Court Melody	10-10-05	6

1999	Clever Remark	10-10-05	5
2000	Trouble Ahead	9-11-04	8
2001	Storm Damage	9-10-07	9
2002	Billingsgate	10-11-01	9
2003	Iris Bleu	7-11-2	14

TOTE GOLD TROPHY (HANDICAP HURDLE)
Newbury 2m 110y

1994	Large Action	6-10-08	11
1995	Mysilv	5-10-08	8
1996	Squire Silk	7-10-12	18
1997	Make a Stand	6-11-07	18
1998	Sharpical	6-11-01	14
1999	Decoupage	7-11-10	18
2000	Geos	5-11-03	17
2001	Landing Light	6-10-02	20
2002	Copeland	7-11-07	16
2003	Spirit Leader	7-10-00	27

HENNESSY COGNAC GOLD CUP
Leopardstown 3m

1994	Jodami	9-12-00	6
1995	Jodami	10-12-00	6
1996	Imperial Call	7-12-00	8
1997	Danoli	9-12-00	8
1998	Dorans Pride	9-12-00	8
1999	Florida Pearl	7-12-00	7
2000	Florida Pearl	8-12-00	7
2001	Florida Pearl	9-12-00	7
2002	Alexander Banquet	9-12-00	5
2003	Beef Or Salmon	7-12-00	5

RACING POST HANDICAP CHASE
Kempton 3m

1994	Antonin	6-10-04	16
1995	Val D'Alene	8-11-02	9
1996	Rough Quest	10-10-08	9
1997	Mudahim	11-10-02	9
1998	Super Tactics	10-10-10	7
1999	Dr. Leunt	8-11-05	8
2000	Gloria Victis	6-11-10	13
2001	Young Spartacus	8-11-03	15
2002	Gunther McBride	7-10-03	14
2003	La Landiere	8-11-07	14

SUNDERLANDS IMPERIAL CUP
(HANDICAP) HURDLE
Sandown 2m 110y

1994	Precious Boy	8-11-07	13
1995	Collier Bay	5-10-02	10
1996	Amancio	5-10-08	11
1997	Carlito Brigante	5-10-00	18
1998	Blowing Wind	5-11-10	15
1999	Regency Rake	7-10-07	9
2000	Magic Combination	7-10-00	18
2001	Ibal	5-9-09	23
2002	Polar Red	5-11-01	16
2003	Korelo	5-11-06	17

IRISH INDEPENDENT ARKLE CHALLENGE
TROPHY (NOVICES) CHASE
(formerly Guinness Arkle Challenge Trophy)
Cheltenham 2m

1994	Nakir	6-11-08	11
1995	Klairon Davis	6-11-08	11
1996	Ventana Canyon	7-11-08	16
1997	Or Royal	6-11-08	9
1998	Champleve	5-11-00	16
1999	Flagship Uberalles	5-11-00	14

2000	Tiutchev	7-11-08	12
2001	Abandoned- Foot & Mouth		
2002	Moscow Flyer	8-11-08	12
2003	Azertyuiop	6-11-08	9

SMURFIT CHAMPION HURDLE
Cheltenham 2m 110y

1994	Flakey Dove	8-11-09	15
1995	Alderbrook	6-12-00	14
1996	Collier Bay	6-12-00	16
1997	Make a Stand	6-12-00	17
1998	Istabraq	6-12-00	18
1999	Istabraq	7-12-00	14
2000	Istabraq	8-12-00	12
2001	Abandoned - Foot & Mouth		
2002	Hors La Loi III	7-12-00	15
2003	Rooster Booster	9-12-00	17

QUEEN MOTHER CHAMPION CHASE
Cheltenham 2m

1994	Viking Flagship	7-12-00	8
1995	Viking Flagship	8-12-00	10
1996	Klairon Davis	7-12-00	7
1997	Martha's Son	10-12-00	6
1998	One Man	10-12-00	8
1999	Call Equiname	9-12-00	13
2000	Edredon Bleu	8-12-00	13
2001	Abandoned - Foot & Mouth		
2002	Flagship Uberalles	8-12-00	12
2003	Moscow Flyer	9-12-00	11

ROYAL & SUNALLIANCE (NOVICES') CHASE
Cheltenham 3m

1994	Monsieur Le Cure	8-11-04	18
1995	Brief Gale	8-10-13	13
1996	Nahthen Lad	7-11-04	12
1997	Hanakham	8-11-04	14
1998	Florida Pearl	6-11-04	10
1999	Looks Like Touble	7-11-04	14
2000	Lord Noelie	7-11-04	9
2001	Abandoned - Foot & Mouth		
2002	Hussard Collonges	7-11-04	19
2003	One Knight	7-11-04	9

JCB TRIUMPH HURDLE
(formerly Daily Express & Elite Racing Club
Triumph Hurdle) Cheltenham 2m 1f (4-y-o)

1994	Mysilv	10-09	28
1995	Kissair	11-00	26
1996	Paddy's Return	11-00	29
1997	Commanche Court	11-00	28
1998	Upgrade	11-00	25
1999	Katarino	11-00	23
2000	Snow Drop	10-09	28
2001	Abandoned - Foot & Mouth		
2002	Scolardy	11-00	28
2003	Spectroscope	11-00	27

TOTE CHELTENHAM GOLD CUP (CHASE)
Cheltenham 3m 2f

1994	The Fellow	9-12-00	15
1995	Master Oats	9-12-00	15
1996	Imperial Call	7-12-00	10
1997	Mr Mulligan	9-12-00	14
1998	Cool Dawn	10-12-00	17
1999	See More Business	9-12-00	12
2000	Looks Like Trouble	8-12-00	12
2001	Abandoned - Foot & Mouth		

2002	Best Mate	7-12-00	18
2003	Best Mate	8-12-00	15

MARTELL CUP CHASE
Aintree 3m 1f

1994	Docklands Express	12-11-05	4
1995	Merry Gale	7-11-09	6
1996	Scotton Banks	7-11-05	6
1997	Barton Bank	11-11-05	5
1998	Escartefigue	6-11-13	8
1999	Macgeorge	9-11-05	5
2000	See More Business	10-12-00	4
2001	First Gold	8-12-00	7
2002	Florida Pearl	10-11-12	6
2003	First Gold	10-11-12	7

MARTELL XO ANNIVERSARY HURDLE
(formerly GLENLIVETANNIVERSARY HURDLE
(4-y-o) Aintree 2m 110y

1994	Tropical Lake	10-09	12
1995	Stompin	11-00	18
1996	Zabadi	11-00	11
1997	Quakers Field	11-00	12
1998	Deep Water	11-00	14
1999	Hors La Loi III	11-04	6
2000	Lord Brex	11-00	12
2001	Bilboa	10-13	14
2002	Quazar	11-04	17
2003	Le Duc	11-00	19

MARTELL MELLING CHASE
Aintree 2m 4f

1994	Katabatic	11-11-10	5
1995	Viking Flagship	8-11-10	6
1996	Viking Flagship	9-11-10	4
1997	Martha's Son	10-11-10	4
1998	Opera Hat	10-11-05	5
1999	Direct Route	8-11-10	6
2000	Direct Route	9-11-10	5
2001	Fadalko	8-11-10	7
2002	Native Upmanship	9-11-10	8
2003	Native Upmanship	10-11-10	6

MARTELL RED RUM CHASE
(LIMITED HANDICAP)
Aintree 2m

1994	Uncle Ernie	9-10-08	8
1995	Coulton	8-11-08	12
1996	Arctic Kinsman	8-11-00	10
1997	Down the Fell	8-10-07	10
1998	Jeffell	8-12-00	5
1999	Flying Instructor	9-11-05	7
2000	Jungli	7-10-07	7
2001	Aghawadda Gold	9-11-02	12
2002	Dark'n Sharp	7-10-08	15
2003	Golden Alpha	9-10-13	16

MARTELL AINTREE HURDLE
Aintree 2m 4f

1994	Danoli	6-11-07	9
1995	Danoli	7-11-07	6
1996	Urubande	6-11-07	8

1997	Bimsey	7-11-07	7
1998	Pridwell	8-11-07	6
1999	Istabraq	7-11-7	7
2000	Mister Morose	10-11-07	10
2001	Barton	8-11-07	8
2002	Ilnamar	6-11-07	14
2003	Sacundai	6-11-07	5

MARTELL GRAND NATIONAL
(HANDICAP CHASE) 4m 4f

1980	Ben Nevis	12-10-12	30
1981	Aldaniti	11-10-13	39
1982	Grittar	9-11-05	39
1983	Corbiere	8-11-04	41
1984	Hallo Dandy	10-10-02	40
1985	Last Suspect	11-10-05	40
1986	West Tip	9-10-11	40
1987	Maori Venture	11-10-13	40
1988	Rhyme 'N Reason	9-11-00	40
1989	Little Polveir	12-10-03	40
1990	Mr Frisk	11-10-06	38
1991	Seagram	11-10-06	40
1992	Party Politics	8-10-07	40
1993	Void Race		
1994	Miinnehoma	11-10-08	36
1995	Royal Athlete	12-10-06	35
1996	Rough Quest	10-10-07	27
1997	Lord Gyllene	9-10-00	36
1998	Earth Summit	10-10-05	37
1999	Bobbyjo	9-10-00	32
2000	Papillon	9-10-12	40
2001	Red Marauder	11-10-11	40
2002	Bindaree	8-10-04	40
2003	Monty's Pass	10-10-07	40

GALA CASINOS DAILY RECORD SCOTTISH
GRAND NATIONAL (HANDICAP CHASE)
Ayr 4m 1f

1994	Earth Summit	6-10-00	22
1995	Willsford	12-10-12	22
1996	Moorcroft Boy	11-10-02	20
1997	Belmont King	9-11-10	17
1998	Baronet	8-10-00	18
1999	Young Kenny	8-11-10	15
2000	Paris Pike	8-11-0	18
2001	Gingembre	7-11-02	30
2002	Take Control	8-10-06	18
2003	Ryalux	10-10-05	19

ATTHERACES GOLD CUP (HANDICAP CHASE)
(formerly WHITBREAD GOLD CUP)
Sandown 3m 5f 110y

1994	Ushers Island	8-10-00	12
1995	Cache Fleur	9-10-01	14
1996	Life of a Lord	10-11-10	17
1997	Harwell Lad	8-10-0	9
1998	Call It A Day	8-10-10	19
1999	Eulogy	9-10-00	19
2000	Beau	7-10-9	20
2001	Ad Hoc	7-10-04	25
2002	Bounce Back	6-10-09	20
2003	Ad Hoc	9-10-10	16

SPLIT SECOND SPEED RATINGS

The following list shows the fastest performances of chasers and hurdlers which have recorded a speed figure of 100 or over during the 2002-2003 season. Additional information in parentheses following the speed figure shows the distance of the race in furlongs, course, state of going and the date on which the figure was achieved.

CHASING

A Piece Of Cake 114 (20f,Ayr,HY,Jan 25)
Abalvino 111 (17f,Nby,S,Feb 28)
Aberfoyle Park 106 (20$\frac{1}{2}$f,Kem,G,Nov 6)
Able Native 101 (17f,Kel,GS,May 1)
Acoustic 103 (24f,Don,G,Jan 24)
Act In Time 104 (26$\frac{1}{2}$f,Nab,S,Nov 6)
Ad Hoc 115 (24$\frac{1}{2}$f,Chl,G,Mar 11)
Aegean 114 (24f,Per,GS,Aug 4)
Aelred 109 (16$\frac{1}{2}$f,Ncs,S,Dec 16)
Agincourt 107 (24f,Lud,S,Jan 16)
Aibitir 109 (24f,Thu,SH,Feb 13)
Air Attache 103 (21$\frac{1}{2}$f,Nab,GF,Jly 28)
Akarus 109 (34f,Utt,S,Mar 15)
Albatros 107 (17f,Gal,Y,Aug 1)
Alcapone 114 (16f,Nav,YS,Nov 3)
Alheri 102 (25$\frac{1}{2}$f,Wcn,F,Oct 10)
All Right Clark 114 (16f,Utt,G,Sep 12)
All Sonsilver 103 (21$\frac{1}{2}$f,Ayr,GS,Feb 23)
Allimac 109 (19f,Her,GF,May 4)
Altregan Boy 103 (28$\frac{1}{2}$f,Mar,S,Dec 5)
Alvaro 102 (25f,Mar,S,Mar 3)
Amberleigh House 109 (20$\frac{1}{2}$f,Ban,G,Mar 22)
Amy Johnson 104 (24f,Naa,S,Nov 23)
Andiamo 105 (22f,Gal,GY,Aug 3)
Andrewjames 104 (24f,Naa,S,Nov 23)
Annaghmore Gale 108 (16f,Pun,F,Sep 29)
Another Artiste 105 (24f,Thu,SH,Feb 13)
Another General 107 (24f,Don,G,Jan 13)
Another Moose 102 (26f,Plu,S,Mar 10)
Another Raleagh 110 (20$\frac{1}{2}$f,Kem,G,Jan 18)
Ansar 109 (17f,Gal,Y,Aug 1)
April Spirit 102 (23$\frac{1}{2}$f,Wor,G,Jly 10)
Arctic Challenge 109 (20$\frac{1}{2}$f,Kem,G,Feb 22)
Arctic Copper 116 (24f,Nav,S,Nov 17)
Arctic Gamble 100 (23$\frac{1}{2}$f,Exe,G,Oct 22)
Arctic Sandy 105 (20$\frac{1}{2}$f,Hex,G,Jun 4)
Arctic Spirit 102 (16$\frac{1}{2}$f,Don,GS,Dec 13)
Ardent Scout 109 (24f,Utt,G,May 4)
Arlequin De Sou 109 (21f,Chl,HY,Jan 1)
Armaturk 103 (17$\frac{1}{2}$f,Exe,G,Nov 5)
Art Stones 100 (21f,Pun,YS,Jan 18)
Asador 104 (19$\frac{1}{2}$f,Chp,HY,Nov 27)
Ashbury Star 104 (18f,Fon,GF,May 6)
Ashgan 106 (23$\frac{1}{2}$f,Wor,G,Sep 14)
Ashgar 103 (26f,Utt,G,May 22)
Ashley Muck 104 (20$\frac{1}{2}$f,Kem,GS,Feb 7)
Ask Henry 104 (22$\frac{1}{2}$f,Nby,GS,Nov 13)
Asparagus 109 (16$\frac{1}{2}$f,Chp,HY,Jan 17)
Atalya 100 (19f,Her,GF,Apr 5)
Atavistic 105 (28f,Str,GS,Oct 31)
Athleague Guest 101 (20f,Utt,S,Nov 8)
Athnowen 111 (16f,Her,G,Feb 10)
Atlantic Power 101 (20$\frac{1}{2}$f,Per,GS,Aug 4)
Atomic Breeze 105 (26f,Crl,GF,Apr 21)
Auburn Spirit 109 (26f,Plu,S,Jan 13)
Audacter 111 (24f,Kem,GF,Oct 26)
Auditty 100 (16f,Hay,GF,Mar 29)
Aura About Him 109 (16f,Pun,SH,Feb 1)

Avalanche 112 (20$\frac{1}{2}$f,Kem,G,Feb 22)
Avanti Express 101 (17$\frac{1}{2}$f,Str,GS,Oct 31)
Azertyuiop 115 (16f,Wcn,GS,Feb 15)

Baccarat 100 (20$\frac{1}{2}$f,Wet,GF,Mar 23)
Bacchanal 118 (24f,Kem,S,Dec 26)
Backdoor Champion 101 (20f,Pun,SH,Feb 1)
Ballinarrid 107 (22f,Gal,GY,Aug 3)
Ballinclay King 118 (21f,Chl,HY,Jan 1)
Bally Lira 107 (26$\frac{1}{2}$f,Chp,HY,Feb 4)
Ballyamber 115 (21f,Leo,S,Jan 12)
Ballybough Rasher 109 (20f,Ain,G,Nov 24)
Ballybrophy 113 (24$\frac{1}{2}$f,Asc,GS,Feb 15)
Ballycassidy 109 (24$\frac{1}{2}$f,Sth,GS,Dec 6)
Ballyconnell 108 (22f,Gal,S,Sep 9)
Ballydine 107 (20f,Gow,YS,Jun 6)
Ballyline 103 (24$\frac{1}{2}$f,Sth,G,May 9)
Ballystone 111 (24f,Mus,GF,Dec 17)
Ballyvalogue 103 (18f,Thu,SH,Feb 13)
Balnagreine 108 (24$\frac{1}{2}$f,Sth,G,May 9)
Banjo Hill 112 (21f,Chl,G,Apr 17)
Barito 105 (20f,Plu,S,Jan 13)
Barren Lands 103 (19f,Her,S,Nov 21)
Barrow Drive 120 (21f,Leo,YS,Feb 9)
Barryscourt Lad 112 (24f,Don,G,Jan 25)
Barton 104 (21f,Chl,G,Mar 13)
Basil 101 (26f,War,S,Jan 23)
Batswing 104 (16f,Ain,G,Apr 3)
Bay Island 104 (24$\frac{1}{2}$f,Ban,S,Oct 28)
Be My Belle 119 (24f,Thu,S,Dec 5)
Be My Better Half 110 (20f,Nav,HY,Mar 8)
Be My Dream 109 (24f,Utt,HY,Jun 6)
Be My Manager 108 (24$\frac{1}{2}$f,Chl,G,Nov 15)
Be My Royal 105 (26$\frac{1}{2}$f,Nby,GS,Nov 30)
Be Upstanding 103 (21$\frac{1}{2}$f,Fak,S,Jan 22)
Bear On Board 108 (24$\frac{1}{2}$f,Ban,S,Mar 5)
Beef Or Salmon 115 (24f,Leo,YS,Feb 9)
Beefy Nova 108 (24f,Hun,G,Mar 12)
Behavingbadly 107 (25f,Ayr,S,Mar 8)
Behrajan 121 (24$\frac{1}{2}$f,Asc,S,Dec 21)
Belisario 108 (20$\frac{1}{2}$f,Wet,G,Feb 26)
Belski 105 (16$\frac{1}{2}$f,Nab,GF,Jly 28)
Benefit 102 (21$\frac{1}{2}$f,Fak,S,Jan 22)
Benson 109 (20$\frac{1}{2}$f,War,GF,Mar 23)
Berlin Blue 106 (24f,Nby,G,Mar 22)
Best Available 104 (19f,Her,GF,May 4)
Best Mate 121 (26$\frac{1}{2}$f,Chl,G,Mar 13)
Bicycle Thief 106 (24$\frac{1}{2}$f,Ban,G,Mar 22)
Big Max 106 (24f,Lud,S,Jan 16)
Billy Nomaite 107 (20f,Mar,GF,Jun 22)
Billy The Snake 116 (19f,Leo,S,Jan 26)
Bindaree 115 (26$\frac{1}{2}$f,Chp,S,Dec 7)
Binny Bay 101 (16$\frac{1}{2}$f,Sed,S,Nov 26)
Bit O Magic 109 (17f,Kel,G,Apr 7)
Black Bullet 107 (16f,Her,S,Mar 7)
Blakeney Coast 100 (20$\frac{1}{2}$f,Hex,G,Apr 14)
Bleu Superbe 110 (16$\frac{1}{2}$f,Tow,G,May 24)
Blitzy Boy 106 (22f,Gal,GY,Aug 3)
Blowing Rock 100 (21f,Utt,GF,Aug 27)
Blowing Wind 106 (21f,Chl,HY,Jan 1)
Bob Justice 108 (17f,Nav,S,May 19)
Bobayaro 101 (25f,Kel,S,Mar 21)
Bobby Grant 116 (24f,Hay,S,Nov 17)
Bohill Lad 105 (16$\frac{1}{2}$f,Nab,GF,Jly 31)
Bold Hunter 100 (17$\frac{1}{2}$f,Ban,G,May 3)

Bold Investor 114 (24f,Kem,S,Dec 26)
Bold King 103 (24f,Tau,F,Apr 3)
Bold Navigator 103 (25f,Hex,G,Oct 12)
Bonus Bridge 111 (19$\frac{1}{2}$f,Exe,GS,Jan 27)
Boogy Woogy 103 (21f,Sed,GF,Oct 1)
Boring Goring 104 (20f,Plu,GF,Oct 7)
Born Flyer 100 (17f,Nav,GY,Mar 22)

Borora King 107 (25f,Fai,S,Jan 19)
Borzov 104 (25f,Fai,GF,Apr 20)
Bouchasson 113 (24f,Per,GS,Aug 4)
Bounce Back 108 (29$\frac{1}{2}$f,San,G,Apr 26)
Bow Strada 112 (16f,Lei,GF,Nov 18)
Bowles Patrol 100 (24f,Hun,GS,Nov 12)
Bramblehill Duke 113 (24$\frac{1}{2}$f,Ban,HY,Nov 29)
Breaking Breeze 109 (19f,Her,GF,Sep 11)
Briar s Mist 103 (24$\frac{1}{2}$f,Ban,G,Mar 22)
Brigade Charge 114 (19f,Leo,S,Jan 26)
Broadbrook Lass 108 (24f,Utt,HY,Jun 6)
Broadgate Flyer 103 (20f,Crl,GF,Apr 19)
Brockton Mist 104 (24f,Hay,G,Nov 7)
Broguestown Breeze 104 (26f,Plu,G,Oct 21)
Broke Road 109 (16$\frac{1}{2}$f,Fak,GS,May 26)
Bronhallow 100 (24f,Hun,GF,Mar 23)
Bronzesmith 105 (16f,Her,G,Nov 7)
Brownie Returns 104 (24f,Naa,S,Nov 23)
Bruthuinne 105 (26f,Plu,G,Oct 21)
Bunratty Castle 111 (20f,Str,GS,Oct 31)
Bush Park 106 (20f,Plu,HY,Dec 4)
Business Class 103 (20f,Mar,G,Apr 26)
Bust Out 114 (17f,Leo,H,Dec 26)
Byron Lamb 106 (17f,Kel,GS,Mar 1)

Cadou Royal 101 (16f,Naa,S,Nov 23)
Cadougold 102 (23$\frac{1}{2}$f,Exe,G,May 1)
Caitriona s Choice 106 (16f,Ayr,HY,Jan 25)
Calon Lan 103 (21$\frac{1}{2}$f,Nab,GF,Jly 28)
Camden Venture 114 (20f,Pun,SH,Feb 2)
Camden West 104 (24f,Naa,S,Jan 25)
Cameron Bridge 105 (16f,Lud,G,Dec 12)
Cameron Jack 101 (16$\frac{1}{2}$f,Hex,HY,Nov 8)
Camp Hill 100 (21$\frac{1}{2}$f,Ayr,GS,Feb 23)
Canadiane 112 (23$\frac{1}{2}$f,Wor,G,Sep 14)
Canon Barney 107 (26f,Utt,S,Mar 15)
Cape Stormer 109 (20$\frac{1}{2}$f,Chl,G,Oct 30)
Captain Clooney 100 (26f,Plu,HY,Dec 4)
Captains Table 109 (16$\frac{1}{2}$f,Don,G,Dec 13)
Captaintwothousand 100 (17$\frac{1}{2}$f,Mar,S,Dec 5)
Carbury Cross 103 (26$\frac{1}{2}$f,Nby,GS,Nov 30)
Cardinal Mark 106 (26f,Crl,HY,Nov 11)
Careysville 101 (24$\frac{1}{2}$f,San,S,Mar 7)
Carina Bay 110 (17f,Gal,Y,Aug 2)
Carnacrack 106 (26f,Crt,G,Jun 8)
Carrick Troop 110 (16f,Wet,GS,Nov 27)
Carryonharry 108 (24f,Kem,G,Feb 22)
Cassia Heights 112 (24f,Hay,S,Nov 30)
Castle Clear 100 (20$\frac{1}{2}$f,Per,GS,Jun 6)
Castle Owen 100 (16f,Per,GS,Jun 6)
Castle Prince 102 (17$\frac{1}{2}$f,Exe,G,Nov 5)
Catchatan 112 (16f,Lei,GS,Dec 27)

Ceanannas Mor 108 (31f,Chl,GS,Nov 15)
Ceannairceach 109 (18f,Pun,S,Nov 2)
Cedar Broom 101 (20¹/₂f,Wor,G,Aug 24)
Cedar Green 108 (26¹/₂f,Fon,GS,Feb 17)
Cedar Square 105 (21¹/₂f,Nab,GS,May 25)
Celibate 118 (21f,Wcn,G,Oct 27)
Celtic Pride 102 (24f,Hay,G,Nov 7)
Cenkos 117 (16f,San,G,Apr 26)
Cesaria 100 (19¹/₂f,Exe,GS,Dec 19)
Chadswell 104 (27f,Sed,S,Nov 26)
Chalcedony 106 (20f,Plu,GF,Oct 7)
Channahrlie 112 (24¹/₂f,Asc,GS,Feb 15)
Chaparro Amargoso 112 (16f,Wol,GS,Jly 5)
Charlieadams 108 (21f,Sed,G,Aug 9)
Charter Royal 100 (16¹/₂f,Sed,S,Nov 26)
Chateau Rose 105 (24¹/₂f,San,S,Mar 7)
Chergan 110 (24f,Mus,GF,Dec 17)
Cherry Tart 104 (20¹/₂f,Per,GS,Jun 6)
Chevalier Bayard 105 (20¹/₂f,Hun,GF,Oct 11)
Chevalier Errant 109 (21¹/₂f,Str,GF,Jun 1)
Chicuelo 111 (20f,Mar,GS,Jly 20)
Chives 123 (29¹/₂f,Chp,HY,Dec 27)
Churchtown Glen 100 (25¹/₂f,Her,GF,May 4)
Cimarrone Cove 111 (24¹/₂f,San,GS,Dec 6)
City Gent 104 (20f,Mar,G,Apr 26)
Clan Royal 105 (16f,San,S,Feb 14)
Classic Lash 100 (20f,Crl,GF,Apr 21)
Clawick Connection 105 (20f,Nav,SH,Jun 9)
Claymore 108 (16f,Utt,HY,Nov 28)
Clear Dawn 108 (24f,Mus,GS,Dec 28)
Clonmel s Minella 115 (19f,Leo,S,Jan 26)
Clonshire Paddy 103 (22¹/₂f,Kel,HY,Dec 2)
Cloone Bridge 100 (25f,Pun,F,Sep 29)
Cobbet 106 (16¹/₂f,Chl,G,Apr 17)
Cobreces 101 (16¹/₂f,Tau,S,Jan 28)
Colombian Green 103 (17¹/₂f,Exe,GS,Dec 6)
Colonel Braxton 113 (24f,Leo,YS,Feb 9)
Colonial Sunset 103 (17f,Plu,S,Feb 10)
Comex Flyer 107 (16¹/₂f,Fak,G,Oct 9)
Commanche Court 116 (26¹/₂f,Chl,G,Mar 13)
Commanche Hero 110 (24f,Hun,G,Mar 12)
Commanche Jim 109 (21f,Fol,S,Dec 2)
Contes 106 (20¹/₂f,Wor,G,Jun 8)
Contract Scotland 102 (20¹/₂f,Wet,GF,Mar 23)
Cool Investment 104 (20f,Plu,HY,Dec 4)
Cool Monty 103 (17¹/₂f,Mar,S,Dec 5)
Coole Spirit 102 (24f,Kem,GS,Jan 27)
Coolteen Hero 101 (25¹/₂f,Wcn,F,Oct 10)
Copernicus 112 (17f,Leo,HY,Dec 29)
Copper Shell 103 (16f,Fol,G,May 3)
Coq Hardi Diamond 108 (24f,Leo,HY,Dec 29)
Coral Island 106 (18¹/₂f,Nby,G,Mar 21)
Corbie s Glen 101 (25f,Kel,GF,Oct 6)
Corkan 111 (24f,Hun,GF,Jun 3)
Corletto 103 (17¹/₂f,Mar,GS,Nov 21)
Count Oski 108 (24¹/₂f,Asc,G,Mar 25)
Courage Under Fire 112 (26¹/₂f,Fon,GS,Nov 11)
Coursing Run 103 (24¹/₂f,Sth,GS,Nov 12)
Courtledge 100 (20f,Plu,G,Apr 29)
Cracking Dawn 107 (24f,Hay,G,Nov 7)
Creative Time 103 (24f,Lud,GS,Jan 3)
Cregg House 107 (16f,Nav,YS,Nov 3)
Cresswell Quay 109 (26¹/₂f,Nab,HY,Nov 19)
Curly Spencer 110 (22¹/₂f,Kel,GS,Mar 1)
Cuthill Hope 113 (22¹/₂f,Kel,S,Nov 2)
Cybele Eria 100 (16f,Lud,G,Mar 16)
Cyfor Malta 111 (21f,Chl,G,Dec 14)

D J Flippance 108 (30f,Ncs,GS,Nov 30)
D Judge 104 (24f,Naa,S,Nov 23)
Dalcassian Buck 100 (19f,Tau,S,Jan 16)
Dalligan 108 (24¹/₂f,Fak,GS,May 26)
Damien s Choice 111 (17f,Kel,G,Apr 7)
Damus 105 (20f,Str,G,Apr 12)
Dan De Man 101 (16¹/₂f,Ncs,GS,Mar 15)
Danaeve 103 (19f,Leo,S,Jan 26)
Dancetillyoudrop 103 (26¹/₂f,Nab,GF,Jly 15)
Dante s Battle 108 (17f,Gal,Y,Aug 2)
Danteco 106 (21f,Sed,GF,Oct 1)
Dantie Boy 105 (19f,Tau,GF,Oct 30)
Dark Magic 102 (22f,Gal,HY,Sep 11)
Dark Room 106 (24f,Lud,S,Jan 16)
Dark n Sharp 109 (16¹/₂f,Chl,G,Mar 13)
Dat My Horse 101 (23¹/₂f,Exe,GS,Dec 19)
Davids Lad 115 (29f,Fai,G,Apr 21)
Davoski 105 (16f,Asc,GS,Nov 2)
Dead-Eyed Dick 102 (23¹/₂f,Exe,GS,Dec 6)
Dealer Del 107 (24f,Tau,GS,Feb 27)
Dealer s Choice 105 (21f,Fol,S,Dec 17)
Dear Deal 108 (26¹/₂f,Fon,GF,May 6)
Deckie 108 (16f,Pun,SH,Dec 8)
Decoded 102 (25f,Kel,GF,Oct 6)
Deep Sunset 100 (20f,Lud,G,Feb 27)
Deep Water 109 (16f,Wet,GF,Mar 17)
Deferlant 108 (20¹/₂f,Wor,GS,Aug 9)
Delgany Royal 112 (24f,Nav,S,Nov 17)
Delilah Blue 106 (20f,Utt,G,May 4)
Denada 104 (26f,War,GS,Dec 7)
Deoch An Dorais 106 (16¹/₂f,Don,G,Dec 13)
Derrintogher Yank 111 (24f,Lud,G,Nov 25)
Desailly 104 (22¹/₂f,Nby,S,Nov 29)
Devil s Run 105 (21f,Sed,S,Mar 11)
Devon View 109 (20¹/₂f,San,G,Apr 26)
Diamond Hall 106 (21f,Chl,G,Apr 17)
Diceman 105 (20f,Ncs,GS,Mar 15)
Dick McCarthy 106 (26¹/₂f,Fon,GF,Apr 24)
Didifon 104 (16¹/₂f,Sed,G,Mar 25)
Die Fledermaus 105 (25f,Wol,G,Jly 15)
Dingo Dancer 109 (19f,Cat,G,Nov 23)
Dionn Righ 103 (27f,Sed,S,Dec 10)
Direct Access 107 (25f,Kel,S,Nov 13)
Dirk Cove 102 (24f,Hun,G,Mar 2)
Dishy 109 (24f,Thu,Y,Feb 27)
Divet Hill 109 (16¹/₂f,Hex,G,Jun 15)
Djeddah 114 (24¹/₂f,Chl,G,Mar 11)
Dominikus 107 (20¹/₂f,Hex,GF,Jun 21)
Don t Tell Jr 100 (24¹/₂f,Fak,GS,Oct 25)
Donadino 111 (17f,Gal,Y,Aug 2)
Donnybrook 107 (24f,Don,G,Jan 25)
Doora Volunteer 108 (20f,Gow,SH,Jan 23)
Dorans Gold 108 (20¹/₂f,Wet,GS,Feb 1)
Double Bogey Blues 101 (25¹/₂f,Her,G,Feb 23)
Douze Douze 111 (20¹/₂f,Hun,GS,Nov 23)
Dragon King 107 (26¹/₂f,Fon,GF,Apr 24)
Dromhale Lady 107 (18f,Thu,SH,Feb 13)
Druid s Glen 110 (24¹/₂f,Sth,GS,Dec 6)
Dual Star 103 (16f,Utt,G,Sep 12)
Duchamp 108 (20¹/₂f,Wet,GS,Nov 2)
Duke Of Buckingham 103 (19f,Tau,GF,Oct 30)
Dungarvans Choice 101 (19¹/₂f,Chp,S,Dec 7)

Dunster Castle 103 (24f,Lud,G,Nov 25)
Dunston Bill 105 (22¹/₂f,Mar,S,Nov 21)
Dutsdale Dancer 108 (20f,Nav,S,Nov 17)

Early Dawn 110 (21f,Sed,GF,May 3)
Easton Gale 104 (24¹/₂f,Fak,GS,Nov 24)
Eau De Cologne 114 (25f,Wet,GF,Apr 21)
Ebony Light 107 (20f,Crl,S,Mar 6)
Echo Du Lac 108 (24¹/₂f,Sth,GS,Jan 30)
Edredon Bleu 117 (17¹/₂f,Exe,G,Nov 5)
Effectual 103 (26¹/₂f,Fon,S,Mar 2)
Ei Ei 110 (17¹/₂f,Mar,GF,Sep 28)
El Bandito 111 (19¹/₂f,Chp,G,Mar 19)
El Cordobes 106 (22¹/₂f,Mar,S,Dec 5)
Elenas River 102 (22¹/₂f,Nby,G,Mar 21)
Eltigri 105 (24f,Nby,S,Dec 28)
Eluna 103 (19¹/₂f,Exe,GS,Jan 27)
Elvis Reigns 105 (17¹/₂f,Crt,HY,Jun 3)
Emperor Ross 112 (20¹/₂f,Per,G,Apr 23)
Emperor s Magic 105 (24¹/₂f,Ban,GF,Apr 12)
Enzo De Baune 103 (20f,Crl,GF,Apr 21)
Eoins Pride 108 (31f,Chl,GS,Nov 15)
Epervier D Or 109 (17¹/₂f,Exe,GS,Dec 6)
Eskimo Jack 114 (18f,Thu,S,Nov 28)
Eskleybrook 114 (16f,Kem,G,Feb 21)
Esperanza Iv 107 (24¹/₂f,Fak,GS,May 26)
Europa 106 (16¹/₂f,Don,G,Jan 25)
Even More 104 (25¹/₂f,Wcn,GS,Feb 6)
Executive Decision 107 (16¹/₂f,Hun,G,Feb 22)
Existential 103 (21¹/₂f,Fak,GS,Oct 25)
Exit Swinger 115 (21f,Chl,HY,Jan 1)
Exit To Wave 120 (24¹/₂f,Asc,S,Dec 21)
Extra Jack 101 (20¹/₂f,Kem,G,Jan 18)
Extra Proud 105 (22¹/₂f,Kel,GF,May 29)

Fadalko 109 (21f,Chl,G,Dec 14)
Fadoudal Du Cochet 112 (16f,Naa,Y,Feb 23)
Fait Le Jojo 110 (16f,Utt,GF,Oct 5)
Falchion 101 (21¹/₂f,Ayr,S,Jan 2)
Fallow Trix 101 (20f,Nav,HY,Mar 8)
Famfoni 109 (31f,Chl,GS,Nov 15)
Family Business 105 (24¹/₂f,Sth,G,May 9)
Fandango De Chassy 102 (26f,Crl,S,Oct 26)
Far Dawn 102 (24¹/₂f,Sth,GF,Mar 18)
Fare Dealing 100 (16¹/₂f,Fak,G,Oct 9)
Farmer Jack 109 (16f,Kem,G,Jan 18)
Fasgo 106 (25f,Naa,GS,Oct 19)
Fatehalkhair 113 (25f,Ain,G,Apr 4)
Favoured Option 113 (25¹/₂f,Her,GF,Apr 5)
Fear Siuil 111 (20f,Str,GF,Jly 14)
Fearless Mel 105 (24¹/₂f,Ban,G,Mar 22)
Felix Darby 109 (29f,War,G,Mar 14)
Fielding s Hay 102 (26f,Utt,G,Apr 21)
Fier Goumier 106 (22f,Gal,Y,Jly 31)
Filscot 107 (24f,Str,G,Jly 27)
Fin Bec 106 (23¹/₂f,Exe,G,May 1)
Finians Ivy 111 (18f,Pun,S,Nov 2)
Fiori 106 (17f,Kel,G,Oct 19)
Fireball Macnamara 103 (21¹/₂f,Fak,GS,Nov 24)
First Gold 117 (25f,Ain,G,Apr 3)
First Love 119 (21f,Fol,S,Feb 11)
First Officer 104 (26f,Plu,GF,Apr 19)
Fisher Street 100 (20¹/₂f,Per,GF,May 15)
Flagship Uberalles 102 (16f,Chl,G,Mar 12)
Flahive s First 105 (17¹/₂f,Crt,G,Aug 26)
Flaxley Wood 105 (21f,Utt,GF,Aug 27)
Flinders Chase 107 (16f,Fol,G,Nov 18)
Florida Pearl 114 (24f,Kem,S,Dec 26)

Fluff N Puff 103 (24f,Lud,G,Nov 25)
Flying High 100 (20¹/₂f,Hex,G,Jun 4)
Foly Pleasant 115 (21f,Chl,G,Dec 14)
Fondmort 118 (21f,Chl,G,Dec 14)
Forest Gunner 106 (24¹/₂f,Fak,GS,Dec 14)
Forrest Tribe 102 (25¹/₂f,Her,GF,May 4)
Fountain Bank 106 (24¹/₂f,Fak,GS,May 26)
Foxchapel King 113 (25f,Fai,S,Nov 30)
Francoskid 108 (24f,Mus,G,Feb 12)
Frantic Tan 114 (29¹/₂f,Chp,HY,Dec 27)
Fred s In The Know 106 (16f,Cat,G,Feb 8)
Free To Run 105 (21f,Sed,G,Aug 9)
French Connection 102 (16f,Utt,G,Sep 12)
French Executive 105 (26f,Plu,GS,Nov 4)
Frezenium 106 (24f,Nav,S,May 19)
Friedhelmo 106 (16f,Fol,G,Nov 18)
Frosty Canyon 119 (29¹/₂f,Chp,HY,Dec 27)
Full Minty 101 (22f,Hay,GS,Feb 8)

Galapiat Du Mesnil 101 (31f,Chl,GS,Nov 15)
Galeaway 105 (26¹/₂f,Fon,GF,Apr 24)
Galeshan 110 (20¹/₂f,Wor,G,Aug 24)
Gallion s Reach 108 (24f,Lud,GF,May 6)
Gardrum Park 104 (24f,Naa,S,Nov 23)
Garolsa 106 (21f,Utt,GF,Jun 30)
Garruth 103 (24f,Tau,S,Feb 13)
Garvivonnian 103 (18f,Thu,S,Nov 28)
Gatflax 106 (17¹/₂f,Str,S,Aug 1)
Gatorade 113 (20¹/₂f,Wor,G,Jun 8)
Gayles And Showers 107 (22¹/₂f,Kel,S,Nov 2)
Gaysun 109 (26¹/₂f,Nab,GF,Jly 15)
General Claremont 102 (31f,Chl,GS,Dec 13)
Gentle Rivage 106 (19¹/₂f,Chp,S,Nov 9)
Geos 112 (19¹/₂f,Asc,GS,Feb 15)
Get Real 114 (16f,Asc,HY,Nov 22)
Get The Point 100 (16f,Fol,G,Mar 16)
Ghadames 102 (20¹/₂f,Sth,GS,May 26)
Ghutah 107 (16¹/₂f,Hun,GF,Jun 3)
Gimme Shelter 101 (32f,Hex,S,Mar 13)
Gimmick 104 (16f,Lud,G,Dec 12)
Gin N Ice 103 (24f,Hun,GF,Jun 3)
Gingembre 119 (25f,Wet,GS,Nov 2)
Gipsy Geof 109 (16f,Fol,G,May 3)
Givenchy De Solzen 108 (17f,Gal,Y,Aug 2)
Glacial River 103 (29f,War,GS,Dec 7)
Glacial Sygnet 107 (20f,Gow,G,Jun 23)
Gladiateur Iv 112 (20¹/₂f,Wor,GF,May 11)
Gladtoknowyou 104 (20¹/₂f,Kem,GS,Jan 27)
Glanamana 105 (26f,War,G,Nov 26)
Glanmerin 104 (20¹/₂f,Wor,G,May 22)
Glenfarclas Boy 103 (16f,Per,GS,Jun 7)
Glens Music 110 (16f,Naa,HY,Mar 9)
Glinger 106 (20¹/₂f,Chl,G,Oct 30)
Glory Storey 112 (24f,Hun,GF,Jun 3)
Glynn Dingle 101 (20¹/₂f,Per,G,Apr 25)
Go Ballistic 102 (25¹/₂f,Chl,G,Dec 13)
Go Roger Go 113 (17f,Leo,HY,Dec 29)
Go White Lightning 106 (24f,Don,G,Jan 13)
Goguenard 118 (20f,Hay,G,Mar 1)
Gola Cher 112 (25¹/₂f,Wcn,G,Nov 9)
Gola Supreme 103 (24¹/₂f,Ban,HY,Nov 29)
Goldbridge 102 (21¹/₂f,Str,G,May 31)
Golden Alpha 113 (16f,Ain,G,Apr 3)
Golden Goal 109 (21f,Wcn,GS,Dec 5)
Golden Rose 104 (20f,Plu,GS,Nov 4)
Golden Storm 105 (22f,Gal,HY,Sep 11)

Goldstreet 105 (16f,Naa,HY,Mar 9)
Good Shuil 114 (27¹/₂f,Chl,GS,Nov 16)
Good Vintage 110 (29f,Fai,G,Apr 21)
Goodnight Mike 101 (20f,Gow,G,Jun 23)
Got One Too 109 (16f,Lei,G,Nov 30)
Gothic Lord 103 (22f,Gal,GY,Aug 4)
Gottabe 106 (20¹/₂f,Wet,GF,May 8)
Governor Daniel 102 (21¹/₂f,Nab,GF,Apr 19)
Gralmano 101 (16f,Cat,G,Nov 23)
Granby Bell 106 (19¹/₂f,Chp,G,Oct 23)
Grand Gousier 100 (20f,Lud,G,Dec 12)
Grand Slam 102 (16¹/₂f,Hex,GF,Sep 15)
Grange Leader 101 (24f,Gow,SH,Jan 23)
Grangewick Flight 106(24f,Crl,G,Mar 28)
Grate Deel 107 (25f,Wet,GS,May 30)
Green Smoke 100 (20f,Ncs,S,Feb 24)
Gregs Way 105 (16f,Crl,GF,Oct 11)
Grey Abbey 116 (25f,Wet,GS,Nov 2)
Ground Ball 116 (21f,Leo,S,Jan 12)
Grouse Hall 107 (20¹/₂f,Wet,GS,Nov 2)
Guid Willie Waught 109 (20f,Str,GF,Jly 14)
Guignol Du Cochet 104 (16f,Wcn,GS,Dec 26)
Guilsborough Gorse 108 (17¹/₂f,Mar,GF,Jun 1)
Gun n Roses II 104 (20f,Hay,G,Mar 1)
Gunner Welburn 119 (29¹/₂f,Chp,HY,Dec 27)
Gunther McBride 112 (24f,Kem,G,Feb 22)
Gus Des Bois 105 (20f,Plu,HY,Jan 23)

Hades De Sienne 101 (24f,Ncs,S,Feb 24)
Hailstorm 102 (24f,Str,S,Aug 10)
Halexy 113 (20¹/₂f,Chl,GS,Nov 17)
Half Barrell 109 (17f,Gal,Y,Aug 2)
Hallyards Gael 103 (20¹/₂f,Wet,GS,May 30)
Hanakham 100 (20¹/₂f,Ban,G,May 3)
Hand Inn Hand 117 (19¹/₂f,Chp,S,Nov 9)
Handyman 111 (23¹/₂f,Exe,G,May 1)
Hanover Square 104 (28f,Str,GS,Oct 31)
Happy Change 103 (16f,Hay,G,Oct 24)
Harbour Pilot 117 (26¹/₂f,Chl,G,Mar 13)
Hard Lines 108 (16¹/₂f,Hex,HY,Nov 8)
Harik 108 (19f,Tau,F,Mar 24)
Harlov 106 (26f,Crl,HY,Nov 28)
Harvis 109 (16f,San,S,Feb 14)
Haut Cercy 118 (24¹/₂f,Chl,G,Mar 11)
Haydn James 107 (20f,Utt,GF,Jun 30)
Hedgehunter 110 (20f,Gow,SH,Jan 23)
Heidi Iii 109 (25f,Wet,GS,Dec 7)
Helvetius 105 (20¹/₂f,Chl,G,Oct 30)
Henrianjames 103 (16¹/₂f,Hex,GF,Oct 4)
Heracles 110 (20¹/₂f,Sth,GS,May 26)
Hermes Iii 109 (21f,Chl,GS,Jan 25)
Hersilia 102 (24f,Per,GS,Jun 7)
Hersov 107 (23¹/₂f,Lei,G,Dec 5)
Hi Lily 100 (20f,Plu,GF,Apr 19)
Hidden Valley 104 (20¹/₂f,War,G,Nov 26)
Hiers De Brouage 105 (19¹/₂f,Exe,G,Mar 18)
High Cotton 107 (24f,Nby,S,Nov 29)
Historg 114 (24¹/₂f,Chl,G,Mar 11)
Hit And Run 103 (16f,Her,G,Jun 4)
Hit Royal 112 (17¹/₂f,Mar,GF,Sep 28)
Hitman 103 (16¹/₂f,War,S,Jan 23)
Hoh No 102 (17f,Plu,GF,Oct 7)
Hombre 104 (16¹/₂f,Sed,HY,Feb 11)
Homme De Fer 105 (24f,Lud,G,Nov 14)
Horus 107 (20f,Nby,GS,Nov 30)
How Ran On 104 (16f,Utt,G,Sep 12)
Hugo De Grez 109 (26f,Crl,HY,Nov 11)

Hunter Gold 101 (24f,Hun,G,Mar 12)
Hunters Creek 101 (21f,Sed,GF,Apr 26)
Hunters Tweed 114 (20¹/₂f,Per,G,Apr 23)
Hurricane Lamp 109 (24f,Str,GF,May 17)
Hussard Collonges 119 (25f,Wet,GS,Nov 2)

I Vehadit 113 (24f,Naa,S,Jan 25)
Ibal 110 (26f,Plu,HY,Jan 23)
Ibin St James 101 (24f,Hun,G,Feb 22)
Ibis Rochelais 109 (21f,Chl,GS,Jan 25)
Ichi Beau 107 (16f,Ayr,G,Apr 12)
Ideal Du Bois Beury 102 (19f,Tau,GS,Nov 28)
Ideal Jack 104 (19f,Tau,S,Jan 16)
Idealko 103 (20f,Lud,G,Mar 16)
Ifni Du Luc 111 (20¹/₂f,Lei,G,Nov 30)
Il Capitano 111 (20¹/₂f,San,GF,Apr 25)
Il Athou 115 (20f,Hay,G,Mar 1)
Illineylad 101 (23¹/₂f,Wor,G,Aug 24)
Impek 119 (16f,Her,G,Nov 7)
Imperial De Thaix 101 (23¹/₂f,Exe,G,Nov 5)
Impertio 102 (24¹/₂f,Ban,S,Mar 5)
Inaki 106 (21¹/₂f,Fak,G,Mar 14)
Inch Perfect 110 (16f,Cat,S,Mar 5)
Indalo 109 (20f,Plu,GS,Feb 24)
Indeed 103 (20¹/₂f,Kem,GS,Feb 7)
Indeed To Goodness 109 (26f,Plu,HY,Jan 23)
Indian Chance 106 (25¹/₂f,Wcn,GS,Jan 18)
Indian Gunner 112 (21f,Wcn,S,Mar 6)
Indian Scout 109 (20f,Hay,G,Nov 30)
Indian Wings 101 (16f,Per,G,Aug 17)
Indien Du Boulay 110 (24f,Mus,GS,Dec 28)
Influence Pedler 102 (24f,Str,G,Jly 27)
Infrasonique 113 (24¹/₂f,Asc,GS,Nov 2)
Innovate 101 (26f,Crl,GF,Apr 21)
Innovative Step 104 (24f,Naa,S,Nov 23)
Ins And Outs 105 (16¹/₂f,Hun,S,Jan 15)
Intelligent 111 (24f,Nav,YS,Feb 16)
Iorana 108 (16f,Wcn,GS,Nov 21)
Iris Bleu 115 (25¹/₂f,Wcn,GS,Feb 15)
Iris Collonges 103 (19f,Her,G,Feb 23)
Iris Royal 112 (24f,Nby,G,Dec 18)
Irish Hussar 115 (25f,Ain,G,Apr 4)
Irish Option 105 (26¹/₂f,Fon,S,Mar 3)
Iron Express 105 (25f,Hex,G,Apr 14)
Isio 110 (16¹/₂f,Don,G,Jan 24)
Island Sound 101 (16f,Wcn,GS,Feb 15)
It Takes Time 117 (25¹/₂f,Chl,G,Dec 13)
It s All A Chance 100 (20¹/₂f,Hex,GF,Sep 15)
It s Beyond Belief 103 (26f,Plu,S,Mar 10)
It s Only Him 109 (18f,Pun,S,Nov 2)
Its Time For A Win 105 (16f,Nav,YS,Nov 3)
Itsonlyme 108 (25¹/₂f,Wcn,G,Nov 9)
Ivanoph 111 (16f,Wcn,GS,Nov 21)
Iverain 110 (25¹/₂f,Chl,G,Dec 13)
Iznogoud 109 (29¹/₂f,San,G,Apr 26)

J J Baboo 105 (24f,Mus,G,Feb 12)
Jack The Bear 109 (26¹/₂f,Nab,S,Nov 6)
Jackson s Hole 100 (27f,Sed,HY,Jan 21)
Jacksonville 100 (21¹/₂f,Ayr,S,Nov 17)
Jaguar Claw 106 (20f,Gow,SH,Jan 23)
Jair Du Cochet 118 (24f,Kem,S,Dec 26)
Jakari 105 (20f,Str,GS,Mar 10)
Jaloux D Estruval 102 (24f,Don,G,Jan 13)
Jamica Plane 104 (18f,Thu,SH,Feb 13)

Jamorin Dancer 103 (17½f,Mar,G,Apr 26)
Jan s Dream 106 (16f,Fol,G,Mar 16)
Janiture 105 (19f,Tau,GS,Nov 14)
Jardin De Beaulieu 104 (20½f,Wet,GS,Dec 7)
Jarro 107 (16f,Wcn,GS,Nov 21)
Jasmin D Oudairies 102 (17f,Nav,GY,Mar 22)
Jasmin Guichois 106 (24½f,Asc,GS,Feb 15)
Jaybejay 107 (16f,Lud,G,Dec 12)
Jazz Duke 101 (26f,Plu,GS,Nov 4)
Jenniferjo 108 (24f,Naa,S,Jan 25)
Jericho Iii 101 (16f,Lei,S,Jan 1)
Jetowa Du Bois Hue 110 (16f,Her,GF,Mar 17)
Jivaros 105 (24f,Hun,G,Mar 2)
Jocks Cross 106 (28½f,Hay,G,Mar 1)
Joe Deane 103 (16f,Lei,S,Feb 12)
Joe Di Capo 102 (24f,Ncs,HY,Jan 29)
Joey Tribbiani 112 (16f,Her,G,Feb 10)
Johnlegood 100 (21f,Chl,G,Apr 17)
Johnny Brushaside 101 (17f,Nav,SH,Jun 9)
Joint Account 110 (25f,Wet,G,May 23)
Joly Bey 112 (24f,Nby,S,Nov 29)
Jonaem 102 (25f,Hex,GF,Jun 1)
Jones Lad 100 (16f,Wor,G,Jly 10)
Jordan s Ridge 107 (16½f,Hex,G,Jun 15)
Jorn Du Soleil 102 (16f,Cat,S,Mar 5)
Jorodama King 102 (24f,Hun,GF,Jun 3)
Joss Naylor 106 (20½f,Ban,S,Dec 18)
Joowoody 108 (25f,Kel,GS,May 1)
Joyeux Royal 104 (17f,Plu,G,Oct 21)
Judaic Ways 108 (24f,Lud,G,Feb 27)
June s River 100 (16½f,Ncs,S,Dec 16)
Jungle Jinks 107 (25f,Wet,G,Feb 26)
Jurado Express 105 (17f,Leo,S,Jan 26)
Juralan 106 (16f,Asc,G,Mar 25)
Jurancon Ii 103 (34f,Utt,S,Mar 15)
Jurassic Scratch 100 (26f,Fol,HY,Jan 24)
Just A Minute 108 (19½f,Exe,GS,Dec 19)
Just For Ger 101 (16f,Ayr,S,Mar 8)
Just Hoping 107 (16½f,Fak,GS,May 26)
Just In Time 103 (17½f,Exe,G,May 1)
Just Jasmine 118 (16f,Asc,HY,Nov 22)
Just Maybe 107 (27f,Tau,S,Jan 16)
Just Reuben 108 (20f,Plu,GS,Feb 24)
Just Strong 106 (25f,Wet,GS,May 30)
Just Two 102 (20f,Nav,HY,Mar 8)
Justin Mac 106 (20½f,Wor,G,Jun 8)
Justjim 103 (20½f,Wor,G,May 22)

Kadarann 113 (20f,Ain,G,Apr 4)
Kadouko 107 (16f,Crl,S,Mar 6)
Kadoun 114 (21f,Leo,HY,Mar 2)
Kaid 109 (20½f,Wor,G,Aug 24)
Kandy Four 105 (20½f,Per,GS,Aug 4)
Karadin 105 (21½f,Nab,GF,Aug 13)
Kassala 106 (16f,Her,GF,Oct 3)
Katarino 115 (21f,Chl,HY,Jan 1)
Katie Buckers 109 (20f,Utt,G,May 4)
Keaneo 100 (20½f,Sth,GS,Nov 12)
Kedon 102 (31f,Chl,GS,Nov 15)
Keen Leader 112 (22f,Hay,S,Nov 17)
Keen To The Last 109 (24½f,Sth,G,May 9)
Keep Smiling 105 (20½f,Ban,GS,Oct 12)
Keeponthesunnyside 108 (22f,Gal,Y,Jly 31)
Keiran 110 (24f,Mus,GF,Dec 17)
Keltic Heritage 105 (24f,Nby,S,Nov 29)
Kemal s Council 107 (24½f,Fak,GS,Dec 14)

Kentford Fern 110 (21f,Utt,S,Mar 15)
Keppler 100 (22f,Gal,S,Sep 9)
Kerry Lads 107 (33f,Ayr,G,Apr 12)
Khatani 108 (20½f,Ban,G,May 3)
Khayali 100 (20½f,Ban,GF,Aug 17)
Kick For Touch 110 (24f,Don,G,Feb 28)
Kilbyrne King 100 (18f,Thu,SH,Feb 13)
Kildorragh 108 (24f,Don,G,Mar 1)
Killultagh Storm 105 (16f,Naa,Y,Feb 23)
Killusty 109 (24½f,San,S,Mar 8)
Kilmoney Rose 101 (24f,Thu,SH,Feb 13)
Kimdaloo 110 (17f,Kel,HY,Nov 19)
Kind Sir 109 (16f,Her,G,Dec 3)
King Of Mommur 102 (24f,Hun,GF,Apr 21)
King Of The Dawn 100 (21f,Fol,S,Jan 14)
King Of The Forest 100 (25f,Hex,HY,Nov 8)
King s Bounty 109 (25f,Wet,GF,Apr 21)
King s Country 104 (16f,Mus,GF,Dec 17)
Kings Glen 102 (21f,Leo,HY,Mar 2)
Kings Mistral 112 (24½f,San,GS,Dec 6)
Kings Valley 100 (20f,Nav,YS,Feb 16)
Kingsmark 123 (24f,Hay,S,Nov 17)
Kingston-Banker 100 (19½f,Chp,G,Mar 19)
Kirmar 112 (24f,Gow,SH,Jan 23)
Kit Smartie 103 (25½f,Chl,G,Dec 13)
Kittenkat 101 (26f,Plu,S,Nov 24)
Klondike Charger 108 (22f,Fon,G,Oct 6)
Knife Edge 115 (17f,Leo,HY,Dec 29)
Knock Knock 116 (29f,Fai,G,Apr 21)
Kock De La Vesvre 102 (20f,Plu,S,Jan 13)
Korakor 114 (20½f,Wet,GS,Nov 2)
Krabloonik 106 (16f,Lud,G,Dec 12)
Kung Hei Fat Choi 102 (25f,Ayr,S,Dec 26)

L Epicurien 106 (21½f,Nab,GS,May 25)
La Colina 102 (17½f,Mar,GS,Nov 21)
La Landiere 114 (21f,Chl,G,Mar 13)
Laazim Afooz 107 (27f,Sed,G,Oct 15)
Lady Cricket 112 (25f,Ain,G,Apr 3)
Lady Felix 103 (24f,Str,G,Apr 12)
Lakeside Lad 104 (24½f,Fak,G,May 8)
Lancastrian Jet 106 (26f,Crl,HY,Nov 11)
Lanmire Glen 104 (16f,Pun,SH,Feb 1)
Lanmire Leader 102 (21f,Fol,S,Dec 2)
Lanmire Tower 107 (24½f,Wcn,GS,Nov 21)
Last Option 106 (24f,Str,GF,May 17)
Lauderdale 111 (17f,Kel,HY,Nov 19)
Le Cabro D Or 107 (26f,Crl,HY,Nov 28)
Le Coudray 115 (17f,Leo,HY,Dec 26)
Le Roi Miguel 119 (19½f,Chp,S,Nov 9)
Le Sauvignon 116 (24f,Kem,S,Dec 26)
Leagues 105 (16½f,Don,G,Dec 13)
Left Bank 102 (24½f,Asc,G,Mar 25)
Lightning Quest 106 (20½f,Per,G,Aug 17)
Lincoln Place 112 (20½f,Hun,GF,Sep 29)
Lindajane 106 (20½f,Hex,G,Jun 4)
Liquor Merchant 101 (22f,Gal,GY,Aug 4)
Lisaan 105 (18f,Thu,S,Nov 28)
Lisdante 112 (23½f,Wor,G,Sep 14)
Lislaughtin Abbey 101 (21½f,Fak,G,Apr 21)
Lismeenan 101 (16f,Her,G,Dec 3)
Little Brown Bear 112 (27f,Sed,G,Sep 6)
Little Ross 101 (16f,Fol,G,Mar 16)
Little Tuska 108 (17½f,Mar,GF,Jun 1)
Lively Dessert 107 (25f,Kel,GS,May 1)
Livingstonebramble 107 (20f,Nav,S,Nov 17)
Log On Intersky 107 (16f,Cat,G,Feb 8)

Logician 116 (16f,Wol,GS,Jly 5)
Looking Forward 103 (21f,Sed,G,Apr 8)
Lord N Master 110 (24½f,San,S,Mar 7)
Lord Broadway 109 (24f,Hun,G,Mar 12)
Lord Capitaine 104 (28f,Sed,G,Mar 25)
Lord Fleet 100 (17½f,Mar,GF,Jun 1)
Lord Grey 100 (16½f,Chl,G,Mar 13)
Lord Jack 107 (20f,Ayr,S,Jan 14)
Lord Maizey 109 (16f,Lei,S,Feb 12)
Lord Moose 105 (24½f,San,S,Mar 8)
Lord North 107 (20½f,Ban,G,May 3)
Lord Of The Turf 115 (24f,Nav,S,Nov 17)
Lord Rapier 113 (25f,Mar,S,Mar 3)
Lord Seamus 100 (24f,Crl,GF,Apr 19)
Lord Strickland 111 (20½f,Wor,G,Jun 8)
Lord York 108 (16f,Asc,G,Mar 25)
Lorgnette 101 (19f,Tau,GS,Nov 14)
Loughbeg Rambler 106 (20½f,Chl,GS,Nov 17)
Lucky Bay 114 (24f,Nby,S,Nov 29)
Lucky Clover 106 (31f,Chl,GS,Nov 15)
Lucky Master 100 (30f,Ban,S,Dec 18)
Lucky Time 102 (16½f,Ncs,G,Apr 29)
Lucys Lad 109 (26½f,Fon,S,Dec 26)
Luke Warm 104 (26½f,Fon,S,Mar 3)
Luzcadou 110 (20f,Ayr,S,Nov 16)

Macgyver 111 (16f,Lei,GS,Dec 27)
Mackinus 106 (20f,Gow,YS,Jun 6)
Macs Gildoran 111 (21f,Chl,G,Mar 13)
Madam Mosso 104 (25½f,Her,S,Mar 7)
Magic Of Sydney 100 (21f,Fol,G,Nov 18)
Maidstone Monument 111 (26½f,Nab,G,Sep 4)
Majestic Bay 110 (24½f,Asc,G,Apr 2)
Major Adventure 109 (24f,Lud,GF,May 6)
Major Sharpe 104 (25½f,Her,G,Jun 4)
Man Murphy 103 (20f,Ncs,GS,Nov 25)
Manodee 103 (24f,Hun,GF,Sep 29)
Maousse Honor 107 (16½f,Nab,GF,Jly 28)
Mapleton 105 (24½f,Sth,G,May 9)
March North 101 (24f,Utt,G,Apr 9)
Marcus Maximus 109 (16f,Lud,G,Dec 12)
Marigliano 102 (16½f,Fak,S,Jan 22)
Marlborough 120 (25f,Wet,GS,Nov 2)
Master Club Royal 108 (27f,Sed,S,Nov 26)
Master Ginger Pop 104 (23½f,Exe,G,Mar 18)
Master Of Illusion 107 (26½f,Nab,S,Nov 6)
Master Ride 102 (23½f,Exe,GS,Jan 27)
Master Tern 117 (25f,Ain,G,Apr 4)
Master Wood 102 (25f,Wet,GS,May 30)
Max Pride 112 (29f,War,GS,Mar 8)
Maxie McDonald 103 (20f,Ain,G,Nov 24)
Maximize 115 (24½f,Chl,G,Mar 11)
Mazileo 109 (24½f,San,GS,Nov 9)
Mercato 101 (16f,Utt,HY,Feb 1)
Merchants Friend 108 (20f,Nby,GS,Nov 13)
Merry Masquerade 101 (25f,Kel,GS,May 1)
Merry Minstrel 106 (16f,Per,G,Apr 24)
Mersey Beat 108 (18f,Fon,GF,May 6)
Michael Mor 109 (24f,Nav,S,Nov 17)
Michael s Princess 103 (23½f,Lei,S,Jan 1)
Midland Flame 110 (20f,Ain,G,Apr 3)
Midnight Gunner 110 (24f,Lud,G,Feb 27)
Mighty Fine 104 (16½f,Sed,S,Nov 26)
Mighty Strong 111 (17½f,Mar,GF,Sep 28)
Millcroft Seaspray 101 (24f,Tau,GS,Dec

12)
Millersford 107 (24f,Utt,S,Jun 13)
Minella Silver 110 (24f,Hay,S,Nov 30)
Mini Sensation 125 (29¹/₂f,Chp,HY,Dec 27)
Minster Glory 101 (16f,Cat,G,Feb 25)
Minster York 107 (20¹/₂f,Per,GF,May 15)
Miss Woodstick 103 (24f,Hun,G,Mar 2)
Mister Bigtime 104 (25¹/₂f,Wcn,GS,Feb 6)
Mister Dave S 105 (25f,Wet,S,Dec 26)
Misty Ramble 102 (27f,Sed,HY,Jan 21)
Misty Ridge 103 (22¹/₂f,Mar,GF,Oct 6)
Modulor 100 (26¹/₂f,Chl,G,Mar 13)
Mohera King 103 (20f,Ayr,S,Mar 7)
Monarch s Pursuit 112 (16f,Wet,GS,Nov 27)
Monkerhostin 107 (16¹/₂f,War,G,Nov 4)
Monkey Island 103 (20¹/₂f,Hex,G,Apr 30)
Monks Error 108 (22f,Gal,GY,Aug 3)
Monsieur Tagel 101 (20f,Lud,G,Dec 12)
Montalcino 113 (18¹/₂f,Nby,S,Dec 28)
Monte Cristo 103 (17f,Plu,S,Nov 24)
Montifault 107 (24f,Nby,G,Mar 22)
Montreal 107 (24f,Kem,G,Feb 22)
Monty s Pass 113 (22f,Gal,Y,Jly 31)
Monty s Quest 106 (25f,Hex,G,Apr 14)
Moon Glow 102 (16¹/₂f,Nab,GF,Aug 26)
Moor Lane 104 (24¹/₂f,Asc,GS,Nov 2)
Moorlands Again 109 (26¹/₂f,Fon,S,Feb 3)
Moral Justice 107 (21f,Utt,GF,Jun 30)
Moral Support 106 (24f,Nby,S,Mar 1)
Morstock 105 (16¹/₂f,Nab,S,May 28)
Moscow Express 106 (20f,Nav,GY,Mar 22)
Moscow Flyer 118 (17f,Leo,HY,Dec 29)
Moss Harvey 107 (21¹/₂f,Fak,GS,Oct 25)
Mothers Help 106 (24f,Hun,GS,Nov 12)
Mount Gay 102 (22¹/₂f,Mar,GF,Aug 31)
Mount Prague 111 (20¹/₂f,Per,G,Apr 23)
Mr Baxter Basics 111 (20¹/₂f,Ban,G,Mar 22)
Mr Ben Gunn 101 (20¹/₂f,Hun,GF,Oct 11)
Mr Bossman 113 (20¹/₂f,Kem,G,Feb 22)
Mr Cospector 105 (26f,War,GS,Dec 7)
Mr Laggan 102 (25f,Hex,GF,Jun 1)
Mr Mahdlo 111 (24f,Utt,S,Jun 13)
Mr Timbrology 100 (19f,Her,S,Nov 21)
Mr Woodentop 101 (25f,Ayr,S,Jan 14)
Mr Woodland 105 (23¹/₂f,Wor,G,Sep 15)
Muharib Lady 100 (26f,Plu,GF,Oct 7)
Mulkev Prince 105 (20f,Lud,GF,Mar 19)
Multi Talented 109 (26f,Plu,HY,Jan 23)
Mumaris 106 (16¹/₂f,Sed,G,Aug 1)
Mumbai 101 (17¹/₂f,Crt,HY,Jun 3)
Mumuqa 106 (16f,Wet,GF,May 8)
Murolook 103 (18f,Thu,SH,Feb 13)
Murt s Man 116 (29¹/₂f,Chp,HY,Dec 27)
Mustang Molly 102 (21¹/₂f,Str,GF,Sep 7)
Mutasarrif 113 (16f,Utt,G,Sep 12)
My Galliano 100 (19f,Tau,GS,Nov 14)
Mytimie 105 (16f,Crl,HY,Nov 11)

Native Beat 105 (19f,Leo,S,Jan 26)
Native Commander 107 (16f,Pun,YS,Jan 18)
Native Fling 111 (16¹/₂f,Chp,HY,Jan 17)
Native Jack 105 (20f,Pun,SH,Feb 1)
Native Performance 106 (22f,Gal,GY,Aug 3)
Native Scout 112 (16f,Utt,S,Dec 20)
Native Sessions 113 (24f,Nav,HY,Mar 8)
Native Speaker 100 (20¹/₂f,San,GS,Nov 9)
Native Upmanship 121 (20f,Ain,G,Apr 4)
Nativetrial 105 (33f,Mar,S,Dec 26)
Navarone 113 (24f,Per,G,Apr 25)

Nearly A Moose 110 (24f,Leo,HY,Dec 28)
Needwood Lion 107 (20¹/₂f,Kem,S,Dec 26)
Nephite 104 (16f,Crl,S,Mar 6)
Never Wonder 100 (23¹/₂f,Exe,G,Oct 22)
New Bird 101 (16f,Ain,G,May 17)
New Rising 101 (26¹/₂f,Fon,HY,Jan 6)
Newby End 100 (25f,Fol,S,Feb 11)
News Maker 106 (24f,Hay,S,Dec 28)
Nick The Jewel 109 (16f,Lud,G,Nov 14)
Nickit 106 (26f,Plu,S,Jan 18)
Night Fighter 102 (16f,Cat,GS,Dec 4)
Nisbet 102 (24f,Mus,G,Feb 12)
No Forecast 110 (20¹/₂f,Chl,GS,Nov 17)
No Kidding 105 (16f,Mus,GF,Dec 17)
No More Hassle 103 (26f,Utt,G,Jun 3)
No Need For Alarm 106 (16¹/₂f,Chp,S,Nov 27)
No Problem 109 (25f,Fai,S,Nov 30)
No Stranger 106 (25f,Fai,S,Jan 19)
No Visibility 103 (16¹/₂f,Tau,S,Jan 28)
Noble Comic 108 (20f,Str,GF,Jly 14)
Noel s Pride 100 (20¹/₂f,Hex,GF,Jun 21)
Nokimover 103 (23f,Utt,G,Jun 3)
Nomadic 110 (20f,Gow,SH,Jan 23)
Nordance Prince 106 (20¹/₂f,Kem,G,Jan 18)
Nordic Prince 113 (24¹/₂f,Sth,GS,Jan 30)
Normarange 103 (25f,Tow,GS,Apr 29)
Northern Fancy 100 (17f,Gal,GY,Aug 3)
Nosam 112 (20¹/₂f,Wet,G,Feb 26)
Noshinannikin 100 (16f,Ain,G,May 17)

Oboedire 102 (24f,Hay,GF,Mar 29)
Occold 110 (24f,Per,GS,Aug 4)
Odagh Odyssey 102 (20¹/₂f,Kem,GS,Feb 7)
Oh So Wisley 101 (24¹/₂f,Sth,GS,Dec 6)
Oliver Cromwell 104 (24f,Tau,S,Feb 13)
On The Run 108 (19f,Her,GF,Sep 11)
One Knight 121 (19¹/₂f,Chp,S,Nov 9)
One Night Out 106 (24f,Kem,S,Dec 26)
Only Once 106 (27f,Sed,HY,Jan 21)
Opal Lou 107 (19¹/₂f,Exe,GS,Dec 19)
Optimistic Chris 111 (17¹/₂f,Mar,GF,Sep 28)
Orange Order 101 (21f,Sed,GF,Jly 17)
Orient Bay 106 (24f,Lud,S,Jan 16)
Oriental Style 106 (20f,Utt,S,Dec 21)
Orswell Crest 109 (24¹/₂f,San,GS,Dec 6)
Our Jolly Swagman 103 (26¹/₂f,Chp,GS,Feb 26)
Over The Burn 102 (25f,Hex,GS,May 4)
Over The Storm 104 (24f,Tau,S,Feb 13)
Over To Bens 100 (22f,Gal,GY,Aug 3)
Over Zealous 113 (29f,War,G,Mar 14)
Ozzie Jones 106 (26¹/₂f,Nab,GF,Jly 15)

Palarshan 115 (16f,Her,G,Nov 7)
Pamela Anshan 106 (19f,Tau,F,Mar 24)
Paperising 108 (25f,Wet,G,May 23)
Pardon What 100 (20¹/₂f,Ban,S,Mar 5)
Parish Oak 106 (20f,Mar,G,Apr 26)
Parlour Game 105 (19¹/₂f,Exe,GS,Dec 19)
Passereau 111 (16f,Utt,G,Sep 12)
Pauls Run 108 (25f,Fai,S,Nov 30)
Pauntley Gofa 102 (20f,Mar,G,Jly 7)
Paxford Jack 109 (25¹/₂f,Chl,S,Dec 31)
Paymaster 102 (20¹/₂f,Hun,GF,Jun 3)
Peccadillo 113 (20¹/₂f,Hun,GF,Sep 29)
Pendle Hill 101 (20f,Ncs,S,Dec 16)
Perange 105 (21¹/₂f,Nab,G,Apr 21)
Perching 105 (26f,Plu,GF,Apr 21)
Percy Parkeeper 106 (16f,Per,GF,Sep 26)
Pertino 107 (16f,Utt,GF,Oct 5)

Pessimistic Dick 113 (26f,Crt,G,Aug 24)
Pettree 106 (24¹/₂f,Sth,GS,Jan 30)
Phar Echo 101 (25f,Hex,G,Apr 30)
Phar From A Fiddle 107 (24f,Per,GS,Aug 4)
Phar From Chance 101 (26¹/₂f,Nab,GF,Aug 13)
Pharaway Citizen 105 (22¹/₂f,Nby,S,Feb 28)
Pharbeitfrome 109 (17¹/₂f,Mar,GF,Jun 1)
Pharpost 104 (22¹/₂f,Nby,S,Feb 28)
Phildari 102 (24f,Hun,GF,Mar 23)
Piccadilly 109 (25f,Mar,GF,Aug 31)
Pikachu Blue 101 (24f,Gow,SH,Jan 23)
Pillaging Pict 114 (22¹/₂f,Kel,GS,Mar 1)
Placid Man 106 (20f,Fon,HY,Jan 6)
Plenty Courage 108 (21f,Sed,GF,May 3)
Polar Champ 111 (26¹/₂f,Nab,G,Jun 10)
Poliantas 121 (21f,Chl,G,Apr 16)
Polish Spirit 103 (21¹/₂f,Str,G,Jly 4)
Political Sox 100 (22¹/₂f,Kel,GF,May 29)
Poly Amanshaa 105 (16¹/₂f,Don,GS,Dec 13)
Port Na Son 105 (22f,Gal,GY,Aug 3)
Possible Pardon 109 (26¹/₂f,Fon,GS,Nov 11)
Power Unit 108 (19f,Tau,S,Jan 16)
Prairie Minstrel 100 (20¹/₂f,Lei,G,Dec 5)
Prancing Blade 118 (23¹/₂f,Wor,G,Sep 14)
Precious Music 107 (24f,Naa,S,Nov 23)
Premier Drive 112 (20f,Ayr,HY,Jan 25)
Prime Target 103 (20f,Nav,HY,Mar 8)
Primitive Way 104 (24f,Per,GF,May 16)
Prince Of Pleasure 114 (22f,Gal,Y,Jly 31)
Prince Sorinieres 105 (24f,Tau,F,Apr 3)
Prince Wot A Mess 100 (25f,Pun,F,Sep 29)
Princess Symphony 100 (29f,Fai,G,Apr 21)
Private Ryan 101 (22f,Gal,Y,Jly 30)
Prominent Profile 105 (18¹/₂f,Nby,G,Dec 18)
Putsometnby 106 (22f,Gal,GY,Aug 4)

Quadco 110 (18f,Thu,S,Nov 28)
Quality First 112 (20f,Hay,G,Mar 1)
Quarterstaff 108 (24f,Crl,G,Mar 28)

Radar 113 (16¹/₂f,Sed,HY,Feb 11)
Raffles Rooster 109 (24f,Don,G,Jan 13)
Rainbow Dance 103 (20¹/₂f,Ban,GS,Oct 12)
Raise A Gale 106 (23¹/₂f,Wor,GF,Jun 19)
Raleagh Native 101 (20f,Plu,G,Apr 29)
Random Harvest 108 (24f,Don,G,Jan 13)
Rathbawn Prince 109 (16f,Naa,Y,Feb 23)
Rathgar Beau 117 (16f,Nav,YS,Feb 16)
Rattothetattat 106 (16f,Pun,YS,Jan 18)
Reach The Clouds 104 (20f,Utt,S,Dec 21)
Red Ark 108 (16¹/₂f,Chl,G,Mar 13)
Red Blazer 110 (20¹/₂f,Hun,GS,Nov 12)
Red Dancer 107 (31f,Chl,GS,Nov 15)
Red Guard 105 (24f,Hun,GF,Apr 21)
Red Hare 103 (24f,Tau,GF,Oct 30)
Red Hot Indian 104 (21¹/₂f,Crt,G,Aug 26)
Red Hustler 103 (16f,Cat,S,Mar 5)
Red Oassis 100 (16f,Her,G,Feb 10)
Red Rampage 100 (20f,Crl,HY,Nov 11)
Red Striker 115 (20f,Hay,G,Mar 1)
Redemption 114 (16f,Asc,HY,Nov 22)
Reflective Way 103 (24f,Per,GS,Jun 6)
Reflex Courier 113 (24f,Hay,S,Nov 30)
Regal Exit 110 (16f,Lud,G,Dec 12)

Regal Holly 111 (21f,Utt,S,Mar 15)
Regal River 112 (23¹/₂f,Lei,S,Jan 1)
Renaloo 109 (16f,Fol,S,Dec 17)
Restless Wind 109 (24f,Hun,GF,Apr 21)
Rhapsody In Blue 107 (24f,Mus,G,Feb 12)
Rheindross 112 (20f,Pun,SH,Feb 2)
Ricardo 112 (16f,Nav,YS,Feb 16)
Ricko 106 (20¹/₂f,Wor,GS,Aug 9)
Ridgewood Water 114 (22f,Gal,Y,Jly 31)
Rigadoon 111 (25f,Mar,GF,Aug 31)
Right N Royal 111 (22f,Gal,GY,Aug 3)
Rigolade 103 (26f,Utt,G,Sep 12)
Rince Ri 113 (24f,Leo,YS,Feb 9)
Rio Diamond 106 (24f,Naa,S,Jan 25)
Risk Accessor 114 (22f,Gal,Y,Jly 31)
Risky Way 105 (16f,Cat,G,Feb 25)
Ritual 110 (16f,Fol,G,Nov 18)
River Amora 100 (20f,Plu,G,Sep 28)
River Bug 103 (26f,Plu,GS,Feb 24)
River Grove 100 (24f,Thu,Y,Feb 27)
River Pilot 103 (16¹/₂f,Chp,HY,Jan 17)
River Slave 111 (23¹/₂f,Lei,S,Jan 1)
River Styx 102 (16f,Hay,G,Oct 24)
River Trix 105 (19¹/₂f,Chp,GF,Apr 22)
Robbo 114 (25f,Ain,G,Apr 4)
Roberty Bob 112 (24¹/₂f,Ban,HY,Nov 29)
Robins Pride 105 (19¹/₂f,Chp,GF,Apr 22)
Rock Rose 106 (24¹/₂f,Asc,GS,Feb 15)
Rockcliffe Gossip 111 (24¹/₂f,Ban,GS,Oct 12)
Rockholm Boy 117 (22f,Gal,Y,Jly 31)
Rockspring Hero 108 (24f,Thu,SH,Feb 13)
Rolfes Delight 104 (25¹/₂f,Wcn,F,Oct 10)
Roller Blade 110 (24f,Kem,GF,Oct 26)
Roman Outlaw 102 (24f,Ncs,HY,Jan 15)
Romantic Hero 103 (20¹/₂f,Lei,S,Jan 29)
Romero 105 (22¹/₂f,Nby,S,Nov 29)
Rosencrantz 112 (20¹/₂f,Wor,G,Jun 8)
Ross Moff 114 (25f,Ain,G,Apr 4)
Roveretto 102 (16f,Mus,G,Jan 17)
Royal Auclair 110 (24¹/₂f,Chl,G,Mar 11)
Royal Barge 112 (25f,Mar,GF,Aug 31)
Royal Beluga 111 (21f,Chl,G,Apr 17)
Royal Event 102 (21¹/₂f,Nab,GS,May 25)
Royal Feelings 101 (24f,Per,GS,Jun 6)
Royal Jake 111 (16f,Pun,SH,Dec 8)
Royal Plaisir 113 (16f,Pun,SH,Dec 8)
Royal Predica 110 (24¹/₂f,Chl,G,Mar 11)
Royale De Vassy 103 (24f,Hay,GS,Jan 18)
Rudi Knight 106 (19¹/₂f,Exe,GS,Jan 27)
Rudi s Pleasure 105 (24f,Thu,SH,Feb 13)
Rudolf Rassendyll 106 (24¹/₂f,San,S,Mar 7)
Rufius 111 (25¹/₂f,Chl,S,Dec 31)
Rugged River 115 (26¹/₂f,Chp,S,Dec 7)
Rule Supreme 116 (21f,Leo,S,Jan 12)
Run For Paddy 107 (24f,Chp,GF,Oct 5)
Runaway Bishop 100 (24¹/₂f,Fak,GS,Dec 14)
Runner Bean 105 (16¹/₂f,Hun,GF,Apr 21)
Running Machine 105 (21f,Fol,S,Feb 11)
Running Man 106 (16f,Kem,GF,Oct 26)
Running Moss 108 (22¹/₂f,Kel,S,Nov 2)
Russell House 106 (24f,Don,G,Jan 24)
Rustic Revelry 105 (21f,Utt,GF,Jun 30)
Ryalux 113 (33f,Ayr,G,Apr 12)

Sabi Sand 103 (24f,Ncs,S,Feb 24)
Saby 102 (16¹/₂f,Nab,G,Apr 21)
Sackville 108 (24f,Mus,G,Feb 28)
Sad Mad Bad 102 (25f,Wet,GS,Dec 7)
Saddlers Mark 106 (18f,Thu,S,Nov 28)
Saffron Sun 107 (23¹/₂f,Exe,G,Mar 18)
Saint Par 112 (21f,Fol,S,Feb 11)

Saint Romble 110 (16f,Asc,GS,Dec 20)
Salford 106 (25¹/₂f,Her,GF,Apr 5)
Samuel Wilderspin 109 (24¹/₂f,Chl,G,Nov 15)
San Francisco 103 (16f,Per,G,Apr 24)
Sandoran 103 (16¹/₂f,Nab,G,Apr 21)
Santella Boy 100 (26¹/₂f,Nab,GF,Aug 5)
Saragann 114 (21f,Chl,HY,Jan 1)
Satchmo 101 (24¹/₂f,Chl,G,Mar 11)
Satcoslam 105 (24f,Leo,HY,Dec 29)
Satshoon 107 (25¹/₂f,Wcn,GS,Nov 21)
Say Again 105 (17f,Leo,HY,Dec 26)
Scallybuck 101 (22f,Gal,GY,Aug 3)
Schwartzhalle 118 (16f,Nav,YS,Feb 16)
Scoring Pedigree 100 (24¹/₂f,Fak,GS,May 26)
Scotmail Boy 104 (20¹/₂f,Wet,G,Feb 26)
Scotmail Lad 111 (22¹/₂f,Kel,GS,Mar 1)
Scots Grey 111 (20¹/₂f,Hun,GS,Nov 12)
Scotton Green 106 (24f,Don,G,Jan 13)
Sea Drifting 109 (21f,Chl,GS,Jan 25)
Sean Connors 112 (16f,Pun,F,Sep 29)
Seattle Art 106 (24f,Per,GS,Aug 4)
Secret Drinker 110 (29f,War,G,Mar 14)
See More Business 118 (26¹/₂f,Chp,S,Dec 7)
See More Perks 106 (22f,Gal,GY,Aug 3)
See You Around 101 (16f,Wcn,GS,Dec 26)
Seebald 120 (20f,Ain,G,Apr 4)
Seixo Branco 105 (17¹/₂f,Mar,S,Dec 26)
Shady Lad 107 (21f,Pun,YS,Jan 18)
Shahboor 104 (16f,Utt,G,Apr 9)
Shamawan 121 (16f,Asc,HY,Nov 22)
Shampooed 103 (18¹/₂f,Nby,G,Dec 18)
Shamsan 106 (20f,Plu,G,Sep 28)
Shannon Quest 107 (16f,Fol,G,May 3)
Shardam 116 (25f,Ain,G,Apr 4)
Shareef 101 (16f,Kem,G,Nov 20)
Sharpastrizam 105 (16f,Per,G,Apr 24)
Shepherds Rest 106 (26f,Utt,G,Jun 3)
Shooting Light 110 (27¹/₂f,Chl,GS,Nov 16)
Shotgun Willy 110 (28¹/₂f,Hay,G,Mar 1)
Shuttleworth 103 (22¹/₂f,Mar,S,Dec 5)
Silent Snipe 107 (25f,Hex,GF,Jun 1)
Simber Hill 109 (26¹/₂f,Nab,G,Sep 4)
Sir Bob 108 (24¹/₂f,Sth,GS,Jan 30)
Sir Cumference 107 (24f,Str,G,Apr 19)
Sir Norman 105 (21¹/₂f,Ayr,S,Nov 17)
Sir Rembrandt 118 (25¹/₂f,Chl,G,Dec 13)
Sir Robbo 103 (25¹/₂f,Her,GF,May 4)
Sir Storm 109 (16f,Wet,HY,Nov 16)
Sir Toby 112 (20¹/₂f,Lei,G,Nov 30)
Sir Valentine 102 (26¹/₂f,Fon,S,Dec 26)
Sir Walter 108 (17¹/₂f,Mar,GF,Jun 1)
Sir Williamwallace 103 (25f,Wol,G,Jly 15)
Sireric 104 (24f,Ncs,HY,Jan 29)
Skinsey Finnegan 111 (16f,Fol,S,Dec 17)
Skippers Cleuch 105 (22¹/₂f,Kel,HY,Nov 19)
Skycab 110 (20¹/₂f,San,G,Apr 26)
Smart Guy 102 (18f,Fon,GF,Apr 24)
Smarty 102 (31f,Chl,GS,Nov 15)
Sniper 103 (21¹/₂f,Crt,G,Aug 26)
Snob Wells 103 (17f,Gal,GY,Aug 3)
Snow Dragon 103 (17f,Gal,Y,Aug 2)
Snow Partridge 101 (24f,Lud,G,Apr 10)
Soeur Fontenail 110 (16f,Wcn,GS,Nov 21)
Solus Dein 101 (22f,Gal,GY,Aug 4)
Some Buzz 108 (16f,Naa,S,Feb 8)
Something Dandy 102 (23¹/₂f,Wor,G,Aug 3)
Son Of Light 106 (26f,Utt,GF,Jly 18)
Sorrento King 108 (21f,Sed,GF,Oct 1)
Sound Of Cheers 104 (16¹/₂f,Hex,G,Mar 29)

Southbay 106 (18f,Thu,SH,Feb 13)
Southern Star 115 (27¹/₂f,Chl,GS,Nov 16)
Southerndown 110 (23¹/₂f,Wor,GF,Jly 17)
Spanish Archer 100 (23¹/₂f,Wor,GF,Jly 17)
Special Agenda 111 (16¹/₂f,Nab,GS,May 25)
Specialize 110 (26f,Crt,G,Aug 24)
Speed Board 104 (24f,Nav,S,May 19)
Spendid 109 (26f,Don,GS,Dec 14)
Spilaw 100 (24f,Hun,G,Mar 12)
Spinofski 109 (25¹/₂f,Wcn,GS,Jan 18)
Splendour 104 (21f,Leo,HY,Mar 2)
Spot The Native 103 (27f,Sed,HY,Jan 21)
Spot Thedifference 110 (29f,Fai,G,Apr 21)
Stage Affair 117 (16f,Nav,YS,Feb 16)
Stanmore 105 (20¹/₂f,Hun,GF,Sep 29)
Star Jack 115 (16f,Wol,GS,Jly 5)
Star Performance 109 (20f,Gow,SH,Jan 23)
Stars Out Tonight 110 (17¹/₂f,Exe,G,Oct 22)
Sterling Stewart 108 (20¹/₂f,Wet,GF,Oct 16)
Stone Cold 111 (20¹/₂f,Wet,G,Feb 26)
Storm Damage 103 (24¹/₂f,San,GS,Nov 9)
Stormez 116 (27¹/₂f,Chl,GS,Nov 16)
Stormhill Stag 104 (19¹/₂f,Exe,G,Mar 18)
Stormy Skye 107 (20f,Plu,GS,Feb 24)
Stratco 103 (23¹/₂f,Exe,G,May 15)
Strawman 102 (18f,Fon,G,Aug 26)
Strong Magic 111 (20¹/₂f,Chl,GS,Nov 17)
Strong Paladin 105 (22f,Fon,G,Oct 6)
Strong Tartan 100 (25f,Kel,G,Oct 19)
Sudden Shock 104 (33f,Ayr,G,Apr 12)
Sullane Storm 103 (24f,Tau,HY,Mar 10)
Sulphur Springs 107 (24f,Str,GF,May 17)
Sunday Habits 105 (26f,Plu,GF,Apr 19)
Sunshine Leader 108 (16f,Wet,HY,Nov 16)
Sunuvugun 100 (25f,Hex,GF,Jun 1)
Super Dollar 100 (17¹/₂f,Str,GF,May 17)
Super Fellow 111 (26¹/₂f,Nab,GF,Aug 5)
Super Nomad 106 (16f,Asc,G,Mar 25)
Superb Leader 103 (17¹/₂f,Ban,G,Mar 22)
Supreme Arrow 105 (18f,Pun,S,Nov 2)
Supreme Catch 105 (20¹/₂f,Hun,GS,Nov 23)
Supreme Fortune 107 (16¹/₂f,Ncs,G,Apr 1)
Supreme Glory 110 (36f,Ain,G,Apr 5)
Supreme Irony 106 (24¹/₂f,Fak,GS,May 26)
Supreme Soviet 108 (24f,Per,GF,May 16)
Surefast 105 (24f,Tau,GS,Feb 27)
Surprising 103 (24f,Hun,S,Jan 15)
Suspendid 104 (20f,Lud,GF,Mar 19)
Swansea Bay 119 (23¹/₂f,Wor,G,Sep 14)
Sweet Deal 105 (20f,Gow,YS,Jun 6)
Swincombe 100 (25¹/₂f,Wcn,GS,Dec 26)

Taakid 107 (21f,Sed,GF,Oct 1)
Takagi 118 (24f,Nav,S,Nov 17)
Take Control 105 (33f,Ayr,G,Apr 12)
Take The Lot 100 (20f,Gow,G,Jun 23)
Take The Stand 105 (26f,Plu,GF,Mar 31)
Tales Of Bounty 105 (24f,Tau,GS,Dec 12)
Tallow Bay 102 (21f,Fol,HY,Jan 24)
Tamango 104 (17¹/₂f,Exe,GS,Dec 6)
Tarasco 106 (17¹/₂f,Mar,GS,Mar 15)

Tarqogan Thyne 108 (24f,Thu,Y,Feb 27)
Tarxien 110 (20¹/₂f,Chl,GS,Nov 16)
Tathmin 103 (23¹/₂f,Wor,GF,Jun 19)
Telemoss 105 (16¹/₂f,Ncs,HY,Jan 15)
Ten Poundsworth 117 (21f,Leo,S,Jan 12)
Tenshookmen 112 (18f,Pun,S,Nov 2)
Tensile 105 (26¹/₂f,Nab,GF,Aug 5)
Test Of Loyalty 102 (17f,Kel,G,Apr 7)
Thari 109 (22f,Gal,S,Sep 9)
Thats All Folks 110 (16¹/₂f,Hex,G,Jun 15)
The Anner Boy 107 (18f,Pun,S,Nov 2)
The Bajan Bandit 108 (22f,Hay,GS,Jan 18)
The Big Un 109 (24f,Hun,G,Mar 12)
The Bunny Boiler 107 (24¹/₂f,Chl,G,Mar 11)
The French Furze 100 (21f,Sed,S,Mar 11)
The Gopher 105 (26f,Plu,G,Sep 28)
The Grey Dyer 107 (20f,Ayr,S,Nov 16)
The Hearty Joker 107 (21f,Fol,GF,Nov 5)
The Hen Hut 101 (22f,Gal,Y,Jly 30)
The Kerry Rebel 102 (24¹/₂f,Ban,G,Sep 14)
The Land Agent 105 (21¹/₂f,Nab,GS,May 25)
The Leader 102 (16f,Fol,HY,Jan 24)
The Manse Brae 104 (20¹/₂f,Ban,G,Sep 14)
The Negotiator 112 (20¹/₂f,Per,G,Apr 23)
The Newsman 106 (21¹/₂f,Str,G,May 31)
The Parsons Dingle 103 (17¹/₂f,Ban,S,Feb 7)
The Premier Cat 113(24f,Nav,YS,Feb 16)
The Quads 108 (31f,Chl,GS,Nov 15)
The Rile 105 (21¹/₂f,Ayr,S,Jan 2)
The Sawdust Kid 109 (26¹/₂f,Fon,G,Aug 26)
The Staggery Boy 105 (16f,Fol,G,Nov 18)
The Villager 112 (19¹/₂f,Exe,GS,Jan 27)
Thrill A Minute 100 (28¹/₂f,Mar,S,Dec 5)
Thyne Will Tell 105 (21¹/₂f,Str,G,Oct 19)
Tik-A-Tai 101 (21¹/₂f,Str,G,Oct 19)
Tim French 101 (20f,Nav,HY,Mar 8)
Timbera 117 (29f,Fai,G,Apr 21)
Time Of Flight 104 (20¹/₂f,Wet,G,Feb 26)
Time To Parlez 110 (26f,Plu,S,Jan 13)
Tino 108 (21f,Fol,GF,Nov 5)
Tiraldo 103 (24f,Str,S,Aug 10)
Tirley Storm 102 (20f,Str,GS,Oct 31)
Tis Gromit 100 (25f,Fol,S,Feb 11)
Tiutchev 117 (19¹/₂f,Asc,GS,Feb 15)
To The Future 103 (25f,Ayr,S,Dec 26)
Tom Costalot 106 (24f,Don,G,Jan 25)
Tom s Prize 110 (25f,Ain,G,Apr 4)
Tomogatchy 105 (20f,Gow,YS,Jun 6)
Tonoco 115 (25f,Wet,GF,Apr 21)
Top Rock 105 (19¹/₂f,Asc,GS,Nov 2)
Torduff Boy 115 (29f,Fai,G,Apr 21)
Torn Silk 102 (23¹/₂f,Wor,S,Jun 9)
Toulouse-Lautrec 103 (20f,Utt,S,Nov 8)
Trading Trouble 101 (20f,Crl,S,Mar 2)
Tresor De Mai 111 (19¹/₂f,Asc,GS,Feb 15)
Tresor Preziniere 101 (16f,Wcn,GF,Mar 20)
Tribal Dancer 110 (24f,Tau,GS,Feb 27)
Tribal King 109 (20¹/₂f,Wet,GS,Nov 2)
Tribal Run 101 (25f,Hex,HY,Nov 8)
Trinitro 108 (31f,Chl,GS,Nov 15)
Trooper 106 (25f,Hex,GF,Jun 1)
Trouble Ahead 112 (20¹/₂f,Per,G,Apr 23)
Trouble Next Door 103 (16f,Wcn,GF,Mar 20)
Truckers Tavern 118 (26¹/₂f,Chl,G,Mar 13)

True Rose 103 (16¹/₂f,Hex,G,Mar 29)
Trusting Tom 108 (20¹/₂f,Wet,GS,Nov 2)
Tudor King 101 (20f,Plu,GF,Apr 19)
Tumbleweed Glen 100 (19f,Her,GF,Apr 21)
Turgeonev 113 (16f,Kem,G,Feb 21)
Turn Two 110 (16f,Naa,S,Feb 8)
Tuska Ridge 107 (24f,Nav,S,May 19)
Tuxedo Junction 105 (20¹/₂f,Wor,G,Jun 8)
Twin Bob 100 (24f,Thu,Y,Feb 27)
Twisted Logic 109 (23¹/₂f,Exe,G,May 1)
Two Tears 103 (24f,Tau,S,Dec 28)
Tysou 108 (16f,Wcn,GF,Mar 20)

Ulusaba 104 (17¹/₂f,Crt,G,Aug 26)
Umbrella Man 105 (16¹/₂f,Don,G,Dec 13)
Un Jour A Vassy 110 (24¹/₂f,Chl,GF,Oct 29)
Uncle Bert 101 (21f,Sed,G,Apr 8)
Uncle Mick 101 (26¹/₂f,Nab,G,Apr 21)
Uncle Teddy 101 (23¹/₂f,Wor,G,Jly 10)
Uncle Wallace 101 (20¹/₂f,Kem,GS,Feb 7)
Upgrade 120 (21f,Wcn,G,Oct 27)

Valley Erne 105 (22f,Gal,Y,Jly 30)
Valley Henry 123 (21f,Wcn,G,Oct 27)
Vanilla Man 111 (20f,Nav,SH,Jun 9)
Verde Luna 105 (26¹/₂f,Fon,GF,Aug 23)
Versicium 100 (17¹/₂f,Str,G,Jly 27)
Victor Laszlo 100 (20¹/₂f,Per,GS,Aug 4)
Village King 106 (24f,Chp,GF,Oct 5)
Villair 102 (20f,Utt,S,Nov 8)
Vincent Van Gogh 100 (24f,Tau,F,Oct 17)
Vol Solitaire 110 (20f,Ayr,G,Apr 12)

Wahiba Sands 112 (16f,San,G,Apr 26)
Wain Mountain 102 (19¹/₂f,Chp,HY,Nov 27)
Walk On By 101 (16¹/₂f,Nab,S,May 28)
Walter Plinge 108 (21f,Sed,GF,May 3)
Walter s Destiny 104 (25¹/₂f,Wcn,GS,Nov 21)
Warrlin 106 (25f,Hex,GS,May 4)
Watership Down 100 (23¹/₂f,Wor,GF,Jly 24)
Wave Rock 110 (21f,Wcn,G,Oct 27)
Weaver George 109 (26f,Crt,G,Aug 24)
Wellie 108 (19¹/₂f,Chp,GF,Apr 22)
Wemyss Quest 104 (20f,Mar,GF,Jun 12)
West Hill Rose 104 (23¹/₂f,Exe,GS,Dec 19)
West Paces 105 (24f,Lud,G,Apr 10)
Western Chief 103 (26¹/₂f,Fon,GF,Aug 23)
What s The Score 109 (21f,Pun,YS,Jan 18)
Whatacharlie 100 (26f,Plu,GF,Apr 21)
Whereareyounow 109 (21f,Chl,GS,Jan 25)
Whitenzo 112 (25f,Ain,G,Apr 4)
Who Dares Wins 106 (26f,Crl,HY,Nov 11)
Wild Spice 111 (25f,Mar,S,Mar 3)
Winchester 108 (19f,Cat,G,Jan 18)
Windle Brook 102 (23¹/₂f,Wor,GF,Jun 29)
Winn s Pride 100 (20¹/₂f,Ban,S,May 18)
Winning Dream 116 (29f,Fai,G,Apr 21)
Wise King 103 (21¹/₂f,Nab,G,Apr 21)
Wonder Weasel 112 (27¹/₂f,Chl,GS,Nov 16)
Wontcostalotbut 103 (26¹/₂f,Fon,G,Dec 10)

Woodfield Gale 105 (19f,Cat,G,Nov 23)
Woodwind Down 105 (16¹/₂f,Sed,G,Aug 1)
Wotsitooya 115 (22f,Gal,Y,Jly 31)
Wrens Island 104 (23¹/₂f,Wor,GF,Jly 24)

Xaipete 110 (16f,Ayr,S,Nov 17)

Yakareem 103 (24f,Lud,F,Oct 10)
Yankee Jamie 105 (21¹/₂f,Ayr,GS,Dec 9)
Yankie Lord 104 (24f,Mus,GF,Dec 17)
Yann s 105 (24f,Tau,S,Feb 13)
Yorkshire Edition 100 (25¹/₂f,Wcn,GF,May 10)
You Re Special 104 (20f,Ncs,GS,Mar 15)
You re Agoodun 115 (24¹/₂f,Asc,GS,Nov 2)
Youlneverwalkalone 121 (24f,Thu,S,Dec 5)
Young Devereaux 109 (16f,Asc,S,Dec 21)
Young Ottoman 111 (24f,Nby,G,Dec 18)
Young Spartacus 112 (20¹/₂f,Chl,G,Mar 12)
Young Thruster 106 (26f,War,G,Nov 26)

Zafarabad 112 (24f,Kem,GF,Oct 26)
Zaffamore 103 (20f,Lud,S,Jan 16)
Zaffaranni 101 (24f,Nby,GS,Nov 13)
Zaggy Lane 108 (24f,Utt,G,May 4)

HURDLES

A Few Bob Back 106 (22¹/₂f,Kel,S,Nov 2)
Abadair 105 (16f,Thu,S,Dec 5)
Abajany 101 (17f,Her,GF,May 4)
Aberdeenshire 110 (16f,Nav,HY,Jly 12)
Aberthatch 104 (16f,Lei,S,Nov 30)
Able Native 109 (16f,Wet,G,Mar 6)
Above The Cut 108 (24f,Mar,G,Jly 7)
Accepting 101 (20f,Ncs,S,Nov 15)
Active Member 104 (16f,Gal,GY,Aug 4)
Ad Hoc 105 (24f,Chl,G,Dec 14)
Adecco 103 (16f,Lud,F,Oct 24)
Adelphi Boy 103 (17¹/₂f,Mar,GF,Jun 12)
Admiral Peary 104 (25¹/₂f,Plu,HY,Dec 4)
Adronikus 104 (17¹/₂f,Mar,GF,Jly 7)
Afro Man 102 (16¹/₂f,Hun,G,Feb 22)
After Me Boys 114 (24f,Ncs,GS,Mar 15)
Agitando 111 (16f,Kem,S,Dec 27)
Aimees Mark 111 (21f,Chl,G,Mar 12)
Airolo 107 (16f,Fai,HY,Mar 1)
Al Towd 107 (24f,Nav,S,Nov 17)
Alakdar 101 (19f,Exe,GF,Apr 15)
Alam 110 (16f,Ayr,S,Jan 2)
Albamores Madam 101 (25¹/₂f,Plu,GF,Mar 31)
Albatros 102 (18f,Fai,GF,Apr 21)
Albrighton 112 (22f,Fai,G,Apr 21)
Aleemdar 108 (16f,Naa,GY,Jly 10)
Alfy Rich 100 (17f,Exe,S,Mar 4)
Alice 102 (21¹/₂f,Sed,G,Aug 1)
All Bleevable 101 (16f,Fak,G,May 8)
All Honey 101 (24f,Lei,S,Nov 30)
Alleged Slave 103 (24f,Chp,HY,Jan 17)
Allude 104 (16¹/₂f,Ain,G,Apr 3)
Almapa 105 (16f,Utt,GF,Jly 18)
Almnadia 106 (17f,Her,GF,Sep 11)
Alpha Blues 105 (18f,Fai,GF,Apr 21)
Alphazar 102 (20f,Pun,YS,Jan 18)
Alpine Slave 107 (18¹/₂f,Fon,S,Mar 2)
Altay 120 (16¹/₂f,Ain,G,Apr 5)
Althrey Ruler 108 (21f,Lud,F,Oct 10)
Althrey Torch 104 (24f,Ban,G,May 3)

Alvaro 104 (26f,Hun,GF,Oct 11)
Alvino 100 (16f,Lud,G,Apr 2)
Always 100 (16f,Thu,S,Nov 28)
Always Game 110 (16f,Gal,S,Sep 9)
Always Rainbows 109 (16f,Wet,GS,Feb 1)
Amacita 101 (17f,Her,GF,Sep 11)
Amandas Princess 103 (20f,Pun,YS,Jan 18)
Amberleigh House 101 (17f,Ban,GS,Feb 7)
Ambidextrous 102 (16f,Utt,GF,Jly 18)
Ambry 112 (16f,Tow,G,May 24)
American President 102 (16f,Wet,S,Dec 26)
Amjad 100 (16¹/₂f,Per,GF,May 16)
Amplifi 105 (16f,Wcn,GS,Jan 18)
An Modh Direach 100 (16f,Fai,G,Apr 22)
Anatar 111 (21f,Chl,G,Mar 12)
Andrew Doble 102 (16f,Sth,GS,Jan 30)
Angel Delight 105 (21f,Kem,GS,Feb 7)
Angel s Folly 109 (16f,Pun,S,Feb 1)
Anna Creevy Lad 104 (16f,Nav,HY,Jly 12)
Anno Jubilo 111 (16f,Nav,HY,Jly 12)
Another Diamond 103 (22¹/₂f,Exe,GF,Apr 8)
Another Dude 102 (19f,Cat,GS,Dec 4)
Anvil Lord 102 (24f,Nav,YS,Nov 3)
Anxious Moments 106 (16f,Leo,S,Jan 12)
Anzal 106 (19f,Exe,GF,Apr 15)
Apadi 105 (16f,Fak,G,Mar 14)
April Allegro 114 (22f,Fai,G,Apr 21)
Aquarius 105 (17f,Tau,F,Oct 17)
Ar Muin Na Muice 108 (21f,Nby,G,Mar 22)
Arabian Moon 108 (18¹/₂f,Fon,G,Oct 6)
Arboreta 101 (20f,Gal,YS,Aug 1)
Arctic Gold 101 (20f,Ncs,G,Apr 1)
Arctic Sky 108 (21f,War,S,Dec 7)
Argento 104 (16f,Hay,S,Dec 28)
Arm And A Leg 100 (17f,Ban,GF,Aug 17)
Arribilo 107 (16¹/₂f,Hun,GF,Apr 21)
Ash Branch 101 (20f,Ban,GF,Aug 17)
Ashgan 107 (20f,Wor,GF,Jly 17)
Ashgar 100 (23f,Wet,HY,Nov 16)
Ashstorm 105 (20f,Leo,YS,Jan 26)
Ashton Vale 101 (17f,Nab,G,Sep 4)
Assured Movements 107 (16f,Tow,GS,Apr 29)
Astafort 100 (16f,Ayr,S,Jan 2)
Aston Mara 102 (20¹/₂f,Utt,G,Jun 3)
Astormydayiscoming 104 (16f,Utt,GF,Oct 5)
Atlantic Crossing 109 (20f,Crl,HY,Nov 28)
Atlantic Rhapsody 105 (16¹/₂f,Hay,G,Aug 3)
Atlastaboy 103 (20f,Hay,S,Nov 30)
Atum Re 107 (16f,Wcn,GS,Feb 15)
Audiostreetdotcom 110 (21f,War,S,Mar 8)
Avalanche 101 (22f,San,HY,Mar 7)
Avebury 105 (17f,Sed,G,Aug 1)
Avitta 108 (16f,Fak,S,Jan 22)
Aye Aye Popeye 106 (16f,Naa,GY,Jly 10)

Baby Gee 103 (16¹/₂f,Don,GS,Feb 28)
Bacchanal 114 (24¹/₂f,Nby,S,Nov 30)
Bachelors Pad 100 (17¹/₂f,Mar,G,Mar 15)
Back In Front 113 (16¹/₂f,Chl,G,Mar 11)
Back Nine 107 (16f,Leo,HY,Mar 2)
Back On Top 108 (20f,Fai,YS,Feb 22)
Backbeat 101 (19f,Nby,S,Feb 28)
Backcraft 105 (16f,Wet,GF,May 8)
Backview 104 (21f,War,HY,Jan 23)

Baclama 105 (20¹/₂f,Utt,G,Jun 3)
Bak To Bill 116 (21f,Kem,G,Feb 22)
Bal De Nuit 107 (17f,Chl,G,Apr 16)
Balakar 109 (16f,War,GF,Mar 23)
Balapour 119 (17f,Chl,G,Mar 13)
Bali Strong 102 (21¹/₂f,Hun,GF,Jun 3)
Balinahinch Castle 108 (25f,War,G,Nov 4)
Balladeer 101 (21f,Kem,GS,Jan 27)
Ballintry Guest 109 (16f,Gal,S,Sep 9)
Ballykettrail 106 (16f,Gal,YS,Jly 31)
Ballylesson 101 (18f,Kel,G,May 29)
Ballylusky 114 (16f,Hay,G,Dec 14)
Ballynattin Blue 104 (24¹/₂f,Ayr,S,Nov 16)
Ballynattin Buck 100 (20f,Leo,HY,Mar 2)
Ballysicyos 105 (24¹/₂f,Kem,S,Dec 27)
Ballystone 102 (24¹/₂f,Crl,S,Oct 26)
Ballyvaddy 107 (20f,Asc,G,Apr 2)
Baloo 104 (24¹/₂f,Utt,G,Sep 12)
Banasan 107 (16f,Nav,YS,Nov 3)
Banjo Hill 104 (18¹/₂f,Fon,G,Aug 26)
Bannow Bay 109 (24f,Leo,HY,Dec 28)
Banogue Lass 106 (16f,Thu,S,Dec 5)
Baracouda 126 (25¹/₂f,Asc,S,Dec 20)
Baranndee 102 (24¹/₂f,Per,GS,Jun 7)
Barcelona 105 (20f,Asc,G,Mar 25)
Barcham Again 107 (21f,Lud,G,Nov 25)
Bareme 112 (16f,Kem,GS,Feb 7)
Barrelbio 104 (20¹/₂f,Per,GF,May 16)
Barresbo 102 (22¹/₂f,Kel,GS,May 1)
Barton Dante 105 (16f,Wet,GF,Mar 17)
Barton Nic 105 (16f,Plu,HY,Feb 10)
Bathwick Annie 108 (20f,Chp,S,Dec 7)
Batman Senora 103 (20f,Ban,GF,Apr 12)
Battle Warning 114 (21f,Kem,G,Feb 22)
Bay Magic 101 (24¹/₂f,Ayr,S,Feb 8)
Be My Destiny 107 (17¹/₂f,Fol,HY,Dec 2)
Be My Friend 111 (17f,Ban,G,Mar 22)
Be Quiet 100 (19f,Naa,S,Jan 25)
Beat The Heat 103 (16f,Cat,G,Jan 18)
Beauly 101 (19f,Exe,GF,Apr 15)
Beaver Lodge 105 (19¹/₂f,Mar,GS,Dec 26)
Bee An Bee 105 (17f,Exe,GS,Dec 19)
Beechcourt 102 (16f,Pun,S,Nov 2)
Beedulup 103 (22f,Crt,G,Aug 24)
Beethoven 104 (20f,Chp,S,Dec 7)
Begsy s Bullet 103 (21¹/₂f,Sed,HY,Jan 21)
Bekstar 102 (20¹/₂f,Sth,GS,Dec 6)
Bell Lane Lad 101 (20f,Ban,GF,Apr 12)
Bellaficient 108 (16f,Naa,S,Feb 8)
Belle D Anjou 102 (17f,Chl,G,Mar 13)
Ben Ewar 104 (20f,Asc,G,Mar 25)
Benbecula 103 (20¹/₂f,San,HY,Mar 8)
Benbyas 114 (16¹/₂f,Chl,GS,Nov 17)
Bengal Boy 100 (16¹/₂f,Per,GF,May 16)
Benrajah 110 (25f,War,GF,Mar 23)
Bentyheath Lane 104 (17f,Ban,GF,Aug 17)
Bergamo 103 (16¹/₂f,Per,GF,Sep 25)
Bering Gifts 106 (16¹/₂f,Hun,GF,Oct 11)
Berkley 107 (24f,Pun,YS,Jan 18)
Bermuda Blue 101 (24¹/₂f,Utt,HY,Jun 6)
Bernardon 110 (16f,Wor,S,Jun 9)
Beseiged 103 (16¹/₂f,Per,GS,Jun 6)
Best Wait 105 (16f,Wcn,GF,Mar 20)
Betabatim 100 (16¹/₂f,Per,GF,May 16)
Better Moment 106 (17f,Nab,GF,Jly 28)
Better Think Again 104 (20f,Fai,YS,Feb 22)
Better Thyne 108 (24¹/₂f,Tau,GS,Dec 12)
Bewleys Hotels 101 (16f,Hay,G,Nov 7)
Beyond Control 105 (22f,San,HY,Mar 7)
Beyond The Pale 105 (16¹/₂f,Nby,HY,Dec 28)
Bhutan 103 (16¹/₂f,Str,GS,Mar 10)
Bid For Fame 105 (21f,Lud,G,Nov 25)

Big Quick 102 (22¹/₂f,Fon,GS,Feb 17)
Bigwig 104 (21f,Plu,S,Jan 13)
Bin It 101 (24¹/₂f,Utt,S,Nov 8)
Binneas 101 (16f,Naa,GY,Jly 10)
Bitter Sweet 106 (16f,Wor,G,Sep 15)
Black Church Lad 106 (16f,Gal,S,Sep 11)
Black Frost 105 (20f,Crl,GF,Apr 21)
Blackchurch Mist 105 (21¹/₂f,Chl,G,Apr 17)
Blame The Ref 114 (22f,Thu,Y,Feb 27)
Blazing Batman 105 (25¹/₂f,Cat,G,Feb 8)
Blood Sub 103 (20¹/₂f,Utt,S,Mar 15)
Blue Irish 105 (27¹/₂f,Sed,G,Oct 31)
Blue Ride 111 (21¹/₂f,Chl,G,Apr 17)
Blue Streak 103 (16f,Plu,GF,Oct 7)
Bluebell Line 100 (16f,Nav,HY,Mar 8)
Blueshaan 107 (17f,Her,GF,May 4)
Blunham Hill 100 (20f,Hay,G,Dec 14)
Bo Dancer 103 (20¹/₂f,Hex,GF,Sep 15)
Bob Ar Aghaidh 103 (20f,Chp,S,Nov 27)
Bob What 113 (16f,Gal,YS,Aug 1)
Bob s Gone 102 (21¹/₂f,Hun,GF,Apr 21)
Bobosh 108 (16¹/₂f,Chl,G,Oct 30)
Bobsbest 105 (17f,Her,GF,May 4)
Bodfari Rose 100 (17f,Ban,S,Nov 29)
Bodfari Signet 112 (20¹/₂f,Per,GF,May 16)
Bohill Lad 104 (19f,Exe,GF,Apr 15)
Bold Cardowan 108 (24f,Hex,GS,May 4)
Bold King 102 (24¹/₂f,Kem,G,Nov 20)
Bolshoi Ballet 106 (16¹/₂f,Nby,S,Mar 1)
Bolt Action 100 (20f,Chp,HY,Dec 27)
Bongo Fury 108 (16¹/₂f,Chl,GS,Nov 16)
Border Star 103 (16¹/₂f,Str,GS,Aug 10)
Borehill Joker 108 (16f,Tow,G,May 24)
Born Flyer 102 (16f,Nav,S,May 19)
Boss Doyle 110 (24f,Leo,HY,Dec 28)
Boss Morton 101 (23f,Wet,GF,Apr 21)
Bound 116 (17f,Chl,G,Dec 13)
Bow Strada 112 (21f,Chl,G,Mar 12)
Box Builder 100 (20¹/₂f,Wet,GS,May 30)
Boy Scout 111 (16f,Pun,F,Sep 29)
Bracey Run 103 (17f,Ban,S,May 18)
Brave Thought 107 (16f,Nav,S,Jan 11)
Brave Vision 104 (16¹/₂f,Kel,G,May 8)
Bravo 103 (20¹/₂f,Hun,GF,Mar 23)
Briar 103 (20¹/₂f,San,HY,Mar 7)
Brief Dance 108 (16f,Wcn,GS,Dec 5)
British Volunteer 107 (21f,Lud,G,Nov 25)
Broadnard 104 (24f,Lei,S,Nov 30)
Brockton Mist 105 (23f,Wet,G,May 23)
Broke Road 105 (16¹/₂f,Str,GF,Apr 27)
Brooklands Lad 103 (19f,Str,GF,Apr 19)
Brooklyn Breeze 108 (20f,Ayr,G,Apr 11)
Brooklyn s Gold 118 (16¹/₂f,Ain,G,Apr 5)
Brooksby Whorlton 103 (21¹/₂f,Sed,S,Dec 10)
Brooksie 104 (17f,Ban,G,May 3)
Broom Close 104 (20f,Crl,S,Oct 26)
Brother Joe 108 (25f,Wet,GS,Nov 2)
Brown Teddy 102 (16¹/₂f,Hun,G,Mar 12)
Brush A King 103 (20¹/₂f,Wet,GF,May 8)
Buckby Lane 106 (21f,Lud,S,Jan 3)
Buckskin Lad 106 (25¹/₂f,Cat,G,Feb 25)
Bude 101 (16f,Lud,G,Mar 16)
Bullfinch 100 (27¹/₂f,Sed,GF,Jly 17)
Bunkum 105 (20f,Chp,HY,Feb 4)
Burning Truth 105 (17f,Her,GF,Oct 3)
Burundi 107 (20¹/₂f,Wet,G,Feb 26)
Bushehr 100 (22¹/₂f,Str,GS,Aug 10)
Bushido 104 (17f,Sed,G,Mar 18)
Busted Flat 109 (23f,Wet,GS,Feb 1)
By Degree 107 (22f,Wcn,GS,Feb 6)

Caballe 103 (17f,Her,G,Feb 10)
Caesar s Palace 106 (24¹/₂f,Sth,GS,May 26)

Cailin s Perk 109 (16f,Leo,S,Jan 12)
Caishill 100 (16f,Thu,S,Nov 28)
Caliban 105 (16f,Hay,G,Nov 30)
Calling Brave 111 (19f,Nby,G,Dec 18)
Camair Crusader 100 (16f,Ncs,G,Apr 29)
Camaraderie 100 (16f,Utt,G,Sep 12)
Cambio 103 (20f,Wor,S,Jun 9)
Camden Tanner 113 (22f,San,HY,Feb 1)
Camdenation 104 (22¹/₂f,Fol,GS,Nov 5)
Cameron Bridge 109 (16f,Wcn,G,Oct 27)
Camp Nou 105 (22f,Nab,HY,Nov 19)
Campaign Trail 103 (17f,Crl,S,Oct 26)
Canada 109 (16¹/₂f,San,HY,Mar 8)
Canadiane 101 (17f,Tau,S,Jan 16)
Canal End 100 (25f,War,G,Mar 14)
Candarli 105 (17f,Exe,G,Mar 18)
Canterbury Jack 103 (24f,Wor,G,Sep 15)
Cape Stormer 102 (22f,Wcn,F,Apr 21)
Capricorn Princess 113 (16f,Utt,G,Apr 9)
Capriolo 105 (18¹/₂f,Fon,GS,Nov 11)
Captain O Neill 101 (20f,Chp,GF,May 8)
Captain Zinzan 101 (16f,Utt,G,Apr 9)
Caracciola 107 (16f,Utt,S,Nov 28)
Caraman 107 (16f,Nav,YS,Feb 16)
Careless 116 (16f,Naa,GY,Jly 10)
Carlesimo 107 (16f,Naa,GY,Jly 10)
Carlovent 113 (24f,Chp,S,Nov 9)
Carlyta 107 (16f,Wcn,GS,Nov 21)
Carneys Cross 109 (20f,Pun,YS,Jan 18)
Carnoustie 100 (17¹/₂f,Fol,GS,Nov 5)
Carpet Princess 105 (16f,Wcn,GS,Nov 21)
Carrigafoyle 101 (16¹/₂f,Don,S,Dec 14)
Case Of Poteen 103 (20f,Ayr,GS,Feb 23)
Cash N Credit 100 (16f,Sth,GF,Mar 18)
Cassinari 102 (20f,Gow,YS,Jun 6)
Castle Clear 110 (20¹/₂f,Per,GF,May 16)
Castle Kevin 108 (22f,Fai,G,Apr 21)
Castle Richard 103 (21¹/₂f,Sed,S,Dec 10)
Castleshane 113 (16f,Wcn,G,Nov 9)
Catalpa Cargo 108 (20f,Fai,HY,Mar 1)
Ceart Go Leor 103 (20f,Fai,G,Apr 22)
Cedar Master 101 (16f,Wor,G,May 22)
Celestial Light 100 (16f,Thu,SH,Feb 13)
Celio 105 (16f,Gal,S,Sep 10)
Celioso 103 (24¹/₂f,Crl,G,Mar 28)
Celtic Star 105 (18¹/₂f,Fon,G,Oct 6)
Celtic Vision 107 (18f,Kel,G,Mar 21)
Central Committee 105 (21¹/₂f,Sed,G,Oct 31)
Central House 120 (16f,Pun,SH,Feb 2)
Ceresfield 102 (16f,Wet,GF,Apr 21)
Cesaria 107 (16¹/₂f,Hun,GS,Nov 23)
Chabrimal Minster 101 (20f,Crl,S,Mar 6)
Chadswell 104 (26f,Crt,HY,Jun 3)
Champagne Lil 104 (24¹/₂f,Per,G,Apr 23)
Champaigne Ronnie 105 (22f,Leo,YS,Jan 26)
Chancy Native 100 (16f,Nav,HY,Jly 12)
Chanoud 103 (18f,Gal,Y,Aug 2)
Chaos Theory 100 (16¹/₂f,Hun,GS,Nov 23)
Charlies Future 108 (19¹/₂f,Tau,HY,Mar 10)
Charmouth Forest 100 (22f,Nab,GF,Apr 19)
Chateau Rose 102 (22¹/₂f,Fon,GS,Nov 11)
Chauvinist 111 (16¹/₂f,Asc,HY,Dec 21)
Chem s Truce 103 (16f,Wet,G,Nov 1)
Chermesina 110 (16f,Nav,S,May 19)
Cherry Hunter 106 (20f,Fai,HY,Mar 1)
Cherry Tart 104 (20¹/₂f,Per,GF,May 16)
Chevet Girl 106 (16f,Wet,G,Nov 1)

Cheyenne Chief 102 (16f,Ncs,S,Nov 15)
Chicago Bulls 106 (20f,Chp,S,Nov 9)
Chief Cashier 112 (16f,Kem,G,Feb 21)
Chief Witness 102 (25f,War,G,Mar 14)
Childer s Road 100 (16f,Gal,S,Sep 11)
Chivite 104 (16f,Fak,G,Mar 14)
Chopneyev 114 (22f,San,HY,Feb 1)
Christopher 105 (17f,Exe,G,May 15)
Christysconcerto 110 (22f,Thu,Y,Feb 27)
Cill Churnain 113 (20f,Wor,G,Sep 14)
Cinnamon Line 102 (24¹/₂f,Tau,S,Jan 28)
Cita Verda 115 (17f,Chl,G,Dec 13)
City Poser 101 (24f,Gal,YS,Aug 1)
Clanwilliam Source 101 (24f,Gal,YS,Aug 1)
Claramanda 104 (16f,Fai,S,Nov 30)
Clarendon 106 (16¹/₂f,Str,GF,Jly 14)
Classic Note 111 (16f,Fai,G,Apr 22)
Classified 113 (21¹/₂f,Chl,GS,Jan 25)
Claude Greengrass 107 (16f,Cat,G,Jan 18)
Clever Thyne 102 (21f,Lud,GS,Nov 14)
Clifton Fox 104 (20f,Chp,HY,Feb 4)
Clifton Mist 104 (19¹/₂f,Tau,S,Dec 28)
Clodoald 109 (16f,Utt,GF,Jly 18)
Clonroche Vinyls 101 (24¹/₂f,Per,G,Apr 23)
Cloone River 113 (16f,Pun,F,Sep 29)
Cloth Of Gold 101 (22f,Nab,G,Jun 14)
Cochis Run 112 (16f,Naa,GY,Jly 10)
Cock A Hoop 101 (24f,Chp,GF,May 8)
Cock Of The North 100 (19¹/₂f,Her,S,Dec 26)
College City 103 (19f,Cat,S,Mar 5)
Colliers Quay 107 (20f,Gal,YS,Aug 1)
Colline De Feu 103 (19f,War,GS,Nov 26)
Colnel Rayburn 110 (16f,Nav,YS,Feb 16)
Colombe D Or 104 (16f,Utt,GF,Jly 18)
Colonel Bradley 106 (19f,Naa,GF,Jly 24)
Colonel Frank 103 (16¹/₂f,Nby,S,Nov 29)
Colonial Rule 102 (21f,War,HY,Jan 23)
Colorado Falls 106 (17¹/₂f,Crt,HY,Jun 3)
Colourful Life 111 (16f,Leo,S,Jan 12)
Columba 104 (18f,Fai,HY,Mar 1)
Columbus 108 (24f,Ban,GF,Apr 12)
Comex Flyer 111 (21f,War,S,Dec 21)
Comfortable Call 105 (17¹/₂f,Mar,G,Apr 26)
Commanche General 103 (21¹/₂f,Mar,GS,Mar 3)
Commanche Hero 105 (22¹/₂f,Fon,GF,May 6)
Commanche Quest 102 (20f,Hay,S,Nov 30)
Commanche Summer 100 (22¹/₂f,Exe,GS,Dec 19)
Commanche Wind 105 (20¹/₂f,Wet,GS,May 30)
Commonchero 105 (16f,Thu,Y,Feb 27)
Compton Amica 104 (19¹/₂f,Tau,HY,Mar 10)
Consalvo 106 (16f,Gal,S,Jly 29)
Contract Scotland 103 (20f,Ncs,G,Apr 29)
Cool Investment 108 (20f,Asc,GS,Nov 2)
Cool Roxy 106 (16f,Fak,GS,Nov 24)
Coolnagorna 120 (21f,Nby,HY,Dec 28)
Coolsan 104 (25f,War,S,Dec 21)
Copeland 105 (16¹/₂f,San,GF,Apr 25)
Copper Moss 104 (16f,Ayr,S,Mar 7)
Copsale Lad 103 (16¹/₂f,Nby,S,Nov 29)
Coquelles 103 (19¹/₂f,Her,G,Feb 23)
Correct And Right 101 (17¹/₂f,Fol,S,Nov 18)
Corrib Supreme 102 (16f,Naa,HY,Mar 9)
Corroboree 103 (16f,Kem,S,Nov 6)

Cosmic Case 105 (16¹/₂f,Per,GF,Sep 25)
Cosmocrat 103 (17f,Chl,GS,Jan 25)
Cotopaxi 104 (20f,Chp,S,Nov 9)
Cottstown Boy 102 (24¹/₂f,Per,GF,May 15)
Coulthard 102 (16¹/₂f,Asc,S,Feb 15)
Court Champagne 104 (20¹/₂f,Utt,G,Apr 21)
Court Of Justice 110 (20f,Ayr,HY,Jan 25)
Covent Garden 118 (18f,Kel,GS,Mar 1)
Cowboyboots 102 (21f,Plu,S,Nov 4)
Crack Regiment 101 (24¹/₂f,Utt,HY,Jun 6)
Cregg House 101 (16f,Nav,S,Jun 9)
Creon 109 (24f,Chp,S,Nov 9)
Cresswell Cherry 102 (21¹/₂f,Mar,G,Oct 19)
Cresswell Gold 100 (20f,Chp,S,Dec 7)
Criaire Princess 102 (22f,Thu,Y,Feb 27)
Crimson Flower 100 (16f,Naa,S,Jun 3)
Crimson Pirate 107 (16¹/₂f,Hun,G,Mar 12)
Croi Bhriste 105 (16f,Naa,YS,Aug 5)
Croker 105 (17f,Ban,GS,Dec 18)
Crownfield 104 (16¹/₂f,Str,GF,Apr 19)
Cruagh Express 105 (16¹/₂f,Str,G,Oct 19)
Crunchy 106 (16f,Cat,S,Mar 5)
Crusset 104 (16f,Naa,Y,Feb 23)
Cruz Santa 108 (24¹/₂f,Utt,G,Sep 12)
Crystal D Ainay 101 (16f,Utt,S,Mar 15)
Cullian 107 (17¹/₂f,Fol,GS,Nov 5)
Cupboard Lover 113 (16f,Kem,G,Feb 21)
Curhubber Girl 107 (20f,Pun,S,Nov 2)
Curly Spencer 100 (20f,Crl,GS,Nov 11)
Curragh Hill 102 (16f,Gal,S,Sep 9)
Curtins Hill 103 (21f,Lud,G,Dec 12)
Cyindien 103 (22¹/₂f,Fol,GS,Nov 5)
Czar Of Peace 109 (16f,Gal,YS,Aug 1)

Dabarpour 104 (16f,War,F,May 11)
Dabus 100 (17¹/₂f,Mar,GF,Aug 31)
Dalian Dawn 112 (16f,Gow,YS,Jun 6)
Dame Fonteyn 100 (16¹/₂f,Chp,HY,Jan 17)
Dance In Tune 107 (17f,Nab,GF,Aug 5)
Dancer Polish 102 (16¹/₂f,Hun,GS,Nov 23)
Dancing Bay 105 (16f,Plu,S,Jan 13)
Dancing Pearl 108 (16f,Sth,GF,Mar 18)
Dancing Water 102 (16¹/₂f,Str,GS,Mar 10)
Dangerousdanmagru 101 (20¹/₂f,Utt,S,Dec 21)
Danimas 102 (16f,Mus,G,Feb 12)
Danse Slave 100 (17f,Her,GF,Mar 17)
Danteco 104 (21¹/₂f,Sed,G,Aug 1)
Dantes Reef 108 (16f,Fai,S,Nov 30)
Dantes Venture 102 (17f,Her,G,Oct 18)
Dantie Boy 104 (19¹/₂f,Tau,F,Mar 24)
Danton 102 (16f,Utt,S,Nov 28)
Daprika 100 (16¹/₂f,Hun,S,Jan 15)
Darapour 109 (20¹/₂f,Sth,GS,Dec 6)
Dardanus 100 (18¹/₂f,Fon,GF,Sep 24)
Darialann 112 (16f,Gal,YS,Jly 31)
Darina s Boy 105 (24f,Ban,S,Mar 5)
Dark Shadows 101 (16¹/₂f,Per,GS,Jun 6)
Dark Trojan 105 (20f,Fai,YS,Feb 22)
Dark n Sharp 116 (16¹/₂f,Chl,GS,Nov 17)
Dashing Home 108 (17f,Chl,G,Mar 13)
Dat My Horse 105 (19¹/₂f,Her,G,Nov 7)
Davenport Milenium 123 (16f,Kem,S,Dec 26)
Davoski 101 (16¹/₂f,Nby,G,Feb 8)
De Oralie 100 (17¹/₂f,Mar,GF,Jun 22)
Deano s Beeno 127 (25¹/₂f,Asc,S,Dec 20)

Deckie 100 (24f,Nav,S,Jun 9)
Deep Sunset 110 (16¹/₂f,San,S,Dec 7)
Deep Water 110 (16f,Ayr,GS,Dec 26)
Deferlant 106 (16f,Fak,GS,Dec 14)
Del Trotter 103 (16f,Ncs,G,Apr 1)
Delaware 108 (22¹/₂f,Str,S,Aug 1)
Delgany Royal 104 (20f,Pun,Y,Mar 16)
Demi Beau 114 (16¹/₂f,Don,GS,Jan 24)
Dene View 105 (19f,Cat,GS,Dec 4)
Deneises Blossom 101 (22f,Crt,G,Jun 8)
Denise Best 100 (20f,Ban,GF,Aug 17)
Deponey 107 (20f,Fai,HY,Mar 1)
Derivative 107 (16f,Utt,S,Nov 28)
Derring Bridge 101 (24¹/₂f,Sth,GS,May 26)
Desert Air 109 (16f,Kem,GS,Feb 7)
Desmond Tutu 109 (16f,Wcn,GS,Jan 18)
Desperate Measures 104 (16¹/₂f,Per,GS,Aug 4)
Detonateur 109 (16¹/₂f,Nby,S,Mar 1)
Diamond Cottage 107 (24f,Hex,GS,May 4)
Diamond Darren 100 (17f,Sed,G,Aug 9)
Diamond Joshua 105 (20¹/₂f,Wet,GF,Mar 23)
Diamonds Will Do 108 (16f,Fak,GS,Dec 14)
Dick Turpin 108 (16f,Plu,S,Feb 24)
Didifon 103 (16f,Ncs,GS,Nov 30)
Dihatjum 102 (16¹/₂f,Str,GF,Jly 14)
Diletia 101 (25¹/₂f,Plu,G,Oct 21)
Direct Bearing 117 (17f,Chl,G,Mar 13)
Dispol Rock 105 (17f,Tau,HY,Mar 10)
Distant Storm 100 (22¹/₂f,Fon,GS,Nov 11)
Distingo 107 (16¹/₂f,Hun,GS,Nov 12)
Diva 113 (16¹/₂f,Hun,GF,Oct 11)
Divet Hill 106 (21¹/₂f,Sed,GF,Jly 17)
Divulge 104 (17f,Sed,G,Aug 1)
Dixcart Valley 101 (25¹/₂f,Cat,G,Feb 8)
Dizzy Tart 104 (17f,Her,G,Feb 23)
Do It On Dani 107 (24f,Mar,GF,Sep 28)
Do L Enfant D Eau 114 (16¹/₂f,Nby,S,Mar 1)
Doc Morrissey 105 (18f,Gal,Y,Aug 2)
Doctor John 103 (16¹/₂f,Don,GS,Jan 24)
Doctor Wood 100 (19¹/₂f,Tau,S,Dec 28)
Doire-Chrinn 101 (16f,Leo,S,Feb 9)
Dollar Law 107 (17f,Chl,GS,Jan 25)
Domenico 109 (16f,Utt,S,Nov 28)
Domquista D Or 106 (17f,Utt,GF,Jly 18)
Don Fernando 103 (17f,Chl,G,Dec 14)
Don Ido 100 (16¹/₂f,Str,G,Oct 19)
Don t Sioux Me 100 (16f,Utt,G,Apr 9)
Donnini 100 (17f,Her,G,May 14)
Donodala 104 (16f,Gal,S,Sep 11)
Dont You Dare 100 (16f,Nav,S,Jun 9)
Double Account 118 (21f,Kem,G,Feb 22)
Double Blade 106 (17f,Sed,GF,Oct 1)
Double Honour 108 (21f,Kem,G,Feb 22)
Douceur Des Songes 102 (16f,Utt,HY,Jun 6)
Downpour 101 (19¹/₂f,Her,GF,May 4)
Dr Charlie 101 (20f,Chp,HY,Feb 4)
Dream Of Nurmi 108 (20¹/₂f,Utt,G,May 4)
Dream On Willie 104 (20f,Crl,HY,Nov 28)
Dream With Me 112 (16¹/₂f,Ain,G,Apr 5)
Drumbo 102 (20f,Fai,YS,Feb 22)
Dubai Seven Stars 120 (24f,Chp,S,Nov 9)
Dublin Native 104 (16f,Nav,HY,Jly 12)
Duchas Macnia 100 (16f,Leo,HY,Mar 2)
Duke Of Earl 100 (16¹/₂f,Hun,GS,Nov 23)
Dun An Doras 105 (17f,Exe,S,Dec 6)
Dungarvans Choice 111 (21f,Nby,S,Feb 28)

Dunlea 109 (21f,Chl,G,Nov 15)
Dunmanus Bay 104 (22¹/₂f,Str,GF,May 17)
Dunraven 107 (16f,Fak,GS,Oct 25)
Durlston Bay 103 (17f,Exe,G,May 15)

Eagles High 102 (16f,Nav,HY,Mar 8)
Easibrook Jane 100 (19f,Exe,S,Mar 4)
East Hill 102 (16f,Kem,G,Nov 20)
East Tycoon 105 (16¹/₂f,Str,GS,Mar 10)
Eastern Tribute 114 (20f,Ayr,HY,Jan 25)
Eastwood Drifter 104 (22¹/₂f,Fon,GF,Aug 23)
Ebinzayd 102 (18f,Kel,GS,May 1)
Ebony Light 100 (20f,Ban,S,Oct 28)
Ede Iff 104 (16f,Wcn,G,Oct 27)
Edmo Heights 118 (16¹/₂f,Ain,G,Apr 5)
Effectual 103 (23¹/₂f,Hay,G,May 4)
Egypt 104 (16¹/₂f,Str,GF,Jly 27)
Ei Ei 107 (16f,Sth,GS,Jan 30)
Eileen Alanna 101 (27¹/₂f,Sed,S,Nov 12)
El Hombre Del Rio 107 (24¹/₂f,Tau,S,Jan 28)
Ela D Argent 106 (16f,Plu,GF,Mar 31)
Ela Re 111 (17¹/₂f,Mar,G,Mar 29)
Elk Run 105 (16f,Naa,GY,Jly 10)
Ellamine 108 (16f,Utt,GF,Aug 27)
Ello Ollie 101 (20f,Ncs,G,Apr 29)
Eluna 105 (21¹/₂f,Chl,G,Apr 17)
Elvis 100 (16f,Plu,GF,Apr 19)
Emmet 111 (18f,Fai,S,Jan 19)
Emotional Moment 114 (21f,Chl,G,Mar 12)
Emperors Guest 106 (16f,Fai,G,Apr 22)
Emphatic 105 (22¹/₂f,Fon,GS,Nov 11)
Empire Park 109 (22f,Nab,S,Nov 6)
En El Em Flyer 102 (25¹/₂f,Plu,HY,Dec 4)
Encore Cadoudal 101 (16¹/₂f,Ain,G,Nov 29)
Endless Magic 106 (20f,Fai,YS,Feb 22)
Enitsag 102 (17f,Ban,GS,Feb 7)
Ennel Boy 103 (24f,Chl,G,Dec 13)
Entertainer 110 (24f,Chp,S,Nov 9)
Environment Audit 102 (16¹/₂f,Hun,G,Mar 2)
Epicure 106 (17f,Nab,GF,Jun 22)
Equivocal 106 (24f,Pun,YS,Jan 18)
Erins Lass 106 (19f,Str,GF,Jly 27)
Erris Express 100 (16¹/₂f,Don,GS,Jan 24)
Escort 103 (24f,Mar,G,Jly 7)
Estival Park 101 (16f,Nav,YS,Feb 16)
Estuary 101 (16¹/₂f,Hun,GF,Aug 26)
Estupendo 102 (22¹/₂f,Fol,HY,Dec 17)
Ettrick 108 (17f,Her,GF,May 4)
Evening Scent 108 (16f,Fai,SH,Dec 1)
Ever Present 107 (17f,Chl,GS,Jan 25)
Ewar Bold 102 (19¹/₂f,Her,G,Jun 4)
Executive Decision 108 (16f,Fak,GS,Dec 14)
Exodous 102 (16¹/₂f,Asc,G,Mar 25)
Exstoto 106 (22f,Wet,GF,Mar 23)
Eye Of The Tiger 106 (20f,Nav,S,Jan 11)
Eyes To The Right 101 (16¹/₂f,Hun,G,Mar 2)

Fabrezan 100 (16f,Kem,G,Nov 20)
Fair And Lively 108 (16f,Nav,HY,Jly 12)
Fair Prospect 102 (20¹/₂f,Utt,G,Apr 9)
Fair Question 106 (17f,Ban,G,Mar 22)
Fairwood Heart 108 (23¹/₂f,Hay,GS,Feb 8)
Falchion 100 (20f,Ayr,GS,Dec 9)
Family Venture 110 (24f,Mus,G,Jan 28)
Fandango De Chassy 103 (25f,War,HY,Jan 23)
Fantasmic 104 (16f,Utt,G,Apr 9)
Fantastic Champion 110

(16f,Kem,GS,Feb 7)
Far Horizon 109 (20f,Asc,S,Dec 20)
Far Pavilions 102 (16f,Cat,GS,Dec 4)
Fare Dealing 106 (20¹/₂f,Sth,GS,Dec 6)
Farinel 118 (24f,Chp,S,Nov 9)
Fashion Victim 105 (21f,Lud,F,Oct 10)
Fast Mix 102 (16f,Plu,HY,Jan 23)
Fatehalkhair 102 (21¹/₂f,Sed,GF,Jly 17)
Father Abraham 106 (18f,Fai,S,Jan 19)
Father D 101 (19f,Exe,GF,Apr 8)
Father Paddy 102 (21¹/₂f,Sed,G,Mar 18)
Feichead Ghra 100 (16f,Naa,S,Feb 8)
Ferdia s Friend 101 (16f,Gal,S,Sep 9)
Field Master 108 (19¹/₂f,Tau,GS,Nov 28)
Fifteen Reds 103 (21¹/₂f,Sed,GF,Jly 17)
Fifth Generation 111 (22¹/₂f,Str,GF,Jly 14)
Find The King 104 (22f,Fai,G,Apr 21)
Firestone 110 (16¹/₂f,Nby,S,Nov 29)
Firey Steel 105 (24f,Pun,YS,Jan 18)
First Embrace 102 (24¹/₂f,Tau,F,Oct 17)
First Truth 110 (17f,Ban,S,May 18)
Fishki s Lad 103 (22¹/₂f,Kel,G,Apr 7)
Flag Fen 105 (16f,Fak,GS,Oct 25)
Flame Creek 124 (17f,Chl,HY,Jan 1)
Flint Knapper 109 (20f,Nav,S,Jun 9)
Florida Coast 113 (16f,Pun,SH,Feb 2)
Florida Rain 103 (19f,Cat,GS,Dec 4)
Florries Son 108 (24f,Hex,GF,Oct 4)
Flossy Tops 101 (20¹/₂f,Wet,HY,Nov 16)
Flying Bold 102 (22f,Nab,GF,Aug 13)
Flying Fortune 101 (24¹/₂f,Nby,G,Mar 21)
Flying Gunner 112 (24f,Chp,S,Nov 9)
Follow Me 101 (21f,Chl,G,Nov 15)
Foreal 101 (20f,Leo,S,Jan 12)
Foreman 112 (21f,Kem,G,Feb 22)
Forest Green Flyer 101 (16f,Lei,HY,Jan 29)
Forest Heath 103 (16¹/₂f,Str,GF,Apr 12)
Forest Ivory 105 (24f,Chp,S,Nov 9)
Forest Tune 106 (16f,Lud,GF,Mar 19)
Fork Lightning 107 (20f,Asc,G,Apr 2)
Formal Bid 108 (20f,Asc,S,Feb 15)
Fortfield 105 (16f,Gow,YS,Jun 6)
Fortunate Dave 105 (16¹/₂f,Hun,G,Mar 2)
Fortune Island 106 (17f,Exe,GS,Feb 23)
Fortune s Fool 101 (17¹/₂f,Mar,G,Apr 26)
Forum Chris 101 (22f,Crt,HY,Jun 3)
Fota Island 121 (20f,Leo,HY,Dec 28)
Four Eagles 107 (16f,Thu,S,Dec 5)
Fox In The Box 104 (20f,Chp,S,Dec 7)
Fragrant Rose 103 (17f,Her,G,Nov 7)
Frankie Anson 103 (23f,Wet,GF,Apr 21)
Frankie s River 101 (20f,Chp,GF,May 8)
Frankincense 103 (21¹/₂f,Sed,HY,Jan 21)
Frazer s Lad 102 (17¹/₂f,Mar,G,Apr 26)
Fred s In The Know 105 (20f,Ayr,S,Nov 17)
Freddie s Comet 100 (17¹/₂f,Mar,GF,Jun 1)
Frederic Forever 104 (16¹/₂f,Chp,GF,Oct 5)
Free Return 103 (19¹/₂f,Her,GF,Sep 11)
Freeline Fantasy 102 (20f,Chp,S,Dec 7)
French Connection 106 (17¹/₂f,Mar,GS,Dec 26)
French Mannequin 103 (16¹/₂f,Str,GF,Apr 12)
Frentzen 100 (26f,Hun,GF,Mar 23)
Friend s Amigo 106 (16f,Fai,SH,Dec 1)
From Little Acorns 100 (21¹/₂f,Sed,GF,May 3)
Frosty Canyon 100 (25f,Wet,GS,Nov 2)
Full Irish 114 (20f,Mar,G,Mar 13)
Full On 102 (21f,Plu,S,Nov 24)
Fundamental 106 (16f,Ayr,GS,Feb 23)

Gabor 102 (16f,Plu,G,Sep 28)
Gaia Grey 101 (23f,Wet,G,May 23)
Gallileo Strike 103 (21f,Chl,G,Nov 15)
Galway Breeze 111 (16f,Gal,YS,Aug 1)
Gangsters R Us 101 (20f,Ayr,HY,Feb 8)
Gargoyle Girl 101 (16¹/₂f,Per,GF,May 15)
Garvivonnian 110 (16f,Gal,YS,Aug 1)
Gastornis 104 (16¹/₂f,Kel,G,Apr 7)
Gatorade 102 (20f,Wor,GF,Aug 24)
Gatso 102 (16f,Gal,S,Sep 10)
Gaudi 106 (20f,Pun,YS,Jan 18)
Gaynor 100 (17f,Nab,GF,Jun 22)
Gemini Guest 104 (16f,Gal,GY,Aug 4)
Gemmas Lady 110 (20f,Pun,YS,Jan 18)
General 113 (17f,Chl,HY,Jan 1)
General Duroc 105 (24¹/₂f,Ayr,S,Mar 8)
Generous Ways 104 (16f,Lud,GF,Mar 19)
Georges Girl 114 (16f,Pun,SH,Feb 2)
Geos 121 (17f,Chl,G,Dec 14)
Ghutah 103 (17f,Exe,F,Oct 1)
Gielgud 103 (19¹/₂f,Her,GF,Apr 21)
Gimme Shelter 104 (24f,Mus,G,Feb 12)
Gimmick 101 (16¹/₂f,Str,GF,Apr 12)
Gin Palace 107 (16f,Kem,G,Jan 18)
Gingko 102 (17f,Ban,G,Mar 22)
Giocomo 107 (20f,Chp,S,Dec 7)
Girl Of Pleasure 100 (16¹/₂f,Str,GS,Aug 10)
Glacial Missile 102 (19¹/₂f,Mar,GF,Aug 31)
Glacial Sunset 104 (24f,Chl,G,Dec 13)
Glen Warrior 104 (24¹/₂f,Tau,S,Jan 28)
Glenbar 107 (24f,Nav,S,Nov 17)
Glencomeragh 107 (18f,Fai,SH,Dec 1)
Glenhaven Nugget 107 (16f,Thu,Y,Feb 27)
Glenmoss Tara 107 (21f,Nby,G,Mar 22)
Glens Music 100 (20f,Nav,S,Jan 11)
Gli Gli 100 (20f,Fai,GF,Apr 20)
Gofagold 102 (18f,Kel,G,May 29)
Going Global 100 (19¹/₂f,Tau,GS,Nov 28)
Golden 101 (16f,Plu,G,Apr 29)
Golden Cross 115 (16f,Leo,S,Feb 9)
Golden Flight 104 (16¹/₂f,Str,GS,Mar 10)
Golden Rod 105 (20¹/₂f,Utt,G,Apr 21)
Golden Thunderbolt 100 (16f,Wet,GF,Apr 21)
Goldstreet 110 (20f,Leo,S,Jan 12)
Golfagent 102 (19f,Str,S,Aug 1)
Gone Far 104 (17f,Chl,GS,Jan 25)
Good Idea 109 (22f,Thu,Y,Feb 27)
Good Thyne Johnny 104 (24¹/₂f,Utt,G,May 22)
Goodonyou-Polly 106 (19f,Naa,GF,Jly 24)
Gospel Song 102 (17¹/₂f,Crt,HY,Jun 3)
Got News For You 107 (24¹/₂f,Tau,GS,Dec 12)
Gotham 101 (16f,Plu,GF,Oct 7)
Governor Daniel 101 (17¹/₂f,Mar,GF,Aug 31)
Graceful Dancer 108 (24¹/₂f,Tau,S,Feb 13)
Gralmano 115 (16f,Hay,G,May 4)
Grattan Lodge 106 (24¹/₂f,Crl,GS,Mar 2)
Grave Doubts 114 (16¹/₂f,Chl,G,Oct 30)
Grayslake 101 (24f,Lud,G,Mar 16)
Great As Gold 102 (17¹/₂f,Mar,GS,Mar 3)
Great Crusader 108 (24¹/₂f,Per,G,Apr 23)
Great Melody 105 (16f,Gal,S,Sep 11)
Green Ideal 111 (16f,Wcn,GS,Feb 6)
Greenback 106 (19¹/₂f,Her,G,Jun 4)
Greenfield 101 (16¹/₂f,Hun,S,Jan 15)
Greenhope 101 (16f,Kem,G,Feb 21)
Gregs Way 110 (19f,Str,GF,Jly 27)
Greywell 114 (16f,Thu,S,Dec 5)
Grimshaw 106 (16f,Naa,GY,Jly 10)

Ground Ball 110 (20f,Pun,Y,Mar 16)
Guard Duty 107 (25¹/₂f,Chl,GS,Nov 16)
Gumley Gale 114 (20¹/₂f,Utt,G,May 4)
Gumption 104 (24¹/₂f,Tau,GS,Feb 27)
Guru 109 (16f,Plu,S,Feb 24)
Gypsy 107 (20¹/₂f,Utt,G,Jun 3)

Haditovski 114 (16¹/₂f,Nby,S,Nov 29)
Hakim 107 (17f,Her,G,Feb 10)
Hale Bopp 108 (17¹/₂f,Fol,HY,Feb 11)
Half An Hour 103 (22f,Wcn,GS,Feb 6)
Half The Pot 111 (22¹/₂f,Fon,S,Mar 2)
Hamadeenah 101 (16f,Utt,G,Sep 12)
Handy Money 105 (17¹/₂f,Mar,S,Dec 5)
Happicat 107 (16f,Hay,G,May 4)
Happy Hussar 104 (22¹/₂f,Exe,GS,Dec 19)
Harchibald 109 (16¹/₂f,Ain,G,Apr 3)
Hardy Duckett 101 (16f,Fai,YS,Feb 22)
Hardy Eustace 124 (20f,Leo,HY,Dec 28)
Harmonic 107 (16f,Fak,G,Oct 9)
Harrovian 100 (16¹/₂f,Kel,S,Nov 13)
Harry The Ear 101 (16f,Gal,Y,Jly 29)
Harry s Dream 103 (19f,Nby,G,Dec 18)
Harvest Time 106 (16f,Gal,S,Sep 11)
Harvis 103 (20f,Hay,GS,Jan 18)
Hasty Prince 102 (16f,Utt,S,Dec 21)
Hat Or Halo 106 (16f,Nav,HY,Jly 12)
Hawadeth 115 (16¹/₂f,Ain,G,Apr 5)
Hawkes Run 103 (20f,Chp,S,Nov 9)
Hayaain 106 (24¹/₂f,Per,GF,May 15)
Haydens Field 114 (24f,Ban,G,May 3)
Heads Onthe Ground 108 (22f,Nav,S,Jan 11)
Healy s Bar 102 (16f,Pun,F,Sep 29)
Healy s Pub 111 (16f,Fai,G,Apr 22)
Heart Midoltian 106 (20f,Gal,YS,Aug 1)
Heavenly Comet 106 (24f,Nav,HY,Mar 8)
Heracles 103 (20f,Wor,G,Jun 8)
Heraclitean Fire 103 (16¹/₂f,Chl,GS,Nov 16)
Here Comes Steve 111 (24f,Ncs,HY,Jan 29)
Hermes Iii 110 (20¹/₂f,Wet,GS,May 30)
Hersilia 100 (24¹/₂f,Utt,G,May 22)
Hey Ref 102 (16f,Hay,GS,Feb 8)
Hi Cloy 115 (20f,Leo,S,Jan 12)
Hi Lily 100 (16f,Utt,HY,Jun 6)
Hidden Genius 102 (20f,Pun,Y,Mar 16)
Hifinanba 102 (16f,Plu,G,Apr 29)
High Drama 100 (17f,Tau,F,Oct 17)
High Hope 101 (16¹/₂f,Nby,G,Dec 18)
High Peak 102 (20f,Mus,G,Jan 28)
High Prospect 113 (16f,Fai,G,Apr 22)
Highbank 105 (17¹/₂f,Mar,G,Mar 15)
Hill Society 103 (20f,Nav,S,Jun 9)
Hilltop Harry 100 (24¹/₂f,Tau,S,Jan 28)
Hip Pocket 109 (21f,Chl,G,Nov 15)
Hirapour 106 (16¹/₂f,Don,GS,Jan 24)
Hirt Lodge 100 (22f,Crt,G,Jun 8)
His Nibs 109 (17¹/₂f,Fol,HY,Dec 2)
His Song 108 (17f,Chl,G,Dec 13)
Hoh Invader 107 (20f,Mus,G,Jan 17)
Holborn Hill 107 (21f,Kem,G,Feb 22)
Hollows Mill 101 (17f,Crl,GF,Apr 21)
Holy Orders 106 (16¹/₂f,Chl,G,Mar 11)
Homeleigh Mooncoin 109 (20f,Wor,GF,Aug 24)
Homer 102 (20f,Ban,GF,Aug 17)
Honey s Gift 102 (16¹/₂f,Hun,G,Mar 2)
Horner Rocks 102 (16f,Pun,S,Nov 2)
Hors La Loi 108 (16f,War,GF,Mar 23)
Hors La Loi Iii 117 (16f,Kem,S,Dec 26)
Hot Bunny 101 (18f,Gal,Y,Aug 2)
Hot Produxion 101 (19f,Nby,G,Mar 22)
Hot Shots 110 (16f,Kem,S,Dec 27)
Hot To Trot 102 (27f,Str,GF,May 17)
Howaya Pet 107 (24f,Nav,HY,Mar 8)
Howdydoody 108 (24¹/₂f,Tau,S,Jan 28)

Howrwenow 102 (20f,Asc,G,Apr 2)
Hugo De Grez 107 (24f,Ncs,GS,Mar 15)
Hugo De Perro 113 (24f,Ncs,GS,Mar 15)
Hume Castle 103 (19f,Naa,G,May 8)
Hunters Bar 112 (16f,Naa,GY,Jly 10)
Hunters Creek 102 (20¹/₂f,Wet,GF,Mar 23)

I Got It 104 (20f,Pun,Y,Mar 16)
I Got Rhythm 105 (16f,Cat,G,Feb 8)
I m On The Line 103 (19f,Naa,G,May 8)
Ice Crystal 104 (20f,Fon,HY,Jan 6)
Ice Saint 102 (19f,Str,GF,Jly 27)
Iceberge 103 (24f,Lud,G,Mar 16)
Ichi Beau 101 (16¹/₂f,Per,G,Apr 24)
Idaho D Ox 118 (16¹/₂f,Ain,G,Apr 5)
Ideal Du Bois Beury 107 (21f,Kem,G,Feb 22)
Ifrane Balima 105 (16f,Lei,HY,Nov 18)
Ikdam Melody 104 (19f,Naa,G,May 8)
Il Capitano 106 (19f,Exe,F,Oct 9)
Il Cavaliere 110 (21f,Kem,G,Jan 18)
Ilabon 104 (16¹/₂f,Nby,G,Mar 22)
Ilnamar 107 (16f,Hay,GS,Jan 18)
Image De Marque II 108 (17f,Chl,G,Mar 13)
Imperial De Thaix 106 (21f,Kem,G,Feb 22)
Impish Jude 111 (17f,Her,G,Feb 10)
Imprevue 102 (20f,Wor,GF,Jly 17)
In Contrast 111 (16¹/₂f,Nby,G,Feb 8)
In Extremis Ii 105 (21¹/₂f,Sed,G,Aug 9)
In Question 102 (21¹/₂f,Hun,GF,Jun 3)
In The Rough 103 (25f,War,HY,Jan 23)
Inca Trail 107 (21f,Lud,S,Jan 3)
Inch Perfect 101 (17f,Sed,G,Apr 8)
Inching Closer 111 (25¹/₂f,Chl,G,Mar 11)
Indien Royal 112 (17f,Chl,G,Apr 16)
Indigo Beach 105 (16f,Fak,G,May 8)
Indium 106 (16¹/₂f,Plu,GF,May 11)
Indoux 105 (20¹/₂f,San,HY,Feb 13)
Inducement 109 (16f,Tow,G,May 24)
Ingenu 107 (20f,Hay,GS,Feb 8)
Inigo Jones 103 (16f,Lud,GF,Mar 19)
Initiative 105 (17f,Sed,GF,Sep 6)
Inn Antique 106 (17f,Sed,S,Nov 12)
Insan Magic 105 (16f,Gal,S,Sep 11)
Intercounty 109 (16f,Thu,S,Dec 5)
Interdit 106 (24f,Ncs,GS,Mar 15)
Intersky Falcon 128 (16f,Kem,S,Dec 26)
Intymcginty 104 (19f,Nby,G,Dec 18)
Investor Relations 101 (17f,Nab,GF,Jun 22)
Inzarmood 102 (17¹/₂f,Crt,GS,Jun 5)
Iorana 106 (16f,Utt,GF,Oct 5)
Ipledgeallegiance 108 (20¹/₂f,Per,GF,May 16)
Ireland s Eye 102 (20¹/₂f,Wet,G,Feb 26)
Iris s Gift 118 (23¹/₂f,Hay,G,Mar 1)
Isam Top 110 (18¹/₂f,Fon,G,Aug 26)
Isard III 110 (20f,Asc,G,Apr 2)
Ishandraz 103 (25¹/₂f,Plu,GF,Mar 31)
Island Faith 106 (21f,Kem,G,Feb 22)
Island Stream 103 (16f,Fak,G,Mar 14)
Ismene 105 (20¹/₂f,Utt,HY,Jun 6)
It Takes Time 110 (25¹/₂f,Chl,GS,Nov 16)
Italian Counsel 108 (18¹/₂f,Fon,G,Aug 26)
Its Wallace Jnr 102 (16f,Wcn,GS,Dec 5)

Jaboune 117 (17f,Chl,G,Mar 13)
Jacdor 115 (17f,Chl,G,Dec 13)
Jack High 107 (19f,Naa,S,Nov 23)
Jack Owen Jack 108 (20f,Gal,YS,Aug 1)
Jackem 103 (23¹/₂f,Fak,G,May 8)
Jacopo 103 (21f,War,S,Mar 8)
Jahash 107 (17f,Chl,GS,Jan 25)
Jalb 111 (16f,Tow,G,May 24)

25)
Lordberniebouffant 102 (24f,Chl,G,Dec 13)
Lords Best 107 (22f,Wcn,GS,Nov 21)
Lorenco Lad 114 (16f,Gal,S,Sep 9)
Lorenzino 104 (22f,San,HY,Feb 1)
Lorgnette 102 (24¹/₂f,Tau,GS,Dec 12)
Lost In The Rain 105 (16f,Leo,S,Feb 9)
Lost The Plot 106 (22¹/₂f,Fon,GF,Sep 24)
Lotomore Lad 106 (24f,Nav,HY,Mar 8)
Lougaroo 101 (16¹/₂f,Chp,HY,Dec 27)
Louisville 101 (16f,Pun,S,Feb 1)
Loup Bleu 100 (17f,Tau,S,Dec 28)
Ludere 101 (24f,Ban,S,Mar 5)
Lunar Crystal 110 (17f,Ban,S,Aug 2)
Lynrick Lady 101 (22¹/₂f,Fol,HY,Dec 17)

Mac Hine 100 (20f,Chp,S,Nov 27)
Macabeo 107 (24f,Nav,S,Nov 17)
Maceo 113 (16¹/₂f,Nby,S,Nov 29)
Macintosh Man 109 (16f,Thu,S,Dec 5)
Macnance 105 (16f,Lei,S,Nov 30)
Maconnor 102 (16¹/₂f,Chp,HY,Feb 4)
Macs Valley 111 (16f,Pun,SH,Feb 2)
Madam Flora 110 (16f,Wcn,GS,Dec 26)
Madam Mosso 105 (24¹/₂f,Utt,HY,Jun 6)
Madam s Man 111 (24f,Ban,G,May 3)
Madge Carroll 110 (21f,War,GS,Nov 26)
Madonna Fan 106 (16f,Gow,YS,Jun 6)
Maggies Well 102 (21¹/₂f,Sed,HY,Jan 21)
Magic Combination 105 (20¹/₂f,Per,G,Aug 17)
Magic To Do 102 (17¹/₂f,Fol,G,May 3)
Magic Waters 101 (20¹/₂f,Wet,G,Feb 26)
Maiden Voyage 102 (20f,Ban,GF,Apr 12)
Majestic 113 (21¹/₂f,Chl,G,Apr 16)
Majestic Bay 105 (22f,Wcn,GS,Nov 21)
Majlis 105 (17f,Chl,HY,Jan 1)
Major Adventure 101 (24f,Mar,GF,Sep 28)
Major Drive 107 (24f,Mus,G,Feb 12)
Malakal 104 (17¹/₂f,Mar,GF,Sep 28)
Malek 105 (20f,Hay,GS,Feb 8)
Mamboesque 106 (19f,Cat,S,Mar 5)
Mamideos 109 (24f,Mar,GF,Oct 6)
Man O Mystery 115 (16¹/₂f,Ain,G,Apr 4)
Mana-Mou Bay 102 (17f,Sed,GF,Apr 26)
Maniatis 100 (16f,Hay,GS,Feb 8)
Maninga 105 (21f,Plu,S,Jan 13)
Manjoe 111 (16f,Thu,S,Dec 5)
Mantilla 100 (19f,Exe,GF,Apr 8)
Maragun 105 (19f,Exe,F,Oct 9)
Maraud 105 (25¹/₂f,Cat,G,Nov 23)
Marble Arch 120 (17f,Chl,G,Dec 14)
Marcus Du Berlais 109 (20f,Fai,YS,Feb 22)
Marcus Maximus 104 (16f,Lud,GF,May 6)
Marcus William 104 (18¹/₂f,Fon,HY,Jan 6)
Mardani 103 (21¹/₂f,Hun,GF,Jun 3)
Marigliano 110 (16f,Fak,GS,Dec 14)
Marigold 109 (18f,Leo,HY,Dec 26)
Mark It 101 (16f,Fak,GS,Nov 24)
Market Legacy 108 (16f,Nav,S,May 19)
Martha Reilly 106 (23f,Wet,GS,Feb 1)
Mason s Arch 108 (22f,Thu,Y,Feb 27)
Master Billyboy 109 (21f,Nby,S,Feb 28)
Master Florian 103 (21f,Plu,S,Nov 24)
Master George 111 (20f,Asc,HY,Nov 22)
Master McGrath 105 (24f,Chp,HY,Jan 17)
Master Papa 101 (16f,Thu,S,Nov 28)
Master T 109 (16¹/₂f,Str,GF,Apr 12)
Master Trix 108 (17¹/₂f,Fol,S,Nov 18)
Material Lady 100 (16f,Naa,GY,Jly 10)

Max Pride 104 (22¹/₂f,Exe,GS,Nov 5)
Maximus 100 (22¹/₂f,Fon,GS,Feb 17)
Maybe The Business 110 (22¹/₂f,Fol,HY,Dec 17)
Mazzini 103 (22¹/₂f,Fon,GF,Aug 23)
Meadows Boy 106 (19¹/₂f,Her,G,Nov 7)
Medallist 100 (17f,Sed,G,Mar 18)
Medelai 100 (17f,Her,GF,May 4)
Megazine 109 (17f,Tau,S,Dec 28)
Meggie s Beau 111 (19¹/₂f,Tau,GS,Feb 27)
Memsahib Ofesteem 105 (21¹/₂f,Chl,G,Apr 17)
Menelek Lord 104 (24¹/₂f,Ayr,S,Mar 8)
Mercato 108 (16¹/₂f,San,HY,Mar 8)
Mercede 104 (17¹/₂f,Crt,GS,Jun 5)
Merchants Friend 104 (16f,Naa,S,Jun 3)
Message Recu 104 (24f,Gal,YS,Aug 1)
Metal Detector 111 (21f,War,S,Mar 8)
Michael Mor 106 (18f,Fai,GF,Apr 21)
Michael s Princess 106 (21f,War,GS,Nov 26)
Mickley 102 (21f,Plu,GF,Oct 7)
Micksie Palmer 104 (16f,Naa,S,Jun 3)
Middlethorpe 107 (16f,Cat,S,Mar 5)
Midnight Coup 104 (21f,Lud,F,Oct 10)
Midnight Creek 103 (16¹/₂f,Kel,HY,Dec 2)
Mighty Minster 101 (16f,Ncs,S,Dec 16)
Mighty Montefalco 106 (24¹/₂f,Utt,GF,Aug 27)
Mike Simmons 104 (19f,War,GS,Nov 26)
Militaire 102 (16f,Wet,GS,Feb 1)
Milkat 107 (16f,Leo,S,Jan 12)
Mill Emerald 108 (20¹/₂f,Utt,G,Jun 3)
Millcroft Seaspray 104 (22f,Nab,HY,Nov 19)
Mind How You Go 112 (17¹/₂f,Mar,G,Mar 29)
Mind Over Matter 101(16f,Thu,S,Nov 28)
Mindanao 105 (16f,Ncs,GS,Nov 25)
Mini Dare 102 (24f,Lud,G,Feb 27)
Minivet 107 (16f,Cat,G,Feb 8)
Minstrel Hall 102 (16f,Ncs,G,Apr 1)
Mirjan 108 (20¹/₂f,Wet,GF,Apr 21)
Mirpour 103 (16f,Fai,S,Nov 30)
Misbehaviour 102 (17f,Her,G,Feb 23)
Mise Rafturai 107 (16f,Fai,G,Apr 22)
Mishead 100 (17¹/₂f,Mar,GF,Jun 1)
Miss Cool 101 (17f,Chl,G,Mar 13)
Miss Divin 109 (16f,Naa,GY,Jly 10)
Miss Janica 100 (19f,Str,S,Aug 1)
Miss Joppy 112 (16f,Thu,S,Dec 5)
Miss Lacroix 105 (19¹/₂f,Her,G,Jun 4)
Miss Rennenski 102 (22f,Crt,G,Aug 24)
Missatrick 107 (16f,Gal,S,Sep 9)
Mistanoora 107 (16¹/₂f,San,S,Nov 9)
Mister Chisum 109 (16f,Ncs,G,Apr 1)
Mister Dave S 104 (27¹/₂f,Sed,G,Mar 25)
Mister Friday 107 (20f,Ayr,GS,Feb 23)
Mister Kilford 112 (16f,Naa,GY,Jly 10)
Mister Magnum 100 (19¹/₂f,Tau,GS,Feb 27)
Mister McGoldrick 108 (16f,Wet,HY,Nov 16)
Mister Putt 105 (16f,Plu,HY,Mar 10)
Mistletoeandwine 102 (20f,Pun,YS,Jan 18)
Misty Ridge 103 (20¹/₂f,Per,G,Aug 17)
Mithak 107 (24f,Lud,S,Jan 16)
Mixsterthetrixster 111 (16¹/₂f,Don,GS,Jan 25)
Momentous Jones 103 (16f,Wcn,GS,Dec 5)
Moneytrain 108 (16f,Lei,HY,Dec 5)
Monger Lane 112 (21¹/₂f,Chl,S,Dec 31)
Monkerhostin 113 (16f,Hay,G,May 4)
Monsieur Tagel 100 (21f,Chl,GF,Oct 29)
Montagnette 101 (24f,Lei,S,Nov 30)

Montayral 101 (20f,Nav,S,Nov 17)
Monte Cristo 109 (16¹/₂f,Hun,GF,Oct 11)
Montessori Mio 103 (17f,Sed,G,Apr 8)
Monty s Double 100 (21f,Lud,GS,Nov 14)
Monty s Quest 100 (20f,Mus,G,Jan 28)
Montys Music 103 (20f,Fai,YS,Feb 22)
Moon Colony 100 (16¹/₂f,Str,GF,Jly 27)
Moon Spinner 106 (16¹/₂f,Hun,GF,Aug 26)
Moonshine Bay 108 (21f,Kem,G,Feb 22)
Moore s Law 110 (20f,Leo,YS,Jan 26)
Moorlands Again 104 (25¹/₂f,Plu,HY,Jan 23)
Moratorium 111 (16f,Gal,YS,Aug 1)
Moscow Fable 105 (16f,Naa,GY,Jly 10)
Moscow Tradition 103 (20f,Chp,S,Dec 7)
Moscow Whisper 100 (20¹/₂f,Per,G,Apr 23)
Moss Harvey 105 (23¹/₂f,Hay,GS,Feb 8)
Mossy Green 106 (19f,Naa,S,Jan 25)
Motcomb Jam 100 (16¹/₂f,Don,GS,Jan 24)
Mounsey Castle 100 (21f,Nby,G,Mar 21)
Mount Gay 104 (20¹/₂f,Per,GS,Aug 4)
Mountgarry 102 (19f,Naa,GF,Jly 24)
Moving Earth 108 (18¹/₂f,Fon,GS,Nov 11)
Moving On Up 113 (16¹/₂f,San,S,Dec 7)
Mr Cavallo 107 (26f,Hun,GF,Sep 29)
Mr Cool 112 (21¹/₂f,Chl,GS,Jan 25)
Mr Fluffy 107 (20f,Wor,G,Jun 8)
Mr Midaz 105 (17f,Sed,G,Mar 8)
Mr Sneaky Boo 110 (22f,Fai,G,Apr 21)
Mr Woodentop 105 (24¹/₂f,Ayr,S,Nov 16)
Mrs Pickles 104 (16¹/₂f,Chp,HY,Jan 17)
Muck Savage 107 (24¹/₂f,Tau,GS,Dec 12)
Mughas 111 (17f,Chl,G,Mar 13)
Muharib Lady 102 (25¹/₂f,Plu,GF,Mar 31)
Mukdar 102 (16f,Lei,HY,Feb 12)
Mulhacen 100 (18¹/₂f,Fon,GF,Apr 24)
Mullacash 111 (18f,Leo,HY,Dec 26)
Mullaghea Boy 106 (16f,Naa,S,Jun 3)
Mulligans Fool 107 (16f,Nav,HY,Jly 12)
Mulligatawny 105 (16¹/₂f,Nby,S,Nov 29)
Munadil 101 (16¹/₂f,Hun,GF,Aug 26)
Munster 105 (20f,Leo,S,Jan 12)
Murchan Benwood 100 (16f,Lei,HY,Feb 12)
Murphy s Cardinal 103 (22¹/₂f,Fol,HY,Jan 24)
Murray River 103 (16¹/₂f,Chp,GF,Apr 22)
Musally 104 (16f,Lud,GF,Mar 19)
Musical Mayhem 106 (25f,Wol,G,Jly 15)
Musimaro 103 (18¹/₂f,Fon,S,Mar 2)
Mutadarra 106 (16f,Wcn,G,Oct 27)
Mutakarrim 116 (16f,Gal,YS,Aug 1)
Mutineer 116 (16f,Leo,S,Feb 9)
My Bold Boyo 103 (17f,Exe,F,Oct 1)
My Galliano 110 (16f,Wcn,G,Oct 27)
My Good Son 109 (22¹/₂f,Str,GF,Jly 14)
My Legal Eagle 106 (17f,Ban,S,May 18)
My Line 105 (17f,Crl,HY,Nov 28)
My Name s Not Bin 102 (22f,Nav,S,Jan 11)
My Native Land 100 (25¹/₂f,Plu,HY,Dec 4)
My Shenandoah 102 (21¹/₂f,Hun,GS,Dec 12)
Mydante 110 (24f,Tow,GS,May 6)
Mylo 102 (17¹/₂f,Crt,G,Jun 8)
Mystic Hill 103 (22¹/₂f,Str,GF,Sep 7)
Mythical King 111 (16¹/₂f,Don,GS,Jan 24)

Nameless Wonder 101 (16¹/₂f,Chl,GS,Nov 16)

Nan Chero 106 (22f,Fai,G,Apr 21)
Narwhal 103 (16¹/₂f,Nby,S,Nov 29)
Nas Na Riogh 116 (16¹/₂f,Chp,HY,Dec 27)
Native Emperor 112 (24¹/₂f,Nby,S,Nov 30)
Native Estates 105 (24f,Leo,S,Jan 12)
Native Fox 105 (19¹/₂f,Her,G,Jun 4)
Native Guide 108 (16f,Nav,YS,Feb 16)
Native Heights 108 (16f,Nav,YS,Feb 16)
Native Jack 114 (20f,Leo,S,Jan 12)
Native Legend 104 (20f,Ayr,GS,Dec 9)
Native Leisure 107 (24f,Nav,S,Nov 17)
Native New Yorker 114 (17f,Chl,GS,Jan 25)
Native Ride 105 (22f,Thu,Y,Feb 27)
Native Sparkle 111 (16f,Nav,YS,Nov 3)
Native Tipp 108 (24f,Pun,S,Feb 1)
Natural 105 (17f,Crl,HY,Nov 28)
Navale 104 (17f,Her,G,Feb 23)
Nawamees 103 (16¹/₂f,Nby,G,Mar 22)
Needwood Spirit 106 (16f,Hay,G,Dec 14)
Negresko 108 (17f,Chl,G,Apr 16)
Neltina 104 (20f,Asc,G,Mar 25)
Nemisto 102 (20f,Asc,S,Dec 20)
Neutron 112 (16f,Wcn,GS,Dec 5)
Never 119 (17f,Chl,G,Dec 14)
New Leader 107 (25f,War,GF,Mar 23)
New Perk 106 (18¹/₂f,Fon,S,Mar 2)
Newhall 117 (16¹/₂f,Ain,G,Apr 5)
Newlands Gold 109 (17f,Chl,G,Mar 13)
Newsplayer 100 (16f,Kem,G,Nov 20)
Newtown Dancer 100 (16f,Wet,GS,Nov 2)
Niagara 106 (16f,Sth,G,May 9)
Nick s Choice 102 (21f,Lud,G,Mar 16)
Nickel Sun 115 (20f,Hay,G,Dec 14)
Night Fighter 104 (17¹/₂f,Crt,G,Aug 24)
Nijinsky Dancer 102 (16f,Fai,SH,Dec 1)
Nil Desperandum 123 (20f,Leo,HY,Dec 28)
Nip On 102 (21¹/₂f,Sed,S,Dec 10)
No Collusion 109 (21¹/₂f,Chl,GF,Apr 16)
No Discount 111 (24f,Nav,YS,Feb 16)
No Picnic 104 (17f,Crl,GS,Mar 2)
No Sam No 100 (22f,Crt,G,Aug 24)
Nobody Told Me 104 (20f,Fai,GF,Apr 20)
Noel s Pride 111 (20f,Wor,GF,Aug 24)
Noisetine 104 (20f,Chp,S,Dec 7)
Non So 117 (17f,Chl,G,Mar 13)
Non Vintage 102 (24f,Mar,G,Jly 7)
Nonantais 112 (19¹/₂f,Tau,GS,Feb 27)
Nonchalant 108 (16f,Nav,YS,Nov 3)
Nordic Prince 106 (24f,Ban,GS,Dec 18)
North Point 103 (16f,Plu,GF,Apr 21)
Norvin 102 (25f,War,GF,Mar 23)
Noshinannikin 104 (20¹/₂f,Wet,GF,Mar 23)
Nouf 103 (17f,Ban,G,May 3)
Nouveau Cheval 101 (20f,Fon,GF,May 6)
Nova Girl 104 (24¹/₂f,Tau,F,Oct 17)
Novi Sad 103 (16¹/₂f,Asc,G,Mar 25)
Nowell House 103 (16f,Ncs,HY,Jan 15)
Numbersixvalverde 110 (16f,Fai,S,Nov 30)
Nutley King 101 (16f,Kem,S,Dec 27)
Nuzum Road Makers 105 (16f,Gal,S,Jly 29)

Occam 105 (17f,Ban,GF,Aug 17)
Ocean Tide 105 (24f,Ban,GS,Dec 18)
October Mist 113 (20f,Hay,G,Dec 14)
Oddlydodd 102 (21¹/₂f,Hun,GF,Apr 21)
Ojays Alibi 103 (17f,Tau,S,Feb 13)
Old California 102 (18¹/₂f,Fon,G,Dec 10)
Old Feathers 109 (21f,Chl,G,Nov 15)

Old Marsh 113 (16f,Kem,G,Feb 21)
Old Rolla 101 (24¹/₂f,Ayr,S,Feb 8)
Old Rouvel 101 (23¹/₂f,Hay,G,May 4)
Oliver Cromwell 102 (24¹/₂f,Kem,S,Dec 27)
Oliverjohn 107 (18f,Fai,SH,Dec 1)
Olivier 101 (21f,Lud,GS,Nov 14)
On The Day 102 (27¹/₂f,Sed,S,Dec 26)
On The Jetty 108 (16f,Nav,YS,Feb 16)
On The Mend 110 (20f,Nav,S,Jan 11)
On The Run 102 (16f,Wol,S,Jly 5)
Onassis 100 (21f,Plu,S,Jan 13)
One For Me 104 (16¹/₂f,Str,G,Oct 19)
Oneway 101 (17f,Ban,GS,Feb 7)
Only Little 106 (17f,Tau,GS,Nov 28)
Only When Provoked 102 (20¹/₂f,Utt,G,Jun 3)
Only Words 105 (17f,Sed,HY,Feb 11)
Only You 100 (20f,Wor,G,May 22)
Ontos 111 (20f,Ayr,HY,Jan 25)
Orangerie 106 (22f,Wcn,GS,Nov 21)
Orchard Fields 101 (23f,Wet,GS,Feb 1)
Ososhot 108 (23f,Wet,GS,Feb 1)
Otahuna 100 (17f,Sed,GF,Sep 6)
Oulton Broad 105 (20¹/₂f,Utt,GF,Jun 30)
Our Armageddon 114 (17¹/₂f,Mar,G,Mar 29)
Our Vic 112 (16f,Wcn,GS,Feb 6)
Out Of The Shadows 106 (16f,Wet,GF,Mar 17)
Over Anxious 112 (19f,Nby,GS,Nov 13)
Over The Bar 111 (24f,Nav,YS,Feb 16)
Over The First 111 (20f,Nav,S,Jan 11)
Over The Hill 106 (27¹/₂f,Sed,G,Oct 31)
Overstrand 102 (17f,Chl,G,Mar 13)
Owen Roe 100 (17f,Her,G,Dec 3)

Pacifyc 102 (22¹/₂f,Str,GF,Jly 14)
Paco Venture 108 (20¹/₂f,Sth,GS,Dec 6)
Pailitas 107 (16¹/₂f,Hun,GF,Jun 3)
Palace Storm 104 (19f,Naa,G,May 8)
Palua 106 (24¹/₂f,Kem,G,Feb 21)
Paperising 108 (20f,Hay,G,Dec 14)
Paperprophet 108 (20f,Mus,GS,Dec 28)
Pardishar 104 (16¹/₂f,Ain,G,May 17)
Paris Pike 103 (24f,Ncs,GS,Mar 15)
Parish Oak 108 (16f,Tow,GS,Apr 29)
Park City 105 (16¹/₂f,Str,GF,Apr 12)
Party Airs 107 (16f,Leo,S,Feb 9)
Patriot Games 102 (20f,Ain,G,Apr 4)
Patrizio 110 (16f,Gow,YS,Jun 6)
Patsy Veale 109 (16f,Gal,YS,Aug 1)
Pauntley Gofa 101 (16f,Lud,GF,May 6)
Pay It Forward 111 (18f,Fai,SH,Dec 1)
Paylander 102 (20f,Fon,GF,Mar 19)
Peacock Theatre 102 (20¹/₂f,Utt,G,Jun 3)
Peartree House 101 (16f,Utt,GF,Aug 27)
Pease Blossom 102 (16f,Naa,S,Feb 8)
Peejay Hobbs 104 (20¹/₂f,Wol,G,Jly 15)
Penny Farthing 107 (16f,Gow,YS,Jun 6)
Penny Pictures 106 (17f,Ban,S,Mar 5)
Pennys From Heaven 104 (17f,Nab,GF,Jly 28)
Pepe Galvez 105 (16¹/₂f,Nby,G,Mar 22)
Peppercorn 101 (16¹/₂f,Nby,S,Nov 30)
Per Amore 103 (16f,Wcn,GS,Nov 21)
Periwinkle Lad 111 (22f,Fai,G,Apr 21)
Perkys Pride 103 (16f,Nav,S,May 19)
Perouse 101 (16¹/₂f,Chp,G,Mar 19)
Persian King 106 (16¹/₂f,Chp,GF,Oct 5)
Persian Waters 112 (21f,Chl,G,Mar 12)
Personal Assurance 103 (16¹/₂f,San,HY,Feb 13)
Pertemps Susie 100 (19f,Exe,GF,Apr 8)
Pertino 108 (16f,Utt,GF,Aug 27)
Peter s Two Fun 104 (20f,Wor,G,Jun 8)
Petolinski 109 (20f,Chp,S,Dec 7)
Phar City 103 (20f,Chp,S,Dec 7)

Phar From Fair 100 (17¹/₂f,Fol,HY,Dec 17)
Phardante Sky 105 (16f,Nav,HY,Jly 12)
Pharlave 106 (16f,Pun,F,Sep 29)
Pharly Reef 105 (16f,Utt,S,Jun 3)
Physical Graffiti 103 (16f,Lei,HY,Feb 12)
Picture Palace 100 (19¹/₂f,Her,G,Feb 23)
Pillar Of Fire 103 (21¹/₂f,Mar,G,Oct 19)
Pillar Rock 107 (16f,Fai,G,Apr 22)
Pip Moss 103 (19¹/₂f,Tau,HY,Mar 10)
Pirandello 110 (16¹/₂f,Str,GF,Apr 12)
Pizarro 113 (21f,Chl,G,Mar 12)
Plenty Courage 104 (22¹/₂f,Kel,G,Apr 7)
Plettenburg Bay 107 (16f,Gal,S,Sep 11)
Pluto 103 (20¹/₂f,Hex,GF,Sep 15)
Plutocrat 111 (20f,Mus,GS,Dec 28)
Poachers Run 101 (21¹/₂f,Sed,GF,Oct 1)
Poachin Again 103 (18f,Leo,HY,Dec 26)
Poc Fada 103 (18f,Gal,Y,Aug 2)
Poker Pal 106 (24f,Pun,SH,Feb 2)
Polar Champ 116 (24f,Chp,S,Nov 9)
Polar Red 115 (17f,Chl,G,Mar 13)
Polish Cloud 103 (16¹/₂f,Nby,S,Mar 1)
Polish Flame 112 (20f,Ayr,HY,Jan 25)
Political Sox 104 (20f,Ayr,S,Mar 8)
Pollster 113 (16f,Nav,S,Jun 9)
Polly Native 103 (16f,Thu,SH,Feb 13)
Polyphony 104 (22¹/₂f,Fon,S,Mar 3)
Poppet 104 (17f,Her,GF,Mar 17)
Porak 106 (16¹/₂f,Asc,GS,Nov 2)
Pornic 104 (16f,Hay,G,Dec 14)
Potoffairies 109 (24f,Nav,S,Nov 17)
Prairie Run 101 (21¹/₂f,Sed,GF,May 3)
Premier Estate 101 (21f,Plu,S,Nov 24)
Pridewood Fuggle 100 (17f,Nab,GF,Jun 22)
Priests Bridge 112 (23¹/₂f,Hay,G,Mar 1)
Prime Attraction 103 (16¹/₂f,Hex,G,Oct 12)
Prime Minister 104 (17f,Her,GF,May 4)
Prince Albert 105 (16f,Fak,G,Oct 9)
Prince Among Men 108 (17f,Her,G,Nov 7)
Prince De Galles 104 (24¹/₂f,Utt,S,Jun 13)
Prince Dimitri 102 (16f,War,S,Dec 21)
Prince May 106 (20f,Leo,S,Jan 12)
Prince Nicholas 101 (26f,Crt,GS,Jun 5)
Prince Slayer 107 (16f,Plu,S,Feb 24)
Princess Lauren 100 (16f,Naa,S,Feb 8)
Princess Sophie 100 (17¹/₂f,Crt,GS,Jun 5)
Princesse Grec 102 (16¹/₂f,Str,GS,Aug 10)
Prokofiev 112 (24f,Chp,S,Nov 9)
Proper Squire 107 (22¹/₂f,Fon,GF,May 6)
Property Partners 104 (20f,Pun,S,Feb 1)
Property Zone 104 (16f,Wet,GF,Mar 17)
Protagonist 105 (17f,Chl,G,Dec 13)
Protocol 108 (17¹/₂f,Mar,GS,Dec 26)
Proverbial Gray 101 (16¹/₂f,Per,GS,Aug 4)
Puck Out 107 (16f,Gal,Y,Jly 29)
Puntal 114 (16f,Sth,G,May 9)
Pure Fun 104 (24f,Lud,F,Oct 10)
Putup Or Shutup 109 (20f,Asc,GS,Nov 2)

Quabmatic 106 (17f,Exe,G,Mar 18)
Quadco 109 (16f,Gal,S,Sep 10)
Quarter Masters 105 (20¹/₂f,Wet,GS,Dec 7)
Quazar 116 (16¹/₂f,Chl,GS,Nov 17)
Quedex 104 (19f,Str,GF,Apr 19)
Queen s Pageant 109 (19¹/₂f,Tau,GS,Nov 28)
Quiet Water 109 (21f,Lud,G,Feb 27)
Quintus 114 (16f,Naa,GY,Jly 10)

Ragdale Hall 107 (19¹/₂f,Her,GF,Sep 11)
Rainbow Chase 102 (16f,Cat,G,Feb 8)
Rainbow Dance 109 (20f,Wor,G,Jun 8)
Rainbow River 109 (16f,Fak,G,Mar 14)
Rainbows Aglitter 108 (17f,Chl,G,Dec 13)
Rakaposhi Raid 107 (24¹/₂f,Per,G,Aug 17)
Ramblees Holly 101 (19¹/₂f,Mar,GF,Oct 6)
Ranelagh Gray 102 (16¹/₂f,Hun,G,Feb 22)
Rapid Deployment 103 (24f,Pun,SH,Feb 2)
Rare Ouzel 110 (21f,Chl,G,Nov 15)
Rathkenny 101 (16f,Thu,Y,Feb 27)
Ratified 102 (24f,Mar,GF,Oct 6)
Raunchy 101 (22f,Crt,G,Aug 26)
Ravenswood 106 (25¹/₂f,Chl,G,Mar 11)
Really 110 (16f,Pun,S,Feb 1)
Reasonable Reserve 107 (24¹/₂f,Per,G,Aug 17)
Recess 105 (16¹/₂f,Chl,GS,Nov 16)
Red Canyon 112 (22¹/₂f,Str,GF,Jly 14)
Red Halo 104 (17f,Ban,S,Aug 2)
Red Hot Robbie 102 (22¹/₂f,Str,G,Oct 31)
Red Lion 101 (16f,Wcn,GS,Feb 15)
Red Marauder 105 (24f,Ncs,S,Feb 24)
Red Socialite 102 (21f,Nby,G,Mar 21)
Red Sun 108 (16¹/₂f,Chl,G,Oct 30)
Red Wine 109 (16¹/₂f,Nby,S,Feb 28)
Redlyn 109 (22f,Thu,Y,Feb 27)
Redouble 100 (19¹/₂f,Tau,GS,Nov 14)
Reflex Blue 108 (21f,Lud,F,Oct 10)
Regal Act 102 (19f,Naa,S,Nov 23)
Regal Exit 104 (16¹/₂f,Nby,G,Feb 8)
Regello 106 (16f,Thu,S,Dec 5)
Regency Red 102 (20¹/₂f,Per,G,Aug 17)
Reggae Rhythm 100 (16¹/₂f,Hun,G,Mar 12)
Reggie Buck 103 (17f,Her,GF,Apr 5)
Remington 104 (16f,Lud,G,Mar 16)
Reminiscer 111 (20f,Pun,YS,Jan 18)
Rescindo 105 (16f,Wcn,GS,Feb 15)
Reverse Swing 108 (16f,Wcn,GS,Nov 21)
Reviewer 110 (16¹/₂f,Nby,S,Mar 1)
Rhinestone Cowboy 114 (16f,Wcn,GS,Feb 15)
Ri Na Realta 105 (19f,Naa,S,Nov 23)
Riccarton 100 (17f,Nab,GF,Jly 28)
Richie s Delight 102 (20f,Wor,G,Aug 3)
Rift Valley 104 (20f,Asc,G,Apr 2)
Right 103 (17f,Ban,GS,Dec 18)
Right Job 113 (16f,Nav,YS,Feb 16)
Rigmarole 115 (16f,Kem,G,Feb 21)
Rigolade 106 (20f,Ban,GF,Aug 17)
Rimosa 100 (17¹/₂f,Mar,GF,Jly 7)
Rising Generation 100 (19¹/₂f,Her,G,Nov 7)
Risky Reef 121 (16¹/₂f,Ain,G,Apr 5)
River Captain 101 (20¹/₂f,Per,G,Aug 17)
River City 108 (17f,Nab,S,Nov 6)
River Ness 108 (21¹/₂f,Sed,G,Oct 15)
River Pirate 100 (16¹/₂f,San,HY,Feb 13)
Robber Baron 104 (19f,Exe,GS,Nov 5)
Robbo 104 (24f,Ncs,S,Feb 24)
Robert The Bruce 106 (20f,Ayr,S,Mar 8)
Robyn Alexander 106 (18¹/₂f,Fon,S,Dec 26)
Rocamadoura 115 (16f,Naa,GY,Jly 10)
Rocastle Lad 106 (17f,Tau,GS,Nov 28)
Rock n Cold 102 (17f,Her,GF,Apr 21)
Rocky Island 105 (20f,Hay,G,Nov 7)
Rodalko 108 (21f,Lud,G,Nov 25)
Rogue Spirit 100 (17¹/₂f,Fol,G,May 3)
Role Model 101 (20f,Wor,G,Aug 3)
Roman Candle 101 (19f,Str,GF,Jly 27)

Roman King 102 (16¹/₂f,Chp,HY,Dec 27)
Romany Hill 101 (22¹/₂f,Str,GS,Aug 10)
Romero 103 (24f,Tow,GS,May 6)
Romil Star 103 (16¹/₂f,Per,GF,May 16)
Rookery Lad 104 (16¹/₂f,Hun,GF,Apr 21)
Rooster Booster 123 (17f,Chl,G,Dec 14)
Rosaker 106 (16f,Fai,SH,Dec 1)
Rosalyons 100 (22¹/₂f,Kel,GS,Mar 1)
Rosarian 109 (24¹/₂f,Nby,G,Mar 21)
Rosco 109 (20f,Asc,G,Apr 2)
Rose D April 107 (17f,Crl,HY,Nov 28)
Rose Tina 101 (21f,Kem,GS,Feb 7)
Rosie Redman 101 (16f,Ncs,S,Dec 16)
Ross Comm 104 (22f,Fai,G,Apr 21)
Rosslea 112 (20¹/₂f,Utt,S,Dec 20)
Rostropovich 110 (24f,Nav,YS,Feb 16)
Rotuma 101 (17f,Sed,G,Mar 18)
Roveretto 108 (22f,Hay,S,Nov 30)
Royal Barge 102 (20f,Ban,GF,Aug 17)
Royal Beluga 100 (17¹/₂f,Mar,GF,Jun 1)
Royal Castle 110 (21¹/₂f,Sed,G,Oct 15)
Royal Destiny 107 (16f,Naa,GY,Jly 10)
Royal Emperor 116 (24f,Ncs,GS,Nov 30)
Royal Hector 100 (16f,Fak,GS,Nov 24)
Royal Wanderer 100 (16¹/₂f,Kel,GF,Oct 6)
Roymillon 108 (26f,Hun,GF,Sep 29)
Rudi Knight 101 (20¹/₂f,Utt,G,May 4)
Rudi s Pleasure 108 (21f,Chl,G,Nov 15)
Rudolf Rassendyll 100 (20¹/₂f,Hun,S,Jan 15)
Rugged Man 100 (17¹/₂f,Crt,HY,Jun 3)
Rum Pointer 110 (22f,Wcn,GS,Dec 26)
Runaway Bishop 107 (24f,Mar,G,Jly 7)
Running Machine 100 (21f,Plu,S,Nov 4)
Running Man 109 (16f,Wcn,G,Nov 9)
Running On 103 (20f,Fai,G,Apr 22)
Running Times 101 (19¹/₂f,Her,G,May 14)
Rushen Raider 101 (24f,Hex,G,May 11)
Russian Court 102 (17f,Ban,GS,Feb 7)
Russian Gigolo 104 (20f,Ban,GS,Oct 12)
Rust En Vrede 100 (16¹/₂f,Str,GF,Apr 12)
Rutledge Red 105 (19¹/₂f,Mar,GF,Oct 6)

Sacundai 102 (20f,Ain,G,Apr 5)
Sadler s Secret 107 (24¹/₂f,Tau,F,Oct 17)
Safari Paradise 115 (21f,Kem,G,Feb 22)
Safe Enough 103 (21f,Plu,GF,Oct 7)
Safe Route 109 (18f,Fai,S,Jan 19)
Sage Dancer 105 (16f,Naa,GY,Jly 10)
Saintsaire 103 (17f,Chl,G,Mar 13)
Saitensohn 115 (19f,Nby,GS,Nov 13)
Salaman 100 (24¹/₂f,Tau,F,Apr 3)
Sally s Twins 105 (24f,Hex,GF,Oct 4)
Sam Rockett 101 (27f,Nab,GF,Jly 31)
Sam s Profiles 104 (20¹/₂f,Utt,G,Apr 21)
Samasakhan 105 (21f,Chl,GS,Nov 17)
Sammy Samba 102 (21f,Lud,F,Oct 24)
Samon 115 (21f,Chl,G,Mar 12)
Samsaam 108 (20f,Asc,G,Apr 2)
San Giorgio 100 (26f,Hun,GF,Sep 29)
Sandholes 111 (20¹/₂f,Per,GF,May 16)
Sandysaran 109 (24f,Pun,S,Feb 1)
Santa Lucia 106 (20f,Mus,G,Jan 17)
Santenay 126 (16f,Kem,S,Dec 26)
Saorsie 101 (17f,Nab,GF,Jly 31)
Saratov 101 (17¹/₂f,Mar,GF,Jun 12)
Sasha Star 102 (16¹/₂f,Hun,GF,Jun 3)
Saspys Lad 111 (16f,Utt,GF,Aug 27)
Satco Express 120 (20f,Leo,HY,Dec 28)
Satcoman 104 (24f,Pun,YS,Jan 18)
Satshoon 103 (24¹/₂f,Tau,S,Jan 28)
Savannah Mo 103 (22f,Ayr,S,Mar 7)
Saxon Mill 109 (17¹/₂f,Mar,S,Dec 5)
Say Again 117 (16f,Gal,YS,Aug 1)

Scarletti 108 (16¹/₂f,Chl,G,Oct 30)
Scarthy Lad 104 (16f,Thu,S,Nov 28)
Scented Air 106 (16¹/₂f,Str,G,Oct 19)
Scotish Law 101 (21f,Lud,GF,Mar 19)
Scottish Memories 113 (20f,Fai,SH,Dec 1)
Scratch The Dove 101 (21f,Kem,GS,Feb 7)
Sea Ferry 107 (24¹/₂f,Tau,GS,Dec 12)
Sea Mark 108 (17¹/₂f,Mar,GF,Jun 1)
Search And Destroy 105 (16¹/₂f,Don,G,Dec 13)
Secret Conquest 100 (17f,Sed,GF,Sep 6)
See The Lady 106 (24f,Pun,S,Feb 1)
See You Sometime 114 (21¹/₂f,Chl,G,Apr 16)
Sel 106 (17¹/₂f,Fol,GS,Nov 5)
Self Defense 122 (16¹/₂f,San,HY,Feb 1)
Sento 105 (22f,Nab,GF,Apr 19)
September Moon 101 (22¹/₂f,Exe,GF,Apr 15)
Serenus 113 (16f,Kem,S,Dec 27)
Set Dance 101 (17¹/₂f,Fol,G,May 3)
Setting Sun 103 (16¹/₂f,Per,GS,Aug 4)
Sh Boom 114 (20¹/₂f,Utt,S,Dec 20)
Shaadiva 100 (18¹/₂f,Fon,GF,Apr 24)
Shaffishayes 103 (17¹/₂f,Mar,G,Mar 15)
Shalako 106 (17f,Tau,GS,Nov 28)
Shalbeblue 100 (16f,Mus,G,Feb 12)
Shamsan 106 (20f,Wor,GF,Jly 17)
Shannon Gale 103 (20f,Pun,Y,Mar 16)
Shannon Light 100 (27f,Nab,S,May 28)
Shannon s Pride 103 (20f,Ayr,GS,Dec 9)
Shared Account 106 (20f,Pun,S,Nov 2)
Sharlom 103 (16f,Utt,GF,Oct 5)
Sharmy 104 (16¹/₂f,Hun,GS,Nov 12)
Sharp Act 101 (16f,Leo,S,Jan 12)
Sharp Belline 109 (24¹/₂f,Sth,GS,May 26)
Sharpaten 110 (16f,Gal,YS,Aug 1)
Shawings 104 (18f,Leo,HY,Dec 26)
She s A Corker 104 (22¹/₂f,Str,GS,Oct 31)
Sheer Frustration 105 (16f,Gal,S,Sep 10)
Sheer Martina 106 (18f,Gal,Y,Aug 2)
Shemdani 104 (16¹/₂f,Asc,S,Feb 15)
Sherbet Lad 105 (20¹/₂f,San,HY,Mar 7)
Shifting Moon 109 (22¹/₂f,Str,GF,Jly 14)
Shirzadiyan 101 (18f,Fai,SH,Dec 1)
Shoshoni Warrior 104 (24¹/₂f,Tau,S,Jan 28)
Show The Way 100 (16¹/₂f,Hun,GF,Aug 26)
Shuil Monty 102 (16f,Naa,GY,Jly 10)
Sikasso 105 (16f,Ncs,S,Dec 16)
Silent Sound 100 (16f,Plu,GF,Mar 31)
Silk Trader 105 (16¹/₂f,Nby,S,Nov 29)
Silken Thyne 105 (23f,Wet,GS,Dec 7)
Silver Birch 106 (20f,Chp,S,Nov 27)
Silver Buzzard 104 (22f,San,HY,Mar 7)
Silver Charmer 105 (19f,Nby,M,Mar 22)
Silver Dagger 102 (16f,Naa,Y,Feb 23)
Silver Gift 106 (26f,Hun,GF,Oct 11)
Silver Knight 113 (24f,Ncs,GS,Mar 15)
Silver Steel 111 (24f,Nav,S,Nov 17)
Silver Swan 105 (20f,Pun,S,Feb 1)
Silvertown 109 (17f,Her,GF,Apr 5)
Simply Supreme 110 (20f,Hay,S,Dec 28)
Sir Alfred 100 (16f,Lud,G,Mar 16)
Sir Lamb 104 (20¹/₂f,Hex,GF,Jun 1)
Sir Ruscott 107 (24f,Lei,S,Nov 30)
Sireric 108 (24f,Ncs,S,Feb 24)
Sister Superior 103 (20¹/₂f,Utt,HY,Jun 6)
Skenfrith 103 (20f,Crl,GF,Apr 21)
Ski Jump 116 (16f,Naa,GY,Jly 10)
Skibb 106 (20f,Pun,Y,Mar 16)
Sky To Sea 105 (16f,Mus,GF,Dec 17)
Slainte 108 (20f,Fai,HY,Mar 1)

Sloane Street 102 (16¹/₂f,Hun,G,Mar 2)

Slooghy 105 (24¹/₂f,Nby,G,Feb 8)

Slush Fund 107 (16f,Nav,YS,Feb 16)

Smiths Landing 106 (20¹/₂f,Hex,G,Mar 29)

Smooth Sailing 100 (16f,Wor,G,May 22)

Smuggler s Song 110 (16f,Naa,S,Feb 8)

Snowmore 103 (20¹/₂f,Sth,GS,Dec 6)

Snowy Ford 107 (20f,Pun,S,Feb 1)

Sockittothem 100 (19f,Naa,GF,Jly 24)

Socrates 108 (16f,Gow,YS,Jun 6)

Sofisio 107 (16f,Utt,GF,Jly 18)

Soho Fields 105 (21f,Lud,G,Feb 27)

Solar System 105 (24f,Leo,S,Jan 12)

Solerina 113 (20f,Leo,YS,Jan 26)

Some Buzz 109 (16f,Fai,G,Apr 22)

Something Dandy 110 (17f,Chl,G,Apr 16)

Son Of A Gun 100 (16f,Fak,G,Mar 14)

Sonevafushi 121 (17f,Chl,HY,Jan 1)

Sonny Jim 101 (18¹/₂f,Fon,S,Feb 3)

Sossus Vlei 102 (16f,Plu,S,Jan 13)

Southerncrosspatch 105 (24¹/₂f,Tau,GS,Dec 12)

Sovereign 106 (19¹/₂f,Her,G,Jun 4)

Sovereign State 103 (16¹/₂f,Per,GS,Aug 4)

Spaghetti Junction 101 (21f,Nby,G,Mar 22)

Spainkris 109 (16f,Ayr,HY,Jan 14)

Special Present 108 (16¹/₂f,Str,GF,Sep 7)

Spectrometer 117 (17f,Chl,G,Dec 13)

Spectroscope 116 (17f,Chl,G,Mar 13)

Spendid 101 (25f,Wet,GS,Nov 2)

Spirit Glen 108 (16f,Fai,S,Nov 30)

Spirit Leader 120 (17f,Chl,G,Mar 13)

Spirit Of Love 106 (22f,Crt,G,Jun 8)

Splendour 106 (24f,Nav,S,Jun 9)

Spoof 100 (27f,Kel,S,Nov 19)

Sporazene 100 (16f,Ayr,G,Apr 12)

Spree Vision 104 (20¹/₂f,Per,G,Aug 17)

Spring Dawn 105 (16¹/₂f,Hun,GS,Nov 12)

Springbok Attitude 101 (17f,Exe,F,Oct 1)

Springfield Scally 122 (24f,Chp,S,Nov 9)

Spud One 108 (16¹/₂f,Hun,G,Feb 22)

Squantum 101 (20f,Pun,S,Feb 1)

Stafford King 106 (20f,Wor,GF,Jun 29)

Stage Affair 112 (16f,Leo,HY,Dec 29)

Stand Aside 104 (20f,Asc,HY,Nov 22)

Standing Bloom 105 (21f,War,HY,Jan 23)

Star Blakeney 101 (22¹/₂f,Utt,GF,Jun 30)

Star Clipper 106 (18f,Fai,S,Nov 30)

Star Councel 110 (24f,Mus,G,Jan 28)

Star Trooper 103 (17f,Sed,S,Dec 26)

Starzaan 112 (16¹/₂f,Ain,G,Apr 3)

Stashedaway 103 (20f,Fai,GF,Apr 20)

Statim 109 (16f,Naa,S,Feb 8)

Steel Band 102 (20f,Fai,HY,Mar 1)

Steel Mill 103 (22¹/₂f,Exe,GS,Nov 5)

Stennikov 102 (19¹/₂f,Mar,G,Oct 19)

Stero Heights 101 (21¹/₂f,Sed,G,Sep 6)

Stoney Path 104 (20f,Wor,G,May 22)

Stormy Beech 107 (17f,Sed,HY,Feb 11)

Stormy Lord 112 (16f,Ayr,GS,Dec 26)

Strait Talking 100 (16f,Fak,G,Apr 21)

Strawberry Hill 103 (17f,Sed,G,Apr 8)

Streamsforth Lad 100 (21f,Lud,GF,Mar 19)

Strictly Speaking 100 (19f,Nby,GS,Nov 13)

Strike Alliance 101 (16f,Naa,YS,Aug 5)

Stromness 109 (24f,Chl,S,Dec 31)

Strong Arrow 101 (23¹/₂f,Fak,G,May 8)

Strong Flow 110 (24¹/₂f,Tau,GS,Feb 27)

Strong Project 106 (24f,Nav,S,Jun 9)

Strong Resolve 105 (16f,Ayr,S,Mar 7)

Subiaco 105 (16¹/₂f,Don,GS,Jan 24)

Sud Bleu 118 (17f,Chl,HY,Jan 1)

Sudden Shock 106 (21¹/₂f,Chl,GS,Jan 25)

Sully Shuffles 105 (24f,Nav,S,Jun 9)

Sullys Hope 115 (17f,Chl,G,Dec 13)

Sum Leader 111 (22f,Fai,G,Apr 21)

Summer Bounty 102 (16¹/₂f,Chl,GS,Nov 16)

Sun Bird 105 (16¹/₂f,Kel,S,Nov 13)

Sun King 106 (17¹/₂f,Mar,GF,Jun 22)

Sunday Rain 110 (16f,Utt,GF,Aug 27)

Sungio 103 (18¹/₂f,Fon,GS,Nov 11)

Sunridge Fairy 107 (17f,Her,GF,Sep 11)

Sunshine Boy 103 (18¹/₂f,Fon,G,Mar 17)

Super Nomad 103 (16f,Cat,G,Feb 8)

Super Sammy 100 (19f,Cat,G,Nov 23)

Superb Leader 100 (17f,Ban,GS,Dec 18)

Supreme Being 103 (20f,Nav,S,Jan 11)

Supreme Fortune 101 (21¹/₂f,Hun,GS,Dec 12)

Supreme Hill 105 (20f,Asc,S,Dec 20)

Supreme Native 105 (16¹/₂f,Chp,GF,Oct 5)

Supreme Optimist 103 (16¹/₂f,Kel,S,Nov 13)

Supreme Piper 105 (19¹/₂f,Tau,S,Jan 16)

Supreme Prince 109 (20f,Chp,S,Nov 9)

Supreme Quest 112 (24f,Ban,G,May 3)

Supreme Toss 111 (21f,War,S,Dec 7)

Supreme Venture 103 (24f,Nav,GY,Mar 22)

Surabaya 104 (26f,Hun,GF,Sep 29)

Sure Future 109 (24¹/₂f,Kem,S,Dec 27)

Surprising 105 (23¹/₂f,Hay,G,May 4)

Swan Hill 100 (20f,Gow,YS,Jun 6)

Swan Knight 103 (16¹/₂f,Str,GS,Mar 10)

Sweet Minuet 101 (18¹/₂f,Fon,GF,Apr 24)

Swift Pearl 109 (20¹/₂f,Per,GS,Aug 4)

Sylva Legend 101 (16¹/₂f,Chp,GF,May 8)

Ta Ta For Now 104 (20¹/₂f,Hex,G,Apr 30)

Tacin 101 (21f,Kem,GS,Jan 27)

Tactful Remark 113 (16f,Wor,S,Jun 9)

Tagar 105 (19f,Nby,GS,Nov 13)

Taillefer 105 (20¹/₂f,San,HY,Feb 14)

Takagi 105 (24f,Nav,GY,Mar 22)

Take A Drop 103 (21f,Chl,GS,Nov 17)

Take Flite 109 (16f,Gal,YS,Aug 1)

Take Heed 105 (16f,Fak,GS,Nov 24)

Takeyourtime 103 (20¹/₂f,Per,GS,Jun 7)

Talarive 117 (18f,Kel,GS,Mar 1)

Tales Of Bounty 102 (25¹/₂f,Chl,GS,Nov 16)

Talking Tactics 103 (16f,Pun,Y,Mar 16)

Tamango 102 (19f,Exe,G,Oct 22)

Taming 109 (16f,Utt,GS,Jun 13)

Tana River 113 (20¹/₂f,San,HY,Mar 8)

Tandys Bridge 109 (20f,Leo,HY,Mar 2)

Tango Royal 104 (16f,Kem,S,Dec 27)

Tanikos 100 (16f,Wet,G,Feb 26)

Tap Dance 103 (21¹/₂f,Sed,G,Aug 1)

Taranges 103 (16f,Naa,S,Jun 3)

Tarboush 102 (16f,Lud,G,Mar 16)

Tardar 108 (21f,Chl,G,Mar 12)

Tathmin 102 (26f,Hun,GF,Oct 11)

Tees Components 117 (24f,Ncs,GS,Nov 30)

Teknash 106 (16f,Pun,S,Nov 2)

Telimar Prince 116 (17f,Chl,G,Dec 13)

Teme Valley 105 (17f,Sed,G,Apr 8)

Temper Lad 105 (22¹/₂f,Fon,GF,May 6)

Temple Dog 105 (16f,Hay,S,Dec 28)

Tensile 108 (20¹/₂f,Utt,GF,Oct 5)

Terek 105 (16¹/₂f,Hun,GS,Nov 12)

Terino 101 (16¹/₂f,Hun,GF,Apr 21)

Texas Ranger 104 (21f,Chl,G,Mar 12)

Thaix 106 (18f,Leo,HY,Dec 26)

Thari 105 (21f,Chl,G,Mar 12)

That s Fine 103 (24¹/₂f,Tau,S,Jan 28)

The Bongo Man 108 (24¹/₂f,Tau,F,Oct 17)

The Bunny Boiler 110 (24f,Nav,S,Nov 17)

The Culdee 105 (22f,Fai,G,Apr 21)

The Dark Flasher 112 (16f,Fai,G,Apr 22)

The Dark Lord 104 (16¹/₂f,Hun,G,Feb 22)

The Flyer 109 (21f,War,S,Dec 21)

The French Furze 119 (16f,Ncs,GS,Nov 30)

The Full Nelson 101 (22¹/₂f,Fon,S,Mar 3)

The Gatherer 107 (17f,Chl,G,Mar 13)

The Gene Genie 101 (17f,Tau,S,Dec 28)

The Granby 106 (24¹/₂f,Don,GS,Mar 1)

The Guy 102 (16f,Nav,S,Jan 11)

The Kew Tour 105 (20¹/₂f,Wet,GF,Mar 23)

The Last Cast 102 (16¹/₂f,San,S,Nov 9)

The Lyme Volunteer 104 (24¹/₂f,Tau,GS,Nov 14)

The Names Bond 102 (17f,Ban,S,Nov 29)

The Nomad 103 (17¹/₂f,Mar,GS,Nov 21)

The Pennys Dropped 109 (17f,Crl,GS,Mar 2)

The Rile 108 (20¹/₂f,Wet,GS,Nov 27)

The River Joker 106 (20¹/₂f,Wet,GS,Dec 7)

The Tall Guy 100 (25¹/₂f,Chl,GF,Oct 29)

The Villager 104 (20f,Chp,G,Oct 23)

Theatre Lane 109 (20f,Pun,YS,Jan 18)

Themanfromcarlisle 100 (20f,Fon,GF,Mar 19)

Therealbandit 103 (22f,Nab,G,Apr 21)

Thesis 105 (17f,Tau,S,Feb 13)

This Thyne 109 (24¹/₂f,Per,G,Aug 17)

Thisthatandtother 115 (16f,Wcn,GS,Jan 18)

Thistlekicker 103 (16¹/₂f,Per,GF,May 15)

Three Lions 112 (17f,Her,G,Feb 10)

Threezedzz 101 (16f,Plu,G,Sep 28)

Through The Rye 119 (17f,Chl,G,Mar 13)

Throwaline 103 (20f,Ayr,G,Apr 11)

Thrower 105 (20¹/₂f,Utt,S,Dec 21)

Thumper 104 (16¹/₂f,Hun,G,Mar 12)

Tiawana 102 (16f,Naa,S,Jun 3)

Tickton Flyer 100 (19f,Cat,GS,Dec 4)

Tiger Grass 108 (24¹/₂f,Per,GF,Sep 26)

Tik-A-Tai 108 (22¹/₂f,Fon,GS,Nov 11)

Tikram 113 (16f,Hay,G,May 4)

Timber King 112 (16f,Gal,YS,Aug 1)

Time N Tide 105 (17f,Ban,S,Nov 29)

Timeless Chick 100 (17f,Her,G,Nov 7)

Timidjar 104 (16¹/₂f,Hun,GF,Apr 21)

Tip Kash 103 (19¹/₂f,Mar,S,Nov 21)

Tissifer 104 (16¹/₂f,Don,GS,Jan 25)

Tobesure 106 (23f,Wet,GS,Feb 1)

Tollbrae 107 (20f,Chp,S,Dec 7)

Tomenoso 110 (16f,Wet,G,Mar 6)

Tommy Trooper 100 (18¹/₂f,Fon,S,Feb 3)

Tony The Piler 104 (20f,Crl,G,Mar 28)

Torose 101 (20f,Gow,YS,Jun 6)

Tory Boy 106 (16¹/₂f,Str,S,Aug 1)

Tosawi 107 (19¹/₂f,Tau,GS,Nov 28)

Toscanini 107 (19f,Exe,S,Mar 4)

Tosheroon 108 (20f,Asc,GS,Nov 2)

Totally Scottish 106 (18f,Kel,G,Mar 21)

Totland Bay 105 (22¹/₂f,Fon,GF,Sep 24)

Touch Of Love 119 (16f,Naa,GY,Jly 10)

Touch Supreme 107 (24f,Nav,S,Nov 17)

Toulon Rouge 101 (21¹/₂f,Sed,HY,Jan 21)

Toulouse 107 (16f,Wcn,GS,Jan 18)

Tourniquet 106 (25f,War,G,Nov 4)

Traditional 102 (16f,Nav,HY,Jly 12)

Trained Bythe Best 104 (20f,Hay,G,Nov 7)
Tramantano 106 (16¹/₂f,Nby,S,Nov 29)
Translucid 106 (16f,War,GS,Nov 26)
Travellers Heir 102 (16¹/₂f,Hun,G,Feb 22)
Treasured Guest 101 (16¹/₂f,Chl,GS,Nov 16)
Tribal County 104 (20f,Crl,S,Mar 6)
Tribal Dancer 109 (24f,Tow,GS,May 6)
Tribal Dispute 105 (16¹/₂f,Kel,G,Apr 7)
Tribal Venture 109 (24f,Chl,G,Apr 17)
Trinity Belle 101 (16f,Plu,S,Nov 24)
Tristan Ludlow 104 (22¹/₂f,Fol,HY,Dec 17)
Trivial 103 (20f,Crl,G,Mar 28)
True Blue Victory 109 (16f,Naa,Y,Feb 23)
True North 112 (24f,Ncs,HY,Jan 29)
True Rose 100 (16¹/₂f,Hex,S,Mar 13)
Trump Card 103 (20f,Mus,G,Jan 17)
Trumpington 100 (22¹/₂f,Str,GS,Aug 10)
Tsunami 103 (17f,Her,G,Feb 10)
Tucacas 109 (16f,Hay,G,May 4)
Tudor King 101 (21f,Lud,F,Oct 24)
Tufty Hopper 103 (27¹/₂f,Sed,S,Nov 26)
Tulach Ard 104 (20f,Crl,GS,Mar 2)
Tullimoss 100 (24f,Mus,G,Feb 12)
Turaath 103 (19¹/₂f,Tau,S,Jan 16)
Turbo 104 (16¹/₂f,Nby,S,Feb 28)
Turtle Dancer 100 (17f,Sed,G,Aug 9)
Turtle Love 104 (17¹/₂f,Mar,G,Apr 26)
Turtleback 117 (17f,Chl,G,Mar 13)
Tuska Ridge 102 (21¹/₂f,Sed,GF,Jly 25)
Tuxedo Junction 106 (17f,Her,GF,May 4)
Tyholland 104 (16f,Naa,S,Feb 8)

Ulusaba 100 (16¹/₂f,Per,GS,Aug 4)
Ulvick Star 104 (26f,Hun,GF,Sep 29)
Uncle Mick 106 (24f,Chp,HY,Nov 27)
Under Construction 104 (17f,Nab,S,Nov 6)
Under The Sand 108 (17f,Chl,GS,Jan 25)
Ungaretti 103 (24f,Lud,G,Feb 27)
Unleash 106 (16¹/₂f,Str,GF,Apr 19)

Valerio 116 (16¹/₂f,Nby,S,Nov 29)
Valeureux 109 (16¹/₂f,Don,GS,Jan 24)
Valfonic 101 (16f,Wor,G,May 22)
Valley Erne 103 (24f,Nav,S,Jun 9)
Valleymore 114 (20f,Hay,GS,Feb 8)
Vanormix 104 (19f,Exe,GS,Feb 23)
Vatirisk 104 (16f,Nav,S,May 19)
Veneguera 100 (21¹/₂f,Hun,GF,Jun 3)
Verde Luna 101 (26f,Hun,GF,Sep 29)
Veridian 104 (17f,Ban,S,May 18)
Vert Espere 111 (20f,Wor,G,Sep 14)
Victor Boy 108 (16f,Gal,S,Sep 10)
Victor Sherlock 116 (16f,Nav,HY,Jly 12)
Viking Buoy 101 (21f,Plu,GF,Apr 21)
Vilprano 106 (24f,Ncs,S,Feb 24)
Virac Boy 102 (22¹/₂f,Fon,S,Mar 3)
Virgin Soldier 108 (17f,Ban,G,Sep 14)
Visibility 116 (16f,Lei,HY,Feb 12)
Vitelucy 107 (16f,Sth,GF,Mar 18)
Volano 106 (17f,Chl,GS,Jan 25)

Wadsworth 102 (18f,Gal,Y,Aug 2)
Waffles Of Amin 106 (17f,Tau,GS,Nov 28)
Wagner 112 (24f,Ncs,GS,Mar 15)
Wainak 105 (16¹/₂f,Per,GS,Aug 4)
Wait For The Will 101 (17¹/₂f,Fol,G,May 3)
Walter Plinge 105 (20¹/₂f,Utt,G,Apr 21)

War Tune 107 (20¹/₂f,Utt,G,Jun 3)
Warjan 110 (17f,Chl,G,Mar 13)
Warrens Castle 111 (20f,Fai,G,Apr 22)
Wartorn 104 (19f,Nby,GS,Nov 13)
Washington Pink 102 (17¹/₂f,Crt,G,Aug 24)
Wave Rock 107 (20¹/₂f,Utt,G,May 22)
We Ll Make It 102 (16¹/₂f,Asc,G,Mar 25)
Wee Danny 102 (22¹/₂f,Str,GF,Jly 14)
Wee Willow 102 (27¹/₂f,Sed,G,Mar 25)
Weet And See 103 (16f,Wol,S,Jly 5)
Welcome To Unos 107 (16f,Cat,G,Feb 8)
Weldunfrank 106 (16¹/₂f,Hun,GF,Jun 3)
Well Chief 115 (17f,Chl,G,Mar 13)
Well Then Now Then 105 (24¹/₂f,Sth,GS,Dec 6)
Welsh Main 105 (16f,Wet,GF,Oct 16)
Wend s Day 106 (16f,Fak,GS,Oct 25)
Wensum Dancer 114 (16f,Naa,GY,Jly 10)
Were Not Stoppin 105 (19f,Str,GF,Jly 27)
Westender 119 (17f,Chl,HY,Jan 1)
Westernmost 105 (17¹/₂f,Crt,G,Jun 8)
Westgate Run 106 (16¹/₂f,Hex,G,Oct 12)
Westmorland 105 (24f,Hex,G,May 11)
What You Know 105 (16f,Wor,G,Sep 14)
What s The Count 104 (21f,Plu,HY,Feb 10)
Which Half 105 (18f,Fai,S,Nov 30)
Whispering John 104 (16f,Wcn,GS,Jan 18)
Whistling Dixie 114 (16f,Hay,G,May 4)
Whitaside 100 (19¹/₂f,Mar,S,Nov 21)
Who Cares Wins 108 (22¹/₂f,Fon,S,Mar 2)
Who s Choice 104 (22f,Nav,S,Jan 11)
Wild Dream 112 (21f,War,GS,Nov 26)
Wild Knight 103 (20f,Chp,S,Dec 7)
Wild Romance 108 (16f,Wcn,GS,Dec 5)
Wildfield Rufo 108 (24¹/₂f,Ayr,HY,Jan 14)
Willy Willy 100 (16f,Plu,GF,Oct 7)
Windy Valley 106 (20f,Wor,GF,Aug 24)
Winged Angel 103 (20¹/₂f,Hex,G,Jun 15)
Wings Of Hope 109 (21f,Lud,F,Oct 10)
Wise Man 103 (22¹/₂f,Kel,G,Mar 21)
Witness Time 100 (20f,Chp,S,Dec 7)
Wonderful Man 102 (16¹/₂f,Per,GF,May 16)
Wontcostalotbut 104 (22¹/₂f,Utt,S,Nov 28)
Woodland Park 100 (23¹/₂f,Fak,G,May 8)
Woodwind Down 107 (20¹/₂f,Hex,GF,Sep 15)
Woodys Deep Ocean 118 (16f,Pun,SH,Feb 2)
Woolley 102 (22¹/₂f,Str,GF,May 17)
World Wide Web 108 (16¹/₂f,Chp,GS,Feb 26)
Wotsitooya 103 (16f,Naa,GY,Jly 10)
Wouldn t You Agree 107 (16f,Gal,GY,Aug 4)
Wrangel 100 (16¹/₂f,Hun,G,Mar 12)
Wun Chai 102 (16¹/₂f,Str,GF,Apr 12)
Wuxi Venture 106 (17f,Ban,GS,Feb 7)

Xaipete 105 (16f,Fak,GS,Oct 25)
Xellance 104 (19¹/₂f,Her,GF,Apr 21)
Xenophon 117 (21f,Chl,G,Mar 12)

Yankee Jamie 111 (24f,Mus,G,Jan 28)
Yayo 105 (16f,Nav,S,Jun 9)
Yellow Soil Star 100 (16f,Nav,HY,Mar 8)
Yeoman s Point 110 (25¹/₂f,Chl,GS,Nov 16)
Yesyes 105 (16f,Plu,S,Nov 24)

Yogi 113 (16f,Naa,HY,Mar 9)
Yorkshire 105 (20f,Chp,GF,May 8)
Young American 113 (20¹/₂f,Utt,G,May 4)
Young Buck 104 (19¹/₂f,Her,G,Jun 4)
Young Dalesman 103 (24f,Mar,GF,Sep 28)
Young Joker 105 (19¹/₂f,Her,GF,Sep 11)

Zaidaan 102 (16f,Wor,G,Sep 14)
Zamat 106 (16¹/₂f,Kel,S,Nov 13)
Zeloso 104 (19¹/₂f,Her,GF,Sep 11)
Zilarator 100 (20¹/₂f,Lei,HY,Dec 27)
Zoffany 101 (16f,Hay,G,Dec 14)
Zoltano 100 (16f,Ayr,HY,Jan 14)
Zsarabak 105 (17f,Ban,G,May 3)

Zurs 106 (17f,Ban,G,Sep 14)

NOTES

Notes